D1524707

PRESENTED

TO ______________________________

____

BY ______________________________

____

ON ______________________________

____

YOUR WORD IS A LAMP TO MY FEET
AND A LIGHT TO MY PATH.

PSALM 119:105

THE

AMPLIFIED

STUDY BIBLE

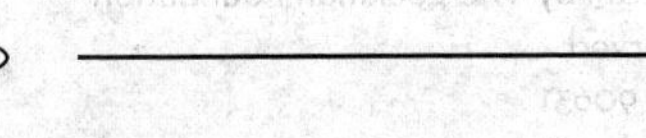

ZONDERVAN®

Published by Zondervan
Grand Rapids, Michigan 49546

www.zondervan.com

Library of Congress Card Catalog Number: 2016943214

Printed in China

---

18 19 20 21 22 /AMC/ 16 15 14 13 12 11 10 9 8 7 6 5 4 3

TABLE OF CONTENTS

THE OLD TESTAMENT

THE NEW TESTAMENT

FOREWORD

Scriptural Promise

"The grass withers, the flower fades,
But the word of our God stands forever."

Isaiah 40:8

The *Amplified* Bible has been produced with the conviction that the words of Scripture as originally penned in the Hebrew, Aramaic, and Greek were inspired by God. Since they are the eternal Word of God, the Holy Scriptures speak with fresh power to each generation, to give wisdom that leads to salvation, that people may serve Christ to the glory of God.

The Fourfold Aim of The Lockman Foundation

1. These publications shall be true to the original Hebrew, Aramaic, and Greek.
2. They shall be grammatically correct.
3. They shall be understandable to the people.
4. They shall give the Lord Jesus Christ His proper place, the place which the Word gives Him; therefore, no translation work will ever be personalized.

THE LOCKMAN FOUNDATION

The Lockman Foundation wishes to express deepest gratitude to all those who have contributed to the development of the 2015 edition of the *Amplified* Bible. Throughout these years of translation many people have shared their time, talent, prayers and very best effort to bring this Bible translation to completion.

It is our prayer that each participant—whether scholar or staff, professor or proofreader, consultant or critical reader—will look at these pages of Scripture and know that each one's contribution is treasured . . . nothing is insignificant when dealing with God's Word.

To quote F. Dewey "Granddad" Lockman (1898–1974), "This work is a symphony, not a solo!" May each of you be specially blessed and always hold a special joy in your heart whenever you read the new *Amplified* Bible 2015. Thank you beloved.

Phoebe McAuley Lambeth
Coordinating Editor

PREFACE

In 1958 The Lockman Foundation and Zondervan Publishing House issued the first edition of the *Amplified* New Testament. In 1962 and 1964 the two-volume *Amplified* Old Testament was released. In 1965 the complete *Amplified* Bible was published, and in 1987 the *Amplified* Bible, *Expanded Edition* was completed. Over fifty years have passed since the *Amplified* New Testament was translated and during that time there have been changes in both the style and usage of the English language; therefore, it seemed appropriate for The Lockman Foundation to revisit this well-loved translation of God's Word. Accordingly, Dr. Robert G. Lambeth, President of The Lockman Foundation, established a translation team and under his leadership the project was developed and completed.

The Lockman Foundation is now pleased to present the *Amplified* Bible of 2015. The English has been updated based on contemporary usage, a substantial number of new amplifications have been added to the Old Testament, and original amplifications have been updated, expanded, refined, or clarified where needed. The translation team has also added a significant number of new footnotes and references.

The result is a translation that is contemporary and firmly based on the foundation established by the *Amplified* Bible of 1965. That original translation project was envisioned and led by Frances Siewert (1881-1967), an amazing and gifted woman who devoted her life to serving the Lord and to making His Word available in an entirely new format. Her contribution to the spread of the Gospel through the *Amplified* Bible is impossible to quantify and her vision continues to speak to the hearts of people today.

The *Amplified* Bible of 2015 has been editorially recast so that a verse may be read either with or without amplification. The basic verse is the literal equivalent translation of the Hebrew, Aramaic, or Greek text. The basic verse is then amplified in a way that permits the reader to have a greater understanding of the relationship between the crispness of contemporary English and the depth of meaning in the biblical languages.

INTRODUCTION

The *Amplified Study Bible* has been designed to provide a foundation for Bible study. It is intended for both beginning and experienced students of the Scriptures who want a Bible that contains the key features of a study Bible combined with the impressive study tools already included in the *Amplified* translation.

The *Amplified*® Translation

First, a word about the *Amplified* translation itself. The *Amplified* Bible is a Literal Equivalent translation that, by using synonyms and definitions, both explains and expands the meaning of words in the text by placing amplification in parentheses, brackets, and after key words. This unique system of translation allows the reader to more completely and clearly grasp the meaning as it was understood in the original languages. Additionally, amplifications provide further theological, historical, and other details for a better understanding of the text.

The appeal and readability of the 2015 edition of the *Amplified* Bible has been broadened by refreshing the English and refining the amplifications for relevance and clarity. The *Amplified* Bible is now easier to read and better than ever to study and understand, as it includes more amplification in the Old Testament and refined amplification in the New Testament. Additionally, the Bible text has been improved to read smoothly with or without amplifications, so the text may be read clearly either way. The same feel and style of amplification has been carefully maintained, so those who read the classic *Amplified* Bible will easily transition to the new text and appreciate its improvements.

Through amplification, the reader gains a better understanding of what the Hebrew and Greek listener instinctively understood (as a matter of course). Take, for example, the Greek word *pisteuo*, which the vast majority of versions render as "believe." That simple translation, however, hardly does justice to the many meanings contained in the Greek *pisteuo*: "to adhere to, cleave to; to trust, to have faith in; to rely on, to depend on." Notice the subtle shades of meaning that are unlocked in John 11:25: "Jesus said to her, 'I am the Resurrection and the Life. Whoever believes in (adheres to, trusts in, relies on) Me [as Savior] will live even if he dies.'"

The Story of the *Amplified* Bible

The story of the *Amplified* Bible is a remarkable story of faith, hope, and love. It's the story of a woman, a foundation, a committee, and a publisher. Commitment, energy, enthusiasm, and giftedness—these are the words that paint the picture, the picture of the making of a translation.

Frances Siewert (Litt. B., B.D., M.A., Litt. D.) was a woman with an intense dedication to the study of the Bible. It was Mrs. Siewert (1881-1967) who laid the foundation of the *Amplified* Bible, devoting her life to a familiarity with the Bible, with the Hebrew and Greek languages, and with the cultural and archaeological background of Biblical times, which would result in the publication of this unique translation.

Every vision needs visionaries willing to follow the cause. The story of this dream is no different. Mrs. Siewert's vision was seen by a California non-profit foundation called The Lockman Foundation, made up of Christian men and women who through their commitment, their expertise, and their financial support undergirded Mrs. Siewert's monumental translation project. The Lockman Foundation's purpose remains today what is was then: to promote Bible translation, Christian evangelism, education, and benevolence.

Commitment, energy, enthusiasm, giftedness—the things visions are made of—describes the efforts of the committee appointed by The Lockman Foundation to carefully review the impressive work of Mrs. Siewert. This Editorial Board, made up of dedicated scholars, lent credibility and organization to this unprecedented attempt to bring out the richness of the Hebrew and Greek languages within the English text itself.

One chapter yet remained to bring the vision into reality. A publishing house in Grand Rapids, Michigan, on its way to becoming a major religious publishing firm, seized the opportunity to participate in a project that all visionaries involved strongly believed would be used by God to change lives. The Zondervan Publishing House joined the team, and the dream became reality with the publication of The *Amplified* New Testament in 1958, followed by the two-volume *Amplified* Old Testament in 1962 and 1964, and the one-volume *Amplified* Bible in 1965.

Since the *Amplified* Bible was first translated, there have been changes in both the style and usage of the English language; therefore, it seemed appropriate for The Lockman Foundation to revisit this well-loved translation of God's Word. Accordingly, Dr. Robert G. Lambeth, President of The Lockman Foundation, established a translation team and under his leadership the project was developed and completed in 2015. The result is a new *Amplified* Bible translation that is contemporary and firmly based on the foundation established by the complete *Amplified* Bible of 1965.

Features of the *Amplified Study Bible*

The features of the *Amplified* Study Bible have been carefully crafted to bring you, the reader, a solid study system with several unique features that allow for deeper study.

The *Amplified* Translation. First, the *Amplified* translation's unique system of punctuation, italics, references, and synonyms unlock subtle shades of meaning as found in the original languages. This translation itself includes an amazing depth of insight into the Word of God. Careful reading of the text will bring deeper understanding of the nuances that the original authors of the Bible intended, bringing greater depth of insight to your personal study.

Study Notes. More than 5000 concise study notes provide helpful, practical, application-oriented comments on passages of Scripture and open the Word so that you can more appropriately apply it to your life. These informative notes are intended not to overpower the words of Scripture, but to come alongside you as the reader to increase your understanding as you consider what God has to say to you today through the power of his living Word.

Theological Notes. Some 330 practical theological notes draw attention to important doctrinal content in the Bible. These notes are signified by a bold Roman heading followed by a dash. They are generally longer notes that highlight important teachings in Scripture that allow you to further unlock the critical teachings of the Bible. Each one of these notes is indexed in two ways in the back matter of this Bible, allowing you as a student of the Bible to read through these notes topically, looking for insights to help you to further appreciate and apply these life-changing teachings.

Book Introductions. These brief introductions to each of the Bible's 66 books help you understand the historical context of each Bible book. Key themes of each book are also highlighted, allowing you to look for these themes as you make your way through each particular book.

Cross References. The cross-reference system provided within the text pages of this study Bible appear in a box at the bottom of each page. These cross references provide a nearly inexhaustible method of understanding the key connections that can be made throughout the Bible text. Each verse that has cross-references associated with it can be further expanded upon and understood through looking up the other passages of Scripture that relate to it, bringing deeper insights to your personal study.

Topical Index. This study feature provides an alphabetical listing of important passages that highlight key concepts in the Bible. Simply look for the Bible topic, person, or word you have in mind, and you'll find more information on that subject area through the referenced passages. The thousands of references in this study tool make this a helpful companion to the other study tools included in this Bible.

Full-color Maps of Bible Lands. Included in the back of this Bible are multiple full-color maps that allow you to understand the locations described within the text of the Bible. These are placed here to add a visual aspect to the study Bible, giving you the opportunity to see and understand more about the context of the history contained within God's Word.

May God bless you as you use the study tools included in this Bible to come to a deeper understanding of, and a more intimate relationship with, the God who has preserved his Word for the instruction, encouragement, and salvation of his people.

> Then [with a deep longing] you will seek Me
> *and* require Me [as a vital necessity] and [you will]
> find Me when you search for Me with all your heart.
>
> Jeremiah 29:13

EXPLANATION OF GENERAL FORMAT

Amplification is indicated within the English text by parentheses, brackets, and italicized conjunctions.

Parentheses in Roman type ( ) supply the definition in context of the preceding name, place, or word. When the *Amplified* Bible is read aloud the definition in context may be skipped over.

Parentheses in **bold** type **( )** indicate a parenthetical phrase that is part of the original language and should be included when Scripture is read aloud.

Brackets in Roman type [ ] contain justified words, phrases, or brief commentary not fully expressed in the preceding English text, but which are validated by the meaning of the original Hebrew, Aramaic, or Greek, or are validated elsewhere by Scripture. The amplifications within brackets serve many purposes. They may expand the depth of meaning in the underlying Hebrew, Aramaic, or Greek word; they may clarify a theological word or concept; they may expand a teaching or principle; they may supply information that helps the reader grasp the context of the passage.

Brackets in **bold** type **[ ]** are footnoted and indicate text not found in early mss or found only in some early mss.

Italicized conjunctions: *and, or, nor* are not in the original text, but are used to connect additional English words indicated by the original Hebrew, Aramaic, or Greek.

Italicized words are not found in the original language, but implied by it.

Proper names of persons, places, or things are often used to replace pronouns. When pronouns are retained in the text they may be followed by a name placed in parentheses.

Pronouns referring to God, the Father; Jesus, the Son; and the Holy Spirit are always capitalized, so that the reader immediately recognizes Deity in the text.

Paragraphs are identified by **bold** verse numbers or **bold** letters. This allows paragraphs to be clearly identified without displaying the verses in paragraph format. The text can still be read or studied by paragraphs, but individual verses are much easier to find when each verse begins on a new line.

Small capital letters are used in the New Testament to indicate Old Testament quotations or obvious references to Old Testament texts. Variations of Old Testament wording are found in New Testament citations depending on whether the New Testament writer translated from a Hebrew text, used existing Greek or Aramaic translations, or restated the material. It should be noted that modern rules for the indication of direct quotations were not used in biblical times; therefore, the ancient writer would use exact quotations or references to quotations without specific indication of such.

The proper name of God in the Old Testament is most significant and understandably so. The most common name for the Deity is God, a translation of the Hebrew word, *Elohim*. One of the titles for God is Lord, a translation of *Adonai*. There is yet another name which is particularly assigned to God as His special or proper name, that is, the four letters YHWH (Exodus 3:14 and Isaiah 42:8). This name has not been pronounced by the Jews because of reverence for the great sacredness of the divine name. Therefore, it has been consistently translated LORD. The only exception to this translation of YHWH is when it occurs in immediate proximity to the word *Lord*, that is, *Adonai*. In that case it is regularly translated GOD in order to avoid confusion. When the name of God appears within parentheses or brackets, the context of the verse determines which name and type style is used.

Verse references are placed in brackets at the end of some verses. If a verse contains more than one Scripture reference, the references are listed in biblical order.

Section headings are included in the text, but are not part of the original language.

ABBREVIATIONS AND SPECIAL MARKINGS

Aram = Aramaic

c = about

DSS = Dead Sea Scrolls

etc. = and so on

e.g. = for example

Gr = Greek translation of O.T. (Septuagint or LXX) or Greek text of N.T.

Heb = Hebrew text, usually Masoretic

i.e., = that is

Lat = Latin

MT = Masoretic text

Syr = Syriac

Lit = A literal translation

Or = An alternate translation justified by the Hebrew, Aramaic, or Greek

ch, chs = chapter, chapters

cf = compare

f, ff = following verse or verses

mg = Refers to a marginal reading on another verse

ms, mss = manuscript, manuscripts

v, vv = verse, verses

THE
OLD TESTAMENT

OLD TESTAMENT OVERVIEW

Genesis: Describes God's creation of the world, the sin of the first humans and the history of the Hebrew people.

Exodus: Israel's miraculous freedom from slavery in Egypt; the giving of the Law and the building of the tabernacle.

Leviticus: Hebrew ceremonial law and rules for living.

Numbers: The story of Israel's wanderings in the wilderness after they disobeyed God.

Deuteronomy: Moses reiterates the Law for the people as they prepare to enter the Promised Land.

Joshua: Israel conquers the Promised Land and the land is divided among the twelve tribes.

Judges: The history of a chaotic period in the life of Israel from Joshua to Samson.

Ruth: A Moabite woman follows her mother-in-law back to Israel and is blessed for her faithfulness.

1 Samuel: The story of Israel during the judgeship of Samuel and the reign of Israel's first king, Saul.

2 Samuel: The reign of King David.

1 and 2 Kings: The history of the nation of Israel from David's death and Solomon's reign to the dividing of the kingdom and the destruction of Judah after the capture of Jerusalem.

1 and 2 Chronicles: The official historical records of Israel and Judah.

Ezra: A small group of Jews returns to Jerusalem from captivity in Babylon to rebuild the temple.

Nehemiah: Another group of Jews returns from captivity and rebuilds the wall around Jerusalem.

Esther: A young Jewish woman becomes queen of Persia and saves the Jewish people from being wiped out by order of the king of Persia.

Job: Pain and patience teach the main character of this book to trust in God alone.

Psalms: A collection songs that were used to worship God. King David wrote many of these Psalms.

Proverbs: Practical wisdom from King Solomon and others.

Ecclesiastes: A poem that leads the reader to examine what's truly important in life.

Song of Solomon: A poetic rendering of love and desire between a husband and wife.

Isaiah: Israel's greatest prophet foretells the birth of Jesus and describes his work.

Jeremiah: Predicts the coming captivity of Judah, what it will suffer, and indicates that God will one day allow the people to return to the land.

Lamentations: Jeremiah's song of sorrow over what Jerusalem will experience.

Ezekiel: Messages of both warning and comfort sent to Jews who were in captivity.

Daniel: Wise Jewish captives remain faithful to God; Daniel prophesies about the future.

Hosea: A picture of God's unfaithful people through the allegory of a faithless wife.

Joel: Predicts Judah's coming judgment with a promise that God will reward faithful people.

Amos: Predicts that Israel and its surrounding neighbors will be punished; points to the Messiah's kingdom.

Obadiah: Predicts the destruction of Edom.

Jonah: A reluctant prophet is sent to proclaim judgment to the Assyrian city of Nineveh.

Micah: Predicts the Babylonian captivity and points toward the birth of the Messiah in Bethlehem.

Nahum: Predicts the destruction of Assyria.

Habakkuk: A prophet chooses to remain faithful in the face of national destruction.

Zephaniah: Predicts the overthrow of Judah because of its unfaithfulness to God.

Haggai: Prophecies about the rebuilding of the temple.

Zechariah: Prophecies about the rebuilding of the temple and the Messiah.

Malachi: A prophet calls the nation of Israel to remain faithful to the Lord.

THE FIRST BOOK OF MOSES,
COMMONLY CALLED

GENESIS

▸ **AUTHOR:** Nowhere in the Book of Genesis is the author named. Although the events of the book end 300 years before Moses was born, the rest of the Bible and most of church historians attribute the authorship of Genesis to Moses. Both the Old and New Testaments have many references to Moses as its author (Ex 7:14; Lev 1:1 – 2; Nu 33:2; Dt 1:1; Da 9:11 – 13; Mal 4:4; Mt 8:4; Mk 12:26; Lk 16:29; Jn 7:19; Ac 26:22; Ro 10:19). Both early Jewish and Christian writers name Moses as the author.

▸ **TIMES:** c. 4000 – 1804 BC ▸ **KEY VERSE:** Ge 3:15

▸ **THEME:** After the initial story of the world's creation, Genesis "("beginnings") covers two basic subjects: God and man. God creates man. Man disobeys God and alienates himself from God. Genesis is the story then of the subsequent interactions between God and man that bring them back together into a right relationship. As such, the book points to the beginnings of the way of change, of restoration, and of a new way of life. Genesis sets the tone for the rest of the Bible with clear teaching on following God's call, believing in His promises, and being obedient to His commands. The main characters who dominate the story are the patriarchs: Abraham, Isaac, Jacob, and Joseph.

The Creation

1 IN THE beginning God (*Elohim*)
created [by forming from nothing]
the heavens and the earth. [Heb 11:3]
2The earth was formless and void *or*
a waste and emptiness, and darkness
was upon the face of the deep [prime-
val ocean that covered the unformed
earth]. The Spirit of God was moving
(hovering, brooding) over the face of
the waters.
3And God said, "Let there be light";
and there was light.
4God saw that the light was good
(pleasing, useful) *and* He affirmed
and sustained it; and God separated
the light [distinguishing it] from the
darkness. [2 Cor 4:6]

1:1 Creation — Biblical revelation begins with a simple, strong, and sublime affirmation. Instead of arguing the existence of God, it declares that the very existence of the universe depends on the creative power of God. The world we live in was created by God and belongs to Him. His absolute ownership requires our faithful stewardship of all things.

1:1 *In the beginning.* No information is given to us about what happened before the creation of the physical universe, though John 1:1 speaks of this time. It is possible that the rise, rebellion, and judgment of Satan transpired before the events of this chapter. ***God.*** This standard Hebrew term for deity *Elohim* is in the form called the plural of majesty or plural of intensity. In contrast to the ordinary plural (gods), this plural means "the fullness of deity" or "God — very God." Furthermore, the use of the plural allows for the later revelation of the Trinity (see 11:7; Mt 28:19; Jn 1:1 – 3).

1:3 *Let there be light.* These words express a principal theme of the Bible: God bringing

---

CHAPTER 1 **1** Jn 1:1,2; Heb 1:10; Ps 8:3; Isa 44:24; Ac 17:24; Rev 4:11 **2** Jer 4:23; Ps 33:6; Isa 40:13,14 **3** Ps 33:9; 2Co 4:6

5 And God called the light day, and the darkness He called night. And there was evening and there was morning, one day.

6 And God said, "Let there be an expanse [of the sky] in the midst of the waters, and let it separate the waters [below the expanse] from the waters [above the expanse]."

7 And God made the expanse [of sky] and separated the waters which were under the expanse from the waters which were above the expanse; and it was so [just as He commanded].

8 God called the expanse [of sky] heaven. And there was evening and there was morning, a second day.

9 Then God said, "Let the waters below the heavens be gathered into one place [of standing, pooling together], and let the dry land appear"; and it was so.

10 God called the dry land earth, and the gathering of the waters He called seas; and God saw that this was good (pleasing, useful) *and* He affirmed and sustained it.

11 So God said, "Let the earth sprout [tender] vegetation, plants yielding seed, and fruit trees bearing fruit according to (limited to, consistent with) their kind, whose seed is in them upon the earth"; and it was so.

12 The earth sprouted *and* abundantly produced vegetation, plants yielding seed according to their kind, and trees bearing fruit with seed in them, according to their kind; and God saw that it was good *and* He affirmed and sustained it.

13 And there was evening and there was morning, a third day.

14 Then God said, "Let there be light-bearers (sun, moon, stars) in the expanse of the heavens to separate the day from the night, and let them be *useful* for signs (tokens) [of God's provident care], and for *marking* seasons, days, and years; [Gen 8:22]

15 and let them be *useful* as lights in the expanse of the heavens to provide light on the earth"; and it was so, [just as He commanded].

16 God made the two great lights—the greater light (the sun) to rule the day, and the lesser light (the moon) to rule the night; *He made* the [galaxies of] stars also [that is, all the amazing wonders in the heavens].

17 God placed them in the expanse of the heavens to provide light upon the earth,

18 to rule over the day and the night, and to separate the light from the darkness; and God saw that it was good *and* He affirmed and sustained it.

19 And there was evening and there was morning, a fourth day.

20 Then God said, "Let the waters swarm *and* abundantly produce living creatures, and let birds soar above the earth in the open expanse of the heavens."

---

light into darkness (see Isa 9:1 – 2). Here, God produced physical light. The New Testament records God sending His Son to be the light of the world (Jn 8:12), bringing release from the spiritual darkness of bondage to sin. In the end, there will no longer be any darkness at all and we will be face to face with the source of light (Rev 21:23).

1:7 *separated the waters.* The description of upper and lower waters is somewhat mysterious; it has been theorized that this is simply a reference to the division between the water of the seas and rivers on the surface of the earth and the water vapor which is part of the atmosphere.

1:11 – 12 *seed ... kind.* God not only created plant life; He also set in motion the process that makes plant life reproduce.

1:14 *for signs (tokens) [of God's provident care], and for marking seasons.* Some have mistakenly viewed these words as a biblical basis for astrology. The signs in this case relate to phases of the moon and the relative positions of stars that mark the passage of time from the vantage point of earth. The two words form a pair that may be translated *seasonal signs*.

1:16 *He made the [galaxies of] stars also.* This is a remarkable statement. In the ancient Middle East, other religions worshiped, deified, and mystified the stars. Israel's neighbors revered the stars and looked to them for guidance. In contrast, the biblical creation story gives the stars only the barest mention, as though the writer shrugged and said, *And, oh, yes, He also made the stars.*

---

5 Ps 74:16 **6** Job 37:18; Jer 10:12 **7** Pr 8:28; Ps 148:4 **9** Job 26:10; Pr 8:29; Jer 5:22; 2Pe 3:5 **11** Heb 6:7; Lk 6:44 **16** Ps 136:8; Ps 8:3; Job 38:7 **18** Jer 31:35

21 God created the great sea monsters
and every living creature that moves,
with which the waters swarmed ac-
cording to their kind, and every winged
bird according to its kind; and God saw
that it was good *and* He affirmed and
sustained it.
22 And God blessed them, saying, "Be
fruitful, multiply, and fill the waters
in the seas, and let birds multiply on
the earth."
23 And there was evening and there
was morning, a fifth day.
24 Then God said, "Let the earth
bring forth living creatures according
to (limited to, consistent with) their
kind: livestock, crawling things, and
wild animals of the earth according to
their kinds"; and it was so [because He
had spoken them into creation].
25 So God made the wild animals of
the earth according to their kind, and
the cattle according to their kind, and
everything that creeps *and* crawls on
the earth according to its kind; and God
saw that it was good (pleasing, useful)
and He affirmed and sustained it.
26 Then God said, "Let Us (Father,
Son, Holy Spirit) make man in Our
image, according to Our likeness [not
physical, but a spiritual personality
and moral likeness]; and let them have
complete authority over the fish of the
sea, the birds of the air, the cattle, and
over the entire earth, and over every-
thing that creeps *and* crawls on the
earth." [Ps 104:30; Heb 1:2; 11:3]
27 So God created man in His own im-
age, in the image *and* likeness of God
He created him; male and female He
created them. [Col 3:9, 10; James 3:8, 9]
28 And God blessed them [granting
them certain authority] and said to
them, "Be fruitful, multiply, and fill the
earth, and subjugate it [putting it under
your power]; and rule over (dominate)
the fish of the sea, the birds of the air,
and every living thing that moves upon
the earth."
29 So God said, "Behold, I have given
you every plant yielding seed that is
on the surface of the entire earth, and
every tree which has fruit yielding
seed; it shall be food for you;
30 and to all the animals on the
earth and to every bird of the air
and to everything that moves on the
ground—to everything in which there
is the breath of life—*I have given* every
green plant for food"; and it was so
[because He commanded it].
31 God saw everything that He had
made, and behold, it was very good
and He validated it completely. And
there was evening and there was
morning, a sixth day.

Such a statement showed great contempt for ancient Babylonian astrology (Ps 29; 93).

1:24 *living creatures.* This expression contains the word sometimes used for the soul, but the word can also mean "life," "being," "living thing," or "person," depending on the context. The same phrase is used for man in 2:7.

1:26 *in Our image.* Since God is spirit (Jn 4:24), there can be no "image" or "likeness" of Him in the normal sense of these words. The traditional view of this passage is that God's image in man is in specific moral, ethical, and intellectual abilities. A more recent view, based on a possible interpretation of Hebrew grammar and the knowledge of the Middle East, interprets the phrase as meaning "Let us make man *as* our image." In ancient times an emperor might command statues of himself to be placed in remote parts of his empire. These symbols would declare that these areas were under his power and reign. So God placed humankind as living symbols of Himself on earth to represent His reign. This interpretation fits well with the command that follows—to reign over all that God has made.

1:28 *fill the earth, and subjugate it.* The word translated *subjugate* means "bring into bondage." This harsh term is used elsewhere of military conquest (Zec 9:15) and of God subduing our iniquities (Mic 7:19). Since this direction was given before the fall, it appears that the need to subjugate the earth is not because of sin but because God left part of the arranging and ordering of the creation as work for mankind to do. Whatever the case, subjugate does not mean "destroy" or "ruin." It does mean to "act as managers who have the authority to run everything as God planned." This command applies equally to male and female.

21 Ps 104:26 **22** Ge 8:17 **26** Ps 100:3; Ecc 7:29; Eph 4:24; Jas 3:9; Ge 9:2; Ps 8:6 **27** 1Co 11:7; Ge 5:2; Mt 19:4
28 Ge 9:1,7; Lev 26:9 **29** Ge 9:3; Ps 104:14,15 **30** Ps 145:15; Job 38:41 **31** Ps 104:24

The Creation of Man and Woman

2 SO THE heavens and the earth
were completed, and all their hosts
(inhabitants).
2 And by the seventh day God com-
pleted His work which He had done,
and He rested (ceased) on the seventh
day from all His work which He had
done. [Heb 4:9, 10]
3 So God blessed the seventh day and
sanctified it [as His own, that is, set it
apart as holy from other days], because
in it He rested from all His work which
He had created and done. [Ex 20:11]
4 This is the history of [the origin of]
the heavens and of the earth when they
were created, in the day [that is, days
of creation] that the LORD God made
the earth and the heavens—
5 no shrub *or* plant of the field was yet
in the earth, and no herb of the field had
yet sprouted, for the LORD God had not
caused it to rain on the earth, and there
was no man to cultivate the ground,
6 but a mist (fog, dew, vapor) used to
rise from the land and water the entire
surface of the ground—
7 then the LORD God formed [that is,
created the body of] man from the
dust of the ground, and breathed into
his nostrils the breath of life; and the
man became a living being [an indi-
vidual complete in body and spirit].
[1 Cor 15:45–49]
8 And the LORD God planted a garden
(oasis) in the east, in Eden (delight,
land of happiness); and He put the man
whom He had formed (created) there.
9 And [in that garden] the LORD God
caused to grow from the ground every
tree that is desirable *and* pleasing to
the sight and good (suitable, pleasant)
for food; the tree of life was also in the
midst of the garden, and the tree of the
[experiential] knowledge (recognition)
of [the difference between] good and
evil. [Rev 2:7; 22:14, 19]
10 Now a river flowed out of Eden to
water the garden; and from there it
divided and became four [branching]
rivers.
11 The first [river] is named Pishon;
it flows around the entire land of
Havilah, where there is gold.
12 The gold of that land is good; bdel-
lium (a fragrant, valuable resin) and
the onyx stone are found there.
13 The name of the second river is
Gihon; it flows around the entire land
of Cush [in Mesopotamia].
14 The third river is named Hiddekel
(Tigris); it flows east of Assyria. And
the fourth river is the Euphrates.
15 So the LORD God took the man [He
had made] and settled him in the Gar-
den of Eden to cultivate and keep it.

2:2 *He rested (ceased) on the seventh day.* God did not rest because of fatigue, but because of His accomplishment. God is never weary (Isa 40:28–29). The verb translated "rested" is related to the word for Sabbath, which means "rest." God's rest on the seventh day showed that He was satisfied with the work He had done.

2:4 *the LORD God.* This is a significant term. The word translated *God* is the same word as in 1:1. The word translated LORD is the proper name of God, Yahweh (or Jehovah; see Ex 3:14–15). The God of chapter 1 and the LORD God of chapter 2 are one and the same.

2:6 *mist.* The precise meaning of this word is uncertain. Obviously it refers to some manner of irrigation before the Lord brought the cycles of rain into being.

2:7 *the breath of life.* Although God created light with a mere word (1:3), He created man by fashioning a body out of mud and clay, transforming the clay into something new, and then breathing life into it. This "breath of life" is something which only God can bestow. Medical knowledge enables doctors to keep a human body "alive," keeping the heart pumping and the vital organs functioning, but it does not enable them to keep or to call back the breath of life. Some have speculated that the "breath of life" is the human soul, but later on, animals are also described as having the "breath . . . of life" in their nostrils (7:22), which would seem to indicate that this is simply a reference to the miracle of living, breathing flesh.

2:15–17 The First Covenant—In biblical times the purpose of a covenant was to establish an agreement between two persons or groups.

CHAPTER 2 **1** Ps 33:6 **2** Ex 20:11; Heb 4:4 **3** Isa 58:13 **4** Ge 1:1 **5** Ge 1:12; Job 38:26-28; Ge 3:23 **7** Ge 3:19,23; Ps 103:14; Job 33:4; Ge 7:22; 1Co 15:45 **8** Isa 51:3; Ge 3:24; Ge 4:16 **9** Eze 31:8; Ge 3:22; Rev 2:7 **11** Ge 25:18 **12** Nu 11:7 **14** Da 10:4

16 And the Lord God commanded the
man, saying, "You may freely (uncon-
ditionally) eat [the fruit] from every
tree of the garden;
17 but [only] from the tree of the
knowledge (recognition) of good and
evil you shall not eat, otherwise on
the day that you eat from it, you shall
most certainly die [because of your
disobedience]."
18 Now the Lord God said, "It is not
good (beneficial) for the man to be
alone; I will make him a helper [one
who balances him—a counterpart who
is] suitable *and* complementary for
him."
19 So the Lord God formed out of the
ground every animal of the field and
every bird of the air, and brought them
to Adam to see what he would call
them; and whatever the man called a
living creature, that was its name.
20 And the man gave names to all
the livestock, and to the birds of the
air, and to every animal of the field;
but for Adam there was not found a
helper [that was] suitable (a compan-
ion) for him.
21 So the Lord God caused a deep
sleep to fall upon Adam; and while he
slept, He took one of his ribs and closed
up the flesh at that place.
22 And the rib which the Lord God
had taken from the man He made
(fashioned, formed) into a woman, and
He brought her *and* presented her to
the man.
23 Then Adam said,

"This is now bone of my bones,
And flesh of my flesh;
She shall be called Woman,
Because she was taken out of
Man."

24 For this reason a man shall leave his
father and his mother, and shall be

The elements of a covenant included a promise on the part of one person and the conditions that needed to be fulfilled, on the part of the other person, in order for the promises to be carried out by both parties to the covenant. The Edenic Covenant is the first covenant mentioned in the Bible. God gave Adam a place in His creation and charged him with the responsibility of caring for the garden. The only condition in the covenant was that Adam could not allow himself to eat of the fruit of the tree of the knowledge of good and evil or he would die. This covenant was terminated by Adam's disobedience which also resulted in man's spiritual and physical death. God then established a new covenant with Adam in Genesis 3:14–21.

2:17 *shall most certainly die.* These emphatic words are made of two forms of the verb meaning "to die." The point is not that the guilty person would drop dead on the instant, but that death would surely happen — there is no escape (Heb 9:27).

2:18 *It is not good.* Until this point, everything in creation was very good.

2:19 *to see what he would call them.* In giving each animal its name, Adam demonstrated his right as God's agent (1:26–28), the one set in place as lord of the created order.

2:20 *helper [that was] suitable (a companion) for him.* Some have felt that calling the woman man's helper indicates that she is inferior in value, but this is far from true. In fact, the term "help" is used to describe God Himself, when He comes to our aid. The word "helper" indicates role, not value or position. The helper Adam needed was not merely a servant or a slave, nor another man exactly like himself. He needed a compliment, equal in value and with the same intelligence, personality, spirituality, and ethical and moral sense; but with different qualities and a different role, a helper who could join with him in his work of subduing the earth.

2:21 *He took one of his ribs.* God's use of Adam's rib was fitting. He might have started over with dust and clay. But by using a part of Adam himself, the identification of Adam with his partner would be ensured. As Martin Luther observed, God might have taken a bone from a toe, and thus signified that Adam was to rule over her; or He might have taken a bone from his head to indicate her rule over him. But by taking a bone from his side, God implied equality and mutual respect.

2:24 *one flesh.* This phrase suggests both a physical, sexual bonding and a lifelong relationship. They are still separate persons, but together they are as one (Eph 5:31). In the New Testament, Jesus refers to this text as the foundation of the biblical view of marriage (Mt 19:5). A married couple functions as "we," rather than "me and

---

17 Ge 3:1,3,11,17; Ge 3:3,19; Ro 6:23 **18** 1Co 11:9; 1Ti 2:13 **19** Ge 1:20,24; Ps 8:6 **21** 1Sa 26:12 **22** Heb 13:4 **23** Ge 29:14; Eph 5:30; 1Co 11:8 **24** Mt 19:5; Eph 5:31

joined to his wife; and they shall be-
come one flesh. [Matt 19:5; 1 Cor 6:16;
Eph 5:31–33]
25 And the man and his wife were
both naked and were not ashamed *or*
embarrassed.

The Fall of Man

3 NOW THE serpent was more crafty
(subtle, skilled in deceit) than any
living creature of the field which the
LORD God had made. And the serpent
(Satan) said to the woman, "Can it
really be that God has said, 'You shall
not eat from any tree of the garden'?"
[Rev 12:9–11]
2 And the woman said to the serpent,
"We may eat fruit from the trees of the
garden,
3 except the fruit from the tree which
is in the middle of the garden. God
said, 'You shall not eat from it nor
touch it, otherwise you will die.' "
4 But the serpent said to the woman,
"You certainly will not die! [2 Cor 11:3]
5 "For God knows that on the day you
eat from it your eyes will be opened
[that is, you will have greater aware-
ness], and you will be like God, know-
ing [the difference between] good and
evil."
6 And when the woman saw that the
tree was good for food, and that it was
delightful to look at, and a tree to be
desired in order to make one wise *and*
insightful, she took some of its fruit
and ate it; and she also gave some to
her husband with her, and he ate.
7 Then the eyes of the two of them
were opened [that is, their awareness in-
creased], and they knew that they were
naked; and they fastened fig leaves to-
gether and made themselves coverings.
8 And they heard the sound of the
LORD God walking in the garden in
the cool [afternoon breeze] of the day,
so the man and his wife hid *and* kept
themselves hidden from the presence
of the LORD God among the trees of
the garden.
9 But the LORD God called to Adam,
and said to him, "Where are you?"
10 He said, "I heard the sound of You
[walking] in the garden, and I was
afraid because I was naked; so I hid
myself."
11 God said, "Who told you that you
were naked? Have you eaten [fruit]
from the tree of which I commanded
you not to eat?"
12 And the man said, "The woman
whom You gave to be with me—she

you." They are a new unit, separate from the family units they each came from. This does not mean that they will no longer relate to their extended families, but that their "one flesh" is a unit distinct from either family.

3:1 ***the serpent.*** With no introduction, Satan appears in the garden of Eden. This is the first clue in Scripture of creation outside the one Adam and Eve experienced. It is interesting to note that Eve expressed no surprise at the serpent speaking to her in intelligible language.

3:3 ***You shall not eat from it, nor touch it.*** Some interpreters suggest that the woman was already sinning by adding to the word of God, for these words were not part of God's instructions in 2:17. Scripture, however, always refers to the eating of the fruit as the sin, and never comments on Eve's addition. Her words reflected the original command well enough, and indeed they would have ensured that the command would be kept.

3:5 ***you will be like God.*** God's fullness of knowledge was only one of the superiorities that set Him apart from the woman. But the serpent combined all of God's superiority over the woman into this one audacious appeal to her pride.

3:6–7 Sin's Consequences—At first Adam's sin does not appear to be all that significant. All he did was take a bite of some fruit. But Scripture takes it very seriously. Adam's sin was one of disobedience and rebellion. God told Adam not to eat the fruit of the "tree of the knowledge of good and evil" under penalty of death (2:17). That action of eating the fruit changed Adam's whole nature as well as his relationship with God. Adam became a sinner and as such he died. His spiritual death was immediate, the physical death progressive. Adam, who began the human race, then became the source of sin for the world. We are all sinners by nature because Adam sinned (Ro 5:12–14). We inherit sin from Adam in our natures in the same way we inherit many of our physical characteristics from our parents. Sin is a universal part of our spiritual inheritance.

25 Ge 3:7,10; Isa 47:3 **CHAPTER 3** **1** Rev 12:9; 2Co 11:3 **4** 2Co 11:3 **6** 1Ti 2:14 **7** Ge 2:25 **8** Job 38:1; Job 31:33; Jer 23:24 **10** Ge 2:25; 1Jn 3:20 **12** Pr 28:13

gave me [fruit] from the tree, and I ate it."

[13]Then the LORD God said to the woman, "What is this that you have done?" And the woman said, "The serpent beguiled *and* deceived me, and I ate [from the forbidden tree]." [2 Cor 11:3; 1 Tim 2:14]

[14]The LORD God said to the serpent,

"Because you have done this,
You are cursed more than all the cattle,
And more than any animal of the field;
On your belly you shall go,
And dust you shall eat
All the days of your life.
15 "And I will put enmity (open hostility)
Between you and the woman,
And between your seed (offspring) and her Seed;
He shall [fatally] bruise your head,
And you shall [only] bruise His heel." [Gal 4:4]

[16]To the woman He said,

"I will greatly multiply
Your pain in childbirth;
In pain you will give birth to children;
Yet your desire *and* longing will be for your husband,
And he will rule [with authority] over you *and* be responsible for you."

[17]Then to Adam the LORD God said, "Because you have listened [attentively] to the voice of your wife, and have eaten [fruit] from the tree about which I commanded you, saying, 'You shall not eat of it';

The ground is [now] under a curse because of you;
In sorrow *and* toil you shall eat [the fruit] of it
All the days of your life.
18 "Both thorns and thistles it shall grow for you;
And you shall eat the plants of the field.
19 "By the sweat of your face
You will eat bread
Until you return to the ground,

3:14–21 The Covenant with Adam—The Adamic Covenant is the second covenant God made with man. It sets forth conditions that will be in effect until the curse of death is lifted (Isa 11:6–10; Ro 8:18–23). In Christ's death and resurrection we have the beginning (firstfruits) of the lifting of the curse. The ultimate lifting of the curse will happen as Christ establishes His final reign on earth.

3:14 *to the serpent.* The Lord turned first to the serpent and brought judgment upon him. God did not excuse the woman because she was deceived, but He did bring the harsher judgment on the one who had deceived her.

3:15 Christ—This passage is sometimes referred to as the "preaching of Messiah in the garden of Eden," because it introduces the One who will deliver mankind from the power of the Tempter. The seed of the serpent, those of the human race who choose evil and thus give themselves into the control of the Evil One, would hate and destroy the Seed of the woman, who was Jesus Christ. But in that very act, Evil condemned itself. Jesus rose triumphant from the grave, having paid the blood atonement for the sin of the world and conquered death forever. Thus the Seed of woman crushed the head of the serpent.

3:16 *Your pain in childbirth.* The woman's joy in conceiving and bearing children would be saddened by the pain of it. ***desire . . . rule.*** The word *desire* can also mean "an attempt to usurp authority or control" as in 4:7. The last two lines of this verse could be paraphrased, "You will now have a tendency to try to dominate your husband and he will have the tendency to act as a tyrant." Each strives for control and neither lives in the best interest of the other (Php 2:3–4). The antidote is in the restoration of mutual respect and dignity through Jesus Christ (Eph 5:21–23).

3:17–19 *The ground is [now] under a curse . . . By the sweat of your face.* Humans sometimes tend to look upon work itself as a curse, but it is important to remember that work in itself is part of the "very good" creation. The curse on the ground simply means that work is now painful and tiresome toil instead of the pure satisfaction that it was designed to be. ***to dust***

---

13 ver. 4; 2Co 11:3; 1Ti 2:14 **14** Isa 65:25 **15** Jn 8:44; Ac 13:10; 1Jn 3:8; Isa 7:14; Lk 1:31,34,35; Ro 16:20; Rev 12:7 **16** Isa 13:8; Jn 16:21; Ge 4:7; 1Co 11:3; Eph 5:22 **17** 1Sa 15:23; Ge 2:17; Ro 8:20; Ecc 2:23 **18** Ps 104:14 **19** 2Th 3:10; Ge 2:7; Job 21:26; Ecc 3:20

For from it you were taken;
For you are dust,
And to dust you shall return."

20 The man named his wife Eve (life
spring, life giver), because she was the
mother of all the living.
21 The LORD God made tunics of [ani-
mal] skins for Adam and his wife and
clothed them.
22 And the LORD God said, "Behold,
the man has become like one of Us
(Father, Son, Holy Spirit), knowing
[how to distinguish between] good and
evil; and now, he might stretch out his
hand, and take from the tree of life as
well, and eat [its fruit], and live [in this
fallen, sinful condition] forever"—
23 therefore the LORD God sent Adam
away from the Garden of Eden, to till
and cultivate the ground from which
he was taken.
24 So God drove the man out; and
at the east of the Garden of Eden He
[permanently] stationed the cherubim
and the sword with the flashing blade
which turned round and round [in ev-
ery direction] to protect *and* guard the
way (entrance, access) to the tree of
life. [Rev 2:7; 22:2, 14, 19]

Cain and Abel

4 NOW THE man Adam knew Eve
as his wife, and she conceived and
gave birth to Cain, and she said, "I
have obtained a man (baby boy, son)
with *the help of* the LORD."
2 And [later] she gave birth to his
brother Abel. Now Abel kept the flocks
[of sheep and goats], but Cain cultivat-
ed the ground.
3 And in the course of time Cain
brought to the LORD an offering of the
fruit of the ground.
4 But Abel brought [an offering of]
the [finest] firstborn of his flock and
the fat portions. And the LORD had
respect (regard) for Abel and for his
offering; [Heb 11:4]
5 but for Cain and his offering He had
no respect. So Cain became extremely
angry (indignant), and he looked an-
noyed *and* hostile.
6 And the LORD said to Cain, "Why
are you so angry? And why do you
look annoyed?
7 "If you do well [believing Me and
doing what is acceptable and pleasing
to Me], will you not be accepted? And
if you do not do well [but ignore My
instruction], sin crouches at your door;
its desire is for you [to overpower you],
but you must master it."
8 Cain talked with Abel his brother
[about what God had said]. And when
they were [alone, working] in the field,
Cain attacked Abel his brother and
killed him. [1 John 3:12]
9 Then the LORD said to Cain, "Where
is Abel your brother?" And he [lied
and] said, "I do not know. Am I my
brother's keeper?"
10 The LORD said, "What have you
done? The voice of your brother's [in-

---

you shall return. The word of God was sure: God had stated that they would certainly die (2:17). Now they were served notice concerning the process of aging and decay that was already at work (5:5; 6:3).

3:22 *tree of life.* Adam and Eve apparently had free access to this tree before the fall, and by continuing to eat its fruit they would live forever. The penalty for sin was not instant death, but banishment from this tree and eventual death and decay. One day this tree will be planted anew and its fruit will be for the healing of the nations (Rev 22:2).

4:3 *Cain brought . . . an offering.* Genesis does not explain how the practice of sacrificial worship began, but it is clear that Adam and Eve's two sons understood the custom. Some people assume that Cain's offering was unsuitable because it was not a blood offering, and blood is required for the forgiveness of sins (Heb 9:22). But nothing in this chapter indicates that Cain and Abel were coming to God for forgiveness. Their sacrifices were acts of worship, and as such a bloodless offering was not necessarily inappropriate (see Lev 6:14 – 23). Apparently the deficiency was in Cain's heart, not in the actual offering. Abel's offering was "more excellent" than Cain's because of his faith in the Lord (Heb 11:4).

4:8 *killed him.* The murder was stunning in its lack of precedent, its suddenness, and its finality. Jesus spoke of this ghastly event as a historical fact (Mt 23:35).

23 Ge 4:2; 9:20 **24** Ge 2:8; Ps 104:4; Heb 1:7 **CHAPTER 4** **3** Nu 18:12 **4** Nu 18:17; Lev 3:16; Heb 11:4
5 Ge 31:2 **8** Mt 23:35 **9** Jn 8:44 **10** Heb 12:24; Rev 6:10

nocent] blood is crying out to Me from the ground [for justice]. [Num 35:33; Deut 21:1–9]
11"And now you are cursed from the ground, which has opened its mouth to receive your brother's [shed] blood from your hand. [Deut 28:15–20]
12"When you cultivate the ground, it shall no longer yield its strength [it will resist producing good crops] for you; you shall be a fugitive and a vagabond [roaming aimlessly] on the earth [in perpetual exile without a home, a degraded outcast]."
13Cain said to the LORD, "My punishment is greater than I can bear.
14"Behold, You have driven me out this day from the face of the land; and from Your face (presence) I will be hidden, and I will be a fugitive and an [aimless] vagabond on the earth, and whoever finds me will kill me."
15And the LORD said to him, "Therefore, whoever kills Cain, a sevenfold vengeance [that is, punishment seven times worse] shall be taken on him [by Me]." And the LORD set a [protective] mark (sign) on Cain, so that no one who found (met) him would kill him. [Gen 4:24]
16So Cain went away from the [manifested] presence of the LORD, and lived in the land of Nod [wandering in exile], east of Eden.
17Cain knew his wife [one of Adam's descendants] and she conceived and gave birth to Enoch; and Cain built a city and named it Enoch, after the name of his son.
18Now to Enoch was born Irad, and Irad became the father of Mehujael, and Mehujael became the father of Methushael, and Methushael became the father of Lamech.
19And Lamech took for himself two wives; the name of the one was Adah, and the name of the other, Zillah.
20Adah gave birth to Jabal; he became the father of those [nomadic herdsmen] who live in tents and have cattle *and* raise livestock.
21His brother's name was Jubal; he became the father of all those [musicians] who play the lyre and flute.
22Zillah gave birth to Tubal-cain, the smith (craftsman) *and* teacher of every artisan in instruments of bronze and iron. The sister of Tubal-cain was Naamah.
23Lamech said to his wives,

"Adah and Zillah,
Hear my voice;
You wives of Lamech,
Listen to what I say;
For I have killed a man [merely] for wounding me,
And a boy [only] for striking (bruising) me.
24 "If Cain is avenged sevenfold [as the LORD said he would be],
Then Lamech [will be avenged] seventy-sevenfold."

25Adam knew [Eve as] his wife again;

4:17 *Cain knew his wife.* The identity of Cain's wife has long been a source of puzzlement and argument to the readers and critics of the Book of Genesis. Some have postulated that God created other humans outside of the garden of Eden, but the Scriptures give no such indication, and in fact Adam refers to his wife as "the mother of all the living" (3:20). It makes the most sense to assume that Cain married one of his sisters. While this idea seems repugnant to us today, it must be remembered that Adam and Eve's children had a near perfect gene pool, and there would not have been any genetic complications with close intermarrying. God's strict prohibition against siblings and other close relatives marrying did not come until much later (Lev 18); even Abraham's wife Sarah was his half sister. ***Enoch.*** The fact that Cain named a city after his son indicates the rapid and dramatic increase in population.

4:25 *Seth.* While it is certain that Adam and Eve had other daughters, and possibly other sons as well, the death of righteous Abel and the banishment of their firstborn, Cain, had left them with no one to carry on their line for good and for the promise of the Messiah. Seth is specifically mentioned among Adam and Eve's children because it would be through his descendants that the Messiah would come. His name is related to a Hebrew verb meaning "to place" or "to set" for he was appointed to take this special place in the plan of God.

---

14 Ps 51:11; Ge 9:6; Nu 35:19,21,27 **15** Ps 79:12 **16** 2Ki 13:23; 24:20; Jer 23:39; 52:3 **17** Ps 49:11 **24** ver. 15 **25** Ge 5:3

and she gave birth to a son, and named him Seth, for [she said], "God has granted another child for me in place of Abel, because Cain killed him."

26 To Seth, also, a son was born, whom he named Enosh (mortal man, mankind). At that [same] time men began to call on the name of the LORD [in worship through prayer, praise, and thanksgiving]. [Joel 2:32; Luke 3:38; Acts 2:21]

Descendants of Adam

5 THIS IS the book (the written record, the history) of the generations of [the descendants of] Adam. When God created man, He made him in the likeness of God [not physical, but a spiritual personality and moral likeness].

2 He created them male and female, and blessed them and named them Mankind at the time they were created.

3 When Adam had lived a hundred and thirty years, he became the father of *a son* in his own likeness, according to his image, and named him Seth.

4 After he became the father of Seth, Adam lived eight hundred years and had *other* sons and daughters.

5 So Adam lived nine hundred and thirty years in all, and he died.

6 When Seth was a hundred and five years old, he became the father of Enosh.

7 Seth lived eight hundred and seven years after the birth of Enosh, and he had *other* sons and daughters.

8 So Seth lived nine hundred and twelve years, and he died.

9 When Enosh was ninety years old, he became the father of Kenan.

10 Enosh lived eight hundred and fifteen years after the birth of Kenan and had *other* sons and daughters.

11 So Enosh lived nine hundred and five years, and he died.

12 When Kenan was seventy years old, he became the father of Mahalalel.

13 Kenan lived eight hundred and forty years after the birth of Mahalalel and had *other* sons and daughters.

14 So Kenan lived nine hundred and ten years, and he died.

15 When Mahalalel was sixty-five years old, he became the father of Jared.

16 Mahalalel lived eight hundred and thirty years after the birth of Jared and had *other* sons and daughters.

17 So Mahalalel lived eight hundred and ninety-five years, and he died.

18 When Jared was a hundred and sixty-two years old, he became the father of Enoch.

19 Jared lived eight hundred years after the birth of Enoch and had *other* sons and daughters.

20 So Jared lived nine hundred and sixty-two years, and he died.

21 When Enoch was sixty-five years old, he became the father of Methuselah.

22 Enoch walked [in habitual fellowship] with God three hundred years after the birth of Methuselah and had *other* sons and daughters.

23 So all the days of Enoch were three hundred and sixty-five years.

4:26 *men began to call on the name of the* LORD. These words can hardly mean that only now did people begin to pray to God. Rather, the verb *call* means "to make proclamation." That is, this is the beginning of preaching, of witnessing, and testifying in the name of the Lord (12:8).

5:3 *a hundred and thirty years.* The long lives of the people of the early chapters of Genesis have led to considerable speculation. One suggestion is that these ages were possible because of tremendously different climate and environmental conditions that were in effect before the flood.

5:5 *and he died.* God created humans for eternity; if Adam and Eve had not disobeyed, they would have lived forever. There is a profound sadness in Adam's death, for it reminds us of Adam's mortality — and hence our own.

5:21 – 24 *because God took him.* Only Enoch and Elijah were taken by God without experiencing death (2Ki 2:11). This was both a testimony of Enoch's deep faith in God (Heb 11:5 – 6) and a strong reminder at the beginning of biblical history that for God's people, there is life in God's presence after our physical bodies have died.

26 Ge 5:6; 1Ki 18:24; Ps 116:17; 1Co 1:2 **CHAPTER 5** **1** Ge 1:26; Eph 4:24; Col 3:10 **2** Ge 1:27 **3** Ge 4:25 **4** 1Ch 1:1; Ge 1:28 **5** Ge 3:19; Heb 9:27 **6** Ge 4:26 **18** Jude 14,15 **22** Ge 6:9; 17:1; 2Ki 20:3; Ps 16:8; Mic 6:8; Mal 2:6

[24]And [in reverent fear and obedi-
ence] Enoch walked with God; and he
was not [found among men], because
God took him [away to be home with
Him]. [Heb 11:5]
[25]When Methuselah was a hundred
and eighty-seven years old, he became
the father of Lamech.
[26]Methuselah lived seven hundred
and eighty-two years after the birth
of Lamech and had *other* sons and
daughters.
[27]So Methuselah lived nine hundred
and sixty-nine years, and he died.
[28]When Lamech was a hundred and
eighty-two years old, he became the
father of a son.
[29]He named him Noah, saying, "This
one shall bring us rest *and* comfort
from our work and from the [dreadful]
toil of our hands because of the ground
which the LORD cursed."
[30]Lamech lived five hundred and
ninety-five years after the birth of Noah
and had *other* sons and daughters.
[31]So all the days of Lamech were sev-
en hundred and seventy-seven years,
and he died.
[32]After Noah was five hundred years
old, he became the father of Shem,
Ham, and Japheth.

The Corruption of Mankind

6 NOW IT happened, when men be-
gan to multiply on the face of the
land, and daughters were born to them,
[2]that the sons of God saw that the
daughters of men were beautiful *and*
desirable; and they took wives for
themselves, whomever they chose *and*
desired.
[3]Then the LORD said, "My Spirit shall
not strive *and* remain with man forev-
er, because he is indeed flesh [sinful,
corrupt—given over to sensual appe-
tites]; nevertheless his days shall yet be
a hundred and twenty years."
[4]There were Nephilim (men of stat-
ure, notorious men) on the earth in
those days—and also afterward—
when the sons of God lived with the
daughters of men, and they gave
birth to their *children.* These were
the mighty men who were of old, men
of renown (great reputation, fame).
[Num 13:33]
[5]The LORD saw that the wickedness
(depravity) of man was great on the
earth, and that every imagination *or*
intent of the thoughts of his heart were
only evil continually.
[6]The LORD regretted that He had
made mankind on the earth, and He
was [deeply] grieved in His heart.
[7]So the LORD said, "I will destroy
(annihilate) mankind whom I have
created from the surface of the earth—
not only man, but the animals and the
crawling things and the birds of the
air—because it [deeply] grieves Me [to
see mankind's sin] *and* I regret that I
have made them."
[8]But Noah found favor *and* grace in
the eyes of the LORD.

6:2 *sons of God . . . daughters of men.* This passage is very difficult to interpret. Some believe that the "sons of God" were the men of the righteous line of Seth, while the "daughters of men" were Cain's offspring. This does not account for the fact that their offspring were giants, men of extraordinary size and talents; it is also problematic in that it assumes that Cain's descendants were universally more sinful than Seth's descendants. Since Noah was the only descendant of Seth who was considered righteous, this is obviously not accurate. A second view is that the "sons of God" were angelic beings. The phrase "sons of God" is used elsewhere in Scripture to refer to angelic beings (Job 1:6), but it seems impossible since angels in heaven do not marry (Mt 22:30). It may be, however, that these "sons of God" were some of the rebellious angels who had joined Satan (Jude 6; 2Pe 2:4); they took on human form (as Satan was apparently able to take on the form of a snake), and out of perverted lust, seduced human women. The problem with this theory is that verse 4 says that these unions produced children. Nothing in the rest of Scripture would indicate that angels reproduce, or that a spirit being could mate with a human being. Nor is there any reference to half-man/half-spirit beings. Whichever view one settles on, it is clear that what happened here was corrupt and one of the reasons for the flood.

24 2Ki 2:11; Heb 11:5 **29** Ge 3:17 **32** Ge 6:10; Ge 10:21 **CHAPTER 6** **1** Ge 1:28 **2** Dt 7:3 **3** Gal 5:16; 1Pe 3:19; Ps 78:39 **5** Ge 8:21 **6** 1Sa 15:11,29; 2Sa 24:16; Mal 3:6; Jas 1:17; Isa 63:10 **8** Ge 19:19; Ex 33:12; Lk 1:30; Ac 7:46

9 These are *the records of* the gen-
erations (family history) of Noah.
Noah was a righteous man [one who
was just and had right standing with
God], blameless in his [evil] genera-
tion; Noah walked (lived) [in habitual
fellowship] with God.
10 Now Noah became the father of
three sons: Shem, Ham, and Japheth.
11 The [population of the] earth
was corrupt [absolutely depraved—
spiritually and morally putrid] in God's
sight, and the land was filled with vio-
lence [desecration, infringement, out-
rage, assault, and lust for power].
12 God looked on the earth and saw
how debased *and* degenerate it was,
for all humanity had corrupted their
way on the earth *and* lost their true
direction.
13 God said to Noah, "I intend to make
an end of all that lives, for through
men the land is filled with violence;
and behold, I am about to destroy them
together with the land.
14 "Make yourself an ark of gopher
wood; make in it rooms (stalls, pens,
coops, nests, cages, compartments)
and coat it inside and out with pitch
(bitumen).
15 "This is the way you are to make
it: the length of the ark shall be three
hundred cubits, its width fifty cubits,
and its height thirty cubits (450' x 75'
x 45').
16 "You shall make a window [for
light and ventilation] for the ark, and
finish it to at least a cubit (eighteen
inches) from the top—and set the [en-
try] door of the ark in its side; and you
shall make it with lower, second and
third decks.
17 "For behold, I, even I, will bring a
flood of waters on the earth, to destroy
all life under the heavens in which
there is the breath *and* spirit of life;
everything that is on the land shall die.
18 "But I will establish My covenant
(solemn promise, formal agreement)
with you; and you shall come into the
ark—you and your [three] sons and
your wife, and your sons' wives with
you.
19 "And of every living thing [found
on land], you shall bring two of every
kind into the ark, to keep them alive
with you; they shall be male and fe-
male.
20 "Of fowls *and* birds according to
their kind, of animals according to
their kind, of every crawling thing of
the ground according to its kind—two
of every kind shall come to you to keep
them alive.

6:11 – 13 Disobedience—In the beginning, God pronounced His creative work good. But with the entrance of sin and decadence on the scene, the world became corrupt in His sight. It was not merely that some individuals or groups had corrupted their ways, but a matter of pervasive perversity. Because sin is repugnant to His holiness, God declared His purpose of destroying both mankind and the earth he had polluted. Defying God's will affects our environment as well as ourselves. Judgment for disobedience is only averted through repentance and fresh submission to God.

6:11 *corrupt*. The verb translated *corrupt* has the idea of being ruined, spoiled, or destroyed. Sinful people were bringing ruin to the world that belonged to the living God (Ps 24:1).

6:14 *ark*. The word *ark* simply means "box," the same word is used for the box in which the baby Moses was placed in the Nile (Ex 2:3), and for the gold-covered chest which contained the stone tablets of the Covenant (Ex 25:10). We usually picture Noah's ark as a huge ship, with curved bow and stern, but it was very likely more like a large box. It was not designed for navigation, but simply to stay safely afloat.

6:15 *cubits*. A cubit was supposed to be the measurement of a man's forearm, from the tip of the bent elbow to the fingertips. This is naturally a somewhat imprecise measurement, but it is generally considered to equal about 18 inches. Hence the ark was about 450 feet long, 75 feet wide, and 45 feet high.

6:17 *I, even I*. The Hebrew text places significant emphasis on the personal role of God in the ensuing storm.

6:18 – 19 *covenant*. This is the first time the word *covenant* is used in the Bible. The details of this covenant were given after the flood (9:9). Here, in the midst of judgment, the Lord stooped down to meet the needs of His servant (Ps 40:1; 113:6) and to enter into a binding oath with him.

9 Ge 7:1; Eze 14:14,20; Heb 11:7; 2Pe 2:5; Ge 5:22 **10** Ge 5:32 **11** Ro 2:13; Eze 8:17 **12** Ps 14:2; 53:2,3 **13** Jer 51:13; 1Pe 4:7; ver. 17 **17** Ge 7:4,21-23; 2Pe 2:5 **18** Ge 7:1,7,13; 1Pe 3:20; 2Pe 2:5 **19** Ge 7:8,9,15,16 **20** Ge 7:9,15

21 “Also take with you every kind of food that is edible, and you shall collect *and* store it; and it shall be food for you and for them.”

22 So Noah did this; according to all that God commanded him, that is what he did.

The Flood

7 THEN THE LORD said to Noah, “Come into the ark, you with all your household, for you [alone] I have seen as righteous (doing what is right) before Me in this generation. [Ps 27:5; 33:18, 19; 2 Pet 2:9]

2 “Of every clean animal you shall take with you seven pair, the male and his female, and of animals that are not clean, two each the male and his female; [Lev 11:1–13]

3 also of the birds of the air, seven pair, the male and the female, to keep the offspring alive on the surface of the earth.

4 “For in seven days I am going to cause it to rain on the earth for forty days and forty nights; and I will destroy (blot out, wipe away) every living thing that I have made from the surface of the earth.”

5 So Noah did all that the LORD commanded him. [Heb 11:7]

6 Noah was six hundred years old when the flood (deluge) of water came on the earth [covering all of the land].

7 Then Noah and his sons and his wife and his sons’ wives with him entered the ark to escape the flood waters. [Matt 24:38; Luke 17:27]

8 Of clean animals and animals that are not clean and birds *and* fowls and everything that crawls on the ground,

9 they came [motivated by God] into the ark with Noah two by two, the male and the female, just as God had commanded Noah.

10 And after the seven days [God released the rain and] the floodwaters came on the earth.

11 In the six hundredth year of Noah’s life, on the seventeenth day of the second month, on that same day all the fountains of the great deep [subterranean waters] burst open, and the windows *and* floodgates of the heavens were opened.

12 It rained on the earth for forty days and forty nights.

13 On the very same day Noah and Shem and Ham and Japheth, the sons of Noah, and Noah’s wife and the three wives of his sons with them, entered the ark,

14 they and every animal according to its kind, all the livestock according to their kinds, every moving thing that crawls on the earth according to its kind, and every bird according to its kind, every winged thing of every sort.

15 So they went into the ark with Noah, two by two of all living beings in which there was the breath *and* spirit of life.

16 Those which entered, male and female of all flesh (creatures), entered as God had commanded Noah; and the LORD closed *the door* behind him.

17 The flood [the great downpour of

7:9 they came [motivated by God] into the ark with Noah. The gathering and cooperation of the animals must have been arranged by God. It appears that after Noah and his wife and sons entered the ark, the animals followed of their own accord.

7:11 fountains of the great deep ... windows and floodgates of the heavens. Until this time, no rain had fallen on the earth, but it was watered by a mist (2:5 – 6). This description of the first rain portrays a thundering, catastrophic event, accompanied by violent upheaval of the earth’s crust and geysers of water bursting from the depths. The violence and the amount of water involved are more than enough to account for many peculiarities of the earth’s surface, such as the formation of the Grand Canyon. The flood also explains the enormous quantity of fossilized remains of plants, animals, and shellfish that are buried in layers of rock over the entire surface of the earth and even on the tops of mountains.

7:16 closed the door behind him. The Lord who had drawn them now closed the door on them. That shut door was a symbol of closure, safety, and God’s deliverance.

22 Heb 11:7; See Ex 40:16; Ge 7:5,9,16 **CHAPTER 7** **1** Mt 24:38; Lk 17:26; Heb 11:7; 1Pe 3:20; 2Pe 2:5; Ge 6:9; Ps 33:18; Pr 10:9; 2Pe 2:9 **2** Lev Ge 11; Lev 10:10; Eze 44:23 **4** ver. 12,17 **5** Ge 6:22 **7** ver. 1 **11** Ge 8:2; Pr 8:28; Eze 26:19; Ge 8:2; Ps 78:23 **12** ver. 4,17 **14** Ge 6:19 **15** Ge 6:20 **16** ver. 2,3 **17** ver. 4,12 rain] was forty days *and* nights on the earth; and the waters increased and lifted up the ark, and it floated [high] above the land.

18 The waters became mighty and increased greatly on the earth, and the ark floated on the surface of the waters.

19 The waters prevailed so greatly *and* were so mighty *and* overwhelming on the earth, so that all the high mountains everywhere under the heavens were covered.

20 [In fact] the waters became fifteen cubits higher [than the highest ground], and the mountains were covered.

21 All living beings that moved on the earth perished—birds and cattle (domestic animals), [wild] animals, all things that swarm *and* crawl on the earth, and all mankind.

22 Everything on the dry land, all in whose nostrils was the breath *and* spirit of life, died.

23 God destroyed (blotted out, wiped away) every living thing that was on the surface of the earth; man and animals and the crawling things and the birds of the heavens were destroyed from the land. Only Noah and those who were with him in the ark remained alive. [Matt 24:37–44]

24 The waters covered [all of] the earth for a hundred and fifty days (five months).

The Flood Abates

8 AND GOD remembered *and* thought kindly of Noah and every living thing and all the animals that were with him in the ark; and God made a wind blow over the land, and the waters receded.

2 Also the fountains of the deep [subterranean waters] and the windows of the heavens were closed, the [pouring] rain from the sky was restrained,

3 and the waters receded steadily from the earth. At the end of a hundred and fifty days the waters had diminished.

4 On the seventeenth day of the seventh month [five months after the rain began], the ark came to rest on the mountains of Ararat [in Turkey].

5 The waters continued to decrease until the tenth month; on the first day of the tenth month the tops of the mountains were seen.

6 At the end of [another] forty days Noah opened the window of the ark which he had made;

7 and he sent out a raven, which flew here and there until the waters were dried up from the earth.

8 Then Noah sent out a dove to see if the water level had fallen below the surface of the land.

9 But the dove found no place on which to rest the sole of her foot, and she returned to him to the ark, for the waters were [still] on the face of the entire earth. So he reached out his hand and took the dove, and brought her into the ark.

10 He waited another seven days and again sent the dove out from the ark.

11 The dove came back to him in the evening, and there, in her beak, was a fresh olive leaf. So Noah knew that the water level had subsided from the earth.

12 Then he waited another seven days and sent out the dove, but she did not return to him again.

13 Now in the six hundred and first year [of Noah's life], on the first day of the first month, the waters were drying up from the earth. Then Noah removed the covering of the ark and looked, and the surface of the ground was drying.

7:19 *the high mountains everywhere under the heavens were covered.* This explicit declaration, accompanied by the assertion in verse 21 that every living thing died, makes it clear that this was no localized event, but in actuality a worldwide catastrophic flood (see 8:5). Jesus affirmed the historicity of the "days of Noah" when he compared them to the end days (Mt 24:37 – 38; Lk 17:26 – 27). Peter similarly used the story of Noah and the flood as a pattern for the final judgment (1Pe 3:20; 2Pe 2:5; 3:5 – 6).

18 Ps 104:26 **21** Ge 6:13,17 **22** Ge 2:7 **23** 1Pe 3:20; 2Pe 2:5 **24** Ge 8:3; 8:4; compared with ver. 11 of this chapter
CHAPTER 8 **1** Ge 19:29; Ex 2:24; 1Sa 1:19; Ps 106:4; Ex 14:21 **2** Ge 7:11; Job 38:37 **3** Ge 7:24 **6** Ge 6:16

14 On the twenty-seventh day of the second month the land was [entirely] dry.

15 And God spoke to Noah, saying,

16 "Go out of the ark, you and your wife and your sons and their wives with you.

17 "Bring out with you every living thing from all flesh—birds and animals and every crawling thing that crawls on the earth—that they may breed abundantly on the earth, and be fruitful and multiply on the earth."

18 So Noah went out, and his wife and his sons and their wives with him [after being in the ark one year and ten days].

19 Every animal, every crawling thing, every bird—and whatever moves on the land—went out by families (types, groupings) from the ark.

20 And Noah built an altar to the LORD, and took of every [ceremonially] clean animal and of every clean bird and offered burnt offerings on the altar.

21 The LORD smelled the pleasing aroma [a soothing, satisfying scent] and the LORD said to Himself, "I will never again curse the ground because of man, for the intent (strong inclination, desire) of man's heart is wicked from his youth; and I will never again destroy every living thing, as I have done.

22 "While the earth remains,
Seedtime and harvest,
Cold and heat,
Winter and summer,
And day and night
Shall not cease."

Covenant of the Rainbow

9 AND GOD blessed Noah and his sons and said to them, "Be fruitful and multiply, and fill the earth.

2 "The fear and the terror of you shall be [instinctive] in every animal of the land and in every bird of the air; and together with everything that moves on the ground, and with all the fish of the sea; they are given into your hand.

3 "Every moving thing that lives shall be food for you; I give you everything, as *I gave* you the green plants *and* vegetables.

4 "But you shall not eat meat along with its life, *that is,* its blood. [Lev 7:26; Acts 15:20; 21:25]

5 "For your lifeblood I will most certainly require an accounting; from every

---

8:14 *the land was [entirely] dry.* After more than a full year, the waters had returned to their place (7:11). As in the beginning, God brought the waters of earth into their place (1:9 – 13). The flood began in Noah's 600th year, in the 2nd month, on day 17 (7:11) and ended in Noah's 601st year, in the 2nd month, on day 27 (8:14).

8:20 *an altar.* This is the first mention of sacrificial worship since the days of Cain and Abel (4:3 – 5); yet we may assume that the principle of sacrificial worship was perpetuated through the line of faithful people (ch. 5).

8:22 *While the earth remains.* The words of this verse are a poem of powerful effect. These words might easily have become a song of faith, the response of the people of God to the promise He made (v. 21). Later in Israel's history, the prophets recalled God's great promise to Noah (Isa 54:9 – 10).

9:1 – 19 God's Promise to Noah — Only when we think of God as Creator, as well as Redeemer, can we begin to understand His covenant of redemption as being related to the covenant of creation (Ge 1:26 – 30; 2:15 – 17). God doesn't abandon His creation. On the contrary, though evil has corrupted it, He graciously (for it is undeserved) establishes a covenantal relationship with Noah's descendants as well as with every beast of the earth. This note of universality is given further expression by Hosea (2:18) and Jonah (4:11). When Paul encourages Roman believers about struggles in this life, he reminds them that they are not alone, but assures them that the whole creation also groans and suffers, eagerly anticipating that final redemption from the curse of sin. The promise given here is to never destroy the earth again by flood (v. 11). The rainbow is then a testimony of the existence of this promise.

9:4 *blood.* This restriction gets more attention in Leviticus (see Lev 17:11 – 12). Blood represents the animal's life. It may be used in sacrifice, for all life belongs to the Lord.

---

16 Ge 7:13 **17** Ge 1:22 **20** Lev Ge 11 **21** Lev 1:9; Eze 20:41; 2Co 2:15; Eph 5:2; Ge 3:17; 6:17; Ge 6:5; Job 14:4; Jer 17:9; Ge 9:11,15 **22** Isa 54:9; Jer 33:20,25 **CHAPTER 9** **1** ver. 7,19; Ge 1:28; 10:32 **2** Ge 1:28; Hos 2:18 **3** Dt 12:15; 14:3,9,11; Ac 10:12,13; Ge 1:29; Ro 14:14,20; 1Co 10:23,26; Col 2:16; 1Ti 4:3,4 **4** Lev 17:10,11,14; Dt 12:23; 1Sa 14:33 **5** Ex 21:28; Ge 4:9,10; Ps 9:12; Ac 17:26

MAJOR COVENANTS IN THE OLD TESTAMENT

COVENANTS	REFERENCE	TYPE	PARTICIPANT	DESCRIPTION
NOAHIC	Ge 9:8–17	Royal Grant	Made with righteous (6:9) Noah (and his descendants and every living thing on earth—all life that is subject to human jurisdiction)	An unconditional divine promise never to destroy all earthly life with some natural catastrophe, the covenant "sign" (9:13,17) being the rainbow in the storm cloud
ABRAHAMIC A	Ge 15:9–21	Royal (land) Grant	Made with "righteous" (his faith was "credited . . . to him as righteousness," v. 6) Abram (and his descendants, v. 16)	An unconditional divine promise to fulfill the grant of the land; a self-maledictory oath symbolically enacted it (v. 17; see note there)
ABRAHAMIC B	Ge 17	Suzerain-vassal	Made with Abraham as patriarchal head of his household	A conditional divine pledge to be Abraham's God and the God of his descendants (cf. "as for me," v. 4; "as for you," v. 9); the condition: total consecration to the Lord as symbolized by circumcision
SINAITIC	Ex 19–24	Suzerain-vassal	Made with Israel as the descendants of Abraham, Isaac and Jacob and as the people the Lord had redeemed from bondage to an earthly power	A conditional divine pledge to be Israel's God (as her protector and the guarantor of her blessed destiny); the condition: Israel's total consecration to the Lord as his people (his kingdom) who live by his rule and serve his purposes in history
PHINEHAS	Nu 25:10–13	Royal Grant	Made with the zealous priest Phinehas	An unconditional divine promise to maintain the family of Phinehas in a "lasting priesthood" (v. 13; implicitly a pledge to Israel to provide her forever with a faithful priesthood)
DAVIDIC	2Sa 7:5–16	Royal Grant	Made with faithful King David after his devotion to God as Israel's king and the Lord's anointed vassal had come to special expression (v. 2)	An unconditional divine promise to establish and maintain the Davidic dynasty on the throne of Israel (implicitly a pledge to Israel) to provide her forever with a godly king like David and through that dynasty to do for her what he had done through David—bring her into rest in the promised land (1Ki 4:20–21; 5:3–4)
NEW	Jer 31:31–34	Royal Grant	Promised to rebellious Israel as she is about to be expelled from the promised land in actualization of the most severe covenant curse (Lev 26:27–39; Dt 28:36–37, 45–68)	An unconditional divine promise to unfaithful Israel to forgive her sins and establish his relationship with her on a new basis by writing his law "on their hearts" (v. 33)—a covenant of pure grace

MAJOR TYPES OF ROYAL COVENANTS/TREATIES IN THE ANCIENT NEAR EAST

ROYAL GRANT (UNCONDITIONAL)	PARITY	SUZERAIN-VASSAL (CONDITIONAL)
A king's grant (of land or some other benefit) to a loyal servant for faithful or exceptional service. The grant was normally perpetual and unconditional, but the servant's heirs benefited from it only as they continued their father's loyalty and service. (Cf. 1Sa 8:14; 22:7; 27:6; Est 8:1.)	A covenant between equals, binding them to mutual friendship or at least to mutual respect for each other's spheres and interests. Participants called each other "brother." (Cf. Ge 21:27; 26:31; 31:44–54; 1Ki 5:12; 15:19; 20:32–34; Am 1:9.)	A covenant regulating the relationship between a great king and one of his subject kings. The great king claimed absolute right of sovereignty, demanded total loyalty and service (the vassal must "love" his suzerain) and pledged protection of the subject's realm and dynasty, conditional on the vassal's faithfulness and loyalty to him. The vassal pledged absolute loyalty to his suzerain—whatever service his suzerain demanded—and exclusive reliance on the suzerain's protection. Participants called each other "lord" and "servant" or "father" and "son." (Cf. Jos 9:6,8; Eze 17:13–18; Hos 12:1.)

Commitments made in these covenants were accompanied by self-maledictory oaths (made orally, ceremonially or both). The gods were called on to witness the covenants and implement the curses of the oaths if the covenants were violated.

animal [that kills a person] I will require it. And from man, from every man's brother [that is, anyone who murders] I will require the life of man. [Ex 21:28, 29]

6 "Whoever sheds man's blood
[unlawfully],
By man (judicial government)
shall his blood be shed,
For in the image of God
He made man. [Rom 13:4]
7 "As for you, be fruitful and
multiply;
Populate the earth abundantly and
multiply in it."

8 Then God spoke to Noah and to his
sons with him, saying,
9 "Now behold, I am establishing My
covenant (binding agreement, solemn
promise) with you and with your de-
scendants after you
10 and with every living creature that
is with you—the birds, the livestock, and
the wild animals of the earth along with
you, of everything that comes out of the
ark—every living creature of the earth.
11 "I will establish My covenant with
you: Never again shall all flesh be cut
off by the water of a flood, nor shall
there ever again be a flood to destroy
and ruin the earth."
12 And God said, "This is the token
(visible symbol, memorial) of the [sol-
emn] covenant which I am making
between Me and you and every living
creature that is with you, for all future
generations;
13 I set My rainbow in the clouds, and
it shall be a sign of a covenant between
Me and the earth.
14 "It shall come about, when I bring
clouds over the earth, that the rainbow
shall be seen in the clouds,
15 and I will [compassionately] remem-
ber My covenant, which is between Me
and you and every living creature of all
flesh; and never again will the water
become a flood to destroy all flesh.
16 "When the rainbow is in the clouds
and I look at it, I will [solemnly] re-
member the everlasting covenant be-
tween God and every living creature
of all flesh that is on the earth."
17 And God said to Noah, "This [rain-
bow] is the sign of the covenant (sol-
emn pledge, binding agreement) which
I have established between Me and all
living things on the earth."
18 The sons of Noah who came out
of the ark were Shem and Ham and
Japheth. Ham would become the father
of Canaan.
19 These are the three sons of Noah,
and from these [men] the whole earth
was populated *and* scattered with in-
habitants.
20 And Noah began to farm *and* cul-
tivate the ground and he planted a
vineyard.
21 He drank some of the wine and
became drunk, and he was uncovered
and lay exposed inside his tent.
22 Ham, the father of Canaan, saw [by
accident] the nakedness of his father,
and [to his father's shame] told his two
brothers outside.
23 So Shem and Japheth took a robe
and put it on both their shoulders, and
walked backwards and covered the
nakedness of their father; their faces
were turned away so that they did not
see their father's nakedness.
24 When Noah awoke from his wine
[induced stupor], he knew what his
younger son [Ham] had done to him.
25 So he said,

"Cursed be Canaan [the son of
Ham];
A servant of servants
He shall be to his brothers."
[Deut 27:16]

9:6 *image of God.* Sin did not destroy man as the image of God. God values human life more highly than animal life because only humankind possesses God's image.

9:9 *covenant.* This is the second occurrence in Genesis of the important concept of covenant (6:18). God promised that He would establish His covenant with Noah and here He accomplished this great work.

6 Ex 21:12,14; Lev 24:17; Mt 26:52; Ge 1:27 **7** ver. 1,19 **9** Ge 6:18; Isa 54:9 **10** Ps 145:9 **11** Isa 54:9 **12** Ge 17:11 **13** Rev 4:3 **15** Lev 26:42,45 **16** Ge 17:13,19; Isa 55:3; Jer 32:40; Heb 13:20 **18** Ge 10:6 **19** Ge 5:32; Ge 10:32; 1Ch 1:4 **20** Ge 3:19,23; 4:2; Pr 12:11 **21** Pr 20:1; 1Co 10:12 **23** Ex 20:12; Gal 6:1 **25** Dt 27:16; Jos 9:23,27; Jos 9:23; 1Ki 9:20,21

[26]He also said,

"Blessed be the LORD,
The God of Shem;
And let Canaan be his servant.
[27]"May God enlarge [the land of] Japheth,
And let him dwell in the tents of Shem;
And let Canaan be his servant."

[28]Noah lived three hundred and fifty years after the flood.
[29]So all the days of Noah were nine hundred and fifty years, and he died.

Descendants of Noah

10 THESE ARE *the records of* the generations (descendants) of Shem, Ham, and Japheth, the sons of Noah; and the sons born to them after the flood:
[2]the sons of Japheth: Gomer, Magog, Madai, Javan, Tubal, Meshech, and Tiras;
[3]the sons of Gomer: Ashkenaz, Riphath, and Togarmah;
[4]the sons of Javan: Elishah, Tarshish, Kittim, and Dodanim.
[5]From these, [the people of] the coastlands of the nations were separated *and* spread into their lands, every one according to his own language, according to their constituent groups (families), *and* into their nations:
[6]the sons of Ham: Cush, Mizraim [from whom descended the Egyptians], Put, and Canaan;
[7]the sons of Cush: Seba, Havilah, Sabtah, Raamah, and Sabteca; and the sons of Raamah; Sheba and Dedan.
[8]Cush became the father of Nimrod; he became a mighty one on the earth.
[9]He was a mighty hunter before the LORD; therefore it is said, "Like Nimrod a mighty hunter before the LORD."
[10]The beginning of his kingdom was Babel and Erech and Accad and Calneh, in the land of Shinar [in Babylonia].
[11]From that land Nimrod went to Assyria, and built Nineveh, and Rehoboth-Ir, and Calah,
[12]and [Nimrod built] Resen, which is between Nineveh and Calah; all these [combined to form] the great city [Nineveh]. [Jon 1:2; 3:2]
[13]Mizraim [the ancestor of the Egyptians] became the father of Ludim, Anamim, Lehabim, Naphtuhim
[14]and Pathrusim and Casluhim—from whom came the Philistines—and Caphtorim.
[15]Canaan became the father of Sidon, his firstborn, and Heth
[16]and the Jebusite and the Amorite and the Girgashite
[17]and the Hivite and the Arkite and the Sinite
[18]and the Arvadite and the Zemarite and the Hamathite. Afterward the families of the Canaanite were spread abroad.
[19]The territory of the Canaanite extended from Sidon as one goes to Gerar, as far as Gaza; and as one goes to Sodom and Gomorrah and Admah and Zeboiim, as far as Lasha.

9:26–27 *Shem.* Shem was given precedence over his brothers. Eber and Abram were descended from Shem (11:10–30), so Shem's blessing is ultimately a blessing on Israel.
9:29 *and he died.* Noah's death was the end of an era. Only he and his family spanned two worlds, that of the earth before and after the flood. His long life (950 years) gave him opportunity to transmit to his many descendants the dramatic story that he had lived out with his family. Peoples in places and cultures the world over have memories and stories of a great flood in antiquity. The details differ, but the stories remain.
10:2 *the sons of Japheth.* The listing of Japheth's descendants is briefer than the others. Among the persons and peoples mentioned is Javan, an ancient name for the Greek people. It is thought that many of Japheth's descendants migrated to Europe.
10:6 *the sons of Ham.* Cush is the ancient name for Ethiopia; Mizraim is a name for Egypt.
10:7–11 *Nimrod.* Like Lamech the descendant of Cain, Nimrod's infamy was proverbial. His territory was in the lands of the east, the fabled ancient cities of Mesopotamia. The prophet Micah would later use the name Nimrod to describe the region of Assyria, which would come under God's judgment (Mic 5:5–6).

26 Ps 144:15; Heb 11:16 **27** Eph 2:13,14; 3:6 **CHAPTER 10** **1** Ge 9:1,7,19 **2** 1Ch 1:5 **5** Ps 72:10; Jer 2:10; 25:22 **6** 1Ch 1:8 **9** Jer 16:16; Mic 7:2; Ge 6:11 **10** Mic 5:6 **14** 1Ch 1:12 **19** Ge 13:12, 14,15,17; 15:18-21

20 These are the descendants of Ham
according to their constituent groups,
according to their languages, by their
lands, and by their nations.
21 Also to Shem, the father of all the
children of Eber [including the He-
brews], the older brother of Japheth,
children were born.
22 The sons of Shem: Elam, Asshur,
Arpachshad, Lud and Aram;
23 the sons of Aram [ancestor of the
Syrians]: Uz, Hul, Gether and Mash.
24 Arpachshad became the father of
Shelah; and Shelah became the father
of Eber.
25 Two sons were born to Eber; the
name of one was Peleg (division), for
[the inhabitants of] the earth were di-
vided in his days; and his brother's
name was Joktan.
26 Joktan became the father of Almo-
dad, Sheleph, Hazarmaveth, Jerah,
27 and Hadoram, Uzal, Diklah,
28 and Obal, Abimael, Sheba,
29 and Ophir, Havilah, and Jobab; all
these were the sons of Joktan.
30 Now their territory extended from
Mesha as one goes toward Sephar, to
the hill country of the east.
31 These are Shem's descendants ac-
cording to their constituent groups
(families), according to their languag-
es, by their lands, according to their
nations.
32 These are the families of the sons
of Noah, according to their descen-
dants, by their nations; and from these
[people] the nations were separated
and spread abroad on the earth after
the flood. [Acts 17:26]

Universal Language, Babel, Confusion

11 NOW THE whole earth spoke
one language and used the same
words (vocabulary).
2 And as people journeyed eastward,
they found a plain in the land of Shinar
and they settled there. [Gen 10:10]
3 They said one to another, "Come,
let us make bricks and fire them
thoroughly [in a kiln, to harden and
strengthen them]." So they used brick
for stone [as building material], and
they used tar (bitumen, asphalt) for
mortar.
4 They said, "Come, let us build a city
for ourselves, and a tower whose top
will reach into the heavens, and let us
make a [famous] name for ourselves,
so that we will not be scattered [into
separate groups] *and* be dispersed over
the surface of the entire earth [as the
LORD instructed]." [Gen 9:1]
5 Now the LORD came down to see
the city and the tower which the sons
of men had built.
6 And the LORD said, "Behold, they
are one [unified] people, and they all
have the same language. This is only
the beginning of what they will do [in
rebellion against Me], and now no evil
thing they imagine they can do will be
impossible for them.
7 "Come, let Us (Father, Son, Holy
Spirit) go down and there confuse *and*

10:21–24 *Eber.* This is the name that gives rise to the term *Hebrew*, which is first used of Abram in 14:13. Eber descended from Shem, the one of Noah's sons who was appointed to carry on the messianic line. Abram was a direct descendant of Eber.

10:32 *the families of the sons of Noah.* Although not every ancient people group is listed in this "Table of the Nations," its clear teaching is that all the varied peoples of the earth, no matter of what land or language, are descended from Noah.

11:2 *the land of Shinar.* This is the region of ancient Babylon in Mesopotamia (10:10), part of modern Iraq.

11:4 Pride—God divided the human race into different language groups because they had refused to obey His command to fill the earth, and had become united for an evil purpose. This does not mean that God wants the world to remain divided. Christ came to reconcile the world to God (2Co 5:19), and when we are in Christ we are not only reconciled to God, but to one another (Eph 2:11–19). The unity God destroyed by judgment at Babel was restored by grace on the day of Pentecost. On that day people from different nations came together to hear the gospel in their own languages.

11:7 *let Us (Father, Son, Holy Spirit) go down.* The plural "Us" in this passage is similar

---

22 1Ch 1:17 **24** Ge 11:12 **25** 1Ch 1:19 **32** ver. 1; Ge 9:19 **CHAPTER 11 4** Dt 1:28 **5** Ge 18:21 **6** Ge 9:19; Ac 17:26; ver. 1; Ps 2:1 **7** Ge 1:26; Ge 42:23; 1Co 14:2,11

mix up their language, so that they will
not understand one another's speech."
8 So the LORD scattered them abroad
from there over the surface of the en-
tire earth; and they stopped building
the city.
9 Therefore the name of the city was
Babel—because there the LORD con-
fused the language of the entire earth;
and from that place the LORD scattered
and dispersed them over the surface of
all the earth.

Descendants of Shem

10 These are *the records of* the gen-
erations of Shem [from whom Abra-
ham descended]. Shem was a hundred
years old when he became the father of
Arpachshad, two years after the flood.
11 And Shem lived five hundred years
after Arpachshad was born, and he
had *other* sons and daughters.
12 When Arpachshad had lived
thirty-five years, he became the father
of Shelah.
13 Arpachshad lived four hundred
and three years after Shelah was born,
and he had *other* sons and daughters.
14 When Shelah had lived thirty
years, he became the father of Eber.
15 Shelah lived four hundred and
three years after Eber was born, and
he had *other* sons and daughters.
16 When Eber had lived thirty-four
years, he became the father of Peleg.
17 And Eber lived four hundred and
thirty years after Peleg was born, and
he had *other* sons and daughters.
18 When Peleg had lived thirty years,
he became the father of Reu.
19 And Peleg lived two hundred and
nine years after Reu was born, and he
had *other* sons and daughters.
20 When Reu had lived thirty-two
years, he became the father of Serug.
21 And Reu lived two hundred and
seven years after Serug was born, and
he had *other* sons and daughters.
22 When Serug had lived thirty years,
he became the father of Nahor.
23 And Serug lived two hundred
years after Nahor was born, and he
had *other* sons and daughters.
24 When Nahor had lived twenty-nine
years, he became the father of Terah.
25 And Nahor lived a hundred and
nineteen years after Terah was born,
and he had *other* sons and daughters.
26 After Terah had lived seventy
years, he became the father of Abram
and Nahor and Haran [his firstborn].
27 Now these are *the records of* the
descendants of Terah. Terah was the
father of Abram (Abraham), Nahor,
and Haran; and Haran was the father
of Lot.
28 Haran died before his father Terah
in the land of his birth, in Ur of the
Chaldeans.
29 Abram and Nahor took wives for
themselves. The name of Abram's wife
was Sarai (later called Sarah), and

---

to the language of 1:26 – 28. The plural pronoun emphasizes the majesty of the speaker.

11:9 ***Babel.*** There is a pun in this name that no Hebrew reader would miss. The verb for *confuse* sounds similar to the name of the city. ***confused . . . scattered.*** Because of their pride and arrogance, God scattered the peoples of the earth and confused their language, but one day peoples of all languages and cultures will unite to celebrate the grace of God's risen Son, lifting their voices together in praise of the Lamb (Rev 5:8 – 14).

11:10 – 25 ***the generations.*** This genealogy shows that Abram was a descendant of Noah through Shem, just as Noah was a descendant of Adam through Seth. It is interesting to note that while the people mentioned in this genealogy lived to be very old, they did not reach the great ages of the peoples before the flood. Instead, their lives appear to be growing progressively shorter.

11:28 ***Ur of the Chaldeans.*** For generations, scholars have believed this to be the famous Ur located near the ancient delta in the Persian Gulf where the Tigris and Euphrates Rivers flow together. More recently, some scholars have noted the tablets at Ebla that speak of an Ur in the region of north Syria and suggest that this is the city of Haran's death.

11:29 ***Sarai.*** The name Sarai means "princess," implying a person of noble birth. Later we learn that Sarai was Abram's half sister (20:12).

8 Lk 1:51; Ge 10:25,32 **9** 1Co 14:23 **10** Ge 10:22; 1Ch 1:17 **12** See Lk 3:36 **16** 1Ch 1:19; Lk 3:35 **20** Lk 3:35 **24** Lk 3:34 **26** Jos 24:2; 1Ch 1:26 **29** Ge 17:15; 20:12; Ge 22:20

the name of Nahor's wife was Milcah,
the daughter of Haran, the father of
Milcah and Iscah.
30 But Sarai was barren; she did not
have a child.
31 Terah took Abram his son, and
Lot the son of Haran, his grandson,
and Sarai his daughter-in-law, his son
Abram's wife; and they went out to-
gether to go from Ur of the Chaldeans
into the land of Canaan; but when they
came to Haran [about five hundred
and fifty miles northwest of Ur], they
settled there.
32 Terah lived two hundred and five
years; and Terah died in Haran.

Abram Journeys to Egypt

12 NOW [in Haran] the LORD had
said to Abram,

"Go away from your country,
And from your relatives
And from your father's house,
To the land which I will show you;
[Heb 11:8–10]
2 And I will make you a great
nation,
And I will bless you [abundantly],
And make your name great
(exalted, distinguished);
And you shall be a blessing [a
source of great good to others];
3 And I will bless (do good for,
benefit) those who bless you,
And I will curse [that is, subject to
My wrath and judgment] the one
who curses (despises, dishonors,
has contempt for) you.
And in you all the families
(nations) of the earth will be
blessed." [Gal 3:8]

4 So Abram departed [in faithful
obedience] as the LORD had directed
him; and Lot [his nephew] left with
him. Abram was seventy-five years
old when he left Haran.
5 Abram took Sarai his wife and Lot
his nephew, and all their possessions
which they had acquired, and the peo-
ple (servants) which they had acquired
in Haran, and they set out to go to the
land of Canaan. When they came to
the land of Canaan,
6 Abram passed through the land
as far as the site of Shechem, to the
[great] terebinth (oak) tree of Moreh.
Now the Canaanites were in the land
at that time.
7 Then the LORD appeared to Abram
and said, "I will give this land to your
descendants." So Abram built an altar
there to [honor] the LORD who had ap-
peared to him.
8 Then he moved on from there to the
mountain on the east of Bethel, and

12:1 – 3 God's Covenant with Abram — The covenant with Abram is the first covenant that pertains to the rule of God. It is unconditional, and depends only on God who obligates Himself in grace, indicated by the unconditional declaration, "I will." The Abrahamic covenant is also the basis of other covenants and it promises blessings in three areas: (1) **national** — "I will make you a great nation," (2) **personal** — "I will bless you [abundantly], and make your name great"; and (3) **universal** — "in you all the families (nations) of the earth will be blessed." The Abrahamic Covenant is an important link in all that God began to do, has done throughout history, and will continue to do until the consummation of history. God blesses Abram and all his descendants through the Messiah, who is Abram's progeny and provides salvation for the entire world.

12:1 *LORD.* Even though the name Yahweh (translated LORD) is not explained until Exodus 3:14 – 15, it is used here to make it clear to the readers that this was the same God who later formed the nation of Israel, and who was the creator (2:4).

12:2 – 3 *I will bless you.* There are seven elements in God's promise to Abram. The number seven is often used in Scripture to suggest fullness and completeness.

12:7 *to your descendants.* The land of Canaan was a gift to the descendants of Abram. God owned the land (Ps 24:1); it was His to do with as He pleased. The people of Canaan had lost their right to occupy the land due to their awful depravity (see 15:16). Thus God declared that this land would become the land of Israel (15:18 – 21; 17:6 – 8).

12:8 *called on the name of the LORD.* This was not a private prayer but a public proclamation. Abram was telling others about the Lord.

30 Ge 16:1,2; Lk 1:36 **31** Ge 12:1; Neh 9:7; Ac 7:4; Ge 10:19 **CHAPTER 12** **1** Ac 7:3; Heb 11:8 **2** Ge 17:6; 18:18; Dt 26:5; 1Ki 3:8; Ge 24:35; Ge 28:4; Gal 3:14 **3** Ge 27:29; Ex 23:22; Nu 24:9; Ge 18:18; 22:18; 26:4; Ps 72:17; Ac 3:25; Gal 3:8 **5** Ge 14:14; Ge 11:31 **6** Heb 11:9; Dt 11:30; Jdg 7:1; Ge 10:18,19 **7** Ge 17:1; Ge 13:15; 17:8; Ps 105:9,11; Ge 13:4 **8** Ge 13:4

pitched his tent, with Bethel on the west
and Ai on the east; and there he built
an altar to the LORD and called on the
name of the LORD [in worship through
prayer, praise, and thanksgiving].
9 Then Abram journeyed on, con-
tinuing toward the Negev (the South
country of Judah).
10 Now there was a famine in the land;
and Abram went down into Egypt to
live temporarily, for the famine in the
land was oppressive *and* severe.
11 And when he was about to enter
Egypt, he said to Sarai his wife, "Listen:
I know that you are a beautiful woman;
12 so when the Egyptians see you,
they will say, 'This is his wife'; and
they will kill me [to acquire you], but
they will let you live.
13 "Please tell them that you are my
sister so that things will go well for
me for your sake, and my life will be
spared because of you."
14 And when Abram entered Egypt,
the Egyptians saw that Sarai was very
beautiful.

12:11 *beautiful woman.* Sarai's physical beauty was remarkable considering her age. She was ten years younger than Abram, or about 65 (12:4; 17:17).

12:13 *my sister.* Sarai *was* Abram's half sister, the daughter of his father but not of his mother (20:12).

9 Ge 13:3 **10** Ge 26:1; Ps 105:13; Ge 43:1 **11** ver. 14; Ge 26:7 **12** Ge 20:11; 26:7 **13** Ge 20:5,13

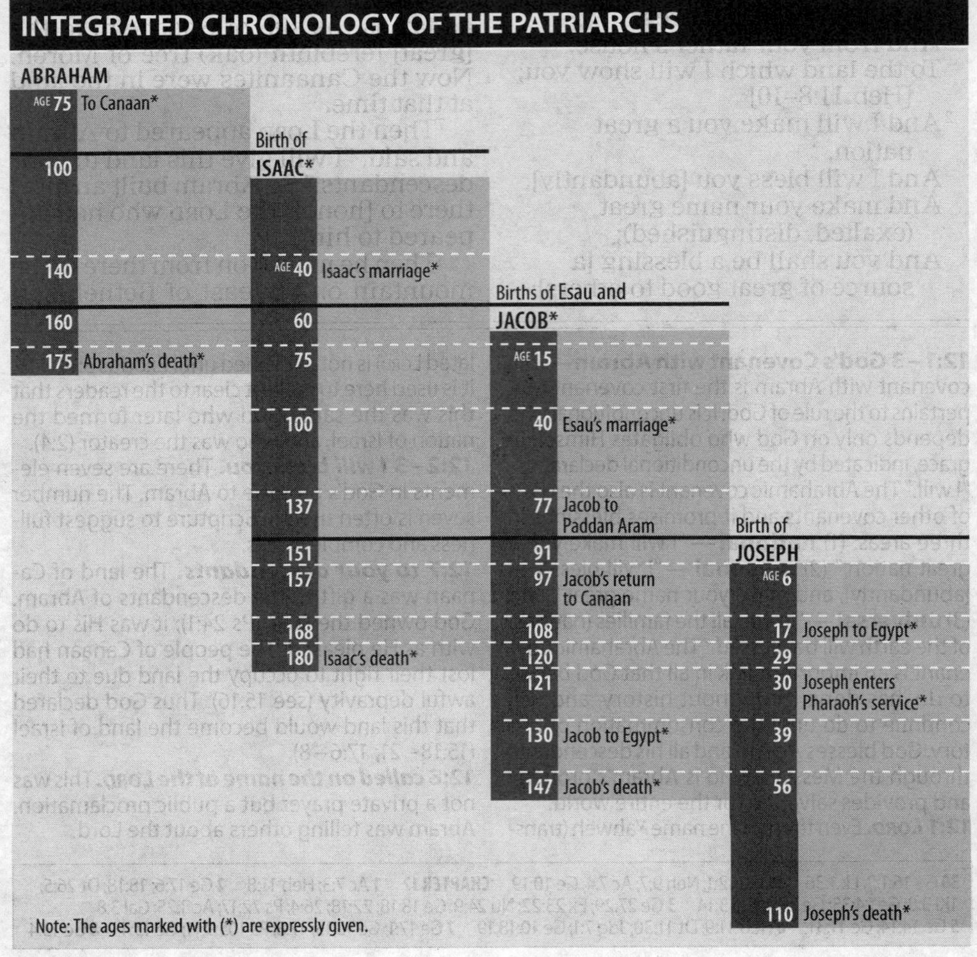

THE TRADITION OF ABRAHAM'S WANDERINGS

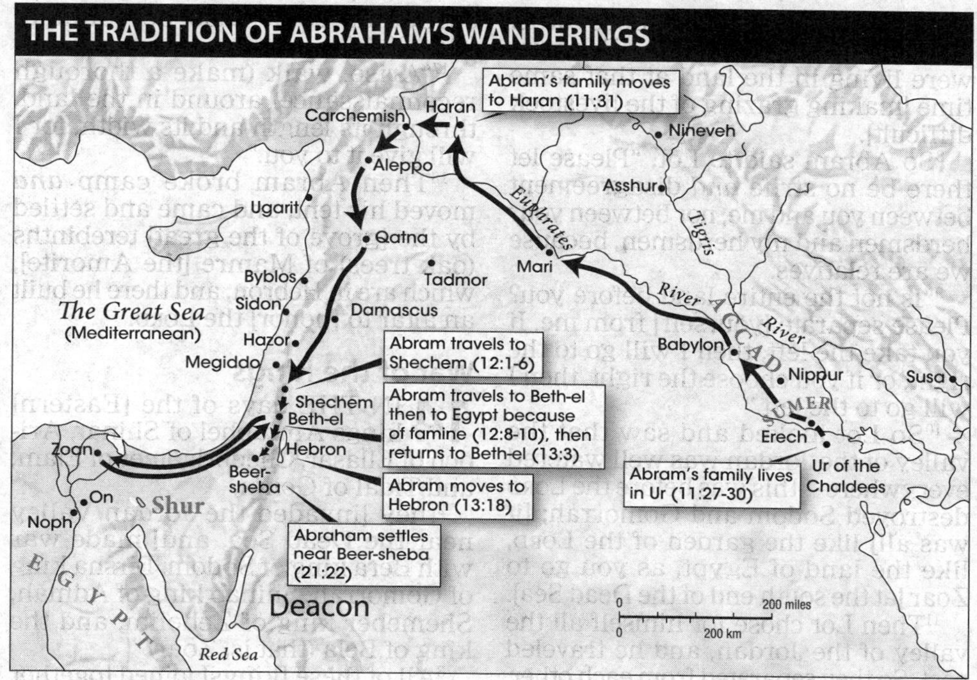

[15]Pharaoh's princes (officials) also saw her and praised her to Pharaoh; and the woman was taken [for the purpose of marriage] into Pharaoh's house (harem).

[16]Therefore Pharaoh treated Abram well for her sake; he acquired sheep, oxen, male and female donkeys, male and female servants, and camels.

[17]But the LORD punished Pharaoh and his household with severe plagues because of Sarai, Abram's wife.

[18]Then Pharaoh called Abram and said, "What is this that you have done to me? Why did you not tell me that she was your wife?

[19]"Why did you say, 'She is my sister,' so that I took her as my wife? Now then, here is your wife; take her and go!"

[20]So Pharaoh commanded his men concerning him; and they escorted him on his way, with his wife and all that he had.

Abram and Lot

13 SO ABRAM went up out of Egypt, he and his wife and all that he had, and Lot [his nephew] with him, into the Negev (the South country of Judah).

[2]Now Abram was extremely rich in livestock and in silver and in gold.

[3]He journeyed on from the Negev as far as Bethel, to the place where his tent had been at the beginning, between Bethel and Ai,

[4]where he had first built an altar; and there Abram called on the name of the LORD [in prayer]. [Gal 3:6–9]

[5]But Lot, who went with Abram, also had flocks and herds and tents.

[6]Now the land was not able to support them [that is, sustain all their grazing and water needs] while they lived near one another, for their possessions were too great for them to stay together.

[7]And there was strife *and* quarreling between the herdsmen of Abram's

---

12:17 *the LORD punished Pharaoh.* This is the first example of the cursing and blessing element of God's promise (see 12:2–3).

13:7 *the Canaanite and the Perizzite.* As in 12:6, the point of this phrase is that the land was already populated; Abram and Lot did not come

16 Ge 20:14 **17** Ge 20:18; 1Ch 16:21; Ps 105:14 **18** Ge 20:9; 26:10 **20** Pr 21:1 **CHAPTER 13** **1** Ge 12:9 **2** Ge 24:35; Ps 112:3; Pr 10:22 **3** Ge 12:8,9 **4** Ge 12:7,8; Ps 116:17 **6** Ge 36:7 **7** Ge 26:20; Ge 12:6

cattle and the herdsmen of Lot's cattle. Now the Canaanite and the Perizzite were living in the land at that same time [making grazing of the livestock difficult].

8 So Abram said to Lot, "Please let there be no strife *and* disagreement between you and me, nor between your herdsmen and my herdsmen, because we are relatives.

9 "Is not the entire land before you? Please separate [yourself] from me. If you take the left, then I will go to the right; or if you choose the right, then I will go to the left."

10 So Lot looked and saw that the valley of the Jordan was well watered everywhere—this was before the LORD destroyed Sodom and Gomorrah; [it was all] like the garden of the LORD, like the land of Egypt, as you go to Zoar [at the south end of the Dead Sea].

11 Then Lot chose for himself all the valley of the Jordan, and he traveled east. So they separated from each other.

12 Abram settled in the land of Canaan, and Lot settled in the cities of the valley and camped as far as Sodom *and* lived there.

13 But the men of Sodom were extremely wicked and sinful against the LORD [unashamed in their open sin before Him].

14 The LORD said to Abram, after Lot had left him, "Now lift up your eyes and look from the place where you are *standing*, northward and southward and eastward and westward;

15 for all the land which you see I will give to you and to your descendants forever. [Acts 7:5]

16 "I will make your descendants [as numerous] as the dust of the earth, so that if a man could count the [grains of] dust of the earth, then your descendants could also be counted. [Gen 28:14]

17 "Arise, walk (make a thorough reconnaissance) around in the land, through its length and its width, for I will give it to you."

18 Then Abram broke camp *and* moved his tent, and came and settled by the [grove of the great] terebinths (oak trees) of Mamre [the Amorite], which are in Hebron, and there he built an altar to [honor] the LORD.

War of the Kings

14 IN THE days of the [Eastern] kings Amraphel of Shinar, Arioch of Ellasar, Chedorlaomer of Elam, and Tidal of Goiim,

2 they [invaded the Jordan Valley near the Dead Sea, and] made war with Bera king of Sodom, Birsha king of Gomorrah, Shinab king of Admah, Shemeber king of Zeboiim, and the king of Bela (that is, Zoar).

3 All of these [kings] joined together [as allies] in the Valley of Siddim (that is, the Sea of Salt).

4 Twelve years they had served Chedorlaomer [the most powerful king in the invading confederacy], but in the thirteenth year they rebelled.

5 In the fourteenth year Chedorlaomer and the [three] kings who were with him attacked and subdued the Rephaim in Ashteroth-karnaim, the Zuzim in Ham, and the Emim in Shaveh-kiriathaim,

6 and the Horites in their mountainous country of Seir, as far as El-paran, which is on the border of the wilderness.

7 Then they turned back and came to En-mishpat (that is, Kadesh), and subdued all the country of the Amalekites, and also the Amorites who lived in Hazazon-tamar.

---

into an empty region but had to compete for land for their rapidly growing herds and flocks.

13:14 – 17 This section forms part of the set of texts that set the stage for the Abrahamic covenant (see the list at 15:1 – 21). This section builds on 12:1 – 3,7 the passage in which God first gave His great promise to Abram.

14:3 ***the Valley of Siddim.*** This valley is most likely submerged under the waters of the Dead Sea today.

8 1Co 6:7 **9** Ge 20:15; 34:10; Ro 12:18 **10** Ge 19:17; Ge 19:24; Ge 2:10; Isa 51:3; Ge 14:2,8; 19:22 **12** Ge 19:29; Ge 14:12; 19:1 **13** Ge 18:20; 2Pe 2:7; Ge 6:11 **14** ver. 11; Ge 28:14 **15** Ge 12:7; 15:18; Dt 34:4; Ac 7:5; 2Ch 20:7; Ps 37:22 **16** Ge 22:17; Ex 32:13 **18** Ge 14:13; Ge 35:27 **CHAPTER 14** **1** Ge 10:10; 11:2; Isa 11:11 **2** Dt 29:23; Ge 19:22 **3** Nu 34:12; Dt 3:17; Jos 3:16 **4** Ge 9:26 **5** Ge 15:20; Dt 2:20; Dt 2:10 **6** Dt 2:12,22 **7** 2Ch 20:2

8 Then the kings of Sodom, Gomorrah, Admah, Zeboiim, and Bela (that is, Zoar) came out; and they joined together for battle with the invading kings in the Valley of Siddim,

9 against Chedorlaomer king of Elam and Tidal king of Goiim and Amraphel king of Shinar and Arioch king of Ellasar—four kings against five.

10 Now the Valley of Siddim was full of tar (bitumen) pits; and as the kings of Sodom and Gomorrah fled, they fell into them. But the remainder [of the kings] who survived fled to the hill country.

11 Then the victors took all the possessions of Sodom and Gomorrah and all their food supply *and* provisions and left.

12 And they also took [captive] Lot, Abram's nephew, and his possessions and left, for he was living in Sodom.

13 Then a survivor who had escaped [from the invading forces on the other side of the Jordan] came and told Abram the Hebrew. Now he was living by the terebinths (oaks) of Mamre the Amorite, brother of Eshcol and brother of Aner—they were allies of Abram.

14 When Abram heard that his nephew [Lot] had been captured, he armed *and* led out his trained men, born in his own house, [numbering] three hundred and eighteen, and went in pursuit as far [north] as Dan.

15 He divided his forces against them by night, he and his servants, and attacked *and* defeated them, and pursued them as far as Hobah, which is north of Damascus.

16 And he brought back all the goods, and also brought back his nephew Lot and his possessions, and also the women, and the people.

Abram and Melchizedek

17 Then after Abram's return from the defeat (slaughter) of Chedorlaomer and the kings who were with him, the king of Sodom went out to meet him at the Valley of Shaveh (that is, the King's Valley).

18 Melchizedek king of Salem (ancient Jerusalem) brought out bread and wine [for them]; he was the priest of God Most High.

19 And Melchizedek blessed Abram and said,

"Blessed (joyful, favored) be
Abram by God Most High,
Creator *and* Possessor of heaven
and earth;
20 And blessed, praised, *and* glorified
be God Most High,
Who has given your enemies into
your hand."

And Abram gave him a tenth of all [the treasure he had taken in battle]. [Heb 7:1–10]

21 The king of Sodom said to Abram, "Give me the people and keep the goods (spoils of battle) for yourself."

14:14 *three hundred and eighteen.* The fact that Abram could find this many fighting men from among his own servants is an indication of the great wealth and honor that the Lord had given him (12:2 – 3).

14:18 *Melchizedek.* This name means "My King is Righteous." Melchizedek was a contemporary of Abram who worshiped the living God. He is described as the "king of Salem," an older shorter name for Jerusalem. The word is based on the root from which the word *shalom* (peace) comes. Melchizedek is a mysterious figure, apparently appearing from nowhere, and with no explanation of his family or background. He is a priest of God Most High, even though there is no indication that he is of Abram's family or even a descendant of Shem. The writer of Hebrews compares Melchizedek with another priest, the Lord Jesus Christ (see Heb 5:9; Ps 110:4).

14:20 *blessed, praised, and glorified be God Most High.* When we bless God, we acknowledge Him as the source of all our blessings (Ps 103:1 – 2). ***a tenth.*** This is the first mention of tithing in the Bible. Even though there is no record of tithing as a command until much later (Dt 14:22), the concept of a tenth belonging to God was apparently known. Abram's gift indicates that he considered Melchizedek a true priest of the living God; in giving this gift Abram was giving to the Lord.

10 Ge 11:3; Ge 19:17,30 **11** ver. 16,21 **12** Ge 12:5; Ge 13:12 **13** Ge 13:18; ver. 24 **14** Ge 13:8; Ge 15:3; Dt 34:1 **15** Isa 41:2,3 **17** 1Sa 18:6; Heb 7:1; 2Sa 18:18 **18** Heb 7:1; Ps 110:4; Heb 5:6; Ac 16:17 **19** Ru 3:10; ver. 22 **20** Ge 24:27; Heb 7:4

22 But Abram said to the king of
Sodom, "I have raised my hand *and*
sworn an oath to the LORD God Most
High, the Creator *and* Possessor of
heaven and earth,
23 that I would not take anything that
is yours, from a thread to a sandal
strap, so you could not say, 'I [the King
of Sodom] have made Abram rich.'
24 "I will take nothing except what
my young men have eaten, and the
share of the spoils belonging to the
men [my allies] who went with me—
Aner, Eshcol, and Mamre; let them
take their share of the spoils."

Abram Promised a Son

15 AFTER THESE things the word
of the LORD came to Abram in a
vision, saying,

"Do not be afraid, Abram,
I am your shield;
Your reward [for obedience] shall
be very great."

2 Abram said, "Lord God, what *reward*
will You give me, since I am [leaving
this world] childless, and he who will
be the owner *and* heir of my house is
this [servant] Eliezer from Damascus?"
3 And Abram continued, "Since You
have given no child to me, one (a ser-
vant) born in my house is my heir."
4 Then behold, the word of the LORD
came to him, saying, "This man
[Eliezer] will not be your heir but he
who shall come from your own body
shall be your heir."
5 And the LORD brought Abram outside
[his tent into the night] and said, "Look
now toward the heavens and count the
stars—if you are able to count them."
Then He said to him, "So [numerous]
shall your descendants be." [Heb 11:12]
6 Then Abram believed in (affirmed,
trusted in, relied on, remained stead-
fast to) the LORD; and He counted
(credited) it to him as righteousness
(doing right in regard to God and man).
[Rom 4:3, 18–22; Gal 3:6; James 2:23]
7 And He said to him, "I am the [same]
LORD who brought you out of Ur of the
Chaldeans, to give you this land as an
inheritance."
8 But Abram said, "Lord GOD, by
what [proof] will I know that I will
inherit it?"
9 So God said to him, "Bring Me a
three-year-old heifer, a three-year-old
female goat, a three-year-old ram, a
turtledove, and a young pigeon."
10 So Abram brought all these to Him
and cut them down the middle, and
laid each half opposite the other; but
he did not cut the birds.
11 The birds of prey swooped down
on the carcasses, but Abram drove
them away.
12 When the sun was setting, a deep

14:22 the LORD God Most High. Abraham identified Yahweh, translated here as "the LORD," with the most high God for whom Melchizedek was priest. This is a clear statement that he and Melchizedek worshiped the same God.
15:1 – 21 This section is one of the texts that present the Abrahamic covenant (see 17:1 – 22; 18:1 – 15; 22:15 – 18; 26:23 – 24; 35:9 – 15; compare also 12:1 – 3, 7; 13:14 – 17).
15:2 Eliezer from Damascus. This man had the honor of being Abram's heir because Abram and Sarai had no child of their own. Some have wondered if Eliezer is also the unnamed servant of Abraham who went on the quest for a wife for Isaac (24:2 – 5).
15:6 Abram believed. Almost ten years had passed since the original promises were given. As Abram grew older and still had no children, it was natural for him to wonder how the promises could be fulfilled. In answer to Abram's questions, God, who had revealed Himself in word, and who had faithfully protected him and sustained him, again pledged His word of promise. Abram believed and his faith was accounted to him as righteousness. Some have thought that in Old Testament times people were saved by their good deeds rather than by faith, but this idea is mistaken. Abram was not saved because of righteous living or obedience, but by believing in God and so being declared righteous by Him. The only valid work is the work of faith (Jn 6:28 – 29; Jas 2:2).
15:9 Bring Me. Abram prepared the sacrifice, but God enacted the sign (v. 17). This emphasizes the unilateral, unconditional nature of the covenant.

22 Da 12:7; ver. 19 **23** See Est 9:15,16 **CHAPTER 15** **1** Da 10:1; Ge 26:24; Da 10:12; Ps 3:3; 84:11; 91:4; Pr 11:18
2 Ac 7:5 **3** Ge 14:14 **4** 2Sa 7:12 **5** Ps 147:4; Jer 33:22; Ex 32:13; Heb 11:12 **6** Ro 4:3,9,22; Gal 3:6; Ps 106:31
7 Ge 12:1; Ge 11:28,31; Ps 105:42,44 **8** See Ge 24:13,14; 1Sa 14:9,10 **10** Jer 34:18; Lev 1:17 **12** Ge 2:21

sleep overcame Abram; and a horror (terror, shuddering fear, nightmare) of great darkness overcame him.

13*God* said to Abram, "Know for sure that your descendants will be strangers [living temporarily] in a land (Egypt) that is not theirs, where they will be enslaved and oppressed for four hundred years. [Ex 12:40]

14"But on that nation whom your descendants will serve I will bring judgment, and afterward they will come out [of that land] with great possessions. [Ex 12:35, 36; Acts 7:6, 7]

15"As for you, you shall [die and] go to your fathers in peace; you shall be buried at a good old age.

16"Then in the fourth generation your descendants shall return here [to Canaan, the land of promise], for the wickedness *and* guilt of the Amorites is not yet complete (finished)." [Josh 24:15]

17When the sun had gone down and a [deep] darkness had come, *there appeared* a smoking brazier and a flaming torch which passed between the [divided] pieces [of the animals]. [Jer 34:18, 19]

18On the same day the LORD made a covenant (promise, pledge) with Abram, saying,

"To your descendants I have given
this land,
From the river of Egypt to the
great river Euphrates—

19[the land of] the Kenites and the Kenizzites and the Kadmonites

20and the Hittites and the Perizzites and the Rephaim,

21the Amorites and the Canaanites and the Girgashites and the Jebusites."

Sarai and Hagar

16 NOW SARAI, Abram's wife, had not borne him any *children,* and she had an Egyptian maid whose name was Hagar.

2So Sarai said to Abram, "See here, the LORD has prevented me from bearing *children.* I am asking you to go in to [the bed of] my maid [so that she may bear you a child]; perhaps I will obtain children by her." And Abram listened to Sarai *and* did as she said.

3After Abram had lived in the land of Canaan ten years, Abram's wife Sarai took Hagar the Egyptian [maid], and gave her to her husband Abram to be his [secondary] wife.

4He went in to [the bed of] Hagar,

15:12 *horror . . . darkness.* These two words give great emphasis to the meaning "an overwhelmingly dark terror." This kind of reaction to the indescribable holiness of the Lord (Isa 6:3; 40:25) is natural — Abram was about to experience the presence of the Almighty. This was a moment of profound dread and holy awe.

15:13 *four hundred years.* Moses wrote down the story of Abram's life from the vantage point of the generation who fulfilled this prophecy (Ex 12:40 – 42).

15:17 *between the [divided] pieces.* This last element has profound implications. In solemn agreements between equals (parity treaties), both parties would pass between the bloody pieces of slain animals and birds. The symbol would be evident to all: "May I become like this if I do not keep my part of the agreement." But Abram was not to walk this grisly pathway. Only God made the journey in the symbols of smoke and fire. The fulfillment of the promise of God to Abram, the Abrahamic covenant, is as sure as the ongoing life of the Lord.

15:18 *this land.* God's promise to Abram included his descendants and the Promised One, the Seed of Genesis 3:15. But the promise also included the land of Canaan. God removed the people of Israel from the land of Canaan several times, but He never revoked His everlasting promise (17:8). The promise will be fulfilled in its fullness when Jesus Christ returns (Isa 9:1 – 7). ***the river of Egypt.*** The "river of Egypt" may refer to the Nile, or it may be what is called today the Wadi el Arish, a smaller watercourse at the natural boundary of Egypt and the land of Israel. ***the great river Euphrates.*** This is the northern arm of the Euphrates in Syria.

15:20 *Rephaim.* A people of unusually tall stature; they are called giants in 2 Samuel 21:15 – 22 (see Nu 13:33; Dt 2:11; 3:11).

16:2 *go in to [the bed of] my maid.* This seems to have been an accepted practice in the ancient middle east. If a woman was unable to bear children, she might use her servant as a surrogate mother, and adopt the child as her own.

13 Ex 1:11; Ac 7:6; Ex 12:40 **14** Ex 6:6; Ex 12:36 **15** Job 5:26; Ac 13:36; Ge 25:8 **16** Ex 12:41; 1Ki 21:26; Mt 23:32 **18** Ge 24:7; Ge 12:7; Ex 23:31; Nu 34:3; Dt 11:24; Jos 1:4 **CHAPTER 16** **1** Ge 15:2,3; Ge 21:9; Gal 4:24 **2** Ge 30:3; Ge 20:18; Ge 30:3,9; Ge 3:17 **3** Ge 12:5 **4** Pr 30:21,23

and she conceived; and when she real-
ized that she had conceived, she looked
with contempt on her mistress [regard-
ing Sarai as insignificant because of
her infertility].
5Then Sarai said to Abram, "May
[the responsibility for] the wrong done
to me [by the arrogant behavior of
Hagar] be upon you. I gave my maid
into your arms, and when she realized
that she had conceived, I was despised
and looked on with disrespect. May
the LORD judge [who has done right]
between you and me."
6But Abram said to Sarai, "Look,
your maid is *entirely* in your hands
and subject to your authority; do as
you please with her." So Sarai treated
her harshly *and* humiliated her, and
Hagar fled from her.
7But the Angel of the LORD found her
by a spring of water in the wilderness,
on the road to [Egypt by way of] Shur.
8And He said, "Hagar, Sarai's maid,
where did you come from and where
are you going?" And she said, "I am
running away from my mistress Sarai."
9The Angel of the LORD said to her,
"Go back to your mistress, and submit
humbly to her authority."
10Then the Angel of the LORD said
to her, "I will greatly multiply your
descendants so that they will be too
many to count."
11The Angel of the LORD continued,

"Behold, you are with child,
And you will bear a son;
And you shall name him Ishmael
(God hears),
Because the LORD has heard
and paid attention to your
persecution (suffering).
12"He (Ishmael) will be a wild
donkey of a man;
His hand *will be* against every
man [continually fighting]
And every man's hand against him;
And he will dwell in defiance of all
his brothers."

13Then she called the name of the LORD
who spoke to her, "You are God Who
Sees"; for she said, "Have I not even
here [in the wilderness] remained alive
after seeing Him [who sees me with
understanding and compassion]?"
14Therefore the well was called Beer-
lahai-roi (Well of the Living One Who
Sees Me); it is between Kadesh and
Bered.
15So Hagar gave birth to Abram's
son; and Abram named his son, to
whom Hagar gave birth, Ishmael (God
hears).
16Abram was eighty-six years old
when Hagar gave birth to Ishmael.

Abraham and the Covenant of Circumcision

17 WHEN ABRAM was ninety-nine
years old, the LORD appeared to
him and said,

"I am God Almighty;
Walk [habitually] before Me [with
integrity, knowing that you are
always in My presence], and
be blameless *and* complete [in
obedience to Me].
2"I will establish My covenant
(everlasting promise) between
Me and you,
And I will multiply you
exceedingly [through your
descendants]."

3Then Abram fell on his face [in wor-
ship], and God spoke with him, saying,

4"As for Me, behold, My covenant is
with you,
And [as a result] you shall be the
father of many nations.

16:11 *Ishmael.* The name Ishmael uses the divine name El, and means "God hears."
17:4 *covenant*. While the peoples who descended directly from Abram (the nation of Israel, the Midianites, Ishmaelites, and Edomites) were certainly numerous, Abram was "father of many" in a much broader sense yet. The message of the New Testament reveals that God's promise to Abram is to be fulfilled in the community of faith in every nation. So certain was the promise,

5 Ge 31:53 **6** 1Pe 3:7; Ex 2:15 **7** Ge 25:18; Ex 15:22 **9** Titus 2:9 **10** Ge 17:20 **11** Lk 1:13,31 **12** Ge 21:20; Ge 25:18 **13** Ge 31:42 **14** Ge 24:62; Nu 13:26 **15** Gal 4:22 **CHAPTER 17** **1** Ge 28:3; Ex 6:3; 2Ki 20:3; Dt 18:13 **2** Ge 12:2 **4** Ro 4:11,12,16

5"No longer shall your name be
Abram (exalted father),
But your name shall be Abraham
(father of a multitude);
For I will make you the father of
many nations.

6"I will make you exceedingly fruitful,
and I will make nations of you, and
kings will come from you.
7"I will establish My covenant be-
tween Me and you and your descen-
dants after you throughout their gen-
erations for an everlasting covenant, to
be God to you and to your descendants
after you. [Gal 3:16]
8"I will give to you and to your de-
scendants after you the land in which
you are a stranger [moving from place
to place], all the land of Canaan, as an
everlasting possession [of property];
and I will be their God." [Acts 7:5]
9Further, God said to Abraham, "As
for you [your part of the agreement],
you shall keep *and* faithfully obey [the
terms of] My covenant, you and your
descendants after you throughout their
generations.
10"This is [the sign of] My covenant,
which you shall keep *and* faithfully
obey, between Me and you and your
descendants after you: Every male
among you shall be circumcised.
11"And you shall be circumcised in
the flesh of your foreskins, and it shall
be the sign (symbol, memorial) of the
covenant between Me and you.
12"Every male among you who is
eight days old shall be circumcised
throughout your generations, [includ-
ing] a *servant* whether born in the
house or one who is purchased with
[your] money from any foreigner, who
is not of your descendants.
13"A *servant* who is born in your
house or one who is purchased with
your money must be circumcised; and
[the sign of] My covenant shall be in
your flesh for an everlasting covenant.
14"And the male who is not circum-
cised in the flesh of his foreskin, that
person shall be cut off from his people;
he has broken My covenant."
15Then God said to Abraham, "As
for Sarai your wife, you shall not call
her name Sarai (my princess), but her
name will be Sarah (Princess).
16"I will bless her, and indeed I will
also give you a son by her. Yes, I will
bless her, and she shall be a *mother
of* nations; kings of peoples will come
from her."
17Then Abraham fell on his face and
laughed, and said in his heart, "Shall
a child be born to a man who is a hun-
dred years old? And shall Sarah, who
is ninety years old, bear *a child*?"

---

that his name was changed to Abraham, as an everlasting reminder of God's gracious covenant. Furthermore, the emphatic "as for me" underscores the identity of the all sufficient God who takes the initiative for establishing the covenantal relationship. This relationship is both spiritual and personal, anticipating the divine pledge, "and I will be their God." The wonder of it all is that we who believe in Jesus Christ are part of that "multitude of nations" who share in the faith of Abraham "who is the father of us all."

17:5 *Abram . . . Abraham.* This name change is significant. Abram means "exalted Father." Abraham means "Father of Many"—a direct reflection of his new role.

17:8 *the land . . . an everlasting possession.* The promise clearly included the Israelite people *and* the land of Canaan. The two are linked in the language of the covenant in chapter 15. Even though God removed Israel more than once from the land, He promised them ultimate possession of Canaan.

17:13 *circumcised.* Circumcision in and of itself did not make people acceptable to God. It was meant as a tangible symbol of God's covenant in their lives, as an outward sign standing for the inward reality of a thorough commitment to God. In the New Testament, the apostle Paul speaks of having a "circumcised heart," pointing to the fact that a circumcised body means nothing if the heart is not in accord (Ro 2:25–29).

17:15 *Sarai . . . Sarah.* Both names come from the same root, meaning "Princess." No explanation is given for the change in Sarah's name, but like the name change from Abram to Abraham (vv. 4–5) the new name accompanied a new relationship with God.

5 Neh 9:7; Ro 4:17 **6** Ge 35:11; Mt 1:6 **7** Gal 3:17; Ge 26:24; 28:13; Ro 9:8 **8** Ge 12:7; Ge 23:4; 28:4; Ex 6:7; Lev 26:12 **10** Ac 7:8 **11** Ro 4:11 **12** Lev 12:3; Lk 2:21 **14** Ex 4:24 **16** Ge 18:10; Ge 35:11; Gal 4:31; 1Pe 3:6 **17** Ge 18:12; 21:6

18 And Abraham said to God, "Oh, that Ishmael [my firstborn] might live before You!"

19 But God said, "No, Sarah your wife shall bear you a son indeed, and you shall name him Isaac (laughter); and I will establish My covenant with him for an everlasting covenant and with his descendants after him.

20 "As for Ishmael, I have heard *and* listened to you; behold, I will bless him, and will make him fruitful and will greatly multiply him [through his descendants]. He will be the father of twelve princes (chieftains, sheiks), and I will make him a great nation. [Gen 25:12–18]

21 "But My covenant [My promise, My solemn pledge], I will establish with Isaac, whom Sarah will bear to you at this time next year."

22 And God finished speaking with him and went up from Abraham.

23 Then Abraham took Ishmael his son, and all *the servants* who were born in his house and all who were purchased with his money, every male among the men of Abraham's household, and circumcised the flesh of their foreskin the very same day, as God had said to him.

24 So Abraham was ninety-nine years old when he was circumcised.

25 And Ishmael his son was thirteen years old when he was circumcised.

26 On the very same day Abraham was circumcised, as well as Ishmael his son.

27 All the men [servants] of his household, both those born in the house and those purchased with money from a foreigner, were circumcised along with him [as the sign of God's covenant with Abraham].

Birth of Isaac Promised

18 NOW THE LORD appeared to Abraham by the terebinth *trees* of Mamre [in Hebron], while he was sitting at the tent door in the heat of the day.

2 When he raised his eyes and looked up, behold, three men were standing [a little distance] from him. When he saw them, he ran from the tent door to meet them and bowed down [with his face] to the ground,

3 and Abraham said, "My lord, if now I have found favor in your sight, please do not pass by your servant [without stopping to visit].

4 "Please let a little water be brought [by one of my servants] and [you may] wash your feet, and recline *and* rest comfortably under the tree.

5 And I will bring a piece of bread to refresh *and* sustain you; after that you may go on, since you have come to your servant." And they replied, "Do as you have said."

6 So Abraham hurried into the tent to Sarah, and said, "Quickly, get ready three measures of fine meal, knead it and bake cakes."

7 Abraham also ran to the herd and brought a calf, tender and choice, and he gave it to the servant [to butcher], and he hurried to prepare it.

8 Then he took curds and milk and the calf which he had prepared, and set it before the men; and he stood beside them under the tree while they ate.

9 Then they said to him, "Where is Sarah your wife?" And he said, "There, in the tent."

10 He said, "I will surely return to you at this time next year; and behold, Sarah your wife will have a son." And

---

17:19 *Isaac.* The name Isaac means "laughter" (see 21:1–6).

18:1 *the LORD appeared.* This was the fifth time the Lord appeared to Abraham since he came into the land of Canaan (12:7; 13:14–17; 15:1–21; 17:1–22).

18:2–3 *three men.* Verse 1 states that the Lord appeared to Abraham, then the next verse refers to "three men." It seems clear from verses 1, 13 and 17 that one of the three was the Lord Himself, and from 19:1 on the other two are referred to as angels. Apparently all three were in human form, and were able to eat the meal that Abraham had prepared. Many have speculated that this was an appearance of the pre-incarnate Christ.

19 Ge 18:10; 21:2; Gal 4:28 **20** Ge 16:10; Ge 25:12,16; Ge 21:18 **21** Ge 21:2 **27** Ge 18:19 **CHAPTER 18** **1** Ge 13:18; 14:13 **2** Heb 13:2; Ge 19:1; 1Pe 4:9 **4** Ge 19:2; 43:24 **5** Jdg 6:18; 13:15; Jdg 19:5; Ps 104:15; Ge 19:8; 33:10 **8** Ge 19:3 **9** Ge 24:67 **10** ver. 14; 2Ki 4:16; Ge 17:19,21; 21:2; Ro 9:9

Sarah was listening at the tent door, which was behind him. [Rom 9:9–12]

11 Now Abraham and Sarah were old, well advanced in years; she was past [the age of] childbearing.

12 So Sarah laughed to herself [when she heard the LORD's words], saying, "After I have become old, shall I have pleasure *and* delight, my lord (husband) being also old?" [1 Pet 3:6]

13 And the LORD asked Abraham, "Why did Sarah laugh [to herself], saying, 'Shall I really give birth [to a child] when I am so old?'

14 "Is anything too difficult *or* too wonderful for the LORD? At the appointed time, when the season [for her delivery] comes, I will return to you and Sarah will have a son." [Matt 19:26]

15 Then Sarah denied it, saying, "I did not laugh"; because she was afraid. And He (the LORD) said, "No, but you did laugh."

16 Then the men got up from there, and looked toward Sodom; and Abraham walked with them to send them on the way.

17 The LORD said, "Shall I keep secret from Abraham [My friend and servant] what I am going to do, [Gal 3:8]

18 since Abraham is destined to become a great and mighty nation, and all the nations of the earth will be blessed through him? [Gen 12:2, 3]

19 "For I have known (chosen, acknowledged) him [as My own], so that he may teach *and* command his children and [the sons of] his household after him to keep the way of the LORD by doing what is righteous and just, so that the LORD may bring upon Abraham what He has promised him."

20 And the LORD said, "The outcry [of the sin] of Sodom and Gomorrah is indeed great, and their sin is exceedingly grave.

21 "I will go down now, and see whether they have acted [as vilely and wickedly] as the outcry which has come to Me [indicates]; and if not, I will know."

22 Now the [two] men (angelic beings) turned away from there and went toward Sodom, but Abraham remained standing before the LORD.

23 Abraham approached [the LORD] and said, "Will You really sweep away the righteous (those who do right) with the wicked (those who do evil)?

24 "Suppose there are fifty righteous [people] within the city; will You really sweep it away and not spare it for the sake of the fifty righteous who are in it?

25 "Far be it from You to do such a thing—to strike the righteous with the wicked, so that the righteous and the wicked are *treated* alike. Far be it from You! Shall not the Judge of all the earth do right [by executing just and righteous judgment]?"

26 So the LORD said, "If I find within the city of Sodom fifty righteous [people], then I will spare the entire place for their sake."

27 Abraham answered, "Now behold, I who am but dust [in origin] and ashes have decided to speak to the Lord. [Gen 3:19; Job 30:19]

28 "If five of the fifty righteous are lacking, will You destroy the entire city for lack of five?" And He said, "If I find [at least] forty-five [righteous people] there, I will not destroy it."

29 Abraham spoke to Him yet again and said, "Suppose [only] forty are found there." And He said, "I will not do it for the sake of the forty [who are righteous]."

30 Then Abraham said [to Him], "Oh, may the Lord not be angry, and I will speak; suppose thirty [righteous

---

18:19 *For I have known (chosen, acknowledged) him.* Some translations say, "I have chosen him." The language speaks of the intimate relationship which motivates the Lord to accomplish His purpose in Abraham (22:12). ***righteous and just.*** One idea in two words—"genuine righteousness."

---

11 Ge 17:17; Ro 4:19; Heb 11:11,12,19; Ge 31:35 **12** Ge 17:17; Lk 1:18; 1Pe 3:6 **14** Nu 11:23; Jer 32:17; Zec 8:6; Mt 3:9; Lk 1:37; ver. 10; Ge 17:21; 2Ki 4:16 **16** Ac 15:3; Ro 15:24; 3 Jn 6 **17** Ps 25:14; Am 3:7; Jn 15:15 **18** Ge 12:3; 22:18; Ac 3:25; Gal 3:8 **19** Dt 4:9,10; 6:7; Jos 24:15; Eph 6:4 **20** Ge 4:10 **21** Ge 11:5; Dt 8:2; 13:3; Jos 22:22; Lk 16:15; 2Co 11:11 **22** Ge 19:1; ver. 1 **23** Heb 10:22; Nu 16:22 **24** Jer 5:1 **25** Job 8:20; Isa 3:10,11; Job 8:3; 34:17; Ps 58:11; 94:2; Ro 3:6 **26** Jer 5:1; Eze 22:30 **27** Lk 18:1; Ge 3:19; Job 4:19; Ecc 12:7; 1Co 15:47,48; 2Co 5:1

people] are found there?" And He said,
"I will not do it if I find thirty there."
31 And he said, "Now behold, I have
decided to speak to the Lord [again].
Suppose [only] twenty [righteous peo-
ple] are found there?" And the Lord
said, "I will not destroy it for the sake
of the twenty."
32 Then Abraham said, "Oh may the
Lord not be angry [with me], and I
will speak only this once; suppose ten
[righteous people] are found there?"
And He said, "I will not destroy it for
the sake of the ten."
33 As soon as He had finished speak-
ing with Abraham the LORD departed,
and Abraham returned to his own
place.

The Doom of Sodom

19 IT WAS evening when the two an-
gels came to Sodom. Lot was sit-
ting at Sodom's [city] gate. Seeing them,
Lot got up to meet them and bowed
down *with his* face to the ground.
2 And he said, "See here, my lords,
please turn aside *and* come into your
servant's house, and spend the night,
and wash your feet; then you may get
up early and go on your way." But they
said, "No, we shall spend the night in
the open plaza [of the city]."
3 However, Lot strongly urged them,
so they turned aside and entered his
house; and he prepared a feast for
them [with wine], and baked unleav-
ened bread, and they ate.
4 But before they lay down [to sleep],
the men of the city, the men of Sodom,
both young and old, surrounded the
house, all the men from every quarter;
5 and they called out to Lot and said
to him, "Where are the men who came
to you tonight? Bring them out to us so
that we may know them [intimately]."
6 But Lot went out of the doorway to
the men, and shut the door after him,
7 and said, "Please, my brothers, do
not do something so wicked.
8 "See here, I have two daughters
who have not known a man [intimate-
ly]; please let me bring them out to
you [instead], and you can do as you
please with them; only do nothing to
these men, because they have in fact
come under the shelter of my roof [for
protection]."
9 But they said, "Get out of the way!"
And they said, "This man (Lot) came
[as an outsider] to live here temporar-
ily, and now he is acting like a judge.
Now we will treat you worse than your
visitors!" So they rushed forward *and*
pressed violently against Lot and came
close to breaking down the door [of
his house].
10 But the men (angels) reached out
with their hands and pulled Lot into
the house with them, and shut the door
[after him].
11 They struck (punished) the men
who were at the doorway of the house
with blindness, from the young men
to the old men, so that they exhausted
themselves trying to find the doorway.
12 And the [two] men (angels) asked
Lot, "Have you any others here [in
Sodom]—a son-in-law, and your sons,
and your daughters? Whomever you
have in the city, take them out of here;
13 for we are destroying this place,
because the outcry [for judgment]
against them has grown so great be-
fore the LORD that the LORD has sent us
to destroy *and* ruin it."
14 So Lot went out and spoke to his
sons-in-law, who were [betrothed, and
legally promised] to marry his daugh-
ters, and said, "Get up, get out of this
place, for the LORD is about to destroy
this city!" But to his sons-in-law he
appeared to be joking.
15 When morning dawned, the angels
urged Lot [to hurry], saying, "Get up!

19:2 *my lords.* This is a greeting of respect for special visitors.
19:5 *know them.* This term usually refers to sexual relations between a man and a woman (4:1), here it is referring to homosexual activity, which God has declared is an abomination (Lev 18:22).

---

32 Jdg 6:39; Jas 5:16 **CHAPTER 19** **1** Ge 18:22; Ge 18:1 **2** Heb 13:2; Ge 18:4; See Lk 24:28 **3** Ge 18:8 **5** Isa 3:9; Jdg 19:22; Ge 4:1; Ro 1:24,27; Jude 7 **6** Jdg 19:23 **8** See Jdg 19:24; See Ge 18:5 **9** 2Pe 2:7,8; Ex 2:14 **12** Ge 7:1; 2Pe 2:7,9 **13** Ge 18:20; 1Ch 21:15 **14** Mt 1:18; Nu 16:21,45; Ex 9:21; Lk 17:28; 24:11 **15** Nu 16:24,26; Rev 18:4

Take your wife and two daughters who
are here [and go], or you will be swept
away in the punishment of the city."
[16]But Lot hesitated *and* lingered. The
men took hold of his hand and the
hand of his wife and the hands of his
two daughters, because the LORD was
merciful to him [for Abraham's sake];
and they brought him out, and left him
outside the city [with his family].
[17]When they had brought them out-
side, one [of the angels] said, "Escape
for your life! Do not look behind you,
or stop anywhere in the entire valley;
escape to the mountains [of Moab], or
you will be consumed *and* swept away."
[18]But Lot said to them, "Oh no, [not
that place] my lords!
[19]"Please listen, your servant has
found favor in your sight, and you have
magnified your lovingkindness (mer-
cy) to me by saving my life; but I can-
not escape to the mountains, because
the disaster will overtake me and I
will be killed.
[20]"Now look, this town [in the dis-
tance] is near *enough for us* to flee to,
and it is small [with only a few people].
Please, let me escape there (is it not
small?) so that my life will be saved."
[21]And the angel said to him, "Behold,
I grant you this request also; I will not
destroy this town of which you have
spoken.
[22]"Hurry and take refuge there, for I
cannot do anything [to punish Sodom]
until you arrive there." For this reason
the town was named Zoar (few, small).
[23]The sun had risen over the earth
when Lot came to Zoar.
[24]Then the LORD rained down brim-
stone (flaming sulfur) and fire on
Sodom and on Gomorrah from the
LORD out of heaven,
[25]and He overthrew (demolished,
ended) those cities, and the entire val-
ley, and all the inhabitants of the cities,
and whatever grew on the ground.
[26]But Lot's wife, from behind him,
[foolishly, longingly] looked [back
toward Sodom in an act of disobedi-
ence], and she became a pillar of salt.
[Luke 17:32]
[27]Abraham started out early the next
morning to the place where he [only the
day before] had stood before the LORD;
[28]and he looked down toward Sodom
and Gomorrah, and toward all the land
of the valley [of the Dead Sea]; and
he saw, and behold, the smoke of the
land went up like the smoke of a kiln
(pottery furnace).
[29]Now when God ravaged *and* de-
stroyed the cities of the plain [of Sid-
dim], He remembered Abraham [and
for that reason], and He sent [Abra-
ham's nephew] Lot out of the midst of
the destruction, when He destroyed the
cities in which Lot had lived.

Lot Is Debased

[30]Now Lot went up from Zoar, and
lived in the mountain together with
his two daughters, for he was afraid
to stay [any longer] in Zoar; and he
lived in a cave with his two daughters.

19:16 *the LORD was merciful to him.* This is the whole point of the story. God could have destroyed the city of Sodom with no word to Lot or Abraham (18:17). But because of His mercy, God's angels grabbed Lot and his family and brought them forcibly to safety. In this passage, Lot appears weak, indecisive, and unsure of whether he really wants to be rescued. However, the New Testament speaks a good word for Lot's character, calling him a "just man" and telling us that he was grieved by the sin he saw in Sodom and Gomorrah (2Pe 2:6–8).

19:22 *Zoar.* This name means "Insignificant in Size."

19:23–26 *brimstone (flaming sulfur) and fire.* This may be simply a supernatural judgment on the cities, but some have also theorized that the fire and brimstone which "rained" down on them may have been from a volcanic eruption. In any case, it is clear that the destruction was a judgment from God, and that it was under His control.

19:26 *pillar of salt.* Near the Dead Sea, which is believed to now cover the site of Sodom and Gomorrah, there are numerous rock salt formations, including pillars about the size of a human. Jesus referred to the fate of Lot's wife as a historical fact (Lk 17:32).

---

16 Lk 18:13; Ps 34:22 **17** 1Ki 19:3; ver. 26; Mt 24:16-18; Lk 9:62; Php 3:13,14 **18** Ac 10:14 **21** Job 42:8,9; Ps 145:19 **22** See Ge 32:25,26; Ex 32:10; Dt 9:14; Mk 6:5; Ge 13:10; 14:2 **24** Dt 29:23; Isa 13:19; Jer 20:16; Eze 16:49,50; Hos 11:8; Lk 17:29; 2Pe 2:6; Jude 7 **25** Ge 14:3; Ps 107:34 **26** Lk 17:32 **27** Ge 18:22 **28** Rev 18:9 **29** Ge 8:1; 18:23 **30** ver. 17,19

31 The firstborn said to the younger, "Our father is aging, and there is not a man on earth [available] to be intimate with us in the customary way [so that we may have children].

32 "Come, let us make our father drunk with wine, and we will lie with him so that we may preserve our family through our father."

33 So they gave their father wine that night, and the firstborn went in and lay with her father; and he did not know when she lay down or when she got up [because he was completely intoxicated].

34 Then the next day, the firstborn said to the younger, "Behold, I lay with my father last night; let us make him drunk with wine tonight also, and then you go in and lie with him, so that we may preserve our family through our father."

35 So they gave their father wine that night also, and the younger got up and lay with him; and *again* he did not know when she lay down or when she got up.

36 Thus both the daughters of Lot conceived by their father.

37 The firstborn gave birth to a son, and named him Moab (from father); he is the father of the Moabites to this day.

38 The younger also gave birth to a son and named him Ben-ammi (son of my people); he is the father of the Ammonites to this day.

Abraham's Deception

20 NOW ABRAHAM journeyed from there toward the Negev (the South country), and settled between Kadesh and Shur; then he lived temporarily in Gerar.

2 Abraham said [again] of Sarah his wife, "She is my sister." So Abimelech king of Gerar sent and took Sarah [into his harem].

3 But God came to Abimelech in a dream during the night, and said, "Behold, you are a dead man because of the woman whom you have taken [as your wife], for she is another man's wife."

4 Now Abimelech had not yet come near her; so he said, "Lord, will you kill a people who are righteous *and* innocent *and* blameless [regarding Sarah]?

5 "Did Abraham not tell me, 'She is my sister?' And she herself said, 'He is my brother.' In the integrity of my heart and innocence of my hands I have done this."

6 Then God said to him in the dream, "Yes, I know you did this in the integrity of your heart, for it was I who kept you back *and* spared you from sinning against Me; therefore I did not give you an opportunity to touch her.

7 "So now return the man's wife, for he is a prophet, and he will pray for you and you will live. But if you do not return *her* [to him], know that you shall die, you and all who are yours (your household)."

8 So Abimelech got up early in the morning and called all his servants and told them all these things; and the men were terrified.

9 Then Abimelech called Abraham and said to him, "What have you done to us? And how have I offended you that you have brought on me and my kingdom a great sin? You have done to me what ought not to be done [to anyone]."

10 And Abimelech said to Abraham, "What have you encountered *or* seen

---

19:36 – 38 *Moab . . . Ben-ammi.* The shameful act of incest led to the births of two sons whose descendants (the Moabites and the Ammonites) would greatly trouble Israel.

20:2 *She is my sister*. The complete truth told in such a way as to deceive or mislead is still a falsehood. Abraham's words were true: "She is my sister," but *the message he intended to convey* was false: "She is not married to me." His intent was deceit and the consequences he reaped were the same as if he had directly lied. A man speaks the real truth when he speaks the truth in his heart (Ps 15:2).

20:3 *God came . . . in a dream.* Presumably, Abimelech was a pagan king. Yet God warned him of the wrong he was about to commit. This

---

31 Ge 16:2,4; 38:8,9; Dt 25:5 **32** Mk 12:19 **37** Dt 2:9 **38** Dt 2:19 **CHAPTER 20** **1** Ge 18:1; Ge 16:7,14; Ge 26:6 **2** Ge 12:13; 26:7; Ge 12:15 **3** Ps 105:14; Job 33:15; ver. 7 **4** Ge 18:23 **5** 2Ki 20:3 **6** Ge 31:7; 35:5; Ex 34:24; 1Sa 25:26,34; Ge 39:9; Lev 6:2; Ps 51:4 **7** 1Sa 7:5; 2Ki 5:11; Job 42:8; Jas 5:14,15; Ge 2:17; Nu 16:32,33 **9** Ge 26:10; Ex 32:21; Jos 7:25; Ge 34:7

ABRAHAM AND ISAAC IN THE LAND OF CANAAN

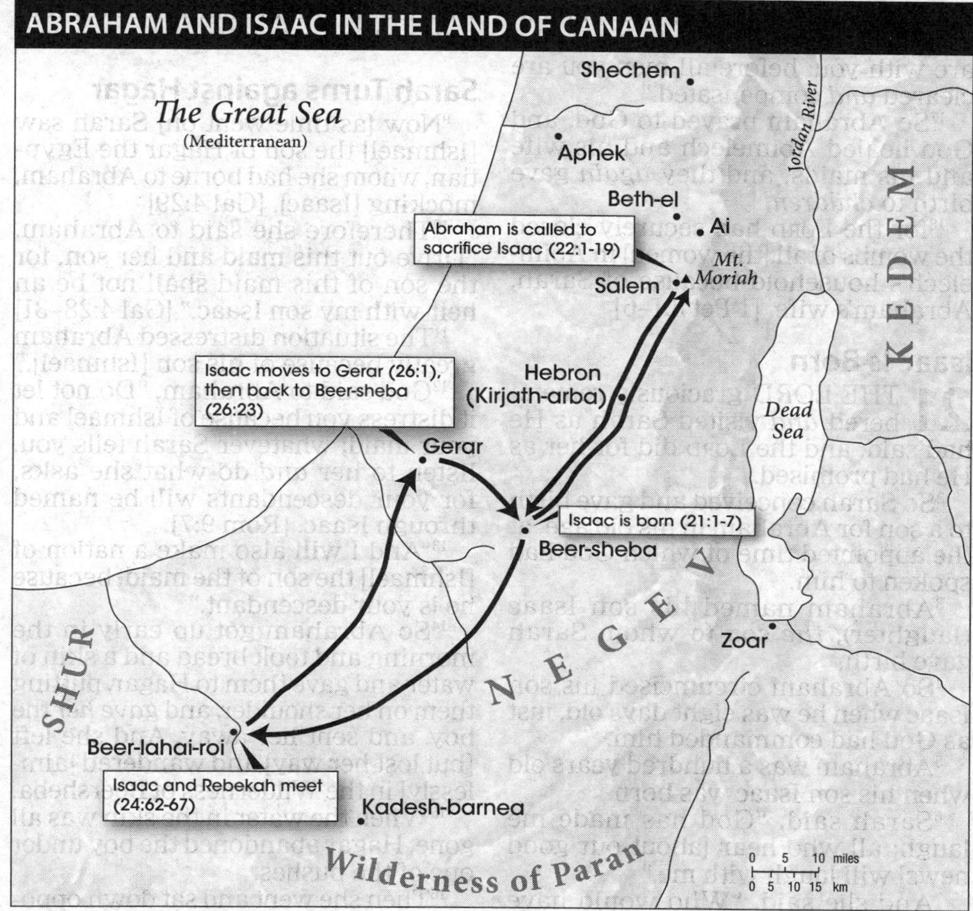

[in us or our customs], that you have
done this [unjust] thing?"
11Abraham said, "Because I thought,
'Surely there is no fear *or* reverence of
God in this place, and they will kill me
because of my wife.'
12"Besides, she actually is my [half]
sister; she is the daughter of my father
[Terah], but not of my mother; and she
became my wife.
13"When God caused me to wander
from my father's house, I said to her,
'This kindness *and* loyalty you can
show me: at every place we stop, say
of me, "He is my brother." ' "
14Then Abimelech took sheep and
oxen and male and female slaves, and
gave them to Abraham, and returned
Sarah his wife to him [as God commanded].
15So Abimelech said, "Behold, my
land is before you; settle wherever you
please."
16Then to Sarah he said, "Look, I
have given this brother of yours a thousand pieces of silver; it is to compensate

is another instance of the protective care that the Lord gives His people (31:24; Nu 22:12–20).
20:12 ***she actually is my [half] sister.*** Later the law would prohibit the marriage of people so closely related, but in the early years of the earth it was apparently acceptable for half siblings to marry (see note on 4:17).

11 Ge 42:18; Ps 36:1; Pr 16:6; Ge 12:12; 26:7 **12** See Ge 11:29 **13** Ge 12:1,9,11; Heb 11:8; Ge 12:13 **14** Ge 12:16 **15** Ge 13:9 **16** Ge 26:11; Ge 24:65

you [for all that has happened] *and* to vindicate your honor before all who are with you; before all men you are cleared *and* compensated."

[17]So Abraham prayed to God, and God healed Abimelech and his wife and his maids, and they *again* gave birth to *children*,

[18]for the LORD had securely closed the wombs of all [the women] in Abimelech's household because of Sarah, Abraham's wife. [1 Pet 3:1–6]

Isaac Is Born

21 THE LORD graciously remembered *and* visited Sarah as He had said, and the LORD did for her as He had promised.

[2]So Sarah conceived and gave birth to a son for Abraham in his old age, at the appointed time of which God had spoken to him.

[3]Abraham named his son Isaac (laughter), *the son* to whom Sarah gave birth.

[4]So Abraham circumcised his son Isaac when he was eight days old, just as God had commanded him.

[5]Abraham was a hundred years old when his son Isaac was born.

[6]Sarah said, "God has made me laugh; all who hear [about our good news] will laugh with me."

[7]And she said, "Who would have said to Abraham that Sarah would nurse children? For I have given birth to a son by him in his old age." [Heb 11:12]

[8]The child [Isaac] grew and was weaned, and Abraham held a great feast on the day that Isaac was weaned.

Sarah Turns against Hagar

[9]Now [as time went on] Sarah saw [Ishmael] the son of Hagar the Egyptian, whom she had borne to Abraham, mocking [Isaac]. [Gal 4:29]

[10]Therefore she said to Abraham, "Drive out this maid and her son, for the son of this maid shall not be an heir with my son Isaac." [Gal 4:28–31]

[11]The situation distressed Abraham greatly because of his son [Ishmael].

[12]God said to Abraham, "Do not let it distress you because of Ishmael and your maid; whatever Sarah tells you, listen to her *and* do what she asks, for your descendants will be named through Isaac. [Rom 9:7]

[13]"And I will also make a nation of [Ishmael] the son of the maid, because he is your descendant."

[14]So Abraham got up early in the morning and took bread and a skin of water and gave them to Hagar, putting them on her shoulder, and *gave her* the boy, and sent her away. And she left [but lost her way] and wandered [aimlessly] in the Wilderness of Beersheba.

[15]When the water in the skin was all gone, Hagar abandoned the boy under one of the bushes.

[16]Then she went and sat down opposite him, about a bowshot away, for she said, "Do not let me see the boy die." And as she sat down opposite him, she raised her voice and wept.

[17]God heard the voice of the boy, and

21:1 *The LORD . . . visited Sarah as He had said.* The Bible stresses that the Lord causes conceptions; that children are a gift of the Lord (Ps 127:3). The verb *visit* is an extraordinary choice here, indicating that the Lord entered directly into the affairs of His people.

21:3 *Isaac.* Isaac means "He (God) Is Laughing (Now)." At one time Abraham and Sarah had both laughed at the improbability of having a son in their old age (17:17; 18:12); now with the birth of the promised child their laughter took on a happier meaning.

21:12 *do what she asks.* As painful as the situation was, God confirmed that Sarah was right that Ishmael would have to leave. Only Isaac was the child of promise, the one through whom the covenant would be fulfilled. This complicated situation was part of the price Abraham had to pay for trying to bring about God's promises in his own time. Nevertheless, God is merciful and He did not abandon Hagar and Ishmael.

21:17 *God heard.* What wonderful words these are! There is no pain of His people that He does not see or hear about (Isa 40:27 – 28; Heb 2:10,18;

---

17 Job 42:9 **18** Ge 12:17 **CHAPTER 21** **1** 1Sa 2:21; Ge 17:19; Gal 4:23,28 **2** Ac 7:8; Gal 4:22; Heb 11:11; Ge 17:21 **3** Ge 17:19 **4** Ac 7:8; Ge 17:10,12 **5** Ge 17:1,17 **6** Ps 126:2; Isa 54:1; Lk 1:58 **7** Ge 18:11,12 **9** Ge 16:1; Ge 16:15; Gal 4:29 **10** Gal 4:30; See Ge 25:6; 36:6,7 **11** Ge 17:18 **12** Ro 9:7,8; Heb 11:18 **13** ver. 18; Ge 16:10; 17:20 **14** Jn 8:35 **17** Ex 3:7

the angel of God called to Hagar from heaven and said to her, "What troubles you, Hagar? Do not be afraid, for God has heard the voice of the boy from where he is [resting].

18"Get up, help the boy up, and hold him by the hand, for I will make him a great nation."

19Then God opened her eyes and she saw a well of water; and she went and filled the [empty] skin with water and gave the boy a drink.

20God was with Ishmael, and he grew *and* developed; and he lived in the wilderness and became an [expert] archer.

21He lived in the wilderness of Paran; and his mother took a wife for him from the land of Egypt.

Covenant with Abimelech

22Now at that time Abimelech and Phicol, the commander of his army, said to Abraham, "God is with you in everything you do;

23so now, swear to me here by God that you will not deal unfairly with me [by breaking any agreements we have] or with my son or with my descendants, but as I have treated you with kindness, you shall do the same to me and to the land in which you have sojourned (temporarily lived)."

24And Abraham said, "I will swear."

25Then Abraham complained to Abimelech about a well of water which the servants of Abimelech had [violently] seized [from him],

26Abimelech said, "I do not know who did this thing. Indeed, you did not tell me, and I did not hear of it until today."

27So Abraham took sheep and oxen and gave them to Abimelech, and the two men made a covenant (binding agreement).

28Then Abraham set apart seven ewe lambs of the flock,

29and Abimelech said to Abraham, "What is the meaning of these seven ewe lambs which you have set apart?"

30Abraham said, "You are to accept these seven ewe lambs from me as a witness for me, that I dug this well."

31Therefore that place was called Beersheba (Well of the Oath or Well of the Seven), because there the two of them swore an oath.

32So they made a covenant at Beersheba; then Abimelech and Phicol, the commander of his army, got up and returned to the land of the Philistines.

33Abraham planted a tamarisk tree at Beersheba, and there he called on the name of the LORD [in prayer], the Eternal God.

34And Abraham lived [as a resident alien] in the land of the Philistines for many days.

The Offering of Isaac

22 NOW AFTER these things, God tested [the faith and commitment of] Abraham and said to him, "Abraham!" And he answered, "Here I am."

2God said, "Take now your son, your only son [of promise], whom you love, Isaac, and go to the region of Moriah, and offer him there as a burnt offering on one of the mountains of which I shall tell you."

3So Abraham got up early in the morning, saddled his donkey, and took two of his young men with him and

---

4:15). Even though Ishmael was not the son of promise, God still had His hand on his life.

21:23 *kindness.* This exceedingly important term, sometimes translated *loyal love* or *lovingkindness* is often used in the Psalms to describe God's character (Ps 100:5). Here we see its proper context in a binding relationship. The term basically describes covenant loyalty (24:12).

21:27 *covenant.* This is a binding agreement between two equals, similar to today's business contracts.

21:28–31 *seven ewe lambs . . . Beersheba.* The Hebrew number seven is similar in sound to the verb meaning "to swear" (v. 24). Thus Beersheba would be the well where they swore and the well of the seven ewe lambs.

21:34 *land of the Philistines.* The name Palestine comes from the word for Philistine.

18 ver. 13 **19** Nu 22:31 **20** Ge 28:15; 39:2,3,21; Ge 16:12 **21** Ge 24:4 **22** Ge 20:2; 26:26; Ge 26:28 **23** Jos 2:12; 1Sa 24:21 **25** See Ge 26:15,18,20-22 **27** Ge 26:31; 31:44; 1Sa 18:3 **29** Ge 33:8 **30** Ge 31:48,52 **31** Ge 26:33 **33** Ge 4:26; Dt 33:27 **CHAPTER 22** **1** 1Co 10:13; Heb 11:17; Jas 1:12; 1Pe 1:7 **2** Heb 11:17; 2Ch 3:1

his son Isaac; and he split the wood for the burnt offering, and then he got up and went to the place of which God had told him.

4 On the third day [of travel] Abraham looked up and saw the place in the distance.

5 Abraham said to his servants, "Settle down *and* stay here with the donkey; the young man and I will go over there and worship [God], and we will come back to you." [Heb 11:17–19]

6 Then Abraham took the wood for the burnt offering and laid it on [the shoulders of] Isaac his son, and he took the fire (firepot) in his own hand and the [sacrificial] knife; and the two of them walked on together.

7 And Isaac said to Abraham, "My father!" And he said, "Here I am, my son." Isaac said, "Look, the fire and the wood, but where is the lamb for the burnt offering?"

8 Abraham said, "My son, God will provide for Himself a lamb for the burnt offering." So the two walked on together.

9 When they came to the place of which God had told him, Abraham built an altar there and arranged the wood, and bound Isaac his son and placed him on the altar, on top of the wood. [Matt 10:37]

10 Abraham reached out his hand and took the knife to kill his son. [Heb 11:17–19]

11 But the Angel of the LORD called to him from heaven and said, "Abraham, Abraham!" He answered, "Here I am."

12 The LORD said, "Do not reach out [with the knife in] your hand against the boy, and do nothing to [harm] him; for now I know that you fear God [with reverence and profound respect], since you have not withheld from Me your son, your only son [of promise]."

13 Then Abraham looked up and glanced around, and behold, behind him was a ram caught in a thicket by his horns. And Abraham went and took the ram and offered it up for a burnt offering (ascending sacrifice) instead of his son.

14 So Abraham named that place The LORD Will Provide. And it is said to this day, "On the mountain of the LORD it will be seen *and* provided."

15 The Angel of the LORD called to Abraham from heaven a second time

16 and said, "By Myself (on the basis of Who I Am) I have sworn [an oath], declares the LORD, that since you have done this thing and have not withheld [from Me] your son, your only son [of promise],

17 indeed I will greatly bless you, and I will greatly multiply your descendants

---

22:5 *worship [God], and we will come back to you.* Abraham's comment to his servants is a significant avowal of his faith in God. Even though he was going to sacrifice his son, he was confident that they both would return.

22:8 *God will provide.* Abraham's faith in God's promise is shown in his response to a very real and terrible test. Many times this is seen as a test of the quality of Abraham's love for God — who would he choose, God or his son? However, there is no sign that Abraham made this mistake. He knew beyond a shadow of doubt that Isaac was given to him directly by God, the son of promise. Therefore it was right that he should love his son of promise as a gift from God. God's covenant said that a great nation would descend from Isaac, therefore it would be so. Abraham's test was not "whom do you love most?" but "do you really believe Me?" The answer was a resounding, "Yes!" Abraham carried his faith to the knife edge on his son's flesh. God had promised, and it would be so, even if Isaac had to be raised from the dead to make His words come to pass (Heb 11:17 – 19).

22:9 *bound Isaac his son.* Surely Isaac could have struggled or run away at this point, but there is no evidence that he did so. Apparently Isaac's faith and trust both in God and in his father was sufficient to stand the test.

22:14 *The Lord Will Provide.* As God provided a ram to take the place of Abraham's son, so one day He would provide His own Son to take our place. Some believe that Mt. Moriah later became part of the city of Jerusalem, and was the site of Solomon's temple.

22:17 *I will greatly bless you.* In the Hebrew, this is stated by doubling the verbs (blessing I will bless you, multiplying I will multiply you), a Hebrew idiom that powerfully emphasizes the certainty of the action.

---

6 Jn 19:17 **9** Heb 11:17; Jas 2:21 **12** 1Sa 15:22; Ge 26:5; Jas 2:22 **16** Ps 105:9; Lk 1:73; Heb 6:13,14 **17** Ge 15:5; Jer 33:22; Ge 13:16; Ge 24:60; Mic 1:9

like the stars of the heavens and like
the sand on the seashore; and your seed
shall possess the gate of their enemies
[as conquerors]. [Heb 6:13, 14; 11:12]
18"Through your seed all the nations
of the earth shall be blessed, because
you have heard *and* obeyed My voice."
[Gen 12:2, 3; 13:16; 22:18; 26:4; 28:14;
Acts 3:25, 26; Gal 3:16]
19So Abraham returned to his ser-
vants, and they got up and went with
him to Beersheba; and Abraham set-
tled in Beersheba.
20Now after these things Abraham
was told, "Milcah has borne children
to your brother Nahor:
21Uz the firstborn and Buz his broth-
er and Kemuel the father of Aram,
22Chesed and Hazo and Pildash and
Jidlaph and Bethuel."
23Bethuel became the father of Re-
bekah. These eight [children] Milcah
bore to Nahor, Abraham's brother.
24Nahor's concubine, whose name
was Reumah, gave birth to Tebah and
Gaham and Tahash and Maacah.

Death and Burial of Sarah

23 SARAH LIVED a hundred and
twenty-seven years; this was the
length of the life of Sarah.
2Sarah died in Kiriath-arba (that is,
Hebron) in the land of Canaan, and
Abraham went to mourn for Sarah
and to weep for her.
3Then Abraham stood up before his
dead [wife's body], and spoke to the
sons of Heth (Hittites), saying,
4"I am a stranger and a sojourner
(resident alien) among you; give (sell)
me property for a burial place among
you so that I may bury my dead [in the
proper manner]."
5The Hittites replied to Abraham,
6"Listen to us, my lord; you are a
prince of God [a mighty prince] among
us; bury your dead in the choicest of
our graves; none of us will refuse you
his grave *or* hinder you from burying
your dead [wife]."
7So Abraham stood up and bowed
to the people of the land, the Hittites.
8And Abraham said to them, "If you
are willing to grant my dead a [proper]
burial, listen to me, and plead with
Ephron the son of Zohar for me,
9so that he may give (sell) me the
cave of Machpelah which he owns—it
is at the end of his field; let him give
it to me here in your presence for the
full price as a burial site [which I may
keep forever among you]."
10Now Ephron was present there
among the sons of Heth; so within
the hearing of all the sons of Heth
and all who were entering the gate of
his city, Ephron the Hittite answered
Abraham, saying,
11"No, my lord, hear me; I give you
the [entire] field, and I also give you the
cave that is in it. In the presence of the
men of my people I give (sell) it to you;
bury your dead [there]."
12Then Abraham bowed down be-
fore the people of the land.
13He said to Ephron in the presence
of the people of the land, "If you will
only please listen to me *and* accept my
offer. I will give you the price of the
field; accept it from me and I will bury
my dead there."
14Ephron replied to Abraham,
15"My lord, listen to me. The land
[you seek] is worth four hundred shek-
els of silver; what is that between you
and me? So bury your dead."

22:18 *seed.* Here this is a grand play on words. The seed was Isaac, and by extension the Jewish nation. Specifically the Seed was one descendant of Abraham, Jesus the Messiah.

23:13 *I will give you the price of the field.* Abraham would not have been offering "money" as we think of it today; minted coins were not invented until at least 650 BC. Instead, trading was done by barter, or with precious metals by weight.

23:15 *what is that between you and me?* The dialogue in this chapter gives a wonderfully detailed example of the bargaining process of the day. Abraham clearly understood Ephron's generous statement as a politely phrased way of setting his price.

18 Ge 12:3; 18:18; 26:4; Ac 3:25; Gal 3:8,9,16,18; ver. 3,10; Ge 26:5 **19** Ge 21:31 **20** Ge 11:29 **21** Job 1:1; Job 32:2 **23** Ge 24:15; Ro 9:10 **CHAPTER 23** **2** Jos 14:15; ver. 19; Ge 13:18 **4** Ge 17:8; 1Ch 29:15; Ps 105:12; Heb 11:9,13; Ac 7:5 **6** Ge 13:2; 14:14; 24:35 **10** Ge 34:20,24; Ru 4:4 **11** See 2Sa 24:21-24 **15** Ex 30:13; Eze 45:12

16 So Abraham listened to Ephron [and agreed to his terms]; and he weighed out for Ephron the [amount of] silver which he had named in the hearing of the Hittites: four hundred shekels of silver, according to the weights current among the merchants.

17 So the field of Ephron in Machpelah, which was to the east of Mamre (Hebron)—the field and the cave which was in it, and all the trees that were in the field and in all its borders around it—were deeded over [legally]

18 to Abraham as his possession in the presence of the Hittites, before all who were entering at the gate of his city.

19 After this, Abraham buried Sarah his wife in the cave of the field of Machpelah to the east of Mamre (that is, Hebron) in the land of Canaan.

20 The field and the cave in it were deeded over to Abraham by the Hittites as a [permanent] possession *and* burial place.

A Bride for Isaac

24 NOW ABRAHAM was old, [well] advanced in age; and the LORD had blessed Abraham in all things.

2 Abraham said to his servant [Eliezer of Damascus], the oldest of his household, who had charge over all that Abraham owned, "Please, put your hand under my thigh [as is customary for affirming a solemn oath], [Gen 15:2]

3 and I will make you swear by the LORD, the God of heaven and the God of earth, that you will not take a wife for my son from the daughters of the Canaanites, among whom I live,

4 but you will [instead] go to my [former] country (Mesopotamia) and to my relatives, and take a wife for my son Isaac [the heir of the covenant promise]."

5 The servant said to him, "Suppose the woman will not be willing to follow me back to this country; should I take your son back to the country from which you came?"

6 Abraham said to him, "See to it that you do not take my son back there!

7 "The LORD, the God of heaven, who took me from my father's house, from the land of my family *and* my birth, who spoke to me and swore to me, saying, 'To your descendants I will give this land'—He will send His angel before you [to guide you], and you will take a wife from there for my son [and bring her here].

8 "If the woman is not willing to follow you [to this land], then you will be free from this my oath *and* blameless; only you must never take my son back there."

9 So the servant put his hand under the thigh of Abraham his master, and swore to him concerning this matter.

10 Then the servant took ten of his master's camels, and set out, taking some of his master's good things with him; so he got up and journeyed to Mesopotamia [between the Tigris and the Euphrates Rivers], to the city of Nahor [the home of Abraham's brother].

11 He made the camels kneel down outside the city by the well of water at the time of the evening when women go out to draw water.

12 And he said, "O LORD, God of my master Abraham, please grant me success today, and show lovingkindness (faithfulness) to my master Abraham.

23:20 field . . . cave . . . were deeded over to Abraham. It is interesting to note that the only piece of the promised land that Abraham ever personally possessed was this field and cave to bury his wife.

24:2 his servant [Eliezer of Damascus], the oldest of his household. Some have thought that this might be Eliezer of Damascus, the one who had been named as Abraham's heir before the births of Ishmael and Isaac.

24:3 the daughters of the Canaanites. This was not an issue of racism, as is sometimes thought — it was theological. The Canaanite peoples worshiped the false gods Baal and Asherah (Dt 7:3).

24:12 O LORD, God of my master Abraham.

16 Jer 32:9 **17** Ge 25:9; 49:30-32; 50:13; Ac 7:16 **20** Jer 32:10,11 **CHAPTER 24** **1** Ge 21:5; ver. 35; Ge 13:2; Ps 112:3; Pr 10:22 **2** Ge 15:2; ver. 10; Ge 39:4-6; Ge 47:29; 1Ch 29:24 **3** Ge 14:22; Dt 6:13; Jos 2:12; Ge 26:35; 28:2; Ex 34:16; Dt 7:3 **4** Ge 28:2; Ge 12:1 **7** Ge 12:1; Ge 12:7; 13:15; 17:8; Ex 32:13; Dt 1:8; 34:4; Ac 7:5; Ex 23:20,23; 33:2; Heb 1:14 **8** Jos 2:17,20 **10** ver. 2; Ge 27:43 **11** Ex 2:16; 1Sa 9:11 **12** ver. 27; Ge 26:24; 32:9; Ex 3:6,15; Neh 1:11; Ps 37:5

13 "Behold, I stand here at the spring
of water, and the daughters of the men
of the city are coming out to draw
water;
14 now let it be that the girl to whom
I say, 'Please, let down your jar so that
I may [have a] drink,' and she replies,
'Drink, and I will also give your camels
water to drink'—may she *be the one*
whom You have selected [as a wife] for
Your servant Isaac; and by this I will
know that You have shown loving-
kindness (faithfulness) to my master."

Rebekah Is Chosen

15 Before Eliezer had finished speak-
ing (praying), Rebekah came out with
her [water] jar on her shoulder. Re-
bekah was the daughter of Bethuel
the son of Milcah, who was the wife
of Abraham's brother Nahor.
16 The girl was very beautiful, a
virgin and unmarried; and she went
down to the spring and filled her jar
and came up.
17 Then the servant ran to meet her,
and said, "Please let me drink a little
water from your jar."
18 And she said, "Drink, my lord";
and she quickly lowered her jar to her
hand, and gave him a drink.
19 When she had given Eliezer a
drink, she said, "I will also draw wa-
ter for your camels until they have
finished drinking."
20 So she quickly emptied her jar into
the trough, and ran again to the well
and drew water for all his camels.
21 Meanwhile, the man stood gazing
at Rebekah in [reverent] silence, [wait-
ing] to know if the LORD had made his
trip successful or not.
22 When the camels had finished
drinking, Eliezer took a gold ring
weighing a half-shekel and two brace-
lets for her hands weighing ten shekels
in gold,
23 and said, "Whose daughter are
you? Please tell me, is there room in
your father's house for us to lodge?"
24 And she said to him, "I am the
daughter of Bethuel, Milcah's son,
whom she bore to [her husband] Na-
hor."
25 Again she said to him, "We have
plenty of both straw and feed, and also
room to lodge."
26 The man bowed his head and wor-
shiped the LORD.
27 He said, "Blessed be the LORD, the
God of my master Abraham, who has
not denied His lovingkindness and
His truth to my master. As for me, the
LORD led me to the house of my mas-
ter's brothers."
28 Then the girl ran and told her moth-
er's household what had happened.
29 Now Rebekah had a brother whose
name was Laban; and Laban ran out
to the man at the well.
30 When he saw the ring and the
bracelets on his sister's arms, and
when he heard Rebekah his sister, say-
ing, "The man said this to me," he went
to Eliezer and found him standing by
the camels at the spring.
31 And Laban said, "Come in, blessed
of the LORD! Why do you stand outside
since I have made the house ready and
have prepared a place for the camels?"
32 So the man came into the house,
and Laban unloaded his camels and
gave them straw and feed, and [he
gave] water to [Eliezer to] wash his

This language does not mean that the servant himself did not believe in God. The servant was making his appeal on the basis of God's covenant loyalty to Abraham.

24:15 Providence — Abraham sent his servant to choose Isaac's bride, confident that his servant would be led by the Lord and that in God's providence he would make the right choice. The servant prayed for very specific guidance, and God sent him Rebekah. He was impressed not only with her physical beauty, but also with her kind, generous, and hospitable character. His decision was confirmed when her parents gave their consent and she agreed to return with him. Today we must remember to seek the Lord's guidance and trust in His providence just as Abraham's servant, Rebekah, and her family did.

13 ver. 43; Ex 2:16 **14** See Jdg 6:17,37; 1Sa 6:7; 14:10; 20:7 **15** Ge 11:29; 22:23 **16** Ge 26:7 **18** 1Pe 3:8 **21** ver. 12,56 **22** Ex 32:2,3; Isa 3:19-21 **24** Ge 22:23 **26** ver. 52; Ex 4:31 **27** Ex 18:10; Ru 4:14; 1Sa 25:32,39; Ge 32:10; Ps 98:3; ver. 48 **29** Ge 29:5 **31** Ge 26:29; Jdg 17:2; Ru 3:10; Ps 115:15 **32** Ge 43:24; Jdg 19:21

feet and the feet of the men who were with him.

33 But when food was set before him, he said, "I will not eat until I have stated my business." And Laban said, "Speak on."

34 So he said, "I am Abraham's servant.

35 "The LORD has greatly blessed my master, and he has become great (wealthy, powerful); He has given him flocks and herds, and silver and gold, and servants and maids, and camels and donkeys.

36 "Now Sarah my master's wife bore a son to my master when she was in her old age, and he has given everything that he has to him.

37 "My master made me swear [an oath], saying, 'You must not take a wife for my son from the daughters of the Canaanites, in whose land I live;

38 but you shall [instead] go to my father's house and to my family and take a wife for my son [Isaac].'

39 "Then I said to my master, 'But suppose the woman will not follow me [back to this land].'

40 "He said to me, 'The LORD, before whom I walk [habitually and obediently], will send His angel with you to make your journey successful, and you will take a wife for my son from my relatives and from my father's house;

41 then you will be free of my oath, when you come to my relatives; and if they do not give her to you, you will [also] be free of my oath.'

42 "I came today to the spring, and said, 'O LORD, God of my master Abraham, if now You will make my journey on which I go successful;

43 please look, I am standing by the spring of water; now let it be that when the maiden [whom You have chosen for Isaac] comes out to draw [water], and to whom I say, "Please, give me a little water to drink from your jar";

44 and if she says to me, "You drink, and I will also draw [water] for your camels"; let that woman be the one whom the LORD has selected *and* chosen [as a wife] for my master's son.'

45 "Before I had finished praying in my heart, behold, Rebekah came out with her [water] jar on her shoulder, and she went down to the spring and drew water. And I said to her, 'Please, let me have a drink.'

46 "And she quickly let down her jar from her *shoulder*, and said, 'Drink, and I will also water your camels'; so I drank, and she also watered the camels.

47 "Then I asked her, 'Whose daughter are you?' She said, 'The daughter of Bethuel, Nahor's son, whom Milcah bore to him'; and I put the ring in her nose, and the bracelets on her arms.

48 "And I bowed down my head and worshiped the LORD, and blessed the LORD, the God of my master Abraham, who had led me in the right way to take the daughter of my master's brother to his son [as a wife].

49 "So now if you are going to show kindness and truth to my master [being faithful to him], tell me; and if not, tell me, that I may turn to the right or to the left [and go on my way]."

50 Then Laban and Bethuel answered, "The matter has come from the LORD; so we dare not speak bad or good [to you about it—we cannot interfere].

51 "Rebekah is before you; take her and go, and let her be the wife of your master's son, as the LORD has spoken."

52 When Abraham's servant heard their words, he bowed himself to the ground [in worship] before the LORD.

53 Then the servant brought out jewelry of silver, jewelry of gold, and articles of clothing, and gave them to Rebekah; he also gave precious things to her brother and her mother.

24:50 *The matter has come from the LORD.* It appears that the family of Bethuel and Laban also worshiped the living God, or at least acknowledged Him along with other gods (see 31:19; Jos 24:2).

33 Job 23:12; Jn 4:34; Eph 6:5-7 **35** ver. 1; Ge 13:2 **36** Ge 21:2; Ge 21:10; 25:5 **37** ver. 3 **38** ver. 4 **39** ver. 5 **40** ver. 7; Ge 17:1 **41** ver. 8 **42** ver. 12 **43** ver. 13 **45** ver. 15; 1Sa 1:13 **47** Eze 16:11,12 **48** ver. 26; Ge 22:23 **49** Ge 47:29; Jos 2:14 **50** Ps 118:23; Mt 21:42; Ge 31:24 **51** Ge 20:15 **52** ver. 26 **53** Ex 3:22; 11:2; 12:35; 2Ch 21:3; Ezr 1:6

54 Then he and the men who were with him ate and drank and spent the night [there]. In the morning when they got up, he said, "Now send me back to my master."

55 But Rebekah's brother and mother said, "Let the girl stay with us a few days—at least ten; then she may go."

56 But Eliezer said to them, "Do not delay me, since the LORD has prospered my way. Send me away, so that I may go back to my master."

57 And they said, "We will call the girl and ask her what she prefers."

58 So they called Rebekah and said, "Will you go with this man?" And she answered, "I will go."

59 So they sent off their sister Rebekah and her nurse [Deborah, as her attendant] and Abraham's servant [Eliezer] and his men.

60 They blessed Rebekah and said to her,

"May you, our sister,
Become [the mother of] thousands
of ten thousands,
And may your descendants
possess (conquer)
The [city] gate of those who hate
them."

61 Then Rebekah and her attendants stood, and they mounted camels and followed the man. So the servant took Rebekah and went on his way.

Isaac Marries Rebekah

62 Now Isaac had returned from going to Beer-lahai-roi (Well of the Living One Who Sees Me), for he was living in the Negev. [Gen 16:14]

63 Isaac went out to bow down [in prayer] in the field in the [early] evening; he raised his eyes and looked, and camels were coming.

64 Rebekah also raised her eyes *and* looked, and when she saw Isaac, she dismounted from her camel.

65 She said to the servant, "Who is that man there walking across the field to meet us?" And the servant said, "He is my master [Isaac]." So she took a veil and covered herself [as was customary].

66 The servant told Isaac everything that he had done.

67 Then Isaac brought her into his mother Sarah's tent, and he took Rebekah [in marriage], and she became his wife, and he loved her; therefore Isaac was comforted after his mother's death.

Abraham's Death

25 ABRAHAM TOOK another wife, whose name was Keturah.

2 She gave birth to Zimran, Jokshan, Medan, Midian, Ishbak, and Shuah.

3 Jokshan was the father of Sheba and Dedan. The sons of Dedan were Asshurim, Letushim, and Leummim.

24:60 *They blessed Rebekah.* These words are not mere sentiment, nor are they a magical charm, but a prayer for God's blessing on her life. ***gate.*** The possession of the gates of one's enemies meant power over them (22:17).

24:67 *he loved her*. The love of Isaac for Rebekah is a wonderful fulfillment and illustration of God's original purpose for marriage. Realizing it was not good for man to be alone (Ge 2:18), the Creator graciously created Eve, a helper for Adam. God Himself then performed history's first wedding. Isaac and Rebekah serve not only as a lovely example of godly marriage, but also as a beautiful picture of the love between Christ and the church in the New Testament. Rebekah, like the church, loved her bridegroom without first seeing him (compare Ge 24:58 with 1Pe 1:8). Like the church, Rebekah was prayed for by her bridegroom (Ge 24:63; Ro 8:34). Isaac, having previously been presented for offering on Mt. Moriah (Ge 22:1–14), was content to await the arrival of his bride. He was an early portrayal of the Son of God who now awaits the arrival of His bride in heaven (Heb 10:12–14).

25:1 *took another wife.* In 1 Chronicles 1:32, Keturah is described as Abraham's concubine. It is not really known exactly what position she had in Abraham's household, or when the relationship began. Her sons had a status similar to that of Ishmael, Abraham's son by Hagar (ch. 16), but without Ishmael's particular blessing (16:10–16).

25:2 *Midian.* This son was the father of the Midianites, some of whom later bought Joseph from his brothers (37:28,36).

54 ver. 56,59 **59** Ge 35:8 **60** Ge 17:16; Ge 22:17 **62** Ge 25:11 **63** Jos 1:8; Ps 1:2; 77:12; 119:15; 143:5 **64** Jos 15:18 **67** Ge 38:12 **CHAPTER 25** **2** 1Ch 1:32

4The sons of Midian were Ephah, Epher, Hanoch, Abida, and Eldaah. All these were the sons of Keturah.

5Now Abraham gave everything that he had to Isaac;

6but to the sons of his concubines [Hagar and Keturah], Abraham gave gifts while he was still living and he sent them to the east country, away from Isaac his son [of promise].

7The days of Abraham's life were a hundred and seventy-five years.

8Then Abraham breathed his last and he died at a good old age, an old man who was satisfied [with life]; and he was gathered to his people [who had preceded him in death]. [Gen 15:15; Heb 11:13–16]

9So his sons Isaac and Ishmael buried him in the cave of Machpelah, in the field of Ephron the son of Zohar the Hittite, which is east of Mamre,

10the field which Abraham purchased from the sons of Heth; there Abraham was buried with Sarah his wife.

11Now after the death of Abraham, God blessed his son Isaac; and Isaac lived at Beer-lahai-roi.

Descendants of Ishmael

12Now these are *the records of* the descendants of Ishmael, Abraham's son, whom Hagar the Egyptian, Sarah's maid, bore to Abraham;

13and these are the names of the [twelve] sons of Ishmael, named in the order of their births: Nebaioth, the firstborn of Ishmael, and Kedar, Adbeel, Mibsam,

14Mishma, Dumah, Massa,

15Hadad, Tema, Jetur, Naphish, and Kedemah.

16These are the sons of Ishmael and these are their names, by their settlements, and by their encampments (sheepfolds); twelve princes (sheiks) according to their tribes. [Foretold in Gen 17:20]

17Ishmael lived a hundred and thirty-seven years; then he breathed his last and died, and was gathered to his people [who had preceded him in death].

18Ishmael's sons (descendants) settled from Havilah to Shur which is east of Egypt as one goes toward Assyria; he settled opposite (east) of all his relatives.

Isaac's Sons

19Now these are *the records of* the descendants of Isaac, Abraham's son: Abraham was the father of Isaac.

20Isaac was forty years old when he married Rebekah, the daughter of Bethuel the Aramean (Syrian) of Paddan-aram, the sister of Laban the Aramean.

21Isaac prayed to the LORD for his wife, because she was unable to conceive children; and the LORD granted his prayer and Rebekah his wife conceived [twins].

22But the children struggled together within her [kicking and shoving one another]; and she said, "If it is so [that the LORD has heard our prayer], why then am I *this way?*" So she went to inquire of the LORD [praying for an answer].

23The LORD said to her,

"[The founders of] two nations are
in your womb;
And the separation of two nations
has begun in your body;
The one people shall be stronger
than the other;
And the older shall serve the
younger."

24When her days to be delivered were fulfilled, behold, there were twins in her womb.

25:11 *God blessed.* God blessed Isaac because He had already established "an everlasting covenant" with him (17:19; Heb 11:17). Later God renewed the covenant with Isaac personally (26:2–5).

25:21 *prayed.* The Hebrew verb here indicates that Isaac prayed passionately for his wife. For examples of passionate prayer, see Ex 8:30; 2Sa 21:14; 24:25.

5 Ge 24:36 **6** Ge 21:14; Jdg 6:3 **8** Ge 15:15; Ge 35:29; 49:33 **9** Ge 35:29; 50:13 **10** Ge 23:16; Ge 49:31 **11** Ge 16:14 **12** Ge 16:15 **13** 1Ch 1:29 **16** Ge 17:20 **17** ver. 8 **18** 1Sa 15:7; Ge 16:12 **19** Mt 1:2 **20** Ge 22:23; Ge 24:29 **21** 1Ch 5:20; 2Ch 33:13; Ezr 8:23; Ro 9:10 **22** 1Sa 9:9; 10:22 **23** Ge 17:16; 24:60; 2Sa 8:14; Ge 27:29; Mal 1:3; Ro 9:12

25 The first came out reddish all over like a hairy garment; and they named him Esau (hairy).

26 Afterward his brother came out, and his hand grasped Esau's heel, so he was named Jacob (one who grabs by the heel, supplanter). Isaac was sixty years old when Rebekah gave birth to them.

27 When the boys grew up, Esau was an able *and* skilled hunter, a man of the outdoors, but Jacob was a quiet *and* peaceful man, living in tents.

28 Now Isaac loved [and favored] Esau, because he enjoyed eating his game, but Rebekah loved [and favored] Jacob.

29 Jacob had cooked [reddish-brown lentil] stew [one day], when Esau came from the field and was famished;

30 and Esau said to Jacob, "Please, let me have a quick swallow of that red stuff there, because I am exhausted *and* famished." For that reason Esau was [also] called Edom (Red).

31 Jacob answered, "First sell me your birthright (the rights of a firstborn)."

32 Esau said, "Look, I am about to die [if I do not eat soon]; so of what use is this birthright to me?"

33 Jacob said, "Swear [an oath] to me today [that you are selling it to me for this food]"; so he swore [an oath] to him, and sold him his birthright.

34 Then Jacob gave Esau bread and lentil stew; and he ate and drank, and got up and went on his way. In this way Esau scorned his birthright. [Heb 12:15–17]

Isaac Settles in Gerar

26 NOW THERE was a famine in the land [of Canaan], besides the previous famine that had occurred in the days of Abraham. So Isaac went to Gerar, to Abimelech king of the Philistines.

2 The LORD appeared to him and said, "Do not go down to Egypt; stay in the land of which I will tell you.

3 "Live temporarily [as a resident] in this land and I will be with you and will bless *and* favor you, for I will give all these lands to you and to your descendants, and I will establish *and* carry out the oath which I swore to Abraham your father. [Gen 22:16–18; Ps 105:9]

4 "I will make your descendants multiply as the stars of the heavens, and will give to your descendants all these lands; and by your descendants shall all the nations of the earth be blessed, [Gen 22:18; Acts 3:25, 26; Gal 3:16]

5 because Abraham listened to *and* obeyed My voice and [consistently] kept My charge, My commandments, My statutes, and My laws."

6 So Isaac stayed in Gerar.

7 The men of the place asked him about his wife, and he said, "She is my sister," for he was afraid to say, "my wife"—thinking, "the men of the place might kill me on account of Rebekah, since she is very beautiful."

25:25 *Esau.* This name sounds like the Hebrew word that means "hairy."

25:26 *Jacob.* The Hebrew word that means "heel" sounds similar to the name Jacob. The name may mean either "He Who Grasps at the Heel (of Another)" or "He (the Lord) Is at His Heels (Is His Protector)."

25:30 *Edom.* This name means "red." The nickname is here connected to the red stew for which he traded his birthright; many have speculated that Esau may have had ruddy skin, or even red hair since the name stuck and even became the name of his land and the nation of his descendants (36:8).

26:1 *Philistines.* The Philistines are thought to have come to the coastland of Canaan following their defeat by the Egyptians around 1200 BC. The Egyptians called them the "Sea Peoples"; they were apparently Greek peoples who migrated eastward (see 1Sa 4:1; 2Sa 5:17).

26:3 *bless and favor you.* The Lord fulfilled His promise to Abraham concerning Isaac (17:19). He established His everlasting covenant with Isaac, just as He had with Abraham.

26:7 *sister.* Rebekah was Isaac's close relative, but she was not his sister (she was his first cousin once removed). Isaac was even more deceitful than his father Abraham (20:2,12).

25 Ge 27:11,16,23 **26** Hos 12:3; Ge 27:36 **27** Ge 27:3,5; Job 1:1,8; Heb 11:9 **28** Ge 27:19,25,31; Ge 27:6 **33** Heb 12:16 **34** Ecc 8:15; Isa 22:13; 1Co 15:32 **CHAPTER 26** **1** Ge 12:10; Ge 20:2 **2** Ge 12:1 **3** Ge 20:1; Ps 39:12; Heb 11:9; Ge 28:15; Ge 12:2; Ge 13:15; Ge 22:16; Ps 105:9 **4** Ge 15:5; 22:17; Ge 12:3; 22:18 **5** Ge 22:16,18 **7** Ge 12:13; 20:2,13; Pr 29:25; Ge 24:16

8 It happened when he had been there a long time, that Abimelech king of the Philistines looked out of a window and saw Isaac caressing Rebekah his wife.

9 Then Abimelech called Isaac and said, "See here, Rebekah is in fact your wife! How did you [dare to] say to me, 'She is my sister'?" And Isaac said to him, "Because I thought I might be killed because of her [desirability]."

10 Abimelech said, "What is this that you have done to us? One of the men [among our people] might easily have been intimate with your wife, and you would have brought guilt on us [before God]."

11 Then Abimelech commanded all his people, "Whoever touches this man [Isaac] or his wife [Rebekah] shall without exception be put to death."

12 Then Isaac planted [seed] in that land [as a farmer] and reaped in the same year a hundred times [as much as he had planted], and the LORD blessed *and* favored him.

13 And the man [Isaac] became great and gained more and more until he became very wealthy *and* extremely distinguished;

14 he owned flocks and herds and a great household [with a number of servants], and the Philistines envied him.

15 Now all the wells which his father's servants had dug in the days of Abraham his father, the Philistines stopped up by filling them with dirt.

16 Then Abimelech said to Isaac, "Go away from here, because you are far too powerful for us."

17 So Isaac left that region and camped in the Valley of Gerar, and settled there.

Quarrel over the Wells

18 Now Isaac again dug [and reopened] the wells of water which had been dug in the days of Abraham his father, because the Philistines had filled them up [with dirt] after the death of Abraham; and he gave the wells the same names that his father had given them.

19 But when Isaac's servants dug in the valley and found there a well of flowing [spring] water,

20 the herdsmen of Gerar quarreled with Isaac's herdsmen, saying, "The water is ours!" So Isaac named the well Esek (quarreling), because they quarreled with him.

21 Then his servants dug another well, and they quarreled over that also, so Isaac named it Sitnah (enmity).

22 He moved away from there and dug another well, and they did not quarrel over that one; so he named it Rehoboth (broad places), saying, "For now the LORD has made room for us, and we shall be prosperous in the land."

23 Then he went up from there to Beersheba.

24 The LORD appeared to him the same night and said,

"I am the God of Abraham your
  father;
Do not be afraid, for I am with you.
I will bless *and* favor you, and
  multiply your descendants,
For the sake of My servant
  Abraham."

25 So Isaac built an altar there and called on the name of the LORD [in prayer]. He pitched his tent there; and there Isaac's servants dug a well.

Covenant with Abimelech

26 Then Abimelech came to him from Gerar with Ahuzzath, his [close friend and confidential] adviser, and Phicol, the commander of his army.

27 Isaac said to them, "Why have you [people] come to me, since you hate me and have sent me away from you?"

26:12 – 13 *blessed.* God's special work for Abraham was extended to the son.
26:25 *called on the name of the LORD.* Isaac followed the practice of his father (12:8). At this altar Isaac not only prayed to the Lord, he also affirmed the reality of the living God in this special land (12:8; 21:33).

10 Ge 20:9 **11** Ps 105:15 **12** Mt 13:8; Mk 4:8; ver. 3; Job 42:12 **13** Ge 24:35; Pr 10:22 **14** Ge 37:11; Ecc 4:4 **15** Ge 21:30 **16** Ex 1:9 **18** Ge 21:31 **20** Ge 21:25 **22** Ge 17:6; 28:3; 41:52; Ex 1:7 **24** Ge 17:7; 24:12; Ge 15:1; ver. 3,4 **25** Ge 12:7; 13:18; Ps 116:17 **26** Ge 21:22 **27** Jdg 11:7; ver. 16

[28]They said, "We see clearly that the
LORD has been with you; so we said,
'There should now be an oath between
us [with a curse for the one who breaks
it], that is, between you and us, and let
us make a covenant (binding agree-
ment, solemn promise) with you,
[29]that you will not harm us, just as
we have not touched you and have
done nothing but good to you and have
sent you away in peace. You are now
the blessed *and* favored of the LORD!' "
[30]Then Isaac held a [formal] banquet
(covenant feast) for them, and they ate
and drank.
[31]They got up early in the morning
and swore oaths [pledging to do noth-
ing but good to each other]; and Isaac
sent them on their way and they left
him in peace.
[32]Now on the same day, Isaac's ser-
vants came and told him about the
well they had dug, saying, "We have
found water."
[33]So he named the well Shibah;
therefore the name of the city is Beer-
sheba to this day. [Gen 21:31]
[34]When Esau was forty years old he
married Judith the daughter of Beeri
the Hittite, and Basemath the daughter
of Elon the Hittite as his wives;
[35]and they were a source of grief to
[Esau's parents] Isaac and Rebekah.

Jacob's Deception

27 NOW WHEN Isaac was old and
his eyes were too dim to see, he
called his elder [and favorite] son Esau
and said to him, "My son." And Esau
answered him, "Here I am."
[2]Isaac said, "See here, I am old; I do
not know when I may die.
[3]"So now, please take your [hunting]
gear, your quiver [of arrows] and your
bow, and go out into the open country
and hunt game for me;
[4]and make me a savory *and* deli-
cious dish [of meat], the kind I love,
and bring it to me to eat, so that my
soul may bless you [as my firstborn
son] before I die."
[5]But Rebekah overheard what Isaac
said to Esau his son; and when Esau
had gone to the open country to hunt
for game that he might bring back,
[6]Rebekah said to Jacob her [younger
and favorite] son, "Listen carefully: I
heard your father saying to Esau your
brother,
[7]'Bring me some game and make me
a savory *and* delicious dish [of meat],
so that I may eat it, and declare my
blessing on you in the presence of the
LORD before my death.'
[8]"So now, my son, listen [carefully]
to me [and do exactly] as I command
you.
[9]"Go now to the flock and bring me
two good *and* suitable young goats,
and I will make them into a savory
dish [of meat] for your father, the kind
he loves [to eat].
[10]"Then you shall bring it to your
father to eat, so that he may bless you
before his death."
[11]Jacob said to Rebekah his mother,
"Listen, Esau my brother is a hairy
man and I am a smooth [skinned] man.
[12]"Suppose my father touches me
and feels my skin; then I will be seen
by him as a cheat (imposter), and I
will bring his curse on me and not a
blessing."
[13]But his mother said to him, "May
your curse be on me, my son; only
listen *and* obey me, and go, bring the
young goats to me."
[14]So Jacob went and got the two

26:34 *Hittite.* Because the Hittites believed in many different gods, Esau's marriages were unacceptable for one belonging to God's covenant family.

27:4 *my soul.* This phrase is simply a substitute for the personal pronoun, "I."

27:8 *listen [carefully] to me [and do exactly] as I command you.* Rebekah certainly appears calculating and devious in this passage, but God had told her before they were even born that the younger son would have precedence over the older (25:23). He had not, however, told her to make sure that it happened, and the results of her deception were family strife and the loss of her younger son.

28 Ge 21:22,23 **29** Ge 24:31; Ps 115:15 **30** Ge 19:3 **31** Ge 21:31 **33** Ge 21:31 **34** Ge 36:2 **35** Ge 27:46; 28:1,8 **CHAPTER 27** **1** Ge 48:10; 1Sa 3:2 **2** Pr 27:1; Jas 4:14 **3** Ge 25:27,28 **4** ver. 27; Ge 48:9,15; 49:28; Dt 33:1 **8** ver. 13 **9** ver. 4 **10** ver. 4 **11** Ge 25:25 **12** ver. 22; Ge 9:25; Dt 27:18 **13** Ge 43:9; 1Sa 25:24; 2Sa 14:9; Mt 27:25 **14** Pr 23:3; Lk 21:34

young goats, and brought them to his
mother; and his mother prepared a
delicious *dish of* food [with a delight-
ful aroma], the kind his father loved
[to eat].
15 Then Rebekah took her elder son
Esau's best clothes, which were with
her in her house, and put them on Ja-
cob her younger son.
16 And she put the skins of the young
goats on his hands and on the smooth
part of his neck.
17 Then she gave her son Jacob the
delicious meat and the bread which
she had prepared.
18 So he went to his father and said,
"My father." And Isaac said, "Here I
am. Who are you, my son?"
19 Jacob said to his father, "I am Esau
your firstborn; I have done what you
told me to do. Now please, sit up and
eat some of my game, so that you may
bless me."
20 Isaac said to his son, "How is it that
you have found the game so quickly, my
son?" And he said, "Because the LORD
your God caused it to come to me."
21 But Isaac [wondered and] said to
Jacob, "Please come close [to me] so
that I may touch you, my son, *and* de-
termine if you are really my son Esau
or not."
22 So Jacob approached Isaac, and
his father touched him and said, "The
voice is Jacob's voice, but the hands
are the hands of Esau."
23 He could not recognize him [as
Jacob], because his hands were hairy
like his brother Esau's hands; so he
blessed him.
24 But he said, "Are you really my son
Esau?" Jacob answered, "I am."
25 Then Isaac said, "Bring the food
to me, and I will eat some of my son's
game, so that I may bless you." He
brought it to him, and he ate; and he
brought him wine and he drank.
26 Then his father Isaac said to him,
"Please come, my son, and kiss me."
27 So he came and kissed him; and
Isaac smelled his clothing and blessed
him and said,

"The scent of my son [Esau]
Is like the aroma of a field which
the LORD has blessed;
28 Now may God give you of the dew
of heaven [to water your land],
And of the fatness (fertility) of the
earth,
And an abundance of grain
and new wine; [Gen 27:39;
Deut 33:13, 28]
29 May peoples serve you,
And nations bow down to you;
Be lord *and* master over your
brothers,
And may your mother's sons bow
down to you.
May those who curse you be
cursed,
And may those who bless you be
blessed."

The Stolen Blessing

30 Now as soon as Isaac had finished
blessing Jacob, and Jacob had scarcely
left the presence of Isaac his father,
Esau his brother came in from his
hunting.
31 Esau also made a delicious dish [of
meat] and brought it to his father and
said to him, "Let my father get up and
eat some of his son's game, so that you
may bless me."
32 Isaac his father said to him, "Who
are you?" And he replied, "I am your
son, your firstborn, Esau."

27:18 – 29 Falsehood — Jacob may have felt justified in deceiving his father, since Esau had already sold him the birthright. Esau had clearly demonstrated his contempt of the position (including the spiritual responsibility) which was his by right, while Jacob valued and desired it. However, lofty purposes and aspirations cannot justify deceit and trickery. We must be content to leave the fulfillment of God's promises in His hand and wait for His time.

27:29 *peoples serve you.* Isaac predicted that Jacob's descendants would obtain supremacy over other peoples. Jesus, as the King of kings, and a descendant of Jacob, ultimately fulfilled this prediction (1Ti 6:14 – 16).

15 ver. 27 **19** ver. 4 **21** ver. 12 **23** ver. 16 **25** ver. 4,10,19,31 **27** SS 4:11; Hos 14:6 **28** Heb 11:20; Dt 33:13,28; 2Sa 1:21; Ps 133:3; Mic 5:7; Ge 45:18; Dt 33:28 **29** Ge 9:25; 25:23; Ge 49:8; Ge 12:3; Nu 24:9; Zep 2:8 **31** ver. 4

33 Then Isaac trembled violently, and
he said, "Then who was the one [who
was just here] who hunted game and
brought it to me? I ate all of it before you
came, and I blessed him. Yes, and he [in
fact] shall be (shall remain) blessed."
34 When Esau heard the words of his
father, he cried out with a great and
extremely bitter cry and said to his
father, "Bless me, even me also, O my
father!" [Heb 12:16, 17]
35 Isaac said, "Your brother came de-
ceitfully and has [fraudulently] taken
away your blessing [for himself]."
36 Esau replied, "Is he not rightly
named Jacob (the supplanter)? For he
has supplanted me these two times:
he took away my birthright, and now
he has taken away my blessing. Have
you not reserved a blessing for me?"
37 But Isaac replied to Esau, "Listen
carefully: I have made Jacob your lord
and master; I have given him all his
brothers *and* relatives as servants; and
I have sustained him with grain and
new wine. What then, can I do for you,
my son?"
38 Esau said to his father, "Have you
only one blessing, my father? Bless me,
even me also, O my father." Then Esau
[no longer able to restrain himself]
raised his voice and wept [loudly].
39 Then Isaac his father answered
and [prophesied and] said to him,

"Your dwelling shall be away from
the fertility of the earth
And away from the dew of heaven
above;
40 But you shall live by your sword,
And serve your brother;
However it shall come to pass
when you break loose [from
your anger and hatred],
That you will tear his yoke off
your neck [and you will be free
of him]."

41 So Esau hated Jacob because of the
blessing with which his father blessed
him; and Esau said in his heart, "The
days of mourning for my father are
very near; then I will kill my brother
Jacob."
42 When these words of her elder son
Esau were repeated to Rebekah, she
sent for Jacob her younger son, and
said to him, "Listen carefully, your
brother Esau is comforting himself
concerning you *by planning* to kill you.
43 "So now, my son, listen *and* do
what I say; go, escape to my brother
Laban in Haran!
44 "Stay with him for a while, until
your brother's anger subsides.
45 "When your brother's anger to-
ward you subsides and he forgets
what you did to him, then I will send
and bring you back from there. Why
should I be deprived of you both in a
single day?"
46 Then Rebekah said to Isaac, "I am
tired of living because of the daughters
of Heth [these insolent wives of Esau].
If Jacob takes a wife from the daugh-
ters of Heth, like these daughters of
the land, what good will my life be to
me?" [Gen 26:34]

Jacob Is Sent Away

28 SO ISAAC called Jacob and
blessed him and charged him,
and said to him, "You shall not marry
one of the women of Canaan.
2 "Arise, go to Paddan-aram, to the
house of Bethuel your mother's father;
and take from there as a wife for your-
self one of the daughters of Laban your
mother's brother.
3 "May God Almighty bless you and
make you fruitful and multiply you, so
that you may become a [great] compa-
ny of peoples.
4 "May He also give the blessing of

27:46 *daughters of Heth.* Intermarrying with the pagan women of Canaan was dangerous because they would bring their pagan gods and pagan worship into their new homes.

28:2 *Paddan-aram.* This is a region of Haran in northern Aram (Syria) near the Euphrates River.
28:3 *God Almighty.* This Hebrew name, *El Shaddai* is used by or in the hearing of Abraham,

33 Ge 28:3,4; Ro 11:29 **34** Heb 12:17 **36** Ge 25:26; Ge 25:33 **37** Fulfilled, 2Sa 8:14; ver. 28 **38** Heb 12:17 **39** ver. 28; Heb 11:20 **40** Ge 25:23; 2Sa 8:14; Ob 18-20; 2Ki 8:20 **41** Ge 37:4,8; Ge 50:3,4,10; Ob 10 **42** Ps 64:5 **43** Ge 11:31 **46** Ge 26:35; 28:8; Ge 24:3 **CHAPTER 28** **1** Ge 27:33; Ge 24:3 **2** Hos 12:12; Ge 25:20; Ge 22:23; Ge 24:29 **3** Ge 17:1,6 **4** Ge 12:2; Ge 17:8

Abraham to you and your descendants
with you, that you may inherit the
[promised] land of your sojournings,
which He gave to Abraham."
5 Then Isaac sent Jacob away, and he
went to Paddan-aram, to Laban, son
of Bethuel the Aramean, the brother
of Rebekah, the mother of Jacob and
Esau.
6 Now Esau noticed that Isaac had
blessed Jacob and sent him to Paddan-
aram to take a wife for himself from
there, and that as he blessed him he
gave him a prohibition, saying, "You
shall not take a wife from the daugh-
ters of Canaan,"
7 and that Jacob obeyed his father
and his mother and had gone to
Paddan-aram.
8 So Esau realized that [his two
wives] the daughters of Canaan dis-
pleased Isaac his father;
9 and [to appease his parents] Esau
went to [the family of] Ishmael and
took as his wife, in addition to the
wives he [already] had, Mahalath the
daughter of Ishmael, Abraham's son,
the sister of Nebaioth [Ishmael's first-
born son].

Jacob's Dream

10 Now Jacob left Beersheba [never
to see his mother again] and traveled
toward Haran.
11 And he came to a certain place and
stayed overnight there because the sun
had set. Taking one of the stones of the
place, he put it under his head and lay
down there [to sleep].
12 He dreamed that there was a lad-
der (stairway) placed on the earth,
and the top of it reached [out of sight]
toward heaven; and [he saw] the angels
of God ascending and descending on it
[going to and from heaven]. [John 1:51]
13 And behold, the LORD stood above
and around him and said, "I am the
LORD, the God of Abraham your [fa-
ther's] father and the God of Isaac; I
will give to you and to your descen-
dants the land [of promise] on which
you are lying.
14 "Your descendants shall be as
[countless as] the dust of the earth,
and you shall spread abroad to the
west and the east and the north and
the south; and all the families (nations)
of the earth shall be blessed through
you and your descendants. [Gen 12:2,
3; 13:16; 22:18; 26:4; Acts 3:25, 26;
Gal 3:8, 16]
15 "Behold, I am with you and will
keep [careful watch over you and
guard] you wherever you may go, and
I will bring you back to this [promised]
land; for I will not leave you until I have
done what I have promised you."
16 Then Jacob awoke from his sleep
and he said, "Without any doubt the
LORD is in this place, and I did not real-
ize it."
17 So he was afraid and said, "How
fearful *and* awesome is this place! This
is none other than the house of God,
and this is the gateway to heaven."
18 So Jacob got up early in the morn-
ing, and took the stone he had put un-
der his head and he set it up as a pillar
[that is, a monument to the vision in his
dream], and he poured [olive] oil on the
top of it [to consecrate it].

Isaac, and Jacob (35:11). God later identified Himself to Moses with this same name (Ex 6:3).

28:9 *Mahalath.* This daughter of Ishmael is probably the same woman as Bashemath (36:3). Her name means "dance."

28:10–15 Jacob's Dream — The ladder of Jacob's dream reminds us of Jesus' words about the angels "ascending and descending on the Son of Man" (Jn 1:51), vividly depicting Himself as the Way into the heavenlies. Certainly Jacob did not deserve such grace after cheating his brother out of the blessings of Isaac. Indeed, he was already suffering by being banished from the fellowship of his family. Nevertheless, God mercifully confirmed the covenant promises made to Abraham and Isaac concerning the land and the descendants. His words, "I am with you and will keep you" speak of God's personal presence for protection and guidance, anticipating Jacob's return to the land, so that all the promises might be fulfilled. Surely the grace of God goes far beyond our small expectations.

8 Ge 24:3; 26:35 **9** Ge 36:3; Ge 25:13 **10** Hos 12:12; Ac 7:2 **12** Ge 41:1; Jn 1:51; Heb 1:14 **13** Ge 35:1; 48:3; Ge 26:24; Ge 13:15; 35:12 **14** Ge 13:16; Ge 13:14; Dt 12:20; Ge 12:3; 18:18; 22:18; 26:4 **15** See ver. 20,21; Ge 48:16; Ge 35:6; Dt 31:6,8; Jos 1:5; 1Ki 8:57; Heb 13:5; Nu 23:19 **16** Ex 3:5; Jos 5:15 **18** Ge 31:13,45; Lev 8:10-12

19He named that place Bethel (the
house of God); the previous name of
that city was Luz (Almond Tree).
20Then Jacob made a vow (promise),
saying, "If God will be with me and
will keep me on this journey that I
take, and will give me food to eat and
clothing to wear,
21and if [He grants that] I return to
my father's house in safety, then the
Lord will be my God.
22"This stone which I have set up as
a pillar (monument, memorial) will be
God's house [a sacred place to me], and
of everything that You give me I will
give the tenth to You [as an offering to
signify my gratitude and dependence on
You]." [Deut 12:8–11; 14:22–26; 26:1–11]

Jacob Meets Rachel

29 THEN JACOB went on his way
and came to the land of the peo-
ple of the East [near Haran].
2As he looked, he saw a well in the
field, and three flocks of sheep lying
there [resting] beside it because the
flocks were watered from that well.
Now the stone on the mouth of the
well [that covered and protected it]
was large,
3and when all the flocks were gath-
ered there, the shepherds would roll
the stone from the mouth of the well,
water the sheep, and [afterward] re-
place the stone on the mouth of the
well.
4Jacob said to them, "My brothers,
where are you from?" And they said,
"We are from Haran."
5So he said to them, "Do you know
Laban the grandson of Nahor [Abra-
ham's brother]?" And they replied, "We
know him."
6And he asked them, "Is it well with
him?" And they said, "He is doing well;
look, here comes his daughter Rachel
with the sheep!"
7Jacob said, "Look, the sun is still
high [overhead]; it is a long time be-
fore the flocks need to be gathered
[in their folds for the night]. Water the
sheep, and go, and return them to their
pasture."
8But they said, "We cannot [leave]
until all the flocks are gathered to-
gether, and the shepherds roll the stone
from the mouth of the well; then we
will water the sheep."
9While he was still speaking with
them, Rachel came with her father's
sheep, for she was a shepherdess.
10When Jacob saw [his cousin] Ra-
chel, the daughter of Laban, his moth-
er's brother, and Laban's sheep, he
came up and rolled the stone away
from the mouth of the well and wa-
tered the flock of Laban, his uncle.
11Then Jacob kissed Rachel [in greet-
ing], and he raised his voice and wept.
12Jacob told Rachel he was her fa-
ther's relative, Rebekah's son; and she
ran and told her father.
13When Laban heard of the arrival
of Jacob, his sister's son, he ran to meet
him, and embraced and kissed him
and brought him to his house. Then
he told Laban all these things.
14Then Laban said to him, "You are
my bone and my flesh." And Jacob
stayed with him a month.
15Then Laban said to Jacob, "Just
because you are my relative, should
you work for me for nothing? Tell me,
what should your wages be?"
16Now Laban had two daughters;
the name of the older was Leah, and
the name of the younger was Rachel.
17Leah's eyes were weak, but Rachel
was beautiful in form and appearance.
18Jacob loved Rachel, so he said, "I
will serve you [as a hired workman] for
seven years [in return] for [the privi-
lege of marrying] Rachel your younger
daughter."

28:22 *the tenth.* Jacob promised to give a tenth of his possessions to God. Abraham had given the same proportion to Melchizedek, the priest of the most high God. Later the Mosaic law required giving a tenth to God (Dt 14:22).

29:6 *Rachel.* This name is a term of endearment meaning "Ewe Lamb."

19 Jdg 1:23,26; Hos 4:15 **20** Ge 31:13; Jdg 11:30; 2Sa 15:8; ver. 15; 1Ti 6:8 **21** Jdg 11:31; 2Sa 19:24,30; Dt 26:17; 2Sa 15:8 **22** Ge 35:7,14; Lev 27:30 **CHAPTER 29** **1** Nu 23:7; Hos 12:12 **6** Ge 43:27 **9** Ex 2:16 **10** Ex 2:17 **11** Ge 33:4; 45:14,15 **12** Ge 13:8; 14:14,16; Ge 24:28 **13** Ge 24:29 **14** Ge 2:23; Jdg 9:2; 2Sa 5:1; 19:12,13 **18** Ge 31:41; 2Sa 3:14

19 Laban said, "It is better that I give
her [in marriage] to you than give her to
another man. Stay *and* work with me."
20 So Jacob served [Laban] for seven
years for [the right to marry] Rachel,
but they seemed like only a few days
to him because of his love for her.

Laban's Treachery

21 Finally, Jacob said to Laban, "Give
me my wife, for my time [of service] is
completed, so that I may take her to me
[as my wife]."
22 So Laban gathered together all the
men of the place and prepared a [wed-
ding] feast [with wine].
23 But in the evening he took Leah
his daughter and brought her to Jacob,
and Jacob went in to [consummate the
marriage with] her.
24 Laban also gave Zilpah his maid to
his daughter Leah as a maid.
25 But in the morning [when Jacob
awoke], it was Leah [who was with
him]! And he said to Laban, "What is
this that you have done to me? Did I
not work for you [for seven years] for
Rachel? Why have you deceived *and*
betrayed me [like this]?"
26 But Laban only said, "It is not
the tradition here to give the youn-
ger [daughter in marriage] before the
older.
27 "Finish the week [of the wedding
feast] for Leah; then we will give you
Rachel also, and in return you shall
work for me for seven more years."
28 So Jacob complied and fulfilled
Leah's week [of celebration]; then La-
ban gave him his daughter Rachel as
his [second] wife.
29 Laban also gave Bilhah his maid to
his daughter Rachel as a maid.
30 So Jacob consummated his mar-
riage *and* lived with Rachel [as his
wife], and he loved Rachel more than
Leah, and he served with Laban for
another seven years.
31 Now when the LORD saw that Leah
was unloved, He made her able to bear
children, but Rachel was barren.
32 Leah conceived and gave birth to
a son and named him Reuben (See, a
son!), for she said, "Because the LORD
has seen my humiliation *and* suffering;
now my husband will love me [since I
have given him a son]."
33 Then she conceived again and gave
birth to a son and said, "Because the
LORD heard that I am unloved, He has
given me this son also." So she named
him Simeon (God hears).
34 She conceived again and gave birth
to a son and said, "Now this time my
husband will become attached to me [as
a companion], for I have given him three
sons." Therefore he was named Levi.
35 Again she conceived and gave
birth to a [fourth] son, and she said,
"Now I will praise the LORD." So she
named him Judah; then [for a time] she
stopped bearing [children].

The Sons of Jacob

30 WHEN RACHEL saw that she
conceived no children for Jacob,
she envied her sister, and said to Jacob,
"Give me children, or else I will die."
2 Then Jacob became furious with
Rachel, and he said, "Am I in the place
of God, who has denied you children?"
3 She said, "Here, take my maid Bil-
hah and go in to her; and [when the
baby comes] she shall deliver it [while
sitting] on my knees, so that by her I
may also have children [to count as
my own]."

29:21–25 Deception — Many times we see God's prohibitions as mere taboos. We somehow imagine that God says no just because He can, instead of acknowledging both His goodwill towards us, and His wisdom. God does not merely prohibit lying because He can, it is because it is destructive. Jacob learned through experience that trickery and deceit bring complicated and painful consequences. False dealing destroys trust in a relationship, and once trust has been broken it is difficult, if not impossible, to entirely restore it.

29:31 ***unloved.*** God was kind to Leah in her predicament. Even though she was the unloved wife, it was through her son Judah that the messianic line was carried out.

20 Ge 30:26; Hos 12:12 **21** Jdg 15:1 **22** Jdg 14:10; Jn 2:1,2 **27** Jdg 14:12 **30** Dt 21:15; Ge 30:26; 31:41; Hos 12:12 **31** Ps 127:3; Ge 30:1 **32** Ex 4:31; Dt 26:7; Ps 25:18 **35** Mt 1:2 **CHAPTER 30** **1** Ge 29:31; Ge 37:11; Job 5:2 **2** Ge 16:2; 1Sa 1:5 **3** Ge 16:2; Ge 50:23; Job 3:12; Ge 16:2

4 So she gave him Bilhah her maid
as a [secondary] wife, and Jacob went
in to her.
5 Bilhah conceived and gave birth to
a son for Jacob.
6 Then Rachel said, "God has judged
and vindicated me, and has heard my
plea and has given me a son [through
my maid]." So she named him Dan
(He judged).
7 Bilhah, Rachel's maid, conceived
again and gave birth to a second son
for Jacob.
8 So Rachel said, "With mighty
wrestlings [in prayer to God] I have
struggled with my sister and have pre-
vailed." So she named him Naphtali
(my wrestlings).
9 When Leah saw that she had
stopped bearing [children], she took
Zilpah her maid and gave her to Jacob
as a [secondary] wife.
10 Zilpah, Leah's maid, gave birth to
a son for Jacob.
11 Then Leah said, "How fortunate!"
So she named him Gad (good fortune).
12 Zilpah, Leah's maid, gave birth to
a second son for Jacob.
13 Then Leah said, "I am happy! For
women will call me happy." So she
named him Asher (happy).
14 Now at the time of wheat harvest
Reuben [the eldest child] went and
found some mandrakes in the field,
and brought them to his mother Leah.
Then Rachel said to Leah, "Please give
me some of your son's mandrakes."
15 But Leah answered, "Is it a small
thing that you have taken my hus-
band? Would you take away my son's
mandrakes also?" So Rachel said, "Ja-
cob shall sleep with you tonight in
exchange for your son's mandrakes."
16 When Jacob came in from the field
in the evening, Leah went out to meet
him and said, "You must sleep with
me [tonight], for I have in fact hired
you with my son's mandrakes." So he
slept with her that night.
17 God listened *and* answered [the
prayer of] Leah, and she conceived
and gave birth to a fifth son for Jacob.
18 Then Leah said, "God has given me
my reward because I have given my
maid to my husband." So she named
him Issachar.
19 Leah conceived again and gave
birth to a sixth son for Jacob.
20 Then Leah said, "God has endowed
me with a good [marriage] gift [for my
husband]; now he will live with me
[regarding me with honor as his wife],
because I have given birth to six sons."
So she named him Zebulun.
21 Afterward she gave birth to a
daughter and named her Dinah.
22 Then God remembered [the
prayers of] Rachel, and God thought
of her and opened her womb [so that
she would conceive].
23 So she conceived and gave birth
to a son; and she said, "God has taken
away my disgrace *and* humiliation."
24 She named him Joseph (may He
add) and said, "May the LORD add to
me another son."

Jacob Prospers

25 Now when Rachel had given birth
to Joseph, Jacob said to Laban, "Send
me away, that I may go back to my own
place and to my own country.
26 "Give me my wives and my chil-
dren for whom I have served you, and
let me go; for you know the work which
I have done for you."
27 But Laban said to him, "If I have
found favor in your sight, *stay with me;*
for I have learned [from the omens in

30:14 *mandrakes.* This is a plant which was regarded as an aid to conception. Its aroma was associated with lovemaking (SS 7:13).
30:22 *remembered . . . thought of her . . . opened.* These three verbs emphasize conception as a gift from God.
30:25 *own place.* Even though Jacob had lived for twenty years with Laban's family, he had not adopted that place as his own. He never forgot that the promise and covenant of God were for the land of Canaan, and he knew that he must return.
30:27 *blessed.* God had promised to bless others through Abraham's descendants (12:2 – 3). Now God blessed Laban through Jacob.

4 Ge 16:3 **6** La 3:59 **8** Mt 4:13 **9** ver. 4 **13** Pr 31:28; Lk 1:48 **14** Ge 25:30 **15** Nu 16:9,13 **20** Mt 4:13 **22** 1Sa 1:19; Ge 29:31 **23** 1Sa 1:6; Isa 4:1; Lk 1:25 **24** Ge 35:17 **25** Ge 24:54,56; Ge 18:33 **26** Ge 29:20,30 **27** Ge 39:3,5; See Ge 26:24

divination and by experience] that the LORD has blessed me because of you."

28 He said, "Name your wages, and I will give it [to you]."

29 Jacob answered him, "You know how I have served you and how your possessions, your cattle *and* sheep *and* goats, have fared with me.

30 "For you had little before I came and it has increased *and* multiplied abundantly, and the LORD has favored you with blessings wherever I turned. But now, when shall I provide for my own household?"

31 Laban asked, "What shall I give you?" Jacob replied, "You shall not give me anything. But if you will do this one thing for me [which I now propose], I will again pasture and keep your flock:

32 Let me pass through your entire flock today, removing from it every speckled and spotted sheep and every dark *or* black one among the lambs and the spotted and speckled among the goats; and those shall be my wages.

33 "So my honesty will be evident for me later, when you come [for an accounting] concerning my wages. Every one that is not speckled and spotted among the goats and dark among the young lambs, *if found* with me, shall be considered stolen."

34 And Laban said, "Good! Let it be done as you say."

35 So on that same day Laban [secretly] removed the male goats that were streaked and spotted and all the female goats that were speckled and spotted, every one with white on it, and all the dark ones among the sheep, and put them in the care of his sons.

36 And he put [a distance of] three days' journey between himself and Jacob, and Jacob was then left in care of the rest of Laban's flock.

37 Then Jacob took branches of fresh poplar and almond and plane trees, and peeled white stripes in them, exposing the white in the branches.

38 Then he set the branches which he had peeled in front of the flocks in the watering troughs, where the flocks came to drink; and they mated *and* conceived when they came to drink.

39 So the flocks mated *and* conceived by the branches, and the flocks gave birth to streaked, speckled, and spotted offspring.

40 Jacob separated the lambs, and [as he had done with the peeled branches] he made the flocks face toward the streaked and all the dark *or* black in the [new] flock of Laban; and he put his own herds apart by themselves and did not put them [where they could breed] with Laban's flock.

41 Furthermore, whenever the stronger [animals] of the flocks were breeding, Jacob would place the branches in the sight of the flock in the watering troughs, so that they would mate *and* conceive among the branches;

42 but when the flock was sickly, he did not put *the branches* there; so the sicker [animals] were Laban's and the stronger Jacob's.

43 So Jacob became exceedingly prosperous, and had large flocks [of sheep and goats], and female and male servants, and camels and donkeys.

Jacob Leaves Secretly for Canaan

31 JACOB HEARD that Laban's sons were saying: "Jacob has taken away everything that was our father's, and from what belonged to our father he has acquired all this wealth *and* honor."

2 Jacob noticed [a change in] the attitude of Laban, and saw that it was not *friendly* toward him as before.

3 Then the LORD said to Jacob, "Return to the land of your fathers and to your people, and I will be with you."

4 So Jacob sent and called Rachel and Leah to his flock in the field,

---

30:37 *branches of fresh poplar.* Just what significance these sticks hold is unknown. Some have theorized that they were simply symbols of Jacob's faith in God. Whatever the case, God blessed Jacob by causing Laban's stock to give birth to speckled and spotted young.

28 Ge 29:15 **29** Ge 31:6,38-40; Mt 24:45; Titus 2:10 **30** 1Ti 5:8 **32** Ge 31:8 **33** Ps 37:6 **37** See Ge 31:9-12 **43** ver. 30; Ge 13:2; 24:35; 26:13,14 **CHAPTER 31** **1** Ps 49:16 **2** Ge 4:5; Dt 28:54 **3** Ge 28:15,20,21; 32:9

5 and he said to them, “I see [a change in] your father’s attitude, that he is not *friendly* toward me as [he was] before; but the God of my father [Isaac] has been with me.

6 “You know that I have served your father with all my strength.

7 “Yet your father has cheated me [as often as possible] and changed my wages ten times; but God did not allow him to hurt me.

8 “If he said, ‘The speckled shall be your wages,’ then the entire flock gave birth to speckled [young]; and if he said, ‘The streaked shall be your wages,’ then the entire flock gave birth to streaked [young].

9 “Thus God has taken away the flocks of your father and given them to me.

10 “And it happened at the time when the flock conceived that I looked up and saw in a dream that the rams which mated [with the female goats] were streaked, speckled, and spotted.

11 “And the Angel of God said to me in the dream, ‘Jacob.’ And I said, ‘Here I am.’

12 “He said, ‘Look up and see, all the rams which are mating [with the flock] are streaked, speckled, and spotted; for I have seen all that Laban has been doing to you.

13 ‘I am the God of Bethel, where you anointed the pillar, and where you made a vow to Me; now stand up, leave this land, and return to the land of your birth.’ ”

14 Rachel and Leah answered him, “Is there still any portion or inheritance for us in our father’s house?

15 “Are we not counted by him as foreigners? For he sold us [to you in marriage], and has also entirely used up our purchase price.

16 “Surely all the riches which God has taken from our father are ours and our children’s. Now then, whatever God has told you to do, do it.”

17 Then Jacob stood [and took action] and put his children and his wives on camels;

18 and he drove away all his livestock and [took along] all his property which he had acquired, the livestock he had obtained and accumulated in Paddan-aram, to go to his father Isaac in the land of Canaan.

19 When Laban had gone to shear his sheep, Rachel [went inside the house and] stole her father’s household gods.

20 And Jacob deceived Laban the Aramean (Syrian) by not telling him that he intended to leave *and* he slipped away secretly.

21 So he fled with everything that he had, and got up and crossed the river [Euphrates], and set his face toward the hill country of Gilead [east of the Jordan River].

Laban Pursues Jacob

22 On the third day [after his departure] Laban was told that Jacob had fled.

23 So he took his relatives with him and pursued him for seven days, and they overtook him in the hill country of Gilead.

24 God came to Laban the Aramean in a dream at night and said to him,

---

31:7 *cheated me*. Jacob had surely lived up to his name, deceiving his old father and tricking his brother out of the birthright. But in Laban he met his match, and tasted some of his own medicine. The consequences of dishonesty reach both ways. Because of his own trickery, Jacob had to flee from his home. He apparently never saw his mother again, and his relationship with his father and his only brother was broken. Lying not only harms the liar, but it also affects those he lies to. Because of Laban’s trickery, Jacob was saddled with an unloved wife, quarreling sons, and consistent domestic strife.

31:19 *household gods*. Laban’s family may have been polytheistic (believing in many gods), as Abraham’s father Terah evidently was (Jos 24:1 – 3). Considering the evidence of verses 25 – 50 it seems likely that they worshiped Yahweh along with other “lesser gods.” In this culture, the possession of the gods was the right of the principal heir. Rachel probably did not steal the idols in order to worship them, but because they represented ownership of her father’s property.

5 ver. 2; ver. 3 **6** ver. 38-41; Ge 30:29 **7** ver. 41; Nu 14:22; Neh 4:12; Job 19:3; Zec 8:23; Ge 20:6; Job 1:10; Ps 37:28; 105:14 **8** Ge 30:32 **9** ver. 1,16 **11** Ge 48:16 **12** Ex 3:7; Ps 139:3; Ecc 5:8 **13** Ge 28:18-20; ver. 3; Ge 32:9 **14** Ge 2:24 **15** Ge 29:15,27; Neh 5:8 **19** Ge 35:2 **21** Ge 46:28; 2Ki 12:17; Lk 9:51,53 **23** Ge 13:8 **24** Ge 20:3; Job 33:15; Mt 1:20; Ge 24:50

“Be careful that you do not speak to
Jacob, either good or bad.”
[25]Then Laban overtook Jacob. Now
Jacob had pitched his tent on the hill,
and Laban with his relatives camped
on the same hill of Gilead.
[26]Then Laban said to Jacob, “What
do you mean by deceiving me *and*
leaving without my knowledge, and
carrying off my daughters as if [they
were] captives of the sword?
[27]“Why did you run away secretly
and deceive me and not tell me, so that
[otherwise] I might have sent you away
with joy and with songs, with [music
on the] tambourine and lyre?
[28]“And why did you not allow me to
kiss my grandchildren and my daugh-
ters [goodbye]? Now you have done a
foolish thing [in behaving like this].
[29]“It is in my power to harm you, but
the God of your father spoke to me last
night, saying, ‘Be careful not to speak
to Jacob, either good or bad.’
[30]“Now [I suppose] you felt you must
go because you were homesick for your
father’s house *and* family; but why did
you steal my [household] gods?”
[31]Jacob answered Laban, “[I left
secretly] because I was afraid, for I
thought you would take your daugh-
ters away from me by force.
[32]“The one with whom you find your
gods shall not live; in the presence of our
relatives [search my possessions and]
point out whatever you find that belongs
to you and take it.” For Jacob did not
know that Rachel had stolen the idols.
[33]So Laban went into Jacob’s tent
and into Leah’s tent and the tent of the
two maids, but he did not find them.
Then he came out of Leah’s tent and
entered Rachel’s tent.
[34]Now Rachel had taken the house-
hold idols and put them in the camel’s
saddlebag and sat on them. Laban
searched through all her tent, but did
not find them.
[35]So Rachel said to her father, “Do
not be displeased, my lord, that I can-
not rise before you, for the manner of
women is on me *and* I am unwell.” He
searched [further] but did not find the
household idols.
[36]Then Jacob became angry and
argued with Laban. And he said to
Laban, “What is my fault? What is
my sin that you pursued me like this?
[37]“Although you have searched
through all my possessions, what have
you found of your household goods?
Put it here before my relatives and your
relatives, so that they may decide [who
has done right] between the two of us.
[38]“These twenty years I *have been*
with you; your ewes and your female
goats have not lost their young, nor
have I eaten the rams of your flocks.
[39]“I did not bring you the torn car-
casses [of the animals attacked by
predators]; I [personally] took the loss.
You required of me [to make good]
everything that was stolen, whether
it occurred by day or night.
[40]“This was my situation: by day the
heat consumed me and by night the
cold, and I could not sleep.
[41]“These twenty years I have been
in your house; I served you fourteen
years for your two daughters and six
years for [my share of] your flocks, and
you have changed my wages ten times.
[42]“If the God of my father, the God
of Abraham, and [the Feared One] of
Isaac, had not been with me, most cer-
tainly you would have sent me away
now empty-handed. God has seen my
affliction *and* humiliation and the [ex-
hausting] labor of my hands, so He
rendered judgment *and* rebuked you
last night.”

The Covenant of Mizpah

[43]Laban answered Jacob, “These
women [that you married] are my
daughters, these children are my
grandchildren, these flocks are [from]
my flocks, and all that you see [here] is

31:44 *covenant*. This instance of a covenant was an agreement between two equals.

26 1Sa 30:2 **28** ver. 55; Ru 1:9,14; 1Ki 19:20; Ac 20:37; 1Sa 13:13; 2Ch 16:9 **29** ver. 53; Ge 28:13; ver. 24 **30** ver. 19; Jdg 18:24 **32** See Ge 44:9 **35** Ex 20:12; Lev 19:32 **39** Ex 22:10; Ex 22:12 **41** Ge 29:27,28; ver. 7 **42** Ps 124:1,2; ver. 53; Isa 8:13; Ge 29:32; Ex 3:7; 1Ch 12:17

mine. But what can I do today to these
my daughters or to their children to
whom they have given birth?
44 "So come now, let us make a cov-
enant, you and I, and let it serve as a
witness between you and me."
45 So Jacob took a stone and set it up
as a [memorial] pillar.
46 Jacob said to his relatives, "Gath-
er stones." And they took stones and
made a mound [of stones], and they ate
[a ceremonial meal together] there on
the mound [of stones]. [Prov 16:7]
47 Laban called it Jegar-sahadutha
(stone monument of testimony in Ar-
amaic), but Jacob called it Galeed.
48 Laban said, "This mound [of
stones] is a witness [a reminder of the
oath taken] today between you and
me." Therefore he [also] called the
name Galeed,
49 and Mizpah (watchtower), for La-
ban said, "May the LORD watch be-
tween you and me when we are absent
from one another.
50 "If you should mistreat (humili-
ate, oppress) my daughters, or if you
should take other wives besides my
daughters, although no one is with us
[as a witness], see *and* remember, God
is witness between you and me."
51 Laban said to Jacob, "Look at this
mound [of stones] and look at this pil-
lar which I have set up between you
and me.
52 "This mound is a witness, and this
pillar is a witness, that I will not pass
by this mound to harm you, and that
you will not pass by this mound and
this pillar to harm me.
53 "The God of Abraham [your father]
and the God of Nahor [my father], and
the god [the image of worship] of their
father [Terah, an idolater], judge be-
tween us." But Jacob swore [only] by
[the one true God] the Fear of his father
Isaac. [Josh 24:2]
54 Then Jacob offered a sacrifice [to the
LORD] on the mountain, and called his
relatives to the meal; and they ate food
and spent the night on the mountain.
55 Early in the morning Laban got up
and kissed his grandchildren and his
daughters [goodbye] and pronounced a
blessing [asking God's favor] on them.
Then Laban left and returned home.

Jacob's Fear of Esau

32 THEN AS Jacob went on his
way, the angels of God met him
[to reassure and protect him].
2 When Jacob saw them, he said,
"This is God's camp." So he named
that place Mahanaim (double camps).
[Gen 32:7, 10]
3 Then Jacob sent messengers ahead
of him to his brother Esau in the land
of Seir, the country of Edom.
4 He commanded them, saying, "This
is what to say to my lord Esau: 'Your
servant Jacob says this, "I have been
living temporarily with Laban, and
have stayed there until now;
5 I have oxen, donkeys, flocks, male
servants, and female servants; and I
have sent [this message] to tell my lord,
so that I may find grace *and* kindness
in your sight." ' "
6 The messengers returned to Jacob,
saying, "We went to your brother Esau,
and now he is coming to meet you, and
there are four hundred men with him."
7 Jacob was greatly afraid and dis-
tressed; and he divided the people
who were with him, and the flocks
and herds and camels, into two camps;
8 and he said, "If Esau comes to the
one camp and attacks it, then the other
camp which is left will escape."
9 Jacob said, "O God of my father

31:49 *Mizpah.* This name means "Outlook Point" and is related to the Hebrew word meaning "to watch." God above had His eyes on both men to make them keep their covenant.

31:53 *The God of Abraham.* The wording in Laban's oath suggests that Abraham, Nahor, and their father Terah all worshiped the same One True God. Joshua records the fact that Terah at least worshiped other gods as well (Jos 24:1 – 3). It is possible that they were henotheistic — worshiping God not as the only God but as the most important and powerful among many.

44 Ge 26:28; Jos 24:27 **45** Ge 28:18 **48** Jos 24:27 **49** Jdg 11:29; 1Sa 7:5 **53** Ge 16:5; Ge 21:23; ver. 42 **55** Ge 28:1; Ge 18:33; 30:25; Nu 24:25 **CHAPTER 32** **1** Ps 91:11; Heb 1:14 **2** Jos 5:14; Ps 103:21; 148:2; Lk 2:13 **3** Ge 33:14,16; Ge 36:6-8; Dt 2:5; Jos 24:4 **4** Pr 15:1 **5** Ge 30:43; Ge 33:8,15 **6** Ge 33:1 **7** Ge 35:3 **9** Ps 50:15; Ge 28:13; Ge 31:3,13

Abraham and God of my father Isaac,
the LORD, who said to me, 'Return to
your country and to your people, and
I will make you prosper,'
10 I am unworthy of all the loving-
kindness *and* compassion and of all the
faithfulness which You have shown to
Your servant. With only my staff [long
ago] I crossed over this Jordan, and now
I have become [blessed and increased
into these] two groups [of people].
11 "Save me, please, from the hand of

32:11 *Save me, please.* Jacob did not pray in generalities. He named his concerns openly, and concluded with another appeal to God's promises. Christians today can likewise base their prayers on God's proven character and His promises in the Bible.

10 Ge 24:27; Job 8:7 **11** Ps 59:1,2; Hos 10:14

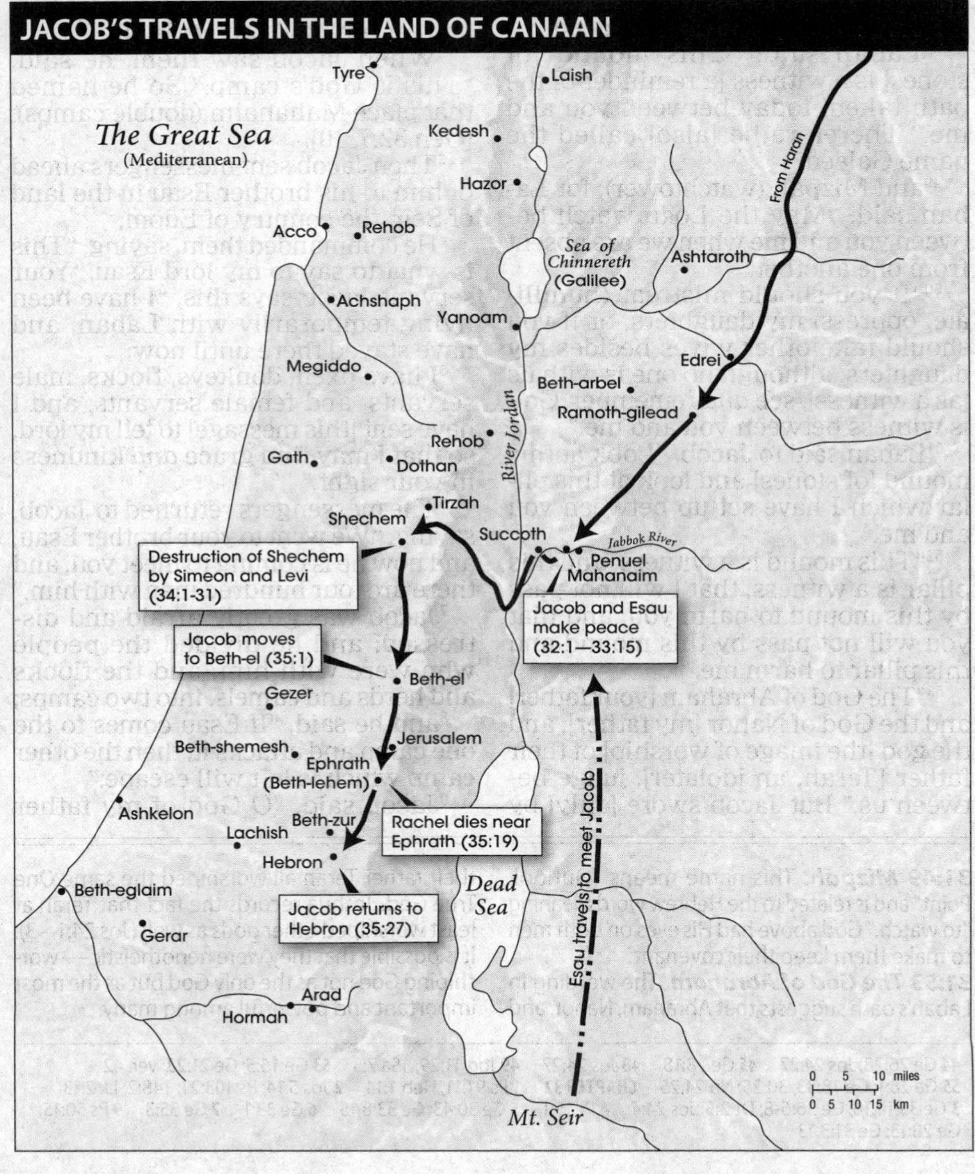

my brother, from the hand of Esau; for
I fear him, that he will come and attack
me and the mothers with the children.
12"And You [LORD] said, 'I will cer-
tainly make you prosper and make
your descendants as [numerous as]
the sand of the sea, which is too great
to be counted.' "
13So Jacob spent the night there.
Then he selected a present for his
brother Esau from the livestock he
had acquired:
14two hundred female goats, twenty
male goats, two hundred ewes, twenty
rams,
15thirty milking camels with their
colts, forty cows, ten bulls, twenty fe-
male donkeys, and ten [donkey] colts.
16He put them into the care of his
servants, every herd by itself, and said
to his servants, "Go on ahead of me,
and put an interval [of space] between
the *individual* herds."
17Then he commanded the one in
front, saying, "When Esau my broth-
er meets you and asks to whom you
belong, and where you are going, and
whose are the *animals* in front of you?
18then you shall say, 'They are your
servant Jacob's; they are a gift sent to my
lord Esau. And he also is behind us.' "
19And so Jacob commanded the sec-
ond and the third as well, and all that
followed the herds, saying, "This is
what you shall say to Esau when you
meet him;
20and you shall say, 'Look, your ser-
vant Jacob is behind us.' " For he said
[to himself], "I will try to appease him
with the gift that is going ahead of me.
Then afterward I will see him; perhaps
he will accept *and* forgive me."
21So the gift [of the herds of live-
stock] went on ahead of him, and he
himself spent that night back in the
camp.
22But he got up that same night and
took his two wives, his two female
servants, and his eleven children, and
waded over the ford of the Jabbok.
23Then he took them and sent them
across the brook. And he also sent
across whatever he had.

Jacob Wrestles

24So Jacob was left alone, and a Man
[came and] wrestled with him until
daybreak.
25When the Man saw that He had not
prevailed against Jacob, He touched
his hip joint; and Jacob's hip was dis-
located as he wrestled with Him.
26Then He said, "Let Me go, for day
is breaking." But Jacob said, "I will
not let You go unless You declare a
blessing on me."
27So He asked him, "What is your
name?" And he said, "Jacob."
28And He said, "Your name shall
no longer be Jacob, but Israel; for you
have struggled with God and with men
and have prevailed." [Hos 12:3, 4]
29Then Jacob asked Him, "Please tell
me Your name." But He said, "Why
is it that you ask My name?" And He
declared a blessing [of the covenant
promises] on Jacob there.
30So Jacob named the place Peniel
(the face of God), *saying*, "For I have
seen God face to face, yet my life has
not been snatched away."
31Now the sun rose on him as he
passed Penuel (Peniel), and he was
limping because of his hip.

32:24 *a Man [came and] wrestled with him.* Some believe that the man who wrestled with Jacob was the pre-incarnate Jesus Christ. Others believe the man was the Angel of God (21:17; 31:11). In any case, Jacob wrestled with a manifestation of God (vv. 28 – 30), and because of God's mercy he survived.

32:28 *Israel.* Before Jacob wrestled with the angel, his name, "One who Supplants," described a man who was deceitful in character. Afterwards he was given the new status of a champion, "One who Strives (or Prevails) with God."

32:30 *God face to face.* The dramatic name ("Face of God") given to the location shows the awesome nature of the encounter. Here God's messenger in human form was the same as God Himself, a fact which Jacob recognized to his amazement. In Hebrew thought, the penalty for seeing God face to face was death (Ex 33:20), yet Jacob had passed through such an experience and had survived.

12 Ge 28:13-15 **13** Ge 43:11; Pr 18:16 **20** Pr 21:14 **22** Dt 3:16 **24** Hos 12:3,4 **25** See Mt 26:41; 2Co 12:7 **26** See Lk 24:28; Hos 12:4 **28** Ge 35:10; 2Ki 17:34; Hos 12:3,4; Ge 25:31; 27:33 **29** Jdg 13:18 **30** Ge 16:13; Ex 24:11; Dt 5:24; Jdg 6:22; Isa 6:5

32Therefore, to this day the Israelites do not eat the tendon of the hip which is on the socket of the thigh, because He touched the socket of Jacob's thigh by the tendon of the hip.

Jacob Meets Esau

33 THEN JACOB looked up, and saw Esau coming with four hundred men. So he divided the children among Leah and Rachel and the two maids.

2He put the maids and their children in front, Leah and her children after them, and Rachel and Joseph last of all.

3Then Jacob crossed over [the stream] ahead of them and bowed himself to the ground seven times [bowing and moving forward each time], until he approached his brother.

4But Esau ran to meet him and embraced him, and hugged his neck and kissed him, and they wept [for joy]. [Luke 15:20]

5Esau looked up and saw the women and the children, and said, "Who are these with you?" So Jacob replied, "They are the children whom God has graciously given your servant."

6Then the maids approached with their children, and they bowed down.

7Leah also approached with her children, and they bowed down. Afterward Joseph and Rachel approached, and they bowed down.

8Esau asked, "What do you mean by all this company which I have met?" And he answered, "[These are] to find favor in the sight of my lord."

9But Esau said, "I have plenty, my brother; keep what you have for yourself."

10Jacob replied, "No, please, if now I have found favor in your sight, then accept my gift [as a blessing] from my hand, for I see your face as if I had seen the face of God, and you have received me favorably.

11"Please accept my blessing (gift) which has been brought to you, for God has dealt graciously with me and I have everything [that I could possibly want]." So Jacob kept urging him and Esau accepted it.

12Then Esau said, "Let us get started on our journey and I will go in front of you [to lead the way]."

13But Jacob replied, "You know, my lord, that the children are frail *and* need gentle care, and the nursing flocks and herds [with young] are of concern to me; for if the men should drive them hard for a single day, all the flocks will die.

14"Please let my lord go on ahead of his servant, and I will move on slowly, governed by the pace of the livestock that are in front of me and according to the endurance of the children, until I come to my lord in Seir [in Edom]."

15Then Esau said, "Please let me leave with you some of the people who are with me." But Jacob said, "What need is there [for it]? Let me find favor in the sight of my lord."

16So Esau turned back [toward the south] that day on his way to Seir.

17But Jacob journeyed [north] to Succoth, and built himself a house and made shelters for his livestock; so the name of the place is Succoth (huts, shelters).

Jacob Settles in Shechem

18When Jacob came from Paddan-aram, he arrived safely *and* in peace at the city of Shechem, in the land of Canaan, and camped in front of the [walled] city.

19Then he bought the piece of land on which he had pitched his tents from the sons of Hamor, Shechem's father, for a hundred pieces of money.

20There he erected an altar and called it El-Elohe-Israel.

33:11 *Please accept my blessing.* Before, Jacob had done all he could to take Esau's blessing (25:29 – 34; 27:1 – 45). Now a wiser man, Jacob wanted to bless his brother with what God had given him.

33:20 *he erected an altar.* The name Jacob gave this altar reflected his mature faith in "God, the God of Israel." The God of Jacob's fathers was now Jacob's personal God, for He had fulfilled His promises and protected him (28:13 – 15).

CHAPTER 33 **1** Ge 32:6 **3** Ge 18:2; 42:6 **4** Ge 32:28; Ge 45:14,15 **5** Ge 48:9; Ps 127:3; Isa 8:18 **8** Ge 32:16; Ge 32:5 **10** Ge 43:3; 2Sa 3:13; 14:24,28,32 **11** Jdg 1:15; 1Sa 25:27; 30:26; 2Ki 5:23 **14** Ge 32:3 **15** Ge 34:11; 47:25; Ru 2:13 **17** Jos 13:27; Jdg 8:5; Ps 60:6 **18** Jn 3:23; Jos 24:1; Jdg 9:1 **19** Jos 24:32; Jn 4:5 **20** Ge 35:7

The Treachery of Jacob's Sons

34 NOW DINAH the daughter of
Leah, whom she had borne to
Jacob, went out [unescorted] to visit
the girls of the land.
2 When Shechem the son of Hamor
the Hivite, prince (sheik) of the land,
saw her, he kidnapped her and lay [in-
timately] with her by force [humbling
and offending her].
3 But his soul longed for and clung to
Dinah daughter of Jacob, and he loved
the girl and spoke comfortingly to her
young heart's wishes.
4 So Shechem said to his father Ha-
mor, "Get me this young woman as a
wife."
5 Now Jacob heard that Shechem had
defiled (violated) Dinah his daughter;
but his sons were in the field with his
livestock, so Jacob said nothing until
they came in.
6 But Shechem's father Hamor went
to Jacob to talk with him.
7 Now when Jacob's sons heard of it
they came in from the field; they were
deeply grieved, and they were very
angry, for Shechem had done a dis-
graceful thing to Israel by lying with
Jacob's daughter, for such a thing is
not to be done.
8 But Hamor conferred with them,
saying, "The soul of my son Shechem
[deeply] longs for your daughter [and
sister]. Please give her to him as his wife.
9 "And [beyond that] intermarry with
us; give your daughters to us [as wives]
and take our daughters for yourselves.
[Ex 34:15, 16; Deut 7:3; Josh 23:12, 13]
10 "In this way you shall live with
us; the country will be open to you;
live and do business in it and acquire
property *and* possessions in it."
11 Shechem also said to Dinah's fa-
ther and to her brothers, "Let me find
favor in your sight, and I will give you
whatever you ask of me.
12 "Demand of me a very large bridal
payment and gift [as compensation
for giving up your daughter and sis-
ter], and I will give you whatever you
tell me; only give me the girl to be my
wife."
13 Jacob's sons answered Shechem
and Hamor his father deceitfully, be-
cause Shechem had defiled *and* dis-
graced their sister Dinah.
14 They said to them, "We cannot do
this thing and give our sister [in mar-
riage] to one who is not circumcised,
because that would be a disgrace to us.
15 "But we will consent to you only
on this *condition:* if you will become
like us, in that every male among you
consents to be circumcised,
16 then we will give our daughters
to you [in marriage], and we will take
your daughters for ourselves, and we
will live with you and become one
people.
17 "But if you do not listen to us *and*
refuse to be circumcised, then we will
take our daughter [Dinah] and go."
18 Their words seemed reasonable to
Hamor and his son Shechem,
19 and the young man did not hesitate
to do the [required] thing, for he was
delighted with Jacob's daughter. Now
he was more respected *and* honored
than all [others] in the household of
his father.
20 Then Hamor and Shechem his son
came to the gate of their [walled] city
[where the leading men would meet]
and spoke with the men of the city,
saying,
21 "These men are peaceful *and*
friendly with us; so let them live in the
land and do business in it, for the land
is large enough [for us and] for them;
let us take their daughters for wives
and let us give them our daughters [in
marriage].
22 "But only on this *condition* will the
men consent to our request that they
live among us and become one people:
that every male among us become cir-
cumcised just as they are circumcised.
23 "Will not their cattle and their pos-
sessions and all their animals be ours
[if we do this]? Let us consent [to do
as they ask], and they will live here
with us."
24 And every [Canaanite] man who
went out of the city gate listened *and*
considered what Hamor and Shechem

CHAPTER 34 **1** Ge 30:21; Titus 2:5 **2** Ge 6:2; Jdg 14:1; Ge 20:2 **4** Jdg 14:2 **5** 1Sa 10:27; 2Sa 13:22 **7** Ge 49:7; 2Sa 13:21; Jos 7:15; Jdg 20:6; Dt 23:17; 2Sa 13:12 **10** Ge 13:9; 20:15; Ge 42:34; Ge 47:27 **12** Ex 22:16,17; Dt 22:29; 1Sa 18:25 **13** See 2Sa 13:24 **14** Jos 5:9 **19** 1Ch 4:9 **24** Ge 23:10,18

said; and every male who was a resident of that city was circumcised.

[25]Now on the third day [after the circumcision], when all the men were [terribly] sore *and* in pain, two of Jacob's sons, Simeon and Levi, Dinah's [full] brothers, took their swords, boldly entered the city [without anyone suspecting them of evil intent], and they killed every male.

[26]They killed Hamor and his son Shechem with the edge of the sword, and took Dinah out of Shechem's house [where she was staying], and left.

[27]Then Jacob's [other] sons came upon those who were killed and looted the town, because their sister had been defiled *and* disgraced.

[28]They took the Canaanites' flocks and their herds and their donkeys, and whatever was in the city and in the field;

[29]they looted all their wealth, and [took captive] all their children and their wives, even everything that was in the houses.

[30]Then Jacob said to Simeon and Levi, "You have ruined me, making me a stench to the inhabitants of the land, the Canaanites and the Perizzites! My men are few in number, and the men of the land will band together against me and attack me; I shall be destroyed, I and my household."

[31]But they said, "Should he [be permitted to] treat our sister as a prostitute?"

Jacob Moves to Bethel

35 THEN GOD said to Jacob, "Go up to Bethel and live there, and make an altar there to God, who appeared to you [in a distinct manifestation] when you fled [years ago] from Esau your brother." [Gen 28:11–22]

[2]Then Jacob said to his household and to all who were with him, "Get rid of the [idols and images of] foreign gods that are among you, and ceremonially purify yourselves and change [into fresh] clothes;

[3]then let us get up and go up to Bethel, and I will make an altar there to God, who answered me in the day of my distress and has been with me wherever I have gone."

[4]So they gave Jacob all the [idols and images of the] foreign gods they had and the rings which were in their ears [worn as charms against evil], and Jacob buried them under the oak tree near Shechem.

[5]As they journeyed, there was a great [supernatural] terror [sent from God] on the cities around them, and [for that reason] the Canaanites did not pursue the sons of Jacob.

[6]So Jacob came to Luz (that is, Bethel), which is in the land of Canaan, he and all the people who were with him.

[7]There he built an altar [to worship the LORD], and called the place El-bethel (God of the House of God), because there God had revealed Himself to him when he escaped from his brother.

[8]Now Deborah, [who once was] Rebekah's nurse, died and was buried below Bethel under the oak; and the name of it was called Allon-bacuth (Oak of Weeping).

Jacob Is Named Israel

[9]Then God [in a visible manifestation] appeared to Jacob again when

---

34:25 *killed every male*. Jacob's sons were correct that God did not want them to intermarry with the pagan Canaanite families. According to later Levitical law, they were even correct that rape was punishable by death. However, their treacherous pretended friendship and the massacre of all the men of Shechem, along with their greedy looting of all the Shechemites' goods, was clearly not a justifiable execution of justice, and God condemned their violence and anger (49:5–7).

35:2 *foreign gods*. Jacob's command included the idols that Rachel had stolen (31:22–35) as well as any idols among his servants. These were not gods Jacob himself had been worshiping, but he had apparently been allowing others in his household to do so.

25 Ge 49:5-7 **30** Ge 49:6; Jos 7:25; Ex 5:21; 1Sa 13:4; Dt 4:27; Ps 105:12 **CHAPTER 35** **1** Ge 28:19; Ge 28:13; Ge 27:43 **2** Ge 18:19; Jos 24:15; Ge 31:19,34; Jos 24:2,23; 1Sa 7:3; Ex 19:10 **3** Ge 32:7,24; Ge 28:20; 31:3,42 **4** Hos 2:13; Jos 24:26; Jdg 9:6 **5** Ex 15:16; Dt 11:25; Jos 2:9; 1Sa 14:15 **6** Ge 28:19,22 **7** Ecc 5:4; Ge 28:13 **8** Ge 24:59 **9** Hos 12:4

he came out of Paddan-aram, and de-
clared a blessing on him. [Gen 32:28]
10 Again God said to him,

"Your name is Jacob;
You shall no longer be called
Jacob,
But Israel shall be your name."

So he was called Israel.
11 And God said to him,

"I am God Almighty.
Be fruitful and multiply;
A nation and a company of nations
shall come from you,
And kings shall be born of your
loins.
12 "The land which I gave Abraham
and Isaac
I will give to you,
and to your descendants after you
I will give the land."

13 Then God ascended from Jacob in the
place where He had spoken with him.
14 Jacob set up a pillar (memorial,
monument) in the place where he had
talked with God, a pillar of stone, and
he poured a drink offering [of wine] on
it; he also poured oil on it [to declare it
sacred for God's purpose].
15 So Jacob named the place where
God had spoken with him, Bethel (the
House of God).
16 Then they journeyed from Bethel;
and when there was still some distance
to go to Ephrath (Bethlehem), Rachel
began to give birth and had difficulty
and suffered severely.
17 When she was in hard labor the
midwife said to her, "Do not be afraid;
you now have another son."
18 And as her soul was departing, (for
she died), she named him Ben-oni (son
of my sorrow); but his father called
him Benjamin (son of the right hand).
19 So Rachel died and was buried
on the way to Ephrath (that is, Beth-
lehem).
20 Jacob set a pillar (memorial, mon-
ument) on her grave; that is the pillar
of Rachel's grave to this day.
21 Then Israel (Jacob) journeyed on
and pitched his tent on the other side
of the tower of Eder [the lookout point
used by shepherds].
22 While Israel was living in that
land, Reuben [his eldest son] went and
lay with Bilhah his father's concubine,
and Israel heard about it.

The Sons of Israel

Now Jacob had twelve sons—
23 The sons of Leah: Reuben, Jacob's
firstborn, then Simeon, Levi, Judah,
Issachar, and Zebulun;
24 and the sons of Rachel: Joseph and
Benjamin;
25 and the sons of Bilhah, Rachel's
maid: Dan and Naphtali;
26 and the sons of Zilpah, Leah's
maid: Gad and Asher. These are the
sons of Jacob born to him in Paddan-
aram.
27 Jacob came to Isaac his father at
Mamre of Kiriath-arba (that is, He-
bron), where Abraham and Isaac had
lived temporarily.
28 Now the days of Isaac were a hun-
dred and eighty years.
29 Isaac's spirit departed and he died
and was gathered to his people [who
had preceded him in death], an old

35:10–12 *Israel shall be your name*. The renewal of God's covenant with Jacob was introduced by confirming Jacob's change of name to Israel, the one who "wrestled with God and prevailed." The promises made to Abraham and Isaac were once again repeated, underscoring the continuity of the covenant. Furthermore, a rather significant phrase is added, "be fruitful and multiply," which incorporated the creation ordinance, thus exhibiting the continuity with the covenant of creation. The covenant Lord is the God of creation and of redemption.

35:16 *Ephrath*. This is an alternative name for the region around Bethlehem (v. 19; 48:7; Ru 1:2; Mic 5:2). The King of Glory would one day be born near the birthplace of Benjamin (Mt 2:1).

35:27 *Jacob came to Isaac his father*. After more than 20 years of exile Jacob finally visited his father. Sadly, his mother Rebekah was probably dead since she is not mentioned.

---

10 Ge 17:5; Ge 32:28 **11** Ge 17:1; 48:3,4; Ex 6:3; Ge 17:5,6,16; 28:3; 48:4 **12** Ge 12:7; 13:15; 26:3,4; 28:13 **13** Ge 17:22 **14** Ge 28:18 **15** Ge 28:19 **17** Ge 30:24; 1Sa 4:20 **19** Ge 48:7; Ru 1:2; Mic 5:2; Mt 2:6 **20** 1Sa 10:2 **21** Mic 4:8 **22** Ge 49:4; 1Ch 5:1 **23** Ge 46:8; Ex 1:2 **27** Ge 13:18; Jos 14:15 **29** Ge 15:15; 25:8; See Ge 25:9; 49:31

man full of days (satisfied, fulfilled);
his sons Esau and Jacob buried him [in
the cave of Machpelah with his parents
Abraham and Sarah].

Esau Moves

36 NOW THESE are *the records of*
the descendants of Esau, (that
is, Edom).
2 Esau took his [three] wives from
the daughters of Canaan: Adah the
daughter of Elon the Hittite, and Ohol-
ibamah the daughter of Anah, the son
of Zibeon the Hivite,
3 and Basemath, Ishmael's daughter,
sister of Nebaioth.
4 Adah bore Eliphaz to Esau, and
Basemath bore Reuel,
5 and Oholibamah bore Jeush, Jalam,
and Korah. These are the sons of Esau
born to him in Canaan.
6 Now Esau took his wives and his
sons and his daughters and all the
members of his household, and his
livestock and all his cattle and all his
possessions which he had acquired in
the land of Canaan, and he went to a
land away from his brother Jacob.
7 For their [great flocks and herds
and] possessions made it impossible
for them to live together [in the same
region]; the land in which they lived
temporarily could not support them
because of their livestock.
8 So Esau lived in the hill country of
Seir; Esau is Edom.

Descendants of Esau

9 These are *the records of* the genera-
tions of Esau the father of the Edomites
in the hill country of Seir.
10 These are the names of Esau's
sons: Eliphaz, the son of Adah, Esau's
wife, and Reuel, the son of Basemath,
Esau's wife.
11 And the sons of Eliphaz were
Teman, Omar, Zepho, Gatam, and
Kenaz.
12 And Timna was a concubine of Eli-
phaz, Esau's son; and she bore Amalek
to Eliphaz. These are the sons of Adah,
Esau's wife.
13 These are the sons of Reuel: Na-
hath, Zerah, Shammah, and Mizzah.
These are the sons of Basemath, Esau's
wife.
14 And these are the sons of Oholi-
bamah, Esau's wife, the daughter of
Anah, the son of Zibeon. She bore to
Esau: Jeush, Jalam, and Korah.
15 These are the *tribal* chiefs of the
sons of Esau: The sons of Eliphaz, the
firstborn of Esau: Chiefs Teman, Omar,
Zepho, Kenaz,
16 Korah, Gatam, and Amalek. These
are the chiefs of Eliphaz in the land of
Edom; they are the sons of Adah.
17 These are the sons of Reuel, Esau's
son: Chiefs Nahath, Zerah, Shammah,
Mizzah. These are the chiefs of Reuel
in the land of Edom; they are the sons
of Basemath, Esau's wife.
18 These are the sons of Oholibamah,
Esau's wife: Chiefs Jeush, Jalam, and
Korah. These are the chiefs born of
Oholibamah, daughter of Anah, Esau's
wife.
19 These are the sons of Esau, (that
is, Edom), and these are their chiefs.
20 These are the sons of Seir the
Horite, the inhabitants of the land:
Lotan, Shobal, Zibeon, Anah,
21 Dishon, Ezer, and Dishan. These
are the chiefs of the Horites, the sons
of Seir in the land of Edom.
22 The sons of Lotan are Hori and
Hemam; and Lotan's sister is Timna.
23 The sons of Shobal are these: Al-
van, Manahath, Ebal, Shepho, and
Onam.
24 These are the sons of Zibeon: Aiah
and Anah. This is the Anah who found
the hot springs in the wilderness as
he pastured the donkeys of Zibeon
his father.
25 The children of Anah are these:

36:12 ***Amalek.*** Esau's grandson Amalek founded a people that later would trouble the Israelites (Nu 14:39–45).

36:40–43 Esau the father of the Edomites — Although Esau was not the heir of God's everlasting covenant with the family of Abraham,

CHAPTER 36 **1** Ge 25:30 **2** Ge 26:34; ver. 25 **3** Ge 28:9 **4** 1Ch 1:35 **7** Ge 13:6,11; Ge 17:8; 28:4 **8** Ge 32:3; Dt 2:5; Jos 24:4; ver. 1 **10** 1Ch 1:35 **12** Ex 17:8,14; Nu 24:20; 1Sa 15:2,3 **20** 1Ch 1:38; Ge 14:6; Dt 2:12,22 **24** See Lev 19:19

Dishon and Oholibamah [Esau's wife], the daughter of Anah.
[26]These are the sons of Dishon: Hemdan, Eshban, Ithran, and Cheran.
[27]Ezer's sons are these: Bilhan, Zaavan, and Akan.
[28]The sons of Dishan are these: Uz and Aran.
[29]The Horite chiefs are these: Chiefs Lotan, Shobal, Zibeon, Anah,
[30]Dishon, Ezer, Dishan. These are the Horite chiefs, according to their various clans in the land of Seir.
[31]And these are the kings who reigned in the land of Edom before any king reigned over the Israelites:
[32]Bela the son of Beor reigned in Edom, and the name of his city was Dinhabah.
[33]Now Bela died, and Jobab the son of Zerah of Bozrah reigned as his successor.
[34]Then Jobab died, and Husham of the land of the Temanites reigned as his successor.
[35]And Husham died, and Hadad the son of Bedad, who defeated Midian in the country of Moab, reigned as his successor. The name of his [walled] city was Avith.
[36]Hadad died, and Samlah of Masrekah succeeded him.
[37]Then Samlah died, and Shaul of Rehoboth on the river [Euphrates] reigned as his successor.
[38]And Shaul died, and Baal-hanan son of Achbor reigned as his successor.
[39]Baal-hanan the son of Achbor died, and then Hadar reigned [as his successor]. His [walled] city was Pau; his wife's name was Mehetabel the daughter of Matred, the daughter of Mezahab.
[40]And these are the names of the *tribal* chiefs of Esau, according to their families and places of residence, by their names: Chiefs Timna, Alvah, Jetheth,
[41]Oholibamah, Elah, Pinon,
[42]Kenaz, Teman, Mibzar,
[43]Magdiel, and Iram. These are the *tribal* chiefs of Edom (that is, of Esau the father of the Edomites), according to their dwelling places in the land of their possession.

Joseph's Dream

37 SO JACOB (Israel) lived in the land where his father [Isaac] had been a stranger (sojourner, resident alien), in the land of Canaan.
[2]These are the generations of Jacob.
Joseph, when he was seventeen years old, was shepherding the flock with his brothers [Dan, Naphtali, Gad, and Asher]; the boy was with the sons of Bilhah and Zilpah, his father's [secondary] wives; and Joseph brought back a bad report about them to their father.
[3]Now Israel (Jacob) loved Joseph more than all his children, because he was the son of his old age; and he made him a [distinctive] multicolored tunic.
[4]His brothers saw that their father loved Joseph more than all of his

God still blessed his family and made them into a nation.

37:1 ***a stranger.*** The Lord had promised that this land would become a permanent possession of Abraham's family (12:7). To the third generation, that promise was still not realized. Jacob and his family were still aliens in the land.

37:2 ***a bad report.*** Since Joseph in general demonstrated his integrity (see ch. 39), he was probably not slandering his brothers, but accurately reporting some negligence on their part.

37:3 ***a [distinctive] multicolored tunic.*** The traditional phrase here is "coat of many colors." The Hebrew phrase may simply mean a garment with long sleeves. The robe was certainly distinctive in some way, and probably costly.

37:4 ***hated him.*** Because fallen and unregenerate man hates God, he displays hatred in his relations with others. The hatred of Joseph's brothers is attributed primarily to the love which Jacob had for his youngest son. As a result of their hatred the brothers were not able to speak kindly to Joseph, and the hatred led to a plot to kill him. Jesus remarked that the world's hatred of His people is a reflection of hatred against Himself (Jn 15:18). Love is the leading characteristic of the godly as hatred is the mark of the worldly person.

31 1Ch 1:43 **37** Ge 10:11 **39** 1Ch 1:50 **40** 1Ch 1:51 **CHAPTER 37** **1** Ge 17:8; 23:4; 28:4; 36:7; Heb 11:9
2 1Sa 2:22-24 **3** Ge 44:20 **4** Ge 27:41; 49:23

brothers; so they hated him and could not [find it within themselves to] speak to him on friendly terms.

[5]Now Joseph dreamed a dream, and he told it to his brothers, and they hated him even more.

[6]He said to them, "Please listen to [the details of] this dream which I have dreamed;

[7]we [brothers] were binding sheaves [of grain stalks] in the field, and lo, my sheaf [suddenly] got up and stood upright *and* remained standing; and behold, your sheaves stood all around my sheaf and bowed down [in respect]."

[8]His brothers said to him, "Are you actually going to reign over us? Are you really going to rule *and* govern us as your subjects?" So they hated him even more for [telling them about] his dreams and for his [arrogant] words.

[9]But Joseph dreamed still another dream, and told it to his brothers [as well]. He said, "See here, I have again dreamed a dream, and lo, [this time I saw] eleven stars and the sun and the moon bowed down [in respect] to me!"

[10]He told it to his father as well as to his brothers; but his father rebuked him and said to him [in disbelief], "What is [the meaning of] this dream that you have dreamed? Shall I and your mother and your brothers actually come to bow down to the ground [in respect] before you?"

[11]Joseph's brothers were envious *and* jealous of him, but his father kept the words [of Joseph] *in mind* [wondering about their meaning].

[12]Then his brothers went to pasture their father's flock near Shechem.

[13]Israel (Jacob) said to Joseph, "Are not your brothers pasturing [the flock] at Shechem? Come, and I will send you to them." And he said, "Here I am [ready to obey you]."

[14]Then Jacob said to him, "Please go and see whether everything is all right with your brothers and all right with the flock; then bring word [back] to me." So he sent him from the Hebron Valley, and he went to Shechem.

[15]Now a certain man found Joseph, and saw that he was wandering around *and* had lost his way in the field; so the man asked him, "What are you looking for?"

[16]He said, "I am looking for my brothers. Please tell me where they are pasturing *our flocks*."

[17]Then the man said, "[They were here, but] they have moved on from this place. I heard them say, 'Let us go to Dothan.' " So Joseph went after his brothers and found them at Dothan.

The Plot against Joseph

[18]And when they saw him from a distance, even before he came close to them, they plotted to kill him.

[19]They said to one another, "Look, here comes this dreamer.

[20]"Now then, come and let us kill him and throw him into one of the pits (cisterns, underground water storage); then we will say [to our father], 'A wild animal killed *and* devoured him'; and we shall see what will become of his dreams!"

[21]Now Reuben [the eldest] heard this and rescued him from their hands and said, "Let us not take his life."

[22]Reuben said to them, "Do not shed his blood, but [instead] throw him [alive] into the pit that is here in the wilderness, and do not lay a hand on him [to kill him]"—[he said this so] that he could rescue him from them and return him [safely] to his father.

[23]Now when Joseph reached his brothers, they stripped him of his tunic, the [distinctive] multicolored tunic which he was wearing;

[24]then they took him and threw him into the pit. Now the pit was empty; there was no water in it.

37:17 ***Dothan.*** This is about ten miles north of Shechem, near Mount Gilboa.

37:21 ***Let us not take his life.*** Reuben, as the firstborn son and principal heir, had the most to lose if Joseph's dreams came true. Yet Reuben intervened to spare Joseph's life. This was something of a contrast with his earlier wicked actions (35:22).

7 Ge 42:6,9; 43:26; 44:14 **9** Ge 46:29 **10** Ge 27:29 **11** Ac 7:9; Da 7:28; Lk 2:19,51 **12** Ge 33:18 **14** Ge 13:18; 35:27 **16** SS 1:7 **17** 2Ki 6:13 **18** 1Sa 19:1; Mt 27:1; Mk 14:1; Ac 23:12 **20** Pr 1:11 **21** Ge 42:22

25 Then they sat down to eat their meal. When they looked up, they saw a caravan of Ishmaelites coming from Gilead [east of the Jordan], with their camels bearing ladanum resin [for perfume] and balm and myrrh, going on their way to carry *the cargo* down to Egypt.

26 Judah said to his brothers, "What do we gain if we kill our brother and cover up his blood (murder)?

27 "Come, let us [instead] sell him to these Ishmaelites [and Midianites] and not lay our hands on him, because he is our brother and our flesh." So his brothers listened to him *and* agreed. [Gen 22:24; 25:2]

28 Then as the Midianite [and Ishmaelite] traders were passing by, the brothers pulled Joseph up and lifted him out of the pit, and they sold him to the Ishmaelites for twenty *shekels* of silver. And so they took Joseph [as a captive] into Egypt.

29 Now Reuben [unaware of what had happened] returned to the pit, and [to his great alarm found that] Joseph was not in the pit; so he tore his clothes [in deep sorrow].

30 He rejoined his brothers and said, "The boy is not there; as for me, where shall I go [to hide from my father]?"

31 Then they took Joseph's tunic, slaughtered a male goat and dipped the tunic in the blood;

32 and they brought the multicolored tunic to their father, saying, "We have found this; please examine it *and* decide whether or not it is your son's tunic."

33 He recognized it and said, "It is my son's tunic. A wild animal has devoured him; Joseph is without doubt torn in pieces!"

34 So Jacob tore his clothes [in grief], put on sackcloth and mourned many days for his son.

35 Then all his sons and daughters attempted to console him, but he refused to be comforted and said, "I will go down to Sheol (the place of the dead) in mourning for my son." And his father wept for him.

36 Meanwhile, in Egypt the Midianites sold Joseph [as a slave] to Potiphar, an officer of Pharaoh and the captain of the [royal] guard.

Judah and Tamar

38 NOW AT that time, Judah left his brothers and went down to [stay with] a certain Adullamite named Hirah.

2 There Judah saw a daughter of Shua, a Canaanite, and he took her [as his wife] and lived with her.

3 So she conceived and gave birth to a son and Judah named him Er.

4 Then she conceived again and gave birth to a son and named him Onan.

5 Again she conceived and gave birth to still another son and named him Shelah. It was at Chezib that she gave birth to him.

6 Now Judah took a wife for Er his firstborn; her name was Tamar.

7 But Er, Judah's firstborn, was evil in the sight of the LORD, and the LORD killed him [in judgment].

37:25 ***Ishmaelites.*** The Ishmaelites of this passage were wandering traders. The name (referring to descendants of Ishmael, the son of Abraham and Hagar) is loosely equivalent with the name Midianite (Midian was another son of Abraham, by Keturah). Probably the families of the two half brothers had a strong alliance and were so closely associated that the names became interchangeable (v. 28).

37:28 ***twenty shekels of silver.*** The standard price for a slave in later Israelite law was 30 pieces of silver.

37:29 ***tore his clothes.*** Tearing one's clothes was a common expression of grief and dismay. Reuben's grief was genuine feeling for his younger brother mixed with fear that he, the oldest brother, would be blamed.

38:1 – 30 At first glance it appears that the story of Judah and Tamar is an intrusion into the story of Joseph, but it is here for a reason. It provides a stunning contrast between the morals of Judah and Joseph. It illustrates the further disintegration of Jacob's family. If this process continued, Jacob's family, the family of promise, would become like the people of Canaan.

---

25 Pr 30:20; See ver. 28,36; Jer 8:22 **26** ver. 20 **27** 1Sa 18:17; Ge 42:21; Ge 29:14 **28** Jdg 6:3; Ps 105:17; Ac 7:9; See Mt 27:9 **29** Job 1:20 **30** Ge 42:13,36 **31** ver. 23 **33** ver. 20 **34** 2Sa 3:31 **35** 2Sa 12:17; Ge 42:38 **36** Ge 39:1 **CHAPTER 38** **1** 2Ki 4:8 **2** Ge 34:2; 1Ch 2:3 **4** Nu 26:19 **5** Nu 26:20 **6** Ge 21:21 **7** Nu 26:19; 1Ch 2:3

[8]Then Judah told Onan, "Go in to
your brother's widow, and perform
your duty as a brother-in-law [under
the levirate marriage custom]; [be her
husband and] raise children for [the
name of] your brother." [Deut 25:5–10]
[9]Onan knew that the child (heir)
would not be his [but his dead broth-
er's]; so whenever he lay with his
brother's widow, he spilled his seed
on the ground [to prevent conception],
so that he would not give a child to his
brother.
[10]But what he did was displeasing
in the sight of the LORD; therefore He
killed him also [in judgment].
[11]Then Judah said to Tamar, his
daughter-in-law, "Remain a widow at
your father's house until Shelah my
[youngest] son is grown"; [but he was
deceiving her] for he thought that [if
Shelah should marry her] he too might
die like his brothers did. So Tamar
went and lived in her father's house.
[12]But quite a while later, Judah's
wife, the daughter of Shua, died; and
when the time of mourning was end-
ed, he went up to his sheepshearers
at Timnah with his friend Hirah the
Adullamite.
[13]Tamar was told, "Listen, your
father-in-law is going up to Timnah
to shear his sheep."
[14]So she removed her widow's
clothes and covered herself with a veil,
and wrapped herself up [in disguise],
and sat in the gateway of Enaim, which
is on the road to Timnah; for she saw
that Shelah had grown up, and she
had not been given to him as a wife
[as Judah had promised].
[15]When Judah saw her, he thought
she was a [temple] prostitute, for she
had covered her face [as such women
did].
[16]He turned to her by the road, and
said, "Please come, let me lie with you";
for he did not know that she was his
daughter-in-law. And she said, "What
will you give me, that you may lie with
me?"
[17]He answered, "I will send you a
young goat from the flock." And she
said, "Will you give me a pledge [as a
deposit] until you send it?"
[18]He said, "What pledge shall I give
you?" She said, "Your seal and your
cord, and the staff that is in your
hand." So he gave them to her and was
intimate with her, and she conceived
by him.
[19]Then she got up and left, and re-
moved her veil and put on her widow's
clothing.
[20]When Judah sent the young goat
by his friend the Adullamite, to get his
pledge [back] from the woman, he was
unable to find her.
[21]He asked the men of that place,
"Where is the temple prostitute who
was by the roadside at Enaim?" They
said, "There was no prostitute here."
[22]So he returned to Judah, and said,
"I cannot find her; also the local men

38:8 *to your brother's widow.* In order to maintain the family line and the name of the deceased, it was the custom in ancient times for the dead man's brother to marry the widow and father a child that would carry on the man's family. This is called *levirate* marriage, from the Latin word meaning "husband's brother." The custom became part of the Mosaic law (Dt 25:5 – 10; Ru 4:1 – 12).

38:15 – 18 Fornication — God designed sexual relations to be enjoyed exclusively within the framework of marriage: one man, for one woman, mutually committed for life. Outside of this framework, all sexual relations are sin. This is not because God wants to deprive His people of pleasure, but because He wants to protect them from the painful and destructive consequences of sin. Sexual union is not only a union of the body, but of the whole person (1Co 6:15 – 20). Illicit sexual relations defile the temple of God, breed both physical and social disease, and serve as a source for many other sins.

38:18 *seal.* This was an ancient means of identification. The seal was distinctively etched in stone, metal, or ivory. To confirm a business transaction, or make an order official, the seal was pressed into soft clay, leaving its distinctive impression. Basically, Judah gave Tamar the equivalent of a modern credit card.

8 Dt 25:5 **9** Dt 25:6 **10** Ge 46:12 **11** Ru 1:13; Lev 22:13 **12** 2Sa 13:39 **13** Jos 15:10,57 **14** Pr 7:12; ver. 11,26 **17** Eze 16:33; ver. 20 **18** ver. 25 **19** ver. 14

said, 'There was no prostitute around
here.' "
23 Then Judah said, "Let her keep
the things (pledge articles) for herself,
otherwise we will be a laughingstock
[searching everywhere for her]. After
all, I sent this young goat, but you did
not find her."
24 About three months later Judah
was told, "Tamar your daughter-in-law
has played the [role of a] prostitute,
and she is with child because of her
immorality." So Judah said, "Bring her
out and let her be burned [to death as
punishment]!"
25 While she was being brought out,
she [took the things Judah had giv-
en her and] sent [them along with a
message] to her father-in-law, saying,
"I am with child by the man to whom
these articles belong." And she added,
"Please examine [them carefully] and
see [clearly] to whom these things be-
long, the seal and the cord and staff."
26 Judah recognized the articles, and
said, "She has been more righteous [in
this matter] than I, because I did not
give her to my son Shelah [as I had
promised]." And Judah did not have
[intimate] relations with her again.
27 Now when the time came for her
to give birth, there were twins in her
womb.
28 And when she was in labor, one
[baby] put out his hand, and the mid-
wife took his hand and tied a scarlet
thread on it, saying, "This one was
born first."
29 But he pulled back his hand, and
his brother was born first. And she
said, "What a breach you have made
for yourself [to be the firstborn]!" So
he was named Perez (breach, break
forth). [Matt 1:3]
30 Afterward his brother who had the
scarlet [thread] on his hand was born
and was named Zerah (brightness).

Joseph's Success in Egypt

39 NOW JOSEPH had been taken
down to Egypt; and Potiphar, an
Egyptian officer of Pharaoh, the cap-
tain of the [royal] guard, bought him
from the Ishmaelites, who had taken
him down there.
2 The LORD was with Joseph, and he
[even though a slave] became a suc-
cessful *and* prosperous man; and he
was in the house of his master, the
Egyptian.
3 Now his master saw that the LORD
was with him and that the LORD caused
all that he did to prosper (succeed) in
his hand. [Gen 21:22; 26:27, 28; 41:38,
39]
4 So Joseph pleased Potiphar *and*
found favor in his sight and he served
him as his personal servant. He made
Joseph overseer over his house, and
he put all that he owned in Joseph's
charge.
5 It happened that from the time that
he made Joseph overseer in his house
and [put him in charge] over all that
he owned, that the LORD blessed the
Egyptian's house because of Joseph; so
the LORD's blessing was on everything
that Potiphar owned, in the house and
in the field.
6 So Potiphar left all that he owned
in Joseph's charge; and with Joseph
there he did not [need to] pay attention
to anything except the food he ate.
Now Joseph was handsome *and*
attractive in form and appearance.
[Gen 43:32]
7 Then after a time his master's wife

38:26 *She has been more righteous.* Judah, one of the heirs of the everlasting covenant with the living God, was put to shame by a Canaanite woman. To his credit, Judah confessed his sins.
38:29 *Perez*. Perez was in the lineage of David, and eventually Jesus the Messiah (Ru 4:18; Mt 1:3).
39:2 *The LORD was with Joseph.* This key phrase of this section is repeated (vv. 21, 23). This phrase indicates that God cared for, protected, and blessed Joseph.
39:4 *found favor.* Joseph's life illustrates the principle that one who is faithful in little will be given charge over much (Mt 25:21; 1Co 4:2).
39:5 *the LORD blessed the Egyptian's house.* God blessed Potiphar's house because of Joseph, just as He had blessed Laban because of Jacob.

24 Jdg 19:2; Lev 21:9; Dt 22:21 **25** Ge 37:32; ver. 18 **26** Ge 37:33; 1Sa 24:17; ver. 14; Job 34:31,32 **29** Ge 46:12; Nu 26:20; 1Ch 2:4; Mt 1:3 **CHAPTER 39** **1** Ge 37:36; Ps:105:17; Ge 37:28 **2** ver. 21; Ge 21:22; 26:24,28; 28:15; 1Sa 16:18; 18:14,28; Ac 7:9 **3** Ps 1:3 **4** ver. 21; Ge 24:2 **5** Ge 30:27 **6** 1Sa 16:12 **7** 2Sa 13:11

looked at Joseph with desire, and she
said, "Lie with me."
8But he refused and said to his mas-
ter's wife, "Look, with me in the house,
my master does not concern himself
with anything; he has put everything
that he owns in my charge.
9"He is not greater in this house than
I am, nor has he kept anything from
me except you, because you are his
wife. How then could I do this great
evil and sin against God [and your
husband]?"
10And so it was that she spoke to
Joseph [persistently] day after day,
but he did not listen to her [plea] to lie
beside her or be with her.
11Then it happened one day that Jo-
seph went into the house to attend to
his duties, and none of the men of the
household was there in the house.
12She caught Joseph by his [outer]
robe, saying, "Lie with me!" But he left
his robe in her hand and ran, and got
outside [the house].
13When she saw that he had left his
robe in her hand and had run outside,
14she called to the men of her house-
hold and said to them, "Look at this,
your master has brought a Hebrew
[into the household] to mock *and* insult
us; he came to me to lie with me, and
I screamed.
15"When he heard me screaming, he
left his robe with me and ran outside
[the house]."
16So she left Joseph's [outer] robe
beside her until his master came home.
17Then she told her husband the
same story, saying, "The Hebrew ser-
vant, whom you brought among us,
came to me to mock *and* insult me;
18then as soon as I raised my voice
and screamed, he left his robe with me
and ran outside [the house]."

Joseph Imprisoned

19And when Joseph's master heard
the words of his wife, saying, "This is
the way your servant treated me," his
anger burned.
20So Joseph's master took him and
put him in the prison, a place where
the king's prisoners were confined; so
he was there in the prison.
21But the LORD was with Joseph and
extended lovingkindness to him, and
gave him favor in the sight of the war-
den.
22The warden committed to Joseph's
care (management) all the prisoners
who were in the prison; so that what-
ever was done there, he was in charge
of it.
23The warden paid no attention to
anything that was in Joseph's care be-
cause the LORD was with him; whatever
Joseph did, the LORD made to prosper.

Joseph Interprets a Dream

40 NOW SOME time later, the cup-
bearer (butler) and the baker for
the king of Egypt offended their lord,
Egypt's king.
2Pharaoh (Sesostris II) was extreme-
ly angry with his two officials, the
chief of the cupbearers and the chief
of the bakers.
3He put them in confinement in the
house of the captain of the guard, in

39:9 *sin against God*. Joseph rejected the solicitation to sin, regarding it both as a wicked act of treachery against his master, and as a defiling and rebellious act before a holy God. Because Joseph's conscience was bound by God and His truth, he was able to resist this evil suggestion more than once. Pleasing God was more important to Joseph than engaging in the pleasures of sin for a season. His fear and reverence of God was the directing power of his life.

39:20 *in the prison*. Surprisingly, Potiphar did not simply kill Joseph outright. It is possible that knowledge of Joseph's character (or his own wife's character) caused him to suspect that the story was not wholly true.

39:21 *lovingkindness*. This word can be translated *loyal love* (Ps 13:5). God faithfully kept His promises by staying with His people (12:1 – 3; 50:24).

39:23 *the LORD made to prosper*. Because of God's blessing, everything Joseph did prospered (Ps 1:1 – 3).

9 Pr 6:29,32; Ge 20:6 **12** Pr 7:13 **17** Ex 23:1; Ps 120:3 **19** Pr 6:34,35 **20** Ps 105:18; 1Pe 2:19; See Ge 40:3,15; 41:14 **21** Ex 3:21; Pr 16:7; Da 1:9; Ac 7:9,10 **22** Ge 40:3,4 **23** ver. 2,3 **CHAPTER 40** **1** Neh 1:11 **2** Pr 16:14 **3** Ge 39:20,23

the same prison where Joseph was
confined.
4 The captain of the guard put Joseph
in charge of them, and he served them;
and they continued to be in custody for
some time.
5 Then the cupbearer and the baker
of the king of Egypt, who were con-
fined in the prison, both dreamed a
dream in the same night, each man
with his [own significant] dream and
each dream with its [personal] inter-
pretation.
6 When Joseph came to them in the
morning and looked at them, [he saw
that] they were sad *and* depressed.
7 So he asked Pharaoh's officials who
were in confinement with him in his
master's house, "Why do you look so
down-hearted today?"
8 And they said to him, "We have
[each] dreamed [distinct] dreams and
there is no one to interpret them." So
Joseph said to them, "Do not interpre-
tations belong to God? Please tell me
[your dreams]."
9 So the chief cupbearer told his
dream to Joseph, and said to him, "In
my dream there was a grapevine in
front of me;
10 and on the vine were three branch-
es. Then as soon as it budded, its blos-
soms burst open, and its clusters pro-
duced ripe grapes [in rapid succession].
11 "Now Pharaoh's cup was in my
hand, and I took the grapes and
squeezed them into Pharaoh's cup;
then I placed the cup into Pharaoh's
hand."
12 Then Joseph said to him, "This
is the interpretation of it: the three
branches represent three days;
13 within three more days Pharaoh
will lift up your head (present you in
public) and restore you to your posi-
tion; and you will [again] put Phar-
aoh's cup into his hand just as [you did]
when you were his cupbearer.
14 "Only think of me when it goes
well with you, and please show me
kindness by mentioning me to Pharaoh
and get me out of this house.
15 "For in fact I was taken (stolen)
from the land of the Hebrews by [un-
lawful] force, and even here I have
done nothing for which they should
put me in the dungeon."
16 When the chief baker saw that the
interpretation [of the dream] was good,
he said to Joseph, "I also dreamed, and
[in my dream] there were three cake
baskets on my head;
17 and in the top basket there were
some of all sorts of baked food for
Pharaoh, but the birds [of prey] were
eating [these foods] out of the basket
on my head."
18 Joseph answered, "This is the in-
terpretation of it: the three baskets
represent three days;
19 within three more days Pharaoh
will lift up your head and will hang you
on a tree (gallows, pole), and [you will
not so much as be given a burial, but]
the birds will eat your flesh."
20 Now on the third day, [which was]
the Pharaoh's birthday, he [released
the two men from prison and] made a
feast for all his servants; and he lifted
up the head of the chief cupbearer and
the head of the chief baker [that is,
presented them in public] among his
servants.
21 He restored the chief cupbearer
to his office, and the cupbearer [once
again] put the cup into Pharaoh's hand;
22 but Pharaoh hanged the chief bak-
er, just as Joseph had interpreted [the
meaning of the dreams] to them.
23 Yet [even after all that] the chief
cupbearer did not remember Joseph,
but forgot [all about] him.

40:8 *interpretations belong to God?* Joseph not only announced his faith, he then quickly acted upon it. Joseph had received dreams and visions as a younger man, and he had understood their meaning (37:5 – 11).

40:22 *Pharaoh hanged the chief baker.* Pharaoh was clearly a ruthless ruler who rewarded those who served him well, but destroyed those he perceived as threats.

8 Ge 41:15; See Ge 41:16; Da 2:11,28,47 **12** ver. 18; Ge 41:12,25; Jdg 7:14; Da 2:36; 4:19; Ge 41:26 **13** 2Ki 25:27; Ps 3:3; Jer 52:31 **14** Lk 23:42; Jos 2:12; 1Sa 20:14,15; 2Sa 9:1; 1Ki 2:7 **15** Ge 39:20 **18** ver. 12 **19** ver. 13 **20** Mt 14:6; Mk 6:21; ver. 13,19; Mt 25:19 **21** ver. 13; Neh 2:1 **22** ver. 19 **23** Job 19:14; Ecc 9:15,16; Am 6:6

Pharaoh's Dream

41 NOW IT happened at the end
of two full years that Pharaoh
dreamed that he was standing by the
Nile.
2 And lo, there came up out of the
Nile seven [healthy] cows, sleek *and*
handsome and fat; and they grazed in
the reed grass [in a marshy pasture].
3 Then behold, seven other cows
came up after them out of the Nile,
ugly and gaunt *and* raw-boned, and
stood by the *fat* cows on the bank of
the Nile.
4 Then the ugly and gaunt *and* raw-
boned cows ate up the seven sleek and
fat cows. Then Pharaoh awoke.
5 Then he fell asleep and dreamed a
second time; and behold, seven ears of
grain came up on a single stalk, plump
and good.
6 Then behold, seven ears [of grain],
thin and dried up by the east wind,
sprouted after them.
7 Then the thin ears swallowed the
seven plump and full ears. And Phar-
aoh awoke, and it was a dream.
8 So when morning came his spirit
was troubled *and* disturbed and he
sent and called for all the magicians
and all the wise men of Egypt. And
Pharaoh told them his dreams, but no
one could interpret them to him.
9 Then the chief cupbearer spoke to
Pharaoh, saying, "I would mention my
faults today.
10 "[Two years ago] Pharaoh was
angry with his servants, and he put
me in confinement in the house of the
captain of the guard, both me and the
chief baker.
11 "We dreamed a dream on the same
night, he and I; each of us dreamed
according to [the significance of] the
interpretation of his own dream.
12 "Now there was with us [in the
prison] a young man, a Hebrew, ser-
vant to the captain of the guard; and
we told him, and he interpreted our
dreams for us, to each man according
to the significance of his own dream.
13 "And just as he interpreted [the
dreams] for us, so it happened; I was
restored to my office [as chief cupbear-
er], and the baker was hanged."

Joseph Interprets

14 Then Pharaoh sent and called for
Joseph, and they hurriedly brought
him out of the dungeon; and when Jo-
seph shaved himself and changed his
clothes [making himself presentable],
he came to Pharaoh.
15 Pharaoh said to Joseph, "I have
dreamed a dream, and there is no one
who can interpret it; and I have heard
it said about you that you can under-
stand a dream and interpret it."
16 Joseph answered Pharaoh, "It is
not in me [to interpret the dream]; God
[not I] will give Pharaoh a favorable
answer [through me]."
17 So Pharaoh said to Joseph, "In my
dream, I was standing on the bank of
the Nile;
18 and seven fat, sleek *and* handsome
cows came up out of the river, and they
grazed in the reed grass [of a marshy
pasture].
19 "Lo, seven other cows came up
after them, very ugly and gaunt [just
skin and bones]; such emaciated an-
imals as I have never seen in all the
land of Egypt.

41:8 *magicians.* The Hebrew term is related to the word for *stylus*, a writing instrument. Thus the magicians were associated in some manner with writing and knowledge, no doubt of the occult. ***wise men.*** These were a class of scholars associated with the courts of the ancient Middle East. They were either functionaries of pagan religions, or merely observers and interpreters of life.

41:14 *shaved.* Egyptian men not only shaved their faces, but their entire bodies and heads. Egyptian officials scorned the "hairy" Canaanites, including the Hebrews (43:32). While he lived in Egypt Joseph apparently adopted the dress and manner of the Egyptians.

41:16 *God.* Joseph praised the power of the living God in the pagan court of Pharaoh. He would not take any credit to himself, nor did he try to use the situation to plead for his own release.

CHAPTER 41 **8** Da 2:1; 4:5,19; Ex 7:11,22; Isa 29:14; Da 1:20; 2:2; 4:7; Mt 2:1 **10** Ge 40:2,3; Ge 39:20 **11** Ge 40:5 **12** Ge 37:36; Ge 40:12 **13** Ge 40:22 **14** Ps 105:20; Da 2:25; 1Sa 2:8; Ps 113:7,8 **15** ver. 12; Da 5:16 **16** Da 2:30; Ac 3:12; 2Co 3:5; Ge 40:8; Da 2:22,28,47; 4:2 **17** ver. 1

20“And the lean and ugly cows ate up
the first seven fat cows.
21“Yet when they had devoured them,
it could not be detected that they had
eaten them, because they were still as
thin *and* emaciated as before. Then
I awoke [but again I fell asleep and
dreamed].
22“I saw in my [second] dream, seven
ears [of grain], plump and good, grow-
ing on a single stalk;
23and lo, seven [other] ears, withered,
thin, and scorched by the east wind,
sprouted after them;
24and the thin ears devoured the sev-
en good ears. Now I told this to the ma-
gicians *and* soothsayers, but there was
no one who could explain it [to me].”
25Then Joseph said to Pharaoh, “The
[two] dreams are one [and the same
and have one interpretation]; God has
shown Pharaoh what He is about to do.
26“The seven good cows are seven
years, and the seven good ears are
seven years; the [two] dreams are one
[and the same].
27“The seven thin and ugly cows that
came up after them are seven years;
and also the seven thin ears, dried up
and scorched by the east wind, they
are seven years of famine *and* hunger.
28“This is the message just as I have
told Pharaoh: God has shown Pharaoh
what He is about to do.
29“Listen very carefully: seven years
of great abundance will come through-
out all the land of Egypt;
30but afterward seven years of fam-
ine *and* hunger will come, and [there
will be such desperate need that] all
the great abundance [of the previous
years] will be forgotten in the land of
Egypt [as if it never happened], and
famine *and* destitution will ravage *and*
destroy the land.
31“So the great abundance will be-
come forgotten in the land because of
that subsequent famine, for it will be
very severe.
32“That the dream was repeated
twice to Pharaoh [and in two differ-
ent ways] indicates that this matter
is fully determined *and* established
by God, and God will bring it to pass
very quickly.
33“So now let Pharaoh [prepare
ahead and] look for a man discerning
and clear-headed and wise, and set
him [in charge] over the land of Egypt
[as governor under Pharaoh].
34“Let Pharaoh take action to ap-
point overseers *and* officials over the
land, and set aside one-fifth [of the
produce] of the [entire] land of Egypt
in the seven years of abundance.
35“Let them gather [as a tax] all [of
the fifth of] the food of these good years
that are coming, and store up grain
under the direction *and* authority of
Pharaoh, and let them guard the food
[in fortified granaries] in the cities.
36“That food shall be put [in stor-
age] as a reserve for the land against
the seven years of famine *and* hunger
which will occur in the land of Egypt,
so that the land (people) will not be
ravaged during the famine.”
37Now the plan seemed good to Phar-
aoh and to all of his servants.

Joseph Is Made a Ruler of Egypt

38So Pharaoh said to his servants,
“Can we find a man like this [a man
equal to Joseph], in whom is the divine
spirit [of God]?”
39Then Pharaoh said to Joseph,
“Since [your] God has shown you all
this, there is no one as discerning *and*
clear-headed and wise as you are.

41:32 *God, and God.* Joseph made it clear that he was speaking about the one God, not the numerous false gods that filled the Egyptian court, or Pharaoh himself who was believed to be a god (22:1; 42:18).

41:38 *in whom is the divine spirit.* Even if he did not follow God himself, Pharaoh was at least acknowledging that Joseph was extraordinarily wise, and that the power of his God was obvious in his life.

41:39 *discerning and clear-headed and wise*. Joseph is an illustration of the instructions Paul

24 ver. 8; Da 4:7 **25** Da 2:28,29,45; Rev 4:1 **27** 2Ki 8:1 **28** ver. 25 **29** ver. 47 **30** ver. 54; Ge 47:13 **32** Nu 23:19; Isa 46:10,11 **34** Pr 6:6-8 **35** ver. 48 **36** Ge 47:15,19 **37** Ps 105:19; Ac 7:10 **38** Nu 27:18; Job 32:8; Pr 2:6; Da 4:8,18; 5:11,14; 6:3

[40]"You shall have charge over my house, and all my people shall be governed according to your word and pay respect [to you with reverence, submission, and obedience]; only in [matters of] the throne will I be greater than you [in Egypt]."

[41]Then Pharaoh said to Joseph, "See, I have set you [in charge] over all the land of Egypt."

[42]Then Pharaoh took off his signet ring from his hand and put it on Joseph's hand, and dressed him in [official] vestments of fine linen and put a gold chain around his neck.

[43]He had him ride in his second chariot; and runners proclaimed before him, "[Attention,] bow the knee!" And he set him over all the land of Egypt.

[44]Moreover, Pharaoh said to Joseph, "*Though* I am Pharaoh, yet without your permission shall no man raise his hand [to do anything] or set his foot [to go anywhere] in all the land of Egypt [all classes of people shall submit to your authority]."

[45]Then Pharaoh named Joseph Zaphenath-paneah; and he gave him Asenath, the daughter of Potiphera, priest of On (Heliopolis in Egypt), as his wife. And Joseph went out over all the land of Egypt [to inspect and govern it].

[46]Now Joseph [had been in Egypt thirteen years and] was thirty years old when he stood before Pharaoh, king of Egypt. Joseph departed from the presence of Pharaoh and went through all the land of Egypt [performing his duties].

[47]In the seven abundant years the earth produced handfuls [for each seed planted].

[48]And Joseph gathered all the [surplus] food of the seven [good] years in the land of Egypt and stored [enormous quantities of] the food in the cities. He stored away in every city the food [collected] from its own surrounding fields.

[49]Thus Joseph gathered *and* stored up grain in great abundance like the sand of the sea, until he stopped counting it, for it could not be measured.

The Sons of Joseph

[50]Now two sons were born to Joseph before the years of famine came, whom Asenath, the daughter of Potiphera, priest of On, bore to him.

[51]Joseph named the firstborn Manasseh (causing to forget), for *he said,* "God has made me forget all my trouble *and* hardship and all [the sorrow of the loss of] my father's household."

[52]He named the second [son] Ephraim (fruitfulness), for "God has caused me to be fruitful *and* very successful in the land of my suffering."

[53]When the seven years of plenty came to an end in the land of Egypt,

[54]the seven years of famine began to come, just as Joseph had said [they would]; the famine was in all the [surrounding] lands, but in the land of Egypt there was bread (food).

[55]So when all the land of Egypt was famished, the people cried out to Pharaoh for food; and Pharaoh said to all the Egyptians, "Go to Joseph; do whatever he says to you."

[56]When the famine was *spread* over all the land, Joseph opened all the storehouses, and sold [surplus grain] to the Egyptians; and the famine grew [extremely] severe in the land of Egypt.

---

gave Colossae: "Conduct yourself with wisdom in your interactions with outsiders" (Col 4:5). Pharaoh recognized that Joseph's wisdom was not the ordinary powers of a clever man, but something unique and outside of himself. Joseph was wise because he listened to God, not just because of his extraordinary intelligence and perspicacity. God's wisdom is moral. It discerns between good and evil. It is seen through prudence in secular affairs and comes through personal experience with the Lord.

41:45 ***Zaphenath-paneah.*** This Egyptian name probably means something like "The God Speaks and Lives." ***Asenath.*** This name means "Belonging to (the Goddess) Neith." ***Potiphera.*** This name means "He Whom Ra (the sun god) Gave." Even though his father-in-law was the priest of a pagan god, Joseph and Asenath's sons were worshipers of the Lord, not Ra.

40 Ps 105:21; Ac 7:10 **41** Da 6:3 **42** Est 3:10; Est 8:15; Da 5:7,29 **43** Est 6:9; Ge 42:6; Ac 7:10 **46** 1Sa 16:21; 1Ki 12:6,8; Da 1:19 **49** Ge 22:17; Jdg 7:12; 1Sa 13:5 **50** Ge 46:20; 48:5 **52** Ge 49:22 **54** Ps 105:16; Ac 7:11; ver. 30 **56** Ge 42:6

57 And [the people of] all countries
came to Egypt to Joseph to buy grain,
because the famine was severe over
all the [known] earth.

Joseph's Brothers Sent to Egypt

42 NOW WHEN Jacob (Israel)
learned that there was grain in
Egypt, he said to his sons, "Why are
you staring at one another [in bewil-
derment and not taking action]?"
2 He said, "I have heard that there is
grain in Egypt; go down there and buy
[some] grain for us, so that we may live
and not die [of starvation]."
3 So ten of Joseph's brothers went
down to buy grain in Egypt.
4 But Jacob did not send Benjamin,
Joseph's [younger] brother, with his
brothers, for he said, "I am afraid that
some harm *or* injury may come to him."
5 So the sons of Israel came [to Egypt]
to buy grain along with the others who
were coming, for famine was in the
land of Canaan *also*.
6 Now Joseph was the ruler over the
land, and he was the one who sold
[grain] to all the people of the land;
and Joseph's [half] brothers came and
bowed down before him with *their*
faces to the ground.
7 When Joseph saw his brothers he
recognized them, but [hiding his iden-
tity] he treated them as strangers and
spoke harshly to them. He said to them,
"Where have you come from?" And
they said, "From the land of Canaan,
to buy food."
8 Joseph recognized his brothers, but
they did not recognize him.
9 Joseph remembered the dreams he
had dreamed about them, and said to
them, "You are spies; you have come
[with a malicious purpose] to observe
the undefended parts of our land."
10 But they said to him, "No, my lord,
for your servants have [only] come to
buy food.
11 "We are all the sons of one man;
we are honest men, your servants are
not spies."
12 Yet he said to them, "No, you have
come to see the undefended parts of
our land."
13 But they said, "Your servants are
twelve brothers [in all], the sons of
one man in the land of Canaan; please
listen: the youngest is with our father
today, and one is no longer alive."
14 Joseph said to them, "It is as I said
to you, you are spies.
15 "In this way you shall be tested:
by the life of Pharaoh, you shall not
leave this place unless your youngest
brother comes here!
16 "Send one of you [back home], and
let him bring your brother [here], while
[the rest of] you remain confined, so
that your words may be tested, [to see]
whether there is any truth in you [and
your story]; or else, by the life of Phar-
aoh, certainly you are spies."
17 Then Joseph put them all in prison
for three days.
18 Now Joseph said to them on the
third day, "Do this and [you may] live,
for I fear God:
19 if you are honest men, let one of
your brothers be confined in your
[place here in] prison; but as for *the
rest of* you, go, carry grain for the fam-
ine in your households,
20 but bring your youngest brother
to me, so your words will be verified
and you will not die." And they did so.
21 And they said to one another, "Tru-
ly we are guilty regarding our brother
[Joseph], because we saw the distress
and anguish of his soul when he plead-

42:4 *Benjamin.* Jacob still played favorites, but this time there is no mention of jealousy among the other brothers as there had been before (37:8).

42:6 *bowed down before him.* God fulfilled the dreams He gave to Joseph at the age of 17 (37:5 – 11).

42:9 *You are spies.* Joseph set out to learn whether his brothers had changed for the better. Would they betray each other when under pressure?

42:18 *I fear God.* Joseph gave his brothers a clue about who he was.

---

57 Dt 9:28 **CHAPTER 42** **1** Ac 7:12 **2** Ge 43:8; Isa 38:1 **4** ver. 38 **5** Ac 7:11 **6** Ge 41:41; Ge 37:7 **9** Ge 37:5,9 **13** Ge 37:30; La 5:7; See Ge 44:20 **15** See 1Sa 1:26; 17:55 **18** Lev 25:43; Neh 5:15 **20** ver. 34; Ge 43:5; 44:23 **21** Job 36:8,9; Hos 5:15; Pr 21:13; Mt 7:2

ed with us [to let him go], yet we would not listen [to his cry]; so this distress *and* anguish has come on us."

22 Reuben answered them, "Did I not tell you, 'Do not sin against the boy'; and you would not listen? Now the accounting for his blood is required [of us for we are guilty of his death]."

23 They did not know that Joseph understood [their conversation], because he spoke to them through an interpreter.

24 He turned away from his brothers and [left the room and] wept; then he returned and talked with them, and took Simeon from them and bound him in front of them [to be kept as a hostage in Egypt].

25 Then Joseph gave orders [privately] that their bags be filled with grain, and that every man's money [used to pay for the grain] be put back in his sack, and that provisions be given to them for the journey. And so this was done for them.

26 They loaded their donkeys with grain and left from there.

27 And at the lodging place, as one *of them* opened his sack to feed his donkey, he saw his money in the opening of his sack.

28 And he said to his brothers, "My money has been returned! Here it is in my sack!" And their hearts sank, and they were afraid *and* turned trembling to one another, saying, "What is this that God has done to us?"

The Return to Canaan

29 When they came to Jacob their father in the land of Canaan, they told him everything that had happened to them, saying,

30 "The man who is the lord of the land spoke harshly to us, and took us for spies of the land.

31 "But we told him, 'We are honest men; we are not spies.

32 'We are twelve brothers, sons of our father; one is no longer alive, and the youngest is with our father today in the land of Canaan.'

33 "And the man, the lord of the country, said to us, 'By this [test] I will know that you are honest men: leave one of your brothers here with me and take *grain for* your starving households and go.

34 'Bring your youngest brother to me; then I will know that you are not spies, but that you are honest men. Then I will return your [imprisoned] brother [back] to you, and you may trade *and* do business in the land.' "

35 Now when they emptied their sacks, every man's bundle of money [paid to buy grain] was in his sack. When they and their father saw the bundles of money, they were afraid.

36 Jacob their father said to them, "You have bereaved me [by causing the loss] of my children. Joseph is no more, and Simeon is no more, and you would take Benjamin [from me]. All these things are [working] against me."

37 Then Reuben spoke to his father, "You may put my two sons to death if I do not bring Benjamin back to you; put him in my care, and I will return him to you."

38 But Jacob said, "My son shall not go down [to Egypt] with you; for his brother is dead, and he alone is left [of Rachel's children]. If any harm *or* accident should happen to him on the journey you are taking, then you will bring my gray hair down to Sheol (the place of the dead) in sorrow."

The Return to Egypt

43 NOW THE famine was very severe in the land [of Canaan].

42:22 ***Did I not tell you.*** Joseph's brothers were fearful because they knew they were guilty before God and that they deserved any punishment that God might choose to send. They must have been troubled by feelings of guilt for years, and even though they did not realize who Joseph really was, they immediately attributed their troubles to their guilt.

42:25 ***money.*** This refers to a certain weight of silver. Coins had not been invented at this time.

22 Ge 37:21; Ge 9:5; 1Ki 2:32; 2Ch 24:22; Ps 9:12; Lk 11:50,51 **25** Mt 5:44; Ro 12:17,20,21 **27** See Ge 43:21 **30** ver. 7 **33** ver. 15,19,20 **34** Ge 34:10 **35** See Ge 43:21 **36** Ge 43:14 **38** ver. 13; Ge 37:33; 44:28; ver. 4; Ge 44:29; Ge 37:35; 44:31 **CHAPTER 43** **1** Ge 41:54,57

2And it happened that when the families of Jacob's sons had finished eating [all of] the grain which they had brought from Egypt, their father said to them, "Go again, buy us a little food."

3But Judah said to him, "The man [representing Pharaoh] solemnly *and* sternly warned us, saying, 'You will not see my face [again] unless your brother is with you.'

4"If you will send our brother with us, we will go down [to Egypt] and buy you food.

5"But if you will not send him, we will not go down there; for the man said to us, 'You will not see my face unless your brother is with you.' "

6And Israel (Jacob) said, "Why did you treat me so badly by telling the man that you had *another* brother?"

7And they said, "The man asked us straightforward questions about ourselves and our relatives. He said, 'Is your father still alive? Have you *another* brother?' And we answered him accordingly. How could we possibly know that he would say, 'Bring your brother down [here to Egypt]'? "

8Judah said to Israel his father, "Send the young man with me and we will get up and go [buy food], so that we may live and not die [of starvation], we as well as you and our little ones.

9"I will be security (a guarantee) for him; you may hold me [personally] responsible for him. If I do not bring him [back] to you and place him [safely] before you, then let me bear the blame before you forever.

10"For if we had not delayed like this, surely by now we would have returned the second time."

11Then their father Israel said to them, "If *it must be* so, then do this; take some of the choicest products of the land in your sacks, and carry it as a present [of tribute] to the man [representing Pharaoh], a little balm and a little honey, aromatic spices *or* gum, resin, pistachio nuts, and almonds.

12"Take double the [amount of] money with you, and take back the money that was returned in the opening of your sacks; perhaps it was an oversight.

13"Take your brother [Benjamin] also, and get up, and go to the man;

14and may God Almighty grant you compassion *and* favor before the man, so that he will release to you your other brother [Simeon] and Benjamin. And as for me, if I am bereaved of my children [Joseph, Simeon, and Benjamin], I am bereaved."

15Then the men took the present, and they took double the [amount of] money with them, and Benjamin; then they left and went down to Egypt and stood before Joseph.

Joseph Sees Benjamin

16When Joseph saw Benjamin with them, he said to the steward of his house, "Bring the men into the house, and kill an animal and make [a meal] ready; for the men will dine with me at noon."

17So the man did as Joseph said, and brought the men to Joseph's house.

18The men were afraid, because they were brought to Joseph's house; and [expecting the worst] they said, "It is because of the money that was returned in our sacks the first time [we came] that we are being brought in, so that he may find a reason to accuse us and assail us, and take us as slaves, and *seize* our donkeys."

19So they approached the steward of Joseph's house, and talked with him at the entrance of the house,

20and said, "Oh, my lord, we indeed came down here the first time to buy food;

21and when we arrived at the inn [after leaving here], we opened our sacks and there was each man's money

---

43:8 *Send the young man with me.* Judah promised that he would keep Benjamin safe. Judah had changed tremendously (38:1). Instead of leaving the family, he protected his brother and was concerned about his father's welfare.

3 Ge 42:20; 44:23 **9** Ge 44:32; Php 18,19 **11** Ge 32:20; Pr 18:16; Ge 37:25; Jer 8:22 **12** Ge 42:25,35 **14** Est 4:16 **16** Ge 24:2; 39:4; 44:1 **20** Ge 42:3,10 **21** Ge 42:27,35

[with which he had paid for grain], in
full, returned in the mouth of his sack.
So we have brought it back [this time].
22“We have also brought down with
us additional money to buy food; we do
not know who put our money [back] in
our sacks [last time].”
23But the steward [encouraged them
and] said, “Peace be to you, do not be
afraid; your God and the God of your
father has [miraculously] given you
treasure in your sacks. I [already] had
your money [which you paid to us].”
Then he brought Simeon out to them.
24Then the steward brought the men
into Joseph’s house and gave them wa-
ter, and they washed [the dust off] their
feet; and he gave their donkeys feed.
25So they prepared the present [of
tribute] for Joseph before his arrival
at noon; for they had heard that they
were to eat a meal there.
26When Joseph came home, they
brought into the house to him the pres-
ent [of tribute] which they had with
them and bowed to the ground before
him.
27He asked them about their well-
being, and said, “Is your old father
well, of whom you spoke? Is he still
alive?”
28And they answered, “Your servant
our father is in good health; he is still
alive.” And they bowed down [their
heads before Joseph] in respect.
29And he looked up and saw his broth-
er Benjamin, his mother’s [only other]
son, and said, “Is this your youngest
brother, of whom you spoke to me?”
And Joseph said, “God be gracious to
you *and* show you favor, my son.”
30Then Joseph hurried out [of the
room] because his heart was deep-
ly touched over his brother, and he
sought *privacy* to weep; so he entered
his chamber and wept there.
31Then he washed his face and came
out, and, restraining himself, said, “Let
the meal be served.”
32So the servants served Joseph by
himself [in honor of his rank], and
his brothers by themselves, and the
Egyptians who ate with him by them-
selves, because [according to custom]
the Egyptians could not eat food with
the Hebrews, for that is loathsome to
the Egyptians.
33Now Joseph’s brothers were seated
[by the steward] before him [in the
order of their birth]—the firstborn
according to his birthright and the
youngest according to his youth; and
the men looked at one another in as-
tonishment [because so much was
known about them].
34Joseph selected *and* sent portions
to them from his own table, but Benja-
min’s portion was five times as much
as any of theirs. So they feasted and
drank freely *and* celebrated with him.

The Brothers Are Brought Back

44 AND HE commanded the stew-
ard of his house, saying, “Fill the
men’s sacks with food, as much as they
can carry, and put every man’s [grain]
money in the mouth of the sack.
2“Put my [personal] cup, the silver
cup, in the mouth of the sack of the
youngest, with his grain money.” And
the steward did as Joseph had told him.
3As soon as the morning was light,
the men were sent away, they and their
donkeys.
4When they had left the city, and
were not yet far away, Joseph said to
his steward, “Get up, follow after the
men; and when you overtake them, say
to them, ‘Why have you repaid evil [to
us] for good [paid to you]?
5‘Is this not my lord’s drinking
cup and the one which he uses for

43:23 *your God and the God of your father.* Surprisingly, the steward expressed his own faith in the God of Joseph and Jacob.

43:26 *bowed.* For the second time (42:6) the brothers of Joseph bowed down to him, just as his dreams had predicted (37:5 – 11).

43:32 *loathsome.* This word can indicate the strongest revulsion, something that might cause physical illness (46:34). The Egyptians (who carefully shaved their entire bodies) may have been repulsed by the “hairy” Hebrews.

24 Ge 18:4; 24:32 **26** Ge 37:7,10 **27** Ge 42:11,13 **28** Ge 37:7,10 **29** Ge 35:17,18; Ge 42:13 **30** 1Ki 3:26; Ge 42:24 **31** ver. 25 **32** Ge 46:34; Ex 8:26 **34** Ge 45:22

divination? You have done [a great and
unforgivable] wrong in doing this.' "
[6]So the steward overtook them and
he said these words to them.
[7]They said to him, "Why does my
lord speak these things? Far be it from
your servants to do such a thing!
[8]"Please remember, the money
which we found in the mouths of our
sacks we have brought back to you
from the land of Canaan. Is it likely
then that we would steal silver or gold
from your master's house?
[9]"With whomever of your servants
your master's cup is found, let him
die, and the rest of us will be my lord's
slaves."
[10]And the steward said, "Now let it
be as you say; he with whom the cup
is found will be my slave, but *the rest
of* you shall be blameless."
[11]Then every man quickly lowered
his sack to the ground and each man
opened his sack [confident the cup
would not be found among them].
[12]The steward searched, beginning
with the eldest and ending with the
youngest, and the cup was found in
Benjamin's sack.
[13]Then they tore their clothes [in
grief]; and after each man had loaded
his donkey again, they returned to
the city.
[14]When Judah and his brothers came
to Joseph's house, he was still there;
and they fell to the ground before him.
[15]Joseph spoke harshly to them,
"What is this thing that you have done?
Do you not realize that such a man as
I can indeed practice divination *and*
foretell [everything you do without
outside knowledge of it]?"
[16]So Judah said, "What can we say to
my lord? What can we reply? Or how
can we clear ourselves, since God has
exposed the sin *and* guilt of your ser-
vants? Behold, we are my lord's slaves,
the rest of us as well as he with whom
the cup is found."
[17]But Joseph said, "Far be it from me
that I should do that; but the man in
whose hand the cup has been found,
he will be my servant; and as for [the
rest of] you, get up and go in peace to
your father."
[18]Then Judah approached him, and
said, "O my lord, please let your ser-
vant say a word to you in private, and
do not let your anger blaze against
your servant, for you are equal to Phar-
aoh [so I speak as if directly to him].
[19]"My lord asked his servants, say-
ing, 'Have you a father or a brother?'
[20]"We said to my lord, 'We have an
old father and a young [brother, Ben-
jamin, the] child of his old age. Now
his brother [Joseph] is dead, and he
alone is left of [the two sons born of]
his mother, and his father loves him.'
[21]"Then you said to your servants,
'Bring him down to me that I may ac-
tually see him.'
[22]"But we said to my lord, 'The young
man cannot leave his father, for if he
should leave his father, his father
would die.'
[23]"You said to your servants, 'Unless
your youngest brother comes with you,
you shall not see my face again.'
[24]"So when we went back to your
servant my father, we told him what
my lord had said.
[25]"Our father said, 'Go back [to
Egypt], and buy us a little food.'
[26]"But we said, 'We cannot go down
[to Egypt]. If our youngest brother is
with us, then we will go down [there];
for we [were sternly told that we]
cannot see the man's face unless our
youngest brother is with us.'

44:15 *can indeed practice divination.* This curious verse is not very clear in meaning. Clearly a God-fearing man like Joseph who knew that only God can interpret dreams and visions (40:8) would not have been one to dabble with the occult. He may just have been trying to frighten his brothers by appearing to know things supernaturally (this would certainly have been backed up by his uncanny knowledge of their birth order in 43:33).

44:17 *get up and go in peace to your father.* Joseph was testing his brothers again, to see if they had changed in their attitude to the son of their father's favorite wife. Would they leave Benjamin a slave in Egypt as they had Joseph?

CHAPTER 44 **8** Ge 43:21 **9** Ge 31:32 **13** Ge 37:29,34; Nu 14:6; 2Sa 1:11 **14** Ge 37:7 **16** ver. 9 **17** Pr 17:15 **18** Ge 18:30,32; Ex 32:22 **20** Ge 37:3 **21** Ge 42:15,20 **23** Ge 43:3,5 **25** Ge 43:2

[27]"Your servant my father said to us,
'You know that my wife [Rachel] bore
me [only] two sons.
[28]'And one [son] went out from me,
and I said, "Surely he is torn to pieces,"
and I have not seen him since.
[29]'If you take this one also from me,
and harm *or* an accident happens to
him, you will bring my gray hair down
to Sheol in sorrow.'
[30]"Now, therefore, when I come to
your servant my father, and the young
man is not with us, since his life is
bound up in the young man's life,
[31]when he sees that the young man
is not *with us*, he will die; and your
servants will bring the gray hair of
your servant our father down to Sheol
in [great] sorrow.
[32]"For your servant became security
for the young man to my father, saying,
'If I do not bring him back to you,
then let me bear the blame before my
father forever.'
[33]"Now, therefore, please let your
servant (Judah) remain here instead
of the youth [to be] a slave to my lord,
and let the young man go home with
his brothers.
[34]"How can I go up to my father if
the young man is not with me—for
fear that I would see the tragedy that
would overtake my [elderly] father [if
Benjamin does not return]?"

Joseph Shows Kindness to His Brothers

45 THEN JOSEPH could not control himself [any longer] in front
of all those who attended him, and he
called out, "Have everyone leave me."
So no man stood there when Joseph
revealed himself to his brothers.
[2]Joseph wept aloud, and the Egyptians
[who had just left him] heard it, and
the household of Pharaoh heard of it.
[3]Then Joseph said to his brothers,
"I am Joseph! Is my father still alive?"
But his brothers were speechless, for
they were stunned *and* dismayed by
[the fact that they were in] Joseph's
presence.
[4]And Joseph said to his brothers,
"Please come closer to me." And they
approached him. And he said, "I am
Joseph your brother, whom you sold
into Egypt.
[5]"Now do not be distressed or angry
with yourselves because you sold me
here, for God sent me ahead of you to
save life *and* preserve our family.
[6]"For the famine has been in the land
these two years, and there are still five
more years in which there will be no
plowing and harvesting.
[7]"God sent me [to Egypt] ahead of
you to preserve for you a remnant on
the earth, and to keep you alive by a
great escape.
[8]"So now it was not you who sent
me here, but God; and He has made
me a father to Pharaoh and lord of all
his household and ruler over all the
land of Egypt.
[9]"Hurry and go up to my father, and
tell him, 'Your son Joseph says this
to you: "God has made me lord of all
Egypt; come down to me, do not delay.
[10]"You shall live in the land of Goshen
[the best pasture land of Egypt], and

45:1 – 4 Real love — A profound comparison can be made between the life of Joseph and the life of Christ. Both Joseph and Jesus were persecuted unjustly (Ge 37:11 – 28; Mt 26:59). Both were lost to their brothers for a while (Ge 45:1 – 15; Ro 10:1 – 4). Both later forgave and restored their repentant brothers (Ge 45:1 – 15; Zec 8:1 – 8).
45:3 *I am Joseph.* Joseph must have said this in Hebrew, finally dropping the ruse of the interpreter (42:23).
45:5 *God sent me*. God often permits the wicked to carry out their evil plans in order to fulfill some larger purpose He has for the objects of their violence and cruelty. Since it is not possible for us to see the whole picture from God's perspective, we must exercise faith and believe that the God of all the earth will do right and that all things do work together for good to those who love God, who are called according to His purpose. Joseph was able to freely forgive his brothers partly because he recognized that their sin had been turned by God into something good.
45:10 *You shall live in the land of Goshen.* This was God's plan. He had told Abraham that his descendants would live in a foreign land (15:13 – 16).

27 Ge 46:19 **28** Ge 37:33 **29** Ge 42:36,38 **30** 1Sa 18:1 **32** Ge 43:9 **33** Ex 32:32 **CHAPTER 45** **3** Ac 7:13 **4** Ge 37:28 **5** Ge 50:20; Ps 105:16,17 **8** Ge 41:43; Jdg 17:10 **10** Ge 47:1

you shall be close to me—you and your children and your grandchildren, your flocks and your herds and all you have.

11 “There I will provide for you *and* sustain you, so that you and your household and all that are yours may not become impoverished, for there are still five years of famine *to come*.” ’

12 “Look! Your eyes see, and the eyes of my brother Benjamin see, that I am speaking to you [personally in your language and not through an interpreter].

13 “Now you must tell my father of all my splendor *and* power in Egypt, and of everything that you have seen; and you must hurry and bring my father down here.”

14 Then he embraced his brother Benjamin's neck and wept, and Benjamin wept on his neck.

15 He kissed all his brothers and wept on them, and afterward his brothers talked with him.

16 When the news was heard in Pharaoh's house that Joseph's brothers had come, it pleased Pharaoh and his servants.

17 Then Pharaoh said to Joseph, “Tell your brothers, ‘Do this: load your animals and return to the land of Canaan [without delay],

18 and get your father and your households and come to me. I will give you the best of the land of Egypt and you will eat the fat (the finest produce) of the land.’

19 “Now you [brothers of Joseph] are ordered [by Pharaoh], ‘Do this: take wagons from the land of Egypt for your little ones and for your wives, and bring your father and come.

20 ‘Do not be concerned with your goods, for the best of all the land of Egypt is yours.’ ”

21 Then the sons of Israel did so; and Joseph gave them wagons according to the command of Pharaoh, and gave them provisions for the journey.

22 To each of them Joseph gave changes of clothing, but to Benjamin he gave three hundred *pieces of* silver and five changes of clothing.

23 To his father he sent the following: ten *male* donkeys loaded with the good things of Egypt, and ten female donkeys loaded with grain and bread and provision for his father [to supply all who were with him] on the journey.

24 So he sent his brothers away, and as they departed, he said to them, “See that you do not quarrel on the journey [about how to explain this to our father].”

25 So they went up from Egypt, and came to the land of Canaan to Jacob their father,

26 and they said to him, “Joseph is still alive, and indeed he is ruler over all the land of Egypt.” But Jacob was stunned *and* his heart almost stopped beating, because he did not believe them.

27 When they told him everything that Joseph had said to them, and when he saw the wagons which Joseph had sent to carry him, the spirit of their father Jacob revived.

28 And Israel (Jacob) said, “It is enough! Joseph my son is still alive. I will go and see him before I die.”

Jacob Moves to Egypt

46 SO ISRAEL set out with all that he had, and came to Beersheba [where both his father and grandfather had worshiped God], and offered sacrifices to the God of his father Isaac. [Gen 21:33; 26:23–25]

2 And God spoke to Israel in visions of the night and said, “Jacob, Jacob!” And he said, “Here I am.”

3 And He said, “I am God, the God of your father; do not be afraid to go

---

46:1 *Israel set out.* Jacob's journey to Egypt began a four-hundred-year sojourn away from the promised land of Canaan. Jacob entered Egypt with his twelve sons and their families; Jacob's descendants would leave Egypt as a small nation.

46:2 *Israel . . . Jacob.* The fact that these names are used interchangeably indicates that the earlier negative connotations of the name Jacob had faded (31:11; 32:28; 35:10).

12 Ge 42:23 **13** Ac 7:14 **18** Ge 27:28; Nu 18:12,29 **22** Ge 43:34 **26** Job 29:24; Ps 126:1; Lk 24:11,41
CHAPTER 46 **1** Ge 21:31,33; 28:10; Ge 26:24,25; 28:13; 31:42 **2** Ge 15:1; Job 33:14,15 **3** Ge 28:13; Ge 12:2; Dt 26:5

down to Egypt, for I will make you
(your descendants) a great nation
there.
4“I will go down with you to Egypt,
and I will also surely bring you (your
people) up again; and Joseph will put
his hand on your eyes [to close them
at the time of your death].”
5So Jacob set out from Beersheba;
and the sons of Israel carried their fa-
ther Jacob and their children and their
wives in the wagons that Pharaoh had
sent to carry him.
6And they took their livestock and
the possessions which they had ac-
quired in the land of Canaan and came
to Egypt, Jacob and all his descendants
with him.
7His sons and his grandsons, his
daughters and his granddaughters,
and all his descendants he brought
with him to Egypt.

Those Who Came to Egypt

8Now these are the names of the sons
of Israel, Jacob and his sons, who went
to Egypt: Reuben, Jacob’s firstborn.
9The sons of Reuben: Hanoch, Pallu,
Hezron, and Carmi.
10The sons of Simeon: Jemuel, Ja-
min, Ohad, Jachin, Zohar, and Shaul
the son of a Canaanite woman.
11The sons of Levi: Gershon, Kohath,
and Merari.
12The sons of Judah: Er, Onan,
Shelah, Perez, and Zerah—but Er and
Onan died in the land of Canaan. And
the sons of Perez were Hezron and
Hamul.
13The sons of Issachar: Tola, Puvah,
Job, and Shimron.
14The sons of Zebulun: Sered, Elon,
and Jahleel.
15These are the sons of Leah, whom
she bore to Jacob in Paddan-aram,
with his daughter Dinah; all of his
sons and daughters *numbered* thirty-
three.
16The sons of Gad: Ziphion, Haggi,
Shuni, Ezbon, Eri, Arodi, and Areli.
17The sons of Asher: Imnah, Ishvah,
Ishvi, Beriah, and Serah their sister.
And the sons of Beriah: Heber and
Malchiel.
18These are the sons of Zilpah, [the
maid] whom Laban gave to Leah his
daughter [when she married Jacob];
and she bore to Jacob these sixteen
persons [two sons and fourteen grand-
children].
19The sons of Rachel, Jacob’s wife:
Joseph and Benjamin.
20Now to Joseph in the land of Egypt
were born Manasseh and Ephraim,
whom Asenath, the daughter of Po-
tiphera, priest of On (Heliopolis in
Egypt), bore to him.
21And the sons of Benjamin: Bela,
Becher, Ashbel, Gera, Naaman, Ehi,
Rosh, Muppim, Huppim, and Ard.
22These are the sons of Rachel,
who were born to Jacob; [there were]
fourteen persons in all [two sons and
twelve grandchildren].
23The son of Dan: Hushim.
24The sons of Naphtali: Jahzeel,
Guni, Jezer, and Shillem.
25These are the sons of Bilhah, [the
maid] whom Laban gave to Rachel his
daughter [when she married Jacob].
And she bore these to Jacob; [there
were] seven persons in all [two sons
and five grandchildren].
26All the persons who came with
Jacob into Egypt—who were his direct
descendants, not counting the wives of
[Jacob or] Jacob’s sons, were sixty-six
persons in all,
27and the sons of Joseph, who were
born to him in Egypt, were two. All
the persons of the house of Jacob [in-
cluding Jacob, and Joseph and his

46:11 ***Gershon, Kohath, and Merari.*** These sons of Levi became the founders of the Levitical families (Ex 6:16 – 19). Aaron and Moses descended from Kohath (Ex 6:20 – 25).

46:26 – 27 ***sixty-six . . . seventy.*** When Joseph, his two sons, and Jacob himself are added, the number of males in Jacob’s family equals seventy.

4 Ge 28:15; 48:21; Ge 15:16; 50:13,24,25; Ex 3:8; Ge 50:1 **5** Ac 7:15; Ge 45:19,21 **6** Dt 26:5; Jos 24:4; Ps 105:23; Isa 52:4 **8** Ex 1:1; Nu 26:5 **10** Ex 6:15 **11** 1Ch 6:1,16 **12** 1Ch 2:3; 4:21; Ge 38:3,7,10; Ge 38:29 **13** 1Ch 7:1 **16** Nu 26:15 **17** 1Ch 7:30 **18** Ge 30:10; Ge 29:24 **19** Ge 44:27 **20** Ge 41:50 **21** 1Ch 7:6; 8:1; Nu 26:38,39, 1Ch 7:12 **23** 1Ch 7:12 **24** 1Ch 7:13 **25** Ge 30:5,7; Ge 29:29 **26** Ex 1:5 **27** Dt 10:22; See Ac 7:14

sons], who came into Egypt, were
seventy.
28Now Jacob (Israel) sent Judah
ahead of him to Joseph, to direct him
to Goshen; and they came into the land
of Goshen.
29Then Joseph prepared his chariot
and went up to meet Israel his father
in Goshen; as soon as he presented
himself before him (authenticating his
identity), he fell on his [father's] neck
and wept on his neck a [very] long
time.
30And Israel said to Joseph, "Now
let me die [in peace], since I have seen
your face [and know] that you are still
alive."
31Joseph said to his brothers and to
his father's household, "I will go up
and tell Pharaoh, and say to him, 'My
brothers and my father's household,
who were in the land of Canaan, have
come to me;
32and the men are shepherds, for
they have been keepers of livestock;
and they have brought their flocks
and their herds and all that they have.'
33"And it shall be that when Pharaoh calls you and says, 'What is your
occupation?'
34you shall say, 'Your servants have
been keepers of livestock from our
youth until now, both we and our fathers [before us],' in order that you may
live [separately and securely] in the
land of Goshen; for every shepherd is
repulsive to the Egyptians."

Jacob's Family Settles in Goshen

47 THEN JOSEPH came and told
Pharaoh, "My father and my
brothers, with their flocks and their
herds and all that they own, have come
from the land of Canaan, and they are
in the land of Goshen."
2He took five men from among his
brothers and presented them to Pharaoh.
3And Pharaoh said to his brothers
[as Joseph expected], "What is your
occupation?" And they said to Pharaoh, "Your servants are shepherds,
both we and our fathers [before us]."
4Moreover, they said to Pharaoh,
"We have come to live temporarily
(sojourn) in the land [of Egypt], for
there is no pasture for the flocks of
your servants [in our land], for the
famine is very severe in Canaan. So
now, please let your servants live in
the land of Goshen."
5Then Pharaoh spoke to Joseph, saying, "Your father and your brothers
have come to you.
6"The land of Egypt is before you;
settle your father and your brothers
in the best of the land. Let them live in
the land of Goshen; and if you know
of any men of ability among them, put
them in charge of my livestock."
7Then Joseph brought Jacob (Israel)
his father and presented him before
Pharaoh; and Jacob blessed Pharaoh.
8And Pharaoh asked Jacob, "How
old are you?"

46:34 *every shepherd is repulsive to the Egyptians.* God used the racial and ethnic prejudice of the Egyptians as a way of preserving the ethnic and spiritual identity of His own people. Jacob's family was already intermarrying with the Canaanites (ch. 38) and was in danger of losing its identity as the people of God.

47:5–6 *Pharaoh.* There is some uncertainty concerning the identity of this Pharaoh. Many believe he was Amenhotep I of the eleventh dynasty. Prior to his reign Egypt had suffered political and economic chaos for 200 years. Irrigation and building projects fell into ruin, and civil war raged. But Pharaoh Amenhotep was able to reunite Egypt, rebuilding the country and developing world trade. One of the reasons for his success no doubt stemmed from the fact that he was a generous man as we are told here. Not only was he generous to his own people, but he was kind to Israel. God had already promised to bless those who blessed the descendants of Abraham (Ge 12:3). The lesson is clear. If a pagan king can experience God's blessing for his liberality, how much more can born-again believers know the riches of heaven for their liberality? Solomon reminds us of this principle: "The generous man [is a source of blessing and] shall be prosperous and enriched" (Pr 11:25).

47:8 *How old are you?* Pharaoh's question

---

28 Ge 31:21; Ge 47:1 **29** Ge 45:14 **30** Lk 2:29,30 **31** Ge 47:1 **33** Ge 47:2,3 **34** ver. 32; Ge 30:35; 34:5; 37:12; Ge 43:32; Ex 8:26 **CHAPTER 47** **1** Ge 46:31; Ge 45:10; 46:28 **2** Ac 7:13 **3** Ge 46:33; Ge 46:34 **4** Ge 15:13; Dt 26:5; Ge 43:1; Ac 7:11; Ge 46:34 **6** Ge 20:15; ver. 4

9 Jacob said to Pharaoh, "The years of my pilgrimage are a hundred and thirty. Few and unpleasant have been the years of my life, and they have not reached the years that my fathers lived during the days of their pilgrimage."

10 And Jacob blessed Pharaoh, and departed from his presence.

11 So Joseph settled his father and brothers and gave them a possession in Egypt, in the best of the land, in the land of Rameses (Goshen), as Pharaoh commanded.

12 Joseph provided *and* supplied his father and his brothers and all his father's household with food, according to [the needs of] their children.

13 Now [in the course of time] there was no food in all the land, for the famine was distressingly severe, so that the land of Egypt and all the land of Canaan languished [in destitution and starvation] because of the famine.

14 Joseph gathered all the money that was found in the land of Egypt and in the land of Canaan [in payment] for the grain which they bought, and Joseph brought the money into Pharaoh's house.

15 And when the money was exhausted in the land of Egypt and in the land of Canaan, all the Egyptians came to Joseph and said, "Give us food! Why should we die before your very eyes? For our money is gone."

16 Joseph said, "Give up your livestock, and I will give you food in exchange for your livestock, since the money is gone."

17 So they brought their livestock to Joseph, and he gave them food in exchange for the horses and the flocks and the herds and the donkeys; and he supplied them with food in exchange for all their livestock that year.

18 When that year was ended, they came to him the next year and said to him, "We will not hide from my lord [the fact] that our money is spent; my lord also has our herds of livestock; there is nothing left in the sight of my lord but our bodies and our lands.

19 "Why should we die before your eyes, both we and our land? Buy us and our land in exchange for food, and we and our land will be servants to Pharaoh. And give us seed [to plant], that we may live and not die, and that the land may not be desolate."

Result of the Famine

20 So Joseph bought all the land of Egypt for Pharaoh; for every Egyptian sold his field because the famine was severe upon them. So the land became Pharaoh's.

21 And as for the people, he relocated them [temporarily] to cities from one end of Egypt's border to the other.

22 Only the land of the priests he did not buy, for the priests had an allotment from Pharaoh, and they lived on the amount which Pharaoh gave them, so they did not sell their land.

23 Then Joseph said to the people, "Look, today I have bought you and your land for Pharaoh; now, here is seed for you, and you shall plant the land.

24 "At harvest time [when you reap the increase] you shall give one-fifth of it to Pharaoh, and four-fifths will be your own to use for seed for the field and as food for you and those of your households and for your little ones."

25 And they said, "You have saved our lives! Let us find favor in the sight of my lord, and we will be Pharaoh's servants."

26 And Joseph made it a law over the land of Egypt—valid to this day—that Pharaoh should have the fifth part [of the crops]; only the land of the priests did not become Pharaoh's.

27 Now [the people of] Israel lived in the country of Egypt, in [the land of] Goshen, and they gained possessions

---

suggests that the long ages of the patriarchal family were truly exceptional, even for this period. Jacob's final 147 years (47:28) were fewer than the 175 years of Abraham (25:7) and the 180 years of Isaac (35:28), but still a significant age.

47:20 *the land.* Pharaoh's ownership of all the land of Egypt would one day lead to gross abuses of power (see the Book of Exodus).

---

9 Ps 39:12; Heb 11:9,13; Job 14:1; Ge 25:7; 35:28 **10** ver. 7 **11** Ex 1:11; 12:37; ver. 6 **13** Ge 41:30; Ac 7:11 **14** Ge 41:56 **15** ver. 19 **22** Ezr 7:24 **25** Ge 33:15 **26** ver. 22 **27** ver. 11; Ge 46:3

and acquired property there and were
fruitful and multiplied greatly.
28 And Jacob lived in the land of
Egypt seventeen years; so the length
of Jacob's life was a hundred and forty-
seven years.
29 And when the time drew near for
Israel to die, he called his son Joseph
and said to him, "If now I have found
favor in your sight, please put your
hand under my thigh and [promise
to] deal loyally and faithfully with me.
Please do not bury me in Egypt,
30 but when I lie down with my fa-
thers [in death], you will carry me out
of Egypt and bury me in their burial
place [at Hebron in the cave of Mach-
pelah]." And Joseph said, "I will do as
you have directed."
31 Then he said, "Swear to me [that
you will do it]." So he swore to him.
Then Israel (Jacob) bowed *in worship*
at the head of the bed.

Israel's Last Days

48 NOW SOME time after these
things happened, Joseph was
told, "Your father is sick." So he took
his two sons Manasseh and Ephraim
with him [to go to Goshen].
2 And when Jacob (Israel) was told,
"Look now, your son Joseph has come
to you," Israel strengthened himself
and sat up on the bed.
3 Then Jacob said to Joseph, "God Al-
mighty appeared to me at Luz (Bethel)
in the land of Canaan and blessed me,
4 and said to me, 'Behold, I will make
you fruitful and numerous, and I will
make you a great company of people,
and will give this land to your descen-
dants after you as an everlasting pos-
session.' [Gen 28:13–22; 35:6–15]
5 "Now your two sons [Ephraim and
Manasseh], who were born to you in
the land of Egypt before I came to you
in Egypt, are mine; Ephraim and Ma-
nasseh shall be mine [that is, adopted
as my heirs and sons as surely], as
Reuben and Simeon are *my sons*.
6 "But other sons who were born to
you after them shall be your own; they
shall be called by the names of their
[two] brothers in their inheritance.
7 "Now as for me, when I came from
Paddan [in Mesopotamia], Rachel died
beside me in the land of Canaan on
the journey, when there was still some
distance to go to Ephrath; and I buried
her there on the way to Ephrath (that
is, Bethlehem)."
8 When Israel [who was almost blind]
saw Joseph's sons, he said, "Who are
these?"
9 Joseph said to his father, "They are
my sons, whom God has given me here
[in Egypt]." So he said, "Please bring
them to me, so that I may bless them."
10 Now Israel's eyes were so dim from
age that he could not see [clearly]. Then
Joseph brought them close to him, and
he kissed and embraced them.
11 Israel said to Joseph, "I never ex-
pected to see your face, but see, God
has shown me your children as well."
12 Then Joseph took the boys [from
his father's embrace], and he bowed
[before him] with his face to the
ground.
13 Then Joseph took them both,
Ephraim with his right hand toward
Israel's left, and Manasseh with his left
hand toward Israel's right, and brought
them close to him.
14 But Israel reached out his right
hand and laid it on the head of
Ephraim, who was the younger, and
his left hand on Manasseh's head,
crossing his hands [intentionally], even
though Manasseh was the firstborn.

47:29 *deal loyally and faithfully with me.* In other words, "demonstrate to me the utmost covenant loyalty." Jacob showed his vigorous faith in God's promises by asking to be buried in the land promised to his descendants.

48:5–7 *Ephraim and Manasseh.* As firstborn, Reuben should have received a double portion of the inheritance, but he had forfeited his birthright by his sins (35:22). By adopting Ephraim and Manasseh as his own sons, Jacob gave the double portion to Joseph.

29 See Dt 31:14; 1Ki 2:1; Ge 24:2; Ge 24:49; See Ge 50:25 **30** 2Sa 19:37; Ge 49:29; 50:5,13 **31** Ge 48:2; 1Ki 1:47; Heb 11:21 **CHAPTER 48** **3** Ge 28:13,19; 35:6,9 **4** Ge 17:8 **5** Ge 41:50; 46:20; Jos 13:7; 14:4 **7** Ge 35:9,16,19 **9** See Ge 33:5; Ge 27:4 **10** Ge 27:1; Ge 27:27 **11** Ge 45:26 **14** ver. 19

15 Then Jacob (Israel) blessed Joseph, and said,

"The God before whom my fathers
Abraham and Isaac walked [in
faithful obedience],
The God who has been my
Shepherd [leading and caring
for me] all my life to this day,
16 The Angel [that is, the LORD
Himself] who has redeemed me
[continually] from all evil,
Bless the boys;
And may my name live on in them
[may they be worthy of having
their names linked with mine],
And the names of my fathers
Abraham and Isaac;
And may they grow into a [great]
multitude in the midst of the
earth."

17 When Joseph saw that his father laid his right hand on Ephraim's head, it displeased him [because he was not the firstborn]; and he grasped his father's hand to move it from Ephraim's head to Manasseh's head.
18 Joseph said to his father, "Not so, my father, for this is the firstborn; place your right hand on Manasseh's head."
19 But his father refused and said, "I know, my son, I know; Manasseh also will become a people and he will be great; but his younger brother shall be greater than he, and his descendants shall become a multitude of nations."
20 Then Jacob blessed them that day, saying,

"By you Israel will pronounce a
blessing, saying,
'May God make you like Ephraim
and Manasseh.' "

And he put Ephraim before Manasseh.
21 Then Israel said to Joseph, "Behold, I am about to die, but God will be with you, and bring you back to [Canaan] the land of your fathers.
22 "Moreover, I have given you [the birthright,] one portion [Shechem, one mountain ridge] more than any of your brothers, which I took [reclaiming it] from the hand of the Amorites with my sword and with my bow." [Gen 33:18, 19; Josh 24:32, 33; John 4:5]

Israel's Prophecy concerning His Sons

49 THEN JACOB called for his sons and said, "Assemble yourselves [around me] that I may tell you what will happen to you *and* your descendants in the days to come.

2 "Gather together and hear, O sons
of Jacob;
And listen to Israel (Jacob) your
father.
3 "Reuben, you are my firstborn;
My might, the beginning of my
strength *and* vigor,
Preeminent in dignity and
preeminent in power [that
should have been your
birthright].
4 "But unstable *and* reckless *and*
boiling over like water [in sinful
lust], you shall not excel *or*
have the preeminence [of the
firstborn],
Because you went up to your
father's bed [with Bilhah];
You defiled it—he went up to my
couch. [Gen 35:22]
5 "Simeon and Levi are brothers
[equally headstrong, deceitful,
vindictive, and cruel];
Their swords are weapons
of violence *and* revenge.
[Gen 34:25–30]
6 "O my soul, do not come into their
secret council;

48:22 one portion [Shechem, one mountain ridge] more. Jacob promised Joseph that he would one day return to the land of Canaan. The promise was fulfilled after Joseph's death (50:24–26).
49:5–7 Simeon and Levi. This prophecy was fulfilled when the Israelites settled in the promised land. Simeon's allotment was scattered within the larger portion of the tribe of Judah, and Levi's allotment was scattered cities throughout the land (Jos 21).

15 Heb 11:21; Ge 17:1 **16** Ge 28:15; Ps 34:22; 121:7; Am 9:12; Ac 15:17 **17** ver. 14 **19** ver. 14; Nu 1:33,35; Dt 33:17 **20** See Ru 4:11,12 **21** Ge 46:4 **22** Jos 24:32; Jn 4:5; Ge 34:28 **CHAPTER 49** **1** Dt 33:1; Am 3:7; Dt 4:30; Isa 39:6; Jer 23:20; Heb 1:2 **3** Ge 29:32 **4** Ge 35:22; Dt 27:20 **5** Ge 29:33,34 **6** Pr 1:15,16; Ps 26:9; Eph 5:11; Ge 34:26

Let not my glory (honor) be united
with their assembly [for I knew
nothing of their plot];
Because in their anger they killed
men [an honored man, Shechem,
and the Shechemites],
And in their self-will they lamed
oxen.
7 "Cursed be their anger, for it was
fierce;
And their wrath, for it was cruel.
I will divide *and* disperse them in
Jacob,
And scatter them in [the midst of
the land of] Israel.

8 "Judah, you are the one whom
your brothers shall praise;
Your hand will be on the neck of
your enemies;
Your father's sons shall bow down
to you.
9 "Judah, a lion's cub;
With the prey, my son, you have
gone high up [the mountain].
He stooped down, he crouched like
a lion,
And like a lion—who dares rouse
him? [Rev 5:5]
10 "The scepter [of royalty] shall not
depart from Judah,
Nor the ruler's staff from between
his feet,
Until Shiloh [the Messiah, the
Peaceful One] comes,
And to Him *shall be* the obedience
of the peoples. [Num 24:17;
Ps 60:7; Ezek 21:27]
11 "Tying his foal to the [strong] vine
And his donkey's colt to the choice
vine,
He washes his clothing in wine
[because the grapevine produces
abundantly],
And his robes in the blood of
grapes. [Is 63:1–3; Zech 9:9;
Rev 19:11–16]
12 "His eyes are darker *and* sparkle
more than wine,
And his teeth whiter than milk.

13 "Zebulun shall dwell at the
seashore;
And he shall be a haven (landing
place) for ships,
And his flank shall be toward
Sidon.

14 "Issachar is [like] a strong-boned
donkey,
Crouching down between the
sheepfolds.
15 "When he saw that the resting
place was good
And that the land was pleasant,
He bowed his shoulder to bear
[burdens],
And became a servant at forced
labor.

16 "Dan shall judge his people,
As one of the tribes of Israel.
17 "Dan shall be a [venomous]
serpent in the way,
A fanged snake in the path,
That bites the horse's heels,
So that his rider falls backward.
18 "I wait for Your salvation, O LORD.

19 "As for Gad—a raiding troop shall
raid him,
But he shall raid at their heels *and*
assault them [victoriously].

20 "Asher's food [supply] shall be rich
and bountiful,
And he shall yield *and* deliver
royal delights.

21 "Naphtali is a doe let loose, [a swift
warrior,]

49:10 *scepter.* With these words, Jacob predicted that a royal line would rise from Judah's descendants. Shiloh is an obscure word, probably meaning "the one to whom it belongs." In other words, Judah's descendants would be the rulers of Israel until the coming of "Shiloh," the One to whom all royal authority belongs. In this context, Shiloh, like "the Seed," is a reference to the coming Messiah.

49:11 – 12 *wine . . . blood.* The imagery in this verse describes the warfare that the Messiah will wage to establish His reign (Ps 2; 110; Rev 19:11 – 21).

8 Dt 33:7; Ps 18:40; 1Ch 5:2 **9** Rev 5:5; Nu 23:24; 24:9 **10** Nu 24:17; Jer 30:21; Ps 60:7; Isa 11:1; Mt 21:9; Isa 60:1-5; Lk 2:30-32 **13** Dt 33:18,19; Jos 19:10,11 **15** 1Sa 10:9 **16** Dt 33:22 **17** Jdg 18:27 **18** Ps 25:5; Isa 25:9 **19** Dt 33:20; 1Ch 5:18 **20** Dt 33:24; Jos 19:24 **21** Dt 33:23

Which yields branched antlers
(eloquent words).

22 "Joseph is a fruitful bough (a main
branch of the vine),
A fruitful bough by a spring (a
well, a fountain);
Its branches run over the wall
[influencing others].
23 "The [skilled] archers have bitterly
attacked *and* provoked him;
They have shot [at him] and
harassed him.
24 "But his bow remained firm *and*
steady [in the Strength that does
not fail],
For his arms were made strong
and agile
By the hands of the Mighty One of
Jacob,
(By the name of the Shepherd,
the Stone of Israel), [Gen 48:15;
Deut 32:4; Is 9:6; 49:26]
25 By the God of your father who will
help you,
And by the Almighty who blesses
you
With blessings of the heavens
above,
Blessings lying in the deep that
couches beneath,
Blessings of the [nursing] breasts
and of the [fertile] womb.
26 "The blessings of your father
Are greater than the blessings of
my ancestors [Abraham and
Isaac]
Up to the utmost bound of the
everlasting hills;
They shall be on the head of
Joseph,
Even on the crown of the head of
him who was the distinguished
one *and* the one who is prince
among (separate from) his
brothers.

27 "Benjamin is a ravenous wolf;
In the morning he devours the
prey,
And at night he divides the spoil."

28 All these are the [beginnings of
the] twelve tribes of Israel, and this
is what their father said to them as
he blessed them, blessing each one
according to the blessing appropriate
to him.
29 He charged them and said to them,
"I am to be gathered to my people; bury
me with my fathers in the cave that is
in the field of Ephron the Hittite,
30 in the cave in the field at Mach-
pelah, east of Mamre, in the land of Ca-
naan, that Abraham bought, along with
the field from Ephron the Hittite, to
possess as a burial site. [Gen 23:17–20]
31 "There they buried Abraham and
Sarah his wife, there they buried Isaac
and Rebekah his wife, and there I bur-
ied Leah—
32 the field and the cave that is in it
was purchased from the sons of Heth."
33 When Jacob (Israel) had finished

49:24 *Shepherd.* The image of God as a shepherd occurs many times in Scripture. This term would have had great significance for a family of shepherds. God shepherded and cared for their families just as they shepherded and cared for their own flocks. God is the one Good Shepherd (Ps 23; Jn 10).

49:28 *the . . . twelve tribes of Israel.* Jacob's blessings are prophecies about the destiny of each tribe. Some of the blessings are obscure, but the blessings on Judah and Joseph are clear prophecies from God about their destinies (compare Moses' blessing of the tribes of Israel, Dt 33).

50:5–6 *swear.* Bound by an oath, Joseph requested leave to bury his father in Canaan in a sepulchre ready for his remains. It seems today that we do not take vows as seriously as Joseph took his promise to his father, and every thing from casual promises to solemn marriage vows are broken with little remorse. Honoring vows, both in small matters and significant, honors God because He asks us to reject "all falsehood [whether lying, defrauding, telling half-truths, spreading rumors, any such as these], speak truth each one" (Eph 4:25). Broken vows result in broken hearts and ruined relationships, blasted memories, ineffective lives and testimonies. Even a foolish or wrong vow cannot be lightly set aside, but must be repented of before God. We must learn to promise wisely, and honor our promises faithfully.

23 Ge 37:4,24; Ps 118:13 **24** Job 29:20; Ps 37:15; Ps 132:2,5; Ge 45:11; 47:12; Ps 80:1; Isa 28:16 **25** Ge 28:13; 35:3; 43:23; Ge 17:1; 35:11; Dt 33:13 **26** Dt 33:15; Hab 3:6; Dt 33:16 **27** Jdg 20:21,25; Nu 23:24; Est 8:11; Eze 39:10; Zec 14:1 **29** Ge 15:15; 25:8; Ge 47:30; 2Sa 19:37; Ge 50:13 **30** Ge 23:16 **31** Ge 23:19; 25:9; Ge 35:29 **33** ver. 29

commanding his sons, he drew his feet into the bed and breathed his last, and was gathered to his people [who had preceded him in death].

Burial Preparations and Mourning for Jacob

50 THEN JOSEPH fell upon his father's face, and wept over him and kissed him [tenderly].
2Then Joseph ordered his servants
the physicians to embalm (mummify) his father. So the physicians embalmed Israel (Jacob).
3Now forty days were required for
this, for that is the customary number of days [of preparation] required for embalming. And the Egyptians wept *and* grieved for him [in public mourning as they would for royalty] for seventy days.
4When the days of weeping *and* pub-
lic mourning for him were past, Joseph spoke to [the nobles of] the house of Pharaoh, saying, "If now I have found favor in your sight, please speak to Pharaoh, saying,
5'My father made me swear [an
oath], saying, "Hear me, I am about to die; bury me in my tomb which I prepared for myself in the land of Canaan." So now let me go up [to Canaan], please, and bury my father; then I will return.' "
6And Pharaoh said, "Go up and bury
your father, as he made you swear."
7So Joseph went up [to Canaan] to
bury his father, and with him went all the officials of Pharaoh, [the nobles of his court and] the elders of his household and all [the nobles and] the elders of the land of Egypt—
8and all the household of Joseph and
his brothers and his father's household. They left only their little ones and their flocks and herds in the land of Goshen.
9Both chariots and horsemen also
went up [to Canaan] with Joseph; and it was a very great company.
10When they came to the threshing
floor of Atad, which is beyond the Jordan, they mourned there with a great lamentation (expressions of mourning for the deceased) and [extreme demonstrations of] sorrow [according to Egyptian custom]; and Joseph

CHAPTER 50 **1** Ge 46:4; 2Ki 13:14 **2** ver. 26; 2Ch 16:14; Lk 24:1; Jn 19:39,40 **3** Nu 20:29; Dt 34:8 **4** Est 4:2 **5** Ge 47:29; 2Ch 16:14; Isa 22:16 **10** Ac 8:2; 1Sa 31:13; Job 2:13

THE TRIBES OF ISRAEL

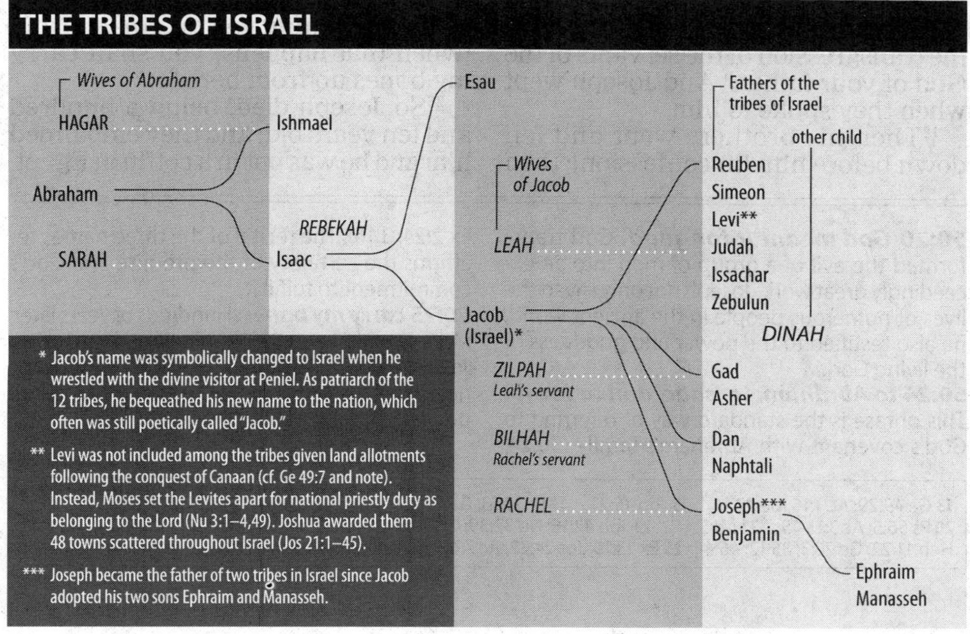

* Jacob's name was symbolically changed to Israel when he wrestled with the divine visitor at Peniel. As patriarch of the 12 tribes, he bequeathed his new name to the nation, which often was still poetically called "Jacob."

** Levi was not included among the tribes given land allotments following the conquest of Canaan (cf. Ge 49:7 and note). Instead, Moses set the Levites apart for national priestly duty as belonging to the Lord (Nu 3:1–4,49). Joshua awarded them 48 towns scattered throughout Israel (Jos 21:1–45).

*** Joseph became the father of two tribes in Israel since Jacob adopted his two sons Ephraim and Manasseh.

observed a seven-day mourning for his father.

11 When the inhabitants of the land, the Canaanites, saw the mourning at the threshing floor of Atad, they said, "This is a grievous mourning for the Egyptians." Therefore the place was named Abel-mizraim (mourning of Egypt); it is west of the Jordan.

Burial at Machpelah

12 So Jacob's sons did for him as he had commanded them;

13 for his sons carried him to the land of Canaan and buried him in the cave of the field of Machpelah, east of Mamre, which Abraham bought along with the field as a burial site from Ephron the Hittite.

14 After he had buried his father, Joseph returned to Egypt, he and his brothers, and all who had gone up with him.

15 When Joseph's brothers saw that their father was dead, they said, "What if Joseph carries a grudge against us and pays us back in full for all the wrong which we did to him?"

16 So they sent *word* to Joseph, saying, "Your father commanded us before he died, saying,

17 'You are to say to Joseph, "I beg you, please forgive the transgression of your brothers and their sin, for they did you wrong." ' Now, please forgive the transgression of the servants of the God of your father." And Joseph wept when they spoke to him.

18 Then his brothers went and fell down before him [in confession]; then they said, "Behold, we are your servants (slaves)."

19 But Joseph said to them, "Do not be afraid, for am I in the place of God? [Vengeance is His, not mine.]

20 "As for you, you meant evil against me, but God meant it for good in order to bring about this present outcome, that many people would be kept alive [as they are this day].

21 "So now, do not be afraid; I will provide for you *and* support you and your little ones." So he comforted them [giving them encouragement and hope] and spoke [with kindness] to their hearts.

Death of Joseph

22 Now Joseph lived in Egypt, he and his father's household, and Joseph lived a hundred and ten years.

23 Joseph saw the third generation of Ephraim's children; also the children of Machir, the son of Manasseh, were born *and* raised on Joseph's knees.

24 Joseph said to his brothers, "I am about to die, but God will surely take care of you and bring you up out of this land to the land which He promised to Abraham, to Isaac, and to Jacob [to give you]."

25 Then Joseph made the sons of Israel (Jacob) swear [an oath], saying, "God will surely visit you *and* take care of you [returning you to Canaan], and [when that happens] you shall carry my bones up from here."

26 So Joseph died, being a hundred and ten years old; and they embalmed him and he was put in a coffin in Egypt.

50:20 *God meant it for good.* God transformed the evil of a group of men into an exceedingly great work. Joseph not only saved the lives of numerous people in the ancient world, he also testified to the power and goodness of the living God.

50:24 *to Abraham, to Isaac, and to Jacob.* This phrase is the standard way of referring to God's covenant with Abraham's family (50:24; Ex 2:24; 3:16). The recital of the three names reaffirms the certainty of the promise and God's commitment to fulfill it.

50:25 *carry my bones.* Hundreds of years later, Moses would keep the Israelites' oath by taking Joseph's bones with the people into the wilderness (Ex 13:19). Finally, Joshua would bury the bones of Joseph at Shechem (Jos 24:32).

13 Ge 49:29; Ac 7:16; Ge 23:16 **15** Job 15:21 **17** Pr 28:13; Ge 49:25 **18** Ge 37:7,10 **19** Ge 45:5; 2Ki 5:7 **20** Ps 56:5; Ac 3:13-15 **21** Mt 5:44 **23** Job 42:16; Nu 32:39; Ge 30:3 **24** Ge 15:14; 46:4; 48:21; Ex 3:16,17; Heb 11:22; Ge 26:3; 35:12; 46:4 **25** Ex 13:19; Jos 24:32; Ac 7:16

THE SECOND BOOK OF MOSES, COMMONLY CALLED

EXODUS

▸ **AUTHOR:** Exodus has been attributed to Moses since the time of Joshua (cf. 20:25; Jos 8:30 – 32), and there is a great deal of both internal and external evidence that supports Moses as the author. The claims in Joshua are backed by similar testimony from Malachi (4:4), the disciples (Jn 1:45), Paul (Ro 10:5), and Christ (Mk 7:10; 12:26; Lk 20:37; Jn 5:46 – 47; 7:19,22 – 23). Portions of the book itself claim the authorship of Moses (ch. 15; 17:8 – 14; 20:1 – 17; 24:4,7,12; 31:18; 34:1 – 27). The author of Exodus must have been a man familiar with the customs and climate of Egypt. Its consistency of style points to a single author and its ancient literary devices support its antiquity.

▸ **TIMES:** c. 1875 – 1445 BC ▸ **KEY VERSES:** Ex 19:5 – 6

▸ **THEME:** The main character of Exodus is clearly Moses. God gives him the job of leading the exodus from Egypt. Moses also takes on the job of establishing, at God's direction, the essential elements of the Jewish patterns of life and worship. He is simultaneously God's designated representative of the people to God and God's messenger and representative to the people. The critical events in Exodus are the Passover and the giving of the Ten Commandments. The remainder of the Old Testament continually refers back to God's deliverance of Israel from Egypt and the law as delivered at Sinai. In these events God's identity and purpose are revealed. There are many signs and wonders of His power. Aspects of His nature and His expectations of the people also become increasingly clear.

Israel Multiplies in Egypt

1 NOW THESE are the names of the sons of Israel who came to Egypt with Jacob; each came with his household:
2Reuben, Simeon, Levi, and Judah;
3Issachar, Zebulun, and Benjamin;
4Dan and Naphtali, Gad, and Asher.
5All the descendants of Jacob were seventy people; Joseph was [already] in Egypt.
6Then Joseph died, and all his brothers and all that generation,
7but the Israelites were prolific and increased greatly; they multiplied and became extremely strong, so that the land was filled with them.
8Now a new king arose over Egypt, who did not know Joseph [nor the history of his accomplishments].
9He said to his people, "Behold, the people of the sons of Israel are too

---

1:1 ***Israel.*** Originally, Israel was called Jacob. His twelve sons became the founders of the twelve tribes of the nation Israel.
1:2 – 4 The sons are listed according to their mothers and their ages. Reuben, Simeon, Levi, Judah, Issachar, and Zebulun were all sons of Leah. Benjamin was the son of Rachel. Dan and Naphtali were sons of Bilhah, the maid of Rachel. Gad and Asher were sons of Zilpah, the maid of Leah (for each son's birth, see Ge 29:31 – 35; 35:16 – 20,23 – 26).
1:8 ***a new king.*** This king did not remember Joseph, his privileged position in the older pharaoh's administration, his administrative skill that

CHAPTER 1 **1** Ge 46:8 **5** Ge 46:26,27 **6** Ge 50:26; Ac 7:15 **7** Ge 46:3; Dt 26:5; Ps 105:24; Ac 7:17 **9** Ps 105:24

many and too mighty for us [they greatly outnumber us].

10 “Come, let us deal shrewdly with them, so that they will not multiply and in the event of war, join our enemies, and fight against us and escape from the land.”

11 So they set taskmasters over them to oppress them with hard labor. And the sons of Israel built Pithom and Raamses as storage cities for Pharaoh.

12 But the more the Egyptians oppressed them, the more they multiplied and expanded, so that the Egyptians dreaded *and* were exasperated by the Israelites.

13 And the Egyptians made the Israelites serve rigorously [forcing them into severe slavery].

14 They made their lives bitter with hard labor in mortar, brick, and all kinds of field work. All their labor was harsh *and* severe.

15 Then the king of Egypt said to the Hebrew midwives, one of whom was named Shiphrah (beauty) and the other named Puah (splendor),

16 “When you act as midwives to the Hebrew women and see them on the birthstool, if it is a son, you shall kill him; but if it is a daughter, she shall live.”

17 But the midwives feared God [with profound reverence] and did not do as the king of Egypt commanded, but they let the boy babies live.

18 So the king of Egypt called for the midwives and said to them, “Why have you done this thing, and allowed the boy babies to live?”

19 The midwives answered Pharaoh, “Because the Hebrew women are not like the Egyptian women; they are vigorous and give birth quickly and their babies are born before the midwife can get to them.”

20 So God was good to the midwives, and the people [of Israel] multiplied and became very strong.

21 And because the midwives feared God [with profound reverence], He established families *and* households for them.

22 Then Pharaoh commanded all his people, saying, “Every son who is born [to the Hebrews] must be thrown into the Nile, but every daughter you shall keep alive.”

The Birth of Moses

2 NOW A man of the house of Levi [the priestly tribe] went and took as his wife a daughter of Levi. [Ex 6:18, 20; Num 26:59]

2 The woman conceived and gave

---

saved the Egyptians from starvation, and his enrichment of the pharaoh's treasury. This pharaoh was probably one of the Hyksos kings who descended from foreign invaders. Ethnically they were a minority in Egypt, and they may have perceived the growing numbers of Hebrews as a personal challenge.

1:11 – 22 ***to oppress them*****.** Long before the sons of Israel came to Egypt, Abraham received a remarkable revelation from the Lord (Ge 15:13 – 16): his descendants would be strangers in a foreign land and would be enslaved and oppressed for four hundred years. “In all their distress He was distressed” (Isa 63:9). At the point when Israel's afflictions became unbearable they cried for help, and God responded in faithfulness to His promise.

1:11 ***Pithom and Raamses*****.** These storage cities are mentioned according to the names by which they were known in later times. The Pharaoh Ramses (whose name presumably relates to the name of one of these cities) was not yet in power.

1:15 ***king of Egypt*****.** This king was probably not the Hyksos king alluded to in verses 8 – 14. This king, perhaps Thutmose I (c. 1539 – 1514 BC), ruled Egypt when Moses was born (2:1 – 10). ***Hebrew midwives*****.** The names of these women (Shiphrah — “beautiful one,” and Puah — “splendid one”) are preserved in this account because they were godly women with a courageous faith. At the same time, the names of the pharaohs — the “important” people of the day — are omitted.

1:17 ***feared*****.** The Hebrew term for “fear” is the word regularly used for piety, obedience, and the true worship of God (20:20; Ge 22:12).

2:2 ***gave birth to a son*****.** This was not their first child, both Miriam and Aaron were older than Moses (v. 4; 7:7).

---

10 Ps 83:3,4; Pr 16:25; Ac 7:19 **11** Ge 15:13; Ex 3:7; Dt 26:6; Ex 5:4,5; Ge 47:11 **14** Ex 2:23; 6:9; Nu 20:15; Ac 7:19,34; Ps 81:6 **17** Pr 16:6; Da 3:16,18; Ac 5:29 **19** See Jos 2:4; 2Sa 17:19,20 **20** Pr 11:18; Ecc 8:12; Isa 3:10; Heb 6:10 **21** See 1Sa 2:35; 2Sa 7:11,13,27,29; 1Ki 11:38; Ps 127:1 **22** Ac 7:19 **CHAPTER 2** **1** Ex 6:20; Nu 26:59; 1Ch 23:14 **2** Ac 7:20; Heb 11:23

birth to a son; and when she saw that
he was [especially] beautiful *and*
healthy, she hid him for three months
[to protect him from the Egyptians].
[Acts 7:20; Heb 11:23]
3When she could no longer hide him,
she got him a basket (chest) made of
papyrus reeds and covered it with tar
and pitch [making it waterproof]. Then
she put the child in it and set it among
the reeds by the bank of the Nile.
4And his sister [Miriam] stood some
distance away to find out what would
happen to him.
5Now the daughter of Pharaoh came
down to bathe at the Nile, and [she, to-
gether with] her maidens walked along
the river's bank; she saw the basket
among the reeds and sent her maid [to
get it], and she brought it *to her*.
6When she opened it, she saw the
child, and behold, the baby was crying.
And she took pity on him and said,
"This is one of the Hebrews' children."
7Then his sister said to Pharaoh's
daughter, "Shall I go and call a wet-
nurse from the Hebrew women to
nurse the child for you?"
8And Pharaoh's daughter said to her,
"Go *ahead*." So the girl went and called
the child's mother.
9Then Pharaoh's daughter said to
her, "Take this child away and nurse
him for me, and I will give you your
wages." So the woman took the child
and nursed him.
10And the child grew, and she
brought him to Pharaoh's daugh-
ter and he became her son. And she
named him Moses, and said, "Because
I drew him out of the water."
11One day, after Moses had grown
[into adulthood], it happened that he
went to his countrymen and looked
[with compassion] at their hard labors;
and he saw an Egyptian beating a He-
brew, one of his countrymen.
12He turned to look around, and see-
ing no one, he killed the Egyptian and
hid him in the sand.
13He went out the next day and saw
two Hebrew men fighting with each
other; and he said to the aggressor,
"Why are you striking your friend?"
14But the man said, "Who made
you a prince and a judge over us? Do
you intend to kill me as you killed the
Egyptian?" Then Moses was afraid
and said, "Certainly this incident is
known."

Moses Escapes to Midian

15When Pharaoh heard about this
matter, he tried to kill Moses. Then
Moses fled from Pharaoh's presence
and took refuge in the land of Midian,
where he sat down by a well.
16Now the priest of Midian had seven

2:6 *one of the Hebrews' children*. A Hebrew baby would have been circumcised on the eighth day. Although circumcision was practiced in Egypt, it was not done to infants. Upon unwrapping the infant's clothing, the women would have seen his special mark.

2:10 *Because I drew him out*. In Hebrew, the name Moses means "he who draws out." In this manner, Moses' name can refer the reader to the living God, who is the true Deliverer, and also to Moses, who was used by God to deliver the Israelites from the Red Sea (chs. 14 – 15). The one who was drawn out of water would be the means of drawing the Israelite nation out of water.

2:11 *after Moses had grown*. The years of Moses' experience in the pharaoh's court are not detailed. Yet Stephen, the New Testament martyr, reported the long-held and surely accurate tradition: "Moses was educated in all the wisdom and culture of the Egyptians, and he was a man of power in words and deeds" (Ac 7:22). The training Moses received was the best education the world had to offer at the time. He would have learned three languages: Egyptian, Akkadian, and Hebrew. When Moses came into the presence of Pharaoh to demand freedom for his people, he was no "uneducated slave," but had received an education on par with the king's.

2:15 *the land of Midian*. This is the region of the Sinai Peninsula and Arabian deserts where the seminomadic Midianites lived (for the Abrahamic origin of this people group, see Ge 25:1).

2:16 *the priest of Midian*. This man appears to have been a foreigner who had come to worship the true and living God.

4 Ex 15:20; Nu 26:59 **5** Ac 7:21 **10** Ac 7:21 **11** Ac 7:23,24; Heb 11:24-26; Ex 1:11 **12** Ac 7:24 **13** Ac 7:26 **14** Ac 7:27,28 **15** Ac 7:29; Heb 11:27; Ge 24:11; 29:2 **16** Ex 3:1; Ge 24:11; 1Sa 9:11

daughters; and they came and drew water [from the well where Moses was resting] and filled the troughs to water their father's flock.

17 Then shepherds came and drove them away, but Moses stood up and helped them and watered their flock.

18 When they came to Reuel (Jethro) their father, he said, "How is it that you have come back so soon today?"

19 They said, "An Egyptian saved us from the shepherds. He even drew water [from the well] for us and watered the flock."

20 Then he said to his daughters, "Where is he? Why have you left the man behind? Invite him to have something to eat."

21 Moses was willing to remain with the man, and he gave Moses his daughter Zipporah [to be his wife].

22 She gave birth to a son, and he named him Gershom (stranger); for he said, "I have been a stranger in a foreign land."

23 Now it happened after a long time [about forty years] that the king of Egypt died. And the children of Israel (Jacob) groaned *and* sighed because of the bondage, and they cried out. And their cry for help because of their bondage ascended to God.

24 So God heard their groaning and God remembered His covenant with Abraham, Isaac, and Jacob (Israel). [Gen 12:1–3; 15:18–21; 17:3–8, 21; 35:10–12]

25 God saw the sons of Israel, and God took notice [of them] *and* was concerned about them [knowing all, understanding all, remembering all]. [Ps 56:8, 9; 139:2]

The Burning Bush

3 NOW MOSES was keeping the flock of Jethro (Reuel) his father-in-law, the priest of Midian; and he led his flock to the west side of the wilderness and came to Horeb (Sinai), the mountain of God.

2 The Angel of the LORD appeared to him in a blazing flame of fire from the midst of a bush; and he looked, and behold, the bush was on fire, yet it was not consumed.

3 So Moses said, "I must turn away [from the flock] and see this great sight—why the bush is not burned up."

4 When the LORD saw that he turned away [from the flock] to look, God called to him from the midst of the bush and said, "Moses, Moses!" And he said, "Here I am."

5 Then God said, "Do not come near; take your sandals off your feet [out of respect], because the place on which you are standing is holy ground."

6 Then He said, "I am the God of your father, the God of Abraham, the God of Isaac, and the God of Jacob." Then Moses hid his face, because he was afraid to look at God.

7 The LORD said, "I have in fact seen

2:19 *An Egyptian.* Moses apparently still dressed and spoke as an Egyptian, rather than as a Hebrew.

2:22 *Gershom.* Gershom means "a stranger there." Moses was doubly removed from his land. He and his people, the Israelites, were strangers in Egypt, and now he was estranged even from his people.

2:23 *the king of Egypt died.* The death of Pharaoh (likely Thutmose III, who died about 1447 BC) meant that Moses could return to Egypt (4:19).

3:1 *Horeb.* This alternate name for Mount Sinai means "desolate place." Yet because of God's appearance on the mountain, this desolate place would become holy. Usually the site of this mountain is identified as Jebel el-Musa, a mountain in the southern Sinai Peninsula.

3:2 *Angel.* The word *angel* simply means "messenger" (Mal 1:1). In the Old Testament, the term "the Angel of the Lord" is used numerous times, and is identified with God as well as being distinguished from Him. In this passage, having mentioned that the Angel of the Lord appeared to Moses, it is immediately established that it was the Lord Himself (v. 4).

3:6 *the God of your father.* God identified Himself as the God worshiped by Abraham, Isaac, and Jacob. In announcing these names, the Lord was assuring Moses that the covenant He had made with them was still intact.

17 Ge 29:10 **18** Nu 10:29; Ex 3:1; 4:18 **20** Ge 31:54 **21** Ex 18:2 **22** Ex 18:3; Ac 7:29 **23** Ac 7:30; Dt 26:7; Ex 3:9; Jas 5:4 **24** Ex 6:5; Ps 105:8,42; Ge 15:14 **25** Ex 4:31; Lk 1:25; Ex 3:7 **CHAPTER 3** **1** Ex 2:16; Ex 18:5; 1Ki 19:8 **2** Dt 33:16; Ac 7:30 **3** Ac 7:31 **4** Dt 33:16 **5** Jos 5:15 **6** Ge 28:13; Ex 4:5; Mt 22:32; Ac 7:32; See 1Ki 19:13 **7** Ex 2:23-25; Ps 106:44; Ex 1:11; Ge 18:21; Ex 2:25

the affliction (suffering, desolation)
of My people who are in Egypt, and
have heard their cry because of their
taskmasters (oppressors); for I know
their pain *and* suffering.
8“So I have come down to rescue
them from the hand (power) of the
Egyptians, and to bring them up from
that land to a land [that is] good and
spacious, to a land flowing with milk
and honey [a land of plenty]—to the
place of the Canaanite, the Hittite, the
Amorite, the Perizzite, the Hivite, and
the Jebusite.
9“Now, behold, the cry of the chil-
dren of Israel has come to Me; and
I have also seen how the Egyptians
oppress them.

The Mission of Moses

10“Therefore, come now, and I will
send you to Pharaoh, and then bring
My people, the children of Israel, out
of Egypt.”
11But Moses said to God, “Who am I,
that I should go to Pharaoh, and that I
should bring the children of Israel out
of Egypt?”
12And God said, “Certainly I will be
with you, and this shall be the sign
to you that it is I who have sent you:
when you have brought the people out
of Egypt, you shall serve *and* worship
God at this mountain.”
13Then Moses said to God, “Behold,
when I come to the Israelites and say
to them, ‘The God of your fathers (an-
cestors) has sent me to you,’ and they
say to me, ‘What is His name?’ What
shall I say to them?”
14God said to Moses, “I AM WHO I
AM”; and He said, “You shall say this to
the Israelites, ‘I AM has sent me to you.’ ”
15Then God also said to Moses,
“This is what you shall say to the Is-
raelites, ‘The LORD, the God of your
fathers, the God of Abraham, the God
of Isaac, and the God of Jacob (Is-
rael), has sent me to you.’ This is My
Name forever, and this is My memo-
rial [name] to all generations.
16“Go, gather the elders (tribal
leaders) of Israel together, and say
to them, ‘The LORD, the God of your
fathers, the God of Abraham, of Isaac,
and of Jacob, appeared to me, saying,
“I am indeed concerned about you
and what has been done to you in
Egypt.
17“So I said I will bring you up out
of the suffering *and* oppression of
Egypt to the land of the Canaanite,
the Hittite, the Amorite, the Perizzite,
the Hivite, and the Jebusite, to a land
flowing with milk and honey.” ’
18“The elders [of the tribes] will lis-
ten *and* pay attention to what you say;
and you, with the elders of Israel, shall
go to the king of Egypt and you shall
say to him, ‘The LORD, the God of the
Hebrews, has met with us; so now,
please, [we ask and plead with you,] let
us go on a three days’ journey into the
wilderness, so that we may sacrifice to
the LORD our God.’
19“But I know that the king of Egypt
will not let you go unless [he is forced]
by a strong hand.
20“So I will reach out My hand and
strike Egypt with all My wonders
which I shall do in the midst of it; and
after that he will let you go.
21“And I will grant this people favor
and respect in the sight of the Egyp-
tians; therefore, it shall be that when
you go, you will not go empty-handed.

3:14 *I AM WHO I AM.* The One who spoke to Moses declared Himself to be the Eternal One—uncaused and independent. Only the Creator of all things can call Himself the *I AM* in the absolute sense; all other creatures are in debt to Him for their existence. But in addition, God the Creator declares His relationship with the people of Israel. The future tense of the Hebrew verb related to God's name is used in verse 12: The I AM *will be* with His people. Thus God declares His covenantal relationship with Israel by His name.

3:15 *The LORD.* LORD in capital letters is the form translators have chosen to represent the Hebrew name YHWH (also transliterated Yahweh, or Jehovah). The Hebrew word meaning "I Am" used in verse 14 is very similar.

8 Ge 50:24; Ex 6:6,8; Dt 1:25; 8:7-9; ver. 17; Ex 13:5; Jer 11:5; Eze 20:6; Ge 15:21 **9** Ex 2:23; Ex 1:11,13,14 **10** Mic 6:4 **11** See Ex 6:12; 1Sa 18:18 **12** Ge 31:3; Jos 1:5; Ro 8:31 **14** Ex 6:3; Jn 8:58; Heb 13:8 **15** Ps 135:13 **16** Ex 4:29; Ex 2:25; Lk 1:68 **17** Ge 15:14,16 **18** Ex 4:31; Ex 5:1,3; Nu 23:3,4,15,16 **19** Ex 5:2 **20** Ex 6:6; 9:15; Dt 6:22; Neh 9:10; Ac 7:36; Ex 12:31 **21** Ex 11:3; 12:36; Pr 16:7

22"But every woman shall [insistently] ask her neighbor and any woman who lives in her house, for articles of silver and articles of gold, and clothing; and you shall put them on your sons and daughters. In this way you are to plunder the Egyptians [leaving bondage with great possessions that are rightfully yours]." [Gen 15:14]

Moses Given Powers

4 THEN MOSES answered [the LORD] and said, "What if they will not believe me or take seriously what I say? For they may say, 'The LORD has not appeared to you.' "

2And the LORD said to him, "What is that in your hand?" And he said, "A staff."

3Then He said, "Throw it on the ground." So Moses threw it on the ground, and it became a [living] serpent [like the royal symbol on the crown of Pharaoh]; and Moses ran from it.

4But the LORD said to Moses, "Reach out your hand and grasp it by the tail." So he reached out his hand and caught it, and it became a staff in his hand—

5["You shall do this," said the LORD,] "so that the elders may believe that the LORD, the God of their fathers, the God of Abraham, the God of Isaac, and the God of Jacob, has [most certainly] appeared to you."

6The LORD also said to him, "Put your hand into your robe [where it covers your chest]." So he put his hand into his robe, and when he took it out, his hand was leprous, as white as snow.

7Then God said, "Put your hand into your robe again." So he put his hand back into his robe, and when he took it out, it was restored [and was] like the rest of his body.

8"If they will not believe you or pay attention to the evidence of the first sign, they may believe the evidence of the second sign.

9"But if they will not believe these two signs or pay attention to what you say, you are to take some water from the Nile and pour it on the dry ground; and the water which you take out of the river will turn into blood on the dry ground."

10Then Moses said to the LORD, "Please, Lord, I am not a man of words (eloquent, fluent), neither before nor since You have spoken to Your servant; for I am slow of speech and tongue."

11The LORD said to him, "Who has made man's mouth? Or who makes the mute or the deaf, or the seeing or the blind? Is it not I, the LORD?

12"Now then go, and I, even I, will be with your mouth, and will teach you what you shall say."

13But he said, "Please my Lord, send *the message* [of rescue to Israel] by [someone else,] whomever else You will [choose]."

Aaron to Speak for Moses

14Then the anger of the LORD was kindled *and* burned against Moses; He said, "Is there not your brother, Aaron the Levite? I know that he speaks fluently. Also, he is coming out to meet you, and when he sees you, he will be overjoyed.

15"You must speak to him and put the words in his mouth; I, even I, will be with your mouth and with his mouth, and I will teach you what you are to do.

16"Moreover, he shall speak for you to the people; he will act as a mouthpiece for you, and you will be as God to him [telling him what I say to you].

17"You shall take in your hand this staff, with which you shall perform the signs [the miracles which prove I sent you]."

18Then Moses went away and returned to Jethro his father-in-law, and said to him, "Please, let me go back so that I may return to my relatives in Egypt, and see if they are still

---

4:6–7 *leprous.* The term *leprosy* included a wide variety of skin diseases.

22 Ex 11:2; Job 27:17; Pr 13:22; Eze 39:10 **CHAPTER 4** **2** ver. 17,20 **5** Ex 19:9; Ex 3:15 **6** Nu 12:10; 2Ki 5:27 **7** Nu 12:13,14; Dt 32:39 **9** Ex 7:19 **10** Ex 6:12; Jer 1:6 **11** Ps 94:9 **12** Isa 50:4; Jer 1:9; Mt 10:19; Mk 13:11; Lk 12:11,12; 21:14,15 **13** See Jnh 1:3 **14** ver. 27; 1Sa 10:2,3,5 **15** Ex 7:1,2; Nu 23:5,12,16; Dt 5:31 **16** Ex 7:1 **17** ver. 2

alive." And Jethro said to Moses, "Go
in peace."
19 Then the LORD said to Moses in
Midian, "Go back to Egypt, for all
the men who were seeking your life
[for killing the Egyptian] are dead."
[Ex 2:11, 12]
20 So Moses took his wife [Zipporah]
and his sons [Gershom and Eliezer]
and seated them on donkeys, and re-
turned to the land of Egypt. Moses also
took the staff of God in his hand.
21 The LORD said to Moses, "When
you return to Egypt, see that you per-
form before Pharaoh all the wonders
(miracles) which I have put in your
hand, but I will harden his heart *and*
make him stubborn so that he will not
let the people go.
22 "Then you shall say to Pharaoh,
'Thus says the LORD, "Israel is My son,
My firstborn.
23 "So I say to you, 'Let My son go
so that he may serve Me'; and if you
refuse to let him go, behold, I will kill
your son, your firstborn." ' "
24 Now it happened at the lodging
place, that the LORD met Moses and
sought to kill him [making him deathly
ill because he had not circumcised one
of his sons]. [Gen 17:9–14]
25 Then Zipporah took a flint knife
and cut off the foreskin of her son and
threw it at Moses' feet, and said, "In-
deed you are a husband of blood to
me!"
26 So He let Moses alone [to recover].
At that time Zipporah said, "*You are*
a husband of blood"—because of the
circumcision.
27 The LORD said to Aaron, "Go into
the wilderness to meet Moses." So he
went and met him at the mountain of
God (Sinai) and kissed him.
28 Moses told Aaron all the words of
the LORD with which He had sent him,
and all the signs that He had com-
manded him to do.
29 Then Moses and Aaron went [into
Egypt] and assembled all the elders of
the Israelites;
30 and Aaron said all the words which
the LORD had spoken to Moses. Then
Moses performed the signs [given to
him by God] before the people.
31 So the people believed; and when
they heard that the LORD was con-
cerned about the Israelites and that
He had looked [with compassion] on
their suffering, then they bowed their
heads and worshiped [the LORD].

Israel's Labor Increased

5 AFTERWARD MOSES and Aaron
came and said to Pharaoh, "Thus
says the LORD, the God of Israel, 'Let

4:19 ***who were seeking your life*.** God promised Abraham that those who persecuted Israel would be judged (Ge 12:3), and it is clear from history that God fulfilled His promise. In Exodus 14, the Egyptians attempted to destroy the Israelites by driving them into the Red Sea, but instead were drowned themselves. Those who threw Daniel to the lions were devoured by those same beasts (Da 6). Haman plotted to destroy all the Jews in Persia, and ended up signing his own death warrant (Est 7). "The LORD keeps all who love Him" (Ps 145:20).
4:21 ***Pharaoh*.** This Pharaoh was most likely Amenhotep II (c. 1447 – 1421). ***I will harden his heart*.** Some interpret these words to mean that God would confirm what Pharaoh had stubbornly determined to do. In the first five plagues, the hardening was attributed to Pharaoh (7:13,22; 8:15,19,32; 9:7). Then for the sixth plague, God hardened a heart that had already rejected Him (9:12). Others insist that God had determined Pharaoh's negative response to Moses long before Pharaoh could harden his heart. These interpreters point to this verse and to 9:16, in which God says that He raised up Pharaoh for the purpose of demonstrating His power.
4:24 ***sought to kill him*.** The precise meaning of this passage is unclear. Apparently someone in Moses' family was not circumcised, despite God's command. It is possible that Moses had kept one of his sons uncircumcised in order to please his Midianite family. (The Midianites practiced adult male circumcision at the time of marriage, rather than infant circumcision as the Hebrews did.) Moses' neglect of the sign of God's covenant was very serious, especially for the future leader of God's people.

---

19 Ex 2:15,23; Mt 2:20 **20** Nu 20:8,9 **21** Ex 3:20; Ex 7:3,13; 9:12,35; Dt 2:30; Jos 11:20; Isa 63:17; Jn 12:40 **22** Hos 11:1; Ro 9:4; 2Co 6:18; Jer 31:9; Jas 1:18 **23** Ex 11:5; 12:29 **24** Nu 22:22; Ge 17:14 **25** Jos 5:2,3 **27** ver. 14; Ex 3:1 **28** ver. 15,16; ver. 8,9 **29** Ex 3:16 **30** ver. 16 **31** ver. 8,9; Ex 3:18; Ex 3:16; Ex 2:25; 3:7; Ge 24:26; 1Ch 29:20 **CHAPTER 5** **1** Ex 10:9

My people go, so that they may celebrate a feast to Me in the wilderness.' "

2 But Pharaoh said, "Who is the LORD that I should obey His voice to let Israel go? I do not know the LORD, nor will I let Israel go."

3 Then they said, "The God of the Hebrews has met with us. Please, let us go on a three days' journey into the wilderness and sacrifice to the LORD our God, so that He does not discipline us with pestilence or with the sword."

4 But the king of Egypt said to Moses and Aaron, "Why do you take the people away from their work? Get back to your burdens!"

5 Pharaoh said, "Look, the people of the land are now many, and you would have them stop their work!"

6 The very same day Pharaoh gave orders to the [Egyptian] taskmasters in charge of the people and their [Hebrew] foremen, saying,

7 "You will no longer give the people straw to make brick as before; let them go and gather straw for themselves.

8 "But the number of bricks which they were making before, you shall [still] require of them; you are not to reduce it in the least. For they are idle *and* lazy; that is why they cry, 'Let us go and sacrifice to our God.'

9 "Let labor be heavier on the men, and let them work [hard] at it so that they will pay no attention to [their God's] lying words."

10 Then the [Egyptian] taskmasters [in charge] of the people and their [Hebrew] foremen went out and said to the people, "Thus says Pharaoh, 'I will not give you any straw.

11 'Go, get straw for yourselves wherever you can find it, but your work [quota] will not be reduced in the least.' "

12 So the people were scattered throughout the land of Egypt to gather stubble to use for straw.

13 And the taskmasters pressured them, saying, "Finish your work, [fulfill] your daily quotas, just as when there was straw [given to you]."

14 And the Hebrew foremen, whom Pharaoh's taskmasters had set over them, were beaten and were asked, "Why have you not fulfilled your required quota of making bricks yesterday and today, as before?"

15 Then the Hebrew foremen came to Pharaoh and cried, "Why do you deal like this with your servants?

16 "No straw is given to your servants, yet they say to us, 'Make bricks!' And look, your servants are being beaten, but it is the fault of your own people."

17 But Pharaoh said, "You are lazy, very lazy *and* idle! That is why you say, 'Let us go *and* sacrifice to the LORD.'

18 "Get out now and get to work; for no straw will be given to you, yet you are to deliver the same quota of bricks."

19 The Hebrew foremen saw that they were in a bad situation because they were told, "You must not reduce [in the least] your daily quota of bricks."

20 When they left Pharaoh's presence, the foremen met Moses and Aaron, who were waiting for them.

21 And the foremen said to them, "May the LORD look upon you and judge you, because you have made us odious (something hated) in the sight of Phar-

---

5:2 *Who is the LORD.* Later these words would haunt Pharaoh (12:31 – 32). Meanwhile, Pharaoh believed himself to be a god in his own right, and certainly felt no need to cave in to the demands of a god who claimed to be the champion of his slave labor force.

5:7 – 9 *let them go and gather straw for themselves*. It is easy to rationalize our cruel treatment of others when it is in our selfish interest to do so. We often hear "Pharaoh's reasoning" about minority peoples or people on welfare today. Of course laziness and discontent is a genuine problem for some who are on welfare, or who feel oppressed (just as it is for some who were born into wealth and privilege), but too often we turn off the concern we should have for the poor and oppressed with the comfortable conviction that somehow they deserve their problems. If we continue in this attitude, we may be sure that God will judge our sin. God cares deeply for the weak, the poor, and the downtrodden; if we are genuine disciples we will share His concern.

2 2Ki 18:35; Job 21:15; Ex 3:19 **3** Ex 3:18 **4** Ex 1:11 **5** Ex 1:7,9 **6** Ex 1:11 **21** Ex 6:9

aoh and his servants, and you have put
a sword in their hand to kill us."
22 Then Moses turned again to the
LORD and said, "O Lord, why have You
brought harm *and* oppression to this
people? Why did You ever send me?
[I cannot understand Your purpose!]
23 "Ever since I came to Pharaoh to
speak in Your name, he has harmed
and oppressed this people, and You
have done nothing at all to rescue Your
people."

God Promises Action

6 THEN THE LORD said to Moses,
"Now you shall see what I will do
to Pharaoh; for under compulsion he
will [not only] let them go, but under
compulsion he will drive them out of
his land."
2 Then God spoke further to Moses and said to him, "I am the LORD.
[Ex 3:14]
3 "I appeared to Abraham, to Isaac,
and to Jacob (Israel) as God Almighty
[El Shaddai], but by My name, LORD,
I did not make Myself known to them
[in acts and great miracles]. [Gen 17:1]
4 "I also established My covenant
with them, to give them the land of
Canaan, the land in which they lived
as strangers (temporary residents, foreigners). [Gen 12:1–3; 13:14–17; 15:18–
21; 17:19; 26:3, 4; 28:13]
5 "And I have also heard the groaning of the sons of Israel, whom the
Egyptians have enslaved, and I have
[faithfully] remembered My covenant
[with Abraham, Isaac, and Jacob].
6 "Therefore, say to the children of
Israel, 'I am the LORD, and I will bring
you out from under the burdens of the
Egyptians, and I will free you from
their bondage. I will redeem *and* rescue you with an outstretched (vigorous, powerful) arm and with great acts
of judgment [against Egypt].
7 'Then I will take you for My people,
and I will be your God; and you shall
know that I am the LORD your God, who
redeemed you *and* brought you out from
under the burdens of the Egyptians.
8 'I will bring you to the land which I
swore to give to Abraham, Isaac, and
Jacob (Israel); and I will give it to you
as a possession. I am the LORD [you
have the promise of My changeless
omnipotence and faithfulness].' "
9 Moses told this to the Israelites, but
they did not listen to him because of
their impatience *and* despondency, and
because of their forced labor.
10 The LORD spoke to Moses, saying,
11 "Go, tell Pharaoh king of Egypt
to let the children of Israel go out of
his land."
12 But Moses said to the LORD, "Look,
[my own people] the Israelites have not
listened to me; so how then will Pharaoh listen to me, for I am unskilled *and*
inept in speech?"
13 Then the LORD spoke to Moses and
Aaron, and gave them a command
concerning the Israelites and Pharaoh
king of Egypt, to bring the Israelites
out of the land of Egypt.

The Heads of Israel

14 These are the heads of their fathers' households. The sons of Reuben,
Israel's (Jacob's) firstborn: Hanoch and
Pallu, Hezron and Carmi; these are the
families of Reuben.
15 The sons of Simeon: Jemuel, Jamin, Ohad, Jachin, Zohar, and Shaul
the son of a Canaanite woman; these
are the families of Simeon.
16 These are the names of the sons
of Levi according to their births: Gershon, Kohath, and Merari; and Levi
lived a hundred and thirty-seven years.

5:23 *speak in Your name.* It seems that Moses expected Pharaoh to cave in as soon as he heard the use of the Lord's name Yahweh (3:13–15; 5:1). Yet God had warned Moses that Pharaoh would do the opposite (3:19; 4:21).

6:4 *My covenant.* This is a reference to the Abrahamic covenant celebrated in Genesis (Ge 12:1–3,7; 15:12–21; 17:1–16; 22:15–18).

6:14–27 *their fathers'.* The family history of Moses, Aaron, and Miriam is important because all of Israel's future priests would come from this family.

CHAPTER 6 **1** Ex 3:19; Ex 12:31,33,39 **3** Ge 17:1; 35:11; 48:3; Ex 3:14; Ps 83:18; Jn 8:58 **4** Ge 15:18; Ge 28:4 **5** Ex 2:24 **6** Ex 3:17; Dt 26:8; Dt 7:8; 1Ch 17:21 **7** Dt 4:20; 2Sa 7:24; Ex 29:45,46; Rev 21:7; Ex 5:4,5 **8** Ge 15:18; 26:3 **9** Ex 5:21 **12** ver. 30; Ex 4:10; Jer 1:6 **14** Ge 46:9; 1Ch 5:3 **15** Ge 46:10; 1Ch 4:24 **16** Ge 46:11; Nu 3:17

17 The sons of Gershon: Libni and Shimei, by their families.

18 The sons of Kohath: Amram (Moses' father), Izhar, Hebron, and Uzziel; and Kohath lived a hundred and thirty-three years.

19 The sons of Merari: Mahli and Mushi. These are the families of Levi according to their generations.

20 Amram married his father's sister Jochebed, and she gave birth to Aaron and Moses; and Amram lived a hundred and thirty-seven years.

21 The sons of Izhar: Korah, Nepheg, and Zichri.

22 The sons of Uzziel: Mishael, Elzaphan, and Sithri.

23 Aaron married Elisheba, the daughter of Amminadab and the sister of Nahshon, and she gave birth to Nadab, Abihu, Eleazar, and Ithamar.

24 The sons of Korah: Assir, Elkanah, and Abiasaph. These are the [extended] families of the Korahites.

25 Eleazar, Aaron's son, married one of the daughters of Putiel, and she gave birth to Phinehas. These are the heads of the fathers' households of the Levites by their families.

26 These are [the same] Aaron and Moses to whom the LORD said, "Bring the children of Israel out of the land of Egypt by their armies."

27 They were the ones who spoke to Pharaoh king of Egypt about bringing the Israelites out of Egypt; these are [the same] Moses and Aaron.

28 Now it happened on the day when the LORD spoke to Moses in the land of Egypt,

29 that He said, "I am the LORD; tell Pharaoh king of Egypt everything that I say to you."

30 But Moses said before the LORD, "Look, I am unskilled *and* inept in speech; how then will Pharaoh listen to me *and* pay attention to what I say?"

"I Will Stretch Out My Hand"

7 THEN THE LORD said to Moses, "Now hear this: I make you as God to Pharaoh [to declare My will and purpose to him]; and your brother Aaron shall be your prophet.

2 "You shall speak all that I command you, and your brother Aaron shall tell Pharaoh to let the children of Israel go out of his land.

3 "And I will make Pharaoh's heart hard, and multiply My signs and My wonders (miracles) in the land of Egypt.

4 "But Pharaoh will not listen to you, and I shall lay My hand on Egypt and bring out My hosts [like a defensive army, tribe by tribe], My people the children of Israel, out of the land of Egypt by great acts of judgment (the plagues).

5 "The Egyptians shall know that I am the LORD, when I stretch out My hand on Egypt and bring out the children of Israel from among them."

6 And Moses and Aaron did so; just as the LORD commanded them, so they did.

7 Now Moses was eighty years old and Aaron eighty-three years old when they spoke to Pharaoh.

Aaron's Rod Becomes a Serpent

8 Now the LORD said to Moses and Aaron,

9 "When Pharaoh says to you, 'Work a miracle [to prove your authority],' then you say to Aaron, 'Take your staff

---

7:1 *your prophet.* As Moses was the prophet of the Lord, so Aaron became Moses' prophet. Aaron would speak for Moses, for a prophet was the "mouth" of the one who sent him.

7:3 *I will make Pharaoh's heart hard.* It was a part of God's plan that Pharaoh would be inflexibly stubborn, thus setting the scene for God to deliver His people by powerful signs and wonders.

7:7 *eighty ... eighty-three.* These men had already lived as long as the average lifetime of our day before their principal life work had begun. Moses and Aaron each lived another forty years as leaders of the nation of Israel.

7:9 – 10 Miracles — A miracle could be defined as the temporary suspension of some natural law (like turning a staff into a snake),

17 1Ch 6:17 **18** 1Ch 6:2,18 **19** 1Ch 6:19; 23:21 **20** Ex 2:1,2 **21** 1Ch 6:37,38 **22** Lev 10:4 **23** Ru 4:19,20; Mt 1:4; Lev 10:1; Nu 3:2; 26:60 **24** Nu 26:11 **25** Nu 25:7,11; Jos 24:33 **26** Ex 7:4; 12:17,51; Nu 33:1 **27** ver. 13; Ex 32:7; 33:1; Ps 77:20 **29** ver. 11; Ex 7:2 **30** ver. 12; Ex 4:10 **CHAPTER 7** **1** Jer 1:10; Ex 4:16 **2** Ex 4:15 **3** Ex 4:21; Ex 11:9; Ex 4:7 **4** Ex 10:1; 11:9; Ex 6:6 **5** ver. 17; Ex 8:22; 14:4,18; Ps 9:16; Ex 3:20 **6** ver. 2 **7** Dt 29:5; 31:2; 34:7; Ac 7:23,30 **9** Isa 7:11; Jn 2:18; 6:30; Ex 4:2,17

and throw it down before Pharaoh, so
that it may become a serpent.' "
[10]So Moses and Aaron came to Phar-
aoh, and did just as the LORD had com-
manded; Aaron threw down his staff
before Pharaoh and his servants, and
it became a serpent.
[11]Then Pharaoh called for the wise
men [skilled in magic and omens]
and the sorcerers [skilled in witch-
craft], and they also, these magicians
(soothsayer-priests) of Egypt, did the
same with their secret arts *and* en-
chantments.
[12]For every man threw down his
staff and they turned into serpents; but
Aaron's staff swallowed up their staffs.
[13]Yet Pharaoh's heart was hardened
and he would not listen to them, just
as the LORD had said.

Water Is Turned to Blood

[14]Then the LORD said to Moses,
"Pharaoh's heart is hard; he refuses
to let the people go.
[15]"Go to Pharaoh in the morning as
he is going out to the water, and wait
for him on the bank of the Nile; and
you shall take in your hand the staff
that was turned into a serpent.
[16]"You shall say to him, 'The LORD, the
God of the Hebrews, has sent me to you,
saying, "Let My people go, so that they
may serve Me in the wilderness. But
behold, you have not listened until now."
[17]'Thus says the LORD, "By this you
shall know *and* recognize *and* ac-
knowledge that I am the LORD: look,
with the staff in my hand I will strike
the water in the Nile, and it shall be
turned to blood.
[18]"The fish in the Nile will die, and
the Nile will become foul, and the
Egyptians will not be able to drink
water from the Nile." ' "
[19]Then the LORD said to Moses, "Say
to Aaron, 'Take your staff and stretch
out your hand over the waters of Egypt,
over their rivers, over their streams,
over their pools, and over all their res-
ervoirs of water, so that they may be-
come blood; and there shall be blood
throughout all the land of Egypt, in
containers both of wood and of stone.' "
[20]So Moses and Aaron did as the
LORD commanded; Aaron lifted up the
staff and struck the waters in the Nile,
in the sight of Pharaoh and in the sight
of his servants, and all the water that
was in the Nile was turned into blood.
[21]The fish in the Nile died, and the
river became foul smelling, and the
Egyptians could not drink its water,
and there was blood throughout all
the land of Egypt.
[22]But the magicians of Egypt did the
same by their secret arts *and* enchant-
ments; so Pharaoh's heart was hard-
ened, and he did not listen to Moses
and Aaron, just as the LORD had said.

---

or the manipulation of natural forces (such as weather) over which humans ordinarily have no jurisdiction. We tend to look for miracles only for their immediate results (healing, retribution, etc.), but in the Bible miracles are always for a "sign." The focus isn't on the actual miracle, but on the supernatural as a sign of God's working in the situation. This is clearly seen in the miracles of Jesus. If His purpose had just been physical healing, He would have set up a clinic and systematically healed everyone. Instead, His miracles were for a sign, to let people know who and what He was (Jn 20:30–31).

7:11 *wise men ... sorcerers ... magicians.* The king's wise men were his counselors, men of learning and insight. In ancient times, the "wise men" of a court were often associated with occult practices. The power of these men may have been in trickery and slight-of-hand illusions, or demonic power. Later the royal courts of Israel had wise men (1Ki 4:34; Pr 25:1), but the black arts of sorcery, divination, and astrology were forbidden (Dt 18:9–14).

7:12 *his staff ... serpents.* The text does not say whether this was a genuine transformation or a trick of Pharaoh's evil sorcerers. Whatever the case, their serpents were no match for the serpent of God's sign.

7:15 *to the water ... the bank of the Nile.* Pharaoh went to the waters of the Nile not to bathe but to be empowered. Pharaoh's bath in the Nile was a sacred Egyptian rite connected to his claim of divinity. The plague on the waters of the Nile was a direct attack on the Egyptian religion.

10 ver. 9; Ex 4:3 **11** Ge 41:8; 2Ti 3:8; ver. 22; Ex 8:7,18 **14** Ex 8:15; 10:1,20,27 **15** ver. 10; Ex 4:2,3 **16** Ex 3:18; Ex 3:12,18; 5:1,3 **17** ver. 5; Ex 5:2; Ex 4:9; Rev 16:4,6 **18** ver. 24 **19** Ex 8:5,6,16; 9:22; 10:12,21; 14:21,26 **20** Ex 17:5; Ps 78:44; 105:29 **21** ver. 18 **22** ver. 11; ver. 3

23Then Pharaoh turned and went
into his house, and he did not take even
this [divine sign] to heart.
24So all the Egyptians dug near the
river for water to drink, because they
could not drink the water of the Nile.
25Seven days passed after the LORD
had struck the Nile.

Frogs over the Land

8 THEN THE LORD said to Moses,
"Go to Pharaoh and say to him,
'Thus says the LORD, "Let My people
go, so that they may serve Me.
2"However, if you refuse to let them
go, hear this: I am going to strike your
entire land with frogs.
3"The Nile will swarm with frogs,
which will come up and go into your
home, into your bedroom and on to
your bed, and into the houses of your
servants and on your people, and into
your ovens and your kneading bowls.
4"So the frogs will come up on you
and on your people and all your ser-
vants." ' "
5Then the LORD said to Moses, "Say
to Aaron, 'Stretch out your hand with
your staff over the rivers, over the
streams *and* canals, over the pools
[among the reeds], and make frogs
come up on the land of Egypt.' "
6So Aaron stretched out his hand
[with his staff] over the waters of
Egypt, and the frogs came up and
covered the land of Egypt.
7But the magicians (soothsayer-
priests) did the same thing with their
secret arts *and* enchantments, and
brought up [more] frogs on the land
of Egypt.
8Then Pharaoh called for Moses and
Aaron and said, "Plead with the LORD
that He may take away the frogs from
me and my people; and I will let the
people go, so that they may sacrifice
to the LORD."
9And Moses said to Pharaoh, "I am
entirely at your service: when shall I
plead [with the Lord] for you and your
servants and your people, so that the
frogs may leave you and your houses
and remain only in the Nile?"
10Then Pharaoh said, "Tomorrow."
Moses replied, "*May it be* as you say,
so that you may know [without any
doubt] *and* acknowledge that there is
no one like the LORD our God.
11"The frogs will leave you and your
houses and leave your servants and
your people; they will remain only in
the Nile."
12So Moses and Aaron left Pharaoh,
and Moses cried out to the LORD [as he
had agreed to do] concerning the frogs
which God had inflicted on Pharaoh.
13The LORD did as Moses asked, and
the frogs died out of the houses, out of
the courtyards *and* villages, and out
of the fields.
14So they piled them up in heaps,
and the land was detestable *and* stank.
15But when Pharaoh saw that there
was [temporary] relief, he hardened his
heart and would not listen *or* pay atten-
tion to them, just as the LORD had said.

7:23 turned and went into his house. Pharaoh showed his utter disdain for the revelation of God's power and his complete lack of concern for the suffering of his own people.

8:7 the magicians ... with their secret arts and enchantments. We do not know how or in what quantities the magicians produced frogs, but doing so hardly helped the situation. Clearly the power they had was not strong enough to counteract the plagues God sent.

8:8 called for Moses and Aaron. Note that Pharaoh did not turn to his magicians to relieve the land of the frogs.

8:15 Instability—The action of this Egyptian Pharaoh is a case study in instability. He gave permission for the people to go and then changed his mind more than once. He alternated between denying the power of God and actually admitting his sin. Pharaoh was a rebel against God, tossed about by his own lack of integrity. Believers can take warning from Pharaoh's behavior. The apostle James informs us that a double-minded man is unstable in all his ways (James 1:8). But stability isn't something we achieve by sheer willpower. Real integrity and stability comes from the security of our relationship with God.

CHAPTER 8 **1** Ex 3:12,18 **2** Ex 7:14; 9:2; Rev 16:13 **3** Ps 105:30 **5** Ex 7:19 **6** Ps 78:45; 105:30 **7** Ex 7:11 **8** Ex 9:28; 10:17 **10** Ex 9:14; Dt 33:26; 2Sa 7:22; 1Ch 17:20; Isa 46:9; Jer 10:6,7 **12** ver. 30; Ex 9:33; 10:18; 32:11; Jas 5:16-18 **15** Ecc 8:11; Ex 7:14

The Plagues of Gnats and Insects

16 Then the LORD said to Moses, “Say to Aaron, ‘Stretch out your staff and strike the dust of the ground, and it will become [biting] gnats (lice) throughout the land of Egypt.’ ”

17 They did so; Aaron stretched out his hand with his staff and struck the dust of the earth, and there were [biting] gnats on man and animal. All the dust of the land became gnats through all the land of Egypt.

18 The magicians (soothsayer-priests) tried by their secret arts *and* enchantments to create gnats, but they could not; and there were gnats on man and animal.

19 Then the magicians said to Pharaoh, “This is the [supernatural] finger of God.” But Pharaoh’s heart was hardened and he would not listen to them, just as the LORD had said.

20 Now the LORD said to Moses, “Get up early in the morning and stand before Pharaoh as he is coming out to the water [of the Nile], and say to him, ‘Thus says the LORD, “Let My people go, so that they may serve Me.

21 “For if you do not let My people go, hear this: I will send swarms of [bloodsucking] insects on you and on your servants and on your people and into your houses; and the houses of the Egyptians will be full of swarms of insects, as well as the ground on which they stand.

22 “But on that day I will separate *and* set apart the land of Goshen, where My people are living, so that no swarms of insects will be there, so that you may know [without any doubt] *and* acknowledge that I, the LORD, am in the midst of the earth.

23 “I will put a division (distinction) between My people and your people. By tomorrow this sign shall be in evidence.” ’ ”

24 Then the LORD did so. And there came heavy *and* oppressive swarms of [bloodsucking] insects into the house of Pharaoh and his servants’ houses; in all the land of Egypt the land was corrupted *and* ruined because of the [great invasion of] insects.

25 Then Pharaoh called for Moses and Aaron and said, “Go, sacrifice to your God [here] in the land [of Egypt].”

26 But Moses said, “It is not right [or even possible] to do that, for we will sacrifice to the LORD our God what is repulsive *and* unacceptable to the Egyptians [that is, animals that the Egyptians consider sacred]. If we sacrifice what is repulsive *and* unacceptable to the Egyptians, will they not riot *and* stone us?

27 “We must go a three days’ journey into the wilderness and sacrifice to the LORD our God as He commands us.”

28 So Pharaoh said, “I will let you go, so that you may sacrifice to the LORD your God in the wilderness; only you shall not go very far away. Plead [with your God] for me.”

29 Moses said, “I am going to leave you, and I will urgently petition (pray, entreat) the LORD that the swarms of insects may leave Pharaoh, his servants, and his people tomorrow; only do not let Pharaoh act deceitfully again by not letting the people go to sacrifice to the LORD.”

30 So Moses left Pharaoh and prayed to the LORD [on behalf of Pharaoh].

31 The LORD did as Moses asked, and removed the swarms of [bloodsucking] insects from Pharaoh, from his servants and from his people; not one remained.

8:18 *The magicians (soothsayer-priests) tried ... enchantments ... but they could not.* Perhaps the lack of announcement meant they had no time to prepare. The magicians could not duplicate God’s work; further proof that this was no trick, but the hand of God.

8:26 *repulsive and unacceptable to the Egyptians.* Moses employed the ethnic and cultural sensibilities of the Egyptians to free the Israelites (Ge 43:32; 46:34). The sacrificial animals of Israel would include sheep, something the Egyptians regarded as detestable.

17 Ps 105:31 **18** Ex 7:11; Da 5:8; 2Ti 3:8,9 **19** 1Sa 6:3,9; Ps 8:3; Mt 12:28; Lk 11:20; ver. 15 **20** Ex 7:15; ver. 1 **22** Ex 9:4,6,26; 10:23; 11:6,7; 12:13 **24** Ps 78:45; 105:31 **26** Ge 43:32; 46:34; Dt 7:25,26; 12:31 **27** Ex 3:18; Ex 3:12 **28** ver. 8; Ex 9:28; 1Ki 13:6 **29** ver. 15 **30** ver. 12

32 But Pharaoh hardened his heart this time also, and he did not let the people go.

Egyptian Cattle Die

9 THEN THE LORD said to Moses, "Go to Pharaoh and tell him, 'Thus says the LORD, the God of the Hebrews: "Let My people go, so that they may serve Me.

2 "But if you refuse to let them go and continue to hold them,

3 now hear this: the hand of the LORD will fall on your livestock which are out in the field, on the horses, the donkeys, the camels, the herds, and the flocks—a horrible plague shall come.

4 "But the LORD will make a distinction between the livestock of Israel and the livestock of Egypt, so that nothing that belongs to the Israelites will die." ' "

5 The LORD set a [definite] time, saying, "Tomorrow the LORD will do this thing in the land."

6 And the LORD did this thing the next day, and all [kinds of] the livestock of Egypt died; but of the livestock of the Israelites, not one died.

7 Then Pharaoh sent [men to investigate], and not even one of the livestock of the Israelites had died. But the heart of Pharaoh was hardened [and his mind was firmly set], and he did not let the people go.

The Plague of Boils

8 Then the LORD said to Moses and Aaron, "Take handfuls of soot from the brick kiln, and let Moses throw it toward the sky in the sight of Pharaoh.

9 "It will become fine dust over the entire land of Egypt, and it will become boils breaking out in sores on man and animal in all the land [occupied by the Egyptians]."

10 So they took soot from the kiln, and stood before Pharaoh; and Moses threw it toward the sky, and it became boils erupting in sores on man and animal.

11 The magicians (soothsayer-priests) could not stand before Moses because of the boils, for the boils were on the magicians as well as on all the Egyptians.

12 But the LORD hardened the heart of Pharaoh, and he did not listen *or* pay attention to them, just as the LORD had told Moses.

13 Then the LORD said to Moses, "Get up early in the morning and stand before Pharaoh and say to him, 'Thus says the LORD, the God of the Hebrews, "Let My people go, so that they may serve Me.

14 "For this time I will send all My plagues on you [in full force,] and on your servants and on your people, so that you may know [without any doubt] *and* acknowledge that there is no one like Me in all the earth.

15 "For by now I could have put out My hand and struck you and your people with a pestilence, and you would then have been cut off (obliterated) from the earth.

16 "But indeed for this very reason I have allowed you to live, in order to show you My power and in order that My name may be proclaimed throughout all the earth. [Rom 9:17–24]

The Plague of Hail

17 "Since you are still [arrogantly] exalting yourself [in defiance] against My people by not letting them go,

---

9:11 *for the boils were on the magicians.* The reference to the hapless magicians is almost humorous. Not only were they powerless, but they also suffered from the plague.

9:16 *for this very reason I have allowed you to live.* God used Pharaoh's stubbornness and disobedience to demonstrate His power. Pharaoh was not only an evil ruler in a powerful state; he was an evil man, ungodly, and unrighteous. Pharaoh set himself up as a god who maintained the stability of his kingdom. The Lord's judgment on him was an appropriate response to this fraud.

9:17 *exalting yourself.* Pharaoh was behaving like the king of Tyrus (Eze 28:1 – 10) and Satan, whom the king of Tyrus emulated (Eze 28:11 – 19).

32 ver. 15; Ex 4:21 **CHAPTER 9** **1** Ex 8:1 **2** Ex 8:2 **3** Ex 7:4 **4** Ex 8:22 **6** Ps 78:50 **7** Ex 7:14; 8:32 **9** Rev 16:2 **10** Dt 28:27 **11** Ex 8:18,19; 2Ti 3:9 **12** Ex 4:21 **13** Ex 8:20 **14** Ex 8:10 **15** Ex 3:20 **16** See Ex 14:17; Pr 16:4; Ro 9:17; 1Pe 2:9

18 hear this: tomorrow about this time
I will send a very heavy *and* dreadful
hail, such as has not been seen in Egypt
from the day it was founded until now.
19 "Now therefore send [a message],
bring your livestock and whatever you
have in the field to safety. Every man
and animal that is in the field and is
not brought home shall be struck by
the hail and shall die." ' "
20 Then everyone among the servants
of Pharaoh who feared the word of the
LORD made his servants and his live-
stock flee into the houses *and* shelters;
21 but everyone who ignored *and* did
not take seriously the word of the LORD
left his servants and his livestock in
the field.
22 Now the LORD said to Moses,
"Stretch out your hand [with your staff]
toward the sky, so that there may be
hail in all the land of Egypt, on man and
on animal and on all the vegetation of
the field, throughout the land of Egypt."
23 Moses stretched out his staff to-
ward the sky, and the LORD sent thun-
der and hail, and lightning (fireballs)
ran down to the earth *and* along the
ground. And the LORD rained hail on
the land of Egypt.
24 So there was hail, and lightning
(fireballs) flashing intermittently in
the midst of the extremely heavy hail,
such as had not been in all the land of
Egypt since it became a nation.
25 The hail struck down everything
that was in the field throughout all the
land of Egypt, both man and animal;
the hail struck *and* beat down all the
plants in the field and shattered every
tree in the field.
26 Only in the land of Goshen, where
the children of Israel lived, was there
no hail.
27 Then Pharaoh sent for Moses and
Aaron, and said to them, "I have sinned
this time; the LORD is righteous, and I
and my people are wicked.
28 "Pray *and* entreat the LORD, for
there has been enough of God's thun-
der and hail; I will let you go, and you
shall stay here no longer."
29 Moses said to him, "As soon as
I leave the city, I will stretch out my
hands to the LORD; the thunder will
cease and there will be no more hail,
so that you may know [without any
doubt] *and* acknowledge that the earth
is the LORD's.
30 "But as for you and your servants,
I know that you do not yet fear the
LORD God."
31 (Now the flax and the barley were
battered *and* ruined [by the hail], be-
cause the barley was in the ear (ripe,
but soft) and the flax was in bud,
32 but the wheat and spelt (coarse
wheat) were not battered *and* ruined,
because they *ripen* late in the season.)
33 So Moses left the city and Phar-
aoh, and stretched out his hands to
the LORD; then the thunder and hail
ceased, and rain no longer poured on
the earth.
34 But when Pharaoh saw that the
rain and the hail and the thunder had
ceased, he sinned again and hardened
his heart, both he and his servants.
35 Pharaoh's heart was hardened,
and he did not let the Israelites go, just
as the LORD had said through Moses.
[Ex 4:21]

The Plague of Locusts

10 THEN THE LORD said to Mo-
ses, "Go to Pharaoh, for I have
hardened his heart and the heart of

9:19 ***bring your livestock.*** The fact that God was judging Pharaoh does not mean that He was unmerciful. The Lord could have destroyed Pharaoh and his people in a moment (v. 15), but instead He warned them of the calamities about to befall them. Apparently some of the Egyptians took the word of the Lord seriously.

9:27 ***I have sinned.*** This was a stunning admission for such a proud man. Sadly, these words of contrition would not hold. Pharaoh repeated them later (10:16–17), only to take them back in the end.

10:1 ***I have hardened his heart.*** Three verbs are used in Exodus to describe God's hardening

22 Rev 16:21 **23** Jos 10:11; Ps 18:13; 78:47; 105:32; 148:8; Isa 30:30; Eze 38:22; Rev 8:7 **25** Ps 105:33 **26** Ex 8:22; 9:4,6; 10:23; 11:7; 12:13; Isa 32:18,19 **27** Ex 10:16; 2Ch 12:6; La 1:18 **28** Ex 8:8,28; 10:17; Ac 8:24 **29** 1Ki 8:22,38; Ps 143:6; Isa 1:15; Ps 24:1; 1Co 10:26,28 **30** Isa 26:10 **31** Ru 1:22; 2:23 **33** ver. 29; Ex 8:12 **35** Ex 4:21
CHAPTER 10 **1** Ex 4:21; 7:14; Ex 7:4

his servants [making them determined
and unresponsive], so that I may exhib-
it My signs [of divine power] among
them,
2 and that you may recount *and* ex-
plain in the hearing of your son, and
your grandson, what I have done [re-
peatedly] to make a mockery of the
Egyptians—My signs [of divine pow-
er] which I have done among them—
so that you may know [without any
doubt] *and* recognize [clearly] that I
am the LORD."
3 So Moses and Aaron went to Phar-
aoh and said to him, "Thus says the
LORD, the God of the Hebrews: 'How
long will you refuse to humble yourself
before Me? Let My people go, so that
they may serve Me.
4 'For if you refuse to let My people
go, then hear this: tomorrow I will
bring [migratory] locusts into your
country.
5 'They shall cover the [visible] sur-
face of the land, so that no one will be
able to see the ground, and they will
eat the rest of what has remained—
that is, the *vegetation* left after the
hail—and they will eat every one of
your trees that grows in the field;
6 your houses and those of all your
servants and of all the Egyptians shall
be filled *with locusts*, as neither your
fathers nor your grandfathers have
seen, from their birth until this day.' "
Then Moses turned and left Pharaoh.
7 Pharaoh's servants said to him,
"How long shall this man be a trap to
us? Let the men go, so that they may
serve the LORD their God. Do you not
realize that Egypt is destroyed?"
8 So Moses and Aaron were brought
back to Pharaoh, and he said to them,
"Go, serve the LORD your God! Who
specifically are the ones that are go-
ing?"
9 Moses said, "We will go with our
young and our old, with our sons and
our daughters, with our flocks and our
herds [all of us and all that we have],
for we must hold a feast to the LORD."
10 Pharaoh said to them, "The LORD
be with you [to help you], if I ever let
you go with your children [because
you will never return]! Look [be fore-
warned], you have an evil plan in mind.
11 "No! Go now, you who are men,
[without your families] and serve the
LORD, if that is what you want." So
Moses and Aaron were driven from
Pharaoh's presence.
12 Then the LORD said to Moses,
"Stretch out your hand over the land
of Egypt for the locusts, so that they
may come up on the land of Egypt and
eat all the plants of the land, all that
the hail has left."
13 So Moses stretched out his staff
over the land of Egypt, and the LORD
brought an east wind on the land all
that day and all that night; when it was
morning, the east wind had brought
the [swarms of] locusts.
14 The locusts came up over all the
land of Egypt and settled down in the
whole territory, a very dreadful mass
of them; never before were there such
locusts as these, nor will there ever
be again.
15 For they covered the [visible] sur-
face of the land, so that the ground was
darkened; and they ate every plant of

---

of Pharaoh's heart. Usually the verb meaning "to make hard" is used (4:21). In 7:3 the verb "to make stiff" is used. Here the Hebrew verb that means "to make heavy" or "to make insensitive" is used.

10:3 *refuse to humble yourself.* Pharaoh's pride was his undoing. He believed himself to be a god and paraded himself like one. God resists the proud but gives grace to the humble (Ps 18:27; 1Pe 5:5).

10:12 – 16 Repentance — In Exodus 9 and 10 there are two vivid examples of "foxhole religion" recorded for us. This kind of "faith" freely acknowledges the person and power of God during a terrible crisis, and then promptly forgets all about Him when the danger passes. Just like little children, we want to avert punishment by saying, "I'm sorry, I'm sorry!" and then go about our business as usual. God is not interested in empty "I've sinned" confessions. Only true repentance from the heart is acceptable to God.

2 Dt 4:9; Ps 44:1; 71:18; 78:5; Joel 1:3 **3** 1Ki 21:29; Job 42:6; Jas 4:10 **4** Pr 30:27; Rev 9:3 **5** Ex 9:32; Joel 1:4; 2:25 **7** Ex 23:33; Jos 23:13; 1Sa 18:21; Ecc 7:26; 1Co 7:35 **9** Ex 5:1 **12** Ex 7:19; ver. 4,5 **14** Ps 78:46; 105:34; Joel 2:2 **15** ver. 5; Ps 105:35

the land and all the fruit of the trees
which the hail had left. There remained
not a green thing on the trees or the
plants of the field throughout all the
land of Egypt.
16Then Pharaoh hurried to call for
Moses and Aaron, and he said, "I have
sinned against the LORD your God and
against you.
17"Now therefore, please forgive my
sin only this once [more], and pray
and entreat the LORD your God, so that
He will remove this [plague of] death
from me."
18Moses left Pharaoh and entreated
the LORD.
19So the LORD shifted *the wind* to a
violent west wind which lifted up the
locusts and drove them into the Red
Sea; not one locust remained within
the border of Egypt.
20But the LORD hardened Pharaoh's
heart [so that it was even more resolved and obstinate], and he did not
let the Israelites go.

Darkness over the Land

21Then the LORD said to Moses,
"Stretch out your hand toward the sky,
so that darkness may come over the
land of Egypt, a darkness which [is so
awful that it] may be felt."
22So Moses stretched out his hand
toward the sky, and for three days a
thick darkness was all over the land
of Egypt [no sun, no moon, no stars].
23The Egyptians could not see one
another, nor did anyone leave his place
for three days, but all the Israelites had
[supernatural] light in their dwellings.
24Then Pharaoh called to Moses,
and said, "Go, serve the LORD; only
your flocks and your herds must be
left behind. Even your children may
go with you."
25But Moses said, "You must also let
us have sacrifices and burnt offerings,
so that we may sacrifice them to the
LORD our God.
26"Therefore, our livestock must also
go with us; not one hoof shall be left
behind, for we must take some of them
to serve the LORD our God. Even we do
not know with what we will serve the
LORD until we arrive there."
27But the LORD hardened Pharaoh's
heart, and he was not willing to let
them go.
28Then Pharaoh said to Moses, "Get
away from me! See that you never enter my presence again, for on the day
that you see my face again you will
die!"
29Then Moses said, "You are correct;
I will never see your face again!"

The Last Plague

11 THEN THE LORD said to Moses,
"I will bring yet one more plague
on Pharaoh and on Egypt; after that he
will let you go. When he lets you go,
he will most certainly drive you out of
here completely.
2"Speak so that all of the people [of
Israel] may hear, and tell every man to
ask from his neighbor, and every woman to ask from her neighbor, articles
of silver, and articles of gold."
3The LORD gave the people favor in
the sight of the Egyptians. Moreover,
the man Moses was greatly esteemed
in the land of Egypt, [both] in the sight
of Pharaoh's servants and in the sight
of the people.

10:20 *But the LORD hardened Pharaoh's heart.* See 3:19; 4:21; 5:2; 7:3,13 – 14.
10:22 *thick darkness.* This calamity was another direct attack on the Egyptian religious system. They worshiped many gods, but none so much as the sun. An enshrouding darkness that lasted three days was a clear statement that their gods, their Pharaoh with his supposed control of nature, and all Pharaoh's counselors were, in reality, helpless before the God of Israel.
10:27 *But the LORD hardened Pharaoh's heart.* See 3:19; 4:21; 5:2; 7:3,13 – 14.
11:3 *favor.* After all that had happened, we might suppose that the Egyptians would have universally hated the Hebrews. Instead, most of the people felt positively towards them, even Pharaoh's own servants.

16 Ex 9:27 **17** Ex 9:28; 1Ki 13:6 **18** Ex 8:30 **19** Joel 2:20 **20** Ex 4:21; 11:10 **21** Ex 9:22 **22** Ps 105:28 **23** Ex 8:22 **24** ver. 8; ver. 10 **27** ver. 20; Ex 4:21; 14:4,8 **29** Heb 11:27 **CHAPTER 11** **1** Ex 12:31,33,39 **2** Ex 3:22; 12:35 **3** Ex 3:21; 12:36; Ps 106:46; 2Sa 7:9; Est 9:4

4 Then Moses said, “Thus says the
LORD: ‘At midnight I am going out into
the midst of Egypt,
5 and all the firstborn in the land [the
pride, hope, and joy] of Egypt shall die,
from the firstborn of Pharaoh who sits
on his throne, to the firstborn of the
slave girl who is behind the hand-mill,
and all the firstborn of cattle as well.
6 ‘There shall be a great cry [of heart-
ache and sorrow] throughout the land
of Egypt, such as has never been be-
fore and such as shall never be again.
7 ‘But not even a dog will threaten
any of the Israelites, whether man or
animal, so that you may know [with-
out any doubt] *and* acknowledge how
the LORD makes a distinction between
Egypt and Israel.’
8 “All these servants of yours will
come down to me and bow down be-
fore me, saying, ‘Get out, you and all
the people who follow you.’ After that I
will leave.” And he left Pharaoh in the
heat of anger.
9 Then the LORD said to Moses, “Phar-
aoh will not listen to you, so that My
wonders (miracles) may be multiplied
in the land of Egypt.”
10 Moses and Aaron did all these
wonders (miracles) before Pharaoh; yet
the LORD hardened Pharaoh’s heart,
and he did not let the Israelites go out
of his land.

The Passover Lamb

12 THE LORD said to Moses and
Aaron in the land of Egypt,
2 “This month shall be the beginning
of months to you; it is to be the first
month of the year to you.
3 “Tell all the congregation of Israel,
‘On the tenth [day] of this month they
are to take a lamb *or* young goat for
themselves, according to [the size of]
the household of which he is the fa-
ther, a lamb *or* young goat for each
household.
4 ‘Now if the household is too small
for a lamb [to be consumed], let him
and his next door neighbor take one
according to the number of people [in
the households]; according to what
each man can eat, you are to divide
the lamb.
5 ‘Your lamb *or* young goat shall be
[perfect] without blemish *or* bodily
defect, a male a year old; you may take
it from the sheep or from the goats.
[1 Pet 1:19, 20]

11:7 *a distinction between Egypt and Israel.* The institution of the Passover accentuated this great distinction. The Lord in His mercy protected His people even as He executed judgment on those who opposed Him.

11:9 – 10 *wonders*. We tend to think that if God would only send a miracle, people would have to believe. Sadly, history shows that this is not true. Often those individuals who have seen God’s mightiest miracles have responded by displaying a total lack of faith. Pharaoh had all the proof one could want of who God was, and did not believe. The Pharisees saw a man raised from the dead, and wanted to kill both the man and his healer (Jn 11:53; 12:9 – 11). God desires us to believe His word by faith, and not be dependent on supernatural and external signs and wonders. Miracles are signs, just as the creation itself is a sign of God’s power and authority (Ro 1:19 – 20), but a person whose heart is hardened toward God will not be any more impressed with a miracle than with a sunset.

12:1 – 14 The Passover — There was only one Passover. The Passover feast has always been one of the primary elements of Jewish religious tradition and is their way of remembering the “pass over” by the Lord, sparing the people of a visit by “the destroyer” (v. 23). By celebrating it, Jews remember one of the key elements of their history. It points to their national identity and to their deliverance as a community of faith. One could say that it was a defining moment of their faith. For the Christian, the event clearly foreshadows the cross of Christ. He is our Passover Lamb who delivers us from death by taking it all on Himself. The parallels between Exodus 12 and the Christian Communion service are noteworthy (1Co 11:23 – 26).

12:2 *the beginning of months to you.* This month, called Abib in 13:4, corresponds to April/May and is also called Nisan. The Hebrew people began to mark time in relation to the time of their departure from Egypt.

12:5 *without blemish.* Sacrifice was not a way to get rid of unwanted animals. Only the very best lambs were suitable. The Passover lamb sacrificed

---

4 Ex 12:12,23,29 **5** Ex 12:12,29; Am 4:10 **6** Ex 12:30; Am 5:17 **7** Ex 8:22; Jos 10:21 **8** Ex 12:33 **9** Ex 3:19; 7:4; 10:1; Ex 7:3 **10** Ex 10:20,27; Ro 2:5; 9:22 **CHAPTER 12** **2** Ex 13:4; Dt 16:1 **5** Lev 22:19-21; Mal 1:8,14; Heb 9:14

[6]'You shall keep it until the four-
teenth day of the same month, then the
whole assembly of the congregation of
Israel is to slaughter it at twilight.
[7]'Moreover, they shall take some
of the blood and put it on the two
doorposts and on the lintel [above the
door] of the houses in which they eat it.
[Matt 26:28; John 1:29; Heb 9:14]
[8]'They shall eat the meat that same
night, roasted in fire, and they shall
eat it with unleavened bread and bitter
herbs.
[9]'Do not eat any of it raw or boiled in
water, but roasted in fire—both its head
and its legs, along with its inner parts.
[10]'You shall let none of the meat re-
main until the morning, and anything

---

for the Israelites was meant as a picture of the coming death of the perfect, sinless Savior, Jesus Christ. **12:8 *unleavened bread and bitter herbs.*** The Passover meal is full of symbolism, the unleavened bread reminded them that the first Passover was eaten in haste, ready for flight. The bitter herbs were a reminder of the bitterness of the slavery from which they were rescued.

6 Lev 23:5; Nu 9:3; Dt 16:1,6 **8** Ex 34:25; Dt 16:3; 1Co 5:8 **9** Dt 16:7 **10** Ex 23:18; 34:25

HEBREW CALENDAR AND SELECTED EVENTS

NUMBER OF MONTH		HEBREW NAME	MODERN EQUIVALENT	BIBLICAL REFERENCES	AGRICULTURE	FESTIVALS**
1 Sacred sequence begins	7	**Aviv; Nisan**	March–April	Ex 12:2; 13:4; 23:15; 34:18; Dt 16:1; Ne 2:1; Est 3:7	Spring (latter) rains; barley and flax harvest begins	Passover; Unleavened Bread; Firstfruits
2	8	**Ziv (Iyyar)***	April–May	1Ki 6:1,37	Barley harvest; dry season begins	
3	9	**Sivan**	May–June	Est 8:9	Wheat harvest	Pentecost (Weeks)
4	10	**(Tammuz)***	June–July		Tending vines	
5	11	**(Av)***	July–August		Ripening of grapes, figs and olives	
6	12	**Elul**	August–September	Ne 6:15	Processing grapes, figs and olives	
7	1 Civil sequence	**Ethanim (Tishri)***	September–October	1Ki 8:2	Autumn (early) rains begin; plowing	Trumpets; Day of Atonement; Tabernacles (Booths)
8	2	**Bul (Marcheshvan)***	October–November	1Ki 6:38	Sowing of wheat and barley	
9	3	**Kislev**	November–December	Ne 1:1; Zec 7:1	Winter rains begin (snow in some areas)	Hanukkah ("Dedication")
10	4	**Tebeth**	December–January	Est 2:16		
11	5	**Shebat**	January–February	Zec 1:7		
12	6	**Adar**	February–March	Ezr 6:15; Est 3:7,13; 8:12; 9:1,15,17,19,21	Almond trees bloom; citrus fruit harvest	Purim
		(Adar Sheni)*— Second Adar	This intercalary month was added about every three years so the lunar calendar would correspond to the solar year.			

*Names of months in parentheses are not in the Bible.

that remains left over until morning, you shall burn completely in the fire.

11 'Now you are to eat it in this manner: [be prepared for a journey] with your loins girded [that is, with the outer garment tucked into the band], your sandals on your feet, and your staff in your hand; you shall eat it quickly—it is the LORD's Passover.

12 'For I [the LORD] will pass through the land of Egypt on this night, and will strike down all the firstborn in the land of Egypt, both man and animal; against all the gods of Egypt I will execute judgments [exhibiting their worthlessness]. I am the LORD.

13 'The blood shall be a sign for you on [the doorposts of] the houses where you live; when I see the blood I shall pass over you, and no affliction shall happen to you to destroy you when I strike the land of Egypt. [1 Cor 5:7; Heb 11:28]

Feast of Unleavened Bread

14 "Now this day will be a memorial to you, and you shall keep it as a feast to the LORD; throughout your generations you are to celebrate it as an ordinance forever.

15 '[In the celebration of the Passover in future years,] seven days you shall eat unleavened bread, but on the first day you shall remove the leaven from your houses [because it represents the spread of sin]; for whoever eats leavened bread on the first day through the seventh day, that person shall be cut off *and* excluded from [the atonement made for] Israel.

16 'On the first day [of the feast] you shall have a holy *and* solemn assembly, and on the seventh day there shall be another holy *and* solemn assembly; no work of any kind shall be done on those days, except for the preparation of food which every person must eat—only that may be done by you.

17 'You shall also observe the Feast of Unleavened Bread, because on this very day I brought your hosts [grouped according to tribal armies] out of the land of Egypt; therefore you shall observe this day throughout your generations as an ordinance forever.

18 'In the first *month,* on the fourteenth day of the month at evening, you shall eat unleavened bread, [and continue] until the twenty-first day of the month at evening.

19 'Seven days no leaven shall be found in your houses; whoever eats what is leavened shall be cut off *and* excluded from [the atonement made for] the congregation of Israel, whether a stranger or native-born. [1 Cor 5:6–8]

20 'You shall eat nothing leavened; in all your dwellings you shall eat unleavened bread.' "

21 Then Moses called for all the elders of Israel and said to them, "Go and take a lamb for yourselves according to [the size of] your families and slaughter the Passover *lamb.*

22 "You shall take a bunch of hyssop, dip it in the blood which is in the basin, and touch some of the blood to the lintel [above the doorway] and to the two doorposts; and none of you shall go outside the door of his house until morning.

A Memorial of Redemption

23 "For the LORD will pass through to strike the Egyptians; and when He sees the blood on the lintel [above the entry way] and on the two doorposts, the LORD will pass over the door and will not allow the destroyer to come into your houses to slay you.

24 "You shall observe this event [concerning Passover] as an ordinance for you and for your children forever.

12:12 *I [the LORD] will pass through . . . will strike down.* The repetition of the pronoun *I* emphasizes that God did this, not an angel or some other agent.

12:13 *sign.* The term "sign" can mean a reminder, memorial, or symbol, as it does here, or a miracle that points to the power of God.

11 Dt 16:5 **12** Ex 11:4,5; Am 5:17; Nu 33:4; Ex 6:2 **14** Ex 13:9; Lev 23:4,5; 2Ki 23:21; ver. 24,43; Ex 13:10 **15** Ex 13:6,7; 23:15; Lev 23:5,6; Dt 16:3,8; 1Co 5:7; Ge 17:14; Nu 9:13 **16** Lev 23:7,8; Nu 28:18,25 **17** Ex 13:3 **18** Lev 23:5; Nu 28:16 **19** Ex 23:15; 34:18 **21** ver. 3; Nu 9:4; Jos 5:10; 2Ki 23:21; Ezr 6:20; Mk 14:12-16 **22** Heb 11:28; ver. 7 **23** ver. 12,13; Eze 9:6; Rev 7:3; 2Sa 24:16; 1Co 10:10; Heb 11:28

25 "When you enter the land which the
LORD will give you, as He has promised,
you shall keep *and* observe this service.
26 "When your children say to you,
'What does this service mean to you?'
27 you shall say, 'It is the sacrifice of the
LORD's Passover, for He passed over the
houses of the Israelites in Egypt when
He struck the Egyptians, but spared our
houses.' " And the people bowed [their
heads] low and worshiped [God].
28 Then the Israelites went and did
[as they had been told]: just as the LORD
had commanded Moses and Aaron, so
they did.
29 Now it happened at midnight that
the LORD struck every firstborn in the
land of Egypt, from the firstborn of
Pharaoh who sat on his throne to the
firstborn of the prisoner who was in
the dungeon, and all the firstborn of
the cattle.
30 Pharaoh got up in the night, he and
all his servants and all the Egyptians,
and there was a great cry [of heartache
and sorrow] in Egypt, for there was no
house where there was not someone
dead.
31 Then he called for Moses and Aar-
on at night and said, "Get up, get out
from among my people, both you and
the Israelites; and go, serve the LORD,
as you said.
32 "Take both your flocks and your
herds, as you have said, and go, and
[ask your God to] bless me also."

Exodus of Israel

33 The Egyptians [anxiously] urged
the people [to leave], to send them out
of the land quickly, for they said, "We
will all be dead."
34 So the people took their dough be-
fore it was leavened, their kneading
bowls being bound up in their clothes
on their shoulders.
35 Now the Israelites had acted in
accordance with the word of Moses;
and they had asked the Egyptians for
articles of silver and articles of gold,
and clothing.
36 The LORD gave the people favor
in the sight of the Egyptians, so that
they gave them what they asked. And
so they plundered the Egyptians [of
those things].
37 Now the Israelites journeyed from
Rameses to Succoth, about six hun-
dred thousand men on foot, besides
[the women and] the children.
38 A mixed multitude [of non-
Israelites from foreign nations] also
went with them, along with both flocks
and herds, a very large number of live-
stock. [Num 11:4; Deut 29:11]
39 And they baked unleavened cakes

12:29–33 *the LORD struck every firstborn.* In the Passover we have a summary of God's eternal plan of salvation. Jesus, the final sacrifice, was killed at the time of the Passover feast; His blood provides salvation from eternal death. Note some similarities between the first and final Passover: (1) the blood of an innocent sacrifice must be shed, (2) the sacrifice must be blameless, and (3) the shed blood must be applied by faith.

12:29 *and all the firstborn of the cattle.* Though not nearly as awful as the death of firstborn children, the death of the livestock was a blow to the Egyptians economically. These deaths were also attacks on the power of their gods (v. 12).

12:32 *and [ask your God to] bless me also.* At last Pharaoh capitulated (10:9,26). The death of his son—and the deaths of firstborn sons everywhere—must have shattered him to the core of his being.

12:36 *plundered the Egyptians.* Newly freed slaves do not usually make their escape with their masters pushing the family silver into their hands. Far from wanting to keep the Israelites in bondage, the rest of Egypt couldn't wait to get rid of them.

12:37 *Rameses.* The reference to Rameses most likely relates to the store city Raamses, mentioned in 1:11, perhaps Tel el-Maskhuta further to the east. ***six hundred thousand men.*** This number of men would indicate a total population of perhaps three million men, women, and children (Nu 1:46).

12:38 *mixed multitude.* Apparently a number of Egyptians and perhaps other non-Hebrews joined the flight out of Egypt. Some of these people later caused trouble when things did not go as smoothly as expected (Nu 11:4).

12:39 *unleavened cakes.* The symbolism in this has to do with the haste of their departure, not (as some have supposed) that there is something

25 Ex 3:8,17 **26** Ex 13:8,14; Dt 32:7; Jos 4:6 **27** ver. 11; Ex 4:31 **28** Heb 11:28 **29** Ex 11:4; Nu 8:17; 33:4; Ps 78:51; 105:36; Ex 4:23; 11:5 **30** Ex 11:6; Pr 21:13; Am 5:17 **31** Ex 11:1; Ps 105:38; Ex 10:9 **32** Ex 10:26; Ge 27:34 **33** Ex 11:8; Ps 105:38; Ge 20:3 **35** Ex 3:22 **36** Ex 3:21; Ge 15:14; Ex 3:22; Ps 105:37 **37** Nu 33:3,5; Ge 47:11; Ge 12:2; Nu 11:21 **39** ver. 33; Ex 6:1

of the dough which they brought from Egypt; it was not leavened, since they were driven [quickly] from Egypt and could not delay, nor had they prepared any food for themselves.

40 Now the period of time the children of Israel lived in Egypt was four hundred and thirty years. [Gen 15:13, 14]

41 At the end of the four hundred and thirty years, to that very day, all the hosts of the Lord [gathered into tribal armies] left the land of Egypt.

Ordinance of the Passover

42 It is a night of watching to be observed for the Lord for having brought them out of the land of Egypt; this [same] night is for the Lord, to be observed *and* celebrated by all the Israelites throughout their generations.

43 The Lord said to Moses and Aaron, "This is the ordinance of the Passover: no foreigner is to eat it;

44 but every man's slave who is bought with money, after you have circumcised him, then he may eat it.

45 "No stranger (temporary resident, foreigner) or hired servant shall eat it.

46 "It is to be eaten inside one house; you shall not take any of the meat outside the house, nor shall you break any of its bones. [John 19:33, 36]

47 "The entire congregation of Israel shall keep *and* celebrate it.

48 "If a stranger living temporarily among you wishes to celebrate the Passover to the Lord, all his males must be circumcised, and then he may participate *and* celebrate it like one that is born in the land. But no uncircumcised person may eat it.

49 "The same law shall apply to the native-born and to the stranger who lives temporarily among you."

50 Then all the Israelites did so; they did just as the Lord had commanded Moses and Aaron.

51 And on that very same day the Lord brought the Israelites out of the land of Egypt by their hosts (tribal armies).

Consecration of the Firstborn

13 THE LORD spoke to Moses, saying,

2 "Sanctify to Me [that is, set apart for My purpose] every firstborn, the first offspring of every womb among the children of Israel, both of man and of animal; it is Mine."

3 Moses said to the people, "Remember [solemnly observe and commemorate] this day on which you came out of Egypt, out of the house of bondage *and* slavery; for by a strong *and* powerful hand the Lord brought you out of this place. And nothing leavened shall be eaten.

4 "On this day in the month Abib, you are about to go onward.

5 "And it shall be when the Lord brings you into the land of the Canaanite, the Hittite, the Amorite, the Hivite, and the Jebusite, which He swore to your fathers to give you, a land [of abundance] flowing with milk and honey, that you shall keep *and* observe this rite (service) in this month.

---

evil in leaven itself. If leaven were intrinsically evil, the Israelites would have been forbidden to eat leaven at any time. In the New Testament, leaven is often used as a symbolic way of speaking about sin, but again, leaven in and of itself is not evil.

12:40 *four hundred and thirty years.* If the exodus took place around 1446 BC, Jacob's arrival in Egypt would have been around 1876 BC.

12:46 *nor shall you break any of its bones.* Not breaking the bones of the lamb foreshadowed Jesus' death. None of the Savior's bones were broken, even though He suffered a horrible death (Ps 34:20; Jn 19:33–36).

13:1–22 *Sanctify to Me.* Before the dramatic story of the crossing of the Red Sea there is a record of foundational institutions that the Lord gave to Israel. These are: (1) the consecration of the firstborn (vv. 1–2); (2) the Feast of Unleavened Bread (vv. 3–10); and (3) the law concerning the firstborn (vv. 11–16). This is followed by the Lord's command to the Israelites to travel in an unexpected direction (vv. 17–22).

40 Ge 15:13; Ac 7:6; Gal 3:17 **41** Ex 7:4 **42** See Dt 16:6 **43** Nu 9:14 **44** Ge 17:12,13 **45** Lev 22:10 **46** Nu 9:12; Jn 19:33,36 **47** ver. 6; Nu 9:13 **48** Nu 9:14 **49** Nu 9:14; 15:15,16; Gal 3:28 **51** ver. 41; Ex 6:26 **CHAPTER 13** **2** ver. 12,13,15; Ex 22:29,30; Nu 3:13; Dt 15:19; Lk 2:23 **3** Ex 12:42; Dt 16:3; Ex 6:1; Ex 12:8 **4** Ex 23:15; 34:18; Dt 16:1 **5** Ex 3:8; Ex 6:8; Ex 12:25,26

6 “For seven days you shall eat un-
leavened bread, and on the seventh
day there shall be a feast to the LORD.
7 “Unleavened bread shall be eaten
throughout the seven days; no leav-
ened bread shall be seen with you,
nor shall there be leaven within the
borders of your territory.
8 “You shall explain this to your son
on that day, saying, ‘It is because of
what the LORD did for me when I came
out of Egypt.’
9 “It shall serve as a sign to you on
your hand (arm), and as a reminder
on your forehead, so that the instruc-
tion (law) of the LORD may be in your
mouth; for with a strong *and* power-
ful hand the LORD brought you out of
Egypt.
10 “Therefore, you shall keep this or-
dinance at this time from year to year.
11 “Now it shall be when the LORD
brings you into the land of the Ca-
naanite, as He swore to you and your
fathers, and gives it to you,
12 you shall set apart *and* dedicate to
the LORD all that first opens the womb.
All the firstborn males of your live-
stock shall be the LORD’s.
13 “Every firstborn of a donkey you
shall redeem by [substituting] a lamb
[as a sacrifice for it], but if you do not
[wish to] redeem it, then you shall
break its neck; and every firstborn
among your sons you shall redeem
[that is, “buy back” from God with a
suitable sacrifice].
14 “And it shall be when your son asks
you in time to come, saying, ‘What
does this mean?’ you shall say to him,
‘With a strong *and* powerful hand the
LORD brought us out of Egypt, from the
house of bondage *and* slavery.
15 ‘For it happened, when Pharaoh
stubbornly refused to let us go, that the
LORD struck every firstborn in the land
of Egypt, both the firstborn of man and
the firstborn of animal. Therefore, I
sacrifice to the LORD all the males, the
first [to be born] of every womb, but
every firstborn of my sons I redeem.’
16 “So it shall serve as a sign *and* a
reminder on your [left] hand (arm) and
as frontlets between your eyes, for by
a strong *and* powerful hand the LORD
brought us out of Egypt.”

God Leads the People

17 So it happened, when Pharaoh let
the people go, God did not lead them by
way of the land of the Philistines, even
though it was nearer; for God said,
“The people might change their minds
when they see war [that is, that there
will be war], and return to Egypt.”
18 But God led the people around by
the way of the wilderness toward the
Red Sea; the sons of Israel went up in
battle array (orderly ranks, marching
formation) out of the land of Egypt.
19 Moses took the bones of Joseph with
him, for Joseph had solemnly ordered
(placed under an oath) the Israelites,

13:9 *sign.* A similar commandment is found in Deuteronomy 6:8. Jews would fasten a small box containing passages of Scripture to their foreheads or arms during prayer, to serve as a memorial. The physical symbol was designed to be a reminder of the inner reality of making God’s law the guiding rule of all we do.
13:13 *firstborn of a donkey.* Donkeys were unclean animals, and could not be used as a sacrifice. Instead they were redeemed with a lamb. Similarly, a firstborn son was redeemed. God would never allow human sacrifice. Later the Lord claimed the Levites for Himself in exchange for the firstborn sons of the people (Nu 3:40 – 51).
13:18 *the way of the wilderness.* The route the Israelites traveled from Egypt to Canaan has been disputed. The traditional route has the people moving in a southerly direction along the western shore of the Sinai Peninsula until they reached Mount Sinai in the far south central region of the peninsula. ***Red Sea.*** This translation comes from the Septuagint (the Greek translation of the Old Testament); the Hebrew phrase means “Sea of Reeds.” This phrase may refer to the ancient northern extension of the Red Sea. Many believe that it was one of the marshy lakes of the region.
13:19 *the bones of Joseph.* The story of the last wish of Joseph and his death is found in Genesis 50:22 – 26.

6 Ex 12:15,16 **7** Ex 12:19 **8** ver. 14; Ex 12:26 **9** See ver. 16; Dt 6:8; Mt 23:5 **10** Ex 12:14,24 **12** ver. 2; Lev 27:26 **13** Ex 34:20; Nu 18:15; Nu 3:46,47; 18:15,16 **14** Ex 12:26; Dt 6:20; Jos 4:6,21; ver. 3 **15** Ex 12:29 **16** ver. 9 **17** Ex 14:11; Nu 14:1-4; Dt 17:16 **18** Ex 14:2; Nu 33:6 **19** Ge 50:25; Jos 24:32

THE EXODUS AND THE ROUTE OF THE WANDERINGS

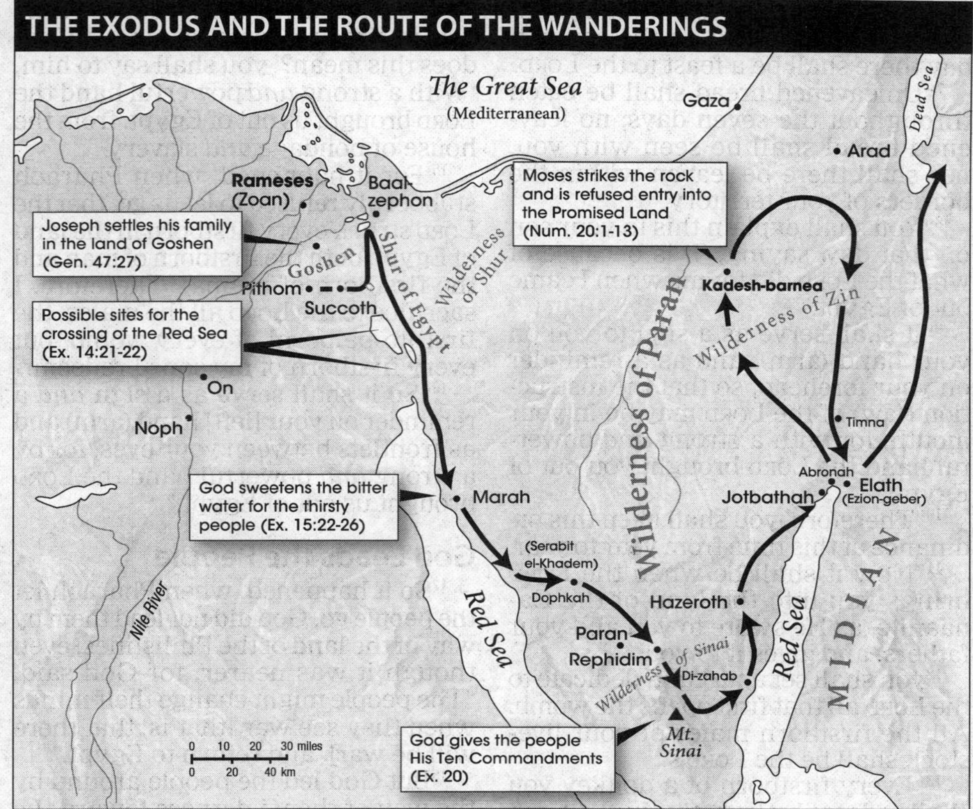

saying, "God will assuredly take care
of you, and you must carry my bones
away from here with you." [Gen 50:25]
20They journeyed from Succoth [in
Goshen] and camped at Etham on the
edge of the wilderness.
21The [presence of the] LORD was
going before them by day in a pillar
(column) of cloud to lead them along
the way, and in a pillar of fire by night
to give them light, so that they could
travel by day and by night.
22He did not withdraw the pillar of
cloud by day, nor the pillar of fire by
night, from going before the people.

Pharaoh in Pursuit

14 NOW THE LORD spoke to Moses,
saying,
2"Tell the sons of Israel to turn back
*and camp in front of Pi-*hahiroth, be-
tween Migdol and the sea. You shall
camp in front of Baal-zephon, opposite
it, by the sea.
3"For Pharaoh will say of the Isra-
elites, 'They are wandering aimlessly
in the land; the wilderness has shut
them in.'
4"I will harden (make stubborn, de-
fiant) Pharaoh's heart, so that he will
pursue them; and I will be glorified *and*
honored through Pharaoh and all his
army, and the Egyptians shall know
[without any doubt] *and* acknowledge
that I am the LORD." And they did so.
5When the king of Egypt was told
that the people had fled, Pharaoh and
his servants had a change of heart to-
ward the people, and they said, "What
is this that we have done? We have let
Israel go from serving us!"
6So Pharaoh harnessed *horses to* his
war-chariots [for battle] and took his
army with him;

20 Nu 33:6 **21** Ex 14:19,24; Nu 9:15; 14:14; Dt 1:33; Neh 9:12; Ps 78:14; 99:7; Isa 4:5; 1Co 10:1 **CHAPTER 14** **2** Ex 13:18; Nu 33:7; Jer 44:1 **3** Ps 71:11 **4** Ex 4:21; 7:3; ver. 17,18; Ex 9:16; Ro 9:17,22,23; Ex 7:5 **5** Ps 105:25

7 and he took six hundred chosen
war-chariots, and all the other war-
chariots of Egypt with fighting chari-
oteers over all of them.
8 The LORD hardened the heart of
Pharaoh, king of Egypt, and he pur-
sued the Israelites, as they were leaving
confidently *and* defiantly. [Acts 13:17]
9 The Egyptians chased them with all
the horses and war-chariots of Phar-
aoh, his horsemen and his army, and
they overtook them as they camped by
the sea, beside Pi-hahiroth, in front of
Baal-zephon.
10 As Pharaoh approached, the Israel-
ites looked up and saw the Egyptians
marching after them, and they were
very frightened; so the Israelites cried
out to the LORD.
11 Then they said to Moses, "Is it be-
cause there are no graves in Egypt
that you have taken us away to die in
the wilderness? What is this that you
have done to us by bringing us out of
Egypt?
12 "Did we not say to you in Egypt,
'Leave us alone; let us serve the Egyp-
tians?' For it would have been better for
us to serve the Egyptians [as slaves]
than to die in the wilderness."

The Sea Is Divided

13 Then Moses said to the people, "Do
not be afraid! Take your stand [be firm
and confident and undismayed] and
see the salvation of the LORD which
He will accomplish for you today; for
those Egyptians whom you have seen
today, you will never see again.
14 "The LORD will fight for you while
you [only need to] keep silent *and* re-
main calm."
15 The LORD said to Moses, "Why do
you cry to Me? Tell the sons of Israel to
move forward [toward the sea].
16 "As for you, lift up your staff and
stretch out your hand over the sea and
divide it, so that the sons of Israel may
go through the middle of the sea on
dry land.
17 "As for Me, hear this: I will harden
the hearts of the Egyptians, and they
will go in [the sea] after them; and I
will be glorified *and* honored through
Pharaoh and all his army, and his war-
chariots and his horsemen.
18 "And the Egyptians shall know
[without any doubt] *and* acknowledge
that I am the LORD, when I am glori-
fied *and* honored through Pharaoh,
through his war-chariots and his char-
ioteers."
19 The angel of God, who had been
going in front of the camp of Israel,
moved and went behind them. The
pillar of the cloud moved from in front
and stood behind them.
20 So it came between the camp of
Egypt and the camp of Israel. It was
a cloud along with darkness [even
by day to the Egyptians], but it gave
light by night [to the Israelites]; so one
[army] did not come near the other all
night.
21 Then Moses stretched out his hand
over the sea; and the LORD swept the
sea back by a strong east wind all that
night and turned the seabed into dry
land, and the waters were divided.
22 The Israelites went into the middle

14:11 – 12 *What is this that you have done to us.* This marks the first of ten episodes of Israel's unbelief, beginning at the Red Sea, and concluding at Kadesh-barnea (Nu 14:22). Because of these ten events an entire generation was prevented from entering the promised land. The New Testament book of Hebrews recalls these events, using the promised land as a picture of heaven and warning that disobedience and unbelief will still keep people out of the final land of "rest" (Heb 4).
14:13 *the salvation of the LORD.* The Hebrew word for salvation comes from a term that has to do with room or space. The people were under great pressure, squeezed between the waters before them and the armies of Pharaoh behind them. Salvation relieved the pressure in a most dramatic way.
14:19 *angel of God.* The term "angel of God" is an alternative expression for the angel of the Lord. The pillar of cloud is later strongly associated with the Lord Himself (33:9 – 11).

7 Ex 15:4 **8** ver. 4; Ex 6:1; 13:9; Nu 33:3 **9** Ex 15:9; Jos 24:6 **10** Jos 24:7; Neh 9:9; Ps 34:17 **11** Ps 106:7,8 **12** Ex 5:21 **13** 2Ch 20:15,17; Isa 41:10 **14** ver. 25; Dt 1:30; Jos 10:14,42; 2Ch 20:29; Isa 31:4; Isa 30:15 **16** ver. 21,26 **17** ver. 8; ver. 4 **18** ver. 4 **19** Ex 13:21; Isa 63:9 **20** See Isa 8:14; 2Co 4:3 **21** Ps 66:6; Ex 15:8; Jos 3:16; Neh 9:11; Ps 74:13; Isa 63:12 **22** Ex 15:19; Ps 66:6; Isa 63:13; 1Co 10:1; Heb 11:29; Hab 3:10

of the sea on dry land, and the waters formed a wall to them on their right hand and on their left.

23 Then the Egyptians pursued them into the middle of the sea, even all Pharaoh's horses, his war-chariots and his charioteers.

24 So it happened at the early morning watch [before dawn], that the LORD looked down on the army of the Egyptians through the pillar of fire and cloud and put them in a state of confusion.

25 He made their chariot wheels hard to turn, and the chariots difficult to drive; so the Egyptians said, "Let us flee from Israel, for the LORD is fighting for them against the Egyptians."

26 Then the LORD said to Moses, "Stretch out your hand over the sea so that the waters may come back over the Egyptians, on their war-chariots and their charioteers."

27 So Moses stretched out his hand over the sea, and the sea returned to its normal flow at sunrise; and the Egyptians retreated right into it [being met by the returning water]; so the LORD overthrew the Egyptians *and* tossed them into the midst of the sea.

28 The waters returned and covered the chariots and the charioteers, and all the army of Pharaoh that had gone into the sea after them; not even one of them survived.

29 But the Israelites walked on dry land in the middle of the sea, and the waters formed a wall to them on their right hand and on their left.

30 The LORD saved Israel that day from the hand of the Egyptians, and Israel saw the Egyptians [lying] dead on the seashore.

31 When Israel saw the great power which the LORD had used against the Egyptians, they feared the LORD [with reverence and awe-filled respect], and they believed in the LORD, and in His servant Moses.

The Song of Moses and Israel

15 THEN MOSES and the children of Israel sang this song to the LORD, singing,

"I will sing to the LORD, for He has
triumphed gloriously;
The horse and its rider He has
thrown into the sea.
2 "The LORD is my strength and my
song,
And He has become my salvation;
This is my God, and I will praise
Him;
My father's God, and I will exalt
Him.
3 "The LORD is a warrior;
The LORD is His name.
4 "Pharaoh's chariots and his army
He has thrown into the sea;
His chosen captains are drowned
in the Red Sea.
5 "The deep [water] covers them;
[Clad in armor] they sank into the
depths like a stone.
6 "Your right hand, O LORD, is
glorious in power;
Your right hand, O LORD, shatters
the enemy.
7 "In the greatness of Your majesty
You overthrow *and* annihilate
those [adversaries] who rise [in
rebellion] against You;

14:25 *the LORD is fighting for them.* This was the confession the Lord demanded; word spread widely that the Lord fought for the Israelites.
14:31 *Israel . . . believed in the LORD.* The same wording is used of Abraham's saving faith in Genesis 15:6 (see also Ro 4). The people were transformed spiritually even as they were delivered physically.
15:2 *My father's God.* The Israelites had worshiped, believed, and obeyed. Today, Christians are part of Abraham's line because they also believe, obey, and worship the same God (Gal 3:6 – 7). Many faithful believers have preceded us.
15:3 *the LORD is His name.* Other supposed gods had secret names that only guilds of priests knew. By knowing a god's secret name, a priest supposedly had special access to that god. But the living God had made His name known to all, and salvation is found in His name alone.

24 See Ps 77:17 **25** ver. 14 **27** Jos 4:18; Ex 15:1,7 **28** Hab 3:8,13; Ps 106:11 **29** ver. 22; Ps 78:52,53 **30** Ps 106:8,10; Ps 59:10 **31** Ex 4:31; Jn 2:11 **CHAPTER 15** **1** Ps 106:12 **2** Ps 18:2; Isa 12:2; Hab 3:18,19; Ge 28:21,22; Ex 3:15,16; Isa 25:1 **3** Rev 19:11; Ex 6:3; Ps 83:18 **4** Ex 14:28; Ex 14:7 **5** Ex 14:28; Neh 9:11 **6** Ps 118:15 **7** Dt 33:26; Ps 59:13; Isa 5:24

You send out Your fury, and it
consumes them like chaff.
8 "With the blast of Your nostrils the
waters piled up,
The flowing waters stood up like a
mound;
The deeps were congealed in the
heart of the sea.
9 "The enemy said, 'I will pursue, I
will overtake, I will divide the
spoil;
My desire shall be satisfied
against them;
I will draw my sword, my hand
shall dispossess them *and* drive
them out.'
10 "You blew with Your wind, the sea
covered them;
[Clad in armor] they sank like lead
in the mighty waters.
11 "Who is like You among the gods,
O LORD?
Who is like You, majestic in
holiness,
Awesome in splendor, working
wonders?
12 "You stretched out Your right
hand,
The sea swallowed them.
13 "You in Your lovingkindness *and*
goodness have led the people
whom You have redeemed;
In Your strength You have guided
them with care to Your holy
habitation.
14 "The peoples have heard [about
You], they tremble;
Anguish *and* fear has gripped the
inhabitants of Philistia.
15 "Then the [tribal] chiefs of Edom
were dismayed *and* horrified;
The [mighty] leaders of Moab,
trembling grips them;
All the inhabitants of Canaan have
melted away [in despair]—
16 Terror and dread fall on them;
Because of the greatness of Your
arm they are as still as a
stone;
Until Your people pass by *and*
[into Canaan], O LORD,
Until the people pass by whom
You have purchased.
17 "You will bring them [into the land
of promise] and plant them on
the mountain (Mt. Moriah in
Jerusalem) of Your inheritance,
The place, O LORD, You have made
for Your dwelling [among
them],
The sanctuary, O Lord, which
Your hands have established.
18 "The LORD shall reign to eternity
and beyond."

19 For the horses of Pharaoh went
with his war-chariots and his chariot-
eers into the sea, and the LORD brought
back the waters of the sea on them, but
the sons of Israel walked on dry land
in the middle of the sea.
20 Then Miriam the prophetess, the
sister of Aaron [and Moses], took a
timbrel in her hand, and all the women

15:11 *Who is like You.* Many times, the Bible uses the language of incomparability to describe the true God. In a world in which there are many supposed gods, the Lord is unique. He alone is God. He is not just better than other gods; there *are* no other gods. No person, god, or thing can be compared to the one true God (Ps 96:4; Isa 40:25–26; Mic 7:18).

15:18 *The LORD shall reign to eternity and beyond.* Ultimately, the salvation of Israel from Egypt points to the coming reign of the living God on earth over His redeemed people. This victory song ends with the assertion of the eternal rule of the Lord, promising the kingdom of God rather than the conquering of neighboring lands. Its emphasis is spiritual, not material. Now that deliverance from slavery in Egypt had been accomplished, the Hebrews would be formed by God into a nation which was designed to be a witness to the rest of the world of God's character and authority.

15:20 *prophetess.* Although there is no record of women serving as priests in ancient Israel, women did serve as prophetesses (Deborah, Jdg 4:4; the wife of Isaiah, Isa 8:3; Huldah, 2Ki 22:14). As a prophetess, Miriam spoke authoritatively from God. However, it is apparent that neither she nor Aaron had the level of intimacy with God that Moses had.

8 Ex 14:21; Ps 78:13 **9** Jdg 5:30; Isa 53:12 **10** Ex 14:21; Ex 14:28 **11** 1Ki 8:23; Isa 6:3; Ps 77:14 **13** Ps 77:15,20; Ps 78:54 **14** Jos 2:9; Ps 48:6 **15** Ge 36:40; Dt 2:4; Nu 22:3; Jos 5:1 **16** Jos 2:9; 1Sa 25:37; Ps 74:2; Jer 31:11; 1Pe 2:9 **17** Ps 44:2; Ps 78:54 **18** Isa 57:15 **19** Ex 14:23; Ex 14:28 **20** Jdg 4:4; Nu 26:59; 1Sa 18:6; Jdg 11:34; 2Sa 6:16; Ps 150:4

followed her with timbrels and dancing. [Mic 6:4]

21 Miriam answered them,

"Sing to the LORD, for He has
triumphed gloriously *and* is
highly exalted;
The horse and its rider He has
hurled into the sea."

The LORD Provides Water

22 Then Moses led Israel from the Red Sea, and they went into the Wilderness of Shur; they went [a distance of] three days (about thirty-three miles) in the wilderness and found no water.

23 Then they came to Marah, but they could not drink its waters because they were bitter; therefore it was named Marah (bitter).

24 The people [grew discontented and] grumbled at Moses, saying, "What are we going to drink?"

25 Then he cried to the LORD [for help], and the LORD showed him a tree, [a branch of] which he threw into the waters, and the waters became sweet.

There the LORD made a statute and an ordinance for them, and there He tested them,

26 saying, "If you will diligently listen *and* pay attention to the voice of the LORD your God, and do what is right in His sight, and listen to His commandments, and keep [foremost in your thoughts and actively obey] all His precepts *and* statutes, then I will not put on you any of the diseases which I have put on the Egyptians; for I am the LORD who heals you."

27 Then the children of Israel came to Elim where there were twelve springs of water and seventy date palms, and they camped there beside the waters.

The LORD Provides Manna

16 THEY SET out from Elim, and all the congregation of Israel came to the Wilderness of Sin, which is between Elim and Sinai, on the fifteenth day of the second month after they left the land of Egypt.

2 The whole congregation of the Israelites [grew discontented and] murmured *and* rebelled against Moses and Aaron in the wilderness,

3 and the Israelites said to them, "Would that we had died by the hand of the LORD in the land of Egypt, when we sat by the pots of meat and ate bread until we were full; for you have brought us out into this wilderness to kill this entire assembly with hunger."

4 Then the LORD said to Moses, "Behold, I will cause bread to rain from heaven for you; the people shall go out and gather a day's portion every day, so that I may test them [to determine] whether or not they will walk [obediently] in My instruction (law).

5 "And it shall be that on the sixth day, they shall prepare to bring in twice as much as they gather daily [so that they will not need to gather on the seventh day]."

6 So Moses and Aaron said to all Israel, "At evening you shall know that the LORD has brought you out of the land of Egypt,

7 and in the morning you will see the glory of the LORD, for He hears your murmurings against the LORD. What are we, that you murmur *and* rebel against us?"

15:24 *grumbled.* The people's recent deliverance from the Egyptian armies makes this complaint seem fickle and a true test of God's mercy. We are like the Israelites far too often, turning from praise to complaint at a moment's notice.
15:27 *Elim.* Elim means "place of trees." The wells and palms of this oasis would have been a welcome relief from the barren wasteland.
16:1 *Wilderness of Sin.* The location of this wasteland is uncertain; its position between Elim and Sinai depends on the location of Mount Sinai. (The name Sin has nothing to do with the English word "sin.")
16:4 *test.* In this sense, to test does not mean "to provide evidence," but "to prove what one really is."
16:5 *twice as much.* Gathering extra food on the sixth day would allow for the Sabbath rest (v. 25).

21 1Sa 18:7; ver. 1 **22** Ge 25:18 **23** Nu 33:8 **24** Ex 16:2 **25** See 2Ki 2:21; See Jos 24:25; Dt 8:2,16; Jdg 3:1,4; Ps 66:10 **26** Dt 7:12,15; Dt 28:27,60; Ex 23:25; Ps 103:3 **27** Nu 33:9 **CHAPTER 16** **1** Nu 33:10,11; Eze 30:15 **2** 1Co 10:10 **3** La 4:9; Nu 11:4 **4** Jn 6:31; Dt 8:2,16 **5** See ver. 22; Lev 25:21 **6** See ver. 12,13; Ex 6:7; Nu 16:28-30 **7** See ver. 10; Isa 35:2; 40:5; Jn 11:4,40; Nu 16:11

The LORD Provides Meat

8 Moses said, "*This will happen* when
the LORD gives you meat to eat in the
evening, and in the morning [enough]
bread to be fully satisfied, because
the LORD has heard your murmurings
against Him; for what are we? Your
murmurings are not against us, but
against the LORD."

9 Then Moses said to Aaron, "Say
to all the congregation of Israel, 'Ap-
proach the LORD, because He has heard
your murmurings.' "

10 So it happened that as Aaron spoke
to the whole congregation of Israel,
they looked toward the wilderness,
and behold, the glory *and* brilliance of
the LORD appeared in the cloud!

11 Then the LORD spoke to Moses,
saying,

12 "I have heard the murmurings of
the Israelites; speak to them, saying,
'At twilight you shall eat meat, and in
the morning you shall be filled with
bread; and you shall know that I am
the LORD your God.' "

13 So in the evening the quails came
up and covered the camp, and in the
morning there was a blanket of dew
around the camp.

14 When the layer of dew evaporated,
on the surface of the wilderness there
was a fine, flake-like thing, as fine as
frost on the ground.

15 When the Israelites saw it, they said
to one another, "What is it?" For they did
not know what it was. And Moses said
to them, "This is the bread which the
LORD has given you to eat. [John 6:31, 33]

16 "This is what the LORD has com-
manded: 'Let every man gather as
much of it as he needs. Take an omer for
each person, according to the number
of people each of you has in his tent.' "

17 The Israelites did so, and some
gathered much [of it] and some [only
a] little.

18 When they measured it with an
omer, he who had gathered a large
amount had no excess, and he who
had gathered little had no lack; every
man gathered according to his need
(family size).

19 Moses said, "Let none of it be left
[overnight] until [the next] morning."

20 But they did not listen to Moses,
and some left a supply of it until morn-
ing, and it bred worms and became
foul *and* rotten; and Moses was angry
with them.

21 So they gathered it every morning,
each as much as he needed, because
when the sun was hot it melted.

The Sabbath Observed

22 Now on the sixth day they gath-
ered twice as much bread, two omers
for each person; and all the leaders of
the congregation came and told Moses.

23 He said to them, "This is what the
LORD has said: 'Tomorrow is a solemn
rest, a holy Sabbath to the LORD'; bake

16:10 *the glory . . . of the LORD.* This is one of the grand appearances of God recorded in Exodus. We do not know exactly what the people saw in the cloud, but the sight certainly made them aware of God's majestic and somewhat ominous presence (Ps 97:2 – 5).

16:14 *a fine, flake-like thing, as fine as frost on the ground.* There have been many attempts to explain manna as a naturally occurring substance that still might be found in the desert, suggesting that it was some kind of plant or animal secretion. However, it is clear from the wording of these verses that this was not so. The description of the manna was necessary precisely because it was *not* a naturally occurring substance, or something they had ever seen before (Nu 11:1 – 15).

16:15 – 18 God's provision — It is easy to think we trust in God and believe He will supply all of our needs when we have food, shelter, and clothing. It is more difficult when the food is low, the clothing has disappeared, and there is no money to pay the rent. Sometimes God allows us to be in this kind of position so that we will have to learn to consciously rely on His providence. When we really place our lives in His hands, we will experience a depth of relationship which is worth far more than all the security in the world.

16:19 *Let none of it be left.* The Israelites' daily dependence on manna was an act of faith in God's provision.

8 See 1Sa 8:7; Lk 10:16; Ro 13:2 **9** Nu 16:16 **10** ver. 7; Ex 13:21; Nu 16:19; 1Ki 8:10,11 **12** ver. 8; ver. 6; ver. 7 **13** Nu 11:31; Ps 78:27,28; 105:40; Nu 11:9 **14** Nu 11:7; Dt 8:3; Neh 9:15; Ps 78:24; 105:40 **15** Jn 6:31,49,58; 1Co 10:3 **16** ver. 36 **18** 2Co 8:15 **23** Ge 2:3; Ex 20:8; 31:15; 35:3; Lev 23:3

and boil what you will bake and boil [today], and all that remains left over put aside for yourselves to keep until morning."

24 They put it aside until morning, as Moses told them, and it did not become foul nor was it wormy.

25 Then Moses said, "Eat that today, for today is a Sabbath to the LORD; today you will not find it in the field.

26 "Six days you shall gather it, but on the seventh day, the Sabbath, there will be none [in the field]."

27 Now on the seventh day some of the people went out to gather, but they found none.

28 Then the LORD said to Moses, "How long do you [people] refuse to keep My commandments and My instructions (laws)?

29 "See, the LORD has given you the Sabbath; therefore He gives you the bread for two days on the sixth day. Let every man stay in his place; no man is to leave his place on the seventh day."

30 So the people rested on the seventh day.

31 The house of Israel called the bread manna; it was like coriander seed, white, and it tasted like flat pastry (wafers) made with honey.

32 Then Moses said, "This is the word which the LORD commands, 'Let an omer of it be kept throughout your generations, that they may see the bread with which I fed you in the wilderness, when I brought you out of the land of Egypt.' "

33 So Moses said to Aaron, "Take a pot and put an omer of manna in it, and place it before the LORD to be kept throughout your generations."

34 As the LORD commanded Moses, so Aaron [eventually] placed it in the presence of the Testimony, to be kept. [Heb 9:4]

35 The Israelites ate manna forty years, until they reached an inhabited land; they ate the manna until they came to the border of the land of Canaan.

36 (Now an omer is the tenth of an ephah.)

Water in the Rock

17 THEN ALL the congregation of the children of Israel moved on from the Wilderness of Sin by stages, according to the commandment of the LORD, and camped at Rephidim, but there was no water for the people to drink.

2 Therefore the people quarreled with Moses and said, "Give us water so we may [have something to] drink." And Moses said to them, "Why do you quarrel with me? Why do you tempt the LORD *and* try His patience?"

3 But the people were thirsty for water; and the people murmured against Moses and said, "Why did you bring us up from Egypt to kill us and our children and our livestock with thirst?"

4 So Moses cried out to the LORD for help, saying, "What shall I do with this people? They are almost ready to stone me."

5 Then the LORD said to Moses, "Pass before the people and take with you some of the elders of Israel; and take in your hand the staff with which you struck the Nile, and go.

6 "Behold, I will stand before you there on the rock at Horeb; there you shall strike the rock, and water will come out of it, so that the people may [have something to] drink." And Moses did so in the sight of the elders of Israel. [1 Cor 10:4]

7 He named the place [where this miracle occurred] Massah (test) and Meribah (contention) because of the quar-

---

16:26 *Six days . . . the Sabbath.* The characteristics of manna were a built-in reminder of the importance of the Sabbath day in the life of the people of Israel.

16:31 *coriander seed . . . honey.* Apparently the manna was very tasty. It must also have been very nutritious since it was the staple of the Israelites for a full generation.

16:32 *kept throughout your generations.* This pot of manna was not only a reminder of God's miraculous provision, but a miracle in itself since it did not spoil as did the extra manna Israelites gathered for themselves.

17:7 *Is the LORD among us.* The people had

24 ver. 20 **26** Ex 20:9,10 **28** 2Ki 17:14; Ps 78:10,22 **31** Nu 11:7,8 **33** Heb 9:4 **34** Ex 25:16,21; 40:20; Nu 17:10; Dt 10:5 **35** Nu 33:38; Jn 6:31,49; Jos 5:12 **CHAPTER 17** **1** Nu 33:12,14 **2** Nu 20:3; Dt 6:16; Ps 78:18,41 **3** Ex 16:2 **4** Ex 14:15; Jn 8:59; 10:31 **5** Eze 2:6; Nu 20:8 **6** Nu 20:10,11 **7** Nu 20:13

reling of the sons of Israel, and because
they tested the [patience of the] LORD,
saying, "Is the LORD among us, or not?"

Amalek Fought

8 Then Amalek [and his people] came
and fought with Israel at Rephidim.
9 So Moses said to Joshua, "Choose
men for us and go out, fight against
Amalek [and his people]. Tomorrow
I will stand on the top of the hill with
the staff of God in my hand."
10 So Joshua did as Moses said, and
fought with Amalek; and Moses, Aar-
on, and Hur went up to the hilltop.
11 Now when Moses held up his hand,
Israel prevailed, and when he lowered
his hand [due to fatigue], Amalek
prevailed.
12 But Moses' hands were heavy *and*
he grew tired. So they took a stone and
put it under him, and he sat on it. Then
Aaron and Hur held up his hands, one
on one side and one on the other side;
so it was that his hands were steady
until the sun set.
13 So Joshua overwhelmed *and* de-
feated Amalek and his people with the
edge of the sword.
14 Then the LORD said to Moses,
"Write this in the book as a memorial
and recite it to Joshua, that I will ut-
terly wipe out the memory of Amalek
[and his people] from under heaven."
[1 Sam 15:2–8]
15 And Moses built an altar and
named it The LORD Is My Banner;
16 saying, "The LORD has sworn [an
oath]; the LORD will have war against
[the people of] Amalek from genera-
tion to generation."

Jethro, Moses' Father-in-law

18 NOW JETHRO (Reuel), the
priest of Midian, Moses' father-
in-law, heard of all that God had done
for Moses and for Israel His people,
and that the LORD had brought Israel
out of Egypt.
2 Then Jethro, Moses' father-in-law,
took Moses' wife Zipporah, after he
had sent her away [from Egypt],
3 along with her two sons, of whom
one was named Gershom (stranger),
for Moses said, "I have been a stranger
in a foreign land."
4 The other [son] was named Eliezer
(my God is help), for *Moses said,* "The
God of my father was my help, and He
rescued me from the sword of Phar-
aoh."
5 Then Jethro, his father-in-law, came
with Moses' sons and his wife to [join]
Moses in the wilderness where he was
camped, at the mountain of God [that
is, Mt. Sinai in Horeb].
6 He sent a message to Moses, "I, your
father-in-law Jethro, am coming to you
with your wife and her two sons [who
are] with her."

---

seen God's power in the plagues, the exodus, the crossing of the Red Sea, and the provision of manna. Every day they saw the pillar of His presence. We can wonder at their lack of faith until we look at our own weakness.

17:8 *Amalek.* The people of Amalek were descendants of Esau, and thus relatives of the Hebrews (Ge 36:12). Their attack on Israel was unprovoked. The Israelites — and the Lord — regarded this attack as particularly heinous (vv. 14 – 16).

17:14 *Write this.* Some people allege that the first five books of the Old Testament were not actually written down until centuries after Moses' death. Others concede that Moses may have written certain small sections, such as the one to which this verse seems to refer (24:4). However, strong tradition supports the assertion that Moses really wrote all of the first five books; ancient Jews, including Jesus, referred to this portion of the Scripture as "the books of Moses."

17:16 *The LORD has sworn.* This Hebrew phrase is somewhat obscure, but appears to mean "Surely there is a hand on the throne of the LORD." In this phraseology, the Creator of the universe is pictured as seated on His throne while raising His hand in a solemn oath. It is a fearful thing for the wicked to fall into the hands of the just and righteous Judge of the universe.

18:6 *her two sons.* Zipporah's two sons stayed with Moses and became part of the families of Israel. However, the subsequent history of the family of Gershom involved a return to idols and inappropriate priesthood (Jdg 18:30).

8 Ge 36:12; Dt 25:17 **9** Ac 7:45; Ex 4:20 **11** Jas 5:16 **14** Ex 34:27; 1Sa 15:3,7; 30:1,17 **CHAPTER 18** **1** Ex 2:16; Ps 106:2,8 **2** Ex 4:26 **3** Ac 7:29; Ex 2:22 **5** Ex 3:1,12

7 So Moses went out to meet his father-in-law, and he bowed down [in respect] and kissed him. They asked each other about their well-being and went into the tent.

8 Moses told his father-in-law about all that the LORD had done to Pharaoh and the Egyptians for Israel's sake, and about all the hardship that had happened during the journey, and how the LORD had rescued them.

9 Jethro rejoiced over all the good things the LORD had done to Israel, in that He had rescued them from the hand of the Egyptians.

10 Jethro said, "Blessed be the LORD, who has rescued you from the hand of the Egyptians and from the hand of Pharaoh, and who has rescued the people from under the hand of the Egyptians.

11 "Now I know that the LORD is greater than all gods; indeed, it was proven when they acted insolently toward Israel [and the LORD showed Himself infinitely superior to all their gods]."

12 Then Jethro, Moses' father-in-law, took a burnt offering and [other] sacrifices [to offer] to God, and Aaron came with all the elders of Israel to eat a meal with Moses' father-in-law before God.

13 Now the next day Moses sat to judge [the disputes] the people [had with one another], and the people stood around Moses from dawn to dusk.

14 When Moses' father-in-law saw everything that he was doing for the people, he said, "What is this that you are doing for the people? Why are you sitting alone [as a judge] with all the people standing around you from dawn to dusk?"

15 Moses said to his father-in-law, "Because the people come to me to ask [about the will] of God.

16 "When they have a dispute they come to me, and I judge between a man and his neighbor and I make known the statutes of God and His laws."

Jethro Counsels Moses

17 Moses' father-in-law said to him, "The thing that you are doing is not good.

18 "You will certainly wear out both yourself and these people who are with you, because the task is too heavy for you [to bear]; you cannot do it alone.

19 "Now listen to me; I will advise you, and may God be with you [to confirm my advice]. You shall represent the people before God. You shall bring their disputes *and* causes to Him.

20 "You shall teach them the decrees and laws. You shall show them the way they are to live and the work they are to do.

21 "Furthermore, you shall select from all the people competent men who [reverently] fear God, men of truth, those who hate dishonest gain; you shall place these over the people as leaders of thousands, of hundreds, of fifties and of tens.

22 "They shall judge the people at all times; have them bring every major dispute to you, but let them judge every minor dispute themselves. So it will be easier for you, and they will bear *the burden* with you.

23 "If you will do this thing and God

18:7 *bowed down [in respect] and kissed him.* The ancient Middle Eastern acts of bowing and kissing were not acts of worship, but signs of respect and reminders of obligations between two people.

18:11 *Now I know that the LORD is greater.* Jethro's words imply that he had once regarded the Lord as one among many gods, or perhaps as the principal deity over the lesser. Here he declares full faith in God as the supreme Deity.

18:21 *hate dishonest gain*. Jethro's five qualifications for judges are similar to the qualifications for elders in the New Testament (1Ti 3:1 – 13). In particular, the men recommended by Jethro were to be God-fearing and haters of dishonesty. As such they would not be susceptible to bribery, and justice would not be perverted. God takes no bribes (Dt 10:17), so neither must a judge. A bribe blinds the eyes. Human justice must reflect divine justice, which is impartial (Ro 2:11).

7 Ge 18:2; Ge 29:13 **8** Ps 81:7 **10** Ge 14:20; 2Sa 18:28 **11** 2Ch 2:5; Ex 1:10,16,22; Lk 1:51 **12** Dt 12:7 **15** Lev 24:12 **16** Ex 24:14; Lev 24:15 **18** Nu 11:14,17 **19** Ex 3:12; Ex 4:16; Nu 27:5 **20** Dt 5:1; Ps 143:8; Dt 1:18 **21** ver. 25; 2Ch 19:5-10; Ac 6:3; 2Sa 23:3; Eze 18:8; Dt 16:19 **22** ver. 26; Lev 24:11; Dt 1:17; Nu 11:17 **23** ver. 18; Ex 16:29; 2Sa 19:39

so commands you, then you will be
able to endure [the responsibility], and
all these people will also go [back] to
their tents in peace."
24 So Moses listened to his father-in-
law and did everything that he had
said.
25 Moses chose able men from all Is-
rael and made them heads over the
people, leaders of thousands, of hun-
dreds, of fifties and of tens [from the
highest to the lowest judicial levels].
26 And they judged the people at all
times; they would bring the difficult
cases to Moses, but every minor dispute
they judged *and* decided themselves.
27 Then Moses said goodbye to his
father-in-law, and Jethro went back to
his own land (Midian).

Moses on Sinai

19 IN THE third month after the
children of Israel had left the
land of Egypt, the very same day, they
came into the Wilderness of Sinai.
2 When they moved out from Rephi-
dim, they came to the Wilderness of
Sinai and they camped there; Israel
camped at the base of the mountain
[of Sinai].
3 Moses went up to God [on the moun-
tain], and the LORD called to him from
the mountain, saying, "Say this to the
house of Jacob and tell the Israelites:
4 'You have seen what I did to the
Egyptians, and how I carried you on
eagles' wings, and brought you to
Myself.
5 'Now therefore, if you will in fact
obey My voice and keep My covenant
(agreement), then you shall be My own
special possession *and* treasure from
among all peoples [of the world], for
all the earth is Mine;
6 and you shall be to Me a kingdom
of priests and a holy nation [set apart
for My purpose].' These are the words
that you shall speak to the Israelites."
7 So Moses called for the elders of the
people, and told them all these words
which the LORD commanded him.
8 All the people answered together
and said, "We will do everything that
the LORD has spoken." And Moses re-
ported the words of the people to the
LORD.
9 The LORD said to Moses, "Behold,
I will come to you in a thick cloud, so
that the people may hear when I speak
with you and may believe *and* trust in
you forever." Then Moses repeated the
words of the people to the LORD.
10 The LORD also said to Moses, "Go to
the people and consecrate them today
and tomorrow [that is, prepare them
for My sacred purpose], and have them
wash their clothes
11 and be ready by the third day, be-
cause on the third day the LORD will
come down on Mount Sinai [in the
cloud] in the sight of all the people.
12 "You shall set barriers for the peo-

19:5–8 God Gives His Covenant—The covenant with Moses is the second covenant that pertains to the rule of God. It is different than the Abrahamic covenant in that it is conditional. It is introduced by the conditional formula "if you will in fact obey My voice . . . you shall be My own special possession and treasure." This covenant was given to the nation Israel so that those who believed God's promises given to Abraham in the Abrahamic Covenant (Ge 12:1–3) would know how they should live. The Mosaic Covenant in its entirety governs three areas of their lives: (1) the commandments governed their personal lives (Ex 20:1–26); (2) the law governed their social lives particularly as they related to one another (Ex 21:1–24:11); and (3) the ordinances governed their religious lives so that the people would know how to approach God (Ex 24:12–31:18). The Mosaic Covenant did not replace the Abrahamic Covenant. It was added alongside the Abrahamic Covenant so that the people of Israel would know how to live until "the seed," Christ, comes and makes the complete and perfect sacrifice. The Mosaic Covenant was never given so that by keeping it people could be saved, but so that they might realize that they cannot do what God wants, even when God writes it down on stone tablets. The law was given that man might realize that he is helpless and that his only hope is to receive the righteousness of God by faith in Jesus (Gal 3:17–24).

---

25 Dt 1:15 **26** ver. 22; Job 29:16 **27** Nu 10:29,30 **CHAPTER 19** **1** Nu 33:15 **2** Ex 17:1,8; Ex 3:1,12 **3** Ac 7:38; Ex 3:4 **4** Dt 29:2; Isa 63:9 **5** Dt 5:2; Dt 7:6; 14:2,21; 1Ki 8:53; Ps 135:4; Ex 9:29; Dt 10:14; Job 41:11; Ps 24:1 **6** Dt 33:2-4; 1Pe 2:5,9; Dt 7:6; Isa 62:12; 1Co 3:17 **8** Dt 5:27 **9** Mt 17:5; Dt 4:12,36; Jn 12:29,30; Ex 14:31 **10** Lev 11:44,45; Heb 10:22; ver. 14 **11** ver. 16,18; Ex 34:5 **12** Heb 12:20

ple all around [the mountain], saying,
‘Beware that you do not go up on the
mountain or touch its border; whoever
touches the mountain must be put to
death.
13‘No hand shall touch him [that
is, no one shall try to save the guilty
party], but the offender must be stoned
or shot through [with arrows]; wheth-
er man or animal [that touches the
mountain], he shall not live.’ When
the ram’s horn sounds a long blast,
they shall come up to the mountain.”
[Num 24:8]
14So Moses went down from the
mountain to the people and sanctified
them [for God’s sacred purpose], and
they washed their clothes.
15He said to the people, “Be prepared
for the third day; do not be intimate
with a woman.”
16So it happened on the third day,
when it was morning, that there were
thunder and flashes of lightning, and a
thick cloud was on the mountain, and
a very loud blast was sounded on a
ram’s horn, so that all the people who
were in the camp trembled.
17Then Moses brought the people
out of the camp to meet God, and they
stood *and* presented themselves at the
foot of the mountain.

The Lord Visits Sinai

18Mount Sinai was wrapped in
smoke because the Lord descended
upon it in fire; its smoke ascended like
the smoke of a furnace, and the whole
mountain quaked violently.
19And it happened, as the blast of
the ram’s horn grew louder and louder,
Moses spoke and God answered him
with [a voice of] thunder. [Deut 4:12]
20The Lord came down on Mount
Sinai, to the top of the mountain; and
the Lord called Moses to the top of the
mountain, and he went up.
21Then the Lord spoke to Moses, “Go
down, warn the people, so that they do
not break through [the barriers around
the mountain] to the Lord to see [Me],
and many of them perish [as a result].
22“Also have the priests who ap-
proach the Lord consecrate (sanctify,
set apart) themselves [for My sacred
purpose], or else the Lord will break
forth [in judgment] against them [and
destroy them].”
23Moses said to the Lord, “The peo-
ple cannot come up to Mount Sinai,
because You warned us, saying, ‘Set
barriers around the mountain and con-
secrate it.’ ”
24Then the Lord said to him, “Go
down and come up again, you and Aar-
on with you; but do not let the priests
and the people break through [the bar-
riers] to come up to the Lord, or He will
break forth [in judgment] against them
[and destroy them].”
25So Moses went down to the peo-
ple and told them [again about God’s
warning].

The Ten Commandments

20 THEN GOD spoke all these
words:
2“I am the Lord your God, who has
brought you out of the land of Egypt,
out of the house of slavery.

19:16 *a very loud blast was sounded on a ram’s horn.* Amazingly, one of the heavenly visitors played the trumpet rather than someone in the camp of Israel (compare Isa 27:13; 1Co 15:52; 1Th 4:16). No wonder they trembled (20:18 – 19).
19:18 *the Lord descended.* Even though we know God is everywhere, language such as this gives us a greater appreciation of His merciful grace.
20:1 *Then God spoke.* The following words of God are known as the law of Moses, but this is only because they were delivered to the people from God through Moses, not because Moses invented them.
20:1 – 17 The Ten Commandments — The first four Commandments (20:1 – 11) lay out the basics of the relationship with God. God is not a mere abstraction or figment of imagination. He is the God who spoke dramatically to the patriarchs and continues to speak to us. Our responsibility is to have a relationship with Him

13 ver. 16,19 **15** 1Co 7:5 **16** Heb 12:18,19; Rev 8:5; Ex 40:34; 2Ch 5:14; Rev 4:1; Heb 12:21 **17** Dt 4:10
18 Dt 4:11; 33:2; Jdg 5:5; Hab 3:3; Ex 3:2; 24:17; 2Ch 7:1-3; Ge 15:17; Ps 144:5; Rev 15:8; Ps 68:8; Jer 4:24; Heb 12:26
19 Heb 12:21; Neh 9:13; Ps 81:7 **21** See Ex 3:5; 1Sa 6:19 **22** Lev 10:3; 2Sa 6:7,8 **23** ver. 12
CHAPTER 20 **1** Dt 5:22 **2** Hos 13:4; Ex 13:3

[3]"You shall have no other gods before Me.
[4]"You shall not make for yourself any idol, or any likeness (form, manifestation) of what is in heaven above or on the earth beneath or in the water under the earth [as an object to worship].
[5]"You shall not worship them nor serve them; for I, the LORD your God, am a jealous (impassioned) God [demanding what is rightfully and uniquely mine], visiting (avenging) the iniquity (sin, guilt) of the fathers on the children [that is, calling the children to account for the sins of their fathers], to the third and fourth generations of those who hate Me, [Is 42:8; 48:11]
[6]but showing graciousness *and* steadfast lovingkindness to thousands [of generations] of those who love Me and keep My commandments.
[7]"You shall not take the name of the LORD your God in vain [that is, irreverently, in false affirmations or in ways that impugn the character of God]; for the LORD will not hold guiltless *nor* leave unpunished the one who takes His name in vain [disregarding its reverence and its power].
[8]"Remember the Sabbath (seventh) day to keep it holy (set apart, dedicated to God).
[9]"Six days you shall labor and do all your work,
[10]but the seventh day is a Sabbath [a day of rest dedicated] to the LORD your God; on that day you shall not do any work, you or your son, or your daughter, or your male servant, or your

---

whereby we explicitly recognize Him, listen to what He says, and then obey. What He wants isn't all that complicated. He is the Creator and Master of the world, as we know it. Any view of God that makes Him less, falls short of what is required to make the relationship between God and man work. For example, if God is not the creator and sustainer of the world, then the perspective of Genesis 1:28 and our responsibility as stewards of His creation don't make much sense.

The last six Commandments (20:12 – 17) give us the basics for living — with our families, our neighbors, and our communities. Disregarding and disobeying any of these commands leads to the breakdown and possible destruction of those relationships. The relationship between a parent and a child can only go downhill if the basic respect for the parent has not been created and maintained. Adultery clearly has enormous potential to destroy a marriage because it creates distrust where trust should be. Trust is one of the foundational blocks of the marriage relationship.

While many would like to say that these Commandments are limiting, confining, and outdated, in reality, they provide the basis for a society to function harmoniously. Only when a culture places limits on itself, is it able to prosper. Followed correctly, these Commandments provide safety and freedom, the same way a fish functions best within the confines of water. In the water it lives and prospers. On land it dies.

20:3 *no other gods.* God is not to be viewed as one god among many, or even as the highest among many. He is the one and only.

20:4 *not make . . . any likeness.* This command has often been misunderstood as a prohibition against all kinds of art. In fact, God used many "likenesses" of created things to beautify His tabernacle, including carved images and woven pictures. The prohibition was not against art, but against attempting to "picture" God. Any statue, icon, painting, or image of any sort which is meant to be a representation of God can only detract from His glory. God does not want His people to worship a picture of "what He might look like," He wants all our worship for Himself alone.

20:5 *a jealous (impassioned) God.* In other words, He has a zeal for the truth that He alone is God, and He is jealous of any rivals.

20:6 *showing graciousness and steadfast lovingkindness to thousands.* The contrasting of the phrases "third and fourth generations" (v. 5) with "thousands" demonstrates that God's mercy is greater than His wrath. The lingering effects of righteousness will last far longer than the lingering effects of wrath.

20:7 *in vain.* Using God's name in vain is trivializing His name by regarding it as insignificant, trying to advance evil purposes by coaxing God to violate His character and purposes, or even simply using it thoughtlessly, without any attempt to realize of whom we are speaking.

20:8 – 11 *Remember the Sabbath (seventh) day.* The word Sabbath means "rest." The command to rest and remember the Lord on the seventh day goes back to the pattern set at the time of creation (Ge 2:2 – 3).

3 Jer 35:15 **4** Dt 27:15 **5** Isa 44:15,19; Dt 4:24; Nu 14:18,33; 1Ki 21:29; Ps 79:8; Jer 32:18 **6** Deut:7:9; Ro 11:28 **7** Mt 5:33; Mic 6:11 **8** Lev 26:2 **9** Eze 20:12; Lk 13:14 **10** Ge 2:2,3; Neh 13:16-19

female servant, or your livestock or
the temporary resident (foreigner) who
stays within your [city] gates.
11“For in six days the LORD made the
heavens and the earth, the sea and
everything that is in them, and He rest-
ed (ceased) on the seventh day. That is
why the LORD blessed the Sabbath day
and made it holy [that is, set it apart
for His purposes].
12“Honor (respect, obey, care for)
your father and your mother, so that
your days may be prolonged in the
land the LORD your God gives you.
13“You shall not commit murder
(unjustified, deliberate homicide).
[Gen 9:6; Ex 21:12, 14, 18]
14“You shall not commit adultery.
[Prov 6:25, 26; Matt 5:27, 28; Rom 1:24;
Eph 5:3]
15“You shall not steal [secretly,
openly, fraudulently, or through care-
lessness]. [Prov 11:1; 16:8; 21:6; 22:16;
Jer 17:11; Mal 3:8]
16“You shall not testify falsely [that
is, lie, withhold, or manipulate the
truth] against your neighbor (any per-
son). [Ex 23:1; Prov 19:9; 24:28]
17“You shall not covet [that is, self-
ishly desire and attempt to acquire]
your neighbor’s house; you shall not
covet your neighbor’s wife, or his male
servant, or his female servant, or his
ox, or his donkey, or anything that
belongs to your neighbor.” [Luke 12:15;
Col 3:5]
18Now all the people witnessed the
thunder and the flashes of lightning
and the sound of the trumpet and
the smoking mountain; and as they
looked, the people were afraid, and
they trembled [and moved backward]
and stood at a [safe] distance.
19Then they said to Moses, “You
speak to us and we will listen, but do
not let God speak to us or we will die.”
20Moses said to the people, “Do not
be afraid; for God has come in order
to test you, and in order that the fear
of Him [that is, a profound reverence
for Him] will remain with you, so that
you do not sin.”
21So the people stood at a [safe] dis-
tance, but Moses approached the thick
cloud where God was.
22Then the LORD said to Moses,
“Thus you shall say to the Israelites,
‘You have seen for yourselves that I
have spoken to you from heaven.
23‘You shall not make *other gods* [to
worship] besides Me; gods of silver or
gods of gold, you shall not make [these
lifeless idols] for yourselves.
24‘You shall make an altar of earth
for Me, and sacrifice on it your burnt
offerings and your peace offerings,
your sheep and your oxen. In every
place where I cause My Name to be
recorded *and* remembered [through
revelation of My divine nature] I will
come to you and bless you.
25‘If you make an altar of stone for
Me, you shall not build it of cut stones,
for if you use a chisel on it, you will
profane it.
26‘Nor shall you go up to My altar on
steps, so that your nakedness will not
be exposed on it.’

20:12 ***Honor (respect, obey, care for) your father and your mother.*** The term “honor” means “to treat with significance.” Many times we equate “honor” with “obey,” but in fact the two are not synonyms. Adult children or children of ungodly parents can find ways to honor when they cannot in good conscience obey.

20:14 ***adultery.*** God regards the sanctity of marriage as a sacred trust similar to the sanctity of life (v. 13). The marriage relationship is a symbol of God’s faithfulness to us.

20:16 ***testify falsely.*** This command is an essential foundation for a just and effective judicial system.

20:20 ***the fear of Him.*** God did not want His people to live in terror of Him, as though He were an irrational, uncontrolled, violent force, ready to be unleashed on innocent people without provocation. Rather, God wanted His people to respect the obvious hazards of wanton sin. Appropriate fear of God in this sense would make them circumspect, reverent, obedient, and worshipful, so that they might not sin.

20:26 ***your nakedness.*** The pagan worship of the Canaanites involved sexually perverse acts. Nothing obscene or unseemly was permitted in the pure worship of the living God.

11 Ge 2:2 **12** Lev 19:3; Dt 5:16; Eph 6:2 **13** Ro 13:9 **14** Dt 5:18 **15** Lev 19:11 **16** Ex 23:1; Dt 5:20 **17** Lk 12:15; Eph 5:3,5; Heb 13:5; Mt 5:28 **18** Heb 12:18; Rev 1:10,12; Ex 19:18 **19** Gal 3:19; Dt 5:25 **20** Isa 41:10,13; Dt 13:3; Pr 16:6; Isa 8:13 **21** Ex 19:16 **22** Dt 4:36 **23** Ex 32:1,2,4 **24** Lev 1:2; Dt 16:6,11; 1Ki 9:3; 2Ch 6:6; Ge 12:2 **25** Dt 27:5

Ordinances for the People

21 “NOW THESE are the ordinanc-
es (laws) which you shall set be-
fore the Israelites:
2“If you purchase a Hebrew servant
[because of his debt or poverty], he
shall serve six years, and in the sev-
enth [year] he shall leave as a free
man, paying nothing. [Lev 25:39]
3“If he came [to you] alone, he shall
leave alone; if he came married, then
his wife shall leave with him.
4“If his master gives him a wife, and
she gives birth to sons or daughters,
the wife and her children shall belong
to her master, and he shall leave [your
service] alone.
5“But if the servant plainly says, ‘I
love my master, my wife and my chil-
dren; I will not leave as a free man,’
6then his master shall bring him
to God [that is, to the judges who act
in God’s name], then he shall bring
him to the door or doorpost. And his
master shall pierce his ear with an
awl (strong needle); and he shall serve
him for life.
7“If a man sells his daughter to be a
female servant, she shall not go free
[after six years] as male servants do.
8“If she does not please her master
who has chosen her for himself [as
a wife], he shall let her be redeemed
[by her family]. He does not have
the authority to sell her to a foreign
people, because he has been unfair
to her.
9“If her master chooses her [as a
wife] for his son, he shall act toward
her as if she were legally his daugh-
ter.
10“If her master marries another
wife, he may not reduce her food, her
clothing, or her privilege as a wife.
11“If he does not do these three
things for her, then shall she leave
free, without *payment of* money.

Personal Injuries

12“Whoever strikes a man so that he
dies must be put to death.
13“However, if he did not lie in wait
[for him], but God allowed him to fall
into his hand, then I will establish
for you a place to which he may es-
cape [for protection until duly tried].
[Num 35:22–28]
14“But if a man acts intentionally
against another and kills him by [de-
sign through] treachery, you are to
take him from My altar [to which he
may have fled for protection], so that
he may be put to death.
15“Whoever strikes his father or his
mother must be put to death.
16“Whoever kidnaps a man, whether
he sells him or is found with him in his
possession, must be put to death.
17“Whoever curses his father or his
mother *or* treats them contemptuously
must be put to death.
18“If men quarrel and one strikes an-
other with a stone or with his fist, and
he does not die but is confined to bed,
19if he gets up and walks around
leaning on his cane, then the one who
struck him shall be left [physically]
unpunished; he must only pay for his
loss of time [at work], and the costs [of
treatment and recuperation] until he is
thoroughly healed.
20“If a man strikes his male or his
female servant with a staff and the
servant dies at his hand, he must be
punished.
21“If, however, the servant survives
for a day or two, the offender shall not
be punished, for the [injured] servant
is his own property.
22“If men fight with each other and
injure a pregnant woman so that she
gives birth prematurely [and the baby
lives], yet there is no *further* injury,
the one who hurt her must be pun-
ished with a fine [paid] to the wom-

21:1 *the ordinances.* This word describes God’s response to a specific action, something like an umpire’s call. The judgments of God set forth here are responses to specific situations; the Ten Commandments are more general laws, a code for living rather than a response to a certain problem.

CHAPTER 21 **1** Dt 4:14 **2** Jer 34:14 **5** Dt 15:16,17 **6** Ex 12:12; Ps 40:6 **7** Neh 5:5 **10** 1Co 7:5 **12** Ge 9:6; Mt 26:52 **13** Dt 19:4,5; 1Sa 24:4,10,18; Nu 35:11; Dt 19:3; Jos 20:2 **14** Dt 19:11,12; Heb 10:26; 1Ki 2:28-34 **16** Dt 24:7; Ge 37:28; Ex 22:4 **17** Mk 7:10 **19** 2Sa 3:29 **22** ver. 30; Dt 22:18,19

an's husband, as much as the judges
decide.
23 "But if there is *any further* injury,
then you shall require [as a penalty]
life for life,
24 eye for eye, tooth for tooth, hand
for hand, foot for foot,
25 burn for burn, wound for wound,
bruise for bruise.
26 "If a man hits the eye of his male
servant or female servant and it is de-
stroyed, he must let the servant go free
because of [the loss of] the eye.
27 "And if he knocks out the tooth of
his male servant or female servant, he
must let the servant go free because of
[the loss of] the tooth.
28 "If an ox gores a man or a woman
to death, the ox must be stoned and
its meat shall not be eaten; but the
owner of the ox shall be cleared [of
responsibility].
29 "But if the ox has tried to gore on
a previous occasion, and its owner has
been warned, but has not kept it con-
fined and it kills a man or a woman,
the ox shall be stoned and its owner
shall be put to death as well.
30 "If a ransom is demanded of him
[in return for his life], then he shall give
whatever is demanded for the redemp-
tion of his life.
31 "If the ox has gored another's son
or daughter, he shall be dealt with ac-
cording to this same rule.
32 "If the ox gores a male or a female
servant, the owner shall give to the
servant's master thirty shekels of silver
[the purchase price for a slave], and the
ox shall be stoned.
33 "If a man leaves a pit open, or digs
a pit and does not cover it, and an ox
or a donkey falls into it,
34 the owner of the pit shall make
restitution; he shall give money to the
animal's owner, but the dead [animal]
shall be his.
35 "If one man's ox injures another's
so that it dies, then they shall sell the
live ox and divide the proceeds equal-
ly; they shall also divide the dead ox
[between them].
36 "Or if it is known that the ox was
previously in the habit of goring, and
its owner has not kept it confined, he
must make restitution of ox for ox, and
the dead [animal] shall be his.

Property Rights

22 "IF A man steals an ox or sheep
and kills or sells it, he shall
make restitution of five oxen for an
ox or four sheep for a sheep.
2 "If a thief is caught breaking in [af-
ter dark] and is struck [by the owner]
so that he dies, there shall be no blood-
guilt for him.
3 "But if the sun has risen, there will
be bloodguilt for him. The thief [if he
lives] must make [full] restitution; if he
has nothing, then he shall be sold [as a
slave to make restitution] for his theft.
4 "If the animal that he stole is found
alive in his possession, whether it is
ox or donkey or sheep, he shall pay
double [for it].
5 "If a man causes a field or vineyard
to be grazed bare or lets his livestock
loose so that it grazes in another man's
field, he shall make restitution from
the best of his own field and the best
of his own vineyard.
6 "If fire breaks out and spreads to
thorn bushes so that the stacked grain
or standing grain or the field is con-
sumed, he who started the fire shall
make full restitution.
7 "If a man gives his neighbor money
or [other] goods to keep [for him while

21:24 *eye for eye, tooth for tooth.* Here we encounter the best known statement of the "law of retaliation." The idea here is not to foster revenge, but to curtail it. The natural, sinful human response is "a head for an eye, a jaw for a tooth, an arm for a hand." This law says "*no more than* eye for eye, tooth for tooth."

22:1–4 *the sun has risen.* There is a difference between struggling with an intruder at the moment when he is caught red-handed, and hunting him down in order to kill him later on. The law made a distinction between self-defense and murder as retaliation.

24 Lev 24:20; Dt 19:21; Mt 5:38 **28** Ge 9:5 **30** ver. 22; Nu 35:31 **32** See Zec 11:12,13; Mt 26:15; 27:3,9; ver. 28
CHAPTER 22 **1** 2Sa 12:6; See Pr 6:31; Lk 19:8 **2** Mt 24:43; Nu 35:27 **3** Ex 21:2 **4** Ex 21:16; See ver. 1,7; Pr 6:31
7 ver. 4

he is away] and it is stolen from the neighbor's house, then, if the thief is caught, he shall pay double [for it].

8 "If the thief is not caught, the owner of the house shall appear before the judges [who act in God's name], to determine whether or not he had stolen his neighbor's goods.

9 "For every offense involving property, whether it concerns ox, donkey, sheep, clothing, or any piece of lost property, which another identifies as his, the case of both parties shall come before the judges [who act in God's name]. Whomever the judges pronounce guilty shall pay double to his neighbor.

10 "If a man gives his neighbor a donkey or an ox or a sheep or any [other] animal to keep [for him], and it dies or is injured or taken away while no one is looking,

11 then an oath before the LORD shall be made by the two of them that he has not taken his neighbor's property; and the owner of it shall accept his word and not require him to make restitution.

12 "But if it is actually stolen from him [when in his care], he shall make restitution to its owner.

13 "If it is torn to pieces [by some predator or by accident], let him bring the mangled carcass as evidence; he shall not make restitution for what was torn to pieces.

14 "And if a man borrows an animal from his neighbor, and it gets injured or dies while its owner is not with it, the borrower shall make full restitution.

15 "But if the owner is with it [when the damage is done], the borrower shall not make restitution. If it was hired, the damage is included in [the price of] its fee.

Various Laws

16 "If a man seduces a virgin who is not betrothed, and lies with her, he must pay a dowry (marriage price) for her to be his wife.

17 "If her father absolutely refuses to give her to him, he must [still] pay money equivalent to the dowry of virgins.

18 "You shall not allow a woman who practices sorcery to live.

19 "Whoever lies with an animal must be put to death. [Lev 18:23]

20 "He who sacrifices to any god, other than to the LORD alone, shall be put under a ban (designated) for destruction (execution).

21 "You shall not wrong a stranger or oppress him, for you were strangers in the land of Egypt.

22 "You shall not harm *or* oppress any widow or fatherless child.

23 "If you harm *or* oppress them in any way, and they cry at all to Me [for help], I will most certainly hear their cry;

24 and My wrath shall be kindled *and* burn; I will kill you with the sword, and your wives shall become widows and your children fatherless.

25 "If you lend money to any one of My people with you who is poor, you shall not act as a creditor (professional moneylender) to him; you shall not charge him interest.

26 "If you ever take your [poor] neighbor's robe in pledge, you must return it to him before sunset,

27 for that is his only covering; it is his clothing for his body. In what shall he sleep? And when he cries to Me [for help], I will hear him, for I am compassionate *and* gracious.

28 "You shall not curse God, nor curse the ruler of your people [since he administers God's law]. [Acts 23:5]

29 "You shall not delay *the offering from* your harvest and your vintage. You shall give (consecrate, dedicate) to Me the firstborn of your sons. [Ex 34:19, 20]

30 "You shall do the same with your oxen *and* with your sheep. It shall be

---

22:18 *You shall not allow a woman who practices sorcery to live.* The Bible does not record any executions of sorcerers or sorceresses, but it does recount the deadly consequences of false worship (ch. 32; Nu 25).

8 Ex 21:6; ver. 28 **9** Dt 25:1; 2Ch 19:10 **11** Heb 6:16 **12** Ge 31:39 **16** Dt 22:28,29 **17** Ge 34:12 **18** 1Sa 28:3 **19** Lev 18:23 **20** Dt 17:2,3,5 **21** Dt 10:19 **22** Jas 1:27 **23** Lk 18:7; Ps 18:6 **24** Ps 69:24; Ps 109:9 **25** Ps 15:5 **26** Dt 24:6 **27** Ex 34:6 **28** Ecc 10:20 **29** Ex 23:16; Ex 13:2,12 **30** Dt 15:19; Lev 22:27

with its mother for seven days; on the
eighth day you shall give it [as an of-
fering] to Me.
31“You shall be holy men to Me;
therefore you shall not eat meat [from
any animal] that has been torn to piec-
es [by predators] in the field; you shall
throw it to the dogs.

Various Laws

23 “YOU SHALL not give a false
report; you shall not join hands
with the wicked to be a malicious wit-
ness [promoting wrong and violence].
2“You shall not follow a crowd to
do [something] evil, nor shall you tes-
tify at a trial *or* in a dispute so as to
side with a crowd in order to pervert
justice;
3nor shall you favor *or* be partial
to a poor man in his dispute [simply
because he is poor].
4“If you meet your enemy's ox or his
donkey wandering off, you must bring
it back to him.
5“If you see the donkey of one who
hates you lying helpless under its load,
you shall not leave the man to deal
with it [alone]; you must help him re-
lease the animal [from its burden].
6“You shall not pervert (bend) the
justice due to your poor in his dispute.
7“Keep far away from a false charge
or action, and do not condemn to death
the innocent or the righteous, for I will
not justify *and* acquit the guilty.
8“You shall not accept a bribe, for
a bribe blinds the clear-sighted and
subverts the testimony *and* the cause
of the righteous.
9“You shall not oppress a stranger,
for you know the soul [the feelings,
thoughts, and concerns] of a stranger,
for you were strangers in Egypt.

The Sabbath and Land

10“You shall sow your land six years
and harvest its yield,
11but the seventh year you shall let
it rest and lie uncultivated, so that the
poor among your people may eat [what
the land grows naturally]; whatever
they leave the animals of the field may
eat. You shall do the same with your
vineyard and olive grove.
12“Six days [each week] you shall do
your work, but on the seventh day you
shall stop [working] so that your ox and
your donkey may settle down *and* rest,
and the son of your female servant, as
well as your stranger, may be refreshed.
13“Now concerning everything
which I have said to you, be on your
guard; do not mention the name of
other gods [either in a blessing or in a
curse]; do not let such speech be heard
[coming] from your mouth.

Three National Feasts

14“Three times a year you shall cele-
brate a feast [dedicated] to Me.
15“You shall observe the Feast of Un-
leavened Bread; for seven days you
shall eat unleavened bread, as I com-
manded you, at the appointed time in
the month of Abib, for in it you came
out of Egypt. No one shall appear be-
fore Me empty-handed [but you shall
bring sacrificial offerings].
16“Also [you shall observe] the Feast
of Harvest (Weeks, Pentecost, or First
Fruits), acknowledging the first fruits
of your labor, of what you sow in the
field. And [third] the Feast of Ingath-
ering (Booths or Tabernacles) at the
end of the year when you gather in
[the fruit of] your labors from the field.
17“Three times a year all your males
shall appear before the Lord GOD.

23:1 *false report.* Malicious talk is everywhere condemned in Scripture (see James 3:1 – 12).

23:3 *favor or be partial to a poor man.* God's support of the poor did not overrule His justice. Here God anticipated that some would use poverty as an excuse for greedy, even criminal, activity.

23:11 *rest and lie uncultivated.* Letting the land rest allowed the poor to glean any produce that might grow during the fallow year. It also gave the land time to rejuvenate for greater productivity in subsequent years. The year of rest was an act of faith, for the Israelites would have to trust God to meet their needs.

23:17 *Lord GOD.* Here two names for God, Adonai (translated as Lord), and Yahweh (translated

31 Lev 19:2; Eze 4:14 **CHAPTER 23** **1** Ps 101:5; Ac 6:11 **2** Ge 7:1; Lev 19:15 **4** Ro 12:20 **5** Dt 22:4 **6** Ecc 5:8
7 Eph 4:25; Mt 27:4; Ro 1:18 **8** Pr 15:27 **9** Ex 22:21 **10** Lev 25:3,4 **12** Lk 13:14 **13** 1Ti 4:16; Nu 32:38
14 Ex 34:23 **15** Ex 12:15; Ex 34:20 **16** Ex 34:22; Dt 16:13 **17** Dt 16:16

18“You shall not offer the blood of
My sacrifice with leavened bread; and
the fat of My feast is not to be left over-
night until morning.
19“You shall bring the choice first
fruits of your ground into the house
of the LORD your God.
“You shall not boil a young goat in
its mother’s milk.

Conquest of the Land

20“Behold, I am going to send an An-
gel before you to keep *and* guard you
on the way and to bring you to the
place I have prepared.
21“Be on your guard before Him, lis-
ten to *and* obey His voice; do not be
rebellious toward Him *or* provoke Him,
for He will not pardon your transgres-
sion, since My Name (authority) is in
Him. [Ex 32:34; 33:14; Is 63:9]
22“But if you will indeed listen to *and*
truly obey His voice and do everything
that I say, then I will be an enemy to
your enemies and an adversary to your
adversaries.
23“When My Angel goes before you
and brings you to [the land of] the
Amorite, the Hittite, the Perizzite, the
Canaanite, the Hivite, and the Jeb-
usite, I will reject them *and* completely
destroy them.
24“You shall not bow down to wor-
ship their gods, nor serve them, nor
do [anything] in accordance with
their practices. You shall completely
overthrow them and break down their
[sacred] pillars *and* images [of pagan
worship].
25“You shall serve [only] the LORD
your God, and He shall bless your
bread and water. I will also remove
sickness from among you.
26“No one shall suffer miscarriage
or be barren in your land; I will fulfill
the number of your days.
27“I will send My terror ahead of you,
and I will throw into confusion all the
people among whom you come, and I
will make all your enemies turn their
backs to you [in flight].
28“I will send hornets ahead of you
which shall drive out the Hivite, the
Canaanite, and the Hittite before you.
29“I will not drive them out before you
in a single year, so that the land does not
become desolate [due to lack of atten-
tion] and the [wild] animals of the field
do not become too numerous for you.
30“I will drive them out before you
little by little, until you have increased
and are strong enough to take posses-
sion of the land.
31“I will establish your borders from
the Red Sea to the Sea of the Philis-
tines (the Mediterranean), and from
the wilderness to the River *Euphrates;*
for I will hand over the residents of the
land to you, and you shall drive them
out before you.
32“You shall not make a covenant
with them or with their gods.
33“They shall not live in your land,
because they will make you sin against
Me; for if you serve their gods, it is
certain to be a trap for you [resulting
in judgment].”

People Affirm Their Covenant with God

24 THEN GOD said to Moses,
“Come up to the LORD, you and
Aaron, Nadab and Abihu (Aaron’s
older sons), and seventy of Israel’s

---

as GOD), are used together. This expression emphasizes God’s sovereignty.

23:20 ***Angel.*** The statement “My Name (authority) is in Him” (v. 21) shows that this messenger is the Angel of the Lord, who is none other than God Himself; with the promise of His presence and protection comes the warning “obey His voice,” for the Lord is a holy God who cannot dwell in the presence of sin. Obedience is the evidence of reality of the covenant relationship. The Angel of the Lord “encamps around those who fear Him” (Ps 34:7).

23:26 ***suffer miscarriage or be barren.*** God reminded His people that He was the one who controlled reproduction — not the fertility cults of the pagan Canaanites.

18 Dt 16:4 **19** Dt 26:10; Dt 14:21 **20** Ex 14:19 **21** Nu 14:11; Ps 78:40,56; Dt 18:19; 1Jn 5:16; Isa 9:6; Jer 23:6 **22** Dt 30:7; Jer 30:20 **23** ver. 20; Jos 24:8 **24** Ex 20:5; Dt 12:30,31; Nu 33:52 **25** Dt 6:13; Mt 4:10; Dt 28:5; Ex 15:26; Dt 7:15 **26** Dt 7:14; 28:4; Mal 3:11; 1Ch 23:1 **27** Dt 2:25; Dt 7:23 **28** Jos 24:12 **29** Dt 7:22 **31** Ge 15:18; Dt 11:24; 1Ki 4:21,24; Jos 21:44 **32** Ex 34:12,15 **33** 1Sa 18:21; Ps 106:36 **CHAPTER 24** **1** Lev 10:1,2; Ex 1:5; Nu 11:16

elders, and you shall worship at a [safe] distance.

[2]"Moses alone shall approach the LORD, but the others shall not come near, nor shall the people come up with him."

[3]Then Moses came and told the people everything that the LORD had said and all the ordinances. And all the people answered with one voice, "Everything the LORD has said we will do."

[4]Moses wrote down all the words of the LORD. Then he got up early in the morning, and built an altar [for worship] at the foot of the mountain with twelve pillars (memorial stones) representing the twelve tribes of Israel.

[5]Then he sent young Israelite men, and they offered burnt offerings and sacrificed young bulls as peace offerings to the LORD.

[6]Moses took half of the blood and put it in large basins, and [the other] half of the blood he sprinkled on the altar.

[7]Then he took the Book of the Covenant and read it aloud to the people; and they said, "Everything that the LORD has said we will do, and we will be obedient."

[8]So Moses took the blood [which had been placed in the large basins] and sprinkled it on the people, and said, "Behold the blood of the covenant, which the LORD has made with you in accordance with all these words." [1 Cor 11:25; Heb 8:6; 10:28, 29]

[9]Then Moses, Aaron, Nadab, and Abihu, and seventy of the elders of Israel went up [the mountainside],

[10]and they saw [a manifestation of] the God of Israel; and under His feet there appeared to be a pavement of sapphire, just as clear as the sky itself. [Ex 33:20–23; Deut 4:12; Ezek 28:14]

[11]Yet He did not stretch out His hand against the nobles of the Israelites; and they saw [the manifestation of the presence of] God, and ate and drank. [Ex 19:21]

[12]Now the LORD said to Moses, "Come up to Me on the mountain and stay there, and I will give you the stone tablets with the law and the commandments which I have written for their instruction." [2 Cor 3:2, 3]

[13]So Moses arose with Joshua his attendant, and he went up to the mountain of God.

[14]And he said to the elders, "Wait here for us until we come back to you. Remember that Aaron and Hur are with you; whoever has a legal matter, let him go to them."

[15]Then Moses went up to the mountain, and the cloud covered the mountain.

[16]The glory *and* brilliance of the LORD rested on Mount Sinai, and the cloud covered it for six days. On the seventh day God called to Moses from the midst of the cloud.

[17]In the sight of the Israelites the appearance of the glory *and* brilliance of the LORD was like consuming fire on the top of the mountain.

[18]Moses entered the midst of the cloud and went up the mountain; and he was on the mountain forty days and forty nights.

24:6 *blood.* This blood anticipated the death of the coming Messiah, Jesus. His blood could do what the blood of bulls and goats could never accomplish; His death opened the way for direct communication with God (12:7; Ro 3:23 – 26; Heb 10:4,10).

24:8 *the blood of the covenant.* Just as their houses were protected from the Passover by the sign of blood (ch. 12), now the people were brought into a covenant relationship with the Lord with a sign of blood. This is a picture of our own relationship with God, brought about by the blood of Jesus (1Pe 1:2).

24:9 – 17 *God of Israel.* This vision of God was a great privilege. The elders of the people saw God standing on a structure resembling a transparent sapphire platform, which emphasized His grandeur. Blue was one of the colors favored by some members of ancient Near Eastern royalty. God's glory is the manifestation of all His divine characteristics, including power and holiness, which for Israel were represented by the billowing consuming fire (Heb 12:29).

24:12 *Come up to Me.* Only Moses could draw near to God at that time. Today, we are all called to draw near to God through Jesus (see Heb 4:14 – 16).

3 ver. 7; Ex 19:8; Dt 5:27; Gal 3:19 **4** Dt 31:9; Ge 28:18 **6** Heb 9:18 **7** Heb 9:19 **8** 1Pe 1:2 **10** Jn 1:18; 1Jn 4:12; Eze 1:26; Rev 4:3; Mt 17:2 **11** Ex 19:21; Ge 32:30; Jdg 13:22; 1Co 10:18 **12** ver. 2,15; Ex 32:15 **13** Ex 32:17 **15** Ex 19:9; Mt 17:5 **16** Ex 16:10 **17** Ex 3:2; Dt 4:36; Heb 12:18,29 **18** Ex 34:28; Dt 9:9

Offerings for the Sanctuary

25 THEN THE LORD spoke to Moses, saying,

2 “Tell the children of Israel to take an offering for Me. From every man whose heart moves him [to give willingly] you shall take My offering.

3 “This is the offering you are to receive from them: gold, silver, and bronze,

4 blue, purple, and scarlet fabric, fine twisted linen, goats’ *hair,*

5 rams’ skins dyed red, porpoise skins, acacia wood,

6 [olive] oil for lighting, balsam for the anointing oil and for the fragrant incense,

7 onyx stones and setting stones for the [priest’s] ephod and for the breastpiece.

8 “Have them build a sanctuary for Me, so that I may dwell among them. [Heb 8:1, 2; 10:1]

9 “You shall construct it in accordance with everything that I am going to show you, as the pattern of the tabernacle and the pattern of all its furniture.

Ark of the Covenant

10 “They shall make an ark of acacia wood two and a half cubits long, one and a half cubits wide, and one and a half cubits high.

11 “You shall overlay the ark with pure gold, overlay it inside and out, and you shall make a gold border (frame) around its top.

12 “You shall cast four gold rings for it and attach them to the four feet, two rings on either side.

13 “You shall make [carrying] poles of acacia wood and overlay them with gold,

14 and put the poles through the rings on the sides of the ark, by which to carry it.

15 “The poles shall remain in the rings of the ark; they shall not be removed from it [so that the ark itself need not be touched].

16 “You shall put into the ark the Testimony (Ten Commandments) which I will give you.

17 “You shall make a mercy seat (cover) of pure gold, two and a half cubits long and one and a half cubits wide.

18 “You shall make two cherubim (winged angelic figures) of [solid] hammered gold at the two ends of the mercy seat.

19 “Make one cherub at each end, making the cherubim *of one piece* with the mercy seat at its two ends.

20 “The cherubim shall have their wings spread upward, covering the mercy seat with their wings and facing each other. The faces of the cherubim are to be *looking downward* toward the mercy seat.

21 “You shall put the mercy seat on the top of the ark, and in the ark you shall put the Testimony which I will give you.

22 “There I will meet with you; from above the mercy seat, from between

---

25:2 *From every man whose heart moves him.* God does not need the gifts of His people, but He desires us to give to Him as an expression of true worship.

25:9 *the pattern.* The language of these verses suggests that there is a heavenly pattern that the earthly tabernacle was designed to resemble (see v. 40; 26:30; 27:8; Ac 7:44; Heb 8:5).

25:10 *ark.* In contrast to the idolatry of Israel’s neighbors, the shrine of the living God had no likeness or idol of any sort (20:2 – 6). ***cubits.*** This measurement was represented by the length of a man’s arm from elbow to extended middle finger. The commonly accepted estimate for the cubit is eighteen inches. Therefore, the ark was about four feet long and two and one quarter feet wide and high.

25:17 *mercy seat.* This English phrase translates a Hebrew noun derived from the verb meaning “atone for,” “to cover over,” or “to make propitiation.” The mercy seat was the lid of the ark, the place where God’s spirit rested.

25:22 *I will speak [intimately] with you.* God dwells with His people in the space-time

CHAPTER 25 **2** Ex 35:5,21; 1Ch 29:3,5,9,14; Ezr 2:68; Neh 11:2; 2Co 8:12; 9:7 **6** Ex 27:20; Ex 30:23; Ex 30:34 **7** Ex 28:4,6; Ex 28:15 **8** Ex 36:1,3,4; Lev 4:6; 10:4; 21:12; Heb 9:1,2; Ex 29:45; 1Ki 6:13; 2Co 6:16; Heb 3:6; Rev 21:3 **9** ver. 40 **10** Ex 37:1; Dt 10:3; Heb 9:4 **15** 1Ki 8:8 **16** Ex 16:34; 31:18; Dt 31:26; 1Ki 8:9; 2Ki 11:12; Heb 9:4 **17** Ex 37:6; Ro 3:25; Heb 9:5 **20** 1Ki 8:7; 1Ch 28:18; Heb 9:5 **21** Ex 26:34; ver. 16 **22** Ex 29:42,43; Nu 7:89; 1Sa 4:4; 2Sa 6:2; 2Ki 19:15; Ps 80:1; Isa 37:16

the two cherubim which are on the ark of the Testimony, I will speak [intimately] with you regarding every commandment that I will give you for the Israelites.

The Table of Bread

23"You shall make a table of acacia wood, two cubits long, one cubit wide, and one and a half cubits high.
24"You shall overlay it with pure gold and make a border of gold around the top of it.
25"You shall make a rim of a hand width around it; you shall make a gold border for the rim around it.
26"You shall make four gold rings for it and fasten them at the four corners that are on the table's four legs.
27"The rings shall be close against the rim as holders for the poles to carry the table.
28"You shall make the poles of acacia wood and overlay them with gold, so that the table may be carried with them.
29"You shall make its plates [for the showbread] and its cups [for incense] and its pitchers and bowls for sacrificial drink offerings; you shall make them of pure gold.
30"You shall set the bread of the Presence (showbread) on the table before Me at all times. [John 6:58]

The Golden Lampstand

31"You shall make a lampstand of pure gold. The lampstand and its base and its shaft shall be made of hammered work; its cups, its calyxes and its flowers shall be *all of one piece* with it.
32"Six branches shall come out of its sides; three branches of the lampstand out of the one side and three branches of the lampstand out of its other side [the shaft being the seventh branch].
33"Three cups shall be made like almond *blossoms,* each with a calyx and a flower on one branch, and three cups made like almond *blossoms* on the other branch with a calyx and a flower—so for the six branches coming out of the lampstand;
34and in the [center shaft of the] lampstand [you shall make] four cups shaped like almond *blossoms,* with their calyxes and their flowers.
35"A calyx shall be under the *first* pair of branches coming out of it, and a calyx under the *second* pair of branches coming out of it, and a calyx under the *third* pair of branches coming out of it, for the six branches coming out of the lampstand.
36"Their calyxes and their branches *shall be of one piece* with it; all of it shall be one piece of hammered work of pure gold.
37"Then you shall make the lamps [of the lampstand] seven *in number* [with one lamp at the top of the shaft]. The priests shall set up its *seven* lamps so that they will light the space in front of it.
38"Its snuffers and their trays shall be of pure gold.
39"It shall be made from a talent (50–80 lbs.) of pure gold, including all these utensils.

---

reality in which He created them, and communes with them in the language with which He endowed them. He is not aloof and He is not silent. His words are an extension of Himself and reflect His nature. They are altogether pure and without blemish, and they are fully authoritative. At the same time, His words reach out to man and are rooted in love, issued from the mercy seat. He speaks them Himself or has them spoken by His authority. He preserves them. He writes them or has them written under His superintendence. God is the ultimate Author of His own Word. This Word is and remains His living and abiding Voice.

25:29 ***pure gold.*** All of the implements for making bread were also to be costly and wonderfully designed to physically represent their holiness. They were "set apart" to God.

25:30 ***the bread of the Presence.*** Twelve loaves representing the twelve tribes of Israel were placed in two rows with six loaves in each row (Lev 24:5–9). It was called bread of the Presence because it was placed symbolically before the face of God.

25:39 ***talent.*** A talent weighed about 75 pounds.

23 Ex 37:10; 1Ki 7:48; 2Ch 4:8; Heb 9:2 **29** Ex 37:16; Nu 4:7 **30** Lev 24:5,6 **31** Ex 37:17; 1Ki 7:49; Zec 4:2; Heb 9:2; Rev 1:12 **33** Ex 37:19 **34** Ex 37:20-22 **37** Ex 27:21; 30:8; Lev 24:3,4; 2Ch 13:11; Nu 8:2

40"See that you make them [exactly]
after their pattern which was shown to
you on the mountain. [Heb 8:5, 6]

Curtains of Linen

26 "MOREOVER, YOU shall make
the tabernacle (sacred tent of
worship) with ten [interior] curtains
of fine twisted linen, and blue, purple, and scarlet fabric; you shall make
them with [embroidered] cherubim,
the handwork of a skillful craftsman.
2"The length of each curtain shall
be twenty-eight cubits, and the width
of each curtain four cubits; all of the
curtains shall measure the same.
3"The five curtains shall be joined
to one another, and *the other* five curtains shall be joined to one another.
4"You shall make loops of blue on
the *outer* edge of the last curtain in the
first set, and likewise in the second set.
5"You shall make fifty loops on the
one curtain, and fifty loops on the edge
of the *last* curtain that is in the second
set. The loops on one curtain correspond to the loops on the other.
6"You shall make fifty gold hooks,
and fasten the curtains together with
the hooks; and the tabernacle shall be
one unit.

Curtains of Goats' Hair

7"Then you shall make [exterior]
curtains of goats' *hair* as a tent over
the tabernacle. You shall make eleven
curtains in all.
8"Each curtain shall be thirty cubits
long and four cubits wide. The eleven
curtains shall all measure the same.
9"You shall join five curtains by
themselves and the *other* six curtains
by themselves, and you shall double
over the sixth curtain at the front of
the tent [to make a closed door].
10"Make fifty loops on the edge of
the outermost curtain in the *first* set,
and fifty loops on the edge of the *outermost* curtain in the second set.
11"You shall make fifty bronze hooks
and put the hooks into the loops and
join the tent together so that it may be
one unit.
12"The overlapping part that is left
over from the tent curtains, the half
curtain that is left over, shall lap over
the back of the tabernacle.
13"The cubit on one side and the cubit
on the other, of what is left over in the
length of the curtains of the tent shall
lap over the sides of the tabernacle on
one side and the other side, to cover it.
14"You shall make a *third* covering
for the tent of rams' skins dyed red,
and a *fourth* covering above that of
porpoise skins.

Boards and Sockets

15"Then you shall make the boards for
the tabernacle of acacia wood, standing
upright [as a trellis-like frame].
16"The length of each board shall be
ten cubits and the width of each board
shall be one and a half cubits.
17"Make two dovetails in each board
for fitting [them] together; you shall do
the same for all the tabernacle boards.
18"You shall make the boards for the
tabernacle [in the following quantities]:
twenty boards for the south side.
19"You shall make forty silver sockets under the twenty boards, two sockets under each board for its two dovetails, and two sockets under another
board for its two dovetails;
20for the north side of the tabernacle
there shall be twenty boards,
21and their forty silver sockets, two
sockets under each board.
22"For the back or west side of the
tabernacle you shall make six boards.
23"Make two boards for the corners
of the tabernacle at the rear [on both
sides].
24"They shall be joined together underneath, and joined together on top
with one ring. So shall it be for both
of them; they shall form the two [rear]
corners.
25"There shall be eight boards and

26:1 *tabernacle.* The word tabernacle simply means "tent."

40 Ex 26:30; Nu 8:4; 1Ch 28:11,19; Ac 7:44; Heb 8:5 **CHAPTER 26** **1** Ex 36:8 **7** Ex 36:14 **14** Ex 36:19

sixteen silver sockets; two sockets under each board.

26“Then you shall make [fifteen] bars of acacia wood: five for the boards of one side of the tabernacle,

27and five bars for the boards of the other side of the tabernacle, and five bars for the boards of the rear end of the tabernacle, for the back wall toward the west.

28“And the middle bar in the center of the boards shall pass through [horizontally] from end to end.

29“You shall overlay the boards with gold and make their rings of gold to hold the bars. You shall overlay the bars with gold.

30“You shall erect the tabernacle according to its plan [the direction corresponding to its meaning and purpose] which has been shown to you on the mountain.

The Veil and Screen

31“You shall make a veil [to divide the two rooms] of blue, purple, and scarlet fabric and fine twisted linen, skillfully worked with cherubim on it.

32“You shall hang it on four pillars (support poles) of acacia wood overlaid with gold, with gold hooks, on four silver sockets.

33“You shall hang the veil from the hooks [that connect the curtains together], and you shall bring the ark of the Testimony there within the veil. The veil shall separate for you the Holy Place and the Holy of Holies.

34“You shall put the mercy seat on the ark of the Testimony in the Holy of Holies.

35“You shall set the table [for the bread] outside the veil [in the Holy Place] on the north side, and the lampstand opposite the table on the south side of the tabernacle.

36“You shall make a screen [to provide a covering] for the doorway of the tent of blue, purple, and scarlet fabric and finely woven [embroidered] linen, the work of an embroiderer. [John 10:9]

37“You shall make five pillars (support poles) of acacia wood to support the hanging curtain and overlay them with gold. Their hooks shall be of gold, and you shall cast five [base] sockets of bronze for them.

The Bronze Altar

27 “AND YOU shall make the altar [for burnt offerings] of acacia wood, five cubits long and five cubits wide; the altar shall be square, and its height shall be three cubits.

2“Make horns (horn-shaped projections) for it on its four corners; the horns shall be of one piece with it, and you shall overlay it with bronze.

3“You shall make pots to remove its ashes, and shovels, basins [to catch the blood of the sacrificed animal], meat-forks, and firepans [to store live coals]. You shall make all its utensils of bronze.

4“Also make a grate for it, a network of bronze; and on the grid you are to make four bronze rings at its four corners.

5“And you shall put it under the ledge of the altar, so that the grid will extend halfway up the altar.

6“You shall make [carrying] poles for the altar, poles of acacia wood, overlaid with bronze.

7“The poles shall be inserted through the rings on the two sides of the altar so that it may be carried. [Num 4:14, 15]

8“You are to make the altar hollow with planks; as you were shown on the mountain [of Sinai], so shall it be made.

Court of the Tabernacle

9“You shall make the court of the tabernacle. The south side of the court is to have curtains of fine twisted linen, a hundred cubits long for one side;

27:9 – 18 *court of the tabernacle*. The courtyard separated the ceremonies of worship from common areas. It was arranged to keep people and stray animals from wandering into the tabernacle. Entering the tent could only be a deliberate act.

30 Ex 25:9,40; 27:8; Ac 7:44; Heb 8:5 **31** Ex 36:35; Lev 16:2; 2Ch 3:14; Mt 27:51; Heb 9:3 **33** Ex 25:16; 40:21; Lev 16:2; Heb 9:2,3 **34** Ex 25:21; 40:20; Heb 9:5 **35** Ex 40:22; Heb 9:2; Ex 40:24 **36** Ex 36:37 **37** Ex 36:38 **CHAPTER 27** **1** Ex 38:1; Eze 43:13 **2** See Nu 16:38 **8** Ex 25:40; 26:30 **9** Ex 38:9

10 it shall have twenty pillars and
twenty bronze sockets; but the hooks
of the pillars and their fasteners shall
be silver;
11 likewise for the north side there
shall be curtains, a hundred *cubits*
long, and its twenty pillars and twenty
bronze sockets; but the hooks of the pil-
lars and their fasteners shall be silver.
12 "For the width of the court on the
west side there shall be curtains of
fifty cubits, with ten pillars (support
poles) and ten sockets.
13 "The width of the court [to the
front], on the east side shall be fifty
cubits.
14 "The curtains for one side [of the
gate] shall be fifteen cubits with three
pillars and three sockets.
15 "On the other side [of the gate] the
curtains shall be fifteen cubits with
three pillars and three sockets.
16 "For the gate of the court there
shall be a screen [to provide a cover-
ing] of twenty cubits, of blue, purple,
and scarlet fabric and finely woven
[embroidered] linen, the work of an
embroiderer, with four pillars and four
[base] sockets.
17 "All the pillars (support poles)
around the court shall be joined togeth-
er with silver rods; their hooks shall be
of silver and their sockets of bronze.
18 "The length of the court shall be
a hundred cubits, and the width fifty
[cubits] throughout, and the height five
cubits of fine twisted linen, and their
sockets of bronze.
19 "All the tabernacle's utensils *and*
instruments used in all its service, and
all its stakes, and all the stakes for the
court, shall be of bronze.
20 "You shall command the Israelites
to provide you with clear oil of beaten
olives for the light, to make a lamp
burn continually [every night].
21 "In the Tent of Meeting [of God with
His people], outside the veil which is in
front of the [ark of the] Testimony [and
sets it apart], Aaron [the high priest]
and his sons shall keep the lamp burn-
ing from evening to morning before the
LORD. It shall be a perpetual statute [to
be observed] throughout their genera-
tions on behalf of the Israelites.

Garments of the Priests

28 "NOW BRING your brother
Aaron near, and his sons with
him from among the sons of Israel, so
that he may serve as priest to Me—
Aaron, Nadab and Abihu, Eleazar and
Ithamar, Aaron's sons.
2 "You are to make sacred garments
[official clothing reserved for holy
services] for Aaron your brother, for
honor and for beauty (ornamentation).
3 "Tell all the skilled *and* talented
people whom I have endowed with
a spirit of wisdom, that they are to
make Aaron's garments to sanctify
him *and* set him apart to serve as a
priest for Me.
4 "These are the garments which
they shall make: a breastpiece and
an ephod [for the breastpiece] and a
robe and a tunic of checkered work, a
turban, and a sash. They shall make
sacred garments for Aaron your broth-
er and his sons, so that he may serve
as a priest to Me.
5 "They are to use the gold and the
blue and the purple and the scarlet
fabric and fine twisted linen [from the
people],
6 and they shall make the ephod of

27:20 ***clear oil of beaten olives.*** All that was used in the tabernacle and sacrifices must be pure and without blemish in order to honor God's holiness. ***a lamp burn continually.*** The oil for the lampstand was the gift of the children of Israel. It had to be pure oil, as a symbol of our need to call upon the Lord from a pure heart (2Ti 2:22). The lamps were to burn continuously, a reminder of the perpetual need of the sinner for the light of God's word, "a lamp to my feet, and a light to my path" (Ps 119:105).
28:3 ***skilled and talented people.*** This expression literally means "those who are wise at heart." The same expression is used of the skillful women who did the weaving (35:25).
28:5 – 14 ***ephod.*** The ephod has been described as a cape or vest made of fine linen with brilliant

20 Lev 24:2 **21** Ex 26:31,33; Ex 30:8; 1Sa 3:3; 2Ch 13:11; Ex 28:43; 29:9,28; Lev 3:17; 16:34; Nu 18:23; 19:21
CHAPTER 28 **1** Nu 18:7; Heb 5:1,4 **2** Ex 29:5,29; 31:10; 39:1,2; Lev 8:7,30; Nu 20:26,28 **3** Ex 31:6; 36:1; Ex 31:3; 35:30,31 **4** ver. 15; ver. 6; ver. 31; ver. 39 **6** Ex 39:2

gold and blue, purple, and scarlet fabric and fine twisted linen, skillfully woven *and* [beautifully] worked.
7"It is to have two shoulder pieces joined to its two [back and front] ends, so that it may be joined together.
8"And the skillfully woven sash, which is on the ephod shall be made of the same material: of gold, of blue, purple, and scarlet fabric and fine twisted linen.
9"You shall take two onyx stones and engrave on them the names of the [twelve] sons of Israel,
10six of their names on one stone and the remaining six names on the other stone, arranged in the order of their births.
11"With the work of a jeweler, like the engravings of a signet, you shall engrave the two stones according to the names of the sons of Israel. You shall have them set in filigree [settings] of gold.
12"You shall put the two stones on the [two] shoulder pieces of the ephod [of the high priest], as memorial stones for Israel; and Aaron shall bear their names on his two shoulders as a memorial before the LORD.
13"You shall make filigree [settings] of gold,
14and you are to make two chains of pure gold like twisted cords, and fasten the corded chains to the *settings*.
15"You are to make a breastpiece of judgment, the work of a skilled *and* talented craftsman; like the work of the ephod you shall make it: of gold, of blue, purple, and scarlet fabric and of fine twisted linen.
16"The breastpiece shall be square and folded double; a span [about nine inches] in length and a span in width.
17"You shall mount on it four rows of stones: the first row shall be a row of ruby, topaz, and emerald;
18the second row a turquoise, a sapphire, and a diamond;
19the third row a jacinth, an agate, and an amethyst;
20and the fourth row a beryl and an onyx and a jasper; they shall be set in gold filigree.
21"The [engraved] stones shall be twelve, according to the names of [the twelve tribes of] the sons of Israel; they shall be like the engravings of a signet, each with its name for the twelve tribes.
22"You shall make for the breastpiece chains of pure gold twisted like cords.
23"You shall make on the breastpiece two rings of gold, and shall put the two rings on the two ends of the breastpiece.
24"You shall put the two twisted cords of gold in the two rings which are on the ends of the breastpiece.
25"The *other* two ends of the two cords you shall fasten in the two filigree *settings* in front, putting them on the shoulder pieces of the ephod.
26"You shall make two gold rings and put them at the two ends of the breastpiece, on its inside edge next to the ephod.
27"You are to make two gold rings and attach them to the lower part of the two shoulder pieces of the ephod in front, close to the place where it is joined, above the skillfully woven sash of the ephod.
28"They shall bind the breastpiece by its rings to the rings of the ephod with a blue cord, so that it will be above the skillfully woven sash of the ephod, so that the breastpiece will not come loose from the ephod.
29"So Aaron shall carry the names of the sons of Israel (Jacob) in the breastpiece of judgment over his heart when he enters the Holy Place, to bring them in continual remembrance before the LORD.
30"In the breastpiece of judgment

---

colors. Its two main sections covered the chest and back, with seams at the shoulders and a band at the waist.
28:16 *span.* The span was determined as the length from the tip of the thumb to the tip of the small finger on an outstretched hand. It is generally estimated as nine inches, or half a cubit.
28:30 *the Urim (Lights) and the Thummim (Perfections).* Together their names may mean "perfect knowledge" or a similar idea. It is not

12 ver. 29; Ex 39:7; See Jos 4:7; Zec 6:14 **15** Ex 39:8 **17** Ex 39:10 **29** ver. 12 **30** Lev 8:8; Nu 27:21; Dt 33:8; 1Sa 28:6; Ezr 2:63; Neh 7:65

you shall put the Urim (Lights) and the
Thummim (Perfections) [to be used
for determining God's will in a mat-
ter]. They shall be over Aaron's heart
whenever he goes before the LORD, and
Aaron shall always carry the judgment
(verdict, judicial decisions) of the sons
of Israel over his heart before the LORD.
31 "And you shall make the robe of
the ephod all of blue.
32 "There shall be an opening at its
top in the center [for the head], with
a binding of woven work around the
opening, like the opening in a coat of
armor, so that it will not tear *or* fray.
33 "You shall make pomegranates
of blue, purple, and scarlet fabric all
around its hem, with gold bells be-
tween them;
34 a golden bell and a pomegranate,
a golden bell and a pomegranate, all
around the [bottom] hem of the robe.
35 "Aaron shall wear the robe when
he ministers, and its sound shall be
heard when he goes [alone] into the
Holy Place before the LORD, and when
he comes out, so that he will not die
there.
36 "You shall also make a plate of
pure gold and engrave on it, like the
engravings of a signet, 'Holy to the
LORD.' [Ex 39:30]
37 "You shall fasten it on the front of
the turban with a blue cord.
38 "It shall be on Aaron's forehead,
and Aaron shall take away the guilt
from the holy things which the sons
of Israel dedicate, with regard to all
their holy gifts. It shall always be on
his forehead, so that they may be ac-
cepted before the LORD. [Luke 24:44;
Heb 8:1, 2]
39 "You shall weave the tunic of
checkered work of fine linen, and
make a turban of fine linen. You shall
make a sash, the work of an embroi-
derer.
40 "For Aaron's sons you shall make
tunics and sashes and [ornamental]
caps, for glory *and* honor and beauty.
41 "You shall put the various articles
of clothing on Aaron your brother and
on his sons with him, and shall anoint
them and ordain and sanctify them,
so that they may serve Me as priests.
42 "You shall make for them [white]
linen undergarments to cover their
bare flesh, reaching from the waist to
the thighs.
43 "The various articles of clothing
shall be on Aaron and on his sons
when they enter the Tent of Meeting,
or when they approach the altar [of
incense] to minister in the Holy Place,
so that they do not incur guilt and die.
It shall be a statute forever to Aaron
and to his descendants after him.

Consecration of the Priests

29 "THIS IS what you shall do to
consecrate Aaron and his sons
so that they may serve Me as priests:
take one young bull and two rams,
without blemish,

---

known exactly what the Urim and Thummim were, or how they were used. Some have suggested that they were two stones used for the casting of lots.

28:42 ***undergarments.*** The command to wear trousers protected the modesty of the priests. Given the sexually preoccupied worship of Israel's neighbors, this provision was decidedly countercultural.

29:1–9 ***consecrate Aaron and his sons.*** The outward purification process was used to symbolize the inward purity which was demanded of the priests of Israel, the intermediaries between the people and their holy God. Obviously the priests were not perfectly pure; it was only God's gracious act of accepting blood sacrifices that allowed the priests to stand in His presence on behalf of the people. The outward washings of the priests showed that they were doing everything possible to live their lives in the way they had been commanded by God. Likewise, in the New Testament era, the only reason that Christians can stand before God as believer-priests is because God graciously accepts Christ's sacrifice on behalf of our sins.

29:1 ***consecrate.*** The priests' actions should mark them as distinct, holy, set aside for God's purposes.

---

31 Ex 39:22 **36** Ex 39:30; Zec 14:20 **38** ver. 43; Lev 10:17; 22:9; Nu 18:1; Isa 53:11; Eze 4:4-6; Jn 1:29; Heb 9:28; 1Pe 2:24; Lev 1:4; 22:27; Isa 56:7 **40** ver. 4; Ex 39:27-29,41; Eze 44:17,18 **41** Ex 29:7; 30:30; 40:15; Lev 10:7; Ex 29:9; Lev 8; Heb 7:28 **42** Ex 39:28; Lev 6:10; 16:4; Eze 44:18 **43** Ex 20:26; Lev 5:1,17; 20:19,20; 22:9; Nu 9:13; 18:22; Ex 27:21; Lev 17:7 **CHAPTER 29** **1** Lev 8:2

2 and unleavened bread and unleav-
ened cakes mixed with oil, and unleav-
ened wafers spread with oil; you shall
make them of fine wheat flour.
3 "You shall put them in one basket,
and present them in the basket along
with the bull and the two rams.
4 "Then bring Aaron and his sons to
the doorway of the Tent of Meeting
[out where the basin is] and wash them
with water.
5 "Then you shall take the garments,
and put on Aaron the tunic and the
robe of the ephod and the ephod and
the breastpiece, and wrap him with
the skillfully woven sash of the ephod;
6 and you shall put the turban on his
head and put the holy crown on the
turban.
7 "Then you shall take the anointing
oil and pour it on his head and anoint
him.
8 "You shall bring his sons and put
tunics on them.
9 "And you shall wrap them with
sashes, Aaron and his sons, and put
the [ornamental] caps on them; and
the priest's office shall be theirs by a
perpetual statute. So you shall ordain
Aaron and his sons.

The Sacrifices

10 "Then you shall bring the bull be-
fore the Tent of Meeting, and Aaron
and his sons shall lay their hands on
the bull's head.
11 "Then you shall kill the bull before
the LORD by the doorway of the Tent
of Meeting.
12 "And you shall take some of the
blood of the bull and with your finger
put it on the horns of the altar [of burnt
offering], and you shall pour out the
remainder of the blood at the base of
the altar.
13 "You shall take all the fat that cov-
ers the intestines and the lobe of the
liver, and the two kidneys and the fat
that is on them, and offer them up in
smoke on the altar.
14 "But the meat of the bull, its hide,
and the contents of its intestines you
shall burn in the fire outside the camp;
it is a sin offering. [Heb 13:11–13]
15 "And you shall take one of the
rams, and Aaron and his sons shall
lay their hands on the head of the ram;
16 then you shall kill the ram and
you shall take its blood and sprinkle
it around the altar [of burnt offering].
17 "Then you shall cut the ram into
pieces, and wash its intestines and
legs, and place them with its pieces
and its head,
18 and you shall burn the whole ram
on the altar. It is a burnt offering to the
LORD: it is a sweet *and* soothing aroma,
an offering by fire to the LORD.
19 "Then you shall take the other ram,
and Aaron and his sons shall lay their
hands on the head of the ram.
20 "Then you shall kill the ram, and
take some of its blood and put it on the
tip of the right ears of Aaron and his
sons and on the thumbs of their right
hands and on the big toes of their right
feet, and sprinkle the [rest of the] blood
around on the altar [of burnt offering].
21 "Then you shall take some of the
blood that is on the altar and some of
the anointing oil, and sprinkle it on
Aaron and his garments and on his
sons and their garments. Now Aaron
and his garments and his sons and
their garments shall be consecrated
(dedicated, made holy, declared sacred
for God's purpose).
22 "You shall also take the fat of the
ram, the fat tail, the fat that covers the
intestines, the lobe of the liver, the two
kidneys with the fat that is on them,
and the right thigh; (for it is a ram of
ordination),
23 and one loaf of bread and one cake

29:9 *ordain*. The verb translated *ordain* in this verse literally means "to fill one's hand." A king was handed a rod as the symbol of his political power; so the hand of the priest was filled with spiritual power.

29:18 *burnt offering*. Aaron and his sons needed to offer sacrifices for themselves as much as for their fellow Israelites (Heb 5:1–4).

2 Lev 2:4; 6:20-22 **4** Ex 40:12; Lev 8:6; Heb 10:22 **5** Ex 28:2; Lev 8:7; Ex 28:8 Lev 8:9 **7** Ex 30:25; Lev 8:12; 10:7; 21:10; Nu 35:25 **8** Lev 8:13 **9** Nu 18:7; Ex 28:41; Lev 8:22; Heb 7:28 **10** Lev 1:4; 8:14 **12** Lev 8:15; Ex 27:2 **13** Lev 3:3 **14** Lev 4:11,12,21; Heb 13:11 **15** Lev 8:18; Lev 1:4-9 **18** Ge 8:21 **19** ver. 3; Lev 8:22 **21** Ex 30:25,31; ver. 1; Heb 9:22 **23** Lev 8:26

of oiled bread and one wafer out of the basket of the unleavened bread that is before the LORD;
[24]and you shall put all these in the hands of Aaron and his sons, and wave them as a wave offering before the LORD.
[25]"Then you shall take them from their hands, add them to the burnt offering, and burn them on the altar for a sweet *and* soothing aroma before the LORD; it is an offering by fire to the LORD.
[26]"Then you shall take the breast of the ram of Aaron's ordination, and wave it as a wave offering before the LORD; and it shall be your (Moses) portion.
[27]"You shall consecrate the waved breast offering [of the ram] used in the ordination and the waved thigh offering of the priests' portion, since it is [a contribution] for Aaron and for his sons.
[28]"It shall be for Aaron and his sons as their due portion from the Israelites forever, for it is a heave offering. It shall be a heave offering to the LORD from the Israelites from the sacrifices of their peace offerings.
[29]"The holy garments of Aaron shall be for his sons after him, to be anointed and ordained in them.
[30]"That son who is [high] priest in his place shall put them on [each day for] seven days when he comes into the Tent of Meeting to minister in the Holy Place.

Food of the Priests

[31]"You shall take the ram of the ordination and boil its meat in a holy place.
[32]"Aaron and his sons shall eat the meat of the ram and the bread in the basket, at the doorway of the Tent of Meeting.
[33]"They shall eat those things by which atonement was made at their ordination and consecration; but a layman shall not eat them, because they are holy [that is, set apart to the worship of God].
[34]"And if any of the meat of ordination or the bread remains until morning, you shall burn it in the fire; it shall not be eaten, because it is holy.
[35]"So you shall do to Aaron and to his sons in accordance with all I have commanded you; during seven days you are to ordain them.
[36]"You shall offer a bull every day as a sin offering for atonement. You shall cleanse the altar *from sin* when you make atonement for it, and you shall anoint it to consecrate it [for God's sacred purpose].
[37]"For seven days you shall make atonement for the altar [of burnt offering] and consecrate it; then the altar shall be most holy. Whatever touches the altar must be holy (set apart for God's service).
[38]"Now this is what you shall offer on the altar: two one year old lambs shall be offered each day, continuously.
[39]"One lamb you shall offer in the morning and the other lamb at twilight;
[40]and with the one lamb there shall be one-tenth of *a measure* of fine flour mixed with one-fourth of a hin of beaten [olive] oil, and one-fourth of a hin of wine for a drink offering [to be poured out].
[41]"And the other lamb you shall offer at twilight, and do with it as with the grain offering of the morning and with the drink offering, for a sweet *and* soothing aroma [to appease God], an offering by fire to the LORD.
[42]"This will be a continual burnt offering throughout your generations at the doorway of the Tent of Meeting before the LORD, where I will meet with you, to speak to you there.

29:24 *wave offering.* This offering made it clear that everything was owed to God, but some was received back as God's gift (Lev 7:30; 10:14).

29:40 *one-tenth of a measure ... hin.* One tenth of a measure was about two quarts; one fourth of a hin was about one quart.

24 Lev 7:30 **25** Lev 8:28 **26** Lev 8:29; Lev 7:33 **27** Lev 7:31,34; Nu 18:11,18; Dt 18:3 **28** Lev 10:15; Lev 7:34 **29** Nu 20:26,28; Nu 18:8 **30** Nu 20:28; Lev 8:35; 9:1,8 **31** Lev 8:31 **32** Mt 12:4 **33** Lev 10:14,15,17; Lev 22:10 **34** Lev 7:18; 8:32 **35** Lev 8:33-35 **36** Heb 10:11; Ex 40:10 **37** Ex 40:10; Mt 23:19 **38** Nu 28:3; 1Ch 16:40; Ezr 3:3; See Da 12:11 **39** Eze 46:13-15 **41** 1Ki 18:29,36; 2Ki 16:15; Ezr 9:4,5; Ps 141:2 **42** Ex 30:8; Ex 25:22

43 “There I will meet with the Israelites, and the Tent of Meeting shall be sanctified by My glory [the Shekinah, God’s dwelling presence].

44 “I will sanctify the Tent of Meeting and the altar [of burnt offering]; also I will sanctify Aaron and his sons to serve as priests to Me.

45 “I will dwell among the sons of Israel and be their God.

46 “They shall know [from personal experience] *and* acknowledge that I am the LORD their God who brought them out of the land of Egypt so that I might dwell among them; I am the LORD their God.

The Altar of Incense

30 “YOU SHALL make an altar upon which to burn incense; you shall make it of acacia wood.

2 “It shall be a cubit long and a cubit wide. It shall be square and it shall be two cubits high. Its horns of one piece with it.

3 “You shall overlay it with pure gold, its top and its sides all around, and its horns; and you shall make a gold molding all around it.

4 “You shall make two gold rings under its molding, make them on the two side walls—on opposite sides—they shall be holders for the poles with which to carry it.

5 “You shall make the poles of acacia wood overlaid with gold.

6 “You shall put the altar of incense [in the Holy Place] in front *and* outside of the veil that screens the ark of the Testimony, before the mercy seat that is over the Testimony, where I will meet with you.

7 “Aaron shall burn sweet *and* fragrant incense on it; he shall burn it every morning when he trims *and* tends the lamps. [Ps 141:2; Rev 5:8; 8:3, 4]

8 “When Aaron sets up the lamps at twilight, he shall burn incense, a perpetual incense before the LORD throughout your generations.

9 “You shall not offer any strange incense on this altar, or burnt offering or meal offering; you shall not pour out a drink offering on it.

10 “Once a year Aaron shall make atonement [for sin] on its horns. He shall make atonement on it with the blood of the sin offering of atonement once a year throughout your generations. It is most holy to the LORD.”

The Ransom Money

11 Then the LORD said to Moses,

12 “When you take the census of the Israelites, each one shall give a ransom for himself to the LORD when you count them, so that no plague will

---

29:45 *dwell among the sons.* Man is God’s special creation, created in His image and likeness. A part of that image and likeness is the uniqueness of personality that allows communion with God. He did not create a race of robots but rather endowed man with a will so that he might choose fellowship with God. In Israel, fellowship with God centered in the tabernacle and especially in the mercy seat which symbolized His presence. Today, believers have fellowship with God through the indwelling of the Holy Spirit. In eternity He will dwell in the midst of His people more fully than ever before.

30:7 *sweet . . . incense.* Burning incense was a privilege restricted to those who were allowed to approach God.

30:9 *strange incense.* The incense offered to God was to be made from a special recipe consecrated to be used only in the worship at the tabernacle. No other incense was acceptable.

30:10 *atonement*. The sacrificial blood of the sin offering (Lev 16:18) was applied to the incense altar to indicate that even this article needed cleansing to preserve its ideal holiness because of man’s willful or accidental sin. The Hebrew word for “atonement” involves the covering or canceling of sin, resulting in the offender being reconciled to God. Without blood being shed there can be no forgiveness (Heb 9:22). The atonement made annually for this small altar is a reminder that everything in God’s service must be holy to the Lord (Zec 14:20).

30:12 *ransom.* The idea is to pay a price for one’s life. The Israelites had to acknowledge that their lives were from God and governed by Him by giving Him an offering of money.

---

43 1Ki 8:11; 2Ch 5:14; Eze 43:5; Hag 2:7,9 **44** Lev 21:15 **45** Ex 25:8; Lev 26:12; Zec 2:10; Jn 14:17,23; Rev 21:3 **46** Ex 20:2 **CHAPTER 30** **1** Ex 37:25; See ver. 7,8,10; Rev 8:3 **6** Ex 25:21,22 **7** ver. 34; 1Sa 2:28; 1Ch 23:13; Lk 1:9; Ex 27:21 **9** Lev 10:1 **10** Lev 16:18 **12** 2Sa 24:2; See Nu 31:50; Mt 20:28; 1Pe 1:18,19; 2Sa 24:15

come on them when you number them.
[Rom 8:1–4]
13“This is what everyone who is
counted shall give [as he joins those
already counted]: a half shekel, ac-
cording to the sanctuary shekel (the
shekel is twenty gerahs); a half shekel
as a contribution to the LORD.
14“Everyone who is counted, from
twenty years old and over, [as he joins
those already counted], shall give this
contribution to the LORD. [Matt 10:24;
1 Pet 1:18, 19]
15“The rich shall not give more and the
poor shall not give less than half a shek-
el, when you give this contribution to the
LORD to make atonement for yourselves.
16“You shall take the atonement
money from the Israelites and use it
[exclusively] for the service of the Tent
of Meeting, so that it may be a memo-
rial for the Israelites before the LORD,
to make atonement for yourselves.”

The Bronze Basin

17Then the LORD said to Moses,
18“You shall also make a basin of
bronze, with a base of bronze, for
washing. You shall put it [outside in
the court] between the Tent of Meeting
and the altar [of burnt offering], and
you shall put water in it.
19“Aaron and his sons shall wash
their hands and their feet.
20“When they enter the Tent of Meet-
ing, they shall wash with water, so
that they will not die. Also, when they
approach the altar to minister, to burn
an offering in the fire to the LORD [they
shall do the same]. [John 13:6–8]
21“They shall wash their hands
and their feet, so that they will not
die; it shall be a perpetual statute for
them, for Aaron and his descendants
throughout their generations.”

The Anointing Oil

22Moreover, the LORD said to Moses,
23“Take for yourself the best spices:
five hundred *shekels* of liquid myrrh,
half as much—two hundred and fifty—
of sweet-scented cinnamon, and two
hundred and fifty of fragrant cane,
24and five hundred *shekels* of cinna-
mon blossom according to the sanctu-
ary shekel, and a hin of olive oil.
25“You shall make of these a holy
anointing oil, a perfume mixture, the
work of a perfumer; it shall be a sacred
anointing oil.
26“You shall anoint the Tent of Meet-
ing with it, and the ark of the Testi-
mony,
27and the table [for the bread] and all
its utensils, and the lampstand and its
utensils, and the altar of incense,
28and the altar of burnt offering
with all its utensils, and the basin [for
cleansing] and its base.
29“You shall consecrate them, that
they may be most holy; whatever
touches them must be holy (set apart
for God).
30“You shall anoint Aaron and his
sons, and consecrate them, that they
may serve as priests to Me.
31“You shall say to the Israelites,
‘This shall be a holy *and* sacred anoint-
ing oil, to Me [alone] throughout your
generations. [Rom 8:9; 1 Cor 12:3]
32‘It shall not be poured on anyone’s
body, nor shall you make any like it in
the same composition. It is holy, and it
shall be sacred to you.
33‘Whoever prepares any like it or
puts any of it on a layman shall be cut
off from his people [excluding him
from the atonement made for them].’ ”

The Incense

34Then the LORD said to Moses, “Take
sweet *and* fragrant spices—stacte, ony-
cha, and galbanum, sweet *and* fragrant
spices with pure frankincense; there
shall be an equal amount of each—
35and make incense with it, a per-
fume, the work of a perfumer, salted,
pure and sacred.

30:19 *wash their hands and their feet.* The continual washing was symbolic of the need to be cleansed from sin regularly.

---

13 Mt 17:24; Nu 3:47; Ex 38:26 **15** Pr 22:2; Eph 6:9 **16** Ex 38:25; Nu 16:40 **18** Ex 38:8; 1Ki 7:38; Ex 40:30 **19** Ex 40:31,32; Ps 26:6; Isa 52:11; Jn 13:10; Heb 10:22 **21** Ex 28:43 **23** SS 4:14; Eze 27:22; Ps 45:8; Pr 7:17; SS 4:14; Jer 6:20 **24** Ps 45:8; Ex 29:40 **25** Ex 37:29; Nu 35:25; Ps 89:20; 133:2 **26** Ex 40:9; Lev 8:10; Nu 7:1 **29** Ex 29:37 **30** Ex 29:7; Lev 8:12,30 **32** ver. 25,37 **33** ver. 38; Ge 17:14; Ex 12:15; Lev 7:20,21 **34** Ex 25:6; 37:29 **35** ver. 25

36 "You shall crush some of it [into a] very fine [powder], and put some of it before the Testimony in the Tent of Meeting, where I will meet with you; it shall be most holy to you.

37 "The incense which you shall make, you shall not make in the same proportions for yourselves; it shall be holy to you for the LORD.

38 "Whoever makes any like it, to use as perfume shall be cut off from his people [excluding him from the atonement made for them]."

The Skilled Craftsmen

31 NOW THE LORD said to Moses,

2 "See, I have called by name Bezalel, son of Uri, the son of Hur, of the tribe of Judah.

3 "I have filled him with the Spirit of God in wisdom *and* skill, in understanding *and* intelligence, in knowledge, and in all kinds of craftsmanship,

4 to make artistic designs for work in gold, in silver, and in bronze,

5 and in the cutting of stones for settings, and in the carving of wood, to work in all kinds of craftsmanship.

6 "And behold, I Myself have appointed with him Oholiab, son of Ahisamach, of the tribe of Dan; to all who are wise-hearted I have given the skill *and* ability to make everything that I have commanded you:

7 the Tent of Meeting, the ark of the Testimony, the mercy seat that is upon it, all the furnishings of the tent—

8 the table [for the bread] and its utensils, the pure *gold* lampstand with all its utensils, the [golden] altar of incense,

9 the [bronze] altar of burnt offering with all its utensils, the basin and its base—

10 the finely worked garments, the holy garments for Aaron the [high] priest and the garments for his sons to minister as priests,

11 and the anointing oil and the sweet *and* fragrant incense for the Holy Place. They are to make *them* according to all that I have commanded you."

The Sign of the Sabbath

12 And the LORD said to Moses,

13 "But as for you, say to the Israelites, 'You shall most certainly observe My Sabbaths, for it is a sign between Me and you throughout your generations, so that you may know [without any doubt] *and* acknowledge that I am the LORD who sanctifies you *and* sets you apart [for Myself].

14 'Therefore, you shall keep the Sabbath, for it is holy to you. Everyone who profanes it must be put to death; for whoever does work on the Sabbath, that person (soul) shall be cut off from among his people [excluding him from the atonement made for them].

15 'For six days work may be done, but the seventh is the Sabbath of complete rest, sacred to the LORD; whoever does work on the Sabbath day must be put to death.

16 'So the Israelites shall observe the Sabbath, to celebrate the Sabbath throughout their generations as a perpetual covenant.'

17 "It is a sign between Me and the Israelites forever; for in six days the LORD made the heavens and the earth, and on the seventh day He ceased and was refreshed."

18 When He had finished speaking

31:3 *filled him with the Spirit of God.* We often think of the "filling of the Spirit" only in connection with Acts 2, but passages such as this one help us to see the continuity of God's work among His people through the ages. In this case, the Spirit empowered uniquely gifted people to design and build a tabernacle befitting a holy and magnificent God.

31:18 *the finger of God.* This verse underscores the divine origin of the law. Scholars of religion have long spoken of Israel's religious ideas as its unique contribution to civilization, much as the Greeks developed philosophy and the Romans displayed a genius for organization and empire-building. Yet such a comparison misses the point of Scripture. The Bible speaks not of the

36 Ex 29:42; Lev 16:2; ver. 32; Ex 29:37; Lev 2:3 **37** ver. 32 **38** ver. 33 **CHAPTER 31** **2** Ex 35:30; 36:1; 1Ch 2:20 **3** Ex 35:31; 1Ki 7:14 **6** Ex 35:34; Ex 28:3; 35:10,35; 36:1 **7** Ex 36:8; Ex 37:1; Ex 37:6 **8** Ex 37:10; Ex 37:17 **9** Ex 38:1; Ex 38:8 **10** Ex 39:1,41; Nu 4:5,6 **11** Ex 30:25,31; Ex 30:34 **13** Lev 19:3,30; 26:2; Eze 20:12,20 **14** Ex 20:8; Dt 5:12; Nu 15:35 **15** Ex 20:9; Ge 2:2 **17** ver. 13; Ge 2:2 **18** Ex 32:15; Dt 4:13; 5:22; 2Co 3:3

with him on Mount Sinai, He gave
Moses the two tablets of the Testimo-
ny, tablets of stone, written with the
finger of God.

The Golden Calf

32 NOW WHEN the people saw that
Moses delayed coming down
from the mountain, they gathered to-
gether before Aaron and said to him,
"Come, make us a god who will go
before us; as for this Moses, the man
who brought us up from the land of
Egypt, we do not know what has be-
come of him."
2So Aaron replied to them, "Take off
the gold rings that are in the ears of
your wives, your sons and daughters,
and bring them to me."
3So all the people took off the gold
rings that were in their ears and
brought them to Aaron.
4And he took *the gold* from their
hands, and fashioned it with an en-
graving tool and made it into a molten
calf; and they said, "This is your god,
O Israel, who brought you up from the
land of Egypt."
5Now when Aaron saw the molten
calf, he built an altar before it; and
Aaron made a proclamation, and
said, "Tomorrow shall be a feast to
the LORD!"
6So they got up early the next day
and offered burnt offerings, and
brought peace offerings; then the peo-
ple sat down to eat and drink, and got
up to play [shamefully—without moral
restraint].
7Then the LORD said to Moses, "Go
down at once, for your people, whom
you brought up from the land of Egypt,
have corrupted themselves.
8"They have quickly turned aside
from the way which I commanded
them. They have made themselves a
molten calf, and have worshiped it and
sacrificed to it, and said, 'This is your
god, O Israel, who brought you up from
the land of Egypt!' "
9The LORD said to Moses, "I have
seen this people, and behold, they are
a stiff-necked (stubborn, rebellious)
people.
10"Now therefore, let Me alone *and*
do not interfere, so that My anger may
burn against them and that I may de-
stroy them; and I will make of you
(your descendants) a great nation."

Moses' Entreaty

11But Moses appeased *and* entreated
the LORD his God, and said, "LORD, why
does Your anger burn against Your
people whom You have brought out
of the land of Egypt with great power
and a mighty hand?
12"Why should the Egyptians say,
'With evil [intent] their God brought
them out to kill them in the mountains
and destroy them from the face of the
earth'? Turn away from Your burning
anger and change Your mind about
harming Your people.
13"Remember Abraham, Isaac, and
Israel (Jacob), Your servants to whom
You swore [an oath] by Yourself, and
said to them, 'I will multiply your de-
scendants as the stars of the heavens,
and all this land of which I have spo-
ken I will give to your descendants,
and they shall inherit it forever.' "

---

genius of Israel, but of the finger of God. The Ten Commandments were not the product of man, but the revelation of the Lord.

32:1–35 The Golden Calf—The story of the Israelites' worship of the golden calf reveals both the unfaithfulness of the Israelites and God's great mercy. Even though the people had so quickly broken their promise to obey Him, God forgave their sin and began again with them.

32:2–3 *gold rings.* These were part of the treasure from Egypt that should have been used for building the tabernacle (35:20–29).

32:4 *a molten calf.* This was an ominous worship symbol. Not only were the cow and the bull worshiped in Egypt, but the bull was a familiar embodiment of Baal seen in Canaan. It appears that the worship of the Lord had been blended with the symbols of Baal and other fertility gods. In this one scene, the people broke the first three of God's commandments.

CHAPTER 32 **1** Ex 24:18; Dt 9:9; Ac 7:40; Ex 13:21 **2** Jdg 8:24-27 **4** Ex 20:23; Dt 9:16; Jdg 17:3,4; 1Ki 12:28; Neh 9:18; Ps 106:19; Ac 7:41 **5** Lev 23:2,4,21,37; 2Ki 10:20; 2Ch 30:5 **6** 1Co 10:7 **7** Dt 9:12; Da 9:24; Ge 6:11,12 **8** Ex 20:3,4,23; 1Ki 12:28 **9** 2Ch 30:8; Isa 48:4; Ac 7:51 **10** Dt 9:14,19; Ex 22:24; Nu 14:12 **11** Dt 9:18,26-29 **12** Nu 14:13; ver. 14 **13** Ge 22:16; Heb 6:13; Ge 12:7; 13:15; 15:7,18; 26:4; 35:11,12

[14]So the LORD changed His mind about the harm which He had said He would do to His people.

[15]Then Moses turned and went down from the mountain with the two tablets of the Testimony in his hand; tablets that were written on both sides—they were written on one side and on the other.

[16]The tablets were the work of God; the writing was the writing of God engraved on the tablets.

[17]Now when Joshua heard the noise of the people as they shouted, he said to Moses, "There is a sound of battle in the camp."

[18]But Moses said,

"It is not the sound of the cry of victory,
Nor is it the sound of the cry of defeat;
But I hear the sound of singing."

Moses' Anger

[19]And as soon as he approached the camp and he saw the calf and the dancing, Moses' anger burned; and he threw the tablets from his hands and smashed them at the foot of the mountain.

[20]Then Moses took the calf they had made and burned it in the fire, and ground it to powder, and scattered it on the surface of the water and made the Israelites drink it.

[21]Then Moses said to Aaron, "What did this people do to you, that you have brought so great a sin on them?"

[22]Aaron said, "Do not let the anger of my lord burn; you know the people yourself, that they are prone to evil.

[23]"For they said to me, 'Make us a god who will go before us; as for this Moses, the man who brought us out of the land of Egypt, we do not know what has become of him.'

[24]"I said to them, 'Let whoever has gold [jewelry], take it off.' So they gave it to me; then I threw it into the fire, and out came this calf."

[25]Now when Moses saw that the people were out of control—for Aaron had let them get out of control to the point of being an object of mockery among their enemies—

[26]then Moses stood in the gate of the camp, and said, "Whoever is on the LORD's side, come to me!" And all the sons of Levi [the priestly tribe] gathered together to him.

[27]He said to them, "Thus says the LORD God of Israel, 'Every man strap his sword on his thigh and go back and forth from gate to gate throughout the camp, and every man kill his brother, and every man his friend, and every man his neighbor [all who continue pagan worship].' "

[28]So the sons of Levi did as Moses instructed, and about three thousand men of the people [of Israel] were killed that day.

[29]Then Moses said [to the Levites], "Dedicate yourselves today to the LORD—for each man has been against his own son and his own brother [in his attempt to escape execution]—so that He may restore *and* bestow His blessing on you this day."

32:14 *the LORD changed His mind.* Here is a wonderful example of the interaction of faithful intercessory prayer and the purpose of the Lord. He uses our prayer combined with His own determination to make His will come to pass.

32:25 – 26 *were out of control.* Obedience to God is many times just the opposite of "what everybody else is doing." Humans are very prone to giving in to peer pressure at the crucial moment. We often care more about what those around us think than about what God thinks. Aaron and the other Levites fell into this trap initially, but when Moses gave them another chance to say where their loyalties really lay, they chose the path of obedience. Even though almost "everybody was doing it," they were willing to say, "No, this is wrong. We were wrong." The Levites were not innocent, but God blessed them for their repentance and their obedience.

32:27 – 28 *his brother ... his friend ... his neighbor.* This terrible massacre is hard for us to reconcile with our feelings, but we must realize that sin is loathsome and deserving of death. The Levites were used by God to execute His judgment in this instance, but they were not given general authority to kill sinners.

14 2Sa 24:16 **15** Dt 9:15 **16** Ex 31:18 **19** Dt 9:16,17 **20** Dt 9:21 **21** Ge 26:10 **22** Ex 14:11 **25** Ex 33:4,5; 2Ch 28:19 **27** Nu 25:5 **29** 1Sa 15:18,22; Pr 21:3; Zec 13:3

30 Then the next day Moses said to
the people, "You have committed a
great sin. Now I will go up to the LORD;
perhaps I can make atonement for your
sin."
31 So Moses returned to the LORD, and
said, "Oh, these people have commit-
ted a great sin [against You], and have
made themselves a god of gold.
32 "Yet now, if You will, forgive their
sin—and if not, please blot me out of
Your book which You have written
(kill me)!"
33 But the LORD said to Moses, "Who-
ever has sinned against Me, I will blot
him out of My book [not you]. [Ps 69:28;
Dan 12:1; Phil 4:3; Rev 3:5]
34 "But now go, lead the people [to the
place] where I have told you. Behold,
My Angel shall go before you; never-
theless, in the day when I punish, I will
punish them for their sin!" [Ex 23:20;
33:2, 3]
35 So the LORD struck the people with
a plague, because of what they had
done with the calf which Aaron had
made [for them].

The Journey Resumed

33 THE LORD spoke to Moses, say-
ing, "Depart, go up from here,
you and the people whom you have
brought from the land of Egypt, to the
land which I swore to Abraham, Isaac,
and Jacob (Israel), saying, 'To your
descendants I will give it.'
2 "I will send an Angel before you and
I will drive out the Canaanite, the Am-
orite, the Hittite, the Perizzite, the Hi-
vite, and the Jebusite. [Ex 23:23; 34:11]
3 "Go up to a land [of abundance]
flowing with milk and honey; for I
will not go up in your midst, because
you are a stiff-necked (stubborn, re-
bellious) people, and I might destroy
you on the way."
4 When the people heard this sad
word, they mourned, and none of them
put on his ornaments.
5 For the LORD had said to Moses,
"Say to the sons of Israel, 'You are
a stiff-necked (stubborn, rebellious)
people! If I should come among you
for one moment, I would destroy you.
Now therefore, [penitently] take off
your ornaments, so that I may know
what to do with you.' "
6 So the Israelites left off all their or-
naments [in repentance], from Mount
Horeb (Sinai) *onward.*
7 Now Moses used to take his own
tent and pitch it outside the camp, far
away from the camp, and he called
it the tent of meeting [of God with
His own people]. And everyone who
sought the LORD would go out to the
[temporary] tent of meeting which was
outside the camp.
8 Whenever Moses went out to the
tent, all the people would rise and
stand, each at his tent door, and look
at Moses until he entered the tent.
9 Whenever Moses entered the tent,
the pillar of cloud would descend and
stand at the doorway of the tent; and
the LORD would speak with Moses.

32:32–33 *blot me out of Your book.* Like Paul many centuries later, Moses could almost wish himself to be cursed, if by being so he could secure the salvation of his people (Ro 9:3).
32:34 *in the day.* This may refer to the day of the Lord, proclaimed by later prophets (Joel 2; Zep 1).
33:5 *stiff-necked.* Contrary to popular belief, God did not choose the Hebrew people because of their righteousness or willingness to serve Him (Dt 9:7). In fact, one of Israel's besetting sins was obstinacy (vv. 3,5), and God saw them as a rebellious and stiff-necked people. The opposite of being obstinate is to "circumcise [that is, remove sin from] your heart" (Dt 10:16). Such a heart is inclined to obey the Word of God. God's presence with His people was in response to His covenantal promise: if they obeyed Him they would be His "special possession and treasure" (Ex 19:5).
33:6 *left off all their ornaments.* These ornaments were probably associated with the idolatrous worship of the golden calf. Their removal was a mark of genuine repentance and renewal.
33:8 *all the people would rise and stand.* In contrast to their former wickedness, the people now responded reverently to the living God.

30 1Sa 12:20,23; 2Sa 16:12; Nu 25:13 **31** Dt 9:18; Ex 20:23 **32** Ps 69:28; Ro 9:3; Da 12:1; Php 4:3; Rev 3:5; 21:27 **33** Lev 23:30; Eze 18:4 **34** Ex 33:2,14; Dt 32:35; Ro 2:5,6 **35** 2Sa 12:9 **CHAPTER 33** **1** Ex 32:7; Ge 12:7 **2** Ex 32:34; Jos 24:11 **3** Ex 3:8; Ex 32:9; Nu 16:21,45 **4** Nu 14:1,39; Ezr 9:3; Est 4:1,4; Eze 24:17,23 **5** See Nu 16:45,46; Ps 139:23 **7** Ex 29:42,43; Dt 4:29 **8** Nu 16:27 **9** Ex 25:22; 31:18; Ps 99:7

10 When all the people saw the pillar of cloud standing at the tent door, all the people would rise and worship, each at his tent door.

11 And so the LORD used to speak to Moses face to face, just as a man speaks to his friend. When Moses returned to the camp, his attendant Joshua, the son of Nun, a young man, would not depart from the tent.

Moses Intercedes

12 Moses said to the LORD, "See, You say to me, 'Bring up this people,' but You have not let me know whom You will send with me. Yet You have said, 'I know you by name, and you have also found favor in My sight.'

13 "Now therefore, I pray you, if I have found favor in Your sight, let me know Your ways so that I may know You [becoming more deeply and intimately acquainted with You, recognizing and understanding Your ways more clearly] and that I may find grace *and* favor in Your sight. And consider also, that this nation is Your people."

14 And the LORD said, "My presence shall go *with you,* and I will give you rest [by bringing you and the people into the promised land]." [Deut 3:20]

15 And Moses said to Him, "If Your presence does not go [with me], do not lead us up from here.

16 "For how then can it be known that Your people and I have found favor in Your sight? Is it not by Your going with us, so that we are distinguished, Your people and I, from all the [other] people on the face of the earth?"

17 The LORD said to Moses, "I will also do this thing that you have asked; for you have found favor (lovingkindness, mercy) in My sight and I have known you [personally] by name." [Rev 2:17]

18 Then Moses said, "Please, show me Your glory!"

19 And God said, "I will make all My goodness pass before you, and I will proclaim the Name of the LORD before you; for I will be gracious to whom I will be gracious, and will show compassion (lovingkindness) on whom I will show compassion." [Rom 9:15, 16]

20 But He said, "You cannot see My face, for no man shall see Me and live!"

21 Then the LORD said, "Behold, there is a place beside Me, and you shall stand there on the rock;

22 and while My glory is passing by, I will put you in a cleft of the rock and *protectively* cover you with My hand until I have passed by.

23 "Then I will take away My hand and you shall see My back; but My face shall not be seen."

The Two Tablets Replaced

34 THEN THE LORD said to Moses, "Cut two tablets of stone like the first, and I will write on these tablets the words that were on the first tablets which you smashed [when you learned of Israel's idolatry].

2 "So be ready by morning, and come up in the morning to Mount Sinai, and present yourself there to Me on the top of the mountain.

3 "No man is to come up with you, nor let any man be seen anywhere on the mountain; nor let flocks or herds feed in front of that mountain."

4 So Moses cut two tablets of stone like the first ones, and he got up early in the morning and went up on Mount Sinai, as the LORD had commanded him, and took the two tablets of stone in his hand.

5 Then the LORD descended in the cloud and stood there with Moses as he proclaimed the Name of the LORD.

33:11 ***his attendant Joshua.*** The word translated *attendant* here does not mean slave, but rather a minister, one who does spiritual service.
33:17 ***I have known you [personally] by name.*** God's grace was accompanied by His intimate knowledge of and care for Moses.
33:22 – 23 ***My hand.*** The use of words such as hand, back, and face is a way of describing God, who is Spirit, in terms familiar to humans.

10 Ex 4:31 **11** Nu 12:8; Dt 34:10; Ex 24:13 **12** Ex 32:34; ver. 17; Jn 10:14,15; 2Ti 2:19 **13** Ex 34:9; Ps 25:4; 27:11; 86:11; 119:33; Dt 9:26,29 **14** Isa 63:9; Jos 21:44 **15** ver. 3 **16** Nu 14:14; Ex 34:10; Dt 4:7,34 **17** Jas 5:16; ver. 12 **18** 1Ti 6:16 **19** Ro 9:15,16,18; Ro 4:4,16 **20** Ge 32:30 **22** Isa 2:21; Ps 91:1,4 **23** Jn 1:18
CHAPTER 34 **1** Ex 32:16,19; ver. 28; Dt 10:2,4 **2** Ex 19:20 **3** Ex 19:12,13,21 **5** Ex 33:19

6 Then the LORD passed by in front of him, and proclaimed, "The LORD, the LORD God, compassionate and gracious, slow to anger, and abounding in lovingkindness and truth (faithfulness);

7 keeping mercy *and* lovingkindness for thousands, forgiving iniquity and transgression and sin; but He will by no means leave *the guilty* unpunished, visiting (avenging) the iniquity (sin, guilt) of the fathers upon the children and the grandchildren to the third and fourth generations [that is, calling the children to account for the sins of their fathers]."

8 Moses bowed to the earth immediately and worshiped [the Lord].

9 And he said, "If now I have found favor *and* lovingkindness in Your sight, O Lord, let the Lord, please, go in our midst, though it is a stiff-necked (stubborn, rebellious) people, and pardon our iniquity and our sin, and take us as Your possession."

The Covenant Renewed

10 Then God said, "Behold, I am going to make a covenant. Before all your people I will do wondrous works (miracles) such as have not been created *or* produced in all the earth nor among any of the nations; and all the people among whom you live shall see the working of the LORD, for it is a fearful *and* awesome thing that I am going to do with you.

11 "Be sure to observe what I am commanding you this day: behold, I am going to drive out the Amorite before you, and the Canaanite, the Hittite, the Perizzite, the Hivite, and the Jebusite.

12 "Watch yourself so that you do not make a covenant (solemn agreement, treaty) with the inhabitants of the land into which you are going, or it will become a [dangerous] trap among you.

13 "But you shall tear down *and* destroy their [pagan] altars, smash in pieces their [sacred] pillars (obelisks, images) and cut down their Asherim

14 —for you shall not worship any other god; for the LORD, whose name is Jealous, is a jealous (impassioned) God [demanding what is rightfully and uniquely His]—

15 otherwise you might make a covenant with the inhabitants of the land and they would play the prostitute with their gods and sacrifice to their gods, and someone might invite you to eat his sacrifice (meal),

16 and you might take some of his daughters for your sons, and his daughters would play the prostitute with their gods and cause your sons also to play the prostitute (commit apostasy) with their gods [that is, abandon the true God for man-made idols].

17 "You shall make for yourselves no molten gods.

18 "You shall observe the Feast of Unleavened Bread (Passover). For seven days you shall eat unleavened bread, as

---

34:6 ***compassionate and gracious ... abounding in lovingkindness and truth.*** God is overwhelmingly gracious. John's description of the coming of Jesus echoes this passage, describing the Messiah as "full of grace and truth" (Jn 1:14,17). To see Jesus is to see the Father (Jn 1:18).

34:7 ***forgiving iniquity.*** God is a God of unlimited grace, mercy, and forgiveness. But man is not automatically forgiven — "He will by no means leave the guilty unpunished." We receive forgiveness from God only when we repent and seek reconciliation with Him. The second covenant with Israel (34:10) included relief from the judgment of the people's sins to allow them to be taught their need and seek forgiveness.

34:15 ***play the prostitute with their gods.*** This is probably more than a figure of speech. Unfaithfulness to the Lord was often manifested in sexual rites with temple prostitutes (male and female), acts of supposed union with Baal, Asherah, and other pagan deities.

34:16 ***take some of his daughters for your sons.*** The quickest way for the Israelites to become corrupted with the false worship of the Canaanites would have been to marry into it.

---

6 Neh 9:17; Joel 2:13; Ro 2:4; Ps 108:4 **7** Ex 20:6; Ps 103:3; 130:4; Da 9:9; Eph 4:32; 1Jn 1:9; Jos 24:19; Job 10:14; Mic 6:11; Na 1:3 **8** Ex 4:31 **9** Ex 33:15,16; Ex 33:3; Ps 33:12; 94:14 **10** Dt 5:2; Dt 4:32; Ps 77:14; Ps 145:6 **11** Dt 6:25; Ex 33:2 **12** Ex 23:32; Ex 23:33 **13** Dt 12:3; 2Ki 18:4; 2Ch 34:3,4 **14** Ex 20:3,5; See Isa 9:6; 57:15; Ex 20:5 **15** ver. 12; Jdg 2:17; Nu 25:2; 1Co 8:4,7,10 **16** Dt 7:3; 1Ki 11:2; Ezr 9:2; Neh 13:25; Nu 25:1,2; 1Ki 11:4 **17** Ex 32:8 **18** Ex 12:15; Ex 13:4

I have commanded you, at the appointed time in the month of Abib; for in the month of Abib you came out of Egypt.

19 "All the firstborn males among your livestock belong to Me, whether cattle or sheep.

20 "You shall redeem the firstborn of a donkey with a lamb; but if you do not redeem it, then you shall break its neck. You shall redeem all the firstborn of your sons. None of you are to appear before Me empty-handed.

21 "You shall work for six days, but on the seventh day you shall rest; [even] in plowing time and in harvest you shall rest [on the Sabbath].

22 "You shall observe *and* celebrate the Feast of Weeks (Harvest, First Fruits, or Pentecost), the first fruits of the wheat harvest, and the Feast of Ingathering (Booths or Tabernacles) at the year's end.

23 "Three times a year all your males shall appear before the Lord GOD, the God of Israel.

24 "For I will drive out *and* dispossess nations before you and enlarge your borders; nor shall any man covet (actively seek for himself) your land when you go up to appear before the LORD your God three times a year.

25 "You shall not offer the blood of My sacrifice with leavened bread, nor shall the sacrifice of the Feast of the Passover (Unleavened Bread) be left over until morning.

26 "You shall bring the very first of the first fruits of your ground to the house of the LORD your God.

"You shall not boil a young goat in his mother's milk [as some pagans do]."

27 Then the LORD said to Moses, "Write these words, for in accordance with these words I have made a covenant with you and with Israel."

28 Moses was there with the LORD forty days and forty nights; he ate no bread and drank no water. And he wrote on the tablets the words of the covenant, the Ten Commandments.

Moses' Face Shines

29 When Moses came down from Mount Sinai with the two tablets of the Testimony in his hand, he did not know that the skin of his face was shining [with a unique radiance] because he had been speaking with God.

30 When Aaron and all the Israelites saw Moses, behold, the skin of his face shone, and they were afraid to approach him.

31 But Moses called to them, and Aaron and all the leaders of the congregation returned to him; and he spoke to them.

32 Afterward all the Israelites approached him, and he commanded them to do everything that the LORD had said to him on Mount Sinai.

33 When Moses had finished speaking with them, he put a veil over his face.

34 But whenever Moses went in before the LORD to speak with Him, he would take off the veil until he came out. When he came out and he told the Israelites what he had been commanded [by God],

35 the Israelites would see the face of Moses, how his skin shone [with a unique radiance]. So Moses put the veil on his face again until he went in to speak with God.

The Sabbath Emphasized

35 MOSES GATHERED all the congregation of the sons of Israel together, and said to them, "These

---

34:28 *forty days and forty nights.* A person can survive without food for weeks, but no one can go entirely without water for more than three or four days. This fact has been used to cast doubt on the truth of this passage, but we must recall that there is no reason to think that God could not keep His servant hydrated in any way He chose.

34:33 *a veil over his face.* Paul taught that Moses wore the veil because the glow faded, a sign of imperfect glory (2Co 3:7,13).

19 Ex 22:29 **20** Ex 13:13; Ex 23:15; Dt 16:16; 1Sa 9:7,8; 2Sa 24:24 **21** Ex 20:9; Lk 13:14 **22** Ex 23:16 **23** Ex 23:14,17 **24** Ex 33:2; Ps 78:55; Dt 12:20; 19:8; See Ge 35:5; Ac 18:10 **25** Ex 23:18; Ex 12:10 **26** Ex 23:19; Ex 23:19 **27** Dt 31:9 **28** Ex 24:18; ver. 1; Ex 31:18; Dt 4:13; 10:2,4 **29** Ex 32:15; Mt 17:2; 2Co 3:7,13 **32** Ex 24:3 **33** 2Co 3:13 **34** 2Co 3:16 **CHAPTER 35** **1** Ex 34:32

are the things which the LORD has commanded you to do:
2“For six days work may be done, but the seventh day shall be a holy day for you, a Sabbath of complete rest to the LORD; whoever does any kind of work on that day shall be put to death.
3“You shall not kindle a fire in any of your dwellings on the Sabbath day.”
4And Moses said to all the congregation of the sons of Israel, “This is the thing which the LORD has commanded:
5‘Take from among you an offering to the LORD. Whoever has a willing heart, let him bring it as the LORD’s offering: gold, silver, and bronze,
6blue, purple, and scarlet fabric, fine linen, goats’ *hair,*
7and rams’ skins dyed red, and skins of porpoises, and acacia wood,
8and [olive] oil for the lighting, and balsam for the anointing oil, and for the fragrant incense,
9and onyx stones and other stones to be set for the ephod and the breastpiece.

Tabernacle Workmen

10‘Let every skilled *and* talented man among you come, and make everything that the LORD has commanded:
11the tabernacle (sacred dwelling of God), its tent and its covering, its hooks, its boards, its bars, its pillars, and its sockets;
12the ark [of the covenant] and its carrying poles, with the mercy seat and the veil (partition curtain) of the screen [to hang between the Holy Place and the Holy of Holies];
13the table and its carrying poles, and all its utensils, and the bread of the [divine] Presence (showbread);
14the lampstand also for the light and its utensils and its lamps, and the oil for the light;
15and the altar of incense and its carrying poles, the anointing oil and the fragrant incense, the screen (curtain) for the doorway at the entrance of the tabernacle;
16the altar of burnt offering with its bronze grating, its carrying poles, and all its utensils, the wash basin and its base (stand);
17the court’s curtains, its support poles and their sockets, and the curtain for the gate of the courtyard;
18the pegs of the tabernacle and the pegs of the court and their cords;
19the finely-woven garments for ministering in the Holy Place, the holy garments for Aaron the priest and the garments for his sons, to minister as priests.’ ”

Gifts Received

20Then all the congregation of the Israelites left Moses’ presence.
21Everyone whose heart stirred him and everyone whose spirit moved him came and brought the LORD’s offering to be used for the Tent of Meeting, for all its service, and for the holy garments.
22Then all whose hearts moved them, both men and women, came and brought brooches, earrings *or* nose rings, signet rings, and necklaces, all jewels of gold; everyone bringing an offering of gold to the LORD.
23Every man who had in his possession blue or purple or scarlet fabric, and fine linen, and goats’ *hair,* and rams’ skins dyed red and porpoise skins, brought them.
24Everyone who could make an offering of silver or bronze brought it as the LORD’s offering; every man who had in his possession acacia wood for any work of the service brought it.
25All the skilled *and* talented women spun thread with their hands, and brought what they had spun, blue and purple and scarlet fabric and fine linen.
26All the women whose heart stirred with a skill spun the goats’ *hair.*
27The leaders brought onyx stones and other stones to be put in settings for the ephod and for the breastpiece,
28and spice and [olive] oil for the light and for the anointing oil and for the fragrant incense.
29The Israelites, all the men and women whose heart moved them to

2 Ex 20:9; Lev 23:3 **3** Ex 16:23 **4** Ex 25:1,2 **5** Ex 25:2 **8** Ex 25:6 **10** Ex 31:6 **11** Ex 26:1,2 **12** Ex 25:10 **13** Ex 25:23; Ex 25:30; Lev 24:5,6 **14** Ex 25:31 **15** Ex 30:1; Ex 30:25; Ex 30:34 **16** Ex 27:1 **17** Ex 27:9 **19** Ex 31:10; 39:1,41; Nu 4:5,6 **21** ver. 5,22,26,29; Ex 36:2 **23** 1Ch 29:8 **25** Ex 28:3; 31:6; 36:1 **27** 1Ch 29:6; Ezr 2:68 **28** Ex 30:23 **29** ver. 21; 1Ch 29:9

bring *material* for all the work which
the LORD had commanded through
Moses to be done, brought a freewill
(voluntary) offering to the LORD.
30 Then Moses said to the Israelites,
"See, the LORD called by name Bezalel
son of Uri, the son of Hur, of the tribe
of Judah;
31 and He has filled him with the
Spirit of God, with wisdom *and* skill,
with intelligence *and* understanding,
and with knowledge in all [areas of]
craftsmanship,
32 to devise artistic designs to work
in gold, silver, and bronze,
33 and in the cutting of stones for set-
ting and in the carving of wood, for
work in every skilled craft.
34 "He has also put in Bezalel's heart
[the willingness] to teach [others the
same skills], both he and Oholiab, son
of Ahisamach, of the tribe of Dan.
35 "He has filled them with skill to do
the work of an engraver, of a designer,
and of an embroiderer, in blue, purple,
and scarlet fabric, and in fine linen, and
of a weaver; makers of every work and
embroiderers of [excellent] designs.

The Tabernacle Underwritten

36 "BEZALEL AND Oholiab, and
every skilled person in whom
the LORD has put ability and under-
standing to know how to do all the
work in the construction of the sanc-
tuary, shall work according to all that
the LORD has commanded."
2 So Moses called Bezalel and Oholi-
ab and every skilled person in whom
the LORD had put ability, everyone
whose heart stirred him, to come to
do the work.
3 They received from Moses all the of-
ferings which the Israelites had brought
for the construction of the sanctuary,
to prepare it for service. And they con-
tinued to bring him freewill (voluntary)
offerings every morning.
4 And all the skilled men who were
doing all the work on the sanctuary
came, each one from the work which
he was doing,
5 and they said to Moses, "The people
are bringing much more than enough
for the construction work which the
LORD commanded us to do."
6 So Moses issued a command, and it
was proclaimed throughout the camp,
"Let neither man nor woman do any
more work for the sanctuary offering."
So the people were restrained from
bringing *anything more;*
7 for the material they had was suffi-
cient and more than enough to do all
the work.

Construction Proceeds

8 All the skilled men among them who
were doing the work on the tabernacle
made ten curtains of fine twisted linen
and blue, purple, and scarlet fabric, with
cherubim [worked into them], the work
of an embroiderer, Bezalel made them.
9 Each curtain was twenty-eight cu-
bits long and four cubits wide; all the
curtains were one size.
10 Bezalel joined five curtains one to
another, and [the other] five curtains
he joined one to another.
11 He made loops of blue on the edge of

35:31–35 *Spirit of God.* The work of the Holy Spirit is often thought to have begun at Pentecost (Ac 2), but in fact the Holy Spirit of God was at work long before that time. The Old Testament shows that He was active in creation (Ge 1:2; Job 33:4). The Spirit came upon men for prophetic utterance (1Sa 10:10) and for all divine revelation (2Sa 23:2). Men were endowed for special functions by the power of the Holy Spirit (Ex 31:3; Jdg 11:29; 13:25; 14:6). Bezalel is a good example of a man indwelt by the Spirit of God in the Old Testament (37:1–9).

36:8–37:29 Servant—Not only ability was required for service in building the tabernacle. God also wanted willing hearts (36:2). Even if we do not feel that we are particularly good at anything, we must remember that every talent we possess, no matter how small, is a gift from God. He gives us these gifts so that we will have something to give back to Him. We should look at ourselves, not saying, "I don't have any great skill, I'll just sit and watch," but rather, "Here's what I have—where shall I start?"

30 Ex 31:2 **34** Ex 31:6 **35** ver. 31; Ex 31:3,6; 1Ki 7:14; 2Ch 2:14; Isa 28:26 **CHAPTER 36** **1** Ex 28:3; 31:6; 35:10,35; Ex 25:8 **2** Ex 35:21,26; 1Ch 29:5 **3** Ex 35:27 **5** 2Co 8:2,3 **8** Ex 26:1

the outermost curtain in the first set; he also did this on the edge of the curtain that was outermost in the second set.

[12]He made fifty loops in the one curtain [of the first set] and fifty loops on the edge of the curtain which was in the second set; the loops were opposite one another.

[13]He made fifty gold hooks and joined the curtains together with the hooks, so that the tabernacle became a unit.

[14]Then he made curtains of goats' *hair* for a tent over the tabernacle; he made eleven curtains in all.

[15]Each curtain was thirty cubits long and four cubits wide; the eleven curtains were of equal size.

[16]Bezalel joined five curtains by themselves and [the other] six curtains by themselves.

[17]He made fifty loops on the edge of the outermost curtain in the *first* set, and he made fifty loops on the edge of the *outermost* curtain of the second set.

[18]He made fifty bronze hooks to join the tent together into a unit.

[19]He made a [third] covering for the tent of rams' skins dyed red, and above it a [fourth] covering of porpoise skins.

[20]Bezalel made boards of acacia wood for the upright framework of the tabernacle.

[21]Each board was ten cubits long and one and a half cubits wide.

[22]Each board had two tenons (dovetails), fitted to one another; he did this for all the boards of the tabernacle.

[23]And [this is how] he made the boards [for frames] for the tabernacle: twenty boards for the south side;

[24]and he made under the twenty boards forty silver sockets; two sockets under one board for its two tenons (dovetails), and two sockets under another board for its two tenons.

[25]For the other side of the tabernacle, the north side, he made twenty boards,

[26]and their forty silver sockets; two sockets under [the end of] each board.

[27]And for the rear of the tabernacle, to the west, he made six [frame] boards.

[28]And he made two boards for each corner of the tabernacle in the rear.

[29]They were separate below, but linked together at the top with one ring; thus he made both of them in both corners.

[30]There were eight boards with sixteen silver sockets, and under [the end of] each board two sockets.

[31]Bezalel made bars of acacia wood, five for the [frame] boards of the one side of the tabernacle,

[32]and five bars for the boards of the tabernacle's other side, and five bars for the boards at the rear side to the west.

[33]And he made the middle bar pass through [horizontally] halfway up the boards from one end to the other.

[34]He overlaid the boards and the bars with gold and made their rings of gold as holders for the bars.

[35]Further, Bezalel made the veil of blue and purple and scarlet fabric, and fine twisted linen; he made it with cherubim, the work of an embroiderer. [Matt 27:50, 51; Heb 10:19–22]

[36]For the veil (partition curtain) he made four support poles of acacia wood and overlaid them with gold; their hooks were gold, and he cast for them four silver sockets.

[37]He made a screen (curtain) for the doorway of the tent, of blue, purple, and scarlet fabric, and fine twisted linen, the work of an embroiderer;

[38]and [he made] the five support poles with their hooks, and overlaid their [ornamental] tops and connecting rings with gold; but their five sockets were bronze.

Construction Continues

37 BEZALEL MADE the ark [of the covenant] of acacia wood—it was two and a half cubits long, and one and a half cubits wide, and one and a half cubits high.

37:1 – 9 *Bezalel.* Bezalel carefully reproduced the pattern given to Moses (25:10 – 22). Obviously this pattern wasn't just a "design suggestion" from God. Each detail had to be just like the plan because each part was a symbol or reminder of their relationship with God, His character, and His holiness.

12 Ex 26:5 **14** Ex 26:7 **19** Ex 26:14 **20** Ex 26:15; Ex 25:5,10; Nu 15:1; Dt 10:3; Jos 2:1 **31** Ex 26:26 **35** Ex 26:31 **37** Ex 26:36 **CHAPTER 37** **1** Ex 25:10

2 And he overlaid it with pure gold inside and out, and made a molding (border) of gold to go all around [the top of it].

3 He cast four rings of gold for it on its four feet, two rings on one side and two rings on the other side.

4 He made carrying poles of acacia wood and overlaid them with gold.

5 He put the carrying poles through the rings at the sides of the ark, to carry it.

6 Bezalel made the mercy seat of pure gold; it was two and a half cubits long, and one and a half cubits wide.

7 He made two cherubim of hammered gold; he made them at the two ends of the mercy seat,

8 one cherub at one end and one cherub at the other end; he made the cherubim [of one piece] with the mercy seat at the two ends.

9 The cherubim spread out their wings upward, covering *and* protecting the mercy seat with their wings, with their faces toward each other; the faces of the cherubim were [looking downward] toward the mercy seat. [Heb 9:23–26]

10 Bezalel made the table [for the bread] of acacia wood; it was two cubits long, a cubit wide, and one and a half cubits high.

11 He overlaid it with pure gold, and made a border of gold for it all around [its top].

12 He made a rim for it [just under the top] a hand width wide all around, and a border of gold around its rim.

13 He cast four rings of gold for it and fastened the rings to the four corners that were at its four legs.

14 Close by the rim were the rings, the holders for the poles [to pass through] to carry the table.

15 Bezalel made the carrying poles of acacia wood to carry the table and overlaid them with gold.

16 He made the utensils which were to be on the table, its dishes and its pans [for bread], its bowls and its jars for pouring drink offerings, of pure gold.

17 Then he made the lampstand (menorah) of pure gold. He made the lampstand of hammered work, its base and its [center] shaft; its cups, its calyxes, and its flowers were *all of one piece* with it.

18 There were six branches coming out of the sides of the lampstand, three branches from one side of *the center shaft* and three branches from the other side of it;

19 three cups shaped like almond *blossoms*, a calyx and a flower in one branch, and three cups shaped like almond *blossoms*, a calyx and a flower in the opposite branch—so for the six branches coming out of *the center shaft of* the lampstand.

20 On *the center shaft of* the lampstand there were four cups shaped like almond *blossoms*, with calyxes and flowers [one at the top];

21 and a calyx was under the *first* pair of branches *coming* out of it, and a calyx under the *second* pair of branches, *coming* out of it, and a calyx under the *third* pair of branches *coming* out of it, for the six branches coming out of the lampstand.

22 Their calyxes and their branches were *of one piece* with it; all of it was a single hammered work of pure gold.

23 He made its seven lamps with its snuffers and its trays of pure gold.

24 He made the lampstand and all its utensils from a talent of pure gold. [John 1:4, 5, 9; 2 Cor 4:6]

25 Then Bezalel made the incense altar of acacia wood; its top was a cubit square and it was two cubits high; the horns were *of one piece* with it.

26 He overlaid it with pure gold, its top, its sides all around and its horns; he also made a rim of gold around it.

27 He made two rings of gold for it under its rim, on its two opposite sides, as holders for the poles [to pass through] to carry it.

28 He made the poles of acacia wood and overlaid them with gold.

29 He also made the holy anointing oil and the pure, fragrant incense of spices, the work of a perfumer.

The Tabernacle Completed

38 THEN BEZALEL made the altar of burnt offering of acacia wood;

6 Ex 25:17 **10** Ex 25:23 **16** Ex 25:29 **17** Ex 25:31 **25** Ex 30:1; 40:26; 1Ki 9:25; 2Ch 29:6,7; Isa 60:6; Heb 7:25 **29** Ex 30:23,34; Ps 133:2; Isa 11:2; 61:1; 1Jn 2:20 **CHAPTER 38** **1** Ex 27:1

its top was square, five cubits long and
five cubits wide, and three cubits high.
2 And he made its horns (horn-shaped projections) on the four corners of it; the horns were *of one piece* with it, and he overlaid it with bronze.
3 He made all the utensils *and* vessels of the altar [of burnt offering], the pots, shovels, basins [to catch the blood of the sacrificed animal], meat hooks and the firepans [to store live coals]. He made all its utensils of bronze.
4 He made for the altar a grating of bronze mesh under its rim, extending halfway up it.
5 He cast four rings for the four corners of the bronze grating as holders for the carrying poles.
6 And he made the carrying poles of acacia wood and overlaid them with bronze.
7 He put the poles through the rings on the sides of the altar, with which to carry it; he made it hollow with planks.
8 Bezalel made the basin and its base of bronze from the mirrors of the attending women who served *and* ministered at the doorway of the Tent of Meeting.
9 Then he made the court: for the south side the curtains of the court were of fine twisted linen, a hundred cubits;
10 their twenty support poles, and their twenty bronze sockets; the hooks of the support poles and their connecting rings were silver.
11 And for the north side [of the court the curtains were also] a hundred cubits; their twenty support poles and their twenty bronze sockets; the hooks of the support poles and their connecting rings were silver.
12 For the west side [of the court] there were curtains of fifty cubits with their ten support poles and their ten sockets; the hooks of the support poles and their connecting rings were silver.
13 For the east side [the front of the courtyard, there were curtains of] fifty cubits.
14 The curtains for one side *of the court gate were* fifteen cubits, with their three support poles and their three sockets;
15 and *the same* for the other side [of the court gate]. Left and right of the court gate there were curtains of fifteen cubits; with their three support poles and their three sockets.
16 All the curtains around the court were of fine twisted linen.
17 The sockets for the support poles were *made of* bronze, the hooks of the support poles and their connecting rings were *made of* silver; and silver overlaid their tops. All the support poles of the court had silver connecting rings.
18 The screen (curtain) for the gate of the courtyard [on the east side] was the work of an embroiderer, in blue, purple, and scarlet fabric, and fine twisted linen; it was twenty cubits long and five cubits high, corresponding to the curtains of the court.
19 Their four support poles and their four sockets were bronze; their hooks were silver, and silver overlaid their tops and their connecting rings.
20 All the pegs for the tabernacle and the court were bronze.

The Cost of the Tabernacle

21 This is the sum of the things for the tabernacle, the tabernacle of the Testimony, as counted according to the command of Moses, for the work of the Levites, under the direction of Ithamar the son of Aaron the priest.
22 Now Bezalel the son of Uri, the

38:22–23 Responsibility — No higher tribute can be paid than "Well done — you've finished." Bezalel and his assistant, Oholiab, were called, Spirit endowed, and commissioned for one work and one work alone. Neither of these individuals ever became celebrities, but God does not measure our effectiveness in His kingdom work by how many times we make the headlines in the local media. God cares about whether we obey Him faithfully, not whether other people approve of us. It is easy to make verbal commitments that sound really good, but God isn't looking for fine words. He complimented Bezalel and Oholiab on finishing their assignment, not on their fine start or their good intentions (39:43).

8 Ex 30:18 **9** Ex 27:9 **20** Ex 27:19 **21** Nu 1:50,53; 9:15; 10:11; 17:7,8; 2Ch 24:6; Ac 7:44; Nu 4:28,33 **22** Ex 31:2,6

son of Hur, of the tribe of Judah, made
everything that the LORD commanded
Moses.
23 With him was Oholiab the son of
Ahisamach, of the tribe of Dan, an
engraver and a skillful craftsman and
an embroiderer in blue and in purple
and in scarlet fabric, and in fine linen.
24 All the gold that was used for the
work, in all the building *and* furnish-
ing of the sanctuary, the gold from
the wave offering, was twenty-nine
talents and seven hundred and thirty
shekels, according to the shekel of the
sanctuary.
25 The silver from those of the con-
gregation who were assembled *and*
counted was 100 talents and 1,775
shekels, according to the shekel of the
sanctuary;
26 a beka for each man (that is, half
a shekel according to the shekel of
the sanctuary) for everyone who was
counted, from twenty years old and
upward, for 603,550 men.
27 The hundred talents of silver were
for casting the sockets of the sanctuary
and the sockets of the veil (partition
curtain); a hundred sockets for the
hundred talents, a talent for a socket.
28 Of the 1,775 *shekels,* he made
hooks for the support poles and over-
laid their tops and made connecting
rings for them.
29 The bronze of the wave offering
was seventy talents and 2,400 shekels.
30 With it Bezalel made the sock-
ets for the doorway of the Tent of
Meeting, and the bronze altar and its
bronze grating, and all the utensils
of the altar,
31 and the sockets of the court all
around and the sockets of the court
gate, and all the pegs of the tabernacle
and all the pegs around the court.

The Priestly Garments

39 MOREOVER, FROM the blue
and purple and scarlet fabric,
they made finely woven garments for
serving *and* ministering in the Holy
Place; they made the holy garments
for Aaron, just as the LORD had com-
manded Moses.
2 Bezalel made the ephod of gold, and
of blue, purple, and scarlet fabric, and
fine twisted linen.
3 Then Bezalel and Oholiab ham-
mered the gold [into thin sheets] and cut
it into threads to work into the blue, pur-
ple, and scarlet fabric, and into the fine
linen, the work of a skilled craftsman.
4 They made attaching shoulder piec-
es for the ephod; it was attached at its
two [upper] edges.
5 The skillfully woven sash with
which to bind it, which was on the
ephod [to hold it in place], was like its
workmanship, of the same material:
of gold and of blue, purple, and scarlet
fabric, and fine twisted linen, just as
the LORD had commanded Moses.
6 They made the onyx stones, set in
settings of gold filigree; they were en-
graved as signets are engraved, with
the names of [the twelve tribes of] the
sons of Israel.
7 And he put them on the shoulder
pieces of the ephod to be memorial
stones (a remembrance) for the sons
of Israel (Jacob), just as the LORD had
commanded Moses.
8 Bezalel made the breastpiece, the
work of a skillful craftsman, like the
workmanship of the ephod: of gold and
of blue, purple, and scarlet fabric, and
fine twisted linen.
9 It was square; they made the breast-
piece folded double, a [hand's] span
long and a [hand's] span wide when
folded double.

38:24 *All the gold.* The weight of all the gold used in the work may have been about a ton. The talent weighed about 75 pounds, and equaled 3,000 shekels.
38:25 *The silver.* The quantity of silver was enormous, about 7,000 pounds.
38:26 *a beka for each man.* The census of Numbers 14:6 puts the number of men over the age of 20 at 603,550.
38:27 – 28 *the sanctuary.* Although the tabernacle was a tent, it was not a makeshift dwelling. It was a glorious shrine that symbolized the presence of the living God in the midst of the people.

24 Ex 30:13,24; Lev 5:15; 27:3,25; Nu 3:47; 18:16 **26** Ex 30:13,15; Nu 1:46 **27** Ex 26:19,21,25,32 **28** Ex 27:17
CHAPTER 39 **1** Ex 35:23; Ex 31:10; 35:19; Ex 28:4 **2** Ex 28:6 **6** Ex 28:9 **7** Ex 28:12 **8** Ex 28:15

10 And they mounted four rows of stones on it. The first row was a row of ruby, topaz, and emerald;

11 and the second row, a turquoise, a sapphire, and a diamond;

12 and the third row, a jacinth, an agate, and an amethyst;

13 and the fourth row, a beryl, an onyx, and a jasper; they were mounted in settings of gold filigree.

14 The stones corresponded to the names of the sons of Israel; they were twelve [in all], corresponding to their names, engraved like a signet, each with its name, for the twelve tribes.

15 And they made on the breastpiece twisted chains like cords of pure gold.

16 They made two settings of gold filigree and two gold rings, and put the two rings on the two ends of the breastpiece.

17 Then they put the two twisted cords of gold in the two rings on the ends of the breastpiece.

18 They put the [other] two ends of the two cords on the two filigree settings, and put them on the shoulder pieces of the ephod at the front of it.

19 They made two rings of gold and put them on the two ends of the breastpiece, on its inner edge which was next to the ephod.

20 Furthermore, they made two [other] gold rings and attached them to the bottom of the two shoulder pieces of the ephod, at the front of it, close to the place where it is joined, above the woven sash of the ephod.

21 They bound the breastpiece by its rings to the rings of the ephod with a blue cord, so that it would lie on the woven sash of the ephod, and so that the breastpiece would not come loose from the ephod, just as the LORD commanded Moses.

22 Then Bezalel made the robe of the ephod of woven work, all of blue;

23 there was an opening [for the head] in the middle of the robe, like the opening in a coat of armor, with a hem around it, so that it would not be frayed *or* torn.

24 On the hem of the robe they made pomegranates of blue, purple, and scarlet fabric, and fine twisted linen.

25 They also made bells of pure gold, and put the bells between the pomegranates around the hem of the robe;

26 a bell and a pomegranate, a bell and a pomegranate, all [the way] around the hem of the robe, for service *and* ministering, just as the LORD commanded Moses.

27 And they made tunics of finely woven linen for Aaron and his sons,

28 and the turban of fine linen, and the ornamental caps of fine linen, and the linen undergarments of fine twisted linen,

29 and the sash of fine twisted linen, and blue, purple, and scarlet fabric, the work of an embroiderer, just as the LORD commanded Moses.

30 They made the plate of the holy crown of pure gold, and wrote on it an inscription, like the engravings of a signet, "Holy to the LORD." [Ex 28:36]

31 They tied a blue cord to it, to fasten it on the turban above, just as the LORD commanded Moses.

32 Thus all the work of the tabernacle of the Tent of Meeting was finished; and the Israelites did according to all that the LORD had commanded Moses; that is what they did.

33 They brought the tabernacle to Moses [for him to inspect]: the tent and all its furnishings, its hooks, its [frame] boards, its bars, its support poles, its sockets *or* bases;

34 and the covering of rams' skins dyed red, and the covering of porpoise skins, and the veil (partition) of the screen (curtain);

38:29 *bronze.* About 5,000 pounds of bronze were used.

39:32 – 43 *that is what they did.* Because it was so important in God's plan for His people, both in the wilderness and today, the tabernacle had to be constructed in exact accordance with the divine pattern. It was the place where His glory would actually dwell and where they could meet Him. Because they had done just as the Lord had commanded, "Moses blessed them." A mood of celebration pervades these verses. One can sense the pride of accomplishment coupled with the reverence for all of these holy objects.

10 Ex 28:17 **14** Rev 21:12 **17** Ex 28:40 **22** Ex 28:31 **25** Ex 28:33 **27** Ex 28:39,40 **28** Ex 28:4,39; Eze 44:18; Ex 28:42 **29** Ex 28:39 **30** Ex 28:36,37 **32** ver. 42,43; Ex 25:40

35 the ark of the Testimony, its carry-
ing poles and the mercy seat;
36 the table and all its utensils and
the bread of the Presence (showbread);
37 the pure *gold* lampstand and its
lamps, with the lamps placed in order,
all its utensils, and the oil for the light;
38 the golden altar [of incense], the
anointing oil and the fragrant incense,
and the [hanging] veil for the doorway
of the tent;
39 the bronze altar [of burnt offering]
and its grating of bronze, its poles and
all its utensils, the basin and its base;
40 the curtains of the courtyard, its
support poles and sockets, and the
screen (curtain) for the courtyard gate,
its cords and pegs, and all the utensils
for the service of the tabernacle, for
the Tent of Meeting [of God with His
people]; [Ex 29:42, 43]
41 the [finely] woven garments for
serving *and* ministering in the Holy
Place, the holy garments for Aaron the
priest, and the garments of his sons to
minister as priests.
42 So the Israelites did all the work
according to all that the LORD had com-
manded Moses.
43 And Moses [carefully] inspected all
the work, and behold, they had done
it; just as the LORD had commanded,
so had they done it. So Moses blessed
them.

The Tabernacle Erected

40 THEN THE LORD spoke to Mo-
ses, saying,
2 "On the first day of the first month
(Abib) you shall set up the tabernacle of
the Tent of Meeting [of God with you].
3 "You shall place the ark of the Tes-
timony there, and you shall screen off
the ark [from the Holy Place of God's
Presence] with the veil (partition cur-
tain). [Heb 10:19–23]
4 "You shall bring in the table [for
the bread] and arrange its setting; you
shall bring in the lampstand and mount
and light its lamps. [Rev 21:23–25]
5 "You shall set the golden altar of
incense in front of the ark of the Tes-
timony [outside the veil], and put the
[hanging] veil at the doorway of the
tabernacle.
6 "You shall set the [bronze] altar of
burnt offering in front of the doorway
of the tabernacle of the Tent of Meeting.
7 "You shall set the basin between the
Tent of Meeting and the altar [of burnt
offering], and put water in it.
8 "You shall set up the courtyard
[curtains] all around and hang up the
screen (curtain) for the gateway of the
courtyard.
9 "Then you shall take the anointing
oil and anoint the tabernacle and all
that is in it, and consecrate it and all its
furniture; and it shall be holy (declared
sacred, separated from secular use).
10 "You shall anoint the altar of burnt
offering and all its utensils, and con-
secrate the altar, and the altar shall
be most holy.
11 "You shall anoint the basin and its
base, and consecrate it.
12 "Then you shall bring Aaron and
his sons to the doorway of the Tent of
Meeting and wash them with water.
[John 17:17–19]
13 "You shall put the holy garments
on Aaron and anoint him and con-
secrate him, that he may serve as a
priest to Me.
14 "You shall bring his sons and put
tunics on them;
15 you shall anoint them just as you
anointed their father, so that they
may serve as priests to Me; and their
anointing shall qualify them for an ev-
erlasting priesthood throughout their
generations."
16 Thus Moses did; in accordance
with all that the LORD commanded
him, so he did.
17 Now it happened on the first day

40:2 *first month.* This was the month of Abib, also called Nisan (12:2; 13:4). The tabernacle was completed nine months after the arrival of the people at Mount Sinai (19:1) and two weeks before the second celebration of the Passover (v. 17).

42 Ex 35:10 **43** Lev 9:22,23; Nu 6:23; Jos 22:6; 2Sa 6:18; 1Ki 8:14; 2Ch 30:27 **CHAPTER 40** **2** Ex 12:2; 13:4; ver. 17; Ex 26:1,30 **3** ver. 21; Ex 26:33; Nu 4:5 **4** ver. 22; Ex 26:35; ver. 23; Ex 25:30; ver. 24,25 **5** ver. 26 **7** ver. 30; Ex 30:18 **9** Ex 30:26 **10** Ex 29:36,37 **12** Lev 8:1-13 **13** Ex 28:41 **15** Nu 25:13 **17** ver. 2; Nu 7:1

of the first month (Abib) in the second year [after the exodus from Egypt], that the tabernacle was erected.

18 Moses erected the tabernacle, laid its sockets, set up its boards, put in its bars and erected its support poles.

19 He spread the tent over the tabernacle and put the covering of the tent over it, just as the LORD had commanded him.

20 He took the Testimony [the stones inscribed with the Ten Commandments] and put it into the ark [of the covenant], and placed the poles [through the rings] on the ark, and put the mercy seat on top of the ark.

21 Moses brought the ark into the tabernacle, and set up a veil (partition) for the screen (curtain), and screened off the ark of the Testimony, just as the LORD had commanded him.

22 Then he put the table in the Tent of Meeting on the north side of the tabernacle, outside the veil.

23 He set the bread [of the Presence] in order on it before the LORD, just as the LORD had commanded him. [John 6:32–35]

24 Then he put the lampstand in the Tent of Meeting, opposite the table, on the south side of the tabernacle.

25 Moses mounted *and* lighted the lamps [on the lampstand] before the LORD, just as the LORD commanded him.

26 He put the golden altar [of incense] in the Tent of Meeting in front of the veil;

27 he burned fragrant incense [as a symbol of prayer] on it, just as the LORD commanded him. [Ps 141:2; Rev 8:3]

28 Then he set up the screen (curtain) at the doorway of the tabernacle.

29 He set the altar of burnt offering before the doorway of the tabernacle of the Tent of Meeting, and offered on it the burnt offering and the grain offering, just as the LORD commanded him.

30 He placed the basin between the Tent of Meeting and the altar [of burnt offering], and put water in it for washing.

31 Then from it Moses and Aaron and his sons washed their hands and their feet.

32 When they entered the Tent of Meeting, and when they approached the altar, they washed, just as the LORD commanded Moses.

33 And he erected the courtyard all around the tabernacle and the altar, and hung the screen (curtain) at the gateway of the courtyard. So Moses finished the work.

The Glory of the LORD

34 Then the cloud [the Shekinah, God's visible, dwelling presence] covered the Tent of Meeting, and the glory *and* brilliance of the LORD filled the tabernacle. [Rev 15:8]

35 Moses was not able to enter the Tent of Meeting because the cloud remained on it, and the glory *and* brilliance of the LORD filled the tabernacle.

36 In all their journeys, whenever the cloud was taken up from over the tabernacle, the Israelites would set out;

37 but if the cloud was not taken up, then they did not journey on until the day when it was taken up.

38 For throughout all their journeys, the cloud of the LORD was on the tabernacle by day, and there was fire in it by night, in the sight of all the house of Israel.

40:20–21 *the Testimony . . . the mercy seat.* The Testimony was the stone tablets of the Ten Commandments (25:16). The mercy seat was the cover of the ark (25:17–22).

40:34 *cloud . . . glory.* When the Lord came near in 19:20, the people were terrified, but this time they were overjoyed. The glory of the Lord filling the tabernacle demonstrated His presence with the Israelites, His significance to them, and His awe-inspiring wonder.

40:35 *the cloud remained on it.* God is not "far away in heaven," occasionally looking at the earth through binoculars. He lives among His people, and He desires to communicate with them (Jn 1:14).

40:38 *the cloud of the LORD.* The Book of Exodus ends with the picture of the gracious God hovering protectively over His people. He allowed His presence to be felt and seen.

20 Ex 25:16 **21** Ex 26:33 **22** Ex 26:35 **23** ver. 4 **24** Ex 26:35 **25** ver. 4; Ex 25:37 **26** ver. 5; Ex 30:6 **27** Ex 30:7 **28** ver. 5; Ex 26:36 **29** ver. 6; Ex 29:38 **30** ver. 7; Ex 30:18 **32** Ex 30:19,20 **33** ver. 8; Ex 27:9,16 **34** Ex 29:43; Lev 16:2; Nu 9:15; 1Ki 8:10,11; 2Ch 5:13; 7:2; Isa 6:4; Hag 2:7,9; Rev 15:8 **35** Lev 16:2; 1Ki 8:11; 2Ch 5:14 **36** Nu 9:17; 10:11; Neh 9:19 **37** Nu 9:19-22 **38** Ex 13:21; Nu 9:15

THE THIRD BOOK OF MOSES, CALLED

LEVITICUS

▸ **AUTHOR:** Moses is declared to be the author of Leviticus fifty-six times within the book. External evidence supporting the authorship of Moses includes 1) a uniform ancient testimony; 2) parallels found in the Ras Shamra Tablets dating from 1400 BC; 3) the testimony of Christ (Mt 8:2 – 4 and Lev 14:1 – 4; Mt 12:4 and Lev 24:9; Lk 2:22).

▸ **TIMES:** c. 1405 BC ▸ **KEY VERSES:** Lev 20:7 – 8

▸ **THEME:** Leviticus is God's guidebook for His newly redeemed people. It shows them how to worship and live holy lives. The instructions for the sacrificial system point to a holy God and what he requires from people who would serve him. The laws of holiness and sanctification provide basic instructions for living in a community. Together the two groups of laws are a framework for relationship between God and man. Blessings result from obedience to these laws and discipline is the result of disobedience.

The Law of Burnt Offerings

1 THE LORD called to Moses and spoke to him from the Tent of Meeting, saying,
2"Speak to the children of Israel and say to them, 'When any one of you brings an offering to the LORD, you shall bring your offering of [domestic] animals from the herd (cattle, oxen) or from the flock (sheep, goats).
3'If his offering is a burnt offering from the herd, he shall offer a male without blemish; he shall offer it at the doorway of the Tent of Meeting so that he may be accepted before the LORD. [Rom 12:1; Phil 1:20]
4"He shall lay his hand on the head of the burnt offering [transferring symbolically his guilt to the sacrifice], that it may be accepted for him to make

---

1:1 – 17 *offering to the LORD.* Leviticus continues the Exodus narrative of the dedication of the tabernacle by indicating how the liberated Israelites are to worship their God. This book deals with the voluntary sacrifices for thanksgiving, communion, or cleansing from sin. These offerings from the herd or flock represented the labor and financial investment of the owner, and were a continual reminder that a price always has to be paid for sin.
1:3 *burnt offering.* The "burnt offering" was the only offering that was entirely consumed on the altar. It foreshadows the total sacrifice of Christ on the cross, as well as representing wholehearted, unreserved worship where nothing is withheld or left over. It reminds us that nothing must be held back for ourselves; it all belongs to Him. ***male without blemish.*** Offering a perfect animal was a real sacrifice, not just "something they didn't really need or want." These perfect animals were valuable for breeding or for sale. The principle still holds. God's people are to offer their best, of their own free will, and with joy.
1:4 *He shall lay his hand on the head of the burnt offering.* Each worshiper brought his or her own offering and laid his own hand on the animal's head. No one could send another to act on his behalf. In the same way, no one today can send someone else to accept Christ's atonement for him; we must each come to Christ ourselves, acknowledging our own sin before Him.

CHAPTER 1 **1** Ex 19:3; Ex 40:34 **2** Lev 22:18,19 **3** Dt 15:21; Eph 5:27; Heb 9:14; 1Pe 1:19 **4** Lev 3:2,8,13; 4:15; Ro 12:1; Php 4:18; 2Ch 29:23,24

atonement on his behalf. [Heb 13:15,
16; 1 Pet 1:2]
[5]‘He shall kill the young bull before
the LORD; and Aaron’s sons the priests
shall present the blood and sprinkle
the blood around on the altar that is
at the doorway of the Tent of Meeting.
[6]‘Then he shall skin the burnt offer-
ing and cut it into pieces.
[7]‘The sons of Aaron the [high] priest
shall put fire on the altar [of burnt of-
fering] and arrange wood on the fire.
[8]‘Then Aaron’s sons the priests shall
arrange the pieces, the head and the
fat, on the wood which is on the fire
that is on the altar.
[9]‘But he shall wash its entrails and
its legs with water. The priest shall
offer all of it up in smoke on the altar
as a burnt offering. It is an offering by
fire, a sweet *and* soothing aroma to
the LORD. [Eph 5:2; Phil 4:18; 1 Pet 2:5]
[10]‘But if his offering is from the flock,
of the sheep or of the goats, as a burnt
offering, he shall offer a male without
blemish.
[11]‘He shall kill it on the north side of
the altar before the LORD, and Aaron’s
sons the priests shall sprinkle its blood
around on the altar.
[12]‘He shall cut it into pieces, with its
head and its fat, and the priest shall
arrange them on the wood which is
on the fire that is on the altar.
[13]‘But he shall wash the entrails and
legs with water. The priest shall offer
all of it, and offer it up in smoke on the
altar. It is a burnt offering, an offering
by fire, a sweet *and* soothing aroma
to the LORD.
[14]‘But if his offering to the LORD is a
burnt offering of birds, then he shall
bring turtledoves or young pigeons as
his offering.
[15]‘The priest shall bring it to the al-
tar, and wring off its head, and offer
it up in smoke on the altar; and its
blood is to be drained out on the side
of the altar.
[16]‘He shall remove its crop with its
feathers and throw it next to the east
side of the altar, in the place for ashes.
[17]‘Then he shall tear it open by its
wings, but shall not sever it. And the
priest shall offer it up in smoke on the
altar, on the wood that is on the fire.
It is a burnt offering, an offering by
fire, a sweet *and* soothing aroma to
the LORD.

The Law of Grain Offerings

2 ‘WHEN ANYONE presents a grain
offering to the Lord, his offering
shall be of fine flour, and he shall pour
[olive] oil over it and put frankincense
on it.
[2]‘He shall bring it to Aaron’s sons the
priests. Out of it he shall take a handful
of the fine flour and oil, with all of its
frankincense, and the priest shall offer
this up in smoke on the altar [of burnt
offering] as the memorial portion of
it. It is an offering by fire, a sweet *and*
soothing aroma to the LORD.
[3]‘What is left of the grain offering
belongs to Aaron and his sons; it is a
most holy part of the offerings to the
LORD by fire.
[4]‘When you bring an offering of
grain baked in the oven, it shall be
unleavened cakes of fine flour mixed
with oil, or unleavened wafers spread
with oil.

1:9 *sweet and soothing aroma.* Never does Scripture represent God as eating the offerings brought to Him, as the pagan gods were thought to do. When a sacrifice was done in faith with a free will, it was accepted by the Lord as desirable, or sweet.

2:1 *oil . . . frankincense.* Olive oil was a primary part of the diet and a prominent symbol of blessing and prosperity. Frankincense was a costly incense from South Arabia and East Africa, an imported luxury that would have to be bought with money. By including frankincense, as well as the animals and grain they could raise on their land, every aspect of Israel’s wealth was made a part of the offerings to God.

2:3 *belongs to Aaron and his sons.* A significant portion of the priest’s daily food came from this part of the grain offering. Only the consecrated priests were allowed to eat it, and only within the tabernacle.

5 Mic 6:6; 2Ch 35:11; Heb 12:24 **7** Ge 22:9 **9** Ge 8:21; Eze 20:28,41; 2Co 2:15 **10** ver. 3 **11** ver. 5; Ex 40:22; Eze 8:5 **14** Lev 5:7 **16** Lev 6:10 **17** Ge 15:10; ver. 9,13 **CHAPTER 2** **1** Lev 6:14; 9:17; Nu 15:4 **2** ver. 9; Lev 5:12; 6:15; 24:7; Isa 66:3; Ac 10:4 **3** Lev 7:9; 10:12,13; Ex 29:37; Nu 18:9 **4** Ex 29:2

5 ‘If your offering is grain baked on a
griddle, it shall be of fine unleavened
flour, mixed with oil.
6 ‘You are to break it into pieces, and
you shall pour oil on it; it is a grain
offering.
7 ‘Now if your offering is grain
cooked in a lidded pan, it shall be made
of fine flour with oil.
8 ‘When you bring the grain offer-
ing that is made of these things to the
LORD, it shall be presented to the priest,
and he shall bring it to the altar [of
burnt offering].
9 ‘The priest shall take from the grain
offering its memorial portion and of-
fer it up in smoke on the altar. It is an
offering by fire, a sweet *and* soothing
aroma to the LORD.
10 ‘What is left of the grain offering
belongs to Aaron and his sons; it is a
most holy part of the offerings to the
LORD by fire.
11 ‘No grain offering that you bring
to the LORD shall be made with leaven,
for you shall not offer up in smoke any
leaven [which symbolizes the spread of
sin] or any honey [which, like leaven, is
subject to fermentation] in any offering
by fire to the LORD. [1 Cor 5:8]
12 ‘As an offering of first fruits you
may offer them [leaven and honey]
to the LORD, but they shall not go up
[in smoke] on the altar as a sweet *and*
soothing aroma.
13 ‘You shall season every grain of-
fering with salt so that the salt (pres-
ervation) of the covenant of your God
will not be missing from your grain
offering. You shall offer salt with all
your offerings. [Mark 9:49, 50]
14 ‘If you bring a grain offering of
early ripened things to the LORD, you
shall bring fresh heads of grain roast-
ed in the fire, crushed grain of new
growth, for the grain offering of your
early ripened things.
15 ‘You shall put oil on it and lay in-
cense on it; it is a grain offering.
16 ‘The priest shall offer up in smoke
its memorial portion, part of the
crushed grain and part of its oil with
all its incense; it is an offering by fire
to the LORD.

The Law of Peace Offerings

3 ‘IF A man’s offering is a sacrifice
of peace offerings, if he offers an
animal from the herd, whether male or
female, he shall offer it without blem-
ish before the LORD.
2 ‘He shall lay his hand on the head
of his offering [transferring symboli-
cally his guilt to the sacrifice] and kill
it at the doorway of the Tent of Meet-
ing; and Aaron’s sons the priests shall
sprinkle the blood around on the altar.
3 ‘From the sacrifice of the peace of-
ferings, an offering by fire to the LORD,
he shall present the fat that covers the

2:8–9 *priest.* There were always two individuals involved when the ancient Hebrew brought his sacrifice to God. One was the offerer himself and the other was the officiating priest, who was the “bridge builder” between men and God. Jesus, as a better priest and a better sacrifice, once for all time bridged the gap between God and man, and through Him we can have direct access to God, to confess our sins and receive forgiveness.

2:11 *leaven.* Leaven and honey were prohibited because both cause fermentation, which represents corruption.

2:13 *salt (preservation) of the covenant of your God.* Salt was to be used in every grain offering. This was a reminder of the covenant that God had made with Israel at Sinai, and was a symbol of faithfulness to God and His covenant. There is an old saying, “he has eaten my salt,” which means that you have taken someone into your home, given them shelter, food, and hospitality. The idea of the “salt” of God’s covenant was a well understood concept.

3:1 *peace offerings.* The Hebrew word for “peace” means “wholeness, completeness, soundness, health.” When a person possesses all of these attributes, he is at peace. The peace offerings were a time of celebrating and enjoying the gift of peace with God. Yet it was only after Christ’s death and resurrection, when He became our perfect peace offering (Col 1:20) that we could really have perfect peace with God. The sacrifices had to be made over and over, but Christ’s death was once, for all time.

3:3–4 *two kidneys with the fat that is on them . . . lobe of the liver.* The fat was one of the

9 ver. 2; Lev 6:15; Ex 29:18 **10** ver. 3 **11** Lev 6:17; See Mt 16:12; Mk 8:15; Lk 12:1; 1Co 5:8; Gal 5:9 **12** Ex 22:29; Lev 23:10,11 **13** Mk 9:49; Col 4:6; Nu 18:19; Eze 43:24 **14** Lev 23:10,14; 2Ki 4:42 **15** ver. 1 **16** ver. 2
CHAPTER 3 **1** Lev 7:11,29; 22:21; Lev 1:3 **2** Ex 29:10; Lev 1:4,5 **3** Ex 29:13,22; Lev 4:8,9

entrails, and all the fat which is on the
entrails,
4 and the two kidneys with the fat
that is on them at the loins, and the
lobe of the liver which he shall remove
with the kidneys.
5 'Aaron's sons shall offer it up in
smoke on the altar [placing it] on the
burnt offering which is on the wood
that is on the fire. It is an offering by
fire, a sweet *and* soothing aroma to
the LORD.
6 'If his peace offering to the LORD is
an animal from the flock, male or fe-
male, he shall offer the animal without
blemish.
7 'If he offers a lamb as his offering,
then he shall present it before the LORD,
8 and he shall lay his hand on the head
of his offering and kill it before the
Tent of Meeting, and Aaron's sons shall
sprinkle its blood around on the altar.
9 'From the sacrifice of peace offer-
ings he shall bring as an offering by
fire to the LORD, its fat, the entire fat
tail which he shall remove close to
the backbone, and the fat that covers
the entrails, and all the fat which is on
the entrails,
10 and the two kidneys with the fat
that is on them at the loins, and the
lobe of the liver, which he shall remove
with the kidneys.
11 'The priest shall offer it up in smoke
on the altar as food, an offering by fire
to the LORD.
12 'If his offering is a goat, he shall
present it before the LORD,
13 and he shall lay his hand on its
head [transferring symbolically his
guilt to the sacrifice], and kill it before
the Tent of Meeting; and the sons of
Aaron shall sprinkle its blood around
on the altar.
14 'Then he shall present from it as
his offering, an offering by fire to the
LORD: the fat that covers the entrails,
and all the fat that is on the entrails,
15 and the two kidneys with the fat
that is on them at the loins, and the
lobe of the liver which he shall remove
with the kidneys.
16 'The priest shall offer them up in
smoke on the altar as food. It is an
offering by fire, a sweet *and* soothing
aroma; all the fat is the LORD's.
17 'It is a permanent statute for your
generations wherever you may be, that
you shall not eat any fat or any blood.' "

The Law of Sin Offerings

4 THEN THE LORD spoke to Moses,
saying,
2 "Speak to the children of Israel, 'If
a person sins unintentionally in any
of the things which the LORD has com-
manded not to be done, and commits
any of them—
3 if the anointed priest sins, bringing
guilt on the people, then he shall offer
to the LORD a young bull without blem-
ish as a sin offering for the sin he has
committed. [Heb 7:27, 28]
4 'He shall bring the bull to the door-
way of the Tent of Meeting before the
LORD, and shall lay his hand on the
bull's head [transferring symbolically
his guilt to the sacrifice] and kill the
bull before the LORD.

---

most prized portions of the meat, and the kidneys were considered the seat of the emotions. The liver was an essential organ for telling the future in the pagan cultures surrounding Israel. Giving all of these things to God symbolized giving Him the best, giving Him the hopes, dreams, and desires of life; recognizing that He alone has control of the future, and that He will reveal it in His own way, at His own time.

3:5 *on the burnt offering.* The peace offering normally followed the burnt offering, which was entirely consumed on the altar. Being reconciled to God through the burnt offering, the worshiper was in a position to fellowship with God. Repentance and reconciliation must always come before genuine fellowship.

3:9 *the entire fat tail.* The tail of the Palestinian broad-tailed sheep is almost entirely fat and can weigh more than 16 pounds. This explains its special mention in the regulations for offering the fat of the sheep.

5 Ex 29:13; Lev 6:12 **6** ver. 1 **11** See Lev 21:6,8,17, 21,22; 22:25; Eze 44:7; Mal 1:7,12 **12** ver. 1,7
16 Lev 7:23,25; 1Sa 2:15; 2Ch 7:7 **17** Lev 6:18; 7:36; 17:7; 23:14; ver. 16; compare with Dt 32:14; Neh 8:10; Ge 9:4; Lev 7:23,26; 17:10,14; Dt 12:16; 1Sa 14:33; Eze 44:7,15 **CHAPTER 4** **2** Lev 5:15,17; Nu 15:22; 1Sa 14:27; Ps 19:12
3 Lev 8:12; Lev 9:2 **4** Lev 1:3,4

5 'Then the anointed priest is to take
some of the bull's blood and bring it
into the Tent of Meeting;
6 and the priest shall dip his finger
in the blood and sprinkle some of it
seven times before the LORD in front
of the veil (curtain) of the sanctuary.
7 'The priest shall also put some of
the blood on the horns of the altar of
fragrant incense which is before the
LORD in the Tent of Meeting. All the
rest of the blood of the bull he shall
pour out at the base of the altar of the
burnt offering which is at the doorway
of the Tent of Meeting.
8 'He shall remove all the fat from
the bull of the sin offering—the fat
that covers the entrails, and all the fat
which is on the entrails,
9 and the two kidneys with the fat
that is on them at the loins, and the
lobe of the liver, which he shall remove
with the kidneys
10 (just as these are removed from the
ox of the sacrifice of peace offerings),
and the priest is to offer them up in
smoke on the altar of burnt offering.
11 'But the hide of the bull and all its
meat, with its head, its legs, its entrails,
and its refuse,
12 that is, *all the rest of* the bull, he
is to bring outside the camp to a clean

4:11 – 12 *all the rest of the bull.* Burning the whole bull ensured that the priest did not profit in any way from his own sin or the atonement for his sin. Carrying it outside the camp was another way of symbolizing the seriousness and pollution of sin.

5 Lev 16:14; Nu 19:4 **7** Lev 8:15; 9:9; 16:18; Lev 5:9 **10** Lev 3:3-5 **11** Ex 29:14; Nu 19:5 **12** Lev 6:11; Heb 13:11

OLD TESTAMENT SACRIFICES

SACRIFICE	OT REFERENCES	ELEMENTS	PURPOSE
Burnt Offering	Lev 1; 6:8–13; 8:18–21; 16:24	Bull, ram or male bird (dove or young pigeon for the poor); wholly consumed; no defect	Voluntary act of worship; atonement for unintentional sin in general; expression of devotion, commitment and complete surrender to God
Grain Offering	Lev 2; 6:14–23	Grain, finest flour, olive oil, incense, baked bread (cakes or wafers), salt; no yeast or honey; accompanied burnt offering and fellowship offering (along with drink offering)	Voluntary act of worship; recognition of God's goodness and provisions; devotion to God
Fellowship Offering	Lev 3; 7:11–34	Any animal without defect from herd or flock; variety of breads	Voluntary act of worship; thanksgiving and fellowship (it included a communal meal)
Sin Offering	Lev 4:1—5:13; 6:24–30; 8:14–17; 16:3–22	1. Young bull: for high priest and congregation 2. Male goat: for leader 3. Female goat or lamb: for common person 4. Dove or pigeon: for the poor 5. Tenth of an ephah of finest flour: for the very poor	Mandatory atonement for specific unintentional sin; confession of sin; forgiveness of sin; cleansing from defilement
Guilt Offering	Lev 5:14—6:7; 7:1–6	Ram	Mandatory atonement for unintentional sin requiring restitution; cleansing from defilement; make restitution; pay 20% fine

When more than one kind of offering was presented (as in Nu 7:13–17), the procedure was usually as follows: (1) sin offering or guilt offering, (2) burnt offering, (3) fellowship offering and grain offering (along with a drink offering). This sequence furnishes part of the spiritual significance of the sacrificial system. First, sin had to be dealt with (sin offering or guilt offering). Second, the worshipers committed themselves completely to God (burnt offering and grain offering). Third, fellowship or communion between the Lord, the priest and the worshiper (fellowship offering) was established. To state it another way, there were sacrifices of expiation (sin offerings and guilt offerings), consecration (burnt offerings and grain offerings) and communion (fellowship offerings—these included vow offerings, thank offerings and freewill offerings).

place where the ashes are poured out,
and burn it on a fire of wood. Where
the ashes are poured out it shall be
burned. [Heb 13:11–13]
13'Now if the whole congregation
of Israel sins unintentionally, and the
matter escapes the notice of the assem-
bly, and they have done any one of the
things which the LORD has command-
ed not to be done, and they become
guilty;
14when the sin which they have com-
mitted becomes known, then the con-
gregation shall offer a young bull of
the herd as a sin offering and bring it
before the Tent of Meeting.
15'Then the elders of the congrega-
tion shall lay their hands on the head
of the bull before the LORD [to transfer
symbolically the congregation's guilt
to the sacrifice], and they shall kill the
bull before the LORD.
16'The anointed priest is to bring
some of the bull's blood to the Tent of
Meeting,
17and the priest shall dip his finger in
the blood, and sprinkle it seven times
before the LORD, in front of the veil
[which screens off the Holy of Holies
and the ark of the covenant].
18'He shall put some of the blood
on the horns of the altar [of incense]
which is before the LORD in the Tent
of Meeting; and he shall pour out all
the rest of the blood at the base of the
altar of burnt offering which is at the
doorway of the Tent of Meeting.
19'He shall remove all its fat from
the bull and offer it up in smoke on
the altar.
20'He shall also do with the bull just
as he did with the bull of the sin offer-
ing; that is what he shall do with this.
So the priest shall make atonement for
[the sin of] the people, and they will
be forgiven.
21'Then the priest is to bring the bull
outside the camp and burn it as he
burned the first bull; it is the sin offer-
ing for the congregation.
22'When a ruler *or* leader sins and
unintentionally does any one of the
things the LORD his God has command-
ed not to be done, and he becomes
guilty,
23if his sin which he has committed
is made known to him, he shall bring
a goat, a male without blemish as his
offering.
24'He shall lay his hand on the head
of the male goat [transferring sym-
bolically his guilt to the sacrifice], and
kill it in the place where they kill the
burnt offering before the LORD; it is a
sin offering.
25'Then the priest is to take some of
the blood of the sin offering with his
finger and put it on the horns of the
altar of burnt offering; and *the rest of*
its blood he shall pour out at the base
of the altar of burnt offering.
26'And he shall offer all its fat up in
smoke on the altar like the fat from
the sacrifice of peace offerings; so the
priest shall make atonement for him
in regard to his sin, and he will be
forgiven.
27'If anyone of the common people
sins unintentionally by doing any of
the things the LORD has commanded
not to be done, and becomes guilty,
28if his sin which he has committed
is made known to him, then he shall
bring a goat, a female without blemish
as his offering for the sin which he has
committed.
29'He shall lay his hand on the
head of the sin offering [transferring

4:13–21 ***the whole congregation***. Interestingly, not only individuals bring a sin offering to God, but the whole congregation as well. We are used to thinking of individuals coming under conviction and repenting, but how can a whole community come to this way of thinking? A congregation or community can begin to realize that they have misrepresented God, or fallen short of their God-given responsibilities, and together repent and ask for forgiveness, even though the members repenting may not have been the actual people who made the bad decisions that created the problem. Groups need to turn around and redirect their actions, just as much as individuals do, and this is one of the ways that God changes whole societies.

13 Nu 15:24; Jos 7:11; Lev 5:2-4,17 **15** Lev 1:4 **16** ver. 5; Heb 9:12-14 **20** ver. 3; Nu 15:25 **22** ver. 2,13 **23** ver. 14; Lev 5:4 **24** ver. 4; Isa 53:6 **25** ver. 30 **26** Lev 3:5; ver. 20; Nu 15:28 **27** ver. 2; Nu 15:27 **28** ver. 23 **29** ver. 4,24

symbolically his guilt to the sacrifice],
and kill it at the place of the burnt
offering.
30'The priest shall take some of its
blood with his finger and put it on the
horns of the altar of burnt offering and
shall pour out all *the rest of* its blood
at the base of the altar.
31'Then he shall remove all its fat,
just as the fat was removed from the
sacrifice of peace offerings; and the
priest shall offer it up in smoke on the
altar as a sweet *and* soothing aroma
to the LORD. In this way the priest shall
make atonement for him, and he will
be forgiven.
32'If he brings a lamb as his offering
for a sin offering, he shall bring a fe-
male without blemish.
33'He shall lay his hand on the head
of the sin offering [transferring sym-
bolically his guilt to the sacrifice], and
kill it as a sin offering in the place
where they kill the burnt offering.
34'The priest is to take some of the
blood of the sin offering with his finger
and put it on the horns of the altar of
burnt offering and all *the rest of* the
blood of the lamb he shall pour out at
the base of the altar.
35'Then he shall remove all its fat,
just as the fat of the lamb is removed
from the sacrifice of the peace offer-
ings, and the priest shall offer it up
in smoke on the altar, on the offer-
ings by fire to the LORD. In this way
the priest shall make atonement for
him in regard to the sin which he has
committed, and he will be forgiven.
[Heb 9:13, 14]

The Law of Guilt Offerings

5 'IF ANYONE sins after he hears
a public adjuration (solemn com-
mand to testify) when he is a witness,
whether he has seen or [otherwise]
known [something]—if he fails to re-
port it, then he will bear his guilt *and*
be held responsible.
2'Or if someone touches any [cer-
emonially] unclean thing—whether
the carcass of an unclean wild animal
or the carcass of an unclean domes-
tic animal or the carcass of unclean
creeping things—even if he is unaware
of it, he has become unclean, and he
will be guilty.
3'Or if he touches human
uncleanness—whatever kind it may
be—and he becomes unclean, but he
is unaware of it, when he recognizes
it, he will be guilty.
4'Or if anyone swears [an oath]
thoughtlessly *or* impulsively aloud
that he will do either evil or good, in
whatever manner a person may speak
thoughtlessly *or* impulsively with an
oath, but he is unaware of it, when he
recognizes it, he will be guilty in one
of these. [Mark 6:23]
5'So it shall be when a person is
guilty in one of these, that he shall
confess the sin he has committed.
6'He shall bring his guilt offering
to the LORD for the sin which he has
committed, a female from the flock,
a lamb or a goat as a sin offering. So
the priest shall make atonement on his
behalf for his sin.
7'But if he cannot afford a lamb, then
he shall bring two turtledoves or two

5:3 *human uncleanness.* Body fluids, a person's waste, and contact with a corpse were all causes of uncleanness. The ancient Israelites knew nothing about microbiology, but God, who knows everything, gave them laws that prevented disease and made them distinct from their neighbors.

5:4 *swears ... but he is unaware of it.* Certainly a person would know when he makes a vow, but he might not be immediately aware of how rash his vow is, or that the long term consequences are undesirable. Whether the vow was made with good intentions, but not carried out, or made with wicked intentions, but not carried out, the person who made the vow is still responsible to repent of his foolishness when he becomes aware of it.

5:7 *two turtledoves.* Part of the purification offering was burned on the altar, and part was not burned. When offering birds, the worshiper brought two in order to accomplish this.

31 Lev 3:14; Lev 3:3; Ge 8:21; Ex 29:18; Lev 1:9; Ezr 6:10; ver. 26 **32** ver. 28 **35** Lev 3:5; ver. 26,31 **CHAPTER 5**
1 1Ki 8:31; Pr 29:24; Mt 26:63; ver. 17; Lev 7:18; 17:16; 19:8; 20:17; Nu 9:13 **2** Lev 11:24, 28,31,39; Nu 19:11,13,16; ver. 17 **3** Lev 12; 13; 15 **4** See 1Sa 25:22; Ac 23:12; See Mk 6:23 **5** Lev 16:21; 26:40; Nu 5:7; Ezr 10:11,12
7 Lev 12:8; 14:21; Lev 1:14

young pigeons as his guilt offering for
his sin to the LORD, one as a sin offering
and the other as a burnt offering.
8‘He shall bring them to the priest,
who shall offer first the one for the sin
offering, and shall nip its head at the
front of its neck, but shall not sever it
[completely].
9‘He shall also sprinkle some of the
blood of the sin offering on the side of
the altar, and the rest of the blood shall
be drained out at the base of the altar;
it is a sin offering.
10‘The second [bird] he shall prepare
as a burnt offering, according to the
ordinance. So the priest shall make
atonement on his behalf for the sin
which he has committed, and it will
be forgiven him.
11‘But if he cannot afford to bring
two turtledoves or two young pigeons,
then he shall bring as his offering for
his sin the tenth part of an ephah of
fine flour as a sin offering; he shall not
put [olive] oil or incense on it, for it is
a sin offering.
12‘He shall bring it to the priest, who
shall take a handful of it as a memorial
portion and offer it up in smoke on the
altar, with the offerings by fire to the
LORD; it is a sin offering.
13‘In this way the priest shall make
atonement for him for the sin which he
has committed in one of these things,
and it will be forgiven him; then *the
rest* shall be for the priest, like the
grain offering.’ ”
14Then the LORD spoke to Moses,
saying,
15“If a person commits a breach of
faith and sins unintentionally against
the holy things of the LORD, then he
shall bring his guilt offering to the
LORD, a ram without blemish from the
flock, valued by you in shekels of sil-
ver, that is, the shekel of the sanctuary,
as a guilt offering.
16“He shall make restitution for the
sin which he has committed against
the holy thing, and shall add a fifth
[of the ram’s value] to it, and give it to
the priest. The priest shall then make
atonement for him with the ram of the
guilt offering, and he shall be forgiven.
17“Now if anyone sins and does any
of the things which the LORD has for-
bidden, though he was not aware of
it, still he is guilty and shall bear his
punishment. [Luke 12:48]
18“He is then to bring to the priest a
ram without blemish from the flock,
according to your valuation, for a guilt
offering. In this way the priest shall
make atonement for him regarding the

5:11 ***tenth part of an ephah.*** This was approximately two quarts.

5:13 ***the rest shall be for the priest.*** Part of the offering was burned on the altar, as was part of the animal sacrifices. The rest belonged to the priests, as did the remainder of the animal sacrifices brought by ordinary citizens, except for their burnt offerings.

5:15 – 6:7 ***person commits a breach of faith.*** The trespass offering covers both offenses against God (5:15 – 19) and against people (6:1 – 7). The offense may be unintentional, or quite deliberate, but regardless of the motive, such actions make the perpetrator guilty. The quickest way to mend relationships with God and with fellow human beings is to honestly admit our guilt and wrongdoing, pay back or repair where we can, and ask forgiveness of those we have sinned against. This responsibility cannot be sidestepped.

5:15 ***commits a breach of faith and sins unintentionally . . . guilt offering.*** This refers both to the objective responsibility of a sinner for his or her actions and the subjective feeling of guilt experienced by the sinner. The offering righted the wrong of the offense and cleared the conscience of the sinner.

5:17 ***though he was not aware of it, still he is guilty.*** Ignorance does not make an offense harmless. The offender was still guilty and bore responsibility for his sin. He might also be troubled in conscience, though he might never learn the exact nature of his offense. This raises the concept that a person can be aware of a break in his fellowship with God, without being sure what caused this break.

5:18 ***error which he committed unintentionally and did not know it.*** This was not a sin of rebellion, but one for which the offender earnestly desired to atone, though he did not know what it was.

8 Lev 1:15 **9** Lev 4:7,18,30,34 **10** Lev 1:14; Lev 4:26 **11** Nu 5:15 **12** Lev 2:2; Lev 4:35 **13** Lev 4:26; Lev 2:3 **15** Lev 22:14; Ezr 10:19; Ex 30:13; Lev 27:25 **16** Lev 6:5; 22:14; 27:13,15, 27,31; Nu 5:7; Lev 4:26 **17** ver. 15; Lev 4:2,13,22,27; ver. 1,2 **18** ver. 15; ver. 16

error which he committed unintention-
ally and did not know it, and he shall
be forgiven.
[19]“It is a guilt offering; he was cer-
tainly guilty before the LORD.”

Guilt Offerings

6 THEN THE LORD spoke to Moses,
saying,
[2]“When anyone sins and acts un-
faithfully against the LORD by deceiv-
ing his neighbor (companion, associ-
ate) in regard to a deposit or a security
entrusted *to him*, or through robbery,
or if he has extorted from his neighbor,
[3]or has found what was lost and lied
about it and sworn falsely, so that he
sins in regard to any one of the things
a man may do—
[4]then if he has sinned and is guilty,
he shall restore what he took by rob-
bery, or what he got by extortion, or the
deposit which was entrusted to him, or
the lost thing which he found,
[5]or anything about which he has
sworn falsely; he shall not only re-
store it in full, but shall add to it one-
fifth more. He shall give it to the one
to whom it belongs on the day of his
guilt offering.
[6]“Then he shall bring to the priest
his guilt offering to the LORD, a ram
without blemish from the flock, as val-
ued by you, as a guilt offering.
[7]“The priest shall make atonement
for him before the LORD, and he will
be forgiven for any one of the things
which he may have done to incur
guilt.”

The Priest’s Part in the Offerings

[8]Then the LORD spoke to Moses,
saying,
[9]“Command Aaron and his sons,
saying, ‘This is the law of the burnt of-
fering: the burnt offering *shall remain*
on the hearth *that is* on the altar all
night until morning and the fire is to
be kept burning on the altar.
[10]‘The priest is to put on his linen
robe, with his linen undergarments
next to his body. Then he shall take up
the ashes of the burnt offering which
the fire has consumed on the altar and
put them beside the altar.
[11]‘Then he shall take off his gar-
ments and put on something else, and
take the ashes outside the camp to a
(ceremonially) clean place.
[12]‘The fire on the altar shall be kept
burning; it shall not [be allowed to] go
out. The priest shall burn wood on it
every morning, and he shall arrange
the burnt offering on it and offer the
fat portions of the peace offerings up
in smoke on it.
[13]‘The fire shall be burning contin-

5:19 *he was certainly guilty before the LORD.* The fact that the priest declared him forgiven, and the peace of conscience that the worshiper had, declares that he was indeed guilty of some trespass; it was not his imagination. It is possible for a Christian to have an overactive conscience that keeps the believer in a constant state of anxiety about unknown sins. It is good to remember that God knows all about this, and if we confess our feelings of guilt, He will either show us our true guilt and grant us forgiveness and a clear conscience, or show us the error in our thinking regarding what He expects from us.

6:5 – 6 *not only restore it.* Restitution and a one-fifth fine were evidence of genuine repentance. Then the offender could bring the ram for the trespass offering and be forgiven for the sin of swearing falsely in God’s name. Jesus preserved this order for the person who remembered at the altar that he had offended his brother (Mt 5:23).

6:10 *undergarments.* The undergarments were linen trousers that prevented immodest exposure as the priest ascended and descended the altar ramp. This modesty communicated to the Israelites that human sexuality could not influence God. That idea was a central feature of Baal worship, which continually tempted the Israelites. The priests of Baal would use obscene gestures and actions in the pagan worship of their depraved god.

6:13 *fire shall be burning continually.* There are at least three reasons the priests are instructed to keep the fire burning. The original fire on the altar came from God, perpetual fire symbolized perpetual worship, and perpetual fire was a reminder of the continual need for atonement and reconciliation with God.

19 Ezr 10:2 **CHAPTER 6** **2** Nu 5:6; Lev 19:11; Ac 5:4; Col 3:9; Ex 22:7,10; Pr 24:28; 26:19 **3** Dt 22:1-3; Ex 22:11; Lev 19:12; Jer 7:9; Zec 5:4 **5** Lev 5:16; Nu 5:7; 2Sa 12:6 **6** Lev 5:15 **7** Lev 4:26 **10** Ex 28:39-41,43; Lev 16:4; Eze 44:17,18; Lev 1:16 **11** Eze 44:19; Lev 4:12 **12** Lev 3:3,9,14

ually on the altar; it shall not [be al-
lowed to] go out.
14 “Now this is the law of the grain of-
fering: the sons of Aaron shall present
it before the LORD in front of the altar.
15 ‘One of them shall take up from it
a handful of the fine flour of the grain
offering with its oil and all the incense
that is on the grain offering, and he
shall offer it up in smoke on the altar,
a sweet *and* soothing aroma, as the
memorial offering to the LORD.
16 ‘What is left of it Aaron and his
sons are to eat. It shall be eaten as
unleavened bread in a holy place; they
are to eat it in the courtyard of the Tent
of Meeting. [1 Cor 9:13, 14]
17 ‘It shall not be baked with leaven
[which represents corruption or sin].
I have given it as their share of My
offerings by fire; it is most holy, like
the sin offering and the guilt offering.
18 ‘Every male among the sons of Aar-
on may eat it [as his share]; it is a perma-
nent ordinance throughout your genera-
tions, from offerings by fire to the LORD.
Whatever touches them will become
consecrated (ceremonially clean).’ ”
19 Then the LORD spoke to Moses,
saying,
20 “This is the offering which Aaron
and his sons are to present to the LORD
on the day when he is anointed: the
tenth of an ephah of fine flour as a
regular grain offering, half of it in the
morning and half of it in the evening.
21 “It shall be prepared with oil on a
griddle. When it is well stirred, you
shall bring it. You shall present the
grain offering in baked pieces as a
sweet *and* soothing aroma to the LORD.
22 “The priest from among the sons
of Aaron who is anointed in his place
shall offer it. By a permanent statute
it shall be entirely offered up in smoke
to the LORD.
23 “So every grain offering of the
priest shall be burned entirely. It shall
not be eaten.”
24 Then the LORD spoke to Moses,
saying,
25 “Speak to Aaron and his sons, say-
ing, ‘This is the law of the sin offering:
the sin offering shall be killed before
the LORD in the [same] place where the
burnt offering is killed; it is most holy.
26 ‘The priest who offers it for sin
shall eat it. It shall be eaten in a holy
place, in the courtyard of the Tent of
Meeting.
27 ‘Whatever touches its meat will
become consecrated (ceremonially
clean). When any of its blood splashes
on a garment, you shall wash what was
splashed on in a holy place.
28 ‘Also the earthenware vessel in
which it was boiled shall be broken;
and if it was boiled in a bronze vessel,
then that vessel shall be scoured and
rinsed in water.
29 ‘Every male among the priests may
eat this offering; it is most holy.
30 ‘But no sin offering from which
any of the blood is brought into the
Tent of Meeting to make atonement in
the Holy Place shall be eaten; it shall
be [completely] burned in the fire.
[Heb 13:11–13]

The Priest’s Part in the Offerings

7 ‘THIS IS the law of the guilt offer-
ing; it is most holy.
2 ‘In the place where they kill the

6:20 *half of it in the morning and half of it in the evening.* The idea of a morning and evening appointment with God is ancient. It is a precious privilege, open to every believer because Jesus opened the door into the presence of God when He died on the cross for our sins.

6:22 *a permanent statute.* This grain offering and the burnt offering were sacrificed daily—with some interruptions, most notably during the exile—until the destruction of the temple in AD 70. Even in the periods of Judah’s worst apostasy, the evidence suggests that the daily offerings continued, though often for incorrect or inadequate reasons (Isa 1:10–17; Jer 7:8–15; Mic 6:6–8).

7:1–7 *guilt offering*. The guilt or trespass offering was “most holy,” showing how seriously

---

14 Lev 2:1; Nu 15:4 **15** Lev 2:2,9 **16** Lev 2:3; Eze 44:29; ver. 26; Lev 10:12,13; Nu 18:10 **17** Lev 2:11; Nu 18:9,10; ver. 25; Ex 29:37; Lev 2:3; 7:1 **18** ver. 29; Nu 18:10; Lev 3:17; Ex 29:37; Lev 22:3-7 **20** Ex 29:2; Ex 16:36 **22** Lev 4:3; Ex 29:25 **25** Lev 4:2; Lev 1:3,5,11; ver. 17 **26** Lev 10:17,18; Nu 18:9,10; Eze 44:28,29; ver. 16 **27** Ex 29:37; 30:29 **28** Lev 11:33; 15:12 **29** ver. 18; Nu 18:10; ver. 25 **30** Lev 4:7,11, 12,18,21; 10:18; 16:27; Heb 13:11 **CHAPTER 7** **1** Lev 5; 6:1-7; Lev 6:17,25; 21:22 **2** Lev 1:3,5,11; 4:24,29,33

burnt offering they are to kill the guilt
offering, and he shall sprinkle its blood
around on the altar.
3 ‘Then he shall offer all its fat, the fat
tail and the fat that covers the entrails,
4 and the two kidneys with the fat
that is on them at the loins, and the
lobe of the liver, which he shall remove
with the kidneys.
5 ‘The priest shall offer them up in
smoke on the altar as an offering by
fire to the LORD; it is a guilt offering.
6 ‘Every male among the priests may
eat it; it shall be eaten in a holy place;
it is most holy.
7 ‘The guilt offering is like the sin
offering, there is one law for [both of]
them: the priest who makes atonement
with it shall have it for himself.
8 ‘The priest who presents any man's
burnt offering shall have for himself
the hide of the burnt offering which
he has presented.
9 ‘Likewise, every grain offering
that is baked in the oven and every-
thing that is prepared in a pan or on a
griddle shall belong to the priest who
presents it.
10 ‘Every grain offering, mixed with
[olive] oil or dry, all the sons of Aaron
may have, one as well as another.
11 ‘Now this is the law of the sacrifice
of peace offerings which shall be pre-
sented to the LORD:
12 ‘If one offers it as a *sacrificial meal
of* thanksgiving, then along with the
sacrifice of thanksgiving he shall offer
unleavened cakes mixed with oil, and
unleavened wafers spread with oil, and
cakes of fine flour mixed with oil.
13 ‘With the sacrifice of his peace
offerings for thanksgiving, he shall
present his offering with cakes of leav-
ened bread.
14 ‘Of this he shall present one [cake]
from each offering as a contribution to
the LORD; it shall belong to the priest
who sprinkles the blood of the peace
offerings.
15 ‘The meat of the sacrifice of thanks-
giving presented as a peace offering
shall be eaten on the day that it is
offered; none of it shall be left until
morning.
16 ‘But if the sacrifice of his offering is
a vow or a freewill offering, it shall be
eaten on the day that he offers his sac-
rifice, and on the next day that which
remains of it may be eaten;
17 but what is left over from the meat
of the sacrifice on the third day shall
be [completely] burned in the fire.
18 ‘If any of the meat of the sacrifice
of his peace offerings is ever eaten
on the third day, then it will not be
accepted, and the one who brought it
will not be credited with it. It shall be
an abhorred (offensive) thing; the one
who eats it shall bear his own guilt.
19 ‘The meat that comes in contact
with anything that is unclean shall
not be eaten; it shall be burned in the
fire. As for other meat, everyone who
is [ceremonially] clean may eat it.
20 ‘But the one who eats meat from
the sacrifice of peace offerings which
belong to the LORD, in his uncleanness,
that person shall be cut off from his
people [excluding him from the atone-
ment made for them].
21 ‘When anyone touches any un-
clean thing—human uncleanness, or
an unclean animal, or any unclean de-
testable thing—and then eats the meat
of the sacrifice of the LORD's peace
offerings, that person shall be cut off
from his people [excluding him from
the atonement made for them].' "
22 Then the LORD spoke to Moses,
saying,
23 "Speak to the children of Israel,
saying, 'You shall not eat any fat from
an ox, a sheep, or a goat.

---

and carefully God considers the acts of reparation made by His people. The priest was to eat it in a holy place. It was his to eat, as part of God's provision for him, but he was to remember where it came from. The price of atonement has never been cheap in God's eyes, even when it was as incomplete as the offering of a goat or lamb.

---

3 Ex 29:13; Lev 3:4,9,10,14-16; 4:8,9 **6** Lev 6:16-18; Nu 18:9,10; Lev 2:3 **7** Lev 6:25,26; 14:13 **9** Lev 2:3,10; Nu 18:9; Eze 44:29 **11** Lev 3:1; 22:18,21; Eze 45:15 **12** Lev 2:4; Nu 6:15 **13** Am 4:5 **14** Nu 18:8,11,19 **15** Lev 22:30 **16** Lev 19:6-8 **18** Nu 18:27; Lev 11:10,11,41; 19:7 **20** Lev 15:3; 1Co 11:28; Ge 17:14 **21** Lev 12; 13; 15; Lev 11:24,28; Eze 4:14; ver. 20 **23** Lev 3:17

24 "The fat of an animal which dies
[of natural causes] and the fat of one
which is torn [to pieces by a predator]
may be put to any other use, but under
no circumstances are you to eat it.
25 'For whoever eats the fat of the an-
imal from which an offering by fire is
presented to the LORD, that person who
eats shall be cut off from his people
[excluding him from the atonement
made for them].
26 'Moreover, you are not to eat any
blood [of any kind], whether of bird or
animal, in any of your dwelling places.
27 'Whoever eats any blood, that per-
son shall be cut off from his people.' "
28 Then the LORD spoke to Moses,
saying,
29 "Speak to the children of Israel,
saying, 'He who offers the sacrifice of
his peace offerings to the LORD shall
bring his offering to the LORD from the
sacrifice of his peace offerings.
30 'With his own hands he is to bring
offerings by fire to the LORD; he shall
bring the fat with the breast, so that
the breast may be presented as a wave
offering before the LORD.
31 'The priest shall offer up the fat in
smoke on the altar, but the breast shall
be for Aaron and his sons.
32 'You shall give the right thigh to
the priest as a contribution from the
sacrifices of your peace offerings.
33 'The son of Aaron who offers the
blood of the peace offerings and the fat
shall have the right thigh as his portion.
34 'For I have taken the breast of the
wave offering and the thigh of the
heave offering from the Israelites, from
the sacrifices of their peace offerings,
and I have given them to Aaron the
priest and to his sons as their perpetual
portion from the Israelites.
35 'This is the *consecrated* portion
from the offerings by fire to the LORD
that was designated for Aaron and his
sons on the day he presented them to
serve as priests to the LORD.
36 'The LORD commanded this to be
given to the priests by the Israelites
on the day that He anointed them. It is
their portion perpetually throughout
their generations.' "
37 This is the law of the burnt offer-
ing, the grain offering, the sin offering,
the guilt offering, the consecration
(ordination) offering, and the sacrifice
of peace offerings,
38 which the LORD commanded Moses
at Mount Sinai on the day He com-
manded the Israelites to present their
offerings to the LORD, in the Wilder-
ness of Sinai.

The Consecration of Aaron and His Sons

8 THEN THE LORD spoke to Moses,
saying,
2 "Take Aaron and his sons with him,
and the garments [which are symbols
of their office], and the anointing oil,
and the bull for the sin offering, and
the two rams, and the basket of un-
leavened bread;
3 and assemble the entire congre-
gation at the doorway of the Tent of
Meeting."
4 Moses did as the LORD commanded
him, and the congregation was as-
sembled at the doorway of the Tent of
Meeting.
5 Moses said to the congregation,
"This is what the LORD has command-
ed us to do."
6 Then Moses brought Aaron and
his sons and washed them with water.
7 He put the undertunic on Aaron,
tied the sash around him, clothed him

7:34 the breast of the wave offering and the thigh of the heave offering. This present was a contribution to the officiating priest as his portion of the peace offerings for thanksgiving. The offering was waved before the Lord as an acknowledgment that He is the giver of all gifts.

8:6–13 Purification—Moses carried out the Lord's command (Ex 29:4) by purifying Aaron and his sons for the priesthood. The purification process began with an outward washing of water which symbolized an inward purity. The believer today also shows his inward reality (his acceptance

26 Ge 9:4; Lev 3:17; 17:10-14; Eze 33:25; Jn 6:53; Ac 15:20,29 **29** Lev 3:1; 22:21; Eze 45:15 **30** Lev 3:3,4,9,14; Ex 29:24,27; Lev 8:27; 9:21; Nu 6:20 **31** Lev 3:5,11,16; ver. 34 **32** ver. 34; Lev 9:21; Nu 6:20 **34** Ex 29:28; Lev 10:14,15; Nu 18:18,19; Dt 18:3 **36** Ex 40:13,15; Lev 8:12,30 **37** Lev 6:9; Lev 6:14; Lev 6:25; ver. 1; Ex 29:1; Lev 6:20; ver. 11 **38** Lev 1:2 **CHAPTER 8** **2** Ex 29:1-3; Ex 28:2,4; Ex 30:24,25 **5** Ex 29:4 **6** Ex 29:4 **7** Ex 29:5; Ex 28:4

in the robe, and put the ephod (an upper vestment) on him. He tied the [skillfully woven] band of the ephod around him, with which he secured it to Aaron.
8 Moses then put the breastpiece on Aaron, and he put in the breastpiece the Urim and the Thummim [the sacred articles the high priest used when seeking God's will concerning the nation].
9 He also put the turban on Aaron's head, and on it, in the front, Moses placed the golden plate, the holy crown, just as the LORD had commanded him.
10 Then Moses took the anointing oil and anointed the tabernacle and all that was in it, and consecrated them.
11 He sprinkled some of the oil on the altar seven times and anointed the altar and all its utensils, and the basin and its stand, to consecrate them.
12 Then he poured some of the anointing oil on Aaron's head and anointed him, to consecrate him.
13 Next Moses brought Aaron's sons forward, put undertunics on them, belted them with sashes, and bound caps on them, just as the LORD had commanded Moses.
14 Then he brought the bull for the sin offering, and Aaron and his sons laid their hands on the head of the bull.
15 Next Moses killed it and took the blood and with his finger put *some of it* around on the horns of the altar and purified it [from sin]. Then he poured out the *rest of the* blood at the base of the altar and consecrated it, to make atonement for it.
16 He took all the fat that was on the entrails, and the lobe of the liver, and the two kidneys with their fat, and Moses offered them up in smoke on the altar.
17 But the bull (the sin offering) and its hide, its meat, and its refuse he burned in the fire outside the camp, just as the LORD had commanded Moses.
18 He brought the ram for the burnt offering, and Aaron and his sons laid their hands on the head of the ram.
19 Moses killed it and sprinkled the blood around on the altar.
20 When he had cut the ram into pieces, Moses offered up the head, the pieces, and the fat in smoke.
21 After he had washed the entrails and the legs in water, Moses offered up the whole ram in smoke on the altar. It was a burnt offering for a sweet *and* soothing aroma, an offering by fire to the LORD, just as the LORD had commanded Moses.
22 Then he brought the second ram, the ram of consecration (ordination), and Aaron and his sons laid their hands on the head of the ram.
23 Moses killed it and took some of its blood and put it on the lobe of Aaron's right ear, and on the thumb of his right hand, and on the big toe of his right foot.
24 He also brought Aaron's sons forward and put some of the blood on the lobes of their right ears, and the thumbs of their right hands, and the big toes of their right feet; and Moses sprinkled the *rest of the* blood around on the altar.
25 He took the fat, the fat tail, all the fat that was on the entrails, the lobe of the liver, and the two kidneys and their fat, and the right thigh;
26 and from the basket of unleavened bread that was before the LORD, he took

---

of Christ and the presence of the Holy Spirit) with his outward actions. These acts of obedience do not create the inward reality, but they confirm it.

8:8 *the Urim and the Thummim.* These were the sacred lots used to determine the will of God. What they looked like and how they were used is not known. Apparently, the high priest phrased questions so the answers would be yes or no, depending on how the lots came up.

8:12 *anointed him.* The high priests of Israel, beginning here with Aaron, were anointed, as were the kings of Israel (1Sa 10:1; 16:13) and at least one of the prophets (1Ki 19:16). Jesus combines in His person the offices of High Priest, King, and Prophet, so He is *the* Anointed One, which is the meaning of the names Messiah (Hebrew) and Christ (Greek).

8 Ex 28:30 **9** Ex 29:6; Ex 28:37 **10** Ex 30:26-29 **12** Ex 29:7; 30:30; Lev 21:10,12; Ps 133:2 **13** Ex 29:8,9 **14** Ex 29:10; Eze 43:19; Lev 4:4 **15** Ex 29:12,36; Lev 4:7; Eze 43:20,26; Heb 9:22 **16** Ex 29:13; Lev 4:8 **17** Ex 29:14; Lev 4:11,12 **18** Ex 29:15 **21** Ex 29:18 **22** Ex 29:19,31 **25** Ex 29:22 **26** Ex 29:23

one unleavened cake, a cake of oiled
bread, and one wafer and put them on
the fat and on the right thigh;
27 and he put all *these things* in Aar-
on's hands and his sons' hands and
presented them as a wave offering be-
fore the LORD.
28 Then Moses took these things
from their hands and offered them up
in smoke on the altar with the burnt
offering. They were a consecration
(ordination) offering for a sweet *and*
soothing aroma, an offering by fire
to the LORD.
29 Moses also took the breast and
presented it as a wave offering before
the LORD; it was Moses' portion of the
ram of consecration (ordination), just
as the LORD had commanded Moses.
30 So Moses took some of the anoint-
ing oil and some of the blood which
was on the altar and sprinkled it on
Aaron and his garments, and also on
his sons and their garments with him;
so Moses consecrated Aaron and his
garments, and his sons and his sons'
garments with him.
31 Then Moses said to Aaron and to
his sons, "Boil the meat at the doorway
of the Tent of Meeting and eat it there
together with the bread that is in the
basket of the consecration (ordination)
offering, just as I commanded, saying,
'Aaron and his sons shall eat it.'
32 "And what remains of the meat and
of the bread you shall burn in the fire.
33 "You shall not go outside the door-
way of the Tent of Meeting for seven
days, until the days of your consecra-
tion (ordination) are ended; for it will
take seven days to consecrate you.
34 "As has been done this day, so the
LORD has commanded to do for your
atonement.
35 "You shall remain day and night
for seven days at the doorway of the
Tent of Meeting, doing what the Lord
has required you to do, so that you
will not die; for so I (Moses) have been
commanded."
36 So Aaron and his sons did all the
things which the LORD had command-
ed through Moses.

Aaron Offers Sacrifices

9 AND IT happened on the eighth
day that Moses called Aaron and
his sons and the elders of Israel;
2 and he said to Aaron, "Take a bull
calf as a sin offering and a ram as a
burnt offering, [each] without blem-
ish, and offer *both* before the LORD.
[Heb 10:10–12]
3 "Then say to the Israelites, 'Take a
male goat as a sin offering, and a calf
and a lamb, both one year old, without
blemish, as a burnt offering,
4 and a bull and a ram as peace offer-
ings to sacrifice before the LORD, and
a grain offering mixed with [olive] oil,
for today the LORD will appear to you.' "
5 So they took what Moses had
commanded to the front of the Tent
of Meeting, and all the congregation
approached and stood before the LORD.
6 Moses said, "This is the thing which
the LORD has commanded you to do, so
that the glory of the LORD may appear
to you."
7 Moses said to Aaron, "Approach the
altar and present your sin offering and
your burnt offering and make atone-
ment for yourself and for the people;
and present the offering of the people
and make atonement for them, just as
the LORD has commanded." [Heb 5:1–
5; 7:27]
8 So Aaron approached the altar
and killed the calf as the sin offering,
which was *designated* for himself.

8:35 *so that you will not die.* This statement was a reminder that it is dangerous to approach God carelessly, without reverence, or ignore His instructions. Two of Aaron's sons failed to heed this warning and died (ch. 10).

9:4 *the LORD will appear to you.* The purpose of all worship is to fellowship with God. The sacrifices were not an end in themselves; they allowed the worshiper to meet with God without being destroyed. The Israelites looked forward and we look back to Christ's atonement, which made the way for us to come freely into God's presence.

27 Ex 29:24 **28** Ex 29:25 **29** Ex 29:26 **30** Ex 29:21; 30:30; Nu 3:3 **31** Ex 29:31,32; 1Sa 2:13-17 **32** Ex 29:34 **33** Ex 29:30,35; Eze 43:25,26 **34** Heb 7:16 **35** Nu 3:7; 9:19; Dt 11:1; 1Ki 2:3 **CHAPTER 9** **1** Eze 43:27 **2** Ex 29:1; Lev 4:3; 8:14; Lev 8:18 **3** Lev 4:23; Ezr 6:17; 10:19 **4** Lev 2:4; ver. 6,23; Ex 29:43 **6** ver. 23; Ex 24:16; 2Ch 5:13,14 **7** Lev 4:3; 1Sa 3:14; Heb 5:3; 7:27; 9:7; Lev 4:16,20; Heb 5:1

9 The sons of Aaron presented the
blood to him; he dipped his finger in
the blood and put *some of it* on the
horns of the altar, and poured out the
rest of the blood at the altar's base;
10 but the fat, the kidneys, and the
lobe of the liver from the sin offering
he offered up in smoke on the altar, just
as the LORD had commanded Moses.
11 And Aaron burned the meat and
the hide in the fire outside the camp.
12 Then he killed the burnt offering;
and Aaron's sons handed the blood
to him and he sprinkled it around on
the altar.
13 They brought the burnt offering
to him piece by piece, with the head,
and Aaron offered them up in smoke
on the altar.
14 He also washed the entrails and
the legs, and offered them up in smoke
with the burnt offering on the altar.
15 Then Aaron presented the people's
offering. He took the goat for the sin
offering of the people, and killed it and
offered it for sin, as *he did* the first.
[Heb 2:16, 17]
16 He also presented the burnt of-
fering and offered it according to the
ordinance.
17 Next Aaron presented the grain
offering and took a handful of it and
offered it up in smoke on the altar in
addition to the burnt offering of the
morning.
18 He also killed the bull and the ram,
the sacrifice of peace offerings which
was for the people; and Aaron's sons
handed the blood to him and he sprin-
kled it around on the altar,
19 As for the portions of fat from the
bull and from the ram—the fat tail, and
the fat covering the internal organs,
and the kidneys, and the lobe of the
liver—
20 they now put the portions of fat on
the breasts; and Aaron offered the fat
up in smoke on the altar.
21 But the breasts and the right thigh
Aaron presented as a wave offering
before the LORD, just as Moses had
commanded.
22 Then Aaron lifted his hands to-
ward the people and blessed them, and
came down [from the altar of burnt
offering] after presenting the sin offer-
ing, the burnt offering, and the peace
offerings.
23 Moses and Aaron went into the
Tent of Meeting, and when they came
out they blessed the people, and the
glory *and* brilliance of the LORD [the
Shekinah cloud] appeared to all the
people [as promised]. [Lev 9:6]
24 Then fire came out from before the
LORD and consumed the burnt offering
and the portions of fat on the altar;
and when all the people saw it, they
shouted and fell face downward [in
awe and worship].

The Sin of Nadab and Abihu

10 NOW NADAB and Abihu, the
sons of Aaron, took their respec-
tive [ceremonial] censers, put fire in
them, placed incense on it and offered
strange (unauthorized, unacceptable)
fire before the LORD, [an act] which He
had not commanded them to do.
2 And fire came out from the pres-
ence of the LORD and devoured them,
and they died before the LORD.

9:15 *the goat for the sin offering.* This goat was offered for atonement of the people as a general acknowledgment that they would always need to make things right with God before they could worship Him, and is referred to again in ch. 16. The bull for the sin offering (4:14) was for a specific sin, rather than dealing with sin nature (that is, our ability to sin).

9:22 *Aaron ... blessed them.* The ultimate function of the priests was to bless the people. The purpose of the priests' sacrifices was to cleanse the priests so they could bless the people, and the purpose of the people's sacrifices was to cleanse the people to receive this blessing from God.

10:1 – 2 *strange (unauthorized, unacceptable) fire.* Aaron and his sons served the Lord as high priests in the worship of the tabernacle. They had been properly appointed, purified, clothed, anointed, and ordained. Initially they did everything that the Lord commanded through

9 Lev 8:15; See Lev 4:7; Heb 9:22,23 **10** Lev 8:16; Lev 4:8 **11** Lev 4:11; 8:17 **12** Lev 1:5; 8:19 **13** Lev 8:20 **14** Lev 8:21 **15** ver. 3; Isa 53:10; Heb 2:17; 5:3 **16** Lev 1:3,10 **17** ver. 4; Lev 2:1,2; Ex 29:38 **18** Lev 3:1 **20** Lev 3:5,16 **21** Ex 29:24; Lev 7:30-34 **22** Nu 6:23; Dt 21:5; Lk 24:50 **23** ver. 6; Nu 14:10 **24** Ge 4:4; Jdg 6:21; 1Ki 18:38; 2Ch 7:1; Ps 20:3; 1Ki 18:39; 2Ch 7:3; Ezr 3:11 **CHAPTER 10** **1** Nu 3:3,4; 1Ch 24:2; Lev 16:12; Ex 30:9 **2** Nu 16:35

3 Then Moses said to Aaron, "This is
what the LORD said:

'I will be treated as holy by those
who approach Me,
And before all the people I will be
honored.' "

So Aaron, therefore, said nothing.
4 Moses called Mishael and Elza-
phan, the sons of Uzziel who was Aar-
on's uncle, and said to them, "Come
here, carry your relatives away from
the front of the sanctuary and *take
them* outside the camp."
5 So they came forward and carried
them, still in their undertunics, outside
the camp, as Moses had said.
6 Then Moses said to Aaron and
to his [younger] sons Eleazar and
Ithamar, "Do not uncover your heads
nor let your hair hang loose nor tear
your clothes [as expressions of mourn-
ing], so that you will not die [also] and
so that He will not express His wrath
and anger toward all the congregation.
But your relatives, the whole house of
Israel, may mourn the burning which
the LORD has brought about.
7 "You shall not even go out of the
doorway of the Tent of Meeting, or you
will die; for the LORD's anointing oil is
upon you." So they did [everything]
according to the word of Moses.
8 Then the LORD spoke to Aaron,
saying,
9 "Do not drink wine or intoxicating
drink, neither you nor your sons with
you, when you come into the Tent of
Meeting, so that you will not die—it is
a permanent statute throughout your
generations—
10 and to make a distinction *and* rec-
ognize a difference between the holy
(sacred) and the common (profane),
and between the [ceremonially] un-
clean and the clean; [Ezek 44:23]
11 and *you are* to teach the Israelites
all the statutes which the LORD has
spoken to them through Moses."
12 Then Moses said to Aaron, and
to his surviving sons, Eleazar and
Ithamar, "Take the grain offering that
is left over from the offerings by fire to
the LORD, and eat it unleavened beside
the altar, for it is most holy.
13 "You shall eat it in a holy place,
because it is your portion and your
sons' portion, from the offerings by
fire to the LORD; for so I have been
commanded.
14 "But the breast of the wave offering
and the thigh of the heave offering you
may eat in a clean place, you and your
sons and daughters with you; for the
breast and the thigh are your portion
and your sons' portion, given out of
the sacrifices of the peace offerings of
the Israelites.
15 "They shall bring the thigh pre-
sented by lifting up and the breast
presented by waving, along with the
offerings by fire of the fat, to present as
a wave offering before the LORD. This
shall be yours and your sons' with you,
as your perpetual portion, just as the
LORD has commanded."
16 But Moses diligently tried to find
the goat [that had been offered] as the
sin offering, and discovered that it had
been burned up [as waste, not eaten]!
So he was angry with Aaron's surviv-
ing sons Eleazar and Ithamar, saying,
17 "Why did you not eat the sin of-
fering in the holy place? For it is most
holy; and God gave it to you to remove
the guilt of the congregation, to make
atonement for them before the LORD.
18 "Behold, its blood was not brought

Moses. But when Nadab and Abihu disobeyed God in the very performance of their duties, the Lord swiftly punished them with a consuming fire. Being blessed with a thriving ministry is no excuse to go off and do things our own way. God doesn't take such actions lightly, and neither should we.

10:3 *I will be treated as holy by those who approach Me.* Although this passage refers specifically to the priests of Israel, it is still a good concept for all believers. We are close to God, we remember that He is holy, that He paid a great price to redeem us, and it is our purpose to glorify Him.

3 Ex 19:22; Isa 52:11; Eze 20:41; Eze 28:22; Ps 39:9 **4** Ex 6:18,22; Nu 3:19,30 **6** Lev 21:10; Nu 6:6,7; Nu 16:22,46; Jos 7:1; 2Sa 24:1 **7** Lev 21:12; Lev 8:30 **9** Lk 1:15; 1Ti 3:3; Titus 1:7 **10** Eze 44:23 **11** Dt 24:8; Neh 8:2,8; Jer 18:18; Mal 2:7 **12** Nu 18:9; Lev 21:22 **13** Lev 2:3; 6:16 **14** Ex 29:24,26,27; Lev 7:31,34; Nu 18:11 **15** Lev 7:29,30 **16** Lev 9:3,15 **17** Lev 6:26,29 **18** Lev 6:30; Lev 6:26,30

into the Holy Place; you certainly should have eaten the goat in the sanctuary, just as I commanded."

[19]Then Aaron said to Moses, "This very day they have [obediently] presented their sin offering and their burnt offering before the LORD, but [such terrible things] as these have happened to me [and to them]; if I [and my sons] had eaten a sin offering today would it have been acceptable *and* pleasing in the sight of the LORD?" [Hos 9:4]

[20]When Moses heard that, he was satisfied.

Laws about Animals for Food

11 THE LORD spoke again to Moses and Aaron, saying to them,

[2]"Speak to the children of Israel, saying, 'Among all the animals which are on the earth, these are the animals which you may eat. [Mark 7:15–19]

[3]'You may eat any animal that has a divided hoof [that is, a hoof split into two parts especially at its distal extremity] and chews the cud.

[4]'Nevertheless, you are not to eat these, among those which chew the cud or divide the hoof: the camel, because it chews the cud but does not divide the hoof; it is [ceremonially] unclean to you.

[5]'And the shaphan, because it chews the cud but does not divide the hoof; it is unclean to you.

[6]'And the hare, because it chews the cud but does not divide the hoof; it is unclean to you.

[7]'And the swine, because it divides the hoof and makes a split hoof, but does not chew the cud; it is unclean to you.

[8]'You shall not eat their meat nor touch their carcasses; they are unclean to you.

[9]'These you may eat, whatever is in the water: whatever has fins and scales in the waters, in the seas, and in the rivers, these you may eat;

[10]but whatever does not have fins and scales in the seas and in the rivers, of all the teeming life in the waters, and of all the living creatures that are in the waters, they are [to be considered] detestable to you. [1 Cor 8:8–13]

[11]'They shall be hated things to you. You may not eat their meat; you shall detest their carcasses.

[12]'Everything in the water that does not have fins and scales is detestable to you.

Avoid the Unclean

[13]'These you shall detest among the birds; they are not to be eaten, for they are hated things: the eagle and the vulture and the buzzard,

[14]the kite, every kind of falcon,

[15]every kind of raven,

[16]the ostrich, the nighthawk, the sea gull, every species of hawk,

[17]the little owl and the cormorant and the great owl,

11:3 *chews the cud.* Ruminants, like cows, sheep, goats, deer, and antelope, eat only plants, mainly grasses and grains. No meat-eating animal chews the cud.

11:4 *the camel.* Some of Israel's neighbors considered the camel a great delicacy.

11:5 – 6 *shaphan ... hare.* The shaphan, or rock hyrax, lives in colonies among the rocks. It is about the size of the rabbit, and like the rabbit, appears to chew constantly, but it is not a true ruminant, nor does it have a hoof.

11:7 *the swine.* The swine is the best known of the unclean animals. We know now that pigs can pass some diseases to humans, and that inadequately cooked meat is one way these diseases are transferred. Pigs were sacrificed to pagan deities, and God was carefully steering His people away from these corrupted cultures.

11:8 *nor touch their carcasses.* In the case of these unclean animals, eating their meat or touching their dead bodies caused the Israelite to be unclean, or ritually impure. However, touching a live animal did not make the Israelites unclean, and they were allowed to use camels and donkeys as beasts of burden.

11:11 – 12 *hated... detestable.* The phrasing is careful, deliberate, and repetitive to remove any possibility of finding any exception anywhere. Abhorrent is a stronger word than "unclean," and implies not just avoidance, but repulsion.

---

19 Lev 9:8,12; Isa 1:11-15 **CHAPTER 11** **2** Dt 14:4; Eze 4:14; Da 1:8; Mt 15:11; Ac 10:12,14; Ro 14:14; Heb 9:10; 13:9 **7** Isa 65:4; 66:3,17 **8** Isa 52:11; Mk 7:2,15,18; Ac 10:14,15; 15:29; 1Co 8:8; Heb 9:10 **9** Dt 14:9 **10** Lev 7:18; Dt 14:3 **13** Dt 14:12

18 the white owl, the pelican, the car-
rion vulture,
19 the stork, all kinds of heron, the
hoopoe, and the bat.
20 'All winged insects that walk on all
fours are detestable to you;
21 yet of all winged insects that walk
on all fours you may eat those which
have legs above their feet with which
to leap on the ground.
22 'Of these you may eat: the whole
species of migratory locust, of bald
locust, of cricket, and of grasshopper.
[Matt 3:4]
23 'But all other winged insects which
are four footed are detestable to you.
24 'By [contact with] these you will be-
come unclean; whoever touches their
carcasses becomes unclean until the
evening (dusk),
25 and whoever picks up any of their
carcasses shall wash his clothes and
be unclean until the evening.
26 'Concerning all the animals which
divide the hoof, but do not have a split
hoof, or which do not chew the cud,
they are unclean to you; whoever
touches them becomes unclean.
27 'Also all *animals* that walk on their
paws, among all *kinds of* animals that
walk on four *legs*, are unclean to you;
whoever touches their carcasses be-
comes unclean until the evening,
28 and the one who picks up their
carcasses shall wash his clothes and
be unclean until the evening; they are
unclean to you.
29 'These also are unclean to you
among the swarming things that crawl
around on the ground [and multiply
profusely]: the mole, the mouse, and
any kind of great lizard,
30 the gecko, the crocodile, the lizard,
the sand reptile, and the chameleon.
31 'These [creatures] are unclean to
you among all that swarm; whoever
touches them when they are dead be-
comes unclean until evening.
32 'Also anything on which one of
them falls after dying becomes un-
clean, whether it is an article of wood
or clothing, or a skin, or a sack—any
article that is used—it must be put in
water, and will be unclean until the
evening; then it becomes clean.
33 'As for any earthenware contain-
er into which any of these [crawling
things] falls, whatever is in it becomes
unclean, and you shall break the con-
tainer.
34 'Any of the food which may be eat-
en, but on which [unclean] water falls,
shall become unclean, and any liquid
that may be drunk in every container
shall become unclean.
35 'Everything that part of their car-
cass falls on becomes unclean; an oven,
or a small stove shall be smashed; they
are unclean, and shall be unclean to you.
36 'Nevertheless a spring or a cis-
tern (reservoir) collecting water shall
be clean; but whoever touches one of
these carcasses shall be unclean.
37 'If a part of their carcass falls on
any seed for sowing which is to be
sown, it is clean;
38 but if water is put on the seed and
a part of their carcass falls on it, it is
unclean to you.
39 'If one of the animals that you may
eat dies [of natural causes], whoever
touches its carcass becomes unclean
until the evening.
40 'And whoever eats some of its meat
shall wash his clothes, and be unclean
until evening; also whoever picks up
its carcass shall wash his clothes, and
be unclean until the evening.
41 'Now everything that swarms on
the ground is detestable; it is not to
be eaten.
42 'Whatever crawls on its belly, and
whatever walks on all fours, and what-
ever has many feet among all things
that swarm on the ground, you shall
not eat; for they are detestable.

11:20 ***walk on all fours.*** This phrase is an idiom for crawling on the ground, as insects do on their six legs. Many insects move about in filth and eat refuse.

11:21 ***legs above their feet.*** The joints are the enlarged third legs of locusts and grasshoppers that enable them to leap. Locusts and grasshoppers do not live in filth or eat dung; they eat only plants.

22 Mt 3:4; Mk 1:6 **25** Lev 14:8; 15:5; Nu 19:10,22; 31:24; Rev 7:14 **29** Isa 66:17 **32** Lev 15:12 **33** Lev 6:28; 15:12; Ps 2:9; Jer 48:38; 2Ti 2:21; Rev 2:27 **40** Lev 17:15; 22:8; Dt 14:21; Eze 4:14; 44:31

43 'Do not make yourselves loathsome (impure, repulsive) by [eating] any swarming thing; you shall not make yourselves unclean by them so as to defile yourselves.

44 'For I am the LORD your God; so consecrate yourselves and be holy, for I am holy. You shall not make yourselves unclean with any of the swarming things that swarm *or* crawls on the ground. [1 Thess 4:7, 8]

45 'For I am the LORD who brought you up from the land of Egypt to be your God; therefore you shall be holy, for I am holy.' " [1 Pet 1:14–16]

46 This is the law regarding the animal and the bird and every living thing that moves in the waters and everything that swarms on the earth,

47 to make a distinction between the [ceremonially] unclean and the [ceremonially] clean, and between the animal that may be eaten and the animal that may not be eaten.

Laws of Motherhood

12 THEN THE LORD spoke to Moses, saying,

2 "Speak to the children of Israel, saying,

'If a woman conceives and gives birth to a male child, she shall be [ceremonially] unclean for seven days, unclean as during her monthly period.

3 'On the eighth day the flesh of the male child's foreskin shall be circumcised.

4 'Then she shall remain [intimately separated] thirty-three days to be purified from the blood; she shall not touch any consecrated thing nor enter the [courtyard of the] sanctuary until the days of her purification are over.

5 'But if she gives birth to a female child, then she shall be unclean for two weeks, as during her monthly period, and she shall remain [intimately separated] sixty-six days to be purified from the blood.

6 'When the days of her purification are completed, whether for a son or for a daughter, she shall bring to the priest at the doorway of the Tent of Meeting a one year old lamb as a burnt offering and a young pigeon or a turtledove as a sin offering;

7 and he shall offer it before the LORD and make atonement for her, and she shall be cleansed from the flow of her blood. This is the law for her who gives birth to a child, whether a male or a female child.

8 'If she cannot afford a lamb then she shall take two turtledoves or young

---

11:44–45 ***be holy.*** Our Lord calls us to personal holiness, and holy living can only come from a life which spends time with the Lord, meditating on who He is, seeking His power to be like Him. We will make mistakes and sin all of our lives, which God never does; when He asks us to be holy because He is holy, it is a goal that we grow toward. Even though we never finish, we still overcome many, many areas of sin, and this growth shows others that we serve a holy God, because they see His characteristics in us.

12:2 ***conceives and gives birth to a . . . child . . . unclean.*** The child did not cause the mother to be unclean. God had ordained and blessed childbirth from the beginning, even before the sin in the garden (Ge 1:28). It was the blood and other fluids in childbirth that made the mother ritually unclean for a period of time, just as other bodily fluids caused people to be unclean.

12:4 ***thirty-three days to be purified from the blood.*** There is a practical as well as a ceremonial aspect to these instructions. The eighth day marked the end of the mother's uncleanness with regard to everyday objects and activities; she would no longer make them unclean by touching them. But her personal uncleanness continued. This corresponds with the medical characteristics of childbirth, and the need for special care and rest for the mother. (There is no reason given why this period is double with the birth of a female child.)

12:8 ***If she cannot afford a lamb.*** Mary, following the birth of Jesus and the days of her purification, went to the temple in Jerusalem and offered a pair of doves because she was poor. ***be clean.*** The law of purification after childbirth demonstrates that all aspects of human existence are touched by sin. Childbirth itself is not sinful, and having children was one of the good commands that the Lord gave Adam and Eve in the garden.

---

43 Lev 20:25 **44** Ex 19:6; Lev 19:2; 20:7,26; Am 3:3; Mt 5:48; 1Th 4:7; 1Pe 1:15,16; Rev 22:11,14 **45** Ex 6:7; 20:2; Ps 105:43-45; Hos 11:1; ver. 44 **47** Lev 10:10; Eze 44:23; Mal 3:18 **CHAPTER 12** **2** Lev 15:19; Job 14:4; Ps 51:5; Lk 2:22; Lev 15:19 **3** Ge 17:12; Lk 1:59; 2:21; Jn 7:22,23; Ro 3:19; Gal 5:3 **6** Lk 2:22 **8** Lev 5:7; Lk 2:24; Lev 4:26

pigeons, one as a burnt offering, the
other as a sin offering; the priest shall
make atonement for her, and she will
be clean.' " [Luke 2:22, 24]

The Test for Leprosy

13 THEN THE LORD spoke to Moses
and to Aaron, saying,
2 "When a man has a swelling on the
skin of his body, a scab, or a bright
spot, and it becomes the infection of
leprosy on the skin of his body, then he
shall be brought to Aaron the priest, or
to one of his sons the priests.
3 "The priest shall look at the dis-
eased spot on the skin of his body, and
if the hair in the infection has turned
white and the infection appears deeper
than the skin of his body, it is an in-
fection of leprosy; when the priest has
looked at him, he shall pronounce him
[ceremonially] unclean.
4 "If the bright spot is white on the
skin of his body and does not appear
to be deeper than the skin, and the hair
on it has not turned white, the priest
shall isolate *the person who has* the
infection for seven days.
5 "The priest shall examine it on the
seventh day, and if in his estimation
the infection has not changed and has
not spread on the skin, then the priest
shall isolate him for seven more days.
6 "The priest shall examine him
again on the seventh day, and if the
infection has a more normal color and
the spot has not spread on the skin,
the priest shall pronounce him clean;
it is *only* a scab; and he shall wash his
clothes and be clean.
7 "But if the scab spreads farther on
the skin after he has shown himself to
the priest for his [ceremonial] cleans-
ing, he shall show himself to the priest
again.
8 "The priest shall look, and if the
scab has spread on the skin, then he
shall pronounce him unclean; it is lep-
rosy.
9 "When a leprous infection is on
a person, he shall be brought to the
priest.
10 "The priest shall examine him, and
if there is a white swelling on the skin
and it has turned the hair white and
there is new raw flesh in the swelling,
11 it is a chronic leprosy on the skin
of his body, and the priest shall pro-
nounce him unclean; he shall not iso-
late him because he is [clearly] un-
clean.
12 "But if the [suspected] leprosy
breaks out farther on the skin, and it
covers all of the skin of the *one who
has the* outbreak—from his head to his
foot—wherever the priest looks,
13 the priest shall examine him. If the
[suspected] leprosy has covered his
entire body, he shall pronounce him
clean of the disease; it has all turned
white, and he is clean.
14 "But whenever raw flesh appears
on him, he shall be unclean.
15 "The priest shall examine the raw
flesh, and he shall pronounce him un-
clean; the raw flesh is unclean, it is
leprosy.
16 "But if the raw flesh turns again
and is changed to white, then he shall
come to the priest,
17 and the priest shall examine him,
and if the diseased part is changed to
white, then the priest shall pronounce
him who had the disease to be clean;
he is clean.
18 "And when there is on the skin
of the body [the scar of] a boil that is
healed,
19 and in the place of the boil there
is a white swelling or a bright spot,
reddish white, then it shall be shown
to the priest;

Yet pain in childbirth was one of the curses of the fall, and this time of purification can be viewed as a reminder that humans are still dealing with a sin nature that needs God's mercy and purification.

13:2 *a man.* The Hebrew word for "a man" means "human being," that is, anyone.

13:11 *shall not isolate him.* Isolation, or quarantine, was for the purpose of protecting the community until a diagnosis was reached. In this case, the patient was already diagnosed as "unclean," which meant he had to live outside the camp (v. 46).

CHAPTER 13 **2** Dt 28:27; Isa 3:17; Dt 17:8,9; 24:8; Mal 2:7; Lk 17:14 **6** Lev 11:25; 14:8 **10** Nu 12:10,12; 2Ki 5:27; 2Ch 26:20 **18** Ex 9:9; 15:26

20 and the priest shall look, and if it looks deeper than the skin and the hair on it has turned white, the priest shall pronounce him unclean; it is the disease of leprosy; it has broken out in the boil.

21 "But if the priest examines it and finds no white hair in it and it is not deeper than the skin and is dull in color, then the priest shall isolate him for seven days.

22 "If it spreads farther on the skin, then the priest shall pronounce him unclean; it is a disease.

23 "But if the bright spot remains where it is and does not spread, it is the scar of the boil, and the priest shall pronounce him clean.

24 "Or if the body has on its skin a burn from fire and the new flesh of the burn becomes a bright spot, reddish white or white,

25 then the priest shall examine it, and if the hair in the bright spot has turned white, and it appears deeper than the skin, then leprosy has broken out in the burn. So the priest shall pronounce him unclean; it is the disease of leprosy.

26 "But if the priest examines it and there is no white hair in the bright spot and it is not deeper than [the rest of] the skin but is dull in color, then the priest shall isolate him for seven days.

27 "And the priest shall examine him on the seventh day; if it is spreading farther on the skin, then the priest shall pronounce him unclean; it is leprosy.

28 "But if the bright spot remains in its place and has not spread in the skin, but is dull in color, it is a swelling from the burn, and the priest shall pronounce him clean; for it is the scar of the burn.

29 "When a man or woman has a disease on the head or in the beard (face),

30 the priest shall examine the diseased place; if it appears to be deeper than the skin, with yellow, thin hair in it, the priest shall pronounce him unclean; it is a scale, it is leprosy of the head or beard.

31 "But if the priest examines the spot infected by the scale, and it does not appear deeper than the skin and there is no black hair in it, the priest shall isolate the *person with the* scaly infection for seven days.

32 "On the seventh day the priest shall examine the diseased spot; if the scale has not spread and has no yellow hair in it, and the scale does not look deeper than the skin,

33 then he shall shave himself, but he shall not shave the scale; and the priest shall isolate the *person with the* scale for seven more days.

34 "Then on the seventh day the priest shall look at the scale; if the scale has not spread on the skin and appears to be no deeper than the skin, the priest shall pronounce him clean; he shall wash his clothes and be clean.

35 "But if the scale spreads farther on the skin after his cleansing,

36 then the priest shall examine him, and if the scale has spread on the skin, the priest need not look for the yellowish hair; he is unclean.

37 "If, in the priest's estimation, the scale has remained [without spreading], and black hair has grown in it, the scale is healed; he is clean, and the priest shall pronounce him clean.

38 "When a man or a woman has bright spots on the skin of the body, *even* white bright spots,

39 then the priest shall look, and if the bright spots on the skin of their bodies is a dull white, it is [only] a rash that has broken out on the skin; he is clean.

40 "If a man loses the hair on his head, he is bald, but he is clean.

41 "And if he loses the hair on front of his head, he is bald on the forehead, but he is clean.

42 "But if there is a reddish-white infection on the bald head or forehead, it is leprosy breaking out on his bald head or forehead.

43 "Then the priest shall examine him, and if the diseased swelling is reddish-white on his bald head or forehead like the appearance of leprosy on the skin of the body,

25 Ex 4:6,7; Nu 12:10; 2Sa 3:29; 2Ki 5:27; Lk 5:12-14 **30** Dt 24:8; Mal 2:7; 1Co 12:9; Dt 28:27; Isa 3:17 **33** Job 1:20; Ro 8:13 **37** Lev 10:10; Jer 15:19; Eze 22:26; 44:23 **40** Isa 15:2; Am 8:10

[44]he is a leprous man; he is unclean; the priest shall most certainly pronounce him unclean; his disease is on his head.

[45]"As for the leper who has the infection, his clothes shall be torn, and the hair of his head shall be uncovered (disheveled), and he shall cover his mustache and call out, 'Unclean! Unclean!'

[46]"He shall remain [ceremonially] unclean as long as the disease is on him; he is unclean. He shall live alone; he shall live outside the camp.

[47]"When a garment has a mark of leprosy in it, whether it is a wool garment or a linen garment, [Jude 23; Rev 3:4]

[48]whether in woven or knitted material or in the warp (lengthwise strands) or woof (crosswise strands) of linen or of wool, or in a skin or on anything made of leather,

[49]if the mark is greenish or reddish in the garment or in the leather or in the warp or woof or in any article made of leather, it is an infestation of leprosy and shall be shown to the priest.

[50]"The priest shall examine the mark and shall quarantine the article with the mark for seven days.

[51]"He shall examine the mark on the seventh day; if it has spread in the garment, whether in the warp or the woof, or in the leather, whatever the leather's purpose, the mark is a malignant leprosy; it is unclean.

[52]"So he shall burn the garment, whether the warp or woof, in wool or linen, or on anything made of leather in which the mark occurs; for it is a malignant leprosy; it shall be burned in the fire.

[53]"But if the priest sees that the mark has not spread in the garment, either in the warp or the woof, or on anything made of leather,

[54]then the priest shall order that they wash the thing in which the mark occurs, and he shall quarantine it for seven more days.

[55]"The priest shall examine the article with the mark after it has been washed, and if the mark has not changed color, even though the mark has not spread, it is unclean; you shall burn it in the fire; it is a corroding mildew, whether on the top or on the front of it.

[56]"If the priest looks and the mark has faded after it is washed, he shall tear it out of the garment, or the leather, or out of the warp or woof.

[57]"If it still appears in the garment, either in the warp or in the woof, or on anything made of leather, it is an outbreak; you shall burn the marked part in the fire.

[58]"The garment, whether the warp or the woof, or anything made of leather from which the mildew has departed after washing, shall then be washed a second time and it will be [ceremonially] clean."

[59]This is the law for a leprous disease in a garment of wool or linen, either in the warp or woof, or on anything made of leather, to pronounce it clean or unclean.

Law of Cleansing a Leper

14 THEN THE LORD spoke to Moses, saying,

13:45–46 *clothes shall be torn . . . mustache.* These actions were signs of mourning, for chronic skin diseases isolated the patients from life and family as if they had died. It is easy to see how leprosy became a metaphor for sin. Like serious skin diseases, sin is dangerous and ultimately fatal, often difficult to diagnose, and incurable without God's intervention.
13:47 *mark of leprosy.* This would include any mold, mildew, or other fungus growths on clothing.
13:50–58 *priest shall examine the mark.* The procedures for diagnosing a problem with a garment were similar to those for diagnosing human skin ailments. The fact that a garment was considered worth saving after a piece had been torn out of it was an economic consideration, reflecting the value of cloth.
14:1–9 *cleansing.* It is likely that the sprigs of hyssop were tied to the cedar with the scarlet thread. With that in one hand and the living bird in the other, the priest would dip them all in the blood and water mixture in the pottery bowl and

45 Eze 24:17,22; Mic 3:7; La 4:15 **46** Nu 5:2; 12:14; 2Ki 7:3; 15:5; 2Ch 26:21; Lk 17:12 **51** Lev 14:44

2 “This shall be the law of the leper on
the day of his [ceremonial] cleansing.
He shall be brought to the priest [at a
meeting place outside the camp];
3 the priest shall go out of the camp
[to meet him]; and the priest shall ex-
amine him, and if the leper has been
healed of the infection of leprosy,
4 then the priest shall give orders to
take two live clean birds and cedar
wood and scarlet string and hyssop for
the one to be cleansed. [Heb 9:19–22]
5 “Next the priest shall order that one
of the birds be killed [as a sacrifice] in
an earthenware container over [fresh]
running water.
6 “As for the live bird, he shall take
it together with the cedar wood and
the scarlet string and the hyssop, and
shall dip them and the live bird in the
blood of the bird sacrificed over the
running water.
7 “He shall sprinkle [the blood] seven
times on the one to be cleansed from
the leprosy and shall pronounce him
[ceremonially] clean. Then he shall let
the live bird go free over the open field.
[Heb 9:13–15]
8 “The one to be cleansed shall wash
his clothes, shave off all his hair, and
bathe in water; and he shall be clean.
After that he may come into the camp,
but he shall stay outside of his tent for
seven days.
9 “On the seventh day he shall shave
off all his hair: he shall shave his head
and his beard and his eyebrows, even
all his hair [on his body]. Then he shall
wash his clothes and bathe his body in
water, and be clean.
10 “Now on the eighth day he shall
take two male lambs without blem-
ish, and a yearling ewe lamb without
blemish, and three-tenths *of an ephah*
of fine flour mixed with [olive] oil as
a grain offering, and one log (about a
pint) of oil;
11 and the priest who cleanses him
shall present the man to be cleansed
and his offerings before the LORD at
the doorway of the Tent of Meeting.
12 “Then the priest shall take one of
the male lambs and offer it as a guilt
offering, with the log of oil, and pre-
sent them as a wave offering before
the LORD.
13 “He shall kill the male lamb in the
place where they kill the sin offering
and the burnt offering, in the sacred
place [the courtyard of the tabernacle];
for the guilt offering, like the sin offer-
ing, belongs to the priest; it is most holy.

---

shake them over the head of the person to be cleansed. It may seem like a rather messy procedure, but being purified from sin has never been a tidy process. In the end, it took Christ's death on the cross to cleanse His followers. The bird which was released is a reminder of the real freedom and joy that any forgiven sinner experiences.

14:2 *He shall be brought to the priest.* The priest was responsible for the diagnosis, and he was the one who administered the sacrifices and rituals that celebrated the return of the person to the community of Israel. Jesus was aware of these laws when he touched the leper and healed him, and then directed the leper to show himself to the priest (Mt 8:4).

14:4 *cedar wood . . . scarlet . . . hyssop.* Cedar is both durable and resistant to decay, scarlet is a reminder of blood, and hyssop is an aromatic herb used for flavor, fragrance, and medicine. Each of these items would have been a reminder of the blood that cleansed, the decay that was stopped, and the sweetness of good health.

14:5 *running water.* This is literally "living water," water from a spring or stream rather than water from a cistern, vessel, or pool. Living water symbolizes life. Jesus told the woman at the well to ask for living water (Jn 4:7 – 14).

14:9 – 32 *shave . . . wash.* What is termed leprosy was apparently a number of skin diseases which were infectious, and thus were an apt picture of sin, which also corrupts the flesh, and is spread through social contact. The picture of isolating, analyzing, and finally cleansing these skin diseases is similar to the process of recognizing, repenting, and being forgiven for sin. Blood is necessary in both cases, and in both cases the touch of the Holy Spirit, symbolized by oil, is present.

14:10 *the eighth day.* The eighth day was the day of circumcision for a newborn male, and the cleansed person was starting again, almost like being born again into the community.

CHAPTER 14 **2** Mt 8:2,4; Mk 1:40,44; Lk 5:12,14; 17:14 **4** Nu 19:6; Heb 9:19; Ps 51:7 **7** Nu 19:18,19; Isa 52:15; Heb 9:13,21; 12:24; 2Ki 5:10,14; Ps 51:2 **8** Lev 13:6; Lev 11:25; Eph 5:26; Heb 10:22; Rev 1:5,6; Nu 12:15 **10** Mt 8:4; Mk 1:44; Lk 5:14; Lev 2:1; Nu 15:4 **12** Lev 5:2,18; 6:6,7; Ex 29:24 **13** Ex 29:11; Lev 1:5; 4:4; Lev 7:7; Lev 2:3; 7:6; 21:22

[14]"The priest shall take some of the
blood of the guilt offering and put it on
the lobe of the right ear of the one to be
cleansed, and on the thumb of his right
hand, and on the big toe of his right foot.
[15]"The priest shall also take some of
the log of oil, and pour it into the palm
of his own left hand;
[16]and the priest shall dip his right
finger in the oil that is in his left palm,
and with his finger sprinkle some of
the oil seven times before the LORD.
[17]"Of the rest of the oil which is in
his palm, the priest shall put some on
the lobe of the right ear of the one to
be cleansed, and on the thumb of his
right hand, and on the big toe of his
right foot, on top of the blood of the
guilt offering.
[18]"The remaining oil that is in the
priest's palm shall be put on the head
of the one to be cleansed. The priest
shall make atonement for him before
the LORD.
[19]"Next the priest shall offer the sin
offering and make atonement for the
one to be cleansed from his unclean-
ness, and afterward kill the burnt
offering.
[20]"The priest shall offer the burnt
offering and the grain offering on the
altar; and the priest shall make atone-
ment for him, and he shall be clean.
[21]"But if the cleansed leper is poor
and his means are insufficient, then he
is to take one lamb as a guilt offering to
be waved to make atonement for him,
and one tenth *of an ephah* of fine flour
mixed with oil as a grain offering, and
a log of oil,
[22]and two turtledoves or two young
pigeons, such as he can afford, one
shall be a sin offering, the other a
burnt offering.
[23]"He shall bring them on the eighth
day for his [ceremonial] cleansing to
the priest at the doorway of the Tent
of Meeting, before the LORD.
[24]"The priest shall take the lamb of
the guilt offering, and the log of oil,
and shall present them as a wave of-
fering before the LORD.
[25]"Next he shall kill the lamb of the
guilt offering; and the priest is to take
some of the blood of the guilt offering
and put it on the lobe of the right ear
of the one to be cleansed, and on the
thumb of his right hand, and on the
big toe of his right foot.
[26]"The priest shall pour some of the
oil into his left palm,
[27]and with his right finger the priest
shall sprinkle some of the oil that is
in his left palm seven times before
the LORD.
[28]"The priest shall put some of the oil
in his palm on the lobe of the right ear
of the one to be cleansed, and on the
thumb of his right hand, and on the big
toe of his right foot, on the places where
he has put the blood of the guilt offering.
[29]"The rest of the oil that is in the
priest's palm shall be put on the head
of the one to be cleansed, to make
atonement for him before the LORD.
[30]"Then he shall offer one of the tur-
tledoves or young pigeons, which are
within his means.
[31]"*He shall offer* what he can afford,
one as a sin offering and the other
as a burnt offering, together with the
grain offering. The priest shall make
atonement before the LORD on behalf
of the one to be cleansed.
[32]"This is the law for the one in
whom there is an infection of leprosy,
whose means are limited for his [cer-
emonial] cleansing."

Cleansing an Infected House

[33]The LORD further spoke to Moses
and Aaron, saying,
[34]"When you come into the land of
Canaan, which I am giving you as a
possession, and I put a mark of leprosy
on a house in your land,

14:21 – 32 *if the cleansed leper is poor.* God's legislation for Israel showed special concern for the poor. In these sacrifices the poor Israelite still had to bring a lamb for the trespass offering, but for the sin offering or burnt offering he was allowed to bring turtledoves or pigeons. The grain offering was reduced from three-tenths to one-tenth of an ephah of fine flour.

14:34 *mark of leprosy on a house.* This is the same term used of serious skin diseases in chapter

14 Ex 29:20; Lev 8:23 **18** Lev 4:26; 5:6 **19** Lev 5:1,6; 12:7 **21** Lev 5:7; 12:8 **22** Lev 12:8; 15:14,15 **23** ver. 10,11 **24** ver. 12 **25** ver. 14,17 **30** ver. 22; Lev 15:14,15 **32** ver. 10 **34** Ge 17:8; Nu 32:22; Dt 7:1; 32:49

35 then the one who owns the house
shall come and tell the priest, 'I have
seen *something that looks like* a mark
of leprosy in my house.'
36 "The priest shall order that they
empty the house before he goes in to
examine the mark, so that everything
in the house will not have to be de-
clared unclean; afterward he shall go
in to see the house.
37 "He shall examine the mark, and
if the mark on the walls of the house
has greenish or reddish depressions
and appears deeper than the surface,
38 the priest shall go out of the house,
to the doorway, and quarantine the
house for seven days.
39 "The priest shall return on the sev-
enth day and look; and if the mark has
spread on the walls of the house,
40 he shall order them to tear out the
contaminated stones and throw them
into an unclean place outside the city.
41 "He shall have the entire inside
area of the house scraped, and the plas-
ter that is scraped off shall be dumped
in an unclean place outside the city.
42 "Then they shall take new stones
and replace the [contaminated] stones,
and he shall take plaster and replaster
the house.
43 "If, however, the mark breaks out
again in the house after he has re-
moved the stones and has scraped and
replastered the house,
44 then the priest shall come and look
again, and if the mark has spread in
the house, it is a malignant leprosy in
the house; it is [ceremonially] unclean.
45 "He shall tear down the house—its
stones and its timber and all the plaster
of the house—and shall take *everything*
outside the city to an unclean place.
46 "Moreover, whoever goes into the
house during the time that it is quaran-
tined becomes unclean until evening.
47 "And whoever lies down in the
house [to rest] shall wash his clothes,
and whoever eats in the house shall
wash his clothes.
48 "But if the priest comes in and in-
spects it and the mark has not spread
in the house after the house has been
replastered, he shall pronounce the
house clean because the mark has not
reappeared.
49 "To cleanse the house then, he shall
take two birds and cedar wood and
scarlet string and hyssop;
50 and he shall kill one of the birds in
an earthenware container over run-
ning water,
51 and he shall take the cedar wood
and the hyssop and the scarlet string,
and the living bird, and dip them in the
blood of the slain bird as well as in the
running water, and sprinkle the house
seven times.
52 "So he shall cleanse the house with
the blood of the bird and with the run-
ning water, along with the live bird and
the cedar wood and the hyssop and the
scarlet string.
53 "But he shall let the live bird go free
outside the city into the open field. So
he shall make atonement for the house,
and it will be clean."
54 This is the law for any mark of
leprosy—even for a scale,
55 and for the leprous garment or
house,
56 and for a swelling, and for a scab,
and for a bright spot on the skin—
57 to teach when they are unclean and
when they are clean. This is the law of
leprosy [in regard to both persons and
property].

Cleansing Unhealthiness

15 THE LORD spoke to Moses and
Aaron, saying,
2 "Speak to the children of Israel,
and say to them, 'When any man has
a bodily discharge, his discharge is
unclean.

---

13. All of these conditions were harmful, whether on human skin, clothing, or the wall of a house.
14:54–57 ***the law for any mark of leprosy.*** The uncleanness of leprosy required action. If it could not be removed, the thing that carried the uncleanness had to be removed from among God's people. In the same way, the uncleanness of sin requires action, but God has provided an infinitely stronger remedy through the blood of Christ.

35 Ps 91:10; Pr 3:33; Zec 5:4 **44** Lev 13:51; Zec 5:4 **49** ver. 4 **53** ver. 20 **54** Lev 13:30 **55** Lev 13:47; ver. 34 **56** Lev 13:2 **57** Dt 24:8; Eze 44:23 **CHAPTER 15** **2** Lev 22:4; Nu 5:2; 2Sa 3:29

3 ‘This shall be [the law concern-
ing] his uncleanness in his discharge:
whether his body allows its discharge
to flow or obstructs its flow; it is un-
cleanness in him.
4 ‘Every bed on which the one who
has the discharge lies becomes un-
clean, and everything on which he sits
becomes unclean.
5 ‘Whoever touches his bed shall
wash his clothes, and bathe in water,
and be unclean until evening;
6 and whoever sits on anything on
which the man with the discharge has
been sitting shall wash his clothes and
bathe in water, and be unclean until
evening.
7 ‘Also whoever touches the man with
the discharge shall wash his clothes
and bathe in water, and be unclean
until evening.
8 ‘And if he who has the discharge
spits on one who is clean, then he shall
wash his clothes and bathe in water,
and be unclean until evening.
9 ‘Any saddle on which the man with
the discharge rides becomes unclean.
10 ‘Whoever touches anything that has
been under him shall be unclean un-
til evening; and whoever carries those
things shall wash his clothes and bathe
in water, and be unclean until evening.
11 ‘Whomever the one with the dis-
charge touches without rinsing his
hands in water shall wash his clothes
and bathe in water, and be unclean
until evening.
12 ‘An earthenware container that the
one with the discharge touches shall be
broken, and every wooden container
shall be rinsed in water.
13 ‘When the man with the discharge
becomes cleansed from his discharge,
he shall count off seven days for his
purification; he shall then wash his
clothes and bathe his body in running
water and will become clean.
14 ‘On the eighth day he shall take
two turtledoves or two young pigeons
and come before the LORD to the door-
way of the Tent of Meeting, and give
them to the priest;
15 and the priest shall offer them,
one as a sin offering and the other as
a burnt offering. So the priest shall
make atonement for the man before the
LORD because of his discharge.
16 ‘Now if any man has a seminal
emission, he shall wash all his body
in water, and be unclean until evening.
17 ‘Every garment and every leath-
er on which there is semen shall be
washed with water, and shall be un-
clean until evening.
18 ‘If a man lies with a woman so that
there is a seminal emission, they shall
both bathe in water and be unclean
until evening.
19 ‘When a woman has a discharge,
if her bodily discharge is blood, she
shall continue in her menstrual im-
purity for seven days; and whoever
touches her shall be unclean until
evening.
20 ‘Everything on which she lies
during her menstrual impurity shall
be unclean; and everything on which
she sits shall be unclean.
21 ‘Anyone who touches her bed shall
wash his clothes and bathe in water,
and be unclean until evening.
22 ‘Whoever touches anything on
which she sits shall wash his clothes
and bathe in water, and be unclean
until evening.
23 ‘And if it is on her bed or on the
thing on which she is sitting, when he
touches it, he shall be unclean until
evening.
24 ‘If a man actually lies with her so
that her menstrual impurity is on him,
he shall be unclean for seven days;
and every bed on which he lies shall
be unclean.

15:18 ***both bathe in water . . . unclean.*** God’s plan from the beginning includes sexual intercourse between a man and his wife; this is not sinful in God’s eyes. The uncleanness and requirements of washing were a ritual cleansing, a reminder of the holiness of God, not a prohibition of intimate relationships.

15:19 ***woman . . . discharge.*** There are rules for cleansing, but no sacrifice was required. Menstruation was not regarded as sinful.

5 Lev 11:25; 17:15 **12** Lev 6:28; 11:32,33 **13** ver. 28; Lev 14:8; Nu 19:11,12 **14** Lev 14:22,23 **15** Lev 14:30,31; Lev 14:19,31 **16** Lev 22:4; Dt 23:10 **18** Ex 19:15; 1Sa 21:4; 1Co 6:18 **19** Lev 12:2 **24** See Lev 20:18

25 'Now if a woman has a flow of
blood for many days, not during the
time of her menstruation, or if she has
a discharge beyond that period, as long
as the impure discharge continues she
shall be as she is in the days of her
[normal] menstrual impurity; she is
unclean. [Matt 9:20]
26 'Every bed on which she lies during
the time of her discharge shall be to her
like the bed of her menstrual impuri-
ty, and whatever she sits on shall be
unclean, like the uncleanness of her
monthly period.
27 'And whoever touches those things
shall be unclean, and shall wash his
clothes and bathe in water, and be un-
clean until evening.
28 'When she is cleansed from her
discharge, then she shall count off for
herself seven days, and after that she
will be clean.
29 'Then on the eighth day she shall
take for herself two turtledoves or two
young pigeons and bring them to the
priest at the doorway of the Tent of
Meeting;
30 and the priest shall offer one as a
sin offering and the other as a burnt
offering; and he shall make atonement
for her before the Lord for her unclean
discharge.'
31 "Thus you shall separate the Isra-
elites from their uncleanness, so that
they do not die in their uncleanness
by their defiling My tabernacle that is
among them."
32 This is the law for the one who
has a discharge and for the one who
has a seminal emission, so that he is
unclean by it;
33 and for the woman who is ill be-
cause of her monthly period, and for
the one who has a discharge, whether
man or woman, or for a man who lies
with a woman who is [ceremonially]
unclean.

Law of Atonement

16 THEN THE Lord spoke to Moses
after the death of the two sons
of Aaron who had died when they [ir-
reverently] approached the presence
of the Lord. [Lev 10:1, 2]
2 The Lord said to Moses,
"Tell Aaron your brother that he
must not enter at any time into the
Holy Place inside the veil (the Holy of
Holies), before the mercy seat which
is on the ark, or he will die, for I will
appear in the cloud over the mercy
seat. [Heb 9:7–15, 25–28]
3 "Aaron [as high priest] shall enter
the Holy Place in this way: with [the
blood of] a young bull as a sin offering
and [the blood of] a ram as a burnt
offering.
4 "He shall put on the holy linen tunic,
and the linen undergarments shall be
next to his body, and he shall be belted

15:25–27 ***blood for many days, not during . . . her menstruation.*** If a woman had a flow of blood at any time other than her normal monthly period, or if this was unusually long, her uncleanness continued the whole time and passed to all she touched. The woman with a hemorrhage who touched Jesus secretly (Lk 8:43–48) was in this situation.

15:28–30 ***cleansed from her discharge.*** The woman was to bring the smallest allowable sacrifice for the atonement of sins she may have committed during the period of her uncleanness.

15:31–33 ***separate . . . from their uncleanness.*** Hygiene and health were important by-products, but the focus of these regulations concerning uncleanness was on keeping God's tabernacle undefiled. Ceremonial laws in regard to natural impurity seem strange to us, because these ceremonies were made obsolete by the perfect sacrifice of Christ. But in the Old Testament one form of blasphemy was the defilement of sanctuary worship by certain forms of ceremonial impurity.

16:2 ***must not enter at any time.*** This refers to the arrogant attitude in which Aaron's sons had approached to offer unauthorized sacrifice. God is Holy, and must not be approached carelessly. After Christ opened the way for all believers to approach God at any time, it is perhaps easy to forget that we still approach with reverence and awe. It was because of the terrible price of the cross that we have this privilege, not because God has suddenly become casual.

---

25 Mt 9:20; Mk 5:25; Lk 8:43 **28** ver. 13-15 **31** Lev 11:47; Dt 24:8; Eze 44:23; Heb 12:15; Nu 5:3; 19:13,20; Eze 5:11; 23:38 **32** ver. 2; ver. 16 **33** ver. 19; ver. 25; ver. 24 **CHAPTER 16** **1** Lev 10:1,2 **2** Ex 30:10; Lev 23:27; Heb 9:7; 10:19; Ex 25:22; 40:34; 1Ki 8:10-12 **3** Ex 25:21; Lev 4:3 **4** Ex 28:39,42,43; Lev 6:10; Eze 44:17,18; Ex 30:20; Lev 8:6,7

with the linen sash, and dressed with
the linen turban (these are the holy
garments). He shall bathe his body in
water and put them on.
5 "He shall take from the congrega-
tion of the Israelites [at their expense]
two male goats as a sin offering and
one ram as a burnt offering.
6 "Then Aaron shall present the bull
as the sin offering for himself, and
make atonement for himself and for
his house.
7 "He shall take the two goats and
present them before the LORD at the
doorway of the Tent of Meeting.
8 "Aaron shall cast lots for the two
goats—one lot for the LORD, the other
lot for the scapegoat.
9 "Then Aaron shall bring the goat
on which the LORD's lot fell and offer
it as a sin offering.
10 "But the goat on which the lot fell
for the scapegoat shall be presented
alive before the LORD to make atone-
ment on it; it shall be sent into the wil-
derness as the scapegoat.
11 "Aaron shall present the bull as
the sin offering for himself and make
atonement for himself and for his
household (the other priests), and he
shall kill the bull as the sin offering
for himself.
12 "He shall take a censer full of burn-
ing coals from the [bronze] altar before
the LORD, and two handfuls of finely
ground sweet incense, and bring it in-
side the veil [into the Most Holy Place],
13 and put the incense on the fire [in
the censer] before the LORD, so that
the cloud of the incense may cover the
mercy seat that is on [the ark of] the
Testimony, otherwise he will die.
14 "He shall take some of the bull's
blood and sprinkle it with his finger on
the east side of the mercy seat; also in
front of the mercy seat he shall sprin-
kle some of the blood with his finger
seven times.
15 "Then he shall kill the goat of the
sin offering that is for [the sins of] the
people and bring its blood within the
veil [into the Most Holy Place] and do
with its blood as he did with the blood
of the bull, and sprinkle it on the mer-
cy seat and in front of the mercy seat.
[Heb 2:17]
16 "So he shall make atonement for
the Holy Place (Holy of Holies) be-
cause of the uncleanness and trans-
gressions of the Israelites, for all their
sins. He shall also do this for the Tent
of Meeting which is among them in the
midst of their uncleanness (impurities).
[Heb 9:22–24]
17 "There shall be no person in the Tent
of Meeting when the high priest goes in
to make atonement in the Holy Place
[within the veil] until he comes out, so
that he may make atonement for himself
(his own sins) and for his household and
for all the congregation of Israel.
18 "Then he shall go out to the altar
[of burnt offering in the court] which is
before the LORD and make atonement
for it, and shall take some of the blood
of the bull and of the goat and put it
on the horns of the altar on all sides.
19 "With his finger he shall sprinkle
some of the blood on the altar of burnt
offering seven times and cleanse it and
consecrate it from the uncleanness of
the Israelites.
20 "When he has finished atoning for
the Holy Place and the Tent of Meeting
and the altar, he shall present the live
goat.

16:6 *for himself.* After atoning for himself, the high priest could offer the sacrifice to atone for the people. The author of Hebrews places great emphasis on this point in discussing the superior priesthood of Jesus, who did not have to offer a sacrifice for Himself before He could be the sacrifice of atonement, one time for all people (Heb 7:26; 9:11–28; 10:19–22).

16:15–19 *the goat ... for [the sins of] the people.* Aaron offered the goat for the people, and the other actions involved in this sacrifice made it clear that the sins of the people had a defiling effect on the tabernacle. If not removed, the sins would have caused the ministry to be ineffective in atoning for the people.

5 See Lev 4:14; Nu 29:11; 2Ch 29:21; Ezr 6:17; Eze 45:22,23 **6** Lev 9:7; Heb 5:2; 7:27,28; 9:7 **10** 1Jn 2:2
12 Lev 10:1; Nu 16:18,46; Rev 8:5; Ex 30:34 **13** Ex 30:7,8; Nu 16:7,18,46; Ex 25:21 **14** Lev 4:5; Heb 9:25; 10:4; Lev 4:6 **15** Heb 2:17; 5:2; 9:7,28; ver. 2; Heb 6:19; 9:3,7,12 **16** See Ex 29:36; Eze 45:18; Heb 9:22,23
17 See Ex 34:3; Lk 1:10 **18** Ex 30:10; Lev 4:7,18; Heb 9:22,23 **19** Eze 43:20 **20** ver. 16; Eze 45:20

[21]"Then Aaron shall lay both of his hands on the head of the live goat, and confess over it all the wickedness of the sons of Israel and all their transgressions in regard to all their sins; and he shall lay them on the head of the goat [the scapegoat, the sin-bearer], and send it away into the wilderness by the hand of a man who is prepared [for the task].

[22]"The goat shall carry on itself all their (the Israelites) wickedness, carrying them to a solitary (infertile) land; and he shall release the goat in the wilderness. [Ps 103:12; Is 53:11, 12; John 1:29]

[23]"Then Aaron shall come into the Tent of Meeting and take off the linen garments which he put on when he went into the Holy Place (Holy of Holies), and shall leave them there.

[24]"He shall bathe his body with water in a holy place and put on his clothes, and come out and offer his burnt offering and that of the people, and make atonement for himself and for the people.

[25]"And he shall offer up in smoke the fat of the sin offering on the altar.

[26]"The man who released the goat as the [sin-bearing] scapegoat shall wash his clothes and bathe his body in water, and afterward he may come into the camp.

[27]"The bull for the sin offering and the goat for the sin offering, whose blood was brought in to make atonement in the Holy Place (Holy of Holies), shall be taken outside the camp; their skins, their meat, and their waste shall be burned in the fire. [Heb 13:11–13]

[28]"Then he who burns them shall wash his clothes and bathe his body with water, and afterward he may come into the camp.

An Annual Atonement

[29]"This shall be a permanent statute for you: in the seventh month (nearly October) on the tenth day of the month you shall humble yourselves [by fasting] and not do any work, whether the native-born or the stranger who lives temporarily among you;

[30]for it is on this day that atonement shall be made for you, to cleanse you; you will be clean from all your sins before the LORD. [Heb 10:1, 2; 1 John 1:7, 9]

16:21 *Aaron shall lay both of his hands on the head of the live goat.* Sending the goat into the wilderness was a public ceremony. Everyone could see Aaron symbolically placing the sins of the people on the goat's head. All of the ways that people could offend God were placed on the head of the goat, which took them away from the camp, away from the people, away from God.

16:22 *goat shall carry on itself.* This is the origin of the common expression "scapegoat." The goat was not guilty of the sins, but he bore them anyway, allowing the guilty to escape the consequences of their sins. In Jesus' bearing the sins of the human race, and in His death outside the city (outside the camp), He fulfilled this annual ritual of the Day of Atonement. Not only was Jesus the perfect High Priest, He was the perfect Sacrifice.

16:29 *in the seventh month.* The Day of Atonement fell between mid-September and mid-October.

16:29–34 The Day of Atonement—This whole process of animal sacrifice seems foreign to us. There is no enjoyment in seeing an animal killed. Special underwear and extra washings do not fit our religious experience. It is easy for us to wonder why this was necessary. What is the big deal anyway? The primary reason we have trouble with this is that we have such a superficial understanding of sin and God's attitude toward it. We tend to think of sin as a kind of correctable mistake, easily taken care of. Why be so upset about it?

The Day of Atonement pointed the Israelites to the seriousness of sin. They were able to see that sin was an affront to God that had to be dealt with. It is like cancer. If it is not treated, death is the ultimate consequence. At its core, sin is rebellion against God. This ceremony stood as a permanent reminder of these truths. It pointed to God's holiness, to the drastic measures needed to deal with sin. Our souls are to be cleansed thoroughly and the sacrifices on the Day of Atonement accomplished this cleansing for the Israelite community. As such it was the most important day in the Jewish religious calendar.

---

21 Isa 53:6 **22** Isa 53:11,12; Jn 1:29; Heb 9:28; 1Pe 2:24 **23** Eze 42:14; 44:19 **24** ver. 3,5 **25** Lev 4:10 **26** Lev 15:5 **27** Lev 4:12,21; 6:30; Heb 13:11 **29** Ex 30:10; Lev 23:27; Nu 29:7 **30** Jer 33:8; Eph 5:26; Heb 9:13,14; 10:1,2; 1Jn 1:7,9

[31]"It is a Sabbath of solemn rest for
you, and you shall humble yourselves;
it is a permanent statute.
[32]"So the priest who is anointed
and ordained to serve *and* minister as
priest in his father's place shall make
atonement: he shall wear the holy linen
garments,
[33]and make atonement for the Holy
Sanctuary, and he shall make atone-
ment for the Tent of Meeting, and
for the altar [of burnt offering in the
court]. He shall also make atonement
for the priests and for all the people of
the assembly.
[34]"This shall be a permanent stat-
ute for you, so that atonement may be
made for the children of Israel for all
their sins once a year." So he did just
as the LORD had commanded Moses.

Blood for Atonement

17 THEN THE LORD spoke to Mo-
ses, saying,
[2]"Speak to Aaron and his sons and
all the children of Israel, and say to
them, 'This is what the LORD has com-
manded, saying,
[3]"Any man from the house of Israel
who kills an ox or lamb or goat in the
camp, or kills it outside the camp
[4]and has not brought it to the door-
way of the Tent of Meeting to offer it
as an offering to the LORD before the
tabernacle of the LORD, that man shall
be guilty of bloodshed. He has shed
blood and shall be cut off from his peo-
ple [excluding him from the atonement
made for them].
[5]"This is so that the sons of Israel
may bring their sacrifices which they
were sacrificing [to idols] in the open
field [where they killed them], that they
may bring them in to the LORD, at the
doorway of the Tent of Meeting to the
priest, and sacrifice them as sacrifices
of peace offerings to the LORD.
[6]"The priest shall sprinkle the blood
on the altar of the LORD at the doorway
of the Tent of Meeting and offer the fat
up in smoke as a sweet *and* soothing
aroma to the LORD.
[7]"So they shall no longer offer their
sacrifices to goat-idols *or* demons *or*
field spirits with which they have
played the prostitute. This shall be a
permanent statute for them throughout
their generations." '
[8]"Then you shall say to them, 'Any
man from the house of Israel or any
of the strangers living temporarily
among you, who offers a burnt offer-
ing or sacrifice
[9]and does not bring it to the doorway
of the Tent of Meeting to offer it to the
LORD shall be cut off from his people
[excluding him from the atonement
made for them].
[10]'Any man from the house of Is-
rael, or any stranger living temporar-
ily among you, who eats any blood,
against that person I shall set My face
and I will cut him off from his people
[excluding him from the atonement
made for them]. [Ezek 33:25]
[11]'For the life of the flesh is in the
blood, and I have given it to you on
the altar to make atonement for your

17:5 *sacrifices . . . in the open field.* Such sacrifices were strictly forbidden. All sacrifices were to be clearly and unequivocally made to God alone, and in His way.
17:7 *to goat-idols or demons . . . played the prostitute.* Pagan deities in the form of goats, like satyrs, were a part of the cultures surrounding the Israelites. Israel's worship of other gods, and God's attitude toward it was likened to the way a husband would feel if his wife became a prostitute. This was a picture of betrayal that the Israelites could understand. ***permanent statute.*** Because this was a permanent rule, it becomes clear that it was not an injunction against slaughtering animals for meat, but referred to sacrifices. When Israel's worship was centered in Jerusalem, some families lived more than a hundred miles from the temple. They could not have traveled so far to kill animals for meat, although they did make the journey for sacrifices.
17:10 *any blood.* Eating blood was forbidden in the strongest possible terms.

31 Lev 23:32 **32** Lev 4:3,5,16; Ex 29:29,30; Nu 20:26,28; ver. 4 **33** ver. 6,16-18,24 **34** Lev 23:31; Nu 29:7; Ex 30:10; Heb 9:7,25 **CHAPTER 17** **3** See Dt 12:5,15,21 **4** Dt 12:5,6,13,14; Ro 5:13; Ge 17:14 **5** Ge 21:33; 22:2; 31:54; Dt 12:2 **6** Lev 3:2; Ex 29:18; Nu 18:17 **7** Dt 32:17; 2Ch 11:15; 1Co 10:20; Ex 34:15; Dt 31:16; Eze 23:8 **8** Lev 1:2,3 **10** Ge 9:4; Dt 12:16,23; 15:23; 1Sa 14:33; Lev 20:3,5,6 **11** Mt 26:28; Ro 3:25; Eph 1:7; Col 1:14,20; 1Pe 1:2; 1Jn 1:7; Heb 9:22

souls; for it is the blood that makes
atonement, by reason of the life [which
it represents].’ [Rom 3:24–26]
12“Therefore I have said to the sons
of Israel, ‘No person among you may
eat blood, nor may any stranger living
temporarily among you eat blood.’
13“So when any Israelite or any
stranger living temporarily among
them, catches any ceremonially clean
animal or bird when hunting, he shall
pour out its blood and cover it with
earth.
14“For in regard to the life of all
flesh, its blood is [the same] as its life;
therefore I said to the Israelites, ‘You
are not to eat the blood of any flesh,
for the life of all flesh is its blood.
Whoever eats it shall be cut off [ex-
cluding him from the atonement made
for them].’
15“Every person who eats an ani-
mal which dies [of natural causes] or
was torn by a predator, whether he
is native-born or a stranger, he shall
wash his clothes and bathe in water,
and be [ceremonially] unclean until
evening; then he will become clean.
[Acts 15:20]
16“But if he does not wash *his clothes*
or bathe his body, he shall bear his
guilt [for it will not be borne by the
sacrifice of atonement].”

Laws on Immoral Relations

18 THEN THE LORD spoke to Mo-
ses, saying,
2“Speak to the children of Israel and
say to them, ‘I am the LORD your God.
3‘You shall not do what is done in
the land of Egypt where you lived, and
you shall not do what is done in the
land of Canaan where I am bringing
you. You shall not follow their statutes
(practices, customs).
4‘You are to follow My judgments
(precepts, ordinances) and keep My
statutes and live by them. I am the
LORD your God.
5‘So you shall keep My statutes and
My judgments, by which, if a person
keeps them, he shall live; I am the LORD.
[Luke 10:25–28; Rom 10:4, 5; Gal 3:12]
6‘No one shall approach any blood
relative of his to uncover nakedness
(have intimate relations). I am the
LORD.
7‘You shall not uncover the naked-
ness of your father, that is, the na-
kedness of your mother. She is your
mother. You shall not uncover her na-
kedness.
8‘You shall not uncover the naked-
ness of your father’s wife; it is your
father’s nakedness.
9‘You shall not uncover the naked-
ness of your sister, *either* the daughter

17:13 *cover it with earth.* Blood was to be treated respectfully, and covering it with earth was a token of burial.

18:2 *the LORD.* This is the translation of the name for God, sometimes called Yahweh, the name by which God revealed Himself to Moses (Ex 6:2 – 8). In using this name, God was basing His claim to the Israelites’ devotion on His willingness to reveal Himself to them, to redeem them and to be their God.

18:4 *My judgments . . . My statutes.* “Judgments” refers to judicial decisions involving situations that might not be addressed in the statutes. “Statutes” are decrees, laws, and acts of a permanent nature.

18:5 *if a person keeps them, he shall live.* God gave the law as a means of life on all levels — physical, moral, spiritual, and relational.

18:6 *No one . . . any blood relative . . . uncover nakedness.* This term covers cases such as incest between father and daughter and between brother and full sister, even though they are absent from the following list. To uncover someone’s nakedness is to have sexual intercourse with that person.

18:7 *You shall not uncover the nakedness of your father.* The point of this passage is that committing incest with the wife of one’s father is symbolically to uncover the father’s nakedness too, because the two are one flesh through marriage.

18:8 *father’s wife.* Even if your father’s wife is not your mother, it is still wrong to have sexual relations with her. In Israel at that time multiple wives or concubines were still part of society, as well as a second wife coming into the family through death or divorce of the first wife.

18:9 *your sister.* Though this may seem redundant, God wanted to make it abundantly clear that a sister who did not share the same pair of

---

13 Lev 7:26; Dt 12:16,24; Eze 24:7 **14** ver. 11,12; Ge 9:4; Dt 12:23 **15** Ex 22:31; Eze 4:14; 44:31; Lev 11:25; Lev 15:5 **16** Lev 5:1 **CHAPTER 18** **2** Ex 6:7; Eze 20:5,7,19,20 **3** Eze 20:7; Ex 23:24 **4** Eze 20:19 **5** Eze 20:11,13,21; Ro 10:5; Gal 3:12; Ex 6:2,6 **7** Lev 20:11 **8** Ge 49:4; Lev 20:11; 1Co 5:1 **9** Lev 20:17

of your father or of your mother, wheth-
er born at home or born elsewhere.
10‘You shall not uncover the naked-
ness of your son’s daughter or your
daughter’s daughter; their nakedness
you shall not uncover, for they are your
own nakedness [that is, your own de-
scendants].
11‘You shall not uncover the naked-
ness of your father’s wife’s daughter;
born to your father, she is your sister.
12‘You shall not uncover the naked-
ness of your father’s sister; she is your
father’s blood relative.
13‘You shall not uncover the naked-
ness of your mother’s sister, for she is
your mother’s blood relative.
14‘You shall not uncover the naked-
ness of your father’s brother’s wife;
you shall not approach his wife; she
is your aunt.
15‘You shall not uncover the naked-
ness of your daughter-in-law; she is
your son’s wife. You shall not uncover
her nakedness.
16‘You shall not uncover the naked-
ness of your brother’s wife; it is your
brother’s nakedness.
17‘You shall not uncover the naked-
ness of a woman and her daughter,
nor shall you take her son’s daughter
or her daughter’s daughter to uncover
their nakedness (have intimate rela-
tions with them); they are [her] blood
relatives; it is an outrageous offense.
18‘You shall not marry a woman in
addition to her sister as a rival while
she is alive, to uncover her nakedness.
19‘Also you shall not approach a
woman to uncover her nakedness
during her menstrual impurity *and*
ceremonial uncleanness.
20‘You shall not have intimate rela-
tions with your neighbor’s wife, to be
defiled with her.
21‘You shall not give any of your
children to offer them [by fire as a
sacrifice] to Molech [the god of the
Ammonites], nor shall you profane the
name of your God [by honoring idols
as gods]. I am the LORD.
22‘You shall not lie [intimately] with
a male as one lies with a female; it is
repulsive. [1 Cor 6:9, 10]
23‘You shall not have intimate rela-
tions with any animal to be defiled with
it; nor shall a woman stand before an
animal to mate with it; it is a perversion.
24‘Do not defile yourselves by any
of these things; for by all these the
nations which I am casting out before
you have become defiled.
25‘For the land has become defiled;
therefore I have brought its punish-
ment upon it, and the land vomits out
its inhabitants.
26‘But as for you, you are to keep My
statutes and My judgments (precepts)
and shall not commit any of these re-
pulsive acts, neither the native-born,
nor the stranger who lives temporarily
among you

---

parents as her brother was still off limits. This would cover husbands of multiple wives and illegitimate children. Sexual sin is serious with long reaching consequences, and it is clearly forbidden within the family.

18:20 *with your neighbor’s wife.* Adultery is forbidden in Exodus 20:14 and its penalty is given in Leviticus 20:10.

18:21 *not give any of your children ... to Molech.* God forbids child sacrifice right along with incest. This is destructive behavior with far reaching consequences, and all followers of the Lord will abhor it as God does.

18:22 *lie [intimately] with a male.* Homosexuality here is labeled as repulsive, something detestable to God both ritually (as a part of the Canaanite religion) and morally. When God is repulsed, it is a clear message that homosexuality is not part of His plan for human relationships.

18:23 *any animal.* Bestiality is labeled a perversion, something out of the natural order and a defilement. It, too, was a feature of some of the religions of Israel’s neighbors.

18:24–30 *defile.* The land had become so defiled by the perverted practices of the Canaanites that it was vomiting them out. For that reason, the land would be available to Israel to settle. The Israelites, however, needed to be careful to live as God’s holy people, or the land would vomit them out as well.

12 Lev 20:19 **14** Lev 20:20 **15** Ge 38:18,26 **16** See Dt 25:5 **17** Lev 20:14 **18** 1Sa 1:6,8 **19** Lev 20:18; Eze 18:6; 22:10 **20** Ex 20:14; Lev 20:10; Dt 5:18; 22:22; Mt 5:27; Ro 2:22; 1Co 6:9; Heb 13:4 **21** Lev 20:2; 2Ki 16:3; 1Ki 11:7,33; Ac 7:43; Lev 19:12; 20:3; Eze 36:20 **22** Lev 20:13; 1Co 6:9; 1Ti 1:10 **23** Ex 22:19; Lev 20:12 **24** Mt 15:18-20; 1Co 3:17; Dt 18:12 **25** Nu 35:34; Eze 36:17; Isa 26:21; Jer 5:9 **26** ver. 5,30

27(for all these repulsive acts have been done by the men who lived in the land before you, and the land has become defiled);

28[do none of these things] so that the land will not vomit you out, should you defile it, as it has vomited out the nation which has been before you.

29'For whoever commits any of these repulsive acts, those persons who do so shall be cut off from among their people [excluding them from the atonement made for them].

30'So keep My command: do not practice any of the repulsive customs which have been practiced before you, so as not to defile yourselves by them; I am the Lord your God.' "

Idolatry Forbidden

19 THEN THE Lord spoke to Moses, saying,

2"Say to all the congregation of the children of Israel, 'You shall be holy, for I the Lord your God am holy. [1 Pet 1:15]

3'Each of you shall respect his mother and his father, and you shall keep My Sabbaths; I am the Lord your God.

4'Do not turn to idols or make for yourselves molten gods (images cast in metal); I am the Lord your God.

5'Now when you offer a sacrifice of peace offerings to the Lord, you shall offer it so that you may be accepted.

6'It shall be eaten the same day you offer it and on the day following; and if anything remains until the third day, it shall be burned in the fire.

7'But if it is eaten at all on the third day, it is repulsive; it will not be accepted [by God as an offering].

8'Everyone who eats it will bear [the responsibility for] his wickedness, for he has profaned a holy thing of the Lord; and that person shall be cut off from his people [excluding him from the atonement made for them].

Various Laws

9'Now when you reap the harvest of your land, you shall not reap to the very corners of your field, nor shall you gather the gleanings (grain left after reaping) of your harvest.

10'And you shall not glean your vineyard, nor shall you gather its fallen grapes; you shall leave them for the poor and for the stranger. I am the Lord your God.

11'You shall not steal, nor deal deceptively, nor lie to one another. [Col 3:9, 10]

12'You shall not swear [an oath] falsely by My name, so as to profane the name of your God; I am the Lord.

13'You shall not oppress *or* exploit your neighbor, nor rob him. You shall not withhold the wages of a hired man overnight until morning.

14'You shall not curse a deaf man nor put a stumbling block before the blind, but you shall fear your God [with profound reverence]; I am the Lord.

15'You shall not do injustice in judgment; you shall not be partial to the poor nor show a preference for the great, but judge your neighbor fairly.

16'You shall not go around as a gossip among your people, and you are not to act against the life of your neighbor [with slander or false testimony]; I am the Lord.

17'You shall not hate your brother in your heart; you may most certainly re-

---

19:3 *keep My Sabbaths.* The weekly Sabbath was an acknowledgment that not everything depended on the Israelites' efforts. It was an acknowledgment of God's lordship and His grace.

19:5 *peace offerings.* The peace offering was a free will offering.

19:10 *for the poor and for the stranger.* Providing for the poor and the alien who could not own land was a priority in ancient Israel. The generosity of God's people was rooted in God's generosity toward the Israelites.

19:16 *gossip.* This person is not just a gossip, but one who is actively seeking to destroy another's reputation.

19:17 *hate . . . in your heart.* Jesus addressed this principle in the Sermon on the Mount (Mt 5:21–24).

28 Jer 9:19 **30** ver. 3 **CHAPTER 19** **2** Lev 11:44 **3** Ex 20:12; Ex 20:8 **4** Ex 20:4; Ex 34:17 **5** Lev 7:16
9 Dt 24:19 **11** Ex 20:15; Eph 4:25 **12** Ex 20:7; Dt 5:11; Mt 5:33; Jas 5:12; Lev 18:21 **13** Mk 10:19; Mal 3:5
14 Deut 27:18 **16** Ex 23:1; Ex 23:1,7; 1Ki 21:13 **17** 1Jn 2:9,11; 3:15; Mt 18:15; Eph 5:11; 1Ti 5:20

buke your neighbor, but shall not incur sin because of him. [Gal 6:1; 1 John 2:9, 11; 3:15]

18 ‘You shall not take revenge nor bear any grudge against the sons of your people, but you shall love your neighbor (acquaintance, associate, companion) as yourself; I am the LORD. [Matt 5:43–46; Rom 12:17, 19]

19 ‘You are to keep My statutes. You shall not breed together two kinds of your cattle; you shall not sow your field with two kinds of seed, nor wear clothing of two kinds of material mixed together.

20 ‘Now if a man has intimate relations with a woman who is a slave acquired for [marriage to] *another* man, but who has not been redeemed nor given her freedom, there shall be punishment [after an investigation]; they shall not be put to death, because she was not free;

21 but he shall bring his guilt offering to the LORD to the doorway of the Tent of Meeting, a ram as a guilt offering.

22 ‘The priest shall make atonement for him with the ram of the guilt offering before the LORD for his sin which he has committed; and he shall be forgiven for his sin.

23 ‘When you enter the land and plant all kinds of trees for food, then you shall consider their fruit forbidden. For three years the fruit shall be forbidden to you; it shall not be eaten.

24 ‘In the fourth year all the fruit shall be holy, an offering of praise to the LORD.

25 ‘In the fifth year you may eat the fruit [of the trees], this is so that their yield may increase for you; I am the LORD your God.

26 ‘You shall not eat *anything* with the blood, nor practice divination [using omens or witchcraft] or soothsaying.

27 ‘You shall not trim *and* round off the side-growth of [the hair on] your heads, nor mar the edges of your beard.

28 ‘You shall not make any cuts on your body [in mourning] for the dead, nor make any tattoo marks on yourselves; I am the LORD.

29 ‘Do not profane your daughter by making her a prostitute, so that the land will not fall to prostitution and become full of wickedness.

30 ‘You shall keep My Sabbaths and revere My sanctuary. I am the LORD.

31 ‘Do not turn to mediums [who pretend to consult the dead] or to spiritists [who have spirits of divination]; do not

---

19:18 *take revenge.* Vengeance belongs to God (Dt 32:35); His vengeance is entirely just. It is easy for human vengeance to be carried out too zealously, leaving the by-products of bitterness and hatred. Instead, we are to do good to those who hate us and pray for those who persecute us (Mt 5:44). ***love.*** The word "love" is first found in Genesis 22:2, where God told Abraham to offer up his son whom he loved as a burnt sacrifice upon Mount Moriah, and the first mention of love in the New Testament is God proclaiming that Jesus is His beloved Son (Mt 3:17). Family love is something people find easy to understand. Even if it is not very strong in one's nuclear family, the longing for love shows us that we understand what it is to be. To take this love one step further, that a parent would allow a child to die for the good of others, stretches the concept of love. And yet it is that very love that caused God to send His Son to die for the whole world.

19:20 *a woman who is a slave.* The slave woman had a low social standing and few rights, and may not have had the freedom to cry out when approached sexually. Therefore, she remained guiltless. Because she was a slave, the man escaped death, but remained guilty before God. Atonement was necessary for him to receive forgiveness.

19:26 *divination.* God, and not a demon or impersonal force, is all powerful and directs the future. Practicing divination reveals a lack of trust in God to bring the best in the future in His timing.

19:27 – 28 *beard . . . cuts on your body . . . nor make any tattoo marks.* The human body was designed by God to be beautiful. Disfiguring the body for the dead, or as a sign of mourning, is dishonoring to God. Some disfiguring was a part of pagan religions, and was forbidden to God's people for any reason.

19:29 *making her a prostitute.* Sexual relations are sacred. Forcing a daughter to violate that sanctity defiled her against her will.

19:31 *mediums . . . spiritists.* In principle this is no different than divination. Its practice involves

---

18 Ro 12:17,19; Mt 5:43 **19** Dt 22:9,10; Dt 22:11 **21** Lev 5:15 **24** Dt 12:17,18; Pr 3:9 **26** Lev 17:10; Dt 18:10,11,14; 1Sa 15:23; 2Ch 33:6; Mal 3:5 **27** Lev 21:5; Isa 15:2; Jer 9:26 **28** Jer 16:6 **29** Dt 23:17 **30** ver. 3; Lev 26:2; Ecc 5:1 **31** Ex 22:18; Isa 8:19; Ac 16:16

seek them out to be defiled by them. I
am the LORD your God.
32 'You shall rise before the gray-
headed and honor the aged, and you
shall fear your God [with profound
reverence]; I am the LORD.
33 'When a stranger resides with you
in your land, you shall not oppress *or*
mistreat him.
34 'But the stranger who resides
with you shall be to you like some-
one native-born among you; and you
shall love him as yourself, for you were
strangers in the land of Egypt; I am the
LORD your God.
35 'You shall do no wrong in judg-
ment, in measurement of weight or
quantity.
36 'You shall have just *and* accurate
balances, just weights, a just ephah,
and a just hin. I am the LORD your God,
who brought you out of the land of
Egypt.
37 'You shall observe *and* keep all My
statutes and all My ordinances and do
them. I am the LORD.' "

On Human Sacrifice and Immoralities

20 THEN THE LORD spoke to Mo-
ses, saying,
2 "Moreover, you shall say to the chil-
dren of Israel,
'Any Israelite or any stranger resid-
ing in Israel who gives any of his chil-
dren to Molech (the god of the Ammon-
ites) [as a human sacrifice] shall most
certainly be put to death; the people of
the land shall stone him with stones.
3 'I will also set My face against that
man [opposing him, withdrawing My
protection from him] and will cut him
off from his people [excluding him
from the atonement made for them],
because he has given some of his chil-
dren to Molech, so as to defile My sanc-
tuary and profane My holy name.
4 'If the people of the land should ever
tolerate that man when he gives any
of his children [as a burnt offering] to
Molech, and fail to put him to death [as
My law requires],
5 then I shall set My face against that
man and against his [extended] family,
and I will cut off from their people both
him and all who follow him in playing
the prostitute (commit apostasy) with
Molech.
6 'As for the person who turns to me-
diums [who consult the dead] or to
spiritists, to play the prostitute after
them, I shall set My face against that
person and will cut him off from his
people [excluding him from the atone-
ment made for them]. [Is 54:5]
7 'You shall consecrate yourselves
therefore, and be holy; for I am the
LORD your God.
8 'You shall keep My statutes and do
them. I am the LORD who sanctifies
you.
9 'If anyone curses his father or moth-
er, he shall most certainly be put to
death; he has cursed his father or moth-
er; his blood is on him [that is, he bears
full responsibility for the consequences].
10 'The man who commits adultery
with another's wife, even his neigh-
bor's wife, the adulterer and the adul-

---

consulting the spirits of the dead, or other spirits, both of which are strictly forbidden. It demonstrates lack of faith and rebellion against God and His ways.

19:35–36 *do no wrong . . . in measurement of weight or quantity.* Injustice in legal transactions or in business are equally wrong. God is just and generous, and His people are to be the same.

20:2–5 *gives any of his children to Molech . . . put to death . . . stone him.* The penalty for child sacrifice, whether carried out by an alien or a citizen of Israel, was death, either carried out by the justice system or by God Himself. Children are a trust and blessing from God, and killing them in a pagan ritual is a wickedness that God will not overlook.

20:8 *who sanctifies you.* To be sanctified is to be "set apart." The worshiper was set apart to God, from all other allegiances.

20:9 *his blood is on him.* This statement assured the executioners that they were not guilty of shedding the offender's blood.

32 1Ti 5:1; ver. 14 **33** Ex 22:21 **34** Ex 12:48; Dt 10:19 **35** ver. 15 **36** Dt 25:13,15 **37** Lev 18:4,5; Dt 4:5,6; 5:1; 6:25 **CHAPTER 20** **2** Lev 18:2; Lev 18:21; 2Ki 23:10; 2Ch 33:6; Jer 7:31 **3** Lev 17:10; Eze 5:11; 23:38,39; Lev 18:21 **4** Dt 17:2,3,5 **5** Lev 17:10; Ex 20:5; Lev 17:7 **6** Lev 19:31 **7** Lev 19:2 **8** Lev 19:37; Ex 31:13 **9** Ex 21:17; Dt 27:16; Pr 20:20; Mt 15:4; ver. 11,12, 13,16,27; 2Sa 1:16 **10** Lev 18:20; Dt 22:22

teress shall most certainly be put to
death. [John 8:4–11]
11 ‘The man who lies [intimately] with
his father’s wife has uncovered his
father’s nakedness; both of them shall
most certainly be put to death; their
blood is on them.
12 ‘If a man lies [intimately] with his
daughter-in-law, both of them shall
most certainly be put to death; they
have committed incest; their blood is
on them.
13 ‘If a man lies [intimately] with a
male as if he were a woman, both men
have committed a detestable (perverse,
unnatural) act; they shall most cer-
tainly be put to death; their blood is
on them.
14 ‘It is immoral *and* shameful if a
man marries a woman and her mother;
all three shall be burned in fire, so that
there will be no immorality among
you. [Josh 7:15, 25]
15 ‘If a man has intimate relations
with an animal, he shall most certain-
ly be put to death; you shall kill the
animal also.
16 ‘If a woman approaches any ani-
mal to mate with it, you shall kill the
woman and the animal; they shall
most certainly be put to death; their
blood is on them.
17 ‘If a man takes his sister, his fa-
ther’s daughter or his mother’s daugh-
ter, so that he sees her nakedness and
she sees his nakedness, it is a disgrace;
and they shall be cut off in the sight of
the sons of their people. He has uncov-
ered his sister’s nakedness; he bears
[responsibility for] his guilt.
18 ‘If a man lies [intimately] with a
woman during her menstrual cycle
and uncovers her nakedness, he has
exposed her flow, and she has uncov-
ered the flow of her blood; both of
them shall be cut off from their people
[excluding them from the atonement
made for them].
19 ‘You shall not uncover the naked-
ness of (have intimate relations with)
your mother’s sister or your father’s
sister, for such a one has uncovered
his blood relative; they will bear their
guilt.
20 ‘If *there is* a man who lies [inti-
mately] with his uncle’s wife, he has
uncovered his uncle’s nakedness; they
will bear their sin. They will die child-
less.
21 ‘If a man takes his brother’s wife,
it is a hated *and* unclean thing; he has
uncovered his brother’s nakedness.
They will be childless.
22 ‘Therefore keep all My statutes and
all My ordinances and do them, so that
the land where I am bringing you to
live may not vomit you out [as it did
those before you]. [Lev 18:28]
23 ‘You shall not follow the statutes
(laws, practices, customs) of the nation
which I am driving out before you; for
they did all these things, and therefore
I have loathed them.
24 ‘But I have said to you, “You are
to inherit *and* take possession of their
land, and I will give it to you to pos-
sess, a land [of plenty] flowing with
milk and honey.” I am the LORD your
God, who has separated you from the
peoples (pagan nations).
25 ‘You are therefore to make a dis-
tinction between the [ceremonially]
clean animal and the unclean, and be-
tween the unclean bird and the clean;
and you shall not make yourselves
detestable by animal or by bird or by
anything that crawls on the ground,
which I have set apart from you as
unclean.
26 ‘You are to be holy to Me; for I the
LORD am holy, and have set you apart
from the peoples (nations) to be Mine.

20:21 *takes his brother’s wife.* It may be assumed that this passage refers to taking his brother’s wife while his brother is still living. Deuteronomy 25:5–10 gives a fairly detailed directive for a brother marrying his brother’s childless widow and giving the firstborn the name of the dead brother, so that his family line will be maintained.

11 Lev 18:8; Dt 27:23 **12** Lev 18:15; Lev 18:23 **13** Lev 18:22; Dt 23:17; Ge 19:5; Jdg 19:22 **14** Lev 18:17; Dt 27:23 **15** Lev 18:23; Dt 27:21 **17** Lev 18:9; Dt 27:22; Ge 20:12 **18** Lev 15:24 **19** Lev 18:12; Lev 18:6 **20** Lev 18:14 **21** Lev 18:16 **22** Lev 18:26; 19:37; Lev 18:25 **23** Lev 18:3,24; Lev 18:27; Dt 9:5 **24** Ex 3:17; 6:8; ver. 26; Ex 19:5; 33:16; Dt 7:6; 14:2; 1Ki 8:53 **25** Lev 11:47; Dt 14:4; Lev 11:43 **26** ver. 7; Lev 19:2; 1Pe 1:16

[27]'A man or woman who is a medium [who pretends to consult the dead] or who is a spiritist shall most certainly be put to death, and be stoned with stones; their blood is on them.' "

Regulations concerning Priests

21 THEN THE LORD said to Moses,
"Speak to the priests, the sons of
Aaron, and say to them:
'No one shall defile himself [that is,
become ceremonially unclean] for the
dead among his people [by touching
a corpse or assisting in preparing it
for burial],
[2]except for his relatives who are
nearest to him, his mother, his father,
his son, his daughter, and his brother,
[3]also his virgin sister, who is near to
him because she has had no husband;
for her he may become unclean.
[4]'He shall not become unclean as a
relative by marriage among his people,
and so profane himself.
[5]'The priests shall not shave their
heads, nor shave off the edges of their
beards, nor make any cuts in their
body.
[6]'They shall be holy to their God and
not profane the name of their God; for
they present the offerings by fire to the
LORD, the food of their God; so they
shall be holy.
[7]'They shall not take [as a wife] a
woman who is a prostitute, nor a wom-
an who is divorced from her husband;
for the priest is holy to his God.
[8]'You shall consecrate him, there-
fore, for he offers the food of your God;
he shall be holy to you; for I the LORD,
who sanctifies you, am holy.
[9]'The daughter of any priest who
profanes herself by prostitution pro-
fanes her father; she shall be burned
in fire. [Josh 7:15, 25]
[10]'But he who is the high priest
among his brothers, on whose head
the anointing oil has been poured and
who has been consecrated to wear
the [sacred] garments, shall not un-
cover his head nor tear his clothes [in
mourning],
[11]nor shall he approach any dead
person, nor defile himself [by doing so,
even] for his father or for his mother;
[12]nor shall he go out of the sanctu-
ary nor profane (make ceremonially
unclean) the sanctuary of his God, for
the consecration of the anointing oil of
his God is on him; I am the LORD.
[13]'He shall take a wife in her vir-
ginity.
[14]'He may not marry a widow or a di-
vorced woman or one who is profaned
by prostitution, but he is to marry a
virgin from his own people, [1 Tim 3:2–
7; Titus 1:7–9]
[15]so that he will not profane *or* dis-
honor his children among his people;
for I am the LORD who sanctifies the
high priest.' "
[16]Then the LORD spoke to Moses,
saying,
[17]"Say to Aaron, 'Throughout their
generations none of your descendants
who has any [physical] defect shall
approach [the altar] to present the food
of his God.
[18]'For no man who has a defect shall
approach [God's altar as a priest]: no
man who is blind or lame, or who has a
disfigured face, or any deformed *limb*,
[19]or a man who has a broken foot or
a broken hand,
[20]or a hunchback or a dwarf, or one
who has a defect in his eye or eczema
or scabs or crushed testicles.
[21]'No man among the descendants of
Aaron the priest who has a [physical]
defect *and* is disfigured *or* deformed is

21:5 *not shave their heads . . . make any cuts in their body.* These were pagan customs, and all Israel was forbidden to observe them (19:27).
21:9 *profanes herself by prostitution.* Prostitution, the ultimate promiscuity, was the opposite of holiness, the ultimate faithfulness. The daughter was to reflect her father's holiness to God.
21:22 *He may eat.* Physical defect did not imply a moral defect. The person afflicted was to receive his food as the other priests did, from the sacrifices.

27 Lev 19:31; ver. 9 **CHAPTER 21** **1** Eze 44:25 **5** Lev 19:27 **6** Lev 18:21; 19:12 **7** Eze 44:22; See Dt 24:1,2 **9** Ge 38:24 **10** Ex 29:29; Lev 8:12; Ex 28:2; Lev 16:32; Lev 10:6 **11** Nu 19:14 **12** Lev 10:7; Ex 28:36; Lev 8:9,12,30 **13** ver. 7; Eze 44:22 **15** ver. 8 **17** Lev 10:3; Nu 16:5 **18** Lev 22:23 **20** Dt 23:1 **21** ver. 6

to approach [the altar] to present the offerings of the LORD by fire. He has a defect; he shall not approach [the altar] to present the food of his God.

22 'He may eat the food of his God, both of the most holy and of the holy things,

23 but he shall not go within the veil or approach the altar [of incense], because he has a defect, so that he will not profane My sanctuaries; for I am the LORD who sanctifies them.' " [Heb 7:28]

24 So Moses spoke to Aaron and to his sons, and to all the Israelites.

Various Rules for Priests

22 THEN THE LORD spoke to Moses, saying,

2 "Tell Aaron and his sons to be careful with the holy things (offerings, gifts) which the children of Israel dedicate to Me, so that they do not profane My holy name; I am the LORD.

3 "Say to them, 'Any one of your descendants throughout your generations who approaches the holy things which the Israelites dedicate to the LORD, while he is [ceremonially] unclean, that person shall be cut off from My presence *and* excluded from the sanctuary; I am the LORD.

4 'No man of the descendants of Aaron who is a leper or has a discharge may eat the holy things [the offerings and the showbread] until he is clean. And whoever touches any person *or* thing made unclean by *contact with* a corpse or a man who has had a seminal emission,

5 or whoever touches any crawling thing by which he is made unclean, or any person by whom he is made unclean, whatever it may be, [Lev 11:24–28]

6 the person who touches any such thing shall be unclean until evening and shall not eat the holy things unless he has bathed his body in water. [Heb 10:22]

7 'When the sun sets, he will be clean, and afterward he may eat the holy things, for it is his food.

8 'He shall not eat that which dies [of natural causes] or is torn by a predator, becoming unclean by it; I am the LORD.

9 'Therefore the priests shall observe My ordinance, so that they will not bear sin because of it and die if they profane it; I am the LORD who sanctifies them.

10 'No layman [that is, someone outside of Aaron's family] is to eat the holy *gift* [which has been offered to God]; a foreigner residing with the priest or a hired man shall not eat the holy thing.

11 'But if a priest buys a slave as his property with his money, the slave may eat the holy thing, and those who are born in the priest's house; they may eat his food.

12 'If a priest's daughter is married to a layman [one not part of the priestly tribe], she shall not eat the offering of the holy things.

13 'But if a priest's daughter is a widow or divorced, and has no child, and returns to her father's house as in her youth, she shall eat her father's food; but no layman shall eat it.

14 'But if a person unknowingly eats a holy *gift* [which has been offered to God], then he shall add one-fifth of

---

22:3 *of your descendants throughout your generations.* This statement made the restriction as broad as possible in any one generation, and as broad as possible through all time. ***cut off from My presence.*** The individual was not executed or banished from the community, but was permanently barred from ministering as a priest.

22:7 *it is his food.* The sacrifices brought by the Israelites were a major part of the daily provisions of the priests.

22:8 *that which dies [of natural causes] or is torn by a predator.* An ordinary Israelite was unclean until evening if he ate such animals (17:15 – 16), but a priest was not to eat them at all.

22:11 *buys a slave . . . the slave may eat.* Strangers, guests, and hired servants were forbidden to eat of the holy gifts, but slaves and their children were considered a part of the priest's family, and could eat of the consecrated food.

22 Lev 2:3,10; 6:17,29; 7:1; 24:9; Nu 18:9; Lev 22:10-12; Nu 18:19 **23** ver. 12 **CHAPTER 22** **2** Nu 6:3; Lev 18:21; Ex 28:38; Nu 18:32; Dt 15:19 **3** Lev 7:20 **4** Lev 15:2; Lev 14:2; 15:13; Nu 19:11; Lev 15:16 **5** Lev 11:24; Lev 15:7,19 **6** Lev 15:5 **7** Lev 21:22; Nu 18:11,13 **8** Ex 22:31; Lev 17:15; Eze 44:31 **9** Ex 28:43 **10** See 1Sa 21:6 **11** Nu 8:11,13 **13** Ge 38:11; Lev 10:14 **14** Lev 5:15,16; Nu 18:11,19

its value to it and give the holy *gift* to the priest.

15 ‘The priests shall not profane the holy things the Israelites offer to the LORD,

16 and so cause them [by neglect of any essential observance] to bear the punishment of guilt when they eat their holy things; for I am the LORD who sanctifies them.’ ”

Flawless Animals for Sacrifice

17 Then the LORD spoke to Moses, saying,

18 “Speak to Aaron and his sons and to all the Israelites and say to them, ‘Any man of the house of Israel or any stranger in Israel who presents his offering, whether to *fulfill* any of their vows or as any of their freewill (voluntary) offerings which they presented to the LORD as a burnt offering—

19 so that you may be accepted—it must be a male without blemish from the cattle, the sheep, or the goats.

20 ‘You shall not offer anything which has a blemish, because it will not be accepted for you. [1 Pet 1:19]

21 ‘Whoever offers a sacrifice of peace offerings to the LORD to fulfill a special vow to the LORD or as a freewill offering from the herd or from the flock, it must be perfect to be accepted; there shall be no blemish in it.

22 ‘Animals *that are* blind or fractured or mutilated, or have a sore or a running wound or an itch or scabs, you shall not offer to the LORD nor make an offering of them by fire on the altar to the LORD.

23 ‘For a freewill offering you may offer either a bull or a lamb which has an overgrown or stunted member (deformity), but for [the payment of] a vow it will not be accepted.

24 ‘You shall not offer to the LORD any animal which has its testicles bruised or crushed or torn or cut off, or sacrifice it in your land.

25 ‘Nor shall you offer as the food of your God any such [animals obtained] from a foreigner, because their corruption *and* blemish makes them unfit; there is a defect in them, they shall not be accepted for you.’ ”

26 Then the LORD spoke to Moses, saying,

27 “When a bull or a sheep or a goat is born, it shall remain for seven days with its mother; and after the eighth day it shall be accepted as an offering by fire to the LORD.

28 “And whether [the mother] is a cow or a sheep, you shall not kill both it and its young in one day.

29 “When you sacrifice an offering of thanksgiving to the LORD, you shall sacrifice it so that you may be accepted.

30 “It shall be eaten on the same day; you shall leave none of it until *the next* morning; I am the LORD.

31 “So you shall keep My commandments and do them; I am the LORD.

32 “You shall not profane My holy name [using it to honor an idol, or treating it with irreverence or contempt or as a byword]; but I will be sanctified (set apart as holy) among the Israelites. I am the LORD, who sanctifies *and* declares you holy,

---

22:18 *stranger in Israel.* Resident aliens in Israel were permitted to worship God with the Israelites, and were subject to the same regulations about sacrifices.

22:21 *it must be perfect to be accepted.* This is a very clear directive, yet the prophet Malachi addressed the problem of defective sacrifices in his day (Mal 1:7 – 14). God called that “despising” His name.

22:31 *commandments*. As Christians, it is important to understand the relationship between grace and law. A focus on the law without grace leads to a rule-oriented life, where our actions may be decent enough, but our heart is hard toward God. But if the focus is only on grace, we may be without the guidelines necessary to keep us from just doing what is right in our own eyes. Certain directives are given to us because even when we are born again, we are not all wise. The best way to balance all of this is to consider the whole counsel of God by reading and seeking to understand the whole Bible.

15 Nu 18:32 **16** ver. 9 **18** Lev 1:2,3,10 **19** Lev 1:3 **20** Dt 15:21; Mal 1:8,14; Eph 5:27; Heb 9:14; 1Pe 1:19 **21** Lev 3:1,6; Nu 15:3,8; Ps 61:8; 65:1; Ecc 5:4,5 **22** ver. 20; Mal 1:8; Lev 1:9,13; 3:3,5 **23** Lev 21:18 **25** Nu 15:15,16; Lev 21:6,17; Mal 1:14 **27** Ex 22:30 **28** Dt 22:6 **29** Lev 7:12; Ps 107:22; 116:17; Am 4:5 **30** Lev 7:15 **31** Lev 19:37; Nu 15:40; Dt 4:40 **32** Lev 18:21; Lev 10:3; Mt 6:9; Lk 11:2; Lev 20:8

33 who brought you out of the land of
Egypt to be your God; I am the LORD."

Laws of Religious Festivals

23 THE LORD spoke again to Moses, saying,
2 "Speak to the children of Israel and
say to them, 'The appointed times (established feasts) of the LORD which you
shall proclaim as holy convocations—
My appointed times are these:

The Sabbath

3 'For six days work may be done, but
the seventh day is the Sabbath of complete rest, a holy convocation (calling
together). You shall not do any work
[on that day]; it is the Sabbath of the
LORD wherever you may be.

The Passover and Unleavened Bread

4 'These are the appointed times of
the LORD, holy convocations which you
shall proclaim at their appointed times:
5 'The LORD's Passover is on the fourteenth day of the first month at twilight.
6 'The Feast of Unleavened Bread to
the LORD is on the fifteenth day of the
same month; for seven days you shall
eat unleavened bread. [1 Cor 5:7, 8]
7 'On the first day you shall have a
holy convocation (calling together);
you shall not do any laborious work
[on that day].
8 'But you shall present an offering
by fire to the LORD for seven days; on
the seventh day there shall be a holy
convocation; you shall not do any laborious work [on that day].' "

The Feast of First Fruits

9 Then the LORD spoke to Moses,
saying,
10 "Speak to the children of Israel
and say to them, 'When you enter the
land which I am giving you and reap
its harvest, you shall bring the sheaf
of the first fruits of your harvest to
the priest.
11 'He shall wave the sheaf before the
LORD so that you may be accepted; the
priest shall wave it on the day after the
Sabbath.
12 'Now on the day when you wave
the sheaf you shall offer a male lamb
one year old without blemish as a
burnt offering to the LORD.
13 'Its grain offering shall be two-tenths of an ephah of fine flour mixed
with [olive] oil, an offering by fire to
the LORD for a sweet *and* soothing
aroma, with its drink offering [to be
poured out], a fourth of a hin of wine.
14 'You shall not eat any bread or
roasted grain or new growth, until
this same day when you bring in the
offering to your God; it is a permanent
statute throughout your generations
wherever you may be.

The Feast of Weeks

15 'You shall count from the day after
the Sabbath, from the day when you
brought in the sheaf (tied bundle of
grain) of the wave offering; there shall

23:3 *six days work may be done.* Work was given to the human race in the garden of Eden. It is one of the ways humans bear the image of God, and is not a curse on the race. Even after the fall it remains God's good gift. ***the Sabbath of complete rest . . . wherever you may be.*** The regular seventh day of rest is for our refreshment, and a day of solemn, joyful worship. It was not to be observed only in the sanctuary, it was to be celebrated in every household. The writer of Hebrews (ch 4) calls belief in the saving work of Jesus, "entering His rest," and compares that to the Sabbath rest.

23:5 *fourteenth day of the first month.* This month would fall between mid-March and mid-April. The Passover celebrated Israel's exodus from Egypt (Ex 12:1 – 28).

23:6 – 8 *Feast of Unleavened Bread.* This festival immediately followed Passover, and later in Israel's history, it involved pilgrimages to the central sanctuary; first in Shiloh, and later in Jerusalem.

23:10 *sheaf of the first fruits.* This bundle of the first harvested barley belonged to God as a special offering, acknowledging God's provision for the harvest.

33 Lev 19:36; Nu 15:41 **CHAPTER 23** **2** ver. 4,37; Ex 32:5; 2Ki 10:20; Ps 81:3 **3** Ex 20:9; 23:12; 31:15; Lev 19:3; Dt 5:13; Lk 13:14 **4** ver. 37; Ex 23:14 **5** Ex 12:6,14,18; 13:3,10; Dt 16:1-8 **7** Ex 12:16; Nu 28:18,25 **10** Ex 34:26; Dt 16:9; Jos 3:15; Ro 11:16; Jas 1:18; Rev 14:4 **11** Ex 29:24 **13** Lev 2:14-16 **15** Ex 34:22; Lev 25:8; Dt 16:9

be seven complete Sabbaths (seven
full weeks).
16‘You shall count fifty days to the
day after the seventh Sabbath; then
you shall present a new grain offering
to the LORD.
17‘You shall bring in from your plac-
es two loaves of bread as a wave offer-
ing, made from two-tenths *of an ephah*
of fine flour; they shall be baked with
leaven as first fruits to the LORD.
18‘And you shall offer with the bread
seven unblemished lambs, one year old,
and one young bull and two rams. They
are to be a burnt offering to the LORD,
with their grain offering and their drink
offerings. It is an offering by fire, a
sweet *and* soothing aroma to the LORD.
19‘And you shall sacrifice one male
goat as a sin offering and two male
lambs, one year old as a sacrifice of
peace offerings.
20‘The priest shall wave them before
the LORD as a wave offering, together
with the bread of the first fruits and
the two lambs. They are to be holy to
the LORD for the priest.
21‘On this same day you shall make
a proclamation, you are to have a holy
convocation (calling together); you
shall not do any laborious work [on
that day]. It is to be a permanent statute
throughout your generations wherever
you may be.
22‘When you reap the harvest of your
land, you shall not reap to the edges of
your field, nor gather the gleaning of
your harvest; you are to leave them for
the poor and for the stranger. I am the
LORD your God.’ ”

16 Ac 2:1; Nu 28:26 **17** Ex 23:16,19; Nu 15:17-21 **19** Lev 4:23,28; Nu 28:30; Lev 3:1 **20** Nu 18:12; Dt 18:4 **22** Lev 19:9

OLD TESTAMENT FESTIVALS AND OTHER SACRED DAYS

NAME	OLD TESTAMENT REFERENCES	OLD TESTAMENT TIME	MODERN EQUIVALENT
Sabbath	Ex 20:8–11; 31:12–17; Lev 23:3; Dt 5:12–15	7th day	Same
Sabbath Year	Ex 23:10–11; Lev 25:1–7	7th year	Same
Year of Jubilee	Lev 25:8–55; 27:17–24; Nu 36:4	50th year	Same
Passover	Ex 12:1–14; Lev 23:5; Nu 9:1–14; 28:16; Dt 16:1–3a,4b–7	1st month (Aviv) 14	March – April
Unleavened Bread	Ex 12:15–20; 13:3–10; 23:15; 34:18; Lev 23:6–8; Nu 28:17–25; Dt 16:3b,4a,8	1st month (Aviv) 15–21	March – April
Firstfruits	Lev 23:9–14	1st month (Aviv) 16	March – April
Weeks (Pentecost) (Harvest)	Ex 23:16a; 34:22a; Lev 23:15–21; Nu 28:26–31; Dt 16:9–12	3rd month (Sivan) 6	May – June
Trumpets (later: Rosh Hashanah–New Year's Day)	Lev 23:23–25; Nu 29:1–6	7th month (Tishri) 1	September – October
Day of Atonement (Yom Kippur)	Lev 16; 23:26–32; Nu 29:7–11	7th month (Tishri) 10	September – October
Tabernacles (Booths) (Ingathering)	Ex 23:16b; 34:22b; Lev 23:33–36a,39–43; Nu 29:12–34; Dt 16:13–15; Zec 14:16–19	7th month (Tishri) 15–21	September – October
Sacred Assembly	Lev 23:36b; Nu 29:35–38	7th month (Tishri) 22	September – October
Purim	Est 9:18–32	12th month (Adar) 14,15	February – March

The Feast of Trumpets

[23]Again the LORD spoke to Moses,
saying,
[24]"Say to the children of Israel, 'On
the first day of the seventh month (al-
most October), you shall observe a day
of solemn sabbatical rest, a memori-
al day announced by the blowing *of
trumpets*, a holy convocation.
[25]'You shall not do any laborious
work [on that day], but you shall pre-
sent an offering by fire to the LORD.' "

The Day of Atonement

[26]The LORD spoke to Moses, saying,
[27]"Also the tenth day of this seventh
month is the Day of Atonement; it shall
be a holy convocation for you, and you
shall humble yourselves [by fasting] and
present an offering by fire to the LORD.

23:24 *the seventh month.* This holiday falls in mid-September. It was a reminder of God's goodness, which was expressed in the covenant, and asked God to continue to remember that covenant.
23:26 – 32 Atonement — The Day of Atonement was a time to set aside all the thoughts and actions that typically fill the day and consider one's relationship with God. This was to be a time of humbleness, which would preclude any self-righteousness or merely comparing oneself with others. It was a time to remember that even people who want to follow God need to have their lives realigned with Him. Christians regularly take time to think of these things as they remember the Lord's death until He comes again, with the bread and the cup of communion.
23:27 *Day of Atonement.* The day was not given this name in chapter 16, but this was the day of all days, when complete atonement was made for all Israel.

24 Nu 29:1; Lev 25:9 **27** Lev 16:30; Nu 29:7

DESCRIPTION	PURPOSE	NEW TESTAMENT REFERENCES
Day of rest; no work	Rest for people and animals	Mt 12:1–14; 28:1; Lk 4:16; Jn 5:9–10; Ac 13:42; Col 2:16; Heb 4:1–11
Year of rest; fallow fields	Rest for land	
Canceled debts; liberation of slaves and indentured servants; land returned to original family owners	Help for poor; stabilize society	
Slaying and eating a lamb, together with bitter herbs and bread made without yeast, in every household	Remember Israel's deliverance from Egypt	Mt 26:17; Mk 14:12–26; Jn 2:13; 11:55; 1Co 5:7; Heb 11:28
Eating bread made without yeast; holding several assemblies; making designated offerings	Remember how the Lord brought the Israelites out of Egypt in haste	Mk 14:1; Ac 12:3; 1Co 5:6–8
Presenting a sheaf of the first of the barley harvest as a wave offering; making a burnt offering and a grain offering	Recognize the Lord's bounty in the land	Ro 8:23; 1Co 15:20–23
A festival of joy; mandatory and voluntary offerings, including the firstfruits of the wheat harvest	Show joy and thankfulness for the Lord's blessing of harvest	Ac 2:1–4; 20:16; 1Co 16:8
An assembly on a day of rest commemorated with trumpet blasts and sacrifices	Present Israel before the Lord for his favor	
A day of rest, fasting and sacrifices of atonement for priests and people and atonement for the tabernacle and altar	Atone for the sins of priests and people and purify the Holy Place	Ro 3:24–26; Heb 9:7; 10:3,19–22
A week of celebration for the harvest; living in booths (temporary shelters) and offering sacrifices	Memorialize the journey from Egypt to Canaan; give thanks for the productivity of Canaan	Jn 7:2,37
A day of convocation, rest and offering sacrifices	Commemorate the closing of the cycle of festivals	
A day of joy and feasting and giving presents	Remind the Israelites of their national deliverance in the time of Esther	

28 "You shall not do any work on this same day, for it is the Day of Atonement, to make atonement on your behalf before the LORD your God.

29 "If there is any person who will not humble himself on this same day, he shall be cut off from his people [excluding him from the atonement made for them].

30 "If there is any person who does any work on this same day, I will destroy that person from among his people.

31 "You shall do no work at all [on that day]. It is a permanent statute throughout your generations wherever you may be.

32 "It is to be to you a Sabbath of complete rest, and you shall humble yourselves. On the ninth day of the month at evening, from evening to evening you shall keep your Sabbath."

The Feast of Booths

33 Again the LORD spoke to Moses, saying,

34 "Say to the children of Israel, 'On the fifteenth day of this seventh month, and for seven days, is the Feast of Booths (Tabernacles) to the LORD.

35 'The first day is a holy convocation (calling together); you shall not do any laborious work [on that day].

36 'For seven days you shall present an offering by fire to the LORD. On the eighth day you shall have a holy convocation and present an offering by fire to the LORD. It is a festive assembly; you shall not do any laborious work [on that day].

37 'These are the appointed times (established feasts) of the LORD, which you shall proclaim to be holy convocations, to present an offering by fire to the LORD, a burnt offering and a grain offering, sacrifices and drink offerings, each on its own day.

38 'This is in addition to the [weekly] Sabbaths of the LORD, and in addition to your gifts and all your vowed offerings and all your freewill offerings, which you give to the LORD.

39 'On exactly the fifteenth day of the seventh month (nearly October), when you have gathered in the crops of the land, you shall celebrate the feast of the LORD for seven days, with a Sabbath rest on the first day and a Sabbath rest on the eighth day.

40 'Now on the first day you shall take for yourselves the foliage of beautiful trees, branches of palm trees, and boughs of thick (leafy) trees, and willows of the brook [and make booths of them]; and you shall rejoice before the LORD your God for seven days.

41 'You shall celebrate it as a feast to the LORD for seven days in the year. It shall be a permanent statute throughout your generations; you shall celebrate it in the seventh month.

42 'You shall live in booths (temporary shelters) for seven days; all native-born in Israel shall live in booths,

43 so that your generations may know that I had the sons of Israel live in booths when I brought them out of the land of Egypt. I am the LORD your God.' "

44 So Moses declared to the Israelites the appointed feasts of the LORD.

The Lamp and the Bread of the Sanctuary

24 THEN THE LORD spoke to Moses, saying,

2 "Command the children of Israel to bring to you clear oil from beaten olives for the light [of the golden lampstand], to make a lamp burn continually.

3 "Outside the veil of the Testimony [between the Holy Place and the Most Holy Place] in the Tent of Meeting, Aaron shall always keep the lamps burning before the LORD from evening until morning; it shall be a permanent statute throughout your generations.

23:40 *boughs of thick (leafy) trees.* This leafy tree is thought to be the myrtle.

29 Ge 17:14 **30** Lev 20:3,5,6 **34** Ex 23:16; Nu 29:12; Dt 16:13; Ezr 3:4; Neh 8:14; Zec 14:16; Jn 7:2 **36** Nu 29:35; Neh 8:18; Jn 7:37; Dt 16:8; 2Ch 7:9 **37** ver. 2,4 **38** Nu 29:39 **39** Ex 23:16; Dt 16:13 **40** Neh 8:15; Dt 16:14,15 **41** Nu 29:12; Neh 8:18 **42** Neh 8:14-16 **43** Dt 31:13 **44** ver. 2 **CHAPTER 24** **2** Ex 27:20

4“He shall keep the lamps burning
on the pure *gold* lampstand before the
LORD continually. [Rev 1:12–18]
5“Then you shall take fine flour and
bake twelve cakes (bread of the Pres-
ence, showbread) with it; two-tenths of
an ephah shall be in each cake (loaf).
6“You shall set the bread of the Pres-
ence (showbread) in two rows, six in
a row, on the pure *gold* table before
the LORD.
7“You shall put pure frankincense
[in two censers, one] beside each row,
so that it may be with the bread as a
memorial portion, an offering by fire
to the LORD.
8“Every Sabbath day Aaron shall ar-
range the showbread before the LORD
continually; it is an everlasting cov-
enant for the Israelites.
9“The bread of the Presence shall be
for Aaron and his sons, and they shall
eat it in a sacred place, for it is for Aar-
on a most holy portion of the offerings
by fire to the LORD, his portion forever.”
10Now the son of an Israelite woman,
whose father was an Egyptian, went
out among the Israelites, and he and a
man of Israel quarreled *and* struggled
with each other in the camp.
11The Israelite woman’s son blas-
phemed the Name [of the LORD] and
cursed. So they brought him to Mo-
ses. (Now his mother’s name was She-
lomith, the daughter of Dibri, of the
tribe of Dan.)
12They put him in custody until the
will *and* command of the LORD might
be made clear to them.
13Then the LORD spoke to Moses,
saying,
14“Bring the one who has cursed [the
LORD] outside the camp, and let all who
heard him lay their hands on his head
[as witnesses to his guilt]; then let all
the congregation stone him.
15“You shall speak to the Israelites,
saying, ‘Whoever curses his God will
bear his sin [through his own death].
16‘Further, the one who blasphemes
the name of the LORD shall most cer-
tainly be put to death; all the congre-
gation shall stone him. The stranger as
well as the native-born shall be put to
death when he blasphemes the Name
[of the LORD].

“An Eye for an Eye”

17‘If a man takes the life of any hu-
man being [unlawfully], he shall most
certainly be put to death.
18‘The one who kills an animal shall
replace it, animal for animal.
19‘If a man injures his neighbor (fel-
low citizen), whatever he has done
shall be done to him:
20fracture for fracture, eye for eye,
tooth for tooth; just as he has injured
a man, so shall the same be done to
him. [Matt 5:38–42; 7:2]
21‘The one who kills an animal shall
replace it; but he who kills a human be-
ing [unlawfully] shall be put to death.
22‘You shall have one standard of law
for the stranger *among you* as well as
for the native, for I am the LORD your
God.’ ”
23Then Moses spoke to the Israelites,
and they brought the one who had
cursed [the LORD] outside the camp
and stoned him with stones. Thus the
Israelites did just as the LORD had com-
manded Moses.

The Sabbatic Year and Year of Jubilee

25 THE LORD spoke to Moses at
Mount Sinai, saying,
2“Speak to the children of Israel and
say to them, ‘When you come into the

24:19 – 20 *eye for eye.* This law is also found in Exodus 21:23 – 25. Its purpose is not to require the injured party to inflict equal bodily harm on the one who had injured him, but to restrict him from inflicting greater harm than he received.

24:22 *one standard of law.* These laws are repeated here in order to answer the question of whether these laws apply to non-Israelites. The answer is yes, they also apply to the stranger in the land.

4 Ex 31:8; 39:37 **5** Ex 25:30 **6** 1Ki 7:48; 2Ch 4:19; 13:11; Heb 9:2 **8** Nu 4:7; 1Ch 9:32; 2Ch 2:4 **9** 1Sa 21:6; Mt 12:4; Mk 2:26; Lk 6:4; Ex 29:33; Lev 8:31 **11** Job 1:5,11,22; Isa 8:21; Ex 18:22,26 **12** Nu 15:34; Ex 18:15; Nu 27:5 **14** Dt 13:9; 17:7 **15** Lev 20:17; Nu 9:13 **16** 1Ki 21:10,13; Mt 12:31; Mk 3:28 **17** Ex 21:12; Nu 35:31; Dt 19:11,12 **18** ver. 21 **19** Ex 21:24; Dt 19:21; Mt 5:38; 7:2 **21** Ex 21:33; ver. 17 **22** Ex 12:49; Lev 19:34; Nu 15:16 **23** ver. 14 **CHAPTER 25** **2** Ex 23:10; See Lev 26:34,35

land which I am giving you, then the
land shall keep a Sabbath to the LORD.
[3]'For six years you shall sow your
field, and for six years you shall prune
your vineyard and gather in its crop.
[4]'But in the seventh year there shall
be a Sabbath of rest for the land, a
Sabbath to the LORD; you shall not sow
[seed in] your field nor prune your
vineyard.
[5]'Whatever reseeds itself (unculti-
vated) in your harvest you shall not
reap, nor shall you gather the grapes
from your uncultivated vine, it shall be
a year of sabbatical rest for the land.
[6]'And all of you shall have for food
whatever the [untilled] land produc-
es during its Sabbath year; yourself,
and your male and female slaves, your
hired servant, and the foreigners who
reside among you,
[7]even your domestic animals and the
[wild] animals that are in your land
shall have all its crops to eat.

The Year of Jubilee

[8]'You are also to count off seven Sab-
baths of years for yourself, seven times
seven years, so that you have the time
of the seven Sabbaths of years, namely,
forty-nine years.
[9]'Then you shall sound the ram's
horn everywhere on the tenth day of
the seventh month (almost October); on
the Day of Atonement you shall sound
the trumpet throughout your land.
[10]'And you shall consecrate the fif-
tieth year and proclaim freedom [for
the slaves] throughout the land to all
its inhabitants. It shall be a Jubilee
(year of remission) for you, and each
of you shall return to his own [ances-
tral] property [that was sold to another
because of poverty], and each of you
shall return to his family [from whom
he was separated by bondage].
[11]'That fiftieth year shall be a Jubilee
for you; you shall not sow [seed], nor
reap what reseeds itself, nor gather the
grapes of the uncultivated vines.
[12]'For it is the Jubilee; it shall be holy
to you; you shall eat its crops out of
the field.
[13]'In this Year of Jubilee each of you
shall return to his own [ancestral]
property.
[14]'If you sell anything to your friend
or buy from your friend, you shall not
wrong one another.
[15]'According to the number of years
after the Jubilee, you shall buy from
your friend. And he is to sell to you
according to the number of years of
crops [which may be harvested before
you must restore the property to him].
[16]'If the years [until the next Jubilee]
are many, you shall increase the price,
but if the years remaining are few, you
shall reduce the price, because it is
the number of crops that he is selling
to you.
[17]'You shall not wrong one another,
but you shall fear your God [with pro-
found reverence]; for I am the LORD
your God.
[18]'Therefore you shall carry out My
statutes and keep My ordinances and
do them, so that you may live securely
on the land.
[19]'Then the land will yield its pro-
duce, so that you can eat your fill and
live securely on it.

25:5 *shall not reap.* Reaping and gathering for storage and selling were not permitted. However, harvesting for daily needs was allowed.

25:10 *freedom.* This word could also be translated "liberty." It meant specifically that all debts were cancelled, all Israelites who had sold themselves into slavery were freed, and all the land reverted to its original owners, from the time the land was divided by Joshua. The same phrase occurs in Isaiah 61:1, the passage Jesus read in the synagogue in Nazareth at the beginning of His earthly ministry. Jesus declares liberty to all who have lost their inheritance and become slaves to sin.

25:11 *Jubilee.* The fiftieth, or jubilee year, followed a Sabbath year of rest, so this meant that there were two years of rest in a row for the land.

25:17 *fear your God.* Fear of God includes respect of man, who is God's highest creation. A deep respect of the life of man, who is created in God's image and likeness, is stressed in Scriptures. This text prohibits taking advantage of or oppressing others, and for the Christian there is

5 2Ki 19:29 **9** Lev 23:24,27 **10** Isa 61:2; 63:4; Jer 34:8,15,17; Lk 4:19; ver. 13; Nu 36:4 **11** ver. 5 **12** ver. 6,7 **13** ver. 10; Lev 27:24; Nu 36:4 **15** Lev 27:18 **17** ver. 14; ver. 43; Lev 19:14,32 **18** Lev 19:37; Lev 26:5; Dt 12:10; Ps 4:8 **19** Lev 26:5; Eze 34:25

20‘And if you say, “What are we going to eat in the seventh year if we do not sow [seed] or gather in our crops?”

21then [this is My answer:] I will order My [special] blessing for you in the sixth year, so that it will produce [sufficient] crops for three years.

22‘When you are sowing the eighth year, you can still eat old things from the crops, eating the old until the ninth year when its crop comes in.

The Law of Redemption

23‘The land shall not be sold permanently, for the land is Mine; you are [only] foreigners and temporary residents with Me. [Heb 11:13; 1 Pet 2:11–17]

24‘So in all the country that you possess, you are to provide for the redemption of the land [in the Year of Jubilee].

25‘If a fellow countryman of yours becomes so poor he has to sell some of his property, then his nearest relative is to come and buy back (redeem) what his relative has sold.

26‘Or in case a man has no relative [to redeem his property], but he has become more prosperous *and* has enough to buy it back,

27then he shall calculate the years since its sale and refund the balance to the man to whom he sold it, and so return to his [ancestral] property. [1 Kin 21:2, 3]

28‘But if he is unable to redeem it, then what he has sold shall remain in the hands of the purchaser until the Year of Jubilee; but at the Jubilee it shall revert, and he may return to his property.

29‘If a man sells a house in a walled city, then his right of redemption remains valid for a full year after its sale; his right of redemption lasts a full year.

30‘But if it is not redeemed for him within a full year, then the house that is in the walled city passes permanently *and* irrevocably to the purchaser throughout his generations. It does not revert back in the Year of Jubilee.

31‘The houses of the villages that have no surrounding walls, however, shall be considered as open fields. They may be redeemed, and revert in the Year of Jubilee.

32‘As for the cities of the Levites, the Levites have a permanent right of redemption for the houses in the cities which they possess.

33‘Therefore, what is [purchased] from the Levites may be redeemed [by a Levite], and the house that was sold in the city they possess reverts in the Year of Jubilee, for the houses in the Levite cities are their [ancestral] property among the Israelites.

34‘But the pasture lands of their cities may not be sold, for that is their permanent possession.

Of Poor Countrymen

35‘Now if your fellow countryman becomes poor and his hand falters with you [that is, he has trouble repaying you for something], then you are to help *and* sustain him, [with courtesy and consideration] like [you would] a stranger or a temporary resident [without property], so that he may live among you. [1 John 3:17]

36‘Do not charge him usurious interest, but fear your God [with profound reverence], so your countryman may [continue to] live among you.

37‘You shall not give him your money at interest, nor your food at a profit.

38‘I am the Lord your God, who brought you out of the land of Egypt to give you the land of Canaan and to be your God.

39‘And if your fellow countryman becomes so poor [in his dealings] with you that he sells himself to you [as payment for a debt], you shall not let him do the work of a slave [who is ineligible for redemption],

---

the added reminder that we are not to injure those “for whom Christ died” (1Co 8:11).
25:23 *temporary residents with Me.* The principle governing all of these laws was that the land did not belong to Israel; it belonged to God.

20 Mt 6:25; ver. 4,5 **21** See Ex 16:29 **22** 2Ki 19:29; Jos 5:11 **23** Dt 32:43; Ps 39:12 **25** Ru 2:20; See Ru 3:2,9,12 **27** ver. 50-52 **28** ver. 13 **32** See Nu 35:2 **34** See Ac 4:36,37 **35** Dt 15:7; Lk 6:35; 1Jn 3:17 **36** Ex 22:25; Dt 23:19; Neh 5:9 **38** Lev 22:32,33 **39** Ex 21:2; Dt 15:12; 1Ki 9:22

40 but he is to be with you as a hired
man, as if he were a temporary resi-
dent; he shall serve with you until the
Year of Jubilee,
41 and then he shall leave you, he and
his children with him, and shall go
back to his own family and return to
the property of his fathers.
42 'For the Israelites are My servants
whom I brought out of the land of
Egypt; they shall not be sold in a slave
sale. [1 Cor 7:23]
43 'You shall not rule over him with
harshness (severity, oppression), but
you are to fear your God [with pro-
found reverence]. [Eph 6:9; Col 4:1]
44 'As for your male and female slaves
whom you may have—you may ac-
quire male and female slaves from the
pagan nations that are around you.
45 'Moreover, from the children of the
strangers who live as aliens among
you, from them you may buy *slaves* and
from their families who are with you,
whom they have produced in your land;
they may become your possession.
46 'You may even bequeath them as
an inheritance to your children after
you, to receive as a possession; you
can use them as permanent slaves. But
in respect to your fellow countrymen,
the children of Israel, you shall not
rule over one another with harshness
(severity, oppression).

Of Redeeming a Poor Man

47 'Now if the financial means of a
stranger or temporary resident among
you become sufficient, and your fellow
countryman becomes poor *in compar-
ison* to him and sells himself to the
stranger who is living among you or
to the descendants of the stranger's
family,
48 then after he is sold he shall have
the right of redemption. One of his
relatives may redeem him:
49 either his uncle or his uncle's son
may redeem him, or one of his blood
relatives from his family may redeem
him; or if he prospers, he may redeem
himself.
50 'Then he [or his redeemer] shall
calculate with his purchaser from
the year when he sold himself to the
purchaser to the Year of Jubilee, and
the [original] price of his sale shall
be adjusted according to the number
of years. The time he was with his
owner shall be considered as that of
a hired man.
51 'If there are still many years [be-
fore the Year of Jubilee], in proportion
to them he must refund [to the purchas-
er] part of the price of his sale for his
redemption *and* release.
52 'And if *only* a few years remain un-
til the Year of Jubilee, he shall so cal-
culate it with him. He is to refund the
proportionate amount for his release.
53 'Like a man hired year by year he
shall deal with him; he shall not rule
over him with harshness in your sight.
54 'Even if he is not redeemed during
these years *and* under these provi-
sions, then he shall go free in the Year
of Jubilee, he and his children with
him.
55 'For the children of Israel are My
servants; My servants, whom I brought
out of the land of Egypt. I am the LORD
your God.

Blessings of Obedience

26 'YOU SHALL not make idols for
yourselves, nor shall you erect
an image, a sacred pillar *or* an obelisk,
nor shall you place any figured stone in
your land so that you may bow down
to it; for I am the LORD your God.
2 'You shall keep My Sabbaths and
have reverence for My sanctuary. I
am the LORD.

25:44–46 *permanent slaves.* The fact that God made laws to govern the current practices of slavery does not mean that He approved of slavery. He made laws about divorce too, but He also said that He hates divorce.

26:1 *figured stone.* A "figured stone" is a sacred pillar, a stone or wooden column erected to represent a pagan god or goddess. It was not a likeness, but a symbol. Together, the four terms used in this verse cover all the possibilities for pagan images.

41 Ex 21:3; ver. 28 **42** ver. 55; Ro 6:22; 1Co 7:23 **43** Eph 6:9; Ex 1:13; Ex 1:17; Dt 25:18; Mal 3:5 **45** Isa 56:3,6 **46** Isa 14:2 **47** ver. 25,35 **48** Neh 5:5 **49** ver. 26 **50** Job 7:1; Isa 16:14 **CHAPTER 26** **1** Ex 20:4,5; Dt 5:8 **2** Lev 19:30

[3]‘If you walk in My statutes and keep
My commandments and [obediently]
do them,
[4]then I will give you rain in its sea-
son, and the land will yield her produce
and the trees of the field bear their fruit.
[5]‘And your threshing season will last
until grape gathering and the grape
gathering [time] will last until plant-
ing, and you will eat your bread and
be filled and live securely in your land.
[6]‘I will also grant peace in the land,
so that you may lie down and there
will be no one to make you afraid. I
will also eliminate harmful animals
from the land, and no sword will pass
through your land.
[7]‘And you will chase your enemies,
and they will fall before you by the
sword.
[8]‘Five of you will chase a hundred,
and a hundred of you will put ten thou-
sand to flight; your enemies will fall
before you by the sword.
[9]‘For I will turn toward you [with fa-
vor and regard] and make you fruitful
and multiply you, and I will establish
and confirm My covenant with you.
[2 Kin 13:23]
[10]‘You will eat the old supply of
[abundant] produce, and clear out the
old [to make room] for the new.
[11]‘I will make My dwelling among
you, and My soul will not reject *nor*
separate itself from you.
[12]‘I will walk among you and be your
God, and you shall be My people.
[13]‘I am the LORD your God, who
brought you out of the land of Egypt
so that you would not be their slaves;
and I broke the bars of your yoke and
made you walk upright [with heads
held high as free men].

Penalties of Disobedience

[14]‘But if you do not obey Me and do
not [obediently] do all these command-
ments,
[15]if, instead, you reject My statutes,
and if your soul rejects My ordinances,
so that you will not [obediently] do all
My commandments, and in this way
break My covenant,
[16]I, in turn, will do this to you: I will
appoint over you sudden terror, con-
sumption, and fever that will waste
away the eyes and cause the soul to
languish also. And you will sow your
seed uselessly, for your enemies will
eat what you plant.
[17]‘I will set My face against you so
that you will be struck down before
your enemies; those who hate you will
rule over you, and you will flee when
no one is pursuing you. [1 Sam 4:10;
31:1]

26:4–5 *rain in its season . . . threshing . . . until grape gathering . . . until planting.* Not only will God provide the rain when needed, He would provide abundant harvests. The grain harvest was finished by early to mid-June, and the grape harvest began about two months later. Having two months to thresh the grain indicated a large harvest. Likewise sowing could not occur until after the first rains softened the ground, usually in mid-October. A two month grape harvest would be a bumper crop. This is the first of the three blessings from God.

26:6–10 *peace in the land.* Neither animal nor human adversaries would be successful against Israel. This is the second of the three blessings from God.

26:11–13 *I will walk among you.* The third blessing was the promise of His presence within Israel, actively walking among them and looking out for their welfare.

26:12–13 *be your God.* The image in these verses is a dramatic one, reminding the Israelites that God would be their intimate associate continually. He would walk with them, support them in times of difficulty and danger, and abundantly provide for both their physical and spiritual needs. To be God's people meant that the Israelites had to obey God's laws scrupulously, to be holy as God is holy, and to be a witness of God among the pagan nations.

26:14–15 *do not [obediently] do all these commandments.* As with the blessings, the curses are presented in an "if-then" format.

26:16–17 *terror, consumption, and fever.* Fear, illness, poor harvest, and enemies in the land would be God's first attempts to draw Israel back to Himself.

3 Dt 28:1-14 **4** Isa 30:23; Ps 67:6; Zec 8:12 **5** Am 9:13; Lev 25:19; Lev 25:18 **6** Isa 45:7; Ps 4:8; Hos 2:18; Zep 3:13; 2Ki 17:25; Eze 14:17 **8** Dt 32:30 **9** Ex 2:25; Ge 17:6,7; Ps 107:38 **10** Lev 25:22 **11** Ex 25:8; Jos 22:19; Ps 76:2; Rev 21:3 **12** 2Co 6:16 **14** Dt 28:15; La 2:17; Mal 2:2 **16** Dt 28:22; 1Sa 2:33; Dt 28:33,51; Job 31:8; Mic 6:15 **17** Lev 17:10; Dt 28:25; Ps 106:41; ver. 36; Ps 53:5

18 'If in spite of all this you still will not listen to Me *and* be obedient, then I will punish you seven times more for your sins.

19 'I will break your pride in your power, and I will make your sky like iron [giving no rain and blocking all prayers] and your ground like bronze [hard to plow and yielding no produce]. [1 Kin 17:1]

20 'Your strength will be spent uselessly, for your land will not yield its produce and the trees of the land will not yield their fruit.

21 'If then, you act with hostility toward Me and are unwilling to obey Me, I will increase the plague on you seven times in accordance with your sins.

22 'I will let loose the [wild] animals of the field among you, which will bereave you of your children and destroy your livestock and make you so few in number that your roads will lie deserted *and* desolate. [2 Kin 17:25, 26]

23 'And if by these things you are not turned to Me, but act with hostility against Me,

24 then I also will act with hostility against you, and I will strike you seven times for your sins.

25 'I will bring a sword on you that will execute vengeance for [breaking] the covenant; and when you gather together in your cities, I will send pestilence (virulent disease) among you, and you shall be handed over to the enemy. [Num 16:49; 2 Sam 24:15]

26 'When I break your staff of bread [that is, cut off your supply of food], ten women will bake your bread in one oven, and they will ration your bread; and you will eat and not be satisfied. [Hag 1:6]

27 'Yet if in spite of this you will not [attentively] listen to Me but act with hostility against me,

28 then I will act with hostility against you in wrath, and I also will punish you seven times for your sins.

29 'You will eat the flesh of your sons and the flesh of your daughters. [2 Kin 6:28, 29]

30 'I will destroy your high places [devoted to idolatrous worship], and cut down your incense altars, and heap your dead bodies upon the [crushed] bodies of your idols, and My soul will detest you [with deep and unutterable loathing]. [2 Kin 23:8, 20]

31 'I will lay waste your cities as well and will make your sanctuaries desolate, and I will not smell your sweet *and* soothing aromas [of offerings by fire]. [2 Kin 25:4–10; 2 Chr 36:19]

32 'I will make the land desolate, and

26:18 – 20 *sky like iron.* The second series of curses were characterized as "seven times more." Rain was essential to the whole nation, both the fall and spring rains.

26:19 *pride in your power.* The pride of power will often cause a person or nation to trust in its own strength and accomplishments rather than to submit to God and give Him the honor and glory. The punishment for this pride was drought — skies like iron, with not even a hint of rain. This can be true on a personal level as well as a national level if one forgets that it is God who has given the position of significance. Then the iron heavens make it seem as if prayers are not heard, and the parched spirit cries out for God's touch again.

26:21 – 22 *increase the plague on you seven times.* The third series of curses are again increased "seven times," so that the land is plagued with wild beasts that attack both their children and their domestic animals.

26:23 – 26 *a sword . . . pestilence . . . handed over to the enemy . . . eat and not be satisfied.* The fourth series of curses are also increased "seven times." When enemies invaded the land, the people living in unwalled villages fled to walled cities, and if the city was besieged, the overcrowding created prime conditions for epidemics and famine.

26:29 *eat the flesh of your sons . . . daughters.* The fifth and final curse, "seven times for your sins," was cannibalism. This actually happened centuries later during a siege of Samaria, and later still in Jerusalem (2Ki 6:28 – 29; La 2:20; 4:10).

26:30 *high places . . . incense altars.* The high places and incense altars were dedicated to the worship of pagan gods.

18 1Sa 2:5 **19** Isa 25:11; Dt 28:23 **20** Ps 127:1; Dt 11:17 **22** Dt 32:24; 2Ch 15:5; Zec 7:14 **23** Jer 2:30; Am 4:6-12 **24** Ps 18:26 **25** Eze 5:17; Dt 28:21 **26** Ps 105:16; Mic 6:14 **28** Jer 21:5; Eze 5:13,15; 8:18 **29** Dt 28:53 **30** 2Ch 34:3; Eze 6:3-6,13 **31** Ps 74:7 **32** Jer 9:11

your enemies who settle in it will be appalled at it.

33 'I will scatter you among the nations and draw out the sword [of your enemies] after you; your land will become desolate and your cities will become ruins. [Ps 44:11–14]

34 'Then the land [of Israel] will enjoy its Sabbaths as long as it lies desolate, while you are in your enemies' land; then the land will rest and enjoy its Sabbaths.

35 'As long as it lies desolate, it will have rest, the rest it did not have on your Sabbaths, while you were living on it. [2 Chr 36:21]

36 'As for those who are left of you, I will bring despair (lack of courage, weakness) into their hearts in the lands of their enemies; the sound of a scattered leaf will put them to flight, and they will flee as if [running] from the sword, and will fall even when no one is chasing them.

37 'They shall stumble over one another as if *to escape* from a sword when no one is chasing them; and you will have no power to stand before your enemies.

38 'You will perish among the nations; the land of your enemies will consume you.

39 'Those of you who are left will rot away because of their wickedness in the lands of your enemies; also because of the wickedness of their forefathers they will rot away like them.

40 'If they confess their wickedness and the wickedness of their forefathers, in their unfaithfulness which they have committed against Me—and also in their acting with hostility toward Me—

41 I also was acting with hostility toward them and brought them into the land of their enemies—then if their uncircumcised (sin-filled) hearts are humbled and they accept the punishment for their wickedness, [2 Kin 24:10–14; Dan 9:11–14]

42 then I will remember My covenant with Jacob, and also My covenant with Isaac, and also My covenant with Abraham, and remember the land. [Ps 106:44–46]

43 'But the land will be abandoned by them and will enjoy its Sabbaths while it lies desolate without them; and they will accept the punishment for their wickedness *and* make amends because they rejected My ordinances and their soul rejected My statutes.

44 'Yet in spite of this, when they are in the land of their enemies, I will not reject them, nor will I so despise them as to destroy them, breaking My covenant with them; for I am the LORD their God. [Deut 4:31–35; Jer 33:4, 5, 23–26; Rom 11:2–5]

45 'But I will, for their sake, [earnestly] remember the covenant with their forefathers, whom I have brought out of the land of Egypt in the sight of the nations, that I might be their God. I am the LORD.' "

46 These are the statutes, ordinances, and laws which the LORD established between Himself and the Israelites through Moses at Mount Sinai.

26:33 *scatter.* This threat was fulfilled in the Babylonian exile of 587 – 536 BC.

26:36 – 37 *despair (lack of courage, weakness) into their hearts.* Survivors would not enjoy relief or peace of mind after escaping the disasters. They would still be timid, even when no one pursued them.

26:38 – 39 *perish among the nations.* Having been exiled to foreign lands, the people were not to think they were beyond God's punitive reach.

26:42 *My covenant.* God's covenant with the patriarchs took precedence over the covenant at Sinai (Gal 3:15 – 18). Even when Israel violated the Sinai covenant, God honored the patriarchal covenant.

26:44 – 45 *I will not reject them . . . remember the covenant.* Ultimately, God's character is grace, mercy, love, and redemption. On that basis, God would remember the covenant and redeem them because He is God.

33 Dt 4:27; Eze 12:15; 20:23; 22:15; Zec 7:14 **34** 2Ch 36:21 **35** Lev 25:2 **36** Eze 21:7,12,15; ver. 17; Pr 28:1 **37** See Jdg 7:22; 1Sa 14:15,16; Isa 10:4; Jos 7:12,13; Jdg 2:14 **39** Dt 28:65; Zec 10:9 **40** Nu 5:7; Neh 9:2; Lk 15:18; 1Jn 1:9 **41** Ac 7:51; Ro 2:29; 2Ch 12:6,7 **42** Ex 2:24; 6:5; Eze 16:60; Ps 136:23 **43** ver. 34,35; ver. 15 **44** Dt 4:31; 2Ki 13:23; Ro 11:2 **45** Ro 11:28; Lev 22:33; 25:38; Ps 98:2; Eze 20:9,14,22 **46** Lev 27:34; Dt 6:1; 12:1; Jn 1:17; Lev 25:1

Rules concerning Valuations

27 AGAIN, THE LORD spoke to Mo-
ses, saying,
2“Speak to the children of Israel and
say to them, ‘When a man makes a
special vow [consecrating himself or
a member of his family], he *shall be*
valued according to your [established
system of] valuation of people belong-
ing to the LORD [that is, the priest ac-
cepts from the man making the vow
a specified amount of money for the
temple treasury in place of the actual
person].
3‘If your valuation is of a male be-
tween twenty and sixty years of age,
then your valuation shall be fifty shek-
els of silver, according to the shekel of
the sanctuary.
4‘Or if the person is a female, then
your valuation shall be thirty shekels.
5‘If the person is between five years
and twenty years of age, then your
valuation for the male shall be twenty
shekels and for the female ten shekels.
6‘But if the child is between one
month and five years of age, then your
valuation shall be five shekels of silver
for the male and three shekels for the
female.
7‘If the person is sixty years old and
above, your valuation shall be fifteen
shekels for the male, and ten shekels
for the female.
8‘But if the person is too poor to pay
your valuation, then he shall be placed
before the priest, and the priest shall
value him; according to the ability of
the one who vowed, the priest shall
value him.
9‘Now if it is an animal of the kind
which men can present as an offering
to the LORD, any such that one gives to
the LORD shall be holy.
10‘He shall not replace it or exchange
it, a good for a bad, or a bad for a good;
but if he does exchange an animal for
an animal, then both the original of-
fering and its substitute shall be holy.
11‘If it is any unclean animal of the
kind which men do not present as an
offering to the LORD, then he shall
bring the animal before the priest,
12and the priest shall value it as ei-
ther good or bad; it shall be as you, the
priest, value it.
13‘But if he ever *wishes to* redeem
it, then he shall add one-fifth of it to
your valuation.
14‘If a man consecrates his house
as sacred to the LORD, the priest shall
appraise it as either good or bad; as
the priest appraises it, so shall it stand.
15‘If the one who consecrates his
house should *wish to* redeem it, then
he shall add one-fifth of your valuation
price to it, so that it may be his.
16‘And if a man consecrates to the
LORD part of a field of his own prop-
erty, then your valuation shall be pro-
portionate to the seed needed for it; a
homer of barley seed shall be valued
at fifty shekels of silver.
17‘If he consecrates his field during
the Year of Jubilee, it shall stand ac-
cording to your valuation.
18‘But if he consecrates his field after
the Jubilee, then the priest shall calcu-
late the price for him in proportion to
the years that remain until the Year of

27:2 – 8 *special vow . . . shall value.* While people could dedicate themselves or their children to the Lord (1Sa 1:11, 22) only the Levites were allowed to serve God as priests. Therefore, those others vowed in service to the Lord had to be redeemed, and the value of his service was given to the sanctuary.

27:8 *too poor.* Fifty shekels might have represented about four years' earnings. If a person was too poor to pay this price, the priest set a price that the person could pay.

27:14 – 24 *consecrates.* Consecrating property to the Lord, and then buying it back with cash if one wants to use it for oneself is a curious idea to modern people. We tend to consider dedication of something to God as using it in a way that pleases Him, and the line between “God's” and “mine” may be very fuzzy. We are familiar with offering praises or tithes to God as worship, but think of the way we handle property as “good” or “poor” stewardship. A passage like this reminds us that we are not to be casual in worship. Are we offering it to God or not? Is it His, or do we want it back at no cost to ourselves?

27:16 *homer of barley.* A homer was a donkey load.

CHAPTER 27 **2** Nu 6:2; See Jdg 11:30,31,39; 1Sa 1:11,28 **3** Ex 30:13 **13** ver. 15,19 **15** ver. 13 **18** Lev 25:15,16

Jubilee; and it shall be deducted from your valuation.

19 'If the one who consecrates the field should ever wish to redeem it, then he shall add one-fifth of the appraisal price to it, so that it may return to him.

20 'If he does not redeem the field, but has sold it to another man, it may no longer be redeemed.

21 'When the field reverts in the Jubilee, the field shall be holy to the LORD, like a field set apart (devoted); the priest shall possess it as his property.

22 'Or if a man consecrates to the LORD a field which he has bought, which is not part of the field of his [ancestral] property,

23 then the priest shall calculate for him the amount of your valuation up to the Year of Jubilee; and the man shall give that [amount] on that day as a holy thing to the LORD.

24 'In the Year of Jubilee the field shall return to the one from whom it was purchased, to whom the land belonged [as his ancestral inheritance].

25 'Every valuation of yours shall be in accordance with the sanctuary shekel; twenty gerahs shall make a shekel.

26 'However, the firstborn among animals, which as a firstborn belongs to the LORD, no man may consecrate, whether an ox or a sheep. It is [already] the LORD's.

27 'If it is among the unclean animals, the owner may redeem it in accordance with your valuation, and add one-fifth to it; or if it is not redeemed, then it shall be sold in accordance with your valuation.

28 'But nothing that a man sets apart [that is, devotes as an offering] to the LORD out of all that he has, of man or of animal or of the fields of his own property, shall be sold or redeemed. Anything devoted to destruction (banned, cursed) is most holy to the LORD.

29 'No one who may have been set apart among men shall be ransomed [from death], he shall most certainly be put to death.

30 'And all the tithe (tenth part) of the land, whether the seed of the land or the fruit of the tree, is the LORD's; it is holy to the LORD. [1 Cor 9:11; Gal 6:6]

31 'If a man wishes to redeem any part of his tithe, he shall add one-fifth to it.

32 'For every tithe of the herd or flock, whatever passes under the [shepherd's] staff, the tenth one shall be holy to the LORD. [2 Cor 9:7–9]

33 'The man is not to be concerned whether *the animal is* good or bad, nor shall he exchange it. But if he does exchange it, then both it and its substitute shall become holy; it shall not be redeemed.' "

34 These are the commandments which the LORD commanded Moses on Mount Sinai for the children of Israel. [Rom 10:4; Heb 4:2; 12:18–29]

27:28 *sets apart.* Setting apart or devoting a possession was a stronger act than dedication. Nothing devoted could be redeemed; persons devoted (under the ban) were to be put to death. No private citizen would have had the power to put himself or anyone else "under the ban."

27:31 *redeem any part of his tithe.* For a person living a distance from the sanctuary, it may have been more practical to redeem the tithe than to bring the crops to the sanctuary.

27:32 *under the [shepherd's] staff.* Sheep and goats were inspected when they passed under the staff that the shepherd placed across the entrance to the fold. This was a time to determine if the animals were under any distress from disease or injury, and was also the time that some of them were set aside for the Lord.

19 ver. 13 **21** Lev 25:10,28,31; ver. 28; Nu 18:14; Eze 44:29 **22** Lev 25:10,25 **23** ver. 18 **24** Lev 25:28 **25** Ex 30:13; Nu 3:47; 18:16; Eze 45:12 **26** Ex 13:2,12; 22:30 **27** ver. 11,12 **28** ver. 21; Jos 6:17-19 **29** Nu 21:2 **30** Ge 28:22; Nu 18:21,24; 2Ch 31:5,6,12; Neh 13:12; Mal 3:8 **31** ver. 13 **32** Jer 33:13; Eze 20:37; Mic 7:14 **33** ver. 10 **34** Lev 26:46

THE FOURTH BOOK OF MOSES, CALLED

NUMBERS

▸ **AUTHOR:** The Jews, Samaritans, and the early church testify to Moses' authorship. Several New Testament passages attribute events cited from Numbers to Moses (Jn 3:14; Ac 7; 13; 1Co 10:1 – 11; Heb 3 – 4; Jn 11), and there are more than eighty claims within Numbers that state that the Lord spoke to Moses (1:1). Numbers 33:2 says that Moses recorded their journeys at the Lord's command. As an eyewitness who kept detailed records, and the central character of the events in the book, no one was better qualified to write this book than Moses.

▸ **TIMES:** c. 1114 – 1405 BC ▸ **KEY VERSES:** Nu 14:22 – 23

▸ **THEME:** At Sinai, this newly resurrected nation of Israel receives its laws, its system of sacrifices, and its national charter. The people then should have been ready to take the next step into the promised land, but they aren't. Numbers largely has Israel in a holding pattern. While the book records further steps taken in organizing the nation, its central narrative is that of the refusal of the people to go into Canaan. But God still doesn't give up on His people. He continues to discipline them in an effort to have a new generation ready to fulfill His plan. In this context Numbers points to God's sovereignty, His patience, and His desire to bless His people.

The Census of Israel's Warriors

1 THE LORD spoke [by special revelation] to Moses in the Wilderness of Sinai in the Tent of Meeting (tabernacle) on the first day of the second month in the second year after the Israelites came out of the land of Egypt, saying,
2 "Take a census of all the congregation of the sons of Israel, by their families (clans), by their fathers' households, according to the number of names, every male, head by head
3 from twenty years old and upward, all in Israel who *are able to* go out to war. You and Aaron shall number them, army by army.
4 "And with you there shall be a man [to assist you] from each tribe, each being the head of his father's household.
5 "These then are the names of the men who shall stand with you: from [the tribe of] Reuben, Elizur the son of Shedeur;
6 from [the tribe of] Simeon, Shelumiel the son of Zurishaddai;
7 from [the tribe of] Judah, Nahshon the son of Amminadab;
8 from [the tribe of] Issachar, Nethanel the son of Zuar;
9 from [the tribe of] Zebulun, Eliab the son of Helon;
10 from the sons (descendants) of

1:1 *Wilderness of Sinai.* The setting of the book of Numbers is the wilderness. Not only did the Israelites live in the wilderness, but they as a nation were traveling through a time of spiritual emptiness. They were starting all over in their relationship with God after a time of slavery. The empty wilderness kept them dependent, and kept them from being distracted with the normal affairs of caring for land and animals.

CHAPTER 1 **1** Ex 19:1; Nu 10:11,12; Ex 25:22 **2** Ex 30:12; 38:26; Nu 26:2,63,64; 2Sa 24:2; 1Ch 21:2

Joseph: from [the tribe of] Ephraim, Elishama the son of Ammihud; from [the tribe of] Manasseh, Gamaliel the son of Pedahzur;

11 from [the tribe of] Benjamin, Abidan the son of Gideoni;

12 from [the tribe of] Dan, Ahiezer the son of Ammishaddai;

13 from [the tribe of] Asher, Pagiel the son of Ochran;

14 from [the tribe of] Gad, Eliasaph the son of Deuel;

15 from [the tribe of] Naphtali, Ahira the son of Enan.

16 "These men were the ones called from the congregation, the leaders of their fathers' (ancestors') tribes; they were the heads of thousands [the highest ranking officers] in Israel."

17 So Moses and Aaron took these men who were designated by name,

18 and assembled all the congregation on the first day of the second month, and they registered by ancestry in their families (clans), by their fathers' households, according to the number of names from twenty years old and upward, head by head,

19 just as the LORD had commanded Moses. So he numbered them in the Wilderness of Sinai.

20 The sons of Reuben, Israel's (Jacob's) firstborn, their generations, by their families (clans), by their fathers' households, according to the number of names, head by head, every male from twenty years old and upward, all who *were able to* go to war:

21 those of the tribe of Reuben numbered 46,500.

22 Of the sons of Simeon, their descendants, by their families (clans), by their fathers' households, their numbered men according to the number of names, head by head, every male from twenty years old and upward, all who *were able to* go to war:

23 those of the tribe of Simeon numbered 59,300.

24 Of the sons of Gad, their descendants, by their families (clans), by their fathers' households, according to the number of names, from twenty years old and upward, all who *were able to* go to war:

25 those of the tribe of Gad numbered 45,650.

26 Of the sons of Judah, their descendants, by their families (clans), by their fathers' households, according to the number of names, from twenty years old and upward, all who *were able to* go to war:

27 those of the tribe of Judah numbered 74,600.

28 Of the sons of Issachar, their descendants, by their families (clans), by their fathers' households, according to the number of names, from twenty years old and upward, all who *were able to* go to war:

29 those of the tribe of Issachar numbered 54,400.

30 Of the sons of Zebulun, their descendants, by their families (clans), by their fathers' households, according to the number of names, from twenty years old and upward, all who *were able to* go to war:

31 those of the tribe of Zebulun numbered 57,400.

32 Of the sons of Joseph: the sons (descendants) of Ephraim, their descendants, by their families (clans), by their fathers' households, according to the number of names, from twenty years old and upward, all who *were able to* go to war:

33 those of the tribe of Ephraim numbered 40,500.

34 Of the sons of Manasseh, their descendants, by their families (clans), by their fathers' households, according to the number of names, from twenty years old and upward, all who *were able to* go to war:

35 those of the tribe of Manasseh numbered 32,200.

36 Of the sons of Benjamin, their descendants, by their families (clans), by their fathers' households, according to the number of names, from twenty years old and upward, all who *were able to* go to war:

37 those of the tribe of Benjamin numbered 35,400.

14 Nu 2:14 **16** Nu 7:2; 1Ch 27:16; Ex 18:21,25 **17** Isa 43:1 **18** Ezr 2:59 **20** Nu 2:10,11; 32:6,15,21,29 **22** Nu 2:12,13; 26:12-14 **24** Nu 2:14,15; 26:15-18; 32:2,29; 34:14 **26** Nu 2:3,4; 26:19-22; 2Sa 24:9 **27** 2Ch 17:14 **28** Nu 2:5,6 **30** Nu 2:7,8; 26:26,27 **32** Nu 2:18,19; 26:35-37 **34** Nu 2:20,21; 26:28-34 **36** Nu 2:22,23; 26:38-41

38Of the sons of Dan, their descen-
dants, by their families (clans), by their
fathers' households, according to the
number of names, from twenty years
old and upward, all who *were able to*
go to war:
39those of the tribe of Dan numbered
62,700.
40Of the sons of Asher, their descen-
dants, by their families (clans), by their
fathers' households, according to the
number of names, from twenty years
old and upward, all who *were able to*
go to war:
41those of the tribe of Asher num-
bered 41,500.
42Of the sons of Naphtali, their de-
scendants, by their families (clans), by
their fathers' households, according
to the number of names, from twenty
years old and upward, all who *were*
able to go to war:
43those of the tribe of Naphtali num-
bered 53,400.
44These were the ones who were
numbered, whom Moses and Aaron
numbered, with the leaders of Israel,
twelve men, each representing his fa-
thers' household.
45So all those numbered of the sons
of Israel, by their fathers' households,
from twenty years old and upward, all
who *were able to* go to war in Israel,
46all who were numbered were
603,550.

Levites Exempted

47The Levites, however, were not
numbered among them by their fa-
thers' tribe.
48For the LORD had said to Moses,
49"Only the tribe of Levi you shall
not number, nor shall you take their
census among the sons of Israel [since
they are unavailable to go to war].
50"But appoint the Levites over the
tabernacle (sanctuary) of the Testi-
mony, and over all its furnishings and
all things that belong to it. They shall
carry the tabernacle [when traveling]
and all its furnishings, and they shall
take care of it and camp around it.
51"When the tabernacle is to go for-
ward, the Levites shall take it down;
and when the tabernacle is to [be set
up for] camp, the Levites shall set it
up. But the layman (non-Levite) who
approaches the tabernacle shall be put
to death.
52"The Israelites shall camp accord-
ing to their armies, every man by his
own camp and every man by his own
[tribal] standard (banner).
53"But the Levites shall camp around
the tabernacle of the Testimony, so that
there will be no wrath against the con-
gregation of the Israelites. The Levites
shall be in charge of the tabernacle of
the Testimony."
54Thus the sons of Israel did *these*
things; according to all that the LORD
had commanded Moses, so they did.

Arrangement of the Camps

2 THE LORD spoke to Moses and
Aaron, saying,
2"The sons of Israel shall camp, each
by his own standard, with the banners
of their fathers' households; they shall
camp around the Tent of Meeting (tab-
ernacle), but at a distance.
3"Those who camp on the east side
toward the sunrise *shall be* of the stan-
dard of the camp of Judah, by their

1:44–46 *all who were numbered.* The number of able-bodied men who were at least twenty years old would indicate a population of between two and five million, including the women, children, and older or infirm men who were not counted in this census.
1:50 *the tabernacle.* The term tabernacle points to the temporary and portable nature of the tent.
2:1–2 *by his own standard.* A person's identity was not only derived from his or her tribe, but also from his or her place in relation to the tabernacle. This is a chapter on design and order; it speaks to the importance of knowing one's duties in relation to the holy and living God.
2:3–9 *on the east side toward the sunrise.* The east side was the favored side, facing the rising sun. The Israelites were not a sea-faring people; in effect they turned their backs to the

---

38 Nu 2:25,26; 26:42,43 **40** Nu 2:27,28; 26:44-47 **44** Nu 26:64 **46** Ex 38:26; See Ex 12:37; Nu 2:32; 26:51 **47** Nu 2:33; See Nu 3; 4; 26:57; 1Ch 6; 21:6 **49** Nu 2:33; 26:62 **50** Ex 38:21; Nu 3:7,8; 4:15,25-27,33; Nu 3:23,29, 35,38 **51** Nu 10:17,21; Nu 3:10,38; 18:22 **52** Nu 2:2,34 **53** ver. 50; Lev 10:6; Nu 8:19; 16:46; 18:5; 1Sa 6:19
CHAPTER 2 **2** Nu 1:52; Jos 3:4 **3** Nu 10:14; Ru 4:20; 1Ch 2:10; Mt 1:4

armies; and Nahshon the son of Am-
minadab shall lead the sons of Judah,
4and his army as numbered totaled
74,600.
5"Next to Judah [on the east side]
the tribe of Issachar shall encamp; and
Nethanel the son of Zuar shall lead the
sons of Issachar,
6and his army as numbered totaled
54,400.
7"Then [also on the east side] the
tribe of Zebulun; and Eliab the son of
Helon shall lead the sons of Zebulun,
8and his army as numbered totaled
57,400.
9"The total of the numbered men [in
the three tribes on the east side] in the
camp of Judah was 186,400, by their
armies. They shall move out first [on
the march].
10"On the south side shall be the
standard of the camp of Reuben, by
their armies; and Elizur the son of
Shedeur shall lead the sons of Reuben,
11and his army as numbered totaled
46,500.
12"Those who camp next to Reuben
[on the south side] shall be the tribe of
Simeon; and Shelumiel the son of Zuri-
shaddai shall lead the sons of Simeon,
13and his army as numbered totaled
59,300.
14"Then [completing the south side]
the tribe of Gad; and Eliasaph the son
of Reuel (Deuel) shall lead the sons
of Gad,
15and his army as numbered totaled
45,650.
16"The total of the numbered men [in
the three tribes on the south side] in the
camp of Reuben was 151,450, by their
armies. They shall move out second
[on the march].
17"Then the Tent of Meeting (taber-
nacle) shall move out with the camp of
the Levites in the middle of the [other]
camps; just as they camp so shall they
move out, every man in his place by
their standards.
18"On the west side shall be the stan-
dard of the camp of Ephraim, by their
armies; and Elishama the son of Am-
mihud shall lead the sons of Ephraim,
19and his army as numbered totaled
40,500.
20"Beside Ephraim [on the west side]
shall be the tribe of Manasseh; and
Gamaliel the son of Pedahzur shall
lead the sons of Manasseh,
21and his army as numbered totaled
32,200.
22"Then [completing the west side
shall be] the tribe of Benjamin; and
Abidan the son of Gideoni shall lead
the sons of Benjamin,
23and his army as numbered totaled
35,400.
24"The total of the numbered men
[of the three tribes on the west side]
in the camp of Ephraim was 108,100,
by their armies. They shall move out
in third place.
25"On the north side shall be the
standard of the camp of Dan, by their
armies; and Ahiezer the son of Ammi-
shaddai shall lead the sons of Dan,
26and his army as numbered totaled
62,700.
27"Encamped next to Dan [on the
north side] shall be the tribe of Asher;
and Pagiel the son of Ochran shall lead
the sons of Asher,
28and his army as numbered totaled
41,500.
29"Then [completing the north side]
comes the tribe of Naphtali; and Ahira
the son of Enan shall lead the sons of
Naphtali,
30and his army as numbered totaled
53,400.
31"The total of the numbered men
[of the three tribes on the north side]
in the camp of Dan was 157,600. They
shall move out last, standard after
standard."
32These are the men of the Israel-
ites [twenty years old and upward] as

---

sea, so the word for "back" could mean "west" or "the sea."

2:17 Tent of Meeting . . . with . . . the Levites in the middle. In the line of march, the tabernacle was in a central position — a symbol not only of Israel's protection of the holy objects, but also of the presence of God among His people.

9 Nu 10:14 **16** Nu 10:18 **17** Nu 10:17,21 **24** Nu 10:22 **29** Ge 30:8; 49:21; 2Ki 15:29; Rev 7:6 **31** Nu 10:25 **32** Ex 38:26; Nu 1:46; 11:21

numbered by their fathers' households. The total of the numbered men of the camps by their armies, 603,550.

33 But the Levites were not numbered with the [other] Israelites, just as the LORD had commanded Moses.

34 Thus the Israelites did [as ordered]; according to everything the LORD had commanded Moses, so they camped by their standards, and so they moved out, everyone with his family (clan), according to his fathers' household.

Levites to Be Priesthood

3 NOW THESE are the *records of the* generations of Aaron and Moses in the day when the LORD spoke [by special revelation] with Moses on Mount Sinai.

2 These are the names of the sons of Aaron: Nadab the firstborn, Abihu, Eleazar, and Ithamar.

3 These are the names of the sons of Aaron, the priests who were anointed, whom Aaron consecrated *and* ordained to minister in the priest's office.

4 But Nadab and Abihu died in the presence of the LORD when they offered strange (unholy, unacceptable, inappropriate) fire before the LORD in the Wilderness of Sinai; and they had no sons. So Eleazar and Ithamar served as priests in the presence *and* under the supervision of Aaron their father. [Lev 10:1–4]

5 Then the LORD spoke to Moses, saying,

6 "Bring the tribe of Levi near and present them before Aaron the priest, so that they may serve him.

7 "They shall carry out the duties for him and for the whole congregation before the Tent of Meeting, doing the service of the tabernacle.

8 "They shall also take care of all the furnishings *and* utensils of the Tent of Meeting, and [attend to] the duties of

---

3:1 – 10 *sons of Aaron.* The priests had privileged access to God. In the New Covenant this is no longer confined only to a particular group of God's people. All Christians comprise God's new temple and constitute "a holy . . . priesthood, to offer spiritual sacrifices [that are] acceptable and pleasing to God through Jesus Christ" (1Pe 2:5).

3:5 – 10 *Aaron and his sons.* The Levites could care for the holy things, but only the priests, who ministered in the tabernacle, drew near to God. Only the high priest entered the most holy place.

33 Nu 1:47 **34** Nu 24:2,5,6 **CHAPTER 3** **2** Ex 6:23 **3** Ex 28:41; Lev 8 **4** Lev 10:1; Nu 26:61; 1Ch 24:2 **6** Nu 8:6; 18:2 **7** See Nu 1:50; 8:11,15,24,26

ENCAMPMENT OF THE TRIBES OF ISRAEL

Nu 2:1–31 Nu 10:11–33

Naphtali Asher Dan*

N W E S

Ephraim* Merarites Judah*

Manasseh Gershonites TABERNACLE Moses and Priests Issachar

Benjamin Kohathites Zebulun

Gad Simeon Reuben*

*Leading tribe of the group

Kohathites carry the tabernacle furnishings | Gershonites and Merarites carry the tabernacle | Levites carry the ark

Dan Ephraim Reuben Judah

Asher Manasseh Simeon Issachar

Naphtali Benjamin Gad Zebulun

MARCHING ORDER OF THE TRIBES

the Israelites, doing the service of the tabernacle.

9 "You shall give the Levites to Aaron and to his sons [as servants and helpers]; they are to be given wholly to him from among the Israelites.

10 "So you shall appoint Aaron and his sons, and they shall observe *and* attend to their priesthood; but the layman (non-Levite) who approaches [the holy things] shall be put to death."

11 Again the LORD spoke to Moses, saying,

12 "Behold, I have taken the Levites from among the sons of Israel instead of *and* as a substitute for every firstborn, that is, the first that opens the womb among the Israelites. So the Levites shall be Mine,

13 for all the firstborn are Mine. On the day that I killed all the firstborn in the land of Egypt, I consecrated for Myself all the firstborn in Israel, both man and animal. They shall be mine; I am the LORD."

14 Then the LORD spoke to Moses in the Wilderness of Sinai, saying,

15 "Number the sons of Levi by their fathers' households, by their families (clans). You shall number every male from a month old and upward."

16 So Moses numbered them just as he was commanded by the word (mouth) of the LORD.

17 These are the [three] sons of Levi by their names: Gershon, Kohath, and Merari.

18 These are the names of the [two] sons of Gershon by their families: Libni and Shimei;

19 and the [four] sons of Kohath by their families: Amram, Izhar, Hebron, and Uzziel;

20 and the [two] sons of Merari by their families: Mahli and Mushi. These are the families of the Levites by their fathers' households.

21 Of Gershon were the families of the Libnites and of the Shimeites. These are the families of the Gershonites.

22 The males who were numbered, every male from a month old and upward totaled 7,500.

23 The families of the Gershonites were to camp behind the tabernacle on the west,

24 and the leader of the fathers' households of the Gershonites was Eliasaph the son of Lael.

Duties of the Priests

25 Now the responsibilities of the sons of Gershon in the Tent of Meeting *involved* the tabernacle and the tent, its covering, and the curtain for the doorway of the Tent of Meeting,

26 and the hangings of the courtyard, the curtain for the doorway of the courtyard which is around the tabernacle and the altar, its tent ropes, and all the service concerning them.

27 Of Kohath were the families of the Amramites, the Izharites, the Hebronites, and the Uzzielites; these are the families of the Kohathites.

28 The males who were numbered, every male from a month old and upward *totaled* 8,600, attending to the duties of the sanctuary.

29 The families of the sons of Kohath were to camp on the south side of the tabernacle,

30 and the leader of the fathers' households of the families of the Kohathites was Elizaphan the son of Uzziel.

31 Now their responsibilities *involved* the ark, the table [on which the bread of the Presence was placed], the lampstand, the altars, the utensils of the sanctuary with which the priests minister, and the curtain, and all the service concerning them.

32 Eleazar, the son of Aaron the priest, was chief of the leaders of the Levites; he supervised those who performed the duties of the sanctuary.

3:11–13 ***I consecrated for Myself.*** God is directly involved in redemption. When God redeemed and saved His people, it was by His own person.

9 Nu 8:19; 18:6 **10** Nu 18:7; ver. 38; Nu 1:51; 16:40 **12** ver. 41; Nu 8:16; 18:6 **13** Ex 13:2; Lev 27:26; Nu 8:17; Lk 2:23; Ex 13:12,15; Nu 8:17 **15** ver. 39; Nu 26:62 **17** Ge 46:11; Ex 6:16; Nu 26:57; 1Ch 6:1,16; 23:6 **18** Ex 6:17 **19** Ex 6:18 **20** Ex 6:19 **23** Nu 1:53 **25** Nu 4:24-26; Ex 25:9; Ex 26:1; Ex 26:7,14; Ex 26:36 **26** Ex 27:9; Ex 27:16; Ex 35:18 **27** 1Ch 26:23 **29** Nu 1:53 **31** Nu 4:15; Ex 25:10; Ex 25:23; Ex 25:31; Ex 27:1; 30:1; Ex 26:32

33 Of Merari were the families of the Mahlites and the Mushites; these are the families of Merari.

34 The males who were numbered, every male from a month old and upward *totaled* 6,200.

35 The leader of the fathers' households of the families of Merari was Zuriel the son of Abihail. The Merarites were to camp on the north side of the tabernacle.

36 Now the appointed responsibilities of the sons of Merari *involved* the frames of the tabernacle, its bars, its pillars, its sockets *or* bases, and all the equipment, and all the service concerning them,

37 and the pillars around the courtyard with their bases and their pegs and their cords (tent ropes).

38 Now those to camp before the tabernacle toward the east, before the Tent of Meeting, toward the sunrise, were to be Moses, and Aaron and his sons, performing the duties of the sanctuary for whatever was required of the Israelites; and the layman (non-Levite) who approached [the sanctuary] was to be put to death.

39 All the men of the Levites whom Moses and Aaron numbered at the command of the LORD, by their families, every male from a month old and upward, were 22,000.

Firstborn Redeemed

40 Then the LORD said to Moses, "Number every firstborn male of the Israelites from a month old and upward, and make a list of their names.

41 "You shall take the Levites for Me instead of *and* as a substitute for all the firstborn among the Israelites. I am the LORD; and *you shall take* the cattle of the Levites instead of *and* as a substitute for all the firstborn among the cattle of the Israelites."

42 So Moses numbered all the firstborn among the Israelites, just as the LORD had commanded him;

43 and all the firstborn males from a month old and upward as numbered were 22,273 [273 more than the Levites].

44 Then the LORD spoke to Moses, saying,

45 "Take the Levites [for Me] instead of all the firstborn among the sons of Israel, and the cattle of the Levites instead of their cattle. And the Levites shall be Mine. I am the LORD.

46 "For the ransom (redemption price) of the 273 of the firstborn of the Israelites who outnumber the Levites,

47 you shall take five shekels apiece, per head, you shall take them in terms of the sanctuary shekel (the shekel is twenty gerahs),

48 and give the money, the ransom (redemption price) of those who outnumber the Levites to Aaron and to his sons."

49 So Moses took the ransom (redemption) money from those who were in excess, beyond those ransomed by the Levites;

50 from the firstborn of the Israelites he took the money in terms of the sanctuary shekel, 1,365 shekels.

51 Then Moses gave the ransom money to Aaron and to his sons at the command of the LORD, just as the LORD had commanded Moses.

3:38 *performing the duties of the sanctuary.* "Performing the duties of the sanctuary" was committed to a particular group of people, and no one else was to intrude on that task. Believers, as part of the body of Christ, also have certain duties. These roles are not rigid, but they are definite, planned, and created by God for the good of the whole church. The teamwork of the whole body creates a harmonious whole, and if one fails in his duty, the whole team suffers (1Co 12).

3:40 – 42 *Number every firstborn male.* When God passed over the homes of the Hebrew families who had obeyed His commands in the Passover (Ex 12:23 – 51), He declared the surviving firstborn Hebrew children — and also the firstborn of animals — to be His. The animals were sacrificed, the firstborn were redeemed (paid for), at first by the Levites who took the place of all the other firstborn, and then by a set sum of money for those that numbered more than the Levites. It is a clear statement of fact that people belong to God.

35 Nu 1:53 **36** Nu 4:31,32 **38** Nu 1:53; Nu 18:5; ver. 7,8; ver. 10 **39** See Nu 26:62 **40** ver. 15 **41** ver. 12,45 **45** ver. 12,41 **46** Ex 13:13; Nu 18:15; ver. 39,43 **47** Lev 27:6; Nu 18:16; Ex 30:13 **50** ver. 46,47 **51** ver. 48

Duties of the Kohathites

4 THEN THE LORD spoke to Moses
and Aaron, saying,
2“Take a census of the sons of Ko-
hath from among the sons of Levi, by
their families (clans), by their fathers’
households,
3from thirty years old and upward,
even to fifty years old, all who enter
the service to do the work in the Tent
of Meeting (tabernacle).
4“This is the work *and* responsibility
of the sons of Kohath in the Tent of
Meeting (tabernacle): the most holy
things.
5“When the camp prepares to move
out, Aaron and his sons shall come
into *the sanctuary* and take down the
veil (curtain) screening off *the Holy of*
Holies, and cover the ark of the testi-
mony with it;
6and they shall put on it a covering of
porpoise skin (fine leather), and shall
spread over that a cloth of pure blue,
and shall insert the carrying poles of
the ark.
7“Over the table of the bread of the
Presence they shall spread a cloth of
blue and put on it the plates, the dishes
[for incense], the sacrificial bowls, the
jars for the drink offering, and the
continual bread [of the Presence] shall
be on it.
8“They shall spread over them a
cloth of scarlet, and cover that with
a covering of porpoise skin, and they
shall insert its carrying poles.
9“Then they shall take a blue cloth
and cover the lampstand for the light,
along with its lamps, its wick cutters,
its trays, and all the oil vessels, by
which it is supplied;
10and they shall put the lampstand
and all its utensils in a covering of
porpoise skin, and shall put it on the
carrying bars.
11“Over the golden [incense] altar
they shall spread a blue cloth, and cov-
er it with a covering of porpoise skin,
and shall insert its carrying poles;
12and they shall take all the utensils
of the service with which they min-
ister in the sanctuary, and put them
in a blue cloth, and cover them with
a covering of porpoise skin, and put
them on the carrying bars.
13“Then they shall clean away the
ashes from the altar [of burnt offering],
and spread a purple cloth over it.
14“They shall also put on it all its
utensils with which they minister in
connection with it: the pans, the meat-
forks, the shovels, the basins, and all
the utensils of the altar; and they shall
spread a covering of porpoise skin
over it, and insert its carrying poles.
15“When Aaron and his sons have
finished covering the sanctuary and
all its furniture, as the camp sets out,
after all that [is done, but not before],
the sons of Kohath shall come to carry
them [using the poles], so that they
do not touch the holy things, and die.
These are the things in the Tent of
Meeting (tabernacle) which the sons
of Kohath are to carry.
16“The responsibility of Eleazar, the
son of Aaron the priest, is the oil for the
light, the fragrant incense, the contin-
ual grain offering, and the anointing
oil—the responsibility of all the taber-
nacle and everything that is in it, with
the sanctuary and its furnishings.”
17Then the LORD spoke to Moses and
Aaron, saying,
18“Do not cut off (eliminate, destroy)
the tribe of the families of the Kohath-
ites [who are only Levites and not
priests], from among the Levites [by

4:3 *from thirty years old.* According to 8:24, the Levites were to be twenty-five years old, which seems like a contradiction to this passage. It is possible that the difference reflects a time of apprenticeship.

4:16 *The responsibility of Eleazar.* God made arrangements for the priest to approach Him in the way He prescribed. If the priests did not do their job, no one else could do it for them. It was a big responsibility, and the well-being of the whole nation depended upon their faithfulness.

CHAPTER 4 **3** See Nu 8:24; 1Ch 23:3,24,27 **4** ver. 15; ver. 19 **5** Ex 26:31; Ex 25:10,16 **6** Ex 25:13 **7** Ex 25:23,29,30 **9** Ex 25:31; Ex 25:37,38 **11** Ex 30:1,3 **15** Nu 7:9; 10:21; Dt 31:9; 2Sa 6:13; 1Ch 15:2,15; 2Sa 6:6,7; 1Ch 13:9,10; Nu 3:31 **16** Ex 25:6; Lev 24:2; Ex 30:34; Ex 29:38; Ex 30:25

exposing them to the sin of touching the most holy things].

19 “But deal with them in this way, so that they may live and not die when they approach the most holy things: Aaron and his sons shall go in and assign each of them to his [specific] work and to his load [to be carried on the march].

20 “But the Kohathites shall not go in to see the holy things, even for an instant, or they will die.”

Duties of the Gershonites

21 Then the LORD spoke to Moses, saying,

22 “Take a census of the sons of Gershon also, by their fathers’ households, by their families.

23 “From thirty years and upward to fifty years old, you shall number them; all who enter for service to do the work in the Tent of Meeting.

24 “This is the service of the families of the Gershonites, in serving and in carrying [when on the march]:

25 they shall carry the tent curtains of the tabernacle, and the Tent of Meeting, its covering and the covering of porpoise skin (fine leather) that is on top of it, and the curtain for the doorway of the Tent of Meeting (tabernacle),

26 and the hangings of the courtyard, and the curtain for the entrance of the gate of the courtyard which is around the tabernacle and the altar, and their tent ropes, and all the equipment for their service; and all that is to be done, they shall perform.

27 “Aaron and his sons shall direct all the service of the sons of the Gershonites, all they have to carry and all they have to do. You shall assign to them as a duty all that they are to carry [on the march].

28 “This is the service of the families of the sons of Gershon in the Tent of Meeting (tabernacle); and their duties *shall be* under the direction of Ithamar the son of Aaron, the [high] priest.

Duties of the Merarites

29 “As for the sons of Merari, you shall number them by their families (clans), by their fathers’ households;

30 from thirty years and upward to fifty years old, you shall number them, everyone who enters the service to do the work of the Tent of Meeting (tabernacle).

31 “This is what they are assigned to carry [on the march], according to all their service in the Tent of Meeting: the boards [for the framework] of the tabernacle and its bars and its pillars and its sockets *or* bases,

32 and the pillars around the courtyard with their sockets *or* bases and their pegs and their cords (tent ropes), with all their equipment and with all their [accessories for] service; and you shall assign *each man* by name the items he is to carry [on the march].

33 “This is the work of the families of the sons of Merari, according to all their tasks in the Tent of Meeting (tabernacle), under the direction of Ithamar the son of Aaron, the priest.”

34 So Moses and Aaron and the leaders of the congregation numbered the sons of the Kohathites by their families (clans) and by their fathers’ households,

35 from thirty years and upward even to fifty years old, everyone who enters the service to do the work in the Tent of Meeting (tabernacle);

36 the men who were numbered by their families were 2,750.

37 These were numbered of the families of the Kohathites, all who did service in the Tent of Meeting (tabernacle), whom Moses and Aaron num-

---

4:21 – 28 *enter for service.* There are various tasks given to us in the kingdom of God which appear to be of minor importance. Daily faithfulness in the little things is the best preparation for greater trusts. Mary, the mother of Jesus, is an example of this. Her response to the angel when she was told that she would be the mother of Jesus was, “Behold, I am the servant of the Lord” (Lk 1:38). She had found favor in the way she conducted her daily life, and God chose her for a unique and blessed role.

19 ver. 4 **20** See Ex 19:21; 1Sa 6:19 **23** ver. 3 **25** Nu 3:25,26 **28** ver. 33 **30** ver. 3 **31** Nu 3:36,37; Ex 26:15 **32** Ex 38:21 **34** ver. 2 **35** ver. 47; Nu 8:24,26; 1Ch 23:24; Lk 3:23; 1Ti 3:6

bered according to the commandment of the LORD through Moses.

38 The men who were numbered of the sons of Gershon, by their families (clans), and by their fathers' households,

39 from thirty years and upward even to fifty years old, everyone who entered the service to do the work in the Tent of Meeting (tabernacle);

40 the men who were numbered by their families, by their fathers' households, were 2,630.

41 These were numbered men of the families of the sons of Gershon, everyone who served in the Tent of Meeting (tabernacle), whom Moses and Aaron numbered just as the LORD had commanded.

42 The men who were numbered of the sons of Merari, by their families (clans), by their fathers' households,

43 from thirty years and upward even to fifty years old, everyone who entered the service for work in the Tent of Meeting (tabernacle);

44 the men who were numbered by their families were 3,200.

45 These are the men who were numbered of the families of the sons of Merari, whom Moses and Aaron numbered in accordance with the commandment of the LORD through Moses.

46 All the men who were numbered of the Levites, whom Moses and Aaron and the leaders of Israel counted by their families (clans) and by their fathers' households,

47 from thirty years and upward even to fifty years old, everyone who could enter to do the work of service and the work of carrying in the Tent of Meeting (tabernacle);

48 the men that were numbered were 8,580.

49 According to the commandment of the LORD through Moses, they were numbered, each *assigned* to his work of serving and carrying. Thus they were numbered by him, just as the LORD had commanded Moses.

On Defilement

5 THE LORD spoke to Moses, saying,

2 "Command the Israelites to send away from the camp every leper and everyone who has a discharge, and whoever is defiled [that is, ceremonially unclean] by [coming in contact with] the dead.

3 "You shall send away both male and female; you shall send them outside the camp so that they will not defile their camp where I dwell in their midst."

4 The Israelites did so, and sent them outside the camp; just as the LORD had said to Moses, so the Israelites did.

5 And the LORD spoke to Moses, saying,

6 "Say to the Israelites, 'When a man or woman commits any of the sins of mankind [against other people], thus breaking faith with the LORD, and that person is guilty,

7 then he shall confess the sin which he has committed, and he shall make restitution for his wrong in full, and add a fifth to it, and give it to [the person] whom he has wronged.

8 'But if the man [who was wronged] has no redeemer (relative) to whom the restitution may be made, it is to be given to the LORD for the priest, besides the ram of atonement with which atonement is made for the offender.

9 'Also every contribution pertaining to all the holy gifts of the Israelites which they offer to the priest, shall be his.

10 'And every man's holy gifts shall be the priest's; whatever any man gives the priest, it becomes his.' "

5:3 *not defile their camp where I dwell.* Ritual purity was important because God wanted the Israelites to remember that He lived among them. They needed to think of Him walking around in the camp and live in such a way that there was not something offensive for God to discover.

5:6 *breaking faith with the LORD.* Not only did God deal with ritual impurity, He was also concerned about how the people treated each other. To label sin as "acting unfaithfully" kept the real issue right in front. When we mistreat our fellow citizens, God cares, and He takes it personally. He made us; He made them. We each belong to Him, and we are not to wrong other people.

41 ver. 22 **45** ver. 29 **47** ver. 3,23,30 **49** ver. 15,24,31; ver. 1,21 **CHAPTER 5** **2** Lev 13:3,46; Lev 15:2; Lev 21:1; Nu 9:6,10; 19:11,13; 31:19 **3** Lev 26:11,12; 2Co 6:16 **6** Lev 6:2,3 **7** Lev 5:5; 26:40; Jos 7:19; Lev 6:5 **8** Lev 6:6,7; 7:7 **9** Ex 29:28; Lev 6:17,18,26; 7:6,7,9,10,14 **10** Lev 10:13

The Adultery Test

11 Then the LORD spoke to Moses,
saying,
12 "Speak to the Israelites and say to
them, 'If any man's wife goes astray
(deviates) and is unfaithful to him,
13 and a man is intimate with her,
and it is hidden from the eyes of her
husband and it is kept secret, although
she has defiled herself, and there is no
witness against her and she has not
been caught in the act,
14 and if a spirit (sense, attitude) of
jealousy comes over him and he is
jealous *and* angry at his wife who has
defiled herself—or if a spirit of jealousy
comes over him and he is jealous of his
wife when she has not defiled herself—
15 then the man shall bring his wife
to the priest, and he shall bring as an
offering for her, a tenth of an ephah
of barley meal; he shall not pour oil
on it nor put frankincense on it [the
symbols of favor and joy], because it is
a grain offering of jealousy, a memo-
rial grain offering, a reminder of [the
consequences of] wickedness.
16 'Then the priest shall have her ap-
proach and have her stand before the
LORD,
17 and the priest shall take holy water
[from the sacred basin] in an earthen-
ware vessel; and he shall take some
of the dust that is on the floor of the
tabernacle and put it in the water.
18 'The priest shall then have the wom-
an stand before the LORD, and let the hair
of the woman's head hang loose, and
put the memorial grain offering in her
hands, which is the jealousy offering,
and in the hand of the priest is to be the
water of bitterness that brings a curse.
19 'Then the priest shall have her
take an oath and say to the woman,
"If no man has lain with you and if you
have not gone astray into uncleanness
[while married], then be immune to this
water of bitterness that brings a curse;
20 but if you have gone astray [while
married] and you have defiled yourself
and a man other than your husband
has been intimate with you"
21 (then the priest shall have the wom-
an swear the oath of the curse, and say
to the woman), "The LORD make you a
curse and an oath among your people
when the LORD makes your thigh waste
away and your abdomen swell;
22 and this water that brings a curse
shall go into your stomach, and make
your abdomen swell and your thigh
waste away." And the woman shall say,
"Amen. Amen (so let it be)."
23 'The priest shall then write these
curses on a scroll and shall wash them
off into the water of bitterness;
24 and he shall make the woman
drink the water of bitterness that
brings a curse, and the water that
brings the curse will go into her and
cause bitterness.
25 'Then the priest shall take the

5:12 *wife goes astray.* The wife belonged to her husband. If she was unfaithful, she could be stoned. If she was not guilty, and he acted on his unsubstantiated suspicions, he would be guilty of murder. The woman had a serious responsibility to her husband because the reliability of family lines depended upon her faithfulness. It is obvious if a woman is pregnant, but it is not obvious who the father is. By bringing the whole sorry problem to God, the Israelites could be sure of justice.

5:15 *bring his wife to the priest.* Determining if a woman had been unfaithful to her husband, when she had not been caught in wrongdoing, was more difficult than detecting skin diseases. But because God was in the camp, the issue could be resolved by the priest, in the presence of God. Again, it reminded the Israelites that nothing was hidden from God.

5:18 *water of bitterness that brings a curse.* This was not a magic potion, but dust from the floor of the tabernacle and holy water. The woman held in her own hands the grain offering for jealousy. These things reminded everyone that they were standing in the presence of God, and that it was He who would determine if the woman bore any guilt.

5:21 *your thigh waste away and your abdomen swell.* These words speak symbolically of a miscarriage (of an illegitimate child) if the woman was pregnant, and the inability to conceive again. In the biblical world, a woman who was unable to bear children was regarded as being under a curse; in this case it would have been true.

---

13 Lev 18:20 **15** Lev 5:11; 1Ki 17:18; Eze 29:16 **21** Jos 6:26; 1Sa 14:24; Neh 10:29; Jer 29:22 **22** Ps 109:18; Dt 27:15 **25** Lev 8:27

grain offering of jealousy out of the woman's hand, and he shall wave the grain offering before the LORD and offer it on the altar.

26 'Then the priest shall take a handful of the grain offering as the memorial portion of it and offer it up in smoke on the altar, and afterward he shall make the woman drink the water.

27 'When he has made her drink the water, then it shall come about, that if she has defiled herself and has been unfaithful to her husband, the curse water will go into her and *cause* bitterness and cause her abdomen to swell and her thigh to waste away, and the woman will become a curse among her people.

28 'But if the woman has not defiled herself and is clean, then she will be free and conceive children.

29 'This is the law of jealousy: when a wife goes astray [while married] and defiles herself,

30 or when a spirit (sense, attitude) of jealousy *and* suspicion comes on a man and he is jealous of his wife; then he shall have the woman stand before the LORD, and the priest shall apply this law to her.

31 'Further, the husband will be free from guilt, but that woman [if guilty] shall bear her guilt.' "

Law of the Nazirites

6 AGAIN THE LORD spoke to Moses, saying,

2 "Say to the sons of Israel, 'When a man or a woman makes a special vow, the vow of a Nazirite, that is, one separated *and* dedicated to the LORD,

3 he shall abstain from wine and strong drink; he shall drink no vinegar, whether made from wine or strong drink, nor shall he drink any grape juice nor eat fresh or dried grapes. [Luke 1:15]

4 'All the time of his separation he shall not eat anything produced from the grapevine, from the seeds even to the skins.

5 'All the time of the vow of his separation no razor shall be used on his head. Until the time of his separation to the LORD is completed, he shall be holy, and shall let the hair of his head grow long.

6 'All the time that he separates himself to the LORD he shall not go near a dead body.

7 'He shall not make himself [ceremonially] unclean for his father, mother, brother, or sister, when they die, because [the responsibility for] his separation to God is on his head.

8 'All the time of his separation he is holy to the LORD.

9 'If a man dies very suddenly beside him, and he defiles his dedicated head, then he shall shave his head on the day that he becomes [ceremonially] clean; he shall shave it on the seventh day [the end of the purification period].

10 'On the eighth day he shall bring two turtledoves or two young pigeons to the priest, to the doorway of the Tent of Meeting (tabernacle).

11 'The priest shall offer the one as a sin offering and the other as a burnt offering and make atonement for him concerning his sin because of the [dead] body. He shall consecrate his head the same day,

12 and he shall dedicate himself to the LORD for the time of his separation and shall bring a male lamb a year old as a guilt offering; but the previous days will be void *and* lost, because his separation was defiled.

5:31 *woman [if guilty] shall bear her guilt.* Throughout the Bible God compares idolatry with marital unfaithfulness, so it is clear that this is a subject that touches close to the heart of every man and woman. God is faithful to His people, and they are to be true to Him. In the same way, as a daily picture of this faithfulness, the husband and wife are to be true and faithful to each other. The law recognizes the volatility of unfaithfulness, provides a limit to unjust accusations, and underlines the seriousness of the moral lapse that comes with adultery. A guilty woman would indeed bear her guilt, but a faithful woman would be exonerated.

6:1 – 8 Self-denial — To serve God by abstaining from legitimate things is the Christian's privilege today as well. It is not that God is looking for sacrifice, but He is looking for a willing heart that will lay aside the good to spend time on the best.

26 Lev 2:2,9 **27** ver. 21 **29** ver. 19 **31** Lev 20:17,19,20 **CHAPTER 6** **2** Lev 27:2; Jdg 13:5; Ac 21:23; Ro 1:1 **3** Am 2:12; Lk 1:15 **5** Jdg 13:5; 16:17; 1Sa 1:11 **6** Lev 21:11; Nu 19:11,16 **7** Lev 21:1,2,11; Nu 9:6 **8** 2Co 6:17,18 **9** Ac 18:18; 21:24 **10** Lev 5:7; 14:22; 15:14,29 **12** Lev 5:6

13 'Now this is the law of the Nazirite when the days of his separation *and* dedication are fulfilled: he shall bring the offering to the doorway of the Tent of Meeting (tabernacle).

14 and he shall offer his gift to the LORD: one male lamb a year old without blemish as a burnt offering, and one female lamb a year old without blemish as a sin offering, and one ram without blemish as a peace offering,

15 and a basket of unleavened bread, cakes of fine flour mixed with oil, and wafers of unleavened bread spread with oil, along with their grain offering and their drink offering.

16 'Then the priest shall present them before the LORD and shall offer the person's sin offering and his burnt offering.

17 'He shall also offer the ram as a sacrifice of peace offerings to the LORD, together with the basket of unleavened bread; the priest shall offer also its grain offering and its drink offering.

18 'The Nazirite shall shave his dedicated head at the doorway of the Tent of Meeting (tabernacle), and take the dedicated hair of his head and put it on the fire which is under the sacrifice of the peace offerings.

19 'The priest shall take the boiled shoulder of the ram, and one unleavened [ring-shaped] loaf out of the basket, and one unleavened flat cake and shall put them on the hands of the Nazirite after he has shaved his dedicated *hair*.

20 'Then the priest shall wave them as a wave offering before the LORD; they are a holy portion for the priest, together with the breast that is waved and the thigh that is offered by lifting up; and afterward the Nazirite may drink wine.'

21 "This is the law for the Nazirite who vows his offering to the LORD for his separation, besides what else he is able to afford, according to the vow which he has vowed; so shall he do according to the law for his separation *and* abstinence [as a Nazirite]." [Acts 21:24, 26]

Aaron's Benediction

22 Then the LORD spoke to Moses, saying,

23 "Speak to Aaron and his sons, saying, 'This is the way you shall bless the Israelites. Say to them:

24 The LORD bless you, and keep you
[protect you, sustain you, and guard you];
25 The LORD make His face shine upon you [with favor],
And be gracious to you
[surrounding you with lovingkindness];
26 The LORD lift up His countenance
(face) upon you [with divine approval],
And give you peace [a tranquil heart and life].'

27 "So Aaron and his sons shall put My name upon the children of Israel, and I will bless them."

Offerings of the Leaders

7 ON THE day that Moses had finished setting up the tabernacle and had anointed and consecrated it and all its furniture, and the altar and all

---

6:21 ***the law for the Nazirite.*** Not to be confused with a Nazarene (one from Nazareth), the Nazirite vows were practiced both in the Old and New Testament. It is likely that John the Baptist was a Nazirite, probably all of his life.

6:23 ***bless the Israelites.*** This special blessing shows the love and mercy of God toward His chosen people. God's keeping power, His shining personal presence, His eye contact, and His own peace would be a blessing that would mark the Israelites as belonging to God Himself, and they would be called with His name.

7:1 ***On the day that Moses had finished setting up the tabernacle.*** This phrasing places the events of this chapter before the taking of the census in chapters 1–4. The tabernacle was completed on the first day of the first month of the second year. The census began one month later.

7:1–11 ***brought their offering.*** The tabernacle from the beginning to the end was constructed

13 Ac 21:26 **14** Lev 4:2,27,32; Lev 3:6 **15** Lev 2:4; Ex 29:2; Nu 15:5,7,10 **18** Ac 21:24 **19** 1Sa 2:15; Ex 29:23,24 **20** Ex 29:27,28 **23** Lev 9:22; Dt 10:8; 21:5; Jos 8:33; 1Ch 23:13 **24** Ps 121:7; Jn 17:11 **25** Ps 31:16; 67:1; 80:3,7,19; 119:135; Da 9:17; Ge 43:29; Ex 33:19; Mal 1:9 **26** Ps 4:6; Jn 14:27; Php 4:7; 2Th 3:16 **27** Dt 28:10; 2Ch 7:14; Isa 43:7; Da 9:18,19; Nu 23:20; Ps 5:12; 67:7; 115:12,13; Eph 1:3 **CHAPTER 7** **1** Ex 40:18; Lev 8:10,11

its utensils; he also anointed them and consecrated them [for holy use].

[2]Then the leaders of Israel, the heads of their fathers' households, made offerings. (These were the leaders of the tribes; they were the ones who were over the men who were numbered.)

[3]They brought their offering before the LORD, six covered carts and twelve oxen; a cart for each two of the leaders and an ox for each one; and they presented them before the tabernacle.

[4]Then the LORD spoke to Moses, saying,

[5]"Accept *these things* from them, so that they may be used in the service of the Tent of Meeting (tabernacle), and give them to the Levites, to each man according to his service."

[6]So Moses took the carts and the oxen and gave them to the Levites.

[7]He gave two carts and four oxen to the sons of Gershon, according to their service [in transporting the tabernacle];

[8]and he gave four carts and eight oxen to the sons of Merari, according to their service [in transporting the tabernacle], under the supervision of Ithamar the son of Aaron, the [high] priest.

[9]But to the sons of Kohath he gave nothing, because they were assigned the care of the holy things which they carried on their shoulders [when the tabernacle was moved].

[10]The leaders offered the dedication *sacrifices* for the altar on the day that it was anointed; and they offered their sacrifice before the altar.

[11]Then the LORD said to Moses, "Let them present their offerings, one leader each day, for the dedication of the altar."

[12]Now the one who presented his offering on the first day was Nahshon the son of Amminadab, of the tribe of Judah;

[13]and his offering was one silver dish, the weight of which was a hundred and thirty *shekels*, one silver basin of seventy shekels, according to the shekel of the sanctuary, both of them full of fine flour mixed with oil as a grain offering;

[14]one golden bowl of ten *shekels*, full of incense;

[15]one young bull, one ram, one male lamb one year old, as a burnt offering;

[16]one male goat as a sin offering;

[17]and for the sacrifice of peace offerings, two oxen, five rams, five male goats, five male lambs one year old. This was the offering of Nahshon the son of Amminadab [from the tribe of Judah].

[18]On the second day Nethanel the son of Zuar, leader [of the tribe] of Issachar, presented [his offering];

[19]he presented as his offering one silver dish, the weight of which was a hundred and thirty *shekels*, one silver basin of seventy shekels, according to the shekel of the sanctuary, both of them full of fine flour mixed with oil as a grain offering;

[20]one golden bowl of ten *shekels*, full of incense;

[21]one young bull, one ram, and one male lamb one year old, as a burnt offering;

[22]one male goat as a sin offering;

[23]and for the sacrifice of peace offerings, two oxen, five rams, five male goats, five male lambs one year old. This was the offering of Nethanel the son of Zuar [from the tribe of Issachar].

[24]On the third day [it was] Eliab the son of Helon, leader [of the tribe] of the sons of Zebulun [who presented his offering];

[25]his offering was one silver dish, the weight of which was a hundred and thirty *shekels*, and one silver basin of seventy shekels, according to the shekel of the sanctuary, both of them

---

and furnished by willing hearts and hands. God wants us to give to His work because we are eager to, not because we are required. Jesus directed, "Give, and it will be given to you ... a good measure — pressed down, shaken together, and running over" (Lk 6:38). We can never out-give God.

---

2 Nu 1:4 **7** Nu 4:23 **8** Nu 4:33; Nu 4:28,33 **9** Nu 4:15; Nu 4:6,8,10,12,14; 2Sa 6:13 **10** See Dt 20:5; 1Ki 8:63; 2Ch 7:5,9; Ezr 6:16; Neh 12:27 **12** Nu 2:3 **13** Ex 30:13; Lev 2:1 **14** Ex 30:34 **15** Lev 1:2; Ex 12:5 **16** Lev 4:23 **17** Lev 3:1

full of fine flour mixed with oil as a
grain offering;
26 one golden bowl of ten *shekels*, full
of incense;
27 one young bull, one ram, one male
lamb one year old, as a burnt offering;
28 one male goat as a sin offering;
29 and for the sacrifice of peace of-
ferings, two oxen, five rams, five male
goats, five male lambs one year old.
This was the offering of Eliab the son
of Helon [from the tribe of Zebulun].
30 On the fourth day [it was] Elizur
the son of Shedeur, leader [of the tribe]
of the sons of Reuben [who presented
his offering];
31 his offering was one silver dish, the
weight of which was a hundred and
thirty *shekels*, and one silver basin
of seventy shekels, according to the
shekel of the sanctuary, both of them
full of fine flour mixed with oil for a
grain offering;
32 one golden bowl of ten *shekels*, full
of incense;
33 one young bull, one ram, one male
lamb one year old, as a burnt offering;
34 one male goat as a sin offering;
35 and for the sacrifice of peace of-
ferings, two oxen, five rams, five male
goats, five male lambs one year old.
This was the offering of Elizur the son
of Shedeur [from the tribe of Reuben].
36 On the fifth day [it was] Shelumiel
the son of Zurishaddai, leader [of the
tribe] of the sons of Simeon [who pre-
sented his offering];
37 his offering was one silver dish, the
weight of which was a hundred and
thirty *shekels*, and one silver basin
of seventy shekels, according to the
shekel of the sanctuary, both of them
full of fine flour mixed with oil as a
grain offering;
38 one golden bowl of ten *shekels*, full
of incense;
39 one young bull, one ram, one male
lamb one year old, for a burnt offering;
40 one male goat as a sin offering;
41 and for the sacrifice of peace of-
ferings, two oxen, five rams, five male
goats, five male lambs one year old.
This was the offering of Shelumiel the
son of Zurishaddai [from the tribe of
Simeon].
42 On the sixth day [it was] Eliasaph
the son of Deuel, leader [of the tribe]
of the sons of Gad [who presented his
offering];
43 his offering was one silver dish
the weight of which was a hundred
and thirty *shekels*, and a silver basin
of seventy shekels, according to the
shekel of the sanctuary, both of them
full of fine flour mixed with oil as a
grain offering;
44 one golden bowl of ten *shekels*, full
of incense;
45 one young bull, one ram, one male
lamb one year old, as a burnt offering;
46 one male goat as a sin offering;
47 and for the sacrifice of peace
offerings, two oxen, five rams, five
male goats, five male lambs one year
old. This was the offering of Eliasaph
the son of Deuel [from the tribe of
Gad].
48 On the seventh day [it was] Elish-
ama the son of Ammihud, leader [of
the tribe] of the sons of Ephraim [who
presented his offering];
49 his offering was one silver dish, the
weight of which was a hundred and
thirty *shekels*, and one silver basin
of seventy shekels, according to the
shekel of the sanctuary, both of them
full of fine flour mixed with oil as a
grain offering;
50 one golden bowl of ten *shekels*, full
of incense;
51 one young bull, one ram, one male
lamb one year old, as a burnt offering;
52 one male goat as a sin offering;
53 and for the sacrifice of peace of-
ferings, two oxen, five rams, five male
goats, five male lambs one year old.
This was the offering of Elishama the
son of Ammihud [from the tribe of
Ephraim].
54 On the eighth day [it was] Gama-
liel the son of Pedahzur, leader [of the
tribe] of the sons of Manasseh [who
presented his offering];
55 his offering was one silver dish the
weight of which was a hundred and
thirty *shekels*, and one silver basin

30 Nu 1:5; 2:10 **36** ver. 41; Nu 1:6; 2:12 **42** Nu 1:14; 2:14 **45** Ps 40:6 **48** Nu 1:10; 2:18 **50** Dt 33:10; Ps 66:15; 141:2; Eze 8:11; Mal 1:11; Lk 1:10; Rev 5:8; 8:3 **54** Nu 1:10; 2:20

of seventy shekels, according to the
shekel of the sanctuary, both of them
full of fine flour mixed with oil as a
grain offering;
56 one golden bowl of ten *shekels*, full
of incense;
57 one young bull, one ram, one male
lamb one year old, as a burnt offering;
58 one male goat as a sin offering;
59 and for the sacrifice of peace of-
ferings, two oxen, five rams, five male
goats, five male lambs one year old.
This was the offering of Gamaliel the
son of Pedahzur [from the tribe of Ma-
nasseh].
60 On the ninth day [it was] Abidan
the son of Gideoni, leader [of the tribe]
of the sons of Benjamin [who present-
ed his offering];
61 his offering was one silver dish, the
weight of which was a hundred and
thirty *shekels*, and one silver basin
of seventy shekels, according to the
shekel of the sanctuary, both of them
full of fine flour mixed with oil as a
grain offering;
62 one golden bowl of ten *shekels*, full
of incense;
63 one young bull, one ram, one male
lamb one year old, as a burnt offering;
64 one male goat as a sin offering;
65 and as the sacrifice of peace offer-
ings, two oxen, five rams, five male
goats, five male lambs one year old.
This was the offering of Abidan the
son of Gideoni [from the tribe of Ben-
jamin].
66 On the tenth day [it was] Ahiezer
the son of Ammishaddai, leader [of the
tribe] of the sons of Dan [who present-
ed his offering];
67 his offering was one silver dish, the
weight of which was a hundred and
thirty *shekels*, and one silver basin
of seventy shekels, according to the
shekel of the sanctuary, both of them
full of fine flour mixed with oil as a
grain offering;
68 one golden bowl of ten *shekels*, full
of incense;
69 one young bull, one ram, one male
lamb one year old, as a burnt offering;
70 one male goat as a sin offering;
71 and for the sacrifice of peace of-
ferings, two oxen, five rams, five male
goats, five male lambs one year old.
This was the offering of Ahiezer the
son of Ammishaddai [from the tribe
of Dan].
72 On the eleventh day [it was] Pagiel
the son of Ochran, leader [of the tribe]
of the sons of Asher [who presented
his offering];
73 his offering was one silver dish, the
weight of which was a hundred and
thirty *shekels*, and one silver basin
of seventy shekels, according to the
shekel of the sanctuary, both of them
full of fine flour mixed with oil as a
grain offering;
74 one golden bowl of ten *shekels*, full
of incense;
75 one young bull, one ram, and one
male lamb one year old, as a burnt
offering;
76 one male goat as a sin offering;
77 and for the sacrifice of peace
offerings, two oxen, five rams, five
male goats, five male lambs one year
old. This was the offering of Pagiel
the son of Ochran [from the tribe of
Asher].
78 On the twelfth day [it was] Ahira
the son of Enan, leader [of the tribe] of
the sons of Naphtali [who presented
his offering];
79 his offering was one silver dish, the
weight of which was a hundred and
thirty *shekels*, and one silver basin
of seventy shekels, according to the
shekel of the sanctuary, both of them
full of fine flour mixed with oil as a
grain offering;
80 one golden bowl of ten *shekels*, full
of incense;
81 one young bull, one ram, one male
lamb one year old, as a burnt offering;
82 one male goat as a sin offering;
83 and for the sacrifice of peace of-
ferings, two oxen, five rams, five male
goats, five male lambs one year old.
This was the offering of Ahira the son
of Enan [from the tribe of Naphtali].
84 This was the dedication offering
for the altar from the leaders of Is-
rael on the day when it was anointed:
twelve dishes of silver, twelve silver
basins, twelve golden bowls;

60 Nu 1:11; 2:22 **66** Nu 1:12; 2:25 **72** Nu 1:13; 2:27 **78** Nu 1:15; 2:29 **84** 2Ch 7:9; Jdg 5:9

85each dish of silver weighing a hundred and thirty *shekels*, each basin seventy [shekels]; all the silver vessels *weighed* 2,400 shekels, according to the shekel of the sanctuary;
86the twelve golden bowls, full of incense, *weighing* ten shekels apiece, according to the shekel of the sanctuary, all the gold of the bowls being a hundred and twenty *shekels;*
87all the oxen for the burnt offering were twelve bulls, the rams twelve, the male lambs one year old twelve, together with their grain offering; and the male goats as a sin offering twelve;
88and all the oxen for the sacrifice of the peace offerings were twenty-four bulls, the rams sixty, the male goats sixty, the male lambs one year old sixty. This was the dedication for the altar [of burnt offering] after it was anointed.
89Now when Moses went into the Tent of Meeting (tabernacle) to speak with the LORD, he heard the voice speaking to him from above the mercy seat (the gold cover) that was on the ark of the Testimony from between the two cherubim; and He spoke [by special revelation] to him.

The Seven Lamps

8 THEN THE LORD spoke to Moses, saying,
2"Speak to Aaron and say to him, 'When you set up *and* light the lamps, the seven lamps will shine in front of the lampstand.' "
3And Aaron did so; he set up the lamps at the front of the lampstand, just as the LORD had commanded Moses.
4Now this was the workmanship of the lampstand: hammered work of gold; from its base to its flowers it was hammered work; according to the pattern which the LORD had shown Moses, so he made the lampstand.

Cleansing the Levites

5Again the LORD spoke to Moses, saying,
6"Take the Levites from among the sons of Israel and cleanse them.
7"This is what you shall do to them to [ceremonially] cleanse them: sprinkle the water of purification on them, and let them use a razor over their whole body and wash their clothes, and they will be clean. [Num 19:17, 18]
8"Then let them take a young bull and its grain offering of fine flour mixed with oil, and you shall take another young bull as a sin offering.
9"You shall present the Levites before the Tent of Meeting (tabernacle), and you shall also assemble the whole congregation of the children of Israel,
10and present the Levites before the LORD, and the Israelites shall lay their hands on the Levites.
11"Aaron shall present the Levites before the LORD as a wave offering from the Israelites, so that they may perform the service of the LORD.
12"Then the Levites shall lay their hands on the heads of the bulls, then you are to offer the one as a sin offering and the other as a burnt offering to the LORD, to make atonement for the Levites.

7:89 *heard the voice.* The tabernacle is referred to as the "tent of meeting," because it was here that the Lord communicated with His people. Moses knew that it was the Lord he was hearing, and he took that word very seriously. The Word of God is still something that God's people can hear, usually through the Bible, sometimes in creation (Ro 1), and sometimes through the work of the Holy Spirit. This is usually a strong impression that God wants you to pay attention to something, wait, change a decision, or pray. The leading of the Holy Spirit will never contradict Scripture, so it is exceedingly important for believers to maintain a familiarity with the Bible, so they can know God and hear Him.

8:10 – 12 *shall lay their hands on.* The sons of Israel who laid their hands on the Levites in this ancient symbol of dedication were showing their support for and agreement with the special role that the Levites had been set aside for. This would be an event that everyone could look back on and remember as an important, solemn time of dedication and asking for God's blessing.

85 Ex 30:13,24; 38:24-26; Lev 5:15; 27:3,25; Nu 3:47 **88** ver. 1 **89** Ex 33:9,11; Ex 25:22 **CHAPTER 8** **2** Ex 25:37; 40:25 **4** Ex 25:31; Ex 25:18; Ex 25:40 **7** Nu 19:9,17,18; Lev 14:8,9 **8** Lev 2:1 **9** See Ex 29:4; 40:12; Lev 8:3 **10** Lev 1:4 **12** Ex 29:10

13“You shall have the Levites stand before Aaron and his sons and present them as a wave offering to the LORD.

14“Thus you shall separate the Levites from among the Israelites, and the Levites shall be Mine [in a very special sense].

15“Then after that the Levites may go in to serve the Tent of Meeting (tabernacle), but you shall cleanse them [first] and present them as a wave offering;

16for they are wholly given to Me from among the Israelites. I have taken them for Myself instead of all who are born first, the firstborn of all the Israelites.

17“For all the firstborn among the Israelites are Mine, among the men and among the animals; on the day that I struck down every firstborn in the land of Egypt, I sanctified *and* set the Israelites apart for Myself.

18“And I have taken the Levites instead of every firstborn among the Israelites.

19“I have given the Levites as a gift to Aaron and to his sons from among the Israelites, to perform the service of the Israelites at the Tent of Meeting (tabernacle) and to make atonement for them, so that there will be no plague among the Israelites if they should approach the sanctuary.”

20Thus Moses and Aaron and all the congregation of the children of Israel did [these things] to the Levites; in accordance with all that the LORD had commanded Moses concerning the Levites, so the Israelites did to them.

21The Levites, too, purified themselves from sin and they washed their clothes; and Aaron presented them as a wave offering before the LORD, and Aaron made atonement for them to cleanse them.

22Then after that the Levites went in to perform their service in the Tent of Meeting before Aaron and his sons; just as the LORD had commanded Moses concerning the Levites, so they did to them.

Retirement

23Now the LORD spoke to Moses, saying,

24“This is what *applies* to the Levites: from twenty-five years old and upward they shall enter to perform service in the work of the Tent of Meeting,

25but at the age of fifty years, they shall retire from the service of the [tabernacle] work and serve no longer.

26They may assist their brothers in the Tent of Meeting to keep an obligation, but they shall do no [heavy or difficult] work. Thus you shall deal with the Levites concerning their obligations.”

The Passover

9 THE LORD spoke to Moses in the Wilderness of Sinai in the first month of the second year after they had come out of the land of Egypt, saying,

2“The sons of Israel are to keep the Passover at its appointed time.

8:16 *wholly given to Me.* The Hebrew words for this phrase are an emphatic doubling: “given, given.”
8:19 *no plague.* God’s holiness would not bear an improper approach. But in His mercy He provided the protective hedge of the Levites, to keep the Israelites from coming near the sanctuary in an unauthorized way, and thus causing a plague.
8:24 *from twenty-five years old.* According to 4:3, the Levites were to be thirty years old, which seems like a contradiction to this passage. It is possible that the difference reflects a time of apprenticeship.
9:1 *the first month of the second year.* This phrasing places the events of this chapter before the taking of the census. (See note for 7:1.)
9:1 – 5 *keep the Passover.* When the first Passover was celebrated in Egypt, the command was given to commemorate it throughout Israel’s generations (Ex 12:14). This would be the second time that the Israelites had observed this special commemorative event. Passover had greater significance than any Israelite of that day could imagine, however wonderful the exodus events were. Redemption from Egypt was a picture of greater redemption yet to be, when the blood of Christ would speak of better things than the

14 Nu 3:45; 16:9 **15** ver. 11,13 **16** Nu 3:12,45 **17** Ex 13:2,12,13,15; Nu 3:13; Lk 2:23 **19** Nu 3:9; Nu 1:53; 16:46; 18:5; 2Ch 26:16 **21** ver. 7 **22** ver. 15; ver. 5 **24** See Nu 4:3; 1Ch 23:3,24,27 **26** Nu 1:53
CHAPTER 9 **2** Ex 12:1; Lev 23:5; Nu 28:16; Dt 16:1,2

3“On the fourteenth day of this month at twilight, you shall keep it at its appointed time; according to all its statutes and ordinances you shall keep it.”

4So Moses told the Israelites to observe the Passover.

5They observed the Passover on the fourteenth day of the first month at twilight in the Wilderness of Sinai; in accordance with all that the LORD had commanded Moses, so the Israelites did.

6But there were certain men who were [ceremonially] unclean because of [touching] the dead body of a man, so they could not observe the Passover on that day; so they came before Moses and Aaron that same day.

7Those men said to Moses, “We are [ceremonially] unclean because of [touching] a dead body. Why are we being restrained from presenting the LORD's offering at its appointed time among the Israelites?”

8Therefore, Moses said to them, “Wait, and I will listen to what the LORD will command concerning you.”

9Then the LORD spoke to Moses, saying,

10“Say to the Israelites, ‘If any one of you or of your descendants becomes [ceremonially] unclean because of [touching] a dead body or is on a distant journey, he may, however, observe the Passover to the LORD.

11‘On the fourteenth day of the second month [thirty days later] at twilight, they shall observe it; they shall eat it with unleavened bread and bitter herbs.

12‘They shall leave none of it until morning nor break any of its bones; in accordance with all the statutes of the Passover they shall observe it. [John 19:36]

13‘But the man who is [ceremonially] clean and is not on a journey, and yet does not observe the Passover, that person shall be cut off from among his people [excluding him from the atonement made for them] because he did not bring the LORD's offering at its appointed time; that man will bear [the penalty of] his sin.

14‘If a stranger lives among you as a resident alien and observes the Passover to the LORD, in accordance with its statutes and its ordinances, so shall he do; you shall have one statute, both for the resident alien and for the native of the land.’ ”

The Cloud on the Tabernacle

15Now on the day that the tabernacle was erected, the cloud [of God's presence] covered the tabernacle, that is, the tent of the Testimony; and in the evening it was over the tabernacle, appearing like [a pillar of] fire until the morning. [Ex 13:21]

16So it was continuously; the cloud covered it *by day*, and the appearance of fire by night.

17Whenever the cloud was lifted from over the tent (tabernacle), afterward the Israelites would set out; and in the place where the cloud stopped, there the Israelites would camp.

18At the LORD's command the Israelites would journey on, and at His command they would camp. As long as the cloud remained over the tabernacle they remained camped.

19Even when the cloud lingered over the tabernacle for many days, the Israelites would keep their obligation to the LORD and not set out.

20Sometimes the cloud remained only a few days over the tabernacle, and in accordance with the command

---

blood applied to the doors in Egypt. Christ is now our eternal Passover (1Co 5:7).

9:12 *nor break any of its bones.* It is fitting to remember that when the Savior was crucified as our “Passover Lamb,” none of His bones were broken (Jn 19:36).

9:15–23 *the cloud.* The cloud was a dramatic symbol of the active presence of God with His people, hovering over them in protection, moving ahead of them for direction, and coming near at night as fire for comfort in the darkness.

5 Jos 5:10 **6** Nu 5:2; 19:11,16; See Jn 18:28; Ex 18:15,19,26; Nu 27:2 **8** Nu 27:5 **11** 2Ch 30:2,15; Ex 12:8 **12** Ex 12:10; Ex 12:46; Jn 19:36; Ex 12:43 **13** Ge 17:14; Ex 12:15; ver. 7; Nu 5:31 **14** Ex 12:49 **15** Ex 40:34; Neh 9:12,19; Ps 78:14; Ex 13:21; 40:38 **17** Ex 40:36; Nu 10:11,33,34; Ps 80:1 **18** 1Co 10:1 **19** Nu 1:53; 3:8

of the LORD they remained camped. Then at His command they set out.

21 If sometimes the cloud remained [over the tabernacle] from evening only until morning, when the cloud was lifted in the morning, they would journey on; whether in the daytime or at night, whenever the cloud was lifted, they would set out.

22 Whether it was two days or a month or a year that the cloud [of the LORD's presence] lingered over the tabernacle, staying above it, the Israelites remained camped and did not set out; but when it was lifted, they set out.

23 At the command of the LORD they camped, and at the command of the LORD they journeyed on; they kept their obligation to the LORD, in accordance with the command of the LORD through Moses.

The Silver Trumpets

10 THE LORD spoke further to Moses, saying,

2 "Make two trumpets of silver; you shall make them of hammered work. You shall use them to summon the congregation and to have the camps move out.

3 "When both are blown, all the congregation [that is, all adult males] shall gather before you at the doorway of the Tent of Meeting (tabernacle).

4 "However, if a single trumpet is blown, then the leaders, heads of the tribes of Israel, shall gather themselves to you.

5 "When you blow an alarm, the camps on the east side [of the tabernacle] shall set out.

6 "When you blow an alarm the second time, then the camps on the south side [of the tabernacle] shall set out. They shall blow an alarm whenever they are to move out [on their journeys].

7 "When the assembly is to be gathered, you shall blow [the trumpets in short, sharp tones], but without sounding an alarm.

8 "The sons of Aaron, the priests, shall blow the trumpets; and the trumpets shall be for you a perpetual statute throughout your generations.

9 "When you go to war in your land against the enemy that attacks you, then sound an alarm with the trumpets, so that you may be remembered before the LORD your God, and you shall be saved from your enemies.

10 "Also in the day of rejoicing, and in your appointed feasts, and at the beginnings of your months, you shall sound the trumpets over your burnt offerings, and over the sacrifice of your peace offerings; and they shall be as a reminder of you before your God. I am the LORD your God."

The Tribes Leave Sinai

11 On the twentieth day of the second month in the second year [since leaving Egypt], the cloud [of the Lord's presence] was lifted from over the tabernacle of the Testimony,

12 and the Israelites set out on their journey from the Wilderness of Sinai, and the cloud [of the LORD's guiding presence] settled down in the Wilderness of Paran.

13 So they moved out for the first time in accordance with the command of the LORD through Moses.

9:23 *At the command.* Like the children of Israel, our existence often seems to us like a wilderness. Most often we want to *move*, to *do*, to know. Without waiting and following God's directions, His Word, His plan, we miss His best, and lessons are lost or delayed. How blessed to wait for God's direction, to obey Him in both stops and starts in all of life! No words spoken, no money spent, no job taken, no engagement ring given or received, without knowing we will be keeping God's charge.

10:2 *two trumpets of silver.* The two silver trumpets were different from the curved ram's horn trumpets (Lev 25:9). Made of hammered silver, these instruments were straight with a flaring bell, like the post horns of medieval Europe. Since they did not have valves, they would have been played like a bugle.

22 Ex 40:36,37 **23** ver. 19 **CHAPTER 10** **2** Isa 1:13 **3** Jer 4:5; Joel 2:15 **4** Ex 18:21; Nu 1:16; 7:2 **5** Nu 2:3 **6** Nu 2:10 **7** ver. 3; Joel 2:1 **8** Nu 31:6; Jos 6:4; 1Ch 15:24; 2Ch 13:12 **9** Nu 31:6; Jos 6:5; 2Ch 13:14; Jdg 2:18; 4:3; 6:9; 10:8,12; Ge 8:1; Ps 106:4 **10** Nu 29:1; Lev 23:24; 1Ch 15:24; ver. 9 **11** Nu 9:17 **12** Ex 40:36; Nu 2:9,16; Ex 19:1; Nu 1:1; 9:5; Ge 21:21; Nu 12:16; 13:3,26 **13** ver. 5,6

14 The standard of the camp of the sons of Judah, according to their armies, moved out first, Nahshon the son of Amminadab was [commander] over its army,

15 and Nethanel the son of Zuar was [commander] over the tribal army of the sons of Issachar;

16 and Eliab the son of Helon was [commander] over the tribal army of the sons of Zebulun.

17 Then the tabernacle was taken down; and the sons of Gershon and the sons of Merari, who were carrying the tabernacle, moved out.

18 Next the standard of the camp of the sons of Reuben, according to their armies, moved out, with Elizur the son of Shedeur [commander] over its army,

19 and Shelumiel the son of Zurishaddai was [commander] over the tribal army of the sons of Simeon,

20 and Eliasaph the son of Deuel was [commander] over the tribal army of the sons of Gad.

21 Then the Kohathites moved out, carrying the holy things, and the tabernacle was set up before they arrived.

22 Next the standard of the camp of the sons of Ephraim moved out, according to their armies, with Elishama the son of Ammihud [commander] over its army,

23 and Gamaliel the son of Pedahzur was [commander] over the tribal army of the sons of Manasseh,

24 and Abidan the son of Gideoni was [commander] over the tribal army of the sons of Benjamin.

25 Then the standard of the camp of the sons of Dan, according to their armies, which formed the rear guard for all the camps, moved out, with Ahiezer the son of Ammishaddai [commander] over its army,

26 and Pagiel the son of Ochran was [commander] over the tribal army of the sons of Asher,

27 and Ahira the son of Enan was [commander] over the tribal army of the sons of Naphtali.

28 This was the order of march of the sons of Israel by their armies as they moved out.

29 Then Moses said to Hobab the son of Reuel the Midianite, Moses' father-in-law, "We are going to the place of which the LORD said, 'I will give it to you.' Come with us, and we will be good to you, for the LORD has promised good [things] concerning Israel."

30 But Hobab [Moses' brother-in-law] said to him, "I will not go; I will return to my own land and to my family."

31 Then Moses said, "Please do not leave us, for you know how we are to camp in the wilderness, and you will serve as eyes for us [as we make our trek through the desert].

32 "So if you will go with us, it shall be that whatever good the LORD does for us, we will do *the same* for you."

33 So they set out from the mountain of the LORD (Sinai) three days' journey; and the ark of the covenant of the LORD went in front of them during the three days' journey to seek out a resting place for them.

34 The cloud of the LORD was over them by day when they set out from the camp.

35 Whenever the ark set out, Moses said,

"Rise up, O LORD!
Let Your enemies be scattered;
And let those who hate You flee
before You." [Ps 68:1, 2]

36 And when the ark rested, Moses said,

"Return, O LORD,
To the myriad (many) thousands of
Israel."

The People Complain

11 NOW THE people became like those who complain *and* whine

10:29 *Reuel.* Also called Jethro (Ex 3:1), Reuel was the priest of Midian who befriended Moses and gave his daughter Zipporah to him as his wife.

11:1 *complain.* Murmuring and complaining demonstrated a lack of trust in God's plan, provision, and judgment. Such attitudes are no

14 Nu 2:3,9; Nu 1:7 **17** Nu 1:51; Nu 4:24,31 **18** Nu 2:16 **21** Nu 4:4,15; 7:9 **22** Nu 2:24 **25** Nu 2:31; Jos 6:9 **28** Nu 2:34 **29** Ex 2:18; Ge 12:7; Jdg 1:16; Ge 32:12; Ex 3:8 **31** Job 29:15 **32** Jdg 1:16 **33** See Ex 3:1; Dt 1:33; Jos 3:3,4,6; Eze 20:6 **34** Ex 13:21; Neh 9:12,19 **35** Ps 68:1,2; 132:8 **CHAPTER 11** **1** Dt 9:22; Ps 78:21; Lev 10:2; 2Ki 1:12

about their hardships, and the LORD
heard it; and when the LORD heard it, His
anger was kindled, and the fire of the
LORD burned among them and devoured
those in the outlying parts of the camp.
2 So the people cried out to Moses,
and when Moses prayed to the LORD,
the fire died out.
3 He named that place Taberah (the
place of burning), because the fire of
the LORD burned among them.
4 The rabble among them [who fol-
lowed Israel from Egypt] had greedy
desires [for familiar and delicious
food], and the Israelites wept again and
said, "Who will give us meat to eat?
5 "We remember the fish we ate free-
ly *and* without cost in Egypt, the cu-
cumbers, melons, leeks, onions, and
garlic.
6 "But now our appetite is gone; there
is nothing at all [in the way of food] to
be seen but this manna."
7 The manna was like coriander
seed, and it looked like bdellium.
8 The people went about and gath-
ered it, and ground it in mills or beat
it in mortars, and boiled it in pots, and
made cakes with it; and it tasted like
cakes baked with fresh [olive] oil.
9 When the dew fell on the camp at
night, the manna fell with it.

The Complaint of Moses

10 Now Moses heard the people weep-
ing [in self-pity] throughout their fam-
ilies, every man at the doorway of his
tent; and the anger of the LORD blazed
hotly, and Moses regarded their be-
havior as evil.
11 So Moses said to the LORD, "Why
have You been so hard on Your ser-
vant? And why have I not found favor
in Your sight, that You have placed
the burden of all these people on me?
12 "Was it I who conceived all these
people? Was it I who brought them
forth, that You should say to me, 'Carry
them in your arms as a nurse carries
the nursing infant, to the land which
You swore to their fathers'?
13 "Where am I to get meat to give to
all these people? For they weep before
me and say, 'Give us meat, so that we
may eat.'
14 "I am not able to carry all these
people alone, because the burden is
too heavy for me.
15 "So if this is the way You are going
to deal with me, please kill me at once,
if I have found favor in your sight, and
do not let me see my wretchedness."

Seventy Elders to Assist

16 Accordingly, the LORD said to Mo-
ses, "Gather for Me seventy men from
among the elders of Israel whom you
know to be the elders of the people and
their officers; bring them to the Tent
of Meeting (tabernacle) and let them
stand there with you.
17 "Then I will come down and speak
with you there, and I will take away
some of the Spirit who is upon you,
and will put *Him* upon them; and they
shall bear the burden of the people
with you, so that you will not have to
bear it all alone.
18 "Say to the people, 'Consecrate (sep-
arate as holy) yourselves for tomorrow,

---

more pleasing to God now than they were then, although He does not discipline complainers with fire from heaven.

11:4 *rabble.* The presence of a mixed multitude, or rabble, indicates that there were people in the camp who had escaped from slavery or poverty in Egypt, but were not Israelites. They seem to have been the instigators of dissatisfaction, who made discomfort an excuse to agitate rebellion against God. God's people have always had the responsibility to keep their ears tuned to God's voice instead of the voices of the unbelievers around them.

11:10 *weeping.* Instead of thankfulness, the Israelites complained against what they had been given and asked for more. This is a serious sin (Ps 78:17), and in response God chastened them. We ought to learn from the example of the Israelites in the wilderness and make thankfulness our lifestyle (Php 4:4).

2 Jas 5:16 **4** As Ex 12:38; Ps 78:18; 1Co 10:6 **5** Ex 16:3 **6** Nu 21:5 **7** Ex 16:14,31 **8** Ex 16:31 **9** Ex 16:13,14 **10** Ps 78:21 **11** Dt 1:12 **12** Isa 40:11; Isa 49:23; 1Th 2:7; Ge 26:3; 50:24; Ex 13:5 **13** Mt 15:33; Mk 8:4 **14** Ex 18:18 **15** See 1Ki 19:4; Jnh 4:3; Rev 3:17 **16** See Ex 24:1,9; Dt 16:18 **17** ver. 25; Ex 19:20; 1Sa 10:6; 2Ki 2:15 **18** Ex 19:10; Ex 16:7; ver. 5; Ac 7:39

and you shall eat meat; for you have wept [in self-pity] in the ears of the LORD, saying, "Who will give us meat to eat? For we were well-off in Egypt." Therefore the LORD will give you meat, and you shall eat.

19'You shall eat, not one day, nor two days, nor five days, nor ten days, nor twenty days,

20but a whole month—until it comes out of your nostrils and is disgusting to you—because you have rejected *and* despised the LORD who is among you, and have wept [in self-pity] before Him, saying, "Why did we come out of Egypt?" ' " [Ps 106:13–15]

21But Moses said, "The people, among whom I am, are 600,000 [fighting men] on foot [besides all the women and children]; yet You have said, 'I will give them meat, so that they may eat it for a whole month!'

22"Should flocks and herds be slaughtered for them, to be sufficient for them? Or should all the fish of the sea be collected for them to be sufficient for them?"

23The LORD said to Moses, "Is the LORD's hand (ability, power) limited (short, inadequate)? You shall see now whether My word will come to pass for you or not." [Is 50:2]

24So Moses went out and spoke to the people the words of the LORD, and he gathered seventy men from among the elders of the people and stationed them around the Tent (tabernacle).

25Then the LORD came down in the cloud and spoke to him; and He took some of the Spirit who was upon Moses and put *Him* upon the seventy elders. When the Spirit rested upon them, they prophesied [praising God and declaring His will], but they did not do it again. [Num 11:29]

26But two men had remained in the camp; one named Eldad and the other named Medad. The Spirit rested upon them (now they were among those who had been registered, but had not gone out to the Tent), and they prophesied in the camp.

27So a young man ran and told Moses and said, "Eldad and Medad are prophesying [extolling the praises of God and declaring His will] in the camp."

28Then Joshua the son of Nun, the attendant of Moses from his youth, said, "My lord Moses, stop them!"

29But Moses said to him, "Are you jealous for my sake? Would that all the LORD's people were prophets and that the LORD would put His Spirit upon them!" [Luke 9:49, 50]

30Then Moses went back into the camp, he and the elders of Israel.

The Quail and the Plague

31Now there went forth a wind from the LORD and it brought quails from the sea, and let *them* fall [so they flew low] beside the camp, about a day's journey on this side and on the other side, all around the camp, about two cubits (three feet) *deep* on the surface of the ground.

32The people spent all that day and all night and all the next day and caught *and* gathered the quail (the one who gathered least gathered ten homers) and they spread them out for themselves around the camp [to cure them by drying].

33While the meat was still between their teeth, before it was chewed, the anger of the LORD was kindled against the people, and the LORD struck them with a very severe plague.

34So that place was named Kibroth-hattaavah (the graves of greediness), because there they buried the people

---

11:26 *Eldad . . . Medad.* These two men prophesied, even though they had not joined the other elders at the tabernacle. They were not obedient, but neither were they presumptuous, and the Lord showed that He still wanted them as leaders.

11:34 *Kibroth-hattaavah.* The place was called "Graves of Craving," for the greedy people buried there.

---

20 Ps 78:29; 106:15; Nu 21:5 **21** Ge 12:2; Ex 12:37; Nu 1:46 **22** See 2Ki 7:2 **23** Isa 50:2; 59:1; Nu 23:19; Eze 12:25 **24** ver. 16 **25** ver. 17; Nu 12:5; See 2Ki 2:15; See 1Sa 10:5,6,10; Joel 2:28; Ac 2:17,18; 1Co 14:1 **26** See 1Sa 20:26; Jer 36:5 **28** See Mk 9:38; Lk 9:49 **29** 1Co 14:5 **31** Ex 16:13; Ps 78:26-28 **32** Ex 16:36; Eze 45:11 **33** Ps 78:30,31 who had been greedy [for more than the manna that God provided them]. [1 Cor 10:1–13]

35From Kibroth-hattaavah the peo-
ple set out for Hazeroth, and they remained at Hazeroth.

The Murmuring of Miriam and Aaron

12 NOW MIRIAM and Aaron spoke against Moses because of the Cushite woman whom he had married (for he had married a Cushite woman);

2and they said, "Has the LORD really
spoken only through Moses? Has He not spoken also through us?" And the LORD heard it.

3(Now the man Moses was very
humble (gentle, kind, devoid of self-righteousness), more than any man who was on the face of the earth.)

4Suddenly the LORD said to Moses,
Aaron, and Miriam, "Come out, you three, to the Tent of Meeting (tabernacle)." And the three of them came out.

5The LORD came down in a pillar of
cloud and stood at the doorway of the tabernacle, and He called Aaron and Miriam, and they came forward.

6And He said,

"Hear now My words:
If there is a prophet among you,
I the LORD will make Myself
known to him in a vision
And I will speak to him in a
dream.
7"But it is not so with My servant
Moses;
He is entrusted *and* faithful in all
My house. [Heb 3:2, 5, 6]
8"With him I speak mouth to mouth
[directly],
Clearly *and* openly and not in
riddles;
And he beholds the form of the
LORD.
Why then were you not afraid
to speak against My servant
Moses?"

9And the anger of the LORD was kin-
dled against Miriam and Aaron, and He departed.

10But when the cloud had withdrawn
from over the tent, behold, Miriam was leprous, as *white as* snow. And Aaron turned *and* looked at Miriam, and, behold, she was leprous.

11Then Aaron said to Moses, "Oh, my
lord, I plead with you, do not account this sin to us, in which we have acted foolishly and in which we have sinned.

12"Oh, do not let her be like one dead,
already half decomposed when he comes from his mother's womb."

13So Moses cried out to the LORD,
saying, "Heal her please, O God, I plead with You!"

14But the LORD said to Moses, "If her
father had but spit in her face, would she not bear her shame for seven days? Let her be shut up outside the camp for seven days, and afterward she may return."

15So Miriam was shut up outside
the camp for seven days, and the people did not move on until Miriam was brought in again [and declared ceremonially clean from her leprosy].

16Afterward the people moved on
from Hazeroth and camped in the Wilderness of Paran.

11:35 *Hazeroth*. This place of rest is called "Enclosures."

12:5 *The LORD came down*. The language of this verse is more directly physical than usual. God came down, stood, and then called Aaron and Miriam forward. God's presence had been in the camp, but this was apparently distinctly more direct.

12:8 *mouth to mouth [directly], Clearly and openly*. Sometimes referred to as "face to face," these verses speak of the completely intimate relationship that God had with Moses.

12:16 *the Wilderness of Paran*. Paran had been the destination of the people since they set out from Mount Sinai. The journey had been marred by discontent, complaining, and rebellion.

---

35 Nu 33:17 **CHAPTER 12** **1** Ex 2:21 **2** Ex 15:20; Mic 6:4; Ge 29:33; Nu 11:1; 2Ki 19:4; Isa 37:4; Eze 35:12,13 **4** Ps 76:9 **5** Nu 11:25; 16:19 **6** Ge 46:2; Job 33:15; Eze 1:1; Da 8:2; 10:8,16; Lk 1:11; Ac 10:11,17; 22:17,18; Ge 31:10; 1Ki 3:5; Mt 1:20 **7** Ps 105:26; Heb 3:2,5; 1Ti 3:11 **8** Ex 33:11; Dt 34:10; 1Co 13:12; Ex 33:19; 2Pe 2:10; Jude 8 **10** Dt 24:9; 2Ki 5:27; 15:5; 2Ch 26:19,20 **11** 2Sa 24:10; Pr 30:32 **12** Ps 88:4 **14** Lev 13:46; Nu 5:2,3 **15** Dt 24:9; 2Ch 26:20,21 **16** Nu 11:35; 33:18

Spies View the Land

13 THEN THE LORD spoke to Moses, saying,

2 “Send men to spy out the land of Canaan, which I am going to give to the sons of Israel. From each of their fathers’ tribes you shall send a man, every one a leader among them.”

3 So Moses sent spies from the Wilderness of Paran at the command of the LORD, all of them men who were heads of the Israelites.

4 These were their names: from the tribe of Reuben, Shammua the son of Zaccur;

5 from the tribe of Simeon, Shaphat the son of Hori;

6 from the tribe of Judah, Caleb the son of Jephunneh;

7 from the tribe of Issachar, Igal the son of Joseph;

8 from the tribe of Ephraim, Hoshea [that is, Joshua] the son of Nun;

9 from the tribe of Benjamin, Palti the son of Raphu;

10 from the tribe of Zebulun, Gaddiel the son of Sodi;

11 from the tribe of Joseph, that is, of the tribe of Manasseh, Gaddi the son of Susi;

12 from the tribe of Dan, Ammiel the son of Gemalli;

13 from the tribe of Asher, Sethur the son of Michael;

14 from the tribe of Naphtali, Nahbi the son of Vophsi;

15 from the tribe of Gad, Geuel the son of Machi.

16 These are the names of the men whom Moses sent to spy out the land; but Moses called Hoshea the son of Nun, Joshua (the LORD is salvation).

17 Moses sent them to spy out the land of Canaan, and said to them, “Go up this way into the Negev (the South country); then go up into the hill country.

18 “See what the land is like and whether the people who live there are strong or weak, few or many,

19 and whether the land in which they live is good or bad, and whether the cities in which they live are [open] camps or fortifications,

20 and what the land is, whether it is fat (productive) or lean, whether there is timber on it or not. Make an effort to get some of the fruit of the land.” Now the time was the time of the first ripe grapes.

21 So they went up and spied out the land from the Wilderness of Zin to Rehob [a town in Lebanon], at Lebo-hamath [in the far north].

22 When they had gone up into the Negev (the South country), they came to Hebron; and Ahiman, Sheshai, and Talmai the descendants of Anak were there. (Now Hebron was built seven years before Zoan in Egypt.)

23 Then they came to the Valley of Eshcol (cluster of grapes), and from there cut down a branch with a single cluster of grapes; and they carried it on a pole between two of them, with some of pomegranates and the figs.

24 That place was called the Valley of Eshcol (cluster of grapes) because of the cluster of grapes which the sons of Israel cut down there.

The Spies’ Reports

25 When they returned from spying out the land, at the end of forty days,

26 they came to Moses and Aaron and to all the congregation of the sons of Israel in the Wilderness of Paran at Kadesh, and brought back word to them and to all the congregation, and showed them the land’s fruit.

27 They reported to Moses and said,

13:16 *Joshua.* Hoshea means “salvation.” Joshua means “the Lord saves.” Moses may have changed Joshua’s name to emphasize that it was the Lord, not any particular leader, that they were dependent on. Jesus is another form of the name Joshua.

13:27 *flow with milk and honey.* This phrase brought visions of pleasure and plenty to the Israelites. Canaan was a good land, a land with pasture for sheep and goats, with orchards and vineyards. The orchards and beekeeping went hand in hand, and thriving orchards meant honey. This was a land that was already developed and prospering.

CHAPTER 13 **2** Nu 32:8; Dt 1:22 **3** Nu 12:16; 32:8; Dt 1:19; 9:23 **6** Nu 34:19; 1Ch 4:15; ver. 30; Nu 14:6,30; Jos 14:6,7,13,14; Jdg 1:12 **8** ver. 16 **16** ver. 8; Ex 17:9; Nu 14:6 **17** ver. 21; Jdg 1:9 **20** Neh 9:25,35; Eze 34:14; Dt 31:6,7,23 **21** Nu 34:3; Jos 15:1; Jos 19:28 **22** Jos 15:13,14; ver. 33; Jos 21:11; Ps 78:12; Isa 19:11 **23** Dt 1:24,25 **26** ver. 3; Nu 20:1; Dt 1:19; Jos 14:6 **27** Ex 3:8; Dt 1:25

“We went in to the land where you sent us; and it certainly does flow with milk and honey, and this is its fruit.

28 “But the people who live in the land are strong, and the cities are fortified (walled) and very large; moreover, we saw there the descendants of Anak [people of great stature and courage].

29 “[The people descended from] Amalek live in the land of the Negev (South country); the Hittite, the Jebusite, and the Amorite live in the hill country; and the Canaanites live by the [Dead] Sea and along the side of the Jordan.”

30 Then Caleb quieted the people before Moses, and said, “Let us go up at once and take possession of it; for we will certainly conquer it.”

31 But the men who had gone up with him said, “We are not able to go up against the people [of Canaan], for they are too strong for us.”

32 So they gave the Israelites a bad report about the land which they had spied out, saying, “The land through which we went, in spying it out, is a land that devours its inhabitants. And all the people that we saw in it are men of great stature.

33 “There we saw the Nephilim (the sons of Anak are part of the Nephilim); and we were like grasshoppers in our own sight, and so we were in their sight.”

The People Rebel

14 THEN ALL the congregation [of Israel] raised their voices and cried out, and the people wept that night.

2 All the Israelites murmured [in discontent] against Moses and Aaron; and the whole congregation said to them, “Oh that we had died in the land of Egypt! Or that we had died in this wilderness!

3 “Why is the LORD bringing us to this land [of Canaan], to fall by the sword? Our wives and children will become plunder. Would it not be better for us to return to Egypt?” [Acts 7:37–39]

4 So they said one to another, “Let us appoint a [new] leader and return to Egypt.”

5 Then Moses and Aaron fell on their faces before all the assembly of the congregation of the Israelites.

6 Joshua the son of Nun and Caleb the son of Jephunneh, who were among those who had spied out the land, tore their clothes [as a sign of grief],

7 and they spoke to all the congregation of the sons of Israel, saying, “The land through which we passed as spies is an exceedingly good land.

8 “If the LORD delights in us, then He will bring us into this land and give it to us, a land which flows with milk and honey.

9 “Only do not rebel against the LORD; and do not fear the people of the land, for they will be our prey. Their protection has been removed from them, and the LORD is with us. Do not fear them.”

10 But all the congregation said to stone Joshua and Caleb with stones. But the glory *and* brilliance of the LORD appeared at the Tent of Meeting (tabernacle) before all the sons of Israel.

Moses Pleads for the People

11 The LORD said to Moses, “How long will these people treat me disrespectfully *and* reject Me? And how long

---

14:3 *Our wives and children will become plunder.* Not only did the Israelites complain against Moses and Aaron, they dishonored God, saying that He would heartlessly bring them to a place where they would die along with their wives and children.

14:11 *How long.* This chapter records perhaps the saddest and most far reaching event in the history of Israel, surpassed only by the crucifixion of their own Messiah. The miracles performed in the exodus did not convince the Israelites of God’s trustworthiness, and the miracles of Christ did not convince the leaders of the day that He was the promised Messiah (Mt 16:1–4).

28 Dt 1:28; ver. 33 **29** Ex 17:8; Jdg 6:3 **30** See Nu 14:6,24 **31** Nu 32:9; Dt 1:28; Jos 14:8 **32** Nu 14:36,37; Am 2:9 **33** Dt 9:2; Isa 40:22; 1Sa 17:42 **CHAPTER 14** **1** Nu 11:4 **2** Ex 16:2; See ver. 28,29 **4** Neh 9:17; See Dt 17:16; Ac 7:39 **5** Nu 16:4,22 **6** Nu 13:6,8 **7** Nu 13:27 **8** Dt 10:15; 2Sa 15:25,26; 1Ki 10:9; Ps 147:11; Nu 13:27 **9** Dt 9:7,23,24; Dt 7:18; Nu 24:8; Ge 48:21; Dt 20:1,3,4; 31:6,8 **10** Ex 17:4; Ex 16:10; Lev 9:23 **11** ver. 23; Ps 95:8; Heb 3:8; Dt 9:23; Ps 78:22,32,42; Jn 12:37

will they not believe in Me, despite all
the [miraculous] signs which I have
performed among them?
12“I will strike them with the pesti-
lence (plague) and dispossess them,
and will make you into a nation greater
and mightier than they.”
13But Moses said to the LORD, “Then
the Egyptians will hear of it, for by
Your strength You brought up these
people from among them,
14and they will tell it to the inhabi-
tants of this land. They have heard that
You, LORD, are among these people [of
Israel], that You, LORD, are seen face
to face, while Your cloud stands over
them; and that You go before them in
a pillar of cloud by day and in a pillar
of fire by night.
15“Now if You kill these people as
one man, then the nations (Gentiles)
that have heard of Your fame will say,
16‘Because the LORD was not able to
bring these people into the land which
He promised to give them, therefore He
slaughtered them in the wilderness.’
17“But now, please, let the power of
the Lord be great, just as You have
declared, saying,
18‘The LORD is slow to anger, and
abundant in lovingkindness, forgiving
wickedness and transgression; but He
will by no means clear *the guilty*, vis-
iting (avenging) the wickedness *and*
guilt of the fathers on the children, to
the third and fourth *generations* [that
is, calling the children to account for
the sins of their fathers].’ [Ex 34:6, 7]
19“Please pardon the wickedness *and*
guilt of these people according to the
greatness of Your lovingkindness, just
as You have forgiven these people,
from Egypt even until now.”

The LORD Pardons and Rebukes

20So the LORD said, “I have pardoned
them according to your word;
21but indeed as I live, all the earth
will be filled with the glory of the LORD.
[Is 6:3; 11:9]
22“Surely all the men who have seen
My glory and My [miraculous] signs
which I performed in Egypt and in the
wilderness, yet have put Me to the test
these ten times and have not listened
to My voice,
23will by no means see the land
which I swore to [give to] their fa-
thers; nor will any who treated me
disrespectfully *and* rejected Me see
it. [Heb 6:4–11]
24“But My servant Caleb, because he
has a different spirit and has followed
Me fully, I will bring into the land into
which he entered, and his descendants
shall take possession of it.
25“Now the Amalekites and the Ca-
naanites live in the valley; tomorrow
turn and set out for the wilderness by
way of the Red Sea.”
26The LORD spoke to Moses and Aar-
on, saying,
27“How long *shall I put up with* this
evil congregation who murmur [in dis-
content] against Me? I have heard the
complaints of the Israelites, which they
are making against Me.
28“Say to them, ‘As I live,’ says the
LORD, ‘just what you have spoken in My
hearing I will most certainly do to you;
29your dead bodies will fall in this
wilderness, even all who were num-

14:19 *Please pardon.* This passage records the divine testing of Moses. God was not speaking lightly when He offered to smite the Israelites and start over with another group, new descendants from Moses. But Moses needed to know his own heart about the Israelites. As frustrating as they had been, they were still a living history of the mighty hand of God, and Moses did not want the story of their rescue to end with annihilation in the wilderness. Moses’ response was what God wanted to hear, and in passionately and humbly asking for their pardon, Moses had no room for bitterness toward the people who were so difficult to lead.

14:23 *will by no means see the land.* God pardoned those who turned against Him, but there was a price to pay. They would not see the land that they had complained was impossible to possess. There is often a lifelong consequence to sin, even with forgiveness.

12 Ex 32:10 **13** Ex 32:12; Eze 20:9,14 **14** Ex 15:14; Ex 13:21; Neh 9:12 **16** Dt 9:28 **18** Ex 34:6,7; Ex 20:5 **19** Ex 34:9; Ps 106:45; Ps 78:38 **20** 1Jn 5:14-16 **21** Ps 72:19 **22** Dt 1:35; Heb 3:17; Ge 31:7 **23** Nu 32:11; Eze 20:15 **24** Jos 14:6,8,9,14; Nu 32:12 **25** Dt 1:40 **27** Ex 16:28; Ex 16:12 **28** ver. 21; Dt 1:35; Heb 3:17; See ver. 2 **29** Nu 1:45; 26:64

bered of you, your entire number from twenty years old and upward, who have murmured against Me. [Heb 3:17–19]

30 ‘Except for Caleb the son of Jephunneh and Joshua the son of Nun, not one of you shall enter the land in which I swore [an oath] to settle you.

31 ‘But your children whom you said would become plunder, I will bring in, and they will know the land which you have despised *and* rejected.

32 ‘But as for you, your dead bodies will fall in this wilderness.

33 ‘Your sons shall be wanderers *and* shepherds in the wilderness for forty years, and they will suffer for your unfaithfulness (spiritual infidelity), until your corpses are consumed in the wilderness.

34 ‘According to the number of days in which you spied out the land [of Canaan], forty days, for each day, you shall bear *and* suffer a year for your sins *and* guilt, for forty years, and you shall know My displeasure [the revoking of My promise and My estrangement because of your sin].

35 ‘I, the LORD, have spoken. I will most certainly do this to all this evil congregation who are gathered together against Me. In this wilderness they shall be consumed [by war, disease, and plagues], and here they shall die.’ ” [1 Cor 10:10, 11]

36 As for the men whom Moses sent to spy out the land, and who returned and made all the congregation murmur *and* complain against him by bringing back a bad report concerning the land,

37 even those [ten] men who brought back the very bad report of the land died by a plague before the LORD. [Heb 3:17–19; Jude 5–7]

38 But Joshua the son of Nun and Caleb the son of Jephunneh remained alive out of those men who went to spy out the land.

Israel Repulsed

39 Moses spoke the Lord’s words to all the Israelites, and the people mourned greatly.

40 They got up early in the morning and went up to the ridge of the hill country, saying, “Look, here we are; we have indeed sinned, but we will go up to the place which the LORD has promised.”

41 But Moses said, “Why then are you transgressing the commandment of the LORD, when it will not succeed?

42 “Do not go up, or you will be struck down before your enemies, for the LORD is not among you.

43 “For the Amalekites and the Canaanites will be there in front of you, and you will fall by the sword, because you have turned away from following the LORD; therefore the LORD will not be with you.”

44 But [in their arrogance] they dared to go up to the ridge of the hill country; however, neither the ark of the covenant of the LORD nor Moses left the camp.

45 Then the Amalekites and the Canaanites who lived in that hill country came down and struck the Israelites and scattered them as far as Hormah.

Laws for Canaan

15 NOW THE LORD spoke to Moses, saying,

2 “Speak to the Israelites and say to them, ‘When you come into the land where you are to live, which I am giving you,

3 then make an offering by fire to the LORD, a burnt offering or a sacrifice to

---

14:45 *Hormah.* The name of this place is very apt; it means “utter destruction.”

15:2 *When you come into the land.* These words may seem inappropriate following God’s punishment for disobedience. But His overall purpose had not changed, and the children would enter the land the parents had rejected.

30 ver. 38; Dt 1:36,38 **31** Dt 1:39; Ps 106:24 **32** 1Co 10:5 **33** Nu 32:13; Ps 107:40; See Dt 2:14; Eze 23:35 **34** Nu 13:25; Ps 95:10; Eze 4:6; See 1Ki 8:56; Heb 4:1 **35** Nu 23:19; ver. 27,29; 1Co 10:5 **36** Nu 13:31,32 **37** 1Co 10:10 **38** Jos 14:6,10 **39** Ex 33:4 **40** Dt 1:41 **41** ver. 25; 2Ch 24:20 **42** Dt 1:42 **43** 2Ch 15:2 **44** Dt 1:43 **45** ver. 43; Dt 1:44; Nu 21:3; Jdg 1:17 **CHAPTER 15** **2** ver. 18; Lev 23:10; Dt 7:1 **3** Lev 1:2,3; Lev 7:16; 22:18,21; Lev 23:8,12,36; Nu 28:19,27; Dt 16:10; Ge 8:21; Ex 29:18

fulfill a special vow, or as a freewill offering or in your appointed feasts, to make a sweet *and* soothing aroma to the LORD, from the herd or from the flock.

4 “The one who presents his offering shall present to the LORD a grain offering of a tenth *of an ephah* of fine flour mixed with a fourth of a hin of oil,

5 and you shall prepare wine for the drink offering, a fourth of a hin, with the burnt offering or for the sacrifice, for each lamb.

6 ‘Or for a ram you shall prepare as a grain offering two-tenths *of an ephah* of fine flour mixed with a third of a hin of oil.

7 ‘And for the drink offering you shall offer a third of a hin of wine, as a sweet *and* soothing aroma to the LORD.

8 ‘When you prepare a bull as a burnt offering or as a sacrifice, in fulfilling a special vow or peace offering to the LORD,

9 then you shall offer with the bull a grain offering of three-tenths *of an ephah* of fine flour mixed with half a hin of oil;

10 and you shall bring as the drink offering one-half a hin of wine as an offering by fire, as a sweet *and* soothing aroma to the LORD.

11 ‘Thus shall it be done for each bull, or for each ram, or for each of the male lambs, or of the goats.

12 ‘According to the number that you prepare, so shall you do to everyone according to their number.

13 ‘All who are native-born shall do these things in this way, in presenting an offering by fire, as a sweet *and* soothing aroma to the LORD.

Law of the Stranger

14 ‘If a stranger lives as a resident alien with you, or whoever may be among you throughout your generations, and he *wishes to* make an offering by fire, as a sweet *and* soothing aroma to the LORD, just as you do, so shall he do.

15 ‘As for the assembly, there shall be one [and the same] statute for you [of the congregation] and for the stranger who is a resident alien with you, a permanent statute throughout your generations; as you are, so shall the stranger be before the LORD.

16 ‘There is to be one law and one ordinance for you and for the stranger who lives with you as a resident alien.’ ”

17 Then the LORD spoke to Moses, saying,

18 “Speak to the Israelites and say to them, ‘When you enter the land to which I am bringing you,

19 then, when you eat the food of the land, you shall lift up an offering (heave offering) to the LORD.

20 ‘You shall lift up a cake *made* of the first of your [ground grain which has been made into] dough as an offering [to the Lord]; as an offering from the threshing floor, so shall you lift it up.

21 ‘From the first of your dough (ground grain) you shall give to the LORD an offering throughout your generations.

22 ‘But when you unintentionally fail and do not observe all these commandments, which the LORD has spoken to Moses,

23 *even* all that the LORD has commanded you through Moses, from the day that the LORD gave command-

---

15:5 *wine.* The wine was poured out on the altar in an accompaniment to the burnt offering. It was another way of giving freely back to God that which the worshiper valued. Paul refers to himself as being poured out like a drink offering (2Ti 4:6). There is a sense of being finished, emptied of himself, and physically spent, as he does his final work. In the same way, the wine was emptied for God; it was used up. It was not waved, nor was a portion saved for the priests.

15:19 – 21 *lift up an offering.* By holding up the very first produce from a harvest, or the first cake made from the first grain of the season, the worshiper thanked God as the giver of all good gifts.

4 Lev 2:1; 6:14; Ex 29:40; Lev 23:13; Lev 14:10; Nu 28:5 **5** Nu 28:7,14 **6** Nu 28:12,14 **8** Lev 7:11 **9** Nu 28:12,14 **11** Nu 28 **15** ver. 29; Ex 12:49; Nu 9:14 **18** ver. 2; Dt 26:1 **19** Jos 5:11,12 **20** Dt 26:2,10; Pr 3:9,10; Lev 2:14; 23:10,16 **22** Lev 4:2

ments and onward throughout your generations,

24 then it shall be, if it was done unintentionally without the knowledge of the congregation, that all the congregation shall offer one young bull as a burnt offering, as a sweet *and* soothing aroma to the LORD, with its grain offering and its drink offering, according to the ordinance, and one male goat as a sin offering.

25 'Then the priest shall make atonement for all the congregation of the sons of Israel, and they will be forgiven, for it was an error and they have brought their offering, an offering by fire to the LORD, and their sin offering before the LORD, for their error.

26 'So all the congregation of the Israelites will be forgiven as well as the stranger who lives among them as a resident alien, because all the people were involved in the error.

27 'Also if one person sins unintentionally, then he shall offer a female goat one year old as a sin offering.

28 'The priest shall make atonement before the LORD for the person who commits an error when he sins unintentionally, making atonement for him so that he may be forgiven.

29 'You shall have one law for him who sins unintentionally, whether he is native-born among the Israelites or a stranger who is living among them as a resident alien.

30 'But the person who does [anything wrong] willfully *and* defiantly, whether he is native-born or a stranger, that one is blaspheming the LORD, and that person shall be cut off from among his people [excluding him from the atonement made for them].

31 'Because he has despised *and* rejected the word of the LORD, and has broken His commandment, that person shall be utterly cut off; [the responsibility for] his wickedness *and* guilt will be upon him.' "

Sabbath-breaking Punished

32 Now while the Israelites were in the wilderness, they found a man who was gathering wood on the Sabbath day.

33 Those who found him gathering wood brought him to Moses and Aaron and to all the congregation;

34 and they put him in custody, because it had not been explained [by God] what should be done to him.

35 Then the LORD said to Moses, "The man shall certainly be put to death. All the congregation shall stone him with stones outside the camp."

36 So all the congregation brought him outside the camp and stoned him to death with stones, just as the LORD had commanded Moses.

37 The LORD said to Moses,

38 "Speak to the sons of Israel and tell them to make for themselves tassels on the hems of their garments throughout their generations, and put a cord of blue on the tassel of each hem.

39 "It shall be a tassel for you to look at and remember all the commandments of the LORD, to do them, so that you do not follow after [the desires of] your own heart and eyes, [desires] after which you used to follow *and* play the prostitute,

40 so that you may remember to do all My commandments and be holy (set apart) to your God.

41 "I am the LORD your God, who

15:30 – 31 *willfully and defiantly.* Moses spoke of unfaithfulness when he reminded the people of their presumption at Kadesh (Dt 1:43). Their presumption was overstepping the limits of what God allowed, and doing it defiantly. If they had trusted God, they would have been happy to do things His way. Christians need to be on guard, lest they too be guilty of presumptuous sin. Consider the words of David, "Also keep back Your servant from presumptuous sins" (Ps 19:13).

15:39 *play the prostitute.* Prostitution of the heart is unfaithfulness to God, in the same way that prostitution is unfaithfulness to the sanctity of marriage.

24 Lev 4:13; ver. 8-10; See Lev 4:23 **25** Lev 4:20 **27** Lev 4:27,28 **28** Lev 4:35 **29** ver. 15 **30** Dt 17:12; Ps 19:13; Heb 10:26 **31** 2Sa 12:9; Pr 13:13; Lev 5:1; Eze 18:20 **32** Ex 31:14,15; 35:2,3 **34** Lev 24:12 **35** Ex 31:14,15; Lev 24:14; 1Ki 21:13; Ac 7:58 **38** Dt 22:12; Mt 23:5 **39** See Dt 29:19; Ps 73:27; 106:39; Jas 4:4 **40** Lev 11:44,45; Ro 12:1; Col 1:22; 1Pe 1:15,16

brought you out of the land of Egypt to
be your God. I am the LORD your God."

Korah's Rebellion

16 NOW KORAH the son of Izhar,
the son of Kohath, the son of
Levi, with Dathan and Abiram the
sons of Eliab, and On the son of Peleth,
descendants of Reuben, took *action*,
2 and they rose up [in rebellion] be-
fore Moses, together with some of the
Israelites, two hundred and fifty lead-
ers of the congregation chosen in the
assembly, men of distinction.
3 They assembled together against
Moses and Aaron, and said to them,
"You have gone far enough, for all the
congregation are holy, every one of
them, and the LORD is among them.
Why then do you exalt yourselves
above the assembly of the LORD?"
4 And when Moses heard this, he fell
face downward;
5 and he spoke to Korah and all his
company, saying, "In the morning the
LORD will show who belongs to Him,
and who is holy, and will bring him
near to Himself; the one whom He will
choose He will bring near to Himself.
[2 Tim 2:19]
6 "Do this: Take censers for your-
selves, Korah and all your company,
7 then put fire in them and place in-
cense on them in the presence of the
LORD tomorrow; and the man whom
the LORD chooses shall be the one who
is holy. You have gone far enough, you
sons of Levi."
8 Then Moses said to Korah, "Hear
now, you sons of Levi,
9 does it seem but a small thing to you
that the God of Israel has separated
you from the congregation of Israel,
to bring you near to Himself, to do the
service of the tabernacle of the LORD,
and to stand before the congregation
to minister to them;
10 and that He has brought you near
[to Him], *Korah* and all your brothers,
sons of Levi with you? Would you seek
the priesthood also?
11 "Therefore you and all your com-
pany are gathered together against the
LORD; but as for Aaron, who is he that
you murmur against him?"
12 Then Moses sent to call Dathan
and Abiram, the sons of Eliab; but they
said [defiantly], "We will not come up.
13 "Is it a small thing that you have
brought us up out of a land [of plenty]
flowing with milk and honey to kill us
in the wilderness, but you would also
lord it over us?
14 "Indeed, you have not brought
us into a land flowing with milk and
honey, nor given us an inheritance of
fields and vineyards. Will you gouge
out the eyes of these men? We will not
come up!"
15 Then Moses became very angry
and said to the LORD, "Pay no attention
to their offering! I have not taken one
donkey from them, nor have I harmed
any one of them."
16 Moses said to Korah, "You and all
your company are to appear before
the LORD tomorrow, both you and they
along with Aaron.
17 "Each of you take his censer and
put incense on it, and each of you bring
his censer before the LORD, two hun-
dred and fifty censers; also you and
Aaron *shall* each *bring* his censer."
18 So they each took his own censer
and put fire on it and laid incense on
it; and they stood at the doorway of
the Tent of Meeting (tabernacle), with
Moses and Aaron.
19 Then Korah assembled all the con-
gregation against Moses and Aaron

16:1 *Korah.* Korah was already set aside in a special position; he was a Levite. His sin was greater than jealousy of his cousins, the priests. He had set himself against God, and led others to do the same.

16:1 – 3 *they rose up.* Churches, organizations, marriages, and homes can all be affected by complaining, by rebelling against those whom God has appointed to lead. Great blessing and joy and guidance come from turning such feelings over to God and obeying Him and those whom He has designated.

CHAPTER 16 **1** Ex 6:21; Nu 26:9; 27:3; Jude 11 **2** Nu 26:9 **3** Ps 106:16; Ex 19:6; Ex 29:45; Nu 14:14; 35:34 **4** Nu 14:5; 20:6 **5** ver. 3; Lev 21:6-8,12,15; Ex 28:1; Nu 17:5; 1Sa 2:28; Eze 40:46; 44:15,16 **9** 1Sa 18:23; Isa 7:13; Nu 3:41,45; 8:14; Dt 10:8 **11** Ex 16:8 **13** Ex 2:14; Ac 7:27,35 **14** Ex 3:8; Lev 20:24 **15** Ge 4:4,5; 1Sa 12:3; Ac 20:33 **16** ver. 6,7; 1Sa 12:3,7 **19** ver. 42; Ex 16:7,10; Lev 9:6,23; Nu 14:10

at the doorway of the Tent of Meeting
(tabernacle). And the glory *and* bril-
liance of the LORD appeared to all the
congregation.
20 Then the LORD spoke to Moses and
Aaron, saying,
21 "Separate yourselves from among
this congregation, so that I may con-
sume them immediately."
22 But they fell on their faces [before
the LORD], and said, "O God, God of
the spirits of all flesh! When one man
sins, will You be angry with the entire
congregation?"
23 Then the LORD spoke to Moses,
saying,
24 "Say to the congregation, 'Get
away from around the tents of Korah,
Dathan, and Abiram.' "
25 Then Moses arose and went to
Dathan and Abiram, and the elders
of Israel followed him.
26 And he said to the congregation,
"Get away from the tents of these wick-
ed men, and touch nothing of theirs, or
you will be swept away in all their sin."
27 So they got back from around the
tents of Korah, Dathan, and Abiram;
and Dathan and Abiram came out and
stood at the doorway of their tents with
their wives and their sons and their
little children.
28 Then Moses said, "By this you shall
know that the LORD has sent me to do
all these works; for I do not act of my
own accord.
29 "If these men die the common
death of all mankind or if what hap-
pens to everyone happens to them,
then [you will know for sure that] the
LORD has not sent me.
30 "But if the LORD creates an entirely
new thing, and the ground opens its
mouth and swallows them up, along
with all that belongs to them, and they
descend alive into Sheol (the nether
world, the place of the dead), then you
will understand that these men have
spurned *and* rejected the LORD!"
31 As soon as Moses finished speak-
ing all these words, the ground under
them split open;
32 and the earth opened its mouth
and swallowed them and their house-
holds, and all the men who support-
ed Korah, with all their possessions.
[Num 26:10, 11]
33 So they and all that belonged to
them went down alive to Sheol; and
the earth closed over them, and they
perished from among the assembly.
34 All Israel who were around them
fled at their outcry, for they said, "The
earth may swallow us *also.*"
35 Fire also came forth from the LORD
and consumed the two hundred and fif-
ty men who were offering the incense.
36 Then the LORD spoke to Moses,
saying,
37 "Tell Eleazar the son of Aaron, the
priest, that he is to pick up the censers
from the midst of the blaze for they
are holy; and you scatter the burning
coals abroad.
38 "As for the censers of these people
who have sinned at the cost of their
lives, have the censers made into ham-
mered sheets as a plating for the altar
[of burnt offering], for they were pre-
sented before the LORD and they are
sacred. They shall be a [warning] sign
to the sons of Israel."
39 So Eleazar the priest took the
bronze censers which the Levites who
were burned had offered, and they
were hammered out [into broad sheets]

16:24 *Get away.* The Lord was giving the people a chance to show to whom they really had allegiance: God, or Korah and his followers.

16:32 *all the men who supported Korah.* The whole families of Dathan and Abiram were swallowed up, but some of Korah's descendants did not follow him, and were not destroyed. Some of them contributed a considerable number of psalms (see Ps 42). God is always merciful, even when dealing with the flagrant troublemakers.

16:37 *pick up the censers.* Just as He spared the relatives of Korah who were not in rebellion, so, also, did He save the censers. They were holy because they had been dedicated to God, but they would not be used as incense burners again.

---

21 ver. 45; See Ge 19:17,22; Jer 51:6; ver. 45; Ex 32:10; 33:5 **22** ver. 45; Nu 14:5; Nu 27:16; Job 12:10; Ecc 12:7; Heb 12:9 **26** Ge 19:12,14 **28** Ex 3:12; Jn 5:36; Nu 24:13; Eze 13:17; Jn 5:30; 6:38 **29** Ex 20:5; 32:34; Job 35:15 **30** Job 31:3; Isa 28:21; ver. 33; Ps 55:15 **31** Nu 26:10; 27:3; Dt 11:6; Ps 106:17 **32** See ver. 17; Nu 26:11; 1Ch 6:22,37 **35** Lev 10:2; Nu 11:1; Ps 106:18; ver. 17 **37** See Lev 27:28 **38** Pr 20:2; Hab 2:10; Nu 17:10; 26:10; Eze 14:8

as a plating for the [bronze] altar [of burnt offering],

40 as a reminder to the sons of Israel so that no layman—that is, one who is not of the descendants of Aaron should approach to offer incense before the LORD; so that he will not become like Korah and as his company—just as the LORD had said to him through Moses.

Murmuring and Plague

41 But on the next day the entire congregation of the Israelites murmured against Moses and Aaron, saying, "You have caused the death of the people of the LORD."

42 When the congregation was assembled against Moses and Aaron, they turned *and* looked at the Tent of Meeting (tabernacle), and behold, the cloud covered it and the glory *and* brilliance of the LORD appeared.

43 Then Moses and Aaron came to the front of the Tent of Meeting (tabernacle),

44 and the LORD spoke to Moses saying,

45 "Get away from among this congregation, so that I may consume them immediately." Then Moses and Aaron fell on their faces [in silence before the LORD].

46 Moses said to Aaron, "Take a censer and put fire in it from the altar and lay incense on it; then bring it quickly to the congregation and make atonement for them, for wrath has gone forth from the LORD; the plague has begun!"

47 So Aaron took the burning censer as Moses commanded, and ran into the midst of the assembly; and behold, the plague had [already] begun among the people; and he put on the incense and made atonement for the people.

48 He stood between the dead and the living, so that the plague was brought to an end.

49 But those who died in the plague were 14,700, besides those who died because of Korah.

50 Then Aaron returned to Moses at the doorway of the Tent of Meeting (tabernacle), for the plague had been brought to an end.

Aaron's Rod Buds

17 THEN THE LORD spoke to Moses, saying,

2 "Speak to the sons of Israel and get rods from them, a rod for each father's household, from all their leaders according to their fathers' households, twelve rods. Write every man's name on his rod,

3 and write Aaron's name on the rod of Levi [his ancestor]; for there is one rod for the head of each of their fathers' households.

4 "You shall then deposit them in the Tent of Meeting (tabernacle) in front of [the ark of] the Testimony, where I meet with you.

5 "It shall be that the rod of the man whom I choose will bud, and I will no longer hear the constant grumblings of the Israelites, who are grumbling against you."

6 So Moses spoke to the Israelites, and each of their leaders gave him a rod, one for each leader according to their fathers' households, twelve rods, and the rod of Aaron was among their rods.

7 So Moses deposited the rods before the LORD in the Tent of the Testimony (tabernacle).

8 Now on the next day Moses went into the Tent of the Testimony, and

---

16:41 *murmured against Moses and Aaron.* Incredibly, even after watching the dramatic destruction of the rebels, the congregation blamed the very leaders who had pleaded for the Lord to spare the rest of the congregation (v. 20). Obviously the people still strongly identified with Korah and his followers, and did not comprehend what they had just witnessed. Witnessing the destructiveness of sin does not always make people wake up and change their ways.

16:48 *He stood between the dead and the living.* Aaron stood between the living and the dead to stop the plague—just like the Savior, who stands in the gap between life and death.

40 Nu 3:10; 2Ch 26:18 **41** Nu 14:2; Ps 106:25 **42** Ex 40:34; ver. 19; Nu 20:6 **45** ver. 21,24; ver. 22; Nu 20:6 **46** Lev 10:6; Nu 8:19; 11:33; 1Ch 27:24 **48** Nu 25:8; Ps 106:30 **CHAPTER 17** **4** Ex 25:22; 29:42,43; 30:36 **5** Nu 16:5; Nu 16:11 **7** Ex 38:21; Nu 18:2; Ac 7:44

the rod of Aaron of the tribe of Levi had sprouted and put out buds and produced blossoms and yielded [ripe] almonds.

[9]Moses brought out all the rods from the presence of LORD to all the Israelites; and they looked, and each man took his rod.

[10]But the LORD said to Moses, "Put Aaron's rod back before the Testimony [in the ark], to be kept as a [warning] sign for the rebellious *and* contentious, so that you may put an end to their murmurings [of discontent] against Me, so that they do not die."

[11]And Moses did so; just as the LORD had commanded him, so he did.

[12]The sons of Israel said to Moses, "Look, we perish, we are doomed, all doomed!

[13]"Everyone who approaches, who approaches the tabernacle of the LORD, must die. Are we to perish completely?"

Duties of Levites

18 SO THE LORD said to Aaron, "You and your sons and your father's household (family) with you shall bear the guilt in connection with the sanctuary [that is, through your service as priests you will atone for the offenses which the people unknowingly commit when brought into contact with the manifestations of God's presence]; and you and your sons with you shall bear the guilt in connection with your priesthood [that is, your own unintentional offenses].

[2]"But bring with you also your brothers, the tribe of Levi, the tribe of your father (ancestor), so that they may join with you and serve you [as assistants], while you and your sons with you are before the Tent of the Testimony [the Holy Place where only priests may go, and the Most Holy Place which only the high priest may enter].

[3]"And the Levites shall attend to your duty [as assistants] and to the duties of all the tent (tabernacle); only they shall not approach the articles of the sanctuary and the altar, or both they and you will die.

[4]"They shall join you and attend to the duties of the Tent of Meeting—all the service of the tent—and no stranger [no layman, anyone who is not a Levite] may approach you [and your sons].

[5]"So you shall attend to the duties of the sanctuary and the duties of the altar [of burnt offering and the altar of incense], so that there will no longer be wrath on the Israelites [as with Korah, Dathan, and Abiram]. [Num 16:42–50]

[6]"Behold, I Myself have taken your fellow Levites from among the sons of Israel; they are a gift to you, given (dedicated) to the LORD, to do the service for the Tent of Meeting (tabernacle).

[7]"Therefore you and your sons with you shall attend to your priesthood for everything concerning the altar [of burnt offering and the altar of incense] and [of the Holy of Holies] within the veil, and you are to serve. I am giving you the priesthood as a bestowed service, but the stranger (outsider, layman) who approaches shall be put to death." [Ex 40:18, 20, 26]

17:12 *we perish.* The Israelites were overshadowed by despondency. Aware of God's righteous judgments against their constant grumbling, they were gripped by fear. They knew they were guilty, they knew that God would punish them, and the warm light of peace had left their lives. When this happens, let us remember that there is still one way back into the sunshine. Repentance leads to the happy experience of the remission of sins and peace with God (Lk 24:47).

17:13 *Are we to perish completely?* Finally the people realized that God had revealed His will through His miraculous actions among them. They suddenly saw their presumption and God's opinion of it.

18:1 *bear the guilt in connection with the sanctuary . . . priesthood.* The priests stood as intermediaries between God and man. If the people had no advocate before the Lord, they would die in their offenses. The priests had a formidable responsibility, for if they did not do their job, the whole community suffered.

10 Heb 9:4; Nu 16:38; ver. 5 **13** Nu 1:51,53; 18:4,7 **CHAPTER 18** **1** Nu 17:13; Ex 28:38 **2** See Ge 29:34; Nu 3:6,7; Nu 3:10 **3** Nu 3:25,31,36; Nu 16:40; Nu 4:15 **4** Nu 3:10 **5** Ex 27:21; 30:7; Lev 24:3; Nu 8:2; Nu 16:46 **6** Nu 3:12,45; Nu 3:9; 8:19 **7** ver. 5; Nu 3:10; Heb 9:3,6

The Priests' Portion

[8]Then the LORD spoke to Aaron,
"Now behold, I [the LORD] have en-
trusted you with My heave offerings,
even all the holy gifts of the Israelites,
I have given them to you as a portion,
and to your sons as a continual allot-
ment. [Lev 7:35]
[9]"This shall be yours of the most
holy things, [reserved] from the fire:
every offering of the people, every
grain offering and sin offering and
guilt offering, which they shall render
(give) to Me, shall be most holy for you
and for your sons.
[10]"You shall eat it as the most holy
thing; every male [of your family]
shall eat it. It shall be holy to you.
[Lev 22:10–16]
[11]"This also is yours: the heave offer-
ing of their gift, including all the wave
offerings of the Israelites. I have given
them to you and to your sons and to
your daughters with you as a continual
allotment; everyone in your household
who is [ceremonially] clean may eat it.
[12]"All the best of the fresh [olive] oil,
and all the best of the new wine and
of the grain, the first fruits of those
which they give to the LORD, I give
them to you.
[13]"The first ripe fruits of all that is
in the land, which they bring to the
LORD, shall be yours; everyone in your
household who is [ceremonially] clean
may eat it.
[14]"Every devoted thing in Israel
[everything that has been promised to
the Lord with an oath] shall be yours.
[15]"Every firstborn of the womb of
all flesh, whether it is man or animal,
which they bring to the LORD, shall be
yours; nevertheless, the firstborn of
man you shall most certainly redeem,
and the firstborn of unclean animals
you shall redeem.
[16]"And their redemption price, from
a month old you shall redeem, accord-
ing to your valuation, for the [fixed]
price of five shekels in silver, in accor-
dance with the shekel of the sanctuary,
which is twenty gerahs.
[17]"But the firstborn of a cow or of
a sheep or of a goat you shall not re-
deem; they are holy [and belong to the
LORD]. You shall sprinkle their blood
on the altar and shall offer up their fat
in smoke as an offering by fire, for a
sweet *and* soothing aroma to the LORD.
[18]"Their meat shall be yours, like the
breast of a wave offering and like the
right thigh.
[19]"All the offerings of the holy things,
which the Israelites offer to the LORD I
have given to you and to your sons and
your daughters with you as a continual
allotment. It is an everlasting covenant
of salt [that cannot be dissolved or vi-
olated] before the LORD to you and to
your descendants with you."
[20]Then the LORD said to Aaron, "You
shall have no inheritance in the land
[of the Israelites], nor have any portion
[of land] among them. I am your por-
tion and your inheritance among the
children of Israel.
[21]"Behold, I have given the Levites all
the tithe in Israel as an inheritance, in
return for their service which they per-
form, the service of the Tent of Meeting
(tabernacle).
[22]"The Israelites shall never again
approach the Tent of Meeting [the cov-
ered sanctuary, the Holy Place, and the
Holy of Holies], or they [who do] will
incur sin and die.
[23]"Only the Levites shall perform the
service of the Tent of Meeting (taberna-
cle), and they shall bear their iniquity;
it shall be a statute forever throughout
your generations, that the Levites shall

18:19 *continual allotment*. The priests lived off the produce of the land as God provided for them through the gifts of His people. Instead of inheriting land, God was their inheritance. They would be well supplied as long as the people were faithful, and this would be a good incentive to the priests to be responsible.

8 Lev 6:16,18; 7:6,32; Nu 5:9; Ex 29:29; 40:13,15 **9** Lev 2:2,3; 10:12,13; Lev 6:25,26; Lev 7:7 **10** Lev 6:16,26 **11** Ex 29:27,28; Lev 22:2,3 **12** Ex 23:19; Neh 10:35,36; Ex 22:29 **13** Ex 23:19; Lev 2:14; Dt 26:2 **14** Lev 27:28 **15** Ex 13:2; Lev 27:26; Nu 3:13; Ex 13:13 **16** Lev 27:6; Ex 30:13 **17** Dt 15:19; Lev 3:2,5 **18** Ex 29:26,28 **19** Lev 2:13; 2Ch 13:5 **20** Dt 10:9; 12:12; 14:27,29; 18:1,2; Jos 13:14,33; 14:3; 18:7; Eze 44:28 **21** ver. 24,26; Lev 27:30,32; Neh 10:37; 12:44; Heb 7:5,8,9; Nu 3:7,8 **22** Nu 1:51; Lev 22:9 **23** Nu 3:7

have no inheritance [of land] among
the children of Israel.
24"But the tithe of the Israelites,
which they present as an offering to
the LORD, I have given to the Levites as
an inheritance; therefore I have said to
them, 'They shall have no inheritance
among the children of Israel.' "
25Then the LORD spoke to Moses,
saying,
26"Moreover, you shall speak to the
Levites and say to them, 'When you
take from the Israelites the tithe which
I have given to you from them as your
inheritance, then you shall present an
offering from it to the LORD, a tithe of
the tithe [paid by the people].
27'Your offering shall be credited to
you as the grain from the threshing
floor or as the full produce from the
wine vat.
28'Likewise you shall also present
an offering to the LORD from all your
tithes, which you receive from the Is-
raelites; and from it you shall give the
LORD's offering to Aaron the priest.
29'Out of all your gifts, you shall
present every offering due to the LORD,
from all the best of it, *even* the sacred
part from them.'
30"Therefore you shall say to them,
'When you have offered the best from
it, then *the rest* shall be credited to the
Levites as the product of the threshing
floor, and as the product of the wine
vat.
31'You may eat it anywhere, you and
[the members of] your households, for
it is your compensation in return for
your service in the Tent of Meeting
(tabernacle).
32'You will bear no sin because of it
when you have offered the best of it;
but you shall not profane the sacred
gifts of the children of Israel, or you
will die [because of it].' "

Ordinance of the Red Heifer

19 THEN THE LORD spoke to Moses
and Aaron, saying,
2"This is the statute of the law which
the LORD has commanded: 'Tell the
Israelites to bring you an unblemished
red heifer in which there is no defect
and on which a yoke has never been
placed.
3'You shall give it to Eleazar the
priest, and it shall be brought outside
the camp and be slaughtered in his
presence.
4'Next Eleazar the priest shall take
some of its blood with his finger and
sprinkle some of it toward the front of
the Tent of Meeting (tabernacle) seven
times.
5'Then the heifer shall be burned in
his sight; its skin, its flesh, its blood,
and its waste, shall be burned (reduced
to ash).
6'The priest shall take cedar wood
and hyssop and scarlet [material] and
cast them into the midst of the burning
heifer.
7'Then the priest shall wash his
clothes and bathe his body in water;
and afterward come into the camp,
but he shall be [ceremonially] unclean
until evening.
8'The one who burns the heifer shall
wash his clothes and bathe his body
in water, and shall be unclean until
evening.
9'Now a man who is [ceremonially]
clean shall collect the ashes of the heif-
er and deposit them outside the camp

19:2 *red heifer.* The animal sacrificed for making the waters of purification was different than sacrifices for sins or thanksgivings. It was a female, not a male, its color was specified, it was killed outside the camp, and cedar and hyssop, used in purification ceremonies, were added to the burning heifer.
19:9 *water to remove impurity.* It is not that this water was "magic," but it was prepared in obedience to God's commands, and was an outward symbol of the inner work that God does to remove impurity. It is important to recognize that the rituals and celebrations were designed by God to create an awareness in His people of their spiritual needs, and ultimately to prepare them for Christ. All of the washings and sacrifices were still powerless to change hearts. That is a spiritual work done by God alone.

26 Neh 10:38 **30** ver. 27 **31** Mt 10:10; Lk 10:7; 1Co 9:13; 1Ti 5:18 **32** Lev 19:8; 22:16; Lev 22:2,15
CHAPTER 19 **2** Dt 21:3; 1Sa 6:7 **3** Lev 4:12,21; 16:27; Heb 13:11 **4** Lev 4:6; 16:14,19; Heb 9:13 **5** Ex 29:14; Lev 4:11,12 **6** Lev 14:4,6,49 **7** Lev 11:25; 15:5 **9** Heb 9:13; ver. 13,20,21

in a clean place, and the congregation of the Israelites shall keep it for water to remove impurity; it is [to be used for] purification from sin.

10 'The one who gathers the ashes of the heifer shall wash his clothes, and be unclean until evening. This shall be a perpetual statute to the Israelites and to the stranger who lives as a resident alien among them.

11 'The one who touches the dead body of any person shall be unclean for seven days.

12 'That one shall purify himself from uncleanness with the water [made with the ashes of the burned heifer] on the third day and on the seventh day, and then he will be clean; but if he does not purify himself on the third day and on the seventh day, he will not be clean.

13 'Whoever touches a corpse, the body of anyone who has died, and does not purify himself, defiles the tabernacle of the LORD; and that person shall be cut off from Israel [that is, excluded from the atonement made for them]. Because the water for impurity was not sprinkled on him, he shall be unclean; his uncleanness is still on him.

14 'This is the law when a man dies in a tent: everyone who comes into the tent and everyone who is in the tent shall be [ceremonially] unclean for seven days.

15 'Every open container [in the tent], which has no covering tied down on it, is unclean.

16 'Also, anyone in the open field who touches one who has been killed with a sword or who has died [of natural causes], or a human bone or a grave, shall be unclean for seven days.

17 'Then for the unclean person they shall take some of the ashes of the heifer burnt for the purification from sin, and running water shall be added to them in a container.

18 'A clean person shall take hyssop and dip it in the water and sprinkle it on the tent and on all the furnishings and on the people who were there, and on the one who touched the bone or the one who was killed or the one who died [naturally] or the grave.

19 'Then the clean person shall sprinkle [the water for purification] on the unclean person on the third day and on the seventh day, and on the seventh day the unclean man shall purify himself, and wash his clothes and bathe himself in water, and shall be [ceremonially] clean at evening.

20 'But the man who is unclean and does not purify himself, that person shall be cut off from among the assembly, because he has defiled the sanctuary of the LORD. The water for purification has not been sprinkled on him; he is unclean.

21 'So it shall be a perpetual statute to them. He who sprinkles the water for impurity [on another] shall wash his clothes, and he who touches the water for impurity shall be unclean until evening.

22 'Furthermore, anything the unclean person touches shall be unclean, and anyone who touches it shall be [ceremonially] unclean until evening.' "

Death of Miriam

20 THEN THE Israelites, the whole congregation, came into the Wilderness of Zin in the first month [in the fortieth year after leaving Egypt]. And

19:20 ***does not purify himself.*** The issues of uncleanness were so serious that the one who applied the waters of purification became unclean also. Refusing to accept the need for cleansing was not just the act of an uncouth person who didn't care about germs. Every time someone dies, it is a reminder that death came into the world through sin (Ro 5:12 – 14). The ritual for cleansing was a way of addressing the fact that it was sin that made this happen: the world is not the way God created it to be, and humans are in continual need of being reconciled to their Creator.

20:1 ***in the first month.*** No year is associated with this month; most likely it is the fortieth year, the end of the sojourn in the wilderness.

11 ver. 16; Lev 21:1; Nu 5:2; 9:6,10; 31:19; La 4:14; Hag 2:13 **12** Nu 31:19 **13** Lev 15:31; ver. 9; Nu 8:7; Lev 7:20; 22:3 **15** Lev 11:32; Nu 31:20 **16** ver. 11 **17** ver. 9 **18** Ps 51:7 **19** Lev 14:9 **20** ver. 13 **22** Hag 2:13; Lev 15:5
CHAPTER 20 **1** Nu 33:36; Ex 15:20; Nu 26:59

the people lived in Kadesh. Miriam
died there and was buried there.
[2]Now there was no water for the con-
gregation, and they gathered together
against Moses and Aaron.
[3]The people contended with Moses,
and said, "If only we had perished
when our brothers perished [in the
plague] before the LORD! [Num 16:49]
[4]"Why have you brought up the as-
sembly of the LORD into this wilderness
to die here, we and our livestock?
[5]"Why have you made us come up
from Egypt, to bring us to this wretch-
ed place? It is not a place of grain or
of figs or of vines or of pomegranates,
and there is no water to drink."
[6]Then Moses and Aaron went from
the presence of the assembly to the
doorway of the Tent of Meeting (tab-
ernacle) and fell on their faces [before
the LORD in prayer]. Then the glory *and*
brilliance of the LORD appeared to them;
[7]and the LORD spoke to Moses, saying,

The Water of Meribah

[8]"Take the rod; and you and your
brother Aaron assemble the congrega-
tion and speak to the rock in front of
them, so that it will pour out its water.
In this way you shall bring water for
them out of the rock and let the con-
gregation and their livestock drink
[fresh water]."
[9]So Moses took the rod from before
the LORD, just as He had commanded
him;
[10]and Moses and Aaron gathered the
assembly before the rock. Moses said
to them, "Listen now, you rebels; must
we bring you water out of this rock?"
[11]Then Moses raised his hand [in an-
ger] and with his rod he struck the rock
twice [instead of speaking to the rock
as the LORD had commanded]. And the
water poured out abundantly, and the
congregation and their livestock drank
[fresh water].
[12]But the LORD said to Moses and
Aaron, "Because you have not believed
(trusted) Me, to treat Me as holy in the
sight of the sons of Israel, you there-
fore shall not bring this assembly into
the land which I have given them."
[Ps 106:32, 33]
[13]These are the waters of Meribah
(contention, strife), where the sons of
Israel contended with the LORD, and
He showed Himself holy among them.
[14]Moses sent messengers from
Kadesh to the king of Edom: "Thus
says your brother Israel, 'You know
all the hardship that has come upon
us [as a nation];
[15]that our fathers (ancestors) went
down to Egypt, and we lived there for
a long time, and the Egyptians treated
[both] us and our fathers badly.

20:2 *no water.* Having no water was the subject of the first crisis that the Israelites had on their journey out of Egypt (Ex 17). The same problem, forty years later, provokes the same ingratitude and anger from the people.

20:11 *struck the rock twice.* The first time God brought water from the rock, He asked Moses to strike it. This time He asked Moses to speak to it. In his anger at the Israelites' attitude, Moses spoke roughly to the Israelites and struck the rock. Even Moses could mess things up by responding in anger.

20:11,23 – 24 *because you [both] rebelled.* Up to this point, Moses' obedience had been impeccable. It may seem that his anger was so understandable that God was overly harsh in His discipline of Moses. But Moses was the only representative of God to the people. It was only with Moses that God had spoken face to face, and Moses had a grave responsibility to only communicate what God actually said. Moses' attitude was displeasing to God, and his actions went beyond what God had directed. Anger and presumption are still two quick ways to break our fellowship with God.

20:13 *Meribah.* This is the same name that was given 40 years earlier to the location of the first water crisis (Ex 17:7). The word means "contention."

20:14 *your brother Israel.* The Edomites were descendants of Jacob's brother Esau. Because of this relationship, Moses had a special basis of appeal, and for the same reason, the Israelites were not to fight the Edomites.

2 Ex 17:1; Nu 16:19,42 **3** Ex 17:2; Nu 14:2; Nu 11:1,33; 14:37; 16:32,35,49 **4** Ex 17:3 **6** Nu 14:5; 16:4,22,45; Nu 14:10 **8** Ex 17:5; Neh 9:15; Isa 43:20; 48:21 **9** Nu 17:10 **10** Ps 106:33 **11** Ex 17:6; Dt 8:15; 1Co 10:4 **12** Dt 1:37; Lev 10:3; Eze 20:41; 36:23; 1Pe 3:15 **13** Dt 33:8; Ps 106:32 **14** Jdg 11:16,17; Dt 2:4; Ob 10,12 **15** Ge 46:6; Ac 7:15; Ex 12:40; Ex 1:11; Dt 26:6; Ac 7:19

16'But when we cried out to the LORD
[for help], He heard us and sent an an-
gel and brought us out of Egypt. Now
look, we are in Kadesh, a city on the
edge of your territory.
17'Please let us pass through your
land. We will not pass through a field
or through a vineyard; we will not even
drink water from a well. We will go
along the king's highway, not turning
[off-course] to the right or to the left
until we have passed through your
territory.' "
18But [the king of] Edom said to him,
"You shall not pass through my territo-
ry, or I will come out against you with
the sword."
19Again, the Israelites said to him,
"We will go by the highway [trade
route], and if I and my livestock drink
any of your water, then I will pay for
it. Only let me pass through on foot,
nothing else."
20But the king of Edom said, "You
shall not pass through [my territory]."
And Edom came out against Israel
with many people and a strong hand.
21Thus [the king of] Edom refused to
give Israel passage through his terri-
tory, so Israel turned away from him.
22Now when they set out from
Kadesh, the Israelites, the whole con-
gregation, came to Mount Hor.

Death of Aaron

23Then the LORD spoke to Moses and
Aaron at Mount Hor, by the border of
the land of Edom, saying,
24"Aaron will be gathered to his peo-
ple [in death]; for he shall not enter the
land which I have given to the children
of Israel, because you [both] rebelled
against My command at the waters of
Meribah. [Num 20:7–12]
25"Take Aaron and Eleazar his son
and bring them up to Mount Hor;
26and strip Aaron of his garments
and put them on Eleazar his son. So
Aaron will be gathered *to his fathers*,
and will die there."
27So Moses did just as the LORD had
commanded; and they went up Mount
Hor in the sight of all the congregation.
28After Moses stripped Aaron of his
[priestly] garments and put them on
Eleazar his son, Aaron died there on
the mountain top. Then Moses and
Eleazar came down from the mountain.
29When all the congregation saw that
Aaron had died, all the house of Israel
wept (mourned) for him thirty days.

Arad Conquered

21 WHEN THE Canaanite, the king
of Arad, who lived in the Negev
(the South country) heard that Israel
was coming by the way of Atharim
[the route traveled by the spies sent out
by Moses], he fought against Israel and
took some of them captive.
2So Israel made a vow to the LORD,
and said, "If You will indeed hand over
these people to me, then I will utterly
destroy their cities."
3The LORD heard the voice of Israel
and handed over the Canaanites; then
they utterly destroyed them and their
cities. So the name of the place was
called Hormah (dedicate to destruction).
4Then they set out from Mount Hor
by the way of the [branch of the] Red
Sea [called the Gulf of Aqabah], to
go around the land of Edom; and the
people became impatient, because [of
the challenges] of the journey.
5So the people spoke against God
and against Moses, "Why have you
brought us out of Egypt to die in the
wilderness? For there is no bread, nor
is there any water, and we loathe this
miserable food."

21:5 *loathe this miserable food.* As the psalmist later observed, "How often they rebelled against Him in the wilderness and grieved Him in the desert!" (Ps 78:40). In their contempt of the food, the people were actually spurning God who had given them this food. It is a sharp reminder to believers to do all things without grumbling (Php 2:14) so the glory of the Lord will be evident to those who are watching.

16 Ex 2:23; 3:7; Ex 3:2; 14:19 **17** See Nu 21:22 **19** Dt 2:6 **20** Jdg 11:17 **21** See Dt 2:27,29; Dt 2:8; Jdg 11:18 **22** Nu 33:37; Nu 21:4 **24** Ge 25:8; Dt 32:50; ver. 12 **25** Nu 33:38; Dt 32:50 **28** Ex 29:29,30; Nu 33:38; Dt 10:6 **29** Dt 34:8 **CHAPTER 21 1** Nu 33:40; Jdg 1:16; Nu 13:21 **2** Ge 28:20; Jdg 11:30; Lev 26:25 **4** Nu 20:22; 33:41; Jdg 11:18 **5** Ps 78:19; Ex 17:3; Nu 11:6

The Bronze Serpent

6 Then the LORD sent fiery (burning)
serpents among the people; and they
bit the people, and many Israelites
died.
7 So the people came to Moses, and
said, "We have sinned, for we have
spoken against the LORD and against
you; pray to the LORD, so that He will
remove the serpents from us." So Mo-
ses prayed for the people.
8 Then the LORD said to Moses, "Make
a fiery *serpent* [of bronze] and set it on
a pole; and everyone who is bitten will
live when he looks at it."
9 So Moses made a serpent of bronze
and put it on the pole, and it happened
that if a serpent had bitten any man,
when he looked to the bronze serpent,
he lived.
10 Now the sons of Israel moved out
and camped at Oboth.
11 They journeyed on from Oboth and
camped at Iye-abarim, in the wilder-
ness facing Moab, toward the sunrise.
12 From there they set out and camped
in the Wadi Zered.
13 From there they journeyed on and
camped on the other side of [the riv-
er] Arnon, which is in the wilderness
that extends from the boundary of the
Amorites; for [the river] Arnon is the
boundary of Moab, between Moab and
the Amorites.
14 That is why it is said in the Book
of the Wars of the LORD:

"Waheb in Suphah,
And the wadis of the Arnon
[River],
15 And the slope of the wadis
That stretches toward the site of Ar
And leans to the border of Moab."

16 From there *the Israelites went on*
to Beer, that is the well where the LORD
said to Moses, "Gather the people to-
gether and I will give them water."
[John 7:37–39]
17 Then Israel sang this song,

"Spring up, O well! Sing to it,
[Rom 14:17]
18 The well which the leaders dug,
Which the nobles of the people
hollowed out
With the scepter and with their
staffs."

And from the wilderness *Israel jour-
neyed* to Mattanah,
19 and from Mattanah to Nahaliel,
and from Nahaliel to Bamoth,
20 and from Bamoth to the valley
that is in the field of Moab, to the top
of Pisgah which looks down on the
wasteland.

Two Victories

21 Then Israel sent messengers to Si-
hon, king of the Amorites, saying,
22 "Let me pass through your land; we
will not turn away [from the road] into
field or vineyard; we will not drink the
water of the wells. We will go by the
king's highway until we have crossed
your border."
23 But Sihon would not allow Israel
to pass through his border. Instead
Sihon gathered all his people together
and went out against Israel into the
wilderness, and came to Jahaz, and
he fought against Israel.
24 Then Israel struck the king of the
Amorites with the edge of the sword
and took possession of his land from

21:8 *fiery serpent . . . will live when he looks at it.* Jesus pointed to this stunning image in His dialogue with Nicodemus (Jn 3:14–15). Jesus was nailed to the cross, and those who look at it—who realize, "the cross is the price for *my* sins"—will receive eternal life. Each Israelite who looked at the bronze snake knew that the snake bites were the penalty for his own sinful attitudes. In both cases, only God has the cure.

21:21 *king of the Amorites.* The Amorites were one of the peoples that God had commissioned Israel to destroy (Ex 33:2; 34:11).

21:21–24 Saying no to God—A stubborn "no" to an innocent and reasonable request can produce a counter-reaction. It is not that it is wrong to ever say "no," but the key fault on the part of the Amorites was a hard-hearted refusal to consider a request that would cost them nothing

---

6 1Co 10:9; Dt 8:15 **7** Ps 78:34; ver. 5; Ex 8:8; 1Sa 12:19; 1Ki 13:6; Ac 8:24 **9** 2Ki 18:4; Jn 3:14,15 **10** Nu 33:43 **11** Nu 33:44 **12** Dt 2:13 **13** Nu 22:36; Jdg 11:18 **15** Dt 2:18,29 **16** Jdg 9:21 **17** Ex 15:1; Ps 105:2; 106:12 **18** Isa 33:22 **20** Nu 23:28 **21** Dt 2:26,27; Jdg 11:19 **22** Nu 20:17 **23** Dt 29:7; Dt 2:32; Jdg 11:20 **24** Dt 2:33; Jos 12:1; Neh 9:22; Ps 135:10; 136:19; Am 2:9

the Arnon to the Jabbok, as far as the Ammonites, for the boundary of the Ammonites was strong.

25 Israel took all these cities, and settled in all the cities of the Amorites, in Heshbon and in all its towns.

26 For Heshbon was the city of Sihon, king of the Amorites, who had fought against the former king of Moab and had taken all his land out of his hand, as far as the Arnon.

27 That is why those who use proverbs say,

"Come to Heshbon,
Let the city of Sihon be built and established.
28 "For fire has gone out of Heshbon,
A flame from the city of Sihon;
It devoured Ar of Moab
And the lords of the heights of the Arnon.
29 "Woe (judgment is coming) to you, Moab!
You are destroyed, O people of [the god] Chemosh!
Moab has given his sons as fugitives [that is, survivors of battle],
And his daughters into captivity
To Sihon king of the Amorites.
30 "We have shot them down [with arrows];
Heshbon is destroyed as far as Dibon,
And we have laid them waste as far as Nophah,
Which reaches to Medeba."

31 Thus Israel settled in the land of the Amorites.

32 Now Moses sent *men* to spy out Jazer, and they overthrew its villages and dispossessed the Amorites who were there.

33 Then they turned and went up by the way of Bashan; and Og the king of Bashan went out against them, he and all his people, to battle at Edrei.

34 But the LORD said to Moses, "Do not fear him, for I have handed over him and all his people and his land to you; and you shall do to him just as you did to Sihon king of the Amorites, who lived at Heshbon."

35 So the sons of Israel killed Og and his sons and all his people, until there was no survivor left to him; and they took possession of his land.

Balak Sends for Balaam

22 THE ISRAELITES journeyed, and camped in the plains of Moab, on the east side of the Jordan [River] across from Jericho.

2 And Balak [the king of Moab] the son of Zippor saw all that Israel had done to the Amorites.

3 So Moab was terrified because of the people, for they were numerous. Moab was overcome with fear because of the sons of Israel.

4 Moab said to the elders of Midian, "Now this horde will lick up all that is around us, just as the ox licks up the grass of the field." And Balak the son of Zippor was the king of Moab at that time.

5 So he sent messengers to Balaam [a famous prophet-diviner] the son of Beor at Pethor, which is by the [Euphrates] River, in the land of the descendants of his people, to call for him, saying, "There is a people who have come out of Egypt; behold, they cover

---

to grant. With God's wisdom, we need to consider our words carefully, and "if possible, as far as it depends on you, live at peace with everyone" (Ro 12:18).

21:27 – 32 *people of [the god] Chemosh.* This song begins with a recital of the earlier victory of the Amorites over the people of Moab and their god Chemosh. After defeating Sihon and the Amorites, Israel became a formidable threat to Moab. The Amorites were pointing out that the Moabites' god did not help them. Now that the Amorites had been defeated, it was clear that the God of Israel was greater than the gods of both the Moabites and the Amorites.

22:5 *Balaam.* Balak hired Balaam to destroy Israel by spiritual means. He thought that Balaam could cause Israel's "gods" to stop protecting them.

28 Jer 48:45,46; Dt 2:9,18; Isa 15:1 **29** Jdg 11:24; 1Ki 11:7,33; 2Ki 23:13; Jer 48:7,13 **30** Jer 48:18,22; Isa 15:2 **32** Nu 32:1; Jer 48:32 **33** Dt 3:1; 29:7; Jos 13:12 **34** Dt 3:2; ver. 24; Ps 135:10; 136:20 **35** Dt 3:3; 29:7; Jos 13:12; Ps 135:10 **CHAPTER 22** **1** Nu 33:48 **2** Jdg 11:25 **3** Ex 15:15 **4** Nu 31:8; Jos 13:21 **5** Dt 23:4; Jos 13:22; 24:9; Neh 13:1,2; Mic 6:5; 2Pe 2:15; Jude 11; Rev 2:14; See Nu 23:7; Dt 23:4

bered of you, your entire number
from twenty years old and upward,
who have murmured against Me.
[Heb 3:17–19]
30‘Except for Caleb the son of Je-
phunneh and Joshua the son of Nun,
not one of you shall enter the land in
which I swore [an oath] to settle you.
31‘But your children whom you said
would become plunder, I will bring in,
and they will know the land which you
have despised *and* rejected.
32‘But as for you, your dead bodies
will fall in this wilderness.
33‘Your sons shall be wanderers *and*
shepherds in the wilderness for forty
years, and they will suffer for your
unfaithfulness (spiritual infidelity),
until your corpses are consumed in
the wilderness.
34‘According to the number of days
in which you spied out the land [of
Canaan], forty days, for each day, you
shall bear *and* suffer a year for your
sins *and* guilt, for forty years, and you
shall know My displeasure [the revok-
ing of My promise and My estrange-
ment because of your sin].
35‘I, the LORD, have spoken. I will
most certainly do this to all this evil
congregation who are gathered togeth-
er against Me. In this wilderness they
shall be consumed [by war, disease,
and plagues], and here they shall die.’ ”
[1 Cor 10:10, 11]
36As for the men whom Moses sent
to spy out the land, and who returned
and made all the congregation mur-
mur *and* complain against him by
bringing back a bad report concern-
ing the land,
37even those [ten] men who brought
back the very bad report of the land
died by a plague before the LORD.
[Heb 3:17–19; Jude 5–7]
38But Joshua the son of Nun and Ca-
leb the son of Jephunneh remained
alive out of those men who went to spy
out the land.

Israel Repulsed

39Moses spoke the Lord’s words to all
the Israelites, and the people mourned
greatly.
40They got up early in the morning
and went up to the ridge of the hill
country, saying, “Look, here we are;
we have indeed sinned, but we will
go up to the place which the LORD has
promised.”
41But Moses said, “Why then are
you transgressing the commandment
of the LORD, when it will not succeed?
42“Do not go up, or you will be struck
down before your enemies, for the
LORD is not among you.
43“For the Amalekites and the Ca-
naanites will be there in front of you,
and you will fall by the sword, because
you have turned away from following
the LORD; therefore the LORD will not
be with you.”
44But [in their arrogance] they dared
to go up to the ridge of the hill coun-
try; however, neither the ark of the
covenant of the LORD nor Moses left
the camp.
45Then the Amalekites and the Ca-
naanites who lived in that hill country
came down and struck the Israelites
and scattered them as far as Hormah.

Laws for Canaan

15 NOW THE LORD spoke to Moses,
saying,
2“Speak to the Israelites and say to
them, ‘When you come into the land
where you are to live, which I am giv-
ing you,
3then make an offering by fire to the
LORD, a burnt offering or a sacrifice to

14:45 *Hormah.* The name of this place is very apt; it means “utter destruction.”
15:2 *When you come into the land.* These words may seem inappropriate following God’s punishment for disobedience. But His overall purpose had not changed, and the children would enter the land the parents had rejected.

30 ver. 38; Dt 1:36,38 **31** Dt 1:39; Ps 106:24 **32** 1Co 10:5 **33** Nu 32:13; Ps 107:40; See Dt 2:14; Eze 23:35 **34** Nu 13:25; Ps 95:10; Eze 4:6; See 1Ki 8:56; Heb 4:1 **35** Nu 23:19; ver. 27,29; 1Co 10:5 **36** Nu 13:31,32 **37** 1Co 10:10 **38** Jos 14:6,10 **39** Ex 33:4 **40** Dt 1:41 **41** ver. 25; 2Ch 24:20 **42** Dt 1:42 **43** 2Ch 15:2 **44** Dt 1:43 **45** ver. 43; Dt 1:44; Nu 21:3; Jdg 1:17 **CHAPTER 15** **2** ver. 18; Lev 23:10; Dt 7:1 **3** Lev 1:2,3; Lev 7:16; 22:18,21; Lev 23:8,12,36; Nu 28:19,27; Dt 16:10; Ge 8:21; Ex 29:18

fulfill a special vow, or as a freewill offering or in your appointed feasts, to make a sweet *and* soothing aroma to the LORD, from the herd or from the flock.

4 'The one who presents his offering shall present to the LORD a grain offering of a tenth *of an ephah* of fine flour mixed with a fourth of a hin of oil,

5 and you shall prepare wine for the drink offering, a fourth of a hin, with the burnt offering or for the sacrifice, for each lamb.

6 'Or for a ram you shall prepare as a grain offering two-tenths *of an ephah* of fine flour mixed with a third of a hin of oil.

7 'And for the drink offering you shall offer a third of a hin of wine, as a sweet *and* soothing aroma to the LORD.

8 'When you prepare a bull as a burnt offering or as a sacrifice, in fulfilling a special vow or peace offering to the LORD,

9 then you shall offer with the bull a grain offering of three-tenths *of an ephah* of fine flour mixed with half a hin of oil;

10 and you shall bring as the drink offering one-half a hin of wine as an offering by fire, as a sweet *and* soothing aroma to the LORD.

11 'Thus shall it be done for each bull, or for each ram, or for each of the male lambs, or of the goats.

12 'According to the number that you prepare, so shall you do to everyone according to their number.

13 'All who are native-born shall do these things in this way, in presenting an offering by fire, as a sweet *and* soothing aroma to the LORD.

Law of the Stranger

14 "If a stranger lives as a resident alien with you, or whoever may be among you throughout your generations, and he *wishes to* make an offering by fire, as a sweet *and* soothing aroma to the LORD, just as you do, so shall he do.

15 'As for the assembly, there shall be one [and the same] statute for you [of the congregation] and for the stranger who is a resident alien with you, a permanent statute throughout your generations; as you are, so shall the stranger be before the LORD.

16 'There is to be one law and one ordinance for you and for the stranger who lives with you as a resident alien.' "

17 Then the LORD spoke to Moses, saying,

18 "Speak to the Israelites and say to them, 'When you enter the land to which I am bringing you,

19 then, when you eat the food of the land, you shall lift up an offering (heave offering) to the LORD.

20 'You shall lift up a cake *made* of the first of your [ground grain which has been made into] dough as an offering [to the Lord]; as an offering from the threshing floor, so shall you lift it up.

21 'From the first of your dough (ground grain) you shall give to the LORD an offering throughout your generations.

22 'But when you unintentionally fail and do not observe all these commandments, which the LORD has spoken to Moses,

23 *even* all that the LORD has commanded you through Moses, from the day that the LORD gave command-

---

15:5 *wine.* The wine was poured out on the altar in an accompaniment to the burnt offering. It was another way of giving freely back to God that which the worshiper valued. Paul refers to himself as being poured out like a drink offering (2Ti 4:6). There is a sense of being finished, emptied of himself, and physically spent, as he does his *final work.* In the same way, the wine was emptied for God; it was used up. It was not waved, nor was a portion saved for the priests.

15:19 – 21 *lift up an offering.* By holding up the very first produce from a harvest, or the first cake made from the first grain of the season, the worshiper thanked God as the giver of all good gifts.

4 Lev 2:1; 6:14; Ex 29:40; Lev 23:13; Lev 14:10; Nu 28:5 **5** Nu 28:7,14 **6** Nu 28:12,14 **8** Lev 7:11 **9** Nu 28:12,14 **11** Nu 28 **15** ver. 29; Ex 12:49; Nu 9:14 **18** ver. 2; Dt 26:1 **19** Jos 5:11,12 **20** Dt 26:2,10; Pr 3:9,10; Lev 2:14; 23:10,16 **22** Lev 4:2

the surface of the land, and they are
living opposite me.
6"Now please come, curse these peo-
ple for me, for they are too powerful
for me; perhaps I will be able to de-
feat them and drive them out of the
land. For I know [your reputation] that
he whom you bless is blessed, and he
whom you curse is cursed."
7So the elders of Moab and of Midian
departed with *fees for* divination (fore-
telling) in hand; and they came to Ba-
laam and told him the words of Balak.
8Balaam said to them, "Spend the
night here and I will bring word back
to you as the LORD may speak to me."
So the leaders of Moab stayed with
Balaam [that night].
9God came to Balaam, and said,
"Who are these men with you?"
10Balaam said to God, "Balak the
son of Zippor, king of Moab, has sent
word to me:
11'Hear this, the people who came
out of Egypt cover the surface of the
land; come now, curse them for me.
Perhaps I may be able to fight against
them and drive them out.' "
12God said to Balaam, "Do not go
with them; you shall not curse the peo-
ple [of Israel], for they are blessed."
13Balaam got up in the morning, and
said to the leaders of Balak, "Go back
to your own land [of Moab], for the
LORD has refused to let me go with
you."
14The leaders of Moab arose and
went to Balak, and said, "Balaam re-
fused to come with us."
15Then Balak again sent leaders,
more numerous and [men who were]
more distinguished than the first ones.
16They came to Balaam, and said
to him, "Thus says Balak the son of
Zippor, 'I beg you, let nothing hinder
you from coming to me.
17'For I will give you a very great
honor and I will do whatever you tell
me; so please come, curse these people
[of Israel] for me.' "
18Balaam answered the servants of
Balak, "Even if Balak were to give me
his house full of silver and gold, I could
not do anything, either small or great,
contrary to the command of the LORD
my God.
19"Now please, you also stay here
tonight, and I will find out what else
the LORD will say to me."
20God came to Balaam at night and
said to him, "If the men have come to
call you, get up and go with them, but
you shall *still* do only what I tell you."
21So Balaam got up in the morning
and saddled his donkey and went with
the leaders of Moab.

The Angel and Balaam

22But God's anger was kindled be-
cause he was going, and the Angel
of the LORD took His stand in the way
as an adversary against him. Now he
was riding on his donkey, and his two
servants were with him.
23When the donkey saw the Angel of
the LORD standing in the way and His
drawn sword in His hand, the donkey
turned off the path and went into the

22:6 *whom you curse is cursed.* The reality is that God's blessing on Israel could not be tampered with. It is important to remember that the Creator God is the source of all blessing and that no evil can stand against God's blessing and protection.

22:8 *as the LORD may speak to me.* Balaam speaks of the Lord as if he were intimate with Him. No doubt he had heard of the Lord, and no doubt the Lord did give him the words to say when Balaam looked at the Israelites. But Balaam did not give the Lord God any greater place in his own life than he gave to pagan gods, as is evidenced by his subsequent actions.

22:18 *the LORD my God.* This is not a confession of faith on Balaam's part, but a bold and false claim to be a medium of Israel's "god." Balaam was motivated by greed, not by a desire to please the Lord (2Pe 2:15; Jude 11).

22:22 *But God's anger was kindled because he was going.* God had given Balaam permission to go, after he asked the second time, and yet God was angry. This is a little puzzling, but if we remember that God is not whimsical, it makes sense. God had already told Balaam "no," and when Balak's leaders came to him again, Balaam came to God again, saying in essence, "but now

---

6 Nu 23:7 **7** 1Sa 9:7,8 **8** ver. 19 **9** ver. 20; Ge 20:3 **12** Nu 23:20; Ro 11:28 **17** ver. 6 **18** Nu 24:13; 1Ki 22:14; 2Ch 18:13 **19** ver. 8 **20** ver. 9; ver. 35; Nu 23:12,26; 24:13 **22** Ex 4:24 **23** See 2Ki 6:17; Da 10:7; Ac 22:9; 2Pe 2:16; Jude 11

field; but Balaam struck the donkey to turn her back toward the path.

24 But the Angel of the LORD stood in a narrow path of the vineyards, with a [stone] wall on this side and a [stone] wall on that side.

25 When the donkey saw the Angel of the LORD, she pressed herself against the wall and crushed Balaam's foot against it, and he struck her again.

26 The Angel of the LORD went further, and stood in a narrow place where there was no room to turn, either to the right or to the left.

27 When the donkey saw the Angel of the LORD, she lay down under Balaam, so Balaam was angry and he struck the donkey [a third time] with his staff.

28 And the LORD opened the mouth of the donkey, and she said to Balaam, "What have I done to you that you have struck me these three times?"

29 Then Balaam said to the donkey, "Because you have made a mockery of me! If there had been a sword in my hand, I would have killed you by now!"

30 The donkey said to Balaam, "Am I not your donkey on which you have ridden all your life until this day? Have I ever been accustomed to do so to you?" And he said, "No."

31 Then the LORD opened Balaam's eyes, and he saw the Angel of the LORD standing in the way with His drawn sword in His hand; and he bowed his head and lay himself face down.

32 The Angel of the LORD said to him, "Why have you struck your donkey these three times? Behold, I have come out to stand against you, because your behavior was obstinate *and* contrary to Me.

33 "The donkey saw Me and turned away from Me these three times. If she had not turned away from Me, I would have certainly killed you now, and let her live."

34 Balaam said to the Angel of the LORD, "I have sinned, for I did not know that You were standing in the way against me. But now, if my going displeases You, I will turn back."

35 The Angel of the LORD said to Balaam, "Go with the men, but you shall speak only what I tell you." So Balaam went along with the leaders of Balak.

36 When Balak heard that Balaam was coming, he went out to meet him at the city of Moab, which is on the border at the Arnon [River], at the farthest end of the border.

37 Balak said to Balaam, "Did I not urgently send *word* to you to call you? Why did you not come to me [immediately]? Am I really unable to honor (pay) you?"

38 So Balaam said to Balak, "Indeed I have come to you now, but am I able to say anything at all? The word that God puts in my mouth, that I shall speak."

39 And Balaam went with Balak, and they came to Kiriath-huzoth.

40 Balak sacrificed oxen and sheep, and sent *some* to Balaam and to the leaders who were with him.

41 Then it came about in the morning that Balak took Balaam and brought him up to the high places of Baal; from there he saw a portion of the Israelites.

The Prophecies of Balaam

23 THEN BALAAM said to Balak, "Build seven altars for me here, and prepare for me seven bulls and seven rams here."

2 Balak did just as Balaam had said, and Balak and Balaam offered a bull and a ram on each altar.

3 Then Balaam said to Balak, "Stand beside your burnt offering and I will

---

there is a lot of money and power available, so let me run this by you again . . ." He was treating the Lord as if He were any little demon god, who is appealed to by money and divination rituals. Balaam did not comprehend that he was dealing with the real powerful, awesome, and almighty God, until he encountered the angel with his drawn sword. God had a plan, and He was going to use Balaam to sabotage Balak's plans in a way that would definitely communicate to Balak exactly who the Israelites' God was, and what His plan was for His people. But Balaam needed to understand that it was the Lord who was in charge, not Balaam and his divination methods.

28 2Pe 2:16 **29** Pr 12:10 **30** 2Pe 2:16 **31** See Ge 21:19; 2Ki 6:17; Lk 24:16,31; Ex 34:8 **32** 2Pe 2:14,15 **34** 1Sa 15:24,30; 26:21; 2Sa 12:13; Job 34:31,32 **35** ver. 20 **36** Ge 14:17; Nu 21:13 **37** ver. 17; Nu 24:11 **38** Nu 23:26; 24:13; 1Ki 22:14; 2Ch 18:13 **41** Dt 12:2 **CHAPTER 23** **1** ver. 29 **2** ver. 14,30 **3** ver. 15; Nu 24:1

go. Perhaps the LORD will come to meet
me; and whatever He shows me I will
tell you." So he went to a desolate hill.
4Now God met Balaam, who said to
Him, "I have prepared seven altars,
and I have offered a bull and a ram
on each altar."
5Then the LORD put a speech in Balaam's mouth, and said, "Return to
Balak, and you shall speak thus."
6Balaam returned to Balak, and behold, he was standing by his burnt sacrifice, he and all the leaders of Moab.
7Balaam took up his [first] discourse
(oracle) and said:

"Balak, the king of Moab, has
brought me from Aram (Syria),
from the mountains of the east,
[saying,]
'Come, curse [the descendants of]
Jacob for me;
And come, [violently] denounce
Israel.'
8 "How shall I curse those whom
God has not cursed?
Or how can I [violently] denounce
those the LORD has not
denounced?
9 "For from the top of the rocks I see
Israel,
And from the hills I look at him.
Behold, the people [of Israel] shall
dwell alone
And will not be reckoned among
the nations.
10 "Who can count the dust (the
descendants) of Jacob
And the number of *even* the fourth
part of Israel?
Let me die the death of the
righteous [those who are upright
and in right standing with God],
And let my end be like his!"
[Ps 37:37; Rev 14:13]

11Then Balak said to Balaam, "What
have you done to me? I brought you to
curse my enemies, but here you have
[thoroughly] blessed them instead!"
12Balaam answered, "Must I not be
obedient *and* careful to speak what the
LORD has put in my mouth?"
13Balak said to him, "Come with me,
I implore you, to another place from
where you can see them, although you
will see only the nearest and not all
of them; and curse them for me from
there."
14So he took Balaam to the field of
Zophim to the top of [Mount] Pisgah,
and built seven altars, and offered a
bull and a ram on each altar.
15Balaam said to Balak, "Stand here
beside your burnt offering while I go
to meet the LORD over there."
16Then the LORD met Balaam and put
a speech in his mouth, and said, "Go
back to Balak and you shall speak thus."
17When Balaam returned to Balak,
he was standing beside his burnt offering, and the leaders of Moab were with
him. And Balak said to him, "What has
the LORD spoken?"
18Balaam took up his [second] discourse (oracle) and said:

"Rise up, O Balak, and hear;
Listen [closely] to me, son of
Zippor.
19 "God is not a man, that He should
lie,
Nor a son of man, that He should
repent.
Has He said, and will He not do it?
Or has He spoken and will He not
make it good *and* fulfill it?
20 "Behold, I have received *His
command* to bless [Israel].
He has blessed, and I cannot
reverse it.

23:5 *the LORD put a speech in Balaam's mouth.* Even though Balaam was not a true servant of God, the words that Balaam spoke were truly God's blessing.
23:7–10 *took up his [first] discourse.* The words that Balaam spoke, however unwillingly, certainly affirmed God's providence for the nation of Israel. It is curious how the Lord used a mercenary and devious diviner to clearly speak the blessing on Israel, but that too was a part of God's providence. Balaam was claiming to speak for the Lord; the Lord would make sure that Balaam indeed spoke for Him.

4 ver. 16 **5** ver. 16; Nu 22:35; Dt 18:18; Jer 1:9 **7** ver. 18; Nu 24:3,15,23; Job 27:1; 29:1; Ps 78:2; Nu 22:6,11,17; 1Sa 17:10 **8** Isa 47:12 **9** Dt 33:28; Ex 33:16; Ezr 9:2; Eph 2:14 **10** Ge 13:16; 22:17; Ps 116:15 **11** Nu 22:11 **12** Nu 22:38 **14** ver. 1,2 **16** ver. 5; Nu 22:35 **18** Jdg 3:20 **19** 1Sa 15:29; Mal 3:6; Jas 1:17 **20** Ge 12:2; 22:17; Nu 22:12

21 "God has not observed wickedness
in Jacob [for he is forgiven],
Nor has He seen trouble in Israel.
The LORD their God is with Israel,
And the shout of their King is
among the people. [Rom 4:7, 8;
1 John 3:1, 2]
22 "God brought them out of Egypt;
They have the strength of a wild ox.
23 "For there is no enchantment *or*
omen against Jacob,
Nor is there any divination against
Israel.
At the proper time it shall be said
to Jacob
And to Israel, what has God done!
24 "Behold, a people rises up like a
lioness
And lifts itself up like a lion;
He will not lie down until he
devours the prey
And drinks the blood of the slain."

25 Then Balak said to Balaam, "Neither curse them at all nor bless them at all!"

26 But Balaam answered Balak, "Did I not say to you, 'All that the LORD speaks, that I must do?' "

27 Then Balak said to Balaam, "Please come; I will take you to another place. Perhaps it will please God to let you curse them for me from there."

28 So Balak brought Balaam to the top of [Mount] Peor, that overlooks the wasteland.

29 And Balaam said to Balak, "Build seven altars for me here, and prepare for me seven bulls and seven rams here."

30 Balak did just as Balaam had said, and offered a bull and a ram on each altar.

The Prophecy from Peor

24 WHEN BALAAM saw that it pleased the LORD to bless Israel, he did not go as he had done each time before [superstitiously] to seek omens *and* signs [in the natural world], but he set his face toward the wilderness (desert).

2 And Balaam raised his eyes and he saw Israel living *in their tents* tribe by tribe; and the Spirit of God came on him.

3 He took up his [third] discourse (oracle) and said:

"The oracle of Balaam the son of
Beor,
And the oracle of the man whose
eye is opened [at last, to see
clearly the purpose and will of
God],
4 The oracle of one who hears the
words of God,
Who sees the vision of the
Almighty,
Falling down, but having his eyes
open *and* uncovered,
5 How fair are your tents, O Jacob,
And your tabernacles, O Israel!
6 "Like valleys that stretch out,
Like gardens beside the river,
Like aloes planted by the LORD,
Like cedars beside the waters.
[Ps 1:3]
7 "Water [that is, great blessings]
will flow from his buckets,
And his offspring *will live* by
many waters,
And his king will be higher than
Agag,
And his kingdom shall be exalted.
8 "God brought Israel out of Egypt;
Israel has strength like the wild
ox;
He will devour [Gentile] nations,
his adversaries (enemies),
And will crush their bones in
pieces,
And shatter them with his arrows.
9 "He bowed down [to rest], he lies
down as a lion;
And as a lioness, who dares to
rouse him?
Blessed [of God] is he who blesses
you,
And cursed [of God] is he who
curses you." [Matt 25:40]

10 Then Balak's anger was kindled against Balaam, and he struck his

21 Ro 4:7,8; Ps 89:15 **22** Nu 24:8; Dt 33:17; Job 39:10 **23** Ps 31:19; 44:1 **24** Ge 49:9; Ge 49:27 **26** ver. 12; Nu 22:38 **27** ver. 13 **28** Nu 21:10 **29** ver. 1 **CHAPTER 24** **1** Nu 23:3,15 **2** Nu 2:2; Nu 11:25; 1Sa 10:10; 19:20,23; 2Ch 15:1 **3** Nu 23:7,18 **4** See 1Sa 19:24; Eze 1:28 **6** Ps 1:3; Jer 17:8; Ps 104:16 **7** Jer 51:13; Rev 17:1,15; 1Sa 15:9; 2Sa 5:12; 1Ch 14:2 **8** Nu 23:22; Nu 14:9; 23:24; Ps 2:9; Jer 50:17; Ps 45:5 **9** Ge 49:9; Ge 12:3 **10** Eze 21:14,17; Nu 23:11; Neh 13:2

hands together; and Balak said to Balaam, "I called you to curse my enemies, but behold, you have done nothing but bless them these three times.
11"Therefore now flee to your place!
I had intended to honor you greatly, but behold, the LORD has held you back from honor."
12Balaam said to Balak, "Did I not tell your messengers whom you had sent to me,
13'Even if Balak would give me his house full of silver and gold, I could not go beyond the command of the LORD, to do either good or bad of my own accord. What the LORD speaks, that I will speak?'
14"And now, look, I am going to my people; come, I will advise you as to what this people [Israel] will do to your people [Moab] in the days to come."
15He took up his [fourth] discourse (oracle) and said:

"The oracle of Balaam the son of
Beor,
The oracle of the man whose eye is
opened,
16The oracle of him who hears the
words of God
And knows the knowledge of the
Most High,
Who sees the vision of the
Almighty,
Falling down, but having his eyes
open *and* uncovered:
17"I see Him, but not now;
I behold Him, but not near.
A star shall come forth from [the
descendants of] Jacob,
A scepter shall rise out of [the
descendants of] Israel
And shall crush the forehead of
Moab
And destroy all the sons of Sheth.
[Matt 2:2; Rom 15:12]
18"Edom shall be [taken as] a
possession,
[Mount] Seir, Israel's enemies, also
will be a possession,
While Israel performs valiantly.
19"One from [the descendants of]
Jacob shall have dominion
And will destroy the remnant from
the city."

20Balaam looked at Amalek and took
up his [fifth] discourse (oracle) and
said:

"Amalek was the first of the
[neighboring] nations [to oppose
the Israelites after they left
Egypt],
But his end shall be destruction."

21And Balaam looked at the Kenites
and took up his [sixth] discourse (oracle) and said:

"Strong is your dwelling place,
And you set your nest in the cliff.
22"Nevertheless the Kenites will be
consumed.
How long will Asshur (Assyria)
keep you (Israel) captive?"

23Then he took up his [seventh] discourse (oracle) and said:

"Alas, who can live unless God has
ordained it?
24"But ships *shall come* from the
coast of Kittim,
And shall afflict Asshur (Assyria)
and Eber;

24:17–19 *I see Him, but not now . . . A star shall come forth from [the descendants of] Jacob.* This poetic language clearly refers to the Messiah. The pagan Balaam had a vision of the coming of the Hebrew Messiah, the Lord Jesus Christ. He was visible from afar, He was like a star, radiant and beautiful. And He is the victor over His enemies, including Moab — the nation that hired Balaam to curse Israel.

24:19 *dominion.* At this point Balaam should have repented of his involvement with Balak. It was clear that the Lord God was in control, not Balaam, and that the Lord's curses were not for hire. This should be a great encouragement to believers in our day, because we can trust in a God who has promised to bless those who trust in Him. Our God will not change His mind and forget those who have put their faith in Him.

24:22 *How long will Asshur (Assyria) keep you (Israel) captive?* Asshur is Assyria. This nation did take the rebellious Northern Kingdom of Israel captive in 772 BC.

11 Nu 22:17,37 **13** Nu 22:18 **14** Mic 6:5; Rev 2:14; Ge 49:1; Da 2:28 **17** Rev 1:7; Mt 2:2; Ge 49:10 **18** 2Sa 8:14 **19** Ge 49:10 **24** Ge 10:4; Ge 10:21,25

So they (the victors) also *will come*
to destruction."

25 Then Balaam arose and departed and returned to his place, and Balak also went on his way.

The Sin of Peor

25 ISRAEL SETTLED *and* remained in Shittim, and the people began to play the prostitute with the women of Moab [by being unfaithful to God].

2 For they invited the Israelites to the sacrifices of their gods, and the Israelites ate [food offered to idols] and bowed down to Moab's gods.

3 So Israel joined themselves to Baal of Peor [in worship]. And the anger of the LORD was kindled against Israel.

4 The LORD said to Moses, "Take all the leaders of the people [who have committed sin with the Moabites], and execute them in broad daylight before the LORD, so that the fierce anger of the LORD may turn away from Israel."

5 So Moses said to the judges of Israel, "Each one of you must kill his men who have joined themselves to Baal of Peor [in worship]."

6 Then one of the Israelites came and presented to his relatives a Midianite woman, in the sight of Moses and the whole congregation of the Israelites, while they were weeping [over God's judgment] at the doorway of the Tent of Meeting (tabernacle).

7 When Phinehas the son of Eleazar, the son of Aaron the priest, saw this, he left the congregation and took a spear in his hand,

8 and he went after the man of Israel into the tent, and pierced both of them through the body, the man of Israel and the woman. Then the plague on the Israelites stopped.

9 Nevertheless, those [Israelites] who died in the plague numbered 24,000.

The Zeal of Phinehas

10 Then the LORD spoke to Moses, saying,

11 "Phinehas the son of Eleazar, the son of Aaron the priest, has turned my wrath away from the Israelites because he was jealous with My jealousy among them, so that I did not destroy the Israelites in My jealousy.

12 "Therefore say, 'Behold, I give to Phinehas My covenant of peace.

13 'And it shall be for him and his descendants after him, a covenant of an everlasting priesthood, because he was jealous (impassioned) for [the unique honor and respect owed to] his God and made atonement for the sons of Israel.' " [Ps 106:28–31]

14 Now the name of the man of Israel who was killed with the Midianite woman was Zimri the son of Salu, a

---

25:1 – 3 *play the prostitute.* Right on the edge of the promised land the Israelites had shown unfaithfulness to God again. It was not just that they had illicit sex with women outside their nation. They had participated in the licentious worship of the Baal of Peor. Worshiping idols on the side is not just a little slip, like eating between meals. They had enough information to know how seriously offended God would be, and they just did not care. Such behavior is always likened to adultery, and this was something that God rebuked His people for repeatedly (Isa 1:21; Jer 3:1; Ezr 16; Hos 2:5).

25:1 *the women of Moab.* What the men of Moab could not do, the women were able to accomplish. They trapped the Israelite men in sexual immorality and false worship. The principle instigator of this sorry affair was none other than Balaam (31:16). Perhaps the most sobering aspect is the fact that the Moabites were descendants of Lot, through his daughter's incestuous relationship with her father, after their long sojourn in Sodom (Ge 19). Sexual perversion had a long history in this group.

25:4 – 5 *fierce anger of the LORD.* This was the most serious challenge to God's authority yet. The people had been seduced into joining the worship of Baal. And it was Baal worship that they had been sent to Canaan to eliminate.

25:7 *Phinehas the son of Eleazar.* For this decisive and courageous act, Phinehas is praised, not only in this book, but in Psalm 106:30 – 31. In the psalm, it says that this act was "credited to him for righteousness."

25 See Nu 31:8 **CHAPTER 25** **1** Nu 33:49; Jos 2:1; 1Co 10:8 **2** Jos 22:17; Hos 9:10; Ex 34:15; Ex 20:5 **3** Ps 106:29 **4** Dt 4:3; ver. 11; Dt 13:17 **5** Ex 18:21; Dt 13:6,9 **6** Joel 2:17 **7** Ps 106:30; Ex 6:25 **8** Ps 106:30 **9** Dt 4:3; 1Co 10:8 **11** Ps 106:30; Ex 20:5; Ps 78:58; Eze 16:38 **12** Mal 2:4,5 **13** See 1Ch 6:4; Ex 40:15; Ac 22:3; Ro 10:2; Heb 2:17

leader of a father's household among the Simeonites.

15 The name of the Midianite woman who was killed was Cozbi the daughter of Zur, who was the tribal head of a father's household in Midian.

16 Then the LORD spoke to Moses, saying,

17 "Provoke hostilities with the Midianites and attack them,

18 for they harass you with their tricks, the tricks with which they have deceived you in the matter [of the Baal] of Peor, and in the matter of Cozbi, the daughter of the leader of Midian, their sister, who was killed on the day of the plague because [of the Baal] of Peor."

Census of a New Generation

26 THEN IT happened after the plague that the LORD said to Moses and Eleazar the son of Aaron the priest,

2 "Take a census of all the [males in the] congregation of the sons of Israel from twenty years old and upward, by their fathers' households, all in Israel who are able to go to war."

3 So Moses and Eleazar the priest spoke with the people in the plains of Moab by the Jordan at Jericho, saying,

4 "*A census of the people shall be taken* from twenty years old and upward, just as the LORD has commanded Moses."

Now the Israelites who came out of the land of Egypt were:

5 Reuben, the firstborn of Israel (Jacob), the sons of Reuben: of Hanoch, the family of the Hanochites; of Pallu, the family of the Palluites;

6 of Hezron, the family of the Hezronites; of Carmi, the family of the Carmites.

7 These are the families (clans) of the Reubenites; and those who were numbered of them were 43,730.

8 The son of Pallu: Eliab.

9 The sons of Eliab: Nemuel and Dathan and Abiram. These are the Dathan and Abiram who were called by the congregation, who contended against Moses and Aaron in the company of Korah, when they contended against the LORD,

10 and the earth opened its mouth and swallowed them up along with Korah, when that company died, when the fire devoured two hundred and fifty men, so that they became a [warning] sign.

11 But Korah's sons did not die [because they did not participate in the rebellion].

12 The sons of Simeon according to their families: of Nemuel, the family of the Nemuelites; of Jamin, the family of the Jaminites; of Jachin, the family of the Jachinites;

13 of Zerah, the family of the Zerahites; of Shaul, the family of the Shaulites.

14 These are the families (clans) of the Simeonites, 22,200.

15 The sons of Gad according to their families: of Zephon, the family of the Zephonites; of Haggi, the family of the Haggites; of Shuni, the family of the Shunites;

16 of Ozni, the family of the Oznites; of Eri, the family of the Erites;

17 of Arod, the family of the Arodites; of Areli, the family of the Arelites.

18 These are the families (clans) of the sons of Gad according to those who were numbered, 40,500.

19 The sons of Judah were Er and Onan, but Er and Onan [were judged by God and] died in the land of Canaan. [Gen 38:7–10]

20 The sons of Judah according to their families: of Shelah, the family of the Shelanites; of Perez, the family of the Perezites; of Zerah, the family of the Zerahites.

26:2 Take a census of all the [males in the] congregation. The plague is over, the old generation has all died. This is a new beginning and a new census. Despite all the people who had died in the wilderness, the total population was not significantly different than the first census.

15 Nu 31:8; Jos 13:21 **17** Nu 31:2 **18** Nu 31:16; Rev 2:14 **CHAPTER 26** **2** Ex 30:12; 38:25,26; Nu 1:2; Nu 1:3 **3** ver. 63; Nu 22:1; 31:12; 33:48; 35:1 **4** Nu 1:1 **5** Ge 46:8; Ex 6:14; 1Ch 5:1 **9** Nu 16:1,2 **10** Nu 16:32,35; Nu 16:38; See 1Co 10:6; 2Pe 2:6 **11** Ex 6:24; 1Ch 6:22 **19** Ge 38:2; 46:12 **20** 1Ch 2:3

21 The sons of Perez: of Hezron, the family of the Hezronites; of Hamul, the family of the Hamulites.

22 These are the families (clans) of Judah according to those who were numbered, 76,500.

23 The sons of Issachar according to their families: of Tola, the family of the Tolaites; of Puvah, the family of the Punites;

24 of Jashub, the family of the Jashubites; of Shimron, the family of the Shimronites.

25 These are the families (clans) of Issachar according to those who were numbered, 64,300.

26 The sons of Zebulun according to their families: of Sered, the family of the Seredites; of Elon, the family of the Elonites; of Jahleel, the family of the Jahleelites.

27 These are the families (clans) of the Zebulunites according to those who were numbered, 60,500.

28 The sons of Joseph according to their families were Manasseh and Ephraim.

29 The sons of Manasseh: of Machir, the family of the Machirites; and Machir was the father of Gilead; of Gilead, the family of the Gileadites.

30 These are the sons of Gilead: of Iezer, the family of the Iezerites; of Helek, the family of the Helekites;

31 of Asriel, the family of the Asrielites; of Shechem, the family of the Shechemites;

32 of Shemida, the family of the Shemidaites; and of Hepher, the family of the Hepherites.

33 Zelophehad the son of Hepher had no sons, but only daughters, and the names of Zelophehad's daughters were Mahlah, Noah, Hoglah, Milcah, and Tirzah.

34 These are the families (clans) of Manasseh; and those who were numbered of them were 52,700.

35 These are the sons of Ephraim according to their families: of Shuthelah, the family of the Shuthelahites; of Becher, the family of the Becherites; of Tahan, the family of the Tahanites.

36 And these are the sons of Shuthelah: of Eran, the family of the Eranites.

37 These are the families (clans) of the sons of Ephraim according to those who were numbered, 32,500. These are the descendants of Joseph according to their families (clans).

38 The sons of Benjamin according to their families: of Bela, the family of the Belaites; of Ashbel, the family of the Ashbelites; of Ahiram, the family of the Ahiramites;

39 of Shephupham, the family of the Shuphamites; of Hupham, the family of the Huphamites.

40 The sons of Bela were Ard and Naaman: *of Ard*, the family of the Ardites; of Naaman, the family of the Naamites.

41 These are the sons of Benjamin according to their families (clans); and those who were numbered, 45,600.

42 These are the sons of Dan according to their families: of Shuham, the family of the Shuhamites. These are the families of Dan according to their families.

43 All the families (clans) of the Shuhamites according to those who were numbered, 64,400.

44 Of the sons of Asher according to their families: of Imnah, the family of the Imnites; of Ishvi, the family of the Ishvites; of Beriah, the family of the Beriites.

45 Of the sons of Beriah: of Heber, the family of the Heberites; of Malchiel, the family of the Malchielites.

46 And the name of the daughter of Asher was Serah.

47 These are the families (clans) of the sons of Asher according to those who were numbered, 53,400.

48 Of the sons of Naphtali according to their families: of Jahzeel, the family of the Jahzeelites; of Guni, the family of the Gunites;

49 of Jezer, the family of the Jezerites; of Shillem, the family of the Shillemites.

50 These are the families (clans) of Naphtali according to their families; and those who were numbered of them were 45,400.

23 Ge 46:13; 1Ch 7:1 **26** Ge 46:14 **28** Ge 46:20 **29** Jos 17:1; 1Ch 7:14,15 **33** Nu 27:1; 36:11 **38** Ge 46:21; 1Ch 7:6 **42** Ge 46:23 **44** Ge 46:17; 1Ch 7:30 **48** Ge 46:24; 1Ch 7:13

51 This was the [total] number of the
[male] Israelites, 601,730 [twenty years
old and upward who were able to go
to war].
52 And the LORD spoke to Moses, say-
ing,
53 "Among these the land shall be
divided as an inheritance according
to the number of names.
54 "To the larger *tribe* you shall give
the larger inheritance, and to the
smaller *tribe* the smaller inheritance;
each *tribe* shall be given its inheri-
tance according to its numbers.
55 "But the land shall be divided by
lot. They shall receive their inheritance
according to the names of the tribes of
their fathers (tribal ancestors).
56 "According to the [location selected
by] lot, their inheritance shall be divid-
ed between the larger and the smaller
[groups]."
57 These are those who were num-
bered of the Levites according to their
families: of Gershon, the family of the
Gershonites; of Kohath, the family of
the Kohathites; of Merari, the family
of the Merarites.
58 These are the families of Levi: the
family of the Libnites, the family of the
Hebronites, the family of the Mahlites,
the family of the Mushites, the family
of the Korahites. And Kohath was the
father of Amram.
59 The name of Amram's wife was
Jochebed, the daughter of Levi, who
was born to Levi in Egypt; and to Am-
ram she bore Aaron, Moses, and Miri-
am their sister.
60 To Aaron were born Nadab, Abihu,
Eleazar, and Ithamar.
61 But Nadab and Abihu died [in the
presence of God] when they offered
[in their ceremonial censers] strange
[unholy, unacceptable, unauthorized]
fire before the LORD. [Lev 10:1–3]
62 Those numbered of the Levites
were 23,000, every male from a month
old and upward; for they were not num-
bered among the sons of Israel, since
no inheritance [of land] was given to
them among the Israelites.
63 These are those numbered by
Moses and Eleazar the priest, who
numbered the sons of Israel [for the
second time] in the plains of Moab by
the Jordan [River] at Jericho.
64 But among these there was not a
man [left] of those numbered by Moses
and Aaron the priest, who numbered
the sons of Israel [for the first time] in
the Wilderness of Sinai.
65 For the LORD had said of them,
"They shall certainly die in the wilder-
ness." And not a man was left of them
except Caleb the son of Jephunneh and
Joshua the son of Nun.

A Law of Inheritance

27 THEN THE [five] daughters of
Zelophehad the son of Hepher,
the son of Gilead, the son of Machir,
the son of Manasseh, from the tribes of
Manasseh [who was] the son of Joseph,
approached [with a request]. These are
the names of his daughters: Mahlah,
Noah, Hoglah, Milcah, and Tirzah.
2 They stood before Moses, Eleazar
the priest, the leaders, and all the con-
gregation at the doorway of the Tent of
Meeting (tabernacle), saying,
3 "Our father died in the wilderness.
He was not among those who assem-
bled together against the LORD in the
company of Korah, but he died for
his own sin [as did all those who re-
belled at Kadesh], and he had no sons.
[Num 14:26–35]
4 "Why should the name of our father
be removed from his family because
he had no son? Give to us a possession
(land) among our father's brothers."

26:51 *This was the [total] number.* The totals of the twelve tribes are very similar. Some had increased, some had decreased. The final figure shows a slight decrease, from 603,550 to 601,730.

27:1–5 *the [five] daughters of Zelophehad.* In ancient Israel, women did not inherit land. Yet because their case made sense, Moses took the issue to the Lord.

51 See Nu 1:46 **53** Jos 11:23; 14:1 **54** Nu 33:54 **55** Nu 33:54; 34:13; Jos 11:23; 14:2 **57** Ge 46:11; Ex 6:16-19; 1Ch 6:1,16 **59** Ex 2:1,2; 6:20 **60** Nu 3:2 **61** Lev 10:1,2; Nu 3:4; 1Ch 24:2 **62** See Nu 3:39; Nu 1:49; Nu 18:20,23,24; Dt 10:9; Jos 13:14,33 **63** ver. 3 **64** Nu 1; Dt 2:14,15 **65** Nu 14:28,29; 1Co 10:5,6; Nu 14:30
CHAPTER 27 **1** Nu 26:33; 36:1,11; Jos 17:3 **3** Nu 14:35; 26:64,65; Nu 16:1,2 **4** Jos 17:4 **5** Ex 18:15,19

[5]So Moses brought their case before
the LORD.
[6]Then the LORD said to Moses,
[7]"The request of the daughters of
Zelophehad is justified. You shall
certainly give them a possession as
an inheritance among their father's
brothers, and you shall transfer their
father's inheritance to them.
[8]"Further, you shall say to the Isra-
elites, 'If a man dies and has no son,
you shall transfer his inheritance to
his daughter.
[9]'If a man has no daughter, then
you shall give his inheritance to his
brothers.
[10]'If a man has no brothers, then you
shall give his inheritance to his father's
brothers.
[11]'If his father has no brothers, then
you shall give his inheritance to his
nearest relative in his own family, and
he shall take possession of it. It shall
be a statute and ordinance to the Isra-
elites, just as the LORD has commanded
Moses.' "
[12]Then the LORD said to Moses, "Go
up to this mountain (Nebo) [in the]
Abarim [range] and look at the land I
have given to the sons of Israel.
[13]"When you have seen it, you too
will be gathered to your people [in
death], just as Aaron your brother was
gathered;
[14]because in the Wilderness of Zin,
during the strife of the congregation,
you rebelled against My command
to treat me as holy [by following My
instruction] before their eyes at the
water." (These are the waters of Mer-
ibah in Kadesh in the Wilderness of
Zin.) [Num 20:10–12]

Joshua to Succeed Moses

[15]Then Moses spoke to the LORD,
saying,
[16]"Let the LORD, the God of the spirits
of all flesh, appoint a man over the
congregation
[17]who will go out and come in before
them, and will lead them out and bring
them in, so that the congregation of
the LORD will not be as sheep without
a shepherd."
[18]The LORD said to Moses, "Take
Joshua the son of Nun, a man in whom
is the Spirit, and lay your hand on him;
[19]and have him stand before Eleazar
the priest and before the whole congre-
gation, and give him a commission in
their sight.
[20]"You shall put some of your au-
thority *and* honor on him, so that all
the congregation of the Israelites will
obey him.
[21]"He shall stand before Eleazar the
priest, who shall inquire before the
LORD for him by the judgment (deci-
sion) of the Urim. At Joshua's com-
mand the people shall go out and at
his command they shall come in, he
and all the congregation of Israel with
him."
[22]Moses did as the LORD command-
ed him. He took Joshua and had him
stand before Eleazar the priest and the
whole congregation,
[23]and Moses laid his hands on Josh-
ua and commissioned him, just as the
LORD had commanded through Moses.

27:7 *The request . . . is justified.* Justice was done to women regarding inheritance because Moses took the case to God, and His truth was used as the foundation for the decree. Only as we base our decisions in life on God's truth, as expressed in the Bible and in Jesus Himself, will we be acting in truth. Any other way can bring injustice and decisions regretted because they spring from error.

27:18 Holy Spirit—Joshua was a "man in whom is the Spirit." In the Old Testament, only a few people had the Holy Spirit. It was not until after Jesus' resurrection that the Holy Spirit indwelt every believer. The way that God speaks to the heart of man, apart from the written Word, has generally been through the quiet voice of the Holy Spirit. Joshua apparently was a man led by the voice of the Spirit of God. He is not pictured as seeing visions or being led by angels, yet his leadership was effective and faithful.

7 Nu 36:2 **11** Nu 35:29 **12** Nu 33:47; Dt 3:27; 32:49 **13** Nu 20:24,28; 31:2; Dt 10:6 **14** Nu 20:12,24; Dt 1:37; 32:51; Ps 106:32; Ex 17:7 **16** Nu 16:22; Heb 12:9 **17** Dt 31:2; 1Sa 8:20; 18:13; 2Ch 1:10; 1Ki 22:17; Zec 10:2; Mt 9:36; Mk 6:34 **18** Ge 41:38; Jdg 3:10; 1Sa 16:13,18; Dt 34:9 **19** Dt 31:7 **20** See Nu 11:17,28; Jos 1:16,17 **21** Jdg 20:18,23,26; 1Sa 23:9; 30:7; Ex 28:30; Jos 9:14; 1Sa 22:10,13,15 **23** Dt 3:28; 31:7

Laws for Offerings

28 THEN THE LORD spoke to Moses, saying,

2 “Command the Israelites and say to them, ‘You shall be careful to present at its appointed time [during the year] My offering, My food for My offerings by fire as a sweet *and* soothing aroma to Me.’

3 “You shall say to the people, ‘This is the offering by fire which you shall present to the LORD every day: two male lambs one year old without blemish as a continual burnt offering.

4 ‘You shall offer one lamb in the morning and you shall offer the other lamb at twilight,

5 also a tenth of an ephah of finely-milled flour as a grain offering, mixed with a fourth of a hin of pressed oil.

6 ‘It is a continual burnt offering which was ordained on Mount Sinai as a sweet *and* soothing aroma, an offering by fire to the LORD.

7 ‘Its drink offering shall be a fourth of a hin for each lamb, in the holy place you shall pour out a strong drink offering to the LORD.

8 ‘The other lamb you shall offer at twilight; as the grain offering of the morning and as its drink offering, you shall offer it, an offering by fire, a sweet *and* soothing aroma to the LORD.

9 ‘Then on the Sabbath day two male lambs one year old without blemish, and two-tenths [of an ephah] of fine flour mixed with oil as a grain offering, and its drink offering.

10 ‘This is the burnt offering of every Sabbath, in addition to the continual burnt offering and its drink offering.

11 ‘Then at the beginning of [each of] your months you shall present a burnt offering to the LORD: two bulls, one ram, seven male lambs one year old without blemish;

12 and three-tenths [of an ephah] of fine flour mixed with oil as a grain offering, for each bull; and two-tenths [of an ephah] of fine flour mixed with oil as a grain offering, for the one ram;

13 and a tenth [of an ephah] of fine flour mixed with oil as a grain offering for each lamb, as a burnt offering of a sweet *and* soothing aroma, an offering by fire to the LORD.

14 ‘Their drink offerings shall be half a hin of wine for a bull, and a third of a hin for a ram, and a fourth of a hin for a lamb. This is the burnt offering of each month throughout the months of the year.

15 ‘And one male goat as a sin offering to the LORD; it shall be offered with its drink offering in addition to the continual burnt offering.

16 ‘The LORD’s Passover shall be on the fourteenth day of the first month [of each year].

17 ‘There shall be a feast on the fifteenth day of this month; unleavened bread shall be eaten for seven days.

18 ‘On the first day there shall be a holy [summoned] assembly; you shall do no laborious work *that day.*

19 ‘But you shall present an offering by fire, a burnt offering to the LORD: two bulls, one ram, and seven male lambs one year old, without blemish.

20 ‘For their grain offering you shall offer fine flour mixed with oil; three-tenths [of an ephah] for the bull, and two-tenths for the ram;

21 you shall offer a tenth [of an ephah] for each of the seven male lambs;

22 and one male goat as a sin offering to make atonement for you.

23 ‘You shall present these in addition to the burnt offering of the morning, which is for a continual burnt offering.

24 ‘In this way you shall present daily, for seven days, the food of the offering by fire, a sweet *and* soothing aroma to the LORD; it shall be presented with its drink offering in addition to the continual burnt offering.

25 ‘On the seventh day you shall have a holy [summoned] assembly; you shall do no laborious work.

CHAPTER 28 **2** Lev 3:11; 21:6,8; Mal 1:7,12 **3** Ex 29:38 **5** Ex 16:36; Nu 15:4; Lev 2:1; Ex 29:40 **6** Ex 29:42; See Am 5:25 **7** Ex 29:42 **10** Eze 46:4 **11** Nu 10:10; 1Sa 20:5; 1Ch 23:31; 2Ch 2:4; Ezr 3:5; Neh 10:33; Isa 1:13,14; Eze 45:17; 46:6; Hos 2:11; Col 2:16 **12** Nu 15:4-12 **15** ver. 22; Nu 15:24 **16** Ex 12:6,18; Lev 23:5; Nu 9:3; Dt 16:1; Eze 45:21 **17** Lev 23:6 **18** Ex 12:16; Lev 23:7 **19** ver. 31; Lev 22:20; Nu 29:8; Dt 15:21 **22** ver. 15 **25** Ex 13:6; Lev 23:8

26 'Also on the day of the first fruits,
when you offer a new grain offering to
the LORD at your *Feast of* Weeks, you
shall have a holy [summoned] assem-
bly; you shall do no laborious work.
27 'You shall present the burnt offer-
ing as a sweet *and* soothing aroma to
the LORD: two young bulls, one ram,
seven male lambs one year old;
28 and their grain offering of fine
flour mixed with oil; three-tenths [of
an ephah] for each bull, two-tenths for
the one ram,
29 a tenth for each of the seven male
lambs,
30 and one male goat to make atone-
ment for you.
31 'In addition to the continual burnt
offering and its grain offering, you
shall present them with their drink of-
ferings. They shall be without blemish.

Offerings of the Seventh Month

29 'ON THE first day of the sev-
enth month, you shall have a
holy [summoned] assembly; you shall
do no laborious work. It will be for
you a day of blowing the trumpets (the
shophar, ram's horn).
2 'You shall offer a burnt offering as a
sweet *and* soothing aroma to the LORD:
one bull, one ram, and seven male
lambs one year old without blemish;
3 also their grain offering, fine flour
mixed with oil, three-tenths [of an
ephah] for the bull, two-tenths for the
ram,
4 and one-tenth [of an ephah] for each
of the seven lambs,
5 and one male goat as a sin offering
to make atonement for you.
6 '*These are* in addition to the burnt
offering of the New Moon and its grain
offering, and the continual burnt of-
fering and its grain offering, and their
drink offerings, according to the ordi-
nance for them, as a sweet *and* sooth-
ing aroma, an offering by fire to the
LORD.
7 'Then on the tenth day of this sev-
enth month you shall have a holy
[summoned] assembly [for the Day
of Atonement]; and you shall humble
yourselves; you shall not do any work.
8 'You shall present a burnt offering
to the LORD as a sweet *and* soothing
aroma: one bull, one ram, and seven
male lambs one year old, which are
without blemish;
9 and their grain offering, fine flour
mixed with oil, three-tenths [of an
ephah] for the bull, two-tenths for the
one ram,
10 a tenth [of an ephah] for each of the
seven lambs,
11 one male goat as a sin offering, in
addition to the sin offering of atone-
ment, and the continual burnt offering
and its grain offering, and their drink
offerings.
12 'Then on the fifteenth day of the
seventh month you shall have a holy

28:26 *Feast of Weeks.* The Feast of Weeks occurred 50 days after Passover and the Feast of Unleavened Bread.

29:1–40 *holy [summoned] assembly.* This chapter regulates offerings to the Lord during the three sacred festivals of the seventh month: the Feast of Trumpets, the Day of Atonement, and the Feast of Tabernacles. The Feast of Trumpets marked the beginning of Israel's civil year. It was a day of preparation for the next two celebrations. The Day of Atonement was a solemn day on which sins were confessed and special sacrifices made for the holy place, the priests, and the people. The Feast of Tabernacles was a time of rejoicing.

29:1 *a day of blowing the trumpets.* The celebration of the Feast of Trumpets involved blowing ram's horns. Later this festival became identified with the New Year festival.

29:11 *offering of atonement.* The Day of Atonement, or Yom Kippur, was regarded as the most holy day of all. Leviticus 16 describes it as a day of fasting, rather than feasting.

29:12 *Feast [of Booths] to the LORD for seven days.* The celebration of the Feast of Booths, or Tabernacles, or Succoth, included both sacrifices and eight days of "no work." In later years Israelites lived in tents or booths during this celebration, to commemorate the years that their ancestors lived in tents in the desert.

26 Ex 23:16; 34:22; Lev 23:10,15; Dt 16:10; Ac 2:1 **27** See Lev 23:18,19 **31** ver. 19 **CHAPTER 29** **1** Lev 23:24 **6** Nu 28:11; Nu 28:3; Nu 15:11,12 **7** Lev 16:29; 23:27; Ps 35:13; Isa 58:5 **8** Nu 28:19 **11** Lev 16:3,5 **12** Lev 23:34; Dt 16:13; Eze 45:25

[summoned] assembly; you shall do
no laborious work, and you shall ob-
serve a Feast [of Booths] to the LORD
for seven days.
13 'You shall present a burnt offer-
ing, an offering by fire as a sweet *and*
soothing aroma to the LORD: thirteen
bulls, two rams, and fourteen male
lambs one year old, which are without
blemish;
14 and their grain offering, fine flour
mixed with oil, three-tenths [of an
ephah] for each of the thirteen bulls,
two-tenths for each of the two rams,
15 and a tenth [of an ephah] for each
of the fourteen lambs;
16 also one male goat as a sin offer-
ing, in addition to the continual burnt
offering, its grain offering and its
drink offering.
17 'Then on the second day [of the
Feast of Booths]: twelve bulls, two
rams, fourteen male lambs one year
old without blemish,
18 with their grain offering and their
drink offerings for the bulls, the rams,
and the lambs, by their number accord-
ing to the ordinance,
19 also one male goat as a sin offer-
ing, in addition to the continual burnt
offering, its grain offering, and their
drink offerings.
20 'Then on the third day [of the Feast
of Booths]: eleven bulls, two rams,
fourteen male lambs one year old with-
out blemish,
21 with their grain offering and drink
offerings for the bulls, the rams, and
the lambs, by their number according
to the ordinance,
22 and one male goat as a sin offering,
in addition to the continual burnt of-
fering, its grain offering, and its drink
offering.
23 'Then on the fourth day [of the
Feast of Booths]: ten bulls, two rams,
and fourteen male lambs one year old
without blemish;
24 their grain offering and their drink
offerings for the bulls, the rams, and
the lambs, by their number according
to the ordinance,
25 and one male goat as a sin offer-
ing, besides the continual burnt offer-
ing, its grain offering, and its drink
offering.
26 'Then on the fifth day [of the Feast
of Booths]: nine bulls, two rams, and
fourteen male lambs one year old with-
out blemish,
27 and their grain offering and drink
offerings for the bulls, the rams, and
the lambs, by their number according
to the ordinance;
28 and one male goat as a sin offer-
ing, in addition to the continual burnt
offering, and its grain offering, and its
drink offering.
29 'Then on the sixth day [of the Feast
of Booths]: eight bulls, two rams, and
fourteen male lambs one year old with-
out blemish;
30 and their grain offering and their
drink offerings for the bulls, the rams,
and the lambs, by their number accord-
ing to the ordinance,
31 and one male goat as a sin offering,
in addition to the continual burnt of-
fering, its grain offering, and its drink
offerings.
32 'Then on the seventh day [of the
Feast of Booths]: seven bulls, two rams,
and fourteen male lambs one year old
without blemish,
33 and their grain offering and drink
offerings for the bulls, the rams, and
the lambs, by their number according
to the ordinance;
34 and one male goat as a sin offer-
ing, in addition to the continual burnt
offering, and its grain offering, and its
drink offering.
35 'On the eighth day you shall have a
solemn assembly [to mark the end of the
feast]; you shall do no laborious work.
36 'You shall present a burnt offering,
an offering by fire, as a sweet *and*
soothing aroma to the LORD: one bull,
one ram, seven male lambs one year
old without blemish;
37 their grain offering and drink of-
ferings for the bull, the ram, and the
lambs, by their number according to
the ordinance,
38 and one male goat as a sin offer-
ing, in addition to the continual burnt
offering, and its grain offering, and its
drink offering.

13 Ezr 3:4; Da 9:24; Heb 7:18,19; 8:13; 10:1-18 **18** ver. 3,4,9,10; Nu 15:12; 28:7,14 **21** ver. 18 **26** Heb 7:26; 1Pe 1:19; Rev 5:6-14 **35** Lev 23:36

39“You shall present these to the LORD
at your appointed times, in addition the
offerings you have vowed and your
freewill offerings, as your burnt offer-
ings, grain offerings, drink offerings,
and as your peace offerings.’ ”
40So Moses spoke to the Israelites in
accordance with everything that the
LORD had commanded him.

The Law of Vows

30 THEN MOSES spoke to the lead-
ers of the tribes of the Israelites,
saying, “This is the thing which the
LORD has commanded:
2“If a man makes a vow to the LORD
or swears an oath to bind himself with
a pledge [of abstinence], he shall not
break (violate, profane) his word; he
shall do according to all that proceeds
out of his mouth.
3“Also if a woman makes a vow to
the LORD and binds herself by a pledge
[of abstinence], while *living* in her fa-
ther’s house in her youth,
4and her father hears her vow and
her pledge by which she has bound
herself, and he offers no objection,
then all her vows shall stand and every
pledge by which she has bound herself
shall stand.
5“But if her father disapproves of
her [making her vow] on the day that
he hears about it, none of her vows or
her pledges by which she has bound
herself shall stand; and the LORD will
forgive her because her father has dis-
approved of her [making the vow].
6“But if she marries while under her
vows or if she has bound herself by a
rash statement,
7and her husband hears of it and
says nothing about it on the day he
hears it, then her vows shall stand and
her pledge by which she bound herself
shall stand.
8“But if her husband disapproves of
her [making her vow or pledge] on the
day that he hears of it, then he shall
annul her vow which she is under and
the rash statement of her lips by which
she bound herself; and the LORD will
forgive her.
9“But the vow of a widow or of a di-
vorced woman, everything by which
she has bound herself, shall stand
against her.
10“However, if she vowed in her hus-
band’s house or bound herself by a
pledge with an oath,
11and her husband heard it, but said
nothing to her and did not disapprove
of her [making the vow], then all her
vows and every pledge by which she
bound herself shall stand.
12“But if her husband absolutely an-
nuls them on the day he heard them,
then whatever proceeds from her lips
concerning her vows or concerning
her pledge shall not stand. Her hus-
band has annulled them, and the LORD
will forgive her.
13“Every vow and every binding oath
to humble herself, her husband may
confirm it or her husband may annul it.
14“But if her husband says nothing
to her [concerning the matter] from
day to day, then he confirms all her
vows or all her pledges which are on
her. He has confirmed them because
he said nothing to her on the day he
heard them.
15“But if he indeed nullifies them
after he hears of them, then he shall
be responsible for *and* bear her guilt
[for breaking her promise].”
16These are the statutes which the
LORD commanded Moses, between a
man and his wife, and between a fa-
ther and his daughter while she is a
youth in her father’s house.

30:2 *If a man makes a vow.* The key issue is clear: One who makes a vow shall not break his word. Vows that are made to the Lord must be carried out.
30:3 *if a woman.* In Israelite culture, an unmarried woman was under the protection of her father. If she made a vow, she might bring her father into an obligation that he did not want to fulfill, or could not fulfill. The same was true of a married woman (v. 6). Her vows would involve her husband, so the husband or father had to agree to the vow.

39 Lev 23:2; 1Ch 23:31; 2Ch 31:3; Ezr 3:5; Neh 10:33; Isa 1:14; Lev 7:11,16; 22:21,23 **CHAPTER 30** **1** Nu 1:4,16; 7:2 **2** Lev 27:2; Dt 23:21; Jdg 11:30,35; Ecc 5:4; Lev 5:4; Mt 14:9; Ac 23:14; Job 22:27; Ps 22:25; 50:14; 66:13,14; 116:14,18; Na 1:15 **8** Ge 3:16

The Slaughter of Midian

31 THE LORD spoke to Moses,
saying,
2 “Take vengeance for the Israelites
on the Midianites; afterward you will
be gathered to your people [in death].”
3 Moses spoke to the people, saying,
“Arm men from among you for war,
so that they may go against Midian to
execute the LORD’s vengeance on Mid-
ian [for seducing Israel to participate
in idolatry]. [Num 25:16–18]
4 “A thousand [fighting men] from
each tribe of all the tribes of Israel you
shall send to the war.”
5 So out of the thousands of Israel, a
thousand from each tribe were select-
ed, twelve thousand armed for war.
6 Moses sent them, a thousand from
each tribe, to the war, and Phinehas
the son of Eleazar the priest, to war
with them, and the sacred vessels [of
the sanctuary] and the trumpets to
blow the alarm in his hand.
7 They made war against Midian, just
as the LORD had commanded Moses,
and they killed every male.
8 They killed the kings of Midian
along with *the rest of* their slain:
Evi and Rekem and Zur [the father
of Cozbi] and Hur and Reba, the five
kings of Midian; also Balaam the son
of Beor they killed with the sword.
[Num 22:31–35; Neh 13:1, 2]
9 The sons of Israel captured the
women of Midian and their children;
and all their cattle, all their livestock,
and all their property they took as
spoil [of war].
10 They burned all the cities where
they lived, and all their encampments
with fire.
11 They took all the plunder and all
the spoils of war, both people and live-
stock.
12 Then they brought the captives, the
spoils, and the plunder to Moses and to
Eleazar the priest and to the congrega-
tion of the Israelites at the camp on the
plains of Moab by the Jordan [River]
across from Jericho.
13 Moses and Eleazar the priest and
all the leaders of the congregation went
out to meet them outside the camp.
14 But Moses was angry with the of-
ficers of the army, the commanders
of thousands and of hundreds, who
served in the war.
15 And Moses said to them, “Have you
let all the women live?
16 “Look, these [are the women who]
caused the Israelites, by the counsel of
Balaam, to trespass against the LORD
in the matter of Peor, and so a plague
came among the congregation of the
LORD. [Num 25:1–9; 31:8]
17 “Now therefore, kill every male
among the children, and kill every
woman who is not a virgin.
18 “But all the young girls who have
not known a man intimately, keep alive
for yourselves [to marry].
19 “Camp outside the camp for seven
days; whoever has killed any person
and whoever has touched any dead
body, purify yourselves and your cap-
tives, on the third day and on the sev-
enth day.
20 “You shall purify every garment
and every article made of leather and
all the things made of goats’ hair, and
every article made of wood.”
21 Then Eleazar the priest said to the
men of war who had gone to battle,
“This is the statute of the law which
the LORD has commanded Moses:

31:2 *Midianites.* The Midianites were descendants of Abraham and his wife Keturah, but were not part of the covenant that God had with Abraham, Isaac, and Jacob.

31:7 – 16 Unfaithfulness — Moses was ordered to campaign against the Midianites because of their wicked involvement in the seduction of Israel (25:17 – 18). He was angry with the officers of the army because they had not carried out the Lord’s directive concerning the women who had caused Israel to act unfaithfully toward the Lord. There was no excuse for the officers’ unfaithfulness. The plague that followed the seduction of Israel should have been enough to make them aware of the great responsibility they had to obey God’s directives.

CHAPTER 31 **2** Nu 25:17; Nu 27:13 **6** Nu 10:9 **7** Dt 20:13; Jdg 21:11; 1Sa 27:9; 1Ki 11:15,16; See Jdg 6:1,2,33 **8** Jos 13:21; Jos 13:22 **11** Dt 20:14 **15** See Dt 20:14; 1Sa 15:3 **16** Nu 25:2; Nu 24:14; 2Pe 2:15; Rev 2:14; Nu 25:9 **17** Jdg 21:11 **19** Nu 5:2; Nu 19:11

[22]only the gold, the silver, the bronze,
the iron, the tin, and the lead,
[23]everything that can stand fire, you
shall pass through fire, and it shall be
clean. Nevertheless, it shall also be
purified with the water of purification
[to remove its impurity]; and all that
cannot stand fire [such as fabrics] you
shall pass through water.
[24]"And you shall wash your clothes
on the seventh day and be clean, and
afterward you may come into the
camp."

Division of the Spoil of War

[25]Then the LORD spoke to Moses,
saying,
[26]"You and Eleazar the priest and
the leaders of the fathers' households
of the congregation are to take a count
of the spoil of war that was captured,
both people and livestock.
[27]"Divide the spoil into two [equal]
parts between those who were in-
volved in the war, that is, those who
went out to battle and all [the rest of]
the congregation.
[28]"Levy a tax for the LORD from the
warriors who went to battle, one in five
hundred of the persons, the oxen, the
donkeys, and the flocks.
[29]"Take this tribute from the war-
riors' half and give it to Eleazar the
priest as an offering to the LORD.
[30]"From the Israelites' half [of the
spoil] you shall take one out of ev-
ery fifty of the persons, the oxen, the
donkeys, the flocks, and of all the live-
stock, and give them to the Levites
who are in charge of the tabernacle
of the LORD."
[31]Moses and Eleazar the priest did
just as the LORD had commanded Mo-
ses.
[32]The plunder that remained from
the spoil of war which the warriors
had taken, was 675,000 sheep,
[33]and 72,000 cattle,
[34]and 61,000 donkeys,
[35]and 32,000 persons in all, of the
[Midianite] women who were virgins.
[36]The half share, the portion of those
who went to war, was 337,500 sheep
in number,
[37]and the LORD's levy (tax) of the
sheep was 675;
[38]the cattle were 36,000, from which
the LORD's levy was 72;
[39]the donkeys were 30,500, from
which the LORD's levy was 61;
[40]the persons were 16,000, from
whom the LORD's levy was 32 persons.
[41]Moses gave the levy which was the
LORD's offering to Eleazar the priest, just
as the LORD had commanded Moses.
[42]As for the Israelites' half, which
Moses separated from that of the war-
riors—
[43]now the congregation's half was
337,500 sheep,
[44]and 36,000 cattle,
[45]and 30,500 donkeys,
[46]and 16,000 people—
[47]and from the Israelites' half, Mo-
ses took one out of every fifty, both of
persons and animals, and gave them
to the Levites, who were in charge of
the tabernacle of the LORD, just as the
LORD had commanded Moses.
[48]Then the officers who were over
the thousands of the army, the com-
manders of thousands and hundreds,
approached Moses,
[49]and they said to him, "Your ser-
vants have counted the warriors under
our command, and not one man of us
is missing.
[50]"So we have brought as an offering
to the LORD what each man obtained—
articles of gold, armlets, bracelets,
signet rings, earrings, necklaces—to
make atonement for ourselves before
the LORD."
[51]Moses and Eleazar the priest took
the gold from them, all the handmade
articles.

31:27 *Divide the spoil.* The division of the prey, or booty, among those who had gone to war and those who had not, set a standard for future battles. The proportion that was regarded as the Lord's also became a standard.

23 Nu 19:9,17 **24** Lev 11:25 **27** Jos 22:8; 1Sa 30:24 **28** See ver. 30,47; Nu 18:26 **30** See ver. 42-47; Nu 3:7,8,25,31,36; 18:3,4 **37** Lev 25:23; Dt 10:14; Job 41:11; Ps 24:1; 50:12; Pr 3:9; Lk 20:25; 1Co 10:26,28 **41** See Nu 18:8,19 **47** ver. 30 **50** Ex 30:12,16

[52]All the gold of the offering which
they presented to the LORD from the
commanders of thousands and of hun-
dreds was 16,750 shekels.
[53]For the men of war had taken plun-
der, every man for himself.
[54]So Moses and Eleazar the priest
received the gold from the command-
ers of thousands and of hundreds, and
brought it into the Tent of Meeting
(tabernacle) as a memorial for the sons
of Israel before the LORD.

Reuben and Gad Settle in Gilead

32 NOW THE sons of Reuben and
the sons of Gad had very large
herds of cattle, and they saw the land of
Jazer and the land of Gilead [on the east
side of the Jordan River], and indeed, the
place was suitable for raising livestock.
[2]So the sons of Gad and of Reuben
came and spoke to Moses, to Eleazar
the priest, and to the leaders of the
congregation, saying,
[3]"[The country around] Ataroth, Di-
bon, Jazer, Nimrah, Heshbon, Elealeh,
Sebam, Nebo, and Beon,
[4]the land which the LORD conquered
before the congregation of Israel, is a
land [suitable] for livestock, and your
servants have [very large herds of]
livestock."
[5]They said, "If we have found favor
in your sight, let this land be given to
your servants as a possession. Do not
take us across the Jordan [River]."
[6]But Moses said to the sons of Gad
and the sons of Reuben, "Shall your
brothers go to war while you sit here?
[7]"Now why are you discouraging the
hearts of the Israelites from crossing
over into the land which the LORD has
given them?
[8]"This is what your fathers did when
I sent them from Kadesh-barnea to see
the land!
[9]"For when they went up to the Val-
ley of Eshcol and saw the land, they
discouraged the hearts of the Israelites
so that they did not go into the land
which the LORD had given them.
[10]"And the LORD's anger was kindled
on that day and He swore an oath,
saying,
[11]'None of the men who came up
from Egypt, from twenty years old
and upward, shall see the land which I
promised to Abraham, to Isaac, and to
Jacob, because they have not followed
Me completely,
[12]except Caleb the son of Jephunneh
the Kenizzite and Joshua the son of
Nun, for they have followed the LORD
completely.'
[13]"So the LORD's anger was kindled
against the sons of Israel (Jacob) and
He made them wander in the wilder-
ness forty years, until the entire gen-
eration of those who had done evil in
the sight of the LORD was destroyed.
[14]"Now look, you [the tribes of Reu-
ben and Gad] have risen up in your
fathers' place, a brood of sinful men,
to add still more to the fierce anger of
the LORD against Israel.
[15]"For if you turn back from follow-
ing Him [completely], He will once
again leave them in the wilderness,
and you will destroy all these people."
[16]But the people of Reuben and Gad
approached Moses and said, "We will
build sheepfolds here for our flocks
and [walled] cities for our children,
[17]but we will be armed and ready
to go to war before the [other tribes of
the] Israelites, until we have brought
them to their place, while our children

31:52 *16,750 shekels.* The officers' gift was over 400 pounds of gold.
32:5 *If we have found favor.* Although an inheritance on the east side of the Jordan was not part of God's promise, the respectful request of the Reubenites and Gadites was granted, because they came humbly, not rebelliously.

32:8–13 *This is what your fathers did.* To discourage obedience of God's orders and so prevent His people from entering upon the full enjoyment of the promises is a serious sin. Let us never forget that without an obedient faith, it is impossible to please God (Heb 11:6).

53 Dt 20:14 **54** Ex 30:16 **CHAPTER 32** **1** Nu 21:32; Jos 13:25; 2Sa 24:5 **4** Nu 21:24,34 **8** Nu 13:3,26; Dt 1:22 **9** Nu 13:24,31; Dt 1:24,28 **10** Nu 14:11,21; Dt 1:34 **11** Nu 14:28,29; Dt 1:35; Nu 14:24,30 **12** Nu 14:24; Dt 1:36; Jos 14:8,9 **13** Nu 14:33-35; Nu 26:64,65 **14** Dt 1:34 **15** Dt 30:17; Jos 22:16,18; 2Ch 7:19 **17** Jos 4:12,13

live in the fortified cities because of
the inhabitants of the land.
18 “We will not return to our homes
until every one of the [other] sons of
Israel has taken possession of his in-
heritance.
19 “For we will not inherit with them
on the west side of the Jordan and
beyond, because our inheritance has
come to us on this side of the Jordan
[River] toward the east.”
20 Moses replied, “If you will do as
you say, if you will arm yourselves
before the LORD for war,
21 and every armed man of yours will
cross the Jordan before the LORD until
He has driven out His enemies before
Him,
22 and the land [west of the Jordan]
is subdued before the LORD, then after-
ward you shall return and be blame-
less [in this matter] before the LORD
and before Israel, and this land [east
of the Jordan] shall be yours as a pos-
session before the LORD.
23 “But if you do not do this, behold, you
will have sinned against the LORD; and
be sure that your sin will find you out.
24 “Build yourselves cities for your
children, and folds for your sheep, and
do that of which you have spoken.”
25 Then the descendants of Gad and of
Reuben said to Moses, “Your servants
will do just as my lord commands.
26 “Our children, our wives, our live-
stock, and all our cattle shall be there
in the cities of Gilead.
27 “But your servants will cross over,
every man armed for war, before the
LORD to the battle, just as my lord says.”
28 So Moses gave the command con-
cerning them to Eleazar the priest,
and to Joshua the son of Nun, and to
the leaders of the fathers’ *households*
of the tribes of the Israelites.
29 Moses said to them, “If the sons of
Gad and the sons of Reuben will cross
over the Jordan with you, every man
armed for battle before the LORD, and
the land is subdued before you, then you
shall give them the land of Gilead [east
of the Jordan River] as a possession;
30 but if they will not cross over with
you armed, they shall have posses-
sions among you in the land of Canaan
[and surrender their right to their land
east of the Jordan River].”
31 The sons of Gad and the sons of
Reuben answered, “As the LORD has
said to your servants, so will we do.
32 “We will cross over armed before
the LORD into the land of Canaan, so
that the possession of our inheritance
on [the east] side of the Jordan may
be ours.”
33 So Moses gave to them, to the sons
of Gad and to the sons of Reuben and
to the half-tribe of Manasseh the son
of Joseph, the kingdom of Sihon, the
king of the Amorites and the kingdom
of Og, the king of Bashan, the land
with its cities and territories, the cities
of the surrounding land.
34 The sons of Gad built Dibon, At-
aroth, Aroer,
35 Atroth-shophan, Jazer, Jogbehah,
36 Beth-nimrah, and Beth-haran, for-
tified (walled) cities, and sheepfolds
for sheep.
37 The sons of Reuben built Heshbon,
Elealeh, Kiriathaim,
38 Nebo, and Baal-meon (their names
being changed) and Sibmah; and they
gave other names to the cities which
they built.
39 The sons of Machir the son of Ma-
nasseh went to Gilead and took it, and
drove out the Amorites who were in it.
40 So Moses gave Gilead to [the tribe
of] Machir the son of Manasseh, and
they settled in it.
41 [The sons of] Jair the son of Ma-
nasseh went and took its towns (tent
villages) and called them Havvoth-jair.

32:31 *so will we do.* Reuben and Gad gladly affirmed their allegiance to the Lord and their consideration of the remainder of the community of Israel. The benevolence of Reuben and Gad is a beautiful picture of the mutual ties between God’s people. Truly, we are one body.

18 Jos 22:4 **19** ver. 33; Jos 12:1; 13:8 **20** Dt 3:18; Jos 1:14; 4:12,13 **22** Dt 3:20; Jos 11:23; 18:1; Jos 22:4; Dt 3:12,15,16,18; Jos 1:15; 13:8,32; 22:4,9 **23** Ge 4:7; 44:16; Isa 59:12 **24** ver. 16,34 **26** Jos 1:14 **27** Jos 4:12 **28** Jos 1:13 **33** Dt 3:12-17; 29:8; Jos 12:6; 13:8; 22:4; Nu 21:24,33,35 **34** Nu 33:45,46; Dt 2:36 **36** ver. 24 **37** Nu 21:27 **38** Isa 46:1; Nu 22:41; See ver. 3; Ex 23:13; Jos 23:7 **39** Ge 50:23 **40** Dt 3:12,13,15; Jos 13:31; 17:1 **41** Dt 3:14; Jos 13:30; 1Ch 2:21; Jdg 10:4; 1Ki 4:13

42 Nobah went and took Kenath and
its villages, and called it Nobah after
his own name.

Review of the Journey from Egypt to Jordan

33 THESE ARE the stages of the
journeys of the Israelites, by
which they came out of the land of
Egypt by their [tribal] armies, under
the leadership of Moses and Aaron.
2 Moses recorded their points of
departure, as the LORD commanded,
stage by stage; and these are their
journeys according to their points of
departure:
3 They set out from Rameses on the
fifteenth day of the first month; on the
day after the Passover the Israelites
moved out triumphantly in the sight
of all the Egyptians,
4 while the Egyptians were burying
all their firstborn whom the LORD had
struck down among them. Upon their
gods the LORD also executed judgments.
5 Then the Israelites moved out from
Rameses [where they had all joined
together], and camped in Succoth.
6 They moved out from Succoth and
camped in Etham, which is on the edge
of the wilderness.
7 They moved out from Etham and
turned back to Pi-hahiroth, east of
Baal-zephon, and they camped before
Migdol.
8 They moved out from before Pi-
hahiroth and passed through the midst
of the [Red] Sea into the wilderness;
and they went a three days' journey in
the Wilderness of Etham and camped
at Marah.
9 They moved out from Marah and
came to Elim; in Elim there were
twelve springs of water and seventy
palm trees, and they camped there.
10 They moved out from Elim and
camped by the Red Sea (Sea of Reeds).
11 They moved out from the Red Sea
and camped in the Wilderness of Sin.
12 They moved out from the Wilder-
ness of Sin and camped at Dophkah.
13 They moved out from Dophkah
and camped at Alush.
14 They moved out from Alush and
camped at Rephidim; now it was there
that the people had no water to drink.
15 They moved out from Rephidim
and camped in the Wilderness of Sinai
[where they remained for about a year].
16 They moved out from the Wilder-
ness of Sinai and camped at Kibroth-
hattaavah.
17 They moved out from Kibroth-
hattaavah and camped at Hazeroth.
18 They moved out from Hazeroth and
camped at Rithmah [near Kadesh, the
place from which the twelve spies were
sent to spy out the land of Canaan].
19 They moved out from Rithmah and
camped at Rimmon-perez.
20 They moved out from Rimmon-
perez and camped at Libnah.
21 They moved out from Libnah and
camped at Rissah.
22 They moved out from Rissah and
camped at Kehelathah.
23 They moved out from Kehelathah
and camped at Mount Shepher.
24 They moved out from Mount She-
pher and camped at Haradah.
25 They moved out from Haradah and
camped at Makheloth.
26 They moved out from Makheloth
and camped at Tahath.
27 They moved out from Tahath and
camped at Terah.
28 They moved out from Terah and
camped at Mithkah.
29 They moved out from Mithkah and
camped at Hashmonah.
30 They moved out from Hashmonah
and camped at Moseroth.
31 They moved out from Moseroth
and camped at Bene-jaakan.
32 They moved out from Bene-jaakan
and camped at Hor-haggidgad.
33 They moved out from Hor-
haggidgad and camped at Jotbathah.
34 They moved out from Jotbathah
and camped at Abronah.
35 They moved out from Abronah and
camped at Ezion-geber [or Elath on the
gulf of Aqabah].

CHAPTER 33 **3** Ex 12:37; Ex 12:2; 13:4; Ex 14:8 **4** Ex 12:29; Ex 12:12; 18:11; Isa 19:1; Rev 12:8 **5** Ex 12:37 **6** Ex 13:20 **7** Ex 14:2,9 **8** Ex 14:22; 15:22,23 **9** Ex 15:27 **11** Ex 16:1 **14** Ex 17:1; 19:2 **15** Ex 16:1; 19:1,2 **16** Nu 11:34 **17** Nu 11:35 **18** Nu 12:16 **30** Dt 10:6 **32** See Ge 36:27; Dt 10:6; 1Ch 1:42; Dt 10:7 **35** Dt 2:8; 1Ki 9:26; 22:48

36 They moved out from Ezion-geber
and camped in the Wilderness of Zin,
which is Kadesh.
37 They moved out from Kadesh and
camped at Mount Hor, on the edge of
the land of Edom.
38 Aaron the priest went up on Mount
Hor at the command of the LORD, and
died there in the fortieth year after
the Israelites came out of the land
of Egypt, on the first day of the fifth
month. [Num 20:23–29]
39 Aaron was a hundred and twenty-
three years old when he died on Mount
Hor.
40 The Canaanite king of Arad, who
lived in the Negev (the South country)
in the land of Canaan, heard that the
sons of Israel were coming.
41 They moved out from Mount Hor
and camped at Zalmonah.
42 Then they moved out from Zalmo-
nah and camped at Punon.
43 They moved out from Punon and
camped at Oboth.
44 They moved out from Oboth and
camped at Iye-abarim, on the border
of Moab.
45 They moved out from Iyim (Iye-
abarim) and camped at Dibon-gad.
46 They moved out from Dibon-gad
and camped at Almon-diblathaim.
47 They moved out from Almon-
diblathaim and camped in the moun-
tains of Abarim, before [Mount] Nebo.
48 They moved out from the moun-
tains of Abarim and camped in the
plains of Moab by the Jordan across
from Jericho [their last stop on the
journey to Canaan].
49 They camped by the Jordan from
Beth-jeshimoth as far as Abel-shittim
in the plains of Moab.

Law of Possessing the Land

50 Then the LORD spoke to Moses
in the plains of Moab by the Jordan
across from Jericho, saying,
51 "Say to the children of Israel,
'When you cross the Jordan into the
land of Canaan,
52 then you shall drive out all the in-
habitants of the land before you and
destroy all their sculpted images, and
destroy all their cast idols and com-
pletely eliminate all their [idolatrous]
high places,
53 and you shall take possession of
the land and live in it, for I have given
the land to you to possess.
54 'You shall inherit the land by lot
according to your families; to the large
tribe you shall give a larger inheri-
tance, and to the small *tribe* you shall
give a smaller inheritance. Wherever
the lot falls to any man, that shall be
[the location of] his [inheritance]. Ac-
cording to the tribes of your fathers
(ancestors) you shall inherit.
55 'But if you do not drive out the in-
habitants of the land from before you,
then those you let remain of them will
be like pricks in your eyes and like
thorns in your sides, and they will at-
tack you in the land in which you live.
56 'And as I [the LORD] planned to do
to them, so I will do to you.' "

Instruction for Apportioning Canaan

34 THEN THE LORD spoke to Mo-
ses, saying,
2 "Command the Israelites, 'When
you enter the land of Canaan, this is
the land that shall be yours as an in-

33:53 *for I have given the land to you to possess.* It was God's land, and He had transferred it from the Canaanites to the Israelites. Though the land was promised to the nation as a gift, it did not come into the possession of the people without their involvement. Israel had to drive out the inhabitants, destroy their high places, their figures, stones, and molten images. Still, the land was God's gracious gift to His people. In spite of all of our striving, we have only what we receive from the hand of the Lord.

33:55 – 56 *But if you do not.* If the idolatrous Canaanites were allowed to live among God's people, they would be a constant enticement to sin. If the Israelites fell into the same sin as the Canaanites, their punishment would be the same.

34:1 – 12 *the land of Canaan according to its boundaries.* Chapter 34 serves as a detailed

36 Nu 20:1; 27:14 **37** Nu 20:22,23; 21:4 **38** Nu 20:25,28; Dt 10:6; 32:50 **40** Nu 21:1 **41** Nu 21:4 **43** Nu 21:10 **44** Nu 21:11; Nu 21:11 **45** Nu 32:34 **46** Jer 48:22; Eze 6:14 **47** Nu 21:20; Dt 32:49 **48** Nu 22:1 **49** Nu 25:1; Jos 2:1 **51** Dt 7:1,2; 9:1; Jos 3:17 **52** Ex 23:24,33; 34:13; Dt 7:2,5; 12:3; Jos 11:12; Jdg 2:2 **54** Nu 26:53-55 **55** Jos 23:13; Jdg 2:3; Ps 106:34,36 **CHAPTER 34** **2** Ge 17:8; Dt 1:7; Ps 78:55; Eze 47:14

heritance, the land of Canaan accord-
ing to its boundaries,
3 your southern region shall be from
the Wilderness of Zin along the side of
Edom, and your southern boundary
from the end of the Salt (Dead) Sea
eastward.
4 'Your boundary shall turn from the
south to the ascent of Akrabbim, and
continue on to Zin, and its limit shall
be south of Kadesh-barnea. Then it
shall go on to Hazar-addar and pass
on to Azmon.
5 'Then the boundary shall turn from
Azmon to the Brook of Egypt (Wadi
el-arish), and its limit shall be at the
[Mediterranean] Sea.
6 'As the western boundary you shall
have the Great [Mediterranean] Sea
and its coastline. This shall be your
western boundary.
7 'And this shall be your north bor-
der: from the Great [Mediterranean]
Sea mark out your boundary line to
Mount Hor;
8 from Mount Hor you shall mark
out your boundary to the entrance of
Hamath, and the limit of the border
shall be at Zedad;
9 then the [northern] boundary shall
go on to Ziphron, and its limit shall
be at Hazar-enan. This shall be your
northern boundary.
10 'You shall mark out your eastern
boundary from Hazar-enan to She-
pham;
11 the [eastern] boundary shall go
down from Shepham to Riblah on the
east side of Ain and shall descend and
reach to the slope on the east of the
Sea of Chinnereth [the Sea of Galilee];
12 and the [eastern] boundary shall
go down to the Jordan [River], and its
limit shall be at the Salt (Dead) Sea.
This shall be your land according to
its boundaries all around.' "
13 So Moses commanded the Israel-
ites, saying, "This is the land you are
to inherit by lot, which the LORD has
commanded to be given to the nine
tribes and the half-tribe [of Manasseh],
14 for the tribe of the sons of Reuben
and the tribe of the sons of Gad have
received *their inheritance* by their fa-
thers' households, and the half-tribe
of Manasseh have received their pos-
session.
15 "The two and a half tribes have
received their inheritance across the
Jordan [River] opposite Jericho, east-
ward toward the sunrise."
16 Then the LORD spoke to Moses,
saying,
17 "These are the names of the men
who shall divide the land among you
as an inheritance: Eleazar the priest
and Joshua the son of Nun.
18 "You shall take one leader from
every tribe to divide the land for the
inheritance.
19 "These are the names of the men:
From the tribe of Judah, Caleb the son
of Jephunneh;
20 from the tribe of the sons of Sime-
on, Samuel the son of Ammihud;
21 from the tribe of Benjamin, Elidad
the son of Chislon;
22 from the tribe of the sons of Dan a
leader, Bukki the son of Jogli;
23 of the sons of Joseph: from the
tribe of the sons of Manasseh a leader,
Hanniel the son of Ephod;
24 from the tribe of the sons of
Ephraim a leader, Kemuel the son of
Shiphtan;
25 from the tribe of the sons of Zeb-
ulun a leader, Elizaphan the son of
Parnach;
26 from the tribe of the sons of Issachar
a leader, Paltiel the son of Azzan;
27 from the tribe of the sons of Asher
a leader, Ahihud the son of Shelomi;

display of the grandeur of the land that God was about to give to His people.

34:16 – 29 *These are the names of the men.* The listing of the men serves several purposes. It gives authenticity to the record, it memorializes these individuals in the history of Israel, and it serves as a legal arrangement so that the transfer of the land to the tribes would be done in order.

3 Jos 15:1; See Eze 47:13; Ge 14:3; Jos 15:2 **4** Jos 15:3; Nu 13:26; 32:8; See Jos 15:3,4 **5** Ge 15:18; Jos 15:4,47; 1Ki 8:65; Isa 27:12 **7** Nu 33:37 **8** Nu 13:21; 2Ki 14:25; Eze 47:15 **9** Eze 47:17 **11** 2Ki 23:33; Jer 39:5,6; Dt 3:17; Jos 11:2; 19:35; Mt 14:34; Lk 5:1 **12** ver. 3 **13** ver. 2; Jos 14:1,2 **14** Nu 32:33; Jos 14:2 **17** Jos 14:1; 19:51 **18** Nu 1:4,16

28 from the tribe of the sons of
Naphtali a leader, Pedahel the son of
Ammihud."
29 These are the [twelve] men whom
the LORD commanded [to work with
Joshua and Eleazar] to divide the in-
heritance to the sons of Israel in the
land of Canaan.

Cities for the Levites

35 THEN THE LORD spoke to Mo-
ses in the plains of Moab by the
Jordan [across from] Jericho, saying,
2 "Command the Israelites to give to
the Levites cities to live in from the
inheritance of their possession; and
you shall give to the Levites pasture
lands around the cities.
3 "The cities shall be theirs to live in;
and their pasture lands shall be for
their cattle and for their herds and for
all their livestock.
4 "The pasture lands around the cit-
ies which you shall give to the Levites
shall reach from the wall of the city
and outward a thousand cubits (1,500
ft.) around.
5 "You shall also measure outside the
city on the east, south, west, and north
sides two thousand cubits (3,000 ft.),
with the city in the center. This shall
belong to the Levites as pasture lands
for the cities.

Cities of Refuge

6 "[Among] the cities which you give
to the Levites shall be the six cities of
refuge, which you shall provide for the
one who commits manslaughter to flee
to; and in addition to them you shall
give forty-two cities [to the Levites].
7 "So you shall give to the Levites
forty-eight cities in all, together with
their pasture lands.
8 "As for the cities which you shall
give from the possession of the Is-
raelites, from the larger *tribes* you
shall take many and from the smaller
tribes few; each *tribe* shall give [at
least some] of its cities to the Levites
in proportion to [the size of] its inher-
itance which it possesses."
9 Then the LORD spoke to Moses,
saying,
10 "Tell the Israelites, 'When you
cross the Jordan [River] into the land
of Canaan,
11 then you shall select for yourselves
cities to be cities of refuge, so that the
one who kills any person unintention-
ally may escape there.
12 'The cities shall be to you as a ref-
uge from the avenger, so that the one
who has caused the death of another
will not be killed until he has had a
[fair] trial before the congregation.
13 'The cities which you are to provide
shall be your six cities of refuge.
14 'You shall provide three cities on
this [east] side of the Jordan [River],
and three [more] cities in the land of
Canaan; they are to be the cities of
refuge.
15 'These six cities shall be a refuge
for the Israelites and for the stranger
and the resident alien among them; so
that anyone who kills a person unin-
tentionally may escape there.
16 'But if he struck his victim down
[intentionally] with an iron object so
that he died, he is a murderer; the
murderer shall certainly be put to
death.
17 'If he struck his victim down [inten-
tionally] with a stone in hand, which
may cause a person to die, and he died,
he is a murderer; the murderer shall
certainly be put to death.
18 'Or if he struck his victim down
[intentionally] with a wooden object
in hand, which may cause a person
to die, and he died, he is a murderer;
the murderer shall certainly be put to
death.
19 'The blood avenger shall himself
put the murderer to death; he shall put
him to death when he meets him.
20 'But if he pushed his victim out of
hatred or threw something at him with
malicious intent, and he died,
21 or if, in enmity, he struck the vic-
tim down with his hand, and he died,
the one that struck the victim shall
certainly be put to death; he is a mur-

CHAPTER 35 **1** See Nu 33:50 **2** Jos 14:3,4; 21:2; See Eze 45:1; 48:8; See Lev 25:34 **6** ver. 13; Dt 4:41; Jos 20:2,7,8; 21:3,13 **7** Jos 21:41 **8** Jos 21:3; Nu 26:54 **10** Dt 19:2; Jos 20:2 **11** Ex 21:13 **12** Dt 19:6; Jos 20:3,5,6 **13** ver. 6 **14** Dt 4:41; Jos 20:8 **15** Nu 15:16 **16** Ex 21:12,14; Lev 24:17; Dt 19:11,12 **19** ver. 21,24,27; Dt 19:6,12; Jos 20:3,5 **20** Ge 4:8; 2Sa 3:27; 20:10; 1Ki 2:31,32; Ex 21:14; Dt 19:11

derer. The blood avenger shall put the murderer to death when he meets him.

22 'But if he pushed the victim suddenly, not in enmity, or threw anything at him without malicious intent,

23 or without seeing him hit him [accidentally] with a stone object that could kill him, and he died, and [the offender] was not his enemy nor intending to harm him,

24 then the congregation shall judge between the offender and the blood avenger according to these ordinances.

25 'The congregation shall rescue the offender from the hand of the blood avenger and return him to his city of refuge, [the place] to which he had escaped; and he shall live there until the death of the high priest who was anointed with the sacred oil.

26 'But if at any time the one guilty of manslaughter comes outside the border of his city of refuge to which he fled,

27 and the blood avenger finds him outside the border of his city of refuge and kills the offender, the blood avenger will not be guilty of murder,

28 because the offender should have remained in his city of refuge until the death of the high priest. But after the high priest's death the offender shall return to the land of his possession.

29 'These things shall be a statute for you throughout your generations wherever you may be.

30 'If anyone kills a person [intentionally], the murderer shall be put to death on the testimony of [two or more] witnesses; but no one shall be put to death on the testimony of [only] one witness.

31 'Moreover, you shall not accept a ransom [in exchange] for the life of a murderer guilty *and sentenced* to death; but he shall certainly be put to death.

32 'You shall not accept a ransom for him who has escaped to his city of refuge, so that he may return to live in his [own] land before the death of the high priest.

33 'So you shall not pollute *and* defile the land in which you live; for [the shedding of innocent] blood pollutes *and* defiles the land. No atonement (expiation) can be made for the land for the [innocent] blood shed in it, except by the blood (execution) of him who shed it.

34 'You shall not defile the land in which you live, in the midst of which I live, for I, the LORD, live among the people of Israel.' "

Inheritance by Marriage

36 THE LEADERS of the fathers' *households* of the family of the sons of Gilead, the son of Machir, the son of Manasseh, of the families of the sons of Joseph, approached and spoke before Moses and before the leaders, the heads of the fathers' *households* of the Israelites,

2 and they said, "The LORD commanded my lord [Moses] to give the land by lot to the sons of Israel as an inheritance, and my lord was commanded by the LORD to give the inheritance of Zelophehad our brother to his daughters.

3 "But if the daughters marry any of the men from any of the *other* tribes of Israel, then their inheritance will be taken away from that of our fathers

---

35:29 – 34 *statute.* The practice of blood vengeance was common in the ancient Near East. Divine law was formulated to control and limit blood vengeance in Israel (vv. 9 – 34). God's Word differed significantly from the surrounding cultures. The difference of practice was due to Israel's unique view of man created in God's image. These directives regarding blood vengeance are referred to here as a "statute," coming from a word meaning "to engrave." The Word of God was written, given to govern and direct their conduct "wherever they may be." We can be truly grateful that the revelation of God comes to us in a permanently accessible form.

35:30 – 34 *If anyone kills a person.* The people were not to confuse accidental manslaughter with premeditated murder.

22 Ex 21:13 **24** ver. 12; Jos 20:6 **25** Jos 20:6; Ex 29:7; Lev 4:3; 21:10 **29** Nu 27:11 **30** Dt 17:6; 19:15; Mt 18:16; 2Co 13:1; Heb 10:28 **33** Ps 106:38; Mic 4:11; Ge 9:6 **34** Lev 18:25; Dt 21:23; Ex 29:45,46
CHAPTER 36 **1** Nu 26:29 **2** Nu 26:55; 33:54; Jos 17:4; Nu 27:1,7; Jos 17:3,4 **3** Nu 27:4

(tribal ancestors) and will be added to
the inheritance of the tribe to which
they belong; so it will be taken away
from our allotted inheritance.
4 "When the [year of] Jubilee of the
Israelites comes, then their inheritance
will be added [permanently] to that of
the tribe to which they belong; so their
inheritance will be taken away from
that of the tribe of our fathers (tribal
ancestors)."
5 Then Moses commanded the Isra-
elites in accordance with the word of
the LORD, saying, "The statement of the
tribe of the sons of Joseph is correct.
6 "This is what the LORD commands
regarding the daughters of Zelophe-
had: 'Let them marry whom they wish;
only they must marry within the fam-
ily of the tribe of their father.'
7 "So no inheritance of the Israelites
shall be transferred from tribe to tribe,
for every one of the Israelites shall hold
to the inheritance of the tribe of his
fathers (tribal ancestors).
8 "Every daughter who possesses
an inheritance [of land] in any one of
the tribes of the Israelites shall marry
[only] a man whose family is of her
father's tribe, so that the Israelites may
each possess the inheritance of his
fathers (tribal ancestors).
9 "So no inheritance shall be trans-
ferred from one tribe to another, but
each of the tribes of the Israelites shall
hold to its own inheritance."
10 The daughters of Zelophehad did
as the LORD commanded Moses.
11 For Mahlah, Tirzah, Hoglah,
Milcah, and Noah, the daughters of
Zelophehad, were married to sons of
their father's brothers.
12 They married into the families of
the descendants of Manasseh the son
of Joseph, and their inheritance re-
mained in the tribe of the family of
their father.
13 These are the commandments and
the ordinances (judgments) which the
LORD commanded through Moses to
the sons of Israel in the plains of Moab
by the Jordan [across from] Jericho.

36:5–13 *within the family of the tribe of their father.* This beautiful example of concern for fair treatment of Zelophehad's daughters, consideration for the well-being of the tribe, and obedience to Moses' decision is a happy ending to this book that is so full of hard-heartedness and disobedience.

4 Lev 25:10 **5** Nu 27:7 **6** ver. 11,12 **7** 1Ki 21:3 **8** 1Ch 23:22 **11** Nu 27:1 **13** Dt 33:4; Nu 26:3; 33:50

THE FIFTH BOOK OF MOSES, CALLED

DEUTERONOMY

▸ **AUTHOR:** Numerous external and internal evidences support the authorship of Moses. The Old Testament attributes Deuteronomy to Moses (Jos 1:7; Jdy 3:4; 1Ki 2:3; 2Ki 14:6; Ezr 3:2; Neh 1:7; Ps 103:7; Da 9:11; Mal 4:4), and there is evidence from Joshua and 1 Samuel to indicate that these laws existed in the form of codified written statutes that influenced the Israelites in Canaan. Christ quoted Deuteronomy when he was being tempted (Mt 4:4,7,10) and attributed it to Moses (Mt 19:7–9; Mk 7:10; Lk 20:28; Jn 5:45–47) as do the more than eighty citations of Deuteronomy in the New Testament. Internally, the book includes about forty claims to Moses as the author (31:24–26; 1:1–5; 4:44–46; 29:1; 31:9). The political and geographic details of Deuteronomy indicate a firsthand knowledge of the events.

▸ **TIMES:** c. 1405 BC ▸ **KEY VERSES:** Dt 30:19–20

▸ **THEME:** Deuteronomy is a series of addresses that Moses gives to the nation of Israel just before it enters the promised land. In many ways it can be seen as the coach's speech given to a team just before it takes the field. The book reviews and reiterates what has been taught in the previous books of Moses in the same way that a coach's last instructions contain a review of the basic game plan and what has been covered in practice. The purpose of that speech is to focus on what to do and then create the motivation to carry it out. For the Israelites much of the previous instruction was somewhat hypothetical. Many of the laws assumed the occupation of the land. Now, as they stand looking over the Jordan River, they're within reach of moving from the hypothetical to the real and practical. God has renewed His marvelous covenant with them. Now is the time to live up to its requirements.

Israel's History after the Exodus

1 THESE ARE the words which Moses spoke to all Israel [while they were still] beyond [that is, on the east side of] the Jordan [River] in the wilderness [across from Jerusalem], in the Arabah [the long, deep valley running north and south from the eastern arm of the Red Sea to beyond the Dead Sea] opposite Suph, between Paran and Tophel and Laban and Hazeroth and Dizahab (place of gold).
2It is [only] eleven days' *journey* from Horeb (Mount Sinai) by way of Mount Seir to Kadesh-barnea [on Canaan's border; yet Israel wandered in the wilderness for forty years before crossing the border and entering Canaan, the promised land].
3In the fortieth year, on the first day of the eleventh month, Moses spoke to the children of Israel in accordance with all that the LORD had commanded him *to say* to them,
4after he had defeated Sihon the king of the Amorites, who lived in Heshbon,

1:2 ***eleven days.*** A journey that might have taken Israel less than two weeks to complete lasted forty years because of unbelief and disobedience (Nu 13–14).

CHAPTER 1 **1** Jos 9:1,10 **2** Nu 13:26; Dt 9:23 **3** Nu 33:38 **4** Nu 21:24,33; Nu 21:33; Jos 13:12

and Og the king of Bashan, who lived
at Ashtaroth in Edrei.
5 Beyond (east of) the Jordan in the
land of Moab, Moses began to explain
this law, saying,
6 "The LORD our God spoke to us at
Horeb, saying, 'You have stayed long
enough on this mountain.
7 'Turn and resume your journey,
and go to the hill country of the Amo-
rites, and to all their neighbors in the
Arabah, in the hill country and in the
lowland (the Shephelah), in the Negev
(South country) and on the coast of
the [Mediterranean] Sea, the land of
the Canaanites, and Lebanon, as far
as the great river, the river Euphrates.
8 'Look, I have set the land before
you; go in and take possession of the
land which the LORD swore (solemnly
promised) to your fathers, to Abraham,
to Isaac, and to Jacob, to give to them
and to their descendants after them.'
9 "I spoke to you at that time, saying,
'I am not able to bear *the burden* of
you alone.
10 'The LORD your God has multiplied
you, and look, today you are as numer-
ous as the stars of heaven.
11 'May the LORD, the God of your
fathers, add to you a thousand times
as many as you are and bless you, just
as He has promised you!
12 'How can I alone bear the weight
and pressure and burden of you and
your strife (contention) *and* complain-
ing?
13 'Choose for yourselves wise, under-
standing, experienced, *and* respected
men from your tribes, and I will ap-
point them as heads (leaders) over you.'
14 "And you answered me, 'The thing
which you have said to do is good.'
15 "So I took the leaders of your tribes,
wise and experienced men, and made
them leaders over you, commanders of
thousands, and hundreds, and fifties,
and tens, and officers (administrators)
for your tribes.
16 "Then I commanded your judges
at that time, saying, 'Hear *the matters*
between your brothers [your fellow
countrymen], and judge righteous-
ly *and* fairly between a man and his
brother, or the stranger (resident alien,
foreigner) who is with him.
17 'You shall not show partiality in
judgment; you shall hear *and* pay
attention to the [cases of the] least
[important] as well as the great. You
shall not fear man, for the judgment
is God's. The case that is too hard for
you [to judge], you shall bring to me,
and I will hear it.'
18 "I commanded you at that time [re-
garding] all the things that you should
do.
19 "Then we set out from Horeb (Si-
nai), and went through all that great
and terrible wilderness which you
saw on the way to the hill country
of the Amorites, just as the LORD our
God commanded us; and we came to
Kadesh-barnea.
20 "And I said to you, 'You have come
to the hill country of the Amorites
which the LORD our God is about to
give us.
21 'Behold, the LORD your God has set
the land before you; go up and take
possession *of it*, just as the LORD, the
God of your fathers, has spoken to you.
Do not fear or be dismayed.'
22 "Then all of you approached me
and said, 'Let us send men [into the
land] before us, so that they may ex-
plore *and* search the area for us, and
bring back to us word regarding the

1:5 *law.* The Hebrew word translated "law" basically means "instruction."
1:13 *wise, understanding.* The qualities of the leaders reflect the attributes of God. Wisdom is the ability to judge fairly and understand and make wise use of facts. Discernment or understanding is the ability to find the hidden or obscure aspects of a situation.
1:20 *Amorites.* The Amorites were one of the groups Israel encountered in their approach to the promised land. This term is often a general designation for the Canaanites.

---

6 Ex 3:1; See Ex 19:1; Nu 10:11 **8** Ge 12:7; 15:18; 17:7,8; 26:4; 28:13 **9** Ex 18:18; Nu 11:14 **10** Ge 15:5; Dt 10:22; 28:62 **11** 2Sa 24:3; Ge 15:5; 22:17; 26:4; Ex 32:13 **12** 1Ki 3:8,9 **15** Ex 18:25; Ex 18:25 **16** Dt 16:18; Jn 7:24; Lev 24:22 **17** Lev 19:15; Dt 16:19; 1Sa 16:7; Pr 24:23; Jas 2:1; 2Ch 19:6; Ex 18:22,26 **19** Nu 10:12; Dt 8:15; Jer 2:6; Nu 13:26 **21** Jos 1:9

way we should go, and the cities we should enter.'

23 "The plan pleased me and I took twelve of your men, one man from each tribe.

24 "They turned and went up into the hill country, and came to the Valley of Eshcol and spied it out.

25 "Then they took some of the fruit of the land in their hands and brought it down to us; and they reported back to us, and said, 'It is a good land which the LORD our God is about to give us.'

26 "Yet you were not willing to go up [to take possession of it], but rebelled against the command of the LORD your God.

27 "You murmured *and* were ill-tempered (discontented) in your tents, and said, 'Because the LORD hates us He has brought us from the land of Egypt to hand us over to the Amorites to destroy us.

28 'Where can we go up? Our brothers (spies) have made our hearts melt [in fear] *and* demoralized us by saying, "The people are bigger and taller than we; the cities are large, and fortified [all the way up] to heaven. And besides, we saw the [giant-like] sons of the Anakim there." '

29 "Then I said to you, 'Do not be shocked, nor fear them.

30 'The LORD your God who goes before you will fight for you Himself, just as He did for you in Egypt before your [very] eyes,

31 and in the wilderness where you saw how the LORD your God carried *and* protected you, just as a man carries his son, all along the way which you traveled until you arrived at this place.'

32 "Yet in spite of this word, you did not trust [that is, confidently rely on and believe] the LORD your God,

33 who went before you along the way, in fire by night and in a cloud by day, to seek a place for you to make camp and to show you the way in which you should go.

34 "And the LORD heard the sound of your words, and He was angry and took an oath, saying,

35 'Not one of these men, this evil generation, shall see the good land which I swore (solemnly promised) to give to your fathers,

36 except Caleb the son of Jephunneh; he shall see it, and to him and to his children I will give the land on which he has walked, because he has followed the LORD completely [and remained true to Him].'

37 "The LORD was angry with me also because of you, saying, 'Not even you shall enter Canaan.

38 'Joshua the son of Nun, who stands before you, he shall enter there. Encourage *and* strengthen him, for he shall cause Israel to inherit it.

39 'Moreover, your little ones whom you said would become prey, and your sons, who today have no knowledge of good or evil, shall enter Canaan, and I will give it to them and they shall possess it.

40 'But as for you, turn around and

1:26–28 *You murmured.* An attitude of complaining and criticism toward the circumstances in our lives keeps us from seeing God's hand in the situation. Our situation may indeed be difficult, but God has promised that He will never leave us nor forsake us. Paul said that he had learned how *to be content in every circumstance.* He made it a habit to give thanks in all things, and knew how to be contented with little, and how to be contented with much. He knew that he could do anything through Christ, who gives us strength (Php 4:13).

1:28 *the [giant-like] sons of the Anakim.* The Anakim were an ancient people known for their great size (Nu 13:28).

1:39 *your little ones whom you said would become prey.* The most outrageous of Israel's complaints against God was that He had wanted their children to die (Nu 14:31). But the Lord demonstrated His love and faithfulness to His people by protecting those younger than 20 so that they could inherit the land.

23 Nu 13:3 **24** Nu 13:22-24 **25** Nu 13:27 **26** Nu 14:1-4; Ps 106:24 **27** Dt 9:28 **28** Nu 13:28,31-33; Dt 9:1,2; Nu 13:28 **30** Ex 14:14; Neh 4:20 **31** Ex 19:4; Dt 32:11,12; Isa 46:3,4; 63:9; Hos 11:3; See Ac 13:18 **32** Ps 106:24; Jude 5 **33** Ex 13:21; Ps 78:14; Nu 10:33; Eze 20:6 **34** Dt 2:14,15 **35** Nu 14:22; Ps 95:11 **36** Nu 14:24; Jos 14:9; Nu 14:24 **37** Nu 20:12; 27:14; Dt 3:26; 4:21; 34:4; Ps 106:32 **38** Nu 14:30; Ex 24:13; 33:11; See 1Sa 16:22; Nu 27:18,19; Dt 31:7,23 **39** Nu 14:31; Nu 14:3; Isa 7:15,16; Ro 9:11 **40** Nu 14:25

set out for the wilderness by way of the
Red Sea (Sea of Reeds).’

41“Then you answered and said to
me, ‘We have sinned against the LORD.
We will go up and fight, just as the
LORD our God has commanded us.’ So
you equipped every man with weapons
of war, and regarded it as easy to go
up into the hill country.

42“But the LORD said to me, ‘Say to
them, “Do not go up and do not fight,
for I am not among you [because of
your rebellion]; otherwise you will be
[badly] defeated by your enemies.” ’

43“So I spoke to you, but you would
not listen. Instead you rebelled against
the command of the LORD, and acted
presumptuously and went up into the
hill country.

44“Then the Amorites who lived in
that hill country came out against you
and chased you as bees do, and struck
you down in Seir as far as Hormah.

45“And you returned and wept before
the LORD; but the LORD would not listen
to your voice nor pay attention to you.

46“So you stayed in Kadesh; many
days you stayed there.

Wanderings in the Wilderness

2 “THEN WE turned and set out for
the wilderness by the way of the
Red Sea, just as the LORD had told me;
and we circled Mount Seir for many
days.

2“And the LORD spoke to me, saying,
3‘You have circled this mountain
long enough; turn northward,

4and command the people, saying,
“You are passing through the territo-
ry of your brothers the sons of Esau
(the Edomites), who live in Seir; and
they will be afraid of you. So be very
careful;

5do not provoke them, for I will not
give you any of their land, not even *as
little as* a footstep, because I have giv-
en Mount Seir to Esau as a possession.

6“You shall buy food from them with
money so that you may [have some-
thing to] eat, and you shall also buy
water from them with money so that
you may [have something to] drink.

7“For the LORD your God has blessed
you in all that you have done; He
has known about your wanderings
through this great wilderness. These
forty years the LORD your God has been
with you; you have lacked nothing.” ’

8“So we passed beyond our brothers
the sons of Esau, who lived in Seir,
away from the Arabah (wilderness)
road, away from Elath and from Ezion-
geber. Then we turned and passed
through by the way of the Wilderness
of Moab.

9“And the LORD said to me, ‘Do not
harass [the descendants of] Moab, nor
provoke them to war, for I will not give
you any of their land as a possession,
because I have given Ar to the sons
(Moab and Ammon) of Lot as a pos-
session.’ [Gen 19:30–38]

10(The Emim lived there in times
past, a people great and numerous,
and as tall as the Anakim.

11These also are regarded as Reph-
aim [an ancient people], as are the
Anakim, but the Moabites call them
Emim.

1:44 *Hormah.* This name means “destruction,” and probably refers to a site south of the Amorite hill country by Kadesh-barnea that was later called by that name.

2:7 *God has blessed.* The Israelites could not have survived forty years in the wilderness without the miraculous provision of God. That care has been an inspiration and encouragement to God’s people throughout history. Those who receive God’s bounty with a thankful heart find that it is enough, no matter how difficult the circumstances, and those who complain never recognize His blessing at all.

2:8 *we turned and passed through by the way.* The Israelites turned away from the way of the Red Sea, on which these cities were located and turned to the wilderness of Moab, which was the area east of Moab (Nu 33:44).

2:9 *Ar.* Ar is a synonym for the region of Moab. The Moabites were related to the Israelites through Lot (Ge 19:37).

41 Nu 14:40 **42** Nu 14:42 **43** Nu 14:44 **44** Ps 118:12 **46** Nu 13:25; 20:1,22; Jdg 11:17 **CHAPTER 2**
1 Nu 14:25; Dt 1:40 **3** See ver. 7,14 **4** Nu 20:14 **5** Ge 36:8; Jos 24:4 **7** Dt 8:2-4 **8** Jdg 11:18; 1Ki 9:26
9 Nu 21:28; Ge 19:36,37 **10** Ge 14:5; Nu 13:22,33; Dt 9:2

12 The Horites also used to live in
Seir, but the sons of Esau dispossessed
them. They destroyed them from be-
fore them and settled in their place,
just as Israel did in the land which the
LORD gave them as their possession.)
13 'Now arise and cross the valley of
the Zered.' So we crossed the Zered
Valley.
14 "Now thirty-eight years passed
from the time we left Kadesh-barnea
until we crossed the Zered Valley, until
that entire generation of the men of
war had died from within the camp,
just as the LORD had sworn to them.
15 "Moreover the hand of the LORD was
against them, to destroy them from with-
in the camp, until they were all dead.
16 "So it came about when all the men
of war had finally died from among
the people,
17 that the LORD spoke to me, saying,
18 'Today you are to pass through Ar,
the border of Moab.
19 'When you come opposite the ter-
ritory of the sons of Ammon, do not
harass them nor provoke them, for I
will not give you any of the land of
the sons of Ammon as a possession,
because I have given it to the sons of
Lot as a possession.'
20 (It is also regarded as the land
of the Rephaim [of giant stature], for
Rephaim used to live there, but the
Ammonites call them Zamzummin,
21 a great, numerous people, and tall
as the Anakim, but the LORD destroyed
them before the sons of Ammon. And
they dispossessed them and settled in
their place,
22 just as He did for the sons of Esau,
who live in Seir, when He destroyed
the Horites from before them; and the
sons of Esau (the Edomites) dispos-
sessed them and settled in their place
[and remain there] even to this day.
23 As for the Avvim, who lived in vil-
lages as far as Gaza, the Caphtorim
(Cretans, later Philistines) who came
from Caphtor (Crete) destroyed them
and settled in their place.)
24 'Now arise, continue on, and go
through the valley of the Arnon. Look,
I have handed over to you Sihon the
Amorite, king of Heshbon, and his
land. Begin! Take possession [of it] and
fight with him in battle.
25 'This day I will begin to put the
dread and the fear of you on the peo-
ples (pagans) under the whole heaven,
who, when they hear the reports about
you, will tremble and be in anguish
because of you.'
26 "So I sent messengers from the Wil-
derness of Kedemoth to Sihon king of
Heshbon with words of peace, saying,
27 'Let me pass through your land
[with my people]. I will travel [with
them] only on the highway; I will not
turn away to the right or to the left.
28 'You will sell me food for money so
that I [along with my people] will eat,
and you will give me water for money
so that I [along with my people] will
drink; only let me [and my people]
travel through [the land] on foot,
29 just as the sons of Esau, who live
in Seir, and the Moabites, who live in
Ar, did for me, until I cross the Jordan
into the land which the LORD our God
is giving us.'
30 "But Sihon king of Heshbon was
not willing for us to travel through his
land; for the LORD your God hardened

2:13 *Zered.* The brook of Zered was east of the Dead Sea at the border between Edom and Moab.
2:15 *hand.* The term "hand" suggests God's personal involvement both in acts of deliverance (Ex 15:6) and in chastisement.
2:23 *Avvim . . . Gaza . . . Caphtorim . . . Caphtor.* The Avvim lived in villages between the Jordan and the Mediterranean coast. Gaza was a Philistine city on the Mediterranean coast. The Caphtorim were a group of tribes that came by sea to the coasts of Canaan and Egypt. Caphtor is possibly the same as Crete (Ge 10:14).
2:24 *Arnon.* The river Arnon was the traditional border between Moab and Ammon.
2:26 *Wilderness of Kedemoth.* This desert within the territory of Sihon was located on its eastern border, east of the Dead Sea.

12 ver. 22; Ge 14:6; 36:20 **13** Nu 21:12 **14** Nu 13:26; Nu 14:33; 26:64; Nu 14:35; Dt 1:34,35; Eze 20:15 **15** Ps 78:33; 106:26 **19** Ge 19:38 **20** Ge 14:5 **21** See ver. 10 **22** Ge 36:8; Ge 14:6; 36:20-30 **23** Jos 13:3; Ge 10:14; Am 9:7 **24** Nu 21:13; Jdg 11:18 **25** Ex 15:14,15 **26** Dt 20:10 **27** Nu 21:21,22; Jdg 11:19 **28** Nu 20:19 **29** See Nu 20:18; Dt 23:3,4; Jdg 11:17 **30** Nu 21:23; Jos 11:20; Ex 4:21

his spirit and made his heart obstinate, in order to hand him over to you, as he is today.

[31]"The LORD said to me, 'Look, I have begun to hand over to you Sihon and his land. Begin! Take possession [of it], so that you may possess his land.'

[32]"Then at Jahaz, Sihon and all his people came out to meet us in battle.

[33]"So the LORD our God handed him over to us [and gave us the victory], and we defeated him and his sons and all his people.

[34]"At the same time we took all his cities and utterly destroyed every city—men, women and children. We left no survivor.

[35]"We took only the cattle as plunder for ourselves and the spoil of the cities which we had captured.

[36]"From Aroer, which is on the edge of the Arnon Valley, and *from* the city which is in the valley, as far as Gilead, there was no city [whose wall was] too high *and* too strong for us; the LORD our God handed over everything to us.

[37]"Only you did not go near the land of the sons of Ammon, all along the river Jabbok and the cities of the hill country, and wherever the LORD our God had forbidden us.

Conquests Recounted

3 "THEN WE turned and went up the road toward Bashan, and at Edrei, Og king of Bashan, with all his people came out to meet us in battle.

[2]"And the LORD said to me, 'Do not fear him, for I have handed him over to you, him and all his people and his land; and you shall do to him just as you did to Sihon king of the Amorites, who lived at Heshbon.'

[3]"So the LORD our God also handed over Og king of Bashan, and all his people, into our hand and we struck him until no survivor was left.

[4]"We captured all his cities at that time; there was not a city which we did not take from them: sixty cities, the whole region of Argob, the kingdom of Og in Bashan.

[5]"All these cities were fortified *and* unassailable with their high walls, gates, and bars; in addition, [there were] a very great number of unwalled villages.

[6]"We utterly destroyed them, just as we did to Sihon king of Heshbon, utterly destroying every city—the men, women, and children.

[7]"But we took all the cattle and the spoil of the cities as plunder for ourselves.

[8]"So we took the land at that time from the hand of the two kings [Sihon and Og] of the Amorites who were beyond the Jordan, from the valley of the Arnon to Mount Hermon

[9](the Sidonians call Hermon Sirion, and the Amorites call it Senir):

[10]all the cities of the plain and all Gilead and all Bashan, as far as Salecah and Edrei, cities of the kingdom of Og in Bashan."

2:32 *Jahaz.* Jahaz was located north of Kedemoth (Isa 15:4).

2:34–35 *utterly destroyed.* By the law of the ban, every living thing, human and animal, was to be put to death. Sometimes, as in this case, the Lord permitted the Israelites to take livestock and property as spoil, and sometimes the Lord permitted the women and children to be spared. Canaanite idolatry had reached such abominable levels that the Lord was not willing to put up with it any longer. He intended to put an end to it, and also to prevent the Israelites from being corrupted by the Canaanites.

2:36–37 *Aroer ... Gilead ... Jabbok.* Aroer was a city on the northern bank of the river Arnon at the border between Sihon and Moab. Gilead was the northern boundary of Sihon. Jabbok was the river Jacob crossed on his way back to Canaan (Ge 32:22).

3:1 *Bashan ... Og.* Bashan was the region east of the Sea of Galilee. The territory of Og may have extended south of the river Yarmuk into Gilead.

3:8 *Mount Hermon.* Mount Hermon is in the mountain range in the north between Canaan and Lebanon.

3:9–11 *Sidonians.* The Sidonians were Phoenicians, a well-known ancient seafaring people.

3:10 *Salecah.* Salecah was a city located at the eastern border of Bashan.

31 Dt 1:8 **32** Nu 21:23 **33** Dt 7:2; 20:16; Nu 21:24; Dt 29:7 **34** Lev 27:28; Dt 7:2,26 **36** Dt 3:12; 4:48; Jos 13:9; Ps 44:3 **37** Ge 32:22; Nu 21:24; Dt 3:16; ver. 5,9,19 **CHAPTER 3** **1** Nu 21:33; Dt 29:7; Dt 1:4 **2** Nu 21:34 **3** Nu 21:35 **4** 1Ki 4:13 **6** Dt 2:24; Ps 135:10-12 **9** Dt 4:48; 1Ch 5:23 **10** Dt 4:49; Jos 12:5; 13:11

11 (For only Og king of Bashan was left of the remnant of the [the giants known as the] Rephaim. Behold, his bed frame was a bed frame of iron; is it not in Rabbah of the Ammonites? It was nine cubits (12 ft.) long and four cubits (6 ft.) wide, using the cubit of a man [the forearm to the end of the middle finger].)

12 "So we took possession of this land at that time. I gave *the territory* from Aroer, which is by the valley of the Arnon, along with half of the hill country of Gilead and its cities to the Reubenites and to the Gadites.

13 "The rest of Gilead and all of Bashan, the kingdom of Og, I gave to the half-tribe of Manasseh, that is, all the region of Argob (concerning all Bashan, it is called the land of Rephaim.

14 Jair the son (descendant) of Manasseh took all the region of Argob as far as the border of the Geshurites and the Maacathites, *that is* Bashan, and called it after his own name, Havvoth (the villages of) Jair, *as it is called* to this day.)

15 "I gave Gilead to Machir [of Manasseh].

16 "To the Reubenites and Gadites I gave *the territory* from Gilead as far as the Valley of Arnon, with the middle of the Valley as a boundary, and as far as the Jabbok River, the boundary of the sons of Ammon;

17 the Arabah also, with the Jordan as its boundary, from Chinnereth (the Sea of Galilee) as far as the sea of the Arabah, the Salt Sea (Dead Sea), at the foot of the slopes of Pisgah on the east.

18 "Then I commanded you [Reuben, Gad, and the half-tribe of Manasseh] at that time, saying, 'The LORD your God has given you this land to possess; all you who are brave men shall cross over [the Jordan] armed before your brothers, the sons of Israel.

19 'But your wives and your children and your cattle—I know that you have much livestock—shall remain in your cities which I have given you,

20 until the LORD gives rest to your fellow countrymen as [He has] to you, and they also possess the land which the LORD your God has given them beyond the Jordan. Then each of you may return to the land (possession) which I have given to you.'

21 "I commanded Joshua at that time, saying, 'Your eyes have seen everything that the LORD your God has done to these two kings [Sihon and Og]; so the LORD shall do the same to all the kingdoms into which you are about to cross.

22 'Do not fear them, for it is the LORD your God who is fighting for you.'

23 "Then I pleaded with the LORD at that time [for His favor], saying,

24 'O Lord GOD, You have only begun to show Your servant Your greatness

---

3:11 *bed frame.* "Bed frame" could also be translated *sarcophagus*, that is, *stone coffin*. ***Rabbah.*** Rabbah was on the site of Amman, the capital of modern Jordan. ***cubit.*** The ordinary cubit is about eighteen inches. Nine cubits is about thirteen feet, and four cubits is about six feet.

3:14 *Geshurites . . . Maachathites.* The Geshurites lived east of the Sea of Galilee and south of Mount Hermon. The Maachathites were descended from Abraham's brother Nahor.

3:17 *Chinnereth*. Chinnereth is another name for the Sea of Galilee.

3:23–25 *pleaded with the LORD.* Moses was a man of prayer and a man of God. He had repeatedly interceded with God for the rebellious Israelites, and God had answered those prayers. Yet this request of Moses to enter the promised land was answered with a decided "no," and with the command not to mention the matter again. We usually don't know why God says "no," to things that seem not only reasonable, but right and good to us. It is hard to give thanks for the answer we did not want, but we must learn that "no" can also be the hand of our loving Heavenly Father. Most of the time we won't see, this side of heaven, how grateful we ought to be for the "no" of God.

3:24 *O Lord GOD.* The Hebrew word for "Lord," or "Master" is followed by the personal name of God (Yahweh, here translated "GOD"). The respect and humbleness in calling God "Master," the long

11 Am 2:9; Ge 14:5; 2Sa 12:26; Jer 49:2; Eze 21:20 **12** Dt 2:36; Jos 12:2; Nu 32:33; Jos 12:6; 13:8 **13** Jos 13:29 **14** 1Ch 2:22; Jos 13:13; 2Sa 3:3; 10:6; Nu 32:41 **15** Nu 32:39 **16** 2Sa 24:5; Nu 21:24; Jos 12:2 **17** Nu 34:11; Nu 34:12; Dt 4:49; Jos 12:3; Ge 14:3 **18** Nu 32:20 **20** Jos 22:4 **21** Nu 27:23 **22** Ex 14:14; Dt 1:30; 20:4 **23** See 2Co 12:8,9 **24** Dt 11:2; Ex 15:11; 2Sa 7:22; Ps 71:19; 86:8; 89:6,8

and Your mighty hand; for what god is
there in heaven or on earth that can do
such works and mighty acts (miracles)
as Yours?
25'I pray, let me go over and see the
good land that is beyond the Jordan,
that good hill country [with Hermon]
and Lebanon.'
26"But the LORD was angry with me
because of you [and your rebellion
at Meribah], and would not listen to
me; and the LORD said to me, 'Enough!
Speak to Me no longer about this mat-
ter. [Num 20:8]
27'Go up to the top of [Mount] Pisgah
and raise your eyes toward the west
and north and south and east, and
see it with your eyes, for you shall not
cross this Jordan.
28'But command Joshua and encour-
age and strengthen him, for he shall
go across and lead this people, and he
will give them the land which you see
as an inheritance.'
29"So we stayed in the Valley oppo-
site Beth-peor.

Israel Urged to Obey God's Law

4 "NOW, O Israel, listen *and* pay at-
tention to the statutes and the judg-
ments (God's legal decisions) which I
am teaching you to do, so that you may
live and go in and take possession of
the land which the LORD, the God of
your fathers, is giving you.
2"You shall not add to the word
which I am commanding you, nor take
away from it, so that you may keep the
commandments of the LORD your God
which I am commanding you.
3"Your eyes have seen what the LORD
did at Baal-peor; for all the men who
followed [and participated in the wor-
ship of] Baal of Peor, the LORD your
God destroyed them from among you,
[Num 25:1–9]
4but you who held tightly to the LORD
your God are alive today, every one
of you.
5"Look, I have taught you statutes
and judgments just as the LORD my
God has commanded me, so that you
may do them in the land which you are
entering to possess.
6"So keep and do them, for that is
your wisdom and your understanding
in the sight of the peoples who will
hear all these statutes and say, 'Surely
this great nation is a wise and under-
standing people.'
7"For what great nation is there that
has a god so near to it as the LORD
our God [is to us] whenever we call
on Him?
8"Or what great nation has statutes
and judgments so righteous (upright,
just) as this whole law which I am plac-
ing before you today?
9"Only pay attention and watch
yourselves closely so that you do not
forget the things which your eyes have
seen and they do not depart from your
heart all the days of your life. Make
them known to your children and

---

companionship revealed in calling God by the covenant name, and the pleading, just to see the promised land, poignantly speak of Moses' longing.

3:29 *Beth-peor.* This was a pagan site dedicated to Baal of Peor (Nu 25:3 – 5) and was the scene of Israel's first disastrous encounter with the sexually centered worship of Baal (4:3).

4:1 *listen.* The exhortation to listen includes an encouragement to obey (4:9; 5:1; 6:3 – 4).

4:6 *in the sight of the peoples.* By living in obedience to God, Israel would become a countercultural force, showing the way of God in both society and government.

4:9 *your children.* One of the purposes of the family is to pass on from generation to generation the acts of God among men. In times where the written record did not exist, or where people could not read, the wonderful acts of God were repeated in stories and conversations. With the Bible readily available, we don't have to rely on our memories alone to recall the things that God has done, but we are still responsible to make these things known to our children. It is also important to tell our children about the times that the Lord has answered our prayers, convicted our conscience, and blessed us with His peace. The best role model a child can have is a parent whose heart is centered on the Lord.

25 Ex 3:8; Dt 4:22 **26** Dt 1:37; 31:2 **27** Nu 27:12 **28** Nu 27:18,23; Dt 31:3,7 **29** Dt 34:6 **CHAPTER 4**
1 Lev 19:37; Dt 5:1; Eze 20:11; Ro 10:5 **2** Jos 1:7 **3** Jos 22:17; Ps 106:28 **6** Job 28:28; Ps 19:7; Pr 1:7 **7** 2Sa 7:23;
Ps 46:1; Isa 55:6 **9** Pr 4:23; Ge 18:19; Dt 6:7; 11:19; Ps 78:5,6; Eph 6:4

your grandchildren [impressing these things on their mind and penetrating their heart with these truths]—

10 *especially* the day you stood before the LORD your God at Horeb (Mount Sinai), when the LORD said to me, 'Assemble the people to Me and I will let them hear My words, so that they may learn to fear Me [with awe-filled reverence and profound respect] all the days they live on the land, and so that they may teach their children.'

11 "You approached and stood at the foot of the mountain, and the mountain burned with fire to the [very] heart of the heavens: darkness, cloud and thick gloom.

12 "Then the LORD spoke to you from the midst of the fire; you heard the sound of the words, but you saw no form—there was only a voice.

13 "So He declared to you His covenant which He commanded you to follow, the Ten Commandments; and He wrote them on two tablets of stone.

14 "The LORD commanded me at that time to teach you the statutes and judgments, so that you might do them in the land which you are going over to possess.

15 "So pay attention *and* watch yourselves carefully—for you did not see any form [of God] on the day the LORD spoke to you at Horeb from the midst of the fire—

16 so that you do not act corruptly and make for yourselves a carved *or* sculpted image [to worship] in the form of any figure, the likeness of male or female,

17 the likeness of any animal that is on the earth, or of any winged bird that flies in the sky,

18 the likeness of anything that crawls on the ground, or of any fish that is in the waters beneath the earth.

19 "And *beware* that you do not raise your eyes toward heaven and see the sun and the moon and the stars, all the host of heaven, and let yourselves be led astray and worship them and serve them, [mere created bodies] which the LORD your God has allotted to [serve and benefit] all the peoples under the whole heaven.

20 "But the LORD has taken you and brought you out of the iron [smelting] furnace, out of Egypt, to be a people for His own possession, as [you are] this day.

21 "Now the LORD was angry with me [at the waters of Meribah] because of you, and He swore [an oath] that I would not cross the Jordan, and that I would not enter the good land which the LORD your God is giving you as an inheritance.

22 "For I am going to die in this land, I am not going to cross the Jordan, but you shall cross over and take possession of this good land.

23 "So be on your guard *and* watch yourselves, so that you do not forget the covenant of the LORD your God which He has made with you, and make for yourselves a carved *or* sculpted image in the form of anything which the LORD your God has forbidden you.

24 "For the LORD your God is a consuming fire; He is a jealous (impassioned)

4:12 heard . . . but you saw no form. The Lord revealed His glory to the Israelites, but they saw no visual image other than darkness and fire. They did hear God's voice, however (v. 15). This verse reminds us that God is Spirit (Jn 4:24).

4:15 – 19 you did not see any form. There was no way of describing or giving shape with any image to the experience of God's presence at Sinai (Ex 20:18). Since Israel had not seen the form of God, they could not represent Him in any way. Although people were created in the likeness of God (Ge 1:26 – 27), no image created in human likeness could represent God, nor could any animal or the majestic heavenly bodies. The Israelites could know God's creation, His power, and His character, but they would have to be satisfied to know Him without any visual image.

4:24 a consuming fire . . . jealous. God is free to destroy disobedient and rebellious people. Israel had witnessed His righteous anger during the wilderness journey as well as in Canaan (Heb 12:19; Nu 16). "Jealous" means that God will tolerate no rivalry or unfaithfulness. This word can also be translated *zealous*. God is zealous for His holiness.

---

10 Ex 19:9,16 **11** Ex 19:18 **12** Dt 5:4,22; Ex 20:22; 1Ki 19:12 **13** Dt 9:9,11; Ex 34:28; Ex 24:12; 31:18 **14** Ex 21:1; Dt 22; Dt 23 **15** Jos 23:11; Isa 40:18 **16** Ex 32:7; ver. 23; Ex 20:4,5; Dt 5:8; Ro 1:23 **19** Dt 17:3; Job 31:26; 2Ki 21:3; Ro 1:25 **20** 1Ki 8:51; Jer 11:4; Ex 19:5; Dt 9:29 **21** Nu 20:12; Dt 1:37; 3:26 **22** See 2Pe 1:13-15; Dt 3:27; Dt 3:25 **23** ver. 9; ver. 16; Ex 20:4,5 **24** Ex 24:17; Dt 9:3; Isa 33:14; Heb 12:29; Ex 20:5; Dt 6:15

God [demanding what is rightfully and uniquely His].

25 “When you become the father of children and grandchildren and have grown old in the land, then if you corrupt yourselves by making a carved *or* sculpted image in the form of anything [for the purpose of worship], and do evil [things] in the sight of the LORD your God, provoking Him to anger,

26 I call heaven and earth as witnesses against you today, that you will soon utterly perish from the land which you are crossing the Jordan to possess. You shall not live long on it, but will be utterly destroyed.

27 “The LORD will scatter *and* disperse you among the peoples (pagan nations), and you will be left few in number among the nations where the LORD drives you.

28 “And there you will serve [false and foreign] gods, the work of human hands, [lifeless images of] wood and stone, which neither see nor hear nor eat nor smell [the offerings of food given to them].

29 “But from there you will seek the LORD your God, and you will find *Him* if you search for Him with all your heart and all your soul.

30 “When you are in distress *and* tribulation and all these things come on you, in the latter days you will return to the LORD your God and listen to His voice.

31 “For the LORD your God is a merciful *and* compassionate God; He will not fail you, nor destroy you, nor forget the covenant with your fathers which He swore to them.

32 “Indeed, ask now about the days that are past, [those days] which were before you, since the day that God created man on the earth, and ask from one end of the heavens to the other. Has *anything* been done like this great thing, or has *anything* been heard like it?

33 “Did [any] people ever hear the voice of God speaking out of the midst of the fire, as you heard, and [still] live?

34 “Or has any [man-made] god ever tried to go and take for himself a nation from within *another* nation by trials, by signs and wonders and by war and by a mighty hand and by an outstretched arm and by great terrors, as the LORD your God did for you in Egypt before your [very] eyes?

35 “It was shown to you so that you might have [personal] knowledge *and* comprehend that the LORD is God; there is no other besides Him.

36 “Out of the heavens He let you hear His voice to discipline *and* admonish you; and on earth He let you see His great fire, and you heard His words from the midst of the fire.

37 “And because He loved your fathers, He chose their descendants who followed them, and brought you from Egypt with His Presence, with His great *and* awesome power,

38 dispossessing *and* driving out from before you nations, [nations that were] greater and mightier than you, to bring you in, to give you their land as an inheritance, as it is this day.

39 Therefore know *and* understand today, and take it to your heart, that the LORD is God in the heavens above and on the earth below; there is no other.

40 “So you shall keep His statutes and His commandments which I am commanding you today, so that it may go

---

4:26 *heaven and earth.* All creation would act as God's witness against a rebellious and obstinate people. God's invisible attributes, His eternal power and divine nature, are all clearly seen in creation (Ro 1:20), so that man is without excuse. The creation belongs to God just as much as man does, and God uses it for His eternal purposes, one of which is to stand as a witness to the disobedient.

4:27 *scatter and disperse you among the peoples.* This is a prophetic warning of the exiles that would take place in 722 and 586 BC.

4:40 *that it may go well with you.* The promise

25 2Ki 17:17 **26** Dt 30:18,19; Isa 1:2; Mic 6:2 **27** Lev 26:33; Neh 1:8 **28** Dt 28:64; 1Sa 26:19; Jer 16:13; Ps 115:4,5; 135:15,16; Isa 44:9; 46:7 **29** Lev 26:39; Dt 30:1-3; 2Ch 15:4; Neh 1:9; Isa 55:6,7 **30** Ge 49:1; Dt 31:29; Jer 23:20; Hos 3:5; Joel 2:12 **31** 2Ch 30:9; Neh 9:31; Ps 116:5; Jnh 4:2 **32** Job 8:8; Mt 24:31 **33** Ex 24:11; 33:20; Dt 5:24,26 **34** Dt 7:19; Ex 7:3; Ex 13:3; Ex 6:6; Dt 26:8; 34:12 **35** Dt 32:39; 1Sa 2:2; Isa 45:5,18; Mk 12:29 **36** Ex 19:9,19; 20:18,22; 24:16; Heb 12:18 **37** Dt 10:15; Ex 13:3,9,14 **38** Dt 7:1; 9:1,4,5 **39** Jos 2:11 **40** Lev 22:31; Dt 5:16; 6:3,18; 12:25,28; 22:7; Eph 6:3

well with you and with your children
after you, and so that you may live long
on the land which the LORD your God
is giving you for all time."
41 Then Moses set apart three cities
[of refuge] beyond the Jordan toward
the rising of the sun (eastward),
42 so that someone who committed
manslaughter could flee there, [that
is, a person] who killed his neighbor
unintentionally and without previously
having hostility toward him, and that
by escaping to one of these cities he
might [claim the right of asylum and]
save his life:
43 Bezer in the wilderness on the pla-
teau for the Reubenites, and Ramoth
in Gilead for the Gadites, and Golan in
Bashan for the Manassites.
44 This is the law which Moses placed
before the sons of Israel;
45 these are the testimonies (legal pro-
visions) and the statutes and the judg-
ments which Moses spoke to the sons
of Israel when they came out of Egypt,
46 beyond the Jordan in the Valley
opposite Beth-peor, in the land of Si-
hon king of the Amorites who lived at
Heshbon, whom Moses and the sons
of Israel defeated when they came out
from Egypt.
47 They took possession of his land
and the land of Og king of Bashan,
the two kings of the Amorites, who
reigned across the Jordan to the east,
48 from Aroer, which is on the edge
of the valley of the [river] Arnon, as
far as Mount Sion (that is, Hermon),
49 with all the Arabah (desert low-
lands) across the Jordan to the east,
even as far as the sea of the Arabah
(the Dead Sea), at the foot of the slopes
of Pisgah.

The Ten Commandments Repeated

5 THEN MOSES summoned all Is-
rael and said to them:
"Hear, O Israel, the statutes and
judgments (legal decisions) which I
am speaking today in your hearing, so
that you may learn them and observe
them carefully.
2 "The LORD our God made a cov-
enant with us at Horeb.
3 "The LORD did not make this cov-
enant with our fathers, but with us, all
of us who are alive here today.
4 "The LORD spoke with you face to
face at the mountain from the midst
of the fire.
5 "I was standing between the LORD
and you at that time, to declare to you
the word of the LORD; for you were
afraid because of the fire and did not
go up the mountain. He said,
6 'I am the LORD your God who
brought you out of the land of Egypt,
out of the house of slavery.
7 'You shall have no other gods be-
fore Me.
8 'You shall not make for yourself an
idol [as an object to worship], or any
likeness (form, manifestation) of what
is in heaven above or on the earth be-
neath or in the water under the earth.
9 'You shall not worship them or serve
them; for I, the LORD your God, am a
jealous (impassioned) God [demand-
ing what is rightfully and uniquely
mine], visiting (avenging) the iniquity
(sin, guilt) of the fathers on the chil-
dren [that is, calling the children to
account for the sins of their fathers],
to the third and the fourth *generations*
of those who hate Me, [Is 42:8; 48:11]
10 but showing graciousness *and*

---

of blessing in the land was conditional—it required obedience.

5:6–21 Commandments—The Ten Commandments are the basis for holy living, not just a list of rules, but an explanation of what God expects of us. Loving God comes first. Setting aside a day to focus on God is essential for maintaining this relationship. The way we feel about God will affect the way we feel about people, and this will have a direct effect on how we treat others. Even though these three ideas summarize the Commandments, it is also essential to examine each individual command and think about how it applies to our lives. It is not easy to faithfully obey these simple statements.

41 Nu 35:6 **42** Dt 19:4 **43** Jos 20:8 **46** Dt 3:29; Nu 21:24; Dt 1:4 **47** Nu 21:35; Dt 3:3,4 **48** Dt 2:36; 3:12; Dt 3:9; Ps 133:3 **49** Dt 3:17 **CHAPTER 5** **2** Ex 19:5; Dt 4:23 **3** See Mt 13:17; Heb 8:9 **4** Ex 19:9,19; 20:22; Dt 4:33,36; 34:10 **5** Ex 20:21; Gal 3:19; Ex 19:16; 20:18; 24:2 **6** Ex 20:2 **7** Ex 20:3 **8** Ex 20:4 **9** Ex 34:7 **10** Jer 32:18; Da 9:4

lovingkindness to thousands [of gener-
ations] of those who love Me and keep
My commandments.
11 ‘You shall not take the name of
the LORD your God in vain [that is,
irreverently, in false affirmations or
in ways that impugn the character of
God]; for the LORD will not hold guilt-
less *nor* leave unpunished the one who
takes His name in vain [disregarding
its reverence and its power].
12 ‘Observe the Sabbath day to keep
it holy (set apart, dedicated to God), as
the LORD your God commanded you.
13 ‘Six days you shall labor and do
all your work,
14 but the seventh day is a Sabbath [a
day of rest dedicated] to the LORD your
God; on that day you shall not do any
work, you or your son or your daughter
or your male servant or your female
servant or your ox or your donkey or
any of your livestock or the stranger
who stays inside your [city] gates, so
that your male servant and your fe-
male servant may rest as well as you.
15 ‘You shall remember [with thought-
ful concern] that you were a slave in
the land of Egypt, and that the LORD
your God brought you out of there with
a mighty hand and by an outstretched
arm; therefore the LORD your God has
commanded you to observe the Sab-
bath day.
16 ‘Honor (respect, obey, care for)
your father and your mother, as the
LORD your God has commanded you,
so that your days [on the earth] may be
prolonged and so that it may go well
with you in the land which the LORD
your God gives you.
17 ‘You shall not murder.
18 ‘You shall not commit adultery.
[Prov 6:25, 26; Matt 5:27, 28; Rom 1:24;
Eph 5:3]
19 ‘You shall not steal. [Prov 11:1; 16:8;
21:6; 22:16; Jer 17:11; Mal 3:8]
20 ‘You shall not give false testimony
[that is, lie, withhold, or manipulate
the truth] against your neighbor (any
person). [Ex 23:1; Prov 19:9; 24:28]
21 ‘You shall not covet [that is, desire
and seek to acquire] your neighbor's
wife, nor desire your neighbor's house,
his field, his male servant or his female
servant, his ox or his donkey or any-
thing that belongs to your neighbor.'
[Luke 12:15; Col 3:5]

Moses Interceded

22 "The LORD spoke these words with
a great voice to all your assembly at
the mountain out of the midst of the
fire, the cloud, and the thick darkness,
and He added no more. He wrote these
commandments on two tablets of stone
and gave them to me.
23 "And when you heard the voice
from the midst of the darkness, while
the mountain was burning with fire,
you approached me, all the leaders
(heads) of your tribes and your elders;
24 and you said, 'Behold, the LORD
our God has shown us His glory and
His greatness, and we have heard His
voice from the midst of the fire; we

5:11 ***take ... in vain.*** Taking the name of the Lord in vain refers to the abuse, misuse, blasphemy, cursing, or manipulation of the Lord's name. Something "vain" is empty or without value, significance, or meaning.

5:12 ***the Sabbath.*** The primary significance of the Sabbath was that it belonged to the Lord.

5:18 ***adultery.*** Adultery was a betrayal not only of a commitment, but of a relationship. Anyone who treated marriage lightly would also treat his or her relationship with God lightly.

5:21 ***covet.*** This command deals specifically with an attitude, rather than an action. Covetousness is self-centered dissatisfaction, which does not reflect loving concern for the well-being of others. Loving God and loving others are closely connected (Mt 22:37 – 39).

5:22 ***wrote these commandments on two tablets of stone and gave them to me.*** The two tablets were two complete copies of the law. Usually two copies were made of ancient Middle Eastern treaties. One was retained by each of the contracting parties. But God gave both copies to Moses, signifying that God Himself would be with the Israelites. God and the Israelites kept their copies in the same place because they lived together.

11 Ex 20:7; Lev 19:12; Mt 5:33 **12** Ex 20:8 **13** Ex 23:12; 35:2; Eze 20:12 **14** Ge 2:2; Ex 16:29; Heb 4:4 **15** Dt 15:15; 16:12; 24:18,22; Dt 4:34,37 **16** Ex 20:12; Lev 19:3; Dt 27:16; Eph 6:2,3; Col 3:20; Dt 4:40 **17** Ex 20:13; Mt 5:21 **18** Ex 20:14; Lk 18:20; Jas 2:11 **19** Ex 20:15; Ro 13:9 **20** Ex 20:16 **21** Ex 20:17; Mic 2:2; Hab 2:9; Lk 12:15; Ro 7:7 **22** Ex 24:12; 31:18; Dt 4:13 **23** Ex 20:18,19 **24** Ex 19:19; Dt 4:33; Jdg 13:22

have seen today that God speaks with
man, yet he [still] lives.
25 'Now then why should we die? For
this great fire will consume us; if we
hear the voice of the LORD our God any
longer, then we will die.
26 'For who is there of all flesh (man-
kind) who has heard the voice of the
living God speaking from the midst of
the fire, as we have, and lived?
27 'You, Moses, go near and listen to
everything that the LORD our God says;
then speak to us everything that the
LORD our God speaks to you, and we
will listen and do it.'
28 "The LORD heard your words when
you spoke to me, and the LORD said
to me, 'I have heard the words of this
people which they have spoken to you.
They have done well in all that they
have spoken.
29 'Oh that they had such a heart in
them, that they would fear [and wor-
ship Me with awe-filled reverence
and profound respect] and keep all
My commandments always, so that it
may go well with them and with their
children forever!
30 'Go and say to them, "Return to
your tents."
31 'But as for you, stand here by Me,
and I will tell you all the command-
ments and the statutes and the judg-
ments which you shall teach them, so
that they may obey them in the land
which I give them to possess.'
32 "Therefore you shall pay attention
and be careful to do just as the LORD
your God has commanded you; you
shall not turn aside to the right or to
the left [deviating from My command-
ments].
33 "You shall walk [that is, live each
and every day] in all the ways which
the LORD your God has commanded
you, so that you may live and so that
it may be well with you, and that you
may live long in the land which you
will possess.

Obey God and Prosper

6 "NOW THIS is the command; the
statutes and the judgments (pre-
cepts) which the LORD your God has
commanded me to teach you, so that
you might do (follow, obey) them in the
land which you are crossing over [the
Jordan] to possess,
2 so that you and your son and your
grandson may fear *and* worship the
LORD your God [with awe-filled rev-
erence and profound respect], to keep
[and actively do] all His statutes and
His commandments which I am com-
manding you, all the days of your life,
so that your days may be prolonged.
3 "Therefore listen, O Israel, and be
careful to do *them*, that it may go well
with you and that you may increase
greatly [in numbers], as the LORD, the
God of your fathers, has promised you,
in a land flowing with milk and honey.
4 "Hear, O Israel! The LORD is our
God, the LORD is one [the only God]!

5:25–26 *why should we die ... LORD our God.* The Israelites' fear was an important part of understanding their sin and need for help in meeting the requirements of God. The living God is powerful, great, and holy, and He wants us to be like Him, so each sinner needs to realize the need for God's mercy.

5:29 *heart in them.* The people were impressed with what they saw and heard, but their hearts were unchanged.

6:2 *fear.* The fear of the Lord includes awe for His greatness and holiness, love for Him, and submission to His will. Initially, the fear of God may involve fright, knowing that God has the right to punish us for our sins. But when we look at his holiness and love, there is a joy in knowing God, who not only sees us for who we really are, but helps us to be who He wants us to be.

6:3 *God of your fathers.* God was their God, generation after generation, and He expected them to follow Him, from generation to generation as well.

6:4–9 Passing on the Faith — In the days leading up to the end of Moses' leadership, he laid out the essentials of raising a family to follow God. Moses knew that these instructions were a foundational element in Israel's future. The only way the Israelites could maintain the land they were going to possess was to make sure that the faith would be passed on to each succeeding

---

25 Dt 18:16 **26** Dt 4:33 **27** Ex 20:19; Heb 12:19 **28** Dt 18:17 **29** Dt 32:29; Ps 81:13; Isa 48:18; Mt 23:37; Lk 19:42; Dt 11:1; Dt 4:40 **31** Gal 3:19 **32** Dt 17:20; 28:14; Jos 1:7; Pr 4:27 **33** Dt 10:12; Jer 7:23; Dt 4:40
CHAPTER 6 **1** Dt 12:1 **2** Dt 10:12,13; Ecc 12:13; Dt 4:40; Pr 3:1,2 **3** Ge 22:17; Ex 3:8 **4** Jn 17:3; 1Co 8:4,6

5"You shall love the LORD your God
with all your heart *and* mind and with
all your soul and with all your strength
[your entire being].
6"These words, which I am commanding you today, shall be [written]
on your heart *and* mind.
7"You shall teach them diligently to
your children [impressing God's precepts on their minds and penetrating
their hearts with His truths] and shall
speak of them when you sit in your
house and when you walk on the road
and when you lie down and when you
get up.
8"And you shall bind them as a sign
on your hand (forearm), and they shall
be used as bands (frontals, frontlets)
on your forehead.
9"You shall write them on the doorposts of your house and on your gates.
10"Then it shall come about when the
LORD your God brings you into the land
which He swore (solemnly promised)
to [give] your fathers—to Abraham,
Isaac, and Jacob—to give you, [a land
with] great and splendid cities which
you did not build,
11and houses full of all good things
which you did not fill, and hewn (excavated) cisterns (wells) which you did
not dig out, and vineyards and olive
trees which you did not plant, and you
eat and are full *and* satisfied,
12then beware that you do not forget the LORD who brought you out of
the land of Egypt, out of the house of
slavery.
13"You shall fear [only] the LORD your
God; and you shall serve Him [with
awe-filled reverence and profound respect] and swear [oaths] by His name
[alone].
14"You shall not follow other gods,
any of the gods of the peoples who
surround you,
15for the LORD your God who is
among you is a jealous (impassioned)
God [demanding what is rightfully and
uniquely His]—otherwise the anger of
the LORD your God will be kindled *and*
burn against you, and He will destroy
you from the face of the earth.
16"You shall not put the LORD your
God to the test, as you tested Him at
Massah. [Ex 17:7]
17"You shall diligently keep [foremost in your thoughts and actively do]
the commandments of the LORD your
God, and His testimonies and His statutes which He has commanded you.
18"You shall do what is right and
good in the sight of the LORD, so that it
may be well with you and that you may

---

generation. Nothing has changed. Today we need to heed the same instructions.

In a family's life the teaching of God is to be a constant, daily effort. God is to be made a part of everyday life. It is the responsibility of a parent to be constantly looking for opportunities to teach children about God's instructions for living. God's instructions should be like clothing. They should be put on the minute we get up and kept on all day. They are to be our constant companions. Sharing our faith should be a natural part of daily communication with our children. We should also remember that these instructions come in the text subsequent to the command to love God with all of our heart and soul and strength. How else can we love Him better than by obeying and following Him and teaching our children to do the same?

6:4 Hear, O Israel. This verse is the celebrated Shema, the basic confession of faith in Judaism (Mt 22:37; Mk 12:29; Lk 10:27). The first word, "hear," is the Hebrew word *shema*. The people are to hear and respond properly to God. He is their God, and He alone is the Lord.

6:5 shall love. Moses repeatedly exhorted the Israelites to respond to God's love with devotion. God commanded His people to choose Him with all their being, and in the process to deny all other supposed deities.

6:8–9 hand ... bands ... doorposts ... gates. In later years the Jews interpreted these instructions by wearing phylacteries (boxes containing Scripture) when they prayed. They attached a small vessel called a mezuzah, which contained these verses, to the doorpost. The purpose of this whole passage is to emphasize that God's ways are to be a part of our conversations, our homes, and every activity. They are to be as close to us and as visible as our hand or our forehead.

5 Mt 22:37; Mk 12:30; 2Ki 23:25 **6** Dt 11:18; Ps 119:11,98 **7** Dt 11:19; Ps 78:4-6 **8** Pr 6:21; 7:3 **9** Dt 11:20; Isa 57:8 **10** Jos 24:13; Ps 105:44 **11** Dt 8:10 **13** Mt 4:10; Lk 4:8; Isa 45:23; 65:16; Jer 4:2 **14** Dt 13:7 **15** Ex 20:5; Dt 4:24; Dt 7:4; 11:17 **16** Mt 4:7; Lk 4:12; 1Co 10:9 **17** Ps 119:4 **18** Ex 15:26; Dt 12:28; 13:18

go in and possess the good land which
the LORD swore to [give] your fathers,
19 by driving out all your enemies from
before you, as the LORD has spoken.
20 "When your son asks you in time
to come, saying, 'What *is the meaning*
of the testimonies and statutes and
judgments (precepts) which the LORD
our God has commanded you?'
21 then you shall say to your son, 'We
were Pharaoh's slaves in Egypt, and
the LORD brought us out of Egypt with
a mighty hand.
22 'Moreover, the LORD showed great
and terrible signs and wonders before
our eyes against Egypt, Pharaoh and
all his household;
23 He brought us out from there in
order to bring us in, to give us the
land which He had sworn to [give] our
fathers.'
24 "So the LORD commanded us to
do all these statutes, to fear [and wor-
ship] the LORD our God [with awe-filled
reverence and profound respect] for
our good always and so that He might
preserve us alive, as it is today.
25 "It will be [considered] righteous-
ness for us [that is, right standing with
God] if we are careful to observe all
this commandment before the LORD our
God—just as He has commanded us.

Warnings

7 "WHEN THE LORD your God
brings you into the land which
you are entering to possess, and has
cleared away many nations before you,
the Hittite and the Girgashite and the
Amorite and the Canaanite and the
Perizzite and the Hivite and the Jeb-
usite, seven nations greater and might-
ier than you,
2 and when the LORD your God gives
them over to you and you defeat them,
then you shall utterly destroy them.
You shall not make a covenant (treaty)
with them nor show mercy *and* com-
passion to them.
3 "You shall not intermarry with
them; you shall not give your daugh-
ter to his son, nor shall you take his
daughter for your son;
4 for they will turn your sons away
from following Me to serve other gods;
then the anger of the LORD will be kin-
dled *and* burn against you and He will
quickly destroy you.
5 "But this is how you shall deal with
them: you shall tear down their al-
tars and smash to pieces their *sacred*
pillars, and cut down their Asherim
(symbols of the goddess Asherah), and
burn their carved *or* sculpted images
in the fire.
6 "For you are a holy people [set
apart] to the LORD your God; the LORD
your God has chosen you out of all the
peoples on the face of the earth to be
a people for His own possession [that
is, His very special treasure].
7 "The LORD did not love you and
choose you because you were great-
er in number than any of the *other*
peoples, for you were the fewest of all
peoples.

6:20–24 *your son asks.* The answer to the Israelite child's question would include four components: we were slaves in Egypt, the Lord brought us out with a mighty hand, He gave us land, and we have a challenge to responsible action. This is a powerful teaching tool, and one that applies to all Christians. We are to teach our children that we were slaves to sin, the Lord Jesus brought us out with a mighty hand, He has given us a Kingdom, and we have a challenge to responsible action.

7:1 *Hittite . . . Girgashite . . . Amorite . . . Canaanite . . . Perizzite . . . Hivite . . . Jebusite.* The Hittites came originally from Asia Minor (Ge 23:10). The Girgashites are an unknown people (Ge 10:16; 1Ch 1:14). The Amorites were the native population of Canaan that had settled in the mountains. The Canaanites were the native population that had settled in the coastland, the Perizzites were the native population that had settled in the hill country, and the Hivites were the native population that had settled south of the Lebanon mountains. The Jebusites (perhaps an offshoot of the Hittites) were the native population settled near what later became Jerusalem.

7:2 *covenant.* Covenant refers to any treaty with the Canaanite nations that might undermine God's covenant with Israel.

19 Nu 33:52,53 **20** Ex 13:14 **21** Ex 13:3 **22** Ex 7; 8; 9; 10 **24** ver. 2; Job 35:7,8; Jer 32:39; Dt 4:1; Ps 41:2 **25** Lev 18:5; Ro 10:3,5 **CHAPTER 7** **1** Dt 31:3; Ex 33:2; Dt 4:38 **2** Dt 23:14; Jos 6:17; 8:24; 9:24; Jos 2:14; Jdg 1:24; 2:2 **3** 1Ki 11:2; Ezr 9:2 **4** Dt 6:15 **5** Ex 23:24; 34:13; Dt 12:2,3 **6** Ps 50:5; Jer 2:3; Ex 19:5; Am 3:2; 1Pe 2:9 **7** Dt 10:22

8 “But because the LORD loves you and is keeping the oath which He swore to your fathers, the LORD has brought you out with a mighty hand and redeemed (bought) you from the house of slavery, from the hand of Pharaoh king of Egypt.

9 “Therefore know [without any doubt] *and* understand that the LORD your God, He is God, the faithful God, who is keeping His covenant and His [steadfast] lovingkindness to a thousand generations with those who love Him and keep His commandments;

10 but repays those who hate Him to their faces, by destroying them; He will not hesitate with him who hates Him, He will repay him to his face.

11 “Therefore, you shall keep (follow, obey) the commandment and the statutes and judgments (precepts) which I am commanding you today.

Promises of God

12 “Then it shall come about, because you listen to these judgments and keep and do them, that the LORD your God will keep with you the covenant and the [steadfast] lovingkindness which He swore to your fathers.

13 “He will love you and bless you and multiply you; He will also bless the fruit of your womb and the fruit of your land, your grain and your new wine and your [olive] oil, the offspring of your cattle and the young of your flock, in the land which He swore to your fathers to give you.

14 “You shall be blessed above all peoples; there will be no male or female barren (childless, infertile) among you or among your cattle.

15 “The LORD will take away from you all sickness; and He will not subject you to any of the harmful diseases of Egypt which you have known, but He will impose them on all [those] who hate you.

16 “And you shall consume all the peoples whom the LORD your God will give over to you; your eye shall not pity them, nor shall you serve their gods, for that would be a [deadly] trap to you.

17 “If you say in your heart, ‘These nations are greater than I am; how can I dispossess them?’

18 you shall not be afraid of them; you shall remember [with confidence] what the LORD your God did to Pharaoh and to all Egypt—

19 the great trials which you saw with your own eyes, and the signs, the wonders, the mighty hand and the outstretched arm by which the LORD your God brought you out. So shall the LORD your God do to all the peoples of whom you are afraid.

20 “Moreover, the LORD your God will send the hornet (His terror) against them, until those who are left and hide themselves from you perish.

21 “You shall not dread them, for the LORD your God is in your midst, a great and awesome God.

22 “The LORD your God will clear away these nations before you little by little; you will not be able to put an end to them quickly, for [if you did] the wild animals would become too numerous for you.

23 “But the LORD your God will hand them over to you, and will confuse them with a great panic until they are destroyed.

24 “And He will hand over their kings to you, and you will make their name perish from under heaven; no man will be able to stand before you until you have destroyed them.

25 “You shall burn the carved *and* sculpted images of their gods in the fire. You shall not covet the silver or gold that is on them, nor take it for yourselves, so that you will not be ensnared by it [in a deadly trap], for it is an abomination (repulsive) to the LORD your God.

7:22 little by little. God's plan was that the land would be conquered in two stages. The first was a broad, rapid conquest under Joshua, and the second was a gradual, area by area conquest.

8 Dt 10:15; Lk 1:55,72,73; Ex 13:3,14 **9** 1Co 1:9; 2Co 1:18; 2Th 3:3; 2Ti 2:13; Heb 11:11; Neh 1:5; Da 9:4 **10** Isa 59:18; Dt 32:35 **12** Dt 28:1; Ps 105:8,9 **13** Jn 14:21; Dt 28:4 **14** Ex 23:26 **15** Ex 15:26; Dt 28:27,60 **16** ver. 2; Dt 19:13,21; Jdg 8:27 **17** Nu 33:53 **18** Dt 31:6; Ps 105:5 **19** Dt 4:34; 29:3 **20** Jos 24:12 **21** Nu 16:3; Jos 3:10; Neh 9:32 **22** Ex 23:29,30 **24** Jos 10:24,25,42; Ex 17:14; Jos 23:9 **25** Ex 32:20; 1Ch 14:12; Jos 7:1,21; Jdg 8:27; Zep 1:3; Dt 17:1

26 "You shall not bring an abomination
(idol) into your house, and like it come
under the ban (doomed to destruction);
you shall utterly detest and you shall ut-
terly hate it, for it is something banned.

God's Gracious Dealings

8 "EVERY COMMANDMENT that
I am commanding you today you
shall be careful to do, so that you may
live and multiply, and go in and pos-
sess the land which the LORD swore [to
give] to your fathers.
2 "And you shall remember [always]
all the ways which the LORD your God
has led you these forty years in the
wilderness, so that He might humble
you and test you, to know what was in
your heart (mind), whether you would
keep His commandments or not.
3 "He humbled you and allowed you
to be hungry and fed you with manna,
[a substance] which you did not know,
nor did your fathers know, so that He
might make you understand [by per-
sonal experience] that man does not
live by bread alone, but man lives by
every *word* that proceeds out of the
mouth of the LORD.
4 "Your clothing did not wear out
on you, nor did your feet swell these
forty years.
5 "Therefore, know in your heart (be
fully cognizant) that the LORD your God
disciplines *and* instructs you just as a
man disciplines *and* instructs his son.
6 "Therefore, you shall keep the com-
mandments of the LORD your God, to
walk [that is, to live each and every
day] in His ways and fear [and wor-
ship] Him [with awe-filled reverence
and profound respect]. [Prov 8:13]
7 "For the LORD your God is bringing
you into a good land, a land of brooks
of water, of fountains and springs,
flowing forth in valleys and hills;
8 a land of wheat and barley, and
vines and fig trees and pomegranates,
a land of olive oil and honey;
9 a land where you will eat bread
without shortage, in which you will
lack nothing; a land whose stones are
iron, and out of whose hills you can
dig copper.
10 "When you have eaten and are sat-
isfied, then you shall bless the LORD
your God for the good land which He
has given you.
11 "Beware that you do not forget the
LORD your God by failing to keep His
commandments and His judgments
(precepts) and His statutes which I am
commanding you today;
12 otherwise, when you have eaten
and are satisfied, and have built good
houses and lived *in them,*
13 and when your herds and flocks
multiply, and your silver and gold mul-
tiply, and all that you have increases,
14 then your heart will become lifted
up [by self-conceit and arrogance] and
you will forget the LORD your God who
brought you from the land of Egypt,
out of the house of slavery.
15 "He led you through the great
and terrible wilderness, *with its* fiery
serpents and scorpions and thirsty
ground where there was no water; it
was He who brought water for you out
of the flinty rock.
16 "He fed you manna in the wilder-
ness, [a substance] which your fathers
did not know, so that He might humble
you [by dependence on Him] and that

8:3 *man does not live by bread alone.* Humans have a spiritual nature that can be satisfied only by the spiritual nutrients of God's Word. Jesus used these words to rebuke Satan when Jesus was tempted in the wilderness (Mt 4:4; Lk 4:1–4). ***proceeds out of the mouth of the LORD.*** The Bible is valuable because it is the word of God. It is inspired by God not only in the sense that it is relating true events, but because God knows the kinds of things that people need to know to follow Him in a world of sin, uncertainty, and death. God's word is man's only wisdom and hope. When people study it, rely on it, and apply it, the word will prove to be both wise and right. For God is as good as His every word, and God's every word is as good as the One from whom it comes.
8:16 *test you, to do good [things] for you.* Through the whole experience in Egypt and the

---

26 Lev 27:28; Jos 6:17; 7:1 **CHAPTER 8** **1** Dt 4:1; 5:32,33; 6:1-3 **2** Dt 1:3; 2:7; Am 2:10; Ex 16:4; Dt 13:3; Jn 2:25 **3** Ex 16:2,3; Ex 16:12,14,35; Mt 4:4; Lk 4:4 **4** Dt 29:5; Neh 9:21 **5** 2Sa 7:14; Ps 89:32; Pr 3:12; Heb 12:5,6; Rev 3:19 **6** Dt 5:33 **7** Dt 11:10-12 **9** Dt 33:25 **10** Dt 6:11,12 **12** Dt 28:47; 32:15; Hos 13:6 **14** 1Co 4:7; Ps 106:21 **15** Isa 63:12-14; Jer 2:6; Nu 21:6; Hos 13:5; Nu 20:11 **16** Ex 16:15; Jer 24:5,6; Heb 12:11

He might test you, to do good [things] for you at the end.

17 “Otherwise, you may say in your heart, ‘My power and the strength of my hand made me this wealth.’

18 “But you shall remember [with profound respect] the LORD your God, for it is He who is giving you power to make wealth, that He may confirm His covenant which He swore (solemnly promised) to your fathers, as it is this day.

19 “And it shall come about if you ever forget the LORD your God and follow other gods and serve them and worship them, I testify against you today that you will most certainly perish.

20 “Like the nations which the LORD causes to perish before you, so shall you perish; because you would not listen to *and* obey the voice of the LORD your God.

Israel Provoked God

9 “HEAR, O Israel! You are crossing the Jordan today to go in to dispossess nations greater and more powerful than you, great cities fortified to heaven,

2 a people great and tall, sons of Anakim, whom you know and of whom you have heard *it said,* ‘Who can stand before the sons of Anak?’

3 “So know today [with confident assurance] that the LORD your God is crossing [the Jordan] before you like a devouring fire. He will destroy them and He will subdue them before you, and you shall drive them out and destroy them quickly, just as the LORD has promised you.

4 “Do not say in your heart when the LORD your God has driven them out before you, ‘Because of my righteousness the LORD has brought me in to possess this land,’ but because of the wickedness of these nations the LORD is dispossessing them before you.

5 “It is not for your righteousness or for the uprightness of your heart that you are going to possess their land, but because of the wickedness of these nations the LORD your God is driving them out before you, and to confirm the oath which the LORD swore to your fathers, to Abraham, Isaac, and Jacob.

6 “Know [without any doubt], that the LORD your God is not giving you this good land to possess because of your righteousness, for you are a stiff-necked (stubborn, obstinate) people.

7 “Remember [with remorse] and do not forget how you provoked the LORD your God to wrath in the wilderness; from the day you left the land of Egypt until you arrived in this place, you have been rebellious against the LORD.

8 “And at Horeb (Sinai) you provoked the LORD to wrath, and the LORD was so angry with you that He would have destroyed you.

9 “When I went up the mountain to receive the tablets of stone, the tablets of the covenant which the LORD made with you, I remained on the mountain forty days and forty nights; I did not eat food or drink water.

---

wilderness, the Lord was leading His children into decisions that would bring out their true nature. Difficult as the tests were, the Lord knew what was necessary to reveal to the Israelites not only His character, but theirs as well.

8:17 *My power.* Moses warned the people that prosperity and wealth often lead to an exaltation of self and a rejection of God.

9:4–6 *to possess this land.* The conquest of Canaan was both a judgment on the wickedness of the native population and a promise fulfilled to Abraham, Isaac, and Jacob (Ge 15:18–21). The land was a gift of grace, not a gift given because of the merits of the Israelites.

9:7 *do not forget.* In addition to remembering the grace of God, the people also had to remember how vulnerable they were to apostasy (1:6–3:29).

9:9 *or drink water.* A person cannot go more than approximately three days without water and survive. God supernaturally preserved Moses during the forty days.

---

17 Dt 9:4 **18** Pr 10:22; Hos 2:8; Dt 7:8,12 **19** Dt 4:26; 30:18 **20** Da 9:11,12 **CHAPTER 9** **1** Dt 11:31; Jos 3:16; 4:19; Dt 4:38; 11:23; Dt 1:28 **2** Nu 13:22, 28,32,33 **3** Dt 31:3; Jos 3:11; Dt 4:24; Heb 12:29; Dt 7:23; Ex 23:31; Dt 7:24 **4** Dt 8:17; Ro 11:6,20; 1Co 4:4,7; Ge 15:16; Lev 18:24; Dt 18:12 **5** Titus 3:5; Ge 12:7; 13:15; 15:7; 17:8; 26:4 **6** ver. 13; Ex 32:9; 33:3; 34:9 **7** Ex 14:11; 16:2; 17:2; Nu 11:4; 20:2; 25:2; Dt 31:27 **8** Ex 32:4; Ps 106:19 **9** Ex 24:12,15; Ex 24:18; 34:28

10 “The LORD gave me the two tab-
lets of stone written with the finger
of God; and on them *were written* all
the words which the LORD had spoken
to you at the mountain from the midst
of the fire on the day of the assembly.
11 “It came about at the end of forty
days and forty nights that the LORD
gave me the two tablets of stone, the
tablets of the covenant.
12 “Then the LORD said to me, ‘Arise,
go down from here quickly, for your
people whom you brought from Egypt
have acted corruptly. They have quick-
ly turned aside from the way which
I commanded them; they have made
(cast) a molten image for themselves.’
13 “Furthermore, the LORD said to me,
‘I have seen this people, and indeed,
they are stiff-necked (stubborn, obsti-
nate) people.
14 ‘Let Me alone, so that I may destroy
them and wipe out their name from
under heaven; and I will make of you a
nation mightier and greater than they.’
15 “So I turned and came down from
the mountain while the mountain was
burning with fire, and the two tablets
of the covenant were in my two hands.
16 “And I saw that you had indeed
sinned against the LORD your God. You
had made for yourselves a molten calf
(idol). You had turned aside quickly
from the way which the LORD had com-
manded you. [Ex 32:1–10]
17 “So I took hold of the two tablets
and threw them from my two hands
and smashed them before your very
eyes!
18 “Then, as before, I fell down before
the LORD for [another] forty days and
forty nights; I did not eat food or drink
water, because of all the sin you had
committed by doing what was evil in
the sight of the LORD to provoke Him
to anger.
19 “For I was afraid of the anger and
absolute fury which the LORD held
against you, [enough divine fury] to
destroy you, but the LORD listened to
me that time also.
20 “The LORD was very angry with
Aaron, angry [enough] to destroy him,
so I also prayed for Aaron at the same
time.
21 “I took your sinful *thing*, the calf
which you had made, and burned it
in the fire and thoroughly crushed it,
grinding the metal thoroughly until it
was as fine as dust; and I threw its dust
into the brook that came down from
the mountain.
22 “At Taberah also and at Massah
and at Kibroth-hattaavah you pro-
voked the LORD to wrath.
23 “And when the LORD sent you from
Kadesh-barnea, saying, ‘Go up and
take possession of the land which I
have given you,’ then you rebelled
against the command of the LORD your
God, and you did not believe *and* rely
on Him, nor did you obey His voice.
24 “You have been rebellious against
the LORD from the [first] day that I
knew you.
25 “So I fell down *and* lay face down
before the LORD forty days and nights
because the LORD had said He would
destroy you.
26 “Then I prayed to the LORD and
said, ‘O Lord GOD, do not destroy Your
people, even Your inheritance, whom

9:10 *finger of God.* The Ten Commandments were written on stone by the hand of God. This visual picture of God writing His words is so personal. There is another time that God writes on tablets, and that is on the tablet of the human heart (2Co 3:3). This, too, is intensely personal and life changing. In the end, His followers can only put the words of the stone tablets into effect after the Spirit of the Living God has written on their hearts.

9:19 *the LORD listened to me.* For Moses' prayer, see verses 26 – 29. Daniel's prayer for the nation resembled Moses' intercession (Da 9:3 – 23).

9:26 – 29 *I prayed.* Moses took God's judgment seriously. Nevertheless he asked God for what he felt was important. He appealed to God's faithfulness, mercy, and honor. It is always all right to beseech the Lord for what seems right to us from our point of view, but as we pray, we remember that God knows more than we do, and we can trust Him to take the best course of action.

10 Ex 31:18; Ex 19:17; 20:1; Dt 4:10; 10:4 **12** Ex 32:7; Dt 31:29; Jdg 2:17 **13** Ex 32:9; ver. 6; Dt 10:16; 31:27; 2Ki 17:14 **14** Ex 32:10; Dt 29:20; Nu 14:12 **15** Ex 32:15; Ex 19:18; Dt 4:11; 5:23 **16** Ex 32:19 **18** Ex 34:28 **19** Ex 32:10,11; Ex 32:14; 33:17; Dt 10:10; Ps 106:23 **21** Ex 32:20; Isa 31:7 **22** Nu 11:1,3,5; Ex 17:7; Nu 11:4,34 **23** Nu 13:3; 14:1; Ps 106:24,25 **24** Dt 31:27 **25** ver. 18 **26** Ex 32:11

You have redeemed through Your greatness, whom You have brought from Egypt with a mighty hand.

27 ‘Remember [with compassion] Your servants, Abraham, Isaac, and Jacob; do not look at the stubbornness of this people or at their wickedness or at their sin,

28 so that the [people of the] land from which You brought us will not say, “Because the LORD was not capable of bringing them into the land which He had promised them and because He hated them He has brought them out to the wilderness [in order] to kill them.”

29 ‘Yet they are Your people and Your inheritance, whom You have brought out by Your great power and by Your outstretched arm.’

The Tablets Rewritten

10 “AT THAT time the LORD said to me, ‘Cut out for yourself two tablets of stone like the first, and come up to Me on the mountain, and make an ark (chest) of wood for yourself.

2 ‘I will write on the tablets the words that were on the first tablets which you shattered, and you shall put them in the ark.’

3 “So I made an ark of acacia wood and cut out two tablets of stone like the first, and went up the mountain with the two tablets in my hand.

4 “The LORD wrote on the tablets, like the first writing, the Ten Commandments which the LORD had spoken to you on the mountain from the midst of the fire on the day of the assembly; then the LORD gave them to me.

5 “Then I turned and came down from the mountain and put the tablets in the ark which I had made; and they are there, just as the LORD commanded me.”

6 (Now the sons of Israel traveled from the wells of the sons of Jaakan to Moserah. There Aaron died and there he was buried and Eleazar his son ministered as priest in his place.

7 From there they traveled to Gudgodah, and from Gudgodah to Jotbathah, a land of brooks of water.

8 At that time the LORD set apart the tribe of Levi to carry the ark of the covenant of the LORD, to stand before the LORD to serve Him and to bless in His name until this day.

9 Therefore, Levi does not have a portion or inheritance [of tribal land] with his brothers; the LORD is his inheritance, as the LORD your God has promised him.)

10 “And I stayed on the mountain, like the first time, forty days and nights, and the LORD listened to me at that time also; the LORD was not willing to destroy you.

11 “Then the LORD said to me, ‘Arise, go on your journey ahead of the people, so that they may go in and take possession of the land which I swore to their fathers to give to them.’

12 “And now, Israel, what does the LORD your God require from you, but to fear [and worship] the LORD your God [with awe-filled reverence and profound respect], to walk [that is, to live each and every day] in all His ways and to love Him, and to serve the LORD your God with all your heart and with all your soul [your choices, your thoughts, your whole being],

13 *and* to keep the commandments of the LORD and His statutes which I am commanding you today for your good?

14 “Behold, the heavens and the highest of heavens belong to the LORD your God, the earth and all that is in it.

15 “Yet the LORD had a delight in loving your fathers *and* set His affection on them, and He chose their descendants after them, you above all peoples, as it is this day.

10:3 *acacia.* The acacia tree is still found in the Sinai peninsula, but in smaller numbers than when the Israelites passed through. Some varieties produce an attractive, highly figured hardwood.

28 Ex 6:6-8; 1Sa 14:25; Ex 32:12; Nu 14:16 **29** Dt 4:20; 1Ki 8:51; Neh 1:10 **CHAPTER 10** **1** Ex 34:1,2; Ex 25:10 **2** Ex 25:16,21 **3** Ex 25:5,10; Ex 34:4 **4** Ex 20:1 **5** Ex 34:29; Ex 40:20; 1Ki 8:9 **6** Nu 33:31; Nu 33:30; Nu 20:28; 33:38 **7** Nu 33:32,33 **8** Nu 3:6; Nu 4:15; Dt 18:5; Nu 6:23; Dt 21:5 **9** Dt 18:1,2; Eze 44:28 **10** Ex 34:28; Dt 9:18,25; Ex 32:14,33,34; 33:17; Dt 9:19 **11** Ex 33:1 **12** Mic 6:8; Dt 6:13; Dt 5:33; Dt 6:5; Mt 22:37 **13** Dt 6:24 **14** 1Ki 8:27; Ex 19:5 **15** Dt 4:37

16 “So circumcise [that is, remove sin from] your heart, and be stiff-necked (stubborn, obstinate) no longer.

17 “For the LORD your God is the God of gods and the Lord of lords, the great, the mighty, the awesome God who does not show partiality nor take a bribe.

18 “He executes justice for the orphan and the widow, and shows His love for the stranger (resident alien, foreigner) by giving him food and clothing.

19 “Therefore, show your love for the stranger, for you were strangers in the land of Egypt.

20 “You shall fear [and worship] the LORD your God [with awe-filled reverence and profound respect]; you shall serve Him and cling to Him [hold tightly to Him, be united with Him], and you shall swear [oaths] by His name.

21 “He is your praise *and* glory; He is your God, who has done for you these great and awesome things which you have seen with your own eyes.

22 “Your fathers went down to Egypt, seventy persons [in all], and now the LORD your God has made you as numerous as the stars of heaven.

Rewards of Obedience

11 “THEREFORE YOU shall love the LORD your God, and always keep His charge, His statutes, His precepts, and His commandments [it is your obligation to Him].

2 “Know this day that I am not *speaking* to your children who have not known [by personal experience] and who have not seen [firsthand] the instruction *and* discipline of the LORD your God—His greatness, His mighty hand and His outstretched arm;

3 and His signs and His works which He did in the midst of Egypt to Pharaoh the king of Egypt and to all his land;

4 and what He did to the army of Egypt, to its horses and its chariots, when He made the water of the Red Sea engulf them as they pursued you, and how the LORD completely destroyed them;

5 and what He did to you in the wilderness until you came to this place;

6 and what He did to Dathan and Abiram, the sons of Eliab, the son of Reuben, when the earth opened its mouth and swallowed them, their households, their tents, and every living thing that followed them, in the midst of all Israel. [Num 26:9, 10]

7 “For your eyes have seen all the great work of the LORD which He did.

8 “Therefore, you shall keep all the commandments which I am commanding you today, so that you may be strong and go in and take possession of the land which you are crossing over [the Jordan] to possess;

9 so that you may live long on the land which the LORD swore (solemnly promised) to your fathers to give to them and to their descendants, a land [of great abundance,] flowing with milk and honey.

10 “For the land which you are entering to possess is not like the land of Egypt from which you have come, where you sowed your seed and watered it with your foot like a garden of vegetables.

11 “But the land into which you are about to cross to possess, a land of hills and valleys, drinks water from the rain of heaven,

12 a land for which the LORD your God

10:19 *show your love for the stranger.* God's good provision for their own needs should have motivated the Israelites to love the stranger among them. To love and provide for the disadvantaged was in fact following God's example.

11:1 *keep His charge.* Loving God is in response to His love for us. We are directed to love God, but God first demonstrates His love for us. He rescued the Israelites from slavery to the Egyptians; He rescues us from slavery to sin (Ro 6:20). Our first response is to return this love He has shown us. Our second response is to keep His commandments, to do the things He says to do. Love oils the wheels of obedience and makes obedience a blessing, not a burden.

11:9 – 12 *not like the land of Egypt.* Agriculture in Egypt depended on irrigation, the annual flooding of the Nile.

---

16 Dt 30:6; Jer 4:4; Ro 2:28,29; Col 2:11; Dt 9:6,13 **17** Da 2:47; Rev 19:16; Dt 7:21; Ac 10:34; Ro 2:11; Eph 6:9; 1Pe 1:17 **18** Ps 68:5 **19** Lev 19:33,34 **20** Mt 4:10; Dt 11:22; Ps 63:11 **21** Ex 15:2; Jer 17:14; Ps 106:21,22 **22** Ge 46:27; Ac 7:14; Ge 15:5 **CHAPTER 11** **1** Dt 10:12; Zec 3:7 **2** Dt 8:5; Dt 5:24 **3** Ps 78:12; 135:9 **4** Ps 106:11 **6** Nu 16:1,31 **7** Dt 5:3; 7:19 **8** Jos 1:6,7 **9** Dt 4:40; Pr 10:27; Dt 9:5; Ex 3:8 **11** Dt 8:7 **12** 1Ki 9:3

cares; the eyes of the LORD your God
are always on it, from the beginning of
the year to the end of the year.
13 “It shall come about, if you listen
obediently *and* pay attention to My
commandments which I command you
today—to love the LORD your God and
to serve Him with all your heart and
with all your soul [your choices, your
thoughts, your whole being]—
14 that He will give the rain for your
land in its season, the early [fall] rain
and the late [spring] rain, so that you
may gather in your grain and your new
wine and your [olive] oil.
15 “And He will give grass in your
fields for your cattle, and you will eat
and be satisfied.
16 “Beware that your hearts are not
deceived, and that you do not turn
away [from the LORD] and serve other
gods and worship them,
17 or [else] the LORD's anger will be
kindled *and* burn against you, and
He will shut up the heavens so that
there will be no rain and the land will
not yield its fruit; and you will perish
quickly from the good land which the
LORD is giving you.
18 “Therefore, you shall impress these
words of mine on your heart and on
your soul, and tie them as a sign on
your hand, and they shall be as bands
(frontals, frontlets) on your forehead.
19 “You shall teach them [diligently]
to your children [impressing God's pre-
cepts on their minds and penetrating
their hearts with His truths], speaking
of them when you sit in your house and
when you walk along the road and when
you lie down and when you rise up.
20 “You shall write them on the door-
posts of your house and on your gates,
21 so that your days and the days of
your children may be multiplied in
the land which the LORD swore to your
fathers to give them, as long as the
heavens are above the earth.
22 “For if you are careful to keep all
this commandment which I am com-
manding you to do, to love the LORD
your God, to walk [that is, to live each
and every day] in all His ways and to
hold tightly to Him—
23 then the LORD will drive out all
these nations from before you, and
you shall dispossess nations greater
and mightier than you.
24 “Every place on which the sole of
your foot treads shall become yours;
your territory shall be from the wilder-
ness to Lebanon, and from the river,
the river Euphrates, as far as the west-
ern sea (the Mediterranean).
25 “No man will be able to stand be-
fore you; the LORD your God will lay
the fear and the dread of you on all the
land on which you set foot, just as He
has spoken to you.
26 “Behold, today I am setting before
you a blessing and a curse—
27 the blessing, if you listen to *and*
obey the commandments of the LORD
your God, which I am commanding
you today;
28 and the curse, if you do not listen
to *and* obey the commandments of the
LORD your God, but turn aside from
the way which I am commanding you
today, by following (acknowledging,
worshiping) other gods which you
have not known.
29 “It shall come about, when the
LORD your God brings you into the land
which you are entering to possess, that
you shall place the blessing on Mount
Gerizim and the curse on Mount Ebal.
[Josh 8:30–35]
30 “Are they not across the Jordan,
west of the road, toward the sunset,
in the land of the Canaanites who live
in the Arabah, opposite Gilgal, beside
the oaks of Moreh?
31 “For you are about to cross the Jor-
dan to go in to possess the land which

11:14 ***early [fall] rain and the late [spring] rain.*** The early rain encouraged the sprouting of seed and new growth. The late rain brought crops to maturity.

13 ver. 22; Dt 6:17; Dt 10:12 **14** Lev 26:4; Dt 28:12; Joel 2:23; Jas 5:7 **15** Ps 104:14; Dt 6:11; Joel 2:19 **16** Dt 29:18; Job 31:27; Dt 8:19 **17** Dt 6:15; 1Ki 8:35; 2Ch 6:26; Dt 4:26; 8:19,20; Jos 23:13,15,16 **18** Dt 6:6; 32:46; Dt 6:8 **19** Dt 4:9,10; 6:7 **20** Dt 6:9 **21** Dt 4:40; Pr 3:2; 4:10; Ps 72:5; 89:29 **22** ver. 13; Dt 6:17; Dt 10:20; 30:20 **23** Dt 4:38; Dt 9:1 **24** Jos 1:3; 14:9; Ge 15:18; Ex 23:31; Nu 34:3 **25** Dt 7:24; Dt 2:25; Ex 23:27 **26** Dt 30:1,15,19 **27** Dt 28:2 **28** Dt 28:15 **29** Dt 27:12,13; Jos 8:33 **30** Ge 12:6; Jdg 7:1 **31** Dt 9:1; Jos 1:11

the Lord your God is giving you, and
you shall possess it and live in it,
[32]and you shall be careful to do all
the statutes and the judgments which
I am setting before you today.

Laws of the Sanctuary

12 "THESE ARE the statutes and
judgments (precepts) which you
shall be careful to do in the land which
the Lord, the God of your fathers, has
given you to possess as long as you live
on the earth.
[2]"You shall utterly destroy all the
places where the nations whom you
shall dispossess serve their gods, on
the high mountains and the hills and
under every green [leafy] tree.
[3]"You shall tear down their altars
and smash their [idolatrous] pillars
and burn their Asherim in the fire; you
shall cut down the carved *and* sculpted
images of their gods and obliterate
their name from that place.
[4]"You shall not act like this toward
the Lord your God.
[5]"But you shall seek *the Lord* at the
place which the Lord your God will
choose out of all your tribes to estab-
lish His Name there for His dwelling
[place], and there you shall come [to
worship Him].
[6]"There you shall bring your burnt
offerings, your sacrifices, your tithes,
the contribution of your hand, your
votive (pledged, vowed) offerings,
your freewill (voluntary) offerings,
and the firstborn of your herd and of
your flock.
[7]"And there you and your house-
holds shall eat before the Lord your
God, and rejoice in all to which you
put your hand, in which the Lord your
God has blessed you.
[8]"You shall not do at all what we are
doing here [in the camp] today, every
man doing whatever is right in his
[own] eyes.
[9]"For you have not yet come to the
resting place and to the inheritance
which the Lord your God is giving you.
[10]"When you cross the Jordan and
live in the land which the Lord your
God is giving you to inherit, and He
gives you rest from all your enemies
around you so that you live in security,
[11]then it shall come about that the
place which the Lord your God will
choose for His Name [and Presence] to
dwell; there you shall bring everything
that I am commanding you: your burnt
offerings, your sacrifices, your tithes
and the [voluntary] contribution of your
hand [as a first gift from the fruits of
the ground], and all your choice votive
offerings which you vow to the Lord.
[12]"And you shall rejoice before the
Lord your God, you and your sons and
your daughters, and your male and
female servants, and the Levite who is
within your [city] gates, since he has
no portion or inheritance with you.

12:1–4 *altars . . . pillars.* The sacred pillars were monuments dedicated to one of the gods. They represented the power of fertility. The poles refer to the altars dedicated to the goddess Asherah, who was frequently associated with Baal.

12:5 *seek.* Whatever one seeks is the object of one's desire and devotion. Once they were settled in the land, the different tribes would be spread out, but they would still find God in their midst, in the place that God chose. This place was to be the object of their desire, God Himself the object of their devotion.

12:6 *sacrifices.* The Hebrew word for sacrifice always designates the offering of an animal. The contribution of the hand was one which the priest lifted up to signify that it was a gift to the Lord (Ex 29:27; Lev 7:34). The priest took his share and the worshiper and his family ate the rest. A votive offering was made in the fulfillment of a vow (Lev 7:16; Nu 6:21). A freewill offering was voluntary (Ex 35:27–29; Lev 7:16).

12:7 *eat . . . rejoice.* The communal offerings were to be eaten and enjoyed by those who offered them. It was a time of celebration before the Lord.

12:8 *whatever is right in his [own] eyes.* In the wilderness the people did not develop a common focus on the Lord. Moses challenged the new generation to act with common faithfulness and obedience.

---

32 Dt 5:32; 12:32 **CHAPTER 12** **1** Dt 6:1; Dt 4:10; 1Ki 8:40 **2** Ex 34:13; Dt 7:5; 2Ki 16:4; 17:10,11; Jer 3:6 **3** Nu 33:52; Jdg 2:2 **4** ver. 31 **5** ver. 11; Dt 26:2; Jos 9:27; 1Ki 8:29; 2Ch 7:12 **6** Lev 17:3,4; ver. 17; Dt 14:22,23; 15:19,20 **7** Dt 14:26; ver. 12,18; Lev 23:40; Dt 16:11,14,15 **8** Jdg 17:6; 21:25 **10** Dt 11:31 **11** ver. 5,14,18,21,26; Dt 14:23; 15:20; 16:2; Jos 18:1; 1Ki 8:29 **12** ver. 7; Dt 10:9; 14:29

13"Be careful that you do not offer
your burnt offerings in every [cultic]
place you see,
14but [only] in the place which the
LORD will choose in one of your tribes,
there you shall offer your burnt offer-
ings, and there you shall do everything
that I am commanding you.
15"However, you may slaughter and
eat meat within any of your [city]
gates, whatever you wish, according
to the blessing of the LORD your God
which He has given you [as His gener-
ous provision for daily life]. The [cere-
monially] unclean and the clean may
eat it, such as the gazelle and the deer.
16"Only you shall not eat the blood;
you are to pour it out on the ground
like water.
17"You are forbidden to eat within
your [city] gates the tithe of your grain
or new wine or oil, or the firstborn
of your herd or flock, or any of your
votive offerings, or your freewill offer-
ings, or the contribution of your hand.
18"But you shall eat them before the
LORD your God in the place which the
LORD your God will choose, you and
your son and your daughter, and your
male and female servants, and the Le-
vite who is within your [city] gates; and
you shall rejoice before the LORD your
God in all that you undertake.
19"Be careful that you do not neglect
the Levite [who serves God] as long as
you live in your land.
20"When the LORD your God extends
your territory, as He promised you, and
you say, 'I will eat meat,' because you
want to eat meat, then you may eat
meat, whatever you wish.
21"If the place which the LORD your
God chooses to put His Name (Pres-
ence) is too far away from you, then
you may slaughter [animals] from your
herd or flock which the LORD has given
you, just as I have commanded you;
and you may eat within your [city]
gates whatever you wish.
22"Just as the gazelle or the deer is
eaten, so you may eat it [but not make
it an offering]; the [ceremonially] un-
clean and the clean alike may eat it.
23"Only be sure that you do not eat
the blood, for the blood is the life (soul),
and you shall not eat the life with the
meat.
24"You shall not eat it; you shall pour
it out on the ground like water.
25"You shall not eat it, so that all
may be well with you and with your
children after you, because you will
be doing what is right in the sight of
the LORD.
26"However, you shall take your holy
things which you have [to offer] and
your votive (pledged, vowed) offerings,
you shall take *them* and go to the place
which the LORD will choose.
27"And you shall offer your burnt
offerings, the meat and the blood, on
the altar of the LORD your God; and the
blood of your sacrifices shall be poured
out on the altar of the LORD your God,
and you shall eat the meat.
28"Be careful to listen to all these
words which I am commanding you,
so that it may be well with you and
with your children after you forever,
because you will be doing what is good
and right in the sight of the LORD your
God.
29"When the LORD your God cuts off
and destroys before you the nations
which you are going in to dispossess,
and you dispossess them and settle in
their land,
30beware that you are not lured (en-
snared) into following them, after they
have been destroyed before you, and

12:17 ***eat within your [city] gates.*** Aspects of God's worship were designed for community celebration, and were not to be done in the privacy of the home.

12:30–31 ***beware that you are not lured.*** For forty years the basic sin which kept Israel out of Canaan was unbelief. However, once they settled in the promised land, the sin that eventually drove them out was idolatry. Idolatry is not only bowing down to a stone or wood image of a god; idolatry

---

13 Lev 17:4 **14** ver. 11 **15** ver. 21; ver. 22; Dt 14:5; 15:22 **16** Ge 9:4; Lev 7:26; 17:10; Dt 15:23; ver. 23 **18** ver. 11,12; Dt 14:23 **19** Dt 14:27 **20** Ge 15:18; 28:14; Ex 34:24; Dt 11:24; 19:8 **22** ver. 15 **23** ver. 16; Ge 9:4; Lev 17:11,14 **25** Dt 4:40; Isa 3:10; Ex 15:26; Dt 13:18; 1Ki 11:38 **26** Nu 5:9,10; 1Sa 1:21,22,24 **27** Lev 1:5,9,13; 17:11 **28** ver. 25 **29** Ex 23:23; Dt 19:1; Jos 23:4

that you do not inquire about their
gods, saying, ‘How did these nations
serve their gods, so that I too may do
likewise?’
31“You shall not behave this way
toward the LORD your God, for they
have done for their gods every repul-
sive thing which the LORD hates; for
they even burn their sons and their
daughters in the fire [as sacrifices] to
their gods.
32“Everything I command you, you
shall be careful to do it; you shall not
add to it nor take away from it.

Shun Idolatry

13 “IF A prophet arises among you,
or a dreamer of dreams, and
gives you a sign or a wonder,
2and the sign or the wonder which he
spoke (foretold) to you comes to pass,
and if he says, ‘Let us follow after other
gods (whom you have not known) and
let us serve *and* worship them,’
3you shall not listen to the words
of that prophet or that dreamer of
dreams; for the LORD your God is test-
ing you to know whether you love the
LORD your God with all your heart *and*
mind and all your soul [your entire
being].
4“You shall walk after the LORD your
God and you shall fear [and worship]
Him [with awe-filled reverence and
profound respect], and you shall keep
His commandments and you shall lis-
ten to His voice, and you shall serve
Him, and cling to Him.
5“But that prophet or that dreamer of
dreams shall be put to death, because
he has counseled rebellion against
the LORD your God who brought you
from the land of Egypt and redeemed
you from the house of slavery, to draw
you away from the way in which the
LORD your God has commanded you
to walk. So you shall remove the evil
from among you.
6“If your brother, the son of your moth-
er, or your son or daughter, or the wife
you cherish, or your friend who is as
[precious to you as] your own life (soul),
entices you secretly, saying, ‘Let us go
and serve other gods’ (*gods* whom nei-
ther you nor your fathers have known,
7of the gods of the peoples who are
around you, near you or far from you,
from one end of the earth to the other),
8you shall not consent to him or
listen to him; and your eye shall not
pity him, nor shall you spare him or
conceal him.
9“Instead, you shall most certainly
execute him; your hand shall be first
[to be raised] against him to put him
to death, and afterwards the hand of
all the people.
10“So you shall stone him to death
with stones, because he has tried to
draw you away from the LORD your
God who brought you from the land
of Egypt, from the house of slavery.

---

takes place every time our trust for our well-being is placed on something that is not the one true God. In the end, idolatry is the ultimate form of unbelief. It mocks God, because it imitates the dependence that people should have on Him, choosing a powerless placebo for the living God. The Lord would remove the temptation of the Canaanite nations, but the Israelites must not become curious and imitate the practices of the vanquished peoples. Calling it a lure was a warning that the temptation to copy would be hidden, a trick, something that would catch them unaware.

13:1 – 2 ***a prophet . . . or a dreamer.*** Both prophecy and dreams were legitimate forms of revelation.

13:3 ***testing you.*** The revelation of God through Moses was the test of any sign or message. When the message deviated from God’s prior revelation, Israel had to discern false teaching.

13:5 ***remove the evil.*** Discipline, punishment, and testing were God’s means of keeping His people pure.

13:9 ***your hand shall be first.*** The relative or friend who brought the charge would lead in the capital punishment of the one who suggested idolatrous practices. With unforgettable words, Jesus emphasized the severity of this offense. Such a person should not have been born (Mt 18:6 – 7).

---

31 Lev 18:3,26,30; Dt 18:10; Jer 32:35; Eze 23:37 **32** Dt 4:2; Jos l:7; Rev 22:18 **CHAPTER 13** **1** Zec 10:2; Mt 24:24; 2Th 2:9 **2** See Dt 18:22; Mt 7:22 **3** Dt 8:2; See Mt 24:24; 2Th 2:11 **4** 2Ki 23:3; 2Ch 34:31; Dt 30:20 **5** Jer 14:15; Zec 13:3; Dt 17:7; 1Co 5:13 **6** Dt 17:2; See Ge 16:5; Dt 28:54; Pr 5:20; 1Sa 18:1,3; 20:17 **8** Pr 1:10 **9** Dt 17:5; Dt 17:7; Ac 7:58

11“Then all Israel will hear and be
afraid, and will never again do such a
wicked thing among you.
12“If you hear [it said] in one of your
cities, which the LORD your God gives
you to live in,
13that some worthless *and* evil men
have gone out from among you and
have tempted the inhabitants of their
city [to sin], saying, ‘Let us go and serve
other gods’ (whom you have not known),
14then you shall investigate and
search out [witnesses] and ask thor-
ough *questions*. If it is true and the
matter is established that this loath-
some thing has been done among you,
15you shall most certainly strike the
inhabitants of that city with the edge
of the sword, utterly destroying it and
all that is in it, even its livestock with
the edge of the sword.
16“Then you shall collect all its spoil
(plunder) into the middle of its open
square and burn the city and set fire
to the spoil as a whole burnt offering
to the LORD your God. It shall be a ruin
forever. It shall not be built again.
17“Nothing from that which is put
under the ban (designated for de-
struction) shall cling to your hand,
so that the LORD may turn away from
His burning anger and show mercy to
you, and have compassion on you and
make you increase, just as He swore
to your fathers,
18because you have listened to *and*
obeyed the voice of the LORD your God,
keeping all His commandments which
I am commanding you today, and do-
ing what is right in the eyes of the LORD
your God.

Clean and Unclean Animals

14 “YOU ARE the sons of the LORD
your God; you shall not cut your-
selves nor shave your forehead for the
sake of the dead,
2for you are a holy people [set apart]
to the LORD your God; and the LORD has
chosen you out of all the peoples who
are on the earth to be a people for His
own possession.
3“You shall not eat anything that is

13:13 *serve other gods.* Falling away from the truth is apostasy. Sometimes this can be fairly subtle, and that is why the word “seduced” is used with this concept. God clearly lays out a test that will always separate the truth from the lie. If someone says, “let us go after other gods …” we know that the speaker is not from God. Our hope is in Christ alone. People do not recognize that they are going after “other gods” because they do not know the one true God. This is why it is so important to faithfully study the Bible, for in it all of the character and actions of God are revealed. We will not be fooled by the counterfeit if we are familiar with the genuine.

13:17 – 18 *turn away from His burning anger and show mercy to you.* This seemingly harsh judgment of evil was an act of obedience. God required the punishment of evildoers so that immoral practices would not spread throughout the land. God would bless the Israelites, and bless the land, but not while the evil practices were still going on.

14:2 God’s Plan and Israel — The modern-day student of the Bible may well ask why so much of Scripture is taken up with the history of a single nation. Certainly many Christians wonder why one nation should be called “God’s chosen people.” The answer to this question is bound up in God’s purpose for Israel. When God promised Abraham that he would become the father of a great nation, He also promised that He would bless all peoples through that nation (Ge 12:1 – 3). Therefore Israel was to be a channel of blessing as well as a recipient. Even their deliverance from Egypt was at least partially designed to show other nations that Israel’s God was the only true God (Ex 7:5; 14:18; Jos 2:9 – 11). It was further prophesied by Isaiah that the Messiah would bring salvation to the Gentiles (Isa 49:6) The Psalms contain many invitations to other nations to come and worship the Lord in Israel (Ps 2:10 – 12; 117:1). Ruth the Moabitess is an example of a foreigner who believed in Israel’s God.

It is clear that God’s promise to Abraham to bless the whole world through him is still being fulfilled. The life, ministry, and death of Jesus Christ and the existence and influence of the church today all came about through God’s choice of Israel. All those the church wins to Christ, whether Jew or Gentile, enter into these great blessings channeled through Israel.

---

11 Dt 19:20 **12** Jdg 20:1,2 **13** 1Jn 2:19; Jude 19; 2Ki 17:21; ver. 2,6 **15** Lev 27:28; Jos 6:17,21 **16** Jos 6:24; Jos 8:28; Jer 49:2 **17** Jos 6:18; Jos 7:26; Ge 22:17; 26:4,24; 28:14 **18** Dt 12:25,28,32 **CHAPTER 14** **1** Ro 8:16; 9:8,26; Gal 3:26; Lev 19:28; 21:5; Jer 16:6; 41:5; 47:5; 1Th 4:13 **2** Lev 20:26; Dt 7:6; 26:18,19 **3** Eze 4:14; Ac 10:13,14

detestable [to the LORD and forbidden
by Him].
4 “These are the animals that you
may eat: the ox, the sheep, the goat,
5 the deer, the gazelle, the roebuck,
the wild goat, the ibex, the antelope
and the mountain sheep.
6 “Among the animals, you may eat
any animal that has the divided hoof
[that is, a hoof] split into two parts
[especially at its distal extremity] and
that chews the cud.
7 “However, you are not to eat any
of these [animals] among those which
chew the cud, or among those that
divide the hoof in two: the camel, the
hare and the shaphan, for though they
chew the cud, they do not split the hoof;
they are unclean for you.
8 “The swine, because it has a divided
hoof but *does* not *chew* the cud; it is
unclean for you. You shall not eat their
meat nor touch their carcasses.
9 “Of all [creatures] that are in the
waters, you may eat these: anything
that has fins and scales you may eat,
10 but you may not eat anything that
does not have fins and scales; it is un-
clean for you.
11 “You may eat any clean bird.
12 “But these are the ones which you
shall not eat: the eagle, the vulture, and
the black buzzard,
13 and the red kite, the falcon, and the
birds of prey of any variety,
14 and every raven of any variety,
15 and the ostrich, the owl, the
seagull, the hawk of any variety,
16 the little owl, the great owl, the
long-eared owl,
17 the pelican, the carrion vulture,
the cormorant,
18 the stork, and the heron of any
variety, and the hoopoe, and the bat.
19 “And all flying insects are unclean
for you; they shall not be eaten.
20 “You may eat any clean bird.
21 “You shall not eat anything that
dies *on its own*. You may give it to the
stranger (resident alien, foreigner) who
is in your [city] gates, so that he may
eat it, or you may sell it to a foreigner
[since they are not under God’s law],
but you are a people holy (set apart) to
the LORD your God. You shall not boil
a young goat *or* a lamb in its mother’s
milk.
22 “Every year you shall certainly
tithe [a tenth] of all the yield of your
seed which is produced by your field.
23 “You shall eat the tithe (tenth) of
your grain, your new wine, your oil,
and the firstborn of your herd and your
flock before the LORD your God in the
place where He chooses to establish
His Name (Presence), so that you may
learn to fear [and worship] the LORD
your God [with awe-filled reverence
and profound respect] always.
24 “If the place where the LORD your
God chooses to set His Name (Pres-
ence) is a great distance from you and
you are not able to carry *your tithe*,
because the LORD your God has blessed
you [with such an abundance],
25 then you shall exchange *your tithe*
for money, and take the money in your
hand and go to the place [of worship]
which the LORD your God chooses.
26 “You may spend the money for
anything your heart desires: for oxen,
or sheep, or wine, or [other] strong
drink, or anything else you want. You
shall eat there in the presence of the
LORD your God and rejoice, you and
your household.
27 “Also you shall not neglect the Le-
vite who is within your [city] gates, for

14:21 not boil . . . in its mother’s milk. Unlike the Canaanites who boiled young goats alive in the milk of their mothers as a sacrifice to fertility gods, Israel was to practice a more humane method of animal sacrifice.

14:22 – 29 tithe [a tenth] of all the yield of your seed. The tithe was to be enjoyed in the presence of the Lord, unless the people had come from a great distance. Then they could exchange it for silver and purchase food and drink with it in Jerusalem.

14:25 money. Money refers to uncoined silver. Coins were not struck until the Persian era.

4 Lev 11:2 **8** Lev 11:26,27 **9** Lev 11:9 **12** Lev 11:13 **19** Lev 11:20; See Lev 11:21 **21** Lev 17:15; 22:8; Eze 4:14; ver. 2; Ex 23:19; 34:26 **22** Lev 27:30; Dt 12:6,17; Neh 10:37 **23** Dt 12:5-7,17,18; Dt 15:19,20 **24** Dt 12:21 **26** Dt 12:7,18; 26:11 **27** Dt 12:12,18,19; Nu 18:20; Dt 18:1,2

he does not have a share [of land] or an inheritance among you.
[28]"At the end of every third year you shall bring out all the tithe of your produce for that year, and shall store it up within your [city] gates.
[29]"The Levite, because he has no share [of land] or an inheritance among you, and the stranger, and the orphan and the widow who are within your [city] gates, shall come and eat and be satisfied, so that the LORD your God may bless you in all the work of your hands.

The Sabbatical Year

15 "AT THE end of every seven years you shall grant a release (remission, pardon) *from debt*.
[2]"This is the regulation for the release: every creditor shall forgive what he has loaned to his neighbor; he shall not require repayment from his neighbor and his brother, because the LORD's release has been proclaimed.
[3]"You may require repayment from a foreigner, but whatever of yours is with your brother [Israelite] your hand shall release.
[4]"However, there will be no poor among you, since the LORD will most certainly bless you in the land which the LORD your God is giving you as an inheritance to possess,
[5]if only you will listen to *and* obey the voice of the LORD your God, to observe carefully all these commandments which I am commanding you today.
[6]"When the LORD your God blesses you as He has promised you, then you will lend to many nations, but you will not borrow; and you will rule over many nations, but they will not rule over you.
[7]"If there is a poor man among you, one of your fellow Israelites, in any of your cities in the land that the LORD your God is giving you, you shall not be heartless, nor close-fisted with your poor brother;
[8]but you shall freely open your hand to him, and shall generously lend to him whatever he needs.
[9]"Beware that there is no wicked thought in your heart, saying, 'The seventh year, the year of release (remission, pardon), is approaching,' and your eye is hostile (unsympathetic) toward your poor brother, and you give him nothing [since he would not have to repay you]; for he may cry out to the LORD against you, and it will become a sin for you.
[10]"You shall freely *and* generously give to him, and your heart shall not be resentful when you give to him, because for this [generous] thing the LORD your God will bless you in all your work and in all your undertakings.
[11]"For the poor will never cease to be in the land; therefore I command you, saying, 'You shall freely open your hand to your brother, to your needy, and to your poor in your land.'
[12]"If your fellow Israelite, a Hebrew man or woman, is sold to you, and serves you for six years, then in the seventh year you shall set him free [from your service].
[13]"When you set him free, you shall not let him go away empty-handed.

15:1 *every seven years.* God taught His people to think in cycles of holy time: six days of work, the seventh to rest; six years of business, the seventh of giving freedom to the poor; six years of agricultural cultivation, and the seventh to let the land lie fallow (Ex 23:10 – 13; Lev 25:1 – 7).
15:7 – 15 *a poor man.* Israel's uniqueness in the ancient world is seen in the laws which connect a right relationship with God and worship of Him with interpersonal relationships. If you love God, you will also treat others well. God is intensely interested in the poor, and it is the responsibility of His people to imitate His concern. The story of the Good Samaritan (Lk 10:30 – 37) is both the simplest and the most profound picture of how this concern works out in real life.
15:7 *not be heartless.* The people's attitude toward the poor should have been a reflection of their gratitude for God's gifts to them.

28 Dt 26:12; Am 4:4 **29** Dt 26:12; ver. 27; Dt 12:12; Dt 15:10; See Mal 3:10 **CHAPTER 15** **1** Ex 21:2; 23:10,11; Lev 25:2,4; Dt 31:10; Jer 34:14 **3** See Dt 23:20 **4** Dt 28:8 **5** Dt 28:1 **6** Dt 28:12,44; Dt 28:13; Pr 22:7 **7** 1Jn 3:17 **8** Lev 25:35; Mt 5:42; Lk 6:34,35 **9** Dt 28:54,56; Mt 20:15; Dt 24:15; Mt 25:41,42 **10** 2Co 9:5,7; Dt 14:29; 24:19 **11** Mt 26:11; Mk 14:7; Jn 12:8 **12** Ex 21:2; Lev 25:39; Jer 34:14

14 “You shall give him generous provisions from your flock, from your threshing floor and from your wine press; you shall give to him as the LORD your God has blessed you.

15 “And you shall remember *and* thoughtfully consider that you were [once] a slave in the land of Egypt, and the LORD your God redeemed you; therefore, I am commanding you these things today.

16 “Now if the servant says to you, ‘I will not leave you,’ because he loves you and your household, since he is doing well with you;

17 then take an awl and pierce it through his ear into the door, and he shall [willingly] be your servant always. Also you shall do the same for your maidservant. [Ex 21:6]

18 “It shall not seem hard to you when you set him free, for he has served you six years *with* double the service of a hired man; so the LORD your God will bless you in everything you do.

19 “You shall consecrate (set apart) to the LORD your God all the firstborn males that are born of your herd and flock. You shall not work with the firstborn of your herd, nor shear the firstborn of your flock.

20 “You and your household shall eat it every year before the LORD your God in the place [for worship] which the LORD chooses.

21 “But if it has any defect *or* injury, *such as* lameness or blindness, or any serious defect, you shall not sacrifice it to the LORD your God.

22 “You shall eat it within your [city] gates; the [ceremonially] unclean and the clean alike *may eat it,* as [if it were] a gazelle or a deer.

23 “Only you shall not eat its blood; you are to pour it out on the ground like water.

The Feast of Passover

16 “OBSERVE THE month of Abib and celebrate the Passover to the LORD your God, for in the month of Abib the LORD your God brought you out of Egypt by night.

2 “You shall sacrifice the Passover [lamb] to the LORD your God from the flock or the herd, in the place where the LORD chooses to establish His Name (Presence).

3 “You shall not eat leavened bread with it; *instead,* for seven days you shall eat the Passover with unleavened bread, the bread of affliction (for you left the land of Egypt in haste); [do this] so that all the days of your life you may remember [thoughtfully] the day when you came out of the land of Egypt.

4 “For seven days no leaven shall be seen with you in all your territory, and none of the meat which you sacrificed the evening of the first day shall remain overnight until morning.

5 “You are not allowed to sacrifice the Passover [lamb] in any of your cities which the LORD your God is giving you;

6 but at the place where the LORD your God chooses to establish His Name (Presence), you shall sacrifice the Passover [lamb] in the evening at sunset, at the time that you came out of Egypt.

7 “You shall cook and eat it in the place which the LORD your God chooses. In the morning you are to return to your tents.

8 “For six days you shall eat unleavened bread, and on the seventh day there shall be a celebration to the LORD your God; so you shall do no work [on that day].

15:19 *shall not work . . . nor shear.* The owners of firstborn male livestock could not profit from the firstborn because they belonged to the Lord.

16:1 *Passover.* Passover was observed on the fourteenth of Abib, or Nissan, which corresponds to our March-April (Ex 12:1 – 21; Lev 23:5 – 8; Nu 28:16 – 25).

16:6 *at sunset.* The twilight sacrifice was in commemoration of the exodus, which occurred at night.

16:9 *sickle to the standing grain.* This took place on the second day of the Feast of the Passover.

---

14 Pr 10:22 **15** Dt 5:15; 16:12 **16** Ex 21:5,6 **18** See Isa 16:14; 21:16 **19** Ex 13:2; 34:19; Lev 27:26; Nu 3:13 **20** Dt 12:5-7,17; 14:23; 16:11,14 **21** Lev 22:20 **22** Dt 12:15,22 **23** Dt 12:16,23 **CHAPTER 16** **1** Ex 12:2; Ex 13:4; Ex 12:29,42 **2** Nu 28:19; Dt 12:5,26 **3** Ex 12:15,19,39; 13:3,6,7; 34:18 **4** Ex 13:7; Ex 12:10; 34:25 **6** Ex 12:6 **7** Ex 12:8,9; 2Ch 35:13; 2Ki 23:23; Jn 2:13; 11:55 **8** Ex 12:16; 13:6; Lev 23:8

The Feast of Weeks

9“You shall count seven weeks for
yourself; you shall begin to count sev-
en weeks from the time you first put
the sickle to the standing grain.
10“Then you shall celebrate the Feast
of Weeks to the LORD your God with a
tribute of a freewill offering from your
hand, which you shall give [to Him]
just as the LORD your God blesses you;
11and you shall rejoice before the
LORD your God, you and your son and
your daughter and your male and
female servants and the Levite who
is within your [city] gates, and the
stranger and the orphan and the wid-
ow who are among you, at the place
where the LORD your God chooses to
establish His Name (Presence).
12“You shall remember that you were
a slave in Egypt, and you shall be care-
ful to obey these statutes.

The Feast of Booths

13“You shall celebrate the Feast of
Booths (Tabernacles) seven days, when
you have gathered in [the grain] from
your threshing floor and [the wine]
from your wine vat.
14“You shall rejoice in your feast,
you and your son and your daughter
and your male and female servants
and the Levite and the stranger and
the orphan and the widow who are
within your city.
15“Seven days you shall celebrate a
feast to the LORD your God in the place
which the LORD chooses, because the
LORD your God will bless you in all
your produce and in all the work of
your hands, so that you will be alto-
gether joyful.
16“Three times a year all your males
shall appear before the LORD your God
in the place which He chooses, at the
Feast of Unleavened Bread (Passover)
and at the Feast of Weeks (Pentecost)
and at the Feast of Booths (Taberna-
cles), and they shall not appear before
the LORD empty-handed.
17“Every man shall give as he is able,
in accordance with the blessing which
the LORD your God has given you.
18“You shall appoint judges and offi-
cers in all your cities (gates) which the
LORD your God is giving you, accord-
ing to your tribes, and they shall judge
the people with righteous judgment.
19“You shall not distort justice; you
shall not be partial, and you shall not
take a bribe, for a bribe blinds the eyes
of the wise and perverts the words of
the righteous.
20“You shall pursue justice, *and only*
justice [that which is uncompromising-
ly righteous], so that you may live and
take possession of the land which the
LORD your God is giving you.
21“You shall not plant for yourself an
Asherah of any kind of tree *or* wood
beside the altar of the LORD your God,
which you shall make.
22“You shall not set up for yourself
a *sacred* pillar which the LORD your
God hates.

Administration of Justice

17 “YOU SHALL not sacrifice to the
LORD your God an ox or sheep
with a blemish or any defect, for that
is a detestable thing to the LORD your
God.
2“If there is discovered among you,

16:13–15 *Feast of Booths.* The harvest festival was a time to celebrate God’s goodness, and to remember how He cared for them when they lived in tents in the wilderness. Today this celebration is called Succoth, from the Hebrew word for booths.

16:19 *not distort justice.* The foundation for a just and honest application of law in human society is God Himself. God entrusts rule to men who function in His place in dispensing justice. To pervert this justice with favoritism or bribes is to malign the character of God, and that is a sin that God always deals with sooner or later.

17:2 *transgressing.* The Hebrew verb for transgressing is used elsewhere to indicate the crossing of a border or stream. Here the word is used to indicate “crossing over” the boundaries that God had set for His people.

9 Ex 23:16; 34:22; Lev 23:15; Ac 2:1 **10** 1Co 16:2 **11** ver. 14; Dt 12:7,12 **12** Dt 15:15 **13** Ex 23:16; Lev 23:34; Nu 29:12 **14** Neh 8:9 **15** Lev 23:39 **16** Ex 23:14; 34:23; Ex 23:15; 34:20 **17** ver. 10 **18** Dt 1:16; 1Ch 23:4; 2Ch 19:5 **19** Ex 23:2,6; Lev 19:15; Dt 1:17; Ex 23:8; Ecc 7:7 **20** Eze 18:5 **21** Ex 34:13; 1Ki 14:15; 16:33; 2Ki 17:16; 21:3; 2Ch 33:3 **22** Lev 26:1 **CHAPTER 17** **1** Dt 15:21; Mal 1:8,13 **2** Dt 13:6; Jos 7:11; 23:16; Jdg 2:20; 2Ki 18:12; Hos 8:1

within any of your cities, which the
Lord your God is giving you, a man or
a woman who does evil in the sight of
the Lord your God, by transgressing
(violating) His covenant,
3 and has gone and served other gods
and worshiped them, or the sun or
the moon or any of the heavenly host,
[doing these things] which I have com-
manded not to do,
4 and if it is told to you and you hear
about it, then you shall investigate
thoroughly [all the charges]. If it is
confirmed beyond doubt that this de-
testable thing has been done in Israel,
5 then you shall bring that man or
that woman who has done this evil
thing to the gates [of your city] and
you shall stone the man or the woman
to death.
6 "On the evidence of two or three
witnesses, he who is to die shall be put
to death; he shall not be put to death
on the evidence of [only] one witness.
7 "The hand of the witnesses shall
be the first against him to put him to
death, and afterward the hand of all
the people. So you shall remove the
evil from among you.
8 "If any case is too difficult for you
to judge—between one kind of homi-
cide and another, between one kind of
lawsuit and another, between one kind
of assault and another, being contro-
versial issues in your courts—then you
shall arise and go to the place which
the Lord your God chooses.
9 "So you shall come to the Levitical
priests or to the judge who is *in office*
at that time, and you shall consult them
and they will declare to you the verdict
in the case.
10 "You shall act in accordance with
the terms of the verdict which they
declare to you from that place which
the Lord chooses. You shall be careful
to act in accordance with all of their
instructions.
11 "You shall act in accordance with
the law which they teach you and the
judgment which they tell you. You
shall not turn aside from their verdict,
to the right or to the left.
12 "The man who acts presumptuous-
ly *and* insolently by not listening to the
priest who stands there to serve the
Lord your God, nor to the judge, that
man shall die; so you shall remove the
evil from Israel.
13 "Then all the people will hear and
be afraid, and will not act presumptu-
ously again.
14 "When you enter the land which
the Lord your God is giving you, and
you take possession of it and live there,
and you say, 'I will set a king over me
like all the nations who are around
me,'
15 you shall most certainly set a king
over you whom the Lord your God
chooses. You shall set a king over you
from among your countrymen (broth-
ers); you may not choose a foreign-
er [to rule] over you who is not your
countryman.
16 "Further, he shall not acquire many

17:4–6 *investigate thoroughly.* An investigation, rather than gossip, determined the truth of any report of idolatry. There must be two or three witnesses for a person to be condemned to death.
17:7 *hand of the witnesses . . . first.* The witnesses participated in the stoning of the guilty because they were responsible for the person's condemnation. Jesus' words about throwing the "first stone" referred to this practice (Jn 8:7).
17:8 *between one kind of homicide and another.* This refers to cases of manslaughter or murder—that is, accidental or intentional homicide.
17:12 *acts presumptuously.* It is presumptuous to ask for judgment and then to refuse to follow the verdict of the priests. It is both asking them to take the weight of the decision and then willfully disregarding that decision.
17:13 *hear.* To hear is to respond and obey.
17:14 *a king.* The regulations that follow anticipate the request that the Israelites would make for a king. At the time of Moses the Israelites were unique among nations. God Himself ruled them through appointed leaders, but there was no king.

3 Dt 4:19; Job 31:26; Jer 7:22,23; 19:5; 32:35 **4** Dt 13:12,14 **5** Lev 24:14; Dt 13:10; Jos 7:25 **6** Nu 35:30; Dt 19:15; Mt 18:16; Jn 8:17; 2Co 13:1; 1Ti 5:19; Heb 10:28 **7** Dt 13:9; Ac 7:58; Dt 13:5; 19:19 **8** 2Ch 19:10; Hag 2:11; Mal 2:7; Ex 21:13, 20,22,28; Dt 12:5; 19:17 **9** Jer 18:18; Dt 19:17; Eze 44:24 **12** Nu 15:30; Dt 18:5,7; Dt 13:5 **13** Dt 13:11; 19:20 **14** 1Sa 8:5,19,20 **15** 1Sa 10:24; 1Ch 22:10; Jer 30:21 **16** 1Ki 4:26; 10:26,28; Isa 31:1; Eze 17:15; Ex 13:17; Nu 14:3; Dt 28:68; Jer 42:15; Hos 11:5

[war] horses for himself, nor make the people return to Egypt in order to acquire horses [to expand his military power], since the LORD said to you, 'You shall never return that way again.'

17"He shall not acquire multiple wives for himself, or else his heart will turn away [from God]; nor [for the same reason] shall he acquire great amounts of silver and gold.

18"Now it shall come about when he sits on the throne of his kingdom, he shall write for himself a copy of this law on a scroll in the presence of the Levitical priests.

19"And it shall be with him and he shall read it all the days of his life, so that he may learn to fear [and worship] the LORD his God [with awe-filled reverence and profound respect], by carefully obeying (keeping foremost in his thoughts and actively doing) all the words of this law and these statutes,

20so that his heart will not be lifted up above his countrymen [by a false sense of self-importance and self-reliance] and that he will not turn away (deviate) from the commandment, to the right or to the left, so that he and his sons may continue [to reign] for a long time in his kingdom in Israel.

Portion of the Levites

18 "THE LEVITICAL priests, the entire tribe of Levi, shall own [privately] no portion [of land] or inheritance with Israel; they shall eat the LORD's offerings by fire and His portion.

2"They shall have no inheritance [of land] among their countrymen (brothers, brethren); the LORD is their inheritance, as He promised them.

3"Now this shall be the priests' portion from the people, from those offering a sacrifice, either an ox or a sheep: they shall give to the priest the shoulder and the two cheeks and the stomach.

4"You shall also give him the first fruits of your grain, your new wine [the first of the season], and your [olive] oil, and the first sheared fleece of your sheep.

5"For the LORD your God has chosen him, him and his sons from all your tribes, to stand and serve in the name of the LORD forever.

6"Now if a Levite comes from any of your cities throughout Israel where he resides, and comes whenever he wishes to [the sanctuary] the place which the LORD chooses;

7then he shall serve in the name of the LORD his God, like all his fellow Levites who stand there before the LORD.

8"They shall have equal portions to eat, except *what they receive* from the sale of their fathers' *estates*. [Jer 32:6–15]

Spiritism Forbidden

9"When you enter the land which the LORD your God is giving you, you shall not learn to imitate the detestable (repulsive) practices of those nations.

10"There shall not be found among you anyone who makes his son or daughter pass through the fire [as a sacrifice], one who uses divination *and* fortune-telling, one who practices witchcraft, or one who interprets omens, or a sorcerer,

11or one who casts a charm *or* spell, or a medium, or a spiritist, or a necromancer [who seeks the dead].

12"For everyone who does these things is utterly repulsive to the LORD; and because of these detestable prac-

18:10 – 12 *pass through the fire . . . sorcerer.* Each of the activities that the Lord forbids in this passage come under the category of occult activities. Passing through the fire was sacrificing a son or daughter to learn about the future or seek favor with a supposed deity. Divination, witchcraft, sorcery, casting spells and interpreting omens, mediums, spiritists, and necromancers (those who call up the dead) are all part of the demonic realm, an attempt to bypass God in foretelling and controlling the future. These activities are detestable to God and should be to His followers as well.

17 See 1Ki 11:3,4 **18** 2Ki 11:12; Dt 31:9; 2Ki 22:8 **19** Ps 119:97,98 **20** Dt 5:32; 1Ki 15:5 **CHAPTER 18** **1** Nu 18:20; 26:62; Dt 10:9; Nu 18:8; 1Co 9:13 **3** Lev 7:30-34 **4** Ex 22:29; Nu 18:12 **5** Ex 28:1; Nu 3:10; Dt 10:8 **6** Nu 35:2; Dt 12:5 **7** 2Ch 31:2 **8** 2Ch 31:4; Neh 12:44 **9** Lev 18:26,27,30; Dt 12:29 **10** Lev 18:21; Dt 12:31; Lev 20:27; Isa 8:19 **11** Lev 20:27; 1Sa 28:7 **12** Lev 18:24; Dt 9:4

tices the LORD your God is driving
them out before you.
13"You shall be blameless (complete,
perfect) before the LORD your God.
14"For these nations which you shall
dispossess listen to those who practice
witchcraft and to diviners *and* fortune-
tellers, but as for you, the LORD your
God has not allowed you to do so.
15"The LORD your God will raise up
for you a prophet like me [Moses] from
among you, from your countrymen
(brothers, brethren). You shall listen
to him. [Matt 21:11; John 1:21]
16"This is according to all that you
asked of the LORD your God at Horeb
(Mount Sinai) on the day of the as-
sembly, saying, 'Let me not hear the
voice of the LORD my God again, nor
see this great fire anymore, so that I
will not die.'
17"The LORD said to me, 'They have
spoken well.
18'I will raise up a prophet from
among their countrymen like you,
and I will put My words in his mouth,
and he shall speak to them all that I
command him.
19'It shall come about that whoever
will not listen to My words which he
shall speak in My name, I Myself will
require it of him [and there will be
consequences].
20'But the prophet who presumes
to speak a word in My name which I
have not commanded him to speak, or
which he speaks in the name of other
gods—that prophet shall die.'
21"If you say in your heart, 'How
will we know *and* recognize the word
which the LORD has not spoken?'
22"When a prophet speaks in the
name of the LORD and the thing does
not happen or come true, that is the
thing which the LORD has not spoken.
The prophet has spoken it presumptu-
ously; you shall not be afraid of him.

Cities of Refuge

19 "WHEN THE LORD your God
cuts off (destroys) the nations
whose land He is giving you, and you
dispossess them and live in their cities
and in their houses,
2you shall designate three cities for
yourself in the central area of the land,
which the LORD your God is giving you
to possess.
3"You shall prepare *and* maintain for
yourself the roads [to these cities], and
divide the territory of your land into
three parts, so that anyone who kills
another unintentionally may escape
there [for asylum].
4"Now this is the case of the offender
(manslayer) who may escape there and
live [protected from vengeance]: when
he kills his neighbor unintentionally,
not having hated him previously—
5as [for example] when *a man* goes
into the forest with his neighbor to
cut wood, and his hand swings the
axe to cut down the tree, but the iron
head slips off the wooden handle and
hits his companion and he dies—the
offender may escape to one of these
cities and live;
6otherwise the avenger of blood
might pursue the offender in the heat
of anger, and overtake him, because
it is a long way, and take his life, even
though he did not deserve to die, since

18:15 *raise up for you a prophet.* A true prophet came from the Lord; no one could become a true prophet by self-will or desire.
18:22 *shall not be afraid of him.* These words of warning for discerning a false prophet were also words of comfort. If the prophet did not come from God, there was no need to become anxious about whatever he might predict.
19:3–4 *divide the territory ... into three parts.* The cities of refuge were intertribal cities. Anyone from any tribe could flee to the city that was closest to him.
19:6 *avenger of blood.* The avenger was possibly a relative commissioned by the elders of the city to execute justice. This Hebrew word is sometimes translated *kinsman redeemer,* and in this verse means "protector of family rights." This individual also stood up for the family to redeem property and persons. The glory of Israel was that its Avenger and Kinsman Redeemer was God Himself (Isa 41:14).

15 Jn 1:45; Ac 3:22 **16** Dt 9:10; Ex 20:19; Heb 12:19 **17** Dt 5:28 **18** Jn 1:45; Ac 3:22; Isa 51:16; Jn 17:8; Jn 4:25; 8:28; 12:49,50 **19** Ac 3:23 **20** Jer 14:14,15; Dt 13:1,2; Jer 2:8 **22** Jer 28:9; See Dt 13:2; ver. 20 **CHAPTER 19** **1** Dt 12:29 **2** Ex 21:13; Nu 35:10,14; Jos 20:2 **4** Nu 35:15; Dt 4:42 **6** Nu 35:12

he did not hate his neighbor before-
hand.
7“Therefore, I command you, saying,
‘You shall set aside three cities [of ref-
uge] for yourself.’
8“If the LORD your God enlarges your
border, as He has sworn to your fathers
to do, and gives you all the land which
He promised to give to your fathers—
9if you keep *and* carefully observe
all these commandments which I am
commanding you today, to love the
LORD your God, and to walk [that is, to
live each and every day] always in His
ways—then you shall add three more
cities [of refuge] for yourself, besides
these three,
10so that innocent blood will not be
shed [by blood avengers] in your land
which the LORD your God is giving
you as an inheritance, and blood guilt
will not be on you [for the death of an
innocent man].
11“But if there is a man who hates
his neighbor and lies in wait *and* am-
bush for him and attacks him and
strikes him down so that he dies, and
the assailant escapes to one of these
cities,
12then the elders of his own city shall
send for him and have him taken back
from there and turn him over to the
avenger of blood, so that he may be
put to death.
13“You shall not pity him [the guilty
one], but you shall purge the blood of
the innocent from Israel, so that it may
go well with you.

Laws of Landmark and Testimony

14“You shall not move your neigh-
bor’s boundary mark, which the
forefathers [who first divided the
territory] have set, in the land which
you will inherit in the land which
the LORD your God is giving you to
possess.
15“A single witness shall not appear
in a trial against a man for any wrong
or any sin which he has committed;
[only] on the testimony *or* evidence of
two or three witnesses shall a charge
be confirmed.
16“If a malicious witness rises up
against a man to [falsely] accuse him
of wrongdoing,
17then both parties to the controver-
sy shall stand before the LORD, before
the priests and the judges who will be
in office at that time.
18“The judges shall investigate thor-
oughly, and if the witness is a false
witness, and he has accused his broth-
er falsely,
19then you shall do to him just as he
had intended to do to his brother. So
you shall remove the evil from among
you.
20“Those who remain will hear and
be afraid, and will never again do such
an evil thing among you.
21“You shall not show pity [to the
guilty one]: *it shall be* life for life, eye
for eye, tooth for tooth, hand for hand,
foot for foot.

19:9 – 13 *keep and carefully observe all these.* The people of Israel were about to enter a land where they would be exposed to ideas and practices in the name of religion that God says are an abomination. The temptation to imitate would be great, but they must not do so. The believer is not different from his world for the sake of difference, but because he must not imitate the things that are inconsistent with a life of fellowship with a holy and just God. Copying the ways of the ungodly not only grieves the Lord, but it mars the picture He is making of Himself *in the lives of those who follow Him.*

19:14 *move your neighbor’s boundary mark.* Removing a landmark was far more than moving a stone. It was changing a property line and in effect cheating some family out of the inheritance of land that God had given them.

19:15 *on the testimony . . . of two or three witnesses.* Requiring two or three witnesses was a safeguard against the dangerous lies of an individual.

19:21 *it shall be life for life, eye for eye.* The law of retribution established the principal that the punishment should not exceed the crime.

8 Ge 15:18; Dt 12:20 **9** Jos 20:7 **11** Nu 35:16,24; Dt 27:24; Pr 28:17 **13** Dt 13:8; Nu 35:33,34; 1Ki 2:31 **14** Dt 27:17; Pr 22:28; Hos 5:10 **15** Nu 35:30; Dt 17:6; Mt 18:16; Jn 8:17; 2Co 13:1; 1Ti 5:19; Heb 10:28 **16** Ps 27:12; 35:11 **17** Dt 17:9; 21:5 **19** Pr 19:5; Da 6:24; Dt 13:5; 17:7; 21:21; 22:21 **20** Dt 17:13; 21:21 **21** ver. 13; Ex 21:23,24; Lev 24:20; Mt 5:38

Laws of Warfare

20 “WHEN YOU go out to battle
against your enemies and see
horses and chariots and people more
numerous than you, do not be afraid
of them; for the LORD your God, who
brought you up from the land of Egypt,
is with you.
2“When you approach the battle, the
priest shall come forward and speak
to the people,
3and shall say to them, ‘Hear, O Is-
rael: you are advancing today to bat-
tle against your enemies. Do not lack
courage. Do not be afraid, or panic, or
tremble [in terror] before them,
4for the LORD your God is He
who goes with you, to fight for you
against your enemies, to save you.’
[1 Sam 17:45]
5“The officers shall also speak to the
soldiers, saying, ‘What man is there
who has built a new house and has not
yet dedicated it? Let him go and return
to his house, otherwise he might die
in the battle and another man would
dedicate it.
6‘What man has planted a vineyard
and has not put it to use [harvesting
its fruit]? Let him go and return to his
house, otherwise he might die in the
battle and another man would begin
to use its fruit.
7‘And who is the man who is en-
gaged (legally promised) to a woman
and has not married her? Let him go
and return to his house, otherwise he
might die in the battle and another
man would marry her.’
8“Then the officers shall speak fur-
ther to the soldiers and say, ‘Who is the
man who is afraid and lacks courage?
Let him go and return to his house, so
that he does not cause his brothers’
courage to fail like his own.’
9“And it shall be when the officers
have finished speaking to the soldiers,
they shall appoint commanders of
armies over them.
10“When you advance to a city to
fight against it, you shall [first] offer
it terms of peace.
11“If that city accepts your terms of
peace and opens *its gates* to you, then
all the people who are found in it shall
become your forced labor and shall
serve you.
12“However, if it does not make peace
with you, but makes war against you,
then you shall lay siege to it.
13“When the LORD your God gives it
into your hand, you shall strike down
all the men in it with the edge of the
sword.
14“Only the women and the children
and the animals and everything that is
in the city, all its spoil, you shall take
as plunder for yourself; and you shall
use the spoil of your enemies which the
LORD your God has given you.
15“That is what you shall do to all
the cities that are very far away from
you, which are not among the cities of
these nations nearby [which you are to
dispossess].
16“Only in the cities of these peoples
that the LORD your God is giving you
as an inheritance, you shall not leave
alive anything that breathes.
17“But you shall utterly destroy them,
the Hittite, the Amorite, the Canaanite,
the Perizzite, the Hivite and the Jeb-
usite, just as the LORD your God has
commanded you,
18so that they will not teach you to act
in accordance with all the detestable

20:5–7 *built a new house . . . planted a vineyard . . . engaged (legally promised) to a woman.* Each of these activities represents a time of planning and preparation that has not yet been fulfilled. The Lord graciously acknowledges that it is right for people to have a chance to enjoy the fruits of their labor before they risk their lives for the nation.

20:8 *afraid and lacks courage.* Unlike the previous situations, the fearful and fainthearted endanger their fellow soldiers. The number of warriors was not as important as the army’s belief that God was fighting for them.

20:17 *utterly destroy.* This was not just a symbolic war; the entire Canaanite population was to be destroyed.

20:18 *they will not teach you.* The principle concern of the Lord was for the welfare of His

---

CHAPTER 20 **1** See Ps 20:7; Isa 31:1; Nu 23:21; Dt 31:6,8; 2Ch 13:12; 32:7,8 **4** Dt 1:30; 3:22; Jos 23:10 **5** See Neh 12:27 **7** Dt 24:5 **8** Jdg 7:3 **10** 2Sa 20:18,20 **13** Nu 31:7 **14** Jos 8:2; Jos 22:8 **16** Nu 21:2,3,35; 33:52; Dt 7:1,2; Jos 11:14 **18** Dt 7:4; 12:30,31; 18:9; Ex 23:33

practices which they have done [in worship and service] for their gods, and in this way cause you to sin against the LORD your God.

19"When you besiege a city for a long time, making war against it in order to capture it, you shall not destroy its [fruit-bearing] trees by swinging an axe against them; for you may eat from them, and you shall not cut them down. For is the tree of the field a man, that it should be besieged (destroyed) by you?

20"Only the trees which you know are not fruit trees shall you destroy and cut down, so that you may build siegeworks against the city that is making war with you until it falls.

Expiation of a Crime

21 "IF SOMEONE is found slain, lying in the field, in the land which the LORD your God gives you to possess, and it is not known who has killed him,

2then your elders and judges shall go out and measure *the distance* to the cities which are around the dead person.

3"It shall be that the elders of the city which is nearest to the dead man shall take a heifer of the herd, one which has not been worked and which has not pulled in a yoke;

4and the elders of that city shall bring the heifer down to a [river] valley with running water, which has not been plowed or planted, and shall break the heifer's neck there in the valley.

5"Then the priests, the sons of Levi, shall approach, for the LORD your God has chosen them to serve Him and to bless in the Name (Presence) of the LORD; and every dispute and every assault (violent crime) shall be settled by them.

6"All the elders of that city nearest to the dead man shall wash their hands over the heifer whose neck was broken in the valley;

7and they shall respond, and say, 'Our hands did not shed this blood, nor did our eyes see it.

8'Forgive Your people Israel whom You have redeemed, O LORD, and do not put the guilt of innocent blood among Your people Israel.' And the guilt of blood shall be forgiven them.

9"So shall you remove the guilt of innocent blood from among you, when you do what is right in the sight of the LORD.

Domestic Relations

10"When you go out to battle against your enemies, and the LORD your God hands them over to you and you lead them away captive,

11and you see a beautiful woman among the captives, and desire her and would take her as your wife,

12then you shall bring her [home] to your house, and she shall shave her head and trim her nails [in preparation for mourning].

13"She shall take off the clothes of her captivity and remain in your house, and weep (mourn) for her father and her mother a full month. After that you may go in to her and be her husband and she shall be your wife.

14"But it shall be that if you have no delight *and* take no pleasure in her, then you shall let her go wherever she wishes. You certainly shall not sell

---

people. The Canaanite population in the land was like a deadly tumor eating away at the body. If the tumor was cut out, the body could live. No one could thrive in that land as a follower of God as long as the Canaanites were there.

21:1 – 9 *someone is found slain.* Although the people were innocent of the act and of any knowledge of the actual death of this individual, the elders must still ask the Lord for forgiveness for the shedding of innocent blood. An honest attempt must be made to find justice and to say, "We know this was wrong." God is teaching His people about an active social conscience in this passage. When we know that an innocent party has been wronged we are not to turn our backs and say that we are not involved. Even the simple act of publicly saying that such action is not pleasing to God is effective in reminding those who hear that God sees all and will judge the perpetrators of sin at some point.

CHAPTER 21 **5** Dt 10:8; 1Ch 23:13; Dt 17:8,9 **6** See Ps 19:12; 26:6; Mt 27:24 **8** Jnh 1:14 **9** Dt 19:13 **13** See Ps 45:10 **14** Ge 34:2; Dt 22:29; Jdg 19:24

her for money; you shall not deal with
her as a slave *or* mistreat her, because
you have humbled her [by forced mar-
riage].
15"If a man has two wives, one loved
and the other unloved, and both the
loved and the unloved have born him
sons, and the firstborn son belongs to
the unloved *wife*,
16then on the day when he wills his
possessions to his sons, he cannot treat
the son of his loved wife as firstborn in
place of the son of the unloved wife—
the [actual] firstborn.
17"Instead he shall acknowledge the
son of the unloved as the firstborn,
by giving him a double portion of all
that he has, for he was the beginning
of his strength (generative power); to
him belongs the right of the firstborn.
18"If any man has a stubborn and
rebellious son who will not obey the
voice of his father or of his mother, and
when they reprimand *and* discipline
him, he will not listen to them,
19then his father and mother shall
take hold of him, and bring him out
to the elders of his city at the gateway
of his hometown.
20"They shall say to the elders of his

21:15 *two wives.* Polygamy was commonly practiced in the cultures of the ancient Middle East and was assumed in the law of Moses. It is apparently something that God allowed, as He did divorce (Mt 19:3–9), but from the beginning it was not that way.
21:16 *firstborn.* A father was expected to show consideration for the firstborn child, regardless of his attitude toward the child's mother.

15 Ge 29:33 **16** 1Ch 5:2; 26:10; 2Ch 11:19,22 **17** See 1Ch 5:1; Ge 49:3; Ge 25:31,33

MAJOR SOCIAL CONCERNS IN THE COVENANT

1. **Personhood**
Everyone's person is to be secure (Ex 20:13; Dt 5:17; Ex 21:16–21,26–32; Lev 19:14; Dt 24:7; 27:18).
2. **False Accusation**
Everyone is to be secure against slander and false accusation (Ex 20:16; Dt 5:20; Ex 23:1–3,6–8; Lev 19:16; Dt 19:15–21).
3. **Women**
No woman is to be taken advantage of within her subordinate status in society (Ex 21:7–11,20,26–32; 22:16–17; Nu 27:1–11; 36:1–12; Dt 21:10–14; 22:13–30; 24:1–5).
4. **Punishment**
Punishment for wrongdoing shall not be excessive so that the culprit is dehumanized (Dt 25:1–3).
5. **Dignity**
Every Israelite's dignity and right to be God's servant are to be honored and safeguarded (Ex 21:2,5–6; Lev 25; Dt 15:12–18).
6. **Inheritance**
Every Israelite's inheritance in the promised land is to be secure (Lev 25; Nu 27:5–7; 36:1–9; Dt 25:5–10).
7. **Property**
Everyone's property is to be secure (Ex 20:15; Dt 5:19; Ex 21:33–36; 22:1–15; 23:4–5; Lev 19:35–36; Dt 22:1–4; 25:13–15).
8. **Fruit of Labor**
Everyone is to receive the fruit of their labors (Lev 19:13; Dt 24:14; 25:4).
9. **Fruit of the Ground**
Everyone is to share the fruit of the ground (Ex 23:10–11; Lev 19:9–10; 23:22; 25:3–55; Dt 14:28–29; 24:19–21).
10. **Rest on Sabbath**
Everyone, down to the humblest servant and the resident foreigner, is to share in the weekly rest of God's Sabbath (Ex 20:8–11; Dt 5:12–15; Ex 23:12).
11. **Marriage**
The marriage relationship is to be kept inviolate (Ex 20:14; Dt 5:18; see also Lev 18:6–23; 20:10–21; Dt 22:13–30).
12. **Exploitation**
No one, however disabled, impoverished or powerless, is to be oppressed or exploited (Ex 22:21–27; Lev 19:14,33–34; 25:35–36; Dt 23:19; 24:6,12–15,17; 27:18).
13. **Fair Trial**
Everyone is to have free access to the courts and is to be afforded a fair trial (Ex 23:6–8; Lev 19:15; Dt 1:17; 10:17–18; 16:18–20; 17:8–13; 19:15–21).
14. **Social Order**
Every person's God-given place in the social order is to be honored (Ex 20:12; Dt 5:16; Ex 21:15,17; 22:28; Lev 19:3,32; 20:9; Dt 17:8–13; 21:15–21; 27:16).
15. **Law**
No one shall be above the law, not even the king (Dt 17:18–20).
16. **Animals**
Concern for the welfare of other creatures is to be extended to the animal world (Ex 23:5,11; Lev 25:7; Dt 22:4,6–7; 25:4).

city, ‘This son of ours is stubborn and rebellious; he will not obey us, he is a glutton and a drunkard.’ [Prov 23:20–22]

21 “Then all the men of his city shall stone him to death; so you shall remove the evil from among you, and all Israel will hear of it and be afraid.

22 “And if a man has committed a sin worthy of death, and he is put to death and [afterward] you hang him on a tree [as a public example], [Josh 10:26, 27]

23 his body shall not hang all night on the tree, but you shall most certainly bury him on the same day (for he who is hanged is cursed by God), so that you do not defile your land which the LORD your God gives you as an inheritance. [Gal 3:13]

Various Laws

22 “YOU SHALL not see your countryman’s ox or his sheep straying away *or* being stolen, and ignore [your duty to help] them; you shall certainly take them back to him. [Prov 24:12]

2 “If your countryman is not nearby or you do not know him, you shall bring the animal to your house, and it shall stay with you until he searches for it; then you shall return it to him.

3 “You shall do this with his donkey or with his garment or with anything that your countryman has lost and you have found. You are not allowed to ignore [your duty to help] them.

4 “You shall not see your countryman’s donkey or his ox fall down along the road, and ignore [your duty to help] them; you shall certainly help him lift it up.

5 “A woman shall not wear a man’s clothing, nor shall a man put on a woman’s clothing; for whoever does these things is utterly repulsive to the LORD your God.

6 “If you happen to come upon a bird’s nest along the road, in any tree or on the ground, with young ones or eggs, and the mother [bird] is sitting on the young or on the eggs, you shall not take the mother with the young.

7 “You shall certainly let the mother go, but you may take the young for yourself, so that it may be well with you and that you may prolong your days.

8 “When you build a new house, you shall make a railing (parapet) around your [flat] roof, so that you do not bring the guilt of [innocent] blood on your house if someone falls from it.

9 “You shall not sow your vineyard with two kinds of seed, or everything produced by the seed which you have sown and the yield of the vineyard will become defiled [and banned for use].

10 “You shall not plow with an ox [a clean animal] and a donkey [an unclean animal] together. [2 Cor 6:14–16]

11 “You shall not wear a fabric made of wool and linen blended together [a fabric pagans believed to be magical]. [Ezek 44:18; Rev 19:8]

12 “You shall make tassels for yourself on the four corners of your outer garment with which you cover yourself. [Num 15:37–40]

21:22 *hang him.* The guilty person was not executed by hanging, but after the person was stoned the corpse was impaled for public viewing as an example.

22:1–4 Kindness — In the same way that God cares for us, we are to care for others. If we see a kindness that we can do for another, we are to do it cheerfully and willingly. Receiving an act of kindness is heartwarming; doing such an act is a great joy.

22:8 *railing.* The battlement was a low wall around the edge of the roof. The rooftop was used as an extra room, and if the home owner did not provide safety measures, he would be responsible for any accidents.

22:11 *wool and linen blended together.* These restrictions were a reminder that the Hebrews were not a mixed people. They were separated to God and they were not to mix with other nations, nor were they to mix two kinds of animals, grain, or fabric. It was part of the concept of purity that governed every aspect of life.

---

21 Dt 13:5; 19:19,20; 22:21,24; Dt 13:11 **22** Dt 19:6; 22:26; Ac 23:29; 25:11,25; 26:31 **23** Jos 8:29; 10:26,27; Jn 19:31; Gal 3:13; Lev 18:25; Nu 35:34 **CHAPTER 22** **1** Ex 23:4 **4** Ex 23:5 **6** Lev 22:28 **7** Dt 4:40 **9** Lev 19:19 **10** See 2Co 6:14-16 **11** Lev 19:19 **12** Nu 15:38

Laws on Morality

13 "If any man takes a wife and goes in to her and then scorns *and* hates her,

14 and charges her [without cause] with shameful behavior and publicly defames her, and says, 'I took this woman, but when I approached her, I did not find in her evidence of virginity,'

15 then the young woman's father and her mother shall get and bring out the evidence of her virginity to the elders of the city at the gate [where court is held].

16 "The father of the young woman shall say to the elders, 'I gave my daughter to this man as a wife, but he hates her *and* has turned against her;

17 and behold, he has made baseless charges against her, saying, "I did not find in your daughter the evidence of her virginity." But this is the evidence of my daughter's virginity.' And they shall spread out the garment before the elders of the city.

18 "Then the elders of that city shall take the man and reprimand him,

19 and they shall fine him a hundred *shekels* of silver and give it to the father of the young woman, because he publicly defamed a virgin of Israel. And she shall remain his wife; he is not allowed to divorce her as long as he lives.

20 "But if this charge is true that the evidence of virginity was not found in the young woman,

21 then they shall bring her out to the doorway of her father's house, and the men of her city shall stone her to death because she has committed a deliberate sin in Israel by playing the prostitute in her father's house. So you shall remove the evil from among you.

22 "If a man is intimate with a woman who is another man's wife, they shall both be put to death, the man who lay with the woman, and the woman. So you shall remove the evil from Israel.

23 "If a young woman who is a virgin is engaged (legally betrothed) to a man, and *another* man finds her in the city and is intimate with her,

24 then you shall bring them both out to the gate of that city and stone them to death—the young woman because she did not cry out for help [though she was] in the city, and the man because he has violated his neighbor's [promised] wife. So you shall remove the evil from among you.

25 "However, if the man finds the girl who is engaged (legally betrothed) in the [open] field, and seizes her and is intimate with her [by force], then only the man who lies with her shall be put to death.

26 "But you shall do nothing to the young woman; she has committed no sin worthy of death, for this is the same as when a man attacks his neighbor and murders him.

27 When he found her in the [open] field, the engaged girl [may have] cried out for help, but there was no one to [hear and] save her.

28 "If a man finds a girl who is a virgin, who is not engaged, and seizes her and is intimate with her and they are discovered,

29 then the man who was intimate with her shall give fifty *shekels* of silver to the girl's father, and she shall become his wife because he has violated her; he can never divorce her.

30 "A man shall not take his father's [former] wife, so that he will not expose his father's wife.

Persons Excluded from the Assembly

23 "HE WHO has been castrated by *having his testicles* crushed or his male organ cut off shall not enter the congregation of the LORD.

2 "A person of illegitimate birth shall

22:14 charges her [without cause] with shameful behavior. Charging her indicated a public accusation. Virginity was highly regarded, for if the legitimacy of children was disputable, inheritance rights and positions in family would also be disputed. It is easy to determine the mother of a child, for pregnancy is obvious, but determining the father of the child was a matter of trust that the wife was faithful to marriage vows.

23:1 *castrated.* An emasculated man had had all or part of the sexual organs removed. This was done to men who were put in charge of harems to prevent

21 Ge 34:7; Jdg 20:6,10; 2Sa 13:12,13; Dt 13:5 **22** Lev 20:10; Jn 8:5; Nu 5:22-27 **23** Mt 1:18,19 **24** Dt 21:14; ver. 21,22; 1Co 5:2,13 **28** Ex 22:16,17 **29** ver. 24 **30** Lev 18:8; 20:11; Dt 27:20; 1Co 5:1; See Ru 3:9; Eze 16:8

not enter the assembly of the LORD;
none of his *descendants,* even to the
tenth generation.
3 "An Ammonite or Moabite shall
not enter the assembly of the LORD;
none of their *descendants,* even to the
tenth generation, shall ever enter the
assembly of the LORD,
4 because they did not meet you with
bread (food) and water on the road as
you came out of Egypt, and because
they hired [to act] against you Balaam
the son of Beor from Pethor of Meso-
potamia, to curse you.
5 "Nevertheless, the LORD your God
was not willing to listen to Balaam, but
the LORD your God turned the curse
into a blessing for you because the
LORD your God has loved you.
6 "You shall never seek their peace
nor their prosperity all your days.
7 "You shall not detest an Edomite,
for he is your brother [Esau's descen-
dant]. You shall not detest an Egyptian,
because you were a stranger (resident
alien, foreigner) in his land.
8 "Their children of the third gener-
ation who are born to them may enter
the assembly of the LORD.
9 "When you go out as an army [to
fight] against your enemies, you shall
keep yourselves from every evil [thing].
10 "If there is any man among you
who is [ceremonially] unclean because
of nocturnal emission, then he must go
outside the camp; he shall not come
back to the camp.
11 "But when evening comes, he shall
bathe in water, and at sundown he may
return to the camp.
12 "You shall also have a place outside
the camp to which you may go,
13 and you shall have a spade among
your tools, and when you [prepare to]
sit down outside [to relieve yourself],
you shall dig *a hole* with it and shall
turn and cover up your waste.
14 "Since the LORD your God walks
in the midst of your camp to rescue
you and to defeat your enemies before
you, therefore your camp must be holy
(undefiled); and He must not see any-
thing indecent among you or He will
turn away from you.
15 "You shall not hand over to his
master a slave who has escaped from
his master to you.
16 "He shall live among you, in the
place he chooses in one of your cities
where it pleases him; you shall not
mistreat *or* oppress him.
17 "There shall be no cult prostitute
among the daughters of Israel, nor
shall there be a cult prostitute (a sod-
omite) among the sons of Israel.
18 "You shall not bring the wages of
a prostitute or the price of a dog [that
is, a male prostitute] into the house of
the LORD your God *as payment* for any
vow, for both of these [the gift and the
giver] are utterly repulsive to the LORD
your God.
19 "You shall not charge interest
to your fellow Israelite—interest on
money, food or anything that may be
loaned for interest.
20 "You may charge interest to a for-
eigner, but to your fellow Israelite you
shall not charge interest, so that the
LORD your God may bless you in all
that you undertake in the land which
you are about to enter to possess.
21 "When you make a vow to the LORD

---

sexual relations with the women. It was also a pagan practice. Genital mutilation was prohibited in Israel.

23:17 ***cult prostitute.*** The cult prostitute was used for the worship of the Canaanite gods and goddesses of fertility. They believed that having intimate relations with the cult prostitutes (either male or female) would bring fertility to their families, fields, and herds. This debased system of worship was one of the reasons God had decided to utterly destroy this group of people.

23:18 ***wages of a prostitute or the price of a dog.*** God did not need or want money earned by such practices that He called abominations. "Dogs" does not refer to the animal. It is still insulting in the Middle East to call a person a dog, and "dogs" are listed with sorcerers, immoral persons, murderers, idolaters, and everyone who loves and practices lying, as those who are outside the heavenly city (Rev 22:15).

23:21 ***vow.*** A vow was purely voluntary, and not

CHAPTER 23 **3** Neh 13:1,2 **4** See Dt 2:29; Nu 22:5,6 **6** Ezr 9:12 **7** Ge 25:24-26; Ob 10,12; Ex 22:21; 23:9; Lev 19:34; Dt 10:19 **10** Lev 15:16 **11** Lev 15:5 **14** Lev 26:12 **15** 1Sa 30:15 **16** Ex 22:21 **17** Lev 19:29; See Pr 2:16; Ge 19:5; 2Ki 23:7 **19** Ex 22:25; Lev 25:36,37 **20** See Lev 19:34; Dt 15:3; Dt 15:10 **21** Nu 30:2; Ecc 5:4,5

your God, you shall not delay to pay
it, for He will most certainly require
it of you, and a delay would cause you
to sin.
22 "But if you refrain from making
a vow, that would not be [counted as]
sin in you.
23 "You shall be careful to perform
that [vow] which passes your lips, just
as you have made a voluntary vow to
the LORD your God, just as you have
promised with your own words (mouth).
24 "When you enter your neighbor's
vineyard, you may eat your fill of
grapes, as many as you please, but
you shall not put any in your basket
[to take with you].
25 "When you come into the stand-
ing grain of your neighbor, you may
pluck the ears of grain with your hand,
but you shall not wield a sickle in your
neighbor's standing grain [to harvest it].

Law of Divorce

24 "WHEN A man takes a wife
and marries her, and it happens
that she loses his favor because he has
found something indecent *or* unac-
ceptable about her, and he writes her
a certificate of divorce, puts it in her
hand and sends her out of his house,
2 and after she leaves his house, she
goes and becomes another man's wife,
3 and if the latter husband turns
against her and writes her a certif-
icate of divorce, puts it in her hand,
and sends her out of his house, or if
the latter husband dies who took her
as his wife,
4 then her former husband who [first]
sent her away may not take her again
as his wife, since she has been defiled;
for that is an outrage before the LORD,
and you shall not bring sin on the land
which the LORD your God gives you as
an inheritance.
5 "When a man takes a new wife, he
shall not go out [to fight] with the army
nor be charged with any duty; he shall
be free at home for one year and shall
bring happiness to his wife whom he
has taken.

Various Laws

6 "No one shall take a handmill or an
upper millstone [used to grind grain
into bread] as security [for a debt], for
he would be taking a [person's] life in
pledge.
7 "If a man is caught kidnapping any
of his countrymen from the sons of
Israel, and he treats him violently or
sells him [as a slave], then that thief
shall die. So you shall remove the evil
from among you.
8 "Be careful during an outbreak of
leprosy, that you diligently observe
and do according to all that the Le-
vitical priests teach you; just as I have
commanded them, so you shall be
careful to do. [Lev 13:14, 15]
9 "Remember [with thoughtful con-
cern] what the LORD your God did to
Miriam on the road as you came out
of Egypt. [Num 12:10]

necessary for the development of godliness. But if a vow was made, it must be kept.

24:1–4 *a certificate of divorce.* Marriage was instituted by God (Ge 2:24). It was intended to be a union of one man and one woman for life. And yet, the Mosaic law allowed divorce, even though God said through His prophet Malachi (Mal 2:16) that He hates divorce. When the Pharisees were asking Jesus about divorce, Jesus explained that it had not been so designed in the beginning, but "because of your hardness of heart" Moses had allowed it. Then Jesus raised the standard set by Moses, saying that those whom God had joined, no man should separate. With the death and resurrection of Christ, all believers receive the Holy Spirit, and it is at this point that hard hearts are changed.

24:4 *defiled.* Returning to her first husband after an intervening marriage might have placed the woman in the same position as an unfaithful wife.

24:6 *millstone.* A pair of millstones was used for grinding grain into flour. The flour was ground between two stones, and to deprive a household of the use of one of the stones was to deprive them of the necessities of daily life.

24:8 *leprosy.* Leprosy refers to a variety of infectious skin diseases. The disease known today as leprosy, Hansen's disease, is different from the diseases described here.

23 Nu 30:2; Ps 66:13,14 **25** Mt 12:1; Mk 2:23; Lk 6:1 **CHAPTER 24** **1** Mt 5:31; 19:7; Mk 10:4 **4** Jer 3:1 **5** Dt 20:7; Pr 5:18 **7** Ex 21:16; Dt 19:19 **8** Lev 13:2; 14:2 **9** See Lk 17:32; 1Co 10:6; Nu 12:10

10“When you lend your neighbor any-
thing, you shall not go into his house to
get his pledge (security deposit).
11“You shall stand outside, and the
man to whom you lend shall bring the
pledge out to you.
12“If the man is poor, you shall not
keep his pledge overnight.
13“You shall certainly restore the
pledge (security deposit) to him at sun-
set, so that he may sleep in his garment
and bless you; and it will be credited to
you as righteousness (right standing)
before the LORD your God.
14“You shall not take advantage of a
hired servant who is poor and needy,
whether [he is] one of your country-
men or one of the strangers (resident
aliens, foreigners) who is in your land
inside your cities.
15“You shall give him his wages on
the day that he earns them before the
sun sets—for he is poor and is counting
on it—so that he does not cry out to
the LORD against you, and it becomes
a sin for you.
16“The fathers shall not be put to
death for [the sins of] their children,
nor shall the children be put to death
for their fathers; [only] for his own sin
shall anyone be put to death.
17“You shall not pervert the justice
due a stranger or an orphan, nor seize
(impound) a widow’s garment as secu-
rity [for a loan].
18“But you shall remember that you
were a slave in Egypt, and the LORD your
God redeemed you from there; therefore
I am commanding you to do this thing.
19“When you reap your harvest in
your field and have forgotten a sheaf
[of grain] in the field, you shall not go
back to get it; it shall be for the strang-
er, for the orphan, and for the widow,
so that the LORD your God may bless
you in all the work of your hands.
20“When you beat [the olives off of]
your olive tree, do not search through
the branches again; [whatever is left]
shall be for the stranger, for the or-
phan, and for the widow.
21“When you gather the grapes of
your vineyard, you shall not glean it
afterward; it shall be for the stranger,
for the orphan, and for the widow.
22“You shall [thoughtfully] remem-
ber [the fact] that you were a slave in
the land of Egypt; therefore I am com-
manding you to do this thing.

Various Laws

25 “IF THERE is a controversy be-
tween men, and they go to court,
and the judges decide [the issue] be-
tween them, and they judge in favor of
the innocent and condemn the guilty,
2then it shall be that if the guilty man
deserves to be beaten, the judge shall
make him lie down and be beaten in
his presence with a [certain] number
of stripes in proportion to his offense.
3“He may have him beaten forty
times, but no more. He is not to be
beaten with more stripes than these
and he is not to be degraded [that is,
treated like an animal] in your sight.
4“You shall not muzzle the ox while
he is threshing [to prevent him from
eating any of the grain]. [1 Cor 9:9, 10;
1 Tim 5:17, 18]
5“If brothers are living together and
one of them dies without a son, the
widow of the deceased shall not be
married outside *the family* to a strang-
er. Her husband’s brother shall be in-
timate with her after taking her as
his wife and perform the duty of a
husband’s brother to her.

25:3 *forty times.* Later Jewish law restricted the number to forty minus one (2Co 11:24) to make sure that the authorities remained within the set limits.

25:4 *not muzzle the ox.* Muzzling kept the animal from eating while it worked. Later the apostle Paul used this law as a principle for providing a living for those who spend their lives preaching the gospel (1Ti 5:18).

25:5 *dies without a son.* The firstborn son of the marriage would be acknowledged as the legal son of the dead brother. Taking a brother’s

13 Ex 22:26; Job 29:11; 2Co 9:13; 2Ti 1:18; Da 4:27 **14** Mal 3:5 **15** Lev 19:13; Jer 22:13; Jas 5:4; Jas 5:4
16 Jer 31:29; Eze 18:20 **17** Pr 22:22; Jer 5:28; Eze 22:29; Zec 7:10; Ex 22:26 **18** ver. 22; Dt 16:12 **19** Lev 19:9; 23:22; Ps 41:1; Pr 19:17 **22** ver. 18 **CHAPTER 25 1** Dt 19:17; Eze 44:24; See Pr 17:15 **2** Lk 12:48; Mt 10:17
3 2Co 11:24; Job 18:3 **4** Pr 12:10; 1Ti 5:18 **5** Mt 22:24; Lk 20:28

6“It shall be that her firstborn [son] will be given the name of the dead brother, so that his name will not be blotted out of Israel.

7“But if the man does not want to marry his brother’s [widowed] wife, then she shall go up to the gate [of the city, where court is held] to the elders, and say, ‘My brother-in-law refuses to continue his brother’s name in Israel; he is not willing to perform the duty of a husband’s brother.’

8“Then the elders of his city will summon him and speak to him. And if he stands firm and says, ‘I do not want to marry her,’

9then his brother’s widow shall approach him in the presence of the elders, and pull his sandal off his foot and spit in his face; and she shall answer and say, ‘So it is done to that man who does not build up his brother’s household.’

10“In Israel his [family] name shall be, ‘The house of him whose sandal was removed.’

11“If [two] men, a man and his countryman, are fighting and the wife of one approaches to rescue her husband from the man who is striking him, and she reaches out with her hand and grabs the aggressor’s genitals,

12then you shall cut off her hand; you shall not show pity [for her].

13“You shall not have in your bag inaccurate weights, a heavy and a light [so you can cheat others].

14“You shall not have in your house inaccurate measures, a large and a small.

15“You shall have a perfect (full) and just weight, and a perfect and just measure, so that your days may be long in the land which the LORD your God gives you.

16“For everyone who does such things, everyone who acts unjustly [without personal integrity] is utterly repulsive to the LORD your God.

17“Remember what Amalek did to you along the road when you came from Egypt,

18how he met you along the road and attacked all the stragglers at your rear when you were tired and weary; and he did not fear God. [Ex 17:14]

19“Therefore when the LORD your God has given you rest from all your surrounding enemies, in the land which the LORD your God gives you as an inheritance to possess, you shall wipe out the memory of Amalek from under heaven; you must not forget.

Offering First Fruits

26 “THEN IT shall be, when you enter the land which the LORD your God gives you as an inheritance, and you take possession of it and live in it,

2that you shall take some of the first of all the produce of the ground which you harvest from the land that the LORD your God gives you, and you shall put it in a basket and go to the place where the LORD your God chooses to establish His Name (Presence).

3“You shall go to the priest who is in office at that time and say to him, ‘I declare this day to the LORD my God that I have entered the land which the LORD swore to our fathers to give us.’

4“Then the priest will take the basket from you and place it before the altar of the LORD your God.

5“And you shall say before the LORD your God, ‘My father [Jacob] was a wandering Aramean, and he [along

---

widow as a second wife provided her with care, and preserved the name, position, and inheritance of the dead brother.

25:7 – 10 *does not want to marry.* Legally the brother-in-law was bound to keep the family name alive. His unwillingness to do so was a public issue, involving the elders of the community. The removal of the sandal was a sign of giving up of one’s rights, and spitting was a strong act of public contempt.

25:19 *wipe out the memory.* The Amalekites would in effect come under the same ban as the Canaanite nations. The fact that they did not fear God made them a stumbling block to any nation that was following God.

26:5 *Aramean.* This is a reference to Jacob, whose parents’ ancestral home was in Aramea (Ge 24:1 – 10).

6 Ge 38:9; Ru 4:10 **7** Ru 4:1,2 **8** Ru 4:6 **9** Ru 4:7; Ru 4:11 **12** Dt 19:13 **13** Lev 19:35,36; Pr 11:1; Eze 45:10; Mic 6:11 **15** Ex 20:12 **16** Pr 11:1; 1Th 4:6 **17** Ex 17:8 **18** Ps 36:1; Pr 16:6; Ro 3:18 **19** 1Sa 15:3; Ex 17:14
CHAPTER 26 **2** Ex 23:19; 34:26; Nu 18:13; Dt 16:10; Pr 3:9; Dt 12:5 **5** Hos 12:12; Ge 43:1,2; 45:7,11; Ge 46:1,6; Ac 7:15; Ge 46:27; Dt 10:22

with his family] went down to Egypt and lived there [as strangers], few in number; but while there he became a great, mighty and populous nation.

6 'And the Egyptians treated us badly and oppressed us, and imposed hard labor on us.

7 'Then we cried out to the LORD, the God of our fathers for help, and He heard our voice and saw our suffering and our labor and our [cruel] oppression;

8 and the LORD brought us out of Egypt with a mighty hand and with an outstretched arm and with great terror [suffered by the Egyptians] and with signs and with wonders;

9 and He has brought us to this place and has given us this land, a land flowing with milk and honey.

10 'And now, look, I have brought the first of the produce of the ground which You, O LORD, have given me.' And you shall place it before the LORD your God, and shall worship before the LORD your God;

11 and you and the Levite and the stranger (resident alien, foreigner) among you shall rejoice in all the good which the LORD your God has given you and your household.

12 "When you have finished paying all the tithe of your produce the third year, [which is] the year of tithing, then you shall give it to the Levite, to the stranger, to the orphan, and to the widow, so that they may eat within the gates of your cities and be satisfied.

13 "You shall say before the LORD your God, 'I have removed the sacred *portion* (the tithe) from my house and also have given it to the Levite, to the stranger, to the orphan, and to the widow, in accordance with all that You have commanded me. I have not transgressed or forgotten any of Your commandments.

14 'I have not eaten from the tithe while mourning, nor have I removed any of it when I was [ceremonially] unclean [making the tithe ceremonially unclean], nor offered any of it to the dead. I have listened to the voice of the LORD my God; I have done *everything* in accordance with all that You have commanded me.

15 'Look down from Your holy dwelling above, from heaven, and bless Your people Israel, and the land which You have given us, as You have sworn to our fathers, a land [of plenty] flowing with milk and honey.'

16 "This day the LORD your God commands you to do these statutes and judgments (precepts). Therefore, you shall be careful to do them with all your heart and with all your soul (your entire being).

17 "Today you have [openly] declared the LORD to be your God, and that you will walk [that is, live each and every day] in His ways and keep His statutes, His commandments, and His judgments (precepts), and listen to His voice.

18 "Today the LORD has declared that you are His people, His treasured possession, just as He promised you, and

---

26:8 *mighty hand . . . outstretched arm.* God with His own hand demonstrated His power to the Egyptians and delivered the Israelites. The idea of God rescuing His people with His mighty arm is repeated in Isaiah 62 and 63.

26:10 *I have brought.* When the worshiper made a statement of what he was doing, (see v. 13) he was taking responsibility for the items he was presenting to the Lord, not just blindly following a set form.

26:15 *Your holy dwelling.* People direct their prayers to heaven, acknowledging at the same time that God is everywhere (Isa 66:1 – 2). Heaven most often refers to the dwelling place of God and the holy angels. Heaven is the place from which Christ came when He came to earth, and He returned there after He was resurrected (Ac 1:11). One day He will come from heaven back to earth (Mt 24:30), and Heaven will ultimately be the home of all believers (1Pe 1:4). Heaven is the place where the will of God is perfectly done, so it is a place of hope and inspiration.

26:16 *with all your heart and with all your soul.* This is a regular emphasis in Deuteronomy. God wants obedience, but He wants it to be the obedience of the engaged heart and mind.

6 Ex 1:11,14 **7** Ex 2:23-25; 3:9; 4:31 **8** Ex 12:37,51; 13:3,14,16; Dt 5:15; Dt 4:34 **9** Ex 3:8 **11** Dt 12:7,12,18; 16:11 **12** Lev 27:30; Nu 18:24; Dt 14:28,29 **13** Ps 119:141, 153,176 **14** Lev 7:20; 21:1,11; Hos 9:4 **15** Isa 63:15; Zec 2:13 **17** Ex 20:19 **18** Ex 6:7; 19:5; Dt 7:6; 14:2; 28:9

that you are to keep all His commandments;

19 and that He will set you high above all the nations which He has made, for praise, fame, and honor: and that you shall be a holy people [set apart and consecrated] to the LORD your God, just as He has spoken."

The Altar at Mount Ebal

27 THEN MOSES and the elders of Israel commanded the people, saying, "Keep (remember, obey) all the commandments which I am commanding you today.

2 "So it shall be on the day when you cross the Jordan to [enter] the land which the LORD your God gives you, that you shall set up for yourself large stones and coat them with plaster (lime, whitewash).

3 "You shall write on the stones all the words of this law when you cross over, so that you may go into the land which the LORD your God gives you, a land [of plenty] flowing with milk and honey, just as the LORD, the God of your fathers has promised you.

4 "Now when you cross the Jordan you shall set up these stones on Mount Ebal, just as I am commanding you today and coat them with plaster.

5 "There you shall build an altar to the LORD your God, an altar of stones; you shall not use an iron tool on them.

6 "You shall build the altar of the LORD your God with whole [uncut] stones, and offer burnt offerings on it to the LORD your God;

7 and you shall sacrifice peace offerings and shall eat there, and shall rejoice before the LORD your God.

8 "And you shall write very clearly on the stones all the words of this law."

9 Then Moses and the Levitical priests said to all Israel, "Be silent and listen, O Israel! This day you have become a people for the LORD your God.

10 "So you shall obey the voice of the LORD your God, and do His commandments and statutes which I am commanding you today."

The Curses of Mount Ebal

11 Moses also commanded the people that day, saying,

12 "These [tribes] shall stand on Mount Gerizim to bless the people when you have crossed the Jordan: Simeon, Levi, Judah, Issachar, Joseph, and Benjamin.

13 "These [tribes] shall stand on Mount Ebal to *pronounce* the curse [for disobedience]: Reuben, Gad, Asher, Zebulun, Dan, and Naphtali.

14 "The Levites shall answer with a loud voice to all the men of Israel:

15 'Cursed is the man who makes a carved or cast image (idol), a repulsive thing to the LORD, the work of the hands of the artisan, and sets it up in secret.' All the people shall answer and say, 'Amen.'

16 'Cursed is he who dishonors (treats with contempt) his father or his mother.' And all the people shall say, 'Amen.'

17 'Cursed is he who moves his neighbor's boundary mark.' And all the people shall say, 'Amen.'

18 'Cursed is he who misleads a blind person on the road.' And all the people shall say, 'Amen.'

19 'Cursed is he who distorts (perverts) the justice due to a stranger, an orphan, and a widow.' And all the people shall say, 'Amen.'

20 'Cursed is he who is intimate with his father's [former] wife, because he

27:7 peace offerings. Many of the sacrifices had to do with sin, repentance, and making things right with God. This particular sacrifice was a time to be thankful and to rejoice in the good care of God.

27:11 – 13 *Mount Gerizim ... Mount Ebal.* Mount Gerizim, the mountain of blessing, is usually covered with vegetation. Mount Ebal, the mountain of cursing, is a barren peak. The visual contrast made a memorable object lesson.

19 Dt 4:7,8; 28:1; Ex 19:6; Dt 7:6; 28:9; 1Pe 2:9 **CHAPTER 27** **2** Jos 4:1; Jos 8:32 **4** Dt 11:29; Jos 8:30,31 **5** Ex 20:25; Jos 8:31 **9** Dt 26:18 **12** Dt 11:29; Jos 8:33; Jdg 9:7 **13** Dt 11:29; Jos 8:33 **14** Dt 33:10; Jos 8:33; Da 9:11 **15** Ex 20:4,23; 34:17; Lev 19:4; 26:1; Dt 4:16,23; 5:8; Isa 44:9; Hos 13:2; See Nu 5:22; Jer 11:5; 1Co 14:16 **16** Ex 20:12; 21:17; Lev 19:3; Dt 21:18 **17** Dt 19:14; Pr 22:28 **18** Lev 19:14 **19** Ex 22:21,22; Dt 10:18; 24:17; Mal 3:5 **20** Lev 18:8; Dt 22:30

has violated what belongs to his father.'
And all the people shall say, 'Amen.'
21 'Cursed is he who is intimate with
any animal.' And all the people shall
say, 'Amen.'
22 'Cursed is he who is intimate with
his [half] sister, whether his father's
or his mother's daughter.' And all the
people shall say, 'Amen.'
23 'Cursed is he who is intimate with
his mother-in-law.' And all the people
shall say, 'Amen.'
24 'Cursed is he who strikes his neigh-
bor in secret.' And all the people shall
say, 'Amen.'
25 'Cursed is he who accepts a bribe to
strike down an innocent person.' And
all the people shall say, 'Amen.'
26 'Cursed is he who does not confirm
the words of this law by doing them
[keeping them, taking them to heart as
the rule of his life].' And all the people
shall say, 'Amen.'

Blessings at Gerizim

28 "NOW IT shall be, if you dil-
igently listen to *and* obey the
voice of the LORD your God, being
careful to do all of His commandments
which I am commanding you today,
the LORD your God will set you high
above all the nations of the earth.
2 "All these blessings will come upon
you and overtake you if you pay atten-
tion to the voice of the LORD your God.
3 "You *will be* blessed in the city, and
you *will be* blessed in the field.
4 "The offspring of your body and the
produce of your ground and the off-
spring of your animals, the offspring
of your herd and the young of your
flock *will be* blessed.
5 "Your basket and your kneading
bowl *will be* blessed.
6 "You *will be* blessed when you come
in and you *will be* blessed when you
go out.
7 "The LORD will cause the enemies
who rise up against you to be defeated
before you; they will come out against
you one way, but flee before you seven
ways.
8 "The LORD will command the bless-
ing upon you in your storehouses and
in all that you undertake, and He will
bless you in the land which the LORD
your God gives you.
9 "The LORD will establish you as a
people holy [and set apart] to Himself,
just as He has sworn to you, if you
keep the commandments of the LORD
your God and walk [that is, live your
life each and every day] in His ways.
10 "So all the peoples of the earth will
see that you are called by the name of
the LORD, and they will be afraid of you.
11 "The LORD will give you great pros-
perity, in the offspring of your body
and in the offspring of your livestock
and the produce of your ground, in
the land which the LORD swore to your
fathers to give you.
12 "The LORD will open for you His
good treasure house, the heavens, to
give rain to your land in its season and
to bless all the work of your hand; and
you will lend to many nations, but you
will not borrow.
13 "The LORD will make you the head
(leader) and not the tail (follower); and
you will be above only, and you will not
be beneath, if you listen *and* pay atten-
tion to the commandments of the LORD
your God, which I am commanding
you today, to observe them carefully.
14 "Do not turn aside from any of the
words which I am commanding you to-

27:26 does not confirm the words of this law by doing them. All of the actions listed in the curses are contrary to the law, as explained in the Book of Leviticus.

28:1 – 9 diligently listen to and obey. This passage repeatedly emphasizes the Israelites' responsibility to obey. God had already saved them from slavery, made them His people, promised to be their God, and to give them a land to dwell in. But the blessings would only come with Israel's obedience. Sadly, Israel failed again and again to follow God. It was only after Christ that the followers of God could have the new Spirit which enabled them to obey from the heart (Ro 7).

21 Lev 18:23 **22** Lev 18:9 **23** Lev 18:17 **24** Ex 20:13; Lev 24:17; Nu 35:31 **25** Ex 23:7,8; Dt 10:17; Eze 22:12 **26** Jer 11:3; Gal 3:10 **CHAPTER 28** **1** Ex 15:26; Lev 26:3; Isa 55:2; Dt 26:19 **2** Zec 1:6 **3** Ps 128:1,4; Ge 39:5 **4** Ge 22:17; 49:25; Dt 7:13; Pr 10:22 **6** Ps 121:8 **7** Lev 26:7,8; 2Sa 22:38,39,41 **8** Lev 25:21; Dt 15:10 **9** Ex 19:5,6; Dt 7:6; 26:18,19 **10** Nu 6:27; 2Ch 7:14; Isa 63:19; Da 9:18,19; Dt 11:25 **11** Dt 30:9; Pr 10:22 **12** Lev 26:4; Dt 11:14; Dt 14:29; Dt 15:6 **13** Isa 9:14,15 **14** Dt 5:32

day, to the right or to the left, to follow
and serve other gods.

Consequences of Disobedience

15 “But it shall come about, if you do
not listen to *and* obey the voice of the
LORD your God, being careful to do all
His commandments and His statutes
which I am commanding you today,
then all these curses will come upon
you and overtake you:
16 “You *will be* cursed in the city and
cursed in the field.
17 “Your basket and your kneading
bowl *will be* cursed.
18 “The offspring of your body and
the produce of your land, the offspring
of your herd and the young of your
flock *will be* cursed.
19 “You *will be* cursed when you come
in and you *will be* cursed when you
go out.
20 “The LORD will send upon you curs-
es, confusion, and rebuke in every-
thing that you undertake to do, until
you are destroyed, perishing quickly
because of the evil of your deeds, be-
cause you have turned away from Me.
21 “The LORD will make the pestilence
and plague cling to you until He has
consumed *and* eliminated you from the
land which you are entering to possess.
22 “The LORD will strike you with con-
sumption [causing you to waste away]
and with fever and with inflammation
and with fiery heat and with the sword
and with blight and with mildew [on
your crops]; and they will pursue you
until you perish.
23 “The heaven which is over your
head shall be bronze [giving no rain
and blocking all prayers], and the
earth which is under you, iron [hard
to plow and yielding no produce].
24 “The LORD will make the rain of
your land powder and dust; from heav-
en it will come down on you until you
are destroyed.
25 “The LORD will cause you to be de-
feated before your enemies; you will
go out against them one way, but flee
before them seven ways, and you will
be *an example of* terror to all the king-
doms of the earth [when they see your
destruction]. [2 Chr 29:8]
26 “Your carcasses will be food for all
the birds of the sky and the beasts of
the earth, and there will be no one to
frighten them away.
27 “The LORD will strike you with the
boils of Egypt and with tumors and
with the scab and the itch that you
cannot heal.
28 “The LORD will strike you with
madness and with blindness and with
bewilderment of heart *and* mind;
29 and you will be groping at noon
[in broad daylight], just as the blind
grope in the darkness, and nothing
you do will prosper; but you will only
be oppressed *and* exploited and robbed
continually, with no one to save you.

28:15 – 19 Disobedience — The price of disobedience is always more than one can imagine in the beginning. It is not only the loss of peace or blessing, great as that may be, but there is also the loss of all that might have been. In God’s plan the obedience is for the benefit of the follower of God, for the benefit of those who are watching and are influenced by this follower, and for the kingdom of God. If the follower disobeys, he may see how his actions affect himself, but he cannot know what other blessings are lost in the wider sphere of his own influence. It is a terrible thing to find oneself in the position of working against God.

28:20 – 57 curses, confusion, and rebuke. Disobedience brings suffering, and this suffering often spills over onto other people, even into future generations. The suffering is a wake-up call, something that is meant to remind the disobedient that they are living against God, and that they need to repent, turn to God, and ask for help. The problem is that often the disobedient have a skewed idea of who God is and what He desires, so they blame God and become more rebellious. There is another kind of suffering as well. This is the suffering of the innocent, as in the case of Job, where God allowed Satan to test him to show Satan that Job really loved God and was not merely faithful because God had blessed him.

---

15 Lev 26:14; La 2:17; Da 9:11; Mal 2:2 **20** Mal 2:2; 1Sa 14:20; Zec 14:13; Isa 30:17; 51:20; 66:15 **21** Lev 26:25 **22** Lev 26:16; Am 4:9 **23** Lev 26:19 **25** Dt 32:30; Isa 30:17; Jer 15:4; 24:9; Eze 23:46 **26** 1Sa 17:44,46; Jer 7:33; 16:4 **27** Ex 15:26; 1Sa 5:6 **28** Jer 4:9 **29** Job 5:14; Isa 59:10

30 “You will be pledged to marry a wife, but another man will be intimate with her [before you]; you will build a house, but you will not live in it; you will plant a vineyard, but you will not use its fruit.

31 “Your ox will be slaughtered before your eyes, but you will not eat any of it; your donkey will be torn away from you, and it will not be returned to you; your sheep will be given to your enemies, and you will have no one to save you.

32 “Your sons and daughters will be given to another people, while your eyes look on and long for them continually; but there will be nothing you can do. [2 Chr 29:9]

33 “A people whom you do not know will eat the produce of your land and all the products of your labors, and you will never be anything but oppressed *and* exploited and crushed continually. [Judg 6:1–6; 13:1]

34 You shall be driven mad by the sight of the things you see.

35 “The LORD will strike you on the knees and on the legs with sore boils that you cannot heal, from the sole of your foot to the crown of your head.

36 “The LORD will bring you and your king, whom you appoint over you, to a nation which you and your fathers have never known; there you will [be forced to] serve other gods, [lifeless gods of] wood and stone. [2 Kin 17:4, 6; 24:12, 14; 25:7, 11; Dan 6:11, 12]

37 “And you will become a horror, a proverb [a mere object lesson], and a taunt [a derisive joke] among all the people to which the LORD drives you.

38 “You will bring out a great quantity of seed to the field, but you will gather in little, because the locusts will consume it. [Hag 1:6]

39 “You will plant vineyards and cultivate them, but you will not drink the wine or gather *the grapes*, because the worm will eat them.

40 “You will have olive trees throughout your territory but you will not anoint yourselves with the oil, because your olives will drop off.

41 “You will have sons and daughters, but they will not be yours [for long], because they will go into captivity. [Lam 1:5]

42 “The cricket will take possession of all your trees and the produce of your ground. [Joel 1:4]

43 “The stranger who lives among you will rise above you higher and higher, and you will go down lower and lower.

44 “He will lend to you [out of his affluence], but you will not lend to him [because of your poverty]; he will be the head, and you the tail.

45 “So all these curses will come on you and pursue you and overtake you until you are destroyed, because you would not obey the voice of the LORD your God by keeping His commandments and His statutes which He has commanded you.

46 They will be a sign and a wonder to you and your descendants forever.

47 “Because you did not serve the LORD your God with a heart full of joy and gladness for the abundance of all things [with which He blessed you],

48 you will therefore serve your enemies whom the LORD sends against you, in hunger and in thirst, in nakedness and in lack of all things; and He will put an iron yoke [of slavery] on your neck until He has destroyed you.

49 “The LORD will bring a nation against you from far away, from the end of the earth, [as swift] as the eagle swoops down [to attack], a nation whose language you will not understand,

50 a defiant nation who will have no

28:30 *marry a wife . . . build a house . . . plant a vineyard.* Each of these momentous events of life were reasons to be excused from service in the army (20:5–7), yet if the Israelites were disobedient, life itself would prevent them from realizing the fruits of their labors.

---

30 Job 31:10; Jer 8:10; Job 31:8; Jer 12:13; Am 5:11; Mic 6:15; Zep 1:13; Dt 20:6 **32** Ps 119:82 **33** Lev 26:16; Jer 5:17 **36** 2Ki 17:4,6; 24:12,14; 2Ch 33:11; Dt 4:28; Jer 16:13 **37** Jer 24:9; Zec 8:13; Ps 44:14 **38** Mic 6:15; Hag 1:6; Joel 1:4 **41** La 1:5 **44** ver. 12; ver. 13 **45** ver. 15 **46** Isa 8:18; Eze 14:8 **47** Neh 9:35-37; Dt 32:15 **48** Jer 28:14 **49** Jer 5:15; 6:22,23; Lk 19:43; Jer 48:40; 49:22; La 4:19; Hos 8:1 **50** 2Ch 36:17; Isa 47:6

respect for the old, nor show favor to
the young,
51and it will eat the offspring of your
herd and the produce of your ground
until you are destroyed, who will leave
you no grain, new wine, or oil, nor the
offspring of your herd or the young of
your flock until they have caused you
to perish.
52"They will besiege you in all your
cities until your high and fortified
walls in which you trusted come down
throughout your land; and they will be-
siege you in all your cities throughout
your land which the LORD your God
has given you.
53"Then you will eat the offspring of
your own body [to avoid starvation],
the flesh of your sons and daughters
whom the LORD your God has given
you, during the siege and the misery
by which your enemy will oppress you.
[2 Kin 6:24–29]
54"The man who is most refined and
well-bred among you will be cruel *and*
hostile toward his brother and toward
the wife he cherishes and toward the
rest of his children who remain,
55so that he will not give *even* one
of them any of the flesh of his chil-
dren which he will eat, because he has
nothing else left, during the siege and
the misery by which your enemy will
oppress you in all your cities.
56"The most refined and well-bred
woman among you, who would not
venture to set the sole of her foot on the
ground because she is so delicate and
pampered, will be cruel *and* hostile
toward the husband she cherishes and
toward her son and daughter,
57and toward her afterbirth that
comes from between her legs and to-
ward the children whom she bears;
for she will eat them secretly for lack
of anything else, during the siege and
the misery by which your enemy will
oppress you in your cities.
58"If you are not careful to do all
the words of this law that are written
in this book, to fear *and* honor with
reverence this glorious and awesome
name, the LORD your God,
59then the LORD will bring extraordi-
nary plagues on you and your descen-
dants, even severe and lasting plagues,
and miserable and chronic sicknesses.
60"Moreover, He will bring on you
all the diseases of Egypt of which you
were afraid, and they will cling to
you.
61"Also the LORD will bring on you
every sickness and every plague which
is not written in this book of this law,
until you are destroyed.
62"Because you did not obey the
voice of the LORD your God, you who
were as numerous as the stars of heav-
en shall be left few in number.
63"It shall come about that just as the
LORD delighted over you to make you
prosper and multiply, so the LORD will
delight over you to bring you to ruin
and destruction; and you will be up-
rooted [violently] from the land which
you are entering to possess.
64"And the LORD will scatter you
among all the nations, from one end
of the earth to the other; and there you
will [be forced to] serve other gods,
[lifeless gods of] wood and stone,
which neither you nor your fathers
have known. [Dan 3:6]
65"Among those nations you will
find no peace (rest), and there will be
no resting place for the sole of your
foot; but there the LORD will give you
a trembling heart, failing eyes, and a
despairing soul.
66"Your life will hang in doubt before
you; night and day you will be filled
with anxiety and have no assurance
of living.
67"In the morning you will say,
'I wish it were evening!' and in the
evening you will say, 'I wish it were

28:52 – 57 *besiege you in all your cities.* Moses forewarned the people of the terrible stresses of sieges (2Ki 6:24 – 31; La 2:20; 4:10). The horrors of hunger and deprivation would lead people to behave in ways that they otherwise could never imagine.

51 ver. 33; Isa 1:7 **52** 2Ki 25:1,2,4 **53** Lev 26:29; 2Ki 6:28,29; Jer 19:9; La 2:20; 4:10 **54** Dt 15:9; Dt 13:6 **56** ver. 54 **57** Ge 49:10 **58** Ex 6:3 **59** Da 9:12 **60** Dt 7:15 **62** Dt 4:27; Dt 10:22; Neh 9:23 **63** Dt 30:9; Jer 32:41; Pr 1:26; Isa 1:24 **64** Lev 26:33; Dt 4:27,28; Neh 1:8; Jer 16:13; ver. 36 **65** Am 9:4; Lev 26:36; Lev 26:16 **67** Job 7:4; ver. 34

morning!'—because of the dread in your heart with which you tremble, and because of the sight of your eyes which you will see.

68 "The LORD will bring you back to Egypt in ships, by the way about which I said to you, 'You will never see it again!' And there you will offer yourselves for sale to your enemies as male and female slaves, but there will be no one to buy you. [Hos 8:13]

The Covenant in Moab

29 THESE ARE the words of the covenant which the LORD commanded Moses to make with the sons of Israel in the land of Moab, in addition to the covenant which He made with them at Horeb (Sinai).

2 Moses summoned all Israel and said to them, "You have seen all that the LORD did before your eyes in the land of Egypt to Pharaoh, to all his servants, and to all his land;

3 the great trials [of Pharaoh] which your eyes have seen, the signs and those great wonders.

4 "Yet to this day the LORD has not given you a heart *and* mind to understand, nor eyes to see, nor ears to hear.

5 "I have led you in the wilderness forty years; your clothes have not worn out on you, and your sandals have not worn out on your feet.

6 "You have not eaten bread, nor have you drunk wine or strong drink, so that you might know that I am the LORD your God [on whom you must depend].

7 "When you reached this place, Sihon the king of Heshbon and Og the king of Bashan came out to meet us in battle, but we defeated them;

8 and we took their land and gave it as an inheritance to the tribe of Reuben, the tribe of Gad, and the half-tribe of Manasseh.

9 "So keep the words of this covenant and obey them, so that you may prosper *and* be successful in everything that you do.

10 "All of you stand today before the LORD your God—your chiefs, your tribes, your elders and your officers, *even* all the men of Israel,

11 your little ones, your wives, and the stranger (resident alien, foreigner) who is in your camps, from the one who chops *and* gathers your firewood to the one who draws your water—

12 so that you may enter into the covenant of the LORD your God, and into His oath *and* agreement which the LORD your God is making with you today,

13 so that He may establish you today as His people and that He may be your God, just as He spoke to you and as He swore to your fathers, to Abraham, Isaac, and Jacob.

14 "It is not with you alone that I am making this covenant and this oath,

15 but with those [future Israelites] who are not here with us today, as well as with those who stand here with us today in the presence of the LORD our God

16 (for you know how we lived in the land of Egypt, and how we passed through the nations along the way;

17 and you have seen their detestable acts and their [repulsive] idols of wood and stone, [lifeless images] of silver and gold, which *they had* with them),

18 so that there will not be among you a man or woman, or family or tribe, whose heart turns away today from the LORD our God, to go and serve the

---

29:9–13 *keep the words of this covenant.* The members of the covenant community included all adults, children, and strangers who had joined the Israelites, as well as those yet to be born.

29:10–15 The Covenant Renewed—As Israel reached the plains of Moab, anticipating their entrance into the promised land, it was important for the people to review and renew their covenantal relationship with God. *So Moses summoned the* people together and challenged them to keep the covenant that God had established with their forefathers. The essential terms of the covenant gave Israel the promised land and prosperity in their possession of it, but only on the condition of their obedience and willingness to walk in God's ways.

29:18 *heart turns away.* To be in the position of once having known the way of the Lord, and then to have turned and followed a path

---

68 Jer 43:7; Hos 8:13; 9:3; Dt 17:16 **CHAPTER 29** **1** Dt 5:2,3 **2** Ex 19:4 **3** Dt 4:34; 7:19 **4** See Isa 6:9,10; 63:17; Jn 8:43; Ac 28:26,27; Eph 4:18 **5** Dt 1:3; 8:2; Dt 8:4 **6** Ex 16:12; Dt 8:3 **7** Nu 21:23,24,33; Dt 2:32 **8** Nu 32:33; Dt 3:12,13 **9** Dt 4:6; 1Ki 2:3; Jos 1:7 **11** See Jos 9:21,23,27 **12** Neh 10:29 **13** Dt 28:9; Ex 6:7; Ge 17:7 **14** Jer 31:31 **15** Ac 2:39; 1Co 7:14 **18** Dt 11:16; Ac 8:23; Heb 12:15

[false] gods of these nations; so that
there will not be among you a root [of
idolatry] bearing poisonous fruit and
wormwood (bitterness).
19"It will happen that when he (a ren-
egade) hears the words of this oath,
and he imagines himself as blessed,
saying, 'I will have peace *and* safety
even though I walk within the stub-
bornness of my heart [rejecting God
and His law], in order that the watered
land dwindles away along with the dry
[destroying everything],'
20the LORD will not be willing to
forgive him, but then the anger of
the LORD and His jealousy will burn
against that man, and every curse
which is written in this book will rest
on him; the LORD will blot out his name
from under heaven.
21"Then the LORD will single him out
for disaster from all the tribes of Israel
[making an example of him], according
to all the curses of the covenant that
are written in this Book of the Law.
22"Now the next generation, your
children who come after you and the
foreigner who comes from a distant
land, when they see the plagues of this
land and the diseases with which the
LORD has afflicted it, will say,
23'The whole land is brimstone and
salt, a burning waste, unsown and
unproductive, and no grass grows in
it; it is like the overthrow of Sodom
and Gomorrah, Admah and Zeboiim,
which the LORD overthrew in His anger
and wrath.'
24"All the nations will say, 'Why has
the LORD done this thing to this land?
Why this great outburst of anger?'
25"Then *people* will say, 'It is because
they abandoned (broke) the covenant
of the LORD, the God of their fathers,
which He made with them when He
brought them out of the land of Egypt.
26'For they went and served other
gods and worshiped them, [false] gods
whom they have not known and whom
He had not allotted (given) to them.
27'So the anger of the LORD burned
against this land, bringing on it every
curse that is written in this book;
28and the LORD uprooted them from
their land in anger and in wrath and in
great indignation, and cast them into
another land, as it is this day.'
29"The secret things belong to the
LORD our God, but the things which
are revealed *and* disclosed belong to
us and to our children forever, so that
we may do all of the words of this law.

---

of disobedience and rebellion is a miserable position. It is the cause of great heartache for the faithful ones who see it happening. The backslider becomes more and more hardened against God, and it will ultimately affect a wider and wider group of people. There is no security or safety while persisting in a course of flagrant and continuous rebellion. ***root [of idolatry] bearing poisonous fruit and wormwood.*** Tolerance for idolatry and pagan practices would always corrupt the community, and therefore the covenant relationship with God.

29:24 – 28 *Why has the LORD done this.* The lesson of faithless Israel would become known among the nations, even as the deliverance of Israel was to be known by them.

29:29 Revelation — Revelation may be defined as that process by which God gives to man truths that he would not otherwise know. The details of the creation story in Genesis 1 and 2 are an example of general revelation. Because man was not created until the sixth day, there was no human to even write about creation until after it happened. God revealed the creation facts to Moses. All created things have an innate knowledge of their Creator through creation itself.

We know God spoke to the human authors of our Bible. We are not sure exactly how it happened, but Scripture gives some examples of specific revelation. God's call to Samuel was in an audible voice he mistook for that of Eli's (1Sa 3). Often God spoke through angels such as when Gabriel was sent to tell Mary she would give birth to the Messiah (Lk 1:26 – 37). On other occasions it appears that God spoke directly to a man, as he did to Noah (Ge 6) and Moses through the burning bush (Ex 3). On still other occasions God communicated through dreams or visions as he did with the wise men (Mt 2:12) and Peter (Ac 10).

One of the most important ways God reveals Himself to people in Scripture is through encounters where God takes on human form called a theophany or Christophany. In Genesis 32 Jacob wrestled with God, and in Joshua 5 Joshua

19 Nu 15:39; Ecc 11:9; Isa 30:1 **20** Eze 14:7; Ps 74:1; Ps 79:5; Eze 23:25; Dt 9:14 **21** Mt 24:51 **23** Jer 17:6; Zep 2:9; Ge 19:24; Jer 20:16 **24** 1Ki 9:8,9; Jer 22:8,9 **27** Da 9:11,13,14 **28** 1Ki 14:15; Ps 52:5; Pr 2:22

Restoration Promised

30 "SO IT shall be when all these
things have come on you, the
blessing and the curse which I have set
before you, and you call them to mind
in all the nations where the LORD your
God has driven you,
2and you have returned to the LORD
your God and have listened to *and*
obeyed His voice with all your heart
and with all your soul, in accordance
with everything that I am command-
ing you today, you and your children,
3then the LORD your God will restore
your fortunes [in your return from ex-
ile], and have compassion on you, and
will gather you together again from
all the peoples (nations) where He has
scattered you.
4"Even if any of your dispersed are
at the ends of the earth, the LORD your
God will gather you together from
there, and from there He will bring
you back.
5"The LORD your God will bring you
into the land which your fathers pos-
sessed, and you will take possession of
it; and He shall make you prosper and
multiply—even more than your fathers.
6"And the LORD your God will cir-
cumcise your heart and the hearts of
your descendants [that is, He will re-
move the desire to sin from your heart],
so that you will love the LORD your God
with all your heart and all your soul,
so that you may live [as a recipient of
His blessing].
7"The LORD your God will inflict all
these curses on your enemies and on
those who hate you, who have perse-
cuted you.
8"And you shall again listen to *and*
obey the voice of the LORD, and do all
His commandments which I command
you today.
9"Then the LORD your God shall
make you abundantly prosperous in
everything that you do, in the offspring
of your body and in the offspring of
your cattle and in the produce of your
land; for the LORD will again delight
over you for good, just as He delighted
over your fathers,
10if you listen to *and* obey the voice
of the LORD your God to keep His com-
mandments and His statutes which are
written in this Book of the Law, and if
you turn to the LORD your God with all
your heart and with all your soul (your
entire being).
11"For this commandment which I
am commanding you today is not too
difficult for you, nor is it out of reach.
12"It is not [a secret hidden] in heav-
en, that you should say, 'Who will go
up to heaven for us and bring it to us,
so that we may hear it and obey it?'
13"Nor is it beyond the sea, that you
should say, 'Who will cross the sea for
us and bring it to us, so that we may
hear it and obey it?'
14"But the word is very near you, in
your mouth and in your heart, so that
you may obey it.

---

encounters a commander of the Lord's that most Bible students take to be a pre-incarnate Christ.

30:1 ***when all these things have come on you.*** God had allowed Moses to foresee Israel's future apostasy and God's dispersal of the people among the nations. Hundreds of years later, these verses must have been both sad and encouraging to the Israelites as they saw the time of their dispersal.

30:6 ***circumcise your heart.*** God's intentions for His people have always been for the whole person to respond to Him. Outward symbols, such as circumcision, were always intended to be the mark of an inner reality, the heart that was tender to the Lord.

30:10 ***this Book of the Law.*** A reference to the Book of Deuteronomy. ***all your heart . . . soul.*** An open heart in the presence God through the law creates a dynamic of "life" and "blessing" (v. 19).

30:11 ***not too difficult for you.*** This is not a mysterious task.

30:12 – 13 ***not [a secret hidden] in heaven . . . beyond the sea.*** Obeying God's law is entirely within the reach of the average person.

30:14 ***very near you.*** The revelation of God, unlike any other book, makes the truth of immediate importance to the reader.

CHAPTER 30 **1** Lev 26:40; Dt 28; Dt 4:29,30; 1Ki 8:47 **2** Neh 1:9; Isa 55:7; La 3:40; Joel 2:12 **3** Ps 106:45; 126:1,4; Jer 29:14; La 3:22,32; Ps 147:2; Jer 32:37; Eze 34:13; 36:24 **4** Dt 28:64; Neh 1:9 **6** Dt 10:16; Jer 32:39; Eze 11:19; 36:26 **9** Dt 28:11; Dt 28:63; Jer 32:41 **11** Isa 45:19 **12** Ro 10:6

Choose Life

15“Listen closely, I have set before
you today life and prosperity (good),
and death and adversity (evil);
16in that I command you today to
love the LORD your God, to walk [that
is, to live each and every day] in His
ways and to keep His commandments
and His statutes and His judgments
(precepts), so that you will live and
multiply, and that the LORD your God
will bless you in the land which you
are entering to possess.
17“But if your heart turns away and
you will not hear *and* obey, but are
drawn away and worship other gods
and serve them,
18I declare to you today that you will
certainly perish. You will not live long
in the land which you cross the Jordan
to enter and possess.
19“I call heaven and earth as wit-
nesses against you today, that I have
set before you life and death, the bless-
ing and the curse; therefore, you shall
choose life in order that you may live,
you and your descendants,
20by loving the LORD your God, by
obeying His voice, and by holding
closely to Him; for He is your life [your
good life, your abundant life, your ful-
fillment] and the length of your days,
that you may live in the land which the
LORD promised (swore) to give to your
fathers, to Abraham, Isaac, and Jacob.”

Moses’ Last Counsel

31 SO MOSES went and spoke
these words to all Israel.
2And he said to them, “I am a hun-
dred and twenty years old today; I am
no longer able to come in and go out
[as your spiritual and military leader],
and the LORD has said to me, ‘You shall
not cross this Jordan.’
3“It is the LORD your God who will
cross ahead of you; He will destroy
these nations before you, and you shall
dispossess them. Joshua is the one who
will go across before you [to lead you],
just as the LORD has said.
4“The LORD will do to them just as
He did to Sihon and Og, the kings of
the Amorites, and to their land, when
He destroyed them.
5“The LORD will hand them over to
you, and you shall do to them in ac-
cordance with all the commandments
which I have commanded you.
6“Be strong and courageous, do not
be afraid or tremble in dread before
them, for it is the LORD your God who
goes with you. He will not fail you or
abandon you.”
7Then Moses called to Joshua and
said to him in the sight of all [the peo-
ple of] Israel, “Be strong and coura-
geous, for you will go with this people
into the land which the LORD has sworn
to their fathers to give them, and you
will give it to them as an inheritance.
8“It is the LORD who goes before you;
He will be with you. He will not fail
you or abandon you. Do not fear or be
dismayed.”
9So Moses wrote this law and gave
it to the priests, the sons of Levi who
carried the ark of the covenant of the
LORD, and to all the elders of Israel.

30:18 *today.* Moses establishes here the best pattern for the preaching of the Word of God. Responses to God should not be delayed. Assuming that there will be a later day to respond to Him is dangerous thinking.

30:19 *life and death.* Biblical teaching is remarkable for the clarity with which it presents the great issues that demand decision. Either we love the Lord and walk in His ways, or we turn from Him to worship idols. We can choose life or death, blessing or cursing. God takes no pleasure in the misery of sinners, but urges us to choose life for our good and the good of unborn generations. The Lord has spoken, and we cannot plead ignorance. ***and your descendants.*** The present generation’s choice always determines the direction of future generations.

31:2–3 *You shall not cross this Jordan.* Moses spoke regretfully of God’s refusal to permit him to enter the promised land, yet he continued to make the most important point of all. The leadership of God Himself would not cease with Moses’ death.

---

15 ver. 1,19; Dt 11:26 **18** Dt 4:26; 8:19 **19** Dt 4:26; 31:28; ver. 15 **20** Ps 27:1; 66:9; Jn 11:25 **CHAPTER 31**
2 Ex 7:7; Dt 34:7; Nu 27:17; 1Ki 3:7; Nu 20:12; 27:13; Dt 3:27 **3** Dt 9:3; Nu 27:21; Dt 3:28 **4** Dt 3:21; Nu 21:24,33
5 Dt 7:2 **6** Jos 10:25; 1Ch 22:13; Dt 1:29; 7:18; Dt 20:4; Jos 1:5; Heb 13:5 **7** ver. 23; Dt 1:38; 3:28; Jos 1:6
8 Ex 13:21; 33:14; Dt 9:3; Jos 1:5,9; 1Ch 28:20 **9** ver. 25; Dt 17:18; Nu 4:15; Jos 3:3; 1Ch 15:12,15

10 Then Moses commanded them, saying, "At the end of *every* seven years, at the time of year when debts are forgiven, at the Feast of Booths (Tabernacles),

11 when all Israel comes to appear before the LORD your God in the place which He chooses, you shall read this law before all [the people of] Israel so that they may hear.

12 "Assemble the people, the men and the women and children and the stranger (resident alien, foreigner) within your cities, so that they may hear and learn and fear the LORD your God [with awe-filled reverence and profound respect], and be careful to obey all the words of this law.

13 "Their children, who have not known [the law], will hear and learn to fear [and worship] the LORD your God, as long as you live in the land which you are crossing the Jordan to possess."

Israel Will Fall Away

14 Then the LORD said to Moses, "Behold, the time for you to die is near; call Joshua, and present yourselves at the Tent of Meeting, so that I may commission him." So Moses and Joshua went and presented themselves at the Tent of Meeting.

15 Then the LORD appeared in the tent in a pillar of cloud, and the pillar of cloud stood beside the doorway of the tent.

16 The LORD said to Moses, "Behold, you are about to lie down [in death] with your fathers; and this people will arise and play the prostitute (commit apostasy) with the foreign gods [of the people] of the land, where they go to be among them. They will abandon (turn away from) Me and break My covenant which I have made with them.

17 "Then My anger will be kindled *and* burn against them in that day, and I will abandon (turn away from) them and hide My face from them. They will be devoured, and many evils and troubles will come on them, so that they will say in that day, 'Is it not because our God is not among us that these evils have come on us?'

18 "But I will certainly hide My face [from them] in that day because of all the evil which they will do, for they will turn to other gods [to worship lifeless idols, to honor handmade relics].

19 "Now then, write this song for yourselves, and teach it to the sons of Israel; put it in their mouth, so that this song may be a witness for Me against the sons of Israel.

20 "For when I bring them into the land which I have sworn to their fathers, a land [of plenty] flowing with milk and honey, and they have eaten and are satisfied and become prosperous, then they will turn to other gods and serve them, and despise *and* reject Me and break My covenant.

21 "Then it shall come about, when many evils and troubles have come on them, that this [sacred] song will confront them as a witness; for it will not be forgotten from the mouth of their descendants. For I know their inclination which is developing even

---

31:12 – 13 Obeying God — Because the Israelites had no books or Bibles, they had to come together to listen to God's word as read by a priest from a scroll. The laws were to be read to the whole assembly including women and children. No doubt memorization was important as a way of impressing the laws on the minds and hearts of the people. But it was not the end. The expected end result of hearing was obedience. Obedience to the Word of God is the only way that the child of God can please God in the new life. "But prove yourselves doers of the word [actively and continually obeying God's precepts], and not merely listeners [who hear the word but fail to internalize its meaning], deluding yourselves [by unsound reasoning contrary to the truth]" (Jas 1:22).

31:16 *play the prostitute.* This expression speaks both of spiritual adultery and physical acts of sexual immorality that were performed in association with the worship of Baal and Asherah, the gods of Canaan.

10 Dt 15:1; Lev 23:34 **11** Dt 16:16; Jos 8:34,35; 2Ki 23:2; Neh 8:1-3 **12** Dt 4:10 **13** Dt 11:2; Ps 78:6,7
14 Nu 27:13; Dt 34:5; Nu 27:19 **15** Ex 33:9 **16** Ex 32:6; Ex 34:15; Jdg 2:17; Dt 32:15; Jdg 2:12; 10:6,13; Jdg 2:20
17 2Ch 15:2; Dt 32:20; Isa 8:17; 64:7; Eze 39:23; Jdg 6:13; Nu 14:42 **18** ver. 17 **19** ver. 26 **20** Dt 32:15; Neh 9:25; Hos 13:6; ver. 16 **21** ver. 17; Hos 5:3; 13:5,6; Am 5:25,26

now, before I bring them into the land which I have sworn *to give them*."

[22]So Moses wrote this song the same day, and taught it to the children of Israel. [Deut 32:1–43]

Joshua Is Commissioned

[23]Then He commanded *and* commissioned Joshua, the son of Nun, and said, "Be strong and courageous, for you will bring the sons of Israel into the land which I have sworn to give them, and I will be with you."

[24]And when Moses completely finished writing the words of this law in a book,

[25]he commanded the Levites who carried the ark of the covenant of the LORD, saying,

[26]"Take this Book of the Law and put it beside the ark of the covenant of the LORD your God, so that it may remain there as a witness against you.

[27]"For I know your rebellion *and* contention and your stubbornness; behold, while I am still alive with you today, you have been rebellious against the LORD; how much more, then, after my death?

[28]"Assemble before me all the elders of your tribes and your officers, so that I may speak these words in their hearing and call heaven and earth as witnesses against them.

[29]"For I know that after my death you will behave corruptly and turn from the way which I have commanded you; and evil will come upon you in the latter days, because you will do evil in the sight of the LORD, provoking Him to anger with the work of your hands."

[30]Then Moses spoke in the hearing of all the congregation of Israel the words of this song, until they were ended:

The Song of Moses

32 "LISTEN, O heavens, and I will speak;
And let the earth hear the words of my mouth.
[2]"Let my teaching drop as the rain,
My speech distill as the dew,
As the light rain upon the tender grass,
And as the spring showers upon the herb.
[3]"For I proclaim the name [and presence] of the LORD;
Ascribe greatness *and* honor to our God!
[4]"The Rock! His work is perfect,
For all His ways are just;
A God of faithfulness without iniquity (injustice),
Just and upright is He.
[5]"They (Israel) have acted corruptly toward Him.
They are not His children, because of their [moral] defect;
But are a perverse and crooked generation.
[6]"Do you thus repay the LORD,
O foolish and unwise people?
Is not He your Father who has acquired you [as His own]?
He has made you and established you [as a nation].
[7]"Remember the days of old,
Consider the years of many generations.
Ask your father, and he will inform you,

31:22 *Moses wrote.* Psalm 90 is also attributed to Moses, and perhaps Psalm 91. Both Psalms are logical meditations for these last chapters of Deuteronomy.

32:7 Remembering the Works of God—The Bible's revelation of God's work in the past provides an informative and exciting panorama of centuries of divine activity toward man.

First, it gives man an education in truths unknowable apart from divine revelation. For example, the creation of man described in Genesis 1 and 2 answers man's most basic questions: "Who am I?" and "Where did I come from?" The only way we can get this information is from God Himself.

Second, the Bible sets forth a significant body of historical evidence for the truth and validity of the Christian faith. These evidences include fulfilled prophecy, the miracles of Christ and Christ's death and resurrection. The believer's

---

23 ver. 14; ver. 7; Jos 1:6 **26** See 2Ki 22:8; ver. 19 **27** Dt 9:24; 32:20; Ex 32:9; Dt 9:6 **28** Dt 30:19; 32:1 **29** Dt 32:5; Jdg 2:19; Hos 9:9; Dt 28:15; Ge 49:1; Dt 4:30 **CHAPTER 32** **1** Isa 1:2 **2** 1Co 3:6; Ps 72:6 **3** 1Ch 29:11 **4** Ps 18:2; 2Sa 22:31; Jer 10:10; Job 34:10 **5** Dt 31:29; Php 2:15 **6** Ps 116:12; Isa 63:16; Ps 74:2; ver. 15 **7** Ex 13:14

Your elders, and they will tell you.
8 "When the Most High gave the nations their inheritance,
When He separated the sons of man,
He set the boundaries of the peoples
According to the number of the sons of Israel.
9 "For the LORD's portion *and* chosen share is His people;
Jacob (Israel) is the allotment of His inheritance.
10 "He found him in a desert land,
In the howling wasteland of a wilderness;
He kept circling him, He took care of him,
He protected him as the apple of His eye.
11 "As an eagle that protects its nest,
That flutters over its young,
He spread out His wings and took them,
He carried them on His pinions. [Luke 13:34]
12 "So the LORD alone led him;
There was no foreign god with him.
13 "He made him (Israel) ride on the high places of the earth,
And he ate the produce of the field;
And He made him suck honey from the rock,
And [olive] oil from the flinty rock,
14 Butter *and* curds of cows, and milk of the flock,
With fat of lambs,
And rams, the breed of Bashan, and goats,
With the finest of the wheat;
And you drank wine, the blood of grapes.

15 "But Jeshurun (Israel) became fat and kicked [at God].
You became fat, thick, sleek, *and* obstinate!
Then he abandoned God who had made him,
And scorned the Rock of his salvation.
16 "They provoked Him to jealousy with strange *gods* [by denying Him the honor and loyalty that is rightfully and uniquely His];
And with repulsive acts they provoked Him to anger.
17 "They sacrificed to demons, not to God,
To gods whom they have not known,

---

faith is thus grounded in historical events and is much more than just "a leap in the dark."

Third, the Bible records examples to help present-day Christians. Israel's failures and the consequences that resulted are used by the New Testament writers as lessons. Believers are urged to avoid grumbling, as Israel did (1Co 10:10 – 11), and the deviant behavior of Sodom and Gomorrah (2Pe 2:4 – 9). Paul is said to be a living example for believers to follow (1Co 4:16; 11:1), as is Jesus' humility in the midst of suffering (1Pe 2:21).

Fourth, the Bible provides encouragement for Christians in their life and witness. If God could use an adulterer and murderer like David, then God can surely use a struggling Christian today if he has David's passion for the Lord. Likewise, if God saved Saul of Tarsus, the chief enemy of the early church (Ac 9:1 – 31), he can certainly save the people with whom Christians daily share their faith.

32:12 *the LORD alone.* Deuteronomy is an extended argument against idolatry and paganism. Clearly the Israelites had no reason to abandon the God of grace and love, who had given them all they needed.

32:15 *Jeshurun.* Jeshurun, a pet name for Israel, means "uprightness." This part of the song contrasts what Israel should have been (upright) and what they became (rebellious). ***he abandoned God.*** A nation or a person who has forsaken God is godless. Because God is the source of blessing, peace, joy, wisdom, and comfort, they have also forsaken all of these attributes. One would think that that would be enough to drive people back to God. But persistence in willful disobedience and willful ignorance of God's ways creates a kind of blindness and deafness that makes people unwilling to turn back. At this point God sometimes hides His face, and they experience greater misfortunes.

32:17 *demons.* Scripture makes it clear that the false gods do not exist as such, and this passage identifies the power behind these gods: demons. It is important to remember this, especially in this era of multiculturalism, when many voices protest the exclusiveness of Christianity.

8 Zec 9:2; Ge 11:8 **9** Ex 19:5 **10** Jer 2:6; Ps 17:8 **11** Isa 31:5 **13** Isa 58:14 **14** Ps 81:16; Ge 49:11 **15** Dt 31:20; Isa 1:4; Isa 51:13; Ps 95:1 **16** 1Co 10:22 **17** Rev 9:20

New *gods* who came lately,
Whom your fathers never feared.
18 "You were unmindful of the Rock who bore you,
And you forgot the God who gave you birth.

19 "The LORD saw it, and rejected them,
Out of indignation with His sons and His daughters.
20 "Then He said, 'I will hide My face from them,
I will see what their end *shall be;*
For they are a perverse generation,
Sons in whom there is no faithfulness.
21 'They have made Me jealous with what is not God;
They have provoked Me to anger with their idols.
So I will make them jealous with those who are not a people;
I will provoke them to anger with a foolish nation.
22 'For a fire is kindled by My anger,
And it burns to the depths of Sheol (the place of the dead, the nether world),
It devours the earth with its yield,
And sets on fire the foundations of the mountains.

23 'I will heap misfortunes on them;
I will use My arrows on them.
24 'They will be wasted by hunger, and consumed by plague
And a bitter destruction;
And I will send the teeth of beasts against them,
With the venom of crawling things of the dust.
25 'Outside the sword will bereave,
And inside [the chambers] terror—
For both young man and virgin,
For the nursing child and the man of gray hair.
26 'I would have said, "I will cut them to pieces [scattering them far away],
I will remove the memory of them from men,"
27 Had I not feared the provocation of the enemy,
That their adversaries would misjudge,
That they would say, "Our [own] hand has prevailed,
And the LORD has not done all this." '

28 "For they are a nation devoid of counsel,
And there is no understanding in them.
29 "O that they were wise, that they understood this,
That they could discern their future *and* ultimate fate!
30 "How could one chase a thousand,
And two put ten thousand to flight,
Unless their Rock had sold them,
And the LORD had given them up?
31 "For their rock is not like our Rock,
Even our enemies themselves judge this.
32 "For their vine is from the vine of Sodom,
And from the fields of Gomorrah;
Their grapes are grapes of poison,
Their clusters, bitter.
33 "Their wine is the venom of serpents,
And the deadly poison of vipers.

34 'Is it not laid up in store with Me,
Sealed up in My treasuries?
35 'Vengeance is Mine, and retribution,

32:29 *discern their . . . ultimate fate.* In this great prophetic song Moses longs for the nation of Israel to turn to God and repent of its wickedness. As history proved, there was continual need for Israel to repent and turn back to God. They did abandon their covenant with God, but God did not abandon them, although He let them reap the consequences of their disobedience. Moses was not the last prophet to long for their repentance, and we can only guess at the heavenly joy Moses felt on the Mount of Transfiguration, seeing Jesus the Christ, who would finally redeem the people (Mk 9).

32:35 *Vengeance is Mine.* Only God who is completely just can judge and make right all the wrongs committed (Ro 12:19–20).

18 Isa 17:10; Jer 2:32 **20** Mt 17:17 **21** Ps 78:58; Ps 31:6; Ro 10:19 **22** La 4:11 **23** Isa 26:15; Ps 7:12,13 **29** Lk 19:42 **30** Ps 44:12 **31** 1Sa 4:8; Jer 40:3 **32** Isa 1:10 **33** Ps 58:4; Ro 3:13 **34** Jer 2:22; Ro 2:5 **35** Heb 10:30; 2Pe 2:3

In due time their foot will slip;
For the day of their disaster is at hand,
And their doom hurries to meet them.'
36 "For the LORD will vindicate His people,
And will have compassion on His servants,
When He sees that their strength (hand) is gone,
And none remains, whether bond or free.
37 "And He will say, 'Where are their gods,
The rock in which they took refuge?
38 'Who ate the fat of their sacrifices,
And drank the wine of their drink offering?
Let them rise up and help you,
Let them be your hiding place!
39 'See now that I, I am He,
And there is no god besides Me;
It is I who put to death and I who give life.
I have wounded and it is I who heal,
And there is no one who can deliver from [the power of] My hand.
40 'Indeed, I lift up My hand to heaven,
And say (swear an oath), as I live forever,
41 If I sharpen the lightning of My sword,
And My hand takes hold of judgment,
I will render vengeance on My adversaries,
And I will repay those who hate Me.
42 'I will make My arrows drunk with blood,
And My sword will devour flesh,
With the blood of the slain and the captives,
From the heads of the leaders of the enemy.'
43 "Rejoice, O nations, with His people;
For He will avenge the blood of His servants,
And will render vengeance on His adversaries,
And will atone for His land *and* His people."

44 Then Moses came and spoke all the
words of this song in the hearing of the
people, he and Joshua the son of Nun.
45 When Moses had finished speak-
ing all these words to all [the people
of] Israel,
46 he said to them, "Take to heart
all the words of warning which I am
speaking to you today; and you shall
command your children to observe
them carefully—to do all the words
of this law.
47 "For it is not an empty *or* trivial
matter for you; indeed it is your [very]

32:36 *have compassion on His servants.* God will discern between the righteous and the wicked (Mal 3:16).

32:39 God's Sovereignty — In his final words to the Israelites, Moses reminds them where they came from. Their history could not be written without God being in the central position. Their future, likewise, was intimately tied to God. To think otherwise would be folly (Dt 32:28 – 29). The basic point is that no matter how you want to look at it, God is in charge. That was the most basic fact in the Israelites' situation.

God's sovereignty is also the central fact in ours. It is not always easy to affirm it. We would much rather see *ourselves* as the central controlling force in our lives. Most of us simply don't like being told what to do or how to live. The problem is that the whole history of man teaches us that when God's laws are not followed, disaster ensues. When we put ourselves in charge, sooner or later we pay the price.

A whole generation of Israelites failed to understand God's sovereignty. As a result, they died in the desert, never having arrived at the promised land. While it is true that they lived out their lives, they surely missed out on what could have been. That fact is the basic backdrop for Moses' last words to the new generation, as they approached the promised land. We dare not ignore the lesson.

32:43 *Rejoice, O nations.* These nations are the Gentiles, invited here to join in worship of the living God. All through history there have been a few who accepted this invitation (such as Ruth), and it was fulfilled in Christ (Ro 15).

---

36 Ps 135:14; Jer 31:20; Joel 2:14; 2Ki 14:26 **37** Jdg 10:14; Jer 2:28 **39** Ps 102:27; Isa 45:5,18,22; 1Sa 2:6; Hos 6:1 **41** Isa 66:16 **42** Jer 46:10; Jer 30:14; La 2:5 **43** Ro 15:10; Rev 19:2; Ps 85:1 **46** Eze 40:4 **47** Pr 3:2; Ro 10:5

life. By [honoring and obeying] this word you will live long in the land, which you are crossing the Jordan to possess."

48 And the LORD said to Moses that very same day,

49 "Go up to this mountain of the Abarim, Mount Nebo, which is in the land of Moab opposite Jericho, and look at the land of Canaan, which I am giving to the sons of Israel as a possession.

50 "Then die on the mountain which you climb, and be gathered to your people [in death], just as Aaron your brother died on Mount Hor and was gathered to his people,

51 because you broke faith with Me among of the sons of Israel at the waters of Meribah-kadesh, in the Wilderness of Zin, and because you did not treat Me as holy among of the sons of Israel. [Num 20:8–12; 27:14]

52 "For you shall see the land opposite you from a distance, but you shall not go there, into the land which I am giving to the children of Israel."

The Blessing of Moses

33 THIS IS the blessing with which Moses the man of God blessed the sons of Israel before his death.

2 He said,

"The LORD came from Sinai,
And dawned on them from Seir;
He shone forth from Mount Paran,
And He came from among ten
thousand holy ones;
At His right hand was a flaming
fire, a law, for them.
3 "Indeed, He loves His people;
All Your holy ones are in Your
hand.
They followed in Your steps;
They accept *and* receive direction
from You.
4 "Moses commanded us with a law,
As a possession for the assembly
of Jacob.
5 "The LORD was King in Jeshurun
(Israel),
When the heads of the people were
gathered,
The tribes of Israel together.
6 "May [the tribe of] Reuben live and
not die out,
But let his men be few."

7 And [Moses said] this of Judah:

"Hear, O LORD, the voice of Judah,
And bring him to his people.
With his hands he contended for
them,
And may You be a help against his
enemies."

8 Of Levi he said,

"Your Thummim and Your Urim
belong to Your godly man
[Aaron],
Whom You tested *and* proved at
Massah,
With whom You contended at the
waters of Meribah; [Num 20:1–13]
9 Who said of his father and mother,
'I did not consider them';
Nor did he acknowledge his
brothers,
Nor did he regard his own sons,

33:1 *Moses the man of God.* In spite of his failure at the waters of Meribah-kadesh, Moses is noted here and throughout the Bible as "the man of God."

33:4 *commanded us with a law.* God chose Israel alone to receive His instructions, yet the law was ultimately for His whole creation, as Jesus demonstrated when He broke down the wall between Jew and Gentile (Ro 3 – 7).

33:9 – 10 *the priests observed Your word.* The Levites were keepers of God's word, even when it meant drawing their swords against their own brothers (Ex 32:25 – 29). This is a degree of testing that most believers will never experience, but Jesus promised that the world would hate His followers, and they would experience opposition even from their own families (Mt 10:22). It is not easy to be a follower of God in a world of sin and death, but the Christian may be assured that as he walks in obedience to God's truth, God "always causes us to triumph in Christ" (2Co 2:14).

48 Nu 27:12,13 **49** Dt 34:1 **50** Nu 20:25,28 **51** Nu 20:11-13; See Lev 10:3 **52** Nu 27:12 **CHAPTER 33** **1** Ge 49:28; Ps 90, title **2** Hab 3:3; Da 7:10; Rev 5:11 **3** Ps 47:4; Hos 11:1; 1Sa 2:9; Lk 10:39; Pr 2:1 **4** Jn 1:17; Ps 119:111 **5** See Ge 36:31; Dt 32:15 **7** Ge 49:8; Ps 146:5 **8** Ex 28:30; Dt 8:2,3,16; Ps 81:7 **9** Ge 29:32; Ex 32:26,27,28; Mal 2:5,6

For the priests observed Your word,
And kept Your covenant.
10 "The priests shall teach Your
ordinances (judgments) to Jacob,
And Your law to Israel.
They shall put incense before You,
And whole burnt offerings on
Your altar.
11 "O LORD, bless Levi's substance
(ability),
And accept *and* take pleasure in
the work of his hands;
Crush *and* shatter the loins of
those who rise up against him,
And of those who hate him, so that
they do not rise *again*."

12 Of Benjamin he said,

"May the beloved of the LORD
dwell in safety by Him;
He shields *and* covers him all the
day long,
And he dwells between His
shoulders."

13 And of Joseph he said,

"Blessed by the LORD be his land,
With the precious things of
heaven, with the dew,
And from the deep *water* that lies
beneath,
14 With the precious fruits of the sun,
And with the precious produce of
the months.
15 "With the best things of the
ancient mountains,
And with the precious things of
the everlasting hills,
16 With the precious things of the
earth and its fullness,
And the favor *and* goodwill of Him
who dwelt in the bush.
Let *these blessings* come upon the
head of Joseph,
And upon the crown of the head of
him who was distinguished [as
a prince] among his brothers.
[Ex 3:4]
17 "His majesty is like a firstborn
young bull,
And his horns like the horns of the
wild ox;
With them he will gore the
peoples,
All of them together, to the ends of
the earth.
And those are the ten thousands of
Ephraim,
And those are the thousands of
Manasseh."

18 Of Zebulun he said,

"Rejoice, Zebulun, in your interests
abroad,
And, Issachar, in your tents [at
home].
19 "They will call the peoples to the
mountain (Mount Carmel);
There they will offer sacrifices of
righteousness;
For they will draw out the
abundance of the seas,
And the hidden treasures of the
sand."

20 Of Gad he said,

"Blessed is the one who enlarges
Gad;
He lurks like a lioness,
And tears the arm and the crown
of the head.
21 "He selected the best [land] for
himself,
For there the leader's portion was
reserved;
Yet he came with the leaders of the
people;
He carried out the justice
(righteous will) of the LORD,
And His ordinances (judgments)
with Israel." [Num 32:29–33]

22 Of Dan he said,

"Dan is a lion's cub,
That leaps forth from Bashan."

33:22 *lion's cub*. This may refer to the small size of the tribe of Dan. Though Dan's land inheritance was close to Judah by the coastal plains, the tribe would not be able to keep their inheritance because of the hostility of the Philistines. Therefore, the Danites would one day migrate to the region of Bashan, south of Mount Hermon (Jdg 18).

10 Lev 10:11; Mal 2:7; Lev 1:9; Ps 51:19 **11** 2Sa 24:23; Eze 20:40 **13** Ge 49:25; Ge 27:28 **15** Ge 49:26; Hab 3:6 **16** Ex 3:2,4; Ge 49:26 **17** 1Ch 5:1; Nu 23:22; Ps 44:5; Ge 48:19 **18** Ge 49:13 **19** Isa 2:3; Ps 4:5 **20** 1Ch 12:8 **21** Nu 32:16,17; Jos 4:12 **22** Jos 19:47

23 Of Naphtali he said,

"O Naphtali, satisfied with favor,
And full of the blessing of the LORD,
Take possession of the sea [of Galilee] and the south."

24 Of Asher he said,

"More blessed than sons is Asher;
May he be favored by his brothers,
And may he dip his foot in oil.
25 "Your strongholds will be iron and bronze,
And as your days are, so will your strength, your rest *and* security be.

26 "There is none like the God of Jeshurun (Israel),
Who rides the heavens to your help,
And through the skies in His majestic glory.
27 "The eternal God is your refuge *and* dwelling place,
And underneath are the everlasting arms;
He drove out the enemy from before you,
And said, 'Destroy!'
28 "So Israel dwells in safety *and* security,
The fountain of Jacob alone *and* secluded,
In a land of grain and new wine;
His heavens also drop down dew.
29 "Happy *and* blessed are you, O Israel;
Who is like you, a people saved by the LORD,
The Shield of your help,
And the Sword of your majesty!
Your enemies will cringe before you,
And you will tread on their high places [tramping down their idolatrous altars]."

The Death of Moses

34 NOW MOSES went up from the
plains of Moab to Mount Nebo,
to the top of Pisgah, that is opposite
Jericho. And the LORD showed him all
the land, from Gilead to Dan,
2 and all Naphtali and the land of
Ephraim and Manasseh, and all the
land of Judah to the western sea (Mediterranean Sea),
3 and the Negev (South country) and
the plain in the Valley of Jericho, the
city of palm trees, as far as Zoar.
4 Then the LORD said to him, "This is
the land which I swore to Abraham,
Isaac, and Jacob, saying, 'I will give
it to your descendants.' I have let you
see it with your eyes, but you shall not
go over there."
5 So Moses the servant of the LORD
died there in the land of Moab, according to the word of the LORD.
6 And He buried him in the valley in
the land of Moab, opposite Beth-peor;
but no man knows where his burial
place is to this day.
7 Although Moses was a hundred
and twenty years old when he died, his
eyesight was not dim, nor his natural
strength abated. [Deut 31:2]
8 So the sons of Israel wept for Moses
in the plains of Moab for thirty days;
then the days of weeping and mourning for Moses were ended.
9 Now Joshua the son of Nun was
filled with the spirit of wisdom, for

34:1 – 2 *Moab . . . Jericho . . . western sea.* Moab was where Moses had given Israel an explanation of the law and led them in a covenant renewal. Jericho was the first city in Canaan to be conquered. The western sea is the Mediterranean.

34:6 *no man knows where his burial place is.* If his burial place had been known, some people would have been tempted to make it a shrine and possibly have begun to worship there.

34:9 *Joshua . . . filled with the spirit of wisdom.* Joshua was the leader chosen to succeed Moses, and God filled him with the spirit of wisdom. But there was another, a prophet like Moses, who would be greater even than Moses. That other was the Lord Jesus Christ (Ac 3:19 – 26).

23 Ge 49:21; See Jos 19:32 **24** Ge 49:20; Job 29:6 **25** Dt 8:9 **26** Ex 15:11; Dt 32:15; Ps 68:4 **27** Ps 90:1; Dt 9:3-5 **28** Jer 23:6; Dt 8:7,8; Ge 27:28 **29** Ps 144:15; 2Sa 7:23; Ps 115:9; Ps 18:44; Dt 32:13 **CHAPTER 34** **1** Nu 27:12; Dt 3:27; Ge 14:14 **2** Dt 11:24 **3** 2Ch 28:15 **4** Ge 12:7; Dt 3:27 **5** Dt 32:50 **6** See Jude 9 **7** Dt 31:2; Gen 27:1 **8** See Ge 50:3,10; Nu 20:29 **9** Isa 11:2; Da 6:3; Nu 27:18,23

Moses had laid his hands on him; so
the sons of Israel listened to him and
did as the LORD commanded Moses.
[10]Since that time no prophet has ris-
en in Israel like Moses, whom the LORD
knew face to face,
[11][none equal to him] in all the signs
and wonders which the LORD sent him
to perform in the land of Egypt against
Pharaoh, all his servants, and all his
land,
[12]and in all the mighty power and all
the great *and* terrible deeds which Mo-
ses performed in the sight of all Israel.

10 Dt 18:15; Ex 33:11; Dt 5:4 **11** Dt 7:19

THE BOOK OF JOSHUA

▸ **AUTHOR:** Jewish tradition seems correct in assigning the authorship of this book to Joshua himself. The unity of style and organization suggest a single authorship for the majority of the book, with the exception of three small portions that may have been added after Joshua's death: Othniel's capture of Kirjath-sepher (15:13 – 19); Dan's migration to the north (19:47); and Joshua's death and burial (24:29 – 33). However, Joshua 24:26 makes this clear statement: "And Joshua wrote these words in the Book of the Law of God."

▸ **TIMES:** c. 1405 – 1398 BC ▸ **KEY VERSE:** Jos 11:23

▸ **THEME:** In the Book of Joshua, the Israelites are commanded to destroy everything and everybody so that they can take full possession of the land. The transition of leadership is from Moses to Joshua. A nomadic people attaches themselves to given tracts of land, and a nation is formed from a wandering tribe as the conquest is completed in 21:43 – 45. We also see how a failure to carry out God's plan completely lays a foundation for future problems.

God's Commission to Joshua

1 NOW IT happened after the death
of Moses the servant of the LORD,
that the LORD spoke to Joshua the son
of Nun, Moses' servant (attendant),
saying, [Deut 34:4–8]
2"Moses My servant is dead; now
therefore arise [to take his place], cross
over this Jordan, you and all this peo-
ple, into the land which I am giving to
them, to the sons of Israel.
3"I have given you every place on
which the sole of your foot treads, just
as I promised to Moses.
4"From the wilderness [of Arabia
in the south] and this Lebanon [in the
north], even as far as the great river,
the river Euphrates [in the east], all
the land of the Hittites (Canaan), and
as far as the Great [Mediterranean]
Sea toward the west shall be your
territory.
5"No man will [be able to] stand be-
fore you [to oppose you] as long as you
live. Just as I was [present] with Moses,
so will I be with you; I will not fail you
or abandon you.
6"Be strong *and* confident and cou-
rageous, for you will give this peo-
ple as an inheritance the land which
I swore to their fathers (ancestors) to
give them.
7"Only be strong and very coura-
geous; be careful to do [everything] in
accordance with the entire law which

1:1 *the servant of the LORD.* In the Hebrew Scripture this is a special title given only to Moses, Joshua (24:29; Jdg 2:8), David (Ps 18: title; 36: title), and the Messiah (Isa 42:19). ***the LORD spoke to Joshua.*** God spoke directly to Joshua encouraging him and urging him to obey all the law. True success cannot occur apart from knowing God personally and doing His will.

1:7 – 8 Perseverance — A successful mission in the service of the Lord is dependent upon courage, meditation, and obedience. Keeping God's words in our hearts molds our character and guides our footsteps.

CHAPTER 1 **1** Ex 24:13; Dt 1:38 **2** Dt 34:5 **3** Dt 11:24 **4** Ge 15:18; Ex 23:31; Nu 34:3-12 **5** Dt 7:24; Ex 3:12; Dt 31:8,23; Jos 3:7; 6:27; Isa 43:2,5; Dt 31:6,8 **6** Dt 31:7,23 **7** Nu 27:23; Dt 31:7; Jos 11:15; Dt 5:32; 28:14

Moses My servant commanded you; do not turn from it to the right or to the left, so that you may prosper *and* be successful wherever you go.

8 "This Book of the Law shall not depart from your mouth, but you shall read [and meditate on] it day and night, so that you may be careful to do [everything] in accordance with all that is written in it; for then you will make your way prosperous, and then you will be successful.

9 "Have I not commanded you? Be strong and courageous! Do not be terrified or dismayed (intimidated), for the LORD your God is with you wherever you go."

Joshua Assumes Command

10 Then Joshua commanded the officers of the people, saying,

11 "Go throughout the camp and command the people, saying, 'Prepare your provisions, for within three days you are to cross this [river] Jordan, to go in to take possession of the land which the LORD your God is giving you to possess [as an inheritance].' "

12 To the Reubenites and to the Gadites and to the half-tribe of Manasseh, Joshua said,

13 "Remember the word which Moses the servant of the LORD commanded you, saying, 'The LORD your God is giving you rest (peace) and will give you this land [east of the Jordan].'

14 "Your wives, your children, and your cattle shall [be allowed to] stay in the land which Moses gave you on this [eastern] side of the Jordan, but you shall go across [the river] before your brothers (the other tribes) armed for battle, all your brave warriors, and you shall help them [conquer and take possession of their land],

15 until the LORD gives your brothers rest, as *He has given* you, and they also take possession of the land which the LORD your God is giving them. Then you shall [be allowed to] return to your own land, and take possession of that which Moses the servant of the LORD gave you beyond the Jordan toward the sunrise."

16 They answered Joshua, saying, "All that you have commanded us we will do, and wherever you send us we will go.

17 "Just as we obeyed Moses in all things, so will we obey you; only may the LORD your God be with you as He was with Moses.

18 "Any man who rebels against your command and does not obey everything that you command him, shall be put to death; only be strong and courageous."

Rahab Shelters Spies

2 JOSHUA THE son of Nun sent two men as scouts secretly from Shittim, saying, "Go, view the land, especially Jericho [the walled city]." So they went

---

1:8 Meditating upon God's Word — Helping people become prosperous and successful is big business. Late night infomercials point to a plethora of techniques for getting rich. Everyone wants to be wealthy. Everyone wants to be successful. These kinds of feelings are particularly strong when starting a new endeavor as Joshua was. At the very beginning of Joshua's leadership of Israel, God lays out for Joshua His key to success, meditating on God's word. Meditate upon the Word of God by rehearsing it in thought over and over in order to understand its implications for the situations of life. The meditation process results in changed thinking, because God's thoughts can literally become our thoughts. Then we are more likely to do what God wants of us. As we live in sync with God's plan for our lives, it follows that we will be more successful and prosperous than if we ignore His teachings.

People spend a large part of their lives in obtaining an education and working at a career in order to be prosperous and successful. Scripture points to itself as the primary means to that end.

1:18 *be strong and courageous.* Joshua's task was not an easy one, for not only must he deal with the ungodly inhabitants of the promised land, he must also provide leadership for his own fearful and complaining people.

2:1 *Rahab.* Rahab was a Canaanite prostitute, yet out of all the populace of Jericho, only she reached out to the living God, and He in turn saved her (6:25).

8 Dt 17:18,19; Ps 1:2 **9** Dt 31:7,8,23; Ps 27:1; Jer 1:8 **11** Dt 9:1; 11:31 **13** Nu 32:20-28; Jos 22:2-4 **15** Jos 22:4 **17** 1Sa 20:13; 1Ki 1:37 **CHAPTER 2** **1** Nu 25:1; Heb 11:31; Jas 2:25; Mt 1:5

and came to the house of a prostitute
named Rahab, and lodged there.
[2]Now the king of Jericho was told,
"Behold, men from the sons of Israel
have come here tonight to spy *and*
search out the land."
[3]So the king of Jericho sent *word*
to Rahab, saying, "Bring out the men
who have come to you, who entered
your house, because they have come
[as spies] to search out all the land."
[4]But the woman had taken the two
men and hidden them; so she said,
"Yes, two men came to me, but I did
not know where they were from.
[5]"When *it was time* to close the
[city] gate at dark, the men left; I do
not know where they went. Pursue
them quickly, for [if you do] you will
overtake them."
[6]But [in fact] she had brought the
scouts up to the roof and had hidden
them under the stalks of flax which she
had laid in order on the roof [to dry].
[7]So the [king's] men pursued them
on the road to the Jordan as far as the
fords [east of Jericho]; as soon as the
pursuers had gone out after them, the
gate [of the city] was shut.
[8]Now before the two men lay down
[to sleep], Rahab came up to them on
the roof,
[9]and she said to the men, "I know
that the LORD has given you the land,
and that the terror *and* dread of you
has fallen on us, and that all the in-
habitants of the land have melted [in
despair] because of you.
[10]"For we have heard how the LORD
dried up the water of the Red Sea for
you when you came out of Egypt, and
what you did to the two kings of the
Amorites who were beyond the Jordan
[on the east], to Sihon and Og, whom
you utterly destroyed.
[11]"When we heard it, our hearts
melted [in despair], and a [fighting]
spirit no longer remained in any man
because of you; for the LORD your God,
He is God in heaven above and on
earth beneath. [Heb 11:31]
[12]"And now, please swear [an oath]
to me by the LORD, since I have shown
you kindness, that you also will show
kindness to my father's household
(family), and give me a pledge of truth
and faithfulness,
[13]and spare my father and my moth-
er and my brothers and my sisters,
along with everyone who belongs to
them, and let us all live."
[14]So the men said to her, "Our lives
for yours if you do not tell [anyone
about] this business of ours; then when
the LORD gives us the land we will show
you kindness and faithfulness [and
keep our agreement with you]."

The Promise to Rahab

[15]Then she let them down by a rope
through the window, for her house was
built into the city wall, so that she was
living on the wall.
[16]And she said to them, "Go [west] to
the hill country, so that the pursuers
[who have headed east] will not en-
counter you; hide yourselves there for
three days until the pursuers return.
Then afterward you can go your way."
[17]The men said to her, "We *shall*

2:4–6 *I do not know where they went.* Rahab lied to the men searching for the Israelite spies, and Joshua praised her, as did the apostle James and the writer of Hebrews (Heb 11:31; Jas 2:25). Throughout both the Old and the New Testament, the commands of God forbid lying, the prophets condemn it, and godly people avoid doing it. Scripture does not address Rahab's sin, but it does praise her for her faith in God. Christians have struggled for centuries over whether lying to save an innocent person's life is acceptable. There does not seem to be a clear cut answer, but Rahab did her best with the knowledge she had to protect the Israelite men.

2:16 *Go [west] to the hill country.* The pursuers had gone down to the Jordan River (v. 7), logically supposing that the spies would be returning to their camp on the eastern side of the river. The only hills near Jericho are to the west, in the opposite direction from the Israelite camp, and further into the land of Canaan.

2 ver. 22 **4** See 2Sa 17:19,20 **6** See Ex 1:17; 2Sa 17:19 **9** Ge 35:5; Ex 23:27; Dt 2:25; 11:25 **10** Ex 14:21; Jos 4:23; Nu 21:24,34,35 **11** Ex 15:14,15; Jos 5:1; 7:5; Isa 13:7; Dt 4:39 **12** See 1Sa 20:14,15,17; See 1Ti 5:8; ver. 18 **14** Jdg 1:24; Mt 5:7 **15** Ac 9:25 **17** Ex 20:7

be blameless *and* free from this oath which you have made us swear,

18 unless, when we come into the land, you tie this cord of scarlet thread in the window through which you let us down, and bring into the house your father and your mother and your brothers and all your father's household [so that they will be safe].

19 "But if anyone goes out the doors of your house into the street, his blood *shall be* on his own head [that is, his own responsibility], and we *shall be* blameless *and* free [from our oath]; however, if a hand is *laid* on anyone who is with you in the house, his blood *shall be* on our head.

20 "But if you tell [anyone] this business of ours, we shall be blameless *and* free from the oath which you made us swear."

21 She said, "According to your words, so be it." Then Rahab sent them off, and they departed; and she tied the scarlet cord in the window.

22 They left and went [on their way] to the hill country [west of Jericho], and stayed there [hidden in the caves] three days until the pursuers returned. The pursuers had searched all along the road but had not found *them*.

23 Then the two men turned back and came down from the hill country and crossed over [the Jordan] and came to Joshua the son of Nun [at Shittim], and told him everything that had happened to them.

24 They said to Joshua, "Certainly the LORD has given all the land into our hands; for all the inhabitants of the land have melted [in despair] because of us."

Israel Crosses the Jordan

3 JOSHUA GOT up early in the morning; then he and all the children of Israel set out from Shittim and came to the Jordan, and they spent the night there before they crossed [the river].

2 And it happened at the end of three days that the officers went throughout the camp,

3 and they commanded the people, "When you see the ark of the covenant of the LORD your God being carried by the Levitical priests, then you shall set out from where you are and follow it.

4 "However, there shall be a distance between you and it of about 2,000 cubits (3,000 ft.) by measurement. Do not come near it, so that you may [be able to see the ark and] know the way you are to go, for you have not passed this way before."

5 Then Joshua said to the people, "Sanctify yourselves [for His purpose], for tomorrow the LORD will do wonders (miracles) among you."

6 Joshua said to the priests, "Take up the ark of the covenant and cross over [the river] ahead of the people." So they took up the ark of the covenant and went on ahead of the people.

7 The LORD said to Joshua, "This day I will begin to magnify *and* exalt you in the sight of all Israel, so that they may know that just as I was with Moses, I will [also] be with you.

8 "You shall command the priests who carry the ark of the covenant, saying, 'When you come to the edge of the waters of the Jordan, you shall stand *still* in the Jordan.' "

9 Joshua said to the Israelites, "Come here, and listen to the words of the LORD your God."

10 Joshua said, "By this you shall know that the living God is among you, and that He will, without fail, drive out from before you the Canaanite, the Hittite, the Hivite, the Perizzite, the Girgashite, the Amorite, and the Jebusite.

3:4 *2,000 cubits.* Two thousand cubits was more than half a mile. God was serious about the people showing due respect for the ark of the covenant.

3:9 Inspiration — God conveyed His message by means of words spoken by a specific chosen person. He descended to the human level and through humanity spoke His word of absolute truth.

18 ver. 12; Jos 6:23 **19** 1Ki 2:32; Mt 27:25 **24** Ex 23:31; Jos 6:2; 21:44 **CHAPTER 3** **1** Jos 2:1 **2** Jos 1:10,11 **3** See Nu 10:33; Dt 31:9,25 **4** Ex 19:12 **5** Ex 19:10,14,15; Lev 20:7; Nu 11:18; Jos 7:13; 1Sa 16:5; Joel 2:16 **6** Nu 4:15 **7** Jos 4:14; 1Ch 29:25; 2Ch 1:1; Jos 1:5 **8** ver. 3; ver. 17 **10** Dt 5:26; 1Sa 17:26; 2Ki 19:4; Hos 1:10; Mt 16:16; 1Th 1:9; Ex 33:2; Dt 7:1; Ps 44:2

11 "Behold, the ark of the covenant
of the Lord of all the earth is crossing
over ahead of you [leading the way]
into the Jordan.
12 "So now take for yourselves twelve
men from the tribes of Israel, one man
from each tribe.
13 "When the soles of the feet of the
priests who carry the ark of the LORD,
the Lord of all the earth, [come to]
rest in the waters of the Jordan, the
waters of the Jordan flowing down
from above will be cut off, and they
will stand in one mass [of water]."
14 So when the people set out from
their tents to cross over the Jordan
with the priests who were carrying
the ark of the covenant before the
people,
15 and when those who were carry-
ing the ark came up to the Jordan,
and the feet of the priests carrying
the ark were submerged at the edge
of the water (for the Jordan overflows
all of its banks throughout the time of
harvest),
16 the waters which were flowing
down from above stopped and rose
up in one mass a great distance away
at Adam, the city that is beside Zare-
than. Those [waters] flowing down-
ward toward the sea of the Arabah, the
Salt Sea, were completely cut off. So
the people crossed [the river] opposite
Jericho. [Ps 114]
17 And while all [the people of] Israel
crossed over on dry ground, the priests
who carried the ark of the covenant of
the LORD stood firm on dry ground in
the midst of the Jordan [riverbed], until
all the nation had finished crossing
over the Jordan.

Memorial Stones from Jordan

4 SO IT was when all the nation had
finished crossing the Jordan, the
LORD said to Joshua,
2 "Take for yourselves the twelve men
[chosen] from among the people, one
man from each tribe,
3 and command them, 'Pick up for
yourselves twelve stones [one each]
from here out of the midst of the Jor-
dan, from the place where the priests'
feet are standing firm; carry them over
with you and lay them down at the
place where you will spend the night
tonight.' "
4 Then Joshua called the twelve men
whom he had appointed from the sons
of Israel, one man from each tribe;
5 and Joshua said to them, "Cross
over again to the ark of the LORD your
God into the midst of the Jordan, and
each of you take up a stone on his
shoulder, according to the number of
the tribes of the sons of Israel,
6 so that this may be a sign among
you; when your children ask later,
'What do these stones mean to you?'
7 then you shall say to them that
the waters of the Jordan were cut off
before the ark of the covenant of the
LORD; when it crossed the Jordan, the
waters of the Jordan were cut off. So
these stones shall become a memorial
for Israel forever."
8 So the [twelve men chosen from
the] sons of Israel did as Joshua com-
manded, and took up twelve stones out
of the midst of the Jordan, according
to the number of the tribes of the sons
of Israel, just as the LORD had spoken
to Joshua; and they carried them over

3:13 *Lord of all the earth.* The term "Adonai," translated "Lord," means "master." It refers to the fact that God is indeed the Sovereign of the entire universe.

3:15 *Jordan overflows.* God did not merely slow the great river to a trickle during a time of drought; he stopped the waters when the river was high. This is significant because it makes the point that a great miracle was involved.

3:16 *Adam.* Adam was a city about 18 miles north of Jericho. The Sea of Arabah is another name for the Dead Sea, into which the Jordan flows from the north. The Dead Sea is the lowest place on earth, 1286 feet below sea level. The phrase "Salt Sea" is added to the name because the sea has no outlet and loses its water by evaporation. The concentration of salt and other minerals is so high that nothing can live in it.

11 ver. 13; Mic 4:13; Zec 4:14; 6:5 **12** Jos 4:2 **13** ver. 15,16; ver. 11; Ps 78:13; 114:3 **14** Ac 7:45 **15** ver. 13; 1Ch 12:15; Jer 12:5; 49:19; Jos 4:18; 5:10,12 **16** 1Ki 4:12; 7:46; Dt 3:17; Ge 14:3; Nu 34:3 **17** See Ex 14:29
CHAPTER 4 **1** Dt 27:2; Jos 3:17 **2** Jos 3:12 **3** Jos 3:13; ver. 19,20 **6** Ex 12:26; 13:14; Dt 6:20 **7** Jos 3:13,16; Ex 12:14; Nu 16:40

with them to the place where they were spending the night and put them down there.

[9]Then Joshua set up [a second monument of] twelve stones in the midst of the Jordan at the place where the feet of the priests who carried the ark of the covenant were standing, and they are there to this day.

[10]For the priests who carried the ark were standing in the midst of the Jordan until everything was finished that the LORD had commanded Joshua to tell the people, in accordance with everything that Moses had commanded Joshua. The people hurried and crossed [the dry riverbed];

[11]and when all the people had finished crossing, the ark of the LORD and the priests crossed over in the presence of the people.

[12]The sons of Reuben and the sons of Gad and half the tribe of Manasseh crossed over armed for battle before the [other] sons of Israel, just as Moses had spoken to them;

[13]about 40,000 [men] armed *and* equipped for war crossed for battle before the LORD to the desert plains of Jericho.

[14]On that day the LORD magnified *and* exalted Joshua in the sight of all Israel; so they feared him [with profound awe and reverence], just as they had feared Moses all the days of his life.

[15]Now the LORD said to Joshua,

[16]"Order the priests carrying the ark of the Testimony to come up out of the Jordan."

[17]So Joshua commanded the priests, saying, "Come up out of the Jordan."

[18]When the priests who carried the ark of the covenant of the LORD had come up from the midst of the Jordan, and the soles of their feet were raised up to the dry land, the waters of the Jordan returned to their place, and flowed over all its banks as before.

[19]Now the people came up from the Jordan on the tenth [day] of the first month and encamped at Gilgal on the eastern border of Jericho.

[20]And those twelve stones which they had taken from the Jordan, Joshua set up in Gilgal.

[21]He said to the sons of Israel, "When your children ask their fathers in time to come, 'What do these stones mean?'

[22]then you shall let your children know, 'Israel crossed this Jordan on dry ground.'

[23]"For the LORD your God dried up the waters of the Jordan for you until you crossed over, just as the LORD your God did to the Red Sea, which He dried up before us until we had crossed;

[24]so that all the peoples of the earth may know [without any doubt] *and* acknowledge that the hand of the LORD is mighty *and* extraordinarily powerful, so that you will fear the LORD your God [and obey and worship Him with profound awe and reverence] forever."

Israel Is Circumcised

5 NOW IT happened when all the kings of the Amorites who were beyond the Jordan to the west, and all the kings of the Canaanites who were by the sea, heard that the LORD had dried up the waters of the Jordan before the Israelites until they had crossed over, their hearts melted [in despair], and

---

4:10 *The people hurried and crossed.* This is a flashback, 3:17 and 4:1 have already told of the crossing over. The purpose is to look back and reflect upon the people's obedience.

4:14 *the LORD magnified and exalted Joshua.* God is once again proclaiming Joshua as the man He has chosen to take Moses' place as leader of His people.

4:16 *Testimony.* In this sense, a "testimony" is a reminder. The ark contained the two stone tablets on which the Ten Commandments were written, reminding people of God's covenant and His law.

4:21 – 24 Fear of God — The Scriptures are full of stories of the acts God performed that built up the respect of the people for Him. The awesome things God did were told to each new generation to develop respect for who God is. This miracle was performed not only for the purpose of getting the Israelites across the Jordan. It was also a sign to all peoples of the power of God.

12 Nu 32:20,27,28 **14** Jos 3:7 **16** Ex 25:16,22 **18** Jos 3:15 **19** Jos 5:9 **20** ver. 3 **21** ver. 6 **22** Jos 3:17 **23** Ex 14:21 **24** 1Ki 8:42,43; 2Ki 19:19; Ex 15:16; 1Ch 29:12; Ex 14:31; Dt 6:2; Jer 10:7 **CHAPTER 5** **1** Nu 13:29; Ex 15:14,15; 1Ki 10:5

there was no [fighting] spirit in them
any longer because of the Israelites
[and what God had done for them].
2 At that time the LORD said to Josh-
ua, "Make for yourself flint knives and
circumcise the [new generation of the]
sons of Israel as [was done] before."
3 So Joshua made flint knives and
circumcised the sons of Israel at
Gibeath-haaraloth.
4 This is the reason why Joshua cir-
cumcised them: all the people who
came out of Egypt who were males,
all the men of war, had died in the
wilderness along the way after they
left Egypt.
5 All the males who came out were
circumcised, but all the males who
were born in the wilderness on the
way as they left Egypt had not been
circumcised.
6 For the Israelites walked forty years
in the wilderness, until all the nation,
that is, the men of war who came out
of Egypt, died because they did not
listen to the voice of the LORD; to them
the LORD had sworn [an oath] that He
would not let them see the land which
He had promised to their fathers to
give us, a land [of abundance] flowing
with milk and honey.
7 So it was their uncircumcised sons
whom He raised up in their place,
whom Joshua circumcised, because
circumcision had not been performed
on the way.
8 Then, when they had finished cir-
cumcising all [the males of] the nation,
they stayed in their places in the camp
until they were healed.
9 Then the LORD said to Joshua, "This
day I have rolled away the reproach
(derision, ridicule) of Egypt from you."
So the name of that place is called
Gilgal (rolling) to this day.
10 While the Israelites camped at Gil-
gal they observed the Passover on the
evening of the fourteenth day of the
month on the desert plains of Jericho.
11 On the day after Passover, on that
very day, they ate some of the produce
of the land, unleavened bread, and
roasted *grain.* [Lev 23:14]
12 And the manna ceased on the day
after they had eaten some of the pro-
duce of the land, so that the Israelites
no longer had manna, but they ate
some of the produce of the land of Ca-
naan during that year.
13 Now when Joshua was by Jericho,
he looked up, and behold, a man was
standing opposite him with his drawn
sword in his hand, and Joshua went to
him and said to him, "Are you for us or
for our adversaries?"
14 He said, "No; rather I have come
now as captain of the army of the
LORD." Then Joshua fell with his face
toward the earth and bowed down, and
said to him, "What does my lord have
to say to his servant?"
15 The captain of the LORD's army said
to Joshua, "Remove your sandals from
your feet, because the place where you
are standing is holy (set apart to the
LORD)." And Joshua did so. [Ex 3:5]

The Conquest of Jericho

6 NOW JERICHO [a fortified city
with high walls] was tightly closed
because [of the people's fear] of the sons
of Israel; no one went out or came in.
2 The LORD said to Joshua, "See, I
have given Jericho into your hand,
with its king and the mighty warriors.
3 "Now you shall march around the
city, all the men of war circling the city

5:2 *as [was done] before.* The generation that left Egypt had been circumcised. However, that generation had died in the wilderness and for some reason they had neglected to circumcise their children, the generation which would enter the promised land.
5:6 *milk and honey.* The land God had promised to Israel was no wilderness, but a land that was fertile for both crops and cattle, and ready to provide for them and supply all their needs.
5:15 *Remove your sandals.* The command for Joshua to remove his sandals was practically identical to the command Moses received at the burning bush (Ex 3:1 – 6). Joshua was confronted with the living God, just as Moses had been (Ex 33:9 – 11).
6:3 *circling the city once.* The city of Jericho

2 Ex 4:25 **4** Nu 14:29; 26:64,65; Dt 2:16 **6** Nu 14:33; Dt 1:3; Nu 14:23; Heb 3:11; Ex 3:8 **7** Nu 14:31; Dt 1:39 **8** See Ge 34:25 **9** Ge 34:14; Jos 4:19 **10** Ex 12:6; Nu 9:5 **12** Ex 16:35 **13** Ge 18:2; 32:24; Ex 23:23; Zec 1:8; Ac 1:10; Nu 22:23 **14** Ge 17:3 **15** Ex 3:5; Ac 7:33 **CHAPTER 6** **2** Jos 2:9,24; 8:1; Dt 7:24

once. You shall do this [once each day] for six days.

4 “Also, seven priests shall carry seven trumpets [made] of rams’ horns ahead of the ark; then on the seventh day you shall march around the city seven times, and the priests shall blow the trumpets.

5 “When they make a long blast with the ram’s horn, and when you hear the sound of the trumpet, all the people shall cry out with a great shout (battle cry); and the wall of the city will fall down in its place, and the people shall go up, each man [going] straight ahead [climbing over the rubble].”

6 So Joshua the son of Nun called for the priests and said to them, “Take up the ark of the covenant, and have seven priests carry seven trumpets *made* of rams’ horns ahead of the ark of the LORD.”

7 He said to the people, “Go forward! March around the city, and let the armed men go ahead of the ark of the LORD.”

8 And it was so, that when Joshua had spoken to the people, the seven priests carrying the seven trumpets *made* of rams’ horns went on before the LORD and blew the trumpets; then the ark of the covenant of the LORD went behind them.

9 The armed men went in front of the priests who blew the trumpets, and the rear guard came after the ark, while the priests continued to blow the trumpets.

10 But Joshua commanded the people, “You shall not shout [the battle cry] nor let your voice be heard nor let a word come out of your mouth, until the day I tell you to shout. Then you shall shout!”

11 So Joshua had the ark of the LORD taken around the city [on the first day], circling it once; then they came back into the camp and spent the night in the camp.

12 Then Joshua got up early in the morning [on the second day], and the priests took up the ark of the LORD.

13 The seven priests carrying the seven trumpets *made* of rams’ horns ahead of the ark of the LORD went on continually, blowing the trumpets; and the armed men went ahead of them and the rear guard came after the ark of the LORD, while the priests continued to blow the trumpets.

14 On the second day they marched around the city once, and returned to the camp; they did this for six days.

15 Then on the seventh day they got up early at daybreak and marched around the city in the same way seven times; only on that day they marched around the city seven times.

16 And the seventh time, when the priests had blown the trumpets, Joshua said to the people, “Shout! For the LORD has given you the city.

17 “The city and everything that is in it shall be under the ban [that is, designated to be destroyed as a form of tribute] to the LORD; only Rahab the prostitute and all [the people] who are with her in her house shall [be allowed to] live, because she hid *and* protected the messengers (scouts) whom we sent.

18 “But as for you, keep yourselves [away] from the things under the ban [which are to be destroyed], so that you do not covet *them* and take some of the things under the ban [for personal gain], and put the camp of Israel under the ban (doomed to destruction), and bring disaster upon it.

---

measured less than half a mile in circumference, so the march would have been completed quickly.

6:6–21 Zeal—Crossing the Jordan marked the beginning step in the fulfillment of God’s promise to give His people the land of Canaan. Immediately the task of conquering Jericho loomed before them. The Lord appeared to Joshua reminding him that God Himself was in charge and the presence of the holy One assured victory (v. 2). The plan for Jericho’s capture was a test of Israel’s zeal for the Lord and seems to have been designed to instill the lesson that submission to God’s directives was key to victory. How different Israel’s history would have been if they had continued to carry out God’s plans fully and zealously! God calls us to the same level of obedience today.

4 See Jdg 7:16,22; Nu 10:8 **9** Nu 10:25 **12** Dt 31:25 **17** Jos 2:4 **18** Dt 7:26; 13:17; Jos 7:1,11,12; Jos 7:25; 1Ki 18:17,18; Jnh 1:12

19“All the silver and gold and articles
of bronze and iron are holy (consecrat-
ed) to the LORD; they shall go into the
treasury of the LORD.”
20So the people shouted [the battle
cry], and the priests blew the trumpets.
When the people heard the sound of
the trumpet, they raised a great shout
and the wall [of Jericho] fell down, so
that the sons of Israel went up into
the city, every man straight ahead
[climbing over the rubble], and they
overthrew the city.
21Then they utterly destroyed every-
thing that was in the city, both man
and woman, young and old, and ox
and sheep and donkey, with the edge
of the sword.
22But Joshua said to the two men
who had spied out the land, “Go into
the prostitute’s house and bring the
woman and all that she has out of
there, as you have sworn to her.”
23So the young men, the spies, went
in and brought out Rahab and her fa-
ther and her mother and her brothers
and everything that she had; they also
brought out all her relatives and allowed
them to stay outside the camp of Israel
[at Gilgal during the time required for
ceremonial cleansing]. [Num 31:19]
24Then they completely burned the
city and everything that was in it. They
put only the silver and the gold, and
the articles of bronze and of iron, into
the treasury of the house (tabernacle)
of the LORD.
25So Joshua spared Rahab the pros-
titute, with her father’s household and
everything that she had; and she has
lived among Israel to this day, because
she hid the messengers (scouts) whom
Joshua sent to spy out Jericho.
26Then Joshua made them take an
oath at that time, saying, “Cursed before
the LORD is the man who rises up and re-
builds this city, Jericho; with *the loss of*
his firstborn he shall lay its foundation,
and with *the loss of* his youngest son
he shall set up its gates.” [1 Kin 16:34]
27So the LORD was with Joshua, and
his fame was in all the land.

Israel Is Defeated at Ai

7 BUT THE sons of Israel acted un-
faithfully *and* violated their obliga-
tion in regard to the things [off limits]
under the ban [those things belonging
to the LORD], for Achan, the son of Car-
mi, the son of Zabdi, the son of Zerah,
from the tribe of Judah, took some of
the things under the ban [for personal
gain]. Therefore the anger of the LORD
burned against the Israelites.
2Now Joshua sent men from Jericho
to Ai, which is near Beth-aven, east of
Bethel, and said to them, “Go up and
spy out the land.” So the men went up
and spied out Ai.
3Then they returned to Joshua and
said to him, “Do not make all the peo-
ple go up [to fight]; have *only* about
two thousand or three thousand men
go up and attack Ai; do not make the
entire army go up there, for they [of
Ai] are few.”
4So about three thousand men from
the sons of Israel went up there, but
they fled [in retreat] from the men of Ai.
5The men of Ai killed about thirty-
six of Israel’s men, and chased them
from the gate as far as [the bluffs of]
Shebarim and struck them down as
they descended [the steep pass], so the
hearts of the people melted [in despair
and began to doubt God’s promise] and
became like water (disheartened).
6Then Joshua tore his clothes and fell
face downward on the ground before

6:26 *Cursed before the LORD.* Joshua’s curse found dramatic fulfillment many centuries later when Hiel of Bethel laid its foundation and rebuilt its gates at great personal cost (1Ki 16:34).

7:6–9 Suffering—Joshua’s prayer was one of despair. Why had God allowed their defeat? Whenever tragedy strikes it is hard to understand why God allowed it to happen to us. In this case it is clearly explained. Achan had greedily taken what was banned by God. Through his sin the whole camp was guilty of deception and thievery. There are other reasons, not related to sin, for God’s permission of tragedy. Sometimes people suffer in order to fulfill a sovereign purpose not immediately apparent.

---

20 ver. 5; Heb 11:30 **21** Dt 7:2 **22** Jos 2:14; Heb 11:31 **23** Jos 2:13 **24** ver. 19 **25** See Mt 1:5 **26** 1Ki 16:34 **27** Jos 1:5; Jos 9:1,3 **CHAPTER 7** **1** Jos 22:20 **4** Lev 26:17; Dt 28:25 **5** Jos 2:9,11; Lev 26:36 **6** Ge 37:29,34; 1Sa 4:12; 2Sa 1:2; 13:19; Neh 9:1; Job 2:12

the ark of the LORD until evening, he and the elders of Israel; and [with great sorrow] they put dust on their heads.

7 Joshua said, "Alas, O Lord GOD, why have You brought this people across the Jordan at all, only to hand us over to the Amorites, to destroy us? If only we had been willing to live beyond the Jordan!

8 "O Lord, what can I say now that [the army of] Israel has turned back [in retreat and fled] before their enemies?

9 "For the Canaanites and all the inhabitants of the land will hear about it, and will surround us and cut off our name from the earth. And what will You do for Your great name [to keep it from dishonor]?"

10 So the LORD said to Joshua, "Get up! Why is it that you have fallen on your face?

11 "Israel has sinned; they have also transgressed My covenant which I commanded them [to keep]. They have even taken some of the things under the ban, and they have both stolen and denied [the theft]. Moreover, they have also put *the stolen objects* among their own things.

12 "That is why the soldiers of Israel could not stand [and defend themselves] before their enemies; they turned their backs [and ran] before them, because they have become accursed. I will not be with you anymore unless you destroy the things under the ban from among you.

13 "Rise up! Consecrate the people and say, 'Consecrate yourselves for tomorrow, for thus says the LORD, the God of Israel: "There are things under the ban among you, O Israel. You cannot stand [victorious] before your enemies until you remove the things under the ban from among you."

14 'In the morning you shall come forward by your tribes. And it shall be that the tribe which the LORD chooses *by lot* shall come forward by families, and the family which the LORD chooses shall come forward by [separate] households, and the household which the LORD chooses shall come forward man by man.

15 'It shall be that the one who is chosen with the things under the ban shall be [killed and his body] burned with fire, he and all that belongs to him, because he has transgressed the covenant of the LORD, and because he has done a disgraceful *and* disobedient thing in Israel.' " [Josh 7:25]

The Sin of Achan

16 So Joshua got up early in the morning and had Israel come forward by tribes, and the tribe of Judah was chosen [by lot].

17 He had the families of Judah come forward, and the family of the Zerahites was chosen; and he had the family of the Zerahites come forward man by man, and Zabdi was chosen.

18 He brought his household forward man by man; and Achan the son of Carmi, son of Zabdi, son of Zerah, of the tribe of Judah, was chosen.

19 Then Joshua said to Achan, "My son, I implore you, give glory to the LORD, the God of Israel, and give praise to Him [in recognition of His righteous judgments]; and tell me now what you have done. Do not hide it from me."

20 So Achan answered Joshua and said, "In truth, I have sinned against the LORD, the God of Israel, and this is what I have done:

21 when I saw among the spoils [in

7:9 ***Your great name.*** Joshua is aware that there is an even larger issue at stake: God's reputation.

7:10 – 15 ***Israel has sinned.*** God had consistent standards for both Israel and the Canaanites. He had ordered Israel to destroy Canaan because of their sin. He could not allow Israel to accommodate sin and corruption, even that of only one man.

7:13 ***until you remove.*** The relationship between obedience and blessing is well illustrated here. Israel would have no further successes until the sin had been uncovered.

7:19 ***give glory to the LORD . . . tell me now what you have done.*** We too dishonor the Lord when we hide our sins, and we honor Him when we confess them.

7 Ex 17:3; Nu 21:5 **9** Dt 32:26; See Ex 32:12; Nu 14:13 **11** ver. 1; Jos 6:17,18; See Ac 5:1,2 **12** See Nu 14:45; Jdg 2:14; Dt 7:26; Jos 6:18; Hag 2:13,14 **13** Ex 19:10; Jos 3:5 **14** Pr 16:33 **15** See 1Sa 14:38,39; ver. 11; Ge 34:7; Jdg 20:6 **18** 1Sa 14:42 **19** See 1Sa 6:5; Jer 13:16; Jn 9:24; Nu 5:6,7; 2Ch 30:22; Ezr 10:10,11; Da 9:4; 1Sa 14:43

Jericho] a beautiful robe from Shinar
(southern Babylon) and two hundred
shekels of silver and a bar of gold
weighing fifty shekels, I wanted them
and took them. Behold, they are hidden
in the ground inside my tent, with the
silver underneath."
22 So Joshua sent messengers, and
they ran to the tent; and they saw the
stolen objects hidden in his tent, with
the silver underneath.
23 And they took them from the tent
and brought them to Joshua and to all
the sons of Israel, and spread them out
before the LORD.
24 Then Joshua and all Israel with
him, took Achan the son of Zerah,
the silver, the [royal] robe, the bar
of gold, his sons, his daughters, his
oxen, his donkeys, his sheep, his tent,
and everything that he had; and they
brought them up to the Valley of Achor
(Disaster).
25 Joshua said, "Why have you
brought disaster on us? The LORD will
bring you disaster this day." Then
all Israel stoned them [to death] with
stones; afterward they burned their
bodies in the fire.
26 Then they piled up over him a great
heap of stones that remains to this
day. Then the LORD turned from the
fierceness of His anger. Therefore the
name of that place has been called the
Valley of Achor (Disaster) to this day.

The Conquest of Ai

8 NOW THE LORD said to Joshua,
"Do not fear or be dismayed (in-
timidated). Take all the men of war
with you and set out, go up to Ai; see,
I have given the king of Ai, his people,
his city, and his land into your hand.
2 "You shall do [the same] to Ai and
its king as you did to Jericho and its
king; [except that] you shall take only
its spoil and its cattle as plunder for
yourselves. Set up an ambush for the
city behind it [on the west side]."
3 So Joshua set out with all the people
of war to go up against Ai; then Joshua
chose thirty thousand valiant men,
and sent them out at night.
4 He commanded them, saying, "Lis-
ten closely, you are going to lie in wait
and ambush the city from behind it. Do
not go very far away from the city, but
all of you be ready.
5 "Then I and all the people who are
with me will approach the city. And
when they come out to meet us [for
battle] as [they did] the first time, we
will run away from them.
6 "They will come out after us until
we have lured them away from the
city, because they will say, 'They are
running from us as [they did] before.'
So we will run from them.
7 "Then you will emerge from the
ambush and take possession of the
city, for the LORD your God will hand
it over to you.
8 "When you have taken the city, you
shall set it on fire; you shall do [exact-
ly] as the LORD commanded. See, I have
commanded you."
9 So Joshua sent them off, and they
went to the place for the ambush and
stayed [hidden] between Bethel and Ai,
on the west side of Ai; but Joshua spent
that night among the people [in Gilgal].
10 Now Joshua got up early in the
morning and assembled the people,

7:25 *stoned them [to death] with stones.* Achan and all that he had were brought out and stoned. This seems like a severe punishment and one that is hard to understand. But it illustrated God's firm insistence on holiness. God could not tolerate the sin Achan had committed and He had to deal with him. It is a sobering thought for us, to remember that often our sins do not affect only ourselves, they also cause others to stumble and fall. We deserve punishment as severe as Achan's, but Jesus Christ took over our penalty and through His blood we can be reconciled to God.

8:1 *Do not fear or be dismayed.* The sins of Achan had broken the special relationship God had established with His people, but God had not abandoned them.

8:7 *the LORD your God will hand it over to you.* Israel was completely dependent on God for their success.

24 ver. 26; Jos 15:7 **25** Jos 6:18; 1Ch 2:7; Gal 5:12; Dt 17:5 **26** Jos 8:29; 2Sa 18:17; La 3:53; Dt 13:17; 2Sa 21:14; ver. 24 **CHAPTER 8** **1** Dt 1:21; 7:18; 31:8; Jos 1:9; Jos 6:2 **2** Jos 6:21; Dt 20:14 **4** Jdg 20:29 **5** Jdg 20:32 **8** 2Sa 13:28

and went up with the elders of Israel before the people to Ai.

11 Then all the fighting men who were with him went up and advanced and arrived in front of the city, and camped on the north side of Ai. Now there was a ravine between them and Ai.

12 And Joshua took about five thousand men and set them in ambush between Bethel and Ai, on the west side of the city.

13 So they stationed the people, all the army—the main encampment that was north of the city, and their rear guard on the west side of the city—and Joshua spent that night in the valley.

14 Now when the king [and the people] of Ai saw it, the men of the city hurried and got up early and went out to meet Israel in battle, the king and all his people at the appointed [time and] place before the desert plain (the Arabah). But he did not know that there was an ambush against him [waiting] behind the city [on the west side].

15 So Joshua and all Israel pretended to be defeated by them, and ran toward the wilderness.

16 Then all the people who were in the city were called together to pursue them, and they pursued Joshua and were lured away from the city.

17 Not a man was left in Ai or Bethel who had not gone out after Israel; so they left the city open *and* unguarded and they pursued Israel.

18 Then the LORD said to Joshua, "Reach out with the spear that is in your hand [and point it] toward Ai, for I will give it into your hand." So Joshua reached out with the spear in his hand [and pointed it] toward the city.

19 The [men in] ambush emerged quickly from their [hiding] place, and when Joshua stretched out his hand they ran and entered the city and captured it, and quickly set the city on fire.

20 When the men of Ai turned back and looked, behold, the smoke of the city was ascending toward the sky, and they had no opportunity to run this way or that way. Then the people who had been running to the wilderness turned back toward the pursuers.

21 When Joshua and all Israel saw that the [men in] ambush had taken the city and that the smoke of the city was ascending, they turned back and struck down the men of Ai.

22 Then the others came out of the city to confront the men of Ai [as they returned], so that they were *trapped* in the midst of Israel, some on this side and some on that side; then Israel struck them until none of them survived or escaped.

23 But they took the king of Ai alive and brought him to Joshua.

24 When Israel had finished killing all the inhabitants of Ai in the field in the wilderness where they pursued them, and they had all fallen by the edge of the sword until they were destroyed, then all Israel returned to Ai and struck it with the edge of the sword.

25 And all who fell that day, both men and women, were twelve thousand, all the people of Ai.

26 For Joshua did not withdraw his hand with which he stretched out the spear until he had utterly destroyed all the inhabitants of Ai.

27 Israel took only the livestock and the spoil of that city as plunder for themselves, according to the word of the LORD which He had commanded Joshua.

28 So Joshua burned Ai and made it a rubbish heap forever, a desolation until this day.

29 He hanged [the body of] the king of Ai on a tree [leaving it there] until evening; at sunset Joshua gave a command and they took the body down

---

8:12–17 Wisdom—The name Ai means "ruin" or "heap." Unlike Jericho, Ai was not a walled city; to Israel it was just a rubble heap. It looked so easy, especially after their resounding victory at Jericho, that they set out to attack without asking for the Lord's direction. In facing tasks that seem well within our powers, we also often forget to ask for the Lord's help. Wisdom in the believer's life demands persistence in depending on the Lord's strength and direction in little problems as well as the big ones.

11 ver. 5 **14** Jdg 20:34; Ecc 9:12 **15** Jdg 20:36 **22** Lev 7:29; Dt 7:2; Job 20:5; Lk 17:26-30; 1Th 5:3
27 Nu 31:22,26; ver. 2 **28** Dt 13:16 **29** Jos 10:26; Dt 21:22,23; Jos 10:27; Jos 7:26; 10:27

from the tree and dumped it at the
entrance of the city gate, and piled a
great heap of stones over it *that stands*
to this day.
30 Then Joshua built an altar to the
LORD, the God of Israel, on Mount Ebal,
31 just as Moses the servant of the LORD
had commanded the sons of Israel, as it
is written in the Book of the Law of Mo-
ses, an altar of uncut stones on which no
one has wielded an iron *tool;* and they
offered on it burnt offerings to the LORD,
and sacrificed peace offerings.
32 And there, in the presence of the
sons of Israel, Joshua wrote on the
stones a copy of the Law of Moses
which *Moses* had written.
33 All Israel, the stranger as well as
the native born [among them], with
their elders and officers and their judg-
es, stood on either side of the ark be-
fore the Levitical priests who carried
the ark of the covenant of the LORD.
Half of them *stood* in front of Mount
Gerizim and half of them in front of
Mount Ebal, just as Moses the servant
of the LORD had commanded at first to
bless the people of Israel.
34 Then afterward Joshua read all
the words of the law, the blessing and
curse, according to all that is written
in the Book of the Law.
35 There was not a word of all that
Moses had commanded which Joshua
did not read before the entire assembly
of Israel, including the women and the
children and the foreigners who were
living among them.

Guile of the Gibeonites

9 NOW WHEN all the kings who
were beyond the Jordan, in the
hill country and in the lowland [at the
western edge of the hills of Judea],
and all along the coast of the Great
[Mediterranean] Sea toward Lebanon,
the Hittite and the Amorite, the Ca-
naanite, the Perizzite, the Hivite and
the Jebusite, heard of this [army and
its victories over Jericho and Ai],
2 they gathered together with one
purpose to fight with Joshua and with
Israel.
3 But when the people of Gibeon [the
Hivites] heard what Joshua had done
to Jericho and Ai,
4 they too acted craftily *and* cunning-
ly, and set out and took along provi-
sions, but took worn-out sacks on their
donkeys, and wineskins (leather bot-
tles) that were worn out and split open
and patched together,
5 and worn-out and patched sandals
on their feet, and worn-out clothes;
and all their supply of food was dry
and had turned to crumbs.
6 They went to Joshua in the camp at
Gilgal and said to him and the men of
Israel, "We have come from a far coun-
try; so now, make a covenant (treaty)
with us."
7 But the men of Israel said to the Hi-
vites, "Perhaps you are living within
our land; how then can we make a
covenant (treaty) with you?"
8 They said to Joshua, "We are your
servants." Then Joshua said to them,
"Who are you, and where do you come
from?"
9 They said to him, "Your servants
have come from a country that is very
far away because of the fame of the
LORD your God; for we have heard the
news about Him and all [the remark-
able things] that He did in Egypt,
10 and everything that He did to the
two kings of the Amorites who were
beyond the Jordan, to Sihon the king of
Heshbon and to Og the king of Bashan
who *lived* in Ashtaroth.
11 "So our elders and all the resi-
dents of our country said to us, 'Take

9:3 *Gibeon.* Gibeon was relatively close to Ai, and about five miles northwest of Jerusalem.
9:6 *We have come from a far country.* Israel was allowed to make treaties with cities that were far away (Ex 34:11 – 12; Dt 20:10 – 18). If the Gibeonites had been telling the truth, a treaty with them would have been permissible.

30 Dt 27:4,5 **31** Ex 20:25; Dt 27:5,6; Ex 20:24 **32** Dt 27:2,8 **33** Dt 31:9,25; Dt 31:12; Dt 11:29; 27:12 **34** Dt 31:11; Neh 8:3; Dt 28:2,15,45; 29:20,21; 30:19 **35** Dt 31:12; ver. 33 **CHAPTER 9** **1** Nu 34:6; Ex 3:17; 23:23 **2** Ps 83:3,5 **3** Jos 10:2; 2Sa 21:1,2; Jos 6:27 **6** Jos 5:10 **7** Jos 11:19; Ex 23:32; Dt 7:2; Jdg 2:2 **8** Dt 20:11 **9** Dt 20:15; Ex 15:14; Jos 2:10 **10** Nu 21:24,33

provisions for the journey and go to meet the sons of Israel and say to them, “We are your servants; now make a covenant (treaty) with us.” ’

12 “This bread of ours was hot (fresh) when we took it along as our provision from our houses on the day we left to come to you; now look, it is dry and has turned to crumbs.

13 “These wineskins which we filled were new, and look, they are split; our clothes and our sandals are worn out because of the very long journey [that we had to make].”

14 So the men [of Israel] took some of their own provisions [and offered them in friendship], and [foolishly] did not ask for the counsel of the LORD.

15 Joshua made peace with them and made a covenant (treaty) with them, to let them live; and the leaders of the congregation [of Israel] swore *an oath* to them.

16 It happened that three days after they had made a covenant (treaty) with them, the Israelites heard that they were [actually] their neighbors and that they were living among them.

17 Then the sons of Israel set out and came to their cities on the third day. Now the cities [of the Hivites] were Gibeon and Chephirah and Beeroth and Kiriath-jearim.

18 But the sons of Israel did not strike them because the leaders of the congregation had sworn to them by the LORD the God of Israel [to spare them]. And all the congregation murmured [expressing great dissatisfaction] against the leaders.

19 But all the leaders said to the whole congregation, “We have sworn to them by the LORD, the God of Israel, so now we cannot touch them.

20 “This [is what] we will do to them: we will let them live, so that the wrath [of God] does not come upon us for [violating] the oath which we have sworn to them.”

21 The leaders said to them, “Let them live [as our slaves].” So they became the cutters *and* gatherers of firewood and water carriers for the entire congregation, just as the leaders had said of them.

22 Joshua called the [Hivite] men and said, “Why did you deceive us, saying, ‘We *live* very far away from you,’ when [in fact] you live among us?

23 “Now therefore, you are cursed, and you shall always be slaves, both cutters *and* gatherers of firewood and water carriers for the house of my God.”

24 They replied to Joshua and said, “Because your servants were told in no uncertain terms that the LORD your God commanded His servant Moses to give you all the land, and to destroy all the land’s inhabitants before you, we feared greatly for our lives because of you, and so we did this [deceptive] thing.

25 “Now look, we are in your hands; do to us as it seems good and right in your sight.”

26 So that is what he did to them; he rescued them from the hands of the Israelites and they did not kill them.

27 Now on that day Joshua made them cutters *and* gatherers of firewood and

---

9:14 *did not ask for the counsel of the LORD.* Significantly, the Israelites did not ask God’s advice about making peace with the Gibeonites, contrary to God’s explicit instructions to Joshua (Nu 27:21).

9:18 Questioning — The congregation rose up and complained to their leaders about making the treaty with Gibeon because they knew the leaders had not consulted the Lord. There is a time to confront leaders, specifically when they sin or when they act in their own wisdom without asking for God’s direction. When the leaders appear to be traveling down the wrong path, the people can always ask respectfully, “Have you consulted the Lord about this? Did you get an answer?”

9:20 *the oath which we have sworn.* Oath taking and swearing was serious business. To take an oath was to give a sacred and unbreakable promise to do a certain thing. Because of the unbreakable nature of an oath, the covenant the Israelites made with the Gibeonites could not be revoked, even though it was obtained under false pretenses.

14 Nu 27:21 **15** Jos 11:19; 2Sa 21:2 **17** Jos 18:25, 26,28; Ezr 2:25 **18** Ps 15:4; Ecc 5:2 **20** See 2Sa 21:1,2,6; Eze 17:13, 15,18,19; Zec 5:3,4; Mal 3:5 **21** Dt 29:11; ver. 15 **22** ver. 6,9; ver. 16 **23** Ge 9:25 **24** Ex 23:32; Dt 7:1,2; Ex 15:14 **25** Ge 16:6 **27** ver. 21,23; Dt 12:5

water carriers for the congregation and
for the altar of the LORD, to this day, in
the place which He would choose.

Five Kings Attack Gibeon

10 WHEN ADONI-ZEDEK king
of Jerusalem heard that Josh-
ua had captured Ai, and had utterly
destroyed it—as he had done to Jeri-
cho and its king, so he had done to Ai
and its king—and that the residents
of Gibeon had made peace with Israel
and were [living] among them,
2he [and his people] feared greatly,
because Gibeon was a great city, like
one of the royal cities, and because it
was greater than Ai, and all its men
were mighty.
3So Adoni-zedek king of Jerusalem
sent *word* to Hoham king of Hebron,
and to Piram king of Jarmuth, to Ja-
phia king of Lachish, and to Debir king
of Eglon, saying,
4"Come up to me and help me, and
let us attack Gibeon [with a combined
army], because it has made peace with
Joshua and with the sons (people) of
Israel."
5Then the five kings of the Amo-
rites, the king of Jerusalem, the king
of Hebron, the king of Jarmuth, the
king of Lachish, and the king of Eglon,

CHAPTER 10 **1** Jos 6:21; Jos 8:22,26,28; Jos 9:15 **2** Ex 15:14-16; Dt 11:25 **4** ver. 1; Jos 9:15 **5** Jos 9:2

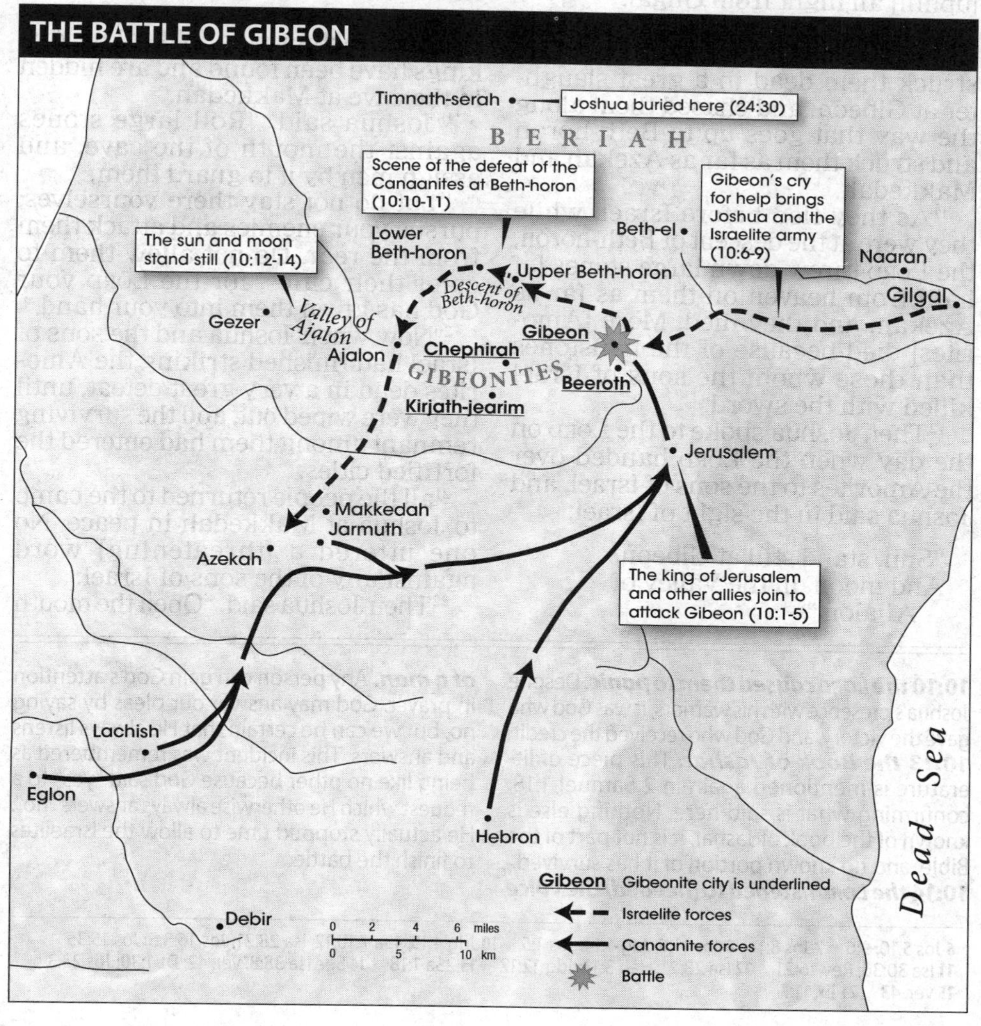

gathered together and went up, they
with all their armies, and they camped
by Gibeon and fought against it.
6 So the men of Gibeon sent *word* to
Joshua at the camp in Gilgal, saying,
"Do not abandon your servants; come
up to us quickly and save us and help
us, for all [five of] the kings of the Am-
orites who live in the hill country have
assembled against us."
7 So Joshua went up from Gilgal, he
and all the people of war with him, and
all the men of valor.
8 The LORD said to Joshua, "Do not
fear them, because I have given them
into your hand; not one of them shall
stand before you."
9 So Joshua came upon them sud-
denly, [surprising them] by marching
[uphill] all night from Gilgal.
10 And the LORD caused them to panic
and be confused before Israel, and He
struck them dead in a great slaugh-
ter at Gibeon, and chased them along
the way that goes up to Beth-horon
and struck them as far as Azekah and
Makkedah.
11 As they fled before Israel, while
they were at the descent of Beth-horon,
the LORD threw down large stones [of
hail] from heaven on them as far as
Azekah, and they died. More [Amo-
rites] died because of the hailstones
than those whom the sons of Israel
killed with the sword.
12 Then Joshua spoke to the LORD on
the day when the LORD handed over
the Amorites to the sons of Israel, and
Joshua said in the sight of Israel,

"Sun, stand still at Gibeon,
And moon, in the Valley of
Aijalon."
13 So the sun stood still, and the
moon stopped,
Until the nation [of Israel] took
vengeance upon their
enemies.

Is it not written in the Book of Jashar?
So the sun stood still in the middle
of the sky and was in no hurry to go
down for about a whole day.
14 There has not been a day like that
before it or after it, when the LORD lis-
tened to (heeded) the voice of a man;
for the LORD was fighting for Israel.
15 Then Joshua and all Israel with
him returned to the camp at Gilgal.

Victory at Makkedah

16 Now these five [Amorite] kings
fled and hid themselves in the cave at
Makkedah.
17 And Joshua was told, "The five
kings have been found and are hidden
in the cave at Makkedah."
18 Joshua said, "Roll large stones
against the mouth of the cave, and
assign men by it to guard them,
19 but do not stay there yourselves;
pursue your enemies and attack them
from the rear. Do not allow them to
enter their cities, for the LORD your
God has given them into your hand."
20 Now when Joshua and the sons of
Israel had finished striking the Amo-
rites dead in a very great defeat, until
they were wiped out, and the surviving
remnant among them had entered the
fortified cities,
21 all the people returned to the camp
to Joshua at Makkedah in peace. No
one uttered a [threatening] word
against any of the sons of Israel.
22 Then Joshua said, "Open the mouth

10:10 *the LORD caused them to panic.* Despite Joshua's presence with his warriors, it was God who gave the victory, and God who received the credit.
10:13 *the Book of Jashar.* This piece of literature is mentioned again in 2 Samuel 1:18, confirming what is said here. Nothing else is known of the book of Jashar, it is not part of the Bible, and no known portion of it has survived.
10:14 *the LORD listened to (heeded) the voice of a man.* Any person can gain God's attention in prayer. God may answer our pleas by saying no, but we can be certain that He always listens and answers. This incident was remembered as being like no other because God said "yes" to a request which He otherwise always answers "no": He actually stopped time to allow the Israelites to finish the battle.

6 Jos 5:10; 9:6 **7** Jos 8:1 **8** Jos 11:6; Jdg 4:14; Jos 1:5 **10** Jdg 4:15; 1Sa 7:10,12; Isa 28:21; Jos 16:3,5; Jos 15:35 **11** Isa 30:30; Rev 16:21 **12** Isa 28:21; Hab 3:11; Jdg 12:12 **13** 2Sa 1:18 **14** See Isa 38:8; ver. 42; Dt 1:30; Jos 23:3 **15** ver. 43 **21** Ex 11:7

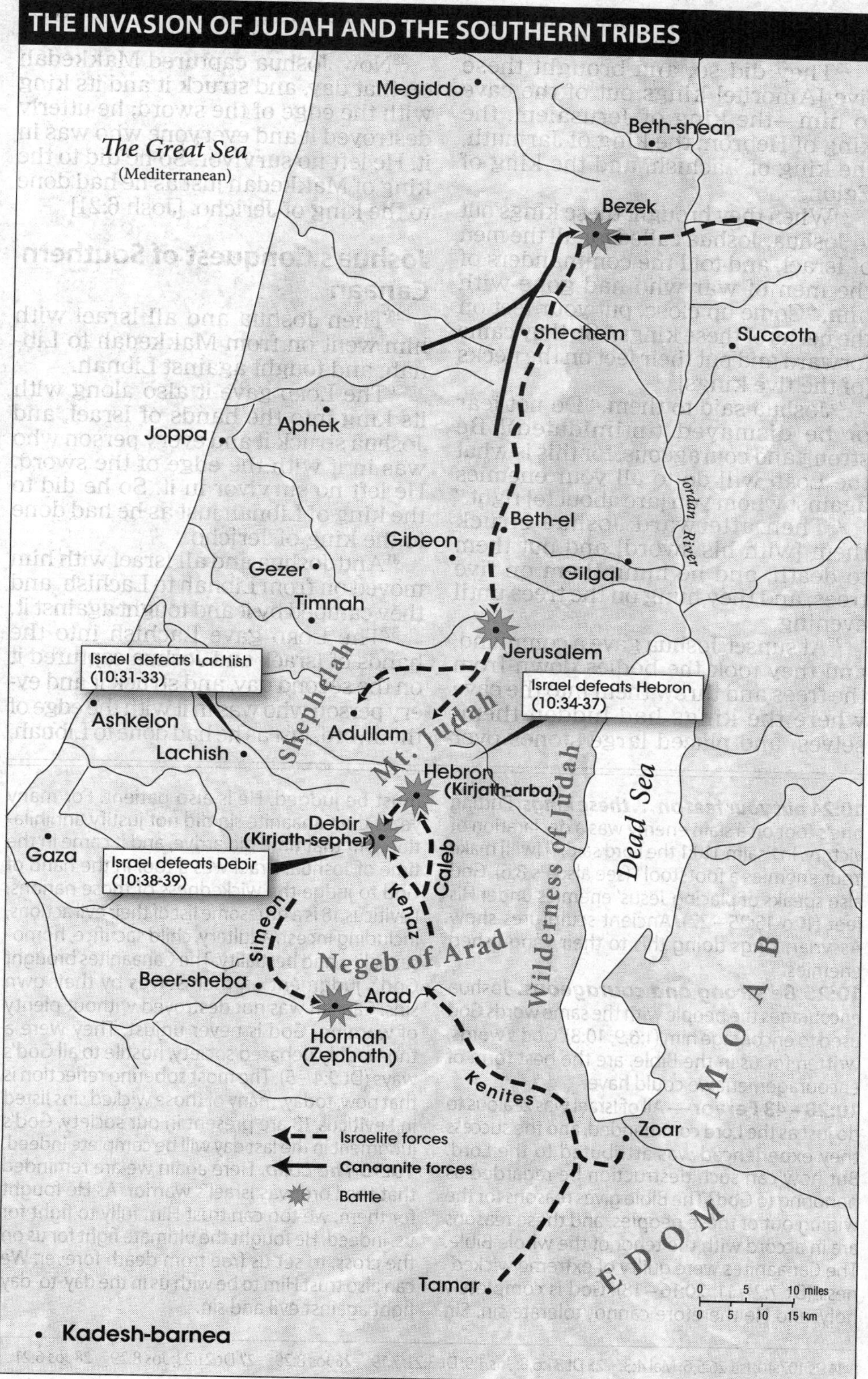
THE INVASION OF JUDAH AND THE SOUTHERN TRIBES
The Great Sea
(Mediterranean)
Megiddo
Beth-shean
Bezek
Shechem
Succoth
Aphek
Joppa
Jordan River
Beth-el
Gibeon
Gilgal
Gezer
Timnah
Jerusalem
Israel defeats Lachish
(10:31-33)
Israel defeats Hebron
(10:34-37)
Ashkelon
Adullam
Shephelah
Mt. Judah
Lachish
Hebron
(Kirjath-arba)
Wilderness of Judah
Dead Sea
Debir
(Kirjath-sepher)
Gaza
Israel defeats Debir
(10:38-39)
Kenaz
Caleb
Simeon
Negeb of Arad
Beer-sheba
Arad
Hormah
(Zephath)
MOAB
Kenites
Zoar
Israelite forces
Canaanite forces
Battle
EDOM
Tamar
0 5 10 miles
0 5 10 15 km
Kadesh-barnea

of the cave and bring out to me those five [Amorite] kings from the cave."

23 They did so, and brought these five [Amorite] kings out of the cave to him—the king of Jerusalem, the king of Hebron, the king of Jarmuth, the king of Lachish, and the king of Eglon.

24 When they brought these kings out to Joshua, Joshua called for all the men of Israel, and told the commanders of the men of war who had gone with him, "Come up close, put your feet on the necks of these kings." So they came forward and put their feet on the necks [of the five kings].

25 Joshua said to them, "Do not fear or be dismayed (intimidated)! Be strong and courageous, for this is what the LORD will do to all your enemies against whom you [are about to] fight."

26 Then afterward Joshua struck them [with his sword] and put them to death, and he hung them on five trees; and they hung on the trees until evening.

27 At sunset Joshua gave a command, and they took the bodies down from the trees and threw them into the cave where the kings had hidden themselves, and placed large stones over the mouth of the cave, [where they remain] to this very day.

28 Now Joshua captured Makkedah on that day, and struck it and its king with the edge of the sword; he utterly destroyed it and everyone who was in it. He left no survivor. So he did to the king of Makkedah just as he had done to the king of Jericho. [Josh 6:21]

Joshua's Conquest of Southern Canaan

29 Then Joshua and all Israel with him went on from Makkedah to Libnah, and fought against Libnah.

30 The LORD gave it also along with its king into the hands of Israel, and Joshua struck it and every person who was in it with the edge of the sword. He left no survivor in it. So he did to the king of Libnah just as he had done to the king of Jericho.

31 And Joshua and all Israel with him moved on from Libnah to Lachish, and they camped by it and fought against it.

32 The LORD gave Lachish into the hands of Israel; and Joshua captured it on the second day, and struck it and every person who was in it with the edge of the sword, just as he had done to Libnah.

10:24 *put your feet on . . . these kings.* Putting one's foot on a slain enemy was a declaration of victory. In Psalm 110:1 the Lord said, "I [will] make Your enemies a footstool" (see also Ps 8:6). God also speaks of placing Jesus' enemies under His feet (1Co 15:25 – 27). Ancient sculptures show Assyrian kings doing this to their vanquished enemies.

10:25 *Be strong and courageous.* Joshua encourages the people with the same words God used to encourage him (1:6,9; 10:8). God's words, written for us in the Bible, are the best form of encouragement we could have.

10:28 – 43 Fervor — All of Israel was zealous to do just as the Lord commanded, and the success they experienced was attributed to the Lord. But how can such destruction be regarded as honoring to God? The Bible gives reasons for the wiping out of these peoples, and these reasons are in accord with the tenor of the whole Bible. The Canaanites were guilty of extreme wickedness (Dt 7:2 – 11; 20:16 – 18). God is completely holy, and He therefore cannot tolerate sin. Sin must be judged. He is also patient. For many years the Canaanite sin did not justify annihilation. But that time did arrive, and it came in the time of Joshua. Israel was a tool in the hand of God to judge the wickedness of those nations. Leviticus 18 is a gruesome list of their evil actions, including incest, adultery, child sacrifice, homosexuality, and bestiality. The Canaanites brought God's judgment on themselves by their own sins. Canaan was not destroyed without plenty of warning. God is never unjust. They were a thoroughly debased society, hostile to all God's ways (Dt 9:4 – 5). The most sobering reflection is that now, today, many of those wicked sins listed in Leviticus 18 are present in our society. God's judgment in the last day will be complete indeed.

10:30 *The LORD.* Here again we are reminded that the Lord was Israel's warrior. As He fought for them, we too can trust Him fully to fight for us. Indeed, He fought the ultimate fight for us on the cross, to set us free from death forever. We can also trust Him to be with us in the day-to-day fight against evil and sin.

24 Ps 107:40; Isa 26:5,6; Mal 4:3 **25** Dt 31:6,8; Jos 1:9; Dt 3:21; 7:19 **26** Jos 8:29 **27** Dt 21:23; Jos 8:29 **28** Jos 6:21

33 Then Horam king of Gezer went
up to help Lachish, and Joshua struck
him and his people down until he had
left him no survivor.
34 And Joshua and all Israel with him
went on from Lachish to Eglon, and
they camped by it and fought against it.
35 They captured it on that day and
struck it with the edge of the sword;
and on that day he utterly destroyed
every person who was in it, just as he
had done to Lachish.
36 Then Joshua and all Israel with
him went up from Eglon to Hebron,
and they fought against it
37 and captured it and struck it and
its king and all its cities and all the
persons who were in it with the edge
of the sword. He left no survivor, just
as he had done to Eglon. He utterly
destroyed it and every person who
was in it.
38 Then Joshua and all Israel with
him returned to Debir, and fought
against it.
39 He captured it with its king and all
its cities, and they struck them with
the edge of the sword, and utterly de-
stroyed every person who was in it. He
left no survivor. Just as he had done to
Hebron, so Joshua did to Debir and its
king, as he had done also to Libnah
and its king.
40 So Joshua struck all the land, the
hill country, the Negev (South coun-
try) and the lowland and the slopes
[that descend to the Dead Sea] and all
their kings. He left no survivor, but
he utterly destroyed all who breathed,
just as the LORD, the God of Israel, had
commanded. [Deut 20:16]
41 Joshua struck them from Kadesh-
barnea even as far as Gaza, and all
the country of Goshen even as far as
Gibeon.
42 Joshua captured all these kings
and their land at one time, because
the LORD, the God of Israel, fought for
Israel.
43 So Joshua and all Israel with him
returned to the camp at Gilgal.

Northern Canaan Taken

11 THEN WHEN Jabin king of
Hazor heard [of Israel's other
victories] he sent *word* to Jobab king
of Madon, and to the king of Shimron,
and to the king of Achshaph,
2 and to the kings who were in the
north, in the hill country, and in the
Arabah [the plain] south of Chinnereth
(the Sea of Galilee) and in the lowland
and on the hills of Dor on the west;
3 to the Canaanite in the east and in
the west, and to the Amorite, the Hit-
tite, the Perizzite, and the Jebusite in
the hill country, and the Hivite at the
foot of [Mount] Hermon in the land of
Mizpeh.
4 They went out, they and all their
armies with them, as many people as
the sand on the seashore, with very
many horses and chariots.
5 So all these kings met and they
came and encamped together at the
waters of Merom, to fight against Israel.
6 Then the LORD said to Joshua, "Do
not be afraid because of them, for to-
morrow by this time I am going to
hand over all of them slain [by the
sword] to Israel; you shall hamstring
(disable) their horses and set fire to
their chariots."
7 So Joshua and all the people of war
with him came against them suddenly
by the waters of Merom, and attacked
them.
8 The LORD handed them over to Is-
rael, who struck them and pursued

11:4 *very many horses and chariots.* In this time in history, horses were used for pulling chariots which accompanied the infantry and carried a rider with a bow or a supply of spears. The enemy of Israel came well armed and with many soldiers to fight—but it made no difference. Again God defeated Israel's enemy. God limited the size of the Israelite army so they would not be depending on military strength, but rather on Him.

11:8 *Great Sidon and Misrephoth-maim.* Great Sidon was a Phoenician city on the Mediterranean coast, and Misrephoth was south of it. The defeat of the Canaanites described here shows them fleeing in all directions.

33 Jos 16:3,10; 1Ki 9:16,17; 1Ch 20:4 **36** See Jos 14:13; 15:13; Jdg 1:10 **38** See Jos 15:15; Jdg 1:11 **40** Dt 20:16,17
41 Ge 10:19; Jos 11:16 **42** ver. 14 **CHAPTER 11** **1** Jos 10:3; Jos 19:15 **2** Nu 34:11; Jos 17:11; Jdg 1:27; 1Ki 4:11
3 Jdg 3:3; Jos 13:11; Ge 31:49 **4** Ge 22:17; 32:12; Jdg 7:12; 1Sa 13:5 **6** Jos 10:8; 2Sa 8:4 **8** Jos 13:6

them as far as Great Sidon and
Misrephoth-maim and eastward as
far as the Valley of Mizpeh; they struck
them down until no survivor was left.
9 Joshua did to them as the LORD had
told him; he hamstrung (disabled) their
horses and set fire to their chariots.
10 At that time Joshua turned back
and captured Hazor and struck its
king dead with the sword; for Hazor
previously was the head of all these
kingdoms.
11 They struck all the people who
were in it with the edge of the sword,
utterly destroying them; there was no
one left who breathed. And he set fire
to Hazor.
12 Joshua captured all the cities of
these kings, and all their kings, and
he struck them with the edge of the
sword, utterly destroying them, just
as Moses the servant of the LORD had
commanded. [Deut 20:16]
13 But Israel did not burn any of the
cities that stood [walled and fortified]
on their mounds, except Hazor alone,
which Joshua burned.
14 The sons of Israel took as their
plunder all the spoil of these cities and
the cattle; but they struck every man
with the edge of the sword, until they
had destroyed them. They left no one
alive.
15 Just as the LORD had commanded
Moses His servant, so Moses had com-
manded Joshua, and so Joshua did; he
left nothing undone of all that the LORD
had commanded Moses.
16 So Joshua took all this land: the hill
country, all the Negev (South country),
all the land of Goshen, the lowland,
the Arabah [plain], the hill country of
Israel and its lowland
17 from Mount Halak, that rises to-
ward Seir [in the south], even as far
as Baal-gad in the Valley of Lebanon
at the foot of Mount Hermon [in the
north]. He captured all their kings and
struck them and put them to death.
18 Joshua waged war with all these
kings a long time [at least five years].
19 There was no city that made peace
with the Israelites except the Hivites
living in Gibeon; they took all *the oth-
ers* in battle.
20 For it was [the purpose] of the LORD
to harden their hearts, to meet Israel
in battle so that Israel would utterly
destroy them, that they would receive
no mercy, but that Israel would destroy
them, just as the LORD had commanded
Moses.
21 Then Joshua came at that time and
cut off the Anakim from the hill coun-
try, from Hebron, from Debir, from
Anab and from all the hill country of
Judah and all the hill country of Israel.
Joshua utterly destroyed them with
their cities.
22 There were no Anakim left in the
land of the children of Israel; only in
Gaza, in Gath, and in Ashdod [of Phi-
listia] some remained.
23 So Joshua took the whole land [of
Canaan], according to all that the LORD
had spoken to Moses, and Joshua gave
it as an inheritance to Israel according
to their divisions by their tribes. So the
land had rest from war.

Kings Defeated by Israel

12 NOW THESE are the kings of
the land whom the sons of Is-
rael defeated, and whose land they
possessed beyond the Jordan toward
the east, from the valley of the [river]

11:16 – 12:24 Zeal — Joshua and the people served as the instruments of divine justice and fulfilled the word spoken to Moses concerning the gift of the land of Canaan. The list of the defeated kings who had banded together against Israel bears testimony to the zeal of Israel for God and the obedience and faithfulness of Joshua. As Christians we can eagerly anticipate the final outcome of world history, when the "kingdom (dominion, rule) of the world has become the kingdom of our Lord and of His Christ" (Rev 11:15).

11:20 *to harden their hearts.* The people whose hearts God hardened were not good people, but people already committed to doing evil.

12 Nu 33:52 **15** Ex 34:11,12; Dt 31:7,8; Jos 1:7 **16** Jos 12:8; Jos 10:41 **17** Jos 12:7; Dt 7:24; Jos 12:7 **19** Jos 9:3,7 **20** Dt 2:30; Jdg 14:4; 1Sa 2:25; Dt 20:16,17 **21** Nu 13:22,33; Dt 1:28; Jos 15:13,14 **22** 1Sa 17:4; Jos 15:46 **23** Nu 34:2; Nu 26:53; Jos 14; 15; ver. 18; Jos 14:15; 21:44; 22:4; 23:1 **CHAPTER 12** **1** Nu 21:24; Dt 3:8,9

Arnon to Mount Hermon, and all the
Arabah [plain] to the east:
2 Sihon king of the Amorites, who
lived in Heshbon, and ruled from Aro-
er, which is on the edge of the valley
of the [river] Arnon, both the middle
of the valley and half of Gilead, and as
far as the brook Jabbok, [which is] the
border of the sons of Ammon;
3 and the Arabah [plain] as far as the
Sea of Chinnereth (Galilee) eastward,
and as far as the sea of the Arabah,
the Salt (Dead) Sea, eastward toward
Beth-jeshimoth, and southward to the
foot of the slopes of [Mount] Pisgah;
4 and the territory of Og king of
Bashan, one of the remnant of the
Rephaim, who lived at Ashtaroth and
at Edrei,
5 and ruled over Mount Hermon and
Salecah and all of Bashan to the border
of the Geshurites and the Maacathites,
and over half of Gilead, *as far as* the
border of Sihon king of Heshbon.

2 Nu 21:24 **3** Dt 3:17; Jos 13:20; Dt 3:17; 4:49 **4** Nu 21:33; Dt 3:4,10,11; Jos 13:12; Dt 1:4 **5** Dt 3:8,10; Jos 13:11; Dt 3:14

THE BATTLE OF THE WATERS AT MEROM

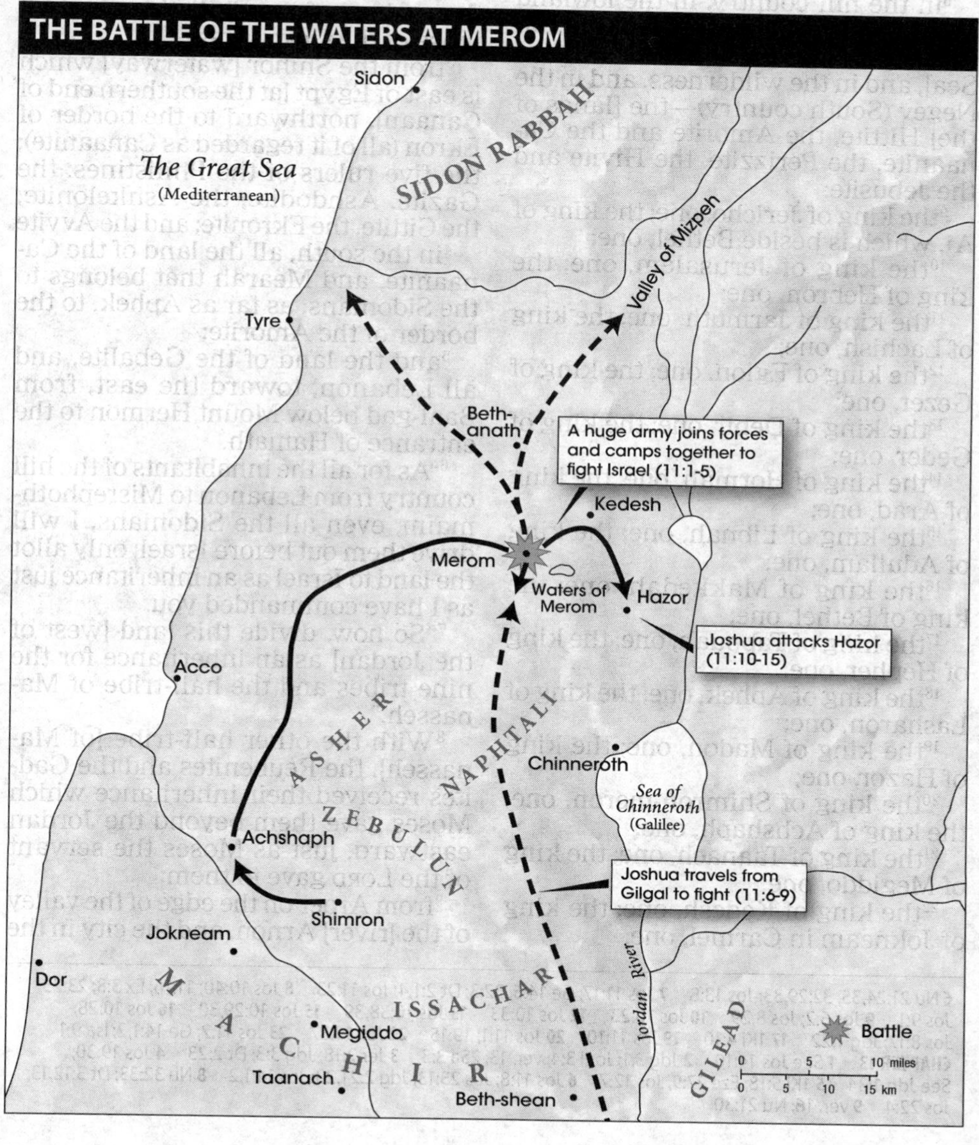

6 Moses the servant of the LORD and
the sons of Israel defeated them; and
Moses the servant of the LORD gave
their land as a possession to the Reu-
benites and the Gadites and the half-
tribe of Manasseh. [Num 21; 32:33;
Deut 2; 3]
7 These are the kings of the land
whom Joshua and the sons of Israel
defeated on the west side of the Jor-
dan, from Baal-gad in the Valley of
Lebanon to Mount Halak, which rises
toward Seir. Joshua gave their land
to the tribes of Israel as a possession
according to their divisions,
8 in the hill country, in the lowland
(foothills), in the Arabah [plain], on
the slopes [descending to the Dead
Sea], and in the wilderness, and in the
Negev (South country)—the [lands of
the] Hittite, the Amorite and the Ca-
naanite, the Perizzite, the Hivite and
the Jebusite:
9 the king of Jericho, one; the king of
Ai, which is beside Bethel, one;
10 the king of Jerusalem, one; the
king of Hebron, one;
11 the king of Jarmuth, one; the king
of Lachish, one;
12 the king of Eglon, one; the king of
Gezer, one;
13 the king of Debir, one; the king of
Geder, one;
14 the king of Hormah, one; the king
of Arad, one;
15 the king of Libnah, one; the king
of Adullam, one;
16 the king of Makkedah, one; the
king of Bethel, one;
17 the king of Tappuah, one; the king
of Hepher, one;
18 the king of Aphek, one; the king of
Lasharon, one;
19 the king of Madon, one; the king
of Hazor, one;
20 the king of Shimron-meron, one;
the king of Achshaph, one;
21 the king of Taanach, one; the king
of Megiddo, one;
22 the king of Kedesh, one; the king
of Jokneam in Carmel, one;
23 the king of Dor in the heights of
Dor, one; the king of Goiim in Gilgal,
one;
24 the king of Tirzah, one: in all,
thirty-one kings.

Canaan Divided among the Tribes

13 NOW JOSHUA was old and ad-
vanced in years, and the LORD
said to him, "You have grown old and
advanced in years, and very substan-
tial portions of the land remain to be
possessed.
2 "This is the land that remains: all
the regions of the Philistines and all
those of the Geshurites;
3 from the Shihor [waterway] which
is east of Egypt [at the southern end of
Canaan], northward to the border of
Ekron (all of it regarded as Canaanite);
the five rulers of the Philistines: the
Gazite, Ashdodite, the Ashkelonite,
the Gittite, the Ekronite; and the Avvite
4 in the south, all the land of the Ca-
naanite, and Mearah that belongs to
the Sidonians, as far as Aphek, to the
border of the Amorite;
5 and the land of the Gebalite, and
all Lebanon, toward the east, from
Baal-gad below Mount Hermon to the
entrance of Hamath.
6 "As for all the inhabitants of the hill
country from Lebanon to Misrephoth-
maim, even all the Sidonians, I will
drive them out before Israel; only allot
the land to Israel as an inheritance just
as I have commanded you.
7 "So now, divide this land [west of
the Jordan] as an inheritance for the
nine tribes and the half-tribe of Ma-
nasseh."
8 With the other half-tribe [of Ma-
nasseh], the Reubenites and the Gad-
ites received their inheritance which
Moses gave them beyond the Jordan
eastward, just as Moses the servant
of the LORD gave to them;
9 from Aroer on the edge of the valley
of the [river] Arnon, and the city in the

6 Nu 21:24,35; 32:29,33; Jos 13:8 **7** Jos 11:17; Ge 14:6; 32:3; Dt 2:1,4; Jos 11:23 **8** Jos 10:40; 11:16; Ex 3:8; 23:23; Jos 9:1 **9** Jos 6:2; Jos 8:29 **10** Jos 10:23 **12** Jos 10:33 **13** Jos 10:38,39 **15** Jos 10:29,30 **16** Jos 10:28; Jos 8:17; Jdg 1:22 **17** 1Ki 4:10 **19** Jos 11:10 **20** Jos 11:1; 19:15 **22** Jos 19:37 **23** Jos 11:2; Ge 14:1,2; Isa 9:1 **CHAPTER 13** **1** See Jos 14:10 **2** Jdg 3:1; Joel 3:4; ver. 13; 2Sa 3:3 **3** Jer 2:18; Jdg 3:3; Dt 2:23 **4** Jos 19:30; See Jdg 1:34 **5** 1Ki 5:18; Eze 27:9; Jos 12:7 **6** Jos 11:8; Jos 23:13; Jdg 2:21,23; Jos 14:1,2 **8** Nu 32:33; Dt 3:12,13; Jos 22:4 **9** ver. 16; Nu 21:30

middle of the valley, and all the plain of Medeba, as far as Dibon;

10 and all the cities of Sihon king of the Amorites, who reigned in Heshbon, as far as the border of the Ammonites;

11 and Gilead, and the territory of the Geshurites and Maacathites, and all Mount Hermon, and all Bashan as far as Salecah;

12 the entire kingdom of Og in Bashan, who reigned in Ashtaroth and Edrei—he alone was left of the remnant of the Rephaim [giants]—for Moses had struck them and dispossessed them.

13 But the sons of Israel did not dispossess the Geshurites or the Maacathites; for Geshur and Maacath live among Israel to this day.

14 It was only to the tribe of Levi that Moses gave no [territory as an] inheritance; the offerings by fire to the LORD, the God of Israel, are their inheritance, as He told him.

15 So Moses gave *an inheritance* to the tribe of the sons of Reuben according to their families.

16 Their territory was from Aroer, which is on the edge of the valley of the [river] Arnon, and the city which is in the middle of the valley and all the plain by Medeba;

17 with Heshbon, and all its cities which are on the plain: Dibon and Bamoth-baal and Beth-baal-meon,

18 and Jahaz and Kedemoth and Mephaath,

19 and Kiriathaim and Sibmah and Zereth-shahar on the hill of the valley,

20 and Beth-peor and the slopes of Pisgah and Beth-jeshimoth,

21 even all the cities of the plain and all the kingdom of Sihon king of the Amorites who reigned in Heshbon, whom Moses struck down along with the leaders of Midian, Evi and Rekem and Zur and Hur and Reba, the princes of Sihon, who lived in the land.

22 The sons of Israel also killed Balaam the son of Beor, the diviner (soothsayer), with the sword among [the rest of] their slain. [Num 31:16]

23 The border of the sons of Reuben was the Jordan. This was the inheritance of the sons of Reuben according to their families, with their cities and villages.

24 Moses also gave *an inheritance* to the tribe of Gad, to the sons of Gad, according to their families.

25 Their territory was Jazer, and all the cities of Gilead, and half the land of the sons of Ammon, as far as Aroer east of Rabbah;

26 and from Heshbon as far as Ramath-mizpeh and Betonim, and from Mahanaim as far as the border of Debir;

27 and in the valley, Beth-haram and Beth-nimrah and Succoth and Zaphon, the rest of the kingdom of Sihon king of Heshbon, with the Jordan as a border, as far as the *lower* end of the Sea of Chinnereth (Galilee) east of the Jordan.

28 This is the inheritance of the sons of Gad according to their families, with their cities and their villages.

29 Moses also gave *an inheritance* to the half-tribe of Manasseh; and it was for the half-tribe of the sons of Manasseh according to their families.

30 Their region extended from Mahanaim, all Bashan, the entire kingdom of Og king of Bashan, and all the towns of Jair, which are in Bashan, sixty cities;

31 also half of Gilead, with Ashtaroth and Edrei, the cities of the kingdom of Og in Bashan; these were for the sons

13:14 ***to the tribe of Levi that Moses gave no [territory as an] inheritance.*** Originally, the tribe of Levi was sentenced to be landless because of Levi's violent behavior (Ge 49:5 – 7). But later the Levites showed their faithfulness to the Lord (Ex 32:25 – 28) and were promised a blessing (Dt 33:8 – 11). Instead of land, the sacrifices of God would be their privileged inheritance.

13:22 ***Balaam the son of Beor.*** Balaam was a pagan fortune teller who had been hired by Balak, king of Moab, to curse the Israelites in the wilderness (Nu 22 – 24).

10 Nu 21:24,25 **11** Jos 12:5 **12** Dt 3:11; Jos 12:4; Nu 21:24,35 **13** ver. 11 **14** Nu 18:20,23,24; Jos 14:3,4; ver. 33 **16** Jos 12:2; Nu 21:28; ver. 9; Nu 21:30 **18** Nu 21:23 **19** Nu 32:37; Nu 32:38 **20** Dt 3:17; Jos 12:3 **21** Dt 3:10; Nu 21:24; Nu 31:8 **22** Nu 22:5; 31:8 **25** Nu 32:35; Compare Nu 21:26,28,29 with Dt 2:19; Jdg 11:13,15; 2Sa 11:1; 12:26 **27** Nu 32:36; Ge 33:17; 1Ki 7:46; Nu 34:11 **30** Nu 32:41; 1Ch 2:23 **31** Jos 12:4; Nu 32:39,40

of Machir the son of Manasseh, for half of the sons of Machir according to their families (clans).

32 These are *the territories* which Moses distributed as an inheritance in the plains of Moab, beyond the Jordan at Jericho to the east.

33 But to the tribe of Levi, Moses did not give an inheritance; the LORD, the God of Israel, is their inheritance, as He told them.

Caleb's Request

14 NOW THESE are *the territories* which the tribes of Israel inherited in the land of Canaan, which Eleazar the priest, and Joshua the son of Nun, and the heads of the households of the tribes of Israel apportioned to them as an inheritance,

2 by the lot of their inheritance, as the LORD had commanded through Moses, for the nine tribes and the half-tribe.

3 For Moses had given an inheritance to the two tribes and the half-tribe beyond the Jordan; but he did not give [any territory as] an inheritance to the Levites among them.

4 For the sons of Joseph were two tribes, Manasseh and Ephraim, and no portion was given in the land to the Levites except cities in which to live, with their pasture lands for their livestock and for their property.

5 The Israelites did just as the LORD had commanded Moses, and they divided the land.

6 Then the [tribe of the] sons of Judah approached Joshua in Gilgal, and Caleb the son of Jephunneh the Kenizzite said to him, "You know the word which the LORD said to Moses the man of God concerning me and you in Kadesh-barnea.

7 "I was forty years old when Moses the servant of the LORD sent me from Kadesh-barnea to scout the land [of Canaan], and I brought a report back to him as it was in my heart.

8 "My brothers (fellow spies) who went up with me made the heart of the people melt with fear; but I followed the LORD my God completely.

9 "So Moses swore [an oath to me] on that day, saying, 'Be assured that the land on which your foot has walked will be an inheritance to you and to your children always, because you have followed the LORD my God completely.' [Deut 1:35, 36]

10 "And now, look, the LORD has let me live, just as He said, these forty-five years since the LORD spoke this word to Moses, when Israel wandered in the wilderness; and now, look at me, I am eighty-five years old today.

11 "I am still as strong today as I was the day Moses sent me; as my strength was then, so is my strength now, for war and for going out and coming in.

12 "So now, give me this hill country about which the LORD spoke that day, for you heard on that day that the [giant-like] Anakim were there, with great fortified cities; perhaps the LORD will be with me, and I shall drive them out just as the LORD said."

13 So Joshua blessed him and gave Hebron to Caleb the son of Jephunneh as an inheritance.

14 Therefore, Hebron became the inheritance of Caleb the son of Jephunneh the Kenizzite to this day, because

---

14:6 *Caleb . . . the Kenizzite.* The Kenizzites were a non-Israelite group descended from Esau through Kenaz (Ge 15:19; 36:11,15,42). It seems that Caleb, one of the most faithful to God of his time, was just a generation removed from a non-Israelite family. Although the Jews are indeed God's chosen people, He loves and honors anyone who obeys His commands.

14:10 – 11 Thankfulness — God's Word is as dependable as its author. His promise to Caleb waited forty-five years for fulfillment, but His blessing was sure. Caleb's view of all God's goodness to him resounded with thankfulness. Being silently thankful is important — God knows our hearts — but thankfulness should also be expressed with words of praise and glorification for the Giver of all good things.

14:14 *he followed the LORD, the God of Israel, completely.* Caleb's wholehearted devotion to God was never a question, even in the

---

33 ver. 14; Jos 18:7; Nu 18:20; Dt 10:9; 18:1,2 **CHAPTER 14** **1** Nu 34:17,18 **2** Nu 26:55; 33:54; 34:13 **3** Jos 13:8,32,33 **4** Ge 48:5; 1Ch 5:1,2 **5** Nu 35:2; Jos 21:2 **6** Nu 32:12; Jos 15:17; Nu 14:24,30; Nu 13:26 **7** Nu 13:6; 14:6 **8** Nu 13:31,32; Nu 14:24; Dt 1:36 **9** Nu 14:23,24; See Nu 13:22 **10** Nu 14:30 **11** See Dt 34:7; Dt 31:2 **12** Nu 13:28,33; Ro 8:31; Jos 15:14; Jdg 1:20 **13** Jos 22:6; Jos 10:37; 15:13 **14** Jos 21:12; ver. 8,9

THE BORDERS OF THE TRIBAL TERRITORIES

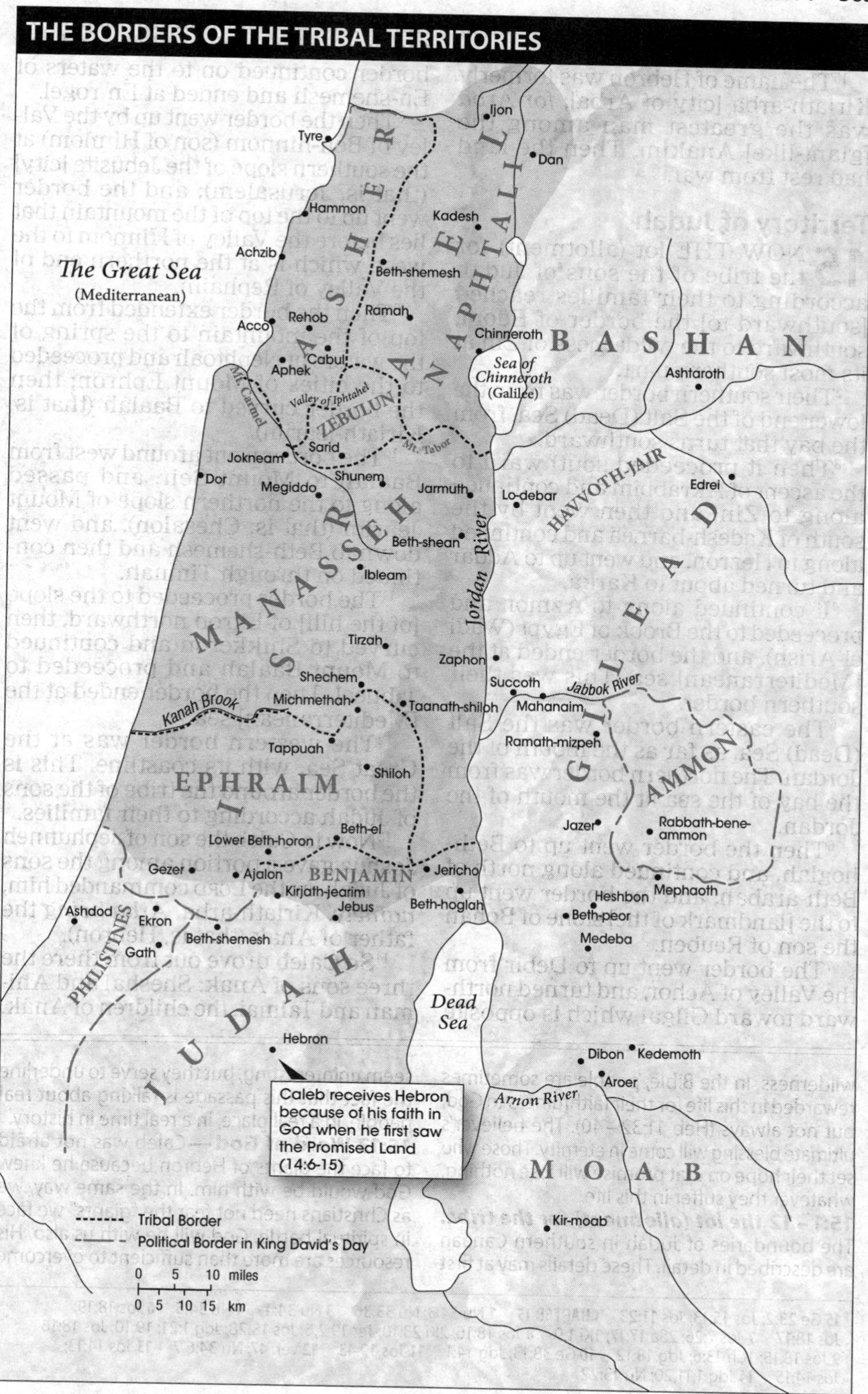

he followed the LORD, the God of Israel, completely.

15 The name of Hebron was formerly Kiriath-arba [city of Arba]; *for Arba* was the greatest man among the [giant-like] Anakim. Then the land had rest from war.

Territory of Judah

15 NOW THE lot (allotment) for the tribe of the sons of Judah according to their families reached [southward to] the border of Edom, southward to the wilderness of Zin at its most southern part.

2 Their southern border was from the lower end of the Salt (Dead) Sea, from the bay that turns southward.

3 Then it proceeded southward to the ascent of Akrabbim and continued along to Zin, and then went by the south of Kadesh-barnea and continued along to Hezron, and went up to Addar and turned about to Karka.

4 It continued along to Azmon and proceeded to the Brook of Egypt (Wadi el-Arish), and the border ended at the [Mediterranean] sea. This was their southern border.

5 The eastern border was the Salt (Dead) Sea, as far as the mouth of the Jordan. The northern border was from the bay of the sea at the mouth of the Jordan.

6 Then the border went up to Beth-hoglah, and continued along north of Beth-arabah, and the border went up to the [landmark of the] stone of Bohan the son of Reuben.

7 The border went up to Debir from the Valley of Achor, and turned northward toward Gilgal which is opposite the ascent of Adummim, which is on the south side of the valley; and the border continued on to the waters of En-shemesh and ended at En-rogel.

8 Then the border went up by the Valley of Ben-hinnom (son of Hinnom) at the southern slope of the Jebusite [city] (that is, Jerusalem); and the border went up to the top of the mountain that lies before the Valley of Hinnom to the west, which is at the northern end of the Valley of Rephaim.

9 Then the border extended from the top of the mountain to the spring of the waters of Nephtoah and proceeded to the cities of Mount Ephron; then the border curved to Baalah (that is, Kiriath-jearim).

10 The border went around west from Baalah to Mount Seir, and passed along to the northern slope of Mount Jearim (that is, Chesalon), and went down to Beth-shemesh and then continued on through Timnah.

11 The border proceeded to the slope [of the hill] of Ekron northward, then curved to Shikkeron and continued to Mount Baalah and proceeded to Jabneel. Then the border ended at the [Mediterranean] sea.

12 The western border was at the Great Sea, with its coastline. This is the border around the tribe of the sons of Judah according to their families.

13 Now to Caleb the son of Jephunneh Joshua gave a portion among the sons of Judah, as the LORD commanded him, *namely,* Kiriath-arba, *Arba being* the father of Anak (that is, Hebron).

14 So Caleb drove out from there the three sons of Anak: Sheshai and Ahiman and Talmai, the children of Anak.

---

wilderness. In the Bible, people are sometimes rewarded in this life for their faithfulness to God, but not always (Heb 11:32–40). The believer's ultimate blessing will come in eternity. Those who set their hope on that promise will lose nothing, whatever they suffer in this life.

15:1–12 *the lot (allotment) for the tribe.* The boundaries of Judah in southern Canaan are described in detail. These details may at first seem uninteresting, but they serve to underline the fact that this passage is talking about real people, in a real place, in a real time in history.

15:13 Word of God — Caleb was not afraid to face the giants of Hebron because he knew God would be with him. In the same way, we as Christians need not fear the "giants" we face in spiritual battle. God will be with us also. His resources are more than sufficient to overcome

15 Ge 23:2; Jos 15:13; Jos 11:23 **CHAPTER 15** **1** Nu 34:3; Nu 33:36 **3** Nu 34:4 **4** Nu 34:5 **6** Jos 18:19; Jos 18:17 **7** Jos 7:26; 2Sa 17:17; 1Ki 1:9 **8** Jos 18:16; 2Ki 23:10; Jer 19:2,6; Jos 18:28; Jdg 1:21; 19:10; Jos 18:16 **9** Jos 18:15; 1Ch 13:6; Jdg 18:12 **10** Ge 38:13; Jdg 14:1 **11** Jos 19:43 **12** ver. 47; Nu 34:6,7 **13** Jos 14:13; Jos 14:15 **14** Jdg 1:11,20; Nu 13:22

15 Then he went up from there against
the people of Debir; Debir was former-
ly named Kiriath-sepher.
16 Caleb said, "I will give Achsah my
daughter as wife to the man who at-
tacks Kiriath-sepher and captures it."
17 And Othniel the son of Kenaz, Ca-
leb's brother, captured it; so he gave
him Achsah his daughter as a wife.
18 Now it came about that when Ach-
sah came *to Othniel*, she persuaded
him [to allow her] to ask her father
for a field. Then she [rode up to Caleb
and] dismounted from her donkey, and
Caleb said to her, "What do you want?"
19 Achsah answered, "Give me a
blessing; since you have given me the
[dry] land of the Negev (South coun-
try), give me springs of water, too." So
he gave her the upper springs and the
lower springs.
20 This is the inheritance of the tribe
of the sons of Judah according to their
families (clans).
21 The cities of the tribe of the sons
of Judah in the extreme south toward
the border of Edom were Kabzeel and
Eder and Jagur,
22 and Kinah and Dimonah and Ada-
dah,
23 and Kedesh and Hazor and Ithnan,
24 Ziph and Telem and Bealoth,
25 and Hazor-hadattah and Kerioth-
hezron (that is, Hazor),
26 Amam and Shema and Moladah,
27 and Hazar-gaddah and Heshmon
and Beth-pelet,
28 and Hazar-shual and Beersheba
and Biziothiah,
29 Baalah and Iim and Ezem,
30 and Eltolad and Chesil and Hor-
mah,
31 and Ziklag and Madmannah and
Sansannah,
32 and Lebaoth and Shilhim and Ain
and Rimmon; in all twenty-nine cities
with their villages.
33 In the lowland: Eshtaol and Zorah
and Ashnah,
34 and Zanoah and En-gannim,
Tappuah and Enam,
35 Jarmuth and Adullam, Socoh and
Azekah,
36 and Shaaraim and Adithaim and
Gederah and Gederothaim; fourteen
cities with their villages.
37 Zenan and Hadashah and Migdal-
gad,
38 and Dilean and Mizpeh and Jok-
theel,
39 Lachish and Bozkath and Eglon,
40 and Cabbon and Lahmas and Chit-
lish,
41 and Gederoth, Beth-dagon and
Naamah and Makkedah; sixteen cities
with their villages.
42 Libnah and Ether and Ashan,
43 and Iphtah and Ashnah and Nezib,
44 and Keilah and Achzib and Mare-
shah; nine cities with their villages.
45 Ekron, with its towns and villages;
46 from Ekron even to the sea, all
that were beside Ashdod, with their
villages;
47 Ashdod, with its towns and its
villages; Gaza, with its towns and its
villages; as far as the Brook of Egypt
(Wadi el-Arish) and the Great [Medi-
terranean] Sea with its coastline.
48 In the hill country: Shamir and
Jattir and Socoh,
49 and Dannah and Kiriath-sannah
(that is, Debir),
50 and Anab and Eshtemoh and
Anim,
51 and Goshen and Holon and Giloh;
eleven cities with their villages.
52 Arab and Dumah and Eshan,
53 and Janum and Beth-tappuah and
Aphekah,
54 and Humtah and Kiriath-arba (that
is, Hebron), and Zior; nine cities with
their villages.
55 Maon, Carmel and Ziph and Jut-
tah,
56 and Jezreel and Jokdeam and Za-
noah,
57 Kain, Gibeah and Timnah; ten cit-
ies with their villages.
58 Halhul, Beth-zur and Gedor,
59 and Maarath and Beth-anoth and
Eltekon; six cities with their villages.
60 Kiriath-baal (that is, Kiriath-
jearim), and Rabbah; two cities with
their villages.
61 In the wilderness [that slopes

15 Jos 10:38; Jdg 1:11 **16** Jdg 1:12 **17** Jdg 1:13; 3:9; Nu 32:12; Jos 14:6 **18** Jdg 1:14; See Ge 24:64; 1Sa 25:23 **19** Ge 33:11 **31** 1Sa 27:6 **33** Nu 13:23 **38** 2Ki 14:7 **47** ver. 4; Nu 34:6 **51** Jos 10:41; 11:16 **54** ver. 13; Jos 14:15 **60** Jos 18:14

downward toward the Dead Sea]:
Beth-arabah, Middin and Secacah,
62 and Nibshan and the City of Salt
and Engedi; six cities with their vil-
lages.
63 But as for the Jebusites, the inhab-
itants of Jerusalem, the [tribe of the]
sons of Judah were not able to drive
them out; so the Jebusites live with the
sons of Judah in Jerusalem to this day.

Territory of Ephraim

16 THEN THE lot (allotment) for
the sons of Joseph went from the
Jordan Valley at Jericho to the waters
of Jericho on the east into the wilder-
ness, going up from Jericho through
the hill country to Bethel.
2 Then it went from Bethel to Luz,
and continued to Ataroth, the border
of the Archites.
3 It went down westward to the ter-
ritory of the Japhletites, as far as the
outskirts of lower Beth-horon, then to
Gezer, and it ended at the sea.
4 The sons of Joseph, Manasseh and
Ephraim, received their inheritance.
5 Now this was the territory of the
sons of Ephraim according to their
families: on the east side the border of
their inheritance was Ataroth-addar,
as far as upper Beth-horon.
6 Then the border went westward at
Michmethath on the north, and turned
eastward to Taanath-shiloh and con-
tinued beyond it to the east of Janoah.
7 It went down from Janoah to At-
aroth and to Naarah, touched Jericho
and ended at the Jordan.
8 The border continued from Tappuah
westward to the Brook Kanah, and it
ended at the [Mediterranean] sea. This
is the inheritance of the tribe of the
sons of Ephraim according to their
families (clans),
9 with the cities which were set apart
for the sons of Ephraim within the in-
heritance of the sons of Manasseh, all
the cities with their villages.
10 But they did not drive out the Ca-
naanites who lived in Gezer, so the
Canaanites live among Ephraim to this
day, and they became forced laborers.

Territory of Manasseh

17 NOW THIS was the lot (allot-
ment) for the tribe of Manasseh,
for he was the firstborn of Joseph. To
Machir the firstborn of Manasseh, the
father of Gilead, were allotted Gilead
and Bashan, because he was a man
of war.
2 So *the lot* was also made for the rest
of the sons of Manasseh according to
their families—for the sons of Abie-
zer and for the sons of Helek and for
the sons of Asriel and for the sons of
Shechem and for the sons of Hepher
and for the sons of Shemida; these
were the male descendants of Manas-
seh the son of Joseph according to their
families (clans).
3 But Zelophehad the son of Hepher,
the son of Gilead, the son of Machir,
the son of Manasseh, had no sons, only
daughters; and these are the names
of his daughters: Mahlah and Noah,
Hoglah, Milcah and Tirzah.
4 They came before Eleazar the priest
and before Joshua the son of Nun and
before the leaders and said, "The LORD
commanded Moses to give us an inher-
itance among our brothers." So accord-
ing to the command of the LORD Joshua

---

the hosts of darkness which confront us in this world (1Jn 4:4).

15:63 *with the sons of Judah.* Judges 1:21 repeats this verse almost verbatim, except that it says Benjamin, not Judah, failed to drive the Jebusites out of Jerusalem. Jerusalem sat astride the boundary between Judah and Benjamin. In the early period, Jerusalem did not belong strictly to either tribe. The tribe of Judah later captured the city from the Jebusites (Jdg 1:8), and from then on it was considered a city of Judah.

17:3 – 6 *Zelophehad . . . had . . . only daughters.* This account serves to show again the theme of the Book of Joshua — that God is faithful to keep His promises. Joshua also was faithful to carry out the commands of God concerning His promise through Moses for the daughters of Zelophehad (Nu 26:33; 27:1 – 11).

---

63 See Jdg 1:8,21; 2Sa 5:6; Jdg 1:21 **CHAPTER 16** **2** Jos 18:13; Jdg 1:26 **3** Jos 18:13; 2Ch 8:5; 1Ki 9:15; 1Ch 7:28 **4** Jos 17:14 **5** Jos 18:13; 2Ch 8:5 **6** Jos 17:7 **7** 1Ch 7:28 **8** Jos 17:9 **9** Jos 17:9 **10** Jdg 1:29; See 1Ki 9:16 **CHAPTER 17** **1** Ge 41:51; 46:20; 48:18; Ge 50:23; Dt 3:15 **2** Nu 26:29-32; 1Ch 7:18; Nu 26:31; Nu 26:32 **3** Nu 26:33; 27:1; 36:2 **4** Jos 14:1; Nu 27:6,7

gave them an inheritance among their
father's brothers.
5 So ten portions fell to Manasseh,
besides the land of Gilead and Bashan,
which is beyond the Jordan [on the
east side of the river],
6 because the daughters of [Zelophe-
had, a descendant of] Manasseh had
received an inheritance among his
[other] sons [whose inheritance went
to their male descendants]. The land of
Gilead belonged to the rest of the sons
of Manasseh. [Num 36:5–12]
7 The territory of Manasseh reached
from Asher to Michmethath which
was east of Shechem; then the border
went southward to the inhabitants of
En-tappuah.
8 The land of Tappuah belonged to
Manasseh, but [the city of] Tappuah
on the border of Manasseh belonged
to the sons of Ephraim.
9 Then the border went down to the
brook of Kanah, south of the brook
(these cities *belonged* to Ephraim,
among the cities of Manasseh), and
Manasseh's border was on the north
side of the brook and it ended at the
sea.
10 The land on the south side *be-
longed* to Ephraim and that on the
north side was Manasseh's, and the sea
was their border; they reached to [the
territory of] Asher on the north and to
[the territory of] Issachar on the east.
11 Also, in Issachar and in Asher, Ma-
nasseh had Beth-shean and its towns
and Ibleam and its towns, and the in-
habitants of Dor and its towns, and the
inhabitants of En-dor and its towns,
and the inhabitants of Taanach and its
towns, and the inhabitants of Megiddo
and its towns; the third is Napheth.
12 But the sons of Manasseh were
not able to [drive out the inhabitants
and] take possession of these cities,
because the Canaanites persisted in
living in that land.
13 When the Israelites became strong,
they put the Canaanites to forced la-
bor, but they did not drive them out
completely.
14 The sons of Joseph spoke to Josh-
ua, saying, "Why have you given us
only one lot and one portion as an
inheritance, when we are a numer-
ous people whom the LORD has so far
blessed?"
15 Then Joshua replied, "If you are
a numerous people, go up to the for-
est and clear ground for yourselves
there in the land of the Perizzites and
the Rephaim, since the hill country of
Ephraim is too narrow for you."
16 The sons of Joseph said, "The hill
country is not enough for us, and all
the Canaanites who live in the valley
have iron chariots, both those who are
in Beth-shean and its towns and those
in the Valley of Jezreel."
17 Joshua said to the house of Joseph,
to Ephraim and to Manasseh, "You
are a numerous people and have great
power; you shall not have *only* one lot,
18 but the hill country shall be yours.
For though it is a forest, you shall clear
it and possess it to its farthest borders;
for you shall drive out the Canaanites,
even though they have iron chariots
and though they are strong."

Rest of the Land Divided

18 THEN THE whole congregation
of the Israelites assembled at Shi-
loh [in the tribal territory of Ephraim],
and set up the Tent of Meeting there;
and the land was subdued before them.
2 There remained among the Isra-
elites seven tribes who had not yet
divided their inheritance.
3 So Joshua asked them, "How
long will you put off entering to take

18:1 *Shiloh.* Shiloh was about 15 miles northwest of Jericho. Here the Israelites set up the tent of meeting (Ex 26). This remained an important religious center for several hundred years (Jdg 18:31; 1Sa 1:9) until the taking of Jerusalem in David's day.

18:3 Unfaithfulness — The seven tribes yet to be settled seemed to have little desire to receive their inheritance and were rebuked for their half-heartedness. They had easily defeated the Canaanites, but they had not followed up on

7 Jos 16:6 **8** Jos 16:8 **9** Jos 16:9 **11** 1Ch 7:29; 1Sa 31:10; 1Ki 4:12 **12** Jdg 1:27,28 **13** Jos 16:10 **14** Jos 16:4; Ge 48:22; Ge 48:19; Nu 26:34,37 **16** Jdg 1:19; 4:3; Jos 19:18; 1Ki 4:12 **18** Dt 20:1 **CHAPTER 18** **1** Jos 19:51; 21:2; 22:9; Jer 7:12; Jdg 18:31; 1Sa 1:3,24; 4:3,4 **3** Jdg 18:9

possession of the land which the LORD, the God of your fathers, has given you?

4 “Provide for yourselves three men from each tribe so that I may send them, and that they may go through the land and write a description of it with regard to their [tribal] inheritance; then they shall return to me.

5 “They shall divide it into seven parts; [the tribe of] Judah shall remain in its territory on the south, and the house of Joseph shall remain in its territory on the north.

6 “You shall describe the land in seven divisions, and bring *the description* here to me. I will cast lots for you here before the LORD our God.

7 “But the Levites have no portion among you, because the priesthood of the LORD is their inheritance. Gad and Reuben and half the tribe of Manasseh also have received their inheritance eastward beyond the Jordan, which Moses the servant of the LORD gave them.”

8 So the men arose and went [on their way], and Joshua commanded those who went to describe the land, saying, “Go and walk throughout the land and describe it, and return to me; and I will cast lots for you here before the LORD in Shiloh.”

9 So the men set out and passed through the land, and described it by cities in seven divisions in a book; and they came back to Joshua to the camp at Shiloh.

10 Joshua cast lots for them in Shiloh before the LORD, and there Joshua divided the land to the sons of Israel, [to each tribe] according to their portions.

The Territory of Benjamin

11 Now the lot (allotment) of the tribe of the sons of Benjamin came up according to their families, and the territory of their lot fell between [the tribes of] the sons of Judah and the sons of Joseph.

12 On the north side their border began at the Jordan, then it went up the slope of Jericho on the north, and up through the hill country westward, and it ended at the Beth-aven wilderness.

13 Then the border continued southward toward Luz, to the slope of Luz (that is, Bethel); then the border went down to Ataroth-addar, by the hill that lies south of lower Beth-horon.

14 The border changed course [from there] and turned around on the western side southward, from the hill that lies to the south opposite Beth-horon; it ended at Kiriath-baal (that is, Kiriath-jearim), a city of [the tribe of] the sons of Judah. This *formed* the western side [of Benjamin’s territory].

15 The southern side was from the edge of Kiriath-jearim, and the border went on westward and went to the source of the waters of Nephtoah.

16 Then the border went down to the edge of the hill overlooking the Valley of Ben-hinnom (son of Hinnom), which is at the north end of the Valley of Rephaim; and it descended to the Valley of Hinnom, south to the slope of the Jebusite, and went on down to En-rogel.

17 Then it turned toward the north and went on to En-shemesh and on to Geliloth, which is opposite the ascent of Adummim, and it went down to the stone of Bohan the son of Reuben.

18 It continued to the north to the side opposite [Beth-] Arabah and went down to the Arabah.

19 The border continued along to the north of the slope of Beth-hoglah; and the border ended at the northern bay of the Salt (Dead) Sea, at the south end of the Jordan. This was the southern border.

20 And the Jordan River was its border on the east side. This was the in-

---

their victories and taken possession of all the land. This laziness was disobedience to God and showed lack of faith in His promises. In our own lives it is fatally easy to begin a work that God sets before us, and then slack off in our faithfulness before it is finished. The believer’s inheritance is reserved in heaven, and cannot be bought by any work of our own. However, God requests holiness of living on our part, and His commands must be obeyed.

5 Jos 15:1; Jos 16:1,4 **6** ver. 10; Jos 14:2 **7** Jos 13:33; Jos 13:8 **12** See Jos 16:1 **13** Ge 28:19; Jdg 1:23; Jos 16:3 **14** See Jos 15:9 **15** Jos 15:9 **16** Jos 15:8; Jos 15:7 **17** Jos 15:6 **18** Jos 15:6

heritance of the sons of Benjamin, ac-
cording to their families and according
to its borders all around.
21 Now the cities of the tribe of the
sons of Benjamin according to their
families were Jericho and Beth-hoglah
and Emek-keziz,
22 and Beth-arabah and Zemaraim
and Bethel,
23 and Avvim and Parah and Ophrah,
24 and Chephar-ammoni and Oph-
ni and Geba; twelve cities with their
villages;
25 Gibeon and Ramah and Beeroth,
26 and Mizpeh and Chephirah and
Mozah,
27 and Rekem and Irpeel and Taralah,
28 and Zelah, Haeleph and the Jeb-
usite (that is, Jerusalem), Gibeah,
Kiriath; fourteen cities with their vil-
lages. This is the inheritance of [the
tribe of] the sons of Benjamin accord-
ing to their families (clans).

Territory of Simeon

19 THEN THE second lot fell to
Simeon, to the tribe of the sons
of Simeon according to their families
(clans), and their inheritance was with-
in the inheritance of the sons of Judah.
2 So they had as their inheritance
Beersheba or Sheba and Moladah,
3 and Hazar-shual and Balah and
Ezem,
4 and Eltolad and Bethul and Hor-
mah,
5 and Ziklag and Beth-marcaboth
and Hazar-susah,
6 and Beth-lebaoth and Sharuhen;
thirteen cities with their villages;
7 Ain, Rimmon and Ether and Ashan;
four cities with their villages;
8 and all the villages which were
around these cities as far as Baalath-
beer, Ramah of the Negev (South coun-
try). This was the inheritance of the
tribe of the sons of Simeon according
to their families.
9 The inheritance of the sons of Sim-
eon *was taken* from the portion of
the sons of Judah, for the share of the
sons of Judah was too large for them;
so the sons of Simeon received an in-
heritance within Judah's inheritance.

Territory of Zebulun

10 The third lot came up for [the tribe
of] the sons of Zebulun according to
their families. The territory of their
inheritance extended to Sarid.
11 Then its border went up westward
and on to Maralah, and reached to
Dabbesheth and reached to the brook
east of Jokneam.
12 Then it turned from Sarid east to-
ward the sunrise as far as the border
of Chisloth-tabor, and it proceeded to
Daberath and on up to Japhia.
13 From there it continued east to-
ward the sunrise to Gath-hepher and to
Eth-kazin, and proceeded to Rimmon
which turns toward Neah.
14 The border circled it on the north
to Hannathon, ending at the Valley of
Iphtahel.
15 Included were Kattah and Nahalal
and Shimron and Idalah and Bethle-
hem; twelve cities with their villages.
16 This was the inheritance of the
sons of Zebulun according to their
families, these cities with their villages.

Territory of Issachar

17 The fourth lot fell to [the tribe of]
Issachar, to the sons of Issachar ac-
cording to their families.
18 Their territory included: Jezreel
and Chesulloth and Shunem,
19 and Hapharaim and Shion and
Anaharath,
20 and Rabbith and Kishion and Ebez,
21 and Remeth and En-gannim and
En-haddah and Beth-pazzez.
22 The border reached to Tabor and
Shahazumah and Beth-shemesh, and
their border ended at the Jordan; six-
teen cities with their villages.
23 This was the inheritance of the tribe
of the sons of Issachar according to their
families, the cities and their villages.

Territory of Asher

24 The fifth lot fell to the tribe of the
sons of Asher according to their families.
25 Their territory was Helkath and
Hali and Beten and Achshaph,
26 and Allammelech and Amad and
Mishal; and on the west it reached to
Carmel and to Shihor-libnath.

28 Jos 15:8 **CHAPTER 19** **1** ver. 9 **2** 1Ch 4:28 **9** ver. 1 **11** Ge 49:13; Jos 12:22

27 Then it turned eastward to Beth-dagon and reached Zebulun and the Valley of Iphtahel northward to Beth-emek and Neiel, and continued in the north to Cabul,

28 and Ebron and Rehob and Hammon and Kanah, as far as Great Sidon.

29 Then the border turned to Ramah, [reaching] to the fortified city of Tyre; and it turned to Hosah, and it ended at the [Mediterranean] sea at the region of Achzib.

30 Included were Ummah, and Aphek and Rehob; twenty-two cities with their villages.

31 This was the inheritance of the tribe of the sons of Asher according to their families, these cities with their villages.

Territory of Naphtali

32 The sixth lot fell to [the tribe of] the sons of Naphtali according to their families.

33 Their border ran from Heleph, from the oak in Zaanannim and Adami-nekeb and Jabneel, as far as Lakkum, and it ended at the Jordan.

34 Then the border turned westward to Aznoth-tabor and went from there to Hukkok; and it reached Zebulun on the south and reached Asher on the west, and to Judah toward the east at the Jordan.

35 The fortified cities were Ziddim, Zer, and Hammath, Rakkath and Chinnereth,

36 and Adamah and Ramah and Hazor,

37 and Kedesh and Edrei and En-hazor,

38 and Yiron and Migdal-el, Horem and Beth-anath and Beth-shemesh; nineteen cities with their villages.

39 This was the inheritance of the tribe of the sons of Naphtali according to their families, the cities and their villages.

Territory of Dan

40 The seventh lot fell to the tribe of the sons of Dan according to their families.

41 The territory of their inheritance included Zorah and Eshtaol and Ir-shemesh,

42 and Shaalabbin and Aijalon and Ithlah,

43 and Elon and Timnah and Ekron,

44 and Eltekeh and Gibbethon and Baalath,

45 and Jehud and Bene-berak and Gath-rimmon,

46 and Me-jarkon and Rakkon, with the territory opposite Joppa.

47 The territory of the sons of Dan went beyond these; so the sons of Dan went up to fight against Leshem (Laish) and captured it. Then they struck it with the edge of the sword and took possession of it and settled there [between the tribes of Naphtali and Manasseh]; they renamed Leshem, Dan, after the name of their father (ancestor) Dan. [Judg 1:34; 18:7–10, 27]

48 This was the inheritance of the tribe of the sons of Dan according to their families (clans), these cities with their villages.

49 When they had finished dividing the land for inheritance by its borders, the Israelites gave an inheritance among them to Joshua the son of Nun.

50 According to the command of the LORD they gave him the city for which he asked—Timnath-serah in the hill country of Ephraim. So he built the city and settled in it.

51 These are the inheritances which Eleazar the priest, Joshua the son of Nun, and the heads of the households of the tribes of the sons of Israel distributed by lot in Shiloh before the LORD at the doorway of the Tent of Meeting. So they finished dividing the land.

19:50 Commandments — The account of the distribution of the land began with the recognition of Caleb's faithfulness to God. The conclusion recognizes Joshua as one who also believed God. Joshua's extreme service and faithfulness was rewarded by the Lord's command. When we delight to obey the word of the Lord, He also delights in giving us the desires of our hearts (Ps 37:4).

28 Jos 11:8; Jdg 1:31 **29** Jdg 1:31 **34** Dt 33:23 **35** Dt 3:17; Jos 11:2; 12:3; Mk 6:53; Lk 5:1 **42** Jdg 1:35
47 See Jdg 18; Jdg 18:29 **50** Jos 24:30; 1Ch 7:24 **51** Nu 34:17; Jos 14:1; Jos 18:1,10

Six Cities of Refuge

20 THE LORD spoke to Joshua,
saying,
2“Speak to the Israelites, saying,
‘Designate the cities of refuge (asylum),
of which I spoke to you through Moses,
3so that the person (manslayer)
who kills any person unintentionally,
without premeditation, may flee there,
and they shall be your refuge from the
blood avenger. [Num 35:10ff]
4‘He shall flee to one of these cities,
and shall stand at the entrance of the
gate of the city and explain his case to
the elders of that city; and they shall
take him into [the protection of] the
city and give him a place [to stay], so
that he may live among them.
5‘If the blood avenger pursues him,
they shall not hand the offender (manslayer)
over to him, because he killed
his neighbor unintentionally *and* without
premeditation and did not hate him
beforehand.
6‘He shall live in that city until he
has stood before the congregation for
judgment [and if acquitted of murder
he must stay there], until the death of
the one who is the high priest in those
days. Then the offender (manslayer)
shall return to his own city and his
own house from which he fled.’ ”
7So they set apart *and* consecrated
Kedesh in Galilee in the hill country of
Naphtali, and Shechem in the hill country
of Ephraim, and Kiriath-arba (that
is, Hebron) in the hill country of Judah.
8Beyond the Jordan east of Jericho,
they designated Bezer in the wilderness
on the plain from the tribe of
Reuben, and Ramoth in Gilead from
the tribe of Gad, and Golan in Bashan
from the tribe of Manasseh.
9These were the appointed cities for
all the Israelites and for the stranger
sojourning (living temporarily) among
them, so that whoever killed any person
unintentionally may flee there,
and not die by the hand of the blood
avenger until he had stood before the
congregation [for judgment].

Forty-eight Cities of the Levites

21 THEN THE heads of the households
of the Levites came to
Eleazar the priest, and Joshua the son
of Nun, and the heads of the households
of the tribes of the sons of Israel.
2They spoke to them at Shiloh in the
land of Canaan, saying, “The LORD
commanded Moses to give us cities
to live in, with their pasture lands for
our cattle.”
3So the sons of Israel gave the Levites
from their inheritance these
[forty-eight] cities and their pasture
lands, in accordance with the command
of the LORD.
4The [first] lot (allotment) came out
for the families of the Kohathites. So
those Levites who were sons (descendants)
of Aaron the priest received
thirteen cities by lot from the tribe of
Judah and from the tribe of Simeon
and from the tribe of Benjamin.
5The rest of the sons of Kohath received
ten cities by lot from the families
of the tribe of Ephraim and from
the tribe of Dan and from the half-tribe
of Manasseh.
6The sons of Gershon received thirteen
cities by lot from the families of
the tribe of Issachar and from the tribe
of Asher and from the tribe of Naphtali
and from the half-tribe of Manasseh
in Bashan.

20:3 *unintentionally.* God’s laws made allowance for motive and intent, just as modern criminal codes distinguish unintentional killing from murder. The blood avenger was a close relative who was the “protector of family rights.” (Ruth 3:13 and 4:1 translate the word used here for “blood avenger” as “close relative”.) God did not give license to take revenge however. He has clearly reserved that task for Himself alone (Dt 32:35; Isa 34:8; Ro 12:19). God’s provision of these cities of refuge put a limit on private acts of vengeance.

20:7 – 8 *set apart and consecrated.* The cities of refuge were evenly distributed so that none was more than a day’s journey from any part of Israel’s land.

21:4 – 8 *by lot.* Even though this seems as if it was done by chance, we know God was in control of every aspect of the inheritance process.

CHAPTER 20 **2** Ex 21:13; Nu 35:6,11,14; Dt 19:2,9 **5** Nu 35:12 **6** Nu 35:12,25 **7** Jos 21:32; 1Ch 6:76; Jos 21:21; 2Ch 10:1; Jos 14:15; 21:11,13; Lk 1:39 **8** Dt 4:43; Jos 21:36; 1Ch 6:78; Jos 21:38; 1Ki 22:3; Jos 21:27 **9** Nu 35:15; ver. 6 **CHAPTER 21** **1** Jos 14:1; 17:4 **2** Jos 18:1; Nu 35:2 **4** ver. 8,19; See Jos 24:33 **5** ver. 20 **6** ver. 27

7 The sons of Merari according to
their families received twelve cities
from the tribe of Reuben and from
the tribe of Gad and from the tribe of
Zebulun.
8 The sons of Israel gave by lot to the
Levites these cities with their pasture
lands, as the LORD had commanded
through Moses.
9 They gave these cities which are
mentioned here by name from the tribe
of the sons of Judah and from the tribe
of the sons of Simeon;
10 and they were for the sons of Aar-
on, one of the families of the Kohath-
ites, of the sons of Levi, because the lot
fell to them first.
11 They gave them [the city of]
Kiriath-arba, *Arba being* the father
of Anak (that is, Hebron) in the hill
country of Judah, with its surrounding
pasture lands.
12 But the fields of the city and its
villages they had given to Caleb the
son of Jephunneh as his property.
13 So to the sons of Aaron the priest
they gave Hebron, the city of refuge for
anyone who committed manslaughter,
with its pasture lands, and Libnah with
its pasture lands,
14 and Jattir with its pasture lands
and Eshtemoa with its pasture lands,
15 and Holon with its pasture lands
and Debir with its pasture lands,
16 and Ain with its pasture lands and
Juttah with its pasture lands *and* Beth-
shemesh with its pasture lands; nine
cities from these two tribes (Judah and
Simeon).
17 From the tribe of Benjamin, Gibeon
with its pasture lands, and Geba with
its pasture lands,
18 Anathoth with its pasture lands
and Almon with its pasture lands; four
cities.
19 All the cities of the sons of Aaron,
the priests, were thirteen cities with
their pasture lands.
20 Then the cities from the tribe of
Ephraim were allotted to the families
of the sons of Kohath, the Levites, *even
to* the rest of the sons of Kohath.
21 They gave them Shechem, the city
of refuge for anyone who committed
manslaughter, with its pasture lands,
in the hill country of Ephraim, and
Gezer with its pasture lands,
22 and Kibzaim with its pasture lands
and Beth-horon with its pasture lands;
four cities.
23 From the tribe of Dan, Eltekeh with
its pasture lands, Gibbethon with its
pasture lands,
24 Aijalon with its pasture lands,
Gath-rimmon with its pasture lands;
four cities.
25 From the half-tribe of Manasseh,
they allotted Taanach with its pasture
lands and Gath-rimmon with its pas-
ture lands; two cities.
26 All the cities with their pasture
lands for the families of the rest of the
sons of Kohath *totaled* ten.
27 To the sons of Gershon, one of
the families of the Levites, *they gave*
from the other half-tribe of Manasseh,
[the city of] Golan in Bashan, the city
of refuge for anyone who committed
manslaughter, with its pasture lands,
and Be-eshterah with its pasture lands;
two cities.
28 From the tribe of Issachar, *they
gave* Kishion with its pasture lands,
Daberath with its pasture lands,
29 Jarmuth with its pasture lands,
and En-gannim with its pasture lands;
four cities.
30 From the tribe of Asher, *they gave*
Mishal with its pasture lands, Abdon
with its pasture lands,
31 Helkath with its pasture lands and
Rehob with its pasture lands; four cit-
ies.
32 From the tribe of Naphtali, *they
gave* Kedesh in Galilee, the city of ref-
uge for anyone who committed man-
slaughter, with its pasture lands and
Hammoth-dor with its pasture lands
and Kartan with its pasture lands;
three cities.
33 All the cities of the Gershonites ac-
cording to their families were thirteen
cities with their pasture lands.
34 To the families of the sons of Me-
rari, the rest of the Levites, *they gave*
from the tribe of Zebulun, Jokneam

7 ver. 34 **8** ver. 3; Nu 35:2 **11** 1Ch 6:55; Jos 15:13,14; Jos 20:7; Lk 1:39 **12** Jos 14:14; 1Ch 6:56 **13** 1Ch 6:57; Jos 15:54; 20:7; Jos 15:42 **14** Jos 15:48; Jos 15:50 **15** Jos 15:49 **16** Jos 15:42; Jos 15:55; Jos 15:10 **17** Jos 18:25 **20** ver. 5; 1Ch 6:66 **21** Jos 20:7 **27** ver. 6; 1Ch 6:71; Jos 20:8 **32** Jos 20:7 **34** ver. 7; See 1Ch 6:77

with its pasture lands and Kartah with
its pasture lands,
35 Dimnah with its pasture lands and
Nahalal with its pasture lands; four
cities.
36 From the tribe of Reuben, *they
gave* Bezer with its pasture lands and
Jahaz with its pasture lands,
37 Kedemoth with its pasture lands
and Mephaath with its pasture lands;
four cities.
38 From the tribe of Gad, *they gave*
Ramoth in Gilead, the city of refuge for
anyone who committed manslaughter,
with its pasture lands and Mahanaim
with its pasture lands,
39 Heshbon with its pasture lands
and Jazer with its pasture lands; four
cities in all.
40 All [these were] the cities of the
sons of Merari according to their fam-
ilies, the rest of the families of the Le-
vites; and their lot was twelve cities.
41 All the cities of the Levites in the
midst of the property of the sons of Is-
rael were forty-eight cities with their
pasture lands.
42 These cities each had its surround-
ing pasture lands; so it was with all
these cities.
43 So the LORD gave Israel all the land
which He had sworn to give to their
fathers (ancestors), and they took pos-
session of it and lived in it.
44 The LORD gave them rest [from
conflict] on every side, in accordance
with everything that He had sworn to
their fathers, and not one of all their
enemies stood before them [in battle];
the LORD handed over all their enemies
to them.
45 Not one of the good promises which
the LORD had spoken to the house of Is-
rael failed; all had come to pass.

Tribes beyond Jordan Return

22 THEN JOSHUA called the Reu-
benites and the Gadites and the
half-tribe of Manasseh,
2 and said to them, "You have kept
all that Moses the servant of the LORD
commanded you, and have listened to
and obeyed my voice in everything
that I commanded you.
3 "You have not deserted your broth-
ers these many days to this day, but
have [carefully] kept the obligation of
the commandment of the LORD your
God.
4 "And now the LORD your God has
given rest to your brothers, as He has
promised them; so turn now and go to
your tents, to the land of your posses-
sion, which Moses the servant of the
LORD gave you beyond the [east side
of the] Jordan.
5 "Only be very careful *and* diligently
observe the commandment and the
law which Moses the servant of the
LORD has commanded you to love the
LORD your God and walk in all His
ways and keep His commandments
and hold fast to Him and serve Him
with all your heart and with all your
soul [your very life]."
6 So Joshua blessed them and sent
them away, and they went to their
tents.
7 Now to the one-half of the tribe of
Manasseh Moses had given *a posses-
sion* in Bashan, but to the other half
Joshua gave *a possession* on the west
side of the Jordan among their broth-
ers. So when Joshua sent them away
to their tents, he blessed them,
8 and he said to them, "Return to
your tents with great riches and with
very much livestock, with silver, gold,
bronze, iron, and with very many

21:43 – 45 *which He had sworn.* Again we see the nature of our God — not only did He keep every promise, He also guaranteed that His people would have rest.

22:5 Perseverance — Past victories do not lessen the responsibility for present faithfulness. Joshua impressed upon the people, especially the tribes of Reuben, Gad, and Manasseh (because they would be living in isolation from the rest of Israel), the urgent need to continue to zealously serve God. Our zeal for the Lord cannot cease because a crisis has passed. There is no certificate of discharge from the army of Christ.

36 Jos 20:8 **38** Jos 20:8 **41** Nu 35:7 **43** Ge 13:15; 15:18; 26:3; 28:4,13 **44** Jos 11:23; 22:4; Dt 7:24 **45** Jos 23:14
CHAPTER 22 **2** Nu 32:20; Dt 3:18; Jos 1:16,17 **4** Nu 32:33 **5** Dt 6:6,17; 11:22; Jer 12:16; Dt 10:12 **6** Ge 47:7; Ex 39:43; Jos 14:13; 2Sa 6:18; Lk 24:50 **7** Jos 17:5 **8** Nu 31:27; 1Sa 30:24

clothes; divide the spoil of your enemies with your brothers (fellow tribesmen)."

9 So the sons (descendants) of Reuben and the sons of Gad and the half-tribe of Manasseh returned *home* and departed from the [other] sons (western tribes) of Israel at Shiloh which is in the land of Canaan, to go to the land of Gilead, to the land of their own which they had possessed, in accordance with the command of the LORD through Moses.

The Offensive Altar

10 When they came to the region of the Jordan which is in the land of Canaan, the sons of Reuben and the sons of Gad and the half-tribe of Manasseh built an altar there by the Jordan, an altar that was great to behold.

11 And the [other] sons of Israel heard it said, "Look, the sons of Reuben and the sons of Gad and the half-tribe of Manasseh have built an altar at the edge of the land of Canaan, in the region [west] of the Jordan, on the side *belonging to* the sons of Israel."

12 When the sons of Israel heard of it, the whole congregation of the Israelites gathered at Shiloh to make war against them.

13 Then the sons of Israel sent Phinehas the son of Eleazar the priest to the sons of Reuben and the sons of Gad and the half-tribe of Manasseh, in the land of Gilead,

14 and with him ten leaders, one leader from each father's household from each of the tribes of Israel; and each one was the head of his father's household among the thousands of Israel.

15 They came to the sons of Reuben and the sons of Gad and the half-tribe of Manasseh, in the land of Gilead, and they said to them,

16 "This is what the entire congregation of the LORD says, 'What is this disloyal *and* unfaithful act which you have committed against the God of Israel, so as to turn away from following the LORD this day, by building yourselves an altar, to rebel against the LORD this day?

17 'Is the wrongdoing (idolatry) of Peor not enough for us, from which we have not cleansed ourselves to this day, even though the affliction [in which twenty-four thousand died] came on the congregation of the LORD, [Num 25:1–9]

18 that you would turn away this day from following the LORD? If you rebel against the LORD today, He will be angry with the entire congregation of Israel tomorrow.

19 'If, however, the land of your possession is unclean, then cross into the land of the possession of the LORD, where the LORD's tabernacle is situated, and settle down among us. But do not rebel against the LORD, or rebel against us by building an altar for yourselves, besides the altar of the LORD our God [at Shiloh].

20 'Did not Achan the son of Zerah act unfaithfully in the things under the ban, and [as a result God's] wrath came on the entire congregation of Israel? And that man did not perish alone in his wrongdoing.' " [Josh 7:1–26]

21 Then the sons of Reuben and the sons of Gad and the half-tribe of Manasseh answered and said to the heads of the families of Israel,

22 "The Mighty One, God, the LORD, the Mighty One, God, the LORD! He

---

22:11 – 12 *have built an altar.* The Bible does not reveal why this altar was built until the events have developed into a full blown crisis. God had commanded Israel not to offer burnt offerings or sacrifices at any location except the tabernacle (Lev 17:8 – 9) and not to worship other gods (Dt 13:12 – 15). The punishment for violating both laws was death. This was why Israel gathered together to go to war against the three apparently erring tribes.

22:16 – 18 *disloyal and unfaithful act.* This is sometimes translated "treacherous" and is the same word used to describe Achan's sin (7:1). No one can sin in isolation. If the tribes of the east of the Jordan were indeed sinning, then the entire nation would feel the effects, as in the case of Achan.

9 Nu 32:1,26,29 **11** Dt 13:12; Jdg 20:12 **12** Jdg 20:1 **13** Dt 13:14; Jdg 20:12; Ex 6:25; Nu 25:7,11-13 **14** Nu 1:4 **16** See Lev 17:8,9; Dt 12:13,14 **17** Nu 25:3,4; Dt 4:3 **18** Nu 16:22 **19** Jos 18:1 **20** Jos 7:1,5 **22** Dt 10:17; Job 10:7; 23:10; Jer 12:3; 2Co 11:11,31

knows, and may Israel itself know. If it was in rebellion, or if in an unfaithful act against the LORD, do not save us this day!
23"If we have built an altar for ourselves to turn away from following the LORD, or if [we did so] to offer a burnt offering or grain offering on it, or if to offer sacrifices of peace offerings on it, may the LORD Himself require it [of us and hold us responsible].
24"But in truth we have done this out of concern, for a reason, saying, 'In time to come your sons (descendants) may say to our sons, "What claim do you have to the LORD, the God of Israel?
25"For the LORD has made the Jordan a border between us and you, you sons of Reuben and sons of Gad; you have no part in the LORD." So your sons (descendants) may cause our sons to stop fearing the LORD.'
26"So we said, 'Let us prepare *and* build an altar, not for burnt offering or for sacrifice,
27but to be a witness between us and you and between the generations after us, that we are to perform the service of the LORD before Him with our burnt offerings, and with our sacrifices and with our peace offerings, so that your sons (descendants) will not say to our sons in time to come, "You have no part in the LORD." '
28"So we said, 'If your descendants should say this to us or to our descendants in time to come, then we can reply, "See the copy of the altar of the LORD which our fathers made, not for burnt offering or for sacrifice, but rather it is a witness between us and you." '
29"Far be it from us that we should rebel against the LORD and turn away from following the LORD this day, by building an altar for burnt offering, for grain offering or for sacrifice, besides the altar of the LORD our God which is before His tabernacle [in Shiloh]."
30So when Phinehas the priest and the leaders of the congregation and heads of the families of Israel who were with him, heard the words which the sons of Reuben and the sons of Gad and the sons of Manasseh spoke, it pleased them.
31Phinehas the son of Eleazar the priest said to the sons of Reuben and the sons of Gad and the sons of Manasseh, "Today we know that the LORD is among us, because you have not committed this unfaithful act against the LORD; indeed you have saved Israel from the hand of the LORD."
32Then Phinehas the son of Eleazar the priest and the leaders returned from the sons of Reuben and the sons of Gad, from the land of Gilead to the land of Canaan, to the sons of Israel, and brought back word to them.
33The report pleased the sons of Israel, and the sons of Israel blessed God; and they said no more about going to battle against them to destroy the land in which the sons of Reuben and the sons of Gad were living.
34The sons of Reuben and the sons of Gad called the altar *Witness;* "For it is a witness between us that the LORD is God."

Joshua's Farewell Address

23 A LONG time after that, when the LORD had given Israel rest from all their enemies on every side, and Joshua had grown old and advanced in years,

---

22:23–28 *out of concern.* The tribes to the east of the Jordan were afraid that geographical distance would isolate them and in time cause the Israelites west of the Jordan to reject them. Thus they built the altar to help prevent the existing unity from being lost. The eastern tribes were careful to label the altar for what it really was — a replica to serve as a witness for future generations.
22:30–31 Prudence — Jumping to conclusions can bring one to the brink of disaster. While their motives were good (maintaining purity), they did not stop to find out what was really going on. This incident provides us with a good example of the importance of communicating before we act. Even when we are dealing with a case of serious sin (as the western tribes thought they were), the first reaction should be to try and persuade the sinner to repent and return to the Lord.

23 Dt 18:19; 1Sa 20:16 **27** ver. 34; Ge 31:48; Jos 24:27; Dt 12:5 **29** Dt 12:13,14 **31** Lev 26:11,12; 2Ch 15:2 **33** 1Ch 29:20; Neh 8:6; Da 2:19; Lk 2:28 **CHAPTER 23** **1** Jos 21:44; 22:4; Jos 13:1

2 that Joshua called all Israel, their elders and their heads and their judges and their officers, and said to them, “I am old and advanced in years.

3 “And you have seen all that the LORD your God has done to all these nations for your sake; for the LORD your God is He who has been fighting for you. [Ex 14:14]

4 “See, I have allotted to you these nations that remain as an inheritance for your tribes, with all the nations which I have cut off, from the Jordan [on the east] to the Great [Mediterranean] Sea toward the setting sun.

5 “The LORD your God will push them away from before you and drive them out of your sight and you will take possession of their land, just as the LORD your God promised you.

6 “Be steadfast *and* very determined to keep and to do everything that is written in the Book of the Law of Moses, so that you do not turn aside from it to the right or the left,

7 so that you do not associate with these nations which remain among you, or mention the name of their gods, or make anyone swear [an oath by them], or serve them, or bow down to them.

8 “But you are to cling to the LORD your God, just as you have done to this day.

9 “For the LORD has driven out great and mighty nations from before you; and as for you, no man has been able to stand [in opposition] before you to this day.

10 “One of your men puts to flight a thousand, for the LORD your God is He who is fighting for you, just as He promised you.

11 “So be very careful *and* watchful of yourselves to love the LORD your God.

12 “For if you ever turn back and cling to the rest of these nations, these that are left among you, and intermarry with them, so that you associate with them and they with you,

13 know *and* understand with certainty that the LORD your God will not continue to drive these nations out from before you; but they will be a snare and trap to you, and a whip on your sides and thorns in your eyes, until you perish from this good land which the LORD your God has given you.

14 “Now behold, today I am going the way of all the earth, and you know in all your hearts and in all your souls that not one word of all the good words which the LORD your God has promised concerning you has failed; all have been fulfilled for you, not one of them has failed.

15 “It shall come about that just as every good word which the LORD your God spoke *and* promised to you has been fulfilled for you, so the LORD will bring upon you every bad thing [about which He warned you], until He has destroyed *and* eliminated you from this good land which the LORD your God has given you.

16 “When you transgress (violate) the covenant of the LORD your God, which He commanded you [to follow], and

---

23:3 *He who has been fighting for you.* This is a reminder that the land belonged to the Lord and that He gave it to Israel.

23:10 *One of your men puts to flight.* The power seen in God’s people was so dramatic it had to be miraculous.

23:11 Duty — Certain outlines of duty are imposed on all mankind (Mic 6:8). We know that one man’s specific duty may differ from another’s, but all share a single common requirement: all must give account before God of what they have done or left undone. The church cannot decide how well each person is performing; there is no “spiritual commitment meter” to give an exact rating of each person’s fulfillment of duty. Each person is responsible to maintain his or her own spiritual life.

23:12 – 13 *intermarry with them.* Years later, Solomon ignored this command and proved how destructive the sin of being unequally yoked could be (1Ki 3:1; 11:1 – 8; 2Co 6:14).

23:16 *perish . . . from the good land.* This warning saw its most dramatic fulfillment when Judah was carried into Babylon because of its repeated

2 Dt 31:28; Jos 24:1; 1Ch 28:1 **3** Ex 14:14; Jos 10:14,42 **4** Jos 13:2,6; 18:10 **5** Ex 23:30; 33:2; 34:11; Dt 11:23; Jos 13:6; Nu 33:53 **6** Jos 1:7; Dt 5:32; 28:14 **7** Ex 23:33; Dt 7:2,3; Pr 4:14; Eph 5:11; Ex 23:13; Jer 5:7; Zep 1:5; See Nu 32:38 **8** Dt 10:20; Jos 22:5 **9** Dt 11:23; Jos 1:5 **10** Lev 26:8; Dt 32:30; Ex 14:14; Dt 3:22 **11** Jos 22:5 **12** 2Pe 2:20,21; Dt 7:3 **13** Jdg 2:3; Ex 23:33; 1Ki 11:4 **14** 1Ki 2:2; Lk 21:33 **15** Dt 28:63; Dt 28:15,16

you go and serve other gods and bow
down to them, then the anger of the
LORD will be kindled against you, and
you shall perish quickly from the good
land which He has given you."

Joshua Reviews Israel's History

24 THEN JOSHUA gathered all
the tribes of Israel to Shechem,
and called for the elders of Israel and
for their heads and for their judges
and for their officers; they presented
themselves before God.
2 Joshua said to all the people, "This
is what the LORD, the God of Israel,
says, 'Your fathers, including Terah,
the father of Abraham and the father
of Nahor, lived beyond the [Euphrates]
River in ancient times; and they served
other gods.
3 'Then I took your father Abraham
from beyond the [Euphrates] River and
led him through all the land of Ca-
naan, and multiplied his descendants,
and I gave him Isaac.
4 'To Isaac I gave Jacob and Esau,
and to Esau I gave [the hill country of]
Mount Seir to possess; but Jacob and
his sons went down to Egypt.
5 'Then I sent Moses and Aaron, and
I plagued Egypt by what I did in its
midst; and afterward I brought you out.
6 'Then I brought your fathers out of
Egypt, and you came to the sea; and the
Egyptians pursued your fathers with
chariots and horsemen to the Red Sea.
7 'When they cried out to the LORD
[for help], He put darkness between
you and the Egyptians, and brought
the sea upon them and covered them;
and your own eyes saw what I did in
Egypt. And you lived in the wilderness
a long time (forty years). [Josh 5:6]
8 'Then I brought you into the land of
the Amorites who lived on the other
side of the Jordan, and they fought
with you; and I gave them into your
hand, and you took possession of their
land and I destroyed them before you.
9 'Then Balak the son of Zippor, king
of Moab, arose and fought against Is-
rael, and he sent and called Balaam
the son of Beor to curse you.
10 'But I would not listen to Balaam.
Therefore he had to bless you, so I saved
you from Balak's hand. [Deut 23:5]
11 'You crossed the Jordan and came
to Jericho; and the citizens of Jericho
fought against you, as did the Amorite
and the Perizzite and the Canaanite
and the Hittite and the Girgashite, the
Hivite and the Jebusite; and so I gave
them into your hand.
12 'I sent the hornet [that is, the terror
of you] before you, which drove the
two kings of the Amorites out before
you; but it was not by your sword or by
your bow. [Ex 23:27, 28; Deut 2:25; 7:20]
13 'I gave you a land for which you
did not labor, and cities which you did
not build, and you live in them; you eat
from vineyards and olive groves which
you did not plant.'
14 "Now, therefore, fear the LORD and
serve Him in sincerity and in truth;
remove the gods which your fathers
served on the other side of the [Eu-
phrates] River and in Egypt, and serve
the LORD.
15 "If it is unacceptable in your sight
to serve the LORD, choose for your-
selves this day whom you will serve:

---

rebellion against God (2Ki 25). The saddest thing is that Israel's rebellion began almost immediately. God lovingly gave them every good thing, but when they disobeyed, they had to be punished.

24:1 *Shechem.* Shechem was a site of ancient religious significance and covenant making going back to Abraham's day (Ge 12:6; 33:18 – 20).

24:13 *a land for which you did not labor.* This fulfills the promise given to Moses in Dt 6:10 – 11. The land was a gift from God to His people. In a similar sense, He has given us another gift for which we did not labor. The gift of salvation, through Jesus Christ, cannot be bought or paid for; it is graciously given from a loving God to those who will accept it.

24:15 *as for me and my house.* Joshua's famous words show the stand we must take — on the side of the living God.

CHAPTER 24 **1** Ge 35:4; Jos 23:2; 1Sa 10:19 **2** Ge 11:26,31; ver. 14 **3** Ge 12:1; Ac 7:2,3; Ps 127:3 **4** Ge 25:24-26; Ge 36:8; Dt 2:5; Ge 46:1,6 **5** Ex 3:10; Ex 7; 8; 9; 10 **6** Ex 12:37,51; Ex 14:2; Ex 14:9 **7** Ex 14:20; Ex 14:27,28; Dt 4:34; Jos 5:6 **8** Nu 21:21,33; Dt 2:32 **9** Jdg 11:25; Nu 22:5 **10** Dt 23:5; Nu 23:11,20 **11** Jos 3:14,17; Jos 6:1; 10:1 **12** Ex 23:28; Dt 7:20; Ps 44:3,6 **13** Dt 6:10,11 **14** Dt 10:12; 1Sa 12:24; Ge 17:1; 20:5; Dt 18:13; 2Co 1:12; ver. 2,23; Eze 20:18; Eze 20:7,8; 23:3 **15** Ru 1:15; 1Ki 18:21; ver. 2; Ex 23:24,32,33; Ge 18:19

whether the gods which your fathers
served that were on the other side of
the River, or the gods of the Amorites
in whose land you live; but as for me
and my house, we will serve the LORD."
16 The people answered, "Far be it
from us to abandon (reject) the LORD
to serve other gods;
17 for the LORD our God is He who
brought us and our fathers up out of
the land of Egypt, from the house of
bondage, and who did these great
signs (miracles) in our sight and kept
us safe all along the way that we went
and among all the peoples among
whom we passed.
18 "The LORD drove all the peoples out
from before us, even the Amorites who
lived in the land. We also will serve the
LORD, for He is our God."
19 Then Joshua said to the people,
"You will not be able to serve the LORD
[if you serve any other gods], for He
is a holy God; He is a jealous God
[demanding what is rightfully and
uniquely His]. He will not forgive your
transgression [of His law] or your sins.
20 "If you do abandon (reject) the
LORD and serve foreign gods, then He
will turn and do you harm and con-
sume *and* destroy you after He has
done you good."
21 The people said to Joshua, "No, but
we will serve [only] the LORD."
22 Joshua then said to the people,
"You are witnesses against yourselves
that you have chosen for yourselves the
LORD, to serve Him." And they said,
"We are witnesses."
23 "Now then, remove the foreign
gods which are among you, and in-
cline your hearts toward the LORD, the
God of Israel."
24 The people said to Joshua, "We will
serve the LORD our God and we will
listen to *and* obey His voice."
25 So Joshua made a covenant with
the people that day, and made for them
a statute and an ordinance at Shechem.
26 And Joshua wrote these words in
the Book of the Law of God. Then he
took a large stone and set it up there
under the oak that was in [the court-
yard of] the sanctuary of the LORD.
27 Joshua then said to all the people,
"Look, this stone shall serve as a wit-
ness against us, for it has heard all the
words of the LORD which He spoke to
us; so it shall be a witness against you,
so that [afterward] you do not deny
your God."
28 Then Joshua sent the people away,
each to [the territory of] his inheri-
tance.

Joshua's Death and Burial

29 It happened after these things that
Joshua the son of Nun, the servant of
the LORD, died, at the age of a hundred
and ten years.
30 They buried him in the territory
of his inheritance in Timnath-serah,
which is in the hill country of Ephraim,
on the north side of Mount Gaash.
31 Israel served the LORD all the days
of Joshua and all the days of the elders
who outlived Joshua, and had known
all the works of the LORD which He had
done for Israel.
32 Now they buried the bones of
Joseph, which the children of Israel
brought up from Egypt, at Shechem,
in the plot of land which Jacob had
bought from the sons of Hamor the
father of Shechem for a hundred pieces
of money; and it became the inheri-
tance of the sons of Joseph.
33 And Eleazar [the priest], the son
of Aaron died; and they buried him
at Gibeah [on the hill] of Phinehas his
son, which had been given to him in
the hill country of Ephraim.

24:32 *the bones of Joseph.* The brief account of the transfer of Joseph's body to Canaan from Egypt notes the fulfillment of Joseph's prophecy hundreds of years before (Ge 50:24 – 25).

19 Mt 6:24; 1Sa 6:20; Ex 20:5; Ex 23:21 **20** 1Ch 28:9; Ezr 8:22; Isa 1:28; Jer 17:13; Jos 23:15; Isa 63:10; Ac 7:42 **22** Ps 119:173 **23** ver. 14; Ge 35:2 **25** Ex 15:25; 2Ki 11:17; ver. 1 **26** Dt 31:24; Jdg 9:6; Ge 28:18; Jos 4:3; Ge 35:4 **27** See Ge 31:48,52; Dt 32:1 **28** Jdg 2:6 **29** Jdg 2:8 **30** Jos 19:50 **31** Jdg 2:7; Dt 11:2 **32** Ge 50:25; Ex 13:19; Ge 33:19 **33** Ex 6:25; Jdg 20:28

THE BOOK OF

JUDGES

▸ **AUTHOR:** Although the author of Judges is anonymous, Jewish tradition contained in the Talmud attributes Judges to Samuel. Samuel lived during the time the book could have been written, and he was a principle character in the transition to the next phase. He would have been aware of the events that occur in the book. Samuel certainly was the crucial link between the period of the judges and the period of the kings. His prophetic ministry clearly fits the moral commentary of Judges, and the consistent style and orderly scheme of the book points to a single compiler.

▸ **TIMES:** c. 1380 – 1045 BC ▸ **KEY VERSES:** Jdg 2:20 – 21

▸ **THEME:** During the Book of Judges, the land wasn't fully conquered. There was political chaos. The Israelites appeared to live mostly in the land between the cities of the Philistines, who dominate them much of the time. Two common phrases occur in the book: The first is the Israelites "did evil in the sight of the Lord." The second is "every man did what was right in his own eyes." In the midst of this situation God raises up judges, who in addition to playing the role of adjudicator, also provide leadership in pulling the tribes together to fight the unconquered nations. Most are reluctant. Nevertheless, God is able to use them and demonstrate His power through these individuals.

Jerusalem Is Captured

1 NOW IT came about after the death
of Joshua, that the sons (descendants) of Israel (Jacob) asked the LORD,
"Who shall go up first for us against
the Canaanites, to fight against them?"
2And the LORD said, "Judah shall go
up [first]; behold, I have given the land
into his hand."
3And [the tribe of the sons of] Judah said to [the tribe of the sons of]
Simeon his brother, "Come up with
me into my allotted territory, so that
we may fight against the Canaanites;
and I likewise will go with you into
your allotted territory." So Simeon
went with him.
4Then Judah went up, and the LORD
gave the Canaanites and the Perizzites
into their hand, and they struck down
in defeat ten thousand men at Bezek.
5Then they found Adoni-bezek in
Bezek and fought against him, and
they struck down in defeat the Canaanites and the Perizzites.
6But Adoni-bezek fled; and they pursued him and caught him and cut off
his thumbs and his big toes.

1:1 *Now . . . after the death of Joshua.* Judges begins as the Book of Joshua does, with reference to the death of the previous leader. Yet no new leader was commissioned to lead Israel after Joshua. The tribe of Judah was designated to lead in the fight against the Canaanites, the first hint of the fulfillment of Jacob's prophecy (Ge 49:8 – 12).

1:3 *Judah . . . Simeon.* History bound the tribes of Judah and Simeon together. They were descended from the same mother (Ge 29:33 – 35), and Simeon had inherited land in Judah's territory (Jos 19:1,9).

1:6 – 7 *thumbs and his big toes.* To cut off a warrior's thumbs and big toes would prevent him from ever engaging in battle again, besides subjecting him to pain and humiliation.

CHAPTER 1 **1** Nu 27:21; Jdg 20:18 **2** Ge 49:8 **3** ver. 17 **4** 1Sa 11:8

7 Adoni-bezek said, “Seventy kings
with their thumbs and big toes cut off
used to gather up *scraps of food* under
my table; as I have done [to others], so
God has repaid me.” So they brought
him to Jerusalem, and he died there.
8 Then the sons of Judah fought
against [Jebusite] Jerusalem and cap-
tured it and struck it with the edge of
the sword and set the city on fire.
9 Afterward the sons of Judah went
down to fight against the Canaanites
who lived in the hill country, in the
Negev (South country) and in the low-
land.
10 So Judah went against the Canaan-
ites who lived in Hebron (the name of
Hebron formerly was Kiriath-arba);
and they defeated Sheshai and Ahi-
man and Talmai.

Capture of Other Cities

11 From there [the tribe of] Judah went
against the inhabitants of Debir (the
name of Debir formerly was Kiriath-
sepher [city of books and scribes]).
12 And Caleb said, “Whoever attacks
Kiriath-sepher and captures it, I will
even give him my daughter Achsah
as a wife.”
13 Othniel the son of Kenaz, Caleb’s
younger brother, captured it; so he
gave him his daughter Achsah as a
wife.
14 When she came *to Othniel*, she
persuaded him to [allow her to] ask
her father [Caleb] for a field. Then she
[rode up to Caleb and] dismounted
from her donkey, and Caleb said to her,
“What do you want?”
15 She said to him, “Give me a blessing;
since you have given me the land of the
Negev (South country), give me springs
of water, too.” So Caleb gave her the
upper springs and the lower springs.
16 The sons of [Jethro] the Kenite,
Moses’ father-in-law, went up from the
City of Palms (Jericho) with the sons
of Judah, to the wilderness of Judah
which is in the Negev (South country)
near Arad; and they went and lived
with the people. [Ex 3:1]
17 Then [the warriors of the tribe of]
Judah went with [the warriors of the
tribe of] Simeon his brother, and they
struck the Canaanites living in Ze-
phath and utterly destroyed it. So the
city was called Hormah (destruction).
18 Also [the warriors of] Judah cap-
tured Gaza with its territory and Ash-
kelon with its territory and Ekron with
its territory.
19 The LORD was with Judah, and [the
tribe of] Judah took possession of the
hill country, but they could not dispos-
sess *and* drive out those inhabiting the
valley because they had iron chariots.
20 Then they gave Hebron to Caleb,
as Moses had said, and he drove out
from there the three sons of Anak.
[Josh 14:6, 9]
21 But the sons of Benjamin did not
drive out the Jebusites who inhabited
Jerusalem; so the Jebusites have lived
with the sons of Benjamin in Jerusa-
lem to this day.

1:8 *Jerusalem.* Jerusalem was captured and burned, but not settled. The complete conquest and settlement of Jerusalem was not accomplished until David’s day (2Sa 5:6 – 10).

1:10 *Hebron.* Hebron, about 20 miles southwest of Jerusalem, was where Abraham settled and built an altar (Ge 13:18).

1:16 *the Kenite.* The Kenites were Midianites, descendants of Abraham’s son by Keturah (Ge 25:1 – 4).

1:18 *Gaza . . . Ashkelon . . . Ekron.* Israel was not able to hold these cities for long. By Samson’s day, all three were in Philistine hands again (14:19; 16:1; 1Sa 5:10).

1:21 Unfaithfulness — This verse duplicates Joshua 15:63 almost exactly, except that in Joshua the tribe of Judah is held responsible. Jerusalem lay on the border between Judah and Benjamin; either or both tribes were responsible for driving out the Canaanites. Their failure to do so was not because the task was too hard, but because they did not really take God’s commands and promises seriously. Jerusalem was not claimed for Israel until David came, a man who trusted the Lord for his victories and obeyed His word. Victories for the Lord are won only through faith.

---

7 Lev 24:19; 1Sa 15:33; Jas 2:13 **8** See Jos 15:63 **9** Jos 10:36; 11:21; 15:13 **10** Jos 14:15; 15:13,14 **11** Jos 15:15 **12** Jos 15:16,17 **13** Jdg 3:9 **14** Jos 15:18,19 **15** Ge 33:11 **16** Jdg 4:11,17; 1Sa 15:6; 1Ch 2:55; Dt 34:3; Nu 21:1; 1Sa 15:6 **17** ver. 3; Nu 21:3; Jos 19:4 **18** Jos 11:22 **19** ver. 2; 2Ki 18:7; Jos 17:16,18 **20** Nu 14:24; Dt 1:36; Jos 14:9,13,14; 15:13,14 **21** See Jos 15:63; 18:28

[22]The house of Joseph also went up against Bethel, and the LORD was with them.

[23]The house of Joseph spied out Bethel (now the name of the city was formerly Luz).

[24]The spies saw a man coming out of the city and they said to him, "Please show us the entrance to the city and we will treat you kindly."

[25]So he showed them the entrance to the city, and they struck the city with the edge of the sword, but they let the man and all his family go free.

[26]The man went into the land of the Hittites and built a city and named it Luz, which is its name to this day.

Places Not Conquered

[27]But [the tribe of] Manasseh did not take possession of Beth-shean and its villages, or Taanach and its villages, or the inhabitants of Dor and its villages, or the inhabitants of Ibleam and its villages, or the inhabitants of Megiddo and its villages; so the Canaanites remained in that land.

[28]It happened when Israel became strong, that they put the Canaanites to forced labor, but they did not drive them out completely.

[29]Neither did [the warriors of] Ephraim drive out the Canaanites who were living in Gezer; so the Canaanites lived in Gezer among them.

[30][The warriors of the tribe of] Zebulun did not drive out the inhabitants of Kitron or of Nahalol; so the Canaanites lived among them and were put to forced labor.

[31][The warriors of the tribe of] Asher did not drive out the inhabitants of Acco, or the inhabitants of Sidon, or of Ahlab, or of Achzib, or of Helbah, or of Aphik, or of Rehob.

[32]So the Asherites lived among the Canaanites, the inhabitants of the land, because they did not drive them out.

[33]Neither did [the warriors of] Naphtali drive out the inhabitants of Beth-shemesh, or the inhabitants of Beth-anath, but they lived among the Canaanites, the inhabitants of the land; and the inhabitants of Beth-shemesh and of Beth-anath became forced labor for them.

[34]Then the Amorites forced the sons of Dan [back] into the hill country, for they would not allow them to come down into the valley;

[35]yet the Amorites persisted in living on Mount Heres (the mountain of the sun), in Aijalon, and in Shaalbim; but when the power of the house (descendants) of Joseph became strong *and* prevailed, they became forced labor.

[36]The border of the Amorites ran from the ascent of Akrabbim, from Sela (rock) and upward.

Israel Rebuked

2 NOW THE Angel of the LORD came up from Gilgal to Bochim. And he said, "I brought you up from Egypt and led you to the land which I swore [to give] to your fathers; and I said, 'I will never break My covenant with you, [Ex 20:2; 23:32]

[2]and as for you, you shall not make a covenant with the inhabitants of this land; you shall tear down their altars.' But you have not obeyed Me; what is this that you have done?

[3]"So I also said, 'I will not drive your enemies out before you; but they will be *like thorns* in your sides and their gods will be a snare to you.' "

[4]When the Angel of the LORD had spoken these words to all the Israelites, the people raised their voices and wept.

1:22 *Bethel.* Bethel means "house of God." It was a site with an honored history, beginning with Abraham's first sacrifice to God (Ge 13:3 – 4) and Jacob's revelation from God there (Ge 31:13).
2:1 *the Angel of the LORD.* The angel of the Lord appears as God's representative here, speaking authoritatively to the people about their covenant disobedience.
2:2 *you shall not make a covenant.* God's commands to make no covenants with pagan nations and to tear down their altars are found in Exodus 23:32; 34:13; Deuteronomy 12:3.

22 ver. 19 **23** Jos 2:1; 7:2; Jdg 18:2; Ge 28:19 **24** Jos 2:12,14 **27** Jos 17:11-13 **29** Jos 16:10; 1Ki 9:16
30 Jos 19:15 **31** Jos 19:24-30 **32** Ps 106:34,35 **33** Jos 19:38; ver. 32; ver. 30 **35** Jos 19:42 **36** Nu 34:4; Jos 15:3
CHAPTER 2 **1** ver. 5; Ge 17:7 **2** Dt 7:2; Dt 12:3; Ps 106:34 **3** Jos 23:13; Jdg 3:6; Ex 23:33; Dt 7:16; Ps 106:36

5 So they named that place Bochim (weepers); and there they offered sacrifices to the LORD.

Joshua Dies

6 And when Joshua had sent the people away, the [tribes of the] Israelites went each to his inheritance, to take possession of the land.

7 The people served the LORD all the days of Joshua and all the days of the elders who outlived Joshua, who had seen all the great work of the LORD which He had done for Israel.

8 Then Joshua the son of Nun, the servant of the LORD, died at the age of a hundred and ten.

9 And they buried him in the territory of his inheritance in Timnath-heres, in the hill country of Ephraim, north of Mount Gaash.

10 Also, all [the people of] that generation were gathered to their fathers [in death]; and another generation arose after them who did not know (recognize, understand) the LORD, nor even the work which He had done for Israel.

Israel Serves Baals

11 Then the Israelites did evil in the sight of the LORD and worshiped *and* served the Baals,

12 and they abandoned the LORD, the God of their fathers, who brought them out of the land of Egypt. They followed other gods from the gods of the peoples who were around them, and they bowed down to them, and offended *and* provoked the LORD to anger.

13 So they abandoned the LORD and served Baal [the pagan god of the Canaanites] and the Ashtaroth.

14 So the anger of the LORD burned against Israel, and He gave them into the hands (power) of plunderers who robbed them; and He sold them into the hands of their surrounding enemies, so that they could no longer stand [in opposition] before their enemies.

15 Wherever they went, the hand of the LORD was against them for evil (misfortune), as the LORD had spoken, and as the LORD had sworn to them, so that they were severely distressed. [Lev 26:14–46]

16 Then the LORD raised up judges who rescued them from the hands of those who robbed them.

17 Yet they did not listen to their judges, for they played the prostitute after other gods and they bowed down to them. They quickly turned aside from the way in which their fathers had walked in obeying the commandments of the LORD; they did not do as *their fathers*.

18 When the LORD raised up judges for them, He was with the judge and He rescued them from the hand of their enemies all the days of the judge; for the LORD was moved to pity by their groaning because of those who oppressed and afflicted them.

19 But when the judge died, they turned back and behaved more corruptly than

---

2:8 – 10 *Then Joshua . . . died.* Most likely the reference to Joshua's death in 1:1 is placed chronologically, and this subsequent passage has been inserted by the author out of sequence. It is a "flashback" that leads into the second major section of the book, emphasizing the spiritual downfall of the nation after their leader was gone.
2:13 *Ashtaroth.* Ashtaroth was a female fertility goddess and a goddess of love and war, closely associated with Baal (10:6; 1Sa 7:4; 12:10).
2:15 *as the LORD had sworn.* God had promised to deliver Israel into the hands of its enemies if the people forsook Him (Dt 28:25; Jos 23:13).
2:18 Pity—God is compassionate toward His people at all times. But God had given notice to His people (Dt 28) that if they disobeyed Him, and did not live according to the covenant, then He would have to discipline them. However, if they did live according to the covenant, then He would bless them as a nation. Throughout Judges the pattern occurred that when the people forgot God another nation would come down upon them as an act of judgment from God. When the nation turned to God, He also would turn and "hear" and "pity" them and bring deliverance. God had not forgotten them when they were in trouble, but He wanted that trouble to cause them to turn to Him.

6 Jos 22:6 **7** Jos 24:31 **8** Jos 24:29 **9** Jos 24:30 **10** Ex 5:2; 1Sa 2:12; 1Ch 28:9; Gal 4:8; Titus 1:16 **12** Dt 31:16; Dt 6:14; Ex 20:5 **13** Jdg 10:6; Ps 106:36 **14** Jdg 3:8; Ps 106:40-42; 2Ki 17:20; Jdg 3:8; Isa 50:1; Lev 26:37; Jos 7:12,13 **15** Lev 26; Dt 28 **16** Jdg 3:9,10,15 **17** Ex 34:15; Lev 17:7 **18** Jos 1:5; Ge 6:6; Ps 106:44 **19** Jdg 3:12

THE LIMITS ON EARLY ISRAELITE CONTROL

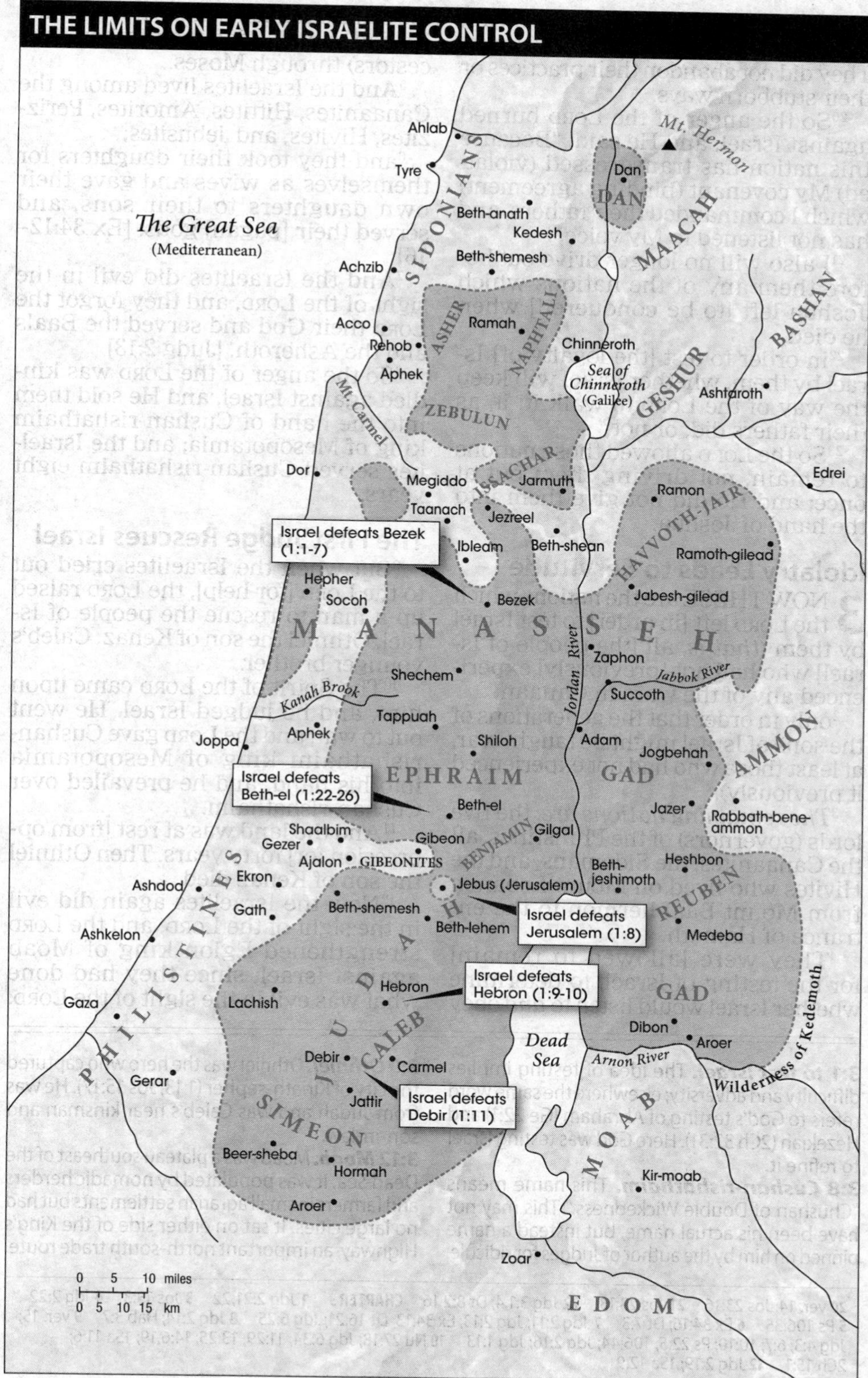

their fathers, in following and serving other gods, and bowing down to them. They did not abandon their practices or their stubborn ways.

20 So the anger of the LORD burned against Israel, and He said, "Because this nation has transgressed (violated) My covenant (binding agreement) which I commanded their fathers, and has not listened to My voice,

21 I also will no longer drive out before them any of the nations which Joshua left [to be conquered] when he died,

22 in order to test [the loyalty of] Israel by them, whether Israel will keep the way of the LORD to walk in it, as their fathers did, or not."

23 So the LORD allowed those nations to remain, not driving them out at once; and He did not give them into the hand of Joshua.

Idolatry Leads to Servitude

3 NOW THESE are the nations which the LORD left [in order] to test Israel by them (*that is,* all [the people of Israel] who had not [previously] experienced any of the wars in Canaan;

2 only in order that the generations of the sons of Israel might be taught war, at least those who had not experienced it previously).

3 *The remaining nations are:* the five lords (governors) of the Philistines, all the Canaanites, the Sidonians, and the Hivites who lived on Mount Lebanon from Mount Baal-hermon to the entrance of Hamath.

4 They were [allowed to remain] for the testing of Israel, to determine whether Israel would listen to *and* obey the commandments of the LORD, which He had commanded their fathers (ancestors) through Moses.

5 And the Israelites lived among the Canaanites, Hittites, Amorites, Perizzites, Hivites, and Jebusites;

6 and they took their daughters for themselves as wives and gave their own daughters to their sons, and served their [pagan] gods. [Ex 34:12–16]

7 And the Israelites did evil in the sight of the LORD, and they forgot the LORD their God and served the Baals and the Asheroth. [Judg 2:13]

8 So the anger of the LORD was kindled against Israel, and He sold them into the hand of Cushan-rishathaim king of Mesopotamia; and the Israelites served Cushan-rishathaim eight years.

The First Judge Rescues Israel

9 But when the Israelites cried out to the LORD [for help], the LORD raised up a man to rescue the people of Israel, Othniel the son of Kenaz, Caleb's younger brother.

10 The Spirit of the LORD came upon him, and he judged Israel. He went out to war, and the LORD gave Cushan-rishathaim king of Mesopotamia into his hand, and he prevailed over Cushan-rishathaim.

11 And the land was at rest [from oppression for] forty years. Then Othniel the son of Kenaz died.

12 Now the Israelites again did evil in the sight of the LORD, and the LORD strengthened Eglon king of Moab against Israel, since they had done what was evil in the sight of the LORD.

3:1 *to test Israel.* The idea of testing implies difficulty and adversity; elsewhere the same word refers to God's testing of Abraham (Ge 22:1) and Hezekiah (2Ch 32:31). Here God was testing Israel to refine it.

3:8 *Cushan-rishathaim.* This name means "Chushan of Double Wickedness." This may not have been his actual name, but instead a name pinned on him by the author of Judges for ridicule.

3:9 *Othniel.* Othniel was the hero who captured the city of Kiriath-sepher (1:13; Jos 15:17). He was from Judah and was Caleb's near kinsman and son-in-law.

3:12 *Moab.* Moab was a plateau southeast of the Dead Sea. It was populated by nomadic herders and farmers in small agrarian settlements but had no large cities. It sat on either side of the King's Highway, an important north-south trade route.

20 ver. 14; Jos 23:16 **21** Jos 23:13 **22** Jdg 3:1,4; Dt 8:2,16 **CHAPTER 3** **1** Jdg 2:21,22 **3** Jos 13:3 **4** Jdg 2:22 **5** Ps 106:35 **6** Ex 34:16; Dt 7:3 **7** Jdg 2:11; Jdg 2:13; Ex 34:13; Dt 16:21; Jdg 6:25 **8** Jdg 2:14; Hab 3:7 **9** ver. 15; Jdg 4:3; 6:7; 10:10; Ps 22:5; 106:44; Jdg 2:16; Jdg 1:13 **10** Nu 27:18; Jdg 6:34; 11:29; 13:25; 14:6,19; 1Sa 11:6; 2Ch 15:1 **12** Jdg 2:19; 1Sa 12:9

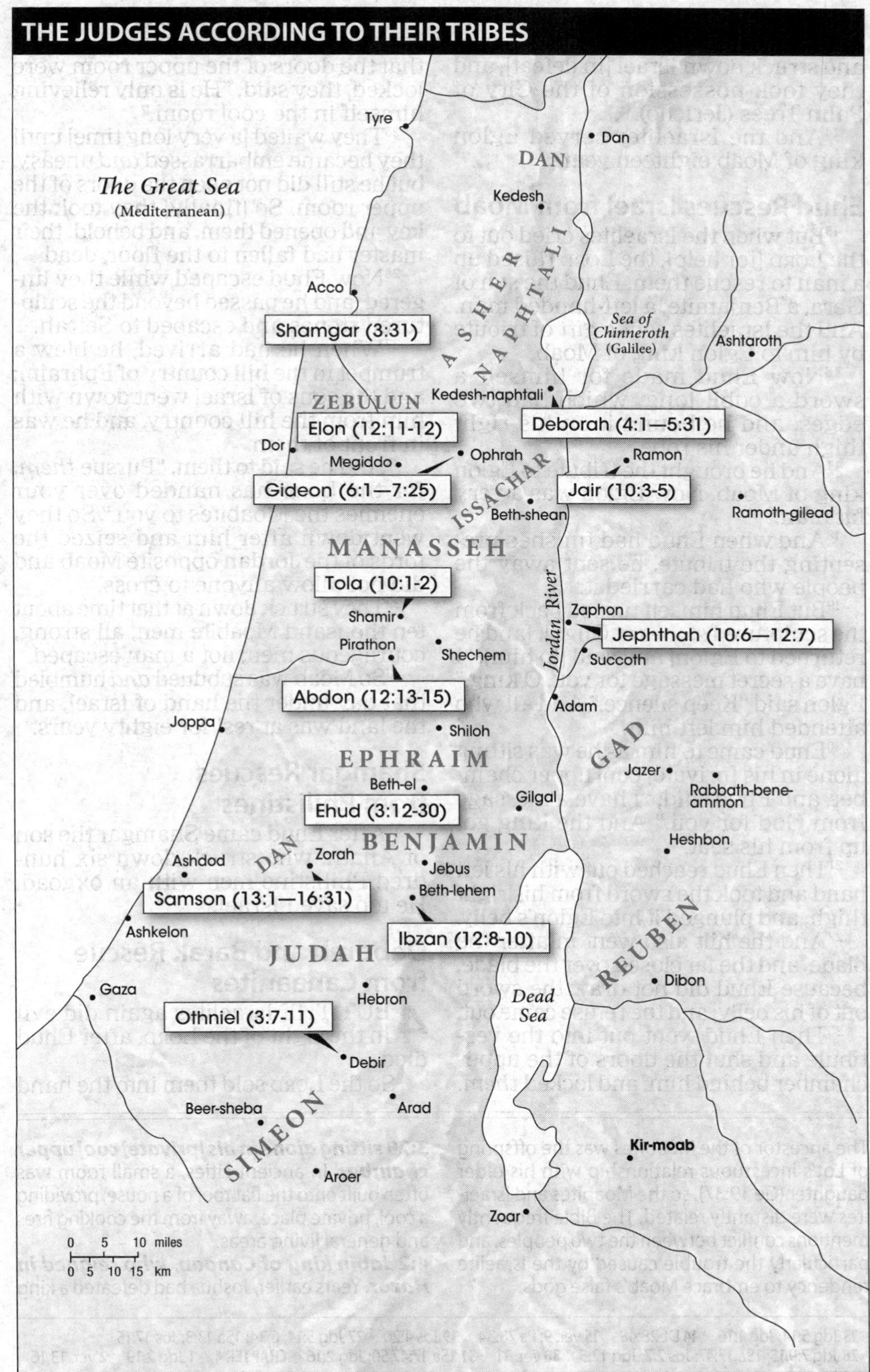
THE JUDGES ACCORDING TO THEIR TRIBES
The Great Sea
(Mediterranean)
Tyre
Dan
DAN
Kedesh
ASHER
NAPHTALI
Sea of Chinneroth
(Galilee)
Acco
Shamgar (3:31)
Ashtaroth
Kedesh-naphtali
ZEBULUN
Deborah (4:1—5:31)
Elon (12:11-12)
Dor
Megiddo
Ophrah
Ramon
Gideon (6:1—7:25)
ISSACHAR
Jair (10:3-5)
Beth-shean
Ramoth-gilead
MANASSEH
Tola (10:1-2)
Jordan River
Shamir
Zaphon
Jephthah (10:6—12:7)
Pirathon
Shechem
Succoth
Abdon (12:13-15)
Adam
Joppa
Shiloh
EPHRAIM
GAD
Jazer
Beth-el
Rabbath-bene-ammon
Gilgal
Ehud (3:12-30)
BENJAMIN
Heshbon
DAN
Zorah
Ashdod
Jebus
Beth-lehem
Samson (13:1—16:31)
Ashkelon
Ibzan (12:8-10)
JUDAH
REUBEN
Gaza
Hebron
Dibon
Dead Sea
Othniel (3:7-11)
Debir
Beer-sheba
Arad
SIMEON
Kir-moab
Aroer
Zoar
0 5 10 miles
0 5 10 15 km

13 And Eglon gathered to him the sons of Ammon and Amalek, and went and struck down Israel [in defeat], and they took possession of the City of Palm Trees (Jericho).

14 And the Israelites served Eglon king of Moab eighteen years.

Ehud Rescues Israel from Moab

15 But when the Israelites cried out to the LORD [for help], the LORD raised up a man to rescue them, Ehud the son of Gera, a Benjamite, a left-handed man. And the Israelites sent *a gift* of tribute by him to Eglon king of Moab.

16 Now Ehud made for himself a sword a cubit long, which had two edges, and he bound it on his right thigh under his robe.

17 And he brought the tribute to Eglon king of Moab. Now Eglon was a very fat man.

18 And when Ehud had finished presenting the tribute, he sent away the people who had carried it.

19 But Ehud himself turned back from the sculptured stones at Gilgal, [and he returned to Eglon] and said [to him], "I have a secret message for you, O king." Eglon said "Keep silence." And all who attended him left him.

20 Ehud came to him as he was sitting alone in his [private] cool upper chamber, and Ehud said, "I have a message from God for you." And the king got up from his seat.

21 Then Ehud reached out with his left hand and took the sword from his right thigh, and plunged it into Eglon's belly.

22 And the hilt also went in after the blade, and the fat closed over the blade, because Ehud did not draw the sword out of his belly; and the refuse came out.

23 Then Ehud went out into the vestibule and shut the doors of the upper chamber behind him, and locked *them.*

24 When Ehud departed, Eglon's servants came. And when they saw that the doors of the upper room were locked, they said, "He is only relieving himself in the cool room."

25 They waited [a very long time] until they became embarrassed *and* uneasy, but he still did not open the doors of the upper room. So [finally] they took the key and opened them, and behold, their master had fallen to the floor, dead.

26 Now Ehud escaped while they lingered, and he passed beyond the sculptured stones and escaped to Seirah.

27 When he had arrived, he blew a trumpet in the hill country of Ephraim; and the sons of Israel went down with him from the hill country, and he was in front of them.

28 And he said to them, "Pursue *them,* for the LORD has handed over your enemies the Moabites to you." So they went down after him and seized the fords of the Jordan opposite Moab and did not allow anyone to cross.

29 They struck down at that time about ten thousand Moabite men, all strong, courageous men; not a man escaped.

30 So Moab was subdued *and* humbled that day under the hand of Israel, and the land was at rest for eighty years.

Shamgar Rescues from Philistines

31 After Ehud came Shamgar the son of Anath, who struck down six hundred Philistine men with an oxgoad. He too saved Israel.

Deborah and Barak Rescue from Canaanites

4 BUT THE Israelites again did evil in the sight of the LORD, after Ehud died.

2 So the LORD sold them into the hand

The ancestor of the Moabites was the offspring of Lot's incestuous relationship with his older daughter (Ge 19:37), so the Moabites and Israelites were distantly related. The Bible frequently mentions conflict between the two peoples, and particularly the trouble caused by the Israelite tendency to embrace Moab's false gods.

3:20 *sitting alone in his [private] cool upper chamber.* In ancient cities, a small room was often built onto the flat roof of a house, providing a cool, private place, away from the cooking fires and general living areas.

4:2 *Jabin king of Canaan, who reigned in Hazor.* Years earlier, Joshua had defeated a king

13 Jdg 5:14; Jdg 1:16 **14** Dt 28:48 **15** ver. 9; Ps 78:34 **19** Jos 4:20 **27** Jdg 5:14; 6:34; 1Sa 13:3; Jos 17:15 **28** Jdg 7:9,15; 1Sa 17:47; Jos 2:7; Jdg 12:5 **30** ver. 11 **31** 1Sa 17:47,50; Jdg 2:16 **CHAPTER 4** **1** Jdg 2:19 **2** ver. 13,16

THE WAR OF EHUD

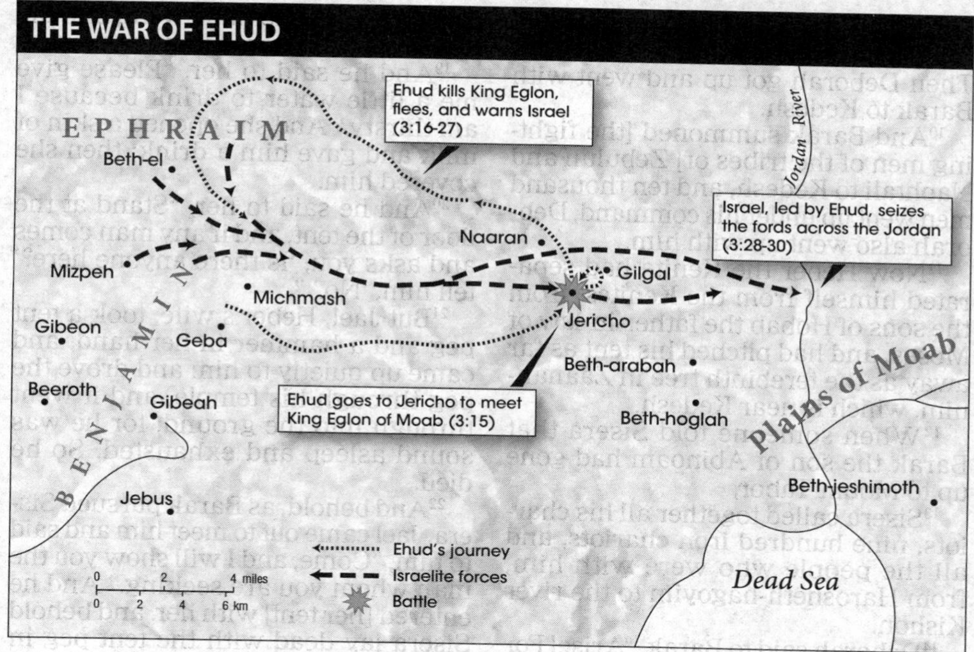

of Jabin king of Canaan, who reigned
in Hazor. The commander of his army
was Sisera, who lived in Harosheth-
hagoyim.
3 Then the Israelites cried out to the
LORD [for help], for Jabin had nine hun-
dred iron chariots and had oppressed
and tormented the sons of Israel se-
verely for twenty years.
4 Now Deborah, a prophetess, the
wife of Lappidoth, was judging Israel
at that time.
5 She used to sit [to hear and decide
disputes] under the palm tree of Deb-
orah between Ramah and Bethel in
the hill country of Ephraim; and the
Israelites came up to her for judgment.
6 Now she sent *word* and summoned
Barak the son of Abinoam from
Kedesh-naphtali, and said to him, "Be-
hold, the LORD, the God of Israel, has
commanded, 'Go and march to Mount
Tabor, and take with you ten thousand
men [of war] from the tribes of Naph-
tali and Zebulun.
7 'I will draw out Sisera, the com-
mander of Jabin's army, with his char-
iots and his infantry to meet you at the
river Kishon, and I will hand him over
to you.' "
8 Then Barak said to her, "If you will
go with me, then I will go; but if you
will not go with me, I will not go."
9 She said, "I will certainly go with
you; nevertheless, the journey that you
are about to take will not be for your

---

of Hazor named Jabin (Jos 11:1 – 15). Probably Jabin was a title rather than a proper name.

4:4 *Deborah.* Deborah is shown in the best light of all the judges in the book. She is called a prophetess (v. 4), and many sought out her decisions (v. 5). For this reason, she is called "a mother in Israel" (5:7). She is probably included among the "leaders" in Israel (5:2), and she instructed Barak in the strategy of the battle (4:9,14). She was also a prominent author of the victory song (5:1) and gave her name to a place in Israel, the palm tree of Deborah (v. 5).

4:9 *will not be for your honor.* Barak clearly respected Deborah as the Lord's spokesperson, and wanted her to be nearby so that he could receive instructions from the Lord. It is not clear whether Deborah's response was a rebuke, or just a statement, but it seems that part of the reason Israel was judged by a woman was because the

3 Jdg 1:19; Jdg 5:8; Ps 106:42 **5** Ge 35:8 **6** Heb 11:32; Jos 19:37 **7** Ex 14:4; Jdg 5:21; 1Ki 18:40; Ps 83:9,10 **9** Jdg 2:14

honor *and* glory, because the LORD will sell Sisera into the hand of a woman." Then Deborah got up and went with Barak to Kedesh.

10 And Barak summoned [the fighting men of the tribes of] Zebulun and Naphtali to Kedesh, and ten thousand men went up under his command; Deborah also went up with him.

11 Now Heber the Kenite had separated himself from the Kenites, from the sons of Hobab the father-in-law of Moses, and had pitched his tent as far away as the terebinth tree in Zaanannim, which is near Kedesh.

12 When someone told Sisera that Barak the son of Abinoam had gone up to Mount Tabor,

13 Sisera called together all his chariots, nine hundred iron chariots, and all the people who were with him, from Harosheth-hagoyim to the river Kishon.

14 Deborah said to Barak, "Arise! For this is the day when the LORD has given Sisera into your hand. Has the LORD not gone out before you?" So Barak went down from Mount Tabor with ten thousand men following him.

15 And the LORD routed Sisera and all his chariots and [confused] all his army with the edge of the sword before Barak; and Sisera dismounted from his chariot and fled away on foot.

16 But Barak pursued the chariots and the army to Harosheth-hagoyim, and the entire army of Sisera fell by the sword; not even one man was left.

17 But Sisera fled on foot to the tent of Jael, the wife of Heber the Kenite, because there was peace between Jabin the king of Hazor and the house of Heber the Kenite.

18 Jael went out to meet Sisera, and said to him, "Turn aside, my lord, turn aside to me! Have no fear." So he turned aside to her [and went] into the tent, and she covered him with a rug.

19 And he said to her, "Please give me a little water to drink because I am thirsty." And she opened a skin of milk and gave him a drink; then she covered him.

20 And he said to her, "Stand at the door of the tent, and if any man comes and asks you, 'Is there anyone here?' tell him, 'No.' "

21 But Jael, Heber's wife, took a tent peg and a hammer in her hand, and came up quietly to him and drove the peg through his temple, and it went through into the ground; for he was sound asleep and exhausted. So he died.

22 And behold, as Barak pursued Sisera, Jael came out to meet him and said to him, "Come, and I will show you the man whom you are seeking." And he entered [her tent] with her, and behold Sisera lay dead with the tent peg in his temple.

23 So on that day God subdued *and* humbled Jabin king of Canaan before the sons of Israel.

24 And the hand of the sons of Israel pressed down heavier and heavier on Jabin king of Canaan, until they had destroyed him.

The Song of Deborah and Barak

5 THEN DEBORAH and Barak the son of Abinoam sang on that day, saying,

2 "For the leaders who took the lead
in Israel,
For the people who volunteered
[for battle],
Bless the LORD!

3 "Hear, O kings; listen, O rulers!
I will sing to the LORD,

men were not listening that closely to God, or willing to take the responsibility. Whatever his stage of spiritual growth was at the time, Barak did obey the Lord and is listed in the Book of Hebrews as a man of great faith (Heb 11:32).

5:2 *took the lead in Israel.* The phrase literally means "the long-haired ones who let their hair hang loose." The precise meaning of the phrase is obscure, but it may mean that loosed locks or flowing hair were signs of great strength or leadership.

5:2–3 Praise — Deborah did not attribute their success to herself or to Barak, or even to Jael, but

10 Jdg 5:18; See Ex 11:8; 1Ki 20:10 **11** Jdg 1:16; Nu 10:29; ver. 6 **14** Dt 9:3; 2Sa 5:24; Ps 68:7; Isa 52:12 **15** Ps 83:9,10; See Jos 10:10 **19** Jdg 5:25 **21** Jdg 5:26 **CHAPTER 5** **1** See Ex 15:1 **2** Ps 18:47; 2Ch 17:16 **3** Dt 32:1,3

I will sing praise to the LORD, the
God of Israel.
4 "LORD, when You went out from
Seir,
When You marched from the field
of Edom,
The earth quaked, the heavens
also dripped,
Yes, the clouds dripped water.
5 "The mountains quaked at the
presence of the LORD,
Yes, this Sinai, at the presence of
the LORD, the God of Israel.

6 "In the days of Shamgar the son of
Anath,
In the days of Jael, the highways
were deserted,
And travelers went by roundabout
ways.
7 "The villagers ceased *to be;* they
ceased in Israel
Until I, Deborah, arose,
Until I arose, a mother in Israel.
8 "They chose new gods;
Then war was in the gates.
Was there a shield or spear seen
Among forty thousand in Israel?
9 "My heart *goes out* to the
commanders of Israel,
The volunteers among the people;
Bless the LORD!
10 "Sing of it, you who ride on white
donkeys,
You who sit on *rich* carpets,
And you who walk by the way.
11 "At the sound of those who divide
flocks among the watering
places,
There they shall recount the
righteous acts of the LORD,
The righteous acts toward His
villagers in Israel.
Then the people of the LORD went
down to the gates.

12 "Awake, awake, Deborah;
Awake, awake, sing a song!
Arise, Barak, and lead away your
captives, you son of Abinoam.
13 "Then down marched the
survivors to the nobles;
The people of the LORD marched
down for Me against the
mighty.
14 "From Ephraim those whose root
is in Amalek *came down,*
After you, Benjamin, with your
relatives;
From Machir came down
commanders *and* rulers,
And from Zebulun those who
handle the scepter of the [office
of] scribe.
15 "And the heads of Issachar *came*
with Deborah;
As Issachar, so was Barak;
Into the valley they rushed at his
heels;
Among the divisions of Reuben
There were great searchings of
heart.
16 "Why [Reuben] did you linger
among the sheepfolds,
To hear the piping for the flocks?
Among the divisions of Reuben
There were great searchings of
heart.
17 "Gilead remained beyond the
Jordan;
And why did Dan live as an alien
on ships?
Asher sat [still] on the seacoast,
And remained by its landings.
[These did not come to battle for
God's people.]

---

to the Lord. He was the one to whom all praise and thanksgiving were directed in the celebration of their victory.

5:7 *a mother in Israel.* This phrase occurs twice in the Old Testament, here and in 2 Samuel 20:19. The title is given to Deborah as one of honor, respect, and prominence.

5:10 *ride on white donkeys . . . walk by the way.* This verse calls all classes of society to bear witness to the mighty acts of God, from the ruling classes, those riding on white donkeys, to the lowest classes, those who walk on the road.

5:17 *live as an alien on ships.* The reference to Dan remaining "on ships" probably reflects the location of their original inheritance, which was along the south-central coastal plain where they would have had access to the sea (Jos 19:40–46). Later they migrated northward, having been forced out of their territory (1:34; 18:1; Jos 19:47).

4 Dt 33:2; Ps 68:8 **5** Ps 97:5; Ex 19:18 **6** Isa 33:8 **7** Isa 49:23 **8** Dt 32:16; 1Sa 13:19,22 **10** Ps 145:5; Jdg 10:4; Ps 107:32 **11** Ps 145:7 **12** Ps 57:8; Ps 68:18 **13** Ps 49:14 **17** See Jos 13:25,31; Jos 19:29

18 "But Zebulun was a people who
risked their lives to the [point of] death;
Naphtali also, on the heights of the field.
19 "The kings came and fought;
Then the kings of Canaan fought
At Taanach by the waters of Megiddo.
Spoils of silver they did not obtain.
20 "From the heavens the stars fought,
From their courses they fought against Sisera.
21 "The torrent Kishon swept the enemy away,
The ancient torrent, the torrent Kishon.
O my soul, march on with strength.
22 "Then the horses' hoofs beat [loudly]
Because of the galloping—the galloping of his valiant *and* powerful steeds.
23 'Curse Meroz,' said the messenger of the LORD,
'Utterly curse its inhabitants;
Because they did not come to the help of the LORD,
To the help of the LORD against the mighty.'
24 "Most blessed of women is Jael,
The wife of Heber the Kenite;
Most blessed is she of women in the tent.
25 "Sisera asked for water and she gave him milk;
She brought him curds in a magnificent bowl.
26 "She reached out her [left] hand for the tent peg,
And her right hand for the workmen's hammer.
Then she struck Sisera, she smashed his head;
And she shattered and pierced his temple.
27 "He bowed, he fell, he lay [still] at her feet;
At her feet he bowed, he fell;
Where he bowed, there he fell dead.
28 "Out of the window she looked down and lamented (cried out in a shrill voice),
The mother of Sisera through the lattice,
'Why is his chariot delayed in coming?
Why have the hoofbeats of his chariots delayed?'
29 "Her wise ladies answered her,
Indeed, she repeated her words to herself,
30 'Are they not finding and dividing the spoil?
A maiden (concubine) or two for every man;
A spoil of dyed garments for Sisera,
A spoil of dyed garments embroidered,
Two pieces of dyed garments embroidered for the neck of the plunderer?'
31 "So let all Your enemies perish, O LORD;
But let those who love Him be like the rising of the sun in its might."

And the land was at rest for forty years.

Israel Oppressed by Midian

6 THEN THE Israelites did evil in the sight of the LORD; and the LORD gave them into the hand of Midian for seven years.

5:26 *Sisera.* The poem describes Sisera's death using graphic, emotive language, which it repeats several times to make the point. Sisera's death was probably a bloodier affair than the prose account indicates.

6:1 *Midian.* Midian was located in the Arabian Peninsula, southeast of Israel and east of the Sinai Peninsula. The Midianites were descendants of Abraham through his wife Keturah (Ge 25:1–2), so they were distantly related to the Israelites. Midianites bought Joseph from his brothers (Ge 37:25–36), welcomed Moses in the wilderness (Ex 2:15–21), and hired Balaam to curse Israel (Nu 22:7). Generally speaking, Israel counted

18 Jdg 4:10 **19** Ps 44:12 **20** Ps 77:17,18; Jdg 4:15 **21** Jdg 4:7 **23** Neh 3:5; 1Sa 18:17 **24** Jdg 4:17; Lk 1:28 **25** Jdg 4:19 **30** Ex 15:9 **31** Ps 83:9,10; 2Sa 23:4; Ps 19:4,5 **CHAPTER 6** **1** Jdg 2:19; Hab 3:7

2 The [powerful] hand of Midian
prevailed against Israel. Because of
Midian the sons of Israel made for
themselves the dens (hideouts) which
were in the mountains, and the caves
and the [mountain] strongholds.
3 For it was whenever Israel had sown
[their seed] that the Midianites would
come up with the Amalekites and the
people of the east and go up against
them.
4 So they would camp against them
and destroy the crops of the land as far
as Gaza, and leave no sustenance in Is-
rael as well as no sheep, ox, or donkey.
5 For they would come up with their
livestock and their tents, and they
would come in as numerous as locusts;
both they and their camels were innu-
merable. So they came into the land to
devastate it.
6 So Israel was greatly impoverished
because of the Midianites, and the Is-
raelites cried out to the LORD [for help].
7 Now it came about when they cried
out to the LORD because of Midian,
8 that the LORD sent a prophet to
the Israelites, and he said to them,
"Thus says the LORD, the God of Is-
rael, 'I brought you up from Egypt and
brought you out of the house of slavery.
9 'And I rescued you from the hand
of the Egyptians and from the hand of
all who oppressed you, and drove them
out before you and gave you their land,
10 and I said to you, "I am the LORD
your God; you shall not fear the gods
of the Amorites in whose land you
live." But you have not listened to *and*
obeyed My voice.' "

Gideon Is Visited

11 Now the Angel of the LORD came
and sat under the terebinth tree at
Ophrah, which belonged to Joash the
Abiezrite, and his son Gideon was
beating wheat in the wine press [in-
stead of the threshing floor] to [hide it
and] save it from the Midianites.
12 And the Angel of the LORD ap-
peared to him and said to him, "The
LORD is with you, O brave man."
13 But Gideon said to him, "Please my
lord, if the LORD is with us, then why has
all this happened to us? And where are
all His wondrous works which our fa-
thers told us about when they said, 'Did
not the LORD bring us up from Egypt?'
But now the LORD has abandoned us
and put us into the hand of Midian."
14 The LORD turned to him and said,
"Go in this strength of yours and save
Israel from the hand of Midian. Have
I not sent you?"
15 But Gideon said to Him, "Please
Lord, how am I to rescue Israel?

Midian among its foes. In this account, the Midianites were menacing Israel, burning, looting, and leaving many near starvation (6:4–5).

6:3 ***Amalekites.*** The Amalekites were a nomadic people who lived in the Sinai desert and the Negev, the desert south of Israel. They were descendants of Esau (Ge 36:12) and they joined the Midianites against Israel.

6:11–16 Doubt—Doubt, at first thought, appears to be an innocuous sin, so harmless that it affects only the attitude of the one who doubts. But doubt is much more serious than this. Doubt of God's Word, planted by the arch deceiver, was at the root of that first sin committed in the garden of Eden. Doubt of God's goodness and truth arose before desire for the forbidden fruit led to disobedience. Doubt of God and doubt of God's Word cause men to make decisions based on human reckonings. Doubts undispelled lead to sin and defeat.

6:11 ***terebinth tree.*** This is a large tree with a thick trunk and heavy branches. Botanically speaking, it is similar to an oak tree, with a majestic appearance. ***wine press.*** A wine press was a square or circular pit carved into rock in which grapes were crushed. Wheat was usually separated on open threshing floors so the wind could carry away the chaff in the winnowing process. The fact that Gideon was forced to thresh wheat hidden inside a winepress—despite the fact that he had access to a threshing floor (v. 37)—is yet another illustration of the desperate state the Israelites were in.

6:13 ***my Lord . . . the LORD.*** "My lord" was a polite form of address, but "the LORD" is the personal name of God (Yahweh).

6:15 ***I am the youngest (smallest) in my father's house.*** Gideon's objection is reminiscent of the words spoken by Moses (Ex 3:11) and Jeremiah (Jer 1:6).

---

2 1Sa 13:6; Heb 11:38 **3** Jdg 3:13; Ge 29:1; Jdg 7:12; 1Ki 4:30; Job 1:3 **4** Lev 26:16; Dt 28:30; Mic 6:15 **5** Jdg 7:12 **6** Hos 5:15 **9** Ps 44:2,3 **10** 2Ki 17:35,37,38; Jer 10:2 **11** Jos 17:2; Heb 11:32 **12** Jdg 13:3; Lk 1:11,28; Jos 1:5 **13** Isa 59:1; Ps 44:1; 2Ch 15:2 **14** 1Sa 12:11; Jos 1:9 **15** See 1Sa 9:21

Behold, my family is the least [significant] in Manasseh, and I am the youngest (smallest) in my father's house."

16 The LORD answered him, "I will certainly be with you, and you will strike down the Midianites as [if they were only] one man."

17 Gideon replied to Him, "If I have found any favor in Your sight, then show me a sign that it is You who speaks with me.

18 "Please do not depart from here until I come back to You, and bring my offering and place it before You." And He said, "I will wait until you return."

19 Then Gideon went and prepared a young goat and unleavened bread from an ephah of flour. The meat he put in a basket and the broth in a pot, and he brought *the food* to Him under the oak (terebinth) and presented it.

20 The Angel of God said to him, "Take the meat and unleavened bread and lay them on this rock, and pour out the broth [over them]." And he did so.

21 Then the Angel of the LORD put out the end of the staff that was in His hand and touched the meat and the unleavened bread; and fire flared up from the rock and consumed the meat and the unleavened bread. Then the Angel of the LORD vanished from his sight.

22 When Gideon realized [without any doubt] that He was the Angel of the LORD, he declared, "Oh no, Lord GOD! For now I have seen the Angel of the LORD face to face [and I am doomed]!"

23 The LORD said to him, "Peace to you, do not be afraid; you shall not die."

24 Then Gideon built an altar there to the LORD and named it The LORD is Peace. To this day it is still in Ophrah, of the Abiezrites.

25 Now on that same night the LORD said to Gideon, "Take your father's bull, the second bull seven years old, and tear down the altar of Baal that belongs to your father, and cut down the Asherah that is beside it;

26 and build an altar to the LORD your God on top of this mountain stronghold [with stones laid down] in an orderly way. Then take the second bull and offer a burnt sacrifice using the wood of the Asherah which you shall cut down."

27 Then Gideon took ten men of his servants and did just as the LORD had told him; but because he was too afraid of his father's household (relatives) and the men of the city to do it during daylight, he did it at night.

The Altar of Baal Destroyed

28 Early the next morning when the men of the city got up, they discovered that the altar of Baal was torn down, and the Asherah which was beside it was cut down, and the second bull was offered on the altar which had been built.

29 So they said to one another, "Who has done this thing?" When they

---

6:16 *I will certainly be with you.* This was the same great promise that God had given to Moses and Joshua previously (Ex 3:12; Jos 1:5–9). This should have greatly encouraged Gideon, but he still had doubts. Often we are quick to judge those who doubt God even when they have first-hand evidence of His mighty works. But we all fail to trust God fully at times. God accomplished His will despite Gideon's weakness, and He can do the same through us.

6:22 *Gideon realized.* When the angel of the Lord vanished, then Gideon realized who it was and feared for his life. This reaction of fear appears to have been rooted in the knowledge that anyone who gazed upon God would die (Ex 33:20).

6:24 *To this day.* This expression lends authenticity to the account. It is the author's way of declaring to later generations that they could verify the story by going and seeing this altar themselves.

6:25 *Asherah.* Asherah was the Canaanite fertility goddess. Sacred wooden poles or groves were erected at places where she was worshiped.

6:26 *the wood of the Asherah.* Gideon's sacrifice was to be a bold statement of the superiority of the Lord over the false gods His people were worshiping.

16 Ex 3:12 **17** ver. 36,37; 2Ki 20:8; Ps 86:17; Isa 7:11 **18** Ge 18:3,5 **19** Ge 18:6-8 **20** Jdg 13:19; See 1Ki 18:33,34 **21** Lev 9:24 **22** Jdg 13:21; Ge 16:13; Ex 33:20; Jdg 13:22 **23** Da 10:19 **24** Jdg 8:32 **25** Ex 34:13; Dt 7:5

searched about and inquired, they were
told, "Gideon the son of Joash did it."
30 Then the men of the city said to
Joash, "Bring out your son, so that he
may be executed, because he has torn
down the altar of Baal and cut down
the Asherah which was beside it."
31 But Joash said to all who stood
against him, "Will you plead for Baal?
Will you save him? Whoever pleads for
Baal shall be put to death while it is
still morning. If Baal is a god, let him
defend himself, because someone has
torn down his altar."
32 Therefore on that day he named
Gideon Jerubbaal, meaning, "Let Baal
plead," because he had torn down his
altar.
33 Then all the Midianites and the
Amalekites and the people of the east
assembled together; and they crossed
over [the Jordan] and camped in the
Valley of Jezreel.
34 So the Spirit of the LORD clothed
Gideon [and empowered him]; and he
blew a trumpet, and the Abiezrites
were called together [as a militia] to
follow him.
35 He sent messengers throughout [the
tribe of] Manasseh, and the fighting
men were also called together to follow
him; and he sent messengers to [the
tribes of] Asher, Zebulun, and Naphtali,
and they came up to meet them.

Sign of the Fleece

36 Then Gideon said to God, "If You
are going to rescue Israel through me,
as You have spoken,
37 behold, I will put a fleece of [freshly
sheared] wool on the threshing floor.
If there is dew only on the fleece, and
it is dry on all the ground [around it],
then I will know that You will rescue
Israel through me, as You have said."
38 And it was so. When he got up ear-
ly the next morning and squeezed the
dew out of the fleece, he wrung from
it a bowl full of water.
39 Then Gideon said to God, "Do not
let your anger burn against me, so that
I may speak once more. Please let me
make a test once more with the fleece;
now let only the fleece be dry, and let
there be dew on all the ground."
40 God did so that night; for it was dry
only on the fleece, and there was dew
on all the ground [around it].

Gideon's 300 Chosen Men

7 THEN JERUBBAAL (that is, Gide-
on) and all the people who were
with him got up early and camped
beside the spring of Harod; and the
camp of Midian was north of them by
the hill of Moreh in the valley.
2 Then the LORD said to Gideon,
"There are too many people with you
for Me to hand over Midian to them,
otherwise Israel will boast [about
themselves] against Me, saying, 'My
own power has rescued me.'
3 "So now, proclaim in the hearing
of the people, 'Whoever is afraid and
trembling, let him turn back and leave
Mount Gilead.' " So twenty-two thou-
sand men returned [home], but ten
thousand remained.

6:36 – 40 Prayer — Gideon had already received an unmistakable message from God, and he had been assured that God would lead him to victory. His prayer and request for a sign were the result of his lack of faith, but in spite of Gideon's wavering, God kindly accommodated his requests. Many people have relied on Gideon's example as a way of seeking guidance from the Lord. Occasionally God has chosen to answer such requests, even as He did for Gideon, because He is compassionate and makes allowances for our weakness, but putting out a fleece is not the action of faith. Isaiah modeled a proper response to God's clearly revealed will: he said, "Here am I. Send me!" (Isa 6:8). So too did the disciples, who dropped their nets immediately and followed Jesus (Mk 1:18).

6:39 *let me make a test once more.* Gideon's desire to test God's sign could have been a violation of the law which prohibited people from testing God (Dt 6:16). Gideon himself was aware that he was doing something unwise, if not sinful, since he asked God not to be angry with him.

7:3 *afraid and trembling.* Mosaic law allowed military exemptions for several classes of people, including those who had just built a home, those who had just planted a vineyard, those engaged to be married, and those who were fearful (Dt 20:5 – 8).

33 ver. 3; Jos 17:16 **34** Jdg 3:10; 1Ch 12:18; 2Ch 24:20; Nu 10:3; Jdg 3:27 **37** See Ex 4:3-7 **39** Ge 18:32
CHAPTER 7 **1** Jdg 6:32 **2** Dt 8:17; 1Co 1:29 **3** Dt 20:8

[4]Then the LORD said to Gideon,
"There are still too many people; bring
them down to the water and I will test
them for you there. Therefore it shall
be that he of whom I say to you, 'This
one shall go with you,' he shall go with
you; but everyone of whom I say to
you, 'This one shall not go with you,'
he shall not go."
[5]So he brought the people down to
the water, and the LORD said to Gideon,
"You shall separate everyone who laps
the water with his tongue as a dog laps,
as well as everyone who kneels down
to drink."
[6]Now the number of those who
lapped [the water], putting their hand
to their mouth, was three hundred
men, but all the rest of the people
kneeled down to drink water.
[7]And the LORD told Gideon, "With
the three hundred men who lapped
I will rescue you, and will hand over
the Midianites to you. Let all the *other*
people go, each man to his home."
[8]So the three hundred men took peo-
ple's provisions [for the journey] and
their trumpets [made of rams' horns]
in their hands. And Gideon sent [away]
all the *other* men of Israel, each to his
tent, but kept the three hundred men.
And the camp of Midian was below
him in the valley.
[9]Now on that same night the LORD

7:4–5 *There are still too many people.* God reduced Gideon's army to emphasize who was really bringing victory.

7 1Sa 14:6 **9** Ge 46:2,3

THE WAR OF GIDEON

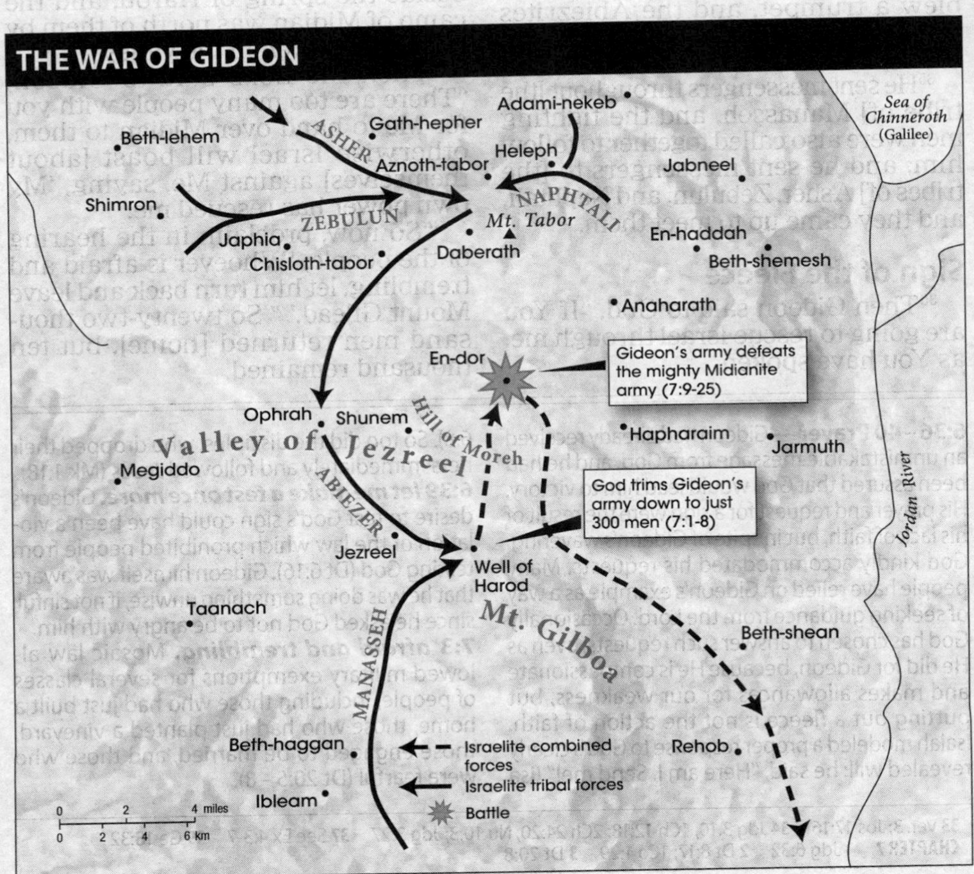

said to Gideon, “Arise, go down against their camp, for I have given it into your hand.

10 “But if you are afraid to go down [by yourself], go with Purah your servant down to the camp,

11 and you will hear what they say; and afterward you will have the courage to go down against the camp.” Then he went down with Purah his servant to the outposts of the army that was in the camp.

12 Now the Midianites and the Amalekites and all the sons of the east were lying [camped] in the valley, as countless as locusts; and their camels were without number, as numerous as the sand on the seashore.

13 When Gideon arrived, there was a man telling a dream to his friend. And he said, “Listen carefully, I had a dream: there was a loaf of barley bread tumbling into the camp of Midian, and it came to the tent and struck it so that it fell, and turned it upside down so that the tent lay flat.”

14 And his friend replied, “This [dream] is nothing less than the sword of Gideon the son of Joash, a man of Israel. God has given Midian and the entire camp into his hand.”

15 When Gideon heard the account of the dream and its interpretation, he bowed down in worship. Then he returned to the camp of Israel and said, “Arise, for the LORD has given the camp of Midian into your hand.”

16 He divided the three hundred men into three companies, and he put trumpets and empty pitchers into the hands of all of them, with torches inside the pitchers.

17 And he said to them, “Look at me, then do likewise. When I come to the edge of the camp, do just as I do.

18 “When I and all who are with me blow the trumpet (ram’s horn), then all around the camp you also blow the trumpets and shout, ‘For the LORD and for Gideon!’ ”

Confusion of the Enemy

19 So Gideon and the hundred men who were with him came to the edge of the camp at the beginning of the middle watch, when the guards had just been changed, and they blew the trumpets and smashed the pitchers that were in their hands.

20 When three companies blew the trumpets and broke the pitchers, they held the torches in their left hands, and the trumpets in their right hands to blow, and they shouted, “A sword for the LORD and for Gideon!”

21 Then each stood in his place around the camp; and the entire [Midianite] army ran, crying out as they fled.

22 When Gideon’s men blew the three hundred trumpets, the LORD set the sword of one [Midianite] against another even throughout the whole army; and the army fled as far as Beth-shittah toward Zererah, as far as the border of Abel-meholah, by Tabbath.

23 The men of Israel were summoned together from [the tribes of] Naphtali and Asher and all Manasseh, and they pursued Midian.

24 Then Gideon sent messengers throughout the hill country of [the tribe of] Ephraim, saying, “Come down against the Midianites and take [control of] the waters before them [thereby cutting off the Midianites], as far as Beth-barah and the Jordan [River].” So all the men of Ephraim were assembled together and they took *control of* the waters, as far as Beth-barah and the Jordan.

25 Then the men of Ephraim took the two leaders of Midian, Oreb and Zeeb, and they killed Oreb at the rock of Oreb, and they killed Zeeb at the wine press of Zeeb, and pursued Midian; and they brought the heads of Oreb and Zeeb to Gideon from across the Jordan.

7:19 *middle watch.* According to Jewish tradition, the hours between sunset and sunrise were divided into three watches, which would put the time of this attack at roughly 10:00 p.m.

11 ver. 13-15; See Ge 24:14; 1Sa 14:9,10 **12** Jdg 6:5,33; 8:10 **21** Ex 14:13,14; 2Ch 20:17; 2Ki 7:7 **22** Jos 6:4,16,20; See 2Co 4:7; Ps 83:9; Isa 9:4; 1Sa 14:20; 2Ch 20:23 **24** Jdg 3:27; Jdg 3:28; Jn 1:28 **25** Jdg 8:3; Ps 83:11; Isa 10:26; Jdg 8:4

Zebah and Zalmunna Routed

8 AND THE men of [the tribe of] Ephraim said to Gideon, "What is this thing that you have done to us, not calling us when you went to fight with Midian?" And they quarreled with him vehemently.

2 But he said to them, "What have I done now [that is so significant] in comparison with you? Is not the gleaning (leftovers) *of the grapes* of [your tribe of] Ephraim better than the vintage (entire harvest) of [my clan of] Abiezer?

3 "God has given the leaders of Midian, Oreb and Zeeb into your hands; and what was I able to do in comparison with you?" Then their anger toward him subsided when he made this statement.

4 So Gideon came to the Jordan and crossed over [the river], he and the three hundred men who were with him—exhausted, yet [still] pursuing [the enemy].

5 He said to the men of Succoth, "Please give loaves of bread to the people who are following me since they are exhausted, and I am pursuing Zebah and Zalmunna, kings of Midian."

6 But the leaders of Succoth said, "Are Zebah and Zalmunna already in your hands, that we should give bread to your army?"

7 Gideon said, "For that [response], when the LORD has handed over Zebah and Zalmunna to me, I will thrash your bodies with the thorns and briars of the wilderness."

8 He went from there up to Penuel and spoke similarly to them; and the men of Penuel answered him just as the men of Succoth had answered.

9 So Gideon said also to the men of Penuel, "When I come again in peace, I will tear down this tower."

10 Now Zebah and Zalmunna were in Karkor with their armies, about fifteen thousand [fighting] men, all who were left of the entire army of the sons of the east; for a hundred and twenty thousand swordsmen had fallen.

11 Gideon went up by the route of those who lived in tents to the east of Nobah and Jogbehah, and he attacked their camp when the camp was unsuspecting.

12 When Zebah and Zalmunna fled, he pursued them and captured the two kings of Midian, Zebah and Zalmunna, and terrified the entire army.

13 Then Gideon the son of Joash returned from the battle by the ascent of Heres.

14 He captured a young man of Succoth and questioned him. And *the youth* wrote down for him [the names of] the leaders of Succoth and its elders, seventy-seven men.

15 He came to the men of Succoth and said, "Look here, Zebah and Zalmunna, about whom you taunted me, saying, 'Are Zebah and Zalmunna now in your hand, that we should give bread to your men who are exhausted?' "

16 He took the elders of the city, and thorns of the wilderness and briars, and with them he punished the men of Succoth.

17 He tore down the tower of Penuel and killed the men of the city.

18 Then Gideon said to Zebah and Zalmunna, "What kind of men were they whom you killed at Tabor?" And they replied, "They were like you, each one of them resembled the son of a king."

19 He said, "They were my brothers,

8:5 *Succoth.* Succoth was east of the Jordan, near the Jabbok River.

8:14 *the youth wrote down for him [the names of] the leaders of Succoth.* Literacy in early civilizations was at first limited to the educated elite, as in Mesopotamia and Egypt. Their writing systems were complex and only a tiny portion of the population could read and write. However, the spread of alphabetic systems vastly simplified the task of reading and writing. Hundreds of potsherds from throughout Palestine have simple inscriptions on them, indicating that some degree of literacy had become widely accessible by Gideon's day.

CHAPTER 8 **1** See Jdg 12:1; 2Sa 19:41 **3** Jdg 7:24,25; Php 2:3; Pr 15:1 **5** Ge 33:17; Ps 60:6 **6** See 1Ki 20:11; See 1Sa 25:11 **7** ver. 16 **8** Ge 32:30; 1Ki 12:25 **9** 1Ki 22:27; ver. 17 **10** Jdg 7:12 **11** Nu 32:35,42; Jdg 18:27; 1Th 5:3 **12** Ps 83:11 **15** ver. 6 **16** ver. 7 **17** ver. 9; 1Ki 12:25 **18** Jdg 4:6; Ps 89:12

the sons of my mother. As the LORD
lives, if only you had let them live, I
would not kill you."
20So [to humiliate them] Gideon said
to Jether his firstborn, "Stand up, and
kill them!" But the youth did not draw
his sword, because he was afraid, for
he was still [just] a boy.
21Then Zebah and Zalmunna said,
"Rise up yourself and strike us; for
as the man is, so is his strength." So
Gideon arose and killed Zebah and
Zalmunna, and took the crescent am-
ulets that were on their camels' necks.
22Then the men of Israel said to Gide-
on, "Rule [as king] over us, both you
and your son, also your son's son, for
you have rescued us from the hand of
Midian."
23But Gideon said to them, "I will not
rule over you, and my son will not rule
over you; the LORD shall rule over you."
24And Gideon said to them, "I would
make a request of you, that each one of
you give me an earring from his spoil."
For the Midianites had gold earrings,
because they were Ishmaelites [who
customarily wore them].
25They answered, "We will certainly
give them *to you.*" And they spread
out a garment, and every one of them
threw an earring there from his spoil.
26And the weight of the golden ear-
rings that he requested was seventeen
hundred *shekels* of gold, apart from
the crescent amulets and pendants and
the purple garments which were worn
by the kings of Midian, and apart from
the chains that were on their camels'
necks.
27Gideon made [all the golden ear-
rings into] an ephod [a sacred, high
priest's garment], and put it in his city
of Ophrah, and all Israel worshiped it
as an idol there, and it became a trap
for Gideon and his household.

Forty Years of Peace

28So Midian was subdued *and* hum-
bled before the sons of Israel, and
they no longer lifted up their heads
[in pride]. And the land was at rest for
forty years in the days of Gideon.
29Jerubbaal (Gideon) the son of
Joash went and lived in his own house.
30Now Gideon had seventy sons born
to him, because he had many wives.
31And his concubine who was in
Shechem also bore him a son, whom
he named Abimelech.
32Gideon the son of Joash died at a
good advanced age and was buried in
the tomb of Joash his father in Ophrah
of the Abiezrites.
33Then it came about, as soon as
Gideon was dead, that the Israelites

8:22 – 23 Self-denial — In the initial flush of victory Gideon was offered hereditary rulership over Israel, which he wisely rejected. God the Lord was Judge with ultimate authority, and He would rule over the people. Gideon knew his place before God. In the same way, we are taught not to think more highly of ourselves than we ought, but "as God has apportioned" (Ro 12:3).

8:22 *Rule [as king] over us.* This request, while understandable from a human perspective, failed to acknowledge that it was God, not Gideon, who had delivered the people.

8:23 *the LORD shall rule over you.* The word order of the Hebrew makes it clear that God's claim was exclusive; it might be paraphrased, "It is the Lord, and no one else, who shall rule over you." This statement is widely assumed to indicate that God intended that Israel should never have a king, but that He would be their only King. However, God had promised Abraham that he would count kings among his descendants (Ge 17:6). The problem was not in the concept of having a king, but in their motivation. They wanted to have a visible, human leader, rather than trusting in God's leadership. The role of a true king would be to lead the people in devotion to God's rule.

8:27 *ephod.* The original ephod was an ornate ceremonial garment worn by the high priest (Ex 29:5). Gideon's motivation for making this golden ephod is unclear, but his imitation of the sacred objects devoted to the worship of God ended up distracting the people and undermining the true worship of God.

8:31 *Abimelech.* This name means "my father is king." Some think that Gideon did become a king in practice if not in name, for he gave his son a royal name and acted as a leader of the people (vv. 24 – 27).

21 Ps 83:11 **23** 1Sa 8:7; 10:19; 12:12 **24** Ge 25:13; 37:25,28 **27** Jdg 17:5; Jdg 6:24; Ps 106:39; Dt 7:16
28 Jdg 5:31 **30** Jdg 9:2,5 **31** Jdg 9:1 **32** Ge 25:8; Job 5:26; ver. 27; Jdg 6:24 **33** Jdg 2:19; Jdg 2:17; Jdg 9:4,46

again played the prostitute with the Baals, and made Baal-berith their god.

34 And the Israelites did not remember the LORD their God, who had rescued them from the hand of all their enemies on every side;

35 nor did they show kindness to the family of Jerubbaal (*that is*, Gideon) in return for all the good that he had done for Israel.

Abimelech's Conspiracy

9 NOW ABIMELECH the son of Jerubbaal (Gideon) went to Shechem to his mother's relatives, and said to them and to the whole clan of the household of his mother's father,

2 "Speak now in the hearing of all the leaders of Shechem, 'Which is better for you, that seventy men, all of the sons of Jerubbaal rule over you, or that one man rule over you?' Also, remember that I am your *own* bone and flesh."

3 So his mother's relatives spoke all these words concerning him so that all the leaders of Shechem could hear; and their hearts were inclined to follow Abimelech, for they said, "He is our relative."

4 And they gave him seventy *pieces* of silver from the house of Baal-berith, with which Abimelech hired worthless and undisciplined men, and they followed (supported) him.

5 Then he went to his father's house at Ophrah and murdered his brothers the sons of Jerubbaal, seventy men, [in a public execution] on one stone. But Jotham the youngest son of Jerubbaal was left *alive*, because he had hidden himself.

6 All the men of Shechem and all of Beth-millo assembled together, and they went and made Abimelech king, by the oak (terebinth) of the pillar (memorial stone) at Shechem.

7 When they told Jotham, he went and stood at the top of Mount Gerizim and shouted to them, "Hear me, O men of Shechem, so that God may hear you.

8 "Once the trees went forth to anoint a king over them, and they said to the olive tree, 'Reign over us!'

9 "But the olive tree said to them, 'Should I give up my fatness by which God and men are honored, and go to wave over the trees?'

10 "Then the trees said to the fig tree, 'You come and reign over us!'

11 "But the fig tree said to them, 'Should I give up my sweetness and my good fruit, and go to wave over the trees?'

12 "Then the trees said to the vine, 'You come and reign over us.'

13 "And the vine replied, 'Should I give up my new wine, which makes God and men happy, and go to wave over the trees?'

14 "Then all the trees said to the bramble, 'You come and reign over us.'

15 "So the bramble said to the trees, 'If in truth you are anointing me king over you, then come and take refuge in my shade; but if not, let fire come out of the bramble and devour the cedars of Lebanon.'

16 "Now then, if you acted in truth

9:1–57 Conspiracy—The seeds of Abimelech's violent grab for power were sown in Israel's persistent infidelity to God, which led to another rejection of the Lord (8:22, 24–27, 33–35).

9:6 oak (terebinth) of the pillar. Sadly, this coronation took place at the same tree where Jacob had put away his foreign gods many years before (Ge 35:4), and where Joshua had commemorated his covenant with God (Jos 24:26).

9:14–15 Pride—The pomp and ceremony that goes with royalty is a source of pride not only for the king but also for his subjects. The idea of having a man from their own tribe ruling the entire nation appealed to the pride of the men of Shechem. Pride led them to surrender their freedom and submit to the rule of man rather than God. It is the cause of many kinds of injustice in society: social, economic, and political. It often leads to war and violence, as it did in this case. Within a brief period of time after Abimelech was anointed king they realized their mistake. The prophecy of Jotham was fulfilled, since fire did come out of the bramble (from Abimelech) to consume the men of Shechem. Pride led to their destruction.

---

34 Ps 78:11,42; 106:13,21 **35** Jdg 9:16-18; Ecc 9:14 **CHAPTER 9** **1** Jdg 8:31 **2** Jdg 8:30; Ge 29:14 **3** Ge 29:15 **4** Jdg 8:33; Jdg 11:3; 2Ch 13:7; Ac 17:5 **5** Jdg 6:24; 2Ki 11:1,2 **7** Dt 11:29; 27:12; Jos 8:33; Jn 4:20 **8** See 2Ki 14:9; Jdg 8:22,23 **9** Ps 104:15 **13** Ps 104:15 **15** Isa 30:2; Da 4:12; Hos 14:7; ver. 20; Nu 21:28; Eze 19:14; 2Ki 14:9; Isa 2:13; 37:24; Eze 31:3 **16** Jdg 8:35

and integrity when you made Abim-
elech king, and if you have dealt well
with Jerubbaal and his house, and
have dealt with him as he deserved—
17 for my father fought for you and
risked his life and rescued you from
the hand of Midian;
18 but you have risen against my fa-
ther's house today and have murdered
his sons, seventy men, on one stone,
and have made Abimelech, son of his
maidservant, king over the people of
Shechem, because he is your relative—
19 if then you have acted in truth and
integrity with Jerubbaal and his house
this day, then rejoice in Abimelech, and
let him also rejoice in you.
20 "But if not, may fire come out from
Abimelech and devour the people of
Shechem and Beth-millo; and may fire
come out from the people of Shechem
and Beth-millo, and devour Abimelech."
21 Then Jotham escaped and fled, and
went to Beer and lived there because
of Abimelech his brother.

Shechem and Abimelech Fall

22 Abimelech ruled over Israel for
three years.
23 Then God sent an evil spirit be-
tween Abimelech and the leaders of
Shechem; and the leaders of Shechem
acted treacherously against Abimelech,
24 so that the violence done to the
seventy sons of Jerubbaal (Gideon)
might come [on the guilty], and that
their [innocent] blood might be laid
on Abimelech their brother, who had
killed them, and on the leaders of
Shechem, who strengthened his hands
(encouraged him) to kill his brothers.
25 The leaders of Shechem set men
in ambush against Abimelech on the
mountaintops, and they robbed all who
passed by them along the road; and it
was reported to Abimelech.
26 Now Gaal the son of Ebed came
with his relatives, and moved into
Shechem; and the leaders of Shechem
trusted him.
27 They went out into the field, gath-
ered the grapes of their vineyard and
trod them, and held a festival; and they
entered the house of their god, and they
ate and drank, and cursed Abimelech.
28 Gaal the son of Ebed said, "Who is
Abimelech, and who is Shechem, that
we should serve him? Is he not [merely]
the son of Jerubbaal and is Zebul not
his lieutenant? Serve the men of Ha-
mor the father (founder) of Shechem.
Why then should we serve Abimelech?
29 "If only this people were under
my authority! Then I would remove
Abimelech and say to him, 'Increase
[the size of] your army and come out
[to fight].' "
30 When Zebul the ruler of the city
heard the words of Gaal the son of
Ebed, his anger burned.
31 He sent messengers to Abimelech
secretly, saying, "Behold, Gaal the son
of Ebed and his relatives have come to
Shechem; and they are stirring up the
city against you.
32 "Now then, get up during the night,
you and the people who are with you,
and set up an ambush in the field.
33 "Then in the morning, at sunrise,
you will get up early and rush upon
and attack the city; and when Gaal
and the people who are with him come
out against you, you shall do to them
whatever you can."
34 So Abimelech and all the people
who were with him got up during the
night, and set up an ambush against
Shechem, in four companies.
35 Now Gaal the son of Ebed came out
and stood in the entrance of the city
gate; then Abimelech and the people
who were with him got up from the
ambush.
36 When Gaal saw the people, he said
to Zebul, "Look, people are coming
down from the mountaintops." But Ze-
bul said to him, "You are *only* seeing
the shadow of the mountains as *if they
were* men."
37 Gaal spoke again and said, "Look!

9:37 *the sorcerers' oak tree.* This term literally means "terebinth tree." It appears to have had some association with occult or magical practices, and this particular terebinth tree was certainly an important landmark (Ge 35:4; Jos 24:26).

18 ver. 5,6 **19** Isa 8:6; Php 3:3 **20** ver. 15,56,57 **21** 2Sa 20:14 **23** 1Sa 16:14; 18:9,10; See 1Ki 22:22; 2Ch 18:22; Isa 19:14; Isa 33:1 **24** 1Ki 2:32; Est 9:25; Mt 23:35,36 **27** ver. 4 **28** 1Sa 25:10; 1Ki 12:16; Ge 34:2,6 **29** 2Sa 15:4

People are coming down from the
highest part of the land, and one com-
pany is coming by way of the sorcer-
ers' oak tree."
38 Then Zebul said to Gaal, "Where
is your [boasting] mouth now, you
who said, 'Who is Abimelech that we
should serve him?' Is this not the peo-
ple whom you despised? Go out now
and fight with them!"
39 So Gaal went out ahead of the
leaders of Shechem and fought with
Abimelech.
40 Abimelech chased him, and he fled
before him; and many fell wounded as
far as the entrance of the gate.
41 Then Abimelech stayed at Aru-
mah, and Zebul drove out Gaal and his
relatives so that they could not remain
in Shechem.
42 The next day the people went out to
the field, and it was reported to Abim-
elech.
43 So he took his people and divided
them into three companies, and set
an ambush in the field; and he looked
and saw the people coming out of the
city. And he rose up against them and
struck them down.
44 Then Abimelech and the company
with him advanced forward and stood
in the entrance of the city gate; the two
other companies attacked all who were
in the field and killed them.
45 Abimelech fought against the city
that entire day. He took the city and
killed the people who were in it; he
demolished the city and sowed it with
salt.
46 When all the leaders of the Tower
of Shechem heard about it, they en-
tered the inner chamber (stronghold)
of the temple of El-berith (the god of a
covenant).
47 Abimelech was told that all the
leaders of the Tower of Shechem were
assembled together.
48 So Abimelech went up to Mount
Zalmon, he and all the people with
him; and Abimelech took an axe in
his hand and cut down a branch from
the trees, picked it up, and laid it on
his shoulder. And he said to the people
with him, "What you have seen me do,
hurry and do just as I have done."
49 So everyone of the people also cut
down his branch and followed Abime-
lech, and they put *the branches* on top
of the inner chamber and set it on fire
over those *inside*, so that all the people
in the Tower of Shechem also died,
about a thousand men and women.
50 Then Abimelech went to Thebez,
and camped against Thebez and took
it.
51 But there was a strong (fortified)
tower in the center of the city, and all
the men and women with all the lead-
ers of the city fled to it and shut them-
selves in; and they went up on the roof
of the tower.
52 So Abimelech came to the tower
and fought against it, and approached
the entrance of the tower to burn it
down with fire.
53 But a certain woman threw an up-
per millstone [down] on Abimelech's
head and crushed his skull.
54 Then he called quickly to the young
man who was his armor bearer, and
said to him, "Draw your sword and
kill me, so that it will not be said of me,
'A woman killed him.' " So the young
man pierced him through, and he died.
55 When the men of Israel saw that
Abimelech was dead, each departed
to his home.
56 In this way God repaid the wicked-
ness of Abimelech, which he had done
to his father [Jerubbaal] by killing his
seventy brothers.
57 Also God repaid all the wickedness
of the men of Shechem on their heads,
and the curse of Jotham the son of

9:45 *sowed it with salt.* Spreading salt on the land turned the area into a barren desert. Salt will kill most vegetation, and it takes a long time for the land to become good again.

9:56 *God repaid the wickedness of Abimelech.* Abimelech was not a true king, he had established his reign through murder and in no way sought to lead the people to the Lord. God did not allow this kind of rebellion to pass unnoticed.

38 ver. 28,29 **45** ver. 20; Dt 29:23; 1Ki 12:25; 2Ki 3:25 **46** Jdg 8:33 **48** Ps 68:14 **53** 2Sa 11:21 **54** 1Sa 31:4
56 ver. 24; Job 31:3; Pr 5:22 **57** ver. 20

Jerubbaal (Gideon) came upon them.
[Judg 9:19, 20]

Oppression of Philistines and Ammonites

10 AFTER ABIMELECH died, Tola
the son of Puah, the son of Dodo,
a man of Issachar, arose to save Israel;
and he lived in Shamir, in the hill coun-
try of Ephraim.
2 Tola judged Israel for twenty-three
years; then he died and was buried in
Shamir.
3 After him, Jair the Gileadite arose,
and he judged Israel for twenty-two
years.
4 He had thirty sons who rode on
thirty donkeys, and they had thirty
towns in the land of Gilead that are
called Havvoth-jair (towns of Jair) to
this day.
5 And Jair died and was buried in
Kamon.
6 Then the Israelites again did what
was evil in the sight of the LORD; they
served the Baals, the Ashtaroth (fe-
male deities), the gods of Aram (Syria),
the gods of Sidon, the gods of Moab,
the gods of the Ammonites, and the
gods of the Philistines. They aban-
doned the LORD and did not serve Him.
7 So the anger of the LORD was kin-
dled against Israel, and He sold them
into the hands of the Philistines and
the Ammonites,
8 and they oppressed and crushed Is-
rael that year. For eighteen years they
oppressed all the Israelites who were
beyond the Jordan in the land of the
Amorites, which is in Gilead.
9 The Ammonites crossed the Jordan
to fight against Judah, Benjamin, and
the house of Ephraim, so that Israel
was greatly distressed.
10 Then the Israelites cried out to
the LORD [for help], saying, "We have
sinned against You, because we have
abandoned (rejected) our God and
have served the Baals."
11 The LORD said to the Israelites, "*Did
I* not *rescue you* from the Egyptians,
the Amorites, the Ammonites, and the
Philistines?
12 "Also when the Sidonians, the Ama-
lekites, and the Maonites oppressed
and crushed you, you cried out to Me,
and I rescued you from their hands.
13 "Yet you have abandoned (rejected)
Me and served other gods; therefore I
will no longer rescue you.
14 "Go, cry out to the gods you have
chosen; let them rescue you in your
time of distress."
15 The Israelites said to the LORD, "We
have sinned, do to us whatever seems
good to You; only please rescue us
this day."
16 So they removed the foreign gods
from among them and served the LORD;
and He could bear the misery of Israel
no longer.
17 Then the Ammonites were as-
sembled together and they camped in

10:6 – 18 Mercy — A lengthy introduction precedes the story of Jephthah. These verses repeat the themes of apostasy and God's unfailing mercy. A new theme here is the emphasis on Israel's confession and repentance (vv. 10,15 – 16).

10:6 *Baals, the Ashtaroth (female deities), the gods of Aram . . . Sidon . . . Moab . . . Ammonites.* This list demonstrates the extent of Israel's idolatry. Not only did the people worship the major Canaanite gods (Baal and Asherah), but they also absorbed the religions of other groups.

10:7 – 8 Suffering — Here, and elsewhere, the Book of Judges underscores the consequences of disobedience. Those consequences are always tragic. The Israelites were never oppressed because they did not have a big enough military, or a strong enough leader, or because God could not protect them. They were oppressed by God's permission because of their disobedience and sin. Defeat and miserable suffering do loom large whenever believers retreat from their exclusive commitment to God. They become their own worst enemy.

10:14 *the gods you have chosen.* This is a response of confrontation. When Israel cried out to God, He reminded them again of their faithless ways.

10:16 *He could bear the misery of Israel no longer.* Not only is God a God of great justice,

CHAPTER 10 **1** Jdg 2:16 **4** Jdg 5:10; 12:14; Dt 3:14 **6** Jdg 2:11; 3:7; 4:1; 6:1; 13:1; Jdg 2:13; Jdg 2:12; 1Ki 11:33; Ps 106:36 **7** Jdg 2:14; 1Sa 12:9 **10** 1Sa 12:10 **11** Ex 14:30; Nu 21:21,24,25; Jdg 3:12,13; Jdg 3:31 **12** Jdg 5:19; Jdg 6:3; Ps 106:42,43 **13** Jer 2:13 **14** Dt 32:37,38 **15** 1Sa 3:18; 2Sa 15:26 **16** 2Ch 7:14; 15:8; Jer 18:7,8; Ps 106:44,45; Isa 63:9 **17** Ge 31:49; Jdg 11:11,29

Gilead. And the sons of Israel assembled and camped at Mizpah.

18The people, the leaders of Gilead (Israel) said to one another, "Who is the man who will begin to fight against the Ammonites? He shall become head over all the inhabitants of Gilead."

Jephthah the Ninth Judge

11 NOW JEPHTHAH the Gileadite was a brave warrior, but he was the son of a prostitute. Gilead was the father of Jephthah.

2Gilead's wife bore him sons, and when his wife's sons grew up, they drove Jephthah out and said to him, "You shall not have an inheritance in our father's house, because you are the son of another woman."

3Then Jephthah fled from his brothers and lived in the land of Tob; and worthless *and* unprincipled men gathered around Jephthah, and went out [on raids] with him.

4Now it happened after a while that the Ammonites fought against Israel.

5When the Ammonites fought against Israel, the elders of Gilead went to get Jephthah from the land of Tob;

6and they said to Jephthah, "Come and be our leader, so that we may fight against the Ammonites."

7But Jephthah said to the elders of Gilead, "Did you not hate me and drive me from the house of my father? Why have you come to me now when you are in trouble?"

8The elders of Gilead said to Jephthah, "This is why we have turned to you now: that you may go with us and fight the Ammonites and become head over all the inhabitants of Gilead."

9So Jephthah said to the elders of Gilead, "If you take me back [home] to fight against the Ammonites and the LORD gives them over to me, will I [really] become your head?"

10The elders of Gilead said to Jephthah, "The LORD is the witness between us; be assured that we will do as you have said."

11So Jephthah went with the elders of Gilead, and the people made him head and leader over them. And Jephthah repeated everything that he had promised before the LORD at Mizpah.

12Now Jephthah sent messengers to the king of the Ammonites, saying, "What is [the problem] between you and me, that you have come against me to fight in my land?"

13The Ammonites' king replied to the messengers of Jephthah, "It is because Israel took away my land when they came up from Egypt, from the [river] Arnon as far as the Jabbok and [east of] the Jordan; so now, return those lands peaceably."

14But Jephthah sent messengers again to the king of the Ammonites,

15and they said to him, "This is what Jephthah says: 'Israel did not take the land of Moab or the land of the Ammonites.

16'For when they came up from Egypt, Israel walked through the wilderness to the Red Sea and came to Kadesh;

17then Israel sent messengers to the king of Edom, saying, "Please let us pass through your land," but the king of Edom would not listen. Also they

---

He is a God of great mercy and compassion. Despite their constant sinning and backsliding, God still loved the Israelites and shared their misery, much as parents are moved by their children's suffering.

11:8 *you may go with us and fight.* This is almost the same phrase that the Israelites used when they asked Samuel for a king (1Sa 8:20).

11:11 *promised before the LORD.* Jephthah's promises "before the Lord" are a strange mixture of faith and foolishness. While Jephthah did acknowledge God, his self-interest and foolishness often overruled his faith. The Book of Hebrews has a more positive view of him. Jephthah is one of those listed "who by faith [that is, with an enduring trust in God and His promises] subdued kingdoms, administered justice, obtained promised blessings . . ." (Heb 11:32 – 33).

18 Jdg 11:8,11 **CHAPTER 11** **1** Jdg 6:12; 2Ki 5:1 **3** Jdg 9:4; 1Sa 22:2 **7** Ge 26:27 **8** Jdg 10:18; Lk 17:4; Jdg 10:18 **10** Jer 42:5 **11** ver. 8; Jdg 10:17; 20:1; 1Sa 10:17; 11:15 **13** Nu 21:24-26; Ge 32:22 **15** Dt 2:9,19 **16** Nu 13:26; 20:1; Dt 1:46 **17** Nu 20:14,18,21; Nu 20:1

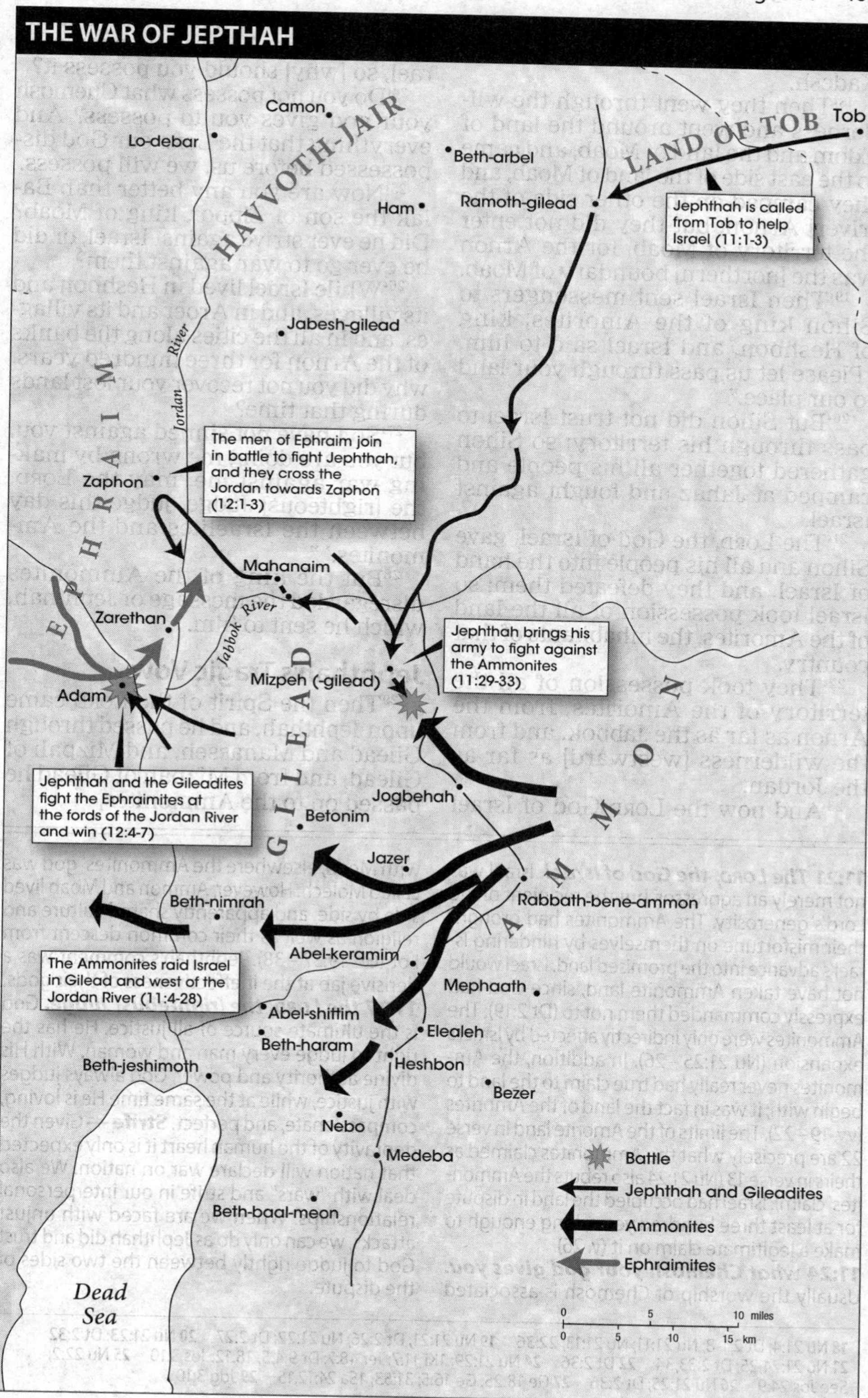
THE WAR OF JEPTHAH
Camon
Lo-debar
HAVVOTH-JAIR
Beth-arbel
LAND OF TOB
Tob
Ham
Ramoth-gilead
Jephthah is called from Tob to help Israel (11:1-3)
Jabesh-gilead
Jordan River
E P H R A I M
The men of Ephraim join in battle to fight Jephthah, and they cross the Jordan towards Zaphon (12:1-3)
Zaphon
Mahanaim
Jabbok River
Zarethan
Jephthah brings his army to fight against the Ammonites (11:29-33)
Mizpeh (-gilead)
Adam
G I L E A D
A M M O N
Jephthah and the Gileadites fight the Ephraimites at the fords of the Jordan River and win (12:4-7)
Jogbehah
Betonim
Jazer
Beth-nimrah
Rabbath-bene-ammon
Abel-keramim
The Ammonites raid Israel in Gilead and west of the Jordan River (11:4-28)
Mephaath
Abel-shittim
Elealeh
Beth-haram
Beth-jeshimoth
Heshbon
Bezer
Nebo
Medeba
Beth-baal-meon
Dead Sea
Battle
Jephthah and Gileadites
Ammonites
Ephraimites
0 5 10 miles
0 5 10 15 km

sent *word* to the king of Moab, but he
would not consent. So Israel stayed at
Kadesh.
18‘Then they went through the wil-
derness and went around the land of
Edom and the land of Moab, and came
to the east side of the land of Moab, and
they camped on the other side of the
[river] Arnon; but they did not enter
the territory of Moab, for the Arnon
was the [northern] boundary of Moab.
19‘Then Israel sent messengers to
Sihon king of the Amorites, king
of Heshbon, and Israel said to him,
“Please let us pass through your land
to our place.”
20‘But Sihon did not trust Israel to
pass through his territory; so Sihon
gathered together all his people and
camped at Jahaz and fought against
Israel.
21‘The LORD, the God of Israel, gave
Sihon and all his people into the hand
of Israel, and they defeated them; so
Israel took possession of all the land
of the Amorites, the inhabitants of that
country.
22‘They took possession of all the
territory of the Amorites, from the
Arnon as far as the Jabbok, and from
the wilderness [westward] as far as
the Jordan.
23‘And now the LORD God of Israel
has dispossessed *and* driven out the
Amorites from before His people Is-
rael, so [why] should you possess it?
24‘Do you not possess what Chemosh
your god gives you to possess? And
everything that the LORD our God dis-
possessed before us, we will possess.
25‘Now are you any better than Ba-
lak the son of Zippor, king of Moab?
Did he ever strive against Israel, or did
he ever go to war against them?
26‘While Israel lived in Heshbon and
its villages, and in Aroer and its villag-
es, and in all the cities along the banks
of the Arnon for three hundred years,
why did you not recover your lost lands
during that time?
27‘So I have not sinned against you,
but you are doing me wrong by mak-
ing war against me; may the LORD,
the [righteous] Judge, judge this day
between the Israelites and the Am-
monites.’ ”
28But the king of the Ammonites
disregarded the message of Jephthah,
which he sent to him.

Jephthah’s Tragic Vow

29Then the Spirit of the LORD came
upon Jephthah, and he passed through
Gilead and Manasseh, and Mizpah of
Gilead, and from Mizpah of Gilead he
passed on to the Ammonites.

11:21 *The LORD, the God of Israel.* Israel was not merely an aggressor, but the recipient of the Lord’s generosity. The Ammonites had brought their misfortune on themselves by hindering Israel’s advance into the promised land. Israel would not have taken Ammonite land, since God had expressly commanded them not to (Dt 2:19). The Ammonites were only indirectly affected by Israel’s expansion (Nu 21:25 – 26). In addition, the Ammonites never really had true claim to the land to begin with; it was in fact the land of the Amorites (vv. 19 – 22). The limits of the Amorite land in verse 22 are precisely what the Ammonites claimed as theirs in verse 13 (Nu 21:24 also rebuts the Ammonites’ claim). Israel had occupied the land in dispute for at least three hundred years, long enough to make a legitimate claim on it (v. 26).

11:24 *what Chemosh your god gives you.* Usually the worship of Chemosh is associated with Moab, elsewhere the Ammonites’ god was called Molech. However, Ammon and Moab lived side by side, and apparently shared culture and religion as well as their common descent from Lot (Ge 19:37 – 38). Jephthah’s comment was a derisive jab at the ineffectiveness of their gods.

11:27 *the LORD, the [righteous] Judge.* God is the ultimate source of all justice. He has the right to judge every man and woman. With His divine authority and power, God always judges with justice, while at the same time He is loving, compassionate, and perfect. **Strife** — Given the depravity of the human heart it is only expected that nation will declare war on nation. We also deal with “wars” and strife in our interpersonal relationships. When we are faced with unjust attacks, we can only do as Jephthah did and trust God to judge rightly between the two sides of the dispute.

18 Nu 21:4; Dt 2:1-8; Nu 21:11; Nu 21:13; 22:36 **19** Nu 21:21; Dt 2:26; Nu 21:22; Dt 2:27 **20** Nu 21:23; Dt 2:32 **21** Nu 21:24,25; Dt 2:33,34 **22** Dt 2:36 **24** Nu 21:29; 1Ki 11:7; Jer 48:7; Dt 9:4,5; 18:12; Jos 3:10 **25** Nu 22:2; See Jos 24:9 **26** Nu 21:25; Dt 2:36 **27** Ge 18:25; Ge 16:5; 31:53; 1Sa 24:12,15 **29** Jdg 3:10

[30]Jephthah made a vow to the LORD
and said, "If You will indeed give the
Ammonites into my hand,
[31]then whatever comes out of the
doors of my house to meet me when I
return in peace from the Ammonites,
it shall be the LORD's, and I will offer
it up as a burnt offering."
[32]Then Jephthah crossed over to the
Ammonites to fight with them; and the
LORD gave them into his hand.
[33]And from Aroer to the entrance of
Minnith he struck them, twenty cities,
and as far as Abel-keramim (brook by
the vineyard), with a very great defeat.
So the Ammonites were subdued *and*
humbled before the Israelites.
[34]Then Jephthah came to his house
at Mizpah, and this is what he saw: his
daughter coming out to meet him with
tambourines and with dancing. And
she was his only child; except for her
he had no son or daughter.
[35]And when he saw her, he tore his
clothes [in grief] and said, "Alas, my
daughter! You have brought me great
disaster, and you are the cause of ruin
to me; for I have made a vow to the
LORD, and I cannot take it back."
[36]And she said to him, "My father,
you have made a vow to the LORD; do to
me as you have vowed, since the LORD
has taken vengeance for you on your
enemies, the Ammonites."
[37]And she said to her father, "Let this
one thing be done for me; let me alone
for two months, so that I may go to the
mountains and weep over my virginity,
I and my companions."
[38]And he said, "Go." So he sent her
away for two months; and she left with
her companions, and wept over her
virginity on the mountains.
[39]At the end of two months she re-
turned to her father, who did to her as
he had vowed; and she had no relations
with a man. It became a custom in
Israel,
[40]that the daughters of Israel went
yearly to tell the story of the daughter
of Jephthah the Gileadite four days in
the year.

Jephthah and His Successors

12 THE MEN of [the tribe of]
Ephraim were summoned [to
action], and they crossed over to Za-
phon and said to Jephthah, "Why did
you cross over to fight with the Am-
monites without calling us to go with

11:31 ***whatever comes out of the doors of my house.*** Some have interpreted Jephthah's vow as a clear intention to offer a human sacrifice. The phrase "to meet me," coupled with coming out of the house seems to refer more appropriately to a human than an animal. Undoubtedly Jephthah knew that human sacrifice was strictly forbidden in Israel (Lev 18:21; 20:2; Dt 12:31; 18:10; Jer 19:5; Eze 20:30 – 31; 23:37 – 39), but his foolishness and lack of faith impelled him to make a reckless vow in order to try to manipulate God.

11:35 ***I have made a vow to the LORD, and I cannot take it back.*** Did Jephthah have to follow through on his vow? Ordinarily the answer would be yes. Vows were made only to God, and they were solemn pledges that had to be kept (Dt 23:21 – 23; Ps 15:4; Ecc 5:4 – 5). But if Jephthah intended his vow to include human sacrifice, he was vowing to sin, an action which could hardly please the Lord.

11:39 ***did to her as he had vowed.*** The text does not explicitly say that he killed his daughter, and some believe that instead he "sacrificed" her by dedicating her to a life of virginity. Human sacrifice was contrary to the law of Moses (Lev 18:21; 20:2 – 5; Dt 12:31; 18:10). Until the wicked reigns of Ahaz and Manasseh centuries later (2Ki 16:3; 21:6), there is no record of human sacrifice in Israel, even by those who followed Baal. The great respect that Jephthah had for God would surely have prevented him from making such a perverse offering. The several references to her virginity seem to support the idea of lifelong celibacy, and the Bible provides evidence that such devoted service for women did exist at the central sanctuary (Ex 38:8; 1Sa 2:22; Lk 2:36 – 37). Jephthah's vow in verse 31 could be translated "shall be the LORD's, *or* I will offer it up as a burnt offering." Thus his vow could be interpreted that if a person came out first, he would dedicate that person to the Lord, or if an animal came out first, he would offer the animal as a burnt sacrifice. As is frequently the case in the Book of Judges, we are given the bare facts of a puzzling story and no comment about what God thought of it.

30 Ge 28:20 **31** See 1Sa 1:11,28; Ps 66:13 **33** Eze 27:17 **34** ver. 11; Jdg 10:17; Ex 15:20; Ps 68:25; Jer 31:4 **35** Ge 37:29,34; Ecc 5:2; Nu 30:2 **36** Nu 30:2; 2Sa 18:19,31 **39** ver. 31; 1Sa 1:22,24 **CHAPTER 12** **1** See Jdg 8:1

you? [For that] we will burn your house down upon you."

2 And Jephthah said to them, "My people and I were in a major conflict with the Ammonites, and when I called you [for help], you did not rescue me from their hand.

3 "So when I saw that you were not coming to help me, I took my life in my hands and crossed over against the Ammonites, and the LORD handed them over to me. So why have you come up to me this day to fight against me?"

4 Then Jephthah assembled all the men of Gilead and fought with [the tribe of] Ephraim; and the men of Gilead defeated Ephraim, because they had said, "You Gileadites are fugitives of Ephraim, in the midst of [the tribes of] Ephraim and Manasseh."

5 And the Gileadites took the fords of the Jordan opposite the Ephraimites; and when *any of* the fugitives of Ephraim said, "Let me cross over," the men of Gilead would say to him, "Are you an Ephraimite?" If he said, "No,"

6 they said to him, "Then say 'Shibboleth.'" And he said, "Sibboleth," for he could not pronounce it correctly. Then they seized him and killed him at the fords of the Jordan. At that time forty-two thousand of the Ephraimites fell.

7 Jephthah judged Israel for six years. Then Jephthah the Gileadite died and was buried in *one of* the cities of Gilead.

8 And after him Ibzan of Bethlehem judged Israel.

9 He had thirty sons, and thirty daughters whom he gave in marriage outside *the family,* and he brought in thirty daughters [-in-law] from outside for his sons. He judged Israel for seven years.

10 Then Ibzan died and was buried at Bethlehem.

11 After him Elon the Zebulunite judged Israel; and he judged Israel for ten years.

12 Then Elon the Zebulunite died and was buried at Aijalon in the land of Zebulun.

13 Now after him Abdon the son of Hillel the Pirathonite judged Israel.

14 He had forty sons and thirty grandsons who rode on seventy donkeys; and he judged Israel for eight years.

15 Then Abdon the son of Hillel the Pirathonite died and was buried at Pirathon in the land of Ephraim, in the hill country of the Amalekites.

Philistines Oppress Again

13 NOW ISRAEL again did what was evil in the sight of the LORD, and the LORD gave them into the hands of the Philistines for forty years.

2 And there was a certain man of Zorah, of the family of the Danites,

12:2 Strife — Gilead and Ephraim grew so hostile that they came to blows, brother fighting against brother. Instead of putting their energy into fighting their common enemy, they were fighting each other. In the same way, today, Christians often react with hurt feelings, pride, and resentment, and prefer to fight against flesh and blood rather than against principalities and powers. The constant infighting Christians indulge in is often a reason for the rest of the world to pass the church off as much ado about nothing.

12:4 *You . . . are fugitives of Ephraim.* This insult may have its roots in the division of the nation into eastern and western groups (5:17; Jos 1:12 – 15). Despite the emphasis in Joshua on the unity of all the tribes (Jos 1:12 – 15; 22:1 – 34), the practical reality in the period of the judges was dramatically different.

12:6 *Shibboleth . . . Sibboleth.* This is the only significant reference to the linguistic differences which apparently existed between the tribes. Today the English word *shibboleth* means an otherwise minor difference that becomes a sticking point because it distinguishes one side from the other.

13:1 – 16:31 Samson — The last of the judges lived at the beginning of the eleventh century BC. He was unusual among the judges in many ways. He did not lead an army, but carried on his campaign against the Philistines singlehandedly. He is mentioned in Hebrews 11:32 in the list of judges who accomplished great things through faith. The Book of Judges, in contrast, paints a darker picture. His checkered history of heroism and moral failure resembles Israel's troubles during the time of the judges.

3 1Sa 19:5; Ps 119:109 **4** See 1Sa 25:10 **5** Jos 22:11; Jdg 3:28 **14** Jdg 5:10; 10:4 **15** Jdg 3:13,27; 5:14
CHAPTER 13 **1** Jdg 2:11; 3:7; 4:1; 6:1; 10:6; 1Sa 12:9 **2** Jos 19:41

whose name was Manoah; and his
wife was infertile and had no *children.*
[3]And the Angel of the LORD appeared
to the woman and said to her, "Behold,
you are infertile and have no *children,*
but you shall conceive and give birth
to a son.
[4]"Therefore, be careful not to drink
wine or [any other] intoxicating drink,
and do not eat anything [ceremonially]
unclean.
[5]"For behold, you shall conceive and
give birth to a son. No razor shall come
upon his head, for the boy shall be a
Nazirite [dedicated] to God from birth;
and he shall begin to rescue Israel from
the hands of the Philistines."
[6]Then the woman went and told her
husband, saying, "A Man of God came
to me and his appearance was like the
appearance of the Angel of God, very
awesome. I did not ask Him where he
came from, and he did not tell me his
name.
[7]"But He said to me, 'Behold, you
shall conceive and give birth to a son,
and now you shall not drink wine or
[any other] intoxicating drink, nor eat
anything [ceremonially] unclean, for
the boy shall be a Nazirite to God from
birth to the day of his death.' "
[8]Then Manoah pleaded with the
LORD and said, "O Lord, please let the
Man of God whom You sent come
again to us and teach us what we are
to do for the boy who is to be born."
[9]And God listened to the voice of
Manoah; and the Angel of God came
again to the woman as she sat in the
field, but Manoah her husband was
not with her.
[10]So the woman ran quickly and told
her husband, "Behold, the Man who
came to me the other day has appeared
to me."
[11]Then Manoah got up and followed
his wife, and came to the Man and said
to him, "Are you the Man who spoke to
this woman?" He said, "I am."
[12]And Manoah said, "Now when
your words come *true,* what shall be
the boy's manner of life, and his vo-
cation?"
[13]The Angel of the LORD said to Ma-
noah, "The woman must pay attention
to everything that I said to her.
[14]"She may not eat anything that
comes from the vine nor drink wine
or [any other] intoxicating drink, nor
eat anything [ceremonially] unclean.
She shall observe everything that I
commanded her."
[15]Then Manoah said to the Angel
of the LORD, "Please let us detain you
and let us prepare a young goat for
you [to eat]."
[16]The Angel of the LORD said to Ma-
noah, "Though you detain me, I will
not eat your food, but if you prepare
a burnt offering, offer it to the LORD."
For Manoah did not know that he was
the Angel of the LORD.
[17]Manoah said to the Angel of the
LORD, "What is your name, so that
when your words come *true,* we may
honor you?"
[18]But the Angel of the LORD said
to him, "Why do you ask my name,
seeing it is wonderful (miraculous)?"
[Is 9:6]
[19]So Manoah took the young goat
with the grain offering and offered it

13:3 *the Angel of the LORD.* The angel of the Lord made a supernatural appearance, described here as "very awesome." Manoah's wife recognized him as "a Man of God." The essential character of the angel, embodied in his name, was not revealed to them (vv. 17 – 18). It seems that the angel of the Lord was God Himself, in a form they could perceive (13:21 – 22; Ge 22:11; Ex 3:14 – 15).
13:5 *Nazirite.* The regulations of the Nazirite vows are found in Numbers 6:1 – 21. Samson's Nazirite service was remarkable in three ways. First, he did not take his vow voluntarily; it was his before birth. Second, his service was to be lifelong, not temporary. Third, he eventually broke every one of its stipulations.
13:6 *Man of God.* This was a term used to describe the prophets (Dt 33:1; 1Ki 17:18). At first Samson's mother may have thought she was talking to a prophet, but His radiant appearance convinced her otherwise.

3 Jdg 6:12; Lk 1:11,13,28,31 **4** ver. 14; Nu 6:2,3; Lk 1:15 **5** Nu 6:5; 1Sa 1:11; Nu 6:2; See 1Sa 7:13; 2Sa 8:1; 1Ch 18:1 **6** Dt 33:1; 1Sa 2:27; 9:6; Mt 28:3; Lk 9:29; Ac 6:15; ver. 17,18 **14** ver. 4 **15** Ge 18:5; Jdg 6:18 **18** Ge 32:29 **19** Jdg 6:19,20

on the rock to the LORD, and He per-
formed miracles while Manoah and
his wife looked on.
20 For when the flame went up toward
heaven from the altar, the Angel of
the LORD ascended in the altar flame.
When Manoah and his wife saw this
they fell on their faces to the ground.
21 The Angel of the LORD did not
appear again to Manoah or his wife.
Then Manoah knew that he was the
Angel of the LORD.
22 So Manoah said to his wife, "We
will certainly die, because we have
seen God."
23 But his [sensible] wife said to him,
"If the LORD had desired to kill us, He
would not have received a burnt of-
fering and a grain offering from our
hands, nor would He have shown us
all these things, nor would He have
announced *such things* as these at
this time."
24 So the woman [in due time] gave
birth to a son and named him Sam-
son; and the boy grew and the LORD
blessed him.
25 And the Spirit of the LORD began
to stir him at times in Mahaneh-dan,
between Zorah and Eshtaol.

Samson's Marriage

14 SAMSON WENT down to Tim-
nah and at Timnah he saw a
woman, one of the daughters of the
Philistines.
2 So he went back and told his father
and his mother, "I saw a woman in Tim-
nah, one of the daughters of the Phi-
listines; now get her for me as a wife."
3 But his father and mother said to
him, "Is there no woman among the
daughters of your relatives, or among
all our people, that you must go to take
a wife from the uncircumcised (pagan)
Philistines?" And Samson said to his
father, "Get her for me, because she
looks pleasing to me."
4 His father and mother did not know
that it was of the LORD, and that He was
seeking an occasion [to take action]
against the Philistines. Now at that time
the Philistines were ruling over Israel.
5 Then Samson went down to Tim-
nah with his father and mother [to
arrange the marriage], and they came
as far as the vineyards of Timnah; and
suddenly, a young lion *came* roaring
toward him.
6 The Spirit of the LORD came upon
him mightily, and he tore the lion apart

13:21–22 *The Angel of the LORD.* Manoah's reaction is similar to the reaction Gideon had when he recognized the angel of the Lord (6:22).
13:25 *the Spirit of the LORD began to stir him.* The Hebrew word translated *stir* can also mean *impel*. The Spirit of the Lord was pushing Samson toward doing the work that God wanted him to do.
14:2 *get her for me as a wife.* Such marriages with foreigners were prohibited for Israelites (Ex 34:16; Dt 7:3).
14:3 *she looks pleasing to me.* Samson's words reveal his self-centered attitude. Instead of seeking to serve God, he was seeking to please himself. Samson's comment here foreshadows the author's summary of the entire period of the judges (17:6; 18:1; 19:1; 21:25). **Unfaithfulness** — The beginning of Samson's downfall was his disobedience to the Lord in his marriage. The theme of marriage within the covenant is common in the Old Testament. From earliest times the people of God were told not to contract marriages with unbelievers (Ge 6:2). When the covenant was renewed prior to the people's entry into Canaanite territory, Joshua warned them not to intermarry; to do so would be evidence of their failure to cling to the Lord (Jos 23:8,12). It is a tragic picture of the decadence of this period to see Samson's unfaithfulness to the Lord in taking a pagan wife. The New Covenant believer remains under the same divine command to marry only in the Lord (1Co 7:39; 2Co 6:14).
14:4 *it was of the LORD.* God would use Samson's defiant wish as a way of defeating the Philistines and providing relief for His people.
14:6 *The Spirit of the LORD came upon him mightily.* The Old Testament speaks numerous times of God's Spirit coming mightily upon individuals, usually to empower them physically for great feats of strength (3:10; 6:34; 11:29). The Spirit empowered others for the important task of speaking God's word (Ge 41:38; Nu 24:2; 1Sa 10:6; 19:20).

20 Lev 9:24; 1Ch 21:16; Eze 1:28; Mt 17:6 **21** Jdg 6:22 **22** Ge 32:30; Ex 33:20; Dt 5:26; Jdg 6:22 **24** Heb 11:32; 1Sa 3:19; Lk 1:80; 2:52 **25** Jdg 3:10; 1Sa 11:6; Mt 4:1; Jos 15:33; Jdg 18:11 **CHAPTER 14** **1** Ge 38:13; Jos 15:10; Ge 34:2 **2** Ge 21:21; 34:4 **3** Ge 24:3,4; Ge 34:14; Ex 34:16; Dt 7:3 **4** Jos 11:20; 1Ki 12:15; 2Ki 6:33; 2Ch 10:15; 22:7; 25:20; Jdg 13:1; Dt 28:48 **6** Jdg 3:10; 13:25; 1Sa 11:6

as one tears apart a young goat, and he
had nothing at all in his hand; but he
did not tell his father or mother what
he had done.
7 So he went down and talked with
the woman; and she looked pleasing
to Samson.
8 When he returned later to take her,
he turned aside to see the carcass of
the lion; and behold, a swarm of bees
and honey were in the body of the lion.
9 So he scraped the honey out into his
hands and went on, eating as he went.
When he came to his father and moth-
er, he gave them *some*, and they ate it;
but he did not tell them he had taken
the honey from the body of the lion.
10 His father went down to the wom-
an, and Samson prepared a feast there,
for that was the customary thing for
young men to do.
11 When the people saw him, they
brought thirty companions (wedding
attendants) to be with him.

Samson's Riddle

12 Then Samson said to them, "Let me
now ask you a riddle; if you can tell me
what it is within the seven days of the
feast, and solve it, then I will give you
thirty linen tunics (undergarments)
and thirty changes of [outer] clothing.
13 "But if you are unable to tell me
[the answer], then you shall give me
thirty linen tunics (undergarments)
and thirty changes of [outer] clothing."
And they said to him, "Ask your riddle,
so that we may hear it."
14 So he said to them,

"Out of the eater came something
to eat,
And out of the strong came
something sweet."

And they could not solve the riddle in
three days.
15 Then on the fourth day they said
to Samson's wife, "Persuade your hus-
band to tell us [through you] the [an-
swer to the] riddle, or we will burn you
and your father's household with fire.
Have you invited us to make us poor?
Is this not *true*?"
16 So Samson's wife wept before him
and said, "You only hate me, you do
not love me; you have asked my coun-
trymen a riddle, and have not told [the
answer] to me." And he said to her,
"Listen, I have not told my father or
my mother [either], so [why] should I
tell you?"
17 However Samson's wife wept be-
fore him seven days while their [wed-
ding] feast lasted, and on the seventh
day he told her because she pressed
him so hard. Then she told the [answer
to the] riddle to her countrymen.
18 So the men of the city said to Sam-
son on the seventh day before sun-
down,

"What is sweeter than honey?
What is stronger than a lion?"

And he said to them,

"If you had not plowed with my
heifer,
You would not have solved my
riddle."

19 Then the Spirit of the LORD came
upon him mightily, and he went down
to Ashkelon and killed thirty of them
and took their gear, and gave changes
of clothes to those who had explained
the riddle. And his anger burned, and
he went up to his father's house.
20 But Samson's wife was *given* to his
companion who had been his friend.

It appears that the work of the Holy Spirit in the Old Testament was primarily a special anointing to accomplish a certain task, and was different from the indwelling Presence that believers enjoy today. Saul (1Sa 10:10; 16:23) and David (1Sa 16:13; Ps 51:11) were both filled with the Holy Spirit when they were anointed as king, but this presence seems to have been directly linked to their obedience.

14:8–9 *carcass of the lion.* Touching the dead lion violated Samson's Nazirite vow (13:5).

14:10 *feast.* The word translated *feast* denotes a banquet with considerable drinking. The passage does not say so, but it is not unlikely that this occasioned another violation of Samson's Nazirite vow (13:5).

12 1Ki 10:1; Eze 17:2; Lk 14:7; Ge 29:27; Ge 45:22; 2Ki 5:22 **15** Jdg 16:5; Jdg 15:6 **16** Jdg 16:15 **19** Jdg 3:10; 13:25 **20** Jdg 15:2; Jn 3:29

Samson Burns Philistine Crops

15 BUT AFTER a while, in the time
of wheat harvest, Samson went
to visit his wife with a young goat [as
a gift of reconciliation]; and he said, "I
will go in to my wife in *her* room." But
her father would not allow him to go in.
2Her father said, "I really thought
you utterly hated her; so I gave her to
your companion. Is her younger sister
not more beautiful than she? Please
take her [as your wife] instead."
3Samson said to them, "This time
I shall be blameless in regard to the
Philistines when I do them harm."
4So Samson went and caught three
hundred foxes, and took torches and
turning *the foxes* tail to tail, he put a
torch between each pair of tails.
5When he had set the torches ablaze,
he let the foxes go into the standing
grain of the Philistines, and he burned
up the heap of sheaves and the stand-
ing grain, along with the vineyards
and olive groves.
6Then the Philistines said, "Who did
this?" And they were told, "Samson,
the son-in-law of the Timnite, because
he took Samson's wife and gave her to
his [chief] companion [at the wedding
feast]." So the Philistines came up and
burned her and her father with fire.
7Samson said to them, "If this is the
way you act, be certain that I will take
revenge on you, and [only] after that
I will stop."
8Then he struck them without mercy,
a great slaughter; and he went down
and lived in the cleft of the rock of Etam.
9Then the [army of the] Philistines
came up and camped in [the tribal
territory of] Judah, and overran Lehi
(Jawbone).
10The men of Judah said, "Why have
you come up against us?" And they
answered, "We have come up to bind
Samson, in order to do to him as he
has done to us."
11Then three thousand men of Judah
went down to the cleft of the rock of
Etam and said to Samson, "Have you
not known that the Philistines are rul-
ers over us? What is this that you have
done to us?" He said to them, "As they
did to me, so I have done to them."
12They said to him, "We have come
down to bind you, so that we may hand
you over to the Philistines." And Sam-
son said to them, "Swear to me that you
will not kill me."
13So they said to him, "No, we will
[only] bind you securely and place you
into their hands; but we certainly will
not kill you." So they bound him with
two new ropes and brought him up
from the rock [of Etam].
14When he came to Lehi, the Philis-
tines came shouting to meet him. And
the Spirit of the LORD came upon him
mightily, and the ropes on his arms
were like flax (linen) that had been
burned, and his bonds dropped off
his hands.
15He found a fresh jawbone of a
donkey, so he reached out his hand
and took it and killed a thousand men
with it.
16Then Samson said,

"With the jawbone of a donkey,
Heaps upon heaps,
With the jawbone of a donkey
I have struck down a thousand
men."

17When he finished speaking, he threw
the jawbone from his hand; and he
named that place Ramath-lehi (hill of
the jawbone).
18Then Samson was very thirsty,
and he called out to the LORD and

15:1 *the time of wheat harvest.* This would have been late May or early June. The wheat harvest was associated with the second of the three great feasts in Israel, the Feast of Weeks, also known as Pentecost (Lev 23:15–22; Dt 16:9–12).
15:13 *two new ropes.* Ropes were made of leather, hair, or plant fibers; one common fiber was flax (Jos 2:6). Being new, these ropes were the strongest possible.
15:15 *a fresh jawbone.* A fresh jawbone would have been tough, resilient, and virtually unbreakable.
15:18 *called out to the LORD.* This is the first record of Samson calling on the Lord.

CHAPTER 15 **2** Jdg 14:20 **6** Jdg 14:15 **9** ver. 19 **11** Jdg 14:4 **14** Jdg 3:10; 14:6 **15** Lev 26:8; Jos 23:10; Jdg 3:31 **18** Ps 3:7

said, "You have given this great vic-
tory through the hand of Your servant,
and now am I to die of thirst and fall
into the hands of the uncircumcised
(pagans)?"
19 So God split open the hollow place
that was at Lehi, and water came out
of it. When Samson drank, his spir-
it (strength) returned and he was
revived. Therefore he named it En-
hakkore (spring which is calling),
which is at Lehi to this day.
20 And Samson judged Israel in the
days of [occupation by] the Philistines
for twenty years. [Judg 17:6]

Samson's Weakness

16 THEN SAMSON went to Gaza
and saw a prostitute there, and
went in to her.
2 The Gazites *were told,* "Samson
has come here." So they surrounded
the place and waited all night at the
gate of the city to ambush him. They
kept quiet all night, saying, "In the
morning, when it is light, we will kill
him."
3 But Samson lay [resting] until mid-
night, then at midnight he got up and
took hold of the doors of the city gate
and the two door-posts, and pulled
them up, [security] bar and all, and he
put them on his shoulders and carried
them up to the top of the hill which is
opposite Hebron.
4 After this he fell in love with a [Phi-
listine] woman [living] in the Valley of
Sorek, whose name was Delilah.
5 So the [five] lords (governors) of
the Philistines came to her and said
to her, "Persuade him, and see where
his great strength *lies* and [find out]
how we may overpower him so that
we may bind him to subdue him. And
each of us will give you eleven hundred
pieces of silver."
6 So Delilah said to Samson, "Please
tell me where your great strength lies
and with what you may be bound and
subdued."
7 Samson said to her, "If they bind
me with seven fresh cords (tendons)
that have not been dried, then I will
be weak and be like any [other] man."
8 Then the Philistine lords brought
her seven fresh cords that had not
been dried, and she bound him with
them.
9 Now she had men lying in ambush
in an inner room. And she said to
him, "The Philistines are upon you,
Samson!" And he broke the cords as
a string of tow breaks when it touches
fire. So [the secret of] his strength was
not discovered.
10 Then Delilah said to Samson, "See
now, you have mocked me and told me
lies; now please tell me [truthfully] how
you may be bound."
11 He said to her, "If they bind me
tightly with new ropes that have not
been used, then I will become weak
and be like any [other] man."
12 So Delilah took new ropes and
bound him with them and said to him,
"The Philistines are upon you, Sam-
son!" And the men lying in ambush
were in the inner room. But he snapped
the ropes off his arms like [sewing]
thread.
13 Then Delilah said to Samson, "Un-
til now you have mocked me and told
me lies; tell me [truthfully] with what
you may be bound." And he said to her,
"If you weave the seven braids of my
hair with the web [and fasten it with
a pin, then I will become weak and be
like any other man."
14 So while he slept, Delilah took the
seven locks (braids) of his hair and
wove them into the web]. And she fas-
tened it with the pin [of the loom] and
said to him, "The Philistines are upon
you, Samson!" And he awoke from
his sleep and pulled out the pin of the
[weaver's] loom and the web.

16:2 *at the gate.* The gates of this time in history were at least two stories high, with guard rooms on either side of a narrow opening. The Philistines waited in the recesses of the gate, hoping to trap Samson.

16:3 *carried them up to the top of the hill.* Given the large size of the doors of a city gate, Samson's feat was astounding. Hebron is 40 miles east of Gaza. Samson's trip would have taken the better part of a day.

19 Ge 45:27; Isa 40:29 **20** Jdg 13:1 **CHAPTER 16** **2** 1Sa 23:26; Ac 9:24 **5** Jdg 14:15

Delilah Extracts His Secret

15 Then she said to him, "How can you say, 'I love you,' when your heart is not with me? You have mocked me these three times and have not told me where your great strength lies."

16 When she pressured him day after day with her words and pleaded with him, he was annoyed to death.

17 Then [finally] he told her everything that was in his heart and said to her, "A razor has never been used on my head, for I have been a Nazirite to God from my mother's womb. If I am shaved, then my strength will leave me, and I will become weak and be like any [other] man."

18 Then Delilah realized that he had told her everything in his heart, so she sent and called for the Philistine lords, saying, "Come up this once, because he has told me everything in his heart." Then the Philistine lords came up to her and brought the money [they had promised] in their hands.

19 She made Samson sleep on her knees, and she called a man and had him shave off the seven braids of his head. Then she began to abuse Samson, and his strength left him.

20 She said, "The Philistines are upon you, Samson!" And he awoke from his sleep and said, "I will go out as I have time after time and shake myself free." For Samson did not know that the LORD had departed from him.

21 Then the Philistines seized him and gouged out his eyes; and they brought him down to Gaza and bound him with [two] bronze chains; and he was *forced to be* a grinder [of grain into flour at the mill] in the prison.

22 But the hair of his head began to grow again after it had been shaved off.

23 Now the Philistine lords gathered together to offer a great sacrifice to Dagon their god, and to celebrate, for they said,

"Our god has given Samson our
enemy into our hands!"

24 When the people saw Samson, they praised their god, for they said,

"Our god has handed over our
enemy to us,
The ravager of our country,
Who has killed many of us."

25 Now when they were in high spirits, they said, "Call for Samson, so that he may amuse us." So they called Samson out of the prison, and he entertained them. They made him stand between the pillars.

26 Then Samson said to the boy who held him by the hand, "Let me feel the pillars on which the [roof of the] house rests, so that I may lean against them."

27 Now the house was full of men and women; all the Philistine lords were there, and on the flat roof were about three thousand men and women who looked on while Samson was entertaining them.

Samson Is Avenged

28 Then Samson called to the LORD and said, "O Lord GOD, please remember me

---

16:16 *pressured him.* Delilah pestered him, just as his wife had done earlier (14:17). Samson's foolishness prevented him from learning the lesson of his earlier experience.

16:19 *and his strength left him.* When he broke the final stipulation of the Nazirite vow by allowing his hair to be cut, the Lord left him and he was captured.

16:20 *Samson did not know.* This is one of the few editorial comments by the author.

16:23 *Dagon.* Dagon was the principal Philistine god. A Philistine temple for Dagon was at Beth-shan, in northern Israel, in the days of Saul (1Sa 31:9 – 10; 1Ch 10:10), and it was in another such temple that the Philistines stored the ark of the covenant for a time (1Sa 5:1 – 7). Dagon was once commonly thought to be a fish god, but modern excavations have shown that he was a god of grain. In fact, one of the Hebrew words for grain is *dagan*.

16:24 *Our god has handed over our enemy to us.* The Philistines viewed their success over Samson as a triumph for their god (Jdg 16:23 – 24). In reality it was the Lord who had delivered Samson into their hands, for "the LORD had departed from him" (v. 20).

---

15 Jdg 14:16 **17** Mic 7:5; Nu 6:5; Jdg 13:5 **19** Pr 7:26,27 **20** Nu 14:9,42,43; Jos 7:12; 1Sa 16:14; 18:12; 28:15,16; 2Ch 15:2 **24** Da 5:4 **25** Jdg 9:27 **27** Dt 22:8 **28** Jer 15:15

and please strengthen me just this one
time, O God, and let me take vengeance
on the Philistines for my two eyes."
29Samson took hold of the two mid-
dle [support] pillars on which the house
rested, and braced himself against
them, one with his right hand and the
other with his left.
30And Samson said, "Let me die with
the Philistines!" And he stretched out
with all his might [collapsing the sup-
port pillars], and the house fell on the
lords and on all the people who were
in it. So the dead whom he killed at his
death were more than those whom he
had killed during his life.
31Then his brothers and his father's
entire [tribal] household came down,
took him, and brought him up; and
they buried him in the tomb of Manoah
his father, [which was] between Zorah
and Eshtaol. So Samson had judged
Israel for twenty years. [Judg 17:6;
Heb 11:32]

Micah's Idolatry

17 THERE WAS a man of the hill
country of Ephraim whose name
was Micah.
2And he said to his mother, "The
eleven hundred *pieces* of silver which
were taken from you, about which you
cursed [the thief] and also spoke about
in my hearing, behold, the silver is
with me; I took it." And his mother
said, "Blessed be my son before the
LORD."
3He returned the eleven hundred
pieces of silver to his mother, and she
said, "I had truly dedicated the silver
from my hand to the LORD for my son
(in his name) to make an image [carved
from wood and plated with silver] and
a cast image [of solid silver]; so now, I
will return it to you."
4So when he returned the silver
to his mother, she took two hundred
pieces of silver and gave them to the
silversmith who made of it an image [of
silver-plated wood] and a cast image
[of solid silver]; and they were in the
house of Micah.
5Now the man Micah had a house of
gods (shrine), and he made an ephod
and teraphim and dedicated *and* in-
stalled one of his sons, who became
his [personal] priest.

16:30 Zeal — The famous lament of David over Saul and Jonathan, "How the mighty have fallen!" (2Sa 1:19,27), could also be applied to Samson. He came from a godly home, but often was overcome by evil passion, pride, and violence. Yet at death his zeal for the Lord brought about a great victory over the Philistines and their god Dagon, and he is listed in Hebrews as a man of faith (Heb 11:32). The plan and purpose of God overruled Samson's folly and the Philistine's arrogance.

16:31 *Samson had judged Israel for twenty years.* The story of the judges concludes with final editorial comments. Samson, the last judge, had been empowered by God's Spirit, just as the first had been. Despite the manifold failings of the judges themselves, God had delivered Israel and caused other nations to bow before Him. Samson's life is ultimately a story about God's faithfulness in spite of human weakness.

17:1 – 21:25 Conclusion — The Book of Judges closes with two appendices (ch. 17 – 18; 19 – 21). They seem to be unrelated to the material preceding them, and to each other. While chapters 2 – 16 describe foreign threats to Israel, these last chapters show an internal breakdown of Israel's worship and unity. Furthermore, the events of these chapters appear to have taken place early in the period of the judges. These chapters may have been written independently of the book's earlier chapters, but there is a certain logic to placing them at the end of the book. The structure highlights the theme of the disintegration of Israel, with the last chapters emphasizing that "every man did what was right in his own eyes" (17:6; 21:25).

17:3 *I had truly dedicated the silver . . . to the LORD.* Micah's mother approved of his action, claiming that these images would be offered on the Lord's behalf. Today the temptation to mix elements of true worship of God with practices unacceptable to Him remains with us, even though it is in different ways.

17:5 *house of gods.* This is literally "a house of God." This was a perversion of the true sanctuary where all worship was to take place. At this time the true "house of God" was at Shiloh (18:31). Micah further violated the law by appointing his own son as his private priest. Micah sinned because his son had not descended from Aaron, nor was he even a Levite (Ex 28:1; 40:12 – 15; Nu 16:39 – 40; 17:8).

31 Jdg 13:25 **CHAPTER 17** **2** Ge 14:19 **3** See Ex 20:4,23; Lev 19:4 **4** Isa 46:6 **5** Jdg 8:27; Ge 31:19,30; Hos 3:4

6 In those days there was no king in
Israel; every man did what was right
in his own eyes.
7 Now there was a young man from
Bethlehem in Judah, from the family [of
the tribe] of Judah, who was a Levite;
and he was staying there [temporarily].
8 Then the man left the town of Beth-
lehem in Judah, to stay wherever he
could find *a place;* and as he jour-
neyed, he came to the hill country of
Ephraim, to the house of Micah.
9 Micah said to him, "Where do you
come from?" And he said to him, "I
am a Levite from Bethlehem in Judah,
and I am going to stay wherever I can
find *a place.*"
10 And Micah said to him, "Live here
with me and be a father and a [person-
al] priest to me, and I will give you ten
pieces of silver each year, a supply of
clothing, and your sustenance (room
and board)." So the Levite went in.
11 The Levite agreed to live with the
man, and the young man became to
Micah like one of his sons.
12 So Micah dedicated (installed) the
Levite, and the young man became his
priest and lived in the house of Micah.
13 Then Micah said, "Now I know
that the LORD will favor me *and* make
me prosper because I have a Levite as
my priest."

Danites Seek Territory

18 IN THOSE days there was no
king in Israel; and in those days
the tribe of the Danites was seeking
an inheritance [of land] for themselves
to live in, for until then an inheritance
had not been allotted to them as a pos-
session among the tribes of Israel.
2 So the sons of Dan sent from the
total number of their [extended] family
five brave men from Zorah and Esh-
taol, to scout the land and to explore it;
and they said to them, "Go, explore the
land." They came to the hill country of
Ephraim, to the house of Micah, and
lodged there.
3 When they passed near Micah's
house, they recognized the voice of
the young man, the Levite, and they
turned aside there and said to him,
"Who brought you here? And what are
you doing in this place? And what do
you have here?"
4 And he said to them, "Micah has
done this and that for me, and he has
hired me and I have become his priest."
5 And they said to him, "Please ask
of God, so that we may know whether
our journey on which we are going will
be successful."
6 The priest said to them, "Go in
peace; the journey on which you are
going is acceptable to the LORD."
7 Then the five men went on and
came to Laish and saw the people who
were there, [how they were] living se-
curely in the style of the Sidonians,
quiet and peaceful; and there was no
oppressive magistrate in the land hu-
miliating *them* in anything, and they
were far from the Sidonians and had
no dealings with anyone.

17:6 *what was right in his own eyes.* This editorial comment is echoed in the last verse of the book (21:25). The author suggests that times were so bad that people did whatever they wanted, not what was right in the Lord's eyes (14:3). We may infer that a king who focused Israel's attention on the Lord would have prevented the outbreaks of sin and oppression so prevalent during the time of the judges.

17:10 *be a father and a [personal] priest to me.* To be called father was a title of honor. Micah wanted the Levite to be his priest, since his background would lend legitimacy to his service. Micah thought this would bring him God's favor (v. 13).

18:1 *Danites.* The Danites were looking for a place to settle because they had been unable to settle effectively in their allotted territory. Compare their allotment in Joshua 19:41 – 47 and their failure to capture it all (1:34 – 35). It seems clear that this story is not placed chronologically, but refers back to the first chapters of Judges. The Danites' migration in search of new land probably would have come soon after the events of 1:34, not some three centuries or more later.

18:7 *Sidonians.* Sidon was a port city northwest of Israel, in what today is Lebanon.

6 Jdg 18:1; 19:1; 21:25; Dt 12:8 **7** See Jos 19:15; Jdg 19:1; Ru 1:1,2; Mic 5:2; Mt 2:1,5,6 **10** Jdg 18:19; Ge 45:8; Job 29:16 **12** ver. 5; Jdg 18:30 **CHAPTER 18** **1** Jdg 17:6; 21:25; Jos 19:47 **2** Jdg 13:25; Nu 13:17; Jos 2:1; Jdg 17:1 **4** Jdg 17:10 **5** 1Ki 22:5; Isa 30:1; Hos 4:12; See Jdg 17:5; ver. 14 **6** 1Ki 22:6 **7** ver. 27,28

[8]The five men came back [home] to
their brothers at Zorah and Eshtaol,
and their brothers said to them, "What
do you *have to report*?"
[9]They said, "Arise, let us go up
against them; for we have seen the
land, and behold, it is very good (fertile).
Will you sit still *and* do nothing?
Do not hesitate to go, to enter, to take
possession of the land.
[10]"When you enter, you will come to
people [feeling] safe and secure with a
spacious land [widely extended on all
sides]; for God has given it into your
hands—a place where there is no lack
of anything that is on the earth."
[11]Then from the [tribal] family of the
Danites, from Zorah and from Eshtaol,
six hundred men armed with weapons
of war set out.
[12]They went up and camped at
Kiriath-jearim in Judah. Therefore they
have called that place Mahaneh-dan to
this day; it is west of Kiriath-jearim.

8 ver. 2 **9** Nu 13:30; Jos 2:23,24; 1Ki 22:3 **10** ver. 7,27; Dt 8:9 **12** Jos 15:60; Jdg 13:25

THE MIGRATION OF THE TRIBE OF DAN

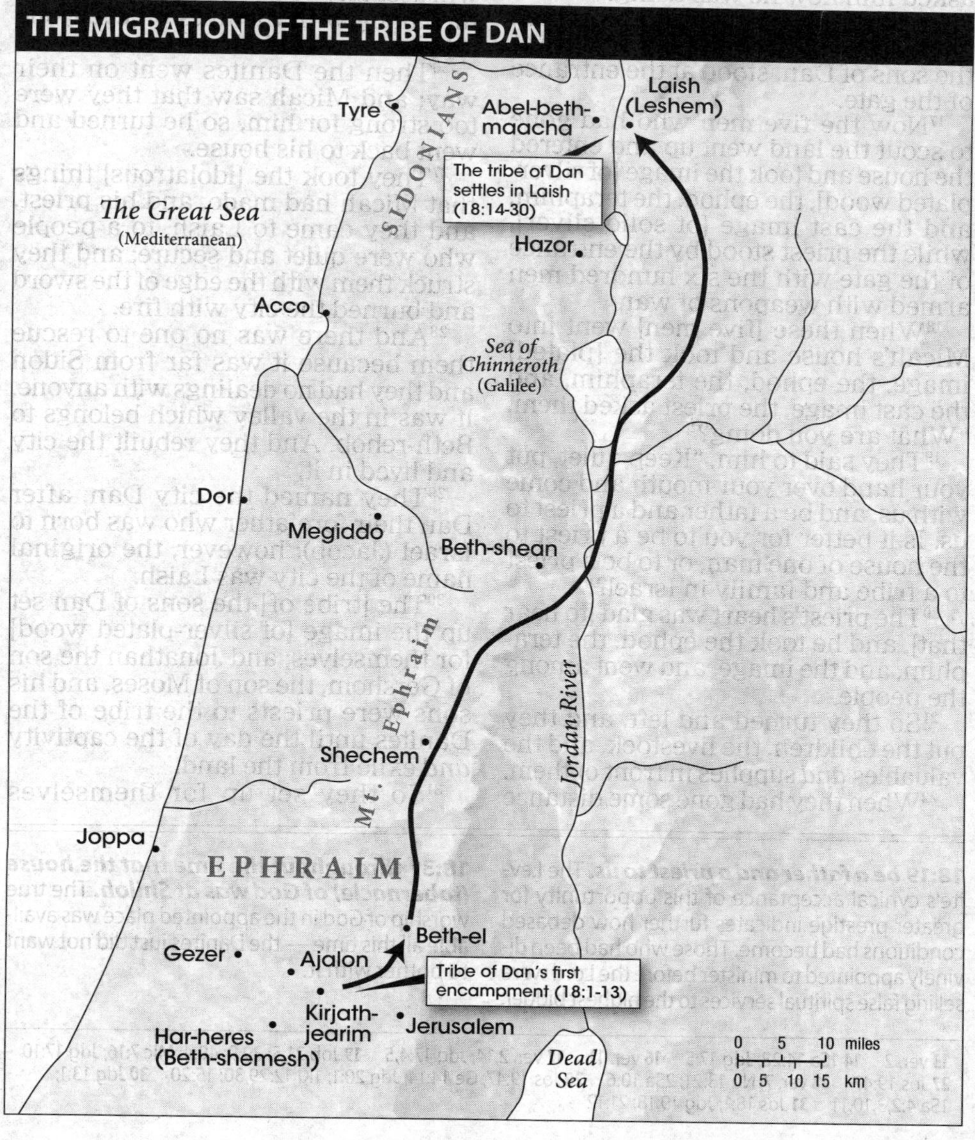

13 They went on from there to the hill country of Ephraim and came to Micah's house.

Danites Take Micah's Idols

14 Then the five men who had gone to scout the country of Laish said to their relatives, "Do you know that there are in these houses an ephod, teraphim, an image [of silver-plated wood], and a cast image [of solid silver]? Now therefore, consider what you should do."

15 So they turned in that direction and came to the house of the young Levite, at the home of Micah, and asked him how he was doing.

16 Now the six hundred men armed with their weapons of war, who were of the sons of Dan, stood at the entrance of the gate.

17 Now the five men who had gone to scout the land went up and entered the house and took the image [of silver-plated wood], the ephod, the teraphim, and the cast image [of solid silver], while the priest stood by the entrance of the gate with the six hundred men armed with weapons of war.

18 When these [five men] went into Micah's house and took the [plated] image, the ephod, the teraphim, and the cast image, the priest asked them, "What are you doing?"

19 They said to him, "Keep quiet, put your hand over your mouth and come with us, and be a father and a priest to us. Is it better for you to be a priest to the house of one man, or to be a priest to a tribe and family in Israel?"

20 The priest's heart was glad [to hear that], and he took the ephod, the teraphim, and the image, and went among the people.

21 So they turned and left, and they put the children, the livestock, and the valuables *and* supplies in front of them.

22 When they had gone some distance from the house of Micah, the men who were [living] in the houses near Micah's house assembled [as a militia] and overtook the sons of Dan.

23 They shouted to the Danites, who turned and said to Micah, "What is your *reason* for assembling [against us]?"

24 He said, "You have taken away my gods which I have made, and the priest, and have gone away; what else do I have left? How can you say to me, 'What is your *reason*?' "

25 The sons of Dan said to him, "Do not let your voice [of complaint] be heard among us, or else angry men will assault you and you will lose your life, along with the lives of [everyone in] your household."

26 Then the Danites went on their way; and Micah saw that they were too strong for him, so he turned and went back to his house.

27 They took the [idolatrous] things that Micah had made, and his priest, and they came to Laish, to a people who were quiet and secure; and they struck them with the edge of the sword and burned the city with fire.

28 And there was no one to rescue them because it was far from Sidon and they had no dealings with anyone. It was in the valley which belongs to Beth-rehob. And they rebuilt the city and lived in it.

29 They named the city Dan, after Dan their forefather who was born to Israel (Jacob); however, the original name of the city was Laish.

30 The [tribe of] the sons of Dan set up the image [of silver-plated wood] for themselves; and Jonathan the son of Gershom, the son of Moses, and his sons were priests to the tribe of the Danites until the day of the captivity *and* exile from the land.

31 So they set up for themselves

18:19 *be a father and a priest to us.* The Levite's cynical acceptance of this opportunity for greater prestige indicates further how debased conditions had become. Those who had been divinely appointed to minister before the Lord were selling false spiritual services to the highest bidder.

18:31 *throughout the time that the house (tabernacle) of God was at Shiloh.* The true worship of God in the appointed place was available all this time — the Danites just did not want to bother with it.

13 ver. 2 **14** 1Sa 14:28; Jdg 17:5 **16** ver. 11 **17** ver. 2,14; Jdg 17:4,5 **19** Job 21:5; 29:9; 40:4; Mic 7:16; Jdg 17:10 **27** Jos 19:47 **28** ver. 7; Nu 13:21; 2Sa 10:6 **29** Jos 19:47; Ge 14:14; Jdg 20:1; 1Ki 12:29,30; 15:20 **30** Jdg 13:1; 1Sa 4:2,3,10,11 **31** Jos 18:1; Jdg 19:18; 21:12

Micah's [silver-plated wooden] image which he had made, *and kept it* throughout the time that the house (tabernacle) of God was at Shiloh.

A Levite's Concubine Degraded

19 NOW IT happened in those days, when there was no king in Israel, that a certain Levite living [as an alien] in the most remote part of the hill country of Ephraim, who took a concubine for himself from Bethlehem in Judah.

[2]But his concubine was unfaithful to him, and left him and went to her father's house in Bethlehem of Judah, and stayed there for a period of four months.

[3]Then her husband arose and went after her to speak kindly *and* tenderly to her in order to bring her back, taking with him his servant and a pair of donkeys. So she brought him into her father's house, and when the father of the girl saw him, he was happy to meet him.

[4]So his father-in-law, the girl's father, detained him; and he stayed there with him for three days. So they ate and drank, and he lodged there.

[5]On the fourth day they got up early in the morning, and the Levite prepared to leave; but the girl's father said to his son-in-law, "Strengthen yourself with a piece of bread, and afterward go your way."

[6]So both men sat down and ate and drank together; and the girl's father said to the man, "Please be willing to spend the night and enjoy yourself."

[7]Then the man got up to leave, but his father-in-law urged him [strongly to remain]; so he spent the night there again.

[8]On the fifth day he got up early in the morning to leave, but the girl's father said, "Please strengthen yourself, and wait until the end of the day." So both of them ate.

[9]When the man and his concubine and his servant got up to leave, his father-in-law, the girl's father, said to him, "Behold, now the day has drawn to a close; please spend the night. Look, now the day comes to an end; spend the night here and celebrate, enjoy yourself. Then tomorrow you may get up early for your journey and go home."

[10]But the man was not willing to stay the night; so he got up and left and came to *a place* opposite Jebus (that is Jerusalem). With him were two saddled donkeys [and his servant] and his concubine.

[11]When they were near Jebus, the day was almost gone, and the servant said to his master, "Please come and let us turn aside into this Jebusite city and spend the night in it."

[12]But his master said to him, "We will not turn aside into a city of foreigners who are not of the sons (descendants) of Israel. We will go on as far as Gibeah."

[13]And he said to his servant, "Come and let us approach one of *these* places: and we will spend the night in Gibeah or in Ramah."

[14]So they passed by and went on their way, and the sun set on them near Gibeah, which belongs to [the tribe of] Benjamin,

[15]and they turned aside there to go in and spend the night in Gibeah. And the Levite went in and sat down in the open square of the city, because no man invited them into his house to spend the night.

[16]Then behold, *there was* an old man *who* was coming out of the field from his work at evening. He was from the hill country of Ephraim but was staying in Gibeah, and the men of the place were sons (descendants) of Benjamin.

19:1 *a concubine.* A concubine was a female servant regarded as a part of the family, often chosen to bear children. Several of the patriarchs had children with concubines: Abraham with Hagar (Ge 16); Jacob with Bilhah and Zilpah (Ge 30:4 – 13).

19:10 *Jebus (that is Jerusalem).* The city of Jerusalem was at this time in the hands of the Jebusites, and it is called a "city of foreigners" in v. 12 (see Jos 15:63).

CHAPTER 19 **1** Jdg 17:6; 18:1; 21:25; Jdg 17:7 **5** Ge 18:5 **10** Jos 18:28 **11** Jos 15:8,63 **12** Jos 18:28 **13** Jos 18:25 **15** Mt 25:43 **16** Ps 104:23

17When he looked up, he saw the traveler [and his companions] in the city square; and the old man said, "Where are you going, and where do you come from?"
18The Levite replied, "We are passing through from Bethlehem [in the territory] of Judah to the most remote part of the hill country of Ephraim; I am from there. I went to Bethlehem of Judah, but I am *now* going [home] to my house, and there is no man [in the city] who will take me into his house [for the night].
19"Yet we have both straw and feed for our donkeys, and also bread and wine for me, and for your handmaid, and for the young man who is with your servant; there is no lack of anything."
20Then the old man said, "Peace be to you. Only *leave* all your needs to me; and do not spend the night in the open square."
21So he brought him into his house and fed the donkeys; and they washed their feet and ate and drank.
22While they were celebrating, behold, men of the city, certain worthless *and* evil men, surrounded the house, pounding on the door; and they spoke to the master of the house, the old man, saying, "Bring out the man who came to your house so that we may have relations with him."
23Then the man, the master of the house, went out and said to them, "No, my fellow citizens, please do not act so wickedly. Since this man has come to my house [as my guest], do not commit this sacrilege.
24"Here is my virgin daughter and this man's concubine. I will bring them out now; abuse *and* humiliate them and do to them whatever you want, but do not commit this act of sacrilege against this man."
25But the men would not listen to him. So the man took the Levite's concubine and brought her outside to them; and they had relations with her and abused her all night until morning; and when daybreak came, they let her go.
26At daybreak the woman came and collapsed at the door of the man's house where her master was, until it was [fully] light.
27When her master got up in the morning and opened the doors of the house and went out to go on his way, he saw his concubine lying at the door of the house, and her hands were on the threshold.
28He said to her, "Get up, and let us go." But there was no answer [for she had died]. Then he put her [body] on the donkey; and the man left and went home.
29When he arrived at his house, he took a knife, and taking hold of his [dead] concubine, he cut her [corpse] limb by limb into twelve pieces, and sent her [body parts] throughout all the territory of Israel.
30All who saw *the dismembered*

19:22 – 30 Perversion — For a man to be raped by a group of town ruffians would be a terrible humiliation; the fact that offering the concubine and the virgin daughter could be considered a solution clearly illustrates the level of perversion and depravity to which the people had sunk. Women were no longer considered the companions and helpers that they were created to be (Ge 2:22 – 24), but as property, to be enjoyed or disposed of at will. The author offers no comment upon the horror perpetrated here, merely stating the cold facts and leaving a strong impression of the heartless and conscienceless state of the people.

19:22 – 26 *men of the city.* This section closely resembles Genesis 19:4 – 9; indeed, the author may have written this story to make the comparison with Sodom unmistakable, as if to say, "Things were as bad as they were in the days of Sodom and Gomorrah."

19:22 *certain worthless and evil men.* This is a phrase describing wicked or worthless people. The name Belial came to designate Satan, as it is used in 2 Corinthians 6:15. ***may have relations with him.*** This same expression is found in Genesis 19:5, where the men of Sodom wanted to force homosexual relations on Lot's guests.

19:30 *Nothing like this has ever happened or been seen.* This phrase is ambiguous. It is

---

18 Jos 18:1; Jdg 18:31; 20:18; 1Sa 1:3,7 **20** Gen 43:23; Jdg 6:23; Ge 19:2 **21** Ge 24:32; 43:24; Ge 18:4; Jn 13:5 **22** Ge 19:4; Jdg 20:5; Hos 9:9; 10:9; Dt 13:13; Gen 19:5; Ro 1:26,27 **23** Ge 19:6,7; 2Sa 13:12 **24** Ge 19:8; Ge 34:2; Dt 21:14 **25** Ge 4:1 **28** Jdg 20:5 **29** Jdg 20:6; See 1Sa 11:7 **30** Jdg 20:7

parts said, "Nothing like this has *ever*
happened or been seen from the day
that the sons of Israel came up from the
land of Egypt to this day. Consider it,
take counsel, and speak [your minds]!"

Resolve to Punish the Guilty

20 THEN ALL the sons of Israel
from Dan [in the north] to Beer-
sheba [in the south], including the land
of Gilead came out, and the congrega-
tion assembled as one man to the LORD
at Mizpah.
[2]The chiefs of all the people of all the
tribes of Israel, presented themselves
in the assembly of the people of God,
four hundred thousand men on foot
who drew the sword.
[3](Now the Benjamites [in whose ter-
ritory the crime was committed] heard
that the [other tribes of the] sons of Is-
rael had gone up to Mizpah.) And the
sons of Israel said, "How did this evil
thing happen?"
[4]So the Levite, the husband of the
woman who was murdered, replied, "I
had come with my concubine to spend
the night in Gibeah, [a town] which
belongs to [the tribe of] Benjamin.
[5]"But the men of Gibeah rose up
against me and surrounded the house
at night because of me. They intended
to kill me, but instead they raped my
concubine [so brutally] that she died.
[6]"So I took my concubine and cut her
[corpse] in pieces and sent her [body
parts] throughout the land of the inher-
itance of Israel; for the men of Gibeah
have committed a lewd and disgraceful
act in Israel.
[7]"Now then, all you sons of Israel, all
of you, give your advice and counsel
here [regarding what should be done]."
[8]Then all the people stood [unified]
as one man, saying, "None of us will go
to his tent, and none of us will return
to his home [until this is settled].
[9]"But now this is the thing which we
will do to Gibeah; *we will go up* by lot
against it,
[10]and we will take ten men out of a
hundred throughout the tribes of Is-
rael, and a hundred out of a thousand,
and a thousand out of ten thousand to
bring provisions for the men, so that
when they come to Gibeah of Ben-
jamin, they may punish them for all
the despicable acts which they have
committed in Israel."
[11]So all the men of Israel assembled
against the city, united as one man.
[12]Then the tribes of Israel sent men
through the entire tribe of Benjamin,
saying, "What is this evil thing that
has been done among you?
[13]"Now therefore, turn over the men
[involved], the worthless *and* wicked
men in Gibeah, so that we may put
them to death and remove *this* wicked-
ness from Israel." But the Benjamites
would not listen to the voice of their
brothers, the sons of Israel.

---

uncertain whether they were horrified by discovering the dismembered body or by learning about the cruel rape and murder.

20:1–2,8 Unity—Both individually and corporately the Israelites of this period were functioning as a law unto themselves. "Every man did what was right in his own eyes" (21:25). One notable exception to this was the response to the loathsome rape and killing of a concubine in the Benjamite territory of Gibeah (19:11–30). The result of this outrageous covenant violation was that all Israel gathered together as one man, and decided that they would not rest until the crime was punished. The people were shocked into unity against sin. It is still true that crises in life often serve to bring people together to work for a common cause or fight against a common enemy. While this can be a good result of difficult times, it is important that God's people be united in serving Him in peace as well as crisis.

20:1 *from Dan [in the north] to Beersheba [in the south].* This is a common expression for the full extent of the land of Israel from north to south.

20:9 *by lot.* God's role is not mentioned here, but one can assume that the people were using lots to seek His will. To their credit, the Israelite tribes were united together as one man, a quality notably absent up to this point in the Book of Judges (v. 11).

CHAPTER 20 **1** ver. 11; Jos 22:12; Jdg 21:5; 1Sa 11:7; Jdg 18:29; 1Sa 3:20; 2Sa 3:10; 24:2; Jdg 10:17; 11:11; 1Sa 7:5; 10:17 **2** Jdg 8:10 **4** Jdg 19:15 **5** Jdg 19:22; Jdg 19:25,26 **6** Jdg 19:29; Jos 7:15 **7** Jdg 19:30 **12** Dt 13:14; Jos 22:13,16 **13** Dt 13:13; Jdg 19:22; Dt 17:12

14 Then the [tribe of the] sons of
Benjamin gathered from the cities to
Gibeah, to go out to battle against the
[other] sons of Israel.
15 And the Benjamites assembled out
of their cities at that time twenty-six
thousand men who drew the sword,
besides the inhabitants of Gibeah, who
assembled seven hundred chosen men.
16 Out of all these people were seven
hundred choice left-handed men; each
one could sling stones at [a target no
wider than] a hair and not miss.
17 Then the men of Israel, other than
Benjamin, assembled four hundred
thousand men who drew the sword;
all of these were men of war.

Civil War, Benjamin Defeated

18 The men of Israel arose and went
up to Bethel and asked of God and
said, "Which of us shall take the lead to
battle against the sons [tribe] of Benja-
min?" And the LORD said, "Judah [shall
go up] first."
19 Then the [fighting men of the]
sons of Israel arose in the morning
and camped against Gibeah.
20 The men of Israel went out to bat-
tle against Benjamin, and assembled
in battle formation against them at
Gibeah.
21 The sons of Benjamin came out of
Gibeah and struck to the ground on
that day twenty-two thousand [fight-
ing] men of Israel.
22 But the people, the [fighting] men
of Israel, took courage *and* strength-
ened themselves and again set their
battle line in the same place where
they formed it the first day.
23 The sons of Israel went up and
wept before the LORD until evening,
and asked of the LORD, "Shall we ad-
vance again to battle against the sons
of our brother Benjamin?" And the
LORD said, "Go up against them."
24 So the sons of Israel came against
the sons of Benjamin the second day.
25 And [the fighting men from the
tribe of] Benjamin went out of Gibeah
against them the second day and again
struck to the ground the sons of Israel,
eighteen thousand men, all of whom
were swordsmen.
26 Then all the sons of Israel and all
the people went up and came to Bethel
and wept; and they sat there before the
LORD and fasted that day until evening
and offered burnt offerings and peace
offerings before the LORD.
27 And the sons of Israel inquired of
the LORD (for the ark of the covenant
of God was there [at Bethel] in those
days,
28 and Phinehas the son of Eleazar,
the son of Aaron, *ministered* before
it in those days), saying, "Shall I yet
again go out to battle against the sons
of my brother Benjamin, or shall I
quit?" And the LORD said, "Go up, for
tomorrow I will hand them over to
you."
29 So Israel set men in ambush
around Gibeah.
30 The [fighting men of the] sons
of Israel went up against the sons of
Benjamin on the third day and placed
themselves in battle formation against
Gibeah as at other times.
31 The Benjamites went out against
their army and were lured away from
the city, and they began to strike and
kill some of the people as at other

20:18 *Judah [shall go up] first.* The book begins and ends with Judah in this prominent position (1:1 – 2). This is no accident, since the end of the book points toward the monarchy, whose true expression would come out of Judah.
20:23 *Go up against them.* The Lord graciously answered the Israelites twice when they called upon Him (v. 18).
20:26 *came to Bethel and wept.* The Israelites suffered a second major defeat (v. 25). The result drove them to fasting and sacrificing at Bethel, something done very rarely in this period.
20:28 *Phinehas.* Phinehas was the grandson of Aaron who had stopped the plague at Peor (Nu 25:6 – 11). The fact that he was still alive shows that the organization of the Book of Judges is not strictly chronological. The author may have placed this account at the end of the book to make the point even more strongly about the spiritual deterioration of the nation.

16 Jdg 3:15; 1Ch 12:2 **18** ver. 23,26; Nu 27:21; Jdg 1:1 **21** Ge 49:27 **23** ver. 26,27 **25** ver. 21 **26** ver. 18
27 Jos 18:1; 1Sa 4:3,4 **28** Jos 24:33; Dt 10:8; 18:5 **29** See Jos 8:4

times, on the highways, one of which
goes up to Bethel and the other to Gibe-
ah, and in the open country, about
thirty men of Israel.
32And the Benjamites said, "They
are defeated before us, as at the first."
But the sons of Israel said, "Let us flee
and lure them away from the city to
the highways."
33Then all the men of Israel got up
from their places and placed them-
selves in battle formation at Baal-
tamar; and the men of Israel [who
were] in ambush rushed from their
place in the plain of Maareh-geba.
34When the ten thousand choice
[fighting] men from all Israel came
against Gibeah, the battle was hard
and fierce; but the Benjamites did
not realize that disaster was about to
strike them.
35And the LORD struck down [the
tribe of] Benjamin before Israel, so that
the sons of Israel destroyed twenty-
five thousand one hundred men of
Benjamin that day, all of whom were
swordsmen.
36So the Benjamites realized that
they were defeated. Then men of Is-
rael gave ground to the Benjamites,
because they relied on the men in am-
bush whom they had placed against
Gibeah.
37Then the men in ambush quick-
ly rushed and attacked Gibeah; and
the men in ambush also deployed and
struck the entire city with the edge of
the sword.
38Now the appointed signal between
the men of Israel and the men in am-
bush was that they would make a great
cloud of smoke rise from the city.
39So the men of Israel turned in the
battle, and Benjamin began to strike
and kill about thirty men of Israel, for
they said, "Certainly they are defeated
before us as in the first battle!"
40But when the [signal] cloud began
to rise out of the city in a column of
smoke, the Benjamites looked behind
them; and behold, the entire city went
up *in smoke* to heaven.
41When the men of Israel turned
back *again*, the men of Benjamin were
terrified, for they saw that disaster had
fallen upon them.
42Therefore, they turned their backs
before the men of Israel [and fled] to-
ward the direction of the wilderness,
but the battle followed *and* overtook
them. As the [fighting men of the] sons
of Benjamin ran among them, the Is-
raelites of the cities came out and de-
stroyed them.
43They surrounded [the men of] Ben-
jamin, pursued them relentlessly, and
overtook them opposite Gibeah toward
the east.
44Thus eighteen thousand men of
Benjamin fell, all of these brave *and*
able warriors.
45The survivors [of Benjamin] turned
and fled toward the wilderness to the
rock of Rimmon, and Israel caught
five thousand of them on the roads and
overtook them at Gidom and killed two
thousand of them.
46So all of Benjamin who fell that
day were twenty-five thousand men
who drew the sword, all of them brave
and able warriors.
47But six hundred men turned and
fled toward the wilderness to the rock
of Rimmon and stayed at the rock of
Rimmon for four months.
48The men of Israel turned back
against [the tribe of] the sons of Ben-
jamin and struck them with the edge
of the sword, both the entire city [of
Gibeah] and the livestock and all that
they found. They also set on fire all the
[surrounding] towns which they found.

Mourning the Lost Tribe

21 NOW THE men of Israel had
sworn [an oath] at Mizpah,
"None of us shall give his daughter
in marriage to [a man of] Benjamin."
2So the people came to Bethel and
sat there before God until evening, and

20:48 *and struck them with the edge of the sword.* The spiritual decay of Israel had resulted in the destruction of its own people with a vengeance once reserved for pagan people.

34 Jos 8:14; Isa 47:11 **36** Jos 8:15 **37** Jos 8:19 **40** Jos 8:20 **45** Jos 15:32 **47** Jdg 21:13 **CHAPTER 21** **1** Jdg 20:1
2 Jdg 20:18,26

lifted up their voices and wept bitterly. [Judg 20:27]
[3]They said, "O LORD, God of Israel, why has this come about in Israel, that there should be today one tribe missing from Israel?"
[4]And the next day the people got up early and built an altar there and offered burnt offerings and peace offerings.
[5]Then the sons of Israel said, "Which one from all the tribes of Israel did not come up in the assembly to the LORD?" For they had taken a great oath concerning him who did not come up to the LORD at Mizpah, saying, "He shall certainly be put to death."
[6]And the sons of Israel felt sorry [and had compassion] for their brother Benjamin and said, "One tribe has been cut off from Israel today.
[7]"What shall we do for wives for those who are left, since we have sworn [an oath] by the LORD that we will not give them any of our daughters as wives?"

Provision for Their Survival

[8]And they said, "Which one is there of the tribes from Israel that did not come up to Mizpah to the LORD?" And behold, [it was discovered that] no one had come to the camp from Jabesh-gilead, to the assembly.
[9]For when the people were assembled, behold, there was not one of the inhabitants of Jabesh-gilead there.
[10]And the congregation sent twelve thousand of the most courageous men there, and commanded them saying, "Go and strike the inhabitants of Jabesh-gilead with the sword, including the women and the children.
[11]"And this is the thing that you shall do; you shall utterly destroy every male and every woman who is not a virgin."
[12]And they found among the inhabitants of Jabesh-gilead four hundred young virgins who had not known a man intimately; and they brought them to the camp at Shiloh, which is in the land of Canaan.
[13]Then the whole congregation sent *word* to the [surviving] sons of Benjamin who were at the rock of Rimmon, and proclaimed peace to them.
[14]So [the survivors of] Benjamin returned at that time, and they gave them the women whom they had kept alive from the women of Jabesh-gilead; but there were not enough [to provide wives] for them.
[15]And the people were sorry [and had compassion] for [the survivors of the tribe of] Benjamin because the LORD had made a gap in the tribes of Israel.
[16]Then the elders of the congregation said, "What shall we do for wives for those [men] who are left, since the women of Benjamin have been destroyed?"
[17]They said, "*There must be* an inheritance for the survivors of Benjamin, so that a tribe will not be wiped out from Israel.
[18]"But we cannot give them wives from our daughters." For the sons of Israel had sworn [an oath], "Cursed is he who gives a wife to [a man from the tribe of] Benjamin."
[19]So they said, "Listen, there is the yearly feast of the LORD at Shiloh, which is on the north side of Bethel, on the east side of the highway that goes up from Bethel to Shechem, and on the south side of Lebonah."

21:6 Repentance—In the midst of this terrible account of great sin within the nation of Israel, we find that the people realized that it was important that none of the tribes should perish. The example set by the nation of Israel is important for believers today. The people of Israel felt sorry for their brothers after the brothers had been disciplined for their great sin. Restoration and continuance of fellowship are important for people who have fallen into sin (2Co 2:6–8; Gal 6:1–2).

21:11 *utterly destroy.* This phrase is found numerous times in the Book of Joshua in regard to the conquest of the Canaanites. However, there is no hint that God supported the bloodbath at Jabesh-gilead.

21:19 *feast of the LORD.* Because of the dancing association, some believe that the yearly

4 2Sa 24:25 **5** Jdg 5:23 **8** 1Sa 11:1; 31:11 **10** ver. 5; Jdg 5:23; 1Sa 11:7 **11** Nu 31:17 **12** Jos 18:1 **13** Jdg 20:47 **15** ver. 6 **18** ver. 1; Jdg 11:35

20 So they instructed the sons of Ben-
jamin, saying, "Go, set an ambush in
the vineyards,
21 and watch; if the daughters of Shi-
loh come out to dance in the dances,
then you shall come out of the vine-
yards and each of you shall catch his
wife from the daughters of Shiloh,
and go to the land of [the tribe of]
Benjamin.
22 "When their fathers or their broth-
ers come to complain to us, we shall
say to them, 'Give them to us volun-
tarily, because we did not take a wife
for each man *of Benjamin* in battle,
nor did you give *wives* to them, for
that would have made you guilty [of
breaking your oath].' "
23 So the sons of [the tribe of] Benja-
min did as instructed and took wives
according to their number, from the
dancers whom they carried away.
Then they went and returned to their
inheritance, and rebuilt the towns and
lived in them.
24 The sons of Israel departed from
there at that time, each man to his tribe
and family, and each man went from
there to his inheritance.
25 In those days [when the judges gov-
erned] there was no king in Israel; every
man did what was right in his own eyes.

---

feast mentioned here was the Passover. Others believe that it was the Feast of Tabernacles, celebrated in the fall, since vineyards are mentioned (vv. 20 – 21). The grape harvest came in the early fall.

21:23 ***took wives according to their number.*** No justification is given for this peculiar abduction except for the supposed needs of the Benjamites. This interesting episode was a way for the rest of Israel to sidestep their oath (v. 1), and try to preserve the tribe of Benjamin.

21:25 ***what was right in his own eyes.*** This statement sums up the whole Book of Judges. What happened was governed by whatever people happened to feel like, rather than by listening to God, and the stories at the end of the book clearly illustrate the results of this mindset.

21 See Ex 15:20; Jdg 11:34; 1Sa 18:6 **23** See Jdg 20:48 **25** Jdg 17:6; 18:1; 19:1; Dt 12:8; Jdg 17:6

THE BOOK OF
RUTH

▸ **AUTHOR:** The Book of Ruth provides a cameo to the other side of the biblical story — the godly remnant who remain true to the laws of God. Although the author of Ruth is not given anywhere in the book, the anonymity should not detract from its spiritual value or literary beauty. Tradition has attributed the writing of Ruth to Samuel, but this is difficult to reconcile with the mention of David when Samuel died before David was installed as king.

▸ **TIMES:** During the Judges ▸ **KEY VERSE:** Ru 1:16

▸ **THEME:** Ruth is a simple yet intriguing short story. Throughout the story, the characters develop and eventually exhibit wisdom, loyalty, and obedience to God and the customs of the day. We see an interesting romance bloom out of most unusual circumstances. It provides a platform for some profound understanding of God's covenant plans with His people, Israel. We see the details of His plan unfold in the lives of a widow, her foreign born daughter-in-law, and a distant relative. We also see the lineage of David and Christ established and blessed.

Naomi Widowed

1 IN THE days when the judges governed [Israel], there was a famine in the land [of Canaan]. And a certain man of Bethlehem in Judah went to live temporarily in the country of Moab with his wife and his two sons.
[2]The man's name was Elimelech and his wife's name was Naomi and his two sons were named Mahlon and Chilion. They were Ephrathites from Bethlehem in Judah. They went to the country of Moab and stayed there.
[3]Then Elimelech, Naomi's husband, died, and she was left [a widow] with her two sons.
[4]They took wives from the Moabite women; the name of the one was Orpah, and the name of the other was Ruth. They lived there about ten years;
[5]and then both Mahlon and Chilion also died, so the woman [Naomi] was left without her two sons and her husband.
[6]Then she set out with her daughters-in-law to return from the country of Moab, for she had heard in Moab how the LORD had taken care of His people [of Judah] in giving them food.
[7]So she left the place where she was living, her two daughters-in-law with her, and they started on the way back to the land of Judah.
[8]But Naomi said to her two daughters-in-law, "Go back, each of you return to your mother's house. May the LORD show kindness to you as you have shown kindness to the dead and to me.
[9]"May the LORD grant that you find

1:4 ***Ruth.*** The name Ruth means "friend" or "compassionate friend." Throughout the account of her life it is easy to see that this name fittingly described Ruth's character.

1:8 ***kindness.*** The Hebrew word translated "kindness" is often used to describe God. It can also be interpreted as "loyal love."

CHAPTER 1 **1** Jdg 2:16; Ge 12:10; 26:1; 2Ki 8:1; Jdg 17:8 **2** Ge 35:19; Jdg 3:30 **6** Ex 4:31; Lk 1:68; Mt 6:11 **8** See Jos 24:15; 2Ti 1:16-18; ver. 5; Ru 2:20 **9** Ru 3:1

rest, each one in the home of her hus-
band." Then she kissed them [good-
bye], and they wept aloud.
10And they said to her, "No, we will
go with you to your people [in Judah]."
11But Naomi said, "Go back, my
daughters, why should you go with
me? Do I still have sons in my womb
that may become your husbands?
12"Go back, my daughters, go, for I
am too old to have a husband. If I said
I have hope, and if I actually had a
husband tonight and even gave birth
to sons,
13would you wait until they were
grown? Would you go without mar-
rying? No, my daughters; for it is
much more difficult for me than for
you, because the LORD's hand has gone
against me."

Ruth's Loyalty

14Then they wept aloud again; and
Orpah kissed her mother-in-law [good-
bye], but Ruth clung to her.
15Then Naomi said, "Look, your
sister-in-law has gone back to her
people and to her gods; turn back *and*
follow your sister-in-law."
16But Ruth said, "Do not urge me
to leave you or to turn back from fol-
lowing you; for where you go, I will
go, and where you lodge, I will lodge.
Your people will be my people, and
your God, my God.
17"Where you die, I will die, and
there I will be buried. May the LORD
do the same to me [as He has done to
you], and more also, if anything but
death separates me from you."
18When Naomi saw that Ruth was
determined to go with her, she said
nothing more.
19So the two of them went on until
they came to Bethlehem. And when
they arrived in Bethlehem, the whole
city was stirred because of them, and
the women asked, "Is this Naomi?"
20She said to them, "Do not call me
Naomi (sweetness); call me Mara (bit-
ter), for the Almighty has caused me
great grief *and* bitterness.
21"I left full [with a husband and two
sons], but the LORD has brought me
back empty. Why call me Naomi, since
the LORD has testified against me and
the Almighty has afflicted me?"
22So Naomi returned from the coun-
try of Moab, and with her Ruth the Mo-
abitess, her daughter-in-law. And they
arrived in Bethlehem at the beginning
of the barley harvest.

Ruth Gleans in Boaz' Field

2 NOW NAOMI had a relative of her
husband, a man of great wealth
and influence, from the family of Elim-
elech, whose name was Boaz.
2And Ruth the Moabitess said to
Naomi, "Please let me go to the field
and glean among the ears of grain af-
ter one [of the reapers] in whose sight
I may find favor." Naomi said to her,
"Go, my daughter."

1:13 *gone against me.* Naomi felt that the Lord was disciplining her. To be a widow in such a time and also without children was very difficult indeed.

1:14 Perseverance — When we sacrifice what would seem to be our best interest for another's welfare, God may unexpectedly use it to uplift and reward us. Ruth's desire to stay with Naomi not only lightened Naomi's lot, but it also brought Ruth into the Messiah's ancestral line.

1:16 – 17 *your God, my God.* Ruth is casting her lot with Naomi, turning her back on all she has known. Most important, she is turning away from the many gods of Moab to the one true God of Israel.

1:22 *Moabitess.* God extended his protection to Ruth even though she was a foreigner and a member of a nation which had been the enemy of God and Israel (Nu 22 – 25).

2:1 *Boaz.* As a relative of Naomi's husband Elimelech, as well as a man of both wealth and good character, Boaz was the ideal person to stand up for the rights of the two widows. In the ancient Middle East, a woman without a husband or father was a woman unprotected and with no way to make a living.

2:2 *glean.* The Law of Moses allowed the poor to glean in the fields of the farmers (Lev 23:22), picking up the loose grain that fell from the sheaves as the reapers gathered them up.

---

11 Ge 38:11; Dt 25:5 **14** Pr 17:17; 18:24 **15** Jdg 11:24; See Jos 24:15,19; 2Ki 2:2; Lk 24:28 **16** 2Ki 2:2,4,6; Ru 2:11,12 **17** 1Sa 3:17; 25:22; 2Sa 19:13; 2Ki 6:31 **18** Ac 21:14 **19** Mt 21:10; See Isa 23:7; La 2:15 **21** Job 1:21 **22** Ex 9:31,32; Ru 2:23; 2Sa 21:9 **CHAPTER 2** **1** Ru 3:2,12; Ru 4:21 **2** Lev 19:9; Dt 24:19

3 So Ruth went and picked up the leftover grain in a field after the reapers; and she happened to stop at the plot of land belonging to Boaz, who was of the family of Elimelech.

4 It was then that Boaz came back from Bethlehem and said to the reapers, "The LORD be with you!" And they answered him, "The LORD bless you!"

5 Then Boaz said to his servant who was in charge of the reapers, "Whose young woman is this?"

6 The servant in charge of the reapers answered, "She is the young Moabite woman who came back with Naomi from the country of Moab.

7 "And she said, 'Please let me glean and gather after the reapers among the sheaves.' So she came and has continued [gathering grain] from early morning until now, except when she sat [resting] for a little while in the [field] house."

8 Then Boaz said to Ruth, "Listen carefully, my daughter. Do not go to glean in another field or leave this one, but stay here close by my maids.

9 "Watch which field they reap, and follow behind them. I have commanded the servants not to touch you. And when you are thirsty, go to the [water] jars and drink from what the servants draw."

10 Then she kneeled face downward, bowing to the ground, and said to him, "Why have I found favor in your eyes that you should notice me, when I am a foreigner?"

11 Boaz answered her, "I have been made fully aware of everything that you have done for your mother-in-law since the death of your husband, and how you have left your father and mother and the land of your birth, and have come to a people that you did not know before.

12 "May the LORD repay you for your kindness, and may your reward be full from the LORD, the God of Israel, under whose wings you have come to take refuge."

13 Then she said, "Let me find favor in your sight, my lord, for you have comforted me and have spoken kindly to your maidservant, though I am not as one of your maidservants."

14 At mealtime Boaz said to her, "Come over here and eat some bread and dip your bread in the vinegar." So she sat beside the reapers; and he served her roasted grain, and she ate until she was satisfied and she had some left [for Naomi].

15 When she got up to glean, Boaz ordered his servants, "Let her glean even among the sheaves, and do not insult her.

16 "Also you shall purposely pull out for her some stalks [of grain] from the sheaves and leave them so that she may collect them, and do not rebuke her."

17 So she gleaned in the field until evening. Then she beat out what she had gleaned, and it was about an ephah of barley.

18 She picked it up and went into the city, and her mother-in-law saw what she had gleaned. Ruth also took out and gave to Naomi what she had saved after she [had eaten and] was satisfied.

19 Her mother-in-law said to her, "Where did you glean today? Where did you work? Blessed be the man who took notice of you." So she told her mother-in-law with whom she had worked and said, "The name of the man with whom I worked today is Boaz."

20 Naomi said to her daughter-in-law, "May he be blessed of the LORD who has not ceased his kindness to the living and to the dead." Again Naomi said to her, "The man is one of our closest relatives, one who has the right to redeem us." [Lev 25:25]

21 Then Ruth the Moabitess said, "He also said to me, 'Stay close to my ser-

---

2:14 – 16 *Come over here and eat some bread.* Boaz not only let Ruth glean, he also amply provided her with food. He went beyond the letter of the law, demonstrating God's compassion and the concern that each believer ought to show for others.

4 Lk 1:28; 2Th 3:16	**6** Ru 1:22	**10** 1Sa 25:23	**11** Ru 1:14,16,17	**12** 1Sa 24:19; Ru 1:16; Ps 17:8	**13** Ge 33:15;
1Sa 1:18; 1Sa 25:41	**14** ver. 18	**18** ver. 14	**19** ver. 10; Ps 41:1	**20** Ru 3:10; 2Sa 2:5; Job 29:13; Pr 17:17; Ru 3:9; 4:6	

vants until they have harvested my entire crop.'"

[22]Naomi said to Ruth, "It is good, my daughter, for you to go out [to work] with his maids, so that others do not assault you in another field."

[23]So she stayed close to the maids of Boaz, gleaning until the end of the barley and wheat harvests. And she lived with her mother-in-law.

Boaz Will Redeem Ruth

3 THEN NAOMI her mother-in-law said to Ruth, "My daughter, shall I not look for security *and* a home for you, so that it may be well with you?

[2]"Now Boaz, with whose maids you were [working], is he not our relative? See now, he is winnowing barley at the threshing floor tonight.

[3]"So wash and anoint yourself [with olive oil], then put on your [best] clothes, and go down to the threshing floor; but stay out of the man's sight until he has finished eating and drinking.

[4]"When he lies down, notice the place where he is lying, and go and uncover his feet and lie down. Then he will tell you what to do."

[5]Ruth answered her, "I will do everything that you say."

[6]So she went down to the threshing floor and did just as her mother-in-law had told her.

[7]When Boaz had eaten and drunk and his heart was happy, he went to lie down at the end of the stack of grain. Then Ruth came secretly, and uncovered his feet and lay down.

[8]In the middle of the night the man was startled and he turned over, and found a woman lying at his feet.

[9]So he said, "Who are you?" And she answered, "I am Ruth your maid. Spread the hem of your garment over me, for you are a close relative *and* redeemer."

[10]Then he said, "May you be blessed by the LORD, my daughter. You have made your last kindness better than the first; for you have not gone after young men, whether poor or rich.

[11]"Now, my daughter, do not be afraid. I will do for you whatever you ask, since all my people in the city know that you are a woman of excellence.

[12]"It is true that I am your close relative *and* redeemer; however, there is a relative closer [to you] than I.

[13]"Spend the night [here], and in the morning if he will redeem you, fine; let him do it. But if he does not wish to redeem you, then, as the LORD lives, I will redeem you. Lie down until the morning."

[14]So she lay at his feet until the morning, but got up before anyone could recognize another; Boaz said, "Do not let it be known that the woman came to the threshing floor [last night]."

[15]He also said, "Give me the shawl you are wearing and hold it out." So Ruth held it and he measured out six measures of barley [into it] and placed it on her. And she went into the city.

[16]When she came home, her mother-in-law said, "How did it go, my

---

3:4 *uncover his feet.* By uncovering Boaz's feet in this manner Ruth was showing her submission to him while also asking him to be her protector.
3:9 *close relative and redeemer.* Ruth reminded Boaz that he was a close relative of her dead husband, and in keeping with the law a close relative was required to be a "kinsman redeemer." This meant that if a man was slain, his kinsman redeemer had to avenge his death. If a man was sold into slavery, his kinsman redeemer paid the price to release him. If a man died childless, his kinsman redeemer had the responsibility to marry his wife and father a child to bear his name (Dt 15:5 – 10). Ruth was placing herself so that Boaz would know that she was willing for him to redeem her.
3:12 *closer [to you] than I.* Boaz remembers that there is yet a closer relative; that relative would have the responsibility and the right to redeem Ruth first. If, however, he did not wish to or was unable to, Boaz would be free to do it himself.

CHAPTER 3 **1** 1Co 7:36; 1Ti 5:8; Ru 1:9 **2** Ru 2:8 **3** 2Sa 14:2 **7** Jdg 19:6,9,22; 2Sa 13:28; Est 1:10 **9** Eze 16:8; ver. 12; Ru 2:20 **10** Ru 2:20; Ru 1:8 **11** Pr 12:4 **12** ver. 9; Ru 4:1 **13** Dt 25:5; Ru 4:5; Mt 22:24; Jdg 8:19; Jer 4:2 **14** Ro 12:17; 14:16; 1Co 10:32; 2Co 8:21; 1Th 5:22

daughter?" And Ruth told her every-
thing that the man had done for her.
17She said, "He gave me these six
measures of barley, and he said to me,
'Do not go back to your mother-in-law
empty-handed.' "
18Then Naomi said, "Sit *and* wait,
my daughter, until you learn how this
matter turns out; for the man will not
rest until he has settled it today."

The Marriage of Ruth

4 THEN BOAZ went up to the city gate
[where business and legal matters
were settled] and sat down, and then
the close relative (redeemer) of whom
Boaz had spoken came by. He said to
him, "Come over here, friend, and sit
down." So he came and sat down.
2Then Boaz took ten men from the
elders of the city and said, "Sit down
here." And they sat down.
3He said to the closest relative (re-
deemer), "Naomi, who has returned
from the country of Moab, must sell
the plot of land which belonged to our
brother Elimelech.
4"So I thought to let you hear of it,
saying, 'Buy it in the presence of those
sitting here, and before the elders of my
people. If you will redeem it, redeem
it; but if not, then tell me, so that I may
know; for there is no one besides you to
redeem it, and I am [next of kin] after
you.'" And he said, "I will redeem it."
5Then Boaz said, "The day that you
buy the field from Naomi, you must also
acquire Ruth the Moabitess, the widow
of the deceased, to restore the name of
the deceased to his inheritance."
6The closest relative (redeemer) said,
"I cannot redeem it for myself, because
[by marrying a Moabitess] I would
jeopardize my own inheritance. Take
my right of redemption (purchase)
yourself, because I cannot redeem it."
[Deut 23:3, 4]
7Now formerly in Israel this was the
custom concerning redeeming and ex-
changing *property.* To confirm a trans-
action, a man pulled off his sandal and
gave it to the other. This was the *way*
of confirming *and* attesting in Israel.
8So, when the closest relative (re-
deemer) said to Boaz, "Buy it for your-
self," he pulled off his sandal [and gave
it to Boaz to confirm the agreement].
9Then Boaz said to the elders and to
all the people, "You are witnesses this
day that I have bought everything that
was Elimelech's and everything that
was Chilion's and Mahlon's from the
hand of Naomi.
10"I have also acquired Ruth the Mo-
abitess, the widow of Mahlon, to be
my wife to restore the name of the
deceased to his inheritance, so that the
name of the deceased will not be cut
off from his brothers or from the gate
of his birthplace. You are witnesses
today."
11All the people at the gate and the
elders said, "We are witnesses. May
the LORD make the woman who is com-
ing into your house like Rachel and
Leah, the two who built the household
of Israel. May you achieve wealth *and*
power in Ephrathah and become fa-
mous in Bethlehem.
12"Further, may your house be like
the house of Perez whom Tamar bore
to Judah, because of the offspring
which the LORD will give you by this
young woman."
13So Boaz took Ruth, and she be-
came his wife. And he went in to her,
and the LORD enabled her to conceive,
and she gave birth to a son.
14Then the women said to Naomi,
"Blessed is the LORD who has not left

4:1 – 2 *the city gate.* The gate of the city was the place where the men congregated and where the officials of a city were to be found. Legal business was typically carried on here where the elders of the city were present to be witnesses.
4:11 *like Rachel and Leah.* The people blessed Ruth and asked the Lord to bless her as he had the founding mothers of the twelve tribes of Israel. Even though she was a Moabitess, Ruth was accepted.
4:14 – 15 *who loves you . . . is better . . . than seven sons.* Ruth, although not knowing the outcome, sowed kindness by staying with Naomi. Because of this she also reaped what she had sown: abundant blessing. She became

18 Ps 37:3,5 **CHAPTER 4** **1** Ru 3:12 **2** 1Ki 21:8; Pr 31:23 **4** Jer 32:7,8; Ge 23:18; Lev 25:25 **5** Ge 38:8; Dt 25:5,6; Ru 3:13; Mt 22:24 **6** Ru 3:12,13 **7** Dt 25:7,9 **10** Dt 25:6 **11** Ps 127:3; 128:3; Dt 25:9; Ge 35:16 **12** 1Ch 2:4; Mt 1:3; 1Sa 2:20 **13** Ru 3:11; Ge 29:31 **14** Lk 1:58

you without a redeemer (grandson, as heir) today, and may his name become famous in Israel.
15"May he also be to you one who restores life and sustains your old age; for your daughter-in-law, who loves you and is better to you than seven sons, has given birth to him."

The Line of David Began Here

16Then Naomi took the child and placed him in her lap, and she became his nurse.
17The neighbor women gave him a name, saying, "A son (grandson) has been born to Naomi." They named him Obed (worshiper). He is the father of Jesse, the father of David [the ancestor of Jesus Christ].
18Now these are the descendants of Perez: Perez was the father of Hezron,
19Hezron was the father of Ram, Ram the father of Amminadab,
20Amminadab the father of Nahshon, Nahshon the father of Salmon,
21Salmon the father of Boaz, Boaz the father of Obed,
22Obed the father of Jesse, and Jesse the father of David [the king of Israel and the ancestor of Jesus Christ].

---

the great-grandmother of King David, and had a place in the genealogy of Christ Jesus. Boaz, as the kinsman redeemer, had to sacrifice his name — the son that was born would bear the family name of Mahlon — but he was also abundantly blessed. Boaz received the admiration of the people (4:11), the beautiful and faithful Ruth became his wife, and together they became ancestors of the great Redeemer, Jesus Christ. This story of Boaz's redemption of the foreign woman points to the wonderful redemption of Jesus for all those who believe in Him.

15 1Sa 1:8 **17** Lk 1:58 **18** 1Ch 2:4 **20** Nu 1:7; Mt 1:4 **22** 1Ch 2:15; Mt 1:6

THE FIRST BOOK OF

SAMUEL

▸ **AUTHOR:** The author of 1 and 2 Samuel is anonymous. Samuel may have written the first portion of the book, but his death recorded in 1 Samuel 25:1 makes it clear that he did not write all of 1 or 2 Samuel. It is very possible that a single compiler, perhaps a member of the prophetic school mentioned in 1 Chronicles 29:29, used the various writings referenced as the chronicles of "Nathan the prophet," "Gad the seer" and "Samuel the seer."

▸ **TIMES:** c. 1105 – 1011 BC ▸ **KEY VERSE:** 1Sa 13:14

▸ **THEME:** First Samuel tells the story of three characters: Samuel, Saul, and David. Saul's story begins the line of Israel's monarchy. His story ends with the end of 1 Samuel. David's starts in 1 Samuel, goes through 2 Samuel and ends in the first few chapters of 1 Kings. All three of the main characters in this book make mistakes that cost them dearly. Samuel has problems with his own sons. The result is the end of the rule of judges. Saul seems to be a classic study in what a poor self-image can do to a person. David's early violence prevents him from being able to build the temple later on when he is king.

Elkanah and His Wives

1 THERE WAS a certain man of
Ramathaim-zophim, of the hill coun-
try of Ephraim, named Elkanah the son
of Jeroham, the son of Elihu, the son of
Tohu, the son of Zuph, an Ephraimite.
2He had two wives, one named Han-
nah and the other named Peninnah.
Peninnah had children, but Hannah
had none.
3This man went up from his city
each year to worship and sacrifice to
the LORD of hosts at Shiloh. Hophni
and Phinehas, the two sons of Eli, were
priests to the LORD there.
4When the day came that Elkanah
sacrificed, he would give portions [of
the sacrificial meat] to Peninnah his
wife and all her sons and daughters.
5But to Hannah he would give a dou-
ble portion, because he loved Hannah,
but the LORD had given her no children.
6Hannah's rival provoked her bit-
terly, to irritate *and* embarrass her,
because the LORD had left her childless.
7So it happened year after year,
whenever she went up to the house of
the LORD, Peninnah provoked her; so
she wept and would not eat.
8Then Elkanah her husband said
to her, "Hannah, why do you cry and
why do you not eat? Why are you so
sad *and* discontent? Am I not better to
you than ten sons?"

1:1 *Elkanah.* Elkanah was a Levite (1Ch 6:26) who lived in a village about five miles north of Jerusalem. He is referred to as an Ephraimite because he lived in the territory of Ephraim.
1:3 *LORD of hosts.* The term "LORD of hosts" refers to God as the One who commands the angelic armies of heaven (1Ki 22:19; Rev 19:14) and the armies of Israel (17:45). ***Shiloh.*** Shiloh, located twenty miles north of Jerusalem, was the religious center for the nation at this time and the location of the tabernacle (Jos 18:1).

CHAPTER 1 **1** 1Ch 6:27,34; Ru 1:2 **3** Ex 23:14; Lk 2:41; Dt 12:5; Jos 18:1 **4** Dt 12:17 **5** Ge 30:2 **6** Job 24:21 **8** Ru 4:15

9 So Hannah got up after eating and
drinking in Shiloh. Now Eli the priest
was sitting on his seat beside the door-
post of the temple (tabernacle) of the
LORD.
10 Hannah was greatly distressed,
and she prayed to the LORD and wept
in anguish.
11 She made a vow, saying, "O LORD
of hosts, if You will indeed look on the
affliction (suffering) of Your maidser-
vant and remember, and not forget
Your maidservant, but will give Your
maidservant a son, then I will give him
to the LORD all the days of his life; a
razor shall never touch his head."
12 Now it happened as she continued
praying before the LORD, that Eli was
watching her mouth.
13 Hannah was speaking in her heart
(mind); only her lips were moving, and
her voice was not heard, so Eli thought
she was drunk.
14 Eli said to her, "How long will you
make yourself drunk? Get rid of your
wine."
15 But Hannah answered, "No, my
lord, I am a woman with a despairing
spirit. I have not been drinking wine
or *any* intoxicating drink, but I have
poured out my soul before the LORD.
[Gen 19:34]
16 "Do not regard your maidservant
as a wicked *and* worthless woman, for
I have spoken until now out of my great
concern and [bitter] provocation."
17 Then Eli answered and said, "Go
in peace; and may the God of Israel
grant your petition that you have asked
of Him."
18 Hannah said, "Let your maid-
servant find grace *and* favor in your
sight." So the woman went on her way
and ate, and her face was no longer
sad.

Samuel Is Born to Hannah

19 The family got up early the next
morning, worshiped before the LORD,
and returned to their home in Ramah.
Elkanah knew Hannah his wife, and
the LORD remembered her [prayer].
20 It came about in due time, after
Hannah had conceived, that she gave
birth to a son; she named him Samuel,
saying, "Because I have asked for him
from the LORD."
21 Then the man Elkanah and all his
household went up to offer to the LORD
the yearly sacrifice and *pay* his vow.

1:9 *Eli.* Eli, Israel's high priest and judge, was from the family of Ithamar, Aaron's fourth son (1Ch 24:1 – 3). The last high priest mentioned before him was Phinehas, the son of Eleazar (Jdg 20:28). It is not known why or how the office of high priest passed from the house of Eleazar to that of Ithamar.

1:11 *vow.* Hannah vowed that the child she would bear would be a servant to the Lord all of his life. Can a parent really make a vow that the child will carry out? Hannah surely both taught Samuel and prayed for him, but it was Samuel who said "yes" to the Lord and to the promise his mother had made. Every single relationship with the Lord is between that individual and the Lord. No one is a follower of God just because his parents are. But there is much that parents can do to encourage and teach their children about loving and serving the Lord, and a heartfelt enthusiastic example is the very best incentive that a parent can provide. ***a razor shall never touch his head.*** The Nazirite vow involved a designated period of time (usually a few weeks or months) during which there was a commitment to refrain completely from wine, from cutting the hair, and touching any dead body. Hannah promised that her son would be a Nazirite for life.

1:17 Petition — The Lord went to great lengths to ensure that Scripture records all the instances in which God heard and answered prayer; unlike the gods of Israel's surrounding nations. In the contest on Mount Carmel, Elijah's prayers were answered while the prayers of the prophets of Baal went nowhere (1Ki 18). The Psalmist says "But certainly God has heard [me]; He has given heed to the voice of my prayer" (Ps 66:19).

Petitions are requests that we pray by faith (Jas 1:6), in the name of Jesus (Jn 14:13). If we pray in this manner, we are assured that God hears us (1Jn 5:14 – 15). We should pray for ourselves, asking for cleansing (1Jn 1:9), and wisdom (Jas 1:5), spiritual leaders (Col 4:3), sick believers (Jas 5:14), rulers (1Ti 2:1 – 3), and even for our enemies (Mt 5:44).

9 1Sa 3:3 **10** Job 7:11 **11** Ge 28:20; Ps 25:18; Ge 8:1; Nu 6:5 **15** Ps 62:8 **16** Dt 13:13 **17** Jdg 18:6; Mk 5:34; Ps 20:4,5 **18** Ru 2:13; Ecc 9:7 **19** Ge 4:1; Ge 30:22 **21** ver. 3

22 But Hannah did not go up, for she
said to her husband, "*I will not go up*
until the child is weaned; and then I
will bring him, so that he may appear
before the LORD and remain there as
long as he lives."
23 Elkanah her husband said to her,
"Do what seems best to you. Wait
until you have weaned him; only may
the LORD establish *and* confirm His
word." So the woman remained [be-
hind] and nursed her son until she
weaned him.
24 Now when she had weaned him,
she took him up with her, along with a
three-year-old bull, an ephah of flour,
and a leather bottle of wine [to pour
over the burnt offering for a sweet
fragrance], and she brought Samuel
to the LORD's house in Shiloh, although
the child was young.
25 Then they slaughtered the bull, and
brought the child to Eli.
26 Hannah said, "Oh, my lord! As
[surely as] your soul lives, my lord, I
am the woman who stood beside you
here, praying to the LORD.
27 "For this child I prayed, and the
LORD has granted me my request which
I asked of Him.
28 "Therefore I have also dedicated
him to the LORD; as long as he lives
he is dedicated to the LORD." And they
worshiped the LORD there.

Hannah's Song of Thanksgiving

2 HANNAH PRAYED and said,

"My heart rejoices *and* triumphs in
the LORD;
My horn (strength) is lifted up in
the LORD,
My mouth has opened wide
[to speak boldly] against my
enemies,
Because I rejoice in Your salvation.
2 "There is no one holy like the
LORD,
There is no one besides You,
There is no Rock like our God.
3 "Do not go on boasting so very
proudly,
Do not let arrogance come out of
your mouth;
For the LORD is a God of
knowledge,
And by Him actions are weighed
(examined).
4 "The bows of the mighty are
broken,
But those who have stumbled
equip themselves with strength.
5 "Those who were full hire
themselves out for bread,
But those who were hungry cease
[to hunger].
Even the barren [woman] gives
birth to seven,
But she who has many children
withers away.
6 "The LORD puts to death and
makes alive;
He brings down to Sheol (the
grave) and raises up [from the
grave].
7 "The LORD makes poor and makes
rich;
He brings low and He lifts up.
8 "He raises up the poor from the
dust,
He lifts up the needy from the ash
heap
To make them sit with nobles,
And inherit a seat of honor *and*
glory;

1:22 *until the child is weaned.* Hebrew children were normally weaned when they were two or three years old.

1:23 *Do what seems best.* According to law, Elkanah could have declared Hannah's vow a rash promise and prohibited her from fulfilling it (Nu 30:10 – 15). When he told her to "do what seems best to you" he was validating her promise to God.

2:1 – 10 Prayer — Hannah's prayer is one of praise to God. We often think of prayer as supplication or intercession, but this is a prayer of rejoicing in the Lord, His salvation, His power to raise up and to shatter, His justice, and His strength. To pray like this requires centering in on who God is, thoughtful recollection of His attributes, and thanksgiving for His work in our lives.

22 Lk 2:22; ver. 11:28; Ex 21:6 **23** Nu 30:7; 2Sa 7:25 **24** Dt 12:5,6,11; Jos 18:1 **25** Lk 2:22 **26** 2Ki 2:2,4,6 **27** Mt 7:7 **28** Ge 24:26,52 **CHAPTER 2 1** Php 4:6; See Lk 1:46; Ps 92:10; Ps 9:14 **2** Ex 15:11; Dt 4:35 **3** Ps 94:4; Jude 15 **4** Ps 37:15 **5** Ps 113:9; Isa 54:1 **6** Job 5:18; Hos 6:1 **7** Job 1:21; Ps 75:7 **8** Lk 1:52; Job 36:7; Job 38:4-6

For the pillars of the earth are the
LORD'S,
And He set the land on them.
9 "He guards the feet of His godly
(faithful) ones,
But the wicked ones are silenced
and perish in darkness;
For a man shall not prevail by
might.
10 "The adversaries of the LORD will
be broken to pieces;
He will thunder against them in
the heavens,
The LORD will judge the ends of the
earth;
And He will give strength to His
king,
And will exalt the horn (strength)
of His anointed." [Luke 1:46]

11 Elkanah [and his wife Hannah] returned to Ramah to his house. But the child [Samuel] served the LORD under the guidance of Eli the priest.

The Sin of Eli's Sons

12 The sons of Eli [Hophni and Phinehas] were worthless (dishonorable, unprincipled) men; they did not know [nor respect] the LORD

13 and the custom of the priests with [the sacrifices of] the people. When any man was offering a sacrifice, the priest's servant would come while the meat was boiling, with a three-pronged [meat] fork in his hand;

14 then he would thrust it into the pan, or kettle, or caldron, or pot; everything that the fork brought up the priest would take for himself. This is what they did in Shiloh to all [the sacrifices of] the Israelites who came there.

15 Also, before they burned (offered) the fat, the priest's servant would come and say to the man who was sacrificing, "Give the priest meat to roast, since he will not accept boiled meat from you, only raw."

16 If the man said to him, "Certainly they are to burn (offer) the fat first, and then you may take as much as you want," then the priest's servant would say, "No! You shall give *it to me* now or I will take it by force."

17 So the sin of the [two] young men [Hophni and Phinehas] was very great before the LORD, for the men treated the offering of the LORD disrespectfully.

Samuel before the LORD as a Boy

18 Now Samuel was ministering before the LORD, as a child dressed in a linen ephod [a sacred item of priestly clothing].

19 Moreover, his mother would make him a little robe and would bring it up to him each year when she came up with her husband to offer the yearly sacrifice.

20 Then Eli would bless Elkanah and his wife and say, "May the LORD give you children by this woman in place of the one she asked for which was dedicated to the LORD." Then they would return to their own home.

21 And [the time came when] the LORD visited Hannah, so that she conceived and gave birth to three sons and two daughters. And the boy Samuel grew before the LORD.

Eli Rebukes His Sons

22 Now Eli was very old; and he heard about everything that his sons were doing to all [the people of] Israel, and how they were lying with the women who served at the entrance to the Tent of Meeting (tabernacle).

23 Eli said to them, "Why do you do such things, the evil things that I hear from all these people?

24 "No, my sons; for the report that I keep hearing from the passers-by among the LORD'S people is not good.

25 "If one man does wrong *and* sins against another, God will intercede (arbitrate) for him; but if a man does

---

2:13–15 *take for himself*. The priests' rightful share of a sacrifice was the breast and the right thigh of the animal (Lev 7:34). Eli's sons sinned by taking any part they wanted and demanding the meat immediately, before the fat consecrated to God had been burned on the altar.

9 Ps 91:11 **10** Ps 2:9; Ps 18:13; Ps 96:13; Ps 89:24 **11** ver. 18; 1Sa 3:1 **12** Jdg 2:10; Ro 1:28 **15** Lev 3:3,4,5,16 **17** Ge 6:11; Mal 2:8 **18** ver. 11; Ex 28:4 **19** 1Sa 1:3 **20** Ge 14:19; 1Sa 1:28 **21** Ge 21:1; ver. 26; Jdg 13:24 **22** Ex 38:8 **25** Nu 15:30; Jos 11:20

wrong to the LORD, who can intercede for him?" But they would not listen to their father, for it was the LORD's will to put them to death.

26 But the boy Samuel continued to grow in stature and in favor both with the LORD and with men.

27 Then a man of God (prophet) came to Eli and said to him, "Thus says the LORD: 'Did I *not* plainly reveal Myself to the house of your father (ancestor) when they were in Egypt *in bondage* to Pharaoh's house?

28 'Moreover, I selected him out of all the tribes of Israel to be My priest, to go up to My altar, to burn incense, to wear an ephod before Me. And [from then on] I gave to the house of your father all the fire *offerings* of the sons of Israel.

29 'Why then do you kick at (despise) My sacrifice and My offering which I commanded in My dwelling place, and honor your sons more than Me, by fattening yourselves with the choicest part of every offering of My people Israel?'

30 "Therefore the LORD God of Israel declares, 'I did indeed say that your house and that of [Aaron] your father would walk [in priestly service] before Me forever.' But now the LORD declares, 'Far be it from Me—for those who honor Me I will honor, and those who despise Me will be insignificant *and* contemptible.

31 'Behold, the time is coming when I will cut off your strength and the strength of your father's house, so that there will not be an old man in your house.

32 'You will look at the distress of *My* house (the tabernacle), in *spite of* all the good which God will do for Israel, and there will never again be an old man in your house.

33 'Yet I will not cut off every man of yours from My altar; your eyes will fail *from weeping* and your soul will grieve, and all those born in your house will die as men [in the prime of life]. [1 Sam 22:17–20]

34 'This will be the sign to you which shall come concerning your two sons, Hophni and Phinehas: on the same day both of them shall die. [1 Sam 4:17, 18]

35 'But I will raise up for Myself a faithful priest who will do according to what is in My heart and in My soul; and I will build him a permanent *and* enduring house, and he will walk before My anointed forever. [1 Sam 2:10]

36 'And it will happen that everyone who is left in your house will come and bow down to him for a piece of silver and a loaf of bread and say, "Please assign me to one of the priest's offices so I may eat a piece of bread." ' "

The Prophetic Call to Samuel

3 NOW THE boy Samuel was attending to the service of the LORD under the supervision of Eli. The word of the LORD was rare *and* precious in those

---

2:30 Godlessness — Whenever a priesthood or church or nation falls into apostasy, the people who should have been served suffer. Eli failed his people far more than his disgraceful sons did, because the Israelites trusted Eli's integrity and his discernment. He should have restrained his sons, and he did not. The price of disobedience is always high, and the spiritual cost to a community that has lost trust in one whom they thought was close to God is greater than most people are willing to calculate.

2:31 – 34 *will not be an old man in your house.* The judgment was partially fulfilled in the massacre of the priests of Nob (22:11 – 19), and was ultimately fulfilled when the priesthood was transferred to the family of Zadok in the time of Solomon (1Ki 2:26 – 27,35).

2:35 *faithful priest.* This term refers to Zadok, who was faithful to God and to the line of David (1Ki 1:7 – 8; 2:26 – 27,35).

3:1 – 19 Listening for God's Call — Samuel heard God's call in an audible voice. That experience is not a common one in the history of those who follow after God. While most of us get a sense of a call by some other means, Samuel's experience does help us to understand what our attitude and response should be.

Samuel's attitude was one of readiness and

---

26 ver. 21; Pr 3:4 **27** 1Ki 13:1; Ex 4:14,27 **28** Ex 28:1,4; Nu 16:5; Lev 2:3,10; 6:16; 7:7,8,34,35; Nu 5:9 **29** Dt 32:15; Dt 12:5 **30** Ex 29:9; Jer 18:9,10; Ps 91:14; Mal 2:9 **31** 1Ki 2:27; See 1Sa 4:11,18,20; 14:3; 22:18 **32** Zec 8:4 **34** 1Ki 13:3; 1Sa 4:11 **35** 1Ki 2:35; Eze 44:15; 2Sa 7:11,27; 1Ki 11:38; Ps 18:50 **36** 1Ki 2:27 **CHAPTER 3** **1** 1Sa 2:11; Ps 74:9; Am 8:11

days; visions [that is, new revelations
of divine truth] were not widespread.
2 Yet it happened at that time, as Eli
was lying down in his own place (now
his eyesight had begun to grow dim
and he could not see *well*).
3 and the [oil] lamp of God had not
yet gone out, and Samuel was lying
down in the temple of the LORD, where
the ark of God was,
4 that the LORD called Samuel, and he
answered, "Here I am."
5 He ran to Eli and said, "Here I am,
for you called me." But Eli said, "I did
not call you; lie down again." So he
went and lay down.
6 Then the LORD called yet again,
"Samuel!" So Samuel got up and went
to Eli and said, "Here I am, for you
called me." But Eli answered, "I did not
call, my son; lie down again."
7 Now Samuel did not yet know [or
personally experience] the LORD, and
the word of the LORD was not yet re-
vealed [directly] to him.
8 So the LORD called Samuel a third
time. And he stood and went to Eli and
said, "Here I am, for you did call me."
Then Eli understood that it was the
LORD [who was] calling the boy.
9 So Eli said to Samuel, "Go, lie down,
and it shall be that if He calls you,
you shall say, 'Speak, LORD, for Your
servant is listening.' " So Samuel went
and lay down in his place.
10 Then the LORD came and stood and
called as at the previous times, "Sam-
uel! Samuel!" Then Samuel answered,
"Speak, for Your servant is listening."
11 The LORD said to Samuel, "Behold,
I am about to do a thing in Israel at
which both ears of everyone who hears
it will ring.
12 "On that day I will carry out
against Eli everything that I have
spoken concerning his house (family),
from beginning to end.
13 "Now I have told him that I am
about to judge his house forever for the
sinful behavior which he knew [was
happening], because his sons were
bringing a curse on themselves [dis-
honoring and blaspheming God] and
he did not rebuke them.
14 "Therefore I have sworn to the
house of Eli that the sinful behavior of
Eli's house (family) shall not be atoned
for by sacrifice or offering forever."
15 So Samuel lay down until morning.
Then he opened the doors of the LORD's
house. But Samuel was afraid to tell
the vision to Eli.
16 But Eli called Samuel and said,
"Samuel, my son." And he answered,
"Here I am."
17 Then Eli said, "What is it that He
said to you? Please do not hide it from
me. May God do the same to you, and
more also, if you hide from me any-
thing of all that He said to you."
18 So Samuel told him everything,
hiding nothing from him. And Eli said,
"It is the LORD; may He do what seems
good to Him."
19 Now Samuel grew; and the LORD
was with him and He let none of his
words fail [to be fulfilled]. [Josh 23:14]
20 And all Israel from Dan [in the
north] to Beersheba [in the south]
knew that Samuel was appointed as
a prophet of the LORD.
21 And the LORD continued to appear
in Shiloh, for the LORD revealed Him-
self to Samuel in Shiloh by the word
of the LORD.

---

eager response with a desire to listen. It is that attitude of listening that was foundational to Samuel's whole life and ministry. Throughout his life we see him listening to God's word and following God's direction. He listened for the general will of God and also had an ear for the more specific directions that God gave him. Sometimes he raised questions about why he was doing a particular thing, but the word from God was paramount. He listened for it and responded to it.

3:14 *shall not be atoned for.* Eli and his sons were guilty of presumptuous sin (Nu 15:30 – 31). For such sin, there was no atoning sacrifice.

3:20 *from Dan [in the north] to Beersheba [in the south].* This expression denotes the whole territory of Israel, from its most northern point to its most southern (Jdg 20:1).

---

3 Ex 27:20; 1Sa 1:9 **7** See Ac 19:2 **11** 2Ki 21:12 **12** 1Sa 2:30-36 **13** 1Sa 2:29-31; Eze 7:3; 18:30; 1Sa 2:12,17,22; 1Sa 2:23,25 **14** Nu 15:30,31 **17** Ru 1:17 **18** Job 1:21; Isa 39:8 **19** 1Sa 2:21; Ge 39:2,21,23; 1Sa 9:6 **20** Jdg 20:1 **21** ver. 1,4

Philistines Take the Ark in Victory

4 AND THE word of [the LORD
through] Samuel came to all Is-
rael. Now Israel went out to meet the
Philistines in battle and they camped
beside Ebenezer while the Philistines
camped at Aphek.
[2]The Philistines assembled in battle
formation to meet Israel, and when the
battle was over, Israel was defeated by
the Philistines, who killed about four
thousand men on the battlefield.
[3]When the people (soldiers) came into
the camp, the elders of Israel said, "Why
has the LORD defeated us today before
the Philistines? Let us bring the ark of
the covenant of the LORD here from Shi-
loh, so that He may come among us and
save us from the hand of our enemies."
[4]So the people sent *word* to Shiloh,
and from there they carried the ark of
the covenant of the LORD of hosts who
sits *above* the cherubim; and the two
sons of Eli, Hophni and Phinehas, were
with the ark of the covenant of God.
[5]So it happened that as the ark of
the covenant of the LORD came into the
camp, all [the people of] Israel shout-
ed with a great shout, and the earth
resounded.
[6]When the Philistines heard the
noise of the shout, they said, "What

4:1 *the Philistines.* Abraham and Isaac had contact with the Philistines as early as the twentieth century BC. With their aggressive invasions and fortress cities, the Philistines established strong political and military control of the southern coastal plain of Palestine. They had iron weapons, and were a significant threat to the Israelites.

4:4 *who sits above the cherubim.* Cherubim are angels generally regarded as guardians of God's holiness (Ge 3:24; Ps 80:1; Ezr 10:9).

4:6–7 *the ark of the LORD had come into the camp. The Philistines were afraid.* Apparently the Philistines viewed the ark as some sort of idol.

CHAPTER 4 1 1Sa 7:12 4 2Sa 6:2; Nu 7:89

THE WANDERINGS OF THE ARK OF THE COVENANT

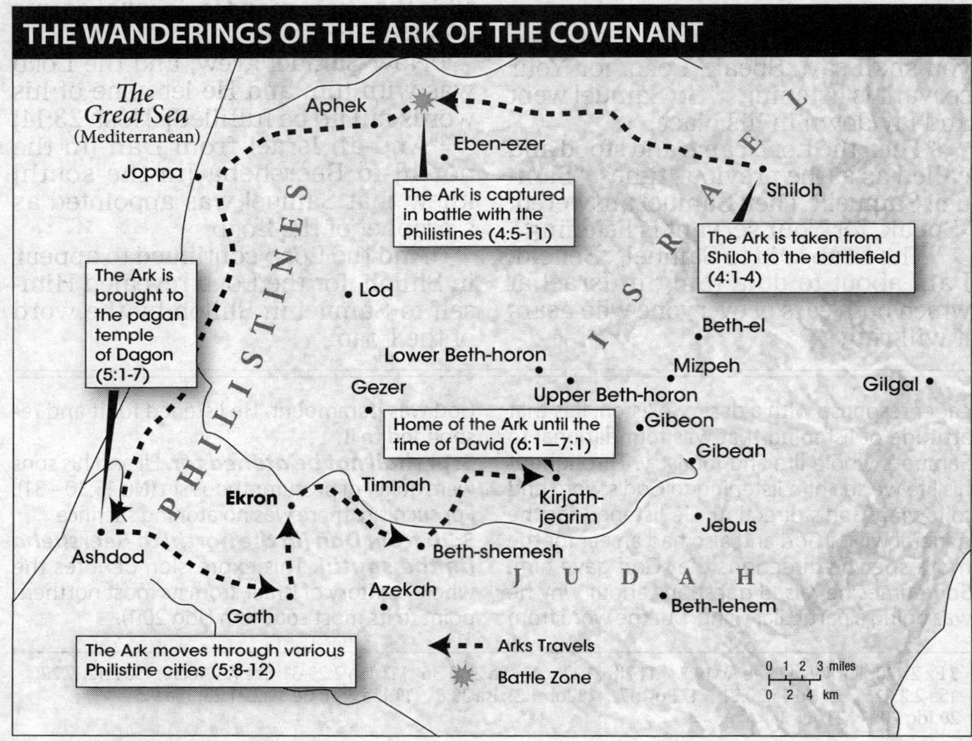

does the noise of this great shout in
the camp of the Hebrews *mean*?" Then
they understood that the ark of the
Lord had come into the camp.
7 The Philistines were afraid, for they
said, "God has come into the camp."
And they said, "Woe [disaster is com-
ing] to us! For nothing like this has
happened before.
8 "Woe to us! Who will rescue us
from the hand of these mighty gods?
These are the gods who struck the
Egyptians with all kinds of plagues
in the wilderness.
9 "Take courage, and be men, O Phi-
listines, so that you do not become ser-
vants to the Hebrews, as they have been
servants to you; act like men and fight!"
10 So the Philistines fought; Israel
was defeated and every man fled to his
tent. It was a very great defeat, for thir-
ty thousand foot soldiers of Israel fell.
11 Also the ark of God was taken;
and the two sons of Eli, Hophni and
Phinehas, were killed. [1 Sam 2:34]
12 Now a man [from the tribe] of
Benjamin ran from the battle line and
came to Shiloh that same day with his
clothes torn and dust on his head [as
signs of mourning over the disaster].
13 When he arrived, Eli was sitting on
his seat by the road, keeping watch, be-
cause his heart was anxious about the
ark of God. When the man arrived to
report [the news] in the city, everyone
in the city cried out [to God, for help].
14 When Eli heard the noise of the
outcry, he asked, "What is the noise
of this uproar?" And the man came
hurriedly and told Eli.
15 Now Eli was ninety-eight years
old; his eyes were dim so that he could
not see.
16 The man said to Eli, "I have come
from the battle line. Indeed, I escaped
from the battle line today." Eli said,
"How did things go, my son?"
17 The messenger replied, "Israel has
fled before the Philistines and there
has also been a great slaughter among
the people. Also your two sons, Hophni
and Phinehas, are dead, and the ark of
God has been taken."
18 When he mentioned the ark of
God, Eli fell off the seat backwards
by the side of the [city] gate. His neck
was broken and he died, for he was
old and heavy. He had judged Israel
for forty years.
19 Now his daughter-in-law, Phinehas'
wife, was pregnant, and was about to
give birth; so when she heard the news
that the ark of God had been taken and
that her father-in-law and her husband
had died, she kneeled down and gave
birth, because her [labor] pains began.
20 And about the time of her death
[following the sudden birth] the wom-
en attending her said to her, "Do not
be afraid, for you have given birth to
a son." But she did not answer or pay
any attention.
21 And she named the boy Ichabod,
saying, "The glory has left Israel," be-
cause the ark of God had been tak-
en and because of [the deaths of] her
father-in-law and her husband.
22 She said, "The glory has left Israel,
for the ark of God has been taken."

Capture of the Ark Provokes God

5 THEN THE Philistines took the ark
of God, and they brought it from
Ebenezer to Ashdod.
2 They took the ark of God and
brought it into the house of Dagon
and set it beside [the image of] Dagon
[their chief idol].
3 When the people of Ashdod got up

4:11 *Also the ark of God was taken.* The loss of the ark, symbolic of God's presence among His people, was a great tragedy for Israel—even worse than the loss of life. The ark probably never returned to Shiloh.
4:21 *Ichabod.* The name Ichabod, meaning "No Glory," reflected Israel's circumstances. The loss of the ark meant the absence of God's glory in Israel.
5:2 *Dagon.* This god appears to be a Philistine adaptation of the Canaanite god Baal. Philistia was in an important grain producing area, and the worship of Dagon was thought to ensure a good crop.

9 1Co 16:13; Jdg 13:1 **10** ver. 2; Lev 26:17; Dt 28:25 **11** 1Sa 2:32; Ps 78:61; 1Sa 2:34; Ps 78:64 **12** 2Sa 1:2; Jos 7:6; 2Sa 13:19; 15:32; Neh 9:1; Job 2:12 **13** 1Sa 1:9 **15** 1Sa 3:2 **16** 2Sa 1:4 **20** Ge 35:17 **21** 1Sa 14:3; Ps 26:8; 78:61
CHAPTER 5 **1** 1Sa 4:1; 7:12 **2** Jdg 16:23 **3** Isa 19:1; 46:1,2; Isa 46:7

early the next day, behold, Dagon had
fallen on his face on the ground be-
fore the ark of the LORD. So they took
Dagon and returned him to his place.
4 But when they got up early the next
morning, behold, Dagon had [again]
fallen on his face on the ground before
the ark of the LORD, and his head and
both palms of his hands were [lying]
cut off on the threshold; only the trunk
[portion] of [the idol of] Dagon was
left on him.
5 This is the reason neither the priests
of Dagon nor any who enter Dagon's
house step on the threshold of Dagon
in Ashdod to this day.
6 Then the hand of the LORD was
heavy on the people of Ashdod, and
He caused them to be dumbfounded
and struck them with tumors, both
Ashdod and its territory.
7 When the men of Ashdod saw what
had happened, they said, "The ark of
the God of Israel must not remain with
us, for His hand is heavy on us and on
Dagon our god."
8 So they sent *word* and gathered all
the lords (governors) of the Philistines
to them and said, "What shall we do
with the ark of the God of Israel?" They
answered, "Let the ark of the God of Is-
rael be brought around to Gath." So they
took the ark of the God of Israel there.
9 But it happened that after they had
taken it *to Gath*, the hand of the LORD
was against the city, causing an ex-
tremely great panic [because of the
deaths from the plague], for He struck
the people of the city, both young and
old, and tumors broke out on them.
10 So they sent the ark of God to Ekron.
And as the ark of God came to Ekron, the
Ekronites cried out, "They have brought
the ark of the God of Israel [from Gath]
to us, to kill us and our people."
11 So they sent *word* and gathered
all the lords of the Philistines and
said, "Send away the ark of the God
of Israel; let it be returned to its own
place, so that it will not kill us and our
people." For there was a deadly panic
throughout the city; the hand of God
was very heavy (severe) there.
12 The men who had not died were
stricken with tumors and the cry of
the city [for help] went up to heaven.

The Ark Returned to Israel

6 NOW THE ark of the LORD had
been in the country of the Philis-
tines for seven months.
2 And the Philistines called for the
priests and the diviners (seers), saying,
"What shall we do with the ark of the
LORD? Let us know how we can send
it *back* to its place."
3 They said, "If you send away the
ark of the God of Israel, do not send it
empty [without a gift]; but be sure to
return [it] to Him [together with] a guilt
offering. Then you will be healed, and
it will be known to you why His hand
is not removed from you."
4 Then they said, "What shall the
guilt offering be which we shall return
to Him?" They answered, "Five golden
tumors and five golden mice, according
to the number of the lords (governors)
of the Philistines, for one plague was
on all of you and on your lords.
5 "So you shall make replicas of your
tumors and of your mice that ravage
the land, and give glory to the God
of Israel; perhaps He will lighten His
hand [of judgment] on you and your
gods and your land.
6 "Why then do you harden your
hearts [allowing pride to cause your
downfall] just as the Egyptians and

5:6–7 Idolatry—The residents of Ashdod made one fatal mistake. They tried to place a false god alongside the true God. These ancient Philistines are not the only ones who have tried this sort of idolatry. People are quick to recognize that there is *"something"* about the Living God, and they want Him. But they want to have God with qualifiers—"God and my career track," "God and my dedication to entertainment," "God and my secret sin," "God and my own way." But God will not share the throne of any man's heart. It has to be God, and God alone.

---

4 Jer 50:2; Eze 6:4,6; Mic 1:7 **5** Zep 1:9 **6** ver. 7,11; Ex 9:3; Ps 32:4; Ac 13:11; 1Sa 6:5; Dt 28:27; Ps 78:66 **9** Dt 2:15; 1Sa 7:13; 12:15; ver. 11; ver. 6; Ps 78:66 **11** ver. 6,9 **CHAPTER 6** **2** Ge 41:8; Ex 7:11; Da 2:2; 5:7; Mt 2:4 **3** Ex 23:15; Dt 16:16; Lev 5:15,16; ver. 9 **4** See ver. 17,18; Jos 13:3; Jdg 3:3 **5** 1Sa 5:6; Jos 7:19; Isa 42:12; Mal 2:2; Jn 9:24; See 1Sa 5:6,11; Ps 39:10; 1Sa 5:3,4,7 **6** Ex 7:13; 8:15; 14:17; Ex 12:31

Pharaoh hardened their hearts? When
He had severely dealt with them *and*
mocked them, did they not allow the
people [of Israel] to go, and they de-
parted?
7 "Now then, make a new cart and
prepare two milk cows on which a
yoke has never been placed; and hitch
the cows to the cart and take their
calves back home, away from them.
8 "Then take the ark of the LORD and
put it on the cart; and put the articles
of gold which you are returning to Him
as a guilt offering in a box beside it.
Then send it away [without a driver].
9 "But watch, if it goes up by the way
of its own territory to Beth-shemesh,
then [you will know that] He has done
us this great evil. But if not, then we
will know that it was not His hand that
struck us; this disaster happened to us
by chance."
10 And the men did so, and took two
milk cows and hitched them to the cart,
and corralled their calves at home.
11 They put the ark of the LORD on the
cart, and the box containing the golden
mice and the replicas of their tumors.
12 And the cows went straight toward
Beth-shemesh along the highway, low-
ing as they went, and did not turn away
to the right or the left. And the Philis-
tine lords (governors) followed them to
the border of Beth-shemesh.
13 Now *the men of* Beth-shemesh
were gathering their wheat harvest
in the valley, and they looked up and
saw the ark and rejoiced to see it.
14 The cart came into the field of Josh-
ua of Beth-shemesh and stopped there.
A large stone was there; and the men
split up the wood of the cart [for fire-
wood] and offered the cows as a burnt
offering to the LORD.
15 The Levites had taken down the
ark of the LORD and the box beside it,
in which were the articles of gold, and
put them on the large stone. And the
men of Beth-shemesh offered burnt
offerings and made sacrifices that day
to the LORD.
16 When the five lords of the Phi-
listines saw what happened, they re-
turned to Ekron that day.
17 These are the golden tumors which
the Philistines returned as a guilt of-
fering to the LORD: one for Ashdod,
one for Gaza, one for Ashkelon, one
for Gath and one for Ekron [the five
chief cities of the Philistines];
18 also the golden mice, *according*
to the number of all the cities of the
Philistines belonging to the five lords,
both fortified cities and [unwalled]
country villages. The large stone on
which the Levites set the ark of the
LORD *remains a witness* to this day in
the field of Joshua of Beth-shemesh.
19 The LORD struck down some of the
men of Beth-shemesh because they
had looked into the ark of the LORD.
He struck down 50,070 men among
the people, and the people mourned
because the LORD had struck the people
with a great slaughter.
20 The men of Beth-shemesh said,
"Who is able to stand before the LORD,
this holy God? And to whom shall He
go up from us?"

6:8 *send it away.* This seemed like a good test to the Philistines. The natural inclination of the cows would be to return home to their calves. If the cows went against their normal instincts, it would show that God was causing them to walk away from their calves.

6:14 *offered the cows as a burnt offering.* The law required that sacrifices be offered only at the central sanctuary (Dt 12:4 – 14). Apparently the people felt that special circumstances required an immediate offering of thanksgiving.

6:19 Presumption — The Israelites who looked into the ark were glad to have it back. Perhaps they thought that the Philistines had looked inside it, and certainly they had more right than the Philistines to gaze upon the holy objects contained in the ark. Their reasons may have seemed good at the moment, but they were ignoring God's specific commands and treating His holiness as unimportant. In the same way today, we can end up trivializing who God is. We can speak frivolously of the things of God, calling Him the "Man upstairs," or being "Sunday Christians." We can presume on our relationship with God without remembering what it cost Jesus to obtain it for us.

7 2Sa 6:3; Nu 19:2 **8** ver. 4,5 **9** Jos 15:10; ver. 3 **16** Jos 13:3 **17** ver. 4 **19** See Ex 19:21; 2Sa 6:7 **20** 2Sa 6:9; Mal 3:2

21 So they sent messengers to the res-
idents of Kiriath-jearim, saying, "The
Philistines have returned the ark of the
LORD. Come down and take it up to you."

Rescue from the Philistines

7 SO THE men of Kiriath-jearim
came and took up the ark of the
Lord and brought it into the house of
Abinadab on the hill, and they conse-
crated Eleazar his son to care for the
ark of the Lord.
2 And from that day the ark re-
mained in Kiriath-jearim for a very
long time, for it was twenty years [until
the reign of King David]; and all the
house of Israel lamented (wailed) *and*
grieved after the LORD. [2 Sam 6:3, 4;
1 Chr 13:5–7]
3 Then Samuel said to all the house
of Israel, "If you are returning to the
LORD with all your heart, remove the
foreign gods and the Ashtaroth (pagan
goddesses) from among you and direct
your hearts to the LORD and serve Him
only; and He will rescue you from the
hand of the Philistines."
4 So the Israelites removed the Baals
and the Ashtaroth and served the LORD
alone.
5 Samuel said, "Gather all Israel to-
gether at Mizpah and I will pray to the
LORD for you."
6 So they gathered at Mizpah, and
drew water and poured it out before
the LORD, and fasted on that day and
said there, "We have sinned against
the LORD." And Samuel judged the Is-
raelites at Mizpah.
7 Now when the Philistines heard
that the Israelites had gathered at
Mizpah, the lords (governors) of the
Philistines went up against Israel. And
when the Israelites heard it, they were
afraid of the Philistines.
8 And the sons of Israel said to Samu-
el, "Do not cease to cry out to the LORD
our God for us, so that He may save us
from the hand of the Philistines."
9 So Samuel took a nursing lamb and
offered it as a whole burnt offering to the
LORD; and Samuel cried out to the LORD
for Israel and the LORD answered him.
10 As Samuel was offering up the burnt
offering, the Philistines approached for
the battle against Israel. Then the LORD
thundered with a great voice that day
against the Philistines and threw them
into confusion, and they were defeated
and fled before Israel.
11 And the men of Israel came out of
Mizpah and pursued the Philistines,
and struck them down as far as [the
territory] below Beth-car.
12 Then Samuel took a stone and set
it between Mizpah and Shen, and he
named it Ebenezer (stone of help), say-
ing, "Thus far the LORD has helped us."
13 So the Philistines were subdued
and they did not come anymore into
Israelite territory. And the hand of the
LORD was against the Philistines all the
days of Samuel.
14 The cities which the Philistines
had taken from Israel were restored
to Israel, from Ekron to Gath; and Is-
rael recovered the cities' territory from
the Philistines. Also there was peace
between Israel and the Amorites.

Samuel's Ministry

15 Now Samuel judged Israel all the
days of his life.
16 He used to go annually on a circuit

7:2 *twenty years.* It was probably twenty years before Samuel called the assembly at Mizpah (v. 5). The ark remained at Kiriath-jearim until David brought it to Jerusalem in the first year of his reign over all Israel.
7:6 *poured it out.* The pouring of water was symbolic of repentance (La 2:19).
7:12 *Ebenezer.* The name Ebenezer means "stone of help." Samuel followed Joshua's practice of commemorating the victories of God for His people with stone markers. Some old gospel hymns refer to an "Ebenezer," meaning a particular notation of something special God has done.
7:14 *Amorites.* This name may refer to the original inhabitants of Canaan (Ge 15:16).

21 Jos 18:14; 1Ch 13:5,6 **CHAPTER 7** **1** 1Sa 6:21; Ps 132:6; 2Sa 6:4 **3** Dt 30:2-10; Isa 55:7; Hos 6:1; Joel 2:12; Ge 35:2; Jos 24:14; Jdg 2:13; 2Ch 30:19; Job 11:13; Dt 6:13; 10:20; Lk 4:8 **4** Jdg 2:11 **5** Jdg 20:1 **6** 2Sa 14:14; Neh 9:1,2; Da 9:3-5; Joel 2:12; Jdg 10:10; Ps 106:6 **8** Isa 37:4 **9** Ps 99:6; Jer 15:1 **10** Jos 10:10; Jdg 4:15; 5:20; 1Sa 2:10; 2Sa 22:14,15 **12** Ge 28:18; Jos 4:9 **13** Jdg 13:1; 1Sa 13:5 **15** 1Sa 12:11; Jdg 2:16

to Bethel, Gilgal, and Mizpah, and he judged Israel in all these places.

17 Then he would return to Ramah, because his home was there; and there he judged Israel, and there he built an altar to the LORD.

Israel Demands a King

8 AND IT came about when Samuel was old that he appointed his sons as judges over Israel.

2 Now the name of his firstborn was Joel, and the name of his second, Abijah; they were judging in Beersheba.

3 His sons, however, did not walk in his ways, but turned aside after dishonest gain, took bribes, and perverted justice.

4 Then all the elders of Israel gathered together and came to Samuel at Ramah

5 and said to him, "Look, you have grown old, and your sons do not walk in your ways. Now appoint us a king to judge us [and rule over us] like all the other nations."

6 But their demand displeased Samuel when they said, "Give us a king to judge *and* rule over us." So Samuel prayed to the LORD.

7 The LORD said to Samuel, "Listen to the voice of the people in regard to all that they say to you, for they have not rejected you, but they have rejected Me from being King over them.

8 "Like all the deeds which they have done since the day that I brought them up from Egypt even to this day—in that they have abandoned (rejected) Me and served other gods—so they are doing to you also.

9 "So now listen to their voice; only solemnly warn them and tell them the ways of the king who will reign over them."

Warning concerning a King

10 So Samuel told all the words of the LORD to the people who were asking him for a king.

11 He said, "These will be the ways of the king who will reign over you: he will take your sons and appoint them for himself to his chariots and among his horsemen and they will run before his chariots.

12 "He will appoint them for himself to be commanders over thousands and over fifties, and *some* to do his plowing and to reap his harvest and to make his implements of war and equipment for his chariots.

13 "He will take your daughters to be perfumers, cooks, and bakers.

14 "He will take the best of your fields, your vineyards, and your olive groves, and give them to his servants.

15 "He will take a tenth of your grain and of your vineyards and give it to his officers and to his servants.

16 "He will take your male servants and your female servants and your best young men and your donkeys and use them for his work.

17 "He will take a tenth of your flocks, and you yourselves shall be his servants.

18 "Then you will cry out on that day because of your king whom you have chosen for yourselves, but the LORD will not answer you on that day [because you have rejected Him as King]."

7:17 *Ramah.* Samuel was back in the town where he was born.

8:5 *appoint us a king.* The reasons given for wanting a king were Samuel's age and his sons' unreliability. This is a sad commentary on Samuel's failure to raise his sons to honor and obey the Lord, particularly considering the example of Eli's sons. But this was not really a reason to ask for a king. The Israelite judges had always been appointed by God, rather than gaining their position by inheritance. There was no reason to think that God would not appoint someone to succeed Samuel.

8:7 *they have rejected Me.* This actually fulfilled the prophecy in Deuteronomy 17:14–20. God knew long ago that the Israelites would choose to be like the other nations and have a king, instead of being ruled more directly by God through judges. He warned them of the pitfalls of having a king, and set out some guidelines for the kings to follow.

---

17 1Sa 8:4; Jdg 21:4 **CHAPTER 8** **1** Dt 16:18; 2Ch 19:5; Jdg 10:4; 12:14, compared with Jdg 5:10 **3** Jer 22:15-17; Ex 18:21; 1Ti 3:3; 6:10; Dt 16:19; Ps 15:5 **5** ver. 19,20; Dt 17:14; Hos 13:10; Ac 13:21 **7** See Ex 16:8; 1Sa 10:19; 12:17,19; Hos 13:10,11 **9** ver. 11 **11** See Dt 17:16; 1Sa 10:25; 1Sa 14:52 **14** 1Ki 21:7; See Eze 46:18 **18** Isa 1:15; Mic 3:4

19 Nevertheless, the people refused to listen to the voice of Samuel, and they said, "No, but there shall be a king over us,

20 so that we too may be like all the nations [around us], that our king may judge [and govern] us and go out before us and fight our battles."

21 Samuel had heard all the words of the people and repeated them to the LORD.

22 And the LORD said to Samuel, "Listen to their request and appoint a king for them." So Samuel said to the men of Israel, "Go, each man to his own city."

Saul's Search

9 THERE WAS a man of [the tribe of] Benjamin whose name was Kish the son of Abiel, the son of Zeror, the son of Becorath, the son of Aphiah, a Benjamite, a mighty man of influence *and* wealth.

2 Kish had a son named Saul, a choice and handsome man; among the sons of Israel there was not a man more handsome than he. From his shoulders and up he was [a head] taller than any of the people.

3 Now the donkeys of Kish, Saul's father, had wandered off *and* were lost. Kish said to his son Saul, "Please take one of the servants with you and arise, go look for the donkeys."

4 And they passed through the hill country of Ephraim and the land of Shalishah, but did not find *them*. Then they passed through the land of Shaalim, but they were not *there* and the land of the Benjamites, but they [still] did not find *them*.

5 When they came to the land of Zuph, Saul said to his servant who was with him, "Come, let us return, otherwise my father will stop *worrying* about the donkeys and become anxious about us."

6 The servant said to him, "Look here, in this city there is a man of God, and the man is held in honor; everything that he says comes true. Now let us go there; perhaps he can advise us about our journey [and tell us where we should go]."

7 Then Saul said to his servant, "But look, if we go [to see him], what shall we bring to the man? For the bread from our sacks is gone and there is no gift to bring to the man of God. What do we have [to offer]?"

8 The servant replied again to Saul, "Here in my hand I have a quarter of a shekel of silver; I will give that to the man of God, and he will advise us as to [where we should go on] our journey [to find the donkeys]."

9 (Formerly in Israel, when a man went to inquire of God, he would say, "Come, let us go to the seer"; for *he who is called* a prophet today was formerly called a seer.)

10 Saul said to his servant, "Well said; come, let us go." So they went to the city where the man of God was living.

11 As they went up the hill to the city, they met some young women going out to draw water, and said to them, "Is the seer (prophet) here?"

12 They answered them, "He is; look, he is ahead of you. Hurry now, for he has come into the city today because the people have a sacrifice on the high place today.

13 "As you enter the city you will find him before he goes up to the high place to eat, for the people will not eat until he comes, because he must ask the blessing on the sacrifice; afterward,

---

8:20 *and fight our battles.* The Israelites were looking for human leadership on the battlefield, instead of recognizing that God would lead them in battle, and win (Ex 15:3; Jdg 7).

9:12 *the high place.* A hill that was used for worship was called "a high place." The Canaanites were known for building their places for worship on hills, and the Israelites apparently used similar sites for worship after the ark was taken from the tabernacle at Shiloh. They believed that the presence of the Lord had departed from the tabernacle, and it was apparently at that point that Shiloh ceased to be a gathering center for the nation.

19 Jer 44:16 **20** ver. 5 **22** ver. 7; Hos 13:11 **CHAPTER 9** **1** 1Sa 14:51; 1Ch 8:33; 9:39 **2** 1Sa 10:23 **4** 2Ki 4:42 **6** Dt 33:1; 1Ki 13:1; 1Sa 3:19 **7** See Jdg 6:18; 13:17; 1Ki 14:3; 2Ki 4:42; 8:8 **9** Ge 25:22; 2Sa 24:11; 2Ki 17:13; 1Ch 26:28; 29:29; 2Ch 16:7,10; Isa 30:10; Am 7:12 **11** Ge 24:11 **12** Ge 31:54; 1Sa 16:2; 1Ki 3:2

those who are invited will eat. So go up
now, for about now you will find him."
14 So they went up to the city. And
as they came into the city, there was
Samuel coming out toward them to go
up to the high place.

God's Choice for King

15 Now a day before Saul came, the
LORD had informed Samuel [of this],
saying,
16 "About this time tomorrow I will
send you a man from the land of Ben-
jamin, and you shall anoint him as
leader over My people Israel; and he
will save My people from the hand of
the Philistines. For I have looked upon
[the distress of] My people, because
their cry [for help] has come to Me."
17 When Samuel saw Saul, the LORD
said to him, "There is the man of whom
I spoke to you. This one shall rule over
My people [as their king]."
18 Then Saul approached Samuel in
the [city] gate and said, "Please tell me
where the seer's house is."
19 Samuel answered Saul, "I am the
seer. Go on ahead of me to the high
place, for you shall eat with me today;
and in the morning I will let you go, and
will tell you all that is on your mind.
20 "As for your donkeys which were
lost three days ago, do not be con-
cerned about them, for they have been
found. And for whom are all things
that are desirable in Israel? Are they
not for you and for all your father's
household (family)?"
21 Saul replied, "Am I not a Benjamite,
of the smallest of the tribes of Israel?
And is not my family the smallest of all
the families of the tribe of Benjamin?
Why then have you spoken this way
to me [as if I were very important]?"
22 Then Samuel took Saul and his ser-
vant and brought them into the hall [at
the high place] and gave them a place
[to sit] at the head of the persons—
about thirty men—who were invited
[while the rest ate outside].
23 Samuel said to the cook, "Bring the
[priests'] portion that I gave you, re-
garding which I told you, 'Set it aside.' "
24 Then the cook lifted up the leg (thigh)
with *the meat* that was on it [indicating
that it was the priest's honored portion]
and placed it before Saul. Samuel said,
"Here is what has been reserved [for
you]. Set it before you and eat, because it
has been kept for you until the appointed
time, ever since I invited the people." So
Saul ate with Samuel that day.
25 When they came down from the
high place into the city, Samuel spoke
with Saul on the roof [of his house].
26 They got up early [the next day];
and at dawn Samuel called Saul [who
was sleeping] on the roof, saying, "Get
up, so that I may send you on your
way." Saul got up, and both he and
Samuel went outside.
27 As they were going down to the
outskirts of the city, Samuel said to
Saul, "Tell the servant to go on ahead
of us so that he may pass by but you
stand still now so that I may proclaim
the word of God to you."

Saul among Prophets

10 THEN SAMUEL took the flask
of oil and poured it on Saul's
head, kissed him, and said, "Has the
LORD not anointed you as ruler over
His inheritance (Israel)?

9:20 Providence — God, in His providence, is directing our lives according to His plan and purpose. Hunting for livestock or having a vehicle break down are normal nuisances, something we can handle, but seldom think about as being the providence of God. Yet if we realize that God has His hand on all of our circumstances, everything that changes our plans puts us into a position to meet, pray for, help, or witness to someone else who would not normally come our way.

9:21 *the smallest of the tribes.* Benjamin was the second smallest tribe at the first census following the exodus (Nu 1:36–37). The tribe was reduced to six hundred fighting men during the punishment of Benjamin for the atrocity at Gibeah (Jdg 19–20).

9:24 *the leg.* Giving Saul the leg was intended to honor him in the presence of the other guests.

10:1 *Has the LORD not anointed you.* The anointing of a ruler was a religious act. That is

15 1Sa 15:1; Ac 13:21 **16** 1Sa 10:1; Ex 2:25; 3:7,9 **17** 1Sa 16:12; Hos 13:11 **20** ver. 3; 1Sa 8:5,19; 12:13
21 1Sa 15:17; Jdg 20:46-48; See Jdg 6:15 **24** Lev 7:32,33; Eze 24:4 **25** Dt 22:8; 2Sa 11:2; Ac 10:9 **CHAPTER 10**
1 1Sa 9:16; 16:13; 2Ki 9:3,6; Ps 2:12; Ac 13:21; Dt 32:9

2 “When you leave me today, you will
meet two men beside Rachel’s tomb in
the territory of Benjamin at Zelzah;
they will say to you, ‘The donkeys you
went to look for have been found. And
your father has stopped caring about
them and is worried about you, saying,
“What shall I do about my son?” ’

3 “Then you will go on further from
there, and you will come to the terebinth
tree of Tabor, and three men going up to
[sacrifice to] God at Bethel will meet you
there, one carrying three young goats,
another carrying three loaves of bread,
and another carrying a jug of wine.

4 They will greet you and give you
two *loaves* of bread, which you will
accept from their hand.

5 “After that you will come to the hill
of God where the garrison of the Phi-
listines is; and when you come there
to the city, you will meet a group of
prophets coming down from the high
place [of worship] with harp, tambou-
rine, flute, and lyre before them, and
they will be prophesying.

6 “Then the Spirit of the LORD will
come upon you mightily, and you will
prophesy with them, and you will be
changed into another man.

7 “When these signs come to you,
do for yourself whatever the situation
requires, for God is with you.

8 “You shall go down ahead of me to
Gilgal; and behold, I will be coming
down to you to offer burnt offerings
and to sacrifice peace offerings. You
shall wait seven days until I come to
you and show you what you must do.”

9 Then it happened when Saul turned
his back to leave Samuel, God changed
his heart; and all those signs came to
pass that day.

10 When they came to the hill [Gibe-
ah], behold, a group of prophets met
him; and the Spirit of God came on
him mightily, and he prophesied [un-
der divine guidance] among them.

11 Now when all who knew Saul pre-
viously saw that he actually proph-
esied now [by inspiration] with the
prophets, the people said one to anoth-
er, “What has happened to [Saul, who
is nobody but] the son of Kish? Is Saul
also among the prophets?”

12 And a man from there answered,
“But who is the father of the others?”
So it became a proverb, “Is Saul also
among the prophets?”

13 When Saul had finished proph-
esying, he went to the high place [of
worship].

14 Saul’s uncle said to him and to his
servant, “Where did you go?” And Saul
said, “To look for the donkeys. And
when we saw that they were nowhere
to be found, we went to Samuel [for
help].”

15 Saul’s uncle said, “Please tell me,
what did Samuel say to you?”

16 And Saul said to his uncle, “He told
us plainly that the donkeys had been
found.” But he did not tell him about
the matter of the kingdom which Sam-
uel had mentioned.

Saul Publicly Chosen King

17 Then Samuel called the people to-
gether to the LORD at Mizpah,

18 and he said to Israel, “Thus says
the LORD, the God of Israel, ‘It was I
who brought Israel up from Egypt,
and I rescued you from the hand of the
Egyptians and from all the kingdoms
that were oppressing you.’

---

why David had such high regard for Saul, refusing to lift a hand against “the LORD’s anointed.” ***His inheritance.*** The land of Israel was God’s gift to His people, but it would return to God’s direct control if the people did not manage it according to God’s laws (Dt 27 – 30).

10:4 ***two loaves of bread.*** The bread that the strangers would offer to Saul would have been bread prepared for use in the worship of God. Giving the bread to Saul was a sacred act, as well as a sign for Saul.

10:9 ***God changed his heart.*** God’s Spirit prepared Saul for the kingship. It probably was not spiritual regeneration in the way it is understood in New Testament times. Saul wanted to worship God, but he continually struggled with wanting to do things his own way.

10:19 Unfaithfulness — This was not the

2 Ge 35:19,20; Jos 18:28 **3** Ge 28:22; 35:1,3,7 **5** 1Sa 13:3; 1Sa 9:12; Ex 15:20,21; 2Ki 3:15; 1Co 14:1 **6** Nu 11:25; 1Sa 16:13; ver. 10; 1Sa 19:23,24 **7** Ex 4:8; Lk 2:12; Jdg 6:12 **8** 1Sa 11:14,15; 1Sa 13:8 **10** ver. 5; 1Sa 19:20 **11** Mt 13:54,55; Jn 7:15; Ac 4:13 **12** Isa 54:13; Jn 6:45 **17** Jdg 11:11; 20:1; 1Sa 7:5,6 **18** Jdg 6:8,9

19“But today you have rejected your
God, who Himself saves you from all
your disasters and distresses; yet you
have said, ‘No! Set a king over us.’
Now then, present yourselves before
the LORD by your tribes and by your
families (clans).”
20And when Samuel brought all the
tribes of Israel near, the tribe of Ben-
jamin was chosen by lot.
21Then he brought the tribe of Ben-
jamin near by their families, and the
family of Matri was chosen by lot. And
Saul the son of Kish was chosen by lot;
but when they looked for him, he could
not be found.
22So they inquired further of the
LORD, “Has the man come here yet?”
And the LORD answered, “He is there,
hiding himself by the provisions *and*
supplies.” [Ex 28:30]
23So they ran and took him from
there, and when he stood among the
people, he was taller than any of the
people from his shoulders upward.
24Samuel said to all the people,
“Do you see him whom the LORD has
chosen? For there is no one like him
among all the people.” So all the people
shouted and said, “*Long* live the king!”
25Then Samuel told the people the re-
quirements of the kingdom, and wrote
them in a book and placed it before the
LORD. And Samuel sent all the people
away, each one to his home.
26Saul also went home to Gibeah;
and the brave men whose hearts God
had touched went with him.
27But some worthless men said,
“How can this man save *and* rescue
us?” And they regarded Saul with con-
tempt and did not bring him a gift. But
he ignored the insult *and* kept silent.

Saul Defeats the Ammonites

11 NOW NAHASH the Ammon-
ite [king] went up and besieged
Jabesh-gilead; and all the men of Jabesh
said to Nahash, “Make a treaty [of
peace] with us and we will serve you.”
2But Nahash the Ammonite told
them, “I will make *a treaty* with you
on this condition, that I will gouge out
the right eye of every one of you, and
make it a disgrace upon all Israel.”
3The elders of Jabesh said to Na-
hash, “Give us seven days so that we
may send messengers throughout the
territory of Israel. Then, if there is no
one to save us, we will come out [and
surrender] to you.”
4Then the messengers came to Gibe-
ah of Saul and told the news to the
people; and all the people raised their
voices and wept aloud.
5Now Saul was coming out of the

---

first time that the Israelites had been unfaithful. Sometimes they could see what God was doing and respond with thanksgiving, and sometimes they seemed to forget everything about Him and go headlong into the very sins He had warned them would bring nothing but disaster. Believers today have the incredible gift of the Holy Spirit to direct them and remind them of the ways of God. It is hard to imagine what it would be like to follow God without the help of the Holy Spirit, the comforter, the helper (Jn 14:25 – 26). It is important to remember that for humanity, unfaithfulness is our middle name, and to thank God for His mercy and grace which provided a way for us to belong to Him.

10:20 ***was chosen.*** Even though Samuel already knew that Saul was to be the king, the designation of Saul as Israel’s first monarch was made by casting lots. The lots were cast like dice, and God’s will was determined by asking yes and no questions. They believed that God controlled all events, including the lots when they were used to seek God.

10:24 ***whom the LORD has chosen.*** Long ago, before they crossed the Jordan, the Lord had told Moses that the Israelites would want a king. At that time the Lord laid out guidelines for the king, and one of them was that the king must be an Israelite chosen by the Lord (Dt 17:14 – 20).

11:1 ***Ammonite.*** The Ammonites, who were descendants of Lot, occupied the fringes of the desert east of the territories of Gad and Manasseh.

11:5 ***out of the field.*** Saul had been appointed king, but he did not assume governmental authority at once. He continued farming until he could answer Israel’s expectations of him by delivering them from their enemies. This pattern was more in the style of the judges of Israel.

---

19 1Sa 8:7,19; 12:12 **20** Ac 1:24,26 **22** 1Sa 23:2,4,10,11 **23** 1Sa 9:2 **24** 2Sa 21:6; 1Ki 1:25,39 **25** 1Sa 8:11 **26** Jdg 20:14; 1Sa 11:4 **27** 1Sa 11:12; Dt 13:13; 2Sa 8:2; 1Ki 4:21; Mt 2:11 **CHAPTER 11** **1** 1Sa 12:12; Jdg 21:8; Ge 26:28; 1Ki 20:34 **2** Ge 34:14; 1Sa 17:26 **4** 1Sa 10:26; 15:34; 2Sa 21:6; Jdg 2:4

field behind the oxen, and he said, "What is *the matter* with the people that they are weeping?" So they told him about the report of the men of Jabesh.
[6]The Spirit of God came upon Saul mightily when he heard these words, and he became extremely angry.
[7]He took a team of oxen and cut them in pieces, and sent them throughout the territory of Israel by the hand of messengers, saying, "Whoever does not come out to follow Saul and Samuel, the same shall be done to his oxen." Then fear of the LORD fell on the people, and they came out [united] as one man [with one purpose].
[8]He assembled *and* counted them at Bezek; and the sons of Israel numbered 300,000, and the men of Judah 30,000.
[9]They said to the messengers who had come, "You shall say to the men of Jabesh-gilead: 'Tomorrow, by the time the sun is hot, you will have help [against the Ammonites].' " So the messengers came and reported this to the men of Jabesh; and they were overjoyed.

6 Jdg 3:10; 6:34; 1Sa 10:10 **7** Jdg 19:29; Jdg 21:5,8,10 **8** Jdg 1:5; 2Sa 24:9

THE SALVATION OF JABESH-GILEAD

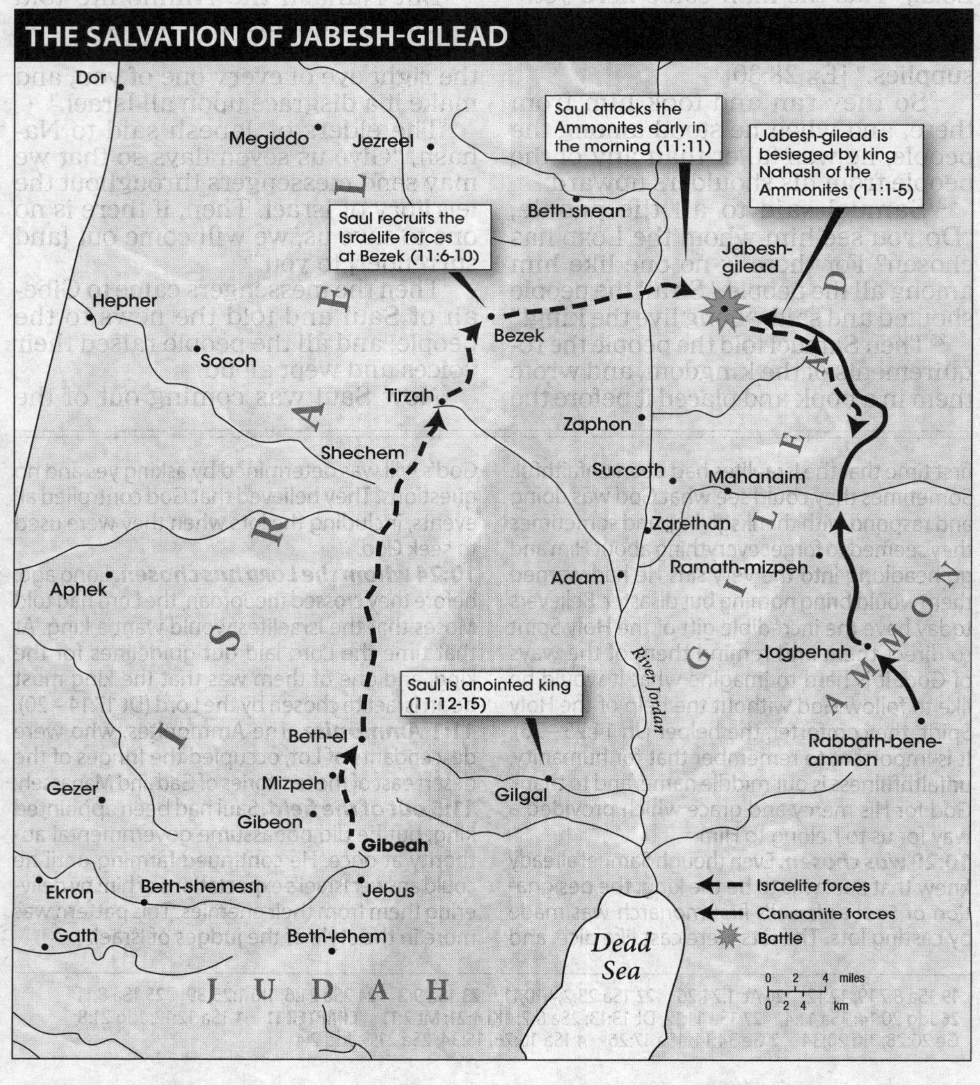

10 So the men of Jabesh said [to Na-
hash the Ammonite], "Tomorrow we
will come out to you [to surrender],
and you may do to us whatever seems
good to you."
11 The next morning Saul put the men
into three companies; and they en-
tered the [Ammonites'] camp during
the [darkness of the early] morning
watch and killed the Ammonites until
the heat of the day; and the survivors
were scattered, and no two of them
were left together.
12 The people said to Samuel, "Who
is the one who said, 'Shall Saul reign
over us?' Bring the men, and we will
put them to death."
13 But Saul said, "No man shall be put
to death this day, for today the LORD
has brought victory to Israel."
14 Samuel said to the people, "Come,
let us go to Gilgal and there restore
the kingdom."
15 So all the people went to Gilgal,
and there they made Saul king before
the LORD in Gilgal. There they also
sacrificed peace offerings before the
LORD; and there Saul and all the men
of Israel rejoiced greatly.

Samuel Addresses Israel

12 THEN SAMUEL said to all Is-
rael, "Behold, I have listened to
your voice in everything that you have
said to me and have appointed a king
over you.
2 "And now, here is the king walking
before you. As for me, I am old and
gray, and here are my sons with you.
I have walked before you from my
childhood to this day.
3 "Here I am; testify against me be-
fore the LORD and [Saul] His anointed
[if I have done someone wrong]. Whose
ox have I taken, or whose donkey have
I taken, or whom have I exploited?
Whom have I oppressed or from whose
hand have I taken a bribe to blind my
eyes [to the truth]? [Tell me and] I will
restore it to you."
4 They said, "You have not exploited
us or oppressed us or taken anything
at all from a man's hand."
5 Samuel said to them, "The LORD is
a witness against you, and [Saul] His
anointed is a witness this day that you
have not found anything in my hand."
And they answered, "*He is* a witness."
6 Then Samuel said to the people,
"It is the LORD who appointed Moses
and Aaron and brought your fathers
(ancestors) up from the land of Egypt.
7 "Now then, take your stand, so that
I may plead *and* contend with you be-
fore the LORD concerning all the righ-
teous acts of the LORD which He did for
you and for your fathers.
8 "When Jacob [and his sons] had
come into Egypt [and later when the
Egyptians oppressed them] and your
fathers cried out to the LORD, then
the LORD sent Moses and Aaron who
brought your fathers out of Egypt and
settled them in this place.
9 "But when they forgot the LORD
their God, He sold them into the hand
of Sisera, commander of Hazor's army,
and into the hand of the Philistines and
of the king of Moab, and they fought
against them.
10 "They cried out to the LORD, say-
ing, 'We have sinned because we
have abandoned (rejected) the Lord
and have served the Baals and the
Ashtaroth; but now rescue us from
the hands of our enemies, and we will
serve You.'
11 "Then the LORD sent Jerubbaal
(Gideon) and Bedan and Jephthah and
Samuel, and He rescued you from the

11:11 *morning watch.* The Israelites divided the night into three watches: nine to twelve, twelve to three, and three to six in the morning.

12:9 *they forgot the LORD their God.* Samuel recounted the nation's apostasy and subsequent divine discipline. Israel was having problems because they had stopped obeying God. It was not because either God or Samuel was inadequate.

10 ver. 3 **11** See 1Sa 31:11; Jdg 7:16 **12** 1Sa 10:27; See Lk 19:27 **13** 2Sa 19:22; Ex 14:13,30; 1Sa 19:5 **14** 1Sa 10:8 **15** 1Sa 10:17; 1Sa 10:8 **CHAPTER 12** **1** 1Sa 8:5,19,20; 1Sa 10:24 **2** Nu 27:17; 1Sa 8:20; 1Sa 8:1,5 **3** 1Sa 24:6; 2Sa 1:14,16; Nu 16:15; Ac 20:33; 1Th 2:5; Dt 16:19 **5** Jn 18:38; Ac 23:9; Ex 22:4 **6** Mic 6:4 **7** Isa 1:18; Mic 6:2,3 **8** Ge 46:5,6; Ex 2:23; Ex 3:10 **9** Jdg 3:7; Jdg 4:2; Jdg 10:7; Jdg 3:12 **10** Jdg 10:10; Jdg 2:13; Jdg 10:15,16 **11** Jdg 6:14,32; Jdg 11:1; 1Sa 7:13

hand of your enemies on every side, and you lived in security.

The King Confirmed

12 "But when you saw that Nahash king of the Ammonites had come against you, you said to me, 'No, but a king shall reign over us'—although the LORD your God was your King.

13 "Now therefore, here is [Saul] the king whom you have chosen, and for whom you asked; behold, the LORD has set a king over you.

14 "If you will fear the LORD [with awe and profound reverence] and serve Him and listen to His voice and not rebel against His commandment, then both you and your king will follow the LORD your God [and it will be well].

15 "But if you do not listen to the LORD's voice, but rebel against His command, then the hand of the LORD will be against you [to punish you], as it was against your fathers.

16 "So now, take your stand and see this great thing which the LORD will do before your eyes.

17 "Is it not [the beginning of the] wheat harvest today? I will call to the LORD and He will send thunder and rain; then you will know [without any doubt], and see that your evil which you have done is great in the sight of the LORD by asking for yourselves a king."

18 So Samuel called to the LORD [in prayer], and He sent thunder and rain that day; and all the people greatly feared the LORD and Samuel.

19 Then all the people said to Samuel, "Pray to the LORD your God for your servants, so that we will not die, for we have added to all our sins *this* evil—to ask for a king for ourselves."

20 Samuel said to the people, "Do not be afraid. You have [indeed] done all this evil; yet do not turn away from following the LORD, but serve the LORD with all your heart.

21 "You must not turn away, for *then you would go* after futile things which cannot profit or rescue, because they are futile.

22 "The LORD will not abandon His people for His great name's sake, because the LORD has been pleased to make you a people for Himself.

23 "Moreover, as for me, far be it from me that I should sin against the LORD by ceasing to pray for you; but I will instruct you in the good and right way.

24 "Only fear the LORD [with awe and profound reverence] and serve Him faithfully with all your heart; for consider what great things He has done for you.

25 "But if you still do evil, both you and your king will be swept away [to destruction]."

War with the Philistines

13 SAUL WAS *thirty* years old when he began to reign, and he reigned *forty*-two years over Israel.

2 Saul chose for himself 3,000 men of Israel; of whom 2,000 were with him in Michmash and in the hill country of Bethel, while 1,000 were with Jonathan at Gibeah of Benjamin. But he sent the rest of the people away, each one to his own tent.

3 Jonathan attacked *and* defeated the

12:17 *wheat harvest.* The season for harvesting wheat in Israel is the months of May and June. ***thunder and rain.*** The land of Israel receives its rainfall during the winter season. For rain to fall during the wheat harvest would be both unusual and detrimental to the harvest.

12:22 *His people.* God's desire to raise up a people for His great name's sake is not based on pride, but on love. He is pleased to show His goodness to the world, and He is willing to reach out to us in spite of our rebellion and foolishness. The whole history of the human race is littered with mankind's failure to acknowledge and follow the living God who created us. But even if we are faithless, God will remain faithful (2Ti 2:13), and that is our great comfort. We cannot even be faithful without His help, but "if God is for us, who can be [successful] against us?" (Ro 8:31).

12 1Sa 11:1; 1Sa 8:5,19; Jdg 8:23; 1Sa 8:7 **13** 1Sa 10:24; 1Sa 8:5; Hos 13:11 **14** Jos 24:14 **15** Lev 26:14; Dt 28:15; Jos 24:20; ver. 9 **16** Ex 14:13 **17** Pr 26:1; Jos 10:12; 1Sa 7:9,10; Jas 5:16-18; 1Sa 8:7 **18** Ex 14:31; Ezr 10:9 **19** Ex 9:28; 10:17; Jas 5:15; 1Jn 5:16 **21** Dt 11:16; Jer 16:19; Hab 2:18; 1Co 8:4 **22** 1Ki 6:13; Jos 7:9; Jer 14:21; Dt 7:7,8 **23** Ac 12:5; Ro 1:9; Col 1:9; 2Ti 1:3; Ps 34:11; Pr 4:11; 1Ki 8:36; 2Ch 6:27; Jer 6:16 **24** Ecc 12:13; Isa 5:12; Dt 10:21 **25** Jos 24:20; Dt 28:36 **CHAPTER 13** **2** 1Sa 10:26 **3** 1Sa 10:5

Philistine garrison which was at Geba,
and the Philistines heard about it. Then
Saul blew the trumpet throughout the
land, saying, "Let the Hebrews hear."
4 All Israel heard that Saul had defeated the Philistine garrison, and also
that Israel had become despicable to
the Philistines. And the people were
summoned to join Saul at Gilgal.
5 Now the Philistines gathered to
fight against Israel, 30,000 chariots
and 6,000 horsemen, and troops in
multitude, like sand on the seashore.
They came up and camped at Michmash, east of Beth-aven.
6 When the men of Israel saw that
they were in a tight situation (for their
troops were hard-pressed), they hid
in caves, in thickets, in cellars, and in
[dry] cisterns (pits).
7 Also *some of* the Hebrews had
crossed the [river] Jordan to the land
of Gad and Gilead. As for Saul, he was
still in Gilgal, and all the people followed
him, trembling [in fear and anticipation].
8 Now Saul waited seven days, according to the appointed time which
Samuel had set, but Samuel had not
come to Gilgal; and the people were
scattering away from Saul.

13:8–9 Presumption — We will never know what would have happened if Saul had waited for Samuel. Whenever we assume we "know better" and take action on our own authority, we cannot know what would have happened if we had followed God's way. Some of the snarls that are the result of stubborn rebellion are often too difficult for us to set right. This is why we must pay such careful attention not only to the direct commandments in the Bible, but to the spirit behind them.

6 Jdg 6:2 **8** 1Sa 10:8

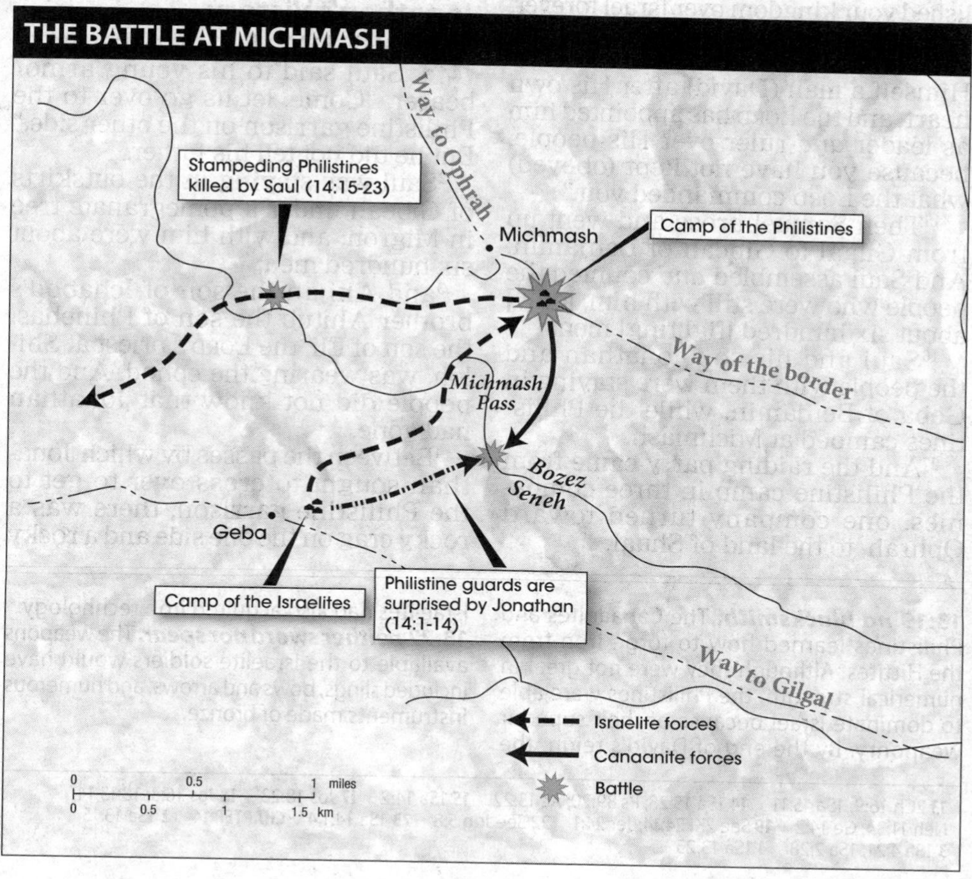

9So Saul said, "Bring me the burnt
offering and the peace offerings." And
he offered the burnt offering [which he
was forbidden to do].
10As soon as he finished offering the
burnt offering, Samuel finally came;
Saul went out to meet and to welcome
him.
11But Samuel said, "What have you
done?" Saul said, "Since I saw that the
people were scattering away from me,
and that you did not come within the
appointed time, and that the Philistines
were assembling at Michmash,
12therefore, I said, 'Now the Philis-
tines will come down against me at
Gilgal, and I have not asked for the
LORD's favor [by making supplication
to Him].' So I forced myself to offer the
burnt offering."
13Samuel said to Saul, "You have
acted foolishly; you have not kept the
commandment of the LORD your God,
which He commanded you, for [if you
had obeyed] the LORD would have estab-
lished your kingdom over Israel forever.
14"But now your kingdom shall not
endure. The LORD has sought out for
Himself a man (David) after His own
heart, and the LORD has appointed him
as leader *and* ruler over His people,
because you have not kept (obeyed)
what the LORD commanded you."
15Then Samuel arose and went up
from Gilgal to Gibeah of Benjamin.
And Saul assembled *and* counted the
people who were still with him, [only]
about six hundred [fighting] men.
16Saul and his son Jonathan and
the people with them were staying in
Geba of Benjamin, while the Philis-
tines camped at Michmash.
17And the raiding party came from
the Philistine camp in three compa-
nies: one company turned toward
Ophrah, to the land of Shual,
18another company turned toward
Beth-horon, and another toward the
border overlooking the Valley of Ze-
boim toward the wilderness.
19Now no blacksmith (metal-worker)
could be found in all the land of Israel,
for the Philistines said, "Otherwise the
Hebrews will make swords or spears."
20So all [the men of] Israel went
down to the Philistines, each to get
his plowshare, pick, axe, or sickle
sharpened.
21The fee [for sharpening] was a pim
(two-thirds of a shekel) for the plow-
shares, the picks, the pitchforks, and
the axes, and to straighten the goads
(cattle prods).
22So it came about on the day of bat-
tle that neither sword nor spear was
found in the hands of any of the people
who were with Saul and Jonathan; but
Saul and Jonathan his son had them.
23And the garrison of the Philistines
went out to the pass at Michmash.

Jonathan's Victory

14 ONE DAY Jonathan the son of
Saul said to his young armor
bearer, "Come, let us go over to the
Philistine garrison on the other side."
But he did not tell his father.
2Saul was staying in the outskirts
of Gibeah under a pomegranate tree
in Migron; and with him were about
six hundred men,
3and Ahijah the son of Ichabod's
brother Ahitub the son of Phinehas,
the son of Eli, the LORD's priest at Shi-
loh, was wearing the ephod. And the
people did not know that Jonathan
had gone.
4Between the passes by which Jona-
than sought to cross over to get to
the Philistine garrison, there was a
rocky crag on the one side and a rocky

13:19 *no blacksmith.* The Canaanites and Philistines learned how to forge iron from the Hittites. Although they were not great in numerical strength, the Philistines were able to dominate Israel because of their superior weaponry. By the end of David's reign, the Israelites had also acquired iron technology.

13:22 *neither sword nor spear.* The weapons available to the Israelite soldiers would have included slings, bows and arrows, and numerous instruments made of bronze.

13 2Ch 16:9; 1Sa 15:11 **14** 1Sa 15:28; Ps 89:20; Ac 13:22 **15** 1Sa 14:2 **17** Jos 18:23 **18** Jos 16:3; 18:13,14; Neh 11:34; Ge 14:2 **19** See 2Ki 24:14; Jer 24:1 **22** See Jdg 5:8 **23** 1Sa 14:1,4 **CHAPTER 14** **2** 1Sa 13:15 **3** 1Sa 4:21; 1Sa 2:28 **4** 1Sa 13:23

crag on the other side; one [crag] was
named Bozez, and the other, Seneh.
5The one crag was on the north in
front of Michmash, and the other on
the south in front of Geba.
6Jonathan said to his young armor
bearer, "Come, let us cross over to the
garrison of these uncircumcised men;
it may be that the LORD will work for
us. For there is nothing to prevent the
LORD from saving, whether by many
or by few."
7And his armor bearer said to him,
"Do everything that is in your heart
(mind); here I am with you in whatever
you think [best]."
8Jonathan said, "See now, we are
going to cross over to the [Philistine]
men and reveal ourselves to them.
9"If they say to us, 'Wait until we
come to you,' then we will stand in our
place and not go up to them.
10"But if they say, 'Come up to us,'
we will go up, for the LORD has handed
them over to us; and this shall be the
sign to us."
11When both of them revealed them-
selves to the garrison of the Philis-
tines, the Philistines said, "Look, the
Hebrews are coming out of the holes
where they have hidden themselves."
12So the men of the garrison re-
sponded to Jonathan and his armor
bearer, "Come up to us and we will
tell you something." Jonathan said to
his armor bearer, "Climb up after me,
for the LORD has given them into the
hands of Israel."
13Then Jonathan climbed up on
his hands and feet, his armor bearer
following after him. The enemy fell
before Jonathan [in combat], and his
armor bearer killed *some of them* af-
ter him.
14That first slaughter which Jona-
than and his armor bearer made was
about twenty men within about half
a [plow] furrow in a plot of land [the
area of which a yoke of oxen could
plow in a day].
15And there was trembling in the
[Philistine] camp, in the field, and
among all the people; even the garri-
son and the raiding party trembled [in
fear], and the earth quaked and it be-
came a trembling *and* terror from God.
16Saul's watchmen in Gibeah of Ben-
jamin looked, and behold, the multi-
tude melted away and they went here
and there.
17Then Saul said to the people with
him, "Take a count and see who has
left us." When they had taken a count,
behold, Jonathan and his armor bearer
were missing.
18Saul said to Ahijah [the priest],
"Bring the ark of God here." For at
that time the ark of God was with the
sons of Israel.
19While Saul talked to the priest,
the commotion in the Philistine camp
continued and increased, so Saul said
to the priest, "Withdraw your hand."
20Then Saul and all the people who
were with him rallied and went into the
battle; and behold, every [Philistine]
man's sword was against his compan-
ion, in wild confusion.
21Now the Hebrews who were with
the Philistines previously, who went
up with them all around in the camp,
they also *turned* to be with the Israel-
ites who were with Saul and Jonathan.
22When all the men of Israel who had
hidden themselves in the hill country
of Ephraim heard that the Philistines
had fled, they too pursued them closely
in the battle.
23So the LORD saved Israel that day,
and the battle spread beyond Beth-aven.

Saul's Foolish Order

24But the men of Israel were hard-
pressed that day, because Saul had
put the people under a curse, saying,
"Cursed be the man who eats food

14:14 ***half a [plow] furrow in a plot of land.*** This can also be translated "half a yoke of land." A yoke of land was the area a pair of oxen could plow in one day.

14:24 ***had put the people under a curse.*** This was not only an oath, but an oath with a curse. Yet food would have helped the soldiers fight with better stamina. Keeping the oath was a matter

6 Jdg 7:4,7; 2Ch 14:11 **10** See Ge 24:14; Jdg 7:11 **15** 2Ki 7:7; Job 18:11; 1Sa 13:17; Ge 35:5 **16** ver. 20 **19** Nu 27:21 **20** Jdg 7:22; 2Ch 20:23 **22** 1Sa 13:6 **23** Ex 14:30; Hos 1:7; 1Sa 13:5 **24** Jos 6:26

before evening, and before I have tak-
en vengeance on my enemies." So none
of the people ate any food.
25 All *the people of* the land came to
a forest, and there was honey on the
ground.
26 When the people entered the forest,
the honey was dripping, but no man
put his hand to his mouth [to taste it],
because the people feared the oath [of
Saul].
27 But Jonathan had not heard when
his father put the people under the
oath. So he put out the end of the staff
that was in his hand and dipped it into
a honeycomb, and then he put his hand
to his mouth, and his energy was re-
stored.
28 But one of the people told him,
"Your father strictly put the people
under an oath, saying, 'Cursed be the
man who eats food today.' " And the
people were exhausted [and hungry].
29 Then Jonathan said, "My father
has troubled the land [with his foolish
curse]. See how my energy is restored
because I tasted a little of this honey.
30 How much better [it would have
been] if only the people had eaten free-
ly today from the spoil of their ene-
mies which they found! For now the
slaughter among the Philistines has
not been great."
31 They struck the Philistines that
day from Michmash to Aijalon. And
the people were very tired.
32 [When night came and the oath
ended] the people rushed greedily
upon the spoil. They took sheep, oxen,
and calves, and slaughtered them on
the ground; and they ate them [raw]
with the blood [still in them].
33 Then Saul was told, "Look, the
people are sinning against the LORD
by eating [the meat] with the blood."
And he said, "You have violated [the
Law] *and* acted treacherously; roll a
large stone to me today." [Lev 7:26, 27]
34 Saul said, "Spread out among the
people and tell them, 'Each one of
you bring me his ox or his sheep, and
butcher it [properly] here and eat; and
do not sin against the LORD by eating
[the meat with] the blood.' " So that
night each one brought his ox with
him and butchered it there.
35 And Saul built an altar to the LORD;
it was the first altar that he built to
the LORD.
36 Then Saul said, "Let us go down
after the Philistines by night and plun-
der them until the morning light, and
let us not leave a man of them [alive]."
They said, "Do whatever seems good
to you." Then the priest said, "Let us
approach God here."
37 Saul asked [counsel] of God, "Shall
I go down after the Philistines? Will
You hand them over to Israel?" But He
did not answer him that day.
38 Then Saul said, "Come here, all
you who are leaders of the people, and
let us find out how this sin [causing
God's silence] happened today.
39 "For as the LORD lives, who saves
Israel, for *even* if *the guilt* is in my son

---

of loyalty to Saul as he avenged his enemies. But the enemies were not Saul's personal enemies, they were the enemies of the whole nation, and the power in the vengeance came from God, not Saul. Saul should have focused the faith of the people on God, not on himself. This oath is an example of poor leadership, foolish vows, and misplaced loyalties. It is easy to get into trouble with an impulsive vow. It may sound very noble and wise in the heat of the moment, but it doesn't turn out to be practical. The kinds of vows that will never get us in trouble are the vows that echo the things that Scripture teaches. Such vows as determining to raise our children for the Lord, promising to stay away from habits that control us, or commitment to pray for certain people will never leave us entangled in promises that we should not have made.

14:32 *rushed greedily upon.* If the soldiers had not been fasting as they fought, they might have had the self-control to properly bleed the animals before they began eating.

14:37 *He did not answer him.* God's silence was taken by Saul as evidence of sin in the camp.

14:39 *he shall most certainly die.* This was Saul's second foolish oath. Saul is not the only one who found himself in trouble because of an impulsive oath. Jephthah made a tragic vow

---

25 Dt 9:28; Mt 3:5; Ex 3:8; Nu 13:27; Mt 3:4 **32** Lev 3:17; 7:26; 17:10; 19:26; Dt 12:16,23,24 **35** 1Sa 7:17
37 1Sa 28:6 **38** Jos 7:14; 1Sa 10:19 **39** 2Sa 12:5

Jonathan, he shall most certainly die."
But not one of all the people answered
him.
[40]Then he said to all the Israelites,
"You shall be on one side; I and my
son Jonathan will be on the other side."
The people said to Saul, "Do what
seems good to you."
[41]Therefore, Saul said to the LORD,
the God of Israel, "Give a perfect lot
[identifying the transgressor]." Then
Saul and Jonathan were selected [by
lot], but the other men went free.
[42]Saul said, "Cast [lots] between me
and my son Jonathan." And Jonathan
was selected.
[43]Saul said to Jonathan, "Tell me
what you have done." So Jonathan told
him, "I tasted a little honey with the
end of the staff that was in my hand.
Here I am, I must die!"
[44]Saul answered, "May God do so
[to me], and more also [if I do not keep
my word], for you shall most certainly
die, Jonathan."
[45]But the people said to Saul, "Must
Jonathan, who has brought about this
great victory in Israel, be put to death?
Far from it! As the LORD lives, not one
hair of his head shall fall to the ground,
for he has worked with God this day."
So the people rescued Jonathan and
he was not put to death.
[46]Then Saul stopped pursuing the
Philistines, and the Philistines went
to their own place.

Constant Warfare

[47]When Saul assumed control of the
kingdom of Israel, he fought against all
his enemies on every side: Moab, the
sons (descendants) of Ammon, Edom,
the kings of Zobah, and the Philistines.
Wherever he turned, he inflicted pun-
ishment.
[48]He acted valiantly and defeated the
Amalekites, and rescued Israel from
the hands of those who had plundered
them.
[49]Now Saul's sons were Jonathan,
Ishvi, and Malchi-shua. The names
of his two daughters *were these*: the
name of the firstborn was Merab, and
the name of the younger, Michal.
[50]The name of Saul's wife was Ahin-
oam the daughter of Ahimaaz. The
commander of his army was named
Abner, the son of Ner, Saul's uncle.
[51]Kish was the father of Saul, and
Ner the father of Abner was the son
of Abiel.
[52]Now the war against the Philis-
tines was severe (brutal, relentless) all
the days of Saul; and whenever Saul
saw any mighty or courageous man,
he recruited him for his staff.

Saul's Disobedience

15 SAMUEL SAID to Saul, "The
Lord sent me to anoint you king
over His people Israel. Now listen *and*
pay close attention to the words of the
Lord.
[2]"Thus says the LORD of hosts
(armies), 'I will punish Amalek for
what he did to Israel, how he set him-
self against him on the way when Is-
rael came up from Egypt.
[3]'Now go and strike Amalek and
completely destroy everything that
they have; do not spare them, but kill
both man and woman, child and in-
fant, ox and sheep, camel and don-
key.' "

(Jdg 11:29–40), John the Baptist was beheaded because of Herod's thoughtless oath (Mt 14:7–9), and a group of Jews bound themselves together with a curse, promising not to eat or drink until they had killed Paul (Ac 23:12). Jesus taught his followers not to swear to foolish vows, but to let their yes be yes, and their no be no (Mt 5:37; Jas 5:12).
14:47 *Moab . . . Ammon.* The Moabites and Ammonites were descendants of Lot (Ge 19:30–38). They occupied regions east of the Jordan and Dead Sea. ***Edom.*** The Edomites were descendants of Esau (Ge 36:8) who ruled over a region southeast of the Dead Sea. ***Zobah.*** This was the Aramean kingdom in the Bekaa valley. ***Philistines.*** The Philistines lived on the coastal plain west of the hill country.
14:48 *Amalekites.* These nomadic desert tribesmen lived south of the hill country.

41 Pr 16:33; Ac 1:24; Jos 7:16; 1Sa 10:20,21 **43** Jos 7:19; ver. 27 **44** Ru 1:17; ver. 39 **45** 2Sa 14:11; 1Ki 1:52; Lk 21:18 **47** 1Sa 11:11; 2Sa 10:6 **48** 1Sa 15:3,7 **49** 1Sa 31:2; 1Ch 8:33 **51** 1Sa 9:1 **52** 1Sa 8:11
CHAPTER 15 **1** 1Sa 9:16 **2** Ex 17:8,14; Nu 24:20; Dt 25:17-19 **3** Lev 27:28,29; Jos 6:17,21

4 So Saul summoned the people and
numbered them at Telaim—200,000
foot soldiers and 10,000 men of Judah.
5 Saul came to the city of Amalek and
set an ambush in the valley.
6 Saul said to the Kenites, "Go, leave,
go down from the Amalekites, so that
I do not destroy you along with them;
for you showed kindness to all the Isra-
elites when they went up from Egypt."
So the Kenites departed from among
the Amalekites.
7 Saul defeated the Amalekites, from
Havilah as far as Shur, which is east
of Egypt.
8 He captured Agag the king of the
Amalekites alive, though he totally
destroyed all [the rest of] the people
with the sword.
9 Saul and the people spared Agag
and the best of the sheep, the oxen,
the fatlings, the lambs, and every-
thing that was good, and they were
not willing to destroy them entirely;
but everything that was undesirable or
worthless they destroyed completely.

Samuel Rebukes Saul

10 Then the word of the LORD came to
Samuel, saying,
11 "I regret that I made Saul king,
for he has turned away from follow-
ing Me and has not carried out My
commands." Samuel was angry [over
Saul's failure] and he cried out to the
LORD all night.
12 When Samuel got up early in the
morning to meet Saul, he was told,
"Saul came to Carmel, and behold, he
set up for himself a monument [com-
memorating his victory], then he turned
and went on and went down to Gilgal."
13 So Samuel came to Saul, and Saul
said to him, "Blessed are you of the
LORD. I have carried out the command
of the LORD."
14 But Samuel said, "What then is this
bleating of the sheep in my ears, and
the lowing of the oxen which I hear?"
15 Saul said, "They have brought
them from the Amalekites, for the
people spared the best of the sheep
and oxen to sacrifice to the LORD your
God; but the rest we have destroyed
completely."
16 Then Samuel said to Saul, "Stop,
and let me tell you what the LORD said
to me last night." Saul said to him,
"Speak."
17 Samuel said, "Is it not true that
even though you were small (insig-
nificant) in your own eyes, you were
made the head of the tribes of Israel?
And the LORD anointed you king over
Israel,
18 and the LORD sent you on a mission,
and said, 'Go, totally destroy the sin-
ners, the Amalekites, and fight against
them until they are eliminated.'
19 "Why did you not obey the voice of
the LORD, but [instead] swooped down
on the plunder [with shouts of victory]
and did evil in the sight of the LORD?"
20 Saul said to Samuel, "I have obeyed
the voice of the LORD, and have gone
on the mission on which the LORD sent
me, and have brought back Agag the
king of Amalek, and have completely
destroyed the Amalekites.
21 "But the people took some of the
spoil, sheep and oxen, the best of the
things [that were] to be totally de-
stroyed, to sacrifice to the LORD your
God at Gilgal."

15:6 *Kenites.* The Kenites were a nomadic offshoot of the Midianites (Nu 10:29). They had been loosely associated with the Israelites since Moses' marriage to the daughter of Jethro, a Kenite (Jdg 1:16; 4:11).

15:22 Obedience — If we love God we are commanded to keep His commandments (Jn 14:15). The problem is, we sometimes fool ourselves. Saul thought he was doing something good for God. He was partially obeying. He killed a lot of the Amalekites, and instead of killing the animals, he sacrificed them. They would still be dead, and it would honor God too. But He was not pleased. Saul did what was "right in his own eyes" but this was not obedience.

6 Nu 24:21; Jdg 1:16; 4:11; Ge 18:25; 19:12,14; Rev 18:4; Ex 18:10,19; Nu 10:29,32 **7** 1Sa 14:48; Ge 2:11; 25:18; Ge 16:7 **8** See 1Ki 20:34,35; See 1Sa 30:1 **9** ver. 3,15 **11** ver. 35; Ge 6:6,7; 2Sa 24:16; Jos 22:16; 1Ki 9:6; ver. 3,9; 1Sa 13:13; ver. 35; 1Sa 16:1 **12** Jos 15:55 **13** Ge 14:19; Jdg 17:2; Ru 3:10 **15** ver. 9,21; Ge 3:12; Pr 28:13 **17** 1Sa 9:21 **20** ver. 13 **21** ver. 15

22 Samuel said,
"Has the LORD as great a delight in
burnt offerings and sacrifices
As in obedience to the voice of the
LORD?
Behold, to obey is better than
sacrifice,
And to heed [is better] than the fat
of rams.
23 "For rebellion is as [serious as]
the sin of divination (fortune-
telling),
And disobedience is as [serious as]
false religion and idolatry.
Because you have rejected the
word of the LORD,
He also has rejected you as king."

24 Then Saul said to Samuel, "I have
sinned; for I have transgressed the
command of the LORD and your words,
because I feared the people and obeyed
their voice.
25 "Now, please, pardon my sin and
return with me, so that I may worship
the LORD."
26 But Samuel said to Saul, "I will not
return with you; for you have rejected
the word of the LORD, and the LORD
has rejected you from being king over
Israel."
27 As Samuel turned to go [away],
Saul grabbed the hem of his robe [to
stop him], and it tore.
28 So Samuel said to him, "The LORD
has torn the kingdom of Israel from
you today and has given it to your
neighbor, who is better than you.
29 "Also the Splendor *and* Glory
and Eminence of Israel will not lie or
change His mind; for He is not a man
that He should change His mind."
30 Saul said, "I have sinned; but please
honor me now before the elders of my
people and before Israel, and go back
with me, so that I may worship the
LORD your God."
31 So Samuel went back following
Saul, and Saul worshiped the LORD.
32 Then Samuel said, "Bring me
Agag, the king of the Amalekites."
And Agag came to him cheerfully.
And Agag said, "Surely the bitterness
of death has come to an end."
33 Samuel said, "As your sword has
made women childless, so shall your
mother be childless among women."
And Samuel cut Agag in pieces before
the LORD in Gilgal.
34 Then Samuel went to Ramah, but
Saul went up to his house in Gibeah
of Saul.
35 Samuel did not see Saul again un-
til the day of his death, for Samuel
grieved over Saul. And the LORD re-
gretted that He had made Saul king
over Israel.

Samuel Goes to Bethlehem

16 THE LORD said to Samuel,
"How long will you grieve for
Saul, when I have rejected him as king
over Israel? Fill your horn with oil and
go; I will send you to Jesse the Beth-
lehemite, for I have chosen a king for
Myself among his sons."
2 But Samuel said, "How can I go?
When Saul hears *about it*, he will kill

15:23 *divination.* Witchcraft, divination, idolatry, and other occult activities are an attempt to manipulate spiritual powers for our own ends. In his rebellion Saul was treating God as if He were a moody, cranky pagan god, who could be thwarted, and then appeased by sacrifices. ***He also has rejected you.*** Saul was rejected because he was still treating God as a force to be used. He was sorry he got caught, but he still thought he was right and could give a quick sacrifice and go on with the plan.

15:35 *see.* God was through with Saul as king, and so was Samuel.

16:2 *I have come to sacrifice to the Lord.* At this time Shiloh was still the designated central location for sacrifices (Dt 12:4 – 14). But with the disruptions of the priesthood, the ark located at Kiriath-jearim (7:2), and the general belief that God had removed His presence from Shiloh, it would not be surprising if the sacrificial system had been interrupted as well. In any case, God did direct Samuel to make this sacrifice at Bethlehem.

22 Isa 1:11-13,16,17; Jer 7:22,23; Mic 6:6-8; Heb 10:6-9; Ecc 5:1; Hos 6:6; Mt 5:24; 9:13; 12:7; Mk 12:33 **23** 1Sa 13:14 **24** See 2Sa 12:13; Ex 23:2; Isa 51:12,13 **26** 1Sa 2:30 **27** See 1Ki 11:30 **28** 1Sa 28:17,18; 1Ki 11:31 **29** Nu 23:19; Eze 24:14; 2Ti 2:13; Titus 1:2 **30** Jn 5:44; 12:43 **33** Ex 17:11; Nu 14:45; See Jdg 1:7 **34** 1Sa 11:4 **35** See 1Sa 19:24; ver. 11; 1Sa 16:1; ver. 11 **CHAPTER 16** **1** 1Sa 15:35; 1Sa 15:23; 1Sa 9:16; 2Ki 9:1; Ps 78:70; Ac 13:22 **2** 1Sa 9:12; 20:29

me." And the LORD said, "Take a heifer
from the herd with you and say, 'I have
come to sacrifice to the Lord.'
3"You shall invite Jesse to the sacri-
fice, and I will show you what you shall
do [after that]; and you shall anoint for
Me the one whom I designate."
4So Samuel did what the LORD said,
and came to Bethlehem. And the elders
of the city came trembling to meet him
and said, "Do you come in peace?"
5And he said, "In peace; I have come
to sacrifice to the LORD. Consecrate
yourselves and come with me to the
sacrifice." He also consecrated Jesse
and his sons and invited them to the
sacrifice.
6So it happened, when they had
come, he looked at Eliab [the eldest
son] and thought, "Surely the LORD's
anointed is before Him."
7But the LORD said to Samuel, "Do
not look at his appearance or at the
height of his stature, because I have
rejected him. For the LORD sees not as
man sees; for man looks at the outward
appearance, but the LORD looks at the
heart."
8Then Jesse called Abinadab and
had him pass before Samuel. But Sam-

16:7 God — Our Creator knows His human creatures intimately, and He is able to discern our thoughts and purposes before we ourselves are aware of them. He always looks beyond appearance and stature to the heart.

3 Ex 4:15; 1Sa 9:16 **4** 1Sa 21:1; 1Ki 2:13; 2Ki 9:22 **5** Ex 19:10 **6** 1Ki 12:26 **7** Ps 147:10; Isa 55:8; 2Co 10:7; 1Ki 8:39 **8** 1Sa 17:13

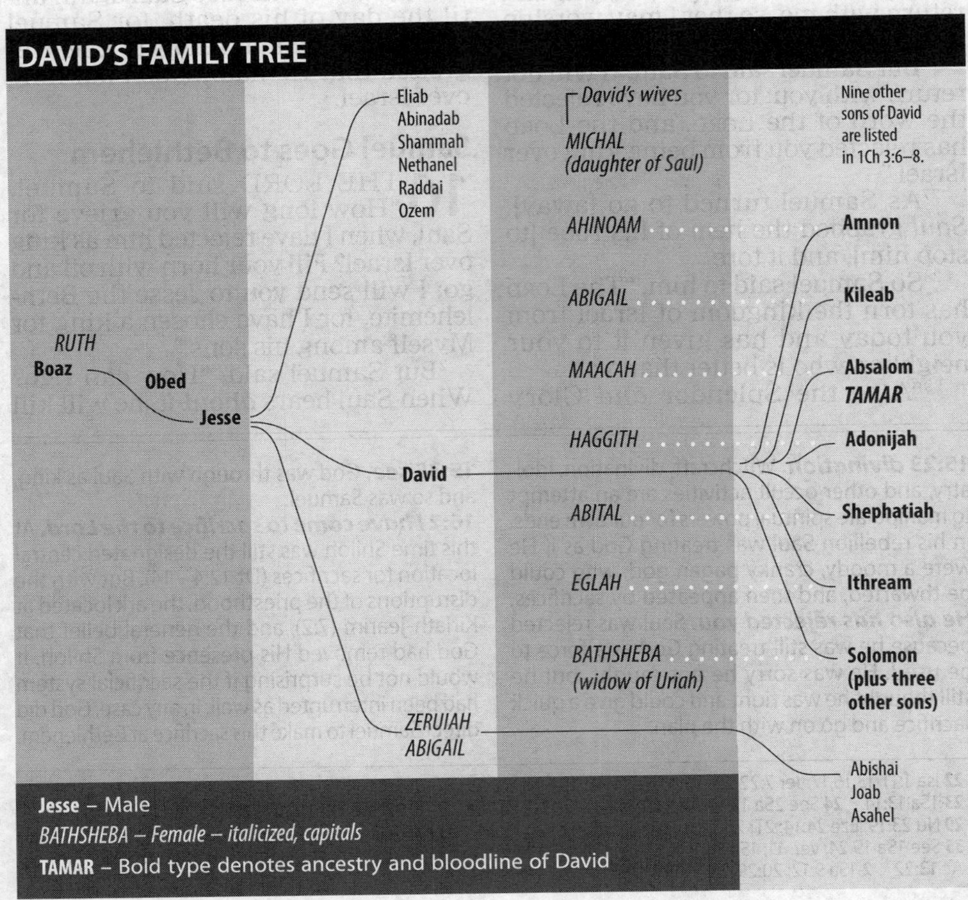

uel said, "The LORD has not chosen this
one either."
9 Next Jesse had Shammah pass by.
And Samuel said, "The LORD has not
chosen him either."
10 Jesse had seven of his sons pass
before Samuel. But Samuel said to
Jesse, "The LORD has not chosen [any
of] these."
11 Then Samuel said to Jesse, "Are all
your sons here?" Jesse replied, "There
is still one left, the youngest; he is tend-
ing the sheep." Samuel said to Jesse,
"Send *word* and bring him; because we
will not sit down [to eat the sacrificial
meal] until he comes here."

David Anointed

12 So Jesse sent *word* and brought him
in. Now he had a ruddy complexion,
with beautiful eyes and a handsome
appearance. The LORD said [to Samuel],
"Arise, anoint him; for this is he."
13 Then Samuel took the horn of oil
and anointed David in the presence of
his brothers; and the Spirit of the LORD
came mightily upon David from that
day forward. And Samuel arose and
went to Ramah.
14 Now the Spirit of the LORD departed
from Saul, and an evil spirit from the
Lord tormented *and* terrified him.
15 Saul's servants said to him, "Be-
hold, an evil spirit from God is tor-
menting you.
16 "Let our lord now command your
servants who are here before you to
find a man who plays skillfully on the
harp; and when the evil spirit from
God is on you, he shall play *the harp*
with his hand, and you will be well."
17 So Saul told his servants, "Find
me a man who plays well and bring
him to me."
18 One of the young men said, "Be-
hold, I have seen a son of Jesse the
Bethlehemite who is a skillful musi-
cian, a brave *and* competent man, a
warrior, discerning (prudent, eloquent)
in speech, and a handsome man; and
the LORD is with him."
19 So Saul sent messengers to Jesse
and said, "Send me David your son,
who is with the flock."
20 Jesse took a donkey [loaded with]
bread and a jug of wine and a young
goat, and sent them to Saul with David
his son.
21 Then David came to Saul and at-
tended him. Saul loved him greatly and
[later] David became his armor bearer.
22 Saul sent *word* to Jesse, saying,
"Please let David be my attendant, for
he has found favor in my sight."
23 So it came about that whenever
the [evil] spirit from God was on Saul,
David took a harp and played it with
his hand; so Saul would be refreshed
and be well, and the evil spirit would
leave him.

16:12 *anoint him.* David was anointed with olive oil. This religious ritual consecrated him to the kingship, although he did not take the role of king for many years. The heart He saw in David is the one He wants to see in all of us. It has purposefulness, intelligence, and willingness to obey. If our heart is centered on God, He can use us to extend His kingdom.

16:14 *departed from Saul.* After the Spirit of God came upon David, Saul was no longer empowered by the Spirit to serve as king. In Old Testament times the Holy Spirit came upon people selectively, usually a king, prophet, or judge. It was only after the resurrection of Jesus that the Holy Spirit came to indwell all believers (Jn 16:5 – 11; Ac 2:4).

16:15 *evil spirit from God.* This affliction is understood in various ways. Perhaps the spirit was a demon that God allowed to harass Saul, in the same way that God allowed Satan to tempt Job (Job 1:8 – 12). Perhaps Saul had a spirit of discontent in his heart, caused by the absence of the Holy Spirit. Perhaps pride, that same sin that caused Satan to fall, was allowed to grow in Saul's heart and dominate his thoughts and actions. Scripture is clear that God is always holy, just, and righteous, so this evil spirit was something that God allowed to come upon Saul, but it was not a part of God.

16:21 *David came to Saul.* David played for Saul, and was his armor bearer. It is unclear exactly how much time David spent with Saul. Probably David at this time continued to come and go from Saul's household to his father's.

9 1Sa 17:13 **11** 1Sa 17:12; 2Sa 7:8 **12** 1Sa 17:42; See 1Sa 9:17 **13** 1Sa 10:1; Nu 27:18; Jdg 11:29; 13:25; 1Sa 10:6,10 **14** Jdg 16:20; Jdg 9:23 **16** ver. 21,22; Ge 41:46; ver. 23; 2Ki 3:15 **18** 1Sa 17:32,34-36; 1Sa 3:19; 18:12,14 **19** ver. 11; 1Sa 17:15 **20** 1Sa 10:27; 17:18 **21** Ge 41:46 **23** ver. 14,16

Goliath's Challenge

17 NOW THE Philistines gathered their armies for battle and were assembled at Socoh, which belongs to Judah; and they camped between Socoh and Azekah, in Ephes-dammim.

2 Saul and the men of Israel were gathered together and they camped in the Valley of Elah, and assembled in battle formation to meet the Philistines.

3 The Philistines were standing on the mountain on one side and Israel was standing on the mountain on the other side, with the valley between them.

4 Then a champion came out from the camp of the Philistines named Goliath of Gath, whose height was six cubits and a span.

5 *He had* a bronze helmet on his head, and wore a coat of scale-armor (overlapping metal plates) which weighed 5,000 shekels of bronze.

6 *He had* bronze shin protectors on his legs and a bronze javelin hung between his shoulders.

7 The [wooden] shaft of his spear was like a weaver's beam; the blade-head of his spear *weighed* six hundred shekels of iron. And a shield-bearer walked in front of him.

8 Goliath stood and shouted to the battle lines of Israel, saying to them, "Why have you come out to draw up for battle? Am I not the Philistine and are you not servants of Saul? Choose a man for yourselves and have him come down to me.

9 "If he is able to fight with me and kill me, then we will become your servants; but if I prevail against him and kill him, then you shall become our servants and serve us."

10 Again the Philistine said, "I defy the battle lines of Israel this day; give me a man so that we may fight together."

11 When Saul and all Israel heard these words of the Philistine, they were dismayed and greatly afraid.

12 Now David was the son of the Ephrathite of Bethlehem in Judah, named Jesse, who had eight sons. Jesse was old in the days of Saul, advanced *in years* among men.

13 His three older sons had followed Saul into battle. The names of his three sons who went to battle were Eliab, the firstborn; next, Abinadab; and third, Shammah.

14 David was the youngest. Now the three oldest followed Saul,

15 but David went back and forth from Saul to tend his father's flock at Bethlehem.

16 The Philistine [Goliath] came out

17:1 ***the Philistines gathered their armies for battle.*** The Philistine and Israelite armies were gathered in the Elah valley, about 15 miles west of David's hometown of Bethlehem. The Philistines were camped on a hill, south of the valley, between the cities of Azekah and Sochoh.
17:2 ***Valley of Elah.*** The valley is an east-west valley, leading from the hill country of Judah toward the lowlands of the Philistines. It had a steep ravine that extended the length of the valley, making it unfit for the Philistine's chariots. Probably the ravine prevented a full-scale assault by the Philistines, causing the long delay before engaging in battle.
17:4 ***champion.*** The champion was a warrior who would fight in single combat as a stand-in for the entire army. The most likely person to take on this champion would be Saul, who, when he was chosen king, stood head and shoulders above his countrymen. ***six cubits and a span.*** The cubit was about 18 inches, and a span was 9 inches. Goliath stood approximately nine feet, nine inches tall.
17:5 ***bronze helmet.*** Ordinary troops had leather helmets. ***coat of scale-armor.*** Goliath's coat of scale-armor was made of overlapping plates of bronze sewn on leather. ***5,000 shekels.*** The coat of armor weighed about 125 pounds.
17:6 ***bronze shin protectors.*** This was armor that protected Goliath's legs. ***bronze javelin.*** The javelin was designed for hurling.
17:7 ***six hundred shekels.*** The spear was a weapon designed for hand-to-hand combat, like a long sword. The head of Goliath's spear weighed about 17 pounds. ***shield-bearer.*** The soldier carried a small round shield, usually worn on the left arm. The shield-bearer carried the much larger, oblong shield.
17:12 ***Ephrathite.*** Ephrath was the early name for Bethlehem.

CHAPTER 17 **1** Jos 15:35 **4** 2Sa 21:19; Jos 11:22 **8** 1Sa 8:17 **9** 1Sa 11:1 **10** ver. 26; 2Sa 21:21 **12** ver. 58; Ru 4:22; 1Sa 16:1,18; Ge 35:19; 1Sa 16:10,11; See 1Ch 2:13-15 **13** 1Sa 16:6,8,9 **15** 1Sa 16:19

morning and evening, and took his
stand for forty days.
17 Then Jesse said to David his son,
"Take for your brothers an ephah of
this roasted grain and these ten loaves
of bread and run quickly to the camp
to your brothers.
18 "Also take these ten cuts of cheese
to the commander of the unit. See how
your brothers are doing and bring
back news of them.
19 "Now they are with Saul and all
the men of Israel in the Valley of Elah,
fighting with the Philistines."

David Accepts the Challenge

20 So David got up early in the morning,
left the flock with a keeper, picked
up *the provisions* and went just as Jesse
had directed him. And he came to
the encampment as the army was going
out in battle formation shouting
the battle cry.
21 Israel and the Philistines drew
up in battle formation, army against
army.
22 Then David left his provisions in
the care of the supply keeper, and ran
to the ranks and came and greeted his
brothers.
23 As he was talking with them, behold,
the champion, the Philistine of
Gath named Goliath, was coming up
from the army of the Philistines, and
he spoke these same words *again;* and
David heard *him.*
24 When the men of Israel all saw the
man, they fled from him, and were
very frightened.
25 The men of Israel said, "Have you
seen this man who is coming up? Surely
he is coming up to defy Israel. The
king will reward the man who kills
him with great riches, and will give
him his daughter [in marriage] and
make his father's house (family) free
[from taxes and service] in Israel."
26 Then David spoke to the men who
were standing by him, "What will be
done for the man who kills this Philistine
and removes the disgrace [of his
taunting] from Israel? For who is this
uncircumcised Philistine that he has
taunted *and* defied the armies of the
living God?"
27 The men told him, "That is what
will be done for the man who kills
him."
28 Now Eliab his oldest brother heard
what he said to the men; and Eliab's
anger burned against David and he
said, "Why have you come down here?
With whom did you leave those few
sheep in the wilderness? I know your
presumption (overconfidence) and the
evil of your heart; for you have come
down in order to see the battle."
29 But David said, "What have I done
now? Was it not just a [harmless] question?"
30 Then David turned away from Eliab
to someone else and asked the same
question; and the people gave him the
same answer as the first time.

David Kills Goliath

31 When the words that David spoke
were heard, the men reported them to
Saul, and he sent for him.
32 David said to Saul, "Let no man's
courage fail because of him (Goliath).
Your servant will go out and fight with
this Philistine."
33 Then Saul said to David, "You are
not able to go against this Philistine to
fight him. For you are [only] a young
man and he has been a warrior since
his youth."
34 But David said to Saul, "Your servant
was tending his father's sheep.
When a lion or a bear came and took
a lamb out of the flock,
35 I went out after it and attacked it
and rescued the lamb from its mouth;
and when it rose up against me, I
seized it by its whiskers and struck
and killed it.
36 "Your servant has killed both the
lion and the bear; and this uncircumcised
Philistine will be like one of

17:17 ***Take for your brothers.*** In ancient times, soldiers usually lived off the land they conquered or depended on personal supplies that they or someone else brought from home.

18 Ge 37:14 **23** ver. 8 **25** Jos 15:16 **26** 1Sa 11:2; 1Sa 14:6; ver. 10; Dt 5:26 **27** ver. 25 **28** Ge 37:4,8,11; Mt 10:36 **29** ver. 17 **30** ver. 26,27 **32** Dt 20:1,3; 1Sa 16:18 **33** See Nu 13:31; Dt 9:2

them, since he has taunted *and* defied
the armies of the living God."
37 David said, "The LORD who rescued
me from the paw of the lion and from
the paw of the bear, He will rescue me
from the hand of this Philistine." And
Saul said to David, "Go, and may the
LORD be with you."
38 Then Saul dressed David in his
garments and put a bronze helmet on
his head, and put a coat of mail (armor)
on him.
39 Then David fastened his sword
over his armor and tried to walk, [but
he could not,] because he was not used
to them. And David said to Saul, "I
cannot go with these, because I am not
used to them." So David took them off.
40 Then he took his [shepherd's] staff
in his hand and chose for himself five
smooth stones out of the stream bed,
and put them in his shepherd's bag
which he had, that is, in his shepherd's
pouch. With his sling in his hand, he
approached the Philistine.
41 The Philistine came and ap-
proached David, with his shield-bearer
in front of him.
42 When the Philistine looked around
and saw David, he derided *and* dis-
paraged him because he was [just] a
young man, with a ruddy *complexion*,
and a handsome appearance.
43 The Philistine said to David, "Am
I a dog, that you come to me with
[shepherd's] staffs?" And the Philistine
cursed David by his gods.
44 The Philistine also said to David,
"Come to me, and I will give your flesh
to the birds of the sky and the beasts
of the field."
45 Then David said to the Philistine,
"You come to me with a sword, a spear,
and a javelin, but I come to you in the
name of the LORD of hosts, the God of
the armies of Israel, whom you have
taunted.
46 "This day the LORD will hand you
over to me, and I will strike you down
and cut off your head. And I will give
the corpses of the army of the Philis-
tines this day to the birds of the sky
and the wild beasts of the earth, so that
all the earth may know that there is a
God in Israel,
47 and that this entire assembly may
know that the LORD does not save with
the sword or with the spear; for the
battle is the LORD's and He will hand
you over to us."
48 When the Philistine rose and came
forward to meet David, David ran
quickly toward the battle line to meet
the Philistine.
49 David put his hand into his bag
and took out a stone and slung it, and
it struck the Philistine on his forehead.
The stone penetrated his forehead, and
he fell face down on the ground.
50 So David triumphed over the Phi-
listine with a sling and a stone, and he
struck down the Philistine and killed
him; but there was no sword in David's
hand.
51 So he ran and stood over the Philis-
tine, grasped his sword and drew it out
of its sheath and killed him, and cut off
his head with it. When the Philistines

17:39–40 Wisdom — David had embarked on a risky venture. It might seem smart to meet Goliath with the best armor, but David had wisdom enough to know that if he was going to attack the giant, it would have to be on his own terms. The years of solitary shepherding had given David the time to practice with his sling, and the opportunity to know that it was the Lord who gave him the strength and the will to kill the predators that threatened his flock. The insight and practices gained through difficult experiences blossom as wisdom. We can look back on these times with thankfulness because that is how God has equipped us for the next task.

17:40 *sling.* A sling was the typical equipment of the shepherd. It was a hollow pocket of leather attached to two cords. Putting a stone in the pouch, the slinger would whirl it around his head to build up momentum. Releasing one of the cords would hurl the stone at its target. It takes skill and practice to be expert with a sling. Slingers were a regular part of armies in the ancient Middle East.

37 2Co 1:10; 2Ti 4:17,18; 1Sa 20:13; 1Ch 22:11,16 **42** 1Co 1:27,28; 1Sa 16:12 **43** 1Sa 24:14; 2Sa 3:8; 9:8; 16:9; 2Ki 8:13 **44** 1Ki 20:10,11 **45** 2Sa 22:33,35; 2Co 10:4; Heb 11:33,34; ver. 10 **46** Dt 28:26; Jos 4:24; 1Ki 8:43; 18:36; 2Ki 19:19; Isa 52:10 **47** Hos 1:7; Zec 4:6; 2Ch 20:15 **50** 1Sa 21:9; See Jdg 3:31; 15:15; 2Sa 23:21 **51** Heb 11:34

saw that their [mighty] champion was
dead, they fled.
52 The men of Israel and Judah stood
with a shout and pursued the Philis-
tines as far as the entrance to the val-
ley and the gates of Ekron. And the
[fatally] wounded Philistines fell along
the way to Shaaraim, even as far as
Gath and Ekron.
53 The sons of Israel returned from
their pursuit of the Philistines and
plundered their camp.
54 Then David took the head of the
Philistine and brought it to Jerusalem,
but he put his weapons in his tent.
55 When Saul saw David going out
against the Philistine, he said to Abner
the captain of the army, "Abner, whose
son is this young man?" And Abner
answered, "By your life, O king, I do
not know."
56 The king said, "Ask whose son the
young man is."
57 When David returned from killing
[Goliath] the Philistine, Abner took
him and brought him before Saul with
the head of the Philistine in his hand.
58 Saul asked him, "Whose son are
you, young man?" And David an-
swered, "*I am* the son of your servant
Jesse of Bethlehem."

Jonathan and David

18 WHEN DAVID had finished
speaking to Saul, the soul of
Jonathan was bonded to the soul of
David, and Jonathan loved him as
himself.
2 Saul took David that day and did
not let him return to his father's house.
3 Then Jonathan made a covenant
with David because he loved him as
himself.
4 Jonathan stripped himself of the
outer robe that he was wearing and
gave it to David, with his armor, includ-
ing his sword, his bow, and his belt.
5 So David went out wherever Saul
sent him, and he acted wisely *and* pros-
pered; and Saul appointed him over
the men of war. And it pleased all the
people and also Saul's servants.
6 As they were coming [home], when
David returned from killing the Phi-
listine, the women came out of all the
cities of Israel, singing and dancing,
to meet King Saul with tambourines,
[songs of] joy, and musical instru-
ments.
7 The women sang as they played
and danced, saying,

"Saul has slain his thousands,
And David his ten thousands."

8 Then Saul became very angry, for
this saying displeased him; and he
said, "They have ascribed to David
ten thousands, but to me they have
ascribed [only] thousands. Now what
more can he have but the kingdom?"
9 Saul looked at David with suspicion
[and jealously] from that day forward.

Saul Turns against David

10 Now it came about on the next
day that an evil spirit from God came
forcefully on Saul, and he raved [mad-
ly] inside his house, while David was
playing *the harp* with his hand, as
usual; and there was a spear in Saul's
hand.
11 Saul hurled the spear, for he
thought, "I will pin David to the wall."
But David evaded him twice.
12 Now Saul was afraid of David, be-
cause the LORD was with him, but had
departed from Saul.
13 So Saul had David removed from

17:55 whose son is this young man. How does this question fit with the fact that David had been serving as a musician in Saul's court and as Saul's armor bearer, and that Saul "loved him greatly" (16:18–23)? Possibly in Saul's unstable mental condition he did not recall David, or perhaps he did not know his name, even if he did recognize him. David was not at court full time until after he had killed Goliath. It would not be unusual for the king to know nothing personal about a servant, even a servant he appreciated.

52 Jos 15:36 **55** See 1Sa 16:21,22 **57** ver. 54 **58** ver. 12 **CHAPTER 18** **1** Ge 44:30; 1Sa 19:2; 20:17; 2Sa 1:26; Dt 13:6 **2** 1Sa 17:15 **6** Ex 15:20; Jdg 11:34 **7** Ex 15:21; 1Sa 21:11; 29:5 **8** Ecc 4:4; 1Sa 15:28 **10** 1Sa 16:14; 1Sa 19:24; 1Ki 18:29; Ac 16:16; 1Sa 19:9 **11** 1Sa 19:10; 20:33 **12** ver. 15,29; 1Sa 16:13,18; 1Sa 16:14; 28:15 **13** ver. 16; Nu 27:17; 2Sa 5:2

his presence and appointed him as
his commander of a thousand; and he
publicly associated with the people.
14David acted wisely *and* prospered
in all his ways, and the LORD was with
him.
15When Saul saw that he was pros-
pering greatly, he was afraid of him.
16But all Israel and Judah loved Da-
vid, because he publicly associated
with them.
17Then Saul said to David, "Behold
I will give you my older daughter
Merab as a wife; only be brave for me
and fight the LORD's battles." For Saul
thought, "My hand shall not be against
him, but let the hand of the Philistines
be against him."
18David said to Saul, "Who am I, and
what is my life or my father's family
in Israel, that I should be the king's
son-in-law?"
19But at the time when Merab, Saul's
daughter, should have been given to
David, she was [instead] given to Adri-
el the Meholathite as a wife.

David Marries Saul's Daughter

20Now Michal, Saul's daughter,
loved David; and when they told Saul,
it pleased him.
21Saul said, "I will give her to him
so that she may become a snare (bad
influence, source of trouble) to him,
and that the hand of the Philistines
may be against him." So Saul said to
David for a second time, "You shall be
my son-in-law today."
22Then Saul commanded his ser-
vants, "Speak to David secretly, say-
ing, 'Listen, the king delights in you,
and all his servants love you; now then,
become the king's son-in-law.' "
23So Saul's servants spoke these
words to David. But David said, "Is it
a trivial thing in your sight to become
a king's son-in-law, seeing that I am a
poor man and insignificant?"
24The servants of Saul told him what
David said.
25Then Saul said, "This is what you
shall say to David: 'The king wants
no dowry except a hundred foreskins
of the Philistines, to take vengeance
on the king's enemies.' " Now Saul's
intention was to cause David's death
at the hand of the Philistines.
26When his servants told David these
words, it pleased him to become the
king's son-in-law. Before the time [for
the marriage] arrived,
27David arose and went, he and his
men, and killed two hundred Philistine
men, and David brought their fore-
skins [as proof of death] and presented
every one of them to the king, so that
he might become the king's son-in-law.
So Saul gave him Michal, his [younger]
daughter, as a wife.
28When Saul saw and knew that the
LORD was with David, and that Michal,
his daughter, loved him,
29Saul was even more afraid of Da-
vid; and Saul became David's constant
enemy.
30Then the Philistine commanders
(princes) came out *to battle*, and it
happened as often as they did, that

18:16 *he publicly associated with them.* David's military activities elevated him to prominence before the people.

18:25 *dowry.* A sum of money, about fifty shekels (Dt 22:29), was paid by the bridegroom to the father of the bride as economic compensation for the loss of a daughter.

18:30 *more wisely . . . than all.* David's wise actions contrast significantly with Saul's foolish actions (13:13).

18:30 Wisdom — David was popular, he had even been privately anointed to be the next king, and Saul had just thrown a spear at him. Yet David did nothing to take justice in his own hands. He remained calm and loyal. It is clear that David decided very early in the time after he was anointed that if he became king, it would have to be totally by the hand of God. He would do nothing to destroy the man that God had previously anointed king. Historically we can see what a very wise choice this was, but it must have been very difficult for David to choose the path of wisdom when he could have raised the power of the people to his side so easily.

14 Ge 39:2,3,23; Jos 6:27 **16** ver. 5 **17** 1Sa 17:25; Nu 32:20,27,29; 1Sa 25:28; ver. 21,25; 2Sa 12:9 **18** See ver. 23; 1Sa 9:21; 2Sa 7:18 **19** 2Sa 21:8; Jdg 7:22 **20** ver. 28 **21** ver. 17; See ver. 26 **25** Ge 34:12; Ex 22:17; 1Sa 14:24; ver. 17 **26** See ver. 21 **27** ver. 13; 2Sa 3:14 **30** 2Sa 11:1; ver. 5

David acted more wisely *and* had more
success than all Saul's servants. So his
name was highly esteemed.

David Protected from Saul

19 NOW SAUL told his son Jona-
than and all his servants to kill
David, but Jonathan, Saul's son, great-
ly delighted in David.
2So he told David, "Saul my father is
seeking to kill you. Now then, please
be on guard in the morning, and stay
in a secret place and hide yourself.
3"As for me, I will go out and stand
beside my father in the field where you
are, and I will speak with my father
about you, and if I learn anything, then
I will tell you."
4Then Jonathan spoke well of David
to Saul his father and said to him, "May
the king not sin against his servant
David, since he has not sinned against
you, and since his deeds have been
very beneficial to you.
5"For he took his life in his hand
and killed the Philistine, and the LORD
brought about a great victory for all Is-
rael; you saw it and rejoiced. Why then
would you sin against innocent blood
by killing David without a cause?"
6Saul listened to Jonathan and swore
[an oath], "As the LORD lives, he shall
not be put to death."
7So Jonathan called David and told
him all these things. And Jonathan
brought David to Saul, and he was in
his presence [serving him] as previ-
ously.
8Then there was war again, and Da-
vid went out and fought with the Phi-
listines and defeated them with a great
slaughter, and they fled before him.
9Then an evil spirit from the LORD
came on Saul as he was sitting in his
house with his spear in his hand, and
David was playing the harp with his
hand.
10Saul tried to pin David to the wall
with the spear, but he escaped from
Saul's presence, so that Saul only stuck
the spear into the wall. Then David
fled and escaped that night.
11Then Saul sent messengers to Da-
vid's house to watch for him, so that
he might kill him in the morning. But
Michal, David's wife, told him, "If you
do not save your life tonight, tomorrow
you will be killed."
12So Michal let David down through
the window, and he fled and escaped.
13And Michal took the household idol
and laid it on the bed, put a pillow of
goats' *hair* at its head, and covered it
with clothes.
14And when Saul sent messengers
to take David, she said, "He is sick."
15Then Saul sent the messengers
[again] to see David, saying, "Bring
him up to me on his bed [if necessary],
so that I may kill him."
16When the messengers came in,
there was the household idol on the bed
with a quilt of goats' *hair* at its head.
17Saul said to Michal, "Why have
you deceived me like this and let my
enemy go, so that he has escaped?"
Michal answered Saul, "He said to me,
'Let me go! Why should I kill you?' "
18So David fled and escaped and
came to Samuel at Ramah, and told
him everything that Saul had done
to him. And he and Samuel went and
stayed in Naioth.
19Saul was told, "David is at Naioth
in Ramah."
20Then Saul sent messengers to take
David; but when they saw the group
of prophets prophesying, and Samuel
standing and presiding over them, the
Spirit of God came on the messengers
of Saul; and they also prophesied.
21When Saul was informed, he
sent other messengers, and they also
prophesied. So Saul sent messengers
again, the third time, and they proph-
esied as well.

19:11 *tomorrow you will be killed.* The story of David's escape is alluded to in the title of Psalm 59.
19:12 *Michal let David down through the window.* Saul had imagined that Michal would be loyal to him and a snare to David. But she loved David, and her loyalty was to her husband.

CHAPTER 19 **2** 1Sa 18:1 **4** Pr 31:8,9; Ge 42:22; Pr 17:13 **5** Jdg 9:17; 1Sa 17:49,50; 1Sa 11:13; 1Ch 11:14; 1Sa 20:32; Mt 27:4 **7** 1Sa 16:21; 18:2,13 **9** 1Sa 16:14; 18:10,11 **11** Ps 59, title **12** See Jos 2:15; Ac 9:24,25 **17** 2Sa 2:22 **20** See Jn 7:32,45; 1Sa 10:5,6; 1Co 14:3,24,25; Nu 11:25; Joel 2:28

22 Then Saul went to Ramah himself and came to the great well that is in Secu; and he asked, "Where are Samuel and David?" And he was told, "They are at Naioth [with the prophets] in Ramah."

23 So he went on to Naioth in Ramah; and the Spirit of God came upon him too, and he went along continually prophesying until he came to Naioth in Ramah.

24 He also took off his [royal] robes [and armor] and prophesied before Samuel and lay down naked all that day and night. So they say, "Is Saul also among the prophets?" [1 Sam 10:10]

David and Jonathan's Covenant

20 DAVID FLED from Naioth in Ramah and he came and said to Jonathan, "What have I done? What is my guilt? What is my sin before (against) your father, that he is seeking my life?"

2 Jonathan said to him, "Far from it! You shall not die. My father does nothing important or insignificant without telling me. So why would he hide this thing from me? It is not so!"

3 But David vowed again, saying "Your father certainly knows that I have found favor in your sight, and he has said, 'Do not let Jonathan know this, or he will be worried.' But truly as the LORD lives and as your soul lives, there is hardly a step between me and death."

4 Then Jonathan said to David, "Whatever you say, I will do for you."

5 David said to Jonathan, "Behold, tomorrow is the New Moon [observance], and I should sit at the table to eat [the sacrificial meal] with the king; but let me go, so that I may hide myself in the field until the third evening.

6 "If your father misses me at all, then say, 'David earnestly asked *permission* from me to go to Bethlehem, his city, because it is the yearly sacrifice there for the entire family.'

7 "If he says, 'All right,' your servant will be safe; but if he is very angry, then be certain that he has decided on evil.

8 "Therefore show kindness to your servant, because you have brought your servant into a covenant of the LORD with you. But if there is iniquity (guilt) in me, kill me yourself; for why should you bring me to your father [to be killed]?"

9 Jonathan said, "Far be it from [happening to] you! In fact, if I indeed learn that my father has decided to harm you, would I not tell you about it?"

10 Then David said to Jonathan, "Who will tell me if your father answers you harshly?"

11 Jonathan said to David, "Come, let us go out into the field [to talk]." So they went out to the field.

12 Then Jonathan said to David, "The LORD, the God of Israel, *is my witness!* When I have sounded out my father about this time tomorrow, or the third day, behold, if he has a good *feeling* toward you, shall I not then send *word* to you and make it known to you?

13 "But if it pleases my father *to do* you harm, may the LORD do so to Jonathan, and more if I do not let you know about it and send you away, so that you may go in safety. And may the LORD be with you as He has been with my father.

14 "If I am still alive, will you not show me the lovingkindness *and* faithfulness of the LORD, so that I will not die?

15 "You shall never cut off your lovingkindness *and* faithfulness from my house, not even when the LORD cuts off every one of the enemies of David from the face of the earth."

20:5 *tomorrow is the New Moon.* The first day of the month, the New Moon, was observed as a religious festival (Nu 10:10; 28:11 – 15). It was celebrated with a sacrificial meal and rest from work.

20:6 *yearly sacrifice.* Apparently Jesse's family gathered for a special time of worship during the New Moon celebration.

23 1Sa 10:10 **24** Isa 20:2; Mic 1:8; See 2Sa 6:14,20; 1Sa 10:11 **CHAPTER 20** **5** Nu 10:10; 28:11; 1Sa 19:2 **6** 1Sa 16:4 **7** See Dt 1:23; 2Sa 17:4; 1Sa 25:17; Est 7:7 **8** Jos 2:14; ver. 16; 1Sa 18:3; 23:18; 2Sa 14:32 **13** Ru 1:17; Jos 1:5; 1Sa 17:37; 1Ch 22:11,16 **15** 2Sa 9:1,3,7; 21:7

16 So Jonathan made a *covenant* with the house of David. [He added,] "May the LORD require it at the hands of David's enemies. [that is, hold them accountable for any harm they inflict on David]."

17 Jonathan made David vow again because of his love for him, for Jonathan loved him as himself.

18 Then Jonathan said to David, "Tomorrow is the New Moon [festival], and you will be missed because your seat will be empty.

19 "When you have stayed for three days, you shall go down quickly and come to the place where you hid yourself on that eventful day [when my father tried to kill you], and shall stay by the stone Ezel.

20 "I will shoot three arrows to the side of it, as though I shot at a target.

21 "And I will send a boy, *saying*, 'Go, find the arrows.' If I specifically say to the boy, 'Look, the arrows are on this side of you, get them,' then come [back to my father's table]; for it is safe for you and there is no danger, as the LORD lives.

22 "But if I say to the boy, 'Look, the arrows are beyond you,' then go, for the LORD has sent you away.

23 "As for the agreement of which you and I have spoken, behold, the LORD is between you and me forever [making sure that we each keep our word]."

24 So David hid in the field; and when the New Moon [festival] came, the king sat down to eat food.

25 The king sat on his seat as on previous occasions, on his seat by the wall; then Jonathan stood up, and Abner [his commander] sat down by Saul's side, but David's place was empty.

26 Yet Saul did not say anything that day, for he thought, "It is an incident [of some kind] and he is not [ceremonially] clean—surely he is unclean."

27 But on the next day, the second *day* of the new moon, David's place was empty [again]; and Saul said to Jonathan his son, "Why has the son of Jesse not come to the meal, either yesterday or today?"

28 Jonathan answered Saul, "David earnestly asked me for permission *to go* to Bethlehem.

29 He said, 'Please let me go because our family is holding a sacrifice in the city, and my brother has commanded me to attend. Now, if I have found favor in your eyes, please let me slip away so that I may see my brothers.' That is why he has not come to the king's table."

Saul Is Angry with Jonathan

30 Then Saul's anger burned against Jonathan and he said to him, "You son of a wayward, rebellious woman! Do I not know that you have chosen the son of Jesse [over me] to your own shame, and to the shame of your mother's nakedness?

31 "For as long as the son of Jesse lives on the earth, neither you [as heir to the throne] nor your kingdom will

---

20:16 – 17 Love — The love and loyalty displayed by Jonathan to David is unparalleled among human relationships in the Bible. He was a living example of the New Testament phrase, "not self-seeking" (1Co 13:5). In protecting David from the murderous plots of Saul, Jonathan was in reality closing the door to his own possible reign over Israel after his father's death. Jonathan knew this, but his faithfulness to David continued until his death on a battlefield (1Sa 31:2).

20:16 *May the LORD require it.* Jonathan prayed that the Lord would hold David accountable to the obligations of the covenant.

20:30 *to the shame of your mother's nakedness.* This was a way of saying that Jonathan shamed his mother who conceived him by maintaining loyalty to David. It was a slur on Jonathan, and a slur on his mother.

20:31 Justice — If David had been taking matters into his own hands, and making moves to secure the kingdom for himself, perhaps Saul would have been justified in seeking David's life. But Saul could charge David with no wrongdoing. Saul was enraged at David, at Jonathan, and in rebellion against God. Because he was driven by anger, Saul could no longer see the injustice in his own thinking.

16 1Sa 25:22; See 1Sa 31:2; 2Sa 4:7; 21:8 **17** 1Sa 18:1 **18** ver. 5 **19** 1Sa 19:2 **21** Jer 4:2 **23** ver. 14,15; See ver. 42 **26** Lev 7:21; 15:5 **28** ver. 6

be established. So now, send [someone]
and bring him to me, for he must die."
32 Jonathan answered Saul his father,
"Why must he be put to death? What
has he done?"
33 Then Saul hurled his spear at him
to strike him down, so Jonathan knew
[without any doubt] that his father had
decided to put David to death.
34 Then Jonathan stood up from the
table in the heat of anger, and ate no
food on that second day of the new
moon (month), for he grieved *and* wor-
ried about David because his father
had dishonored him.
35 In the morning Jonathan went out
to the field for the meeting with David,
and a young boy was with him.
36 And he said to his boy, "Run, please
find the arrows which I am about to
shoot." As the boy ran, he shot an ar-
row past him.
37 When the boy came to the place
where Jonathan had shot the arrow,
Jonathan called to him, "Is the arrow
not beyond you?"
38 And Jonathan called out after the
boy, "Hurry, be quick, do not stay!" So
Jonathan's boy picked up the arrow
and came back to his master.
39 But the boy was not aware of any-
thing; only Jonathan and David knew
about the matter.
40 Jonathan gave his weapons to his
boy and said to him, "Go, take them
to the city."
41 As soon as the boy was gone, Da-
vid got up from the south side [beside
the mound of stones] and fell on his
face to the ground [in submission and
respect], and bowed three times. Then
they kissed one another and wept to-
gether, but David *wept* more.
42 Jonathan told David, "Go in safety,
inasmuch as we have sworn to each
other in the name of the LORD, saying,
'The LORD shall be between me and
you, and between my descendants and
yours forever.' " Then he stood and left,
while Jonathan went into the city.

David Takes Consecrated Bread

21 THEN DAVID went to Nob to
Ahimelech the priest; and Ahim-
elech came trembling [in fear] to meet
David and said to him, "Why are you
alone, and no one with you?"
2 David said to Ahimelech the priest,
"The king has commissioned me with
a matter and has told me, 'Let no one
know anything about the matter for
which I am sending you and with
which I have commissioned you. I have
directed the young men to a certain
place.'
3 "Now what [food] do you have on
hand? Give me five loaves of bread, or
whatever can be found."
4 The priest answered David, "There
is no ordinary (unconsecrated) bread
on hand, but there is consecrated
bread; [you may have it] if only the
young men have kept themselves from
women."
5 David answered the priest, "Be
assured that women have been kept
from us in these three days since I
set out, and the bodies of the young
men were consecrated (ceremonially
clean), although it was an ordinary
(unconsecrated) journey; so how much
more will their vessels be holy today?"
6 So the priest gave him the conse-
crated *bread;* for there was no bread
there except the bread of the Presence

21:1 *Nob.* Nob was a Levitical community in Benjamin where the tabernacle was located after it was in Shiloh. ***Ahimelech.*** Ahimelech, the great-grandson of Eli, was serving as high priest.

21:4 *no ordinary (unconsecrated) bread.* Ahimelech explained that the only bread available was holy bread, sometimes called the "showbread," which had been displayed before the Lord in the tabernacle (Ex 25:30; Lev 24:5 – 9). According to God's law, this bread could be eaten only by priests.

21:6 *gave him the consecrated bread.* This was the bread that had been displayed before the Lord for a week, and was removed for fresh bread. In giving the bread to David, Ahimelech broke the Law, yet in his compassion he kept the spirit of the Law. Jesus referred to this incident when He explained to the Pharisees that it was all right to pick grain to eat on the Sabbath (Mt 12:2 – 4).

32 1Sa 19:5; Mt 27:23; Lk 23:22 **33** 1Sa 18:11; ver. 7 **42** 1Sa 1:17 **CHAPTER 21** **1** 1Sa 16:4 **4** Ex 25:30; Lev 24:5; Mt 12:4; Ex 19:15; Zec 7:3 **5** 1Th 4:4; Lev 8:26 **6** Mt 12:3,4; Mk 2:25,26; Lk 6:3,4; Lev 24:8,9

which was removed from before the
LORD in order to put hot bread *in its*
place when it was taken away.
7 Now one of Saul's servants was
there that day, detained before the
LORD; his name was Doeg the Edomite,
the chief of Saul's shepherds.
8 David said to Ahimelech, "Do you
not have a sword or spear here on
hand? For I brought neither my sword
nor my [other] weapons with me, be-
cause the king's business was urgent."
9 Then the priest said, "The sword
of Goliath the Philistine, whom you
killed in the Valley of Elah, is here
wrapped in a cloth behind the ephod;
if you would take it for yourself, do so.
For there is no other here except for it."
And David said, "There is none like
that; give it to me."
10 Then David arose and fled from
Saul that day, and went to Achish king
of Gath.
11 The servants of Achish said to him,
"Is this not David the king of the land?
Did they not sing in praise of this one
as they danced, saying,

'Saul has slain his thousands,
And David his ten thousands'?"

12 David took these words to heart and
was greatly afraid of Achish king of
Gath.
13 So [fearing for his life] he changed
his behavior in their sight, and acted
insanely in their hands, and he scrib-
bled on the doors of the gate, and
drooled on his beard.
14 Then Achish said to his servants,
"Look, you see that the man is insane.
Why have you brought him to me?
15 "Do I lack madmen, that you bring
this one to behave like a madman in
my presence? Shall this one come into
my house?"

The Priests Slain at Nob

22 SO DAVID departed from there
and escaped to the cave of Adul-
lam; and when his brothers and all his
father's house heard about it, they went
down there to him.
2 Everyone who was suffering hard-
ship, and everyone who was in debt,
and everyone who was discontented
gathered to him; and he became cap-
tain over them. There were about four
hundred men with him.
3 And David went from there to Miz-
pah of Moab; and he said to the king
of Moab, "Please let my father and my
mother come [out of Judah] and stay
with you until I know what God will
do for me."
4 Then he left them with the king of
Moab; and they stayed with him all the
time that David was in the stronghold.
5 Then the prophet Gad said to Da-
vid, "Do not stay in the stronghold;
leave, and go into the land of Judah."
So David left and went into the forest
of Hereth.
6 But Saul heard that David and the
men who were with him had been
discovered. Now Saul was in Gibeah,
sitting under the tamarisk tree on the
high place with his spear in his hand,
and all his servants were standing
around him.
7 Saul said to his servants who were
standing around him, "Listen now,
you Benjamites! Will the son of Jesse

21:7 *detained before the LORD.* Apparently Doeg, although he was not an Israelite, was at the tabernacle under a spiritual vow.

21:10 *Achish . . . Gath.* Achish ruled the city of Gath, one of the five major cities of the Philistines (6:17).

21:12 – 13 *Achish king of Gath.* These verses provide the background for Psalms 34 and 56. In Psalm 34 Achish is referred to as Abimilech, which was apparently a dynastic title used by the Philistine rulers (Ge 26:1).

22:1 *cave of Adullam.* The cave near the city of Adullam was about ten miles southeast of Gath and sixteen miles southwest of Jerusalem. It was here that David composed Psalm 142, and possibly Psalm 57.

22:2 *Everyone who was suffering hardship . . . debt.* The men who gathered around David were not so much taking sides with him as escaping Saul. The sense of desolation in Psalm 142:4 reflects David's feeling of being all alone. ***became captain over them.*** Nevertheless, David organized them, governed them, and made them into a loyal and obedient unit.

7 1Sa 22:9; Ps 52, title **9** 1Sa 17:2,50; See 1Sa 31:10 **11** Ps 56, title; 1Sa 18:7; 29:5 **12** Lk 2:19 **13** Ps 34, title
CHAPTER 22 **1** Ps 57, title; 142, title; 2Sa 23:13 **2** Jdg 11:3 **5** 2Sa 24:11; 1Ch 21:9; 2Ch 29:25 **7** 1Sa 8:14

also give every one of you fields and
vineyards? Will he make you all com-
manders of thousands and hundreds?
8“For all of you have conspired against
me so that no one informs me when
my son [Jonathan] makes *a covenant*
with the son of Jesse. None of you cares
about me or informs me that my son has
stirred up my servant against me to lie
in ambush, as *he does* this day?”
9Then Doeg the Edomite, who was
standing with Saul’s servants, replied,
“I saw the son of Jesse coming to Nob,
to Ahimelech [the priest] the son of
Ahitub.
10“Ahimelech inquired of the LORD
for him, and gave him provisions and
the sword of Goliath the Philistine.”
11Then the king sent someone to
call Ahimelech the priest, the son of
Ahitub, and all his father’s household,
the priests who were at Nob; and all of
them came to the king.
12Then Saul said, “Listen now, son
of Ahitub.” He replied, “Here I am [at
your service], my lord.”
13Saul said to him, “Why have you
and the son of Jesse conspired against
me, in that you have given him bread
and a sword and have inquired of God
for him, so he would rebel against me
by lying in ambush, as *he does* this
day?”
14Then Ahimelech answered the
king, “And who among all your ser-
vants is as faithful *and* trustworthy
as David, who is the king’s son-in-law,
and who is captain over your guard
[and your confidant], and is honored
in your house?
15“Did I *just* begin to inquire of God
for him today? Far be it from me! Do
not let the king impute any *guilt* to
his servant or to any of the household
of my father, for your servant knows
nothing at all about this entire matter.”
16But Saul said, “Be assured that you
shall die, Ahimelech, you and all your
father’s household (extended family).”
17And the king said to the guards
who stood around him, “Turn around
and kill the priests of the LORD, be-
cause their loyalty also is with David,
and because they knew that he was
fleeing and did not inform me.” But the
servants of the king were not willing
to put out their hands to attack the
LORD’s priests.
18So the king said to Doeg, “You
turn around and attack the priests.”
And Doeg the Edomite turned and
attacked the priests, and that day he
killed eighty-five men who wore the
[priest’s] linen ephod.
19And he struck Nob the city of the
priests with the edge of the sword, both
men and women, children and infants;
also *he struck* oxen and donkeys and
sheep with the edge of the sword.
20But one of the sons of Ahimelech
the son of Ahitub, named Abiathar,
escaped and fled to David.
21Abiathar told David that Saul had
murdered the LORD’s priests.
22Then David said to Abiathar, “I
knew that day, when Doeg the Edomite
was there, that he would certainly tell
Saul. I have brought about *the death*
of everyone in your father’s household
(extended family).
23“Stay with me; do not be afraid, for
he who seeks my life seeks your life,
but you are safe with me.”

David Rescues Keilah

23 THEN THEY told David, say-
ing, “Behold, the Philistines are
fighting against Keilah and are plun-
dering (robbing) the threshing floors
[of the grain].”
2So David inquired of the LORD, say-
ing, “Shall I go and attack these Phi-
listines?” And the Lord said to David,

22:18 ***Doeg.*** Only Doeg, who was a descendant of Esau, but not an Israelite, was willing to kill the priests of the living God.

22:22 ***I have brought about the death.*** David felt responsible for the death of the priests and their families because he knew that he was jeopardizing them by receiving help from them. He knew Doeg would betray him, and he felt that he should have done something to prevent this or to warn the priests.

8 1Sa 18:3; 20:30 **9** 1Sa 21:7; Ps 52, title; ver. 1-3; 1Sa 21:1; 1Sa 14:3 **10** Nu 27:21; 1Sa 21:6,9 **17** See Ex 1:17 **18** See 1Sa 2:31 **19** ver. 9,11 **20** 1Sa 23:6; 1Sa 2:33 **23** 1Ki 2:26 **CHAPTER 23** **1** Jos 15:44 **2** ver. 4,6,9; 1Sa 30:8; 2Sa 5:19,23

"Go and attack the Philistines and save
Keilah."
[3]But David's men said to him, "Listen, we are afraid here in Judah. How much more then if we go to Keilah against the battle lines of the Philistines?"
[4]Then David inquired of the LORD again. And the LORD answered him, "Arise, go down to Keilah, for I will hand over the Philistines to you."
[5]So David and his men went to Keilah and fought the Philistines; he drove away their cattle and struck them with a great slaughter. So David rescued the inhabitants of Keilah.
[6]When Abiathar the son of Ahimelech fled to David at Keilah, he came down with an ephod in his hand.
[7]Now when Saul was informed that David had come to Keilah, Saul said, "God has handed him over to me, for he shut himself in by entering a city that has double gates and bars."
[8]So Saul summoned all the people (soldiers) for war, to go down to Keilah to besiege David and his men.
[9]But David knew that Saul was plotting evil against him; and he said to Abiathar the priest, "Bring the ephod here."
[10]Then David said, "O LORD, the God of Israel, Your servant has heard for certain that Saul intends to come to Keilah, to destroy the city on my account.

6 1Sa 22:20 **9** Nu 27:21; 1Sa 30:7 **10** 1Sa 22:19

THE EVENTS OF DAVID'S WANDERINGS

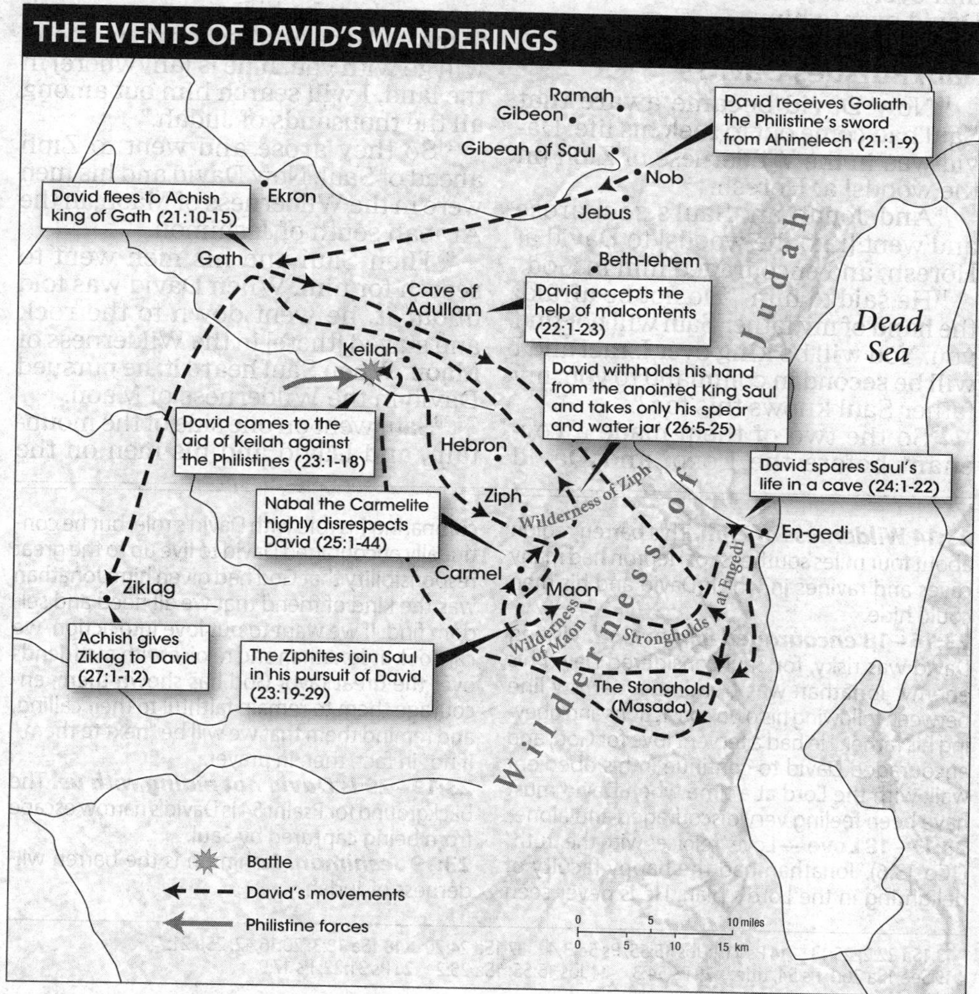

11“Will the men of Keilah hand me over to him? Will Saul come down just as Your servant has heard? O LORD, God of Israel, I pray, tell Your servant.” And the LORD said, “He will come down.”

12Then David asked, “Will the men of Keilah surrender me and my men to Saul?” The LORD said, “They will surrender you.”

13Then David and his men, about six hundred, arose and left Keilah, and they went wherever they could go. When Saul was told that David had escaped from Keilah, he gave up the pursuit.

14David stayed in the wilderness in strongholds, in the hill country of the Wilderness of Ziph. Saul searched for him every day, but God did not hand David over to him.

Saul Pursues David

15Now David became aware that Saul had come out to seek his life. David was in the Wilderness of Ziph [in the woods] at Horesh.

16And Jonathan, Saul’s son, arose and went [into the woods] to David at Horesh, and encouraged him in God.

17He said to him, “Do not be afraid; the hand of my father Saul will not find you. You will be king over Israel and I will be second in command to you; my father Saul knows this too.”

18So the two of them made a covenant before the LORD; and David stayed [in the woods] at Horesh and Jonathan went to his house.

19Then the Ziphites came to Saul at Gibeah, saying, “Is David not hiding with us in strongholds of Horesh, on the hill of Hachilah, which is south of Jeshimon?

20“Now then, O king, come down [to Ziph] in accordance with all your heart’s desire to do so [and capture him]; and our part shall be to hand him over to the king.”

21Saul said, “May you be blessed by the LORD, because you have had compassion on me.

22“Go now, be very persistent and investigate, and see where his haunt is and who has seen him there; for I am told he is very cunning.

23“So look, and take note of all the places where he hides and come back to me with the established facts, then I will go with you. If he is [anywhere] in the land, I will search him out among all the thousands of Judah.”

24So they arose and went to Ziph ahead of Saul. Now David and his men were in the Wilderness of Maon, in the Arabah south of Jeshimon.

25Then Saul and his men went to search for him. When David was told *about it*, he went down to the rock and stayed [there] in the Wilderness of Maon. When Saul heard it, he pursued David in the Wilderness of Maon.

26Saul went on one side of the mountain, and David and his men on the

---

23:14 *Wilderness of Ziph.* This barren region about four miles southeast of Hebron had many caves and ravines in which David and his men could hide.

23:16–18 *encouraged him in God.* Visiting David was risky, for Saul considered David his enemy. Jonathan was treading a narrow line between following his own convictions and obeying his father. He had a fervent love for God, and encouraged David to continue in his obedient walk with the Lord at a time when David must have been feeling very discouraged and alone.

23:17–18 Love—Love “rejoices with the truth” (1Co 13:6). Jonathan had the happy faculty of delighting in the Lord’s plan. He is never seen comparing his role with David’s role, but he continually encouraged David to live up to the great responsibility that God had given him. Jonathan was the kind of friend that we all need and seldom find. If we want to put love into action, we can look at Jonathan and rejoice with our friends over the great favor God has shown them, encourage them to remain faithful to their calling, and remind them that we will be “next to them,” if not in fact, then in prayer.

23:19–29 *Is David not hiding with us.* The background for Psalm 54 is David’s narrow escape from being captured by Saul.

23:19 *Jeshimon.* Jeshimon is the barren wilderness of Judah.

13 1Sa 22:2; 25:13 **14** Ps 11:1; Jos 15:55; Ps 54:3,4 **17** 1Sa 24:20 **18** 1Sa 18:3; 20:16,42; 2Sa 21:7 **19** See 1Sa 26:1; Ps 54, title **20** Ps 54:3 **24** Jos 15:55; 1Sa 25:2 **26** Ps 31:22; Ps 17:9

other side of the mountain. And David
was hurrying to get away from Saul,
for Saul and his men were surrounding
David and his men to capture them.
27 But a messenger came to Saul, say-
ing, "Hurry and come, because the
Philistines have attacked the land."
28 So Saul returned from pursuing
David and went to meet the Philistines;
therefore they called that place the
Rock of Escape.
29 David went up from there and
stayed in the strongholds of Engedi.

David Spares Saul's Life

24 WHEN SAUL returned from
following the Philistines, he was
told, "Behold, David is in the Wilder-
ness of Engedi."
2 Then Saul took three thousand cho-
sen men out of all Israel and went to
search for David and his men in front
of the Rocks of the Wild Goats.
3 On the way he came to the sheep-
folds where there was a cave; and Saul
went in to relieve himself. Now David
and his men were sitting in the cave's
innermost recesses.
4 David's men said to him, "Behold,
this is the day of which the LORD said
to you, 'Behold, I will hand over your
enemy to you, and you shall do to him
as seems good to you.' " Then David
arose [in the darkness] and stealthily
cut off the hem (edge) of Saul's robe.
5 Afterward, David's conscience
bothered him because he had cut off
the hem of Saul's *robe*.
6 He said to his men, "The LORD for-
bid that I should do this thing to my
master, the LORD's anointed, to put out
my hand against him, since he is the
anointed of the LORD."
7 So David strongly rebuked his men
with these words and did not let them
rise up against Saul. Saul got up, left
the cave and went on his way.
8 Then David also got up afterward
and went out of the cave and called
after Saul, saying, "My lord the king!"
And when Saul looked behind him, Da-
vid bowed with his face to the ground
and lay himself face down.
9 David said to Saul, "Why do you
listen to the words of men who say,
'David seeks to harm you?'
10 "Behold, your eyes have seen today
how the LORD had given you into my
hand in the cave. Some told me to kill
you, but I spared you; I said, 'I will not
reach out my hand against my lord, for
he is the LORD's anointed.'
11 "Look, my father! Indeed, see the
hem of your robe in my hand! Since I
cut off the hem of your robe and did
not kill you, know and understand
[without question] that there is no evil
or treason in my hands. I have not
sinned against you, though you are
lying in wait to take my life.
12 "May the LORD judge between me
and you; and may the LORD avenge
me on you; but my hand shall not be
against you.
13 "As the proverb of the ancients says,

24:3 *sheepfolds.* At night shepherds in the wild area would gather their sheep into a protective rock enclosure. A low stone wall would keep the sheep from wandering, and the shepherd would position himself at the entrance to keep guard. Often a cave with a wall built across its mouth served as a sheepfold.

24:10 – 12 Mercy — David does not say the words, "I forgive you," in this passage, but he speaks as one who has forgiven Saul for his foolish and violent acts against himself. A big part of forgiving an unrepentant individual is deliberately putting the whole situation in God's hands, knowing that it is only God who can judge rightly. God will vindicate the innocent, and punish the guilty, if necessary.

24:12 *my hand shall not be against you.* David knew that the Lord had anointed him to be the king to succeed Saul, and Saul knew it too. Saul, probably thinking of how he himself would have responded, was sure that David would seize power and oust him with trickery and violence. David had to prove to Saul that he was not going to harm him, and the only way to do this was to turn down every opportunity he had to kill the king. It was God's job, and His alone, to arrange the transfer of power from Saul to David.

---

27 See 2Ki 19:9 **29** 2Ch 20:2 **CHAPTER 24** **1** 1Sa 23:28 **2** Ps 38:12 **3** ver. 10; Jdg 3:24; Ps 57, title; 142, title **4** 1Sa 26:8 **5** 2Sa 24:10 **6** 1Sa 26:11 **7** Ps 7:4; Mt 5:44; Ro 12:17,19 **9** Ps 141:6; Pr 16:28; 17:9 **11** Ps 7:3; 35:7; 1Sa 26:20 **12** Ge 16:5; Jdg 11:27; 1Sa 26:10; Job 5:8

'Out of the wicked comes wickedness';
but my hand shall not be against you.
[14]"After whom has the king of Israel
come out? Whom do you pursue [with
three thousand men]? A dead dog, a
single flea?
[15]"May the LORD be the judge and
render judgment between me and you;
and may He see and plead my cause
and vindicate me *by saving me* from
your hand." [Ps 142]
[16]When David had finished saying
these words to Saul, Saul said, "Is this
your voice, my son David?" Then Saul
raised his voice and wept.
[17]He said to David, "You are more
righteous *and* upright [in God's eyes]
than I; for you have done good to me,
but I have done evil to you.
[18]"You have declared today the good
that you have done to me, for when the
LORD put me into your hand, you did
not kill me.
[19]"For if a man finds his enemy, will
he let him go away unharmed? So may
the LORD reward you with good in re-
turn for what you have done for me
this day.
[20]"Now, behold, I know that you will
certainly be king and that the king-
dom of Israel will be established in your
hand.
[21]"So now swear to me by the LORD
that you will not cut off my descen-
dants after me and that you will not
destroy my name from my father's
household (extended family)."
[22]David gave Saul his oath; and Saul
went home, but David and his men
went up to the mountain stronghold.

Samuel's Death

25 NOW SAMUEL died; and all
Israel assembled and mourned
for him, and they buried him at his
house in Ramah. Then David left and
went down to the Wilderness of Paran.

Nabal and Abigail

[2]Now *there was* a man in Maon
whose business *and* possessions were
in Carmel; and the man was very rich.
He had three thousand sheep and a
thousand goats, and he was shearing
his sheep in Carmel
[3](now the man's name was Nabal
and his wife's name was Abigail. She
was intelligent and beautiful in ap-
pearance, but the man was harsh and
evil in his dealings; he was a Calebite).
[4]David heard in the wilderness that
Nabal was shearing his sheep.
[5]So David sent ten young men; and
David said to the young men, "Go up
to Carmel and go to Nabal, and greet
him in my name;
[6]and this is what you shall say, 'Have
a long life! Peace be to you, and peace
to your house, and peace to all that
you have.
[7]'Now I have heard that you have
shearers. Now your shepherds have
been with us and we have not harmed
them, nor were they missing anything
all the time they were in Carmel.
[8]'Ask your young men and they will
tell you. Therefore let my young men
find favor in your sight [and be well-
treated], for we have come on a good
(festive) day. Please, give whatever you
find at hand to your servants and to
your son David.' "
[9]When David's young men came,
they spoke to Nabal according to all
these words in the name of David; then
they waited.
[10]But Nabal answered David's ser-
vants and said, "Who is David? And
who is the son of Jesse? There are

24:22 ***David gave Saul his oath.*** David agreed to Saul's requests, and he kept his promise (2Sa 9:1 – 13; 21:1 – 14), as Saul knew he would. However, David had no great confidence in the lasting value of Saul's expressions of remorse, so David remained in hiding.

25:2 ***Maon.*** Located in the Judean hill country, Maon was about eight miles south of Hebron. ***Carmel.*** Carmel was located on the edge of the Judean wilderness, about a mile north of Maon. ***shearing his sheep.*** Like the times of harvest, sheep shearing was a festive occasion.

14 1Sa 17:43; 2Sa 9:8; 1Sa 26:20 **15** ver. 12; 2Ch 24:22; Ps 35:1; 43:1; Mic 7:9 **16** 1Sa 26:17 **17** 1Sa 26:21; Ge 38:26; Mt 5:44 **18** 1Sa 26:23 **20** 1Sa 23:17 **21** Ge 21:23; 2Sa 21:6,8 **22** 1Sa 23:29 **CHAPTER 25** **1** 1Sa 28:3; Nu 20:29; Dt 34:8; Ge 21:21; Ps 120:5 **2** 1Sa 23:24; Jos 15:55 **4** Ge 38:13; 2Sa 13:23 **6** 1Ch 12:18; Lk 10:5 **7** ver. 15,21 **8** Neh 8:10; Est 9:19 **10** Jdg 9:28

many servants today, each of whom is breaking away from his master.

11 "So should I take my bread and my water and my meat that I have slaughtered for my shearers, and give it to men when I do not know where they are from?"

12 So David's young men made their way back and returned; and they came and told him everything that was said [to them by Nabal].

13 David said to his men, "Each man put on your sword." So each man put on his sword. David also put on his sword, and about four hundred men went up behind David while two hundred stayed *back* with the provisions and supplies.

14 But one of *Nabal's* young men told Abigail, Nabal's wife, "Listen, David sent messengers out of the wilderness to bless (greet) our master, and he shouted at them [in contempt].

15 "But *David's* men were very good to us, and we were not harmed *or* treated badly, nor did we miss anything as long as we were with them, when we were in the fields.

16 "They were a wall [of protection] to us both night and day, all the time that we were with them tending the sheep.

17 "Now then, know this and consider what you should do, for evil is [already] planned against our master and against all his household; but he is such a worthless *and* wicked man that one cannot speak [reasonably] to him."

Abigail Intercedes

18 Then Abigail hurried and took two hundred *loaves* of bread, two jugs of wine, five sheep already prepared [for roasting], five measures of roasted grain, a hundred clusters of raisins, and two hundred cakes of figs, and loaded them on donkeys.

19 She said to her young men (servants), "Go on ahead of me; behold, I am coming after you." But she did not tell her husband Nabal.

20 It happened that as she was riding on her donkey and coming down by [way of] the hidden part of the mountain, that suddenly David and his men were coming down toward her, and she met them.

21 Now David had said, "Surely in vain I have protected *and* guarded all that this man has in the wilderness, so that nothing was missing of all that belonged to him; and he has repaid me evil for good.

22 "May God do so to the enemies of David, and more also, if by morning I leave [alive] even one male of any who belong to him."

23 When Abigail saw David, she hurried and dismounted from the donkey, and kneeled face downward before David and bowed down to the ground [in respect].

24 Kneeling at his feet she said, "My lord, let the blame *and* guilt be on me alone. And please let your maidservant speak to you, and listen to the words of your maidservant.

25 "Please do not let my lord pay attention to this worthless man, Nabal, for as his name is, so is he. Nabal (fool) is his name and foolishness (stupidity) is with him; but I your maidservant did not see my lord's young men whom you sent.

26 "So now, my lord, as the LORD lives, and as your soul lives, since the LORD has prevented you from shedding blood, and from avenging yourself by your own hand, now then let your enemies and those who seek to do evil to my lord, be as [self-destructive as] Nabal.

27 "Now this gift, which your maidservant has brought my lord, let it be given to the young men who accompany *and* follow my lord.

28 "Please forgive the transgression of your maidservant; for the LORD will

---

25:21 *repaid me evil for good.* Saul had returned David evil for good, and David refrained from retaliation. But Nabal's insult did not meet with such forbearance. David's fierce response is actually a response of the natural man, and as such gives an even better understanding of the force of David's commitment to restrain his natural response to Saul for the sake of his Lord.

---

11 Jdg 8:6 **13** 1Sa 30:24 **15** ver. 7 **16** Ex 14:22; Job 1:10 **17** 1Sa 20:7; Dt 13:13; Jdg 19:22 **18** Ge 32:13; Pr 18:16; 21:14 **19** Ge 32:16,20 **21** Ps 109:5 **22** Ru 1:17; 1Sa 3:17; 20:13,16; ver. 34; 1Ki 14:10; 21:21; 2Ki 9:8 **23** Jos 15:18; Jdg 1:14 **26** 2Ki 2:2; ver. 33; Ge 20:6; Ro 12:19; 2Sa 18:32 **27** Ge 33:11; 1Sa 30:26; 2Ki 5:15 **28** 2Sa 7:11,27; 1Ki 9:5; 1Ch 17:10,25; 1Sa 18:17; 1Sa 24:11

certainly make my lord a secure *and*
enduring house, because my lord is
fighting the battles of the LORD, and
evil will not be found in you all your
days.
29“Should anyone rise up to pursue
you and to seek your life, then the life
of my lord will be bound in the [pre-
cious] bundle of the living with the
LORD your God; but the lives of your
enemies—those He will hurl out as
from the center of a sling.
30“And it will happen when the LORD
does for my lord according to all the
good that He has spoken (promised)
concerning you, and appoints you rul-
er over Israel,
31that this [incident] will not cause
grief or [bring] a troubled conscience
to my lord, both by having shed blood
without cause and by my lord having
avenged himself. When the LORD deals
well with my lord, then remember
[with favor] your maidservant.”
32David said to Abigail, “Blessed be
the LORD, the God of Israel, who sent
you to meet me this day.
33“And blessed be your discretion
and discernment, and blessed be you,
who has kept me from bloodshed this
day and from avenging myself by my
own hand.
34“Nevertheless, as the LORD the God
of Israel lives, who has prevented me
from harming you, if you had not come
quickly to meet me, most certainly
by the morning light there would not
have been left to Nabal so much as
one male.”
35So David accepted what she had
brought to him and said to her, “Go
up to your house in peace. See, I have
listened to you and have granted your
request.”
36Then Abigail came to Nabal, and
he was holding a feast in his house [for
the shearers], like the feast of a king.
And Nabal’s mood was joyous because
he was very drunk; so she told him
nothing at all until the morning light.
37But in the morning, when Nabal
was sober, and his wife told him these
things, his heart died within him and
he became [paralyzed and helpless]
like a stone.
38About ten days later, the LORD
struck Nabal and he died.

David Marries Abigail

39When David heard that Nabal was
dead, he said, “Blessed be the LORD,
who has pleaded the cause of my re-
proach [suffered] at the hand of Nabal
and has kept His servant from [retaliat-
ing with] evil. For the Lord has returned
the wickedness of Nabal on his own
head.” Then David sent word to Abigail,
proposing to take her as his wife.
40When the servants of David came
to Abigail at Carmel, they said to her,
“David sent us to you to take you [to
him] to be his wife.”

25:29 *bound in the [precious] bundle of the living with the LORD your God.* This metaphor reflects the custom of binding valuables in a bundle to protect them from injury. The point here is that God cares for His own as a man cares for his valuable treasure.

25:30–31 Prudence—Abigail’s courageous and gracious intervention saved not only her own household, but all that David had worked so hard to maintain during the years he was a fugitive. It takes more strength of character to restrain oneself than to lash out and return sting for sting. But the bitterness of grief that follows a vicious tongue or a vicious deed is a far heavier burden than suffering an injustice.

25:33 *blessed be your discretion and discernment, and blessed be you.* David responds to the wisdom of Abigail’s entreaty, and he also shows that he knows she came to him without regard to personal risk. Abigail laid out the facts and David responded to her godly counsel because he was accustomed to listening to the Lord, and recognized that she was representing God’s point of view.

25:39 *the Lord has returned the wickedness.* David was very thankful that the Lord had kept him from taking revenge on Nabal, for that would have been evil. But David was also thankful that the Lord, in His justice, had seen fit to punish Nabal. For David this would have been a reminder of his situation with Saul. David was not to touch the Lord’s anointed, and the Lord would indeed at some point deal with Saul for trying to take David’s life.

29 Jer 10:18 **32** Ge 24:27; Ex 18:10; Lk 1:68 **33** ver. 26 **34** ver. 26; ver. 22 **35** 1Sa 20:42; 2Sa 15:9; 2Ki 5:19; Lk 7:50; 8:48; Ge 19:21 **36** 2Sa 13:23 **39** ver. 32; Pr 22:23; ver. 26,34; 1Ki 2:44

41And she stood and bowed with her
face to the ground and said, "Behold,
your maidservant is [ready to be] a
maid to wash the feet of the servants
of my lord."
42Then Abigail quickly got up, and
rode on a donkey, with five of her
maidens who attended her; and she
followed the messengers of David and
became his wife.
43David had also taken Ahinoam
of Jezreel, and they both became his
wives.
44But Saul had given Michal his
[younger] daughter, David's wife, to
Palti the son of Laish, who was from
Gallim.

David Again Spares Saul

26 THE ZIPHITES came to Saul
at Gibeah, saying, "Is David not
hiding on the hill of Hachilah, *east of*
Jeshimon?"
2So Saul arose and went down to
the Wilderness of Ziph, taking with
him three thousand chosen men of Is-
rael, to search for David [there] in the
wilderness of Ziph.
3Saul camped on the hill of Hachi-
lah, which is beside the road east of
Jeshimon, but David stayed in the wil-
derness. When he saw that Saul came
into the wilderness after him,
4David sent out spies, and he learned
that Saul was definitely coming.
5So David arose and went to the
place where Saul had camped, and
saw the spot where Saul lay, as well as
Abner the son of Ner, the commander
of his army; and Saul was lying inside
the circle of the camp, with the army
camped around him.
6Then David said to Ahimelech the
Hittite and to Abishai the son of Zerui-
ah, brother of Joab, "Who will go down
with me to Saul in the camp?" And
Abishai said, "I will go down with you."
7So David and Abishai went to the
army during the night, and there was
Saul lying asleep inside the circle of
the camp with his spear stuck in the
ground by his head; and Abner and the
people were lying around him.
8Then Abishai said to David, "God
has given your enemy into your hand
this day; now then, please let me strike
him with the spear *driving it* to the
ground with one stroke, and I will not
strike him the second time."
9But David said to Abishai, "Do not
kill him, for who can put out his hand
against the LORD's anointed [king] and
be guiltless (innocent)?"
10David also said, "As the LORD lives,
most certainly the LORD will strike him
[in His own time and way], or his day
will come and he will die, or he will
go down into battle and be carried off
[dead].
11"The LORD forbid that I would put
out my hand against the LORD's anoint-
ed; but now take the spear that is by
his head and the jug of water, and let
us go."
12So David took the spear and the jug
of water from *beside* Saul's head, and
they left, and no one saw or knew nor
did anyone awaken, because they were
all *sound* asleep, for a deep sleep from
the LORD had fallen on them.
13Then David crossed over to the
other side and stood on the top of the
mountain at a distance, with a large
area between them.
14David called to the army and to
Abner the son of Ner, "Will you not

26:2 *Ziph.* Ziph was four miles southeast of Hebron, which would have been about 4 or 5 miles from Maon, where Nabal lived.
26:6 *Abishai.* Abishai was David's nephew (1Ch 2:16).
26:10 *the LORD will strike him [in His own time and way], or . . . he will die.* David had just been reminded that the Lord could and would deal with his enemies, which strengthened him for his next encounter with Saul. David had not trusted in the value of Saul's expressions of remorse, but it must have been discouraging even so, to be faced with the same relentless pursuit, the same dogged determination to kill him, even though David repeatedly said he would not stretch out his hand against Saul, the king who had been anointed by God.

43 Jos 15:56; 1Sa 27:3; 30:5 **44** 2Sa 3:14; Isa 10:30 **CHAPTER 26** **1** 1Sa 23:19; Ps 54, title **5** 1Sa 14:50; 17:55 **6** 1Ch 2:16; Jdg 7:10,11 **9** 1Sa 24:6,7; 2Sa 1:16 **10** 1Sa 25:38; Lk 18:7; Ro 12:19; See Ge 47:29; Dt 31:14; Job 7:1; 14:5; 1Sa 31:6 **11** 1Sa 24:6,12 **12** Ge 2:21; 15:12

answer, Abner?" Abner replied, "Who
are you who calls [and disturbs] the
king?"
15 David said to Abner, "Are you not a
[brave] man? Who is like you in Israel?
Why then have you not guarded your
lord the king? For one of the people
came [into your camp] to kill the king
your lord.
16 "This thing that you have done is
not good. As the LORD lives, you surely
deserve to die, because you have not
guarded your lord, the LORD's anointed.
And now, see where the king's spear
is, and the jug of water that was by
his head."
17 Then Saul recognized David's
voice and said, "Is this your voice, my
son David?" And David said, "It is my
voice, my lord the king!"
18 And David said, "Why is my lord
pursuing his servant? For what have
I done? Or what evil is in my hand?
19 "Now therefore, please let my lord
the king hear the words of his servant.
If the LORD has incited you against me,
let Him accept an offering [from me];
but if it is men, may they be cursed
before the LORD, because they have
driven me out this day to keep me from
sharing in the inheritance of the LORD,
saying, 'Go, serve other gods.'
20 "Now then, do not let my blood fall
to the ground away from the presence
of the LORD; for the king of Israel has
come out to search for a single flea,
just as when one hunts a [defenseless]
partridge in the mountains."
21 Then Saul said, "I have sinned.
Return, my son David, for I will not
harm you again because my life was
precious in your sight this day. Hear
me, I have played the fool and have
done a very great wrong [to you]."
22 David answered, "Look, here is the
king's spear! Now let one of the young
men come over and get it.
23 "The LORD will repay each man for
his righteousness and his faithfulness;
for the LORD handed you over to me
today, but I refused to put out my hand
against the LORD's anointed.
24 "Now behold, just as your life was
precious in my sight this day, so let
my life be precious in the sight of the
LORD, and may He rescue me from all
distress."
25 Then Saul said to David, "May you
be blessed, my son David; you will
both accomplish much and certainly
prevail." So David went on his way,
and Saul returned to his place.

David Flees to the Philistines

27 BUT DAVID said in his heart,
"Now I will die one day by the
hand of Saul. There is nothing better
for me than to escape to the land of
the Philistines. Then Saul will give up
searching for me inside the borders of
Israel, and I will escape from his hand
[once and for all]."
2 So David and the six hundred men
who were with him arose and crossed
over to Achish the son of Maoch, king
of Gath.
3 And David lived with Achish at
Gath, he and his men, each man with
his household, and David with his two
wives, Ahinoam the Jezreelitess, and

26:19 *If the LORD has incited you.* David knew that God could bring adverse events into someone's life to turn him to the Lord. If Saul was pursuing David because God wanted him to, God would accept a sin offering from David. But if men had stirred up Saul to kill David, that would be wicked injustice. In that case, David had no hesitation in asking God to curse them. For in driving David out of his homeland, he was effectively cut off from the inheritance of the Lord, which would include the land, the blessings on the land and people, and the special ways God had ordained for worship and sacrifice.

26:20 *partridge.* A partridge was known to flee for safety by running rather than fighting. David was reminding Saul that he was not fighting against the king.

26:23 Righteousness — One mark of a righteous person is that he can walk away from a situation where he has a golden chance to get in the last kick. And as he walks away, he says, "Father, forgive him, for he does not know what he is doing." David never lost sight of the fact that this business of being king was God's plan, not his own.

17 1Sa 24:16 **18** 1Sa 24:9,11 **19** 2Sa 16:11; 24:1; Dt 4:28; 2Sa 14:16; 20:19 **20** 1Sa 24:14 **21** 1Sa 15:24; 24:17; 1Sa 18:30 **23** Ps 7:8; 18:20 **25** Ge 32:28 **CHAPTER 27** **2** 1Sa 25:13; 1Sa 21:10 **3** 1Sa 25:43

Abigail the Carmelitess, [who was] Nabal's widow.
[4]When Saul was told that David had fled to Gath, he no longer searched for him.
[5]Then David said to Achish, "If I have found favor in your sight, let me be given a place [of my own] in one of the cities in the country, so that I may live there; for why should your servant live in the royal city with you?"
[6]Then Achish gave David [the town of] Ziklag that day. Therefore Ziklag has belonged to the kings of Judah to this day.
[7]The number of days that David lived in the country of the Philistines was a year and four months.
[8]Now David and his men went up and raided the Geshurites, the Girzites, and the Amalekites [the enemies of Israel that Joshua had failed to annihilate]; for they had inhabited the land from ancient times, as one comes to Shur even as far as the land of Egypt. [Deut 25:19; Josh 13:1, 2, 13]
[9]David attacked the land and did not leave a man or a woman alive, but he took the sheep, the cattle, the donkeys, the camels, and the clothing, and returned to Achish.
[10]When Achish asked, "Where did you raid today?" David replied, "Against the Negev (the South country) of Judah, and against the Negev of the Jerahmeelites, and against the Negev of the Kenites."
[11]David did not leave a man or a woman alive to bring *news* to Gath, saying [to himself], "Otherwise they will tell about us, saying, 'This is what David has done, and this has been his practice all the time that he has lived in the country of the Philistines.' "
[12]Achish believed David, saying, "He has certainly become hated by his people in Israel; so he will always be my servant."

Saul and the Spirit Medium

28 IN THOSE days the Philistines gathered their forces for war to fight against Israel. Achish said to David, "Understand for certain that you and your men will go out with me to battle."
[2]David said to Achish, "All right, you shall know what your servant can do." So Achish said to David, "Therefore I will make you my bodyguard for life."
[3]Now Samuel had died, and all Israel had mourned for him and buried him

---

27:5 *let me be given a place [of my own] in one of the cities.* David was probably wanting more independence of movement in his own city and freedom from daily involvement with Achish's household and religious practices. This request was also a good way to find out how much Achish trusted him. If Achish was willing for David to live independently, he was not likely to be treating David as a spy or enemy.

27:10 *the Negev (the South country) of Judah.* The Negev was a dry pastoral region, south of Hebron.

27:12 *he will always be my servant.* It seems that David was double dealing with Achish in a way that was dishonest, and indeed he was. But Achish was not David's friend. He was the sworn enemy of David's people and all that David held dear. Achish intended to use David's military expertise for his own ends. This account does not say what God, whose very character is truth, thought about David's strategy. It is clear that God continued to protect and bless David during this very vulnerable time, and the raiding that David had done was continuing the commission the Lord had given the Israelites when they first came into the land.

28:2 *you shall know what your servant can do.* In this case, David is purposely ambiguous. He states that his prowess is well known, without saying that he commits this skill to Achish. David could not refuse Achish's offer without risking his life. He trusted the Lord to rescue him from this compromising situation.

28:3 *Samuel had died.* No one could go to Samuel for advice or direction from the Lord. ***mediums and the spiritists.*** The term "mediums" refers to necromancers, those who presume to communicate with the dead. "Spiritists" is a general term for those who have contact with spirits. In keeping with God's law, persons associated with necromancy and spiritism had been expelled from the land (Ex 22:18; Lev 19:31; Dt 18:9 – 14).

6 See Jos 15:31; 19:5 **8** Jos 13:2; Jos 16:10; Jdg 1:29; Ex 17:16; See 1Sa 15:7,8; Ge 25:18 **10** See 1Ch 2:9,25; Jdg 1:16 **CHAPTER 28** **1** 1Sa 29:1 **3** 1Sa 5:1; See ch 1:19; ver. 9; Ex 22:18; Lev 19:31; 20:2; Dt 18:10,11

in Ramah, his own city. And Saul had
removed the mediums and the spirit-
ists (soothsayers) from the land.
4 The Philistines assembled and
came and camped at Shunem; and
Saul gathered all the Israelites and
they camped at Gilboa.
5 When Saul saw the Philistine army,
he was afraid and badly shaken.
6 So Saul inquired of the LORD, but
the LORD did not answer him, either by
dreams or by Urim [used like lots by
the priest to determine the will of God]
or by prophets. [Prov 1:24–30]
7 Then Saul said to his servants, "Find
for me a woman who is a medium [be-
tween the living and the dead], so that
I may go to her and ask her advice."
His servants said to him, "There is a
woman who is a medium at En-dor."
8 So Saul disguised himself by wear-
ing different clothes, and he left with
two men, and they came to the woman
at night. He said *to her*, "Conjure up
for me, please, and bring up [from the
dead] for me [the spirit] whom I shall
name to you."
9 But the woman said to him, "See
here, you know what Saul has done,
how he has cut off (eliminated) those
who are mediums and spiritists from
the land. So why are you laying a trap
for my life, to cause my death?"
10 Then Saul swore [an oath] to her
by the LORD, saying, "As the LORD lives,
no punishment shall come upon you
for this."
11 So the woman said, "Whom shall I
bring up for you?" He said, "Bring up
Samuel for me."
12 When the woman saw Samuel, she
screamed with a loud voice; and she
said to Saul, "Why have you deceived
me? You are Saul!"
13 The king said to her, "Do not be
afraid; but [tell me] what do you see?"
The woman said to Saul, "I see a divine
[superhuman] being coming up from
the earth."
14 He said to her, "What is his appear-
ance?" And she said, "An old man is
coming up, wrapped in a robe." Then
Saul knew that it was Samuel, and he
bowed with his face to the ground and
paid respect [to him].
15 Then Samuel said to Saul, "Why
have you disturbed me by bringing
me up?" Saul answered, "I am greatly
distressed; for the Philistines are mak-
ing war against me, and God has left
me and no longer answers me, either
through prophets or by dreams; there-

28:6 *Saul inquired of the LORD.* It sounds as if Saul was desperate to hear from the Lord. But he had never said, "Whatever You want, Lord, I will do it." Saul knew that he had been rejected by God as king, and if he wanted to repent, Saul could have admitted to God that he was not fit to be king, and asked God to turn the kingdom over to the man of His choice. But Saul wanted to be king, and to hear from God, and have David ejected, and have the Philistines leave him alone, none of which was possible for a man who had decided to deliberately disobey the Lord.

28:7 – 11 Unfaithfulness — It started with disobeying God's directions about fighting with the Amalekites, and it ended with a witch. Saul apparently never saw himself as a rebel. He knew that the Lord had rejected him, but he thought that it was unjust. Rejecting God is the beginning of a downward spiral, and finally the man who had hounded the mediums from the land was asking a witch for guidance because he had no hope of hearing from God.

28:10 *Saul swore [an oath] to her by the LORD.* While engaging in a practice that was essentially a denial of God's control of everything, Saul swore in God's name that he would protect the woman.

28:12 *When the woman saw Samuel.* The appearance of Samuel has been interpreted in various ways. Some think that a demon impersonated Samuel, and others think that Saul was tricked into believing it was Samuel. It seems best to follow the early view that this was a genuine appearance of Samuel, which God Himself brought about. Several points favor this interpretation. The medium herself was surprised and frightened by his appearance. Saul identified the figure as Samuel. The message Samuel spoke was clearly from God. The text says the figure was Samuel. There is no inherent difficulty with God bringing back the spirit of Samuel from heaven and allowing him to appear to Saul — in spite of the woman's evil profession.

4 Jos 19:18; 2Ki 4:8; 1Sa 31:1 **5** Job 18:11 **6** 1Sa 14:37; Pr 1:28; La 2:9; Nu 12:6; Ex 28:30; Nu 27:21; Dt 33:8 **8** Dt 18:11; 1Ch 10:13; Isa 8:19 **9** ver. 3 **13** Ex 22:28 **14** 1Sa 15:27; 2Ki 2:8,13 **15** Pr 5:11-13; 14:14; 1Sa 18:12; ver. 6

fore I have called you to make known to me what I should do."

16 Samuel said, "Why then do you ask me, since the LORD has left you and has become your enemy?

17 "The LORD has done [to you] just as He said through me [when I was with you]; for the LORD has torn the kingdom out of your hand and given it to your neighbor, to David. [1 Sam 15:22–28]

18 "Because you did not obey the voice of the LORD and did not execute His fierce wrath on Amalek, therefore the LORD has done this thing to you this day.

19 "Moreover, the LORD will also put Israel along with you into the hands of the Philistines, and tomorrow you and your sons will be with me [among the dead]. Indeed, the LORD will put the army of Israel into the hands of the Philistines."

20 Then Saul immediately fell full length on the earth [floor of the medium's house], and was very afraid because of Samuel's words; and he was thoroughly exhausted because he had not eaten all day and all night.

21 The woman came to Saul and saw that he was greatly troubled, and she said to him, "Look, your maidservant has obeyed you, and I have taken my life in my hand and have listened to everything you said to me.

22 "So now, please listen to the voice of your maidservant, and let me set a piece of bread before you, and eat, so that you may have strength when you go on your way."

23 But he refused and said, "I will not eat." But his servants together with the woman urged him, and he [finally] listened to them. So he got up from the ground and sat on the bed.

24 The woman had a fattened calf in the house; she quickly killed it, and took flour, kneaded it and baked unleavened bread.

25 She brought it before Saul and his servants, and they ate. Then they got up and went away that night.

The Philistines Mistrust David

29 NOW THE Philistines gathered all their forces at Aphek, while Israel camped by the spring in Jezreel.

2 As the Philistine lords (governors) were proceeding on [marching] by hundreds and by thousands, and David and his men were proceeding on in the rear with Achish [the king of Gath],

3 the Philistine commanders [having noticed David] said, "What are these Hebrews *doing here?*" Achish said to the Philistine commanders, "Is this not David, the servant of Saul king of Israel, who has been with me these days and years, and I have found no fault in him from the day he deserted *to me* to this day?"

4 But the Philistine commanders were angry with Achish and they said to him, "Make this man return, so that he may go back to his place where you have assigned him, and do not let him go down to battle with us, or in the battle he may [turn and] become our adversary. For how could David reconcile himself to his lord [Saul]? *Would it* not be with the heads of these [Philistine] men?

5 "Is this not David, of whom they used to sing in dances,

'Saul killed his thousands,
And David his ten thousands'?"

6 Then Achish called David and said to him, "As the LORD lives, you *have been* upright (righteous), and your behavior in the army is pleasing in my sight. For from the day you came to me to this day I have found no evil in you.

28:19 *with me.* The words "with me" refer to the grave. This text is not intended to provide a final answer concerning Saul's spiritual status. At the very least, it does indicate the reality of life after death.

29:6 *you have been upright.* David had not been honest with Achish, but he had not turned his hand against Achish personally.

17 1Sa 15:28 **18** 1Sa 15:9; 1Ki 20:42; 1Ch 10:13; Jer 48:10 **21** Jdg 12:3; 1Sa 19:5; Job 13:14 **CHAPTER 29**
1 1Sa 28:1; 1Sa 4:1 **2** 1Sa 28:1,2 **3** See 1Sa 27:7; Da 6:5 **4** 1Ch 12:19; As 1Sa 14:21 **5** 1Sa 18:7; 21:11
6 2Sa 3:25; 2Ki 19:27; ver. 3

Nevertheless, the [Philistine] lords do
not approve of you.
[7]“So return now and go in peace
[to your place], so that you do not dis-
please the Philistine lords.”
[8]David said to Achish, “But what
have I done? What have you found in
your servant from the day when I [first]
came before you to this day, that I may
not go and fight against the enemies
of my lord the king?”
[9]Achish answered David, “I know
that you are blameless in my sight,
like an angel of God; nevertheless the
commanders of the Philistines have
said, ‘He must not go up with us to
the battle.’
[10]“So now, get up early in the morn-
ing with your master’s servants who
have come with you, and as soon as
you are up in the morning and have
light, leave.”
[11]So David and his men got up ear-
ly to leave in the morning, to return
to the land of the Philistines. But the
Philistines went up to Jezreel [to fight
against Israel].

David’s Victory over the Amalekites

30 NOW IT happened when Da-
vid and his men came [home] to
Ziklag on the third day, [they found]
that the Amalekites had made a raid
on the Negev (the South country) and
on Ziklag, and had overthrown Ziklag
and burned it with fire;
[2]and they had taken captive the
women [and all] who were there, both
small and great. They killed no one,
but carried them off [to be used as
slaves] and went on their way.
[3]When David and his men came
to the town, it was burned, and their
wives and their sons and their daugh-
ters had been taken captive.
[4]Then David and the people who
were with him raised their voices and
wept until they were too exhausted to
weep [any longer].
[5]Now David’s two wives had been
captured, Ahinoam the Jezreelitess
and Abigail the widow of Nabal the
Carmelite.
[6]Further, David was greatly dis-
tressed because the people spoke of
stoning him, for all of them were em-
bittered, each man for his sons and
daughters. But David felt strength-
ened *and* encouraged in the LORD his
God.
[7]David said to Abiathar the priest,
Ahimelech’s son, “Please bring me
the ephod.” So Abiathar brought him
the ephod.
[8]David inquired of the LORD, say-
ing, “Shall I pursue this band [of raid-
ers]? Will I overtake them?” And He
answered him, “Pursue, for you will
certainly overtake them, and you will
certainly rescue [the captives].”
[9]So David went, he and the six hun-
dred men who were with him, and came
to the brook Besor; there those [who
could not continue] remained behind.
[10]But David pursued [the Amalek-
ites], he and four hundred men, for two

29:7 *return.* This was the God-orchestrated escape from a compromising situation that David was confident God would provide. ***go in peace.*** This farewell was more than a courtesy. Achish was releasing David from any further obligation that he had incurred when Achish had made David his vassal in Ziklag.

29:9 – 10 Prudence — Achish saw David as an angel of God. There must have been something in the way that David conducted himself that showed even a pagan Philistine that David belonged to the God of Israel, and that this was a good place to be. David was being very careful in how he dealt with the Philistine. He could not endanger the people who depended on him, nor be unfaithful to his Lord. Only God can help us when we have to live in such a difficult situation.

30:1 *Amalekites.* The Amalekites were a nomadic people who roamed the dry land south of the hill country. For their attack on the Israelites after the exodus from Egypt (Ex 17:8 – 13), they were placed under divine judgment (Dt 25:19).

30:7 *ephod.* The Urim and Thummim were attached to the ephod. The Lord could be consulted by the means of the Urim and Thummim, but the Bible does not say how this worked.

30:10 *too exhausted.* The weariness of David’s men was due to the fact that they had traveled

9 2Sa 14:17,20; 19:27; ver. 4 **11** 2Sa 4:4 **CHAPTER 30** **1** See 1Sa 15:7; 27:8 **5** 1Sa 25:42,43; 2Sa 2:2 **6** Ex 17:4; Ps 42:5; 56:3,4,11; Hab 3:17,18 **7** 1Sa 23:6,9 **8** 1Sa 23:2,4 **10** ver. 21

hundred who were too exhausted to
cross the brook Besor stayed *behind*.
11They found an Egyptian [who had
collapsed] in the field and brought him
to David, and gave him bread and he
ate, and they gave him water to drink,
12and they gave him a piece of a
fig cake and two clusters of raisins;
and when he had eaten, his energy
returned, for he had not eaten bread or
had any water to drink for three days
and three nights.
13David said to him, "To whom do
you belong, and where are you from?"
He said, "I am a young man from
Egypt, a servant of an Amalekite; and
my master abandoned me [as useless]
when I fell sick three days ago.
14"We made a raid on the Negev of
the Cherethites, and on that which be-
longs to Judah, and on the Negev of
Caleb, and we burned Ziklag with fire."
15Then David said to him, "Will you
take me down to this band [of raid-
ers]?" And he said, "Swear to me by
God that you will not kill me or turn
me over to the hand of my master, and
I will bring you down to this band."
16When he brought David down, the
Amalekites had disbanded *and* spread
over all the land, eating and drinking
and dancing because of all the great
spoil they had taken from the land of
the Philistines and from the land of
Judah.
17Then David [and his men] struck
them down [in battle] from twilight
until the evening of the next day; and
not a man of them escaped, except four
hundred young men who rode camels
and fled.
18So David recovered all that the
Amalekites had taken, and rescued
his two wives.
19Nothing of theirs was missing
whether small or great, sons or daugh-
ters, spoil or anything that had been
taken; David recovered it all.
20So David captured all the flocks
and herds [which the enemy had], and
[the people] drove those animals be-
fore him and said, "This is David's
spoil."

The Spoils Are Divided

21David came to the two hundred
men who were so exhausted that they
could not follow him and had been
left at the brook Besor [with the pro-
visions]. They went out to meet David
and the people with him, and when
he approached the people, he greeted
them.
22Then all the wicked and worth-
less men among those who went with
David said, "Because they did not go
with us, we will give them none of the
spoil that we have recovered, except
that each man may take his wife and
children away and leave."
23David said, "You must not do so,
my brothers, with what the LORD has
given us. He has kept us safe and has
handed over to us the band [of Ama-
lekites] that came against us.
24"And who will listen to you in re-
gard to this matter? For as is the share
of him who goes down into the battle,
so shall his share be who stays by the
provisions and supplies; they shall
share alike."
25So from that day forward he made
it a statute and an ordinance for Israel
to this day.
26When David came to Ziklag, he
sent part of the spoil to the elders of
Judah, his friends, saying, "Here is a
blessing (gift) for you from the spoil of
the enemies of the LORD:
27For those in Bethel, Ramoth of the
Negev, Jattir,
28Aroer, Siphmoth, Eshtemoa,
29Racal, the cities of the Jerah-
meelites, the cities of the Kenites,
30Hormah, Bor-ashan, Athach,

about 80 miles from Aphek to Ziklag (29:1; 30:1), only to set off immediately in pursuit of the Amalekites.
30:26 ***sent part of the spoil to the elders of Judah.*** This goodwill gesture helped David reestablish his relationships among the leaders of Judah after his stay in Philistine territory.

12 1Sa 25:18; 2Ki 20:7; Jdg 15:19; 1Sa 14:27 **14** ver. 16; 2Sa 8:18; 1Ki 1:38,44; Eze 25:16; Zep 2:5; Jos 14:13; 15:13 **16** 1Th 5:3 **19** ver. 8 **21** ver. 10 **22** Dt 13:13; Jdg 19:22 **24** See Nu 31:27; Jos 22:8 **27** Jos 19:8; Jos 15:48 **28** Jos 13:16; Jos 15:50 **29** 1Sa 27:10; Jdg 1:16 **30** Jdg 1:17

[31]Hebron, and for [those elders in] all the places where David himself and his men were accustomed to go."

Saul and His Sons Slain

31 NOW THE Philistines fought against Israel, and the men of Israel fled before them and fell slain on Mount Gilboa.
[2]The Philistines overtook Saul and his sons; and they killed Jonathan and Abinadab and Malchi-shua, Saul's sons.
[3]The battle went heavily against Saul, and the archers hit him; and he was severely wounded by the archers.
[4]Saul said to his armor bearer, "Draw your sword and pierce me through with it, otherwise these uncircumcised [Philistines] will come and pierce me through and abuse *and* mock me." But his armor bearer would not, because he was terrified [of doing such a thing]. So Saul took his sword and fell on it.
[5]When his armor bearer saw that Saul was dead, he also fell on his sword and died with him.
[6]So Saul, his three sons, his armor bearer, and all his men died together on that day.
[7]When the men of Israel who were on the other side of the valley [of Jezreel], and those who were beyond the Jordan, saw that the *other* men of Israel had fled and that Saul and his sons were dead, they abandoned the cities and fled; then the Philistines came and lived in them.
[8]The next day, when the Philistines came to plunder the dead, they found Saul and his three sons fallen on Mount Gilboa.
[9]So they cut off Saul's head and stripped off his weapons *and* armor and sent them throughout the land of the Philistines, to bring the good news to the house of their idols and to the people.
[10]And they put Saul's weapons *and* armor in the temple of the Ashtaroth (female goddesses), and they fastened his body to the wall of Beth-shan.
[11]When the inhabitants of Jabesh-gilead heard what the Philistines had done to Saul,
[12]all the brave men stood and walked all night, and they took the bodies of Saul and his sons from the wall of Beth-shan, and they came to Jabesh and cremated them there.
[13]They took their bones and buried them under the tamarisk tree at Jabesh, and fasted [as a sign of mourning and respect] for seven days.

30:31 ***Hebron.*** Hebron was a Levitical city, and a city of refuge, and it was soon to become David's capital (2Sa 5:3).

31:2 ***Saul and his sons.*** Saul's fourth son, Ishbosheth, was apparently not present at this battle, since Abner promoted him to king after Saul's death (2Sa 2:8 – 10).

31:6 ***all his men.*** This does not refer to the whole army, but rather to men who were particularly associated with Saul, such as his royal body guards.

31:11 ***inhabitants of Jabesh-gilead.*** The inhabitants of this town had been delivered from the threats of Nahash the Ammonite by Saul in his first military campaign as king of Israel (11:1 – 11).

31:13 ***and fasted [as a sign of mourning and respect] for seven days.*** In ancient Israel, fasting was a way of expressing sorrow in mourning. With their fasting, the men of Jabesh showed their respect for Israel's first king.

31 Jos 14:13; 2Sa 2:1 **CHAPTER 31** **1** 1Ch 10:1-12; 1Sa 28:4 **2** 1Sa 14:49 **3** See 2Sa 1:6 **4** See Jdg 9:54; 1Sa 14:6; 2Sa 1:14; 1Sa 14:6 **9** 2Sa 1:20 **10** 1Sa 21:9; Jdg 2:13; 2Sa 21:12; Jos 17:11; Jdg 1:27 **11** 1Sa 11:3,9,11 **12** See 1Sa 11:1-11; 2Sa 2:4-7; 2Ch 16:14; Jer 34:5; Am 6:10 **13** 2Sa 21:12-14; Ge 50:10

THE SECOND BOOK OF

SAMUEL

▸ **AUTHOR:** No author is mentioned anywhere in this book. Although the traditional view is that Samuel wrote 2 Samuel, it was probably compiled by one man who combined the written chronicles of "Nathan the prophet" and "Gad the seer" (1Ch 29:29). In addition to these written sources, the compiler evidently used another source called the "Book of Jashar" (1:18).

▸ **TIMES:** c. 1011 – 971 BC ▸ **KEY VERSES:** 2Sa 7:12 – 13

▸ **THEME:** Second Samuel begins with Saul's death and David's ascension to the throne of Judah. A few years later he becomes the king of all of Israel. During his reign there were many problems, most of which can be traced back to David's own behavior. He abuses power and plays favorites with his sons. The result is much personal sorrow and the seeds of discord that follow in succeeding generations. Second Samuel gives us a full picture of a king, a poet, a soldier, and a sinner who yearns after God's own heart and follows where He leads.

David Learns of Saul's Death

1 NOW IT happened after the death
of Saul, when David had returned
from the slaughter of the Amalekites,
that he stayed two days in Ziklag.
2On the third day a man came [un-
expectedly] from Saul's camp with his
clothes torn and dust on his head [as in
mourning]. When he came to David, he
bowed to the ground and lay himself
face down [in an act of great respect
and submission].
3Then David asked him, "Where do
you come from?" He said, "I have es-
caped from the camp of Israel."
4David said to him, "How did it go?
Please tell me." He answered, "The
people have fled from the battle. Also,
many of the people have fallen and are
dead; Saul and Jonathan his son are
also dead."
5So David said to the young man
who informed him, "How do you
know Saul and his son Jonathan are
dead?"
6And the young man who told him
explained, "By chance I happened to be
on Mount Gilboa, and there was Saul
leaning on his spear, and the chariots
and horsemen [of the Philistines] were
close behind him.
7"When he turned to look behind
him, he saw me, and called to me. And
I answered, 'Here I am.'
8"He asked me, 'Who are you?' I an-
swered him, 'I am an Amalekite.'
9"He said to me, 'Stand up facing me
and kill me, for [terrible] agony has
come over me, yet I still live [and I will
be taken alive].'
10"So I stood facing him and killed
him, because I knew that he could not
live after he had fallen. Then I took
the crown which was on his head and
the band which was on his arm, and
I have brought them here to my lord."
[1 Sam 31:4]
11Then David grasped his own
clothes and tore them [in mourning];
so did all the men who were with him.

1:2 *clothes torn and dust on his head.* Dust or ashes on the head, torn clothing, and sack cloth were all signs of mourning.

CHAPTER 1 **1** 1Sa 30:17,26 **2** 2Sa 4:10; 1Sa 4:12 **6** 1Sa 31:1; See 1Sa 31:2-4 **10** Jdg 9:54 **11** 2Sa 3:31; 13:31

[12]They mourned and wept and fasted until evening for Saul and Jonathan his son, and for the LORD's people and the house of Israel, because they had fallen by the sword [in battle].
[13]David said to the young man who informed him, "Where are you from?" He answered, "I am the son of a foreigner (resident alien, sojourner), an Amalekite."
[14]David said to him, "How is it that you were not afraid to put out your hand to destroy the LORD's anointed?"
[15]David called one of the young men and said, "Go, execute him." So he struck the Amalekite and he died.
[16]David said to the [fallen] man, "Your blood is on your own head, for your own mouth has testified against you, saying, 'I have killed the LORD's anointed.' "

David's Dirge for Saul and Jonathan

[17]Then David sang this dirge (funeral song) over Saul and his son Jonathan,
[18]and he told *them* to teach the sons of Judah, *the song of* the bow. Behold, it is written in the Book of Jashar:

[19]"Your glory *and* splendor, O Israel,
is slain upon your high places!
How the mighty have fallen!
[20]"Tell it not in Gath,
Proclaim it not in the streets of Ashkelon,
Or the daughters of the Philistines will rejoice,
The daughters of the uncircumcised (pagans) will exult.
[21]"O mountains of Gilboa,
Let not dew or rain be upon you, nor fields with offerings;
For there the shield of the mighty was defiled,
The shield of Saul, [dry, cracked] not anointed with oil.
[22]"From the blood of the slain, from the fat of the mighty,
The bow of Jonathan did not turn back,
And the sword of Saul did not return empty.
[23]"Saul and Jonathan, beloved and lovely *and* friends in their lives,
And in their death they were not separated;
They were swifter than eagles,
They were stronger than lions.
[24]"O daughters of Israel, weep over Saul,
Who clothed you luxuriously in scarlet,
Who put ornaments of gold on your apparel.
[25]"How the mighty have fallen in the midst of the battle!
Jonathan lies slain upon your high places.
[26]"I am distressed for you, my brother Jonathan;
You have been a good friend to me.
Your love toward me was more wonderful
Than the love of women.

1:12 *fasted.* Spiritual fasting is abstaining from food to devote time and energy to prayer. Sometimes people plan a time of fasting, and sometimes it just comes upon them because overwhelming spiritual needs supersede all thought of food. This was a time of true calamity for Israel, even though it solved a problem for David. He was personally very grieved, for he had known the man Saul as he could have been, and he had lost Jonathan, the best friend he would ever have. His future as king seemed assured, but the task of uniting the nation would be very difficult.

1:14 *the LORD's anointed.* David's use of the phrase "the LORD's anointed" indicates that even though Saul was his enemy, David honored the position that Saul had as God's representative. David repeatedly refused to harm Saul because of this (1Sa 24:6; 26:9).

1:15 *struck the Amalekite.* The Amalekite had probably been hoping for a reward from David. His story was a lie (1Sa 31), and this lie cost him his life. David's execution of the Amalekite was a strong testimony to those under his command that he had no part in Saul's death and did not reward it in any way.

14 Nu 12:8; 1Sa 31:4; 1Sa 24:6; 26:9; Ps 105:15 **15** 2Sa 4:10,12 **16** 1Sa 26:9; 1Ki 2:32,33,37; ver. 10; Lk 19:22 **18** 1Sa 31:3; Jos 10:13 **19** ver. 27 **20** 1Sa 31:9; Mic 1:10; See Jdg 16:23; See Ex 15:20; Jdg 11:34; 1Sa 18:6; 1Sa 31:4 **21** 1Sa 31:1; Jdg 5:23; Job 3:3,4; Jer 20:14; 1Sa 10:1 **22** 1Sa 18:4 **23** Jdg 14:18 **26** 1Sa 18:1,3; 19:2; 20:17,41; 23:16

27 “How the mighty have fallen,
And the weapons of war have
perished!”

David Made King over Judah

2 SO IT happened after this that David inquired of the LORD, saying, “Shall I go up into one of the cities of Judah?” And the LORD said to him, “Go up.” David asked, “Where shall I go?” And He said, “To Hebron.”

2 So David went up there [to Hebron] with his two wives also, Ahinoam of Jezreel and Abigail the widow of Nabal of Carmel [in Judah].

3 And David brought up his men who were with him, each one with his household; and they lived in the cities of Hebron.

4 Then the men of Judah came and there they anointed David king over the house of Judah.

Then they told David, “It was the men of Jabesh-gilead who buried Saul.” [1 Sam 31:11–13]

5 So David sent messengers to the men of Jabesh-gilead, and said to them, “May you be blessed by the LORD because you showed this graciousness *and* loyalty to Saul your lord (king), and buried him.

6 “Now may the LORD show lovingkindness and truth *and* faithfulness to you. I too will show this goodness to you, because you have done this thing.

7 “So now, let your hands be strong and be valiant; for your lord Saul is dead, and also the house of Judah has anointed me king over them.”

Ish-bosheth Made King over Israel

8 Now [Saul’s cousin] Abner the son of Ner, commander of Saul’s army, had taken Ish-bosheth the son of Saul and brought him over to Mahanaim.

9 He made him king over Gilead, over the Ashurites, over Jezreel, over Ephraim, over Benjamin, even over all Israel [except Judah].

10 Ish-bosheth, Saul’s son, was forty years old when he became king over Israel, and he reigned for two years. But the house of Judah followed David.

11 And the time that David was king in Hebron over the house of Judah was seven years and six months.

Civil War

12 Now Abner the son of Ner and the servants of Ish-bosheth the son of Saul went out from Mahanaim to Gibeon.

13 Joab [David’s nephew] the son of Zeruiah and the servants of David also went out and met them by the pool of Gibeon. They sat down, with one group on one side of the pool and the other group on the other side of the pool.

14 Then Abner said to Joab, “Let the young men now stand and have a contest before us.” And Joab said, “Let them stand.”

15 So they stood up and went over by number, twelve for Benjamin and Ish-bosheth the son of Saul, and twelve of the servants of David.

16 Each one of them seized his opponent by the head and *thrust* his sword into his opponents side; so they fell down together. Therefore that place was called Helkath-hazzurim [that is, the Field of Sides], which is in Gibeon.

17 There was a very fierce battle that day, and Abner and the men of Israel were beaten before the servants of David.

18 Three sons of Zeruiah [the half sister of David] were there: Joab, Abishai, and Asahel. Now Asahel was as light *and* swift-footed as one of the [wild] gazelles in the field.

2:5 *graciousness.* David was grateful to the men who had shown kindness to Saul. This acknowledgement was not an act of politeness, but came from David’s own heart of compassion. Saul repeatedly demonstrated that he considered himself above correction, but David was careful to maintain an attitude of kindness and humility.

2:18 *Joab, Abishai, and Asahel.* The three brothers were David’s nephews, children of his sister Zeruiah (1Ch 2:13–16).

27 ver. 19 **CHAPTER 2** **1** Jdg 1:1; 1Sa 23:2,4,9; 30:7,8; ver. 11; 1Sa 30:31; 2Sa 5:1,3; 1Ki 2:11 **2** 1Sa 30:5 **3** 1Sa 27:2,3; 30:1; 1Ch 12:1 **4** ver. 11; 2Sa 5:5; 1Sa 31:11,13 **5** Ru 2:20; 3:10 **6** 2Ti 1:16,18 **8** 1Sa 14:50 **11** 2Sa 5:5; 1Ki 2:11 **12** Jos 18:25 **13** Jer 41:12 **18** 1Ch 2:16; 1Ch 12:8; Ps 18:33

19 Asahel pursued Abner and did not turn to the right or to the left as he followed him.

20 Then Abner looked behind him and said, "Is that you, Asahel?" He answered, "It is I."

21 So Abner said to him, "Turn to your right or to your left, and grab one of the young men and take his armor for yourself." But Asahel was not willing to turn away from pursuing Abner.

22 Abner repeated again, "Turn away from following me. Why should I have to strike you to the ground? How would I be able to face Joab your brother [and look him in the eye]?"

23 But Asahel refused to turn away; so Abner struck him in the abdomen with the butt end of his spear, and the spear came out his back; and he fell there and died on that spot. And it came about that everyone who came to the place where Asahel fell and died, stood still [and reflected].

24 But Joab and Abishai [Asahel's brothers] pursued Abner. When the sun was going down, they came to the hill of Ammah, which is in front of Giah on the way to the wilderness of Gibeon.

25 And the sons of [the tribe of] Benjamin gathered together behind Abner and became one troop, and took their stand on the top of a hill.

26 Then Abner called to Joab, "Must the sword devour forever? Do you not know that it will be bitter in the end? How long [will it be] before you tell the people to stop pursuing their brothers?"

27 Joab said, "As God lives, if you had not spoken, then the people certainly would have stopped pursuing their brothers in the morning."

28 So Joab blew the trumpet; and all the people halted and no longer pursued Israel, nor did they fight anymore.

29 Then Abner and his men went through the Arabah (desert region) all that night, crossed the Jordan, went through Bithron and walked the whole morning and came to Mahanaim [where Ish-bosheth ruled Israel].

30 Joab returned from pursuing Abner; and when he had gathered all the people together, nineteen of David's servants were missing, besides Asahel.

31 But the servants of David had struck down many of Benjamin and Abner's men; *so that* three hundred and sixty men died.

32 And they picked up [the body of] Asahel and buried him in the tomb of his father in Bethlehem. Then Joab and his men walked all night and they arrived in Hebron at daybreak.

The House of David Strengthened

3 THERE WAS a long war between the house of Saul and the house of David; but David grew steadily stronger, while the house of Saul grew weaker and weaker [to the point of being powerless].

2 Sons were born to David in Hebron: his firstborn was Amnon, by Ahinoam of Jezreel;

3 his second, Chileab, by Abigail the widow of Nabal of Carmel; the third, Absalom the son of [his wife] Maacah, daughter of Talmai the king of Geshur;

4 the fourth, Adonijah the son of [his wife] Haggith; the fifth, Shephatiah the son of [his wife] Abital;

2:19 *Asahel pursued Abner.* Asahel did not have a personal grudge against Abner. This was a military move. If Abner, the chief military leader, was dead, Ish-bosheth's power base would dissolve.

3:1 Strife — Finally David was in a position to push to establish his kingdom. It was still a contest of power and loyalty. An important question had to be settled: Is the king chosen by God? Or is the one who seizes the power the king? David knew he had to establish himself both politically and militarily, but he wanted to show, even in battle, that he trusted God to establish his kingdom.

3:2 *Sons were born to David.* David began his reign in Judah with two wives, Ahinoam and Abigail. His wife Michal, the daughter of Saul, had been given to another when David fled from Saul. In Hebron David married four more wives, in spite of the warning from Moses that a king should not "acquire multiple wives for himself" (Dt 17:17).

3:3 *Chileab.* Chileab is also called Daniel (1Ch 3:1).

23 2Sa 3:27; 4:6; 20:10 **27** ver. 14; Pr 17:14 **CHAPTER 3** **2** 1Ch 3:1-4; 1Sa 25:43 **3** 1Sa 27:8; 2Sa 13:37
4 1Ki 1:5

5and the sixth, Ithream, by David's
wife Eglah. These [sons] were born to
David in Hebron.

Abner Joins David

6Now while war continued between
the houses of Saul and David, Abner
was proving himself strong in the
house of Saul.
7Now Saul had a concubine whose
name was Rizpah the daughter of
Aiah; and Ish-bosheth said to Abner,
"Why have you gone in to my father's
concubine?"
8Then Abner was very angry at the
words of Ish-bosheth, and he said, "Am
I a dog's head [a despicable traitor] that
belongs to Judah? Today I show loyalty
and kindness to the house of Saul your
father, to his brothers and his friends,
by not having you handed over to David;
and yet you charge me today with
guilt concerning this woman.
9"May God do so to Abner, and more
also, if I do not do for David just as the
LORD has sworn to him,
10to transfer the kingdom from the
house of Saul, and establish the throne
of David over Israel and Judah from
Dan [in the north] to Beersheba [in
the south]."
11And Ish-bosheth could not say another
word to Abner, because he was
afraid of him.
12Then Abner sent messengers to
David [who was] in his place [at Hebron],
saying, "Whose is the land?
Make your covenant (treaty) with me,
and behold, my hand shall be with you
to bring all Israel over to you."
13David said, "Good! I will make a
covenant (treaty) with you, but I require
one thing of you: you shall not see my
face unless you first bring Michal, Saul's
daughter, when you come to see me."
14So David sent messengers to Ish-bosheth,
Saul's son, saying, "Give me
my wife Michal, to whom I was betrothed
for [the price of] a hundred
foreskins of the Philistines."
15So Ish-bosheth sent and took her
from her husband, from Paltiel the son
of Laish [to whom Saul had given her].
16But her husband went with her,
weeping continually behind her as far
as Bahurim. Then Abner told him, "Go,
return." And he did so.
17Abner talked with the elders (tribal
leaders) of Israel, saying, "In times past
you were seeking for David to be king
over you.
18"Now then, do it [and make him
king]! For the LORD has spoken of David,
saying, 'By the hand of My servant
David I will save My people Israel
from the hand of the Philistines
and the hand of all their enemies.' "
[1 Sam 9:16]

3:5 *born to David in Hebron.* These six sons, each from a different mother, constituted the royal family during David's reign over the house of Judah. The dynastic lists in Chronicles include four sons of David by Bathsheba (1Ch 3:5) and nine other sons whose mothers are not named (1Ch 3:6–8).

3:7 *gone in to my father's concubine.* The royal harem was the property of the king's successor. Taking a king's concubine was tantamount to claiming the throne.

3:8 *dog's head.* In the ancient Middle East dogs were scavengers, living off dead animals and garbage, and were viewed with contempt. ***to Judah.*** The tribe of Judah was the enemy of Ish-bosheth. In essence Abner was saying, "Do you think I am the scum of the enemy?"

3:13 *Michal.* David's first wife, Michal (1Sa 18:17–27), was left in Gibeah when David fled from Saul's court (1Sa 19:11–27). Saul then gave his daughter Michal, perhaps out of spite, to a man named Palti (1Sa 25:44). This request of David's was certainly in line with his rights as a husband who had given a proper dowry for his bride, and it was also a political statement. He was asserting his power over the house of Saul. (See note for 3:7.)

3:16 *her husband went with her.* Michal's husband wept. Nothing is said of Michal's feelings, or of David's. A king did not leave his wife with another man, for that was in the same category as another man taking the king's concubines. How he, or anyone else felt about it, had no bearing on the situation. (See note for 3:7.)

7 2Sa 21:8,10; 2Sa 16:21 **8** Dt 23:18; 1Sa 24:14; 2Sa 9:8; 16:9 **9** Ru 1:17; 1Ki 19:2; 1Sa 15:28; 16:1,12; 28:17; 1Ch 12:23 **10** Jdg 20:1; 2Sa 17:11; 1Ki 4:25 **13** Ge 43:3; 1Sa 18:20 **14** 1Sa 18:25,27 **15** 1Sa 25:44 **16** 2Sa 19:16 **18** ver. 9

19 Abner also spoke to [the men of]
Benjamin. Then he also went to tell Da-
vid at Hebron everything that seemed
good to Israel and to the entire house
of Benjamin.
20 So Abner came to David at Hebron,
and [brought] twenty men along with
him. And David prepared a feast for
Abner and the men with him.
21 Abner said to David, "Let me stand
up and go, and gather all Israel to my
lord the king, so that they may make
a covenant (treaty) with you, and that
you may reign over all that your soul
desires." So David sent Abner away,
and he went in peace.
22 Then the servants of David came
with Joab from a raid and brought a
great quantity of spoil with them; but
Abner was not with David at Hebron,
because David had sent him away, and
he had gone in peace.
23 When Joab and all the army that
was with him arrived, they told Joab,
"Abner the son of Ner came to the king,
and he has sent him away, and he has
gone in peace."
24 Then Joab came to the king and
said, "What have you done? Behold,
Abner came to you; why did you send
him away, so that he is already gone?
25 "You know Abner the son of Ner,
that he [only] came to deceive you
[with flattering words] and to learn of
your going out and coming in, and to
find out what you are doing."

Joab Murders Abner

26 When Joab left David, he sent mes-
sengers after Abner, and they brought
him back from the well of Sirah; but
David knew nothing [about Joab's ac-
tion].
27 So when Abner returned to He-
bron, Joab took him aside to the middle
of the gate to speak to him privately,
and there he struck Abner in the ab-
domen so that he died, to avenge the
blood of Asahel, Joab's brother.
28 Afterward, when David heard of it,
he said, "I and my kingdom are forever
innocent before the LORD of the blood
of Abner the son of Ner.
29 "Let the guilt fall on the head of
Joab and on all his father's house (fam-
ily); and may there never disappear
from the house of Joab one who suffers
with a discharge or one who is a leper
or one who walks with a crutch [being
unfit for war], or one who falls by the
sword, or one who lacks food."
30 So Joab and Abishai his brother
murdered Abner because he had killed
their brother Asahel in the battle at
Gibeon.

David Mourns Abner

31 Then David said to Joab and to
all the people with him, "Tear your
clothes, put on sackcloth, and mourn
before Abner." And King David walked
behind the bier.
32 They buried Abner in Hebron; and
the king raised his voice and wept at
the grave of Abner, and all the people
wept.
33 And the king sang a dirge (funeral
song) over Abner and said,

"Should Abner [the great warrior]
die as a fool dies?
34 "Your hands were not bound, nor
your feet put in fetters;
As a man falls before the wicked,
so you have fallen."

And all the people wept again over
him.
35 All the people came to urge David
to eat food while it was still day; but
David took an oath, saying, "May God
do so to me, and more also, if I taste
bread or anything else before the sun
sets."
36 And all the people took notice of it
and it pleased them, just as everything
that the king did pleased all the people.
37 So all the people and all Israel
understood that day that it had not

3:22 *gone in peace.* The words "gone in peace" are repeated (v. 21), to emphasize that the hostilities between David and Abner had been resolved.

19 1Ch 12:29 **21** ver. 10,12; 1Ki 11:37 **25** 1Sa 29:6; Isa 37:28 **27** 1Ki 2:5; 2Sa 20:9,10; 2Sa 4:6; 2Sa 2:23 **29** 1Ki 2:32,33; Lev 15:2 **30** 2Sa 2:23 **31** Jos 7:6; 2Sa 1:2,11; Ge 37:34 **33** 2Sa 13:12,13 **35** 2Sa 12:17; Jer 16:7; Ru 1:17; 2Sa 1:12

been the will of the king to put Abner
the son of Ner to death.
38Then the king said to his servants,
"Do you not know that a prince and a
great man has fallen this day in Israel?
39"Today I am weak, though anoint-
ed king; these men, the sons of Zerui-
ah, are too difficult for me. May the
LORD repay the evildoer [Joab] in ac-
cordance with his wickedness!"

Ish-bosheth Murdered

4 WHEN SAUL'S son Ish-bosheth
[king of Israel], heard that Abner
had died in Hebron, he lost courage,
and all Israel was horrified.
2Saul's son had two men who were
commanders of [raiding] bands [of
soldiers]. One was named Baanah and
the other Rechab, the sons of Rimmon
the Beerothite of the sons (tribe) of
Benjamin (for Beeroth is also consid-
ered part of [the tribe of] Benjamin,
3and the Beerothites fled to Gittaim,
and have been resident aliens there to
this day).
4Jonathan, Saul's son, had a son
whose feet were crippled. He was five
years old when the news [of the deaths]
of Saul and Jonathan came from Jez-
reel. And the boy's nurse picked him up
and fled; but it happened that while she
was hurrying to flee, he fell and became
lame. His name was Mephibosheth.
5So the sons of Rimmon the Bee-
rothite, Rechab and Baanah, left and
came to the house of Ish-bosheth in the
heat of the day while he was taking his
midday rest.
6They came into the interior of
the house as if to get wheat [for the
soldiers], and they struck him in the
stomach. Then Rechab and Baanah his
brother escaped [unnoticed].
7Now when they entered the house
he was lying on his bed in his bed-
room. They [not only] struck and killed
him, [but] they also beheaded him.
Then they took his head and traveled
all night by way of the Arabah.
8They brought the head of Ish-
bosheth to David at Hebron, and said to
the king, "Look, the head of Ish-bosheth
the son of Saul, your enemy, who sought
your life; thus the LORD has granted my
lord the king vengeance this day on
Saul and on his descendants."
9David replied to Rechab and
Baanah his brother, the sons of Rim-
mon the Beerothite, and said to them,
"As the LORD lives, who has redeemed
my life from every adversity,
10when a man told me, 'Behold, Saul
is dead,' thinking that he was bringing
good news, I seized and killed him in
Ziklag, to reward him for his news.
11"How much more, when wicked
men have killed a righteous *and* just
man in his own house on his bed, shall
I not require his blood from your hand
and remove you from the earth?"
12So David commanded his young
men, and they killed them and cut off
their hands and feet and hung them
beside the pool in Hebron. But they
took Ish-bosheth's head and buried it
in Hebron in the tomb of Abner [his
relative].

4:8–10 *brought the head of Ish-bosheth to David.* Ish-bosheth was Jonathan's brother. Whether or not they looked alike, David had no desire to have the head of his beloved friend's brother brought to him as a prize. Once again, greed for a reward overcame prudence, and the plotters lost their lives on their own testimony.

4:9–12 Strife—Once again David was faced with the question: Who was going to establish his kingdom? In David's mind the answer could only be "God." David wanted to meet his adversary honestly on the field of battle or over a flag of truce, but he would have nothing to do with murder. There was another compelling reason for David to conduct himself honorably. David was closely associated with Ish-bosheth as the brother of his wife and of his best friend, and he did not find it easy to be at war with him.

4:11 *righteous and just man.* Ish-bosheth had accepted what he considered to be his rightful role as the next king after his father, Saul. Apparently, even in David's mind, Ish-bosheth's supposition was reasonable.

39 2Sa 19:7; See 2Sa 19:13; 1Ki 2:5,6,33,34; 2Ti 4:14 **CHAPTER 4** **1** Ezr 4:4; Isa 13:7; Mt 2:3 **2** Jos 18:25 **3** Neh 11:33 **4** 2Sa 9:3; 1Sa 29:1,11 **6** 2Sa 2:23 **8** 1Sa 19:2,10,11 **9** Ge 48:16; 1Ki 1:29 **10** 2Sa 1:2,4,15 **11** Ge 9:5,6 **12** 2Sa 1:15; 2Sa 3:32

David King over All Israel

5 THEN ALL the tribes of Israel came
to David at Hebron and said, "Behold, we are your bone and your flesh.
2"In times past, when Saul was king
over us, it was you who led Israel out [to war] and brought Israel in [from battle]. And the LORD told you, 'You shall shepherd My people Israel and be ruler over them.' " [1 Sam 15:27–29; 16:1]
3So all the elders (tribal leaders)
of Israel came to the king at Hebron, and King David made a covenant with them at Hebron before the LORD; and they anointed him king over Israel.
4David was thirty years old when
he became king, and he reigned forty years.
5In Hebron he reigned over Judah
seven years and six months, and in Jerusalem he reigned thirty-three years over all Israel and Judah.
6Now the king and his men went to
Jerusalem against the Jebusites, the inhabitants of the land, who said to David, "You shall not enter here, for the blind and the lame [even the weakest among us] will turn you away"; they thought, "David cannot come in here [because the walls are impenetrable]."
7Nevertheless, David captured the
stronghold (fortress) of Zion, that is, the City of David.
8Then David said on that day, "Who-
ever strikes the Jebusites, let him go up through the [underground] water shaft to strike the lame and the blind, who are detested by David's soul [because of their arrogance]." So [for that reason] they say, "The blind or the lame (Jebusites) shall not come into the [royal] house [of Israel]." [1 Chr 11:6]
9So David lived in the stronghold
and called it the City of David. And he built all around [the surrounding area] from the Millo [fortification] and inward.
10David became greater and greater,
for the LORD, the God of hosts (armies), was with him.
11Now Hiram the king of Tyre sent
messengers to David with cedar trees, carpenters, and stonemasons; and they built a house (palace) for David.
12And David knew that the LORD had
established him as king over Israel, and that He had exalted his kingdom for His people Israel's sake.
13David took more concubines and
wives from Jerusalem, after he came

5:3 *anointed him king over Israel.* This was the third time that David was anointed as king. The first time was in anticipation of his rule (1Sa 16:13), the second time was acknowledgment of his rule over Judah (2:4), and the third time acknowledged his rule over the entire nation.
5:6 *went to Jerusalem.* The city of Jerusalem was strategically located on a hill, just south of Mount Moriah, with steep cliffs on all sides except the north, making it a natural fortress. It was near the border of Judah and Benjamin. Jerusalem became the site of the temple, and the place, more than any other place on earth, which was identified with the Jewish people. It was there that Jesus was crucified, and it is there that He will come again (Zec 14:4). ***the blind and the lame.*** Jerusalem was so strategically situated that the "blind and the lame" would be enough to defeat David.
5:7 *Zion.* The word Zion originally applied to the Jebusite stronghold, which became the City of David after its capture. As the city expanded to the north, encompassing Mount Moriah, the temple mount came to be called Zion (Ps 78:68 – 69). Eventually the term was used as a synonym for Jerusalem (Isa 40:9).
5:8 *water shaft.* The water shaft or tunnel extended about 230 feet up from the Gihon spring to the top of the hill where the Jebusite fortress was situated (2Ch 32:30). The tunnel gave the city a secure water supply in the event of a siege.
5:11 *cedar trees.* Most buildings in Israel were made of stone. The use of cedar added elegance to David's palace.
5:13 *took more concubines and wives.* These marriages probably reflect David's involvement in international treaties and alliances which were sealed with the marriage of a king's daughter to the other participant in the treaty. Concubines, wives who did not have the legal rights of a true marriage, were a part of a royal harem. The status of kings in ancient times was often measured in part by the size of their harem. But Israel's kings had been warned not to acquire many wives (Dt 17:17).

CHAPTER 5 **1** 1Ch 11:1; Ge 29:14 **2** 1Sa 18:13; 1Sa 16:1 **3** 1Ch 11:3; 2Ki 11:17; Jdg 11:11; 1Sa 23:18 **4** 1Ch 26:31; 29:27 **5** 2Sa 2:11; 1Ch 3:4 **6** Jdg 1:21; Jos 15:63; Jdg 1:8; 19:11,12 **7** 1Ki 2:10; 8:1 **8** 1Ch 11:6-9 **9** ver. 7 **11** 1Ki 5:2 **13** Dt 17:17; 1Ch 3:9

from Hebron; and more sons and daughters were born to him.
[14]And these are the names of those who were born to him in Jerusalem: Shammua, Shobab, Nathan, Solomon,
[15]Ibhar, Elishua, Nepheg, Japhia,
[16]Elishama, Eliada, and Eliphelet.

War with the Philistines

[17]When the Philistines heard that David had been anointed king over Israel, all the Philistines went up to look for him, but he heard about it and went down to the stronghold.
[18]Now the Philistines had come and spread out [for battle] in the Valley of Rephaim.
[19]David inquired of the LORD, saying, "Shall I go up against the Philistines? Will You hand them over to me?" And the LORD said to David, "Go up, for I will certainly hand them over to you."
[20]So David came to Baal-perazim, and he defeated them there, and said, "The LORD has broken through my enemies before me, like a breakthrough of water." So he named that place Baal-perazim (master of breakthroughs).
[21]The Philistines abandoned their [pagan] idols there, so David and his men took them away [to be burned].
[22]The Philistines came up once again and spread out in the Valley of Rephaim.
[23]When David inquired of the LORD, He said, "You shall not go up, but circle around behind them and come at them in front of the balsam trees.
[24]"And when you hear the sound of marching in the tops of the balsam trees, then you shall pay attention *and* act promptly, for at that time the LORD will have gone out before you to strike the army of the Philistines."
[25]David did just as the LORD had commanded him, and struck down the Philistines from Geba as far as Gezer.

Peril in Moving the Ark

6 AGAIN DAVID gathered together all the chosen men of Israel, thirty thousand.
[2]And David arose and went with all those who were with him to Baale-judah [Kiriath-jearim], to bring up from there [to Jerusalem] the ark of God which is called by the Name—the very Name of the LORD of hosts, who dwells enthroned *above* the cherubim.
[3]They placed the ark of God on a new cart and brought it out of the house of Abinadab, which was on the hill; and Uzzah and Ahio, sons of Abinadab, were leading the new cart.
[4]So they brought it with the ark of God from the house of Abinadab, which was on the hill; and Ahio was walking in front of the ark. [1 Sam 7:2]
[5]Meanwhile, David and all the house of Israel were celebrating *and* dancing before the LORD with all kinds of *instruments made of* fir *or* cypress wood, with lyres, harps, tambourines, castanets, and cymbals.
[6]When they came to Nacon's threshing floor, Uzzah reached out [with his hand] to the ark of God and took hold of it, because the oxen [stumbled and] nearly overturned it.

5:18 ***Valley of Rephaim.*** This valley extends southwest from Jerusalem toward the coastal plain, and is a strategic approach to the city.
5:21 ***abandoned their [pagan] idols.*** The Philistines would have regarded their gods as being defeated by the God of Israel.
6:2 ***Baale-judah.*** The name means "Masters of Judah," and the city was also called Baalah and Kiriath-jearim. It was here that the ark had been left after it was returned by the Philistines in the days when Samuel was a young man and there was no king (1Sa 7:1–2). ***cherubim.*** Cherubim are angelic beings generally regarded as guardians of God's holiness (Ex 25:22).
6:3 ***placed the ark of God on a new cart.*** The law was specific that the ark was to be carried by the sons of Kothath, not by a cart or any other vehicle (Ex 25:14–15; Nu 7:8–9).
6:6–8 Respect for the Ark—It is easy to understand David's anger at God. Uzzah's death seems quite unnecessary. It looks like his motives were in fact good ones. Reading about this event elicits fear and questioning. Why? We can't see how the punishment fits the crime. This seems

14 1Ch 3:5 **17** 1Ch 11:16; 2Sa 23:14 **18** Jos 15:8; Isa 17:5 **19** 1Sa 23:2,4 **20** Isa 28:21 **21** Dt 7:5,25 **22** 1Ch 14:13 **23** ver. 19 **24** 2Ki 7:6; Jdg 4:14 **25** Jos 16:10 **CHAPTER 6** **2** 1Ch 13:5,6; 1Sa 4:4; Ps 80:1 **4** 1Sa 7:1

7And the anger of the LORD burned
against Uzzah, and God struck him
there for his irreverence; and he died
there by the ark of God.
8David became angry *and* grieved
and offended because of the LORD's
outburst against Uzzah, and that place
has been called Perez-uzzah (outburst
against Uzzah) to this day.
9So David was afraid of the LORD
that day; and he said, "How can the
ark of the LORD come to me?"
10David was unwilling to move the
ark of the LORD into the City of David
with him; instead he took it aside to the
house of Obed-edom the Gittite.
11So the ark of the LORD remained
in the house of Obed-edom the Git-
tite for three months, and the LORD
blessed Obed-edom and all his house-
hold (family).

The Ark Is Brought to Jerusalem

12Now King David was told, "The
LORD has blessed the house of Obed-
edom and all that belongs to him, be-
cause of the ark of God." So David
went and brought up the ark of God
from the house of Obed-edom into
the City of David with rejoicing *and*
gladness.
13And when those who were carry-
ing the ark of the LORD [by its poles]
had gone six paces, he sacrificed an
ox and a fatling.
14And David was dancing before
the LORD with great enthusiasm, and
David was wearing a linen ephod [a
priest's upper garment].
15So David and all the house of
Israel were bringing the ark of the
LORD up [to the City of David] with
shouts [of joy] and with the sound of
the trumpet.
16Then, as the ark of the LORD came
into the City of David, Michal, Saul's
daughter [David's wife], looked down
from the window above and saw King
David leaping and dancing before the
LORD; and she felt contempt for him in
her heart [because she thought him
undignified].
17They brought in the ark of the LORD
and set it in its place inside the tent
which David had pitched for it; and Da-

---

incredibly arbitrary. How can we possibly understand the mystery that's involved here? Why such tragedy in the midst of this celebration?

The instructions on handling the ark are found in Numbers 4:15,19–20. There it says if you touch the holy things you die. We still don't understand why, but obviously there was more to the ark than anybody could imagine and no human could control it or use it. It was God's, made to be representative of His holiness and glory. God placed such power in the ark that a human would be overwhelmed by it.

We have such a poor sense of the holiness of God that we only see this event from our perspective. Fear and awe must be a part of a healthy relationship with God. While God is love, He is also to be feared.

6:6 *threshing floor.* A threshing floor was a place for processing grain, separating kernels from the chaff (Ru 3:2).

6:7 *for his irreverence.* God had warned His people that not even the Kohathites of the tribe of Levi could touch the holy objects of the tabernacle. All of the holy objects were to be covered by the priests before the sons of Kohath came to carry them "so that they do not touch the holy things, and die" (Nu 4:15).

6:10 *Obed-edom.* Obed-edom was a Levite of the family of Korah, and later one of the doorkeepers for the tabernacle (1Ch 15:18,24; 26:4–8). ***the Gittite.*** He was called the Gittite because he was from the Levitical city of Gath-rimmon (Jos 21:24).

6:14 *linen ephod.* The linen ephod was a short sleeveless garment worn by priests (1Sa 2:18). David wore it to honor the Lord because of his worshipful activities that day (v. 13).

6:17 *the tent which David had pitched for it.* There are no descriptive details of this tent. It is not clear exactly what happened to the tabernacle after it was moved from Shiloh to Nob (1Sa 5; 21:1–5). At the time that David bought the threshing floor from Araunah (24:21–25) the tabernacle of the Lord, which Moses had made in the wilderness, and the altar of burnt offering were in the high place of Gibeon (1Ch 21:29), which was about six miles northwest of Jerusalem.

7 1Sa 6:19 **9** Ps 119:120 **10** 1Ch 13:13 **11** 1Ch 13:14; Ge 39:5 **12** 1Ch 15:25 **13** Nu 4:15; Jos 3:3; 1Ch 15:2,15; See 1Ki 8:5 **14** Ps 30:11; 1Sa 2:18 **15** 1Ch 15:28 **17** 1Ch 16:1; 1Ch 15:1; Ps 132:8; 1Ki 8:5,62,63

vid offered burnt offerings and peace
offerings before the LORD.
18When David had finished offering
the burnt offerings and peace offer-
ings, he blessed the people in the name
of the LORD of hosts (armies),
19and distributed to all the people,
the entire multitude of Israel, both
to men and women, to each a [ring-
shaped] loaf of bread, a cake of dates,
and a cake of raisins. Then all the peo-
ple departed, each to his house.
20Then David returned to bless his
household. But [his wife] Michal the
daughter of Saul came out to meet Da-
vid and said, "How glorious *and* distin-
guished was the king of Israel today,
who uncovered himself *and* stripped
[off his kingly robes] in the eyes of his
servants' maids like one of the riffraff
who shamelessly uncovers himself!"
21So David said to Michal, "It was
before the LORD [that I did this], who
chose me above your father and all his
house, to appoint me as ruler over Is-
rael, the people of the LORD. Therefore
I will celebrate [in pure enjoyment]
before the LORD.
22"Yet I will demean myself *even*
more than this, and will be humbled
(abased) in my own sight [and yours,
as I please], but by the maids whom
you mentioned, by them I shall be held
in honor."
23Michal the daughter of Saul had no
child to the day of her death.

David Plans to Build a Temple

7 WHEN KING David lived in his
house (palace) and the LORD had
given him rest from all his surround-
ing enemies,
2the king said to Nathan the prophet,
"See now, I dwell in a house of cedar,
but the ark of God dwells within tent
curtains."
3And Nathan said to the king, "Go,
do everything that is in your heart, for
the LORD is with you."
4But it happened that night that the
word of the LORD came to Nathan, say-
ing,
5"Go and tell My servant David,
'Thus says the LORD, "Should you be
the one to build Me a house in which
to dwell?
6"For I have not dwelt in a house
since the day I brought the sons (de-
scendants) of Israel up from Egypt,
even to this day; but I have been mov-
ing about in a tent, even in a taber-
nacle.
7"Wherever I have gone with all the
Israelites, did I speak a word to any
from the tribes of Israel, whom I com-
manded to shepherd My people Israel,
asking, 'Why have you not built Me a
house of cedar?' " '

God's Covenant with David

8"So now, say this to My servant
David, 'Thus says the LORD of hosts,

6:18 – 19 *peace offerings.* A distinctive feature of the peace offering was that a portion of it would be eaten by the worshiper as a fellowship meal before the Lord.

6:20 – 23 *uncovered himself.* The love and respect that Michal once had for David was gone. She ridiculed his enthusiasm as he worshiped the Lord, and for David that was not an attitude he could overlook. It is difficult to comprehend the complexities of a marriage where multiple wives and concubines are a part of the picture, and the wife is viewed as chattel before she is viewed as a person. As in so many places in the Bible, the picture is drawn, but without comment on what God thought. Jesus clarifies this a little when He comments on the hardness of hearts, and says, "from the beginning it has not been this way" (Mt 19:8).

7:2 *Nathan.* Nathan was a personal advisor to David. As a prophet, he spoke for God, advising David on religious matters. He also chronicled the reigns of David and Solomon (1Ch 29:29).

7:4 – 17 The Covenant with David — The Davidic covenant contains God's promise to Israel and to David. God promised Israel that Palestine would always be their place (vs. 10). He also promised that David would have an unending dynasty and an everlasting kingdom. This promise is fulfilled in Christ. Both Matthew and Luke, in their Gospels, trace Jesus' ancestry back to David.

---

18 1Ki 8:55 **19** 1Ch 16:3 **20** Ps 30, title; ver. 14,16; Jdg 9:4 **21** 1Sa 13:14 **23** See 1Sa 15:35; Isa 22:14
CHAPTER 7 **1** 1Ch 17:1 **2** 2Sa 5:11; See Ac 7:46; Ex 26:1 **5** 1Ki 5:3; 8:19; 1Ch 22:8 **6** 1Ki 8:16; Ex 40:18,19,34
7 Lev 26:11; Dt 23:14; Mt 2:6; Ac 20:28 **8** 1Sa 16:11,12

"I took you from the pasture, from
following the sheep, to be ruler over
My people Israel.
9"I have been with you wherever you
have gone, and have cut off all your
enemies from before you; and I will
make you a great name, like that of
the great men of the earth.
10"I will appoint a place for My
people Israel and will plant them, so
that they may live in a place of their
own and not be disturbed again. The
wicked will not afflict them again, as
formerly,
11even from the day that I appointed
judges over My people Israel; and I will
give you rest from all your enemies.
The LORD also declares to you that
He will make a house (royal dynasty)
for you.
12"When your days are fulfilled and
you lie down [in death] with your fa-
thers (ancestors), I will raise up your
descendant after you, who shall be
born to you, and I will establish his
kingdom.
13"He [is the one who] shall build a
house for My Name *and* My Presence,
and I will establish the throne of his
kingdom forever.
14"I will be his Father, and he shall
be My son. When he commits iniq-
uity (wrongdoing), I will discipline
him with the rod of men and with the
strokes of the sons of man.
15"But My lovingkindness *and* mer-
cy will not depart from him, as I took
it from Saul, whom I removed from
before you.
16"Your house (royal dynasty) and
your kingdom will endure forever be-
fore Me; your throne will be estab-
lished forever."'"
17Nathan spoke to David in accor-
dance with all these words and all of
this vision.

David's Prayer

18Then King David went in and sat
[in prayer] before the LORD, and said,
"Who am I, O Lord GOD, and what
is my house (family), that You have
brought me this far?
19"Yet this was very insignificant in
Your eyes, O Lord GOD, for You have
spoken also of Your servant's house
(royal dynasty) in the distant future.
And this is the law *and* custom of man,
O Lord GOD.
20"What more can David say to You?
For You know (acknowledge, choose)
Your servant, O Lord GOD.
21"Because of Your word (promise),
and in accordance with Your own
heart, You have done all these great
and astounding things to let Your ser-
vant know (understand).
22"Therefore You are great, O Lord
GOD; for there is none like You, and
there is no God besides You, according
to all that we have heard with our ears.
23"What one nation on earth is like
Your people Israel, whom God went to
redeem for Himself as a people and to
make a name for Himself, and to do
great and awesome things for Your-
self and for Your land, before Your
people whom You have redeemed for
Yourself from Egypt, *from* nations and
their gods?
24"You established for Yourself Your
people Israel as Your people forever,
and You, O LORD, have become their
God.
25"Now, O LORD God, confirm forever
the word [of the covenant] that You

7:13 *the throne of his kingdom forever.* This is not to say that Solomon would rule forever. Rather, the right to rule, represented by the image of the throne, would always belong to his descendants. Further, there would always be a male heir who would be able to rule. Ultimately this promise is fulfilled in Christ (Mt 1).

7:19 *in the distant future.* God extended the promise concerning David's dynasty far into the future. All of human history leads inevitably to the rule of Christ on earth. This is its destiny, its prophetic fulfillment, the final meaning of all history.

9 1Sa 18:14; 2Sa 5:10; 1Sa 31:6 **10** Ps 44:2; 80:8; Jer 24:6; Ps 89:22 **11** Jdg 2:14; 1Sa 12:9; ver. 27; Ex 1:21 **12** 1Ki 2:1; Dt 31:16; Ps 132:11 **13** 1Ki 5:5; 8:19; ver. 16 **14** Heb 1:5; Ps 89:30 **15** 1Sa 15:23,28; 16:14 **16** ver. 13; Jn 12:34 **18** Ge 32:10 **19** Isa 55:8 **20** Ps 139:1 **22** 1Ch 16:25; 2Ch 2:5; Jer 10:6; Dt 3:24; 4:35; 32:39 **23** Ps 147:20; Dt 9:26 **24** Dt 26:18; Ps 48:14

have spoken in regard to Your servant
and his house (royal dynasty); and do
just as You have spoken,
[26]so that Your Name may be magni-
fied forever, saying, 'The LORD of hosts
(armies) is God over Israel;' and may
the house (royal dynasty) of Your ser-
vant David be established before You.
[27]"For You, O LORD of hosts, God of
Israel, have revealed this to Your ser-
vant, saying, 'I will build you a house
(royal dynasty).' For that reason Your
servant has found courage to pray this
prayer to You.
[28]"And now, O Lord GOD, You are
God, and Your words are truth, and
You have promised this good thing to
Your servant.
[29]"Therefore now, may it please You
to bless the house (royal dynasty) of
Your servant, so that it may continue
forever before You; for You, O Lord
GOD, have spoken it, and with Your
blessing may the house of Your servant
be blessed forever."

David's Triumphs

8 NOW IT came about after this that
David defeated the Philistines and
subdued (humbled) them, and he took
control of Metheg-ammah [the main
city] from the hand of the Philistines.
[2]He defeated Moab, and measured
them with a length of rope, making
them lie down on the ground; he mea-
sured two lengths to [choose those to]
put to death, and one full length to
[choose those to] be kept alive. And the
[surviving] Moabites became servants
to David, bringing tribute.
[3]Then David defeated Hadadezer
the son of Rehob, king of Zobah, as he
went to restore his power at the River
[Euphrates].
[4]David captured from him 1,700
horsemen and 20,000 foot soldiers.
David also hamstrung all the chariot
horses (making them lame), but re-
served *enough* of them for a hundred
chariots.
[5]When the Arameans (Syrians) of
Damascus came to help Hadadezer,
king of Zobah, David struck down
22,000 Arameans.
[6]Then David put garrisons among
the Arameans in Damascus, and the
Arameans became his servants and
brought tribute. The LORD helped Da-
vid wherever he went.
[7]David took the shields of gold that
were carried by the servants of Hadad-
ezer, and brought them to Jerusalem.
[8]And from Betah and Berothai, cit-
ies of Hadadezer, King David took an
immense quantity of bronze.
[9]When Toi king of Hamath heard
about David's defeat of all the forces
of Hadadezer,
[10]Toi sent Joram his son to King Da-
vid to greet and congratulate him for
his battle and defeat of Hadadezer; for
Hadadezer had been at war with Toi.
Joram brought with him articles of
silver, gold, and bronze [as gifts].

7:27 *prayer.* David was a king for God, not for himself. It is not likely that he was totally without pride in his position, but he did not seem to be a man who was full of himself. His purpose in wanting to build the temple was to glorify God whom he loved, not to glorify himself. David's prayer of worship and thanksgiving is an intimate key that shows how he was able to keep himself both willing and trusting as he followed God.

7:28 *You are God, and Your words are truth.* This is David's theme, throughout his life, and this is why he was a man after God's heart (1Sa 13:14).

8:2 *Moabites.* The Moabites were descendants of the incestuous relationship between Lot and his older daughter (Ge 19:36 – 37).

8:4 *hamstrung.* David disabled the horses by cutting the back sinews of the hind legs to prevent them from being used for military activity (Jos 11:6,9).

8:5 *Damascus.* Damascus was located at an oasis near the foot of the Anti-Lebanon mountains and was one of the most strategically located cities of the ancient world. Damascus lay at the crossroads of the two main international highways; the Via Maris, leading south and west to Egypt, and the King's Highway, leading from the east side of the Jordan south to Arabia.

8:8 *Berothai.* This city was about 30 miles northwest of Damascus.

---

28 Jn 17:17 **29** 2Sa 22:51 **CHAPTER 8** **2** Nu 24:17; See 1Sa 10:27 **3** 2Sa 10:6; Ps 60, title; See Ge 15:18
4 Jos 11:6,9 **5** 1Ki 11:23 **6** ver. 14; 2Sa 7:9 **7** See 1Ki 10:16 **10** 1Ch 18:10

11King David also dedicated these [gifts] to the LORD, along with the silver and gold that he had dedicated from all the nations which he subdued:

12from Aram (Syria), Moab, the Ammonites, the Philistines, and Amalek, and from the spoil of Hadadezer the son of Rehob, king of Zobah.

13So David made a name *for himself* when he returned from killing 18,000 Arameans (Syrians) in the Valley of Salt.

14He put garrisons in Edom; in all Edom he put garrisons, and all the Edomites became servants to David. And the LORD helped him wherever he went.

15So David reigned over all Israel, and continued to administer justice and righteousness for all his people.

16Joab the son of Zeruiah was [commander] over the army; Jehoshaphat the son of Ahilud was recorder (secretary);

17Zadok the son of Ahitub and Ahimelech the son of Abiathar were the [chief] priests, and Seraiah was the scribe;

18Benaiah the son of Jehoiada was [head] over both the Cherethites and Pelethites [the king's bodyguards]; and David's sons were chief [confidential] advisers (officials) [to the king]. [1 Chr 18:17]

David's Kindness to Mephibosheth

9 AND DAVID said, "Is there still anyone left of the house (family) of Saul to whom I may show kindness for Jonathan's sake?"

2There was a servant of the house of Saul whose name was Ziba, so they called him to David. And the king said to him, "Are you Ziba?" He said, "*I am* your servant."

3And the king said, "Is there no longer anyone *left* of the house (family) of Saul to whom I may show the goodness *and* graciousness of God?" Ziba replied to the king, "There is still a son of Jonathan, [one] whose feet are crippled." [1 Sam 20:14–17]

4So the king said to him, "Where is he?" And Ziba replied to the king, "He is in the house of Machir the son of Ammiel, in Lo-debar."

5Then King David sent *word* and had him brought from the house of Machir the son of Ammiel, from Lo-debar.

6Mephibosheth the son of Jonathan, the son of Saul, came to David and fell face down and lay himself down [in respect]. David said, "Mephibosheth." And he answered, "Here is your servant!"

7David said to him, "Do not be afraid, for I will certainly show you kindness for the sake of your father Jonathan, and will restore to you all the land of your grandfather Saul; and you shall always eat at my table."

8Again Mephibosheth lay himself face down and said, "What is your servant, that you would be concerned for a dead dog like me?"

9Then the king summoned Ziba, Saul's servant, and said to him, "I have given your master's grandson everything that belonged to Saul and to all his house (family).

8:15 *David reigned over all Israel.* As a result of David's conquests, the sovereignty of Israel extended from the Gulf of Aqaba and the River of Egypt to the Euphrates River — the very region God had promised Abraham (Ge 15:18).

9:1 – 13 *kindness.* David wrote in Psalm 23:5, "You prepare a table before me in the presence of my enemies." And that is just what David did for Mephibosheth, for the sake of his father Jonathan. Jonathan and David had been separated by the hostility that Saul had for David, and as far as Mephibosheth would have understood, David was an enemy to the house of Saul. But the bond of love and friendship that David and Jonathan had was greater than the hostility of Saul, and David was faithful to honor those bonds.

9:4 *Machir the son of Ammiel.* Machir was a man, apparently of wealth and position, who extended hospitality to David during Absalom's revolt (17:27 – 29). He showed himself to be a man of kindness who was willing to help someone in need, even if it might not be politically expedient.

11 1Ki 7:51 **13** 2Ki 14:7; See 1Ch 18:12; Ps 60, title **14** Ge 27:29,37,40; Nu 24:18 **16** 2Sa 19:13; 20:23; 1Ch 11:6; 1Ki 4:3 **17** 1Ch 24:3 **18** 1Ch 18:17; 1Sa 30:14 **CHAPTER 9** **1** 1Sa 18:3; Pr 27:10 **2** 2Sa 16:1; 19:17,29 **3** 1Sa 20:14; 2Sa 4:4 **4** 2Sa 17:27 **8** 2Sa 16:9 **9** 2Sa 16:4; 19:29

THE KINGDOM IN DAVID'S DAYS

10“You and your sons and your ser-
vants shall cultivate the land for him,
and you shall bring in *the produce,*
so that your master’s grandson may
have food to eat; but Mephibosheth,
your master’s grandson, shall always
eat at my table.” Now Ziba had fifteen
sons and twenty servants.
11Then Ziba said to the king, “Your
servant will do according to everything
that my lord the king commands.” So
Mephibosheth ate at David’s table as
one of the king’s sons.
12Mephibosheth had a young son
whose name was Mica. And all who
lived in Ziba’s house were servants to
Mephibosheth.
13So Mephibosheth lived in Jeru-
salem, for he always ate at the king’s
table. And he was lame in both feet.

Ammon and Aram Defeated

10 NOW IT happened later that [Na-
hash] the king of the Ammonites
died, and his son Hanun became king
in his place.
2Then David said, “I will show kind-
ness to Hanun the son of Nahash, just
as his father did to me.” So David sent
[a letter along with] some of his ser-
vants to console him in regard to his
father’s death; and David’s servants
came into the land of the Ammonites.
3But the princes of the Ammonites
[were suspicious and] said to Hanun
their lord, “Do you think that David
is honoring your father because he
has sent comforters to you? Has David
not sent his servants to you in order
to search the city, to spy it out and
overthrow it?”
4So Hanun took David’s servants
and shaved off half their beards, and
cut off their robes in the middle as far
as their hips, and sent them away.
5When David was informed, he sent
[messengers] to meet them [before they
reached Jerusalem], for the men were
greatly ashamed *and* humiliated. And
the king said, “Stay at Jericho until
your beards grow, and *then* return.”
6When the Ammonites saw that
they had become an object of hatred
to David, they sent *word* and hired the
Arameans (Syrians) of Beth-rehob and
the Arameans of Zobah, 20,000 foot
soldiers, and the king of Maacah with
1,000 men, and the men of Tob with
12,000 men [to fight for them].
7When David heard about it, he sent
Joab and the entire army, the strong
and brave men.
8The Ammonites came out and lined
up for battle at the entrance of the [city]
gate, but the Arameans of Zobah and
Rehob and the men of Tob and Maacah
were [stationed] by themselves in the
field.
9Now when Joab saw that the bat-
tlefront was against him in front and
in the rear, he selected some of all the
choice men in Israel and set them in

9:11 *as one of the king’s sons.* David kept his promise to Jonathan. The two young men had vowed that the Lord would be between them, and between their descendants forever (1Sa 20:42). It was a way of saying that the Lord would always be in their relationships with each other, keeping them loyal, kind, honest, and willing to bear each other’s burdens. Now Jonathan’s son was provided for as one of David’s sons.
10:1 *the king of the Ammonites.* The king of Ammon was probably the same Nahash who was defeated by Saul at Jabesh-gilead (1Sa 11:1 – 11).
10:2 *as his father did to me.* The occasion of Nahash’s kindness is not recorded. One possibility is that Nahash, an enemy of Saul, had given aid to David during his war with Ish-bosheth (2:8 – 4:12).
10:6 *Beth-rehob and . . . Zobah.* These two Aramean city-states were located north of Israel. ***Maacah.*** The small Aramean kingdom east of the Jordan was part of the territory assigned to the half-tribe of Manasseh (Jos 12:5; 13:11) ***Tob.*** Tob was also an area east of the Jordan, but not a part of Israel (Jdg 11:3).
10:8 *at the entrance of the [city] gate.* Some cities had multiple gates. If attackers broke through one gate, they would find another gate in front of them. The Ammonites fought near the entrance of the city so they could retreat behind the city gates if the battle turned against them. The mercenary soldiers were in more exposed positions in the field.

10 ver. 7,11,13; 2Sa 19:28; 2Sa 19:17 **12** 1Ch 8:34 **13** ver. 7,10; 2Ki 25:29; ver. 3 **CHAPTER 10** **1** 1Ch 19:1
4 Isa 20:4; 47:2 **6** Ge 34:30; Ex 5:21; 1Sa 13:4; 2Sa 8:3,5 **7** 2Sa 23:8 **8** ver. 6

battle formation to meet the Arameans
(Syrians).
10But he placed the rest of the men
in the hand of his brother Abishai, and
he placed them in battle formation to
meet the Ammonites.
11Joab said [to Abishai], "If the Ar-
ameans are too strong for me, then you
shall help me; but if the Ammonites
are too strong for you, I will come to
help you.
12"Be courageous, and let us show
ourselves courageous for the benefit
of our people and the cities of our God.
And may the LORD do what is good in
His sight."
13So Joab and the people who were
with him approached the battle against
the Arameans, and they fled before
him.
14When the Ammonites saw that
the Arameans had fled, they also
fled before Abishai and entered the
city. So Joab returned from *battling*
against the Ammonites and came to
Jerusalem.
15When the Arameans saw that they
were defeated by Israel, they gathered
together.
16Hadadezer sent *word* and brought
out the Arameans who were beyond
the River [Euphrates]; and they came
to Helam; and Shobach the command-
er of the army of Hadadezer led them.
17When David was informed, he
gathered all Israel together and crossed
the Jordan, and came to Helam. Then
the Arameans assembled in battle
formation to meet David and fought
against him.
18But the Arameans fled before Is-
rael, and David killed 700 Aramean
charioteers and 40,000 horsemen, and
struck Shobach the commander of
their army, and he died there.
19When all the kings serving Hadad-
ezer saw that they had been defeated
by Israel, they made peace with Israel
and served them. So the Arameans
(Syrians) were afraid to help the Am-
monites anymore.

Bathsheba, David's Great Sin

11 THEN IT happened in the spring,
at the time when the kings go out
to battle, that David sent Joab and his
servants with him, and all [the fighting
men of] Israel, and they destroyed the
Ammonites and besieged Rabbah. But
David remained in Jerusalem.
2One evening David got up from his
couch and was walking on the [flat]
roof of the king's palace, and from
there he saw a woman bathing; and
she was very beautiful in appearance.
3David sent *word* and inquired about
the woman. *Someone* said, "Is this not
Bathsheba, the daughter of Eliam, the
wife of Uriah the Hittite?"
4David sent messengers and took
her. When she came to him, he lay
with her. And when she was purified
from her uncleanness, she returned to
her house.
5The woman conceived; and she sent
word and told David, "I am pregnant."
6Then David sent *word* to Joab, *say-
ing,* "Send me Uriah the Hittite." So
Joab sent Uriah to David.
7When Uriah came to him, David
asked him how Joab was, how the peo-
ple were doing, and how the war was
progressing.
8Then David said to Uriah, "Go

10:10 *Abishai.* Abishai was one of David's mighty men (23:18). He was a brave warrior (1Sa 26:6 – 9) and a successful commander (1Ch 18:12 – 13), but was impetuous and perhaps even bloodthirsty (16:9; 19:21). He had played a part in the murder of Abner.

11:1 *in the spring, at the time when the kings go out to battle.* Spring was a good time to mount a campaign. They could be assured of good weather and an abundance of food along the way.

11:2 *from there he saw a woman bathing.* She was probably in the enclosed courtyard of her home, a place of privacy, not visible from the street.

11:5 *The woman conceived.* The law commanded both parties in an adulterous relationship to be put to death (Lev 20:10). In practice, a woman who became pregnant might be forced to bear the shame and guilt alone (Jn 8:1 – 11).

---

12 Dt 31:6; 1Sa 4:9; 1Co 16:13; 1Sa 3:18 **19** 2Sa 8:6 **CHAPTER 11** **1** 1Ch 20:1 **2** Dt 22:8; Ge 34:2; Job 31:1; Mt 5:28 **3** 2Sa 23:39 **4** Ps 51, title; Jas 1:14; Lev 15:19,28; 18:19 **8** Ge 18:4; 19:2

down to your house, and wash your feet (spend time at home)." Uriah left the king's palace, and a gift from the king was sent out after him.
[9]But Uriah slept at the entrance of the king's palace with all the servants of his lord, and did not go down to his house.
[10]When they told David, "Uriah did not go down to his house," David said to Uriah, "Have you not [just] come from a [long] journey? Why did you not go to your house?"
[11]Uriah said to David, "The ark and Israel and Judah are staying in huts (temporary shelters), and my lord Joab and the servants of my lord are camping in the open field. Should I go to my house to eat and drink and lie with my wife? By your life and the life of your soul, I will not do this thing."
[12]Then David said to Uriah, "Stay here today as well, and tomorrow I will let you leave." So Uriah remained in Jerusalem that day and the next.
[13]Now David called him [to dinner], and he ate and drank with him, so that he made Uriah drunk; in the evening he went out to lie on his bed with the servants of his lord, and [still] did not go down to his house.
[14]In the morning David wrote a letter to Joab and sent it with Uriah.
[15]He wrote in the letter, "Put Uriah in the front line of the heaviest fighting and leave him, so that he may be struck down and die."
[16]So it happened that as Joab was besieging the city, he assigned Uriah to the place where he knew the [enemy's] valiant men were *positioned*.
[17]And the men of the city came out and fought against Joab, and some of the people among the servants of David fell; Uriah the Hittite also died.
[18]Then Joab sent *word* and informed David of all the events of the war.
[19]And he commanded the messenger, "When you have finished reporting all the events of the war to the king,
[20]then if the king becomes angry and he says to you, 'Why did you go so near to the city to fight? Did you not know that they would shoot [arrows] from the wall?
[21]'Who killed Abimelech the son of Jerubbesheth (Gideon)? Was it not a woman who threw an upper millstone on him from the wall so that he died at Thebez? Why did you go so near the wall?' Then you shall say, 'Your servant Uriah the Hittite is also dead.'" [Judg 9:35, 53]
[22]So the messenger left, and he came and told David everything that Joab had sent him *to report*.
[23]The messenger said to David, "The men indeed prevailed against us and came out to us in the field, but we were on them *and* pushed them as far as the entrance of the [city] gate.
[24]"Then the archers shot at your servants from the wall. Some of the king's servants are dead, and your servant Uriah the Hittite is also dead."
[25]Then David said to the messenger, "Tell Joab this, 'Do not let this thing disturb you, for the sword devours one [side] as well as another. Strengthen your battle against the city and overthrow it'; and so encourage Joab."
[26]When Uriah's wife [Bathsheba] heard that her husband Uriah was dead, she mourned for her husband.
[27]And when the time of mourning was past, David sent *word* and had her brought to his house, and she became his wife and bore him a son. But the thing that David had done [with Bathsheba] was evil in the sight of the LORD.

Nathan Rebukes David

12 AND THE LORD sent Nathan [the prophet] to David. He came and said to him,

"There were two men in a city, one
rich and the other poor.
[2]"The rich man had a very large
number of flocks and herds,

11:21 *Was it not a woman.* The story referred to here is recorded in Judges 9:50 – 55. For a soldier to die at the hand of a woman was at best, shameful, if not a point of ridicule (Jdg 4:17 – 24). It seems that Joab was letting David know that he knew David's real reasons for wanting Uriah dead.

11 2Sa 7:2,6; 2Sa 20:6 **13** Ge 19:33,35; ver. 9 **14** See 1Ki 21:8,9 **15** 2Sa 12:9 **21** Jdg 6:32; 9:53 **27** 2Sa 12:9
CHAPTER 12 **1** Ps 51, title; See 2Sa 14:5; 1Ki 20:35-41; Isa 5:3

3 But the poor man had nothing but
one little ewe lamb
Which he had purchased and
nourished;
And it grew up together with him
and his children.
It ate his food, drank from his cup,
it lay in his arms,
And was like a daughter to him.
4 "Now a traveler (visitor) came to
the rich man,
And to avoid taking one from his
own flock or herd
To prepare [a meal] for the traveler
who had come to him,
He took the poor man's ewe lamb
and prepared it for his guest."
5 Then David's anger burned intensely
against the man, and he said to Na-
than, "As the LORD lives, the man who
has done this deserves to die.
6 "He shall make restitution for the
ewe lamb four times as much [as the
lamb was worth], because he did this
thing and had no compassion."
7 Then Nathan said to David, "You
are the man! Thus says the LORD, the
God of Israel, 'I anointed you as king
over Israel, and I spared you from the
hand of Saul.
8 'I also gave you your master's house,
and put your master's wives into your
care *and* under your protection, and I
gave you the house (royal dynasty) of
Israel and of Judah; and if *that had*
been too little, I would have given you
much more!
9 'Why have you despised the word
of the LORD by doing evil in His sight?
You have struck down Uriah the Hit-
tite with the sword and have taken his
wife to be your wife. You have killed
him with the sword of the Ammonites.
[Lev 20:10; 24:17]
10 'Now, therefore, the sword shall
never depart from your house, because
you have despised Me and have taken
the wife of Uriah the Hittite to be your
wife.'
11 "Thus says the LORD, 'Behold, I will
stir up evil against you from your own
household; and I will take your wives
before your eyes and give them to your
companion, and he will lie with your
wives in broad daylight.
12 'Indeed you did it secretly, but I
will do this thing before all Israel, and
in broad daylight.' " [2 Sam 16:21, 22]
13 David said to Nathan, "I have
sinned against the LORD." And Na-
than said to David, "The LORD also
has allowed your sin to pass [without
further punishment]; you shall not
die. [Ps 51]
14 "Nevertheless, because by this
deed you have given [a great] oppor-
tunity to the enemies of the LORD to
blaspheme [Him], the son that is born
to you shall certainly die."
15 Then Nathan went [back] to his
home.

12:7 *You are the man.* It took courage and a strong commitment to the Lord for Nathan to speak these words to the king. Nathan's rebuke was centered on who the Lord is, and what the Lord expects of His servants. It was the word of the Lord that convicted David, not the force of Nathan's character or rhetoric.

12:9 *despised the word of the LORD.* David had broken the commandments about coveting, adultery, and murder (Ex 20:13–17). The word despised means "to think lightly of."

12:13 *I have sinned against the LORD.* David did not attempt to rationalize his sin or make an excuse for himself. A fuller expression of David's confession is found in Psalm 51. ***you shall not die.*** David deserved death (Lev 20:10; Nu 35:31–33), but God's grace is able to circumvent His own plan for punishment.

12:14 Adultery — Adultery is forbidden in the Ten Commandments (Ex 20:14), and it is not difficult to think of a long list of the messy problems that accompany adultery. But adultery is not just a problem involving other people. It is also a problem with God. It is a direct and deliberate disobedience of a nonnegotiable command. This kind of disobedience is also a choice to stop listening to God in other areas — not because He won't communicate, but because we won't. We don't want to ask for help because we don't want to hear Him say, "And what about the affair with ___?" Adultery is more expensive than we can calculate.

6 Ex 22:1; Lk 19:8 **7** 1Sa 16:13 **9** See 1Sa 15:19; Nu 15:31; 2Sa 11:15-17,27 **10** Am 7:9 **11** Dt 28:30; 2Sa 16:22 **12** 2Sa 16:22 **13** See 1Sa 15:24; 2Sa 24:10; Job 7:20; Pr 28:13; 2Sa 24:10; Job 7:21; Mic 7:18; Zec 3:4 **14** Isa 52:5; Eze 36:20,23; Ro 2:24

Loss of a Child

And the LORD struck the child that Uriah's widow bore to David, and he was very sick.

16 David therefore appealed to God for the child [to be healed]; and David fasted and went in and lay all night on the ground.

17 The elders of his household stood by him [in the night] to lift him up from the ground, but he was unwilling [to get up] and would not eat food with them.

18 Then it happened on the seventh day that the child died. David's servants were afraid to tell him that the child was dead, for they said, "While the child was still alive, we spoke to him and he would not listen to our voices. How then can we tell him the child is dead, since he might harm himself [or us]?"

19 But when David saw that his servants were whispering to one another, he realized that the child was dead. So David said to them, "Is the child dead?" And they said, "He is dead."

20 Then David got up from the ground, washed, anointed *himself* [with olive oil], changed his clothes, and went into the house of the LORD and worshiped. Then he came [back] to his own house, and when he asked, they set food before him and he ate.

21 Then his servants said to him, "What is this thing that you have done? While the child was alive you fasted and wept, but when the child died, you got up and ate food."

22 David said, "While the child was still alive, I fasted and wept; for I thought, 'Who knows, the LORD may be gracious to me and the child may live.'

23 "But now he is dead; why should I [continue to] fast? Can I bring him back again? I will go to him [when I die], but he will not return to me."

Solomon Born

24 David comforted his wife Bathsheba, and went to her and lay with her; and she gave birth to a son, and David named him Solomon. And the LORD loved the child;

25 and He sent *word* through Nathan the prophet, and he named him Jedidiah (beloved of the LORD) for the sake of the LORD [who loved the child].

War Again

26 Now Joab fought against Rabbah of the Ammonites and captured the royal city.

27 Joab sent messengers to David and said, "I have fought against Rabbah; I have even taken the city of waters.

28 "So now, assemble the rest of the men, and camp against the city and capture it, or I will take the city myself, and it will be named after me."

29 So David gathered all the men together and went to Rabbah, then fought against it and captured it.

30 And he took the crown of their king from his head; it weighed a talent of gold, and [set in it was] a precious stone; and it was *placed* on David's head. And he brought the spoil out of the city in great amounts.

31 He also brought out the people who were there, and put them to [work with] the saws and sharp iron instruments and iron axes, and made them work at the brickkiln. And he did this to all the Ammonite cities. Then David and all the men returned to Jerusalem.

Amnon and Tamar

13 IT HAPPENED afterwards that Absalom the son of David had a beautiful sister whose name was Tamar, and Amnon [her half brother] the son of David was in love with her.

12:24 *Solomon.* The name Solomon is related to the Hebrew word for *peace.*

12:25 *Jedidiah.* The name Jedidiah means "beloved of the Lord." The Hebrew name is related to David's name, meaning "beloved." This name, coming from the prophet Nathan, surely must have comforted David and Bathsheba with assurance of God's forgiveness.

12:30 *a talent of gold.* The crown weighed about 75 pounds.

13:1 Temptation — Not all temptation is equal. Some kinds of temptations are easily squelched,

---

16 2Sa 13:31 **20** Job 1:20 **22** See Isa 38:1,5; Jnh 3:9 **23** Job 7:8-10 **24** Mt 1:6; 1Ch 22:9 **26** 1Ch 20:1; Dt 3:11 **30** 1Ch 20:2 **CHAPTER 13** **1** 2Sa 3:2,3; 1Ch 3:9

2 Amnon was so frustrated because
of his [half-] sister Tamar that he made
himself sick, for she was a virgin, and
Amnon thought it impossible for him
to do anything to her.
3 But Amnon had a friend whose
name was Jonadab the son of Shimeah,
David's brother; and Jonadab was a
very shrewd (cunning) man.
4 He said to Amnon, "Why are you,
the king's son, so depressed morning
after morning? Will you not tell me?"
And Amnon said to him, "I am in love
with Tamar, my [half-] brother Absa-
lom's sister."
5 Jonadab said to him, "Go to bed and
pretend you are sick; and when your
father [David] comes to see you, say
to him, 'Just let my sister Tamar come
and serve me food, and let her prepare
it in my sight, so that I may see it and
eat it from her hand.' "
6 So Amnon lay down and pretended
to be sick; and when the king came
to see him, Amnon said to the king,
"Please let my sister Tamar come and
make me a couple of cakes in my sight,
so that I may eat from her hand."
7 Then David sent *word* to the house
for Tamar, saying, "Go now to your
brother Amnon's house, and prepare
some food for him."
8 So Tamar went to her brother Am-
non's house, and he was in bed. And
she took dough and kneaded it, and
made cakes in his sight, and baked
them.
9 She took the pan and dished them
out before him, but he refused to eat.
And Amnon said, "Have everyone
leave me." So everyone left him [except
Tamar].
10 Then Amnon said to Tamar, "Bring
the food into the bedroom, so that I
may eat from your hand." So Tamar
took the cakes she had made and
brought them into the bedroom to her
[half-] brother Amnon.
11 When she brought them to him
to eat, he took hold of her and said,
"Come, lie with me, my sister."
12 She replied, "No, my brother! Do
not violate me, for such a thing is not
done in Israel; do not do this disgrace-
ful thing! [Gen 34:7]
13 "As for me, how could I get rid of
my shame *and* disgrace? And you, you
will be considered one of the fools in
Israel. So now, just speak to the king
[about taking me as your wife], for he
will not withhold me from you."
14 But he would not listen to her; and
since he was stronger than she, he
violated her and lay with her.
15 Then Amnon became extremely
hateful toward her, for his hatred to-
ward her was greater than the love
which he had for her. And Amnon said
to her, "Get up and get out!"
16 But she said, "No, because this
wrong of sending me away is worse
than the other that you have done to
me!" But he would not listen to her.
17 Instead, he called his young man
who was his personal servant and said,
"Now throw this woman out of my
presence and bolt the door behind her."
18 Now Tamar was wearing a [long-
sleeved] robe of various colors; for
that is how the virgin daughters of

and others must be fought with vigilance and every ounce of energy that we have. The battle begins in the mind, and one of the first steps in combating temptation is to make up one's mind that the answer must be "no." Once we begin thinking of how nice it would be to give in, the temptation has a foothold that can grow into full blown sin. God always provides a way out, but we have to want to take that way (1Co 10:13).

13:4 *I am in love with Tamar, my [half-] brother Absalom's sister.* Such relationships are clearly forbidden in the law (Lev 18:9, 29; 20:17). The lust that he conceived in his heart gave birth to sin, and that sin, when accomplished, brought death (Jas 1:15). Amnon did die, but even worse, his heart was hardened so that he did not care what he had done to Tamar. For her, the price of his wickedness was very high.

13:17 *throw this woman out.* It is difficult to translate the contempt which Amnon had for Tamar. His order to his servant suggests the words and tone used when asking a servant to dump trash. If she had not been his sister, Amnon would have been forced to marry her (Dt 22:28 – 29).

3 See 1Sa 16:9 **6** Ge 18:6 **9** Ge 45:1 **11** Ge 39:12 **12** Lev 18:9,11; 20:17; Ge 34:7; Jdg 19:23; 20:6 **13** See Lev 18:9,11 **14** Dt 22:25; See 2Sa 12:11 **18** Ge 37:3; Jdg 5:30

the king dressed themselves in robes.
Then Amnon's personal servant took
her out and bolted the door behind her.
19 So Tamar put dust on her head [in
grief] and tore the long-sleeved robe
which she had on, and she put her hand
on her head and went away crying out
[for help].
20 So her brother Absalom said to her,
"Has your brother Amnon been with
you? But now keep silent, my sister; he
is your brother; do not take this matter
to heart." So Tamar remained secluded
in her brother Absalom's house.
21 Now when King David heard about
all these things, he was very angry
[but failed to take any action].
22 But Absalom did not speak to Am-
non either good or bad; for Absalom
hated Amnon because he had violated
his sister Tamar.
23 Now it came about after two full
years that Absalom had sheepshear-
ers at Baal-hazor near Ephraim, and
Absalom invited all the king's sons
[to a party].

Absalom Avenges Tamar

24 Absalom came to [his father] the
king and said, "Behold, your servant
has sheepshearers; please let the king
and his servants go with your servant."
25 But the king said to Absalom, "No,
my son, we should not all go, for we will
be a burden to you." Although Absalom
[strongly] urged David, still he would
not go, but he gave him his blessing.
26 Then Absalom said, "If not, then
at least let my brother Amnon go with
us." And the king said to him, "Why
should he go with you?"
27 But Absalom urged him [again],
and he let Amnon and all the king's
sons go with him.
28 Now Absalom commanded his ser-
vants, "Notice carefully, when Am-
non's heart is joyous with wine, and
when I say to you, 'Strike Amnon,'
then kill him. Do not be afraid; have
I not commanded you myself [and in
doing so have I not taken full respon-
sibility for his death]? Be courageous
and brave."
29 So the servants of Absalom did
to Amnon just as Absalom had com-
manded. Then all the king's sons got
up, and every man mounted his mule
and fled.
30 Now it happened while they were
on the way [back home], that the [exag-
gerated] report came to David, "Absa-
lom has killed all the king's sons, and
not one of them is left."
31 Then the king stood and tore his
clothes and lay on the ground [in
mourning]; and all his servants were
standing by with their clothes torn.
32 But Jonadab the son of Shimeah,
David's brother, responded, "Do not
let my lord assume that all the king's
sons have been put to death; for only
Amnon is dead. This *act of revenge*
has been on Absalom's mind since the
day Amnon violated his sister Tamar.

13:19 *dust on her head . . . tore the long-sleeved robe . . . put her hand on her head.* All of these gestures, as well as her public weeping, were traditional signs of mourning. Amnon had wantonly destroyed her, and there was nothing anyone could do to set her life right. Women who have been raped often feel abandoned by society, and the very people who should have protected them are oblivious to their need for comfort. Rape is a private crime, and yet it is also a very public menace. It is difficult to redress the wrongs caused by rape without subjecting the victim to more publicity than is comfortable for someone who has already been severely traumatized.

13:21 *very angry.* David was angry, but he took no steps to discipline his son. Perhaps he felt he could not enforce exile on his son (Lev 18:9,29; 20:17), when the Lord had forgiven him in a similar circumstance. The big difference between David and Amnon was that David acknowledged his sin and was remorseful and repentant.

13:23 *Ephraim.* This does not refer to the tribal area, but to a city about 13 miles north of Jerusalem (Jn 11:54).

13:29 *mule.* The mule, the offspring of a donkey and a horse, combines the size and strength of a horse with the surefootedness and endurance of a donkey. Although the Israelites were forbidden to breed such hybrids (Lev 19:19), mules were imported into Israel. They were the preferred mount of royalty during this period. (18:9; 1Ki 1:33).

---

19 Jos 7:6; 2Sa 1:2; Job 2:12; Jer 2:37 **22** Ge 24:50; 31:24; Lev 19:17,18 **23** See Ge 38:12,13; 1Sa 25:4,36
28 Jdg 19:6,9,22; Ru 3:7; 1Sa 25:36; Est 1:10 **31** 2Sa 1:11; 2Sa 12:16 **32** ver. 3

33"So now, do not let my lord the
king take the report to heart that all
the king's sons are dead; for Amnon
alone is dead."
34Now Absalom fled. And the young
man who kept watch looked up, and
behold, many people were coming
from the road behind him by the side
of the mountain.
35And Jonadab said to the king,
"Look, the king's sons are coming.
It has turned out just as your servant
said."
36And when he finished speaking,
the king's sons came, and they raised
their voices and wept; and the king and
all his servants also wept very bitterly.
37But Absalom fled and went to [his
mother's father] Talmai the son of Ammihud,
king of Geshur. And David
mourned for his son every day.
38So Absalom fled and went to Geshur,
and was there for three years.
39And *the heart of* King David
longed to go to Absalom; for he was
comforted regarding Amnon, since
he was dead.

The Woman of Tekoa

14 NOW JOAB the son of Zeruiah
knew that the king's heart
longed for Absalom.
2So Joab sent *word* to Tekoa and had
a wise woman brought from there and
told her, "Please pretend to be a mourner,
and put on mourning clothes, and
do not anoint yourself with oil, but act
like a woman who has for many days
been in mourning for the dead.
3"Then go to the king and speak to
him in this way." So Joab told her what
to say.
4When the woman of Tekoa spoke
to the king, she bowed with her face to
the ground and lay herself down, and
said, "Help, O king."
5The king asked her, "What is the
matter?" She said, "Truly I am a widow;
my husband is dead.
6"Your maidservant had two sons,
but the two of them struggled *and*
fought in the field. There was no one
to separate them, so one struck the
other and killed him.
7"Now behold, the entire family has
risen against your maidservant, and
they say, 'Hand over the one who killed
his brother, so that we may put him to
death [to pay] for the life of his brother
whom he killed and destroy the heir
also.' By doing this they will extinguish
my coal that is left, leaving my
husband without a name or a remnant
(heir) on the face of the earth."
8Then David said to the woman, "Go
to your home, and I will give orders
concerning you."
9The woman of Tekoa said to the
king, "My lord, O king, the guilt is on
me and on my father's house, but the
king and his throne are guiltless."
10The king said, "If anyone speaks
to you [about this matter], bring him
to me [for judgment], and he will not
touch you again."
11Then she said, "Please let the king
remember the LORD your God, so that
the avenger of blood will not continue
to destroy, otherwise they will destroy
my son." And David said, "As the LORD
lives, not a single hair [from the head]
of your son shall fall to the ground."
12Then the woman said, "Please let

13:37 *Talmai.* Talmai was Absalom's grandfather, the father of David's wife Maacah (3:3). He ruled as king of the territory of Geshur, northeast of the Sea of Galilee.

14:7 *extinguish my coal that is left.* The woman used a graphic picture of the extinction of her family. The demise of a family name and the end of a surviving remnant or family line were crucial matters to the Hebrew people.

14:11 *avenger of blood.* The Hebrew phrase, "avenger of blood" or "redeemer of blood" is closely related to the term "kinsman redeemer." The kinsman redeemer is the protector of family rights. Here, the protector of the family would be expected to bring vengeance on one who had taken the life of a family member. Cities of refuge had been established under Moses for protection from a blood avenger in cases where the killing was accidental (Nu 35:9 – 34).

33 2Sa 19:19 **34** ver. 38 **37** 2Sa 3:3 **38** 2Sa 14:23,32; 15:8 **39** Ge 38:12 **CHAPTER 14** **1** 2Sa 13:39 **2** 2Ch 11:6; See Ru 3:3 **3** ver. 19; Ex 4:15 **4** 1Sa 20:41; 2Sa 1:2; See 2Ki 6:26,28 **5** See 2Sa 12:1 **9** Ge 27:13; 1Sa 25:24; Mt 27:25; 2Sa 3:28,29; 1Ki 2:33 **11** Nu 35:19; 1Sa 14:45; Ac 27:34

your maidservant speak *one more* word to my lord the king." He said, "Speak."

13 The woman said, "Now why have you planned such a thing against God's people? For in speaking this word the king is like a guilty man, in that the king does not bring back his banished one.

14 "For we will certainly die and are like water that is spilled on the ground and cannot be gathered up again. Yet God does not [simply] take away life, but devises plans so that the one who is banished is not driven away from Him.

15 "Now I came to speak of this matter to my lord the king because the people have made me afraid. So your maidservant thought, 'I will just speak to the king; perhaps the king will do what his maidservant requests.

16 'For the king will hear and save his maidservant from the hand of the man who would destroy me and my son together from the inheritance of God.'

17 "Then your maidservant said, 'Please let the word of my lord the king be comforting, for my lord the king is as the angel of God to discern good and evil. May the LORD your God be with you.' "

18 Then the king answered and said to the woman, "Do not hide from me anything that I ask you." And the woman said, "Let my lord the king please speak."

19 The king said, "Is the hand of Joab with you in all of this?" And the woman answered, "As your soul lives, my lord the king, no one can turn to the right or to the left from anything that my lord the king has said. Indeed, it was your servant Joab who commanded me; he put all these words in the mouth of your maidservant.

20 "In order to change the appearance of things [between Absalom and you, his father] your servant Joab did this thing. But my lord has wisdom like the wisdom of the angel of God, to know everything that is in the earth."

Absalom Is Recalled

21 Then the king said to Joab, "Listen, I will most certainly do this thing; now go, bring back the young man Absalom."

22 Joab bowed his face toward the ground and lay himself down and blessed the king. Then Joab said, "Today your servant knows that I have found favor in your sight, my lord, O king, in that the king has done the request of his servant."

23 So Joab got up, went to Geshur, and brought Absalom to Jerusalem.

24 However, the king said, "Let him go to his own house, and do not let him see my face." So Absalom went

---

14:14 Restoration — The wise woman from Tekoa spoke compellingly of Absalom's (the banished one's) need to make things right with God. David, whose heart was leaning toward his son, was touched, and he brought Absalom back. But no restoration took place. Neither Absalom nor David discussed how they had failed to seek justice according to law in the case of Amnon and Tamar. Restoration is only possible if we are willing to look sin in the face and acknowledge the need to repent before God and turn to new and righteous ways.

It is difficult to know exactly what the woman is saying to David, because she is speaking with double meanings. On the surface is her made-up story, which is supposed to speak allegorically to David. In this instance she is referring to the fact that because "her son" did not kill "his brother" in pre-meditated murder, he should have found safety in a city of refuge. Absalom, however, did kill his brother in pre-meditated murder. The mitigating factor is that Amnon should have been banished for his rape of Tamar, and the king, Tamar's first protector, had done nothing. Absalom was the next in line as near relative of Tamar, so there was some justice in his desire to bring Amnon to account.

14:19 *hand of Joab.* The exact extent of the under-game Joab was playing is not explained. Joab had been a difficult force in David's life (13:37–39). Joab had killed Abner in a way that David considered unjust, and it was Joab who arranged Uriah's death for David. These factors, and the fact that Joab was in some way sponsoring Absalom's return, made the relationship between David and Joab uneasy. The old trust was gone.

14:24 *do not let him see my face.* Absalom was allowed to return, but his position was not restored. There were issues of justice that had

---

13 Jdg 20:2; 2Sa 13:37,38 **14** Job 34:15; Heb 9:27; Nu 35:15,25,28 **17** ver. 20; 2Sa 19:27 **19** ver. 3 **20** ver. 17; 2Sa 19:27 **23** 2Sa 13:37 **24** Ge 43:3; 2Sa 3:13

to his own house and did not see the
king's face.
25 Now in all Israel there was no man
as handsome as Absalom, so highly
praised [for that]; from the sole of his
foot to the crown of his head there was
no blemish in him.
26 When he cut the hair of his head
(for at the end of each year he cut it,
because its weight was heavy on him)
he weighed the hair of his head at 200
shekels by the king's weight.
27 To Absalom were born three sons
and one daughter whose name was
Tamar; she was a beautiful woman.
28 Absalom lived two full years in
Jerusalem, without seeing the king's
face.
29 So Absalom sent for Joab, to send
him to the king, but he would not come
to him; even when he sent again a sec-
ond time, he [still] would not come.
30 Therefore Absalom said to his ser-
vants, "See, Joab's property is near
mine, and he has barley there; go and
set it on fire." So Absalom's servants
set the field on fire.
31 Then Joab took action and went
to Absalom at his house and said to
him, "Why did your servants set my
field on fire?"
32 Absalom answered Joab, "I sent for
you, saying, 'Come here, so that I may
send you to the king to ask, "Why have
I come [back] from Geshur? It would
be better for me to still be there." ' Now
then, let me see the king's face, and if
there is guilt in me, let him put me to
death."
33 So Joab came to the king and told
him. Then David called for Absalom,
and he came to the king and bowed his
face to the ground before the king; and
the king kissed Absalom.

Absalom's Conspiracy

15 AFTER THIS, Absalom provided
for himself a chariot and horses,
and fifty men as runners before him.
2 He would get up early and stand
beside the road to the gate [of the city,
where court was held]; and when any
man who had a dispute came to the
king for judgment, Absalom would call
to him, "From what city are you?" And
he would say, "Your servant is from
one of the tribes of Israel."
3 Then Absalom would say to him,
"See, your claims are good and right,
but there is no man appointed as the
king's agent to listen to you."
4 Moreover Absalom would say, "Oh,
that I were appointed judge in the land!
Then every man who had a dispute
could come to me and I would get jus-
tice for him."
5 And whenever a man approached
to bow down before him, he would put
out his hand, take hold of him, and
kiss him.
6 This is how Absalom dealt with
everyone in Israel who came to the

---

not been settled. One was David's apparent indifference to the sin of Amnon, and the other was whether Amnon's death was an act of justice or an act of murder. It never pays to let matters of justice remain undecided for a long period of time. It creates bitterness and disrespect for the authorities whose job it is to decide matters of justice, and the people involved become set in their attitudes in a way that makes repentance and restitution virtually impossible.

14:26 ***200 shekels.*** The weight of Absalom's hair was about 5 pounds.

14:27 ***three sons.*** Apparently Absalom's sons did not live to maturity. When he set up a pillar in Jerusalem to memorialize his name, he said it was because he had no son.

14:32 ***Come here.*** Apparently Joab did not sponsor Absalom to the extent of acting as a go-between with his father. Absalom responded with the attitude of a superior to an inferior, not what one might expect from the king's son to his father's highest ranking officer. It seems from the fearless and high handed way in which he answered Joab that Absalom was already seeing himself as his father's successor.

15:4 ***I would get justice for him.*** Administration of justice, the proper relationship between people in society according to God's standard of righteousness, was a major concern of the Old Testament rulers and prophets (8:15; 1Ki 3:28; Isa 1:17; Am 5:24). Absalom is playing on the people's emotions, and perhaps justifying himself in his actions against Amnon as well.

---

25 Isa 1:6 **27** See 2Sa 18:18 **28** ver. 24 **33** Ge 33:4; 45:15; Lk 15:20 **CHAPTER 15** **1** 2Sa 12:11; 1Ki 1:5 **4** Jdg 9:29 **6** Ro 16:18

king for judgment. So Absalom stole
the hearts of the men of Israel.

7And after four years, Absalom said
to the king, "Please let me go and pay
my vow which I have made to the LORD
at Hebron [my birthplace].

8"For your servant made a vow while
I lived at Geshur in Aram (Syria), 'If the
LORD will in fact bring me back to Je-
rusalem, then I will serve the Lord [by
offering a sacrifice of thanksgiving].' "

9And [David] the king said to him,
"Go in peace." So he arose and went
to Hebron.

10But Absalom sent spies throughout
all the tribes of Israel, saying, "As soon
as you hear the sound of the trumpet, you
shall say, 'Absalom is king in Hebron.' "

11Then two hundred men from Jeru-
salem who were invited [as guests to
his sacrificial feast] went with Absa-
lom. They went innocently and knew
nothing [about his plan against David].

12And Absalom sent for Ahithophel
the Gilonite, David's counselor, from
his city Giloh, while he was offering
sacrifices. And the conspiracy grew
strong, for the people with Absalom
increased continually.

David Flees Jerusalem

13Then a messenger came to David,
saying, "The hearts of the men of Israel
are with Absalom."

14David said to all his servants who
were with him at Jerusalem, "Arise,
let us flee, or none of us will escape
from Absalom! Go in haste, or he will
overtake us quickly and bring disaster
on us and strike the city with the edge
of the sword."

15The king's servants said to him,
"Listen, your servants *are ready to do*
whatever my lord the king decides."

16So the king left, and all his house-
hold with him. But the king left be-
hind ten women *who were* concubines
to take care of the house (palace).
[2 Sam 12:11; 20:3]

17The king left, and all the people
with him, and they stopped at the last
house.

18All of David's servants passed on
beside him, and all the Cherethites,
Pelethites and the Gittites, six hundred
men who had come with him from
Gath, passed on before the king.

19Then the king said to Ittai the Git-
tite, "Why should you go with us, too?
Go back and stay with the king [of
your own country], for you are a for-
eigner and an exile as well; *return* to
your own place.

20"You came *only* yesterday, so should
I make you wander with us today while
I go where I will? Return and take your
brothers back with you also. May loving-
kindness and faithfulness be with you."

21But Ittai answered the king, "As
the LORD lives, and as my lord the king

15:13 *The hearts of the men of Israel.* When David's power in Judah was confined to Hebron (ch. 2) he was resented by the supporters of Saul in the rest of the country. Old suspicions and resentments can be stoked again by a person who knows how to use people to his own advantage — a disreputable quality in which Absalom excelled.

15:15 *your servants are ready.* The loyalty of David's servants must have been a real encouragement in a time of such disloyalty from David's own family.

15:18 *Cherethites, Pelethites.* The Cherethites and Pelethites were elite units of David's army. These trusted troops of David were not Israelites, but mercenaries from a variety of nations, possibly Crete and Philistia. They had been with David for years, owed him their loyalty, and would defend him and his family to the death. ***Gittites.*** The Gittites were probably Philistine mercenary soldiers who were among David's original followers from Gath (1Sa 22:1 – 2).

15:19 – 21 Righteousness — Making the choice to stand with the right man, even when it looked like he might spend the rest of his life in exile was not practical, but it was right. We will all have to make choices to tell the truth, stand up for honorable actions, or support someone who is right but not powerful. Taking the right path does not mean it will be easy, but when we are on the right path, God is with us, "Even … through the [sunless] valley of the shadow of death" (Ps 23:4).

15:21 *whether for death or life.* David rewarded Ittai's loyalty when he made Ittai commander of a third of the army (18:2).

---

7 1Sa 16:1 **8** 1Sa 16:2; Ge 28:20,21; 2Sa 13:38 **11** 1Sa 9:13; 16:3,5; Ge 20:5 **12** Ps 41:9; 55:12-14; Jos 15:51; Ps 3:1 **13** ver. 6; Jdg 9:3 **14** 2Sa 19:9; Ps 3, title **16** Ps 3, title; 2Sa 16:21,22 **18** 2Sa 8:18 **19** 2Sa 18:2 **20** 1Sa 23:13 **21** Ru 1:16,17

lives, most certainly wherever my lord the king may be, whether for death or life, there will your servant be also."

22 So David said to Ittai, "Go on and cross over [the Brook Kidron]." So Ittai the Gittite crossed over with all his men and all the little ones who were with him.

23 While all the country was weeping with a loud voice, all the people crossed over. The king also crossed the Brook Kidron, and all the people went on toward the way of the wilderness [that lies between Jerusalem and the Jordan River].

24 Now Zadok also *came,* and all the Levites with him carrying the ark of the covenant of God. And they set down the ark of God, and Abiathar [the priest] came up [and officiated] until all the people had finished passing from the city.

25 Then the king told Zadok, "Take the ark of God back to [its rightful place in] the city [of Jerusalem, the capital]. If I find favor in the LORD's sight, He will bring me back again and let me see both it and His dwelling place (habitation).

26 "But if He should say, 'I have no delight in you,' then here I am; let Him do to me what seems good to Him."

27 The king also said to Zadok the priest, "Are you not a seer? Return to the city in peace [you and Abiathar], and your two sons with you, your son Ahimaaz and Jonathan the son of Abiathar.

28 "See, I am going to wait at the fords [of the Jordan] in the wilderness until word comes from you to inform me."

29 So Zadok and Abiathar brought the ark of God back to Jerusalem, and they stayed there.

30 And David went up the ascent of the *Mount of* Olives, weeping as he went, with his head covered and walking barefoot [in despair]. And all the people who were with him covered their heads and went up, weeping as they went.

31 David was told, "Ahithophel [your counselor] is among the conspirators with Absalom." David said, "O LORD, I pray You, turn Ahithophel's counsel into foolishness."

32 It happened when David came to the summit [of the Mount of Olives], where he worshiped God, behold, Hushai the Archite came to meet him with his tunic torn and dust on his head [as if in mourning].

33 David said to him, "If you go on with me, you will be a burden to me.

34 "But if you return to the city, and say to Absalom, 'I will be your servant, O king; as I have been your father's servant in the past, so I will be your servant now;' then you can thwart (make useless) the advice of Ahithophel for me.

35 "Are not Zadok and Abiathar the priests with you there? So it shall be that every word you hear from the king's palace, you shall report it to them.

36 "Their two sons are there with them, Ahimaaz, Zadok's son and Jonathan, Abiathar's son; and by them you shall send to me everything that you hear."

15:23 *Brook Kidron.* The Brook Kidron is a small stream that flows through the valley separating Jerusalem and the Mount of Olives during the rainy season (October through March). ***way of the wilderness.*** The way of the wilderness refers to the road leading through the wilderness of Judah to Jericho and down to the fords of the Jordan.

15:25 *He will bring me back again.* David committed the entire situation to the care and will of the Lord.

15:31 *Ahithophel.* Ahithophel was Bathsheba's grandfather (11:3; 23:34). A wise counselor (16:23), he had been in David's service (v. 12) but had switched his allegiance to Absalom. David's prayer was for his enemy to be confused. The name Ahithophel may mean "Brother of Folly."

15:34 *thwart (make useless) the advice.* David had committed the entire situation to the care and will of the Lord, but he was acting wisely to protect himself and to provide a source of information as well as an inside confederate to confound the enemy.

23 2Sa 16:2 **25** Ps 43:3 **26** Nu 14:8; 2Sa 22:20; 1Ki 10:9; 2Ch 9:8; Isa 62:4; 1Sa 3:18 **27** 1Sa 9:9; See 2Sa 17:17 **28** 2Sa 17:16 **30** 2Sa 19:4; Est 6:12; Isa 20:2,4; Jer 14:3,4; Ps 126:6 **31** Ps 3:1,2; 55:12; 2Sa 16:23; 17:14,23 **32** Jos 16:2; 2Sa 1:2 **33** 2Sa 19:35 **34** 2Sa 16:19 **35** 2Sa 17:15,16 **36** ver. 27

37So Hushai, David's friend, returned
to the city, and [at about the same time]
Absalom came into Jerusalem.

Ziba, a False Servant

16 WHEN DAVID was a little past
the summit [of the Mount of Ol-
ives], behold, Ziba, the servant of Me-
phibosheth, met him with a team of
saddled donkeys, and on them were
two hundred loaves of bread, a hun-
dred clusters of raisins, a hundred
summer fruits, and a jug of wine.
2The king said to Ziba, "Why do you
have these?" Ziba said, "The donkeys
are for the king's household (family)
to ride on, the bread and summer fruit
for the young men to eat, and the wine
is for anyone to drink who becomes
weary in the wilderness."
3Then the king said, "And where is
your master's son [Mephibosheth]?"
Ziba said to the king, "Behold, he re-
mains in Jerusalem, for he said, 'Today
the house of Israel will give me back
the kingdom of my father.' "
4Then the king said to Ziba, "Behold,
everything that belonged to Mephib-
osheth is [now] yours." Ziba said, "I
bow down [in honor and gratitude];
let me find favor in your sight, O my
lord the king."

David Is Cursed

5When King David came to Ba-
hurim, a man named Shimei, the son
of Gera, came out from there. He was
of the family of Saul's household and
he was cursing continually as he came
out.
6He threw stones at David and at all
the servants of King David; yet all the
people and all the warriors *remained*
on his right and on his left.
7This is what Shimei said as he cursed:
"Get out, get out, you man of bloodshed,
you worthless *and* useless man!
8"The LORD has returned upon you
all the bloodshed of the house of Saul,
in whose place you have reigned; and
the LORD has given the kingdom into
the hands of Absalom your son. And
behold, you are *caught* in your own
evil, for you are a man of bloodshed!"
9Then Abishai [David's nephew],
the son of Zeruiah, said to the king,
"Why should this dead dog (despicable
person) curse my lord the king? Let me
go over and take off his head."
10But the king said, "What business
is this of yours, O sons of Zeruiah? If
Shimei is cursing because the LORD
said to him, 'Curse David,' then who
should say, 'Why have you done so?' "
11Then David said to Abishai and to
all his servants, "Look, my son [Absa-
lom] who came from my own body, is
seeking my life; how much more [rea-
son] now [does] this Benjamite [have to
curse me]? Let him alone and let him
curse, for [it could be that] the LORD
has told him [to do it].
12"Perhaps the LORD will look on the
wrong done to me [by Shimei, if he is
acting on his own]; and [in that case
perhaps] the Lord will this day return
good to me in place of his cursing."

16:1 *Ziba.* A longtime servant of both Saul and Mephibosheth, Ziba was expressing his loyalty to King David.
16:5 *Bahurim.* Bahurim was near Jerusalem, east of the Mount of Olives (3:16). ***cursing continually.*** These were not simple insults or the words of someone with a foul mouth. Shimei was asking God to destroy David (Nu 22:6).
16:6 *threw stones.* Throwing stones is a gesture of contempt, as if the fleeing king were merely a stray dog. Stones can also be deadly, as is shown by the fact that stoning was a normal means of capital punishment among the Hebrews (1Ki 21:13).
16:9 – 13 Forbearance — David was more aware of his failure as a father than his dignity as a king. David knew that both Moses and Saul had been disciplined by God, and he certainly did not rule out the idea that both Absalom's rebellion and Shimei's cursing might be part of a lesson that God had for him. He was willing to endure both while he waited to see how God would work things out.
16:10 *What business is this of yours.* This idiom means that David did not share the feelings and views of Abishai.

37 2Sa 16:16; 1Ch 27:33; 2Sa 16:15 **CHAPTER 16** **1** 2Sa 15:30,32; 2Sa 9:2 **2** 2Sa 15:23; 17:29 **3** 2Sa 19:27 **5** 2Sa 19:16; 1Ki 2:8,44 **7** Dt 13:13 **8** Jdg 9:24,56,57; 1Ki 2:32,33; See 2Sa 1:16; 3:28,29; 4:11,12 **9** 1Sa 24:14; 2Sa 9:8; Ex 22:28 **10** 2Sa 19:22; 1Pe 2:23; See 2Ki 18:25; La 3:38; Ro 9:20 **11** 2Sa 12:11; Ge 15:4 **12** Ro 8:28

13 So David and his men went on the
road; and Shimei went along on the hill-
side close beside David and cursed as he
went and threw stones and dust at him.
14 The king and all the people who
were with him arrived [at the Jordan
River] weary, and he refreshed himself
there.

Absalom Enters Jerusalem

15 Then Absalom and all the people,
the men of Israel, entered Jerusalem,
and Ahithophel with him.
16 Now it happened when Hushai the
Archite, David's friend, came to Absa-
lom, Hushai said to him, "*Long* live the
king! *Long* live the king!"
17 Absalom said to Hushai, "Is this
your loyalty to your friend? Why did
you not go with your friend?"
18 Hushai said to Absalom, "No! For
whomever the LORD and this people
and all the men of Israel have chosen
[as king], I will be his, and I will re-
main with him.
19 "Besides, whom should I serve?
Should I not *serve* in the presence of
David's son? As I have served in your
father's presence, so I shall serve in
your presence."
20 Then Absalom said to Ahithophel,
"Give *me* your advice. What should
we do?"
21 Ahithophel said to Absalom, "Go
in to your father's concubines, whom
he has left behind to take care of the
house; then all Israel will hear that
you have made yourself odious to your
father. Then the hands of all who are
with you will be strengthened [by your
boldness and audacity]."
22 So they pitched a tent for Absa-
lom on the roof [of the king's palace],
and Absalom went in to his father's
concubines in the sight of all Israel.
[2 Sam 12:11, 12]
23 The advice of Ahithophel, which he
gave in those days, was as if a man had
consulted the word of God; that is how
all Ahithophel's counsel was *regarded*
by both David and Absalom.

Hushai's Counsel

17 THEN, AHITHOPHEL said to
Absalom, "Please let me choose
12,000 men, and I will set out and pur-
sue David tonight.
2 "I will strike while he is weary and
exhausted, and terrify him; and all the
people with him will flee [in terror].
Then I will attack the king alone,
3 and I will bring all the people [who
follow David] back to you. The return
of everyone depends on the [death of
the] man you are seeking; then all the
people will be at peace [and accept
you as king]."
4 So the plan pleased Absalom and
all the elders of Israel.
5 Nevertheless, Absalom said, "Now
call Hushai the Archite also, and let us
hear what he has to say."
6 When Hushai came to Absalom,
Absalom said to him, "Ahithophel has
advised this [plan of action]. Should
we do what he says? If not, you speak
[and explain why not]."
7 So Hushai said to Absalom,
"Ahithophel has not given good advice
this time."
8 And Hushai said, "You know your
father and his men, that they are brave
men, and they are enraged *and* fierce,
like a bear deprived of her cubs in the
field. Your father is a [shrewd] man
of war, and will not spend the night
with the people [knowing that you
seek his life].
9 "Behold, he has hidden himself
[even] now in one of the ravines or in
another place; and when some of your

16:21 – 22 *concubines.* In ancient times taking over a king's harem was a recognized means of claiming the throne. Once Absalom violated David's concubines, he was set on a course of sure and final alienation from his father. Putting his tent on the roof was a public and insolent act.
17:2 *I will attack the king alone.* In a battle, it is a little rash to promise to kill only one person. Ahithophel was suggesting that David's companions and troops would switch their loyalty to Absalom if David were killed.
17:8 *bear deprived of her cubs.* There is no more dangerous foe in the woods than a mother bear who believes her cubs to be in danger.

15 2Sa 15:37 **16** 2Sa 15:37 **17** 2Sa 19:25; Pr 17:17 **19** 2Sa 15:34 **21** 2Sa 15:16; 20:3; Ge 34:30; 1Sa 13:4; 2Sa 2:7; Zec 8:13 **22** 2Sa 12:11,12 **23** 2Sa 15:12 **CHAPTER 17** **2** See Dt 25:18; 2Sa 16:14; Zec 13:7 **8** Hos 13:8

troops fall at the first attack, whoever hears *about it* will say, 'There has been a defeat among the people who follow Absalom.'

10 "And even the one who is brave, whose heart is like the heart of a lion, will completely lose heart *and* melt away; for all Israel knows that your father is a mighty man, and that those who are with him are brave men.

11 "But I advise that all [the men of] Israel be summoned to you, from Dan [in the north] to Beersheba [in the south], like the sand that is by the sea in abundance, and that you personally go into battle.

12 "So shall we come upon David in one of the places where he can be found, and we *will fall* on him as the dew falls [unseen and unheard] on the ground; and of him and of all the men who are with him, not even one will be left.

13 "If he retreats into a city, then all Israel shall bring ropes to that city, and we will drag it into the ravine until not even a pebble [of it] is found there."

14 Then Absalom and all the men of Israel said, "The advice of Hushai the Archite is better than that of Ahithophel." For the LORD had ordained to thwart the good advice of Ahithophel, so that the LORD could bring disaster upon Absalom.

Hushai's Warning Saves David

15 Then Hushai said to Zadok and Abiathar the priests, "This is the advice that Ahithophel gave to Absalom and the elders of Israel, and this is the advice that I have given.

16 "Now then, send *word* quickly and tell David, 'Do not spend the night at the fords [on the west side of the Jordan] in the wilderness, but by all means cross over [to the east side of the river], or else the king and all the people with him will be destroyed [if Ahithophel is allowed by Absalom to lead an attack].' "

17 Now Jonathan and Ahimaaz [the priests' sons] were staying at En-rogel, and a maidservant [appearing to go for water] would go and tell them [what was happening], and they would go [secretly] and inform King David; for they could not [allow themselves to] be seen coming into the city [of Jerusalem].

18 But a boy saw them and told Absalom; so the two of them left quickly and came to the house of a man in Bahurim, who had a well in his courtyard, and [with his permission] they went down into it.

19 And the woman [of the house] took a covering and spread it over the mouth of the well and scattered grain on it; so nothing was discovered.

20 Then Absalom's servants came to the woman at the house and asked, "Where are Ahimaaz and Jonathan?" And the woman said to them, "They have crossed over the brook." When they searched and could not find them, they returned to Jerusalem.

21 After they left, Jonathan and Ahimaaz came up out of the well and went and informed King David, and said to David, "Arise and cross over the Jordan River quickly, for Ahithophel has advised [an attack] against you."

22 Then David and all the people who were with him departed and crossed over the Jordan. By daybreak, not even one was left who had not crossed the Jordan.

23 Now when Ahithophel saw that his advice had not been followed, he saddled his donkey and set out and went to his home, to his city. Then he put his household in order, and hanged himself. So he died and was buried in the tomb of his father.

24 Then David came to Mahanaim.

17:22 *crossed the Jordan*. Although the Jordan was not a large river, crossing it provided a barrier between him and his enemies. The tribal allotments included land on both sides of the Jordan, but there was always an emotional understanding that the "real" land of Israel was west of the Jordan. David was truly an exile.

10 Jos 2:11 **11** Jdg 20:1; Ge 22:17 **14** 2Sa 15:31,34 **15** 2Sa 15:35 **16** 2Sa 15:28 **17** 2Sa 15:27,36; Jos 2:4; Jos 15:7; 18:16 **18** 2Sa 16:5 **19** See Jos 2:6 **20** See Ex 1:19; Jos 2:4,5 **21** ver. 15,16 **23** 2Sa 15:12; Mt 27:5 **24** Ge 32:2; Jos 13:26; 2Sa 2:8

And Absalom crossed over the Jordan, he and all the men of Israel with him.
25Absalom put Amasa in command of the army instead of Joab. Now Amasa was the son of a man named Ithra the Israelite, who had married Abigail the daughter of Nahash, [the half sister of David and] the sister of Zeruiah, Joab's mother.
26So Israel and Absalom camped in the land of Gilead.
27When David came to Mahanaim, Shobi the son of Nahash from Rabbah of the Ammonites, and Machir the son of Ammiel from Lo-debar, and Barzillai the Gileadite from Rogelim
28brought beds, basins, pottery, wheat, barley, flour, roasted grain, broad beans, lentils, and [other] roasted *grain*,
29honey, cream, sheep, and cheese of the herd, for David and the people who were with him, to eat; for they said, "The people are hungry and weary and thirsty in the wilderness."

Absalom's Death

18 DAVID NUMBERED the men who were with him and set over them commanders of thousands and commanders of hundreds.
2Then David sent the army out, a third under the command of Joab, a third under Abishai the son of Zeruiah, Joab's brother, and a third under the command of Ittai the Gittite. And the king said to the men, "I myself will certainly go out [to fight] with you."
3But the men said, "You should not go out [to battle with us]. For if in fact we retreat, they will not care about us; even if half of us die, they will not care about us. But you are worth ten thousand of us. So now it is better that you be *ready* to help us from the city [of Mahanaim]."
4Then the king said to them, "I will do whatever seems best to you." So the king stood beside the gate [of Mahanaim], and all the army went out in groups of hundreds and of thousands.
5The king commanded Joab and Abishai and Ittai, saying, "*Deal* gently with the young man Absalom for my sake." And all the men heard when the king gave orders to all the commanders about Absalom.
6So the men went out into the field against Israel, and the battle was *fought* in the forest of Ephraim.
7The men of Israel [who supported Absalom] were defeated there by the men of David, and a great slaughter took place there that day, 20,000 men.
8For the battle there was spread out over the surface of the entire countryside, and the [hazards of the] forest devoured more men that day than did the sword.
9Now Absalom met the servants of David. Absalom was riding on his mule, and the mule went under the thick branches of a massive tree, and his head was caught in [the thick branches of] the tree; and he was left hanging [in midair] between heaven and earth, while the mule that had been under him kept going.
10A certain man saw it and informed Joab, saying, "I saw Absalom hanging in a tree."
11Joab said to the man who informed him, "You saw *him!* Why then did you not strike him there to the ground? I

17:27 *Shobi . . . Barzillai.* The gifts of these three men showed a real understanding of the material needs of the exiles, and this act of kindness must have been very encouraging to them. ***Machir.*** Jonathan's son Mephibosheth was living with Machir when David found him (9:4).
18:3 – 4 Wisdom — One facet of good leadership is the ability to delegate authority to others and leave the results in the hands of God. Waiting in safety was not David's idea, but it seemed best to others, so David agreed. David's strength as a leader lay in having the hearts of his followers, and they in turn put his safety as a high priority. These loyal men did not think that God was done with David as king, and David needed their wisdom.
18:9 *massive tree.* This strong, massive tree, sometimes translated terebrinth or elm, was native to the land of Israel and grew to a height of about 35 feet.

25 1Ch 2:16,17 **27** See 2Sa 10:1; 12:29; 2Sa 9:4; 2Sa 19:31,32; 1Ki 2:7 **29** 2Sa 16:2 **CHAPTER 18** **2** 2Sa 15:19 **3** 2Sa 21:17 **5** ver. 12 **6** Jos 17:15,18

would have given you ten *pieces* of silver and a belt."

12 The man told Joab, "Even if I were to feel the weight of a thousand *pieces* of silver in my hands, I would not put out my hand against the king's son; for we all heard the king command you, Abishai, and Ittai, saying, 'Protect the young man Absalom, for my sake.'

13 "Otherwise, if I had acted treacherously against his life (for nothing is hidden from the king) you yourself would have taken sides against me."

14 Joab said, "I will not waste time with you." So he took three spears in his hand and thrust them through the heart of Absalom while he was still alive [and caught] in the midst of the tree.

15 And ten young men, Joab's armor bearers, surrounded and struck Absalom and killed him.

16 Then Joab blew the trumpet [to signal the end of the combat], and the men returned from pursuing Israel, for Joab held them back.

17 They took [down the body of] Absalom and threw him into a deep pit in the forest and set up a huge mound of stones over him. Then all Israel fled, everyone to his own tent.

18 Now Absalom in his lifetime had taken and set up for himself a memorial pillar which is in the King's Valley, for he said, "I have no son to keep my name in remembrance." He named the memorial pillar after himself, and to this day it is called Absalom's Monument.

David Is Grief-stricken

19 Then Ahimaaz the son of Zadok, said, "Let me run and bring the king news that the LORD has vindicated him *by rescuing him* from [the power of] his enemies."

20 But Joab told him, "You are not the man to carry news [to King David] today, but you shall carry news another day. On this day you shall carry no news, because the king's son is dead."

21 Then Joab said to the Cushite (Ethiopian), "Go, tell the king what you have seen." And the Cushite bowed to Joab and ran.

22 Then Ahimaaz the son of Zadok said again to Joab, "But whatever happens, please let me also run after the Cushite." Joab said, "Why should you run, my son, seeing you will have no messenger's reward for going [because you have only bad news]?"

23 "But whatever happens, Let me run." So Joab said to him, "Run." Then Ahimaaz ran by the way of the plain [of the Jordan River] and outran the Cushite.

24 Now David was sitting between the two gates; and the lookout went up to the roof of the gate by the wall, and when he raised his eyes and looked, he saw a man running alone.

25 The lookout called *down* and told the king. The king said, "If he is alone, he has good news to tell." And he came nearer and nearer.

26 Then the lookout saw another man running, and he called to the gatekeeper and said, "Look, *another* man running alone." The king said, "He also is bringing good news."

27 The lookout said, "I think the man in front runs like Ahimaaz the son of Zadok." The king said, "He is a good man and is coming with good news."

28 And Ahimaaz called out and said to the king, "All is well." And he bowed before the king with his face to the ground and said, "Blessed be the LORD your God, who has handed over the men who lifted up their hands [to fight] against my lord the king."

29 The king asked, "Is the young man Absalom safe?" Ahimaaz answered, "When Joab sent the king's servant, and your servant, I saw a great turmoil, but I do not know what *it was about.*"

30 The king told him, "Step aside; stand here." And he stepped aside and stood still.

31 Behold, the Cushite (Ethiopian) arrived, and said, "Let my lord the

---

18:23 *by the way of the plain.* The plain was the floor of the Jordan valley. Ahimaaz took a longer route, but avoided the hilly terrain on the road taken by the Cushite.

12 ver. 5 **17** Jos 7:26 **18** Ge 14:17; See 2Sa 14:27 **24** 2Ki 9:17

king receive good news, for the LORD
has vindicated you today *by rescuing*
you from the hand (power) of all those
who stood against you."
32The king asked the Cushite, "Is the
young man Absalom [my son] safe?"
The Cushite replied, "May the enemies
of my lord the king, and all those who
rise against you to do evil, be [dead]
like that young man is."
33The king was deeply moved and
went to the upper room over the gate
and wept [in sorrow]. And this is what
he said as he walked: "O my son Absalom, my son, my son Absalom! How
I wish that I had died instead of you,
O Absalom, my son, my son!"

Joab Reproves David's Lament

19 IT WAS told to Joab, "Behold, the
king is weeping and mourning
for Absalom."
2So the victory on that day was
turned into mourning for all the people, for the people heard it said on that
day, "The king grieves for his son."
3The people stole into the city [of Mahanaim] that day, as people who are
humiliated *and* ashamed steal away
when they retreat in battle.
4But the king covered his face and
cried out with a loud voice, "O my son
Absalom, O Absalom, my son, my son!"
5Then Joab came into the house to
the king and said, "Today you have put
all your servants to shame who this
day have saved your life and the lives
of your sons and your daughters, and
the lives of your wives and concubines.
6"For you love those who hate you
and hate those who love you. For you
have shown today that commanders
and servants are nothing to you; for
today I know that if Absalom had lived
and all the rest of us had died today,
then you would be pleased.
7"So now stand up, go out and speak
kindly *and* encouragingly to your servants; for I swear by the LORD that
if you do not go out, not a man will
stay with you tonight. And this will
be worse for you than all the evil that
has come upon you from your youth
until now."

David Restored as King

8Then the king stood and sat at the
gate [of Mahanaim]. And they told all
the people, "The king is sitting at the
gate," and all the people came before
the king.
But Israel [Absalom's troops] had
fled, every man to his tent.
9All the people were quarreling
throughout the tribes of Israel, saying,
"The king rescued us from the hands
of our enemies, and he saved us from
the hands of the Philistines, but now he
has fled out of the land from Absalom.
10"And Absalom, whom we anointed
over us, has died in battle. So now, why
are you [leaders] doing nothing about
bringing back the king?"
11Then King David sent *word* to Zadok and to Abiathar the priests, saying, "Say to the elders of Judah, 'Why
are you the last to bring the king back
to his house [in Jerusalem], since the

18:33 *O my son Absalom.* David's grief can be understood by any parent who has lost a child to vice or crime. Absalom was a rebel, but he had been a little boy born to David in the early years as king in Hebron, and for David he would always be that beloved son. Absalom deserved to die, and David knew it, but he still longed for things to have turned out differently. In a few short years the repercussions of his sin with Bathsheba had destroyed the lives of Amnon, Tamar, and Absalom.

18:33 Despondency—In many ways mental suffering is more intense and devastating than physical suffering. It was hard for David to even imagine taking up life again and going back to Jerusalem as king. It is only the Lord who can give courage in such moments, and He often does it by reminding us of who He is, what He has done in the past, and what He promises to do in the future. Sandwiched in these certainties, we can begin to see that His hand is on us even in our grief.

19:11 *elders of Judah.* David asked his friends, the priests, to begin the movement to invite David back to his throne. Apparently he did not want to come into Jerusalem without public support for his rule.

33 2Sa 19:4 **CHAPTER 19** **3** ver. 32 **4** 2Sa 15:30; 2Sa 18:33 **9** 2Sa 15:14

word of all Israel has come to the king,
and to his house?
12 ‘You are my brothers (relatives,
relations); you are my bone and my
flesh. Why then are you the last to
bring back the king?’
13 “Say to Amasa [the commander
of Absalom’s troops], ‘Are you not my
bone and my flesh? May God do so to
me, and more also, if you will not be
commander of my army from now on
in place of Joab.’ ”
14 In this way he changed the hearts
of all the men of Judah as one man, so
they sent *word* to the king, “Return,
you and all your servants.”
15 So David returned and came to the
Jordan. And [supporters from] Judah
came to Gilgal to meet the king, to
escort him across the Jordan.
16 Then Shimei the son of Gera, a
Benjamite of Bahurim, hurried and
came down with the men [from the
tribe of] of Judah to meet King David,
17 and a thousand men [from the
tribe] of Benjamin with him. And Ziba,
the servant of the house of Saul, and
his fifteen sons and twenty servants
with him, rushed down to the Jordan
before the king.
18 Then they [repeatedly] crossed the
ford to bring over the king’s household
(family), and to do what pleased him.
And Shimei the son of Gera fell down
before the king as he was about to
cross the Jordan,
19 and said to the king, “Let not my
lord consider me guilty, nor remember
what your servant did wrong on the
day my lord the king left Jerusalem,
so that the king would take it to heart.
20 “For your servant knows that I
have sinned; therefore, behold, I have
come today, the first of all the house
of Joseph to come down to meet my
lord the king.”
21 But Abishai the son of Zeruiah
said, “Should not Shimei be put to
death for this, because he cursed the
LORD’s anointed?”
22 David said, “What business is this
of yours, you sons of Zeruiah, that you
should be an adversary to me today?
Should anyone be put to death in Israel
today? For do I not know that today I
am king over Israel?”
23 Therefore the king said to Shimei,
“You shall not be put to death.” And
so the king gave him his promise.
[1 Kin 2:44–46]
24 Then Mephibosheth the [grand]
son of Saul came down to meet the
king, but he had not cared for his feet,
nor trimmed his mustache, nor washed
his clothes from the day the king left
until the day he returned in peace *and*
safety.
25 And when he came to Jerusalem
to meet the king, the king said to him,
“Why did you not go with me, Mephib-
osheth?”
26 He said, “My lord the king, my
servant [Ziba] betrayed me; for I said,
‘Saddle a donkey for me so that I may
ride on it and go with the king,’ for
your servant is lame [but he took
the donkeys and left without me].
[2 Sam 16:1–4]
27 “Further, he has slandered your
servant to my lord the king; but my
lord the king is like the angel of God;
so do what is good in your eyes.

19:13 *Amasa.* David’s nephew Amasa had commanded the army of Absalom (17:25). When David offered him the position of commander it was probably intended to secure Amasa’s allegiance as well as discipline Joab for killing Absalom against David’s orders.

19:23 *the king gave him his promise.* The king was willing to accept Shimei as a loyal subject if he continued in his loyalty, and he swore that he would not kill Shimei. Apparently David did not trust Shimei, for he later directed Solomon to kill him (1Ki 2:8) along with others that he considered dangerous to Solomon’s reign. David could not put Shimei to death himself because of his oath, but his son could do it if there was just cause.

19:27 *do what is good in your eyes.* David did not try to decide whether it was Ziba or Mephibosheth who was telling the truth. He commanded that they divide the land. Each was provided for; neither was validated in his claims.

12 2Sa 5:1 **13** 2Sa 17:25; Ru 1:17 **14** Jdg 20:1 **15** Jos 5:9 **16** 2Sa 16:5; 1Ki 2:8 **17** 2Sa 9:2,10; 16:1,2
19 1Sa 22:15; 2Sa 16:5,6; 2Sa 13:33 **20** See 2Sa 16:5 **21** Ex 22:28; 1Sa 26:9 **22** 2Sa 16:10; 1Sa 11:13
23 1Ki 2:8,9,37,46 **24** 2Sa 9:6 **25** 2Sa 16:17 **27** 2Sa 16:3; 2Sa 14:17,20

[28]"For were not all of my father's
household (family) nothing but dead
men before my lord the king; yet you
set your servant among those who ate
at your own table. So what right do I
still have to cry out anymore to the
king [for help]?"
[29]The king said to him, "Why speak
anymore of your affairs? I have said,
'You and Ziba shall divide the land.' "
[30]Mephibosheth said to the king,
"Let him even take it all, since my lord
the king has returned to his own house
in safety *and* peace."
[31]Now Barzillai the Gileadite came
down from Rogelim and went on to
the Jordan with the king to escort him
over the Jordan.
[32]Barzillai was a very old man,
eighty years old; and he had provided
the king with food while he stayed at
Mahanaim, for he was a very great *and*
wealthy man.
[33]The king said to Barzillai, "Cross
over with me and I will provide for you
in Jerusalem with me."
[34]But Barzillai said to the king, "How
much longer have I to live, that I should
go up with the king to Jerusalem?
[35]"I am this day eighty years old.
Can I [be useful to advise you to] discern between good and bad? Can your
servant taste what I eat or drink? Can
I still hear the voices of singing men
and women? Why then should your
servant be an added burden to my lord
the king?
[36]"Your servant would merely cross
over the Jordan with the king. Why
should the king compensate me with
this reward?
[37]"Please let your servant return,
so that I may die in my own city [and
be buried] by the grave of my father
and mother. But here is your servant
Chimham [my son]; let him cross over
with my lord the king, and do for him
what seems good to you." [1 Kin 2:7]
[38]The king answered, "Chimham
shall cross over with me, and I will
do for him what seems good to you;
and whatever you ask of me, I will do
for you."
[39]So all the people crossed over the
Jordan. When the king had crossed
over, he kissed Barzillai and blessed
him, and he returned to his place.
[40]Then the king went on to Gilgal,
and Chimham went on with him; and
all the people of Judah and also half the
people of Israel accompanied the king.
[41]And all the men of Israel came to
the king and said to him, "Why have
our brothers (relatives), the men [from
the tribe] of Judah, stolen you away
and brought the king and his household and all David's men with him over
the Jordan [instead of waiting for us
to arrive]?"
[42]Then all the men of Judah answered the men of Israel, "Because
the king is a close relative to us. So
why then are you angry about this
matter? Have we eaten at all at the
king's *expense*? Or has anything been
taken for us?"
[43]Then the men of Israel answered
the men of Judah, "We have ten [tribes']
shares in the king, and we have more
claim on David than you. Why then
did you treat us with contempt *and*
ignore us [by rushing ahead]? Were
we not the first to speak of bringing
back our king?" But the words of the
men of Judah were harsher than those
of the men of Israel.

Sheba's Revolt

20 THERE HAPPENED to be
there a worthless *and* wicked
man named Sheba the son of Bichri, a
Benjamite. He blew a trumpet [to call
Israel to revolt] and said,

"We have no portion in David
And no inheritance in the son of
Jesse,
Every man to his tents, O Israel!"

19:36 Love — Barzillai's acts of hospitality were acts of love: love for the Lord, and love for his king (Mk 9:41). Such true acts of kindness may bring a reward, but the real reward is the pleasure that comes with giving.

28 2Sa 9:7,10,13 **31** 1Ki 2:7 **32** 2Sa 17:27 **35** Ps 90:10 **37** 1Ki 2:7; Jer 41:17 **39** Ge 31:55 **41** ver. 15 **42** ver. 12 **43** See Jdg 8:1; 12:1 **CHAPTER 20** **1** 2Sa 19:43; 1Ki 12:16; 2Ch 10:16

2 So all the men of Israel deserted David and followed Sheba the son of Bichri; but the men of Judah stayed faithfully with their king, from the Jordan to Jerusalem.

3 Then David came to his house (palace) at Jerusalem, and the king took the ten women, his concubines whom he had left to take care of the house, and placed them under guard and provided for them, but did not go in to them. So they were confined, and lived as widows until the day of their death.

4 Now the king said to Amasa [the commander of his army], "Summon the [fighting] men of Judah to me within three days, and be present here yourself."

5 So Amasa went to summon [the fighting men of] Judah, but he delayed longer than the time which David had set for him.

6 And David said to Abishai [his nephew], "Now Sheba the son of Bichri will do us more harm than Absalom did. Take your lord's servants and pursue him, so that he does not find fortified cities for himself and escape from our sight."

7 So Joab's men went after him, along with [David's bodyguards] the Cherethites and Pelethites and all the warriors; they went out from Jerusalem to pursue Sheba the son of Bichri.

8 When they were at the great stone in Gibeon, Amasa came to meet them. Now Joab was wearing his military uniform, and over it he had a belt with a sheathed sword strapped around his hips; and as he went forward, it fell out.

9 Joab said to Amasa, "Is it going well with you, my brother?" And with his right hand Joab took hold of Amasa by the beard [as if] to kiss him [in greeting].

Amasa Murdered

10 But Amasa [who had replaced Joab as David's commander] was off guard *and* not attentive to the sword in Joab's hand. So Joab struck Amasa in the abdomen with the sword, spilling his intestines to the ground. Without another blow Amasa died. Then Joab and Abishai his brother pursued Sheba the son of Bichri.

11 Now one of Joab's young men stood by him and said, "Whoever favors Joab and is for David, let him follow Joab!"

12 But Amasa was wallowing in his blood in the middle of the highway. And when the man saw that all the people who came by stopped [to look], he moved Amasa from the highway into the field and threw a garment over him when he saw that everyone who came by Amasa stopped.

Revolt Put Down

13 When [the body of] Amasa was removed from the highway, everyone followed after Joab to pursue Sheba the son of Bichri.

14 Now Joab went through all the tribes of Israel to Abel, even Beth-maacah, and all the Berites; and they assembled and also went after Sheba.

15 And the army of Joab came and besieged Sheba in Abel Beth-maacah, and they built up an assault ramp against the city, and it stood against the outer rampart; and all the people who were with Joab were wreaking destruction to make the wall fall.

16 Then a wise woman cried out from

20:6 *us more harm.* Sheba's revolt had more potential for destroying David's reign than Absalom's revolt because it was based on long-standing tribal animosity between Judah and the tribe of Benjamin.

20:9 *my brother.* This was not the first time Joab had killed a man while pretending to have a friendly word with him (3:27). The text does not say whether he suspected Amasa of treachery in his delay, or if Joab was acting out of jealousy, protecting his own long standing position of leader of David's army.

20:13 – 22 Strife — Once again David had an opportunity to demonstrate that it was God who had chosen him to be king. If a leader has to contend for his position he is sure to leave rebellion and destruction in his wake.

3 2Sa 15:16; 16:21,22 **4** 2Sa 19:13 **6** 2Sa 11:11; 1Ki 1:33 **7** 2Sa 8:18; 1Ki 1:38 **9** Mt 26:49; Lk 22:47 **10** 1Ki 2:5; 2Sa 2:23 **14** 2Ki 15:29; 2Ch 16:4 **15** 2Ki 19:32

the city, "Hear, hear! Tell Joab, 'Come here so that I may speak to you.' "

17 So when he approached her, the woman asked, "Are you Joab?" He answered, "I am." Then she said to him, "Listen to the words of your maidservant." He answered, "I am listening."

18 Then she said, "In the past people used to say, 'They will certainly ask *advice* at Abel,' and so they settled *the dispute.*

19 "I am one of the peaceable and faithful in Israel. You are seeking to destroy a city, and a mother in Israel. Why would you swallow up (devour) the inheritance of the LORD?"

20 Joab answered, "Far be it, far be it from me that I would swallow up or destroy!

21 "That is not true. But a man of the hill country of Ephraim, Sheba the son of Bichri by name, has lifted up his hand [in rebellion] against King David. Only hand him over, and I will leave the city." And the woman said to Joab, "Behold, his head shall be thrown to you over the wall."

22 Then the woman in her wisdom went to all the people [to inform them of the agreement]. And they beheaded Sheba the son of Bichri and threw his head [down] to Joab. So he blew the trumpet [signaling the end of the attack], and they dispersed from the city, every man to his own tent. And Joab returned to Jerusalem to [David] the king. [Eccl 9:13–16]

23 Now Joab was [commander] over the entire army of Israel; Benaiah the son of Jehoiada was [commander] over the Cherethites and Pelethites [the king's bodyguards];

24 Adoram was over the forced labor; Jehoshaphat the son of Ahilud was recorder;

25 Sheva was the scribe; and Zadok and Abiathar were priests;

26 also Ira the Jairite was a priest to David.

Gibeonite Revenge

21 THERE WAS famine in the days of David for three consecutive years; and David sought the presence (face) of the LORD [asking the reason]. The LORD replied, "It is because of Saul and his bloody house, because he put the Gibeonites to death."

2 So the king called the Gibeonites and spoke to them (now the Gibeonites were not of the sons (descendants) of Israel but of the remnant (survivors) of the Amorites. The Israelites had sworn [an oath] to [spare] them, but Saul in his zeal for the sons of Israel and Judah had sought to strike down the Gibeonites).

3 So David said to the Gibeonites, "What should I do for you? How can I make it good so that you will bless the LORD's inheritance (Israel)?"

4 The Gibeonites said to him, "We will not accept silver or gold belonging to Saul or his household (descendants); nor is it for us to put any man to death in Israel." David said, "I will do for you whatever you say."

5 So they said to the king, "The man who consumed us and planned to exterminate us from remaining in any territory of Israel,

6 let seven men [chosen] from his sons (descendants) be given to us and we will hang them before the LORD [that is, put them on display, impaled with broken legs and arms] in Gibeah of Saul, the chosen one of the LORD." And the king said, "I will give them."

7 But the king spared Mephibosheth the son of Jonathan, the son of Saul, because of the LORD's oath that was between David and Saul's son Jonathan.

8 So the king took the two sons of Rizpah the daughter of Aiah, whom she bore to Saul, Armoni and Mephibosheth, and the five sons of Merab the daughter of Saul, whom she had borne to Adriel the son of Barzillai the Meholathite.

21:1 *because he put the Gibeonites to death.* When the Israelites first came into the promised land under the leadership of Joshua, the Gibeonites had deceived them into making a treaty that guaranteed their protection and security (Jos 9:3–27). Saul had broken that agreement.

19 1Sa 26:19; 2Sa 21:3 **22** Ecc 9:14,15 **23** 2Sa 8:16,18 **24** 1Ki 4:6; 2Sa 8:16; 1Ki 4:3 **25** 2Sa 8:17; 1Ki 4:4 **26** 2Sa 23:38 **CHAPTER 21** **2** Jos 9:3,15-17 **3** 2Sa 20:19 **6** 1Sa 10:26; 1Sa 10:24 **7** 1Sa 18:3; 20:8,15 **8** 2Sa 3:7

9 He handed them over to the Gibeonites, and they hanged them on the hill before the LORD, and the seven died together. They were put to death in the first days of the grain harvest, the beginning of the barley harvest [in the spring].

10 Rizpah the daughter of Aiah took sackcloth and spread it out for herself on the rock, from the beginning of harvest [in the spring] until [the autumn] rain fell on them; and she allowed neither the birds of the sky to rest on their bodies by day, nor the beasts of the field [to feed on them] by night.

11 David was told what Rizpah the daughter of Aiah, the concubine of Saul, had done.

12 Then David went and took the bones of Saul and Jonathan his son from the men of Jabesh-gilead, who had stolen them from the open square of Beth-shan, where the Philistines had hanged them on the day when the Philistines had killed Saul in Gilboa.

13 He brought up the bones of Saul and of Jonathan his son from there, and they gathered the bones of those who had been hanged [with their arms and legs broken].

14 They buried the bones of Saul and Jonathan his son in the country of Benjamin in Zela, in the tomb of Kish his father; and they did all that the king commanded. After that, God was moved by prayer for the land.

15 Now the Philistines were at war again with Israel. David went down with his servants, and as they fought against the Philistines, David became weary.

16 Then Ishbi-benob, who was among the descendants of the giant, the weight of whose spear was three hundred *shekels* (six pounds) of bronze, was armed with a new *sword,* and he intended to kill David.

17 But Abishai the son of Zeruiah came to David's aid, and struck and killed the Philistine. Then David's men swore to him, "You shall not go out again with us to battle, so that you do not extinguish the lamp of Israel."

18 After this, there was war again with the Philistines at Gob (Gezer). At that time Sibbecai the Hushathite killed Saph (Sippai), who was among the descendants of the giant.

19 There was war with the Philistines again at Gob, and Elhanan the son of Jaare-oregim, a Bethlehemite, killed Goliath the Gittite, whose spear shaft was like a weaver's beam.

20 There was war at Gath again, where there was a man of *great* stature who had six fingers on each hand and six toes on each foot, twenty-four in number; he also was a descendant of the giants.

21 And when he taunted *and* defied Israel, Jonathan the son of Shimei, David's brother, killed him.

22 These four [warriors] were descended from the giant in Gath, and they fell by the hands of David and his servants.

David's Psalm of Rescue

22 DAVID SPOKE the words of this song to the LORD when the LORD

21:10 ***Rizpah.*** Rizpah remained near the bodies, protecting them from scavengers, from the barley harvest to the early rains (late April to October). This heartbreaking devotion from the mother of two of the slain men commended her to David, and finally the bones of Saul and all of his sons were buried in the family grave site.

21:14 ***God was moved by prayer for the land.*** It is hard to understand why the death of the descendants of Saul as payment for his treachery was something that would be connected to God hearing prayers for famine. Saul was described as rebellious, and apparently his disobedience was more far reaching than is recorded in Scripture. Possibly the men who were killed had been implicated in killing the Gibeonites. Even if we do not understand, we can always be sure that God is just and God is righteous.

21:16 ***giant.*** The giants were the Rephaim, a people living in Canaan who were noted for their large size.

22:1 ***words of this song.*** This psalm later became part of the congregational worship of Israel (Ps 18), but it began as David's personal and earnest expression of praise to the Lord.

9 2Sa 6:17 **10** ver. 8; 2Sa 3:7; See Dt 21:23 **12** 1Sa 31:11-13 **14** Jos 18:28; See Jos 7:26; 2Sa 24:25 **17** 2Sa 18:3; 1Ki 11:36 **18** 1Ch 20:4; 1Ch 11:29 **19** See 1Ch 20:5 **20** 1Ch 20:6 **21** 1Sa 16:9 **22** 1Ch 20:8 **CHAPTER 22** **1** Ex 15:1; Jdg 5:1; Ps 18, title; 34:19

rescued him from the hands of all his
enemies and from the hand of Saul.
2He said:

"The LORD is my rock and my
fortress [on the mountain] and
my rescuer; [1 Sam 23:14, 25, 28]
3My God, my rock, in whom I take
refuge;
My shield and the horn of my
salvation, my stronghold and
my refuge,
My Savior—You save me from
violence. [Gen 15:1]
4"I call on the LORD, who is worthy
to be praised,
And I am saved from my enemies.
5"For the waves of death
encompassed me;
The torrents of destruction
overwhelmed *and* terrified me.
6"The cords of Sheol surrounded me;
The snares of death confronted me.
7"In my distress I called upon the
LORD;
I cried out to my God,
And from His temple [in the
heavens] He heard my voice;
My cry for help *came* into His
ears.
8"Then the earth shook and
quaked,
The foundations of the heavens
trembled
And were shaken, because He was
angry.
9"Smoke went up out of His
nostrils,
And devouring fire from His
mouth;
Coals were kindled by it.
10"He bowed the heavens also, and
came down
With thick darkness under His
feet.
11"He rode on a cherub and flew;
He appeared upon the wings of the
wind.
12"He made darkness canopies
around Him,
A mass of waters, thick clouds of
the skies.
13"Out of the brightness before Him
Coals of fire were set aflame.
14"The LORD thundered from
heaven,
And the Most High uttered His
voice.
15"He sent out arrows and scattered
them;
Lightning, and confused them.
16"The channels of the sea appeared,
The foundations of the world were
uncovered
At the rebuke of the LORD,
At the blast of the breath of His
nostrils.
17"He sent from above, He took me;
He drew me out of great waters.
18"He rescued me from my strong
enemy,
From those who hated me, for they
were too mighty for me.
19"They came upon me in the day of
my calamity,
But the LORD was my support.
20"He also brought me out to an
open place;
He rescued me because He
delighted in me.
21"The LORD has dealt with me
according to my righteousness;
According to the cleanness of my
hands He has rewarded me.
22"For I have kept the ways of the
LORD,
And have not acted wickedly
against my God.

22:3 *the horn of my salvation.* The horn of an animal is used for protection and defense, so it is a good word picture for a sign of might and power.
22:6 *Sheol.* Sheol is used in Hebrew poetry as a synonym for death. In the Old Testament, Sheol is described as a place of dust, referring to death (Job 17:16), a place of decay (Ps 16:10), and as a pit (Isa 14:15).

22:22 *I have kept the ways of the LORD.* David did not keep the ways of the Lord perfectly. His sins have been written down for the whole world to know throughout the ages. But he never forgot the Lord, always knew that what he did mattered to God, and always turned his steps back to the Lord when he went astray. Like Paul, David ran the race in such a way as to get the prize (1Co 9:24).

2 Dt 32:4 **3** Heb 2:13; Ge 15:1; Lk 1:69; Pr 18:10; Ps 9:9; Jer 16:19 **6** Ps 116:3 **7** Ps 116:4; Ex 3:7 **8** Ps 77:18; Job 26:11 **9** Ps 97:3 **10** Isa 64:1; Ex 20:21 **11** Ps 104:3 **12** Ps 97:2 **13** ver. 9 **14** 1Sa 2:10 **15** Ps 7:13 **16** Ex 15:8 **17** Ps 144:7 **18** ver. 1 **20** Ps 31:8; 2Sa 15:26 **21** Ps 7:8; Ps 24:4 **22** Ps 119:3

23 "For all His judgments (legal
decisions) were before me,
And from His statutes I did not
turn aside.
24 "I was also blameless before Him,
And kept myself from
wrongdoing.
25 "Therefore the LORD has
rewarded me according to my
righteousness,
According to my cleanness in His
sight.
26 "With the loving *and* loyal You
show Yourself loving *and* loyal,
With the blameless You show
Yourself blameless.
27 "With the pure You show Yourself
pure,
With the perverted You show
Yourself astute.
28 "And You save the afflicted people;
But Your eyes are on the haughty
whom You abase (humiliate).
29 "For You, O LORD, are my lamp;
The LORD illumines *and* dispels my
darkness.
30 "For by You I can run upon a troop;
By my God I can leap over a wall.
31 "As for God, His way is blameless
and perfect;
The word of the LORD is tested.
He is a shield to all those who take
refuge *and* trust in Him.
32 "For who is God, besides the LORD?
And who is a rock, besides our
God? [1 Sam 2:2]
33 "God is my strong fortress;
He sets the blameless in His way.
34 "He makes my feet like the doe's
feet [firm and swift];
He sets me [secure and confident]
on my high places.
35 "He trains my hands for war,
So that my arms can bend (pull
back) a bow of bronze.
36 "You have also given me the shield
of Your salvation,
And Your help *and* gentleness
make me great.
37 "You enlarge my steps under me,
And my feet have not slipped.
38 "I pursued my enemies and
destroyed them,
And I did not turn back until they
were consumed (eliminated).
39 "I consumed them and shattered
them, so that they did not rise;
They fell under my feet.
40 "For You have surrounded me with
strength for the battle;
You have subdued under me those
who stood against me.
41 "You have also made my enemies
turn their backs to me [in
retreat],
And I destroyed those who hated
me.
42 "They looked, but there was no
savior *for them*—
Even to the LORD [they looked], but
He did not answer them.
43 "Then I beat them as [small as] the
dust of the earth;
I crushed and stamped them as the
mire (dirt, mud) of the streets.
44 "You also have rescued me from
strife with my [own] people;
You have kept me as the head of
the nations.
People whom I have not known
served me.
45 "Foreigners pretend obedience to
me;
As soon as they hear [me], they
obey me.
46 "Foreigners lose heart;
They come trembling out of their
strongholds.
47 "The LORD lives, and blessed be my
rock,
And exalted be my God, the rock
of my salvation.
48 "It is God who executes vengeance
for me,

22:34 *doe's feet.* The type of deer indicated in this passage is noted for its swiftness, agility, and sure-footedness.

22:35 *bend (pull back) a bow of bronze.* It would take unusual strength to bend a bronze bow (Job 20:24).

22:47 *The LORD lives.* This shout of exaltation is the heart cry of every follower of God. The

23 Dt 7:12 **24** Job 1:1 **25** ver. 21 **26** Mt 5:7 **27** Lev 26:23 **28** Ps 72:12; Job 40:11 **31** Da 4:37; Ps 12:6 **32** Isa 45:5,6 **33** Ps 27:1; Isa 12:2; Heb 13:21; Ps 101:2,6 **34** 2Sa 2:18; Isa 33:16 **35** Ps 144:1 **37** Pr 4:12 **39** Mal 4:3 **40** Ps 18:32; Ps 44:5 **41** Ge 49:8 **42** Pr 1:28 **43** Ps 18:42; Isa 10:6 **44** 2Sa 3:1; Dt 28:13; Isa 55:5 **46** Mic 7:17 **47** Ps 89:26 **48** Ps 144:2

And brings down [and disciplines]
the peoples under me,
49 Who also brings me out from my
enemies.
You even lift me above those who
rise up against me;
You rescue me from the violent man.
50 "For this I will give thanks *and*
praise You, O LORD, among the
nations;
I will sing praises to Your name.
51 "He is a tower of salvation *and*
great deliverance to His king,
And shows lovingkindness to His
anointed,
To David and his offspring
forever."

David's Last Song

23 NOW THESE are the last words of David.

David the son of Jesse declares,
The man who was raised on high
declares,
The anointed of the God of Jacob,
And the sweet psalmist of Israel,
2 "The Spirit of the LORD spoke by me,
And His word was on my tongue.
3 "The God of Israel,
The Rock of Israel spoke to me,
'He who rules over men righteously,
Who rules in the fear of God,
4 Is like the morning light *when* the
sun rises,
A morning without clouds,
When the fresh grass *springs* out
of the earth
Through sunshine after rain.'
5 "Truly is not my house so [blessed]
with God?
For He has made an everlasting
covenant with me,
Ordered in all things, and secured.
For will He not cause to grow *and*
prosper
All my salvation and my every wish?
Will He not make it grow *and*
prosper?
6 "But the wicked *and* worthless are
all to be thrown away like thorns,
Because they cannot be taken with
the hand;
7 "But the man who touches them
Must be armed with iron and the
shaft of a spear,
And they are utterly burned *and*
consumed by fire in their place."

His Mighty Men

8 These are the names of the mighty
men (warriors) whom David had:
Josheb-basshebeth, a Tachemonite,
chief of the captains, *also called* Adino

---

difference between the Living God and the dead idols that entrapped so many in the countries around him stood out very strongly to David.

22:51 *His anointed.* David was anointed by God to be king of Israel. He was set aside for a certain job. Jesus is the ultimate Anointed One, which is the meaning of the Hebrew name Messiah and the Greek name Christ.

23:1 *sweet psalmist of Israel.* Of the 150 psalms in the Book of Psalms, 73 are attributed to David by the text. No person in Scripture is more closely associated with music in the worship of the Lord than King David. He left behind a beautiful record of his heartfelt love of the Lord, his struggles, and his victories.

23:3–4 Fear of God—For centuries certain dynasties of rulers in Europe claimed the divine right to rule. Certainly the Bible teaches that government is ordained of God (Ro 13). But it also teaches that rulers have a deep stewardship responsibility. They are to rule men in the fear of God. Over and over again it is shown that God sets rulers in place, and also deposes those who consistently rebel against Him.

23:5 *everlasting covenant.* David celebrates his everlasting covenant (7:12–16) here and in Psalm 89.

23:6–7 *the wicked and worthless.* This is an expression of contempt and scorn, the phrase that Shimei hurled at David when David was fleeing from the rebellion of his son Absalom (16:7). The expression was also used to describe Sheba, the scoundrel from the tribe of Benjamin (20:1). David anticipated God's judgment on the ungodly, who are likened to thorns fit only to be burned.

23:8 *mighty men.* The term "mighty men" suggests that these were the elite of David's troops, possibly his personal body guards. These men were heroes in the full sense of the word. Their listing must have inspired others to attain such accomplishments.

---

49 Ps 140:1 **50** Ro 15:9 **51** Ps 144:10; Ps 89:20; Ps 89:29 **CHAPTER 23** **1** Ps 78:70; 1Sa 16:12,13; Ps 89:20
2 2Pe 1:21 **3** Dt 32:4; Ex 18:21 **5** Ps 89:29

the Eznite (spear) because of the eight hundred men killed [by him] at one time. [1 Chr 11:11]

9 Next to him was Eleazar the son of Dodo the son of Ahohi. He was one of the three mighty men with David when they taunted *and* defied the Philistines assembled there for battle, and the men of Israel had gone.

10 Eleazar stood up and struck down the Philistines until his hand was weary and clung to the sword. The LORD brought about a great victory that day; the people returned after him only to take the spoil [of the slain].

11 Next to Eleazar was Shammah the son of Agee the Hararite. The Philistines were gathered into an army where there was a plot of ground full of lentils, and the people [of Israel] fled from the Philistines.

12 But he took his stand in the center of the plot and defended it and struck down the Philistines; and the LORD brought about a great victory.

13 Then three of the thirty chief men went down and came to David at harvest time in the cave of Adullam, while an army of Philistines was encamped in the Valley of Rephaim.

14 David was then in the stronghold, and the garrison of the Philistines was then in Bethlehem.

15 And David had a craving and said, "Oh that someone would give me water to drink from the well of Bethlehem, which is by the gate!"

16 So the three mighty men broke through the camp of the Philistines, and drew water from the well of Bethlehem by the gate, and carried and brought it to David. But he would not drink it, but poured it out [in worship] to the LORD.

17 And he said, "Far be it from me, O LORD, that I should drink this. [Is it not the same as] the blood of the men who went at the risk of their lives?" So he would not drink it. These things the three mighty men did.

18 Now Abishai the brother of Joab the son of Zeruiah was chief of the thirty. He wielded his spear against three hundred men and killed them, and gained a reputation beside the three.

19 He was the most honored of the thirty, so he became their commander; however, he did not attain to the [greatness of the] three.

20 Then Benaiah the son of Jehoiada, the son of a valiant man of Kabzeel, who had done many notable acts, killed two [famous] warriors of Moab. He also went down and killed a lion in the middle of a pit on a snowy day.

21 And he killed an Egyptian, an impressive *and* handsome man. The Egyptian had a spear in his hand, but Benaiah went down to him with a club, snatched the spear out of the Egyptian's hand and killed the man with his own spear.

22 These things Benaiah the son of Jehoiada did, and gained a reputation beside the three mighty men.

23 He was honored among the thirty, but he did not attain to the [greatness of the] three. David appointed him over his guard.

24 Asahel the brother of Joab was one of the thirty; *then* Elhanan the son of Dodo of Bethlehem,

25 Shammah of Harod, Elika of Harod,

26 Helez the Paltite, Ira the son of Ikkesh of Tekoa,

27 Abiezer of Anathoth, Mebunnai the Hushathite,

23:13 – 14 ***Valley of Rephaim.*** This valley was a route to Jerusalem. ***Bethlehem.*** David's hometown (1Sa 16:1 – 3) was about six miles south of Jerusalem.

23:15 ***give me water to drink from the well of Bethlehem.*** Anyone who has grown up with an especially good well for drinking water can identify with David's craving. The taste of the water from the well at "home" seems more thirst quenching, more heartening, than any other.

23:16 ***poured it out [in worship] to the LORD.*** David was deeply moved by this act of loyalty. He could have let it make him feel important, but instead he dedicated the water to the Lord, knowing that no man's craving should be satisfied at the risk of another man's life.

9 1Ch 11:12 **11** 1Ch 11:27; See 1Ch 11:13,14 **13** 1Ch 11:15; 1Sa 22:1; 2Sa 5:18 **14** 1Sa 22:4,5 **17** Lev 17:10 **18** 1Ch 11:20 **20** Jos 15:21; Ex 15:15 **23** 2Sa 8:18; 20:23 **24** 2Sa 2:18 **25** See 1Ch 11:27

[28]Zalmon the Ahohite, Maharai of Netophah,
[29]Heleb the son of Baanah of Netophah, Ittai the son of Ribai of Gibeah of the Benjamites,
[30]Benaiah of Pirathon, Hiddai of the brooks of Gaash,
[31]Abi-albon the Arbathite, Azmaveth the Barhumite,
[32]Eliahba of Shaalbon, the sons of Jashen, Jonathan,
[33]Shammah the Hararite, Ahiam the son of Sharar the Ararite,
[34]Eliphelet the son of Ahasbai the son of Maacah, Eliam the son of Ahithophel of Giloh,
[35]Hezro (Hezrai) of Carmel, Paarai the Arbite,
[36]Igal the son of Nathan of Zobah, Bani the Gadite,
[37]Zelek the Ammonite, Naharai of Beeroth, armor bearer of Joab the son of Zeruiah,
[38]Ira the Ithrite, Gareb the Ithrite,
[39]Uriah the Hittite—thirty-seven in all.

The Census Taken

24 NOW AGAIN the anger of the LORD burned against Israel, and He incited David against them to say, "Go, count [the people of] Israel and Judah."
[2]So the king said to Joab the commander of the army who was with him, "Go now through all the tribes of Israel, from Dan [in the north] to Beersheba [in the south], and conduct a census of the people, so that I may know the number of the people."
[3]But Joab said to the king, "May the LORD your God add to the people a hundred times as many as there are, and let the eyes of my lord the king see it; but why does my lord the king want to do this thing?"
[4]Nevertheless, the king's word prevailed against Joab and the commanders of the army. So they went from the king's presence to take a census of the people of Israel.
[5]They crossed over the Jordan and camped in Aroer, on the south side of the city which is in the middle of the river valley [of the Arnon] toward Gad, and on toward Jazer.
[6]Then they came to Gilead and to the land of Tahtim-hodshi, and they came to Dan-jaan and around to Sidon,
[7]and they came to the stronghold of Tyre and to all the cities of the Hivites and Canaanites, and they went out to the south of Judah, to Beersheba.
[8]So when they had gone about through all the land [taking the census], they came to Jerusalem at the end of nine months and twenty days.
[9]And Joab gave the sum of the census of the people to the king. In Israel there were 800,000 valiant men who drew the sword, and the men of Judah were 500,000.
[10]But David's heart (conscience) troubled him after he had counted the people. David said to the LORD, "I have sinned greatly in what I have done. But now, O LORD, please take away the sin of Your servant, for I have acted very foolishly."
[11]When David got up in the morning,

24:3 *why does my lord the king want to do this thing.* God was angry with Israel, and the numbering and resulting pestilence were a part of His plan to deal with Israel in such a way that they did not become complacent. This incident is not well explained in Scripture. Joab knew that David was acting presumptuously, but at this point David could not see it. Perhaps the census showed a lack of trust in the Lord, and a sense that the might of the nation rested in its armed men.

24:9 *men who drew the sword.* The numbers given refer only to men of military age. It is impressive that the division of Israel and Judah was so well established. This division would in the end result in a divided kingdom.

24:10 *David's heart (conscience) troubled him.* The text does not state precisely what David's sin was. His heart was always sensitive to God's will, and he quickly confessed his sin and sought restoration with the Lord.

30 Jdg 2:9 **38** 2Sa 20:26 **39** 2Sa 11:3,6 **CHAPTER 24** **1** 2Sa 20:1; 1Ch 27:23,24 **2** Jdg 20:1; Jer 17:5 **5** Dt 2:36; Jos 13:9,16; Nu 32:1,3 **6** Jos 19:47; Jdg 18:29; Jos 19:28; Jdg 18:28 **9** See 1Ch 21:5 **10** 1Sa 24:5; 2Sa 12:13; 1Sa 13:13 **11** 1Sa 22:5; 1Sa 9:9; 1Ch 29:29

the word of the LORD came to the
prophet Gad, David’s seer, saying,
12“Go and say to David, ‘Thus says
the LORD, “I am giving you three
choices; select one of them for your-
self, and I will do it to you.” ’ ”
13So Gad came to David and told
him, and said to him, “Shall seven
years of famine come to you in your
land? Or will you flee three months
before your enemies as they pursue
you? Or shall there be three days of
pestilence (plague) in your land? Now
consider this and decide what answer
I shall return to Him who sent me.”
14Then David said to Gad, “I am in
great distress. Let us fall into the hands
of the LORD, for His mercies are great,
but do not let me fall into the hands
of man.”

Pestilence Sent

15So the LORD sent a pestilence
(plague) [lasting three days] upon Israel
from the morning until the appointed
time, and seventy thousand men of the
people from Dan to Beersheba died.
16When the [avenging] angel
stretched out his hand toward Jerusa-
lem to destroy it, the LORD relented from
the disaster and said to the angel who
destroyed the people, “It is enough!
Now relax your hand.” And the angel
of the LORD was by the threshing floor
of Araunah the Jebusite.
17When David saw the angel who was
striking down the people, he spoke to
the LORD and said, “Behold, I [alone] am
the one who has sinned and done wrong;
but these sheep (people of Israel), what
have they done [to deserve this]? Please
let Your hand be [only] against me and
my father’s house (family).”

David Builds an Altar

18Then Gad [the prophet] came to
David that day and said to him, “Go
up, set up an altar to the LORD on the
threshing floor of Araunah the Jeb-
usite [where you saw the angel].”
19So David went up according to
Gad’s word, as the LORD commanded.
20Araunah looked down and saw
the king and his servants crossing
over toward him; and he went out and
bowed before the king with his face
toward the ground.
21Araunah said, “Why has my lord
the king come to his servant?” And
David said, “To buy the threshing floor
from you, to build an altar to the LORD,
so that the plague may be held back
from the people.”
22Araunah said to David, “Let my
lord the king take and offer up what-
ever seems good to him. Look, here
are oxen for the burnt offering, and
threshing sledges and the yokes of the
oxen for the wood.
23“All of this, O king, Araunah gives
to the king.” And Araunah said to the
king, “May the LORD your God be fa-
vorable to you.”
24But the king said to Araunah, “No,
but I will certainly buy it from you for
a price. I will not offer burnt offer-
ings to the LORD my God which cost
me nothing.” So David purchased the
threshing floor and the oxen for fifty
shekels of silver.
25David built an altar to the LORD
there, and offered burnt offerings
and peace offerings. So the LORD was
moved [to compassion] by [David’s]
prayer for the land, and the plague was
held back from Israel.

24:24 *threshing floor.* The threshing floor was located on Mount Moriah, where Abraham had bound Isaac (Ge 22:2). Later, Solomon would build the temple at this site (1Ki 6:1; 1Ch 21:27 – 22:1; 2Ch 3:1). ***fifty shekels of silver.*** The fifty shekels of silver paid only for the threshing floor, the oxen, and the implements. The land that surrounded the threshing floor would cost considerably more — six hundred shekels, or 15 pounds of gold (1Ch 21:25).

24:25 *burnt offerings and peace offerings.* The burnt offering was the principal atoning sacrifice for unintentional sins (Lev 1:1 – 17; 6:8 – 13). It was completely consumed on the altar, except for the hide, which was given to the officiating priest. The peace offering was an optional sacrifice, which did not form any part of the regular offerings required in the tabernacle or temple. It was a voluntary expression of thanksgiving or worship (Lev 3:1 – 17; 7:11 – 34).

13 See 1Ch 21:12 **14** Ps 103:8,13,14; 119:156; See Isa 47:6; Zec 1:15 **15** 1Ch 21:14; 27:24 **16** Ex 12:23; Ge 6:6; 1Sa 15:11; Joel 2:13,14; 2Ch 3:1 **17** 1Ch 21:17 **18** 1Ch 21:18 **21** See Ge 23:8-16; Nu 16:48,50 **22** 1Ki 19:21 **23** Eze 20:40,41 **24** See 1Ch 21:24,25 **25** 2Sa 21:14; ver. 21

THE FIRST BOOK OF THE
KINGS

▸ **AUTHOR:** Both 1 and 2 Kings emphasize God's righteous judgment on idolatry and immorality. The style of these books is similar to that found in Jeremiah. The author of 1 Kings is unknown, but evidence supports the Talmudic tradition that Kings was written by Jeremiah. Clearly, the author was a prophet/historian as evidenced in the prophetic exposé of apostasy.

▸ **TIMES:** c. 971 – 851 BC ▸ **KEY VERSES:** 1Ki 9:4 – 5

▸ **THEME:** First Kings continues the saga of the kings of Israel after David. Solomon's reign and the details of the building of the temple take up a major portion of 1 Kings. After Solomon, the kingdom divides, and we have parallel narratives of the Northern Kingdom, Israel, and the Southern Kingdom, Judah. The book covers a span of about 120 years. During these years, idolatry becomes the norm, and God is largely forgotten. After Solomon, the main character of the book is Elijah the prophet.

David in Old Age

1 NOW KING David was old, ad-
vanced in years; they covered him
with clothes, but he could not get warm.
2 So his servants said to him, "Let
a young virgin be found for my lord
the king and let her attend him and
become his nurse; let her lie against
your chest, so that my lord the king
may feel warm."
3 So they searched for a beautiful girl
throughout the territory of Israel, and
found Abishag the Shunammite, and
brought her to the king.
4 The girl was very beautiful; and she
became the king's nurse and served
him, but the king was not intimate
with her.
5 Then Adonijah the son of [David's
wife] Haggith exalted himself, saying,
"I [the eldest living son] will be king."
So [following Absalom's example]
he prepared for himself chariots and
horsemen, and fifty men to run before
him. [2 Sam 15:1]
6 His father [David] had never re-
buked him at any time by asking,
"Why have you done this?" Adonijah
was also a very handsome man, and
he was born after Absalom.
7 He had conferred with Joab the
son of Zeruiah [David's half sister]
and with Abiathar the priest; and they
followed Adonijah and helped him.
8 But Zadok the priest, Benaiah the
son of Jehoiada, Nathan the prophet,

1:1 *King David was old.* David was about seventy years old at the time of his death (2Sa 5:4; 1Ch 29:26 – 28), and the long years of warfare had doubtlessly taken their physical toll.

1:5 *Adonijah.* The name Adonijah means "the LORD is my Lord." Amnon and Absalom both experienced violent deaths (2Sa 13:28 – 29; 18:14). Chiliab, his second son, apparently died at an early age. Adonijah was David's oldest surviving son.

1:6 *had never rebuked him.* While David had been a most capable leader and a man of deep spiritual sensitivity, he had not exercised proper parental discipline of his children (2Sa 13:21 – 39; 14:18 – 24).

CHAPTER 1 **3** Jos 19:18 **5** 2Sa 3:4 **6** 2Sa 3:3; 1Ch 3:2 **7** 2Sa 20:25; 1Ki 2:22,28 **8** 1Ki 4:18; 2Sa 23:8

CHRONOLOGY OF FOREIGN KINGS

This is a chronology of selected foreign kings mentioned in this study Bible.

ARAM	Ben-Hadad I	c. 895 – 860*
	Ben-Hadad II	c. 860 – 843
	Hazael	c. 843 – 796
	Ben-Hadad III	c. 796 – 770
	Rezin	740s – 732
ASSYRIA	Tiglath-Pileser III	745 – 727
	Shalmaneser V	727 – 722
	Sargon II	721 – 705
	Sennacherib	705 – 681
	Esarhaddon	681 – 669
	Ashurbanipal	669 – 627
BABYLONIA	Marduk-Baladan II	722 – 710, 703
	Nebuchadnezzar II	605 – 562
	Amel-Marduk	562 – 560
	Nabonidus	556 – 539
	Belshazzar (Coregency with Nabonidus)	553(?) – 539
EGYPT	Ahmose I	1550 – 1525**
	Thutmose II	1491 – 1479
	Thutmose III	1479 – 1425
	Tutankhamun	1333 – 1323
	Seti I	1289 – 1278
	Rameses II	1279 – 1212
	Merneptah	1212 – 1202
	Siamun	978 – 959
	Psusennes II	959 – 945
	Shishak I	945 – 924
	Osorkon I	924 – 889
	Shabako	716 – 702
	Shebitku	701 – 690
	Tirhakah	690 – 664
	Necho II	610 – 595
	Psammeticus II	595 – 589
	Hophra	589 – 570
PERSIA	Cyrus the Great	559 – 530
	Cambyses II	530 – 522
	Darius I the Great	522 – 486
	Xerxes (Ahasuerus)	486 – 465
	Artaxerxes I	465 – 424
	Darius II	423 – 404

*All dates are BC and are those of the kings' reigns.

**The earlier Egyptian dates assigned here are less certain than the later ones; there were also a few coregencies.

Shimei, Rei, and David's most formidable warriors did not side with Adonijah [in his desire to become king].

9 Adonijah sacrificed sheep and oxen and fattened steers by the Stone of Zoheleth, which is beside [the well] En-rogel; and he invited all his brothers, the king's sons, and all the men of Judah, the king's servants [to this feast]. [2 Sam 15:7–12]

10 But he did not invite Nathan the prophet, Benaiah, the most formidable warriors, or his brother Solomon.

Nathan and Bathsheba

11 Then Nathan spoke to Bathsheba the mother of Solomon, "Have you not heard that Adonijah the son of Haggith has become king, and David our lord does not know about it?

12 "Come now, please let me advise you and save your life and the life of your son Solomon. [2 Sam 12:24, 25]

13 "Go at once to King David and say to him, 'Did you not, my lord, O king, swear to your maidservant, saying, "Solomon your son shall certainly be king after me, and he shall sit on my throne"? Why then has Adonijah become king?'

14 "Behold, while you are still there speaking with the king, I will come in after you and confirm your words."

15 So Bathsheba went to the king in his bedroom. Now the king was very old *and* weak, and Abishag the Shunammite was attending the king.

16 So Bathsheba bowed down and paid respect to the king. And the king said, "What do you wish?"

17 She said to him, "My lord, you swore by the LORD your God to your maidservant, *saying*, 'Solomon your son shall certainly be king after me and he shall sit on my throne.'

18 "But now, behold, Adonijah is [acting as] king; and now [as things stand], my lord the king, you do not know it.

19 "He has sacrificed oxen and fattened steers and sheep in abundance, and has invited all the king's sons and Abiathar the priest and Joab the commander of the army [to a feast], but he did not invite your servant Solomon.

20 "Now as for you, my lord the king, the eyes of all Israel are on you [waiting for you] to tell them who shall sit on the throne of my lord the king after him.

21 "Otherwise it will come about when my lord the king lies down [in death] with his fathers, that I and my son Solomon will be considered political enemies."

22 While she was still speaking with the king, Nathan the prophet came in.

23 The king was told, "Here is Nathan the prophet." And when he came before the king, he bowed before the king with his face to the ground.

24 Then Nathan said, "My lord the king, have you said, 'Adonijah shall be king after me, and he shall sit on my throne'?

25 "Because he has gone down today [to En-Rogel] and has sacrificed oxen and fattened steers and sheep in abundance, and has invited all the king's sons, the commanders of the army and Abiathar the priest [to this feast]; and [right now] they are eating and drinking in his presence; and they say, '*Long* live King Adonijah!'

26 "But he has not invited me, your servant, nor Zadok the priest, nor Benaiah the son of Jehoiada, nor your servant Solomon.

27 "If this thing has been done by my lord the king, why have you not shown your servants who shall sit on the throne of my lord the king after him?"

1:11 – 14 Wisdom — In Old Testament times, messages from God were often given through personal prophecy. Today, believers do not often receive messages through prophecy. God has given the higher privilege of direct access to His wisdom through the ministry of the indwelling Holy Spirit in all who believe. Today believers have access to God's wisdom through His Word, His indwelling Spirit, and counsel from mature Christians.

1:11 *Nathan.* It is a mark of David's integrity that Nathan, who had confronted him with his terrible sin with Bathsheba, was still welcome in the royal household (2Sa 12:1 – 15).

11 2Sa 3:4 **13** 1Ch 22:9 **17** ver. 13,30 **19** ver. 7-9,25 **21** Dt 31:16; 1Ki 2:10 **25** ver. 19; 1Sa 10:24

28 King David answered, "Call Bath-
sheba to me." And she came into the
king's presence and stood before him.
29 Then the king swore an oath and
said, "As the LORD lives, who has re-
deemed my soul from all distress,
30 even as I swore to you by the LORD,
the God of Israel, saying, 'Solomon
your son shall certainly be king after
me, and he shall sit on my throne in
my place'; I will indeed do so this *very*
day."
31 Bathsheba bowed down with her
face to the ground, and laid herself face
down before the king and said, "May
my lord King David live forever!"
32 Then King David said, "Call Zadok
the priest, Nathan the prophet, and
Benaiah the son of Jehoiada to me."
And they came before the king.
33 The king told them, "Take the ser-
vants of your lord with you and have
Solomon my son ride on my own mule,
and bring him down to [the spring at]
Gihon [in the Kidron Valley].
34 "Let Zadok the priest and Nathan
the prophet anoint him there as king
over Israel. Then blow the trumpet and
say, '*Long* live King Solomon!'
35 "Then you shall come up [to Jeru-
salem] after him, and he shall come
and sit on my throne and he shall
reign *as king* in my place; for I have
appointed him to be ruler over Israel
and Judah."
36 Benaiah [the overseer of the king's
bodyguards], the son of Jehoiada an-
swered the king and said, "Amen! (So
be it!) May the LORD, the God of my
lord the king, say so too.
37 "Just as the LORD has been with
my lord the king, so may He be with
Solomon, and make his throne great-
er than the throne of my lord King
David!"

Solomon Anointed King

38 So Zadok the priest, Nathan the
prophet, Benaiah the son of Jehoiada,
the Cherethites, and the Pelethites [the
king's bodyguards] went down [from
Jerusalem] and had Solomon ride on
King David's mule, and brought him
to [the spring at] Gihon.
39 Zadok the priest took a horn of
[olive] oil from the [sacred] tent and
anointed Solomon. They blew the
trumpet, and all the people said, "*Long*
live King Solomon!"
40 All the people went up after him,
and they were playing on flutes and
rejoicing with great joy, so that the
earth shook *and* seemed to burst open
with their [joyful] sound.
41 Now Adonijah and all the guests
who were with him heard it as they
finished eating. When Joab heard the
trumpet sound, he said, "Why is the
city in such an uproar?"
42 While he was still speaking, be-
hold, Jonathan the son of Abiathar
the priest arrived. And Adonijah said,
"Come in, for you are a valiant *and*
trustworthy man and you bring good
news." [2 Sam 17:17–21]
43 But Jonathan replied to Adonijah,
"No, *on the contrary,* our lord King
David has made Solomon king!
44 "The king has sent him with Za-
dok the priest, Nathan the prophet,
Benaiah the son of Jehoiada, the Cher-
ethites, and the Pelethites; and they
have had him ride on the king's [own
royal] mule.

1:29 *who has redeemed my soul.* In these words of praise, David celebrated the innumerable times that the Lord had acted on his behalf, to deliver him from his enemies and from his own sins. Some of David's psalms were written in connection with those times of God's deliverance (Ps 40; 142).

1:38 *the Cherethites, and the Pelethites.* These two groups were part of David's bodyguard (2Sa 8:18; 15:18; 20:7). Their association with David stretched back to his days among the Philistines, with whom the Cherethites are usually identified (1Sa 30:13–14; Eze 25:16; Zep 2:5).

1:39 *Zadok . . . anointed Solomon.* Every priestly anointing would recall the words of Psalm 2, in accordance with the words of the Davidic covenant of 2 Samuel 7. The anointing announced that the anointed one was now the adopted son of the living God.

29 2Sa 4:9 **30** ver. 17 **31** Neh 2:3; Dan 2:4 **33** 2Sa 20:6; 2Ch 32:30 **34** 1Sa 10:1; 16:3,12; 2Sa 2:4; 5:3; 1Ki 19:16; 2Ki 9:3; 11:12; 2Sa 15:10; 2Ki 9:13; 11:14 **37** Jos 1:5,17; 1Sa 20:13; ver. 47 **38** 2Sa 8:18; 23:20-23 **39** Ex 30:23,25,32; Ps 89:20; 1Ch 29:22; 1Sa 10:24 **42** 2Sa 18:27

45“Also, Zadok the priest and Nathan the prophet have anointed him king in Gihon, and they have come up from there celebrating, so the city is in an uproar. This is the noise which you have heard.

46“Besides, Solomon has taken his seat on the throne of the kingdom.

47“Moreover, the king’s servants came to bless (congratulate) our lord King David, saying, ‘May your God make the name of Solomon better (more famous) than your name and make his throne greater than your throne.’ And the king bowed himself [before God] upon the bed.

48“The king has also said this: ‘Blessed be the LORD, the God of Israel, who has granted one [of my descendants] to sit on my throne today and *allowed* my eyes to see it.’ ”

49Then all Adonijah’s guests were terrified [of being branded as traitors] and stood up *and* left the feast, and each one went on his way.

50And Adonijah feared Solomon, and he got up and went [to the tabernacle on Mt. Zion] and took hold of the horns of the altar [seeking asylum].

51Now Solomon was told, “Behold, Adonijah is afraid of King Solomon, and behold, he has grasped the horns of the altar [seeking God’s protection], saying, ‘King Solomon must swear to me today that he will not kill his servant with the sword.’ ”

52Solomon said, “If he [proves he] is a worthy man, not *even* one of his hairs shall fall to the ground; but if wickedness is found in him, he shall die.”

53So King Solomon sent [soldiers], and they brought Adonijah down from the altar [that was in front of the tabernacle]. And he came and bowed down to King Solomon, and Solomon said to him, “Go to your house.”

David’s Charge to Solomon

2 WHEN DAVID’S time to die approached, he gave instructions to Solomon his son, saying,

2“I am going the way of all the earth [as dust to dust]. Be strong and prove yourself a man.

3“Keep the charge of the LORD your God, [that is, fulfill your obligation to] walk in His ways, keep His statutes, His commandments, His precepts, and His testimonies, as it is written in the Law of Moses, so that you may succeed in everything that you do and wherever you turn,

4so that the LORD may fulfill His promise concerning me, saying, ‘If your sons are careful regarding their way [of life], to walk before Me in truth with all their heart *and* mind and with all their soul, you shall not fail to have a man (descendant) on the throne of Israel.’

1:50 *took hold of the horns of the altar.* This action was in keeping with the traditional function of the altar as a haven of refuge for those who had committed unintentional crimes (Ex 21:12 – 14).

1:53 Forgiveness — Solomon chose to forgive Adonijah for his attempted usurpation of the throne, realizing that Adonijah had legitimate reason to think that he should be the next king. Wiser than his years, young Solomon overlooked the offense of his brother rather than bring any reproach on his reign at this early stage. Sadly, Adonijah proved himself unworthy of his pardon, making another attempt to take the throne after his father David was dead.

2:4 *you shall not fail to have a man (descendant) on the throne.* God had made an unconditional covenant with David (2Sa 7:12 – 16; 1Ch 17:11 – 14; Ps 89), granting him a continual posterity and a royal dynasty. Although the Davidic covenant was an everlasting sacred promise, individual kings through their evil behavior could fail to receive the benefits of the covenant. The line of promise would be preserved, but the time would come when the promised Ruler would not be on an earthly throne (Hos 3:4). God’s prophets predict that the heir to the throne of David will yet reign over a repentant, regathered, and restored Israel (Jer 33:19 – 26; Eze 34:22 – 31) in fulfillment of the promises of the covenants (Eze 37:21 – 28; Mic 7:18 – 20). The New Testament reveals that all this will be realized in Jesus Christ, the Savior King (Ac 3:25 – 26; 15:16 – 17; Gal 3:26 – 29; Rev 3:21), who is David’s Heir in the ultimate sense (Ac 2:22 – 36).

46 1Ch 29:23 **47** ver. 37; Ge 47:31 **48** 1Ki 3:6; Ps 132:11,12 **50** 1Ki 2:28 **52** 1Sa 14:45; 2Sa 14:11 **CHAPTER 2** **1** Ge 47:29; Dt 31:14 **2** Jos 23:14; Dt 17:19,20 **3** Dt 29:9; Jos 1:7; 1Ch 22:12,13 **4** 2Sa 7:25; Ps 132:12; 2Ki 20:3; 2Sa 7:12,13; 1Ki 8:25

5 “Now you also know what Joab the son of Zeruiah [my sister] did to me, and what he did to the two commanders of the armies of Israel, to Abner the son of Ner and to Amasa the son of Jether, [both of] whom he murdered; avenging the blood of war in [a time of] peace. And he put the [innocent] blood of war [of Abner and Amasa] on his belt that was around his waist, and on his sandals on his feet.

6 “So act in accordance with your wisdom, but do not let his gray head go down to Sheol (the place of the dead) in peace.

7 “But be gracious *and* kind to the sons of Barzillai the Gileadite, and let them be among those who [have the honor to] eat at your table; for they met me [with kindness] when I fled from your brother Absalom. [2 Sam 17:27–29]

8 “And look, you have with you Shimei the son of Gera, the Benjamite of Bahurim; he is the one who cursed me with a sinister curse the day I went to Mahanaim. But he came down to meet me at the Jordan [on my return], and I swore to him by the LORD, saying, ‘I will not put you to death with the sword.’

9 “But now do not let him go unpunished, for you are a wise man; and you will know what to do to him, and you will bring his gray head down to Sheol [covered] with blood.”

Death of David

10 So David lay down with his fathers [in death] and was buried in the City of David.

11 The time that David reigned over Israel was forty years: he reigned seven years in Hebron and thirty-three years in Jerusalem.

12 Then Solomon sat on the throne of David his father, and his kingdom was firmly established.

13 Now Adonijah the son of [David and] Haggith came to Bathsheba the mother of Solomon. She said, “Do you come in peace?” And he said, “In peace.”

14 Then he said, “I have something *to say* to you.” And she said, “Speak.”

15 So he said, “You know that the kingdom belonged to me [as the eldest living son] and all Israel looked to me *and* expected me to be king. However, the kingdom has passed [from me] and became my brother’s, for it was his from the LORD.

16 “So now I am making one request of you; do not refuse me.” And she said to him, “Speak.”

17 He said, “Please speak to King Solomon, for he will not refuse you; *ask* that he may give me Abishag the Shunammite as a wife.” [1 Kin 1:1–4]

18 Bathsheba replied, “Very well; I will speak to the king for you.”

Adonijah Executed

19 So Bathsheba went to King Solomon to speak to him for Adonijah. And the king rose to meet her, bowed before her, and sat down on his throne; then he had a throne set for her, the king’s mother, and she sat on his right.

20 Then she said, “I am making one small request of you; do not refuse me.” And the king said to her, “Ask, my mother, for I will not refuse you.”

21 So she said, “Let Abishag the Shunammite be given to your brother Adonijah as a wife.”

22 King Solomon answered and said to his mother, “And why are you asking for Abishag the Shunammite for Adonijah? Ask the kingdom for him also—since he is my older brother—[ask it] for him and for Abiathar the

---

2:5–8 *Joab . . . Shimei.* David knew that these two men would cause trouble for Solomon if they were not dealt with. Joab had murdered two generals (2Sa 3:27; 20:10), killed David’s son Absalom (2Sa 18:14), and joined Adonijah’s conspiracy (1:7,19). Shimei had cursed the king and treated him shamefully as he was fleeing from Absalom (2Sa 16:5–13; 19:16–23).

5 2Sa 3:39; 18:5,12,14; 2Sa 3:27; 2Sa 20:10 **6** ver. 9; Pr 20:26 **7** 2Sa 19:31,38; 2Sa 9:7,10; 19:28; 2Sa 17:27 **8** 2Sa 16:5; 2Sa 19:18; 2Sa 19:23 **9** Ex 20:7; Job 9:28; Ge 42:38; 44:31 **10** 1Ki 1:21; Ac 2:29; 13:36; 2Sa 5:7 **11** 2Sa 5:4; 1Ch 29:26,27 **12** 1Ch 29:23; 2Ch 1:1 **13** 1Sa 16:4,5 **15** 1Ch 22:9,10; 28:5-7; Da 2:21 **17** 1Ki 1:3,4 **19** Ex 20:12; See Ps 45:9 **22** 1Ki 1:7

priest and Joab the son of Zeruiah [his supporters]!"

23 Then King Solomon swore by the LORD, saying, "May God do the same to me, and more also, if Adonijah has not requested this [deplorable] thing against his own life.

24 "So now, as the LORD lives, who has established me and set me on the throne of David my father, and who has made me a house as He promised, Adonijah shall indeed be put to death today."

25 So King Solomon sent Benaiah the son of Jehoiada, and he struck Adonijah and he died.

26 Then the king said to Abiathar the priest, "Go to Anathoth to your own fields, for you certainly deserve to die; but I will not put you to death this day, because you carried the ark of the Lord GOD before my father David, and you suffered everything that my father endured."

27 So Solomon dismissed Abiathar [a descendant of Eli] from being priest to the LORD, fulfilling the word of the LORD, which He had spoken concerning the house (descendants) of Eli in Shiloh. [1 Sam 2:27–36]

Joab Executed

28 Now the news reached Joab, for Joab had supported *and* followed Adonijah, although he had not followed Absalom. So Joab fled to the [sacred] tent of the LORD and took hold of the horns of the altar [to seek asylum].

29 King Solomon was told that Joab had fled to the tent of the LORD and was at that moment beside the altar. Then Solomon sent Benaiah the son of Jehoiada, saying, "Go, strike him down."

30 So Benaiah came to the tent of the LORD and told Joab, "This is what the king commands, 'Come out *of there.*'" But Joab said, "No, for I will die here." Then Benaiah brought word to the king again, saying, "This is what Joab said, and this is how he answered me."

31 The king said to him, "Do as he has said. Strike him down and bury him, so that you may remove from me and from my father's house the innocent blood which Joab shed.

32 "The LORD will return his bloody deeds upon his own head, because he struck down two men more righteous and honorable than he and killed them with the sword, without my father David knowing: Abner the son of Ner, commander of the army of Israel, and Amasa the son of Jether, commander of the army of Judah.

33 "So shall their blood return on the head of Joab and the heads of his descendants forever. But for David, his descendants, his house, and his throne, may there be peace from the LORD forever."

34 So Benaiah the son of Jehoiada went up [to the tabernacle] and struck and killed Joab, and he was buried at his own house in the wilderness [of Judah].

35 The king appointed Benaiah the son of Jehoiada over the army in Joab's place, and appointed Zadok the priest in place of Abiathar.

Shimei Executed

36 Now the king sent *word* and called for Shimei and said to him, "Build yourself a house in Jerusalem and live there. Do not go from there to any other place.

37 "For on the day you leave and cross over the Brook Kidron, know for certain that you shall surely die; your blood shall be on your own head."

2:27 *Abiathar.* This act fulfilled God's word to Eli, removing the last of his descendants from serving before the Lord (1Sa 2:30 – 33). When Abiathar was removed from office, his influence was greatly restricted. Solomon spared his life in recognition of his past service to God and David (2Sa 15:24,29; 1Ch 15:11 – 15).

2:28 *horns of the altar.* Because Joab was a murderer (2Sa 3:27; 18:14; 20:10), he could not claim the protective sanctity of the horns of the altar, and could not escape execution.

2:35 *Zadok.* Zadok was a descendant of Eleazar, the son of Aaron (1Ch 6:4 – 8).

23 Ru 1:17 **24** 2Sa 7:11,13; 1Ch 22:10 **26** Jos 21:18; 1Sa 23:6; 2Sa 15:24,29; 1Sa 22:20,23; 2Sa 15:24 **27** 1Sa 2:31-35 **28** 1Ki 1:7; 1Ki 1:50 **31** Ex 21:14; Nu 35:33; Dt 19:13; 21:8,9 **32** Jdg 9:24,57; 2Ch 21:13; 2Sa 3:27; 2Sa 20:10 **33** 2Sa 3:29; Pr 25:5 **35** Nu 25:11-13; 1Sa 2:35; See 1Ch 6:53; 24:3; ver. 27 **36** ver. 8; 2Sa 16:5 **37** 2Sa 15:23; Lev 20:9; Jos 2:19; 2Sa 1:16

[38]Shimei said to the king, "The word
(ruling) is good. As my lord the king has
said, so will your servant do." So Shimei
lived in Jerusalem for many days.
[39]But it happened after three years,
that two of Shimei's servants ran away
to Achish the son of Maacah, the king
of Gath. And Shimei was told, "Behold,
your [runaway] servants are in Gath."
[40]So Shimei arose, saddled his don-
key, and went to Gath to [King] Achish
to look for his servants. And Shimei
went and brought them *back* from Gath.
[41]Now Solomon was told that Shimei
had gone from Jerusalem to Gath, and
had returned.
[42]So the king sent *word* and called
for Shimei and said to him, "Did I not
make you swear by the LORD and sol-
emnly warn you, saying, 'Know for
certain that on the day you leave [Je-
rusalem] and go anywhere, you shall
surely die'? And you said to me, 'The
word (ruling) I have heard is good.'
[43]"Why then have you not kept the
oath of the LORD, and the command
which I gave you?"
[44]The king also said to Shimei, "You
are aware in your own heart of all the
evil you did to my father David; so the
LORD shall return your evil on your
own head.
[45]"But King Solomon shall be
blessed, and the throne of David shall
be established before the LORD forever."
[46]So the king commanded Benaiah
the son of Jehoiada, and he went out
and struck down Shimei, and he died.

So the kingdom was established in the hands of Solomon.

Solomon's Rule Consolidated

3 NOW SOLOMON became a son-
in-law to Pharaoh king of Egypt
[and formed an alliance] by taking
Pharaoh's daughter [in marriage]. He
brought her to the City of David [where
she remained temporarily] until he
had finished building his own house
(palace) and the house of the LORD and
the wall around Jerusalem.
[2]But [in the meantime] the people
were still sacrificing [to God] on the
high places (hilltops) [as the pagans
did to their idols], for there was no
[permanent] house yet built for the
Name of the LORD.
[3]Now Solomon loved the LORD, walk-
ing [at first] in the statutes of David
his father, except [for the fact that]
he sacrificed and burned incense in
the high places [ignoring the law that
required all sacrifices to be offered at
the tabernacle]. [Lev 17:3, 4]
[4]The king went to Gibeon [near Je-
rusalem, where the tabernacle and the
bronze altar stood] to sacrifice there,
for that was the great high place. Sol-
omon offered a thousand burnt offer-
ings on that altar.
[5]In Gibeon the LORD appeared to
Solomon in a dream at night; and God
said, "Ask [Me] what I shall give you."

Solomon's Prayer

[6]Then Solomon said, "You have
shown Your servant David my father
great lovingkindness, because he
walked before You in faithfulness and
righteousness and with uprightness of
heart toward You; and You have kept
for him this great lovingkindness, in
that You have given him a son to sit on
his throne, as it is today.
[7]"So now, O LORD my God, You have
made Your servant king in place of Da-
vid my father; and as for me, I am but a
little boy [in wisdom and experience];
I do not know how to go out or come

3:1 *became a son-in-law.* In the ancient Middle East, political alliances were often ratified by the marriage of the son of one king to the daughter of another. Except in unusual circumstances, the pharaohs of Egypt did not observe this custom. Therefore, the giving of Pharaoh's daughter to Solomon attested to the Israelite king's growing prestige and importance to the Egyptians.

3:7 *but a little boy.* The term "boy" often refers to a servant or to an inexperienced person still in training for a profession. With proper humility, Solomon stressed his relative youth and inexperience.

39 1Sa 27:2 **44** 2Sa 16:5; Eze 17:19 **45** Pr 25:5 **46** ver. 12; 2Ch 1:1 **CHAPTER 3** **1** 1Ki 7:8; 9:24; 2Sa 5:7; 1Ki 7:1; 1Ki 6; 1Ki 9:15,19 **2** Lev 17:3-5; Dt 12:2,4,5; 1Ki 22:43 **3** Dt 6:5; 30:16,20; Ro 8:28; 1Co 8:3; ver. 6,14 **4** 2Ch 1:3; 1Ch 16:39; 2Ch 1:3 **5** 1Ki 9:2; 2Ch 1:7; Nu 12:6; Mt 1:20 **6** 2Ch 1:8; 1Ki 2:4; 9:4; 2Ki 20:3; 1Ki 1:48 **7** Nu 27:17

in [that is, how to conduct business as a king].

8“Your servant is among Your people whom You have chosen, a great people who are too many to be numbered or counted.

9“So give Your servant an understanding mind *and* a hearing heart [with which] to judge Your people, so that I may discern between good and evil. For who is able to judge *and* rule this great people of Yours?” [James 1:5]

God’s Answer

10Now it pleased the Lord that Solomon had asked this thing.

11God said to him, “Because you have asked this and have not asked for yourself a long life nor for wealth, nor for the lives of your enemies, but have asked for yourself understanding to recognize justice,

12behold, I have done as you asked. I have given you a wise and discerning heart (mind), so that no one before you was your equal, nor shall anyone equal to you arise after you.

13“I have also given you what you have not asked, both wealth and honor, so that there will not be anyone equal to you among the kings, for all your days.

14“If you walk in My ways, keeping My statutes and My commandments, as your father David did, then I will lengthen your days.”

15Then Solomon awoke, and he realized that it was a dream. He came [back] to Jerusalem and stood before the ark of the covenant of the LORD; he offered burnt offerings and peace offerings, and he prepared a feast for all his servants. [2 Sam 6:17]

Solomon Wisely Judges

16Then two women who were prostitutes came to the king and stood before him.

17And the one woman said, “O my lord, this woman and I live in the same house; and I gave birth to a child while she was in the house.

18“And on the third day after I gave birth, this woman also gave birth. And we were [alone] together; no one else was with us in the house, just we two.

19“Now this woman’s son died during the night, because she lay on him [and smothered him].

20“So she got up in the middle of the night and took my son from [his place] beside me while your maidservant was asleep, and laid him on her bosom, and laid her dead son on my bosom.

21“When I got up in the morning to nurse my son, behold, he was dead. But when I examined him carefully in the morning, behold, it was not my son, *the one* whom I had borne.”

22Then the other woman said, “No! For my son is the one who is living, and your son is the dead one.” But the first woman said, “No! For your son is the dead one, and my son is the living one.” [This is how] they were speaking before the king.

23Then the king said, “This woman says, ‘This is my son, the one who is

---

3:14 Obedience — Because he loved God above all at this time of his life (v. 3), and chose wisdom and discernment for his office, Solomon received even more — riches and honor and distinction. Obedient in many ways, he was accordingly blessed by God. When commands are given by a loving, caring person, obedience must result in blessing. God repeatedly stated this principle (Dt 5:29 – 6:24). Saul, David, and Solomon all lost blessing because of disobedience. This was not because of narrowness or rigidity on God’s part. He does not give us commands to make our lives harder, or to be harsh and demanding. His commands have blessings built in — He is showing us the best way to live.

3:15 *ark of the covenant.* Although David had brought the ark of the covenant to Jerusalem (2Sa 6), the tabernacle and its furnishings remained in Gibeon, which served as an important worship center (v. 4, 2Ch 1:3 – 5). After its capture by the Philistines (1Sa 5 – 6), the ark never returned to the tabernacle. The ark was not in the holy of holies again until it was placed in Solomon’s temple.

8 Dt 7:6; Ge 13:16; 15:5 **9** 2Ch 1:10; Pr 2:3-9; Jas 1:5; Ps 72:1,2; Heb 5:14 **11** Jas 4:3 **12** 1Jn 5:14,15; 1Ki 4:29-31; Ecc 1:16 **13** Mt 6:33; Eph 3:20; 1Ki 4:21,24 **14** 1Ki 15:5; Ps 91:16; Pr 3:2 **15** Ge 41:7; Ge 40:20; 1Ki 8:65; Est 1:3; Da 5:1; Mk 6:21 **16** Nu 27:2

alive, and your son is the dead one';
and the other woman says, 'No! For
your son is the dead one, and my son
is the one who is alive.' "
24 Then the king said, "Bring me a
sword." So they brought a sword be-
fore the king.
25 Then the king said, "Cut the living
child in two, and give half to the one
[woman] and half to the other."
26 Then the woman whose child was
the living one spoke to the king, for
she was deeply moved over her son,
"O my lord, give her the living child,
and by no means kill him." But the
other said, "He shall be neither mine
nor yours; cut *him!*"
27 Then the king said, "Give the first
woman [who is pleading for his life]
the living child, and by no means kill
him. She is his mother."
28 When all [the people of] Israel
heard about the judgment which the
king had made, they [were in awe and
reverently] feared the king, for they
saw that the wisdom of God was with-
in him to administer justice.

Solomon's Officials

4 KING SOLOMON was king over
all [the people of] Israel.
2 These were his [chief] officials:
Azariah the son of Zadok was the *high*
priest;
3 Elihoreph and Ahijah the sons of
Shisha, were scribes; Jehoshaphat the
son of Ahilud was the recorder [of im-
portant events];
4 Benaiah the son of Jehoiada was
in command of the army; Zadok and
Abiathar were priests;
5 Azariah the son of Nathan was
in charge of the deputies; Zabud the
son of Nathan was priest and was the
king's friend [and trusted advisor];
6 Ahishar was in charge of the house-
hold (palace); and Adoniram the son of
Abda was in charge of the forced labor.
7 Solomon had twelve deputies over
all Israel, who secured provisions for
the king and his household; each man
had to provide for a month in the year.
8 These were their names: Ben-hur,
in the hill country of [the tribe of]
Ephraim;
9 Ben-deker in Makaz and Shaalbim
and Beth-shemesh and Elon-beth-
hanan;
10 Ben-hesed, in Arubboth (to him
belonged Socoh and all the land of
Hepher);
11 Ben-abinadab, in all the hills of
Dor (Taphath, Solomon's daughter,
was his wife);
12 Baana the son of Ahilud, in Ta-
anach, Megiddo, and all Beth-shean
which is beside Zarethan below Jez-
reel, from Beth-shean to Abel-meholah
as far as beyond Jokmeam;
13 Ben-geber, in Ramoth-gilead (the
villages of Jair the son of Manasseh,
which are in Gilead belonged to him,
also the region of Argob, which is in
Bashan, sixty great cities with walls
and bronze bars);
14 Ahinadab the son of Iddo, in Ma-
hanaim;
15 Ahimaaz, in [the tribe of] Naphtali
(he also married Basemath, Solomon's
daughter);
16 Baana the son of Hushai, in [the
tribe of] Asher and Bealoth;
17 Jehoshaphat the son of Paruah, in
[the tribe of] Issachar;
18 Shimei the son of Ela, in [the tribe
of] Benjamin;
19 Geber the son of Uri, in the land

3:28 *wisdom ... justice.* These important qualities which marked Solomon's reign would characterize the rule of Israel's Messiah in a far greater way (Isa 11:1 – 5). David's final words to Solomon were, "act in accordance with your wisdom" (2:6). Wisdom does not dwell as a recluse among books in the study. Rather, wisdom stands with confidence at the crossroads of life. Solomon's wisdom was decisive. Through God he was able to observe the actions of others and in this way have a revelation of the truth.

4:7 – 19 *twelve deputies.* These men were responsible for handling lesser administrative tasks and raising revenue for the crown. The districts did not follow tribal boundaries.

4:18 *Shimei.* This is not the same Shimei who cursed David (2Sa 16:5 – 13), but probably the man mentioned in 1:8 as a supporter of Solomon.

26 Ge 43:30; Isa 49:15; Jer 31:20; Hos 11:8 **28** ver. 9,11,12 **CHAPTER 4** **3** 2Sa 8:16; 20:24 **4** 1Ki 2:35; See 1Ki 2:27 **5** ver. 7; 2Sa 8:18; 20:26; 2Sa 15:37; 16:16; 1Ch 27:33 **6** 1Ki 5:14 **13** Nu 32:41; Dt 3:4 **19** Dt 3:8

of Gilead, the country of Sihon king of the Amorites and of Og king of Bashan; and *he was* the only officer who was in the land.

Solomon's Power, Wealth and Wisdom

20 [The people of] Judah and Israel were as numerous as the sand that is in abundance by the sea; they were eating and drinking and rejoicing.
21 Now Solomon reigned over all the kingdoms from the [Euphrates] River to the land of the Philistines and to the border of Egypt; they brought tribute (money) and served Solomon all the days of his life.
22 Solomon's food [for the royal household] for one day was thirty kors of finely milled flour, sixty kors of wheat flour,
23 ten fat oxen, twenty pasture-fed oxen, a hundred sheep not counting fallow deer, gazelles, roebucks, and fattened fowl.
24 For he was ruling over everything west of the [Euphrates] River, from Tiphsah to Gaza, over all the kings west of the [Euphrates] River; and he had peace on all sides around him.
25 Judah and Israel lived in security, every man under his vine and fig tree [in peace and prosperity], from Dan [in the north] to Beersheba [in the south], during all the days of Solomon. [Mic 4:3, 4]
26 Solomon also had 40,000 stalls of horses for his chariots, and 12,000 horsemen.
27 Those deputies provided food for King Solomon and for all [the staff] who came to King Solomon's table, each in his month; they let nothing be lacking.
28 They also brought the barley and straw for the horses and swift steeds (warhorses, chargers) to the place where it was needed, each man according to his assignment.
29 Now God gave Solomon [exceptional] wisdom and very great discernment and breadth of mind, like the sand of the seashore.
30 Solomon's wisdom surpassed the wisdom of all the sons of the east and all the wisdom of Egypt.
31 For he was wiser than all [other] men, [wiser] than Ethan the Ezrahite, and Heman, Calcol, and Darda, the sons of Mahol. His fame was *known* in all the surrounding nations.
32 He also spoke 3,000 proverbs, and his songs were 1,005.
33 He spoke of trees, from the cedar which is in Lebanon to the hyssop [vine] that grows on the wall; he spoke also of animals, of birds, of creeping things, and fish.
34 People came from all the peoples (nations) to hear the wisdom of Solomon, and from all the kings of the earth who had heard of his wisdom.

Alliance with King Hiram

5 HIRAM KING of Tyre sent his servants to Solomon when he heard that they had anointed him king in

---

4:20 *as numerous as the sand.* God fulfilled His promise to make Abraham's descendants numerous (Ge 15:5,18). Solomon's empire extended far beyond the traditional boundaries of Israel. Through this greatly expanded empire, Hebrew people not only traveled to far-flung regions, but they took with them their knowledge of the living God.
4:22 *kors.* A kor was the same size as a homer (Eze 45:14); at between six and seven bushels, it was the normal load for a donkey.
4:29 *wisdom.* The three terms used in this verse underscore Solomon's depth of understanding. He was not merely intelligent, able to understand facts and logic; he was also given the ability to apply his intelligence to problems which defy logic, possessing a rare understanding of human beings with all their emotional and spiritual complexities.
4:32–34 *proverbs . . . songs.* Solomon was the author of a large part of the Book of Proverbs. He is also traditionally assigned the authorship of the Song of Solomon, Psalms 72 and 127, and Ecclesiastes.
5:1 *Hiram.* This Phoenician king ruled over Tyre for 34 years (978–944 BC).

20 Ge 22:17; 1Ki 3:8; Pr 14:28; Ps 72:3,7; Mic 4:4 **21** 2Ch 9:26; Ps 72:8; Ge 15:18; Jos 1:4; Ps 68:29; 72:10,11 **24** Ps 72:11; 1Ch 22:9 **25** See Jer 23:6; Mic 4:4; Zec 3:10; Jdg 20:1 **26** 1Ki 10:26; 2Ch 1:14; See Dt 17:16 **27** ver. 7 **29** 1Ki 3:12 **30** Ge 25:6; See Ac 7:22 **31** 1Ki 3:12; 1Ch 15:19; Ps 89, title; See 1Ch 2:6; 6:33; 15:19; Ps 88, title **32** Pr 1:1; Ecc 12:9; SS 1:1 **34** 1Ki 10:1; 2Ch 9:1,23 **CHAPTER 5** **1** 2Sa 5:11; 1Ch 14:1; Am 1:9

place of his father, for Hiram had always been a friend of David.

2 Then Solomon sent *word* to Hiram, saying,

3 "You know that David my father could not build a house (temple) for the Name (Presence) of the LORD his God because of the wars which surrounded him, until the LORD put his enemies under his feet. [2 Sam 7:4ff; 1 Chr 22:8]

4 "But now that the LORD my God has given me rest [from war] on every side, there is neither adversary nor misfortune [confronting me].

5 "Behold, I intend to build a house (temple) to the Name of the LORD my God, just as the LORD said to my father David: 'Your son whom I will put on your throne in your place shall build the house for My Name *and* Presence.'

6 "So now, command that they cut cedar trees from Lebanon for me, and my servants will join your servants, and I will give you whatever wages you set for your servants. For you know that there is no one among us who knows how to cut timber like the men of Sidon."

7 When Hiram heard the words of Solomon, he rejoiced greatly and said, "Blessed be the LORD this day, who has given David a wise son [to be king] over this great people."

8 So Hiram sent *word* to Solomon, saying, "I have heard *the message* which you sent to me; I will do everything you wish concerning the cedar and cypress timber.

9 "My servants will bring the logs down from Lebanon to the [Mediterranean] sea, and I will have them made into rafts *to go* by sea to the place (port) that you direct me; then I will have them broken up there, and you shall carry *them* away. Then you shall return the favor by providing food for my household."

10 So Hiram gave Solomon all the cedar and cypress timber he desired,

11 and Solomon gave Hiram 20,000 kors of wheat as food for his household, and 20 kors of pure [olive] oil. Solomon gave all these to Hiram each year.

12 The LORD gave Solomon wisdom, just as He promised him; and there was peace between Hiram and Solomon, and the two of them made a treaty.

Conscription of Laborers

13 King Solomon levied forced laborers from all Israel; and the forced laborers numbered 30,000 men.

14 He sent them to Lebanon, 10,000 a month in shifts; one month they were in Lebanon and two months at home. Adoniram was in charge of the forced laborers.

15 Solomon had 70,000 burden bearers (transporters) and 80,000 stonemasons in the hill country [of Judah],

16 besides Solomon's 3,300 chief deputies who were in charge of the project and who were in charge of the people doing the work.

17 The king gave orders, and they

5:7 *Blessed be the LORD.* Acknowledging the deities of another people is well known in the Bible (Da 3:28) and other ancient Middle Eastern literature. It does not necessarily imply that Hiram was expressing faith in God.

5:13 *levied . . . 30,000 men.* Solomon's long and extensive use of this type of social conscription to accomplish his vast building projects became a source of considerable difficulty for his successor, Rehoboam (12:4).

6:1 *four hundred and eightieth year.* Many scholars take this date as the key date for establishing the time of the exodus. The division of the kingdom at the death of Solomon can be dated at 930 BC (11:41 – 43). Allowing forty years for Solomon's rule (11:42), the fourth year of his reign would be 966 BC. If the exodus took place 480 years before 966 BC, its date was 1446 BC.

6:2 *house . . . for the LORD.* Solomon followed the floor plan of the tabernacle, but doubled its dimensions. Solomon's temple was constructed on Mount Moriah, the mountain where Abraham was told to offer Isaac as a sacrifice (2Ch 3:1; Ge 22:2), on the site of the threshing floor of Araunah where God had spoken to David (2Sa 24:24). ***cubits.*** The standard cubit was about 18 inches.

6:11 *word of the LORD.* This message to Solomon might have come by means of a prophet. On other occasions, Solomon had more personal encounters with the Lord (3:5; 9:2; 11:11).

2 2Ch 2:3 **3** 1Ch 22:8; 28:3 **4** 1Ki 4:24; 1Ch 22:9 **5** 2Ch 2:4; 2Sa 7:13; 1Ch 17:12 **6** 2Ch 2:8,10 **9** See Ezr 3:7; Eze 27:17; Ac 12:20 **11** See 2Ch 2:10 **12** 1Ki 3:12 **14** 1Ki 4:6 **15** 1Ki 9:21; 2Ch 2:18 **17** 1Ch 22:2

quarried great stones, valuable stones, to lay the foundation of the house (temple) with cut stones.

18 So Solomon's builders and Hiram's builders and the men of Gebal cut *and* chiseled *the stones*, and prepared the timber and the stones to build the house (temple).

The Building of the Temple

6 NOW IT came about in the four hundred and eightieth year after the Israelites came out of the land of Egypt, in the fourth year of Solomon's reign over Israel, in the month of Ziv (April-May) which is the second month, that he began to build the Lord's house (temple).

2 The length of the house which King Solomon built for the LORD was sixty cubits (90 ft.), its width twenty (30 ft.), and its height thirty cubits (45 ft.).

3 The porch in front of the main room of the house (temple) was twenty cubits long, corresponding to the width of the house, and its depth in front of the house was ten cubits.

4 He also made framed (artistic) window openings for the house.

5 Against the wall of the house he built extensions around the walls of the house, around both the main room (Holy Place) and the Holy of Holies; and he made side chambers all around.

6 The lowest story was five cubits wide, the middle was six cubits wide, and the third was seven cubits wide; for he made offsets (niches) *in the walls* all around on the outside of the house so that *the supporting beams* would not be inserted into the walls of the house.

7 While it was being built, the house was built of stone prepared *and* finished (precut) at the quarry, and no hammer, axe, or iron tool of any kind was heard in the house while it was under construction.

8 The entrance to the lowest side chamber was on the right [or south] side of the house; and they would go up winding stairs to the middle [level], and from the middle to the third.

9 So Solomon built the house (temple) and finished it, and roofed the house with beams and boards of cedar.

10 Then he built the extensions [of rooms] against the entire house, each [story] five cubits high; and they were attached to the house with timbers of cedar.

11 Now the word of the LORD came to Solomon, saying,

12 "*Concerning* this house which you are building, if you will walk in My statutes and execute My precepts and keep all My commandments by walking in them, then I will carry out My word (promises) with you which I made to David your father.

13 "I will dwell among the sons (descendants) of Israel, and will not abandon My people Israel."

14 So Solomon built the house (temple) and finished it.

15 He built the walls of the interior of the house [that is, the Holy Place and the Holy of Holies] with boards of cedar, from the floor of the house to the rafters of the ceiling. He overlaid the interior with wood, and he overlaid the floor of the house with boards of cypress.

16 He built twenty cubits on the rear of the house with boards of cedar from the floor to the ceiling; he built its interior as the [inner] sanctuary, the Holy of Holies.

17 The [rest of the] house, that is, the temple in front of *the Holy of Holies*, was forty cubits long.

18 The cedar on the house within had wood carvings *in the shape* of gourds and open flowers. Everything was cedar; no stone was visible.

19 Then he prepared the Holy of Holies

6:19 *ark of the covenant*. The ark of the covenant (Dt 10:8) was so named because it housed the two stone tablets of the covenant — the Ten Commandments (Dt 10:1 – 5). The ark symbolized the presence of the sovereign God in the midst of His people (8:10 – 11; Jos 3:13).

CHAPTER 6 **1** 2Ch 3:1,2; Ac 7:47 **2** See Eze 41:1 **4** See Eze 40:16 **5** See Eze 41:6; ver. 16,19-21,31 **7** See Dt 27:5,6 **9** ver. 14,38 **12** 1Ki 2:4; 9:4; 2Sa 7:13; 1Ch 22:10 **13** Ex 25:8; 2Co 6:16; Rev 21:3; Dt 31:6 **16** Ex 26:33; Lev 16:2; 1Ki 8:6; 2Ch 3:8; Eze 45:3

within the house in order to put the ark of the covenant of the LORD there.

20 The Holy of Holies was twenty cubits in length, twenty cubits in width, and twenty cubits in height (a cube), and he overlaid it with pure gold. He also overlaid the cedar altar [with gold].

21 Solomon overlaid the interior of the house with pure gold, and he drew chains of gold across the front of the Holy of Holies (inner sanctuary), and he overlaid it with gold.

22 Then he overlaid the entire house with gold, until the whole house was finished. He also overlaid the entire [incense] altar which was by the Holy of Holies with gold.

23 Within the Holy of Holies he made two cherubim (sculptured figures) of olive wood, each ten cubits high.

24 One wing of the cherub was five cubits long, and the other wing was *also* five cubits long; it was ten cubits from the tip of one wing to the tip of the other.

25 The [wingspan of the] other cherub was also ten cubits. The measurements and cut (shape) of the two cherubim were the same;

26 the height of the one cherub was ten cubits, as was the other.

27 He put the cherubim [above the ark] inside the innermost room of the house, and their wings were spread out so that the wing of the one touched one wall, and the wing of the other cherub was touching the other wall; and their inner wings were touching each other in the middle of the house.

28 Solomon also overlaid the cherubim with gold.

29 He carved all the walls of the house all around with carved engravings of cherubim, palm-shaped decorations, and open flowers, [both] the inner and the outer *sanctuaries*.

30 He overlaid the floor of the house with gold, [both] the inner and outer *sanctuaries*.

31 For the entrance of the Holy of Holies he made two [folding] doors of olive wood, the lintel (header above the door) and five-sided doorposts (frames).

32 So *he made* two doors of olive wood, and he carved on them carvings of cherubim, palm-shaped decorations, and open flowers; and overlaid them with gold; and he hammered out overlays of gold on the cherubim and palm decorations.

33 Also he made for the entrance of the [outer] sanctuary (the Holy Place) four-sided doorposts (frames) of olive wood

34 and two doors of cypress wood; the two leaves of the one door turned on pivots *and* were folding, and the two leaves of the other door also turned on pivots.

35 He carved cherubim, palm-shaped decorations, and open flowers *on the doors*, and overlaid them with gold evenly applied on the carved work.

36 He built the inner courtyard with three rows of cut stone and a row of cedar beams.

37 In the fourth year [of King Solomon's reign] the foundation of the LORD's house was laid, in the [second] month, Ziv (April-May).

38 In the eleventh year [of King Solomon's reign] in the month of Bul (October-November), that is, the eighth month, the house was finished

---

6:20 *Holy of Holies.* The Holy of Holies was a cube of thirty feet. ***gold.*** The amount of gold used in this room was about 21 tons or 600 talents (2Ch 3:8).

6:23 *cherubim.* Cherubim are mighty angelic beings; they were often depicted in the furnishings of the tabernacle and temple. Not a great deal is known about their nature. Cherubim were set to guard the entrance to the garden of Eden (Ge 3:24). The only extensive description of their appearance is in the Book of Ezekiel (Eze 1:5 – 14; 10:1).

6:31 *doors of olive wood.* A veil or curtain was hung here as well (Ex 26:31 – 36; 2Ch 3:14).

6:38 Worship — in the midst of Solomon's building project he received a prophetic revelation from the Lord (vv. 11 – 14) in which a promise and a condition were prominent: the Lord would fulfill His promise to David if Solomon obeyed His laws. The temple was the external sign that the Lord would keep His covenant of grace and dwell among the people. Worship can never be divorced from obedience to God's laws in everyday life.

22 Ex 30:1,3,6 **23** Ex 37:7-9; 2Ch 3:10-12 **27** Ex 25:20; 37:9; 2Ch 5:8 **34** Eze 41:23-25 **37** ver. 1 **38** Compare; ver. 1

throughout all its parts and in accordance with all its specifications. So he built it in seven years.

Solomon's Palace

7 NOW SOLOMON built his own house (palace) in thirteen years, and he finished all of his house [in that time].

2 He also built the House of the Forest of Lebanon; its length was a hundred cubits (150 ft.), its width fifty cubits (75 ft.), and its height thirty cubits (45 ft.), upon four rows of cedar pillars, with cedar beams upon the pillars.

3 And it was covered with cedar [as a roof] on the supporting beams that were upon the forty-five pillars, fifteen in each row.

4 *There were artistic window* frames in three rows, and window was opposite window in three tiers.

5 All the doorways and doorposts [and windows] had squared [artistic] frames, and window was opposite window in three tiers.

6 He also made the Hall of Pillars; its length was fifty cubits (75 ft.) and its width thirty cubits (45 ft.). There was a porch in front, and pillars and a threshold in front of them.

7 He made the hall for the throne where he was to judge, the Hall of Judgment; it was paneled with cedar from [one] floor to [another] floor.

8 His house where he was to live, the other courtyard behind the hall, was of similar workmanship. Solomon also made a house like this hall for Pharaoh's daughter, whom he had married.

9 All these were of expensive stones, of stone cut according to measure, sawed with saws, inside and outside; even from the foundation to the coping, and from the outside to the great courtyard.

10 The foundation was of expensive stones, large stones, stones of ten cubits and stones of eight cubits.

11 And above [the foundation] were expensive stones, stones cut according to measure, and cedar.

12 So the great courtyard all around had three rows of cut stone and a row of cedar beams like the inner courtyard of the house of the LORD, and the porch of the house.

Hiram's Work in the Temple

13 Now King Solomon sent *word* and brought Hiram [a skilled craftsman] from Tyre.

14 He was the son of a widow from the tribe of Naphtali, and his father was a man of Tyre, a craftsman in bronze. Hiram was filled with wisdom, understanding, and skill for doing any [kind of] work in bronze. So he came to King Solomon and did all his [bronze] work.

15 He cast the two pillars of bronze; the one pillar was eighteen cubits high, and a [measuring] line of twelve cubits measured the circumference of both.

16 He also made two capitals (crowns) of cast bronze to put on the tops of the pillars; the height of one capital was five cubits, and the height of the other capital was five cubits.

17 *There were* nets of network (latticework) and twisted threads (wreaths) of chainwork for the capitals which were on the tops of the pillars, seven for one capital and seven for the other.

18 So Hiram made the pillars [in this manner], and two rows around on the one network to cover the capitals which were on the top of the

---

7:1 – 2 *House of the Forest of Lebanon.* This building was also apparently used as an armory (10:16 – 17; Isa 22:8).

7:13 – 14 *Hiram.* Hiram (called Huram in some translations) was of mixed parentage. His father was a Phoenician artisan who had married a widow from the tribe of Naphtali (2Ch 2:14). Like his father, Hiram had become a master craftsman; his contributions to the work on the temple were extensive.

7:16 *five cubits.* Jeremiah 52:22 agrees with this measurement, but 2 Kings 25:17 records the height as three cubits. This apparent discrepancy may just be a difference in whether the capitals of the pillars were included in the measurement height.

CHAPTER 7 **1** 1Ki 9:10; 2Ch 8:1 **8** 1Ki 3:1; 2Ch 8:11 **12** Jn 10:23; Ac 3:11 **14** 2Ch 2:14; 2Ch 4:16; Ex 31:3; 36:1 **15** 2Ki 25:17; 2Ch 3:15; 4:12; Jer 52:21

pomegranates; and he did the same
for the other capital.
19 The capitals which were upon the
top of the pillars in the porch were of
lily work (design), four cubits.
20 The capitals were on the two pillars
and also above and close to the rounded
projection which was beside the net-
work. There were two hundred pome-
granates in rows around both capitals.
21 Hiram set up the pillars at the
porch of the temple; he set up the right
pillar and named it Jachin (may he
establish), and he set up the left pillar
and named it Boaz (in it is strength).
22 On the tops of the pillars was lily
work (design). So the work of the pil-
lars was finished.
23 Now he made the Sea (basin) of
cast *metal,* ten cubits from brim to
brim, circular in form, five cubits high
and thirty cubits in circumference.
[Ex 30:17–21; 2 Chr 4:6]
24 Under its brim were gourds en-
circling it ten to a cubit, completely
surrounding the Sea; the gourds were
in two rows, cast in one piece with it.
25 It stood on twelve oxen, three fac-
ing north, three west, three south, and
three east; the Sea *was set* on top of
them, and all their rear parts *pointed*
inward.
26 It was a hand width thick, and its
brim was made like the brim of a cup,
like a lily blossom. It held two thou-
sand baths.
27 Then Hiram made ten bronze
stands [for smaller basins]; the length
of each stand was four cubits, its width
was four cubits and its height was
three cubits.
28 This was the design of the stands:
they had borders between the frames.
29 On the borders between the frames
were lions, oxen, and cherubim; and on
the frames there was a pedestal above.
Beneath the lions and oxen were bor-
ders of hanging work.
30 Now each stand had four bronze
wheels with bronze axles, and its four
feet had supports [for a basin]. Beneath
the basin were cast supports with bor-
ders at each side.
31 Its opening inside the crown at the
top *measured* a cubit, and its opening
was round like the design of a pedes-
tal, a cubit and a half. Also on its open-
ing were carvings, and their borders
were square, not round.
32 Underneath the borders were four
wheels, and the axles of the wheels
were on the stand. And the height of
a wheel was a cubit and a half.
33 The wheels were made like a char-
iot wheel: their axles, their rims, their
spokes, and their hubs were all cast.
34 Now there were four supports at
the four corners of each stand; the sup-
ports were part of the stand itself.
35 On the top of the stand there was
a circular piece half a cubit high, and
on the top of the stand its supports and
borders were part of it.
36 And on the surface of its supports
and its borders Hiram engraved cher-
ubim, lions, and palm-shaped decora-
tions, according to the [available] space
for each, with borders all around.
37 He made the ten stands like this:
they all had one casting, one measure,
and one form.
38 Then he made ten basins of bronze;
each basin held forty baths and was
four cubits, and there was one basin
on each of the ten stands.
39 Then he placed the bases, five on
the right [or south] side of the house
and five on the left [or north] side;
and he set the Sea [of cast metal] on
the right side of the house toward the
southeast.
40 Now Hiram made the basins and
the shovels and the bowls. So Hiram
finished all the work which he did
for King Solomon on the house of the
LORD:

7:21 *Jachin . . . Boaz.* Jachin can mean "He will establish." The name Boaz may mean "in Him is strength." Another possible meaning is "He is quick." These two pillars were placed near the porch in front of the temple (2Ch 3:17).

7:40 – 47 Service — When talents and skills are used in God's service, no work is insignificant. All is deserving of our best because it is done for God (Mt 10:42). For this task Hiram was filled with wisdom, understanding, and skill (v. 14).

20 See 2Ch 3:16; 4:13; Jer 52:23 **21** 2Ch 3:17 **23** 2Ki 25:13; 2Ch 4:2; Jer 52:17 **24** 2Ch 4:3 **25** 2Ch 4:4,5; Jer 52:20 **26** See 2Ch 4:5 **29** Ge 3:24; 1Ki 6:27; Ps 18:10; Eze 1:10; 41:18,19; Rev 4:6-8 **38** 2Ch 4:6

41the two pillars and the [two] bowls
of the capitals which were on the top of
the two pillars, and the two networks
to cover the two bowls of the capitals
which were on top of the pillars;
42and the four hundred pomegran-
ates for the two networks, two rows
of pomegranates for each network to
cover the two bowls of the capitals that
were on the tops of the pillars;
43the ten stands and the ten basins
on the stands;
44one Sea (basin), and the twelve
oxen under the Sea;
45the pails, the shovels, and the
bowls; all these utensils which Hiram
made for King Solomon in the house
of the LORD were of polished bronze.
46In the plain of the Jordan [River]
the king cast them, in the clay ground
between Succoth and Zarethan.
47Solomon left all the utensils *un-
weighed*, because there were so many;
the weight of the bronze could not be
determined.
48Solomon made all the [other] fur-
niture which was in the house of the
LORD: the [incense] altar of gold; the
table of gold on which was the bread
of the Presence;
49the lampstands of pure gold, five
on the right side and five on the left, in
front of the Holy of Holies (inner sanc-
tuary); with the flowers, the lamps, and
the tongs of gold;
50the cups, snuffers, bowls, spoons,
firepans—of pure gold; and the hinges
of gold [both] for the doors of the inner
house, the Holy of Holies, and for the
doors of the house, the main room [the
Holy Place].
51So all the work that King Sol-
omon did on the house of the LORD
was completed. Solomon brought in
the things which David his father had
dedicated—the silver, the gold, and
the utensils—and he put them in the
treasuries of the LORD's house.

The Ark Brought into the Temple

8 THEN SOLOMON assembled the
elders of Israel and all the heads of
the tribes, the leaders of the fathers'
households of the sons of Israel, to
King Solomon in Jerusalem, to bring
up the ark of the covenant of the Lord
from the City of David, which is Zion.
2All the men of Israel assembled
before King Solomon at the feast in
the month of Ethanim (September-
October), that is, the seventh month.
3All the elders of Israel came, and
the priests carried the ark.
4They brought up the ark of the
LORD and the Tent of Meeting and all
the holy utensils that were in the tent;
the priests and the Levites brought
them up.
5King Solomon and all the congre-
gation of Israel, who had assembled
before him, were with him before the
ark, sacrificing sheep and oxen, so
many that they could not be counted
or numbered.
6Then the priests brought the ark of
the covenant of the LORD to its place,
into the inner sanctuary of the house,

This description is similar to the description of Bezalel's work on the tabernacle (Ex 31:2–6). The Holy Spirit is the source of natural gifts as well as the supernatural gifts used in the service of the Lord.

7:48 *the [other] furniture*. The furnishings of the temple were designed to correspond with similar furnishings in the tabernacle (Ex 25; 30). Although Solomon made ten tables and lampstands instead of one, their functions remained the same, all ten being considered one unit (2Ch 29:18).

7:51 *David*. David's personal example of giving (1Ch 29:1–9) provided a high model of godly concern in leadership.

8:1 *ark of the covenant*. The ark had been in Jerusalem for some time (2Sa 6), and now it was finally in its proper setting. With the erection of the temple and the placement of the ark, the division of spiritual activities between Gibeon, the location of the tabernacle, and Jerusalem, where the ark had resided in a temporary shelter, was now at an end. The pattern of central worship set up in the wilderness could once again be observed (Dt 12:1–4).

41 ver. 17,18 **45** Ex 27:3; 2Ch 4:16 **46** 2Ch 4:17; Ge 33:17; Jos 3:16 **48** Ex 37:25; Ex 37:10; Lev 24:5-8
51 2Sa 8:11 **CHAPTER 8** **1** 2Ch 5:2; 2Sa 6:17; 2Sa 5:7; 6:12,16 **2** Lev 23:34; 2Ch 7:8 **3** Nu 4:15 **4** 2Ch 1:3
5 2Sa 6:13 **6** 2Sa 6:17; Ex 26:33,34; 1Ki 6:19; 1Ki 6:27

into the Holy of Holies, under the
wings of the cherubim.
7 For the cherubim spread their two
wings over the place of the ark, and
the cherubim covered the ark and its
[carrying] poles from above.
8 The poles were so long that the ends
of the poles were visible from the Holy
Place that was in front of the Holy of
Holies, but they were not visible from
the outside; they are there to this day
(the date of this writing).
9 There was nothing in the ark except
the two tablets of stone which Moses
put there at Horeb (Sinai), where the
LORD made a covenant with the Isra-
elites when they came out of the land
of Egypt. [Deut 10:2–5]
10 Now it happened that when the
priests had come out of the Holy Place,
the cloud filled the LORD's house,
11 so the priests could not stand [in
their positions] to minister because of
the cloud, for the glory *and* brilliance
of the LORD had filled the LORD's house
(temple).

Solomon Addresses the People

12 Then Solomon said,

"The LORD has said that He would
dwell in the thick darkness [of
the cloud].
13 "I have certainly built You a lofty
house,
A place for You to dwell in
forever."

14 Then the king turned around and
blessed all the assembly of Israel, while
all the assembly of Israel was standing.
15 He said, "Blessed be the LORD, the
God of Israel, who spoke with His
mouth to my father David and has
fulfilled it with His hand, saying,
16 'Since the day that I brought My
people Israel out of Egypt, I did not
choose a [particular] city out of all
the tribes of Israel *in which* to build
a house so that My Name (Presence)
would be in it, but I chose David to be
over My people Israel.'
17 "Now it was [determined] in the
heart of my father David to build a
house (temple) for the Name of the
LORD, the God of Israel.
18 "But the LORD said to my father
David, 'Because it was in your heart
to build a house for My Name, you did
well, in that it was in your heart.
19 'Nevertheless, you shall not build
the house, but your son, who shall be
born to you, it is he who shall build it
for My Name [and My Presence].'
20 "Now the LORD has fulfilled His
word which He spoke; I have risen in
the place of my father David and have
taken my seat on the throne of Israel,
just as the LORD promised, and have
built the house (temple) for the Name
of the LORD, the God of Israel.
21 "There I have made a place [in the
Holy of Holies] for the ark, in which
is the covenant (solemn agreement)
of the LORD, which He made with our
fathers when He brought them out of
the land of Egypt." [Ex 34:28]

The Prayer of Dedication

22 Then Solomon stood [in the court-
yard] before the altar of the LORD in
the presence of all the assembly of Is-
rael and spread out his hands toward
heaven.

8:9 *two tablets of stone.* The two tablets upon which the Ten Commandments were inscribed were known as the "tablets of the covenant" (Dt 9:9) and were kept in the ark (Dt 10:1 – 5,8) along with the jar of manna (Ex 16:33 – 34) and Aaron's rod that budded (Nu 17:10).

8:10 – 11 *the cloud.* This visible presence of God's dwelling with His people — sometimes called the "shekinah glory" — had also covered the tabernacle when it was inaugurated (Ex 40:34 – 35).

8:20 *the LORD has fulfilled.* Israel's God is a keeper of promises. His promise to give Abraham's descendants a land (Ge 15:13 – 14,18 – 21; Jos 14:12 – 15) had been provisionally realized (Jos 21:43 – 45). Solomon also appropriated God's promise to David (2Sa 7:12 – 18). Subsequent kings in the Davidic line could likewise by faith enjoy the blessings of God promised in the Davidic covenant (Ps 89:3 – 4,19 – 24,27 – 37).

8 Ex 25:14 **9** Ex 25:21; Dt 10:2; Dt 10:5; Heb 9:4; Ex 40:20; Ex 34:27,28 **10** Ex 40:34 **12** 2Ch 6:1; Ps 18:11 **13** 2Sa 7:13; Ps 132:14 **14** 2Sa 6:18 **15** Lk 1:68; 2Sa 7:5,25 **16** ver. 29; 1Sa 16:1; 2Sa 7:8; 1Ch 28:4 **17** 2Sa 7:2 **18** 2Ch 6:8,9 **19** 2Sa 7:5,12,13 **20** 1Ch 28:5,6 **21** ver. 9; Dt 31:26 **22** 2Ch 6:12; Ex 9:33; Ezr 9:5

[23]He said, "O LORD, the God of Israel,
there is no God like You in heaven
above or on earth below, who keeps the
covenant and shows lovingkindness to
Your servants who walk before You
with all their heart;
[24]You who have kept what You prom-
ised to Your servant my father David.
You have spoken with Your mouth and
have fulfilled Your word with Your
hand, as it is this day.
[25]"Now therefore, O LORD, the God
of Israel, keep for Your servant my
father David that which You promised
him when You said, 'You shall not be
without a man (descendant) to sit on
the throne of Israel, if only your sons
take heed to their way [of life] to walk
before Me [according to my laws] as
you have done.'
[26]"Now, O God of Israel, please let
Your word which You have spoken
to Your servant David my father be
confirmed.
[27]"But will God indeed dwell on the
earth? Behold, heaven and the highest
heaven cannot contain You; how much
less this house which I have built!
[28]"Yet graciously consider the prayer
of Your servant and his supplication,
O LORD my God, to listen to the [loud]
cry and to the prayer which Your ser-
vant prays before You today;
[29]that Your eyes may be open to-
ward this house night and day, toward
the place of which You have said, 'My
Name (Presence) shall be there,' that
You may listen to the prayer which
Your servant shall pray toward this
place.
[30]"Listen to the prayer of Your ser-
vant and of Your people Israel which
they pray toward this place. Hear in
heaven, Your dwelling place; hear and
forgive.
[31]"If a man sins against his neighbor
and is made to take an oath [of inno-
cence] and he comes to take the oath
before Your altar in this house (temple),
[32]then hear from heaven and act and
judge Your servants, condemning the
wicked by bringing his guilt on his
own head, and justifying the righteous
by rewarding him in accordance with
his righteousness.
[33]"When Your people Israel are de-
feated before an enemy because they
have sinned against You, and *then*
they turn to You again and praise Your
Name and pray and ask for Your favor
and compassion in this house (temple),
[34]then hear in heaven, and forgive
the sin of Your people Israel, and bring
them back to the land which You gave
their fathers.
[35]"When the heavens are shut up

8:27 *God.* God is infinite; no mere building, no matter how wonderful, can contain Him. God rules from heaven in a realm far superior to anything that man can imagine. Unlike the pagan gods who were thought to actually live in the temples built for them, He is not limited by time or space (Ac 7:48; 17:24). Yet God has committed Himself to fellowship with men, walking among them on the earth and being their God. Incredibly, He has chosen to dwell in the hearts of human beings. The true believer is the temple that God desires (1Co 3:16 – 19).

8:29 – 30 The Temple in the Life of Israel — Once Solomon built the temple, it became the primary location for the ceremonial worship of Israel. But it was also to be a house of prayer (Isa 56:7), a special place where God's people could rightly maintain their individual relationships with God. The temple was a place for repentance and forgiveness (Lk 18:10 – 14). It was a place for petitions to be brought to God. The temple was the central point of worship and life for Israel. Even today in many European towns, beautiful church buildings stand in the town square as a testament to the centrality that the church once had in the life of the community.

Too often we fall into a practice that makes ceremony itself the central thing or, in some cases, the only thing. Here, we can see what mattered most was not the ritualistic practices but communication with God. This passage and others like it give clarity to many of the claims of the prophets mentioned later in Scripture. If the people had been praying and listening to God as a part of the act of worship, surely they would have been more obedient to His commands, especially in view of the fact that prophets continually rebuked them.

23 Ex 15:11; 2Sa 7:22; Dt 7:9; Neh 1:5; Da 9:4; Ge 17:1; 1Ki 3:6; 2Ki 20:3 **25** 2Sa 7:12,16; 1Ki 2:4 **26** 2Sa 7:25 **27** 2Ch 2:6; Isa 66:1; Jer 23:24; Ac 7:49; 17:24; 2Co 12:2 **29** Dt 12:11; Da 6:10 **30** Neh 1:6 **31** Ex 22:11 **32** Dt 25:1 **33** Lev 26:17; Dt 28:25; Lev 26:39 **35** Lev 26:19; Dt 28:23

and there is no rain because they have
sinned against You, and they pray to-
ward this place and praise Your name
and turn from their sin when You af-
flict them,
36 then hear in heaven and forgive the
sin of Your servants and of Your people
Israel; indeed, teach them the good
way in which they should walk (live).
And send rain on Your land which
You have given to Your people as an
inheritance.
37 "If there is famine in the land, or
if there is pestilence (plague), blight,
mildew, migratory locusts, or grass-
hoppers, if their enemy besieges them
in the land of their cities, whatever
affliction *or* plague, whatever sickness
[there is],
38 whatever prayer or pleading is
made by any individual, or by Your
people Israel, each knowing the afflic-
tion of his own heart, and spreading
his hands out toward this house;
39 then hear in heaven Your dwelling
place, and forgive and act and give to
each according to his ways, whose
heart (mind) You know, for You and
You alone know the hearts of all the
children of men,
40 so that they may fear You [with
reverence and awe] all the days that
they live in the land which You have
given to our fathers.
41 "Moreover, concerning a foreigner
who is not of Your people Israel, but
comes from a far (distant) country for
the sake of Your name [to plead with
You]
42 (for they will hear of Your great
name, Your strong hand [of power],
and outstretched arm); when he comes
and prays toward this house (temple),
43 hear in heaven, Your dwelling
place, and do according to all for which
the foreigner calls upon (prays to) You,
so that all peoples of the earth may
know Your name and fear You [with
reverence and awe], as *do* Your people
Israel, and that they may know [with-
out any doubt] that this house which
I have built is called by Your name.
44 "When Your people go out to battle
against their enemy, by whatever way
You send them, and they pray to the
LORD toward the city which You have
chosen and the house that I have built
for Your Name *and* Presence,
45 then hear in heaven their prayer
and their pleading, and maintain their
right *and* defend their cause.
46 "When they sin against You (for
there is no man who does not sin) and
You are angry with them and hand
them over to the enemy, so that they
are carried away captive to the ene-
my's land, [whether] far away or near;
47 if they take it to heart in the land
where they have been taken captive,
and they repent and pray to You in the
land of their captors, saying, 'We have
sinned and done wrong and we have
acted wickedly;'
48 if they return to You with all their
heart and with all their soul in the land
of their enemies who have taken them
captive, and they pray to You toward
their land [of Israel] which You gave
to their fathers, the city [of Jerusalem]
which You have chosen, and the house
which I have built for Your Name *and*
Presence;
49 then hear their prayer and their
supplication in heaven Your dwelling
place, and maintain their right *and*
defend their cause,
50 and forgive Your people who have
sinned against You and all the trans-
gressions which they have committed
against You, and make them *objects of*
compassion before their captors, that
they will be merciful to them
51 (for they are Your people and Your
heritage, whom You brought out of

8:41 *foreigner.* Unlike God's people or resident aliens within the commonwealth of Israel (Dt 10:18–19), foreigners had no particular claim on the ear of God. But the Israelites expected foreigners to be drawn to God by the way His people worshiped Him.

---

36 Ps 25:4; 27:11; 94:12; 1Sa 12:23 **37** Lev 26:16,25,26 **39** 1Sa 16:7; 1Ch 28:9; Ps 11:4; Jer 17:10; Ac 1:24 **40** Ps 130:4 **42** Dt 3:24 **43** 1Sa 17:46; 2Ki 19:19; Ps 102:15 **46** 2Ch 6:36; Ecc 7:20; Jas 3:2; 1Jn 1:8,10; Lev 26:34,44; Dt 28:36,64 **47** Lev 26:40; Neh 1:6; Ps 106:6; Da 9:5 **48** Jer 29:12-14; Da 6:10 **50** Ezr 7:6; Ps 106:46 **51** Dt 9:29; Neh 1:10; Dt 4:20; Jer 11:4

Egypt, from the midst of the iron furnace [of slavery and oppression]),
[52]that Your eyes may be open to the supplication of Your servant and to the supplication of Your people Israel, to listen to them *and* be attentive to them whenever they call to You.
[53]"For You singled them out from all the peoples of the earth as Your heritage, just as You declared through Moses Your servant, when You brought our fathers out of Egypt, O Lord GOD."

Solomon's Benediction

[54]When Solomon finished offering this entire prayer and supplication to the LORD, he arose from before the LORD's altar, where he had knelt down with his hands stretched toward heaven.
[55]And he stood and blessed all the assembly of Israel with a loud voice, saying,
[56]"Blessed be the LORD, who has given rest to His people Israel, in accordance with everything that He promised. Not one word has failed of all His good promise, which He spoke through Moses His servant.
[57]"May the LORD our God be with us as He was with our fathers; may He not leave us nor abandon us [to our enemies],
[58]that He may guide our hearts to Himself, to walk in all His ways [following Him] and to keep His commandments, His statutes, and His precepts which He commanded our fathers.
[59]"Let these words of mine, with which I have made supplication before the LORD, be near to the LORD our God day and night, so that He will maintain the cause *and* right of His servant and of His people Israel as each day requires,
[60]so that all the peoples of the earth may know that the LORD is God; there is no one else.
[61]"Therefore, your hearts are to be wholly devoted to the LORD our God, to walk in His statutes and to keep His commandments, as [you are doing] today."

Dedicatory Sacrifices

[62]Then the king and all [the people of] Israel with him [repeatedly] offered sacrifice before the LORD.
[63]Solomon offered as peace offerings to the LORD: 22,000 oxen and 120,000 sheep. So the king and all the Israelites dedicated the house (temple) of the LORD.
[64]On that same day the king consecrated the middle of the courtyard that was in front of the house (temple) of the LORD; for he offered there the burnt offerings, the grain offerings, and the fat of the peace offerings, because the bronze altar that was before the LORD was too small to hold [all] the burnt offerings, the grain offerings and the fat of the peace offerings.
[65]So at that time Solomon held the feast, and all Israel with him, a great assembly, from the entrance of Hamath [on the northern border of Israel] to the Brook of Egypt [at Israel's southern border], before the LORD our God, for seven days and seven *more* days

---

8:54 *arose ... had knelt down.* Chronicles adds that Solomon's prayer and blessing were accompanied by heavenly fire that consumed the sacrifice on the altar (2Ch 7:1 – 3).

8:58 Regeneration — Solomon prayed for an ability given by God that would allow the people to live according to the covenant which had been given at the time of Moses. Solomon was aware that the nation's history was full of examples of the people turning away from God and from His written revelation. Ultimately, the promise of God to the nation of Israel was that there would be a new covenant given to them which would be internalized and which would be brought about by the Holy Spirit (Jer 31) — the new covenant which was ratified in Jesus' blood (1Co 11:25). Believers today have a power which enables us to live according to God's Word — the Holy Spirit who is the agent of our regeneration.

8:60 *all the peoples of the earth.* This verse does not limit God to the Jews but includes the Gentiles as well.

53 Ex 19:5; Dt 9:26,29 **55** 2Sa 6:18 **56** Dt 12:10; Jos 21:45; 23:14 **57** Dt 31:6; Jos 1:5 **58** Ps 119:36 **60** Jos 4:24; 1Sa 17:46; Dt 4:35,39 **61** 1Ki 11:4; 15:3,14; 2Ki 20:3 **62** 2Ch 7:4 **64** 2Ch 7:7; 2Ch 4:1 **65** ver. 2; Lev 23:34; Nu 34:8; Jos 13:5; Jdg 3:3; 2Ki 14:25; Ge 15:18; Nu 34:5; 2Ch 7:8

[beyond the prescribed period for the
Feast of Booths], fourteen days in all.
66 On the eighth (fifteenth) day he
sent the people away and they blessed
the king. Then they went to their tents
joyful and in good spirits because of
all the goodness which the LORD had
shown to David His servant and Israel
His people.

God's Promise and Warning

9 NOW IT happened when Solomon
had finished building the house
(temple) of the LORD and the king's
house (palace), and all else which he
was pleased to do,
2 that the LORD appeared to Solomon
a second time, just as He had appeared
to him at Gibeon.
3 The LORD told him, "I have heard
your prayer and supplication which
you have made before Me; I have con-
secrated this house which you have
built by putting My Name *and* My
Presence there forever. My eyes and
My heart shall be there perpetually.
4 "As for you, if you walk (live your
life) before Me, as David your father
walked, in integrity of heart and in
uprightness, acting in accordance with
everything that I have commanded
you, and will keep My statutes and
My precepts,
5 then I will establish the throne of
your kingdom over Israel forever, just
as I promised your father David, say-
ing, 'You shall not be without a man
(descendant) on the throne of Israel.'
6 "But if you or your sons turn away
from following Me, and do not keep
My commandments and My statutes
which I have set before you, but go and
serve other gods and worship them,
7 then I will cut off Israel from the
land which I have given them, and
I will cast out of My sight the house
which I have consecrated for My Name
and Presence. Then Israel will become
a proverb (a saying) and a byword (ob-
ject of ridicule) among all the peoples.
8 "This house (temple) will become
a heap of ruins; everyone who passes
by will be appalled and sneer and say,
'Why has the LORD done such a thing
to this land and to this house?'
9 "And they [who know] will say, 'Be-
cause they abandoned the LORD their
God, who brought their fathers out
of the land of Egypt, and they have
chosen other gods and have worshiped
and served them; that is the reason
the LORD has brought on them all this
adversity.' "

Cities Given to Hiram

10 Now at the end of twenty years,
in which Solomon had built the two
houses, the temple of the LORD and the
palace of the king
11 (Hiram king of Tyre had supplied
Solomon with as much cedar and cy-
press timber [from Lebanon] and gold
as he desired), at that time King Sol-
omon gave Hiram twenty cities in the
land of Galilee (northern Israel).
12 So Hiram came from Tyre to see
the cities which Solomon had given
him, and they did not please him.
13 He said, "What are these cities
[good for] which you have given me,
my brother?" So they have been called
the land of Cabul (like nothing, unpro-
ductive) to this day.
14 And Hiram sent to the king 120
talents of gold.
15 Now this is the account of the
forced labor which King Solomon con-
scripted to build the house of the LORD,

9:2 *second time.* God had appeared previously to Solomon in Gibeon (3:4 – 15). The Lord's warning was a necessary reminder for Solomon, who eventually did compromise the conditions required for enjoying God's blessing (11:1 – 11).

9:12 *they did not please him.* Hiram's displeasure with Solomon's gift would later result in Solomon's redeeming the towns by repaying the debt in another manner (2Ch 8:1 – 2).

9:14 *120 talents.* A talent was said to be the full load one man could easily carry. It was equal to three thousand shekels, or about 70 pounds.

66 2Ch 7:9 **CHAPTER 9** **1** 2Ch 7:11; 1Ki 7:1; 2Ch 8:6 **2** 1Ki 3:5 **3** 2Ki 20:5; Ps 10:17; 1Ki 8:29; Dt 11:12 **4** Ge 17:1; 1Ki 15:5 **5** 2Sa 7:12,16; 1Ki 2:4; 1Ch 22:10 **6** 2Sa 7:14; 2Ch 7:19,20 **7** 2Ki 17:23; 25:21; Jer 7:14; Dt 28:37 **8** 2Ch 7:21; Dt 29:24-26; Jer 22:8,9 **10** 1Ki 6:37,38; 7:1; 2Ch 8:1 **11** 2Ch 8:2 **13** Jos 19:27 **15** 1Ki 5:13; ver. 24; 2Sa 5:9; Jos 19:36; Jos 17:11; Jos 16:10

his own house, the Millo (fortification),
the wall of Jerusalem, [and the fortress
cities of] Hazor, Megiddo, and Gezer.
[16]*For* Pharaoh king of Egypt had
gone up and taken Gezer, burned it
with fire and killed the Canaanites
who lived in the city, and he had giv-
en it as a dowry to his daughter, Sol-
omon's wife.
[17]So Solomon rebuilt [and fortified]
Gezer and Lower Beth-horon,
[18]Baalath and Tamar in the wilder-
ness, in the land *of Judah*,
[19]and all the storage cities [for surplus
provisions] which Solomon had, and
the cities for his chariots and cities for
his horsemen, and whatever it pleased
Solomon to build in Jerusalem, in Leb-
anon, and in all the land under his rule.
[20]*As for* all the people who were left
of the Amorites, Hittites, Perizzites,
Hivites, and Jebusites, who were not of
the sons (descendants) of Israel,
[21]their children who were left after
them in the land, whom the Israelites
were unable to completely destroy,
from them Solomon levied (conscript-
ed) forced laborers, even to this day
(the date of this writing).
[22]But Solomon did not make slaves
of the sons of Israel; for they were men
of war (soldiers), his servants, his of-
ficers, his captains, his chariot com-
manders, and his horsemen.
[23]These were the chief officers who
were over Solomon's work, five hun-
dred and fifty, who ruled over the peo-
ple doing the work.
[24]As soon as Pharaoh's daughter
came up from the City of David to her
house which Solomon had built for her,
then he built the Millo (fortification).
[25]Three times a year [during the ma-
jor annual festivals] Solomon offered
burnt offerings and peace offerings on
the altar he had built to the LORD, and
he burned incense with them before
the LORD. So he finished the house [of
the LORD].
[26]King Solomon built a fleet of ships
in Ezion-geber, which is near Eloth on
the shore of the Red Sea (Sea of Reeds),
in the land of Edom.
[27]And Hiram [king of Tyre] sent his
servants with the fleet, sailors who
knew the sea, along with the servants
of Solomon.
[28]They came to Ophir and took four
hundred and twenty talents of gold from
there, and brought it to King Solomon.

The Queen of Sheba

10 NOW WHEN the queen of Sheba
heard of the fame of Solomon
concerning the name of the LORD, she
came to test him with riddles.
[2]So she came to Jerusalem with a
very large caravan (entourage), with
camels carrying spices, a great quantity
of gold, and precious stones. When she
came to Solomon, she spoke with him
about everything that was on her mind
[to discover the extent of his wisdom].
[3]Solomon answered all her ques-
tions; there was nothing hidden from

9:16 ***Gezer.*** Gezer had been a strong Canaanite city, a part of Ephraim's territorial assignment. Ephraim had never taken Gezer; however, Egypt had conquered the city. Its key location on the edge of the lowlands west of Jerusalem made it a splendid gift for Pharaoh to give on the occasion of his daughter's marriage to Solomon.

9:26 ***Ezion-geber.*** Ezion-geber was at the head of the modern Gulf of Aqaba. Its key location as an outlet to the Red Sea and the regions beyond made it commercially important to Solomon and to Hiram, his Phoenician trading partner (2Ch 8:17–18).

9:28 ***Ophir.*** The exact location of Ophir is a mystery. Some have speculated that it may have been in Africa, since it was reached by sea (1Ki 22:48). It was certainly a celebrated gold area, the source of much of the wealth David and Solomon used to pay for their vast building projects (1Ch 29:4).

10:1 ***Sheba.*** Located in southwestern Arabia (present-day Yemen), Sheba was the homeland of the Sabeans, a people whose far-flung commercial enterprises stretched from Syria to east Africa to distant India. The Sabeans dealt in such precious commodities as gold, gemstones, perfumes, and rare spices.

16 Jos 16:10 **17** Jos 16:3; 2Ch 8:5 **18** Jos 19:44; 2Ch 8:4,6 **19** 1Ki 4:26; ver. 1 **20** 2Ch 8:7 **21** Jdg 3:1; Jos 15:63; 17:12; Jdg 1:28; Ezr 2:55,58; Neh 7:57 **22** Lev 25:39 **23** See 2Ch 8:10 **24** 1Ki 3:1; 2Ch 8:11; 1Ki 7:8; 2Sa 5:9; 1Ki 11:27; 2Ch 32:5 **25** 2Ch 8:12,13,16 **26** 2Ch 8:17,18; Nu 33:35; Dt 2:8; 1Ki 22:48 **27** 1Ki 10:11 **28** Job 22:24
CHAPTER 10 **1** 2Ch 9:1; Mt 12:42; Lk 11:31; See Jdg 14:12; Pr 1:6

the king which he did not explain to her.

4When the queen of Sheba had seen all the wisdom of Solomon, and the house (palace) which he had built,

5the food on his table, the seating of his servants (court officials), the attendance of his waiters and their attire, his cupbearers, his stairway by which he went up to the house (temple) of the LORD, she was breathless *and* awed [by the wonder of it all].

6Then she told the king, "The report which I heard in my own land about your words and wisdom is true!

7"I did not believe the report until I came and saw it with my own eyes. Behold, the half of it was not told to me. You exceed in wisdom and prosperity the report which I heard.

8"How blessed (fortunate, happy) are your men! How blessed are these your servants who stand continually before you, hearing your wisdom!

9"Blessed be the LORD your God who delighted in you to set you on the throne of Israel! Because the LORD loved Israel forever, He made you king to execute justice and righteousness."

10She gave the king a hundred and twenty talents of gold and a very great *quantity* of spices and precious stones. Never again did such an abundance of spices come in [to Israel] as that which the queen of Sheba gave King Solomon.

11Also the ships of Hiram, which brought gold from Ophir, brought in from Ophir a great *quantity* of almug wood (sandalwood) and precious stones.

12From the almug wood (sandalwood) the king made pillars for the house of the LORD and for the king's palace, and also lyres and harps for the singers. Such almug wood did not come in [to Israel] *again*, nor has it been seen to this day.

13King Solomon [in turn] gave to the queen of Sheba everything that she wanted, whatever she asked, besides what he gave to her from his royal bounty. So she returned to her own country, she and her servants.

Wealth, Splendor and Wisdom

14Now the weight of the gold that came to Solomon in one [particular] year was six hundred and sixty-six talents of gold,

15besides *the taxes* from the traders and from the wares of the merchants, and [the tribute money] from all the kings of the Arabs (Bedouins) and the governors of the country.

16King Solomon made two hundred large shields of beaten (hammered) gold; six hundred *shekels of* gold went into each shield.

17*He made* three hundred *smaller* shields of beaten gold; three minas of gold went into each shield. The king put them in the House of the Forest of Lebanon [the king's armory].

18Also the king made a great throne of ivory and overlaid it with the finest gold.

19The throne had six steps, and a round top *was attached* to the throne from the back. On either side of the seat were armrests, and two lions stood beside the armrests.

20Twelve lions stood there, one on either end of each of the six steps; there was nothing like it made for any other kingdom.

21All King Solomon's drinking vessels were of gold, and all vessels of the House of the Forest of Lebanon were of pure gold. None were of silver; it was not considered valuable in the days of Solomon.

22For the king had at sea the [large cargo] ships of Tarshish with the ships of Hiram. Once every three years the ships of Tarshish came bringing gold, silver, ivory, monkeys, and peacocks.

23So King Solomon exceeded all the

10:9 *Blessed be the LORD your God.* The queen's acknowledgement of Solomon's God and the Lord's covenant faithfulness towards Israel does not necessarily mean that she made a commitment of personal faith in the Lord. She may simply have been expressing respect for Solomon's God (see 5:7).

5 1Ch 26:16 **8** Pr 8:34 **9** 1Ki 5:7; 2Sa 8:15; Ps 72:2; Pr 8:15 **10** Ps 72:10,15 **11** 1Ki 9:27 **12** 2Ch 9:11; 2Ch 9:10 **15** 2Ch 9:24; Ps 72:10 **17** 1Ki 14:26; 1Ki 7:2 **18** 2Ch 9:17 **21** 2Ch 9:20 **22** Ge 10:4; 2Ch 20:36 **23** 1Ki 3:12,13; 4:30

kings of the earth in wealth and in
wisdom.
24All the earth was seeking the pres-
ence of Solomon, to hear his wisdom
which God had put in his mind.
25Every man brought a gift [of trib-
ute]: articles of silver and gold, gar-
ments, weapons, spices, horses, and
mules, so much year by year.
26Now Solomon collected chariots
and horsemen; he had 1,400 chariots
and 12,000 horsemen, which he sta-
tioned in the chariot cities and with
the king in Jerusalem.
27The king made silver *as common*
in Jerusalem as stones, and cedars as
plentiful as the sycamore trees that are
in the lowland.
28Solomon's horses were imported
from Egypt and from Kue, and the
king's merchants acquired them from
Kue, for a price. [Deut 17:15, 16]
29A chariot could be imported from
Egypt for six hundred *shekels* of silver,
and a horse for a hundred and fifty;
and in the same way they exported
them, by the king's merchants, to all
the kings of the Hittites and to the
kings of Aram (Syria).

Solomon Turns from God

11 NOW KING Solomon [defiant-
ly] loved many foreign women
along with the daughter of Pharaoh:
Moabite, Ammonite, Edomite, Sido-
nian, and Hittite women,
2from the very nations of whom the
LORD said to the Israelites, "You shall
not associate with them, nor shall they
associate with you, for the result will
be that they will turn away your hearts
to follow their gods." Yet Solomon
clung to these in love. [Deut 17:17]
3He had seven hundred wives, prin-
cesses, and three hundred concubines,
and his wives turned his heart away
[from God].
4For when Solomon was old, his
wives turned his heart away after oth-
er gods; and his heart was not com-
pletely devoted to the LORD his God,
as was the heart of his father David.

10:26 *1,400 chariots.* Shalmaneser III of Assyria reported that at the battle of Qarqar (853 BC) he faced a combined enemy chariot force of 3,900, some two thousand of which were supplied by Israel.

10:27 *silver . . . cedars.* Under Solomon, Israel enjoyed its greatest period of prosperity. This time of prosperity and peace also must have allowed for the growth of scholarship and for arts and music.

11:1 – 4 Unfaithfulness — Solomon was affected by the contemporary practices of the surrounding culture. Entering into a political marriage was a means to consolidate a relationship with a neighboring monarch, and Solomon followed this custom at the expense of obedience to God. Unfaithfulness creeps into our lives when our hearts are more closely attuned to contemporary culture and peer pressure than to the voice of God. The heinousness of Solomon's unfaithfulness stands in contrast with the abundance of God's favor and the plainness of His commands (vv. 9 – 10).

11:1 – 2 Materialism — Even before Israel crossed over the Jordan and entered the promised land, God had given special instructions for the nation's future kings, warning them against materialism: they were not to collect horses, women, or gold for themselves (Dt 17:16 – 17). However, King Solomon did all three, resulting in his downfall. He owned many horses (4:26); he gathered hundreds of wives and concubines (v. 3); and he possessed much gold and silver (10:14 – 27). The gathering of material wealth, when gained honestly, is not prohibited in the Bible. Improper love of possessions, however, is idolatry. We can own things, but things must not own us.

11:1 *many foreign women.* Taking foreign wives violated the Lord's prohibitions against marrying Canaanite women (v. 2; Ex 34:12 – 17; Dt 7:1 – 3); taking many wives violated the standard of monogamy established at the beginning (Ge 2:24 – 25), and resulted in rampant polygamy, something God had also forbidden to Israel's future kings (Dt 17:17).

11:3 *seven hundred . . . three hundred.* If the reference to 60 queens and 80 concubines in Song of Solomon 6:8 is to Solomon's wives, it represents a much earlier period in Solomon's reign.

11:4 *not completely devoted.* Although it is true that David did not always live up to God's standards, he was loyal to God and trusted Him implicitly, even when he was rebuked for his sins (2Sa 12:13; Ps 32:1 – 5; 53:1 – 5).

---

26 1Ki 4:26; 2Ch 1:14; 9:25; Dt 17:16 **27** 2Ch 1:15-17 **28** Dt 17:16; 2Ch 1:16; 9:28 **29** Jos 1:4; 2Ki 7:6 **CHAPTER 11**
1 Neh 13:26; Dt 17:17 **2** Ex 34:16; Dt 7:3,4 **4** Dt 17:17; Neh 13:26; 1Ki 8:61; 1Ki 9:4

[5]For Solomon went after Ashtoreth,
the [fertility] goddess of the Sido-
nians, and after Milcom the horror
(detestable idol) of the Ammonites.
[1 Kin 9:6–9]
[6]Solomon did evil [things] in the
sight of the LORD, and did not follow
the LORD fully, as his father David *had*
done.
[7]Then Solomon built a high place
for [worshiping] Chemosh the horror
(detestable idol) of Moab, on the hill
which is east of Jerusalem, and for
Molech the horror (detestable idol) of
the sons of Ammon.
[8]And he did the same for all of his
foreign wives, who burned incense and
sacrificed to their gods.
[9]So the LORD became angry with
Solomon because his heart was turned
away from the LORD, the God of Israel,
who had appeared to him twice,
[10]and had commanded him concern-
ing this thing, that he should not fol-
low other gods; but he did not observe
(remember, obey) what the LORD had
commanded.
[11]Therefore the LORD said to Sol-
omon, "Because you have done this
and have not kept My covenant and
My statutes, which I have commanded
you, I will certainly tear the kingdom
away from you and give it to your ser-
vant.
[12]"However, I will not do it in your
lifetime, for the sake of your father
David, but I will tear it out of the hand
of your son (Rehoboam).
[13]"However, I will not tear away all
the kingdom; I will give one tribe (Ju-
dah) to your son for the sake of My
servant David and for the sake of Je-
rusalem which I have chosen."

God Raises Adversaries

[14]Then the LORD stirred up an ad-
versary against Solomon, Hadad the
Edomite; he was of royal descent in
Edom.
[15]For it came about, when David was
in Edom, and Joab the commander of
the army had gone up to bury those
killed [in battle] and had struck down
every male in Edom
[16](for Joab and all [the army of] Is-
rael stayed there six months, until he
had killed every male in Edom),
[17]that Hadad escaped to Egypt, he
and some Edomites from his father's
servants with him, while Hadad was
[still] a little boy.
[18]They set out from Midian [south of
Edom] and came to Paran, and took
men with them from Paran and came
to Egypt, to Pharaoh king of Egypt,
who gave [young] Hadad a house and
ordered food *and* provisions for him
and gave him land.
[19]Hadad found great favor with
Pharaoh, so that he gave Hadad in
marriage the sister of his own wife, the
sister of Tahpenes the queen.
[20]The sister of Tahpenes gave birth
to Genubath, Hadad's son, whom Tah-
penes weaned in Pharaoh's house; and
Genubath was in Pharaoh's household
among the sons of Pharaoh.
[21]But when Hadad heard in Egypt
that David had died and that Joab the
commander of the army was dead,
Hadad said to Pharaoh, "Let me leave,
so that I may go to my own country."
[22]Then Pharaoh said to him, "But
what have you lacked with me that
now you ask to go to your own coun-
try?" He replied, "Nothing; neverthe-
less you must let me go."

11:7 *high place.* The use of high places in association with the worship of foreign gods shows the terrible danger that the high places presented to Israel (3:2–4; 14:23; Mic 1:3). ***Molech.*** The worship of Molech was associated with Baal worship and with human sacrifice (Jer 7:31–32; 19:5–6; 32:35).
11:13 *one tribe.* The one tribe left to the house of David was Judah, the principal tribe of the Southern Kingdom. By this time, Simeon had assimilated with Judah (12:17–21).
11:14 *Hadad the Edomite.* Hadad was one of the survivors who had escaped when David defeated the Edomite army (2Sa 8:13–14). Pharaoh's ready reception and favorable treatment of Hadad probably had political ramifications, the pharaoh seeing him as a potential future ally on Israel's border.

5 ver. 33; Jdg 2:13; 2Ki 23:13 **7** Nu 33:52; Nu 21:29; Jdg 11:24; 2Ki 23:13 **9** 1Ki 3:5; 9:2 **10** 1Ki 6:12; 9:6 **11** ver. 31; 1Ki 12:15,16 **13** 2Sa 7:15; 1Ki 12:20; Dt 12:11 **14** 1Ch 5:26 **15** 2Sa 8:14; 1Ch 18:12; Nu 24:19; Dt 20:13 **21** 1Ki 2:10,34

23 God also stirred up *another* adversary for Solomon, Rezon the son of Eliada, who had fled from his master, Hadadezer king of Zobah.

24 Rezon gathered men to himself and became leader of a marauding band, after David killed those *in Zobah*. They went to Damascus and stayed there and they reigned in Damascus. [2 Sam 10:8, 18]

25 So Rezon was an adversary to Israel all the days of Solomon, along with the evil that Hadad *inflicted*. Rezon hated Israel and reigned over Aram (Syria).

26 Jeroboam, Solomon's servant, the son of Nebat, an Ephrathite of Zeredah whose mother's name was Zeruah, a widow, also rebelled against the king.

27 Now this is the reason why he rebelled against the king: Solomon built the Millo (fortification) and he repaired *and* closed the breach of the city of his father David.

28 The man Jeroboam was a brave warrior and when Solomon saw that the young man was industrious, he put him in charge of all the forced labor of the house of Joseph.

29 It came about at that time, when Jeroboam left Jerusalem, that the prophet Ahijah the Shilonite met him on the road. Now Ahijah had covered himself with a new cloak; and the two of them were alone in the field.

30 Then Ahijah took hold of the new cloak which he was wearing and tore it into twelve pieces.

31 He said to Jeroboam, "Take ten pieces for yourself; for thus says the LORD, the God of Israel, 'Behold, I am going to tear the kingdom from the hand of Solomon and give you ten tribes—

32 but he [and his descendants] shall have one tribe (Benjamin was annexed to Judah), for the sake of My servant David and for the sake of Jerusalem, the city which I have chosen out of all the tribes of Israel—

33 because they have abandoned Me and have worshiped Ashtoreth the goddess of the Sidonians, Chemosh the god of the Moabites, and Milcom the god of the sons of Ammon; and they have not walked in My ways *and* followed My commandments, doing what is right in My sight and *keeping* My statutes and My ordinances as did his father David.

34 'However, I will not take the entire kingdom out of his hand; but I will make him ruler all the days of his life for the sake of My servant David, whom I chose because he kept My commandments and My statutes.

35 'But I will take the kingdom out of his son's hand and give it to you: ten tribes.

36 'Yet to his son I will give one tribe, so that My servant David may have a lamp always before Me in Jerusalem, the city where I have chosen to put My Name *and* Presence.

37 'I will take you [Jeroboam], and you shall reign over whatever your soul desires; and you shall be king over Israel (the ten northern tribes).

38 'Then it shall be, that if you listen to all that I command you and walk in My ways, and do what is right in My sight, keeping *and* observing My statutes and My commandments, as My servant David did, then I will be

---

11:26 *Jeroboam*. At first a trusted official for Solomon (v. 28), Jeroboam came under his wrath and fled to Egypt. Eventually, Jeroboam was instrumental in bringing about the prophesied schism of the country (12:2 – 19). He became the first king of the Northern Kingdom (12:20).

11:31 – 32 *ten tribes . . . one tribe*. The twelfth tribe might be Simeon, which was absorbed by Judah; it is also possible that Benjamin existed for some time as a "buffer state" between Israel and Judah, linked at times with the Southern Kingdom (2Ch 11:3).

11:36 *a lamp*. This is an image of one of the divinely intended functions of the kings of ancient Israel. In the midst of the darkness of a pagan world, the Davidic kings were to be a lamp to the nations, in anticipation of the coming Messiah who would be the Light of the World (Jn 1:1 – 9; 2Sa 21:17; 2Ki 8:19; 2Ch 21:7).

23 2Sa 8:3 **24** 2Sa 8:3; 10:8,18 **26** 1Ki 12:2; 2Ch 13:6; 2Sa 20:21 **27** 1Ki 9:24 **29** 1Ki 14:2 **30** See 1Sa 15:27; 24:5 **31** ver. 11,13 **33** ver. 5-7 **35** 1Ki 12:16,17 **36** 1Ki 15:4; 2Ki 8:19 **38** Jos 1:5; 2Sa 7:11,27

with you and build you an enduring
house, as I built for David, and I will
give Israel to you.
39 ‘And in this way I will afflict the
descendants of David for this (their
sin), but not forever.’ ”
40 So Solomon attempted to kill Jer-
oboam; but Jeroboam set out and es-
caped to Egypt, to Shishak king of
Egypt, and stayed in Egypt until Sol-
omon died.

The Death of Solomon

41 The rest of the acts of Solomon—
and all that he did, and his wisdom—
are they not written in the book of the
acts of Solomon?
42 The time Solomon reigned in Jeru-
salem over all Israel was forty years.
43 And Solomon slept [in death] with
his fathers and was buried in the city
of his father David. Rehoboam his son
reigned in his place.

King Rehoboam Acts Foolishly

12 REHOBOAM WENT to She-
chem, for all Israel had come to
Shechem to make him king.
2 Now when Jeroboam the son of
Nebat heard about it, he was living in
Egypt (for he was still in Egypt, where
he had fled from King Solomon).
3 So they sent *word* and called for
him, and Jeroboam and all the as-
sembly of Israel came and spoke to
Rehoboam, saying,
4 “Your father made our yoke (bur-
den) heavy; so now lighten the hard
labor and the heavy yoke your father
imposed on us, and we will serve you.”
5 Rehoboam replied to them, “Leave
for three days, then come back to me
[for my decision].” So the people left.
6 King Rehoboam consulted with the
elders who had served *and* advised his
father Solomon while he was still alive
and said, “How do you advise me to
answer this people?”
7 They spoke to him, saying, “If you
will be a servant to this people today,
and will serve them and grant their
request, and speak good words to
them, then they will be your servants
forever.”
8 But he ignored the advice which
the elders gave him and consulted the
young men who grew up with him and
served him.
9 He said to them, “What do you ad-
vise that we answer this people who
have said to me, ‘Lighten the yoke (bur-
den) which your father put on us’?”
10 The young men who had grown up
with him answered, “This is what you
should say to this people who told you,
‘Your father made our yoke heavy, but
as for you, make our yoke lighter’—say
this to them: ‘My little finger is thicker
than my father’s loins [and my reign
will be even more severe].
11 ‘And now, whereas my father load-
ed you with a heavy yoke, I will add to
your yoke. My father disciplined you
with whips, but I will discipline you
with scorpions.’ ”
12 Jeroboam and all the people came
back to Rehoboam on the third day,
just as the king had instructed, saying,
“Return to me on the third day.”
13 The king answered the people
harshly and ignored the advice which
the elders had given him,

11:40 *Shishak.* Shishak (or Sheshonq I, 945–924 BC) was the first pharaoh of Egypt's strong twenty-second dynasty. Ironically, this future destroyer of Israel appears here as a protector of one of its future kings.

11:41 *the book of the acts of Solomon.* This book is mentioned only here; compare the references to the Book of the Chronicles of the Kings of Israel (14:19) and the Book of the Chronicles of the Kings of Judah (14:29). It is likely that the author of the books of Kings drew on these sources.

12:1 *Shechem.* Shechem was an important center of Israelite activity. It was the first place mentioned in Canaan with reference to Abraham (Ge 12:6). It was also one of the Levitical cities of refuge (Nu 35:6). By going for his coronation to a place with ancient ties to the history of his people, and which was situated in the region of the northern tribes, Rehoboam doubtless believed that he was making a strategic move.

41 2Ch 9:29 **42** 2Ch 9:30 **43** 2Ch 9:31; Mt 1:7 **CHAPTER 12** **1** 2Ch 10:1 **2** 1Ki 11:26; 1Ki 11:40 **4** 1Sa 8:11-18; 1Ki 4:7 **7** 2Ch 10:7; Pr 15:1

14 and spoke to them in accordance
with the advice of the young men, say-
ing, "My father made your yoke heavy,
but as for me, I will add to your yoke;
my father disciplined you with whips,
but I will discipline you with scorpions."
15 So the king did not listen to the
people; for the situation was from the
LORD, so that He might fulfill His word
which He spoke through Ahijah the
Shilonite to Jeroboam the son of Nebat.
[1 Kin 11:29–33]

The Kingdom Divided; Jeroboam Rules Israel

16 So when all [the ten northern tribes
of] Israel saw that the king did not lis-
ten to them, the people replied to the
king, saying,

"What portion do we have in
David?
We have no inheritance in the son
of Jesse;
To your tents, O Israel!
Look now after your own house,
David!"

Then Israel went back to their tents.
17 But as for the sons (descendants)
of Israel who lived in the cities of Ju-
dah [including Benjamin], Rehoboam
reigned over them.
18 Then King Rehoboam sent
Adoram, who was in charge of the
forced labor [to represent him], and
all Israel stoned him to death. And
King Rehoboam quickly mounted his
chariot to escape to Jerusalem.
19 So Israel (the ten northern tribes)
has rebelled against the house (royal
line) of David to this day (the date of
this writing).
20 It came about when all Israel heard
that Jeroboam had returned, that they
sent *word* and called him to the as-
sembly and made him king over all Is-
rael. None followed the house of David
except the tribe of Judah [including
Benjamin].
21 Now when Rehoboam arrived in
Jerusalem, he assembled all the [fight-
ing men from the] house of Judah, with
the tribe of Benjamin, 180,000 chosen
warriors, to fight against the house of
Israel to bring the kingdom back to
Rehoboam the son of Solomon.
22 But the word of God came to She-
maiah the man of God, saying,
23 "Tell Rehoboam the son of Sol-
omon, king of Judah, and all the house
(fighting men) of Judah and Benjamin
and the rest of the people,
24 'Thus says the LORD, "You shall not
go up and fight against your brothers,
the sons of Israel. Let every man return

12:15 *from the LORD.* Even at this crucial time of national schism, God was sovereignly working through human events to accomplish His will, which had been made known through earlier prophecy (11:29–39). ***might fulfill His word.*** All things derive their origin and destiny from God. They are determined, controlled, and directed from beginning to end by His wise and sovereign counsel. His plan encompasses everything that comes to pass, including all ends and all the ways and means to those ends. His plan also incorporates the folly of men in their deliberations, advice, and decisions, without compelling them to it by external constraint. In fact, God's Word reveals the solemn truth that His plan encompasses even the sin, ungodliness, and evil of men in their motivations and aspirations, their thoughts, words, and deeds, without eliminating their full responsibility for it (Ac 2:22–23; 4:27–28).
12:16 *What portion do we have in David?* The ancient rivalry felt by the northern tribes now came to a peak in resentment against the tribe of Judah and the house of David.
12:17 *cities of Judah.* The southern section of the land also included the tribal allotment of Simeon. But Simeon by this time had been absorbed by Judah, their allotment was "within the inheritance of the sons of Judah" (Jos 19:1).
12:20 *made him king.* The coronation of Jeroboam had been prophesied by Ahijah the prophet of the Lord (11:29–31). Nonetheless, the actual coronation apparently was done apart from priest or prophet of the Lord; there was no divine anointing, no true religious ceremony. Only the kings of the Southern Kingdom would have the sanction of the Davidic covenant (2Sa 7).
12:22 *Shemaiah.* According to 2 Chronicles 12:15, Iddo the prophet and Shemaiah together wrote a history of Rehoboam's reign.

15 ver. 24; Jdg 14:4; 2Ch 10:15; 22:7; 25:20; 1Ki 11:11,31 **16** 2Sa 20:1 **17** 1Ki 11:13,36 **18** 1Ki 4:6; 5:14 **19** 2Ki 17:21 **20** 1Ki 11:13,32 **21** 2Ch 11:1 **22** 2Ch 11:2 **24** ver. 15

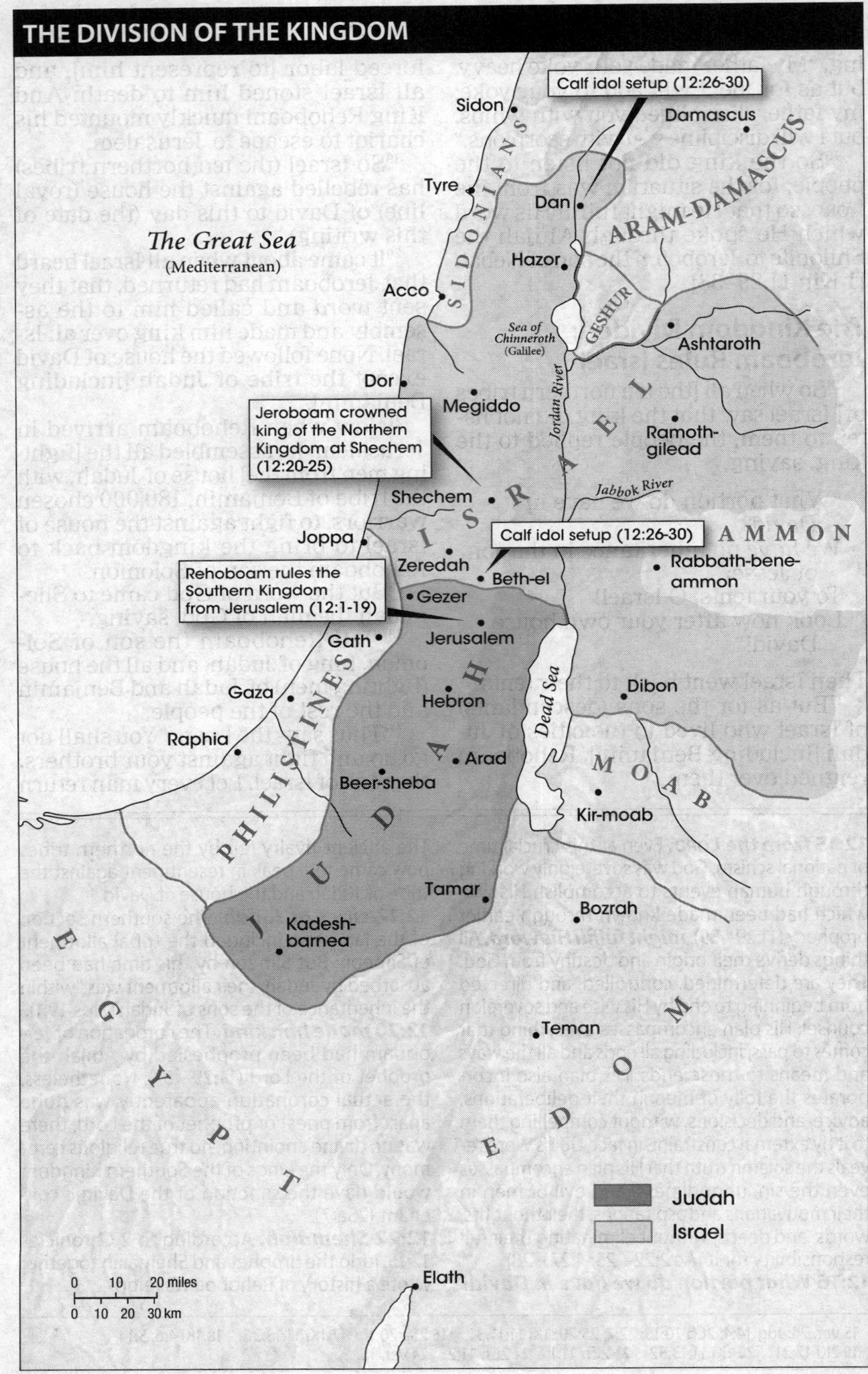
THE DIVISION OF THE KINGDOM
Calf idol setup (12:26-30)
Sidon
Damascus
SIDONIANS
ARAM-DAMASCUS
Tyre
Dan
The Great Sea
(Mediterranean)
Hazor
Acco
GESHUR
Sea of Chinneroth (Galilee)
Ashtaroth
Jordan River
Dor
ISRAEL
Megiddo
Jeroboam crowned king of the Northern Kingdom at Shechem (12:20-25)
Ramoth-gilead
Jabbok River
Shechem
Calf idol setup (12:26-30)
AMMON
Joppa
Zeredah
Rabbath-bene-ammon
Rehoboam rules the Southern Kingdom from Jerusalem (12:1-19)
Beth-el
Gezer
Jerusalem
Gath
Dead Sea
Gaza
Hebron
Dibon
PHILISTINES
Raphia
Arad
Beer-sheba
MOAB
JUDAH
Kir-moab
Tamar
Bozrah
Kadesh-barnea
EGYPT
EDOM
Teman
Judah
Israel
0 10 20 miles
0 10 20 30 km
Elath

to his house, for this thing has come
about from Me." ' " So they listened to
the word of the LORD and returned to
go home, in accordance with the word
of the LORD.

Jeroboam's Idolatry

25 Then Jeroboam built Shechem [as
his royal city] in the hill country of
Ephraim and lived there. He went out
from there and rebuilt Penuel [as a
stronghold].
26 Jeroboam [doubted God's promise
to him and] said in his heart, "Now the
kingdom will return to the house of
David. [1 Kin 11:38]
27 "If these people go up to the house
of the LORD in Jerusalem to offer sac-
rifices, then their heart will turn to
their lord, to Rehoboam king of Judah;
and they will kill me and return to
Rehoboam king of Judah."
28 So the king took counsel [and fol-
lowed bad advice] and made two calves
of gold. And he said to the people, "It
is too much for you to go [all the way]
up to Jerusalem; behold your gods,
O Israel, who brought you up out of
the land of Egypt."
29 He set the one [golden calf] in Beth-
el, and the other he put in Dan.
30 Now this thing became a sin [for
Israel]; because the people went *to
worship* before the one [or the other
of them] as far as Dan.
31 And Jeroboam also made houses
on high places, and he made priests
from all people who were not of the
sons (descendants) of Levi.
32 Jeroboam held a feast on the fif-
teenth day of the eighth month, like
the feast which is *kept* in Judah, and
he went up to the altar; he did this in
Bethel, sacrificing to the calves which
he had made. And he stationed in Beth-
el the priests of the high places which
he had made. [Lev 23:34]
33 So he went up to the altar which
he had made in Bethel on the fifteenth
day of the eighth month, in the month
which he had devised in his own heart
[in defiance of God's commandments];
and he held a feast for the Israelites
and he went up to the altar to burn
incense [in defiance of God's law.]

Jeroboam Warned, Stricken

13 NOW BEHOLD, there came a
man of God from Judah to Bethel
by the word (command) of the LORD,
while Jeroboam was standing by the
altar [which he had built] to burn in-
cense.
2 The man cried out against the [idol-
atrous] altar by the word of the LORD,
"O altar, altar, thus says the Lord: 'Be-
hold, a son shall be born to the house
of David, Josiah by name; and on you
shall he sacrifice [the bodies of] the
priests of the high places who burn

12:28 *two calves of gold.* Not only would they strike a familiar chord from Israel's history, but the two calves would arouse the interest of the remaining Canaanites in the Northern Kingdom. The result of Jeroboam's action was religious confusion and apostasy; this was the first time that a deliberate attempt had been made to establish a heterodox doctrine, an unauthorized variation of the true religion. It appears that Jeroboam was doing the same thing that Aaron did, presenting the calves as representations of God, and thus luring people away from true worship.
12:29 *Bethel.* Bethel was north of Jerusalem in Benjamite territory; it had enjoyed a prominent place in Israelite history throughout the earlier patriarchal period (Ge 28:10 – 21). Dan was in the north; before its capture by the Danites it had a reputation as a center for pagan worship (Jdg 18:30). Jeroboam's choice of these two sites was a brilliant move. He had one site in the northernmost part of his kingdom and another in the southernmost part; both had long ties to Israel's past, and eliminated the need for long, tedious treks to Jerusalem.
12:31 *not of the sons (descendants) of Levi.* Jeroboam's new religious institutions included starting a new religious order that did not include the Levites; setting up shrines at high places (3:2 – 3); and replacing the Feast of Tabernacles with a fall festival of the eighth month. His various attempts at religious innovation would quickly incur God's wrath and earn him a reputation that would live in infamy (13:33 – 34; 22:52).

---

25 See Jdg 9:45; Jdg 8:17 **27** Dt 12:5,6 **28** 2Ki 10:29; 17:16; Ex 32:4,8 **29** Ge 28:19; Hos 4:15; Jdg 18:29 **30** 1Ki 13:34; 2Ki 17:21 **31** 1Ki 13:32; Nu 3:10; 1Ki 13:33; 2Ki 17:32; 2Ch 11:14,15 **32** Lev 23:33,34; Nu 29:12; 1Ki 8:2,5; Am 7:13 **33** Nu 15:39; 1Ki 13:1 **CHAPTER 13** **1** 2Ki 23:17; 1Ki 12:32,33 **2** 2Ki 23:15,16

incense on you, and human bones shall
be burned on you.' "
[3]And he gave a sign the same day,
saying, "This is the sign which the
LORD has spoken: 'Behold, the altar
shall be split apart and the ashes
that are on it shall be poured out.' "
[2 Kin 23:15, 16]
[4]When the king heard the words
which the man of God cried out against
the altar in Bethel, Jeroboam put out
his hand from the altar, saying, "Seize
him!" And his hand which he had put
out against him withered, so that he
was unable to pull it back to himself.
[5]The altar also was split apart and
the ashes were poured out from the
altar in accordance with the sign which
the man of God had given by the word
of the LORD.
[6]The king answered and said to the
man of God, "Please entreat [the favor
of] the LORD your God and pray for me,
that my hand may be restored to me."
So the man of God entreated the LORD,
and the king's hand was restored to
him and became as it was before.
[7]And the king said to the man of
God, "Come home with me and refresh
yourself, and I will give you a reward."
[8]But the man of God said to the king,
"*Even* if you were to give me half your
house (wealth), I would not go with
you, nor would I eat bread or drink
water in this place.
[9]"For I was commanded by the word
of the LORD, 'You shall not eat bread or
drink water, nor shall you return by the
way you came.' "
[10]So he went another way and did
not return by the way that he came
to Bethel.

The Disobedient Prophet

[11]Now there was an old prophet liv-
ing in Bethel; and his sons came and
told him everything that the man of
God had done that day in Bethel; they
also told their father the words which
he had spoken to the king.
[12]Their father asked them, "Which
way did he go?" For his sons had seen
which way the man of God who came
from Judah had gone.
[13]He said to his sons, "Saddle the
donkey for me." So they saddled the
donkey for him and he rode away on it,
[14]and he went after the man of God.
And he found him sitting under an
oak (terebinth) tree, and he said to
him, "Are you the man of God who
came from Judah?" And he said, "I
am."
[15]Then he said to him, "Come home
with me and eat bread."
[16]He said, "I cannot return with you
nor go in with you, nor will I eat bread
or drink water with you in this place.
[17]"For I was told by the word of the
LORD, 'You shall not eat bread nor

13:4–5 *Seize him!* The life and character of Jeroboam stands in stark contrast to that of King David. When David was told that he would become king, he never forgot that it was God who gave him the position, and God who would maintain it. Jeroboam, however, seemed to think that he would only stay in office by his own efforts. When David was confronted with his sin by Nathan the prophet, he humbly confessed (2Sa 12:13). The wicked Jeroboam sought to arrest his accuser.

13:6 *the LORD your God.* This language may be simply deferential to the prophet, but here it may indicate recognition by Jeroboam that he was no longer really serving the living God.

13:7–8 *reward.* The prophet was not just being ungracious, he was following a direct command from God. In biblical times, sharing a meal was more than just a social custom. It implied an intimate fellowship. Great religious ceremonies from the Passover to the Lord's Table center on people eating together. The prophet did not want his act of mercy to suggest that God accepted Jeroboam's deviant worship, or leave the impression that a touch from God could be bought and paid for. Giving a gift can be an easy way to avoid the really important matter of changing lives and lifestyles. If a person is convinced that by his giving he is rewarding a church or a pastor, then it becomes impossible for that church or pastor to have any kind of prophetic ministry to that individual. Instead, they become his debtor.

13:11 *an old prophet.* This prophet was clearly an apostate. He had not spoken against Jeroboam; instead, he boldly lied to the Lord's true prophet.

3 Isa 7:14; Jn 2:18; 1Co 1:22 **6** Ex 8:8; 9:28; 10:17; Nu 21:7; Ac 8:24; Jas 5:16 **7** 1Sa 9:7; 2Ki 5:15 **8** Nu 22:18; 24:13 **9** 1Co 5:11 **16** ver. 8:9 **17** 1Ki 20:35; 1Th 4:15

drink water there, nor shall you return
by going the way that you came.' "
18 He answered him, "I too am a
prophet, as you are; and an angel
spoke to me by the word of the LORD,
saying, 'Bring him back with you to
your house, so that he may eat bread
and drink water.' " *But* he lied to him.
19 So the man of God went back with
him, and ate bread in his house and
drank water.
20 Now it happened as they were sit-
ting at the table, that the word of the
LORD came to the prophet who had
brought him back.
21 And he cried out to the man of God
who had come from Judah, "Thus says
the LORD, 'Because you have disobeyed
the word of the LORD and have not kept
the commandment which the LORD
your God commanded you,
22 but have come back and have eaten
bread and drunk water in the place
of which the LORD said to you, "You
shall not eat bread nor drink water";
your body shall not come to the tomb
of your fathers (ancestors).' "
23 After the prophet of the house had
eaten bread and after he had drunk,
he saddled the donkey for the prophet
whom he had brought back.
24 Now when he had gone, a lion met
him by the road and killed him, and his
body was thrown in the road, with the
donkey standing beside it; the lion was
also standing beside the body.
25 And there were men passing by,
and they saw the body thrown in the
road, and the lion standing beside the
body. So they came and told about it
in the city [of Bethel] where the old
prophet lived.
26 When the prophet who had brought
him back from the road heard about it,
he said, "It is the man of God who was
disobedient to the word of the LORD;
therefore the LORD has given him to
the lion, which has torn him and killed
him, in accordance with the word of
the LORD which He spoke to him."
27 And he said to his sons, "Saddle the
donkey for me." And they saddled it.
28 And he went and found the body
thrown on the road, and the donkey
and the lion standing beside the body;
the lion [miraculously] had not eaten
the body or attacked the donkey.
29 Then the prophet picked up the
body of the man of God and laid it on
the donkey and brought it back, and
he came into the city (Bethel) of the
old prophet to mourn and to bury him.
30 And he laid the body in his own
grave, and they mourned over him,
saying, "Alas, my brother!"
31 Then after he had buried him, he
said to his sons, "When I am dead,
bury me in the grave in which the man
of God is buried; lay my bones beside
his bones.
32 "For the words which he cried out
by the word of the LORD against the
altar in Bethel and against all the hous-
es of the high places which are in the
cities of Samaria shall certainly come
to pass."
33 After this event, Jeroboam [still] did
not turn from his evil way, but again
made priests for the high places from
among all the people. He ordained
anyone who was willing, so that there
would be priests for the high places.
34 And this thing (idol worship) be-
came the sin of the house of Jeroboam

13:19 *went back with him.* The man of God had withstood Jeroboam's persuasions; he probably came expecting just such pressure. Sadly, he made the mistake of letting down his guard when he had passed the test he was expecting. There is never any excuse for violating God's clear instructions, and he paid a terrible price for his disobedience.

13:24 *a lion.* The way the lion stood by both the man of God and his donkey shows that the lion did not kill for food but was God's executioner (vv. 25–26,28).

13:32 *cities of Samaria.* The city of Samaria did not, in fact, come into being for nearly half a century (16:24), but the author mentions it here from his own later perspective.

13:33 *evil way.* Rather than learning from the report of this incident, Jeroboam was even more set in his evil ways. His apostasy would earn for him his reputation as the one who "made Israel to sin" (16:26).

24 1Ki 20:36 **30** Jer 22:18 **31** 2Ki 23:17,18 **32** ver. 2; 2Ki 23:16,19; See 1Ki 16:24 **33** 1Ki 12:31,32; 2Ch 11:15; 13:9 **34** 1Ki 12:30; 1Ki 14:10

to blot it out and eliminate it from the face of the earth.

Ahijah Prophesies against the King

14 AT THAT time Abijah the son [and crown prince, heir] of Jeroboam became sick.

2 Jeroboam said to his wife, "Please get up and disguise yourself, so that people will not know that you are Jeroboam's wife, and go to Shiloh. Ahijah the prophet is there, the one who told me that *I would be* king over this people.

3 "Take with you ten loaves of bread, *some* cakes, and a bottle of honey, and go to him. He will tell you what will happen to the boy."

4 Jeroboam's wife did so. She got up and went [twenty miles] to Shiloh, and came to the house of Ahijah. Now Ahijah could not see, because his eyes were dim from old age.

5 And the LORD said to Ahijah, "Behold, the wife of Jeroboam is coming to inquire of you about her son, because he is sick. You shall say such and such to her, for when she arrives, she will pretend to be another woman."

6 So when Ahijah heard the sound of her feet as she came in the doorway, he said, "Come in, wife of Jeroboam. Why do you pretend to be another woman? For I have been sent to you [by God] with a harsh *message*.

7 "Go, tell Jeroboam, 'This is what the LORD, the God of Israel, says: "Because I exalted you from among the people and made you leader over My people Israel,

8 and tore the kingdom away from the house of David and gave it to you—but you have not been like My servant David, who kept My commandments and followed Me with all his heart, to do only what was right in My eyes,

9 but have done more evil than all [the kings] who were before you; for you have gone and made for yourself other gods and molten images to provoke Me to anger, and have cast Me behind your back—

10 therefore behold, I am bringing evil on the house (royal line) of Jeroboam, and I will cut off (destroy) from Jeroboam every male, both bond and free, in Israel, and will *utterly* sweep away the house of Jeroboam as one sweeps away dung until it is all gone.

11 "The dogs will eat [the carcass of] anyone belonging to Jeroboam who dies in the city, and the birds of the sky will eat [the carcass of] anyone who dies in the field, for the LORD has spoken it." ' [Deut 28:26]

12 "Now as for you (Jeroboam's wife), arise, go to your own house. When your feet enter the city, the child [Abijah] will die.

13 "All Israel shall mourn for him and bury him, for he alone of Jeroboam's *family* will come to [be placed in] the grave, because in him there was found something good *and* pleasing toward the LORD, the God of Israel, in the house of Jeroboam.

14 "Moreover, the LORD will raise up for Himself a king over Israel who will cut off the house (royal line) of Jeroboam this day and from now on.

15 "The LORD will strike Israel, as a reed is shaken in the water; and He will uproot Israel from this good land which He gave to their fathers, and He

---

14:4 *Shiloh.* Located about twenty miles north of Jerusalem, Shiloh had been the religious center for the nation during the time of the judges and was the location of the tabernacle (Jos 18:1; 1Sa 1:3). The city was destroyed by the Philistines after the loss of the ark (1Sa 4:1 – 11; Jer 7:12 – 15). ***could not see.*** Although he was blind, Ahijah could "see" by means of the revelation of the living God.
14:11 *dogs.* Dogs were scavengers, and in the Middle East they came to symbolize the dregs of society (2Ki 8:13).
14:14 *cut off the house.* As prophesied here, the end of Jeroboam's reign would soon be accomplished (15:27 – 16:7).
14:15 *Asherim.* This word refers to the wooden poles or images associated with the worship of the goddess Asherah (Jdg 3:7; 2Ki 23:4). Her worship would become one of the sins that would

CHAPTER 14 **2** 1Ki 11:31 **3** See 1Sa 9:7,8 **4** 1Ki 11:29 **7** See 2Sa 12:7,8 **8** 1Ki 11:31; 1Ki 11:33,38; 15:5 **9** 1Ki 12:28; 2Ch 11:15; Neh 9:26; Ps 50:17 **10** 1Ki 15:29; 1Ki 21:21; 2Ki 9:8; Dt 32:36; 2Ki 14:26 **11** 1Ki 16:4; 21:24 **12** ver. 17 **13** 2Ch 12:12; 19:3 **14** 1Ki 15:27-29 **15** 2Ki 17:6; Ps 52:5; Jos 23:15,16; 2Ki 15:29; Ex 34:13; Dt 12:3

will scatter them beyond the [Euphra-
tes] River, because they have made
their Asherim, provoking the LORD
to anger.
16“He will give up Israel because of
the sins of Jeroboam which he has
committed, and with which he has
made Israel sin [by leading them into
idolatry].”
17So Jeroboam’s wife arose and
left and came to Tirzah [the king’s
residence]. As she was entering the
threshold of the house, the child [Abi-
jah] died.
18And all Israel buried him and
mourned for him, in accordance
with the word of the LORD which He
spoke through His servant Ahijah the
prophet.
19Now as for the rest of the acts of
Jeroboam, how he made war and how
he reigned, behold, they are written
in the Book of the Chronicles of the
Kings of Israel.
20The time that Jeroboam reigned
was twenty-two years, and he slept
with his fathers [in death]; and Nadab
his son reigned in his place.

Rehoboam Misleads Judah

21Now Rehoboam the son of Sol-
omon reigned in Judah. Rehoboam
was forty-one years old when he be-
came king, and he reigned seventeen
years in Jerusalem, the city the LORD
had chosen from all the tribes of Israel
in which to put His Name (Presence).
His mother’s name was Naamah the
Ammonitess.
22And [the people of] Judah did evil
in the sight of the LORD. They provoked
Him to jealousy more than all that
their fathers had done, with their sins
which they had committed.
23For they also built for themselves
high places [to worship idols] and *sa-
cred* pillars and Asherim [for the god-
dess Asherah]. *These were* on every
high hill and under every luxuriant
tree.
24There were also male cult pros-
titutes in the land. They committed
all the repulsive acts of the nations
which the LORD dispossessed before
the Israelites.
25Now in the fifth year of King
Rehoboam, Shishak king of Egypt
[Jeroboam’s brother-in-law] came up
against Jerusalem.
26He took away the treasures of the
house (temple) of the LORD and the
treasures of the king’s house; he took
away everything, he even took all the
shields of gold which Solomon had
made.
27So King Rehoboam made bronze
shields to replace them and handed
them over to the captains of the palace
guard who guarded the doorway of the
king’s house.

---

bring about the downfall of the Northern Kingdom (2Ki 17:9 – 11).

14:17 *Tirzah.* Famed for its beauty (SS 6:4), Tirzah was a royal retreat and the capital of the Northern Kingdom’s first two dynasties (15:33).

14:19 *the Book of the Chronicles of the Kings of Israel.* This book is mentioned 15 times in Kings. Apparently it was an official record of events in the Southern Kingdom down to the days of Jehoiakim. This work should not be confused with the biblical books of Chronicles, which were written much later, after the exile.

14:20 *Jeroboam.* Each of the subsequent kings of Israel was judged against the example of the wickedness of Jeroboam (15:34). Only with Ahab was a worse pattern set (16:31).

14:23 *high places.* The high places were a problem throughout the history of Judah and Israel (Mic 1:3). At times, the worship offered on them may have been done sincerely, in true worship of God (3:2 – 4; 2Ki 12:3). But these were also the places in which Canaanite worship rites were practiced, and images set up to honor Baal and Asherah. Even when the worship on the high places was not mixed with pagan rituals, it was not in accord with the law of Moses (see 2Ch 1:3).

14:24 *repulsive acts.* This is an exceedingly strong term; it describes perverted activities that impelled God to dispossess the Canaanite peoples from their land (Dt 18:9 – 12).

14:26 *treasures of the house (temple) of the LORD.* The sacking of the temple is particularly shocking when we think of the long and detailed

16 1Ki 12:30; 13:34; 15:30,34; 16:2 **17** 1Ki 16:6,8; ver. 12 **18** ver. 13 **19** 2Ch 13:2 **21** 2Ch 12:13; 1Ki 11:36; ver. 31 **22** 2Ch 12:1; Dt 32:21 **23** Dt 12:2; Eze 16:24,25; 2Ki 17:9,10; Isa 57:5 **24** Dt 23:17; 1Ki 15:12; 2Ki 23:7 **25** 1Ki 11:40; 2Ch 12:2 **26** 2Ch 12:9-11; 1Ki 10:17

RULERS OF THE DIVIDED KINGDOM OF ISRAEL AND JUDAH

DATA AND DATES IN ORDER OF SEQUENCE

	SCRIPTURE	KINGS	SYNCHRONISM OR CORRELATION	LENGTH OF REIGN	HISTORICAL DATA	DATES
1.	*1Ki 12:1–24 1Ki 14:21–31*	***Rehoboam** (Judah)*		*17 years*		*930-913*
2.	1Ki 12:25—14:20	**Jeroboam I** (Israel)		22 years		930-909
3.	*1Ki 15:1–8*	***Abijah** (Judah)*	*18th of Jeroboam*	*3 years*		*913-910*
4.	*1Ki 15:9–24*	***Asa** (Judah)*	*20th of Jeroboam*	*41 years*		*910-869*
5.	1Ki 15:25–31	**Nadab** (Israel)	2nd of Asa	2 years		909-908
6.	1Ki 15:32—16:7	**Baasha** (Israel)	3rd of Asa	24 years		908-886
7.	1Ki 16:8–14	**Elah** (Israel)	26th of Asa	2 years		886-885
8.	1Ki 16:15–20	**Zimri** (Israel)	27th of Asa	7days		885
9.	1Ki 16:21–22	**Tibni** (Israel)			Overlap with Omri	885-880
10.	1Ki 16:23–28	**Omri** (Israel)	27th of Asa 31st of Asa	12 years	Made king by the people Overlap with Tibni Official reign = 11 actual years Sole reign	885 885-880 885-874 880-874
11.	1Ki 16:29—22:40	**Ahab** (Israel)	38th of Asa	22 years	Official reign = 21 actual years	874-853
12.	*1Ki 22:41–50*	***Jehoshaphat** (Judah)*	*4th of Ahab*	*25 years*	*Coregency with Asa Official reign Sole reign Has Jehoram as regent*	*872-869 872-848 869-853 853-848*
13.	1Ki 22:51—2Ki 1:18	**Ahaziah** (Israel)	17th of Jehoshaphat	2 years	Official reign = 1 year actual reign	853-852
14.	2Ki 1:17 2Ki 3:1—8:15	**Joram** (Israel)	2nd of Jehoram 18th of Jehoshaphat	12 years	Official reign = 11 actual years	852 852-841
15.	*2Ki 8:16–24*	***Jehoram** (Judah)*	*5th of Joram*	*8 years*	*Coregency with Jehoshaphat Sole reign Official reign = 7 actual years*	*853-848 848-841 848-841*
16.	*2Ki 8:25–29 2Ki 9:29*	***Ahaziah** (Judah)*	*12th of Joram 11th of Joram*	*1 year*	*Nonaccession-year reckoning Accession-year reckoning*	*841 841*
17.	2Ki 9:30—10:36	**Jehu** (Israel)		28 years		841-814
18.	*2Ki 11*	***Athaliah** (Judah)*		*7 years*		*841-835*
19.	*2Ki 12*	***Joash** (Judah)*	*7th of Jehu*	*40 years*		*835-796*
20.	2Ki 13:1–9	**Jehoahaz** (Israel)	23rd of Joash	17 years		814-798
21.	2Ki 13:10–25	**Jehoash** (Israel)	37th of Joash	16 years		798-782

*Italics denote rulers of **Judah**.* Non-italic type denotes rulers of **Israel**.

SCRIPTURE		KINGS	SYNCHRONISM OR CORRELATION	LENGTH OF REIGN	HISTORICAL DATA	DATES
22.	*2Ki 14:1–22*	***Amaziah** (Judah)*	*2nd of Jehoash*	*29 years*		*796-767*
					Overlap with Azariah	*792-767*
23.	2Ki 14:23–29	**Jeroboam II** (Israel)		41 years	Coregency with Jehoash	793-782
					Total reign	793-753
			15th of Amaziah		Sole reign	782-753
24.	*2Ki 15:1–7*	***Azariah** (Judah) (= **Uzziah**)*	*27th of Jeroboam*		*Overlap with Amaziah*	*792-767*
				52 years	*Total reign*	*792-740*
					Sole reign	*767-750*
25.	2Ki 15:8–12	**Zechariah** (Israel)	38th of Azariah	6 months		753
26.	2Ki 15:13–15	**Shallum** (Israel)	39th of Azariah	1 month		752
27.	2Ki 15:16–22	**Menahem** (Israel)	39th of Azariah	10 years	Ruled in Samaria	752-742
28.	2Ki 15:23–26	**Pekahiah** (Israel)	50th of Azariah	2 years		742-740
29.	2Ki 15:27–31	**Pekah** (Israel)			In Gilead; overlapping years	752-740
				20 years	Total reign	752-732
			52nd of Azariah		Sole reign	740-732
30.	*2Ki 15:32–38*	***Jotham** (Judah)*	*2nd of Pekah*		*Coregency with Azariah*	*750-740*
	2Ki 15:30			*16 years*	*Official reign*	*750-735*
					Reign to his 20th year	*750-732*
31.	*2Ki 16*	***Ahaz** (Judah)*			*Total reign*	*735-715*
			17th of Pekah			*735*
				16 years	*From 20th of Jotham*	*732-715*
32.	2Ki 15:30	**Hoshea** (Israel)			20th of Jotham	732
	2Ki 17		12th of Ahaz	9 years		732-722
33.	2Ki 18:1—20:21	***Hezekiah** (Judah)*	3rd of Hoshea	29 years		715-686
					Coregency with Ahaz	729-715
34.	*2Ki 21:1–18*	***Manasseh** (Judah)*			*Coregency with Hezekiah*	*697-686*
				55 years	*Total reign*	*697-642*
35.	*2Ki 21:19–26*	***Amon** (Judah)*		*2 years*		*642-640*
36.	*2Ki 22:1—23:30*	***Josiah** (Judah)*		*31 years*		*640-609*
37.	*2Ki 23:31–33*	***Jehoahaz** (Judah)*		*3 months*		*609*
38.	*2Ki 23:34—24:7*	***Jehoiakim** (Judah)*		*11 years*		*609-598*
39.	*2Ki 24:8–17*	***Jehoiachin** (Judah)*		*3 months*		*598-597*
40.	*2Ki 24:18—25:26*	***Zedekiah** (Judah)*		*11 years*		*597-586*

Adapted from *The Mysterious Numbers of the Hebrew Kings* by Edwin R. Thiele. ©1983 by Zondervan. Used by permission.

28 And as often as the king went
into the house of the LORD, the guards
would carry them and bring them back
into the guardroom.
29 Now as for the rest of the acts of
Rehoboam, and everything that he did,
are they not written in the Book of the
Chronicles of the Kings of Judah?
30 There was also war between Re-
hoboam and Jeroboam continually.
31 And Rehoboam slept with his fa-
thers [in death] and was buried with
his fathers in the City of David. His
mother's name was Naamah the Am-
monitess. Abijam (Abijah) his son be-
came king in his place.

Abijam Reigns over Judah

15 IN THE eighteenth year of King
Jeroboam the son of Nebat, Abi-
jam became king over Judah.
2 He reigned three years in Jerusa-
lem. His mother was Maacah [grand]
daughter of Abishalom (Absalom).
3 He walked in all the sins [of idol
worship] that his father [Rehoboam]
committed before him; and his heart
was not entirely devoted to the LORD
his God, like the heart of his father
(forefather) David.
4 Nevertheless, for David's sake the
LORD his God gave him a lamp (de-
scendant on the throne) in Jerusalem,
setting up his son after him and estab-
lishing Jerusalem,
5 because David did what was right
in the eyes of the LORD, and had not
turned aside from anything that He
commanded him all the days of his life,
except in the matter of [the betrayal of]
Uriah the Hittite.
6 There was war between Rehoboam
[Abijam's father] and Jeroboam all the
days of Rehoboam's life.
7 Now as for the rest of the acts of
Abijam and everything that he did,
are they not written in the Book of
the Chronicles of the Kings of Judah?
And there was war between Abijam
and Jeroboam.

Asa Succeeds Abijam

8 Abijam slept with his fathers [in
death] and they buried him in the City
of David. Asa his son became king in
his place.
9 So in the twentieth year of Jero-
boam king of Israel, Asa began to
reign as king over Judah.
10 He reigned forty-one years in Je-
rusalem. His [great-grand]mother was
Maacah the daughter of Abishalom
(Absalom). [1 Kin 15:2]
11 Asa did what was right in the eyes
of the LORD, as did his father (forefa-
ther) David.

---

description of Solomon's building and furnishing of the house of the Lord.

15:2 *Maacah.* Elsewhere she is described as "the daughter of Uriel of Gibeah" (2Ch 13:2), and "the daughter of Absalom" (2Ch 11:21). It is thought that she was the granddaughter of Absalom; the daughter of Uriel of Gibea and Absalom's daughter Tamar (2Sa 14:27). She was the favorite of Rehoboam's many wives. The fact that she is mentioned in connection with both her son Abijam and her grandson Asa (vv. 10,12) makes it appear that she was an important figure, probably wielding a good deal of influence.

15:4 *for David's sake.* That is, because of God's love for David and the promise He had made to him (2Sa 7). ***lamp.*** This is one of the lovely images of God's intended blessing on the Davidic house.

15:5 Perseverance—The lamp of God was still shining in Jerusalem during the reign of Abijam, even though he was not wholly devoted to the Lord, nor was his father who reigned before him. In spite of the sins of Abijam and his father, God continued to let His light shine in Jerusalem for the sake of David, whose heart was all for the Lord. In a similar way, our actions will affect the generations which follow us. If we are committed to God's ways, and willing to stand for what is right, our children will benefit; if we selfishly follow our own pleasures, our children often are left picking up the pieces.

15:10 *His [great-grand]mother was Maacah.* It is important to remember that many times the Hebrews used the terms "father, mother, son, daughter" loosely, to indicate ancestry rather than exact generation (v. 3).

29 2Ch 12:15 **30** 1Ki 12:24; 15:6; 2Ch 12:15 **31** 2Ch 12:16; ver. 21; Mt 1:7 **CHAPTER 15** **1** 2Ch 13:1 **2** 2Ch 11:20-22 **3** 1Ki 11:4; Ps 119:80 **4** 1Ki 11:32,36; 2Ch 21:7 **5** 1Ki 14:8; 2Sa 11:4,15; 12:9 **6** 1Ki 14:30 **7** 2Ch 13:2,3,22 **8** 2Ch 14:1 **11** 2Ch 14:2

12 He expelled the male cult prosti-
tutes (sodomites) from the land and
removed all the idols that his fathers
[Solomon, Rehoboam, and Abijam]
had made. [1 Kin 11:5–11; 14:22]
13 He also deposed his [great-grand]
mother Maacah from *being* queen
mother, because she had made a hor-
rid (obscene, vulgar) image for [the
goddess] Asherah. Asa cut down her
horrid image, and burned it by the
Brook Kidron.
14 But the high places [of idol wor-
ship] were not removed. Nevertheless,
Asa's heart was entirely devoted to the
LORD all his days.
15 He brought the things which his
father had dedicated and the things
which he had dedicated into the house
of the LORD—silver, gold, and utensils
and accessories.
16 Now there was war between Asa
and Baasha king of Israel all their
days.
17 Baasha king of Israel went up
against Judah and fortified Ramah
[north of Jerusalem], in order to pre-
vent *anyone* from going out or coming
in to Asa king of Judah.
18 Then Asa took all the silver and
gold left in the treasuries of the house
of the LORD and the treasuries of the
palace of the king and handed them
over to his servants. And King Asa
sent them to Ben-hadad the son of Tab-
rimmon, the son of Hezion, king of
Aram (Syria), who lived in Damascus,
saying,
19 "*Let there be* a treaty between me
and you, *as there was* between my
father and your father. Behold, I have
sent you a gift of silver and gold; go,
break your treaty with Baasha king
of Israel, so that he will withdraw
from me."
20 So Ben-hadad listened to king Asa
and sent the commanders of his armies
against the cities of Israel, and con-
quered Ijon, Dan, Abel-beth-maacah,
and all Chinneroth [the region of the
Sea of Galilee], along with all the land
of Naphtali.
21 When Baasha heard about it, he
stopped fortifying Ramah and stayed
in Tirzah.
22 Then King Asa made a proclama-
tion to all Judah—none was exempt—
and they carried away the stones of
Ramah and its timber with which
Baasha had built [the fortifications].
And King Asa built with them [border
fortresses at] Geba of Benjamin and
Mizpah.

Jehoshaphat Succeeds Asa

23 Now as for the rest of all the acts
of Asa, all his might, everything that

15:13 *He also deposed.* Asa's many spiritual activities (2Ch 14:2 – 5; 15:1 – 18) are telescoped into a few statements here. Although the reforms mentioned took place early in Asa's reign (2Ch 14:2 – 5), the chronicler indicates that the deposing of Maacah took place in the fifteenth year of his rule (895 BC). Maacah's removal came as a result of a time of covenant renewal (2Ch 15:1 – 16) and a consequent reaction against her vile idolatry.

15:14 *high places.* In some instances, the high places were places where the Lord was worshiped (1Sa 9:12); in other cases they were used for pagan purposes (2Ch 14:2 – 3).

15:17 *Ramah.* Ramah was about five and a half miles north of Jerusalem on the main north-south commercial route through the land, and it was therefore of great importance to both kingdoms. It gave east-west access to both the foothills of Ephraim and the Mediterranean coast, so it was of strategic military importance as well. Baasha was striking a blow for control of the center of the land.

15:18 – 19 Unfaithfulness — Asa's life was a mixture of good and evil, faithfulness and faithlessness. He took a stand against the rampant idolatry, removing male cult prostitutes and idolatrous worship, and even demoting his own grandmother to reduce her evil influence (v. 13). Yet later in his life, he signally failed to trust God for either safety or health. When Baasha, king of Israel, attacked him, he sought help from the Syrians (vv. 17 – 18) rather than from God, and resented and rejected the prophetic rebuke he received (2Ch 16:7 – 10). Near the end of his life, Asa suffered a crippling disease in his feet; yet even in this "he did not seek the LORD, but [relied only on] the physicians" (2Ch 16:12).

---

12 1Ki 14:24; 22:46 **13** 2Ch 15:16; Ex 32:20 **14** 1Ki 22:43; 2Ch 15:17,18; See ver. 3 **17** 2Ch 16:1; Jos 18:25; See 1Ki 12:27 **18** 2Ch 16:2; 1Ki 11:23,24 **20** 2Ki 15:29; Jdg 18:29; 2Sa 20:14 **22** 2Ch 16:6; Jos 21:17; Jos 18:26 **23** 2Ch 16:12

he did, and the cities which he built, are they not written in the Book of the Chronicles of the Kings of Judah? But during the time of his old age he had a foot disease.
[24]Asa slept with his fathers [in death] and was buried with his fathers in the city of his father David. Jehoshaphat his son reigned in his place.

Nadab, then Baasha, Rules over Israel

[25]Now Nadab the son of Jeroboam began to reign over Israel in the second year of Asa king of Judah, and he reigned over Israel for two years.
[26]He did evil in the sight of the LORD and walked in the way of his father [Jeroboam] and in his sin [of idolatry], with which he made Israel sin.
[27]Baasha the son of Ahijah of the house (tribe) of Issachar conspired against Nadab, and Baasha struck him down at Gibbethon, which belonged to the Philistines, while Nadab and all Israel were laying siege to Gibbethon.
[28]So Baasha killed Nadab in the third year of Asa king of Judah, and reigned in his place.
[29]As soon as he was king, Baasha struck down all the household of Jeroboam. He did not leave for Jeroboam anyone alive, but he destroyed them in accordance with the word of the LORD which He had spoken through His servant Ahijah the Shilonite—[1 Kin 14:9–16]
[30]because of the sins committed by Jeroboam and which he made Israel commit, and because he provoked the LORD God of Israel to anger.
[31]Now as for the rest of Nadab's acts and everything that he did, are they not written in the Book of the Chronicles of the Kings of Israel?

War with Judah

[32]There was war between Asa and Baasha king of Israel all their days.
[33]In the third year of Asa king of Judah, Baasha the son of Ahijah became king over all Israel in Tirzah [the capital city], *and reigned* twenty-four years.
[34]He did evil in the sight of the LORD and walked in the way of Jeroboam and in his sin [of idolatry] with which he made Israel sin.

Prophecy against Baasha

16 NOW THE word of the LORD came to Jehu the son of Hanani against Baasha, saying,
[2]"Because I exalted you [Baasha] from the dust and made you leader over My people Israel, and you walked in the way of Jeroboam and made My people Israel sin, provoking Me to anger with their sins [of idol worship],
[3]behold, I am going to sweep away Baasha and his household (family), and I will make your house (royal line) like that of Jeroboam the son of Nebat.
[4]"The dogs will eat anyone belonging to Baasha who dies in the city, and the birds of the sky will eat anyone belonging to him who dies in the field."
[5]Now as for the rest of the acts of Baasha, what he did and his might, are they not written in the Book of the Chronicles of the Kings of Israel?

The Israelite Kings

[6]Baasha slept with his fathers [in death] and was buried in Tirzah. Elah his son became king in his place.
[7]Moreover, the word of the LORD

15:25 ***Nadab.*** His name means "Generous" or "Noble," but he did not live up to his name.
15:29 ***in accordance with the word of the LORD.*** The death of Nadab was in line with the prophetic fulfillment of God's judgment on the house of Jeroboam (14:9,16). Nonetheless, the manner of his death was condemned by God through His prophet Jehu (16:7).

16:1 – 7 ***Jehu.*** This Jehu is not to be confused with Jehu the king of Israel (2Ki 9:2). Jehu the prophet came from the Southern Kingdom; his long prophetic ministry lasted into the days of Jehoshaphat. Like his father before him, he confronted sin fearlessly, even in the royal house (2Ch 16:7 – 10).

24 2Ch 17:1 **26** 1Ki 12:30; 14:16 **27** 1Ki 14:14; Jos 19:44 **29** 1Ki 14:10,14 **30** 1Ki 14:9,16 **32** ver. 16 **34** 1Ki 12:28,29; 13:33; 14:16 **CHAPTER 16** **1** ver. 7; 2Ch 19:2; 20:34 **2** 1Ki 14:7; 1Ki 15:34 **3** ver. 11; 1Ki 14:10; 15:29 **4** 1Ki 14:11 **5** 2Ch 16:1 **6** 1Ki 14:17; 15:21 **7** ver. 1; 1Ki 15:27,29; See Hos 1:4

came against Baasha and his house-
hold through the prophet Jehu the son
of Hanani, both for all the evil that
Baasha did in the sight of the LORD in
provoking Him to anger with the work
of his hands (idolatry), in being like
the house of Jeroboam, and because
he [willingly] destroyed it (the family
of Jeroboam).
8 In the twenty-sixth year of Asa king
of Judah, Elah the son of Baasha be-
came king over Israel in Tirzah, *and
reigned* two years.
9 His servant Zimri, commander of
half his chariots, conspired against
Elah. Now Elah was in Tirzah, getting
drunk in the house of Arza, who was
in charge of the [king's] household in
Tirzah.
10 Then Zimri came in and struck and
killed Elah in the twenty-seventh year
of Asa king of Judah, and became king
in his place.
11 When he became king, as soon
as he sat on his throne, he killed the
entire household of Baasha; he did not
leave a single male [alive], either of his
relatives or his friends.
12 Thus Zimri destroyed the entire
household of Baasha, in accordance
with the word of the LORD which He
spoke against Baasha through Jehu
the prophet, [1 Kin 16:3]
13 for all the sins of Baasha and the
sins of Elah his son, which they com-
mitted, and made Israel commit, pro-
voking the LORD God of Israel to anger
with their idols.
14 Now as for the rest of the acts of
Elah and everything that he did, are
they not written in the Book of the
Chronicles of the Kings of Israel?
15 In the twenty-seventh year of Asa
king of Judah, Zimri reigned [over
Israel] for seven days at Tirzah. Now
the troops were camped against Gib-
bethon, [a city] which belonged to the
Philistines,
16 and the people who were camped
heard it said, "Zimri has conspired and
has also struck down the king." So all
Israel made Omri, the commander of
the army, king over Israel that day in
the camp.
17 Then Omri went up from Gibbe-
thon, and all Israel with him, and they
besieged Tirzah.
18 When Zimri saw that the city was
taken, he went into the fortress of the
king's palace; and *while inside,* he set
fire to the king's palace and died,
19 because of the sins he had commit-
ted, doing evil in the sight of the LORD,
by walking in the way of Jeroboam,
and because of his sin he caused Is-
rael to sin.
20 Now as for the rest of the acts of
Zimri, and his [treasonous] conspira-
cy which he committed, are they not
written in the Book of the Chronicles
of the Kings of Israel?
21 Then the people of Israel were di-
vided in half. Half of the people fol-
lowed Tibni the son of Ginath, to make
him king, and the *other* half followed
Omri.
22 But the people who followed Omri
prevailed over the people who followed
Tibni the son of Ginath. So Tibni died
and Omri became king.
23 In the thirty-first year of Asa king
of Judah, Omri became king over Is-
rael *and reigned* for twelve years. He
reigned six years at Tirzah.
24 Omri bought the hill Samaria from
Shemer for two talents of silver, and
he built *a city* on the hill [and fortified
it], and named the city which he built
Samaria, after the owner of the hill,
Shemer.
25 But Omri did evil in the sight of the
LORD, and acted more wickedly than
all who *came* before him.
26 He walked in all the ways of Jero-
boam the son of Nebat and in his sin,

16:10 *Zimri.* Zimri's treacherous act was the prophesied judgment on Baasha and Elah for their wickedness.

16:23 *Omri.* Omri's exploits are commemorated in the Moabite Stone and the Assyrian annals. Indeed, he was so important to the Assyrians that they called Israel "the House of Omri" long after his death. Yet the author of Kings describes little of Omri's achievements, because he did evil in the eyes of the Lord.

9 2Ki 9:31 **11** 1Sa 25:22 **12** ver. 3; ver. 1 **13** Dt 32:21; 1Sa 12:21; Isa 41:29; Jnh 2:8; 1Co 8:4; 10:19 **15** 1Ki 15:27 **19** 1Ki 12:28; 15:26,34 **24** See 1Ki 13:32; 2Ki 17:24; Jn 4:4 **25** Mic 6:16 **26** ver. 19; ver. 13

which he made Israel commit, provok-
ing the LORD God of Israel, [to anger]
with their idols.
27Now as for the rest of the acts of
Omri which he did, and his might
which he showed, are they not writ-
ten in the Book of the Chronicles of
the Kings of Israel?
28So Omri slept with his fathers [in
death] and was buried in Samaria.
Ahab his son became king in his place.
29Ahab the son of Omri became king
over Israel in the thirty-eighth year of
Asa king of Judah, and Ahab the son
of Omri reigned over Israel in Samaria
for twenty-two years.
30Ahab the son of Omri did evil in
the sight of the LORD more than all [the
kings] who were before him.
31It came about, as if it had been a
trivial thing for Ahab to walk in the
sins of Jeroboam the son of Nebat,
that he married Jezebel the daughter
of Ethbaal king of the Sidonians, and
went and served Baal and worshiped
him.
32So he erected an altar for Baal in
the house of Baal which he built in
Samaria.
33Ahab also made the Asherah.
Ahab did more to provoke the LORD
God of Israel than all the kings of Is-
rael who were before him.
34In his days, Hiel the Bethelite re-
built Jericho. He laid its foundations
with the *loss of* Abiram his firstborn,
and set up its gates with the *loss of* his
youngest son Segub, in accordance
with the word of the LORD, which He
spoke through Joshua the son of Nun.
[Josh 6:26]

Elijah Predicts Drought

17 NOW ELIJAH the Tishbite, who
was of the settlers of Gilead, said
to Ahab, "As the LORD, the God of Israel
lives, before whom I stand, there shall
be neither dew nor rain these years,
except by My word." [Deut 11:16, 17]
2And the word of the LORD came to
him, saying,
3"Go from here and turn eastward
and hide yourself by the brook Cherith,
which is east of the Jordan [River].
4"You shall drink from the brook,
and I have commanded the ravens to
sustain you there [with food]."
5So he went and did in accordance
with the word of the LORD; he went and
lived by the brook Cherith, which is
east of the Jordan.
6And the ravens brought him bread
and meat in the morning, and bread
and meat in the evening; and he would
drink from the brook.
7It happened after a while that the
brook dried up, because there was no
rain in the land.

16:30 *Ahab.* In Ahab we come to the very lowest point in the degeneration of the spiritual life of the kings of Israel. Each of the kings of the Northern Kingdom had been guilty of walking in the steps of Jeroboam, but Ahab's sins made Jeroboam's look trivial. His greatest crime was his promotion of Baal worship as the state religion. **16:31 *Jezebel.*** Ahab's marriage to Jezebel was politically important and demonstrated the rising prominence of Israel's third dynasty. Her father was both king and priest of Baal in Sidon; similarly, Jezebel was princess and priestess of Baal. Her Phoenician name was Abizebel, meaning "My Father [Baal] is Noble." The Hebrew scribes purposely dropped a letter from her name, calling her Jezebel, "Lacking Honor." ***went and served Baal and worshiped him.*** Ahab completely abandoned even a skewed worship of God, and became a full-fledged worshiper of Baal.

16:34 *rebuilt Jericho.* Jericho had been semi-occupied at various times (Jdg 3:13), but not as a permanently occupied fortified city. Either Hiel offered his sons as foundation sacrifices, or they died in some mishap. However it happened, Joshua's curse was carried out.

17:1 *Elijah.* No prophet had arisen since Moses who was like Elijah. His name means "The Lord is God," a statement which was the core of his message to the unbelieving nation. ***dew nor rain.*** Elijah's pronouncement was an immediate challenge: Baal was supposed to govern the weather, but Elijah was declaring him powerless before the Living God.

17:6 *ravens.* It is interesting to note that ravens were considered unclean birds (Lev 11:15).

---

31 Dt 7:3; Jdg 18:7; 1Ki 21:25,26; 2Ki 10:18; 17:16 **32** 2Ki 10:21,26,27 **33** 2Ki 13:6; 17:10; 21:3; Jer 17:2; ver. 30; 1Ki 21:25 **34** Jos 6:26 **CHAPTER 17** **1** 2Ki 3:14; Dt 10:8; Jas 5:17; Lk 4:25

8 Then the word of the LORD came to him, saying,

9 "Arise, go to Zarephath, which belongs to Sidon, and stay there. Behold, I have commanded a widow there to provide for you."

10 So he set out and went to Zarephath, and when he came to the gate of the city, behold, a widow was there gathering sticks [for firewood]. He called out to her and said, "Please bring me a little water in a jar, so that I may drink."

11 As she was going to get it, he called to her and said, "Please bring me a piece of bread in your hand."

12 But she said, "As the LORD your God lives, I have no bread, only a handful of flour in the bowl and a little oil in the jar. See, I am gathering a few sticks so that I may go in and bake it for me and my son, that we may eat it [as our last meal] and die."

13 Elijah said to her, "Do not fear; go and do as you have said. Just make me a little bread from it first and bring it out to me, and afterward you may make one for yourself and for your son.

14 "For this is what the LORD God of Israel says: 'The bowl of flour shall not be exhausted nor shall the jar of oil be empty until the day that the LORD sends rain [again] on the face of the earth.' "

15 She went and did as Elijah said. And she and he and her household ate for *many* days.

16 The bowl of flour was not exhausted nor did the jar of oil become empty, in accordance the word of the LORD which He spoke through Elijah.

Elijah Raises the Widow's Son

17 It happened after these things, that the son of the woman, the mistress of the house, became sick; and his illness was so severe that there was no breath left in him.

18 So she said to Elijah, "What [problem] is there between you and me, O man of God? Have you come to me to bring my sin to mind and to put my son to death?"

19 He said to her, "Give me your son." Then he took him from her arms and carried him up to the upper room where he was living, and laid him on his own bed.

20 He called to the LORD and said, "O LORD my God, have You brought further tragedy to the widow with whom I am staying, by causing her son to die?"

21 Then he stretched himself out upon the child three times, and called to the LORD and said, "O LORD my God, please let this child's life return to him."

22 The LORD heard the voice of Elijah, and the life of the child returned to him and he revived.

23 Elijah took the child and brought him down from the upper room into the [lower part of the] house and gave him to his mother; and Elijah said, "See, your son is alive."

24 Then the woman said to Elijah, "Now I know that you are a man of God and that the word of the LORD in your mouth is truth."

Obadiah Meets Elijah

18 NOW IT happened after many days that the word of the Lord came to Elijah in the third year, saying,

---

17:9 *Zarephath.* Zarephath was in Phoenician territory, seven miles south of Sidon, the stronghold of Baal. The Lord's sustaining Elijah first by a raven and then by a widow provided the prophet with a dramatic test of faith at the outset of his ministry. The widow, too, would be taught the value of trusting in God alone.

17:14 *shall not be exhausted.* While an apostate Israelite nation suffered because of the drought, God supplied the daily necessities to a non-Israelite who willingly took Him at His word. Both the prophet and the widow were reminded of the value of personal trust in Him who alone is sufficient to meet every need (Php 4:19).

17:17 – 23 Resurrection — Resurrection from the dead was not a miracle ordinary people expected to see, even from a prophet of God. This widow, however, would have had reason to hope for God's help. She had opened her home to Elijah, and she had seen firsthand His power and the results of complete trust in Him. Yet it was not until she had seen the miracle of her son brought back to life that she expressed faith in God.

9 Ob 20 **18** See Lk 5:8 **21** 2Ki 4:34,35 **22** Heb 11:35 **24** Jn 3:2; 16:30 **CHAPTER 18** **1** Lk 4:25; Jas 5:17; Dt 28:12

"Go, show yourself to Ahab, and I will
send rain on the face of the earth."
2So Elijah went to show himself to
Ahab. Now the famine was severe in
Samaria.
3Ahab called Obadiah who was the
governor of his house. (Now Obadiah
feared the LORD greatly;
4for when Jezebel destroyed the
prophets of the LORD, Obadiah took
a hundred prophets and hid them by
fifties in a cave, and provided them
with bread and water.)
5Then Ahab said to Obadiah, "Go
into the land to all the sources of water
and to all the streams; perhaps we may
find grass and keep the horses and
mules alive, and not have to kill some
of the cattle."
6So they divided the land between
them to survey it. Ahab went one way
by himself and Obadiah went another
way by himself.
7As Obadiah was on the way, behold,
Elijah met him. He recognized him
and fell face downward [out of respect]
and said, "Is it you, my lord Elijah?"
8He answered him, "It is I. Go tell
your master, 'Elijah is here.' "
9But he said, "What sin have I com-
mitted, that you would hand over your
servant to Ahab to put me to death?
10"As the LORD your God lives, there
is no nation or kingdom where my
master has not sent *messengers* to seek
you; and when they said, 'He is not
here,' Ahab made the kingdom or na-
tion swear that they had not found you.
11"And now you are saying, 'Go, tell
your master, "Behold, Elijah [is here]." '
12"And as soon as I leave you, the
Spirit of the LORD will carry you to a
place I do not know; so when I come to
tell Ahab and he does not find you, he
will kill me. Yet your servant has [rev-
erently] feared the LORD from my youth.
13"Has it not been told to my lord
[Elijah] what I did when Jezebel killed
the prophets of the LORD, how I hid a
hundred of the LORD's prophets by fif-
ties in a cave, and provided them with
bread and water?
14"And now you are saying, 'Go, tell
your master, "Elijah is here" '; and he
will kill me."
15Elijah said, "As the LORD of hosts
(armies) lives, before whom I stand,
I will certainly show myself to Ahab
today."
16So Obadiah went to meet Ahab
and told him; and Ahab went to meet
Elijah.
17When Ahab saw Elijah, Ahab said
to him, "Are you the one who is bring-
ing disaster on Israel?"
18Elijah said, "I have not brought
disaster on Israel, but you and your
father's household *have*, by abandon-
ing (rejecting) the commandments of
the LORD and by following the Baals.
19"Now then, send *word* and gather to
me all Israel at Mount Carmel, together
with the 450 prophets of Baal and the
400 prophets of [the goddess] Asherah,
who eat at [Queen] Jezebel's table."

God or Baal on Mount Carmel

20So Ahab sent *word* to all the Is-
raelites and assembled the [pagan]
prophets together at Mount Carmel.
21Elijah approached all the people
and said, "How long will you hesitate
between two opinions? If the LORD is
God, follow Him; but if Baal, follow

18:3 *Obadiah.* Although tradition has sometimes identified them, this Obadiah is probably not the author of the prophetic book of that name. It is clear that this Obadiah was a man of great faith, whose heroic actions give us a more balanced picture of the situation people of faith endured in Israel at this time.

18:18 *the Baals.* The wording indicates that Ahab had a practice of attending services at various local shrines where this deity was worshiped.

18:19 *Baal ... Asherah.* The worship of Baal and Asherah held a constant fascination for Israel from earliest times (Ex 34:13; Nu 25; Jdg 2:13) and eventually caused Israel's demise (2Ki 17:16 – 18).

18:21 *two opinions.* We are confronted today with a choice no less momentous than the Israelites' choice between the Lord and Baal. Here is a broad road that leads down to destruction; there, a way narrow and difficult that leads upward to life (Mt 7:13 – 14). God doesn't share devotion

12 2Ki 2:16; Eze 3:12,14; Mt 4:1; Ac 8:39 **17** 1Ki 21:20; Jos 7:25; Ac 16:20 **18** 2Ch 15:2 **19** Jos 19:26; 1Ki 16:33 **20** 1Ki 22:6 **21** 2Ki 17:41; Mt 6:24; See Jos 24:15

him." But the people [of Israel] did not
answer him [so much as] a word.
22 Then Elijah said to the people, "I
alone remain a prophet of the LORD,
while Baal's prophets are 450 men.
23 "Now let them give us two oxen,
and let them choose one ox for them-
selves and cut it in pieces, and lay it on
the wood, but put no fire *under it*. I will
prepare the other ox and lay it on the
wood, and I will not put a fire *under it*.
24 "Then you call on the name of your
god, and I will call on the name of the
LORD; and the god who answers by
fire, He is God." And all the people
answered, "It is well spoken."
25 Elijah said to the prophets of Baal,
"Choose one bull for yourselves and
prepare it first, since there are many
of you; and call on the name of your
god, but put no fire *under it*."
26 So they took the bull that was giv-
en to them and prepared it, and called
on the name of Baal from morning
until noon, saying, "O Baal, hear *and*
answer us." But there was no voice
and no one answered. And they leaped
about the altar which they had made.
27 At noon Elijah mocked them, say-
ing, "Cry out with a loud voice, for he
is a god; either he is occupied, or he
is out [at the moment], or he is on a
journey. Perhaps he is asleep and must
be awakened!"
28 So they cried out with a loud voice
[to get Baal's attention] and cut them-
selves with swords and lances in ac-
cordance with their custom, until the
blood flowed out on them.
29 As midday passed, they played the
part of prophets *and* raved dramat-
ically until the time for offering the
evening sacrifice; but there was no
voice, no one answered, and no one
paid attention.
30 Then Elijah said to all the people,
"Come near to me." So all the peo-
ple approached him. And he repaired
and rebuilt the [old] altar of the LORD
that had been torn down [by Jezebel].
[1 Kin 18:13; 19:10]
31 Then Elijah took twelve stones in
accordance with the number of the
tribes of the sons of Jacob, to whom
the word of the LORD had come, say-
ing, "Israel shall be your name."
[Gen 32:28]
32 So with the stones Elijah built an
altar in the name of the LORD. He made
a trench around the altar large enough
to hold two measures of seed.
33 Then he laid out the wood and cut
the ox in pieces and laid it on the wood.
34 And he said, "Fill four pitchers with
water and pour it on the burnt offering
and the wood." And he said, "Do it the
second time." And they did it the sec-
ond time. And he said, "Do it the third
time." And they did it a third time.
35 The water flowed around the al-
tar, and he also filled the trench with
water.

Elijah's Prayer

36 At the time of the offering of the
evening sacrifice, Elijah the proph-
et approached [the altar] and said,
"O LORD, the God of Abraham, Isaac,
and Israel (Jacob), let it be known to-
day that You are God in Israel and that

---

with anything or anyone. We have to make the choice to be on God's side; we cannot serve two masters. We will either gratify self, conforming to the corrupt pattern of this present age, or glorify Him who alone is worthy of worship.

18:27 ***out [at the moment], or he is on a journey.*** "On a journey" is a euphemism with the same meaning as our euphemism "using the restroom." Elijah was piling on the sarcasm — a god is not supposed to have embarrassing bodily functions.

18:30 ***repaired and rebuilt the [old] altar.*** This was an earlier altar that had been used by the true people of God. Elijah avoided all contact with the altar that was associated with Baal.

18:36 ***LORD, the God of Abraham, Isaac, and Israel.*** This phrase, so characteristic of worship in the early period (Ge 50:24; Ex 3:6), reminded Elijah's hearers that the God who had made the covenant with Abraham was still the God of the Northern Kingdom, and the nation's only hope of life, protection, and blessing (Dt 30:20).

22 1Ki 19:10,14; ver. 19 **24** ver. 38; 1Ch 21:26 **26** Ps 115:5; Jer 10:5; 1Co 8:4 **28** Lev 19:28; Dt 14:1 **29** 1Co 11:4,5; ver. 26 **30** 1Ki 19:10 **31** Ge 32:28; 2Ki 17:34 **32** Col 3:17 **33** Lev 1:6-8; See Jdg 6:20 **35** ver. 32,38 **36** Ex 3:6; 1Ki 8:43; 2Ki 19:19; Nu 16:28

I am Your servant and that I have done
all these things at Your word.
37“Answer me, O LORD, answer me,
so that this people may know that You,
O LORD, are God, and that You have
turned their hearts back [to You].”
38Then the fire of the LORD fell and
consumed the burnt offering and the
wood, and *even* the stones and the
dust; it also licked up the water in the
trench.
39When all the people saw it, they fell
face downward; and they said, “The
LORD, He is God! The LORD, He is God!”
40Then Elijah said to them, “Seize
the prophets of Baal; do not let one of
them escape.” They seized them; and
Elijah brought them down to the brook
Kishon, and [as God’s law required]
killed them there. [Deut 13:5, 12–15;
18:20]
41Now Elijah said to Ahab, “Go up,
eat and drink, for there is the sound
of the roar *of an abundance* of rain.”
42So Ahab went up to eat and to
drink. And Elijah went up to the top
of Carmel; and he crouched down to
the earth and put his face between
his knees,
43and he said to his servant, “Go up,
look toward the sea.” So he went up
and looked and said, “There is nothing.”
Elijah said, “Go back” seven
times.
44And at the seventh *time* the servant
said, “A cloud as small as a man’s
hand is coming up from the sea.” And
Elijah said, “Go up, say to Ahab, ‘Prepare
your chariot and go down, so that
the rain shower does not stop you.’ ”
45In a little while the sky grew dark
with clouds and wind, and there were
heavy showers. And Ahab mounted
and rode [his chariot] and went [inland]
to Jezreel.
46Then the hand of the LORD came
upon Elijah [giving him supernatural
strength]. He girded up his loins and
outran Ahab to the entrance of Jezreel
[nearly twenty miles].

Elijah Flees from Jezebel

19 NOW AHAB told Jezebel all that
Elijah had done, and how he had
killed all the prophets [of Baal] with
the sword.
2Then Jezebel sent a messenger to
Elijah, saying, “So may the gods do
to me, and even more, if by this time
tomorrow I do not make your life like
the life of one of them.”
3And Elijah was afraid and arose
and ran for his life, and he came to
Beersheba which belongs to Judah,
and he left his servant there.
4But he himself traveled a day’s journey
into the wilderness, and he came
and sat down under a juniper tree and
asked [God] that he might die. He said,
“It is enough; now, O LORD, take my
life, for I am no better than my fathers.”
5He lay down and slept under the
juniper tree, and behold, an angel
touched him and said to him, “Get up
and eat.”
6He looked, and by his head there
was a bread cake baked on hot coal,
and a pitcher of water. So he ate and
drank and lay down again.
7Then the angel of the LORD came
again a second time and touched him
and said, “Get up, and eat, for the jour-

18:46 *girded up his loins.* Elijah tucked his garment into his sash, enabling him to run freely the 13 miles to Jezreel.
19:3 *ran for his life.* One may ask why a man who had seen God’s mighty power should give way to fear, but we must realize that God did not criticize Elijah for his reaction. Elijah was not a superhero but a man with a nature like ours (Jas 5:17). He had seen a great victory on Mount Carmel, but he also knew that Jezebel was still in power, the faith of the people was still weak, at best, and his life truly was in danger. To run for his life did not necessarily indicate lack of trust; running is sometimes just the act of prudence.
19:5 *Get up and eat.* God’s response to Elijah’s fear and discouragement was to give him the very tangible, physical encouragement of food and rest.
19:7 *the angel of the LORD.* This term sometimes refers to God Himself (Ex 3:2–6); other times it seems to refer simply to a heavenly messenger (2Ki 1:3; 19:35).

38 Lev 9:24; Jdg 6:21; 1Ch 21:26; 2Ch 7:1 **39** ver. 24 **40** 2Ki 10:25; Dt 13:5; 18:20 **42** Jas 5:17,18 **46** 2Ki 4:29; 9:1 **CHAPTER 19** **1** 1Ki 18:40 **2** Ru 1:17; 1Ki 20:10; 2Ki 6:31 **4** Nu 11:15; Jnh 4:3,8

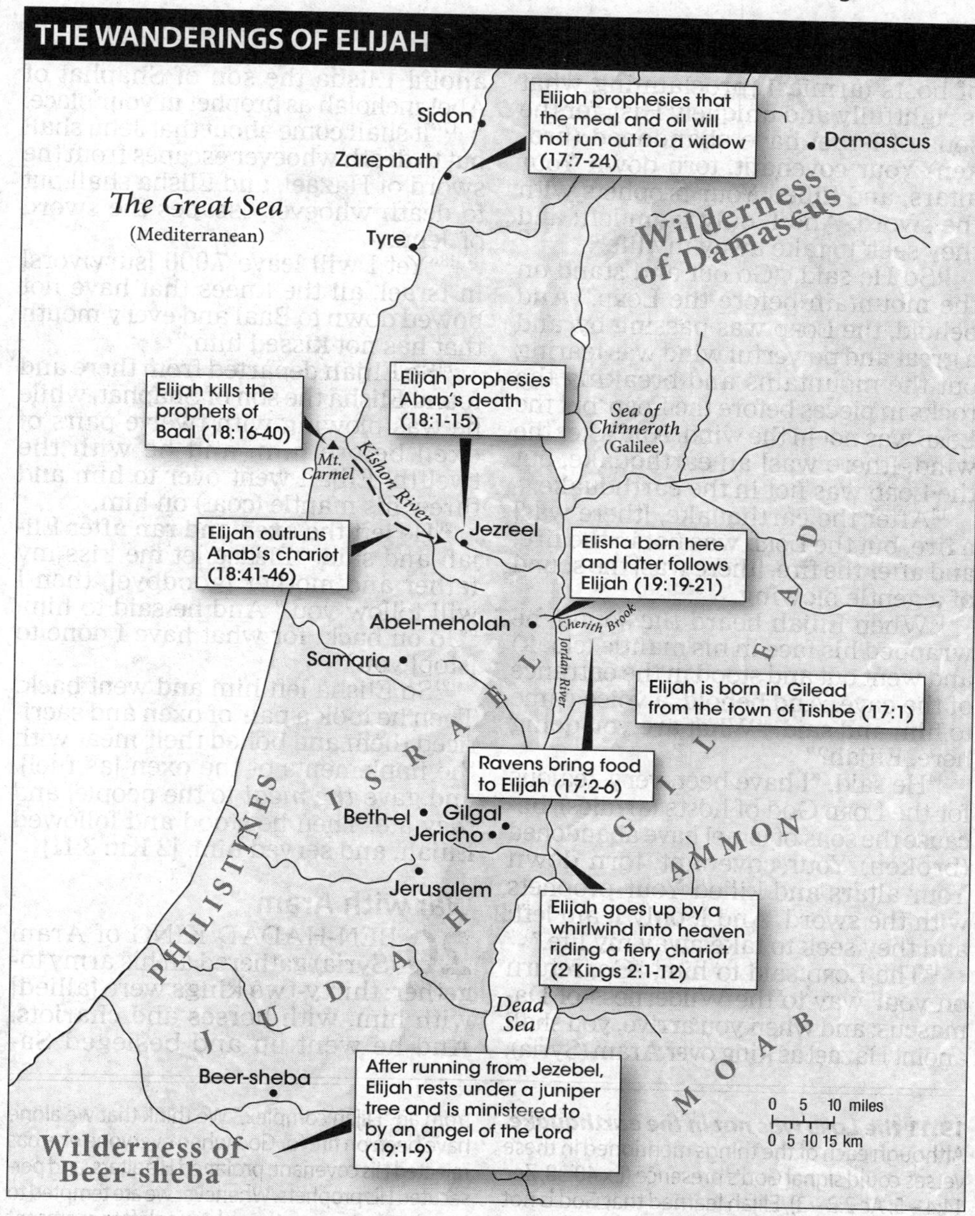

ney is too long for you [without adequate sustenance]."

[8]So he got up and ate and drank, and with the strength of that food he traveled forty days and nights to Horeb (Sinai), the mountain of God.

Elijah at Horeb

[9]There he came to a cave and spent the night in it; and behold, the word of the LORD *came* to him, and He said to him, "What are you doing here, Elijah?"

19:8 *Horeb.* The name Horeb refers to Mount Sinai itself, "the mountain of God" (Ex 3:1).

8 Ex 34:28; Dt 9:9,18; Mt 4:2; Ex 3:1

10 He said, "I have been very zeal-
ous (impassioned) for the LORD God
of hosts (armies) [proclaiming what
is rightfully and uniquely His]; for the
sons of Israel have abandoned (bro-
ken) Your covenant, torn down Your
altars, and killed Your prophets with
the sword. And I, only I, am left; and
they seek to take away my life."
11 So He said, "Go out and stand on
the mountain before the LORD." And
behold, the LORD was passing by, and
a great and powerful wind was tearing
out the mountains and breaking the
rocks in pieces before the LORD; but the
LORD was not in the wind. And after the
wind, [there was] an earthquake, but
the LORD was not in the earthquake.
12 After the earthquake, [there was]
a fire, but the LORD was not in the fire;
and after the fire, [there was] the sound
of a gentle blowing.
13 When Elijah heard *the sound*, he
wrapped his face in his mantle (cloak)
and went out and stood in the entrance
of the cave. And behold, a voice came
to him and said, "What are you doing
here, Elijah?"
14 He said, "I have been very zealous
for the LORD God of hosts (armies), be-
cause the sons of Israel have abandoned
(broken) Your covenant, torn down
Your altars and killed Your prophets
with the sword. And I, only I, am left;
and they seek to take away my life."
15 The LORD said to him, "Go, return
on your way to the Wilderness of Da-
mascus; and when you arrive, you shall
anoint Hazael as king over Aram (Syria);
16 and you shall anoint Jehu the son
of Nimshi as king over Israel; and
anoint Elisha the son of Shaphat of
Abel-meholah as prophet in your place.
17 "It shall come about that Jehu shall
put to death whoever escapes from the
sword of Hazael, and Elisha shall put
to death whoever escapes the sword
of Jehu.
18 "Yet I will leave 7,000 [survivors]
in Israel, all the knees that have not
bowed down to Baal and every mouth
that has not kissed him."
19 So Elijah departed from there and
found Elisha the son of Shaphat, while
he was plowing with twelve pairs *of
oxen* before him, and he with the
twelfth. Elijah went over to him and
threw his mantle (coat) on him.
20 He left the oxen and ran after Eli-
jah and said, "Please let me kiss my
father and mother [goodbye], then I
will follow you." And he said to him,
"Go on back; for what have I done to
[stop] you?"
21 So Elisha left him and went back.
Then he took a pair of oxen and sacri-
ficed them and boiled their meat with
the implements of the oxen [as fuel],
and gave *the meat* to the people, and
they ate. Then he stood and followed
Elijah, and served him. [2 Kin 3:11]

War with Aram

20 BEN-HADAD KING of Aram
(Syria) gathered all his army to-
gether; thirty-two kings were [allied]
with him, with horses and chariots.
And he went up and besieged Sa-

19:11 ***the LORD was not in the earthquake.*** Although each of the things mentioned in these verses could signal God's presence (Ex 40:38; Zec 14:4 – 5; Ac 2:2 – 3), Elijah learned that God is not just the God of the spectacular.

19:12 ***gentle blowing.*** This is often translated "a still small voice." Elijah had called for fire and national revival. What Elijah did not see was that God was already quietly at work in the lives of many people (v. 18).

19:18 ***have not bowed down.*** In times of widespread drift and deliberate deviation from biblical standards of doctrine and ethics, it is easy to suffer from an "Elijah complex." We think that we alone have been on fire for God when everyone else has rejected His covenant, profaned His altars, and persecuted His prophets. Whenever we are tempted to imagine that we are the only ones left to represent the cause of the gospel, we are also open to the dangers of self-pity and self-righteousness. But we are not alone when we belong to the family of God. In every age, God has preserved faithful people who rejoice in Him and are on fire for the truth.

20:1 ***Ben-hadad.*** Ben-hadad II (860 – 842 BC) was king of Aram, the ancient name for the area which is Syria today.

10 Ro 11:3; Nu 25:11,13; Ps 69:9; 1Ki 18:4; 1Ki 18:22; Ro 11:3 **11** Ex 24:12; Eze 1:4; 37:7 **13** Ex 3:6; Isa 6:2; ver. 9 **14** ver. 10 **15** 2Ki 8:12,13 **16** 2Ki 9:1-3; Lk 4:27 **17** 2Ki 8:12; 9:14; 10:6; 13:3; See Hos 6:5 **18** Ro 11:4; See Hos 13:2 **20** Mt 8:21,22; Lk 9:61,62 **21** 2Sa 24:22

maria [Israel's capital], and fought against it.

2 Then he sent messengers to the city to Ahab king of Israel; and he said to him, "Thus says Ben-hadad:

3 'Your silver and your gold are mine; your wives and your children, even the fairest, also are mine [as conditions of peace].' "

4 The king of Israel [conceded his defeat and] answered, "By your word, my lord, O king, I am yours, and all that I have."

5 The messengers returned and said, "Thus says Ben-hadad: 'I indeed sent *word* to you, saying, "You shall give me your silver, your gold, your wives, and your children,"

6 but about this time tomorrow I will send my servants to you, and they will search your house and the houses of your servants; and they will take with their hands (confiscate) whatever is desirable in your eyes and carry it away.' "

7 Then the king of Israel summoned all the elders of the land and said, "Please observe and see how this man is seeking our destruction. For he sent *messengers* to me for my wives, my children, my silver, and my gold, and I did not refuse him."

8 All the elders and all the people said to him, "Do not listen or consent [to this additional demand]."

9 So he said to Ben-hadad's messengers, "Tell my lord the king, 'Every *demand* you first sent to your servant I will do, but I cannot do this [additional] thing [as a condition of peace].' " And the messengers left; then they brought him word again.

10 Ben-hadad sent *word* to him and said, "May the gods do so to me, and more also, if there is enough dust left of Samaria for handfuls for all the [armed] people who follow me."

11 The king of Israel answered, "Tell him, 'A man who puts on [his armor to go to battle] should not boast like the man who takes it off [after the battle has been won].' "

12 When Ben-hadad heard this message, as he and the kings were drinking in the temporary shelters, he said to his servants, "Station *yourselves.*" So they stationed *themselves* against the city [of Samaria].

Ahab Victorious

13 Then a prophet approached Ahab king of Israel and said, "Thus says the LORD: 'Have you seen all this great army? Behold, I will hand them over to you, and you shall know [without any doubt] that I am the LORD.' "

14 Ahab said, "By whom?" And he said, "Thus says the LORD: 'By the young men [the attendants or bodyguards] of the governors of the districts.' " Then Ahab said, "Who shall begin the battle?" And he answered, "You."

15 Then Ahab assembled *and* counted the young men of the governors of the districts, and there were 232. After them he assembled *and* counted all the people, all the sons of Israel, 7,000. [1 Kin 19:18]

16 They went out at noon, while Ben-hadad was getting drunk in the temporary shelters, he and the thirty-two kings who were helping him.

17 The young men of the governors of the districts went out first; and Ben-hadad sent *men* out and they told him, saying, "Men have come out of Samaria."

18 And he said, "Whether they have come out for peace or for war, take them alive."

19 So these young men of the governors of the districts went out of the city, and the army followed them.

20 And each one killed his man; and the Arameans (Syrians) fled and Israel pursued them. Ben-hadad king of Aram escaped on a horse with horsemen.

20:2 *Ahab.* When he is associated with his wicked wife Jezebel, Ahab appears as thoroughly evil. But in this chapter he appears as a capable leader in a time of international turmoil, and as a person who had some sense of the power and presence of God (vv. 13–14).

20:13 *a prophet.* This prophet was not named, but his true message reminds us that there were

CHAPTER 20 **10** 1Ki 19:2 **12** ver. 16 **13** ver. 28 **16** ver. 12; 1Ki 16:9

21 The king of Israel went out and struck [the riders of] the horses and chariots, and killed the Arameans in a great slaughter.

22 Then the prophet approached the king of Israel and said to him, "Go, strengthen yourself and observe and see what you have to do; for at the first of next year the king of Aram (Syria) will come up against you."

23 Now the servants of the king of Aram said to him, "Israel's god is a god of the hills; that is why they were stronger than we. But let us fight against them in the plain, and surely we will be stronger than they.

24 "Do this: remove the [thirty-two allied] kings, each from his place, and put captains in their place,

25 and assemble an army like the army that you have lost *in battle*, horse for horse and chariot for chariot. Then we will fight against them in the plain, and surely we shall be stronger than they." And he listened to their words and did so.

Another Aramean War

26 At the first of the year [in spring], Ben-hadad assembled *and* counted the Arameans (Syrians) and went up to Aphek [east of the Sea of Galilee] to fight against Israel.

27 The sons of Israel were counted and given provisions, and they went to meet them. The Israelites camped before the enemy like two little flocks of goats [with everything against them, except God], and the Arameans filled the country.

28 A man of God approached and said to the king of Israel, "Thus says the LORD, 'Because the Arameans have said, "The LORD is a god of the hills, but He is not a god of the valleys," I will give this great army into your hand, and you shall know [by experience] that I am the LORD.' " [Phil 4:13]

29 So they camped opposite each other for seven days. Then on the seventh day the battle began, and the sons of Israel killed 100,000 of the Aramean foot soldiers in a single day.

30 But the rest ran to the city of Aphek, and the [city] wall fell on 27,000 of the men who were left. Ben-hadad escaped and came into the city, going into an inner chamber [to hide].

31 But his servants said to him, "We have heard that the kings of the house (royal line) of Israel are merciful kings. Please let us put sackcloth around our loins and ropes on our necks [as symbols of submission], and go out to the king of Israel; perhaps he will spare your life."

32 So they put sackcloth around their loins and ropes on their necks, and came to the king of Israel and said, "Your servant Ben-hadad says, 'Please let me live.' " And Ahab asked, "Is he still alive? He is my brother."

33 Now the men took it as a *good* omen, and quickly understanding his meaning said, "Yes, your brother Ben-hadad *lives*." Then the king said, "Go, bring him." Then Ben-hadad came out to him, and Ahab had him come up into the chariot.

34 Ben-hadad [tempting him] said to

---

still many prophets who were faithful to the Lord (18:13; 20:35).

20:23 *god of the hills.* The Aramean advisors reflected traditional ancient Middle Eastern theological concepts. Their gods were limited to certain geographical locations.

20:26 *Aphek.* This is not the Philistine city where the ark was lost (1Sa 4:1), but another location just east of the Jordan in northern Gilead. They were launching their second campaign in the Jordan Valley, but they would learn that the power of the living God is not limited to the mountains as they had hoped.

20:28 *not a god of the valleys.* The God of Israel is Lord of the universe, and there is no limit to His power and authority. Not only are we responsible to Him as individuals, but so are the social, economic, and political institutions of the world. Just as it was presumption for the Arameans to think that God was bound by geography, it is also presumption to think that if we follow the laws of morality in our private lives, we can violate them in our social, economic, and political relationships. Separation of church and state should not mean separation of God and state. The nation that violates the moral laws of God will eventually suffer defeat.

22 2Sa 11:1 **26** Jos 13:4 **28** ver. 13 **31** Ge 37:34 **34** 1Ki 15:20

him, "I will restore the cities which my
father took from your father; and you
may set up bazaars (shops) of your
own in Damascus, as my father did in
Samaria." Then, *Ahab replied,* "I will
let you go with this covenant (treaty)."
So he made a covenant with him and
let him go.
[35]Now a certain man of the sons of
the prophets said to another by the
word of the LORD, "Please strike me."
But the man refused to strike him.
[36]Then the prophet said to him, "Be-
cause you have not obeyed the voice of
the LORD, behold, as soon as you leave
me, a lion will kill you." And as soon
as he left him, a lion found him and
killed him.
[37]Then the prophet found another
man and said, "Please strike me." So
the man struck him hard, wounding
him.
[38]So the prophet left and waited for
King Ahab by the road, and disguised
himself [as a wounded soldier] with a
bandage over his eyes.
[39]As the king passed by, the prophet
called out to the king and said, "Your
servant went out into the middle of
the battle, and behold, a man turned
aside and brought a man to me and
said, 'Guard this man; if for any reason
he is missing, then your life shall be
required for his life, or else you shall
pay a talent of silver.'
[40]"But while your servant was busy
here and there, he [escaped and] was
gone." And the king of Israel said to
him, "Such is your own judgment (ver-
dict); you have determined it."
[41]Then the prophet quickly removed
the bandage from his eyes, and [Ahab]
the king of Israel recognized him as
one of the prophets.
[42]He said to the king, "Thus says the
LORD: 'Because you have released from
your hand the man [Ben-hadad] whom
I had devoted to destruction, your life
shall be *required* for his life, and your
people for his people.' "
[43]So the king of Israel went to his
house resentful and sullen, and came
to Samaria. [1 Kin 22:34–36]

Ahab Covets Naboth's Vineyard

21 NOW IT came about after these
things that Naboth the Jezreelite
had a vineyard in Jezreel, close beside
the [winter] palace of Ahab king of
Samaria;
[2]Ahab spoke to Naboth, saying,
"Give me your vineyard, so that I may
have it for a garden of vegetables *and*
herbs, because it is near my house. I
will give you a better vineyard for it,
or, if you prefer, I will give you what it
is worth in money."
[3]But Naboth said to Ahab, "The LORD
forbid me that I should give the inher-
itance of my fathers to you."
[4]So Ahab [already upset by the
Lord's message] came into his house
[feeling more] resentful and sullen be-
cause of what Naboth the Jezreelite
had said to him; for he had said, "I
will not give you the inheritance of my
fathers." And he lay down on his bed
and turned away his face, and would
not eat any food.
[5]Then Jezebel his wife came to him
and asked him, "Why is your spirit so
troubled that you have not eaten?"
[6]And he said to her, "Because I spoke
to Naboth the Jezreelite and said to
him, 'Give me your vineyard for mon-
ey; or if you prefer, I will give you *an-
other* vineyard for it.' But he answered,
'I will not give you my vineyard.' "

20:43 *resentful and sullen.* Rather than repenting of his sin, Ahab felt ill-used by God and resented his punishment, adamantly refusing to change his ways.

21:1 *Samaria.* Samaria was Ahab's capital city; sometimes its name is used to represent all Israel (2Ki 1:3; 2Ch 24:23; Jnh 3:6).

21:2 *Give me your vineyard.* All the land was the Lord's, who granted it to each Israelite tribe and family, and provisions were made so that the land could not be permanently sold out of the family to whom it had been given (Lev 25:23–28; Nu 36:2–9). In this sense, the vineyard was not Naboth's to dispose of. It belonged to his descendants as much as it did to him.

35 2Ki 2:3,5,7,15; 1Ki 13:17,18 **36** 1Ki 13:24 **39** See 2Sa 12:1; 2Ki 10:24 **42** 1Ki 22:31-37 **43** 1Ki 21:4
CHAPTER 21 **2** 1Sa 8:14 **3** Lev 25:23; Nu 36:7; Eze 46:18

[7]Jezebel his wife said to him, "Do
you now reign over Israel? Get up, eat
food, and let your heart rejoice; I will
give you the vineyard of Naboth the
Jezreelite."
[8]So she wrote letters in Ahab's name
and sealed them with his seal, and sent
them to the elders and nobles who lived
with Naboth in his city.
[9]Now in the letters she wrote, "Pro-
claim a fast and seat Naboth at the
head of the people;
[10]and seat two worthless *and* un-
principled men opposite him, and have
them testify against him, saying, 'You
cursed God and the king.' Then take
him out and stone him to death."

Jezebel's Plot

[11]So the men of his city, the elders
and the nobles who lived there, did as
Jezebel had sent *word* to them, just as
it was written in the letters which she
had sent to them.
[12]They proclaimed a fast and seated
Naboth at the head of the people.
[13]Two worthless *and* unprincipled
men came in and sat down opposite
him; and they testified against Naboth
before the people, saying, "Naboth
cursed *and* renounced God and the
king." Then they brought him outside
the city and stoned him to death.
[14]Then they sent *word* to Jezebel,
saying, "Naboth has been stoned to
death."
[15]When Jezebel heard that Naboth
had been stoned and was dead, she
said to Ahab, "Arise, take possession
of the vineyard of Naboth the Jez-
reelite which he refused to sell you,
because Naboth is no longer alive,
but dead."
[16]When Ahab heard that Naboth
was dead, he arose to go down to the
vineyard of Naboth the Jezreelite, to
take possession of it.
[17]Then the word of the LORD came to
Elijah the Tishbite, saying,
[18]"Arise, go down to meet Ahab king
of Israel, who is in Samaria. Behold, he
is in the vineyard of Naboth, where he
has gone to take possession of it.
[19]"You shall speak to him, saying,
'Thus says the LORD: "Have you mur-
dered and also taken possession [of
the victim's property]?" ' And you shall
speak to him, saying, 'Thus says the
Lord: "In the place where dogs licked
up the blood of Naboth, dogs will lick
up your blood as well." ' "
[20]Ahab said to Elijah, "Have you
found me, O my enemy?" And he an-
swered, "I have found you, because
you have sold yourself to do evil in the
sight of the LORD.
[21]"Behold [says the LORD], I am bring-
ing evil (catastrophe) on you, and will
utterly sweep you away, and will cut
off from Ahab every male, both bond
and free in Israel;
[22]and I will make your house (de-
scendants) like that of Jeroboam the
son of Nebat, and like the house of
Baasha the son of Ahijah, for provok-
ing Me to anger and making Israel sin.
[23]"The LORD also spoke in regard
to Jezebel, saying, 'The dogs will eat
[the body of] Jezebel in the district of
Jezreel.'
[24]"The dogs will eat anyone belong-
ing to Ahab who dies in the city, and

21:13 *outside the city.* God's law was followed in the manner and place of his death (Lev 24:14 – 16,23), although his execution was an outrage, based on false testimony, lies, greed, and refusal to honor the laws concerning the land.

21:19 *Have you murdered.* In Genesis 9:6 the principle was established that those who shed human blood must have their blood shed by other humans. Ahab had previously allowed his wicked wife Jezebel to plot the murder of an innocent landowner in order to obtain his vineyard. As a result, God determined that both Ahab and Jezebel would die bloody deaths, and this is exactly what happened (22:34 – 38; 2Ki 9:30 – 37). How tragic that these two brilliant, capable, and talented members of royalty, whose lives could have brought so much blessing to Israel, would instead bring about their own downfall by choosing the path of wickedness rather than the path of life.

10 Ex 22:28; Lev 24:15,16; Ac 6:11; Lev 24:14 **12** Isa 58:4 **13** See 2Ki 9:26 **17** Ps 9:12 **18** 1Ki 13:32; 2Ch 22:9 **19** 1Ki 22:38 **20** 1Ki 18:17; 2Ki 17:17; Ro 7:14 **21** 1Ki 14:10; 2Ki 9:8; 1Sa 25:22; 1Ki 14:10 **22** 1Ki 15:29; 1Ki 16:3,11 **23** 2Ki 9:36 **24** 1Ki 14:11; 16:4

the birds of the air will eat anyone who dies in the field." [1 Kin 14:11; 16:4]

25 There certainly was no one like Ahab who sold himself to do evil in the sight of the LORD, because Jezebel his wife incited him.

26 He acted very repulsively in following idols, in accordance with everything the Amorites had done, whom the LORD expelled [from the land] before the sons of Israel.

27 Now when Ahab heard these words [of Elijah], he tore his clothes, put on sackcloth and fasted, and he lay in sackcloth and went about dejectedly (mourning).

28 Then the word of the LORD came to Elijah the Tishbite, saying,

29 "Do you see how Ahab has humbled himself before Me? Because he has humbled himself before Me, I will not bring the evil (catastrophe) in his lifetime, but in his son's days I will bring evil upon his house."

Ahab's Third Campaign against Aram

22 ARAM (SYRIA) and Israel continued without war for three years.

2 In the third year Jehoshaphat king of Judah came down to the king of Israel.

3 Now the king of Israel said to his servants, "Do you know that Ramoth in Gilead is ours, yet we are still doing nothing to take it from the hand of the king of Aram?"

4 And Ahab said to Jehoshaphat, "Will you go with me to battle at Ramoth-gilead?" Jehoshaphat said to the king of Israel, "I am as you are, my people as your people, my horses as your horses."

5 But Jehoshaphat said to the king of Israel, "Please inquire first for the word of the LORD."

6 Then the king of Israel gathered the prophets together, about four hundred men, and said to them, "Shall I go to battle against Ramoth-gilead, or should I not?" And they said, "Go up, for the LORD has handed it over to the king."

7 But Jehoshaphat [doubted and] said, "Is there not another prophet of the LORD here whom we may ask?"

8 The king of Israel said to Jehoshaphat, "There is one more man, Micaiah the son of Imlah, by whom we may inquire of the LORD, but I hate him, because he never prophesies good *news* for me, but *only* evil." But Jehoshaphat said, "May the king not say that [Micaiah only tells bad news]."

9 Then the king of Israel summoned an officer and said, "Bring quickly Micaiah the son of Imlah."

10 Now the king of Israel and Jehoshaphat king of Judah were each sitting on his throne, dressed in *their* [royal] robes, [in an open place] at the threshing floor at the entrance of the gate of Samaria; and all the prophets were prophesying before them.

11 Then Zedekiah the son of Chenaanah made for himself horns of iron and said, "Thus says the LORD: 'With these you will gore the Arameans (Syrians) until they are destroyed.' "

12 All the prophets were prophesying in the same way [to please Ahab], saying, "Go up to Ramoth-gilead and be successful, for the LORD will hand it over to the king."

Micaiah Predicts Defeat

13 Then the messenger who went to summon Micaiah said to him, "Listen

---

21:27 *when Ahab heard these words.* The vacillating nature of Ahab's conduct is seen clearly in verses 25 – 29. He did great evil, under the influence of his evil wife. Nevertheless, he could at times display real courage (22:34 – 35) and even real humility before God (v. 29). His life is a sad picture of what happens when we are ruled by our own passions rather than by God.

22:4 *Jehoshaphat.* Jehoshaphat was the fourth king of the Southern Kingdom. He was related to Ahab through the marriage of his son Jehoram to Ahab's daughter Athaliah (2Ki 8:18 – 27).

22:9 *Micaiah.* The prophet Micaiah is not known except in connection with this incident (2Ch 18:8 – 27).

---

25 1Ki 16:30; 1Ki 16:31 **26** Ge 15:16; 2Ki 21:11 **27** Ge 37:34 **29** 2Ki 9:25 **CHAPTER 22** **2** 2Ch 18:2 **3** Dt 4:43 **4** 2Ki 3:7 **6** 1Ki 18:19 **7** 2Ki 3:11

carefully, the words of the prophets
are unanimously favorable to the king.
Please let your words be like the word
of one of them, and speak favorably."
14But Micaiah said, "As the LORD
lives, I will speak what the LORD says
to me."
15So when he came to the king, the
king said to him, "Micaiah, shall we
go against Ramoth-gilead in battle, or
shall we not?" And he answered him,
"Go up and be successful, for the LORD
will hand it over to the king."
16But the king [doubted him and]
said to him, "How many times must
I make you swear to tell me nothing
but the truth in the name of the LORD?"
17And he said,

"I saw all Israel
Scattered upon the mountains,
Like sheep that have no shepherd.
And the LORD said,
'These have no master.
Let each of them return to his
house in peace.' "

18Then the king of Israel said to Je-
hoshaphat, "Did I not tell you that he
would not prophesy good concerning
me, but evil?"
19Micaiah said, "Therefore, hear the
word of the LORD. I saw the LORD sit-
ting on His throne, and all the host
(army) of heaven standing by Him on
His right hand and on His left.
20"The LORD said, 'Who will entice
Ahab to go up and fall at Ramoth-
gilead?' And one said this, while an-
other said that.
21"Then a spirit came forward and
stood before the LORD and said, 'I will
entice him.'
22"The LORD said to him, 'How?'
And he said, 'I will go out and be a
deceiving spirit in the mouth of all his
prophets.' Then the LORD said, 'You
are to entice him and also succeed.
Go and do so.'
23"Now then, behold, the LORD has
put a deceiving spirit in the mouth of
all these prophets; and the LORD has
proclaimed disaster against you."
24But Zedekiah the son of Che-
naanah approached and struck Mica-
iah on the cheek and said, "How did
the Spirit of the LORD pass from me to
speak to you?"
25Micaiah said, "Behold, you shall
see on that day [of the king's defeat]
when you enter an inner room [looking
for a place] to hide yourself."
26Then the king of Israel said, "Take
Micaiah and return him to Amon, the
governor of the city, and to Joash, the
king's son,
27and say, 'Thus says the king, "Put
this man in prison, and feed him spar-
ingly with the bread and water until I
return safely." ' "
28Micaiah said, "If you indeed return
safely, the LORD has not spoken by me."
Then he said, "Listen, all you people."

Defeat and Death of Ahab

29So [Ahab] the king of Israel and
Jehoshaphat the king of Judah went
up to Ramoth-gilead.
30The king of Israel said to Je-

22:14 *I will speak what the LORD says to me.* Unless a prophecy is truly directed by God, it is valueless. Micaiah's response was what one would expect from a godly man, but his first statement to Ahab (v. 15) is a little puzzling. It seems that Micaiah was playing with Ahab a little, pointing out to him the futility of asking for favorable prophecy rather than true prophecy. It seems obvious that Micaiah (or God through Micaiah), was in no way deceiving Ahab, since Ahab was instantly aware that he had not been given a real prophecy.

22:16–17 *truth.* All of us wish to hear good news, not bad. We want to hear the favorable, the acceptable, the words that bring us happiness and do not condemn. It can be tempting to speak only what will be well-received even if it is not true, but neither God nor man is served by untruth. While the truth should always be spoken in love (Eph 4:15), it must be the sole content of what we say. The prophet had to speak only the truth, or he would no longer have been a prophet — his words were the words of the Lord spoken in His name. Our words should be true because, if we are His people, we speak in His name.

14 Nu 22:38 **17** Mt 9:36 **19** Isa 6:1; Da 7:9; Job 1:6; 2:1; Da 7:10; Zec 1:10; Mt 18:10; Heb 1:7,14 **22** Jdg 9:23; Job 12:16; Eze 14:9; 2Th 2:11 **23** Eze 14:9 **24** 2Ch 18:23 **28** Nu 16:29; Dt 18:20-22 **30** 2Ch 35:22

hoshaphat, "I will disguise myself and enter the battle, but you put on your [royal] clothing." So the king of Israel disguised himself and went into the battle.

31 Now the king of Aram (Syria) had commanded the thirty-two captains of his chariots, saying, "Do not fight with [anyone, either] small or great, but with [Ahab] the king of Israel alone."

32 When the captains of the chariots saw Jehoshaphat, they said, "Surely it is the king of Israel." They turned to fight against him, and Jehoshaphat shouted out [in fear].

33 When the captains of the chariots saw that it was not the king of Israel, they turned back from pursuing him.

34 But one man drew a bow at random and struck the king of Israel in a joint of the armor. So he said to the driver of his chariot, "Turn around and take me out of the fight, because I have been seriously wounded."

35 The battle raged that day, and [Ahab] the king was propped up in his chariot facing the Arameans (Syrians). And in the evening he died, and the blood from his wound ran down into the bottom of the chariot.

36 Then about sundown a resounding cry passed throughout the army, saying, "Every man to his city and every man to his own country!"

37 So the king died and was brought to Samaria, and they buried the king in Samaria.

38 They washed the chariot by the pool [on the outskirts] of Samaria, where the prostitutes bathed, and the dogs licked up his blood, in accordance with the word of the LORD which He had spoken. [1 Kin 21:19]

39 Now the rest of Ahab's acts, and everything that he did, the ivory palace which he built and all the cities which he built, are they not written in the Book of the Chronicles of the Kings of Israel?

40 So Ahab slept with his fathers [in death], and Ahaziah his son became king in his place.

The New Rulers

41 Now Jehoshaphat the son of Asa became king over Judah in the fourth year of Ahab king of Israel.

42 Jehoshaphat was thirty-five years old when he became king, and he reigned twenty-five years in Jerusalem. His mother's name was Azubah the daughter of Shilhi.

43 He walked in all the ways of Asa his father, without turning from them, doing right in the sight of the LORD. However, the high places were not removed; the people still sacrificed and burned incense on the high places.

44 Jehoshaphat also made peace with the king of Israel.

45 Now the rest of the acts of Jehoshaphat, his might which he displayed and how he made war, are they not written in the Book of the Chronicles of the Kings of Judah?

46 And the remnant of the sodomites (male cult prostitutes) who remained in the days of his father Asa, Jehoshaphat expelled from the land.

47 Now there was no king in Edom; a deputy (governor) was [serving as] king.

48 Jehoshaphat had [large cargo] ships of Tarshish constructed to go to Ophir for gold, but they did not go, because the ships were wrecked at Ezion-geber.

49 Then Ahaziah the son of Ahab said to Jehoshaphat, "Let my servants go with your servants in the ships," But Jehoshaphat was unwilling *and* refused.

22:38 *the dogs licked up his blood.* Elijah's grisly prophecy concerning the house of Ahab came to pass here (21:19 – 24).

22:39 *ivory palace.* Archeological excavations at Samaria have illustrated the nature of Ahab's palace, a house with luxurious decorations made of ivory.

22:46 *remnant of the sodomites.* Apparently male prostitution was a part of the debased religious practices of Baal worship (14:24).

32 2Ch 18:31; Pr 13:20 **38** 1Ki 21:19 **39** Am 3:15 **41** 2Ch 20:31 **43** 2Ch 17:3; 1Ki 14:23; 15:14; 2Ki 12:3 **44** 2Ch 19:2; 2Co 6:14 **46** 1Ki 14:24; 15:12 **47** Ge 25:23; 2Sa 8:14; 2Ki 3:9; 8:20 **48** 2Ch 20:35; 1Ki 10:22; 2Ch 20:37; 1Ki 9:26

[50]Jehoshaphat slept with his fathers
[in death] and was buried with his fa-
thers in the city of his father David,
and Jehoram his son became king in
his place.
[51]Ahaziah the son of Ahab became
king over Israel in Samaria in the sev-
enteenth year of Jehoshaphat king of
Judah, and he reigned over Israel for
two years.
[52]He did evil in the sight of the LORD
and walked in the [idolatrous] way of
his father [Ahab] and of his mother
[Jezebel], and in the way of Jeroboam
the son of Nebat, who made Israel sin.
[53]He served Baal and worshiped
him, and he provoked the LORD God
of Israel to anger, in accordance with
everything that his father [Ahab] had
done.

22:53 Conclusion — The story does not end here but is continued in 2 Kings. The division of the Book of Kings is not original, but was done for convenience when the Bible was translated into Greek in the 2nd century BC.

50 2Ch 21:1 **51** ver. 40 **52** 1Ki 15:26 **53** Jdg 2:11; 1Ki 16:31

THE SECOND BOOK OF THE
KINGS

▸ **AUTHOR:** This book, thought to originally be part of 1 Kings, is similar to the Book of Jeremiah. It has been observed that the omission of Jeremiah's ministry in the account of King Josiah and his successors may indicate that Jeremiah himself was the recorder of the events. The last two chapters were evidently added to the book after the Babylonian captivity and written by someone other than Jeremiah.

▸ **TIMES:** 853 – 560 BC ▸ **KEY VERSES:** 2Ki 17:22 – 23

▸ **THEME:** Both Elijah in 1 Kings and Elisha in 2 Kings are prime examples of how prophets functioned in Israel. They fearlessly confronted kings. They were involved in miracles. Both seemed to always be involved in the middle of some political controversy. Most importantly, they called on God and got results. In 2 Kings, Israel's story begins with the reign of Ahab's son, Ahaziah, continues with the capture and deportation of Israel to Assyria in 722 BC, and ends with Judah's fall in 587 BC, when Nebuchadnezzar burns the temple and palace in Jerusalem and deports many people back to Babylon.

Ahaziah's Messengers Meet Elijah

1 NOW MOAB rebelled against Is-
rael after the death of Ahab.
[2]Ahaziah [the king of Israel] fell
through the lattice (grid) in his up-
per chamber which was in Samaria,
and became sick [from the injury]. So
he sent messengers, saying to them,
"Go, inquire of Baal-zebub, the god
of Ekron, if I will recover from this
sickness."
[3]But the angel of the LORD said to Eli-
jah the Tishbite, "Arise, go up to meet
the messengers of the king of Samaria,
and say to them, 'Is it because there
is no God in Israel that you are going
to inquire of Baal-zebub, the god of
Ekron?'
[4]"Therefore this is what the LORD
says: 'You [Ahaziah] will not leave
the bed on which you lie, but you will
certainly die.' " So Elijah departed.
[5]When the messengers returned to
Ahaziah, he said to them, "Why have
you returned [so soon]?"
[6]They replied, "A man came up to
meet us and said to us, 'Go, return to the
king who sent you and tell him, "Thus
says the LORD: 'Is it because there is no
God in Israel that you send to inquire
of Baal-zebub, the god of Ekron? There-
fore you will not leave the bed on which
you lie, but you will certainly die.' " ' "

1:2 ***Ahaziah.*** The account of his brief, wicked reign begins in 1 Kings 22:51. The division of the Book of Kings into two parts was for the convenience of the translators, as is indicated by the fact that Ahaziah's reign carries over from one book to the other without a break.

1:6 Unbelief — Just as in the days of Ahaziah, men and women today often will turn to everything but the one genuine source of truth. But because there is no help or life or power in man's gods, man's ideas and philosophies, belief in them will end only in wasted, ineffective lives, and eventually in eternal death. True joy and meaning in life can only be found through trust in God.

CHAPTER 1 **1** 2Sa 8:2; 2Ki 3:5 **2** 1Sa 5:10

7 The king asked them, "What was the appearance of the man who came up to meet you and said these things to you?"

8 They answered him, *"He was* a hairy man with a [wide] leather band bound around his loins." And Ahaziah said, "It is Elijah the Tishbite."

9 Then the king sent to Elijah a captain of fifty with his fifty [fighting men to seize the prophet]. And he went up to him, and behold, he was sitting on the top of a hill. And the captain said to him, "Man of God, the king says, 'Come down.' "

10 Elijah replied to the captain of fifty, "So if I am a man of God, then let fire come down from heaven and consume you and your fifty [fighting men]." Then fire fell from heaven and consumed him and his fifty.

11 So King Ahaziah again sent to him another captain of fifty with his fifty [fighting men]. And he said to him, "Man of God, thus says the king, 'Come down quickly.' "

12 Elijah answered them, "If I am a man of God, let fire come down from heaven and consume you and your fifty [fighting men]." And the fire of God came down from heaven and consumed him and his fifty.

13 So Ahaziah again sent a captain of a third fifty with his fifty [fighting men]. And the third captain of fifty went up and came bowed down on his knees before Elijah, and begged him [for compassion] and said to him, "O man of God, please let my life and the lives of your servants, these fifty, be precious in your sight.

14 "Behold, fire came down from heaven and consumed the first two captains of fifty with their fifties; but now let my life be precious in your sight."

15 The angel of the LORD said to Elijah, "Go down with him; do not be afraid of him." So he stood and went down with him to the king.

16 Then Elijah said to Ahaziah, "Thus says the LORD: 'Since you have sent messengers to inquire of Baal-zebub, god of Ekron—is it because there is no God in Israel to inquire of His word?—therefore you will not leave the bed on which you lie, but will certainly die.' "

Jehoram Reigns over Israel

17 So Ahaziah [the son of King Ahab] died in accordance with the word of the LORD which Elijah had spoken. And because he had no son, Jehoram [his younger brother] became king [of Israel, the northern kingdom] in his place in the second year of Jehoram the son of Jehoshaphat, king of Judah [the southern kingdom].

18 Now the rest of the acts of Ahaziah which he did, are they not written in the Book of the Chronicles of the Kings of Israel?

Elijah Taken to Heaven

2 WHEN THE LORD was about to take Elijah up to heaven by a whirlwind, Elijah and Elisha were traveling from Gilgal.

2 And Elijah said to Elisha, "Please stay here, for the LORD has sent me to Bethel." But Elisha replied, "As the LORD lives and as your soul lives, I will not leave you." So they went down to Bethel.

3 Now the sons of the prophets who were at Bethel came out to Elisha and said to him, "Do you know that the LORD will take your master away from you today?" He said, "Yes, I know it; be quiet [about it]."

1:8 *a hairy man.* This may refer to Elijah's garments, but the usual translation of "hairy man" is supported by the ancient versions.
1:10 *fire . . . from heaven.* Heavenly fire could signal divine judgment (Ge 19:24). Elijah had already called down such fire in his contest with the prophets of Baal (1Ki 18:36–38). If this fire was lightning, the episode would have been a particularly significant slap in the face of their religion, showing that Baal was not the god of the storm he was reputed to be. The God of Israel was — and is — the Lord of creation.
2:3 *take . . . away.* The same Hebrew word is used for Enoch's entrance to heaven (Ge 5:24). The work that God was about to do had been divinely revealed to many of God's servants

8 See Zec 13:4; Mt 3:4 **10** Lk 9:54 **13** 1Sa 26:21; Ps 72:14 **CHAPTER 2** **1** Ge 5:24; 1Ki 19:21 **2** See Ru 1:15,16; ver. 4,6; 1Sa 1:26; 2Ki 4:30 **3** ver. 5,7,15; 1Ki 20:35; 2Ki 4:1,38; 9:1

THE ACTIVITIES OF ELISHA

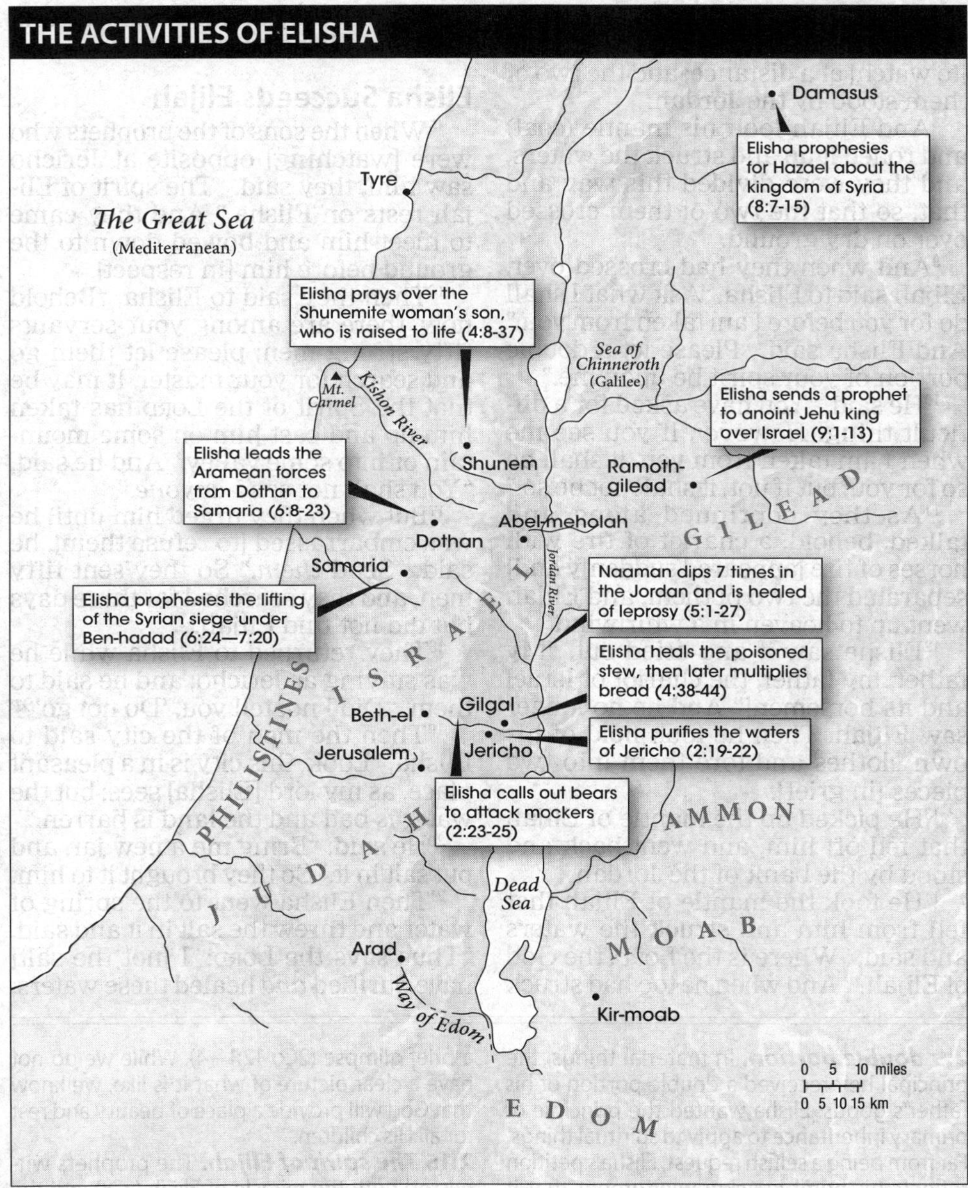

⁴Elijah said to him, "Elisha, please
stay here, for the LORD has sent me to
Jericho." But he said, "As the LORD lives
and as your soul lives, I will not leave
you." So they came to Jericho.
5The sons of the prophets who were
at Jericho approached Elisha and said
to him, "Do you know that the LORD
will take your master away from you
today?" And he answered, "Yes, I
know it; be quiet [about it]."
6Elijah said to him, "Please stay
here, for the LORD has sent me to the
Jordan." But he said, "As the LORD lives
and as your soul lives, I will not leave
you." So the two of them went on.

(vv. 3,5). This widespread knowledge of God's purpose would protect against later denials by cynical persons that the event had ever taken place.

[7]Fifty men of the sons of the prophets also went and stood opposite them [to watch] at a distance; and the two of them stood by the Jordan.
[8]And Elijah took his mantle (coat) and rolled it up and struck the waters, and they were divided this way and that, so that the two of them crossed over on dry ground.
[9]And when they had crossed over, Elijah said to Elisha, "Ask what I shall do for you before I am taken from you." And Elisha said, "Please let a double portion of your spirit be upon me."
[10]He said, "You have asked for a difficult thing. *However,* if you see me when I am taken from you, it shall be so for you; but if not, it shall not be so."
[11]As they continued along and talked, behold, a chariot of fire with horses of fire [appeared suddenly and] separated the two of them, and Elijah went up to heaven in a whirlwind.
[12]Elisha saw it and cried out, "My father, my father, the chariot of Israel and its horsemen!" And he no longer saw Elijah. Then he took hold of his own clothes and tore them into two pieces [in grief].
[13]He picked up the mantle of Elijah that fell off him, and went back and stood by the bank of the Jordan.
[14]He took the mantle of Elijah that fell from him and struck the waters and said, "Where is the LORD, the God of Elijah?" And when he too had struck the waters, they divided this way and that, and Elisha crossed over.

Elisha Succeeds Elijah

[15]When the sons of the prophets who were [watching] opposite at Jericho saw him, they said, "The spirit of Elijah rests on Elisha." And they came to meet him and bowed down to the ground before him [in respect].
[16]Then they said to Elisha, "Behold now, there are among your servants fifty strong men; please let them go and search for your master. It may be that the Spirit of the LORD has taken him up and cast him on some mountain or into some valley." And he said, "You shall not send *anyone.*"
[17]But when they urged him until he was embarrassed [to refuse them], he said, "Send *them.*" So they sent fifty men, and they searched for three days but did not find Elijah.
[18]They returned to Elisha while he was staying at Jericho; and he said to them, "Did I not tell you, 'Do not go'?"
[19]Then the men of the city said to Elisha, "Look, this city is in a pleasant place, as my lord [Elisha] sees; but the water is bad and the land is barren."
[20]He said, "Bring me a new jar, and put salt in it." So they brought it to him.
[21]Then Elisha went to the spring of water and threw the salt in it and said, "Thus says the LORD: 'I [not the salt] have purified *and* healed these waters;

2:9 *double portion.* In material things, the principal heir received a double portion of his father's goods. Elisha wanted the principle of primary inheritance to apply to spiritual things. Far from being a selfish request, Elisha's petition reflects his humble acknowledgment that if Elijah's ministry were to continue through him, it would take special God-given spiritual power.
2:11 *heaven.* The Bible does not give very much information about exactly what happens to the believer after death. Elijah is described as being "caught up to heaven," and it is assumed that he went to the same place to which Enoch had been taken up (Heb 11:5). Jesus assured the thief on the cross that he would be in "paradise" with Him (Lk 23:43), a place of which Paul also had a brief glimpse (2Co 12:1 – 4). While we do not have a clear picture of what it is like, we know that God will provide a place of beauty and rest for all His children.
2:15 *The spirit of Elijah.* The prophets witnessed both the miracle of Elijah (v. 8) and the similar miracle of Elisha. In this way there would be common agreement that Elisha was the successor of Elijah. They bowed, not in worship, but in respect and submission to the will of God.
2:17 *he was embarrassed.* Although these words may indicate Elisha's sense of shame on behalf of his disciples for their disbelief, the use of the phrase elsewhere indicates that it means Elisha was worn out, no longer willing to resist (8:11). He came to the point where he gave in to their request.

8 ver. 14; Ex 14:21; Jos 3:16 **11** 2Ki 6:17; Ps 104:4 **12** 2Ki 13:14 **14** ver. 8 **15** ver. 7 **16** See 1Ki 18:12; Eze 8:3; Ac 8:39; 2Ki 1:17 **21** See Ex 15:25; 2Ki 4:41; 6:6; Jn 9:6

there shall no longer be death or bar-
renness because of it.' "
22So the waters have been purified to
this day, in accordance with the word
spoken by Elisha.
23Then Elisha went up from Jeri-
cho to Bethel. On the way, young boys
came out of the city and mocked him
and said to him, "Go up, you baldhead!
Go up, you baldhead!"
24When he turned around and
looked at them, he cursed them in the
name of the LORD. Then two female
bears came out of the woods and tore
to pieces forty-two of the boys.
25Elisha went from there to Mount
Carmel, and from there he returned
to Samaria.

Jehoram Meets Moab Rebellion

3 JEHORAM THE son of Ahab be-
came king over Israel in Samaria
in the eighteenth year of Jehoshaphat
king of Judah, and reigned twelve
years.
2He did evil in the sight of the LORD,
but not like his father and mother; for
he put away the *sacred* pillar of Baal
that his father had made.
3Nevertheless, he continued in the
[idolatrous] sins of Jeroboam the son
of Nebat, who made Israel sin; he did
not depart from them.
4Mesha the king of Moab was a sheep
breeder, and he used to pay [an annual
tribute] to the king of Israel 100,000
lambs and the wool of 100,000 rams.
5But when Ahab died, the king of
Moab rebelled against the king of Is-
rael.
6So King Jehoram left Samaria at
that time and assembled all [the fight-
ing men of] Israel.
7Then he went and sent *word* to Je-
hoshaphat king of Judah, saying, "The
king of Moab has rebelled against me.
Will you go with me to fight against
Moab?" And he replied, "I will go; I am
as you are, my people as your people,
my horses as your horses."
8Jehoram said, "Which way shall
we go up?" Jehoshaphat answered,
"The way through the Wilderness of
Edom."
9So the king of Israel went with the
king of Judah and the king of Edom.
They made a circuit of seven days'
journey, but there was no water for
the army or for the cattle that followed
them.
10Then the king of Israel said, "We
are doomed, for the LORD has called
these three kings to be handed over
to Moab."
11But Jehoshaphat said, "Is there no
prophet of the LORD here from whom
we may inquire of the LORD?" One of
the servants of the king of Israel an-
swered, "Elisha the son of Shaphat
is here, who used to pour water over
Elijah's hands."
12Jehoshaphat said, "The word of the
LORD is with him." So the king of Israel
and Jehoshaphat and the king of Edom
went down to Elisha.

2:23 *Go up, you baldhead!* The words of these youths indicate their disbelief of Elijah's "going up" into heaven and their disrespect for God's prophet. God did not tolerate blasphemy against Himself by the demeaning of Elijah's departure, or the abuse of his prophet, whom He had called for an important task at a critical period in Israel's history.
3:2 *sacred pillar of Baal.* Probably this was a stone pillar or statue erected by Ahab and bearing an inscription and image of the god Baal. Although it was put away temporarily, it apparently was not destroyed, because it later became one of the objects of Jehu's purge (10:26–27).
3:4 *Mesha the king of Moab.* The existence of this Moabite king is confirmed by an inscription on a pillar known as the Moabite Stone. The inscription indicates that Omri had conquered the plains of Moab north of the Arnon River, and that the area remained under Israelite control throughout Ahab's reign. Thus the events of this chapter probably took place after Jehoram's accession and shortly before Jehoshaphat's death in 847 BC. ***sheep breeder.*** This Hebrew word is used only of Mesha and of Amos, the prophet (Am 1:1).
3:7 *Will you go with me.* Because Jehoshaphat was related to the throne of the Northern Kingdom through the marriage of his son Jehoram to Ahab's daughter Athaliah, it could be presumed that he would be available as an ally.

CHAPTER 3 **2** 1Ki 16:31,32 **3** 1Ki 12:28,31,32 **4** See Isa 16:1 **5** 2Ki 1:1 **7** 1Ki 22:4 **11** 1Ki 22:7 **12** 2Ki 2:25

13 Now Elisha said to the king of Is-
rael, "What *business* do you have with
me? Go to the prophets of your [wick-
ed] father [Ahab] and to the prophets
of your [pagan] mother [Jezebel]." But
the king of Israel said to him, "No, for
the LORD has called these three kings
together to be handed over to Moab."
14 Elisha said, "As the LORD of hosts
(armies) lives, before whom I stand,
were it not that I have regard for Je-
hoshaphat king of Judah, I would not
look at you nor see you [king of Israel].
15 "But now bring me a musician."
And it came about while the musician
played, that the hand (power) of the
LORD came upon Elisha.
16 He said, "Thus says the LORD,
'Make this valley (the Arabah) full of
trenches.'
17 "For thus says the LORD, 'You will
not see wind or rain, yet that valley
will be filled with water, so you and
your cattle and your *other* animals
may drink.
18 'This is but a simple thing in the
sight of the LORD; He will also hand
over the Moabites to you.
19 'You shall strike every fortified city
and every choice (principal) city, and
cut down every good tree and stop up
all sources of water, and ruin every
good piece of land with stones.' "
20 It happened in the morning, when
the sacrifice was offered, that suddenly
water came [miraculously] from the
area of Edom, and the country was
filled with water.
21 Now all the Moabites heard that
the [three] kings had come up to fight
against them, and all who were able to
put on armor, as well as those who were
older, were summoned and stood [to-
gether in battle formation] at the border.
22 When they got up early the *next*
morning, the sun shone on the water,
and the Moabites saw the water across
from *them* as red as blood.
23 And they said, "This is blood!
Clearly the kings have fought together,
and have killed one another. Now then,
Moab, to the spoil [and the plunder of
the dead soldiers]!"
24 But when they came to the camp
of Israel, the Israelites rose up and
struck the Moabites, so that they fled
before them; and they went forward
into the land, killing the Moabites [as
they went].
25 They destroyed the [walls of the]
cities, and each man threw a stone on
every piece of good land, covering it
[with stones]. And they stopped up all
the springs of water and cut down all
the good trees, until they left *nothing*
in Kir-hareseth [Moab's capital city]
but its stones. Then the [stone] slingers
surrounded the city and destroyed it.
26 When the king of Moab saw that
the battle was too fierce for him, he
took with him seven hundred swords-
men to break through to the king of
Edom; but they could not.
27 Then the king of Moab took his
eldest son, who was to reign in his
place, and offered him [publicly] as
a burnt offering [to Chemosh] on the
[city] wall [horrifying everyone]. And
there was great wrath against Israel,
and Israel's allies [Judah and Edom]
withdrew from King Jehoram and re-
turned to their own land.

The Widow's Oil

4 NOW ONE of the wives *of a man* of
the sons of the prophets cried out to
Elisha [for help], saying "Your servant
my husband is dead, and you know
that your servant [reverently] feared
the LORD; but the creditor is coming to

3:14 *I would not look at you.* As a devotee of Baal, Jehoram had no claim on the favor of God. Nevertheless, he would enjoy the benefits of God's grace toward Jehoshaphat.
3:20 *filled with water.* The dry stream beds can easily overflow their banks in downpours of rain. Even distant areas can be flooded by water from faraway mountain streams swelled by heavy rains.
4:1 *one of the wives.* The fate of widows was perilous in the ancient Middle East. A practical test of biblical piety was to observe how those in power treated widows and orphans (Job 24:21; Ps 146:9).

13 Eze 14:3; Jdg 10:14; Ru 1:15; 1Ki 18:19 **14** 1Ki 17:1; 2Ki 5:16 **15** See 1Sa 10:5; Eze 1:3; 3:14,22; 8:1 **16** 2Ki 4:3 **20** Ex 29:39,40 **25** Isa 16:7,11 **27** Am 2:1; 2Ki 8:20 **CHAPTER 4** **1** 1Ki 20:35; See Lev 25:39; Mt 18:25

take my two sons to be his slaves [in
payment for a loan].”
2 Elisha said to her, “What shall I do
for you? Tell me, what do you have [of
value] in the house?” She said, “Your
maidservant has nothing in the house
except a [small] jar of [olive] oil.”
3 Then he said, “Go, borrow contain-
ers from all your neighbors, empty
containers—and not *just* a few.
4 “Then you shall go in and shut the
door behind you and your sons, and
pour out [the oil you have] into all these
containers, and you shall set aside
each one when it is full.”
5 So she left him and shut the door
behind her and her sons; they were
bringing her *the containers* as she
poured [the oil].
6 When the containers were all full,
she said to her son, “Bring me another
container.” And he said to her, “There
is not a one left.” Then the oil stopped
[multiplying].
7 Then she came and told the man of
God. He said, “Go, sell the oil and pay
your debt, and you and your sons can
live on the rest.”

The Shunammite Woman

8 Now there came a day when Elisha
went over to Shunem, where there was
a prominent *and* influential woman,
and she persuaded him to eat a meal.
Afterward, whenever he passed by, he
stopped there for a meal.
9 She said to her husband, “Behold,
I sense that this is a holy man of God
who frequently passes our way.
10 “Please, let us make a small, fully-
walled upper room [on the housetop]
and put a bed there for him, with a
table, a chair, and a lampstand. Then
whenever he comes to *visit* us, he can
turn in there.”
11 One day he came there and turned
in to the upper room and lay down to
rest.
12 And he said to Gehazi his servant,
“Call this Shunammite.” So he called
her and she stood before him.
13 Now he said to Gehazi, “Say to
her now, ‘You have gone to all this
trouble for us; what can I do for you?
Would you *like* to be mentioned to the
king or to the captain of the army?’ ”
She answered, “I live among my own
people [in peace and security and need
no special favors].”
14 Later Elisha said, “What then is to
be done for her?” Gehazi answered,
“Well, she has no son and her husband
is old.”
15 He said, “Call her.” So Gehazi
called her, and she [came and] stood
in the doorway.
16 Elisha said, “At this season next
year, you will embrace a son.” She said,
“No, my lord. O man of God, do not lie
to your maidservant.”
17 But the woman conceived and gave
birth to a son at that season the next
year, just as Elisha had said to her.

The Shunammite’s Son

18 When the child was grown, the day
came that he went out to his father, to
the reapers.
19 But he said to his father, “My head,
my head.” The man said to his servant,
“Carry him to his mother.”
20 When he had carried and brought
him to his mother, he sat on her lap
until noon, and *then* he died.
21 She went up and laid him on the
bed of the man of God, and shut *the*

4:10 *small, fully-walled upper room.* The flat roofs of houses in this time were used as extra living space, and often a small room would be built on the roof which could be reached from outside. This accommodated a guest while providing privacy. Recognizing Elisha as one of God’s chosen servants, the Shunammite woman was especially concerned that the normal measures of hospitality be applied even more fully.

4:12 – 13 Thankfulness — Both Elijah and the Shunammite woman illustrate the vitally important teaching of Scripture: Be thankful; be ready both to receive and to give; express your thankfulness always with words and deeds. Too many blessings, kind words, and thoughtful actions go thankless until it is too late. The kindness and love expressed to Elijah registered in his heart and mind. His loving question should be our question in response to kindness: “What can I do for you?”

3 See 2Ki 3:16 **8** Jos 19:18 **16** Ge 18:10,14; ver. 28

door [of the small upper room] behind him and left.

22 Then she called to her husband and said, "Please send me one of the servants and one of the donkeys, so that I may run to the man of God and return."

23 He said, "Why are you going to him today? It is neither the New Moon nor the Sabbath." And she said, "*It will be* all right."

24 Then she saddled the donkey and said to her servant, "Drive [the animal] fast; do not slow down the pace for me unless I tell you."

25 So she set out and came to the man of God at Mount Carmel.

When the man of God saw her at a distance, he said to Gehazi his servant, "Look, there is the Shunammite *woman*.

26 "Please run now to meet her and ask her, 'Is it well with you? Is it well with your husband? Is it well with the child?' " And she answered, "It is well."

27 When she came to the mountain to the man of God, she took hold of his feet. Gehazi approached to push her away; but the man of God said, "Let her alone, for her soul is desperate *and* troubled within her; and the LORD has hidden *the reason* from me and has not told me."

28 Then she said, "Did I ask for a son from my lord? Did I not say, 'Do not give me false hope'?"

29 Then he said to Gehazi, "Gird up your loins (prepare now!) and take my staff in your hand, and go [to the woman's house]; if you meet any man [along the way], do not greet him and if a man greets you, do not [stop to] answer him; and lay my staff on the face of the boy [as soon as you reach the house]."

30 The mother of the child said, "As the LORD lives and as your soul lives, I will not leave you." So Elisha arose and followed her.

31 Gehazi went on ahead of them and laid the staff on the boy's face, but there was no sound or response [from the boy]. So he turned back to meet Elisha and told him, "The boy has not awakened (revived)."

32 When Elisha came into the house, the child was dead and lying on his bed.

33 So he went in, shut the door behind the two of them, and prayed to the LORD.

34 Then he went up and lay on the child and put his mouth on his mouth, his eyes on his eyes, and his hands on his hands. And as he stretched himself out on him *and* held him, the boy's skin became warm. [1 Kin 17:21]

35 Then he returned and walked in the house once back and forth, and went up [again] and stretched himself out on him; and the boy sneezed seven times and he opened his eyes.

36 Then Elisha called Gehazi and said, "Call this Shunammite." So he called her. And when she came to him, he said, "Pick up your son."

37 She came and fell at his feet, bowing herself to the ground [in respect and gratitude]. Then she picked up her son and left.

4:23 *New Moon ... Sabbath.* There was no work on these days, so they would be more suitable for going to see the prophet (Ex 20:9 – 12; Am 8:5).

4:27 *the LORD has hidden.* The prophets did not know everything, but only what God made known to them (5:26).

4:33 *prayed to the LORD.* Elisha's actions demonstrate that his faith was in the person and power of God alone, and not in the staff that symbolized his prophetic office. The restoration of the boy's life is a demonstration that life itself is in the hands of God.

4:36 Resurrection — When the writer of Hebrews tells us about those "women [who] received back their dead by resurrection" (Heb 11:35), he is probably referring to the two women about whom we read in 1 Kings 17:8 – 24 and 2 Kings 4:8 – 37. Many similarities can be seen between these two resurrection miracles, but it is clear that neither prophet followed a "resurrection formula." God is not bound to follow certain procedures or respond to incantations. Instead, He heals whom He will, in what way He wills.

25 2Ki 2:25 **28** ver. 16 **29** 1Ki 18:46; 2Ki 9:1; Lk 10:4; See Ex 7:19; 14:16; 2Ki 2:8,14; Ac 19:12 **30** 2Ki 2:2 **31** Jn 11:11 **33** ver. 4; Mt 6:6; 1Ki 17:20 **34** 1Ki 17:21; Ac 20:10 **35** 1Ki 17:21; 2Ki 8:1,5 **37** 1Ki 17:23; Heb 11:35

The Poisonous Stew

38 Elisha came back to Gilgal during a famine in the land. The sons of the prophets were sitting before him, and he said to his servant, "Put on the large pot and cook stew for the sons of the prophets."

39 Then one [of them] went into the field to gather herbs, and found a wild vine and gathered from it a lapful of wild gourds, and came and cut them up into the pot of stew, although they did not know *what they were.*

40 So they served it for the men to eat. But as they ate the stew, they cried out, "O man of God, there is death in the pot." And they could not eat it.

41 But he said, "Bring flour." And he threw it into the pot and said, "Serve it for the people so that they may eat." Then there was nothing harmful in the pot.

42 Now [at another time] a man from Baal-shalisha came and brought the man of God bread of the first fruits, twenty loaves of barley bread, and fresh ears of grain [in the husk] in his sack. And Elisha said, "Give it to the people [affected by the famine] so that they may eat."

43 His servant said, "How am I to set [only] this before a hundred [hungry] men?" He said, "Give it to the people so that they may eat, for thus says the LORD, 'They shall eat and have *some* left.' "

44 So he set it before them, and they ate and left *some*, in accordance with the word of the LORD.

Naaman Is Healed

5 NOW NAAMAN, commander of the army of the king of Aram (Syria), was *considered* a great man by his king, and was highly respected because through Naaman the LORD had given victory to Aram (Syria). He was also a man of courage, *but he was* a leper.

2 The Arameans (Syrians) had gone out in bands [as raiders] and had taken captive a little girl from the land of Israel; and she waited on Naaman's wife [as a servant].

3 She said to her mistress, "I wish that my master [Naaman] were with the prophet who is in Samaria! Then he would heal him of his leprosy."

4 Naaman went in and told his master [the king], "The girl who is from the land of Israel said such and such."

5 Then the king of Aram (Syria) said, "Go now, and I will send a letter to the king of Israel (Jehoram the son of Ahab)." So he left and took with him ten talents of silver and 6,000 *shekels* of gold, and ten changes of clothing.

6 And he brought the letter to the king of Israel. It said, "And now when this letter comes to you, I will have sent my servant Naaman to you, so that you may heal him of his leprosy."

7 When the king of Israel read the letter, he tore his clothes [in shock and outrage at the request] and said, "Am I God, to kill and to make alive, that this man sends to me [a request] to heal a man of his leprosy? Just consider [what he is asking] and see how he is seeking an opportunity [for a battle] with me."

8 Now when Elisha the man of God heard that the king of Israel had torn his clothes, he sent *word* to the king, asking, "Why have you torn your clothes? Just let Naaman come to me, and he shall know that there is a [true] prophet in Israel."

4:41 *flour.* The flour had no magical properties; Elisha's faith in the living God effected the miraculous cure.

5:1 *king of Aram.* The king of Aram (or Syria) was Ben-hadad II (860–842 BC). He was a constant threat against the Northern Kingdom and would lead an invasion against it later (6:24–7:20).

5:3 *the prophet ... in Samaria.* Although Elisha traveled frequently and may sometimes have lived at Mount Carmel (4:25), he apparently maintained a residence in the capital city of Samaria (2:25; 6:9–7:20).

5:7 *tore his clothes.* While such letters of introduction were common in the ancient Middle East, Ben-hadad's frequent forays against Israel made the king suspicious that the Arameans were seeking a pretext for another attack. Tearing one's robes was a sign of grief or agitation.

38 2Ki 2:1; 2Ki 8:1; 2Ki 2:3; Lk 10:39; Ac 22:3 **40** Ex 10:17 **41** See Ex 15:25; 2Ki 2:21; 5:10; Jn 9:6 **42** 1Sa 9:4; 1Sa 9:7; 1Co 9:11; Gal 6:6 **43** Lk 9:13; Jn 6:9; Lk 9:17; Jn 6:11 **44** Mt 14:20; 15:37; Jn 6:13 **CHAPTER 5** **1** Lk 4:27; Ex 11:3 **5** 1Sa 9:8; 2Ki 8:8,9 **7** Ge 30:2; Dt 32:39; 1Sa 2:6

9So Naaman came with his horses
and chariots and stopped at the en-
trance of Elisha's house.
10Elisha sent a messenger to him,
saying, "Go and wash in the Jordan
seven times, and your flesh will be
restored to you and *you will* be clean."
11But Naaman was furious and went
away and said, "Indeed! I thought 'He
would at least come out to [see] me and
stand and call on the name of the LORD
his God, and wave his hand over the
place [of leprosy] and heal the leper.'
12"Are not Abana and Pharpar, the
rivers of Damascus [in Aram], better
than all the waters of Israel? Could I
not wash in them and be clean?" So he
turned and went away in a rage.
13Then his servants approached and
said to him, "My father, if the prophet
had told you *to do some* great thing,
would you not have done it? How much
more then, when he has said to you,
'Wash, and be clean?' "
14So he went down and plunged him-
self into the Jordan seven times, just as
the man of God had said; and his flesh
was restored like that of a little child
and he was clean.

Gehazi's Greed

15Then Naaman returned to the man
of God, he and all the people in his
group, and stood before him. He said,
"Behold, I know that there is no God in
all the earth, except in Israel; so now
accept a blessing *and* gift from your
servant."
16But Elisha said, "As the LORD lives,
before whom I stand, I will accept
nothing." He urged him to take it, but
Elisha refused.
17Naaman said, "If not, then please,
let your servant be given a load of
earth for a team of mules; for [from
this day on] your servant will no longer
offer a burnt offering nor a sacrifice to
other gods, but only to the LORD, [the
God of Israel].
18"In this matter may the LORD par-
don your servant: when my master
[the king] goes into the house of [his
god] Rimmon to worship there, and
he leans on my hand and I bow in the
house of Rimmon, when I bow down
in the house of Rimmon, may the LORD
pardon your servant in this matter [of
attending the king when he worships]."
19Elisha said to him, "Go in peace."
So Naaman departed and was a good
distance away from him,
20when Gehazi, the servant of Eli-
sha the man of God, said, "My master
has spared this Naaman the Aramean
(Syrian), by not accepting from him
what he brought. As the LORD lives, I
will run after him and get something
from him."
21So Gehazi pursued Naaman. When
Naaman saw someone running after
him, he got down from the chariot to
meet him and said, "Is all well?"
22And he said, "All is well. My mas-
ter has sent me to say, 'Just now two
young men of the sons of the prophets
have come to me from the hill country
of Ephraim. Please give them a talent
of silver and two changes of clothes.' "
23Naaman said, "Please take two
talents." And he urged him [to accept],
and tied up two talents of silver in two
bags with two changes of clothes and
gave them to two of his servants; and
they carried them in front of Gehazi.
24When he came to the hill, he took
them from their hand and put them
in the house [for safekeeping]; and he
sent the men away, and they left.
25Then he went in and stood before

5:10 ***wash in the Jordan.*** Elisha's instructions illustrate the fact that simple obedience to God's will, even if it is not what we imagined, is the only road to receiving God's blessings.
5:15 ***no God . . . except in Israel.*** Naaman is an unusual example of a foreigner who came to faith in God.
5:17 ***earth.*** Naaman's unusual request may refer back to God's instructions to the Israelites in the desert (Ex 20:24). Altars built for the worship of the Lord were to be made of earth or undressed stones, perhaps to avoid the possibility of the altar itself becoming an object of veneration.
5:23 ***talents.*** A talent was an enormous amount of silver — equal to 3,000 shekels, or about 75 pounds.

10 See 2Ki 4:41; Jn 9:7 **14** Job 33:25; Lk 4:27 **15** Dan 2:47; 3:29; 6:26,27; Ge 33:11 **16** 2Ki 3:14; Ge 14:23; See Mt 10:8; Ac 8:18,20 **18** 2Ki 7:2,17

his master. Elisha asked him, "Where
have you been, Gehazi?" He said,
"Your servant went nowhere."
26Elisha said to him, "Did my heart
not go *with you*, when the man turned
from his chariot to meet you? Is it a
[proper] time to accept money and
clothing and olive orchards and vine-
yards and sheep and oxen and male
and female servants?
27"Therefore, the leprosy of Naaman
shall cling to you and to your descen-
dants forever." So Gehazi departed
from his presence, a leper *as white* as
snow. [Ex 4:6; Num 12:10]

The Axe Head Recovered

6 NOW THE sons of the prophets
said to Elisha, "Look now, the place
where we live near you is too small
for us.
2"Please let us go to the Jordan [Riv-
er] and let each man take from there
a beam [for the building]; and let us
make a place there for ourselves where
we may live." And he answered, "Go."
3Then one said, "Please be willing
to go with your servants." So he an-
swered, "I shall go."
4So he went with them; and when
they came to the Jordan, they cut down
[some of] the trees.
5But it happened that as one was
cutting down a beam, the axe head
fell into the water; and he cried out
and said, "Oh no, my master! It was
borrowed!"
6The man of God said, "Where did it
fall?" When he showed him the place,
Elisha cut off a stick and threw it in
there, and made the iron [axe head] float.
7He said, "Pick it up for yourself."
So he reached out with his hand and
took it.

The Arameans Plot to Capture Elisha

8Now the king of Aram (Syria) was
making war against Israel, and he con-
sulted with his servants, saying, "My
camp shall be in such and such a place."
9The man of God sent *word* to the
king of Israel saying, "Be careful not
to pass by this place, because the Ar-
ameans are pulling back to there."
10Then the king of Israel sent *word*
to the place about which Elisha had
warned him; so he guarded himself
there repeatedly.
11Now the heart of the king of Aram
(Syria) was enraged over this thing. He
called his servants and said to them,
"Will you not tell me which of us is
helping the king of Israel?"
12One of his servants said, "None [of
us is helping him], my lord, O king; but
Elisha, the prophet who is in Israel,
tells the king of Israel the words that
you speak in your bedroom."
13So he said, "Go and see where he is,
so that I may send [men] and seize him."
And he was told, "He is in Dothan."
14So he sent horses and chariots and
a powerful army there. They came by
night and surrounded the city.
15The servant of the man of God got
up early and went out, and behold,
there was an army with horses and

5:26–27 Worldliness—Naaman, in gratitude, urged Elisha to receive a gift, but Elisha steadfastly refused. The prophet wanted the new convert to understand clearly that the God of Israel cannot be bribed. His gifts are bestowed because of His gracious heart. Gehazi's sin was serious—it involved covetousness, lying, misrepresentation of the prophet and, more importantly, brought disgrace on the name of the God of Israel. Gehazi was acting in his own self-interest rather than for the cause of God. When we choose according to the values of unregenerate men, we are worldly and damage the interests of God's kingdom.

5:26 *Did my heart not go with you.* The use of the term *heart* suggests not only Elisha's knowledge but also his strong feelings for Gehazi.

6:6 *made the iron [axe head] float.* At a time when most tools were still made of bronze, an iron blade was valuable.

6:13 *Dothan.* Dothan was in the central highlands of Israel. It is mentioned only here and in Genesis 37:17, when Joseph was sold to the Midianites.

6:15 *servant of the man of God.* Since Gehazi had become a leper (5:27), this is probably another servant. However, Gehazi is mentioned again in 8:4 as one who was still faithfully representing the miracles done through Elisha.

27 1Ti 6:10; Ex 4:6; Nu 12:10; 2Ki 15:5 **CHAPTER 6** **1** 2Ki 4:38 **6** 2Ki 2:21 **13** Ge 37:17

chariots encircling the city. Elisha's
servant said to him, "Oh no, my mas-
ter! What are we to do?"
16 Elisha answered, "Do not be afraid,
for those who are with us are more
than those who are with them."
17 Then Elisha prayed and said,
"LORD, please, open his eyes that he
may see." And the LORD opened the
servants eyes and he saw; and behold,
the mountain was full of horses and
chariots of fire surrounding Elisha.
18 When the Arameans came down
to him, Elisha prayed to the LORD and
said, "Please strike this people (nation)
with blindness." And God struck them
with blindness, in accordance with
Elisha's request.
19 Then Elisha said to the Arameans,
"This is not the way, nor is this the city.
Follow me and I will lead you to the
man whom you are seeking." And he
led them to Samaria.
20 When they had come into Samaria,
Elisha said, "LORD, open the eyes of
these *men,* so that they may see." And
the LORD opened their eyes and they
saw. Behold, they were in the midst
of Samaria.
21 When the king of Israel (Jehoram)
saw them, he said to Elisha, "My father,
shall I kill them? Shall I kill them?"
22 Elisha answered, "You shall not
kill them. Would you kill those you
have taken captive with your sword
and bow? Serve them bread and water,
so that they may eat and drink, and go
back to their master [King Ben-hadad]."
23 So the king prepared a great feast
for them; and when they had eaten and
drunk he sent them away, and they
went to their master. And the maraud-
ing bands of Aram did not come into
the land of Israel again.

The Siege of Samaria—Cannibalism

24 But it came about after this, that
Ben-hadad king of Aram (Syria) gath-
ered his whole army together and went
up and besieged Samaria.
25 Now there was a great famine in
Samaria; and they besieged it until
a donkey's head was sold for eighty
shekels of silver, and a fourth of a kab
of dove's dung for five *shekels* of silver.
26 As the king of Israel (Jehoram)
was passing by on the [city] wall a
woman cried out to him, "Help, my
lord, O king!"
27 He said, "If the LORD does not help
you, from where shall I get you help?
From the threshing floor, or from the
wine press?"
28 And the king said to her, "What is
the matter with you?" She answered,
"This woman said to me, 'Give your

6:16–17 Understanding the Big Picture—Spiritually, we don't often make the personal progress we should. We fall back into old patterns of behavior too easily. We feel like God has left us out there alone to fight with our internal weaknesses as well as external forces that often seem to overpower us.

We're like Elisha's servant who couldn't see the full reality. We don't have a big enough vision to see what God is doing around us and in us. We're too wrapped up in our own physical and emotional reality. We're so full of ourselves that there's no room for God and the new vision He can bring to our lives.

Curiously, this story doesn't contain any record of the servant's response to what he saw. Did that new vision dramatically change his life? Did he forever understand the extent of God's protective care? Maybe that happened, or maybe like most of us, he was only able to catch a glimpse. We must live by faith that the full reality is represented by those brief and beautiful glimpses of the bigger picture.

6:19 *I will lead you.* Elisha's words are technically true, although he was undoubtedly misleading and deceiving the Arameans. The fact that he did not use his unfair advantage to kill Israel's enemies is worthy of notice.

6:25 *donkey's head.* Donkeys were unclean for food (Lev 11:3). ***dove's dung.*** It is not known whether this term is meant to refer to the actual manure of doves or pigeons, or whether it is a slang term for some kind of bean or seed (some translations say "seed pods" or "locust beans").

6:28 *eat him.* Israel had been warned that national disobedience could reduce the people to such a loathsome deed (Lev 26:29; Dt 28:53–57).

16 2Ch 32:7; Ps 55:18; Ro 8:31 **17** 2Ki 2:11; Ps 34:7; 68:17; Zec 1:8; 6:1-7 **18** Ge 19:11 **22** Ro 12:20 **23** ver. 8,9; 2Ki 5:2

son so we may eat him today, and we will eat my son tomorrow.'

29"So we cooked my son and ate him. The next day I said to her, 'Give your son so that we may eat him'; but she had hidden her son."

30When the king heard the woman's words, he tore his clothes—now he was still walking along on the wall—and the people looked [at him], and he had on sackcloth underneath [his royal robe] next to his skin.

31Then he said, "May God do so to me and more also, if the head of Elisha the son of Shaphat remains on him today!"

32Now Elisha was sitting in his house, and the elders were sitting with him. And *the king* sent a man ahead of him [to behead Elisha]; but before the messenger arrived, Elisha told the elders, "Do you see how this son of [Jezebel] a murderer has sent [a man] to remove my head? Look, when the messenger comes, shut the door and hold it securely against him. Is not the sound of his master's feet [just] behind him?"

33While Elisha was still talking with them, the messenger came down to him [followed by the king] and the king said, "This evil [situation] is from the LORD! Why should I wait for [help from] the LORD any longer?"

Elisha Promises Food

7 THEN ELISHA said, "Hear the word of the LORD. Thus says the LORD, 'Tomorrow about this time a measure of finely-milled flour will sell for a shekel, and two measures of barley for a shekel, at the gate of Samaria.' "

2Then the royal officer on whose arm the king leaned answered the man of God and said, "If the LORD should make windows in heaven [for the rain], could this thing take place?" Elisha said, "Behold, you will see it with your own eyes, but [because you doubt] you will not eat of it."

Four Lepers Relate Arameans' Flight

3Now four men who were lepers were at the entrance of the [city's] gate; and they said to one another, "Why should we sit here until we die?

4"If we say, 'We will enter the city'—then the famine is in the city and we will die there; and if we sit still here, we will also die. So now come, let us go over to the camp of the Arameans (Syrians). If they let us live, we will live; and if they kill us, we will only die."

5So they got up at twilight to go to the Aramean camp. But when they came to the edge of the camp, there was no one there.

6For the LORD had caused the Aramean army to hear the sound of chariots, and the sound of horses, the sound of a great army. They had said to one another, "The king of Israel has hired against us the kings of the Hittites, and the kings of the Egyptians, to come [and fight] against us."

7So the Arameans set out and fled during the twilight, and left their tents, horses, and donkeys, *even left* the camp just as it was, and fled for their lives.

8When these lepers came to the edge of the camp, they went into one tent and ate and drank, and carried away from there silver, gold, and clothing, and went and hid them. Then they went back and entered another tent and carried [some valuable things] from there *also*, and went and hid them.

9Then they said one to another, "We are not doing the right thing. This is a

7:3 *lepers.* Because lepers were excluded from the city (Lev 13:4–6; Nu 5:2–3), and avoided by all, they probably were ignored by the invaders and had been left to their fate. If the ordinary people of the city were suffering from hunger, these men must have been in even worse plight. They concluded that they had nothing to lose by going to the other side.

7:9 *good news.* Good news and good fortune had to be shared (Pr 15:27; 21:17), and the men feared that failure to do so might merit divine punishment.

29 Lev 26:29; Dt 28:53,57 **30** 1Ki 21:27 **31** Ru 1:17; 1Ki 19:2 **32** Eze 8:1; 20:1; Lk 13:32; 1Ki 18:4 **33** Job 2:9
CHAPTER 7 **1** ver. 18,19 **2** ver. 17,19,20; Mal 3:10 **3** Lev 13:46 **6** 2Sa 5:24; 2Ki 19:7; Job 15:21; 1Ki 10:29
7 Ps 48:4-6; Pr 28:1

day of good news, yet we are keeping
silent. If we wait until the morning
light, some punishment [for not re-
porting this now] will come on us. So
now come, let us go and tell the king's
household."
10 So they came and called to the
gatekeepers of the city. They told them,
"We went to the camp of the Arameans
(Syrians), and behold, there was no one
there, nor the sound of man there—
only the horses and donkeys tied up,
and the tents [had been left] just as
they were."
11 Then the gatekeepers called out
and it was reported to the king's house-
hold inside [the city].
12 Then the king got up in the night
and said to his servants, "I will tell you
what the Arameans have done to us.
They know that we are hungry; so they
have left the camp to hide themselves
in the open country, thinking, 'When
they come out of the city, we shall take
them alive and get into the city.' "
13 One of his servants replied, "Please
let some *men* take five of the horses
which remain inside the city. Consider
this: [if they are caught then at worst]
they will be like all the people of Israel
who are left in the city; [even if they
are killed then] they will be like all
the people of Israel who have already
died. So let us send [them] and see
[what happens]."
14 So they took two chariots with
horses, and the king sent them after
the Aramean army, saying, "Go and
see."

The Promise Fulfilled

15 They went after them to the Jordan,
and all the road was entirely littered
with clothing and equipment which
the Arameans (Syrians) had thrown
away when they hurriedly fled. And
the messengers returned and told the
king.
16 Then the people [of Israel] went
out and plundered the camp of the
Arameans. So [goods were so plen-
tiful that] a measure of finely-milled
flour [was sold] for a shekel, and two
measures of barley for a shekel, in
accordance with the word of the LORD
[as spoken through Elisha]. [2 Kin 7:1]
17 Now the king had appointed the
royal officer on whose arm he leaned
to be in charge of the [city] gate; and
the [starving] people trampled him
at the gate [as they struggled to get
through for food], and he died, just as
the man of God had foretold when the
king came down to him.
18 It happened just as [Elisha] the
man of God had spoken to the king,
saying, "Two measures of barley will
be sold for a shekel and a measure
of finely-milled flour for a shekel to-
morrow about this time at the gate of
Samaria."
19 The royal officer had answered the
man of God and said, "Now behold,
[even] if the LORD should make win-
dows in heaven, could such a thing
happen?" And Elisha had answered,
"You will see it with your own eyes,
but [because of your doubt] you will
not eat it." [2 Kin 7:2]
20 And so it happened to him; for the
people trampled him at the gate, and
he died.

The King Restores the Shunammite's Land

8 NOW ELISHA had said to the
[Shunammite] woman whose son
he had restored to life, "Prepare and
go, you and your household, and stay
temporarily wherever you can; for
the LORD has called for a famine, and
moreover, it will come on the land [and
continue] for seven years."
2 So the woman set out and did every-

8:1 Kindness — Performing an act of kindness can be compared to throwing sand in the wind. You can be sure some of it will come back to you. The woman mentioned here could give glowing testimony to this. She had been led to feed and house the prophet Elisha (4:8–10), and this act of kindness produced good fruit. Through Elisha's prayers, her child was born and restored (ch. 4), and now Elisha warned her of the coming famine. God always remembers our acts of kindness (Mal 3:16). In fact, the only thing God "forgets" about us is our confessed sins (Jer 31:34).

16 ver. 1 **17** ver. 2 **18** ver. 1 **CHAPTER 8** **1** 2Ki 4:35; Ps 105:16; Hag 1:11

thing in accordance with the word of the man of God. She and her household went and stayed temporarily as foreigners in the land of the Philistines for seven years.

3 At the end of the seven years the woman returned from the land of the Philistines; and she went to appeal to the king [of Israel] for her house and for her land.

4 Now the king was talking with Gehazi, the servant of the man of God, saying, "Tell me all the great things that Elisha has done."

5 And [just] as Gehazi was telling the king how Elisha had restored the dead to life, behold, the woman whose son he had restored to life appealed to the king for her house and for her land. And Gehazi said, "My lord, O king, this is the woman and this is her son, whom Elisha restored to life."

6 When the king asked the woman, she told him [everything]. So the king appointed for her a certain high official, saying, "Restore everything that was hers, including all the produce of the field since the day that she left the land until now."

Elisha Predicts Evil from Hazael

7 Now Elisha came to Damascus, and Ben-hadad king of Aram (Syria) was sick; and he was told, "The man of God has come here."

8 And the king said to Hazael, "Take a gift with you and go to meet the man of God, and inquire of the LORD by him, saying, 'Will I recover from this illness?' "

9 So Hazael went to meet Elisha and took a gift with him of every good thing of Damascus, forty camels' loads; and he came and stood before him and said, "Your son Ben-hadad king of Aram has sent me to you, asking, 'Will I recover from this illness?' "

10 And Elisha said to him, "Go, say to him, 'You will certainly recover,' but the LORD has shown me that he will certainly die."

11 Elisha stared steadily at Hazael until he was embarrassed, and then the man of God wept.

12 Hazael said, "Why are you weeping, my lord?" He answered, "Because I know the evil that you will do to the sons (descendants) of Israel. You will set their strongholds on fire, kill their young men with the sword, smash their children to pieces, and rip up their pregnant women."

13 Then Hazael said, "*Surely not!* For what is your servant, *who is nothing more than* a dog, that he would do this monstrous thing?" And Elisha answered, "The LORD has shown me that you will be king over Aram."

14 Then Hazael departed from Elisha and came to his master, who said to him, "What did Elisha say to you?" And he answered, "He told me you would certainly recover."

15 But the next day Hazael took the bedspread and dipped it in water and

---

8:3 *she went to appeal.* The Shunammite woman had not renounced or sold her property, but merely had left during the previous famine. Moreover, she had returned within seven years (Dt 15:1 – 6; Ru 4:3 – 4). Since the property was still legally hers, she pressed her claim to the king himself.

8:4 *Gehazi.* At this point, Gehazi was still faithful to the ministry of Elisha.

8:6 *Restore everything.* We get a complex picture of King Jehoram. At times he was so angry with Elisha that he wished him dead (6:31), yet even then he was in mourning for his people. In this section, his righteous judgment should be contrasted with the wretched behavior of the wicked Ahab (1Ki 21:1 – 16).

8:10 *You will certainly recover.* Elisha was answering Ben-hadad's exact question: his illness was not deadly, in the natural course of things, he would have recovered. However, Elisha also knew that Ben-hadad's life would be taken by his servant Hazael.

8:11 *embarrassed.* Elisha had reached the end of his ability to resist his emotions and wept over the suffering that Hazael would bring.

8:13 *dog.* In the ancient Middle East, dogs were despised as scavengers and unclean animals. Shalmaneser III of Assyria noted Hazael's accession to the throne with the words: "Hazael, son of nobody, seizes the throne."

---

4 2Ki 5:27 **5** 2Ki 4:35 **8** 1Ki 19:15; 1Sa 9:7; 1Ki 14:3; 2Ki 5:5; 2Ki 1:2 **10** ver. 15 **11** Lk 19:41 **12** 2Ki 10:32; 12:17; 13:3,7; Am 1:3; 2Ki 15:16; Hos 13:16; Am 1:13 **13** 1Sa 17:43; 1Ki 19:15

covered the king's face, so that he died. And Hazael became king in his place.

Another Jehoram Reigns in Judah

16 Now in the fifth year of Joram (Jehoram) the son of Ahab king of Israel, when Jehoshaphat was king of Judah, Jehoram the son of Jehoshaphat king of Judah became king.

17 He was thirty-two years old when he became king, and he reigned for eight years in Jerusalem.

18 He walked in the ways of the kings of Israel, just as the house of Ahab had done, for [Athaliah] the daughter of Ahab became his wife. He did evil in the sight of the LORD.

19 Yet for the sake of His servant David the LORD was not willing to destroy Judah, since He had promised to give him a lamp (enthroned descendant) through his sons always.

20 In his days Edom revolted from the rule of Judah, and set up a king over themselves.

21 So Jehoram [king of Judah] went over to Zair [in Edom] with all his chariots. He set out by night and struck down the Edomites who had surrounded him and the captains of his chariots; but the people [of his army] fled to their tents.

22 So Edom revolted against Judah to this day. Then Libnah revolted at the same time.

23 The rest of the acts of Jehoram and everything that he did, are they not written in the Book of the Chronicles of the Kings of Judah?

Ahaziah Succeeds Jehoram in Judah

24 Jehoram slept with his fathers [in death] and was buried with them in the City of David. Ahaziah his son became king in his place.

25 In the twelfth year of Joram (Jehoram) the son of Ahab king of Israel, Ahaziah the son of Jehoram king of Judah began to reign.

26 Ahaziah was twenty-two years old when he became king, and he reigned one year in Jerusalem. His mother's name was Athaliah, the granddaughter of Omri king of Israel.

27 He walked in the ways of the house of Ahab and did evil in the sight of the LORD, as *did* the house of Ahab, for he was a son-in-law of the house of Ahab.

28 Ahaziah went with Joram the son of Ahab to battle against Hazael king of Aram (Syria) in Ramoth-gilead; and the Arameans wounded Joram.

29 King Joram returned to Jezreel to be healed of the wounds which the Arameans had inflicted on him at Ramah when he fought against Hazael king of Aram. And Ahaziah the son of Jehoram king of Judah went down to see Joram the son of Ahab in Jezreel, because he was sick.

Jehu Reigns over Israel

9 NOW ELISHA the prophet called one of the sons of the prophets and said to him, "Gird up your loins (prepare for action), take this flask of oil in your hand and go to Ramoth-gilead.

2 "When you arrive there, look for

8:16–19 Apostasy—The complete picture of Jehoram's shameful apostasy is presented by the chronicler (2Ch 21:2–26). There were two powerful influences in Jehoram's life, one good and one evil; sadly, the evil influence prevailed. His father, Jehoshaphat, was one of the few godly kings of Judah, but Jehoram's wife was Athaliah, daughter of Jezebel, who influenced him to worship Baal (v. 18). Jehoram's life of unfaithfulness earned God's judgment, and he died a lonely and miserable death. Nevertheless, the Lord remained committed to His covenant promise (v. 19). Human unfaithfulness cannot destroy God's purpose of salvation.

8:16 *Joram . . . Jehoram.* These are variant spellings of the same name; the two kings were brothers-in-law since Jehoram of Judah had married the sister of Joram of Israel.

8:27 *the ways of the house of Ahab.* The lowest point of Israel's religious apostasy was reached in the reign of Ahab and his wicked wife Jezebel (1Ki 16:31).

9:2 *Jehu.* The name Jehu means "the Lord is He."

16 2Ch 21:3 **17** 2Ch 21:5 **18** ver. 26 **19** 2Sa 7:13; 1Ki 11:36; 15:4; 2Ch 21:7 **20** Ge 27:40; 2Ki 3:27; 2Ch 21:8-10; 1Ki 22:47 **22** 2Ch 21:10 **24** 2Ch 22:1 **26** See 2Ch 22:2 **27** 2Ch 22:3,4 **28** 2Ch 22:5 **29** 2Ki 9:15; 2Ki 9:16; 2Ch 22:6,7 **CHAPTER 9** **1** 1Ki 20:35; 2Ki 4:29; Jer 1:17; 2Ki 8:28,29 **2** ver. 5,11

Jehu the son of Jehoshaphat the son of Nimshi, and go in and have him arise from among his brothers, and take him into an inner room.

3“Then take the flask of oil and pour it on his head and say, ‘Thus says the LORD: “I have anointed you king over Israel.” ’ Then open the door and flee and do not delay.”

4So the young man, the servant of the prophet, went to Ramoth-gilead.

5When he arrived, the captains of the army were sitting [outside]; and he said, “I have a message for you, O captain.” Jehu said, “To which one of us?” And he said, “For you, O captain.”

6So Jehu got up, and they went into the house. And he poured the oil on Jehu’s head and said to him, “Thus says the LORD, the God of Israel: ‘I have anointed you king over the people of the LORD, over Israel.

7‘You shall strike the house of Ahab your master, so that I may avenge the blood of My servants the prophets, and the blood of all the servants of the LORD, [who have died] at the hands of Jezebel.

8‘For the entire house of Ahab shall perish, and I will cut off from Ahab every male, both bond and free, in Israel.

9‘I will make the house of Ahab like the house of Jeroboam the son of Nebat, and like the house of Baasha the son of Ahijah. [1 Kin 21:22]

10‘And the dogs will eat Jezebel in the territory of Jezreel, and there will be no one to bury her.’ ” Then he opened the door and fled. [2 Kin 9:33–37]

11When Jehu came out to the servants of his master, one said to him, “Is all well? Why did this madman come to you?” And he said to them, “You know [very well] the man and his talk.”

12And they said, “It is a lie; tell us now.” And he said, “Thus and thus he spoke to me, saying, ‘Thus says the LORD: “I have anointed you king over Israel.” ’ ”

13Then they hurried and each man took his garment and placed it [as a cushion] under Jehu on the top of the [outside] stairs, and blew the trumpet, saying, “Jehu is king!”

Jehoram (Joram) Is Assassinated

14So Jehu the son of Jehoshaphat, the son of Nimshi, conspired against Joram [to dethrone and kill him]. Now Joram with all Israel was protecting Ramoth-gilead against Hazael king of Aram (Syria),

15but King Joram had returned to Jezreel to heal from the wounds which the Arameans had inflicted on him when he fought with Hazael king of Aram. So Jehu said, “If this is your intent, let no one survive and leave the city (Ramoth-gilead) to go and tell *of the plan* in Jezreel [the capital].”

16So Jehu rode in a chariot and went to Jezreel, for Joram was lying there. And Ahaziah king of Judah had come down to see Joram.

17Now the watchman was standing on the tower in Jezreel and he saw the crowd with Jehu as he approached, and said, “I see a company.” And Joram said, “Send a horseman to meet them and have him ask, ‘Do you come in peace?’ ”

18So the horseman went to meet him and said, “Thus says the king: ‘Do you come in peace?’ ” And Jehu said, “What have you to do with peace? Rein in behind me.” And the watchman reported, “The messenger approached them, but he has not returned.”

19Then Joram sent out a second horseman, who approached them and said, “Thus says the king: ‘Do you come in peace?’ ” Jehu replied, “What have you to do with peace? Rein in behind me.”

9:6 *poured the oil.* The last part of the Lord’s threefold command to Elijah had been carried out (1Ki 19:15 – 21; 2Ki 8:7 – 13). In the Old Testament, anointing was customarily reserved for a king (2Sa 2:4) or the high priest (Ex 40:13).

9:13 *garment.* This action was a mark of homage fit for a king (Mt 21:8). This scene is reminiscent of the anointing of King Solomon (1Ki 1:34).

3 1Ki 19:16 **6** 1Ki 19:16; 2Ch 22:7 **7** 1Ki 18:4; 21:15 **8** 1Ki 14:10; 21:21; 1Sa 25:22; Dt 32:36 **9** 1Ki 14:10; 15:29; 21:22; 1Ki 16:3,11 **10** ver. 35,36; 1Ki 21:23 **11** Jer 29:26; Jn 10:20; Ac 26:24; 1Co 4:10 **13** Mt 21:7 **15** 2Ki 8:29 **16** 2Ki 8:29

20 And the watchman reported, "He
approached them, but he has not re-
turned; and the driving [of the chariot]
is like that of Jehu the son of Nimshi,
for he drives furiously."
21 Then Joram said, "Harness [the
chariot]." When they harnessed his
chariot *horses*, Joram king of Israel
and Ahaziah king of Judah went out,
each in his chariot, and they went out
to meet Jehu and met him on the prop-
erty of Naboth the Jezreelite.
22 When Joram saw Jehu, he said,
"Do you come in peace, Jehu?" And
he answered, "What peace [can ex-
ist] as long as the fornications of your
mother Jezebel and her sorceries are
so many?"
23 So Joram reined [his chariot]
around and fled, and he said to Ahazi-
ah, "Treachery *and* betrayal, Ahaziah!"
24 But Jehu drew his bow with his
full strength and shot Joram between
his shoulders; and the arrow went out
through his heart and he sank down
in his chariot.
25 Then Jehu said to Bidkar his offi-
cer, "Pick him up and throw him on
the property of the field of Naboth the
Jezreelite; for I remember when you
and I were riding together after his
father Ahab, that the LORD uttered this
prophecy against him:
26 'I certainly saw the blood of
Naboth and the blood of his sons yes-
terday,' says the LORD, 'and I will repay
you on this property,' says the LORD.
Now then, pick him up and throw him
into the property [of Naboth], in ac-
cordance with the word of the LORD."
[1 Kin 21:15–29]

Jehu Assassinates Ahaziah

27 When Ahaziah the king of Judah
saw this, he fled by the way of the
garden house. Jehu pursued him and
said, "Shoot him too, [while he is] in the
chariot." *So they shot him* at the ascent
to Gur, which is by Ibleam. And Aha-
ziah fled to Megiddo and died there.
28 Then his servants carried him in
a chariot to Jerusalem and buried him
in his grave with his fathers in the City
of David.
29 In the eleventh year of Joram, the
son of Ahab, Ahaziah became king
over Judah.
30 So when Jehu came to Jezreel, Jez-
ebel heard about it, and she painted her
eyes and adorned her head and looked
down from the [upper] window.
31 As Jehu entered in at the gate, she
said, "Is it well, Zimri, your master's
murderer?" [1 Kin 16:9, 10]
32 Then Jehu raised his face toward
the window and said, "Who is on my
side? Who?" And two or three officials
looked down at him.

Jezebel Is Killed

33 And he said, "Throw her down." So
they threw her down, and some of her
blood spattered on the wall and on the
horses, and he trampled her underfoot.
34 When he came in, he ate and
drank, and said, "See now to this
cursed woman and bury her, for she
is a king's daughter."
35 They went to bury her, but they
found nothing left of her except the
skull and the feet and the palms of
her hands.
36 So they returned and told Jehu.
Then he said, "This is the word of the
LORD, which He spoke through His
servant Elijah the Tishbite, saying, 'In
the property of Jezreel the dogs shall
eat the flesh of Jezebel. [1 Kin 21:23]
37 'The corpse of Jezebel will be like

9:21 *the property of Naboth.* Ahab's dynasty ended on the very stolen property that occasioned the divine sentence of judgment (1Ki 21:17 – 24). Ahab's unlawful seizure of the land of Naboth was regarded as one of his most heinous crimes.

9:22 *fornications of . . . Jezebel.* Jezebel's spiritual adultery had brought vile demonic practices into the kingdom and sealed its doom (1Ki 21:25 – 26). As God had said, such activities would surely bring about the nation's demise (Dt 28:25 – 26). Jehu justified his actions as a judgment on Jezebel's sins.

9:23 *Treachery.* In reality, Joram and Ahaziah were the true traitors, the ones who had led the people in rebellion against God and sealed their own doom by their disobedience.

21 2Ch 22:7 **25** 1Ki 21:29 **30** Eze 23:40 **31** 1Ki 16:9-20 **34** 1Ki 16:31 **36** 1Ki 21:23 **37** Ps 83:10

dung on the surface of the field in the
property of Jezreel, so they cannot say,
"This is Jezebel." ' "

Judgment upon Ahab's House

10 AHAB HAD seventy sons [and
grandsons] in Samaria. So Jehu
wrote letters and sent them to Samaria,
to the rulers of Jezreel, to the elders,
and to the guardians of *the children of*
Ahab, saying,
2 "Now as soon as this letter comes
to you, since your master's sons (male
descendants) are with you, as well as
chariots and horses and a fortified city
and weapons,
3 select the best and most capable
of your master's sons, and set him on
his father's throne, and fight for your
master's [royal] house."
4 But they were extremely afraid
and said, "Look, the two kings did
not stand before Jehu; so how can we
stand?"
5 And the one who was in charge of
the household, and the one who was
overseer of the city, the elders, and the
guardians [of the children] sent *word*
to Jehu, saying, "We are your servants
and we will do whatever you tell us,
but we will not make any man king;
do what is good in your eyes."
6 Then Jehu wrote a second letter
to them, saying, "If you are with me
and will obey me, take the heads of
your master's sons, and come to me
at Jezreel tomorrow about this time."
Now the [dead] king's sons, seventy
persons, were with the great men of
the city, who were rearing them.
7 When the letter came to them, they
took the king's sons and slaughtered
them, seventy persons, and put their
heads in baskets, and sent them to
Jehu at Jezreel.
8 When a messenger came and told
him, "They have brought the heads of
the king's sons," he said, "Put them in
two heaps at the entrance of the city
gate until morning."
9 The next morning he went out and
stood and said to all the people, "You
are just *and* innocent; behold, I con-
spired against [Joram] my master and
killed him, but who killed all these?
10 "Know then [without any doubt]
that there shall fall to the earth noth-
ing of the word of the LORD, which
the LORD spoke concerning the house
of Ahab, for the LORD has done what
He said through His servant Elijah."
[1 Kin 19:17]
11 So Jehu killed all who remained of
the house of Ahab in Jezreel, and all
his great men and his familiar friends
and his priests, until he left him with-
out a survivor.
12 And he set out and went to Sa-
maria. On the way as he was at the
place of the sand heaps [meeting place]
for the shepherds,
13 Jehu met the relatives of Ahazi-
ah king of Judah and said, "Who are
you?" They answered, "We are the rel-
atives of Ahaziah; and we came down
to greet the royal princes and the sons
of the queen mother [Jezebel]."
14 Then Jehu said, "Take them alive."
So they took them alive and [later]
slaughtered them at the well by the
place of the sand heaps, forty-two men;
he left none of them [alive].

10:1 *seventy sons.* Ahab's "seventy sons" probably included the children of his concubines, as well as grandchildren.

10:9 Righteousness — Jehu declared Ahab's "great men" (v. 6) "innocent" of the death of Ahab's seventy sons, or as the Hebrew word translates literally, "just" or "righteous." They were righteous in the same sense that Jehu himself was (v. 30), in that God had ordered the death of Ahab's family and they were actually carrying out God's orders. However, this did not mean that these men could be considered righteous in any other sense. They had already thrown in their lot with Ahab and his wicked ways; they were his "great men," and as such, they had to meet the same fate as the rest of his family (v. 11). They had almost accidentally been obedient to God's will, but their hearts were still for the enemy.

10:10 *the LORD has done what He said.* Evaluating Jehu is difficult. His praise for the ministry of the prophets of God and his stated respect for the word of God commend him to us, but later he did not exhibit faithfulness to the Lord (10:31).

CHAPTER 10 **7** 1Ki 21:21 **9** 2Ki 9:14,24 **10** 1Sa 3:19; Jer 44:28; 1Ki 21:19,21,29 **13** 2Ki 8:29; 2Ch 22:8

15 When Jehu went on from there, he met Jehonadab the son of Rechab *coming* to meet him. He greeted him and said to him, "Is your heart right, as my heart is with yours?" Jehonadab answered, "It is." *Jehu said* "If it is, give me your hand." He gave him his hand, and Jehu pulled him up into the chariot.

16 And he said, "Come with me and see my zeal for the LORD." So he had Jehonadab in his chariot.

17 When Jehu came to Samaria, he killed everyone who remained of Ahab's family in Samaria, until he had destroyed all of them, in accordance with the word of the LORD which He spoke to Elijah.

Jehu Destroys Baal Worshipers

18 Jehu assembled all the people and said [in pretense] to them, "Ahab served Baal a little; Jehu will serve him much [more].

19 "Now, summon unto me all the prophets of Baal, all his worshipers and all his priests. Let no one be missing, for I have a great sacrifice for Baal; whoever is missing shall not live." But Jehu did it with trickery, in order to destroy the worshipers of Baal.

20 Jehu said, "Consecrate a festive assembly (celebration) for Baal." And they proclaimed it.

21 Then Jehu sent throughout Israel, and all the worshipers of Baal came; there was no one left who did not come. They went to the house (temple) of Baal, and the house of Baal was filled from one end to the other.

22 He said to the man in charge of the wardrobe, "Bring out garments for all the worshipers of Baal." And he brought the garments out to them.

23 Then Jehu with Jehonadab the son of Rechab went into the house of Baal; and he said to the worshipers of Baal, "Search carefully and see that there are no servants of the LORD here with you, but only the worshipers of Baal."

24 Then they went in to offer sacrifices and burnt offerings.

Now Jehu had stationed eighty men outside for himself and said, "If any of the men whom I have brought into your hands escape, the one who lets him go shall forfeit his own life for that man's life."

25 Then it came about, as soon as he had finished offering the burnt offering, that Jehu said to the guards and to the royal officers, "Go in and kill them; let no one come out." And they killed them with the edge of the sword; and the guard and the royal officers threw *their bodies* out, and went to the inner room of the house of Baal.

26 They brought out the *sacred* pillars (obelisks) of the house of Baal and burned them.

27 They also tore down the *sacred* pillar of Baal and tore down the house of Baal, and made it into a latrine [forever unclean] to this day.

28 Thus Jehu eradicated Baal from Israel.

29 However, Jehu did not turn from the [idolatrous] sins of Jeroboam the son of Nebat, who made Israel sin, that is, [led them to worship] the golden calves which were at Bethel and Dan. [1 Kin 12:28ff]

10:15 *Jehonadab.* The name Jehonadab means "The Lord is noble." He was an ascetic, nomadic Rechabite. These people were known for their faithfulness to God and to the austere regulations laid down by Jehonadab (Jer 35:1 – 16).

10:21 – 24 Worship — At times Israel imported pagan ideas and practices into their worship and attempted to mix them with the worship of the Lord. The extremity of this apostasy was reached when Ahab erected an altar for Baal, the fertility god of the Canaanites, in a temple built for Baal in Samaria (1Ki 16:32). The participants in Baal worship engaged not only in immoral sexual orgies but in the detestable practice of child sacrifice (Nu 25:1 – 8; Jer 19:5). God could not tolerate such behavior and Jehu's purge was the punishment that He had promised for disobedience.

10:21 *house (temple) of Baal.* This was the temple constructed by Ahab (1Ki 16:32).

10:29 *the golden calves.* Jehu's destruction of Baal worship was a political act. His continuing of the state worship policies established by Jeroboam clearly shows his disregard for true spiritual revival in Israel.

15 Jer 35:6; 1Ch 2:55; Ezr 10:19 **16** 1Ki 19:10 **17** 2Ki 9:8; 2Ch 22:8; 1Ki 21:21 **18** 1Ki 16:31,32 **19** 1Ki 22:6 **21** 1Ki 16:32 **24** 1Ki 20:39 **26** 1Ki 14:23 **27** Ezr 6:11; Da 2:5; 3:29 **29** 1Ki 12:28,29

30 The LORD said to Jehu, "Because
you have done well in executing what
is right in My eyes, and have done
to the house of Ahab in accordance
with everything that was in My heart,
your sons (descendants) shall sit on Is-
rael's throne to the fourth generation."
[2 Kin 15:12]
31 But Jehu did not take care to walk
in the law of the LORD, the God of Is-
rael, with all his heart; he did not turn
from the sins of Jeroboam, who made
Israel sin.
32 *So* in those days the LORD began
to cut off *portions* of Israel; Hazael [of
Aram] defeated them throughout the
territory of Israel:
33 from the Jordan eastward, all the
land of Gilead, the Gadites and the
Reubenites and the Manassites, from
Aroer, which is by the Arnon River,
even Gilead and Bashan.

Jehoahaz Succeeds Jehu

34 Now the rest of the acts of Jehu
and everything that he did and all his
might, are they not written in the Book
of the Chronicles of the Kings of Israel?
35 Jehu slept with his fathers [in
death], and they buried him in Sa-
maria. Jehoahaz his son became king
in his place.
36 The time that Jehu reigned over
Israel in Samaria was twenty-eight
years.

Athaliah Queen of Judah

11 WHEN ATHALIAH the mother
of Ahaziah [king of Judah] saw
that her son was dead, she arose and
destroyed all the royal offspring.
2 But Jehosheba, the daughter of
King Joram [of Judah and half] sister
of Ahaziah, took Joash the son of Aha-
ziah and abducted him from among
the king's sons who were to be killed,
and hid him and his nurse in the bed-
room. So they hid him from Athaliah,
and he was not put to death.
3 Joash was hidden with his nurse
in the house (temple) of the LORD for
six years, while Athaliah reigned over
the land.
4 Now in the seventh year Jehoiada
[the priest, Jehosheba's husband] sent
for the captains of hundreds of the
Carites and of the guard and brought
them to him to the house of the LORD.
Then he made a covenant with them
and put them under oath in the house
of the LORD, and showed them the
king's [hidden] son.
5 He commanded them, saying, "This
is the thing that you shall do: a third of
you who come in [reporting for duty]
on the Sabbath shall keep watch over
the king's house
6 (a third shall also be at the [city]
gate Sur, and a third at the gate behind
the guards); so you shall keep watch
over the palace [from three posts] for
defense.
7 "Two units of you, all those who
go out [off duty] on the Sabbath, shall
also keep watch over the house (tem-
ple) of the LORD for [the protection of]
the king.
8 "You shall surround the [young]
king, each man with weapons in his
hand; and whoever comes through the
ranks shall be put to death. You are to
be with the king when he goes out and
when he comes in."
9 The captains of hundreds acted in

10:32 *the LORD began to cut off portions of Israel.* The attacks of Hazael were part of God's judgment on Israel.
11:1 *Athaliah.* This name means "the LORD is exalted." Sadly, she did not live up to her name, and instead exalted herself.
11:2 *Jehosheba.* Josephus says that Jehosheba was Ahaziah's half sister. As the wife of the high priest Jehoida, her marriage, and her relation to the royal house made it possible for her to rescue and hide her nephew Joash.
11:3 *was hidden . . . in the house (temple) of the LORD.* Joash was to inherit the promises of the Davidic covenant. His righteous reign may be attributed in part to his early years spent in the house of the Lord and to the godly instruction and protection of his aunt Jehosheba and her husband.
11:9 *acted in accordance with everything . . . the priest commanded.* The remarkably willing obedience of the royal guard would seem to indicate that even her own followers were disgusted by Athaliah's wickedness.

30 See ver. 35; 2Ki 13:1,10; 14:23; 15:8,12 **31** 1Ki 14:16 **32** 2Ki 8:12 **33** Am 1:3 **CHAPTER 11** **1** 2Ch 22:10; 2Ki 8:26 **4** 2Ch 23:1 **5** 1Ch 9:25 **9** 2Ch 23:8

accordance with everything that Jehoiada the priest commanded; and each of them took his men who were to come in (on duty) on the Sabbath, with those who were to go out (off duty) on the Sabbath, and they came to Jehoiada the priest.

10 The priest gave to the captains of hundreds the spears and shields that had been King David's, which were in the house of the LORD.

11 And the guards stood, each man with weapons in his hand, from the right side to the left side of the temple area, by the altar [in the courtyard] and by the temple [proper], all around the king.

12 Then Jehoiada brought out the king's son and put the crown on him and gave him the Testimony [a copy of the Mosaic Law]; and they made him king and anointed him, and they clapped their hands and said, "*Long* live the king!"

13 When Athaliah heard the sound of the guards and of the people, she went into the house of the LORD to the people.

14 When she looked, behold, there stood the [young] king [on the platform] by the pillar, as was customary [on such occasions], and the captains and the trumpeters were beside the king; and all the people of the land rejoicing and blowing the trumpets. Then Athaliah tore her clothes and cried, "Treason! Treason!"

15 Then Jehoiada the priest commanded the captains of hundreds appointed over the army and said to them, "Take her out between the ranks, and whoever follows her put to death with the sword." For the priest had said, "Let her not be put to death in the house (temple) of the LORD."

16 So they seized her, and she went through the horses' entrance to the king's house (palace), and she was put to death there.

17 Then Jehoiada made a covenant between the LORD, the king, and the people, that they would be the LORD's people—also between the king and the people [to be his subjects].

18 Then all the people of the land went to the house of Baal and tore it down. They utterly smashed his altar and his images to pieces, and they put Mattan the priest of Baal to death in front of the altars. And [Jehoiada] the priest appointed officers over the house of the LORD.

19 Then he took the captains of hundreds, the Carites (royal bodyguards), the guard, and all the people of the land; and they brought the [young] king down from the house of the LORD, and came by way of the guards' gate to the king's house. And [little] Joash sat on the throne of the kings.

20 So all the people of the land rejoiced and the city [of Jerusalem] was quiet. For they had put Athaliah to death with the sword at the king's house.

21 Jehoash (Joash) was seven years old when he became king.

Joash (Jehoash) Reigns over Judah

12 IN THE seventh year of Jehu [king of Israel], Jehoash became king [over Judah], and he reigned forty years in Jerusalem. His mother's name was Zibiah of Beersheba.

11:12 *gave him the Testimony.* Deuteronomy prescribed the duties of the king with regard to the preservation of God's law (Dt 17:18). By putting a copy of the Law in Joash's hand and the crown on his head, Jehoiada presented him as the rightful heir to the throne. The term "testimony" recalls the covenant, emphasizing that Joash's coronation was given both its scriptural warrant and its rightful connection to the Davidic covenant.

11:17 *covenant.* Covenant renewal was particularly necessary after the usurpation by the wicked Athaliah.

11:20 *rejoiced . . . quiet.* The joy of the people and the peacefulness of the land were marks of God's blessing to the restored Davidic dynasty.

11:21 *Jehoash.* This variant spelling is used interchangeably with Joash.

10 2Sa 8:7 **12** 1Sa 10:24 **13** 2Ch 23:12 **14** 2Ki 23:3; 2Ch 34:31 **17** 2Ch 23:16; 2Sa 5:3 **18** 2Ki 10:26; Dt 12:3; 2Ch 23:17; 2Ch 23:18 **21** 2Ch 24:1 **CHAPTER 12** **1** 2Ch 24:1

2 Jehoash did right in the sight of the
LORD all his days in which Jehoiada the
priest instructed him.
3 Only the high places were not re-
moved; the people were still sacrific-
ing and burning incense [to the LORD]
on the high places [rather than at the
temple].

The Temple to Be Repaired

4 Jehoash said to the priests, "All the
money for the dedicated things which
is brought into the house of the LORD, in
current money, *both* the money of each
man's assessment [for all those bound
by vows], *and* all the money which any
man's heart prompts him to bring into
the house (temple) of the LORD,
5 let the priests receive such contri-
butions for themselves, each from his
acquaintance; and they shall repair
any breach in the house *of the LORD*,
wherever a breach is found."
6 But it came about in the twenty-third
year of [the reign of] King Jehoash, that
the priests *still* had not repaired the
damages of the *LORD's* house.
7 Then King Jehoash called for Je-
hoiada the priest and the [other] priests
and said to them, "Why are you not
repairing the damage of the house
(temple)? Now then, do not take any
more money from your acquaintances,
but turn it all over for [the repair of]
the damages of the house." [You are no
longer responsible for this work. I will
take it into my own hands.]
8 So the priests agreed that they
would receive no [more] money from
the people, nor [be responsible to] re-
pair the damages of the house.
9 Then Jehoiada the priest took a chest
and bored a hole in its lid and set it be-
side the altar, on the right side as one
enters the house of the LORD; and the
priests who guarded the door put in the
chest all the money that was brought [by
the people] into the house of the LORD.
10 And whenever they saw that there
was a large amount of money in the
chest, the king's scribe and the high
priest came up and tied it in bags and
counted the money that was found in
the house of the LORD.
11 Then they gave the money, which
was weighed out into the hands of
those who were doing the work, who
had the oversight of the house of the
LORD; and they paid it out to the car-
penters and builders who worked on
the house (temple) of the LORD,
12 and to the masons and stonecut-
ters, and to buy timber and hewn (cut)
stone to repair any breach in the house
of the LORD, and for all that was laid
out for repairing the house.
13 However, there were not made for
the house of the LORD basins of silver,
snuffers, bowls, trumpets, any gold
containers or [other] silver containers,
from the money that was brought into
the house of the LORD;
14 but they gave that to those who did
the work, and with it they repaired the
house of the LORD.
15 Moreover, they did not require an
accounting from the men into whose
hands they placed the money to be paid
to those who did the work, for they
acted in good faith.
16 Money from the guilt offerings and
money from the sin offerings was not
brought into the house of the LORD [for
repairs]; it was for the priests.
17 Then Hazael king of Aram (Syr-
ia) went up, fought against Gath [in
Philistia], and captured it. And Hazael
resolved to go up to Jerusalem.

12:2 ***all his days in which Jehoiada the priest instructed him.*** Sadly, after Jehoiada's death Joash's reign took a different turn; nonetheless, he was one of the few kings of Judah who showed some signs of righteousness.

12:3 ***high places.*** Although the high places seem to have been used at times for the worship of the true God, they were also strongly associated with Canaanite religious rites (1Ki 3:2 – 4; 14:23). Apostasy would become a besetting sin later in Joash's reign (2Ch 24:17 – 19,24).

12:17 ***Hazael king of Aram.*** The Aramean invasion recorded here took place late in Joash's reign. The king fell into apostasy and this invasion came as a judgment of his wickedness.

3 1Ki 15:14; 22:43; 2Ki 14:4 **4** 2Ki 22:4; Ex 30:13; Ex 35:5; 1Ch 29:9 **6** 2Ch 24:5 **7** 2Ch 24:6 **9** 2Ch 24:8
13 See 2Ch 24:14 **15** 2Ki 22:7 **16** Lev 5:15,18; Lev 7:7; Nu 18:9 **17** 2Ki 8:12; See 2Ch 24:23

18 So Jehoash the king of Judah took all the sacred things that Jehoshaphat and Jehoram and Ahaziah, his fathers, kings of Judah, had dedicated, and his own sacred things and all the gold that was found in the treasuries of the house (temple) of the LORD and of the king's house, and sent them to Hazael king of Aram; and Hazael departed from Jerusalem. [1 Kin 15:18]

Joash (Jehoash) Succeeded by Amaziah in Judah

19 Now the rest of the acts of Joash and everything that he did, are they not written in the Book of the Chronicles of the Kings of Judah?

20 His servants arose and formed a conspiracy [against him] and struck down Joash [in revenge] at the house of Millo, [on the way] that goes down to Silla. [2 Chr 24:22–25]

21 For Jozacar (Jozachar) the son of Shimeath and Jehozabad the son of Shomer, his servants, struck him and he died; and they buried Joash with his fathers in the City of David. Amaziah his son became king in his place.

Kings of Israel: Jehoahaz and Joash (Jehoash)

13 IN THE twenty-third year of Joash the son of Ahaziah, king of Judah, Jehoahaz the son of Jehu became king over Israel in Samaria, *and he reigned* seventeen years.

2 He did evil in the sight of the LORD, and followed the [idolatrous] sins of Jeroboam the son of Nebat, who made Israel sin; he did not turn from them.

3 So the anger of the LORD was kindled *and* burned against Israel, and He handed them over time and again to Hazael the king of Aram (Syria), and of Ben-hadad the son of Hazael.

4 But Jehoahaz sought the favor of the LORD, and the LORD listened to him; for He saw the oppression of Israel, how the king of Aram oppressed them.

5 Then the LORD gave Israel a savior [to rescue them and give them peace], so that they escaped from under the hand of the Arameans; and the sons (descendants) of Israel lived in their tents as before.

6 Yet they did not turn from the [idolatrous] sins of the [royal] house of Jeroboam, who made Israel sin; but walked in them. And the Asherah [set up by Ahab] also remained standing in Samaria [Israel's capital].

7 For he left to Jehoahaz [king of Israel] an army of no more than fifty horsemen, ten chariots, and 10,000 footmen, for the king of Aram (Ben-hadad) had destroyed them and made them like dust to be trampled.

8 Now the rest of the acts of Jehoahaz, everything that he did and his might, are they not written in the Book of the Chronicles of the Kings of Israel?

9 Jehoahaz slept with his fathers [in death], and they buried him in Sa-

---

12:20 ***struck down Joash.*** Joash had been severely wounded in Hazael's invasion (2Ch 24:24–25), and then fell victim to dissent and unpopularity that culminated in his assassination. Because of Joash's apostasy and murder of Zechariah, Jehoiada's son (2Ch 24:17–22), the king was not laid to rest in the royal tombs (2Ch 24:25).

13:2 ***evil . . . the [idolatrous] sins of Jeroboam.*** After the end of the house of Omri in Jehu's purge, the kings of Israel reverted to the level of syncretism that had been established by Jeroboam I, indulging in a skewed religion in which worship of the Lord was mixed with idolatry.

13:4 ***sought the favor of the LORD.*** Although Jehoahaz did not follow the Lord exclusively, God graciously heard his genuine plea for help. In His long-suffering mercy, God often deals patiently with people and blesses them in spite of their failures (1Ki 21:25–29; 2Pe 3:9).

13:6 Unbelief — No one is bound to continue following a path of sin. We always have the option of turning to God. However, the tendency to maintain things as they are and have been, to resist change no matter how urgently needed or how right it may be, or how much good it promises, is powerful. We cling to the known, the familiar, no matter how unsatisfying and ineffective it may be or how unhappy it may make us. Changing direction is not easy or painless, but the good news is that it really can be done. God is loving and forgiving, and when we repent of sin, He gives us the power to overcome it.

18 1Ki 15:18; 2Ki 18:15,16 **20** 2Ki 14:5; 2Ch 24:25 **21** 2Ch 24:27 **CHAPTER 13** **3** Jdg 2:14; 2Ki 8:12 **4** Ps 78:34; Ex 3:7; 2Ki 14:26 **5** See ver. 25; 2Ki 14:25,27 **6** 1Ki 16:33 **7** Am 1:3

maria; Joash his son became king in
his place.
10 In the thirty-seventh year of Joash
king of Judah, Jehoash (Joash) the son
of Jehoahaz became king over Israel
in Samaria, *and reigned* sixteen years.
11 He did evil in the sight of the LORD;
he did not turn away from all the [idol-
atrous] sins of Jeroboam the son of
Nebat, who made Israel sin; but he
walked in them.
12 Now the rest of the acts of Joash,
everything that he did, and his might
with which he fought against Amaziah
king of Judah, are they not written in
the Book of the Chronicles of the Kings
of Israel?
13 Joash slept with his fathers [in
death], and Jeroboam [II] sat on his
throne. Joash was buried in Samaria
with the kings of Israel.

Death of Elisha

14 Now Elisha had become sick with
the illness by which he would die. And
Joash the king of Israel came down
to him and wept over him and said,
"O my father, my father, the chariot of
Israel and its horsemen!" [2 Kin 2:12]
15 And Elisha said to him, "Take a
bow and arrows." So he took a bow
and arrows.
16 Then he said to the king of Israel,
"Put your hand on the bow." And he
put his hand on it, and Elisha put his
hands on the king's hands.
17 And he said, "Open the window to
the east," and he opened it. Then Elisha
said, "Shoot!" And he shot. And Elisha
said, "The LORD's arrow of victory, the
arrow of victory over Aram (Syria); for
you will strike the Arameans in Aphek
until you have destroyed them."
18 Then he said, "Take the arrows,"
and he took them. And Elisha said to
the king of Israel, "Strike the ground,"
and he struck *it* three times and
stopped.
19 So the man of God was angry with
him and said, "You should have struck
five or six times; then you would have
struck down Aram until you had de-
stroyed it. But now you shall strike
Aram *only* three times."
20 Elisha died, and they buried him.
Now marauding bands of Moabites
would invade the land in the spring
of the year.
21 And it happened that as a man was
being buried [on an open bier], they
saw a marauding band [coming]; and
they threw the man into Elisha's grave.
But when the [body of the] man [was
being let down and] touched the bones
of Elisha he revived and stood up on
his feet.
22 Hazael the king of Aram oppressed
Israel all the days of Jehoahaz.
23 But the LORD was gracious to them
and had compassion on them and
turned toward them for the sake of
His covenant with Abraham, Isaac,
and Jacob, and He was unwilling to
destroy them, and did not cast them
from His presence until now. [Mal 3:6]
24 Hazael king of Aram (Syria) died;
Ben-hadad his son became king in
his place.
25 Then Jehoash (Joash) the son of
Jehoahaz recovered from Ben-hadad
the son of Hazael the cities which he
had taken from Jehoahaz his father
by war. Three times Joash defeated
Ben-hadad and recovered the cities of
Israel. [2 Kin 13:19]

13:14 *O my father.* The grief of Jehoash at the impending death of Elisha shows that, like his father Jehoahaz, this Israelite king possessed some genuine spirituality. The line of Jehu had its good moments and received some reward from the Lord (10:30). However, none of this line or any other of the kings of Israel served God with all their hearts.

13:18 *he struck it three times and stopped.* Jehoash's half-hearted compliance with Elisha's instructions exposed his weak faith and illustrated God's unfavorable evaluation of his character (v. 11).

13:21 *he revived.* There was no magic in Elisha's bones; this was a demonstration of the power of God associated with His servant.

13:23 *had compassion on them.* This glimpse of the wonderful mercy of the living God is like a drink of fresh water in the midst of the sad tale of the Northern Kingdom.

12 2Ki 14:15; See ver. 14,25; 2Ki 14:9; 2Ch 25:17 **14** 2Ki 2:12 **17** 1Ki 20:26 **19** ver. 25 **22** 2Ki 8:12 **23** Ex 2:24,25; Ex 32:13 **25** ver. 18,19

Amaziah Reigns over Judah

14 IN THE second year of Joash
the son of Jehoahaz, king of Is-
rael, Amaziah the son of Joash king of
Judah became king.
2He was twenty-five years old when
he became king, and he reigned twenty-
nine years in Jerusalem. His mother's
name was Jehoaddin of Jerusalem.
3He did right in the sight of the LORD,
though not like David his father (ances-
tor). He acted in accordance with every-
thing that his father Joash had done.
4However, the high places were not
removed; the people were still sac-
rificing and burning incense on the
high places.
5As soon as the kingdom was firmly
in Amaziah's hand, he executed his
servants who had killed his father the
king. [2 Kin 12:20]
6But he did not put the sons of the
murderers to death, in compliance
with what is written in the Book of the
Law of Moses, in which the LORD com-
manded, saying, "The fathers shall not
be put to death for the sons, nor shall
the sons be put to death for the fathers;
but each shall be put to death [only] for
his own sin." [Deut 24:16]
7Amaziah killed 10,000 [men] of
Edom in the Valley of Salt, and took
Sela (rock) by war, and renamed it
Joktheel, to this day.
8Then Amaziah sent messengers to
Jehoash (Joash) the son of Jehoahaz,
the son of Jehu, king of Israel, say-
ing, "Come, let us face each other [in
combat]."
9Jehoash the king of Israel sent *word*
to Amaziah king of Judah, saying, "The
[little] thorn-bush in Lebanon sent *word*
to the [tall] cedar in Lebanon, saying,
'Give your daughter to my son as wife.'
But a wild beast that was in Lebanon
passed by and trampled the thorn-bush.
10"You have indeed defeated Edom,
and your heart has lifted you up [in
pride]. Enjoy your glory but stay at
home; for why should you plunge into
misery so that you, even you, would
fall [at my hand], and Judah with you?"
11But Amaziah would not listen. So
Jehoash king of Israel went up; and he
and Amaziah king of Judah faced each
other [in combat] at Beth-shemesh,
which belongs to Judah.
12Judah was defeated by Israel, and
every man fled to his tent.
13Then Jehoash king of Israel cap-
tured Amaziah the king of Judah, the
son of Jehoash (Joash), the son of Aha-
ziah, at Beth-shemesh, and came to Je-
rusalem and broke through the wall of
Jerusalem from the Gate of Ephraim to
the Corner Gate, 400 cubits (600 feet).
14He seized all the gold and silver
and all the utensils found in the house
(temple) of the LORD and in the trea-
suries of the king's house, as well as
hostages, and returned to Samaria.

Jeroboam II Succeeds Jehoash (Joash) in Israel

15Now the rest of the acts of Jehoash
which he did, and his might and how
he fought with Amaziah the king of

14:1 *Amaziah.* The name Amaziah means "the LORD is Mighty." He was one of the few godly kings in the kingdom of Judah.

14:4 *high places.* Like his father Joash before him (12:3), Amaziah allowed worship at the high places to continue. This practice blossomed into open idolatry in the reigns of subsequent kings (16:4; 21:3).

14:9 – 10 Pride — Amaziah's conquest of the formidable city of Sela atop the seemingly unapproachable cliffs of the Wadi Musa was a monumental accomplishment. Rather than recognize God's hand in this feat, Amaziah became proud and fell into spiritual compromise (2Ch 25:5 – 16). A little success can sometimes be a dangerous thing. Failure to acknowledge God's power leads to personal pride, and such pride leads inevitably to downfall. God will not share His glory.

14:11 *Beth-shemesh.* The name of the city means "House of the Sun," indicating that there had once been a temple to the sun god there in Canaanite times. Beth-shemesh was in the Valley of Sorek, about 15 miles west of Jerusalem. This was the town where the holy ark was taken after its "wanderings" among the Philistines.

14:17 *fifteen years.* The notice of fifteen years of

CHAPTER 14 **1** 2Ki 13:10; 2Ch 25:1 **4** 2Ki 12:3 **5** 2Ki 12:20 **6** Dt 24:16; Eze 18:4,20 **7** 2Ch 25:11; 2Sa 8:13; Ps 60, title; Jos 15:38 **8** 2Ch 25:17,18 **9** See Jdg 9:8; 1Ki 4:33 **10** Dt 8:14; 2Ch 32:25; Eze 28:2,5,17; Hab 2:4 **11** Jos 19:38; 21:16 **13** Neh 8:16; 12:39; Jer 31:38; Zec 14:10 **14** 1Ki 7:51 **15** 2Ki 13:12

Judah, are they not written in the Book of the Chronicles of the Kings of Israel?
16Jehoash slept with his fathers [in death] and was buried in Samaria with the kings of Israel. His son Jeroboam [II] became king in his place.

Azariah (Uzziah) Succeeds Amaziah in Judah

17Amaziah the son of Joash king of Judah lived for fifteen years after the death of Jehoash the son of Jehoahaz king of Israel.
18The rest of the acts of Amaziah, are they not written in the Book of the Chronicles of the Kings of Judah?
19Now a conspiracy was formed against him in Jerusalem, and Amaziah fled [south] to Lachish; but they sent [men] after him to Lachish and killed him there.
20Then they carried him on horses and he was buried at Jerusalem with his fathers in the City of David.
21And all the people of Judah took Azariah, who was [only] sixteen years old, and made him king in place of his father Amaziah.
22He built Elath and restored it to Judah after the king [his father Amaziah] slept with his fathers [in death].
23In the fifteenth year of Amaziah the son of Joash king of Judah, Jeroboam [II] the son of Joash (Jehoash) king of Israel became king in Samaria, *and reigned* forty-one years.
24He did evil in the sight of the LORD; he did not turn from all the [idolatrous] sins of Jeroboam [I] the son of Nebat, who made Israel sin.
25Jeroboam restored Israel's border from the entrance of Hamath to the Sea of the Arabah (Dead Sea), in accordance with the word of the LORD, the God of Israel, which He spoke through His servant Jonah the son of Amittai, the prophet who was from Gath-hepher.
26For the LORD saw the affliction (suffering) of Israel as very bitter; there was no one left, bond or free, nor any helper for Israel.
27But the LORD had not said that He would blot out the name of Israel from under the heavens, so He saved them by the hand of Jeroboam [II] the son of Joash [king of Israel].

Zechariah Reigns over Israel

28The rest of the acts of Jeroboam [II], all that he did, his might, how he fought, and how he recovered Damascus and Hamath for Israel, *which had belonged* to Judah, are they not written in the Book of the Chronicles of the Kings of Israel?
29Jeroboam [II] slept with his fathers [in death], even with the kings of Israel. Zechariah his son became king in his place.

Series of Kings: Azariah (Uzziah) over Judah

15 IN THE twenty-seventh year of Jeroboam [II] king of Israel, Azariah (Uzziah) the son of Amaziah king of Judah became king.
2He was sixteen years old when he became king, and he reigned fifty-two

---

life for Amaziah suggests he was released after the death of Jehoash for an additional period (782–867 BC). If so, he reigned alongside his son Azariah (or Uzziah), whose 52-year reign began in 792 BC (15:2).

14:23 *forty-one years.* Jeroboam II had a very long reign. His 41 years included 10 years as coregent with his father Jehoash (792–782 BC).

14:25 *Jonah.* Once again a prophet of God gave direction to a king. The reference to Jonah here provides the historical setting for the famous prophet (Jnh 1:1).

14:28 *his might.* The Scriptures emphasize Jeroboam's military prowess. Yet Jeroboam's might may have also been economic. The well-known Samaritan Ostraca, which may date from this period, record the delivery to Samaria of fine oil and barley produced on the royal estates.

14:29 *Zechariah.* The brief reign of Zechariah is noted in 15:8–12. He was the fourth in the line of Jehu to reign in Israel, in fulfillment of God's gracious promise to Jehu (10:30).

15:1 *Azariah.* Also called Uzziah (2Ch 26:1), this king is credited with 52 years of reign. This figure includes 10 years during which his father Amaziah was held captive (792–782 BC). The latter part of Azariah's reign was tainted by his

17 2Ch 25:25 **19** 2Ch 25:27; Jos 10:31 **22** 2Ki 16:6; 2Ch 26:2 **25** Nu 13:21; 34:8; Dt 3:17; Jnh 1:1; Mt 12:39,40; Jos 19:13 **26** 2Ki 13:4; Dt 32:36 **27** 2Ki 13:5 **28** 2Sa 8:6; 1Ki 11:24; 2Ch 8:3 **CHAPTER 15** **1** 2Ki 14:21; 2Ch 26:1,3,4; 2Ch 26:1

years in Jerusalem. His mother's name
was Jecoliah of Jerusalem.
3 He did right in the sight of the LORD,
in accordance with all that his father
Amaziah had done.
4 Only [the altars on] the high plac-
es were not removed; the people still
sacrificed and burned incense on the
high places [instead of worshiping God
at the temple].
5 And the LORD struck (afflicted) the
king, and he was a leper until the day
of his death, and lived in a separate
house. Jotham the king's son was in
charge of the household, judging the
people of the land. [2 Chr 26:16–21]
6 Now the rest of Azariah's acts, and
everything that he did, are they not
written in the Book of the Chronicles
of the Kings of Judah?
7 Azariah slept with his fathers [in
death], and they buried him with his
fathers in the City of David. His son
Jotham became king in his place.

Zechariah over Israel

8 In the thirty-eighth year of Azariah
king of Judah, Zechariah the son of
Jeroboam [II] became king over Israel
in Samaria for six months.
9 He did evil in the sight of the LORD,
just as his fathers had done; he did not
turn from the sins of Jeroboam [I] the
son of Nebat, who made Israel sin.
10 But Shallum the son of Jabesh con-
spired against Zechariah and struck
and killed him in the presence of the
people and reigned in his place.
11 Now the rest of the acts of Zech-
ariah, behold, they are written in the
Book of the Chronicles of the Kings
of Israel.
12 This is [the fulfillment of] the word
of the LORD which He spoke to Jehu,
saying, "Your sons (descendants) shall
sit on the throne of Israel to the fourth
generation." And so it came to pass.
[2 Kin 10:30]
13 Shallum the son of Jabesh became
king in the thirty-ninth year of Uzzi-
ah (Azariah) king of Judah, and he
reigned one month in Samaria.
14 For Menahem the son of Gadi went
up from Tirzah and came to Samaria,
and struck and killed Shallum the son
of Jabesh in Samaria and became king
in his place.
15 The rest of Shallum's acts, and his
conspiracy which he made, they are
written in the Book of the Chronicles
of the Kings of Israel.
16 Then Menahem struck [the town
of] Tiphsah and all who were in it and
its borders from Tirzah; [he attacked
it] because they did not surrender *to
him;* so he struck it and ripped up all
the women there who were pregnant.

Menahem over Israel

17 In the thirty-ninth year of Aza-
riah king of Judah, Menahem the son
of Gadi became king over Israel, *and
reigned* ten years in Samaria.
18 He did evil in the sight of the LORD;
for all his days he did not turn from the
sins of Jeroboam the son of Nebat, who
caused Israel to sin.
19 Pul, [Tiglath-pileser III] king of As-
syria, came against the land [of Israel],
and Menahem gave Pul a thousand

---

intrusion into the priestly office (2Ch 26:16 – 19), an act that resulted in his being stricken with leprosy (v. 5). This condition put his son Jotham on the throne to rule with him and handle public matters relative to the royal office. The nature of Jotham's duties (v. 5), the assigning of a full 52 years of reign to Azariah, and Isaiah's dating of his call to the year of Azariah's (or Uzziah's) death (Isa 6:1) may indicate that Azariah retained the power of the throne until the end.

15:5 *leper.* The events that brought about this affliction are described in 2Ch 26:16 – 21.

15:12 *fourth generation.* Jehu had been promised a continuing posterity into the fourth generation as a reward for carrying out his divine commission (10:30), but after the death of Zachariah in 752 BC, Israel plunged into a period of degeneracy, bloody conspiracies and international intrigue that would bring about its demise in 722 BC.

15:17 *Menahem.* This wicked king came into power by assassination and established his authority by brutal acts against humanity. Ironically, his name means "comforter."

15:19 *Pul.* Pul is a second Babylonian name for the Assyrian king Tiglath-pileser III (745 – 727 BC;

4 ver. 35; 2Ki 12:3; 14:4 **5** 2Ch 26:19-21; Lev 13:46 **7** 2Ch 26:23 **10** Am 7:9 **12** 2Ki 10:30 **13** Mt 1:8,9 **14** 1Ki 14:17 **16** 1Ki 4:24; 2Ki 8:12 **19** 1Ch 5:26; Isa 66:19; Hos 8:9; 2Ki 14:5

talents of silver [as a bribe], so that he might help him to strengthen his control of the kingdom.

20 Menahem exacted the money from Israel, from all the wealthy, influential men, fifty shekels of silver from each man to give to the king of Assyria. So the king of Assyria turned back and did not stay there in the land.

21 Now the rest of Menahem's acts, and everything that he did, are they not written in the Book of the Chronicles of the Kings of Israel?

22 And Menahem slept with his fathers [in death]; his son Pekahiah became king in his place.

Pekahiah over Israel

23 In the fiftieth year of Azariah king of Judah, Pekahiah the son of Menahem became king over Israel, *and reigned* two years in Samaria.

24 He did evil in the sight of the LORD; he did not turn from the [idolatrous] sins of Jeroboam [I] the son of Nebat, who made Israel sin.

25 But Pekah the son of Remaliah, his officer, conspired against Pekahiah and struck him in Samaria, in the citadel of the king's house, with Argob and Arieh; and with Pekah were fifty Gileadites. So he killed Pekahiah and became king in his place.

26 Now the rest of the acts of Pekahiah, all that he did, they are written in the Book of the Chronicles of the Kings of Israel.

Pekah over Israel

27 In the fifty-second year of Azariah king of Judah, Pekah the son of Remaliah became king over Israel, *and reigned* twenty years in Samaria.

28 He did evil in the sight of the LORD; he did not turn from the [idolatrous] sins of Jeroboam [I] the son of Nebat, who made Israel sin.

29 In the days of Pekah king of Israel, Tiglath-pileser king of Assyria came and took Ijon, Abel-beth-maacah, Janoah, Kedesh, Hazor, Gilead, and Galilee, all the land of [the tribe of] Naphtali, and he carried the people captive to Assyria.

30 Hoshea the son of Elah conspired against Pekah the son of Remaliah [of Israel]; he struck and killed him, and became king in his place in the twentieth year of Jotham the son of Uzziah [king of Judah].

31 Now the rest of Pekah's acts, and everything that he did, they are written in the Book of the Chronicles of Israel's Kings.

Jotham over Judah

32 In the second year of Pekah the son of Remaliah king of Israel, Jotham the son of Uzziah king of Judah became king.

1Ch 5:26). Although he came to the throne as a usurper from the ranks of the military, he would prove a competent king. Under Tiglath-pileser III and his successors, Assyria became the dominant power in the Middle East for well over a century (747 – 612 BC).

15:23 *Pekahiah.* Pekahiah means "the Lord has opened the eyes." After an evil reign of two years, a usurper "closed his eyes" for him.

15:25 Murder — Sometimes a corrupt leader needs to be taken out of power, but when this is done by coup and murder, the new leader ends up being just as bad as the old one. He lives in fear that someone will do the same thing to him; in an attempt to keep his position, he will exercise the same control and perpetrate the same kind of abuses as the leader he deposed. A vicious cycle is begun, as we can see from the succession of murders and new kings in Israel. Anytime leadership changes through conniving and coup, even if actual murder is not part of the picture, problems in trust and confidence will result.

15:27 *Pekah.* Because Hoshea's nine-year reign (17:1) began in 732 BC, Pekah's twenty years must have included a time of kingship in his own district during the unsettled days of Shallum, Menahem, and Pekahiah (752 – 740 BC). Apparently Pekah rode the crest of anti-Assyrian sentiment.

15:30 *Hoshea . . . conspired.* The annals of Tiglath-pileser III record Hoshea's heavy tribute and the Assyrian king's claim that he himself set the new Israelite king in office.

15:32 *Jotham.* Jotham's reign was partly righteous. After the purge of Ahaziah and Athaliah (9:27 – 29; 11:13 – 16), the kings of Judah who reigned in relative righteousness were Joash (12:2 – 3), Amaziah (14:3 – 4), and Azariah (15:3 – 4).

27 Isa 7:1 **29** 1Ch 5:26; Isa 9:1; 1Ki 15:20 **32** 2Ch 27:1

33 When he was twenty-five years
old, he became king [over Judah], and
he reigned sixteen years in Jerusa-
lem. His mother's name was Jerusha
daughter of Zadok.
34 He did what was right in the sight
of the LORD, in accordance with every-
thing that his father Uzziah had done.
35 Only [the altars on] the high plac-
es were not removed; the people still
sacrificed and burned incense on the
high places [rather than in the temple].
He built the upper gate of the house of
the LORD.
36 Now the rest of the acts of Jotham,
and all that he did, are they not writ-
ten in the Book of the Chronicles of
Judah's Kings?
37 In those days the LORD began send-
ing Rezin the king of Aram (Syria)
and [Israel's king] Pekah the son of
Remaliah against Judah.
38 Jotham slept with his fathers [in
death], and was buried with them in
the City of David his father (ancestor).
Ahaz his son became king in his place.

Ahaz Reigns over Judah

16 IN THE seventeenth year of Pe-
kah the son of Remaliah, Ahaz
the son of Jotham, king of Judah, be-
came king.
2 Ahaz was twenty years old when he
became king, and he reigned sixteen
years in Jerusalem. He did not do what
was right in the sight of the LORD his
God, as his father (ancestor) David
had done.
3 Instead he walked in the way of the
[idolatrous] kings of Israel, and even
made his son pass through the fire [as
a human sacrifice], in accordance with
the repulsive [and idolatrous] practices
of the [pagan] nations whom the LORD
drove out before the Israelites.
4 He also sacrificed and burned in-
cense on the high places and on the
hills and under every green tree.
5 Then Rezin the king of Aram (Syr-
ia) and Pekah the son of Remaliah,
king of Israel, came up to Jerusalem
to wage war. They besieged Ahaz, but
could not overcome *and* conquer him.
6 At that time Rezin king of Aram
recovered Elath [in Edom] for Aram,
and drove the Jews away from it. The
Arameans came to Elath, and live
there to this day.

Ahaz Seeks Help of Assyria

7 So Ahaz sent messengers to Tiglath-
pileser king of Assyria, saying, "I am
your servant and son. Come up and
rescue me from the hand of the kings
of Aram and of Israel, who are rising
up against me."
8 And Ahaz took the silver and gold
that was found in the house of the
LORD and in the treasuries of the king's
house, and sent a gift to the king of
Assyria.
9 So the king of Assyria listened to
him; and he went up against Damas-
cus and captured it, and carried *its
people* away into exile to Kir, and put
Rezin [king of Aram] to death.

Damascus Falls

10 Now King Ahaz went to Damascus
to meet Tiglath-pileser the king of As-

A positive righteousness would be modeled by Hezekiah (18:3 – 6) and again by Josiah (22:2).
16:1 *Ahaz . . . became king.* The seventeenth year of Pekah was 736 – 735 BC. Ahaz's 16-year reign apparently ended in 720 BC. If so, like Jotham before him, Ahaz must have lived on another four years after giving up his rule. Hezekiah's first year of independent rule began in 715 BC, 14 years before Sennacherib's invasion of Judah and his siege of Jerusalem in 701 BC.
16:3 *made his son pass through the fire.* According to the author of Chronicles, this rite was connected with the Baal worship practiced in the valley of the son of Hinnom (2Ch 28:2 – 3). Ahaz was an apostate who personally led his people in the religious worship practices of Canaan.
16:7 *sent messengers . . . king of Assyria.* Tiglath-pileser's records list the tribute of both Hoshea and Ahaz.
16:10 – 16 Vanity — The king of Israel was commanded to pattern his reign according to God's Word, but Ahaz apparently thought his

34 ver. 3 **35** ver. 4; 2Ch 27:3 **37** 2Ki 16:5; Isa 7:1; ver. 27 **CHAPTER 16** **1** 2Ch 28:1 **3** Lev 18:21; 2Ch 28:3; Ps 106:37,38; Dt 12:31 **4** Dt 12:2; 1Ki 14:23 **5** Isa 7:1,4 **6** 2Ki 14:22 **7** 2Ki 15:29 **8** 2Ki 12:18; See 2Ch 28:21 **9** Foretold; Am 1:5

syria, and saw the *pagan* altar which was at Damascus. Then King Ahaz sent a model of the altar to Urijah the priest along with a [detailed] pattern for all its construction.
[11]So Urijah the priest built an altar; in accordance with everything that King Ahaz had sent from Damascus, that is how Urijah the priest made it before King Ahaz returned from Damascus.
[12]When the king came from Damascus, he saw the altar; then the king approached the altar and offered [sacrifices] on it,
[13]and burned his burnt offering and his grain offering, and poured out his drink offering, and sprinkled the blood of his peace offerings on the altar.
[14]He brought the bronze altar, which was before the LORD, from the front of the house (temple), from between the [new] altar and the house of the LORD, and put it on the north side of the [new] altar.
[15]Then King Ahaz commanded Urijah the priest, saying, "Upon the great [new] altar, burn the morning burnt offering and the evening grain offering, and the king's burnt offering and his grain offering, with the burnt offering of all the people of the land and their grain offering and their drink offerings; and sprinkle on the new altar all the blood of the burnt offering and all the blood of the sacrifice. But the [old] bronze altar shall be kept for me to use to examine the sacrifices."
[16]Urijah the priest acted in accordance with everything that King Ahaz commanded.
[17]Then King Ahaz cut away the frames of the basin stands [in the temple], and removed the basin from [each of] them; and he took down the [large] Sea from the bronze oxen which were under it, and put it on a plastered stone floor.
[18]He removed from the house of the LORD the covered way for the Sabbath which they had built in the house, and the outer entrance of the king, because of the king of Assyria [who might confiscate them].

Hezekiah Reigns over Judah

[19]Now the rest of the acts of Ahaz, are they not written in the Book of the Chronicles of the Kings of Judah?
[20]So Ahaz slept with his fathers [in death] and was buried with his fathers in the City of David; and his son Hezekiah became king in his place.

Hoshea Reigns over Israel

17 IN THE twelfth year of Ahaz king of Judah, Hoshea the son of Elah became king over Israel in Samaria, *and reigned* for nine years.
[2]He did evil in the sight of the LORD, but not as the kings of Israel who came before him.
[3]Shalmaneser [V] king of Assyria came up against him, and Hoshea became his servant and paid him tribute (money).
[4]But the king of Assyria discovered a conspiracy in Hoshea, who sent messengers to So, king of Egypt, and offered no tribute to the king of Assyria, as *he had done* year by year; therefore the king of Assyria arrested him and bound him in prison.

---

own ideas were better. Once the Word of God has been set aside, there is no stopping point for presumptuous spirituality and immoral activities. Such practices may be aesthetically and humanly pleasing, but Jesus designated them as vain worship because they are based upon precepts and traditions of men, rather than on God's holy and sufficient Word (Mt 15:7–9).

16:18 *because of the king of Assyria.* Ahaz was more interested in imitating the foreign king than in following God. His use of the altar to make sacrifices to God and his many other religious innovations underscored Ahaz's essential paganism (2Ch 28:2–4,22–25). He went so far in his apostasy as to shut the doors of the temple (2Ch 28:24).

17:1 *twelfth year.* Hoshea became king in 732 BC, so the twelve years of Ahaz indicate a period of coregency with his father Jotham.

17:3 *Shalmaneser.* Shalmaneser V succeeded Tiglath-pileser III as king of Assyria in 727 BC.

12 2Ch 26:16,19 **14** 2Ch 4:1 **15** Ex 29:39-41 **17** 2Ch 28:24; 1Ki 7:27,28; 1Ki 7:23,25 **20** 2Ch 28:27
CHAPTER 17 **3** 2Ki 18:9

5Then the king of Assyria invaded
all the land [of Israel] and went up
to Samaria and besieged it for three
years.

Israel Captive

6In the ninth year of Hoshea, the
king of Assyria took Samaria and car-
ried [the people of] Israel into exile to
Assyria, and settled them in Halah and
in Habor, by the river of Gozan, and in
the cities of the Medes.

Why Israel Fell

7Now this came about because the
Israelites had sinned against the LORD
their God, who had brought them up
from the land of Egypt, from under
the hand of Pharaoh king of Egypt;
and they had feared [and worshiped]
other gods
8and walked in the customs of the
[pagan] nations whom the LORD had
driven out before the sons (descen-
dants) of Israel, and *in the pagan cus-
toms of* the kings of Israel which they
had introduced.
9The Israelites ascribed things to
the LORD their God which were not
true. They built for themselves high
places [of worship] in all their towns,
from [the lonely] lookout tower to the
[populous] fortified city.
10They set up for themselves *sacred*
pillars (memorial stones) and Asherim
on every high hill and under every
green tree.
11There they burned incense on all
the high places, just as the [pagan]
nations whom the LORD had deported
before them; and they did evil *and* con-
temptible things, provoking the LORD
[to anger].
12And they served idols, of which the
LORD had said to them, "You shall not
do this thing."
13Yet the LORD warned Israel and
Judah through all His prophets and ev-
ery seer, saying, "Turn from your evil
ways and keep My commandments
and My statutes, in accordance with
all the Law which I commanded your
fathers, and which I sent to you by My
servants the prophets."
14However they did not listen, but
stiffened their necks as did their fa-
thers who did not believe (trust in, rely
on, remain steadfast to) the LORD their
God.
15They rejected His statutes and His
covenant which He made with their
fathers, as well as His warnings that he
gave them. And they followed vanity
[that is, false gods, idols] and became
vain (empty-headed). They followed
the [pagan practices of the] nations
which surrounded them, although the

17:7 *Israelites had sinned.* The reason for the fall of Samaria and the end of the Northern Kingdom was clearly its spiritual failure; they had turned away from the living God.

17:14–18 Israel's Disobedience — These verses are a good summary of the spiritual departure from God that led to Israel's eventual downfall. The people of Israel didn't listen and three specific results are recorded:

1. The Israelites refused to believe. All the fulfilled promises, all the history of God's saving acts were simply ignored. It didn't matter what God had done. They had ears to hear and eyes to see, yet failed to do so.

2. They rejected God's laws and covenant. They willfully turned their backs on the way of living that God had directed them toward.

3. They worshiped idols. They actually worshiped anything and everything but what they were instructed to worship. In spite of God's clear mandate to them to have no other gods before Him, the Israelites were easily influenced by any culture they came in contact with.

The common denominator here is the will. This was willful rebellion. We are no different. Every day each of us, by an act of our own will, does something disobedient. We worry unnecessarily, we have fears for aspects of our lives that we know God has promised to protect and care for. Sometimes we simply don't care what God has said. We'd rather do what we want because it feels good or because His way is too difficult. We are truly sinners in need of a forgiving God.

---

5 2Ki 18:9 **6** 2Ki 18:10,11; Hos 13:16, Foretold; Lev 26:32,33; Dt 28:36,64; 29:27,28; 1Ch 5:26 **8** Lev 18:3; Dt 18:9; 2Ki 16:3 **9** 2Ki 18:8 **10** 1Ki 14:23; Isa 57:5; Ex 34:13; Dt 16:21; Mic 5:14; Dt 12:2; 2Ki 16:4 **12** Ex 20:3,4; Lev 26:1; Dt 5:7,8; Dt 4:19 **13** 1Sa 9:9; Jer 18:11; 25:5; 35:15 **14** Dt 31:27; Pr 29:1 **15** Dt 29:25; Dt 32:21; 1Ki 16:13; 1Co 8:4; Ps 115:8; Ro 1:21; Dt 12:30,31

LORD had commanded that they were
not to do as they did.
[16]They abandoned all the command-
ments of the LORD their God and made
for themselves cast images of two
calves; and they made an Asherah
[idol] and worshiped all the [starry]
host of heaven and served Baal.
[17]They made their sons and their
daughters pass through the fire [as hu-
man sacrifices], and used divination [to
foretell the future] and enchantments;
and they sold themselves to do evil in
the sight of the LORD, provoking Him
to anger.
[18]Therefore the LORD was very angry
with Israel and removed them from
His sight; none [of the tribes] was left
except the tribe of Judah.
[19]Judah did not keep the command-
ments of the LORD their God either, but
walked in the customs which Israel
introduced.
[20]So the LORD rejected all the descen-
dants of Israel (Jacob) and [repeatedly]
afflicted them and handed them over
to plunderers, until He had cast them
out of His sight.
[21]When He had torn Israel from
the [royal] house of David, they made

17:21 *Jeroboam drove Israel away from following the LORD.* Jeroboam had initiated the false worship that set the standard for all of Israel's idolatrous activities. The worship of the calves at Dan and Bethel, and Israel's fascination with Baal worship (1Ki 12:28–29; 16:32–33), are repeatedly cited as the chief causes of Israel's spiritual defeat and political collapse.

16 Ex 32:8; 1Ki 12:28; 1Ki 14:15; 1Ki 16:31; 22:53; 2Ki 11:18 **17** Lev 18:21; 2Ki 16:3; Eze 23:37; Dt 18:10; 1Ki 21:20 **18** 1Ki 11:13,32 **19** Jer 3:8 **20** 2Ki 13:3; 15:29 **21** 1Ki 11:11,31; 1Ki 12:20,28

THE RISE OF THE KINGDOM OF ASSYRIA

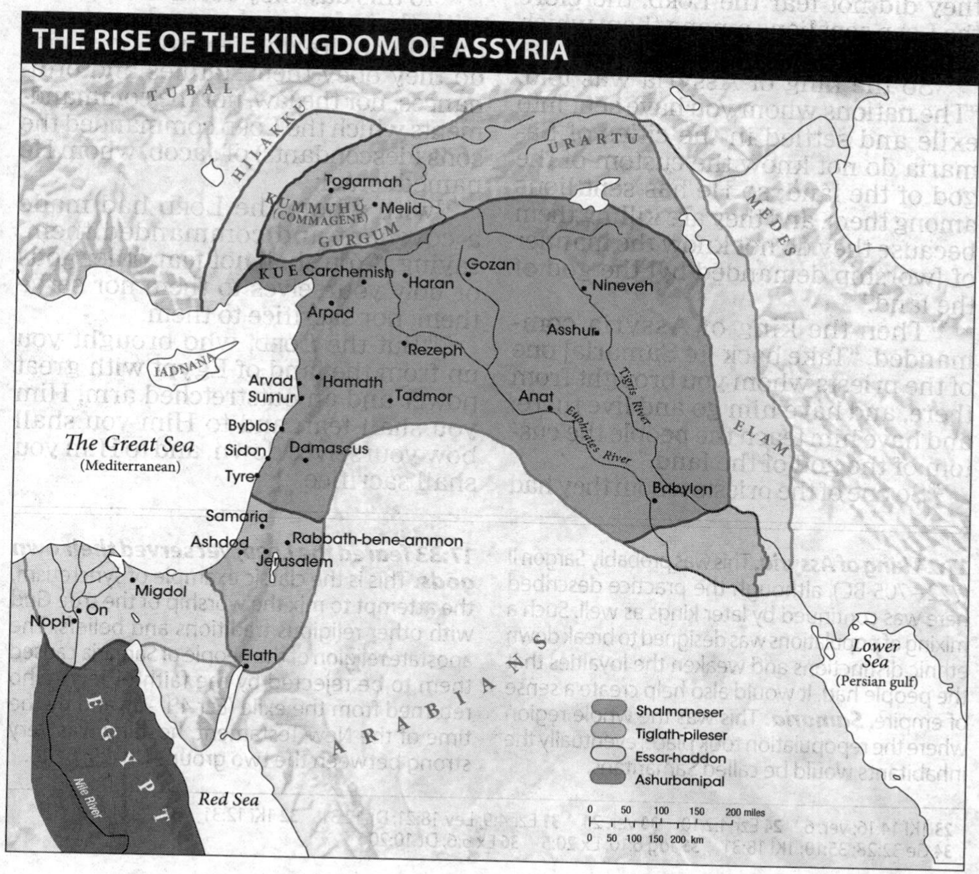

Jeroboam the son of Nebat king. And Jeroboam drove Israel away from following the LORD and made them commit a great sin.

22 For the Israelites walked in all the [idolatrous] sins which Jeroboam committed; they did not turn from them

23 until the LORD removed Israel from His sight, just as He had foretold through all His servants the prophets. So Israel went into exile from their own land to Assyria to this day [the date of this writing].

Cities of Israel Filled with Strangers

24 The king of Assyria brought *men* from Babylon and from Cuthah and from Avva and from Hamath and Sepharvaim, and settled them in the cities of Samaria in place of the sons (people) of Israel. They took possession of Samaria and lived in its cities.

25 Now when they began to live there, they did not fear the LORD; therefore the LORD sent lions among them which killed some of them.

26 So the king of Assyria was told, "The nations whom you have sent into exile and settled in the cities of Samaria do not know the custom of the god of the land; so He has sent lions among them, and they are killing them because they do not know the manner of [worship demanded by] the god of the land."

27 Then the king of Assyria commanded, "Take back [to Samaria] one of the priests whom you brought from there, and have him go and live there; and have him teach the people the custom of the god of the land."

28 So one of the priests whom they had exiled from Samaria came [back] and lived in Bethel and taught them how they should fear [and worship] the LORD.

29 But every nation still made gods of its own and put them in the houses (shrines) of the high places which the Samaritans had made, every nation in the cities where they lived.

30 The men of Babylon made Succoth-benoth, the men of Cuth made Nergal, the men of Hamath made Ashima,

31 the Avvites made Nibhaz and Tartak; and the Sepharvites burned their children in the fire to Adrammelech and Anammelech, the gods of Sepharvaim.

32 They also feared the LORD and appointed from among themselves priests of the high places, who sacrificed for them in the houses of the high places.

33 They feared the LORD, yet served their own gods, following the custom of the nations from among whom they had been sent into exile.

34 To this day they act in accordance with their former [pagan] customs: they do not [really] fear the LORD, nor do they obey their statutes and ordinances, nor the law, nor the commandments which the LORD commanded the sons (descendants) of Jacob, whom He named Israel;

35 with whom the LORD had made a covenant and commanded them, saying, "You shall not fear other gods or bow yourselves to them nor serve them, nor sacrifice to them.

36 "But the LORD, who brought you up from the land of Egypt with great power and an outstretched arm, Him you shall fear, and to Him you shall bow yourselves down, and to Him you shall sacrifice.

17:24 *king of Assyria.* This was probably Sargon II (722 – 705 BC), although the practice described here was continued by later kings as well. Such a mixing of populations was designed to break down ethnic distinctions and weaken the loyalties that the people had. It would also help create a sense of empire. ***Samaria.*** This was the whole region where the repopulation took place; eventually the inhabitants would be called Samaritans.

17:33 *feared the LORD, yet served their own gods.* This is the classic example of syncretism, the attempt to mix the worship of the true God with other religious traditions and beliefs. The apostate religion of the people of Samaria caused them to be rejected by the faithful Jews who returned from the exile (Ezr 4:1 – 5), and by the time of the New Testament, hostility was very strong between the two groups (Jn 4:9; 8:48).

23 1Ki 14:16; ver. 6 **24** Ezr 4:2,10 **30** ver. 24 **31** Ezr 4:9; Lev 18:21; Dt 12:31 **32** 1Ki 12:31 **33** Zep 1:5 **34** Ge 32:28; 35:10; 1Ki 18:31 **35** Jdg 6:10; Ex 20:5 **36** Ex 6:6; Dt 10:20

37 "The statutes and the ordinances and the law and the commandment which He wrote for you [by the hand of Moses], you shall observe and do forever. You shall not fear (worship, serve) other gods.

38 "The covenant that I have made with you, you shall not forget; you shall not fear other gods.

39 "But the LORD your God you shall fear [and worship]; then He will rescue you from the hands of all your enemies."

40 However, they did not listen, but they acted in accordance with their former custom.

41 So these nations [superficially] feared the LORD; they also served their idols, as did their children and their children's children, just as their fathers did, so do they to this day [the date of this writing].

Hezekiah Reigns over Judah

18 NOW IT came about in the third year of Hoshea the son of Elah king of Israel, Hezekiah the son of Ahaz king of Judah became king.

2 He was twenty-five years old when he became king, and he reigned twenty-nine years in Jerusalem. His mother's name was Abi the daughter of Zechariah.

3 Hezekiah did right in the sight of the LORD, in accordance with everything that David his father (ancestor) had done.

4 He removed the high places [of pagan worship], broke down the images (memorial stones) and cut down the Asherim. He also crushed to pieces the bronze serpent that Moses had made, for until those days the Israelites had burned incense to it; and it was called Nehushtan [a bronze sculpture]. [Num 21:8]

5 Hezekiah trusted in *and* relied confidently on the LORD, the God of Israel; so that after him there was no one like him among all the kings of Judah, nor *among those* who were before him.

6 For he clung to the LORD; he did not turn away from [faithfully] following Him, but he kept His commandments, which the LORD had commanded Moses.

Hezekiah Victorious

7 And the LORD was with Hezekiah; he was successful wherever he went. And he rebelled against the king of Assyria and refused to serve him.

8 He defeated the Philistines as far as Gaza [the most distant city] and its borders, from the [isolated] lookout tower to the [populous] fortified city.

9 Now in the fourth year of King Hezekiah, which was the seventh of Hoshea the son of Elah king of Israel,

---

18:1 *the third year of Hoshea.* The 29 years of Hezekiah's reign thus included a period of coregency with his father Ahaz before he ruled independently (715 – 699 BC). The name Hezekiah means "the Lord has strengthened."

18:3 *Hezekiah did right in the sight of the LORD.* Hezekiah was the first king since David who served the Lord with all his heart.

18:4 *high places.* Consistently, the kings who preceded Hezekiah are criticized by the author for not destroying the high places (15:34 – 35). While there were traditions of worship of the true God at these locations, far too often they became sites for the licentious worship of Baal and Asherah. Hezekiah's reforms included not only the destruction of the pagan cult objects introduced in the days of his apostate father Ahaz, but the bronze serpent that had been preserved since the days of Moses (2Ch 29 – 31). Symbols all too easily can be made into objects of veneration.

18:5 *no one like him.* Hezekiah's faith was unparalleled by any other king who had preceded him after the time of David; Josiah's adherence to the law would be extolled in a similar manner (23:25).

18:6 Obedience — The obedience of Hezekiah provides a powerful lesson for all of God's people. He "clung" to the Lord, staying true to God and His commandments. He must have faced strong opposition as he eliminated practices which had been going on for generations, and destroyed objects which had long been considered sacred, but he knew that God's approval was more important than human approbation. In the same way, we must be willing to serve God before we please those around us.

37 Dt 5:32 **38** Dt 4:23 **41** ver. 32,33 **CHAPTER 18** **1** 2Ch 28:27; 29:1 **4** 2Ch 31:1; Nu 21:9 **5** 2Ki 19:10; Job 13:15; Ps 13:5; 2Ki 23:25 **6** Dt 10:20; Jos 23:8 **7** 2Ch 15:2; 1Sa 18:5,14; Ps 60:12; 2Ki 16:7 **8** 1Ch 4:41; Isa 14:29; 2Ki 17:9 **9** 2Ki 17:3

Shalmaneser the king of Assyria went
up against Samaria and besieged it.
10 At the end of three years they cap-
tured it; in the sixth year of Hezekiah,
which was the ninth year of Hoshea
the king of Israel, Samaria was taken.
11 Then the king of Assyria sent Is-
rael into exile to Assyria, and put them
in Halah, and on the Habor, the river
of [the city of] Gozan, and in the cities
of the Medes,
12 because they did not obey the voice
of the LORD their God, but broke His
covenant, everything that Moses the
servant of the LORD had commanded;
and they would not listen nor do it.

Invasion of Judah

13 In the fourteenth year of King Hez-
ekiah, Sennacherib king of Assyria
went up against all the fortified cities
of Judah [except Jerusalem] and cap-
tured them.
14 Then Hezekiah king of Judah sent
word to the king of Assyria at Lachish,
saying, "I have done wrong. Withdraw
from me; whatever you impose on me
I will bear." So the king of Assyria
imposed on Hezekiah king of Judah [a
tribute tax of] three hundred talents of
silver and thirty talents of gold.
15 Hezekiah gave him all the silver
that was found in the house (temple)
of the LORD, and in the treasuries of
the king's house (palace).
16 At that time Hezekiah cut away
the gold framework from the doors of
the temple of the LORD and from the
doorposts which he had overlaid, and
gave it to the king of Assyria.
17 Then the king of Assyria sent the
Tartan and the Rab-saris and the Rab-
shakeh [his highest officials] with a
large army, from Lachish to King Hez-
ekiah at Jerusalem. They went up and
came to Jerusalem, and when they
went up and arrived, they stood by
the aqueduct of the upper pool, which
is on the road of the Fuller's Field.
[2 Chr 32:9–19; Is 36:1–22]
18 When they called for the king,
Eliakim the son of Hilkiah, who was
in charge of the [king's] household,
and Shebna the scribe, and Joah the
son of Asaph the secretary went out
to [meet] them.
19 Then the Rabshakeh said to them,
"Say to Hezekiah, 'Thus says the great
king, the king of Assyria, "What is
[the reason for] this confidence that
you have?
20 "You say (but they are only empty
words) '*I have* counsel and strength for
the war.' Now on whom do you rely,
that you have rebelled against me?
21 "Now pay attention: you are rely-
ing on Egypt, on that staff of crushed
reed; if a man leans on it, it will *only*
go into his hand and pierce it. So is
Pharaoh king of Egypt to all who trust
and rely on him.
22 "But if you tell me, 'We trust in *and*
rely on the LORD our God,' is it not He
whose high places and altars Hezekiah
has removed, and has said to Judah
and Jerusalem, 'You shall worship
[only] before this altar in Jerusalem'?
23 "Now then, make a bargain with
my lord the king of Assyria, and I will
give you two thousand horses, if on
your part you can put riders on them.
24 "How then can you drive back *even*
one official of the least of my master's
servants, when you rely on Egypt for
chariots and horsemen?

18:13 *fourteenth year.* Hezekiah's fourteenth year of sole rule was 701 BC. The details of the generally rebellious situation that provoked Sennacherib to invade the western portion of his empire are recounted in his annals, where Hezekiah is particularly mentioned for his involvement in the whole affair.

18:17 *Tartan ... Rab-saris ... Rabshakeh.* These titles suggest persons of high station in Assyria.

18:20 *on whom do you rely?* Perhaps Hezekiah's reputation for trusting in God was already widely known (v. 5). Trusting became the focal point of the Assyrian's psychological warfare (vv. 19–22,24–30).

18:21 *crushed reed.* Actually, Sennacherib's warning against confidence in Egypt was well taken, the point having been made previously by Isaiah (Isa 30:3–5; 31:1–3).

10 2Ki 17:6 **11** 2Ki 17:6; 1Ch 5:26 **13** 2Ch 32:1; Isa 36:1 **15** 2Ki 16:8 **17** Isa 7:3 **19** 2Ch 32:10 **21** Eze 29:6,7 **22** ver. 4; 2Ch 31:1; 32:12

[25]"Now have I come up against this
place to destroy it without the LORD's
approval? The LORD said to me, 'Go up
against this land and destroy it.' " ' "
[26]Then Eliakim the son of Hilkiah,
and Shebna and Joah, said to the Rab-
shakeh, "Please speak to your servants
in the Aramaic (Syrian) language, be-
cause we understand it; and do not
speak with us in the Judean (Hebrew)
language in the hearing of the people
who are on the wall."
[27]But the Rabshakeh said to them,
"Has my master sent me *only* to your
master and to you to say these things?
Has he not sent me to the men who sit
on the wall, [who are doomed by the
siege] to eat their own excrement and
drink their own urine along with you?"
[28]Then the Rabshakeh stood and
shouted out with a loud voice in Judean
(Hebrew), "Hear the word of the great
king, the king of Assyria.
[29]"Thus says the king, 'Do not let
Hezekiah deceive you, for he will not
be able to rescue you from my hand;
[30]nor let Hezekiah make you trust
in *and* rely on the LORD, saying, "The
LORD will certainly rescue us, and this
city [of Jerusalem] will not be given
into the hand of the king of Assyria."
[31]'Do not listen to Hezekiah, for thus
says the king of Assyria: "Surrender
to me and come out to [meet] me, and
every man may eat from his own vine
and fig tree, and every man may drink
the waters of his own well,
[32]until I come and take you away to
a land like your own land, a land of
grain and new wine, a land of bread
and vineyards, a land of olive trees and
honey, so that you may live and not
die." Do not listen to Hezekiah when
he misleads *and* incites you, saying,
"The LORD will rescue us!"
[33]'Has any one of the gods of the
nations ever rescued his land from the
hand of the king of Assyria?
[34]'Where are the gods of Hamath
and Arpad [in Aram]? Where are the
gods of Sepharvaim, Hena, and Ivvah
[in the valley of the Euphrates]? Have
they rescued Samaria (Israel's capital)
from my hand?
[35]'Who among all the gods of the
lands have rescued their lands from
my hand, that the LORD would rescue
Jerusalem from my hand?' "
[36]But the people kept silent and did
not answer him, for the king had com-
manded, "Do not answer him."
[37]Then Eliakim the son of Hilkiah,
who was in charge of the [royal] house-
hold, and Shebna the scribe and Joah
the son of Asaph the secretary, came
to Hezekiah with their clothes torn [in
grief and despair] and told him what
the Rabshakeh had said.

Isaiah Encourages Hezekiah

19 WHEN KING Hezekiah heard it,
he tore his clothes and he covered
himself with sackcloth and went into the
house (temple) of the LORD. [Is 37:1–13]
[2]Then he sent Eliakim who was in
charge of his household, Shebna the

18:25 *The LORD said to me.* The Assyrians may have been aware of prophecies concerning the judgment of Judah and Jerusalem and Assyria's own role as God's avengers (Isa 10:5 – 11). The remark was intended to introduce stark terror into the hearts of the people of Jerusalem (2Ch 32:18) by pointing out that now even their God was against them.

18:25 Self-righteousness — The Assyrians were God's instrument for punishing Israel (Isa 10:5 – 10), but this fact was not due to any righteousness or virtue on Assyria's part. Rather, their attitude was blasphemous and proud (19:22). The lesson for the powerful king of Assyria is the lesson for kings, nations, and all individuals: no one may boast before the Lord (1Co 1:29).

18:33 *the gods of the nations.* Rabshekah's assertion that none of the gods of the nations who had opposed Assyria had withstood the Assyrian king is another aspect of the continued psychological warfare and evidence of Rabshekah's awareness of Isaiah's prophetic words (Isa 10:7 – 11).

19:2 *Isaiah.* The ministry of the great prophet Isaiah had begun in the year that Uzziah (or Azariah) died (Isa 6:1), nearly four decades earlier (740 BC). Once Isaiah had sought out Judah's godless King Ahaz to minister to him (Isa 7:3); now the prophet was being sought by the godly Hezekiah

---

29 2Ch 32:15 **32** Dt 8:7,8 **33** 2Ki 19:12; 2Ch 32:14; Isa 10:10,11 **34** 2Ki 19:13 **35** Da 3:15 **37** Isa 33:7
CHAPTER 19 **1** Isa 37:1 **2** Lk 3:4

scribe, and the elders of the priests, covered with sackcloth, to Isaiah the prophet the son of Amoz.
[3]They said to him, "Thus says Hezekiah, 'This is a day of distress *and* anxiety, of punishment and humiliation; for children have come to [the time of their] birth and there is no strength to rescue them.
[4]'It may be that the LORD your God will hear all the words of the Rabshakeh, whom his master the king of Assyria has sent to taunt *and* defy the living God, and will rebuke the words which the LORD your God has heard. So offer a prayer for the remnant [of His people] that is left [in Judah].' "
[5]So the servants of King Hezekiah came to Isaiah.
[6]Isaiah said to them, "Say this to your master: 'Thus says the LORD, "Do not be afraid because of the words that you have heard, with which the servants of the king of Assyria have reviled (blasphemed) Me.
[7]"Behold, I will put a spirit in him so that he will hear a rumor and return to his own land. And I will make him fall by the sword in his own land." ' "

Sennacherib Defies God

[8]So the Rabshakeh returned and found the king of Assyria fighting against Libnah [a fortified city of Judah]; for he had heard that the king had left Lachish.
[9]When the king heard them say concerning Tirhakah king of Ethiopia, "Behold, he has come out to make war against you," he sent messengers again to Hezekiah, saying,
[10]"Say this to Hezekiah king of Judah, 'Do not let your God on whom you rely deceive you by saying, "Jerusalem shall not be handed over to the king of Assyria."
[11]'Listen, you have heard what the Assyrian kings have done to all the lands, destroying them completely. So will you be spared?
[12]'Did the gods of the nations whom my forefathers destroyed rescue them—Gozan and Haran [of Mesopotamia] and Rezeph and the people of Eden who were in Telassar?
[13]'Where is the king of Hamath, the king of Arpad [of northern Syria], the king of the city of Sepharvaim, and of Hena and Ivvah?' "

Hezekiah's Prayer

[14]Hezekiah received the letter from the hand of the messengers and read it. Then he went up to the house (temple) of the LORD and spread it out before the LORD. [Is 37:14–20]
[15]Hezekiah prayed before the LORD and said, "O LORD, the God of Israel,

(the details of 18:13 – 20:19 are also recorded in Isa 36 – 39).

19:4 *hear . . . taunt and defy.* The first verb does not suggest that God is unaware of the words of Rabshekah. Rather, the words describe God as determining to redress the wrong.

19:6 *Do not be afraid.* Isaiah's prophecy was one of comfort. Not only would Sennacherib fail to conquer Jerusalem, but he would face a violent death upon his return home. Both points of this prophetic message would come true, although Sennacherib was not assassinated until 20 years later (c. 681 BC). In his annals Sennacherib boasts of five more campaigns; however, he makes no mention of any other invasions of Judah.

19:9 *Tirhakah king of Ethiopia.* Since Tirhakah did not become king until 690 BC, there is an apparent problem with the chronology of this verse. However, it is possible that the biblical author merely calls Tirhakah by the title he was best known by at the time of writing.

19:12 *Eden.* This is not the Eden of Genesis, but an area known today as Bit-Adini, south of Haran (Eze 27:23; Am 1:5).

19:15 *You have made the heavens and the earth.* The conflict mentioned in this chapter involves far more than the kings of Egypt, Assyria, or Judah. The warfare is one in which the gods of the pagan world would dishonor the true and living God of Israel. Hezekiah's prayer was addressed to the God who alone is sovereign over all the kingdoms of the world. His sovereignty is related to the fact of creation; He is the God who made heaven and earth. The heathen gods are born in corrupted human imaginations, and backed by a rebellious angel (Satan), but God is the one who owns and controls the universe.

4 2Sa 16:12; 2Ki 18:35; Ps 50:21 **6** Isa 37:6; 2Ki 18:17 **7** ver. 35-37; Jer 51:1 **8** 2Ki 18:14 **9** See 1Sa 23:27
10 2Ki 18:5 **12** 2Ki 18:33,34; Eze 27:23 **13** 2Ki 18:34 **14** Isa 37:14 **15** Ps 80:1; Isa 44:6

who is enthroned *above* the cherubim
[of the ark in the temple], You are the
God, You alone, of all the kingdoms of
the earth. You have made the heavens
and the earth.
16 "O LORD, bend down Your ear and
hear; LORD, open Your eyes and see;
hear the [taunting] words of Sennach-
erib, which he has sent to taunt *and*
defy the living God.
17 "It is true, LORD, that the Assyrian
kings have devastated the nations and
their lands
18 and have thrown their gods into the
fire, for they were not [real] gods but
[only] the work of men's hands, wood
and stone. So they [could destroy them
and] have destroyed them.
19 "Now, O LORD our God, please, save
us from his hand so that all the king-
doms of the earth may know [without
any doubt] that You alone, O LORD,
are God."

God's Answer through Isaiah

20 Then Isaiah the son of Amoz sent
word to Hezekiah, saying, "Thus says
the LORD, the God of Israel: 'I have
heard your prayer to Me regard-
ing Sennacherib king of Assyria.'
[Is 37:21–38]
21 "This is the word that the LORD has
spoken against him:

'The virgin daughter of Zion
Has despised you and mocked you;
The daughter of Jerusalem
Has shaken her head behind you!
22 'Whom have you taunted and
blasphemed?
Against whom have you raised
your voice,
And haughtily lifted up your
eyes?
Against the Holy One of Israel!
23 'Through your messengers you
have taunted *and* defied the Lord,
And have said [boastfully], "With
my many chariots
I came up to the heights of the
mountains,
To the remotest parts of Lebanon;
I cut down its tall cedar trees and
its choicest cypress trees.
I entered its most distant lodging,
its densest forest.
24 "I dug *wells* and drank foreign
waters,
And with the sole of my feet I
dried up
All the rivers of [the Lower Nile of]
Egypt."
25 'Have you not heard [asks the God
of Israel]?
Long ago I did it;
From ancient times I planned it.
Now I have brought it to pass,
That you [king of Assyria] should
[be My instrument to] turn
fortified cities into ruinous
heaps.
26 'Therefore their inhabitants were
powerless,
They were shattered [in spirit] and
put to shame;
They were like plants of the field,
the green herb,
As grass on the housetops is
scorched before it is grown up.
27 'But I [the LORD] know your sitting
down [O Sennacherib],
Your going out, your coming in,
And your raging against Me.
28 'Because of your raging against
Me,
And because your arrogance *and*
complacency have come up to
My ears,
I will put My hook in your nose,
And My bridle in your lips,
And I will turn you back [to
Assyria] by the way that you
came.

19:21 ***daughter of Zion.*** As elsewhere in the Old Testament (Zep 3:14), this phrase should be written "daughter Zion," without the "of." Zion (Jerusalem) is like a daughter to God, whom He will protect and guard as only a father would.

19:22 ***Holy One of Israel.*** This title is characteristic of Isaiah's own manner of referring to God. He uses the phrase 26 times (Isa 6:3). Sennacherib needed to know that his boastful pride blasphemed the sovereign and holy God of all nations.

16 Ps 31:2; 2Ch 6:40; ver. 4 **18** Jer 10:3 **19** Ps 83:18 **20** Isa 37:21; Ps 65:2 **21** La 2:13; Ps 22:7,8 **22** Jer 51:5 **23** 2Ki 18:17; Ps 20:7 **25** Isa 45:7; Isa 10:5 **26** Ps 129:6 **27** Ps 139:1 **28** Eze 29:4; ver. 33,36

29 'Then this shall be the sign [of these
things] to you [Hezekiah]: this year
you will eat what grows of itself, in the
second year what springs up voluntar-
ily, and in the third year sow and reap,
plant vineyards, and eat their fruit.
30 'The survivors who remain of the
house of Judah will again take root
downward and bear fruit upward.
31 'For a remnant will go forth from
Jerusalem, and [a band of] survivors
from Mount Zion. The zeal of the LORD
of hosts shall perform this.
32 'Therefore thus says the LORD con-
cerning the king of Assyria: "He will
not come to this city [Jerusalem] nor
shoot an arrow there; nor will he come
before it with a shield nor throw up a
siege ramp against it.
33 "By the way that he came, by the
same way he will return, and he will
not come into this city," ' declares the
LORD.
34 'For I will protect this city to save
it, for My own sake and for My servant
David's sake.' "
35 Then it came to pass that night,
that the angel of the LORD went forth
and struck down 185,000 [men] in the
camp of the Assyrians; when *the sur-
vivors* got up early in the morning, be-
hold, all [185,000] of them were dead.
36 So Sennacherib king of Assyria
left and returned *home,* and lived at
Nineveh.
37 It came about as he was wor-
shiping in the house of Nisroch his
god, that his sons Adrammelech and
Sharezer killed him with a sword; and
they escaped to the land of Ararat. And
Esarhaddon his son became king in
his place.

Hezekiah's Illness and Recovery

20 IN THOSE days [when Sennach-
erib first invaded Judah] Heze-
kiah became deathly ill. The prophet
Isaiah the son of Amoz came and said
to him, "Thus says the LORD, 'Set your
house in order, for you shall die and not
recover.' " [2 Chr 32:24–26; Is 38:1–8]
2 Then Hezekiah turned his face to
the wall and prayed to the LORD, saying,
3 "Please, O LORD, remember now
[with compassion] how I have walked
before You in faithfulness *and* truth
and with a whole heart [entirely de-
voted to You], and have done what is
good in Your sight." And Hezekiah
wept bitterly.
4 Before Isaiah had gone out of the
middle courtyard, the word of the LORD
came to him, saying,
5 "Go back and tell Hezekiah the
leader of My people, 'Thus says the
LORD, the God of David your father
(ancestor): "I have heard your prayer,
I have seen your tears. Behold, I am
healing you; on the third day you shall
go up to the house of the LORD.
6 "I will add fifteen years to your life
and save you and this city [Jerusalem]
from the hand of the king of Assyr-
ia; and I will protect this city for My
own sake and for My servant David's
sake." ' "
7 Then Isaiah said, "Bring a cake of
figs. And they brought it and placed it

19:30 *survivors . . . will again take root.* The promises in these verses were both for the immediate situation and ultimately for the final regathering of the Jewish people into their land in the time of the coming Messiah.

19:32 *not come to this city.* While Sennacherib later boasted of taking some 46 Judean cities, with reference to Jerusalem he could only report that he made Hezekiah "prisoner in Jerusalem, his royal residence, like a bird in a cage." God's defense and deliverance of Jerusalem demonstrated His faithfulness to the Davidic covenant.

19:37 *killed him with a sword.* The events depicted here took place 20 years after God's deliverance of Jerusalem. When his father was assassinated, Esarhaddon took the throne and ruled from 681 to 668 BC.

20:3 *I have walked before You.* Hezekiah's prayer recognized that although all of life is in God's hands, God is also a rewarder of those who faithfully serve Him (Dt 5:30 – 33; 30:15 – 16).

20:7 *cake of figs.* The practice of applying figs to an ulcerated sore is well attested in the records of the ancient Middle East, being mentioned as early as 2000 BC.

---

30 2Ch 32:22 **31** Isa 9:7 **34** 2Ki 20:6; 1Ki 11:12 **35** Isa 37:36 **36** Ge 10:11 **37** 2Ch 32:21; ver. 7; Ezr 4:2 **CHAPTER 20**
1 Isa 38:1 **3** Neh 13:22 **5** 1Sa 9:16; 10:1; 2Ki 19:20; Ps 65:2; Ps 39:12; 56:8 **6** 2Ki 19:34 **7** Isa 38:21

on the [painful] inflammation, and he recovered."

8 Hezekiah said to Isaiah, "What will be the sign that the LORD will [completely] heal me, and that I shall go up to the house of the LORD on the third day?"

9 Isaiah said, "This will be the sign to you from the LORD, that He will do the thing that He has spoken: shall the shadow [indicating the time of day] go forward ten steps, or go backward ten steps?"

10 Hezekiah answered, "It is easy for the shadow to go forward ten steps; no, but let the shadow turn backward ten steps."

11 So Isaiah the prophet called out to the LORD, and He brought the shadow on the steps ten steps backward by which it had gone down on the sundial of Ahaz.

Hezekiah Shows Babylon His Treasures

12 At that time Berodach-baladan a son of Baladan, king of Babylon, sent letters and a gift to Hezekiah, for he had heard that Hezekiah had been sick. [Is 39:1–8]

13 Hezekiah listened to *and* welcomed them and [foolishly] showed them all his treasure house—the silver and gold and spices and precious oil and his armory and everything that was found in his treasuries. There was nothing in his house (palace) nor in all his realm that Hezekiah did not show them.

14 Then Isaiah the prophet came to King Hezekiah and said to him, "What did these men say [that would cause you to do this for them]? From where have they come to you?" Hezekiah said, "They have come from a far country, from Babylon."

15 Isaiah said, "What have they seen in your house?" Hezekiah answered, "They have seen everything that is in my house (palace). There is nothing in my treasuries that I have not shown them."

16 Then Isaiah said to Hezekiah, "Hear the word of the LORD.

17 'Behold, the time is coming when everything that is in your house, and that your fathers have stored up until this day, will be carried to Babylon; nothing will be left,' says the LORD.

18 'And some of your sons (descendants) who will be born to you will be taken away [as captives]; and they will become eunuchs in the palace of the king of Babylon.' "

19 Then Hezekiah said to Isaiah, "The word of the LORD which you have spoken is good." For he thought, "Is it not good, if [at least] there will be peace and security in my lifetime?"

20 The rest of the acts of Hezekiah and all his might, and how he made the [Siloam] pool and the aqueduct and brought water into the city, are they not

---

20:12 *Berodach-baladan.* This was a Chaldean king who twice ruled in Babylon (721 – 710,703 BC). A perennial enemy of Assyria, he was twice defeated by them and cast out from Babylon. His search for allies in his resistance to Assyria may have occasioned the embassy to Hezekiah, especially because he had heard of Hezekiah's miraculous deliverance from the Assyrian army (2Ch 32:31).

20:13 *showed them all his treasure house.* One of the remarkable features of the Bible is the fact that it does not gloss over the faults of its best heroes and heroines. This account of the foolishness of Hezekiah follows immediately on the narrative of his great trust in the Lord (vv. 1 – 11).

20:16 – 18 Vanity — How much better for Israel's welfare if Hezekiah had been interested in introducing the Babylonian envoys to his God rather than to the treasures of the nation. The prophet's rebuke confirms that Hezekiah's action arose from a vain desire to impress the Babylonians with the externals of his kingdom. Human pride, and the vain hope that deliverance will come from man, must be forsaken if God's blessing is to be experienced.

20:19 *The word of the LORD . . . is good.* Hezekiah's response seems a little heartless. He did verbally acknowledge God's right to decide, but it does not appear that he had any real sense of the trouble his folly would bring on the people.

20:20 *the [Siloam] pool and the aqueduct.* Hezekiah dug a tunnel between the spring of Gihon and the Pool of Siloam to bring a ready

---

8 See Jdg 6:17,37,39; Isa 7:11,14; 38:22 **9** See Isa 38:7,8 **11** See Isa 38:8 **12** Isa 39:1 **13** 2Ch 32:27,31 **15** ver. 13 **17** 2Ki 24:13; 25:13; Jer 27:21; 52:17 **18** 2Ki 24:12; 2Ch 33:11 **19** 1Sa 3:18; Job 1:21; Ps 39:9 **20** 2Ch 32:32; Neh 3:16; 2Ch 32:30

written in the Book of the Chronicles
of the Kings of Judah?
21 Hezekiah slept with his fathers [in
death], and Manasseh his son became
king in his place.

Manasseh Succeeds Hezekiah

21 MANASSEH WAS twelve years
old when he became king, and
he reigned for fifty-five years in Jeru-
salem. His mother's name was Heph-
zibah.
2 He did [great] evil in the sight of
the LORD, in accordance with the [idol-
atrous] repulsive acts of the [pagan]
nations whom the LORD dispossessed
before the sons (descendants) of Israel.
3 For he rebuilt the high places [for
the worship of pagan gods] which his
father Hezekiah had destroyed; and
he set up altars for Baal and made
an [image of] Asherah, just as Ahab
king of Israel had done, and he wor-
shiped all the [starry] host of heaven
and served them.
4 And he built [pagan] altars in the
house (temple) of the LORD, of which
the LORD had said, "In Jerusalem I will
put My Name (Presence)."
5 And he built altars for all the host
of heaven in the two courtyards of the
house of the LORD.
6 He made his son pass through the
fire *and* burned him [as an offering to
Molech]; he practiced witchcraft and
divination, and dealt with mediums
and soothsayers. He did great evil in
the sight of the LORD, provoking *Him
to anger.*
7 He made a carved image of the
[goddess] Asherah and set it up in the
house (temple), of which the LORD said
to David and to his son Solomon, "In
this house and in Jerusalem [in the
tribe of Judah], which I have chosen
from all the tribes of Israel, I will put
My Name forever.
8 "And I will not make the feet of Is-
rael wander anymore from the land
which I gave their fathers, if only they
will be careful to act in accordance
with everything that I have command-
ed them, and with all the law that My
servant Moses commanded them."
9 But they did not listen; and Manas-
seh seduced them to do more evil than
the nations whom the LORD destroyed
before the sons (descendants) of Israel.

The King's Idolatries Rebuked

10 Now the LORD spoke through His
servants the prophets, saying,
11 "Because Manasseh king of Judah
has committed these repulsive acts,
having done more evil than all the Am-
orites did who were before him, and
has also made Judah sin with his idols;
12 therefore thus says the LORD, the
God of Israel: 'Behold, I am bringing
such catastrophe on Jerusalem and
Judah, that everyone who hears of
it, both of his ears will ring [from the
shock].
13 'I will stretch over Jerusalem the
measuring line of Samaria and the
plummet of the house of Ahab; and I
will wipe Jerusalem clean just as one

---

supply of water within the eastern wall of Jerusalem. This tunnel is still in existence, a crooked shaft 1,750 feet long.

21:1 ***Manasseh.*** This wicked king's fifty-five year reign was the longest of any of the kings of the divided kingdom. Externally, the period was one of political stability. It is known as the Assyrian Peace, an era in which the kings Esarhaddon (681 – 668 BC) and Ashurbanipal (668 – 626 BC) reigned and brought the Assyrian Empire to its zenith. However, the length of Manasseh's reign does not indicate a good rule, but rather God's persevering mercy and faithfulness to the Davidic covenant (2Ch 33:10 – 13).

21:3 ***host of heaven.*** Worship of heavenly bodies was strictly forbidden (Dt 4:19; 17;2 – 7) and was condemned strongly by Israel's prophets (Isa 47:13; Am 5:26). Yet Manasseh paid no attention to either the law or the prophets (2Ch 33:2 – 10).

21:4 ***altars in the house (temple) of the LORD.*** All that had been accomplished by the godly kings of Judah was undone by this reprobate. But wicked as Manasseh was, God heard his prayer when he repented (2Ch 33:12 – 16).

---

21 2Ch 32:33 **CHAPTER 21** **1** 2Ch 33:1 **2** 2Ki 16:3 **3** 2Ki 18:4; 1Ki 16:32; Dt 4:19; 17:3; 2Ki 17:16 **4** Jer 32:34; 2Sa 7:13; 1Ki 8:29; 9:3 **6** Lev 18:21; 20:2; 2Ki 16:3; 17:17; Lev 19:26,31; Dt 18:10,11; 2Ki 17:17 **7** 2Sa 7:13; 1Ki 8:29; 9:3; 2Ki 23:27; Jer 32:34 **8** 2Sa 7:10 **9** Pr 29:12 **11** 2Ki 23:26,27; 24:3,4; Jer 15:4; 1Ki 21:26; ver. 9 **12** 1Sa 3:11; Jer 19:3 **13** See Isa 34:11; La 2:8; Am 7:7,8

wipes a [dirty] bowl clean, wiping it
and turning it upside down.
14“I will abandon the remnant (re-
mainder) of My inheritance and hand
them over to their enemies; and they
will become plunder and spoil to all
their enemies,
15because they have done evil in My
sight, and have been provoking Me to
anger, since the day their fathers came
from Egypt to this day.’ ”
16Moreover, Manasseh shed a very
great quantity of innocent blood, until
he had filled Jerusalem from one end
to another; besides his sin with which
he made Judah sin, by doing evil in
the sight of the LORD. [2 Chr 33:1–10]
17Now the rest of the acts of Manas-
seh, everything that he did, and the
sin that he committed, are they not
written in the Book of the Chronicles
of the Kings of Judah?
18Manasseh slept with his fathers [in
death] and was buried in the garden of
his own house, in the garden of Uzza.
And his son Amon became king in
his place.

Amon Succeeds Manasseh

19Amon was twenty-two years old
when he became king, and he reigned
two years in Jerusalem. His mother's
name was Meshullemeth the daughter
of Haruz of Jotbah.
20He also did evil in the sight of the
LORD, just as his father Manasseh had
done. [2 Kin 23:26, 27; 24:3, 4]
21He walked in all the [evil] ways
that his father had walked; and he
served the idols that his father had
served, and worshiped them;
22he abandoned the LORD, the God
of his fathers, and did not walk in the
way of the LORD.
23But the servants of Amon con-
spired against him and killed the king
in his own house (palace).
24Then the people of the land [of Ju-
dah] killed all those who had conspired
against King Amon, and the people of
the land made his son Josiah king in
his place.
25Now the rest of the acts of Amon
which he did, are they not written in
the Book of the Chronicles of the Kings
of Judah?
26He was buried in his tomb in the
garden of Uzza, and his son Josiah
became king in his place.

Josiah Succeeds Amon

22 JOSIAH WAS eight years old
when he became king, and
reigned for thirty-one years in Jeru-
salem. His mother's name was Jedidah
daughter of Adaiah of Bozkath.
2He did what was right in the sight
of the LORD and walked in all the ways
of his father (ancestor) David, and did
not turn aside to the right or to the left.
3In the eighteenth year of King Jo-
siah, the king sent Shaphan the son
of Azaliah, the son of Meshullam the
scribe to the house of the LORD, saying,

21:15 *since the day.* The story of the Old Testament is not a record of God's anger, but of His mercy and the delay of His just wrath.

21:23 *conspired against him.* No reason is assigned for the conspiracy that brought about Amon's assassination. While it may have had some connection with the international crisis that precipitated Ashurbanipal's renewed attention to the west, Amon's own wickedness may have provided sufficient cause.

22:1 *Josiah.* The name Josiah means "The Lord Supports." Like the name of Cyrus (Isa 44:28; 45:1) and of the city of Bethlehem (Mic 5:2), the name Josiah was announced by a prophet long before the time of his birth (1Ki 13:1 – 2).

22:2 *did not turn aside.* Not many rulers can rival Josiah's thirty-eight years of perseverance in righteousness. Some begin with high ideals and a commitment to do what is right in the sight of the Lord, but they soon learn that compromise is the art of politics. Compromise can be right and good. We ought to think more highly of others than ourselves and be willing to let go of our own preferences and opinions for the good of others. However, good can never result from compromising God's revealed ethics, morality, and justice. We must learn to live like Josiah, putting obedience to God before comfort and popular acceptance.

---

16 2Ki 24:4 **17** 2Ch 33:11-19 **18** 2Ch 33:20 **19** 2Ch 33:21-23 **20** ver. 2 **22** 1Ki 11:33 **23** 2Ch 33:24,25 **26** Mt 1:10 **CHAPTER 22** **1** 2Ch 34:1; Jos 15:39 **2** Dt 5:32 **3** 2Ch 34:8

4“Go up to Hilkiah the high priest, so
that he may count the entire amount
of money brought into the house of
the LORD, which the doorkeepers have
collected from the people. [2 Kin 12:4]
5“And have them deliver it to the
hands of the workmen who have been
appointed over the house of the LORD,
and have them give it to the workmen
who are in the house of the LORD to
repair the damages of the house—
6that is, [have them give the money]
to the carpenters and the builders and
the masons—and to buy timber and
cut stones to repair the house (temple).
7“However, no accounting shall be
required of them for the money placed
in their hands, because they act faith-
fully.”

The Lost Book

8Hilkiah the high priest said to
Shaphan the scribe, “I have found the
Book of the Law in the house (temple)
of the LORD.” Hilkiah gave the book to
Shaphan, and he read it.
9Shaphan the scribe came to the
king and brought back word to him:
“Your servants have emptied out the
money that was found in the house,
and have placed it in the hands of the
workmen who have been appointed
over the house of the LORD.”
10Then Shaphan the scribe told the
king, “Hilkiah the priest has given me
a book.” And Shaphan read it [aloud]
before the king.
11Now when the king heard the
words of the Book of the Law, he tore
his clothes.
12Then the king commanded Hilkiah
the priest, Ahikam the son of Shaphan,
Achbor the son of Micaiah, Shaphan
the scribe, and Asaiah the servant of
the king, saying,
13“Go, inquire of the LORD for my
sake and for the sake of the people and
for all Judah concerning the words of
this book which has been found, for
great is the wrath of the LORD which
has been kindled against us, because
our fathers have not listened to *and*
obeyed the words of this book, so as
to act in accordance with everything
that is written concerning us.”

Huldah Predicts

14So Hilkiah the priest, Ahikam,
Achbor, Shaphan, and Asaiah went
to Huldah the prophetess, the wife of
Shallum the son of Tikvah, the son of
Harhas, keeper of the wardrobe (she
was living in Jerusalem, in the Second
Quarter [the new part of the city]); and
they spoke to her.
15She said to them, “Thus says the
LORD, the God of Israel: ‘Tell the man
who sent you to me,
16thus says the LORD: “Behold, I am
bringing a catastrophe on this place
(Judah) and on its inhabitants, [accord-
ing to] all the words of the book which
the king of Judah has read.
17“Because they have abandoned (re-
jected) Me and have burned incense to
other gods, that they might provoke
Me to anger with all the work of their
hands, therefore My wrath burns
against this place, and it will not be
quenched.” ’
18“But to the king of Judah who sent
you to inquire of the LORD, you shall
say this to him: ‘Thus says the LORD
God of Israel, “*Regarding* the words
which you have heard,
19because your heart was tender

22:4 *Hilkiah the high priest.* This man was a major figure in the revival of true religion that young Josiah accomplished. The work of restoring the temple was under his direction.

22:8 *the Book of the Law.* This may mean either parts or all of the Pentateuch. Although it was placed by the side of the ark of the covenant (Dt 31:26), it may have been lost, set aside, or hidden during the wicked reigns of Manasseh and Amon.

22:14 *Huldah the prophetess.* Huldah is one of only a few women mentioned in Scripture as a prophetess. She served at the same time as other godly prophets, such as Jeremiah and Zephaniah, and some have suggested that her husband Shallum was a relative of Jeremiah (Jer 32:7 – 12).

4 2Ki 12:4; 2Ki 12:9 **5** 2Ki 12:11,12,14 **7** 2Ki 12:15 **8** Dt 31:24; 2Ch 34:14 **12** 2Ch 34:20 **13** Dt 29:27 **14** 2Ch 34:22 **16** Dt 29:27; Da 9:11-14 **17** Dt 29:25-27 **18** 2Ch 34:26 **19** Ps 51:17; Isa 57:15; 1Ki 21:29; Lev 26:31,32; Jer 26:6; 44:22

(receptive, penitent) and you humbled yourself before the LORD when you heard what I said against this place and against its inhabitants, that they should become a desolation and a curse, and because you have torn your clothes and wept before Me, I have heard you," declares the LORD.

20"Therefore, behold, [King Josiah,] I will gather you to your fathers, and you will be taken to your grave in peace, and your eyes will not see all the evil (catastrophe) which I will bring on this place." ' " So they brought back word to the king.

Josiah's Covenant

23 KING JOSIAH sent *word* and they brought to him all the elders of Judah and of Jerusalem.

2The king went up to the house of the LORD, and with him all the men of Judah and all the inhabitants of Jerusalem, the priests, the prophets, and all the people, both small and great; and he read in their hearing all the words of the book of the covenant which was found in the house (temple) of the LORD.

3The king stood by the pillar and made a covenant before the LORD, to walk after the LORD and to keep His commandments, His testimonies, and His statutes with all his heart and soul, to confirm the words of this covenant that were written in this book. And all the people entered into the covenant.

Reforms under Josiah

4Then the king commanded Hilkiah the high priest and the priests of the second rank and the doorkeepers to bring out of the temple of the LORD all the articles made for Baal, for [the goddess] Asherah, and for all the [starry] host of heaven; and he burned them outside Jerusalem in the fields of the Kidron, and carried their ashes to Bethel [where Israel's idolatry began]. [1 Kin 12:28, 29]

5He got rid of the idolatrous priests whom the kings of Judah had ordained to burn incense [to pagan gods] in the high places in Judah's cities and all around Jerusalem—also those who burned incense to Baal, to the sun, to the moon, to the constellations [of the zodiac], and to all the [starry] host of heaven.

6Josiah brought out the Asherah from the house of the LORD to the Brook Kidron outside Jerusalem, and burned it there, and ground it to dust, and threw its dust on the graves of the common people [who had sacrificed to it].

7And he tore down the houses of the [male] cult prostitutes, which were at the house (temple) of the LORD, where the women were weaving [tent] hangings for the Asherah [shrines].

8Then Josiah brought all the [idolatrous] priests from the cities of Judah, and desecrated the high places where the priests had burned incense [to idols], from Geba to Beersheba, [that

---

23:2 *he read . . . the words of the book.* Like Moses (Ex 24:3–8) and Joshua (Jos 8:34–35) before him, Josiah followed the ancient standard for godly leadership (Dt 17:18–20; 31:9–13) and assembled the people to renew the covenant.

23:3 Knowing the Will of God—Christians often act as if learning the will of God is some mysterious process fraught with the danger of making all kinds of mistakes. This passage points to the fact that most of what we need to know about the will of God is contained in the Scriptures. The best place to *learn* the will of God is from reading the Bible. The only way to *do* the will of God is to obey the teaching of the Bible. God may have more specific plans for each of us, but His basic plan for all of us is to do what He says as revealed in His written word.

23:5 *idolatrous priests.* This term is also used by Zephaniah to describe the priests who led the rites associated with Baal and with star worship of various kinds (Zep 1:4). These priests had been appointed by Judah's past kings but functioned outside the divinely established priesthood.

23:6 *the Asherah.* Although they had been destroyed by Hezekiah, these wooden images had been reintroduced by Manasseh (21:7) and also by Amon (21:21).

---

20 Ps 37:37; Isa 57:1,2 **CHAPTER 23** **1** 2Ch 34:29,30 **2** 2Ki 22:8 **3** 2Ki 11:14,17 **4** 2Ki 21:3,7 **5** 2Ki 21:3 **6** 2Ki 21:7; 2Ch 34:4 **7** 1Ki 14:24; 15:12; Eze 16:16 **8** 1Ki 15:22

is, north to south]; and he tore down the high places of the gates which were at the entrance of the gate of Joshua the governor of the city, which were on one's left at the city gate.

9 However, the priests of the high places were not allowed to go up to the altar of the LORD in Jerusalem [to serve], but they ate unleavened bread among their brothers.

10 Josiah also defiled Topheth, which is in the Valley of Ben-hinnom (son of Hinnom), so that no man could make his son or his daughter pass through the fire [as a burnt offering] for Molech. [Ezek 16:21]

11 And he got rid of the horses that the kings of Judah had given [in worship] to the sun at the entrance of the house of the LORD, by the chamber of Nathan-melech the official, which was in the annex; and he burned the chariots of the sun.

12 The altars [dedicated to the starry host of heaven] which were on the roof, the upper chamber of Ahaz, which the kings of Judah had made, and the altars which Manasseh had made in the two courtyards of the house of the LORD, the king tore down; and he smashed them there and threw their dust into the Brook Kidron.

13 The king desecrated the high places which were opposite [east of] Jerusalem, which were on the right (south) of the mount of corruption which Solomon the king of Israel had built for Ashtoreth the repulsiveness of the Sidonians, for Chemosh the repulsiveness of Moab, and for Milcom the repulsiveness of the sons (descendants) of Ammon.

14 He broke in pieces the *sacred* pillars (cultic memorial stones, images) and cut down the Asherim and replaced them with human bones [to desecrate the places forever].

15 Further, the altar that was at Bethel, the high place which Jeroboam the son of Nebat, who made Israel sin, had made, even that altar and the high place he tore down. Then he demolished its stones, ground them to dust, and burned the Asherah.

16 And as Josiah turned, he saw the graves that were there on the mountain, and he sent *men* and had the bones taken from the graves, and burned them on the altar and [thereby] desecrated it, in accordance with the word of the LORD which the man of God prophesied, who proclaimed these things [about this altar, naming Josiah before he was born]. [1 Kin 13:2–5]

17 Then Josiah said, "What is this monument (gravestone) that I see?" The men of the city told him, "It is the grave of the man of God who came from Judah and proclaimed these things which you have done to the altar of Bethel."

18 He said, "Let him alone; let no one disturb his bones." So they left his bones undisturbed, with the bones of the prophet who came from Samaria. [1 Kin 13:31, 32]

19 Josiah also removed all the houses of the high places which were in the cities of Samaria, which the kings of Israel had made provoking the LORD [to anger]; and he did to them just as he had done [to those] in Bethel.

20 All the priests of the high places

23:10 ***Topheth.*** This appears to have been a place in the valley of Hinnom where human sacrifices were made to Molech (Jer 7:31–32; 32:35). ***pass through the fire [as a burnt offering] for Molech.*** Some think that Molech was a god of the Ammonites (1Ki 11:5), or that Molech was the name of a type of child sacrifice associated with Baal worship (Jer 19:5–6). Evidence of such child sacrifice has been found in the excavations at the Phoenician city of Carthage.

23:18 ***the prophet who came from Samaria.*** The prophet from Samaria was the old prophet of Bethel (1Ki 13:11). Samaria is the name for an entire area, not just the city that was later the capital of the Northern Kingdom (1Ki 13:32; 16:23–24). After the death of the man of God who had denounced Jeroboam's altar at Bethel, the aged prophet of Bethel requested that at his death he should be buried in Bethel beside that prophet of Judah.

9 See Eze 44:10-14; 1Sa 2:36 **10** Isa 30:33; Jer 7:31; 19:6,11-13; Jos 15:8; Lev 18:21; Dt 18:10; Eze 23:37,39 **12** See Jer 19:13; Zep 1:5; 2Ki 21:5 **13** 1Ki 11:7 **14** Ex 23:24; Dt 7:5,25 **15** 1Ki 12:28,33 **16** 1Ki 13:2 **17** 1Ki 13:1,30 **18** 1Ki 13:31 **19** See 2Ch 34:6,7 **20** 1Ki 13:2; Ex 22:20; 1Ki 18:40; 2Ki 11:18; 2Ch 34:5

who were there he slaughtered on the
altars, and burned human bones on
them [to desecrate the places forever].
Then he returned to Jerusalem.

Passover Reinstituted

21Then the king commanded all the
people, saying, "Celebrate the Passover
to the LORD your God as it is written in
this book of the covenant."
22Indeed, such a Passover as this
had not been held since the days of
the judges who judged Israel, nor in
all the days of the kings of Israel and
the kings of Judah.
23But in the eighteenth year of King
Josiah, this Passover to the LORD was
kept in Jerusalem.
24Moreover, Josiah removed the me-
diums and the soothsayers and the
teraphim (household gods) and the
idols and all the repulsive things that
were seen in Judah and in Jerusalem,
so that he might fulfill the words of the
law written in the book which Hilkiah
the priest found in the house (temple)
of the LORD.
25Before him there was no king like
Josiah who turned to the LORD with
all his heart and all his soul and all
his might, in accordance with all the
Law of Moses; nor did anyone like him
arise after him.
26However, the LORD did not turn
from the fierceness of His great wrath
which was kindled against Judah be-
cause of all the despicable acts with
which Manasseh had provoked Him.
27The LORD said, "I will also remove
Judah from My sight, just as I have
removed Israel; and will reject this city
which I have chosen, this Jerusalem,
and the house, of which I said, 'My
Name [and the pledge of My Presence]
shall be there.' "

Jehoahaz Succeeds Josiah

28Now the rest of the acts of Josiah,
everything that he did, are they not
written in the Book of the Chronicles
of the Kings of Judah?
29In his days Pharaoh Neco (Necho)
king of Egypt went up to the king of
Assyria to the river Euphrates [to help
him fight Nabopolassar the king of
Babylon]. King Josiah went out to
meet him, but Pharaoh killed Josiah
at Megiddo when he saw him.
30Josiah's servants carried his dead
body in a chariot from Megiddo,

23:22 *such a Passover.* The restoration of religious places was part of the revival of spiritual worship. Although Hezekiah had held a Passover (2Ch 30), he had done so with some modification of the law (2Ch 30:13 – 20). Accordingly, Josiah's meeting of the strict requirements of the law (2Ch 35:1 – 19) was truly unparalleled since the days of the judges.

23:25 *there was no king like Josiah.* Like his grandfather Hezekiah, who was famed for being without equal in his trust of the Lord (18:5), Josiah was truly a righteous king. Because of their outstanding examples of godliness, the authors of Kings and Chronicles devote considerable space to their reigns.

23:26 – 27 Unfaithfulness — The revival under Josiah, recorded in chapters 22 and 23, was like a stay of execution. It gave Judah some additional time but it was too little, too late. The die had been cast in Manasseh's reign as God threatened to wipe out Jerusalem "as one wipes a [dirty] bowl" (21:13) because Manasseh did more evil than the other nations whom the Lord had destroyed. In the light of Jeremiah 18:7 – 8 we must assume that Josiah's people responded only externally to God's principles and not from the heart. Unfaithfulness was deeply rooted, and professions of religion could not change them from the inside.

23:29 *Pharaoh Neco.* During the long years of Josiah's reign (640 – 609 BC), Assyrian power had steadily crumbled until, as Nahum had predicted, Nineveh itself had fallen (612 BC). The surviving Assyrian forces had regrouped at Haran. Because Egypt was a long-standing ally of Assyria, Neco journeyed northward to help the beleaguered Assyrians. Josiah's deployment of his forces to the valley of Megiddo was an attempt to prevent the Egyptians from aiding the Assyrian forces at Haran. Although Pharaoh Neco was delayed sufficiently so that Haran was lost to the Assyrians, Josiah's action ultimately cost him his life (2Ch 35:20 – 25).

21 2Ch 35:1; Ex 12:3; Lev 23:5; Nu 9:2; Dt 16:2 **22** 2Ch 35:18,19 **24** Lev 19:31; 20:27; Dt 18:11 **25** 2Ki 18:5 **26** 2Ki 21:11,12; 24:3,4; Jer 15:4 **27** 2Ki 17:18,20; 18:11; 21:13; 1Ki 8:29; 9:3; 2Ki 21:4,7 **29** 2Ch 35:20; Zec 12:11; 2Ki 14:8 **30** 2Ch 35:24; 2Ch 36:1

brought him to Jerusalem, and buried
him in his own tomb. Then the people
of the land took Jehoahaz the son of
Josiah and anointed him and made
him king in his father's place.
31 Jehoahaz was twenty-three years
old when he became king, and he
reigned for [only] three months in Je-
rusalem. His mother's name was Ha-
mutal daughter of Jeremiah of Libnah.
32 He did evil in the sight of the LORD,
in accordance with everything that his
forefathers had done.
33 Pharaoh Neco imprisoned him at
Riblah in the land of Hamath, so that
he would not reign in Jerusalem, and
imposed a fine on the land of a hundred
talents of silver and a talent of gold.

Jehoiakim Made King by Pharaoh

34 Pharaoh Neco made Eliakim the
son of Josiah king in place of his fa-
ther Josiah, and changed his name to
Jehoiakim. But he took Jehoahaz and
brought him to Egypt, where he died.
35 Jehoiakim gave the silver and the
gold to Pharaoh, but he taxed the land
to give the money as Pharaoh com-
manded. He collected the silver and
gold from the people of the land, from
everyone according to his assessment,
to give it to Pharaoh Neco.
36 Jehoiakim was twenty-five years
old when he became king, and he
reigned for eleven years in Jerusa-
lem. His mother's name was Zebidah
daughter of Pedaiah of Rumah.
37 He did evil in the sight of the LORD,
in accordance with everything that his
forefathers had done.

Babylon Controls Jehoiakim

24 IN HIS days, Nebuchadnezzar
king of Babylon came up, and
Jehoiakim became his servant for
three years; then he turned and re-
belled against him.
2 The LORD sent marauding bands
of Chaldeans, Arameans (Syrians),
Moabites, and Ammonites against Je-
hoiakim. And He sent them against
Judah to destroy it, in accordance with
the word of the LORD which He spoke
through His servants the prophets.
3 Surely this came on Judah at the
command of the LORD, to remove them
from His sight because of the sins of
[King] Manasseh, in accordance with
everything that he had done,
4 and also for the innocent blood that
he shed, for he filled Jerusalem with
innocent blood; and the LORD would
not pardon it.
5 Now the rest of the acts of Jehoia-
kim, and everything that he did, are
they not written in the Book of the
Chronicles of the Kings of Judah?

Jehoiachin Reigns

6 So Jehoiakim slept with his fathers
[in death], and his son Jehoiachin be-
came king in his place.
7 The king of Egypt did not come out
of his land again, because the king of
Babylon had taken everything that
belonged to the king of Egypt, from the
river of Egypt to the river Euphrates.

23:31 *Jehoahaz.* Jehoahaz, also called Shallum (Jer 22:11), was Josiah's third son (24:18; 1Ch 3:15).
23:34 *brought him to Egypt, where he died.* The curse for Judah's disobedience was beginning to fall (Dt 28:64–48).
23:37 *He did evil.* Jehoiakim's short reign was noted for its extreme wickedness (2Ch 36:5–8). Jeremiah depicts him as a despicable monster who took advantage of his people (Jer 22:13–14,17), filled the land with every sort of vice and violence (Jer 18:18–20), and opposed all that was holy (Jer 25:1–7). Unlike his father Josiah, who led the nation in reformation at the hearing of the Word of God (22:11; 23:1–25), Jehoiakim went so far as to cut up and burn a scroll of Scripture (Jer 36:21–24) and to kill Urijah, a true prophet of God (Jer 26:20–23).
24:2 *Chaldeans.* This name originally applied to certain inhabitants of southern Mesopotamia, but by this time the term had come to be identified with the Babylonians, and Babylonia was called Chaldea. After the fall of the Babylonian Empire, the term Chaldean came to mean "soothsayer" (Da 2:2).

31 2Ki 24:18 **33** 2Ki 25:6; Jer 52:27 **34** 2Ch 36:4; 2Ki 24:17; Da 1:7; Mt 1:11; Jer 22:11; Eze 19:3 **35** ver. 33 **36** 2Ch 36:5 **CHAPTER 24** **1** 2Ch 36:6; Jer 25:1,9; Da 1:1 **2** Jer 25:9; 32:28; Eze 19:8; 2Ki 20:17; 21:12-14; 23:27 **3** 2Ki 21:2,11; 23:26 **4** 2Ki 21:16 **6** See 2Ch 36:6,8; Jer 22:18; 36:30 **7** Jer 37:5,7; Jer 46:2

[8]Jehoiachin was eighteen years old when he became king, and he reigned [only] three months in Jerusalem. His mother's name was Nehushta daughter of Elnathan of Jerusalem.
[9]He did evil in the sight of the LORD, in accordance with everything that his father had done.

Deportation to Babylon

[10]At that time the servants of Nebuchadnezzar king of Babylon went up to Jerusalem, and the city came under siege.
[11]Nebuchadnezzar king of Babylon came to the city while his servants were besieging it.
[12]Jehoiachin king of Judah surrendered to the king of Babylon, he and his mother and his servants and his captains and his [palace] officials. So the king of Babylon took him prisoner in the eighth year of his [own] reign.
[13]He carried out of there (Jerusalem) all the treasures of the house (temple) of the LORD, and the treasures of the house (palace) of the king, and cut in pieces all the articles of gold in the temple of the LORD, which Solomon king of Israel had made, just as the LORD had said.
[14]He led away into exile all Jerusalem and all the captains and all the brave men, ten thousand captives, and all the craftsmen and the smiths. None remained except the poorest people of the land.
[15]Nebuchadnezzar led Jehoiachin away into exile to Babylon; also he took the king's mother and the king's wives and his officials and the leading men of the land [including Ezekiel] as exiles from Jerusalem to Babylon. [Ezek 1:1]
[16]And the king of Babylon brought as exiles to Babylon all the brave men, seven thousand [of them], and the craftsmen and the smiths, a thousand [of them], all strong and fit for war.

Zedekiah Made King

[17]Then the king of Babylon made Mattaniah, Jehoiachin's uncle, king in his place, and changed his name to Zedekiah.
[18]Zedekiah was twenty-one years old when he became king, and he reigned for eleven years in Jerusalem. His mother's name was Hamutal daughter of Jeremiah of Libnah. [2 Kin 23:31]
[19]He did evil in the sight of the LORD, in accordance with everything that Jehoiakim had done.
[20]Because of the anger of the LORD *these things* happened in Jerusalem and Judah, and it [finally] came to the point that He cast them from His presence. And Zedekiah rebelled against the king of Babylon.

24:8 *Jehoiachin.* Because the scriptural description of Jehoiachin seems to represent him as a mature young man (Jer 22:24 – 30; Eze 19:6), Jehoiachin's age at accession was probably eighteen rather than eight, as given elsewhere in some manuscripts (compare 2Ch 36:9).

24:12 *Jehoiachin.* Jehoiakim apparently had died before Nebuchadnezzar arrived at Jerusalem, because it was Jehoiachin who was carried off captive with other leaders of Judah (such as Ezekiel; Eze 1:1). Jeremiah called him "Jeconiah" and "Coniah" (Jer 22:24 – 28).

24:14 – 16 *led away.* The people of Israel lost their freedom and independence because of their own perpetually iniquitous ways. To be exiled is to be torn away from everything familiar, from everything traditional, from all identifiable scenery, and forced to live in a place where one has no identity and no roots. The people's whole sense of national identity was bound to their land, the place God had given them, and to be torn from that land was the ultimate evidence that God had rejected them.

24:15 *led Jehoiachin away into exile.* Jehoiachin's captivity was prophesied in Jeremiah 22:24 – 27. Jehoiachin's eventual release is recorded in 25:27 – 30 and Jeremiah 52:31 – 34.

24:17 *Mattaniah.* This was Josiah's youngest son (1Ch 3:15). He reigned until the fall of Jerusalem in 586 BC.

---

8 2Ch 36:9 **10** Da 1:1 **12** Jer 24:1; 29:1,2; Eze 17:12; Jer 25:1; 2Ki 25:27; Jer 52:28 **13** 2Ki 20:17; Isa 39:6; Da 5:2,3; Jer 20:5 **14** Jer 24:1; Jer 52:28; 1Sa 13:19,22; 2Ki 25:12 **15** 2Ch 36:10; Est 2:6; Jer 22:24 **16** Jer 52:28 **17** Jer 37:1; 1Ch 3:15; 2Ch 36:10; 2Ch 36:4 **18** 2Ch 36:11; Jer 52:1; 2Ki 23:31 **19** 2Ch 36:12 **20** 2Ch 36:13; Eze 17:15

Nebuchadnezzar Besieges Jerusalem

25 NOW IN the ninth year of Zedekiah's reign, on the tenth day of the tenth month, Nebuchadnezzar king of Babylon came, he with all his army, against Jerusalem, and camped against it and built siege works surrounding it.

2 The city came under siege [for nearly two years] until the eleventh year of King Zedekiah.

3 On the ninth day of the *fourth* month the famine [caused by the siege] was severe in the city; there was no food for the people of the land.

4 Then the city [wall] was broken into [and conquered]; all the men of war *fled* by night by way of the gate between the two walls by the king's garden, though the Chaldeans (Babylonians) were all around the city. And they went by way of the Arabah (the plain of the Jordan).

5 The army of the Chaldeans pursued the king and overtook him in the plains of Jericho. Then his entire army was dispersed from him.

6 So they seized the king (Zedekiah) and brought him to the king of Babylon at Riblah [on the Orontes River], and sentence was passed on him.

7 They slaughtered the sons of Zedekiah before his eyes, then put out the eyes of Zedekiah and bound him [hand and foot] with bronze fetters and brought him to Babylon. [Jer 34:3; Ezek 12:13]

Jerusalem Burned and Plundered

8 On the seventh day of the fifth month in the nineteenth year of King Nebuchadnezzar of Babylon, Nebuzaradan, captain of the bodyguard, a servant of the king of Babylon, came to Jerusalem.

9 He burned the house (temple) of the LORD, the king's house, and all the houses of Jerusalem; every great house he burned down.

10 All the army of the Chaldeans (Babylonians) who *were with* the captain of the bodyguard tore down the walls around Jerusalem.

11 Then Nebuzaradan the captain of the bodyguard deported [into exile] the rest of the people who were left in the city and the deserters who had joined the king of Babylon, and the rest of the multitude.

12 But the captain of the bodyguard left some of the unimportant *and* poorest people of the land to be vineyard workers and farmers.

13 Now the Chaldeans (Babylonians) smashed the bronze pillars which were in the house of the LORD and their bases and the bronze sea (large basin) which were in the house of the LORD, and carried the bronze to Babylon.

14 They took away the pots, the shovels, the snuffers, the spoons, and all the bronze articles which were used in the *temple* service,

15 the captain of the bodyguard also took away the firepans and basins, anything made of fine gold and anything made of fine silver.

16 The two pillars, the one sea (large basin), and the bases which Solomon had made for the house of the LORD, the bronze of all these articles was incalculable.

17 The height of the one pillar was eighteen cubits (27 ft.), and a capital of bronze was on top of it. The height of the capital was three cubits (4.5 ft.); a network (lattice work) and pome-

---

25:7 ***put out the eyes.*** The last thing Zedekiah saw was the reward of his sinful folly—the horrible spectacle of his own loved ones being put to death. He would carry this picture with him until his own death in a Babylonian prison (Jer 52:11).

25:10 ***tore down the walls.*** These walls would lie in ruins for a century and a half (Neh 2:11–6:16).

25:17 ***three cubits.*** This may be the height of the capitals not including the ornamental work; 1Ki 7:16 and Jer 52:22 say five cubits.

CHAPTER 25 **1** 2Ch 36:17; Jer 34:2; Eze 24:1 **3** Jer 39:2 **4** Jer 39:2; 39:4-7; Eze 12:12 **6** 2Ki 23:33; Jer 52:9 **7** Jer 39:7 **8** Jer 52:12; 2Ki 24:12; Jer 39:9 **9** 2Ch 36:19; Jer 39:8; Am 2:5 **10** Neh 1:3; Jer 52:14 **11** Jer 39:9 **12** 2Ki 24:14 **13** Jer 27:19; 52:17; 1Ki 7:15; 1Ki 7:27; 1Ki 7:23 **14** Ex 27:3; 1Ki 7:45 **16** 1Ki 7:47 **17** 1Ki 7:15; Jer 52:21

granates around the capital were all of
bronze. And the second pillar had the
same as these, with a network.
18The captain of the bodyguard took
[captive] Seraiah the chief priest, Zeph-
aniah the second priest, and the three
doorkeepers [of the temple].
19And from the city [of Jerusalem]
he took an officer who was in com-
mand of the men of war, and five men
from the king's personal advisors
who were found in the city, and the
scribe of the captain of the army who
mustered the people of the land [for

25:18 ***Seraiah.*** Although Seraiah was executed (v. 21), his son Jehozadak was deported (1Ch 6:15). Through Jehozadak's line would come Ezra, the priest and great reformer, who one day would return to Jerusalem and take up Seraiah's work (Ezr 7:1).

18 Jer 52:24; 1Ch 6:14; Ezr 7:1; Jer 21:1 **19** Jer 52:25

THE CAMPAIGN OF NEBUCHADNEZZAR AGAINST JUDAH

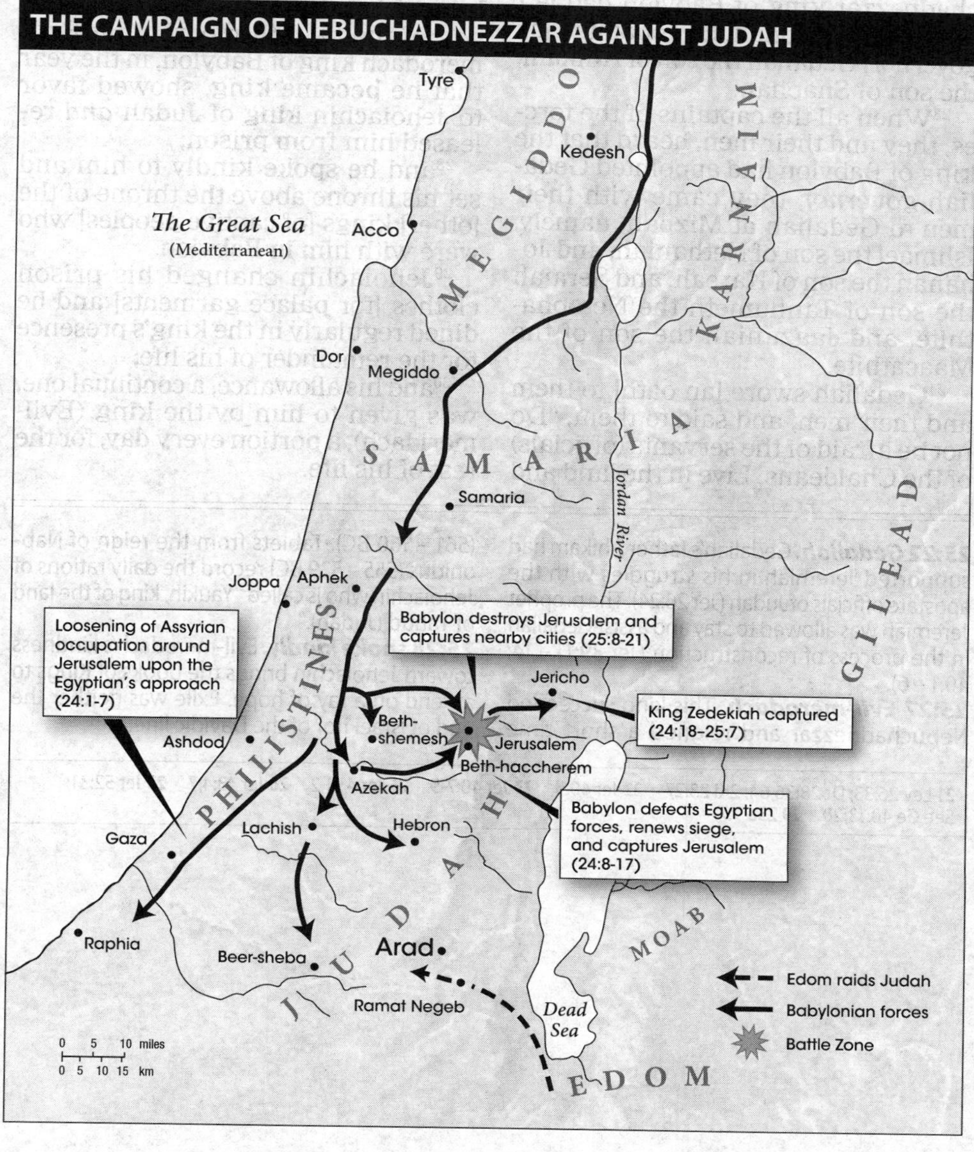

military service] and sixty men from the people of the land who were found in the city.
[20]Nebuzaradan the captain of the bodyguard took them and brought them to the king of Babylon at Riblah.
[21]Then the king of Babylon struck them down and killed them at Riblah in the land of Hamath [north of Damascus]. So Judah was taken into exile from its land.

Gedaliah Made Governor

[22]Now over the people whom Nebuchadnezzar king of Babylon had left in the land of Judah, he appointed [as governor] Gedaliah the son of Ahikam, the son of Shaphan.
[23]When all the captains of the forces, they and their men, heard that the king of Babylon had appointed Gedaliah *governor,* they came with their men to Gedaliah at Mizpah, namely, Ishmael the son of Nethaniah, and Johanan the son of Kareah, and Seraiah the son of Tanhumeth the Netophathite, and Jaazaniah the son of the Maacathite.
[24]Gedaliah swore [an oath] to them and their men, and said to them, "Do not be afraid of the servants (officials) of the Chaldeans. Live in the land and serve the king of Babylon, and it will be well with you."
[25]But in the seventh month Ishmael the son of Nethaniah, the son of Elishama, of the royal family [who had a claim to be governor], came with ten men and struck and killed Gedaliah and the Jews and the Chaldeans who were with him at Mizpah.
[26]Then all the people, both small and great, and the captains of the forces set out and went to Egypt; for they were afraid of the Chaldeans (Babylonians).
[27]Now it came about in the thirty-seventh year of the exile of Jehoiachin king of Judah, on the twenty-seventh day of the twelfth month, that Evil-merodach king of Babylon, in the year that he became king, showed favor to Jehoiachin king of Judah *and* released him from prison;
[28]and he spoke kindly to him and set his throne above the throne of the [other] kings [of captive peoples] who were with him in Babylon.
[29]Jehoiachin changed his prison clothes [for palace garments] and he dined regularly in the king's presence for the remainder of his life;
[30]and his allowance, a continual one, was given to him by the king (Evil-meridach), a portion every day, for the rest of his life.

25:22 *Gedaliah.* Gedaliah's father Ahikam had supported Jeremiah in his struggles with the apostate officials of Judah (Jer 26:24). The prophet Jeremiah was allowed to stay and assist Gedaliah in the process of reconstruction (Jer 39:11 – 14; 40:1 – 6).
25:27 *Evil-merodach.* This king succeeded Nebuchadnezzar and reigned a short time (561 – 560 BC). Tablets from the reign of Nabonidus (555 – 539 BC) record the daily rations of Jehoiachin who is called "Yaukin, king of the land of Yahud (Judah)."
25:28 *spoke kindly.* Evil-merodach's kindness toward Jehoiachin brings the books of Kings to an end on a ray of hope. Exile was neither the end of Israel nor of the Davidic line.

21 Lev 26:33; Dt 28:36,64; 2Ki 23:27 **22** Jer 40:5 **23** Jer 40:7-9 **25** Jer 41:1,2 **26** Jer 43:4,7 **27** Jer 52:31; See Ge 40:13,20 **29** 2Sa 9:7

THE FIRST BOOK OF THE

CHRONICLES

▸ **AUTHOR:** Tradition in the Jewish Talmud supports Ezra the priest as the author of 1 Chronicles. The content points to priestly authorship because of the emphasis on the temple, the priesthood, and the theocratic line of David in the Southern Kingdom of Judah. Ezra was an educated scribe (Ezr 7:6), and according to the apocryphal book of 2 Maccabees 2:13 – 15, Nehemiah collected an extensive library which was available to Ezra for his use in compiling Chronicles.

▸ **TIMES:** c. 1004 – 971 BC ▸ **KEY VERSES:** 1Ch 7:11 – 14

▸ **THEME:** First Chronicles is largely a retelling of the texts of 1 and 2 Samuel with administrative details and the roles that the various tribes and alliances played in the events of the nation. We don't see the family conflict with Michal when the ark is brought to Jerusalem or the affair with Bathsheba and its fallout. When it comes to succession, all we are told is that David chose Solomon to succeed him. This is a primary document of the history of Israel.

Genealogy from Adam

1 ADAM [HIS genealogical line],
Seth, Enosh,
[2]Kenan, Mahalalel, Jared,
[3]Enoch, Methuselah, Lamech,
[4]Noah, [and his sons] Shem, Ham,
and Japheth.
[5]The sons (descendants) of Japheth:
Gomer, Magog, Madai, Javan, Tubal,
Meshech, and Tiras.
[6]The sons of Gomer: Ashkenaz,
Diphath, and Togarmah.
[7]The sons of Javan: Elishah, Tarshish, Kittim, and Rodanim.
[8]The sons of Ham: Cush, Mizraim,
Put, and Canaan.
[9]The sons of Cush: Seba, Havilah,
Sabta, Raama, and Sabteca. The sons
of Raamah: Sheba and Dedan.
[10]Cush became the father of Nimrod;
he began to be a mighty one upon the
earth.
[11]Mizraim became the father of the
people of Lud, Anam, Lehab, Naphtuh,
[12]Pathrus, and Casluh, from whom
came the Philistines, and Caphtor.
[13]Canaan became the father of Sidon
his firstborn, and Heth,
[14]the Jebusites, Amorites, Girgashites,
[15]Hivites, Arkites, Sinites,
[16]Arvadites, Zemarites, and Hamathites.
[17]The sons of Shem: Elam, Asshur,
Arpachshad, Lud, Aram, Uz, Hul,
Gether, and Meshech.
[18]Arpachshad became the father of
Shelah, and Shelah became the father
of Eber.
[19]To Eber were born two sons: the
name of the one was Peleg, because

1:1 ***Adam [his genealogical line], Seth, Enosh.*** Including the names of these pre-flood people along with the rest of the genealogical record indicates that the chronicler had no question of their historical identity.

1:18 ***Eber.*** Eber was the ancestor of Abraham, Isaac, and Jacob. The name Hebrew, a derivative of Eber's name, was applied to the Israelites.

1:19 ***the earth was divided.*** This refers to the division of the earth's population by the scattering of the human race following the judgment of God on the tower of Babel.

CHAPTER 1 **1** Ge 4:25,26; 5:3,9 **5** Ge 10:2 **8** Ge 10:6 **10** Ge 10:8,13 **12** Dt 2:23 **13** Ge 10:15 **17** Ge 10:22; 11:10

in his days [the population of] the
earth was divided [according to its
languages], and his brother's name
was Joktan.
20 Joktan became the father of Almodad,
Sheleph, Hazarmaveth, Jerah,
21 Hadoram, Uzal, Diklah,
22 Ebal, Abimael, Sheba,
23 Ophir, Havilah, and Jobab. All
these were the sons of Joktan.
24 Shem [his genealogical line], Arpachshad,
Shelah,
25 Eber, Peleg, Reu,
26 Serug, Nahor, Terah,
27 Abram, the same as Abraham.

Descendants of Abraham

28 The sons of Abraham: Isaac [by
his wife Sarah] and Ishmael [by Hagar
her maid].
29 These are their descendants: The
firstborn of Ishmael, Nebaioth; then
Kedar, Adbeel, Mibsam,
30 Mishma, Dumah, Massa, Hadad,
Tema,
31 Jetur, Naphish, and Kedemah.
These are the sons of Ishmael.
32 Now the sons of Keturah, Abraham's
concubine: she gave birth to
Zimran, Jokshan, Medan, Midian, Ishbak,
and Shuah. The sons of Jokshan:
Sheba and Dedan.
33 The sons of Midian: Ephah, Epher,
Hanoch, Abida, and Eldaah. All these
are the sons [and grandsons] of Keturah.
34 Abraham became the father of
Isaac. The sons of Isaac: Esau and Israel
(Jacob).
35 The sons of Esau: Eliphaz, Reuel,
Jeush, Jalam, and Korah.
36 The sons of Eliphaz: Teman, Omar,
Zephi, Gatam, Kenaz, Timna, and
Amalek.
37 The sons of Reuel: Nahath, Zerah,
Shammah, and Mizzah.
38 The sons of Seir: Lotan, Shobal, Zibeon,
Anah, Dishon, Ezer, and Dishan.
39 The sons of Lotan: Hori and
Homam; and Timna was Lotan's sister.
40 The sons of Shobal: Alian, Manahath,
Ebal, Shephi, and Onam. The
sons of Zibeon: Aiah and Anah.
41 The son of Anah: Dishon. The sons
of Dishon: Hamran, Eshban, Ithran,
and Cheran.
42 The sons of Ezer: Bilhan, Zaavan,
and Jaakan. The sons of Dishan: Uz
and Aran.
43 These are the kings who reigned
in the land of Edom before any king
reigned over the sons (descendants) of
Israel (Jacob): Bela the son of Beor; the
name of his city was Dinhabah.
44 When Bela died, Jobab the son of Zerah
of Bozrah became king in his place.
45 When Jobab died, Husham of the
land of the Temanites became king in
his place.
46 When Husham died, Hadad [I of
Edom] the son of Bedad, who defeated
Midian in the field of Moab, became
king in his place; the name of his city
was Avith.
47 When Hadad [I] died, Samlah of
Masrekah became king in his place.
48 When Samlah died, Shaul of Rehoboth
on the River [Euphrates] became
king in his place.
49 When Shaul died, Baal-hanan
the son of Achbor became king in his
place.
50 When Baal-hanan died, Hadad [II]
became king in his place; the name of
his city was Pai; his wife's name was
Mehetabel daughter of Matred, the
daughter of Mezahab.

1:36 ***Timna.*** Timna was Eliphaz's concubine (Ge 36:12). Her son Amalek was the founder of the Amalekites, a people that became one of Israel's most persistent enemies (Ex 17:8 – 16; Dt 25:17 – 19; 1Sa 15:1 – 3).
1:38 ***Seir.*** Seir was the patriarchal name of the pre-Edomite population in the region east and south of the Dead Sea (Ge 36:20 – 30). ***Lotan.*** Lotan was Temna's brother, and Temna was the concubine of Esau's son. This is how the people of Seir and the descendants of Esau were related, and together these two people groups became the kingdom of Edom.
1:43 ***the kings . . . of Edom.*** Although the kings of Edom ruled in succession, they were not part of a dynasty. Apparently Edom did not have a capital, and its kings ruled from their own cities.

20 Ge 10:26 **24** Ge 11:10; Lk 3:36 **25** Ge 11:15 **27** Ge 17:5 **28** Ge 21:2; Ge 16:11,15 **29** Ge 25:13-16 **32** Ge 25:1 **34** Ge 21:2; 25:25,26 **35** Ge 36:9,10 **38** Ge 36:20 **41** Ge 36:25 **43** Ge 36:31 **48** Ge 36:37

51 Hadad died also.
The chiefs of Edom were: chiefs
Timna, Aliah, Jetheth,
52 Oholibamah, Elah, Pinon,
53 Kenaz, Teman, Mibzar,
54 Magdiel, and Iram. These are the
chiefs of Edom.

Genealogy: Twelve Sons of Jacob (Israel)

2 THESE ARE the sons of Israel:
Reuben, Simeon, Levi, Judah, Is-
sachar, Zebulun,
2 Dan, Joseph, Benjamin, Naphtali,
Gad, and Asher.
3 The sons of Judah: Er, Onan, and
Shelah; the three were born to him by
Shua's daughter the Canaanitess. Er,
Judah's eldest, was evil in the LORD's
sight, and He put him to death.
4 Tamar, Judah's daughter-in-law,
bore him Perez and Zerah. Judah's
sons were five in all. [Gen 38]
5 The sons of Perez: Hezron and
Hamul.
6 The sons of Zerah: Zimri, Ethan,
Heman, Calcol, and Dara—five in all.
[1 Kin 4:31]
7 The son of Carmi: Achar, the trou-
bler of Israel, who violated the ban [by
taking things from Jericho that had
been banned]. [Josh 7:1]
8 The son of Ethan: Azariah.

Genealogy of David

9 The sons of Hezron who were born
to him: Jerahmeel, Ram, and Chelubai
[that is, Caleb].
10 Ram became the father of Am-
minadab, and Amminadab became
the father of Nahshon, leader of the
sons of Judah.
11 Nahshon became the father of Sal-
ma, Salma became the father of Boaz,
12 Boaz became the father of Obed,
and Obed became the father of Jesse.
13 Jesse became the father of Eliab
his firstborn, Abinadab the second,
Shimea the third,
14 Nethanel the fourth, Raddai the fifth,
15 Ozem the sixth, David the seventh.
16 Their sisters were Zeruiah and Ab-
igail. The sons of Zeruiah: Abishai,
Joab, and Asahel, three.
17 Abigail gave birth to Amasa, and
the father of Amasa was Jether the
Ishmaelite.
18 And Caleb the son of Hezron had
sons by his wife Azubah and by Jeri-
oth. Azubah's sons were: Jesher, Sho-
bab, and Ardon.
19 Azubah died, and Caleb married
Ephrath, who bore him Hur.
20 Hur became the father of Uri, and
Uri became the father of Bezalel [the
skillful craftsman who made the fur-
nishings of the tabernacle]. [Ex 31:2–5]
21 Later, when Hezron was sixty
years old, he married the daughter of
Machir the father of Gilead, and she
bore him Segub.
22 Segub became the father of Jair,
who [later] had twenty-three cities in
the land of Gilead.
23 But Geshur and Aram took from
them Havvoth-jair, with Kenath and
its villages, sixty towns *in all*. All these
were the sons (descendants) of Machir,
the father of Gilead.

1:51 *chiefs.* The word "chiefs" usually referred to military leaders (Ge 36:40 – 43).

2:1 – 55 Family — The Hebrew nation, descended through Abraham, kept one of the most carefully preserved family records of all time. To be associated with the family of Israel was to be identified with the God of Israel, and the history of this people is closely associated with the things that God taught each of these ancestors.

2:10 *Nahshon.* This genealogy is selective, focusing on the members important to the lineage of David. Nahshon was head of the tribe of Judah at the time of the wilderness march from Sinai to Kadesh Barnea (Nu 1:7; 2:3; 7:12). He was more than five generations removed from Judah.

2:16 *sisters.* Sisters are not usually mentioned in ancient genealogies. However this genealogy pays particular attention to the family of David, and as his sister's sons were important members of his military units, the sisters are listed.

2:18 *Caleb.* This Caleb is not the famous companion of Joshua (Nu 13:6; Jos 14:6 – 7), who lived several centuries later during the conquest of Canaan.

51 Ge 36:40 **CHAPTER 2** **1** Ge 29:32; 30:5; 35:18,22; 46:8 **3** Ge 38:3; 46:12; Nu 26:19; Ge 38:2; Ge 38:7 **4** Ge 38:29,30 **5** Ge 46:12; Ru 4:18 **6** 1Ki 4:31 **7** See 1Ch 4:1; Jos 6:18; 7:1 **10** Ru 4:19,20; Mt 1:4; Nu 1:7; 2:3 **13** 1Sa 16:6 **16** 2Sa 2:18 **17** 2Sa 17:25 **19** ver. 50 **20** Ex 31:2 **21** Nu 27:1 **23** Nu 32:41; Dt 3:14; Jos 13:30

[24]After Hezron died in Caleb-
ephrathah, Abijah, Hezron's wife, bore
him Ashhur the father of Tekoa.
[25]The sons of Jerahmeel the first-
born of Hezron: Ram the firstborn,
Bunah, Oren, Ozem, and Ahijah.
[26]Jerahmeel had another wife,
named Atarah; she was the mother
of Onam.
[27]The sons of Ram the firstborn of
Jerahmeel were: Maaz, Jamin, and
Eker.
[28]The sons of Onam: Shammai and
Jada. The sons of Shammai: Nadab
and Abishur.
[29]The name of Abishur's wife was
Abihail; she bore him Ahban and
Molid.
[30]The sons of Nadab: Seled and Ap-
paim. Seled died childless.
[31]The son of Appaim: Ishi. The son
of Ishi: Sheshan. The son of Sheshan:
Ahlai.
[32]The sons of Jada the brother of
Shammai: Jether and Jonathan. Jether
died childless.
[33]The sons of Jonathan: Peleth and
Zaza. These were the sons (descen-
dants) of Jerahmeel.
[34]Sheshan had no sons—only daugh-
ters. But Sheshan had a servant, an
Egyptian, whose name was Jarha.
[35]So Sheshan gave his daughter to
Jarha his servant as a wife; she bore
him Attai.
[36]Attai became the father of Na-
than, and Nathan became the father
of Zabad.
[37]Zabad became the father of Ephlal,
and Ephlal became the father of Obed.
[38]Obed became the father of Jehu,
and Jehu became the father of Aza-
riah.
[39]Azariah became the father of
Helez, and Helez became the father
of Eleasah.
[40]Eleasah became the father of Sis-
mai, and Sismai became the father of
Shallum.
[41]Shallum became the father of Jeka-
miah, and Jekamiah became the father
of Elishama.
[42]The sons of Caleb, the brother of
Jerahmeel: Mesha his firstborn was
the father of Ziph; and his son Mare-
shah was the father of Hebron.
[43]The sons of Hebron: Korah,
Tappuah, Rekem, and Shema.
[44]Shema became the father of Ra-
ham, the father of Jorkeam. And Re-
kem became the father of Shammai.
[45]The son of Shammai was Maon;
Maon became the father of Bethzur.
[46]Ephah, Caleb's concubine, gave
birth to Haran, Moza, and Gazez; Ha-
ran became the father of Gazez.
[47]The sons of Jahdai: Regem,
Jotham, Geshan, Pelet, Ephah, and
Shaaph.
[48]Maacah, Caleb's concubine, gave
birth to Sheber and Tirhanah.
[49]She also bore Shaaph the father
of Madmannah and Sheva the father
of Machbena and of Gibea; and the
daughter of Caleb was Achsah.
[50]These were the sons (descendants)
of Caleb.
The sons of Hur, the firstborn of
Ephrathah: Shobal the father of
Kiriath-jearim,
[51]Salma the father of Bethlehem and
Hareph the father of Beth-gader.
[52]Shobal the father of Kiriath-
jearim had [other] sons (descendants):
Haroeh, half of the Manahathites [in
Judah],
[53]and the families of Kiriath-jearim:
the Ithrites, Puthites, Shumathites,
and Mishraites. From these came the
Zorathites and the Eshtaolites.
[54]The sons (descendants) of Salma:
Bethlehem, the Netophathites, Atroth-
beth-joab, and half of the Manaha-
thites, the Zorites.
[55]The families of scribes who lived
at Jabez: the Tirathites, Shimeathites,
and Sucathites. These are the Kenites
who came from Hammath, the father
of the house of Rechab.

2:51 *father of Bethlehem.* The chronicler recorded Caleb's genealogy because of the significance of Bethlehem, the birthplace of King David. One of Caleb's descendants, Salma, was the founder of Bethlehem.

24 1Ch 4:5 **31** See ver. 34,35 **36** 1Ch 11:41 **49** Jos 15:17 **55** Jdg 1:16; Jer 35:2

Family of David

3 THESE WERE the sons of David
who were born to him in Hebron:
the firstborn was Amnon, by Ahin-
oam the Jezreelitess; second, Daniel
(Chileab), by Abigail the Carmelitess;
2 third, Absalom the son of Maacah,
daughter of Talmai king of Geshur;
fourth, Adonijah, the son of Haggith;
3 fifth, Shephatiah, by Abital; sixth,
Ithream, by his wife Eglah.
4 These six were born to David in
Hebron; he reigned there seven years
and six months, and in Jerusalem he
reigned thirty-three years.
5 These were born to David in Je-
rusalem: Shimea (Shammua), Sho-
bab, Nathan, Solomon—four by Bath-
shua (Bathsheba) daughter of Ammiel
(Eliam);
6 then Ibhar, Elishama (Elishua),
Eliphelet (Elpelet),
7 Nogah, Nepheg, Japhia,
8 Elishama, Eliada (Beeliada), and
Eliphelet—nine *in all.*
9 All *these were* the sons of David,
besides the sons of the concubines; and
Tamar was their sister.
10 Solomon's son was Rehoboam.
Abijah was his son, Asa his son, Je-
hoshaphat his son,
11 Joram (Jehoram) his son, Ahaziah
his son, Joash his son,
12 Amaziah his son, Azariah his son,
Jotham his son,
13 Ahaz his son, Hezekiah his son,
Manasseh his son,
14 Amon his son, Josiah his son.
15 The sons of Josiah: firstborn, Jo-
hanan; second, Jehoiakim (Eliakim);
third, Zedekiah; fourth, Shallum (Je-
hoahaz).
16 The sons (descendants) of Jehoi-
akim: Jehoiachin (Jeconiah) his son,
Zedekiah his son.
17 The sons (descendants) of Jehoia-
chin (Jeconiah) the prisoner: Shealtiel
his son,
18 Malchiram, Pedaiah, Shenazzar,
Jekamiah, Hoshama and Nedabiah.
19 The sons of Pedaiah: Zerubbabel
and Shimei. The sons of Zerubbabel:
Meshullam and Hananiah, and She-
lomith was their sister;
20 and Hashubah, Ohel, Berechiah,
Hasadiah, and Jushab-hesed—five *in
all.*
21 The sons of Hananiah: Pelatiah
and Jeshaiah, the sons of Rephaiah,
the sons of Arnan, the sons of Obadi-
ah, the sons of Shecaniah.
22 The sons (descendants) of Sheca-
niah: Shemaiah. The sons of Shema-
iah: Hattush, Igal, Bariah, Neariah,
and Shaphat—six *in all.*
23 The sons of Neariah: Elioenai, Hiz-
kiah, and Azrikam—three *in all.*
24 The sons of Elioenai: Hodaviah,
Eliashib, Pelaiah, Akkub, Johanan,
Delaiah, and Anani—seven *in all.*

Descendants of Judah

4 THE SONS of Judah: Perez, Hez-
ron, Carmi, Hur, and Shobal.
2 Reaiah the son of Shobal became the
father of Jahath, and Jahath became
the father of Ahumai and Lahad. These
were the families of the Zorathites.

3:1 – 5 *sons of David.* The fact that David had six sons by six wives in Hebron does not condone polygamy. David had apparently followed the custom of marrying the daughters of neighboring kings to create allies, in spite of the warning Moses gave for the kings to avoid accumulating many wives (Dt 17:17). Jesus refers back to creation when He addresses the concept of single partners for life (Mt 19:1 – 12), so it is clear that even though some polygamy was practiced, it has never been God's plan for marriage.

3:19 *Pedaiah.* Zerubbabel here is designated as a son of Pedaiah, but elsewhere (Ezr 3:2; 8; 5:2; Neh 12:1; Hag 1:12; 14; 2:2; 23) as a son of Pedaiah's brother Shealtiel (v. 17). It is likely that Shealtiel had died while Zerubbabel was young, and that the youth was raised by his uncle Pedaiah. This relationship may explain Luke's statement that Zerubbabel was "the son of Shealtiel" (Lk 3:27), who was a descendant of David through his son Nathan.

4:1 *sons of Judah.* The chronicler here refers to other persons and events relative to Judah's genealogy (2:3 – 17). In the list in this verse Perez is Judah's son, Hezron is his grandson, Carmi his nephew, Hur the grandson of Hezron, and Shobal the grandson of Hur.

CHAPTER 3 **1** 2Sa 3:2; Jos 15:56 **3** 2Sa 3:5 **4** 2Sa 2:11; 2Sa 5:5 **5** 1Ch 14:4; 2Sa 12:24 **8** See 2Sa 5:14-16 **9** 2Sa 13:1 **10** 1Ki 11:43 **16** Mt 1:11; 2Ki 24:17, being his uncle **17** Mt 1:12 **22** Ezr 8:2 **CHAPTER 4** **1** Ge 46:12

3 These were the sons of Etam: Jezreel, Ishma, and Idbash; and the name of their sister was Hazzelelponi.

4 Penuel was the father of Gedor, and Ezer the father of Hushah. These were the sons of Hur, the eldest of Ephrathah (Ephrath), the father of Bethlehem.

5 Ashhur, the father of Tekoa, had two wives, Helah and Naarah.

6 Naarah bore him Ahuzzam, Hepher, Temeni and Haahashtari. These were Naarah's sons.

7 The sons of Helah: Zereth, Izhar, and Ethnan.

8 Koz fathered Anub, Zobebah, and the families of Aharhel the son of Harum.

9 Jabez was more honorable than his brothers; but his mother named him Jabez, saying, "Because I gave birth to him in pain."

10 Jabez cried out to the God of Israel, saying, "Oh that You would indeed bless me and enlarge my border [property], and that Your hand would be with me, and You would keep me from evil so that it does not hurt me!" And God granted his request.

11 Chelub the brother of Shuhah became the father of Mehir, the father of Eshton.

12 Eshton became the father of Beth-rapha, Paseah, and Tehinnah the father of Ir-nahash. These are the men of Recah.

13 The sons of Kenaz: Othniel and Seraiah. The sons of Othniel: Hathath and Meonothai.

14 Meonothai became the father of Ophrah, and Seraiah became the father of Joab the father of Ge-harashim [the Valley of Craftsmen, so named] because they were craftsmen.

15 The sons of Caleb [Joshua's companion] the son of Jephunneh: Iru, Elah, and Naam. The son of Elah: Kenaz.

16 The sons of Jehallelel: Ziph, Ziphah, Tiria, and Asarel.

17 The sons of Ezrah: Jether, Mered, Epher, and Jalon. These are the sons of Bithia daughter of Pharaoh, whom Mered took: she conceived *and gave birth to* Miriam, Shammai, and Ishbah the father of Eshtemoa.

18 Mered's Jewish wife gave birth to Jered the father of Gedor, Heber the father of Soco, and Jekuthiel the father of Zanoah.

19 The sons of the wife of Hodiah, the sister of Naham, were: the fathers of Keilah the Garmite and Eshtemoa the Maacathite.

20 The sons of Shimon: Amnon, Rinnah, Benhanan, and Tilon. The sons of Ishi: Zoheth and Ben-zoheth.

21 The sons of Shelah son of Judah: Er the father of Lecah and Laadah the father of Mareshah, and the families of the house of the linen workers at Beth-ashbea;

22 and Jokim, the men of Cozeba, Joash, and Saraph, who ruled in Moab, and Jashubi-lehem. These are ancient words (genealogical records).

23 These were the potters and those who lived [among plantations and hedges] at Netaim and Gederah; they lived there with the king for his work.

4:4 *Ephrathah.* Ephrathah is the wife of the early Caleb (2:19) and the mother of Hur, whose son Salma was the "father of Bethlehem." The names of Bethlehem and Ephrath are closely connected (Ge 35:19; Ru 4:11), and the birthplace of the anticipated Messiah is called Bethlehem Ephrathah (Mic 5:2).

4:9 – 10 Providence — This passage does not say why or how Jabez was more honorable than his brothers. At the least, he recognized that God is the source of all blessings, and Jabez asked God to bless him. James said that we have not because we ask not (Jas 4:2 – 3), and then goes on to address the issue of selfish motives in prayer. Paul encourages believers not to be anxious, but to make our requests to God, with prayer and thanksgiving (Php 4:6). It is clear that it is right to ask God for the things that we believe are good, to thank Him for them, and to keep in mind that we can trust Him to meet all of our needs.

4:15 *Caleb.* This is the Caleb who was the friend and colleague of Joshua (Jos 14:6 – 7).

4:21 *Er.* The fact the Shelah named his son "Er" indicates that he followed the levirate custom of raising up a child in the name of a deceased brother (Ge 38:6 – 11).

4 1Ch 2:50 **5** 1Ch 2:24 **9** Ge 34:19 **13** Jos 15:17 **14** Neh 11:35 **21** Ge 38:1,5

Descendants of Simeon

24 The sons of Simeon: Nemuel, Jamin, Jarib, Zerah, and Shaul;

25 Shallum was Shaul's son, Mibsam his son, Mishma his son.

26 The sons of Mishma: Hammuel his son, Zaccur his son, Shimei his son.

27 Shimei had sixteen sons and six daughters; but his brothers did not have many sons, neither did all their family multiply like the sons of Judah.

28 They lived at Beersheba, Moladah, Hazar-shual,

29 Bilhah, Ezem, Tolad,

30 Bethuel, Hormah, Ziklag,

31 Beth-marcaboth, Hazar-susim, Beth-biri, and at Shaaraim. These were their cities until the reign of David.

32 *These were* their villages: Etam, Ain, Rimmon, Tochen, and Ashan—five cities—

33 and all their villages that were around these towns as far as Baal. These were their settlements, and they have their genealogical record.

34 Meshobab, Jamlech, Joshah the son of Amaziah,

35 Joel, Jehu the son of Joshibiah, the son of Seraiah, the son of Asiel,

36 also Elioenai, Jaakobah, Jeshohaiah, Asaiah, Adiel, Jesimiel, Benaiah,

37 Ziza the son of Shiphi, the son of Allon, the son of Jedaiah, the son of Shimri, the son of Shemaiah;

38 these mentioned by name were leaders in their families; and their fathers' houses increased greatly [so they needed more land].

39 So they journeyed to the entrance of Gedor, to the east side of the valley, to seek pasture for their flocks.

40 They found rich, good pasture, and the [cleared] land was wide, quiet, and peaceful; for those who had lived there previously came from Ham [and had left it a better place for those who came after them].

41 These, registered by name, came in the days of Hezekiah king of Judah, and they attacked their tents and the Meunites (foreigners) who were found there, and utterly destroyed them to this day; and they settled in their place, because there was pasture there for their flocks.

42 From them, from the sons of Simeon, five hundred men went to Mount Seir, with Pelatiah, Neariah, Rephaiah, and Uzziel, the sons of Ishi, as their leaders.

43 They destroyed the remnant of the Amalekites who escaped, and they have lived there to this day (the date of this writing).

Descendants of Reuben

5 NOW [WE come to] the sons of Reuben the firstborn of Israel—for Reuben was the eldest, but because he defiled his father's bed [with Bilhah his father's concubine], his birthright was given to [Manasseh and Ephraim] the sons of Joseph [the favorite] son of Israel, so that he is not enrolled in the genealogy according to the birthright. [Gen 35:22; 48:15–22; 49:3, 4]

2 Though Judah prevailed over his brothers, and from him came [David] the leader [and eventually the Messiah], yet the birthright was Joseph's—[Gen 49:10; Mic 5:2]

3 the sons of Reuben the firstborn of Israel: Hanoch, Pallu, Hezron, and Carmi.

4 The sons of Joel: Shemaiah his son, Gog his son, Shimei his son,

---

4:24 *Simeon.* The tribe of Simeon had no land allotted to them (Jos 19:1 – 9) because they were a small tribe. They settled in the territory of Judah.

5:9 entrance into . . . the river Euphrates. The Reubenites had pushed east into the wilderness, so they were the first to be deported by the Assyrians (v. 6).

5:25 Unbelief — In marriage, adultery is the ultimate breach of trust, breaking a solemn promise of faithfulness and commitment. These tribes of Israel acted just like adulterers when they chose idols instead of the living God. Like a prostitute who has chosen crudity, vulgarity, and cheap finery instead of the steady faithful love and fine clothing from her husband, so Israel had believed a lie and abandoned their covenant with the living God.

28 Jos 19:2 **41** 2Ki 18:8 **43** See 1Sa 15:8; 30:17; 2Sa 8:12 **CHAPTER 5** **1** Ge 29:32; 49:3; Ge 35:22; 49:4; Ge 48:15,22 **2** Ge 49:8,10; Ps 60:7; 108:8; Mic 5:2; Mt 2:6 **3** Ge 46:9; Ex 6:14; Nu 26:5

5 Micah his son, Reaiah his son, Baal his son,

6 Beerah his son, whom Tilgath-pilneser king of Assyria carried away into exile; he was a leader of the tribe of Reuben.

7 And his brothers (relatives) by their families, in the genealogy of their generations, were the chief Jeiel, and Zechariah,

8 Bela the son of Azaz, the son of Shema, the son of Joel, who lived in Aroer as far as Nebo and Baal-meon.

9 To the east Bela settled as far as the entrance into the desert from the river Euphrates, because their cattle had multiplied in the land of Gilead.

10 In the days of King Saul they made war with the Hagrites, who fell by their hands; and they lived in their tents throughout all the land east of Gilead.

Descendants of Gad

11 The sons of Gad lived opposite them in the land of Bashan, as far as Salecah:

12 Joel was the chief, Shapham the second, then Janai and Shaphat in Bashan.

13 Their relatives from the households of their fathers: Michael, Meshullam, Sheba, Jorai, Jacan, Zia, and Eber—seven *in all*.

14 These were the sons of Abihail the son of Huri, the son of Jaroah, the son of Gilead, the son of Michael, the son of Jeshishai, the son of Jahdo, the son of Buz;

15 Ahi the son of Abdiel, the son of Guni, was chief in their fathers' households.

16 They lived in Gilead, in Bashan and in its towns, and in all the [surrounding] pasture lands of Sharon, as far as their borders.

17 All these were enrolled in the genealogies in the days of Jotham king of Judah and in the days of Jeroboam [II] king of Israel.

18 The sons of Reuben, the Gadites, and the half-tribe of Manasseh—valiant men able to bear shield and sword, and to shoot with the bow, and skillful in war—were 44,760 who went to war.

19 And these Israelites, [on the east side of the Jordan River] made war with the Hagrites [a tribe of northern Arabia], Jetur, Naphish, and Nodab.

20 They were given help against them, and the Hagrites were handed over to them, and all who were *allied* with them; for they cried out to God [for help] in the battle; and He granted their entreaty because they relied on *and* trusted in Him.

21 These Israelites took away their livestock: their 50,000 camels, and 250,000 sheep, and 2,000 donkeys; and 100,000 people.

22 For a great number fell mortally wounded, because the battle was of God. And these Israelites settled in their territory until the exile [by Assyria more than five centuries later]. [2 Kin 15:29]

Descendants of Manasseh

23 Now the sons (people) of the half-tribe of Manasseh lived in the land; their settlements spread from Bashan to Baal-hermon and Senir and Mount Hermon.

24 These were the heads of their fathers' households: Epher, Ishi, Eliel, Azriel, Jeremiah, Hodaviah, and Jahdiel, warriors of valor [willing and able to encounter danger], famous men, and heads of the households of their fathers.

25 But they acted treacherously against the God of their fathers and played the prostitute with the gods of the peoples of the land, whom God had destroyed before them.

26 So the God of Israel stirred up the spirit of Pul, king of Assyria, [that is,] the spirit of Tilgath-pilneser king of

5:26 *Tilgath-pilneser.* The famous king Tiglath-pilneser, who reigned around 745–727 BC, has gone down in Assyrian annals as one of the most powerful rulers of the neo-Assyrian period (v. 6).

7 See ver. 17 **8** Jos 13:15,16 **9** Jos 22:9 **10** Ge 25:12 **11** Jos 13:11,24 **16** 1Ch 27:29 **17** 2Ki 15:5,32; 14:16,28 **19** Ge 25:15; 1Ch 1:31 **20** See ver. 22; Ps 22:4,5 **22** 2Ki 15:29; 17:6 **25** 2Ki 17:7 **26** 2Ki 15:19; 2Ki 15:29; 2Ki 17:6; 18:11

Assyria, and he carried them away into exile—the Reubenites, the Gadites, and the half-tribe of Manasseh—and brought them to Halah, Habor, Hara, and the river Gozan, [where they remain] to this day.

Genealogy: The Priestly Line

6 THE SONS of Levi: Gershom, Kohath and Merari.
2The sons of Kohath: Amram, Izhar, Hebron, and Uzziel.
3The sons of Amram: Aaron, Moses and Miriam. And the sons of Aaron: Nadab, Abihu, Eleazar, and Ithamar.
4Eleazar became the father of Phinehas, Phinehas became the father of Abishua,
5and Abishua became the father of Bukki, and Bukki became the father of Uzzi,
6and Uzzi became the father of Zerahiah, and Zerahiah became the father of Meraioth,
7Meraioth became the father of Amariah, and Amariah became the father of Ahitub,
8and Ahitub became the father of Zadok, and Zadok became the father of Ahimaaz,
9and Ahimaaz became the father of Azariah, and Azariah became the father of Johanan,
10and Johanan became the father of Azariah (it was he who was priest in the house (temple) which Solomon built in Jerusalem)
11and Azariah became the father of Amariah, and Amariah became the father of Ahitub,
12and Ahitub became the father of Zadok, and Zadok became the father of Shallum,
13and Shallum became the father of Hilkiah, and Hilkiah became the father of Azariah,
14and Azariah became the father of Seraiah, and Seraiah became the father of Jehozadak;
15and Jehozadak went into captivity when the LORD sent [the people of] Judah and Jerusalem into exile by the hand of Nebuchadnezzar.
16The sons of Levi: Gershom, Kohath, and Merari.
17These are the names of the sons of Gershom: Libni and Shimei.
18The sons of Kohath: Amram, Izhar, Hebron, and Uzziel.
19The sons of Merari: Mahli and Mushi. These are the families of the Levites according to their fathers.

6:1 – 60 Family — Families are usually marked by certain traits or characteristics. Because the Levites were the designated priests, they had a special responsibility to have a reputation for uprightness and faithfulness, but all Israelites were a representation of God to the nations around them. If we are a part of the family of God, we should ask ourselves if we look like God. When people see us, do they see His characteristics?
6:1 *Levi.* All religious personnel involved in tabernacle or temple ministry had to be members of the tribe of Levi. Aaron himself was a Levite, and from the beginning of the priesthood his descendants were designated as the only ones who could serve as high priests (6:16 – 25; Ex 28:1).
6:2 – 4 *Kohath.* This son of Levi was the one to whom the office of priest became exclusively connected. Every priest had to be a Levite, but not every Levite could become a priest. The high priests were descended from Aaron, Kohath's grandson. ***Eleazar.*** Beginning with Eleazar, the genealogy traces the line of high priests through Jehozadak, the priest who went into Babylonian exile with his people (v. 15). ***Ithamar.*** Another line of high priests began with Ithamar, including such persons as Eli, Ahimelech, and Abiathar. In the days of David the priestly service was divided between the Eleazar and the Ithamar priests. Solomon rejected the Ithamar priesthood, and accepted only the priests descended from Eleazar (1Ki 2:26 – 27). From Eleazar to Jehozadak, there were at least 22 high priests in unbroken succession.
6:8 *Zadok.* This priest, not the same person as the Zadok of verse 12, was the one selected by David to serve along with Ahimelech the son of Abiathar as high priest (2Sa 8:17).
6:14 *Jehozadak.* The last priest in the list was carried into Babylon (v. 15). He was the father of Joshua, the priest who returned from Babylon with Zerubbabel to rebuild the temple and reestablish the Jewish community (Hag 1:12,14).
6:17 *Gershom.* The purpose of this genealogy is to list the principal offspring of the sons of Levi who were not priests, but servants in the temple.

CHAPTER 6 **1** Ge 46:11; Ex 6:16; Nu 26:57; 1Ch 23:6 **2** See ver. 22 **3** Lev 10:1 **8** 2Sa 8:17; 2Sa 15:27 **10** See 2Ch 26:17,18; 1Ki 6; 2Ch 3 **11** See Ezr 7:3 **14** Neh 11:11 **15** 2Ki 25:18 **16** Ex 6:16

[20]Of Gershom: Libni his son, Jahath
his son, Zimmah his son,
[21]Joah his son, Iddo his son, Zerah
his son, Jeatherai his son.
[22]The sons of Kohath: Amminadab
his son, Korah his son, Assir his son,
[23]Elkanah his son, Ebiasaph his son,
Assir his son,
[24]Tahath his son, Uriel his son, Uzzi-
ah his son, and Shaul his son.
[25]The sons of Elkanah: Amasai and
Ahimoth.
[26]*As for* Elkanah, the sons of El-
kanah: Zophai his son and Nahath
his son,
[27]Eliab his son, Jeroham his son,
Elkanah [Samuel's father] his son.
[28]The sons of Samuel: Joel the first-
born and Abijah the second.
[29]The sons of Merari: Mahli, Libni
his son, Shimei his son, Uzza his son,
[30]Shimea his son, Haggiah his son,
Asaiah his son.
[31]Now these are those whom David
appointed over the service of song in
the house of the LORD after the ark [of
the covenant] rested *there.*
[32]They ministered with singing
before the tabernacle of the Tent of
Meeting, until Solomon had built the
LORD's house (temple) in Jerusalem,
performing their service in due order.
[33]These men and their sons served
from the Kohathites: Heman the sing-
er, the son of Joel, the son of Samuel
[the great prophet and judge],
[34]the son of Elkanah [III], the son
of Jeroham, the son of Eliel, the son
of Toah,
[35]the son of Zuph, the son of El-
kanah [II], the son of Mahath, the son
of Amasai,
[36]the son of Elkanah [I], the son of
Joel, the son of Azariah, the son of
Zephaniah,
[37]the son of Tahath, the son of Assir,
the son of Ebiasaph, the son of Korah,
[38]the son of Izhar, the son of Ko-
hath, the son of Levi, the son of Israel
(Jacob).
[39]Heman's [tribal] brother Asaph
stood at his right hand: Asaph the son
of Berechiah, the son of Shimea,
[40]the son of Michael, the son of Baa-
seiah, the son of Malchijah,
[41]the son of Ethni, the son of Zerah,
the son of Adaiah,
[42]the son of Ethan, the son of Zim-
mah, the son of Shimei,
[43]the son of Jahath, the son of Ger-
shom, the son of Levi.
[44]Their relatives the sons of Merari
stood at the left hand: Ethan the son
of Kishi, the son of Abdi, the son of
Malluch,
[45]the son of Hashabiah, the son of
Amaziah, the son of Hilkiah,
[46]the son of Amzi, the son of Bani,
the son of Shemer,
[47]the son of Mahli, the son of Mushi,
the son of Merari, the son of Levi.
[48]Their relatives the Levites [who
were not descended from Aaron] were
appointed for all *the other kinds of*
service of the tabernacle of the house
of God.

Descendants of Aaron

[49]But [the line of] Aaron and his sons
made offerings on the altar of burnt
offering and on the altar of incense,
ministering for all the work of the Holy
of Holies (Most Holy Place), and [they
did so] to make atonement for Israel,
according to all that Moses, God's ser-
vant, had commanded.
[50]These are the sons of Aaron: Elea-
zar his son, Phinehas his son, Abishua
his son,
[51]Bukki his son, Uzzi his son, Zera-
hiah his son,
[52]Meraioth his son, Amariah his son,
Ahitub his son,

6:22 *Amminidab.* Amminidab is another name for Ishar (v. 18) who otherwise appears as the father of Korah (6:37 – 38; Ex 6:21; Nu 16:1).

6:28 *Samuel.* Samuel's ancestors were described as Ephraimites (1Sa 1:1). Although Samuel was an Ephraimite because he lived in a city in the tribal territory of Ephraim, this genealogy makes it clear that he was a Levite. Levites lived in their own cities among all the tribes, because they did not receive a land inheritance. As a Levite, he could be trained under Eli (1Sa 2:11), and later officiate at public services that included sacrifices (1Sa 9:13; 10:8).

20 ver. 42 **25** See ver. 35,36 **31** 1Ch 16:1 **37** Ex 6:24 **41** See ver. 21 **49** Lev 1:9; Ex 30:7

53Zadok his son, Ahimaaz his son.
54Now these are their settlements
according to their camps within
their borders: to the sons of Aaron
of the families of the Kohathites (for
theirs was the *first* allocation by lot)
[Josh 21:10]
55to them they gave Hebron in the
land of Judah and its surrounding pas-
ture land;
56but the fields of the city and its
villages they gave to Caleb the son of
Jephunneh.
57To the sons of Aaron they gave
the *following* cities of refuge: Hebron,
Libnah with its pasture lands, Jat-
tir, Eshtemoa with its pasture lands,
[Josh 21:13]
58Hilen with its pasture lands, Debir
with its pasture lands,
59Ashan with its pasture lands, and
Beth-shemesh with its pasture lands;
60and from the tribe of Benjamin:
Geba, Alemeth, and Anathoth, with
their pasture lands. All their cities
throughout their families were thir-
teen cities.
61Then to the rest of the sons of Ko-
hath *were given* ten cities by lot from
the family of the tribe [of Ephraim and
of Dan and], from the half-tribe, the
half of Manasseh. [Josh 21:5]
62To the sons of Gershom, according
to their families, *were given* thirteen
cities from the tribes of Issachar, Ash-
er, Naphtali, and [the other half of]
Manasseh in Bashan.
63To the sons of Merari *were given*
twelve cities by lot, according to their
families, from the tribes of Reuben,
Gad, and Zebulun.
64So the sons of Israel gave to the
Levites these cities with their pasture
lands.
65They gave by lot from the tribes of
the sons of Judah, Simeon, and Benja-
min these cities which are mentioned
by name.
66Some of the families of the sons
of Kohath had cities of their [allotted]
territory from the tribe of Ephraim.
67They gave to the Levites the *follow-
ing* cities of refuge: Shechem in the hill
country of Ephraim with its pasture
lands, Gezer with its pasture lands;
68Jokmeam and Beth-horon with
their pasture lands,
69Aijalon and Gath-rimmon, with
their pasture lands;
70and from the half-tribe of Manas-
seh [these cities], with their pasture
lands: Aner and Bileam, for the rest
of the families of the sons of Kohath.
71To the sons of Gershom *were giv-
en* from the family of the half-tribe
of Manasseh: Golan in Bashan and
Ashtaroth, with their pasture lands;
72from the tribe of Issachar: Kedesh
and Daberath with their pasture lands,
73Ramoth and Anem with their pas-
ture lands;
74from the tribe of Asher: Mashal
and Abdon with their pasture lands,
75Hukok and Rehob with their pas-
ture lands;
76and from the tribe of Naphta-
li: Kedesh in Galilee, Hammon, and
Kiriathaim with their pasture lands.

6:57 *Hebron.* The law specified that if a person killed another unintentionally he could find sanctuary in one of six specified cities, and there wait in safety for the trial (Nu 35:6 – 27). No one could take revenge as long as he was in the city of refuge. These six cities were included among the 48 Levitical cities, and Hebron, located in Judah, was one of them.

6:61 – 7:27 Family — In any family record, some of the names have strong memories associated with them. The reputations may be good or bad, but they are all a part of the family reputation. It is comforting to know that the family that produced Saul, the unfaithful king, is the same line that produced Saul, who became the faithful apostle Paul.

6:67 *Shechem.* Shechem was both a Levitical city and a city of refuge. Shechem was especially significant in Israel. It was the site of Abraham's first altar in Canaan (Ge 12:6 – 7), the place where Jacob bought a piece of land (Ge 33:19), and the location of the first capital of the Northern Kingdom (1Ki 12:25).

6:76 *Kedesh.* Kedesh was another of the six cities of refuge. It was the most northern of the three west of the Jordan.

54 Jos 21 **55** Jos 21:11,12 **56** Jos 14:13; 15:13 **57** Jos 21:13 **61** ver. 66; Jos 21:5 **63** Jos 21:7,34 **66** ver. 61 **67** Jos 21:21 **71** Jos 21:27 **72** Jos 21:28

77 To the rest of *the Levites*, the sons of Merari *were given*, from the tribe of Zebulun: Rimmono and Tabor, with their pasture lands;

78 and on the other side of the Jordan at Jericho, on the east side of the Jordan *the Levites were given*, from the tribe of Reuben: Bezer in the wilderness and Jahzah with their pasture lands,

79 Kedemoth and Mephaath with their pasture lands;

80 from the tribe of Gad: Ramoth in Gilead and Mahanaim with their pasture lands,

81 Heshbon and Jazer with their pasture lands.

Descendants of Issachar

7 THE SONS of Issachar were: Tola, Puah, Jashub, and Shimron—four *in all*.

2 The sons of Tola: Uzzi, Rephaiah, Jeriel, Jahmai, Ibsam, and Samuel, heads of their fathers' households. *The sons* of Tola were courageous men in their generations; their number in the days of David was 22,600.

3 The son of Uzzi: Izrahiah. The sons of Izrahiah: Michael, Obadiah, Joel, Isshiah; all five of them were chief men.

4 With them by their generations according to their fathers' households were 36,000 troops of the army for war, for they had many wives and children.

5 Their relatives among all the families of Issachar, courageous men, registered by genealogies, were 87,000 in all.

Descendants of Benjamin

6 *The sons of* Benjamin were three: Bela, Becher, and Jediael.

7 The sons of Bela were five: Ezbon, Uzzi, Uzziel, Jerimoth, and Iri. They were heads of the households of their fathers, courageous men. By their genealogies they were 22,034.

8 The sons of Becher: Zemirah, Joash, Eliezer, Elioenai, Omri, Jeremoth, Abijah, Anathoth, and Alemeth, all these were sons of Becher.

9 They were registered by their genealogies according to their generations, as heads of their fathers' households, courageous men, 20,200 *in number*.

10 The son of Jediael: Bilhan. The sons of Bilhan: Jeush, Benjamin, Ehud, Chenaanah, Zethan, Tarshish, and Ahishahar.

11 All these were the sons of Jediael, according to the heads of their fathers' households, 17,200 courageous men of valor, fit for military service.

12 Shuppim and Huppim were the sons of Ir, and Hushim the son of Aher.

Sons of Naphtali

13 The sons of Naphtali: Jahziel, Guni, Jezer, and Shallum, the sons of Bilhah.

Descendants of Manasseh

14 The sons of Manasseh: Asriel, whom his Aramean concubine bore; she gave birth to Machir the father of Gilead.

15 Machir took as a wife the sister of Huppim and Shuppim; her name was Maacah. The name of a second [descendant, the first being Gilead], was Zelophehad; and Zelophehad had [only] daughters. [Num 27:1–7]

16 Maacah the wife of Machir gave birth to a son; she named him Peresh. The name of his brother was Sheresh; his sons were Ulam and Rakem.

17 The son of Ulam: Bedan. These were the sons of Gilead the son of Machir, the son of Manasseh.

6:78 ***Bezer.*** Bezer was also a city of refuge, the farthest south of those east of the Jordan.

6:80 ***Ramoth in Gilead.*** Another city of refuge, Ramoth, was directly east of the Jordan. In this way the cities of refuge were distributed throughout the land so that any Israelite could be within a few miles of one of them. All six cities were assigned to the Levites, with Hebron designated for the priests (Dt 17:8 – 13; 19:17 – 21).

7:14 ***Manasseh . . . Machir.*** Manasseh was the son of Joseph, and his son was Machir. Machir's daughter became the wife of Judah's grandson Hezron (2:2), which joined the two tribes of Judah and Manasseh.

7:15 ***Zelophehad had [only] daughters.*** This man had no sons, so Moses made provision for inheritance rights for daughters in such cases (Nu 36:1 – 9).

CHAPTER 7 **1** Ge 46:13; Nu 26:23 **2** 2Sa 24:1,2; 1Ch 27:1 **6** Ge 46:21; Nu 26:38; 1Ch 8:1 **17** 1Sa 12:11

18 His sister Hammolecheth gave birth to Ishhod and Abiezer and Mahlah.
19 The sons of Shemida were: Ahian, Shechem, Likhi, and Aniam.

Descendants of Ephraim

20 The sons of Ephraim: Shuthelah and Bered his son, Tahath [I] his son, Eleadah his son, Tahath [II] his son,
21 Zabad his son, Shuthelah his son, and Ezer and Elead were killed by men who were natives of Gath, because they came down to take their livestock.
22 Their father Ephraim mourned for many days, and his relatives came to comfort him.
23 Then he went in to his wife, and she conceived and gave birth to a son, and he named him Beriah (on misfortune), because tragedy had come on his house.
24 Beriah's daughter was Sheerah, who built both Lower and Upper Beth-horon, and also Uzzen-sheerah.
25 Rephah was his son *along* with Resheph; Resheph's son was Telah, Tahan his son,
26 Ladan his son, Ammihud his son, Elishama his son,
27 Non (Nun) his son, and Joshua [Moses' successor] his son.
28 Their possessions and settlements were Bethel and its towns, and eastward Naaran, and westward Gezer, and Shechem, and as far as Ayyah with all their towns,
29 and along the borders of the sons of Manasseh, Beth-shean, Taanach, Megiddo, Dor, with all their towns. In these [places] lived the sons of Joseph the son of Israel (Jacob).

Descendants of Asher

30 The sons of Asher: Imnah, Ishvah, Ishvi, and Beriah; and Serah their sister.
31 The sons of Beriah: Heber and Malchiel, who was the father of Birzaith.
32 Heber became the father of Japhlet, Shomer, Hotham, and Shua their sister.
33 The sons of Japhlet: Pasach, Bimhal, and Ashvath. These were the sons of Japhlet.
34 The sons of Shemer (Shomer) [his brother]: Ahi and Rohgah, Jehubbah, and Aram.
35 The sons of his brother Helem (Hotham): Zophah, Imna, Shelesh, and Amal.
36 The sons of Zophah: Suah, Harnepher, Shual, Beri, Imrah,
37 Bezer, Hod, Shamma, Shilshah, Ithran, and Beera.
38 The sons of Jether: Jephunneh, Pispa, and Ara.
39 The sons of Ulla: Arah, Hanniel, and Rizia.
40 All these were sons (descendants) of Asher, heads of their fathers' houses, choice men, courageous men, chiefs of the leaders. Their number, enrolled by genealogies for service in war, was 26,000 men.

Genealogy from Benjamin

8 BENJAMIN BECAME the father of Bela his firstborn, Ashbel the second, Aharah the third,
2 Nohah the fourth and Rapha the fifth.
3 Bela had sons: Addar, Gera, Abihud,
4 Abishua, Naaman, Ahoah,
5 Gera, Shephuphan, and Huram.
6 These are the sons of Ehud: These are the heads of the fathers' *households* of the inhabitants of Geba; they were exiled to Manahath:
7 Naaman, Ahijah, and Gera—he forced them into exile; he became the father of Uzza and Ahihud.
8 Shaharaim became the father of children in the country of Moab after he had sent away (divorced) Hushim and Baara his wives.
9 By Hodesh his wife he became the father of Jobab, Zibia, Mesha, Malcam,

---

7:20–21 ***Tahath... Shuthelah.*** The repetition of these two names illustrates the custom of sons being named for their grandfathers or more remote ancestors.

8:1 ***Benjamin.*** The reason for this second and much more detailed genealogy of Benjamin is its focus on the genealogy of King Saul (vv. 29–40).

8:9 ***Mesha.*** There was a well-known Moabite

---

20 Nu 26:35 **29** Jos 17:7,11 **30** Ge 46:17; Nu 26:44 **CHAPTER 8** **1** Ge 46:21; Nu 26:38; 1Ch 7:6 **6** 1Ch 2:52

[10]Jeuz, Sachia, and Mirmah. These
were his sons, heads of fathers' *house-
holds.*
[11]By Hushim he became the father
of Abitub and Elpaal.
[12]The sons of Elpaal: Eber, Misham,
and Shemed, who built Ono and Lod,
with its towns;
[13]and Beriah and Shema, who were
heads of fathers' *households* of the
inhabitants of Aijalon, who drove out
the inhabitants of Gath;
[14]and Ahio, Shashak, and Jeremoth.
[15]Zebadiah, Arad, Eder,
[16]Michael, Ishpah, and Joha *were* the
sons of Beriah.
[17]Zebadiah, Meshullam, Hizki, Heber,
[18]Ishmerai, Izliah, and Jobab were
the sons of Elpaal.
[19]Jakim, Zichri, Zabdi,
[20]Elienai, Zillethai, Eliel,
[21]Adaiah, Beraiah, and Shimrath
were the sons of Shimei.
[22]Ishpan, Eber, Eliel,
[23]Abdon, Zichri, Hanan,
[24]Hananiah, Elam, Anthothijah,
[25]Iphdeiah and Penuel were the sons
of Shashak.
[26]Shamsherai, Shehariah, Athaliah,
[27]Jaareshiah, Elijah, and Zichri were
the sons of Jeroham.
[28]These [men] were heads of the fa-
thers' *households,* according to their
generations, chief men who lived in
Jerusalem.
[29]Now in Gibeon, *Jeiel,* the father
of Gibeon lived, and his wife's name
was Maacah;
[30]and his firstborn son was Abdon,
then Zur, Kish, Baal, Nadab,
[31]Gedor, Ahio, and Zecher.
[32]Mikloth became the father of
Shimeah. They also lived with their
relatives in Jerusalem opposite their
other relatives.

Genealogy from King Saul

[33]Ner became the father of Kish,
and Kish became the father of [King]
Saul, and Saul became the father of
Jonathan, Malchi-shua, Abinadab and
Eshbaal (Ish-bosheth).
[34]The son of Jonathan was Merib-
baal (Mephibosheth), and Merib-baal
became the father of Micah.
[35]The sons of Micah: Pithon, Melech,
Tarea, and Ahaz.
[36]Ahaz became the father of Je-
hoaddah, and Jehoaddah became the
father of Alemeth, Azmaveth, and
Zimri; and Zimri became the father
of Moza.
[37]Moza became the father of Binea;
Raphah was his son, Eleasah his son,
Azel his son.
[38]Azel had six sons, and these were
their names: Azrikam, Bocheru, Ish-
mael, Sheariah, Obadiah, and Hanan.
All these were the sons of Azel.
[39]The sons of Eshek his brother:
Ulam his firstborn, Jeush the second,
and Eliphelet the third.
[40]The sons of Ulam were courageous
men, archers, and had many sons and
grandsons—150 *in all.* All these were
of the sons (descendants) of Benjamin.

---

king named Mesha. Both the Scriptures (2Ki 3:4) and the Moabite Stone attest to this fact. The reference here to Mesha as a son of Shaharaim and Hodesh, his Moabite wife (v. 8), suggests that the illustrious Moabite king may have had a Benjamite father, but the evidence is not conclusive.

8:28 *chief men ... lived in Jerusalem.* This city was not taken by David until approximately 1004 BC, so the line of Benjamin was traced to at least that time. Even after David took the city, there may have been Benjamites who still lived there, for David gave Benjamites positions of responsibility in his government (11:31; 12:1 – 7,29).

8:30 *Kish.* Kish was the father of Saul (v. 33; 9:39). In this passage the relationship between Jeiel and Kish is unclear because Kish is also named as the son of Ner (v. 33). However, in 9:35 – 39 the lineage is clearly traced from Jeiel to Ner to Kish and finally to Saul.

8:32 *Jerusalem.* Jerusalem remained under Jebusite control until David conquered it (2Sa 5:6 – 19). Perhaps at this time the Benjamites lived among the Jebusites.

8:33 *Eshbaal.* Eshbaal was evidently Saul's youngest son, since he was not named in the genealogies of the beginning of Saul's reign (1Sa 14:49). Usually called Ishbosheth, which means "man of shame," he reigned for a short time after his father's death (2Sa 2:10).

13 ver. 21 **29** 1Ch 9:35 **34** 2Sa 9:12

People of Jerusalem

9 SO ALL Israel was enrolled by genealogies; and they are written in
the Book of the Kings of Israel. And
Judah was carried away into exile to
Babylon because of their unfaithfulness [to God].
2Now the first [of the returned exiles] who lived [again] in their possessions in their cities were Israel, the
priests, the Levites, and the Nethinim
(temple servants).
3Some of the sons (people) of Judah,
Benjamin, Ephraim, and Manasseh
lived in Jerusalem:
4Uthai the son of Ammihud, the son
of Omri, the son of Imri, the son of Bani,
of the sons of Perez the son of Judah.
5From the Shilonites: Asaiah the
firstborn and his sons.
6From the sons of Zerah: Jeuel and
their relatives, 690 [of them].
7From the sons of Benjamin: Sallu
the son of Meshullam, the son of Hodaviah, the son of Hassenuah;
8Ibneiah the son of Jeroham, Elah
the son of Uzzi, the son of Michri, and
Meshullam son of Shephatiah, the son
of Reuel, the son of Ibnijah;
9and their relatives according to
their generations, 956. All these men
were heads of fathers' *households* according to their fathers' houses.
10Of the priests: Jedaiah, Jehoiarib,
Jachin,
11Azariah the son of Hilkiah, the
son of Meshullam, the son of Zadok,
the son of Meraioth, the son of Ahitub,
the chief officer of the house of God;
12and Adaiah the son of Jeroham, the
son of Pashhur, the son of Malchijah;
Maasai the son of Adiel, the son of
Jahzerah, the son of Meshullam, the
son of Meshillemith, the son of Immer;
13and their relatives, heads of their
fathers' households, 1,760—very able
men for the work of the service of the
house of God.
14Of the Levites: Shemaiah the son of
Hasshub, the son of Azrikam, the son
of Hashabiah, of the sons of Merari;
15and Bakbakkar, Heresh, Galal,
and Mattaniah son of Mica, the son
of Zichri, the son of Asaph;
16and Obadiah the son of Shemaiah,
the son of Galal, the son of Jeduthun,
and Berechiah the son of Asa, the son
of Elkanah, who lived in the villages
of the Netophathites [near Jerusalem].
17The gatekeepers were: Shallum,
Akkub, Talmon, Ahiman, and their
relatives (Shallum the chief
18who until now *was assigned* to
the king's gate on the east side) they
were the gatekeepers for the camp of
the Levites.
19Shallum the son of Kore, the son
of Ebiasaph, the son of Korah, and
his relatives of his father's house, the
Korahites, were in charge of the work
of the service, doorkeepers of the Tent;
and their fathers had been in charge
of the camp of the LORD, keepers of
the entrance.
20Phinehas the son of Eleazar was
ruler over them in times past, and the
LORD was with him.
21Zechariah son of Meshelemiah

9:1 Unfaithfulness—Blatant disobedience always leads to disaster. God is serious about working righteousness in our lives, and He knows the changes that both trials and blessings can bring to our hearts. He will not leave us in a state of lethargy and peace if we need to be ignited. Sometimes He will test us to see if we are serious about walking with Him. Like the Israelites, we need to ask ourselves if we are obedient or compromising.

9:2 *Israel.* The deportation of Israel by the Assyrians from 734 to 722 BC resulted in Israel's dispersion throughout the eastern Mediterranean world. However, it is apparent from this verse that some of them joined their Judean brethren in the return from Babylon after 539 BC.

9:3 *Ephraim, and Manasseh.* Both of these tribes were from the Northern Kingdom, or Israel. This is another confirmation that the returning community included Israelites as well as Judeans. It is very possible that some of those in the northern tribes, who had remained faithful to the Lord, may have migrated into Judah before Assyria took Israel captive.

9:19 *Korah.* As descendants of Kohath (Ex 6:18), Korah and his line had close connections with the priesthood. They could not be priests, but they ministered closely with the temple, first as carriers of the holy objects (Nu 4:5–15), and later as gatekeepers.

CHAPTER 9 **1** Ezr 2:59 **2** Ezr 2:70; Neh 7:73; Jos 9:27; Ezr 2:43; 8:20 **3** Neh 11:1 **10** Neh 11:10 **20** Nu 31:6

was gatekeeper at the entrance of the Tent of Meeting.
22 All those chosen to be gatekeepers at the thresholds were 212. They were enrolled by their genealogies in their villages [around Jerusalem], these men [whose grandfathers] David and Samuel the seer had appointed to their official duty.
23 So they and their sons were in charge of the gates of the house of the LORD, that is, the house of the tabernacle, as guards.
24 The gatekeepers were *stationed* on the four sides —on the east, west, north, and south.
25 Their relatives in their villages were to come in every seven days from time to time to be with them;
26 for these Levites, the four chief gatekeepers, had an official duty, and were in charge of the chambers and treasuries of the house of God.
27 They spent the night around the house of God, for the [night] watch was theirs, and they were in charge of opening *the house* morning after morning.
28 Now some of them were in charge of the serving utensils, being required to count them when they brought them in or took them out.
29 Some of them also were appointed over the furniture and over all the [sacred] utensils of the sanctuary, as well as over the fine flour and the wine and the [olive] oil and the frankincense and the spices.
30 Other sons of the priests prepared the mixture of spices.
31 Mattithiah, one of the Levites, the firstborn of Shallum the Korahite, was responsible for the things baked in pans.
32 Some of their Kohathite relatives were in charge of the showbread to prepare it every Sabbath.
33 Now these are the singers, heads of the fathers' *households* of the Levites, *living* in the *temple* chambers, free *from other service* because they were on duty day and night.
34 These were heads of fathers' *households* of the Levites according to their generations, chief men, who lived in Jerusalem.

Ancestry and Descendants of Saul

35 Jeiel the father of Gibeon lived in Gibeon, and his wife's name was Maacah,
36 and his firstborn son was Abdon, then Zur, Kish, Baal, Ner, Nadab,
37 Gedor, Ahio, Zechariah, and Mikloth.
38 Mikloth became the father of Shimeam. They also lived with their relatives in Jerusalem, opposite their *other* relatives.
39 Ner became the father of Kish, and Kish became the father of [King] Saul, and Saul became the father of Jonathan, Malchi-shua, Abinadab, and Esh-baal.
40 The son of Jonathan was Merib-baal (Mephibosheth); Merib-baal became the father of Micah.
41 The sons of Micah: Pithon, Melech, Tahrea [and Ahaz].
42 Ahaz became the father of Jarah, and Jarah became the father of Alemeth, Azmaveth, and Zimri; and Zimri became the father of Moza,
43 Moza became the father of Binea and Rephaiah his son, Eleasah his son, Azel his son.
44 Azel had six sons, and these are their names: Azrikam, Bocheru, Ishmael, Sheariah, Obadiah, and Hanan. These were the sons of Azel.

Defeat and Death of Saul and His Sons

10 NOW THE Philistines fought against Israel; and the men of Israel fled from them and fell slain on Mount Gilboa.
2 The Philistines followed closely after Saul and his sons *and* overtook them, and the Philistines killed Jonathan, Abinadab, and Malchi-shua, the sons of Saul.
3 The battle became heavy against Saul, and the archers found him; and he was [mortally] wounded by the archers.

22 1Ch 26:1,2; 1Sa 9:9 **25** 2Ki 11:5 **30** Ex 30:23 **31** Lev 2:5; 6:21 **32** Lev 24:8 **33** 1Ch 6:31; 25:1 **35** 1Ch 8:29 **39** 1Ch 8:33 **41** 1Ch 8:35 **CHAPTER 10** **1** 1Sa 31:1,2

[4]Then Saul said to his armor bearer, "Draw your sword and run me through with it, otherwise these uncircumcised [Philistines] will come and abuse *and* humiliate me." But his armor bearer would not, for he was terrified. So Saul took his own sword and fell on it.
[5]When his armor bearer saw that Saul was dead, he also fell on his sword and died.
[6]So Saul died with his three sons and all *those* of his house died together.
[7]When all the men of Israel who were in the valley saw that the army had fled, and that Saul and his sons were dead, they abandoned their cities and fled; and the Philistines came and lived in them.
[8]It came about the next day, when the Philistines came to strip (plunder) the slain, that they found Saul and his sons fallen on Mount Gilboa.
[9]So they stripped Saul and took his head and his armor and sent *messengers* around the land of the Philistines to bring the good news to their idols and to the people.
[10]They put Saul's armor in the house of their gods and nailed up his head in the house (temple) of Dagon.

Jabesh-gilead's Tribute to Saul

[11]When all Jabesh-gilead heard about everything that the Philistines had done to Saul,
[12]all the brave men arose, took away the body of Saul and the bodies of his sons and brought them to Jabesh, and they buried their bones under the oak in Jabesh; then they fasted seven days. [1 Sam 31:12]
[13]So Saul died for his trespass which he committed against the LORD, for his failure to keep the word of the LORD; and also because he consulted a medium [regarding a spirit of the dead], to inquire *of her*,
[14]and did not inquire of the LORD [instead]. Therefore the LORD killed him and turned the kingdom over to David the son of Jesse. [1 Sam 28:6]

David Made King over All Israel

11 THEN ALL Israel gathered to David at Hebron, saying, "Behold, we are your bone and your flesh. [2 Sam 2:8–10]
[2]"In times past, even when Saul was king, it was you who led out and brought in Israel; and the LORD your God said to you, 'You shall shepherd My people Israel, and you shall be prince *and* leader over My people Israel.' "
[3]So all the elders of Israel came to the king at Hebron, and David made a covenant (solemn agreement) with them there before the LORD; and they anointed him king over Israel, in accordance with the word of the LORD through Samuel. [1 Sam 16:1, 12, 13]

10:4 ***uncircumcised.*** For the Hebrew, circumcision was a sign of God's promise through Abraham to them. The uncircumcised were those outside the promise, often their enemies. ***abuse.*** The abuse of the Philistines might take the form of cutting off Saul's thumbs and big toes, which would leave him disabled and humiliated (Jdg 1:6–7). Whatever they did would have been meant to belittle Saul, his kingdom, and his God. ***was terrified.*** The armor bearer was not afraid of Saul. He was afraid of God. He was afraid of killing one who had been anointed king over Israel and who belonged to God who had set him apart. ***sword and fell on it.*** Suicide was very rare among Hebrews of Old Testament times.

10:10 ***Dagon.*** Dagon was worshiped by the Philistines and other peoples in Syria and northwest Mesopotamia as the god of gain. Apparently the Philistines celebrated military victory by bringing a trophy of their success back to their temple where it could be displayed as a tribute to the might of their god.

10:14 ***the LORD killed him.*** This statement is shocking in its bluntness. In the final analysis, Saul's death was not by his own hand, but by the hand of God. The Lord let Saul pursue a course that led to death.

11:1–2 Unity — The history of events between the death of Saul and the beginning of David's reign over all Israel is omitted by the chronicler, but is narrated in 2 Samuel 2–4. The fighting between the house of David and the house of Saul continued until Saul's son Ishbosheth was killed. Israel could not be unified as long as some were

---

10 1Sa 31:10 **13** 1Sa 13:13; 15:23; 28:7 **14** 1Sa 15:28; 2Sa 3:9,10; 5:3 **CHAPTER 11** **1** 2Sa 5:1 **2** Ps 78:71
3 2Sa 5:3; 1Sa 16:1,12,13

Jerusalem, Capital City

4 Then David and all Israel went to Jerusalem (that is Jebus); and the Jebusites, the inhabitants of the land, were there.

5 Then the Jebusites said to David, "You shall not come in here." But David captured the stronghold of Zion (that is, the City of David).

6 Now David said, "Whoever strikes down a Jebusite first shall be chief and commander." Joab the son of Zeruiah [David's half sister] went up first, and so he was made chief.

7 Then David lived in the stronghold; so it was called the City of David.

8 He built the city around it, from the Millo (fortification) to the surrounding area; and Joab repaired the rest of the [old Jebusite] city.

9 David became greater and greater, for the LORD of hosts was with him.

David's Mighty Men

10 Now these are the chiefs of David's mighty men, who strongly supported him in his kingdom, together with all Israel, to make him king, in accordance with the word of the LORD concerning Israel.

11 This is the list of David's mighty men: Jashobeam, the son of a Hachmonite, the chief of the thirty [heroes]. He lifted up his spear against three hundred whom he killed at one time.

12 Next to him [in rank] was Eleazar the son of Dodo the Ahohite, who was one of the three mighty men.

13 He was with David at Pasdammim [where David had killed Goliath] and there the Philistines were gathered together for battle, and there was a plot of ground full of barley; and the people [of Israel] fled before the Philistines.

14 But they took their stand in the midst of that plot and defended it, and killed the Philistines; and the LORD rescued them by a great victory. [2 Sam 23:9, 10]

15 Three of the thirty chief men went down to the rock to David, into the cave of Adullam, while the army of the Philistines was camped in the Valley of Rephaim.

16 David was then in the stronghold, while the garrison of the Philistines was in Bethlehem.

17 David had a craving and said, "Oh that someone would give me a drink of water from the well of Bethlehem, which is next to the gate!"

18 Then the three [mighty men] broke through the camp of the Philistines and drew water out of the well of Bethlehem which was next to the gate, and brought it to David. But David would not drink it; he poured it out to the LORD [as an offering];

19 and he said, "Far be it from me before my God that I would do this thing! Shall I drink the blood of these men who have put their lives in jeopardy? For they brought it at the risk of their lives." So he would not drink it. These things the three mighty men did.

20 Abishai the brother of Joab was chief of the [other] three, and he lifted up his spear against three hundred and killed them, and he had a name as well as the three.

21 Of the three in the second [rank]

---

trying to be loyal to Saul. God had already rejected Saul and chosen David, but until Saul's house was gone, the people could not focus on God's choice for king. We as believers often find ourselves in a state of disunity because we are mixed up with our own agendas instead of seeing God's plan.

11:8 ***He built the city.*** Once David occupied Mount Ophel, the original and very small area of Jerusalem, he greatly enlarged it by building retaining walls along the Kidron valley to the east and south and the Tyropoeon valley to the west. Between these walls and the top of the hill he built terraces, so that various buildings could be constructed there.

11:18 ***poured it out to the LORD.*** Even though he had been longing for a drink from his "home well," David never considered sending any of his brave supporters to get it for him. When they risked their lives to bring it to him, David responded by pouring it on the ground, as if it had been a blood offering for God. The Israelites were strictly forbidden to eat blood (Lev 3:17; Dt 12:23), and David considered this water to be in the same category. Only God should receive such a sacrifice (Ge 35:14).

---

4 2Sa 5:6; Jdg 1:21; 19:10 **10** 2Sa 23:8; 1Sa 16:1,12 **14** Jdg 1:21; 19:10 **15** 2Sa 23:13; 1Ch 14:9 **20** 2Sa 23:18 **21** 2Sa 23:19

he was the most honored and became
their captain; however, he did not
attain to the *first* three [Jashobeam,
Eleazar, and Shammah].
22 Benaiah the son of Jehoiada, the son
of a courageous man of Kabzeel who had
done great things, killed the two *sons of*
Ariel of Moab. Also he went down and
killed a lion in a pit on a snowy day.
23 He killed an Egyptian also, a man
of *great* stature, five cubits tall. In
the Egyptian's hand was a spear like
a weaver's beam, and Benaiah went
down to him with [only] a staff (rod) and
grabbed the spear from the Egyptian's
hand and killed him with his own spear.
24 Benaiah the son of Jehoiada did
these *things*, and had a name as well
as the three mighty men.
25 He was honored among the thirty,
but he did not attain to [the rank of] the
[first] three. David appointed him over
his bodyguard.
26 Now the mighty men of the armies
were: Asahel the brother of Joab, El-
hanan the son of Dodo of Bethlehem,
27 Shammoth the Harorite, Helez the
Pelonite,
28 Ira the son of Ikkesh of Tekoa, Abi-
ezer of Anathoth,
29 Sibbecai the Hushathite, Ilai the
Ahohite,
30 Maharai the Netophathite, Heled
the son of Baanah the Netophathite,
31 Ithai the son of Ribai of Gibeah of
the Benjamites, Benaiah the Pirathonite,
32 Hurai of the brooks of Gaash, Abiel
the Arbathite,
33 Azmaveth the Baharumite, Eliah-
ba the Shaalbonite,
34 the sons of Hashem the Gizonite,
Jonathan the son of Shagee the Ha-
rarite,
35 Ahiam the son of Sacar the Hara-
rite, Eliphal the son of Ur,
36 Hepher the Mecherathite, Ahijah
the Pelonite,
37 Hezro the Carmelite, Naarai the
son of Ezbai,
38 Joel the brother of Nathan, Mibhar
the son of Hagri,
39 Zelek the Ammonite, Naharai the
Berothite, the armor bearer of Joab
the son of Zeruiah [David's half sister],
40 Ira the Ithrite, Gareb the Ithrite,
41 Uriah the Hittite [Bathsheba's hus-
band], Zabad the son of Ahlai,
42 Adina the son of Shiza the Reu-
benite, a chief of the Reubenites, and
thirty [heroes] with him,
43 Hanan the son of Maacah, and
Joshaphat the Mithnite,
44 Uzzia the Ashterathite, Shama and
Jeiel the sons of Hotham the Aroerite,
45 Jediael the son of Shimri, and his
brother Joha, the Tizite,
46 Eliel the Mahavite, Jeribai and
Joshaviah the sons of Elnaam, Ithmah
the Moabite,
47 Eliel and Obed and Jaasiel the Me-
zobaite.

David's Supporters in Ziklag

12 THESE ARE the ones who came
to David at Ziklag, while he still
concealed himself from Saul the son of
Kish; they were among the courageous
men who helped him in battle.
2 They were armed with bows, and
could use the right hand or the left to
sling stones and *shoot* arrows from the
bow; *they were* Saul's relatives from
[the tribe of] Benjamin.
3 The chief was Ahiezer and then
Joash, the sons of Shemaah of Gibeah;
Jeziel and Pelet the sons of Azmaveth;
Beracah, and Jehu of Anathoth,
4 Ishmaiah of Gibeon, a mighty man
among the thirty, and [a leader] over
them; Jeremiah, Jahaziel, Johanan,
Jozabad of Gederah,
5 Eluzai, Jerimoth, Bealiah, Shema-
riah, Shephatiah the Haruphite,
6 Elkanah, Isshiah, Azarel, Joezer,
and Jashobeam, the Korahites,
7 and Joelah and Zebadiah the sons
of Jeroham of Gedor.

11:23 *five cubits*. The Egyptian was about seven and a half feet tall.
11:41 *Uriah*. This is the same Uriah who was the husband of Bathsheba. The fact that Uriah was one of the mighty men of valor, who did so much to establish David as king, makes David's betrayal of Uriah doubly tragic (2Sa 11).

22 2Sa 23:20 **26** 2Sa 23:24 **CHAPTER 12** **1** 1Sa 27:2; 27:6 **2** Jdg 20:16

8Courageous men from the Gadites
came over to David in the stronghold
in the wilderness, men trained for war,
who could handle shield and spear,
whose faces were like the faces of li-
ons, and who were swift as gazelles
on the mountains.
9Ezer was the first, Obadiah the sec-
ond, Eliab the third,
10Mishmannah the fourth, Jeremiah
the fifth,
11Attai the sixth, Eliel the seventh,
12Johanan the eighth, Elzabad the
ninth,
13Jeremiah the tenth, Machbannai
the eleventh.
14These from the sons (descendants)
of Gad were captains of the army; he
who was least was equal to a hun-
dred, and the greatest was equal to a
thousand.
15These are the men who crossed
over the Jordan in the first month
when it had overflowed all its banks
and they put to flight all those in the
valleys, east and west.
16Then some of the men of Benjamin
and Judah came to the stronghold to
David.
17David went out to meet them and
said to them, "If you have come peace-
fully to me to help me, my heart shall be
united with you; but if *you have come* to
betray me to my adversaries, since there
is no violence *or* wrong in my hands,
may the God of our fathers look on
[what you are doing] and punish [you]."
18Then the [Holy] Spirit came on
Amasai, who was chief of the thirty,
and he said,

"We are yours, O David,
And with you, O son of Jesse!
Peace, peace be to you,
And peace be to him who helps you;
For your God helps you."

Then David accepted *and* received them
and made them officers of his troops.
19Some [of the men] of Manasseh
also defected to David when he came
with the Philistines to go to battle
against Saul. But David's men did not
[actually] assist the Philistines, for the
lords (governors) of the Philistines af-
ter consultation sent him away, saying,
"At *the cost of* our heads he may defect
to his master Saul." [1 Sam 29:2–9]
20As David went to Ziklag, *these
men* defected to him from Manasseh:
Adnah, Jozabad, Jediael, Michael, Joz-
abad, Elihu, and Zillethai, captains of
thousands who belonged to Manasseh.
21They helped David against the
band of raiders, for they were all cou-
rageous men, and [all seven] became
commanders in his army.
22For day by day men kept coming
to David to help him, until there was
a great army, like the army of God.

Supporters Gathered at Hebron

23These are the numbers of the
[armed] units equipped for war who
came to David at Hebron to turn [over]
the kingdom of Saul to him, in accor-
dance with the word of the LORD.
24Those of the tribe of Judah who
carried shield and spear were 6,800,
armed for war;
25of the tribe of Simeon, brave war-
riors, 7,100;
26of the tribe of Levi, 4,600.
27Jehoiada was the leader of [the house
of] Aaron, and with him were 3,700,
28and Zadok, a courageous young
man, and twenty-two captains from
his father's house.
29Of the tribe of Benjamin, the rel-
atives of [King] Saul, 3,000; for until

12:2 *Saul's relatives from [the tribe of] Benjamin.* There is a curious little play on words here. Benjamin means "son of the right hand." These Benjamites could shoot and sling with either the right hand or the left hand, which made them particularly versatile in battle. They were more than "sons of the right hand" to David. They were "sons of the left hand" as well.

12:15 *in the first month.* The first month was Nisan, corresponding approximately to April, the time of spring rains. Ordinarily a person could not cross the Jordan at flood stage, but the fact that the Gadites were not stopped by the floods is a testimony of their unusual courage.

12:28 *Zadok.* This Zadok was probably the same Zadok who was first appointed by David as priest

---

8 2Sa 2:18 **15** Jos 3:15 **18** 2Sa 17:25 **19** 1Sa 29:2; 1Sa 29:4 **21** 1Sa 30:1,9,10 **23** 2Sa 2:3; 1Ch 10:14; 1Sa 16:1 **28** 2Sa 8:17 **29** 2Sa 2:8,9

now the majority of them had kept
their allegiance to the house of Saul.
[30]Of the tribe of Ephraim, 20,800,
courageous men, famous in their fa-
thers' houses.
[31]Of the half-tribe of Manasseh,
18,000, who were designated by name
to come and make David king.
[32]Of the tribe of Issachar, men who
understood the times, with knowl-
edge of what Israel should do, two
hundred chiefs; and all their relatives
were at their command;
[33]of the tribe of Zebulun, there were
50,000 in military service who could
draw up in battle formation with all
kinds of weapons of war and helped
David, men with an undivided heart.
[34]Of the tribe of Naphtali, *there
were* 1,000 captains, and with them
37,000 [of the rank and file armed]
with shield and spear.
[35]Of the tribe of Dan, 28,600 men
who could draw up in battle formation.
[36]Of the tribe of Asher, 40,000 men
in military service, able to draw up
in battle formation.
[37]From the other side [east] of the
Jordan *River*, of [the tribes of] Reuben
and Gad and the half-tribe of Ma-
nasseh, 120,000 men, *armed* with all
kinds of weapons of war for the battle.
[38]All these, being men of war ar-
rayed in battle formation, came to
Hebron with a perfect (committed)
heart to make David king over all
Israel; and all the rest of Israel were
also of one mind to make David king.
[39]They were there with David for
three days, eating and drinking, for
their relatives had prepared for them.
[40]Also those who were [living]
near them [from] as far as [the tribes
of] Issachar, Zebulun, and Naphta-
li, brought food on donkeys, camels,
mules, and oxen, abundant supplies of
flour, cakes of figs and raisins, wine,
[olive] oil, oxen, and sheep, for there
was joy in Israel.

Peril in Transporting the Ark

13 DAVID CONSULTED with the
captains of the thousands and
the hundreds, even with every leader.
[2]David said to all the assembly of Is-
rael, "If it seems good to you, and if it is
from the LORD our God, let us send *word*
everywhere to our fellow countrymen
who remain in all the land of Israel, and
to the priests and Levites who are with
them in their cities with pasture lands,
so that they may meet with us;
[3]and let us bring back the ark of our
God to us, for we did not seek it during
the days of Saul."
[4]Then all the assembly agreed to do
so, for the thing was right in the eyes
of all the people.
[5]So David gathered all Israel togeth-
er, from the Shihor [watercourse] of
Egypt, to the entrance of Hamath [in
the north], to bring the ark of God from
Kiriath-jearim.
[6]David and all Israel went up to Baa-
lah, *that is*, to Kiriath-jearim, which

---

at Gibeon (16:39). The office of priest was not incompatible with that of warrior, as Phinehas showed (Nu 25:6 – 9; Jos 22:13 – 30).

12:32 Wisdom — The men of Issachar were dealing with the issue of "the Lord's anointed." There was no longer any question that David was the Lord's choice, and that Saul had been replaced, but the timing was crucial. It would do no good to anoint David if it took rebellion and treason to place him on the throne. Men who gain power by trickery usually assume that others will be ready to do likewise, and dishonesty and intrigue are not a good foundation for a God-honoring nation. It is sometimes hard to wait for God's timing, or even hard to tell just what His timing is, but if we ask for wisdom, He will give it to us (Jas 1:5).

13:3 the ark of our God. This was the ark of the covenant that contained a copy of the Ten Commandments (Ex 25:10 – 22). Besides holding the stone tablets, the ark represented the presence of the living God among the Israelites.

13:5 Commitment — One of David's first official actions upon becoming king was to bring the ark of God to Jerusalem. The ark had been in Kiriath-jearim since the time it was returned by the Philistines when Samuel was a boy (1Sa 6:20 – 7:1). Moving the ark to Jerusalem was a sign of David's commitment to place the Lord first in his reign.

13:6 the LORD who sits enthroned above the cherubim. On each side of the ark of the covenant were two cherubim. They extended their wings over the cover, also called the mercy

32 Est 1:13 **CHAPTER 13** **2** 1Sa 31:1; Isa 37:4 **3** 1Sa 7:1,2 **5** 1Sa 7:5; Jos 13:3; 1Sa 6:21; 7:1 **6** Jos 15:9,60; 1Sa 4:4; 2Sa 6:2

belongs to Judah, to bring up from
there the ark of God the LORD who sits
enthroned *above* the cherubim, *the ark*
which is called by *His* name.
7 They carried the ark of God on
a new cart and brought it out of the
house of Abinadab, and Uzza and Ahio
[his brother] drove the cart.
8 David and all Israel celebrated [joy-
fully] before God with all their might,
with songs, lyres, harps, tambourines,
cymbals, and trumpets.
9 When they came to the threshing
floor of Chidon, Uzza put out his hand
to hold *and* steady the ark, for the oxen
[that were drawing the cart] nearly
overturned it.
10 The anger of the LORD burned
against Uzza, and He struck him down
because he touched the ark; and there
he died before God. [Num 4:15]
11 David became angry because of the
LORD's outburst against Uzza; so that
place is called Perez-uzza to this day.
12 David was afraid of God that day,
and he said, "How can I bring the ark
of God *home* with me?"
13 So David did not bring the ark with
him to the City of David, but took it
aside to the house of Obed-edom the
Gittite. [Josh 21:20, 24; 1 Chr 15:24]
14 So the ark of God remained with
the family of Obed-edom in his house
three months; and the LORD blessed the
house of Obed-edom and all that he had.

David's Family Enlarged

14 NOW HIRAM king of Tyre sent
messengers to David with cedar
timbers, masons and carpenters, to
build a house (palace) for him.
2 And David understood that the
LORD had established *and* confirmed
him as king over Israel, for his king-
dom was highly exalted for the sake
of His people Israel.
3 Then David took more wives at Je-
rusalem, and he became the father of
more sons and daughters.
4 Now these are the names of the
children born [to him] in Jerusalem:
Shammua, Shobab, Nathan, Solomon,
5 Ibhar, Elishua, Elpelet,
6 Nogah, Nepheg, Japhia,
7 Elishama, Beeliada, and Eliphelet.

Philistines Defeated

8 When the Philistines heard that
David had been anointed king over
all Israel, they all went up in search of
David; and he heard about it and went
out against them.
9 Now the Philistines had come and
made a raid in the Valley of Rephaim.
10 So David inquired of God, "Shall I
go up against the Philistines? And will
You hand them over to me?" Then the
LORD said to him, "Go up, and I will
hand them over to you."
11 So Israel came up to Baal-perazim,
and David defeated the Philistines
there. Then David said, "God has
broken through my enemies by my
hand, like the breakthrough of wa-
ters." Therefore they named that place
Baal-perazim.
12 The Philistines abandoned their
gods (idols) there; so David gave a
command and they were burned in
a fire [as the Law of Moses required].
[Deut 7:5]

---

seat (Ex 25:17 – 22), and the glory of God was perceived as sitting on top of the ark, as a King sits on a throne. ***which is called by His name.*** In Deuteronomy, the presence of God is often spoken of as the presence of His name (Dt 12:1 – 14).

13:9 ***threshing floor of Chidon.*** Also called "Nacon's threshing floor" (2Sa 6:6), this hard flat surface was used for separating the grain kernels from the straw and husks.

13:11 ***Perez-uzza.*** Perez-uzza means "outbreak against Uzza." The ark should have been carried on poles by Levites (Nu 4:14 – 15). This direction for transporting the holy things was very clear, and should have been remembered.

14:1 – 2 ***Hiram king of Tyre.*** A powerful ruler of the Phoenician city-state of Tyre, Hiram is mentioned in the Scriptures and in other sources. He was a contemporary of both David and Solomon. He helped build David's house, and he also supplied material for the temple and other building projects in Solomon's reign (1Ki 9:10).

14:3 ***took more wives.*** See the note for 3:1 – 5.

14:4 ***children.*** The first four listed here are all sons of Bathsheba (3:5).

7 See Nu 4:15; 1Sa 7:1 **8** 2Sa 6:5 **10** Nu 4:15; 1Ch 15:13,15; Lev 10:2 **14** 2Sa 6:11; As Ge 30:27; 1Ch 26:5
CHAPTER 14 **1** 2Sa 5:11 **4** 1Ch 3:5 **8** 2Sa 5:17 **9** 1Ch 11:15

13 The Philistines again made a raid
in the valley.
14 So David inquired again of God,
and God said to him, “Do not go up
after them; circle around behind them
and come at them in front of the bal-
sam trees.
15 “It shall be when you hear the
sound of marching in the tops of the
balsam trees, then you shall go out to
battle, for God has gone out before you
to strike the Philistine army.”
16 So David did just as God had com-
manded him, and they struck down the
army of the Philistines from Gibeon as
far as Gezer.
17 Then David’s fame spread into all
the lands; and the LORD caused all na-
tions to fear him.

Plans to Move the Ark to Jerusalem

15 *DAVID* BUILT houses for him-
self in the City of David; and he
prepared a place for the ark of God and
pitched a tent for it.
2 Then David said, “No one is to carry
the ark of God except the Levites; for
the LORD chose them to carry the ark
of God and to minister to Him forever.”
3 And David assembled all Israel at
Jerusalem to bring up the ark of the
LORD to the place which he had pre-
pared for it.
4 David gathered together the sons of
Aaron and the Levites:
5 of the sons of Kohath, Uriel the
chief, with 120 of his relatives;
6 of the sons of Merari, Asaiah the
chief, with 220 of his relatives;
7 of the sons of Gershom, Joel the
chief, with 130 of his relatives;
8 of the sons of Elizaphan, Shemaiah
the chief, with 200 of his relatives;
9 of the sons of Hebron, Eliel the
chief, with 80 of his relatives;
10 of the sons of Uzziel, Amminadab
the chief, with 112 of his relatives.
11 Then David called for Zadok
and Abiathar the priests, and for the
Levites—Uriel, Asaiah, Joel, Shema-
iah, Eliel, and Amminadab,
12 and he said to them, “You are the
heads of the fathers’ *households* of the
Levites; consecrate yourselves, both
you and your relatives, so that you
may bring up the ark of the LORD God
of Israel, to *the place* that I have pre-
pared for it.
13 “Because you did not [carry it as
God directed] the first time, the LORD
our God made an [angry] outburst
against us, for we did not seek Him

15:1 *place for the ark.* The place for the ark was in the tent in the City of David. The original tabernacle built in Moses’ day had been placed at Shiloh (Jos 18:1). It remained there until the capture of the ark by the Philistines (1Sa 4:1 – 11), when it was evidently moved to Nob, just two miles from Jerusalem (1Sa 21:1 – 6). Then it was moved to a high place at Gibeon (2Ch 1:3), about two miles north of Saul’s city Gibeah. When David became king he left the Mosaic tabernacle at Gibeon and appointed the priest Zadok to attend to its ministry (16:39). Even after he had built a new tabernacle on Mount Zion and brought the ark into it, the original tent remained at Gibeon. Solomon brought the ark from Mount Zion and the tabernacle of Moses from Gibeon and placed them in the new temple he had built on Mount Moriah (2Ch 5:4 – 5).

15:2 *No one . . . except the Levites.* According to the provisions of the Law, the ark was to be carried only by the Levites, by means of poles inserted through corner rings (Nu 4:14 – 15).

15:11 *Zadok.* The other line of the priesthood descended from Aaron’s son Eleazar, and included Zadok (6:8). During David’s time representatives of both Ithamar and Eleazar served. Zadok served at the tabernacle at Gibeon, and Abiathar served as chief priest at Jerusalem. When Solomon became king, Abiathar was deposed and Zadok ministered as high priest at the temple (1Ki 2:26 – 27, 35). The dismissal of Abiathar as priest was in accordance with the Lord’s word to Eli because of the unfaithfulness of Eli’s sons (1Sa 2:27 – 36). ***Abiathar.*** The transition from the rule of Saul to David involved a transition from the old Mosaic tabernacle to the new place David had established on Mount Zion in preparation for the temple (v. 1). Abiathar’s father, the priest Ahimelech, was in charge of the old tabernacle when it left Shiloh and was moved to Nob (1Sa 21:1). Ahimelech was Eli’s great-grandson (1Sa 14:3; 22:9). Eli is considered to have been a descendant of Aaron’s son Ithamar.

13 2Sa 5:22 **14** 2Sa 5:23 **17** Jos 6:27; 2Ch 26:8; Dt 2:25; 11:25 **CHAPTER 15** **1** 1Ch 16:1 **2** Nu 4:2,15; Dt 10:8; 31:9 **3** 1Ki 8:1; 1Ch 13:5 **8** Ex 6:22 **9** Ex 6:18 **13** 2Sa 6:3; 1Ch 13:7; 1Ch 13:10,11 in accordance with the ordinance." [Num 1:50; 1 Chr 13:7–10]

[14]So the priests and the Levites consecrated (dedicated) themselves to bring up the ark of the LORD God of Israel.

[15]The Levites carried the ark of God on their shoulders with the poles, as Moses commanded in accordance with the word of the LORD.

[16]Then David told the chiefs of the Levites to appoint their relatives as the singers, with instruments of music—harps, lyres, and cymbals—to play loudly *and* to raise sounds of joy [with their voices].

[17]So the Levites appointed Heman the son of Joel, and from his relatives, Asaph the son of Berechiah; and from the sons of Merari their relatives, Ethan the son of Kushaiah,

[18]and with them their relatives of the second rank: Zechariah, Ben, Jaaziel, Shemiramoth, Jehiel, Unni, Eliab, Benaiah, Maaseiah, Mattithiah, Eliphelehu, and Mikneiah, Obed-edom, and Jeiel, the gatekeepers.

[19]So the singers, Heman, Asaph, and Ethan *were appointed* to sound aloud the bronze cymbals;

[20]and Zechariah, Aziel, Shemiramoth, Jehiel, Unni, Eliab, Maaseiah, and Benaiah [were to play] with harps *tuned* to Alamoth [that is, a high pitch];

[21]and Mattithiah, Eliphelehu, Mikneiah, Obed-edom, Jeiel, and Azaziah were to lead with lyres set to Sheminith [that is, the eighth string, a low pitch].

[22]Chenaniah, leader of the Levites, was *in charge of* the singing; he gave instruction in singing because he was skilled.

[23]Berechiah and Elkanah were gatekeepers for the ark.

[24]Shebaniah, Joshaphat, Nethanel, Amasai, Zechariah, Benaiah, and Eliezer the priests blew the trumpets before the ark of God. Obed-edom and Jehiah (Jeiel) were also gatekeepers for the ark.

[25]So David, with the elders of Israel and the captains over thousands, went to bring up the ark of the covenant of the LORD from the house of Obed-edom with joy.

[26]Because God was helping the Levites who carried the ark of the covenant of the LORD [to do it carefully and safely], they sacrificed seven bulls and seven rams.

[27]David was clothed with a robe of fine linen, as were all the Levites who carried the ark, and the singers and Chenaniah, director of the music of the singers. David also wore an ephod (a priestly upper garment) of linen.

[28]Thus all Israel brought up the ark of the covenant of the LORD with shouting, and with the sound of the horn, with trumpets, with loud-sounding cymbals, with harps and lyres.

[29]It happened that as the ark of the covenant of the LORD came to the

---

15:17 ***Heman.*** The musician Heman was the grandson of the prophet Samuel (6:33). He is probably the same Heman who appears in the superscription of Psalm 88. ***Asaph.*** Asaph was leader of the Gershoite Levites (6:39–43). Asaph and his sons ministered primarily as singers (25:1–2; 2Ch 20:14) and composers, as their superscriptions suggest (Ps 50; 73–83). ***Ethan.*** Ethan was the head of the Merarite division of musicians (6:44). He may be the composer of Psalm 89.

15:20 ***with harps tuned to Alamoth.*** The meaning of "alamoth" is uncertain. It may mean a soprano voice, or a high pitch.

15:21 ***lyres set to Sheminith.*** The meaning of "sheminith" is uncertain, but it is apparently a musical term, perhaps derived from the Hebrew word for eighth, referring to musical scales.

15:24 ***Obed-edom.*** It is likely that Obed-Edom in this verse was the same person who had custody of the ark in the months before it was brought to Jerusalem (13:13–14). He apparently was a Levite and certainly a righteous man.

15:29 ***Michal [David's wife] the daughter of Saul.*** Michal was David's first wife, whom he married before Saul started pursuing him (1Sa 18:27; 19:11–17). When David was hiding from Saul, Michal was given in marriage to another (1Sa 25:44). One of the conditions of David's peace agreement with Abner was that Michal be returned to him (2Sa 3:13–16). The Bible does

---

15 Ex 25:14; Nu 4:15; 7:9 **17** 1Ch 6:33; 1Ch 6:39; 1Ch 6:44 **20** Ps 46, title **24** Nu 10:8; Ps 81:3 **25** 2Sa 6:12,13; 1Ki 8:1 **28** 1Ch 13:8 **29** 2Sa 6:16

City of David, Michal [David's wife] the daughter of Saul, looking down through a window, saw King David leaping and dancing [in celebration]; and she despised him in her heart.

A Tent for the Ark

16 SO THEY brought the ark of God and set it inside the tent which David had pitched for it, and they offered burnt offerings and peace offerings before God.

2 When David had finished offering the burnt offerings and the peace offerings, he blessed the people in the name of the LORD.

3 He distributed to everyone in Israel, both man and woman, to everyone a loaf of bread, a portion *of meat,* and a raisin cake.

4 He appointed some of the Levites to minister before the ark of the LORD and to profess [God's name] and to thank and praise the LORD, the God of Israel:
5 Asaph the chief, and second to him Zechariah, *then* Jeiel (Jaaziel), Shemiramoth, Jehiel, Mattithiah, Eliab, Benaiah, Obed-edom, and Jeiel with musical instruments, harps and lyres; also Asaph *played* loud-sounding cymbals;
6 and Benaiah and Jahaziel the priests *blew* trumpets continually before the ark of the covenant of God.

7 Then on that day David first entrusted to Asaph and his relatives to give thanks to the LORD [as their chief task].

Psalm of Thanksgiving

8 O give thanks to the LORD, call on His name;
Make His deeds known among the peoples.
9 Sing to Him, sing praises to Him;
Speak of all His wonders.
10 Glory in His holy name;
Let the hearts of those who seek the LORD rejoice.
11 Seek the LORD and His strength;
Seek His face continually [longing to be in His presence].
12 Remember [with gratitude] His marvelous deeds which He has done,
His miracles and the judgments from His mouth,
13 O seed of Israel His servant,
Children of Jacob, His chosen ones!
14 He is the LORD our God;
His judgments are in all the earth.
15 Be mindful of His covenant forever,
The promise which He commanded *and* established to a thousand generations,
16 *The covenant* which He made with Abraham,
And His oath (sworn promise) to Isaac.

---

not say why Michal despised David, but it seems probable that the real source of her attitude was bitterness about her life. If she had no understanding of God's hand in her life and the life of the nation, seeing David's joyful abandonment before the Lord would have been galling.

16:3 *He distributed.* David's distribution of food was in line with the nature of the peace offerings. Such offerings often accompanied occasions of praise and thanksgiving such as this one. They were unique in that they provided a common meal in which all participated before God — the offerer, his family and friends, and the priests (Lev 7:11 – 14; 28 – 34; Dt 12:17 – 19).

16:4 *Levites.* The appointment of Levites described here was of a more permanent nature than that of 15:1 – 24, which concerned the immediate task of moving the ark into Jerusalem. Some of the same persons were involved, as verses 5 and 6 make clear.

16:7 *to give thanks to the LORD.* David's musical abilities are well-known, both as a harpist (1Sa 16:18) and as the writer of many of the psalms. This psalm consists of three different parts. Each portion correlates with part of another psalm. Verses 8 – 22 correspond with Psalm 105:1 – 15; verses 23 – 33 with Psalm 96:1 – 13; and verses 34 – 36 with Psalm 106:1,47 – 48.

16:12 – 16 Obedience — "Remember [with gratitude] His marvelous deeds ... Be mindful of His covenant forever ..." and for those of us who are believers, we proclaim "[the fact of] the Lord's death until He comes [again]" (1Co 11:23 – 26). Remembering is connected to obedience, only when we remember His commands can we obey Him.

CHAPTER 16 **1** 2Sa 6:17-19 **4** Ps 38; 70, title **7** See 2Sa 23:1 **8** Ps 105:1-15 **16** Ge 17:2; 26:3; 28:13; 35:11

17 He confirmed it as a statute to
Jacob,
And to Israel as an everlasting
covenant, [Gen 35:11, 12]
18 Saying, "To you I will give the land
of Canaan,
As the portion of your possession
and inheritance."
19 When you were few in number,
Even a very few, and strangers in it,
20 When they wandered from nation
to nation,
And from *one* kingdom to another
people,
21 He allowed no man to oppress *or*
exploit them,
And, He reproved *and* punished
kings for their sakes, *saying*,
[Gen 12:17; 20:3; Ex 7:15–18]
22 "Do not touch My anointed ones,
And do My prophets no harm."
[Gen 20:7]
23 Sing to the LORD, all the earth;
Proclaim the good news of His
salvation from day to day.
24 Declare His glory among the
nations,
His marvelous works among all
peoples.
25 For great is the LORD, and greatly
to be praised;
He is also to be feared [with awe-
filled reverence] above all gods.
26 For all the gods of the peoples are
[lifeless] idols,
But the LORD made the heavens.
27 Splendor and majesty are [found]
in His presence;
Strength and joy are [found] in His
place (sanctuary).
28 Ascribe to the LORD, O families of
the peoples,
Ascribe to the LORD glory *and*
honor and strength.
29 Ascribe to the LORD the glory *and*
honor due His name;
Bring an offering [of thanksgiving],
and come before Him;
Worship the LORD in the splendor
of holiness.
30 Tremble [reverently] before Him,
all the earth;
The world is firmly established, it
will not be moved.
31 Let the heavens be glad, and let
the earth rejoice;
And let them say among the
nations, "The LORD reigns."
32 Let the sea roar, and all the things
that fill it;
Let the field rejoice, and all that is
in it.
33 Then the trees of the forest will
sing for joy before the LORD;
For He comes to judge *and* govern
the earth.

16:22 *anointed.* In this context "anointed ones" means those set apart for God's service, not necessarily literally anointed with oil.

16:29 The Meaning of Worship — Worship refers to the honor and praise given in thought or deed to a person or thing. The Bible teaches that God alone is worthy of worship (Ps 29:2). But it also records accounts of those who worshiped inappropriately: people (Ac 14:8–18); false gods (2Ki 10:19); images and idols (Isa 2:8); heavenly bodies (2Ki 21:3); Satan (Rev 13:4); and demons (Rev 9:20).

True worship involves at least three important elements:

Reverence. This includes the honor and respect directed toward the Lord in thought and feeling. Jesus said that those who worship God must do so "in spirit and truth" (Jn 4:24). The term spirit speaks of the personal nature of worship. It is from my person to God's person and involves the intellect, emotions, and will. The word truth speaks of the content of worship. God is pleased when we worship Him, understanding His true character.

Public expression. This was particularly prevalent in the Old Testament because of the sacrificial system. For example, when a believer received a particular blessing for which he wanted to thank God, it was not sufficient to say it privately; he expressed his thanks publicly with a thank-offering (Lev 7:12).

Service. The words for worship in both Testaments originally referred to the labor of slaves for the master. Worship especially includes the joyful service which Christians render to Christ their Master. The concept of worship involves much more than church attendance once or twice a week. It involves an entire life of obedience, service, and praise to God.

16:33 *trees . . . sing.* This is a figure of speech called personification, in which inanimate things are spoken of as if they had human characteristics. Because the whole creation was negatively

19 Ge 34:30 **21** Ge 12:17; 20:3; Ex 7:15-18 **22** Ps 105:15 **23** Ps 96:1 **26** Lev 19:4

[34]O give thanks to the LORD, for *He is* good;
For His lovingkindness endures forever.
[35]Then say, "Save us, O God of our salvation;
Gather us together and rescue us from the nations,
That we may give thanks to Your holy name,
And glory in Your praise."
[36]Blessed be the LORD, the God of Israel,
Forever and ever.

And all the people said, "Amen," and praised the LORD.

Worship before the Ark

[37]So David left Asaph and his relatives there before the ark of the covenant of the LORD to minister before the ark continually, as each day's work required;
[38]and Obed-edom with his sixty-eight relatives; also Obed-edom the son of Jeduthun, and Hosah, were to be gatekeepers.
[39]*David left* Zadok the priest and his relatives the priests before the dwelling place (tabernacle) of the LORD in the high place which was at Gibeon, [1 Chr 21:29]
[40]to offer burnt offerings to the LORD on the altar of burnt offering continually, morning and evening, in accordance with all that is written in the Law of the LORD, which He commanded Israel.
[41]With them were Heman and Jeduthun, and the rest who were chosen and designated by name, to give thanks to the LORD, for His lovingkindness endures forever.
[42]With them were Heman and Jeduthun *with* trumpets and cymbals for those who *were to* sound aloud, and instruments for [accompanying] the songs of God. And the sons of Jeduthun were to be at the gate.
[43]Then all the people departed, each to his house, and David returned [home] to bless his household.

God's Covenant with David

17 AS DAVID sat in his house (palace), he said to Nathan the prophet, "Behold, I live in a house of cedars, while the ark of the covenant of the LORD is under tent curtains."
[2]Then Nathan said to David, "Do all that is in your heart, for God is with you."
[3]But it came about that same night that the word of God came to Nathan, saying,
[4]"Go and tell David My servant, 'Thus says the LORD, "You shall not build a house for Me to dwell in;

---

affected by the fall of humanity into sin, it could not be restored to perfection and could not truly rejoice until humanity was redeemed. ***He comes.*** When the Lord returns to the earth, all creation will burst out in praise.

16:38 *Obed-edom.* There are two men by this name in this verse. The first is the Obed-edom whose house sheltered the ark for three months (13:14) and who was a doorkeeper (15:24). The second was also a gatekeeper, a son of Jeduthun.

16:39 *Zadok.* Until the temple of Solomon was completed, there were two legitimate places for community worship — the Mosaic tabernacle at Gibeon, and David's tabernacle on Mount Zion. Zadok, a descendant of Eleazer, served at Gibeon, while Abiathar, a descendant of Ithamar, served at Jerusalem (see note for 15:11).

16:41 *Jeduthun.* This was probably another name for the musician Ethan, who is usually named together with Asaph and Heman (15:17; 19; 6:33,39,44).

16:42 *instruments for the songs of God.* It is difficult to overemphasize the importance of music in Old Testament worship. The Book of Psalms in itself, and constant references to choral and orchestral ministry demonstrate the significance of music as the people worshiped their Creator (9:33; 15:16 – 24; 16:4 – 6; 25:1 – 31)

17:1 *Nathan the prophet.* Nathan was a prophet at the time of both David and Solomon. He was closely connected with both kings, and was trusted as a faithful spokesman of God (2Sa 7:2 – 3; 12:1 – 15; 1Ki 1:8 – 38; 45; 2Ch 29:25). The "chronicles of Nathan the prophet" provided a source for the composition of the books of Chronicles (29:29; 2Ch 9:29). ***a house of cedars.*** Cedar paneling was too expensive to be used in an ordinary home.

34 Ps 106:1; 107:1; 118:1; 136:1 **35** Ps 106:47,48 **36** 1Ki 8:15; Dt 27:15 **39** 1Ch 21:29; 2Ch 1:3; 1Ki 3:4 **40** Ex 29:38; Nu 28:3 **41** ver. 34; 2Ch 5:13; 7:3; Ezr 3:11; Jer 33:11 **43** 2Sa 6:19,20 **CHAPTER 17** **1** 2Sa 7:1

5 for I have not dwelt in a house since the day that I brought Israel up [from Egypt] until this day, but I have gone from tent to tent and from *one* dwelling place *to another.*

6 "Wherever I have walked with all Israel, did I say a word to any of the judges of Israel, whom I commanded to shepherd My people, saying, 'Why have you not built for Me a house of cedar?' " '

7 "Now, therefore, this is what you shall say to My servant David: 'Thus says the LORD of hosts, "I took you from the pasture, from following the sheep, to be leader over My people Israel.

8 "I have been with you wherever you have gone, and I have cut off all your enemies from before you; and I will make your name like the name of the great ones of the earth.

9 "I will appoint a place for My people Israel, and will plant them, so that they may live in their own place and not be moved again [nor tremble with fear]; and the wicked will not waste (persecute) them anymore, as formerly,

10 since the time that I commanded judges to be over My people Israel. And I will humble *and* subdue all your enemies.

"Furthermore, I tell you that the LORD will build you a house (a blessed posterity).

11 "And it shall come to pass that when your days are completed and you must go to be with your fathers [in death], I will raise up *one of* your descendants after you, one of your own sons; and I will establish his kingdom.

12 "He shall build Me a house, and I will establish his throne forever. [1 Chr 28:7]

13 "I will be his father and he shall be My son; and I will not take My steadfast love *and* mercy away from him, as I took it from him (King Saul) who was before you. [Heb 1:5, 6]

14 "But I will settle him in My house and in My kingdom forever, and his throne shall be established forevermore." ' " [Is 9:7]

15 According to all these words and according to all this vision, so Nathan spoke to David.

David's Prayer in Response

16 Then David the king went in and sat before the LORD and said, "Who am I, O LORD God, and what is my house *and* family that You have brought me this far?

17 "This was a small thing in Your eyes, O God; but You have spoken of Your servant's house for a great while to come, and have regarded me according to the standard *and* estate of a man of high degree (prominence), O LORD God.

18 "What more can David say to You for the honor *granted to* Your servant? For You know Your servant.

19 "O LORD, for Your servant's sake, and in accordance with Your own heart, You have accomplished all this greatness, to make known all these great things.

20 "O LORD, there is no one like You, nor is there any God except You, according to all that we have heard with our ears.

21 "And what one nation on the earth is like Your people Israel, whom God went to redeem for Himself as a people, to make a name for Yourself by great and awesome *and* terrible things, by driving out nations from before Your people, whom You redeemed out of Egypt?

22 "You made Your people Israel Your

17:9 *I will appoint a place.* This did not mean that Israel would move to another land, but it was a restating of God's promise that they were meant to inherit the land (Ge 13:14 – 17; 15:18 – 21; 17:8; Ex 3:16 – 17; 6:8; Dt 1:8; Jos 1:2 – 5).

17:16 – 18 Thankfulness — As with David, God's willingness to bless us is not because we are great but because He is good. His purpose is for us to be like Him, and to bless us and establish us forever with Him through Christ (Jn 14).

17:20 *any God except You.* This is a clear assertion of the uniqueness of Israel's God. Statements such as "all gods" and "the gods of the peoples" in David's song of thanksgiving (16:25 – 26) must be understood in the light of this clear confession that there is only one living God.

13 2Sa 7:14,15 **14** Lk 1:33 **16** 2Sa 7:18

own people forever, and You, LORD,
became their God.
[23]"Therefore now, O LORD, let the
word which You have spoken concerning Your servant and his house endure
forever, and do as You have said.
[24]"Let Your name [and the character
that it denotes] endure and be magnified forever, saying, 'The LORD of hosts
is the God of Israel, yes, a God to Israel;
and the house of Your servant David
is established before You.'
[25]"For You, O my God, have revealed
to Your servant that You will build for
him a house (descendants); therefore
Your servant has found *courage* to
pray before You.
[26]"And now, O LORD, You are God,
and you have spoken *and* promised
this good thing to Your servant.
[27]"Therefore may it please You to
bless the house (descendants) of Your
servant, that it may continue before
You forever; for what You bless,
O LORD, is blessed forever."

David's Kingdom Strengthened

18 AFTER THIS it came about that David defeated and subdued the Philistines, and he took Gath and its villages out of the hand of the Philistines.
[2]He defeated Moab, and the Moabites
became David's servants and brought
tribute (gifts).
[3]David also defeated Hadadezer
king of Zobah *as far as* Hamath, as
he went to establish his dominion to
the Euphrates River.
[4]David took from him 1,000 chariots,
7,000 horsemen, and 20,000 foot soldiers (infantrymen). David also hamstrung [nearly] all the chariot horses
[to make them lame and useless], but
left enough of them for 100 chariots.
[5]When the Arameans (Syrians) of
Damascus came to help Hadadezer
king of Zobah, David killed 22,000 of
the Arameans.
[6]Then David put *military outposts*
among the Arameans in Damascus;
and the Arameans became David's
servants and brought tribute. Thus the
LORD helped David wherever he went.
[7]David took the shields of gold which
were carried by the servants of Hadadezer and brought them to Jerusalem.
[8]Likewise from Tibhath and from
Cun, cities of Hadadezer, David
brought a very large amount of bronze,
with which Solomon later made the
bronze Sea (large basin), the pillars,
and the utensils of bronze. [1 Kin 7:13–47; 2 Chr 4:2–18]
[9]When Tou king of Hamath heard
how David had defeated all the army
of Hadadezer king of Zobah,
[10]he sent Hadoram his son to King
David to greet him and to bless (congratulate) him, because he had fought
against Hadadezer and had defeated
him; for Hadadezer had been at war
with Tou. And *Hadoram brought* all
kinds of articles of gold and silver and
bronze.
[11]King David also dedicated these
to the LORD [setting them apart for sacred use], with the silver and the gold
which he brought from all the nations:
from Edom, Moab, the Ammonites, the
Philistines, and from Amalek.
[12]Also Abishai the son of Zeruiah
[David's half sister] defeated 18,000
Edomites in the Valley of Salt.
[13]He put military outposts in Edom,
and all the Edomites became David's
servants. Thus the LORD helped David
wherever he went.
[14]So David reigned over all Israel

18:1 *took Gath.* This is the only record of David taking a Philistine city, although he had defeated the Philistines many times in battle. Gath was the Philistine city closest to Israelite territory, so it posed the greatest threat to Israel.
18:2 *Moab.* David's great-grandmother Ruth was a Moabitess (Ru 4:13 – 17), and David had sent his own family to Moab for protection when he was hiding from Saul (1Sa 22:3 – 4). Yet Moab had been an enemy of Israel (Nu 23), and would be again (Eze 25:9).
18:11 *dedicated these to the LORD.* The fact that David dedicated all the spoils of war to God suggests that he viewed the battles as campaigns initiated and led by God. When Solomon built the temple, he brought all the dedicated things into the temple treasuries (2Ch 5:1).

CHAPTER 18 **1** 2Sa 8:1 **8** 1Ki 7:15,23; 2Ch 4:12,15,16 **12** 2Sa 8:13 **13** 2Sa 8:14

and administered justice and righ-
teousness for all his people.
15 Joab the son of Zeruiah was in com-
mand of the army, and Jehoshaphat
the son of Ahilud was the recorder;
16 Zadok the son of Ahitub and Abim-
elech the son of Abiathar were the
priests, and Shavsha was secretary
(state scribe);
17 and Benaiah the son of Jehoiada
was in charge of the Cherethites and
the Pelethites [David's bodyguards],
and the sons of David were chiefs at
the king's side.

David's Messengers Abused

19 NOW IT came about after this,
that Nahash king of the Ammon-
ites died, and his son became king in
his place.
2 David said, "I will be kind (gracious)
to Hanun son of Nahash, because his
father was kind to me." So David sent
messengers to comfort him concerning
[the death of] his father. And the ser-
vants of David came to the land of the
Ammonites to comfort Hanun.
3 But the leaders of the Ammonites
said to Hanun, "Do you think that
David has sent people to console *and*
comfort you because he honors your
father? Have his servants not come to
you to search and to overthrow and to
spy out the land?"
4 Therefore Hanun took David's ser-
vants, shaved them [cutting off half
their beards], and cut off their garments
in the middle as far as their buttocks,
and sent them away [in humiliation].
5 When David was told how the men
were treated, he sent *messengers* to
meet them, for they were very humil-
iated *and* ashamed [to return]. So the
king said, "Stay in Jericho until your
beards grow [back], and *then* return."
6 When the Ammonites saw that they
had made themselves hateful to David,
Hanun and his people sent 1,000 tal-
ents of silver to hire for themselves
chariots and horsemen from Meso-
potamia, Aram-maacah, and Zobah.
7 So they hired for themselves 32,000
chariots and the king of Maacah and
his troops, who came and camped
before Medeba. And the Ammonites
gathered together from their cities and
came to battle.
8 When David heard *about it*, he sent
Joab and all the army of courageous
men.
9 The Ammonites came out and lined
up in battle formation at the entrance
of the city [Medeba], while the kings
who had come were by themselves in
the open country.

Ammon and Aram Defeated

10 Now when Joab saw that the battle
was set against him in the front and in
the rear, he chose *warriors* from all the
choice men of Israel and put them in for-
mation against the Arameans (Syrians).
11 The rest of the soldiers he placed
in the hand of Abishai his brother, and
they lined up against the Ammonites.
12 He said, "If the Arameans are too
strong for me, then you shall help me;
but if the Ammonites are too strong
for you, I will help you.
13 "Be strong and let us show ourselves
courageous for the sake of our people
and for the cities of our God; and may
the LORD do what is good in His sight."
14 So Joab and the people who were
with him approached the Arameans
for battle, and they fled before him.

18:17 *Cherethites . . . Pelethites.* These were companies of soldiers, probably mercenaries from Philistia (Eze 25:16; 1Sa 30:14; 2Sa 15:18).

19:1 *Nahash.* Nahash was reigning in Saul's earliest years (1Sa 11:1); the present incident must have occurred early in David's reign at Jerusalem.

19:3 Slander — The delegation was treated scandalously, and David's motives were slanderously attacked. Of course there were no grounds for such suspicions. Men who themselves act basely toward their neighbors are most likely to suspect such behavior in others. One of the marks of a godly person is that he does not slander with his tongue (Ps 15:3).

19:4 *shaved . . . cut off.* Hebrew men were proud of their beards and scrupulously modest in their attire. The Ammonites had humiliated David's men in the most offensive way possible.

19:6 *1,000 talents.* A talent is about 75 pounds.

---

17 2Sa 8:18 **CHAPTER 19** **1** 2Sa 10:1 **6** 1Ch 18:5,9

15 When the Ammonites saw that the
Arameans fled, they also fled before
Abishai, Joab's brother, and entered
the city [Medeba]. Then Joab came to
Jerusalem.
16 When the Arameans (Syrians) saw
that they had been defeated by Israel,
they sent messengers and brought out
the Arameans who were beyond the
[Euphrates] River, with Shophach the
commander of the army of Hadadezer
leading them.
17 When this was told to David, he
gathered all Israel and crossed the Jordan, and came upon them and drew up
in formation against them. So when
David drew up in battle array against
the Arameans, they fought against him.
18 But the Arameans fled before Israel, and David killed of the Arameans
7,000 charioteers and 40,000 foot soldiers, and put to death Shophach the
commander of the army.
19 When the servants of Hadadezer
saw that they had been defeated by Israel, they made peace with David and
became subject to *and* served him. And
the Arameans (Syrians) were not willing to help the Ammonites anymore.

War with Philistine Giants

20 THEN IT happened at the end
of the year, at the time when
kings go out *to battle,* Joab led out
the army and ravaged *and* devastated the land of the Ammonites, and
came and besieged Rabbah. But David
stayed at Jerusalem [with Bathsheba].
Joab struck Rabbah and overthrew it.
[2 Sam 12:24–29]
2 David took the crown of their
king from his head and found that it
weighed a talent of gold and that there
was a precious stone in it; so it was
set on David's head. He also brought
a very great amount of spoil (plunder)
out of the city [of Rabbah].
3 He brought out the people who were
in it, and put them [to work] with saws,
iron picks, and axes. David dealt *in
this way* with all the Ammonite cities.
Then David and all the people returned
to Jerusalem.
4 Now it came about after this that
war broke out at Gezer with the Philistines; then Sibbecai the Hushathite
killed Sippai, one of the descendants
of the giants, and they were subdued.
5 There was war again with the Philistines, and Elhanan the son of Jair
killed Lahmi the brother of Goliath the
Gittite, the shaft of whose spear was
like a weaver's beam.
6 Again there was war at Gath, where
there was a man of *great* stature who
had twenty-four fingers and toes, six
fingers on each hand and six *toes on
each foot;* and he also was descended
from the giants.
7 When he taunted Israel, Jonathan
the son of Shimea, David's brother,
killed him.
8 These were descended from the
giants in Gath, and they fell by the
hand of David and by the hand of his
servants.

Census Brings Pestilence

21 SATAN [THE adversary] stood
up against Israel and incited
David to count [the population of]
Israel.

19:19 ***became subject to and served him.*** "Subject to" signifies national subservience to a greater power, in this case, Israel.
20:1 ***David stayed at Jerusalem.*** This is the time that David committed adultery with Bathsheba (2Sa 11). The chronicler omits this story, not because it is unsavory, but because it has no bearing on his theme. He is showing how the Davidic dynasty was the fulfillment of God's promises.
20:2 ***crown.*** The crown David took was ceremonial and not for wearing, since it weighed about 75 pounds. David put the crown on his head to demonstrate that he had vanquished the Ammonites and now reigned over them as well.
20:7 ***Shimea.*** This was David's older brother, the third son of Jesse (2:13).
20:8 ***the giants in Gath.*** Goliath was from Gath (1Sa 17:4).
21:1 Temptation by Satan — The role of Satan as the Christian's opponent is well summed up by the meaning of the name Satan, which means "adversary." He is also called "the devil," meaning "accuser." He can appear as a dragon (Rev 12:3-4,9) or as a beautifully deceptive "angel

CHAPTER 20 **1** 2Sa 11:1; 12:26 **2** 2Sa 12:30,31 **4** 2Sa 21:18; 1Ch 11:29 **6** 2Sa 21:20 **CHAPTER 21** **1** 2Sa 24:1

[2]So David said to Joab and the leaders of the people, "Go, count Israel from Beersheba to Dan, and bring me their total, so that I may know it."
[3]Joab said, "May the LORD add to His people a hundred times as many as they are! But, my lord the king, are they not all my lord's servants? Why then does my lord require this? Why will he bring guilt on Israel?"
[4]But the king's word prevailed over Joab. So Joab left and went throughout all Israel and came to Jerusalem.
[5]Then Joab gave the total of the census of the people to David. And all Israel were 1,100,000 men who drew the sword; and in Judah 470,000 men who drew the sword.
[6]But he did not count Levi and Benjamin among them, because the king's order was detestable to Joab.
[7]Now God was displeased with this act [of arrogance and pride], and He struck Israel.
[8]Then David said to God, "I have sinned greatly because I have done this thing. But now, I beseech You, take away the wickedness *and* guilt of Your servant, for I have acted very foolishly."
[9]And the LORD said to Gad, David's seer,
[10]"Go and tell David, saying, 'Thus says the LORD, "I offer you three *choices;* choose for yourself one of them, which I will do to you [as punishment for your sin]." ' "
[11]So Gad came to David and said to him, "Thus says the LORD: 'Choose for yourself
[12]either three years of famine, or

---

of light" (2Co 11:14). He stands hatefully opposed to all the work of God and promotes defiance among men (Job 2:4–5). When Satan sinned he was expelled from heaven (Lk 10:18), although apparently he still had some access to God (Job 2:4–5). A multitude of angels joined him in his rebellion and subsequently became the demons mentioned often in the biblical record (Mt 12:24; Rev 12:7). Although Satan's doom was secured by Jesus' death on the cross (Jn 16:11), he will continue to hinder God's program until he and his angels are destroyed (Mt 25:41).

The terrifying work of Satan in the unbeliever is described in Scripture as follows: he blinds their minds (2Co 4:4); he takes the Word of God from their hearts (Lk 8:12); and he controls them (Ac 13:8). In regard to Christians, Satan may accuse them (Rev 12:10), devour their testimony for Christ (1Pe 5:8–9), deceive them (Col 2:8), hinder their work (1Th 2:18), tempt them to immorality (1Co 7:5), and even be used by God to discipline Christians (1Co 5:5; 2Co 12:7).

The Christian's response to Satan is to recognize his power and deception (2Co 2:11; Eph 6:11), to adhere steadfastly to the faith (1Pe 5:9) to resist him openly (Jas 4:7), and not to give him opportunities. In practice, the best way to oppose him is to be a growing Christian. Believers can respond to temptation by Satan with confidence. We know that nothing can separate us from the love of God (Ro 8:38–39). Also in light of Satan's tremendous power to blind men to the gospel, Christians must always be aggressively and compassionately witnessing to the lost in order to snatch them from his control.

21:2 ***So David said.*** Samuel attributed David's impulse to number the people to God Himself (2Sa 24:1) while here it is attributed to Satan (v. 1). The apparent contradiction can be resolved by recognizing that though Satan is the author of all evil, he cannot exercise his evil intentions apart from the permission of God. Moreover, God could use Satan to accomplish His own purposes of judgment (1Ki 22:19–23; Job 1) or discipline (as here with David). ***Go, count.*** David's plan to take a census was not evil in itself, for the Lord Himself at other times had commanded the Israelites to be counted (Nu 1). The problem seems to have been David's presumptuous attitude. He apparently wanted to have a number to look at, instead of remembering that no matter how many or few were the Israelites, their strength was always in the Lord. ***Beersheba to Dan.*** This was the traditional way of describing all of Israel from south to north. The distance is about 150 miles.

21:3 ***bring guilt.*** Joab's warning was David's chance to repent of his intention to number the people for his own purposes. God does not entice us to evil (Jas 1:13–15; 4:7–8), and even though God was using Satan in this situation, David was still the one who decided to sin (v. 17). God knew what was in David's heart, and either through Joab's rebuke or through David carrying out his sinful thoughts, God intended to deal with David's attitude.

21:9 ***seer.*** Gad was a prophet, one who received revelations from the Lord (1Sa 22:5).

2 1Ch 27:23 **6** 1Ch 27:24 **8** 2Sa 24:10; 2Sa 12:13 **9** See 1Sa 9:9 **12** 2Sa 24:13

three months to be swept away before your enemies, while the sword of your enemies overtakes you, or else three days of the sword of the LORD and plague in the land, and the angel of the LORD bringing destruction throughout all the territory of Israel.' Now therefore, consider what answer I shall return to Him who sent me."
13David said to Gad, "I am in great distress; please let me fall into the hands of the LORD, for His mercies are very great; but do not let me fall into the hand of man."
14So the LORD sent a plague on Israel, and 70,000 men of Israel fell.
15God sent an angel to Jerusalem to destroy it; and as he was destroying it, the LORD looked, and relented concerning the catastrophe and said to the destroying angel, "It is enough; now remove your hand [of judgment]." And the angel of the LORD was standing by the threshing floor of Ornan the Jebusite.
16Then David raised his eyes and saw the angel of the LORD standing between earth and heaven, having a drawn sword in his hand stretched out over Jerusalem. Then David and the elders, covered in sackcloth, fell on their faces.
17David said to God, "Is it not I who commanded the people to be counted? I am the one who has sinned and done evil; but as for these sheep [the people of Israel], what have they done? O LORD my God, please let Your hand be against me and my father's house, but not against Your people that they should be plagued."

David's Altar

18Then the angel of the LORD commanded Gad to say to David, that David should go up and build an altar to the LORD on the threshing floor of Ornan the Jebusite.
19So David went up at Gad's word, which he spoke in the name of the LORD.
20Now Ornan was threshing wheat, and he turned back and saw the angel; and his four sons who were with him hid themselves.
21As David came to Ornan, Ornan looked and saw him, and went out from the threshing floor and bowed down before David with his face to the ground.
22Then David said to Ornan, "Give me the site of this threshing floor, so that I may build an altar on it to the LORD. You shall charge me the full price for it, so that the plague may be averted from the people."
23Ornan said to David, "Take it for yourself; and let my lord the king do what is good in his eyes. See, I will give you the oxen also for burnt offerings and the threshing sledges (heavy wooden platforms) for wood and the wheat for the grain offering; I give it all."
24But King David said to Ornan, "No, I will certainly pay the full price; for I will not take what is yours for the LORD, nor offer a burnt offering which costs me nothing."
25So David gave Ornan 600 shekels of gold by weight for the site. [2 Chr 3:1]
26Then David built an altar to the LORD there and presented burnt offerings and peace offerings. And he called on the LORD, and He answered him with fire from heaven on the altar of burnt offering.
27Then the LORD commanded the [avenging] angel, and he put his sword back into its sheath.
28At that time, when David saw that the LORD had answered him on the

---

21:15 ***Jerusalem to destroy it.*** When God saw David's repentance and heard his intercessory prayer (v. 17), He relented and stopped the destroying angel. God responded to David's heartfelt prayer. One of the most important aspects of intercessory prayer is how it turns the heart of the one praying toward God, and aligns the intercessor with God's attitudes and purposes.

21:24 ***which costs me nothing.*** David showed a clear perception of the essence of sacrifice. Every prayer, every sacrifice must come from the heart and labor of the one who offers these things to God. No one can have a relationship with God for or on behalf of someone else.

15 2Sa 24:16; See Ge 6:6 **16** 2Ch 3:1 **18** 2Ch 3:1 **25** 2Sa 24:24 **26** Lev 9:24; 2Ch 3:1; 7:1

threshing floor of Ornan the Jebusite,
he sacrificed there.
29 For the tabernacle of the LORD,
which Moses made in the wilderness,
and the altar of burnt offering were at
that time in the high place at Gibeon.
30 But David could not go before it
to inquire of God, for he was terrified
by the sword of the angel of the LORD.

David Prepares for Temple Building

22 THEN DAVID said, "This is the
house of the LORD God, and this
is the altar of burnt offering for Israel."
2 So David gave orders to gather the
foreigners who were in the land of
Israel, and he assigned stonecutters
to hew out stones to build the house
of God.
3 David prepared large quantities of
iron to make nails for the doors of the
gates and for the clamps (trusses), and
more bronze than could be weighed;
4 and cedar trees beyond number,
for the Sidonians and Tyrians brought
large quantities of cedar timber to
David.
5 David said, "Solomon my son is
young and inexperienced, and the
house that is to be built for the LORD
shall be exceedingly magnificent, fa-
mous, and an object of glory *and* splen-
dor throughout all lands [of the earth].
So now I will make preparations for it."
Therefore, David made ample prepa-
rations before his death.

Solomon Charged with the Task

6 Then he called for Solomon his son
and ordered him to build a house for
the LORD, the God of Israel.
7 David said to Solomon, "My son, I
had intended to build a house for the
Name (Presence) of the LORD my God.
8 "But the word of the LORD came
to me, saying, 'You have shed much
blood and have waged great wars; you
shall not build a house for My Name,
because you have shed so much blood
on the earth before me.
9 'Behold, a son will be born to you,
who will be a man of peace. I will give
him rest from all his enemies on every
side; for his name shall be Solomon,
and I will give peace and quiet to Israel
in his days. [2 Sam 12:24, 25]
10 'He shall build a house for My
Name (Presence). He shall be My son
and I will be his father; and I will es-
tablish his royal throne over Israel
forever.'
11 "Now, my son, may the LORD be
with you so that you may be successful
and build the house of the LORD your
God, just as He has spoken concern-
ing you.
12 "Only may the LORD give you wis-
dom and understanding, and give you
charge over Israel, so that you may
keep the law of the LORD your God.
13 "Then you will prosper, if you are
careful to observe *and* fulfill the stat-
utes and ordinances which the LORD

21:29 *tabernacle . . . which Moses made.* The Old Testament account does not fully trace the movement of the tabernacle after Shiloh, but it did end up first at Nob and finally at Gibeon (15:1).

22:1 *This is the house of the LORD God.* As long as the ark remained at Kiriath-jearim and the tabernacle of Moses was at Nob and Gibeon, it was impossible for worship to be carried out in the manner originally intended. When the house of God was built, the ark and the altar would be together once again.

22:5 *young and inexperienced.* Solomon was born about halfway through David's reign. At the time that David began to gather building materials, Solomon was probably not over 18 years old.

22:13 Zeal—David says in Psalm 71, "O God, You have taught me from my youth, and I still declare your wondrous works" (v. 17). Wherever he went, David proclaimed the goodness and majesty of God, and now he saw the temple and the centrality of worship as the pinnacle of his service for God. He could encourage Solomon to proceed with confidence because he knew he was doing God's will.

29 1Ch 16:39; 1Ki 3:4; 1Ch 16:39; 2Ch 1:3 **CHAPTER 22** **1** Dt 12:5; 2Sa 24:18; 1Ch 21:18, 19,26,28; 2Ch 3:1 **2** 1Ki 9:21 **3** ver. 14; 1Ki 7:47 **4** 1Ki 5:6 **5** 1Ch 29:1 **7** 2Sa 7:2; 1Ki 8:17; 1Ch 17:1; 28:2; Dt 12:5,11 **8** 1Ki 5:3 **9** 1Ch 28:5; 1Ki 4:25; 5:4 **10** 2Sa 7:13; 1Ki 5:5; 1Ch 17:12,13; 28:6; Heb 1:5 **11** ver. 16 **12** 1Ki 3:9,12 **13** Jos 1:7,8; 1Ch 28:7; Dt 31:7,8; Jos 1:6,7,9; 1Ch 28:20

commanded Moses concerning Israel. Be strong and courageous, do not fear nor be dismayed.

14 “Now listen, with great trouble I have prepared *and* provided for the house of the LORD 100,000 talents of gold, 1,000,000 talents of silver, and bronze and iron beyond weighing, for they are great in quantity. I have also prepared *and* provided timber and stone, and you may add to them.

15 “Further, you have workmen in abundance: stonecutters and stonemasons and carpenters, and all men who are skillful in every kind of work.

16 “As for the gold, the silver, the bronze, and the iron, there is no limit. So arise and begin working, and may the LORD be with you.”

17 David also commanded all the leaders of Israel to help Solomon his son, *saying*,

18 “Is not the LORD your God with you? And has He not given you rest *and* peace on every side? For He has given the inhabitants of the land into my hand, and the land is subdued before the LORD and before His people.

19 “Now set your heart and your soul to seek (inquire of, require as your vital necessity) the LORD your God. Arise and build the sanctuary of the LORD God, so that you may bring the ark of the covenant of the LORD and the holy articles *and* utensils of God into the house built for the Name (Presence) of the LORD.”

Solomon Reigns

23 WHEN DAVID reached old age, he made his son Solomon king over Israel.

2 And he assembled together all the leaders of Israel with the priests and Levites.

Offices of the Levites

3 The Levites thirty years old and upward were counted, and their number man by man was 38,000.

4 Of these 24,000 were to oversee *and* inspect the work of the house of the LORD and 6,000 were to be administrators and judges,

5 and 4,000 were gatekeepers, and 4,000 [musicians] were to praise the LORD with the instruments which David made for giving praise.

6 And David organized them into divisions according to the sons of Levi: Gershon, Kohath, and Merari.

Gershonites

7 Of the Gershonites: Ladan (Libni) and Shimei.

8 The sons of Ladan: Jehiel the first and Zetham and Joel—three *in all*.

9 The sons of Shimei: Shelomoth, Haziel, and Haran—three *in all*. These were the heads of the fathers' *households* of Ladan.

10 The sons of Shimei: Jahath, Zina (Zizah), Jeush, and Beriah. These were the four sons of Shimei.

11 Jahath was the first and Zizah the second; but Jeush and Beriah did not have many sons [not enough for a father's house or clan], so they were [counted together] as one father's household, one working group.

Kohathites

12 The sons of Kohath: Amram, Izhar, Hebron, and Uzziel—four *in all*.

13 The sons of Amram: Aaron and Moses. Aaron was set apart to consecrate him as most holy, he and his sons forever, to burn incense before the LORD, attend to His service, and to bless [worshipers] in His name forever.

22:18 ***subdued before the LORD.*** The conquest of the land began in Joshua's time and was completed under David. It had been a long process, including times of great disobedience and others of great faith. There is an element of submission in this statement, relating both to the Israelites and the land itself.

23:1 ***his son Solomon king.*** This phrasing suggests that this is an official appointment, perhaps in the role of coregent with David. It was later ratified by the whole nation (29:22).

14 As ver. 3 **16** ver. 11 **18** Dt 12:10; Jos 22:4; 2Sa 7:1; 1Ch 23:25 **19** 2Ch 5:7; 1Ki 5:3 **CHAPTER 23** **1** 1Ki 1:33 **3** Nu 4:3 **4** Dt 16:18; 2Ch 19:8 **5** 2Ch 29:25,26 **6** Ex 6:16; Nu 26:57; 2Ch 8:14 **7** 1Ch 26:21 **12** Ex 6:18 **13** Ex 6:20; Ex 28:1; Heb 5:4; Ex 30:7; 1Sa 2:28; Dt 21:5; Nu 6:23

14 But as for Moses the man of God,
his sons were counted among the tribe
of Levi.
15 The sons of Moses: Gershom and
Eliezer.
16 The son of Gershom: Shebuel the
chief.
17 The son of Eliezer was Rehabiah
the chief. Eliezer had no other sons,
but Rehabiah's sons were very many
[in number].
18 The son of Izhar: Shelomith the
chief.
19 The sons of Hebron: Jeriah the
first, Amariah the second, Jahaziel
the third, and Jekameam the fourth.
20 The sons of Uzziel: Micah the first
and Isshiah the second.

Merarites

21 The sons of Merari: Mahli and
Mushi. The sons of Mahli: Eleazar
and Kish.
22 Eleazar died and had no sons, but
daughters only, and their relatives, the
sons of Kish, took them as wives.
23 The sons of Mushi: Mahli, Eder,
and Jeremoth—three *in all*.

Duties Revised

24 These were the Levites by their fa-
thers' households, the heads of the fa-
thers' *households* of those registered,
according to the number of names of
the individuals who were the servants
of the house of the LORD, from twenty
years old and upward.
25 For David said, "The LORD God of Is-
rael, has given peace *and* rest to His peo-
ple, and He dwells in Jerusalem forever.
26 "Also, the Levites will no longer
need to carry the tabernacle and all
its utensils for its service."
27 For by the last words of David,
the Levites from twenty years old and
above were counted.
28 For their duty is to assist [the
priests] the sons of Aaron in the ser-
vice of the house of the LORD, in [caring
for] the courtyards, the chambers, the
purifying of all holy things, and any
work of the service of the house of
God,
29 and with the showbread, and the
fine flour for a grain offering, and un-
leavened wafers, or *what is baked in*
the pan or what is well-mixed, and all
measures of volume and size [as the
Law of Moses required].
30 They are to stand every morning
to thank and praise the LORD, and like-
wise at evening,
31 and to offer all burnt sacrifices to
the LORD on the Sabbaths, the new
moons, and the festivals by number
according to the ordinance concerning
them, continually before the LORD.
32 So they shall be responsible for
the Tent of Meeting, the Holy Place,
and the sons of Aaron their relatives,
for the service of the house of the
LORD.

Divisions of Levites

24 THE DIVISIONS of the descen-
dants of Aaron *were these:* the
sons of Aaron were Nadab, Abihu,
Eleazar, and Ithamar.
2 But Nadab and Abihu died before
their father and had no sons; there-

23:26 *no longer need to carry.* When the tabernacle was replaced by a permanent building, the role of the Levites changed. This is another aspect of the subdued land. The Israelites were there to stay.

23:30 Praise—This is a beautiful picture of daily praise, thanking the Lord for the day that begins and the day that ends. As believers, we don't need someone else to thank the Lord on our behalf. We need to praise Him. The value of praise is that it lifts our hearts to God's heart. It keeps us thinking about Him and worshiping Him. Life can be almost overwhelming at times, and a habit of praising God lifts our thoughts above our troubles and focuses on who He is and what He has done.

23:32 *Holy Place.* This referred to the outer room of the tabernacle. The Most Holy Place was only approached by the high priest.

24:1 *sons of Aaron.* (See note after 6:2–4; 15:11.)

14 1Ch 26:23 **15** Ex 18:3,4 **16** 1Ch 26:24 **17** 1Ch 26:25 **19** 1Ch 24:23 **21** 1Ch 24:26; 1Ch 24:29 **22** 1Ch 24:28; Nu 36:6 **23** 1Ch 24:30 **24** Nu 10:17,21; Nu 1:3; Ezr 3:8 **25** 1Ch 22:18 **26** Nu 4:5 **29** Ex 25:30; Lev 6:20; Lev 2:4; Lev 2:5,7; Lev 19:35 **31** Nu 10:10; Lev 23:4 **32** Nu 1:53; 3:6-9 **CHAPTER 24** **1** Lev 10:1,6; Nu 26:60 **2** Nu 3:4; 26:61

fore Eleazar and Ithamar served as
priests.
3David, with Zadok of the sons of
Eleazar and Ahimelech of the sons of
Ithamar, divided them according to
their offices for their *assigned* duties.
4Since there were more chief men
found among the descendants of Elea-
zar than among the descendants of
Ithamar [because of Eli's misfortunes,
and Saul's massacre of the priests at
Nob], they were divided in this way:
sixteen heads of fathers' households
of the descendants of Eleazar and
eight of the descendants of Ithamar,
corresponding to their fathers' house-
holds.
5So they were divided by lot, one
group with the other; for they were
officers of the sanctuary and officers
(high priests) of God, both from the
descendants of Eleazar and from the
descendants of Ithamar.
6Shemaiah, the son of Nethanel the
scribe, from the Levites, recorded them
in the presence of the king, the officers,
Zadok the priest, Ahimelech the son
of Abiathar [the priest who escaped
Saul's massacre at Nob], and the heads
of the fathers' *households* of the priests
and of the Levites; one father's house-
hold taken for Eleazar and one taken
for Ithamar.
7The lots fell, the first one to Jehoiar-
ib, the second to Jedaiah,
8the third to Harim, the fourth to
Seorim,
9the fifth to Malchijah, the sixth to
Mijamin,
10the seventh to Hakkoz, the eighth
to Abijah,
11the ninth to Jeshua, the tenth to
Shecaniah,
12the eleventh to Eliashib, the twelfth
to Jakim,
13the thirteenth to Huppah, the four-
teenth to Jeshebeab,
14the fifteenth to Bilgah, the six-
teenth to Immer,
15the seventeenth to Hezir, the eigh-
teenth to Happizzez,
16the nineteenth to Pethahiah, the
twentieth to Jehezkel,
17the twenty-first to Jachin, the
twenty-second to Gamul,
18the twenty-third to Delaiah, the
twenty-fourth to Maaziah.
19These were their offices *and* posi-
tions for their service in the house of
the LORD according to the ordinance
given to them by their father (ancestor)
Aaron, just as the LORD God of Israel
had commanded him.
20Now as for the rest of the sons of
Levi: of the sons of Amram: Shubael;
of the sons of Shubael: Jehdeiah.
21Of Rehabiah: of the sons of Reha-
biah: Isshiah the first.
22Of the Izharites: Shelomoth; of the
sons of Shelomoth, Jahath.
23The sons *of Hebron:* Jeriah *the
first,* Amariah the second, Jahaziel
the third, Jekameam the fourth.
24Of the sons of Uzziel, Micah; of the
sons of Micah, Shamir.
25The brother of Micah, Isshiah; of
the sons of Isshiah, Zechariah.
26The sons of Merari: Mahli and
Mushi; the sons of Jaaziah, Beno.
27The sons of Merari: by Jaaziah
were Beno, Shoham, Zaccur, and Ibri.
28By Mahli: Eleazar, who had no
sons.
29By Kish: the sons of Kish, Jer-
ahmeel.
30The sons of Mushi: Mahli, Eder,
and Jerimoth. These were the sons of
the Levites according to their fathers'
households.
31These also cast lots as did their
relatives the sons of Aaron in the pres-
ence of David the king, Zadok, Ahim-
elech, and the heads of the fathers'
households of the priests and of the
Levites—the head of father's *house-
holds* as well as those of his younger
brother.

24:10 *Abijah.* This Abijah may be the ancestor of Zacharias, father of John the Baptist, who is named in Luke 1:5.

24:20 – 21 *sons of Levi.* The nonpriestly Levites also were divided by clan to determine their service rotation.

10 Neh 12:4,17; Lk 1:5 **19** 1Ch 9:25 **21** 1Ch 23:17 **23** 1Ch 23:19; 26:31 **26** Ex 6:19; 1Ch 23:21 **28** 1Ch 23:22
30 1Ch 23:23

Number and Services of Musicians

25 MOREOVER, DAVID and the commanders of the army selected for the [temple] service some of the sons of Asaph, Heman, and Jeduthun, who were to prophesy with lyres, harps, and cymbals. The list of the musicians who performed their service was *as follows:*

2 Of the sons of Asaph: Zaccur, Joseph, Nethaniah, and Asharelah; the sons of Asaph were under the direction of Asaph, who prophesied under the direction of the king.

3 Of Jeduthun, the sons of Jeduthun: Gedaliah, Zeri, Jeshaiah, Shimei, Hashabiah, and Mattithiah, six, under the direction of their father Jeduthun, who prophesied with the lyre in thanksgiving and praise to the LORD.

4 Of Heman, the sons of Heman: Bukkiah, Mattaniah, Uzziel, Shebuel, Jerimoth, Hananiah, Hanani, Eliathah, Giddalti, Romamti-ezer, Joshbekashah, Mallothi, Hothir, and Mahazioth.

5 All these [men] were the sons of Heman the king's seer to exalt him in accordance with the words of God; for God gave Heman fourteen sons and three daughters. [Ps 68:25]

6 All these were under the direction of their father to sing in the house of the LORD, with cymbals, harps, and lyres, for the service of the house of God. Asaph, Jeduthun, and Heman were under the order *and* direction of the king.

7 So their number [who led the remainder of the 4,000], with their relatives who were trained in singing to the LORD, all who were skillful, was 288. [1 Chr 23:5]

Divisions of Musicians

8 The musicians cast lots for their duties, everyone alike, the small (younger) as well as the great (older), the teacher *as well* as the student.

9 The first lot for Asaph fell to Joseph; the second to Gedaliah, to him, his relatives and his sons, twelve;

10 the third to Zaccur, his sons and his relatives, twelve;

11 the fourth to Izri, his sons and his relatives, twelve;

12 the fifth to Nethaniah, his sons and his relatives, twelve;

13 the sixth to Bukkiah, his sons and his relatives, twelve;

14 the seventh to Jesharelah, his sons and his relatives, twelve;

15 the eighth to Jeshaiah, his sons and his relatives, twelve;

16 the ninth to Mattaniah, his sons and his relatives, twelve;

17 the tenth to Shimei, his sons and his relatives, twelve;

18 the eleventh to Azarel, his sons and his relatives, twelve;

19 the twelfth to Hashabiah, his sons and his relatives, twelve;

20 the thirteenth to Shubael, his sons and his relatives, twelve;

21 the fourteenth to Mattithiah, his sons and his relatives, twelve;

22 the fifteenth to Jeremoth, his sons and his relatives, twelve;

23 the sixteenth to Hananiah, his sons and his relatives, twelve;

24 the seventeenth of Joshbekashah, his sons and his relatives, twelve;

25 the eighteenth to Hanani, his sons and his relatives, twelve;

26 the nineteenth to Mallothi, his sons and his relatives, twelve;

27 the twentieth to Eliathah, his sons and his relatives, twelve;

28 the twenty-first to Hothir, his sons and his relatives, twelve;

29 the twenty-second to Giddalti, his sons and his relatives, twelve;

30 the twenty-third to Mahazioth, his sons and his relatives, twelve;

31 the twenty-fourth to Romamti-ezer, his sons and his relatives, twelve.

25:1 *prophesy with lyres, harps, and cymbals.* The role of prophet was not limited to a prediction or proclamation in words. Vocal and instrumental music could be a kind of prophetic message, usually in the form of praise (1Sa 10:5 – 6). **25:2 *under the direction of the king.*** This underscored the leading role that David took in the religious life of the nation.

CHAPTER 25 **1** 1Ch 6:33,39,44 **6** ver. 2 **8** 2Ch 23:13

Divisions of the Gatekeepers

26 FOR THE divisions of the gate-
keepers: Of the Korahites: Me-
shelemiah the son of Kore, of the sons
of Asaph.
2 Meshelemiah had sons: Zechariah
the firstborn, Jediael the second, Zeb-
adiah the third, Jathniel the fourth,
3 Elam the fifth, Jehohanan the sixth,
Eliehoenai the seventh.
4 Obed-edom had sons: Shemaiah the
firstborn, Jehozabad the second, Joah
the third, Sacar the fourth, Nethanel
the fifth,
5 Ammiel the sixth, Issachar the sev-
enth, Peullethai the eighth; for God had
blessed him.
6 Also to his son Shemaiah sons were
born who ruled over the house of their
father, for they were courageous men
of ability.
7 The sons of Shemaiah: Othni,
Rephael, Obed, and Elzabad, whose
brothers were courageous *and* able
men, Elihu and Semachiah.
8 All these were sons of Obed-edom
[in whose house the ark was kept], they
and their sons and relatives, strong
and able men for the service—sixty-
two from Obed-edom. [1 Chr 13:13, 14]
9 Meshelemiah had sons and rela-
tives, eighteen courageous men.
10 Also Hosah, one of the sons of Me-
rari, had sons: Shimri the first *and*
chief (although he was not the first-
born, his father made him first),
11 Hilkiah the second, Tebaliah the
third, Zechariah the fourth; the sons
and relatives of Hosah were thirteen
in all.
12 To these divisions of the gatekeep-
ers, the chief men, *were given* duties,
like their relatives, to minister in the
house of the LORD.
13 They cast lots, the small (younger)
and great (older) alike, in accordance
with their fathers' households, for ev-
ery gate.
14 The lot for the east [gates] fell to
Shelemiah. They cast lots also for his
son Zechariah, a wise counselor, and
his lot came out for the north [gates].
15 To Obed-edom [it came out] for the
south [gates], and the storehouse *was
allotted* to his sons.
16 To Shuppim and Hosah [the lot
fell] for the west [gates], by the gate of
Shallecheth, on the ascending high-
way, division by division.
17 On the east were six Levites, on the
north four a day, on the south four a
day, and two by two at the storehouse.
18 At the colonnade on the west side
[of the outer court of the temple] *there
were* four at the road and two at the
colonnade.
19 These were the divisions of the
gatekeepers among the Korahites and
the sons of Merari.

Keepers of the Treasure

20 Of the Levites, Ahijah was in
charge of the treasuries of the house
of God and the treasuries of the ded-
icated gifts.
21 The sons of Ladan, the sons of
the Gershonites belonging to Ladan,
namely, the Jehielites, *were* the heads
of the fathers' *households*, belonging
to Ladan the Gershonite.
22 The sons of Jehieli, Zetham and
his brother Joel, were in charge of the
treasuries of the house of the LORD.
23 Of the Amramites, Izharites, He-
bronites, and Uzzielites:
24 Shebuel the son of Gershom, the
son of Moses, was supervisor over the
treasuries.
25 His relatives by Eliezer were his
son Rehabiah, his son Jeshaiah, his
son Joram, his son Zichri, and his son
Shelomoth.

26:1 – 32 Duty — Our duties include all of the activities required to fulfill an assigned service. We are not praised for doing these jobs, and sometimes only the Lord sees what we have done. The temple servants knew that their jobs were "for" the Lord, but they were not personally very visible among the hundreds who did similar tasks. From the gatekeepers to the guardians of the treasures, faithfulness was the moral obligation, or duty, of each officer. For us as believers, the moral obligation is the same. We are never off duty.

26:14 *lot for the east*. The east Gate was the most important because it led straight into the main entrance of the temple.

CHAPTER 26 **10** 1Ch 16:38 **20** 1Ch 28:12; Mal 3:10 **24** 1Ch 23:16 **25** 1Ch 23:18

26 This Shelomoth and his relatives were in charge of all the treasuries of the dedicated gifts which King David, the heads of the fathers' *households*, the commanders of thousands and hundreds, and the commanders of the army, had dedicated.

27 From spoil won in battles they dedicated *gifts* to maintain *and* repair the house of the LORD.

28 Also all that Samuel the seer had dedicated, and Saul the son of Kish, Abner the son of Ner and Joab the son of Zeruiah, everyone who had dedicated *anything*, this was in the care of Shelomoth and his relatives.

Outside Duties

29 Of the Izharites: Chenaniah and his sons were *appointed* to outside duties for Israel, as administrators and judges.

30 Of the Hebronites: Hashabiah and his relatives, 1,700 capable men, were in charge of the affairs of Israel west of the Jordan, for all the work of the LORD and the service of the king.

31 Of the Hebronites: Jerijah was the chief (these Hebronites were examined according to their descendants and fathers' *households* in the fortieth [and final] year of David's reign, and men of courage *and* ability were found among them at Jazer in Gilead)

32 and Jerijah's relatives, 2,700 capable men, were heads of fathers' *households;* and King David made them overseers of the Reubenites, the Gadites, and the half-tribe of Manasseh, for everything pertaining to God and to the king.

Commanders of the Army

27 THIS IS the list of the sons (descendants) of Israel, the heads of fathers' *households*, the commanders of thousands and of hundreds, and their officers who served the king in all matters of the divisions which came in and went out month by month throughout the year, each division *numbering* 24,000:

2 Jashobeam the son of Zabdiel was in charge of the first division for the first month; and in his division were 24,000.

3 *He was* descended from Perez, *and was* chief of all the commanders of the army for the first month.

4 Dodai the Ahohite and his division was in charge of the division for the second month, Mikloth was the chief officer; and in his division were 24,000.

5 The third commander of the army for the third month was Benaiah, the son of Jehoiada the priest, as chief; and in his division were 24,000.

6 This is the Benaiah who was the mighty man of the thirty and was in charge of the thirty; and Ammizabad his son was *over* his division.

7 The fourth, for the fourth month was Asahel the brother of Joab, and Zebadiah his son after him; and in his division were 24,000.

8 The fifth, for the fifth month was the commander Shamhuth the Izrahite; and in his division were 24,000.

9 The sixth, for the sixth month was Ira the son of Ikkesh the Tekoite; and in his division were 24,000.

10 The seventh, for the seventh month

27:1 *heads of fathers' households, the commanders.* Apparently a professional standing army is being described here, one that was divided into twelve corps.

27:2 *Jashobeam.* A connection can be made here to the list of David's mighty men, which is also headed by Jashobeam (11:11–12). He was one of "the three," which meant that he was regarded as unusually heroic.

27:4 *Dodai.* Dodai's son Eleazar was the second of the mighty men included in the first trio along with Jashobeam (11:12).

27:5 *Benaiah.* As the son of a priest, Benaiah was from the tribe of Levi. In the earlier list of mighty men he was celebrated for killing a lion and a gigantic Egyptian (11:22–23). Because of this kind of courage, he was honored among the thirty mighty men, though he was not one of "the three" (11:24). Later he was named as commander of the entire Israelite army (2Ki 4:4).

27:7 *Asahel.* David's nephew Asahel (2:15–16) was among the thirty mighty men, but did not achieve a position among "the three" (11:26).

28 1Sa 9:9 **29** 1Ch 23:4 **31** 1Ch 23:19; See Jos 21:39 **32** 2Ch 19:11 **CHAPTER 27** **2** 2Sa 23:8; 1Ch 11:11 **6** 2Sa 23:20,22,23; 1Ch 11:22 **7** 2Sa 23:24; 1Ch 11:26 **9** 1Ch 11:28 **10** 1Ch 11:27

was Helez the Pelonite of the sons
of Ephraim; and in his division were
24,000.
11 The eighth, for the eighth month
was Sibbecai the Hushathite of the
Zerahites; and in his division were
24,000.
12 The ninth, for the ninth month was
Abiezer of Anathoth, a Benjamite; and
in his division were 24,000.
13 The tenth, for the tenth month was
Maharai from Netophah of the Zera-
hites; and in his division were 24,000.
14 The eleventh, for the eleventh
month was Benaiah the Pirathonite
of the sons of Ephraim; and in his di-
vision were 24,000.
15 The twelfth, for the twelfth month
was Heldai the Netophathite of Oth-
niel; and in his division were 24,000.

Chief Officers of the Tribes

16 Now in charge of the tribes of Is-
rael [were the following]: chief officer
of the Reubenites was Eliezer the son
of Zichri; of the Simeonites, Shepha-
tiah the son of Maacah;
17 of Levi, Hashabiah the son of Kem-
uel; of Aaron, Zadok;
18 of Judah, Elihu, one of David's
brothers; of Issachar, Omri the son of
Michael;
19 of Zebulun, Ishmaiah the son of
Obadiah; of Naphtali, Jeremoth the
son of Azriel;
20 of the Ephraimites, Hoshea the son
of Azaziah; of the half-tribe of Manas-
seh, Joel the son of Pedaiah;
21 of the half-tribe of Manasseh in
Gilead, Iddo the son of Zechariah; of
Benjamin, Jaasiel the son of Abner;
22 of Dan, Azarel the son of Jeroham.
These were the leaders of the tribes
of Israel.
23 But David did not count those
twenty years of age and under, for
the LORD had said he would multiply
Israel as the stars of heaven.
24 Joab the son of Zeruiah began a
census but did not finish; and because
of this, [God's] wrath came on Israel,
and the number was not recorded in
the chronicles of King David.

Various Overseers

25 Azmaveth the son of Adiel was
in charge of the king's storerooms;
and Jonathan the son of Uzziah was
in charge of the storehouses in the
country, in the cities, in the villages,
and in the towers.
26 Ezri the son of Chelub was in
charge of those who did the work of
the field, tilling the soil.
27 Shimei the Ramathite was in
charge of the vineyards; Zabdi the
Shiphmite was in charge of the pro-
duce of the vineyards for the wine
cellars.
28 Baal-hanan the Gederite was in
charge of the olive and sycamore trees
in Shephelah (the lowlands); and Joash
was in charge of the stores of [olive] oil.
29 Shitrai the Sharonite was in
charge of the cattle grazing in Sharon;
Shaphat the son of Adlai was in charge
of the cattle in the valleys.
30 Obil the Ishmaelite was in charge
of the camels; and Jehdeiah the Meron-
othite was in charge of the donkeys.
31 Jaziz the Hagrite was in charge of
the flocks. All these were overseers
and stewards of the property which
belonged to King David.

Counselors

32 Also Jonathan, David's uncle,
was a counselor *and* advisor, a man
of understanding *and* wisdom, and a
scribe; and Jehiel the son of Hachmoni

27:11 – 12 *Sibbecai . . . Abiezer.* These two men were also members of the elite thirty mighty men. (11:28 – 29).
27:18 *Elihu.* This brother of David is usually called Eliab (1Sa 16:6).
27:29 *Sharonite.* A fertile plain between Israelite and Philistine territory, Sharon was ideal for grazing cattle and sheep. It is appropriate that someone from Sharon, who knew the land and all its seasonal changes, should be in charge of the livestock.
27:30 *Ishmaelite.* As inhabitants of the desert, the Ishmaelites were at home with the breeding and use of camels.

11 2Sa 21:18 **12** 1Ch 11:28 **13** 2Sa 23:28; 1Ch 11:30 **14** 1Ch 11:31 **17** 1Ch 26:30 **18** 1Sa 16:6 **23** Ge 15:5 **24** 2Sa 24:15; ch 21:7

attended (tutored) the king's sons. [2 Kin 10:6]
33 Ahithophel was counselor to the king; and Hushai the Archite was the king's companion *and* friend.
34 Ahithophel was succeeded by Jehoiada the son of Benaiah and by Abiathar; and Joab was the commander of the king's army.

David's Address about the Temple

28 DAVID ASSEMBLED at Jerusalem all the leaders (officials) of Israel, the leaders of the tribes, and the commanders of the divisions that served the king, and the commanders of thousands, and the commanders of hundreds, and the overseers of all the property and livestock of the king and his sons, with the palace officers and the mighty men, and all the brave warriors.
2 Then David the king rose to his feet and said, "Hear me, my brothers [in arms] and my people. I had intended to build a permanent home for the ark of the covenant of the LORD and as a footstool for our God, and I prepared materials for the building.
3 "But God said to me, 'You shall not build a house for My Name (Presence), because you are a man of war and have shed blood.'
4 "However, the LORD, the God of Israel, chose me from all in my father's house to be king over Israel forever. For He has chosen Judah to be the leader; and in the house (tribe) of Judah he chose the house of my father; and among the sons of my father He was pleased to make me king over all Israel.
5 "Of all my sons (for the LORD has given me many sons) He has chosen my son Solomon to sit on the throne of the kingdom of the LORD over Israel.
6 "He said to me, 'Solomon your son shall build My house and My courts; for I have chosen him to be a son to Me, and I will be a father to him.
7 'I will establish his kingdom forever if he loyally *and* continually obeys My commandments and My ordinances, as is done today.'
8 "Now therefore, in the sight of all Israel, the assembly of the LORD, and in the hearing of our God, observe and seek after all the commandments of the LORD your God so that you may

---

28:2 *footstool.* The word "footstool" is a metaphor describing either the ark of the covenant or the tabernacle as the earthly base of God's activity. The words make a little picture of God on His throne in heaven, resting his feet on the earth. **28:4–6 Government of Israel**—The government of Israel was under two important headings: the laws, and the leaders. **The laws**—The "commandments," especially the Ten Commandments, revealed God's holiness and set up a divine standard of righteousness for the people to follow (Ex 20:1–17). The judgments governed the social life of the people (Ex 21). The ordinances included the sacrifices that showed that blood must be shed for the forgiveness of sins (Lev 1–17). **The leaders**—At first Moses was the primary leader; then he was replaced by Joshua. After Joshua's death the nation was governed for many years by judges who were usually raised up by God to oppose a specific enemy. Finally, at the people's request, God granted them a king, thus establishing the monarchy (1Sa 8:6–17).

Through most of Israel's history four leadership roles can be seen:

The king was the Lord's representative who ruled the people, but only as the Lord's servant. He led in war (1Sa 8:20) and made judicial decisions (2Sa 15:2); but could not make law, since he himself was under the law (Dt 17:14–20).

The priest taught the Lord's laws and officiated at the offering of sacrifices (Lev 1:5).

The prophet was the man of God who spoke for God and gave divine pronouncements for the present or the future.

The wise man produced literary works stressing practical wisdom (Pr 1:1), taught discipline of character to the young (Pr 22:17), and gave counsel to the king (2Sa 16:20).

28:6 *be a son to Me, and I will be a father to him.* This remarkable statement not only shows that the Davidic kings enjoyed unparalleled access to the Lord as his adopted sons (17:3; Ps 2:7), but it anticipates the absolute sonship of the Son of David, Jesus Christ (Ac 13:33; Heb 1:5).

---

33 2Sa 15:12; 2Sa 15:37; 16:16 **34** 1Ki 1:7; 1Ch 11:6 **CHAPTER 28** **1** 1Ch 27:16; 1Ch 27:1,2; 1Ch 27:25; 1Ch 11:10 **2** 2Sa 7:2; Ps 99:5; 132:7 **3** 2Sa 7:5,13; 1Ki 5:3; 1Ch 17:4; 22:8 **4** 1Sa 16:7-13; Ge 49:8; 1Ch 5:2; 1Sa 16:1; 1Sa 16:12,13 **5** 1Ch 3:1; 23:1; 1Ch 22:9 **6** 2Sa 7:13,14; 1Ch 22:9,10; 2Ch 1:9 **7** 1Ch 22:13

possess the good land and leave it as an inheritance to your sons after you forever.

9 “As for you, Solomon my son, know the God of your father [have personal knowledge of Him, be acquainted with, and understand Him; appreciate, heed, and cherish Him] and serve Him with a blameless heart and a willing mind; for the LORD searches all hearts *and* minds, and understands every intent *and* inclination of the thoughts. If you seek Him [inquiring for and of Him and requiring Him as your first and vital necessity] He will let you find Him; but if you abandon (turn away from) Him, He will reject you forever.

10 “Consider this carefully, for the LORD has chosen you to build a house for the sanctuary. Be courageous *and* strong and do it.”

11 Then David gave to his son Solomon the plan for the porch *of the temple,* its buildings, its treasuries, its upper chambers, its inner rooms, and for the place for the [ark and its] mercy seat;

12 and the plan of all that he had in mind, for the courts of the house of the LORD, and for all the surrounding rooms, for the storerooms of the house of God and for the storerooms for the dedicated gifts *and* offerings;

13 *the plan* for the divisions of the priests and the Levites and for all the work of the service in the house of the LORD and for all the utensils for service in the house of the LORD;

14 for the golden *utensils,* the weight of gold and silver for all the gold and silver articles for every kind of service;

15 and the weight *of gold* for the golden lampstands and their golden lamps, with the weight of each lampstand and its lamps; and the *weight of silver* for the silver lampstands, with the weight of each lampstand and its lamps according to the use of each lampstand;

16 the gold by weight for each table of showbread, and the silver for the tables of silver;

17 and the forks, the basins, and the pitchers of pure gold; and for the golden bowls with the weight for each bowl; and for the silver bowls with the weight for each bowl;

18 and for the altar of incense refined gold by weight; and gold for the model of the chariot of the cherubim that spread *their wings* and covered the ark of the LORD’s covenant.

19 “All *this,” said David,* “the LORD made me understand in writing by His hand upon me, all the work *and* details [to be done] according to this plan.”

20 Then David said to his son Solomon, “Be strong and courageous, and take action; do not fear nor be dismayed, for the LORD God, my God, is with you. He will not fail you nor abandon you [but will guide you in the construction] until you have finished all the work for the service of the house of the LORD.

21 “And see, [you have] the divisions of the priests and Levites for all the service of God’s house, and every willing, skillful man will be with you in all the kinds of work for any kind of service. Also the officers and all the people will be entirely at your command.”

Offerings for the Temple

29 AND KING David said to all the assembly, “My son Solomon, whom alone God has chosen, is still young and inexperienced and the work

---

28:19 *by His hand upon me.* The plans for the temple were from God, just as the plans of the tabernacle of Moses were. This was extremely important, for God had stressed the necessity of making the tabernacle exactly according to His instructions (Ex 38:22; 39:5 – 7,42 – 43). The Israelites would need to know that this permanent building was God’s plan, not just David’s.

28:20 *Be strong and courageous.* David’s charge to Solomon is very similar to the charge given to Joshua when Moses handed over the leadership of Israel to him (Jos 1:6 – 9).

9 Jer 9:24; Hos 4:1; Jn 17:3; 2Ki 20:3; 1Sa 16:7; 1Ki 8:39; 1Ch 29:17; Jer 11:20; 17:10; 20:12; Rev 2:23; 2Ch 15:2 **10** ver. 6 **11** ver. 19; See Ex 25:40 **12** 1Ch 26:20 **18** Ex 25:18-22; 1Sa 4:4; 1Ki 6:23 **19** ver. 11,12; See Ex 25,40 **20** Dt 31:7,8; Jos 1:6,7,9; 1Ch 22:13; Jos 1:5 **21** 1Ch 24; 25; 26; Ex 35:25,26 **CHAPTER 29** **1** 1Ki 3:7; 1Ch 22:5; Pr 4:3 **2** See Isa 54:11,12; Rev 21:18

is great; for the temple is not for man
but for the LORD God.
2“So with all my ability I have pro-
vided for the house of my God the gold
for the *things of* gold, silver for the
things of silver, bronze for the *things*
of bronze, iron for the *things of* iron,
and wood for the *things of* wood, *as*
well as onyx stones and stones to be
inlaid, stones of antimony (a brittle,
silvery-white metal) and stones of var-
ious colors, and all kinds of precious
stones and alabaster in abundance.
3“Moreover, because I delight in the
house of my God, the [personal] treasure
that I have of gold and silver, I give to the
house of my God, in addition to all that I
have already provided for the holy house:
4*namely,* 3,000 talents of gold from
the gold of Ophir, and 7,000 talents of
refined silver, to overlay the walls of
the buildings;
5gold for the *things of* gold, silver for
the *things of* silver, that is, for all the
work to be done by craftsmen. Now
who is willing to consecrate himself
today to the LORD?”
6Then the rulers of the fathers' *house-*
holds, and leaders of the tribes of Israel,
and the commanders of thousands and
of hundreds, with the overseers of the
king's work, offered willingly
7and gave for the service of the house
of God: 5,000 talents and 10,000 darics
of gold, and 10,000 talents of silver, and
18,000 talents of bronze, and 100,000
talents of iron.
8Whoever had *precious* stones gave
them to the treasury of the house of the
LORD, in the care of Jehiel the Gershonite.
9Then the people rejoiced because
they had given willingly, for with a
whole *and* blameless heart they had
offered freely to the LORD. King David
also rejoiced greatly.

David's Prayer

10Therefore David blessed the LORD
in the sight of all the assembly and
said, “Blessed (praised, adored, and
thanked) are You, O LORD God of Israel
(Jacob) our father, forever and ever.
11“Yours, O LORD, is the greatness
and the power and the glory and the
victory and the majesty, indeed every-
thing that is in the heavens and on the
earth; Yours is the dominion *and* king-
dom, O LORD, and You exalt Yourself
as head over all.
12“Both riches and honor *come* from
You, and You rule over all. In Your
hand is power and might; and it is in
Your hands to make great and to give
strength to everyone.
13“Now therefore, our God, we thank
You, and praise Your glorious name.
14“But who am I, and who are my
people, that we should be able to offer
as generously as this? For all things
come from You, and from Your own
hand we have given to You.
15“For we are sojourners before You,
and tenants, as all our fathers were;
our days on the earth are like a shad-
ow, and there is no hope [of remaining].

29:4 Generosity—It is extremely difficult to assign a modern monetary value to ancient goods and services, but we might compare David's gift for the temple to approximately one billion, eight-hundred thousand dollars in gold, and eighty-four million in silver. This kind of personal wealth is astounding, but for David, its value was significant only as provision for the temple for the Lord. He never lost sight of the fact that both honor and riches come from God. They are His to give, His to use, and His to remove.

29:7 *5,000 talents.* This represents about 190 tons of gold. *10,000 darics.* This is about 185 pounds of gold. *18,000 talents.* This was equivalent to about 675 tons. *100,000 talents.* This was approximately 3,750 tons.

29:10 *blessed the LORD.* David modeled before the people the worship of the living God. He started with praise for God's goodness, greatness, and glory, and then acknowledged his place under the care and blessing of God.

29:14–15 All That We Have—Even though David was king and could accumulate whatever he wanted, he was more conscious of the need to give, particularly to God. How can anyone strive to accumulate, if you know in the long run that none of what you've gathered is really yours? Generosity is the natural outcome of a right perspective on possessions.

4 1Ki 9:28 **6** 1Ch 27:1; 1Ch 27:25 **8** 1Ch 26:21 **9** 2Co 9:7 **11** Mt 6:13; 1Ti 1:17; Rev 5:13 **12** Ro 11:36
15 Ps 39:12; Heb 11:13; 1Pe 2:11; Job 14:2; Ps 90:9

16"O LORD our God, all this abun-
dance that we have prepared to build
You a house for Your holy Name, it is
from Your hand, and is all Your own.
17"I know also, my God, that You test
the heart and delight in uprightness
and integrity. In the uprightness of
my heart I have willingly offered all
these *things*. So now with joy I have
seen Your people who are present
here, make their offerings willingly
and freely to You.
18"O LORD, God of Abraham, Isaac,
and Israel, our fathers, keep forever
such purposes *and* thoughts in the
minds of Your people, and direct their
hearts toward You;
19and give to my son Solomon a
perfect heart to keep Your command-
ments, Your testimonies, and Your
statutes, and to do all [that is neces-
sary] to build the temple [for You], for
which I have made provision."
20Then David said to all the assem-
bly, "Now bless (praise, thank) the
LORD your God." And all the assem-
bly blessed the LORD, the God of their
fathers, and bowed down and honored
the LORD and to the king [as His earth-
ly representative].

Sacrifices

21The next day they offered sacrifices
and burnt offerings to the LORD: 1,000
bulls, 1,000 rams, and 1,000 lambs, with
their drink offerings (libations) and
sacrifices in abundance for all Israel.
22They ate and drank that day before
the LORD with great rejoicing.

Solomon Again Made King

They made Solomon the son of Da-
vid king a second time, and anointed
him as ruler for the LORD and Zadok
as [high] priest.
23Then Solomon sat on the throne of
the LORD as king in place of David his
father; and he prospered, and all Israel
obeyed him.
24All of the leaders and warriors,
and also all the sons of King David,
pledged allegiance to King Solomon.
25The LORD highly exalted Solomon
in the sight of all Israel, and bestowed
on him royal majesty which had not
been on any king before him in Israel.
26Thus David the son of Jesse
reigned over all Israel.
27The time that he reigned over Is-
rael was forty years; he reigned seven
years in Hebron and thirty-three years
in Jerusalem.

Death of David

28He died in a good old age [his
seventy-first year], full of days (satis-
fied), riches and honor. Solomon his
son reigned in his place.
29Now the acts of King David, from
first to last, are written in the chron-
icles (records) of Samuel the seer, in
the chronicles of Nathan the prophet,
and in the chronicles of Gad the seer,
30with [accounts of] all his reign,
and his power, and the times *and* cir-
cumstances which came on him, on
Israel, and on all the kingdoms of the
[surrounding] lands.

Verse 15 points to two other elements that indicate a basis for generosity. David understood where his real home was, namely with God. If a king regards himself as an alien in his own land, how much more should we? Somehow he resisted the temptation to regard the land as his to do with as he wished. He understood the brevity of life. Why spend time accumulating when we can't take it with us? Living with this perspective allows us to be transparent before God. We can be in sync with God because we're keeping nothing from him. What we have has value only as it furthers the kingdom, and God is quite capable of supplying everything we need to be able to live.

It also means we're functioning clearly in the context of the biblical mandate of stewardship. We're here to have dominion (Ge 1:28) but with the end that God is honored by what we do.

29:18 *God of Abraham, Isaac, and Israel*. These familiar words identify the Israelites with the promises of God to their forefathers, and to the God of those promises.

29:22 *king a second time*. This refers to the ratification of Solomon's kingship (see note on 23:1).

29:23 *throne of the LORD*. The position of king may have passed from David to Solomon, but the throne was the Lord's. Eventually Jesus, the Son of David and the Son of God, would sit on that throne and reign forever (Lk 1:32).

17 1Sa 16:7; 1Ch 28:9; Pr 11:20 **19** Ps 72:1; ver. 2; 1Ch 22:14 **22** 1Ki 1:35,39 **24** Ecc 8:2 **25** 1Ki 3:13; 2Ch 1:12; Ecc 2:9 **27** 2Sa 5:4; 1Ki 2:11; 2Sa 5:5 **28** Ge 25:8; 1Ch 23:1 **30** Da 2:21

THE SECOND BOOK OF THE

CHRONICLES

▸ **AUTHOR:** The sources of 1 and 2 Chronicles include multiple official and prophetic records. In addition to these, the author-compiler had access to genealogical lists and documents, such as the message and letters of Sennacherib (2Ch 32:10 – 17). It seems likely that Ezra was the author as Jewish tradition suggests.

▸ **TIMES:** c. 991 – 538 BC ▸ **KEY VERSE:** 2Ch 7:14

▸ **THEME:** Second Chronicles begins with Solomon's reign and ends with the fall of Jerusalem. It covers more extensively the details involved in the building and dedication of the temple. The kings of Judah are detailed down through the last king, Zedekiah, who is exiled to Babylon in 587 BC. It largely ignores what happens in the Northern Kingdom after the split into two nations.

Solomon Worships at Gibeon

1 SOLOMON THE son of David established himself securely over his
kingdom, and the LORD his God was with
him and made him exceedingly great.
[2]Solomon spoke to all Israel, to the
commanders of thousands and of hundreds and to the judges and to every
leader in all Israel, the heads of the
fathers' (ancestors') *households*.
[3]Then Solomon and all the assembly
went to the high place at Gibeon [to
offer sacrifices, where the Canaanites
had habitually worshiped], for God's
Tent of Meeting was there, which Moses the servant of the LORD had made
in the wilderness.
[4]But David had brought up the ark of
God from Kiriath-jearim to the place
he had prepared for it, because he had
pitched a tent for it in Jerusalem.
[5]Now the bronze altar, which Bezalel
the son of Uri, the son of Hur, had made
was there before the tabernacle of the
LORD, and Solomon and the assembly
sought it out.
[6]And Solomon went up to the bronze
altar before the LORD at the Tent of
Meeting, and offered a thousand burnt
offerings on it.
[7]That night God appeared to Solomon and said to him, "Ask what I
shall give to you."

Solomon's Prayer for Wisdom

[8]Then Solomon said to God, "You
have shown great lovingkindness *and*
mercy to my father David, and have
made me king in his place.
[9]"Now, O LORD God, Your promise
to my father David is fulfilled, for You
have made me king over a people as
numerous as the dust of the earth.
[10]"Give me wisdom and knowledge,

1:3 *high place.* In the Old Testament the high places were usually associated with pagan worship (Nu 22:41). The Israelites were specifically charged to destroy these places of worship so that they would not become a snare and lead them into idol worship (Nu 33:53; Dt 12:3). Nevertheless, Israelites often chose the high places to worship (1Sa 9:12). The high place at Gibeon was the location of the Mosaic tabernacle and the great bronze altar throughout David's reign (see note for 1Ki 14:23).

1:10 *go out and come in.* This figure of speech

CHAPTER 1 **1** 1Ki 2:46; Ge 39:2; 1Ch 29:25 **2** 1Ch 27:1 **3** 1Ki 3:4; 1Ch 16:39; 21:29 **4** 2Sa 6:2,17; 1Ch 15:1 **5** Ex 27:1,2; 38:1,2; Ex 31:2 **6** 1Ki 3:4 **7** 1Ki 3:5 **8** 1Ch 28:5 **9** 1Ki 3:7,8 **10** 1Ki 3:9; Nu 27:17; Dt 31:2

so that I may go out and come in [per-
forming my duties] before this people,
for [otherwise] who can rule *and* ad-
minister justice to this great people of
Yours?"
11God replied to Solomon, "Because
this was in your heart and you did not
ask for riches, possessions or honor
and personal glory, or the life of those
who hate you, nor have you even asked
for long life, but you have asked for
wisdom and knowledge for yourself
so that you may rule *and* administer
justice to My people over whom I have
made you king,
12wisdom and knowledge have been
granted you. I will also give you rich-
es, possessions, and honor, such as
none of the kings who were before you
has possessed nor will those who will
come after you."
13So Solomon went from the high
place at Gibeon, from the Tent of Meet-
ing, to Jerusalem. And he reigned over
Israel.

Solomon's Wealth

14Solomon acquired chariots and
horsemen; he had 1,400 chariots and
12,000 horsemen, and he stationed them
in the cities [suited for the use] of chari-
ots and with the king at Jerusalem.
15The king made silver and gold as
plentiful *and* common in Jerusalem
as stones, and he made cedar as plen-
tiful as the sycamore-fig trees in the
lowland.
16Solomon's horses were imported
from Egypt and from Kue. The king's
merchants purchased them [in large
numbers] from Kue at a price.
17And they imported chariots from
Egypt for 600 *shekels* of silver apiece,
and horses for 150 apiece; and in the
same way they exported horses to all
the kings of the Hittites and the kings
of the Arameans (Syrians).

Solomon Will Build a Temple and Palace

2 NOW SOLOMON decided to build a
house (temple) for the Name of the
LORD, and a royal palace for himself.
2So Solomon assigned 70,000 men
to carry loads, 80,000 men to quarry
stone in the mountains, and 3,600 to
supervise them.
3Then Solomon sent *word* to Hiram
king of Tyre, saying, "As you dealt with
my father David and sent him cedars to

---

refers to the totality of Solomon's life. As king he would lead by example as well as by edict.

1:11 – 12 Wisdom — There's significance here in what Solomon didn't ask for. He didn't ask for honor, money, a long life, or the death of his enemies. He didn't ask for the things that would be on the top of most people's lists. He didn't ask for what would make life comfortable and easy. He asked for what would make life good. He asked for wisdom with an eye toward how he would rule, knowing that the quality of his reign largely depended on the quality of his judgments in dealing with people and issues. His priority was his service to others rather than doing what was supposedly best for his personal well being.

What would be an equivalent today? A corporate executive wanting to know how to make his company contribute for the good of society as opposed to focusing exclusively on profit. A manager being more interested in seeing his staff happy and functioning well rather than getting ahead himself. A father being interested in seeing his family be healthy rather than getting his own.

1:14 *chariots.* A chariot force of 1,400 units was a significant achievement for Israel, a nation located primarily in hilly terrain where chariots were of limited value. ***horsemen.*** Moses warned the future kings not to multiply horses for themselves, nor were they to send people back to Egypt to multiply horses (Dt 17:16). The number of horses that Solomon had for his 1,400 chariots was probably about 4,000.

1:17 *600 shekels of silver.* It is often difficult to assign a price in modern currency to the goods and services of the ancient world. This verse suggests that a chariot cost as much as four horses. ***they exported.*** Solomon had a thriving business in horses and chariots. Because Israel was on the route between Asia and Africa, such goods would go through Israel and become subject to Solomon's heavy import and export taxes.

2:3 *Hiram king of Tyre.* Hiram was the same Phoenician ruler who had provided men and materials for David's palace.

11 1Ki 3:11-13 **12** 1Ch 29:25; 2Ch 9:22; Ecc 2:9 **14** 1Ki 4:26; 10:26; 2Ch 9:25 **15** 1Ki 10:27; 2Ch 9:27; Job 22:24 **16** 1Ki 10:28; 2Ch 9:28 **CHAPTER 2** **1** 1Ki 5:5 **2** ver. 18; 1Ki 5:15 **3** 1Ch 14:1

build himself a house in which to live,
[please] do the same for me.
4"Observe, I am about to build a
house for the Name of the LORD my
God, dedicated to Him, to burn fra-
grant incense [of sweet spices] before
Him, to set out the showbread con-
tinually, and to offer burnt offerings
morning and evening, on Sabbaths,
New Moons, and on the festivals of
the LORD our God, as *ordained* forever
in Israel.
5"The house I am going to build will
be great, for our God is greater than
all the gods.
6"But who is able to build a house for
Him, since the heavens and [even] the
highest heavens cannot contain Him?
Who am I to build a house for Him,
except [as a place] to burn *incense* be-
fore Him?
7"Now send me a man who is skilled
to work in gold, silver, bronze, and
iron, and in purple, crimson, and blue
fabrics, and who knows how to make
engravings, *to work* with the skilled
men who are with me in Judah and
Jerusalem, whom my father David
provided.
8"Send me also cedar, cypress, and
algum timber, for I know that your
servants know how to cut timber in
Lebanon. And indeed my servants *will
work* with your servants
9to prepare for me an abundance of
timber, because the house I am about
to build will be great and wonderful.
10"And I will give to your servants
who cut timber, 20,000 measures of
crushed wheat and 20,000 measures of
barley, and 20,000 baths of wine and
20,000 baths of [olive] oil."

Hiram to Assist

11Then Hiram, king of Tyre replied
in a letter sent to Solomon: "Because
the LORD loves His people, He has
made you king over them."
12Hiram said also, "Blessed be the
LORD, the God of Israel, who made
heaven and earth, who has given King
David a wise son, endowed with dis-
cretion and understanding, who will
build a house for the LORD and a royal
palace for himself.
13"Now I am sending a skilled man,
endowed with understanding, Huram-
abi,
14the son of a Danite woman and a
Tyrian father. He is trained to work in
gold, silver, bronze, iron, stone, and
wood; in purple, blue, and crimson
fabrics, and in fine linen. He is able
to make any kind of engraving and
to carry out any design given him. *He
will work* with your skilled men and
those of my lord, David your father.
15"Now then, let my lord send to his
servants the wheat, the barley, the oil,
and the wine of which he has spoken.
16"We will cut whatever timber you
need from Lebanon and bring it to you
on rafts by sea to Joppa, so that you
may take it up to Jerusalem."

2:5 *our God is greater than all the gods.* Solomon's statement means that God is the only true God, not that He is the greatest among many lesser ones. All pagan "gods" are not gods at all (1Co 8:4–5; 10:20).

2:6 Heaven — God is omnipresent. This means that He is everywhere present at all times. There are no bounds or limitations to his presence. But in a special sense, God does have a center for His existence. This is described by Solomon as the "highest heavens," an expression also used by Moses (Dt 10:14). His title "Lord of hosts" (1Sa 1:3) suggests that the dwelling of God is populated by angels and other heavenly beings. It is here that His throne is situated (Isa 6:1). In this sphere His will is done perfectly (Da 4:35).

2:10 *wheat... barley.* The amount of wheat and barley was about 125,000 bushels, or 3,750 tons of each. ***wine... oil.*** Twenty thousand baths of wine and oil was approximately 115,000 gallons of each.

2:12 Prudence — The wisdom and generosity of King Hiram toward Solomon showed him to be a prudent king. He wanted things to go well for Solomon because he liked and respected his father David, and good neighbors created stability for both nations.

2:14 *Danite woman.* His mother was an Israelite from the tribe of Dan.

---

4 ver. 1; Ex 30:7; Ex 25:30; Lev 24:8; Nu 28:3,9,11 **5** Ps 135:5 **6** 1Ki 8:27; Isa 66:1 **7** 1Ch 22:15 **8** 1Ki 5:6 **10** 1Ki 5:11 **11** 1Ki 10:9; 2Ch 9:8 **12** 1Ki 5:7; Ge 1; 2; Ac 4:24; 14:15; Rev 10:6 **14** 1Ki 7:13 **15** ver. 10 **16** 1Ki 5:8,9

17 Then Solomon took a count of all
the aliens in the land of Israel, like the
census that his father David had taken;
and they were found to be 153,600.
18 He assigned 70,000 of them to car-
ry loads and 80,000 to quarry stone in
the mountain, and 3,600 as overseers
to make the people work.

The Temple Construction in Jerusalem

3 THEN SOLOMON began to build
the house of the LORD in Jerusa-
lem on Mount Moriah, where the LORD
appeared to his father David, in the
place that David had prepared, on the
threshing floor of Ornan the Jebusite.
[1 Chr 21:20–22]
2 Solomon began to build on the sec-
ond day of the second month in the
fourth year of his reign.

Dimensions and Materials of the Temple

3 Now this is the [measurement of
the] foundation which Solomon laid for
the house of God: the length in cubits—
by the old standard of measure—was
sixty cubits (90 ft.), and the width was
twenty cubits (30 ft.).
4 The porch in front of the house
was as long as the width of the house,
twenty cubits, and the height was 120
cubits. He overlaid it inside with pure
gold.
5 He overlaid the main room [the
Holy Place] with cypress wood and
overlaid it with fine gold, and decorat-
ed it with palm trees and chains.
6 And he adorned the house with pre-
cious stones; and the gold was gold
from Parvaim.
7 He also overlaid the house [the
Holy Place] with gold—the beams, the
thresholds, and its walls and its doors;
and he carved cherubim on the walls.
8 Now he made the room of the Holy
of Holies: its length equaling the width
of the house was twenty cubits, and
its width was twenty cubits; and he
overlaid it with 600 talents of fine gold.
9 The weight of the nails was fifty
shekels of gold. He also overlaid the
upper rooms with gold.
10 And in the Holy of Holies he made
two sculptured cherubim, and overlaid
them with gold.
11 The wingspan of the cherubim was
twenty cubits: one wing of one cherub
was five cubits, reaching to the wall
of the house, and its other wing, of
five cubits, touched the other cherub's
wing.
12 The wing of the other cherub, of
five cubits, touched the wall of the
house; and its other wing of five cubits
touched the wing of the first cherub.
13 The wings of these cherubim ex-
tended twenty cubits. The cherubim
stood on their feet, their faces toward
the Holy Place (the main room).

3:1 *Mount Moriah.* This was the mountain where Abraham brought his son Isaac to sacrifice him (Ge 22) and where the Lord provided a ram instead. It was suitable that this place where Abraham showed such incredible obedience should be the site of the temple that dealt with the issues of sacrifice and sin. ***threshing floor of Ornan.*** It was here that David saw the angel of death and prayed for the people (2Sa 24).

3:2 *second day of the second month.* The second month fell in our month of April.

3:3 *cubits — by the old standard of measure.* The Israelites had two standard cubits, one about 17 inches and the other about 20 inches. The temple was probably made on the cubit that measured a little over 17 inches, which means that its foundation was approximately 90 feet long and 30 feet wide. The tabernacle that Moses made in the wilderness was about 45 feet long and 15 feet wide (Ex 26:15 – 37). More details of the temple are in 1 Kings 5 – 7.

3:5 *main room.* This room was the holy place, or sanctuary (1Ki 6:17).

3:8 *Holy of Holies.* The "holy of holies" was the inner sanctuary where the ark of the covenant was kept. This room was cubical, 30 feet on a side. ***600 talents.*** The room was overlaid with about 23 tons of gold.

3:9 *nails . . . gold.* Gold by itself is too soft to use for nails, so the nails mentioned here must have been plated with gold, as the weight would indicate.

3:13 *twenty cubits.* The wings of the cherubim spanned the entire width of the room.

---

17 As ver. 2; 1Ki 5:13; 2Ch 8:7,8; 1Ch 22:2 **18** As it is; ver. 2 **CHAPTER 3** **1** 1Ki 6:1; Ge 22:2; 1Ch 21:18; 22:1
3 1Ki 6:2 **4** 1Ki 6:3 **5** 1Ki 6:15 **10** 1Ki 6:23

14 He made the veil [between the Holy
Place and the Holy of Holies] of blue,
purple, and crimson colors, and fine
linen, and embroidered cherubim on it.
15 He also made two pillars for the
front of the house, thirty-five cubits
high, and the capital on the top of each
one was five cubits.
16 He made chains [like a necklace] in
the inner sanctuary and put them on
the tops of the pillars; and he made a
hundred pomegranates and put them
on the chains.
17 He erected the pillars in front of the
temple, one on the right, the other on
the left, and named the one on the right
Jachin (may He establish) and the one
on the left Boaz (in Him is strength).

Furnishings of the Temple

4 THEN SOLOMON made an altar
of bronze, twenty cubits in length,
twenty cubits in width, and ten cubits
in height.
2 He also made the Sea [that is, the
large basin used for ceremonial wash-
ing] of cast metal, ten cubits from brim
to brim, circular in form, and five cu-
bits in height, and its circumference
was thirty cubits.
3 Under it and entirely encircling it
were figures of oxen, ten to a cubit.
The oxen were in two rows, cast in
one piece.
4 It stood on twelve oxen, three facing
north, three facing west, three facing
south, three facing east; and the Sea
was set on top of them and all their
hindquarters turned inward.
5 It was a handbreadth (the width of
the four fingers) thick; its brim was
made like the brim of a cup, like a
lily blossom. It could hold 3,000 baths
(measures).
6 He also made ten [portable] basins
in which to wash, and he put five on
the right (south) side and five on the
left (north). They would rinse things
for the burnt offering in them, but the
Sea was for the priests to wash in.
7 And he made ten golden lamp-
stands just as directed and set them
in the temple, five on the right side and
five on the left.
8 He made also ten tables and placed
them in the temple, five on the right side
and five on the left side, and he made
a hundred [ceremonial] basins of gold.
9 Moreover, he made the courtyard of
the priests, and the great courtyard [for
the people] and doors for the courtyard,
and he overlaid their doors with bronze.

3:14 *the veil.* The veil was a heavy curtain between the holy place and the holy of holies. It shielded the ark and cherubim from view, and as God was visualized as sitting on the mercy seat under the wings of the cherubim (see note on 1Ch 13:6), it also shielded even the priests from the most intimate presence of God. The veil between the holy place and the holy of holies was ripped in two when Jesus died on the cross (Mt 27:51). The tearing of the temple curtain is seen as a symbol that through Jesus, believers have direct access to the Lord God (Heb 6:19; 9:1 – 10:20).

3:15 *thirty-five cubits ... five cubits.* The pillars were about 53 feet tall with a 7 foot capital on top.

4:2 *the Sea.* The Sea was a receptacle for water corresponding to the much smaller bronze basin of the Mosaic tabernacle (Ex 30:17 – 21). The basin provided water for the priests to wash their hands and feet in preparation for ministering at the altar. The Sea served the same purpose. It was huge — 15 feet in diameter and 45 feet in circumference.

4:5 *3,000 baths.* When filled with about 27,000 gallons of water the Sea would have weighed about 108 tons.

4:6 *ten [portable] basins.* Each laver held 40 baths, or about 230 gallons (1Ki 7:38). They could accommodate large animals, such as oxen. The law of burnt offerings required certain parts of the animal to be washed in water before it was placed on the altar (Lev 1:9,13).

4:7 *ten golden lampstands.* The wilderness tabernacle had only one lampstand (Ex 25:31), but the temple had ten.

4:8 *ten tables.* There had been only one table in the tabernacle (Ex 25:23). The increase reflects the grandeur of the temple, as well as the large number of people to be served.

4:9 *courtyard of the priests.* There were areas in and about the temple that only the priests

---

14 Ex 26:31; Mt 27:51; Heb 9:3 **15** 1Ki 7:15; Jer 52:21 **16** 1Ki 7:20 **17** 1Ki 7:21 **CHAPTER 4** **1** Ex 27:1,2; 2Ki 16:14; Eze 43:13,16 **2** 1Ki 7:23 **3** 1Ki 7:24-26 **5** See 1Ki 7:26 **6** 1Ki 7:38 **7** 1Ki 7:49; Ex 25:31; 1Ch 28:12,19 **8** 1Ki 7:48 **9** 1Ki 6:36

[10]He set the Sea on the right side at the southeast corner [of the house].

[11]And Huram also made the pails [for ashes], the shovels, and the basins. So Huram finished the work that he did for King Solomon in the house of God:

[12]the two pillars, the bowls, the capitals on top of the two pillars, and the two lattice works to cover the two bowls of the capitals which were on top of the pillars,

[13]and the four hundred pomegranates for the two lattice works, two rows of pomegranates for each lattice to cover the two bowls of the capitals on the pillars.

[14]He also made the stands and he made the basins on the stands;

[15]and the one Sea with the twelve oxen under it.

[16]The pails, the shovels, and the meat-forks, and all the utensils Huram-abi made of polished bronze for King Solomon for the house of the LORD.

[17]The king cast them on the plain of the Jordan, in the clay ground between Succoth and Zeredah.

[18]Solomon made all these utensils in such great quantity that the weight of the bronze could not be determined.

[19]Solomon also made all the articles that were in the house of God: the golden altar, and the tables for the bread of the Presence (showbread),

[20]and the lampstands with their lamps of pure gold, to burn in front of the inner sanctuary (the Holy of Holies) as directed;

[21]the flowers, the lamps, and the tongs of gold, of purest gold;

[22]and the snuffers, the basins, the dishes [for incense], and the firepans, of pure gold; and for the entrance of the house (temple), the inner doors for the Holy of Holies and the doors of the Holy Place (main room), were of gold.

The Ark Is Brought into the Temple

5 THUS ALL the work that Solomon did for the house of the LORD was finished. He brought in the things that his father David had dedicated, and he put the silver and the gold and all the utensils in the treasuries of the house of God.

[2]Then Solomon assembled the elders of Israel and all the heads of the tribes, the leaders of the fathers' *households* of the Israelites, in Jerusalem to bring the ark of the covenant of the LORD up from the City of David, which is Zion.

[3]All the men of Israel gathered before the king at the feast in the seventh month.

---

could enter. One of these was the area immediately surrounding it and enclosed by a separating wall, the "courtyard of the priests." ***great courtyard.*** The great court was an outer area where the people in general could go.

4:14 *stands.* The stands were mobile with four bronze wheels (1Ki 7:27 – 37).

4:17 *cast them . . . in the clay ground.* Many bronze products were made at a place in the Jordan valley about 35 miles north of the Dead Sea. Archaeologists have uncovered evidence of this work in an area where the clay is suitable for bronze casting.

4:19 *golden altar.* This altar was used for offering incense (Ex 30:1 – 10; 1Ki 7:48). It was in the holy place just in front of the veil.

4:22 *inner doors.* The tabernacle had a veil between the "holy of holies" where the ark was, and the "house," or holy place. Solomon's temple had a set of doors there as well.

5:2 *ark of the covenant.* Though David had built a tabernacle, or tent, on Mount Zion to house the ark (1Ch 15:1), it was still separate from the original tabernacle and bronze altar at Gibeon. Completing Solomon's temple made it possible for the ark and the altar to be in the same place for the first time since the Israelites lost the ark to the Philistines during the days when the tabernacle was at Shiloh and Samuel was a little boy (1Sa 4 – 6).

5:3 *feast.* Since this was the seventh month, the feast was the Feast of Tabernacles. This was an appropriate occasion for moving the ark to a permanent location because the feast commemorated Israel's wandering in the wilderness when the ark had no permanent place (Lev 23:39 – 43).

10 1Ki 7:39 **11** See 1Ki 7:40 **12** 1Ki 7:41 **13** See 1Ki 7:20 **14** 1Ki 7:27,43 **16** 1Ki 7:14,45 **17** 1Ki 7:46 **18** 1Ki 7:47 **19** 1Ki 7:48-50; Ex 25:30 **20** Ex 27:20,21 **21** Ex 25:31 **CHAPTER 5** **1** 1Ki 7:51 **2** 1Ki 8:1; 2Sa 6:12 **3** 1Ki 8:2; See 2Ch 7:8-10

4And all the elders of Israel came,
and the Levites took up the ark.
5The Levitical priests brought up
the ark, the Tent of Meeting, and all
the holy utensils that were in the Tent.
6And King Solomon and all the as-
sembly of Israel who gathered together
with him before the ark were sacrific-
ing so many sheep and oxen that they
could not be counted or numbered.
7Then the priests brought the ark of
the covenant of the LORD to its place, to
the inner sanctuary of the house, into
the Holy of Holies, under the wings of
the cherubim;
8for the cherubim spread out their
wings over the place of the ark, mak-
ing a covering above the ark and its
carrying poles.
9The poles were so long that the ends
of the poles of the ark were visible from
the front of the Holy of Holies (inner
sanctuary), but were not visible from
the outside. They are there to this day.
10There was nothing in the ark ex-
cept the two tablets [of the Ten Com-
mandments] which Moses put there at
Mount Horeb, when the LORD made a
covenant with the Israelites, when they
came out of Egypt. [Ex 31:18]

The Glory of God Fills the Temple

11When the priests came out of the
Holy Place (for all the priests who were
present had sanctified themselves [sep-
arating themselves from everything
unclean], without regard to their as-
signed divisions),
12and all of the Levitical singers,
Asaph, Heman, and Jeduthun, with
their sons and relatives, clothed in fine
linen, with cymbals, harps, and lyres
were standing at the east end of the
altar, and with them a hundred and
twenty priests blowing trumpets
13in unison when the trumpeters and
singers were to make themselves heard
with one voice praising and thanking
the LORD, and when they raised their
voices accompanied by the trumpets
and cymbals and [other] instruments
of music, and when they praised the
LORD, *saying,* "For *He* is good, for His
mercy *and* lovingkindness endure for-
ever," then the house of the LORD was
filled with a cloud,
14so that the priests could not remain
standing to minister because of the
cloud; for the glory *and* brilliance of
the LORD filled the house of God.

Solomon's Dedication

6 THEN SOLOMON said,
"The LORD has said that He would
dwell in the thick cloud.
2"I have built You a lofty house,
A place for You to dwell forever."
3Then the king turned around and
blessed the entire assembly of Israel,
while they were all standing.
4And he said, "Blessed be the LORD,
the God of Israel, who spoke with His
mouth to my father David and has ful-
filled with His hands *what He prom-
ised,* saying,
5'Since the day that I brought My
people out of the land of Egypt, I did
not choose a city among all the tribes

5:5 *Tent.* This tent was the Mosaic tabernacle. Solomon ended worship at the high place at Gibeon by dismantling the tabernacle and bringing it and all its furnishings to Jerusalem.
5:9 *to this day.* The ark was supposed to remain safely in the temple forever. At the time of the writing of this book (probably between 460 and 430 BC), the temple had been destroyed and the ark was gone. No one knows what happened to the ark after Nebuchadnezzar destroyed Jerusalem in 586 BC.
5:12 *Asaph, Heman, and Jeduthun.* These men were the heads of the divisions of Levitical musicians (1Ch 6:33; 39, 44; 25:1).
5:13 Praise—Praise and worship are simply recognizing the perfections and worthiness of the Lord. His lovingkindness never runs out or diminishes. Everyday his mercy and grace exist in perfection on our behalf. A time for daily praise is one of the best ways to grow closer to God.
6:2 *place for You to dwell forever.* It did not occur to Solomon that one day the glory of the Lord would depart from this temple and it would be destroyed (Ezr 10:18).

10 Dt 10:2,5; 2Ch 6:11 **12** 1Ch 25:1; 1Ch 15:24 **13** Ps 136; See 1Ch 16:34,41 **14** Ex 40:35; 2Ch 7:2
CHAPTER 6 **1** 1Ki 8:12; Lev 16:2

of Israel *in which* to build a house so
that My Name (Presence) might be
there, nor did I choose any man to be
a leader over My people Israel;
6 but I have chosen Jerusalem that
My Name might be there, and I have
chosen David to be over My people
Israel.'
7 "Now it was in the heart of my father David to build a house for the
Name of the LORD, the God of Israel.
8 "But the LORD said to my father David, 'Because it was in your heart to
build a house for My Name, you did
well that it was in your heart.
9 'Nevertheless you shall not build
the house, but your son who will be
born to you, he shall build the house
for My Name.'
10 "Now the LORD has fulfilled His
word which He spoke; for I have risen
in place of my father David and I sit on
the throne of Israel, just as the LORD
promised, and have built the house for
the Name of the LORD, the God of Israel.
11 "There I have placed the ark [the
symbol of His Presence] in which is
the covenant of the LORD [the Ten Commandments], which He made with the
people (descendants) of Israel."

Solomon's Prayer of Dedication

12 Then Solomon stood before the
altar of the LORD in the presence of the
entire assembly of Israel and spread
out his hands.
13 For Solomon had made a bronze
platform, five cubits square and three
cubits high, and had set it in the midst
of the courtyard; and he stood on it,
and he knelt down on his knees in
the presence of all the assembly of Israel and spread out his hands toward
heaven,
14 and he said, "O LORD, God of Israel,
there is no god like You in heaven or
on the earth, keeping covenant and
showing mercy *and* lovingkindness to
Your servants who walk before You [in
obedience] with all their heart,
15 [You] who have kept Your promise
to Your servant David, my father, that
which You told him; You have spoken
with Your mouth and have fulfilled it
with Your hand, as it is today.
16 "Now therefore, O LORD, the God of
Israel, keep with Your servant David,
my father, that which You promised
him, saying, 'You shall not fail to have
a man to sit on the throne of Israel,
provided your sons are careful to walk
in My law as you, [David,] have walked
before Me.'
17 "Now then, O LORD, the God of Israel, let Your word which You have
spoken to Your servant David be confirmed (verified).
18 "But will God actually dwell with
mankind on the earth? Behold, heaven
and the highest heaven cannot contain
You; how much less this house which
I have built!
19 "Yet have regard for the prayer of
Your servant and for his supplication,
O LORD my God, to listen to the cry
and to the prayer which Your servant
prays before You,
20 that Your eyes may be open toward
this house day and night, toward the
place in which You have said that *You
would* put Your Name (Presence), to
listen to the prayer which Your servant
shall pray toward this place.
21 "So listen to the requests of Your
servant and Your people Israel when
they pray toward this place. Hear from
Your dwelling place, from heaven; and
when You hear, forgive.

6:14 *there is no god like You.* Solomon's acclamation is echoed by every child of God who reflects on God's faithfulness and mercy to those who "walk before Him" with "all their heart." It is not that Solomon considered other gods to be valid, but he was in a position to see the kind of trust that pagans put in their gods, and how whimsical and unfaithful these "gods" were.

6:16 *provided your sons . . . walk in My law.* Solomon was recognizing that the covenant was dependent on the people remaining faithful to God, and he wanted his line to walk with God as David had. Even though future generations did not imitate David, God's faithfulness was carried out through Jesus, the son of David (Mt 9:27; 15:22; 22:41–45).

6 2Ch 12:13; 1Ch 28:4 **7** 2Sa 7:2; 1Ch 17:1; 28:2 **11** 2Ch 5:10 **12** 1Ki 8:22 **14** Ex 15:11; Dt 4:39; 7:9
15 1Ch 22:9 **16** 2Sa 7:12,16; 1Ki 2:4; 6:12; 2Ch 7:18; Ps 132:12 **18** 2Ch 2:6; Isa 66:1; Ac 7:49

22 “If a man sins against his neighbor, and he is required to take an oath, and he comes and takes the oath before Your altar in this house,

23 then hear from heaven and act and judge Your servants, punishing the wicked by bringing his conduct on his own head, and providing justice to the righteous by giving to him in accordance with his righteousness (innocence).

24 “If Your people Israel have been defeated by an enemy because they have sinned against You, and they return *to You* and confess Your name, and pray and make supplication before You in this house,

25 then hear from heaven and forgive the sin of Your people Israel, and bring them again to the land which You gave to them and to their fathers.

26 “When the heavens are shut up and there is no rain because Your people have sinned against You, and they pray toward this place and confess Your name, and turn from their sin when You afflict *and* humble them;

27 then hear in heaven and forgive the sin of Your servants and Your people Israel, indeed, teach them the good way in which they should walk. And send rain on Your land which You have given to Your people as an inheritance.

28 “If there is famine in the land, if there is pestilence, if there is blight or mildew, if there are [migratory] locusts or grasshoppers, if their enemies besiege them in the land of their cities, whatever plague or whatever sickness *there is*,

29 then whatever prayer or request is made by any man or all of Your people Israel, each knowing his own suffering and his own pain, and stretching out his hands toward this house,

30 then hear from heaven, Your dwelling place, and forgive, and render to each in accordance with all his ways, whose heart You know; for You alone know the hearts of the sons of men,

31 so that they may fear You, to walk in Your ways [in obedience to You] as long as they live in the land which You have given to our fathers.

32 “Also in regard to the foreigner who is not from Your people Israel, but has come from a far country for the sake of Your great name and Your mighty power and Your outstretched arm—when they come and pray toward this house,

33 then hear from heaven, from Your dwelling place, and do according to all for which the foreigner calls to You, so that all the peoples of the earth may know Your name, and fear You [reverently and worshipfully], as *do* Your people Israel, and that they may know that this house which I have built is called by Your Name.

34 “When Your people go out to war against their enemies, by the way that You send them, and they pray to You facing this city [Jerusalem] which You have chosen and the house which I have built for Your Name,

35 then hear from heaven their prayer and their request, and maintain their cause *and* do justice.

36 “When they sin against You (for there is no man who does not sin) and

---

6:23 *hear from heaven.* Solomon's request that God hear from heaven underscored God's transcendence. Although God had chosen to be present on earth at the temple, He is also beyond the limits of the temple building.

6:25 *bring them again.* This statement is a hint of the future captivity and deportation of God's disobedient people (Dt 28:29–30). When the exile to Babylon became a reality, the temple was destroyed and no one could pray at that place as before. But even in those days, God's people directed their prayer toward Jerusalem (Da 6:10).

6:32–33 *in regard to the foreigner.* God made His covenant exclusively with Israel, the nation descended from Abraham, but He did so for the purpose of attracting the nations to Himself, the Creator of all people. A foreigner who embraced the Lord as God would be numbered among God's people.

6:36 *there is no man who does not sin.* This statement is repeated in the New Testament (Ro 3:23; 1Jn 1:8–10). ***take them away captive.*** Solomon's speech anticipated the possibility of exile (v. 25), something that had already taken place by the time Chronicles was written.

26 1Ki 17:1 **28** 2Ch 20:9 **30** 1Ch 28:9 **32** Jn 12:20; Ac 8:27 **36** Pr 20:9; Ecc 7:20; Jas 3:2; 1Jn 1:8

You are angry with them and hand
them over to an enemy, so that they
take them away captive to a land far
away or near,
37 if they take it to heart in the land
where they have been taken captive,
and repent and pray to You in the land
of their captivity, saying, 'We have
sinned, we have done wrong and have
acted wickedly';
38 if they return to You with all their
heart and with all their soul in the land
of their captivity, and pray facing their
land which You have given to their
fathers and toward the city which You
have chosen, and toward the house
which I have built for Your Name;
39 then hear from heaven, from Your
dwelling place, their prayer and re-
quests, and maintain their cause *and*
do justice and forgive Your people who
have sinned against You.
40 "Now, O my God, I pray, let Your
eyes be open and Your ears attentive
to the prayer *offered* in this place.
41 "Now then arise, O LORD God, [and
come] to Your resting place, You and
the ark of Your strength *and* pow-
er. Let Your priests, O LORD God, be
clothed with salvation and let Your
godly ones rejoice in [Your] goodness.
42 "O LORD God, do not turn away
and reject the face of Your anointed;
remember *Your* lovingkindness *and*
faithfulness to Your servant David."

The Shekinah Glory

7 WHEN SOLOMON had finished
praying, fire came down from
heaven and consumed the burnt offer-
ing and the sacrifices, and the [Shek-
inah] glory *and* brilliance of the LORD
filled the house. [Lev 9:24]
2 The priests could not enter the
house of the LORD because the glory
and brilliance of the LORD had filled
the LORD's house.
3 When all the people of Israel saw
how the fire came down and *saw* the
glory *and* brilliance of the LORD upon
the house, they bowed down on the
stone pavement with their faces to
the ground, and they worshiped and
praised the LORD, *saying*, "For He is
good, for His mercy *and* lovingkind-
ness endure forever."

7:1 Miracles — This event marks the third of four events when supernatural fire fell from heaven. The first occurred during the dedication of the tabernacle in the days of Moses (Lev 9:24). The second happened when David dedicated a piece of ground to the Lord that later became the site of Solomon's temple (1Ch 21:26). The final occurrence transpired on Mount Carmel when Elijah prayed for fire to consume his offering (1Ki 18:38). We often think that a miracle will convince an unbeliever of the reality of the living God, and sometimes it does. But sensing the presence of God, or seeing His work, does not equal believing. The Israelites often backslid, even after miraculous events, and even the miracles of Jesus did not convince all that He was the Messiah (Mt 11:20 – 24).

7:3 Need for Worship — The first reason for *worship is simply* that God commands it (1Ch 16:29; Mt 4:10). The first four of the Ten Commandments charge men and women to worship the one true God and Him alone (Ex 20:3 – 10). To allow anything or anyone other than God to have a position of lordship over us constitutes gross disobedience to the will of God and incurs His terrible wrath (Ex 20:5; Dt 27:15). Eventually all peoples will bow to God anyway, even if they do so unwillingly (Php 2:10).

An equally important reason for worship is that God is worthy of our worship. He designed us for worship. He alone possesses the attributes that merit our worship and service. Among these are goodness (Ps 100:5), mercy (Ex 4:31), holiness (Ps 99:5,9), and creative power (Rev 4:11). When men of biblical times clearly saw the unveiled glory of God, they could not help but fall prostrate in worship. Examples of this response can be seen in the actions of Moses (Ex 34:5 – 8), Isaiah (Isa 6), Paul (Ac 9:3 – 6), and John (Rev 1:9 – 17).

A final reason for worship is that men and women need to give it. People cannot find personal fulfillment apart from the glad submission of themselves in worshipful obedience to God. He is the Creator and they are the creatures (Rev 4:11). We are made to worship God. If we do anything less, we fail to be who God created us to be. One who worships God not only participates in the occupation of heaven (Rev 7:9 – 12), but also finds joyful satisfaction in the present time (Ro 12:2; Col 3:24).

41 Ps 132:8-10,16; 1Ch 28:2; Neh 9:25 **42** Ps 132:1; Isa 55:3 **CHAPTER 7** **1** 1Ki 8:54; Lev 9:24; Jdg 6:21; 1Ki 18:38; 1Ch 21:26; 1Ki 8:10,11 **2** 2Ch 5:14 **3** 2Ch 5:13; Ps 136:1; 1Ch 16:41; 2Ch 20:21

Sacrifices Offered

4 Then the king and all the people
offered a sacrifice before the LORD.
5 King Solomon offered a sacrifice
of 22,000 oxen and 120,000 sheep. In
this way the king and all the people
dedicated God's house.
6 The priests stood at their posts
[ready for service], and the Levites
also, with the musical instruments of
the LORD which King David had made
to praise the LORD, *saying*, "For His
lovingkindness *and* mercy endure for-
ever," whenever David offered praise
through their ministry. The priests
were opposite the Levites blowing the
trumpets and all Israel was standing.
7 Moreover, Solomon consecrated
the middle of the courtyard that was
in front of the house of the LORD, for it
was there that he offered burnt offer-
ings and the fat of the peace offerings
because the bronze altar which he had
made was not sufficient to hold the
burnt offerings, the grain offerings,
and the fat [all together].

The Feast of Dedication

8 At that time Solomon observed the
feast for seven days, and all Israel with
him, a very large assembly, from the
entrance of Hamath to the Brook of
Egypt.
9 On the eighth day they held a cel-
ebration, for they had observed the
dedication of the altar for seven days,
and the feast for seven days.
10 And on the twenty-third day of the
seventh month Solomon sent the peo-
ple to their tents, rejoicing and happy
in heart because of the goodness that
the LORD had shown to David, to Sol-
omon, and to His people Israel.

God's Promise and Warning

11 And so Solomon finished the house
(temple) of the LORD and the palace
of the king. He successfully accom-
plished all that he had planned to do in
the house of the LORD and in his palace.
12 Then the LORD appeared to Sol-
omon by night and said to him: "I have
heard your prayer and have chosen
this place for Myself as a house of sac-
rifice.
13 "If I shut up the heavens so that no
rain falls, or if I command locusts to
devour the land, or if I send pestilence
and plague among My people,
14 and My people, who are called by
My Name, humble themselves, and
pray and seek (crave, require as a ne-
cessity) My face and turn from their
wicked ways, then I will hear [them]
from heaven, and forgive their sin and
heal their land.
15 "Now My eyes will be open and
My ears attentive to prayer *offered* in
this place.
16 "For now I have chosen and sanc-
tified *and* set apart for My purpose
this house that My Name may be here
forever, and My eyes and My heart will
be here perpetually.

7:8 *feast.* The feast was the Feast of Tabernacles, which began on the fifteenth day of the seventh month and continued through the twenty-second day (see note for 5:3). ***Hamath . . . Brook of Egypt.*** These geographical locations specify the extent of Solomon's early kingdom from north to south.

7:9 *dedication of the altar.* This is the same dedication referred to in 5:3.

7:10 *sent the people to their tents.* The people returned to their huts, or booths, where they stayed as a part of the Feast of Tabernacles. Few if any Israelites used tents for their housing at this time.

7:11 *house of the LORD . . . palace of the king.* Since it took Solomon 13 years to build his palace and 20 years in all to build both it and the temple, these events are half-way through Solomon's 40-year reign.

7:14 Prayer — This promise to hear, if the people will pray, is directly linked to the covenant promises that God made with the Israelites (Dt 28 – 30). Blessings were linked to obedience, curses linked to rebellion, and the promise that God would hear if they repented was the reminder that God had eternal commitment to them. Even nations outside this covenant have taken great comfort in remembering this promise. God always hears the sincere prayers of His people, and Christians are directed to pray for the leaders of the nations (1Ti 2:1 – 2).

4 1Ki 8:62,63 **6** 1Ch 15:16; 2Ch 5:12 **7** 1Ki 8:64 **8** 1Ki 8:65; Jos 13:3 **10** 1Ki 8:66 **11** 1Ki 9:1 **12** Dt 12:5 **13** 2Ch 6:26,28 **14** Jas 4:10; 2Ch 6:27,30 **15** 2Ch 6:40 **16** 1Ki 9:3; 2Ch 6:6

17 “As for you [Solomon], if you will walk before me as your father David walked, and do everything that I have commanded you, and observe My statutes and My ordinances, [1 Kin 11:1–11]

18 then I will establish your royal throne just as I covenanted with your father David, saying, ‘You will not fail to have a man as ruler in Israel.’

19 “But if you [people] turn away and abandon My statutes and My commandments which I have set before you, and you go and serve other gods and worship them,

20 then I will uproot Israel from My land which I have given them; and I will cast this house, which I have consecrated for My Name, out of My sight, and will make it a proverb and an object of scorn among all nations. [Jer 24:9, 10]

21 “And as for this house, which was so exalted, everyone who passes by it will be astonished *and* appalled and say, ‘Why has the LORD done thus to this land and to this house?’

22 “Then people will say, ‘It is because they abandoned the LORD, the God of their fathers, who brought them out of the land of Egypt, and they adopted other gods, and worshiped them and served them; therefore He has brought all this adversity *and* evil on them.’ ”

Solomon’s Activities and Accomplishments

8 NOW IT came about at the end of the twenty years, in which Solomon had built the house of the LORD and his own house (palace),

2 that he built *and* fortified the cities which Huram (Hiram) had given to him, and settled the Israelites there.

3 Then Solomon went to Hamath-zobah and captured it.

4 He built Tadmor in the wilderness, and all his storage cities in Hamath.

5 He also built upper Beth-horon and lower Beth-horon, fortified cities with walls, gates, and bars [to lock the gates];

6 and Baalath and all the storage cities that Solomon had, and all the cities for his chariots and the cities for his horsemen, and all that Solomon desired to build in Jerusalem, in Lebanon, and in all the land under his rule.

7 All the people who were left of the Hittites, the Amorites, the Perizzites, the Hivites, and the Jebusites, who were not of Israel,

8 *but were* descendants of those who were left in the land, whom the Israelites had not destroyed—Solomon brought them up as forced laborers to this day.

9 But Solomon did not make slaves of the Israelites for his work; they were men of war, his chief captains, and commanders of his chariots and his horsemen.

10 These were the chief officers of King Solomon, two hundred and fifty [in authority] who ruled over the people.

11 Then Solomon brought the daughter of Pharaoh up from the City of David into the house (palace) he had built for her, for he said, “My wife shall not live in the house of David king of Israel, because the places where the ark of the LORD has entered are holy.”

12 Then Solomon offered burnt offerings to the LORD on the altar of the LORD which he had built in front of the porch [of the temple],

13 a certain number every day, of-

8:4 ***Tadmor.*** Solomon built and fortified cities such as Tadmor because they were on vital caravan routes. These fortified cities provided protection to his caravans and became the customs points at which Solomon collected taxes. ***storage cities.*** Facilities were scattered throughout Solomon’s outlying provinces to provide warehouses for his armies and merchantmen, as well as to store produce and other tributes paid by the vassal states (1Ki 9:19).

8:5 ***upper Beth-horon and lower Beth-horon.*** These cities were strategically located near the border between Judah and the northern tribal districts, along a major mountain pass to the Mediterranean (Jos 10:10; 1Sa 13:18).

17 1Ki 9:4 **18** 2Ch 6:16 **19** Lev 26:14,33; Dt 28:15,36,37 **21** Dt 29:24 **CHAPTER 8** **1** 1Ki 9:10 **4** 1Ki 9:17 **7** 1Ki 9:20 **10** See 1Ki 9:23 **11** 1Ki 3:1; 7:8; 9:24 **13** Ex 29:38; Nu 28:3,9,11,26; 29:1; Ex 23:14; Dt 16:16

fering them up as Moses commanded
for the Sabbaths, the New Moons, and
the three annual feasts—the Feast
of Unleavened Bread, the Feast of
Weeks, and the Feast of Booths (Tab-
ernacles).
14 Now in accordance with the or-
dinance of his father David, he ap-
pointed the divisions of the priests for
their service, and the Levites for their
duties of praise and ministering *and*
serving before the priests as every day
required, and the gatekeepers by their
divisions at every gate; for David the
man of God had so commanded.
15 And they did not deviate from
the commandment of the king to the
priests and Levites in any respect or in
regard to the storehouses *or* treasuries.
16 Thus all the work of Solomon was
carried out from the day the founda-
tion of the house of the LORD was laid
until it was finished. So the house of
the LORD was completed.
17 Then Solomon went to Ezion-geber
and to Eloth on the shore of the [Red]
Sea in the land of Edom.
18 And Huram (Hiram) sent him,
by his servants, ships and servants
familiar with the sea; and they went
with Solomon's servants to Ophir, and
took from there four hundred and fifty
talents of gold, and brought them to
King Solomon.

Visit of the Queen of Sheba

9 WHEN THE queen of Sheba heard
of the fame of Solomon, she came
to Jerusalem to test Solomon with
riddles. She was accompanied by a
very large number of attendants, with
camels bearing spices (balsam oil) and
a large amount of gold and precious
stones. And when she came to Sol-
omon, she talked with him about all
that was on her mind.
2 Solomon answered all her ques-
tions; nothing was hidden from him
which he did not make clear to her.
3 So when the queen of Sheba saw
the [depth of] Solomon's wisdom, and
the house which he had built,
4 and the food of his table, the [vast]
seating order of his officials, the atten-
dance *and* service of his ministers and
their attire, his cupbearers and their
attire, and his stairway by which he
went up to the house of the LORD, she
was breathless.
5 She said to the king, "The report
which I heard in my own land regard-
ing your [accomplishments and your]
words and your wisdom was true,
6 but I did not believe the reports until
I came and saw it with my own eyes.
Behold, the half of the greatness of
your wisdom was not told to me; you
have surpassed the report that I heard.
7 "Blessed *and* fortunate are your
people, how blessed *and* fortunate are
these servants of yours who stand be-
fore you continually and hear your
wisdom!
8 "Blessed be the LORD your God,
who delighted in you, setting you on
His throne as king for the LORD your
God; because your God loved Israel,
establishing them forever, therefore He
made you king over them, to do justice
and righteousness."
9 Then she gave the king a hundred
and twenty talents of gold, a very large
amount of spices (balsam oil) and pre-
cious stones; there was no such spice
[anywhere] like that which the queen
of Sheba gave to King Solomon.
10 The servants of Huram and those
of Solomon, who brought gold from

8:18 *Huram.* The Phoenicians were world famous mariners, so when Solomon undertook a merchant marine enterprise he called once more on his good friend Huram (also spelled Hiram), king of Tyre. ***Ophir.*** A source of finest gold (1Ch 29:4); the location of Ophir is not known, except that it was reached by sea. People have speculated that it may have been in South Arabia, India, or Africa.

9:1 *Sheba.* Sheba was more than a thousand miles south of Israel, at the southern end of the Arabian Peninsula.

9:8 *Blessed be the LORD your God.* The language of politeness in the ancient world does not necessarily suggest that the Queen of Sheba was converted. Visiting dignitaries customarily praised the god of the host nation.

14 1Ch 24:3; 1Ch 25:1; 1Ch 9:17; 26:1 **17** 1Ki 9:26 **18** 1Ki 9:27; 2Ch 9:10,13 **CHAPTER 9** **1** 1Ki 10:1; Mt 12:42; Lk 11:31 **10** 2Ch 8:18

Ophir, also brought almug trees and
precious stones.
11 From the almug timber the king
made stairways for the house of the
LORD and for the king's palace, and lyres
and harps for the singers; none like that
was seen before in the land of Judah.
12 King Solomon gave to the queen
of Sheba all [the things] she desired,
whatever she asked, besides *a return
for* what she had brought to the king.
So she returned to her own land with
her servants.

Solomon's Wealth and Power

13 Now the weight of gold which came
to Solomon in one year was 666 talents,
14 besides what the traders and mer-
chants brought; and all the kings of
Arabia and the governors of the coun-
try brought gold and silver to Solomon.
15 King Solomon made two hundred
large shields of beaten gold, using six
hundred *shekels of* beaten gold on each
large shield.
16 And *he made* three hundred [small-
er] shields of beaten gold, using three
hundred shekels of gold on each shield;
and the king put them in the house of
the Forest of Lebanon.
17 Moreover, the king made a great
throne of ivory and overlaid it with
pure gold.
18 *There were* six steps to the throne
and a golden footstool attached to the
throne, and arms on each side of the seat,
with two lions standing beside the arms.
19 Also, twelve lions were standing
there, one on each side of the six steps.
Nothing like it had ever been made for
any [other] kingdom.
20 All King Solomon's drinking ves-
sels were of gold, and all the vessels of
the house of the Forest of Lebanon were
of pure gold; silver was not considered
valuable in the days of Solomon.
21 For the king's ships went to Tar-
shish with the servants of Huram; once
every three years the ships of Tarshish
came bringing gold and silver, ivory
and apes and peacocks.
22 So King Solomon surpassed all
the kings of the earth in wealth and
wisdom.
23 And all the kings of the earth were
seeking the presence of Solomon, to
hear his wisdom which God had put
into his heart.
24 Each man brought his gift, articles
of silver and gold, garments, weapons,
spices, horses and mules, so much year
by year.
25 Now Solomon had 4,000 stalls
for horses and chariots, and 12,000
horsemen, and he stationed them in
the chariot cities or with the king at
Jerusalem. [Deut 17:16, 17]
26 He ruled over all the kings from the
Euphrates River to the land of the Philis-
tines, and as far as the border of Egypt.
27 The king made silver in Jerusalem
as common as stones, and cedar wood
as plentiful as the sycamore-fig trees
that are in the lowland.
28 And they were importing horses
for Solomon from Egypt and from all
[the other] countries.
29 Now the rest of the acts of Solomon,
from the first to the last, are they not
written in the records of Nathan the
prophet, and in the prophecy of Ahijah

9:13 *666 talents.* Solomon's annual income in gold amounted to 25 tons. This figure probably reflects the annual revenues of the entire nation through taxes.

9:14 *kings . . . governors . . . brought.* The gold and silver that the kings and governors brought to Solomon was tribute, a form of taxation on vassal states, not a voluntary gift.

9:15 *shields of beaten gold.* The shields of beaten gold were for decorative or ceremonial purpose, not the armory. Gold was too expensive, too heavy, and too soft to use in battle.

9:26 *to the land of the Philistines.* Most of the kings of Israel had continuing trouble with the Philistines, even though they were able to subdue every other surrounding neighbor. David had some success against the Philistines (1Ch 18:1), and later Jehoshaphat managed to exact tribute from some of them (17:11).

9:29 *Nathan the prophet.* This is the same Nathan that rebuked David for his adultery and murder (2Sa 12:1 – 15). He was a confidant and counselor to both David and Solomon (1Ki 1:8 – 11). ***Ahijah . . . Iddo.*** Ahijah and Iddo were contemporaries who compiled the accounts of both Jeroboam and Rehoboam (12:15).

25 1Ki 4:26; 10:26; 2Ch 1:14 **26** 1Ki 4:21; Ge 15:18; Ps 72:8 **27** 1Ki 10:27; 2Ch 1:15 **28** 1Ki 10:28; 2Ch 1:16
29 1Ki 11:41; 1Ki 11:29; 2Ch 12:15; 13:22

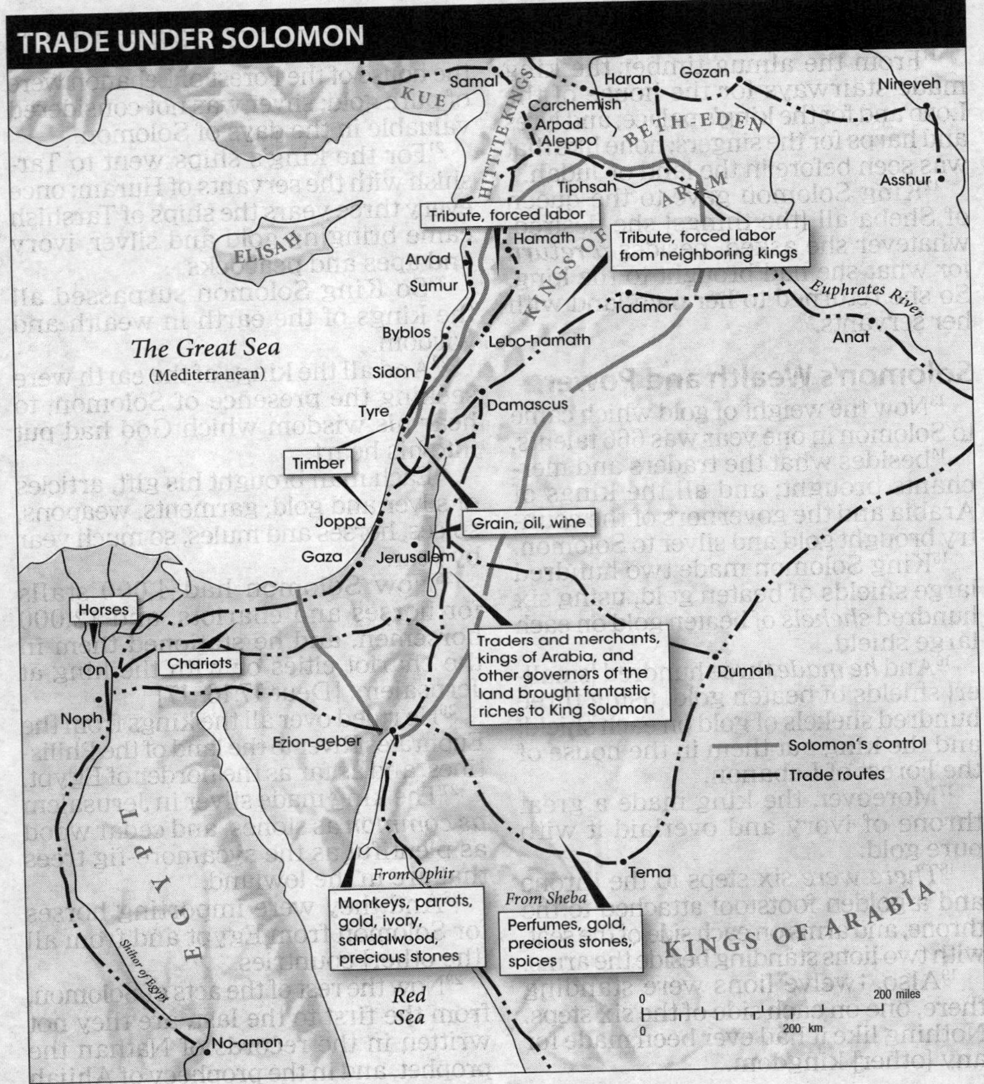

the Shilonite, and in the visions of Iddo
the seer concerning Jeroboam the son
of Nebat?
30Solomon reigned forty years in
Jerusalem over all Israel.

Death of Solomon

31And Solomon slept with his fathers
[in death]; he was buried in the city of
his father David. Rehoboam his son
reigned in his place.

Rehoboam's Reign of Folly

10 THEN REHOBOAM went to
Shechem, because all Israel had
come to Shechem to make him king.
2When Jeroboam the son of Nebat
heard *about the new king* (for he was

9:31 ***Rehoboam.*** Rehoboam was a son of Solomon by his wife Naamah of Ammon (12:13). He was 41 when he began to rule, so he must have been born during the period when Solomon ruled alongside David (1Ch 29:22–23).

10:1 ***Shechem.*** Rehoboam probably chose

30 1Ki 11:42,43 **CHAPTER 10** **1** 1Ki 12:1 **2** 1Ki 11:40

in Egypt, where he had fled from the
presence of King Solomon), Jeroboam
returned from Egypt. [1 Kin 11:26–40]
3 And the people sent *messengers*
and summoned him. So when Jero-
boam and all Israel came, they spoke
to Rehoboam, saying,
4 "Your father [King Solomon] made
our yoke hard (heavy, difficult); so now
lighten the hard service of your father
and his heavy yoke which he put on us,
and we will serve you."
5 Rehoboam replied, "Come back to
me again in three days." So the people
departed.
6 Then King Rehoboam consulted
with the elders who had served his
father Solomon [as advisers] while he
was alive, asking, "What advice do you
give me in answer to these people?"
7 They answered him, saying, "If you
are kind to these people and please
them and speak good words to them,
then they will be your servants forever."
8 But the king rejected the advice
which the elders gave him, and consult-
ed with the young men who grew up
with him and served him [as advisers].
9 He asked them, "What advice do
you give to us regarding the answer to
these people, who have spoken to me,
saying, 'Lighten the yoke which your
father put on us'? "
10 The young men who grew up with
him told him, "Tell the people who said to
you, 'Your father made our yoke heavy,
but you make it lighter for us': 'My little
finger is thicker than my father's loins!
11 'Now my father loaded you with
a heavy yoke, but I will add [more
weight] to your yoke. My father disci-
plined you with whips, but I *will dis-*
cipline you with scorpions (extremely
painful scourges).' "
12 So on the third day Jeroboam and
all the people returned to Rehoboam
just as the king had directed, saying,
"Return to me on the third day."
13 The king answered them harshly,
for King Rehoboam rejected the coun-
sel of the elders.
14 He spoke to them in accordance
with the advice of the young men,
saying, "My father made your yoke
heavy, but I will add to it; my father
disciplined you with whips, but I *will*
discipline you with scorpions."
15 So the king did not listen to the
people, for the turn of events was from
God that the LORD might fulfill His
word, which He had spoken through
Ahijah the Shilonite to Jeroboam the
son of Nebat. [1 Kin 11:29–39]
16 When all Israel saw that the king
did not listen *and* pay attention to
them, the people answered him,

"What portion do we have in
David?
We have no inheritance in the son
of Jesse.

Shechem as the place to be crowned because a rift had begun to develop between the northern and southern tribes (1Ki 11:26–40).

10:4 Wisdom — Bravado is different than wisdom. Saying that one is going to be tough is different than being wise. Short of despotic force, no king can rule a people who do not trust him, and even if there is not outright rebellion, the resistance makes an unhappy nation. Like many other people, Rehoboam mistook conciliation for weakness, and lost his chance to have influence with most of the nation. It is important to remember that the outcome of this encounter was just what God wanted. Rehoboam was reaping the fruits of his father's (and his own) indifference to God.

10:15 the turn of events was from God. Human foolishness and decisions often achieve God's purposes. Solomon's defection from God late in his reign had already disqualified his descendants from ruling over all Israel (1Ki 11:9–13). Rehoboam initiated the split with his own foolish actions.

11:13 all their districts. Though Israel and Judah had split into two kingdoms, the priests and Levites of Israel sided with Judah. One reason for this was that they knew that Rehoboam was of the lineage of David, and therefore part of God's covenant promise to David. Another reason was that Jeroboam had established his own religious cult, which had no need for the true priests of God (1Ki 12:24–33).

11:16 followed them to Jerusalem. Once the legitimate religious leaders had left Israel, the worshipers of God in the Northern Kingdom could no longer worship in good conscience, so they either made pilgrimages to Jerusalem, or moved there (1Ki 12:25–33). At the time of the

15 1Sa 2:25; 1Ki 12:15,24; 1Ki 11:29

Every man to your tents, O Israel;
Now, [Rehoboam, descendant of]
David, see to your own house."

So all Israel went to their tents.
17But as for the Israelites who lived
in Judah's cities, Rehoboam ruled over
them.
18Then King Rehoboam sent Hadoram,
who was over the forced labor, and the
Israelites stoned him and he died. And
King Rehoboam hurried to mount his
[royal] chariot to escape to Jerusalem.
19And Israel has rebelled against the
house of David to this day.

Rehoboam Reigns over Judah and Builds Cities

11 NOW WHEN Rehoboam came
to Jerusalem, he assembled the
house of Judah and Benjamin, 180,000
chosen warriors to fight against [the
ten tribes of] Israel to restore the king-
dom to Rehoboam.
2But the word of the LORD came to
Shemaiah the man of God, saying,
3"Say to Rehoboam the son of Sol-
omon, king of Judah, and to all Israel
in Judah and Benjamin,
4'Thus says the LORD: "You shall not
go up nor fight against your brothers
(countrymen); return, every man to his
house, for this thing is from Me." ' "
And they listened to *and* obeyed the
words of the LORD and turned back
from going against Jeroboam.
5Rehoboam lived in Jerusalem and
built [fortified] cities for defense in
Judah.
6He built Bethlehem, Etam, Tekoa,
7Beth-zur, Soco, Adullam,
8Gath, Mareshah, Ziph,
9Adoraim, Lachish, Azekah,
10Zorah, Aijalon, and Hebron, which
are fortified cities in Judah and Ben-
jamin.
11He strengthened the fortresses and
put officers in them, with supplies of
food, [olive] oil, and wine.
12And in each city he put [large]
shields and spears, and made them
very strong. So he held Judah and
Benjamin.
13Further, the priests and the Levites
who were in all Israel took their stand
with Rehoboam from all their districts.

Jeroboam Appoints False Priests

14For the Levites left their pasture
lands and their property and came to
Judah and Jerusalem, because Jero-
boam and his sons had excluded them
from serving as priests to the LORD.
15Jeroboam appointed his own
priests for the high places, for the sa-
tyrs (goat demons) and calves (idols)
which he had made. [1 Kin 12:28]
16Those from all the tribes of Israel
who set their hearts on seeking the
LORD God of Israel followed them to
Jerusalem, to sacrifice to the LORD God
of their fathers.
17So they strengthened the kingdom
of Judah and supported Rehoboam the
son of Solomon for three years; for
they walked in the way of David and
Solomon for three years.

Rehoboam's Family

18Rehoboam took as his wife Mahal-
ath, the daughter of Jerimoth the son
of David, and of Abihail the daughter
of Eliab the son of Jesse.
19She bore him sons: Jeush, Shema-
riah, and Zaham.
20After her he took Maacah the
daughter (granddaughter) of Absalom,
and she bore him Abijah, Attai, Ziza,
and Shelomith.
21Rehoboam loved Maacah the daugh-
ter (granddaughter) of Absalom more
than all his wives and concubines—for
he had taken eighteen wives and sixty
concubines, and he fathered twenty-
eight sons and sixty daughters.
22Rehoboam appointed Abijah the

Babylonian captivity (36:10) the Northern Kingdom was already captured by Assyria (2Ki 17), but there were many representatives from the northern tribes living in Judah.

11:22 ***Abijah.*** Rehoboam named his son Abijah as the next king to ensure a smooth succession

19 1Ki 12:19 **CHAPTER 11** **1** 1Ki 12:21 **2** 2Ch 12:15 **14** Nu 35:2; 2Ch 13:9 **15** 1Ki 12:31; 13:33; 14:9; Hos 13:2; Lev 17:7; 1Co 10:20; 1Ki 12:28 **16** See 2Ch 15:9; 30:11,18 **17** 2Ch 12:1 **20** 1Ki 15:2; She is called Michaiah the daughter of Uriel, 2Ch 13:2 **22** See Dt 21:15-17

son of Maacah the chief leader among his brothers, because he *intended* to make him king.

23 He acted wisely and distributed some of his sons throughout the territories of Judah and Benjamin to all the fortified cities. He gave them abundant provisions, and he sought many wives *for them*.

Shishak of Egypt Invades Judah

12 WHEN THE kingdom of Rehoboam was established and strong, he and all Israel with him abandoned the law of the LORD.

2 And it came about in King Rehoboam's fifth year, because they had been unfaithful to the LORD, that Shishak king of Egypt came up against Jerusalem

3 with 1,200 chariots and 60,000 horsemen. The people who came with him from Egypt were beyond counting—the Lubim, the Sukkiim, and the Ethiopians.

4 Shishak took the fortified cities of Judah and came as far as Jerusalem.

5 Then Shemaiah the prophet came to Rehoboam and the leaders of Judah who had gathered at Jerusalem because of Shishak, and said to them, "Thus says the LORD: 'You have abandoned (turned away from) Me, so I have abandoned you into the hands of Shishak.' "

6 Then the leaders of Israel and the king humbled themselves and said, "The LORD is righteous."

7 When the LORD saw that they humbled themselves, the word of the LORD came to Shemaiah, saying, "They have humbled themselves so I will not destroy them, but I will grant them some *measure* of a remnant [that escapes]; and My wrath shall not be poured out on Jerusalem by means of Shishak.

8 "Nevertheless they will become his slaves, so that they may know [the difference between] My service and the service of the kingdoms of the countries."

Plunder Impoverishes Judah

9 So Shishak king of Egypt went up against Jerusalem; he took the treasures of the house of the LORD and the treasures of the king's house (palace). He took everything. He even took the shields of gold which Solomon had made.

10 In their place King Rehoboam made shields of bronze and entrusted them to the care of the officers of the guard who guarded the door of the king's house.

11 And whenever the king entered the house of the LORD, the guards came and carried the shields and *then* brought them back into the guards' room.

12 When Rehoboam humbled himself, the wrath of the LORD turned away from him, so as not to destroy him completely; and also conditions were good in Judah.

13 So King Rehoboam established himself in Jerusalem and reigned.

---

following his death. Abijah probably served under or alongside Rehoboam, just as Solomon had served under David (1Ch 23:1).

12:2 *Egypt.* Egypt was beginning to recover from a long period of decline and wanted to reestablish control over Israel. God used their ambitions to discipline Rehoboam for abandoning the Lord.

12:3 *Lubim . . . Sukkiim.* The Lubim were the Libyans, and the Sukkiim were other desert tribes, probably from western Libya. ***Ethiopians.*** These famous warriors, sometimes referred to as Cushites, originated in the lands south of Egypt.

12:6 Righteousness — The king and princes of Judah recognized that the Lord was righteous, even in leaving them in the hands of Shishak. What they did not know, was the difference between being the "vassal" of the righteous Lord, and the vassal of the unrighteous Shishak. Like the Israelites, we count on the righteousness and graciousness of the Lord toward us. It is good to know that He is unfailing in His lovingkindness, but it is not something to presume upon, as if our conforming to His image does not really matter.

12:9 *took the treasures.* Judah was now a vassal state of Egypt.

CHAPTER 12 **1** 2Ch 11:17; 1Ki 14:22-24 **2** 1Ki 14:24,25 **3** 2Ch 16:8 **5** 2Ch 11:2 **6** Jas 4:10; Ex 9:27 **7** 1Ki 21:28,29 **8** See Isa 26:13; Dt 28:47,48 **9** 1Ki 14:25,26; 1Ki 10:16,17; 2Ch 9:15,16 **10** 1Ki 14:27 **13** 1Ki 14:21; 2Ch 6:6

Rehoboam was forty-one years old
when he began to reign, and he reigned
seventeen years in Jerusalem, the city
in which the LORD had chosen from all
the tribes of Israel to put His Name.
And his mother was Naamah the Am-
monitess.
14He did evil because he did not set
his heart to seek *and* worship *and* hon-
or the LORD.
15Now the acts of Rehoboam, from
the first to the last, are they not written
in the records of Shemaiah the proph-
et and of Iddo the seer, according to
genealogical enrollment? *There were*
wars between Rehoboam [of Judah]
and Jeroboam [of Israel] continually.
16And Rehoboam slept with his fa-
thers [in death] and was buried in the
City of David; and Abijah his son be-
came king in his place.

Abijah Succeeds Rehoboam

13 IN THE eighteenth year of King
Jeroboam, Abijah became king
over Judah.
2He reigned three years in Jerusa-
lem. His mother's name was Micaiah
the daughter of Uriel of Gibeah.
And there was war between Abijah
and Jeroboam [of Israel].
3Abijah began the battle with an
army of brave soldiers, 400,000 cho-
sen men. Jeroboam drew up in battle
formation against him with 800,000
chosen men, valiant men.

Civil War

4Then Abijah stood on Mount Ze-
maraim, which is in the hill country
of Ephraim, and said, "Listen to me,
Jeroboam and all Israel:
5"Do you not know that the LORD
God of Israel, gave rule over Israel
forever to David and to his sons by a
covenant of salt [a permanent pact, ex-
tending to each generation of Israel]?
[Num 18:19]
6"Yet Jeroboam the son of Nebat, a
servant of Solomon the son of David,
rose up and rebelled against his lord
[the king],
7and worthless (unprincipled, un-
ethical) men gathered around him,
useless *and* wicked men, who proved
too strong for Rehoboam the son of
Solomon when Rehoboam was young
and timid, and could not assert himself
against them.
8"And now you intend to assert your-
selves against the kingdom of the LORD
which is in the hands of the sons of
David, since you are a great multitude
and have with you the golden calves
(idols) which Jeroboam made for you
as gods.
9"Have you not driven out the priests
of the LORD, the sons of Aaron and the

13:2 *His mother's name was Micaiah.* Micaiah is a variation of "Maacah." She is the daughter of "Uriel of Gibeah" in this passage, as well as the "daughter of Absalom" (11:21). It is thought that she was the granddaughter of Absalom, the daughter of Uriel of Gibeah and Absalom's daughter Tamar (2Sa 14:27). The terms "father, mother, son, daughter" were often used in talking of ancestors instead of generations. Jesus is referred to as the "son of David" (Mt 9:27; 15:22; 22:42), which is clearly a reference to his ancestry.
13:5 *covenant of salt.* Salt was a preservative and symbolized durability, so a covenant of salt was one that would not be broken. Sometimes covenant makers each took a pinch of salt and mixed it, to show that just as the salt could not be separated, so the promise could not be set aside.
13:6 *Yet Jeroboam.* The throne had been promised to David's line forever, yet the promise was contingent on the faithfulness of his descendents (7:18 – 19). Because Solomon had turned from God, part of the kingdom was taken from him, and Jeroboam was chosen by God through the prophet Ahijah to rule over the part of the kingdom that was taken from Solomon (10:2). So far this story mirrors the events in the lives of Saul and David. But unlike David, Jeroboam did not wait for the Lord to deliver the promised kingdom to him. Jeroboam took his place by force, and immediately turned from God. His name became a byword, synonymous with "bad king." (See also 1Ki 11 – 14.)
13:7 *when Rehoboam was young and timid.* Abijah's version of the nation's division put his father in a relatively good light. Rehoboam was 41 years old when he became king (12:13).

15 2Ch 9:29; 13:22; 1Ki 14:30 **CHAPTER 13** **1** 1Ki 15:1 **2** See 2Ch 11:20 **4** Jos 18:22 **5** 2Sa 7:12,13,16; Nu 18:19 **6** 1Ki 11:26; 12:20 **7** Jdg 9:4 **8** 1Ki 12:28; 14:9; Hos 8:6 **9** 2Ch 11:14,15; Ex 29:35

Levites, and made priests for your-
selves like the peoples of *other* lands?
So whoever comes to consecrate him-
self with a young bull and seven rams,
even he may become a priest of non-
existent gods (idols).
10 “But as for us, the LORD is our God,
and we have not abandoned (turned
away from) Him. The sons of Aaron
are ministering to the LORD as priests,
and the Levites attend to their service.
11 “Every morning and every evening
they offer the burnt offerings and the
fragrant incense to the LORD; and the
showbread is set on the clean table [of
pure gold], and the golden lampstand
with its lamps is ready to light every
evening; for we keep the charge of the
LORD our God [that is, the obligation we
have to Him], but you have abandoned
(turned away from) Him.
12 “Behold, God is with us at our head,
and His priests [are here] with their
signal trumpets to sound an alarm
against you. O sons of Israel, do not
fight against the LORD God of your
fathers, for you cannot succeed.”
13 But Jeroboam had set an ambush
to come from the rear, so that Israel
was in front of Judah and the ambush
was behind them.
14 When [the men of] Judah turned
around, they were attacked from both
front and rear; so they cried out to the
LORD [for help], and the priests blew
the trumpets.
15 Then the men of Judah raised a
war cry; and as they shouted, God
struck Jeroboam and all Israel [with
defeat] before Abijah and Judah.
16 And the sons of Israel fled before
Judah, and God handed over the sons
of Israel to them.
17 Abijah and his people inflicted on
them a great defeat, so that 500,000
chosen men of Israel fell slain.
18 Thus the sons of Israel were sub-
dued (humbled) at that time, and the
sons of Judah prevailed because they
relied on the LORD, the God of their
fathers.
19 Abijah pursued Jeroboam and cap-
tured [several] cities from him: Bethel,
Jeshanah, and Ephraim (Ephron), with
their villages.

Death of Jeroboam

20 Jeroboam did not recover strength
again during the time of [the reign of]
Abijah. And the LORD struck him and
he died.
21 But Abijah became powerful. He
took fourteen wives for himself and
fathered twenty-two sons and sixteen
daughters.
22 Now the rest of the acts of Abijah,
and his ways and his sayings, are writ-
ten in the writing of the prophet Iddo.

Asa Succeeds Abijah in Judah

14 SO ABIJAH slept with his fa-
thers [in death], and they buried
him in the City of David; and Asa his
son became king in his place. The land
was at peace for ten years during his
days.
2 Asa did what was good and right in
the sight of the LORD his God.
3 He removed the foreign altars and
high places and tore down the [pagan]
pillars (obelisks, memorial stones), and
cut to pieces the Asherim [the symbols
of the goddess Asherah].
4 And he commanded Judah to
seek the LORD God of their fathers [to

14:2 – 4 Faithfulness — King Asa chose to be faithful to God as he began his reign. His people enjoyed ten years of peace because of Asa's obedience. For each one of us there is a peace that comes with faithfulness to God. This does not necessarily mean that outer circumstances are uncomplicated, but in our hearts the peace of God can still reign. Like Asa, our actions affect the lives of those around us. We are created to have an eternal relationship with God, and that begins in the life of faith, believing that He is who He says He is and that we need Him. "Now faith is the assurance of things hoped for, and the evidence of things not seen" (Heb 11:1).

14:3 *pillars.* Sacred pillars were stone posts associated with Canaanite fertility rites. ***Asherim.*** Asherah was a Canaanite goddess associated with Baal worship. Asherim were the poles, trees, or groves that were symbolic parts of Asherah worship.

---

11 2Ch 2:4; Lev 24:6; Ex 27:20,21; Lev 24:2,3 **12** Nu 10:8 **15** 2Ch 14:12 **18** 1Ch 5:20; Ps 22:5 **19** Jos 15:9 **20** 1Sa 25:38; 1Ki 14:20 **22** 2Ch 12:15 **CHAPTER 14** **1** 1Ki 15:8 **3** See 1Ki 15:14; 2Ch 15:17; Ex 34:13; 1Ki 11:7

inquire of and for Him and seek Him
as a vital necessity], and to observe
the law [given to Moses] and the com-
mandment.
5 Asa also removed the [idolatrous]
high places and the incense altars from
all the cities of Judah. The kingdom
was at rest *and* undisturbed under
his reign.
6 He built fortified cities in Judah,
since the land was at rest, and there
was no one at war with him in those
years, because the LORD had given him
rest.
7 So he said to Judah, "Let us build
these cities and surround them with
walls, towers, gates and bars [to se-
cure the doors]. The land is still ours
because we have sought the LORD our
God; we have sought Him [longing for
Him with all our heart] and He has
given us peace on every side." So they
built and prospered.
8 Now Asa had an army of 300,000
men from Judah, who carried large
shields and spears, and 280,000 from
Benjamin, who carried shields and
drew bows, all courageous men.
9 Now Zerah the Ethiopian (Cushite)
came out against Judah with an army
of a million men and three hundred
chariots, and he came as far as Mare-
shah.
10 Then Asa went out against him,
and they drew up in battle formation in
the Valley of Zephathah at Mareshah.
11 Asa called out to the LORD his God,
saying, "O LORD, there is no one be-
sides You to help *in the battle* between
the powerful and the weak; so help us,
O LORD our God, for we trust in *and*
rely on You, and in Your name we have
come against this multitude. O LORD,
You are our God; let not man prevail
against You."
12 So the LORD struck the Ethiopians
[with defeat] before Asa and Judah,
and the Ethiopians fled.
13 Asa and the people who were with
him pursued them as far as Gerar; and
so many Ethiopians fell that none of
them *were found* alive; for they were
destroyed before the LORD and His
army. And they carried away a very
large amount of spoil.
14 They attacked *and* destroyed all
the cities around Gerar, for the dread
of the LORD had fallen on them. They
plundered all the cities, for there was
a large amount of spoil in them.
15 They also struck down the people
[living] in tents who had livestock, and
took captive large numbers of sheep
and camels. Then they returned to
Jerusalem.

The Prophet Azariah Warns Asa

15 NOW THE Spirit of God came on
Azariah the son of Oded,
2 and he went out to meet Asa and
said to him, "Hear me, Asa, and all
Judah and Benjamin: the LORD is with
you while you are with Him. If you
seek Him [inquiring for and of Him,
as your soul's first necessity], He will
let you find Him; but if you abandon
(turn away from) Him, He will aban-
don (turn away from) you.
3 "Now for a long time Israel was
without the true God and without a
teaching priest, and without [God's]
law.
4 "But when they were in their trouble
and distress they turned to the LORD
God of Israel, and [in desperation ear-
nestly] sought Him, and He let them
find Him.
5 "In those times there was no peace
for him who went out or for him who

14:9 *Zerah the Ethiopian.* Since Egypt was strong at this time (12:3) and fully in control of its own territory, it is likely that Zerah and his large army were mercenaries of the Egyptian king Osorkon I (914 – 874 BC), successor of Shishak. ***Mareshah.*** Mareshah was one of Asa's important fortified cities, about 25 miles southwest of Jerusalem (11:8). It was near the Via Maris, the coastal highway connecting Egypt and Canaan, making it strategically important.
14:13 *Gerar.* Gerar was at the frontier between Egypt and Canaan and might have been in Egyptian territory at this time.

9 2Ch 16:8; Jos 15:44 **11** Ex 14:10; 2Ch 13:14; Ps 22:5; 1Sa 14:6 **12** 2Ch 13:15 **13** Ge 10:19; 20:1 **14** Ge 35:5; 2Ch 17:10 **CHAPTER 15** **1** Nu 24:2; Jdg 3:10; 2Ch 20:14 **2** Jas 4:8; ver. 4,15; 1Ch 28:9; 2Ch 33:12,13; Jer 29:13; Mt 7:7; 2Ch 24:20 **3** Hos 3:4; Lev 10:11 **4** Dt 4:29

came in, for great suffering came on
all the inhabitants of the lands.
6 "Nation was crushed by nation, and
city by city, for God troubled them with
every kind of distress.
7 "But as for you, be strong and do
not lose courage, for there is reward
for your work."

Asa's Reforms

8 And when Asa heard these words,
the prophecy of Azariah the son of
Oded the prophet, he took courage and
removed the repulsive idols from all
the land of Judah and Benjamin and
from the cities which he had captured
in the hill country of Ephraim. Then
he restored the altar [of burnt offering]
of the LORD which was in front of the
porch [of the temple] of the LORD.
9 He gathered all Judah and Benjamin
and the strangers who were with
them out of Ephraim, Manasseh, and
Simeon, for they came over to Asa
from Israel in large numbers when
they saw that the LORD his God was
with him.
10 So they assembled at Jerusalem in
the third month of the fifteenth year of
Asa's reign.
11 They sacrificed to the LORD on
that day from the spoil they had
brought—700 oxen and 7,000 sheep.
12 They entered into a covenant (solemn
agreement) to seek the LORD God
of their fathers with all their heart
and soul;
13 and that whoever would not seek
the LORD God of Israel, was to be put
to death, whether young or old, man
or woman.
14 They swore an oath to the LORD
with a loud voice, with [jubilant] shouting,
with trumpets, and with horns.
15 All Judah rejoiced over the oath,
for they had sworn with all their heart
and had sought Him with their whole
heart, and He let them find Him. So
the LORD gave them rest on every side.
16 He also removed Maacah, King
Asa's mother, from *the position of*
queen mother, because she had made a
repulsive image for [the goddess] Asherah.
Asa cut down her idol, crushed it,
and burned it at the Brook Kidron.
17 But the high places [of pagan worship]
were not removed from Israel.
Nevertheless Asa's heart was blameless
all his days.
18 He brought the things that his father
[Abijah] had dedicated and those
things that he had dedicated into the
house of God—silver and gold and
utensils.
19 And there was no war until the
thirty-fifth year of Asa's reign.

Asa Wars against Baasha

16 IN THE thirty-sixth year of Asa's
reign Baasha king of Israel came
up against Judah and fortified Ramah
in order to prevent *anyone* from going
out or coming in to [meet with] Asa
king of Judah.
2 Then Asa brought out silver and
gold from the treasuries of the house
of the LORD and from the king's house,
and sent them to Ben-hadad king of
Aram (Syria), who lived in Damascus,
saying,
3 "*Let there be* a treaty between you
and me, as there was between my father
and your father. Look, I am sending
you silver and gold; go, break your

15:10 *third month.* This quite likely locates this festival at the time of the firstfruits, the Feast of Pentecost (Lev 23:15 – 21; Nu 28:26 – 31).
15:16 *Maacah.* It appears that "mother" is used in the sense of ancestress; Maacah was the mother of Asa's father, Abijah (13:2). Still, Asa demoted her from her position as queen mother because she set up pagan idols — a courageous and delicate task for anyone, even a king.
15:17 Perseverance — Asa started his reign with a determination to serve the Lord and to abolish idol worship. Oded the prophet spurred him on to finish the job, to get rid of idols in his land and the land just captured. Paul talks about fighting the good fight, finishing the course, keeping the faith (2Ti 4:7). We all need people like Oded in our lives, who encourage us to keep on being faithful. In the same manner, we need to encourage others to persevere to the end.

6 Mt 24:7 **8** 2Ch 13:19 **9** 2Ch 11:16 **11** 2Ch 14:15; 2Ch 14:13 **12** 2Ki 23:3; 2Ch 34:31; Neh 10:29 **13** Ex 22:20; Dt 13:5,9,15 **15** ver. 2 **16** 1Ki 15:13 **17** 2Ch 14:3,5; 1Ki 15:14 **CHAPTER 16** **1** 1Ki 15:17; 2Ch 15:9

treaty with Baasha king of Israel, so
that he will withdraw from me."
4 Ben-hadad listened to King Asa and
sent the commanders of his armies
against the cities of Israel; and they
attacked *and* conquered Ijon, Dan,
Abel-maim, and all the storage cities
of Naphtali.
5 When Baasha heard about it, he
ceased fortifying Ramah and stopped
his work.
6 Then King Asa brought all Judah,
and they carried away the stones of
Ramah and its timber with which Baa-
sha had been building, and with them
he fortified Geba and Mizpah.

Asa Imprisons the Prophet

7 At that time Hanani the seer came
to Asa king of Judah and said to him,
"Because you relied on the king of
Aram (Syria) and did not rely on the
LORD your God, the army of the king
of Aram (Syria) has escaped out of
your hand.
8 "Were not the Ethiopians and Lu-
bim a huge army with a great number
of chariots and horsemen? Yet because
you relied on the LORD, He placed them
in your hand.
9 "For the eyes of the LORD move to
and fro throughout the earth so that
He may support those whose heart is
completely His. You have acted fool-
ishly in this; therefore, from now on
you will have wars."
10 Then Asa was angry with the seer
and put him in prison [in the stocks],
for he was enraged with him because
of this. And at the same time Asa op-
pressed some of the people.
11 Now the acts of Asa, from the first
to the last, are written in the Book of
the Kings of Judah and Israel.
12 In the thirty-ninth year of his reign
Asa developed a disease in his feet.
His disease was severe, yet even in his
illness he did not seek the LORD, but
[relied only on] the physicians.
13 So Asa slept with his fathers [in
death], dying in the forty-first year of
his reign.
14 They buried him in his own tomb
which he had cut out for himself in the
City of David, and they laid him on a
bier which he had filled with various
kinds of spices blended by the perfum-
ers' art; and they made a very great
fire in his honor.

Jehoshaphat Succeeds Asa

17 JEHOSHAPHAT HIS son then
became king [of Judah] in Asa's
place, and strengthened his position
over Israel.
2 He placed troops in all the fortified
cities of Judah, and set garrisons in
the land of Judah and in the cities of
Ephraim which his father Asa had
captured.

His Good Reign

3 The LORD was with Jehoshaphat
because he followed the example of
his father (ancestor) David. He did not
seek [to follow] the Baals [the false
gods],
4 but sought the God of his father,
and walked in (obeyed) His command-
ments, and did not act as Israel did.
5 Therefore the LORD established the
kingdom in his hand; and all Judah
brought tribute to Jehoshaphat, and he
had great wealth and honor.
6 His heart was encouraged *and* he
took great pride in the ways of the
LORD; moreover, he again removed the
high places [of pagan worship] and the
Asherim from Judah.

16:6 *Geba and Mizpah.* Geba was just east of Ramah, and Mizpah was between Ramah and Bethel. Fortifying these two cities effectively stopped Israel from rebuilding Ramah because it was now between two of Asa's fortresses.

16:7–9 *Hanani the seer.* Hanani was probably the father of another prophet, Jehu, who once challenged King Jehoshaphat of Judah (19:2; 20:34).

17:2 *cities of Ephraim.* Ephraim is a synonym for Israel. The cities referred to here are mentioned also in 15:8.

7 1Ki 16:1; 2Ch 19:2; Isa 31:1; Jer 17:5 **8** 2Ch 14:9; 2Ch 12:3 **9** Job 34:21; Pr 5:21; 15:3; Jer 16:17; 32:19; Zec 4:10; 1Sa 13:13; 1Ki 15:32 **10** 2Ch 18:26; Jer 20:2; Mt 14:3 **11** 1Ki 15:23 **12** Jer 17:5 **13** 1Ki 15:24 **14** Ge 50:2; Mk 16:1; Jn 19:39,40; 2Ch 21:19; Jer 34:5 **CHAPTER 17** **1** 1Ki 15:24 **2** 2Ch 15:8 **4** 1Ki 12:28 **5** 1Sa 10:27; 1Ki 10:25; 1Ki 10:27; 2Ch 18:1 **6** 1Ki 22:43; 2Ch 15:17; 19:3; 20:33

[7]Then in the third year of his reign
he sent his officials, Ben-hail, Obadiah,
Zechariah, Nethanel, and Micaiah, to
teach in the cities of Judah;
[8]and with them were the Levites—
Shemaiah, Nethaniah, Zebadiah,
Asahel, Shemiramoth, Jehonathan,
Adonijah, Tobijah, and Tobadonijah;
and with them the priests Elishama
and Jehoram.
[9]They taught in Judah *having* the
Book of the Law of the LORD with them;
they went throughout all the cities of
Judah and taught among the people.
[10]Now the dread of the LORD was
on all the kingdoms of the lands sur-
rounding Judah, so that they did not
make war against Jehoshaphat.
[11]Some of the Philistines brought
gifts and silver as tribute to Je-
hoshaphat; the Arabians also brought
him flocks: 7,700 rams and 7,700 male
goats.
[12]So Jehoshaphat became greater
and greater. He built fortresses and
storage cities in Judah.
[13]He had large supplies in the cities
of Judah, and soldiers, courageous
men, in Jerusalem.
[14]This was the number of them by
their fathers' (ancestors') households:
of Judah, the commanders of thou-
sands, Adnah the commander, and
with him 300,000 courageous men;
[15]and next to him was Jehohanan
the commander, and with him 280,000;
[16]and next to him Amasiah the son of
Zichri, who volunteered for the LORD,
and with him 200,000 courageous men;
[17]and of Benjamin: Eliada, a brave
man, and with him 200,000 men armed
with bow and shield;
[18]and next to him was Jehozabad,
and with him 180,000 armed *and* ready
for military service.
[19]These are the ones who were in the
service of the king, besides those he
had placed in fortified cities through-
out Judah.

Jehoshaphat Allies with Ahab

18 NOW JEHOSHAPHAT had
great wealth and honor, and was
allied by marriage with Ahab.
[2]Some years later he went down to
[visit] Ahab in Samaria. And Ahab
slaughtered many sheep and oxen for
him and the people who were with
him, and induced him to go up against
Ramoth-gilead.
[3]Ahab king of Israel said to Je-
hoshaphat king of Judah, "Will you
go with me to [fight against] Ramoth-
gilead?" He answered, "I am as you
are, and my people as your people
[your hopes and concerns are ours];
we will be with you in the battle."
[4]Further, Jehoshaphat said to the
king of Israel, "Please inquire first for
the word of the LORD."
[5]Then the king of Israel assembled
the prophets, four hundred men, and
said to them, "Shall we go against
Ramoth-gilead to battle, or shall I re-
frain?" And they said, "Go up, for God
will hand it over to the king."
[6]But Jehoshaphat said, "Is there no
prophet of the LORD still here by whom
we may inquire?"
[7]The king of Israel said to Je-
hoshaphat, "There is still one man by
whom we may inquire of the LORD,
but I hate him, for he never prophesies
[anything] good for me, but always
evil. He is Micaiah the son of Imla"
And Jehoshaphat said, "Let not the

17:13 – 18 *soldiers, courageous men.* Jehoshaphat's men were grouped into three divisions of Judeans with a total number of 780,000 and two divisions of Benjamites numbering 380,000. The Hebrew word for thousand can mean family, or clan (Jdg 6:15; 1Sa 10:19; Mic 5:2). In that case, the 780,000 would be 780 companies, and the 380,000 would be 380 companies, and the total warriors would be nearer to 78,000 and 38,000.

18:2 *Ramoth-gilead.* This important city was some 35 miles east of Beth-shan, and was controlled by the Arameans. It was also one of the Israelite cities of refuge (Jos 20:8; 1Ch 6:80).

18:5 *the prophets.* These prophets were probably prophets of Baal or Asherah (1Ki 18:19), the Canaanite gods worshiped by Ahab's wife Jezebel.

7 2Ch 15:3 **9** 2Ch 35:3; Neh 8:7 **10** Ge 35:5 **11** 2Sa 8:2 **16** Jdg 5:2,9 **19** ver. 2 **CHAPTER 18 1** 2Ch 17:5; 2Ki 8:18 **2** 1Ki 22:2 **4** 1Sa 23:2,4,9; 2Sa 2:1

king say so [perhaps this time it will
be different]."

Ahab's False Prophets Assure Victory

8 Then the king of Israel called for
an officer and said, "Bring Micaiah
the son of Imla quickly."
9 Now the king of Israel and Je-
hoshaphat the king of Judah were
sitting, each on his throne, arrayed
in their robes; they were sitting at the
threshing floor at the entrance of the
gate of Samaria; and all the prophets
were prophesying before them.
10 Zedekiah the son of Chenaanah
had made horns of iron for himself;
and said, "Thus says the LORD: 'With
these you shall gore the Arameans
(Syrians) until they are destroyed.' "
11 All the prophets prophesied this,
saying, "Go up to Ramoth-gilead and
succeed; the LORD will hand it over to
the king."

Micaiah Brings Word from God

12 The messenger who went to call
Micaiah said to him, "Listen, the words
of the prophets are of one accord, *fore-
telling a* favorable *outcome* for the
king. So just let your word be like one
of them and speak favorably."
13 But Micaiah said, "As the LORD
lives, I will [only] speak what my God
says."
14 When he came to the king, the
king said to him, "Micaiah, shall we
go to Ramoth-gilead to battle, or shall
I refrain?" And he said, "Go up and
succeed, for they will be handed over
to you."
15 Then the king said to him, "How
many times must I warn you (make
you swear an oath) to tell me nothing
but the truth in the name of the LORD?"
16 Then Micaiah said,

"I saw all [the people of] Israel
Scattered on the mountains,
As sheep that have no shepherd;
And the LORD said,
'These have no master.
Let each one return to his house in
peace.' "

17 Then the king of Israel said to Je-
hoshaphat, "Did I not tell you that he
would not prophesy good in regard to
me, but [only] evil?"
18 So Micaiah said, "Therefore, hear
the word of the LORD: I saw the LORD
sitting on His throne, and all the host
(army) of heaven standing on His right
and on His left.
19 "Then the LORD said, 'Who will
entice Ahab king of Israel to go up and
fall [defeated] at Ramoth-gilead?' And
one said this and another said that.
20 "Then a spirit came forward and
stood before the LORD and said, 'I will
entice him.' The LORD said to him, 'By
what means?'
21 "He said, 'I will go out and be a
deceptive spirit in the mouth of all his
prophets.' Then the LORD said, 'You
are to entice him and also succeed.
Go and do so.'
22 "Now, you see, the LORD put a decep-
tive spirit in the mouth of these prophets
of yours; and the LORD has [actually]
proclaimed disaster against you."
23 Then Zedekiah the son of Che-
naanah came up and struck Micaiah
on the cheek and said, "Which way
did the Spirit of the LORD go [when he
departed] from me to speak to you?"

18:11 *prophesied.* The true prophet's words come directly from God, and they show God's thoughts, and sometimes His plans. These false prophets were speaking authoritatively, probably accompanied with such ravings and demonstrations as would show their power and ability to see the future (1Ki 18:26–29).

18:15 *nothing but the truth.* Ahab knew from experience that his prophets told him what they thought he wanted to hear, not the truth. Because their prophecies agreed with Micaiah's, he knew that Micaiah must have been mocking when he prophesied success.

18:22 *deceptive spirit.* The spirits who stood before the Lord were both angels and demons, none of whom could act without God's permission. God allowed this spirit to work in the mouths of the false prophets to accomplish His own purposes of judgment (1Ch 21:1; Job 1).

13 Nu 22:18,20,35; 23:12,26; 24:13; 1Ki 22:14 **20** Job 1:6 **22** Job 12:16; Isa 19:14; Eze 14:9 **23** Jer 20:2; Mk 14:65; Ac 23:2

24 Micaiah said, "Behold, you will see on that day when you go into an inner room [desperately trying] to hide yourself."

25 Then the king of Israel said, "Take Micaiah and return him to Amon the governor of the city and to Joash the king's son,

26 and say, 'Thus says the king: "Put this man in prison and feed him just enough bread and water to survive until I return in peace (safely)." ' "

27 But Micaiah said, "If you actually return in peace, the LORD has not spoken by me." And he added, "Listen [to what I have said], you people, all of you."

Ahab's Defeat and Death

28 So [Ahab] the king of Israel and Jehoshaphat king of Judah went up against Ramoth-gilead.

29 The king of Israel said to Jehoshaphat, "I will disguise myself and will go into battle, but you put on your [royal] robes." So the king of Israel disguised himself, and they went into the battle.

30 Now the king of Aram (Syria) had commanded the captains of his chariots, saying, "Do not fight with the small or the great, but only with the king of Israel."

31 So when the captains of the chariots saw Jehoshaphat [of Judah], they said, "It is the king of Israel!" So they turned to fight against him, but Jehoshaphat called out [for God's help], and the LORD helped him; and God diverted them away from him.

32 When the captains of the chariots saw that it was not the king of Israel, they turned back from pursuing him.

33 Then a certain man drew his bow at random and struck [Ahab] the king of Israel between the scales of *his* armor. So Ahab said to his chariot driver, "Turn around and take me out of the battle, because I am seriously wounded."

34 The battle raged that day, and the king of Israel propped himself up in his chariot in front of the Arameans (Syrians) until the evening, and at sunset he died.

Jehu Rebukes Jehoshaphat

19 JEHOSHAPHAT THE king of Judah returned safely to his house (palace) in Jerusalem.

2 Jehu the son of Hanani the seer went out to meet him and said to King Jehoshaphat, "Should you help the ungodly and love those who hate the LORD and in doing so *bring* wrath from the LORD on yourself?

3 "But there are *some* good things found in you, for you have removed the Asherim (idols) from the land and you have set your heart to seek God [with all your soul's desire]."

4 So Jehoshaphat lived in Jerusalem, and he went out again among the people from Beersheba to the hill country of Ephraim and brought them back to the LORD, the God of their fathers.

Reforms Instituted

5 He appointed judges in the land in all the fortified cities of Judah, city by city,

6 and he said to the judges, "Be careful what you do, for you do not judge for man, but for the LORD who is with you in the matter of judgment.

7 "So now let the fear (reverent awe) of the LORD be on you [to keep you from making unjust decisions]; be careful in what you do, for there is no injustice

---

18:33 *at random.* From the human perspective, this was a chance shot. From God's perspective, chance had no part in it. Ahab's disguise could not foil God's plan.

19:3 Repentance — Repentance is never by word only. It is always followed by actions which show that the attitude of repentance is really present. Part of repentance is acknowledging that God is right and that He knows how we should live. It was the change in Jehoshaphat's actions that proved his change of heart.

19:4 *hill country of Ephraim.* The mountains of Ephraim became the northern border of Judah after the division into two kingdoms. This is another way of saying that the whole country was brought back to the Lord.

26 2Ch 16:10 **CHAPTER 19** **2** 1Sa 9:9; Ps 139:21; 2Ch 32:25 **3** 2Ch 17:4,6; 2Ch 30:19; Ezr 7:10 **6** Dt 1:17; Ps 82:1; Ecc 5:8 **7** Dt 32:4; Ro 9:14; Dt 10:17; Job 34:19; Ac 10:34; Ro 2:11; Gal 2:6; Eph 6:9; Col 3:25

with the LORD our God, or partiality, or acceptance of a bribe."

8 In Jerusalem also Jehoshaphat appointed some of the Levites, priests, and heads of the fathers' *households* of Israel to *render* the judgment of the LORD and to judge disputes among the inhabitants of Jerusalem.

9 Then the king commanded them, "Do this in the fear of the LORD, faithfully and wholeheartedly.

10 "Whenever any dispute comes to you from your brothers (relatives) who live in their cities, between blood and blood, between law and commandment, or between statutes and judgments, you are to warn [and instruct] them so that they may not be guilty before the LORD; otherwise [God's] wrath will come on you and your brothers. Do this and you will not be guilty.

11 "Behold, Amariah the chief priest will be over you in all matters of the LORD, and Zebadiah the son of Ishmael, the governor of the house of Judah, in all the king's matters; and the Levites will serve you as officers. Deal courageously, and may the LORD be with the upright."

Judah Invaded

20 NOW IT happened after this that the Moabites and the Ammonites, together with some of the Meunites, came to make war against Jehoshaphat.

2 Then it was reported to Jehoshaphat, "A great multitude has come against you from beyond the [Dead] Sea, out of Aram (Syria); and behold, they are in Hazazon-tamar (that is, Engedi)."

3 Then Jehoshaphat was afraid and set himself [determinedly, as his vital need] to seek the LORD; and he proclaimed a fast throughout all Judah.

4 So [the people of] Judah gathered together to seek help from the LORD; indeed they came from all the cities of Judah to seek the LORD [longing for Him with all their heart].

Jehoshaphat's Prayer

5 Then Jehoshaphat stood in the assembly of Judah and Jerusalem, in the house of the LORD in front of the new courtyard,

6 and said, "O LORD, God of our fathers, are You not God in heaven? And do You not rule over all the kingdoms of the nations? Power and might are in Your hand, there is no one able to take a stand against You.

7 "O our God, did You not drive out the inhabitants of this land before Your people Israel and give it forever to the descendants of Your friend Abraham?

8 "They have lived in it, and have built You a sanctuary in it for Your Name, saying,

9 'If evil comes on us, or the sword of judgment, or plague, or famine, we will stand before this house and before You (for Your Name *and* Your Presence is in this house) and we will cry out to You in our distress, and You will hear and save us.'

10 "Now behold, the sons of Ammon and Moab and Mount Seir, whom You would not allow Israel to invade when they came from the land of Egypt (for they turned away from them and did not destroy them), [Deut 2:9]

11 here they are, rewarding us by coming to drive us out of Your possession which You have given us as an inheritance.

12 "O our God, will You not judge them? For we are powerless against this great multitude which is coming against us. We do not know what to do, but our eyes are on You."

13 So all Judah stood before the LORD, with their infants, their wives, and their children.

Jahaziel Answers the Prayer

14 Then in the midst of the assembly the Spirit of the LORD came upon Jahaziel the son of Zechariah, the son

---

20:14 ***Jahaziel.*** As a member of the Asaph division of the Levites (1Ch 6:39; 15:17 – 19; 16:7) Jahaziel was probably a musician. The spiritual work of the musicians was closely linked with prophecy (1Ch 25:1).

8 Dt 16:18; 2Ch 17:8 **9** 2Sa 23:3 **10** Dt 17:8; Nu 16:46; Eze 3:18 **11** 1Ch 26:30; 2Ch 15:2 **CHAPTER 20**
2 Ge 14:7; Jos 15:62 **3** 2Ch 19:3; Ezr 8:21; Jer 36:9; Jnh 3:5 **6** Ps 47:2,8; Da 4:17; 1Ch 29:12; Ps 62:11; Mt 6:13
7 Ge 17:7; Ex 6:7; Ps 44:2; Isa 41:8; Jas 2:23 **9** 1Ki 8:33,37; 2Ch 6:28-30; 2Ch 6:20 **10** Dt 2:4,9,19; Nu 20:21
11 Ps 83:12 **12** 1Sa 3:13; Ps 25:15; 121:1,2; 123:1,2; 141:8 **14** Nu 11:25,26; 24:2; 2Ch 15:1

of Benaiah, the son of Jeiel, the son of Mattaniah, a Levite of the sons of Asaph.

15He said, "Listen carefully, all [you people of] Judah, and you inhabitants of Jerusalem, and King Jehoshaphat. The LORD says this to you: 'Be not afraid or dismayed at this great multitude, for the battle is not yours, but God's.

16'Go down against them tomorrow. Behold, they will come up by the ascent of Ziz, and you will find them at the end of the river valley, in front of the Wilderness of Jeruel.

17'You *need* not fight in this *battle;* take your positions, stand and witness the salvation of the LORD who is with you, O Judah and Jerusalem. Do not fear or be dismayed; tomorrow go out against them, for the LORD is with you.' "

18Jehoshaphat bowed with his face to the ground, and all Judah and the inhabitants of Jerusalem fell down before the LORD, worshiping Him.

19The Levites, from the sons of the Kohathites and the sons of the Korahites, stood up to praise the LORD God of Israel, with a very loud voice.

Enemies Destroy Themselves

20So they got up early in the morning and went out into the Wilderness of Tekoa; and as they went out, Jehoshaphat stood and said, "Hear me, O Judah, and you inhabitants of Jerusalem! Believe *and* trust in the LORD your God and you will be established (secure). Believe *and* trust in His prophets and succeed."

21When he had consulted with the people, he appointed those who sang to the LORD and those who praised Him in their holy (priestly) attire, as they went out before the army and said, "Praise *and* give thanks to the LORD, for His mercy *and* lovingkindness endure forever."

22When they began singing and praising, the LORD set ambushes against the sons of Ammon, Moab, and Mount Seir, who had come against Judah; so they were struck down [in defeat].

23For the sons of Ammon and Moab [suspecting betrayal] rose up against the inhabitants of Mount Seir, completely destroying them; and when they had finished with the inhabitants of Seir, they helped to destroy one another.

24When [the men of] Judah came to the lookout tower of the wilderness, they looked toward the multitude, and behold, they were dead bodies lying on the ground, and no one had escaped.

25When Jehoshaphat and his people came to take their spoil, they found much among them, *including* equipment, garments, and valuable things which they took for themselves, more than they could carry away; so much that they spent three days gathering the spoil.

Triumphant Return to Jerusalem

26Then on the fourth day they assembled in the Valley of Beracah, for it was there that they blessed the LORD. For that reason they named that place "The Valley of Beracah (blessing)" until today.

27Then they returned to Jerusalem with joy, every man of Judah and

---

20:19 *Kohathites . . . Korahites.* The Kohathites were members of the Levitical division of Heman the singer (1Ch 6:33). The Korahites were a subdivision of the Kohathites (1Ch 6:37,39) who were employed as gatekeepers to the temple.

20:21 Thankfulness—More necessary than guns for soldiers, more important than strategy, is the giving of thanks to God. Judah faced a literal, physical battle involving great odds. They sent their singers out first, singing praises to God and thanking Him for His everlasting lovingkindness. Is this the way we face battles in our lives? Do we first thank God for who He is, what He has done, and for His faithfulness to us?

20:26 *Valley of Beracah.* The Judeans renamed Ziz "The valley of Beracah," meaning "blessing," to remind themselves of God's goodness.

15 Ex 14:13,14; Dt 1:29,30; 31:6,8; 2Ch 32:7 **17** Ex 14:13,14; Nu 14:9; 2Ch 15:2; 32:8 **18** Ex 4:31 **20** Isa 7:9
21 1Ch 16:29; 1Ch 16:34; Ps 136:1; 1Ch 16:41; 2Ch 5:13 **22** Jdg 7:22; 1Sa 14:20 **27** Neh 12:43

Jerusalem, led by Jehoshaphat, for the LORD had made them rejoice over their enemies.

28 They came to Jerusalem with harps, lyres, and trumpets to the house (temple) of the LORD.

29 And the fear of God came on all the kingdoms of those countries when they heard that the LORD had fought against the enemies of Israel.

30 So the kingdom of Jehoshaphat was quiet, for his God gave him rest on all sides.

31 Now Jehoshaphat reigned over Judah. He was thirty-five years old when he became king, and he reigned in Jerusalem for twenty-five years. His mother's name was Azubah the daughter of Shilhi.

32 He walked in the way of his father Asa and did not depart from it, doing what was right in the sight of the LORD.

33 Only the high places [for pagan sacrifices] were not removed, for the people had not yet set their hearts firmly on the God of their fathers.

34 Now the rest of the acts of Jehoshaphat, from the first to the last, behold, they are written in the records of Jehu the son of Hanani, which are recorded in the Book of the Kings of Israel.

Alliance Displeases God

35 After [all] this Jehoshaphat king of Judah made an alliance with Ahaziah king of Israel, and he acted wickedly in doing so.

36 He joined him in building ships to go to Tarshish [for trade], and they built them in Ezion-geber.

37 Then Eliezer the son of Dodavahu of Mareshah prophesied against Jehoshaphat, saying, "Because you have allied yourself with Ahaziah, the LORD has broken down what you have built." So the ships were wrecked and were unable to go to Tarshish.

Jehoram Succeeds Jehoshaphat in Judah

21 JEHOSHAPHAT SLEPT with his fathers [in death] and was buried with them in the City of David; and his son Jehoram became king in his place.

2 He had brothers, the sons of Jehoshaphat: Azariah, Jehiel, Zechariah, Azaryahu, Michael, and Shephatiah. All of these were the sons of Jehoshaphat king of Israel.

3 Their father gave them many gifts of silver, gold, and valuable things, in addition to fortified cities in Judah; but he gave the kingdom to Jehoram because he was the firstborn.

4 When Jehoram had ascended over the kingdom of his father and made himself secure, he killed all his brothers with the sword [to eliminate any rivals], and some of the leaders of Israel as well.

5 Jehoram was thirty-two years of age when he became king, and he reigned eight years in Jerusalem.

6 He walked in the way of the kings of Israel, just as the house of Ahab had done (for he married the daughter of Ahab), and he did what was evil in the sight of the LORD.

7 Yet the LORD would not destroy the house of David because of the covenant which He had made with David, and because He had promised to give a lamp to him and to his sons forever. [2 Sam 7:12–17; 1 Kin 11:36; Ps 132:17]

Revolt against Judah

8 In the days of Jehoram Edom revolted against the rule of Judah and set up a king over themselves.

9 Then Jehoram crossed over [the Jordan River] with his commanders

---

20:34 *Jehu.* The son of the prophet Hanani, Jehu was a prophet himself (19:2). He is mentioned in 1 Kings in connection with the kings of Israel, and was therefore a good source of information about both the Northern and Southern Kingdoms.

20:35 *Ahaziah.* Ahaziah was the son of Ahab. He succeeded his father and reigned for two years (1Ki 22:51). Ahaziah was injured in a fall and turned to the Philistine gods rather than to the Lord for healing (2Ki 1:2).

29 2Ch 17:10 **30** 2Ch 15:15; Job 34:29 **31** 1Ki 22:41 **33** See 2Ch 17:6; 2Ch 12:14; 19:3 **34** 1Ki 16:1,7 **35** 1Ki 22:48,49 **37** 1Ki 22:48; 2Ch 9:21 **CHAPTER 21** **1** 1Ki 22:50 **6** 2Ch 22:2 **7** 2Sa 7:12,13; 1Ki 11:36; 2Ki 8:19; Ps 132:11 **8** 2Ki 8:20

and all his chariots, and rose up by
night and struck down the Edomites
who were surrounding him and the
commanders of the chariots.
[10]So Edom revolted against the rule
of Judah to this day. Then Libnah re-
volted at the same time against Je-
horam's rule, because he had aban-
doned (turned away from) the LORD
God of his fathers.
[11]Moreover, he made [idolatrous]
high places in the hill country of Ju-
dah, and caused the inhabitants of
Jerusalem to be unfaithful [to God],
and he led Judah astray [compelling
the people's cooperation].
[12]Then a letter came to Jehoram from
Elijah the prophet, saying, "Thus says
the LORD God of David your father (an-
cestor): 'Because you have not walked
in the ways of your father Jehoshaphat
nor in the ways of Asa king of Judah,
[13]but have walked in the way of the
kings of Israel, and caused Judah and
the inhabitants of Jerusalem to be
unfaithful [to God] as the house of
Ahab was unfaithful, and you have
also murdered your brothers, your fa-
ther's house (your own family), who
were better than you,
[14]behold, the LORD is going to strike
your people, your sons, your wives,
and all your possessions with a great
disaster;
[15]and you will suffer a severe illness,
an intestinal disease, until your intes-
tines come out because of the sickness,
day after day.' "
[16]Then the LORD stirred up against
Jehoram the spirit (anger) of the Phi-
listines and of the Arabs who bordered
the Ethiopians.
[17]They came against Judah and
invaded it, and carried away all the
possessions found in the king's house
(palace), together with his sons and
his wives; so there was not a son left
to him except Jehoahaz, the youngest
of his sons.
[18]After all this, the LORD struck Je-
horam with an incurable intestinal
disease.
[19]Now it came about in the course
of time, at the end of two years, that
his intestines came out because of his
disease and he died in excruciating
pain. And his people did not make a
funeral fire *to honor* him, like the fire
for his fathers.
[20]Jehoram was thirty-two years old
when he became king, and he reigned
in Jerusalem eight years; and he de-
parted with no one's regret (sorrow).
They buried him in the City of David,
but not in the tombs of the kings.

Ahaziah Succeeds Jehoram in Judah

22 THEN THE inhabitants of Jeru-
salem made Ahaziah, his youn-
gest son, king in his place, because the
band of men (raiders) who came with
the Arabs to the camp had killed all
the older *sons*. So Ahaziah the son of
Jehoram king of Judah began to reign.
[2]Ahaziah was twenty-two years old
when he became king and he reigned
one year in Jerusalem. His mother's
name was Athaliah, a granddaughter
of Omri. [2 Kin 8:26]
[3]He also walked in the ways of the
house of Ahab, for his mother was his
adviser [and she encouraged him] to
act wickedly.

21:11 *be unfaithful.* Israel's relationship with God was like a marriage relationship. Worship of other gods was a violation in the same way that prostitution violates a marriage. It not only says that the true husband is not worthy of respect, it is a rejection of the whole idea of the faithfulness and care of the true husband.
21:12 *Elijah the prophet.* Though 1 and 2 Kings pay considerable attention to Elijah (1Ki 17:1 – 2Ki 2:18), the books of Chronicles mention him only here. He had been taken up into heaven after King Ahaziah's death (2Ki 1:17; 2:1).
21:20 *tombs of the kings.* These tombs were a royal cemetery in Jerusalem where most of the kings of David's dynasty were buried. (Asa was an exception, 16:14.)
22:1 *Ahaziah.* Ahaziah of Judah was the namesake of his uncle from Israel. His father Jehoram had married a sister of Ahab's son Ahaziah (1Ki 22:40; 2Ki 8:18).

11 Lev 20:5 **13** ver. 11; Ex 34:15; Dt 31:16; 1Ki 16:31-33; 2Ki 9:22; ver. 4 **15** ver. 18,19 **17** 2Ch 24:7 **18** ver. 15 **19** 2Ch 16:14 **CHAPTER 22** **1** ver. 6; 2Ch 21:17; 2Ch 21:17 **2** 2Ki 8:26; 2Ch 21:6

[4]So he did evil in the sight of the LORD like the house of Ahab, for they were his advisers after the death of his father, resulting in his destruction.

Ahaziah Allies with Jehoram of Israel

[5]He also walked in accordance with their advice, and he went with Jehoram the son of Ahab king of Israel to wage war against Hazael king of Aram (Syria) at Ramoth-gilead. And the Arameans wounded Joram (Jehoram). [2 Kin 8:28ff]

[6]Then he returned to Jezreel to recover from the wounds they had inflicted on him at Ramah when he fought against Hazael king of Aram. And Ahaziah, the son of Jehoram king of Judah, went down to see Jehoram the son of Ahab in Jezreel, because he was sick.

[7]But the downfall of Ahaziah was ordained by God, in that he went to Joram (Jehoram). For when he arrived there he went out [as an ally] with Jehoram against Jehu the son of Nimshi, whom the LORD had anointed to destroy the house of Ahab.

Jehu Murders Leaders of Judah

[8]It came about that when Jehu was executing judgment on the house of Ahab, he found the leaders of Judah and the sons of Ahaziah's [murdered] brothers ministering to Ahaziah, and he killed them.

[9]Jehu also searched for Ahaziah, who was hiding in Samaria; he was captured, brought to Jehu, and put to death. They buried him, for they said, "*After all*, he is the grandson of Jehoshaphat, who sought the LORD with all his heart." So the house of Ahaziah had no one *left* to retain the power to rule over the kingdom.

[10]Now when Athaliah the mother of Ahaziah saw that her son was dead, she rose and destroyed all the royal family of the house of Judah.

[11]But Jehoshabeath, the king's daughter, took Joash the [infant] son of Ahaziah and stole him away from among the king's sons who were being put to death, and she placed him and his nurse in the bedroom. So Jehoshabeath, the daughter of King Jehoram [of Judah] and wife of Jehoiada the priest, hid Joash from [his grandmother] Athaliah so that she did not murder him (for Jehoshabeath was the sister of Ahaziah).

[12]Joash was hidden with them in the house (temple) of God for six years, and Athaliah reigned over the land.

Jehoiada Sets Joash on the Throne of Judah

23 IN THE seventh year Jehoiada [the priest] summoned his courage and took the captains of hundreds: Azariah the son of Jeroham, Ishmael the son of Johanan, Azariah the son of Obed, Maaseiah the son of Adaiah, and Elishaphat the son of Zichri, *and they entered* into a covenant with him.

[2]They went throughout Judah and gathered the Levites out of all the

---

22:5 *Jehoram the son of Ahab.* Jehoram succeeded his brother Ahaziah because Ahaziah had no son of his own (2Ki 1:17). He is also called Joram, a short form of Jehoram, to distinguish him from his brother-in-law Jehoram who was king of Judah. ***Hazael.*** Hazael was the king of Damascus who came to power after assassinating Ben-hadad (2Ki 8:7 – 15). Elijah had prophesied that this would come about and had even commissioned Elisha to anoint Hazael to his new position (1Ki 19:15). Elisha wept after he had anointed Hazael, for he knew that Hazael would cruelly kill many Israelites. ***Ramoth-gilead.*** Ahab and Jehoshaphat had tried to recover this city from Aramean domination 12 years earlier (18:3).

22:10 *the royal family.* Most of the royal heirs that Athaliah murdered were her own grandchildren. She wanted to stamp out the Davidic dynasty and bring Judah back under Israelite control. Satan had been diligent in his attempts to thwart the plans of God, and because the Davidic line was directly linked to the Messiah, this would have been a strategic move. It is not unlike the murder of the baby boys by Herod at the time of Jesus' birth (Mt 2:10 – 18).

5 2Ki 8:28 **6** 2Ki 9:15 **7** Jdg 14:4; 1Ki 12:15; 2Ch 10:15; 2Ki 9:21; 2Ki 9:6,7 **8** 2Ki 10:10,11; 2Ki 10:13,14
9 2Ki 9:27; 2Ch 17:4 **10** 2Ki 11:1 **CHAPTER 23** **1** 2Ki 11:4

cities of Judah, and the heads of the *households of the* fathers (ancestors) in Israel, and they came to Jerusalem.

3 Then all the assembly made a covenant in the house of God with the king [that is, with the child Joash, to overthrow Athaliah by proclaiming his sovereignty]. And Jehoiada [the priest] said to them, "Behold, the king's son [Joash] shall reign, as the LORD has said in regard to the sons of David.

4 "This is what you shall do: a third of you, of the priests and Levites who are resuming service on the Sabbath, shall be gatekeepers,

5 a [second] third *shall be* at the king's house (palace), and a [final] third at the Gate of the Foundation; and all the people shall be in the courtyards of the house of the LORD.

6 "But let no one enter the house (temple) of the LORD except the priests and the Levites who minister; they may enter, for they are holy. And let all the people carefully observe the law of the LORD.

7 "The Levites shall surround the [young] king, every man with his weapons in his hand; and whoever comes into the temple [breaking through the ranks of the guard to get near Joash] is to be killed. You are to be with the king when he comes in [from the temple chamber where he is hiding] and when he goes out."

8 So the Levites and all Judah acted in accordance with everything that Jehoiada the priest had commanded; and every man took his men who were to resume duty on the Sabbath, with those who were to go off duty on the Sabbath, for Jehoiada the priest did not dismiss [any of] the divisions [from their duties].

9 Then Jehoiada the priest gave to the captains of hundreds the spears and the large and small shields which had been King David's, which were in the house of God.

10 He stationed all the people around the king [as guards for him], every man with his weapon in his hand, from the right side to the left side of the house (temple), by the altar and by the house.

11 Then they brought out the king's son and put the crown on him, and *gave him* the testimony [a copy of the Mosaic Law] and made him king. And Jehoiada and his sons anointed him and said, "*Long* live the king!" [Ex 25:16, 21]

Athaliah Killed

12 When Athaliah heard the sound of the people running and praising the king, she went into the house of the LORD to [see what] the people [were doing].

13 She looked, and there was the [young] king, standing by his pillar at the entrance, and the captains and the trumpeters were beside him. And all the people of the land were rejoicing and blowing trumpets, and the singers with their musical instruments were directing the [singing of] praise. Then Athaliah tore her clothes and cried, "Treason! Treason!"

14 So Jehoiada the priest brought out the captains of hundreds who were appointed over the army and said to them, "Bring her out between the ranks [of soldiers]; and whoever follows her shall be put to death with the sword." For the priest had said, "Do not let her be put to death in the temple of the LORD."

15 So they seized Athaliah, and when she arrived at the entrance of the Horse Gate of the king's house (palace), they put her to death there.

23:3 Unity — Unity is only unity when we are "the same" on issues of the truth. The removal of Athaliah could not have occurred without the cooperation and teamwork of everyone. Knowing that they were doing God's will gave them great courage.

23:11 *the testimony.* The testimony was a copy of the Law of Moses, part of which outlined the king's covenant privileges and duties (Dt 17:18–20; 1Ch 29:19). ***anointed him.*** Anointing was a sign and seal of the king's appointment by God (1Sa 16:3; 1Ki 1:39).

3 2Sa 7:12; 1Ki 2:4; 9:5; 2Ch 6:16; 7:18; 21:7 **4** 1Ch 9:25 **6** 1Ch 23:28,29 **8** See 1Ch 24; 25 **11** Dt 17:18 **13** 1Ch 25:8 **15** Neh 3:28

Reforms Carried Out

[16]Then Jehoiada made a covenant between himself, all the people, and the king, that they would be the LORD's people.

[17]Then all the people went to the house of Baal and tore it down, and they smashed its altars and its images to pieces, and killed Mattan, the priest of Baal, in front of the altars.

[18]Also Jehoiada placed the offices *and* officers of the house of the LORD under the authority of the Levitical priests, whom David had [previously] assigned over the house of the LORD, to offer the burnt offerings of the LORD, as it is written in the Law of Moses, with rejoicing and singing in accordance with the order of David.

[19]Jehoiada stationed the gatekeepers [at the gates] of the house of the LORD, so that no one would enter *who was* in any way unclean.

[20]He took the captains of hundreds, the nobles, the rulers of the people, and all the people of the land, and brought the king down from the house of the LORD; and they came through the upper gate to the king's house (palace) and set the king on the throne of the kingdom.

[21]So all the people of the land rejoiced, and the city was quiet after Athaliah had been put to death with the sword.

Young Joash Influenced by Jehoiada

24 JOASH WAS seven years old when he became king, and he reigned for forty years in Jerusalem. His mother's name was Zibiah from Beersheba.

[2]Joash did what was right in the sight of the LORD all the days of Jehoiada the priest [his uncle].

[3]Jehoiada took two wives for him, and he fathered sons and daughters.

Faithless Priests

[4]Now it came about after this that Joash decided to restore the house (temple) of the LORD.

[5]He gathered the priests and the Levites and said to them, "Go out to the cities of Judah and collect money from all Israel to repair the house of your God from year to year; and see that you do it quickly." But the Levites did not act quickly.

[6]So the king called for Jehoiada the high *priest* and said to him, "Why have you not required the Levites to bring in from Judah and Jerusalem the tax for the tent of the testimony which was *authorized by* Moses, the servant of the LORD and *the servant* of the assembly of Israel?"

[7]For the sons of Athaliah, that wicked woman, had broken into the house of God and also had used all the holy *and* dedicated things of the house of the LORD for the Baals.

Temple Repaired

[8]So at the king's command they made a chest and set it outside by the gate of the house of the LORD.

[9]Then they made a proclamation in Judah and Jerusalem to bring in for the LORD the tax that Moses the servant of God imposed on Israel in the wilderness.

[10]All the officers and all the people rejoiced and brought their tax and dropped it into the chest until they had finished [and the chest was full].

[11]It came about that whenever the Levites brought the chest to the king's official, and whenever they saw that there was a large amount of money, the king's secretary and the chief priest's representative would come and empty the chest, and take it, and return it to its place. They did this day after day and collected a large amount of money.

24:7 *dedicated things.* The dedicated things included gold, silver, and other valuables collected as tribute from defeated enemies and presented to God as spoils of war, acknowledging that the victory was His and for His purposes (2Sa 8:10 – 11).

17 Dt 13:9 **18** 1Ch 23:6,30,31; 24:1; Nu 28:2 **19** 1Ch 26:1 **20** 2Ki 11:19 **CHAPTER 24** **1** 2Ki 11:21; 12:1 **2** See 2Ch 26:5 **5** 2Ki 12:4 **6** 2Ki 12:7; Ex 30:12-14,16; Nu 1:50; Ac 7:44 **7** 2Ch 21:17; 2Ki 12:4 **8** 2Ki 12:9 **9** ver. 6 **11** 2Ki 12:10

12 The king and Jehoiada gave it to
those who did the work of the ser-
vice of the house of the LORD; and
they would hire masons and carpen-
ters (craftsmen) and also those who
worked in iron and bronze to repair
and restore the house of the LORD.
13 So the workmen labored, and the
repair work progressed in their hands;
and they restored *and* organized the
house of God in accordance with its
specifications and strengthened it.
14 When they had finished, they
brought the rest of the money before
the king and Jehoiada; and it was
[melted down and] made into utensils
for the house of the LORD, utensils for
ministering and for burnt offerings,
and bowls and utensils of gold and
silver. And they offered burnt offerings
in the house of the LORD continually all
the days of Jehoiada.
15 Now when Jehoiada grew old and
was full of days, he died. He was a hun-
dred and thirty years old at his death.
16 They buried him in the City of Da-
vid among the kings, because he had
done good [things] in Israel and toward
God and His house.
17 Now after the death of Jehoiada
[the priest, who had hidden Joash],
the officials of Judah came and bowed
down to King Joash; then the king
listened to them.
18 They abandoned the house of the
LORD, the God of their fathers, and
served the Asherim and the idols; so
[God's] wrath came on Judah and Je-
rusalem for their sin *and* guilt.
19 Yet God sent prophets among them
to bring them back to the LORD; these
prophets testified against them, but
they would not listen.

Joash Murders Son of Jehoiada

20 Then the Spirit of God came over
Zechariah the son of Jehoiada the
priest, and he stood above the people
and said to them, "This is what God
has said: 'Why do you transgress the
commandments of the LORD so that
you cannot prosper? Because you have
abandoned (turned away from) the
LORD, He has also abandoned (turned
away from) you.' "
21 So they conspired against Zecha-
riah and stoned him [to death] at the
command of the king, in the courtyard
of the house of the LORD.
22 Thus Joash the king did not re-
member the kindness which Jehoiada,
Zechariah's father, had shown him, but
he murdered his son. And when Zecha-
riah was dying, he said, "May the LORD
see this and require an accounting!"

Aram Invades and Defeats Judah

23 Now it happened at the end of the
year, that the army of Aram (Syria)
went up against Joash. They came to
Judah and Jerusalem and killed all the
leaders among the people and sent all
their spoil to the king of Damascus.
24 Though the army of the Arameans
came with a small company of men,
the LORD handed over a very large
army into their hands, because Joash

24:14 *all the days of Jehoiada.* As long as Jehoiada remained alive, Judah enjoyed a revival of the true worship of God.

24:20 – 21 *Zechariah the son of Jehoiada.* This priest is not the prophet of the same name who wrote the Book of Zechariah, nor is he the Zacharias mentioned by Jesus (Mt 23:35). Zechariah, whose father rescued the young Joash, may even have been raised like a brother to King Joash. The "Zechariah, son of Berechiah," that Jesus refers to was probably the prophet who wrote the Book of Zechariah (Zec 1:7), although the reference to his death is found only in the Gospels.

24:22 Martyrs — Zechariah is one of the pre-Christian martyrs who gave his life for his faith in God. Some of these faithful ones are listed in Hebrews 11, some are known only to God. Jesus predicted that those killed for their faith would actually increase in the last days (Mt 10:21; 24:9) and during the coming great tribulation, the ranks of the martyrs will swell to unprecedented size (Rev 7:14). The "offense" of martyrs is their relationship with God; their comfort is that God knows, and He keeps them faithful to the end (2Ti 4:8).

24:24 *executed judgment.* God arranged for Israel's defeat and Josiah's death in fulfillment of Zechariah's dying cry for justice (v. 22). Judgment

---

14 See 2Ki 12:13 **18** 1Ki 14:23; Jdg 5:8; 2Ch 19:2; 28:13; 29:8; 32:25 **19** 2Ch 36:15; Jer 7:25,26; 25:4 **20** Nu 14:41; 2Ch 15:2 **21** Mt 23:35; Ac 7:58,59 **23** 2Ki 12:17 **24** Lev 26:8; Dt 32:30; Isa 30:17; Lev 26:25; Dt 28:25; 2Ch 22:8; Isa 10:5

and Judah had abandoned (turned away from) the LORD, the God of their fathers. So the Arameans executed judgment against Joash.

25 When they left Joash (for they left him very ill), his own servants conspired against him because of the blood of the son of Jehoiada the priest, and they murdered him on his bed. So he died, and they buried him in the City of David, but they did not bury him in the tombs of the kings.

26 The conspirators against Joash were Zabad the son of Shimeath the Ammonitess, and Jehozabad the son of Shimrith the Moabitess.

27 Now as to his sons and the many prophecies uttered against him and the rebuilding of the house of God, they are written in the commentary on the Book of Kings. Then his son Amaziah became king in his place.

Amaziah Succeeds Joash in Judah

25 AMAZIAH WAS twenty-five years old when he became king, and he reigned for twenty-nine years in Jerusalem. His mother's name was Jehoaddan of Jerusalem.

2 He did right in the sight of the LORD, yet not wholeheartedly.

3 When his kingdom was firmly established, he killed his servants who had struck down his father the king.

4 But he did not kill their children; for *he did* as it is written in the Law, in the Book of Moses, where the LORD commanded, "The fathers shall not die for the children, nor the children die for the fathers, but each shall be put to death for his own sin."

Amaziah Defeats Edomites

5 Amaziah assembled [the men of] Judah and appointed them in accordance with *their* fathers' (ancestors') households under commanders of thousands and of hundreds throughout Judah and Benjamin. He numbered them from twenty years old and above and found there to be 300,000 choice men fit for war and *able to* handle spear and shield.

6 He also hired 100,000 brave warriors from Israel for a hundred talents of silver.

7 But a man of God came to him, saying, "O king, do not let this army of Israel go with you, for the LORD is not with Israel *nor with* any of the sons of Ephraim.

8 "But if you do go [in spite of this warning], be strong *and* courageous for battle; yet God will cause you to stumble *and* fall before the enemy, for God has power to help and to cause *people* to stumble."

9 Amaziah said to the man of God, "But what *shall we* do about the hundred talents which I gave to the troops of Israel?" The man of God answered, "The LORD is able to give you much more than this."

10 So Amaziah dismissed the troops that came to him from Ephraim, to go home. So their anger was kindled *and* burned greatly against Judah, and they returned home in the heat of anger.

11 Now Amaziah took courage and led his people out to the Valley of Salt, and he struck down 10,000 of the men of Seir (Edom).

12 The sons of Judah also captured 10,000 alive and brought them to the top of the cliff. They threw them down from the top of the cliff and they were all crushed to pieces.

13 But the troops whom Amaziah sent back, *those* not allowed to go with him to battle, attacked *and* raided the cities

---

for evil does not always come so quickly, but it is just as inevitable, no matter how long it is delayed.

25:7 *do not let this army of Israel go with you.* As long as Israel was in rebellion against God, He would not bless any alliance with them. ***Ephraim.*** Ephraim was the dominant tribe in Israel, so the whole kingdom was sometimes referred to as Ephraim (Hos 4:15–19).

25:11 *Valley of Salt.* This valley was probably in the desert south of the Dead Sea. ***men of Seir.*** These people were Edomites, descendants of Esau.

25 2Ki 12:20; ver. 21 **27** 2Ki 12:18; 2Ki 12:21 **CHAPTER 25** **1** 2Ki 14:1 **2** ver. 14; See 2Ki 14:4 **3** 2Ki 14:5 **4** Dt 24:16; 2Ki 14:6; Jer 31:30; Eze 18:20 **5** Nu 1:3 **8** 2Ch 20:6 **9** Pr 10:22 **11** 2Ki 14:7

of Judah, from Samaria to Beth-horon,
and struck down 3,000 men and took
a large amount of spoil.

Amaziah Rebuked for Idolatry

14 After Amaziah came back from the
slaughter of the Edomites, he brought
the gods of the sons of Seir, and set
them up to be his gods, bowed before
them, and burned incense to them.
15 So the anger of the LORD burned
against Amaziah, and He sent him a
prophet who said to him, "Why have
you desired the gods of the people who
did not save their own people from
your hand?"
16 As he was talking, the king said
to him, "Have we made you the king's
counselor? Stop! Why should you
be put to death?" Then the prophet
stopped and said, "I know that God
has decided to destroy you because
you have done this and have ignored
my advice."

Amaziah Defeated by Joash of Israel

17 Then Amaziah king of Judah took
counsel and sent *word* to Joash the son
of Jehoahaz the son of Jehu, king of
Israel, saying, "Come [to battle], let us
face each other." [2 Kin 14:8–20]
18 Then Joash king of Israel sent *word*
to Amaziah king of Judah, saying,
"The [little] thorn bush in Lebanon
sent *word* to the [great] cedar in Leb-
anon, saying, 'Give your daughter to
my son in marriage.' But a wild beast
in Lebanon passed by and trampled
down the thorn bush.
19 "You say, 'See, I have struck down
and defeated Edom.' Your heart lifts
you up to boast [about your victory].
Now stay at home; why should you
meddle *and* court disaster so that you,
even you, will fall and Judah with you?"
20 But Amaziah would not listen, for
it was from God, so that He might hand
Judah over *to Joash* because they had
desired the gods of Edom.
21 So Joash king of Israel went up;
and he and Amaziah king of Judah
faced one another at Beth-shemesh,
which belonged to Judah.
22 And Judah was defeated by Israel,
and they fled, every man to his tent.
23 Then Joash king of Israel captured
Amaziah king of Judah, the son of
Joash the son of Jehoahaz (Ahaziah),
at Beth-shemesh, and brought him to
Jerusalem and broke down the wall of
Jerusalem from the Ephraim Gate to
the Corner Gate, 400 cubits.
24 *He took* all the gold and silver and
all the utensils which were found in the
house of God with [the doorkeeper]
Obed-edom, and the treasures of the
king's house (palace), and the hostag-
es, and returned to Samaria.
25 And Amaziah the son of Joash
king of Judah lived fifteen years after
the death of Joash the son of Jehoahaz
king of Israel.
26 Now the rest of the acts of Amazi-
ah, from the first to the last, are they
not written in the Book of the Kings of
Judah and Israel?
27 Now from the time that Amaziah
turned away from following the LORD,
they conspired against him in Jerusa-
lem, and he fled to Lachish; but they
sent *men* after him to Lachish and
killed him there.

25:18 *thorn bush . . . cedar.* The thorn bush represents Amaziah, and the cedar, Joash. It was arrogant for the weak, insignificant Amaziah to suppose that he could defeat Joash. ***wild beast.*** The wild beast that tramples the bush represents the war that Amaziah was so eager to pursue.

25:19 Vanity—Those who reject God's counsel in favor of their own way are taking counsel against Him; their devising is in vain and will come to nothing (Ps 2:12). Refusing God's counsel, though seeking counsel from others, Amaziah decided to challenge the king of Israel to war (v. 17). It is hard to imagine how he thought he could succeed under such circumstances. One of the delusions that goes with rejection of God is a false confidence in ones' own powers of understanding.

25:27 *Lachish.* The fact that Amaziah reached the city of Lachish on the border with Philistia, some 25 miles from Jerusalem, suggests that he may have been seeking sanctuary among the Philistines.

14 See 2Ch 28:23; Ex 20:3,5 **15** Ps 96:5; ver. 11 **16** 1Sa 2:25 **17** 2Ki 14:8,9 **20** 1Ki 12:15; 2Ch 22:7; ver. 14 **23** See 2Ch 21:17; 22:1,6 **25** 2Ki 14:17

28 Then they brought him on horses and buried him with his fathers in the City of [David in] Judah.

Uzziah Succeeds Amaziah in Judah

26 THEN ALL the people of Judah took Uzziah, who was sixteen years old, and made him king in place of his father Amaziah.

2 He built Eloth and restored it to Judah after the king [Amaziah] slept with his fathers [in death].

3 Uzziah was sixteen years old when he became king, and he reigned fifty-two years in Jerusalem. His mother's name was Jechiliah of Jerusalem.

4 He did right in the sight of the LORD, in accordance with everything that his father Amaziah had done.

5 He continued to seek God in the days of Zechariah, who had understanding through the vision of God; and as long as he sought (inquired of, longing for) the LORD, God caused him to prosper.

Uzziah Succeeds in War

6 He went out and made war against the Philistines, and broke through the wall of Gath, the wall of Jabneh, and the wall of Ashdod; and he built cities near Ashdod and [elsewhere] among the Philistines.

7 God helped him against the Philistines, and against the Arabs who lived in Gur-baal, and the Meunites.

8 The Ammonites paid tribute (money) to Uzziah, and his fame spread abroad, even as far as the border of Egypt, for he became very strong.

9 Uzziah also built towers in Jerusalem at the Corner Gate, the Valley Gate, and at the corner buttress [of the wall], and fortified them.

10 He also built towers in the wilderness and dug many cisterns, for he had a great deal of livestock, both in the lowlands and in the plain. *He also had* farmers and vinedressers in the hill country and in the fertile fields, for he loved the soil.

11 Moreover, Uzziah had an army ready for battle, which went into combat by divisions according to the number of their muster as recorded by Jeiel the scribe and Maaseiah the official, under the direction of Hananiah, one of the king's commanders.

12 The total number of the heads of the fathers' households, of valiant men, was 2,600.

13 Under their command was an army of 307,500, who could wage war with great power, to help the king against the enemy.

14 Moreover, Uzziah prepared shields, spears, helmets, body armor, bows, and sling stones for the entire army.

15 In Jerusalem he made machines of war invented by skillful men to be put on the towers and on the [corner] battlements for the purpose of shooting arrows and large stones. And his fame spread far, for he was marvelously helped until he was strong.

Pride Is Uzziah's Undoing

16 But when Uzziah became strong, he became so proud [of himself and his accomplishments] that he acted corruptly, and he was unfaithful *and* sinned against the LORD his God, for he went into the temple of the LORD to burn incense on the altar of incense. [Num 3:38]

17 Then Azariah the priest went in after him, and with him eighty priests of the LORD, men of courage.

18 They opposed King Uzziah and said to him, "It is not for you, Uzziah, to burn incense to the LORD, but for the priests, the sons of Aaron who have been consecrated to burn incense. Get out of the sanctuary, for you have been

---

26:2 *Eloth.* On the eastern arm of the Red Sea, Eloth was technically in Edomite territory (8:17), but it was regularly under Israel or Judah throughout Old Testament times (21:8–10).

26:15 *machines.* This is one of the earliest references to catapults, which seem to have been defensive weapons, since their users were on the towers and in the corners.

CHAPTER 26 **1** 2Ki 14:21,22; 15:1 **5** See 2Ch 24:2; Ge 41:15; Da 1:17; 10:1 **6** Isa 14:29 **7** 2Ch 21:16 **8** 2Sa 8:2; 2Ch 17:11 **9** 2Ki 14:13; Neh 3:13,19,32; Zec 14:10 **16** Dt 32:15; 8:14; 2Ch 25:19; 2Ki 16:12,13 **17** 1Ch 6:10 **18** Nu 16:40; 18:7; Ex 30:7,8

unfaithful and will have no honor from
the LORD God."
[19]Then Uzziah, with a censer in his
hand to burn incense, was enraged;
and while he was enraged with the
priests, leprosy broke out on his fore-
head before the priests in the house
of the LORD, beside the incense altar.
[20]As Azariah the chief priest and all
the priests looked toward him, behold,
he was leprous on his forehead; and
they hurried him out of there, and he
also hurried to get out because the
LORD had stricken him.
[21]King Uzziah was a leper to the day
of his death; and, being a leper, he lived
in a separate house, for he was exclud-
ed from the house of the LORD. And his
son Jotham took charge of the king's
household, judging *and* governing the
people of the land.
[22]Now the rest of the acts of Uzziah,
from the first to the last, Isaiah the proph-
et, the son of Amoz, has written. [Is 1:1]
[23]So Uzziah slept with his fathers [in
death], and they buried him with his
fathers in the burial field of the kings
[outside the royal tombs], for they said,
"He is a leper." And his son Jotham
became king in his place.

Jotham Succeeds Uzziah in Judah

27 JOTHAM WAS twenty-five
years old when he became king,
and he reigned for sixteen years in
Jerusalem. His mother's name was
Jerushah the daughter of Zadok.
[2]He did right in the sight of the LORD,
in accordance with everything that his
father Uzziah had done; however, he did
not enter the temple of the LORD. But the
people continued behaving corruptly.
[3]He built the upper gate of the house
of the LORD, and did extensive building
on the wall of Ophel.
[4]Moreover, he built cities in the hill
country of Judah, and in the forests he
built fortresses and towers.
[5]He also fought with the king of the
Ammonites and prevailed over them.
As a result the Ammonites gave him
during that year a hundred talents of
silver and ten thousand measures each
of wheat and of barley. The Ammon-
ites also paid him that much in the
second year and third year.
[6]So Jotham grew powerful, because
he directed his ways before the LORD
his God.
[7]Now the rest of the acts of Jotham,
and all his wars and his ways, behold,
they are written in the Book of the
Kings of Israel and Judah.
[8]He was twenty-five years old when
he became king, and he reigned for
sixteen years in Jerusalem.
[9]And Jotham slept with his fathers
[in death], and they buried him in the
City of David. Ahaz his son became
king in his place.

Ahaz Succeeds Jotham in Judah

28 AHAZ WAS twenty years old
when he became king, and he
reigned for sixteen years in Jerusalem.

26:19 *leprosy.* Leprosy was any kind of serious skin condition (Lev 13:1 – 14:32). Today the term "leprosy" refers technically only to Hansen's disease. The Law viewed leprosy as a breach of God's own holiness; it was a graphic symbol of defilement.
26:22 *Isaiah.* Isaiah the prophet witnessed the last years of Uzziah, but very little about Uzziah is included in the Book of Isaiah. The books of Kings and Chronicles frequently refer to further details written about the kings, but they were not part of the Scripture, so we know very little about these records.
27:1 *sixteen years.* Jotham's sixteen years began eleven years before Uzziah died. This suggests that Uzziah had leprosy for more than a decade before he died.
27:3 *upper gate.* This gate connected the temple and the royal palace. ***wall of Ophel.*** Ophel was the original Jebusite area of Jerusalem. Its walls dated back hundreds of years and must have required regular maintenance.
27:6 Truth — In the face of deep moral corruption among his people, Jotham set his course to act on God's truth. There is always blessing in obedience, even if the blessing is not the sort that the rest of the world can see.
28:1 *did not do right in the sight of the LORD.*

19 Nu 12:10; 2Ki 5:27 **20** As Est 6:12 **21** 2Ki 15:5; Lev 13:46; Nu 5:2 **22** Isa 1:1 **23** 2Ki 15:7; Isa 6:1
CHAPTER 27 **1** 2Ki 15:32 **2** 2Ki 15:35 **9** 2Ki 15:38 **CHAPTER 28** **1** 2Ki 16:2

He did not do right in the sight of the LORD, as his father (forefather) David *had done.*
[2]Instead he walked in the ways of the kings of Israel, and even made cast images for the Baals.
[3]And he burned incense in the Valley of Ben-hinnom and burned his sons [as an offering], in accordance with the repulsive acts of the [pagan] nations whom the LORD had driven out before the sons (descendants) of Israel.
[4]He also sacrificed and burned incense on the high places [of pagan worship], on the hills and under every green tree.

Judah Is Invaded

[5]Therefore the LORD his God handed over Ahaz to the king of Aram (Syria), who defeated him and led away a great number [of the people] as captives, and brought them to Damascus. And he was also handed over to the king of Israel, who struck Judah with a great slaughter.
[6]For Pekah son of Remaliah killed 120,000 in Judah in one day, all courageous men, because they had abandoned (turned away from) the LORD God of their fathers.
[7]And Zichri, a warrior of Ephraim, killed Maaseiah the king's son, and Azrikam the governor of the house, and Elkanah, who was second [in power] to the king.
[8]And the sons of Israel led away captive 200,000 of their kinsmen [of Judah]—women, sons, and daughters—and they also took a great quantity of spoil from them and brought it to Samaria.
[9]But a prophet of the LORD was there, whose name was Oded; and he went out to meet the army that was returning to Samaria and said to them, "Behold, because the LORD, the God of your fathers, was angry with Judah, He handed them over to you; but you have killed them in a rage that has reached as far as heaven.
[10]"And now you intend to subjugate the people of Judah and Jerusalem as male and female slaves for yourselves. But are you yourselves not guilty *of transgressions* against the LORD your God?
[11]"Now therefore, hear me and return the captives whom you have captured from your brothers (fellow descendants of Israel, i.e. Jacob), for the burning anger of the LORD is against you."
[12]Then some of the heads of the Ephraimites (Israel)—Azariah the son of Johanan, Berechiah the son of Meshillemoth, Jehizkiah the son of Shallum, and Amasa the son of Hadlai—took a stand against those who were returning from the battle,
[13]and said to them, "You must not bring the captives in here; for we are guilty before the LORD *already,* and

---

During Ahaz's reign Isaiah and Micah prophesied in Judah, and Hosea prophesied in Israel.

28:3 ***Valley of Ben-hinnom.*** This valley was just outside the western wall of Jerusalem. It was a dumping ground for all kinds of refuse, much of which was burned. The valley itself became a symbol of impurity. It was used as a site of pagan worship, including human sacrifice (2Ki 23:10; Jer 7:31–32; 19:2–6; 32:35). ***repulsive acts of the [pagan] nations.*** Worshipers of the Ammonite god Molech practiced human and child sacrifice (Lev 18:21; 20:2–5; Dt 12:31).

28:4 ***every green tree.*** Canaanite nature cults focused on evergreens, probably as symbols of *perpetual fertility (see note on 14:3).*

28:6 ***Pekah.*** Pekah, who assassinated Pekahiah son of Menahem so that he could become king of Israel (2Ki 15:23–27), reigned for 20 years. He was murdered in a plot headed by Hoshea, the last king of Israel. ***because they had abandoned (turned away from) the LORD God.*** Pekah was not offended by Judah's godlessness and did not himself initiate this purge. God used Pekah to carry out His judgment.

28:9 ***Oded.*** The prophet Oded is mentioned only here. ***killed them in a rage.*** God used the Israelite armies to carry out His judgment on Judah (v. 6), but He never intended for the Israelites to enjoy it.

28:13 ***our guilt is so great.*** Within ten years the Assyrians would capture Samaria and deport all of the Israelites, treating them far more cruelly than

---

2 Ex 34:17; Lev 19:4; Jdg 2:11 **3** 2Ki 23:10; Lev 18:21; 2Ki 16:3; 2Ch 33:6 **5** Isa 7:1; 2Ki 16:5,6 **6** 2Ki 15:27
8 2Ch 11:4 **9** Isa 10:5; 47:6; Eze 25:12,15; 26:2; Ob 10; Zec 1:15; Ezr 9:6; Rev 18:5 **10** Lev 25:39,42, 43,46
11 Jas 2:13

what you intend to *do will* add more
to our sins and our guilt. For our guilt
is so great that His burning anger is
against Israel."
[14]So the armed men [of Israel] left
the captives and the spoil [of Judah] be-
fore the officers and all the assembly.
[15]Then the men who were designated
by name rose up and took the captives,
and from the spoil they clothed all
those who were naked; they clothed
them and gave them sandals, and fed
them and gave them [something to]
drink, anointed them [with oil, as was
a host's duty], and led all the feeble
ones on donkeys, and they brought
them to Jericho, the City of Palm Trees,
to their brothers (fellow descendants of
Israel, i.e. Jacob). Then they returned
to Samaria. [Luke 10:25–37]

Compromise with Assyria

[16]At that time King Ahaz sent *word*
to the king of Assyria [to ask him] for
help.
[17]For the Edomites had come again
and attacked Judah and led away cap-
tives.
[18]The Philistines had also invaded
the cities of the low country and of the
Negev (the South country) of Judah,
and had taken Beth-shemesh, Aijalon,
Gederoth, and Soco with their villag-
es, and also Timnah with its villages,
and Gimzo with its villages, and they
settled there.
[19]For the LORD humbled Judah be-
cause of Ahaz king of Israel, for Ahaz
had allowed unrestrained *and* undisci-
plined behavior in Judah and had been
very unfaithful to the LORD.
[20]So Tilgath-pilneser king of Assyria
came against him and harassed him
instead of strengthening *and* support-
ing him.
[21]Although Ahaz took a portion [of
treasure] from the house of the LORD
and from the house (palace) of the king
and from the leaders, and gave it [as
tribute] to the king of Assyria, it did
not help Ahaz.
[22]In the time of his distress, this
same King Ahaz became yet more
unfaithful to the LORD.
[23]For he sacrificed to the gods of Da-
mascus, which had defeated him, and
he said, "Since the gods of the kings of
Aram (Syria) helped them, I will sacri-
fice to them so that they may help me."
But they became the ruin *and* downfall
of him and all of Israel.
[24]Then Ahaz collected the utensils
of the house of God and he cut them
in pieces; and he shut the doors of the
house of the LORD and made altars for
himself in every corner of Jerusalem.

---

they were treating the Judeans. The Israelites brought this judgment on themselves not only by this incident, but by the whole course of the history of their unfaithfulness to God.

28:16 *king of Assyria*. The kings of Assyria were Tiglath-pileser III, Shalamaneser V, and Sargon II.

28:18 *Beth-shemesh . . . Gimzo*. All these places were near valleys that led up to central Judah from the surrounding plains. Control of them meant control of Judah itself. Because Ahaz understood this, he appealed to Assyria.

28:20 *Tilgath-pilneser*. Tilgath-pilneser brought the Mesopotamian influence over the countries of the eastern Mediterranean to its highest point. He undertook a campaign against Arpad in Syria and terrorized Menahem of Israel so much that Menahem paid him a huge bribe to be left alone (2Ki 15:19). Tilgath returned to the west again, and Ahaz scrambled for protection against Syria and Israel (2Ki 16:5 – 7; Isa 7:1 – 2). The Assyrians overran Damascus and replaced the assassinated Pekah of Israel with Hoshea (2Ki 15:30), but they did not assist Ahaz. The king of Judah's troubles with the Edomites, Philistines, Arameans, and even the Israelites (Isa 7:1) were over for the time being, but at great cost.

28:23 Unbelief — Looking to the gods of his enemies, foolishly believing that the gods had aided his enemies in their victory, Ahaz went farther from God into unbelief. Ahaz committed two grievous sins. He ascribed to another source what was God's doing, and he placed his faith in what was imagined, to bring success to himself. There is never a time when God is out of control. Even if things do not turn out the way we wish they would, we can be sure that if we keep our minds and attitudes in line with God's ways, we will eventually see these events from His perspective.

15 ver. 12; 2Ki 6:22; Lk 6:27; Ro 12:20; Dt 34:3; Jdg 1:16 **16** 2Ki 16:7 **18** Eze 16:27,57 **19** 2Ch 21:2; Ex 32:25
20 2Ki 15:29; 16:7-9 **23** See 2Ch 25:14; Jer 44:17,18 **24** See 2Ch 29:3,7

25 In every city of Judah he made
high places to burn incense to other
gods, provoking to anger the LORD, the
God of his fathers.
26 Now the rest of his acts and of all
his ways, from the first to the last, be-
hold, they are written in the Book of
the Kings of Judah and Israel.
27 And Ahaz slept with his fathers [in
death], and they buried him in the city,
in Jerusalem, but they did not bring
him into the tombs of the kings of Is-
rael. And his son Hezekiah reigned in
his place.

Hezekiah Succeeds Ahaz in Judah

29 HEZEKIAH BECAME king
when he was twenty-five years
old, and he reigned twenty-nine years
in Jerusalem. His mother's name was
Abijah the daughter of Zechariah.
2 He did right in the sight of the LORD,
in accordance with everything that
David his father (forefather) had done.
3 In the first year of his reign, in the
first month, he opened the doors of the
house of the LORD [which his father
had closed] and repaired them [and
replaced the gold overlay]. [2 Kin 18:16]
4 He brought in the priests and
Levites and gathered them into the
square on the east.

Reforms Begun

5 Then he said to them, "Levites, lis-
ten to me! Now consecrate (dedicate)
yourselves and consecrate the house
of the LORD, the God of your fathers,
and get the filth [of idol worship] out
of the Holy Place.
6 "For our fathers have been unfaith-
ful and have done evil in the sight of
the LORD our God, and they have aban-
doned Him and have turned their faces
away from the dwelling place of the
LORD, and have turned their backs [to-
ward Him].
7 "They have also closed the doors
of the [temple] porch and put out the
lamps, and they have not burned in-
cense nor offered burnt offerings in
the Holy Place to the God of Israel.
[2 Kin 16:10–16]
8 "Therefore the wrath of the LORD
has been against Judah and Jerusa-
lem, and He has made them an object
of terror, of horror, and of hissing, just
as you see with your own eyes.
9 "For behold, our fathers have fallen
by the sword, and our sons and our
daughters and our wives are in cap-
tivity because of this.
10 "Now it is in my heart to make a
covenant (solemn agreement) with the
LORD God of Israel, so that His burning
anger will turn away from us.
11 "My sons, do not be negligent *and*
careless now, for the LORD has chosen
you to stand in His presence, to attend
to His service, and to be His ministers
and burn incense."
12 Then the Levites arose: Mahath the
son of Amasai and Joel the son of Aza-
riah, from the sons of the Kohathites;
from the sons of Merari: Kish the son
of Abdi, Azariah the son of Jehallelel;
from the Gershonites: Joah the son of
Zimmah and Eden the son of Joah;
13 from the sons of Elizaphan: Shim-
ri and Jeiel; from the sons of Asaph:
Zechariah, and Mattaniah;
14 from the sons of Heman: Jehiel and
Shimei; and from the sons of Jeduthun:
Shemaiah and Uzziel.
15 They gathered their brothers (fel-
low Levites) together, consecrated
themselves, and went in to cleanse
the house of the LORD, as the king had
commanded by the words of the LORD.
16 The priests went into the inner part
of the house of the LORD to cleanse it,
and every unclean thing they found in

29:9 *in captivity.* Under the wicked leadership of Ahaz, many of the people of Judah had been taken captive by Rezin of Damascus and Pekah of Israel (28:5–8).

29:12 *Kohathites . . . Merari . . . Gershonites.* Hezekiah summoned the leaders of the three major Levitical clans, two leaders from each clan.

26 2Ki 16:19,20 **CHAPTER 29** **1** 2Ki 18:1; 2Ch 26:5 **3** ver. 7; See 2Ch 28:24 **5** 1Ch 15:12; 2Ch 35:6 **6** Jer 2:27; Eze 8:16 **7** 2Ch 28:24 **8** 2Ch 24:18; 1Ki 9:8; Jer 18:16; 19:8; 25:9,18; 29:18 **9** 2Ch 28:5,6,8,17 **10** 2Ch 15:12 **11** Nu 3:6; 8:14; 18:2,6 **15** ver. 5; 1Ch 23:28

the temple of the LORD they brought out
to the courtyard of the LORD's house.
Then the Levites received it to take
out to the Kidron Valley [for disposal].
17 Now they began the consecration
on the first [day] of the first month, and
on the eighth day of the month they
came to the porch of the LORD. Then for
eight days they consecrated the house
of the LORD, and on the sixteenth day
of the first month they finished.
18 Then they went inside to King Hez-
ekiah and said, "We have cleansed the
entire house (temple) of the LORD, the
altar of burnt offering with all of its
utensils, and the table of showbread
with all its utensils.
19 "Moreover, we have prepared and
consecrated all the utensils which King
Ahaz had discarded during his reign
in his unfaithfulness; and behold, they
are in front of the altar of the LORD."

Hezekiah Restores Temple Worship

20 Then King Hezekiah arose early
and assembled the officials of the city,
and went up to the house of the LORD.
21 They brought seven bulls, seven
rams, seven lambs, and seven male
goats for a sin offering for the kingdom,
the sanctuary, and Judah. He com-
manded the priests, the sons of Aaron,
to offer them on the altar of the LORD.
22 So they slaughtered the bulls, and
the priests took the blood and sprinkled
it on the altar. They also slaughtered the
rams and sprinkled the blood on the
altar; then they slaughtered the lambs
and sprinkled the blood on the altar.
23 Then they brought the male goats
for the sin offering before the king and
the assembly, and they laid their hands
on them [to symbolize the transference
of their sin].
24 The priests slaughtered them and
cleansed the altar from sin with their
blood to atone for all Israel, because
the king commanded that the burnt
offering and the sin offering *be made*
for all Israel.
25 Hezekiah stationed the Levites in
the house of the LORD with cymbals,
with harps, and with lyres, in accor-
dance with the command of David
[his ancestor] and of Gad the king's
seer, and of Nathan the prophet; for the
command was from the LORD through
His prophets.
26 The Levites stood with the *musical*
instruments of David, and the priests
with the trumpets.
27 Then Hezekiah gave the order to
offer the burnt offering on the altar.
And when the burnt offering began,
the song to the LORD also began with
the trumpets *accompanied* by the in-
struments of David, king of Israel.
28 The entire congregation wor-
shiped, the singers also sang, and the
trumpets sounded; all this *continued*
until the burnt offering was finished.
29 When the burnt offerings were
completed, the king and all who were
present with him bowed down and
worshiped [God].
30 Also King Hezekiah and the offi-
cials ordered the Levites to exclaim
praises to the LORD with the words of
David and of Asaph the seer. And they
exclaimed praises with joy, and bowed
down and worshiped.
31 Then Hezekiah said, "Now you
have consecrated yourselves to the

29:21 *bulls . . . rams . . . lambs . . . goats.* The law required the sacrifice of these animals for atonement of sin in general (Lev 1:3 – 13). On the other hand, the sacrifice of goats atoned for specific sins (Lev 4:1 – 5:13). Here the priests offered seven of each kind to signify the wholeness of their repentance.

29:24 *all Israel.* The repetition of "all Israel" here suggests that Hezekiah meant to include all twelve tribes, including the Northern Kingdom (30:1 – 9).

29:30 *the words of David and of Asaph.* This refers to the psalms of David and Asaph (1Ch 6:39; 15:17; 16:5; 25:1), many of them in the Book of Psalms. The people of Judah used these psalms for community worship and private meditation.

29:31 *thank offerings.* Sometimes called "peace" or "fellowship" offerings, thank offerings celebrated the relationship gained by the offerings of atonement (v. 21 – 24; Lev 3:1 – 17; 7:11 – 36). The thank offerings included people

19 2Ch 28:24 **21** Lev 4:3,14 **22** Lev 8:14,15,19,24; Heb 9:21 **23** Lev 4:15,24 **24** Lev 14:20 **25** 1Ch 16:4; 25:6; 1Ch 23:5; 25:1; 2Ch 8:14; 2Sa 24:11; 2Ch 30:12 **26** 1Ch 23:5; Am 6:5; Nu 10:8,10; 1Ch 15:24; 16:6 **27** 2Ch 23:18 **29** 2Ch 20:18 **31** Lev 7:12

LORD; approach and bring sacrifices and thank offerings into the house of the LORD." And the assembly brought in sacrifices and thank offerings, and all those who were willing *brought* burnt offerings. [Ex 35:5, 22]

32 The number of the burnt offerings which the assembly brought was 70 bulls, 100 rams, and 200 lambs. All these were for a burnt offering to the LORD.

33 The consecrated things were 600 bulls and 3,000 sheep.

34 But there were too few priests and they were unable to skin all the burnt offerings; so until the *other* priests had consecrated themselves, their brothers, the Levites, helped them until the work was done. For the Levites were more upright in heart *and* more conscientious than the priests in consecrating themselves.

35 There were also many burnt offerings with the fat of the peace offerings and with the drink offerings for the burnt offerings. So the service of the house of the LORD was established again.

36 Then Hezekiah and all the people rejoiced because of what God had prepared for the people, for the thing came about suddenly.

All Israel Invited to the Passover

30 HEZEKIAH SENT *word* to all Israel and to Judah and also wrote letters to Ephraim and Manasseh to come to the house of the LORD at Jerusalem to celebrate the Passover *Feast* to the LORD God of Israel.

2 For the king and his officials and all the assembly in Jerusalem had decided to celebrate the Passover in the second month, [Num 9:10, 11]

3 since they could not celebrate it at that time because a sufficient number of priests had not consecrated themselves, nor had the people assembled at Jerusalem.

4 Thus the [decision to set a] new time pleased the king and the entire assembly.

5 So they decided to circulate a proclamation throughout Israel, from Beersheba to Dan, that the people were to come to celebrate the Passover to the LORD God of Israel, at Jerusalem. For they had not celebrated it in great numbers as it was prescribed [for a long time].

6 So the runners went throughout Israel and Judah with the letters from the hand of the king and his officials, in accordance with the command of the king, saying, "O sons (descendants) of Israel, return to the LORD God of Abraham, Isaac, and Israel (Jacob), so that He will return to those of you who escaped and are left from the hand (power) of the kings of Assyria.

7 "Do not be like your fathers and your brothers, who were unfaithful to the LORD God of their fathers, so that He made them a horror (lifeless, desolate), just as you see.

8 "Now do not stiffen your neck [becoming obstinate] like your fathers, but yield to the LORD and come to His sanctuary which He has sanctified *and* set apart forever, and serve the LORD your God, so that His burning anger will turn away from you.

9 "For if you return to the LORD, your brothers (relatives) and your children will find compassion in the presence of those who led them away captive and will return to this land. For the LORD your God is gracious and merciful, and He will not turn His face away from you if you return to Him."

---

and priests in a great banquet together, all in fellowship with God.

29:34 *too few priests.* Under Ahaz the priests and Levites had been stripped of their duties. Now, 20 years later, there were not enough priests.

30:1 *sent word to all Israel.* Though the kingdom of Israel had split more than two centuries before, Hezekiah never lost sight of the fact that God's covenant was made with all twelve tribes and that His promises included them all (Eze 37:15 – 28).

30:8 *come to His sanctuary.* People who were not priests were not allowed to enter the temple. This phrase is a figure of speech for serving the Lord.

30:9 *if you return to the LORD.* Hezekiah was referring to the covenant (Dt 28 – 30) which promised that obedience would lead to blessing

34 2Ch 35:11; 2Ch 30:3; Ps 7:10 **35** Lev 3:16; Nu 15:5,7,10 **CHAPTER 30** **2** Nu 9:10,11 **3** Ex 12:6,18; 2Ch 29:34 **6** Jer 4:1; Joel 2:13; 2Ki 15:19 **7** Eze 20:18; 2Ch 29:8 **8** Dt 10:16; 2Ch 29:10 **9** Ps 106:46; Ex 34:6; Isa 55:7

10 So the runners (couriers) passed
from city to city through the country
of Ephraim and Manasseh, as far as
Zebulun; but the people laughed at
them with scorn and mocked them.
11 Yet *some of* the men of Asher, Ma-
nasseh, and Zebulun humbled them-
selves and came to Jerusalem.
12 Also the hand of God was on Ju-
dah to give them one heart to do that
which the king and the officials had
commanded by the word of the LORD.

Passover Reinstituted

13 Now many people were gathered at
Jerusalem to celebrate the Feast of Un-
leavened Bread in the second month;
it was a very large assembly.
14 They took action and removed the
[pagan] altars which were in Jerusa-
lem; they also removed all the incense
altars and threw them into the Brook
Kidron [the dumping place for the ash-
es of such repulsive things].
15 Then they slaughtered the Pass-
over *lambs* on the fourteenth day of
the second month. And the priests and
the Levites were ashamed of them-
selves, and consecrated themselves
and brought burnt offerings to the
house of the LORD.
16 They stood at their accustomed
stations, in accordance with the Law
of Moses, the man of God. The priests
sprinkled the blood [which they re-
ceived] from the hand of the Levites
[on the altar].
17 For there were many in the assem-
bly who had not consecrated them-
selves [that is, become ceremonially
clean and free from all sin]; so the
Levites had to slaughter the Passover
lambs for everyone who was not clean,
in order to make them holy for the LORD.
18 For the majority of the people, many
from Ephraim and Manasseh, Issachar
and Zebulun, had not purified them-
selves, and yet they ate the Passover
contrary to what had been prescribed.
For Hezekiah had prayed for them, say-
ing, "May the good LORD pardon
19 everyone who sets his heart to seek
God—the LORD God of his fathers—
even though it is not in accordance
with the [ceremonial] purification
[rules] of the sanctuary."
20 So the LORD listened to Hezekiah
and healed the people [of their un-
cleanness].
21 The Israelites who were present
in Jerusalem celebrated the Feast of
Unleavened Bread for seven days
with great joy. The Levites and priests
praised the LORD day after day, *singing*
to the LORD with loud instruments.
22 Hezekiah spoke encouragingly to
all the Levites who showed good un-
derstanding *in the things* of the LORD.
So the people ate for the appointed
seven days, sacrificing peace offerings
and giving thanks to the LORD God of
their fathers.
23 Then the whole assembly decided
to celebrate [the feast] for another sev-
en days; and they celebrated it *another*
seven days with joy.
24 For Hezekiah king of Judah gave
to the assembly 1,000 bulls and 7,000
sheep, and the officials gave the as-
sembly 1,000 bulls and 10,000 sheep.
And a large number of priests conse-
crated themselves [for service].
25 All the assembly of Judah rejoiced,
with the priests and the Levites and all

---

in the land, and disobedience would result in exile.

30:10 *as far as Zebulun.* Zebulun was probably the northernmost territory of Israel at this time because Naphtali had been taken by Tiglath-pileser III (2Ki 15:29).

30:17 *Levites had to slaughter.* Traditionally the slaughter of the Passover lamb was performed by the head of the family (Ex 12:3–6). But on this occasion many were not ritually purified, and the Levites acted on their behalf.

30:22 *who showed good understanding.* The Levites' ministry included teaching (17:8–10). The people of Israel had had virtually no consistent teaching of God's revelation for 200 years, apart from the witness of the prophets such as Elijah, Elisha, Hosea, and Amos.

30:25 *sojourners.* The sojourners were aliens who lived in Israel and Judah and who could come to the festivals because they adhered to God and the Law (Dt 16:11; 26:11; 29:11; 31:12).

10 2Ch 36:16 **11** ver. 18,21; 2Ch 11:16 **12** Php 2:13; 2Ch 29:25 **14** 2Ch 28:24 **15** 2Ch 29:34 **17** 2Ch 29:34 **18** ver. 1,11; Ex 12:43 **19** 2Ch 19:3 **21** Ex 12:15; 13:6 **22** Dt 33:10; 2Ch 17:9; 35:3; Ezr 10:11 **23** See 1Ki 8:65 **24** 2Ch 35:7,8; 2Ch 29:34 **25** ver. 11,18

the assembly that came from Israel, both the sojourners (resident aliens, foreigners) who came from the land of Israel and those living in Judah.

[26]So there was great joy in Jerusalem, because there had been nothing like this in Jerusalem since the time of Solomon the son of David, king of Israel.

[27]Then the priests and Levites stood and blessed the people; and their voice was heard and their prayer came up to His holy dwelling place, to heaven.

Idols Are Destroyed

31 NOW WHEN all of this was finished, all Israel who were present went out to the cities of Judah, and smashed the [pagan] pillars (obelisks, memorial stones) in pieces, cut down the Asherim (wooden symbols of a female deity), and tore down the high places and the altars [of idolatry] throughout all Judah and Benjamin, as well as in Ephraim and Manasseh, until they had destroyed them all. Then all the sons (descendants) of Israel returned to their own cities, each to his own property.

[2]And Hezekiah appointed the divisions of the priests, and the Levites by their divisions, each in accordance with his service, both the priests and Levites, for burnt offerings and for peace offerings, to minister and to give thanks and to praise in the gates of the camp of the LORD.

Reforms Continued

[3]Hezekiah also *appointed* the king's [personal] portion of his goods: for the morning and evening burnt offerings, and the burnt offerings for the Sabbaths and for the New Moons and for the appointed feasts, as it is written in the Law of the LORD.

[4]He also told (ordered) the people living in Jerusalem to give the portion that was due to the priests and Levites, so that they might [be free to] devote themselves to the Law of the LORD.

[5]As soon as the *king's* order spread, the Israelites gave in abundance the first fruits of grain, new wine, [olive] oil, honey, and of all the produce of the field; and they brought in the tithe of everything abundantly.

[6]The sons of Israel and Judah who lived in the cities of Judah also brought in the tithe of oxen and sheep, and the tithe of sacred gifts which were consecrated to the LORD their God, and placed them in heaps.

[7]In the third month [at the end of wheat harvest] they began to make the heaps, and they finished them in the seventh month.

[8]When Hezekiah and the rulers came and saw the heaps, they blessed the LORD and His people Israel.

[9]Then Hezekiah questioned the priests and Levites about the heaps.

[10]Azariah the high priest of the house of Zadok answered him, "Since

---

30:26 Heaven — Solomon asked God to hear the prayers of the people as they directed their prayers toward the temple in Jerusalem, and to respond from His dwelling in heaven (2Ch 6:21). The people, nearly 200 years after Solomon made this prayer, sought the Lord, and He heard them. There is great joy among the people when they realize that God hears them from heaven, and there is great joy in heaven when one sinner repents (Lk 15:7).

31:2 *Hezekiah appointed.* The long interruption (28:24) of Judah's official worship in the time of Ahaz brought chaos to their religious life. David had originally organized the Levitical system, but because of the years of neglect, Hezekiah had to reorganize it.

31:3 *New Moons.* The new moon celebrations came at the appearance of the new moon, the beginning of another month (Nu 28:11 – 15). ***appointed feasts.*** The fixed festivals were the Passover and Feast of Unleavened Bread (Lev 23:4 – 8); Feast of Firstfruits or Pentecost (Lev 23:15 – 22); and the Feast of Tabernacles (Lev 23:33 – 43).

31:5 *first fruits.* The early harvests of grain, particularly barley, were being reaped at this time. The Passover had been held a month late (30:2) and it was now the third month. The first fruits began appearing at the time of the late Passover, and the harvests were fully gathered in some 50 days later, at the time of Pentecost (Lev 23:9 – 22). ***the tithe.*** A tenth of the harvest belonged to the Levites (Nu 18:21 – 24).

27 Nu 6:23 **CHAPTER 31** **1** 2Ki 18:4 **2** 1Ch 23:6; 24:1; 1Ch 23:30,31 **3** Nu 28; 29 **4** Nu 18:8; Neh 13:10; Mal 2:7 **5** Ex 22:29; Neh 13:12 **6** Lev 27:30; Dt 14:28 **10** Mal 3:10

SENNACHERIB'S CAMPAIGN IN PHILISTIA AND JUDAH

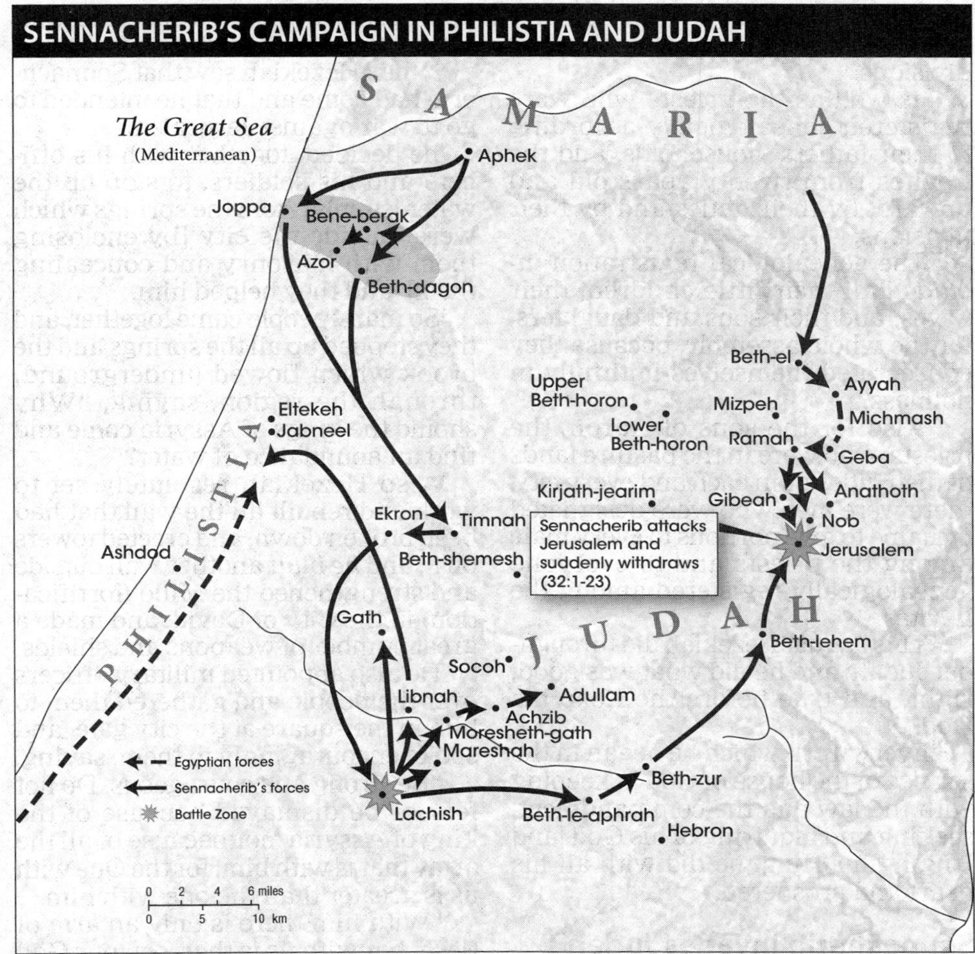

the people began to bring the offerings into the house of the LORD, we have had enough to eat with plenty left over, for the LORD has blessed His people, and this great quantity is left over."
11Then Hezekiah told them to prepare rooms [for storage] in the house of the LORD, and they prepared them.
12They faithfully brought in the contributions, the tithes, and the sacred (dedicated) things. Conaniah the Levite was in charge of them, and Shimei his brother was second [in authority].
13Jehiel, Azaziah, Nahath, Asahel, Jerimoth, Jozabad, Eliel, Ismachiah, Mahath, and Benaiah were overseers directed by Conaniah and Shimei his brother by the appointment of King Hezekiah, and Azariah was the *chief* officer of the house of God.
14Kore the son of Imnah the Levite, keeper of the East Gate, was in charge of the voluntary offerings to God, to apportion the contributions for the LORD and the most holy things.
15Under his authority were Eden, Miniamin, Jeshua, Shemaiah, Amariah, and Shecaniah in the cities of the priests, to distribute faithfully *their portions* to their brothers (relatives) by divisions, whether great or small,
16without regard to their genealogical registration, to the males from thirty years old and upward—everyone who entered the house of the LORD for

12 Neh 13:13 **15** Jos 21:9

his daily obligations—for their service in accordance with their duties by their divisions;

17 as well as the priests who were registered genealogically according to their fathers' households, and the Levites from twenty years old and upward, by their duties and by their divisions.

18 The genealogical registration *included* all their little children, their wives, and their sons and daughters, for the whole assembly, because they consecrated themselves faithfully in holiness.

19 Also for the sons of Aaron, the priests, who were in the pasture lands of their cities or in each and every city, there were men who were designated by name to give portions to every male among the priests and to everyone genealogically registered among the Levites.

20 This is what Hezekiah did throughout Judah; and he did what was good, right, and true before the LORD his God.

21 Every work which he began in the service of the house of God in keeping with the law and the commandment, seeking *and* inquiring of his God [and longing for Him], he did with all his heart and prospered.

Sennacherib Invades Judah

32 AFTER THESE things and this faithfulness, Sennacherib king of Assyria came and invaded Judah and besieged the fortified cities, intending to take them for himself.

2 When Hezekiah saw that Sennacherib had come and that he intended to go to war against Jerusalem,

3 he decided, together with his officers and his soldiers, to stop up the water [supply] from the springs which were outside the city [by enclosing them with masonry and concealing them], and they helped him.

4 So many people came together, and they stopped up all the springs and the brook which flowed [underground] through the region, saying, "Why should the kings of Assyria come and find an abundance of water?"

5 Also Hezekiah resolutely set to work and rebuilt all the wall that had been broken down, and erected towers on it, and *he built* another wall outside and strengthened the Millo (fortification) in the City of David, and made a great number of weapons and shields.

6 He also appointed military officers over the people and gathered them to him in the square at the city gate, and spoke encouragingly to them, saying,

7 "Be strong and courageous. Do not fear or be dismayed because of the king of Assyria, nor because of all the army that is with him; for the One with us is greater than the one with him.

8 "With him there is only an arm of flesh, but with us is the LORD our God to help us and to fight our battles." And the people relied on the words of Hezekiah king of Judah.

31:17 *genealogically . . . by their divisions.* All temple servants had to descend from Levi, but the priests had to trace their genealogy specifically to Aaron (1Ch 6:49 – 53).

32:1 *Sennacherib.* In Hezekiah's fourteenth year, Sennacherib invaded Judah and eventually laid siege to Jerusalem (2Ki 18:13 – 17). One of the most imperialistic of Assyria's kings, Sennacherib undertook many military campaigns to the west. In his own inscriptions he boasts of having taken many of Judah's cities, a claim supported by the parallel account in 2 Kings.

32:3 *stop up the water.* Hezekiah managed to stop the water by concealing the springs outside the city and then digging a tunnel to bring them to the Pool of Siloam inside the city walls. Hezekiah hid the source of water and made it unavailable to the enemy (2Ki 20:20). The Siloam Inscription describes how workmen constructed the 1,800 foot tunnel connecting the springs of Gihon to the Pool of Siloam.

32:5 *strengthened the Millo.* Millo means landfill and refers to extensive terracing that surrounded the ancient hills of Ophel and Mount Zion. The work of extending the hills of Jerusalem was first undertaken by David (1Ch 11:7 – 8) and continued by Solomon (1Ki 9:15).

---

17 1Ch 23:24,27 **19** Lev 25:34; Nu 35:2; ver. 12-15 **20** 2Ki 20:3 **CHAPTER 32** **1** 2Ki 18:13; Isa 36:1
5 Isa 22:9,10; 2Ch 25:23; 2Sa 5:9; 1Ki 9:24 **7** Dt 31:6; 2Ch 20:15; 2Ki 6:16 **8** Jer 17:5; 1Jn 4:4; 2Ch 13:12; Ro 8:31

Sennacherib Undermines Hezekiah

9 After this, Sennacherib king of Assyria, while he was at Lachish [besieging it] with all his forces, sent his servants to Jerusalem, to Hezekiah king of Judah, and to all Judah who were at Jerusalem, saying,

10 "Thus says Sennacherib king of Assyria, 'In what do you trust that you are remaining in Jerusalem under siege?

11 'Is not Hezekiah misleading you in order to let you die by famine and thirst, *while* saying, "The LORD our God will rescue us from the hand of the king of Assyria?"

12 'Has the same Hezekiah not taken away his [Baal's] high places and his altars, and commanded Judah and Jerusalem, "You shall worship before [only] one altar and burn incense on it"?

13 'Do you not know what I and my fathers (ancestors) have done to all the peoples of the [other] lands? Were the gods of the nations of those lands able to rescue their lands from my hand at all?

14 'Who [was there] among all the gods of those nations that my fathers utterly destroyed who was able to rescue his people from my hand, that your God should be able to rescue you from my hand?

15 'So now, do not let Hezekiah deceive or mislead you like this, and do not believe him, for no god of any nation or kingdom has been able to rescue his people from my hand or the hand of my fathers. How much less will your God rescue you from my hand!' "

16 And his servants said *even* more against the LORD God and against His servant Hezekiah.

17 The Assyrian king also wrote letters insulting *and* taunting the LORD God of Israel, and speaking against Him, saying, "As the gods of the nations of other lands have not rescued their people from my hand, so the God of Hezekiah will not rescue His people from my hand."

18 They shouted it loudly in the language of Judah to the people of Jerusalem who were on the wall, to frighten and terrify them, so that they might take the city [without a long siege].

19 They spoke of the God of Jerusalem as [they spoke of] the gods of the peoples of the earth, [which are only] the work of the hands of men.

Hezekiah's Prayer Is Answered

20 But Hezekiah the king and the prophet Isaiah the son of Amoz prayed about this and cried out to heaven [for help].

21 And the LORD sent an angel who destroyed every brave warrior, commander, and officer in the camp of the king of Assyria. So the king returned to his own land in shame. And when he entered the house (temple) of his god, some of his own children killed him there with the sword. [2 Kin 19:35–37]

22 Thus the LORD saved Hezekiah and the inhabitants of Jerusalem from the hand of Sennacherib the king of Assyria and from the hand of all *others*, and He gave them rest on every side.

23 And many brought gifts to the LORD at Jerusalem and valuable presents to Hezekiah king of Judah; so from then on he was exalted in the sight of all nations.

32:9 *while he was at Lachish [besieging it]*. Both the Old Testament and Assyrian inscriptions document the siege against Lachish, an important fortified city west of Jerusalem and near the great coastal route (11:9). Its capture by Assyria would cut off access to Jerusalem from the west and would give Assyria control of the coast.

32:18 *in the language of Judah*. Aramaic had become the language of international communication and diplomacy and there was no reason to continue the dialogue in Hebrew except to traumatize the people.

32:20 *the prophet Isaiah*. By now the prophet Isaiah had been involved in public ministry to the kings of Judah for nearly 40 years (26:22; Isa 6:1). He had considerable prestige and was especially important as a counselor of young Hezekiah (Isa 37:1 – 7).

9 2Ki 18:17 **10** 2Ki 18:19 **11** 2Ki 18:30 **12** 2Ki 18:22 **13** 2Ki 18:33-35 **15** 2Ki 18:29 **17** 2Ki 19:9; 2Ki 19:12 **18** 2Ki 18:28 **19** 2Ki 19:18 **20** 2Ki 19:15; 2Ki 19:2,4 **21** 2Ki 19:35 **23** 2Ch 17:5; 2Ch 1:1

24 In those days Hezekiah became
terminally ill; and he prayed to the
LORD, and He answered him and gave
him a [miraculous] sign.
25 But Hezekiah did nothing [for
the LORD] in return for the benefit *be-
stowed* on him, because his heart had
become proud; therefore *God's* wrath
came on him and on Judah and Jeru-
salem.
26 However, Hezekiah humbled his
proud heart, both he and the inhabi-
tants of Jerusalem, so that the wrath of
the LORD did not come on them during
the days of Hezekiah.
27 Now Hezekiah had immense
wealth and honor; and he made for
himself treasuries for silver, gold, pre-
cious stones, spices, shields, and all
kinds of delightful articles,
28 and storehouses for the produce of
grain, new wine, and [olive] oil, and
stalls for all kinds of cattle, and sheep-
folds for the flocks.
29 Moreover, he made cities for him-
self and *acquired* an abundance of
flocks and herds, for God gave him
very many possessions.
30 This same Hezekiah also stopped
up the upper outlet of the waters of
Gihon and channeled them down to
the west side of the City of David. Hez-
ekiah succeeded in everything that
he did.
31 And so *in the matter of* the envoys
of the rulers of Babylon, who were sent
to him to inquire about the wonder that
had happened in the land, God left
him *alone only* to test him, in order to
know everything that was in his heart.
[Is 39:1–7]
32 Now the rest of the acts of Hezekiah
and his godly achievements, behold,
they are written in the vision of Isaiah
the prophet, the son of Amoz, in the
Book of the Kings of Judah and Israel.
33 So Hezekiah slept with his fathers
[in death] and they buried him in the
upper section of the tombs of the de-
scendants of David; and all Judah and
the inhabitants of Jerusalem honored
him at his death. And his son Manas-
seh became king in his place.

Manasseh Succeeds Hezekiah in Judah

33 MANASSEH WAS twelve years
old when he became king, and
he reigned for fifty-five years in Je-
rusalem.
2 But he did evil in the sight of the
LORD, like the repulsive acts of the [pa-
gan] nations whom the LORD dispos-
sessed before the sons (descendants)
of Israel.
3 For he rebuilt the [idolatrous] high
places which his father Hezekiah had
torn down; and he set up altars for
the Baals and made the Asherim, and
worshiped all the host of heaven [the
sun, the moon, stars and planets] and
served them. [Deut 4:19]
4 He built [pagan] altars in the house
of the LORD, of which the LORD had
said, "My Name shall be in Jerusalem
forever."
5 He built altars for all the host of
heaven in the two courts of the house
of the LORD.
6 He made his sons pass through
the fire [as an offering to his gods]

32:25 *his heart had become proud.* Hezekiah had received Babylonian envoys who had come to congratulate him on his recovery, and probably to enlist his support in their struggle against Assyria (2Ki 20:12 – 19). Their visit ignited his desire to show off the treasures of his kingdom, and this treasure was eventually seized by the same Babylonians (2Ki 20:16 – 18; Isa 39:6 – 7).
32:31 *test.* This test was not for God's benefit, but for Hezekiah's.

33:4 *My Name shall be in Jerusalem.* The point was that God had the exclusive right to inhabit the temple, as opposed to the deities Manasseh introduced (v. 5).
33:6 *pass through the fire.* Like Ahaz, Manasseh practiced human sacrifice, going so far as to offer up his own children (28:3). ***divination . . . sorcery.*** Divination and sorcery attempt to bring about desired results by employing magical or mystical rituals. ***mediums and spiritists.***

24 2Ki 20:1; Isa 38:1 **25** Ps 116:12; 2Ch 26:16; Hab 2:4; 2Ch 24:18 **26** Jer 26:18; 2Ki 20:19 **29** 1Ch 29:12 **30** Isa 22:9,11 **31** 2Ki 20:12; Isa 39:1; Dt 8:2 **32** Isa 36; 37; 38; 39; 2Ki 18; 19; 20 **33** 2Ki 20:21; Pr 10:7
CHAPTER 33 **1** 2Ki 21:1 **2** Dt 18:9; 2Ch 28:3 **3** 2Ki 18:4; 2Ch 30:14; 31:1; Dt 16:21; Dt 17:3 **4** Dt 12:11; 1Ki 8:29; 9:3; 2Ch 6:6; 7:16 **5** 2Ch 4:9 **6** Lev 18:21; Dt 18:10; 2Ki 23:10; 2Ch 28:3; Eze 23:37,39; 2Ki 21:6

in the Valley of Ben-hinnom; and he
practiced witchcraft, used divination,
and practiced sorcery, and dealt with
mediums and spiritists. He did much
evil in the sight of the LORD, provoking
Him to anger.
7 Then he set the carved image of the
idol which he had made in the house
of God, of which God had said to Da-
vid and to Solomon his son, "In this
house and in Jerusalem, which I have
chosen from all the tribes of Israel, I
will put My Name [and the symbol of
my Presence] forever;
8 and I will not again remove Israel
from the land which I appointed for
your fathers, if they will only be care-
ful to do everything that I have com-
manded them in regard to all the law,
the statutes, and the ordinances *given*
through Moses."
9 So Manasseh caused Judah and
the inhabitants of Jerusalem to sin,
by doing more evil than the [pagan]
nations whom the LORD had destroyed
before the sons of Israel.

Manasseh's Idolatry Rebuked

10 Now the LORD spoke to Manasseh
and to his people, but they paid no
attention.
11 So the LORD brought the command-
ers of the army of the king of Assyria
against them, and they captured Ma-
nasseh with hooks [through his nose
or cheeks] and bound him with bronze
[chains] and took him to Babylon.
12 But when he was in distress, he
sought the LORD his God and humbled
himself greatly before the God of his
fathers.
13 When he prayed to Him, He was
moved by his entreaty and heard his
pleading, and brought him back to
Jerusalem to his kingdom. Then Ma-
nasseh knew that the LORD is God.
14 After this he built an outer wall for
the City of David on the west side of Gi-
hon, in the river valley, to the entrance
of the Fish Gate; and he encircled the
Ophel *with it* and made it very high.
Then he put military commanders in
all the fortified cities of Judah.
15 He also removed the foreign gods
and the idol from the house of the
LORD, as well as all the altars which
he had built on the mountain of the
house of the LORD and in Jerusalem;
and he threw them outside the city.
16 Then he set up the altar of the LORD
and sacrificed peace offerings and
thank offerings on it; and he ordered
Judah to serve the LORD God of Israel.
[Ex 35:5, 22]
17 Yet the people still sacrificed on
the high places, *but* only to the LORD
their God.
18 Now the rest of the acts of Manas-
seh, and his prayer to his God, and the
words of the seers who spoke to him
in the name of the LORD God of Israel,
behold, they are among the records of
the kings of Israel.
19 His prayer also and how God heard
him, and all his sin, his unfaithfulness,
and the sites on which he built high
places and set up the Asherim and
the carved images, before he humbled

Mediums are those who claim to contact and consult with the dead. Spiritists are the "knowing ones" whose specialty is also communication with the dead in the hope of acquiring information inaccessible to the living. All such practices were common among Canaanite and other pagan religions and were to be strictly avoided by God's people (Dt 13:1 – 6; 18:9 – 14).

33:11 *Babylon.* For some time Babylon had been part of the Assyrian Empire, though it had broken free on occasion, especially under the leadership of Berodach-Baladan, Hezekiah's contemporary (2Ki 20:12). Ashurbanipal brought Babylon back under Assyrian domination. He was the king who took Manasseh to Babylon as a prisoner.

33:14 *outer wall for the City of David.* The term "City of David" originally referred to Mount Zion alone (1Ch 11:5) but eventually designated the entire city, including Mount Ophel, the original Jebusite settlement. ***Gihon.*** Gihon was the spring that was the main source of water for Jerusalem. It was in the Kidron valley near the northeastern brow of Mt. Zion. ***Fish Gate.*** The fish gate was in the center of the wall north of the temple. Manasseh's construction was a total distance of about 750 yards.

7 2Ki 21:7 **8** 2Sa 7:10 **11** Dt 28:36; Job 36:8; Ps 107:10,11 **12** 1Pe 5:6 **13** 1Ch 5:20; Ezr 8:23; Ps 9:16; Da 4:25 **14** 1Ki 1:33; 2Ch 27:3 **15** ver. 3,5,7 **16** Lev 7:12 **17** 2Ch 32:12 **18** 1Sa 9:9

himself, behold, they are written in the records of the Hozai.

20 So Manasseh slept with his fathers [in death], and they buried him in [the garden of] his own house. And his son Amon became king in his place.

Amon Becomes King in Judah

21 Amon was twenty-two years old when he became king, and he reigned for two years in Jerusalem.

22 But he did evil in the sight of the LORD, just as his father Manasseh had done. Amon sacrificed to all the carved images which his father Manasseh had made, and he served them.

23 Further, he did not humble himself before the LORD as his father Manasseh [finally] had done, but Amon multiplied his guilt *and* his sin.

24 And his servants conspired against him and killed him in his own house (palace).

25 But the people of the land struck down all those who had conspired against King Amon, and they made his son Josiah king in his place.

Josiah Succeeds Amon in Judah

34 JOSIAH WAS eight years old when he became king, and he reigned for thirty-one years in Jerusalem.

2 He did what was right in the sight of the LORD, and walked in the ways of David his father (forefather) and did not turn aside either to the right or to the left.

3 For in the eighth year of his reign, while he was still young (sixteen), he began to seek after *and* inquire of the God of his father David; and in the twelfth year he began to purge Judah and Jerusalem of the high places, the Asherim, and the carved and cast images.

4 They tore down the altars of the Baals in his presence; he cut to pieces the incense altars that were high above them; he also smashed the Asherim and the carved images and the cast images to pieces, and ground them to dust and scattered it on the graves of those who had sacrificed to them.

5 Then Josiah burned the bones of the [pagan] priests on their altars and purged *and* cleansed Judah and Jerusalem.

6 In the cities of Manasseh, Ephraim, Simeon, and as far as Naphtali, in their surrounding ruins,

7 he tore down the altars and beat *and* crushed the Asherim and the carved images into powder, and cut to pieces all the incense altars throughout the land of Israel. Then he returned to Jerusalem.

Josiah Repairs the Temple

8 In the eighteenth year of Josiah's reign, when he had purged the land and the [LORD's] house, he sent Shaphan the son of Azaliah, and Maaseiah the governor of the city, and Joah the son of Joahaz the recorder (secretary), to repair the house of the LORD his God.

9 When they came to Hilkiah the high priest, they delivered the money that had been brought into the house of God, which the Levites, who guarded

---

33:20 *buried him in [the garden of] his own house.* Manasseh had truly converted (v. 13), but his prior sin had been so heinous that he was denied burial in the royal cemetery.
34:3 *carved and cast images.* (See note for 14:3).
34:5 *burned the bones of the [pagan] priests.* This act of Josiah, which took place at Bethel, fulfilled the words of the prophet of Judah in the days of Jeroboam I, king of Israel (1Ki 13:1 – 2; 2Ki 23:15 – 16). The prophet had mentioned Josiah by name three hundred years before.

34:8 *Shaphan.* Shaphan was a scribe or secretary of the king (v. 15). He was responsible for state records that must have included the original temple plans and specifications. The temple was repaired strictly according to its original pattern. ***Joahaz the recorder (secretary).*** The recorder kept the royal diaries. Official happenings were duly noted and recorded for posterity. The work of men like Joahaz provided sources for later historians such as the author of Chronicles (1Ch 18:15).

20 2Ki 21:18 **21** 2Ki 21:19 **23** ver. 12 **24** 2Ki 21:23,24 **CHAPTER 34** **1** 2Ki 22:1 **3** 2Ch 15:2; 1Ki 13:2; 2Ch 33:17,22 **4** Lev 26:30; 2Ki 23:4; 2Ki 23:6 **5** 1Ki 13:2 **7** Dt 9:21 **8** 2Ki 22:3

the doors, had collected from Manas-
seh and Ephraim, and from all the
remnant of Israel, and from all Judah
and Benjamin, and the inhabitants of
Jerusalem.
[10]Then they gave it to the workmen
who were appointed over the house of
the LORD, and the workmen who were
working in the house of the LORD gave
it [to others] to repair and restore the
house (temple).
[11]They in turn gave it to the car-
penters and builders to buy quarried
stone and timber for couplings (truss-
es, braces) and to make beams for the
houses which the kings of Judah had
let go to ruin.
[12]The men did the work faithfully
with foremen over them to supervise
and inspect [their work]: Jahath and
Obadiah, the Levites of the sons of
Merari, and Zechariah and Meshul-
lam of the sons of the Kohathites, and
the Levites, all who were skillful with
musical instruments.
[13]*They were* also in charge of the
burden bearers [who carried heavy
loads], and supervised all the workmen
in any kind of service; and some of the
Levites were scribes and officials and
gatekeepers.

Hilkiah Discovers Lost Book of the Law

[14]When they were bringing out the
money which had been brought into
the house of the LORD, Hilkiah the
priest found the Book of the Law of
the LORD *given* by Moses.
[15]Hilkiah told Shaphan the scribe,
"I have found the Book of the Law in
the house of the LORD." And he gave
the book to Shaphan.
[16]Shaphan brought the book to the
king, but [first] reported further to
him, "Your servants are doing every-
thing that was entrusted to them.
[17]"They have emptied out the money
that was found in the house of the LORD,
and have delivered it into the hands of
the overseers and the workmen."
[18]Then Shaphan the scribe told the
king, "Hilkiah the priest has given me
a book." And Shaphan read from it in
the presence of the king.
[19]When the king heard the words of
the Law, he tore his clothes.
[20]Then the king commanded Hilki-
ah, Ahikam the son of Shaphan, Ab-
don the son of Micah, Shaphan the
scribe, and Asaiah a servant of the
king, saying,
[21]"Go, inquire of the LORD for me and
for those who are left in Israel and in
Judah in regard to the words of the
book which has been found; for great
is the wrath of the LORD which has been
poured out on us because our fathers
have not kept *and* obeyed the word of
the LORD, to act in accordance with
everything that is written in this book."

Huldah, the Prophetess, Speaks

[22]So Hilkiah and those whom the
king had told went to Huldah the
prophetess, the wife of Shallum the
son of Tokhath, the son of Hasrah,
keeper of the wardrobe (now she lived
in Jerusalem, in the Second Quarter);
and they spoke to her about this.
[23]And she answered them, "Thus
says the LORD, the God of Israel: 'Tell
the man who sent you to me,
[24]thus says the LORD: "Behold, I am
bringing evil on this place and on its
inhabitants, all the curses that are writ-
ten in the book which they have read
in the presence of the king of Judah.
[25]"Because they have abandoned (re-
jected) Me and have burned incense to
other gods, in order to provoke Me to
anger with all the works of their hands,

34:22 *Huldah the prophetess.* Huldah is one of four female prophets named in the Old Testament. The other three are Miriam (Ex 15:20), Deborah (Jdg 4:4), and Noadiah (Neh 6:14).

34:24 *all the curses that are written in the book.* Both Deuteronomy and Leviticus had long lists of blessings for obedience and curses for rebellion, which were part of the conditions attached to the covenant with Israel (Dt 28–30).

34:25 Apostasy — In all of life, no greater sin, no more serious or sadder error could be made than to forsake God and believe other gods. Such

9 See 2Ki 12:4 **13** 1Ch 23:4,5 **14** 2Ki 22:8 **22** 2Ki 22:14

My wrath will be poured out on this place and it will not be extinguished.” ’

26 “But you shall say the following to King Josiah of Judah, who sent you to inquire of the LORD: ‘Thus says the LORD God of Israel, *concerning* the words which you have heard,

27 “Because your heart was gentle *and* penitent and you humbled yourself before God when you heard His words against this place and its inhabitants, and humbled yourself before Me, and tore your clothes and wept before Me, I also have heard you,” declares the LORD.

28 “Behold, I will gather you to your fathers [in death], and you shall be gathered to your grave in peace, and your eyes shall not see all the evil which I am going to bring on this place and on its inhabitants.” ’ ” So they brought back word to the king.

29 Then the king sent *word* and gathered all the elders of Judah and Jerusalem.

30 And the king went up to the house of the LORD with all the men of Judah, the inhabitants of Jerusalem, the priests, the Levites, and all the people, from the greatest to the least; and he read aloud so they could hear all the words of the Book of the Covenant which was found in the house of the LORD.

Josiah's Good Reign

31 Then the king stood in his place and made a covenant before the LORD—to walk after (obey) the LORD, and to keep His commandments, His testimonies, and His statutes with all his heart and with all his soul, to perform the words of the covenant written in this book.

32 Further, he made all who were present in Jerusalem and Benjamin stand [with him, in confirmation of it]. So the inhabitants of Jerusalem acted in accordance with the covenant of God, the God of their fathers.

33 Josiah removed all the [pagan] repulsive things from all the lands belonging to the sons (descendants) of Israel, and made all who were present in Israel serve the LORD their God. Throughout his lifetime they did not turn from following the LORD God of their fathers.

The Passover Observed Again

35 JOSIAH CELEBRATED the Passover to the LORD in Jerusalem; they slaughtered the Passover *lambs* on the fourteenth *day* of the first month.

2 He appointed the priests to their positions and encouraged them in the service of the house of the LORD.

3 To the Levites who taught all Israel and were holy to the LORD he said, “Put the holy ark in the house (temple) which Solomon the son of David king of Israel built; it shall not be a burden [carried] on your shoulders any longer. Now serve the LORD your God and His people Israel.

4 “Prepare *yourselves* according to your fathers' (ancestors') households by your divisions, in accordance with the instructions of David king of Israel, and the instructions of his son Solomon.

5 “And stand in the holy place [of the priests] according to the sections of the fathers' households of your fellow

---

an act cuts one off from all of the loving care, the wisdom, and discipline of the Creator God. Apostasy grieves God, and it grieves those who love God.

34:31 ***a covenant . . . to walk after (obey) the LORD.*** Very few of the kings of Judah promised to follow the Lord as Josiah did. After David, only Joash, Hezekiah, and Josiah made such public commitments (23:3; 29:10; 1Ch 17:7–14).

35:3 ***Put the holy ark in the house (temple) . . . it shall not be a burden [carried] on your shoulders.*** The ark had apparently been removed from the temple. Who removed it and when or why is not known, but plenty of wicked kings could have done it. Manasseh's vehement opposition to God must have kept the ark in constant jeopardy, so perhaps it had been removed for protection. The only proper way to carry the ark was on the shoulders of the priests (Nu 4:5; 6:1).

29 2Ki 23:1 **31** 2Ki 11:14; 23:3; 2Ch 6:13 **33** 1Ki 11:5; Jer 3:10 **CHAPTER 35** **1** 2Ki 23:21,22; Ex 12:6; Ezr 6:19 **2** 2Ch 23:18; Ezr 6:18; 2Ch 29:5,11 **3** Dt 33:10; See 2Ch 34:14; 2Ch 5:7 **4** 1Ch 9:10; 1Ch 23; 24; 25; 26; 2Ch 8:14 **5** Ps 134:1

kinsmen the lay people, and according
to the Levites, by division of [the fam-
ilies of] a father's household.
6"Slaughter the Passover *lambs* and
consecrate yourselves, and prepare
for your fellow countrymen to carry
out (obey) the word of the LORD *given*
by Moses."
7Then Josiah contributed to the lay
people, to all who were present, flocks
of lambs and young goats number-
ing 30,000, all as Passover offerings,
and 3,000 bulls—these were from the
king's property.
8His officers also contributed a
voluntary offering to the people, the
priests and the Levites. Hilkiah, Zech-
ariah, and Jehiel, the officials of the
house of God, gave to the priests for
the Passover offerings 2,600 *from the
flocks* [of lambs and young goats], and
300 bulls.
9Conaniah also, and Shemaiah and
Nethanel, his brothers, and Hashabiah
and Jeiel and Jozabad, officers of the
Levites, contributed to the Levites for
the Passover offerings 5,000 *from the
flocks* [of lambs and young goats], and
500 bulls.
10When the service was ready, the
priests stood in their [assigned] places
and the Levites by their divisions, in
accordance with the king's command.
11They slaughtered the Passover
lambs, and while the priests sprinkled
the blood *received* from their hand, the
Levites skinned *the animals*.
12Then they removed the burnt of-
ferings, to distribute them to the sec-
tions of the fathers' households of the
lay people to offer to the LORD, as it is
written in the Book of Moses. *They did*
the same with the bulls.
13So they roasted the Passover *lambs*
on the fire according to the ordinance;
and they cooked the holy offerings in
pots, in kettles, and in pans, and quick-
ly brought them to all the lay people.
14Afterward the Levites prepared
for themselves and for the priests, be-
cause the priests, the sons of Aaron,
were busy offering the burnt offerings
and the fat until night; so the Levites
prepared for themselves and for the
priests, the sons of Aaron.
15The singers, the sons of Asaph,
were also in their places in accordance
with the command of David, Asaph,
Heman, and Jeduthun the king's seer;
and the gatekeepers at each gate did
not need to leave their service, because
their kinsmen the Levites prepared
for them.
16So all the service of the LORD was
prepared on that day to celebrate the
Passover, and to offer burnt offerings
on the altar of the LORD, in accordance
with the command of King Josiah.
17Thus the sons of Israel who were
present celebrated the Passover at
that time, and the Feast of Unleavened
Bread for seven days.
18No Passover like it had been cele-
brated in Israel since the days of Samu-
el the prophet; nor had any of the kings
of Israel celebrated such a Passover as
Josiah did with the priests, the Levites,
all Judah and Israel who were present,
and the inhabitants of Jerusalem.
19In the eighteenth year of Josiah's
reign this Passover was celebrated.

Josiah Dies in Battle

20After all this, when Josiah had pre-
pared the temple, Neco king of Egypt
came up to make war at Carchemish

35:6 *Slaughter the Passover lambs.* The Levites were standing in for the people in the sacrifice of the Passover lambs. This became the tradition from that time on, with the result that the priests gained influence and power.

35:13 *holy offerings.* The other holy offerings, distinguished from the Passover offering, were the cattle slaughtered for thank, or peace, offerings (v. 7).

35:18 *since the days of Samuel the prophet.* It had been almost four hundred years since the days of Samuel.

35:20 *to make war at Carchemish.* Carchemish was one of the last strongholds of Assyria to resist the onslaught of the rising neo-Babylonian kingdom. The Babylonians and Medes were on their way to subdue Haran and Carchemish. Neco, more afraid of the Babylonians than the

6 2Ch 29:5,15 **7** 2Ch 30:24 **10** Ezr 6:18 **11** 2Ch 29:22; See 2Ch 29:34 **12** Lev 3:3 **13** Ex 12:8,9; Dt 16:7; 1Sa 2:13-15 **15** 1Ch 25:1; 1Ch 9:17,18; 26:14 **17** Ex 12:15; 13:6; 2Ch 30:21 **18** 2Ki 23:22,23 **20** 2Ki 23:29

on the Euphrates, and Josiah went out to meet him.

[21]But Neco sent messengers to Josiah, saying, "What business do we have with each other, O King of Judah? *I am* not *coming* against you today, but against the house with which I am at war, and God has ordered me to hurry. Stop for your own sake from *interfering with* God who is with me, so that He will not destroy you."

[22]Yet Josiah would not turn away from him, but disguised himself in order to fight against him. He did not listen to the words of Neco from the mouth of God, but came to fight against him on the plain of Megiddo.

[23]The archers shot King Josiah, and the king said to his servants, "Take me away, for I am badly wounded."

[24]So his servants took him out of the chariot and carried him in the second chariot which he had, and brought him to Jerusalem where he died and was buried in the tombs of his fathers. All Judah and Jerusalem mourned for Josiah.

[25]Then Jeremiah sung a lament (funeral song) for Josiah, and all the male and female singers have spoken about Josiah in their laments to this day. They made the songs an ordinance in Israel; behold, they are written in the Lamentations. [Lam 4:20]

[26]Now the rest of the acts of Josiah and his deeds of devotion *and* godly achievements as written in the Law of the LORD,

[27]and his acts, from the first to the last, behold, they are written in the Book of the Kings of Israel and Judah.

Jehoahaz, Jehoiakim, then Jehoiachin Rule

36 THEN THE people of the land took Joahaz the son of Josiah, and made him king in Jerusalem in place of his father.

[2]Joahaz was twenty-three years old when he became king, and he reigned [only] three months in Jerusalem.

[3]Then the king of Egypt deposed him at Jerusalem, and imposed a fine on the land of a hundred talents of silver and one talent of gold.

[4]The king of Egypt made Eliakim, the brother *of Joahaz,* king over Judah and Jerusalem, and changed his name to Jehoiakim. But Neco took Joahaz his brother, and brought him to Egypt.

[5]Jehoiakim was twenty-five years old when he became king, and he reigned for eleven years in Jerusalem; and he did evil in the sight of the LORD his God.

[6]Nebuchadnezzar king of Babylon came up against him and bound him with bronze [chains] to take him to Babylon.

Assyrians, was hoping to get to Carchemish in time to assist his Assyrian allies in their time of need. Josiah was an ally of Babylon, so he went to Megiddo to intercept the Egyptians.

35:21 *God has ordered me.* God sometimes spoke to pagan rulers about a course of action He wanted them to take (36:22; Ge 20:6; 41:25; Da 2:28). Necho did not know the source of his divine leading, but God did direct him, displaying His sovereignty over even the wicked and unbelieving powers of this world (Isa 44:28–45).

35:22 *Megiddo.* The major route from Egypt to the upper Euphrates was the Via Maris, or Way of the Sea. This route went up the coast of Israel before turning inland through the mountain pass at Megiddo. It crossed the plain of Jezreel, crossed the Jordan near the Sea of Galilee, and went on through Damascus where it joined the north-south route to upper Syria. If Josiah could control the pass at Megiddo, he could control the movement of traffic on that vital route.

36:3 *king of Egypt.* After Assyria's defeat at Haran and Carchemish, the Egyptian army withdrew south of the Euphrates, dominating Syria and Judah. Judah became an Egyptian vassal state, which explains why Neco could depose Jehoahaz and require tribute.

36:6 *Nebuchadnezzar.* Nebuchadnezzar was leading a campaign against Carchemish when he succeeded his father. He drove Egypt out of Syria and Judah and took some Jewish captives, including Daniel, back to Babylon (Da 1:1). At the same time, Jehoiakim changed his loyalty from Neco to Nebuchadnezzar and remained a trusted vassal for three years (2Ki 24:1). But then Jehoiakim rebelled against Babylon, and in about

---

24 2Ki 23:30; Zec 12:11 **25** La 4:20; See Mt 9:23; Jer 22:20 **CHAPTER 36** **1** 2Ki 23:30 **5** 2Ki 23:36,37
6 2Ki 24:1; Foretold, Hab 1:6; Jer 36:30

7 Nebuchadnezzar also brought some of the articles of the house (temple) of the Lord to Babylon and put them in his temple there.

8 Now the rest of the acts of Jehoiakim and the repulsive acts which he committed, and what was found against him, behold, they are written in the Book of the Kings of Israel and Judah. And his son Jehoiachin became king in his place.

9 Jehoiachin was eight[teen] years old when he became king, and he reigned for three months and ten days in Jerusalem, and he did evil in the sight of the Lord. [2 Kin 24:8]

Captivity in Babylon Begun

10 Now at the turn of the year [in the spring], King Nebuchadnezzar sent *word* and had him brought to Babylon with the valuable articles of the house of the Lord, and made his brother Zedekiah king over Judah and Jerusalem.

Zedekiah Rules in Judah

11 Zedekiah was twenty-one years old when he became king, and he reigned for eleven years in Jerusalem.

12 He did evil in the sight of the Lord his God; he did not humble himself before Jeremiah the prophet, *who spoke* for the Lord.

13 He also rebelled against King Nebuchadnezzar who had made him swear *allegiance* by God. He stiffened his neck and hardened his heart against turning to the Lord God of Israel.

14 Also, all the officials of the priests and the people were very unfaithful, *following* all the repulsive acts of the [pagan] nations; and they defiled the house of the Lord which He had sanctified in Jerusalem.

15 The Lord, the God of their fathers, sent *word* to them again and again by His messengers, because He had compassion on His people and on His dwelling place.

16 But they kept mocking the messengers of God and despising His words and scoffing at His prophets until the wrath of the Lord arose against His people, until there was no remedy *or* healing.

17 Therefore He brought the king of the Chaldeans against them, who killed their young men with the sword in the house of their sanctuary, and had no compassion on young man or

---

602 BC Nebuchadnezzar returned to Jerusalem to punish him. ***to take him to Babylon.*** Jehoiakim was not actually taken to Babylon since he reigned until 598 BC and died of natural causes in Jerusalem (Jer 22:18).

36:7 *brought some of the articles of the house (temple) of the Lord.* The Babylonian king looted the temple of much of its treasure, fulfilling the prophecy made to Hezekiah a century earlier (32:31). ***his temple.*** His temple was the temple of the Babylonian's patron god Marduk.

36:10 *Zedekiah.* Zedekiah was the youngest of the four sons of Josiah, and the third to rule over Judah (v. 1). He became king by Nebuchadnezzar's appointment, showing Judah's status as a Babylonian vassal (v. 3).

36:12 *Jeremiah.* Jeremiah was the famous prophet who composed the Book of Jeremiah, which included his words to Zedekiah (Jer 21:3 – 7; 32:5).

36:14 *all the repulsive acts of the [pagan] nations.* This statement refers primarily to idolatry and all the immorality and perversity that went with it. God's covenant with Israel required them to be different from the nations in this key respect (Ex 23:24; Lev 26:1; Dt 4:15 – 20,25 – 28; 18:9 – 14; 27:14 – 15).

36:16 Unbelief — There is a line of divine patience that a nation can cross, bringing doom upon that country. In 586 BC Judah stepped over that mark. Prior to this God had graciously given His people many opportunities to repent of their unbelief. When we earnestly pray for our country as commanded by God (1Ti 2:1 – 2) we are asking to be kept from overstepping the limit of God's patience. About three thousand years ago, Solomon succinctly said, "Righteousness [moral and spiritual integrity and virtuous character] exalts a nation, but sin is a disgrace to any people." (Pr 14:34).

36:17 *king of the Chaldeans.* The Chaldean, or Babylonian, king was Nebuchadnezzar, who reigned from 605 to 562 BC. He became an instrument of God's judgment all through Judah's last years and well into the Exile (Da 2:37 – 38; 5:18 – 19).

7 2Ki 24:13; Da 1:1,2 **9** 2Ki 24:8 **10** 2Ki 24:10-17; Da 1:1,2; Jer 37:1 **11** 2Ki 24:18; Jer 52:1 **13** 2Ki 17:14 **15** Jer 25:3,4 **16** Jer 5:12; Pr 1:25; Jer 38:6; Mt 23:34; Ps 79:5 **17** Dt 28:49; 2Ki 25:1; Ezr 9:7; Ps 74:20

virgin, old man or infirm; He gave
them all into his hand.
[18]And as for all the articles of the
house of God, great and small, and
the treasures of the house of the LORD,
and the treasures of the king and of
his officials, he brought them all to
Babylon.
[19]Then they burned the house of God
and tore down the wall of Jerusalem,
and burned all its fortified buildings
with fire, and destroyed all its valuable
articles.
[20]He deported to Babylon those who
had escaped from the sword; and they
were servants to him and to his sons
until the kingdom of Persia was estab-
lished there,
[21]to fulfill the word of the LORD by
the mouth of Jeremiah, until the land
had restored its Sabbaths; for as long
as the land lay desolate it kept Sabbath
until seventy years were complete.
[Lev 25:4; 26:43; Jer 25:11; 29:10]

Cyrus Permits Return

[22]Now in the first year of Cyrus king
of Persia—in order to fulfill the word of
the LORD by the mouth of Jeremiah—
the LORD stirred up the spirit of Cyrus
king of Persia, so that he sent a proc-
lamation throughout his kingdom, and
also *put it* in writing, saying,
[23]"Thus says Cyrus king of Persia:
'The LORD, the God of heaven, has giv-
en me all the kingdoms of the earth,
and He has appointed me to build Him
a house in Jerusalem, which is in Ju-
dah. Whoever there is among you of
all His people, may the LORD his God
be with him, and let him go up [to
Jerusalem]!' "

36:20 ***until the kingdom of Persia.*** Cyrus conquered Babylon in 539 BC and allowed the Jews to return to Jerusalem the following year.
36:21 ***Jeremiah.*** In two places (Jer 25:12; 29:10) Jeremiah predicted the Exile and its length (Da 9:2). ***Sabbath.*** According to the Law of Moses, the land was to lie fallow every seventh year (Lev 25:4). Judah's exile in Babylon allowed the land to enjoy the sabbaths it had missed because of disobedience (Lev 26:33 – 35).
36:22 ***the first year of Cyrus.*** The first year refers to the first year of Cyrus' rule over Babylon, not his first year over Media and Persia. He began to rule Media and Persia in 550 BC. Twelve years later he brought Babylon under his control and issued his famous decree, known from the Old Testament (Ezr 1:2 – 4) and from his own records, the Cylinder of Cyrus. Jeremiah's seventy years were from about 609 to 539 BC. ***the LORD stirred up.*** Cyrus was both a mighty monarch and the instrument by whom God delivered His people from exile, returned them to their land, and rebuilt the temple (Isa 44:28 – 45). Like many rulers who encountered the Living God, Cyrus recognized and even extolled His power as the God of Israel, but this was not the same as abandoning all other gods and following the Lord alone.
36:23 Providence — God is the Lord of the universe. He not only rules over those who are called by His name, but He also moves upon the hearts and minds of others whom He chooses to use in the fulfillment of His purpose. It was part of God's plan for the Jews to be taken captive by Babylon, and for Babylon to be taken by Persia. Cyrus had been chosen and ordained for his role in returning the Jews to their own land, and was even called by name by Isaiah the prophet (Isa 44:28; 45:1). It is not always possible to understand the things that the Lord is doing, but we can still rejoice in His providence, confident that the Judge of all the earth will do right (Ge 18:25).

18 2Ki 25:13 **19** 2Ki 25:9; Ps 79:1,7 **20** 2Ki 25:11; Jer 27:7 **21** Jer 26:6,7; Lev 26:34; Da 9:2; Lev 25:4,5
22 Ezr 1:1; Jer 29:10; Isa 44:28 **23** Ezr 1:2,3

THE BOOK OF

EZRA

▸ **AUTHOR:** Although Ezra is not specifically named as the author, Jewish tradition attributes the book to him. This seems appropriate as portions of the book are written in the first person, from Ezra's point of view (7:28 – 9:15). Similar to Chronicles, this book has a strong priestly emphasis. Ezra was a direct descendant of Aaron through Eleazar, Phinehas, and Zadok, and so came from a long and illustrious priestly line. It is believed that Ezra had access to the extensive library of written documents gathered by Nehemiah and that this was one of the sources used in writing this book as well as Chronicles.

▸ **TIMES:** c. 538 – 457 BC ▸ **KEY VERSE:** Ezr 1:3

▸ **THEME:** Many scholars think Ezra and Nehemiah belong together as one book. Together they tell parts of the same story. The exile is over and the temple is to be rebuilt along with the wall of Jerusalem despite considerable opposition. While Nehemiah's perspective is that of a civil servant and building contractor, Ezra is a teacher of the law and a priest, and as such, provides leadership by bringing God's Word to the people and by restoring proper worship. When the people respond to the Word and reestablish their relationship with God through worship, the building process is renewed and completed.

Proclamation of Cyrus

1 NOW IN the first year of Cyrus king of Persia [that is, the first year he ruled Babylon], in order to fulfill the word of the LORD by the mouth of Jeremiah [the prophet], the LORD stirred up (put in motion) the spirit of Cyrus king of Persia, so that he sent a proclamation throughout all his kingdom, and also *put it* in writing, saying: [Jer 29:10–14]
2 "Thus says Cyrus king of Persia, 'The LORD, the God of heaven, has given me all the kingdoms of the earth and He has appointed me to build Him a house at Jerusalem, which is in Judah.
3 'Whoever there is among you of all His people, may his God be with him! Let him go up to Jerusalem, which is in Judah and rebuild the house of the LORD, the God of Israel; He is God who is in Jerusalem.
4 "In any place where a survivor (Jewish exile) may live, let the men

---

1:1 ***first year of Cyrus.*** This refers to the first year of Cyrus' reign over Babylon. Cyrus the Great, the founder of the Persian Empire and the Achaemenid dynasty, conquered Babylon in 539 BC. The events in the Book of Ezra were taking place at the same time as the latter part of the Book of Daniel, after the overthrow of Belshazzar by the Medes and Persians, and the absorption of Babylon into the Persian Empire (Da 5:28,30 – 31; 6:28). ***Jeremiah.*** Jeremiah had prophesied that the Babylonian captivity would last 70 years (Jer 25:11; 29:10) after which the Lord would judge Babylon (Jer 25:12 – 14). ***he sent a proclamation.*** One hundred and forty years before Cyrus the Great was even born, Isaiah the prophet called him by name, foretelling the decree he would issue allowing the Israelites to return to their homeland (Isa 44:28; 45:14).

1:4 ***let the men (Gentiles) of that place support him.*** The assistance that the Israelites were to receive from their non-Jewish neighbors in

CHAPTER 1 **1** 2Ch 36:22,23; Ezr 5:13,14 **2** Isa 44:28; 45:1,13 **3** Da 6:26

(Gentiles) of that place support him
with silver and gold, with goods and
cattle, together with freewill offerings
for the house of God in Jerusalem.' "

Holy Articles Restored

5Then the heads of the fathers'
households of Judah and Benjamin,
and the priests and Levites, all those
whose spirits God had stirred up, arose
to go up and rebuild the house of the
LORD which is in Jerusalem.
6All those who were around them
encouraged them with articles of silver,
with gold, with goods, with cattle, and
with valuable things, in addition to all
that was given as a freewill offering.
7Also King Cyrus brought out the
articles of the house of the LORD, which
Nebuchadnezzar had carried away
from Jerusalem [when he captured
that city] and had put in the house of
his gods.
8And Cyrus, king of Persia, had
Mithredath the treasurer bring them
out, and he counted them out to Shesh-
bazzar, the governor (leader) of Judah.
9And they counted: 30 dishes (ba-
sins) of gold, 1,000 dishes of silver, 29
duplicates;
1030 [small] gold bowls, 410 [small]
silver bowls of a second *kind*, and 1,000
other articles.
11All the articles of gold and of silver
totaled 5,400. All these Sheshbazzar
[the governor] brought up with the
exiles who went from Babylon up to
Jerusalem.

---

rebuilding the temple was similar to the help an earlier generation received from the Egyptians before the exodus (Ex 12:33–36). In a sense, the return to Jerusalem to rebuild the temple was a second exodus (Isa 43:14–21; 48:20–21).

1:7 *which Nebuchadnezzar had carried away.* See 2 Kings 24:1–7,11–13; 25:8–17; 2 Chronicles 36:5–19; Daniel 1:2.

1:8 *Sheshbazzar.* Ezra 5:2 and 5:16 appear to identify Sheshbazzar and Zerubbabel as one and the same person. The name Sheshbazzar occurs in only two passages (vv. 8–11; 5:14–16) and both times are related to official Persian actions. It is possible, and considered likely, that Sheshbazzar was the Persian name for Zerubbabel.

2:2 *Nehemiah ... Mordecai.* The Nehemiah

5 Php 2:13 **7** Ezr 5:14; 6:5; 2Ki 24:13; 2Ch 36:7 **8** See Ezr 5:14

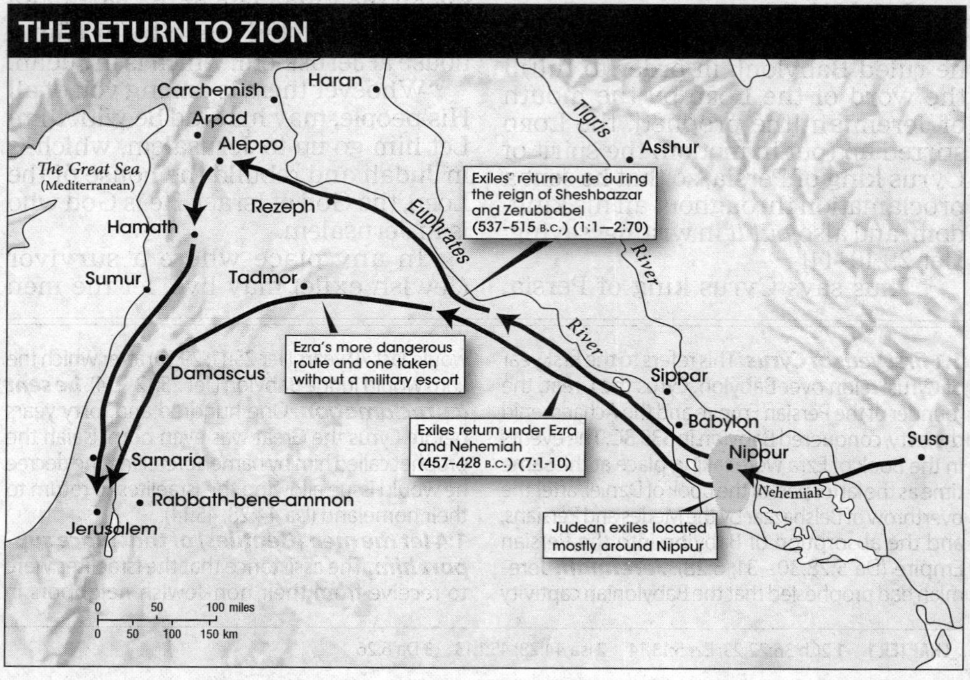

Number of Those Returning

2 NOW THESE are the people of the
province [of Judah] who came up
from the captivity of the exiles, whom
Nebuchadnezzar the king of Babylon
had deported to Babylon, and who re-
turned to Jerusalem and Judah, each
to his own city.
2 These came with Zerubbabel:
Jeshua, Nehemiah, Seraiah, Reelaiah,
Mordecai, Bilshan, Mispar, Bigvai, Re-
hum, Baanah.
The number of the men of the people
of Israel:
3 the sons (descendants) of Parosh,
2,172;
4 the sons of Shephatiah, 372;
5 the sons of Arah, 775;
6 the sons of Pahath-moab of the sons
of Jeshua and Joab, 2,812;
7 the sons of Elam, 1,254;
8 the sons of Zattu, 945;
9 the sons of Zaccai, 760;
10 the sons of Bani, 642;
11 the sons of Bebai, 623;
12 the sons of Azgad, 1,222;
13 the sons of Adonikam, 666;
14 the sons of Bigvai, 2,056;
15 the sons of Adin, 454;
16 the sons of Ater of Hezekiah, 98;
17 the sons of Bezai, 323;
18 the sons of Jorah, 112;
19 the sons of Hashum, 223;
20 the sons of Gibbar, 95;
21 the men of Bethlehem, 123;
22 the men of Netophah, 56;
23 the men of Anathoth, 128;
24 the sons of Azmaveth, 42;
25 the sons of Kiriath-arim, Chephi-
rah and Beeroth, 743;
26 the sons of Ramah and Geba, 621;
27 the men of Michmas, 122;
28 the men of Bethel and Ai, 223;
29 the sons of Nebo, 52;
30 the sons of Magbish, 156;
31 the sons of the other Elam, 1,254;
32 the sons of Harim, 320;
33 the sons of Lod, Hadid and Ono, 725;
34 the men of Jericho, 345;
35 the sons of Senaah, 3,630.

Priests Returning

36 The priests: the sons of Jedaiah of
the house of Jeshua, 973;
37 the sons of Immer, 1,052;
38 the sons of Pashhur, 1,247;
39 the sons of Harim, 1,017.

Levites Returning

40 The Levites: the sons of Jeshua and
Kadmiel, of the sons of Hodaviah, 74.
41 The singers: the sons of Asaph, 128.
42 The sons of the gatekeepers: of
Shallum, Ater, Talmon, Akkub, Hatita,
and Shobai, in all 139.
43 The temple servants: the sons of
Ziha, Hasupha, Tabbaoth,
44 the sons of Keros, Siaha, Padon,
45 the sons of Lebanah, Hagabah,
Akkub,
46 the sons of Hagab, Shalmai, Hanan,
47 the sons of Giddel, Gahar, Reaiah,
48 the sons of Rezin, Nekoda, Gazzam,
49 the sons of Uzza, Paseah, Besai,
50 the sons of Asnah, Meunim, Neph-
isim,
51 the sons of Bakbuk, Hakupha,
Harhur,
52 the sons of Bazluth, Mehida, Harsha,
53 the sons of Barkos, Sisera, Temah,

---

mentioned here is not the same man who rebuilt the walls of Jerusalem 90 years later. The Mordecai in this verse is also considered to be a different man than the one who figured so prominently in the Book of Esther.

2:40 – 42 *The Levites . . . The singers . . . The sons of the gatekeepers.* The Levites assisted the priests in the temple and in teaching the people the Law. The singers were also Levites and had the responsibility of praising God with music (1Ch 15:16). Although only 128 singers returned to Jerusalem, at one time there had been as many as four thousand who praised the Lord with musical instruments in Solomon's temple (1Ch 23:5). The temple servants were another set of Levites who prevented unauthorized people from entering the restricted area of the temple.

2:43 *The temple servants.* In 1 Chronicles 9:2, the temple servants, also called the Nethinim, are distinguished from the priests and the Levites. Jewish tradition identifies the Nethinim with the Gibeonites who had been assigned by Joshua to assist the Levites in more menial tasks (Jos 9:27).

CHAPTER 2 **1** Neh 7:6; 2Ki 24:14-16; 25:11; 2Ch 36:20 **5** See Neh 7:10 **6** Neh 7:11 **31** See ver. 7 **36** 1Ch 24:7 **37** 1Ch 24:14 **38** 1Ch 9:12 **39** 1Ch 24:8 **43** 1Ch 9:2

CHRONOLOGY: EZRA–NEHEMIAH

Dates below are given according to a Nisan-to-Nisan Jewish calendar (see chart, p. 113).
Roman numerals represent months; Arabic numerals represent days.

540 BC
530
520
510
500
490
480
470
460
450
440
430

YEAR	MONTH	DAY	EVENT	REFERENCE
539 BC	Oct.	12	Capture of Babylon	Da 5:30
538 537	Mar. to Mar.	24 11	Cyrus's first year	Ezr 1:1–4
537(?)			Return under Sheshbazzar	Ezr 1:11
537	VII		Building of altar	Ezr 3:1
536	II		Work on temple begun	Ezr 3:8
536–530			Opposition during Cyrus's reign	Ezr 4:1–5
530–520			Work on temple ceased	Ezr 4:24
520	VI = Sept.	24 21	Work on temple renewed under Darius	Ezr 5:2; Hag 1:14
516	XII = Mar.	3 12	Temple completed	Ezr 6:15
458	I = Apr.	1 8	Ezra departs from Babylon	Ezr 7:6–9
	V = Aug.	1 4	Ezra arrives in Jerusalem	Ezr 7:8–9
	IX = Dec.	20 19	People assemble	Ezr 10:9
	X = Dec.	1 29	Committee begins investigation	Ezr 10:16
457	I = Mar.	1 27	Committee ends investigation	Ezr 10:17
445 444	Apr. to Apr.	13 2	20th year of Artaxerxes I	Ne 1:1
444	I = Mar.–Apr.		Nehemiah approaches the king	Ne 2:1
	Aug.(?)		Nehemiah arrives in Jerusalem	Ne 2:11
	VI = Oct.	25 2	Completion of wall	Ne 6:15
	VII = Oct. to Nov.	8 5	Public assembly	Ne 7:73—8:1
	VII = Oct.	15-22 22-28	Festival of Tabernacles	Ne 8:14
	VII = Oct.	24 30	Day of Fasting	Ne 9:1
433 432	Apr. to Apr.	1 19	32nd year of Artaxerxes; Nehemiah's recall and return	Ne 5:14; 13:6

[54]the sons of Neziah, Hatipha.
[55]The sons of [King] Solomon's servants: the sons of Sotai, Hassophereth (Sophereth), Peruda,
[56]the sons of Jaalah, Darkon, Giddel,
[57]the sons of Shephatiah, Hattil, Pochereth-hazzebaim, Ami.
[58]All the temple servants and the sons of Solomon's servants totaled 392.
[59]Now these are the ones who came up from Tel-melah, Tel-harsha, Cherub, Addan, and Immer, but they could not provide evidence of their fathers' households and their descendants, whether they were of Israel:
[60]the sons of Delaiah, Tobiah, and Nekoda, 652.

Priests Removed

[61]Of the sons of the priests: the sons of Hobaiah, of Hakkoz, and of Barzillai, who took a wife from the daughters of Barzillai the Gileadite, and he was known by their name. [2 Sam 17:27, 28; 19:31–39]
[62]These searched [for their names] among those registered in the genealogies, but they were not found; so they *were excluded* from the priesthood as [ceremonially] unclean.
[63]The governor told them that they should not eat of the most holy things [the priests' food] until a priest stood up with Urim and Thummim [who by consulting these articles in his breastplate could determine God's will in the matter].
[64]The whole assembly totaled 42,360,
[65]besides their male and female servants who numbered 7,337; and [among them] they had 200 male and female singers.
[66]Their horses totaled 736; their mules, 245;
[67]their camels totaled 435; their donkeys, 6,720.
[68]Some of the heads of the fathers' *households* (extended families), when they arrived at the house of the LORD in Jerusalem, made voluntary contributions for the house of God to rebuild it on its [old] foundation.
[69]They gave according to their ability to the treasury for the work, 61,000 drachmas of gold, 5,000 minas of silver, and 100 priestly [linen] garments.
[70]So the priests, the Levites, some of the people, the singers, the gatekeepers, and the temple servants settled in their [own] cities, and all Israel [gradually settled] into their cities.

Altar and Sacrifices Restored

3 WHEN THE seventh month came and the sons of Israel were in the cities, the people gathered together as one man to Jerusalem.
[2]Then Jeshua the son of Jozadak and his brothers the priests, and Zerubbabel the son of Shealtiel and his brothers arose, and they built the altar of the God of Israel, to offer burnt offerings on it, as it is written in the Law of Moses, the man of God.
[3]So they set up the altar on its [old] foundation, for they were terrified

---

2:63 *Urim and Thummim.* The Urim and Thummim were somehow used to determine God's will (Ex 28:30). It is not known exactly what they were, but it has been speculated that they were special sacred stones, used for casting lots.

2:64 *42,360.* The individual numbers listed in chapter 2 add up to only 29,818. The difference is accounted for because the larger total includes women, who are not named in the lists.

2:65 *male and female singers.* These men and women are thought to be other than the choir of the temple (v. 41). They were probably professional singers employed for banquets and feasts (2Ch 35:25; Ecc 2:7 – 8). It could be that some of the Jews achieved prosperity and a degree of luxury in Babylon. They had not, after all, been enslaved in exile, but only restricted from returning to their land.

3:1 *seventh month.* The seventh month was a sacred month to the Jewish people. The first day of the month was the Feast of Trumpets (Nu 29:1 – 6), the tenth day was the Day of Atonement (Nu 29:7 – 11), and the fifteenth day was the Feast of Tabernacles (Nu 29:12 – 38).

3:2 – 3 *Jeshua.* This is believed to be the same person as the priest Joshua mentioned by the prophets Haggai and Zechariah (Hag 1:1; Zec 3:1).

---

55 1Ki 9:21 **58** Jos 9:21,27; 1Ch 9:2; 1Ki 9:21 **61** 2Sa 17:27 **62** Nu 3:10 **63** Lev 22:2,10,15,16; Ex 28:30; Nu 27:21 **64** Neh 7:66 **68** Neh 7:70 **69** 1Ch 26:20 **70** Ezr 6:16,17; Neh 7:73 **CHAPTER 3** **2** Dt 12:5 **3** Nu 28:3

because of the peoples of the lands; and they offered burnt offerings on it to the LORD, morning and evening.

4 They celebrated the Feast of Booths, as it is written, and offered the fixed number of daily burnt offerings, in accordance with the ordinances, as each day required;

5 and afterward, there was the continual burnt offering, the offering at the New Moons, and at all the appointed festivals of the LORD that were consecrated, and the offerings of everyone who made a voluntary offering to the LORD.

6 From the first day of the seventh month they began to offer burnt offerings to the LORD, but the foundation of the temple of the LORD had not been laid.

7 They gave money to the masons and to the carpenters, and gave food, drink, and [olive] oil to the people from Sidon and Tyre, to bring cedar wood from Lebanon to the seaport of Joppa, in accordance with the authorization they had from Cyrus king of Persia.

Temple Restoration Begun

8 In the second year of their coming to God's house at Jerusalem, in the second month, Zerubbabel the son of Shealtiel and Jeshua the son of Jozadak began [the work], with the rest of their brothers—the priests and Levites and all who came to Jerusalem from the captivity. They appointed the Levites, from twenty years old and upward, to oversee the work of the house of the LORD.

9 Then Jeshua with his sons and brothers stood united with Kadmiel and his sons, the sons of Judah and the sons of Henadad with their sons and brothers the Levites, to oversee the workmen in the house of God.

10 Now when the builders had laid the foundation of the temple of the LORD, the priests stood in their apparel with trumpets, and the Levites, the sons of Asaph, with their cymbals, to praise the LORD in accordance with the directions of David king of Israel.

11 They sang [responsively], praising and giving thanks to the LORD, *saying*, "For He is good, for His lovingkindness (mercy) toward Israel *endures* forever." And all the people shouted with a great shout when they praised the LORD because the foundation of the house of the LORD was laid.

12 But many of the priests and Levites and heads of fathers' *households*, the old men who had seen the first house (temple), wept with a loud voice when the foundation of this house was laid before their eyes, while many shouted aloud for joy,

13 so that the people could not distinguish the sound of the shout of joy from the sound of the weeping of the people, for the people shouted with a loud shout, and the sound was heard far away.

Adversaries Hinder the Work

4 NOW WHEN [the Samaritans] the adversaries of Judah and Benjamin heard that the exiles from the captivity were building a temple to the LORD God of Israel,

2 they came to Zerubbabel [who was

3:4 *Feast of Booths.* The Feast of Booths, or Tabernacles, was a feast instituted as a remembrance of the earlier generations' wanderings in the wilderness (Nu 29:13 – 38).

3:11 Patience — In spite of Israel's history of sin, leading to the broken empire, captivity, exile, the destruction of the temple and walls of Jerusalem, God still had not forgotten His people. Joy filled the hearts of the Israelites, for God's love had endured. Patiently, faithfully, He was keeping every promise. He is equally faithful and patient to each of us, even though we so often miss the mark. He does not give us up, but showers us with benefits and never ceases to show us His unchanging persistent love.

4:1 *the adversaries of Judah.* The enemies of Judah were the Samaritans. Esarhaddon (v. 2), who ruled Assyria from 681 – 669 BC, had transported the conquered people of the Northern Kingdom to other lands. He then brought people

4 Neh 8:14; Zec 14:16; Ex 23:16; Nu 29:12 **5** Ex 29:38; Nu 28:3, 11,19,26 **7** 1Ki 5:6,9; 2Ch 2:10; Ac 12:20; 2Ch 2:16; Ac 9:36; Ezr 6:3 **8** 1Ch 23:24,27 **9** Ezr 2:40 **10** 1Ch 16:5; 6:31; 16:4; 25:1 **11** Ex 15:21; 2Ch 7:3; Neh 12:24; 1Ch 16:34; Ps 136:1; 1Ch 16:41; Jer 33:11 **CHAPTER 4** **1** See ver. 7-9 **2** ver. 10; 2Ki 17:24,32,33; 19:37

now governor] and to the heads of the fathers' *households* and said to them, "Let us build with you, for we seek your God [and worship] just as you do; and we have sacrificed to Him since the days of Esarhaddon king of Assyria, who brought us up here." [2 Kin 17:24–29]
[3]But Zerubbabel and Jeshua and the rest of the heads of fathers' *households* of Israel said to them, "You have nothing in common with us in building a house to our God; but we ourselves will together build to the LORD God of Israel, just as King Cyrus, the king of Persia, has commanded us."
[4]Then [the Samaritans and others of] the people of the land discouraged the people of Judah, and frightened them [to deter them] from building,
[5]and hired advisers [to work] against them to frustrate their plans during the entire time that Cyrus king of Persia reigned, [and this lasted] even until the reign of Darius king of Persia.
[6]Now in the reign of Ahasuerus (Xerxes), in the beginning of his reign, the Samaritans wrote [to him] an accusation against the inhabitants of Judah and Jerusalem [who had returned from exile].
[7]Later, in the days of [King] Artaxerxes, Bishlam, Mithredath, Tabeel and the rest of their associates wrote to Artaxerxes king of Persia; and the text of the letter was written in Aramaic and translated *from* Aramaic.

The Letter to King Artaxerxes

[8]Rehum the [Persian] commander [of the Samaritans] and Shimshai the scribe wrote a letter against Jerusalem to Artaxerxes the king as follows—
[9]then *wrote* Rehum the [Persian] commander, Shimshai the scribe, and the rest of their associates, the judges, the lesser governors, the officials, the secretaries, the men of Erech, the Babylonians, the men of Susa, that is, the Elamites,
[10]and the rest of the nations whom the great and noble Osnappar deported and settled in the city of Samaria, and in the rest of the region west of the [Euphrates] River. Now
[11]this is a copy of the letter which they sent to him:
"To King Artaxerxes from your servants, the men in the region west of the [Euphrates] River; and now:
[12]Let it be known to the king that the Jews who came up from you have come to us at Jerusalem. They are rebuilding this rebellious and evil city and are finishing its walls and repairing the foundations.
[13]"Now let it be known to the king, that if that city is rebuilt and the walls are finished, then they will not pay tax, custom, or toll, and the revenue of the kings will be diminished.
[14]"Now because we are in the service of the palace, and it is not proper for us to witness the king's dishonor, for that reason we have sent *word* and informed the king,
[15]in order that a search may be made in the record books of your fathers. And you will discover in the record books and learn that this is a rebellious city, damaging to kings and provinces, and that in the past they have incited rebellion within it. That is why that city was laid waste (destroyed).
[16]"We are informing the king that if that city is rebuilt and its walls

---

from elsewhere into Palestine. These foreigners intermarried with the Hebrews who were left in the land. Their offspring became the Samaritans mentioned in the New Testament.

4:4–5 Persecution — Israel encountered hostility when they returned to their land. At first glance it might seem that Israel was at fault for turning down help. These people said they had been offering sacrifices to Jehovah. This did not mean, however, that they had ceased to serve their idols (2Ki 17:29–35). Whatever their hidden reasons for offering help, it would not have been in favor of the Israelites. Their underlying hostility became obvious as they succeeded in hindering the work on the temple.

4:6 *Ahasuerus.* When Darius I died (486 BC) his son Ahasuerus reigned (485–465 BC). Ahasuerus' Greek name was Xerxes. This is the same king who appears in the Book of Esther.

3 Neh 2:20; Ezr 1:1-3 **4** Ezr 3:3 **9** 2Ki 17:30,31 **10** ver. 1; ver. 11,17; ch 7:12 **13** Ezr 7:24

finished, it will mean that you will
have no possession in *the province*
west of the [Euphrates] River."

The King Replies and Work Stops

17 *Then* the king sent an answer to
Rehum the [Persian] commander, to
Shimshai the scribe, and to the rest of
their colleagues who live in Samaria
and in the rest of *the provinces* west of
the River: "Peace (Greetings). And now,
18 The document which you sent to us
has been translated and read before me.
19 "I have issued a command and a
search has been made, and it has been
discovered that this city [Jerusalem] in
earlier times has revolted against the
kings, and that rebellion and sedition
have been perpetrated in it.
20 "There have also been mighty
kings over Jerusalem who have ruled
over all *the provinces* west of the [Euphrates]
River, and tax, custom, and
toll were paid to them.
21 "So, now issue a decree to make
these men stop [work], so that this city
is not rebuilt until a [new] command is
issued by me.
22 "Beware of being negligent in
carrying out this *matter.* Why should
damage increase to the detriment of
the kings?"
23 Then as soon as the copy of King
Artaxerxes' document was read before
Rehum and Shimshai the scribe, and
their colleagues, they went up hurriedly
to Jerusalem to the Jews, and made
them stop [work] by force of arms.
24 Then the work on the house of God
in Jerusalem stopped. It was suspended
until the second year of the reign of
Darius king of Persia.

Temple Work Resumed

5 NOW WHEN the prophets, Haggai
the prophet and Zechariah, the son
(grandson) of Iddo, prophesied to the
Jews who were in Judah and Jerusalem
in the name of the God of Israel,
whose Spirit was over them,
2 then Zerubbabel the son of Shealtiel
[heir to the throne of Judah] and
Jeshua the son of Jozadak arose and
began to rebuild the house of God in
Jerusalem; and the prophets of God
[Haggai and Zechariah] were with
them, supporting *and* encouraging
them. [Hag 1:12–14; Matt 1:12, 13]
3 At that time Tattenai, the governor
of *the province* on the west side of the
[Euphrates] River, and Shethar-bozenai
and their colleagues came to them and
said, "Who issued you a decree *and*
authorized you to rebuild this temple
and to restore this wall (shrine)?"
4 Then, accordingly, we told them the
names of the men who were reconstructing
this building.
5 But the eye of their God was on the
elders of the Jews, so they [Tattenai
and the others] did not stop them until
a report could come before Darius, and
then an answer was returned by letter
concerning it.

Adversaries Write to Darius

6 *This is* a copy of the letter that Tattenai,
governor of *the province* west
of the [Euphrates] River, and Shethar-bozenai
and his associates, the officials
who were west of the River, sent
to Darius the king.
7 They sent a report to him in which
it was written: "To Darius the king,
all peace.
8 "Let it be known to the king that we
have gone to the province of Judah, to
the house of the great God. It is being
built with huge stones, with beams
laid in the walls; and this work goes
on with diligence *and* care and is succeeding
in their hands.
9 "Then we asked those elders, 'Who
issued you a decree to rebuild this temple
and to finish this structure?'

4:21 *this city is not rebuilt.* The Persian king Artaxerxes ordered the Jewish people to cease their work on the temple. Years later at the request of Nehemiah the decision was reviewed (Neh 2:1 – 8).

4:24 *Darius king of Persia.* This is not the same Darius as the Darius of Daniel 5 and 6.

20 1Ki 4:21; Ps 72:8; Ge 15:18; Jos 1:4 **CHAPTER 5** **1** Hag 1:1; Zec 1:1 **2** Ezr 3:2 **3** ver. 6; Ezr 6:6; ver. 9 **4** ver. 10 **5** See Ezr 7:6,28; Ps 33:18; Ezr 6:6 **6** Ezr 4:9 **9** ver. 3,4

[10]"We also asked them their names
so that we might notify you, and so
that we might record the names of the
men in charge.
[11]"They replied, 'We are servants
of the God of heaven and earth, and
are rebuilding the temple which was
erected many years ago, which a great
king of Israel built and finished.
[12]'But because our fathers provoked
the God of heaven to wrath, He handed
them over to Nebuchadnezzar king of
Babylon, the Chaldean, who destroyed
this temple and exiled the people to
Babylon.
[13]'But in the first year of Cyrus king
of Babylon, [the same] King Cyrus
issued a decree to rebuild this house
of God.
[14]'Also the gold and silver utensils of
the house of God which Nebuchadnez-
zar had taken from the temple in Jeru-
salem and had brought into the temple
of Babylon, King Cyrus took from the
temple of Babylon and had them given
to a man whose name was Sheshbaz-
zar, whom he had appointed governor.
[15]'And Cyrus said to him, "Take
these utensils, go and deposit them in
the temple in Jerusalem, and let the
house of God be rebuilt on its site."
[16]'Then that Sheshbazzar came and
laid the foundations of the house of
God in Jerusalem; and from then until
now it has been under construction
and is not yet completed.'
[17]"So now, if it pleases the king, let
a search be conducted in the king's
treasure house [in the royal archives]
there in Babylon to see if it is true that
a decree was issued by King Cyrus to
rebuild this house of God at Jerusalem;
and let the king send us his decision
concerning this matter."

Darius Finds Cyrus' Decree

6 THEN KING Darius issued a de-
cree, and a search was conducted
in Babylon in the archives where the
treasures [and records] were stored.
[2]In Ecbatana in the fortress (palace)
in the province of Media, a scroll was
found on which this was recorded:
"Memorandum—
[3]"In the first year of King Cyrus,
Cyrus the king issued a decree: '*Con-
cerning* the house of God in Jerusalem,
let the temple (house), the place where
sacrifices are offered, be rebuilt and
let its foundations be strongly laid, its
height and its width each 60 cubits,
[4]with three layers of huge stones and
one layer of timbers. Let the cost be
paid from the royal treasury.
[5]'Also let the gold and silver uten-
sils of the house of God, which Neb-
uchadnezzar took from the temple in
Jerusalem and brought to Babylon,
be returned and brought back to their
[proper] places in the temple in Jeru-
salem; and you shall put them in the
house of God.'
[6]"Now *therefore,* Tattenai, governor
of *the province* west of the [Euphra-
tes] River, Shethar-bozenai and your
associates, the officials who are west
of the River, keep far away from there.
[7]"Leave the work on this house of
God alone; let the governor of the
Jews and the Jewish elders rebuild
this house of God on its site.
[8]"Also, I issue a decree as to what
you are to do for these Jewish elders
for the rebuilding of this house of God:
the full cost is to be paid to these peo-
ple from the royal treasury out of the
taxes of *the provinces* west of the Riv-
er, and that without delay.
[9]"Whatever is needed, including

5:12 *our fathers provoked the God of heaven.* Although the Jewish people acknowledged that Nebuchadnezzar destroyed the first temple they traced the cause not to his power, but to their sin and God's judgment.
6:2 *Ecbatana.* This city was the summer residence of the Persian kings.
6:3 *its height and its width each 60 cubits.* Though the complete dimensions are not given, it is likely that the second temple was built on the foundation stones that were still in place from the time of Solomon (1Ki 6:2).
6:8 – 10 *Also.* Not only could Tattenai not stop reconstruction of the temple, he also had to fund its completion.

11 1Ki 6:1 **12** 2Ch 36:16,17; 2Ki 24:2; 25:8,9,11 **13** Ezr 1:1 **14** Ezr 1:7,8; 6:5; Hag 1:14; 2:2,21 **16** Ezr 3:8,10; Ezr 6:15 **17** Ezr 6:1,2 **CHAPTER 6** **1** Ezr 5:17 **4** 1Ki 6:36 **5** Ezr 1:7,8; 5:14 **6** Ezr 5:3

young bulls, rams, and lambs for the burnt offerings to the God of heaven, and wheat, salt, wine, and anointing oil, according to the request of the priests at Jerusalem, let it all be given to them daily without fail,

10so that they may offer pleasing (sweet-smelling) sacrifices to the God of heaven and pray for the life of the king and his sons.

11"I have also issued a decree that *if there is* any man who violates this edict, a beam of timber shall be pulled from his house [and set up]; then he shall be impaled on it, and his house shall be turned into a refuse heap for this [violation].

12"May the God who has caused His Name to dwell there overthrow any king or people who attempts to alter *this command*, so as to destroy this house of God in Jerusalem. I, Darius, have issued this decree; let it be carried out quickly *and* with due diligence."

The Temple Completed and Dedicated

13Then Tattenai, governor of *the province* west of the [Euphrates] River, with Shethar-bozenai and their associates carried out the decree with due diligence, just as King Darius had sent *and* commanded.

14And the Jewish elders built and prospered through the prophesying of Haggai the prophet and Zechariah the son of Iddo. They finished their building as commanded by the God of Israel and in accordance with the decree of Cyrus and Darius and Artaxerxes king of Persia.

15This temple was finished on the third day of the month of Adar, in the sixth year of the reign of King Darius.

16And all Israel—the priests, the Levites, and the rest of the [former] exiles—celebrated the dedication of this house of God with joy.

17They offered at the dedication of this house of God 100 bulls, 200 rams, 400 lambs, and, as a sin offering for all Israel, 12 male goats, according to the number of Israel's tribes.

18Then they appointed the priests to their divisions and the Levites in their orders for the service of God at Jerusalem, as it is written in the book of Moses.

The Passover Observed

19The [former] exiles kept the Passover on the fourteenth [day] of the first month.

20For the priests and the Levites had purified themselves together; all of them were [ceremonially] clean. So they slaughtered the Passover *lamb* for all the exiles, for their brothers the priests, and for themselves.

21The *Passover* was eaten by the sons (descendants) of Israel (Jacob) who returned from exile and by all those who had separated themselves from the [ceremonial] uncleanness of the nations of the land to *join* them, *in order* to seek the LORD God of Israel.

22They observed the Feast of Unleavened Bread for seven days with joy, for the LORD had caused them to rejoice and had turned the heart of the king of Assyria toward them, so that he encouraged them *and* strengthened

---

6:16 *celebrated the dedication . . . with joy.* Some have suggested that Psalms 145 – 148 were used to celebrate the completion of the rebuilding of the temple.

6:19 *kept the Passover.* This celebration must have been exceptionally memorable; it was the first time since the captivity that the people were able to celebrate according to the law, with sacrifices offered in the temple (v. 20).

6:21 *the [ceremonial] uncleanness of the nations of the land.* The term "nations of the land" probably refers to the people who had been transplanted into Palestine by the Assyrians.

6:22 Providence — The situation the Jews faced seemed hopeless. But God in His providence caused Cyrus to look favorably upon the Jews and allow them to return to their homeland. What seemed impossible became possible through God. Sometimes it is easy for us to forget that even in the worst of times and circumstances God is still on His throne.

10 Ezr 7:23 **11** Da 2:5; 3:29 **12** 1Ki 9:3 **14** Ezr 5:1,2; ver. 3; Ezr 1:1; 5:13; Ezr 4:24; Ezr 7:1 **16** 1Ki 8:63; 2Ch 7:5 **17** Ezr 8:35 **18** 1Ch 24:1; 1Ch 23:6; Nu 3:6; 8:9 **19** Ex 12:6 **20** 2Ch 30:15; 2Ch 35:11 **21** Ezr 9:11 **22** Ex 12:15; 13:6; 2Ch 30:21; 35:17; Pr 21:1; 2Ki 23:29; 2Ch 33:11; Ezr 1:1

their hands in the work of the house
of God, the God of Israel.

Ezra Journeys from Babylon to Jerusalem

7 NOW AFTER this, in the reign of
Artaxerxes I [son of Ahasuerus
(Xerxes)] king of Persia, Ezra the son
(descendant) of Seraiah, the son of
Azariah, the son of Hilkiah,
2the son of Shallum, the son of Za-
dok, the son of Ahitub,
3the son of Amariah, the son of Aza-
riah, the son of Meraioth,
4the son of Zerahiah, the son of Uzzi,
the son of Bukki,
5the son of Abishua, the son of
Phinehas, the son of Eleazar, the son
of Aaron the chief priest—
6this Ezra went up from Babylon.
He was a scribe skilled in the Law (the
five books) of Moses, which the LORD
God of Israel had given; and the king
granted him everything that he asked,
for the hand of the LORD his God was
on him.
7Some of the sons of Israel, with
some of the priests and Levites, the
singers and gatekeepers, and the tem-
ple servants also went up [from Bab-
ylon] to Jerusalem in the seventh year
of King Artaxerxes.
8Ezra came to Jerusalem in the fifth
month of the seventh year of the king.
9For on the first of the first month
he started out from Babylon, and on
the first of the fifth month he arrived
in Jerusalem, because the good hand
of his God was on him.
10For Ezra had set his heart (re-
solved) to study *and* interpret the Law
of the LORD, and to practice it and teach
His statutes and ordinances in Israel.

King's Decree on Behalf of Ezra

11Now this is a copy of the decree
that King Artaxerxes gave to Ezra the
priest, the scribe [who was] learned in
the words of the commandments of
the LORD and of His statutes to Israel:
12"Artaxerxes, king of kings, to Ezra
the priest, the scribe of the Law of the
God of heaven, perfect *peace* (greet-
ings). And now
13I have issued a decree that all of
the people of Israel and their priests
and the Levites in my kingdom who
are willing to go to Jerusalem, may
go with you.
14"For you are sent by the king and
his seven advisers to inquire about
Judah and Jerusalem in accordance
with the Law of your God, which is in
your hand,
15and to bring [with you] the silver
and gold which the king and his advis-
ers have freely offered to the God of
Israel, whose dwelling is in Jerusalem,

7:1 – 5 *after this.* The events of chapter 6 took place during the reign of King Darius. The temple was completed and dedicated in 515 BC. Chapter 7 jumps forward many years to the reign of Artaxerxes (464 – 424 BC). Thus, between chapters 6 and 7 there is a gap of approximately 60 years. During this period, the events of the Book of Esther took place.

7:6 *a scribe skilled in the Law (the five books) of Moses.* A scribe was one who copied and studied the law. After the exile, the office of scribe came into prominence, in some ways replacing the prophet in importance, and eventually eclipsing the role of the priest. In the Gospels, numerous references are made to the scribes as ones who were considered spiritual leaders of the people.

7:9 *first month . . . fifth month.* The first month corresponds to March-April, the fifth month to July-August. ***the good hand of his God.*** Ezra was grateful for God's protection even more since the route he traveled was dangerous because of rebellion in Egypt and the fact that spring was the time armies began their campaigns.

7:9 – 10 Obedience — Ezra followed God's command and made his paramount exercise the study, practice, and teaching of God's law. The "good hand of his God" was upon Ezra, for he "had set his heart (resolved) to study and interpret the Law of the LORD." That same command is for us also. We don't always know when we as Christians are being watched by others, but if we are diligent to obey, our lives will point to Christ.

CHAPTER 7 **1** Neh 2:1; 1Ch 6:14 **6** ver. 11,12; Ezr 8:22 **7** Ezr 8:1; See Ezr 8:15; Ezr 2:43; 8:20 **9** Neh 2:8,18 **10** Ps 119:45; ver. 6,25; Dt 33:10; Neh 8:1-8; Mal 2:7 **12** Eze 26:7; Da 2:37; Ezr 4:10 **14** Est 1:14 **15** 2Ch 6:2; Ps 135:21

16 and all the silver and gold which you find in the whole province of Babylon, along with the freewill offering of the people and of the priests for the house of their God in Jerusalem.

17 "Therefore with this money, you shall diligently buy bulls, rams, and lambs, with their grain offerings and drink offerings, and offer them on the altar of the house of your God which is in Jerusalem.

18 "And whatever seems good to you and to your brothers to do with the rest of the silver and the gold, you may do in accordance with the will of your God.

19 "As for the utensils which are given to you for the service of the house of your God, deliver [those] in full before the God of Jerusalem.

20 "The rest of the things required for the house of your God, which you may have occasion to provide, provide it from the royal treasury.

21 "And I, Artaxerxes the king, issue a decree to all the treasurers *in the provinces* west of the [Euphrates] River, that whatever Ezra the priest, the scribe of the Law of the God of heaven, may require of you, it shall be done diligently *and* at once—

22 *even* up to 100 talents of silver, 100 kors (measures) of wheat, 100 baths of wine, 100 baths of [olive] oil, and salt as needed.

23 "Whatever is commanded by the God of heaven, let it be done diligently *and* with enthusiasm for the house of the God of heaven, so that there will not be wrath against the kingdom of the king and his sons.

24 "We also inform you that it is not authorized to impose tax, tribute, or toll on any of the priests, Levites, singers, doorkeepers, temple servants or *other* servants of this house of God.

25 "You, Ezra, are to appoint magistrates and judges in accordance with the wisdom *and* instruction of your God which is in your hand, so that they may judge all the people who are in *the province* west of the [Euphrates] River; *appoint* those who know the laws of your God; and you may teach anyone who does not know *them*.

26 "Whoever does not observe *and* practice the law of your God and the law of the king, let judgment be executed upon him strictly *and* promptly, whether it be for death or banishment or confiscation of property or imprisonment."

The King's Kindness

27 Blessed be the LORD, the God of our fathers [said Ezra], who put *such a thing* as this in the king's heart, to adorn *and* glorify the house of the LORD in Jerusalem,

28 and has extended His mercy *and* lovingkindness to me before the king, his advisers, and all the king's mighty officials. I was strengthened *and* encouraged, for the hand of the LORD my God was upon me, and I gathered together outstanding men of Israel to go up with me [to Jerusalem].

People Who Went with Ezra

8 THESE ARE the heads of their fathers' *households* and *this is* the genealogy of those who went up with me from Babylon in the reign of King Artaxerxes:

2 of the sons of Phinehas, Gershom; of the sons of Ithamar, Daniel; of the sons of David, Hattush;

3 of the sons of Shecaniah *who was* of the sons of Parosh, Zechariah, and with him were registered 150 men by genealogy;

4 of the sons of Pahath-moab, Eliehoenai son of Zerahiah, with 200 men;

5 of the sons of Zattu, Shecaniah son of Jahaziel, with 300 men;

6 of the sons of Adin, Ebed son of Jonathan, with 50 men;

7 of the sons of Elam, Jeshaiah son of Athaliah, with 70 men;

7:22 *100 talents of silver.* One hundred talents of silver weighed nearly four tons. One hundred kors of wheat amounted to about 625 bushels; one hundred baths of oil equaled about six hundred gallons each.

16 Ezr 8:25; 1Ch 29:6,9 **17** Nu 15:4-13; Dt 12:5,11 **25** Ex 18:21,22; Dt 16:18; ver. 10; 2Ch 17:7; Mal 2:7; Mt 23:2,3 **27** 1Ch 29:10; Ezr 6:22 **28** Ezr 9:9; ver. 6,9; See Ezr 5:5; 8:18 **CHAPTER 8** **2** 1Ch 3:22 **3** Ezr 2:3

[8]of the sons of Shephatiah, Zebadiah
son of Michael, with 80 men;
[9]of the sons of Joab, Obadiah son of
Jehiel, with 218 men;
[10]of the sons of Bani, Shelomith son
of Josiphiah, with 160 men;
[11]of the sons of Bebai, Zechariah son
of Bebai, with 28 men;
[12]of the sons of Azgad, Johanan son
of Hakkatan, with 110 men;
[13]of the sons of Adonikam, the last to
come, their names are Eliphelet, Jeiel,
and Shemaiah, with 60 men;
[14]and of the sons of Bigvai, Uthai and
Zabbud, with 70 men.

Ezra Sends for Levites

[15]Now I gathered them together at
the river that runs to Ahava, where we
camped for three days. I observed the
people and the priests, and I did not
find any Levites there.
[16]So I sent for Eliezer, Ariel, Shema-
iah, Elnathan, Jarib, Elnathan, Na-
than, Zechariah, and Meshullam, [who
were] leading men, and also for Joiarib
and Elnathan, [who were] teachers.
[17]And I sent them to Iddo, the leading
man at the place Casiphia, telling them
what to say to Iddo and his brothers,
the temple servants at the place Ca-
siphia, *that is,* to bring us servants
(ministers) for the house of our God.
[18]And as the good hand of our God
was upon us, they brought us a man of
understanding (insight) from the sons
of Mahli, the son of Levi, the son of Is-
rael, *named* Sherebiah, with his sons
and his brothers (relatives), 18 men;
[19]and Hashabiah, and with him Je-
shaiah of the sons of Merari, with his
brothers (relatives) and their sons, 20
men;
[20]also 220 of the temple servants,
whom David and the leaders had set
apart [with their descendants] for the
service of the Levites. They were all
designated by name.

Protection of God Invoked

[21]Then I proclaimed a fast there at
the river Ahava, so that we might hum-
ble ourselves before our God to seek
from Him a safe journey for us, our
children, and all our possessions.
[22]For I was ashamed to request troops
and horsemen from the king to protect
us from the enemy along the way, be-
cause we had told the king, "The hand
of our God is favorable toward all those
who seek Him, but His power and His
anger are against all those who aban-
don (turn away from) Him."
[23]So we fasted and sought [help
from] our God concerning this [mat-
ter], and He heard our plea.
[24]Then I set apart twelve leading
priests, Sherebiah, Hashabiah, and ten
of their brothers (relatives),
[25]and I weighed out to them the sil-
ver, the gold, and the utensils, the of-
fering for the house of our God which
the king, his advisers, his officials,
and all Israel who were present there
had offered.
[26]I weighed into their hands 650 tal-
ents of silver, and silver utensils *worth*
100 talents, and 100 talents of gold;
[27]also 20 bowls of gold *worth* 1,000
darics, and two utensils of fine shiny
bronze, precious as gold.
[28]Then I said to them, "You are holy
to the LORD, the utensils are holy, and
the silver and the gold are a freewill of-
fering to the LORD God of your fathers.
[29]"Guard and keep them until you
weigh them before the leading priests
and the Levites and the leaders of the
fathers' *households* of Israel in Jeru-
salem, in the chambers of the house
of the LORD."
[30]So the priests and the Levites

8:17 ***Casiphia.*** The significance of Casiphia is uncertain, but it is thought that there may have been a Jewish sanctuary or temple there.

8:22 ***seek Him.*** Ezra knew that God would protect him; he wasn't afraid to "stick his neck out" even though it might have been more comfortable to have the security of soldiers as escorts. In our own lives, it is the same. Our responsibility is obedience, no matter what. Our safety is God's responsibility.

15 See Ezr 7:7 **18** Neh 8:7; 9:4,5 **20** See Ezr 2:43 **21** 2Ch 20:3; Lev 16:29; 23:29; Isa 58:3,5; Ps 5:8 **22** 1Co 9:15; Ezr 7:6,9,28; Ps 33:18,19; 34:15,22; Ro 8:28; Ps 34:16; 2Ch 15:2 **23** 1Ch 5:20; 2Ch 33:13; Isa 19:22 **25** Ezr 7:15,16 **28** Lev 21:6-8; Dt 33:8; Lev 22:2,3; Nu 4:4,15,19,20

received the weighed out silver and
gold, and the utensils, to bring them
to Jerusalem to the house of our God.
31 We set out from the river Ahava on
the twelfth [day] of the first month to
go to Jerusalem; and the hand of our
God was upon us, and He rescued us
from the hand of the enemy and those
who lay in ambushes along the way.
32 So we came to Jerusalem and re-
mained there for three days.

Treasure Placed in the Temple

33 On the fourth day the silver and
the gold and the utensils were weighed
out in the house of our God into the
hand of Meremoth the son of Uriah the
priest, and with him was Eleazar the
son of Phinehas; and with them were
the Levites—Jozabad the son of Jeshua
and Noadiah the son of Binnui.
34 Every piece was counted and
weighed, and all the weight was re-
corded at that time.
35 Also the [former] exiles who had
come from the captivity offered burnt
offerings to the God of Israel: 12 bulls
for all Israel, 96 rams, 77 lambs, and
12 male goats for a sin offering. All
this was a burnt offering to the LORD.
36 And they delivered the king's
edicts to the king's satraps (lieuten-
ants) and to the governors west of the
[Euphrates] River, and they supported
the people and God's house.

Mixed Marriages

9 WHEN THESE things were com-
pleted, the officials came to me
and said, "The people of Israel and
the priests and Levites have not sep-
arated themselves from the peoples
of the lands, but have committed the
repulsive acts of the Canaanites, Hit-
tites, Perizzites, Jebusites, Ammonites,
Moabites, Egyptians, and Amorites.
2 "For they have taken some of their
daughters *as wives* for themselves and
for their sons, so that the holy race
has intermingled with the peoples of
the lands. Indeed, the officials and
chief men have been foremost in this
unfaithful act *and* direct violation [of
God's will]." [Deut 7:3, 4]
3 When I heard this, I tore my cloth-
ing and my robe [in grief], I pulled out
some of the hair from my head and my
beard, and sat down appalled [at the
shame of it].
4 Then everyone who trembled at the
words of the God of Israel because of
the unfaithfulness of the exiles gath-
ered to me as I sat appalled until the
evening offering.

Prayer of Confession

5 At the evening offering I arose from
my [time of] humiliation *and* penitence
and having torn my clothing and my
robe, I fell on my knees and stretched
out my hands to the LORD my God,
6 and I said, "O my God, I am ashamed
and embarrassed to lift up my face to
You, my God, for our wrongdoings
have risen higher than our heads and
our guilt has grown to the heavens.
7 "Since the days of our fathers to this
day we have been exceedingly guilty;
and on account of our wrongdoings we,
our kings, and our priests have been
handed over to the kings of the lands,
to the sword, to captivity, to plundering,
and to complete shame, as it is today.
8 "But now for a brief moment grace
has been [shown to us] from the LORD
our God, who has left us a surviving
remnant and has given us a peg (se-
cure hold) in His holy place, that our
God may enlighten our eyes and give
us a little reviving in our bondage.
9 "For we are slaves; yet our God has
not abandoned us in our bondage, but

9:2 taken some of their daughters as wives for themselves. Intermarrying with people who did not worship the One True God was expressly forbidden (Ex 34:16; Dt 7:3). While there are instances of marriages to non-Israelites being blessed (Rahab, Ruth), these were cases where the woman had clearly taken a stand as a believer in Yahweh, renouncing her old religion.

31 Ezr 7:6,9,28 **32** Neh 2:11 **33** ver. 26,30 **35** Ezr 6:17 **36** Ezr 7:21 **CHAPTER 9** **1** Ezr 6:21; Neh 9:2; Dt 12:30,31 **2** Ex 34:16; Dt 7:3; Ex 22:31; Dt 7:6; 2Co 6:14 **3** Job 1:20; Ps 143:4 **4** Ezr 10:3; Ex 29:39 **5** Ex 9:29 **6** Da 9:7,8; Ps 38:4; 2Ch 28:9; Rev 18:5 **7** Ps 106:6; Da 9:5,6; Dt 28:36; Neh 9:30; Da 9:7,8 **8** Ps 34:5 **9** Neh 9:36; Ps 136:23; Ezr 7:28; Isa 5:2

has extended lovingkindness to us before the kings of Persia, to revive us to rebuild the house of our God, to repair the site of its ruins and to give us a wall [of protection] in Judah and Jerusalem.
10"Now, O our God, what shall we say after this? For we have abandoned (turned away from) Your commandments,
11which You have commanded by Your servants the prophets, saying, 'The land which you are entering to possess is a defiled land with the uncleanness of the peoples of the lands, through their repulsive acts which have filled it from one end to the other *along* with their impurity.
12'So now do not give your daughters to their sons or take their daughters for your sons; and never seek their peace or their prosperity, so that you may be strong and eat the good *things* of the land and leave it as an inheritance to your children forever.'
13"And after everything that has come upon us for our evil deeds and for our great guilt, since You our God have punished us less than our wrongdoings *deserve,* and have given us survivors like these,
14shall we again break Your commandments and intermarry with the peoples who practice these repulsive acts? Would You not be angry with us to the point of total destruction, so that there would be no remnant nor survivor? [Deut 7:2–4]
15"O LORD God of Israel, You are [uncompromisingly] just (righteous), for we have been left as survivors, as it is this day. Behold, we are before You in our guilt, for no one can stand before You because of this."

Reconciliation with God

10 NOW WHILE Ezra was praying and confessing, weeping and laying himself face down before the house of God, a very large group from Israel, of men, women, and children, gathered to him, for the people wept bitterly.
2Shecaniah the son of Jehiel, of the sons of Elam, said to Ezra, "We have been unfaithful to our God and have married foreign women from the peoples of the land; yet now there is hope for Israel in spite of this.
3"Therefore let us now make a covenant with our God to send away all the [foreign] wives and their children, in accordance with the advice of my

---

9:13 – 14 *punished us less than our wrongdoings deserve.* Israel was guilty and deserved whatever punishment God gave them. God would have been just in consuming them, even to the point of leaving no remnant or survivor. But in His great mercy, God provided a way out for Israel. In an even greater way, He provided a way out for all mankind. Sin is always sin, no matter how small it may seem to us. God would be justified in destroying us all for only one sin. God is just. This means that He cannot tolerate sin even a little bit. But He is also more loving, kind, and compassionate than we can comprehend. In His mercy, He provided the way out. He sent His son to pay the price of our sin for us. In this way His justice was satisfied, and at the same time His love provided a way to save us.

9:15 *we have been left as survivors.* It is true that Israel was rebellious and evil at times in her history. Kings and Chronicles record how wicked they had become. But the people who returned to rebuild the temple were a chastened and different generation from the one taken into captivity. The men and women who went back were determined to obey God's laws and would not tolerate idolatry. While the returning Jews succeeded in ridding themselves of heathen idol worship, they created another problem. They set in motion a legalistic system that culminated with a people who valued their interpretation of the law over the Scriptures. The condition progressed until Jesus spoke out against their extremism and their lack of mercy and compassion (Mt 23:1 – 36).

10:3 Fear of God — When one thinks of fear, usually what comes to mind is dread and alarm — an unpleasant emotion caused by the anticipation of danger or a threat. But the fear of God is another thing. We tremble and obey Him, not out of dread but out of deep reverence for an almighty God. The covenant the men of Israel made with God was the most binding form of covenant a person could make. They were pledging "in the fear of God" to do as they promised.

12 Ex 23:32; Dt 7:3; 23:6; Pr 20:7 **13** Ps 103:10 **14** Jn 5:14; 2Pe 2:20; Neh 13:23; Dt 9:8 **15** Neh 9:33; Da 9:14; Ro 3:19; 1Co 15:17 **CHAPTER 10** **1** Da 9:20; 2Ch 20:9 **2** Neh 13:27 **3** 2Ch 34:31; Ezr 9:4; Dt 7:2,3

lord and of those who tremble [in reverent obedience] at the commandment of our God; and let it be done in accordance with the Law.
4"Stand up, for it is your duty, and we will be with you. Be brave and act."
5Then Ezra stood and made the leaders of the priests, the Levites, and all Israel, take an oath that they would act in accordance with this proposal; so they took the oath.
6Then Ezra got up from before the house of God and went into the chamber of Jehohanan the son of Eliashib [and spent the night there]. He did not eat bread nor drink water, for he was mourning over the [former] exiles' faithlessness.
7They made a proclamation throughout Judah and Jerusalem to all the [former] exiles, that they were to assemble at Jerusalem,
8and that whoever would not come within three days, by order of the counsel of the leaders and the elders, all his possessions *and* property would be forfeited and he himself would be excluded from the assembly of the exiles.
9So all the men of Judah and Benjamin gathered at Jerusalem within three days. It was the twentieth [day] of the ninth month, and all the people sat in the open square *in front of* the house of God, trembling because of [the seriousness of] this matter and because of the heavy rain.
10Then Ezra the priest stood up and said to them, "You have been unfaithful [to God] and have married foreign (pagan) women, adding to the guilt of Israel.
11"So now, make confession to the LORD God of your fathers and do His will. Separate yourselves from the peoples of the land and from [your] foreign wives."
12Then all the assembly replied with a loud voice, "It is our responsibility to do just as you have said.
13"But there are many people and it is the season of heavy rain; so we are unable to stand outside. Nor *can* the task *be done* in a day or two, for we have transgressed greatly in this matter.
14"Let our leaders stand for *and* represent the entire assembly; let all those in our cities who have married foreign wives come at appointed times, together with the elders and judges of each city, until the burning anger of our God over this matter is turned away from us."
15Only Jonathan the son of Asahel and Jahzeiah the son of Tikvah opposed this, and Meshullam and Shabbethai the Levite supported them.
16Then the [former] exiles did so. Ezra the priest and men *who were* heads of fathers' *households* were selected, according to their fathers' households, each of them by name; and they sat down on the first day of the tenth month to investigate the matter.
17And by the first day of the first month they finished *investigating* all the men married to foreign wives.

List of Offenders

18Now among the sons of the priests who had married foreign women were found: of the sons of Jeshua [the high priest] the son of Jozadak, and his brothers—Maaseiah, Eliezer, Jarib, and Gedaliah.
19They vowed to send away their [pagan] wives, and being guilty, *they each offered* a ram of the flock for their offense.
20Of the sons of Immer: Hanani and Zebadiah;
21and of the sons of Harim: Maaseiah, Elijah, Shemaiah, Jehiel, and Uzziah;
22and of the sons of Pashhur: Elioenai, Maaseiah, Ishmael, Nethanel, Jozabad, and Elasah.
23Of the Levites: Jozabad, Shimei,

10:9 *the ninth month.* The ninth month, Chislev, corresponds to November-December.

4 1Ch 28:10 **5** Neh 5:12 **6** Dt 9:18 **9** See 1Sa 12:18 **11** Jos 7:19; Pr 28:13; ver. 3 **14** 2Ch 30:8 **19** 2Ki 10:15; 1Ch 29:24; 2Ch 30:8; Lev 6:4,6

Kelaiah, that is, Kelita, Pethahiah, Judah, and Eliezer.
[24]Of the singers: Eliashib; and of the gatekeepers: Shallum, Telem, and Uri.
[25]Of Israel, of the sons of Parosh: Ramiah, Izziah, Malchijah, Mijamin, Eleazar, Malchijah (Hashabiah), and Benaiah;
[26]and of the sons of Elam: Mattaniah, Zechariah, Jehiel, Abdi, Jeremoth, and Elijah;
[27]and of the sons of Zattu: Elioenai, Eliashib, Mattaniah, Jeremoth, Zabad, and Aziza;
[28]and of the sons also of Bebai: Jehohanan, Hananiah, Zabbai, and Athlai;
[29]and of the sons of Bani: Meshullam, Malluch, Adaiah, Jashub, Sheal, and Jeremoth;
[30]and of the sons of Pahath-moab: Adna, Chelal, Benaiah, Maaseiah, Mattaniah, Bezalel, Binnui, and Manasseh;
[31]and of the sons of Harim: Eliezer, Isshijah, Malchijah, Shemaiah, Shimeon,
[32]Benjamin, Malluch, and Shemariah;
[33]of the sons of Hashum: Mattenai, Mattattah, Zabad, Eliphelet, Jeremai, Manasseh, and Shimei;
[34]of the sons of Bani: Maadai, Amram, Uel,
[35]Benaiah, Bedeiah, Cheluhi,
[36]Vaniah, Meremoth, Eliashib,
[37]Mattaniah, Mattenai, Jaasu,
[38]Bani, Binnui, Shimei,
[39]Shelemiah, Nathan, Adaiah,
[40]Machnadebai, Shashai, Sharai,
[41]Azarel, Shelemiah, Shemariah,
[42]Shallum, Amariah, and Joseph.
[43]Of the sons of Nebo: Jeiel, Mattithiah, Zabad, Zebina, Jaddai, Joel, and Benaiah.
[44]All these had married foreign women, and some of them had wives *by whom* they had children.

THE BOOK OF

NEHEMIAH

▸ **AUTHOR:** It is apparent that much of this book came from Nehemiah's personal memoirs. The account is extremely vivid and frank. Obviously, 1:1 – 7:5; 12:27 – 43; and 13:4 – 31 are the "words of Nehemiah." Some scholars state that Nehemiah composed the above portions and compiled the rest. Others feel that Ezra wrote 7:6 – 12:26 and 12:44 – 13:3, then put together the rest using Nehemiah's diary. Nehemiah 7:5 – 73 and Ezra 2:1 – 70 are almost identical, but both lists may have been pulled from an existing record of the same period.

▸ **TIMES:** 444 – 425 BC ▸ **KEY VERSE:** Neh 6:15

▸ **THEME:** Nehemiah's role in rebuilding the temple and the walls of Jerusalem is more political than physical, as he deals with the new political situation arising in Persia and in Jerusalem. He also serves as the general contractor who pulls together the raw materials and the workers while orchestrating the rebuilding process. Within all his work, there is an underlying understanding that he has been called by God to do this work and is fulfilling God's purposes. When the people don't follow through with adhering to the law, Nehemiah is just as forceful as Ezra in calling the people back to repentance and obedience.

Nehemiah's Grief for the Exiles

1 THE WORDS of Nehemiah son of
Hacaliah:
Now it happened in the month of
Chislev, in the twentieth year [of the
Persian king], as I was in the capitol
of Susa,
2Hanani, one of my brothers, and
some men from Judah came; and I
asked them about the surviving Jews
who had escaped and survived the
captivity, and about Jerusalem.
3They said to me, "The remnant
there in the province who survived the
captivity are in great distress and reproach; the wall of Jerusalem is broken
down and its [fortified] gates have been
burned (destroyed) by fire."
4Now it came about when I heard
these words, I sat down and wept and
mourned for days; and I was fasting
and praying [constantly] before the
God of heaven.
5And I said, "Please, O LORD God of
heaven, the great and awesome God,
who keeps the covenant and loving-

1:1 *Nehemiah.* Nehemiah, whose name means "The Lord Comforts," was a highly placed statesman associated with Ezra in the work of reestablishing the people of Judah in the promised land. ***the twentieth year.*** This is a reference to the twentieth year of rule of Artaxerxes I Longimanus (456 – 424 BC). It was he who had commissioned Ezra to return to Jerusalem (Ezr 7:1). ***capitol of Susa.*** The capitol, or fortified royal palace, was built on an acropolis about 150 miles north of the Persian Gulf, in present day Iran. This is the city where Daniel received his vision about the rams and goats (Da 8:2) and the home of Mordecai and Esther (Est 1:2).

1:2 *men from Judah . . . Jerusalem.* The journey from Susa to Jerusalem, which covered nearly one thousand miles, probably took about four months.

1:5 Obedience — The covenant of God with the Israelites had been made with the understanding that obedience would bring God's great

CHAPTER 1 **1** Neh 10:1 **3** Neh 2:17; 2Ki 25:10 **5** Da 9:4; Ex 20:6

kindness for those who love Him and
keep His commandments,
6 please let Your ear be attentive and
Your eyes open to hear the prayer of
Your servant which I am praying be-
fore You, day and night, on behalf of
Your servants, the sons (descendants)
of Israel (Jacob), confessing the sins of
the sons of Israel which we have com-
mitted against You; I and my father's
house have sinned.
7 "We have acted very corruptly
against You and have not kept the
commandments, nor the statutes, nor
the ordinances which You commanded
Your servant Moses. [Deut 6:1–9]
8 "Please remember the word which
You commanded Your servant Mo-
ses, saying, 'If you are unfaithful *and*
violate your obligations to Me I will
scatter you [abroad] among the peo-
ples; [Lev 26:33]
9 but if you return to Me and keep My
commandments and do them, though
those of you who have been scattered
are in the most remote part of the heav-
ens, I will gather them from there and
will bring them to the place where I
have chosen for My Name to dwell.'
[Deut 30:1–5]
10 "Now they are Your servants and
Your people whom You have redeemed
by Your great power and by Your
strong hand.
11 "Please, O Lord, let Your ear be
attentive to the prayer of Your servant
and the prayer of Your servants who
delight to [reverently] fear Your Name
[Your essence, Your nature, Your at-
tributes, with awe]; and make Your
servant successful this day and grant
him compassion in the sight of this
man [the king]."
For I was cupbearer to the king [of
Persia].

Nehemiah's Prayer Answered

2 IN THE month of Nisan, in the
twentieth year of King Artaxer-
xes, when wine was *placed* before him,
I took the wine and gave it to the king.
Now I had not [previously] been sad in
his presence.
2 So the king said to me, "Why do you
look sad when you are not sick? This
is nothing but sadness of heart." Then
I was very frightened,
3 and I said to the king, "Let the king
live forever. Why should my face not
be sad when the city, the place of my
fathers' tombs, lies desolate and its
gates have been consumed by fire?"
4 The king said to me, "What do you
request?" So I prayed to the God of
heaven.
5 I said to the king, "If it pleases the
king, and if your servant has found
favor in your presence, [I ask] that you
send me to Judah, to the city of my
fathers' tombs, so that I may rebuild it."
6 The king, beside whom the queen
was sitting, asked me, "How long will
your journey take, and when will you
return?" So it pleased the king to send
me, and I gave him a definite time [for
my return].

---

blessings, and the result of rebellion would be curses, one of which was captivity (Dt 28–30). God had been patient for a long time, but eventually the nation was overpowered, and many of the people taken into captivity. Nehemiah acknowledged not only the necessity of obedience, but the confidence that he had that God would answer his prayer because God said He would hear and bless the obedient.

1:11 *cupbearer to the king.* As the king's cupbearer, Nehemiah held an honored position. His constant proximity to the king of Persia made him privy to the state secrets and personal affairs of the king.

2:2 *you look sad.* Persian monarchs believed that just being in their presence would make any person happy. Yet, Nehemiah was about to request the emperor's permission to go to Jerusalem, suggesting that he would rather be somewhere other than in the emperor's presence. In addition to this, it was Artaxerxes himself who had ordered the work on the wall to be stopped (Ezr 4:21–23). Nehemiah had reason to be afraid.

2:4 *I prayed.* Even though Nehemiah had come into the presence of the king, he never left the presence of God.

---

6 1Ki 8:28,29; 2Ch 6:40; Da 9:17,18; Da 9:20 **7** Ps 106:6; Da 9:5; Dt 28:15 **8** Lev 26:33; Dt 4:25-27; 28:64 **9** Lev 26:39; Dt 4:29-31; 30:2; Dt 30:4 **10** Dt 9:29; Da 9:15 **11** ver. 6; Isa 26:8; Heb 13:18; Neh 2:1 **CHAPTER 2** **1** Ezr 7:1; Neh 1:11 **2** Pr 15:13 **3** 1Ki 1:31; Da 2:4; 5:10; 6:6,21; Neh 1:3 **6** Neh 5:14; 13:6

7 Then I said to the king, "If it pleases
the king, let letters be given to me for the
governors *of the provinces* beyond the
[Euphrates] River, so that they will allow
me to pass through until I reach Judah,
8 and a letter to Asaph, the keeper of
the king's forest, so that he will give
me timber to construct beams for the
gates of the fortress which is by the
temple, and for the city wall and for
the house which I will occupy." And the
king granted me *what I asked*, for the
good hand of my God was upon me.
9 Then I came to the governors *of
the provinces* beyond the [Euphrates]
River and gave them the king's letters.
Now the king had sent officers of the
army and horsemen with me.
10 When Sanballat the Horonite and
Tobiah the Ammonite official heard
this, it caused them great displeasure
that someone had come to see about the
welfare *and* prosperity of the Israelites.

Nehemiah Inspects Jerusalem's Walls

11 So I came to Jerusalem and was
there for three days.
12 Then I got up in the night, I and a
few men with me. I did not tell anyone
what my God was putting in my heart
to do for Jerusalem, and there was
no animal with me except the one on
which I was riding [so as not to attract
attention].
13 So I went out at night by the Valley
Gate toward the Dragon's Well and
to the Refuse Gate and inspected the
walls of Jerusalem which were broken
down and its gates which were con-
sumed by fire.
14 Then I passed over to the Fountain
Gate and to the King's Pool, but there
was no place for the animal that I was
riding to pass.
15 So I went up at night by the ravine
[of Kidron] and inspected the wall;
then I turned back and entered [the
city] by the Valley Gate, and returned.
16 The officials did not know where
I had gone or what I had done; nor
had I yet told the Jews, the priests, the
nobles, the officials, or the rest who
did the work.
17 Then I said to them, "You see the
bad situation that we are in—how Je-
rusalem is desolate *and* lies in ruins
and its gates have been burned with
fire. Come, and let us rebuild the wall
of Jerusalem, so that we will no longer
be a disgrace."
18 Then I told them how the hand of
my God had been favorable to me and
also about the words that the king had
spoken to me. And they said, "Let us
rise up and build." So they thoroughly
supported the good *work*.
19 But when Sanballat the Horonite
and Tobiah the Ammonite official and
Geshem the Arab heard about it, they
mocked us and regarded us with con-
tempt and said, "What is this thing you
are doing? Are you rebelling against
the king?"
20 I answered them, "The God of
heaven [has appointed us for His pur-
pose and] will give us success; there-
fore we His servants will arise and
build, but you have no portion, right,
or memorial in Jerusalem."

Builders of the Walls

3 THEN ELIASHIB the high priest
rose up with his brothers the
priests and built the Sheep Gate. They
consecrated it and set up its doors; and
they consecrated the wall [westward]
to the Tower of the Hundred, as far as
the Tower of Hananel.
2 Next to Eliashib the men of Jericho

2:8 *the king's forest . . . timber.* Jerusalem had plenty of limestone for building projects, but timber was scarce.

2:10 *the Ammonite.* At the time of Nehemiah, the Ammonites (Ge 19:38) had pushed west into the land vacated by Judah. The prospect of a strong Jewish community in newly fortified Jerusalem would have seemed threatening.

2:18 *God had been favorable.* Nehemiah emphasized that it was not just his own idea to rebuild the wall of Jerusalem. The idea had come to him from the Lord (v. 8,12).

8 Neh 3:7; ver. 18; Ezr 5:5; 7:6,9,28 **11** Ezr 8:32 **13** 2Ch 26:9; Neh 3:13; ver. 17; Neh 1:3 **14** Neh 3:15 **15** 2Sa 15:23; Jer 31:40 **17** Neh 1:3; Ps 44:13; 79:4; Jer 24:9; Eze 5:14,15; 22:4 **18** ver. 8; 2Sa 2:7 **19** Neh 6:6 **20** Ezr 4:3 **CHAPTER 3** **1** Neh 12:10; Jn 5:2; Neh 12:39; Jer 31:38; Zec 14:10 **2** Ezr 2:34

built, and next to them Zaccur the son
of Imri built.
[3]Now the sons of Hassenaah built the
Fish Gate; they laid its beams and set
up its doors with its bolts and its bars.
[4]Next to them Meremoth the son of
Uriah, the son of Hakkoz, made re-
pairs. Next to him Meshullam the son
of Berechiah, the son of Meshezabel,
made repairs. And next to him Zadok
the son of Baana *also* made repairs.
[5]Next to him the men of Tekoa made
repairs, but their nobles did not sup-
port the work of their overseers.
[6]Joiada the son of Paseah and Me-
shullam the son of Besodeiah repaired
the Old Gate. They laid its beams and set
up its doors with its bolts and its bars.
[7]Next to them Melatiah the Gibeon-
ite and Jadon the Meronothite, the men
of Gibeon and of Mizpah, made repairs
for the official seat (Jerusalem resi-
dence) of the governor [of the province]
beyond the [Euphrates] River.

3 2Ch 33:14; Neh 12:39; Zep 1:10; See Neh 6:1; 7:1 **5** Jdg 5:23 **6** Neh 12:39 **7** Neh 2:8

JERUSALEM IN THE DAYS OF THE RETURN

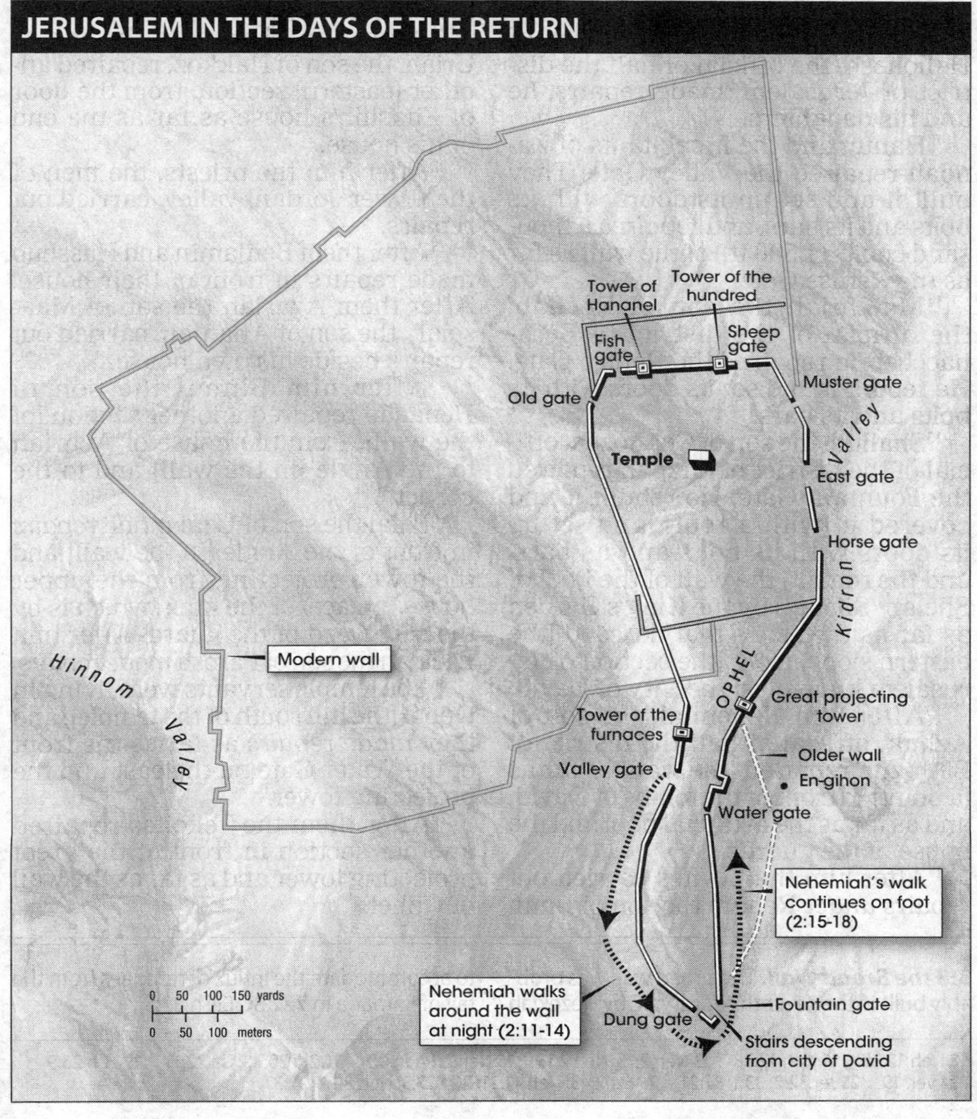

8 Next to them Uzziel the son of Harhaiah, one of the goldsmiths, made repairs. Next to him Hananiah, one of the perfumers, made repairs, and they restored Jerusalem as far as the Broad Wall.

9 Next to them Rephaiah the son of Hur, official of half the district of Jerusalem, made repairs.

10 Next to them Jedaiah the son of Harumaph made repairs opposite his own house. And next to him Hattush the son of Hashabneiah made repairs.

11 Malchijah the son of Harim and Hasshub the son of Pahath-moab repaired another section and the Tower of the Furnaces.

12 Next to him Shallum the son of Hallohesh, the official of half the district of Jerusalem, made repairs, he and his daughters.

13 Hanun and the inhabitants of Zanoah repaired the Valley Gate. They built it and set up its doors with its bolts and its bars, and *repaired* a thousand cubits (1,500 ft.) of the wall as far as the Refuse Gate.

14 Malchijah the son of Rechab, the official of the district of Beth-haccherem repaired the Refuse Gate. He rebuilt it and set its doors with its bolts and its bars.

15 Shallum the son of Col-hozeh, official of the district of Mizpah repaired the Fountain Gate. He rebuilt it and covered it [with a roof], and set up its doors with its bolts and its bars, and [he rebuilt] the wall of the Pool of Shelah (Siloam) by the King's Garden as far as the stairs that descend [the eastern slope] from [the section of Jerusalem known as] the City of David.

16 After him Nehemiah the son of Azbuk, official of half the district of Beth-zur, repaired [the wall] as far as [a point] in front of the tombs of David, and as far as the artificial pool and the house of the guards.

17 After him the Levites carried out repairs *under* Rehum the son of Bani. Next to him Hashabiah, official of half the district of Keilah, carried out repairs for his district.

18 After him their brothers carried out repairs *under* Bavvai the son of Henadad, official of [the other] half of the district of Keilah.

19 Next to him Ezer the son of Jeshua, the official of Mizpah, repaired another section [northward] in front of the ascent to the armory at the Angle [in the wall].

20 After him Baruch son of Zabbai zealously repaired another section [toward the hill], from the Angle [in the wall] to the door of the house of Eliashib the high priest.

21 After him Meremoth the son of Uriah, the son of Hakkoz, repaired another [eastern] section, from the door of Eliashib's house as far as the end of his house.

22 After him the priests, the men of the [lower Jordan] valley, carried out repairs.

23 After them Benjamin and Hasshub made repairs in front of their house. After them Azariah the son of Maaseiah, the son of Ananiah, carried out repairs beside his own house.

24 After him Binnui the son of Henadad repaired another section [of the wall], from the house of Azariah to the Angle [in the wall] and to the corner.

25 Palal the son of Uzai *made repairs* in front of the Angle [in the wall] and the tower projecting from the upper house (palace) of the king, which is by the courtyard of the guard. After him Pedaiah the son of Parosh *made repairs.*

26 The temple servants were living in Ophel [the hill south of the temple], and they *made repairs* as far as the front of the Water Gate on the east and the projecting tower.

27 After them the Tekoites repaired another section in front of the great projecting tower and as far as the wall of Ophel.

3:8 *the Broad Wall.* The broad wall was probably built in the seventh century BC by Hezekiah to accommodate the influx of refugees from the fall of Samaria in 722 BC (2Ch 32:5).

8 Neh 12:38 **11** Neh 12:38 **13** Neh 2:13; Neh 2:13 **15** Neh 2:14; Jn 9:7 **16** 2Ki 20:20; Isa 22:11 **19** 2Ch 26:9 **24** ver. 19 **25** Jer 32:2; 33:1; 37:21 **26** Ezr 2:43; Neh 11:21; 2Ch 27:3; Neh 8:1,3; 12:37

28 Above the Horse Gate the priests made repairs, each one in front of his own house.

29 After them Zadok the son of Immer carried out repairs in front of his house. After him Shemaiah the son of Shecaniah, keeper of the East Gate, repaired *the wall*.

30 After him Hananiah the son of Shelemiah, and Hanun the sixth son of Zalaph, repaired another section. After him Meshullam the son of Berechiah carried out repairs in front of his own quarters.

31 After him Malchijah, one of the goldsmiths, carried out repairs as far as the house of the temple servants and of the merchants, in front of the Inspection Gate and as far as the upper room of the corner.

32 Between the upper room of the corner and the Sheep Gate the goldsmiths and merchants carried out repairs.

Work Is Ridiculed

4 BUT WHEN Sanballat heard that we were rebuilding the wall, he became furious, completely enraged, and he ridiculed the Jews.

2 He spoke before his brothers and the army of Samaria, "What are these feeble Jews doing? Can they restore it for themselves? Can they offer sacrifices? Can they finish in a day? Can they revive the stones from the heaps of dust *and* rubbish, even the ones that have been burned?"

3 Now Tobiah the Ammonite was beside him, and he said, "Even what they are building—if a fox should get up on it, he would break down their stone wall."

4 [And Nehemiah prayed] Hear, O our God, how we are despised! Return their taunts on their own heads. Give them up as prey in a land of captivity.

5 Do not forgive their wrongdoing and do not let their sin be wiped out before You, for they have offended the builders [and provoked You].

6 So we built the wall and the entire wall was joined together to half its *height*, for the people had a heart to work.

7 But when Sanballat, Tobiah, the Arabs, the Ammonites, and the Ashdodites heard that the repair of the walls of Jerusalem went on, and that the breaches were being closed, they were very angry.

8 They all conspired together to come and to fight against Jerusalem, and to cause a disturbance in it.

Discouragement Overcome

9 But we prayed to our God, and because of them we set up a guard against them day and night.

10 Then [the leaders of] Judah said,

"The strength of the burden
bearers is failing,
And there is much rubble;
We ourselves are unable
To rebuild the wall."

11 Our enemies said, "They will not know or see us until we are among them, kill them and put a stop to the work."

12 When the Jews who lived near them came, they said to us ten times (repeatedly), "From every place you turn, they will come up against us."

13 So I stationed *armed men* behind the wall in the lowest places, at the open positions [where it was least protected]; and I stationed the people in families with their swords, spears, and bows.

14 When I saw *their fear*, I stood and said to the nobles and officials and the rest of the people: "Do not be afraid

4:2 *revive the stones.* When limestone is subjected to intense heat, it becomes unsuitable for building. The stones from the burned wall would not be useable.

4:9 Prayer—It is difficult to work in a hostile environment. Ambition, courage, and preparation are important in a situation like this, and so is prayer. If we are not careful to ask God to protect us, our fear can cripple us as much as the animosity of our enemies. No matter how prepared we may be for a crisis, the power of God is the ultimate factor in determining whether we win or lose.

28 2Ki 11:16; 2Ch 23:15; Jer 31:40 **CHAPTER 4** **1** Neh 2:10,19 **3** Neh 2:10,19 **4** Ps 123:3,4; Ps 79:12; Pr 3:34 **5** Ps 69:27,28; 109:14,15; Jer 18:23 **7** ver. 1 **8** Ps 83:3-5 **9** Ps 50:15 **14** Nu 14:9; Dt 1:29; Dt 10:17; 2Sa 10:12

of them; [confidently] remember the Lord who is great and awesome, and [with courage from Him] fight for your brothers, your sons, your daughters, your wives, and for your homes."
15Now when our enemies heard that we knew about *their plot against us*, and that God had frustrated their plan, we all returned to the wall, each one to his work.
16From that day on, half of my servants carried on the work while the other half held the spears, shields, bows, and breastplates; and the captains were behind the whole house of Judah.
17Those who were rebuilding the wall and those who carried burdens loaded themselves *so that everyone* worked with one hand and held a weapon with the other.
18Every builder *had* his sword secured at his side as he built. And the one who sounded the trumpet [to summon the troops] stood at my side.
19I said to the nobles, the officials and the rest of the people, "The work is great and extensive, and we are separated on the wall, far from one another.
20"Wherever you hear the sound of the trumpet, gather to us there. Our God will fight for us."
21So we carried on with the work with half of them holding spears from dawn until the stars came out.
22At that time I also said to the people, "Let each man with his servant spend the night inside Jerusalem so that they may serve as a guard for us at night and a laborer during the day."
23So neither I, my brothers (relatives), my servants, nor the men of the guard who followed me, none of us took off our clothes; each took his weapon [even] to the water.

Usury Abolished

5 NOW THERE was a great outcry of the [poorer] people and their wives against their Jewish brothers [to whom they were deeply in debt].
2For there were some who were saying, "We, *along with* our sons and our daughters, are many; therefore allow us to get grain, so that we may eat and survive."
3There were *others* who were saying, "We are mortgaging our fields, our vineyards, and our houses to buy grain because of the famine."
4There were also *others* who were saying, "We have borrowed money on our fields and vineyards for the [Persian] king's [heavy] tax.
5"Now our flesh (skin) is the same as that of our brothers (relatives), and our children are like their children, yet here we are forcing (selling) our sons and our daughters to be slaves; and some of our daughters are forced into bondage *already*, and we are powerless [to redeem them] because our fields and vineyards belong to others."
6Then I was very angry when I heard their outcry and these words [of accusation].
7I thought it over and then challenged the nobles and the rulers. I said to them, "You are exacting usury (excessive interest) from your own brother (relative)." So I held a great assembly to confront them.
8I said to them, "According to our ability we have redeemed (purchased back) our Jewish brothers who were sold to the [Gentile] nations; now would you even sell your brothers, that they might be sold to us?" Then they were silent and could not find a [single] word *to say*.
9So I said, "What you are doing is

5:7 *exacting usury.* It was not wrong to lend money to a fellow Jew, or even to lend money at interest to a non-Jewish person, but it was forbidden to charge interest to a fellow Jew (Ex 22:25; Dt 23:19–20). The people had already fallen back into disobedience.

5:9 Fear of God — Fear of God is the knowledge that God has the right to judge our actions for good or evil. It is the basis for keeping the commandments which concern other men. We do not murder because it is taking the life of one who bears the image and likeness of God. We deal honestly with one another, we do not covet our neighbor's possessions, or abridge any of his rights, because those things are given to him by God, and our neighbor belongs to God who

15 Job 5:12 **20** Ex 14:14,25; Dt 1:30; 3:22; 20:4; Jos 23:10 **CHAPTER 5** **1** Isa 5:7; Lev 25:35-37; Dt 15:7 **5** Isa 58:7; Ex 21:7; Lev 25:39 **7** Ex 22:25; Lev 25:36; Eze 22:12 **8** Lev 25:48 **9** Lev 25:36; 2Sa 12:14; Ro 2:24; 1Pe 2:12

not good. Should you not walk in the fear of our God to prevent the taunting by the [pagan] nations, our enemies?

10“And likewise I, my brothers, and my servants are lending them money and grain. Please, let us stop [charging] this interest. [Ex 22:25]

11“Please, give back to them this very day their fields, their vineyards, their olive groves, and their houses, and also a hundredth part of the money, the grain, the new wine, and the oil that you are lending them.”

12Then they said, “We will give it back and not require anything from them. We will do exactly as you say.” Then I called the priests and took an oath from them that they would act in accordance with this promise.

13I also shook out the front of my garment and said, “So may God shake out every man from his house and from his possessions who does not keep this promise; like this may he be shaken out and emptied.” And all the assembly said, “Amen!” And they praised the LORD. Then the people acted in accordance with this promise.

Nehemiah’s Example

14Moreover, from the day that I was appointed to be their governor in the land of Judah, from the twentieth year to the thirty-second year of King Artaxerxes, for twelve years, neither I nor my relatives have eaten the governor’s food *allowance*.

15But the former governors who were [in office] before me put heavy burdens on the people and took food and wine from them in addition to forty shekels of silver [as an excessive monthly salary]; even their servants assumed authority over the people. But I did not do so because of the [reverent] fear of God.

16I also applied myself to the work on this wall; we did not buy any land, and all my servants were gathered together there for the work.

17Moreover, there were at my table a hundred and fifty Jews and officials, besides those who came to us from the nations that were around us.

18Now the following were prepared for each day: one ox and six choice sheep; also fowls (poultry) were prepared for me; and in intervals of ten days all sorts of wine *was provided* in abundance. Yet for all this, I did not demand the governor’s food *allowance*, because the servitude was heavy on this people.

19Remember me, O my God, for good, *according to* all I have done for this people. [Heb 6:10]

The Enemy’s Plot

6 NOW WHEN Sanballat, Tobiah, Geshem the Arab, and the rest of our enemies heard that I had rebuilt the wall, and that there was no breach left in it, although at that time I had not set up doors in the gates,

2Sanballat and Geshem sent *word* to me, saying, “Come, let us meet together at Chephirim in the plain of Ono.” But they were planning to harm me.

3So I sent messengers to them, saying, “I am doing a great work and cannot come down. Why should the work stop while I leave to come down to [meet with] you?”

4They sent *word* to me four times in this way, and I answered them in the same way.

5Then Sanballat sent his servant to me in the same way the fifth time, with an open letter in his hand.

---

created him. If we do not walk in the fear of the Lord, we demonstrate our pride and presumption to those who are watching us.

5:11 *hundredth part.* This is probably a reference to the interest the nobles and rulers had been charging.

5:15 *former governors.* Several former governors had paid their own expenses with the people’s taxes. During his twelve year administration (444 – 432 BC), Nehemiah did not collect taxes from the people, although as the governor he had the right to.

6:2 *the plain of Ono.* The plain of Ono was about twenty miles northwest of Jerusalem.

12 Ezr 10:5; Jer 34:8,9 **13** Mt 10:14; Ac 13:51; 18:6; 2Ki 23:3 **14** Neh 13:6; 1Co 9:4,15 **15** 2Co 11:9; 12:13; ver. 9 **17** 2Sa 9:7; 1Ki 18:19 **18** 1Ki 4:22; ver. 14,15 **19** Neh 13:22 **CHAPTER 6** **1** Neh 2:10,19; Neh 3:1,3 **2** Pr 26:24,25; 1Ch 8:12; Neh 11:35; Ps 37:12,32

[6]In it was written, "It is reported among the [neighboring] nations, and Gashmu is saying that you and the Jews are planning to revolt, and that is the reason you are rebuilding the wall. And according to these reports, you are to be their king.

[7]"Also [it is reported that] you have appointed prophets to make a proclamation concerning you in Jerusalem, saying, 'There is a king in Judah!' And now these things will be reported to the [Persian] king. So come now, and let us consult together."

[8]I sent *a message* to him, saying, "Such things as you are saying have not been done; you are inventing them in your own mind."

[9]For they all wanted to frighten us, thinking, "They will become discouraged with the work and it will not be done." But now, [O God,] strengthen my hands.

[10]When I went into the house of Shemaiah the son of Delaiah, the son of Mehetabel, who was confined at home, he said, "Let us meet [and take refuge] together in the house of God, within the temple, and let us shut the doors of the temple, because they are coming to kill you, and they are coming to kill you at night."

[11]But I said, "Should a man like me flee [in fear and hide]? Should someone like me enter the temple [for sanctuary] to save his life? I will not go."

[12]Then I realized that God had not sent him, but he spoke this prophecy against me because Tobiah and Sanballat had hired him.

[13]He was hired for this reason, that I would be frightened and do as he said and sin, so that they would have [grounds to make] a malicious report in order to censure *and* disgrace me.

[14]Remember, O My God, Tobiah and Sanballat in regard to these actions of theirs, and also [remember] the prophetess Noadiah and the rest of the prophets who were *trying to* frighten me.

The Wall Is Finished

[15]So the wall was finished on the twenty-fifth [day] of [the month] Elul, in fifty-two days.

[16]When all our enemies heard *about it*, and all the [Gentile] nations around us saw it, they lost their confidence; for they recognized that this work had been accomplished with the help of our God.

[17]Moreover, in those days many letters went from the nobles of Judah to Tobiah, and Tobiah's *letters* came to them.

[18]For many in Judah were bound by oath to him because he was the son-in-law of Shecaniah the son of Arah, and his son Jehohanan had married the daughter of Meshullam the son of Berechiah.

[19]Also, they were speaking about Tobiah's good deeds in my presence, and reporting to him what I said. Then Tobiah sent letters to frighten me.

Census of First Returned Exiles

7 NOW WHEN the wall had been rebuilt and I had set up the doors, and the gatekeepers, singers, and Levites had been appointed,

[2]I put my brother Hanani, with Hananiah the commander of the fortress,

---

6:10 *Shemaiah.* Shemaiah was a false prophet, not the Levite of the same name who helped build the wall (3:29) or the priest who sealed the covenant with Nehemiah (10:8). Whether he was pretending to represent God, or was speaking with "authority" because he claimed that he had inside information, Shemaiah's strategy was to get Nehemiah sidetracked.

6:16 Providence — The fact that the Jews were able to finish the wall so quickly and with such singleness of purpose said even to their enemies that it was God who had helped them. God always provides everything we need to do His work. It is when we get off on our own agendas that we are short of energy and resources. Like Nehemiah, we need to pray for God's direct guidance, and then pray to keep our focus on His plan.

7:1 *gatekeepers, singers, and Levites.* The Levites were assistants to the priests (Nu 18:1 – 4) who guarded and cleaned the sanctuary. The gatekeepers and singers were also Levites (1Ch 9:17 – 19; 26:12 – 19).

---

6 Neh 2:19 **12** Eze 13:22 **14** Neh 13:29; Eze 13:17 **16** Neh 2:10; 4:1,7; 6:1; Ps 126:2 **CHAPTER 7** **1** Neh 6:1 **2** Neh 2:8; Ex 18:21

in charge of Jerusalem, for Hananiah
was a more faithful and God-fearing
man than many [of the others].
3I said to them, "Do not let the gates
of Jerusalem be opened until the sun is
hot; and while the watchmen are still
standing *guard,* have them shut and
bar the doors. Appoint guards from
the residents of Jerusalem, each at his
post [on the wall], and each in front of
his own house."
4Now the city was spacious and
large, but there were few people in it
and the houses had not [yet] been built.
5Then my God put it into my heart to
assemble the nobles, the officials, and
the people to be registered by genealo-
gy. Then I found the register of the gene-
alogy of those who came [from Babylon]
first, and I found the following record:
6These are the sons (descendants,
people) of the province who came up
from the captivity of the exiles whom
Nebuchadnezzar the king of Babylon
had deported [to Babylon]; they re-
turned to Jerusalem and to Judah, each
to his city,
7the ones who came with Zerub-
babel, Jeshua, Nehemiah, Azariah,
Raamiah, Nahamani, Mordecai,
Bilshan, Mispereth, Bigvai, Nehum,
and Baanah.
The men of the people of Israel num-
bered:
8the sons of Parosh, 2,172;
9the sons of Shephatiah, 372;
10the sons of Arah, 652;
11the sons of Pahath-moab of the
sons of Jeshua and Joab, 2,818;
12the sons of Elam, 1,254;
13the sons of Zattu, 845;
14the sons of Zaccai, 760;
15the sons of Binnui, 648;
16the sons of Bebai, 628;
17the sons of Azgad, 2,322;
18the sons of Adonikam, 667;
19the sons of Bigvai, 2,067;
20the sons of Adin, 655;
21the sons of Ater, of Hezekiah, 98;
22the sons of Hashum, 328;
23the sons of Bezai, 324;
24the sons of Hariph, 112;
25the sons of Gibeon, 95;
26the men of Bethlehem and Neto-
phah, 188;
27the men of Anathoth, 128;
28the men of Beth-azmaveth, 42;
29the men of Kiriath-jearim, Chephi-
rah and Beeroth, 743;
30the men of Ramah and Geba, 621;
31the men of Michmas, 122;
32the men of Bethel and Ai, 123;
33the men of the other Nebo, 52;
34the sons of the other Elam, 1,254;
35the sons of Harim, 320;
36the sons of Jericho, 345;
37the sons of Lod, Hadid and Ono, 721;
38the sons of Senaah, 3,930.
39*These are* the priests: the sons of
Jedaiah of the house of Jeshua, 973;
40the sons of Immer, 1,052;
41the sons of Pashhur, 1,247;
42the sons of Harim, 1,017.
43*These are* the Levites: the sons
of Jeshua, of Kadmiel, of the sons of
Hodevah, 74.
44The singers: the sons of Asaph, 148.
45The gatekeepers: the sons of Shal-
lum, the sons of Ater, the sons of Tal-
mon, the sons of Akkub, the sons of
Hatita, and the sons of Shobai, 138.
46The temple servants: the sons of
Ziha, the sons of Hasupha, the sons
of Tabbaoth,
47the sons of Keros, the sons of Sia,
the sons of Padon,
48the sons of Lebana, the sons of
Hagaba, the sons of Shalmai,
49the sons of Hanan, the sons of Gid-
del, the sons of Gahar,

7:3 *gates.* The gates of a city normally opened at sunrise. If an enemy mounted a surprise attack at sunrise, he would find a city just beginning to wake up. By keeping the gates closed a little longer, the city was safer.

7:4 *few people.* For the size of the city, Jerusalem was under-populated. Even though it had been 90 years since people had returned under Zerubbabel to live there, Jerusalem still had a lot of undeveloped space within the walls renewed by Nehemiah.

7:5 *my God put it into my heart.* Nehemiah attributed to the Lord the idea of a census that would show the distribution of the population. If he knew the population pattern in the capital and the countryside, he could then determine which districts could best afford to lose a portion of their inhabitants to Jerusalem.

6 Ezr 2:1 **34** See ver. 12 **39** 1Ch 24:7 **40** 1Ch 24:14 **41** See 1Ch 9:12; 24:9 **42** 1Ch 24:8

50 the sons of Reaiah, the sons of Re-
zin, the sons of Nekoda,
51 the sons of Gazzam, the sons of
Uzza, the sons of Paseah,
52 the sons of Besai, the sons of Meu-
nim, the sons of Nephushesim,
53 the sons of Bakbuk, the sons of
Hakupha, the sons of Harhur,
54 the sons of Bazlith, the sons of Me-
hida, the sons of Harsha,
55 the sons of Barkos, the sons of Sis-
era, the sons of Temah,
56 the sons of Neziah, the sons of
Hatipha.
57 The sons of Solomon's servants: the
sons of Sotai, the sons of Sophereth,
the sons of Perida,
58 the sons of Jaala, the sons of Dar-
kon, the sons of Giddel,
59 the sons of Shephatiah, the sons
of Hattil, the sons of Pochereth-
hazzebaim, the sons of Amon.
60 All the temple servants and the sons
of Solomon's servants, *totaled* 392.
61 And these were the ones who came
up from Tel-melah, Tel-harsha, Cher-
ub, Addon and Immer; but they [had
no birth records and] could not prove
their fathers' houses or their descent,
whether they were of Israel:
62 the sons of Delaiah, the sons of
Tobiah, the sons of Nekoda, 642.
63 Of the priests: the sons of Hobaiah,
the sons of Hakkoz, and the sons of
Barzillai, who [was so named because
he had] married one of the daughters
of Barzillai, the [well-known] Gilead-
ite, and was named after them.
64 These men searched for their an-
cestral registration *among* those re-
corded in the genealogies, but it was not
located; so they were *excluded* from the
priesthood as [ceremonially] unclean.
65 The governor told them that they
should not eat any of the most holy
food until a priest arose with Urim and
Thummim [to determine God's will in
the matter].

Total of People and Gifts

66 The entire assembly together was
42,360,
67 besides their male and their female
servants, of whom *there were* 7,337;
and they had 245 male and female
singers.
68 Their horses were 736; their mules,
245;
69 *their* camels, 435; *their* donkeys,
6,720.
70 Some from among the heads of
fathers' *households* gave to the work.
The governor gave to the treasury
1,000 gold drachmas, 50 basins, 530
priests' garments.
71 Some of the heads of fathers'
households gave to the treasury for
the work 20,000 gold drachmas and
2,200 silver minas.
72 And what the rest of the people
gave was 20,000 gold drachmas, 2,000
silver minas, and 67 priests' garments.
73 So the priests, the Levites, the
gatekeepers, the singers, some of the
people, the temple servants, along with
all Israel, lived in their cities.
And when the seventh month came,
the sons (descendants) of Israel (Jacob)
were in their cities.

Ezra Reads the Law

8 THEN ALL the people gathered
together as one man at the open
square in front of the Water Gate; and
they asked Ezra the scribe to bring the
Book of the Law of Moses which the
LORD had given to Israel.
2 So Ezra the priest brought the Law
before the assembly of men, women
and all who *could* listen with under-
standing, on the first day of the sev-
enth month.
3 Then he read from it, in front of the
open square which was in front of the
Water Gate, from early morning until
midday, in the presence of the men and

7:70 *drachmas.* One thousand gold drachmas would weigh about nine pounds.

8:2 *men, women and all who could listen with understanding.* This is a more specific list of those gathered than is usual. "All who could listen" includes older children, as well as adults. ***first day of the seventh month.*** The wall had been completed on the twenty-fifth day of the sixth month (6:15) so this event took place just a few days after the completion of the wall.

8:3 Reading God's Word — There are many parts of the world today that still have limited

61 Ezr 2:59 **70** Neh 8:9 **71** Ezr 2:69 **73** Ezr 3:1 **CHAPTER 8** **1** Ezr 3:1; Neh 3:26; Ezr 7:6 **2** Dt 31:11,12; Lev 23:24

women, those who could understand;
and all the people listened carefully to
the Book of the Law.
4 Ezra the scribe stood on a [large]
wooden platform which they had con-
structed for this purpose. And beside him
[on the platform] stood Mattithiah, She-
ma, Anaiah, Uriah, Hilkiah, and Maase-
iah on his right; and Pedaiah, Mishael,
Malchijah, Hashum, Hashbaddanah,
Zechariah, and Meshullam on his left.
5 Ezra opened the book in the sight
of all the people, for he was standing
above them; and when he opened it,
all the people stood up.
6 Then Ezra blessed the LORD, the
great God. And all the people an-
swered, "Amen, Amen!" while lifting
up their hands; and they knelt down
and worshiped the LORD with *their*
faces toward the ground.
7 Also Jeshua, Bani, Sherebiah, Ja-
min, Akkub, Shabbethai, Hodiah,
Maaseiah, Kelita, Azariah, Jozabad,
Hanan, Pelaiah, and the Levites, ex-
plained the Law to the people, and the
people *remained* in their places.
8 So they read from the Book of the
Law of God, translating and explain-
ing it so that the people understood
the reading.

"This Day Is Holy"

9 Then Nehemiah, who was the gov-
ernor, and Ezra the priest and scribe,
and the Levites who taught the people
said to all the people, "This day is holy
to the LORD your God; do not mourn or

---

access to the Bible and below average literacy rates. Even if they could obtain a Bible they might not be able to read it. Other areas of the world have a well-educated population and freedom to pursue any religion they choose. Throughout much of history, the only access to Scripture was through someone who read it in a public or church setting. Today most of the western world has access to audio tapes of the Bible or to numerous printed versions. Here are some suggestions to aid you in receiving the greatest benefit from reading or listening to the Bible:

Read the Bible prayerfully. Ask the Spirit of God to meet your heart's need as you read (Ps 119:18).

Read the Bible thoughtfully. Think about the meaning and implications of what you are reading.

Read the Bible carefully. Take careful note not only of the words that are used but also of how they relate to one another.

Read the Bible repeatedly. It may be of great help to read the same portion over and over again each day for a month's time. This is a good way for the words to take root in your heart. If you are reading a short book, read it every day. Divide longer books up into manageable portions of two or three chapters and read that portion through every day.

Read the Bible extensively. Sometimes it is of great help to read through large portions of the Word of God at one sitting. If you do this, do it at a time when you are alert and not likely to be disturbed during your reading.

Read the Bible regularly. It is good to have a particular time every day when you habitually give yourself to the reading of the Word of God.

Read the Bible faithfully. Inevitably there will be days when you will fail to read the Bible. Do not let your momentary lapse discourage you. Faithfully resume your practice of reading God's Word.

Read the Bible obediently. Because the Bible is God's Word written to you, it is essential to obey it (Ex 12:24).

Read the Bible thankfully. Thank God for the gift He has given us in Scripture. Thank Him that you have the freedom or the opportunity to read the Bible at all.

8:5 *all the people stood up.* Standing signified their reverence for the Word. This gesture later became characteristic of the Jewish people in synagogue services.

8:6 *lifting up their hands.* The people answered "Amen" and lifted their hands, indicating their participation with Ezra in prayer.

8:9 – 10 Repentance — Once the people understood the Word of God, they wept. They had heard the high standard of the law, recognized their low standing before the Lord, and were convicted. Weeping and sorrow for sin are part of repentance. But the other part of repentance is change. With change comes joy. The joy of the Lord is the joy that springs up in our hearts because of our relationship to the Lord. It is a God-given gladness found when we are in communion with God. When our goal is to know more about the Lord, the by-product is His joy.

8:9 God's Word Convicts — One of the great proofs that the Bible is really God's inspired Word is its unique ability to convict men and women

---

5 Jdg 3:20 **6** 1Co 14:16; La 3:41; 1Ti 2:8; Ex 4:31; 12:27; 2Ch 20:18 **7** Lev 10:11; Dt 33:10; 2Ch 17:7; Mal 2:7
9 Ezr 2:63; Neh 7:65; 10:1; Lev 23:24; Nu 29:1; Dt 16:14; Ecc 3:4

weep." For all the people were weeping when they heard the words of the Law.

10Then Ezra said to them, "Go [your way], eat the rich festival food, drink the sweet *drink*, and send portions to him for whom nothing is prepared; for this day is holy to our Lord. And do not be worried, for the joy of the LORD is your strength *and* your stronghold."

11So the Levites quieted all the people, saying, "Be still, for the day is holy; do not be worried."

12Then all the people went on their way to eat, to drink, to send portions [of food to others] and to celebrate a great festival, because they understood the words which had been communicated to them.

Feast of Booths Restored

13On the second day, all of the heads of fathers' *households* of all the people, the priests, and the Levites, were gathered before Ezra the scribe to gain insight into the words of the Law (divine instruction).

14They found written in the Law how the LORD had commanded through Moses that the Israelites should live in booths (huts) during the feast of the seventh month.

15So they proclaimed and published an announcement in all their cities and in Jerusalem, saying, "Go out to the hills and bring olive branches, wild olive, myrtle, palm, and other leafy branches to make booths, as it is written." [Lev 23:39, 40]

16So the people went out and brought them and made booths for themselves, each on the roof *of his house*, and in their courtyards and the courtyards of God's house, and in the open square of the Water Gate and in the square of the Gate of Ephraim.

17The entire assembly of those who had returned from the captivity made booths and lived in them. Indeed since the days of Joshua the son of Nun until that *very* day, the Israelites had not done so. And there was great rejoicing *and* celebration.

18Every day, from the first day to the last, Ezra read from the Book of the Law of God. They celebrated the feast for seven days; on the eighth day *there was* a [closing] solemn assembly in accordance with the ordinance.

The People Confess Their Sin

9 NOW ON the twenty-fourth day of this month the Israelites assembled with fasting and in sackcloth and with dirt on their heads.

2The descendants of Israel (Jacob) separated themselves from all foreigners, and stood and confessed their sins and the wrongdoings of their fathers.

---

of their sins. There are many biblical stories that point to this phenomenon where people realize the extent of their sin and the need to repent of it.

Under Josiah's rule a copy of God's Word is found in the temple. When it is read, both the king and the people are convicted of their sins in not keeping God's law. Afterwards a great revival occurs (2Ch 34:14–28).

When Nehemiah returns to Israel to help the returning Jews rebuild the gates of Jerusalem, he assembles the people and has the Scriptures read to them for three hours a day. This soon causes them to confess their sin (Neh 9:3).

In the New Testament we see many instances where the Holy Spirit uses God's Word to convict people of their sin. At Pentecost Peter uses the Scriptures to rebuke Israel for crucifying its Messiah. The result of his sermon is three thousand souls being convicted and accepting Christ (Ac 2:37,41).

8:17 *since the days of Joshua.* The reference here is to the construction of booths. The people of Israel had celebrated the Feast of Tabernacles since the days of Joshua (1Ki 8:65; 2Ch 7:9; Ezr 3:4).

9:1 *the twenty-fourth day of this month.* The people's public worship had begun on the first day of the seventh month (8:2). More than three weeks later, the people were still engaged in public worship. ***fasting and in sackcloth and with dirt.*** These are all traditional signs of mourning.

9:2 *separated ... from all foreigners.* The separation was a sacred separation from foreign persons who worshiped other gods and whose practices might have brought harm to the integrity of the worship of the Lord.

---

10 Est 9:19; Rev 11:10 **12** ver. 10; ver. 7,8 **14** Lev 23:34,42; Dt 16:13 **15** Lev 23:4; Dt 16:16; Lev 23:40
16 Dt 22:8; Neh 12:37; 2Ki 14:13; Neh 12:39 **17** 2Ch 30:21 **18** Dt 31:10; Lev 23:36; Nu 29:35 **CHAPTER 9**
1 Neh 8:2; Jos 7:6; 1Sa 4:12; 2Sa 1:2; Job 2:12 **2** Ezr 10:11; Neh 13:3,30

3 While they stood in their places, they read from the Book of the Law of the LORD their God for a fourth of the day and for *another* fourth [of it] they confessed [their sins] and worshiped the LORD their God.
4 On the platform of the Levites stood Jeshua, Bani, Kadmiel, Shebaniah, Bunni, Sherebiah, Bani, and Chenani, and they called out with a loud voice to the LORD their God.
5 Then the Levites—Jeshua, Kadmiel, Bani, Hashabneiah, Sherebiah, Hodiah, Shebaniah, and Pethahiah—said, "Stand up and bless (praise, honor) the LORD your God from everlasting to everlasting.

May Your glorious name be
blessed
And exalted above all blessing and
praise."
6 [And Ezra said],
"You are the LORD, You alone;
You have made the heavens,
The heaven of heavens with all
their host (the heavenly bodies),
The earth and everything that is
on it,
The seas and everything that is in
them.
You give life to all of them,
And the heavenly host is bowing
down [in worship] to You.
7 "You are the LORD God,
Who chose Abram
And brought him out of Ur of the
Chaldees,
And gave him the name Abraham.
8 "You found his heart to be faithful
before You,
And You made a covenant with
him
To give him the land of the
Canaanite,
Of the Hittite, of the Amorite,
Of the Perizzite, the Jebusite, and
the Girgashite—
To give it to his descendants.
And You have fulfilled Your
promise,
For You are righteous *and* just.

9 "You saw our fathers' affliction in
Egypt,
And You heard their cry by the
Red Sea (Sea of Reeds).
10 "Then You performed signs and
wonders against Pharaoh,
Against all his servants and all the
people of his land;
For You knew that they behaved
arrogantly toward them (the
Israelites),
And You made a name for
Yourself, as it is to this day.
11 "You divided the sea before them,
So that they passed through the
midst of the sea on dry land;
You hurled their pursuers into the
depths,
Like a stone into mighty *and*
raging waters.

9:3 *confessed.* When this word is used with God as its object, as in this verse, it refers to the praise of God. They were acknowledging His attributes and worthiness of praise.

9:6 *You are the LORD, You alone.* One of the fundamental teachings of Scripture is that God is not one among many. He alone is the living God (Dt 6:4).

9:7 *You are the LORD God.* The word order of the Hebrew text is striking: "You are He, Yahweh (the) God." The use of the definite article marks Him as "the true God."

9:9 *our fathers' affliction in Egypt.* The Book of Exodus tells about the plight of the Israelites in Egypt and their complaint to the Lord for deliverance. It then speaks of God's mercy in His response to the people's need. This verse suggests that before the people expressed their hurt, the Lord was already aware of their troubles.

9:11 Persecution — No one asks for or welcomes persecution. But history has borne out the fact that when believers are persecuted they draw close to the Lord. They are keenly aware that they are dependent on Him for strength, endurance, and even sustenance. Some of the sweetest times with the Lord are the times when unbelievers pity us for our tribulation. Times of rest bring independence of spirit. This is when it helps to go back and remember the things that the Lord has done in the past and rejoice, and to remember that He is sufficient for future persecution as well.

3 Neh 8:7,8 **5** 1Ch 29:13 **6** 2Ki 19:15,19; Ps 86:10; Isa 37:16,20; Ge 1:1; Ex 20:11; Rev 14:7; Dt 10:14; 1Ki 8:27; Ge 2:1; Ps 36:6 **7** Ge 11:31; Ge 17:5 **8** Ge 15:6; Ge 15:18; Jos 23:14 **9** Ex 2:25; 14:10 **10** Ex 7-10,12,14; Ex 18:11; Jer 32:20 **11** Ex 14:21; Ps 78:13; Ex 15:5

12 "And with a pillar of cloud You led
them by day,
And with a pillar of fire by night
To light the way for them
In which they were to go.
13 "Then You came down on Mount
Sinai,
And spoke with them from
heaven;
And You gave them fair
ordinances and true laws,
Good statutes and
commandments.
14 "So You made known to them
Your holy Sabbath,
And gave them commandments,
statutes, and law,
Through Your servant Moses.
15 "You gave them bread from
heaven for their hunger,
And brought water for them out of
a rock for their thirst,
And You told them to enter and
take possession of
The land that You swore to give
them. [John 6:31–34]

16 "But they, our fathers, acted
arrogantly;
They stiffened their necks
and would not heed Your
commandments.
17 "They refused to listen *and* obey,
And did not remember Your
wondrous acts which You had
performed among them;
So they stiffened their necks and
[in their rebellion] appointed a
leader in order to return them to
slavery in Egypt.
But You are a God of forgiveness,
Gracious and merciful *and*
compassionate,
Slow to anger and abounding in
lovingkindness;
And You did not abandon them.
[Num 14:4]
18 "Even when they had made for
themselves
A calf of cast metal
And said, 'This is your god
Who brought you up from Egypt,'
And committed great [and
contemptible] blasphemies,

19 You, in Your great mercy *and*
compassion,
Did not abandon them in the
wilderness;
The pillar of the cloud did not
leave them by day,
To lead them in the way,
Nor the pillar of fire by night,
to light for them the way they
should go.
20 "You [also] gave Your good Spirit
to instruct them,
You did not withhold Your manna
from their mouth,
And You gave them water for their
thirst.
21 "Indeed, for forty years You
sustained them in the
wilderness; they lacked nothing,
Their clothes did not wear out, and
their feet did not swell.
22 "You also gave them kingdoms
and peoples,
And You allotted *the kingdoms* to
them as a boundary.
So they took possession of the land
of Sihon king of Heshbon
And the land of Og king of Bashan.
23 "You made their children as
numerous as the stars of heaven,
And You brought them into the
land
Which You told their fathers to
enter and possess.
24 "So their sons (descendants) went
in and took possession of the
land;
And You subdued before them
the inhabitants of the land, the
Canaanites,
And You gave them into their
hand, with their kings and the
peoples of the land,
To do with them as they pleased.
25 "They captured fortified cities and
a fertile land.
They took possession of houses
full of all good things,
Hewn cisterns, vineyards, olive
groves,
And fruit trees in abundance.
So they ate and were filled and
became fat,

12 Ex 13:21 **13** Ex 20:1; Ro 7:12 **14** Ge 2:3; Ex 20:8 **15** Ex 16:14; Jn 6:31; Ex 17:6; Dt 1:8 **16** Ps 106:6; Dt 31:27 **17** Ps 78:11; Nu 14:4; Joel 2:13 **18** Ex 32:4 **19** Ps 106:45; 1Co 10:1 **20** Nu 11:17; Isa 63:11; Ex 16:15; Jos 5:12; Ex 17:6 **21** Dt 2:7; 8:4; 29:5 **22** Nu 21:21 **23** Ge 22:17 **24** Jos 1:2; Ps 44:2,3 **25** Nu 13:27; Dt 6:11; Dt 32:15; Hos 3:5

And they reveled *and* were
delighted in Your great
goodness.
26 "Yet they were disobedient and
rebelled against You,
And cast Your law behind their
backs
And killed Your prophets who
warned them
To return to You;
And they committed great [and
contemptible] blasphemies.
27 "Therefore You handed them over
to their enemies who oppressed
them.
But when they cried out to You in
the time of their suffering *and*
distress,
You heard them from heaven,
and according to Your great
compassion You gave them
people to rescue *them*.
Who rescued them from the hand
of their enemies.
28 "But as soon as they had rest, they
again did evil before You;
Therefore You abandoned them
into the hand of their enemies,
so that they ruled over them.
Yet when they turned and cried
out again to You, You heard
them from heaven,
And You rescued them many
times in accordance with Your
compassion,
29 And You admonished them *and*
warned them to turn them back
to Your law.
Yet they acted presumptuously
and arrogantly and did not
heed Your commandments, but
sinned against Your ordinances,
Which by keeping, a man will live.
But they turned a stubborn
shoulder, stiffened their neck,
and would not listen.
30 "Yet You were patient with them
for many years,
And admonished them *and*
warned them by Your Spirit
through Your prophets;
Still they would not listen.
Therefore You gave them into the
hand (power) of the peoples of
the lands.
31 "Yet in Your great compassion You
did not utterly destroy them or
abandon them,
For You are a gracious and
merciful God.
32 "Now therefore, our God, the
great, the mighty, and the
awesome God, who keeps the
covenant and lovingkindness,
Do not let all the hardship seem
insignificant before You,
Which has come upon us, our
kings, our princes, our priests,
our prophets, our fathers and on
all Your people,
Since the time of the kings of
Assyria to this day.
33 "However, You are just *and*
righteous in everything that has
come upon us;
For You have dealt faithfully, but
we have acted wickedly.
34 Our kings, our princes, our priests,
and our fathers have not kept
Your law
Or paid attention to Your
commandments and Your
warnings which You have given
them.

9:26 *killed Your prophets.* Jesus also directed this charge against the rebellious people of his time (Mt 23:31).
9:30 – 31 Patience — Nehemiah writes, "You were patient with them." This is the same eternal God who still patiently bears with His people. Even as born again believers we struggle with sin, and we are thankful that He is patient with us as we grow in the grace and knowledge of our Lord and Savior, Jesus Christ (2Pe 3:18). This patience does not mean that He is tolerant of sin, but that He knows that it takes perseverance to walk as a Christian. He gives us time to grow. Indeed, God is patient to the whole world, not wishing for any to perish, but for all to come to repentance (2Pe 3:9).
9:32 *Now.* *Now* refers to the time of the great revival under Ezra (8:1 – 2). ***covenant.*** God's covenant and loyalty are unbreakable (2Ti 2:11 – 13).

26 Jdg 2:11; 1Ki 14:9; Ps 50:17; 1Ki 18:4 **27** Jdg 2:14; Ps 106:41; Ps 106:44; Jdg 2:18 **28** Jdg 3:11; Ps 106:43 **29** Lev 18:5; Ro 10:5; Gal 3:12 **30** 2Ki 17:13; 2Ch 36:15; Jer 7:25; Ac 7:51; 1Pe 1:11; 2Pe 1:21; Isa 5:5 **31** Jer 4:27 **32** Ex 34:6,7; 2Ki 17:3 **33** Ps 119:137; Da 9:14; Ps 106:6; Da 9:5,6,8

[35]"But they, in their kingdom,
With Your great goodness which You gave them,
With the broad and rich land which You set before them,
Did not serve You or turn from their wicked deeds.
[36]"Behold, we are slaves today,
And as for the land which You gave our fathers, to eat of its fruit and its goodness,
Behold, we are slaves in it.
[37]"Its abundant produce is for the kings
Whom You have set over us because of our sins;
They also rule over our bodies
And over our cattle as they please,
So we are in great distress.

A Covenant Results

[38]"Now because of all this
We are making an agreement in writing;
And on the sealed document *are the names* of our princes, our Levites, and our priests."

Signers of the Document

10 NOW *THESE were the names* on the sealed document: Nehemiah the governor, the son of Hacaliah. And Zedekiah,
[2]Seraiah, Azariah, Jeremiah,
[3]Pashhur, Amariah, Malchijah,
[4]Hattush, Shebaniah, Malluch,
[5]Harim, Meremoth, Obadiah,
[6]Daniel, Ginnethon, Baruch,
[7]Meshullam, Abijah, Mijamin,
[8]Maaziah, Bilgai, Shemaiah—these
were the priests.
[9]And the Levites: Jeshua the son
of Azaniah, Binnui of the sons of
Henadad, Kadmiel,
[10]and their brothers: Shebaniah, Ho-
diah, Kelita, Pelaiah, Hanan,
[11]Mica, Rehob, Hashabiah,
[12]Zaccur, Sherebiah, Shebaniah,
[13]Hodiah, Bani, Beninu.
[14]The leaders of the people: Parosh,
Pahath-moab, Elam, Zattu, Bani,
[15]Bunni, Azgad, Bebai,
[16]Adonijah, Bigvai, Adin,
[17]Ater, Hezekiah, Azzur,
[18]Hodiah, Hashum, Bezai,
[19]Hariph, Anathoth, Nebai,
[20]Magpiash, Meshullam, Hezir,
[21]Meshezabel, Zadok, Jaddua,
[22]Pelatiah, Hanan, Anaiah,
[23]Hoshea, Hananiah, Hasshub,
[24]Hallohesh, Pilha, Shobek,
[25]Rehum, Hashabnah, Maaseiah,
[26]Ahiah, Hanan, Anan,
[27]Malluch, Harim, Baanah.

Obligations of the Document

[28]Now the rest of the people—the
priests, the Levites, the gatekeepers,
the singers, the temple servants, and
all those who had separated them-
selves from the peoples of the lands
to the Law of God, their wives, their
sons, their daughters, all those who
had knowledge and understanding—
[29]are joining with their fellow Is-
raelites, their nobles, and are taking
on themselves a curse and an oath to
walk in God's Law, which was given
through Moses the servant of God, and
to keep and to observe all the com-
mandments of GOD our Lord, and His
ordinances and statutes:
[30]and that we will not give our
daughters [as wives] to the peoples

9:38 *because of all this.* The psalm ends in action, not just sentiment. The intent was to bring the participants in this time of worship and remembrance to a commitment to change behavior and to pledge to mirror God's faithfulness.
10:1 *these were the names on the sealed document.* The way a person in official capacity "signed" a document in the ancient world was similar to the use of a wax seal. A personally distinctive seal was pressed into soft clay. The pattern of the seal identified the official who had issued the document.
10:30 *will not give our daughters.* Marriage with non-Jewish people was strictly forbidden in Scriptures (Ex 34:12–16; Dt 7:3; Jos 23:12–13; Jdg 3:6). Ezra had dealt very decisively with those who had married foreign wives, and this was still in their memory (Ezr 9–10).

35 Dt 28:47 **36** Dt 28:48; Ezr 9:9 **37** Dt 28:33,51; 28:48 **38** 2Ki 23:3; 2Ch 29:10; Ezr 10:3 **CHAPTER 10** **1** Neh 1:1 **2** Neh 12:1-21 **14** Ezr 2:3; Neh 7:8 **28** Ezr 2:36-43; 9:1; Neh 13:3 **29** Dt 29:12; Ps 119:106; 2Ki 23:3; 2Ch 34:31 **30** Ex 34:16; Dt 7:3; Ezr 9:12

of the land or take their daughters for
our sons.
31 As for the peoples of the land who
bring merchandise or any grain on the
Sabbath day to sell, we will not buy
from them on the Sabbath or on a holy
day; and we will give up *raising crops*
during the seventh year [leaving the
land uncultivated], and *forgive* every
debt. [Ex 23:10, 11; Deut 15:1, 2]
32 Also we pledge ourselves to con-
tribute yearly one third of a shekel for
the service [expenses] of the house of
our God:
33 for the showbread; for the contin-
ual grain offerings and the continual
burnt offerings; [for the offerings on]
the Sabbaths, the New Moons, the
[feasts at] appointed times; for the holy
things, for the sin offerings to make
atonement for Israel; and for all the
work of the house of our God.
34 We have also cast lots—the priests,
the Levites, and the people—for [con-
tributing] the supply of wood, to bring
it to the house of our God, according
to our fathers' households, at set times
annually, to burn on the altar of the
LORD our God, as it is written in the
Law;
35 and [we obligate ourselves] to bring
the first fruits of our ground and the
first fruits of all the fruit of every tree
to the house of the LORD annually,
36 as well as the firstborn of our sons
and of our cattle, as is written in the
Law, and the firstborn of our herds
and flocks, to bring to the house of our
God, for the priests who minister in the
house of our God.
37 We will bring the first [and best] of
our dough, our contributions, the fruit
of every tree, the new wine and the [ol-
ive] oil to the priests, to the chambers
of the house of our God, and the tithe
of our ground to the Levites, for the
Levites are the ones who receive the
tithes in all the rural towns.
38 The priest, the son of Aaron, shall
be with the Levites when they receive
tithes, and they shall bring one-tenth
of the tithes up to the house of our God,
to the chambers of the storehouse.
39 For the Israelites and the sons of
Levi shall bring the offering of the
grain, the new wine, and the oil to the
chambers; the utensils of the sanctu-
ary, the priests who are ministering,
the gatekeepers, and the singers are
there. In this manner, we will not ne-
glect the house of our God.

Time Passes; Heads of Provinces

11 NOW THE leaders of the people
lived in Jerusalem; but the rest of
the people cast lots to bring one [per-
son] out of ten to live in Jerusalem, the
holy city, while nine-tenths *remained*
in the *other* cities.
2 And the people blessed all the men
who volunteered to live in Jerusalem.
3 These are the heads of the prov-
inces who lived in Jerusalem, but in
the cities of Judah everyone lived on
his property in their cities—the Israel-
ites, the priests, the Levites, the temple
servants, and the descendants of Sol-
omon's servants.
4 And some of the sons of Judah and
some of the sons of Benjamin lived in
Jerusalem. From the sons of Judah:
Athaiah the son of Uzziah, the son of
Zechariah, the son of Amariah, the son
of Shephatiah, the son of Mahalalel, of
the sons of Perez;
5 Maaseiah the son of Baruch, the
son of Col-hozeh, the son of Hazaiah,
the son of Adaiah, the son of Joiarib,
the son of Zechariah, the son of the
Shilonite.

11:1 *cast lots.* Casting lots was considered a good way to determine God's will when there was no other clear direction. Solomon wrote, "The lot is cast into the lap, but its every decision is from the LORD" (Pr 16:33). ***one [person] out of ten.*** This was the proportion determined in order to bring the population of Jerusalem to the level deemed necessary for its strength and viability.

31 Ex 20:10; Lev 23:3; Dt 5:12; Ex 23:10; Lev 25:4; Dt 15:1; Neh 5:12 **33** Lev 24:5; 2Ch 2:4; See Nu 28; 29 **34** Neh 13:31; Isa 40:16; Lev 6:12 **35** Ex 23:19; Lev 19:23; Nu 18:12 **36** Ex 13:2,12,13; Lev 27:26,27; Nu 18:15,16 **37** Lev 23:17; Nu 15:19; 18:12; Dt 18:4; 26:2; Lev 27:30; Nu 18:21 **38** Nu 18:26; 1Ch 9:26; 2Ch 31:11 **39** Dt 12:6,11; 2Ch 31:12; Neh 13:12; Neh 13:10,11 **CHAPTER 11** **1** ver. 18; Mt 4:5; 27:53 **2** Jdg 5:9 **3** 1Ch 9:2,3; Ezr 2:43; Ezr 2:55 **4** 1Ch 9:3

6 All the sons of Perez who lived at Jerusalem were 468 able men.

7 These are the sons of Benjamin: Sallu the son of Meshullam, the son of Joed, the son of Pedaiah, the son of Kolaiah, the son of Maaseiah, the son of Ithiel, son of Jeshaiah;

8 and after him Gabbai and Sallai, 928.

9 Joel the son of Zichri was their overseer, and Judah the son of Hassenuah was second in command of the city.

10 Of the priests: Jedaiah the son of Joiarib, Jachin,

11 Seraiah the son of Hilkiah, the son of Meshullam, the son of Zadok, the son of Meraioth, the son of Ahitub, the leader of the house of God,

12 and their brothers (relatives, fellow workers) who did the work of the house, 822; and Adaiah the son of Jeroham, the son of Pelaliah, the son of Amzi, the son of Zechariah, the son of Pashhur, the son of Malchijah,

13 and his brothers, heads of fathers' *households*, 242; and Amashsai the son of Azarel, the son of Ahzai, the son of Meshillemoth, the son of Immer,

14 and their brothers, brave men, 128. Their overseer was Zabdiel the son of Haggedolim [one of the great men].

15 Now from the Levites: Shemaiah the son of Hasshub, the son of Azrikam, the son of Hashabiah, the son of Bunni;

16 and Shabbethai and Jozabad, from the leaders of the Levites, who were in charge of the outside work of the house of God;

17 Mattaniah the son of Mica, the son of Zabdi, the son of Asaph, who was the leader to begin the thanksgiving in prayer, and Bakbukiah, second among his brothers; and Abda the son of Shammua, the son of Galal, the son of Jeduthun.

18 All the Levites in the holy city *totaled* 284.

19 The gatekeepers: Akkub, Talmon, and their kinsmen, who kept watch at the gates, *totaled* 172.

Outside Jerusalem

20 Now the rest of Israel, the priests and the Levites, were in all the cities of Judah, each on his own inheritance.

21 But the temple servants were living in Ophel; Ziha and Gishpa were in charge of the temple servants.

22 The overseer of the Levites in Jerusalem was Uzzi the son of Bani, the son of Hashabiah, the son of Mattaniah, the son of Mica, from Asaph's sons, who were the singers in regard to the work of the house of God.

23 For *there was* a command from the [Persian] king regarding the singers, *as to their* daily task.

24 Pethahiah the son of Meshezabel, of the sons of Zerah the son of Judah, was the king's representative in all matters concerning the people.

25 As for the villages with their fields, some sons (descendants) of Judah lived in Kiriath-arba and its towns, Dibon and its towns, and Jekabzeel and its villages,

26 in Jeshua, in Moladah, in Bethpelet,

27 in Hazar-shual and in Beersheba and its towns,

28 in Ziklag and in Meconah and its towns,

29 in En-rimmon, in Zorah, and in Jarmuth,

30 Zanoah, Adullam, and their villages, Lachish and its fields, and Azekah

---

11:25 ***Kiriath-arba.*** Kiriath-arba is another name for Hebron.
12:1 ***Zerubbabel.*** The return of Zerubbabel is recorded in Ezra 1 – 6. ***Jeshua.*** Jeshua is Joshua the priest. ***Ezra.*** This is not the priest who wrote the book of the same name.
12:22 ***Darius.*** Darius refers to Darius II (Nothus), who ruled Persia from 423 to 405 BC.
12:23 ***the Book of the Chronicles.*** The Book of the Chronicles was not the biblical book, but an official record of the heads of the fathers' houses.
12:27 ***dedication of the wall.*** After the completion of Jerusalem's wall (ch. 6), the people repented and renewed their commitment to the Lord (ch. 8 – 10). The repopulation of Jerusalem was ordered, so the dedication was delayed.

10 1Ch 9:10 **16** 1Ch 26:29 **18** ver. 1 **21** See Neh 3:26 **23** See Ezr 6:8,9; 7:20 **24** 1Ch 18:17; 23:28 **25** Jos 14:15

and its towns. So they camped from
Beersheba as far as the Hinnom Valley.
[31]The sons (descendants) of Benja-
min also *lived* from Geba *onward,* at
Michmash, Aija, Bethel and its towns,
[32]at Anathoth, Nob, Ananiah,
[33]Hazor, Ramah, Gittaim,
[34]Hadid, Zeboim, Neballat,
[35]Lod, and Ono, the Valley of the
Craftsmen.
[36]And certain divisions of the Le-
vites in Judah belonged to Benjamin.

Priests and Levites who Returned to Jerusalem with Zerubbabel

12 NOW THESE are the priests
and Levites who came up with
Zerubbabel the son of Shealtiel and
with Jeshua: Seraiah, Jeremiah, Ezra,
[2]Amariah, Malluch, Hattush,
[3]Shecaniah, Rehum, Meremoth,
[4]Iddo, Ginnethoi, Abijah,
[5]Mijamin, Maadiah, Bilgah,
[6]Shemaiah, Joiarib, Jedaiah,
[7]Sallu, Amok, Hilkiah, and Jedaiah.
These were the heads of the priests and
their kinsman in the days of Jeshua.
[8]The Levites were Jeshua, Binnui,
Kadmiel, Sherebiah, Judah, and Mat-
taniah who was in charge of the songs
of thanksgiving *and* praise, he and his
brothers.
[9]Also Bakbukiah and Unni, their
brothers, stood opposite them in their
divisions of service.
[10]Now Jeshua became the father of
Joiakim, Joiakim of Eliashib, Eliashib
of Joiada,
[11]and Joiada became the father of
Jonathan, and Jonathan of Jaddua.
[12]And in the days of Joiakim, the
priests, the heads of fathers' *house-
holds* were: of Seraiah, Meraiah; of
Jeremiah, Hananiah;
[13]of Ezra, Meshullam; of Amariah,
Jehohanan;
[14]of Malluchi, Jonathan; of Sheba-
niah, Joseph;
[15]of Harim, Adna; of Meraioth,
Helkai;
[16]of Iddo, Zechariah; of Ginnethon,
Meshullam;
[17]of Abijah, Zichri; of Miniamin and
of Moadiah, Piltai;
[18]of Bilgah, Shammua; of Shemaiah,
Jehonathan;
[19]of Joiarib, Mattenai; of Jedaiah,
Uzzi;
[20]of Sallai, Kallai; of Amok, Eber;
[21]of Hilkiah, Hashabiah; of Jedaiah,
Nethanel.

The Chief Levites

[22]As for the Levites in the days of
Eliashib, Joiada, Johanan, and Jaddua,
the heads of fathers' *households* were
registered; so were the priests, during
the reign of Darius the Persian.
[23]The sons of Levi, heads of fathers'
households, were recorded in the Book
of the Chronicles until the days of Jo-
hanan the son of Eliashib.
[24]The heads of the Levites were
Hashabiah, Sherebiah, and Jeshua
the son of Kadmiel, and their brothers
opposite them, to praise and to give
thanks, as commanded by David the
man of God, [one] division [singing] in
response to [the men in the opposite]
division.
[25]Mattaniah, Bakbukiah, Obadi-
ah, Meshullam, Talmon, and Akkub
were gatekeepers keeping watch at the
storehouses of the gates.
[26]These men *served* in the days of
Joiakim the son of Jeshua, the son of
Jozadak, and in the days of Nehemiah
the governor and Ezra the priest and
scribe.

Dedication of the Wall

[27]Now at the dedication of the wall of
Jerusalem they sought out the Levites
from all their places in order to bring
them to Jerusalem to celebrate the ded-
ication with gladness, with hymns of
thanksgiving, and with songs *to the
accompaniment* of cymbals, harps,
and lyres.
[28]So the sons of the singers gathered
together from the district around Je-
rusalem, and from the villages of the
Netophathites,
[29]from Beth-gilgal and from the
fields of Geba and Azmaveth, for the

35 1Ch 4:14 **CHAPTER 12** **1** Ezr 2:1,2; See Neh 10:2-8 **4** Lk 1:5 **7** Ezr 3:2; Hag 1:1; Zec 3:1 **8** Neh 11:17 **23** 1Ch 9:14 **24** 1Ch 23; 25; 26; Ezr 3:11 **26** Neh 8:9; Ezr 7:6,11 **27** Dt 20:5; Ps 30, title; 1Ch 25:6; 2Ch 5:13; 7:6

singers had built villages for them-
selves around Jerusalem.
30 The priests and the Levites puri-
fied themselves; they also purified the
people, the gates, and the wall.

Procedures for the Temple

31 Then I had the leaders of Judah
come up on the wall, and I appointed
two large thanksgiving choirs, the first
one proceeding to the right on top of
the wall toward the Refuse Gate.
32 Hoshaiah and half of the leaders
of Judah followed them,
33 with Azariah, Ezra, Meshullam,
34 Judah, Benjamin, Shemaiah, and
Jeremiah,
35 and some of the priests' sons with
trumpets, and Zechariah the son of
Jonathan, the son of Shemaiah, the
son of Mattaniah, the son of Micaiah,
the son of Zaccur, the son of Asaph,
36 and his brothers, Shemaiah, Az-
arel, Milalai, Gilalai, Maai, Nethanel,
Judah, and Hanani, with the musical
instruments of David the man of God.
And Ezra the scribe went in front of
them.
37 At the Fountain Gate they went
directly up the steps of the City of Da-
vid by the stairway of the wall above
David's house to the Water Gate on
the east.
38 The second choir went to the left; I
followed with half of the people on the
wall, above the Tower of the Furnaces,
to the Broad Wall,
39 and above the Gate of Ephraim,
and by the Old Gate, by the Fish Gate,
by the Tower of Hananel and the Tower
of the Hundred, as far as the Sheep
Gate; and they stopped at the Gate of
the Guard.
40 Then the two choirs stood in the
house of God. So did I, and half of the
officials with me;
41 and the priests Eliakim, Maaseiah,
Miniamin, Micaiah, Elioenai, Zechari-
ah and Hananiah, with trumpets;
42 and Maaseiah, Shemaiah, Eleazar,
Uzzi, Jehohanan, Malchijah, Elam,
and Ezer. And the singers sang, with
Jezrahiah as their leader.
43 Also on that day they offered great
sacrifices and rejoiced because God
had given them great joy; the women
and children also rejoiced, so that the
joy of Jerusalem was heard from far
away.
44 On that day men were appoint-
ed over the chambers for the stores,
the contributions, the first fruits, and
the tithes, to gather into them from
the fields of the cities the portions re-
quired by the law for the priests and
the Levites; for Judah rejoiced over the
priests and Levites who served.
45 And they performed the worship of
their God and the service of purifica-
tion; so did the singers and gatekeep-
ers, as David and his son Solomon had
commanded.
46 For in the days of David and Asaph,
in ancient times, there were leaders of
singers, songs of praise and hymns of
thanksgiving to God.
47 So in the days of Zerubbabel and
[later of] Nehemiah, all Israel would
give the daily portions for the sing-
ers and the gatekeepers; and they set
apart the consecrated *portion* for the
Levites, and the Levites set apart the

12:31 – 46 Praise — Nehemiah choreographed a dramatic demonstration of praise, thanksgiving, and celebration on top of the wall. It was a wholehearted celebration to the Lord, and a visible victory dance before Israel's enemies. This time of praise had been preceded by repentance and reorganization of their duties to the temple and the city of Jerusalem. Praise that rises deep in the heart is always praise that comes from knowing that we are in good standing with God. We have repented of our sins and set our hearts and minds on obedience. God is good, His ways are infinitely right, and He is worthy of all of our enthusiastic worship.

12:43 *sacrifices.* The sacrifices offered at the dedication of the wall probably were not burnt offerings, but peace offerings in which the people shared a common meal. The dedication was an occasion for great rejoicing, and men, women, and children took part.

---

31 See ver. 38; Neh 2:13; 3:13 **35** Nu 10:2,8 **36** 1Ch 23:5 **37** Neh 2:14; 3:15; Neh 3:15; Neh 3:26; 8:1,3,16
38 See ver. 31; Neh 3:11; Neh 3:8 **39** 2Ki 14:13; Neh 8:16; Neh 3:6; Neh 3:3; Neh 3:1; Neh 3:32; Jer 32:2
44 2Ch 31:11,12; Neh 13:5, 12,13 **45** 1Ch 25; 26 **46** 1Ch 25:1 **47** Nu 18:21,24; Nu 18:26

consecrated *portion* for the sons of Aaron [the priests].

Foreigners Excluded

13 ON THAT day they read aloud from the book of Moses so that the people could hear [its words], and in it was found written that no Ammonite or Moabite could ever enter the assembly of God,

[2]because they did not meet the Israelites with bread and water, but hired Balaam against them to curse them. Yet our God turned the curse into a blessing. [Num 22:3–11; Deut 23:5, 6]

[3]When the Jews heard the law, they separated from Israel all who were of foreign descent.

Tobiah Expelled and the Temple Cleansed

[4]Now prior to this, Eliashib the priest, who was appointed over the chambers of the house of our God, and was related to Tobiah [our adversary],

[5]had prepared for Tobiah a large room (chamber) where previously they had put the grain offerings, the frankincense, the utensils, and the tithes of grain, new wine, and [olive] oil which were given by commandment for the Levites, the singers, and gatekeepers, and the contributions for the priests.

[6]But during all this *time* I was not at Jerusalem, for in the thirty-second year of Artaxerxes [Persian] king of Babylon I went to the king. Then after some time I asked for a leave [of absence] from the king,

[7]and I came to Jerusalem. Then I discovered the evil [thing] that Eliashib had done for Tobiah by preparing a room for him in the courtyards of the house of God.

[8]It was very displeasing to me, so I threw all of Tobiah's household furnishings out of the room.

[9]Then I gave an order, and they cleaned the rooms; and I put back there the utensils of the house of God with the grain offerings and the frankincense.

Tithes Restored

[10]I also discovered that the portions due the Levites had not been given *to them*, so that the Levites and the singers who did the work had gone away, each one back to his own field.

[11]Then I reprimanded the officials and said, "Why is the house of God neglected?" So I gathered the Levites and singers together and restored them at their posts.

[12]Then all Judah brought the tithe of the grain, the new wine, and the oil to the storehouses.

[13]I appointed [as treasurers] over the storehouses: Shelemiah the priest, Zadok the scribe, and Pedaiah of the Levites; assisting them was Hanan son of Zaccur, the son of Mattaniah; for they were considered faithful *and* reliable, and their task was to distribute [supplies] to their brothers (fellow Levites).

[14]O my God, remember me concerning this and do not wipe out my loyal deeds *and* kindnesses which I have done for the house of my God and for its services.

Sabbath Restored

[15]In those days I saw some in Judah who were treading wine presses on the Sabbath, and bringing in sheaves *or* sacks of grain and loading them on donkeys, as well as wine, grapes, figs, and all kinds of loads, which they brought into Jerusalem on the Sabbath day. So I protested *and* warned them on the day they sold the produce.

[16]Also men of Tyre were living there who brought fish and all kinds of merchandise, and they were selling them to the people of Judah on the Sabbath, even in Jerusalem.

[17]Then I reprimanded the nobles of Judah, and said to them, "What is this evil thing that you are doing—profaning the Sabbath day?

13:4 – 9 *Tobiah.* Tobiah was an Ammonite (2:10).

CHAPTER 13 **1** Dt 31:11,12; 2Ki 23:2; Neh 8:3,8; 9:3; Isa 34:16; Dt 23:3,4 **2** Nu 22:5; Jos 24:9,10; Nu 23:11; 24:10; Dt 23:5 **3** Neh 9:2; 10:28 **5** Neh 12:44; Nu 18:21,24 **6** Neh 5:14 **7** ver. 1,5 **9** 2Ch 29:5 **10** Mal 3:8; Nu 35:2 **11** ver. 17,25; Neh 10:39 **12** Neh 10:38 **13** 2Ch 31:12; Neh 12:44; 1Co 4:2 **14** Neh 5:19 **15** Ex 20:10; Neh 10:31; Jer 17:21

18 “Did your fathers (ancestors) not do
the same, and did our God not bring all
this trouble on us and on this city? Yet
you are adding to the wrath on Israel
by profaning the Sabbath.”
19 Now when it began to get dark at
the gates of Jerusalem before the Sab-
bath [began], I commanded that the
doors be shut and not be opened until
after the Sabbath. Then I stationed
some of my servants at the gates so
that no load [of merchandise] would
enter [Jerusalem] on the Sabbath day.
20 So once or twice the merchants
and sellers of every kind of merchan-
dise spent the night outside Jerusalem.
21 But I warned them, saying, “Why
do you spend the night by the wall? If
you do so again, I will use force against
you.” From that time on, they did not
come on the Sabbath.
22 And I commanded the Levites to
purify themselves and come and guard
the gates to keep the Sabbath day holy.
O my God, remember me *concerning*
this also and have compassion on me
according to the greatness of Your
lovingkindness.

Mixed Marriages Forbidden

23 In those days I also saw Jews who
had married women from Ashdod,
Ammon, and Moab.
24 As for their children, half spoke
in the language of Ashdod, and none
of them knew how to speak [Hebrew]
the language of Judah, but only the
language of his own people.
25 So I contended with them and
cursed them and struck some of them
and pulled out their hair, and made
them swear by God, saying, “You shall
not give your daughters [in marriage] to
their sons, nor take [any of] their daugh-
ters for your sons or for yourselves.
26 “Did not Solomon king of Israel sin
[greatly against God] regarding these
things? Yet among the many nations
there was no king like him. He was
loved by his God, and God made him
king over all Israel; nevertheless the
foreign women caused even him to
sin [by turning to other gods and so,
judged by God, he lost his kingdom].
[1 Kin 11:1–11]
27 “Do we then hear about you that
you have done all this great evil, act-
ing unfaithfully against our God by
marrying foreign (pagan) women?”
28 One of the sons of Joiada, the son
of Eliashib the high priest, was a son-
in-law of Sanballat the Horonite, so I
chased him away from me.
29 O my God, remember them, be-
cause they have defiled the priesthood
and the covenant of the priesthood and
the Levites.
30 Thus I cleansed *and* purified them
from everything foreign (pagan), and
I defined the duties of the priests and
Levites, each one in his task;
31 and *I provided* for the wood offer-
ing at appointed times and for the first
fruits. O my God, [please] remember
me for good [and imprint me on Your
heart].

13:23–24 *Jews who had married women from Ashdod, Ammon, and Moab.* The problem of Jews marrying foreigners had been dealt with thirty years before by Ezra (Ezr 9–10).

13:25 *cursed them and struck . . . them and pulled out their hair.* It is unnerving to read this list of verbs and imagine the scene. These were not the dispassionate remarks of someone giving a seminar. Nehemiah forced them to comply to the will of God in this matter. After all, this was the principal issue that had led to Israel's captivity in the beginning.

13:28 *son-in-law of Sanballat.* The marriage was particularly offensive because it formed a treasonable alliance with Israel's enemies and compromised the purity of the high priesthood.

18 Jer 17:21 **19** Lev 23:32; Jer 17:21 **22** Neh 12:30 **23** Ezr 9:2 **25** Pr 28:4; Ezr 10:5; Neh 10:29 **26** 1Ki 11:1; 2Sa 12:24; 1Ki 11:4 **27** Ezr 10:2 **28** Neh 12:10,22 **29** Neh 6:14; Mal 2:4,11,12 **30** Neh 10:30; Neh 12:1 **31** Neh 10:34; ver. 14,22

THE BOOK OF

ESTHER

▸ **AUTHOR:** Even though the author's identity is not given in the text, it is obvious from the intimate knowledge of Persian customs and etiquette, the palace in Susa, and the details of the reign of King Ahasuerus, that the author lived in Persia during this period. The love expressed here for the Jewish people and the author's knowledge of Jewish customs further suggests Jewish authorship. It is also thought that this Persian Jew was either an eyewitness to the events or knew an eyewitness. It may be that this author had access to the detailed records kept by Mordecai.

▸ **TIMES:** c. 483 – 473 BC ▸ **KEY VERSE:** Est 4:14

▸ **THEME:** Esther is unique among the Scriptures for two reasons: God is not mentioned by name once, and the heroine is a woman who is part of the harem of a foreign king. The events of the book take place about 30 years before Nehemiah, after the temple in Jerusalem was rebuilt but before the walls were refinished. Esther probably helped to pave the way for Nehemiah's work. The book fits well within the tapestry of the Old Testament. Just as in so many other Old Testament narratives, God provides the means to preserve His people in the face of a severe crisis. It is still read aloud as part of the Purim celebration by Jewish people.

The Banquets of the King

1 IT WAS in the days of Ahasuerus
(Xerxes) who reigned from India
to Ethiopia (Cush) over 127 provinces,
2 in those days when King Ahasuerus
sat on his royal throne which was at
the citadel in Susa [the capital of the
Persian Empire],
3 in the third year of his reign he
held a banquet for all his officials and
his attendants. The army *officers* of
Persia and Media, the nobles and the
officials of the provinces were there in
his presence.
4 And he displayed the riches of his
glorious kingdom and the splendor of
his great majesty for many days, 180
days *in all.*
5 When these days were completed,
the king held a banquet for all the peo-
ple who were present at the citadel in
Susa [the capital], from the greatest [in
importance] to the least, a seven-day
feast in the courtyard of the garden of
the king's palace.
6 *There were curtains* (draperies) of
fine white and violet linen fastened
with cords of fine purple linen to silver
rings and marble columns. The couch-
es of gold and silver *rested* on a mosaic
floor of porphyry, marble, mother-of-
pearl, and precious *colored* stones.
7 Drinks were served in various

1:1 *Ahasuerus.* The kingdom of Ahasuerus extended from India (the region drained by the Indus River) to Ethiopia (northern Sudan). The Persian Kingdom under Ahasuerus was divided into smaller areas called provinces and larger divisions called satrapies.

1:6 *white and violet.* These were the royal colors of the Persians.

CHAPTER 1 **1** Ezr 4:6; Da 9:1; Est 8:9; Da 6:1 **2** 1Ki 1:46; Neh 1:1 **3** Ge 40:20; Est 2:18 **6** Est 7:8; Am 2:8; 6:4

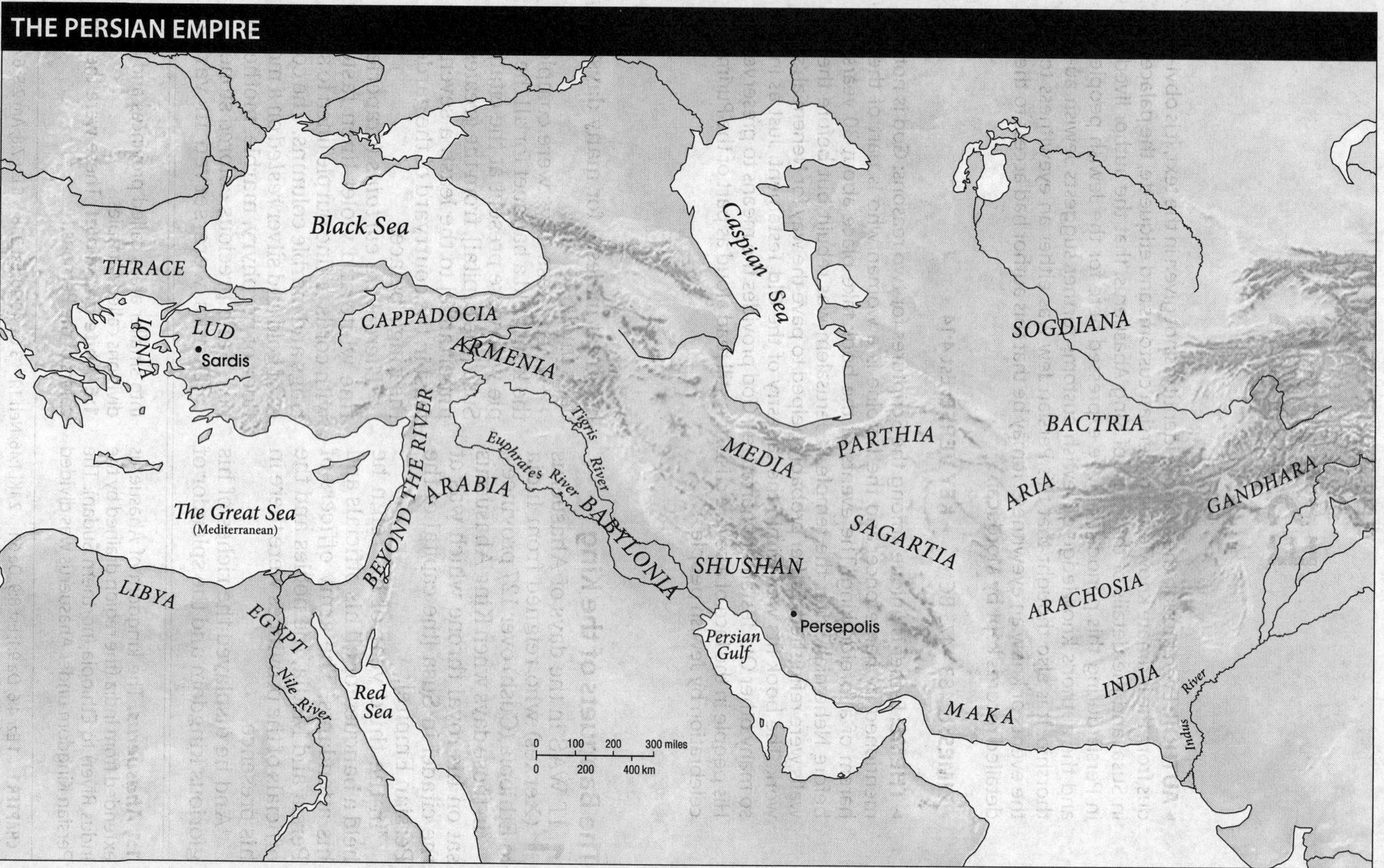
THE PERSIAN EMPIRE
Black Sea
Caspian Sea
THRACE
IONIA
LUD
Sardis
CAPPADOCIA
ARMENIA
SOGDIANA
BACTRIA
PARTHIA
MEDIA
Tigris River
Euphrates River
ARABIA
BEYOND THE RIVER
The Great Sea
(Mediterranean)
BABYLONIA
ARIA
GANDHARA
SAGARTIA
SHUSHAN
ARACHOSIA
LIBYA
EGYPT
Nile River
Red Sea
Persian Gulf
Persepolis
INDIA
Indus River
MAKA
0 100 200 300 miles
0 200 400 km

kinds of golden goblets, and the royal
wine was plentiful, in accordance with
the generosity of the king.
[8]The drinking was *carried on* in accordance with the law; no one was
compelled [to drink], for the king had
directed each official of his household
to comply with each guest's wishes.
[9]Queen Vashti also held a [separate]
banquet for the women in the palace
of King Ahasuerus.

Queen Vashti's Refusal

[10]On the seventh day, when the king's
heart was joyful with wine (in high
spirits), he commanded Mehuman,
Biztha, Harbona, Bigtha, Abagtha,
Zethar, and Carkas, the seven eunuchs
who served in the presence of King
Ahasuerus [as his attendants],
[11]to bring Queen Vashti before the
king, wearing her royal crown (high
turban), to display her beauty before
the people and the officials, for she
was lovely to see.
[12]But Queen Vashti refused to come
at the king's command, which was
delivered [to her] by the eunuchs. So
the king became extremely angry and
burned with rage.
[13]Then the king spoke to the wise
men who understood the times [asking
for their advice]—for it was the custom
of the king *to speak* before all those
who were familiar with law and legal
matters—
[14]and who were close to him [as advisors]: Carshena, Shethar, Admatha,
Tarshish, Meres, Marsena, and Memucan, the seven officials of Persia and
Media who had access to the king and
were ranked highest in the kingdom.
[15][He said,] "According to the law,
what is to be done with Queen Vashti
because she did not obey the command
of King Ahasuerus *which was conveyed* by the eunuchs?"
[16]And Memucan answered in the
presence of the king and the officials, "Vashti the queen has not only
wronged the king but [also] all the officials (royal representatives) and all the
peoples who are in all the provinces of
King Ahasuerus.
[17]"For the queen's conduct will become known to all women, causing
them to look on their husbands with
contempt (disrespect), since they will
say, 'King Ahasuerus commanded
Queen Vashti to be brought before him,
but she did not come.'
[18]"This [very] day the ladies of Persia and Media who have heard of the
queen's refusal will speak [in the same
way] to all the king's officials, and
there will be plenty of contempt and
anger.
[19]"If it pleases the king, let a royal
command be issued by him and let it be
written in the laws of the Persians and
Medes so that it cannot be repealed
or modified, that Vashti is no longer
to come before King Ahasuerus; and
let the king give her royal position to
another who is better *and* more worthy
than she.
[20]"So when the king's great decree is
proclaimed throughout his [extensive]
kingdom, all women will give honor to
their husbands, from the great to the
insignificant."
[21]This statement (advice) pleased the
king and the officials, and the king did
what Memucan proposed.
[22]So he sent letters to all the royal provinces, to each province in its
own script and to each people in their
own language, saying that every man
should be the master *and* rule in his
own home and that he should speak

1:8 *no one was compelled.* The usual Persian custom was that guests at a banquet were required to drink each time the king raised his cup.
1:10 *eunuchs.* These eunuchs were servants who were castrated for the purpose of acting as harem attendants. They would have had the physical strength and stamina of any man, but not be a sexual threat to the king's women.
1:16–18 *Memucan.* Acting as spokesman for the others, Memucan responded shrewdly by enlarging the offense beyond a personal affront to the king. The Hebrew word used for contempt occurs only here in the Old Testament. It is related to the verb translated "despise."

10 Est 7:9 **13** Jer 10:7; Da 2:12; Mt 2:1; 1Ch 12:32 **14** Ezr 7:14; 2Ki 25:19 **17** Eph 5:33 **20** Eph 5:33; Col 3:18; 1Pe 3:1 **22** Est 8:9; Eph 5:22-24; 1Ti 2:12

[in the household] in the language of his own people.

Vashti's Successor Sought

2 AFTER THESE things, when the wrath of King Ahasuerus (Xerxes) had subsided, he remembered Vashti and what she had done and what had been decreed against her.

2 Then the king's attendants, who served him, said, "Let beautiful young virgins be sought for the king.

3 "Let the king appoint administrators in all the provinces of his kingdom, and have them gather all the beautiful young virgins to the citadel in Susa, into the harem, under the custody of Hegai, the king's eunuch, who is in charge of the women; and let their beauty preparations be given *to them.*

4 "Then let the young woman who pleases the king be queen in place of Vashti." This pleased the king, and he did accordingly.

5 There was a certain Jew in the citadel of Susa whose name was Mordecai the son of Jair, the son of Shimei, the son of Kish, a Benjamite,

6 who had been deported from Jerusalem with the captives who had been exiled with Jeconiah king of Judah, whom Nebuchadnezzar the king of Babylon had exiled.

7 He was the guardian of Hadassah, that is Esther, his uncle's daughter, for she had no father or mother. The young woman was beautiful of form and face; and when her father and mother died, Mordecai took her in as his own daughter.

Esther Finds Favor

8 So it came about when the king's command and his decree were proclaimed and when many young women were gathered together in the citadel of Susa into the custody of Hegai, that Esther was taken to the king's palace [and placed] in the custody of Hegai, who was in charge of the women.

9 Now the young woman pleased Hegai and found favor with him. So he quickly provided her with beauty preparations and her [portion of] food, and he gave her seven choice maids from the king's palace; then he transferred her and her maids to the best *place* in the harem.

10 Esther did not reveal [the Jewish background of] her people or her family, for Mordecai had instructed her not to do so.

11 Every day Mordecai [who was an attendant in the king's court] walked back and forth in front of the courtyard of the harem to learn how Esther was getting along and what was happening to her.

12 Now when it was each young woman's turn to go before King Ahasuerus, after the end of her twelve months under the regulations for the women—for the days of their beautification were completed as follows: six months with oil of myrrh and six months with [sweet] spices *and* perfumes and the beauty preparations for women—

13 then the young woman would go before the king in this way: anything that she wanted was given her to take

---

2:5 *Kish.* Some think this may have been the Kish who was the father of King Saul (1Sa 9:1–2). It was not uncommon to refer to someone as "the son of" a more distant ancestor (Mt 15:22).
2:6 *who had been deported.* This verse is a little confusing, as the Hebrew text does not indicate the subject of the verb "had been carried away." It seems highly unlikely that it could be Mordecai, because if he had been among those carried to Babylon, he would probably not be alive in the time of Ahasuerus. If the name Kish does not refer to a more distant ancestor, he may have been the one taken into captivity. Whatever the case, it is obvious that Mordecai and his family were among those descended from the captives taken to Babylon in the days of Nebuchadnezzar.
2:7 *Hadassah.* Hadassah is a Hebrew name that means "Myrtle." Esther is a Persian name meaning "star." Jewish people in that time customarily had two names when they lived in places other than Israel. One would be their secular name, which was understood by their adopted culture, and the other would be their sacred name, given in Hebrew.
2:8 *Esther was taken.* We cannot determine whether Esther went willingly or reluctantly to the palace complex. But perhaps God was already preparing her for the work he had for her to do.

CHAPTER 2 **1** Est 1:19,20 **6** 2Ki 24:14,15; 2Ch 36:10,20; Jer 24:1 **7** ver. 15 **8** ver. 3 **9** ver. 3,12 **10** ver. 20

with her from the harem into the king's palace.

14 In the evening she would go in and the next morning she would return to the second harem, to the custody of Shaashgaz, the king's eunuch who was in charge of the concubines. She would not return to the king unless he delighted in her and she was summoned by name.

15 Now *as for* Esther, the daughter of Abihail the uncle of Mordecai who had taken her in as his [own] daughter, when her turn came to go in to the king, she requested nothing except what Hegai the king's eunuch [and attendant] who was in charge of the women, advised. And Esther found favor in the sight of all who saw her.

16 So Esther was taken to King Ahasuerus, to his royal palace in the tenth month, that is, the month of Tebeth (Dec-Jan), in the seventh year of his reign.

Esther Becomes Queen

17 Now the king loved Esther more than all the *other* women, and she found favor and kindness with him more than all the [other] virgins, so that he set the royal crown on her head and made her queen in the place of Vashti.

18 Then the king held a great banquet, Esther's banquet, for all his officials and his servants; and he made a festival for the provinces and gave gifts in accordance with the resources of the king.

19 And when the virgins were gathered together the second time, Mordecai was sitting at the king's gate.

20 Esther had not revealed her family or her people [that is, her Jewish background], just as Mordecai had instructed her; for Esther did what Mordecai told her just as when she was under his care.

Mordecai Saves the King

21 In those days, while Mordecai was sitting at the king's gate, Bigthan and Teresh, two of the king's eunuchs who guarded the door, became angry and conspired to attack King Ahasuerus.

22 But the plot became known to Mordecai, who informed Queen Esther, and Esther told the king in Mordecai's name.

23 Now when the plot was investigated and found *to be true,* both men were hanged on the gallows. And it was recorded in the Book of the Chronicles in the king's presence.

Haman's Plot against the Jews

3 AFTER THESE things King Ahasuerus (Xerxes) promoted Haman, the son of Hammedatha the Agagite, and advanced him and established his authority over all the officials who were with him.

2 All the king's servants who were at the king's gate [in royal service]

2:14 *concubines.* These women lived unfortunate, though highly pampered lives. If the king never called them again, they were destined to remain secluded in the harem for the rest of their lives.

2:21 *sitting at the king's gate.* In ancient cities, the gates were the "courthouse" of the town, where official business was carried out (Dt 22:13 – 15). The "king's gate" may have served a similar purpose.

3:1 *the Agagite.* Some believe Agagite is a reference to the historical district of Agag within the Persian Empire. Others believe this term more likely links Haman's descent to the Amalekites. These descendants of Esau (Ge 36:12) were ancient enemies of the Hebrews (Ex 17:8). Agag, a king of the Amalekites, was captured by King Saul (1Sa 15:8). If Haman was descended from the Amalekites, and Mordecai from the family of Saul (v. 5), then the irritation Haman had for Mordecai could have been a symptom of a long-standing family hostility.

3:2 *bowed down . . . paid homage to.* It is not known whether the bowing was required as an act of worship to the king's man, or merely as an overt sign of deep respect. If such obeisance indicated worship, Mordecai's reason for refusal is obvious. If it was merely a sign of respect, he may not have been able to bring himself to show such honor to one who was an ancestral enemy.

15 ver. 7 **18** Est 1:3 **19** ver. 21; Est 3:2 **20** ver. 10 **22** Est 6:2 **23** Est 6:1 **CHAPTER 3** **1** Nu 24:7; 1Sa 15:8 **2** Est 2:19; ver. 5; Ps 15:4

bowed down and honored *and* paid homage to Haman; for this is what the king had commanded in regard to him. But Mordecai [a Jew of the tribe of Benjamin] neither bowed down nor paid homage [to him].

3 Then the king's servants who were at the king's gate said to Mordecai, "Why are you disregarding the king's command?"

4 Now it happened when they had spoken to him day after day and he would not listen to them, that they told Haman to see whether Mordecai's reason [for his behavior] would stand [as valid]; for he had told them that he was a Jew.

5 When Haman saw that Mordecai neither bowed down nor paid homage to him, he was furious.

6 But he disdained laying hands on Mordecai alone, for they had told him *who* the people of Mordecai were (his nationality); so Haman determined to destroy all the Jews, the people of Mordecai, who *lived* throughout the kingdom of Ahasuerus.

7 In the first month, the month of Nisan (Mar-Apr), in the twelfth year of King Ahasuerus, Haman cast Pur, that is, the lot, cast before him day after day [to find a lucky day to approach the king], month after month, until the twelfth month, the month of Adar (Feb-Mar).

8 Then Haman said to King Ahasuerus, "There is a certain people scattered [abroad] and dispersed among the peoples in all the provinces of your kingdom; their laws are different from *those* of all *other* people, and they do not observe the king's laws. Therefore it is not in the king's interest to [tolerate them and] let them stay *here*.

9 "If it pleases the king, let it be decreed that they be destroyed, and I will pay ten thousand talents of silver into the hands of those who carry out the *king's* business, to put into the king's treasuries."

10 Then the king removed his signet ring from his hand [that is, the special ring which was used to seal his letters] and gave it to Haman, the son of Hammedatha the Agagite, the enemy of the Jews.

11 The king said to Haman, "The silver is given to you, and the people *also*, to do with them as you please."

12 Then the king's scribes (secretaries) were summoned on the thirteenth day of the first month, and it was written just as Haman commanded to the king's satraps (chief rulers), and to the governors who were over each province and to the officials of each people, each province according to its script (writing), each people according to their own language; being written in the name of King Ahasuerus and sealed with the king's signet ring.

13 Letters were sent by couriers to all the king's provinces to destroy, to kill and to annihilate all the Jews, both young and old, women and children, in one day, the thirteenth [day] of the

---

3:5–6 *furious.* If Haman was of Amalekite ancestry, it could be that this was the cause of his deep hatred. Also, it is possible that Haman simply could not stand to see anyone who did not properly respect his position.

3:7 *Pur, that is, the lot.* The casting of lots was common in ancient times. Haman's casting a lot at the beginning of the year to determine the best time to destroy the Jewish people fits in with the culture of the day, as the Babylonians believed that the gods gathered at the beginning of each year to establish the destiny of human beings. The word *pur* is the basis for the name of the new feast in chapter 9.

3:8 Slander—Haman was sly. He devised an accusation to convince the king that the Jews were a dangerous and treasonous people. His accusation contained a clever mixture of truth and falsehood. The laws of the Jewish people were admittedly different, but this was not unusual, nor was it a threat to Persia, which contained many minorities. Not only was accusing the whole Jewish nation of civil disobedience a lie, it was also intended to lead to something much worse: murder.

3:10 *signet ring.* The king's signet ring symbolized his authority. He would have used this signet as a stamp to authorize official documents.

---

3 ver. 2 **5** ver. 2; Est 5:9; Da 3:19 **6** Ps 83:4 **7** Est 9:24 **8** Ezr 4:13; Ac 16:20 **10** Ge 41:42; Est 8:2,8
12 Est 8:9; Est 1:22; 1Ki 21:8; Est 8:8,10 **13** Est 8:10; Est 8:12; Est 8:11

twelfth month, which is the month of Adar (March 7, 473 B.C.), and to seize their belongings as plunder.

14 A copy of the edict to be decreed as law in every province was published to all the peoples, so that they would be ready for this day.

15 The couriers went out hurriedly by order of the king, and the decree was issued at the citadel in Susa. And while the king and Haman sat down to drink, the city of Susa was perplexed [by the unusual and alarming decree].

Esther Learns of Haman's Plot

4 NOW WHEN Mordecai learned of everything that had been done, he tore his clothes [in mourning], and put on sackcloth and ashes, and went out into the center of the city and cried out loudly and bitterly.

2 He went [only] as far as the king's gate, because no one was to enter the king's gate dressed in sackcloth.

3 In each and every province that the decree and law of the king reached, there was great mourning among the Jews, with fasting, weeping and wailing; and many lay on sackcloth and ashes.

4 When Esther's maids and her eunuchs came and told her [what had happened], the queen was seized by great fear. She sent garments to clothe Mordecai so that he would remove his sackcloth, but he did not accept them.

5 Then Esther summoned Hathach, one of the king's eunuchs, whom the king had appointed to attend her, and ordered him *to go* to Mordecai to find out what this issue was and why it had come about.

6 So Hathach went out to Mordecai in the [open] square of the city, which was in front of the king's gate.

7 Mordecai told him everything that had happened to him, and the exact amount of money that Haman had promised to pay to the king's treasuries for the destruction of the Jews.

8 Mordecai also gave him a copy of the text of the decree which had been issued in Susa for the Jews destruction, so that he might show Esther and explain it to her, and order her to go in to the king to seek his favor and plead with him for [the lives of] her people.

9 Hathach came back and told Esther what Mordecai had said.

10 Then Esther spoke to Hathach and ordered him *to reply* to Mordecai, saying:

11 "All the king's servants and the people of the king's provinces know that for any man or woman who comes to the king to the inner court without being summoned, he has but one law, that he is to be put to death, unless the king holds out to him the golden scepter so that he may live. And as for me, I have not been summoned to come to the king for these [last] thirty days."

12 So they told Mordecai what Esther had said.

13 Then Mordecai told them to reply to Esther, "Do not imagine that you in the king's palace can escape any more than all the Jews.

14 "For if you remain silent at this

3:15 *Haman sat down to drink.* Haman was so unconcerned about the death sentence he was placing on the Jewish people that he sat down comfortably to relax while the city was in confusion.

4:1 – 2 *sackcloth and ashes.* Sackcloth and ashes were used as a visible sign of mourning, indicating a sense of desolation.

4:3 *fasting.* It is interesting to note that throughout the entire Book of Esther, God is not mentioned by name even once. One assumes that Esther's fasting was accompanied by prayer, but it is never mentioned. Fasting was a religious custom, and we know the Jews relied on God for their safety. Many think the author of Esther was writing the story to a secular audience, and this is the reason for God's actual name being left out.

4:11 *I have not been summoned.* Esther understood that Mordecai was asking her to risk her life. She would be taking her life into her hands to go uncalled to the king in any circumstances; the fact that she had not been called for a month probably meant that she was even more unsure of her reception.

4:14 *for such a time as this.* Even though this verse does not directly mention God, Mordecai obviously believed that Esther was made queen through God's design, and she would be acting as God's agent to deliver His people.

14 Est 8:13,14 **15** See Est 8:15; Pr 29:2 **CHAPTER 4** **1** 2Sa 1:11; Jos 7:6; Eze 27:30; Ge 27:34 **7** Est 3:9 **8** Est 3:14,15 **11** Est 5:1; Da 2:9; Est 5:2; 8:4

time, liberation and rescue will arise
for the Jews from another place, and
you and your father's house will perish
[since you did not help when you had
the chance]. And who knows whether
you have attained royalty for such a
time as this [and for this very pur-
pose]?"

Esther Plans to Intercede

15 Then Esther told them to reply to
Mordecai,
16 "Go, gather all the Jews that are
present in Susa, and observe a fast
for me; do not eat or drink for three
days, night or day. I and my maids also
will fast in the same way. Then I will
go in to [see] the king [without being
summoned], which is against the law;
and if I perish, I perish."
17 So Mordecai went away and did ex-
actly as Esther had commanded him.

Esther Plans a Banquet

5 ON THE third day [of the fast] Es-
ther put on her royal robes and
stood in the inner court of the king's
palace opposite his [throne] room. The
king was sitting on his royal throne,
facing the [main] entrance of the pal-
ace.
2 When the king saw Esther the
queen standing in the court, she found
favor in his sight; and the king extend-
ed to her the golden scepter which was
in his hand. So Esther approached and
touched the top of the scepter.
3 Then the king said to her, "What is
troubling you, Queen Esther? What is
your request? It shall be given to you,
up to half of the kingdom."
4 Esther said, "If it pleases the king,
may the king and Haman come this
day to the banquet that I have prepared
for him."
5 Then the king said, "Bring Haman
quickly so that we may do as Esther
says." So the king and Haman came
to the banquet which Esther had pre-
pared.
6 As they drank their wine at the ban-
quet, the king said to Esther, "What
is your petition? It shall be granted to
you. And what is your request? Even to
half of the kingdom it shall be done."
7 Then Esther replied, "My petition
and my request is this:
8 if I have found favor in the sight
of the king, and if it pleases the king
to grant my petition and to do as I re-
quest, may the king and Haman come
to the banquet that I will prepare for
them; and tomorrow I will do as the
king says [and express my request]."

Haman's Pride

9 Haman went away that day joyful
and in good spirits. But when he saw
Mordecai at the king's gate refusing to
stand up or show fear before him, he
was filled with rage toward Mordecai.
10 Nevertheless, Haman controlled
himself and went home. There he sent
for his friends and his wife Zeresh.
11 Then Haman recounted to them the
glory of his riches, the large number of
his sons, and every *instance* in which
the king had magnified him and how
he had promoted him over the officials
and servants of the king.
12 Haman also said, "Even Queen Es-
ther let no one but me come with the
king to the banquet she had prepared;
and tomorrow also I am invited by her
[together] with the king.
13 "Yet all of this does not satisfy me

4:16 Self-denial — Even though Esther must have been afraid, knowing that she was breaking the law, she decided to trust God. Her statement "if I perish, I perish," was not despair, but willingness to act however God willed, recognizing that the consequences were in His hands. Self-denial is not easy, but God never fails His children.

5:2 *she found favor in his sight.* When Esther illegally entered the king's court, he was pleased by her appearance and decided to overlook her offense. In this scene we again see the hand of God.

5:8 *tomorrow I will do as the king says.* Why did Esther delay in telling the king her real request? Perhaps she was afraid, and used the intervening time to strengthen her courage. But it seems that here also is God's hand, for the delay provided time for the king's sleepless night and the events that followed.

---

16 See Est 5:1; See Ge 43:14 **CHAPTER 5** **1** See Est 4:16; See Est 4:11; 6:4 **2** Pr 21:1; Est 4:11; 8:4 **3** Mk 6:23 **6** Est 7:2; Est 9:12 **9** Est 3:5 **10** 2Sa 13:22 **11** Est 9:7

as long as I see Mordecai the Jew sitting at the king's gate."
[14]Then his wife Zeresh and all his friends said to him, "Have a gallows fifty cubits high made, and in the morning ask the king to have Mordecai hanged on it; then go joyfully to the banquet with the king." And the advice pleased Haman, so he had the gallows made.

The King Plans to Honor Mordecai

6 ON THAT night the king could not sleep; so he ordered that the book of records *and* memorable deeds, the chronicles, be brought, and they were read before the king.
[2]It was found written there how Mordecai had reported that Bigthana and Teresh, two of the king's eunuchs who were doorkeepers, had planned to attack King Ahasuerus (Xerxes).
[3]The king said, "What honor or distinction has been given Mordecai for this?" Then the king's servants who attended him said, "Nothing has been done for him."
[4]So the king said, "Who is in the court?" Now Haman had just entered the outer court of the king's palace to ask the king about hanging Mordecai on the gallows which he had prepared for him.
[5]The king's servants said to him, "Look, Haman is standing in the court." And the king said, "Let him come in."
[6]So Haman came in and the king said to him, "What is to be done for the man whom the king desires to honor?" Now Haman thought to himself, "Whom would the king desire to honor more than me?"
[7]So Haman said to the king, "For the man whom the king desires to honor,
[8]let a royal robe be brought which the king has worn, and the horse on which the king has ridden, and on whose head a royal crown has been placed;
[9]and let the robe and the horse be handed over to one of the king's most noble officials. Let him dress the man whom the king delights to honor [in the royal robe] and lead him on horseback through the open square of the city, and proclaim before him, 'This is what shall be done for the man whom the king desires to honor.' "

Haman Must Honor Mordecai

[10]Then the king said to Haman, "Quickly take the royal robe and the horse, as you have said, and do this for Mordecai the Jew, who is sitting at the king's gate. Leave out nothing of all that you have said."
[11]So Haman took the royal robe and the horse and dressed Mordecai, and led him *on horseback* through the open square of the city, proclaiming before him, "This is what shall be done for the man whom the king desires to honor."
[12]Then Mordecai returned to the king's gate. But Haman hurried to his [own] house, mourning and with his head covered [in sorrow].
[13]Then Haman told Zeresh his wife and all his friends everything that had happened to him. Then his wise counselors and his wife Zeresh said to him, "If Mordecai, before whom you have begun to fall *in status,* is of Jewish heritage, you will not overcome him, but will certainly fall before him."
[14]While they were still speaking with

5:14 *gallows.* The gallows height, 50 cubits, was about 75 feet.
6:1 *the king could not sleep.* Within this chapter we observe a series of events that point unmistakably to God's sovereign hand. Only because of the "chance happening" of his sleepless night did the king learn of Mordecai's past loyalty.
6:4 *Now Haman had just entered the outer court.* Here again is the Lord's hand at work on behalf of his people. No sooner had Mordecai's reward been discussed than Haman appeared in the court.
6:10 *Jew.* The term "Jew," derived from Judah, came into use during the exile because the people were primarily from the Southern Kingdom of Judah.

14 Est 7:9; Est 6:4; Est 7:10 **CHAPTER 6** **1** Est 2:23 **4** See Est 5:1; Est 5:14 **8** 1Ki 1:33 **9** Ge 41:43 **12** 2Ch 26:20; 2Sa 15:30; Jer 14:3,4 **14** Est 5:8

him, the king's eunuchs (attendants) arrived and hurriedly brought Haman to the banquet which Esther had prepared.

Esther's Plea

7 SO THE king and Haman came to drink *wine* with Esther the queen.

2And the king said to Esther on the second day also as they drank their wine, "What is your petition, Queen Esther? It shall be granted to you. And what is your request? Even to half of the kingdom, it shall be done."

3Then Queen Esther replied, "If I have found favor in your sight, O king, and if it pleases the king, let my life be spared as my petition, and my people [be spared] as my request;

4for we have been sold, I and my people, to be destroyed, killed and wiped out of existence. Now if we had only been sold as slaves, men and women, I would have remained silent, for our hardship would not be sufficient to burden the king [by even mentioning it]."

5Then King Ahasuerus (Xerxes) asked Queen Esther, "Who is he, and where is he, who dares to do such a thing?"

6Esther said, "An adversary and an enemy is Haman, this evil man." Then Haman became terrified before the king and queen.

Haman Is Hanged

7Then in his fury, the king stood up from drinking wine *and went* into the palace garden [to decide what he should do]; but Haman stayed to plead for his life from Queen Esther, for he saw that harm had been determined against him by the king.

8When the king returned from the palace garden to the place where they were drinking wine, Haman was falling on the couch where Esther was. Then the king said, "Will he even *attempt to* assault the queen with me in the palace?" As the king spoke those words, the servants covered Haman's face [in preparation for execution].

9Then Harbonah, one of the eunuchs serving the king said, "Now look, there are gallows fifty cubits (75 ft.) high standing at Haman's house, which Haman made for Mordecai, whose good warning saved the king." And the king said, "Hang him on it."

10So they hanged Haman on the gallows that he had prepared for Mordecai. Then the king's anger subsided.

Mordecai Promoted

8 ON THAT day King Ahasuerus (Xerxes) gave the house of Haman, the enemy of the Jews, to Queen Esther; and Mordecai came before the king, because Esther had disclosed what [relation] he was to her.

2The king took off his signet ring which he had taken away from Haman, and gave it to Mordecai. And Esther put Mordecai in charge of the house of Haman.

3Then Esther spoke again to the king and fell down at his feet and wept and implored him to avert the evil *plot* of Haman the Agagite and his plan which he had devised against the Jews [because the decree to annihilate the Jews was still in effect].

4Then the king held out to Esther the golden scepter. So Esther arose and stood before the king.

5Then she said, "If it pleases the king and if I have found favor before him and the matter is proper in the king's view and I am pleasing in his sight, let it be written to revoke the letters devised by Haman the son of Hammedatha, the Agagite, which he wrote [in order] to destroy the Jews who are in all the king's provinces.

7:3 *my people [be spared] as my request.* Esther disclosed her real identity to the king in her plea for the lives of her people.

7:6 *Haman, this evil man.* In Haman's evil plan to kill his enemy he had unwittingly threatened the queen's life.

7:8 *covered Haman's face.* The covering of his face signified that he was condemned to death.

8:2 *he had taken away from Haman.* Mordecai was given Haman's position as prime minister.

CHAPTER 7 **2** Est 5:6 **4** Est 3:9 **8** Est 1:6; Job 9:24 **9** Est 1:10; Est 5:14; Ps 7:16; Pr 11:5,6 **10** Ps 37:35,36; Da 6:24 **CHAPTER 8** **1** Est 2:7 **2** Est 3:10 **4** Est 4:11; 5:2

6 "For how can I endure to see the tragedy that will happen to my people? Or how can I endure to see the destruction of my kindred?"

7 Then King Ahasuerus said to Queen Esther and to Mordecai the Jew, "Behold, I have given Esther the house of Haman, and they have hanged him on the gallows because he stretched out his hand against the Jews.

The King's Decree Avenges the Jews

8 "Also, concerning the Jews, write as you see fit, in the king's name, and seal it with the king's signet ring—for a decree which is written in the king's name and sealed with the king's signet ring may not be revoked."

9 So the king's scribes were called at that time in the third month (that is, the month of Sivan) on the twenty-third day; and it was written in accordance with everything that Mordecai commanded, to the Jews, to the chief rulers (satraps), and the governors and officials of the provinces which *extended* from India to Ethiopia (Cush), 127 provinces, to every province in its own script (writing), and to every people in their own language and to the Jews according to their script and their language.

10 He wrote [a decree] in the name of King Ahasuerus, and sealed it with the king's ring, and sent letters by couriers on horseback, riding on the royal [mail] relay horses, the offspring of the racing mares.

11 In it the king granted the Jews who were in every city *the right* to assemble and to defend their lives; to destroy, to kill, and to annihilate any armed force that might attack them, their little children, and women; and to take the enemies' goods as plunder,

12 on one day in all the provinces of King Ahasuerus, the thirteenth [day] of the twelfth month (that is, the month of Adar).

13 A copy of the edict was to be issued as a law in every province and as a proclamation to all peoples, so that the Jews would be ready on that day, to avenge themselves on their enemies.

14 So the couriers, who were mounted on the royal relay horses, left quickly, urged on by the king's command; and the decree was issued at the citadel in Susa [the capital].

15 Then Mordecai departed from the presence of the king in royal apparel of blue and white, with a large crown of gold and with a robe of fine linen and purple wool; and the city of Susa shouted and rejoiced.

16 For [at this time] the Jews had light [a dawn of new hope] and gladness and joy and honor.

17 In each and every province and in each and every city, wherever the king's command and his decree arrived, the Jews *celebrated with* gladness and joy, a feast and a holiday. And many among the peoples of the land became Jews, for the fear of the Jews [and their God] had fallen on them.

The Jews Destroy Their Enemies

9 NOW IN the twelfth month (that is, the month of Adar) on the thirteenth day when the king's command and edict were about to be executed, on the [very] day when the enemies of the Jews had hoped to gain power over them [and slaughter them], it happened the other way around so that the Jews themselves gained power over those who hated them.

2 The Jews assembled in their cities throughout the provinces of King Ahasuerus (Xerxes) to apprehend those who wanted to do them harm;

8:8 *may not be revoked.* In the Persian Empire, a royal decree could not be altered, but a second one could be written that effectively invalidated the first.
8:17 *became Jews.* This is the only place in the Old Testament that refers to conversion to Judaism. Before, a person was a Jew if he or she was born so, and now it appears as a religion to which one could convert.

6 Neh 2:3; Est 7:4 **7** ver. 1; Pr 13:22 **8** See Est 1:19; Da 6:8,12,15 **9** Est 3:12; Est 1:1; Est 1:22; 3:12 **10** 1Ki 21:8; Est 3:12,13 **11** See Est 9:10,15,16 **12** Est 3:13; 9:1 **13** Est 3:14,15 **15** See Est 3:15; Pr 29:2 **16** Ps 97:11 **17** 1Sa 25:8; Ps 18:43; Ge 35:5; Ex 15:16; Dt 2:25; 11:25; Est 9:2 **CHAPTER 9** **1** Est 8:12; Est 3:13; 2Sa 22:41 **2** ver. 16; Est 8:11; Ps 71:13,24; Est 8:17

and no one could stand before them, for the fear of them [and their God] had fallen on all the peoples.

3 Even all the officials of the provinces and the chief rulers (satraps) and the governors and those who attended to the king's business supported the Jews [in defeating their enemies], because the fear of Mordecai [and his God's power] had fallen on them.

4 For Mordecai was great *and* respected in the king's palace, and his fame spread throughout all the provinces; for the man Mordecai became greater and greater.

5 So the Jews struck all their enemies with the sword, killing and destroying them; and they did what they pleased to those who hated them.

6 At the citadel in Susa the Jews killed and destroyed five hundred men,

7 and [they killed] Parshandatha, Dalphon, Aspatha,

8 Poratha, Adalia, Aridatha,

9 Parmashta, Arisai, Aridai, and Vaizatha,

10 the ten sons of Haman the son of Hammedatha, the Jews' enemy; but they did not lay their hands on the plunder.

11 On that day the number of those who were killed at the citadel in Susa was reported to the king.

12 The king said to Queen Esther, "The Jews have killed and destroyed five hundred men and the ten sons of Haman at the citadel in Susa. What then have they done in the rest of the king's provinces! Now what is your petition? It shall be granted to you. What is your further request? It shall also be done."

13 Esther replied, "If it pleases the king, let it be granted to the Jews who are in Susa to act tomorrow also in accordance with the decree of today; and let [the dead bodies of] Haman's ten sons be hanged on the gallows." [Esth 9:10]

14 So the king commanded it to be done; the decree was given in Susa, and they hanged [the bodies of] Haman's ten sons.

15 The Jews who were in Susa also gathered together on the fourteenth day of the month of Adar and killed three hundred men in Susa, but they did not lay their hands on the plunder.

16 Now the rest of the Jews who were in the king's provinces assembled, to defend their lives and rid themselves of their enemies, and kill 75,000 of those who hated them; but they did not lay their hands on the plunder.

17 *This was done* on the thirteenth day of the month of Adar, and on the fourteenth day they rested and made it a day of feasting and rejoicing.

18 But the Jews who were in Susa assembled on the thirteenth and on the fourteenth of the same month, and on the fifteenth day they rested and made it a day of feasting and rejoicing.

19 Therefore the Jews of the villages, who live in the rural [unwalled] towns, make the fourteenth day of the month of Adar a holiday for rejoicing and feasting and sending choice portions *of food* to one another.

The Feast of Purim Instituted

20 Now Mordecai recorded these events, and he sent letters to all the Jews who lived in all the provinces of King Ahasuerus, both near and far,

21 obliging them to celebrate the fourteenth day of the month of Adar, and the fifteenth day of the same month, annually,

22 because on those days the Jews rid themselves of their enemies, and as the month which was turned for them from grief to joy and from mourning into a holiday; that they should make them days of feasting and rejoicing and sending choice portions *of food* to one another and gifts to the poor.

9:7 – 10 *ten sons of Haman*. The patterns of reprisal and revenge were so deeply engrained in the culture of the ancient Middle East that the survival of even one of these sons might mean trouble for the next generation of Jews.

4 2Sa 3:1; 1Ch 11:9; Pr 4:18 **10** Est 5:11; Job 18:19; 27:13-15; Ps 21:10; See Est 8:11 **12** Est 5:6; 7:2 **13** Est 8:11; 2Sa 21:6,9 **15** ver. 2; Est 8:11; ver. 10 **16** ver. 2; Est 8:11; See Est 8:11 **18** ver. 11,15 **19** Dt 16:11,14; Est 8:17; ver. 22; Neh 8:10,12 **22** ver. 19; Neh 8:10

[23]So the Jews undertook what they
had started to do, and what Mordecai
had written to them.
[24]For Haman the son of Hammedatha, the Agagite, the enemy of all
the Jews, had plotted against the Jews
to destroy them and had cast Pur, that
is, the lot, [to find the right time] to
disturb and destroy them.
[25]But when it came before the king,
he commanded in writing that Haman's wicked scheme which he had
devised against the Jews was to return
on his own head, and that he and his
sons should [endure what he planned
for the Jews and] be hanged on the
gallows.
[26]Therefore they called these days
Purim after the name Pur (lot). And
because of all the instructions in this
letter, and what they had faced in this
regard and what had happened to them,
[27]the Jews established and made it a
custom for themselves and for their descendants and for all who joined them,
so that they would not fail to celebrate
these two days as it was written and at
the appointed time annually.
[28]So these days were to be remembered and celebrated throughout every
generation, every family, every province and every city; and these days of
Purim were not to cease from among
the Jews, nor their memory fade from
their descendants.
[29]Then Queen Esther, the daughter of
Abihail, with Mordecai the Jew, wrote
with full power *and* authority to confirm this second letter about Purim.
[30]He sent letters to all the Jews, to the
127 provinces of the kingdom of Ahasuerus, in words of peace and truth,
[31]to establish these days of Purim [to
be observed] at their appointed times,
just as Mordecai the Jew and Queen
Esther had established for them, and
as they had established for themselves
and for their descendants with instructions regarding their times of fasting
and their lamentations (expressions of
needing help).
[32]The command of Esther established these customs for Purim, and it
was written in the book [of the royal
archives].

Mordecai's Greatness

10 KING AHASUERUS (Xerxes)
imposed a tax on the land and
on the coastlands of the sea.
[2]And all the accomplishments of his
authority and strength, and the full
account of the greatness of Mordecai
to which the king had raised him, are
they not written in the Book of the
Chronicles of the Kings of Media and
Persia?
[3]For Mordecai the Jew was second
only to King Ahasuerus, and great
among the Jews and in favor with his
many fellow people, for he worked for
the good of his people and spoke for
the welfare *and* peace of his whole
nation.

9:26–28 *Purim*. Purim (from the word *pur*, referring to the lots Haman cast to determine the best day for destroying the Jews; 3:7) reminds the Jews of God's deliverance from their day of destruction.

24 Est 3:6,7 **25** ver. 13,14; Est 7:5; 8:3; Est 7:10; Ps 7:16 **26** ver. 20 **27** Est 8:17; Isa 56:3,6; Zec 2:11 **29** Est 2:15; See Est 8:10; ver. 20 **30** Est 1:1 **31** Est 4:3,16 **CHAPTER 10** **1** Ge 10:5; Ps 72:10; Isa 24:15 **2** Est 8:15; 9:4 **3** Ge 41:40; 2Ch 28:7; Neh 2:10; Ps 122:8,9

THE BOOK OF JOB

▸ **AUTHOR:** The author of Job is unknown and there are no textual hints as to his identity. The non-Hebraic cultural background may point to a Gentile authorship, but an interesting school of thought maintains that Moses may have written this book. The land of Uz (1:1) is directly adjacent to Midian, where Moses lived for 40 years. Perhaps the oldest book of the Bible, set in the time of the patriarchs (Abraham, Isaac, Jacob, and Joseph), it is conceivable that Moses obtained a record of the dialogue left by Job or Elihu.

▸ **TIMES:** Unknown ▸ **KEY VERSE:** Job 13:15

▸ **THEME:** There are many things that set Job apart from the rest of Scripture. Its dramatic format is unique. It is a story that is not part of the flow of the history of Israel. And the thematic focus is narrower than other books of its size. A classic work of literature, its primary subject matter is the most basic question man has of God: Why do we suffer? The Book of Job is the biblical text that addresses this issue head on, and the dramatic nature of the story intensifies the conflict of ideas and understanding between God and man.

Job's Character and Wealth

1 THERE WAS a man in the land of
Uz whose name was Job; and that
man was blameless and upright, and
one who feared God [with reverence]
and abstained from *and* turned away
from evil [because he honored God].
2 Seven sons and three daughters
were born to him.
3 He also possessed 7,000 sheep,
3,000 camels, 500 yoke (pairs) of oxen,
500 female donkeys, and a very great
number of servants, so that this man
was the greatest [and wealthiest and
most respected] of all the men of the
east (northern Arabia).
4 His sons used to go [in turn] and
feast in the house of each one on his

1:1 *Uz.* The precise location of Uz is unknown, but it may have been near Edom. Some of the other towns and peoples mentioned in this book are known to have been located near Edom, so it is logical to assume that Uz was in the same area.

1:2 Why Do We Suffer? — Scripture points us to multiple reasons for suffering. Here, as in Job's case, suffering somehow is involved in God's purposes, and we are to learn from it. The New Testament echoes this teaching in James 1 where it says to "Consider it nothing but joy, my brothers and sisters, whenever you fall into various trials. Be assured that the testing of your faith [through experience] produces endurance [leading to spiritual maturity, and inner peace]" (Jas 1:2–3). Suffering also happens as a result of our own sin. David suffered many family trials because of his sin with Bathsheba. Other times we suffer directly because of our faith, as martyrs have done for centuries. Sometimes living out our faith comes in direct conflict with the ruling powers, and we suffer because of it. Still other times we suffer because we live in a fallen world where things go wrong or natural disasters occur.

Both Peter and Paul advise us to commit our pain and suffering to God, realizing He is faithful to work out all things for our good and God's glory (Ro 8:28; 1Pe 4:9). This lesson is often learned over a whole lifetime as we see in numerous Psalms and in the lives of many biblical characters.

CHAPTER 1 **1** 1Ch 1:17; Eze 14:14; Jas 5:11; Ge 17:1; Pr 16:6

day, and they would send *word* and in-
vite their three sisters to eat and drink
with them. [Gen 21:8; 40:20]
5 When the days of their feasting
were over, Job would send [for them]
and consecrate them, rising early in
the morning and offering burnt offer-
ings *according to* the number of them
all; for Job said, "It may be that my
sons have sinned and cursed God in
their hearts." Job did this at all [such]
times.
6 Now there was a day when the
sons of God (angels) came to present
themselves before the LORD, and Satan
(adversary, accuser) also came among
them. [Rev 12:10]
7 The LORD said to Satan, "From
where have you come?" Then Satan
answered the LORD, "From roaming
around on the earth and from walking
around on it."
8 The LORD said to Satan, "Have you
considered *and* reflected on My servant
Job? For there is none like him on the
earth, a blameless and upright man,
one who fears God [with reverence]
and abstains from *and* turns away
from evil [because he honors God]."
9 Then Satan answered the LORD,
"Does Job fear God for nothing?
10 "Have You not put a hedge [of pro-
tection] around him and his house and
all that he has, on every side? You have
blessed the work of his hands [and
conferred prosperity and happiness
upon him], and his possessions have
increased in the land.
11 "But put forth Your hand now and
touch (destroy) all that he has, and he
will surely curse You to Your face."
12 Then the LORD said to Satan, "Be-
hold, all that Job has is in your power,
only do not put your hand on *the man*
himself." So Satan departed from the
presence of the LORD.

Satan Allowed to Test Job

13 Now there was a day when Job's
sons and daughters were eating and
drinking wine in their oldest brother's
house,
14 and a messenger came to Job and
said, "The oxen were plowing and the
donkeys were feeding beside them,
15 and the Sabeans attacked *and*
swooped down on them and took
away the animals. They also killed the

1:6 *the sons of God.* Celestial beings or angels are called "sons of God" because they had no parents. They were created by God to serve Him (2:1; 4:18; Ps 103:20). This can also mean a group of saints (Ge 6:2). Adam was also called "the son of God" (Lk 3:38) because God was his Creator rather than having a human father and mother. Here Satan is said to be among them. ***Satan.*** At some point after creation, Satan, who was the highest created angel (Eze 28:12 – 15), aspired to be as God Himself (Isa 14:13 – 14). As a result, he was barred from his heavenly position (Eze 28:16) and took a large number of angels with him in his rebellion, over whom he rules as "prince" (Mt 12:24). Jesus says that He saw Satan fall from heaven (Lk 10:18), but this chapter in Job, and the incident of the lying spirit with the false prophets of Ahab (2Ch 18:8 – 22), indicate that Satan still had access to heaven and heavenly counsels. God can and does limit Satan (1:12). The cross defeated Satan (Jn 12:31), but the final judgment will not occur until the end of the millennium (Rev 20:10). In the meantime, Satan tries to thwart and defeat the work of God. God sometimes uses Satan to teach a lesson (1Ch 21; 2Co 12:7 – 10), but it is still God who is in control.

1:7 *the LORD.* The Hebrew word Yahweh, usually translated "the LORD," is the personal name of the true God of the Old Testament (Ex 3:14 – 15). It is the particular name of God in covenantal relations with His people Israel (Ex 6:1 – 6; 19:3 – 8).

1:8 *a blameless and upright man.* The Lord was not saying that Job was sinless, but He was saying that Job had his priorities right. Job feared the Lord and it showed in his life.

1:10 *hedge.* No harm could come to Job unless the Lord permitted it (v. 12). Believers today should take great comfort from the biblical teaching that the Lord protects His people — whether by a cloud (Ex 14:19 – 20), or by a wall of fiery chariots (2Ki 6:17), or through guardian angels (Heb 1:14).

1:11 *curse.* The sin of cursing God is a pivotal issue for the Book of Job. Job feared that his children might think or speak irreverently of God (v. 5). But Satan asserted that Job would "surely curse" God if his prosperity and blessings were removed. Even Job's wife urged him to "curse God and die" (2:9).

1:15 *Sabeans.* The Sabeans were nomadic

---

5 Job 42:8; 1Ki 21:10 **6** Job 2:1 **7** 1Pe 5:8 **10** Ps 34:7; Isa 5:2; Ps 128:1,2; Pr 10:22 **11** Job 2:5; 19:21; Isa 8:21; Mal 3:13,14 **13** Ecc 9:12

servants with the edge of the sword,
and I alone have escaped to tell you."
16While he was still speaking, another
[messenger] also came and said, "The
fire of God (lightning) has fallen from
the heavens and has burned up the sheep
and the servants and consumed them,
and I alone have escaped to tell you."
17While he was still speaking, another [messenger] also came and said, "The Chaldeans formed three bands and made a raid on the camels and have taken them away and have killed the servants with the edge of the sword, and I alone have escaped to tell you."
18While he was still speaking, another [messenger] also came and said, "Your sons and your daughters were eating and drinking wine in their oldest brother's house,
19and suddenly, a great wind came from across the desert, and struck the four corners of the house, and it fell on the young people and they died, and I alone have escaped to tell you."
20Then Job got up and tore his robe and shaved his head [in mourning for the children], and he fell to the ground and worshiped [God].
21He said,

"Naked (without possessions) I
came [into this world] from my
mother's womb,
And naked I will return there.
The LORD gave and the LORD has
taken away;
Blessed be the name of the LORD."

22Through all this Job did not sin nor did he blame God.

Job Loses His Health

2 AGAIN THERE was a day when the sons of God (angels) came to present themselves before the LORD, and Satan (adversary, accuser) also came among them to present himself before the LORD.
2The LORD said to Satan, "From where have you come?" Then Satan answered the LORD, "From roaming around on the earth and from walking around on it."
3The LORD said to Satan, "Have you considered *and* reflected on My servant Job? For there is none like him on the earth, a blameless and upright man, one who fears God [with reverence] and abstains from *and* turns away from evil [because he honors God]. And still he maintains *and* holds tightly to his integrity, although you incited Me against him to destroy him without cause."
4Satan answered the LORD, "Skin for skin! Yes, a man will give all he has for his life.
5"But put forth Your hand now, and touch his bone and his flesh [and severely afflict him]; and he will curse You to Your face."
6So the LORD said to Satan, "Behold, he is in your hand, only spare his life."
7So Satan departed from the presence of the LORD and struck Job with *loathsome* boils *and* agonizingly painful sores from the sole of his foot to the crown of his head.
8And Job took a piece of broken pottery with which to scrape himself, and he sat [down] among the ashes (rubbish heaps).
9Then his wife said to him, "Do you still cling to your integrity [and your faith and trust in God, without blaming Him]? Curse God and die!"
10But he said to her, "You speak as one of the [spiritually] foolish wom-

---

raiders from Sheba, probably located in southwestern Arabia, in present-day Yemen.

1:17 *Chaldeans.* The Chaldeans were part of various west Semitic marauding tribes active in the middle Euphrates from the twelfth to the ninth centuries BC. They migrated eastward into Assyria and then Babylonia, and were the forerunners of the Chaldean or neo-Babylonian dynasty established by Nebuchadnezzar's father.

2:10 *good ... adversity and disaster.* This comment of Job's is one of the central themes of the whole book. A person of faith will trust in God through prosperity or adversity, even if they are unable to understand why bad things happen (Hab 3:17 – 19).

18 ver. 4,13 **20** Ge 37:29; Ezr 9:3; 1Pe 5:6 **21** Ps 49:17; Ecc 5:15; 1Ti 6:7; Ecc 5:19; Jas 1:17; Ge 31:16; Eph 5:20; 1Th 5:18 **22** Job 2:10 **CHAPTER 2** **1** Job 1:6 **2** Job 1:7 **3** Job 1:1,8; Job 27:5,6; Job 9:17 **5** Job 1:11; Job 19:20 **6** Job 1:12 **7** Isa 1:6 **8** 2Sa 13:19; Job 42:6; Eze 27:30; Mt 11:21 **10** Job 1:21; Heb 12:6; Jas 5:10,11; Job 1:22; Ps 39:1

en speaks [ignorant and oblivious to God's will]. Shall we indeed accept [only] good from God and not [also] accept adversity *and* disaster?" In [spite of] all this Job did not sin with [words from] his lips.

11 Now when Job's three friends heard of all this adversity that had come upon him, each one came from his own place, Eliphaz the Temanite, Bildad the Shuhite, and Zophar the Naamathite; for they had made an appointment together to come to sympathize with him and to comfort him.

12 When they looked from a distance and did not recognize him [because of his disfigurement], they raised their voices and wept; and each one tore his robe [in grief] and they threw dust over their heads toward the sky [in sorrow].

13 So they sat down on the ground with Job for seven days and seven nights and no one spoke a word to him, for they saw that his pain was very great.

Job's Lament

3 AFTER THIS, Job opened his mouth and cursed the day of his *birth.*

2 And Job said,

3 "Let the day on which I was born
perish,
And the night which announced:
'There is a man-child conceived.'
4 "May that day be darkness;
Let God above not care about it,
Nor light shine on it.
5 "Let darkness and gloom claim it
for their own;
Let a cloud settle upon it;
Let all that blackens the day
terrify it (the day that I was
born).
6 "As for that night, let darkness
seize it;
Let it not rejoice among the days
of the year;
Let it not be counted in the number
of the months.
7 "Behold, let that night be barren
[and empty];
Let no joyful voice enter it.
8 "Let those curse it who curse the
day,
Who are skilled in rousing up
Leviathan.
9 "Let the stars of its early dawn be
dark;
Let *the morning* wait in vain for
the light,
Let it not see the eyelids of
morning (the day's dawning),
10 Because it did not shut the doors of
my *mother's* womb,
Nor hide trouble from my eyes.
11 "Why did I not die at birth,
Come forth from the womb and
expire?
12 "Why did the knees receive me?
And why the breasts, that I would
nurse?
13 "For now I would have lain down
and been quiet;
I would have slept then, I would
have been at rest [in death],
14 With kings and counselors of the
earth,
Who built up [now desolate] ruins
for themselves;

2:11 ***Temanite . . . Shuhite . . . Naamathite.*** A Temanite was probably an Edomite from Teman in northern Edom, and a Naamathite probably came from Naameh, a mountainous area in northwestern Arabia. From this context, it can be assumed that a Shuhite was also a person from a certain town, unknown in modern times.
3:1 ***cursed the day.*** The Hebrew word for "cursed," meaning "to hold in contempt," is elsewhere employed of cursing God (Ex 22:28; Lev 24:15) or cursing one's parents (Ex 21:17). Job expressed a strong malediction against the day of his birth and the night of his conception, but he did not commit blasphemy. He did not curse the Chaldeans, or Sabeans, much less God. Neither did he express thoughts of suicide.
3:8 ***curse.*** Job employed two separate Hebrew words translated "curse," different from the term in verse 1. He wished that the popular magicians who cast spells on the day for their clients could have cast a spell on his day so that he never could have been born. He was not endorsing pagan magic, but was speaking vividly and forcefully to express his agony and despair.

11 Ge 36:11; Jer 49:7; Ge 25:2; Job 42:11; Ro 12:15 **12** Neh 9:1; La 2:10; Eze 27:30 **13** Ge 50:10 **CHAPTER 3**
3 Jer 20:14 **5** Job 10:21; Jer 13:16; Am 5:8 **8** Jer 9:17 **11** Job 10:18 **12** Ge 30:3 **14** Job 15:28

[15]Or with princes who had gold,
Who filled their houses with silver.
[16]"Or like a miscarriage which is hidden *and* put away, I would not exist,
Like infants who never saw light.
[17]"There [in death] the wicked cease from raging,
And there the weary are at rest.
[18]"There the prisoners rest together;
They do not hear the taskmaster's voice.
[19]"The small and the great are there,
And the servant is free from his master. [Jer 20:14–18]

[20]"Why is the light given to him who is in misery,
And life to the bitter in soul,
[21]Who wait for death, but it does not come,
And dig (search) for death more [diligently] than for hidden treasures,
[22]Who rejoice exceedingly,
And rejoice when they find the grave?
[23]"*Why is the light of day given* to a man whose way is hidden,
And whom God has hedged in?
[24]"For my groaning comes at the sight of my food,
And my cries [of despair] are poured out like water.
[25]"For the thing which I greatly fear comes upon me,
And that of which I am afraid has come upon me.
[26]"I am not at ease, nor am I quiet,
And I am not at rest, and yet trouble still comes [upon me]."

Eliphaz: Innocent Do Not Suffer

4 THEN ELIPHAZ the Temanite answered and said,
[2]"If we dare to converse with you, will you be impatient [or offended]?
But who can restrain himself from speaking?
[3]"Behold, you have admonished *and* instructed many,
And you have strengthened weak hands.
[4]"Your words have helped the one who was stumbling to stand,
And you have strengthened feeble knees.
[5]"But now adversity comes upon you, and you are impatient *and* intolerant;
It touches you, and you are horrified.
[6]"Is not your fear *of God* your confidence,
And [is not] the integrity *and* uprightness of your ways your hope?

[7]"Remember now, who, being innocent, ever perished?
Or where [and in what circumstances] were those upright *and* in right standing with God destroyed?
[8]"As I have seen, those who plow wickedness
And those who sow trouble *and* harm harvest it.
[9]"By the breath of God they perish,
And by the blast of His anger they are consumed.
[10]"The roaring of the lion and the voice of the *fierce* lion,

3:20–22 *wait for death.* Even though Job longed for death, he was not considering suicide. The context of the other passages indicates that Job merely wished that the Lord would let him die (7:15–21; 10:18–22).

3:23 *whom God has hedged in.* The irony is that Job perceived God's hedge as keeping him from a desirable death instead of seeing it as God's protection of his life.

4:7 *who, being innocent, ever perished.* Eliphaz concluded that since Job was suffering, he must have sin in his life. Eliphaz supported the retribution doctrine: God supports the righteous but abandons the wicked.

4:8 *sow trouble and harm harvest it.* It can be true that planting wicked actions will yield a crop of trauma, but the converse is not necessarily true. Hard times can come to anyone, and the crop that is harvested in hard times depends on whether or not we continue to follow God in times of trouble.

16 Ps 58:8 **18** Job 39:7 **20** Jer 20:18; 2Ki 4:27 **21** Rev 9:6; Pr 2:4 **23** La 3:7 **CHAPTER 4** **3** Isa 35:3
4 Isa 35:3 **6** Job 1:1; Pr 3:26 **7** Ps 37:25 **8** Pr 22:8 **10** Ps 58:6

And the teeth of the young lions
are broken.
11 "The lion perishes for lack of prey,
And the cubs of the lioness are
scattered.

12 "Now a word was secretly brought
to me,
And my ear received a whisper of it.
13 "Amid disquieting thoughts from
the visions of the night,
When deep sleep falls on men,
14 Dread and trembling came upon
me,
Which made all my bones shake.
15 "Then a spirit passed before my
face;
The hair on my skin stood on end!
16 "The spirit stood still, but I could
not discern its appearance;
A form was before my eyes;
There was silence, and then I
heard a voice, saying:
17 'Can [mortal] man be just before
God *or* be more righteous than
He?
Can a man be pure before his
Maker *or* be more cleansed than
He? [1 John 1:7; Rev 1:5]
18 'God puts no trust *or* confidence,
even in His [heavenly] servants,
And He charges His angels with
error.
19 'How much more [will He blame
and charge] those who dwell in
houses (bodies) of clay,
Whose foundations are in the dust,
Who are crushed like a moth.
20 'Between morning and evening
they are broken in pieces *and*
destroyed;
Unobserved *and* unnoticed, they
perish forever.
21 'Is not their tent-cord drawn up
within them [so that the tent
collapses]?
Do they not die, and yet without
[acquiring] wisdom?'

God Is Just

5 "CALL NOW—is there anyone
who will answer you?
And to which of the holy ones
(angels) will you turn?
2 "For anger slays the foolish man,
And jealousy kills the simple
(naive).
3 "I have seen the foolish taking root
[and outwardly prospering],
But I cursed his dwelling
immediately [for his destruction
was certain].
4 "His children are far from safety
[and included in their father's
ruin],
They are oppressed *and* crushed
in the [court of justice in the
city's] gate,
And there is no one to rescue
them.
5 "The hungry devour his harvest
And take it even [when it grows]
among the thorns;
The trap opens for [his] wealth.
6 "For affliction does not come forth
from the dust,
Nor does trouble spring forth from
the ground.
7 "For man is born for trouble,
[As naturally] as sparks fly
upward.

8 "As for me, I would seek God *and*
inquire of Him,
And I would commit my cause to
God;
9 Who does great and unsearchable
things,
Marvelous things without number.
10 "He gives rain upon the earth

4:13 *visions of the night*. Eliphaz appealed to a vision to authenticate his theology, but all dreams do not come from God. The "reader" of this book has different information, for God pulled aside the curtain of heaven to reveal the true background for Job's troubles.

4:19 Death — We live in houses of clay, and our foundations are in the dust. We may presume upon tomorrow, having illusions of permanence, but suddenly the cords of our tent are pulled up and our existence collapses. We perish, more readily than a moth encircling a flame. Surely the transience of life, the reality of death, and the certainty of judgment should move us to pray that the Eternal God will teach us to number our days so we can use them wisely (Ps 90:12). This awareness gives us a sense of urgency in turning from sin and serving our Savior.

11 Ps 34:10 **13** Job 33:15 **14** Hab 3:16 **18** Job 15:15 **20** Ps 90:5,6 **CHAPTER 5** **3** Jer 12:2,3

And sends waters upon the fields,
11 So that He sets on high those who are lowly,
And He lifts to safety those who mourn.
12 "He frustrates the devices *and* schemes of the crafty,
So that their hands cannot attain success *or* achieve anything of [lasting] worth.
13 "He catches the [so-called] wise in their own shrewdness,
And the advice of the devious is quickly thwarted. [1 Cor 3:19, 20]
14 "In the daytime they meet in darkness,
And at noon they grope as in the night.
15 "But God saves [the innocent] from the sword of the mouth of the devious,
And the poor from the hand of the mighty.
16 "So the helpless have hope,
And injustice shuts its mouth.

17 "Behold, how happy *and* fortunate is the man whom God reproves,
So do not despise *or* reject the discipline of the Almighty [subjecting you to trial and suffering].
18 "For He inflicts pain, but He binds up *and* gives relief;
He wounds, but His hands also heal.
19 "He will rescue you from six troubles;
Even in seven, evil will not touch you.
20 "In famine He will redeem you from death,
And in war from the power of the sword.
21 "You will be hidden from the scourge of the tongue,
And you will not be afraid of destruction when it comes.
22 "You will laugh at violence and famine,
And you will not be afraid of the wild beasts of the earth.
23 "For you will be in harmony with the stones of the field,
And the beasts of the field will be at peace with you.
24 "You will know also that your tent is secure *and* at peace,
And you will visit your dwelling and fear no loss [nor find anything amiss].
25 "You will know also that your descendants will be many,
And your offspring as the grass of the earth.
26 "You will come to your grave in old age,
Like the stacking of grain [on the threshing floor] in its season.
27 "Behold this; we have investigated it, *and* it is true.
Hear *and* heed it, and know for yourself [for your own good]."

Job's Friends Are No Help

6 THEN JOB answered and said,
2 "Oh, that my grief could actually be weighed
And placed in the balances together with my tragedy [to see if my grief is the grief of a coward]!

5:17 *discipline.* Eliphaz insinuated that since Job's suffering was a result of God's discipline for his sin, Job should not reject what God was trying to teach him. While it is true that God sometimes disciplines people for their own good (Pr 3:11 – 12; Heb 12:7), Eliphaz was suggesting that trouble in one's life necessarily means that one is being disciplined. Once again, the reader of this book has insight that the participants in the story do not have. Job's troubles do indeed teach him more about God, but the troubles originated because God was showing Satan that His followers are not following Him for what they get, but because of who He is.

5:23 *in harmony with the stones of the field.* Stones in the field are a significant hindrance to farming, just as wild animals or lack of rain are a hindrance. Eliphaz was saying that one who accepts the discipline of the Almighty will not find himself fighting the elements of nature. It is true that God is a deliverer, a healer, and one who disciplines his followers. We can safely trust Him to care for us. But having disaster, wounds, or failure is not necessarily a sign of God's discipline.

11 Ps 113:7 **12** Neh 4:15 **15** Ps 35:10 **16** 1Sa 2:8 **17** Ps 94:12 **18** 1Sa 2:6 **19** Ps 34:19; Ps 91:10 **20** Ps 33:19 **21** Ps 31:20 **22** Isa 11:9 **23** Ps 91:12 **25** Ps 112:2; Ps 72:16 **26** Pr 10:27 **27** Ps 111:2

3 "For now it would be heavier than
the sand of the sea;
Therefore my words have been
incoherent,
4 Because the arrows of the
Almighty are within me,
My spirit drinks their poison;
The terrors of God are arrayed
against me.
5 "Does the wild donkey bray when
he has grass?
Or does the ox low over his fodder?
6 "Can something that has no taste
to it be eaten without salt?
Or is there any flavor in the white
of an egg?
7 "My soul refuses to touch them;
Such things are like loathsome food
to me [sickening and repugnant].
8 "Oh that my request would come
to pass,
And that God would grant me the
thing that I long for!
9 "I wish that it would please God to
crush me,
That He would let loose His hand
and cut me off.
10 "Then I would still have
consolation,
And I would jump for joy amid
unsparing pain,
That I have not denied *or* hidden
the words of the Holy One.
11 "What strength do I have left, that
I should wait [and hope]?
And what is ahead of me, that I
should be patient *and* endure?
12 "Is my strength *and* endurance
that of stones,
Or is my flesh made of bronze?
13 "Is it that I have no help within
myself,
And that success *and* wisdom have
been driven from me?
14 "For the despairing man *there
should be* kindness from his
friend;
So that he does not abandon
(turn away from) the fear of the
Almighty.
15 "My brothers have acted
deceitfully like a brook,
Like the torrents of brooks that
vanish,
16 Which are dull *and* dirty because
of ice,
And into which the snow melts
and hides itself;
17 When it is warm, they are silent
and cease to flow;
When it is hot, they vanish from
their place.
18 "The paths of their course wind
along,
They go up into nothing *and* perish.
[Your counsel is as helpful to me
as a dry streambed in the heat
of summer.]
19 "The caravans of Tema looked [for
water],
The caravans of Sheba waited for
them [in vain].
20 "They were put to shame *and*
disappointed because they had
trusted [that they would find
water];
They came there and were
ashamed.
21 "Indeed, you have now become
like a dried-up stream,
You see a terror [believing me
to be a victim of the wrath
of God] and are afraid [to be
compassionate].

6:9 Prayer — Job thought it would be better to die than to endure all the pain and suffering that resulted from the tragedies he had experienced. He could not know that the fact that he was alive was actually because God had protected him. This prayer should be a great comfort to believers. We cannot always see God's hedge of protection in a traumatic situation. We can cry out for relief, when God wants us to endure. He knows far more about our situation than we do, and we can trust Him, even as we anguish over unanswered prayer.

6:10 *I would still have consolation.* Job's single comfort was that he had not denied God, even though he believed that God was the one who had wounded him.

6:15 *torrents of brooks that vanish.* A brook is a stream that only carries water during the rainy season. Other times of the year it is a dry path. Job was likening his friends to a dry stream.

CHAPTER 6 **4** Ps 38:2; 88:15 **10** Ac 20:20; Lev 19:2; Isa 57:15 **14** Pr 17:17 **15** Ps 38:11; Jer 15:18 **19** Ge 25:15; Ps 72:10 **20** Jer 14:3 **21** Job 13:4; Ps 38:11

22 "Did I ever say, 'Give me
something,'
Or, 'Pay a bribe for me from your
wealth,'
23 Or, 'Rescue me from the
adversary's hand,'
Or, 'Redeem me from the hand of
the tyrants'?

24 "Teach me, and I will be silent;
And show me how I have erred.
25 "How painful are words of
honesty.
But what does your argument
prove?
26 "Do you intend to reprove my
words [with a convincing
argument],
When the words of one in despair
belong to the wind [and go
ignored]?
27 "You would cast *lots* (gamble) over
the fatherless
And bargain away your friend.
28 "Now please look at me,
And *see* if I lie to your face [for you
know that I would not].
29 "Turn away [from your suspicion],
let there be no injustice;
Turn away, my righteousness *and*
vindication is still in it.
30 "Is there injustice *or* malice on my
tongue?
Can my palate not discern what is
destructive?

Job's Life Seems Futile

7 "IS NOT man forced to labor on
earth?
And are not his days like the days
of a hired man?
2 "As a slave earnestly longs for the
shade,
And as a hired man eagerly awaits
his wages,
3 So am I allotted months of futility
and suffering,
And [long] nights of trouble *and*
misery are appointed to me.
4 "When I lie down I say,
'When shall I arise [and the night
be gone]?'
But the night continues,
And I am continually tossing until
the dawning of day.
5 "My body is clothed with worms
and a crust of dust;
My skin is hardened [and broken
and loathsome], and [breaks out
and] runs.
6 "My days are swifter than a
weaver's shuttle,
And are spent without hope.

7 "Remember that my life is but
breath [a puff of wind, a sigh];
My eye will not see good again.
8 "The eye of him who sees me
[now] will see me no more;
Your eyes *will be* upon me, but I
will not be.
9 "As a cloud vanishes and is gone,
So he who goes down to Sheol (the
nether world, the place of the
dead) does not come up.
10 "He will not return again to his
house,
Nor will his place know about him
anymore.

11 "Therefore I will not restrain my
mouth;
I will speak in the anguish of my
spirit,
I will complain in the bitterness of
my soul [O Lord].
12 "Am I the sea, or the sea monster,
That You set a guard over me?
13 "When I say, 'My bed will comfort
me,
My couch will ease my complaint,'
14 Then You frighten me with dreams
And terrify me through visions,
15 So that I would choose suffocation,

6:24 *show me how I have erred.* If Job's friends could show him error in his ways, Job was willing to listen. The problem was that Job's friends were reasoning backwards. They were assuming that they knew his error, based on the extent of Job's suffering. But they had their formula wrong. Sinners may suffer, but suffering does not equal sin or the Lord's discipline.

7:6 *hope.* Job's choice of the word "hope" in the context of the weaver's shuttle may convey a double meaning. The Hebrew word for "hope" sounds like the Hebrew word that means "thread" or "cord."

27 Ps 57:6 **29** Job 17:10 **CHAPTER 7** **1** Job 14:5 **3** Job 29:2 **4** Dt 28:67 **5** Isa 14:11 **6** Job 9:25 **7** Ps 78:39 **8** Job 20:9 **9** 2Sa 12:23 **10** Job 8:18 **11** Ps 39:1,9; 1Sa 1:10 **13** Job 9:27

Death rather than my pain.
16 "I waste away *and* loathe my life; I
will not live forever.
Let me alone, for my days are
but a breath [futile and without
substance].
17 "What is man that You [should]
magnify him [and think him
important]?
And that You are concerned about
him? [Ps 8:4]
18 "And that You examine him every
morning
And try *and* test him every moment?
19 "Will You never turn Your gaze
away from me [it plagues me],
Nor let me alone until I swallow
my spittle?
20 "If I have sinned, what [harm]
have I done to You,
O Watcher of mankind?
Why have You set me as a target
for You,
So that I am a burden to myself?
21 "Why then do You not pardon my
transgression
And take away my sin *and* guilt?
For now I will lie down in the dust;
And You will seek me [diligently],
but I will not be."

Bildad Says God Rewards the Good

8 THEN BILDAD the Shuhite answered and said,

2 "How long will you say these
things?
And will the words of your mouth
be a mighty wind?
3 "Does God pervert justice?
Or does the Almighty pervert
righteousness?
4 "If your children have sinned
against Him,
Then He has handed them over to
the power of their transgression
and punished them.
5 "If you would [diligently] seek God
And implore the compassion *and*
favor of the Almighty,
6 Then, if you are pure and upright,
Surely now He will awaken for you
And restore your righteous place.
7 "Though your beginning was
insignificant,
Yet your end will greatly increase.
8 "Inquire, please, of past generations,
And consider *and* apply yourself to
the things searched out by their
fathers.
9 "For we are *only* of yesterday and
know nothing,
Because our days on earth are
[like] a shadow [just a breath or
a vapor].
10 "Will they (the fathers) not teach
you *and* tell you,
And utter words from their hearts
[the deepest part of their nature]?
11 "Can the papyrus grow up without
a marsh?
Can the rushes *or* reed grass grow
without water?
12 "While it is still green (in flower)
and not cut down,
Yet it withers before any *other*
plant [when without water].
13 "So are the paths of all who forget
God;

7:20 *what [harm] have I done to You.* Job, too, was assuming that his troubles came from God. Job did not believe that he had sinned in a way that would cause God to bring trouble on him. This may sound presumptuous, as if Job thought he was without any sin at all. But we remember that God Himself referred to Job as upright and blameless. God was not finding fault with the way that Job was living out his life of faith in God.

8:3 *Does God pervert justice?* Bildad was saying that Job and his children received what they deserved.

8:6 *if you are pure and upright.* This was actually the way God described Job (1:8; 2:3). Bildad's concept that one must "get right with God" was not erroneous. But his error was his assumption that loss of possessions was equal with loss of God's favor.

8:13 *So are the paths of all who forget God.* Bildad falsely deduced that one can always determine the cause by looking at the effect. We can know that the people around us suffer, but it is not given to us to know the spiritual causes, if any, behind this suffering.

16 Job 10:1; Job 14:6; Ps 62:9 **17** Ps 8:4 **20** Ps 36:6; Ps 21:12; La 3:12 **CHAPTER 8** **3** Ge 18:25 **4** Job 1:5,18 **5** Job 11:13 **8** Dt 4:32 **9** Ge 47:9; 1Ch 29:15; Job 7:6 **12** Ps 129:6; Jer 17:6 **13** Job 11:20; Pr 10:28

And the hope of the godless will
perish,
14 For his confidence is fragile *and*
breaks,
And his trust is [like] a spider's web.
15 "He trusts in his house, but it does
not stand;
He holds tightly to it, but it does
not endure.
16 "He thrives *and* prospers [like a
green plant] before the sun,
And his branches spread out over
his garden.
17 "His [godless] roots are wrapped
around a pile of rocks,
And he gazes at a house of stones.
18 "If he is snatched from his place
[in the garden],
Then his place will forget him,
saying, 'I have never seen you.'
19 "Behold, this is the joy of His way;
And from out of the dust others
will spring up *and* grow [to take
his place].
20 "Behold, God will not reject a *man
of* integrity,
Nor will He strengthen *or* support
evildoers.
21 "He will yet fill your mouth with
laughter
And your lips with joyful shouting
[if you are found blameless].
22 "Those who hate you will be
clothed with shame,
And the tents of the wicked will be
no longer."

Job Says There Is No Arbitrator between God and Man

9 THEN JOB answered and said,

2 "Yes, I know it is true.
But how can a mortal man be right
before God?
3 "If one should want to contend *or*
dispute with Him,
He could not answer Him once in
a thousand *times*.
4 "*God* is wise in heart and mighty
in strength;
Who has [ever] defied *or*
challenged Him and remained
unharmed?
5 "*It is God* who removes the
mountains, and they do not
know it,
When He overturns them in His
anger;
6 Who shakes the earth out of its
place,
And its pillars tremble;
7 Who commands the sun, and it
does not shine;
Who seals up the stars [from view];
8 Who alone stretches out the
heavens
And tramples down the waves of
the sea;
9 Who made [the constellations] the
Bear, Orion, and the Pleiades,
And the [vast starry] spaces of the
south;
10 Who does great things, [beyond
understanding,] unfathomable,
Yes, marvelous *and* wondrous
things without number.
11 "Behold, He passes by me, and I do
not see Him;
He moves past me, but I do not
perceive Him.
12 "Behold, He snatches away; who
can restrain *or* turn Him back?
Who will say to Him, 'What are
You doing?'
13 "God will not turn back His anger;
The [proud] helpers of Rahab [the
arrogant monster of the sea]
bow under Him.
14 "How can I answer Him [and plead
my case],
Choosing my words [to reason]
with Him?
15 For though I were righteous, I
could not answer.
I must appeal for mercy to my
Opponent *and* Judge.

9:3 *If one should want to contend or dispute with Him.* The word "contend" indicates a legal argument, not a quarrel. Job was seeking justice. He did not think he had sinned (as his friends indicated) so that God would punish him.

15 Job 27:18 **18** Job 7:10; Ps 37:36 **19** Ps 113:7 **22** Ps 35:26; 109:29 **CHAPTER 9** **2** Ps 143:2; Ro 3:20 **4** Job 36:5 **6** Isa 2:19,21; Hag 2:6; Heb 12:26; Job 26:11 **8** Ge 1:6; Ps 104:2,3 **9** Ge 1:16; Am 5:8 **10** Ps 71:15 **11** Job 23:8,9 **12** Isa 45:9; Jer 18:6; Ro 9:20 **13** Job 26:12 **15** Job 10:15

16 "If I called and He answered me,
I could not believe that He was
listening to my voice.
17 "For He bruises me with a tempest
And multiplies my wounds without
cause.
18 "He will not allow me to catch my
breath,
But fills *and* saturates me with
bitterness.
19 "If it is a matter of strength *and*
power, behold, *He is* mighty!
And if of justice, who can summon
and challenge Him?
20 "Though I am innocent *and* in
the right, my own mouth would
pronounce me guilty;
Though I am blameless, He would
denounce me as guilty.
21 "[Though] I am blameless,
I do not care about myself;
I despise my life.
22 "It is *all* one; therefore I say,
'He destroys [both] the blameless
and the wicked.'
23 "When [His] scourge kills
suddenly,
He mocks at the despair of the
innocent.
24 "The earth is given into the hands
of the wicked;
He covers the faces of its judges
[so that they are blind to justice].
If it is not He, then who is it
[that is responsible for all this
injustice]?
25 "Now my days are swifter than a
runner;
They vanish, they see no good.
26 "They pass by like the [swift] boats
made of reeds,
Like an eagle that swoops down
on its prey.
27 "If I say, 'I will forget my
complaint,
I will leave off my sad appearance,
and be cheerful *and* brighten
up,'
28 I am afraid of all my pains *and*
worries [yet to come];
I know that You will not acquit me
and leave me unpunished.
29 "I am accounted wicked *and* held
guilty;
Why then should I labor in vain [to
appear innocent]?
30 "If I were to wash myself with
snow
And cleanse my hands with lye,
31 You would still plunge me into the
pit,
And my own clothes would hate
me [and refuse to cover my foul
body].
32 "For God is not a [mere] man, as I
am, that I may answer Him,
That we may go to court *and*
judgment together.
33 "There is no arbitrator between us,
Who could lay his hand upon us
both [would that there were].
[1 Tim 2:5]
34 "Let Him take His rod away from
me,
And let not the dread *and* fear of
Him terrify me.
35 "*Then* I would speak [my defense]
and not fear Him;
But I am not like that in myself.

Job Despairs of God's Dealings

10 "I AM disgusted with my life
and loathe it!
I will give free expression to my
complaint;
I will speak in the bitterness of my
soul.

9:17 *bruises me with a tempest.* Job saw God as Lord of the heavens (v. 7–8) and assumed that it was God who sent the tempest that destroyed his children. Job did not know that it was Satan who sought to destroy him, and that God drew a line of protection around him.

10:1–3 Affliction — In the face of his adversities, Job despaired of life, but he continued to plead with God in prayer for an answer. Job's friends saw all suffering in a mathematical equation with sin. If these friends were right, that would reduce our relationship with God to a formula that says, "If you are good, God will rescue you, and if you are bad, God will abandon you to suffering." The converse of that statement says, "If you are suffering, you are bad, and because I am not suffering, I am good." It is often in the converse that a formula is shown to be faulty.

17 Job 2:3 **22** Ecc 9:2,3; Eze 21:3 **25** Job 7:6,7 **26** Hab 1:8 **27** Job 7:13 **28** Ps 119:120; Ex 20:7 **30** Jer 2:22 **32** Ecc 6:10; Isa 45:9; Ro 9:20 **33** 1Sa 2:25 **34** Job 13:20; Ps 39:10 **CHAPTER 10** **1** 1Ki 19:4; Jnh 4:3; Job 7:11

2 "I will say to God, 'Do not
condemn me [and declare me
guilty]!
Show me why You contend *and*
argue *and* struggle with me.
3 'Does it indeed seem right to You
to oppress,
To despise *and* reject the work of
Your hands,
And to look with favor on the
schemes of the wicked?
4 'Do You have eyes of flesh?
Do You see as a man sees?
5 'Are Your days as the days of a
mortal,
Are Your years as man's years,
6 That You seek my guilt
And search for my sin?
7 'Although You know that I am not
guilty *or* wicked,
Yet there is no one who can rescue
me from Your hand.

8 'Your hands have formed and
made me altogether.
Would You [turn around and]
destroy me?
9 'Remember now, that You have
made me as clay;
So will You turn me into dust
again?
10 'Have You not poured me out like
milk
And curdled me like cheese?
11 '[You have] clothed me with skin
and flesh,
And knit me together with bones
and sinews.
12 'You have granted me life and
lovingkindness;
And Your providence (divine care,
supervision) has preserved my
spirit.
13 'Yet these [present evils] You have
hidden in Your heart [since my
creation]:
I know that this was within You
[in Your purpose and thought].
14 'If I sin, then You would take note
and observe me,
And You would not acquit me of
my guilt.
15 'If I am wicked, woe to me [for
judgment comes]!
And if I am righteous, I dare not
lift up my head.
For I am sated *and* filled with
disgrace and the sight of my
misery.
16 'Should I lift my head up, You
would hunt me like a lion;
And again You would show Your
marvelous power against me.
17 'You renew Your witnesses against
me
And increase Your indignation
and anger toward me;
Hardship after hardship is with me
[attacking me time after time].

18 'Why then did You bring me out of
the womb?
Would that I had perished and no
eye had seen me!
19 'I should have been as though I
had not existed;
[I should have been] carried from
the womb to the grave.'
20 "Would He not let my few days
alone,
Withdraw from me that I may
have a little cheer
21 Before I go—and I shall not return—
To the land of darkness and the
deep shadow [of death],
22 The [sunless] land of utter gloom
as darkness *itself*,
[The land] of the shadow of death,
without order,
And [where] it shines as [thick]
darkness."

Who can really claim to be good? We are all sinners in need of a savior.

10:7 *I am not guilty or wicked . . . there is no one who can rescue.* Job thought that God was unjust in oppressing him, yet he realized that there is no one higher than God to deliver him from God. Job's thinking was twisted in much the same way that his friends' was. He was equating innocence with peace, and he could not imagine any reason why God would not rescue him.

10:18 *bring me out of the womb.* Job wondered how the God who so carefully fashioned him in the womb (v. 9–11) could turn against him. This was the desperate cry of a sufferer blind to the fact that God was working good out of all the tragic events of his life.

4 1Sa 16:7 **8** Ps 119:73 **9** Ge 2:7; Isa 64:8 **10** Ps 139:14-16 **14** Ps 139:1 **15** Isa 3:11; Job 9:12,15; Ps 25:18 **16** Isa 38:13; La 3:10 **18** Job 3:11 **20** Ps 39:5; Job 7:16,19 **21** Ps 88:12; Ps 23:4

Zophar Rebukes Job

11 THEN ZOPHAR the Naamathite
answered and said,
2 "Shall a multitude of words not be answered?
And should a talkative man [making such a long-winded defense] be acquitted?
3 "Should your boasts *and* babble silence men?
And shall you scoff and no one put you to shame?
4 "For you have said, 'My teaching (doctrine) [that God knowingly afflicts the righteous] is pure,
And I am innocent in your eyes.' [Job 10:7]
5 "But oh, that God would speak,
And open His lips [to speak] against you,
6 And [that He would] show you the secrets of wisdom!
For sound wisdom has two sides.
Know therefore that God forgets a part of your wickedness *and* guilt.

7 "Can you discover the depths of God?
Can you [by searching] discover the limits of the Almighty [ascend to His heights, extend to His widths, and comprehend His infinite perfection]?
8 "*His wisdom* is as high as the heights of heaven. What can you do?
It is deeper than Sheol (the nether world, the place of the dead). What can you know?
9 "It is longer in measure [and scope] than the earth,
And broader than the sea.
10 "If God passes by or arrests,
Or calls an assembly [of judgment], who can restrain Him?
[If He is against a man, who can call Him to account for it?]
11 "For He recognizes *and* knows false *and* worthless men,
And He sees wickedness, will He not consider it?
12 "But a hollow (empty-headed) man will become intelligent *and* wise
[Only] when the colt of a wild donkey is born as a man.

13 "If you direct your heart [on the right path]
And stretch out your hands to Him,
14 If sin is in your hand, put it far away [from you],
And do not let wrongdoing dwell in your tents;
15 Then, indeed, you could lift up your face [to Him] without *moral* defect,
And you would be firmly established *and* secure and not fear.
16 "For you would forget your trouble;
You would remember it as waters that have passed by.
17 "And your life would be brighter than the noonday;
Darkness [then] would be like the morning.
18 "Then you would trust [with confidence], because there is hope;
You would look around you and rest securely.

11:4 *My teaching (doctrine) . . . is pure.* Zophar exaggerated what Job had said about his innocence (9:14 – 21) to make Job look foolish.
11:7 *Can you discover the depths of God?* Zophar was correct in saying that understanding the depths of God is beyond man. But the fact that we cannot know everything about God does not mean that we cannot know anything about Him, nor that it is wrong to try to know and understand Him better.
11:13 *stretch out your hands to Him.* Stretching out the hands was a posture of prayer as well as of praise (Ps 134:2). Assuming that Job was suffering because of his iniquity, this was not bad advice.
11:15 *secure and not fear.* There is peace and comfort for those who have repented of their sin and turned to God. This is true and important to remember. But Zophar's presupposition that iniquity causes suffering kept him from understanding what Job's struggle was.

CHAPTER 11 **4** Job 6:30 **6** Ezr 9:13 **7** Ecc 3:11 **10** Job 9:12; Rev 3:7 **11** Ps 10:14 **12** Ro 1:22 **13** 1Sa 7:3; Ps 88:9 **14** Ps 101:3 **15** Job 22:26; Ps 119:6; 1Jn 3:21 **16** Isa 65:16 **17** Ps 37:6; Pr 4:18; Isa 58:8,10 **18** Lev 26:5,6; Ps 3:5; Pr 3:24

19 "You would lie down with no one
to frighten you,
And many would entreat *and* seek
your favor.
20 "But the eyes of the wicked will
fail,
And they will not escape [the
justice of God];
And their hope is to breathe their
last [and die]."

Job Chides His Accusers

12 THEN JOB responded,
2 "No doubt you are the [only wise]
people [in the world],
And wisdom will die with you!
3 "But I have intelligence *and*
understanding as well as you;
I am not inferior to you.
Who does not know such things
as these [of God's wisdom and
might]?
4 "I am a joke to my friends;
I, one whom God answered when
he called upon Him—
A just and blameless man is a joke
[and laughed to scorn].
5 "He who is at ease has contempt
for misfortune,
But misfortune is ready [and
anxiously waiting] for those
whose feet slip.
6 "The tents of the destroyers
prosper;
And those who provoke God are
[apparently] secure,
Whom God brings into their
power.

7 "Now ask the animals, and let
them teach you [that God does
not deal with His creatures
according to their character];
And ask the birds of the air, and
let them tell you;
8 Or speak to the earth [with its
many forms of life], and it will
teach you;
And let the fish of the sea declare
[this truth] to you.
9 "Who among all these does not
recognize [in all these things
that good and evil are randomly
scattered throughout nature and
human life]
That the hand of the LORD has
done this,
10 In whose hand is the life of every
living thing,
And the breath of all mankind?
11 "Does the ear not put words to the
test,
Just as the palate tastes its food
[distinguishing between the
desirable and the undesirable]?
12 "With the aged [you say] is
wisdom,
And *with* long life is
understanding.

Job Speaks of the Power of God

13 "But [only] with Him are [perfect]
wisdom and might;
He [alone] has [true] counsel and
understanding.
14 "Behold, He tears down, and it
cannot be rebuilt;
He imprisons a man, and there can
be no release.
15 "Behold, He restrains the waters,
and they dry up;
Again, He sends the waters
out, and they overwhelm *and*
devastate the earth.
16 "With Him are might and sound
wisdom,
The misled and the misleader are
His [and in His power].
17 "He makes [great and scheming]
counselors walk barefoot
And makes fools of judges.
18 "He loosens the bond of kings
And binds their loins with a
loincloth.
19 "He makes priests walk barefoot,
And He overturns men firmly
seated *and* secure.
20 "He deprives the trusted ones of
speech

12:13 ***He [alone] has [true] counsel and understanding.*** Job was sure that he did not understand what was happening to him, but he knew that God did know the answer.

20 Lev 26:16; Dt 28:65; Job 18:14; Pr 11:7 **CHAPTER 12** **4** Job 21:3; Ps 91:15 **5** Pr 14:2 **6** Jer 12:1; Mal 3:15 **15** 1Ki 8:35; Ge 7:11 **20** Job 32:9

And takes away the discernment
and discretion of the aged.
21 "He pours contempt on princes
and nobles
And loosens the belt of the strong
[disabling them].
22 "He uncovers mysteries [that
are difficult to grasp and
understand] out of the darkness
And brings black gloom *and* the
shadow of death into light.
23 "He makes nations great, and He
destroys them;
He enlarges nations, and leads
them away [captive].
24 "He removes intelligence *and*
understanding from the leaders
of the people of the earth
And makes them wander *and*
move blindly in a pathless waste.
25 "They grope in darkness without
light,
And He makes them stagger like a
drunken man."

Job Says His Friends' Proverbs Are Ashes

13 [JOB CONTINUED:] "Behold,
my eye has seen all *this*,
My ear has heard and understood it.
2 "What you know I also know;
I am not inferior to you.
3 "But I wish to speak to the
Almighty,
And I desire to argue with God.
4 "But you smear me with lies [you
defame my character most
untruthfully];
You are all worthless physicians
and have no remedy to offer.
5 "Oh, that you would be completely
silent,
And that *silence* would be your
wisdom!
6 "Please hear my argument
And listen to the pleadings of my
lips.
7 "Will you speak what is unjust for
God,
And speak what is deceitful for
Him?
8 "Will you show partiality for Him
[and be unjust to me so that you
may gain favor with Him]?
Will you contend *and* plead for
God?
9 "Will it be well for you when He
investigates you [and your
tactics against me]?
Or will you deceive Him as one
deceives a man?
10 "He will surely reprimand you
If you secretly show partiality.
11 "Will not His majesty terrify you,
And will not the dread of Him fall
upon you?
12 "Your memorable sayings are
[worthless, merely] proverbs of
ashes;
Your defenses are defenses of
[crumbling] clay.

Job Is Sure He Will Be Vindicated

13 "Be silent before me so that I may
speak;
And let happen to me what may.
14 "Why should I take my flesh in my
teeth
And put my life in my hands
[incurring the wrath of God]?
15 "Even though He kills me;
I will hope in Him.
Nevertheless, I will argue my ways
to His face.
16 "This also will be my salvation,
For a godless man may not come
before Him.
17 "Listen diligently to my speech,
And let my declaration fill your
ears.
18 "Behold now, I have prepared my
case;
I know that I will be vindicated.

13:4 *smear me with lies.* Job's friends were accusing him of hidden sin, offering a false formula for peace with God, and assuming that they had a greater understanding both of Job and of God's ways than they really did. False doctrine, even if held with sincerity, is still a lie.
13:12 *memorable sayings . . . defenses.* The quickest way to make ourselves look silly is to try

21 Ps 107:40; Da 2:21 **23** Ps 107:38; Isa 9:3 **24** Ps 107:4 **25** Job 5:14; Ps 107:27 **CHAPTER 13** **2** Job 12:3 **3** Job 23:3 **4** Job 6:21 **5** Pr 17:28 **7** Job 36:4 **14** Job 18:4 **15** Ps 23:4; Pr 14:32; Job 27:5

19 "Who will argue *and* contend with me?
For then I would be silent and die.
20 "Only [O Lord,] do not do two things to me,
And then I will not hide myself from Your face:
21 Withdraw Your hand from me *and* remove this bodily suffering,
And let not the dread of You terrify me.
22 "Then [Lord,] call, and I will answer;
Or let me speak, and then reply to me.
23 "How many are my iniquities and sins [that so much sorrow should come to me]?
Make me recognize *and* understand my transgression and my sin. [Rom 8:1]
24 "Why do You hide Your face [as if offended]
And consider me Your enemy?
25 "Will You cause a windblown leaf to tremble?
Will You pursue the chaff of the dry stubble?
26 "For You write bitter things against me [in Your indictment]
And make me inherit *and* suffer for the iniquities of my youth.
27 "You also put my feet in the stocks [as punishment]
And [critically] observe all my paths;
You set a circle *and* limit around the soles of my feet [which I must not overstep],
28 While I waste away like a rotten thing,
Like a garment that is moth-eaten.

Job Speaks of the Finality of Death

14 "MAN, WHO is born of a woman,
Is short-lived and full of turmoil.
2 "Like a flower he comes forth and withers;
He also flees like a shadow and does not remain.
3 "You also open Your eyes upon him
And bring him into judgment with Yourself.
4 "Who can make a clean thing out of the unclean?
No one! [Is 1:18; 1 John 1:7]
5 "Since his days are determined,
The number of his months is with You [in Your control],
And You have made his limits so he cannot pass [his allotted time].
6 "[O God] turn your gaze from him so that he may rest,
Until he fulfills his day [on earth] like a hired man.

7 "For there is hope for a tree,
If it is cut down, that it will sprout again,
And that the shoots of it will not cease *nor* fail, [but there is no such hope for man].
8 "Though its roots grow old in the earth
And its stump dies in the dry soil,
9 Yet at the scent of water [the stump of the tree] will flourish
And bring forth sprigs *and* shoots like a seedling.
10 "But [the brave, strong] man must die and lie face down;
Man breathes his last, and where is he?
11 "As water evaporates from the sea,
And a river drains and dries up,

---

to explain something that we don't understand. Prayer is far more helpful than worthless counsel.

13:21 *Withdraw Your hand ... terrify me.* Job was not cocky as he turned to plead his case before God. His requests were safe and wise for any believer who struggles with what life has handed him. Job asked God not to give up on him, and he asked God to keep him from being overpowered by the terror and majesty of God. Job knew very well that he was far below God, and that all that God is and does could be totally overwhelming to him.

---

19 Isa 50:8 **20** Job 9:34 **21** Ps 39:10 **24** Dt 32:20; Isa 8:17; Dt 32:42; Job 16:9; La 2:5 **25** Isa 42:3 **26** Job 20:11; Ps 25:7 **27** Job 33:11 **CHAPTER 14** **1** Ecc 2:23 **2** Job 8:9; Ps 90:5,6 **3** Ps 144:3; 143:2 **4** Ps 51:2,5,10; Jn 3:6; Ro 5:12; Eph 2:3 **5** Job 7:1 **6** Job 7:16,19; Ps 39:13; Job 7:1

[12] So man lies down and does not
rise [again].
Until the heavens are no longer,
The dead will not awake nor be
raised from their sleep.
[13] "Oh, that You would hide me in
Sheol (the nether world, the
place of the dead),
That You would conceal me until
Your wrath is past,
That You would set a definite time
and then remember me [and in
Your lovingkindness imprint me
on your heart]!
[14] "If a man dies, will he live again?
I will wait all the days of my
struggle
Until my change *and* release
will come. [John 5:25; 6:40;
1 Thess 4:16]
[15] "[Then] You will call, and I will
answer You;
You will long for [me] the work of
Your hands.
[16] "But now You number [each of] my
steps;
You do not observe *nor* take note
of my sin.
[17] "My transgression is sealed up in a
bag,
And You cover my wickedness
[from Your view].
[18] "But as a mountain, if it falls,
crumbles into nothing,
And as the rock is moved from its
place,
[19] Water wears away the stones,
Its floods *and* torrents wash away
the soil of the earth,
So You [O Lord] destroy the hope
of man.
[20] "You prevail forever against him
and overpower him, and he
passes on;
You change his appearance
and send him away [from the
presence of the living].
[21] "His sons achieve honor, and he
does not know it;
They become insignificant, and he
is not aware of it.
[22] "But his body [lamenting its decay]
grieves in pain over it,
And his soul mourns over [the loss
of] himself."

Eliphaz Says Job Presumes Much

15 THEN ELIPHAZ the Temanite
answered [Job] and said,
[2] "Should a wise man [such as
you] utter such windy *and* vain
knowledge [as we have just
heard]
And fill himself with the east wind
[of withering, parching, and
violent accusations]?
[3] "Should he rebuke *and* argue with
useless talk?
Or with words in which there is no
benefit?
[4] "Indeed, you are doing away with
fear,
And you are diminishing
meditation before God.
[5] "For your guilt teaches your
mouth,
And you choose [to speak] the
language of the crafty *and*
cunning.
[6] "Your own mouth condemns you,
and not I;
Yes, your own lips testify against
you.
[7] "Were you the first man to be born
[the original wise man],

14:13 ***hide me . . . until Your wrath is past.*** Job's wish for the grave to be a temporary hiding place from God's wrath differed dramatically from his earlier remarks concerning the grave (7:9 – 10; 10:18 – 22). He attributed the cause of his suffering to God's wrath because he assumed the retribution dogma that the righteous are always blessed and the wicked will eventually experience God's judgment. It did not occur to Job that he was being tested.

14:14 ***live again.*** Job had some understanding of the eternality of man's soul. The answer to his question comes in the New Testament with an emphatic "Yes!" by Jesus (Jn 11:23 – 26; 1Co 15:3 – 57).

12 Isa 51:6; Ac 3:21; Ro 8:20; 2Pe 3:7; Rev 20:11; 21:1 **14** Job 13:15 **15** Job 13:22 **16** Job 10:6,14; Pr 5:21; Jer 32:19 **17** Dt 32:34; Hos 13:12 **21** Ecc 9:5; Isa 63:16 **CHAPTER 15** **6** Lk 19:22 **7** Ps 90:2; Pr 8:25

Or were you created before the hills?
8 "Do you hear the secret counsel of God,
And do you limit [the possession of] wisdom to yourself?
9 "What do you know that we do not know?
What do you understand that is not equally clear to us?
10 "Among us are both the gray-haired and the aged,
Older than your father.
11 "Are the consolations of God [as we have interpreted them to you] too trivial for you,
[Or] were we too gentle toward you [in our first speech] to be effective?
12 "Why does your heart carry you away [allowing you to be controlled by emotion]?
And why do your eyes flash [in anger or contempt],
13 That you should turn your spirit against God
And let *such* words [as you have spoken] go out of your mouth?
14 "What is man, that he should be pure *and* clean,
Or he who is born of a woman, that he should be righteous *and* just?
15 "Behold, God puts no trust in His holy ones (angels);
Indeed, the heavens are not pure in His sight—
16 How much less [pure and clean is] the one who is repulsive and corrupt,
Man, who drinks unrighteousness *and* injustice like water!

What Eliphaz Has Seen of Life

17 "I will tell you, listen to me;
And what I have seen I will also declare;
18 What wise men have [freely] told,
And have not hidden [anything passed on to them] from their fathers,
19 To whom alone the land was given,
And no stranger passed among them [corrupting the truth].
20 "The wicked man writhes with pain all his days,
And numbered are the years stored up for him, the ruthless one.
21 "A [dreadful] sound of terrors is in his ears;
While at peace *and* in a time of prosperity the destroyer comes upon him [the tent of the robber is not at peace].
22 "He does not believe that he will return out of the darkness [for fear of being murdered],
And he is destined for the sword [of God's vengeance].
23 "He wanders about for food, saying, 'Where is it?'
He knows that the day of darkness *and* destruction is already at hand.
24 "Distress and anxiety terrify him,
They overpower him like a king ready for battle.
25 "Because he has stretched out his hand against God
And behaves arrogantly against the Almighty,
26 Running *and* charging headlong against Him

15:21 *[dreadful] sound of terrors.* Eliphaz began his subtle argument to prove that Job was a wicked man. He alluded to Job's dread, the same word translated *feared* in 3:25, as an implicit indicator that Job was wicked.
15:24 *Distress . . . terrify.* In contrast to 14:20 where Job complained to God that He overpowered people, Eliphaz said that the wicked man's (by implication, Job's) own fears overpower him. Eliphaz's statement may have been true, but that did not mean it applied to Job. Job did not understand God's ways correctly, but neither did Eliphaz. Job was overpowered by Satan's attacks, and he could not see what God was doing. Eliphaz assumed that because Job was overpowered, it was because he had behaved arrogantly towards God.

8 Ro 11:34; 1Co 2:11 **9** Job 13:2 **10** Job 32:6,7 **14** Job 14:4; Pr 20:9; Ecc 7:20; 1Jn 1:8,10 **15** Job 4:18; 25:5 **16** Job 4:19; Ps 14:3; 53:3; Job 34:7; Pr 19:28 **18** Job 8:8 **19** Joel 3:17 **20** Ps 90:12 **21** 1Th 5:3 **23** Ps 59:15; 109:10; Job 18:12

With his ornamented *and* massive
shield;
27 For he has covered his face with
his fat,
Adding layers of fat to his thighs
[giving himself up to pleasures],
28 And he has lived in desolate [God-
forsaken] cities,
In houses which no one should
inhabit,
Which were destined to become
heaps [of ruins];
29 He will not become rich, nor will
his wealth endure;
And his grain will not bend to the
earth *nor* his possessions be
extended on the earth.
30 "He will not escape from darkness
[fleeing disaster];
The flame [of God's wrath] will
wither his branch,
And by the blast of His mouth he
will go away.
31 "Let him not trust in vanity
(emptiness, futility) and be led
astray;
For emptiness will be his reward
[for such living].
32 "It will be fulfilled while he still
lives,
And his branch will not be green
[but shall wither away].
33 "He will fail to bring his grapes to
maturity [leaving them to wither
unnourished] on the vine,
And will cast off blossoms [and
fail to bring forth fruit] like the
olive tree.
34 "For the company of the godless is
barren,
And fire consumes the tents of
bribery (wrong and injustice).
35 "They conceive mischief and bring
forth wickedness,
And their inmost soul prepares
deceit *and* fraud."

Job Says Friends Are Sorry Comforters

16 THEN JOB answered and said,
2 "I have heard many such things;
Wearisome *and* miserable
comforters are you all.
3 "Is there no end to [your futile]
words of wind?
Or what plagues you [so much]
that you [so boldly] answer [me
like this]?
4 "I also could speak like you,
If you were in my place;
I could compose *and* join words
together against you
And shake my head at you.
5 "[But instead] I could strengthen
and encourage you with [the
words of] my mouth,
And the consolation *and* solace
of my lips would soothe your
suffering *and* lessen your
anguish.

Job Says God Shattered Him

6 "If I speak [to you miserable
comforters], my pain is not
relieved;
And if I refrain [from speaking],
what [pain or anguish] leaves
me?
7 "But now God has exhausted me.
You [O Lord] have destroyed all
my family *and* my household.
8 "You have taken a firm hold on me
and have shriveled me up,

15:31 *trust in vanity.* Eliphaz was entirely right in his comments about the fruitlessness of a wicked life, and that the Lord will bring the wicked into judgment. But Eliphaz did not have the concept that in this life the wicked can appear to prosper, and the righteous can appear to struggle. Judgment may not fall in this life.

15:34 *fire consumes.* In mentioning the fire that consumes the tents of the wicked, Eliphaz implied that the fire of God that destroyed Job's sheep and servants (1:16) was a direct result of Job's corruption.

16:7–17 Afflictions — One of the clear lessons of the Book of Job is that it is possible to give false and insensitive counsel to one who is experiencing affliction and testing. When we suffer, some of the lessons learned are for us, some of the lessons are for others who are watching, and some are for the Kingdom of God. We may not know in this life what all of the implications are. Our afflictions are

27 Ps 17:10 **31** Isa 59:4 **32** Job 22:16; Ps 55:23 **35** Ps 7:14; Isa 59:4; Hos 10:13 **CHAPTER 16** **2** Job 13:4 **4** Ps 22:7; 109:25; La 2:15

It has become a witness [against me];
And my leanness [and infirmity] rises up [as evidence] against me,
It testifies to my face [about my guilt].
9 "His wrath has torn me and hunted me down,
He has gnashed at me with his teeth;
My adversary sharpens His gaze *and* glares [with piercing eyes] at me.
10 "They have gaped at me with their mouths,
With contempt they have struck me on the cheek;
They massed themselves together [and conspired] against me. [Ps 22:13; 35:21]
11 "God hands me over to criminals
And tosses me [headlong] into the hands of the wicked.
12 "I was [living] at ease, but He crushed me *and* broke me apart,
And He has seized me by the neck and has shaken me to pieces;
He has also set me up as His target.
13 "His arrows surround me.
He pierces my kidneys (vital organs) without mercy;
He pours out my gall on the ground.
14 "He attacks me, making wound after wound;
He runs at me like a warrior.
15 "I have sewed sackcloth over my skin [as a sign of mourning]
And have defiled my horn (symbol of strength) in the dust.
16 "My face is red *and* swollen with weeping,
And on my eyelids is the shadow of death [my eyes are dimmed],
17 Although there is no violence *or* wrongdoing in my hands,
And my prayer is pure.

18 "O earth, do not cover my blood,
And let there be no [resting] place for my cry [where it will cease being heard].
19 "Even now, behold, my Witness is in heaven,
And my Advocate [who vouches and testifies for me] is on high. [Rom 1:9]
20 "My friends are scoffers [who ridicule];
My eye pours out tears to God.
21 "Oh, that a man would mediate *and* plead with God [for me]
Just as a man [mediates and pleads] with his neighbor *and* friend. [1 Tim 2:5]
22 "For when a few years are past,
I shall go the way of no return.

Job Says He Has Become a Byword

17 "MY SPIRIT is broken, my days are extinguished,
The grave is *ready* for me.
2 "Surely there are mockers *and* mockery with me,
And my eye gazes on their obstinacy *and* provocation.

3 "Give me a pledge (guarantee, promise) with Yourself [acknowledge my innocence before my death];
Who is there that will be my guarantor *and* give security for me?

---

designed by God to drive us out of ourselves to the Eternal God who is our refuge and who supports us with His everlasting arms (Dt 33:27). As friends of the afflicted, we must be sympathetic, loving, and kind, remembering that often only God has the answers. If we have suffered similarly, we have comfort to offer (2Co 1:6 – 7), and if we have not suffered similarly, we can support our friends in prayer and practical service.

16:21 *a man would mediate and plead.* Job was expressing the need for an intercessor. This need anticipated Jesus Christ, who is our Intercessor (Heb 7:25) and Advocate (1Jn 2:1).

17:3 *pledge.* In another legal metaphor, Job appealed to God by laying down a pledge, that is, by providing bail. The use of the same metaphor in Psalms 119:121 – 122 to indicate the psalmist's request for relief from his "oppressors"

9 Job 10:16,17; Job 13:24 **10** Ps 22:13; La 3:30; Mic 5:1 **11** Job 1:15,17 **12** Job 7:20 **15** Job 30:19; Ps 7:5 **18** Job 27:9; Ps 66:18 **19** Ro 1:9 **21** Job 31:35; Ecc 6:10; Isa 45:9; Ro 9:20 **22** Ecc 12:5 **CHAPTER 17** **1** Ps 88:3,4 **2** 1Sa 1:6 **3** Pr 17:18

4 "But You [Lord] have closed their hearts to understanding,
Therefore You will not exalt them [by giving a verdict against me].
5 "He who denounces *and* informs against his friends for a share *of the spoil,*
The eyes of his children will also languish *and* fail.

6 "But He has made me a byword *and* mockery among the people,
And I have become one in whose face people spit.
7 "My eye has grown dim (unexpressive) because of grief,
And all my [body's] members are [wasted away] like a shadow.
8 "The upright will be [astonished and] appalled at this,
And the innocent will stir himself up against the godless *and* polluted.
9 "Nevertheless the righteous will hold to his ways,
And he who has clean hands will grow stronger and stronger. [Ps 24:4]
10 "But as for all of you, come back again,
Even though I do not find a wise man among you.
11 "My days are past, my purposes *and* plans are frustrated *and* torn apart;
The wishes of my heart [are broken].
12 "These [thoughts try to] make the night into the day;
'The light is near,' *they say* in the presence of darkness [but they pervert the truth].
13 "But if I look to Sheol (the nether world, the place of the dead) as my home,
If I make my bed in the darkness,
14 If I call out to the pit (grave), 'You are my father';
And to the worm [that feeds on decay], 'You are my mother and my sister [because I will soon be closest to you],'
15 Where now is my hope?
And who regards *or* considers *or* is even concerned about my hope?
16 "Will my hope go down with me to Sheol (the nether world, the place of the dead)?
Shall we go down together in the dust?"

Bildad Speaks of the Wicked

18 THEN BILDAD the Shuhite answered and said,
2 "How long will you hunt for words *and* continue these speeches?
Do some clear thinking *and* show understanding and then we can talk.
3 "Why are we regarded as beasts,
As if [we are] stupid (senseless) in your eyes?
4 "You who tear yourself apart in anger,
Is the earth to be abandoned for your sake,
Or the rock to be moved out of its place?
5 "Indeed, the light of the wicked will be put out,
And the flame of his fire will not shine. [Prov 13:9; 24:20]
6 "The light will be dark in his tent,
And his lamp beside him will be put out. [Ps 18:28]
7 "The vigorous stride will be shortened,

---

may suggest that Job was pleading for God to *demonstrate confidence in his innocence.*

17:9 the righteous will hold to his ways. Job seems to be entertaining a little sarcasm here. He had referred to himself as a byword, one at whom men spit. Then he said that the righteous will grow stronger, which was not a reference to himself, even though he still did not think he deserved the trouble that had fallen upon him. He was probably referring to his friends, who considered themselves righteous, with clean hands, and who repeatedly strengthened their position and arguments.

18:4 who tear yourself apart in anger. This may be Bildad's response to Job's allegation that God had torn Job in His anger (16:13).

---

6 Job 30:9 **7** Ps 6:7; 31:9 **9** Ps 24:4 **10** Job 6:29 **11** Job 7:6 **16** Jnh 2:6; Job 3:17-19 **CHAPTER 18**
3 Ps 73:22 **4** Job 13:14 **5** Pr 13:9 **6** Job 21:17; Ps 18:28 **7** Job 5:13

And his own counsel *and* the
scheme [in which he trusted]
will bring his downfall.
8 "For the wicked is thrown into a
net by his own feet (wickedness),
And he steps on the webbing [of
the lattice-covered pit].
9 "A snare catches him by the heel,
And a trap snaps shut on him.
10 "A noose is hidden for him on the
ground,
And a trap for him on the path.
11 "Terrors frighten him on every side
And chase at his heels.
12 "The strength [of the wicked] is
famished *and* weakened,
And disaster is ready at his side [if
he stops].
13 "His skin is devoured by disease;
The firstborn of death [the worst
of diseases] consumes his limbs.
14 "He is torn from his tent which he
trusted [for safety],
And he is marched *and* brought to
the king of terrors (death).
15 "Nothing of his dwells in his tent;
Brimstone (burning sulfur) is
scattered over his dwelling [to
purify it].
16 "The roots [of the wicked] are
dried up below,
And above, his branch is cut off
and withers.
17 "Memory of him perishes from the
earth,
And he has no name on the street.
18 "He is driven *and* propelled from
light into darkness,
And chased from the inhabited
world.
19 "He has no offspring or prosperity
among his people,
Nor any survivor where he
sojourned.
20 "Those in the west are astonished
and appalled at his fate,
And those in the east are seized
with horror.
21 "Surely such are the dwellings of
the wicked *and* the ungodly,
And such is the place of him who
does not know *or* recognize *or*
honor God."

Job Feels Insulted

19 THEN JOB answered and said,
2 "How long will you torment *and*
exasperate me
And crush me with words?
3 "These ten times you have insulted
me;
You are not ashamed to wrong me
[and harden your hearts against
me].
4 "And if it were true that I have
erred,
My error would remain with me
[and I would be conscious
of it].
5 "If indeed you [braggarts] vaunt
and magnify yourselves over me
And prove my disgrace
(humiliation) to me,
6 Know then that God has wronged
me *and* overthrown me
And has closed His net around me.

Everything Is Against Him

7 "Behold, I cry out, 'Violence!' but I
am not heard;
I shout for help, but there is no
justice.

18:8 – 10 *net ... trap.* Six different Hebrew synonyms for various types of nets and traps emphasize the many imminent dangers that God has designed for the wicked to ensure that they will be caught in their wickedness.

18:21 *wicked.* Bildad believed that the evidence he had exhibited in verses 5 – 20 implicated Job himself as the wicked one. Bildad was right that, in the end, the wicked will perish dramatically. But in this life they are not necessarily judged. If it were that simple, that the wicked never prospered and the righteous always thrived, people might try to be followers of God just for the blessings. The whole thrust of the Book of Job is that God Himself is reason enough to follow God, whether or not there is prosperity (1:9 – 11).

19:7 Despondency — The despondency of Job was a swollen river into which many streams had poured. He had experienced the loss of family, property, and health. His wife and friends had

---

8 Job 22:10; Ps 9:15; 35:8 **9** Job 5:5 **11** Job 20:25; Jer 6:25; 20:3,4 **12** Job 15:23 **14** Job 11:20; Ps 112:10; Pr 10:28 **16** Job 29:19; Isa 5:24; Am 2:9; Mal 4:1 **17** Ps 34:16; 109:13; Pr 2:22; 10:7 **19** Isa 14:22; Jer 22:30 **21** Jer 9:3; 1Th 4:5 **CHAPTER 19** **5** Ps 38:16

8 "He has walled up my way so that
I cannot pass,
And He has set darkness upon my
paths.
9 "He has stripped me of my honor
And removed the crown from my
head.
10 "He breaks me down on every
side, and I am gone;
He has uprooted my hope like a
tree.
11 "He has also kindled His wrath
[like a fire] against me
And He considers *and* counts me
as one of His adversaries.
12 "His troops come together
And build up their way *and* siege
works against me
And camp around my tent.

13 "He has put my brothers far from
me,
And my acquaintances are
completely estranged from me.
14 "My relatives have failed [me],
And my intimate friends have
forgotten me.
15 "Those who live [temporarily]
in my house and my maids
consider me a stranger;
I am a foreigner in their sight.
16 "I call to my servant, but he does
not answer;
I have to implore him with words.
17 "My breath is repulsive to my wife,
And I am loathsome to my own
brothers.
18 "Even young children despise me;
When I get up, they speak against
me.
19 "All the men of my council hate me;
Those I love have turned against
me.
20 "My bone clings to my skin and to
my flesh,
And I have escaped [death] by the
skin of my teeth.
21 "Have pity on me! Have pity on
me, O you my friends,
For the hand of God has touched me.
22 "Why do you persecute me as God
does?
Why are you not satisfied with my
flesh (anguish)?

Job Says, "My Redeemer Lives"

23 "Oh, that the words I now speak
were written!
Oh, that they were recorded in a
scroll!
24 "That with an iron stylus and
[molten] lead
They were engraved in the rock
forever!
25 "For I know that my Redeemer *and*
Vindicator lives,
And at the last He will take His
stand upon the earth. [Is 44:6;
48:12]
26 "Even after my [mortal] skin is
destroyed [by death],
Yet from my [immortal] flesh I will
see God,
27 Whom I, even I, will see for myself,
And my eyes will see Him and not
another!
My heart faints within me.
28 "If you say, 'How shall we
[continue to] persecute him?'

---

misunderstood him. The suffering saint felt tormented, crushed with the irrelevant words of critics who should have comforted instead of corrected him. Crying out for help, Job received none and came to the conclusion that there is no justice anywhere. The interesting thing about Job *is that while he may have despaired of hearing* from God, he never doubted that God was there and knew what was going on.

19:8 *He has walled up my way.* Job felt fenced in by God, when it was really Satan who had been mistreating him (1:10; 3:23). The only fence from God was a hedge of protection.

19:25 *I know that my Redeemer and Vindicator lives.* Job's longing for a mediator (9:33) and his desire for someone to plead on his behalf with God (16:19–21) may suggest that he was thinking of someone other than God. Here was a strong, resolute hope for a mediator between God and humanity. Ultimately Job's longing for a vindicator or mediator was fulfilled in Jesus Christ (1Ti 2:5).

19:26 *from my [immortal] flesh I will see God.* Job was stating his strong belief in the eternality of the soul, and even of the resurrected body, although it was not until Christ's resurrection that followers of the Living God understood all the implications of this belief (1Co 15:12–19).

11 Job 13:24 **18** 2Ki 2:23 **19** Ps 55:13 **20** Ps 102:5 **22** Ps 69:26 **26** Ps 17:15; 1Co 13:12

And 'What pretext for a case
against him can we find [since
we claim the root of these
afflictions is found in him]?'
29 "*Then* beware *and* be afraid of the
sword [of divine vengeance] for
yourselves,
For wrathful are the punishments
of that sword,
So that you may know there is
judgment."

Zophar Says, "The Triumph of the Wicked Is Short"

20 THEN ZOPHAR the Naamathite
answered and said,

2 "Therefore my disquieting
thoughts make me answer,
Because of the uneasiness that is
within me.
3 "I have heard the reproof which
insults me,
But the spirit of my understanding
makes me answer.
4 "Do you not know this from the
old days,
Since the time that man was
placed on the earth,
5 That the triumphing of the wicked
is short,
And the joy of the godless is only
for a moment? [Ps 37:35, 36]
6 "Though his pride reaches the
heavens
And his head touches the clouds,
7 *Yet* he perishes forever like his
own refuse;
Those who have seen him will say,
'Where is he?'
8 "He flies away like a dream and
cannot be found;
Yes, he is chased away like a
vision of the night.
9 "The eye which saw him sees him
no longer,
Neither does his [accustomed]
place behold him any longer.
10 "His sons favor the poor [and pay
his obligations],
And his hands give back his [ill-
gotten] wealth.
11 "His bones are full of youthful
strength
But it lies down with him in the
dust.
12 "Though evil *and* wickedness are
sweet in his mouth
And he hides it under his tongue,
13 Though he desires it and will not
let it go
But holds it in his mouth,
14 *Yet* his food turns [to poison] in
his stomach;
It is the venom of vipers within
him.
15 "He swallows [his ill-gotten]
riches,
But will vomit them up;
God will drive them out of his
belly.
16 "He sucks the poison of vipers
[which ill-gotten wealth
contains];
The viper's tongue slays him.
17 "He does not look at the rivers,
The flowing streams of honey and
butter [to enjoy his wealth].
18 "He gives back what he has
labored for *and* attained
And cannot swallow it [down to
enjoy it];
As to the riches of his labor,
He cannot even enjoy them.
19 "For he has oppressed and
neglected the poor;
He has violently taken away
houses which he did not build.
20 "Because he knew no quietness *or*
calm within him [because of his
greed],
He does not retain anything he
desires.
21 "There is nothing left of what he
devoured;

19:29 *be afraid of the sword.* Job anticipated the reaction of his friends to his stated confidence that someday he would see God face-to-face.
20:7 *refuse.* The word "refuse" may also be translated *dung.* This was a scathing comment.

20:20 *he knew no quietness.* In stating that the wicked person knows no quietness, Zophar implied that Job had received what he deserved.

CHAPTER 20 **5** Ps 37:35 **6** Isa 14:13,14; Ob 3,4 **8** Ps 73:20 **11** Job 13:26; Job 21:26 **17** Ps 36:8; Jer 17:8
20 Ecc 5:13

Therefore his prosperity does not
endure.
[22]"In the fullness of his excess (great
abundance) he will be in trouble;
The hand of everyone who suffers
will come against him [he is
miserable on every side].
[23]"When he fills his belly,
God will send His fierce anger on
him
And will rain it upon him while he
is eating. [Num 11:33; Ps 78:26–31]
[24]"He may flee from the iron
weapon,
But the bow of bronze will pierce
him through.
[25]"*The arrow* is drawn forth and
it comes out of his back [after
passing through his body];
Yes, the glittering point comes out
of his gall.
Terrors march in upon him;
[26]Complete darkness (misfortune) is
held in reserve for his treasures.
An unfanned fire will devour him;
It will consume the survivor in his
tent.
[27]"The heavens will reveal his
wickedness *and* guilt,
And the earth will rise up against
him.
[28]"The produce *and* increase of
his house will depart [with the
victors];
His possessions will be dragged
away in the day of God's wrath.
[29]"This is the wicked man's portion
from God,
And the heritage decreed *and*
appointed to him by God."

Job's Dialogue Regarding the Wicked

21 THEN JOB answered and said,
[2]"Listen carefully to my speech,
And let this be the consolation.
[3]"Bear with me, and I also will
speak;
And after I have spoken, you may
[continue to] mock [me].
[4]"As for me, is my complaint to man
or about him?
And why should I not be impatient
and my spirit troubled?
[5]"Look at me and be astonished
and appalled;
And put your hand over your
mouth.
[6]"Even when I remember, I am
troubled *and* afraid;
Horror *and* trembling take hold of
my flesh.
[7]"Why do the wicked *still* live,
Become old, and become mighty
in power?
[8]"Their children *and* descendants
are established with them in
their sight,
And their offspring before their
eyes.
[9]"Their houses are safe from fear;
And the rod of God is not on them.
[10]"His bull breeds and does not fail;
His cow calves and does not
miscarry.

20:27 heavens will reveal his wickedness and guilt. Zophar apparently reversed Job's appeal to the earth and heavens (16:18–19) for vindication. He argued that the heavens and earth would bear witness not to Job's innocence, but to his guilt.

20:29 heritage . . . appointed to him by God. In contrast to his previous words (11:13–20), Zophar seemed to be suggesting that it was too late for Job to repent. It is true, as Zophar says (v. 5) that the wicked and godless will be judged. But that does not mean either that Job was one of the wicked, or that the judgment of the wicked would be in this life (Lk 16:19–25).

21:7 wicked still live. With a rhetorical question, Job began exposing the loopholes in the retribution dogma—the belief that suffering always indicates God's punishment of a person. Other biblical writers also agonized over the prosperity of the wicked (Ps 37; 73; Jer 12:1–4), but Scriptures affirm that God is controlling everything to accomplish His good purpose (Ro 8:28).

21:9 safe from fear. Job reacted to Eliphaz's argument (15:21–24) that although the wicked live peacefully for a while, they live in terror of inevitable destruction.

24 Isa 24:18; Am 5:19 **25** Job 16:13; Job 18:11 **26** Ps 21:9 **29** Job 27:13 **CHAPTER 21** **3** Job 16:10 **5** Jdg 18:19; Job 40:4 **7** Job 12:6; Ps 73:3,12; Jer 12:1 **9** Ps 73:5 **10** Ex 23:26

11 "They send forth their little ones
like a flock,
And their children skip about.
12 "They lift up their voices *and* sing
to the tambourine and the lyre
And rejoice to the sound of the
flute.
13 "They fully enjoy their days in
prosperity,
And so go down to Sheol (the
nether world, the place of the
dead) in a [peaceful] moment.
14 "Yet they say to God, 'Depart from
us,
For we do not desire the
knowledge of Your ways.
15 'Who [and what] is the Almighty,
that we should serve Him?
And what would we gain if we
plead with Him?' [Ex 5:2]
16 "*But* notice, the prosperity *of the
wicked* is not in their hand (in
their power);
The counsel of the wicked [and
the mystery of God's dealings
with the ungodly] is far from my
comprehension.
17 "How often [then] is it that the
lamp of the wicked is put out,
And that their disaster falls on
them?
Does God distribute pain *and*
destruction *and* sorrow [to them]
in His anger? [Luke 12:46]
18 "Are they like straw before the
wind,
And like chaff that the storm
steals *and* carries away?
19 "*You say,* 'God stores away
[the punishment of] man's
wickedness for his children.'
Let God repay him so that he may
know *and* experience it.
20 "Let his own eyes see his
destruction,
And let him drink of the wrath of
the Almighty.
21 "For what pleasure does he have in
his house *and* family after he is
dead,
When the number of his months
[of life] is cut off?
22 "Can anyone teach God
knowledge,
Seeing that He judges those on
high? [Rom 11:34; 1 Cor 2:16]
23 "One dies in his full strength,
Being wholly at ease and quiet *and*
satisfied;
24 His pails are full of milk [his sides
are filled out with fat],
And the marrow of his bones is
moist,
25 Whereas another dies with a bitter
soul,
Never even tasting pleasure *or*
good fortune.
26 "Together they lie down in the
dust,
And the worms cover them.
27 "Behold, I know your thoughts,
And the plots by which you would
wrong me.
28 "For you say, 'Where is the house
of the noble man?
And where is the tent, the dwelling
place of the wicked?'
29 "Have you not asked those who
travel this way,
And do you not recognize their
witness?
30 "That evil men are [now] reserved
for the day of disaster *and*
destruction,
They will be led away on the day
of [God's] wrath?
31 "*But* who will confront him with
his actions *and* rebuke him face
to face,
And who will repay him for what
he has done?
32 "When he is carried to his grave,
A guard will keep watch over his
tomb.

21:17 ***lamp of the wicked is put out.*** The rhetorical questions introduced by "how often" expected the answer, "not very often." Job challenged Bildad's belief that the wicked person's light does go out (18:5 – 6).

21:19 ***wickedness for his children.*** Job denied the dogma that even if a wicked person prospers temporarily, his children will be punished. Job's position is sustained by other passages in the Bible (Dt 24:16; Jn 9:1 – 3).

13 Job 36:11 **14** Job 22:17 **15** Ex 5:2; Mal 3:14 **16** Ps 1:1; Pr 1:10 **17** Lk 12:46 **18** Ps 1:4 **19** Ex 20:5 **20** Ps 75:8; Isa 51:17 **22** Isa 40:13 **26** Ecc 9:2 **30** Pr 16:4

33 "The [dirt] clods of the valley are
sweet to him [and gently cover
him],
Moreover, all men will follow after
him [to a grave],
While countless ones go before
him.
34 "How then can you vainly comfort
me with empty words,
Since your answers remain
untrue?"

Eliphaz Accuses and Exhorts Job

22 THEN ELIPHAZ the Temanite
answered and said,
2 "Can a vigorous man be of use to
God,
Or a wise man be useful to
himself? [Ps 16:2; Luke 17:10]
3 "Is it any pleasure *or* joy to
the Almighty that you are
righteous?
Or is it of benefit to Him that
you make your ways perfect?
[Is 62:3; Zech 2:8; Mal 3:17;
Acts 20:28]
4 "Is it because of your fear of Him
that He corrects you,
That He enters into judgment
against you?
5 "Is not your wickedness great,
And your sins without end?
6 "For you have taken pledges of
your brothers without cause,
And stripped men naked.
7 "You have not given water to the
weary to drink,
And you have withheld bread from
the hungry. [Matt 25:42]
8 "But the land is possessed by the
man with power,
And the favored *and* honorable
man dwells in it.
9 "You have sent widows away
empty-handed,
And the arms (strength) of the
fatherless have been broken.
10 "Therefore snares surround you,
And sudden dread terrifies *and*
overwhelms you;
11 Or darkness, so that you cannot
see,
And a flood of water covers you.

12 "Is not God in the height of
heaven?
And behold the distant stars, how
high they are!
13 "You say, 'What does God know
[about me]?
Can He judge through the thick
darkness?
14 'Thick clouds are a hiding place
for Him, so that He cannot see,
And He walks on the vault (circle)
of the heavens.'
15 "Will you keep to the ancient path
That wicked men walked [in the
time of Noah], [2 Pet 2:5]
16 Men who were snatched away
before their time,
Whose foundations were poured
out like a river?
17 "They said to God, 'Depart from
us!
What can the Almighty do for us
or to us?'
18 "Yet He filled their houses with
good *things;*
But the counsel of the wicked *and*
ungodly is far from me.

22:2 *man be of use to God.* The implication of Eliphaz's rhetorical question — that man cannot put God under any obligation that God must repay — was a valid theological principle that the Lord Himself corroborates in 41:11. However, his application of that principle to Job's circumstances (vv. 3 – 5) was invalid, for it was based on the faulty assumption that the righteous are always blessed and the wicked always experience God's judgment on earth.

22:3 – 4 *righteous . . . fear.* The same Hebrew root words ("integrity" and "fear of God") had earlier been used by Eliphaz in his courteous remarks about Job (4:6). In these verses Eliphaz is being sarcastic.

22:6 – 9 *naked . . . weary . . . widows.* These trumped up charges were categorically denied by Job (29:11 – 17; 31:13 – 22), and God's own witness to Satan revealed to the reader that the charges were false (1:8)

22:18 *the counsel of the wicked . . . is far from me.* Eliphaz was repeating Job (21:16).

---

33 Heb 9:27 **CHAPTER 22** **2** Ps 16:2 **6** Ex 22:26 **7** Dt 15:7 **11** Ps 69:1,2 **13** Ps 73:11 **16** Job 15:32 **17** Job 21:14

19 "The righteous see it and are glad;
And the innocent mock *and* laugh at them, *saying*,
20 'Surely our adversaries are cut off *and* destroyed,
And fire has consumed their abundance.'

21 "Now yield *and* submit yourself to Him [agree with God and be conformed to His will] and be at peace;
In this way [you will prosper and great] good will come to you.
22 "Please receive the law *and* instruction from His mouth
And establish His words in your heart *and* keep them. [Ps 119:11]
23 "If you return to the Almighty [and submit and humble yourself before Him], you will be built up [and restored];
If you remove unrighteousness far from your tents,
24 And place your gold in the dust,
And *the gold of* Ophir among the stones of the brooks [considering it of little value],
25 And make the Almighty your gold
And your precious silver,
26 Then you will have delight in the Almighty,
And you will lift up your face to God.
27 "You will pray to Him, and He will hear you,
And you will pay your vows.
28 "You will also decide *and* decree a thing, and it will be established for you;
And the light [of God's favor] will shine upon your ways.
29 "When you are cast down *and* humbled, you will speak with confidence,
And the humble person He will lift up *and* save.
30 "He will even rescue the one [for whom you intercede] who is not innocent;
And he will be rescued through the cleanness of your hands."
[Job 42:7, 8]

Job Says He Longs for God

23 THEN JOB answered and said,
2 "Even today my complaint is contentious;
His hand is heavy despite my groaning.
3 "Oh, that I knew where I might find Him,
That I might [even] come to His seat!
4 "I would present my cause before Him
And fill my mouth with arguments.
5 "I would learn the words which He would answer,
And understand what He would say to me.
6 "Would He contend against me with His great power?
No, surely He would give attention to me. [Is 27:4, 5; 57:16]
7 "There the righteous and upright could reason with Him;
So I would be acquitted forever by my Judge.

8 "Behold, I go forward (to the east), but He is not there;
I go backward (to the west), but I cannot perceive Him;
9 To the left (north) He turns, but I cannot behold Him;
He turns to the right hand (south), but I cannot see Him.
10 "But He knows the way that I take [and He pays attention to it].
When He has tried me, I will come forth as [refined] gold [pure and luminous]. [Ps 17:3; 66:10; James 1:12]
11 "My feet have carefully followed His steps;
I have kept His ways and not turned aside.

22:30 *cleanness of your hands.* This was actually fulfilled through Job's prayer for the three friends (42:8–10).

19 Ps 58:10 **21** Isa 27:5 **22** Ps 119:11 **24** 2Ch 1:15 **26** Job 27:10 **27** Isa 58:9 **29** 1Pe 5:5 **CHAPTER 23** **6** Isa 57:16 **8** Job 9:11 **10** Ps 139:1-3; Ps 17:3; 66:10; Jas 1:12 **11** Ps 44:18

12 "I have not departed from the
commandment of His lips;
I have kept the words of His mouth
more than my necessary food.
13 "But He is unique *and*
unchangeable, and who can
turn Him?
And *what* His soul desires, that He
does.
14 "For He performs what is planned
(appointed) for me,
And He is mindful of many such
things.
15 "Therefore I would be terrified at
His presence;
When I consider [all of this], I
tremble in dread of Him.
16 "For God has made my heart faint,
And the Almighty has terrified me,
17 But I am not silenced by the
darkness [of these woes that fell
on me],
Nor by the thick darkness which
covers my face.

Job Says God Seems to Ignore Wrongs

24 "WHY DOES the Almighty
not set seasons for judgment?
Why do those who know Him not
see His days [for punishment of
the wicked]? [Acts 1:7]
2 "Some remove the landmarks;
They [violently] seize and pasture
flocks [appropriating land and
flocks openly].
3 "They drive away the donkeys of
the orphans;
They take the widow's ox for a
pledge.
4 "They crowd the needy off the road;
The poor of the land all hide
themselves.
5 "Behold, as wild donkeys in the
desert,
The poor go to their work,
diligently seeking food;
As bread for their children in the
desert.
6 "They harvest their fodder in a
field [that is not their own],
And glean the vineyard of the
wicked.
7 "They spend the night naked,
without clothing,
And have no covering against the
cold.
8 "They are wet from the rain of the
mountains
And cling to the rock for lack of
shelter.
9 "Others snatch the fatherless
[infants] from the breast [to sell
or make them slaves],
And against the poor they take a
pledge [of clothing].
10 "They cause *the poor* to go about
naked without clothing,
And they take away the sheaves
[of grain] from the hungry.
11 "Within the walls [of the wicked]
the poor make [olive] oil;
They tread [the grapes in] the wine
presses, but thirst.
12 "From the [populous and crowded]
city men groan,
And the souls of the wounded cry
out for help;
Yet God [seemingly] does not pay
attention to the wrong [done to
them].

13 "Others have been with those who
rebel against the light;
They do not want to know its ways
Nor stay in its paths.
14 "The murderer rises at dawn;
He kills the poor and the needy,
And at night he becomes a thief.
15 "The eye of the adulterer waits for
the twilight,
Saying, 'No eye will see me,'
And he covers his face.
16 "In the dark they dig into [the
penetrable walls of] houses;

23:13 *unique.* When Job contemplated the unique power and sovereign freedom of God, he was terrified (13:21).
24:2 *remove the landmarks.* Removing landmarks was tantamount to stealing land. The landmarks set boundaries, and moving them would have been like moving surveyor's stakes (Dt 27:17).

12 Jn 4:32,34 **13** Ps 115:3 **14** 1Th 3:3 **16** Ps 22:14 **CHAPTER 24** **1** Ac 1:7 **2** Dt 19:14; 27:17; Pr 22:28; 23:10; Hos 5:10 **3** Dt 24:6,10,12,17; Job 22:6 **4** Pr 28:28 **7** Ex 22:26; Dt 24:12,13; Job 22:6 **8** La 4:5 **14** Ps 10:8 **15** Pr 7:9; Ps 10:11 **16** Jn 3:20

They shut themselves up by day;
They do not know the light [of day].
17 "For the morning is the same to him as the thick darkness [of midnight];
For he is familiar with the terrors of thick darkness.

18 "They are insignificant on the surface of the water;
Their portion is cursed on the earth;
They do not turn toward the vineyards.
19 "Drought and heat consume the snow waters;
So does Sheol (the nether world, the place of the dead) [consume] *those who* have sinned.
20 "A mother will forget him;
The worm feeds on him until he is no longer remembered.
And wickedness will be broken like a tree [which cannot be restored]. [Prov 10:7]
21 "He preys on the barren (childless) woman
And does no good for the widow.
22 "Yet God draws away the mighty by His power;
He rises, but no one has assurance of life.
23 "God gives them security, and they are supported;
And His eyes are on their ways.
24 "They are exalted for a little while, and then they are gone;
Moreover, they are brought low and like everything [they are] gathered up *and* taken out of the way;
Even like the heads of grain they are cut off.
25 "And if this is not so, who can prove me a liar
And make my speech worthless?"

Bildad Says Man Is Inferior

25 THEN BILDAD the Shuhite answered and said,
2 "Dominion and awe belong to God;
He establishes peace *and* order in His high places.
3 "Is there any number to His [vast celestial] armies?
And upon whom does His light not rise?
4 "How then can man be justified *and* righteous with God?
Or how can he who is born of a woman be pure *and* clean? [Ps 130:3; 143:2]
5 "Behold, even the moon has no brightness [compared to God's majesty and glory]
And the stars are not pure in His sight,
6 How much less man, *that* maggot,
And the son of man, *that* worm!"

Job Rebukes Bildad

26 BUT JOB answered and said,
2 "What a help you are to the weak (powerless)!
How you have saved the arm that is without strength!
3 "How you have counseled the one who has no wisdom!
And how abundantly you have provided sound wisdom *and* helpful insight!
4 "To whom have you uttered [these] words?
And whose spirit [inspired what] came forth from you?

24:16 *dig into [the penetrable walls of] houses.* The walls of houses were built of mud bricks, through which thieves could dig.
24:24 *brought low.* Job was not so much arguing that the wicked would not prosper (vv. 18 – 25), as he was saying that everyone is brought low.
25:6 *worm.* What a contrast to the words of God (Ge 1:26 – 31) when He made humans in His own image and declared them "very good." Bildad was conscious of the great gap between God and man, but unlike Job, he did not feel that he could make the connection of communication that Job was striving for.
26:4 *whose spirit [inspired what] came forth from you.* The contrast between Bildad's comments about God (ch. 25) and Job's worshipful declaration of God's majesty (vv. 7 – 14) indicate the difference in the level of their understanding of who God is.

20 Pr 10:7 **23** Ps 11:4; Pr 15:3 **CHAPTER 25** **3** Jas 1:17 **4** Job 4:17; 15:14

The Greatness of God

5 "The spirits of the dead tremble
Underneath the waters and their inhabitants.
6 "Sheol (the nether world, the place of the dead) is naked before God,
And Abaddon (the place of destruction) has no covering [from His eyes].
7 "*It is* He *who* spreads out the north over emptiness
And hangs the earth on nothing.
8 "He wraps the waters in His clouds [which otherwise would spill on earth all at once],
And the cloud does not burst under them.
9 "He covers the face of the full moon
And spreads His cloud over it.
10 "He has inscribed a circular limit (the horizon) on the face of the waters
At the boundary between light and darkness.
11 "The pillars of the heavens tremble
And are terrified at His rebuke.
12 "He stirred up the sea by His power,
And by His understanding He smashed [proud] Rahab.
13 "By His breath the heavens are cleared;
His hand has pierced the [swiftly] fleeing serpent. [Ps 33:6]
14 "Yet these are just the fringes of His ways [mere samples of His power],
The faintest whisper of His voice!
Who can contemplate the thunder of His [full] mighty power?"

Job Affirms His Righteousness

27 JOB CONTINUED his discourse and said,
2 "As God lives, who has taken away my right *and* denied me justice,
And the Almighty, who has caused bitterness *and* grief for my soul,
3 As long as my life is within me,
And the breath of God is [still] in my nostrils,
4 My lips will not speak unjustly,
Nor will my tongue utter deceit.
5 "Far be it from me that I should admit you are right [in your accusations against me];
Until I die, I will not remove my integrity from me.
6 "I hold fast my uprightness *and* my right standing with God and I will not let them go;
My heart does not reproach me for any of my days.

The State of the Godless

7 "May my enemy be as the wicked,
And he who rises up against me be as the unrighteous (unjust).
8 "For what is the hope of the godless, even though he has gained [in this world],
When God takes his life?
9 "Will God hear his cry
When trouble *and* distress come upon him?
10 "Will he take delight in the Almighty?

26:6 Sheol (the nether world, the place of the dead) is naked. This is the place of the dead and "destruction," which were fearful hidden concepts to Job and his contemporaries, but they held no secrets for the all-knowing God.
26:7 hangs the earth on nothing. Job's comments on the suspension of the earth, the manner of clouds (v. 8), and the horizon (v. 10) speak much for his powers of observation as well as the inspiration of Scripture.
27:2 who has caused bitterness and grief for my soul. Though Job repeatedly complained of a bitter spirit (7:11; 10:1), the Lord did not cause him to respond that way. Job's responses only exposed the attitude that lay deep within his being. The message of the Lord for Job was that no matter what the circumstances, one should resolutely trust in God (40:8; 42:1 – 6).
27:5 admit you are right. Job maintained that his friends were erroneous in their reasoning, and to agree with them would be to compromise his integrity.

6 Ps 22:6 **CHAPTER 26** **6** Ps 139:8; Pr 15:11; Heb 4:13 **7** Job 9:8; Ps 24:2; 104:2 **8** Pr 30:4 **10** Job 38:8; Ps 33:7; 104:9 **12** Ex 14:21; Isa 51:15; Jer 31:35 **13** Ps 33:6; Isa 27:1 **CHAPTER 27** **2** Job 34:5 **5** Job 2:9; 13:15 **6** Job 2:3; Ac 24:16 **8** Mt 16:26; Lk 12:20 **9** Job 35:12; Pr 1:28; 28:9; Isa 1:15; Jer 14:12; Eze 8:18; Mic 3:4; Jn 9:31; Jas 4:3 **10** See Job 22:26,27

Will he call on God at all times?
11 "I will teach you regarding the hand (power) of God;
I will not conceal what is with the Almighty [God's actual treatment of the wicked].
12 "Behold, all of you have seen it;
Why then do you act vainly *and* foolishly [cherishing worthless concepts]?
13 "This [which I am about to explain] is the portion of a wicked man from God,
And the inheritance which tyrants *and* oppressors receive from the Almighty:
14 "Though his children are many, they are destined for the sword;
And his descendants will not have sufficient bread.
15 "Those who survive him will be buried because of the plague,
And [their] widows will not be able to weep.
16 "Though he heaps up silver like dust
And piles up clothing like clay,
17 He may prepare it, but the just will wear it
And the innocent will divide the silver.
18 "He builds his house like a spider's web,
Like a (temporary) hut which a watchman makes.
19 "He lies down rich, but never will again;
He opens his eyes, and it is gone.
20 "Terrors overtake him like a [suddenly rising] flood;
A windstorm steals him away in the night.
21 "The east wind lifts him up, and he is gone;
It sweeps him out of his place.
22 "For it will hurl [thunderbolts of God's wrath] at him unsparingly *and* without compassion;
He flees in haste from its power.
23 "People will clap their hands at him [to mock and ridicule him]
And hiss him out of his place.

Job Tells of Earth's Treasures

28 "SURELY THERE is a mine for silver,
And a place where they refine gold.
2 "Iron is taken out of the earth,
And copper is smelted from the stone ore.
3 "*Man* puts an end to darkness [by bringing in a light],
And to the farthest bounds he searches out
The rock buried in gloom and deep shadow.
4 "He breaks open (mine) shafts far away from where people live,
[In places] forgotten by the [human] foot;
They dangle [in the mines] and hang away from men.
5 "[As for] the earth, out of it comes food,
But underneath [its surface, down deep] it is turned over as fire.
6 "Its stones are the bed of sapphires;
It holds dust of gold.
7 "The path [deep within] no bird of prey knows,
And the falcon's eye has not caught sight of it.
8 "The proud beasts [and their young] have not walked on it,
Nor has the *fierce* lion passed over it.
9 "Man puts his hand on [and tears apart] the flinty rock;
He overturns the mountains at the base [looking for treasure].
10 "He cuts out channels *and* passages among the rocks;
And his eye sees every precious thing.

27:12 *act vainly and foolishly.* Job maintained that the actions of his friends were foolish, considering the knowledge of God that they should have had.
27:13 *portion of a wicked man.* Job likened the foolishness of his friends to wickedness, and indeed it is wicked to knowingly misrepresent God. The rest of the chapter is a satirical paraphrase of the friends' teaching about the fate of the wicked (24:18–25), which Job has thrown back in his friends' faces.

13 Job 20:29 **14** Dt 28:41; Est 9:10; Hos 9:13 **15** Ps 78:64 **17** Pr 28:8; Ecc 2:26 **18** Isa 1:8; La 2:6 **20** Job 18:11

11 "Man dams up the streams from
flowing [so that they do not
trickle into the mine],
And what is hidden he brings out
to the light.

The Search for Wisdom Is Harder

12 "But where can wisdom be found?
And where is the place of
understanding?
13 "Man does not know the value of
it;
Nor is it found in the land of the
living.
14 "The deep says, 'It is not in me';
And the sea says, 'It is not with
me.'
15 "It cannot be obtained for pure
gold,
Nor can silver be weighed as its
price.
16 "It cannot be valued in [terms of]
the gold of Ophir,
In the precious onyx *or* beryl, or
the sapphire.
17 "Gold and glass cannot equal
wisdom,
Nor can it be exchanged for
articles of fine gold.
18 "No mention of coral and crystal
can be made;
For the possession of wisdom is
even above [that of] rubies *or*
pearls.
19 "The topaz of Ethiopia cannot
compare with it,
Nor can it be valued in pure gold.
20 "From where then does wisdom
come?
And where is the place of
understanding?
21 "It is hidden from the eyes of all
the living
And concealed from the birds of
the heavens.
22 "Abaddon (the place of
destruction) and Death say,
'We have [only] heard a report of it
with our ears.'
23 "God understands the way [to
wisdom]
And He knows its place [for
wisdom is with God alone].
24 "For He looks to the ends of the
earth
And sees everything under the
heavens.
25 "When He gave weight *and*
pressure to the wind
And allotted the waters by
measure,
26 When He made a limit for the rain
And a way for the thunderbolt,
27 Then He saw wisdom and
declared it;
He established it and searched it out.
28 "But to man He said, 'Behold, the
reverential *and* worshipful fear
of the Lord—that is wisdom;
And to depart from evil is
understanding.'"

Job's Past Was Glorious

29 AND JOB again took up his discussion and said,
2 "Oh, that I were as in the months
of old,
As in the days when God watched
over me, [Eccl 7:10]
3 When His lamp shone upon my
head
And by His light I walked through
darkness;
4 As I was in the prime of my days,
When the friendship *and* counsel
of God were over my tent,
5 When the Almighty was still
with me
And my boys were around me,

28:13 – 19 *not.* Every verse in this whole stanza has the Hebrew word for "not" at least once, stressing the absence of wisdom or even the desire for wisdom. The rhetorical questions concerning the whereabouts of wisdom and understanding (v. 12) receive an emphatic answer: not anywhere in the land of the living or dead.

28:28 *fear of the LORD.* To fear God is to acknowledge that God has the right to judge our actions for good or evil. Job had talked a lot about injustice and his innocence, but he was solidly aware that only God has wisdom, and in the end, his fear of the Lord was greater than his protestations of blamelessness.

CHAPTER 28 **12** Ecc 7:24 **13** Pr 3:15 **14** ver. 22; Ro 11:33 **15** Pr 3:13-15; 8:10,11,19 **20** ver. 12 **22** ver. 14 **24** Pr 15:3 **25** Ps 135:7 **26** Job 38:25 **28** Dt 4:6; Pr 1:7 **CHAPTER 29** **3** Job 18:6 **4** Ps 25:14

6 When my steps [through rich
pastures] were washed with
butter *and* cream [from my
livestock],
And the rock poured out for me
streams of oil [from my olive
groves].
7 "When I went out to the gate of the
city,
When I took my seat [as a city
father] in the square,
8 The young men saw me and hid
themselves,
The aged arose *and* stood
[respectfully];
9 The princes stopped talking
And put their hands on their
mouths;
10 The voices of the nobles were
hushed,
And their tongues stuck to the roof
of their mouths.
11 "For when an ear heard [my name
mentioned], it called me happy
and fortunate;
And when an eye saw [me], it
testified for me [approvingly],
12 Because I rescued the poor who
cried for help,
And the orphan who had no helper.
13 "The blessing of him who was
about to perish came upon me,
And I made the widow's heart sing
for joy.
14 "I put on righteousness, and it
clothed me;
My justice was like a robe and a
turban!
15 "I was eyes to the blind
And I was feet to the lame.
16 "I was a father to the needy;
I investigated the case I did not
know [and assured justice].
17 "And I smashed the jaws of the
wicked
And snatched the prey from his
teeth.
18 "Then I said, 'I shall die in my nest,
And I shall multiply my days as
the sand.
19 'My root is spread out *and* open to
the waters,
And the dew lies all night upon my
branch.
20 'My glory *and* honor are fresh in
me [being constantly renewed],
And my bow gains [ever] new
strength in my hand.'

21 "They listened to me and waited
And kept silent for my counsel.
22 "After I spoke, they did not speak
again,
And my speech dropped upon
them [like a refreshing shower].
23 "They waited for me [and for my
words] as for the rain,
And they opened their mouths as
for the spring rain.
24 "I smiled at them when they did
not believe,
And they did not diminish the
light of my face.
25 "I chose a way for them and sat as
chief,
And dwelt as a king among his
soldiers,
As one who comforts mourners.

Job's Present State Is Humiliating

30 "BUT NOW those younger
than I mock *and* laugh at me,
Whose fathers I refused to put
with the sheepdogs of my flock.
2 "Indeed, how could the strength of
their hands profit me?
Vigor had perished from them.
3 "They are gaunt with want and
famine;
They gnaw the dry *and* barren
ground by night in [the gloom
of] waste and desolation.

29:12 ***rescued the poor.*** Considering Job's account of his life when he was prosperous, Eliphaz's accusations of Job sending the widows away empty and crushing the orphans (22:9) was a calculated insult.

29:14 ***put on righteousness . . . a turban.*** This vivid portrait of Job was a stark contrast to his present condition, with his flesh being "clothed" in worms and dust.

6 Ge 49:11; Dt 32:13; Job 20:17; Ps 81:16 **9** Job 21:5 **10** Ps 137:6 **12** Ps 72:12; Pr 21:13; 24:11 **14** Dt 24:13; Isa 59:17; 61:10; Eph 6:14; 1Th 5:8 **15** Nu 10:31 **16** Pr 29:7 **17** Ps 58:6; Pr 30:14 **18** Ps 30:6 **19** Job 18:16; Ps 1:3; Jer 17:8 **20** Ge 49:24 **23** Zec 10:1

4 "They pluck [and eat] saltwort
(mallows) among the bushes,
And their food is the root of the
broom shrub.
5 "They are driven from the
community;
They shout after them as after a
thief.
6 "They must dwell on the slopes of
wadis
And in holes in the ground and in
rocks.
7 "Among the bushes they cry out
[like wild animals];
Beneath the prickly scrub they
gather *and* huddle together.
8 "*They are the* sons of [worthless
and nameless] fools,
They have been driven out of the
land.

9 "And now I have become [the
subject of] their taunting;
Yes, I am a byword *and* a
laughingstock to them.
10 "They hate me, they stand aloof
from me,
And do not refrain from spitting in
my face.
11 "For God has loosed His bowstring
[attacking me] and [He has]
afflicted *and* humbled me;
They have cast off the bridle [of
restraint] before me.
12 "On my right the [rabble] brood
rises;
They push my feet away, and
they build up their ways of
destruction against me [like an
advancing army].
13 "They break up *and* clutter my
path [upsetting my plans],
They profit from my destruction;
No one restrains them.
14 "As *through* a wide breach they
come,
Amid the crash [of falling walls]
they roll on [over me].
15 "Terrors are turned upon me;
They chase away my honor *and*
reputation like the wind,
And my prosperity has passed
away like a cloud.

16 "And now my soul is poured out
within me;
The days of affliction have seized
me.
17 "My bones are pierced [with
aching] in the night season,
And *the pains* that gnaw me take
no rest.
18 "By the great force [of my disease]
my garment (skin) is disfigured
and blemished;
It binds about me [choking me]
like the collar of my coat.
19 "God has cast me into the mire
[a swampland of crisis],
And I have become [worthless]
like dust and ashes.
20 "I cry to You for help, [Lord,] but
You do not answer me;
I stand up, but You [only] gaze
[indifferently] at me.
21 "You have become harsh *and* cruel
to me;
With the might of Your hand You
[keep me alive only to]
persecute me.
22 "You lift me up on the wind and
cause me to ride [upon it];
And You toss me about in the
tempest *and* dissolve me in the
storm.
23 "For I know that You will bring me
to death
And to the house of meeting
[appointed] for all the living.

24 "However, does not one falling in
a heap of ruins stretch out his
hand?
Or in his disaster [will he not]
therefore cry out for help?

30:11 *loosed His bowstring.* A bow that is not strung up is not ready for use. This was a terrible contrast to his former life, described in 29:20, where Job referred to himself as having his bowstring renewed. A bow that is being used has its string replaced regularly so that the bow can operate at its maximum strength.
30:21 *might of Your hand.* Job blamed God's strong hand, which Satan could not move, for calamities that were actually caused by the hand of Satan (1:11 – 12; 18 – 19).

CHAPTER 30 **9** Job 17:6; Ps 35:15; 69:12; La 3:14 **10** Nu 12:14; Dt 25:9; Isa 50:6; Mt 26:67; 27:30 **11** See Job 12:18 **12** Job 19:12 **16** Ps 42:4 **23** Heb 9:27

25 "Did I not weep for one whose
life was hard *and* filled with
trouble?
Was not my heart grieved for the
needy?
26 "When I expected good, then came
evil [to me];
And when I waited for light, then
came darkness.
27 "I am seething within *and* my
heart is troubled and cannot rest;
Days of affliction come to meet me.
28 "I go about mourning without
comfort [my skin blackened by
disease, not by the heat of the
sun];
I stand up in the assembly *and* cry
out for help.
29 "I am a brother to [howling] jackals,
And a companion to ostriches
[which scream dismally].
30 "My skin falls from me in
blackened flakes,
And my bones are burned with
fever.
31 "Therefore my lyre (harp) is *used*
for [the sound of] mourning,
And my flute for the [sound of the]
voices of those who weep.

Job Asserts His Integrity

31 "I HAVE made a covenant
(agreement) with my eyes;
How then could I gaze [lustfully]
at a virgin?
2 "For what is the portion I would
have from God above,
And what heritage from the
Almighty on high?
3 "Does not tragedy fall [justly] on
the unjust
And disaster to those who work
wickedness?
4 "Does not God see my ways
And count all my steps?
5 "If I have walked with falsehood,
Or if my foot has chased after
deceit,
6 Oh, let Him weigh me with
accurate scales,
And let God know my integrity.
7 "If my step has turned away from
the way [of God],
Or if my heart has [covetously]
followed my eyes,
Or if any spot [of guilt] has stained
my hands,
8 Then let me plant and [let] another
eat [from the results of my
labor],
And let my crops be uprooted *and*
ruined.
9 "If my heart has been enticed *and* I
was made a fool by a woman,
Or if I have [covetously] lurked at
my neighbor's door [until his
departure],
10 Let my wife grind [meal, like a
bond slave] for another [man],
And let others kneel down over
her.
11 "For *adultery* is a heinous *and*
lustful crime;
Moreover, it would be a sin
punishable by the judges.
[Deut 22:22; John 8:5]
12 "For it is a fire which consumes
to Abaddon (destruction, ruin,
final torment);
And [illicit passion] would burn
and rage *and* uproot all my
[life's] increase [destroying
everything].
13 "If I have despised *and* rejected
the claim of my male or female
servants
When they filed a complaint
against me,
14 What then could I do when God
arises [to judge me]?
When He calls me to account,
what will I answer Him?
[Ps 44:21]
15 "Did not He who made me in the
womb make my servant,

31:5 *If.* The word "if" was a part of a formula used by accused persons to swear their innocence. The full oath formula was, in effect, "If I am guilty of this crime, may God impose that curse." Because of hesitation about speaking a curse, the person swearing the oath would normally use an

25 Ps 35:13; Ro 12:15 **26** Jer 8:15 **28** Ps 42:9 **29** Ps 102:6; Mic 1:8 **30** Ps 119:83; La 4:8; Ps 102:3 **CHAPTER 31** **1** Mt 5:28 **2** Job 20:29 **4** 2Ch 16:9; Pr 5:21; Jer 32:19 **7** See Nu 15:39; Ecc 11:9; Eze 6:9; Mt 5:29 **8** Lev 26:16; Dt 28:30,38 **10** 2Sa 12:11; Jer 8:10 **11** Ge 38:24; Lev 20:10; See ver. 28 **14** Ps 44:21 **15** Job 34:19

And did not the same One
fashion us both in the womb?
[Prov 14:31; 22:2; Mal 2:10]

16 "If I have withheld from the poor
what *they* desired,
Or have caused the eyes of the
widow to look in vain [for relief],
17 Or have eaten my morsel [of food]
alone,
And did not share it with the orphan
18 (But from my youth the orphan
grew up with me as with a
father,
And from my mother's womb I
have been the widow's guide),
19 If I have seen anyone perish for
lack of clothing,
Or any poor person without
covering,
20 If his loins have not thanked *and*
blessed me [for clothing them],
And if he was not warmed with
the fleece of my sheep,
21 If I have lifted my hand against the
orphan,
Because I saw [that the judges
would be] my help at the
[council] gate,
22 Then let my shoulder fall away
from its socket,
And my arm be broken off at the
elbow.
23 "For tragedy from God is a terror
to me,
And because of His majesty *and*
exaltation I can do nothing [nor
endure facing Him]. [Is 13:6;
Joel 1:15]

24 "If I have put my trust *and*
confidence in gold,
Or have declared fine gold my
hope *and* assurance,
25 If I gloated *and* rejoiced because
my wealth was great,
And because my [powerful] hand
[alone] had obtained so much,
26 If I beheld the sun [as an object of
worship] when it shone
Or the moon going in its splendor,
27 And my heart became secretly
enticed [by them],
And my hand threw a kiss from
my mouth [in respect to them],
28 This also would have been
[a heinous] sin *calling for*
judgment,
For I would have denied God
above. [Deut 4:19; 17:2–7]

29 "Have I rejoiced at the destruction
of the enemy [who hated me],
Or exulted [in malicious triumph]
when evil overtook him?
30 "No, I have not allowed my mouth
to sin
By cursing my enemy *and* asking
for his life.
31 "I assure you, the men of my tent
have said,
'Who can find one [in need] who
has not been satisfied with his
meat'?
32 "The stranger has not lodged in
the street,
Because I have opened my door to
the traveler.
33 "Have I concealed my
transgressions like Adam *or* like
other men,
By hiding my wickedness in my
bosom,
34 Because I feared the great
multitude,
And the contempt of families
terrified me,
So that I kept silence *and* did not
acknowledge my sin and did not
go out of the door?
35 "Oh, that I had one to listen to me!
Look, here is my signature (mark);
Let the Almighty answer me!
Let my adversary write out His
indictment [and put His vague
accusations in tangible form].
36 "Surely I would [proudly] bear it
on my shoulder,

---

abbreviated version. By contrast, Job used the full formula four times, which demonstrated his confidence that he would be acquitted.

31:27 *my hand threw a kiss from my mouth.* This phrase refers to the apparent ancient custom of kissing the hand as a prelude to the superstitious and idolatrous act of throwing a kiss to the heavenly bodies.

20 Dt 24:13 **21** Job 22:9 **23** Isa 13:6 **24** Mk 10:24 **25** Ps 62:10 **26** Eze 8:16 **29** Pr 17:5 **30** Mt 5:44 **32** Ge 19:2,3 **33** Pr 28:13 **34** Ex 23:2 **35** Job 13:22

And bind the scroll around my head like a crown.
37 "I would count out to Him the number of my steps [with every detail of my life],
Approaching His presence as *if I were* a prince.

38 "For if my land has cried out against me,
And its furrows weep together;
39 If I have eaten its fruits without paying for them,
Or have caused its [rightful] owners to lose their lives,
40 Let thorns grow instead of wheat,
And stinkweed *and* cockleburs instead of barley."

So the words of Job [with his friends] are finished.

Elihu Rebukes Job

32 SO THESE three men ceased
answering Job, because he was
righteous in his own eyes [and could
not be persuaded otherwise by them].
2 But Elihu the son of Barachel the
Buzite, of the family of Ram, became
indignant. His indignation was kin-
dled *and* burned *and* he became upset
with Job because he justified himself
rather than God [and even expressed
doubts about God's character].
3 Elihu's anger burned against Job's
three friends because they had found
no answer [and were unable to deter-
mine Job's error], and yet they had
condemned Job *and* declared him to
be in the wrong [and responsible for
his own afflictions].
4 Now Elihu had waited to speak to
Job because the others were years old-
er than he.
5 And when Elihu saw that there was
no answer in the mouths of these three
men, he burned with anger.
6 Then Elihu the son of Barachel the
Buzite said,

"I am young, and you are aged;
For that reason I was anxious and dared not tell you what I think.
7 "I thought age should speak,
And a multitude of years should teach wisdom.
8 "But there is [a vital force and] a spirit [of intelligence] in man,
And the breath of the Almighty gives them understanding. [Prov 2:6]
9 "Those [who are] abundant *in years* may not [always] be wise,
Nor may the elders [always] understand justice.
10 "Therefore I say, 'Listen to me;
I also will give you my opinion [about Job's situation] *and* tell you plainly what I think.'

11 "You see, I waited for your words,
I listened to your [wise] reasons,
While you pondered *and* searched out what to say.
12 "I even paid close attention to [what] you [said],
Indeed, not one of you convinced Job [nor could you refute him],
Not one of you supplied [satisfactory] answers to his words.
13 "Beware if you say,
'We have found wisdom;

32:1 *righteous in his own eyes.* Job's friends accused him of self-righteousness because of his denial of the sins they ascribed to him. Job considered himself blameless (and so did God), but he was not without sin. Job needed to see how he compared to God's utter holiness, in spite of the fact that he had none of the unconfessed sins that his friends accused him of.

32:2 *indignation was kindled.* Elihu's first mistake was in dealing with a delicate situation while he was angry. He did use the same arguments as the three friends, but he did not understand the whole situation any better than they did. Only the reader is aware of the counsel that took place in heaven (ch. 1).

33:12 *in this you are not right or just.* Elihu was correct in saying that God was not answerable to Job. God does not ever have to explain Himself to us, even though He often graciously does so. Job had great respect for God, and understood the fear of the Lord (28:28). He was persistent in asking God for an answer, and in the end, God did reply.

39 Jas 5:4; 1Ki 21:19 **40** Ge 3:18 **CHAPTER 32** **1** Job 33:9 **8** Pr 2:6 **9** 1Co 1:26 **13** Jer 9:23

God thrusts Job down [justly], not
man [for God alone is dealing
with him].'
14 "Now Job has not directed his
words against me [therefore I
have no reason to be offended],
Nor will I answer him with
arguments like yours. [I speak
for truth, not for revenge.]

15 "They (Job's friends) are dismayed
and embarrassed, they no
longer answer;
The words have moved away *and*
failed them," [says Elihu].
16 "And shall I wait, because they say
nothing,
But stand still and say no more?
17 "I too will give my share of
answers;
I too will express my opinion *and*
share my knowledge.
18 "For I am full of words;
The spirit within me constrains
me.
19 "My belly is like unvented wine;
Like new wineskins it is about to
burst.
20 "I must speak so that I may get
relief;
I will open my lips and answer.
21 "I will not [I warn you] be partial
to any man [that is, let my
respect for you mitigate what I
say];
Nor flatter any man.
22 "For I do not know how to flatter,
[in an appropriate way, and I
fear that],
My Maker would soon take me
away.

Elihu Claims to Speak for God

33 "HOWEVER, JOB, please
listen to my words,
And pay attention to everything I
say.
2 "Behold, I have opened my mouth
[to begin my speech];
My tongue in my mouth is going to
speak.
3 "My words will express the
uprightness of my heart,
And my lips will speak what they
know with utter sincerity.
4 "The Spirit of God has made me,
And the breath of the Almighty
gives me life [which inspires
me].
5 "Answer me, if you can;
Set yourselves before me, take
your stand.
6 "Behold, I belong to God like you;
I too was formed out of the clay.
7 "Behold, I will not make you afraid
or terrified of me [for I am only
mortal and not God],
Nor should any pressure from me
weigh heavily upon you.

8 "Surely you have spoken in my
hearing,
And I have heard the sound of
your words, saying:
9 'I am pure, without transgression;
I am innocent and there is no guilt
in me.
10 'Behold, God finds pretexts
against me;
He counts me as His enemy.
11 'He puts my feet in the stocks [to
hinder and humiliate me];
He [suspiciously] watches all my
paths,' [you say].
12 "Look, let me answer you, in this
you are not right *or* just;
For God is greater *and* far superior
to man.

13 "Why do you complain against
Him?
That He does not answer [you
with] all His doings.
14 "For God speaks once,
And *even* twice, yet no one notices
it [including you, Job].
15 "In a dream, a vision of the night
[one may hear God's voice],
When deep sleep falls on men
While slumbering upon the bed,
16 Then He opens the ears of men
And seals their instruction,
17 That He may turn man aside *from*
his conduct,
And keep him from pride;
18 He holds back his soul from the pit
[of destruction],

CHAPTER 33 **4** Ge 2:7 **6** Job 9:32,33 **7** Job 9:34 **9** Job 10:7 **10** Job 16:9 **11** Job 13:27 **13** Isa 45:9
14 Ps 62:11 **15** Nu 12:6 **16** Job 36:10,15

And his life from passing over
into Sheol (the nether world, the
place of the dead).

19 "Man is also disciplined with pain
on his bed,
And with unceasing complaint in
his bones,
20 So that his life makes him loathe
food,
And his soul [loathe] even his
favorite dishes.
21 "His flesh is so wasted away that it
cannot be seen,
And his bones which were not
seen now stick out.
22 "Then his soul draws near to the
pit [of destruction],
And his life to those who bring
death (the destroyers).

23 "If there is an angel as a mediator
for him,
One out of a thousand,
To explain to a man what is right
for him [that is, how to be in
right standing with God],
24 Then the angel is gracious to him,
and says,
'Spare him from going down to the
pit [of destruction];
I have found a ransom [a
consideration, or reason for
redemption, an atonement]!'
25 "Let his flesh be restored *and*
become fresher than in youth;
Let him return to the days of his
youthful strength.
26 "He will pray to God, and He shall
be favorable to him,
So that he looks at His face with
joy;
For God restores to man His
righteousness [that is, his right
standing with God—with its
joys].
27 "He sings out to other men,
'I have sinned and perverted that
which was right,
And it was not proper for me!
28 'God has redeemed my life from
going to the pit [of destruction],
And my life shall see the light.' "

29 [Elihu comments,] "Behold, God
does all these *things* twice, yes,
three times, with a man,
30 To bring his life back from the pit
[of destruction],
That he may be enlightened with
the light of the living.
31 "Pay attention, Job, listen to me;
Keep silent, and I will speak.
32 "If you have anything to say,
answer me;
Speak, for I desire to justify you.
33 "If not [and you have nothing to
say], listen to me;
Keep silent, and I will teach you
wisdom."

Elihu Vindicates God's Justice

34 ELIHU CONTINUED *his discourse* and said,

2 "Hear my words, you wise men,
And listen to me, you who have [so
much] knowledge.
3 "For the ear puts words to the test
As the palate tastes food.
4 "Let us choose for ourselves that
which is right;
Let us know among ourselves
what is good.
5 "For Job has said, 'I am righteous
[and innocent],
But God has taken away my right;
[Job 33:9]
6 Although I am right, I am
accounted a liar.
My wound is incurable, *though I
am* without transgression.'
7 "What man is like Job,
Who drinks up derision like water,

33:29–30 *To bring his life back from the pit.* Again, one of Job's advisors had some correct understanding of God, but he mistakenly applied it to Job. It is true that the chastening of pain or trouble sometimes causes men to turn to God and repent of wickedness. But Job's problem was not perverting what was right (v. 27). For him, the answer for the purpose of his pain could not be "to bring his life back from the pit." Without claiming that Job was sin free, God had called him blameless and upright (1:8).

20 Ps 107:18 **27** 2Sa 12:13; Pr 28:13; Lk 15:21; 1Jn 1:9; Ro 6:21 **28** Isa 38:17 **30** Ps 56:13 **33** Ps 34:11
CHAPTER 34 **3** Job 6:30; 12:11 **5** Job 33:9; Job 27:2 **6** Job 9:17 **7** Job 15:16

8 Who goes in company with those
who do evil
And walks with wicked men?
9 "For he has said, 'It profits a man
nothing
When he takes delight *and* is
pleased with God *and* obeys
Him.'

10 "Therefore hear me, you men of
understanding.
Far be it from God that He would
do wickedness,
And from the Almighty to do
wrong.
11 "For God pays a man according to
his work,
And He will make every man find
[appropriate] *compensation*
according to his way.
12 "Surely God will not act wickedly,
Nor will the Almighty pervert
justice.
13 "Who put God in charge over the
earth?
And who has laid *on Him* the
whole world?
14 "If God should determine to do so,
If He should gather to Himself
[that is, withdraw from man]
His [life-giving] spirit and His
breath,
15 All flesh would perish together,
And man would return to dust.
[Ps 104:29; Eccl 12:7]

16 "If *you now have* understanding,
hear this;
Listen to the sound of my words.
17 "Shall one who hates justice [and
is an enemy of right] govern?
And will you condemn Him who is
just *and* mighty?
18 "God who says to a king, 'You are
worthless *and* vile,'
Or to princes *and* nobles, 'You are
wicked *and* evil'?
19 "Who is not partial to princes,
Nor does He regard the rich above
the poor,
For they all are the work of His
hands.
20 "In a moment they die, even at
midnight
The people are shaken and pass
away,
And the powerful are taken away
without a [human] hand.

21 "For God's eyes are on the ways of
a man,
And He sees all his steps.
[Ps 34:15; Prov 5:21; Jer 16:17]
22 "There is no darkness nor deep
shadow
Where the evildoers may hide
themselves.
23 "For He sets no appointed time for
a man,
That he should appear before Him
in judgment.
24 "He breaks mighty men without
inquiry,
And sets others in their place.
[Dan 2:21]
25 "Therefore He knows of their
works,
And He overthrows them in the
night,
So that they are crushed *and*
destroyed.
26 "He strikes them like the wicked
In a public place,
27 Because they turned aside from
following Him
And would not consider *or* show
regard for any of His ways,
[1 Sam 15:11]
28 So that they caused the cry of the
poor to come to Him,

34:8 *walks with wicked men.* There was no justice in this charge against Job.
34:12 *act wickedly . . . pervert justice.* Elihu was unhappy with Job's persistent charges that God was unjust (9:22 – 24; 24:1 – 25), and this was a proper concern. The judge of all the earth will always do right (Rev 15:3).
34:16 *hear this.* As indicated by the singular Hebrew verb translated "hear," Elihu was addressing Job directly in verses 16 – 33.
34:24 *breaks mighty men.* Job was a mighty man who was broken. Elihu's implication is that Job was a worker of iniquity (v. 22).

9 Mal 3:14 **10** Job 8:3 **11** Ps 62:12; Pr 24:12; Mt 16:27 **12** Job 8:3 **14** Ps 104:29 **15** Ge 3:19 **17** 2Sa 23:3 **18** Ex 22:28 **19** Dt 10:17; Job 31:15 **20** Ex 12:29 **21** Job 31:4 **22** Ps 139:12; Am 9:2,3 **24** Da 2:21 **27** 1Sa 15:11; Ps 28:5; Isa 5:12 **28** Jas 5:4; Ex 22:23

And He heard the cry of the
afflicted. [Ex 22:23; James 5:4]
29 "When He keeps quiet, who then
can condemn?
When He hides His face
[withdrawing His favor and
help], who then can behold Him
[and make supplication to Him],
Whether it be a nation or a man by
himself?—
30 So that godless men would not
rule
Nor be snares for the people.

31 "For has anyone said to God,
'I have endured *my chastisement;*
I will not offend *anymore;*
32 Teach me what I do not see [in
regard to how I have sinned];
If I have done wrong (injustice,
unrighteousness),
I will not do it again'?
33 "Shall God's retribution [for your
sins] be on your terms, because
you refuse to accept it?
For you must do the choosing, and
not I;
Therefore say what you
[truthfully] know.
34 "Men of understanding will tell me,
Indeed, every wise man who hears
me [will agree],
35 'Job speaks without knowledge,
And his words are without wisdom
and insight.
36 'Job ought to be tried to the limit
Because he answers like wicked
men!
37 'For he adds rebellion [in
his unsubmissive, defiant
attitude toward God] to his
[unacknowledged] sin;
He claps his hands among us [in
open mockery and contempt of
God],
And he multiplies his words [of
accusation] against God.' "

Elihu Sharply Reproves Job

35 ELIHU CONTINUED speaking
[to Job] and said,
2 "Do you think this is according to
[your] justice?
Do you say, 'My righteousness is
more than God's'?
3 "For you say, 'What advantage
have you [by living a righteous
life]?
What profit will I have, more [by
being righteous] than if I had
sinned?'
4 "I will answer you,
And your companions with you.
5 "Look to the heavens and see;
And behold the skies which are
[much] higher than you.
6 "If you have sinned, what do you
accomplish against Him?
And if your transgressions are
multiplied, what have you done
to Him?
7 "If you are righteous, what do you
give God,
Or what does He receive from your
hand?
8 "Your wickedness *affects only* a
man such as you,
And your righteousness *affects
only* a son of man [but it cannot
affect God, who is sovereign].
9 "Because of the multitudes of
oppressions *the people* cry out;
They cry for help because of the
[violent] arm of the mighty.
10 "But no one says, 'Where is God
my Maker,
Who gives songs [of rejoicing] in
the night, [Acts 16:25]

34:37 *adds rebellion . . . to his [unacknowledged] sin.* Job was stubborn, but he was not rebellious. He was willing to accept punishment if he deserved it (31:5 – 6).

35:6 *If you have sinned.* This is the same argument used by Eliphaz (22:2). The point that Elihu was making here and through verse 8, is that God's stature is not affected either by the sinfulness or righteousness of man. He cannot be diminished by sin nor made greater by righteousness. This is a true and important point. But it leaves out the understanding that God created man to be in His image, and He does care about the actions of man. God wants men to live blamelessly (ch. 1), and it is good to want to please God.

30 1Ki 12:28,30 **35** Job 35:16 **CHAPTER 35** **3** Job 21:15 **4** Job 34:8 **5** Job 22:12 **6** Pr 8:36; Jer 7:19
7 Ps 16:2; Pr 9:12 **9** Job 34:28 **10** Isa 51:13; Ps 42:8; Ac 16:25

11 Who teaches us more than the
beasts of the earth
And makes us wiser than the birds
of the heavens?'
12 "The people cry out, but He does
not answer
Because of the pride of evil men.
13 "Surely God will not listen to an
empty cry [which lacks trust],
Nor will the Almighty regard it.
14 "Even though you say that you do
not see Him [when missing His
righteous judgment on earth],
Yet your case is before Him, and
you must wait for Him!
15 "And now, because He has not
[quickly] punished in His anger,
Nor has He acknowledged
transgression *and* arrogance
well [and seems unaware of
the wrong of which a person is
guilty],
16 Job uselessly opens his mouth
And multiplies words without
knowledge [drawing the
worthless conclusion that
the righteous have no more
advantage than the wicked]."

Elihu Speaks of God's Dealings with Men

36 ELIHU CONTINUED and said,
2 "Bear with me a little longer, and I
will show you,
That there is yet more to say on
God's behalf.
3 "I will bring my knowledge from
afar,
And will ascribe righteousness to
my Maker.
4 "For truly my words are not false;
He who is perfect in knowledge is
with you.
5 "Behold, God is mighty, and yet
does not despise *anyone* [nor
regard any as trivial];
He is mighty in the strength *and*
power of understanding.
6 "He does not prolong the life of the
wicked,
But gives the afflicted their justice.
7 "He does not withdraw His eyes
from the righteous [those in
right standing with Him];
But with kings upon the throne
He has seated them forever, and
they are exalted.
8 "And if they are bound in bonds [of
adversity],
And held by cords of affliction,
[Ps 107:10, 11]
9 Then He declares to them [the true
character of] their deeds
And their transgressions, that
they have acted arrogantly [with
presumption and notions of self-
sufficiency].
10 "He opens their ears to instruction
and discipline,
And commands that they return
from evil.
11 "If they hear and serve *Him*,
They will end their days in
prosperity
And their years in pleasantness
and joy.
12 "But if they do not hear *and* obey,
they will die by the sword [of
God's destructive judgments]
And they will die [in ignorance]
without [true] knowledge.

35:12 Pride—Elihu accused Job of pride because Job had declared his own righteousness (32:1). But Elihu's presumption and self-righteousness became even more excessive than Job's as he developed his pompous speech against Job (36:4). Later Elihu would understand that God had accepted Job, while his "friends" were condemned. Even knowledge about God and commitment to God can become a source of pride that blinds us to other things that God is doing, both in ourselves and in others.

35:13 *an empty cry.* Elihu was assuming that Job had no answer from God because God knew that Job's cry was empty.

36:2 *say on God's behalf.* Elihu believed that he was speaking for God and that he was setting Job straight. It is interesting to note that God asked Job to pray for the other three friends (42:7–10), but no word, either of censure or praise, was said about Elihu.

36:6–14 *does not prolong the life of the wicked.* Elihu repeats the concept that the wicked are judged by being cut off and the repentant are rewarded.

---

11 Ps 94:12 **12** Pr 1:28 **13** Isa 1:15; Jer 11:11 **14** Job 9:11; Ps 37:5,6 **15** Ps 89:32 **16** Job 34:35
CHAPTER 36 **5** Job 9:4 **7** Ps 33:18; 113:8 **8** Ps 107:10 **10** Job 33:16 **11** Job 21:13; Isa 1:19,20

13 "But the godless in heart store up
anger [at the divine discipline];
They do not cry [to Him] for help
when He binds them [with cords
of affliction]. [Rom 2:5]
14 "They die in youth,
And their life *ends* among the cult
prostitutes. [Deut 23:17]
15 "He rescues the afflicted in their
affliction,
And opens their ears [so that they
pay attention to His voice] in
times of oppression.
16 "Then indeed, He enticed you
from the mouth of distress *and*
confinement,
Into a broad place where there is
no constraint *or* distress;
And that which was set on your
table was full of fatness (rich
food).
17 "But you [Job] were full of
judgment on the wicked,
Judgment and justice take hold *of
you.*
18 "Do not let wrath entice you into
scoffing;
And do not let the greatness *and*
the extent of the ransom turn
you aside.
19 "Will your wealth [be sufficient to]
keep you from [the confinement
of] distress,
Or will all the force of your
strength do it?
20 "Do not long for the night,
When people vanish from their
places.
21 "Take heed *and* be careful, do not
turn to wickedness,
For you have chosen this [the vice
of complaining against God]
rather than [learning from]
affliction.
22 "Behold, God is exalted in His
power;
Who is a ruler *or* a teacher like
Him?
23 "Who has appointed God His way,
And who can say [to Him], 'You
have done wrong'?
24 "Remember that you should
magnify God's work,
Of which men have sung.
25 "All men have seen God's work;
Man looks at it from a distance.
26 "Behold, God is exalted, and we do
not know *Him;*
The number of His years is
unsearchable. [1 Cor 13:12]
27 "For He draws up the drops of
water,
They distill rain from the mist,
28 Which the clouds pour down,
They drop abundantly upon
mankind."
29 "Can anyone understand the
spreading of the clouds
Or the thundering of His pavilion?
[Ps 18:11; Is 40:22]
30 "Behold, He spreads His lightning
around Him [against the dark
clouds],
And He covers the depths of the sea.
31 "For by these [mighty acts] He
judges the peoples;

36:23 *You have done wrong.* This is probably the most accurate warning that Elihu gives to Job. Even though Job was sure that God would vindicate his actions (and the reader knows that God saw Job as blameless and upright), he could not defend his position without telling God that He had done wrong. God cannot sin, nor will He tempt people to sin.

36:24 *magnify God's work.* This is the best advice that Elihu gave Job, and indeed, it was something that Job had already done (26:5 – 14; 28:1 – 28). Exalting God for who He is and what He has done is one of the best ways to gain perspective when we are in trouble or despair.

36:26 *Behold, God is exalted.* As Elihu begins to praise God, his anger with Job disappears, and he speaks accurately and joyfully of the things that he knows about God. From here to the end of chapter 37 Elihu is praising God. The speeches of Elihu are the most difficult of the friends' admonitions to analyze, and scholars are not in total agreement about which charges by Elihu are discerning and which charges are misapplied "conventional wisdom." Like all mixtures of truth and misunderstanding, Elihu's discourse needs careful sorting.

13 Ro 2:5 **14** Ps 55:23 **16** Ps 18:19; 31:8; Ps 23:5; Ps 36:8 **18** Ps 49:7 **19** Pr 11:4 **21** Ps 66:18; Heb 11:25 **22** Isa 40:13; 1Co 2:16 **23** Job 34:13; Job 34:10 **24** Ps 92:5; Rev 15:3 **26** 1Co 13:12; Ps 90:2; Heb 1:12 **27** Ps 147:8 **28** Pr 3:20 **30** Job 37:3 **31** Job 37:13; Ac 14:17

He gives food in abundance.
32 "He covers *His* hands with the lightning,
And commands it to strike the mark.
33 "His thundering voice declares [awesomely] His presence;
The cattle also are told of His coming storm.

Elihu Says God has Authority over the Storm

37 "INDEED, AT *His* thundering my heart trembles
And leaps out of its place.
2 "Listen carefully to the thunder of His voice,
And the rumbling that goes out of His mouth!
3 "He lets it loose under the whole heaven,
And His lightning to the ends of the earth.
4 "After it, His voice roars;
He thunders with the voice of His majesty,
And He does not restrain
His lightning [against His adversaries] when His voice is heard.
5 "God thunders marvelously with His voice;
He does great things which we cannot comprehend.
6 "For He says to the snow, 'Fall on the earth';
And [He speaks] to the showers and to the downpour [of His mighty rains], 'Be strong.'
7 "God seals (brings to a standstill, stops) [by severe weather] the hand of every man,
That all men [whom He has made] may know His work [that is, His sovereign power and their subjection to it].
8 "Then the beast goes into its lair
And remains in its hiding place.
9 "Out of its chamber comes the storm,
And cold from the north wind.
10 "Ice is made by the breath of God,
And the expanse of the waters is frozen. [Ps 147:17, 18]
11 "He loads the thick cloud with moisture;
He disperses the cloud of His lightning.
12 "Its direction is turned around by His guidance,
That it may do whatever He commands it
On the face of the inhabited earth.
13 "Whether [it be] for correction, or for His earth [generally]
Or for [His] mercy *and* lovingkindness, He causes it to happen. [Ex 9:18, 23; 1 Sam 12:18, 19]

14 "Listen to this, Job;
Stand still and consider the wonders of God.
15 "Do you know how God establishes *and* commands them,
And makes the lightning of His [storm] cloud shine?
16 "Do you know about the layers of thick clouds [and how they are balanced and poised in the heavens],
The wonderful works of Him who is perfect in knowledge,
17 You whose garments are hot,
When He quiets the earth [in sultry summer] with the [oppressive] south wind?
18 "Can you, with Him, spread out the sky,
Strong as a molten mirror?
19 "Tell us [Job] what words [of man] shall we say to such a Being;

37:7 *seals (brings to a standstill, stops) [by severe weather] the hand of every man.* God uses the winter storm to stop man so that he cannot work, but instead may recognize the work of God.
37:12 *guidance.* This is a nautical term which literally means "steerings" or "rope-pullings" (Pr 15) and portrays God as the wise Captain who skillfully charts the course for the clouds, which respond obediently to His hand at the helm.
37:18 *Strong as a molten mirror.* Ancient mirrors were firm and unbreakable because they were made of polished bronze.

32 Ps 147:8 **33** 1Ki 18:41 **CHAPTER 37** **4** Ps 29:3 **5** Job 5:9 **6** Ps 147:16 **7** Ps 109:27 **8** Ps 104:22 **10** Ps 147:17 **12** Ps 148:8 **13** Ex 9:18; Job 38:26; 2Sa 21:10; 1Ki 18:45 **14** Ps 111:2 **16** Job 36:29; Job 36:4 **18** Ge 1:6; Isa 44:24

We cannot state *our case* because
of darkness [that is, our
ignorance in the presence of the
unsearchable God].
20 "So shall it be told Him that I wish
to speak?
Or should a man say that he would
be swallowed up [and destroyed
by God]?

21 "Now people cannot look at the
light when it is bright in the
skies [without being blinded],
When the wind has passed and
cleared them.
22 "Out of the north comes golden
splendor [and people can hardly
look on it];
Around God is awesome splendor
and majesty [far too glorious for
man's eyes].
23 "The Almighty—we cannot find
Him;
He is exalted in power
And He will not do violence to [nor
disregard] justice and abundant
righteousness. [1 Tim 6:16]
24 "Men therefore fear Him;
He does not regard *nor* respect
any who are wise in heart [in
their own understanding and
conceit]." [Matt 10:28]

God Speaks Now to Job

38 THEN THE LORD answered Job
out of the whirlwind and said,
2 "Who is this that darkens counsel
[questioning my authority and
wisdom]
By words without knowledge?
[Job 35:16]
3 "Now gird up your loins like a man,
And I will ask you, and you
instruct Me!
4 "Where were you when I laid the
foundation of the earth?
Tell *Me*, if you know *and* have
understanding.
5 "Who determined the
measurements [of the earth], if
you know?
Or who stretched the [measuring]
line on it?
6 "On what were its foundations
fastened?
Or who laid its cornerstone,
7 When the morning stars sang
together
And all the sons of God (angels)
shouted for joy?

8 "Or who enclosed the sea with
doors
When it burst forth and went out
of the womb;
9 When I made the clouds its garment
And thick darkness its swaddling
band,
10 And marked for it My [appointed]
boundary
And set bars and doors [defining
the shorelines], [Jer 5:22]
11 And said, 'This far you shall come,
but no farther;
And here your proud waves shall
stop'? [Ps 89:9; 93:4]

God's Mighty Power

12 "*Since* your days began, have you
ever commanded the morning,
And caused the dawn to know its
place,

37:24 *nor respect . . . wise in heart.* Even though Elihu had claimed earlier to be one who "is perfect in knowledge" (36:4), he knew that God does not give preferential treatment, even to the wise.

38:2 *words without knowledge.* The theme of the first speech of the Lord is given here. Job did not know what he was talking about. God quite quickly points out that there is a wide gap in understanding between God and man. God was not saying that Job had sinned in the way that his friends had accused him, but He was saying that Job had been presumptuous with his superficial knowledge of divine things. Job, along with his friends, had to learn that suffering may serve a purpose known only to God. In that case, a follower of God will submit even to loss and trauma, without complaint, for the glory of God.

38:10 *My [appointed] boundary.* If God controls the sea and places boundaries on it, He can place boundaries on anything else that will affect mankind.

23 1Ti 6:16; Job 36:5 **24** Mt 10:28; Mt 11:25 **CHAPTER 38** **1** Ex 19:16 **2** Job 34:35; 1Ti 1:7 **3** Job 40:7 **4** Ps 104:5; Pr 8:29 **7** Job 1:6 **8** Ge 1:9 **10** Job 26:10 **11** Ps 89:9 **12** Ps 148:5

13 So that light may take hold of the
corners of the earth
And shake the wickedness out of it?
14 "The earth is changed like clay
into which a seal is pressed;
And the things [of the earth]
stand out like a [multi-colored]
garment.
15 "Their light is withheld from the
wicked,
And the uplifted arm is broken.
16 "Have you entered *and* explored
the springs of the sea
Or [have you] walked in the
recesses of the deep?
17 "Have the gates of death been
revealed to you,
Or have you seen the gates of deep
darkness?
18 "Have you understood the expanse
of the earth?
Tell *Me*, if you know all this.
19 "Where is the way *where* light
dwells?
And as for darkness, where is its
place,
20 That you may take it to its territory
And that you may know the paths
to its house?
21 "You [must] know, since you were
born then,
And because you are so extremely
old!
22 "Have you entered the storehouses
of the snow,
Or have you seen the storehouses
of the hail,
23 Which I have reserved for the time
of trouble,
For the day of battle and war?
[Ex 9:18; Josh 10:11; Is 30:30;
Rev 16:21]
24 "Where is the way that the light is
distributed,
Or the east wind scattered over the
earth?
25 "Who has prepared a channel for the
torrents of rain *and* for the flood,
Or a path for the thunderbolt,
26 To bring rain on the uninhabited
land,
And on the desert where no man
lives,
27 To satisfy the barren and desolate
ground
And to make the seeds of grass to
sprout?
28 "Has the rain a father?
Or who has begotten the drops
of dew?
29 "Out of whose womb has come
the ice?
And the frost of heaven, who has
given it birth?
30 "Water becomes like stone [and
hides itself],
And the surface of the deep is
frozen *and* imprisoned.
31 "Can you bind the chains of [the
cluster of stars called] Pleiades,
Or loose the cords of [the
constellation] Orion?
32 "Can you lead forth a constellation
in its season,
And guide [the stars of] the Bear
with her sons?
33 "Do you know the ordinances of
the heavens,
Or [can you] establish their rule
over the earth?
34 "Can you lift up your voice to the
clouds,
So that an abundance of water will
cover you?
35 "Can you send forth lightnings
that they may go
And say to you, 'Here we are'?
36 "Who has put wisdom in the
innermost being [of man, or in
the layers of clouds]
Or given understanding to the
mind [of man, or to the heavenly
display]?

38:26 *where no man lives.* Though God utilizes meteorological elements to intervene in human affairs, He also uses them in areas that lie outside the human realm, for the sake of the land itself.

38:32 *the Bear.* This is a reference to the constellation known as Ursa Major, also called the Big Dipper or Great Bear.

13 Ps 104:35 **15** Job 18:5; Ps 10:15 **16** Ps 77:19 **17** Ps 9:13 **22** Ps 135:7 **23** Ex 9:18; Jos 10:11; Isa 30:30; Eze 13:11,13; Rev 16:21 **25** Job 28:26 **27** Ps 107:35 **28** Ps 147:8; Jer 14:22 **29** Ps 147:16 **30** Job 37:10 **31** Job 9:9; Am 5:8 **33** Jer 31:35 **36** Job 32:8; Ps 51:6; Ecc 2:26

37 "Who can count the clouds by
[earthly] wisdom,
Or pour out the water jars of the
heavens,
38 When the dust hardens into a mass
And the clods stick together
[because of the heat]?

39 "Can you [Job] hunt the prey for
the lion,
Or satisfy the appetite of the
young lions
40 When they crouch in their dens
And lie in wait in their lair?
41 "Who provides prey for the raven
When its young cry to God
And wander about without food?

God Speaks of Nature and Its Beings

39 "DO YOU know the time when
the wild goats of the rock give
birth [to their young]?
Do you observe the calving of the
deer?
2 "Can you count the months that
they carry offspring,
Or do you know the time when
they give birth?
3 "They kneel down, they bring
forth their young,
They cast out their labor pains.
4 "Their young ones become strong,
they grow up in the open field;
They leave and do not return to
them.

5 "Who sent out the wild donkey
free [from dependence on man]?
And who has loosed the bonds of
the wild donkey [to survive in
the wild],
6 To whom I gave the wilderness as
his home
And the salt land as his dwelling
place?
7 "He scorns the tumult of the city,
And does not hear the shouting of
the taskmaster.
8 "He explores the mountains as his
pasture
And searches after every green
thing.
9 "Will the wild ox be willing to
serve you,
Or remain beside your manger at
night?
10 "Can you bind the wild ox with
a harness [to the plow] in the
furrow?
Or will he plow the valleys for you?
11 "Will you trust him because his
strength is great
And leave your labor to him?
12 "Will you have faith *and* depend
on him to return your grain
And gather it from your threshing
floor?

13 "The [flightless] wings of the
ostrich wave joyously;
With the pinion (shackles, fetters)
and plumage of love,
14 For she leaves her eggs on the
ground
And warms them in the dust,
15 Forgetting that a foot may crush
them,
Or that the wild beast may trample
them.
16 "She treats her young cruelly, as if
they were not hers;
Though her labor is in vain
because she is unconcerned [for
the safety of her brood],
17 For God has made her forget
wisdom,
And has not given her a share of
understanding.
18 "Yet when she lifts herself on high,
[So swift is she that] she laughs at
the horse and his rider.

19 "Have you given the horse his
might?
Have you clothed his neck with
quivering *and* a shaking mane?

39:1 *Do you know.* God continues His probing of Job. He has shown His control of the earth and seas, the elements and the heavens, and now He shows the splendor and mysteries of the wild forces of nature, which are also all in God's control.

39:5 *loosed the bonds of the wild donkey.* God shows his compassion even for beasts of burden. This contrasts sharply with Job's complaints about God not noticing the oppression by the wicked (24:1 – 12).

39 Ps 104:21; 145:15 **41** Ps 147:9; Mt 6:26 **CHAPTER 39** **1** Ps 29:9 **6** Job 24:5; Jer 2:24; Hos 8:9 **9** Nu 23:22; Dt 33:17 **16** La 4:3 **17** Job 35:11

20 "Have you [Job] made him leap
like a locust?
The majesty of his snorting
[nostrils] is terrible.
21 "He paws in the valley and rejoices
in his strength;
He goes out to meet the weapons
[of armed men].
22 "He laughs at fear and is not
dismayed;
And [in battle] he does not turn
back from the sword.
23 "The quiver rattles against him,
[As do] the flashing spear and the
lance [of his rider].
24 "With fierceness and rage he races
to devour the ground,
And he does not stand still at the
sound of the [war] trumpet.
25 "As often as the trumpet sounds he
says, 'Aha!'
And he smells the battle from far
away,
And *senses* the thunder of the
captains and the war cry.

26 "Is it by your understanding that
the hawk soars,
Stretching his wings toward the
south [as winter approaches]?
27 "Is it at your command that the
eagle mounts up
And makes his nest on high [in an
inaccessible place]?
28 "On the cliff he dwells and
remains [securely],
Upon the point of the rock and the
inaccessible stronghold.
29 "From there he spies out the prey;
His eyes see it from far away.
30 "His young ones suck up blood;
And where the slain are, there is he."

Job: What Can I Say?

40 THEN THE LORD said to Job,
2 "Will the faultfinder contend with
the Almighty?
Let him who disputes with God
answer it."

3 Then Job replied to the LORD and
said,

4 "Behold, I am of little importance
and contemptible; what can I
reply to You?
I lay my hand on my mouth.
[Ezra 9:6; Ps 51:4]
5 "I have spoken once, but I will not
reply again—
Indeed, twice [I have answered],
and I will add nothing further."

God Questions Job

6 Then the LORD answered Job out of
the whirlwind, saying,

7 "Now gird up your loins (prepare
yourself) like a man,
And I will ask you, and you
instruct Me.
8 "Will you really annul My
judgment *and* set it aside as
void?
Will you condemn Me [your God]
that you may [appear to] be
righteous *and* justified?
9 "Have you an arm like God,
And can you thunder with a voice
like His?

10 "Adorn yourself with eminence
and dignity [since you question
the Almighty],
And array yourself with honor and
majesty.
11 "Pour out the overflowings of your
wrath,
And look at everyone who is proud
and make him low.
12 Look at everyone who is proud,
and humble him,
And [if you are so able] tread down
the wicked where they stand.
13 "[Crush and] hide them in the dust
together;

39:30 *where the slain are, there is he.* The animals that feed on the blood of the slain prevent the spread of disease. This too, is part of God's intricate plan.
40:8 *condemn Me [your God] that you may [appear to] be righteous.* Because Job had been arguing against the inflexible retribution dogma, which views suffering as God's punishment for sin, Job had to condemn God in order to maintain his own innocence.

21 Jer 8:6 **27** Jer 49:16; Ob 4 **30** Mt 24:28; Lk 17:37 **CHAPTER 40** **2** Job 33:13 **4** Ezr 9:6; Job 42:6; Ps 51:4; Job 29:9; Ps 39:9 **6** Job 38:1 **7** Job 38:3; Job 42:4 **8** Ps 51:4; Ro 3:4 **9** Job 37:4; Ps 29:3,4 **10** Ps 93:1; 104:1 **12** Isa 2:12; Da 4:37

Shut them up in the hidden place
[the house of death].
14 "[If you can do all this, Job,
proving your divine power] then
I [God] will also praise you *and*
acknowledge
That your own right hand can
save you.

God's Power Shown in Creatures

15 "Behold now, Behemoth, which I
created as well as you;
He eats grass like an ox.
16 "See now, his strength is in his loins
And his power is in the muscles
and sinews of his belly.
17 "He sways his tail like a cedar;
The tendons of his thighs are twisted
and knit together [like a rope].
18 "His bones are tubes of bronze;
His limbs are like bars of iron.

19 "He is the first [in magnitude and
power] of the works of God;
[Only] He who made him can bring
near His sword [to master him].
20 "Surely the mountains bring him
food,
And all the wild animals play there.
21 "He lies down under the lotus
plants,
In the hidden shelter of the reeds
in the marsh.
22 "The lotus plants cover him with
their shade;
The willows of the brook surround
him.
23 "If a river rages *and* overflows, he
does not tremble;
He is confident, though the Jordan
[River] swells and rushes
against his mouth.
24 "Can anyone capture him when he
is on watch,
Or pierce his nose with barbs [to
trap him]?

God's Power Shown in Creatures

41 "CAN YOU draw out
Leviathan with a fishhook?
Or press down his tongue with a
cord?
2 "Can you put a rope [made] of
rushes into his nose
Or pierce his jaw through with a
hook?
3 "Will he make many supplications
to you [begging to be spared]?
Or will he speak soft words to
you [to coax you to treat him
kindly]?
4 "Will he make a covenant *or* an
arrangement with you?
Will you take him for your servant
forever?
5 "Will you play with him as with a
bird?
Or will you bind him [and put him
on a leash] for your maidens?
6 "Will traders bargain over him?
Will they divide him up among the
merchants?
7 "Can you fill his skin with
harpoons,
Or his head with fishing spears?
8 "Lay your hand on him;
Remember the battle [with him];
you will not do such [an ill-
advised thing] again!
9 "Behold, his [assailant's] hope
and expectation [of defeating
Leviathan] is false;
Will not one be overwhelmed even
at the sight of him?
10 "No one is so fierce [and
foolhardy] that he dares to stir
up Leviathan;
Who then is he who can stand
before Me [or dares to contend
with Me, the beast's creator]?
11 "Who has first given to Me that I
should repay him?

40:15 *Behemoth.* Suggestions for the identity of this beast include the elephant, the hippopotamus, or a dinosaur. The name means "great beast," and the description most nearly fits a dinosaur, as neither the elephant nor the hippo has a tail like a cedar.

41:1 *Leviathan.* The identity of Leviathan, which is a transliteration for the Hebrew word "sea monster," or "sea serpent," is disputed. His description (vv. 12 – 18) sounds like the traditional dragon. He is a sea animal, an uncontrollable giant.

20 Ps 104:14 **CHAPTER 41** **1** Ps 104:26; Isa 27:1 **2** Isa 37:29 **11** Ro 11:35; Ex 19:5; Dt 10:14; Ps 24:1; 50:12; 1Co 10:26,28

Whatever is under the whole
heaven is Mine. [Who can
have a claim against Me who
made the unmastered beast?]
[Rom 11:35]

12 "I will not keep silence concerning
his limbs,
Nor his mighty strength, nor his
orderly frame.
13 "Who can penetrate *or* strip off his
outer armor?
Who can come to his jaws with a
double bridle?
14 "Who can open the doors (jaws) of
his face?
Around his [open jaws and] teeth
there is terror.
15 "His strong scales are his pride,
Bound together as with a tight
seal.
16 "One is so near to another
That no air can come between
them.
17 "They are joined one to another;
They stick together and cannot be
separated.
18 "His sneezes flash forth light,
And his eyes are like the [reddish]
eyelids of the dawn.
19 "Out of his mouth go burning
torches,
And sparks of fire leap out.
20 "Out of his nostrils smoke goes
forth
As from a boiling pot and [as
from] *burning* rushes.
21 "His breath kindles coals,
And a flame goes forth from his
mouth.
22 "In Leviathan's neck resides
strength,
And dismay *and* terror dance
before him.
23 "The folds of his flesh are joined
together,
Firm on him and immobile [when
he moves].
24 "His heart is as hard as a stone,
Indeed, as solid as a lower
millstone.
25 "When he raises himself up, the
mighty are afraid;
Because of the crashing they are
bewildered.
26 "The sword that reaches him
cannot avail,
Nor [does] the spear, the dart, or
the javelin.
27 "He considers iron as straw,
Bronze as rotten wood.
28 "The arrow cannot make him flee;
Slingstones are treated as stubble
by him.
29 "Clubs [also] are regarded as
stubble;
He laughs at the rushing *and* the
rattling of the javelin.
30 "His underparts are like sharp
pieces of broken pottery;
He moves across *and* spreads out
[grooves] like a threshing sledge
on the mire (muddy river banks).
31 "He makes the deep water boil like
a pot;
He makes the sea like a [foaming]
pot of ointment.
32 "Behind him he makes a shining
wake;
One would think the deep to be
gray-haired [with foam].
33 "Upon earth there is nothing like
him—no equal exists,
A creature made without fear.
34 "He looks on everything that is
high [without terror];
He is monarch over all the sons
of pride. [And now, Job, who
are you who does not dare to
disturb the beast, yet who dares
resist Me, the beast's creator?
Everything under the heavens is
Mine; therefore, who can have a
claim against God?]"

Job's Confession

42 THEN JOB answered the LORD
and said,
2 "I know that You can do all things,
And that no thought *or* purpose of
Yours can be restrained.
3 "[You said to me] 'Who is this that
darkens *and* obscures counsel
[by words] without knowledge?'
Therefore [I now see] I have
[rashly] uttered that which I did
not understand,
Things too wonderful for me,
which I did not know. [Job 38:2]

CHAPTER 42 **2** Ge 18:14; Mt 19:26; Mk 10:27; 14:36; Lk 18:27 **3** Job 38:2; Ps 40:5; 131:1; 139:6

4 'Hear, please, and I will speak;
I will ask You, and You instruct
[and answer] me.'
5 "I had heard of You [only] by the
hearing of the ear,
But now my [spiritual] eye sees
You.
6 "Therefore I retract [my words and
hate myself]
And I repent in dust and ashes."

God Displeased with Job's Friends

7 It came about that after the LORD had spoken these words to Job, that the LORD said to Eliphaz the Temanite, "My wrath is kindled against you and against your two friends, for you have not spoken of Me what is right, as My servant Job has.

8 "Now therefore, take for yourselves seven bulls and seven rams, and go to My servant Job, and offer up a burnt offering for yourselves, and My servant Job will pray for you. For I will accept him [and his prayer] so that I may not deal with you *according to your* folly, because you have not spoken of Me the thing that is right, as My servant Job has."

9 So Eliphaz the Temanite and Bildad the Shuhite and Zophar the Naamathite went and did as the LORD told them; and the LORD accepted Job's prayer.

God Restores Job's Fortunes

10 The LORD restored the fortunes of Job when he prayed for his friends, and the LORD gave Job twice as much as he had before. [Deut 30:1–3; Ps 126:1, 2]

11 Then all his brothers and sisters and all who had known him before came to him, and they ate bread with him in his house; and they consoled him and comforted him over all the [distressing] adversities that the LORD had brought on him. And each one gave him a piece of money, and each a ring of gold.

12 And the LORD blessed the latter days of Job more than his beginning; for he had 14,000 sheep, 6,000 camels, 1,000 yoke of oxen, and 1,000 female donkeys. [Job 1:3]

13 He had seven sons and three daughters.

14 And he called the name of the first [daughter] Jemimah, and the name of the second Keziah, and the name of the third Keren-happuch.

15 In all the land there were found no women so fair as the daughters of Job; and their father gave them an inheritance among their brothers.

16 After this, Job lived 140 years, and saw his sons and his grandsons, four generations.

17 So Job died, an old man and full of days. [James 5:11]

42:4 *instruct [and answer] me.* Job was completely done with his complaints of injustice. He knew that his presuppositions were wrong, and that he needed God's wisdom.

42:5 Conviction — Job was not convicted of a particular sin, but of too small a view of God. In the Bible, the revelation of the character and person of God is the criterion for proper self-evaluation (Isa 6:5). Job regretted that his trust in God had been so imperfect, for he now understood God in a new way.

42:6 *repent in dust and ashes.* Dust and ashes were a sign of mourning. Job could not retract more fully.

42:7 *spoken of Me . . . as My servant Job has.* Even though God had just shown Job his presumption, God still validated Job's doggedly held position that God had not brought suffering on him because of sin in his life.

42:10 *restored the fortunes of Job when he prayed.* Not only did God deal with Job's presumption and the wrong ideas of his friends, but He provided the perfect way to restore their relationship with each other, as well as with God.

4 Job 38:3; 40:7 **6** Ezr 9:6; Job 40:4 **8** Nu 23:1; Mt 5:24; Ge 20:17; Jas 5:15,16; 1Jn 5:16 **10** Ps 14:7; 126:1; Isa 40:2 **11** See Job 19:13 **12** Job 8:7; Jas 5:11; See Job 1:3 **13** Job 1:2 **16** Job 5:26; Pr 3:16 **17** Ge 25:8

THE

PSALMS

▸ **AUTHOR:** Seventy-five of the psalms in the book are designated as Davidic: 3–9; 11–32; 34–41; 51–65; 68–70; 86; 101; 103; 108–110; 122; 124; 131; 133; and 138–145. The New Testament tells us that the "anonymous" psalms 2 and 95 were also written by David. In addition to these, 12 are by Asaph, a priest who headed the service of music; ten are by the sons of Korah, a guild of singers and composers; two are by Solomon, Israel's most powerful king; one is by Moses; one by Heman, a wise man; and one is by Ethan, another wise man. The remaining fifty psalms are anonymous, but tradition attributes them to Ezra.

▸ **TIMES:** c. 1410–430 BC ▸ **KEY VERSE:** Ps 19:14

▸ **THEME:** A collection of songs that literally covers hundreds of years of Jewish history from the patriarchs down through the postexilic period, the Book of Psalms is practical and personal as well as scenic and magnificently beautiful. The Psalms teach us how to pray, how to grieve, how to rejoice, and how to worship. Any Christian who makes building a relationship with God a priority in his or her life will find great spiritual nourishment in the Psalms. It is the prayer book for all who believe in the God of the universe. Jesus used it as such, and so should we.

THE DESIGN AND MESSAGE OF THE PSALTER

The Psalms exhibit numerous structural features that contribute to their overall theme: instruction in the godly life under the reign of God

BOOK I

Ps 1–2 Introduction, framed by two *'ashre* ("Blessed is/are") declarations
- 1 Evokes instructions of *Torah* [Law] and *Ḥokmah* [Wisdom]
- 2 Evokes Former and Latter Prophets (Yahweh and his anointed, Israel's only hope in the turmoil of history)

Thus 1. The Psalter must be read in the context of the rest of the OT canon.
2. As the portal to the temple of the Psalter, these two psalms teach that those who would appropriate the prayers and praises of the Psalter must fit the profile of the framing declarations; their lives must be shaped by Law and godly Wisdom, and they must "take refuge" in Yahweh and his anointed—the two basic components of "the fear of Yahweh."

Ps 3–14

64 lines
- 3 Plea for deliverance from foes
- 4 Plea for relief in time of drought
- 5 Plea for deliverance from foes
- 6 Plea for healing
- 7 Plea for deliverance from foes
- **8 Praise of the Creator (the glory of God bestowed on humans)**

64 lines
- 9 Plea for deliverance from hostile nations
- 10 Plea for deliverance from the wicked
- 11 Trust in Yahweh's righteous rule
- 12 Plea for help in an ungodly time
- 13 Plea for deliverance from serious illness and enemies
- **14 The folly of humankind ("The LORD looks down . . . to see . . . All have turned away")**

Ps 15–24
- **15 Who has access to the temple?**
  - 16 Confession of trust in Yahweh
    - 17 Plea for deliverance from foes
      - 18 Royal praise for deliverance
        - **19 Yahweh's glory in Creation and Torah** (The summer sun moving across the face of the sky from east to west)
      - 20–21 Prayer for king's victory; praise for victory
    - 22 Plea for deliverance from foes
  - 23 Confession of trust in Yahweh
- **24 Who may ascend the holy hill?**

Ps 25–33

25 Alphabetic acrostic (22 verses long)
Prayer for covenant mercies
26 Prayer of a "blameless" person
27 Appeal against false accusers
"Be strong and take heart
and wait for the LORD."
28 Prayer of one going "down to the pit"
29 Praise of the King of creation
(The winter thunderstorm moving across the face of the sky from west to east)
30 Praise of one spared from going "down to the pit"
31 Appeal against false accusers
"Be strong and take heart,
all you who hope in the LORD."
32 Blessedness of a penitent person
33 Twenty-two verses long
Praise for God's good rule

Ps 34–37

34 Alphabetic acrostic
Instruction in godly wisdom
35 Appeal against malicious slanderers
36 Appeal against threats of godless, wicked people
37 Alphabetic acrostic
Instruction in godly wisdom

Ps 38–41

38 Prayer for relief from serious illness and enemies: a confession of sin
39 Prayer for relief from serious illness and enemies: a confession of sin
40 Prayer for relief from troubles (serious illness?) and enemies: a confession of sin
41 Prayer for relief from serious illness and enemies: a confession of sin
40:4 *'Ashre* "Blessed is the one who trusts in the LORD."
41:1 *'Ashre* "Blessed are those who have regard for the weak."

BOOK II

Ps 42–45 Three prayers with a royal psalm attached (see Ps 69–72)

42 Prayer of individual ("Why have you forgotten me" in the face of the oppression of enemies?)
43 Continuation of Ps 42
44 Prayer of the community ("Why do you hide your face and forget our . . . oppression?")
45 Song in praise of the king on a day of his glory (wedding to a foreign princess)
(" . . . ride forth . . . in the cause of truth, humility and justice")
("Your throne . . . will last for ever and ever")

Ps 46–48 In celebration of the security of Zion

46 Zion's security
47 Zion's Great King triumphant over all nations
48 Zion's security

Ps 49–53 The proper posture before God

49 The folly of those who "trust in their wealth and boast of their great riches"
50 God calls his people to account
51 Humble prayer for forgiveness and cleansing
52 The folly of the one who "trusted in his great wealth" and those who "boast of evil"
53 The folly of those who live as if there is no God (repeat of Ps 14)

Ps 54–60 Seven prayers at the center of Book II

54 Prayer of individual for help against enemies
55 Prayer for help: a conspiracy <u>in Jerusalem</u> ("they prowl about on its walls")
("words. . .are drawn **swords**")
56 Prayer for help against enemies
57 Prayer for deliverance from enemies
("tongues are sharp **swords**")
58 Prayer for the heavenly Judge to set right what human rulers have not
59 Prayer for help: enemies <u>surround Jerusalem</u> ("They . . . prowl about the city")
("spew . . . words from their lips . . . sharp as **swords**")
60 Prayer of community for help after suffering devastating defeat
("You have rejected us" and "no longer go out with our armies")

Ps 61–64 Four royal prayers with interweaving themes

61 Appeal for restoration to God's presence ("rock," "refuge," "strong tower," "in the shelter of your wings")
62 Appeal for deliverance from arrogant foes ("rock," "fortress," "mighty rock," "refuge"; "You reward everyone according to what they have done")
63 Appeal for God's refreshing presence when threatened by enemies ("sing in the shadow of your wings"; "Those who want to kill me . . . will go down to the depths of the earth")
64 Appeal for God's protection against conspirators ("The righteous will rejoice in the LORD and will take refuge in him")

Ps 65–68 God's "awesome and righteous deeds" evoke the praise of "all...the earth"

65 God's blessing the earth into fruitfulness is highlighted ("the hope of all the ends of the earth")
66 God's saving acts on behalf of Israel are highlighted ("Shout for joy to God, all the earth!")
67 God's blessing the earth into fruitfulness is highlighted ("all the peoples praise . . . all the ends of the earth . . . fear")
68 God's saving acts in behalf of Israel are highlighted ("kings . . . bring you gifts . . . Sing to God, you kingdoms of the earth")

Ps 69–72 Three prayers with a royal psalm attached (see Ps 42–45)

69 A king's prayer for deliverance when under vicious attack
70 A short prayer (repeat of Ps 40; see introduction to Ps 71)
71 A king's prayer for God's help in old age when under attack
72 A prayer that the king be specially gifted to rule justly
("... endure . . . through all generations")
("... all nations . . . be blessed through him")

BOOK III

Made up of three groups of six psalms (73–78), five psalms (79–83), six psalms (84–89)

Ps 73–78

73 Instruction based on individual experience
74 Communal prayer: God has "rejected" his people
75 Praise to God: His "Name is near," and he cuts off the horns of the wicked but causes the "horns of the righteous" to be "lifted up"
76 Celebration: God's "name is great" in Israel; he "breaks the spirit of [enemy] rulers"
77 Individual prayer: God has rejected him
78 Instruction based on communal experience

Ps 79–83

79 Communal prayer: when invaded by fierce enemies
80 Prayer for God to restore his people after they have been ravaged by enemies
81 Exhortation to Israel: "If Israel would only follow my ways, how quickly I would subdue their enemies"
82 Prayer for God to judge the wicked rulers of the earth
83 Communal prayer: when attacked by coalition of enemies

Ps 84–89

84 Expression of yearning for "the courts of the LORD" and prayer for God to "look with favor" on "our shield," "your anointed"

85 Prayer for God to "restore" his people from some situation of distress
86 Individual prayer for God's help when under attack by enemies
87 Song celebrating God's special love for Zion and care for its citizens
88 Individual prayer for God to remove his wrath and deliver from death
89 Prayer for God to rescue his people, to remember his covenant with David

BOOKS IV AND V

Ps 90–100 Eleven psalms framed by "Lord [Adonai] . . . our dwelling place throughout all generations" (90:1) and "The Lord [Yahweh] . . . his love . . . faithfulness continues through all generations" (100:5)

90 Plaintive prayer concerning the mortality of those who have long had the Lord as their "dwelling place"
91 Assurances for those who make the Most High their "dwelling" place (v. 9; cf. v. 1): "With long life I will satisfy" them (v. 16)
92 Celebration of Yahweh's righteous rule and its result (what the "senseless. . . do not know"): "evildoers. . . will be destroyed forever" but "the righteous. . . will still bear fruit in old age"
93 Celebration of the invincible reign of Yahweh
94 Appeal to Yahweh to deal judicially with those who perpetrate injustices and oppression: "Take notice, you senseless ones among the people"
95 Call for the delivered covenant community to joyfully worship Yahweh their God (and warning not to repeat earlier rebelliousness)
96 Call to all nations to worshipfully celebrate the universal reign of Yahweh
97 Joyful celebration of Yahweh's universal reign—whose throne is founded on "righteousness and justice"
98 Call to all nations to worshipfully praise Yahweh for his saving acts in behalf of Israel
99 Joyful celebration of Yahweh's universal reign, especially for what he has done for Israel
100 Concluding exhortation to worshipfully praise Yahweh, Israel's Maker and "good" Shepherd-King

Ps 101–110 A "little psalter" framed by two royal psalms

101 A royal pledge to reign righteously
102 Individual lament
103 Praise of Yahweh for his "great. . . love"
104 Praise of Yahweh the Creator
105 Recital of Israel's saving history
106 Recital of Israel's history of rebellion
107 Call for praise of Yahweh who hears cries of distress
108 Praise of Yahweh for his "great. . . love"
109 Individual lament
110 Prophecies concerning the Messianic King-Priest

Ps 111–119 The "Egyptian Hallel" framed by 111/112 and 119

111/112 Formal and thematic twins: Righteous God (111:3) and God-fearing persons, "who find great delight in his [God's] commands" (112:1)

Egyptian Hallel
113
114
115
116
117
118
Psalms used in Israel's great annual festivals

119 Prayer of one who finds "delight" in God's "commands" (v. 35)

Ps 120–137 Songs of ascents plus two appendices

120–134 The Songs of Ascents
135–136 Hymns traditionally associated by the Jews with the songs of ascents
137 Song of love for Zion by one returned from Babylonian exile (brings closure to the preceding collection)

Ps 138–145 Eight psalms assigned to David: prayers framed by praise

138 Praise of Yahweh: "When I called, you answered"; "May all the kings . . . praise you . . . for [your] glory"
139 Acknowledgment of total nakedness before the omniscient and omnipresent God
140–144 Five prayers for deliverance from:
140: evildoers, "the violent. . . the wicked"
141: evildoers
142: pursuers who "are too strong for me"
143: enemies
144: foreigners
145 (Acrostic) Praise of Yahweh, "the King": who "is near to all who call on him"; "All your works . . . tell of the glory of your kingdom . . . so that all . . . may know of . . . the glorious splendor of your kingdom"

Ps 146–150 Five Hallelujah psalms that serve as the concluding doxology for the entire Psalter (see Introduction: Collection, Arrangement and Date)

MESSIANIC PSALMS

PSALM	SUBJECT	MESSIANIC	NT PROOF	FURTHER (CONTEXTUAL) EVIDENCE
Christ spoken of in the third person				
Ps 8	Humiliation and glory	Ps 8:4b–8	Heb 2:5–10; 1Co 15:27	All things are under their feet (Ps 8:6). In him humanity's role as ruler over other creatures comes to fulfillment.
Ps 72	Rule	Ps 72:6–17	Heb 2:5–10; 1Co 15:27	Transition to the future (Ps 72:5). His reign is forever (v. 7). Territory (v. 8). All worship him (vv. 9–11).
Ps 89	Of David	Ps 89:3–4, 28–29, 34–36	Ac 2:30	David's line is eternal (Ps 89:4, 29, 36–37).
Ps 109	Judas cursed	Ps 109:6–19	Ac 1:16–20	Adversaries (pl.) in Ps 109:4–5 shift in v. 6 to one preeminent betrayer. The plural is resumed in v. 20.
Ps 132	Of David	Ps 132:11–12	Ac 2:30	David's line is eternal (Ps 132:12).
Christ addressed in the second person				
Ps 45	Throne forever	Ps 45:6–7	Heb 1:8–9	He is deity (Ps 45:6), yet not the Father (Ps 45:7).
Ps 102	Eternity	Ps 102:25–27	Heb 1:10–12	Address to Yahweh (Ps 102:1–22); to El, a change (Ps 102:24), applied to Christ.
Ps 110	Ascension and priesthood	Ps 110:1–7	Mt 22:43–45; Ac 2:33–35; Heb 1:13; 5:6–10; 6:20; 7:24	He is David's Lord (Ps 110:1). Eternal priest (Ps 110:4).
Christ speaks in the first person				
Ps 2	Kiss the Son	Ps 2:1–11	Ac 4:25–28; 13:33; Heb 1:5; 5:5	The speaker is God's only Son (Ps 2:7).
Ps 16	No decay	Ps 16:10	Ac 2:24–31; 13:35–37	He possesses more than David — no decay (Ps 16:10).
Ps 22	Passion	Ps 22:1–31	Mt 27:35–46; Jn 19:23–25; Heb 2:12	Not seeing decay cannot apply to David; nor pierced hands and feet (Ps 22:16); nor lots cast for his garments (Ps 22:18).
Ps 40	Incarnation	Ps 40:6–8	Heb 10:5–10	Praises in Ps 40:1–5 are interrupted by a descriptive section (vv. 6–8). David did not always delight to do God's will, but Christ did (v. 8).
Ps 69	Judas cursed	Ps 69:25	Ac 1:16–20	The specific "deserted" place lies between generalizations in Ps 69:24 and 26, narrowed down to Judas.

BOOK ONE

Psalm 1

The Righteous and the Wicked Contrasted.

[1]BLESSED [fortunate, prosperous, and favored by God] is the man who does not walk in the counsel of the wicked [following their advice and example],
Nor stand in the path of sinners,
Nor sit [down to rest] in the seat of scoffers (ridiculers).
[2]But his delight is in the law of the LORD,
And on His law [His precepts and teachings] he [habitually] meditates day and night. [Rom 13:8–10; Gal 3:1–29; 2 Tim 3:16]
[3]And he will be like a tree *firmly* planted [and fed] by streams of water,
Which yields its fruit in its season;
Its leaf does not wither;
And in whatever he does, he prospers [and comes to maturity]. [Jer 17:7, 8]
[4]The wicked [those who live in disobedience to God's law] are not so,
But they are like the chaff [worthless and without substance] which the wind blows away.
[5]Therefore the wicked will not stand [unpunished] in the judgment,
Nor sinners in the assembly of the righteous.
[6]For the LORD knows *and* fully approves the way of the righteous,
But the way of the wicked shall perish.

Psalm 2

The Reign of the LORD's Anointed.

[1]WHY ARE the nations in an uproar [in turmoil against God],
And why do the people devise a vain *and* hopeless plot?
[2]The kings of the earth take their stand;
And the rulers take counsel together

1:1 Success — Psalm 1 sets the tone for the whole Book of Psalms. It contrasts the ways of life of the blessed man and the wicked man. Being blessed or successful is not a once for all time, dramatic event, but rather a lifetime of choosing to follow God and His commandments. Success happens when we move from grudging acceptance to enthusiastic delight in absorbing and then following God's laws and mandates. Nothing provides more resources. No motivational speakers will set us on a better course. No degrees will give us more of a life-changing education.

At first glance this kind of lifestyle may not look like the most exciting way to live. We can go through life, plodding along this way, without anybody even noticing. It's a lifestyle that doesn't fill up trophy cases or result in monuments being created. It can, however, end with "Well done, thou good and faithful servant" from our Lord. The excitement is in the results of being in a position to help family and friends grow. Success comes from being in a relationship with God that means fruitfulness by His definition.

1:1 ***Blessed [fortunate, prosperous, and favored by God] is the man.*** Hebrew wisdom literature and poetry is filled with descriptions of two favorite characters: "the righteous man" and "wisdom" (often personified as "she"). In this context, "the righteous man" is a literary tool used to represent those who love and desire to please God, rather than an actual individual.
1:2 ***meditates.*** Biblical meditation is focusing the mind on Scripture or the attributes and actions of God.
1:3 ***he prospers.*** This is not a guarantee of the future financial worth of the righteous; rather, the righteous person is always useful and productive to the Lord.
1:6 ***knows and fully approves the way.*** The verb "knows" in this context refers not just to God's awareness, but to an intimate, personal knowledge (101:4). God is intimately involved with the way of the righteous, but has no connection with the way of the ungodly, except in judgment (146:9).
2:1 ***Why are the nations in an uproar.*** David, the human author of this psalm (Ac 4:24–26), was

PSALM 1 **1** Pr 4:14; Ps 26:4; Jer 15:17 **2** Ps 119:35; Jos 1:8; Ps 119:1 **3** Jer 17:8; Eze 47:12; Ge 39:3; Isa 3:10 **4** Job 21:18; Isa 17:13 **6** Ps 37:18; 2Ti 2:19 **PSALM 2** **1** Ac 4:25 **2** Jn 1:41

Against the LORD and His
Anointed (the Davidic King, the
Messiah, the Christ), saying,
[Acts 4:25–27]
3 "Let us break apart their [divine]
bands [of restraint]
And cast away their cords [of
control] from us."

4 He who sits [enthroned] in the
heavens laughs [at their
rebellion];
The [Sovereign] Lord scoffs at
them [and in supreme contempt
He mocks them].
5 Then He will speak to them in His
[profound] anger
And terrify them with His
displeasure, saying,
6 "Yet as for Me, I have anointed *and*
firmly installed My King
Upon Zion, My holy mountain."

7 "I will declare the decree of the
LORD:
He said to Me, 'You are My Son;
This day [I proclaim] I have
begotten You. [2 Sam 7:14;
Heb 1:5; 3:5, 6; 2 Pet 1:17, 18]
8 'Ask of Me, and I will assuredly
give [You] the nations as Your
inheritance,
And the ends of the earth as Your
possession.
9 'You shall break them with a rod
of iron;
You shall shatter them [in pieces]
like earthenware.' " [Rev 12:5;
19:15]

10 Now therefore, O kings, act
wisely;
Be instructed *and* take warning,
O leaders (judges, rulers) of the
earth.
11 Worship the LORD *and* serve
Him with reverence [with awe-
inspired fear and submissive
wonder];
Rejoice [yet do so] with trembling.
12 Kiss (pay respect to) the Son, so
that He does not become angry,
and you perish in the way,
For His wrath may soon be
kindled *and* set aflame.
How blessed [fortunate, prosperous,
and favored by God] are all those
who take refuge in Him!

Psalm 3

Morning Prayer of Trust in God.

A Psalm of David.
When he fled from Absalom his son.

1 O LORD, how my enemies have
increased!
Many are rising up against me.
2 Many are saying of me,
"There is no help [no salvation] for
him in God." *Selah.*

3 But You, O LORD, are a shield for
me,
My glory [and my honor], and the
One who lifts my head.
4 With my voice I was crying to the
LORD,
And He answered me from His
holy mountain. *Selah.*
5 I lay down and slept [safely];
I awakened, for the LORD sustains
me.
6 I will not be intimidated *or* afraid
of the ten thousands
Who have set themselves against
me all around.

---

probably referring to the nations that confronted him and his legitimate heirs to the throne of Israel. But the Davidic kings were mere shadows of the coming great King, the Savior Jesus. Consequently, in a larger sense, this verse refers to any attack on Jesus and His divine kingdom. This assault occurred in its most dramatic form at the cross, but resistance to God's kingdom has continued.
2:12 *Kiss (pay respect to) the Son.* All peoples are presented with a clear choice. They can either love and respect the Lord's anointed, and so experience His great blessing, or they can refuse to submit, and incur God's wrath.
3 title *When he fled from Absalom.* The history behind this psalm is recorded in 1 Samuel 15.
3:2 *Selah.* This is probably a literary or musical term, perhaps indicating a pause in the lyrics for a musical interlude.

3 Lk 19:14 **4** Ps 37:13; Pr 1:26 **6** 2Sa 5:7 **7** Ac 13:33 **8** Ps 22:27 **9** Ps 89:23; Rev 2:27 **11** Heb 12:28; Php 2:12 **12** Jn 5:23; Rev 6:16; Ps 34:8; Isa 30:18; Ro 9:33 **PSALM 3** **Title** 2Sa 15–18 **1** 2Sa 15:12 **2** Ps 71:11 **3** Ps 28:7; Ps 27:6 **4** Ps 34:4; Ps 2:6 **5** Lev 26:6; Pr 3:24 **6** Ps 27:3

TYPES OF HEBREW PARALLELISM

TYPE	CHARACTERISTIC	EXAMPLE
I. Synonymous	Repetition of same thought	
Identical	Each element is synonymous	Ps 24:1 The earth is the Lord's, and everything in it, the world, and all who live in it.
Similar	Each element is similar	Ps 19:2 Day after day they pour forth speech; night after night they reveal knowledge.
Incomplete	Second element of previous line is repeated	Jer 17:9 The heart is deceitful above all things and beyond cure. Who can understand it?
Continued	Second element is repeated and built upon	Ps 24:5 They will receive blessing from the Lord, and vindication from God their Savior.
II. Antithetic	Parallel by contrast (by use of the opposite)	Ps 1:6 For the Lord watches over the way of the righteous, but the way of the wicked leads to destruction.
III. Synthetic	Building on a thought	
Completion	Completes a thought	Ps 2:6 I have installed my king on Zion, my holy mountain.
Comparison	Draws an analogy	Pr 15:17 Better a small serving of vegetables with love than a fattened calf with hatred.
Reason	Gives a reason	Pr 26:4 Do not answer a fool according to his folly, or you yourself will be just like him.
Conceptual	Use of theme element	Ps 1:1 Blessed is the one who does not walk in step with the wicked or stand in the way that sinners take or sit in the company of mockers.
IV. Climactic	Builds on same word or phrase	Ps 29:1 Ascribe to the Lord, you heavenly beings, ascribe to the Lord glory and strength.
V. Emblematic	Use of simile or metaphor	Ps 42:1 As the deer pants for streams of water, so my soul pants for you, my God. Pr 25:25 Like cold water to a weary soul is good news from a distant land.

[7]Arise, O LORD; save me, O my God!
For You have struck all my enemies on the cheek;
You have shattered the teeth of the wicked.
[8]Salvation belongs to the LORD;
May Your blessing be upon Your people. *Selah.*

Psalm 4

Evening Prayer of Trust in God.

To the Chief Musician; on stringed instruments. A Psalm of David.

[1]ANSWER ME when I call, O God of my righteousness!
You have freed me when I was hemmed in *and* relieved me when I was in distress;
Be gracious to me and hear [and respond to] my prayer.
[2]O sons of men, how long will my honor *and* glory be [turned into] shame?
How long will you [my enemies] love worthless (vain, futile) things and seek deception *and* lies? *Selah.*
[3]But know that the LORD has set apart for Himself [and dealt wonderfully with] the godly man [the one of honorable character and moral courage—the one who does right].
The LORD hears *and* responds when I call to Him.
[4]Tremble [with anger or fear], and do not sin;
Meditate in your heart upon your bed and be still [reflect on your sin and repent of your rebellion]. [Eph 4:26] *Selah.*
[5]Offer righteous sacrifices;
Trust [confidently] in the LORD.
[6]Many are saying, "Oh, that we might see some good!"
Lift up the light of Your face upon us, O LORD.
[7]You have put joy in my heart,
More than [others know] when their wheat and new wine have yielded abundantly.
[8]In peace [and with a tranquil heart] I will both lie down and sleep,
For You alone, O LORD, make me dwell in safety *and* confident trust.

Psalm 5

Prayer for Protection from the Wicked.

To the Chief Musician; on wind instruments. A Psalm of David.

[1]LISTEN TO my words, O LORD,
Consider my groaning *and* sighing.
[2]Heed the sound of my cry for help, my King and my God,
For to You I pray.
[3]In the morning, O LORD, You will hear my voice;
In the morning I will prepare [a prayer and a sacrifice] for You and watch *and* wait [for You to speak to my heart].
[4]For You are not a God who takes pleasure in wickedness;

3:7 *struck . . . on the cheek.* In the poetic imagery that David uses, his enemies are like powerful beasts whose strength is in their jaws and whose terror is in their teeth. God's strike at the source of their strength means that they are no longer a threat.

4:1 *O God of my righteousness.* This phrase can also be translated "O my righteous God." It has two meanings: only God is righteous, and all of a person's righteousness is found in Him alone.

4:4 *Tremble [with anger or fear], and do not sin.* These words are cited by Paul in the New Testament, translated "Be angry [at sin—at immorality, at injustice, at ungodly behavior], yet do not sin" (Eph 4:26). This is a good description of what righteous indignation should look like.

4:7 *their wheat and new wine.* The joy God gives transcends the joy of the harvest. Agricultural produce, the result of abundant rain on fertile soil, was a blessing of God on His people. But there is something greater than full barns and overflowing cisterns—the joy of God's presence.

7 Job 16:10; La 3:30 **8** Isa 43:11 **PSALM 4** **3** 2Ti 2:19; 2Pe 2:9 **4** Eph 4:26; Ps 77:6 **5** Dt 33:19; Ps 50:14; Ps 37:3 **6** Nu 6:26 **7** Isa 9:3 **8** Ps 3:5; Lev 25:18 **PSALM 5** **2** Ps 3:4 **3** Ps 30:5

No evil [person] dwells with You.
[5]The boastful *and* the arrogant will not stand in Your sight;
You hate all who do evil.
[6]You destroy those who tell lies;
The LORD detests *and* rejects the bloodthirsty and deceitful man.
[7]But as for me, I will enter Your house through the abundance of Your steadfast love *and* tender mercy;
At Your holy temple I will bow [obediently] in reverence for You.

[8]O LORD, lead me in Your righteousness because of my enemies;
Make Your way straight (direct, right) before me.
[9]For there is nothing trustworthy *or* reliable *or* truthful in what they say;
Their heart is destruction [just a treacherous chasm, a yawning gulf of lies].
Their throat is an open grave;
They [glibly] flatter with their [silken] tongue. [Rom 3:13]
[10]Hold them guilty, O God;
Let them fall by their own designs *and* councils!
Cast them out because of the abundance of their transgressions,
For they are mutinous *and* have rebelled against You.

[11]But let all who take refuge *and* put their trust in You rejoice,
Let them ever sing for joy;
Because You cover *and* shelter them,
Let those who love Your name be joyful *and* exult in You.
[12]For You, O LORD, bless the righteous man [the one who is in right standing with You];
You surround him with favor as with a shield.

Psalm 6

Prayer for Mercy in Time of Trouble.

To the Chief Musician; on stringed instruments, set [possibly] an octave below. A Psalm of David.

[1]O LORD, do not rebuke *or* punish me in Your anger,
Nor discipline me in Your wrath.
[2]Have mercy on me *and* be gracious to me, O LORD, for I am weak (faint, frail);
Heal me, O LORD, for my bones are dismayed *and* anguished.
[3]My soul [as well as my body] is greatly dismayed.
But as for You, O LORD—how long [until You act on my behalf]?

[4]Return, O LORD, rescue my soul;
Save me because of Your [unfailing] steadfast love *and* mercy.
[5]For in death there is no mention of You;
In Sheol (the nether world, the place of the dead) who will praise You *and* give You thanks?

[6]I am weary with my groaning;
Every night I soak my bed with tears,

5:7 *Your holy temple.* David was a leader in reforming the worship of God in Jerusalem, and he established a structure for the worship that would take place in the temple to be built by Solomon. David uses the word "temple" in anticipation of the future glorious building; all later generations of Hebrew worshipers would understand their own worship better because of the use of this word in these psalms.

5:9 *Their throat is an open grave.* Paul echoed the words of these verses in describing the depravity of all people (Ro 3:13).

6:4 *because of Your [unfailing] steadfast love and mercy.* Perhaps the most significant single term in the Hebrew text regarding the character of God is the word rendered "mercy" here. The Hebrew word describes what some prefer to call the "loyal love" or "lovingkindness" of God.

6:6–7 *grief.* The sighing and tears of this psalm are to be understood as responses to the psalmist's physical afflictions experienced at the hands of his enemies, and also to reflect the seriousness with which he felt the weight and burden of

---

6 Rev 21:8; Ps 55:23 **8** Ps 25:5 **9** Lk 11:44; Ro 3:13; Ps 62:4 **11** Isa 65:13 **PSALM 6 Title** 1Ch 15:21; Ps 12, Title
2 Hos 6:1 **5** Ps 30:9

I drench my couch with my
weeping.
7 My eye grows dim with grief;
It grows old because of all my
enemies.

8 Depart from me, all you who do evil,
For the LORD has heard the voice
of my weeping. [Matt 7:23;
Luke 13:27]
9 The LORD has heard my
supplication [my plea for grace];
The LORD receives my prayer.
10 Let all my enemies be ashamed
and greatly horrified;
Let them turn back, let them
suddenly be ashamed [of what
they have done].

Psalm 7

The LORD Implored to Defend the Psalmist against the Wicked.

An Ode of David, [perhaps in a wild, irregular, enthusiastic strain,] which he sang to the LORD concerning the words of Cush, a Benjamite.

1 O LORD my God, in You I take
refuge;
Save me and rescue me from all
those who pursue me,
2 So that my enemy will not tear me
like a lion,
Dragging me away while there is
no one to rescue [me].

3 O LORD my God, if I have done
this,
If there is injustice in my hands,
4 If I have done evil to him who was
at peace with me,
Or without cause robbed him who
was my enemy,
5 Let the enemy pursue me and
overtake me;
And let him trample my life to the
ground
And lay my honor in the dust.
Selah.

6 Arise, O LORD, in Your anger;
Lift up Yourself against the rage of
my enemies;
Rise up for me; You have
commanded judgment *and*
vindication.
7 Let the assembly of the nations be
gathered around You,
And return on high over them.
8 The LORD judges the peoples;
Judge me, O LORD, *and* grant
me justice according to my
righteousness and according to
the integrity within me.
9 Oh, let the wickedness of the
wicked come to an end, but
establish the righteous [those in
right standing with You];
For the righteous God tries the
hearts and minds. [Rev 2:23]
10 My shield *and* my defense depend
on God,
Who saves the upright in heart.
11 God is a righteous judge,
And a God who is indignant every
day.

12 If a man does not repent, God will
sharpen His sword;
He has strung *and* bent His
[mighty] bow and made it ready.
13 He has also prepared [other]
deadly weapons for Himself;
He makes His arrows fiery shafts
[aimed at the unrepentant].
14 Behold, the [wicked and irreverent]
man is pregnant with sin,
And he conceives mischief and
gives birth to lies.

---

his own sinfulness. All affliction is not directly related to sin; however, it is an occasion when a spiritual accounting with God should be taken and in which the believer should be inclined to strengthen himself in God.

7:1 *in You I take refuge.* The dominant message in the Book of Psalms is twofold: (1) God is good, and (2) life is difficult. The life of faith is lived between these two realities.

7:12 *If a man does not repent.* God abhors sin, but He is also merciful, giving people the opportunity to repent before they are punished for their wickedness.

7:14 *he conceives mischief.* These words are

7 Job 17:7 **8** Mt 25:41; Ps 3:4 **PSALM 7** **Title** Hab 3:1; 2Sa 16 **1** Ps 31:15 **2** Isa 38:13; Ps 50:22 **3** 2Sa 16:7; 1Sa 24:11 **4** 1Sa 24:7 **6** Ps 94:2; Ps 44:23 **8** Ps 18:20 **9** 1Sa 16:7 **10** Ps 125:4 **12** Dt 32:41 **14** Job 15:35

[15]He has dug a pit and hollowed it out,
And has fallen into the [very] pit which he made [as a trap].
[16]His mischief will return on his own head,
And his violence will come down on the top of his head [like loose dirt].
[17]I will give thanks to the LORD according to His righteousness *and* justice,
And I will sing praise to the name of the LORD Most High.

Psalm 8

The LORD's Glory and Man's Dignity.

To the Chief Musician; set to a Philistine lute [or perhaps to a particular Hittite tune]. A Psalm of David.

[1]O LORD, our Lord,
How majestic *and* glorious *and* excellent is Your name in all the earth!
You have displayed Your splendor above the heavens.
[2]Out of the mouths of infants and nursing babes You have established strength
Because of Your adversaries,
That You might silence the enemy *and* make the revengeful cease. [Matt 21:15, 16]
[3]When I see *and* consider Your heavens, the work of Your fingers,
The moon and the stars, which You have established,
[4]What is man that You are mindful of him,
And the son of [earthborn] man that You care for him?
[5]Yet You have made him a little lower than God,
And You have crowned him with glory and honor.
[6]You made him to have dominion over the works of Your hands;
You have put all things under his feet, [1 Cor 15:27; Eph 1:22, 23; Heb 2:6–8]
[7]All sheep and oxen,
And also the beasts of the field,
[8]The birds of the air, and the fish of the sea,
Whatever passes through the paths of the seas.
[9]O LORD, our Lord,
How majestic *and* glorious *and* excellent is Your name in all the earth!

Psalm 9

A Psalm of Thanksgiving for God's Justice.

To the Chief Musician; on Muth-labben. A Psalm of David.

[1]I WILL give thanks *and* praise the LORD, with all my heart;
I will tell aloud all Your wonders *and* marvelous deeds.

---

echoed in the apostle James' description of the progress of sin (Jas 1:14–15).

8:5 *a little lower than God.* Mankind stands at the summit of God's creation. The Septuagint, an ancient Greek translation of the Old Testament, translates the Hebrew word meaning "God" (*elohim*) as "angels." The author of Hebrews bases his argument in 2:5–9 on this translation, and both readings are true. God made man (human beings) in His own image, just a little lower than angels. God created human beings as majestic creatures who were to rule over His creation. In our fallen state, we are profoundly disfigured, a perversion of the majesty God intended. However, Jesus restores those who put their trust in Him. In Christ, we recover majesty; in Him, we become the people that God wants us to be. Whenever we feel worthless, the words of this psalm should encourage us. We and all other human beings are valuable because God Himself created us in His own glorious image.

8:9 *O LORD, our Lord.* The first word is the divine name Yahweh. The second Hebrew word translated "our Lord" speaks of the One in control: "our Sovereign."

9:1 *with all my heart.* Real praise is not half-hearted; it involves one's whole being (146:2). The words of these two verses are characteristic of the

15 Job 4:8 **16** Est 9:25 **PSALM 8 Title** Ps 81, Title; 84, Title **1** Ps 148:13; Ps 113:4 **2** 1Co 1:27; Ps 44:16 **3** Ps 111:2 **4** Job 7:17 **6** Ge 1:26; Heb 2:8 **9** ver. 1

[2]I will rejoice and exult in you;
I will sing praise to Your name,
O Most High.
[3]When my enemies turn back,
They stumble and perish before
You.
[4]For You have maintained my right
and my cause;
You have sat on the throne judging
righteously.
[5]You have rebuked the nations, You
have destroyed the wicked *and*
unrepentant;
You have wiped out their name
forever and ever.
[6]The enemy has been cut off *and*
has vanished in everlasting
ruins,
You have uprooted their cities;
The very memory of them has
perished.
[7]But the LORD will remain *and* sit
enthroned forever;
He has prepared *and* established
His throne for judgment.
[Heb 1:11]
[8]And He will judge the world in
righteousness;
He will execute judgment for the
nations with fairness (equity).
[Acts 17:31]
[9]The LORD also will be a refuge *and*
a stronghold for the oppressed,
A refuge in times of trouble;
[10]And those who know Your name
[who have experienced Your
precious mercy] will put their
confident trust in You,
For You, O LORD, have not
abandoned those who seek You.
[Ps 42:1]
[11]Sing praises to the LORD, who
dwells in Zion;
Declare among the peoples His
[great and wondrous] deeds.
[12]For He who avenges blood
[unjustly shed] remembers them
(His people);
He does not forget the cry of the
afflicted *and* abused.
[13]Have mercy on me *and* be gracious
to me, O LORD;
See how I am afflicted by those
who hate me,
You who lift me up from the gates
of death,
[14]That I may tell aloud all Your
praises,
That in the gates of the daughter of
Zion (Jerusalem)
I may rejoice in Your salvation *and*
Your help.
[15]The nations have sunk down in the
pit which they have made;
In the net which they hid, their
own foot has been caught.
[16]The LORD has made Himself
known;
He executes judgment;
The wicked are trapped by the
work of their own hands.
Higgaion (meditation) Selah.
[17]The wicked will turn to Sheol (the
nether world, the place of the
dead),
Even all the nations who forget
God.
[18]For the poor will not always be
forgotten,
Nor the hope of the burdened
perish forever.
[19]Arise, O LORD, do not let man
prevail;
Let the nations be judged before
You.
[20]Put them in [reverent] fear of You,
O LORD,
So that the nations may know they
are but [frail and mortal] men.
Selah.

---

praise of God in the Psalms. He is to be praised for His works and His name. His name represents who He is; His works represent what He does.
9:10 *those who know Your name.* Those in Old Testament times who "knew the name of the Lord" were those who looked forward with saving faith to God's promised redemption, just as we look back with saving faith to the redemption accomplished.
9:14 *the daughter of Zion.* This endearing term for Jerusalem indicated the close relationship and nurturing care God had for His people.

PSALM 9 **2** Ps 5:11; Ps 83:18 **5** Pr 10:7 **7** Heb 1:11 **8** Ps 96:13 **9** Ps 32:7 **10** Ps 91:14 **11** Ps 107:22 **12** Ge 9:5 **14** Ps 13:5 **15** Ps 7:15,16 **16** Ex 7:5; Ps 92:3 **17** Job 8:13 **18** Ps 12:5; Pr 23:18

Psalm 10

A Prayer for the Overthrow of the Wicked.

[1] WHY DO You stand far away,
O LORD?
Why do You hide [Yourself, veiling
Your eyes] in times of trouble?
[2] In pride *and* arrogance the wicked
hotly pursue *and* persecute the
afflicted;
Let them be caught in the plots
which they have devised.

[3] For the wicked boasts *and* sings
the praises of his heart's desire,
And the greedy man curses and
spurns [and even despises] the
LORD.
[4] The wicked, in the haughtiness
of his face, will not seek *nor*
inquire for *Him;*
All his thoughts are, "There
is no God [so there is no
accountability or punishment]."

[5] His ways prosper at all times;
Your judgments [LORD] are on
high, out of his sight [so he
never thinks about them];
As for all his enemies, he sneers at
them.
[6] He says to himself, "I will not be
moved;
For throughout all generations
I will not be in adversity [for
nothing bad will happen to me]."
[7] His mouth is full of curses and
deceit (fraud) and oppression;
Under his tongue is mischief and
wickedness [injustice and sin].
[8] He lurks in ambush in the villages;
In hiding places he kills the
innocent;
He lies in wait for the unfortunate
[the unhappy, the poor, the
helpless].
[9] He lurks in a hiding place like a
lion in his lair;
He lies in wait to catch the
afflicted;
He catches the afflicted when he
draws him into his net.
[10] He crushes [his prey] and
crouches;
And the unfortunate fall by his
mighty *claws.*
[11] He says to himself, "God has
[quite] forgotten;
He has hidden His face; He will
never see my deed."

[12] Arise, O LORD! O God, lift up Your
hand [in judgment];
Do not forget the suffering.
[13] Why has the wicked spurned *and*
shown disrespect to God?
He has said to himself, "You will
not require me to account."
[14] You have seen it, for You have noted
mischief and vexation (irritation)
to take it into Your hand.
The unfortunate commits *himself*
to You;
You are the helper of the
fatherless.
[15] Break the arm of the wicked and
the evildoer,
Seek out his wickedness until You
find no more.

[16] The LORD is King forever and ever;
The nations will perish from His
land.
[17] O LORD, You have heard the desire
of the humble *and* oppressed;
You will strengthen their heart,
You will incline Your ear to hear,

10:1 *Why.* Psalm 10 is found as the second half of Psalm 9 in the Septuagint, the ancient Greek translation of the Hebrew Scripture.

10:3 *the greedy.* The verb "to boast," as translated here, is most commonly rendered "praise." The wicked offer praise, but not to the Lord. Rather, their hearts offer praise and worship to their own covetous desires. Their desires know no divinely set limits, since the wicked do not seek Him, but live with the conscious thought that there is no God (v. 4).

10:11 *God has [quite] forgotten.* The wicked behave the way they do because they doubt that the Lord knows, cares, or will act. They want to believe that there will be no final judgment, so they feel free to do as they please. But the truth is that God will establish justice.

PSALM 10 **2** Ps 7:16 **3** Ps 94:4; Pr 28:4 **4** Ps 14:1 **6** Ecc 8:11; Isa 56:12; Rev 18:7 **7** Ro 3:14 **11** Job 22:13 **12** Mic 5:9 **14** 2Ti 1:12; Ps 68:5 **16** Ps 29:10

[18] To vindicate *and* obtain justice for
the fatherless and the oppressed,
So that man who is of the earth
will no longer terrify them.

Psalm 11

The LORD a Refuge and Defense.

To the Chief Musician. *A Psalm* of David.

[1] IN THE LORD I take refuge [and
put my trust];
How can you say to me, "Flee like
a bird to your mountain;
[2] For look, the wicked are bending
the bow;
They take aim with their arrow on
the string
To shoot [by stealth] in darkness at
the upright in heart.
[3] "If the foundations [of a godly
society] are destroyed,
What can the righteous do?"

[4] The LORD is in His holy temple; the
LORD's throne is in heaven.
His eyes see, His eyelids test the
children of men. [Acts 7:49;
Rev 4:2]
[5] The LORD tests the righteous and
the wicked,
And His soul hates the
[malevolent] one who loves
violence. [James 1:12]
[6] Upon the wicked (godless) He will
rain coals of fire;
Fire and brimstone and a
dreadful scorching wind will
be the portion of their cup [of
doom].
[7] For the LORD is [absolutely]
righteous, He loves
righteousness (virtue, morality,
justice);
The upright shall see His face.

Psalm 12

God, a Helper against the Treacherous.

To the Chief Musician; set an octave below.
A Psalm of David.

[1] SAVE *AND* help *and* rescue, LORD,
for godly people cease to be,
For the faithful vanish from
among the sons of men.
[2] They speak deceitful *and*
worthless words to one
another;
With flattering lips and a double
heart they speak.
[3] May the LORD cut off all flattering
lips,
The tongue that speaks great
things [in boasting];
[4] Who have said, "With our tongue
we will prevail;
Our lips are our own; who is lord
and master over us?"
[5] "Because of the devastation of
the afflicted, because of the
groaning of the needy,
Now I will arise," says the LORD; "I
will place him in the safety for
which he longs."

[6] The words *and* promises of the
LORD are pure words,
Like silver refined in an earthen
furnace, purified seven times.

11:1 *In the LORD I take refuge.* In contrast to the surrounding psalms of lament (9;10;12), this psalm expresses great trust in the Almighty Lord. **11:3 *If the foundations [of a godly society] are destroyed.*** The wicked may taunt, but in fact the foundations are not destroyed and will never be. **11:5 *The LORD tests.*** Undergoing trials and suffering is not necessarily a mark of sin or of God's disfavor. Such tests will show the true allegiance of our hearts.

12:2 *deceitful and worthless words.* The very foundation of a nation is undermined when falsehood prevails. Every aspect of life — home, business, social life — is based on truth. Falsehood breeds suspicion and distrust, which will destroy the very fabric of society and civilization. **12:6 *pure words.*** In contrast to the idle words of the wicked, the words of God are altogether trustworthy. The eternal and steadfast nature of the Lord Himself stands behind His words. He will establish justice just as He has promised to David (v. 5).

18 Ps 82:3 **PSALM 11** **1** Ps 56:11 **2** Ps 64:3,4 **3** Ps 82:5 **4** Ps 33:13; 34:15,16 **5** Ge 22:1 **6** Ge 43:34; 1Sa 1:4; Ps 75:8 **7** Ps 45:7 **PSALM 12** **Title** Ps 6, Title **2** Ps 10:7 **6** 2Sa 22:31; Ps 18:30; Pr 30:5

7 You, O LORD, will preserve *and* keep them;
You will protect him from this [evil] generation forever.
8 The wicked strut about [in pompous self-importance] on every side,
As vileness is exalted *and* baseness is prized among the sons of men.

Psalm 13

Prayer for Help in Trouble.

To the Chief Musician. A Psalm of David.

1 HOW LONG, O LORD? Will You forget me forever?
How long will You hide Your face from me?
2 How long must I take counsel in my soul,
Having sorrow in my heart day after day?
How long will my enemy exalt himself *and* triumph over me?

3 Consider and answer me, O LORD my God;
Give light (life) to my eyes, or I will sleep the *sleep of* death,
4 And my enemy will say, "I have overcome him,"
And my adversaries will rejoice when I am shaken.

5 But I have trusted *and* relied on *and* been confident in Your lovingkindness *and* faithfulness;
My heart shall rejoice *and* delight in Your salvation.
6 I will sing to the LORD,
Because He has dealt bountifully with me.

Psalm 14

Folly and Wickedness of Men.

To the Chief Musician.
A Psalm of David.

1 THE [SPIRITUALLY ignorant] fool has said in his heart, "There is no God."
They are corrupt, they have committed repulsive *and* unspeakable deeds;
There is no one who does good. [Rom 3:10]
2 The LORD has looked down from heaven upon the children of men
To see if there are any who understand (act wisely),
Who [truly] seek after God, [longing for His wisdom and guidance].
3 They have all turned aside, together they have become corrupt;
There is no one who does good, not even one. [Rom 3:11, 12]

4 Have all the workers of wickedness *and* injustice no knowledge,
Who eat up my people as they eat bread,
And do not call upon the LORD?
5 There they tremble with great fear,
For God is with the [consistently] righteous generation.
6 You [evildoers] shamefully plan against the poor,
But the LORD is his safe refuge.

7 Oh, that the salvation of Israel would come out of Zion!

13:1 ***How long, O LORD?*** The Lord allows David to pour out his anxiety before Him. But by the end of David's prayer, the Lord has granted him a correct perspective on his situation. David's only option is to trust in the sovereign mercy of his loving God.

13:5 ***Your lovingkindness and faithfulness.*** These words refer to God's loyal love, His faithfulness to His commitment to take care of His people.

14:1 ***fool.*** This word does not refer to mental inability, but to moral and spiritual insensitivity. A fool is one who lives a life of "practical atheism," the view that even if there is a God, it really does not matter to one's life.

14:4 ***no knowledge.*** The wicked lack knowledge of God's truth. Although people may be brilliant in their chosen fields, they can still be morally insensitive and spiritually closed to the issues that have eternal consequences.

PSALM 13 **1** Job 13:24 **3** Ezr 9:8; Jer 51:39 **PSALM 14** **1** Ps 10:4 **2** Ps 33:13 **4** Isa 64:7 **6** Ps 9:9 **7** Ps 53:6; Job 42:10

When the LORD restores His
captive people,
Then Jacob will rejoice, Israel will
be glad. [Rom 11:25–27]

Psalm 15

Description of a Citizen of Zion.

A Psalm of David.

1 O LORD, who may lodge [as a
guest] in Your tent?
Who may dwell [continually] on
Your holy hill?
2 He who walks with integrity *and*
strength of character, and
works righteousness,
And speaks *and* holds truth in
his heart.
3 He does not slander with his
tongue,
Nor does evil to his neighbor,
Nor takes up a reproach against
his friend;
4 In his eyes an evil person is
despised,
But he honors those who fear
the LORD [and obediently
worship Him with awe-inspired
reverence and submissive
wonder].
He keeps his word even to his own
disadvantage and does
not change it [for his own
benefit];
5 He does not put out his money at
interest [to a fellow Israelite],
And does not take a bribe against
the innocent.
He who does these things will
never be shaken. [Ex 22:25, 26]

Psalm 16

The LORD, the Psalmist's Portion in Life and Deliverer in Death.

A Mikhtam of David [probably intended
to record memorable thoughts].

1 KEEP *AND* protect me, O God, for
in You I have placed my trust
and found refuge.
2 I said to the LORD, "You are my
Lord;
I have no good besides You."
3 As for the saints (godly people)
who are in the land,
They are the majestic *and* the
noble *and* the excellent ones in
whom is all my delight.
4 The sorrows [pain and suffering]
of those who have chosen
another *god* will be multiplied
[because of their idolatry];
I will not pour out their drink
offerings of blood,
Nor will I take their names upon
my lips.

5 The LORD is the portion of my
inheritance, my cup [He is all I
need];
You support my lot.
6 The [boundary] lines [of the land]
have fallen for me in pleasant
places;
Indeed, my heritage is beautiful
to me.

7 I will bless the LORD who has
counseled me;
Indeed, my heart (mind) instructs
me in the night.
8 I have set the LORD continually
before me;

15:1 *who may lodge [as a guest] in Your tent.* No one except Jesus the Messiah is righteous enough to approach God. But there have always been those who stand before God as forgiven sinners, whose righteousness comes as a gift from God. We may come boldly into God's presence because our sins have been covered by Christ's blood.
15:2 *He who walks with integrity ... and works righteousness.* The Lord commands us to be holy (1Pe 1:15 – 16), and He also gives us the power to become holy (2Th 2:16 – 17).
16:5 *my inheritance.* This phrase refers to the promised land. God had given this inheritance to His people (Dt 6:1 – 3). However, there was a greater inheritance for the Levites, who did not receive a share in the land (Nu 26:62); their share of the inheritance was in the Lord. David had an ancestral inheritance in the land. As king, he also had extensive royal holdings. But he realized that

PSALM 15 **1** Ps 24:3 **3** Ex 23:1 **4** Est 3:2 **5** 2Pe 1:10 **PSALM 16** **Title** Ps 56-60 **2** Job 35:7 **4** Ex 23:13

Because He is at my right hand, I
will not be shaken.
9 Therefore my heart is glad and
my glory [my innermost self]
rejoices;
My body too will dwell
[confidently] in safety,
10 For You will not abandon me to
Sheol (the nether world, the
place of the dead),
Nor will You allow Your Holy One
to undergo decay. [Acts 13:35]
11 You will show me the path
of life;
In Your presence is fullness
of joy;
In Your right hand there are
pleasures forevermore.
[Acts 2:25–28, 31]

Psalm 17

Prayer for Protection against Oppressors.

A Prayer of David.

1 HEAR THE just (righteous)
cause, O LORD; listen to my loud
[piercing] cry;
Listen to my prayer, that comes
from guileless lips.
2 Let my verdict of vindication come
from Your presence;
May Your eyes look with equity
and behold things that are just.
3 You have tried my heart;
You have visited me in the
night;
You have tested me and You find
nothing [evil in me];
I intend that my mouth will not
transgress.
4 Concerning the deeds of men, by
the word of Your lips
I have kept away from the paths of
the violent.
5 My steps have held closely to Your
paths;
My feet have not staggered.
6 I have called upon You, for You,
O God, will answer me;
Incline Your ear to me, hear my
speech.
7 Wondrously show Your [marvelous
and amazing] lovingkindness,
O Savior of those who take refuge
at Your right hand
From those who rise up *against
them.*
8 Keep me [in Your affectionate
care, protect me] as the apple of
Your eye;
Hide me in the [protective] shadow
of Your wings
9 From the wicked who despoil *and*
deal violently with me,
My deadly enemies who surround
me.
10 They have closed their unfeeling
heart [to kindness and
compassion];

---

no inheritance was greater than his relationship with Almighty God.

16:10 *Sheol.* This is the Hebrew word for "the grave," or the realm of the dead. Not much is known of the ancient Hebrew's concept of life after death. "The grave" or Sheol seems to be a dreaded place, shrouded in mystery.

17:3 *tried my heart.* David knew that God had done what he was requesting even before he asked. That is, God knew David's needs and what was in his heart. David's prayer helped him to focus on the source of his strength and to reaffirm his determination to live a pure life.

17:4 God's Word Corrects—There are many symbols for God's Word that can be found in the Bible itself. It can be thought of as a mirror (Jas 1:23–25), a seed (1Pe 1:23), a lamp (Ps 119:105), a sword (Eph 6:17), and even food (Heb 5:12–14). But the Bible also serves as a measuring rod that can be used as a standard against which to measure our beliefs.

God Himself sometimes uses His Word to correct us as He did with David. "You have dealt well with Your servant, O Lord, according to Your promise ... Before I was afflicted I went astray, but now I keep and honor Your word [with loving obedience]" (Ps 119:65,67).

There are times when God's Word can correct believers when they are in honest and unintentional error. Aquila and Priscilla, a godly Christian couple, used the Scriptures to help a young preacher named Apollos (Ac 18:24–28). Paul does the same thing for some former disciples of John the Baptist that he met in the city of Ephesus (Ac 19:1–7).

10 Ps 49:15 **11** Mt 7:14 **PSALM 17** **3** Job 23:10 **5** Ps 119:133 **6** Ps 116:2 **10** 1Sa 2:3

With their mouths they
speak proudly *and* make
presumptuous claims.
[11] They track us down *and* have
now surrounded us in our
steps;
They set their eyes to force us to
the ground,
[12] He is like a lion eager to tear [his
prey],
And like a young lion lurking in
hiding places.

[13] Arise, O LORD, confront him, cast
him down;
Save my soul from the wicked
with Your sword,
[14] From men with Your hand,
O LORD,
From men of the world [these
moths of the night] whose
portion [of enjoyment] is in this
life—idle and vain,
And whose belly You fill with Your
treasure;
They are satisfied with children,
And they leave what they have left
[of wealth] to their children.
[15] As for me, I shall see Your face in
righteousness;
I will be [fully] satisfied when I
awake [to find myself] seeing
Your likeness.

Psalm 18

David Praises the LORD for Rescuing Him.

To the Chief Musician. A Psalm of David, the servant of the LORD, who spoke the words of this song to the LORD on the day when the LORD rescued him from the hand of all his enemies and from the hand of Saul. And he said:

[1] "I LOVE You [fervently and
devotedly], O LORD, my
strength."
[2] The LORD is my rock, my fortress,
and the One who rescues me;
My God, my rock *and* strength in
whom I trust *and* take refuge;
My shield, and the horn of my
salvation, my high tower—my
stronghold. [Heb 2:13]
[3] I call upon the LORD, who is
worthy to be praised;
And I am saved from my enemies.
[Rev 5:12]
[4] The cords of death surrounded me,
And the streams of ungodliness
and torrents of destruction
terrified me.
[5] The cords of Sheol (the nether
world, the place of the dead)
surrounded me;

17:14 *whose portion [of enjoyment] is in this life.* The wicked live their lives with only the pursuit of the pleasures of this world in mind. The righteous should not try to obtain what this life can offer, but instead pursue God and His ways.

17:15 *I shall see Your face.* In the Old Testament there is no well-developed theology of heaven, yet there are times when the faith of the writer rises to utter statements of hope of resurrection and of life eternal with God. It would appear that such a view was always a part of godly faith, even though dim in comparison with the later revelation through Christ. Both Psalms 16 and 17 are testimonies to a growing faith that entrance into God's presence would be the fruit of a relationship with God in this life. The afflictions on earth cause faith to look forward to a time after this life when one will behold God's face in righteousness, and faith in God will be vindicated by seeing God.

18:1 *I love You [fervently and devotedly], O LORD.* Twice in the Psalms the poet declares a love for God (116:1). Here an unusual word for love is used, referring to compassion as deep as a mother's love. The text for this psalm is also found in 2 Samuel 22.

18:2 *The LORD is my rock.* This is a particularly apt image for David, who many times had to hide in the mountains for security (1Sa 26:1,20).

18:5–6 *distress.* As the title of Psalm 18 indicates, this poem of praise was composed in the midst of very trying times (2Sa 22:1). Once again, David had become the object of Saul's uncontrollable rage; in his bouts of paranoia, Saul mistakenly suspected that David was laying the foundation of a revolt against his own royal position. How foolish David would have been had he said, "In my distress I took the matter into my own hands." Rather he said, "In my distress I called upon the LORD." We have no other option when caught in our distressing situations. Otherwise we compound the suffering.

---

15 1Jn 3:2; Ps 4:6,7; 16:11 **PSALM 18** **Title** Ps 36, Title; 2Sa 22 **1** Ps 144:1 **2** Heb 2:13 **3** Ps 76:4 **4** Ps 116:3

The snares of death confronted me.
6 In my distress [when I seemed surrounded] I called upon the LORD
And cried to my God for help;
He heard my voice from His temple,
And my cry for help came before Him, into His *very* ears.

7 Then the earth shook and quaked,
The foundations of the mountains trembled;
They were shaken because He was indignant *and* angry.
8 Smoke went up from His nostrils,
And fire from His mouth devoured;
Coals were kindled by it.
9 He bowed the heavens also and came down;
And thick darkness was under His feet.
10 And He rode upon a cherub (storm) and flew;
And He sped on the wings of the wind.
11 He made darkness His hiding place (covering); His pavilion (canopy) around Him,
The darkness of the waters, the thick clouds of the skies.
12 Out of the brightness before Him passed His thick clouds,
Hailstones and coals of fire.
13 The LORD also thundered in the heavens,
And the Most High uttered His voice,
Hailstones and coals of fire.
14 He sent out His arrows and scattered them;
And *He sent* an abundance of lightning flashes and confused *and* routed them [in defeat].
15 Then the stream beds of the waters appeared,
And the foundations of the world were laid bare
At Your rebuke, O LORD,
At the blast of the breath of Your nostrils.
16 He reached from on high, He took me;
He drew me out of many waters.
17 He rescued me from my strong enemy,
And from those who hated me, for they were too strong for me.
18 They confronted me in the day of my disaster,
But the LORD was my support.
19 He brought me out into a broad place;
He rescued me because He was pleased with me *and* delighted in me.

20 The LORD dealt with me according to my righteousness (moral character, spiritual integrity);
According to the cleanness of my hands He has rewarded me.
21 For I have kept the ways of the LORD,
And have not wickedly departed from my God.
22 For all His ordinances were before me,
And I did not put away His statutes from me.
23 I was blameless before Him,
And I kept myself free from my sin.
24 Therefore the LORD has rewarded me according to my righteousness (moral character, spiritual integrity),
According to the cleanness of my hands in His sight.
25 With the kind (merciful, faithful, loyal) You show Yourself kind,
With the blameless You show Yourself blameless,
26 With the pure You show Yourself pure,
And with the crooked You show Yourself astute.

18:11–12 *darkness . . . brightness.* The references to darkness speak of the hiddenness of God. He cannot be completely understood by those whom He has created. The references to brightness speak of God's holiness.

7 Ac 4:31 **9** Ps 144:5 **10** Ps 99:1; Ps 104:3 **11** Ps 97:2 **12** Ps 97:3 **13** Ps 29:3 **14** Jos 10:10; Ps 144:6; Isa 30:30 **16** Ps 144:7 **19** Ps 31:8; 118:5 **20** 1Sa 24:19 **24** 1Sa 26:23 **25** 1Ki 8:32 **26** Lev 26:23,24,27,28; Pr 3:34

[27]For You save an afflicted *and*
humble people,
But bring down those [arrogant
fools] with haughty eyes.
[28]For You cause my lamp to be
lighted *and* to shine;
The LORD my God illumines my
darkness.
[29]For by You I can crush a troop,
And by my God I can leap over a
wall.
30 As for God, His way is blameless.
The word of the LORD is tested [it is
perfect, it is faultless];
He is a shield to all who take
refuge in Him.
[31]For who is God, but the LORD?
Or who is a rock, except our God,
[32]The God who encircles me with
strength
And makes my way blameless?
[33]He makes my feet like hinds' feet
[able to stand firmly and tread
safely on paths of testing and
trouble];
He sets me [securely] upon my
high places.
[34]He trains my hands for war,
So that my arms can bend a bow
of bronze.
[35]You have also given me the shield
of Your salvation,
And Your right hand upholds *and*
sustains me;
Your gentleness [Your gracious
response when I pray] makes
me great.
[36]You enlarge the path beneath me
and make my steps secure,
So that my feet will not slip.
37 I pursued my enemies and
overtook them;
And I did not turn back until they
were consumed.
[38]I shattered them so that they were
not able to rise;
They fell [wounded] under my feet.
[39]For You have encircled me with
strength for the battle;
You have subdued under me those
who rose up against me.
[40]You have also made my enemies
turn their backs to me [in defeat],
And I silenced *and* destroyed those
who hated me.
[41]They cried for help, but there was
no one to save them—
Even to the LORD [they cried], but
He did not answer them.
[42]Then I beat them fine as the dust
before the wind;
I emptied them out as the dirt of
the streets.
43 You have rescued me from the
contentions of the people;
You have placed me as the head of
the nations;
A people whom I have not known
serve me.
[44]As soon as they hear me, they
respond *and* obey me;
Foreigners feign obedience to me.
[45]Foreigners lose heart,
And come trembling out of their
strongholds.
46 The LORD lives, blessed be my rock;
And may the God of my salvation
be exalted,
[47]The God who avenges me,
And subdues peoples (nations)
under me.
[48]He rescues me from my enemies;
Yes, You lift me up above those
who rise up against me;

18:35 ***the shield of Your salvation.*** The use of battle armor as an image of God's provision for the righteous is found in both the Old and New Testaments (Eph 6:10–20).

18:41 ***They cried . . . to the LORD.*** Apparently, in the extremes of battle, the enemies of David found no help from their gods, so they screamed aloud to David's God for deliverance. But God would not answer them. There is only one prayer from the wicked to which He gladly listens — the prayer of repentance.

18:43 ***head of the nations.*** David gained his empire by the work of the Lord on his behalf. But David's empire was only a picture of the kingdom of God that will one day be governed by David's greater Son, the Lord Jesus.

27 Ps 101:5; Pr 6:17 **28** Job 18:6 **30** Dt 32:4; Da 4:37; Rev 15:3; Ps 12:6; 119:140; Pr 30:5; Ps 17:7 **31** Dt 32:31,39; 1Sa 2:2; Ps 86:8; Isa 45:5 **32** Ps 91:2 **33** 2Sa 2:18; Hab 3:19; Dt 32:13; 33:29 **34** Ps 144:1 **36** Pr 4:12 **41** Job 27:9; Pr 1:28; Jer 11:11 **42** Zec 10:5 **43** 2Sa 8; Isa 52:15 **45** Mic 7:17 **47** Ps 47:3 **48** Ps 59:1

You deliver me from the man of
violence.
49 Therefore will I give thanks *and*
praise You, O LORD, among the
nations,
And sing praises to Your name.
[Rom 15:9]
50 He gives great triumphs to His king,
And shows steadfast love *and*
mercy to His anointed,
To David and his descendants
forever. [2 Sam 22:2–51]

Psalm 19

The Works and the Word of God.

To the Chief Musician. A Psalm of David.

1 THE HEAVENS are telling of the
glory of God;
And the expanse [of heaven] is
declaring the work of His hands.
[Rom 1:20, 21]
2 Day after day pours forth speech,
And night after night reveals
knowledge.
3 There is no speech, nor are there
[spoken] words [from the stars];
Their voice is not heard.
4 Yet their voice [in quiet evidence]
has gone out through all the
earth,
Their words to the end of the world.
In them *and* in the heavens He
has made a tent for the sun,
[Rom 10:18]
5 Which is as a bridegroom coming
out of his chamber;
It rejoices as a strong man to run
his course.
6 The sun's rising is from one end of
the heavens,
And its circuit to the other end of
them;
And there is nothing hidden from
its heat.

7 The law of the LORD is perfect
(flawless), restoring *and*
refreshing the soul;
The statutes of the LORD are
reliable *and* trustworthy,
making wise the simple.
8 The precepts of the LORD are right,
bringing joy to the heart;
The commandment of the LORD is
pure, enlightening the eyes.
9 The fear of the LORD is clean,
enduring forever;
The judgments of the LORD
are true, they are righteous
altogether.
10 They are more desirable than gold,
yes, than much fine gold;
Sweeter also than honey and the
drippings of the honeycomb.
11 Moreover, by them Your servant is
warned [reminded, illuminated,
and instructed];
In keeping them there is great
reward.
12 Who can understand his errors *or*
omissions? Acquit me of hidden
(unconscious, unintended)
faults.

18:49 *among the nations.* By proclaiming the victories of God to the nations, the poets were calling for the nations to respond in faith. How fitting that Paul would cite this verse (or its parallel in 2Sa 22:50) in Romans 15:9 as an indicator of God's ongoing intention to bring His salvation to all people.

19:1 *The heavens are telling.* All of creation reveals God's glory and majesty (Ro 1:18 – 20).

19:4 *a tent for the sun.* In the ancient Middle East, the sun was often thought of as a god. In this poem, the sun is but the stunning workmanship of the Creator, glorifying the God who made it.

19:7 – 8 *The law of the LORD.* The world reveals God's glory, and the Word reveals His saving grace. God's law (or teaching) is described as "perfect," which is best understood here as "complete." This law needs no alteration in part or in whole. It has power to bring deep and radical change in the inner life or soul. It is God's great instrument in conversion (Jas 1:18; 1Pe 1:23). The Word of God is spoken of as God's "testimony" because it is His own instruction concerning His person and purpose. In Scripture, God testifies concerning Himself, His Son, and sinners. God's Word is sure (2Pe 1:19), and may be trusted because He is faithful (1Ti 1:15). To those wise in their own eyes, the truth of God is hidden (Mt 11:25), but to the simple the Scriptures give wisdom that leads to salvation (2Ti 3:15).

P. 1972

49 Ro 15:9 **50** Ps 144:10 **PSALM 19** **1** Isa 40:22 **4** Ro 10:18 **5** Ecc 1:5 **7** Ps 111:7

13 Also keep back Your servant
from presumptuous (deliberate,
willful) *sins;*
Let them not rule *and* have control
over me.
Then I will be blameless
(complete),
And I shall be acquitted of great
transgression.
14 Let the words of my mouth and the
meditation of my heart
Be acceptable *and* pleasing in Your
sight,
O LORD, my [firm, immovable]
rock and my Redeemer.

Psalm 20

Prayer for Victory over Enemies.

To the Chief Musician. A Psalm of David.

1 MAY THE LORD answer you
(David) in the day of trouble!
May the name of the God of Jacob
set you *securely* on high [and
defend you in battle]!
2 May He send you help from the
sanctuary (His dwelling place)
And support *and* strengthen you
from Zion!
3 May He remember all your meal
offerings
And accept your burnt offering.
Selah.
4 May He grant you your heart's
desire
And fulfill all your plans.
5 We will sing joyously over your
victory,
And in the name of our God we
will set up our banners.
May the LORD fulfill all your
petitions.
6 Now I know that the LORD saves
His anointed;
He will answer him from His holy
heaven
With the saving strength of His
right hand.
7 Some *trust* in chariots and some
in horses,
But we will remember *and* trust in
the name of the LORD our God.
8 They have bowed down and fallen,
But we have risen and stood
upright.
9 O LORD, save [the king];
May the King answer us in the day
we call.

Psalm 21

Praise for Help.

To the Chief Musician. A Psalm of David.

1 O LORD the king will delight in
Your strength,
And in Your salvation how greatly
will he rejoice!
2 You have given him his heart's
desire,
And You have not withheld the
request of his lips. *Selah.*
3 For You meet him with blessings
of good things;
You set a crown of pure gold on
his head.
4 He asked life of You,
And You gave it to him,
Long life forever and evermore.
5 His glory is great because of Your
victory;
Splendor and majesty You bestow
upon him.
6 For You make him most blessed
[and a blessing] forever;

19:14 *my Redeemer.* God is the One who purchases our freedom from any bondage or slavery. The principal meaning of the word is "defender of family rights."

20:5 *victory.* In the immediate context, victory is used to describe daily deliverance from the rigors of the battle and the triumph over the enemy. But the Lord's deliverance of us from our spiritual troubles should prompt the same type of praise.

20:6 *His right hand.* This is a slogan that describes God's powerful deliverance of the Israelites from Egypt (17:7; 44:3; 118:16; Ex 15:6).

21:2 *his heart's desire.* The Lord gives people their aspirations when they are derived from a fundamental desire for God's honor and glory (20:4; 37:4; 145:19).

14 Isa 47:4 **PSALM 21** **4** Ps 61:5,6

You make him joyful with the joy
of Your presence. [Gen 12:2]
7 For the king [confidently] trusts in
the LORD,
And through the lovingkindness
(faithfulness, goodness) of the
Most High he will never be
shaken.
8 Your hand will reach out *and*
defeat all your enemies;
Your right hand will reach those
who hate you.
9 You will make them as [if in] a
blazing oven in the time of your
anger;
The LORD will swallow them up in
His wrath,
And the fire will devour them.
10 Their offspring You will destroy
from the earth,
And their descendants from the
sons of men.
11 For they planned evil against You;
They devised a [malevolent] plot
And they will not succeed.
12 For You will make them turn their
backs [in defeat];
You will aim Your bowstring [of
divine justice] at their faces.
13 Be exalted, LORD, in Your
strength;
We will sing and praise Your
power.

Psalm 22

A Cry of Anguish and a Song of Praise.

To the Chief Musician; set to [the tune of] Aijeleth Hashshahar (The Doe of the Dawn). A Psalm of David.

1 MY GOD, my God, why have You
forsaken me?
Why are You so far from helping
me, and from the words of my
groaning? [Matt 27:46]
2 O my God, I call out by day, but
You do not answer;
And by night, but I find no rest *nor*
quiet.
3 But You are holy,
O You who are enthroned in [the
holy place where] the praises of
Israel [are offered].
4 In You our fathers trusted
[leaned on, relied on, and were
confident];
They trusted and You rescued
them.
5 They cried out to You and were
delivered;
They trusted in You and were not
disappointed *or* ashamed.

6 But I am [treated as] a worm
[insignificant and powerless]
and not a man;
I am the scorn of men and
despised by the people.
[Matt 27:39–44]
7 All who see me laugh at me *and*
mock me;
They [insultingly] open their lips,
they shake their head, *saying,*
[Matt 27:43]
8 "He trusted *and* committed
himself to the LORD, let Him save
him.
Let Him rescue him, because He
delights in him." [Matt 27:39, 43;
Mark 15:29, 30; Luke 23:35]
9 Yet You are He who pulled me out
of the womb;
You made me trust when on my
mother's breasts.
10 I was cast upon You from birth;
From my mother's womb You have
been my God.

21:9 *the time of your anger.* This may refer to any period of God's judgment, but compare to "the day of the Lord" (Joel 2:1; Zep 1:14).

22:1 *My God, my God, why have You forsaken me?* David used these words to express a painful sense of separation from God at a time of great trouble (38:21). These were the very words used by Christ while in agony on the cross (Mt 27:46; Mk 15:34).

22:6 *despised by the people.* When David was at his lowest, his enemies ridiculed his faith in the Lord. These words also describe the experience of the Savior who endured the verbal abuse of His tormentors (Mt 27:27 – 31,39 – 44).

PSALM 22 **1** Mk 15:34 **3** Dt 10:21 **5** Isa 49:23 **6** Job 25:6; Isa 53:3 **7** Mt 27:39; Job 16:4 **8** Mt 27:43; Ps 91:14 **9** Ps 71:6 **10** Isa 46:3

11 Do not be far from me, for trouble
is near;
And there is no one to help.
12 Many [enemies like] bulls have
surrounded me;
Strong *bulls* of Bashan have
encircled me. [Ezek 39:18;
Amos 4:1]
13 They open wide their mouths
against me,
Like a ravening and a roaring lion.
14 I am poured out like water,
And all my bones are out of joint.
My heart is like wax;
It is melted [by anguish] within
me.
15 My strength is dried up like a
fragment of clay pottery;
And my [dry] tongue clings to my
jaws;
And You have laid me in the dust
of death. [John 19:28]
16 For [a pack of] dogs have
surrounded me;
A gang of evildoers has encircled
me,
They pierced my hands and my
feet. [Is 53:7; John 19:37]
17 I can count all my bones;
They look, they stare at me.
[Luke 23:27, 35]
18 They divide my clothing among
them
And cast lots for my garment.
[John 19:23, 24]
19 But You, O LORD, do not be far
from me;
O You my help, come quickly to
my assistance.
20 Rescue my life from the sword,
My only *life* from the paw of the
dog (the executioner).
21 Save me from the lion's mouth;
From the horns of the wild oxen
You answer me.
22 I will tell of Your name to my
countrymen;
In the midst of the congregation
I will praise You. [John 20:17;
Rom 8:29; Heb 2:12]
23 You who fear the LORD [with awe-
inspired reverence], praise Him!
All you descendants of Jacob,
honor Him.
Fear Him [with submissive wonder],
all you descendants of Israel.
24 For He has not despised nor
detested the suffering of the
afflicted;
Nor has He hidden His face from
him;
But when he cried to Him for help,
He listened.
25 My praise will be of You in the
great assembly.
I will pay my vows [made in the
time of trouble] before those
who [reverently] fear Him.
26 The afflicted will eat and be
satisfied;
Those who [diligently] seek Him
and require Him [as their
greatest need] will praise the
LORD.
May your hearts live forever!
27 All the ends of the earth will
remember and turn to the LORD,
And all the families of the nations
will bow down *and* worship
before You,
28 For the kingship *and* the kingdom
are the LORD's
And He rules over the nations.
29 All the prosperous of the earth
will eat and worship;

22:15 *my [dry] tongue clings to my jaws.* Jesus' words "I am thirsty" (Jn 19:28) also expressed the pain of terrible thirst.
22:16 *They pierced my hands and my feet.* This verse explicitly predicts the crucifixion of the Lord Jesus Christ. The words were a figure of speech for David, but they were literally true for Jesus.
22:18 *cast lots for my garment.* This text was directly fulfilled by the soldiers who gambled at the foot of the cross for the possession of Jesus' robe (Mt 27:35).
22:27 *all the families of the nations.* This is speaking of the eventual spread of the gospel of redemption to the whole world, fulfilling God's promise to bless all nations through Abraham's descendants (Ge 12:3).

12 Ps 68:30 **13** La 2:16 **14** Da 5:6 **15** Pr 17:22; Jn 19:28 **16** Mt 27:35 **17** Lk 23:27,35 **18** Lk 23:34
20 Ps 35:17 **21** 2Ti 4:17; Isa 34:7 **22** Heb 2:12; Ro 8:29 **23** Ps 135:19 **24** Heb 5:7 **25** Ps 35:18; Ecc 5:4
28 Mt 6:13 **29** Ps 45:12; Isa 26:19

All those who go down to the dust
(the dead) will bow before Him,
Even he who cannot keep his soul
alive.
30 Posterity will serve Him;
They will tell of the Lord to the
next generation.
31 They will come and declare His
righteousness
To a people yet to be born—that
He has done it [and that it is
finished]. [John 19:30]

Psalm 23

The LORD, the Psalmist's Shepherd.

A Psalm of David.

1 THE LORD is my Shepherd [to
feed, to guide and to shield me],
[Ezek 34:11–31]
I shall not want.
2 He lets me lie down in green
pastures;
He leads me beside the still *and*
quiet waters. [Rev 7:17]
3 He refreshes *and* restores my soul
(life);
He leads me in the paths of
righteousness
for His name's sake.

4 Even though I walk through the
[sunless] valley of the shadow of
death,
I fear no evil, for You are with me;
Your rod [to protect] and Your
staff [to guide], they comfort *and*
console me.
5 You prepare a table before me in
the presence of my enemies.
You have anointed *and* refreshed
my head with oil;
My cup overflows.
6 Surely goodness and mercy *and*
unfailing love shall follow me all
the days of my life,
And I shall dwell forever
[throughout all my days] in the
house *and* in the presence of the
LORD.

Psalm 24

The King of Glory Entering Zion.

A Psalm of David.

1 THE EARTH is the LORD's, and
the fullness of it,
The world, and those who dwell in
it. [1 Cor 10:26]
2 For He has founded it upon the
seas
And established it upon the
streams *and* the rivers.
3 Who may ascend onto the
mountain of the LORD?
And who may stand in His holy
place?

23:1 *The LORD is my Shepherd.* Even though the word "king" does not appear in it, this psalm is a description of what it means to be a good ruler. Moreover, the psalm prophetically speaks of Jesus. He is the Good Shepherd whose flock trusts in Him (Jn 10:1 – 18) and the King whose perfect rule will be established (Lk 23:2 – 3).

23:4 *the [sunless] valley of the shadow of death.* The awareness of our own mortality often comes with sickness, trials, and hardship. But the Lord our protector can lead us through these dark and difficult valleys to eternal life with Him. There is no need to fear death's power (1Co 15:25 – 27). Our Lord has already traveled this road and come through the valley of darkness. Because He lives, we too shall live. Death is not our final destiny.

23:6 *in the house and in the presence of the LORD.* God's promise for the Israelites was not just for the enjoyment of this life in the land of promise; it was also for the full enjoyment of the life to come in His presence (16:9 – 11;17:15; 49:15).

24:1 Affirming God's Ownership of the World — Whose world is this anyway? David, of course, who lived in the hills with the animals, had a firm answer. It is God's world. This statement should shape our thinking about a great deal of life. We should have a heightened sense of stewardship to care for God's creation. We should look to God more to understand what is important and what is not important. Seeing God's creation every day should help make praise and thanksgiving a way of life. It should also help us desire to understand God's redemptive acts in history and in our lives.

30 Ps 87:6 **31** Ps 78:6 **PSALM 23** **1** Isa 40:11; Jn 10:11; Php 4:19 **2** Eze 34:14; Rev 7:17 **3** Ps 5:8

[4]He who has clean hands and a
pure heart,
Who has not lifted up his soul to
what is false,
Nor has sworn [oaths] deceitfully.
[Matt 5:8]
[5]He shall receive a blessing from
the LORD,
And righteousness from the God
of his salvation.
[6]This is the generation (description)
of those who diligently seek
Him *and* require Him as their
greatest need,
Who seek Your face, even [as did]
Jacob. [Ps 42:1] *Selah.*
[7]Lift up your heads, O gates,
And be lifted up, ancient doors,
That the King of glory may come in.
[8]Who is the King of glory?
The LORD strong and mighty,
The LORD mighty in battle.
[9]Lift up your heads, O gates,
And lift them up, ancient doors,
That the King of glory may come in.
[10]Who is [He then] this King of
glory?
The LORD of hosts,
He is the King of glory [who
rules over all creation with His
heavenly armies]. *Selah.*

Psalm 25

Prayer for Protection, Guidance and Pardon.

A Psalm of David.

[1]TO YOU, O LORD, I lift up my soul.
[2]O my God, in You I [have
unwavering] trust [and I rely on
You with steadfast confidence],
Do not let me be ashamed *or* my
hope in You be disappointed;
Do not let my enemies triumph
over me.
[3]Indeed, none of those who
[expectantly] wait for You will
be ashamed;
Those who turn away from what
is right *and* deal treacherously
without cause will be ashamed
(humiliated, embarrassed).
[4]Let me know Your ways, O LORD;
Teach me Your paths.
[5]Guide me in Your truth and teach
me,
For You are the God of my
salvation;
For You [and only You] I wait
[expectantly] all the day long.
[6]Remember, O LORD, Your
[tender] compassion and Your
lovingkindnesses,
For they have been from of old.
[7]Do not remember the sins of my
youth or my transgressions;
According to Your lovingkindness
remember me,
For Your goodness' sake, O LORD.
[8]Good and upright is the LORD;
Therefore He instructs sinners in
the way.
[9]He leads the humble in justice,
And He teaches the humble His
way.
[10]All the paths of the LORD are
lovingkindness *and* goodness
and truth *and* faithfulness
To those who keep His covenant
and His testimonies.
[11]For Your name's sake, O LORD,
Pardon my wickedness *and* my
guilt, for they are great.
[12]Who is the man who fears the
LORD [with awe-inspired
reverence and worships Him
with submissive wonder]?

24:4 ***clean hands and a pure heart.*** God looks at a person's actions and also at the attitudes of the heart.

24:9 ***That the King of glory may come in.*** When Jesus came, the meaning of this ancient poem became clear (Mt 21:1 – 10; Rev 19:11 – 16).

25:3 ***who [expectantly] wait for You.*** Waiting on the Lord is the equivalent of hoping in Him (25:5; 40:1).

25:7 ***sins of my youth.*** Both the sins of immaturity and the transgressions of adulthood need forgiveness (1Jn 1:9).

---

4 Job 10:21,22; Ps 44:19; Ps 3:6; Isa 43:2 **5** Ps 92:10 **PSALM 24** **1** Ex 9:29; Job 41:11 **3** Ps 15:1 **4** Job 17:9; 1Ti 2:8; Mt 5:8; Ps 15:4 **6** Ps 27:8 **7** Isa 26:2; Ps 97:6; Hag 2:7; Mal 3:1 **PSALM 25** **1** Ps 86:4 **2** Ps 34:8; Isa 28:16; Ps 13:4 **4** Ex 33:13; Ps 5:8 **6** Ps 103:17; Isa 63:15 **7** Job 13:26; Jer 3:25; Ps 51:1 **11** Ps 31:3; 79:9; Ro 5:20 **12** Ps 37:23

He will teach him [through His
word] in the way he should
choose.
13 His soul will dwell in prosperity
and goodness,
And his descendants will inherit
the land.
14 The secret [of the wise counsel] of
the LORD is for those who fear
Him,
And He will let them know His
covenant *and* reveal to them
[through His word] its [deep,
inner] meaning. [John 7:17; 15:15]
15 My eyes are continually toward
the LORD,
For He will bring my feet out of
the net.

16 Turn to me [LORD] and be gracious
to me,
For I am alone and afflicted.
17 The troubles of my heart are
multiplied;
Bring me out of my distresses.
18 Look upon my affliction and my
trouble,
And forgive all my sins.
19 Look upon my enemies, for they
are many;
They hate me with cruel *and*
violent hatred.
20 Guard my soul and rescue me;
Do not let me be ashamed *or*
disappointed,
For I have taken refuge in You.
21 Let integrity and uprightness
protect me,
For I wait [expectantly] for You.
22 O God, redeem Israel,
Out of all his troubles.

Psalm 26

Protestation of Integrity and Prayer for Protection.

A Psalm of David.

1 VINDICATE ME, O LORD, for I
have walked in my integrity;
I have [relied on and] trusted
[confidently] in the LORD without
wavering *and* I shall not slip.
2 Examine me, O LORD, and try me;
Test my heart and my mind.
3 For Your lovingkindness is before
my eyes,
And I have walked [faithfully] in
Your truth.
4 I do not sit with deceitful *or*
unethical *or* worthless men,
Nor seek companionship with
pretenders (self-righteous
hypocrites).
5 I hate the company of evildoers,
And will not sit with the wicked.
6 I will wash my hands in
innocence,
And I will go about Your altar,
O LORD,
7 That I may proclaim with the voice
of thanksgiving
And declare all Your wonders.

8 O LORD, I love the habitation of
Your house
And the place where Your glory
dwells.
9 Do not sweep my soul away with
sinners,
Nor [sweep away] my life with
men of bloodshed,

25:14 *for those who fear Him.* Those who fear the Lord pay attention to His instructions and thus learn the secrets of God's wisdom (111:10; Pr 1:7; 3:32).

25:19 *They hate me.* This psalm is a prayer for forgiveness, instruction, and protection from the forces of darkness which are oppressing the writer. His most prominent trial is hostility from enemies. The animosity which the psalmist encountered was not primarily personal, but was the result of his identification with God's cause. Therefore, he could ask the Lord to look upon Him and vindicate him in the face of his afflictions. The writer's suffering had its roots in the origins of redemptive history (Ge 3:15) — there would be enmity between the seed of the woman and the seed of the serpent, between the godly and the ungodly. Jesus also reminded his disciples that hatred directed against his servants on His account was to be expected (Jn 15:18 – 20).

26:3 *Your lovingkindness.* The loyal love (13:5) of God is the recurring focus of the Book of Psalms.

26:9 *Do not sweep my soul away.* On the basis of his protests of integrity (vv. 1 – 2), David prays

13 Pr 19:23; Ps 37:11 **14** Pr 3:32; Jn 7:17 **15** Ps 141:8 **16** Ps 69:16 **18** 2Sa 16:12 **22** Ps 130:8 **PSALM 26** **1** Ps 7:8; 2Ki 20:3; Ps 28:7; Pr 29:25 **2** Ps 17:3 **3** 2Ki 20:3 **4** Ps 1:1 **5** Ps 31:6; Ps 1:1 **6** Ps 73:13 **8** Ps 27:4 **9** Ps 28:3

[10]In whose hands is a wicked scheme,
And whose right hand is full of bribes.
[11]But as for me, I shall walk in my integrity;
Redeem me and be merciful *and* gracious to me.
[12]My foot stands on a level place;
In the congregations I will bless the LORD.

Psalm 27

A Psalm of Fearless Trust in God.

A Psalm of David.

[1]THE LORD is my light and my salvation—
Whom shall I fear?
The LORD is the refuge *and* fortress of my life—
Whom shall I dread?
[2]When the wicked came against me to eat up my flesh,
My adversaries and my enemies, they stumbled and fell.
[3]Though an army encamp against me,
My heart will not fear;
Though war arise against me,
Even in this I am confident.
[4]One thing I have asked of the LORD, and that I will seek:
That I may dwell in the house of the LORD [in His presence] all the days of my life,
To gaze upon the beauty [the delightful loveliness and majestic grandeur] of the LORD
And to meditate in His temple. [Ps 16:11; 18:6; 65:4; Luke 2:37]
[5]For in the day of trouble He will hide me in His shelter;
In the secret place of His tent He will hide me;
He will lift me up on a rock.
[6]And now my head will be lifted up above my enemies around me,
In His tent I will offer sacrifices with shouts of joy;
I will sing, yes, I will sing praises to the LORD.

[7]Hear, O LORD, when I cry aloud;
Be gracious *and* compassionate to me and answer me.
[8]*When You said,* "Seek My face [in prayer, require My presence as your greatest need]," my heart said to You,
"Your face, O LORD, I will seek [on the authority of Your word]."
[9]Do not hide Your face from me,
Do not turn Your servant away in anger;
You have been my help;
Do not abandon me nor leave me,
O God of my salvation!
[10]Although my father and my mother have abandoned me,
Yet the LORD will take me up [adopt me as His child]. [Ps 22:10]

[11]Teach me Your way, O LORD,
And lead me on a level path
Because of my enemies [who lie in wait].
[12]Do not give me up to the will of my adversaries,
For false witnesses have come against me;
They breathe out violence.
[13]*I would have despaired* had I not believed that I would see the goodness of the LORD
In the land of the living.
[14]Wait for *and* confidently expect the LORD;
Be strong and let your heart take courage;
Yes, wait for *and* confidently expect the LORD.

---

for divine discrimination (4:3). God distinguishes those who have responded to His grace from those who have not.

27:6 *sacrifices with shouts of joy.* These are praise offerings that the believers bring to God to celebrate the blessings He gives them (Heb 13:15).

27:14 *Wait for and confidently expect the LORD.* To wait for the Lord is to demonstrate confident expectation. The Hebrew word for "wait" may also be translated "hope." To hope in God is to wait for His timing and His action (40:1; Isa 40:31).

10 1Sa 8:3 **12** Ps 40:2; Ps 27:11; Ps 111:1 **PSALM 27 1** Isa 60:19; Ex 15:2; Ps 62:2 **2** Ps 14:4 **3** Ps 3:6 **4** Ps 26:8; Lk 2:37; Ps 90:17 **5** Ps 91:1; Ps 40:2 **6** Ps 3:3 **9** Ps 69:17 **10** Isa 49:15 **11** Ps 25:4 **13** Eze 26:20

Psalm 28

A Prayer for Help, and Praise for Its Answer.

A Psalm of David.

1 TO YOU I call, O LORD,
My rock, do not be deaf to me,
For if You are silent to me,
I will become like those who go down to the pit (grave).
2 Hear the voice of my supplication (specific requests, humble entreaties) as I cry to You for help,
As I lift up my hands *and* heart toward Your innermost sanctuary (Holy of Holies).
3 Do not drag me away with the wicked
And with those who do evil,
Who speak peace with their neighbors,
While malice *and* mischief are in their hearts.
4 Repay them according to their work and according to the evil of their practices;
Repay them according to the deeds of their hands;
Repay them what they deserve. [2 Tim 4:14; Rev 18:6]
5 Because they have no regard for the works of the LORD
Nor the deeds of His hands,
He will tear them down and not rebuild them.

6 Blessed be the LORD,
Because He has heard the voice of my supplication.
7 The LORD is my strength and my [impenetrable] shield;
My heart trusts [with unwavering confidence] in Him, and I am helped;
Therefore my heart greatly rejoices,
And with my song I shall thank Him *and* praise Him.
8 The LORD is their [unyielding] strength,
And He is the fortress of salvation to His anointed.
9 Save Your people and bless Your inheritance;
Be their shepherd also, and carry them forever.

Psalm 29

The Voice of the LORD in the Storm.

A Psalm of David.

1 ASCRIBE TO the LORD, O sons of the mighty,
Ascribe to the LORD glory and strength.
2 Ascribe to the LORD the glory due His name;
Worship the LORD in the beauty *and* majesty of His holiness [as the creator and source of holiness].

3 The voice of the LORD is upon the waters;
The God of glory thunders;
The LORD is over many waters.
4 The voice of the LORD is powerful;

28:1 *the pit.* This is one of the terms for death in the Psalms (55:23; 143:7).

28:5 *they have no regard.* The language here is similar to that of Paul in Romans 1:18 – 32. One day even the wicked will have to acknowledge God as their Creator and give Him the glory He deserves.

28:8 *His anointed.* This term acknowledges God's covenant with David, His promise that He would be David's God and David would be His representative. This passage became a heritage of the monarchy, a treasure for each godly king in the Davidic line to go back to for strength and encouragement.

29:1 *O sons of the mighty.* This means "O sons of gods." This Hebrew phrase refers to spiritual beings who are in the presence of God (see Job 1:6).

29:2 Worship by Israel — The central aspect of Israel's worship was the object of their worship, the Lord. While other nations paid homage to many gods, including inanimate objects such as trees and stones, Israel worshiped the one true God. This worship could be private, as a family or corporate as a congregation.

Israel's worship occurred in many different contexts and many different elements. It included offering sacrifices (1Sa 1:3), adopting a reverent

PSALM 28 **1** Ps 83:1; Ps 88:4 **2** Ps 5:7; Ps 138:2 **3** Ps 12:2 **4** Rev 18:6 **5** Isa 5:12 **7** Ps 18:2; 13:5 **8** Ps 20:6 **9** Dt 9:29; Ezr 1:4 **PSALM 29** **1** 1Ch 16:28 **2** 2Ch 20:21 **3** Job 37:4,5

The voice of the LORD is full of
majesty.
5 The voice of the LORD breaks the
cedars;
Yes, the LORD breaks in pieces the
cedars of Lebanon.
6 He makes Lebanon skip like a calf,
And Sirion (Mount Hermon) like a
young, wild ox.
7 The voice of the LORD rakes flames
of fire (lightning).
8 The voice of the LORD shakes the
wilderness;
The LORD shakes the wilderness of
Kadesh.
9 The voice of the LORD makes the
doe labor *and* give birth
And strips the forests bare;
And in His temple all are saying,
"Glory!"
10 The LORD sat *as King* at the flood;
Yes, the LORD sits as King forever.
11 The LORD will give [unyielding and
impenetrable] strength to His
people;
The LORD will bless His people
with peace.

Psalm 30
Thanksgiving for Deliverance from Death.

A Psalm; a Song at the Dedication of the House (Temple). *A Psalm* of David.

1 I WILL extol *and* praise You,
O LORD, for You have lifted me up,
And have not let my enemies
rejoice over me.
2 O LORD my God,
I cried to You for help, and You
have healed me.
3 O LORD, You have brought my life
up from Sheol (the nether world,
the place of the dead);
You have kept me alive, so that
I would not go down to the pit
(grave).
4 Sing to the LORD, O you His godly
ones,
And give thanks at the mention of
His holy *name*.
5 For His anger is but for a moment,
His favor is for a lifetime.
Weeping may endure for a night,
But a shout of joy comes in the
morning. [2 Cor 4:17]
6 As for me, in my prosperity I said,
"I shall never be moved."
7 By Your favor *and* grace, O LORD,
you have made my mountain
stand strong;
You hid Your face, and I was
horrified.
8 I called to You, O LORD,
And to the Lord I made
supplication (specific request).
9 "What profit is there in my blood
(death), if I go down to the pit
(grave)?
Will the dust praise You? Will it
declare Your faithfulness [to
man]?
10 "Hear, O LORD, be gracious *and*
show favor to me;
O LORD, be my helper."
11 You have turned my mourning
into dancing for me;

---

posture (2Ch 7:6), verbal praise — either spoken (1Ch 16:7) or sung (Ps 57:7), instrumental praise (Ps 150:3–5), prayer (2Ch 6:14–42), and the great feasts (Lev 23; 25).

The first place of worship for the people of Israel was the tabernacle constructed by Moses (Ex 25; 27; 30–31; 35; 40). Solomon's temple in Jerusalem became the permanent place for the central worship of the whole nation when it was completed. The New Testament teaching is that there is no limitation on location for worship. Access to God is direct and immediate (1Co 6:19).

29:10 *at the flood.* God is the true victor over all. He even controlled the waters at the height of their destructive power during the flood.

30:3 *from Sheol.* David is not reporting a resurrection, but a deliverance from a nearly fatal illness. As in 28:1, the psalmist describes death as a great pit into which a person drops into the enveloping darkness of the unknown.

30:10 *my helper.* "Helper" can also be translated "power" or "shield (33:20). Jesus promised His disciples that the Holy Spirit would be their Helper (Jn 14:16).

5 Isa 2:13 **6** Ps 114:4; Dt 3:9 **8** Nu 13:26 **10** Ps 10:16 **11** Ps 28:8 **PSALM 30 Title** Dt 20:5 **1** Ps 28:9; Ps 25:2 **3** Ps 86:13 **5** Ps 103:9; 63:3 **7** Ps 104:29 **9** Ps 6:5

You have taken off my sackcloth
and clothed me with joy,
12 That my soul may sing praise to
You and not be silent.
O LORD my God, I will give thanks
to You forever.

Psalm 31

A Psalm of Complaint and of Praise.

To the Chief Musician. A Psalm of David.

1 IN YOU, O LORD, I have placed my
trust *and* taken refuge;
Let me never be ashamed;
In Your righteousness rescue me.
2 Incline Your ear to me, deliver me
quickly;
Be my rock of refuge,
And a strong fortress to save me.
3 Yes, You are my rock and my
fortress;
For Your name's sake You will
lead me and guide me.
4 You will draw me out of the net that
they have secretly laid for me,
For You are my strength *and* my
stronghold.
5 Into Your hand I commit my spirit;
You have redeemed me, O LORD,
the God of truth *and* faithfulness.
[Luke 23:46; Acts 7:59]

6 I hate those who pay regard to
vain (empty, worthless) idols;
But I trust in the LORD [and rely
on Him with unwavering
confidence].
7 I will rejoice and be glad in Your
steadfast love,
Because You have seen my
affliction;
You have taken note of my life's
distresses,
8 And You have not given me into
the hand of the enemy;
You have set my feet in a broad
place.

9 Be gracious *and* compassionate to
me, O LORD, for I am in trouble;
My eye is clouded *and* weakened
by grief, my soul and my body
also.
10 For my life is spent with sorrow
And my years with sighing;
My strength has failed because of
my iniquity,
And even my body has wasted
away.
11 Because of all my enemies I
have become a reproach *and*
disgrace,
Especially to my neighbors,
And an object of dread to my
acquaintances;
Those who see me on the street
run from me.
12 I am forgotten like a dead man, out
of mind;
I am like a broken vessel.
13 For I have heard the slander *and*
whispering of many,
Terror is on every side;
While they schemed together
against me,
They plotted to take away my life.
[Jer 20:10]
14 But as for me, I trust [confidently]
in You *and* Your greatness,
O LORD;
I said, "You are my God."
15 My times are in Your hands;
Rescue me from the hand of my
enemies and from those who
pursue *and* persecute me.
16 Make Your face shine upon Your
servant;
Save me in Your lovingkindness.

31:1 *I have placed my trust.* This is a psalm of lament, yet David expresses deep trust in God in spite of his afflictions.
31:5 *Into Your hand I commit my spirit.* With these words, David expressed his complete dependence on God. These very words were spoken by Jesus on the cross shortly before His death (Lk 23:46), and by Stephen when he was stoned (Ac 7:59).
31:15 *My times are in Your hands.* Even when we cannot understand the "why," we can trust that God is in control of when each life begins and ends, and also of our times of suffering.

PSALM 31 **1** Ps 22:5 **2** Ps 71:2 **3** Ps 18:2; 23:3 **5** Lk 23:46 **6** Jnh 2:8 **7** Jn 10:27 **8** Dt 32:30 **9** Ps 6:7 **11** Isa 53:4; Job 19:13; Ps 64:8 **12** Ps 88:4,5 **13** Jer 20:10; La 2:22; Mt 27:1 **16** Ps 4:6

17 Let me not be put to shame,
O LORD, for I call on You;
Let the wicked (godless) be put
to shame, let them be silent in
Sheol (the nether world, the
place of the dead).
18 Let the lying lips be mute,
Which speak insolently *and*
arrogantly against the
[consistently] righteous
With pride and contempt.

19 How great is Your goodness,
Which You have stored up for
those who [reverently] fear You,
Which You have prepared for
those who take refuge in You,
Before the sons of man!
20 In the secret place of Your
presence You hide them from the
plots *and* conspiracies of man;
You keep them secretly in a shelter
(pavilion) from the strife of
tongues.
21 Blessed be the LORD,
For He has shown His marvelous
favor *and* lovingkindness to
me [when I was assailed] in a
besieged city.
22 As for me, I said in my alarm,
"I am cut off from Your eyes."
Nevertheless You heard the voice
of my supplications (specific
requests)
When I cried to You [for help].
23 O love the LORD, all you His godly
ones!
The LORD preserves the faithful
[those with moral and spiritual
integrity]
And fully repays the [self-
righteousness of the]
arrogant.
24 Be strong and let your hearts take
courage,
All you who wait for *and*
confidently expect the LORD.

Psalm 32

Blessedness of Forgiveness and of Trust in God.

A Psalm of David. A skillful song,
or a didactic *or* reflective poem.

1 BLESSED [FORTUNATE,
prosperous, favored by God]
is he whose transgression is
forgiven,
And whose sin is covered.
2 Blessed is the man to whom
the LORD does not impute
wickedness,
And in whose spirit there is no
deceit. [Rom 4:7, 8]

3 When I kept silent *about my sin,*
my body wasted away
Through my groaning all the day
long.
4 For day and night Your hand [of
displeasure] was heavy
upon me;
My energy (vitality, strength)
was drained away as with
the burning heat of summer.
Selah.
5 I acknowledged my sin to You,
And I did not hide my wickedness;

31:22 *I said in my alarm.* The psalmist's emotional response was to accuse God of abandoning him instead of asking for help, yet God still answered his true need.
32:1 *Blessed.* "Blessed" means "happy." It is appropriate that this word is used both of the righteous (1:1) and of the forgiven.
32:3 *kept silent.* When we refuse to admit our sin, we will suffer. David realized that it was not just his feelings that were assaulting him, but the heavy hand of God (38:1,6–8). No matter who else is hurt, the principal offense of any sin is always against the Lord.

32:5 What Should be Done About Sin—There are only two things that the believer should do about his sin: confess it and forsake it. He should never condone or attempt to excuse his sin. Here David confesses his sin and experiences forgiveness. Similarly 1 John 1:9 makes the same point. When the believer confesses his sin, he has the assurance that God "is faithful" (He can be counted on to keep His word) and "just" (He is just in dealing with our sins because He paid the price for them) "and will forgive our sins and cleanse us continually from all unrighteousness." God is able to cleanse us completely from anything

17 Ps 25:2; Ps 115:17 **18** Ps 120:2; 94:4 **19** Isa 64:4 **20** Ps 27:5; Job 5:21 **21** Ps 17:7; 1Sa 23:7 **22** Ps 116:11; La 3:54 **23** Ps 34:9 **24** Ps 27:14 **PSALM 32** **1** Ps 85:2 **2** 2Co 5:19; Jn 1:47 **4** Job 33:7 **5** Pr 28:13

I said, "I will confess [all] my
transgressions to the LORD";
And You forgave the guilt of my
sin. *Selah.*
6 Therefore, let everyone who
is godly pray to You [for
forgiveness] in a time when
You [are near and] may be
found;
Surely when the great waters
[of trial and distressing times]
overflow they will not reach [the
spirit in] him.
7 You are my hiding place; You,
LORD, protect me from trouble;
You surround me with songs
and shouts of deliverance.
Selah.
8 I will instruct you and teach you in
the way you should go;
I will counsel you [who are willing
to learn] with My eye upon
you.
9 Do not be like the horse or
like the mule which have no
understanding,
Whose trappings include bridle
and rein to hold them in check,
Otherwise they will not come near
to you.
10 Many are the sorrows of the
wicked,
But he who trusts in *and* relies on
the LORD shall be surrounded
with compassion *and*
lovingkindness.
11 Be glad in the LORD and rejoice,
you righteous [who actively seek
right standing with Him];
Shout for joy, all you upright in
heart.

Psalm 33
Praise to the Creator and Preserver.

1 REJOICE IN the LORD, you
righteous ones;
Praise is becoming *and*
appropriate for those who are
upright [in heart—those with
moral integrity and godly
character].
2 Give thanks to the LORD with the
lyre;
Sing praises to Him with the harp
of ten strings.
3 Sing to Him a new song;
Play skillfully [on the strings] with
a loud *and* joyful sound.
4 For the word of the LORD is right;
And all His work is done in
faithfulness.
5 He loves righteousness and justice;
The earth is full of the
lovingkindness of the LORD.
6 By the word of the LORD were the
heavens made,
And all their host by the breath of
His mouth. [Gen 1:1–3; Job 38:4–
11; Heb 11:3; 2 Pet 3:5]
7 He gathers the waters of the sea
together as in a wineskin;
He puts the deeps in storehouses.
8 Let all the earth fear *and* worship
the LORD;
Let all the inhabitants of the world
stand in awe of Him.
9 For He spoke, and it was done;
He commanded, and it stood fast.
10 The LORD nullifies the counsel of
the nations;

---

that is inconsistent with His own moral character. Having received forgiveness and cleansing, the believer is to forsake his sin and yield himself completely to God. In so doing, the believer is restored to full fellowship with God.

32:9 *bridle and rein . . . Otherwise they will not come near to you.* God does not want to drive His people with rules and regulations, the "bridle and rein" of righteousness. Rather, He wants His people to follow Him willingly, that they desire above all to please Him, not just to appease Him.

33:5 *The earth is full.* In spite of the fallen nature of our world, much of the creation remains as it was in the beginning: "very good" (Ge 1:31). We do have to deal with evil, but every time we see the goodness of God's creation we should rejoice.

33:9 *He spoke, and it was done.* The creation account in Genesis 1 describes God's spoken word as the controlling element in creation; John 1 shows that Word to be Jesus Christ, God's Son.

6 1Ti 1:16; Isa 55:6 **7** Ps 9:9; Ex 15:1 **9** Pr 26:3; Job 35:11 **10** Ro 2:9; Pr 16:20 **11** Ps 64:10 **PSALM 33**
1 Ps 32:11; Ps 147:1 **2** Ps 92:3 **3** Ps 96:1 **5** Ps 11:7; Ps 119:64 **6** Heb 11:3; Job 26:13 **7** Job 26:10 **9** Ge 1:3
10 Isa 8:10

He makes the thoughts *and* plans
of the people ineffective.
11 The counsel of the LORD stands
forever,
The thoughts *and* plans of His
heart through all generations.
12 Blessed [fortunate, prosperous,
and favored by God] is the
nation whose God is the LORD,
The people whom He has chosen
as His own inheritance.
[Deut 32:8, 9]

13 The LORD looks [down] from
heaven;
He sees all the sons of man;
14 From His dwelling place He looks
closely
Upon all the inhabitants of the
earth—
15 He who fashions the hearts of
them all,
Who considers *and* understands
all that they do.
16 The king is not saved by the great
size of his army;
A warrior is not rescued by his
great strength.
17 A horse is a false hope for
victory;
Nor does it deliver anyone by its
great strength.

18 Behold, the eye of the LORD is
upon those who fear Him [and
worship Him with awe-inspired
reverence and obedience],
On those who hope [confidently]
in His compassion *and*
lovingkindness,
19 To rescue their lives from death
And keep them alive in famine.
20 We wait [expectantly] for the LORD;
He is our help and our shield.
21 For in Him our heart rejoices,
Because we trust [lean on, rely on,
and are confident] in His holy
name.
22 Let Your [steadfast]
lovingkindness, O LORD, be
upon us,
In proportion as we have hoped in
You.

Psalm 34

The LORD, a Provider and the One Who Rescues Me.

A Psalm of David; when he pretended to be insane before Abimelech, who drove him out, and he went away.

1 I WILL bless the LORD at all
times;
His praise shall continually be in
my mouth.
2 My soul makes its boast in the
LORD;
The humble *and* downtrodden will
hear it and rejoice.
3 O magnify the LORD with me,
And let us lift up His name
together.

4 I sought the LORD [on the authority
of His word], and He answered
me,
And delivered me from all my
fears. [Ps 73:25; Matt 7:7]
5 They looked to Him and were
radiant;
Their faces will never blush in
shame *or* confusion.
6 This poor man cried, and the LORD
heard him
And saved him from all his
troubles.

33:15 *He who fashions the hearts . . . Who considers.* When we are troubled and weary and suffering, we can never say that God does not notice or understand. He made us carefully, and He continues to watch over all that we do.
33:18 *hope.* Those who hoped for the Lord's lovingkindness were looking forward in faith to the promised redemption, the ultimate fulfillment of the covenants, just as believers today who have the same hope, based on faith in Christ's finished work of redemption.
34:1 *at all times.* The determination of David to praise God is similar to the words of Paul in 1 Thessalonians 5:18. The story behind this psalm may be found in 1 Samuel 21:10–15.

11 Job 23:13 **12** Ex 19:5; Dt 7:6 **13** Job 28:24; Ps 11:4 **15** Jer 32:19 **16** Ps 44:6 **17** Ps 20:7; Pr 21:31 **18** Job 36:7; Ps 34:15; Ps 147:11 **19** Job 5:20 **20** Ps 130:6 **21** Jn 16:22 **PSALM 34** **1** Eph 5:20 **2** Jer 9:24; Ps 119:74 **3** Lk 1:46 **4** Mt 7:7 **6** Ps 3:4; ver. 17,19

7 The angel of the LORD encamps
around those who fear Him
[with awe-inspired reverence
and worship Him with
obedience],
And He rescues [each of] them.
[2 Kin 6:8–23; Ps 18:1; 145:20]
8 O taste and see that the LORD [our
God] is good;
How blessed [fortunate,
prosperous, and favored by God]
is the man who takes refuge in
Him. [1 Pet 2:2, 3]
9 O [reverently] fear the LORD, you
His saints (believers, holy ones);
For to those who fear Him there is
no want.
10 The young lions lack [food] and
grow hungry,
But they who seek the LORD will
not lack any good thing.
11 Come, you children, listen to me;
I will teach you to fear the LORD
[with awe-inspired reverence
and worship Him with
obedience].
12 Who is the man who desires life
And loves many days, that he may
see good?
13 Keep your tongue from evil
And your lips from speaking
deceit.
14 Turn away from evil and do good;
Seek peace and pursue it.
15 The eyes of the LORD are toward
the righteous [those with moral
courage and spiritual integrity]
And His ears are open to their cry.
16 The face of the LORD is against
those who do evil,
To cut off the memory of them
from the earth. [1 Pet 3:10–12]
17 When *the righteous* cry [for help],
the LORD hears
And rescues them from all their
distress *and* troubles.
18 The LORD is near to the
heartbroken
And He saves those who are
crushed in spirit (contrite in
heart, truly sorry for their sin).
19 Many hardships *and* perplexing
circumstances confront the
righteous,
But the LORD rescues him from
them all.
20 He keeps all his bones;
Not one of them is broken.
[John 19:33, 36]
21 Evil will cause the death of the
wicked,
And those who hate the righteous
will be held guilty *and* will be
condemned.
22 The LORD redeems the soul of His
servants,
And none of those who take refuge
in Him will be condemned.

Psalm 35

Prayer for Rescue from Enemies.

A Psalm of David.

1 CONTEND, O LORD, with those
who contend with me;
Fight against those who fight
against me.
2 Take hold of shield and buckler
(small shield),
And stand up for my help.
3 Draw also the spear and javelin to
meet those who pursue me.

34:7 *The angel of the LORD.* This term is often used interchangeably with the name of God (Ex 3). When we realize that God Himself is watching over us, there is no need to fear.
34:9 *O [reverently] fear the LORD.* This is a call to awe, wonder, worship, and reverence (Pr 1:7). To fear God is to respond to Him in obedience.
34:20 *keeps all his bones.* John 19:33 – 36 shows that the words of this verse were fulfilled in detail in the death of Jesus. Despite the terrible suffering that the Savior endured, none of His bones were broken.
35:2 *stand up for my help.* David did not hesitate to call upon God for vindication, comfort, and justice. He placed complete dependence on the Lord.

7 Da 6:22; 2Ki 6:17 **8** 1Pe 2:3; Ps 2:12 **10** Ps 84:11 **11** Ps 32:8 **12** 1Pe 3:10 **14** Ps 37:27; Heb 12:14 **15** Job 36:7 **16** Lev 17:10; Pr 10:7 **17** Ps 145:19 **18** Ps 145:18; Isa 57:15 **19** Pr 24:16; ver. 6,17 **20** Jn 19:36 **21** Ps 94:23 **22** 1Ki 1:29; Ps 71:23 **PSALM 35** **1** Ps 43:1; Ex 14:25 **2** Isa 42:13

Say to my soul, "I am your salvation."
4 Let those be ashamed and
dishonored who seek my life;
Let those be turned back [in
defeat] and humiliated who plot
evil against me.
5 Let them be [blown away]
like chaff before the wind
[worthless, without substance],
With the angel of the LORD driving
them on.
6 Let their way be dark and slippery,
With the angel of the LORD
pursuing *and* harassing them.
7 For without cause they hid their
net for me;
Without cause they dug a pit [of
destruction] for my life.
8 Let destruction come upon my
enemy by surprise;
Let the net he hid for me catch him;
Into that very destruction let him
fall.

9 Then my soul shall rejoice in the
LORD;
It shall rejoice in His salvation.
10 All my bones will say, "LORD, who
is like You,
Who rescues the afflicted from
him who is too strong for him [to
resist alone],
And the afflicted and the needy
from him who robs him?"
11 Malicious witnesses rise up;
They ask me of things that I do not
know.
12 They repay me evil for good,
To the sorrow of my soul.
13 But as for me, when they were
sick, my clothing was sackcloth
(mourning garment);
I humbled my soul with fasting,
And I prayed with my head bowed
on my chest.
14 I behaved as if grieving for my
friend or my brother;
I bowed down in mourning, as one
who sorrows for his mother.
15 But in my stumbling they rejoiced
and gathered together [against
me];
The slanderers whom I did not
know gathered against me;
They slandered *and* reviled me
without ceasing.
16 Like godless jesters at a feast,
They gnashed at me with their
teeth [in malice].

17 LORD, how long will You look on
[without action]?
Rescue my life from their
destructions,
My only *life* from the young lions.
18 I will give You thanks in the great
congregation;
I will praise You among a mighty
people.
19 Do not let those who are
wrongfully my enemies rejoice
over me;
Nor let those who hate me
without cause wink their eye
[maliciously]. [John 15:24, 25]
20 For they do not speak peace,
But they devise deceitful words
[half-truths and lies] against
those who are quiet in the land.
21 They open their mouths wide
against me;
They say, "Aha, aha, our eyes have
seen it!"

35:8 *Let destruction come upon my enemy.* David's response is certainly not an example of turning the other cheek or loving his enemies (Mt 5:39,44), but it shows David's keen awareness of the battle between good and evil, the reality of wickedness, and his understanding that wickedness is an abomination to the Lord.

35:18 *congregation.* Three times a year, at three of the great annual feasts, all males were required to appear before the Lord in Jerusalem. Each brought his offering to the Lord on these occasions. When they came accompanied by their families, as was often the case, Jerusalem was flooded by a vast horde of people intent upon worshiping God. David viewed speaking before this "great congregation" or the assembly of Israel as the ultimate opportunity for testimony. A constant testimony is given to the world by believers as they give voice to praise Him for His watchful care over them.

35:19 *hate me without cause.* This passage was fulfilled in the suffering of Jesus, the Savior (Jn 15:23–25).

---

4 Ps 70:2,3 **5** Job 21:18; Ps 1:4 **6** Ps 73:18 **7** Ps 9:15 **8** 1Th 5:3 **10** Ex 15:11 **12** Jn 10:32 **13** Job 30:25
15 Job 30:1,8; Job 16:9 **16** Job 16:9; La 2:16 **17** Hab 1:13; Ps 22:20 **19** Ps 13:4; Job 15:12; Ps 69:4 **21** Ps 22:13; 40:15

22 You have seen this, O LORD; do not
keep silent.
O Lord, do not be far from me.
23 Wake Yourself up, and arise to my
right
And to my cause, my God and my
Lord.
24 Judge me, O LORD my God,
according to Your righteousness
and justice;
And do not let them rejoice over
me.
25 Do not let them say in their heart,
"Aha, that is what we wanted!"
Do not let them say, "We have
swallowed him up *and*
destroyed him."
26 Let those be ashamed and
humiliated together who rejoice
at my distress;
Let those be clothed with shame
and dishonor who magnify
themselves over me.
27 Let them shout for joy and rejoice,
who favor my vindication *and*
want what is right for me;
Let them say continually, "Let
the LORD be magnified, who
delights *and* takes pleasure in
the prosperity of His servant."
28 And my tongue shall declare Your
righteousness (justice),
And Your praise all the day long.

Psalm 36

Wickedness of Men and Lovingkindness of God.

To the Chief Musician. *A Psalm* of David the servant of the LORD.

1 TRANSGRESSION SPEAKS
[like an oracle] to the wicked
(godless) [deep] within his heart;
There is no fear (dread) of God
before his eyes. [Rom 3:18]
2 For he flatters *and* deceives
himself in his own eyes
Thinking that his sinfulness will
not be discovered and hated [by
God].
3 The words of his mouth are
wicked and deceitful;
He has ceased to be wise *and* to do
good.
4 He plans wrongdoing on his bed;
He sets himself on a path that is
not good;
He does not reject *or* despise evil.
5 Your lovingkindness *and*
graciousness, O LORD, extend to
the skies,
Your faithfulness [reaches] to the
clouds.
6 Your righteousness is like the
mountains of God,
Your judgments are like the great
deep.
O LORD, You preserve man and
beast.
7 How precious is Your
lovingkindness, O God!
The children of men take refuge in
the shadow of Your wings.
8 They drink their fill of the
abundance of Your house;
And You allow them to drink from
the river of Your delights.
9 For with You is the fountain of
life [the fountain of life-giving
water];
In Your light we see light.
[John 4:10, 14]
10 O continue Your lovingkindness to
those who know You,
And Your righteousness
(salvation) to the upright in
heart.
11 Do not let the foot of the proud
[person] overtake me,
And do not let the hand of the
wicked drive me away.

35:26 *ashamed.* The phrase "be ashamed" does not refer just to simple embarrassment, but to the revelation of the complete emptiness of wickedness before the judgment seat of God. **36:1 *no fear (dread) of God.*** Underlying wickedness is a complete disregard for the reality of God in a person's life and in the world. **36:9 *fountain of life.*** God's salvation and continuing mercy to His people are often described in terms of life-giving water (Isa 12:3; Jer 2:13; Jn 4:1 – 14).

22 Ex 3:7; Ps 28:1; Ps 10:1 **23** Ps 44:23 **24** 2Th 1:6 **25** La 2:16 **26** Ps 109:29 **27** Ro 12:15 **PSALM 36** **1** Ro 3:18 **3** Jer 4:22 **4** Pr 4:16; Isa 65:2 **6** Ro 11:33 **7** Ps 17:8 **8** Ps 65:4; Job 20:17; Rev 22:1 **9** Jer 2:13; 1Pe 2:9

[12]There those who [are perverse
and] do evil have fallen;
They have been thrust down and
cannot rise.

Psalm 37

Security of Those Who Trust in the LORD, and Insecurity of the Wicked.

A Psalm of David.

[1]DO NOT worry because of
evildoers,
Nor be envious toward
wrongdoers;
[2]For they will wither quickly like
the grass,
And fade like the green herb.
[3]Trust [rely on and have
confidence] in the LORD and do
good;
Dwell in the land and feed
[securely] on His faithfulness.
[4]Delight yourself in the LORD,
And He will give you the desires
and petitions of your heart.
[5]Commit your way to the LORD;
Trust in Him also and He will do it.
[6]He will make your righteousness
[your pursuit of right standing
with God] like the light,
And your judgment like [the
shining of] the noonday [sun].

[7]Be still before the LORD; wait
patiently for Him *and* entrust
yourself to Him;
Do not fret (whine, agonize)
because of him who prospers in
his way,
Because of the man who carries
out wicked schemes.
[8]Cease from anger and abandon
wrath;
Do not fret; *it leads* only to evil.
[9]For those who do evil will be cut
off,
But those who wait for the LORD,
they will inherit the land.
[Is 57:13c]
[10]For yet a little while and the
wicked one will be gone
[forever];
Though you look carefully where he
used to be, he will not be [found].
[Heb 10:36, 37; Rev 21:7, 8]
[11]But the humble will [at last] inherit
the land
And will delight themselves in
abundant prosperity *and* peace.
[Ps 37:29; Matt 5:5]

[12]The wicked plots against the
righteous
And gnashes at him with his teeth.
[13]The Lord laughs at him [the
wicked one—the one who
oppresses the righteous],
For He sees that his day [of defeat]
is coming.
[14]The wicked have drawn the sword
and bent their bow
To cast down the afflicted and the
needy,
To slaughter those who are upright
in conduct [those with personal
integrity and godly character].
[15]The sword [of the ungodly] will
enter their own heart,
And their bow will be broken.

[16]Better is the little of the righteous
[who seek the will of God]
Than the abundance (riches)
of many wicked (godless).
[1 Tim 6:6, 7]

37:1 *Do not worry.* When the wicked seem to prosper, the psalmist calls for patience, a renewed sense of dependence on the Lord, and a new sense of pleasure in knowing Him.
37:4 *the desires and petitions of your heart.* Many times, we read this verse as a promise that God will give us anything that we want because He wants us to be happy. In reality, this verse goes much deeper. When we truly delight in God, He plants in our hearts godly desires that He delights to fulfill.
37:7 *Be still before the LORD . . . Do not fret.* This is not a call to stop caring and go to sleep, but to depend actively on the living Lord, leaving our lives and times in His hands.
37:13 *He sees that his day [of defeat] is coming.* The wicked sometimes appear to prosper, but from God's perspective, the flourishing of the wicked is short (Ecc 3:16 – 17).

PSALM 37 **1** Ps 73:3; Pr 23:17 **2** Ps 90:5,6 **4** Isa 58:14 **5** Ps 55:22; Mt 6:25 **6** Job 11:17 **7** La 3:26 **8** Ps 73:3; Eph 4:26 **9** Isa 57:13 **10** Heb 10:36; Job 7:10 **11** Mt 5:5 **12** Ps 35:16 **13** Ps 2:4; 1Sa 26:10 **15** Ps 9:16 **16** Pr 15:16

17 For the arms of the wicked will be
broken,
But the LORD upholds *and* sustains
the righteous [who seek Him].
18 The LORD knows the days of the
blameless,
And their inheritance will
continue forever.
19 They will not be ashamed in the
time of evil,
And in the days of famine they
will have plenty *and* be satisfied.
20 But the wicked (ungodly) will
perish,
And the enemies of the LORD will
be like the glory of the pastures
and like the fat of lambs [that is
consumed in smoke],
They vanish—like smoke they
vanish away.
21 The wicked borrows and does not
pay back,
But the righteous is gracious *and*
kind and gives.
22 For those blessed by God will [at
last] inherit the land,
But those cursed by Him will be
cut off. [Is 57:13c]
23 The steps of a [good and
righteous] man are directed *and*
established by the LORD,
And He delights in his way [and
blesses his path].
24 When he falls, he will not be
hurled down,
Because the LORD is the One who
holds his hand *and* sustains him.
25 I have been young and now I am
old,
Yet I have not seen the righteous
(those in right standing with
God) abandoned
Or his descendants pleading for
bread.
26 All day long he is gracious and
lends,
And his descendants are a
blessing.

27 Depart from evil and do good;
And you will dwell [securely in the
land] forever.
28 For the LORD delights in justice
And does not abandon His saints
(faithful ones);
They are preserved forever,
But the descendants of the wicked
will [in time] be cut off.
29 The righteous will inherit the land
And live in it forever.
30 The mouth of the righteous
proclaims wisdom,
And his tongue speaks justice *and*
truth.
31 The law of his God is in his heart;
Not one of his steps will slip.
32 The wicked lies in wait for the
righteous
And seeks to kill him.
33 The LORD will not leave him in his
hand
Or let him be condemned when he
is judged.
34 Wait for *and* expect the LORD and
keep His way,
And He will exalt you to inherit
the land;
[In the end] when the wicked are
cut off, you will see it.

35 I have seen a wicked, violent man
[with great power]
Spreading *and* flaunting himself
like a cedar in its native soil,
36 Yet he passed away, and lo, he was
no more;

37:21 ***the righteous is gracious and kind and gives.*** There are many contrasts between the wicked and the righteous in the wisdom psalms; this one is based on contrasting attitudes toward possessions (15:5; 112:5). Jesus said that such generous givers would be rewarded with "good measure — pressed down, shaken together, and running over" (Lk 6:38).

37:25 ***pleading for bread.*** Some interpret these words as referring to spiritual famine — the righteous will never be deprived of the Lord's presence (Jn 6:35). However, many have taken these words literally and experienced God's miraculous provision for their material needs.

37:27 ***Depart from evil.*** In this life people must choose either to cling to God and righteousness or to pursue evil.

17 Ps 10:15 **18** Ps 1:6; Isa 60:21 **19** Ps 33:19 **20** Ps 102:3 **21** Ps 112:5,9 **22** Pr 3:33 **23** 1Sa 2:9 **24** Pr 24:16 **25** Job 15:23 **26** Dt 15:8 **27** Ps 34:14 **28** Isa 30:18; Ps 21:10 **29** Pr 2:21 **30** Mt 12:35 **31** Dt 6:6 **32** Ps 10:8 **33** 2Pe 2:9; Ps 109:31 **34** Ps 27:14; Ps 52:5,6 **35** Job 5:3 **36** Job 20:5

I sought him, but he could not be
found.
37 Mark the blameless man [who is
spiritually complete], and behold
the upright [who walks in moral
integrity];
There is a [good] future for
the man of peace [because
a life of honor blesses one's
descendants].
38 As for transgressors, they will be
completely destroyed;
The future of the wicked will be
cut off.
39 But the salvation of the righteous
is from the LORD;
He is their refuge *and* stronghold
in the time of trouble.
40 The LORD helps them and rescues
them;
He rescues them from the wicked
and saves them,
Because they take refuge in Him.

Psalm 38

Prayer in Time of Discipline.

A Psalm of David; to bring
to remembrance.

1 O LORD, do not rebuke me in
Your wrath,
Nor discipline me in Your burning
anger.
2 For Your arrows have sunk into
me *and* penetrate deeply,
And Your hand has pressed down
on me *and* greatly disciplined me.
3 There is no soundness in my flesh
because of Your indignation;
There is no health in my bones
because of my sin.
4 For my iniquities have gone over
my head [like the waves of a
flood];
As a heavy burden they weigh too
much for me.
5 My wounds are loathsome and foul
Because of my foolishness.
6 I am bent over and greatly bowed
down;
I go about mourning all day long.
7 For my sides are filled with
burning,
And there is no health in my flesh.
8 I am numb and greatly bruised
[deadly cold and completely
worn out];
I groan because of the disquiet *and*
moaning of my heart.
9 Lord, all my desire is before You;
And my sighing is not hidden from
You.
10 My heart throbs violently, my
strength fails me;
And as for the light of my eyes,
even that has also gone from me.
11 My loved ones and my friends
stand aloof from my plague;
And my neighbors stand far away.
[Luke 23:49]
12 Those who seek my life lay snares
for me,
And those who seek to injure me
threaten mischievous things *and*
destruction;
They devise treachery all the day
long.
13 But I, like a deaf man, do not hear;
I am like a mute man who does not
open his mouth.
14 Yes, I am like a man who does not
hear,
In whose mouth are no arguments.
15 For in You, O LORD, I hope;
You will answer, O Lord my God.
16 For I pray, "May they not rejoice
over me,
Who, when my foot slips, would
boast against me."

37:39 *salvation.* The principal issue here is not regeneration, but sanctification — the daily deliverance of God's people from temptation and evil.
38:1 *do not rebuke me.* David is not saying, "Don't tell me I'm wrong," but "Have mercy on my sinfulness." David's penitent psalms can serve as a model for our own prayers of confession.
38:14 *a man who does not hear.* David was determined not to present an opportunity for his enemies to condemn the name of the Lord. His silence foreshadowed the silence of Jesus before His accusers (Mk 14:61).

37 Isa 32:17 **38** Ps 1:4 **39** Ps 3:8; 9:9 **40** Isa 31:5; 1Ch 5:20 **PSALM 38** **Title** Ps 70, Title **1** Ps 6:1 **2** Job 6:4; Ps 32:4 **3** Ps 6:2 **4** Ezr 9:6; Mt 11:28 **6** Ps 35:14; Job 30:28 **7** Job 7:5 **8** Job 3:24 **10** Ps 6:7 **11** Ps 31:11; Lk 10:31; Lk 23:49 **12** 2Sa 17:1; 2Sa 16:7 **13** 2Sa 16:10; Ps 39:2,9 **15** Ps 39:7 **16** Ps 13:4; Ps 35:26

17 For I am ready to fall;
My sorrow is continually before me.
18 For I do confess my guilt *and* iniquity;
I am filled with anxiety because of my sin. [2 Cor 7:9, 10]
19 But my [numerous] enemies are vigorous and strong,
And those who hate me without cause are many.
20 They repay evil for good, they attack *and* try to kill me,
Because I follow what is good.
21 Do not abandon me, O LORD;
O my God, do not be far from me.
22 Make haste to help me,
O Lord, my Salvation.

Psalm 39

The Vanity of Life.

To the Chief Musician; for Jeduthun. A Psalm of David.

1 I SAID, "I will guard my ways
That I may not sin with my tongue;
I will muzzle my mouth
While the wicked are in my presence."
2 I was mute and silent [before my enemies],
I refrained *even* from good,
And my distress grew worse.
3 My heart was hot within me.
While I was musing the fire burned;
Then I spoke with my tongue:
4 "LORD, let me know my [life's] end
And [to appreciate] the extent of my days;
Let me know how frail I am [how transient is my stay here].
5 "Behold, You have made my days as [short as] hand widths,
And my lifetime is as nothing in Your sight.
Surely every man at his best is a mere breath [a wisp of smoke, a vapor that vanishes]! [Eccl 1:2] *Selah.*
6 "Surely every man walks around like a shadow [in a charade];
Surely they make an uproar for nothing;
Each one builds up *riches*, not knowing who will receive them. [Eccl 2:18, 19; 1 Cor 7:31; James 4:14]
7 "And now, Lord, for what do I expectantly wait?
My hope [my confident expectation] is in You.
8 "Save me from all my transgressions;
Do not make me the scorn *and* reproach of the [self-righteous, arrogant] fool.
9 "I am mute, I do not open my mouth,
Because it is You who has done it.
10 "Remove Your plague from me;
I am wasting away because of the conflict *and* opposition of Your hand.
11 "With rebukes You discipline man for sin;
You consume like a moth what is precious to him;
Surely every man is a mere breath [a wisp of smoke, a vapor that vanishes]. *Selah.*
12 "Hear my prayer, O LORD, and listen to my cry;
Do not be silent at my tears;
For I am Your temporary guest,
A sojourner like all my fathers.
13 "O look away from me, that I may smile *and* again know joy
Before I depart and am no more."

38:18 *I do confess.* David's silence was only before his enemies; to the Lord he willingly confessed his sins.
39:1 *I will guard my ways.* David determined to be silent in suffering so that he would not speak out foolishly.
39:9 *You who has done it.* David knows that his only chance of deliverance is in God. But he also believes that his trouble has come from God. He is in a quandary. Should he ask for God's help, or should he ask for God to leave him alone?
39:13 *O look away from me.* If God is not going to deliver him, the despondent psalmist

18 Pr 28:13; 2Co 7:9 **20** Ps 35:12 **21** Ps 35:22 **PSALM 39** **Title** 1Ch 16:41; Ps 62, Title; 77, Title **1** 1Ki 2:4 **2** Ps 38:13 **6** Lk 12:20 **8** Ps 44:13 **9** Lev 10:3; Job 2:10 **11** Job 13:28 **12** Ge 47:9 **13** Job 10:20; Job 14:10

Psalm 40
God Sustains His Servant.

To the Chief Musician.
A Psalm of David.

1 I WAITED patiently *and*
expectantly for the LORD;
And He inclined to me and heard
my cry.
2 He brought me up out of a horrible
pit [of tumult and of destruction],
out of the miry clay,
And He set my feet upon a rock,
steadying my footsteps *and*
establishing my path.
3 He put a new song in my mouth, a
song of praise to our God;
Many will see and fear [with great
reverence]
And will trust confidently in the
LORD. [Ps 5:11]

4 Blessed [fortunate, prosperous,
and favored by God] is the
man who makes the LORD his
trust,
And does not regard the proud nor
those who lapse into lies.
5 Many, O LORD my God, are the
wonderful works which You
have done,
And Your thoughts toward us;
There is none to compare with You.
If I would declare and speak of
your wonders,
They would be too many to count.

6 Sacrifice and meal offering You
do not desire, *nor* do You delight
in them;
You have opened my ears *and*
given me the capacity to hear
[and obey Your word];
Burnt offerings and sin offerings
You do not require. [Mic 6:6–8]
7 Then I said, "Behold, I come [to the
throne];
In the scroll of the book it is
written of me.
8 "I delight to do Your will, O my God;
Your law is within my heart."
[Jer 31:33; Heb 10:5–9]

---

asks God to leave him alone. It is rare outside the Book of Job to find language such as this (Job 7:19). The pain of the psalmist was so far from being resolved that he remained in despair until the last verse. Yet the fact that God saves those who call upon Him is described again and again in the Book of Psalms (22:31; 118:21).

40:1 *I waited patiently.* The verb "to wait" expresses a confident trust or faith in the Lord (130:5). David knows that salvation comes only from the Almighty (3:8).

40:6 *You have opened my ears.* God allows us to hear His words, and He also gives us understanding and wisdom to internalize and apply them.

40:7 *Behold, I come.* According to Hebrews 10:4 – 7, Jesus spoke these words to the Father.

40:8 To Know God's Will — Knowing the will of God is not simply a vehicle for finding the right vocation for a life's work. While vocation is important, it is only a small part of God's will. The will of God must be thought of in more comprehensive terms. The will of God is for everyone to live in such a way as to bring honor and glory to God. For different people God may have very different things in mind. We must continually stay in God's Word so that He can make clear to us what His will is for us. We must also be still, listen, and know that He is God.

The first step towards understanding God's will is believing in Christ (Jn 3:14 – 16). If we do not accept this gift from God, we will not be saved from judgment (Mt 7:21). Second, Scripture teaches us that it is God's will for every believer to be sanctified (2Th 2:13 – 17). Third, the Bible declares God's will as it must be applied to our lives (Dt 29:29). This fact involves commands to be obeyed, principles to be followed, prohibitions of things to be avoided and living examples to be imitated or shunned. God takes great joy in those who cheerfully do His will.

Although the Bible is a comprehensive revelation of God's will, there are always decisions wemake that Scripture does not directly address. In order to know God's will in these situations we need to be in fellowship with the Lord (1Jn 1:6 – 7), seek principles from the Word (1Co 10:6), obtain advice from godly counselors (Pr 11:14), use common sense, and remember that God works through our own minds and He desires for us to do His will (Php 2:13).

PSALM 40 **1** Ps 27:14 **2** Ps 69:2,14; 27:5 **3** Ps 33:3 **4** Ps 34:8 **5** Job 9:10; Isa 55:8 **8** Jn 4:34; Ps 37:31; Jer 31:33

[9]I have proclaimed good news of
righteousness [and the joy that
comes from obedience to You] in
the great assembly;
Behold, I will not restrain my
lips [from proclaiming Your
righteousness],
As You know, O LORD.
[10]I have not concealed Your
righteousness within my
heart;
I have proclaimed Your
faithfulness and Your
salvation.
I have not concealed Your
lovingkindness and Your
truth from the great assembly.
[Acts 20:20, 27]
[11]Do not withhold Your compassion
and tender mercy from me,
O LORD;
Your lovingkindness and Your truth
will continually preserve me.
[12]For innumerable evils have
encompassed me;
My sins have overtaken me, so
that I am not able to see.
They are more numerous than the
hairs of my head,
And my heart has failed me.
[13]Be pleased, O LORD, to save me;
O LORD, make haste to help me.
[14]Let those be ashamed and
humiliated together
Who seek my life to destroy it;
Let those be turned back [in
defeat] and dishonored
Who delight in my hurt.
[15]Let those be appalled *and* desolate
because of their shame
Who say to me, "Aha, aha
[rejoicing in my misfortune]!"
[16]Let all who seek You rejoice and
be glad in You;
Let those who love Your salvation
say continually,
"The LORD be magnified!"
[17]Even though I am afflicted and
needy,
Still the Lord takes thought *and* is
mindful of me.
You are my help and my
rescuer.
O my God, do not delay. [Ps 70:1–5;
1 Pet 5:7]

Psalm 41

The Psalmist in Sickness Complains of Enemies and False Friends.

To the Chief Musician.
A Psalm of David.

[1]BLESSED [BY God's grace and
compassion] is he who considers
the helpless;
The LORD will save him in the day
of trouble.
[2]The LORD will protect him and
keep him alive;
And he will be called blessed in
the land;
You do not hand him over to the
desire of his enemies.
[3]The LORD will sustain *and*
strengthen him on his sickbed;
In his illness, You will restore him
to health.
[4]As for me, I said, "O LORD, be
gracious to me;
Heal my soul, for I have sinned
against You."

40:9 *assembly.* In Psalm 35 David prayed for deliverance from his enemies and promised to give God praise before "the great assembly," the assembly of Israel, for that deliverance. Psalm 40 is a joyful account of his deliverance from trouble, and his witness of God's righteousness before the people. The believer is obligated to speak of God's righteous acts toward him, so that others may hear of the goodness and glory of God.

40:11 *tender mercy.* This term refers to God's affection for us. David is asking God to surround him with warmth and comfort that is practically maternal.

41:4 *for I have sinned.* In the context of this psalm, this is a general acknowledgement of sin and the need for God's forgiveness and restoration (1Jn 1:9).

9 Ps 22:22; 119:13 **10** Ac 20:20 **11** Ps 43:3 **12** Ps 38:4 **13** Ps 70:1 **14** Ps 35:4 **15** Ps 73:19 **16** Ps 70:4; Ps 35:27 **17** Ps 70:5 **PSALM 41** **2** Ps 27:12

5 My enemies speak evil of me,
saying,
"When will he die and his name
perish?"
6 And when one comes to see me, he
speaks empty words,
While his heart gathers malicious
gossip [against me];
When he goes away, he tells it
[everywhere].
7 All who hate me whisper together
about me;
Against me they devise my hurt
[imagining the worst for me],
saying,
8 "A wicked thing is poured out
upon him *and* holds him;
And when he lies down, he will
not rise up again."
9 Even my own close friend in
whom I trusted,
Who ate my bread,
Has lifted up his heel against me
[betraying me]. [John 13:18]

10 But You, O LORD, be gracious
to me and restore me
[to health],
So that I may repay them.
11 By this I know that You favor *and*
delight in me,
Because my enemy does not shout
in triumph over me.
12 As for me, You uphold me in my
integrity,
And You set me in Your presence
forever.
13 Blessed be the LORD, the God of
Israel,
From everlasting to everlasting
[from this age to the next, and
forever].
Amen and Amen (so be it).

BOOK TWO

Psalm 42

Thirsting for God in Trouble and Exile.

To the Chief Musician. A skillful song, *or* a didactic *or* reflective poem, of the sons of Korah.

1 AS THE deer pants [longingly] for
the water brooks,
So my soul pants [longingly] for
You, O God.
2 My soul (my life, my inner self)
thirsts for God, for the living God.
When will I come and see the face
of God? [Ps 63:1, 2; John 7:37;
1 Thess 1:9, 10]
3 My tears have been my food day
and night,
While they say to me all day long,
"Where is your God?"
4 These things I [vividly] remember
as I pour out my soul;
How I used to go along before
the great crowd of people and
lead them in procession to the
house of God [like a choirmaster
before his singers, timing the
steps to the music and the chant
of the song],
With the voice of joy and
thanksgiving, a great crowd
keeping a festival.

5 Why are you in despair, O my soul?
And why have you become restless
and disturbed within me?
Hope in God *and* wait expectantly
for Him, for I shall again praise
Him
For the help of His presence.

41:9 ***Even my own close friend.*** Jesus quoted this verse, noting its fulfillment in Judas (Jn 13:18).
41:13 ***Blessed.*** This psalm begins with a blessing of God on the righteous; it ends with the righteous blessing their Lord. This word "blessed" is different from the word in verse 1. Here the word identifies the Lord as the source of our blessing.
42:4 ***I used to go along before the great crowd . . . to the house of God.*** This psalm was written in exile. The psalmist is remembering with longing and tears the times when he was able to worship God in Jerusalem.
42:5 ***I shall again praise Him.*** As is common in the Psalms, the poet is not describing an act of private devotion, but of public praise of the goodness of God. This is praise in words and songs that would be repeated in the midst of the congregation (22:22; Eph 5:19; Heb 13:15).

9 2Sa 15:12; Job 19:19; Ps 55:12; Ob 7; Jn 13:18 **12** Job 36:7; Ps 34:15 **13** Ps 106:48 **PSALM 42** **2** Ps 63:1
3 Ps 80:5 **4** Job 30:16; Isa 30:29 **5** ver. 11; La 3:24

6 O my God, my soul is in despair
within me [the burden more
than I can bear];
Therefore I will [fervently]
remember You from the land of
the Jordan
And the peaks of [Mount] Hermon,
from Mount Mizar.
7 Deep calls to deep at the
[thundering] sound of Your
waterfalls;
All Your breakers and Your waves
have rolled over me.
8 Yet the LORD will command His
lovingkindness in the daytime,
And in the night His song will be
with me,
A prayer to the God of my life.

9 I will say to God my rock, "Why
have You forgotten me?
Why do I go mourning because of
the oppression of the enemy?"
10 As a crushing of my bones [with a
sword], my adversaries taunt me,
While they say continually to me,
"Where is your God?"
11 Why are you in despair, O my
soul?
Why have you become restless
and disquieted within me?
Hope in God *and* wait expectantly
for Him, for I shall yet praise Him,
The help of my countenance and
my God.

Psalm 43

Prayer for Rescue.

1 JUDGE *AND* vindicate me,
O God; plead my case against an
ungodly nation.
O rescue me from the deceitful
and unjust man!
2 For You are the God of my
strength [my stronghold—in
whom I take refuge]; why have
You rejected me?
Why do I go mourning because of
the oppression of the enemy?

3 O send out Your light and Your
truth, let them lead me;
Let them bring me to Your holy
hill
And to Your dwelling places.
4 Then I will go to the altar of God,
To God, my exceeding joy;
With the lyre I will praise You,
O God, my God!

5 Why are you in despair, O my soul?
And why are you restless *and*
disturbed within me?
Hope in God *and* wait expectantly
for Him, for I shall again praise
Him,
The help of my [sad] countenance
and my God.

Psalm 44

Former Times of Help and Present Troubles.

To the Chief Musician. *A Psalm* of the sons of Korah. A skillful song, *or* a didactic *or* reflective poem.

1 WE HAVE heard with our ears,
O God,
Our fathers have told us
The work You did in their days,
In the days of old.
2 You drove out the [pagan] nations
with Your own hand;
Then you planted *and* established
them (Israel);
[It was by Your power that] You
uprooted the [pagan] peoples,

42:6 *the land of the Jordan ... peaks of [Mount] Hermon.* These are references to the promised land, from which the people were exiled. **43:1 *Judge and vindicate me.*** It is believed that Psalm 43 is a continuation of Psalm 42. **43:5 *in despair.*** Psalms 42 and 43 reflect a uniform feeling of being cut off from God, rejected and forsaken by Him. There is a common refrain in both psalms in which the author reasons with himself in order to surmount his feelings of depression and loneliness. Prayer is still possible when God seems to be absent, and we can hope in God in the face of present affliction because faith enables the believer to give thanks before the answer is experienced.

7 Ps 88:7 **8** Job 35:10 **9** Ps 38:6 **10** Joel 2:17; Mic 7:10 **11** Ps 43:5 **PSALM 43** **1** Ps 26:1; 35:1 **2** Ps 42:9 **3** Ps 40:11; 57:3; Ps 3:4 **5** Ps 42:5,11 **PSALM 44** **1** Ex 12:26; Ps 78:3 **2** Ex 15:17; Dt 7:1; Ps 80:8

Then You spread them abroad.
[3]For our fathers did not possess the land [of Canaan] by their own sword,
Nor did their own arm save them,
But Your right hand and Your arm and the light of Your presence,
Because You favored *and* delighted in them.

[4]You are my King, O God;
Command victories *and* deliverance for Jacob (Israel).
[5]Through You we will gore our enemies [like a bull];
Through Your name we will trample down those who rise up against us.
[6]For I will not trust in my bow,
Nor will my sword save me.
[7]But You have saved us from our enemies,
And You have put them to shame *and* humiliated those who hate us.
[8]In God we have boasted all the day long,
And we will praise *and* give thanks to Your name forever. *Selah.*

[9]But now You have rejected us and brought us to dishonor,
And You do not go out with our armies [to lead us to victory].
[10]You make us turn back from the enemy,
And those who hate us have taken spoil for themselves.
[11]You have made us like sheep to be eaten [as mutton]
And have scattered us [in exile] among the nations.
[12]You sell Your people cheaply,
And have not increased Your wealth by their sale.
[13]You have made us the reproach *and* taunt of our neighbors,
A scoffing and a derision to those around us.
[14]You make us a byword among the nations,
A laughingstock among the people.
[15]My dishonor is before me all day long,
And humiliation has covered my face,
[16]Because of the voice of the taunter and reviler,
Because of the presence of the enemy and the avenger.

[17]All this has come upon us, yet we have not forgotten You,
Nor have we been false to Your covenant [which You made with our fathers].
[18]Our heart has not turned back,
Nor have our steps wandered from Your path,
[19]Yet You have [distressingly] crushed us in the place of jackals
And covered us with [the deep darkness of] the shadow of death.

[20]If we had forgotten the name of our God
Or stretched out our hands to a strange god,
[21]Would not God discover this?
For He knows the secrets of the heart.

44:4 ***You are my King.*** In this community lament, it is striking that here the speaker is singular. It may be that these words are spoken by Israel's king to the King of glory. As the king of the nation, it was appropriate for him to lead the people in asking for God's renewed favor.
44:9 ***You have rejected us.*** The army of Israel was not just a group of soldiers. They were the warriors of the Almighty; their victories were the victories of God, and their defeats were losses that He allowed them to endure. If He ceased accompanying them to battle, they were doomed to failure.
44:17 ***we have not forgotten You.*** The faithful remnant had to bear the punishment of exile as well as the wicked. Human beings are so interwoven that it is impossible to sin alone. Inevitably others will have to share the burden of our just punishment.

3 Dt 8:17; Jos 24:12; Dt 7:7,8 **4** Ps 74:12 **5** Da 8:4 **6** Ps 33:16 **7** Ps 40:14 **8** Ps 34:2; Jer 9:24 **9** Ps 60:1 **10** Lev 26:17; Dt 28:25 **11** Ro 8:36; Dt 28:64; Ps 60:1 **12** Isa 52:3,4; Jer 15:13 **13** Dt 28:37 **14** Jer 24:9; Job 16:4; Ps 22:7 **16** Ps 8:2 **17** Da 9:13 **18** Job 23:11 **19** Isa 34:13; Ps 23:4 **20** Dt 6:14; Ps 88:9 **21** Job 31:14; Ps 139:1

[22]But for Your sake we are killed all
the day long;
We are considered as sheep to be
slaughtered. [Rom 8:35–39]
[23]Awake! Why do You sleep, O Lord?
Awaken, do not reject us forever.
[24]Why do You hide Your face
And forget our affliction and our
oppression?
[25]For our life has melted away into
the dust;
Our body clings to the ground.
[26]Rise up! Come be our help,
And ransom us for the sake of
Your steadfast love.

Psalm 45

A Song Celebrating the King's Marriage.

To the Chief Musician; set to the [tune of] "Lilies." A Psalm of the sons of Korah. A skillful song, *or* a didactic *or* reflective poem. A Song of Love.

[1]MY HEART overflows with a
good theme;
I address my psalm to the King.
My tongue is like the pen of a
skillful writer.
[2]You are fairer than the sons of men;
Graciousness is poured upon Your
lips;
Therefore God has blessed You
forever.
[3]Strap Your sword on *Your* thigh,
O mighty One,
In Your splendor and Your majesty!
[4]And in Your majesty ride on
triumphantly
For the cause of truth and humility
and righteousness;
Let Your right hand guide You to
awesome things.
[5]Your arrows are sharp;
The peoples (nations) fall under You;
Your arrows pierce the hearts of
the King's enemies.
[6]Your throne, O God, is forever and
ever;
The scepter of uprightness is the
scepter of Your kingdom.
[7]You have loved righteousness
(virtue, morality, justice) and
hated wickedness;
Therefore God, your God, has
anointed You
Above Your companions with the
oil of jubilation. [Heb 1:8, 9]
[8]All Your garments are *fragrant*
with myrrh, aloes *and* cassia;
From ivory palaces stringed
instruments have made You glad.
[9]Kings' daughters are among Your
noble ladies;
At Your right hand stands the
queen in gold from Ophir.
[10]Hear, O daughter, consider
and incline your ear [to my
instruction]:

44:22 as sheep. These words predict another beloved Son of the Most High who would also feel cast off by the Lord (Isa 53:7; Ro 8:36).
45:3 O mighty One. In the ancient Middle East the king was supposed to be a great warrior. The model in Israel was David, the celebrated champion who defeated the giant Goliath (1Sa 17). The term "mighty One" is also a messianic title.
45:6 – 7 O God . . . God, your God. The words "thy throne" indicate the messianic direction of the psalm. Here the King is addressed as God, yet it is "God, your God" who anointed Him. The writer to the Hebrews used these verses to assert Jesus' deity (Heb 1:8 – 9).
45:7 righteousness. A person is known by his loves and his hates. If a person "loves" something, he will "hate" its opposite. One who loves justice will hate oppression. One who loves truth will hate falsehood. One who loves kindness will hate cruelty. The psalm deliberately uses very strong verbs: *loved* righteousness, *hated* wickedness. We might prefer to be a bit more moderate and tone down the language, but the Scripture calls us to disengage ourselves radically from wickedness, for it is both a virus and a vice. ***anointed You.*** Anointing set aside a particular person for special service to God. In Old Testament times, those who were anointed for special service foreshadowed the Anointed One, the Messiah.
45:9 Ophir. Possibly located in southern Arabia or in Africa (2Ch 8:17 – 18), this place was known in the Old Testament world as a source of fine gold.

22 Ro 8:36 **23** Ps 7:6 **24** Job 13:24; Ps 13:1 **25** Ps 119:25 **PSALM 45** **Title** Ps 69, Title; 80, Title **2** Lk 4:22 **3** Isa 49:2; Heb 4:12; Rev 1:16; Isa 9:6 **4** Rev 6:2 **6** Ps 93:2; Heb 1:8 **7** Ps 33:5; Isa 61:1; 1Ki 1:39; Ps 79:4; Ps 21:6 **8** SS 1:3 **9** 1Ki 2:19 **10** See Dt 21:13

Forget your people and your
father's house;
11 Then the King will desire your
beauty;
Because He is your Lord, bow
down *and* honor Him.
12 The daughter of Tyre will come
with a gift;
The rich among the people will
seek your favor.

13 Glorious is the King's daughter
within [the palace];
Her robe is interwoven with gold.
[Rev 19:7, 8]
14 She will be brought to the King in
embroidered garments;
The virgins, her companions who
follow her,
Will be brought to You.
15 With gladness and rejoicing will
they be led;
They will enter into the King's palace.

16 In place of your fathers will be
your sons;
You shall make princes in all the
land.
17 I will make Your name to be
remembered in all generations;
Therefore the peoples will praise
and give You thanks forever and
ever.

Psalm 46

God the Refuge of His People.

To the Chief Musician. *A Psalm* of the sons of Korah, set to soprano voices. A Song.

1 GOD IS our refuge and strength
[mighty and impenetrable],
A very present *and* well-proved
help in trouble.
2 Therefore we will not fear, though
the earth should change
And though the mountains be
shaken *and* slip into the heart of
the seas,
3 Though its waters roar and foam,
Though the mountains tremble at
its roaring. *Selah.*

4 There is a river whose streams
make glad the city of God,
The holy dwelling places of the
Most High.
5 God is in the midst of her [His
city], she will not be moved;
God will help her when the
morning dawns.
6 The nations made an uproar, the
kingdoms tottered *and* were
moved;
He raised His voice, the earth
melted.
7 The LORD of hosts is with us;
The God of Jacob is our stronghold
[our refuge, our high tower].
Selah.

8 Come, behold the works of the
LORD,
Who has wrought desolations *and*
wonders in the earth.
9 He makes wars to cease to the end
of the earth;
He breaks the bow into pieces and
snaps the spear in two;
He burns the chariots with fire.
10 "Be still and know (recognize,
understand) that I am God.
I will be exalted among the nations!
I will be exalted in the earth."
11 The LORD of hosts is with us;
The God of Jacob is our stronghold
[our refuge, our high tower].
Selah.

45:14 *embroidered garments.* In the ancient world, the beauty of the bride's gowns might be an expression of her family's wealth, their pride in her, and their love for her.
46:2 *though the earth should change.* God is a refuge for His people against everything actual or imagined.
46:5 *God is in the midst of her.* We do not have an absentee deliverer, a defense that is only sometimes present. The Lord lives with His people and His protection can be counted on.
46:10 *Be still and know (recognize, understand) that I am God.* This call for stillness before the Lord is not preparation for worship, but for impending judgment (Hab 2:20; Zep 1:7; Zec 2:13).

11 Ps 95:6; Isa 54:5 **12** Isa 49:23 **13** Isa 61:10 **14** SS 1:4 **16** 1Pe 2:9; Rev 1:6; 20:6 **PSALM 46 Title** Ps 48; 66; 1Ch 15:20 **1** Dt 4:7 **3** Ps 93:3,4 **4** See Isa 8:7; Ps 48:1,8; Isa 60:14 **5** Isa 12:6; Eze 43:7 **6** Ps 2:1; Jos 2:9 **8** Ps 66:5 **9** Isa 2:4; Ps 76:3; Eze 39:9 **10** Isa 2:11,17

Psalm 47

God the King of the Earth.

To the Chief Musician.
A Psalm of the sons of Korah.

[1]O CLAP your hands, all you people;
Shout to God with the voice of triumph *and* songs of joy.
[2]For the LORD Most High is to be feared [and worshiped with awe-inspired reverence and obedience];
He is a great King over all the earth.
[3]He subdues peoples under us
And nations under our feet.
[4]He chooses our inheritance for us,
The glory *and* excellence of Jacob whom He loves. [1 Pet 1:4, 5] *Selah.*

[5]God has ascended amid shouting,
The LORD with the sound of a trumpet.
[6]Sing praises to God, sing praises;
Sing praises to our King, sing praises.
[7]For God is the King of all the earth;
Sing praises in a skillful psalm *and* with understanding.
[8]God reigns over the nations;
God sits on His holy throne.
[9]The princes of the people have gathered together as the people of the God of Abraham,
For the shields of the earth belong to God;
He is highly exalted.

Psalm 48

The Beauty and Glory of Zion.

A Song; a Psalm of the sons of Korah.

[1]GREAT IS the LORD, and greatly to be praised,
In the city of our God, His holy mountain.
[2]Fair *and* beautiful in elevation, the joy of all the earth,
Is Mount Zion [the City of David] in the far north,
The city of the great King.
[Matt 5:35]
[3]God, in her palaces,
Has made Himself known as a stronghold.

[4]For, lo, the kings assembled themselves,
They [came and] passed by together.
[5]They saw it, then they were amazed;
They were stricken with terror, they fled in alarm.
[6]Panic seized them there,
And pain, as that of a woman in childbirth.
[7]With the east wind
You shattered the ships of Tarshish.

47:4 *whom He loves.* To love means "to make one's choice in." God had chosen the Israelites to be His holy people and, in that way, He loved them. In His dialogue with Nicodemus, Jesus explained that God's love extended to all the nations as well as to Israel (Jn 3:16).
47:9 *the people of the God of Abraham.* This is the prophetic picture of the ultimate fulfillment of the Abrahamic covenant (Ge 12:1 – 3). One day all the peoples of the earth who have come to faith in God through Jesus will discover that they are one people. They are all the true seed of Abraham because they, like Abraham, believed in God (Ge 15:6; Gal 3:5 – 8).
48:1 *Great is the LORD.* Psalm 48 unites with Psalms 46 and 47 to form three great psalms of praise to God for His kingship and His love for the holy city of Jerusalem. This emphasis on Jerusalem has led many scholars to speak of these psalms as "Songs of Zion." ***the city of our God.*** The city of Jerusalem had a particularly dear place in the heart of God's people (1Ki 14:21). The city was holy because of the presence of God in the temple.
48:2 *the joy of all the earth.* As is strongly established in the Book of Psalms, the purpose of God's work in Israel was to draw all nations to Himself. ***city of the great King.*** Jesus quoted these words in Mt 5:35, speaking of Jerusalem.

PSALM 47 **1** Isa 55:12 **2** Dt 7:21; Ps 76:12; Mal 1:14 **3** Ps 18:47 **4** 1Pe 1:4 **5** Ps 68:33 **7** Zec 14:9; 1Co 14:15

8 As we have heard, so have we seen
In the city of the LORD of hosts, in
the city of our God:
God will establish her forever.
Selah.

9 We have thought of Your
lovingkindness, O God,
In the midst of Your temple.
10 As is Your name, O God,
So is Your praise to the ends of the
earth;
Your right hand is full of
righteousness (rightness,
justice).
11 Let Mount Zion be glad,
Let the daughters of Judah rejoice
Because of Your [righteous]
judgments.
12 Walk about Zion, go all around
her;
Count her towers,
13 Consider her ramparts,
Go through her palaces,
That you may tell the next
generation [about her glory].
14 For this is God,
Our God forever and ever;
He will be our guide even until
death.

Psalm 49

The Folly of Trusting in Riches.

To the Chief Musician.
A Psalm of the sons of Korah.

1 HEAR THIS, all peoples;
Listen carefully, all inhabitants of
the world,
2 Both low and high,
Rich and poor together:
3 My mouth will speak wisdom,
And the meditation of my heart
will be understanding.
4 I will incline my ear *and* consent
to a proverb;
On the lyre I will unfold my
riddle.

5 Why should I fear in the days of
evil,
When the wickedness of those
who would betray me surrounds
me [on every side],
6 Even those who trust in *and* rely
on their wealth
And boast of the abundance of
their riches?
7 None of them can by any means
redeem [either himself or] his
brother,
Nor give to God a ransom for
him—
8 For the ransom of his soul is too
costly,
And he should cease *trying*
forever—
9 So that he should live on
eternally,
That he should never see the
pit (grave) *and* undergo
decay.

10 For he sees *that even* wise men
die;
The fool and the stupid alike
perish
And leave their wealth to others.
[Eccl 2:12–16]
11 Their inward thought is that their
houses will continue forever,
And their dwelling places to all
generations;
They have named their lands after
their own names [ignoring
God].
12 But man, with all his [self] honor
and pomp, will not endure;
He is like the beasts that
perish.

48:12 *Walk about Zion.* Praising the city of Zion was another way of praising God, whose dwelling was there.

49:4 *riddle.* This word refers to a perplexing moral problem. How do the righteous come to terms with oppressive rich people who seem to have no thought for God?

49:6 *those who trust in and rely on their wealth.* The accumulation of material wealth is of no value in the life to come (Mk 10:23). Money

8 1Ch 16:31; Ps 93:1; Rev 19:6 **9** Ps 89:18 **PSALM 48** **1** Ps 46:4; Isa 2:2,3; Mic 4:1; Zec 8:3 **2** Ps 50:2; Jer 3:19; Isa 14:13; Mt 5:35 **4** 2Sa 10:6,14,16,18,19 **6** Ex 15:15 **7** Eze 27:26; Jer 18:17 **9** Ps 26:3 **10** Dt 28:58 **PSALM 49** **4** Ps 78:2; Mt 13:35 **6** Mk 10:24 **7** Job 36:18 **8** Mt 16:26 **9** Ps 89:48 **10** Ecc 2:16; Ecc 2:18 **11** Ge 4:17

13 This is the fate of those who are
foolishly confident,
And of those after them who
approve [and are influenced by]
their words. *Selah.*
14 Like sheep they are appointed
for Sheol (the nether world, the
place of the dead);
Death will be their shepherd;
And the upright shall rule over
them in the morning,
And their form *and* beauty shall
be for Sheol to consume,
So that they have no dwelling [on
earth].
15 But God will redeem my life from
the power of Sheol,
For He will receive me. *Selah.*

16 Be not afraid when [an ungodly]
man becomes rich,
When the wealth *and* glory of his
house are increased;
17 For when he dies he will carry
nothing away;
His glory will not descend after
him.
18 Though while he lives he counts
himself happy *and*
prosperous—
And though people praise you
when you do well for
yourself—
19 He shall go to the generation of
his fathers;
They shall never again see the
light.
20 A man [who is held] in honor,
Yet who lacks [spiritual]
understanding *and* a teachable
heart, is like the beasts that
perish.

Psalm 50

God the Judge of the Righteous and the Wicked.

A Psalm of Asaph

1 THE MIGHTY One, God, the
LORD, has spoken,
And summoned the earth from the
rising of the sun to its setting
[from east to west].
2 Out of Zion, the perfection of
beauty,
God has shone forth.
3 May our God come and not keep
silent;
Fire devours before Him,
And around Him a mighty tempest
rages.
4 He summons the heavens above,
And the earth, to judge His
people:
5 "Gather My godly ones to Me,
Those who have made a covenant
with Me by sacrifice."
6 And the heavens declare His
righteousness,
For God Himself is judge. *Selah.*

7 "Hear, O My people, and I will
speak;
O Israel, I will testify against you:
I am God, your God.
8 "I do not reprove you for your
sacrifices;
Your burnt offerings are
continually before Me.
9 "I will accept no young bull from
your house
Nor male goat from your folds.

---

can never buy redemption. Only God has the power to deliver us from death and hell.

49:14 *Death will be their shepherd.* Death is the great leveler. People who have beauty, riches (vv. 16 – 17), and power in this world will lose them all at death. They will be stripped of everything except their character or soul. This is why the Scriptures exhort us to pursue character development — God's law, holiness, wisdom, and *knowledge* — more than anything else.

50:1 *The mighty One, God, the LORD.* These three titles give a stunning introduction to the poem, a grand display of God Himself in the midst of His people.

50:8 *reprove you for your sacrifices.* The sacrifices were commanded by God in Leviticus, but the people had difficulty keeping a godly perspective on the nature of sacrifices. God did not need their offerings — He is already the owner of all the earth. The sacrifices were for their sakes, so that they would understand that sin equals death, and atonement comes by blood.

13 Lk 12:20 **14** Ps 47:3; Da 7:22; Mal 4:3; Job 4:21 **15** Hos 13:14 **18** Dt 29:19 **19** Job 33:30 **20** Ecc 3:19
PSALM 50 Title 1Ch 15:17; 2Ch 29:30 **1** Isa 9:6 **2** Ps 80:1 **3** Ps 97:3; Da 7:10 **4** Dt 4:26 **5** Dt 33:3; Ex 24:7
6 Ps 75:7 **7** Ex 20:2 **8** Jer 7:22; Hos 6:6 **9** Ac 17:25

10 "For every beast of the forest is Mine,
And the cattle on a thousand hills.
11 "I know every bird of the mountains,
And everything that moves in the field is Mine.
12 "If I were hungry, I would not tell you,
For the world and all it contains are Mine. [1 Cor 10:26]
13 "Shall I eat the flesh of bulls
Or drink the blood of male goats?
14 "Offer to God the sacrifice of thanksgiving
And pay your vows to the Most High;
15 Call on Me in the day of trouble;
I will rescue you, and you shall honor *and* glorify Me."

16 But to the wicked God says:
"What right have you to recite My statutes
Or to take My covenant on your lips?
17 "For you hate instruction *and* discipline
And cast My words behind you [discarding them].
18 "When you see a thief, you are pleased with him *and* condone his behavior,
And you associate with adulterers.
19 "You give your mouth to evil
And your tongue frames deceit.
20 "You sit and speak against your brother;
You slander your own mother's son.
21 "These things you have done and I kept silent;
You thought that I was just like you.
Now I will reprimand *and* denounce you and state *the case* in order before your eyes.

22 "Now consider this, you who forget God,
Or I will tear you in pieces, and there will be no one to rescue [you].
23 "He who offers a sacrifice of praise *and* thanksgiving honors Me;
And to him who orders his way rightly [who follows the way that I show him],
I shall show the salvation of God."

Psalm 51

A Contrite Sinner's Prayer for Pardon.

To the Chief Musician. A Psalm of David; when Nathan the prophet came to him after he had sinned with Bathsheba.

1 HAVE MERCY on me,
O God, according to Your lovingkindness;
According to the greatness of Your compassion blot out my transgressions.
2 Wash me thoroughly from my wickedness *and* guilt

50:12 ***If I were hungry, I would not tell you.*** God doesn't hunger for food — and even if He did, He would not need His people to bring it to Him. He hungers for the righteousness of His people. **50:18** ***associate with adulterers.*** In this psalm the Lord brings a legal case against His people for violations of the covenant (v. 4). Verses 7 – 15 address the formalists, whose major emphasis is on the outward and external observances of the ceremonial law. Verses 16 – 23 are spoken to wicked members of the community who do not put God's commandments into practice in everyday life. The believer's attitude toward evil is to be one of total rejection: "Do not love the world [of sin that opposes God and His precepts], nor the things that are in the world" (1Jn 2:15). There is no neutrality in regard to the moral law, and no approval can be given to those who disobey God's law (Ro 1:32).

51:1 ***Have mercy on me.*** This psalm is associated with one of the hardest experiences of David's life, the aftermath of his affair with Bathsheba. For the account of David's sin and the prophet Nathan's rebuke, see 2 Samuel 11:1 – 12:15. ***the greatness of Your compassion.*** David's call for mercy is the only appropriate request for a confessing sinner. No sinner should ask for justice, for that would mean judgment and ruin.

12 Job 41:11 **14** Heb 13:15; Dt 23:21 **15** Job 22:27; Ps 22:23 **17** Ro 2:21; Neh 9:26 **18** Ro 1:32; 1Ti 5:22 **19** Ps 52:2 **21** Ecc 8:11; Ps 10:11; 90:8 **22** Job 8:13; Ps 9:17; Isa 51:13 **23** Ps 27:6; Gal 6:16
PSALM 51 **Title** 2Sa 12:1; 11:2,4 **1** Isa 43:25; Col 2:14 **2** Heb 9:14; 1Jn 1:7

And cleanse me from my sin.
[3]For I am conscious of my transgressions *and* I acknowledge them;
My sin is always before me.
[4]Against You, You only, have I sinned
And done that which is evil in Your sight,
So that You are justified when You speak [Your sentence]
And faultless in Your judgment. [Rom 3:4]

[5]I was brought forth in [a state of] wickedness;
In sin my mother conceived me [and from my beginning I, too, was sinful]. [John 3:6; Rom 5:12; Eph 2:3]
[6]Behold, You desire truth in the innermost being,
And in the hidden part [of my heart] You will make me know wisdom.
[7]Purify me with hyssop, and I will be clean;
Wash me, and I will be whiter than snow.
[8]Make me hear joy and gladness *and* be satisfied;
Let the bones which You have broken rejoice.
[9]Hide Your face from my sins
And blot out all my iniquities.

[10]Create in me a clean heart, O God,
And renew a right *and* steadfast spirit within me.
[11]Do not cast me away from Your presence
And do not take Your Holy Spirit from me.
[12]Restore to me the joy of Your salvation
And sustain me with a willing spirit.
[13]Then I will teach transgressors Your ways,
And sinners shall be converted *and* return to You.

[14]Rescue me from bloodguiltiness, O God, the God of my salvation;
Then my tongue will sing joyfully of Your righteousness *and* Your justice.
[15]O Lord, open my lips,
That my mouth may declare Your praise.
[16]For You do not delight in sacrifice, or else I would give it;
You are not pleased with burnt offering. [1 Sam 15:22]

51:4 *Against You.* David had sinned against Bathsheba, Uriah, and the nation he was called to rule. But none of these indictments were as serious as David's offense against God.

51:5 *wickedness.* The psalmist should not be misunderstood as teaching that the pollution of human nature results from anything inherently corrupt in sexual relations between husband and wife. We are male and female by the sovereign will and creative power of God (Ge 1:27). What David confesses, however, is the reality of human depravity (Ro 5:12). We are inclined to gratify the cravings of our sinful nature, following its desires and thoughts, contradicting God's commands. This is why we must experience radical regeneration by the supernatural power of the Holy Spirit. Apart from that rebirth, we can neither see nor enter the kingdom of God (Jn 3:3 – 5).

51:7 *hyssop.* Here David refers to the ritual acts of cleansing described in the law of Moses (Lev 14:4; Nu 19:6).

51:10 – 13 Confession — Confession leads to forgiveness, but what does that look like? Psalm 51 gives us a picture. The results of forgiveness are a clean heart, a renewed spirit, a restored relationship with God, and a joyful experience of God's salvation. God cleans us up. He makes us presentable. He reorients us towards Himself, helping us to focus on what is right. By forgiving us, God crosses over the canyon of sin that separates us from Him. When you put all this together there is great cause for joy on our part. Forgiveness is more than a theological abstract. It makes the salvation experience deeply personal and emotional in every sense. It takes that which is wrong in our life and makes it right.

51:16 *You do not delight in sacrifice.* God's pleasure is not in the sacrificed animal, but in the willing obedience of His people (Ge 4:1 – 7; Jn 4:21 – 24; Ro 12:1 – 2). The motions of sacrifice not accompanied by a contrite heart are not acceptable to God (Isa 1:12 – 20).

4 2Sa 12:13; Lk 15:21; Ro 3:4 **5** Job 14:4; Job 14:4 **7** Lev 14:4; Heb 9:19; Isa 1:18 **8** Mt 5:4 **9** Jer 16:17 **10** Eze 18:31; Ac 15:19 **11** Gen 4:14; Lk 11:13; Eph 4:30 **12** 2Co 3:17 **14** 2Sa 12:9; Ps 35:28 **16** 1Sa 15:22; Ps 40:6; Isa 1:11; Jer 7:22

[17]My [only] sacrifice [acceptable] to
God is a broken spirit;
A broken and contrite heart
[broken with sorrow for sin,
thoroughly penitent], such,
O God, You will not despise.
[18]By Your favor do good to Zion;
May You rebuild the walls of
Jerusalem.
[19]Then will You delight in the
sacrifices of righteousness,
In burnt offering and whole burnt
offering;
Then young bulls will be offered
on Your altar.

Psalm 52

Futility of Boastful Wickedness.

To the Chief Musician. A skillful song, *or* a didactic *or* reflective poem. *A Psalm* of David, when Doeg the Edomite came and told Saul, "David has come to the house of Ahimelech."

[1]WHY DO you boast of evil,
O mighty man?
The lovingkindness of God
endures all day long.
[2]Your tongue devises destruction,
Like a sharp razor, working
deceitfully.
[3]You love evil more than good,
And falsehood more than
speaking what is right. *Selah.*
[4]You love all words that devour,
O deceitful tongue.
[5]But God will break you down
forever;
He will take you away and tear
you away from your tent,
And uproot you from the land of
the living. *Selah.*
[6]The righteous will see it and fear,
And will [scoffingly] laugh,
saying,
[7]"Look, [this is] the man who would
not make God his strength [his
stronghold and fortress],
But trusted in the abundance of his
riches,
Taking refuge in his wealth."
[8]But as for me, I am like a green
olive tree in the house of God;
I trust [confidently] in the
lovingkindness of God forever
and ever.
[9]I will thank You forever, because
You have done it, [You have
rescued me and kept me safe].
I will wait on Your name, for it is
good, in the presence of Your
godly ones.

Psalm 53

Folly and Wickedness of Men.

To the Chief Musician; in a mournful strain. A skillful song, *or* didactic *or* reflective poem of David.

[1]THE [empty-headed] fool has said
in his heart, "There is no God."
They are corrupt *and* evil, and
have committed repulsive
injustice;
There is no one who does good.
[2]God has looked down from heaven
upon the children of men
To see if there is anyone who
understands,
Who seeks after God [who
requires Him, who longs for
Him as essential to life].
[3]Every one of them has turned
aside *and* fallen away;

52:2 *Your tongue.* This phrase refers to more than just words. These people used language as a weapon, for they believed that the gods could empower their words to a devastating effect.
52:6 *see it and fear.* This fear is a deepened respect for God and a sense of awe before His throne.
52:8 *a green olive tree.* An olive tree was a symbol of beauty. In Romans 11:16 – 24, the olive tree is used as a symbol of the Gentiles who are grafted into the root — the people of God or the church.
53:1 *The [empty-headed] fool.* In the Bible, the term "fool" does not indicate mental incompetence, but moral and spiritual insensitivity.

17 Ps 34:18; Isa 57:15 **19** Ps 4:5; Mal 3:3 **PSALM 52 Title** 1Sa 22:9; Eze 22:9 **1** 1Sa 21:7 **2** Ps 50:19; Ps 57:4 **3** Jer 9:4,5 **5** Pr 2:22 **6** Job 22:19; Ps 37:34; Mal 1:5; Ps 58:10 **7** Ps 49:6 **8** Jer 11:16; Hos 14:6 **9** Ps 54:6 **PSALM 53 1** Ro 3:10 **2** Ps 33:13; 2Ch 15:2

Together they have become filthy
and corrupt;
There is no one who does good, no,
not even one. [Rom 3:10–12]
4 Have workers of wickedness
no knowledge *or* no
understanding?
They eat up My people *as though*
they ate bread
And have not called upon God.
5 There they were, in great terror
and dread, where there had been
no terror *or* dread;
For God scattered the bones of him
who besieged you;
You have put them to shame,
because God has rejected them.
6 Oh, that the salvation of Israel
would come out of Zion!
When God restores [the fortunes
of] His people,
Let Jacob rejoice, let Israel be glad.

Psalm 54

Prayer for Defense against Enemies.

To the Chief Musician; with stringed instruments. A skillful song, *or* a didactic *or* reflective poem, of David, when the Ziphites went and told Saul, "David is hiding among us."

1 SAVE ME, O God, by Your name;
And vindicate me by Your
[wondrous] power.
2 Hear my prayer, O God;
Listen to the words of my mouth.
3 For strangers have risen against me
And violent men have sought my
life;
They have not set God before
them. *Selah.*
4 Behold, God is my helper *and* ally;
The Lord is the sustainer of my
soul [my upholder].
5 He will pay back the evil to my
enemies;
In Your faithfulness destroy them.
6 With a freewill offering I will
sacrifice to You;
I will give thanks *and* praise Your
name, O LORD, for it is good.
7 For He has rescued me from every
trouble,
And my eye has looked *with
satisfaction* (triumph) on my
enemies.

Psalm 55

Prayer for the Destruction of the Treacherous.

To the Chief Musician; with stringed instruments. A skillful song, *or* a didactic *or* reflective poem, of David.

1 LISTEN TO my prayer, O God,
And do not hide Yourself from my
plea.
2 Listen to me and answer me;
I am restless *and* distraught in my
complaint and distracted
3 Because of the voice of the enemy,
Because of the pressure of the
wicked;

53:5 *scattered the bones.* This is a prophetic pronouncement of the final judgment on the wicked.

54:3 *They have not set God before them.* In one of the dark moments of David's life, when the insanely jealous King Saul was bent on destroying him, David was able to lift his heart in supplication, trust, and praise to God. He had been hiding with his men in the hill country south of Jeshimon, but his location was betrayed to Saul by the people of Ziph (1Sa 23:19; 26:1). These were the "strangers" who doubtless stood to profit from David's death. They had no regard for covenant law, which bade the Israelites to love their neighbors as themselves (Lev 19:18). Nor did they love the Lord their God wholeheartedly (Dt 6:5), but instead turned their hands against His anointed. Betrayal is a supreme act of treachery, whether in terms of a human being such as David, or of Jesus (Lk 22:48), the anointed Son of God. As such, it merits the most severe punishment from God (Mk 14:21).

54:5 *He will pay back.* David did not take vengeance into his own hands. Only the Lord can take revenge.

4 Jer 4:22 **5** Lev 26:17; Eze 6:5 **6** Ps 14:7 **PSALM 54 Title** 1Sa 23:19 **3** Ps 86:14 **4** Ps 118:7 **5** Ps 89:49 **6** Ps 52:9 **7** Ps 59:10 **PSALM 55 2** Isa 38:14 **3** 2Sa 16:7,8

For they bring down trouble on me,
And in anger they persecute me.

4 My heart is in anguish within me,
And the terrors of death have
fallen upon me.
5 Fear and trembling have come
upon me;
Horror has overwhelmed me.
6 And I say, "Oh, that I had wings
like a dove!
I would fly away and be at rest.
7 "I would wander far away,
I would lodge in the [peace of the]
wilderness. *Selah.*
8 "I would hurry to my refuge [my
tranquil shelter far away]
From the stormy wind *and* from
the tempest."

9 Confuse [my enemies], O Lord,
divide their tongues [destroying
their schemes],
For I have seen violence and strife
in the city.
10 Day and night they go around her
walls;
Wickedness and mischief are in
her midst.
11 Destruction is within her;
Oppression and deceit do not
depart from her streets *and*
market places.

12 For it is not an enemy who taunts
me—
Then I could bear it;
Nor is it one who has hated me
who insolently exalts himself
against me—
Then I could hide from him.
13 But it is you, a man my equal *and*
my counsel,
My companion and my familiar
friend;
14 We who had sweet fellowship
together,
Who walked to the house of God
in company.
15 Let death come deceitfully upon
them;
Let them go down alive to Sheol
(the nether world, the place of
the dead),
For evil [of every kind] is in their
dwelling *and* in their hearts, in
their midst.

16 As for me, I shall call upon God,
And the LORD will save me.
17 Evening and morning and at noon
I will complain and murmur,
And He will hear my voice.
18 He has redeemed my life in peace
from the battle that was
against me,
For there were many against me.
19 God will hear and humble them,
Even He who sits enthroned from
old— *Selah.*
Because in them there has been no
change [of heart],
And they do not fear God [at all].
20 He [my companion] has put out his
hands against those who were at
peace with him;
He has broken his covenant [of
friendship and loyalty].
21 The words of his mouth were
smoother than butter,
But his heart was hostile;
His words were softer than oil,
Yet they were drawn swords.
22 Cast your burden on the LORD
[release it] and He will sustain
and uphold you;
He will never allow the righteous
to be shaken (slip, fall, fail).
[1 Pet 5:7]

55:4 *terrors of death.* David's intense pain can be felt in his strong language. The phrase "terrors of death" is unusual. The Hebrew word for "terror" or "dread" is first used in Scripture to describe the horror that Abraham felt in the unnatural darkness that seized him as God was about to come near (Ge 15:12). The word also described the horrors that would fall on the people of Canaan when the Lord gave the land to the Israelites (Ex 15:16). To strengthen this feeling, David speaks of fear and trembling and an overwhelming horror (Eze 7:18).

55:15 *Let them go down alive to Sheol.* David could express his emotions to God in prayer, but judgment or revenge was in God's hands (Ro 12:19).

55:22 *Cast your burden on the LORD.* The Lord is the one constant in life, and the one true Friend.

4 Ps 116:3 **9** Jer 6:7 **12** Ps 41:9; 35:26 **13** 2Sa 15:12; Ps 41:9; Jer 9:4 **14** Ps 42:4 **15** Nu 16:30 **17** Lk 18:1 **18** 2Ch 32:7,8 **19** Dt 33:27 **20** Ac 12:1; Ps 7:4 **21** Ps 28:3 **22** Ps 37:5; Mt 6:25; Ps 37:24

[23]But You, O God, will bring
down the wicked to the pit of
destruction;
Men of blood and treachery will
not live out half their days.
But I will [boldly and
unwaveringly] trust in You.

Psalm 56

Supplication for Rescue and Grateful Trust in God.

To the Chief Musician; set to [the tune of] "Silent Dove Among Those Far Away." A Mikhtam of David. [A record of memorable thoughts] when the Philistines seized him in Gath.

[1]BE GRACIOUS to me, O God, for
man has trampled on me;
All day long the adversary
oppresses *and* torments me.
[2]My enemies have trampled upon
me all day long,
For they are many who fight
proudly against me.
[3]When I am afraid,
I will put my trust *and* faith in You.
[4]In God, whose word I praise;
In God I have put my trust;
I shall not fear.
What can mere man do to me?
[5]All day long they twist my words
and say hurtful things;
All their thoughts are against me
for evil.
[6]They attack, they hide *and* lurk,
They watch my steps,
As they have [expectantly] waited
to take my life.
[7]Cast them out because of their
wickedness.
In anger bring down the peoples,
O God!
[8]You have taken account of my
wanderings;
Put my tears in Your bottle.
Are they not recorded in Your book?
[9]Then my enemies will turn back in
the day when I call;
This I know, that God is for me.
[Rom 8:31]
[10]In God, *whose* word I praise,
In the LORD, *whose* word I praise,
[11]In God have I put my trust *and*
confident reliance; I will not be
afraid.
What can man do to me?
[12]Your vows are *binding* upon me,
O God;
I will give thank offerings to You.
[13]For You have rescued my soul
from death,
Yes, and my feet from stumbling,
So that I may walk before God
In the light of life.

Psalm 57

Prayer for Rescue from Persecutors.

To the Chief Musician; set to [the tune of] "Do Not Destroy." A Mikhtam of David. [A record of memorable thoughts of David] when he fled from Saul in the cave.

[1]BE GRACIOUS to me, O God, be
gracious *and* merciful to me,
For my soul finds shelter *and*
safety in You,

56:1 *Be gracious to me.* David cried out to God because of his overwhelming sense of loss during his time as a fugitive in a foreign land (1Sa 21:10–15).
56:8 *Put my tears in Your bottle.* Nothing that happens to us escapes God's notice and care; not a tear falls to the ground that He does not remember. When we suffer, it is a great comfort to know that God is *for* us—everything that we live through will be put to use for our good.
57 title *Saul in the cave.* The narrative of David's life indicates that he twice hid in caves—once in Adullam (1Sa 22:1–5) which was the setting of Psalm 142, and once in En Gedi (1Sa 24:1–7), the setting of this poem. In En Gedi, David spared Saul's life even though he had a perfect chance to put Saul out of the way and claim the kingship for himself.
57:1–3 *I will cry to God.* Although he had lived a righteous life, David still realized that he did not deserve the protection of God and that if his life was saved it would be by the grace of God. He trusted God to care for him just as a mother hen protects her young by covering them with her wings.

23 Ps 5:6; Job 15:32; Pr 10:27; Ecc 7:17 **PSALM 56 Title** 1Sa 21:11 **1** Ps 57:1 **2** Ps 57:3 **4** Ps 118:6; Isa 31:3 **6** Ps 59:3; Ps 71:10 **9** Ro 8:31 **13** Ps 116:8; Job 33:30 **PSALM 57 Title** 1Sa 22:1; Ps 142, Title **1** Ps 17:8; Isa 26:20

And in the shadow of Your
wings I will take refuge *and* be
confidently secure
Until destruction passes by.
2 I will cry to God Most High,
Who accomplishes *all things* on
my behalf [for He completes my
purpose in His plan].
3 He will send from heaven and
save me;
He calls to account him who
tramples me down. *Selah.*
God will send out His
lovingkindness and His truth.

4 My life is among lions;
I must lie among those who
breathe out fire—
The sons of men whose teeth are
spears and arrows,
And their tongue a sharp sword.
5 Be exalted above the heavens,
O God;
Let Your glory *and* majesty be
over all the earth.
6 They set a net for my steps;
My very life was bowed down.
They dug a pit before me;
Into the midst of it they themselves
have fallen. *Selah.*

7 My heart is steadfast, O God, my
heart is steadfast *and* confident!
I will sing, yes, I will sing praises
[to You]!
8 Awake, my glory!
Awake, harp and lyre!
I will awaken the dawn.
9 I will praise *and* give thanks to
You, O Lord, among the people;
I will sing praises to You among
the nations.
10 For Your faithfulness *and*
lovingkindness are great,
reaching to the heavens,
And Your truth to the clouds.
11 Be exalted above the heavens,
O God;
Let Your glory *and* majesty be
over all the earth.

Psalm 58

Prayer for the Punishment of the Wicked.

To the Chief Musician; set to [the tune of]
"Do Not Destroy." A Mikhtam of David.
[A record of memorable thoughts of David.]

1 DO YOU indeed speak
righteousness, O gods (heavenly
beings)?
Do you judge fairly, O sons of
men? [Ps 82:1, 2]
2 No, in your heart you devise
wrongdoing;
On earth you deal out the violence
of your hands.
3 The wicked are estranged from
the womb;
These go astray from birth,
speaking lies [even twisted
partial truths].
4 Their poison is like the venom of a
serpent;
They are like the deaf horned
viper that stops up its ear,
5 So that it does not listen to the
voice of charmers,
Or of the skillful enchanter casting
[cunning] spells.
6 O God, break their teeth in their
mouth;
Break out the fangs of the young
lions, O LORD.
7 Let them flow away like water that
runs off;

57:5 *Be exalted.* One of the ways in which God exalts Himself is by graciously delivering the needy.
57:7 *My heart is steadfast.* Just as Paul was able to say that he had kept the faith (2Ti 4:7), David rejoiced that his trust in God had remained strong.
58:1 *O gods.* This may also be translated "mighty ones" or "judges." Although they were merely humans, the wicked judges were behaving as though they claimed divine authority.
58:6 *break their teeth.* The wicked are pictured as having powerful teeth, as though they were carnivores, eating the righteous alive. Here David asks God to shatter their teeth, symbolizing the destruction of the power of the wicked over the poor and defenseless.

2 Ps 138:8 **3** Ps 43:3 **4** Pr 30:14 **5** Ps 108:5 **6** Ps 9:15 **7** Ps 108:1 **8** Ps 16:9 **9** Ps 108:3 **10** Ps 103:11 **11** ver. 5 **PSALM 58** **Title** Ps 57, Title **3** Isa 48:8 **4** Ecc 10:11 **6** Job 4:10

When he aims his arrows, let them
be as headless shafts.
8 *Let them be* as a snail which melts
away (secretes slime) as it goes
along,
Like the miscarriage of a woman
which never sees the sun.
9 Before your cooking pots can feel
the *fire of* thorns [burning under
them as fuel],
He will sweep them away with a
whirlwind, the green and the
burning ones alike.

10 The [unyieldingly] righteous
will rejoice when he sees the
vengeance [of God];
He will wash his feet in the blood
of the wicked.
11 Men will say, "Surely there is a
reward for the righteous;
Surely there is a God who judges
on the earth."

Psalm 59

Prayer for Rescue from Enemies.

To the Chief Musician; set to [the tune of] "Do Not Destroy." A Mikhtam of David, [a record of memorable thoughts] when Saul sent men to watch his house in order to kill him.

1 DELIVER ME from my enemies,
O my God;
Set me *securely* on an inaccessibly
high place away from those who
rise up against me.
2 Deliver me from those who
practice wrongdoing,
And save me from bloodthirsty
men.
3 Look! They lie in wait for my life;
Fierce *and* powerful men [are
uniting together to] launch an
attack against me,
Not for my wrongdoing nor for
any sin of mine, O LORD.
4 They run and set themselves
against me though there is no
guilt in me;
Stir Yourself to meet *and* help me,
and see [what they are doing]!
5 You, O LORD God of hosts, the God
of Israel,
Arise to punish all the nations;
Spare no one *and* do not
be merciful to any who
treacherously plot evil. *Selah.*
6 They return at evening, they howl
and snarl like dogs,
And go [prowling] around the city.
7 Look how they belch out [insults]
with their mouths;
Swords [of sarcasm, ridicule,
slander, and lies] are in their lips,
For *they say*, "Who hears us?"
8 But You, O LORD, will laugh at
them [in scorn];
You scoff at *and* deride all the
nations.

9 O [God] my strength, I will watch
for You;
For God is my stronghold [my
refuge, my protector, my high
tower].
10 My God in His [steadfast]
lovingkindness will meet me;
God will let me look *triumphantly*
on my enemies [who lie in wait
for me].

58:10 *wash his feet in the blood of the wicked.* We know that it is wrong to rejoice in the downfall of another human being; the picture of the righteous wading in the blood of their fallen enemies is hard for modern Western Christians to understand. Jesus clearly taught that our attitude towards our enemies should be one of compassion and forgiveness (Mt 5:43 – 48; Lk 23:34), but this does not mean that we should take a soft attitude towards sin. Wickedness grieves and angers God, and when wickedness has finally been dealt with, we will rejoice.

59:1 *Deliver me from my enemies.* The story behind this psalm of lament is found in 1 Samuel 19:9 – 17.

59:3 *Not for my wrongdoing.* There were times in David's life when he knew that he was suffering because of sin in his life (Ps 32:1 – 7), but at other times he was hounded by wicked persons even though he was innocent.

59:6 *dogs.* Dogs were unclean animals, semi-wild scavengers rather than the beloved pets of our own day. To call someone a dog or compare him to a dog was a profound insult.

8 Job 3:16 **9** Pr 10:25 **10** Ps 68:23 **11** Ps 92:15 **PSALM 59 Title** Ps 57, Title; 1Sa 19:11 **3** Ps 56:6 **4** Ps 35:23 **6** ver. 14 **7** Ps 57:4; Pr 12:18; Ps 10:11 **8** Pr 1:26 **9** Ps 62:2 **10** Ps 21:3; 54:7

11 Do not kill them, or my people will
forget;
Scatter them *and* make them
wander [endlessly] back and
forth by Your power, and bring
them down,
O Lord our shield!
12 For the sin of their mouths and the
words of their lips,
Let them even be trapped in their
pride,
And on account of the curses and
lies which they tell.
13 Destroy *them* in wrath, destroy
them so that they may be no
more;
Let them know that God rules over
Jacob (Israel)
To the ends of the earth. *Selah.*
14 They return at evening, they howl
and snarl like dogs,
And go [prowling] around the
city.
15 They wander around for food [to
devour]
And growl all night if they are not
satisfied.
16 But as for me, I will sing of Your
mighty strength *and* power;
Yes, I will sing joyfully of Your
lovingkindness in the morning;
For You have been my stronghold
And a refuge in the day of my
distress.
17 To You, O [God] my strength, I will
sing praises;
For God is my stronghold [my
refuge, my protector, my high
tower], the God who shows me
[steadfast] lovingkindness.

Psalm 60

Lament over Defeat in Battle, and Prayer for Help.

To the Chief Musician; set to [the tune of] "The Lily of the Testimony." A Mikhtam of David [intended to record memorable thoughts and] to teach; when he struggled with the Arameans of Mesopotamia and the Arameans of Zobah, and when Joab returned and struck twelve thousand Edomites in the Valley of Salt.

1 O GOD, You have rejected us
and cast us off. You have
broken [down our defenses and
scattered] us;
You have been angry; O restore us
and turn again to us.
2 You have made the land quake,
You have split it open;
Heal its rifts, for it shakes *and*
totters.
3 You have made Your people
experience hardship;
You have given us wine to drink
that makes us stagger *and* fall.
4 You have set up a banner for those
who fear You [with awe-inspired
reverence and submissive
wonder—a banner to shield
them from attack],
A banner that may be displayed
because of the truth. *Selah.*
5 That Your beloved ones may be
rescued,
Save with Your right hand and
answer us.

6 God has spoken in His holiness [in
His promises]:

59:11 *Do not kill them . . . Scatter.* The imprecation or curse in this verse is unusual. Instead of asking for the destruction of the wicked, the psalmist asks for them to be scattered, to be made fugitives. This would be a constant reminder of the consequences of evil.

59:16 – 17 *I will sing.* David knew that King Saul had sent a murder squad to track him down and kill him. Yet he arose in the morning with joy in his heart and a song on his lips. This was in contrast to his enemies, who would return to the city each evening after a long, fruitless search for David. They were nervous, irritable, and arrogant.

60:1 *You have broken [down our defenses and scattered] us.* This is a poetic description of an otherwise unknown defeat of the armies of Israel in a battle that was part of the campaign against Aram of Zobah and his Mesopotamian allies (2Sa 8). The defeat was so startling that it caused the people of Israel to feel as though God had made the earth tremble.

60:5 *Your beloved ones.* This term is particularly endearing (Isa 5:1; Jer 11:15). God did not merely act for His people out of duty, He loved them.

12 Pr 12:13 **14** ver. 6 **15** Job 15:23 **17** Ps 18:1 **PSALM 60** **Title** Ps 80; 2Sa 8:3; 1Ch 18:3 **1** Ps 44:9
2 2Ch 7:14 **3** Ps 71:20; Jer 25:15 **4** Ps 20:5 **5** Ps 108:6 **6** Ps 89:35; Jos 1:6; Ge 12:6; Jos 13:27

"I will rejoice, I will divide [the
land of] Shechem and measure
out the Valley of Succoth [west
to east].
7 "Gilead is Mine, and Manasseh is
Mine;
Ephraim is My helmet;
Judah is My scepter.
8 "Moab is My washbowl;
Over Edom I shall throw My shoe
[in triumph];
Over Philistia I raise the shout [of
victory]."

9 Who will bring me into the
besieged city [of Petra]?
Who will lead me to Edom?
10 Have You not rejected us, O God?
And will You not go out with our
armies?
11 Give us help against the enemy,
For the help of man is worthless
(ineffectual, without purpose).
12 Through God we will have victory,
For He will trample down our
enemies.

Psalm 61

Confidence in God's Protection.

To the Chief Musician; on stringed instruments. *A Psalm* of David.

1 HEAR MY cry, O God;
Listen to my prayer.
2 From the end of the earth I call
to You, when my heart is
overwhelmed *and* weak;
Lead me to the rock that is higher
than I [a rock that is too high to
reach without Your help].
3 For You have been a shelter *and* a
refuge for me,
A strong tower against the enemy.
4 Let me dwell in Your tent forever;
Let me take refuge in the shelter of
Your wings. *Selah.*

5 For You have heard my vows,
O God;
You have given me the inheritance
of those who fear Your name
[with reverence].
6 You will prolong the king's life
[adding days upon days];
His years will be like many
generations.
7 He will sit enthroned forever
before [the face of] God;
Appoint lovingkindness and truth
to watch over *and* preserve him.
8 So I will sing praise to Your name
forever,
Paying my vows day by day.

Psalm 62

God Alone a Refuge from Treachery and Oppression.

To the Chief Musician; to Jeduthun [Ethan, the noted musician, founder of an official musical family]. A Psalm of David.

1 FOR GOD alone my soul *waits* in
silence;
From Him comes my salvation.
2 He alone is my rock and my
salvation,
My defense *and* my strong
tower; I will not be shaken *or*
disheartened.
3 How long will you attack a man

60:8 *Moab . . . Edom . . . Philistia.* These traditional enemies of Israel were also enemies of God. The Lord would not allow them to disturb His people.

60:12 *we will have victory.* As the title records, this was what happened. David's general Joab led the battle, and under God's hand Israel's enemies were soundly defeated. When the help of man proves useless, often God dramatically provides strength and power so that our boast is solely in Him.

61:2 *the rock that is higher than I.* The imagery of God as a Rock for the believer was introduced by Moses (Dt 32:4) and is developed elsewhere in the Psalms (62:2; 71:3; 144:1).

61:6 *like many generations.* This phrase refers to David's long rule, but more literally prophesies the eternal rule of Jesus, the King of kings.

62 title *Jeduthun.* Jeduthun was appointed by David as one of those in charge of the music associated with worship (1Ch 16:41 – 42).

7 Dt 33:17; Ge 49:10 **8** 2Sa 8:1 **10** Ps 108:11; Jos 7:12 **12** Nu 24:18 **PSALM 61** **3** Pr 18:10 **4** Ps 91:4 **7** Ps 40:11 **PSALM 62** **Title** 1Ch 25:1 **1** Ps 33:20 **3** Isa 30:13

So that you may murder him, all of you,
Like a leaning wall, like a tottering fence?
4 They consult only to throw him down from his high position [to dishonor him];
They delight in lies.
They bless with [the words of] their mouths,
But inwardly they curse. *Selah.*

5 For God alone my soul waits in silence *and* quietly submits to Him,
For my hope is from Him.
6 He only is my rock and my salvation;
My fortress *and* my defense, I will not be shaken *or* discouraged.
7 On God my salvation and my glory rest;
He is my rock of [unyielding] strength, my refuge is in God.
8 Trust [confidently] in Him at all times, O people;
Pour out your heart before Him.
God is a refuge for us. *Selah.*

9 Men of low degree are only a breath (emptiness), and men of [high] rank are a lie (delusion).
In the balances they go up [because they have no measurable weight or value];
They are together lighter than a breath.
10 Do not trust in oppression,
And do not vainly hope in robbery;
If riches increase, do not set your heart on them.

11 God has spoken once,
Twice I have heard this:
That power belongs to God.
12 Also to You, O Lord, belong lovingkindness *and* compassion,
For You compensate every man according to [the value of] his work. [Jer 17:10; Rev 22:12]

Psalm 63

The Thirsting Soul Satisfied in God.

A Psalm of David; when he was in the wilderness of Judah.

1 O GOD, You are my God; with deepest longing I will seek You;
My soul [my life, my very self] thirsts for You, my flesh longs *and* sighs for You,
In a dry and weary land where there is no water.
2 So I have gazed upon You in the sanctuary,
To see Your power and Your glory. [Ps 42:1, 2]
3 Because Your lovingkindness is better than life,
My lips shall praise You.
4 So will I bless You as long as I live;
I will lift up my hands in Your name.
5 My soul [my life, my very self] is satisfied as with marrow and fatness,
And my mouth offers praises [to You] with joyful lips.

6 When I remember You on my bed,
I meditate *and* thoughtfully focus on You in the night watches,
7 For You have been my help,
And in the shadow of Your wings [where I am always protected] I sing for joy.

62:8 *Trust . . . O people.* David addresses the righteous with his lesson of reliance on God. What is true for David is extended to all in the believing community.
62:11 *once, Twice.* It is a convention of wisdom literature to use a number and then raise it by one (Pr 30:15–31), emphasizing the certainty of the point made.
63 title *in the wilderness of Judah.* This possibly refers to an incident during the period when Saul was chasing David (1Sa 22–24).
63:2 *in the sanctuary.* The sanctuary had been at Nob (1Sa 21:1), and it was there that David had sought the presence of the Lord. Later it was moved to Jerusalem (76:1–2).
63:4 *lift up my hands.* To lift the hands to the Lord expresses dependence on Him, coupled with an acknowledgement of His power, wonder, and majesty.

4 Ps 28:3 **7** Jer 3:23 **8** 1Sa 1:15; La 2:19 **9** Ps 39:5; Isa 40:17 **10** Lk 12:15 **11** Job 33:14 **12** Mt 16:27
PSALM 63 **Title** 1Sa 22:5 **1** Ps 42:2 **2** Ps 27:4 **6** Ps 42:8

[8]My soul [my life, my very self]
clings to You;
Your right hand upholds me.

[9]But those who seek my life to
destroy it
Will [be destroyed and] go into
the depths of the earth [into the
underworld].
[10]They will be given over to the
power of the sword;
They will be a prey for foxes.
[11]But the king will rejoice in God;
Everyone who swears by Him
[honoring the true God,
acknowledging His authority
and majesty] will glory,
For the mouths of those who speak
lies will be stopped.

Psalm 64

Prayer for Protection from Secret Enemies.

To the Chief Musician. A Psalm of David.

[1]HEAR MY voice, O God, in my
complaint;
Guard my life from the terror of
the enemy.
[2]Hide me from the secret counsel
and conspiracy of the ungodly,
From the scheming of those who
do wrong,
[3]Who have sharpened their tongues
like a sword.
They aim venomous words as
arrows,
[4]To shoot from ambush at the
blameless [one];
Suddenly they shoot at him,
without fear.
[5]They encourage themselves in
[their pursuit of] an evil agenda;
They talk of laying snares secretly;
They say, "Who will discover us?"
[6]They devise acts of injustice,
saying,
"We are ready with a well-
conceived plan."
For the inward thought and
the heart of a man are deep
(mysterious, unsearchable).

[7]But God will shoot them with an
[unexpected] arrow;
Suddenly they will be wounded.
[8]So they will be caused to stumble;
Their own tongue is against them;
All who gaze at them will shake
the head [in scorn].
[9]Then all men will fear [God's
judgment];
They will declare the work of God,
And they will consider *and* wisely
acknowledge what He has done.
[10]The righteous will rejoice in the
LORD and take refuge in Him;
All the upright in heart will glory
and offer praise.

Psalm 65

God's Abundant Favor to Earth and Man.

To the Chief Musician.
A Psalm of David. A Song.

[1]TO YOU belongs silence
[the submissive wonder of
reverence], and [it bursts into]
praise in Zion, O God;
And to You the vow shall be
performed.
[2]O You who hear prayer,
To You all mankind comes.
[3]Wickedness *and* guilt prevail
against me;
Yet as for our transgressions,
You forgive them [removing them
from Your sight].

63:8 *Your right hand.* The same power of God that delivered Israel from Egypt (Ex 15:6) would support David — and all other believers in their daily lives.
64:10 *take refuge in Him.* By placing our problems into God's hands, we can rest in His sovereign will for our lives. Concerns about the future can be cast aside, for the Lord controls our future and has good plans for us (Ro 8:28).
65:3 *You forgive them.* David speaks of a coming day when sin will be dealt with fully, when redemption will be completely paid. This took place in the death and resurrection of Jesus Christ (Eph 1:7).

11 Dt 6:13 **PSALM 64** **3** Ps 58:7 **5** Ps 10:11 **8** Ps 31:11 **9** Jer 50:28; 51:10 **PSALM 65** **1** Ps 62:1 **2** Isa 66:23 **3** Heb 9:14

4 Blessed is the one whom You
choose and bring near
To dwell in Your courts.
We will be filled with the goodness
of Your house,
Your holy temple.

5 By awesome *and* wondrous things
You answer us in righteousness,
O God of our salvation,
You who are the trust *and* hope of
all the ends of the earth and of
the farthest sea;
6 Who creates the mountains by His
strength,
Being clothed with power,
7 Who stills the roaring of the seas,
The roaring of their waves,
And the tumult of the peoples,
8 So they who dwell at the ends *of
the earth* stand in awe of Your
signs [the evidence of Your
presence]. [Mark 4:36–41]
You make the dawn and the sunset
shout for joy.

9 You visit the earth and make it
overflow [with water];
You greatly enrich it;
The stream of God is full of water;
You provide their grain, when You
have prepared the earth.
10 You water its furrows abundantly,
You smooth its ridges;
You soften it with showers,
You bless its growth.
11 You crown the year with Your
bounty,
And Your paths overflow.
12 The pastures of the wilderness
drip [with dew],
And the hills are encircled with
joy.
13 The meadows are clothed with
flocks
And the valleys are covered with
grain;
They shout for joy and they sing.

Psalm 66

Praise for God's Mighty Deeds and for His Answer to Prayer.

To the Chief Musician. A Song. A Psalm.

1 SHOUT JOYFULLY to God, all the
earth;
2 Sing of the honor *and* glory *and*
magnificence of His name;
Make His praise glorious.
3 Say to God, "How awesome *and*
fearfully glorious are Your
works!
Because of the greatness of
Your power Your enemies will
pretend to be obedient to You.
4 "All the earth will [bow down to]
worship You [in submissive
wonder],
And will sing praises to You;
They will praise Your name in
song." *Selah.*

5 Come and see the works of God,
He is awesome in His deeds
toward the children of men.
6 He turned the sea into dry land;
They crossed through the river on
foot;
There we rejoiced in Him.
[Ex 14–15]
7 Who rules by His might forever,
His eyes keep watch on the
nations;
Do not let the rebellious exalt
themselves. *Selah.*

8 Bless our God, O peoples,
And make the sound of His praise
be heard abroad,

65:9 *You visit the earth.* Rainfall is seen here as a gracious visitation of God. This is in keeping with the provisions of God's covenant with Israel (Dt 28:12). These words have some fulfillment every time the rains bring productivity to the earth.
66:1 *all the earth.* As in Psalm 100:1, the call is not only for the people of Israel, but for the peoples of all the earth to join in the praises of the living God, the Most High (Ps 87:7; 96:1–6; 117:1).
66:2 *the honor and glory and magnificence of His name.* The Lord's name describes His character, so honoring God's name is honoring God Himself (Ex 3:14–15).
66:8 *Bless our God.* To bless God is to identify Him as the source of our blessing.

4 Ps 33:12; 4:3; Ps 36:8 **6** Ps 93:1 **7** Mt 8:26; Isa 17:13 **9** Jer 5:24; Ps 46:4 **13** Isa 55:12 **PSALM 66** **1** Ps 100:1 **3** Ps 65:5 **4** Ps 117:1 **6** Ex 14:21

9 Who keeps us among the
living,
And does not allow our feet to
slip *or* stumble.
10 For You have tested us, O God;
You have refined us as silver is
refined.
11 You brought us into the net;
You laid a heavy burden [of
servitude] on us.
12 You made men (charioteers) ride
over our heads [in defeat];
We went through fire and through
water,
Yet You brought us out into a
[broad] *place of* abundance [to
be refreshed].
13 I shall come into Your house with
burnt offerings;
I shall pay You my vows,
14 Which my lips uttered
And my mouth spoke as a promise
when I was in distress.
15 I shall offer to You burnt offerings
of fat lambs,
With the [sweet] smoke of rams;
I will offer bulls with male goats.
Selah.

16 Come and hear, all who fear
God [and worship Him with
awe-inspired reverence and
obedience],
And I will tell what He has done
for me.
17 I cried aloud to Him;
He was highly praised with my
tongue.
18 If I regard sin *and* baseness in my
heart [that is, if I know it is there
and do nothing about it],
The Lord will not hear [me];
[Prov 15:29; 28:9; Is 1:15;
John 9:31; James 4:3]
19 But certainly God has heard [me];
He has given heed to the voice of
my prayer.
20 Blessed be God,
Who has not turned away my
prayer
Nor His lovingkindness
from me.

Psalm 67

The Nations Exhorted to Praise God.

To the Chief Musician; on stringed instruments. A Psalm. A Song.

1 GOD BE gracious *and* kind-
hearted to us and bless us,
And make His face shine [with
favor] on us— *Selah.*
2 That Your way may be known on
earth,
Your salvation *and* deliverance
among all nations.
3 Let the peoples praise You, O God;
Let all the peoples praise You.
4 Let the nations be glad and sing
for joy,
For You will judge the people fairly
And guide the nations on earth.
Selah.
5 Let the peoples praise You, O God;
Let all the peoples praise You.
6 The earth has yielded its harvest
[as evidence of His approval];
God, our God, blesses us.
7 God blesses us,

66:13 *Your house.* This term refers to the temple in Jerusalem where God lived among His people.
66:16 *all who fear God.* Those who fear God are those who respond in awe and wonder to Him.
66:18 *regard sin and baseness.* Ongoing sin tolerated in a believer's life is one of the main things that blocks effective prayer and hinders growth.
67:1 *His face shine.* In the language of Aaron's benediction (Nu 6:24–26), the psalmist calls for God to smile on His people.
67:2 *known on earth.* From the beginning God had intended to bring His blessing to all nations, in fulfillment of the provisions of the Abrahamic covenant (Ge 12:3). This passage anticipates the thrust of world mission that is found in the New Testament (Mt 28:18–20; Ac 1:8).
67:6 *yielded its harvest.* The coming of God's kingdom on earth will be marked by a magnificent increase in production. The curse on the land (Ge 3:17–19; Ro 8:22) will be lifted at that time.

10 Ps 17:3; Isa 48:10; Zec 13:9; 1Pe 1:7 **11** La 1:13 **12** Isa 51:23; Isa 43:2 **13** Ecc 5:4 **18** Isa 1:15; Jn 9:31; Jas 4:3 **19** Ps 116:1,2 **PSALM 67** **1** Nu 6:25; Ps 4:6 **2** Ac 18:25; Isa 52:10; Titus 2:11 **4** Ps 96:10 **6** Lev 26:4; Ps 85:12; Eze 34:27

And all the ends of the earth shall
fear Him [with awe-inspired
reverence and submissive
wonder].

Psalm 68

The God of Sinai and of the Sanctuary.

To the Chief Musician.
A Psalm of David. A Song.

1 LET GOD arise, and His enemies
be scattered;
Let those who hate Him flee before
Him.
2 As smoke is driven away, so drive
them away;
As wax melts before the fire,
So let the wicked *and* guilty perish
before [the presence of] God.
3 But let the righteous be glad; let
them be in good spirits before
God,
Yes, let them rejoice with delight.
4 Sing to God, sing praises to His
name;
Lift up *a song* for Him who rides
through the desert—
His name is the LORD—be in good
spirits before Him.

5 A father of the fatherless and
a judge *and* protector of the
widows,
Is God in His holy habitation.
6 God makes a home for the lonely;
He leads the prisoners into
prosperity,
Only the stubborn *and* rebellious
dwell in a parched land.
7 O God, when You went out before
Your people,
When You marched through the
wilderness, *Selah.*
8 The earth trembled;
The heavens also poured down
rain at the presence of God;
Sinai itself trembled at the
presence of God, the God of
Israel.
9 You, O God, sent abroad plentiful
rain;
You confirmed Your inheritance
when it was parched *and* weary.
10 Your flock found a dwelling place
in it;
O God, in Your goodness You
provided for the poor.

11 The Lord gives the command [to
take Canaan];
The women who proclaim the
good news are a great host
(army);

12 "The kings of the [enemies']
armies flee, they flee,
And the beautiful woman who
remains at home divides the
spoil [left behind]."
13 When you lie down [to rest] among
the sheepfolds,
You [Israel] are like the wings of
a dove [of victory] overlaid with
silver,
Its feathers glistening with gold
[trophies taken from the enemy].
14 When the Almighty scattered [the
Canaanite] kings in the land of
Canaan,
It was snowing on Zalmon.

68:1 *Let God arise.* This psalm is based in part on the Song of Deborah in Judges 5. The presence of the wicked on the earth is an assault on God's holiness and a constant threat to the righteous. Only God's mercy compels Him to delay His judgment (75:2).
68:5–6 *father.* The view of God as Father is not as fully developed in the Old Testament as it is in the New Testament. This passage affords some insight into the character of God as Father. He is not seen in these verses as the Almighty God destroying His foes. He is pictured rather as the Father helping His children in need. He delights in kindly works which bring a happy existence to His children.
68:11 *The women who proclaim the good news.* This may refer to the women who gave praise to God under the direction of Miriam (Ex 15:20–21).
68:14 *the Almighty.* This translates the name "Shaddai," a title that refers to the majesty and strength of the Lord (91:1).

PSALM 68 **1** Nu 10:35; Isa 33:3 **2** Isa 9:18; Hos 13:3; Mic 1:4 **3** Ps 32:11 **4** Dt 33:26; Ex 6:3 **5** Ps 10:14 **6** 1Sa 2:5; Ps 107:4-7; Ac 12:6; Ps 107:34 **7** Ex 13:21; Jdg 4:14 **9** Dt 11:11 **10** Dt 26:5; Ps 74:19 **12** Nu 31:8; Jos 10:16 **13** Ps 81:6; Ps 105:37 **14** Jos 10:10

15 A mountain of God is the
mountain of Bashan;
A [high] mountain of many
summits is Mount Bashan
[rising east of the Jordan].
16 Why do you look with envy,
mountains with many peaks,
At the mountain [of the city of
Zion] which God has desired for
His dwelling place?
Yes, the LORD will dwell *there*
forever.
17 The chariots of God are myriads,
thousands upon thousands;
The Lord is among them as He
was at Sinai, in holiness.
18 You have ascended on high, You
have led away captive *Your*
captives;
You have received gifts among
men,
Even from the rebellious also, that
the LORD God may dwell there.
[Eph 4:8]

19 Blessed be the Lord, who bears
our burden day by day,
The God who is our salvation!
Selah.
20 God is to us a God of acts of
salvation;
And to GOD the Lord belong
escapes from death [setting us
free].
21 Surely God will shatter the head of
His enemies,
The hairy scalp of one who goes
on in his guilty ways.
22 The Lord said, "I will bring your
enemies back from Bashan;
I will bring them back from the
depths of the [Red] Sea,
23 That your foot may crush them in
blood,
That the tongue of your dogs
may have its share from your
enemies."

24 They have seen Your [solemn]
procession, O God,
The procession of my God, my
King, into the sanctuary [in
holiness].
25 The singers go in front, the players
of instruments last;
Between them the maidens
playing on tambourines.
26 Bless God in the congregations,
[give thanks, gratefully praise
Him],
The LORD, *you who are* from
[Jacob] the fountain of Israel.
27 The youngest is there, Benjamin,
ruling them,
The princes of Judah and their
company [the southern tribes],
The princes of Zebulun and
the princes of Naphtali [the
northern tribes].

28 Your God has commanded your
strength [your power in His
service and your resistance to
temptation];
Show Yourself strong, O God, who
acted on our behalf.
29 Because of Your temple at
Jerusalem
[Pagan] kings will bring gifts to
You [out of respect].
30 Rebuke the beasts [living] among
the reeds [in Egypt],
The herd of bulls (the leaders) with
the calves of the peoples;
Trampling underfoot the pieces of
silver;
He has scattered the peoples who
delight in war.

68:18 ***You have led away captive Your captives.*** Paul quotes this verse in Ephesians 4:8, applying it to Jesus Christ. ***received gifts.*** When God delivered His people from Egypt, He brought them out with great treasures from the Egyptians (Ex 12:35 – 36). These gifts were used by the people of Israel to build the tabernacle (Ex 35:20 – 29), where the Lord promised to dwell.

68:29 ***kings will bring gifts to You.*** Royal guests came to Solomon with gifts (1Ki 10:1 – 10); but the ultimate prophetic fulfillment of this verse was in the kings who came to Jerusalem to bring gifts to the infant Jesus (Mt 2:1 – 12). One day all kings will show their obedience and humility before Jesus, the great King (2:10 – 12; 76:11).

16 Dt 12:5; 1Ki 9:3 **17** Dt 33:2 **18** Eph 4:8; Jdg 5:12; Ac 2:4,33; 1Ti 1:13; Ps 78:60 **20** Dt 32:39 **21** Hab 3:13; Ps 55:23 **22** Nu 21:33; Ex 14:22 **23** Ps 58:10; 1Ki 21:19 **25** 1Ch 13:8 **26** Dt 33:28; Isa 48:1 **27** 1Sa 9:21 **28** Ps 42:8 **29** Ps 72:10 **30** Ps 22:12; 2Sa 8:2

[31] Princes *and* envoys shall come
from Egypt;
Ethiopia will quickly stretch out
her hands [with the offerings of
submission] to God.

[32] Sing to God, O kingdoms of the
earth,
Sing praises to the Lord! *Selah.*

[33] To Him who rides in the highest
heavens, the ancient heavens,
Behold, He sends out His voice, a
mighty *and* majestic voice.

[34] Ascribe strength to God;
His majesty is over Israel
And His strength is in the skies.

[35] O God, *You are* awesome *and*
profoundly majestic from Your
sanctuary;
The God of Israel gives strength
and power to His people.
Blessed be God!

Psalm 69

A Cry of Distress and Imprecation on Adversaries.

To the Chief Musician; set to [the tune of] "Lilies." *A Psalm* of David.

[1] SAVE ME, O God,
For the waters have threatened my
life [they have come up to my
neck].

[2] I have sunk in deep mire, where
there is no foothold;
I have come into deep waters,
where a flood overwhelms me.

[3] I am weary with my crying; my
throat is parched;
My eyes fail while I wait [with
confident expectation] for my
God.

[4] Those who hate me without cause
are more than the hairs of my
head;
Those who would destroy me are
powerful, being my enemies
wrongfully;
I am forced to restore what I did
not steal. [John 15:25]

[5] O God, You know my folly;
My wrongs are not hidden from
You.

[6] Do not let those who wait
[confidently] for You be
ashamed through me, O Lord
GOD of hosts;
Do not let those who seek You
[as necessary for life itself] be
dishonored through me, O God
of Israel,

[7] Because for Your sake I have
borne reproach;
Confusion *and* dishonor have
covered my face.

[8] I have become estranged from my
brothers
And an alien to my mother's sons.
[John 7:3–5]

[9] For zeal for Your house has
consumed me,
And the [mocking] insults of those
who insult You have fallen on
me. [John 2:17; Rom 15:3]

[10] When I wept *and* humbled myself
with fasting,

69:1 ***the waters have threatened my life.*** This highly messianic psalm presents a remarkable description of the suffering of Jesus Christ. Psalm 22 describes Jesus' physical sufferings, while Psalm 69 focuses more on His emotional and spiritual suffering. Yet, like Psalm 22, this psalm was written by David approximately a thousand years before the events it describes. Both psalms begin with the sufferings of David but have their full meaning in the sufferings of Jesus. For these reasons, the apostles in the New Testament acknowledge that David was a prophet of God (Ac 2:30).

69:4 ***without cause.*** The Savior suffered affliction even though He was holy, harmless, and undefiled, and so no amount of holiness in His followers can prevent the enmity of a wicked world (Jn 15:19). In the Sermon on the Mount, Jesus promised blessing and a great reward to His followers who suffered for the sake of righteousness, a cause which is identified with Christ's own person (Mt 5:10 – 11). Peter must have taken seriously Jesus' words on this subject, for he reminds believers that if they are reviled for the name of Christ, it is a blessing which indicates that the Spirit of God is resting upon them (1Pe 4:14).

69:9 ***zeal for Your house has consumed me.*** Like Phinehas in Numbers 25, David describes himself as a zealot for the house of the Lord.

31 Isa 19:21; 45:14; Ps 44:20 **33** Ps 18:10 **34** Ps 29:1 **35** Ps 76:12 **PSALM 69** **Title** Ps 45, Title **1** Jnh 2:5 **2** Ps 40:2 **3** Ps 6:6; Ps 119:82; Isa 38:14 **4** Ps 35:19; Jn 15:25 **8** Isa 53:3 **9** Jn 2:17; Ro 15:3 **10** Ps 35:13

It became my reproach.
11 When I made sackcloth my
clothing [as one in mourning],
I became a byword [a mere object
of scorn] to them.
12 They who sit in the [city's] gate
talk about me *and* mock me,
And I am the song of the
drunkards.
13 But as for me, my prayer is to You,
O LORD, at an acceptable *and*
opportune time;
O God, in the greatness of Your
favor *and* in the abundance of
Your lovingkindness,
Answer me with truth [that is, the
faithfulness of Your salvation].
14 Rescue me from the mire and do
not let me sink;
Let me be rescued from those
who hate me and from the deep
waters.
15 Do not let the floodwater
overwhelm me,
Nor the deep waters swallow me up,
Nor the pit [of Sheol] shut its
mouth over me.
16 Answer me, O LORD, for Your
lovingkindness is sweet *and*
good *and* comforting;
According to the greatness of Your
compassion, turn to me.
17 Do not hide Your face from Your
servant,
For I am in distress; answer me
quickly.
18 Draw near to my soul and redeem it;
Ransom me because of my
enemies [so that they do not
delight in my distress].
19 You know my reproach and my
shame and my dishonor [how I
am insulted];
My adversaries are all before You
[each one fully known].
20 Reproach *and* insults have broken
my heart and I am so sick.
I looked for sympathy, but there
was none,
And for comforters, but I found
none.
21 They (self-righteous hypocrites)
also gave me gall [poisonous
and bitter] for my food,
And for my thirst they gave me
vinegar to drink. [Matt 27:34, 48]
22 May their table [with all its
abundance and luxury] become
a snare [to them];
And when they are in peace
[secure at their sacrificial
feasts], *may it become* a trap.
23 May their eyes be dimmed so that
they cannot see,
And make their loins shake
continually [in terror and
weakness].
24 Pour out Your indignation on
them,
And let [the fierceness of] Your
burning anger overtake them.
25 May their encampment be
desolate;
May no one dwell in their tents.
[Matt 23:38; Acts 1:20]
26 For they have persecuted him
whom You have struck,
And they tell of the pain of those
whom You have pierced *and*
wounded.
27 Add [unforgiven] iniquity to their
iniquity [in Your book],
And may they not come into Your
righteousness.
28 May they be blotted out of the
book of life [and their lives come
to an end]

Jesus' cleansing of the temple was a fulfillment of these words (Jn 2:17).

69:21 *gall.* "Gall" is commonly employed in Scripture as a synonym for poison, or bitterness. When Jesus hung on the cross, He actually was offered some sour wine mixed with gall (probably the bitter herb myrrh), a drink given occasionally to relieve the crucified person's thirst and pain (Mt 27:34).

69:25 May their encampment be desolate. These words were fulfilled in Judas Iscariot. See Acts 1:20, in which the words of this verse are joined to the words of 109:8.

11 Jer 24:9 **12** Job 30:9 **13** Isa 49:8 **14** Ps 144:7; ver. 1,2,15 **15** Nu 16:33 **16** Ps 25:16 **17** Ps 27:9 **19** Ps 22:6,7; Isa 53:3 **20** Isa 63:5; Job 16:2 **21** Mt 27:34; Mk 15:23; Jn 19:29 **22** Ro 11:9 **23** Isa 6:9,10; Ro 11:10 **24** 1Th 2:16 **25** Mt 23:38 **26** Isa 53:4 **27** Ro 1:28; Isa 26:10 **28** Ex 32:32; Php 4:3; Eze 13:9

And may they not be recorded
with the righteous (those in
right standing with God).
[Rev 3:4, 5; 20:12, 15; 21:27]

29 But I am sorrowful and in pain;
May Your salvation, O God, set me
[securely] on high.
30 I will praise the name of God with
song
And magnify Him with
thanksgiving.
31 And it will please the LORD better
than an ox
Or a young bull with horns and
hoofs.
32 The humble have seen it and are
glad;
You who seek God [requiring Him
as your greatest need], let your
heart revive *and* live. [Ps 22:26;
42:1]
33 For the LORD hears the needy
And does not despise His *who are*
prisoners.

34 Let heaven and earth praise Him,
The seas and everything that
moves in them.
35 For God will save Zion and rebuild
the cities of Judah,
That His servants may remain
there and possess it.
36 The descendants of His servants
will inherit it,
And those who love His name will
dwell in it.

Psalm 70

Prayer for Help against Persecutors.

To the Chief Musician. *A Psalm* of
David, to bring to remembrance.

1 O GOD, *come quickly* to save me;
O LORD, come quickly to help me!
2 Let those be ashamed and
humiliated
Who seek my life;
Let them be turned back and
humiliated
Who delight in my hurt.
3 Let them be turned back because
of their shame *and* disgrace
Who say, "Aha, aha!"

4 May all those who seek You [as
life's first priority] rejoice and be
glad in You;
May those who love Your salvation
say continually,
"Let God be magnified!"
5 But I am afflicted and needy;
Come quickly to me, O God!
You are my help and my rescuer;
O LORD, do not delay.

Psalm 71

Prayer of an Old Man for Rescue.

1 IN YOU, O LORD, I have put my trust
and confidently taken refuge;
Let me never be put to shame.
2 In Your righteousness deliver me
and rescue me;
Incline Your ear to me and save me.
3 Be to me a rock of refuge *and* a
sheltering stronghold to which I
may continually come;
You have given the commandment
to save me,
For You are my rock and my
fortress.
4 Rescue me, O my God, from the
hand of the wicked (godless),
From the grasp of the unrighteous
and ruthless man.
5 For You are my hope;
O Lord GOD, *You are* my trust *and*
the source of my confidence
from my youth.

70:2 *be ashamed and humiliated.* David prays that those who rejoice in his misery will be proven wrong in their assumption that the Lord is unable to help His people. In this way, the Lord's deliverance of David will result in God's name being glorified — both by the joy of God's people and the shame of His enemies.

71:2 *Your righteousness.* The psalmist is concerned with his own plight and also with the character of God. The psalmist's point is that God

30 Ps 28:7 **31** Ps 50:13 **32** Ps 34:2; Ps 22:26 **33** Eph 3:1 **34** Ps 96:11; 148:1; Isa 44:23; Isa 55:12 **35** Ps 51:18; Isa 44:26 **36** Ps 102:28 **PSALM 70** **Title** Ps 38, Title **1** Ps 40:13 **2** Ps 35:4,26 **3** Ps 40:15 **5** Ps 40:17; Ps 141:1 **PSALM 71** **1** Ps 25:2,3 **2** Ps 31:1; Ps 17:6 **3** Ps 31:2,3; 44:4 **4** Ps 140:1,4 **5** Jer 17:7

6 Upon You have I relied *and* been
sustained from my birth;
You are He who took me from my
mother's womb *and* You have
been my benefactor from that
day.
My praise is continually of You.

7 I am as a wonder to many,
For You are my strong refuge.
8 My mouth is filled with Your
praise
And with Your glory all day long.
9 Do not cast me off *nor* send me
away in the time of old age;
Do not abandon me when my
strength fails *and* I am weak.
10 For my enemies have spoken
against me;
Those who watch for my life have
consulted together,
11 Saying, "God has abandoned him;
Pursue and seize him, for there is
no one to rescue *him*."

12 O God, do not be far from me;
O my God, come quickly to help me!
13 Let those who attack my life be
ashamed and consumed;
Let them be covered with reproach
and dishonor, who seek to injure
me.
14 But as for me, I will wait *and* hope
continually,
And will praise You yet more and
more.
15 My mouth shall tell of Your
righteousness
And of Your [deeds of] salvation
all day long,
For their number is more than I
know.
16 I will come with the mighty acts
of the Lord God [and in His
strength];
I will make mention of Your
righteousness, Yours alone.

17 O God, You have taught me from
my youth,
And I still declare Your wondrous
works *and* miraculous deeds.
18 And even when I am old and gray-
headed, O God, do not abandon
me,
Until I declare Your [mighty]
strength to this generation,
Your power to all who are to
come.

19 Your righteousness, O God,
reaches to the [height of the]
heavens,
You who have done great things;
O God, who is like You, [who is
Your equal]?
20 You who have shown me many
troubles and distresses
Will revive *and* renew me again,
And will bring me up again from
the depths of the earth.
21 May You increase my greatness
(honor)
And turn to comfort me.

22 I will also praise You with the
harp,
Your truth *and* faithfulness, O my
God;
To You I will sing praises with the
lyre,
O Holy One of Israel.
23 My lips will shout for joy when I
sing praises to You,
And my soul, which You have
redeemed.
24 My tongue also will speak of Your
righteousness all day long;
For they are ashamed, for they
are humiliated who seek my
injury.

---

could display His righteousness by answering the needs of the psalmist, whose life had been lived in constant trust in God.

71:7 *a wonder.* The poet declares that the work of God in his life has made him a special sign to the people, similar to the great miracles of God through Moses and Aaron in Egypt (Ex 7:3; 11:9).

71:22 *the harp . . . the lyre.* The psalmist praised God with music, both vocal and instrumental. His worship came from his inner being ("my soul," v. 23) which was filled with praises to the living God. No matter what form our worship takes, it is worthless unless it comes from the heart.

6 Ps 22:9,10; Isa 46:3 **7** Isa 8:18 **8** Ps 35:28 **9** ver. 18 **10** 2Sa 17:1; Mt 27:1 **12** Ps 35:22; 70:1 **13** ver. 24 **15** Ps 35:28; 40:5 **18** ver. 9 **19** Ps 57:10; Ps 35:10 **20** Ps 60:3; Hos 6:1,2 **22** Ps 92:1-3; 2Ki 19:22; Isa 60:9 **23** Ps 103:4

Psalm 72
The Reign of the Righteous King.

A Psalm of Solomon.

[1]GIVE THE king [knowledge of] Your judgments, O God,
And [the spirit of] Your righteousness to the king's son [to guide all his ways].
[2]May he judge Your people with righteousness,
And Your afflicted with justice. [1 Kin 3:1–5]
[3]The mountains will bring peace *and* prosperity to the people,
And the hills, in [the establishment of] righteousness.
[4]May he bring justice to the poor among the people,
Save the children of the needy
And crush the oppressor,
[5]Let them fear You [with awe-inspired reverence and worship You with obedience] while the sun endures,
And as long as the moon [reflects light], throughout all generations.
[6]May he come down like rain on the mown grass,
Like showers that water the earth.
[7]In his days may the righteous flourish,
And peace abound until the moon is no more. [Is 11:1–9]
[8]May he also rule from sea to sea
And from the River [Euphrates] to the ends of the earth. [Zech 14:9]
[9]The nomads of the desert will bow before him,
And his enemies will lick the dust.
[10]The kings of Tarshish and of the islands will bring offerings;
The kings of Sheba and Seba will offer gifts.
[11]Yes, all kings will bow down before him,
All nations will serve him. [Ps 138:4]
[12]For he will rescue the needy when he cries for help,
The afflicted *and* abused also, and him who has no helper.
[13]He will have compassion on the poor and needy,
And he will save the lives of the needy.
[14]He will redeem their life from oppression *and* fraud and violence,
And their blood will be precious in His sight.
[15]So may he live, and may the gold of Sheba be given to him;
And let them pray for him continually;
Let them bless *and* praise him all day long.
[16]There will be an abundance of grain in the soil on the top of the mountains;
Its fruit will wave like [the cedars of] Lebanon,
And those of the city will flourish like grass of the earth.
[17]May his name endure forever;
May his name continue as long as the sun;

72:1 ***Give the king [knowledge of] Your judgments.*** Solomon's prayer for his own godly reign is an intensely messianic poem, speaking in ideal terms of the coming of the great King. The psalm calls for a good king to govern Israel under God's blessing. Ultimately this king is the Savior Jesus.
72:8 ***May he also rule from sea to sea.*** The promises of God to Abraham included a promise that his descendants would have dominion over the land of Canaan (Ge 15:18 – 21). These verses expand the geographical dimensions to include the entire earth.
72:14 ***He will redeem their life.*** This verse points to Jesus' death on the cross, when He paid the price to redeem us from the oppression of sin.
72:17 ***May his name endure forever.*** The name of the great King will be regarded as the greatest in the universe. Paul speaks this way of Jesus' name in Philippians 2:9 – 11.

PSALM 72 **Title** Ps 127, Title **2** Isa 32:1 **3** Ps 85:10; Isa 32:17 **4** Isa 11:4 **5** ver. 7:17 **6** Hos 6:3 **7** Isa 2:4; Jer 33:6; Lk 1:33 **8** Ex 23:31; Zec 9:10 **9** Ps 74:14; Isa 49:23 **10** 2Ch 9:21 **11** Isa 49:23 **12** Job 29:12 **14** Ps 116:15 **16** 1Ki 4:20 **17** Ps 89:36; Ge 12:3; Jer 4:2; Lk 1:48

And let men bless themselves by
him;
Let all nations call him blessed.

18 Blessed be the LORD God, the God
of Israel,
Who alone does wonderful things.
19 Blessed be His glorious name
forever;
And may the whole earth be filled
with His glory.
Amen and Amen.

20 The prayers of David son of Jesse
are ended.

BOOK THREE

Psalm 73

The End of the Wicked Contrasted with That of the Righteous.

A Psalm of Asaph.

1 TRULY GOD is good to Israel,
To those who are pure in heart.
2 But as for me, my feet came close
to stumbling,
My steps had almost slipped.
3 For I was envious of the arrogant
As I saw the prosperity of the
wicked.
4 For there are no pains in their death,
Their body is fat *and* pampered.
5 They are not in trouble *as other*
men,
Nor are they plagued like mankind.
6 Therefore pride is their necklace;
Violence covers them like a
garment [like a long, luxurious
robe].
7 Their eye bulges from fatness
[they have more than the heart
desires];
The imaginations of their mind
run riot [with foolishness].
8 They mock and wickedly speak of
oppression;
They speak loftily [with malice].
9 They set their mouth against the
heavens,
And their tongue swaggers
through the earth. [Rev 13:6]

10 Therefore his people return to this
place,
And waters of abundance [offered
by the irreverent] are [blindly]
drunk by them.
11 They say, "How does God know?
Is there knowledge [of us] with the
Most High?"
12 Behold, these are the ungodly,
Who always prosper *and* are at
ease [in the world]; they have
increased in wealth.

72:20 *The prayers of David . . . are ended.* The superscription of this psalm attributes it to Solomon. It is possible that Solomon wrote this poem as the close of a collection of his father's psalms. Other psalms were later added to this original collection.

73:1 Walking in the Spirit—An important prerequisite to walking in the Spirit is the confession of sin. Sin must be confessed in order to restore fellowship and to continue receiving God's forgiveness (1Jn 1:5–10). Confession means that we agree with God about our sin. That involves much more than simply acknowledging the sin. Confession requires an attitude of sorrow for the sin and a willingness to turn from it. It does not mean that we will never commit the same sin again, but it does mean that the attitude of repentance towards the sin is present.

Confession should be made at the moment the Christian becomes aware of sin. The Scriptures actually mention two specific times for confession: before the close of the day (Eph 4:26) and before the Lord's Supper (1Co 11:27–32). Failure to do the latter is a special cause for discipline from the Lord.

Confession of sin should involve only those who have knowledge of the sin. This means that private sins should be confessed privately; sins between individuals confessed between those involved (Mt 5:23–24); and public sins confessed publicly (Mt 18:17). Public confession is normally made for the edification of the church (1Co 14:26).

73:3 *For I was envious.* This psalmist is open with the readers concerning his own weakness and doubts; he also shows that he came to the right conclusion in the end: to trust God.

73:12 *prosper and are at ease [in the world].* It often does appear that ungodly people get

---

18 1Ch 29:10; Ex 15:11 **19** Neh 9:5; Nu 14:21; Hab 2:14 **PSALM 73** **Title** Ps 50, Title **3** Job 21:7; Ps 37:1 **5** Job 21:9 **6** Ps 109:18 **7** Jer 5:28 **8** Ps 53:1; Jude 16 **9** Rev 13:6 **10** Ps 75:8 **11** Job 22:13

13 Surely then in vain I have cleansed
my heart
And washed my hands in
innocence. [Mal 3:14]
14 For all the day long have I been
stricken,
And punished every morning.
15 If I had said, "I will say this," [and
expressed my feelings],
I would have betrayed the
generation of Your children.
16 When I considered how to
understand this,
It was too great an effort for me
and too painful
17 Until I came into the sanctuary of
God;
Then I understood [for I
considered] their end.
18 Surely You set the wicked-minded
and immoral on slippery places;
You cast them down to destruction.
19 How they are destroyed in a
moment!
They are completely swept away
by sudden terrors!
20 Like a dream [which seems real]
until one awakens,
O Lord, when stirred, [You
observe the wicked], You will
despise their image.
21 When my heart was embittered
And I was pierced within [as with
the fang of an adder],
22 Then I was senseless and ignorant;
I was like a beast before You.
23 Nevertheless I am continually with
You;
You have taken hold of my right
hand.
24 You will guide me with Your counsel,
And afterward receive me to
honor *and* glory.
25 Whom have I in heaven [but You]?
And besides You, I desire nothing
on earth.
26 My flesh and my heart may fail,
But God is the rock *and* strength
of my heart and my portion
forever.
27 For behold, those who are far from
You will perish;
You have destroyed all those
who are unfaithful *and* have
abandoned You.
28 But as for me, it is good for me to
draw near to God;
I have made the Lord GOD my
refuge *and* placed my trust in
Him,
That I may tell of all Your works.

Psalm 74

An Appeal against the Devastation of the Land by the Enemy.

A skillful song, *or* a didactic *or* reflective poem, of Asaph.

1 O GOD, why have You rejected us
forever?
Why does Your anger smoke
against the sheep of Your
pasture?

---

away with everything, ending up on the top of the heap and leaving the godly wondering whether their own acts of righteous living are without meaning or purpose.

73:15 ***betrayed.*** Even as he struggled with the apparent lack of reward for righteousness, Asaph knew in his heart that such thoughts were wrong. Even when we can't understand the surface facts, God's witness in our spirits lets us know when we are moving down the wrong track.

73:22 ***like a beast before You.*** An animal has no sense of eternity or divine perspective. When the psalmist wondered about the value of righteousness, his thinking was based only on the present, like an animal, rather than understanding the bigger picture as a being with an eternal soul.

73:28 ***it is good for me to draw near to God.*** There are those who may enjoy great wealth and notoriety today, but nothing they have or do will last forever. Compared to a relationship with the living God, nothing else matters.

74:1 ***anger.*** The Babylonian destruction of the temple in 586 BC occasioned a crisis of faith among the ancient covenant people. Since the temple served as the external sign of God's covenant with Israel, its destruction may have caused

13 Job 34:9; Mal 3:14; Ps 26:6 **16** Ecc 8:17 **17** Ps 77:13; Ps 37:38 **18** Ps 35:6 **20** Job 20:8; Ps 90:5 **22** Ps 92:6; Pr 30:2 **24** Ps 32:8; 48:14 **25** Php 3:8 **26** Ps 84:2; 119:81 **27** Ps 119:155 **28** Heb 10:22
PSALM 74 **1** Ps 44:9,23; Jer 31:37; Dt 29:20; Ps 95:7

[2] Remember Your congregation,
which You have purchased of old,
Which You have redeemed to be the tribe of Your inheritance;
Remember Mount Zion, where You have dwelt.
[3] Turn your footsteps [quickly] toward the perpetual ruins;
The enemy has damaged everything within the sanctuary.
[4] In the midst of Your meeting place Your enemies have roared [with their battle cry];
They have set up their own emblems for signs [of victory].
[5] It seems as if one had lifted up
An axe in a forest of trees [to set a record of destruction].
[6] And now all the carved work [of the meeting place]
They smash with hatchets and hammers.
[7] They have burned Your sanctuary to the ground;
They have profaned the dwelling place of Your name.
[8] They said in their heart, "Let us completely subdue them."
They have burned all the meeting places of God in the land.
[9] We do not see our symbols;
There is no longer any prophet [to guide us],
Nor does any among us know for how long.
[10] O God, how long will the adversary scoff?
Is the enemy to revile Your name forever?
[11] Why do You withdraw Your hand, even Your right hand [from judging the enemy]?
Remove Your hand from Your chest, destroy *them!*
[12] Yet God is my King of old,
Working salvation in the midst of the earth.
[13] You divided the [Red] Sea by Your strength;
You broke the heads of the sea monsters in the waters. [Ex 14:21]
[14] You crushed the heads of Leviathan (Egypt);
You gave him as food for the creatures of the wilderness. [Job 41:1]
[15] You broke open fountains and streams;
You dried up ever-flowing rivers. [Ex 17:6; Num 20:11; Josh 3:13]
[16] The day is Yours, the night also is Yours;
You have established *and* prepared the [heavenly] light and the sun.
[17] You have defined *and* established all the borders of the earth [the divisions of land and sea and of the nations];
You have made summer and winter. [Acts 17:26]
[18] Remember this, O LORD, the enemy has scoffed,
And a foolish *and* impious people has spurned Your name.
[19] Oh, do not hand over the soul of your turtledove to the wild beast;
Do not forget the life of Your afflicted forever.

---

the impression that God's promise to David had been canceled (2Sa 7:12 – 14). The psalmist is deeply conscious that God is angry with the nation, and the reason for His anger is unmistakably clear. The people had forsaken the covenant, and worshiped and served other gods (Dt 29:25 – 26). God's anger reminds us of His eternal hatred of all unrighteousness. It is the holiness of God stirred into an appropriate response to sin.

74:12 *my King of old.* The Lord is King by virtue of His creation of the earth (Ps 93). He is King because of His special relationship with Israel (44:4; 99:1 – 3). And He is the coming King who will reign over all (96:13; 97:1 – 6; 98:6 – 9).

74:14 *Leviathan.* This creature was used to poetically describe various evil forces over which God has ultimate control and victory. Eventually the Leviathan (Job 41:1 – 10) became a symbol for Satan (Isa 27:1) who is "the dragon, that old serpent" (Rev 20:2).

74:15 *dried up ever-flowing rivers.* God enabled His people to cross over the Red Sea (Ex 14) and the river Jordan (Jos 3).

4 Da 6:27 **8** Ps 83:4 **9** Am 8:11 **11** La 2:3 **12** Ps 44:4 **13** Ex 14:21; Isa 51:9,10; Eze 29:3 **14** Nu 14:9 **15** Ex 17:5,6; Nu 20:11; Jos 3:13 **17** Ge 8:22 **18** ver. 22; Ps 39:8 **19** SS 2:14; Ps 68:10 **20** Ge 17:7,8; Ps 106:45

20 Consider the covenant [You made
with Abraham],
For the dark places of the land
are full of the habitations of
violence.
21 Let not the oppressed return
dishonored;
Let the afflicted and needy praise
Your name.
22 Arise, O God, plead Your own
cause;
Remember how the foolish man
scoffs at You all day long.
23 Do not forget the [clamoring]
voices of Your adversaries,
The uproar of those who rise
against You, which ascends
continually [to Your ears].

Psalm 75

God Abases the Proud, but Exalts the Righteous.

To the Chief Musician; set to [the tune of] "Do Not Destroy." A Psalm of Asaph. A Song.

1 WE GIVE thanks *and* praise to
You, O God, we give thanks,
For Your [wonderful works declare
that Your] name is near;
People declare Your wonders.
2 "When I select an appointed
time,
I will judge with equity," [says the
LORD].
3 "The earth and all the inhabitants
of it melt [in tumultuous
times].
It is I who will steady its pillars.
Selah.
4 "I said to the arrogant, 'Do not
boast;'
And to the wicked, 'Do not lift up
the horn [of self-glorification].
5 'Do not lift up your [defiant and
aggressive] horn on high,
Do not speak with a stiff neck.' "
6 For not from the east, nor from the
west,
Nor from the desert comes
exaltation. [Is 14:13]
7 But God is the Judge;
He puts down one and lifts up
another.
8 For a cup [of His wrath] is in the
hand of the LORD, and the wine
foams;
It is well mixed *and* fully spiced,
and He pours out from it;
And all the wicked of the earth
must drain it and drink down
to its dregs. [Ps 60:3; Jer 25:15;
Rev 14:9, 10; 16:19]
9 But as for me, I will declare it *and*
rejoice forever;
I will sing praises to the God of
Jacob.
10 All the horns of the wicked He will
cut off,
But the horns of the righteous will
be lifted up.

Psalm 76

The Victorious Power of the God of Jacob.

To the Chief Musician; on stringed instruments. A Psalm of Asaph. A Song.

1 GOD IS known in Judah;
His name is great in Israel.
2 His tabernacle is in Salem
(Jerusalem);
His dwelling place is in Zion.
3 There He broke the flaming
arrows,
The shield, the sword, and the
weapons of war. *Selah.*

75:2 *When I select an appointed time.* God will not be rushed, even by His devoted followers. When we grow impatient to see justice done, we must remember that God has a better sense of time than we do.

75:8 *a cup.* This is not a cup of blessing, but of the Lord's wrath. The biblical image of wine and judgment goes back to Jacob's blessing on Judah (Ge 49:11) and is referred to in Christ's judgment as depicted in Revelation 19:13–15.

76:2 *Salem.* Salem is the shortened form of the name Jerusalem.

22 Ps 89:51 **PSALM 75 Title** Ps 57, Title **4** Zec 1:21 **7** Ps 50:6; 1Sa 2:7; Da 2:21 **8** Job 21:20; Jer 25:15; Rev 14:10; 16:19; Pr 23:30; Ps 73:10 **10** Ps 101:8; Jer 48:25; Ps 89:17; 148:14 **PSALM 76 1** Ps 48:1 **3** Ps 46:9; Eze 39:9

[4]You are glorious *and* resplendent,
More majestic than the mountains of prey.
[5]The stouthearted have been stripped of their spoil,
They have slept the sleep [of death];
And none of the warriors could use his hands.
[6]At Your rebuke, O God of Jacob,
Both rider and horse were cast into a dead sleep [of death].
[Ex 15:1, 21; Nah 2:13; Zech 12:4]
[7]You, even You, are to be feared [with the submissive wonder of reverence];
Who may stand in Your presence when once You are angry?
[8]You caused judgment to be heard from heaven;
The earth feared and was quiet
[9]When God arose to [establish] judgment,
To save all the humble of the earth. *Selah.*
[10]For the wrath of man shall praise You;
With a remnant of wrath You will clothe *and* arm Yourself.
[11]Make vows to the LORD your God and fulfill them;
Let all who are around Him bring gifts to Him who is to be feared [with awe-inspired reverence].
[12]He will cut off the spirit of princes;
He is awesome *and* feared by the kings of the earth.

Psalm 77

Comfort in Trouble from Recalling God's Mighty Deeds.

To the Chief Musician; according to Jeduthun [one of David's three chief musicians, founder of an official musical family]. A Psalm of Asaph.

[1]MY VOICE rises to God, and I will cry aloud;
My voice rises to God, and He will hear me.
[2]In the day of my trouble I [desperately] sought the Lord;
In the night my hand was stretched out [in prayer] without weariness;
My soul refused to be comforted.
[3]I remember God; then I am disquieted *and* I groan;
I sigh [in prayer], and my spirit grows faint. *Selah.*
[4]You have held my eyelids open;
I am so troubled that I cannot speak.
[5]I have considered the ancient days,
The years [of prosperity] of long, long ago.
[6]I will remember my song in the night;
I will meditate with my heart,
And my spirit searches:
[7]Will the Lord reject forever?
And will He never be favorable again?
[8]Has His lovingkindness ceased forever?

76:6 *rider and horse.* This verse is referring to the defeat of the army of Pharaoh (Ex 14:13–29; 15).
76:7 *to be feared.* For the righteous, the fear of God is a response of awe, wonder, adoration, and worship. For the wicked, the fear of God is terror, for there is no escape from Him (14:5).
76:11 *bring gifts.* As one might bring gifts to a king, so the righteous should bring their gifts to God — the ultimate gift being the dedication of their lives to the service of God (Ro 12:1).
77:3 *remember . . . disquieted.* What he knew of God contrasted with what he was experiencing. The more the psalmist thought about these things, the more troubled he became.
77:7–8 *Will the Lord reject forever?* Even though we have put our faith in Christ and committed ourselves to obeying His will, this doesn't automatically guarantee total and perpetual immunity from trouble. There will be seasons when God seems remote and we begin to wonder about God's unfailing love. It is in these times that we must hold most firmly to what we know about God, rather than what we feel. God has neither forgotten to show mercy nor stifled His compassion.

4 Eze 38:12 **5** Isa 46:12; Ps 13:3; Jer 51:39 **6** Ex 15:1,21; Eze 39:20; Na 2:13; Zec 12:4 **7** Na 1:6 **8** Ex 19:10; 2Ch 20:29,30 **9** Ps 9:7-9; 72:4 **10** Ps 65:7; Da 3:28 **11** Ecc 5:4-6; 2Ch 32:22,23; Ps 68:29 **12** Ps 68:35
PSALM 77 Title Ps 39, Title; 62, Title **1** Ps 3:4 **2** Ps 50:15; Isa 26:9,16 **3** Ps 143:4 **5** Dt 32:7; Ps 143:5; Isa 51:9 **6** Ps 42:8; Ps 4:4 **7** Ps 74:1; 85:1 **8** Ro 9:6

Have His promises ended for all
time?
9 Has God forgotten to be gracious?
Or has He in anger withdrawn His
compassion? *Selah.*
10 And I said, "This is my grief,
That the right hand of the Most
High has changed [and His
lovingkindness is withheld]."

11 I will [solemnly] remember the
deeds of the LORD;
Yes, I will [wholeheartedly]
remember Your wonders of old.
12 I will meditate on all Your works
And thoughtfully consider all Your
[great and wondrous] deeds.
13 Your way, O God, is holy [far from
sin and guilt].
What god is great like our God?
14 You are the [awesome] God who
works [powerful] wonders;
You have demonstrated Your
power among the people.
15 You have with Your [great] arm
redeemed Your people,
The sons of Jacob and Joseph.
Selah.

16 The waters [of the Red Sea] saw
You, O God;
The waters saw You, they were in
anguish;
The deeps also trembled.
17 The clouds poured down water;
The skies sent out a sound [of
rumbling thunder];
Your arrows (lightning) flashed
here and there.
18 The voice of Your thunder was in
the whirlwind;
The lightnings illumined the world;
The earth trembled and shook.
19 Your way [of escape for Your
people] was through the sea,
And Your paths through the great
waters,
And Your footprints were not
traceable.
20 You led Your people like a flock
By the hand of Moses and Aaron
[to the promised goal].

Psalm 78

God's Guidance of His People in Spite of Their Unfaithfulness.

A skillful song, *or* a didactic *or* reflective poem, of Asaph.

1 LISTEN, O my people, to my
teaching;
Incline your ears to the words of
my mouth [and be willing to
learn].
2 I will open my mouth in a parable
[to instruct using examples];
I will utter dark *and* puzzling
sayings of old [that contain
important truth]— [Matt 13:34, 35]
3 Which we have heard and
known,
And our fathers have told us.
4 We will not hide them from their
children,

77:11 *I will [solemnly] remember.* Asaph did not *feel* any more at peace, but he made a conscious decision to turn from his pain and focus his thoughts on the person, works, and wonders of God. When we are in distress, we often feel that it is our right to vent our frustrations and complaints as long as we still feel them, but God doesn't call us to be driven by feelings. Instead, we have to consciously decide to praise God, trusting that the feelings will follow.

77:20 *You led Your people like a flock.* Lost in contemplation of the greatness of God, the poet seems thoroughly distracted from his pain. He does not mention it again, not daring to compare it to the greatness of the Almighty.

78:1 *my teaching.* The psalmist uses the vocabulary of the wisdom school to establish himself. "My teaching" or "my law" is the familiar word *Torah*. The wisdom writers used this word to indicate insight; their instruction is always in accord with the law of Moses (Pr 1:8; 3:1; 4:2).

78:2 *dark and puzzling sayings.* These are riddles, or instructions with a deeper meaning beyond the surface.

78:4 Israel's History—The biblical history of Israel covers 1,800 years and represents a marvelous panorama of God's gracious working through promise, miracle, blessing, and judgment. Israel begins as only a promise to Abraham (Ge 12:2). For over four hundred years the people of Israel

9 Isa 49:15 **10** Ps 31:22 **11** Ps 143:5 **13** Ps 73:17; Ex 15:11 **15** Ex 6:6; Dt 9:29 **16** Ex 14:21 **17** 2Sa 22:15 **18** 2Sa 22:8 **19** Hab 3:15; Ex 14:28 **20** Ex 13:21; Isa 63:11,12 **PSALM 78 Title** Ps 74, Title **1** Isa 51:4 **2** Mt 13:35 **3** Ps 44:1 **4** Dt 6:7; Joel 1:3; Ex 13:8,14

But [we will] tell to the generation
to come the praiseworthy deeds
of the LORD,
And [tell of] His great might *and*
power and the wonderful works
that He has done.

5 For He established a testimony (a
specific precept) in Jacob
And appointed a law in Israel,
Which He commanded our fathers
That they should teach to their
children [the great facts of God's
transactions with Israel],
6 That the generation to come might
know them, that the children
still to be born
May arise and recount them to
their children,
7 That they should place their
confidence in God
And not forget the works of God,
But keep His commandments,
8 And not be like their fathers—
A stubborn and rebellious
generation,
A generation that did not prepare
its heart to know *and* follow
God,
And whose spirit was not faithful
to God.

9 The sons of Ephraim were armed
as archers and carrying bows,
Yet they turned back in the day of
battle.
10 They did not keep the covenant of
God
And refused to walk according to
His law;
11 And they forgot His [incredible]
works
And His miraculous wonders that
He had shown them.
12 He did marvelous things in the
sight of their fathers
In the land of Egypt, in the field of
Zoan [where Pharaoh resided].
13 He divided the [Red] Sea and
allowed them to pass through it,
And He made the waters stand
up like [water behind] a dam.
[Ex 14:22]
14 In the daytime He led them with a
cloud
And all the night with a light of
fire. [Ex 13:21; 14:24]
15 He split rocks in the wilderness
And gave *them* abundant [water
to] drink like the ocean depths.
16 He brought streams also from the
rock [at Rephidim and Kadesh]

---

maintain their belief in that promise while in bondage in Egypt. Finally, in God's perfect timing, He brings the nation out of Egypt with the greatest series of miracles recorded in the Old Testament (Ex 7 – 15). This event is called the exodus, meaning a *going out*. It is the formative event in the history of the nation. It was a great act of redemption and in the Old Testament is the foremost example of God's care for His people (Ps 77:14 – 20; 78:12 – 55; Hos 11:1).

Once God had redeemed Israel He established His covenant with them at Mount Sinai (Ex 19:5 – 8). From that point on He has been their God and they, His people. The covenant foretells gracious blessings for obedience and severe judgments for disobedience. The rest of Israel's history demonstrates the certainty of that prophecy. Throughout periods of conquest, judges, monarchy, exile, restoration, and Gentile domination, Israel was blessed when she obeyed and judged when she disobeyed. The nation is finally destroyed in AD 70, although this event is not described in the New Testament. Many prophecies appear to promise a future redemption (Ro 11:26).

There are at least three good reasons to study the history of Israel:

It sets forth examples to be followed or avoided (1Co 10:6).

It shows God's control of historical events (Ps 78).

It serves as a model for all ages of God's kindness and mercy towards his people (Ps 78).

78:5 – 7 *testimony*. The history of Israel is told in a series of cycles with steps in each cycle ranging from a firm, dependent hope in God to deep apostasy. One generation would seek the works of God, hope in Him, and follow Him. The next generation would forget the mighty works of God and depart from reliance and confidence in Him. To avert this endless round of making the same mistakes, God commanded His people to make His laws a regular part of their everyday lives (Dt 6:4 – 9), so that they could not forget.

78:9 *Ephraim . . . turned back*. The poet may be referring to Ephraim's conflict with Jephthah (Jdg 12:1 – 7).

5 Ps 147:19; Dt 4:9 **6** Ps 102:18 **8** 2Ki 17:14; Ex 32:9; ver. 37 **10** 2Ki 17:15 **11** Ps 106:13 **12** Ex 7-12; Nu 13:22 **13** Ex 14:21; Ex 15:8 **14** Ex 13:21 **15** Nu 20:11 **16** Dt 9:21

And caused waters to run down
like rivers. [Ex 17:6; Num 20:11]
17 Yet they still continued to sin
against Him
By rebelling against the Most
High in the desert.
18 And in their hearts they put God to
the test
By asking for food according to
their [selfish] appetite.
19 Then they spoke against God;
They said, "Can God prepare [food
for] a table in the wilderness?
20 "Behold, He struck the rock so that
waters gushed out
And the streams overflowed;
Can He give bread also?
Or will He provide meat for His
people?"
21 Therefore, when the LORD heard,
He was full of wrath;
A fire was kindled against Jacob,
And His anger mounted up
against Israel,
22 Because they did not believe in
God [they did not rely on Him,
they did not adhere to Him],
And they did not trust in His
salvation (His power to save).
23 Yet He commanded the clouds
from above
And opened the doors of heaven;
24 And He rained down manna upon
them to eat
And gave them the grain of
heaven. [Ex 16:14; John 6:31]
25 Man ate the bread of angels;
God sent them provision in
abundance.
26 He caused the east wind to blow in
the heavens
And by His [unlimited] power He
guided the south wind.
27 He rained meat upon them like the
dust,
And winged birds (quail) like the
sand of the seas. [Num 11:31]
28 And He let them fall in the midst
of their camp,
Around their tents.
29 So they ate and were well filled,
He gave them what they craved.
30 Before they had satisfied their
desire,
And while their food was in their
mouths, [Num 11:33]
31 The wrath of God rose against them
And killed some of the strongest
of them,
And subdued the choice young
men of Israel.
32 In spite of all this they still sinned,
For they did not believe in His
wonderful *and* extraordinary
works.
33 Therefore He consumed their days
like a breath [in emptiness and
futility]
And their years in sudden terror.
34 When He killed [some of] them,
then those remaining sought
Him,
And they returned [to Him] and
searched diligently for God [for
a time].
35 And they remembered that God
was their rock,
And the Most High God their
Redeemer.
36 Nevertheless they flattered Him
with their mouths
And lied to Him with their tongues.
37 For their heart was not steadfast
toward Him,
Nor were they faithful to His
covenant. [Acts 8:21]
38 But He, the source of compassion
and lovingkindness, forgave
their wickedness and did not
destroy them;
Many times He restrained His anger
And did not stir up all His wrath.

78:29 *He gave them what they craved.* When we turn our hearts toward the Lord, our desires will change to match His will. Then He delights to give us our desires because they are right things which will lead to wholeness and goodness (37:4). Without God, we don't have the wisdom to know what we should long for.

78:38 *the source of compassion and lovingkindness.* The awesome transcendence of the Lord is complemented in this section (v. 35) by an emphasis on His compassionate mercy.

17 Heb 3:16 **18** Ex 16:2 **19** Nu 11:4 **20** Nu 20:11 **21** Nu 11:1 **22** Heb 3:18 **23** Mal 3:10 **24** Jn 6:31 **26** Nu 11:31 **29** Nu 11:20 **30** Nu 11:33 **32** Nu 14; 16; 17; ver. 22 **33** Nu 14:29 **34** Hos 5:15 **35** Dt 32:4,15,31; Isa 41:14; 63:9 **36** Eze 33:31 **38** Nu 14:18,20; Isa 48:9; 1Ki 21:29

[39]For He [graciously] remembered
that they were mere [human]
flesh,
A wind that goes and does not
return.
[40]How often they rebelled against
Him in the wilderness
And grieved Him in the desert!
[41]Again and again they tempted God,
And distressed the Holy One of
Israel.
[42]They did not remember [the
miracles worked by] His
[powerful] hand,
Nor the day when He redeemed
them from the enemy,
[43]How He worked His miracles in
Egypt
And His wonders in the field of
Zoan [where Pharaoh resided],
[44]And turned their rivers into blood,
And their streams, so that they
could not drink.
[45]He sent among them swarms of
flies which devoured them,
And frogs which destroyed them.
[46]He also gave their crops to the
grasshopper,
And the fruit of their labor to the
locust.
[47]He destroyed their vines with
[great] hailstones
And their sycamore trees with frost.
[48]He gave over their cattle also to
the hailstones,
And their flocks *and* herds to
thunderbolts. [Ex 9:18–21]
[49]He sent upon them His burning
anger, [Ex 12:23]
His fury and indignation and
distress,
A band of angels of destruction
[among them].
[50]He leveled a path for His anger [to
give it free run];
He did not spare their souls from
death,
But turned over their lives to the
plague.
[51]He killed all the firstborn in Egypt,
The first and best of their strength
in the tents [of the land of the
sons] of Ham.
[52]But God led His own people
forward like sheep
And guided them in the wilderness
like [a good shepherd with] a
flock.
[53]He led them safely, so that they did
not fear;
But the sea engulfed their enemies.
[Ex 14:27, 28]
[54]So He brought them to His holy
land,
To this mountain [Zion] which His
right hand had acquired.
[55]He also drove out the nations
before the sons of Israel
And allotted *their land* as an
inheritance, measured out *and*
partitioned;
And He had the tribes of Israel
dwell in their tents [the
tents of those who had been
dispossessed].
[56]Yet they tempted and rebelled
against the Most High God
And did not keep His testimonies
(laws).
[57]They turned back and acted
unfaithfully like their fathers;
They were twisted like a warped
bow [that will not respond to the
archer's aim].
[58]For they provoked Him to
[righteous] anger with their high
places [devoted to idol worship]
And moved Him to jealousy with
their carved images [by denying
Him the love, worship, and
obedience that is rightfully and
uniquely His].
[59]When God heard this, He was
filled with [righteous] wrath;
And utterly rejected Israel, [greatly
hating her ways],
[60]So that He abandoned the
tabernacle at Shiloh,

78:58 ***high places.*** These places of worship were associated with the Canaanite worship of Baal and other fertility gods.

78:60 ***the tabernacle at Shiloh.*** This reference to Shiloh, the place where the tabernacle was set up in the time of Eli, places the time of

39 Ps 103:14; Jn 3:6; Job 7:7,16 **40** Ps 95:8-10; Heb 3:16 **41** Nu 14:22; Dt 6:16 **44** Ex 7:20; Ps 105:29 **45** Ex 8:24; Ps 105:31; Ex 8:6 **47** Ex 9:23,25; Ps 105:33 **48** Ex 9:23-25 **51** Ex 12:29; Ps 106:22 **52** Ps 77:20 **53** Ex 14:19,27 **54** Ex 15:17; Ps 44:3 **55** Ps 44:2; Jos 13:7 **56** Jdg 2:11 **57** Eze 20:27; Hos 7:16 **58** Dt 32:16,21; Jdg 2:12; Dt 12:2

The tent in which He had dwelled
among men,
61 And gave up His strength *and*
power (the ark of the covenant)
into captivity,
And His glory into the hand of
the enemy (the Philistines).
[1 Sam 4:21]
62 He also handed His people over to
the sword,
And was infuriated with His
inheritance (Israel). [1 Sam 4:10]
63 The fire [of war] devoured His
young men,
And His [bereaved] virgins had no
wedding songs.
64 His priests [Hophni and Phinehas]
fell by the sword,
And His widows could not weep.
[1 Sam 4:11, 19, 20]

65 Then the Lord awakened as from
sleep,
Like a [mighty] warrior who
awakens from the sleep of wine
[fully conscious of his power].
66 He drove His enemies backward;
He subjected them to lasting
shame *and* dishonor.
67 Moreover, He rejected the tent of
Joseph,
And did not choose the tribe
of Ephraim [in which the
tabernacle stood].
68 But He chose the tribe of Judah [as
Israel's leader],
Mount Zion, which He loved [to
replace Shiloh as His capital].
69 And He built His sanctuary
[exalted] like the heights [of the
heavens],
Like the earth which He has
established forever.
70 He also chose David His servant
And took him from the sheepfolds;
[1 Sam 16:11, 12]
71 From tending the ewes with
nursing young He brought him
To shepherd Jacob His people,
And Israel His inheritance.
[2 Sam 7:7, 8]
72 So David shepherded them
according to the integrity of his
heart;
And guided them with his skillful
hands.

Psalm 79

A Lament over the Destruction of Jerusalem, and Prayer for Help.

A Psalm of Asaph.

1 O GOD, the nations have invaded
[the land of Your people] Your
inheritance;
They have defiled Your sacred
temple;
They have laid Jerusalem in ruins.
2 They have given the dead bodies
of Your servants as food to the
birds of the heavens,
The flesh of Your godly ones to the
beasts of the earth.
3 They have poured out their blood
like water all around Jerusalem,
And there was no one to bury
them.
4 We have become an object of
taunting to our neighbors
[because of our humiliation],
A derision and mockery to those
who encircle us.

---

disobedience described here in the latter period of the judges (1Sa 1:3).

78:61 ***gave up His strength and power (the ark of the covenant) into captivity.*** This term is an unusual way of speaking of the ark of the covenant which was lost to the Philistines during the battle of Aphek (1Sa 4:1 – 11). At this time the suffering of the people was acute, including even the deaths of priests (1Sa 4:17 – 18).

78:68 ***Mount Zion, which He loved.*** The description of the sanctuary in verses 68 – 69 suggests that this psalm was written after Solomon's temple was built.

78:71 ***To shepherd Jacob His people.*** The shepherding attributed to David is an ideal; it will be fully realized in the Savior King, Jesus, the true Good Shepherd (Mt 2:6; Jn 10:1 – 18).

79:1 ***Your sacred temple.*** The destruction described in this verse may be what the Babylonians did in 586 BC.

61 Jdg 18:30 **62** 1Sa 4:10 **63** Jer 7:34 **64** 1Sa 22:18; Job 27:15 **65** Isa 42:13 **66** 1Sa 5:6 **68** Ps 87:2 **70** 1Sa 16:11,12 **71** Isa 40:11; 2Sa 5:2 **72** 1Ki 9:4 **PSALM 79 1** Ps 74:2; Mic 3:12 **2** Jer 7:33

[5]How long, O LORD? Will You be
angry forever?
Will Your jealousy [which cannot
endure a divided allegiance]
burn like fire?
[6]Pour out Your wrath on the
[Gentile] nations that do not
know You,
And on the kingdoms that do not
call on Your name. [2 Thess 1:8]
[7]For they have devoured Jacob
And made his pasture desolate.

[8]O do not remember against us the
sins *and* guilt of our forefathers.
Let Your compassion *and* mercy
come quickly to meet us,
For we have been brought very low.
[9]Help us, O God of our salvation,
for the glory of Your name;
Rescue us, forgive us our sins for
Your name's sake.
[10]Why should the [Gentile] nations
say, "Where is their God?"
Let there be known [without delay]
among the nations in our sight
[and to this generation],
Your vengeance for the blood of
Your servants which has been
poured out.
[11]Let the groaning *and* sighing of
the prisoner come before You;
According to the greatness of Your
power keep safe those who are
doomed to die.
[12]And return into the lap of our
neighbors sevenfold
The taunts with which they have
taunted You, O Lord.
[13]So we Your people, the sheep of
Your pasture,
Will give You thanks forever;
We will declare *and* publish
Your praise from generation to
generation.

Psalm 80

God Implored to Rescue His People from Their Calamities.

To the Chief Musician; set to [the tune of] "Lilies, a Testimony." A Psalm of Asaph.

[1]HEAR US O Shepherd of Israel,
You who lead Joseph like a flock;
You who sit enthroned above
the cherubim [of the ark of the
covenant], shine forth!
[2]Before Ephraim and Benjamin and
Manasseh, stir up Your power
And come to save us!
[3]Restore us, O God;
Cause Your face to shine on us
[with favor and approval], and
we will be saved.
[4]O LORD God of hosts,
How long will You be angry with
the prayers of Your people?
[5]You have fed them the bread of
tears,
And You have made them drink
[bitter] tears in abundance.
[6]You make us an object of
contention to our neighbors,
And our enemies laugh [at our
suffering] among themselves.
[7]Restore us, O God of hosts;
And cause Your face to shine on us
[with favor and approval], and
we will be saved.

79:6 *Pour out Your wrath.* An imprecation or curse on one's enemies is often found in the psalms of lament (Ps 137:7 – 9). Vengeance is left to the Lord, but such a call for vengeance is based in part on the covenant provisions that God had established with Abraham. God had promised to curse those who cursed Abraham's descendants (Ge 12:2 – 3).
79:12 *return into the lap of our neighbors sevenfold The taunts.* While the Israelites' cries for vengeance seem to be missing the concept of "love your neighbor," it is clear that they understand both the seriousness of the offense against God and also the fact that it is God, not they, who must avenge.
80:1 *Shepherd of Israel.* The concept of God as the Good Shepherd who cares for His people is clearly shown by Jesus in John 10:1 – 18. ***sit enthroned above the cherubim.*** In the most holy place, the ark of the covenant was topped by the mercy seat on which were two cherubim, heavenly symbols of the throne of God (Ex 25:22).

5 Ps 74:1,9; Zep 3:8 **6** Jer 10:25; Rev 16:1; Isa 45:4,5; 2Th 1:8; Ps 53:4 **8** Isa 64:9 **9** Jer 14:7 **10** Ps 42:10
11 Ps 102:20 **12** Ge 4:15; Isa 65:6,7; Jer 32:18; Lk 6:38; Ps 74:18 **13** Ps 74:1; 95:7; Isa 43:21 **PSALM 80**
Title Ps 45, Title; 69, Title **1** Ps 77:20; Dt 33:2; Ps 50:2 **3** La 5:21; Nu 6:25; Ps 4:6 **5** Ps 42:3; Isa 30:20

[8]You uprooted a vine (Israel) from
Egypt;
You drove out the [Canaanite]
nations and planted the vine [in
Canaan].
[9]You cleared away *the ground*
before it,
And it took deep root and filled the
land.
[10]The mountains were covered with
its shadow,
And its branches were like the
cedars of God.
[11]Israel sent out its branches to the
[Mediterranean] Sea,
And its branches to the
[Euphrates] River. [1 Kin 4:21]
[12]Why have You broken down its
walls *and* hedges,
So that all who pass by pick its
fruit?
[13]A boar from the woods eats it
away,
And the insects of the field feed
on it.
[14]Turn again [in favor to us], O God
of hosts;
Look down from heaven and see,
and take care of this vine,
[15]Even the stock which Your right
hand has planted,
And [look down on] the son
that You have reared *and*
strengthened for Yourself.
[16]It is burned with fire, it is cut down;
They perish at the rebuke of Your
[angry] appearance.
[17]Let Your hand be upon the man of
Your right hand,
Upon the son of man whom You
have made strong for Yourself.
[18]Then we shall not turn back from
You;
Revive us and we will call on Your
name.
[19]Restore us, O LORD God of
hosts;
Cause Your face to shine on us
[in favor and approval], and we
shall be saved.

Psalm 81

God's Goodness and Israel's Waywardness.

To the Chief Musician; set to the Philistine lute. *A Psalm* of Asaph.

[1]SING ALOUD to God our
strength;
Shout for joy to the God of Jacob
(Israel).
[2]Raise a song, sound the timbrel,
The sweet sounding lyre with the
harp.
[3]Blow the trumpet at the New
Moon,
At the full moon, on our feast
day.
[4]For this is a statute for Israel,
An ordinance of the God of
Jacob.
[5]He established it for a testimony in
Joseph
When He went throughout the
land of Egypt.
I heard the language [of One
whom] I did not know, *saying*,
[6]"I removed the burden from his
shoulder;
His hands were freed from the
basket.
[7]"You called in [the time of] trouble
and I rescued you;
I answered you in the secret place
of thunder;

80:8 *You uprooted a vine (Israel) from Egypt*. The picture of Israel as God's vine recurs other places in Scripture (see, for example, Isa 5:1 – 25). In the New Testament, Jesus used the same metaphor to describe the relationship of God with all who trust in Him (Jn 15:1 – 8).
81:3 *at the New Moon*. The New Moon festival is mentioned in association with the Feast of Trumpets (Nu 29:6). Regulations for this festival can be found in the instructions to the Levites during the time of David (1Ch 23:31) and Solomon (2Ch 2:4). This psalm seems to be a basic instruction on the festival. The language and regulations are as solemn as any in the Torah.
81:7 *I answered you*. The Lord's appearance to Moses on Mount Sinai was God's great revelation of Himself (Ex 19:20).

8 Isa 5:1,7; Jer 2:21; Eze 15:6; Ps 44:2 **12** Isa 5:5; Na 2:2 **14** Isa 63:15 **16** Ps 39:11; 76:7 **17** Ps 89:21
PSALM 81 **Title** Ps 8, Title **5** Ps 114:1 **7** Ex 2:23; Ps 50:15; Ex 19:19; Ex 17:6,7

I tested you at the waters of
Meribah. [Num 20:3, 13, 24]
Selah.
8 "Hear, O My people, and I will
admonish you—
O Israel, if you would listen
to Me!
9 "Let there be no strange god
among you,
Nor shall you worship any foreign
god.
10 "I am the LORD your God,
Who brought you up from the land
of Egypt.
Open your mouth wide and I will
fill it.
11 "But My people would not listen to
My voice,
And Israel did not [consent to]
obey Me.
12 "So I gave them up to the
stubbornness of their heart,
To walk in [the path of] their own
counsel. [Acts 7:42, 43; 14:16;
Rom 1:24, 26]
13 "Oh, that My people would listen
to Me,
That Israel would walk in My
ways!
14 "Then I would quickly subdue *and*
humble their enemies
And turn My hand against their
adversaries;
15 Those who hate the LORD would
pretend obedience to Him *and*
cringe before Him,
And their time *of punishment*
would be forever.
16 "But I would feed Israel with the
finest of the wheat;
And with honey from the rock I
would satisfy you."

Psalm 82

Unjust Judgments Rebuked.

A Psalm of Asaph.

1 GOD STANDS in the divine
assembly;
He judges among the gods (divine
beings).
2 How long will you judge unjustly
And show partiality to the wicked?
Selah.
3 Vindicate the weak and
fatherless;
Do justice *and* maintain the
rights of the afflicted and
destitute.
4 Rescue the weak and needy;
Rescue them from the hand of the
wicked.
5 The rulers do not know nor do
they understand;
They walk on in the darkness [of
complacent satisfaction];
All the foundations of the earth
[the fundamental principles of
the administration of justice] are
shaken.
6 I said, "You are gods;
Indeed, all of you are sons of
the Most High. [Gen 6:1–4;
John 10:34–36; Rom 13:1, 2]
7 "Nevertheless you will die like
men
And fall like any one of the
princes."
8 Arise, O God, judge the
earth!
For to You belong all the
nations. [Matt 28:18–20;
Rev 11:15]

81:9 *no strange god.* Asaph, the chief musician during David's reign, reviews the goodness of God and His marvelous deliverance of Israel from the land of bondage (Ex 7 – 12). The plagues sent upon Egypt were meant to accomplish a purpose: first, to show to God's people the power of the true God; and second, to demonstrate to the Egyptians the total inability of their false gods. In spite of these dramatic object lessons against idolatry, Israel began worshiping pagan images almost as soon as they left Egypt.

82:6 *You are gods.* Jesus quoted this verse in His exchange with the religious authorities who wanted to stone Him for declaring Himself to be the Son of God (Jn 10:31 – 35). The word translated "gods" here is the same word that is used in verse 1. This word (*elohim*) is used to refer to the one God, to false gods, to angels, or to "mighty ones" (that is, the judges).

8 Ps 50:7 **9** Dt 32:12; Isa 43:12 **10** Ex 20:2; Ps 103:5 **11** Ex 32:1; Dt 32:15 **12** Ac 7:42 **13** Dt 5:29; 32:29; Isa 48:18 **15** Ro 1:30 **16** Dt 32:14; Job 29:6 **PSALM 82** **1** 2Ch 19:6; ver. 6 **2** Dt 1:17 **3** Jer 22:3 **4** Job 29:12; Pr 24:11 **5** Mic 3:1; Ps 11:3 **6** Ex 22:28; Jn 10:34 **7** Ps 49:12 **8** Mic 7:2,7; Ps 2:8; Rev 11:15

Psalm 83

God Implored to Confound His Enemies.

A Song. A Psalm of Asaph.

1 DO NOT keep silent, O God;
Do not hold Your peace or be still, O God.
2 For behold, Your enemies are in tumult,
And those who hate You have raised their heads [in hatred of You]. [Acts 4:25, 26]
3 They concoct crafty schemes against Your people,
And conspire together against Your hidden *and* precious ones.
4 They have said, "Come, and let us wipe them out as a nation;
Let the name of Israel be remembered no more."
5 For they have conspired together with one mind;
Against You they make a covenant—
6 The tents of Edom and the Ishmaelites,
Of Moab and the Hagrites,
7 Gebal and Ammon and Amalek,
Philistia with the inhabitants of Tyre.
8 Assyria also has joined with them;
They have helped the children of Lot [the Ammonites and the Moabites] *and* have been an arm [of strength] to them. *Selah.*

9 Deal with them as [You did] with Midian,
As with Sisera and Jabin at the brook of Kishon, [Judg 4:12–24]
10 Who were destroyed at En-dor,
Who became like dung for the earth.
11 Make their nobles like Oreb and Zeeb
And all their princes like Zebah and Zalmunna, [Judg 7:23–25; 8:10–21]
12 Who said, "Let us possess for ourselves
The pastures of God."

13 O my God, make them like whirling dust,
Like chaff before the wind [worthless and without substance].
14 Like fire consumes the forest,
And like the flame sets the mountains on fire,
15 So pursue them with Your tempest
And terrify them with [the violence of] Your storm.
16 Fill their faces with shame *and* disgrace,
That they may [persistently] seek Your name, O LORD.
17 Let them be ashamed and dismayed forever;
Yes, let them be humiliated and perish,
18 That they may know that You alone, whose name is the LORD,
Are the Most High over all the earth.

Psalm 84

Longing for the Temple Worship.

To the Chief Musician; set to a Philistine lute. A Psalm of the sons of Korah.

1 HOW LOVELY are Your dwelling places,
O LORD of hosts!

83:6 *tents of Edom.* The place names in this passage refer to nations on the borders of Israel and Judah. The Hagrites may have come from Arabia (1Ch 5:10,19–20).

83:9 *Sisera.* God's victory over Sisera was accomplished through Deborah and Barak (Jdg 4–5). The same God who had battled Israel's enemies in the past would fight all those who might oppose His people in the future.

83:16 *That they may [persistently] seek Your name.* Asaph's first call for God to shame Israel's enemies is redemptive — that the nations might hear, feel shame, repent, and seek the Lord. Yet, if they continued in their wicked path, they would be further confounded and would one day face God in judgment.

84:1 *How lovely are Your dwelling places.* This psalm celebrates God's presence in

---

PSALM 83 **1** Ps 28:1 **2** Ps 2:1; 81:15 **3** Ps 27:5 **4** Jer 11:19 **6** See 2Ch 20:1,10,11 **9** Jdg 4:15 **10** Zep 1:17 **11** Jdg 8:12 **13** Isa 17:13; Ps 35:5 **14** Dt 32:22 **18** Ps 59:13; Ex 6:3; Ps 92:8 **PSALM 84** **Title** Ps 8, Title **1** Ps 27:4

[2]My soul (my life, my inner self)
longs for and greatly desires the
courts of the LORD;
My heart and my flesh sing for joy
to the living God.
[3]The bird has found a house,
And the swallow a nest for herself,
where she may lay her young—
Even Your altars, O LORD of hosts,
My King and my God.
[4]Blessed *and* greatly favored are
those who dwell in Your house
and Your presence;
They will be singing Your praises
all the day long. *Selah.*

[5]Blessed *and* greatly favored is the
man whose strength is in You,
In whose heart are the highways
to Zion.
[6]Passing through the Valley of
Weeping (Baca), they make it a
place of springs;
The early rain also covers it with
blessings.
[7]They go from strength to strength
[increasing in victorious
power];
Each of them appears before God
in Zion.

[8]O LORD God of hosts, hear my
prayer;
Listen, O God of Jacob! *Selah.*
[9]See our shield, O God,
And look at the face of Your
anointed [the king as Your
representative].

[10]For a day in Your courts is better
than a thousand [anywhere else];
I would rather stand [as a
doorkeeper] at the threshold of
the house of my God
Than to live [at ease] in the tents of
wickedness.
[11]For the LORD God is a sun and
shield;
The LORD bestows grace *and* favor
and honor;
No good thing will He withhold
from those who walk uprightly.
[12]O LORD of hosts,
How blessed *and* greatly favored
is the man who trusts in You
[believing in You, relying on
You, and committing himself
to You with confident hope and
expectation].

Psalm 85

Prayer for God's Mercy upon the Nation.

To the Chief Musician.
A Psalm of the sons of Korah.

[1]O LORD, You have [at last] shown
favor to Your land [of Canaan];
You have restored [from Babylon]
the captives of Jacob (Israel).
[2]You have forgiven the wickedness
of Your people;
You have covered all their sin.
Selah.

Jerusalem, the city where His temple was built. Today it is not necessary to go to Jerusalem to draw near to God, for God is near to those who trust in His Son (Mt 28:18 – 20).

84:6 *the Valley of Weeping (Baca).* The "Valley of Weeping" refers to the various difficulties that one might face on a pilgrimage. With God, even times of hardship and sorrow can become times of great joy and blessing.

84:9 *Your anointed.* The two phrases "our shield" and "Your anointed" both point to the same person, the king of Israel (89:3 – 4). These anointed kings foreshadowed the coming Messiah — the Anointed One.

84:11 *No good thing will He withhold.* When we go through times of darkness and difficulty, it sometimes seems that God is not giving us what we need. However, God is far wiser than we can ever be, and He never withholds what is good from us. When it seems that He does, we must assume that what we want would not actually be a good thing for us to have.

85:1 *You have restored [from Babylon] the captives.* The setting for this psalm appears to be the restoration of the people of God following a great catastrophe — perhaps the Babylonian captivity.

85:2 – 3 *You have forgiven.* In all its forms, from hideous to petty, sin alienates people from God and is deserving of His punishment. The wonderful message of the Bible is that God will forgive even the most despicable sinner if that

2 Ps 42:1,2 **6** 2Sa 5:23 **7** Pr 4:18; Dt 16:16 **9** ver. 11 **11** Isa 60:19; Ge 15:1; Ps 115:9; Pr 2:7; Ps 34:9 **12** Ps 2:12
PSALM 85 **Title** Ps 42, Title **1** Ezr 1:11; Jer 30:18; Eze 39:25; Joel 3:1

[3]You have withdrawn all Your wrath,
You have turned away from Your burning anger.
[4]Restore us, O God of our salvation,
And cause Your indignation toward us to cease.
[5]Will You be angry with us forever?
Will You prolong Your anger to all generations?
[6]Will You not revive us *and* bring us to life again,
That Your people may rejoice in You?
[7]Show us Your lovingkindness, O LORD,
And grant us Your salvation.

[8]I will hear [with expectant hope] what God the LORD will say,
For He will speak peace to His people, to His godly ones—
But let them not turn again to folly.
[9]Surely His salvation is near to those who [reverently] fear Him [and obey Him with submissive wonder],
That glory [the manifest presence of God] may dwell in our land.
[10]Steadfast love and truth *and* faithfulness meet together;
Righteousness and peace kiss each other.
[11]Truth springs from the earth,
And righteousness looks down from heaven.
[12]Indeed, the LORD will give what is good,
And our land will yield its produce.
[13]Righteousness will go before Him
And will make His footsteps into a way [in which to walk].

Psalm 86
A Psalm of Supplication and Trust.

A Prayer of David.

[1]INCLINE YOUR ear, O LORD, and answer me,
For I am distressed and needy [I long for Your help].
[2]Protect my life (soul), for I am godly *and* faithful;
O You my God, save Your servant, who trusts in You [believing in You and relying on You, confidently committing everything to You].
[3]Be gracious *and* merciful to me, O Lord,
For to You I cry out all the day long.
[4]Make Your servant rejoice,
For to You, O Lord, I lift up my soul [all that I am—in prayer].
[5]For You, O Lord, are good, and ready to forgive [our sins, sending them away, completely letting them go forever and ever];
And abundant in lovingkindness *and* overflowing in mercy to all those who call upon You.
[6]Hear, O LORD, my prayer;
And listen attentively to the voice of my supplications (specific requests)!
[7]In the day of my trouble I will call upon You,
For You will answer me.
[8]There is no one like You among the gods, O Lord,
Nor are there any works [of wonder and majesty] like Yours.

---

sinner repents and turns from wickedness. God's forgiveness is not just an arbitrary overlooking of our sin, but a judicial act whereby He applies the penalty paid by His son to our account. Our sins are thus covered by Jesus' blood, and God considers us righteous.

85:10 *Steadfast love and truth and faithfulness meet together.* Kindness without truth is hypocrisy, while truth without love and mercy is cruel. Only when the two meet can we experience wholeness and healing.

86:1 *Incline Your ear.* David's dramatic phrase captures the grandeur of God on high and his own humble position on the earth below.

86:8 *among the gods.* The ancient nations took their sense of identity in part from their ties to

4 Ps 80:7 **5** Ps 79:5 **6** Hab 3:2 **8** Hab 2:1; Zec 9:10; 2Pe 2:20 **9** Isa 46:13; Zec 2:5 **10** Ps 72:3; Isa 32:17; Lk 2:14 **12** Ps 84:11; Jas 1:17 **13** Ps 89:14 **PSALM 86** **3** Ps 56:1; 57:1 **4** Ps 25:1; 143:8 **5** Ps 130:7; 145:9; Joel 2:13 **8** Ex 15:11; Ps 89:6; Dt 3:24

9 All nations whom You have made
shall come and kneel down in
worship before You, O Lord,
And they shall glorify Your name.
10 For You are great and do
wondrous works!
You alone are God.

11 Teach me Your way, O LORD,
I will walk *and* live in Your truth;
Direct my heart to fear Your name
[with awe-inspired reverence
and submissive wonder].
[Ps 5:11; 69:36]
12 I will give thanks *and* praise You,
O Lord my God, with all my
heart;
And will glorify Your name
forevermore.
13 For great is Your lovingkindness
and graciousness toward me;
And You have rescued my life
from the depths of Sheol [from
death].
14 O God, arrogant *and* insolent men
have risen up against me;
A band of violent men have sought
my life,
And they have not set You before
them.
15 But You, O Lord, are a God [who
protects and is] merciful and
gracious,
Slow to anger and abounding in
lovingkindness and truth.
16 Turn to me, and be gracious to me;
Grant Your strength [Your
might and the power to resist
temptation] to Your servant,
And save the son of Your handmaid.
17 Show me a sign of [Your] goodwill,
That those who hate me may see it
and be ashamed,
Because You, O LORD, helped and
comforted me.

Psalm 87

The Privileges of Citizenship in Zion.

A Psalm of the sons of Korah. A Song.

1 HIS FOUNDATION is on the holy
mountain.
2 The LORD loves the gates of Zion
More than all the dwellings of
Jacob (Israel).
3 Glorious things are spoken of you,
O city of God [Jerusalem]. *Selah.*
4 "I will mention Rahab (Egypt) and
Babylon among those who know
Me—
Behold, Philistia and Tyre with
Ethiopia (Cush)—
'This one was born there.' "
5 But of Zion it will be said, "This one
and that one were born in her,"
And the Most High Himself will
establish her.

---

their supposed gods. When the nations found out that their "gods" did not exist, they would have to acknowledge that the Lord alone is God. Here David envisions other nations worshiping the true God and thus anticipates the missionary thrust of the New Testament (Ps 117:1; Mt 28:18 – 20).

86:13 ***You have rescued my life.*** The cold hand of death knocks at everyone's door, whether we dwell in a luxury condominium with security guards or a tenement surrounded by urban blight. The good news, however, is that the Lord has not left us at the mercy of death, but has provided for the deliverance of our souls from the depths of the grave. We can face the future confidently, knowing that, when our bodies die, our spirits will be with Christ, and that one day we shall also experience the resurrection of the body by His mighty power (Php 3:20 – 21).

87:1 ***His foundation.*** God Himself established Zion (or Jerusalem) as the center of true worship. He ordained Solomon to build a temple there so that He could live among the Israelites (1Ki 6:13). Zion is holy because of God's declaration (1Ki 11:13), His promise, the worship given Him there (1Ki 8:14 – 66), the future work of the Savior there (Mt 21:4 – 11), and the future rule of the King there (Rev 21).

87:4 ***Rahab.*** Rahab is a symbolic name for Egypt (Isa 30:7) that has negative connotations, alluding to the arrogance of the Egyptians. ***Babylon.*** Babylon was the proverbial seat of apostasy and idolatry (Ge 10:10).

87:5 ***born in her.*** Despite their foreign heritage, the people who worshiped God were considered to have been born in Zion. It appears that this is referring to a spiritual birth, foreshadowing Jesus' teaching about being born again (Jn 3:1 – 8).

9 Ps 22:31; Isa 43:7; Rev 15:4 **10** Ex 15:11; Ps 72:18; Dt 6:4; Mk 12:29 **11** Ps 25:4 **15** Ex 34:6; Neh 9:17; Ps 103:8; Joel 2:13 **PSALM 87** **2** Ps 78:68 **3** See Isa 60

[6]The LORD will count, when He
registers the peoples,
"This one was born there." *Selah.*
[7]The singers as well as the players
of flutes *will say,*
"All my springs *and* sources of joy
are in you [Jerusalem, city of
God]."

Psalm 88

A Petition to Be Saved from Death.

A Song. A Psalm of the sons of Korah. To the Chief Musician; set to chant mournfully. A didactic *or* reflective poem of Heman the Ezrahite.

[1]O LORD, the God of my salvation,
I have cried out [for help] by day
and in the night before You.
[Luke 18:7]
[2]Let my prayer come before You
and enter into Your presence;
Incline Your ear to my cry!
[3]For my soul is full of troubles,
And my life draws near the grave
(Sheol, the place of the dead).
[4]I am counted among those who go
down to the pit (grave);
I am like a man who has no
strength [a mere shadow],
[5]Cast away [from the living] *and*
abandoned among the dead,
Like the slain who lie in a
[nameless] grave,
Whom You no longer remember,
And they are cut off from Your
hand.
[6]You have laid me in the lowest pit,
In dark places, in the depths.
[7]Your wrath has rested heavily
upon me,
And You have afflicted me with all
Your waves. [Ps 42:7] *Selah.*
[8]You have put my friends far from
me;
You have made me an object of
loathing to them.
I am shut up and I cannot go out.
[9]My eye grows dim with sorrow.
O LORD, I have called on You every
day;
I have spread out my hands to You
[in prayer].
[10]Will You perform wonders for the
dead?
Shall the departed spirits arise
and praise You? *Selah.*
[11]Will Your lovingkindness be
declared in the grave
Or Your faithfulness in Abaddon
(the underworld)?
[12]Will Your wonders be known in
the darkness?
And Your righteousness in the
land of forgetfulness [where the
dead forget and are forgotten]?
[13]But I have cried out to You,
O LORD, for help;
And in the morning my prayer will
come to You.
[14]O LORD, why do You reject me?
Why do You hide Your face from
me? [Matt 27:46]
[15]I was afflicted and close to death
from my youth on;
I suffer Your terrors; I am
overcome.
[16]Your fierce wrath has swept over
me;
Your terrors have destroyed me.
[17]They have surrounded me like
flood waters all day long;
They have completely
encompassed me.
[18]Lover and friend You have placed
far from me;
My familiar friends are in
darkness.

---

88 title *Heman.* Heman is identified in 1 Kings 4:31 as a gifted wise man, and in 1 Chronicles 15:16 – 19 as one of the musically gifted Levites who ministered in worship during the time of David.
88:1 *God of my salvation.* Even in the midst of despair, Heman confesses his faith in God's saving goodness.

88:3 *grave.* This is also translated "Sheol," which is the Hebrew word for "hell." It is often linked with the term "pit" as a symbol of the end of earthly existence. The Old Testament has very little to say about what happens to a soul after death, but it is clear that to go to Sheol is the end of all we know.

6 Eze 13:9 **PSALM 88 Title** 1Ki 4:31; 1Ch 2:6 **1** Ps 27:9 **3** Ps 107:18 **4** Ps 28:1 **5** Isa 53:8 **7** Ps 42:7 **8** Job 19:13; La 3:7 **9** Ps 38:10; 86:3; 143:6 **10** Ps 6:5; Isa 38:18 **12** Job 10:21 **13** Ps 5:3 **14** Job 13:24; Ps 13:1 **15** Job 6:4 **17** Ps 22:16 **18** Job 19:13

Psalm 89

The LORD's Covenant with David, and Israel's Afflictions.

A skillful song, *or* a didactic *or* reflective poem, of Ethan the Ezrahite.

1 I WILL sing of the goodness *and* lovingkindness of the LORD forever;
With my mouth I will make known Your faithfulness from generation to generation.
2 For I have said, "Goodness *and* lovingkindness will be built up forever;
In the heavens [unchangeable and majestic] You will establish Your faithfulness."
3 [God has said] "I have made a covenant with My chosen one;
I have sworn to David My servant,
4 I will establish your seed forever
And I will build up your throne for all generations." [Is 9:7; Jer 33:14–26; Luke 1:32, 33; Gal 3:16] *Selah.*

5 The heavens (angels) praise Your wonders, O LORD,
Your faithfulness also in the assembly of the holy ones.
6 For who in the heavens can be compared to the LORD?
Who among the divine beings is like the LORD,
7 A God greatly feared *and* reverently worshiped in the council of the holy [angelic] ones,
And awesome above all those who are around Him?
8 O LORD God of hosts, who is like You, O mighty LORD?
Your faithfulness surrounds You [as an intrinsic, unchangeable part of Your very being].
9 You rule the swelling of the sea;
When its waves rise, You still them. [Ps 65:7; 107:29; Mark 4:39]
10 You have crushed Rahab (Egypt) like one who is slain;
You have scattered Your enemies with Your mighty arm.

11 The heavens are Yours, the earth also is Yours;
The world and all that is in it, You have founded *and* established them. [Gen 1:3]
12 The north and the south, You have created them;
Mount Tabor and Mount Hermon shout for joy at Your name.
13 You have a strong arm;
Mighty is Your hand, Your right hand is exalted.
14 Righteousness and justice are the foundation of Your throne;
Lovingkindness and truth go before You.
15 Blessed *and* happy are the people who know the joyful sound [of the trumpet's blast]!
They walk, O LORD, in the light *and* favor of Your countenance!
16 In Your name they rejoice all the day,
And in Your righteousness they are exalted.
17 For You are the glory of their strength [their proud adornment],
And by Your favor our horn is exalted.
18 For our shield belongs to the LORD,
And our king to the Holy One of Israel.

89:1 *the goodness and lovingkindness of the LORD.* The lovingkindness of the Lord in this psalm centers on the covenant that He made with David, promising him an eternal dynasty (2Sa 7).
89:6 *divine beings.* This phrase may mean "sons of gods" or "heavenly beings." The reference could be to other supposed gods or to angels, members of the heavenly court (Job 1:6).
89:13 *a strong arm.* God is the great Deliverer; He brandished His arm and hand in delivering His people from Egypt (Ex 6:6; 15:6).
89:18 *the Holy One of Israel.* This is the title that Isaiah used to describe God, following his experience of God's holiness in his memorable vision of God's throne (Isa 6:1 – 5).

PSALM 89 **Title** 1Ki 4:31; 1Ch 2:6 **1** Ps 101:1; Ps 119:90 **2** Ps 119:89 **3** 1Ki 8:16; 1Ch 28:4; 2Sa 7:13 **4** Lk 1:33 **5** Ps 19:1 **7** Ps 76:7,11 **9** Ps 65:7 **10** Ps 87:4 **11** Ge 1:1 **12** Jos 19:22; 12:1 **15** Ps 98:6

19 Once You spoke in a vision to Your godly ones,
And said, "I have given help to one who is mighty [giving him the power to be a champion for Israel];
I have exalted one chosen from the people.
20 "I have found David My servant;
With My holy oil I have anointed him, [Acts 13:22]
21 With whom My hand shall be established *and* steadfast;
My arm also shall strengthen him.
22 "The enemy will not outwit him,
Nor will the wicked man afflict *or* humiliate him.
23 "I will crush his adversaries before him,
And strike those who hate him.
24 "My faithfulness and My steadfast lovingkindness shall be with him,
And in My name shall his horn be exalted [great power and prosperity shall be conferred upon him].
25 "I will also set his hand on the [Mediterranean] sea,
And his right hand on the rivers [the tributaries of the Euphrates].
26 "He will cry to Me, 'You are my Father,
My God, and the rock of my salvation.'
27 "I will also make him My firstborn (preeminent),
The highest of the kings of the earth. [Rev 1:5]
28 "My lovingkindness I will keep for him forevermore,
And My covenant will be confirmed to him.
29 "His descendants I will establish forever,
And his throne [will endure] as the days of heaven. [Is 9:7; Jer 33:14–26; Gal 3:16]
30 "If his children turn away from My law
And do not walk in My ordinances,
31 If they break My statutes
And do not keep My commandments,
32 Then I will punish their transgression with the rod [of discipline],
And [correct] their wickedness with stripes. [2 Sam 7:14]
33 "Nevertheless, I will not break off My lovingkindness from him,
Nor allow My faithfulness to fail.
34 "My covenant I will not violate,
Nor will I alter the utterance of My lips.
35 "Once [for all] I have sworn by My holiness, [My vow which cannot be violated];
I will not lie to David.
36 "His descendants shall endure forever
And his throne [will continue] as the sun before Me. [Is 9:7; Jer 33:14–26; Gal 3:16]
37 "It shall be established forever like the moon,
And the witness in the heavens is ever faithful." [Rev 1:5; 3:14]
Selah.

38 But [in apparent contradiction of all this] You [the faithful LORD] have cast off and rejected;
You have been full of wrath against Your anointed.
39 You have spurned *and* repudiated the covenant with Your servant;
You have profaned his crown [by casting it] in the dust.
40 You have broken down all his [city] walls;
You have brought his strongholds to ruin.
41 All who pass along the road rob him;
He has become the scorn of his neighbors.

89:29 *descendants . . . throne.* These words echo the covenant God made with David (2Sa 7:8 – 17).

89:34 *My covenant I will not violate.* God is determined to complete, fulfill, and accomplish His grand plan for David's dynasty (2Sa 7:1 – 24).

19 1Ki 11:34 **20** 1Sa 16:1 **21** Ps 80:17 **22** 2Sa 7:10 **23** 2Sa 7:9 **24** 2Sa 7:15 **26** 1Ch 22:10; 2Sa 22:47 **27** Col 1:15; Nu 24:7 **28** Isa 55:3 **29** Jer 33:17; Dt 11:21 **30** 2Sa 7:14; Ps 119:53; Jer 9:13 **32** 2Sa 7:14 **33** 2Sa 7:15 **35** Am 4:2 **36** Lk 1:33; Ps 72:17 **38** 1Ch 28:9; Dt 32:19 **39** La 5:16 **41** Ps 44:13

42 You have exalted the right hand of his foes;
You have made all his enemies rejoice.
43 Also, You have turned back the edge of his sword
And have not made him [strong enough] to stand in battle.
44 You have put an end to his splendor
And have hurled his throne to the ground.
45 You have shortened the days of his youth;
You have covered him with shame. *Selah.*

46 How long, O LORD?
Will You hide Yourself forever?
Will Your wrath burn like fire?
47 Remember how fleeting my lifetime is;
For what vanity, [for what emptiness, for what futility, for what wisp of smoke] You have created all the sons of men!
48 What man can live and not see death?
Can he rescue his soul from the [powerful] hand of Sheol (the nether world, the place of the dead)? *Selah.*

49 O Lord, where are Your former lovingkindnesses [so abundant in the days of David and Solomon],
Which You swore to David in Your faithfulness?
50 Remember, O Lord, the reproach of Your servants [scorned, insulted, and disgraced];
How I bear in my heart the reproach of all the many peoples,
51 With which Your enemies have taunted, O LORD,
With which they have mocked the footsteps of Your anointed.
52 Blessed be the LORD forevermore!
Amen and Amen.

BOOK FOUR

Psalm 90

God's Eternity and Man's Transitoriness.

A Prayer of Moses the man of God.

1 LORD, YOU have been our dwelling place [our refuge, our sanctuary, our stability] in all generations.
2 Before the mountains were born
Or before You had given birth to the earth and the world,
Even from everlasting to everlasting, You are [the eternal] God.
3 You turn man back to dust,
And say, "Return [to the earth], O children of [mortal] men!"
4 For a thousand years in Your sight
Are like yesterday when it is past,
Or as a watch in the night.
[2 Pet 3:8]
5 You have swept them away like a flood, they fall asleep [forgotten as soon as they are gone];
In the morning they are like grass which grows anew—
6 In the morning it flourishes and springs up;
In the evening it wilts and withers away.
7 For we have been consumed by Your anger

89:49–51 ***Which You swore to David.*** The writer complains that God has not been keeping His promises to David (2Sa 7:1–24). As a result, His people are experiencing harsh treatment from their enemies. There is no resolution to this psalm; it ends with the people, the king, and the psalmist in distress. Yet the inclusion of this psalm among the praises of Israel suggests that God did answer this prayer of His people, just as He did in the case of Psalm 60.

90:1 ***LORD.*** This is not God's personal name (Ex 3:14–15), but a Hebrew word celebrating His majestic authority.

90:4 ***a thousand years ... like yesterday.*** A thousand years may seem long at the time, but in comparison with God's eternal existence, they are nothing.

90:7 ***Your anger.*** The unbelieving Israelites in the wilderness experienced God's anger (Nu

46 Ps 79:5 **47** Job 7:7 **48** Ps 49:9; Heb 11:5 **49** 2Sa 7:15; Ps 54:5 **50** Ps 69:9,19 **51** Ps 74:22 **52** Ps 41:13
PSALM 90 **Title** Dt 33:1 **1** Eze 11:16 **2** Pr 8:25 **3** Ge 3:19 **4** 2Pe 3:8 **5** Ps 73:20; Isa 40:6

And by Your wrath we have been
terrified.
8 You have placed our wickedness
before you,
Our secret *sins* [which we tried
to conceal, You have placed]
in the [revealing] light of Your
presence.
9 For all our days pass away in Your
wrath;
We have finished our years like a
whispered sigh. [Num 14:26–35]
10 The days of our life are seventy
years—
Or even, if because of strength,
eighty years;
Yet their pride [in additional years]
is only labor and sorrow,
For it is soon gone and we fly
away.
11 Who understands the power of
Your anger? [Who connects this
brevity of life among us with
Your judgment of sin?]
And Your wrath, [who connects it]
with the [reverent] fear that is
due You?
12 So teach us to number our days,
That we may cultivate *and* bring to
You a heart of wisdom.
13 Turn, O LORD [from Your fierce
anger]; how long will it be?
Be compassionate toward Your
servants—revoke Your sentence.
14 O satisfy us with Your
lovingkindness in the morning
[now, before we grow older],
That we may rejoice and be glad
all our days.
15 Make us glad in proportion to the
days You have afflicted us,
And the years we have suffered
evil.
16 Let Your work [the signs of Your
power] be revealed to Your
servants
And Your [glorious] majesty to
their children.
17 And let the [gracious] favor of the
Lord our God be on us;
Confirm for us the work of our
hands—
Yes, confirm the work of our
hands.

Psalm 91

Security of the One Who Trusts in the LORD.

1 HE WHO dwells in the shelter of
the Most High
Will remain secure *and* rest in
the shadow of the Almighty
[whose power no enemy can
withstand].
2 I will say of the LORD, "He is my
refuge and my fortress,
My God, in whom I trust [with
great confidence, and on whom
I rely]!"
3 For He will save you from the trap
of the fowler,
And from the deadly pestilence.

13–14). An entire generation spent their lives wandering because of their unbelief and rebellion.

90:10 ***seventy years . . . eighty years.*** The point here is not to set a maximum, but to present a context for the brevity of human life. No matter how long people live, death is inevitable.

90:12 Counting Our Days—This prayer of Moses, probably written near the end of his life, gives us some excellent insight into living. We need to seek wisdom, be sober-minded and diligent, and seek to use our time wisely, living in light of the Lord's commands.

Life is often painful, sometimes very painful but survivable.

We perpetually fall short of God's plan for us. We are loved by an all-powerful yet merciful God who knows all about us.

The only true satisfaction is in knowing and obeying God.

Serve God to your fullest because your time here on earth is short.

90:17 ***Confirm for us the work of our hands.*** We need to have a sense of lasting meaning in our lives, something that will continue to the next generation.

91:1 ***in the shelter.*** The person who trusts in God is the one who lives close to Him. ***Most High.*** This title emphasizes God's majesty and is parallel to the term "Almighty." Together, the terms "most High" and "Almighty" speak of God as a mountain-like majesty.

8 Ps 50:21; 19:12 **12** Ps 39:4 **13** Dt 32:36; Ps 135:14 **14** Ps 85:6 **16** Hab 3:2 **17** Ps 27:4; Isa 26:12
PSALM 91 **1** Ps 31:20; Ps 17:8 **2** Ps 142:5 **3** Ps 124:7

[4]He will cover you *and* completely
protect you with His pinions,
And under His wings you will find
refuge;
His faithfulness is a shield and a
wall.
[5]You will not be afraid of the terror
of night,
Nor of the arrow that flies by day,
[6]Nor of the pestilence that stalks in
darkness,
Nor of the destruction (sudden
death) that lays waste at noon.
[7]A thousand may fall at your side
And ten thousand at your right
hand,
But danger will not come near you.
[8]You will only [be a spectator as
you] look on with your eyes
And witness the [divine]
repayment of the wicked [as you
watch safely from the shelter of
the Most High].
[9]Because you have made the LORD,
[who is] my refuge,
Even the Most High, your dwelling
place, [Ps 91:1, 14]
[10]No evil will befall you,
Nor will any plague come near
your tent.
[11]For He will command His angels
in regard to you,
To protect *and* defend *and*
guard you in all your ways [of
obedience and service].
[12]They will lift you up in their
hands,
So that you do not [even] strike
your foot against a stone.
[Luke 4:10, 11; Heb 1:14]
[13]You will tread upon the lion and
cobra;
The young lion and the serpent
you will trample underfoot.
[Luke 10:19]
[14]"Because he set his love on Me,
therefore I will save him;
I will set him [securely] on high,
because he knows My name
[he confidently trusts and relies
on Me, knowing I will never
abandon him, no, never].
[15]"He will call upon Me, and I will
answer him;
I will be with him in trouble;
I will rescue him and honor him.
[16]"With a long life I will satisfy him
And I will let him see My
salvation."

Psalm 92

Praise for the LORD's Goodness.

A Psalm. A Song for the Sabbath day.

[1]IT IS a good *and* delightful thing
to give thanks to the LORD,
To sing praises to Your name,
O Most High,
[2]To declare Your lovingkindness in
the morning
And Your faithfulness by night,
[3]With an instrument of ten strings
and with the harp,
With a solemn sound on the lyre.
[4]For You, O LORD, have made me
glad by Your works;
At the works of Your hands I
joyfully sing.
[5]How great are Your works,
O LORD!
Your thoughts are very deep
[beyond man's understanding].

91:4 *pinions . . . wings.* Just as chicks take refuge under the wings of the mother hen, so we can take refuge in God's enveloping care.
91:7 *A thousand may fall at your side.* The Israelites in Egypt were spared the danger that touched their neighbors (Ex 9:26; 10:23; 11:7); similarly, believers in the Lord are protected from Satan's attacks.
91:11 *command His angels in regard to you.* These words were used by Satan to tempt the Savior (Mt 4:5–6).
91:13 *lion and cobra.* The animal and snake imagery in this verse pictures all kinds of evil that might threaten believers.
91:14 *he set his love on Me.* The word used here is not the usual Hebrew word for love. It has the idea of "holding close to," or even "hugging tightly in love" (Dt 7:8; 10:15).

4 Ps 17:8 **5** Job 5:19; Ps 112:7; Pr 3:23; Isa 43:2 **8** Mal 1:5 **9** ver. 2; Ps 90:1 **10** Pr 12:21 **11** Ps 34:7; 71:3; Mt 4:6; Lk 4:10; Heb 1:14 **12** Job 5:23; Ps 37:24 **14** Ps 9:10 **15** Ps 50:15; Isa 43:2; 1Sa 2:30
PSALM 92 **1** Ps 147:1 **2** Ps 89:1 **3** 1Ch 23:5; Ps 33:2 **5** Ps 40:5; Isa 28:29; Ro 11:33

6 A senseless man [in his crude
and uncultivated state] knows
nothing,
Nor does a [self-righteous] fool
understand this:
7 That though the wicked sprout up
like grass
And all evildoers flourish,
They will be destroyed forever.
8 But You, LORD, are on high
forever.
9 For behold, Your enemies, O LORD,
For behold, Your enemies will
perish;
All who do evil will be scattered.
10 But my horn [my emblem of
strength and power] You have
exalted like that of a wild ox;
I am anointed with fresh oil [for
Your service].
11 My eye has looked on my foes;
My ears hear of the evildoers who
rise up against me.
12 The righteous will flourish like the
date palm [long-lived, upright
and useful];
They will grow like a cedar in
Lebanon [majestic and stable].
13 Planted in the house of the LORD,
They will flourish in the courts of
our God.
14 [Growing in grace] they will
still thrive *and* bear fruit *and*
prosper in old age;
They will flourish *and* be vital and
fresh [rich in trust and love and
contentment];
15 [They are living memorials] to
declare that the LORD is upright
and faithful [to His promises];
He is my rock, and there is no
unrighteousness in Him.
[Rom 9:14]

Psalm 93

The Majesty of the LORD.

1 THE LORD reigns, He is clothed
with majesty *and* splendor;
The LORD has clothed and
encircled Himself with
strength;
the world is firmly established, it
cannot be moved.
2 Your throne is established from of
old;
You are from everlasting.
3 The floods have lifted up, O LORD,
The floods have lifted up their
voice;
The floods lift up their pounding
waves.
4 More than the sounds of many
waters,
More than the mighty breakers of
the sea,
The LORD on high is mighty.
5 Your precepts are fully confirmed
and completely reliable;
Holiness adorns Your house,
O LORD, forever.

Psalm 94

The LORD Implored to Avenge His People.

1 O LORD God, You to whom
vengeance belongs,

92:6 *A senseless man . . . a [self-righteous] fool.* A foolish or senseless person is not someone with limited intelligence, but rather a person who is spiritually obtuse — someone who ignores God and refuses to accept responsibility.
92:10 *my horn [my emblem of strength and power] You have exalted.* This is a figure of speech for the psalmist's eventual triumph, the celebration of the psalmist's strength.
92:12 *flourish like the date palm.* This promise does not refer to success as the world counts it — the righteous are not often wealthy or powerful — but rather to spiritual success. Those who are committed to following God's ways will be so alive spiritually that even in old age they will appear young and vibrant.
93:1 *has clothed and encircled Himself with strength.* This language describes the victor of one-on-one combat. God is dressed in the garments of victory.
93:4 *The LORD on high is mighty.* The Creator King is infinite in power; no force in the universe competes with Him.

6 Ps 73:22 **7** Job 12:6; 21:7; Ps 37:1,2; Jer 12:1,2; Mal 3:15 **8** Ps 83:18 **9** Ps 68:1 **10** Ps 89:17; 23:5 **11** Ps 54:7; 59:10 **12** Ps 52:8; Isa 65:22; Hos 14:5,6 **13** Ps 100:4 **15** Dt 32:4; Ro 9:14 **PSALM 93** **1** Ps 96:10; 97:1; Isa 52:7; Rev 19:6; Ps 104:1; Ps 65:6 **2** Ps 45:6; Pr 8:22 **4** Ps 65:7; 89:9 **PSALM 94** **1** Na 1:2

O God, You to whom vengeance
belongs, shine forth [in
judgment]!
2 Rise up, O Judge of the earth;
Give to the proud a fitting
compensation.
3 O LORD, how long will the wicked,
How long will the wicked rejoice
in triumph?
4 They pour out *words,* speaking
arrogant things;
All who do evil boast proudly.
[Jude 14, 15]
5 They crush Your people, O LORD,
And afflict *and* abuse Your
heritage.
6 They kill the widow and the alien
And murder the fatherless.
7 Yet they say, "The LORD does not
see,
Nor does the God of Jacob (Israel)
notice it."
8 Consider thoughtfully, you
senseless (stupid ones) among
the people;
And you [dull-minded] fools,
when will you become wise *and*
understand?
9 He who made the ear, does He not
hear?
He who formed the eye, does He
not see?
10 He who instructs the nations,
Does He not rebuke *and* punish,
He who teaches man knowledge?
11 The LORD knows the thoughts of
man,
That they are a mere breath (vain,
empty, futile). [1 Cor 3:20]
12 Blessed [with wisdom and
prosperity] is the man whom
You discipline *and* instruct,
O LORD,
And whom You teach from Your
law,
13 That You may grant him [power to
calm himself and find] peace in
the days of adversity,
Until the pit is dug for the wicked
and ungodly.
14 For the LORD will not abandon His
people,
Nor will He abandon His
inheritance.
15 For judgment will again be
righteous,
And all the upright in heart will
follow it.
16 Who will stand up for me against
the evildoers?
Who will take a stand for
me against those who do
wickedness?
17 If the LORD had not been my help,
I would soon have dwelt in [the
land of] silence.
18 If I say, "My foot has slipped,"
Your compassion *and*
lovingkindness, O LORD, will
hold me up.
19 When my anxious thoughts
multiply within me,
Your comforts delight me.
20 Can a throne of destruction be
allied with You,
One which frames *and* devises
mischief by decree [under the
sacred name of law]?

94:2 *Judge of the earth.* Even when the poets call out for divine vengeance, they recognize that God decides when to exercise His wrath and judgment. God's law clearly states that vengeance belongs to Him (Dt 32:35).

94:6 *kill the widow and the alien.* The Israelites had been commanded to comfort widows and orphans and to welcome strangers, as long as those strangers obeyed the law of God (Ex 22:21 – 22).

94:12 *Blessed [with wisdom and prosperity] is the man whom You discipline and instruct.* The word "blessed" means "happy." Discipline doesn't usually seem to us to be a reason for joy, but we must realize that God's discipline is always for our ultimate good, and thus shows the depth of His love for us (Heb 12:7 – 11).

94:13 *the pit is dug for the wicked.* "Pit" is one of the words used as a synonym for Sheol (16:10). Digging the "pit" is a way of describing the preparations for the final judgment of the wicked (Rev 20:11 – 15).

94:14 *the LORD will not abandon His people.* God will not forget His people any more than He will forget or deny Himself (2Ti 2:13).

94:18 *Your compassion and lovingkindness.* God's "compassion" or "lovingkindness" refers to His loyal, covenant love.

---

2 Ps 7:6; Ge 18:25 **3** Job 20:5 **4** Ps 31:18; Jude 15 **7** Ps 10:11 **8** Ps 73:22; 92:6 **9** Ex 4:11 **10** Job 35:11; Isa 28:26 **11** 1Co 3:20 **12** Job 5:17; Heb 12:5 **14** 1Sa 12:22; Ro 11:1 **17** Ps 124:1,2 **18** Ps 38:16 **20** Am 6:3; Isa 10:1

21 They band themselves together
against the life of the righteous
And condemn the innocent to
death.
22 But the LORD has become my high
tower *and* defense,
And my God the rock of my
refuge.
23 He has turned back their own
wickedness upon them
And will destroy them by means
of their own evil;
The LORD our God will wipe them
out.

Psalm 95

Praise to the LORD, and Warning against Unbelief.

1 O COME, let us sing joyfully to the
LORD;
Let us shout joyfully to the rock of
our salvation.
2 Let us come before His presence
with a song of thanksgiving;
Let us shout joyfully to Him with
songs.
3 For the LORD is a great God
And a great King above all gods,
4 In whose hand are the depths of
the earth;
The peaks of the mountains are
His also.
5 The sea is His, for He made it [by
His command];
And His hands formed the dry
land. [Gen 1:9]
6 O come, let us worship and bow
down,
Let us kneel before the LORD our
Maker [in reverent praise and
prayer].
7 For He is our God
And we are the people of His
pasture and the sheep of His
hand.
Today, if you will hear His voice,
[Heb 3:7–11]
8 Do not harden your hearts *and*
become spiritually dull as at
Meribah [the place of strife],
And as at Massah [the place
of testing] in the wilderness,
[Ex 17:1–7; Num 20:1–13;
Deut 6:16]
9 "When your fathers tested Me,
They tried Me, even though they
had seen My work [of miracles].
10 "For forty years I was grieved *and*
disgusted with that generation,
And I said, 'They are a people who
err in their heart,
And they do not acknowledge *or*
regard My ways.'
11 "Therefore I swore [an oath] in My
wrath,
'They absolutely shall not enter
My rest [the land of promise].' "
[Heb 4:3–11]

Psalm 96

A Call to Worship the LORD the Righteous Judge.

1 O SING to the LORD a new song;
Sing to the LORD, all the earth!
2 Sing to the LORD, bless His name;
Proclaim good news of His
salvation from day to day.

95:1 – 7 ***shout joyfully.*** Along with others (Ps 96 – 100), this song was probably sung at the dedication of the temple after it was restored by Ezra and Nehemiah. It was a time of great celebration. The hearts of the people were filled with joy as they sang and shouted to God, whom they declared to be the great King above all gods.
95:6 ***worship . . . bow down . . . kneel.*** These words amplify each other and call for a reflective, humble approach to God. Worship is joyful and can be done with abandon (v. 1 – 5); but at other times worship may be quiet reverence of the Almighty (Ps 134).
95:7 – 11 ***For He is our God.*** This whole section is quoted in Hebrews 3:7 – 11, with a notable introduction: "Therefore, just as the Holy Spirit says." This phrase reminds us that the words of the Psalms, which are the response of the worshiping Israelite community, are also the oracles of God.
95:8 ***Meribah.*** This word would remind the Israelites of a time when they had doubted the Lord's provision (Ex 17:7; Nu 20:13).

21 Mt 27:1; Pr 17:15 **22** Ps 59:9 **23** Ps 7:16; Pr 2:22 **PSALM 95** **1** Ps 100:1; Dt 32:15; 2Sa 22:47 **3** Ps 96:4 **5** Ge 1:9,10 **6** Php 2:10 **7** Ps 79:13; 100:3; Heb 3:7 **8** Ex 17:2,7 **9** Ps 78:18; 1Co 10:9; Nu 14:22 **10** Heb 3:10 **11** Heb 4:3,5 **PSALM 96** **1** 1Ch 16:23-33

3 Declare His glory among the nations,
His marvelous works *and* wonderful deeds among all the peoples.
4 For great is the LORD and greatly to be praised;
He is to be feared above all gods. [Deut 6:5; Rev 14:7]
5 For all the gods of the peoples are [worthless, lifeless] idols,
But the LORD made the heavens.
6 Splendor and majesty are before Him;
Strength and beauty are in His sanctuary.

7 Ascribe to the LORD, O families of the peoples,
Ascribe to the LORD glory and strength.
8 Ascribe to the LORD the glory of His name;
Bring an offering and come into His courts.
9 Worship the LORD in the splendor of holiness;
Tremble [in submissive wonder] before Him, all the earth.
10 Say among the nations, "The LORD reigns;
Indeed, the world is firmly *and* securely established, it shall not be moved;
He will judge *and* rule the people with fairness." [Rev 11:15; 19:6]

11 Let the heavens be glad, and let the earth rejoice;
Let the sea roar, and all the things it contains;
12 Let the field be exultant, and all that is in it.
Then all the trees of the forest will sing for joy
13 Before the LORD, for He is coming,
For He is coming to judge the earth.
He will judge the world with righteousness
And the peoples in His faithfulness. [1 Chr 16:23–33; Rev 19:11]

Psalm 97

The LORD's Power and Dominion.

1 THE LORD reigns, let the earth rejoice;
Let the many islands *and* coastlands be glad.
2 Clouds and thick darkness surround Him [as at Sinai];
Righteousness and justice are the foundation of His throne. [Ex 19:9]
3 Fire goes before Him
And burns up His adversaries on all sides.
4 His lightnings have illuminated the world;
The earth has seen and trembled.
5 The mountains melted like wax at the presence of the LORD,
At the presence of the Lord of the whole earth.

96:3 ***all the peoples.*** This is a bold declaration that one day the message of God's mercy will be known the world over, the fulfillment of God's covenant promise to Abraham that through his descendants all nations of the earth would be blessed (Ge 12:1–3).
96:7 ***O families of the peoples.*** The allusion to the Abrahamic covenant continues (vv. 2–3; Ge 12:1–3).
96:10 ***The LORD reigns.*** This key phrase was the counter-cultural cry of ancient Israelites in a world that believed that gods could rise and fall. In contrast, the living God remains Ruler for all eternity.
96:11–13 ***Let the heavens be glad . . . for He is coming.*** All creation groans under the curse, but when Christ returns, "the creation itself will also be freed from its bondage to decay [and gain entrance] into the glorious freedom of the children of God" (Ro 8:21).
97:2 ***Clouds and thick darkness.*** These words may be rephrased as "impenetrable clouds," an indicator of the final judgment and God's awesome power (Joel 2:2; Zep 1:15).

4 Ps 145:3; Ps 18:3; Ps 95:3 **5** Jer 10:11; Ps 115:15; Isa 42:5 **6** Ps 29:2 **7** Ps 29:1,2 **9** Ps 29:2 **10** Ps 97:1; 67:4 **11** Ps 69:34; 98:7 **13** Rev 19:11 **PSALM 97** **1** Ps 96:10; Isa 60:9 **2** Ps 18:11; Ps 89:14 **3** Ps 18:8 **4** Ex 19:18 **5** Mic 1:4

[6]The heavens declare His
righteousness,
And all the peoples see His glory
and brilliance.
[7]Let all those be [deeply] ashamed
who serve carved images,
Who boast in idols.
Worship Him, all you gods!
[Heb 1:6]
[8]Zion heard this and was glad,
And the daughters (cities) of Judah
rejoiced [in relief]
Because of Your judgments,
O LORD.
[9]For You are the LORD Most High
over all the earth;
You are exalted far above all
gods.
[10]You who love the LORD, hate
evil;
He protects the souls of His godly
ones (believers),
He rescues them from the hand of
the wicked. [Rom 8:13–17]
[11]Light is sown [like seed] for the
righteous *and* illuminates their
path,
And [irrepressible] joy [is spread]
for the upright in heart [who
delight in His favor and
protection].
[12]Rejoice in the LORD, you righteous
ones [those whose moral and
spiritual integrity places them in
right standing with God],
And praise *and* give thanks at
the remembrance of His holy
name.

Psalm 98
A Call to Praise the LORD for His Righteousness.

A Psalm.

[1]O SING to the LORD a new song,
For He has done marvelous *and*
wonderful things;
His right hand and His holy arm
have gained the victory for Him.
[2]The LORD has made known His
salvation;
He has [openly] revealed His
righteousness in the sight of the
nations. [Luke 2:30, 31]
[3]He has [graciously] remembered
His lovingkindness and His
faithfulness to the house of
Israel;
All the ends of the earth have
witnessed the salvation of our
God. [Acts 13:47; 28:28]
[4]Shout joyfully to the LORD, all the
earth;
Shout [in jubilation] and sing for
joy and sing praises.
[5]Sing praises to the LORD with the
lyre,
With the lyre and the sound of
melody.
[6]With trumpets and the sound of
the horn
Shout with joy before the King, the
LORD.
[7]Let the sea thunder *and* roar, and
all the things it contains,
The world and those who dwell in it.

97:7 *Worship Him, all you gods.* One day, people will be forced to acknowledge that God is the only one worthy of worship, as they see that the very things they devoted themselves to in rejection of God must bow down to the Creator as Lord.
97:10 *hate.* The righteousness of God evokes a response either of delight or of shame because of sin (Isa 6:5). The subjects of the kingdom, the lovers of God, follow Him by loving what He loves and hating what He hates. "The [reverent] fear and worshipful awe of the LORD includes the hatred of evil" (Pr 8:13). Sin is portrayed in Scripture as an active and powerful force in unrelenting pursuit of its victims (Ge 4:7; 1Pe 5:8), and the believer is called to total war against it.
98:1 *His right hand.* The "right hand" of the Lord is a way of referring to His great salvation of Israel from Egypt (Ex 15:6; Dt 4:34). The phrase is like a slogan for the Lord's redemption.
98:2 *[openly] revealed His righteousness in the sight of the nations.* God's salvation was designed to be a witness to the nations (Dt 4:6).

6 Ps 19:1 **7** Ex 20:4; Lev 26:1; Heb 1:6 **9** Ps 83:18; Ex 18:11; Ps 95:3 **10** Ps 34:14; Am 5:15; Pr 2:8; Ps 37:39; Da 3:28 **11** Job 22:28; Pr 4:18 **12** Ps 33:1; 30:4 **PSALM 98** **1** Ps 96:1; Isa 42:10; Ex 15:11; Ps 77:14; Ex 15:6; Isa 63:5 **2** Isa 52:10; Lk 2:30; Isa 62:2 **3** Lk 1:54; Isa 49:6 **4** Ps 95:1 **6** Nu 10:10

[8]Let the rivers clap their hands;
Let the mountains sing together
for joy *and* delight
[9]Before the LORD, for He is coming
to judge the earth;
He will judge the world with
righteousness
And the peoples with fairness.

Psalm 99

Praise to the LORD for His Fidelity to Israel.

[1]THE LORD reigns, let the peoples
tremble [with submissive
wonder]!
He sits enthroned above the
cherubim, let the earth shake!
[2]The LORD is great in Zion,
And He is exalted *and* magnified
above all the peoples.
[3]Let them [reverently] praise Your
great and awesome name;
Holy is He. [Rev 15:4]
[4]The strength of the King loves
justice *and* righteous judgment;
You have established fairness;
You have executed justice and
righteousness in Jacob (Israel).
[5]Exalt the LORD our God
And worship at His footstool;
Holy is He.
[6]Moses and Aaron were among His
priests,
And Samuel was among those
who called on His name;
They called upon the LORD and He
answered them.
[7]He spoke to them in the pillar of
cloud;
They kept His testimonies
And the statutes that He gave
them. [Ps 105:9, 10]
[8]You answered them, O LORD our
God;
You were a forgiving God to them,
And yet an avenger of their *evil*
practices.
[9]Exalt the LORD our God
And worship at His holy hill [Zion,
the temple mount],
For the LORD our God is holy.

Psalm 100

All Men Exhorted to Praise God.

A Psalm of Thanksgiving.

[1]SHOUT JOYFULLY to the LORD,
all the earth.
[2]Serve the LORD with gladness *and*
delight;
Come before His presence with
joyful singing.
[3]Know *and* fully recognize with
gratitude that the LORD Himself
is God;
It is He who has made us, not we
ourselves [and we are His].
We are His people and the sheep
of His pasture. [Eph 2:10]
[4]Enter His gates with a song of
thanksgiving
And His courts with praise.

98:9 *for He is coming.* Creation rejoices at the coming of the Lord because when He establishes His kingdom, the curse will be lifted, and all creation will be freed from its slavery to corruption (Ro 8:21 – 22).
99:1 *cherubim.* Cherubim are the angels most closely related to the glory of God. Two gold cherubim graced the mercy seat of the ark of the covenant (Ex 25:18 – 22).
99:3 *name; Holy is He.* To be holy is to be "distinct from," "separated," "set apart." This is the principal Hebrew word used to describe the transcendence of God (113:4 – 6).
99:5 *His footstool.* The footstool of the Lord is sometimes said to be the earth (Isa 66:1); but more specifically, Zion is the Lord's footstool (132:7; Isa 60:13). When the Israelites came to the temple in Jerusalem to worship, they pictured themselves as being at the feet of the Creator.
100:1 *Shout joyfully.* This command is addressed not just to Israel but to all the earth. The Israelites were to be a people who would attract the nations to worship God.
100:3 *the LORD Himself is God.* These words reflect the great confession of faith in Dt 6:4 – 9.

8 Isa 55:12 **9** Ps 96:10 **PSALM 99** **1** Ex 25:22 **2** Ps 97:9 **4** Job 36:5-7 **5** Ps 132:7; Lev 19:2 **6** Jer 15:1; Ex 14:15; 1Sa 7:9 **7** Ex 33:9 **8** Nu 14:20; Dt 9:20 **9** Ps 34:3 **PSALM 100** **Title** Ps 145, Title **1** Ps 95:1 **3** Eph 2:10; Eze 34:31 **4** Ps 116:17

Be thankful to Him, bless *and* praise His name.
5 For the LORD is good;
His mercy *and* lovingkindness are everlasting,
His faithfulness [endures] to all generations.

Psalm 101

The Psalmist's Profession of Uprightness.

A Psalm of David.

1 I WILL sing of [steadfast] lovingkindness and justice;
To You, O LORD, I will sing praises.
2 I will behave wisely *and* follow the way of integrity.
When will You come to me?
I will walk in my house in integrity *and* with a blameless heart.
3 I will set no worthless *or* wicked thing before my eyes.
I hate the practice of those who fall away [from the right path];
It will not grasp hold of me.
4 A perverse heart shall depart from me;
I will not tolerate evil.
5 Whoever secretly slanders his neighbor, him I will silence;
The one who has a haughty look and a proud (arrogant) heart I will not tolerate.

6 My eyes will be on the faithful (honorable) of the land, that they may dwell with me;
He who walks blamelessly is the one who will minister to *and* serve me.
7 He who practices deceit will not dwell in my house;
He who tells lies *and* half-truths will not continue [to remain] in my presence.
8 Morning after morning I will destroy all the wicked in the land,
That I may cut off from the city of the LORD all those who do evil.

Psalm 102

Prayer of an Afflicted Man for Mercy on Himself and on Zion.

A Prayer of the afflicted; when he is overwhelmed and pours out his complaint to God.

1 HEAR MY prayer, O LORD,
And let my cry for help come to You!
2 Do not hide Your face from me in the day of my distress!
Incline Your ear to me;
In the day when I call, answer me quickly.
3 For my days have vanished in smoke,
And my bones have been scorched like a hearth.
4 My heart has been struck like grass and withered,
Indeed, [absorbed by my heartache] I forget to eat my food.
5 Because of the sound of my groaning [in suffering and trouble]
My bones cling to my flesh.
6 I am like a [mournful] vulture of the wilderness;
I am like a [desolate] owl of the wasteland.

100:5 *the LORD is good.* The shout of the goodness of God in this verse is buttressed by an appeal to His lovingkindness and faithfulness. The Hebrew root word for "faithfulness" comes from the word meaning "to be established" or "to be confirmed." From this word also comes the word "amen," meaning "surely" or "truly." God's goodness is based on His loyal love and His truth.

101:1 *lovingkindness and justice.* God's loyal love is coupled with justice. He does not allow sin to go unnoticed or unpunished, either in His children or in those who oppress them.

101:6 *My eyes will be on the faithful.* David made a covenant with his eyes (Job 31:1) to observe the righteous and sustain them in their walk.

5 Ps 136:1 **PSALM 101** **2** 1Sa 18:14; 1Ki 11:4 **3** Ps 97:10; Jos 23:6 **4** Ps 119:115 **5** Pr 6:17 **8** Ps 75:10; Jer 21:12; Ps 48:2,8 **PSALM 102** **Title** Ps 61:2 **1** Ps 18:6 **2** Ps 69:17; 71:2 **3** Jas 4:14; Job 30:30; Ps 31:10 **4** Ps 37:2 **5** Job 19:20 **6** Job 30:29; Isa 34:11

7 I am sleepless *and* lie awake
[mourning],
I have become like a lonely bird on
a housetop.
8 My enemies taunt me all day long;
Those who ridicule me use my
name as a curse.
9 For I have eaten ashes like bread,
And have mingled my drink with
tears [Is 44:20]
10 Because of Your indignation and
Your wrath,
For You have lifted me up and
thrown me away.
11 My days are like an evening
shadow that lengthens *and*
vanishes [with the sun];
And as for me, I wither away like
grass.
12 But You, O LORD, are enthroned
forever [ruling eternally as
sovereign];
And [the fame and glory of]
Your name [endures] to all
generations.
13 You will arise and have
compassion on Zion,
For it is time to be gracious *and*
show favor to her;
Yes, the appointed time [the
moment designated] has come.
[Ps 12:5; 119:126]
14 For Your servants find
[melancholy] pleasure in the
stones [of her ruins]
And feel pity for her dust.
15 So the nations will fear the name
of the LORD,
And all the kings of the earth [will
recognize] Your glory. [Ps 96:9]
16 For the LORD has built up Zion;
He has appeared in His glory *and*
brilliance;
17 He has regarded the prayer of the
destitute,
And has not despised their prayer.
18 Let this be recorded for the
generation to come,
That a people yet to be created will
praise the LORD.
19 For He looked down from His holy
height [of His sanctuary],
From heaven the LORD gazed on
the earth,
20 To hear the sighing of the prisoner,
To set free those who were
doomed to death,
21 So that people may declare the
name of the LORD in Zion
And His praise in Jerusalem,
22 When the peoples are gathered
together,
And the kingdoms, to serve the
LORD.
23 He has exhausted my strength
[humbling me with sorrow] in
the way;
He has shortened my days.
24 I said, "O my God, do not take me
away in the midst of my days;
Your years are [eternal]
throughout all generations.
25 "At the beginning You founded the
earth;
The heavens are the work of Your
hands.
26 "Even they will perish, but You
endure;
Yes, all of them will wear out like
a garment.
Like clothing You will change
them and they shall be changed.
27 "But You remain the same,
And Your years will never end.
[Heb 1:10–12]
28 "The children of Your servants
will continue,
And their descendants will be
established before You."

102:12 *enthroned forever.* Our days may be just a passing shadow, but God is King forever. He is gracious, loves His people, and promises to favor them.
102:15 *the nations will fear.* A time will come when the Lord will rule over all the earth.

102:25 *At the beginning.* God is eternal and His works are from ancient times. The writer of the Book of Hebrews applies these words of creation and eternality to the Son (vv. 25–27; Heb 1:10–12).

7 Ps 77:4; Ps 38:11 **8** Ac 26:11; 23:12 **9** Ps 42:3 **10** Ps 30:7 **11** Ecc 6:12; Isa 40:6-8; Jas 1:10 **12** Ps 9:7; 135:13 **13** Isa 60:10; 40:2 **14** Ps 79:1 **15** 1Ki 8:43 **16** Isa 60:1,2 **17** Neh 1:6 **18** Ro 15:4; Ps 22:31 **19** Dt 26:15 **20** Ps 79:11 **21** Ps 22:22 **23** Job 21:21 **24** Isa 38:10; Ps 90:2 **25** Heb 1:10 **26** Isa 34:4 **27** Mal 3:6; Heb 13:8 **28** Ps 69:36

Psalm 103

Praise for the LORD's Mercies.

A Psalm of David.

[1] BLESS *AND* affectionately praise
the LORD, O my soul,
And all that is [deep] within me,
bless His holy name.
[2] Bless *and* affectionately praise the
LORD, O my soul,
And do not forget any of His
benefits;
[3] Who forgives all your sins,
Who heals all your diseases;
[4] Who redeems your life from the pit,
Who crowns you [lavishly] with
lovingkindness and tender mercy;
[5] Who satisfies your years with
good things,
So that your youth is renewed like
the [soaring] eagle. [Is 40:31]

[6] The LORD executes righteousness
And justice for all the oppressed.
[7] He made known His ways [of
righteousness and justice] to
Moses,
His acts to the children of Israel.
[8] The LORD is merciful and gracious,
Slow to anger and abounding in
compassion *and* lovingkindness.
[James 5:11]
[9] He will not always strive *with us*,
Nor will He keep *His anger*
forever.
[10] He has not dealt with us according
to our sins [as we deserve],
Nor rewarded us [with
punishment] according to our
wickedness.
[11] For as the heavens are high above
the earth,
So great is His lovingkindness
toward those who fear *and*
worship Him [with awe-filled
respect and deepest reverence].
[12] As far as the east is from the west,
So far has He removed our
transgressions from us.
[13] Just as a father loves his
children,
So the LORD loves those who
fear *and* worship Him [with
awe-filled respect and deepest
reverence].
[14] For He knows our [mortal] frame;
He remembers that we are
[merely] dust.

[15] As for man, his days are like
grass;
Like a flower of the field, so he
flourishes.
[16] For the wind passes over it and it
is no more,
And its place knows it no longer.
[17] But the lovingkindness of the LORD
is from everlasting to everlasting
on those who [reverently] fear
Him,
And His righteousness to
children's children, [Deut 10:12]
[18] To those who honor *and* keep His
covenant,
And remember to do His
commandments [imprinting His
word on their hearts].

[19] The LORD has established His
throne in the heavens,
And His sovereignty rules over all
[the universe].

103:1 *Bless and affectionately praise the LORD.* To bless the Lord is to remember that He is the source of all our blessings. The psalmist blesses the Lord with his entire being (146:2).
103:3 *heals all your diseases.* This cannot be seen as a promise that the godly will never suffer from disease. Many believers have suffered and died of illnesses, despite repeated prayers for healing. Even though He does not always choose to heal, God is the source of all healing. This verse could also be seen as a parallel construction, coupling pardon from iniquity with healing from the disease of sin.
103:8 *merciful and gracious.* This is a basic description of God in the Old Testament (86:15; Ex 34:6–7). If God dealt with us according to our sins, no one could stand before Him (130:3).
103:11 *as the heavens are high above the earth.* There is no way to compare the divine with the mortal; the mercy of God is greater than the heavens.
103:17 *the lovingkindness of the LORD.* God's loyal love is forever.

PSALM 103 **1** Ps 104:1 **3** Ps 130:8; Isa 33:24; Ex 15:26 **4** Ps 5:12 **5** Isa 40:31 **7** Ps 147:19 **8** Ex 34:6,7 **9** Ps 30:5 **10** Ezr 9:13 **12** Isa 43:25 **13** Mal 3:17 **14** Ecc 12:7 **15** 1Pe 1:24; Job 14:1,2 **16** Job 7:10 **18** Dt 7:9 **19** Ps 47:2; Da 4:25

20 Bless the LORD, you His angels,
You mighty ones who do His commandments,
Obeying the voice of His word!
21 Bless the LORD, all you His hosts,
You who serve Him and do His will.
22 Bless the LORD, all you works of His, in all places of His dominion;
Bless *and* affectionately praise the LORD, O my soul!

Psalm 104

The LORD's Care over All His Works.

1 BLESS *AND* affectionately praise the LORD, O my soul!
O LORD my God, You are very great;
You are clothed with splendor and majesty,
2 [You are the One] who covers Yourself with light as with a garment,
Who stretches out the heavens like a tent curtain,
3 Who lays the beams of His upper chambers in the waters [above the firmament],
Who makes the clouds His chariot,
Who walks on the wings of the wind,
4 Who makes winds His messengers,
Flames of fire His ministers. [Heb 1:7]

5 He established the earth on its foundations,
So that it will not be moved forever and ever. [Job 38:4, 6]
6 You covered it with the deep as with a garment;
The waters were standing above the mountains. [Gen 1:2; 2 Pet 3:5]
7 At Your rebuke they fled;
At the sound of Your thunder they hurried away.
8 The mountains rose, the valleys sank down
To the place which You established for them.
9 You set a boundary [for the waters] that they may not cross over,
So that they will not return to cover the earth.

10 You send springs into the valleys;
Their waters flow among the mountains.
11 They give drink to every beast of the field;
The wild donkeys quench their thirst there.
12 Beside them the birds of the heavens have their nests;
They lift up their voices *and* sing among the branches. [Matt 13:32]
13 He waters the mountains from His upper chambers;
The earth is satisfied with the fruit of His works.

14 He causes grass to grow for the cattle,
And all that the earth produces for cultivation by man,
So that he may bring food from the earth—
15 And wine which makes the heart of man glad,

103:20–22 *Bless the LORD.* The poet began the psalm with a call to his own inner being to respond with praise to God (v. 1); he concludes the psalm with a call to heaven and earth to join him.

104:2 *covers Yourself with light.* God is Spirit (Jn 4:24), and descriptions of Him vary throughout the Bible. One strong description of Him is "light" (1Jn 1:5). Here, light is described as the garment that enfolds His wonder. The first act of God in Genesis was the command for light (Ge 1:3).

104:5 *established the earth on its foundations.* The poet retells the story of creation from Genesis 1.

104:6 *covered it with the deep.* The term "deep" is the same word used in Genesis 1:2.

104:9 *set a boundary.* God promised that never again would the entire earth be covered as in the flood (Ge 8:21–22).

104:15 *wine ... oil ... bread.* It is clear that the earth was created for human beings and filled with good things for our sake.

20 Ps 148:2; Mt 6:10 **21** Ge 32:2; Heb 1:14 **PSALM 104** **1** Ps 103:1 **2** Da 7:9; Isa 40:22 **3** Am 9:6; Isa 19:1; Ps 18:10 **4** Heb 1:7 **5** Job 26:7 **6** Ge 7:19 **8** Ge 8:5 **9** Job 26:10; Ge 9:11 **13** Ps 147:8; Jer 10:13 **14** Ge 1:29; Job 28:5; Ps 136:25 **15** Jdg 9:13

So that he may make his face
glisten with oil,
And bread to sustain *and*
strengthen man's heart.
16 The trees of the LORD drink their
fill,
The cedars of Lebanon which He
has planted,
17 Where the birds make their
nests;
As for the stork, the fir trees are
her house.
18 The high mountains are for the
wild goats;
The rocks are a refuge for the
shephanim.
19 He made the moon for the seasons;
The sun knows the [exact] place of
its setting.
20 You [O LORD] make darkness and
it becomes night,
In which prowls about every wild
beast of the forest.
21 The young lions roar after their
prey
And seek their food from God.
22 When the sun arises, they
withdraw
And lie down in their dens.
23 Man goes out to his work
And remains at his labor until
evening.
24 O LORD, how many *and* varied are
Your works!
In wisdom You have made them
all;
The earth is full of Your riches *and*
Your creatures.
25 There is the sea, great and broad,
In which are swarms without
number,
Creatures both small and great.
26 There the ships [of the sea] sail,
And Leviathan [the sea monster],
which You have formed to play
there.
27 They all wait for You
To give them their food in its
appointed season.
28 You give it to them, they gather it
up;
You open Your hand, they are
filled *and* satisfied with good
[things].
29 You hide Your face, they are
dismayed;
You take away their breath, they
die
And return to their dust.
30 You send out Your Spirit, they are
created;
You renew the face of the
ground.

31 May the glory of the LORD endure
forever;
May the LORD rejoice *and* be glad
in His works—
32 He looks at the earth, and it
trembles;
He touches the mountains, and
they smoke.
33 I will sing to the LORD as long as I
live;
I will sing praise to my God while I
have my being.
34 May my meditation be sweet *and*
pleasing to Him;
As for me, I will rejoice *and* be
glad in the LORD.
35 Let sinners be consumed from the
earth,
And let the wicked be no
more.
Bless *and* affectionately praise
the LORD, O my soul.
Praise the LORD! (Hallelujah!)

104:19 *He made the moon for the seasons.* In the ancient world, the heavenly bodies (sun, moon, and stars) were often worshiped as gods. God makes it clear that, far from being objects of worship, these things were created and set in place specifically for humans. The moon is not our god but our servant, set in place to keep track of times and seasons.

104:27 *They all wait for You.* All creation depends on the Creator for birth, life, and sustenance. Even death is controlled by the Sovereign One.

104:31 *May the LORD rejoice and be glad in His works.* The Lord considered His creation "good" from the beginning (Ge 1:31), and His pleasure in it remains (Pr 8:30–31).

19 Ge 1:14 **20** Isa 45:7 **21** Job 38:39 **23** Ge 3:19 **24** Pr 3:19 **26** Job 41:1 **27** Ps 136:25 **29** Job 34:15; Ecc 12:7 **30** Isa 32:15; Eze 37:9 **31** Ge 1:31 **32** Hab 3:10; Ps 144:5 **33** Ps 63:4 **35** Ps 37:38; Pr 2:22

Psalm 105

The LORD's Wonderful Works in Behalf of Israel.

[1]O GIVE thanks to the LORD, call
upon His name;
Make known His deeds among the
people.
[2]Sing to Him, sing praises to Him;
Speak of all His wonderful acts
and devoutly praise them.
[3]Glory in His holy name;
Let the hearts of those who seek
and require the LORD [as their
most essential need] rejoice.
[4]Seek *and* deeply long for the LORD
and His strength [His power,
His might];
Seek *and* deeply long for His face
and His presence continually.
[5]Remember [with awe and
gratitude] the wonderful things
which He has done,
His amazing deeds and the
judgments uttered by His mouth
[on His enemies, as in Egypt],
[Ps 78:43–51]
[6]O you offspring of Abraham, His
servant,
O you sons of Jacob, His chosen
ones!
[7]He is the LORD our God;
His judgments are in all the earth.
[8]He has remembered His covenant
forever,
The word which He commanded
and established to a thousand
generations,
[9]*The covenant* which He made with
Abraham,
And His sworn oath to Isaac,
[Luke 1:72, 73]
[10]Which He confirmed to Jacob as a
statute,
To Israel as an everlasting
covenant,
[11]Saying, "To you I will give the land
of Canaan
As the measured portion of your
inheritance."
[12]When there were only a few men
in number,
Very few [in fact], and strangers
in it;
[13]And they wandered from one
nation to another,
From one kingdom to another
people,
[14]He allowed no man to oppress
them;
He rebuked kings for their sakes,
saying, [Gen 12:17; 20:3–7]
[15]"Do not touch My anointed ones,
And do My prophets no harm."
[1 Chr 16:8–22]
[16]And He called for a famine upon
the land [of Egypt];
He cut off every source of bread.
[Gen 41:54]
[17]He sent a man before them,
Joseph, who was sold as a slave.
[Gen 45:5; 50:20, 21]
[18]His feet they hurt with shackles;
He was put in chains of iron,
[19]Until the time that his word
[of prophecy regarding his
brothers] came true,
The word of the LORD tested *and*
refined him.
[20]The king sent and released him,

105:5 *Remember [with awe and gratitude] the wonderful things.* The psalmist calls to memory what God did for His people in fulfillment of the covenant with Abraham (Ge 12:1 – 3; 22:16 – 18).
105:8 *He has remembered.* The words of the original promise to Abraham set out the Lord's obligation in strong terms (Ge 12:1 – 3).
105:13 – 15 *wandered ... rebuked kings for their sakes.* The descendants of Abraham have more than once been strangers in a foreign land, but each time the Lord has preserved their identity as a people and has rescued them from destruction. He saved them from the hand of Pharaoh (Exodus), and from the Persians (Esther). Today, the Jews are again scattered, but even though many have forgotten their God, they still do not forget that they are Jews. God's miraculous preservation of the identity of His people indicates that He is not yet finished with them.
105:17 *Joseph.* The story of Joseph's life is told in Genesis 37 – 50.

PSALM 105 **1** 1Ch 16:8; Isa 12:4; Ps 145:5 **2** Ps 119:27 **4** Ps 27:8 **5** Ps 77:11 **7** Isa 26:9 **8** Lk 1:72 **9** Ge 17:2; 22:16 **11** Ge 13:15; 15:18 **12** Ge 34:30; Dt 7:7; Heb 11:9 **14** Ge 35:5; Ge 12:17 **16** Ge 41:54; Lev 26:26; Isa 3:1 **17** Ge 45:5; Ge 37:28 **18** Ge 40:15 **19** Ge 41:25 **20** Ge 41:14

The ruler of the peoples [of Egypt],
and set him free.
21 He made Joseph lord of his house
And ruler of all his possessions,
[Gen 41:40]
22 To imprison his princes at his will,
That he might teach his elders
wisdom.
23 Israel also came into Egypt;
Thus Jacob sojourned in the land
of Ham. [Gen 46:6]
24 There the LORD greatly increased
[the number of] His people,
And made them more powerful
than their enemies.

25 He turned the heart [of the
Egyptians] to hate His people,
To deal craftily with His servants.
26 He sent Moses His servant,
And Aaron, whom He had chosen.
27 They exhibited His wondrous
signs among them,
Great miracles in the land of Ham
(Egypt).
28 He sent [thick, oppressive] darkness
and made *the land* dark;
And Moses and Aaron did not
rebel against His words.
[Ex 10:22; Ps 99:7]
29 He turned Egypt's waters into
blood
And caused their fish to die.
[Ex 7:20, 21]
30 Their land swarmed with frogs,
Even in the chambers of their
kings. [Ex 8:6]
31 He spoke, and there came swarms
of flies
And gnats in all their territory.
[Ex 8:17, 24]
32 He gave them hail for rain,
With flaming fire in their land.
[Ex 9:23, 25]
33 He struck their vines also and
their fig trees,
And shattered the [ice-laden] trees
of their territory. [Ps 78:47]
34 He spoke, and the [migratory]
locusts came,
And the young locusts, even
without number, [Ex 10:4, 13, 14]
35 And ate up all the vegetation in
their land,
And devoured the fruit of their
ground.
36 He also struck down all the
firstborn in their land,
The first fruits *and* chief substance
of all their strength. [Ex 12:29;
Ps 78:51]

37 He brought the sons of Israel out
[of Egypt] with silver and gold,
And among their tribes there
was not one who stumbled.
[Ex 12:35]
38 Egypt was glad when they
departed,
For the dread *and* fear of them
had fallen on the Egyptians.
[Ex 12:33]
39 The LORD spread a cloud as a
covering [by day],
And a fire to illumine the night.
[Ex 13:21]
40 The Israelites asked, and He
brought quail,
And satisfied them with the bread
of heaven. [Ex 16:12–15]
41 He opened the rock and water
flowed out;
It ran in the dry places like a river.
[Ex 17:6; Num 20:11]
42 For He remembered His holy word
To Abraham His servant;
[Gen 15:14]
43 He brought out His people with joy,
And His chosen ones with a joyful
shout,
44 He gave them the lands of the
nations [of Canaan],

105:26 – 36 He sent Moses. The full story of the Israelites' slavery in Egypt and the plagues God sent upon the Egyptians is told in Exodus 1 – 11.
105:44 *gave them the lands of the nations.* It is believed that this psalm may have been composed after the return from exile in Babylon. A celebration of God's gift of land would have been a tremendous source of encouragement to the people who had just returned to Israel.

21 Ge 41:40 **23** Ge 46:6; Ps 78:51 **24** Ex 1:7 **25** Ex 1:8 **26** Ex 3:10 **27** Ex 7-12; Ps 106:22 **28** Ex 10:22; Ps 99:7 **29** Ex 7:20; Ps 78:44 **30** Ex 8:6; Ps 78:45 **31** Ex 8:17; Ps 78:45 **32** Ex 9:23; Ps 78:48 **33** Ps 78:47 **34** Ex 10:4; Ps 78:46 **36** Ex 12:29; Ps 78:51; Ge 49:3 **37** Ex 12:35 **38** Ex 12:33 **39** Ex 13:21; Neh 9:12 **40** Ex 16:12; Ps 78:18,24 **41** Ex 17:6; Ps 78:15; 1Co 10:4 **42** Ge 15:14 **44** Jos 13:7

So that they would possess *the fruits of* those peoples' labor, [Deut 6:10, 11]
45 So that they might observe His precepts
And keep His laws [obediently accepting and honoring and valuing them].
Praise the LORD! (Hallelujah!)

Psalm 106

Israel's Rebelliousness and the LORD's Deliverances.

1 PRAISE THE LORD! (Hallelujah!)
Oh give thanks to the LORD, for He is good;
For His mercy *and* lovingkindness endure forever! [1 Chr 16:34]
2 Who can put into words the mighty deeds of the LORD?
Or who can proclaim all His praise [that is due Him]?
3 Blessed are those who observe justice [by honoring God's precepts],
Who practice righteousness at all times.

4 Remember me, O LORD, when You favor Your people.
Visit me with Your salvation [when You rescue them],
5 That I may see the prosperity of Your chosen ones,
That I may rejoice in the gladness of Your nation,
That I may glory with Your inheritance.

6 We have sinned like our fathers;
We have committed iniquity, we have behaved wickedly. [Lev 26:40–42]
7 Our fathers in Egypt did not understand *nor* appreciate Your miracles;
They did not remember the abundance of Your mercies *nor* imprint Your lovingkindnesses on their hearts,
But they were rebellious at the sea, at the Red Sea. [Ex 14:21]
8 Nevertheless He saved them for His name's sake,
That He might make His [supreme] power known.
9 He rebuked the Red Sea, and it dried up;
And He led them through the depths as through a pasture. [Ex 14:21]
10 So He saved them from the hand of the one that hated them,
And redeemed them from the hand of the [Egyptian] enemy. [Ex 14:30]
11 And the waters covered their adversaries;
Not one of them was left. [Ex 14:27, 28; 15:5]
12 Then Israel believed in [the validity of] His words;
They sang His praise.

13 But they quickly forgot His works;
They did not [patiently] wait for His counsel *and* purpose [to be revealed regarding them],
14 But lusted intensely in the wilderness
And tempted God [with their insistent desires] in the desert. [Num 11:4]
15 So He gave them their request,
But sent a wasting disease among them. [Ps 78:29–31]

16 They envied Moses in the camp,
And Aaron [the high priest], the holy one of the LORD, [Num 16:1–32]

106:6 *sinned like our fathers.* It is easy to point out the places where people have gone wrong in the past and to marvel at their stupidity and rebellion, but we have to point the finger at ourselves as well.
106:12 *Then Israel believed.* The people had faithlessly rebelled, but God graciously rescued them anyway, proving that His word is true and worth believing.
106:13 *they quickly forgot.* Faith which is only active in the face of abundant proof is weak and short-lived.
106:15 *He gave them their request.* When the people rebelliously kept asking for their

45 Dt 4:1; 6:21-25 **PSALM 106** **1** 1Ch 16:34 **3** Ps 15:2; Gal 6:9 **4** Ps 119:132 **6** Da 9:5 **7** Ex 14:11 **8** Ex 9:16 **9** Ex 14:21; Ps 18:15; Na 1:4; Isa 63:11 **10** Ex 14:30 **11** Ex 14:27 **12** Ex 15:1 **13** Ex 15:24 **14** 1Co 10:6 **15** Nu 11:31; Isa 10:16 **16** Nu 16:1

17 Therefore the earth opened and
swallowed Dathan,
And engulfed the company of
Abiram. [Num 16:31, 32]
18 And a fire broke out in their
company;
The flame consumed the wicked.
[Num 16:35, 46]

19 They made a calf in Horeb (Sinai)
And worshiped a cast image.
[Ex 32:4]
20 Thus they exchanged [the true
God who was] their glory
For the image of an ox that eats
grass.
21 They forgot God their Savior,
Who had done such great things in
Egypt,
22 Wonders in the land of Ham,
Awesome things at the Red Sea.
23 Therefore He said He would
destroy them,
[And He would have done so] had
not Moses, His chosen one,
stepped into the gap before Him,
To turn away His wrath from
destroying them. [Ex 32:10, 11, 32]
24 Then they despised the pleasant
land [of Canaan];
They did not believe in His word
nor rely on it,
25 But they sulked *and* complained in
their tents;
They did not listen to the voice of
the LORD.
26 Therefore He lifted up His hand
[swearing] to them,
That He would cause them to fall
in the wilderness,
27 And that He would cast out their
descendants among the nations
And scatter them in the lands [of
the earth].

28 They joined themselves also to [the
idol] Baal of Peor,
And ate sacrifices offered to the
dead.
29 Thus they provoked Him to anger
with their practices,
And a plague broke out among
them.
30 Then Phinehas [the priest] stood
up and interceded,
And so the plague was halted.
[Num 25:7, 8]
31 And that was credited to him for
righteousness,
To all generations forever.

32 They provoked Him to anger at the
waters of Meribah,
So that it went hard with Moses on
their account; [Num 20:3–13]
33 Because they were rebellious
against His Spirit,
Moses spoke recklessly with his
lips.

34 They did not destroy the [pagan]
peoples [in Canaan],
As the LORD commanded them,

---

own desires, God finally let them have their own way — and also let them take the consequences. We don't have to fear that we might accidentally pray for something wrong and then receive a bad gift from the Lord. Even when we pray wrongly, if our hearts are turned towards God, He will redirect our desires and teach us the better way (37:4). However, it is sin if we keep praying for something when we already know that He said no, and we may have to bear consequences that we never dreamed of.

106:20 *exchanged [the true God who was] their glory.* These words are echoed by Paul in Romans 1:22–23.

106:24–25 *They did not believe.* The Old Testament books of Exodus and Joshua illustrate God's plan of salvation. The first relates how Israel was brought out of the land of bondage, and the second describes how they were brought into the land of blessing. The wilderness route they traveled was of His choosing, but not the aimless wandering which followed. That sad 40-year episode was a direct result of their sin of unbelief.

106:28 *Baal of Peor.* After Balaam was prevented from cursing the Israelites, he suggested that the Moabites could destroy the Israelites in another way, by leading them into sin against their God (Nu 25).

106:34 *not destroy the [pagan] peoples.* If Israel had obeyed and the Canaanites had been driven out, the people might never have succumbed to the idolatry that marked their existence for hundreds of years.

17 Dt 11:6 **18** Nu 16:35,46 **19** Ex 32:4 **20** Jer 2:11; Ro 1:23 **21** Ps 78:11 **22** Ps 78:51 **23** Ex 32:10; Dt 9:19; Eze 22:30 **24** Dt 8:7; Eze 20:6; Heb 3:18 **25** Nu 14:2 **26** Eze 20:15; Nu 14:29 **27** Lev 26:33 **28** Hos 9:10 **30** Nu 25:7 **31** Nu 25:11 **32** Nu 20:3; Ps 81:7 **33** Nu 20:10 **34** Jdg 1:21; Dt 7:2; Jdg 2:2

35 But they mingled with the
[idolatrous] nations
And learned their ways,
36 And served their idols,
Which became a [dreadful] snare
to them.
37 They even sacrificed their sons
and their daughters to demons
[Deut 32:17; 2 Kin 16:3]
38 And shed innocent blood,
Even the blood of their sons and of
their daughters,
Whom they sacrificed to the idols
of Canaan;
And the land was polluted with
their blood.
39 In this way they became unclean
in their practices;
They played the prostitute in their
own deeds [by giving their
worship, which belongs to God
alone, to other "gods"].
40 Therefore the anger of the LORD
was kindled against His people
And He detested His own
inheritance. [Deut 32:17]
41 He gave them into the hands of the
nations,
And those who hated them ruled
over them.
42 Their enemies also oppressed them,
And they were subdued under
the [powerful] hand of their
enemies.
43 Many times He rescued them;
But they were rebellious in their
counsel,
And sank down in their
wickedness.
44 Nevertheless He looked
[sympathetically] at their distress
When He heard their cry;
45 And He remembered His covenant
for their sake,
And relented [rescinding their
sentence] according to the
greatness of His lovingkindness
[when they cried out to Him],
46 He also made them *objects* of
compassion
Among those who had carried them
away captive. [2 Kin 25:27–30]
47 Save us, O LORD our God,
And gather us from among the
nations,
That we may give thanks to Your
holy name
And glory in praising You.
48 Blessed be the LORD, the God of
Israel,
From everlasting even to
everlasting.
And let all the people say, "Amen."
Praise the LORD! (Hallelujah!)
[1 Chr 16:35, 36]

BOOK FIVE

Psalm 107

The LORD Rescues People from Many Troubles.

1 O GIVE thanks to the LORD, for He
is good;
For His compassion *and*
lovingkindness endure forever!
2 Let the redeemed of the LORD say so,
Whom He has redeemed from the
hand of the adversary,
3 And gathered them from the lands,
From the east and from the west,
From the north and from the south.
4 They wandered in the wilderness
in a [solitary] desert region;
And did not find a way to an
inhabited city.

106:45 *He remembered His covenant.* God's wrath must always be seen in the context of His loyal love and His long forbearance. Even when the people brought down His wrath by their sins, He remained faithful to the covenant.

107:1 *His compassion and lovingkindness endure forever.* God's "loyal love" or "mercies" will never end. He is always willing to restore those who call on Him.

35 Jdg 3:5,6; Isa 2:6 **36** Jdg 2:12; Dt 7:16 **37** 2Ki 16:3; Lev 17:7 **38** Nu 35:33 **39** Eze 20:18; Lev 17:7; Nu 15:39; Eze 20:30 **40** Jdg 2:14; Dt 9:29 **41** Jdg 2:14; Neh 9:27 **43** Jdg 2:16; Neh 9:27 **44** Jdg 10:10 **45** Lev 26:41; Jdg 2:18; Ps 69:16 **46** Ezr 9:9; Jer 42:12 **47** 1Ch 16:35 **48** Ps 41:13 **PSALM 107** **1** Ps 106:1; Ps 119:68 **2** Ps 106:10 **3** Ps 106:47 **4** Dt 32:10

[5]Hungry and thirsty,
They fainted.
[6]Then they cried out to the LORD in
their trouble,
And He rescued them from their
distresses.
[7]He led them by the straight way,
To an inhabited city [where they
could establish their homes].
[8]Let them give thanks to the LORD
for His lovingkindness,
And for His wonderful acts to the
children of men!
[9]For He satisfies the parched throat,
And fills the hungry appetite with
what is good.

10 Some dwelt in darkness and in the
deep (deathly) darkness,
Prisoners [bound] in misery and
chains, [Luke 1:79]
[11]Because they had rebelled against
the precepts of God
And spurned the counsel of the
Most High.
[12]Therefore He humbled their heart
with hard labor;
They stumbled and there was no
one to help.
[13]Then they cried out to the LORD in
their trouble,
And He saved them from their
distresses.
[14]He brought them out of darkness
and the deep (deathly) darkness
And broke their bonds apart.
[Ps 68:6; Acts 12:7; 16:26]
[15]Let them give thanks to the LORD
for His lovingkindness,
And for His wonderful acts to the
children of men!
[16]For He has shattered the gates of
bronze
And cut the bars of iron apart.

17 Fools, because of their rebellious
way,
And because of their sins, were
afflicted.
[18]They detested all kinds of food,
And they drew near to the gates of
death.
[19]Then they cried out to the LORD in
their trouble,
And He saved them from their
distresses.
[20]He sent His word and healed them,
And rescued them from their
destruction. [2 Kin 20:4, 5;
Matt 8:8]
[21]Let them give thanks to the LORD
for His lovingkindness,
And for His wonderful acts to the
children of men! [Heb 13:15]
[22]And let them offer the sacrifices of
thanksgiving,
And speak of His deeds with
shouts of joy!

23 Those who go down to the sea in
ships,
Who do business on great waters;
[24]They have seen the works of the
LORD,
And His wonders in the deep.
[25]For He spoke and raised up a
stormy wind,
Which lifted up the waves of the
sea.
[26]They went up toward the heavens
[on the crest of the wave], they
went down again to the depths
[of the watery trough];
Their courage melted away in their
misery.
[27]They staggered and trembled like
a drunken man,
And were at their wits' end [all
their wisdom was useless].
[28]Then they cried out to the LORD in
their trouble,
And He brought them out of their
distresses.
[29]He hushed the storm to a gentle
whisper,
So that the waves of the sea were
still. [Ps 65:7; 89:9; Matt 8:26]

107:9 ***He satisfies the parched throat.*** Only God can fulfill the spiritual longings of the human soul.
107:17 ***Fools.*** This harsh word emphasizes moral failure (Pr 1:7; 15:5). These people deserved the trouble they suffered, yet they too may call upon the Lord, and He will deliver and restore them.

6 Ps 50:15; Hos 5:15 **7** Ezr 8:21 **8** ver. 15,21 **9** Ps 34:10; Lk 1:53 **10** Lk 1:79; Job 36:8 **11** La 3:42; Ps 73:24; Lk 7:30; Ac 20:27 **12** Ps 22:11; Isa 63:5 **14** Ps 68:6; Ac 12:7 **15** ver. 8,21,31 **16** Isa 45:2 **17** La 3:39 **18** Job 33:20,22; Ps 9:13 **20** Mt 8:8; Ps 30:2; 103:3; Job 33:28; Ps 30:3; 49:15 **22** Lev 7:12; Ps 116:17; Heb 13:15; Ps 9:11; 73:28; 118:17 **25** Jnh 1:4 **26** Ps 22:14 **28** ver. 6,13,19 **29** Ps 89:9; Mt 8:26

30 Then they were glad because of
the calm,
And He guided them to their
desired haven (harbor).
31 Let them give thanks to the LORD
for His lovingkindness,
And for His wonderful acts to the
children of men!
32 Let them exalt Him also in the
congregation of the people,
And praise Him at the seat of the
elders.

33 He turns rivers into a wilderness,
And springs of water into a thirsty
ground; [1 Kin 17:1, 7]
34 A productive land into a [barren]
salt waste,
Because of the wickedness of
those who dwell in it. [Gen 13:10;
14:3; 19:25]
35 He turns a wilderness into a pool
of water
And a dry land into springs of
water; [Is 41:18]
36 And there He has the hungry dwell,
So that they may establish an
inhabited city,
37 And sow fields and plant vineyards,
And produce an abundant harvest.
38 Also He blesses them so that they
multiply greatly,
And He does not let [the number
of] their cattle decrease.
39 When they are diminished and
bowed down (humbled)
Through oppression, misery, and
sorrow,
40 He pours contempt on princes
And makes them wander in a
pathless wasteland.
41 Yet He sets the needy securely on
high, away from affliction,
And makes their families like a
flock.
42 The upright see it and rejoice;
But all unrighteousness shuts its
mouth.
43 Who is wise? Let him observe *and*
heed these things;
And [thoughtfully] consider the
lovingkindness of the LORD.

Psalm 108

Praise and Supplication to God for Victory.

A Song. A Psalm of David.

1 O GOD, my heart is steadfast [with
confident faith];
I will sing, I will sing praises, even
with my soul.
2 Awake, harp and lyre;
I will awaken the dawn!
3 I will praise *and* give thanks to
You, O LORD, among the people;
And I will sing praises to You
among the nations.
4 For Your lovingkindness is great
and higher than the heavens;
Your truth *reaches* to the skies.
[Ps 57:7–11]
5 Be exalted [in majesty], O God,
above the heavens,
And Your glory above all the earth.
6 That Your beloved [ones] may be
rescued,
Save with Your right hand, and
answer me!

7 God has spoken in His holiness:
"I will rejoice, I will portion out
Shechem [as I divide Canaan
among My people],

107:33 *He turns rivers into a wilderness.* During the reign of King Ahab of the Northern Kingdom of Israel, God sentenced the land to three years of drought because of their Baal worship (1Ki 17:1 – 7).
107:43 *Who is wise.* There is no wisdom apart from centering in on and responding to the love of God. The psalmist exhorts the readers to review God's history of delivering those in trouble and to praise His great love.

108 title *A Song.* This psalm is actually a medley of two other psalms of David. Verses 1 – 5 are from 57:7 – 11, and verses 6 – 13 are from 60:5 – 12. David is the author of both of these psalms, and 108 is attributed to him as well, even though the arrangement may have been someone else's.
108:7 *I will rejoice.* The remarkable fact about these words is that they are spoken by God. The Lord has pleasure in delivering His people and

31 ver. 8,15,21 **32** Ps 22:22,25 **33** 1Ki 17:1,7 **34** Ge 13:10; 14:3; 19:25 **35** Ps 114:8; Isa 41:18 **38** Ge 12:2; 17:16,20; Ex 1:7 **39** 2Ki 10:32 **40** Job 12:21,24 **41** 1Sa 2:8; Ps 113:7,8; Ps 78:52 **42** Job 5:15,16; Job 5:16; Ps 63:11; Pr 10:11; Ro 3:19 **43** Ps 64:9; Jer 9:12; Hos 14:9 **PSALM 108** **1** Ps 57:7 **2** Ps 57:8-11 **5** Ps 57:5,11 **6** Ps 60:5

And measure out the Valley of
Succoth.
8 "Gilead is Mine, Manasseh is Mine;
Ephraim also is the helmet of
My head [My stronghold, My
defense];
Judah is My scepter. [Gen 49:10]
9 "Moab is My washbowl;
Over Edom I will throw My shoe
[to show Edom is Mine];
Over Philistia I will shout [in
triumph]."

10 Who will bring me into the
fortified city [of Petra]?
Who will lead me to Edom?
11 Have You not rejected us, O God?
And will You not go out, O God,
with our armies?
12 Give us help against the adversary,
For deliverance by man is in vain
[a worthless hope].
13 With God we will do valiantly,
For it is He who will trample down
our enemies. [Ps 60:5–12]

Psalm 109

Vengeance Invoked upon Adversaries.

To the Chief Musician. A Psalm of David.

1 O GOD of my praise!
Do not keep silent,
2 For the mouth of the wicked and
the mouth of the deceitful are
opened against me;
They have spoken against me with
a lying tongue.
3 They have also surrounded me
with words of hatred,
And have fought against me
without a cause.
4 In return for my love, they
attack me,
But I am in prayer.
5 They have repaid me evil for good,
And hatred for my love.

6 Appoint a wicked man against him,
And let an attacker stand at his
right hand [to kill him].
7 When he enters into dispute, let
wickedness come about.
Let his prayer [for help] result
[only] in sin.
8 Let his days be few;
And let another take his office.
[Acts 1:20]
9 Let his children be fatherless
And his wife a widow.
10 Let his children wander and beg;
Let them seek their food *and* be
driven far from their ruined
homes. [Gen 4:12]
11 Let the creditor seize all that
he has,
And let strangers plunder the
product of his labor.
12 Let there be no one to extend
kindness to him,
Nor let anyone be gracious to his
fatherless children.
13 Let his descendants be cut off,
And in the following generation let
their name be blotted out.

14 Let the wickedness of his fathers
be remembered by the LORD;
And do not let the sin of his
mother be blotted out.
15 Let them be before the LORD
continually,

---

giving them victory. He celebrates His deliverance of them.

109:8 ***let another take his office.*** These words (along with 69:25) are quoted in Acts 1:20 as having been fulfilled in the replacement of Judas Iscariot.

109:9 ***fatherless . . . a widow.*** The curses that the psalmist wants to call down on his enemies seem very harsh and unforgiving. It is hard to understand how we should take this kind of language, in the face of Christ's teaching about loving our enemies and doing good to those who hurt us. However, two important points are clear: the psalmist left vengeance in the hands of the Lord, and he also clearly understood the reality of wickedness. We must remember that forgiveness is not saying, "It wasn't really bad." True forgiveness does not pretend that sin did not happen; it recognizes evil, and then releases the desire for vengeance into God's hands. God has promised that He will judge the wicked in the end.

8 Ge 49:10 **10** Ps 60:9 **13** Ps 60:12 **PSALM 109** **1** Ps 83:1 **3** Ps 35:7; 69:4; Jn 15:25 **5** Ps 35:7,12; 38:20 **6** Zec 3:1 **7** Pr 28:9 **8** Ac 1:20 **9** Ex 22:24 **11** Job 5:5; 18:9 **13** Job 18:19; Ps 37:28; Pr 10:7 **14** Ex 20:5; Neh 4:5; Jer 18:23 **15** Job 18:17; Ps 34:16

That He may cut off their memory
from the earth;
16 Because the man did not
remember to show kindness,
But persecuted the suffering and
needy man,
And the brokenhearted, to put
them to death.
17 He also loved cursing, and it came
[back] to him;
He did not delight in blessing, so it
was far from him.
18 He clothed himself with cursing as
with his garment,
And it seeped into his inner self
like water
And like [anointing] oil into his
bones.
19 Let it be to him as a robe with
which he covers himself,
And as a sash with which he is
constantly bound.
20 Let this be the reward of my
attackers from the LORD,
And of those who speak evil
against my life.

21 But You, O GOD, the Lord, show
kindness to me, for Your name's
sake;
Because Your lovingkindness
(faithfulness, compassion) is
good, O rescue me;
22 For I am suffering and needy,
And my heart is wounded within
me.
23 I am vanishing like a shadow
when it lengthens *and* fades;
I am shaken off like the locust.
24 My knees are unsteady from
fasting;
And my flesh is gaunt and without
fatness.
25 I also have become a reproach *and*
an object of taunting to others;
When they see me, they shake
their heads [in derision].
[Matt 26:39]

26 Help me, O LORD my God;
Save me according to Your
lovingkindness—
27 And let them know that this is
Your hand;
You, LORD, have done it.
28 Let them curse, but You bless.
When adversaries arise, let them
be ashamed,
But let Your servant rejoice.
29 Let my attackers be clothed with
dishonor,
And let them cover themselves
with their own shame as with a
robe.
30 I will give great praise *and* thanks
to the LORD with my mouth;
And in the midst of many I will
praise Him.
31 For He will stand at the right hand
of the needy,
To save him from those who judge
his soul.

Psalm 110

The LORD Gives Dominion to the King.

A Psalm of David.

1 THE LORD (Father) says to my
Lord (the Messiah, His Son),
"Sit at My right hand
Until I make Your enemies
a footstool for Your feet
[subjugating them into complete
submission]." [Josh 10:24;
Matt 26:64; Acts 2:34;
1 Cor 15:25; Col 3:1; Heb 12:2]

109:27 *let them know.* Even in the psalmist's intense emotional state, he wants to see the name of God defended, proclaimed, and honored.

110:1 *The LORD.* "LORD" is the translation of the Hebrew name Yahweh (I AM) and refers to God the Father. According to Jesus' interpretation of the passage (Mt 22:41–45; Mk 12:35–37; Lk 20:41–44), the second *Lord* is a reference to the Son of God in heaven in the presence of the Father. David himself confesses the Son to be his Lord—that is, his master or sovereign. ***at My right hand.*** This position of high honor beside the Father was given to the Savior upon

16 Ps 34:18 **17** Pr 14:14; Eze 35:6 **18** Nu 5:22 **23** Ps 102:11 **24** Heb 12:12 **25** Ps 22:6,7; Mt 27:39
27 Job 37:7 **28** 2Sa 16:11; Isa 65:14 **29** Ps 35:26; 132:18 **30** Ps 35:18; 111:1 **31** Ps 16:8; 73:23
PSALM 110 **1** Mt 22:44; Mk 12:36; Lk 20:42; Ac 2:34; 1Co 15:25

[2]The LORD will send the scepter
of Your strength from Zion,
saying,
"Rule in the midst of Your
enemies." [Rom 11:26, 27]
[3]Your people will offer themselves
willingly [to participate in Your
battle] in the day of Your
power;
In the splendor of holiness, from
the womb of the dawn,
Your young men are to You as
the dew.
[4]The LORD has sworn [an oath]
and will not change His
mind:
"You are a priest forever
According to the order of
Melchizedek." [Heb 5:10; 7:11,
15, 21]
[5]The LORD is at Your right
hand,
He will crush kings in the day
of His wrath.
[6]He will execute judgment [in
overwhelming punishment]
among the nations;
He will fill them with corpses,
He will crush the chief men over
a broad country. [Ezek 38:21,
22; 39:11, 12]
[7]He will drink from the brook
by the wayside;
Therefore He will lift up His head
[triumphantly].

Psalm 111

The LORD Praised for His Goodness.

[1]PRAISE THE LORD! (Hallelujah!)
I will give thanks to the LORD with
all my heart,
In the company of the upright and
in the congregation.
[2]Great are the works of the LORD,
Studied by all those who delight in
them.
[3]Splendid and majestic is His work,
And His righteousness endures
forever.
[4]He has made His wonderful acts to
be remembered;
The LORD is gracious and merciful
and full of loving compassion.
[5]He has given food to those who
fear Him [with awe-inspired
reverence];
He will remember His covenant
forever. [Deut 10:12; Ps 96:9]
[6]He has declared *and* made known
to His people the power of His
works,
In giving them the heritage of the
nations.
[7]The works of His hands are truth
and [absolute] justice;
All His precepts are sure
(established, reliable,
trustworthy).

His resurrection and ascension (Ac 2:33 – 36; 1Co 15:20 – 28; Col 3:1; Heb 1:13). The Savior placing His feet on His foes depicts the utter defeat of the enemies of Christ (1Co 15:25 – 26; Eph 1:22 – 23).

110:3 *In the splendor of holiness.* This description of the people who join the King in His great battle fits with Revelation 19:14.

110:4 *a priest.* God is seen appointing the coming Messiah to be a priest (Heb 7). This was a source of confusion for Jews, as demonstrated by the questions that the New Testament Jews had about the Messiah. Some Dead Sea Scrolls give evidence that more than one Messiah was anticipated. According to Scripture, the Messiah would be a descendant of David (Isa 9:7), but this prophecy presents Him as a priest. This might seem to be a contradiction because true priests had to be descendants of Aaron, but the Messiah is presented as a priest by divine declaration rather than human descent. ***Melchizedek.*** Melchizedek is first mentioned in Genesis 14:18 – 20. He was a true priest of the Most High God, unrelated to Abraham and living hundreds of years before Aaron. He became a prototype of the Messiah, whose priesthood was not based on connection with the line of Aaron but was by divine decree (Heb 5:5 – 11; 6:20; 7:1 – 28).

111:1 *Praise the LORD.* This translates the Hebrew word *hallelujah.*

3 Jdg 5:2; Ps 96:9 **4** Nu 23:19 **5** Ps 16:8; Ps 2:5,12; Ro 2:5 **6** Ps 68:21; Hab 3:13 **7** Isa 53:12
PSALM 111 **1** Ps 35:18; 89:5; 107:32 **2** Job 38-41; Ps 92:5; Ps 143:5 **3** Ps 145:4 **4** Ps 86:5; 103:8
5 Mt 6:26 **7** Rev 15:3; Ps 19:7

8 They are upheld forever and ever;
They are done in [absolute] truth
and uprightness.
9 He has sent redemption to His
people;
He has ordained His covenant
forever;
Holy and awesome is His name—
[inspiring reverence and godly
fear].
10 The [reverent] fear of the LORD is
the beginning (the prerequisite,
the absolute essential, the
alphabet) of wisdom;
A good understanding *and* a
teachable heart are possessed
by all those who do *the will of
the LORD*;
His praise endures forever.
[Job 28:28; Prov 1:7; Matt 22:37,
38; Rev 14:7]

Psalm 112

Prosperity of the One Who Fears the LORD.

1 PRAISE THE LORD! (Hallelujah!)
Blessed [fortunate, prosperous,
and favored by God] is the man
who fears the LORD [with awe-
inspired reverence and worships
Him with obedience],
Who delights greatly in His
commandments. [Deut 10:12]
2 His descendants will be mighty on
earth;
The generation of the upright will
be blessed.
3 Wealth and riches are in his house,
And his righteousness endures
forever.
4 Light arises in the darkness for the
upright;
He is gracious and compassionate
and righteous (upright—in right
standing with God).
5 It is well with the man who is
gracious and lends;
He conducts his affairs with
justice. [Ps 37:26; Luke 6:35;
Col 4:5]
6 He will never be shaken;
The righteous will be remembered
forever. [Prov 10:7]
7 He will not fear bad news;
His heart is steadfast, trusting
[confidently relying on and
believing] in the LORD.
8 His heart is upheld, he will not
fear
While he looks [with satisfaction]
on his adversaries.
9 He has given freely to the poor;
His righteousness endures forever;
His horn will be exalted in honor.
[2 Cor 9:9]
10 The wicked will see it and be
angered,
He will gnash his teeth and melt
away [in despair and death];
The desire of the wicked will
perish *and* come to nothing.

111:9 *redemption.* The psalmists constantly look back to the exodus, but they also speak of that which was still to come—the redemption of mankind through the Messiah.
111:10 *fear of the LORD.* The fear of the Lord describes an obedient response of wonder and awe before the Most High God.
112:1 *Praise the LORD.* Like Psalm 111, this psalm begins with the Hebrew word "hallelujah." It then picks up where Psalm 111 left off. ***Blessed.*** This word, meaning "manifestly happy," is the same word which begins the Book of Psalms.
112:2 *His descendants will be mighty.* Compare the blessings of this psalm with the curses placed on the wicked in 109:6–13.
112:9 *given freely to the poor.* The gracious and compassionate nature of God is also seen in His people, especially in their acts of benevolence toward the poor. The poor are the materially destitute and helpless segments of society—widows, orphans, and aliens—whose rights are more easily violated. Scripture tells us that giving to the poor is lending to the Lord and will be repaid by the Lord (Pr 19:17). To give freely to the poor literally means "to scatter" God's gifts, which suggests that the poor will be provided for and that abundance will come to the giver as well (2Co 9:8–9). ***His horn.*** The horn is a symbol of power. When used for a righteous person, it speaks of prominence and a lasting sense of worth in his or her life.

8 Isa 40:8; Rev 15:3 **9** Lk 1:68; Lk 1:49 **10** Ecc 12:13 **PSALM 112** **1** Ps 119:16 **2** Ps 102:28 **3** Mt 6:33 **4** Job 11:17; Ps 97:11 **5** Ps 37:26; Eph 5:15; Col 4:5 **6** Pr 10:7 **7** Pr 1:33; Ps 57:7; Ps 64:10 **8** Pr 1:33; Ps 59:10; 118:7 **9** 2Co 9:9; Ps 75:10 **10** Lk 13:28; Ps 37:12; 58:7,8; Pr 11:7

Psalm 113

The Lord Exalts the Humble.

1 PRAISE THE LORD! (Hallelujah!)
Praise, O servants of the LORD,
Praise the name of the LORD.
2 Blessed be the name of the LORD
From this time forth and forever.
3 From the rising of the sun to its
setting
The name of the LORD is to be
praised [with awe-inspired
reverence].
4 The LORD is high above all
nations,
And His glory above the
heavens.

5 Who is like the LORD our God,
Who is enthroned on high,
6 Who humbles Himself to regard
The heavens and the earth?
[Ps 138:6; Is 57:15]
7 He raises the poor out of the dust
And lifts the needy from the ash
heap,
8 That He may seat them with
princes,
With the princes of His people.
9 He makes the barren woman live
in the house
As a joyful mother of children.
Praise the LORD! (Hallelujah!)

Psalm 114

God's Rescue of Israel from Egypt.

1 WHEN ISRAEL came out of
Egypt,
The house of Jacob from a people
of strange language,
2 Judah became His sanctuary,
And Israel His dominion.
[Ex 29:45, 46; Deut 27:9]

3 The [Red] Sea looked and fled;
The Jordan turned back. [Ex 14:21;
Josh 3:13, 16; Ps 77:16]
4 The mountains leaped like
rams,
The [little] hills, like lambs.
5 What ails you, O sea, that you
flee?
O Jordan, that you turn back?
6 O mountains, that you leap like
rams,
O [little] hills, like lambs?

7 Tremble, O earth, at the presence
of the Lord,
At the presence of the God of
Jacob (Israel),
8 Who turned the rock into a pool of
water,
The flint into a fountain of water.
[Ex 17:6; Num 20:11]

113:1 ***Praise the LORD.*** This psalm of descriptive praise begins and ends with the Hebrew word "hallelujah." This psalm, along with Psalm 114, is traditionally read before the Passover meal.
113:2 ***the name of the LORD.*** In biblical times there was a close association between a person's name and identity. Praising the name of God centers one's thoughts on His character.
113:4 ***high above all nations.*** Unlike the manmade gods of the ancient Middle East, the Lord is not limited to a certain tribe or territory. Not only is He supreme over all nations, but His glory cannot be contained in the universe.
113:6 ***humbles Himself.*** God is not some far distant deity who set the world in motion and then went about His business. Instead, He is deeply involved in the lives of the people He created and loves us so much that He came down from His high position to save us (Php 2:5–9).
113:9 ***barren woman.*** In that time and culture, a barren woman was without significance and without joy. The joy of a barren woman who has been given children is a picture of the joy we receive when God stoops down to touch us.
114:1 ***of Egypt.*** This psalm recalling the salvation of Israel from Egypt is traditionally read along with Psalm 113 before the Passover meal.
114:2 ***Judah became His sanctuary.*** This verse anticipates the New Testament sense of God living among His people (Eze 37:26–27; 2Co 6:16–18).

PSALM 113 **1** Ps 135:1 **2** Da 2:20 **3** Isa 59:19; Mal 1:11 **4** Ps 97:9; 99:2; 8:1 **5** Ps 89:6 **6** Ps 11:4; 138:6; Isa 57:15 **7** 1Sa 2:8; Ps 107:41 **8** Job 36:7 **9** 1Sa 2:5; Ps 68:6; Isa 54:1; Gal 4:27 **PSALM 114** **1** Ex 13:3; Ps 81:5 **2** Ex 6:7; Dt 27:9 **3** Ex 14:21; Ps 77:16; Jos 3:13 **4** Ps 29:6; 68:16 **5** Hab 3:8 **8** Ex 17:6; Nu 20:11; Ps 107:35

Psalm 115

Pagan Idols Contrasted with the LORD.

1 NOT TO us, O LORD, not to us,
But to Your name give glory
Because of Your lovingkindness,
because of Your truth *and* faithfulness.
2 Why should the nations say,
"Where, now, is their God?"
3 But our God is in heaven;
He does whatever He pleases.
4 The idols [of the nations] are silver and gold,
The work of man's hands.
5 They have mouths, but they cannot speak;
They have eyes, but they cannot see;
6 They have ears, but they cannot hear;
They have noses, but they cannot smell;
7 They have hands, but they cannot feel;
They have feet, but they cannot walk;
Nor can they make a sound with their throats.
8 Those who make them will become like them,
Everyone who trusts in them.
[Ps 135:15–18]

9 O Israel, trust *and* take refuge in the LORD! [Be confident in Him, cling to Him, rely on His word!]
He is their help and their shield.
10 O house of Aaron, trust in the LORD;
He is their help and their shield.
11 You who [reverently] fear the LORD, trust in LORD;
He is their help and their shield.
12 The LORD has been mindful of us;
He will bless,
He will bless the house of Israel;
He will bless the house of Aaron.
13 He will bless those who fear *and* worship the LORD [with awe-inspired reverence and submissive wonder],
Both the small and the great.
[Ps 103:11; Rev 11:18; 19:5]
14 May the LORD give you [great] increase,
You and your children.
15 May you be blessed of the LORD,
Who made heaven and earth.

16 The heavens are the heavens of the LORD,
But the earth He has given to the children of men.
17 The dead do not praise the LORD,
Nor do any who go down into silence;
18 But as for us, we will bless *and* affectionately and gratefully praise the LORD
From this time forth and forever.
Praise the LORD! (Hallelujah!)

Psalm 116

Thanksgiving for Rescue from Death.

1 I LOVE the LORD, because He hears [and continues to hear]
My voice and my supplications (my pleas, my cries, my specific needs).
2 Because He has inclined His ear to me,
Therefore I will call on Him as long as I live.

115:1 *to Your name give glory.* This community psalm of praise focuses on the glory of the Lord in the salvation of His people. It is one of the Passover Psalms (115 – 118; 136), traditionally read or sung after the Passover meal.
115:4 – 8 *idols.* Like the prophets (Isa 40:18 – 20; Jer 10:1 – 10), the psalms are derisive toward the idols of the nations.
115:18 *Praise the LORD.* Many of the Passover Psalms (115 – 117) conclude with the Hebrew word "hallelujah."
116:1 *I love the LORD.* This messianic psalm is one of the Passover psalms (113 – 118). It was probably recited by Jesus on the night of His arrest, the night He celebrated the Passover with His disciples (Lk 22:15).

PSALM 115 **1** Isa 48:11; Eze 36:32 **2** Ps 42:3,10; 79:10; Joel 2:17 **3** 1Ch 16:26; Ps 135:6; Da 4:35 **4** Dt 4:28; Ps 135:15; Jer 10:3 **8** Ps 135:18; Isa 44:9-11 **9** Ps 118:2,3; 33:20 **13** Ps 128:1 **15** Ge 14:19; 1:1; Ps 96:5 **17** Ps 6:5; 88:10-12; Isa 38:18 **18** Ps 113:2; Da 2:20 **PSALM 116** **1** Ps 18:1

[3]The cords *and* sorrows of death
encompassed me,
And the terrors of Sheol came
upon me;
I found distress and sorrow.
[4]Then I called on the name of the
LORD:
"O LORD, please save my life!"

[5]Gracious is the LORD, and
[consistently] righteous;
Yes, our God is compassionate.
[6]The LORD protects the simple
(childlike);
I was brought low [humbled
and discouraged], and He
saved me.
[7]Return to your rest, O my soul,
For the LORD has dealt bountifully
with you. [Matt 11:29]
[8]For You have rescued my life from
death,
My eyes from tears,
And my feet from stumbling *and*
falling.
[9]I will walk [in submissive wonder]
before the LORD
In the land of the living.
[10]I believed [and clung to my God]
when I said,
"I am greatly afflicted." [2 Cor 4:13]
[11]I said in my alarm,
"All men are liars."

[12]What will I give to the LORD [in
return]
For all His benefits toward me?
[How can I repay Him for His
precious blessings?]
[13]I will lift up the cup of salvation
And call on the name of the LORD.
[14]I will pay my vows to the LORD,
Yes, in the presence of all His
people.
[15]Precious [and of great consequence]
in the sight of the LORD
Is the death of His godly ones [so
He watches over them].
[16]O LORD, truly I am Your servant;
I am Your servant, the son of Your
handmaid;
You have unfastened my chains.
[17]I will offer to You the sacrifice of
thanksgiving,
And will call on the name of the
LORD.
[18]I will pay my vows to the LORD,
Yes, in the presence of all His
people,
[19]In the courts of the LORD's house
(temple)—
In the midst of you, O Jerusalem.
Praise the LORD! (Hallelujah!)

Psalm 117

A Psalm of Praise.

[1]O PRAISE the LORD, all you nations!
Praise Him, all you people!
[Rom 15:11]
[2]For His lovingkindness prevails
over us [and we triumph and
overcome through Him],
And the truth of the LORD endures
forever.
Praise the LORD! (Hallelujah!)

Psalm 118

Thanksgiving for the LORD's Saving Goodness.

[1]O GIVE thanks to the LORD, for He
is good;
For His lovingkindness endures
forever.

116:3 *sorrows of death.* These words point prophetically to the Savior's anguish on the cross (Mt 27:27–35).

116:10 *I believed . . . I said.* This belief is the hope of eternal life articulated in verse 9. Paul quotes this verse (translated "I believed, and therefore have I spoken") as proof of the scriptural hope of the resurrection (2Co 4:13).

116:13 *the cup of salvation.* This psalm is traditionally read after the Passover meal, following the third cup of wine, called the cup of salvation. How appropriate that this Passover psalm would call to mind God's cup of salvation the very night that the Savior was betrayed (Mt 26:27; Lk 22:14–22).

118:1 *give thanks.* This is the climax of the group of psalms called the Passover psalms.

3 Ps 18:4-6 **5** Ps 103:8; Ezr 9:15; Neh 9:8; Ps 119:137; 145:17 **7** Jer 6:16; Mt 11:29; Ps 13:6; 119:17 **8** Ps 56:13 **9** Ps 27:13 **10** 2Co 4:13 **11** Ps 31:22; Ro 3:4 **14** ver. 18; Ps 22:25; Jnh 2:9 **15** Ps 72:14 **16** Ps 119:125; 143:12; Ps 86:16 **17** Lev 7:12; Ps 50:14; 107:22 **19** Ps 96:8; 100:4 **PSALM 117** **1** Ro 15:11 **2** Ps 100:5 **PSALM 118** **1** 1Ch 16:8; Ps 106:1; 107:1

2 Oh let Israel say,
"His lovingkindness endures forever."
3 Oh let the house of Aaron say,
"His lovingkindness endures forever."
4 Oh let those who [reverently] fear the LORD, say,
"His lovingkindness endures forever."

5 Out of my distress I called on the LORD;
The LORD answered me and set me free.
6 The LORD is on my side; I will not fear.
What can [mere] man do to me? [Heb 13:6]
7 The LORD is on my side, He is among those who help me;
Therefore I will look [in triumph] on those who hate me.
8 It is better to take refuge in the LORD
Than to trust in man.
9 It is better to take refuge in the LORD
Than to trust in princes.

10 All nations encompassed me;
In the name of the LORD I will surely cut them off.
11 They encompassed me, yes, they surrounded me [on every side];
In the name of the LORD I will cut them off.
12 They swarmed around me like bees;
They flare up *and* are extinguished like a fire of thorns;
In the name of the LORD I will surely cut them off. [Deut 1:44]
13 You [my enemy] pushed me violently so that I was falling,
But the LORD helped me.
14 The LORD is my strength and song,
And He has become my salvation.

15 The sound of joyful shouting and salvation is in the tents of the righteous:
The right hand of the LORD does valiantly.
16 The right hand of the LORD is exalted;
The right hand of the LORD does valiantly.
17 I will not die, but live,
And declare the works *and* recount the illustrious acts of the LORD.
18 The LORD has disciplined me severely,
But He has not given me over to death. [2 Cor 6:9]

19 Open to me the [temple] gates of righteousness;
I shall enter through them, I shall give thanks to the LORD.
20 This is the gate of the LORD;
The righteous will enter through it. [Ps 24:7]
21 I will give thanks to You, for You have heard *and* answered me;

These psalms were probably sung by Jesus on the night before His death.

118:2 *His lovingkindness endures forever.* This refrain praises God's loyal, merciful, covenant love throughout the psalm.

118:9 *trust in princes.* Although relying on other people is part of living, our ultimate trust can only be placed in the Lord God. Even powerful rulers are limited by their own mortality (146:3).

118:13 *the LORD helped me.* Compare this to Paul's words in 2 Timothy 4:17 – 18. Deliverance always comes from God.

118:14 *my strength and song.* These words are a quotation from "the Song of Moses" (Ex 15:2); they are also quoted in Isaiah 12:2. The God who delivered the Israelites by dividing the waters of the Red Sea was ready to deliver the psalmist from trouble.

118:19 *Open to me the [temple] gates of righteousness.* The poet draws on the wording and imagery of Psalm 24. There is only One who can enter the gates of the Lord of His own accord — Jesus, the perfect King of glory.

118:20 *gate of the LORD.* The literal reference may be to the gate of Jerusalem, the city of God — or even to a gate of the temple. Jesus declared that He was the gate or door leading to salvation (Jn 10:9).

2 Ps 115:9 **5** Ps 120:1; 18:19 **6** Ps 27:1; Heb 13:6 **7** Ps 54:4; Ps 59:10 **8** Ps 40:4; 62:8,9 **9** Ps 146:3 **11** Ps 88:17 **12** Dt 1:44; Ecc 7:6; Na 1:10 **14** Ex 15:2; Isa 12:2 **16** Ex 15:6 **17** Ps 6:5; Hab 1:12; Ps 73:28 **18** 2Co 6:9 **19** Isa 26:2 **20** Ps 24:7; Isa 35:8; Rev 22:14 **21** Ps 116:1; ver. 14

And You have become my
salvation [my Rescuer, my
Savior].
22 The stone which the builders
rejected
Has become the chief corner
stone.
23 This is from the LORD *and* is His
doing;
It is marvelous in our eyes.
[Matt 21:42; Acts 4:11; 1 Pet 2:7]
24 This [day in which God has saved
me] is the day which the LORD
has made;
Let us rejoice and be glad in it.
25 O LORD, save now, we beseech
You;
O LORD, we beseech You, send now
prosperity *and* give us success!
26 Blessed is the one who comes in
the name of the LORD;
We have blessed you from the
house of the LORD [you who come
into His sanctuary under His
guardianship]. [Mark 11:9, 10]
27 The LORD is God, and He has given
us light [illuminating us with
His grace and freedom and joy].
Bind the festival sacrifices with
cords to the horns of the altar.
28 You are my God, and I give thanks
to You;
[You are] my God, I extol You.
29 O give thanks to the LORD, for He
is good;
For His lovingkindness endures
forever.

Psalm 119

Meditations and Prayers Relating to the Law of God.

א

Aleph.

1 HOW BLESSED *and* favored by
God are those whose way is
blameless [those with personal
integrity, the upright, the
guileless],
Who walk in the law [and who
are guided by the precepts and
revealed will] of the LORD.
2 Blessed *and* favored by God are
those who keep His testimonies,
And who [consistently] seek Him
and long for Him with all their
heart.
3 They do no unrighteousness;

118:22 *the chief corner stone.* The potent imagery of this verse depicts Jesus' rejection by many (Isa 53:3; Mk 8:31; Lk 9:22; 17:25). Jesus elaborated on this prophetic verse with the parable of the vineyard owner. In this parable, the rejection included the murder of the owner's son — a reference to God's only Son (Mk 12:1 – 12). But, even though the Savior was rejected, He was elevated to the right hand of God (Ac 7:56). The cross, the symbol of Jesus' rejection, has become the symbol of our salvation (1Co 1:18; Heb 12:2).
118:25 *save now.* These words are familiar to us in the transliteration of the Hebrew word "hosanna." The words are so significant that, if the people had not shouted them aloud (Mt 21:16) when Jesus entered Jerusalem, the stones would have had to shout them (Lk 19:40).
118:26 *Blessed is the one who comes.* These are the very words that the people used to bless Jesus as He rode into Jerusalem the week before the Passover (Mt 21:9; Mk 11:9; Lk 19:38).
119:1 *blessed . . . are those whose way is blameless.* This very lengthy poem is an acrostic. For each of the 22 consonants in the Hebrew alphabet, there are eight verses beginning with that letter. Within the psalm, eight words for God's law occur again and again: law, testimonies, promise, precepts, statutes, commandments, judgments, word. These words elaborate the application of the law of God to daily life and to Israel's destiny. ***the law . . . of the LORD.*** The Hebrew word *torah*, translated "law," basically means "instruction" or "direction." Broadly, it refers to all God's instructions from Moses to the prophets. More strictly, it refers to the first five books of the Old Testament. The law was never designed as a means of salvation; no one could be saved by keeping it. Instead, the law was the means for the Israelites to learn how to live as God's holy people. The psalmists consistently describe the law of God as a great blessing, for it was God's gracious revelation to His people for their own good (Dt 6:1 – 3). In the law, God mercifully pointed out the right path to follow. Only mistaken legalistic interpretations of the law prompted the negative statements in the New Testament.

22 Mt 21:42; Mk 12:10; Lk 20:17; Ac 4:11 **26** Mt 21:9; Mk 11:9; Lk 19:38; See Zec 4:7 **27** Est 8:16; 1Pe 2:9
28 Ex 15:2; Isa 25:1 **29** ver. 1 **PSALM 119** **1** Ps 128:1 **3** 1Jn 3:9; 5:18

They walk in His ways.
[1 John 3:9; 5:18]
4 You have ordained Your
precepts,
That we should follow them with
[careful] diligence.
5 Oh, that my ways may be
established
To observe *and* keep Your statutes
[obediently accepting and
honoring them]!
6 Then I will not be ashamed
When I look [with respect] to all
Your commandments [as my
guide].
7 I will give thanks to You with an
upright heart,
When I learn [through discipline]
Your righteous judgments [for
my transgressions].
8 I shall keep Your statutes;
Do not utterly abandon me
[when I fail].

ב

Beth.

9 How can a young man keep his
way pure?
By keeping watch [on himself]
according to Your word
[conforming his life to Your
precepts].
10 With all my heart I have sought
You, [inquiring of You and
longing for You];
Do not let me wander from
Your commandments [neither
through ignorance nor by willful
disobedience]. [2 Chr 15:15]
11 Your word I have treasured *and*
stored in my heart,
That I may not sin against You.
12 Blessed *and* reverently praised are
You, O LORD;
Teach me Your statutes.
13 With my lips I have told of
All the ordinances of Your mouth.
14 I have rejoiced in the way of Your
testimonies,
As much as in all riches.
15 I will meditate on Your precepts
And [thoughtfully] regard Your
ways [the path of life established
by Your precepts]. [Ps 104:34]
16 I will delight in Your statutes;
I will not forget Your word.

ג

Gimel.

17 Deal bountifully with Your servant,
That I may live and keep Your
word [treasuring it and being
guided by it day by day].
[Ps 119:97–101]

119:9 – 11 ***Your word.*** The Lord designs that His Word should bring purity (v. 9), security (v. 23), freedom (v. 45), hope (v. 49), life (v. 50), light (v. 105), and peace (v. 165).

119:9 God's Word Cleanses — One of the pieces of furniture in the Old Testament tabernacle was called the bronze laver (Ex 38:8). It was a huge upright bronze bowl filled with water, resting upon a pedestal. The priests would often stop at this laver to perform their ritualistic cleansings. The Word of God is like this laver. Only the Word can remove the filth and dirt from our hearts (1Pe 1:22) just as the bronze laver removed the physical impurities from the priests.

How can the Bible cleanse us? It can cleanse us from wrong thoughts (Ps 19:12; Ps 51:10; Php 4:8 – 9). It can help eliminate fear (Jdg 1:9). It can cleanse us from wrong actions (1Jn 1:9). Jesus directly promises all this: "You are already clean because of the word which I have given you" (Jn 15:3).

119:11 Memorizing Scripture — The Bible recognizes the importance of Scripture memorization. By memorizing the Word, we have access to it no matter where we are or what our circumstances. The following benefits can be cited:

It keeps us from sinning (Ps 119:11).

It provides comfort in times of trouble (Ps 119:52,92).

It provides daily sustenance for the spiritual life (Dt 8:3).

It provides continual and ready guidance in all the situations of life (Pr 6:20 – 23).

It provides the basis for formal and informal instruction of your children (Dt 6:6 – 7).

119:16 ***statutes.*** The Hebrew word translated "statutes" refers to something marked out as a boundary, something inscribed or engraved. Hence the word speaks of the permanence of the law, which God Himself had engraved in stone (Ex 24:12). The same word is often translated "decree" (2:7).

---

6 Job 22:26; 1Jn 2:28 **7** ver. 171 **10** 2Ch 15:15; ver. 21,118 **11** Ps 37:31; Lk 2:19 **12** ver. 26,33; Ps 25:4
13 Ps 34:11 **15** ver. 23,48; Ps 1:2 **16** Ps 1:2 **17** Ps 116:7

[18]Open my eyes [to spiritual truth]
so that I may behold
Wonderful things from Your law.
[19]I am a stranger on the earth;
Do not hide Your commandments
from me. [Gen 47:9; 1 Chr 29:15;
Ps 39:12; 2 Cor 5:6; Heb 11:13]
[20]My soul is crushed with longing
For Your ordinances at all times.
[21]You rebuke the presumptuous *and*
arrogant, the cursed *ones*,
Who wander from Your
commandments.
[22]Take reproach and contempt away
from me,
For I observe Your testimonies.
[23]Even though princes sit and talk to
one another against me,
Your servant meditates on Your
statutes.
[24]Your testimonies also are my
delight
And my counselors.

ד

Daleth.

[25]My earthly life clings to the dust;
Revive *and* refresh me according
to Your word. [Ps 143:11]
[26]I have told of my ways, and You
have answered me;
Teach me Your statutes.
[27]Make me understand the way of
Your precepts,
So that I will meditate (focus my
thoughts) on Your wonderful
works. [Ps 145:5, 6]
[28]My soul dissolves because of grief;
Renew *and* strengthen me
according to [the promises of]
Your word.
[29]Remove from me the way of
falsehood *and* unfaithfulness,
And graciously grant me Your law.
[30]I have chosen the faithful way;
I have placed Your ordinances
before me.
[31]I cling tightly to Your testimonies;
O LORD, do not put me to shame!
[32]I will run the way of Your
commandments [with purpose],
For You will give me a heart that is
willing.

ה

He.

[33]Teach me, O LORD, the way of Your
statutes,
And I will [steadfastly] observe it
to the end.
[34]Give me understanding [a
teachable heart and the ability
to learn], that I may keep Your
law;
And observe it with all my heart.
[Prov 2:6; James 1:5]
[35]Make me walk in the path of Your
commandments,
For I delight in it.
[36]Incline my heart to Your
testimonies
And not to *dishonest* gain *and*
envy. [Ezek 33:31; Mark 7:21, 22;
1 Tim 6:10; Heb 13:5]
[37]Turn my eyes away from vanity
[all those worldly, meaningless
things that distract—let Your
priorities be mine],
And restore me [with renewed
energy] in Your ways.
[38]Establish Your word *and* confirm
Your promise to Your servant,
As that which produces [awe-
inspired] reverence for You.
[Deut 10:12; Ps 96:9]
[39]Turn away my reproach which I
dread,
For Your ordinances are good.

119:22 *testimonies.* The Hebrew word translated "testimonies" is derived from the verb meaning "to witness" or "to testify." It refers to the Ten Commandments, called the "two tablets of the testimony" (Ex 31:18). The commandments were a testimony because they were a witness to the Israelites of their faithfulness or unfaithfulness to the covenant (Dt 31:26).

119:37 *Your ways.* The will of God is like a path leading to life; His ways are a reflection of His good character.

19 Ge 47:9; 1Ch 29:15; Ps 39:12; 2Co 5:6; Heb 11:13 **20** Ps 42:1,2; 63:1; 84:2 **21** ver. 10,110 **22** Ps 39:8 **23** ver. 15 **24** ver. 77,92 **25** Ps 44:25; Ps 143:11 **26** Ps 25:4; 27:11; 86:11 **27** Ps 145:5,6 **28** Ps 107:26 **32** 1Ki 4:29; Isa 60:5; 2Co 6:11 **33** ver. 12; Mt 10:22; Rev 2:26 **35** ver. 16 **36** Eze 33:31; Mk 7:21; Lk 12:15; Heb 13:5 **37** Isa 33:15; Pr 23:5 **38** 2Sa 7:25

40 I long for Your precepts;
Renew me through Your righteousness.

ו
Vav.

41 May Your lovingkindness also come to me, O LORD,
Your salvation according to Your promise;
42 So I will have an answer for the one who taunts me,
For I trust [completely] in Your word [and its reliability].
43 And do not take the word of truth utterly out of my mouth,
For I wait for Your ordinances.
44 I will keep Your law continually,
Forever and ever [writing Your precepts on my heart].
45 And I will walk at liberty,
For I seek *and* deeply long for Your precepts.
46 I will also speak of Your testimonies before kings
And shall not be ashamed. [Ps 138:1; Matt 10:18, 19; Acts 26:1, 2]
47 For I shall delight in Your commandments,
Which I love.
48 And I shall lift up my hands to Your commandments,
Which I love;
And I will meditate on Your statutes.

ז
Zayin.

49 Remember [always] the word *and* promise to Your servant,
In which You have made me hope.
50 This is my comfort in my affliction,
That Your word has revived me *and* given me life. [Rom 15:4]
51 The arrogant utterly ridicule me,
Yet I do not turn away from Your law.
52 I have remembered [carefully] Your ancient ordinances, O LORD,
And I have taken comfort.
53 Burning indignation has seized me because of the wicked,
Who reject Your law.
54 Your statutes are my songs
In the house of my pilgrimage.
55 O LORD, I remember Your name in the night,
And keep Your law.
56 This has become mine [as the gift of Your grace],
That I observe Your precepts [accepting them with loving obedience].

ח
Heth.

57 The LORD is my portion;
I have promised to keep Your words.
58 I sought Your favor with all my heart;
Be merciful *and* gracious to me according to Your promise.
59 I considered my ways
And turned my feet to [follow and obey] Your testimonies.
60 I hurried and did not delay
To keep Your commandments.
61 The cords of the wicked have encircled *and* ensnared me,
But I have not forgotten Your law.
62 At midnight I will rise to give thanks to You
Because of Your righteous ordinances.
63 I am a companion of all who [reverently] fear You,
And of those who keep *and* honor Your precepts.

119:45 *at liberty.* Many think of laws, instructions, and commandments as limiting and restricting, but the law of God paradoxically frees us. It frees us from sin (v. 133) and gives us the peace that comes from following the Lord's instructions (v. 165).

119:56 *precepts.* This Hebrew word means "an appointed thing," "something for which one is given charge." The word has the same idea as "commandment" for both words assume that the One who commands has the authority to "take charge" or "appoint" (v. 4).

40 ver. 20; ver. 25,37 **41** ver. 77; Ps 106:4 **46** Ps 138:1; Mt 10:18; Ac 26 **47** ver. 16 **48** ver. 15 **49** ver. 74,81 **50** Ro 15:4 **51** Jer 20:7; ver. 157; Job 23:11; Ps 44:18 **53** Ezr 9:3 **55** Ps 63:6 **57** Ps 16:5; Jer 10:16; La 3:24 **58** ver. 41 **59** Lk 15:17 **62** Ac 16:25

64 The earth, O Lord, is full of Your lovingkindness *and* goodness;
Teach me Your statutes.

ט
Teth.

65 You have dealt well with Your servant,
O Lord, according to Your promise.
66 Teach me good judgment (discernment) and knowledge,
For I have believed *and* trusted *and* relied on Your commandments.
67 Before I was afflicted I went astray,
But now I keep *and* honor Your word [with loving obedience].
68 You are good and do good;
Teach me Your statutes.
69 The arrogant have forged a lie against me,
But I will keep Your precepts with all my heart.
70 Their heart is insensitive like fat [their minds are dull and brutal],
But I delight in Your law.
71 It is good for me that I have been afflicted,
That I may learn Your statutes.
72 The law from Your mouth is better to me
Than thousands of gold and silver *pieces*.

י
Yodh.

73 Your hands have made me and established me;
Give me understanding *and* a teachable heart, that I may learn Your commandments.
74 May those who [reverently] fear You see me and be glad,
Because I wait for Your word.
75 I know, O Lord, that Your judgments are fair,
And that in faithfulness You have disciplined me. [Heb 12:10]
76 O may Your lovingkindness *and* graciousness comfort me,
According to Your word (promise) to Your servant.
77 Let Your compassion come to me that I may live,
For Your law is my delight.
78 Let the arrogant be ashamed *and* humiliated, for they sabotage me with a lie;
But I will meditate on Your precepts.
79 May those who fear You [with submissive wonder] turn to me,
Even those who have known Your testimonies.
80 May my heart be blameless in Your statutes,
So that I will not be ashamed.

כ
Kaph.

81 My soul languishes *and* grows weak for Your salvation;
I wait for Your word.
82 My eyes fail [with longing, watching] for [the fulfillment of] Your promise,
Saying, "When will You comfort me?"
83 For I have become like a wineskin [blackened and shriveled] in the smoke [in which it hangs],
Yet I do not forget Your statutes.
84 How many are the days of Your servant [which he must endure]?
When will You execute judgment on those who persecute me? [Rev 6:10]
85 The arrogant (godless) have dug pits for me,
Men who do not conform to Your law.

119:70 *delight.* This is not the delight of a passive observer, but the delight of a disciple who has staked his life and security on a cause or principle.
119:82 *Your promise.* The Hebrew term for "promise" is derived from the verb "to say." The term is a general word for God's law, encompassing everything that the Lord has promised and spoken.

64 Ps 33:5; ver. 12,26 **67** ver. 71; Jer 31:18; Heb 12:11 **68** Ps 106:1; 107:1; Mt 19:17; ver. 12,26 **69** Job 13:4; Ps 109:2 **70** Ps 17:10; Isa 6:10; Ac 28:27; ver. 35 **71** ver. 67; Heb 12:10 **72** Ps 19:10; Pr 8:10,11,19 **73** Job 10:8; Ps 100:3; 138:8; 139:14; ver. 34,144 **74** Ps 34:2; ver. 49,147 **75** Heb 12:10 **77** ver. 41; ver. 24,47 **78** Ps 25:3; ver. 86; ver. 23 **81** Ps 73:26; 84:2; ver. 74,114 **82** ver. 123; Ps 69:3 **83** Job 30:30 **84** Ps 39:4; Rev 6:10 **85** Ps 35:7; Pr 16:27

86 All Your commandments are
faithful *and* trustworthy.
They have persecuted me with a
lie; help me [LORD]!
87 They had almost destroyed me
on earth,
But as for me, I did not turn away
from Your precepts.
88 According to Your steadfast love
refresh me *and* give me life,
So that I may keep *and* obey the
testimony of Your mouth.

ל

Lamedh.

89 Forever, O LORD,
Your word is settled in
heaven [standing firm and
unchangeable]. [Ps 89:2;
Matt 24:34, 35; 1 Pet 1:25]
90 Your faithfulness *continues* from
generation to generation;
You have established the earth,
and it stands [securely].
91 They continue this day according
to Your ordinances,
For all things [all parts of the
universe] are Your servants.
[Jer 33:25]
92 If Your law had not been my
delight,
Then I would have perished in my
time of trouble.
93 I will never forget Your precepts,
For by them You have revived me
and given me life.
94 I am Yours, save me [as Your own];
For I have [diligently] sought Your
precepts *and* required them [as
my greatest need]. [Ps 42:1]
95 The wicked wait for me to
destroy me,
But I will consider Your
testimonies.
96 I have seen that all [human]
perfection has its limits [no
matter how grand and perfect
and noble];
Your commandment is
exceedingly broad *and* extends
without limits [into eternity].
[Rom 3:10–19]

מ

Mem.

97 Oh, how I love Your law!
It is my meditation all the day.
[Ps 1:2]
98 Your commandments make me
wiser than my enemies,
For Your words are always
with me.
99 I have better understanding *and*
deeper insight than all my
teachers [because of Your word],
For Your testimonies are my
meditation. [2 Tim 3:15]
100 I understand more than the aged
[who have not observed Your
precepts],
Because I have observed *and* kept
Your precepts.
101 I have restrained my feet from
every evil way,
That I may keep Your word.
[Prov 1:15]
102 I have not turned aside from Your
ordinances,
For You Yourself have taught me.
103 How sweet are Your words to my
taste,
Sweeter than honey to my mouth!
[Ps 19:10; Prov 8:11]
104 From Your precepts I get
understanding;
Therefore I hate every false way.

נ

Nun.

105 Your word is a lamp to my feet
And a light to my path. [Prov 6:23]
106 I have sworn [an oath] and have
confirmed it,
That I will keep Your righteous
ordinances. [Neh 10:29]

119:97 ***how I love Your law.*** Fundamentally, the psalmist's attraction to the law is the result of his love for God Himself, his Teacher (vv. 102,132).

119:105 ***a light to my path.*** God's word is a guide for everyday living.

86 ver. 78; Ps 35:19 **88** ver. 40 **89** Ps 89:2; Mt 24:34; 1Pe 1:25 **91** Jer 33:25 **92** ver. 24 **96** Mt 5:18
97 Ps 1:2 **98** Dt 4:6 **99** 2Ti 3:15 **100** Job 32:7-9 **101** Pr 1:15 **103** Ps 19:10; Pr 8:11 **104** ver. 128 **105** Pr 6:23
106 Neh 10:29

[107] I am greatly afflicted;
Renew *and* revive me [giving me life], O LORD, according to Your word.
[108] Accept *and* take pleasure in the freewill offerings of my mouth, O LORD,
And teach me Your ordinances. [Hos 14:2; Heb 13:15]
[109] My life is continually in my hand,
Yet I do not forget Your law.
[110] The wicked have laid a snare for me,
Yet I do not wander from Your precepts.
[111] I have taken Your testimonies as a heritage forever,
For they are the joy of my heart. [Deut 33:4]
[112] I have inclined my heart to perform Your statutes
Forever, even to the end.

ס
Samekh.

[113] I hate those who are double-minded,
But I love *and* treasure Your law.
[114] You are my hiding place and my shield;
I wait for Your word. [Ps 32:7; 91:1]
[115] Leave me, you evildoers,
That I may keep the commandments of my God [honoring and obeying them]. [Ps 6:8; 139:19; Matt 7:23]
[116] Uphold me according to Your word [of promise], so that I may live;
And do not let me be ashamed of my hope [in Your great goodness]. [Ps 25:2; Rom 5:5; 9:33; 10:11]
[117] Uphold me that I may be safe,
That I may have regard for Your statutes continually.
[118] You have turned Your back on all those who wander from Your statutes,
For their deceitfulness is useless.
[119] You have removed all the wicked of the earth like dross [for they have no value];
Therefore I love Your testimonies.
[120] My flesh trembles in [reverent] fear of You,
And I am afraid *and* in awe of Your judgments.

ע
Ayin.

[121] I have done justice and righteousness;
Do not leave me to those who oppress me.
[122] Be the guarantee for Your servant for good [as Judah was the guarantee for Benjamin];
Do not let the arrogant oppress me. [Gen 43:9]
[123] My eyes fail [with longing, watching] for [the fulfillment of] Your salvation,
And for [the fulfillment of] Your righteous word.
[124] Deal with Your servant according to Your [gracious] lovingkindness,
And teach me Your statutes.
[125] I am Your servant; give me understanding [the ability to learn and a teachable heart]
That I may know Your testimonies.
[126] It is time for the LORD to act;
They have broken Your law.
[127] Therefore I love Your commandments more than gold,
Yes, more than refined gold.
[128] Therefore I esteem as right all Your precepts concerning everything;
I hate every false way.

פ
Pe.

[129] Your testimonies are wonderful;
Therefore my soul keeps them.

119:127 *commandments.* This word alludes to God's authority to govern His people. The commandments of God help believers to find their way in a world that is filled with confusion, sin, and error.

107 ver. 88 **108** Hos 14:2; Heb 13:15; ver. 12,26 **109** Job 13:14 **110** Ps 140:5; ver. 10,21 **111** Dt 33:4; ver. 77,92 **112** ver. 33 **114** Ps 32:7; ver. 81 **115** Ps 6:8; Mt 7:23 **116** Ps 25:2; Ro 5:5 **118** ver. 21 **119** Eze 22:18 **120** Hab 3:16 **122** Heb 7:22 **123** ver. 81,82 **124** ver. 12 **125** Ps 116:16 **127** Ps 19:10 **128** ver. 104

[130]The unfolding of Your [glorious] words give light;
Their unfolding gives understanding to the simple (childlike).
[131]I opened my mouth and panted [with anticipation],
Because I longed for Your commandments.
[132]Turn to me and be gracious to me *and* show me favor,
As is Your way to those who love Your name.
[133]Establish my footsteps in [the way of] Your word;
Do not let any human weakness have power over me [causing me to be separated from You].
[134]Redeem me from the oppression of man;
That I may keep Your precepts. [Luke 1:74]
[135]Make Your face shine [with pleasure] upon Your servant,
And teach me Your statutes. [Ps 4:6]
[136]My eyes weep streams of water
Because people do not keep Your law.

צ
Tsadhe.

[137]Righteous are You, O LORD,
And upright are Your judgments.
[138]You have commanded Your testimonies in righteousness
And in great faithfulness.
[139]My zeal has [completely] consumed me,
Because my enemies have forgotten Your words.
[140]Your word is very pure (refined);
Therefore Your servant loves it.
[141]I am small and despised,
But I do not forget Your precepts.
[142]Your righteousness is an everlasting righteousness,
And Your law is truth. [Ps 19:9; John 17:17]
[143]Trouble and anguish have found me,
Yet Your commandments are my delight *and* my joy.
[144]Your righteous testimonies are everlasting;
Give me understanding [the ability to learn and a teachable heart] that I may live.

ק
Qoph.

[145]I cried with all my heart; answer me, O LORD!
I will observe Your statutes.
[146]I cried to You; save me
And I will keep Your testimonies.
[147]I rise before dawn and cry [in prayer] for help;
I wait for Your word.
[148]My eyes anticipate the night watches *and* I awake before the call of the watchman,
That I may meditate on Your word.
[149]Hear my voice according to Your [steadfast] lovingkindness;
O LORD, renew *and* refresh me according to Your ordinances.
[150]Those who follow after wickedness approach;
They are far from Your law.
[151]You are near, O LORD,
And all Your commandments are truth.
[152]Of old I have known from Your testimonies
That You have founded them forever. [Luke 21:33]

119:136 *streams of waters.* One of the earmarks of a true believer is the remorse and sorrow that is felt when the person sins and fails to keep God's law.
119:149 *renew and refresh.* With these words, the psalmist begs God to transform him, to breathe new life back into his soul. The psalmist does not want his obedience to be mechanical; he asks for a renewed spirit. The basis for his plea is God's covenantal love and His just nature.

130 Ps 19:7 **131** ver. 20 **132** Ps 106:4; 2Th 1:6 **133** Ps 17:5; Ps 19:13; Ro 6:12 **134** Lk 1:74 **135** Ps 4:6; ver. 12,26 **136** Jer 9:1; Eze 9:4 **137** Neh 9:33 **138** Ps 19:7-9 **139** Ps 69:9; Jn 2:17 **140** Ps 12:6 **142** Ps 19:9 **143** ver. 77 **144** ver. 34,73 **147** Ps 5:3; ver. 74 **148** Ps 63:1,6 **149** ver. 40 **151** Ps 145:18; ver. 142 **152** Lk 21:33

ר

Resh.

[153] Look upon my agony and
rescue me,
For I do not forget Your law.
[154] Plead my cause and redeem me;
Revive me *and* give me life
according to [the promise of]
Your word.
[155] Salvation is far from the wicked,
For they do not seek Your statutes.
[156] Great are Your tender mercies *and*
steadfast love, O LORD;
Revive me *and* give me life
according to Your ordinances.
[157] Many are my persecutors and my
adversaries,
Yet I do not turn away from Your
testimonies.
[158] I see the treacherous and loathe
them,
Because they do not respect
Your law.
[159] Consider how I love Your precepts;
Revive me *and* give me life,
O LORD, according to Your
lovingkindness.
[160] The sum of Your word is truth
[the full meaning of all Your
precepts],
And every one of Your righteous
ordinances endures forever.

ש

Shin.

[161] Princes persecute me without cause,
But my heart stands in [reverent]
awe of Your words [so I
can expect You to help me].
[1 Sam 24:11, 14; 26:18]
[162] I rejoice at Your word,
As one who finds great treasure.
[163] I hate and detest falsehood,
But I love Your law.
[164] Seven times a day I praise You,
Because of Your righteous
ordinances.
[165] Those who love Your law have
great peace;
Nothing makes them stumble.
[Prov 3:2; Is 32:17]
[166] I hope *and* wait [with complete
confidence] for Your salvation,
O LORD,
And I do Your commandments.
[Gen 49:18]
[167] My soul keeps Your testimonies
[hearing and accepting and
obeying them];
I love them greatly.
[168] I keep Your precepts and Your
testimonies,
For all my ways are [fully known]
before You.

ת

Tav.

[169] Let my [mournful] cry come before
You, O LORD;
Give me understanding [the ability
to learn and a teachable heart]
according to Your word [of
promise].
[170] Let my supplication come before
You;
Deliver me according to Your word.
[171] Let my lips speak praise [with
thanksgiving],
For You teach me Your statutes.
[172] Let my tongue sing [praise for the
fulfillment] of Your word,
For all Your commandments are
righteous.
[173] Let Your hand be ready to
help me,
For I have chosen Your precepts.
[174] I long for Your salvation, O LORD,
And Your law is my delight.
[175] Let my soul live that it may praise
You,
And let Your ordinances help me.

119:159 ***lovingkindness.*** The "lovingkindness" of God is a recurring theme in the Book of Psalms, describing His loyal, covenant love and merciful care of His people.

119:162 ***rejoice.*** Jesus also described the "kingdom of God" as a great treasure, one so valuable that it would be worth selling everything one had in order to possess it (Mt 13:44–46).

153 La 5:1 **154** 1Sa 24:15; ver. 40 **155** Job 5:4 **156** ver. 149 **157** Ps 44:18 **158** Eze 9:4 **159** ver. 88 **160** Jn 17:17 **161** 1Sa 24:11 **165** Pr 3:2; Isa 32:17 **166** Ge 49:18 **168** Pr 5:21 **169** ver. 144 **171** ver. 7 **173** Jos 24:22 **174** ver. 166; ver. 16,24

176 I have gone astray like a lost
sheep;
Seek Your servant, for I do not
forget Your commandments.
[Is 53:6; Luke 15:4; 1 Pet 2:25]

Psalm 120

Prayer for Breaking Away from the Treacherous.

A Song of Ascents.

1 IN MY trouble I cried to the
LORD,
And He answered me.
2 Rescue my soul, O LORD, from
lying lips,
And from a deceitful tongue.
3 What shall be given to you, and
what more shall be done
to you,
You deceitful tongue?—
4 Sharp arrows of the warrior,
With the burning coals of the
broom tree.
5 Woe to me, for I sojourn in
Meshech,
and I live among the tents of
Kedar [among hostile people]!
[Gen 10:2; 25:13; Jer 49:28, 29]
6 Too long my soul has had its
dwelling
With those who hate peace.
7 I am for peace, but when I speak,
They are for war.

Psalm 121

The LORD the Keeper of Israel.

A Song of Ascents.

1 I WILL lift up my eyes to the hills
[of Jerusalem]—
From where shall my help come?
[Jer 3:23]
2 My help comes from the LORD,
Who made heaven and earth.
3 He will not allow your foot
to slip;
He who keeps you will not
slumber. [1 Sam 2:9; Ps 127:1;
Prov 3:23, 26; Is 27:3]
4 Behold, He who keeps Israel
Will neither slumber [briefly] nor
sleep [soundly].
5 The LORD is your keeper;
The LORD is your shade on your
right hand. [Is 25:4]
6 The sun will not strike you
by day,
Nor the moon by night. [Ps 91:5;
Is 49:10; Rev 7:16]
7 The LORD will protect you from
all evil;
He will keep your life.
8 The LORD will guard your
going out and your coming in
[everything that you do]
From this time forth and forever.
[Deut 28:6; Prov 2:8; 3:6]

119:176 *like a lost sheep.* Jesus, the Messiah, described Himself as the Good Shepherd who would lay down His own life in order to protect and rescue His sheep (Jn 10:11). He affirmed that God does indeed seek lost sinners in order to bring them to Himself (Lk 15:3–7).

120:1 *In my trouble I cried.* This psalm is the first of a group of psalms called the Songs of Ascent (120–134). This group of hymns was probably used by pilgrims making their way to Jerusalem to worship the Lord during the three annual feasts—Passover, Pentecost, and Tabernacles (Lev 23). Since Jerusalem is on a high hill, a traveler always goes "up" to Jerusalem; hence the term "songs of ascent."

120:5 *Meshech . . . Kedar.* These seem to be examples of the pagan peoples among whom the psalmist had to live.

121:1 *my eyes to the hills.* This Song of Ascent (see Ps 120) dramatically pictures a traveler approaching the city of Jerusalem.

121:2 *from the LORD.* As comforting as the sight of the holy city would be to a pilgrim, the psalmist emphasizes the real reason for rejoicing: God's tender care for His people. ***Who made.*** We might have expected the psalmist to emphasize God as a loving heavenly Father or a tender and compassionate Savior, but instead he ascribes our everlasting safety to the God of creation. God owns the world because He made it; nothing that happens is beyond Him.

121:6 *Nor the moon by night.* There is never a time when the Lord is "off duty" and does not see what is happening to His people.

176 Isa 53:6 **PSALM 120** **1** Jnh 2:2 **5** Ge 10:2; Eze 27:13; Ge 25:13; 1Sa 25:1; Jer 49:28 **PSALM 121** **1** Jer 3:23 **2** Ps 124:8 **3** 1Sa 2:9; Ps 127:1; Isa 27:3 **5** Isa 25:4; Ps 16:8 **6** Ps 91:5; Isa 49:10 **7** Ps 41:2 **8** Dt 28:6

Psalm 122

Prayer for the Peace of Jerusalem.

A Song of Ascents. Of David.

1 I WAS glad when they said
to me,
"Let us go to the house of the
LORD." [Is 2:3; Zech 8:21]
2 Our feet are standing
Within your gates, O Jerusalem,
3 Jerusalem, that is built
As a city that is firmly joined
together;
4 To which the [twelve] tribes go up,
even the tribes of the LORD,
[As was decreed as] an ordinance
for Israel,
To give thanks to the name of the
LORD.
5 For there the thrones of judgment
were set,
The thrones of the house of David.

6 Pray for the peace of Jerusalem:
"May they prosper who love you
[holy city].
7 "May peace be within your
walls
And prosperity within your
palaces."
8 For the sake of my brothers and
my friends,
I will now say, "May peace be
within you."
9 For the sake of the house of
the LORD our God [which is
Jerusalem],
I will seek your (the city's) good.

Psalm 123

Prayer for the LORD's Help.

A Song of Ascents.

1 UNTO YOU I lift up my eyes,
O You who are enthroned in the
heavens!
2 Behold, as the eyes of servants
look to the hand of their master,
And as the eyes of a maid to the
hand of her mistress,
So our eyes look to the LORD our
God,
Until He is gracious *and* favorable
toward us.

3 Be gracious to us, O LORD, be
gracious *and* favorable toward us,
For we are greatly filled with
contempt.
4 Our soul is greatly filled
With the scoffing of those who are
at ease,
And with the contempt of the
proud [who disregard God's law].

Psalm 124

Praise for Rescue from Enemies.

A Song of Ascents. Of David.

1 "IF IT had not been the LORD who
was on our side,"
Let Israel now say,
2 "If it had not been the LORD who
was on our side
When men rose up against us,

122:1 *I was glad.* This third Song of Ascent (see Ps 120) describes the joy of the pilgrim on arriving at Jerusalem to worship God.
122:4 *the [twelve] tribes go up.* This refers to the three annual feasts of ancient Israel (Lev 23), as well as to any time that an individual or family needed to worship the Lord in the holy city.
122:5 *thrones of judgment.* Jerusalem was not only the central place for worship, it was also the site where civil judgments and decisions were made. Religious and civil issues were closely intertwined in the law of God.
122:6 *the peace of Jerusalem.* True peace will only come when the Prince of Peace returns to establish His rule (Ps 98:5 – 6; Rev 21:9 – 27)
123:2 *as the eyes of servants.* Good servants keep watch over their masters, anticipating their wants and keeping themselves in constant readiness to obey orders. In the same way, we should keep ourselves focused on pleasing God. The more we look at Him, the more we become like Him (2Co 3:18).
124:1 *the LORD who was on our side.* It is because God is "on our side" that He sent His Son to save the world (Jn 3:16).

PSALM 122 1 Isa 2:3; Zec 8:21 3 See 2Sa 5:9 4 Ex 23:17; Dt 16:16; Ex 16:34 5 Dt 17:8; 2Ch 19:8 6 Ps 51:18 9 Neh 2:10 **PSALM 123** 1 Ps 121:1; 141:8; Ps 2:4; 11:4; 115:3 **PSALM 124** 1 Ps 129:1

[3]Then they would have [quickly] swallowed us alive,
When their wrath was kindled against us;
[4]Then the waters would have engulfed us,
The torrent would have swept over our soul;
[5]Then the raging waters would have swept over our soul."

[6]Blessed be the LORD,
Who has not given us as prey to be torn by their teeth.
[7]We have escaped like a bird from the snare of the fowlers;
The trap is broken and we have escaped.
[8]Our help is in the name of the LORD,
Who made heaven and earth.

Psalm 125

The LORD Surrounds His People.

A Song of Ascents.

[1]THOSE WHO trust in *and* rely on the LORD [with confident expectation]
Are like Mount Zion, which cannot be moved but remains forever.
[2]As the mountains surround Jerusalem,
So the LORD surrounds His people
From this time forth and forever.
[3]For the scepter of wickedness shall not rest on the land of the righteous,
So that the righteous will not reach out their hands to do wrong.

[4]Do good, O LORD, to those who are good
And to those who are upright in their hearts.
[5]But as for those who turn aside to their crooked ways [in unresponsiveness to God],
The LORD will lead them away with those who do evil.
Peace be upon Israel.

Psalm 126

Thanksgiving for Return from Captivity.

A Song of Ascents.

[1]WHEN THE LORD brought back the captives to Zion (Jerusalem),
We were like those who dream [it seemed so unreal]. [Ps 53:6; Acts 12:9]
[2]Then our mouth was filled with laughter
And our tongue with joyful shouting;
Then they said among the nations,
"The LORD has done great things for them."
[3]The LORD has done great things for us;
We are glad!

[4]Restore our captivity, O LORD,
As the stream-beds in the South (the Negev) [are restored by torrents of rain].
[5]They who sow in tears shall reap with joyful singing.
[6]He who goes back and forth weeping, carrying his bag of seed [for planting],
Will indeed come again with a shout of joy, bringing his sheaves with him.

124:6 *Blessed be the LORD.* To bless God is to identify Him as the source of our blessings (103:2).
125:2 *the mountains surround Jerusalem.* Jerusalem is built on one of seven mountain peaks in the region. The mountains provided some protection for the city, since any invading army would have to march through difficult terrain to reach the city.
126:1 *brought back the captives.* This seventh Song of Ascent (see Ps 120) comes from the time of the restoration of Jerusalem, following the Babylonian captivity.
126:4 *Restore our captivity.* The people who returned were a small percentage of those who had been exiled; the people still prayed that God would complete the restoration of His people to their land.

3 Ps 56:1,2; 57:3; Pr 1:12 **7** Ps 91:3; Pr 6:5 **8** Ps 121:2; Ge 1:1; Ps 134:3 **PSALM 125** **3** Pr 22:8; Isa 14:5 **5** Pr 2:15; Ps 128:6 **PSALM 126** **1** Ps 53:6; Ps 85:1; Hos 6:11; Joel 3:1; Ac 12:9 **2** Job 8:21 **5** See Jer 31:9

Psalm 127

Prosperity Comes from the LORD.

A Song of Ascents. Of Solomon.

1 UNLESS THE LORD builds the house,
They labor in vain who build it;
Unless the LORD guards the city,
The watchman keeps awake in vain. [Ps 121:1, 3, 5]
2 It is vain for you to rise early,
To retire late,
To eat the bread of anxious labors—
For He gives [blessings] to His beloved *even in his* sleep.

3 Behold, children are a heritage *and* gift from the LORD,
The fruit of the womb a reward. [Deut 28:4]
4 Like arrows in the hand of a warrior,
So are the children of one's youth.
5 How blessed [happy and fortunate] is the man whose quiver is filled with them;
They will not be ashamed
When they speak with their enemies [in gatherings] at the [city] gate.

Psalm 128

Blessedness of the Fear of the LORD.

A Song of Ascents.

1 BLESSED [HAPPY and sheltered by God's favor] is everyone who fears the LORD [and worships Him with obedience],
Who walks in His ways *and* lives according to His commandments. [Ps 1:1, 2]
2 For you shall eat the fruit of [the labor of] your hands,
You will be happy *and* blessed and it will be well with you.
3 Your wife shall be like a fruitful vine
Within the innermost part of your house;
Your children will be like olive plants
Around your table.
4 Behold, for so shall the man be blessed *and* divinely favored
Who fears the LORD [and worships Him with obedience].

5 May the LORD bless you from Zion [His holy mountain],
And may you see the prosperity of Jerusalem all the days of your life;
6 Indeed, may you see your [family perpetuated in your] children's children.
Peace be upon Israel!

Psalm 129

Prayer for the Overthrow of Zion's Enemies.

A Song of Ascents.

1 "MANY TIMES they have persecuted me (Israel) from my youth,"
Let Israel now say,
2 "Many times they have persecuted me from my youth,
Yet they have not prevailed against me.

127:1 *Unless the LORD.* This psalm, the eighth Song of Ascent (see Ps 120), is one of only two psalms attributed to Solomon (see Ps 72).
127:2 *bread of anxious labors.* This phrase captures the essence of those removed from a sense of the Lord in their lives. The food that should give them strength for life and a zest for living only maintains their miserable state.
127:5 *at the [city] gate.* The gate was the place where the elders of the city met and where citizens would convene (Ru 4:1 – 12).
128:1 *Blessed.* This word describes the happiness of those who trust in the Lord and do His will (127:5). ***fears.*** The fear of God is an attitude of respect, a response of reverence and wonder. It is the only appropriate response to our Creator and Redeemer.
128:2 *the fruit of [the labor of] your hands.* There is a reward in work and a satisfaction in labor that is a blessing of God (Ecc 3:9 – 13).
129:1 – 4 *Many times.* The psalm begins with

PSALM 127 **1** Ps 121:3-5 **2** Ge 3:17,19 **3** Ge 33:5; 48:4; Jos 24:3,4; Dt 28:4 **5** Job 5:4; Pr 27:11
PSALM 128 **1** Ps 119:1 **2** Isa 3:10 **3** Eze 19:10; Ps 52:8; 144:12 **5** Ps 134:3 **6** Ge 50:23; Job 42:16; Ps 125:5 **PSALM 129** **1** Eze 23:3; Hos 2:15; Ps 124:1

3 "The [enemies, like] plowers
plowed on my back;
They made their furrows [of
suffering] long [in Israel]."
4 The LORD is righteous;
He has cut in two the [thick] cords
of the wicked [which enslaved
the people of Israel].

5 May all who hate Zion
Be put to shame and turned
backward [in defeat].
6 Let them be like the grass on the
housetops,
Which withers before it grows up,
7 With which the reaper does not fill
his hand,
Nor the binder of sheaves his arms,
8 Nor do those who pass by say,
"The blessing of the LORD be
upon you;
We bless you in the name of the
LORD."

Psalm 130

Hope in the LORD's Forgiving Love.

A Song of Ascents.

1 OUT OF the depths [of distress] I
have cried to You, O LORD.
2 Lord, hear my voice!
Let Your ears be attentive
To the voice of my
supplications.
3 If You, LORD, should keep an
account of our sins *and* treat us
accordingly,
O Lord, who could stand [before
you in judgment and claim
innocence]? [Ps 143:2; Rom 3:20;
Gal 2:16]
4 But there is forgiveness with
You,
That You may be feared *and*
worshiped [with submissive
wonder]. [Deut 10:12]

5 I wait [patiently] for the
LORD, my soul [expectantly]
waits,
And in His word do I
hope.
6 My soul waits for the
Lord
More than the watchmen for
the morning;
More than the watchmen for
the morning.
7 O Israel, hope in the LORD;
For with the LORD there is
lovingkindness,
And with Him is abundant
redemption.
8 And He will redeem Israel
From all his sins.

---

a liturgy of suffering, as the people of God acknowledge that throughout their history in the land they have been under constant assault by various peoples.

129:6 *grass on the housetops.* Sod was sometimes used on the roofs of the houses. After a spring rain, there might be grass growing on the housetop, but this was not grass that flourished; it lacked roots and soon withered under the summer heat.

130:1 *Out of the depths.* The placement of this penitential psalm is fitting. We must not be so interested in the destruction of the wicked (Ps 129) that we fail to understand our own heart before the Lord.

130:3 *sins.* Does the Lord keep a record of our sins? The answer is both yes and no. At the end of all things, Christ will sit on the judgment seat, the books will be opened, and everyone will be judged according to the actual record (Rev 20:11 – 15). However, if we cry to Him for mercy now in this life, we shall find forgiveness. Then the record of our sins will be cast away into the depth of God's forgetfulness. They are covered by the blood of Jesus.

130:4 *forgiveness . . . That You may be feared.* God's provision for forgiveness is not to be taken lightly (Ro 6:1 – 2). The truly forgiven sinner realizes the magnitude of God's grace, remains grateful for Jesus' sacrifice for sins, and lives in the fear or awe of God (Ps 128).

130:8 *He will redeem.* God had redeemed the people from slavery in Egypt; the psalmist also looked forward to the time when He would redeem the people from slavery to their own sinful natures, through the death and resurrection of Jesus Christ (Gal 3:13).

6 Ps 37:2 **8** Ru 2:4; Ps 118:26 **PSALM 130** **1** La 3:55; Jnh 2:2 **3** Ps 143:2; Ro 3:20 **4** Ex 34:7; 1Ki 8:40; Ps 2:11; Jer 33:8 **5** Ps 27:14; Isa 8:17; Ps 119:81 **6** Ps 119:147 **7** Ps 131:3; Ps 86:5; Isa 55:7 **8** Ps 103:3,4; Mt 1:21

Psalm 131

Childlike Trust in the Lord.

A Song of Ascents. Of David.

1 LORD, MY heart is not proud, nor my eyes haughty;
Nor do I involve myself in great matters,
Or in things too difficult for me.
2 Surely I have calmed and quieted my soul;
Like a weaned child [resting] with his mother,
My soul is like a weaned child within me [composed and freed from discontent].
3 O Israel, hope in the Lord
From this time forth and forever.

Psalm 132

Prayer for the Lord's Blessing Upon the Sanctuary.

A Song of Ascents.

1 O LORD, remember on David's behalf
All his hardship *and* affliction;
2 How he swore to the Lord
And vowed to the Mighty One of Jacob:
3 "I absolutely will not enter my house,
Nor get into my bed—
4 I certainly will not permit my eyes to sleep
Nor my eyelids to slumber,
5 Until I find a place for the Lord,
A dwelling place for the Mighty One of Jacob (Israel)." [Acts 7:46]
6 Behold, we heard of it at Ephrathah;
We found it in the field of Jaar. [1 Sam 6:21]
7 Let us go into His tabernacle;
Let us worship at His footstool.
8 Arise, O Lord, to Your resting place,
You and the ark [the symbol] of Your strength.
9 Let Your priests be clothed with righteousness (right living),
And let Your godly ones shout for joy.
10 For the sake of Your servant David,
Do not turn away the face of Your anointed.
11 The Lord swore to David
A truth from which He will not turn back:
"One of your descendants I will set upon your throne. [Ps 89:3, 4; Luke 1:69; Acts 2:30, 31]
12 "If your children will keep My covenant
And My testimony which I will teach them,
Their children also shall sit upon your throne forever."

131:1 *my heart is not proud.* David presents himself with genuine humility, a delicate balance between self-abasement and arrogant pride. From the life of David, we know that he was not always able to keep this balance. But it was his desire, and at times — by God's grace — a reality in his life.

131:2 *Like a weaned child.* A weaned child is comforted just by the presence of his mother, without crying for the more tangible comfort of milk as a younger baby does.

132:1 *remember.* This psalm was one of the 15 Songs of Ascent sung by pilgrims as they approached the holy city to worship. Each year, as they marched and sang, they anticipated that perhaps this was the year that this prophecy would be fulfilled. ***David's . . . hardship and affliction.*** If this psalm was written during the period after the exile, these words have a significant meaning. During the years between the return of the people to Jerusalem and the birth of Jesus, there would have been a growing desire on the part of godly people for the Lord to restore David's kingdom in fulfillment of His promise.

132:6 *Ephrathah.* This name refers to the region of Bethlehem (Ru 1:2).

132:12 *sit upon your throne forever.* The ultimate fulfillment of God's covenant with David (2Sa 7:8 – 16) is in Jesus Christ, the Son of David (Lk 1:32 – 33; Ac 2:30).

PSALM 131 **1** Ro 12:16; Job 42:3; Ps 139:6 **2** Mt 18:3; 1Co 14:20 **3** Ps 130:7 **PSALM 132** **2** Ps 65:1; Ge 49:24 **4** Pr 6:4 **5** Ac 7:46 **6** 1Sa 17:12; 7:1; 1Ch 13:5 **7** Ps 5:7; 99:5 **8** Nu 10:35; 2Ch 6:41; Ps 78:61 **9** Job 29:14; Isa 61:10 **11** Ps 89:3,4; 2Sa 7:12; 1Ki 8:25

13 For the LORD has chosen Zion;
He has desired it for His dwelling place:
14 "This is My resting place forever" [says the LORD];
"Here will I dwell, for I have desired it.
15 "I will abundantly bless her provisions;
I will satisfy her poor with bread.
16 "Her priests also I will clothe with salvation,
And her godly ones will shout aloud for joy.
17 "There I will make the horn (strength) of David grow;
I have prepared a lamp for My anointed [fulfilling the promises]. [1 Kin 11:36; 15:4; 2 Chr 21:7; Luke 1:69]
18 "His enemies I will clothe with shame,
But upon himself shall his crown shine."

Psalm 133

The Excellency of Brotherly Unity.

A Song of Ascents. Of David.

1 BEHOLD, HOW good and how pleasant it is
For brothers to dwell together in unity!
2 It is like the precious oil [of consecration] poured on the head,
Coming down on the beard,
Even the beard of Aaron,
Coming down upon the edge of his [priestly] robes [consecrating the whole body]. [Ex 30:25, 30]
3 It is like the dew of [Mount] Hermon
Coming down on the hills of Zion;
For there the LORD has commanded the blessing: life forevermore.

Psalm 134

Greetings of Night Watchers.

A Song of Ascents.

1 BEHOLD, BLESS *and* praise the LORD, all servants of the LORD (priests, Levites),
Who stand *and* serve by night in the house of the LORD. [1 Chr 9:33]
2 Lift up your hands to the sanctuary
And bless the LORD.
3 May the LORD bless you from Zion,
He who made heaven and earth.

Psalm 135

Praise the LORD's Wonderful Works. Vanity of Idols.

1 PRAISE THE LORD! (Hallelujah!)
Praise the name of the LORD;
Praise Him, O servants of the LORD (priests, Levites),
2 You who stand in the house of the LORD,
In the courts of the house of our God,
3 Praise the LORD, for the LORD is good;
Sing praises to His name, for it is gracious *and* lovely.

132:16 *joy.* God's presence is a source of joy to the upright. God had chosen Zion as His resting place, and His godly ones shouted "aloud for joy." When God rules on the throne of the human spirit, joy reigns within.
132:17 *horn ... lamp.* The words "horn" and "lamp" speak of the Messiah's authority and righteousness (Isa 11:1 – 5).
133:3 *the dew of [Mount] Hermon.* This high mountain to the north of Israel received such large amounts of water that it seemed to be a source of moisture for the lands below.
134:1 *all servants of the LORD.* This psalm concludes the Songs of Ascent. The people who had come to worship at the temple were getting ready to go home, but the priests would remain at the holy temple, continuing to lift up worship to the Lord.

13 Ps 48:1,2 **14** Ps 68:16 **15** Ps 147:14 **16** 2Ch 6:41; Hos 11:12 **17** Eze 29:21; Lk 1:69; 1Ki 11:36 **18** Ps 35:26; 109:29 **PSALM 133** **1** Ge 13:8; Heb 13:1 **2** Ex 30:25 **3** Dt 4:48; Lev 25:21; Dt 28:8; Ps 42:8 **PSALM 134** **1** Ps 135:1,2; 1Ch 9:33 **2** 1Ti 2:8 **3** Ps 124:8; 128:5; 135:21 **PSALM 135** **1** Ps 113:1; 134:1 **2** Lk 2:37; Ps 116:19 **3** Ps 119:68; 147:1

4 For the LORD has chosen [the
descendants of] Jacob for
Himself,
Israel for His own special treasure
and possession. [Deut 7:6]

5 For I know that the LORD is great
And that our Lord is above all gods.
6 Whatever the LORD pleases, He
does,
In the heavens and on the earth, in
the seas and all deeps—
7 Who causes the clouds to rise from
the ends of the earth;
Who makes lightning for the rain,
Who brings the wind from His
storehouses;
8 Who struck the firstborn of Egypt,
Both of man and animal;
[Ex 12:12, 29; Ps 78:51; 136:10]
9 Who sent signs and wonders into
your midst, O Egypt,
Upon Pharaoh and all his
servants.
10 Who struck many nations
And killed mighty kings,
11 Sihon, king of the Amorites,
Og, king of Bashan,
And all the kingdoms of Canaan;
12 And He gave their land as a
heritage,
A heritage to Israel His people.
13 Your name, O LORD, endures
forever,
Your fame *and* remembrance,
O LORD, [endures] throughout all
generations.
14 For the LORD will judge His people
And He will have compassion
on His servants [revealing His
mercy]. [Heb 10:30]
15 The idols of the nations are silver
and gold,
The work of men's hands.
16 They have mouths, but they do
not speak;
They have eyes, but they do
not see;
17 They have ears, but they do
not hear,
Nor is there any breath in their
mouths.
18 Those who make idols are like
them [absolutely worthless—
spiritually blind, deaf, and
powerless];
So is everyone who trusts in *and*
relies on them. [Ps 115:4–8]

19 O house of Israel, bless *and* praise
the LORD [with gratitude];
O house of Aaron, bless the LORD;
20 O house of Levi, bless the LORD;
You who fear the LORD [and
worship Him with obedience],
bless the LORD [with grateful
praise]! [Deut 6:5; Ps 31:23]
21 Blessed be the LORD from Zion,
Who dwells [with us] at
Jerusalem.
Praise the LORD! (Hallelujah!)

Psalm 136
Thanks for the LORD's Goodness to Israel.

1 GIVE THANKS to the LORD, for
He is good;
For His lovingkindness
(graciousness, mercy,
compassion) endures forever.
2 Give thanks to the God of gods,
For His lovingkindness endures
forever.
3 Give thanks to the Lord of lords,
For His lovingkindness endures
forever.

135:8 *the firstborn of Egypt.* The defeat of Egypt was solely the work of the Lord. Israel was merely His instrument; the battle belonged to Him (Ex 12:12; 15:3).

135:15 *idols of the nations.* The people who returned from Babylon had had their fill of the worship of idols; at long last, the people of Israel were ready to worship the only true God.

135:19 *bless and praise the LORD.* To bless the Lord is to identify Him as the source of all blessings and to be grateful for all that He has given.

136:1 *mercy.* This word, also translated "lovingkindness" or "loyal love," is the most significant term used in the Psalms to describe the character of God. His love is forever; it is part of His eternal character.

4 Ex 19:5; Dt 7:6,7 **5** Ps 95:3; 97:9 **6** Ps 115:3 **7** Jer 10:13; Job 28:25; Zec 10:1; Job 38:22 **8** Ex 12:12; Ps 78:51 **9** Ex 7-10; Ps 136:15 **10** Nu 21:24; Ps 136:17 **11** Jos 12:7 **12** Ps 78:55; 136:21,22 **13** Ex 3:15; Ps 102:12 **14** Dt 32:36 **15** Ps 115:4-8 **19** Ps 115:9 **21** Ps 134:3 **PSALM 136** **1** Ps 106:1; 1Ch 16:34 **2** Dt 10:17

4 To Him who alone does great wonders,
For His lovingkindness endures forever;
5 To Him who made the heavens with skill,
For His lovingkindness endures forever;
6 To Him who stretched out the earth upon the waters,
For His lovingkindness endures forever;
7 To Him who made the great lights,
For His lovingkindness endures forever;
8 The sun to rule over the day,
For His lovingkindness endures forever;
9 The moon and stars to rule by night,
For His lovingkindness endures forever;

10 To Him who struck the firstborn of Egypt,
For His lovingkindness endures forever; [Ex 12:29]
11 And brought Israel out from among them,
For His lovingkindness endures forever; [Ex 12:51; 13:3, 17]
12 With a strong hand and with an outstretched arm,
For His lovingkindness endures forever;
13 To Him who divided the Red Sea into parts,
For His lovingkindness endures forever; [Ex 14:21, 22]
14 And made Israel pass through the midst of it,
For His lovingkindness endures forever;
15 But tossed Pharaoh and his army into the Red Sea,
For His lovingkindness endures forever;
16 To Him who led His people through the wilderness,
For His lovingkindness endures forever;
17 To Him who struck down great kings,
For His lovingkindness endures forever;
18 And killed mighty kings,
For His lovingkindness endures forever; [Deut 29:7]
19 Sihon, king of the Amorites,
For His lovingkindness endures forever; [Num 21:21–24]
20 And Og, king of Bashan,
For His lovingkindness endures forever; [Num 21:33–35]
21 And gave their land as a heritage,
For His lovingkindness endures forever;
22 Even a heritage to Israel His servant,
For His lovingkindness endures forever; [Josh 12:1]

23 Who [faithfully] remembered us in our lowly condition,
For His lovingkindness endures forever;
24 And has rescued us from our enemies,
For His lovingkindness endures forever;
25 Who gives food to all flesh,
For His lovingkindness endures forever;
26 Give thanks to the God of heaven,
For His lovingkindness (graciousness, mercy, compassion) endures forever.

136:4–9 *great wonders.* God's creation of the universe is the grand display of His wisdom. The heavens give a clear presentation of the glory of God (19:1–6). Romans 1:20 teaches that God's "invisible attributes" are clearly seen through the things He has made.

136:23 *remembered us.* It is possible that these words suggest the return of the people of Judah and Jerusalem to their land following the Babylonian captivity.

4 Ps 72:18 **5** Ge 1:1; Pr 3:19; Jer 51:15 **6** Ge 1:9; Ps 24:2; Jer 10:12 **7** Ge 1:14 **8** Ge 1:16 **10** Ex 12:29; Ps 135:8 **11** Ex 12:51 **12** Ex 6:6 **13** Ex 14:21; Ps 78:13 **15** Ex 14:27; Ps 135:9 **16** Ex 13:18 **17** Ps 135:10 **18** Dt 29:7 **19** Nu 21:21 **20** Nu 21:33 **21** Jos 12:1; Ps 135:12 **23** Ge 8:1; Dt 32:36; Ps 113:7 **25** Ps 104:27; 145:15

Psalm 137

An Experience of the Captivity.

1 BY THE rivers of Babylon,
There we [captives] sat down and wept,
When we remembered Zion [the city God imprinted on our hearts].
2 On the willow trees in the midst of Babylon
We hung our harps.
3 For there they who took us captive demanded of us a song with words,
And our tormentors [who made a mockery of us demanded] amusement, *saying*,
"Sing us one of the songs of Zion."
4 How can we sing the LORD's song
In a strange *and* foreign land?
5 If I forget you, O Jerusalem,
Let my right hand forget [her skill with the harp].
6 Let my tongue cling to the roof of my mouth
If I do not remember you,
If I do not prefer Jerusalem
Above my chief joy. [Ezek 3:26]

7 Remember, O LORD, against the sons of Edom,
The day of [the fall of] Jerusalem,
Who said "Down, down [with her]
To her very foundation."
8 O daughter of Babylon, you devastator,
How blessed will be the one
Who repays you [with destruction] as you have repaid us. [Is 13:1–22; Jer 25:12, 13]
9 How blessed will be the one who seizes and dashes your little ones
Against the rock.

Psalm 138

Thanksgiving for the LORD's Favor.

A Psalm of David.

1 I WILL give You thanks with all my heart;
I sing praises to You before the [pagan] gods.
2 I will bow down [in worship] toward Your holy temple
And give thanks to Your name for Your lovingkindness and Your truth;
For You have magnified Your word together with Your name.
3 On the day I called, You answered me;
And You made me bold *and* confident with [renewed] strength in my life.

4 All the kings of the land will give thanks *and* praise You, O LORD,

---

137:1 *Babylon.* Babylon was one of the great empires in world history. When this psalm was written, the Jews were living there in exile.
137:5 *If I forget you.* The love of the people for Jerusalem was not just for the place, but for its function in their lives. The place was holy because it was the dwelling place of God and the place of worship and sacrifice for sins.
137:9 *How blessed will be.* The idea of rejoicing and happiness at the violence depicted here is hard to swallow. Like some of the other difficult stories recorded in Scripture (see the Book of Judges), this imprecatory psalm is included with no comments about how God viewed the psalmist's emotion. Elsewhere in Scripture, we receive strict commands condemning taking vengeance into our own hands (Ro 12:19 – 21), rejoicing when others suffer (Ob 12), and refusing to forgive (Mt 5:43 – 45; 6:14 – 15). However, none of these passages are saying that we should pretend that evil doesn't exist. This psalmist's violent reaction to evil should remind us of how seriously God takes sin. He will not allow wickedness to go unpunished.
138:1 *before the [pagan] gods.* David is so confident in his faith in the Lord that he is determined to take the name of God into foreign territory.
138:2 *Your holy temple.* The use of the word "temple" does not rule out David as the author of this or similar poems (15:1). The Hebrew term is a general one that would fit whatever building was in use in David's day.

PSALM 137 **3** Ps 79:1 **6** Eze 3:26 **7** Jer 49:7; La 4:22; Eze 25:12; Ob 10 **8** Isa 13:1,6; Jer 25:12; Jer 50:15; Rev 18:6 **9** Isa 13:16 **PSALM 138** **1** Ps 119:46 **2** Ps 28:2; 1Ki 8:29; Ps 5:7; Isa 42:21 **4** Ps 102:15

When they have heard of the
promises of Your mouth [which
were fulfilled].
5 Yes, they will sing of the ways of
the LORD [joyfully celebrating
His wonderful acts],
For great is the glory *and* majesty
of the LORD.
6 Though the LORD is exalted,
He regards the lowly [and invites
them into His fellowship];
But the proud *and* haughty
He knows from a distance.
[Prov 3:34; James 4:6; 1 Pet 5:5]

7 Though I walk in the midst of
trouble, You will revive me;
You will stretch out Your hand
against the wrath of my
enemies,
And Your right hand will save me.
[Ps 23:3, 4]
8 The LORD will accomplish that
which concerns me;
Your [unwavering]
lovingkindness, O LORD,
endures forever—
Do not abandon the works of Your
own hands. [Ps 57:2; Phil 1:6]

Psalm 139

God's Omnipresence and Omniscience.

To the Chief Musician. A Psalm of David.

1 O LORD, you have searched me
[thoroughly] and have known
me.
2 You know when I sit down and
when I rise up [my entire life,
everything I do];
You understand my thought from
afar. [Matt 9:4; John 2:24, 25]
3 You scrutinize my path and my
lying down,
And You are intimately acquainted
with all my ways.
4 Even before there is a word on my
tongue [still unspoken],
Behold, O LORD, You know it all.
[Heb 4:13]
5 You have enclosed me behind and
before,
And [You have] placed Your hand
upon me.
6 Such [infinite] knowledge is too
wonderful for me;
It is too high [above me], I cannot
reach it.

7 Where can I go from Your Spirit?
Or where can I flee from Your
presence?
8 If I ascend to heaven, You are
there;
If I make my bed in Sheol (the
nether world, the place of the
dead), behold, You are there.
[Rom 11:33]
9 If I take the wings of the dawn,
If I dwell in the remotest part of
the sea,
10 Even there Your hand will lead me,
And Your right hand will take
hold of me.
11 If I say, "Surely the darkness will
cover me,
And the night will be the only light
around me,"
12 Even the darkness is not dark to
You *and* conceals nothing from
You,
But the night shines as bright as
the day;

138:6 *the lowly.* When man is boastful and conceited before God, he separates himself from God. Yet God bends with a special concern toward those who are humble before Him.
138:8 *lovingkindness ... endures forever.* God's loyal covenant love will never be rescinded or forgotten.
139:5 *You have enclosed me behind and before.* The purpose of God's intimate knowledge of His servants is protective and helpful, not judgmental and condemning.
139:7 – 12 *You are there.* The believer can rejoice and rest in the knowledge that God is present in every place and every situation in life.
139:12 *Darkness and light are alike to you.* God can see what is happening to us even under cover of darkness. Nothing can conceal His people from Him.

6 Ps 113:5,6; Isa 57:15; Pr 3:34; Jas 4:6; 1Pe 5:5 **7** Ps 23:3,4 **8** Ps 57:2; Php 1:6; Job 10:3,8 **PSALM 139**
1 Ps 17:3; Jer 12:3 **2** 2Ki 19:27; Mt 9:4; Jn 2:24 **3** Job 31:4 **4** Heb 4:13 **6** Job 42:3; Ps 40:5 **7** Jer 23:24; Jnh 1:3 **8** Am 9:2; Pr 15:11 **12** Job 34:22

Darkness and light are alike *to You.* [Dan 2:22]
13 For You formed my innermost parts;
You knit me [together] in my mother's womb.
14 I will give thanks *and* praise to You, for I am fearfully and wonderfully made;
Wonderful are Your works,
And my soul knows it very well.
15 My frame was not hidden from You,
When I was being formed in secret,
And intricately *and* skillfully formed [as if embroidered with many colors] in the depths of the earth.
16 Your eyes have seen my unformed substance;
And in Your book were all written
The days that were appointed *for me,*
When as yet there was not one of them [even taking shape].
17 How precious also are Your thoughts to me, O God!
How vast is the sum of them! [Ps 40:5]
18 If I could count them, they would outnumber the sand.
When I awake, I am still with You.
19 O that You would kill the wicked, O God;
Go away from me, therefore, men of bloodshed. [Is 11:4]
20 For they speak against You wickedly,
Your enemies take *Your name* in vain. [Jude 15]
21 Do I not hate those who hate You, O LORD?
And do I not loathe those who rise up against You?
22 I hate them with perfect *and* utmost hatred;
They have become my enemies.
23 Search me [thoroughly], O God, and know my heart;
Test me and know my anxious thoughts;
24 And see if there is any wicked *or* hurtful way in me,
And lead me in the everlasting way.

Psalm 140

Prayer for Protection against the Wicked.

To the Chief Musician. A Psalm of David.

1 RESCUE ME, O LORD, from evil men;
Protect me from violent men.
2 They devise evil things in their hearts;
They continually [gather together and] stir up wars.
3 They sharpen their tongues like a serpent's;
Poison of a viper is under their lips. [Rom 3:13] *Selah.*

139:14 God's Omniscience — He is the God who knows. He knows everything that has happened and will happen. He understands all of nature perfectly. In fact He knows everything there is to know. God knows so much that it would be impossible to overstate what He knows. The proper theological term for this attribute of God is *omniscience.*

God knows all of our thoughts, motives, and deeds. God knows us better than we know ourselves. We are all uneasy with the fact that God knows us so well. Like Adam and Eve, we fear the exposure of our sin.

There is, however, great reason to rejoice in the fact that God knows us so well. He loves us in spite of what He knows about us; in the middle of our sin He still loves us. He knows the worst things there are to know about us and still wants to save us. He also knows the best things about us. When everyone else misunderstands us, He understands us fully. Finally, God knows what we will be. He has a marvelous end in mind that should give us great comfort no matter what our present state.

139:16 *in Your book.* The idea is that all human beings, and the structure and meaning of each person's life, are all established from the beginning by God.

139:23 *Search me [thoroughly], O God.* It is only when we are aware of our sins that we can repent of them and be healed.

15 Job 10:8,9 **17** Ps 40:5 **19** Isa 11:4; Ps 119:115 **20** Jude 15 **21** 2Ch 19:2 **23** Job 31:6 **24** Ps 5:8
PSALM 140 **2** Ps 56:6 **3** Ps 58:4

4 Keep me, O LORD, from the hands
of the wicked;
Protect me from violent men
Who intend to trip up my steps.
5 The proud have hidden a trap for
me, and cords;
They have spread a net by the
wayside;
They have set traps for me.
Selah.

6 I said to the LORD, "You are my
God;
Listen to the voice of my
supplications, O LORD.
7 "O GOD the Lord, the strength of
my salvation,
You have covered my head in the
day of battle.
8 "Do not grant, O LORD, the desires
of the wicked;
Do not further their evil device,
that they not be exalted. *Selah.*

9 "Those who surround me raise
their heads;
May the mischief of their own lips
come upon them.
10 "Let burning coals fall upon them;
Let them be thrown into the fire,
Into deep [water] pits from which
they cannot rise.
11 "Do not let a slanderer be
established in the earth;
Let evil quickly hunt the violent
man [to overthrow him and stop
his evil acts]."

12 I know [with confidence] that the
LORD will maintain the cause of
the afflicted,
And [will secure] justice for the
poor.
13 Surely the righteous will give
thanks to Your name;
The upright will dwell in Your
presence.

Psalm 141

An Evening Prayer for Sanctification and Protection.

A Psalm of David.

1 LORD, I call upon You; hurry
to me.
Listen to my voice when I call to
You.
2 Let my prayer be counted as
incense before You;
The lifting up of my hands as the
evening offering. [1 Tim 2:8;
Rev 8:3, 4]
3 Set a guard, O LORD, over my
mouth;
Keep watch over the door of my
lips [to keep me from speaking
thoughtlessly].
4 Do not incline my heart to [consent
to or tolerate] any evil thing,
Or to practice deeds of wickedness
With men who plan *and* do evil;
And let me not eat of their
delicacies (be tempted by their
gain).

5 Let the righteous [thoughtfully]
strike (correct) me—it is a
kindness [done to encourage my
spiritual maturity].
It is [the choicest anointing] oil on
the head;
Let my head not refuse [to accept
and acknowledge and learn
from] it;

140:6 *You are my God.* David confessed his complete trust in the Lord even though he was surrounded by people plotting his destruction. On the basis of his trust, he pled with the Lord to deliver him.
140:10 *Let burning coals fall.* David recalls the judgment of Sodom and Gomorrah (Ge 19:12–29) and asks God to once again judge the enemies of the righteous.
140:12 *justice for the poor.* The cause of the poor and afflicted is of special interest to the Lord. He promises to uphold and comfort them (41:1; 72:4; 109:31; Lk 4:18; 6:20).
141:2 *as incense.* The prayers of God's people are also compared to incense in Revelation 8:3–4.
141:3 *Set a guard . . . over my mouth.* David recognized how terribly easy it is to sin in what we say (Pr 30:32–33; Jas 3:1–12).
141:5 *Let the righteous [thoughtfully] strike (correct) me—it is a kindness.* The rebuke of a righteous person, even if it is painful at the time, is designed to bring about good. Sometimes

4 Ps 71:4 **5** Jer 18:22 **8** Dt 32:27 **9** Ps 7:16 **10** Ps 11:6 **12** Ps 9:4 **PSALM 141** **1** Ps 70:5 **2** Rev 5:8; Rev 8:3; 1Ti 2:8; Ex 29:39 **4** Pr 23:6 **5** Pr 9:8

For still my prayer is against their
wicked deeds. [Prov 9:8; 19:25;
25:12; Gal 6:1]
6 Their [wicked, godless] judges are
thrown down the sides of the
rocky cliff,
And they [who followed them]
will hear my words, for they are
pleasant (just).
7 As when the one plows and breaks
open the ground [and the soil
scatters behind him],
Our bones have been scattered
at the mouth of Sheol [by
the injustices of the wicked].
[2 Cor 1:9]

8 For my eyes are toward You,
O God, the Lord;
In You I take refuge; do not
pour out my life *nor* leave me
defenseless.
9 Keep me from the jaws of the trap
which they have set for me,
And from the snares of those who
do evil.
10 Let the wicked fall into their own
nets,
While I pass by *and* safely escape
[from danger].

Psalm 142

Prayer for Help in Trouble.

A skillful song, *or* a didactic *or* reflective poem, of David; when he was in the cave. A Prayer.

1 I CRY aloud with my voice to the
Lord;
I make supplication with my voice
to the Lord.
2 I pour out my complaint before Him;
I declare my trouble before Him.
3 When my spirit was overwhelmed
and weak within me [wrapped
in darkness],
You knew my path.
In the way where I walk
They have hidden a trap for me.
4 Look to the right [the point of
attack] and see;
For there is no one who has regard
for me [to act in my favor].
Escape has failed me *and* I have
nowhere to run;
No one cares about my life.

5 I cried out to You, O Lord;
I said, "You are my refuge,
My portion in the land of the
living.
6 "Give attention to my cry,
For I am brought very low;
Rescue me from my persecutors,
For they are stronger than I.
7 "Bring my soul out of prison
(adversity),
So that I may give thanks *and*
praise Your name;
The righteous will surround me
[in triumph],
For You will look after me."

Psalm 143

Prayer for Help and Guidance.

A Psalm of David.

1 HEAR MY prayer, O Lord,
Listen to my supplications!
Answer me in Your faithfulness,
and in Your righteousness.
2 And do not enter into judgment
with Your servant,

being "nice" isn't really the kindest thing we can do for someone.

141:8 *my eyes are toward You.* If we focus on the strength of wickedness, we will be overcome with fear. If we focus on ourselves, we will become absorbed in our difficulties or exalt ourselves in our victories. Only when we focus on God can we achieve balance and health.

142 title *when he was in the cave.* This may refer to one of two occasions when David hid from King Saul in a cave: at En Gedi (57; 1Sa 24), and at Adullam (1Sa 22:1).

142:5 *You are my refuge.* Sometimes God allows us to go through times when we have no one at our right hand, "no one who has regard for me," just so that we will be very aware of our need for God.

143:2 *no man living is righteous or justified.* This is not so much a confession as an observation that everyone is sinful.

8 Ps 25:15 **9** Ps 119:110 **10** Ps 35:8 **PSALM 142 Title** Ps 57, Title; 1Sa 22:1 **2** Isa 26:16 **3** Ps 143:4; Ps 140:5 **4** Ps 69:20; 31:11 **5** Ps 46:1; La 3:24; Ps 27:13 **6** Ps 116:6 **7** Ps 34:2; Ps 13:6 **PSALM 143 1** Ps 31:1 **2** Job 14:3; Ex 34:7

For in Your sight no man living is
righteous *or* justified. [Ps 130:3;
Rom 3:20–26; Gal 2:16]
3 For the enemy has persecuted me,
He has crushed my life down to
the ground;
He has made me dwell in dark
places, like those who have been
long dead.
4 Therefore my spirit is
overwhelmed *and* weak within
me [wrapped in darkness];
My heart grows numb within me.

5 I remember the days of old;
I meditate on all that You have
done;
I ponder the work of Your hands.
6 I reach out my hands to You;
My throat *thirsts* for You, as a
parched land [thirsts for water].
Selah.

7 Answer me quickly, O LORD, my
spirit fails;
Do not hide Your face from me,
Or I will become like those who go
down into the pit (grave).
8 Let me hear Your lovingkindness
in the morning,
For I trust in You.
Teach me the way in which I
should walk,
For I lift up my soul to You.
9 Rescue me, O LORD, from my
enemies;
I take refuge in You.

10 Teach me to do Your will [so that I
may please You],
For You are my God;
Let Your good Spirit lead me on
level ground.

11 Save my life, O LORD, for Your
name's sake;
In Your righteousness bring my
life out of trouble.
12 In your lovingkindness, silence
and destroy my enemies
And destroy all those who afflict
my life,
For I am Your servant.

Psalm 144

Prayer for Rescue and Prosperity.

A Psalm of David.

1 BLESSED BE the LORD, my Rock
and my great strength,
Who trains my hands for war
And my fingers for battle;
2 My [steadfast] lovingkindness and
my fortress,
My high tower and my rescuer,
My shield and He in whom I take
refuge,
Who subdues my people under me.
3 LORD, what is man that You take
notice of him?
Or the son of man that You think
of him? [Job 7:17; Ps 8:4; Heb 2:6]
4 Man is like a mere breath;
His days are like a shadow that
passes away.

5 Bow Your heavens, O LORD, and
come down;
Touch the mountains, and they
will smoke.
6 Flash lightning and scatter my
enemies;

143:3 ***in dark places.*** To live in dark places is similar to being in the pit (v. 7); this is the reason for the parallel to those who are already dead (Job 10:21 – 22).

143:11 ***for Your name's sake.*** The requests of the psalmists are often tied to various character traits of God. When we pray "in Jesus name," we pray both in the authority of His name and in the character it represents.

144:4 ***like a shadow.*** Human life apart from God is presented in the darkest terms by the Word of God. Briefly stated, it is short and full of trouble (Job 14:1), uncertain (Lk 12:16 – 20), and empty (Ecc 1:2). In contrast, Paul the apostle describes the life of the redeemed as being like a victorious soldier, a winning athlete, a successful farmer, a diligent student, and a useable vessel (2Ti 2). The redeemed life is marked by peace and purpose now, and eternity with Christ later.

144:11 ***hand of falsehood.*** The principal lie of the enemy was that the Lord could not save His people (Isa 36:18 – 20).

4 Ps 77:3 **5** Ps 77:5 **6** Ps 88:9; 63:1 **7** Ps 28:1 **8** Ps 46:5; Ps 25:1 **10** Ps 25:4,5; Neh 9:20; Isa 26:10 **11** Ps 119:25 **12** Ps 54:5 **PSALM 144** **1** 2Sa 22:35; Ps 18:34 **3** Job 7:17; Ps 8:4; Heb 2:6 **4** Job 4:19; Ps 102:11 **5** Ps 18:9; Ps 104:32 **6** Ps 18:13

Send out Your arrows and confuse
and embarrass *and* frustrate
them.
7 Stretch out Your hand from
above;
Set me free and rescue me from
great waters,
Out of the hands of [hostile]
foreigners [who surround us]
8 Whose mouths speak deceit
[without restraint],
And whose right hand is a right
hand of falsehood.

9 I will sing a new song to You,
O God;
Upon a harp of ten strings I will
sing praises to You,
10 Who gives salvation to kings,
Who sets David His servant free
from the evil sword.
11 Set me free and rescue me
from the hand of [hostile]
foreigners,
Whose mouth speaks deceit
[without restraint],
And whose right hand is a right
hand of falsehood.
12 Let our sons in their youth be like
plants full grown,
And our daughters like corner
pillars fashioned for a palace;
13 Let our barns be full, supplying
every kind of produce,
And our flocks bring forth
thousands and ten thousands in
our fields;
14 Let our cattle bear
Without mishap and without
loss,
And let there be no outcry in our
streets!
15 How blessed *and* favored are the
people in such circumstance;
How blessed [fortunate,
prosperous, and favored] are
the people whose God is the
LORD!

Psalm 145

The LORD Extolled for His Goodness.

A Psalm of praise. Of David.

1 I WILL exalt You, my God,
O King,
And [with gratitude and
submissive wonder] I will
bless Your name forever and
ever.
2 Every day I will bless You *and*
lovingly praise You;
Yes, [with awe-inspired reverence]
I will praise Your name forever
and ever.
3 Great is the LORD, and highly to be
praised,
And His greatness is [so vast and
profound as to be] unsearchable
[incomprehensible to man].
[Job 5:9; 9:10; Rom 11:33]
4 One generation shall praise Your
works to another,
And shall declare Your mighty
and remarkable acts.
5 On the glorious splendor of Your
majesty
And on Your wonderful works,
I will meditate.
6 People will speak of the power of
Your awesome acts,
And [with gratitude and
submissive wonder] I will tell
of Your greatness.
7 They will overflow [like a
fountain] when they speak
of Your great *and* abundant
goodness
And will sing joyfully of Your
righteousness.

8 The LORD is gracious and full of
compassion,
Slow to anger and abounding in
lovingkindness.
9 The LORD is good to all,

144:15 *How blessed.* The blessing that David describes refers both to external well-being and to internal peace.
145:8 *gracious and full of compassion.* In contrast to the popular image of God as stern and critical, God is full of compassion for erring humans — so much so that He sent His own Son to redeem them (Jn 3:16).

8 Ps 12:2 **9** Ps 33:2,3 **10** Ps 18:50 **12** Ps 128:3 **15** Ps 33:12 **PSALM 145** **Title** Ps 100, Title **3** Ps 147:5; Ro 11:33 **4** Isa 38:9 **8** Nu 14:18 **9** Na 1:7

And His tender mercies are over
all His works [the entirety of
things created].
10 All Your works shall give thanks
to You *and* praise You, O LORD,
And Your godly ones will bless
You.
11 They shall speak of the glory of
Your kingdom
And talk of Your power,
12 To make known to the sons of men
Your mighty acts
And the glorious majesty of Your
kingdom.
13 Your kingdom is an everlasting
kingdom,
And Your dominion *endures*
throughout all generations.
[Dan 7:14, 27]

14 The LORD upholds all those [of His
own] who fall
And raises up all those who are
bowed down.
15 The eyes of all look to You [in
hopeful expectation],
And You give them their food in
due time.
16 You open Your hand
And satisfy the desire of every
living thing.

17 The LORD is [unwaveringly]
righteous in all His ways
And gracious *and* kind in all His
works.
18 The LORD is near to all who call
on Him,
To all who call on Him in truth
(without guile).
19 He will fulfill the desire of those
who fear *and* worship Him [with
awe-inspired reverence and
obedience];
He also will hear their cry and will
save them.
20 The LORD keeps all who love Him,
But all the wicked He will destroy.
21 My mouth will speak the praise of
the LORD,
And all flesh will bless *and*
gratefully praise His holy name
forever and ever.

Psalm 146

The LORD an Abundant Helper.

1 PRAISE THE LORD! (Hallelujah!)
Praise the LORD, O my soul!
2 While I live I will praise the LORD;
I will sing praises to my God as
long as I live.
3 Do not trust in princes,
In mortal man, in whom there is
no salvation (help).
4 When his spirit leaves him, he
returns to the earth;
In that very day his thoughts *and*
plans perish. [1 Cor 2:6]
5 How blessed *and* graciously
favored is he whose help is the
God of Jacob (Israel),
Whose hope is in the LORD his
God, [Gen 32:30]
6 Who made heaven and earth,
The sea, and all that is in them,
Who keeps truth *and* is faithful
forever, [Gen 1:3]
7 Who executes justice for the
oppressed,
Who gives food to the hungry.
The LORD sets free the prisoners.

8 The LORD opens *the eyes of* the
blind;

145:13 *an everlasting kingdom.* The rule of God is eternal, and the message of His wonders needs to be delivered to all people in the present time.

145:17 *righteous . . . gracious and kind.* The pairing of these terms is a powerful description of the character of God. Righteousness alone would lead to our destruction because of our sin, but God is also kind and gracious and has arranged a way for us to be saved.

146:3 *in princes.* Even the best of people are not adequate help in times of terrible stress.

146:5 *hope.* Most men are aware that there is more in life than they are getting out of it. They try many things to satisfy their desire for a fuller life. But like Solomon, who gives his testimony in the Book of Ecclesiastes, they find that "things" do not satisfy. Blessedness, or fullness of life, comes to those who have a relationship with God and hope of eternal life with Him.

10 Ps 19:1 **13** 1Ti 1:17 **14** Ps 146:8 **15** Ps 104:27; Ps 136:25 **16** Ps 104:21 **18** Dt 4:7; Jn 4:24 **20** Ps 31:23
PSALM 146 **1** Ps 103:1 **2** Ps 104:33 **3** Isa 2:22 **4** Ecc 12:7; 1Co 2:6 **5** Jer 17:7 **6** Rev 14:7 **7** Ps 103:6; Ps 107:9; Ps 107:10 **8** Mt 9:30; Lk 13:13

The LORD lifts up those who are
bowed down;
The LORD loves the righteous [the
upright in heart]. [Luke 13:13;
John 9:7, 32]
9 The LORD protects the strangers;
He supports the fatherless and the
widow;
But He makes crooked the way of
the wicked.
10 The LORD shall reign forever,
Your God, O Zion, to all
generations.
Praise the LORD! (Hallelujah!)
[Ps 10:16; Rev 11:15]

Psalm 147

Praise for Jerusalem's Restoration and Prosperity.

1 PRAISE THE LORD!
For it is good to sing praises to our
[gracious and majestic] God;
Praise is becoming *and*
appropriate.
2 The LORD is building up
Jerusalem;
He is gathering [together] the
exiles of Israel.
3 He heals the brokenhearted
And binds up their wounds
[healing their pain and
comforting their sorrow].
[Ps 34:18; Is 57:15; 61:1;
Luke 4:18]
4 He counts the number of the stars;
He calls them all by their names.
5 Great is our [majestic and mighty]
Lord and abundant in strength;
His understanding is inexhaustible
[infinite, boundless].
6 The LORD lifts up the humble;
He casts the wicked down to the
ground.

7 Sing to the LORD with thanksgiving;
Sing praises to our God with the
lyre,
8 Who covers the heavens with
clouds,
Who provides rain for the earth,
Who makes grass grow on the
mountains.
9 He gives to the beast its food,
And to the young ravens that for
which they cry.
10 He does not delight in the strength
(military power) of the horse,
Nor does He take pleasure in the
legs (strength) of a man.
11 The LORD favors those who
fear *and* worship Him [with
awe-inspired reverence and
obedience],
Those who wait for His mercy *and*
lovingkindness. [Ps 145:20]

12 Praise the LORD, O Jerusalem!
Praise your God, O Zion!
13 For He has strengthened the bars
of your gates,
He has blessed your children
within you.
14 He makes peace in your borders;
He satisfies you with the finest of
the wheat.
15 He sends His command to the
earth;
His word runs very swiftly.
16 He gives [to the earth] snow like
[a blanket of] wool;
He scatters the frost like ashes.
17 He casts out His ice like
fragments;
Who can stand before His cold?

146:10 *reign forever.* God's reign is both present and eternal.
147:2 *building up Jerusalem.* The few people who had returned from captivity faced an immense task. They needed to remember that the work was God's and He would see that it was accomplished.
147:3 *heals the brokenhearted.* God's principle work is always within the human heart (51:10–12).
147:6 *lifts up the humble.* God's greatness may be approached only by the humble (Jas 4:6).
147:9 *beast its food.* Jesus describes God's care as extending even to sparrows (Mt 10:29).
147:10 *He does not delight.* The joy that God finds in His "very good" creation (Ge 1) does not compare with the delight that He takes in humans whose hearts are turned to Him.

9 Dt 10:18; Ps 68:5; Ps 147:6 **10** Ex 15:18; Ps 10:16 **PSALM 147 1** Ps 92:1; Ps 135:3; Ps 33:1 **2** Ps 102:16; Dt 30:3 **3** Ps 51:17 **4** Isa 40:26 **5** Ps 48:1; Na 1:3; Isa 40:28 **6** Ps 146:8 **8** Job 38:26; Ps 104:13 **9** Job 38:41; Ps 104:27; Mt 6:26 **10** Ps 33:16; Hos 1:7 **14** Isa 60:17,18; Ps 132:15 **15** Ps 107:20 **16** Job 37:6

18 He sends out His word and melts
the ice;
He causes His wind to blow and
the waters to flow.
19 He declares His word to Jacob,
His statutes and His ordinances to
Israel. [Mal 4:4]
20 He has not dealt this way with any
[other] nation;
They have not known [understood,
appreciated, heeded, or
cherished] His ordinances.
Praise the LORD! (Hallelujah!)
[Ps 79:6; Jer 10:25]

Psalm 148

The Whole Creation Invoked to Praise the LORD.

1 PRAISE THE LORD!
Praise the LORD from the heavens;
Praise Him in the heights!
2 Praise Him, all His angels;
Praise Him, all His hosts (armies)!
3 Praise Him, sun and moon:
Praise Him, all stars of light!
4 Praise Him, highest heavens,
And the waters above the heavens!
5 Let them praise the name of the
LORD,
For He commanded and they were
created.
6 He has also established them
forever and ever;
He has made a decree which shall
not pass away.

7 Praise the LORD from the earth,
Sea monsters and all deeps;
8 Lightning and hail, snow and fog;
Stormy wind, fulfilling His orders;
9 Mountains and all hills;
Fruitful trees and all cedars;
10 Beasts and all cattle;
Creeping things and winged birds;
11 Kings of the earth and all people;
Princes and all judges of the earth;
12 Both young men and virgins;
Old men and children.

13 Let them praise the name of the
LORD,
For His name alone is exalted *and*
supreme;
His glory *and* majesty are above
earth and heaven.
14 He has lifted up a horn for His
people [giving them strength,
prosperity, dignity, and
preeminence],
Praise for all His godly ones;
For the people of Israel, a people
near to Him.
Praise the LORD! (Hallelujah!)
[Ps 75:10; Eph 2:17]

Psalm 149

Israel Invoked to Praise the LORD.

1 PRAISE THE LORD!
Sing to the LORD a new song,
And praise Him in the
congregation of His godly ones
(believers).
2 Let Israel rejoice in their Maker;
Let Zion's children rejoice in their
King. [Zech 9:9; Matt 21:5]
3 Let them praise His name with
dancing;
Let them sing praises to Him with
the tambourine and lyre.

147:19 *His word.* God's word goes throughout His creation, causing snow, frost, hail, wind, and every other aspect of weather to obey His command. He has also given His Word to His people. Will we obey as the wind does, or will we be the only element of creation that is unresponsive to Him?
148:5 *He commanded and they were created.* The reality of God as Creator of the universe is the basis of His claim on our lives.

148:14 *a people near to Him.* When we consider the meaning of God's holiness (99:1; Isa 6:3) and the reality of His power, the marvel that He approaches us to mercifully provide for us becomes overwhelming.
149:1 *in the congregation.* One of the primary emphases in the Book of Psalms is that the praise of God is to take place in the center of the worshiping community. Praise unites the people of God (33:1 – 3).

18 Job 37:10 **19** Dt 33:4; Ps 76:1; Mal 4:4 **20** Ro 3:1,2 **PSALM 148** **4** 1Ki 8:27; 2Co 12:2; Ge 1:7 **5** Ge 1:1,6; Ps 33:6,9 **6** Ps 89:37; Jer 33:25 **7** Isa 43:20 **8** Ps 147:15-18 **9** Isa 44:23 **13** Isa 12:4; Ps 113:4 **14** Ps 75:10; Ps 149:9; Eph 2:17 **PSALM 149** **1** Ps 33:3; Isa 42:10 **2** Job 35:10; Ps 100:3; Isa 54:5; Zec 9:9; Mt 21:5 **3** Ps 81:2

[4]For the LORD takes pleasure in His people;
He will beautify the humble with salvation.

[5]Let the godly ones exult in glory;
Let them sing for joy on their beds.
[6]Let the high praises of God be in their throats,
And a two-edged sword in their hands, [Heb 4:12; Rev 1:16]
[7]To execute vengeance on the nations
And punishment on the peoples,
[8]To bind their kings with chains
And their nobles with fetters of iron,
[9]To execute on them the judgment written.
This is the honor for all His godly ones.
Praise the LORD! (Hallelujah!)

Psalm 150

A Psalm of Praise.

[1]PRAISE THE LORD!
Praise God in His sanctuary;
Praise Him in His mighty heavens.
[2]Praise Him for His mighty acts;
Praise Him according to [the abundance of] His greatness. [Deut 3:24; Ps 145:5, 6]

[3]Praise Him with trumpet sound;
Praise Him with harp and lyre.
[4]Praise Him with tambourine and dancing;
Praise Him with stringed instruments and flute.
[5]Praise Him with resounding cymbals;
Praise Him with loud cymbals.
[6]Let everything that has breath *and* every breath of life praise the LORD!
Praise the LORD! (Hallelujah!)

149:5 ***the godly ones.*** This term refers to those who demonstrate in their lives the characteristics of the God whom they serve.
149:6 ***two-edged sword.*** The focus of the psalm switches from the congregation at worship to the army in training. Israel's army was to be the vanguard for the battle of the Lord. Their training was to have a strong component of praise and worship to God.
150:1 ***Praise the LORD.*** This psalm is a development of the Hebrew word "hallelujah," meaning "praise the Lord." **Praise** — To praise God is to acknowledge who He is in all His glory. While thanksgiving is given to acknowledge what God has done, praise is given to declare who God is. Here are some facts about praise:

God alone is worthy of our praise (Ps 18:3; 113:3).

It is His will for us to praise Him (Ps 50:23).

Praise should be continuous (Ps 34:1; 71:6) and also public (Ps 22:25).

We are to praise God for His holiness (2Ch 20:21), grace (Eph 1:6), goodness (Ps 135:3), and kindness (Ps 138:2).

All nature praises God (Ps 148).

The sun, moon, and stars praise Him (Ps 19:1).

The angels praise Him (Ps 148:2).

150:6 ***everything that has breath.*** The very breath that God gives us should be used to praise Him. As long as we live we should praise our Creator (146:1 – 2). By His breath God created all things (33:6), and by our breath we should adore Him. The Book of Psalms begins with God's blessing on the righteous (1:1) and concludes with all of creation blessing its loving Creator.

4 Ps 35:27; Ps 132:16 **5** Job 35:10 **6** Heb 4:12; Rev 1:16 **9** Dt 7:1,2; Ps 148:14 **PSALM 150** **2** Ps 145:5; Dt 3:24 **3** Ps 81:2 **4** Ex 15:20; Ps 33:2; Isa 38:20 **5** 1Ch 15:16,19,28

THE

PROVERBS

▸ **AUTHOR:** Solomon's name appears at the beginning of the three sections that he wrote: 1 – 9; 10:1 – 22:16; and 25 – 29. Only about 800 of the more than 3000 proverbs attributed to Solomon are recorded here. It is likely that Solomon collected and edited proverbs other than his own. The collection of Solomonic proverbs in chapters 25 – 29 was assembled by the scribes of King Hezekiah. Some of the sayings in Proverbs are quite similar to those found in *The Wisdom of Amenemope,* a document of teachings on civil service by an Egyptian who probably lived between 1000 BC and 600 BC.

▸ **TIMES:** c. 950 – 700 BC ▸ **KEY VERSES:** Pr 3:5 – 6

▸ **THEME:** The Proverbs are part of what is commonly called the wisdom literature of the Bible. Each society needs a way to pass on what it understands to be the best way to live to succeeding generations. Biblical wisdom literature provided that means for the Jewish community. The Proverbs contain nuggets of truth that endure not only in the Jewish culture, but also make sense today. It contains basic wisdom on how to deal with the most common everyday issues that we face. Transcending personality and culture, the simple truth is that if people followed the advice of Proverbs, many of their problems would be reduced dramatically.

The Usefulness of Proverbs

1 THE PROVERBS (truths obscurely
expressed, maxims) of Solomon
son of David, king of Israel:
2 To know [skillful and godly]
wisdom and instruction;
To discern *and* comprehend the
words of understanding *and*
insight,
3 To receive instruction in wise
behavior *and* the discipline of
wise thoughtfulness,
Righteousness, justice, and
integrity;
4 That prudence (good judgment,
astute common sense) may
be given to the naive *or*
inexperienced [who are easily
misled],
And knowledge and discretion
(intelligent discernment) to the
youth,
5 The wise will hear and increase
their learning,
And the person of understanding
will acquire wise counsel *and*
the skill [to steer his course
wisely and lead others to the
truth], [Prov 9:9]

1:2 – 3 *To know . . . To discern . . . To receive.* These verbs refer to the ways we acquire wisdom. Wisdom refers to skill. Instruction could also be translated discipline; it refers to the process of receiving knowledge and applying it to daily life.

1:3 *Righteousness, justice, and integrity.* Biblical wisdom also has a moral context. It involves all of life and may often involve a change of behavior and a commitment to justice.

1:4 *knowledge and discretion (intelligent discernment) to the youth.* The young have little experience and are more likely to make mistakes. A wise person has learned by experience how to

CHAPTER 1 **1** 1Ki 4:32; Ecc 12:9 **5** Pr 9:9

THE WISE MAN ACCORDING TO PROVERBS: AN OUTLINE

I. HIS CHARACTER

A. He Is Teachable, Not Intractable
  1. He receives and loves instruction (18:15; 19:20)
  2. He grows in wisdom (1:5; 9:9; 10:14)

B. He Is Righteous, Not Wicked
  1. He fears the Lord (1:7; 14:16; see below under relationship to the Lord)
  2. He hates what is false (13:5)
  3. He shuns evil (3:7; 14:16; 16:6)
  4. He does what is righteous (2:20)
  5. He speaks the truth (22:21)

C. He Is Humble, Not Proud (15:33)

D. He Is Self-controlled, Not Rash
  1. His temperament
    a. He is self-controlled (29:11)
    b. He has a calm spirit (17:27)
    c. He is slow to become angry (29:8,11)
  2. His actions
    a. He is cautious, not rash (19:2)
    b. He thinks before he acts (13:16; 14:8)
    c. He thinks before he speaks (12:23; 15:2)

E. He Is Forgiving, Not Vindictive
  1. He is patient (19:11)
  2. He is concerned about goodwill/peace (14:9)
  3. He forgives those who wrong him (10:12; 17:9)
  4. He is not vindictive (20:22; 24:29)

II. HIS RELATIONSHIPS

A. To the Lord
  1. He fears the Lord (9:10; 14:16; 15:33)
  2. He trusts in the Lord (3:5; 16:3,20)
  3. He is ever mindful of the Lord (3:6)
  4. He chooses the Lord's way/wisdom (8:10–11; 17:24)
  5. He submits to the Lord's discipline (1:2–3; 3:11)
  6. He confesses his sin to the Lord (28:13)

B. To His Family
  1. To his parents
    a. He respects them (17:6; contrast 30:17)
    b. He listens to them (23:22; cf. 1:8; 4:1)
    c. He seeks to bring them honor and joy
      (1) By being wise (10:1; 15:20; 29:3)
      (2) By being righteous (23:24)
      (3) By being diligent (10:5)
  2. To his wife
    a. He appreciates her
      (1) As a gift from the Lord (18:22; 19:14)
      (2) As his crowning glory (12:4; 31:10–31)
    b. He praises her (31:28)
    c. He trusts her (31:11)
    d. He is faithful to her (5:15–20)
  3. To his children
    a. He loves them (3:12; 13:24)
    b. He is concerned about them (1:8—9:18)
    c. He trains them (22:6)
      (1) Reasons for training them
        (a) Own peace of mind and joy (29:17)
        (b) Child's honor and well-being (1:8–9; 4:9; 19:18; 23:13–14)
      (2) By teaching/instructing them (1:10; chs. 5–7; 28:7; cf. 4:1–9)
      (3) By disciplining them
        (a) By verbal correction (13:1)
        (b) By physical discipline (13:24; 23:13–14)
    d. He provides for their
      (1) Physical needs (21:20; cf. 27:23–27)
      (2) Spiritual heritage (14:26; 20:7)

C. To His Friends and Neighbors
  1. To his friends
    a. He values them (27:10)
    b. He is constant to them (17:17; 18:24)
    c. He gives them counsel (27:9,17; cf. 27:6; 28:23)
  2. To his neighbors
    a. He fulfills his obligations to them (3:27–28)
    b. He strives for peace with them (3:29–30)
    c. He does not outstay his welcome (25:17)
    d. He does not deceive or mislead them (16:29; 26:18–19)

III. HIS WORDS

A. The Power and Limitations of His Words
  1. Their power
    a. The power of life and death (12:6; 13:14; 15:4; 18:21)
    b. The power to heal or to wound (11:9,11; 12:18; 15:4,30; 16:24)
  2. Their limitations
    a. Cannot substitute for deeds (14:23)
    b. Cannot alter the facts (26:23–26)
    c. Cannot compel response (29:19)

B. The Character of His Words
  1. They are honest, not false (12:22; 16:13)
  2. They are few, not many (10:19)
    a. Not boastful (27:2)
    b. Not argumentative (17:14)
    c. Not contentious (29:9)
    d. Not a slanderer
      (1) Revealing secrets (11:13; 20:19)
      (2) Spreading gossip (10:18; 26:20–22)
  3. They are calm, not emotional
    a. Rational (15:28; 17:27)
    b. Gentle and peaceful (15:1,18)
    c. Persuasive (25:15)
  4. They are apt, not untimely (15:23; 25:11)

C. The Source of His Words
  1. His heart/character (compare 4:23 with Mt 12:33–35)
    a. Positively, he is righteous (cf. 10:11; 13:14)
    b. Negatively, he is not
      (1) Proud (13:10; cf. 6:16–19)
      (2) Hateful (26:24,28)
  2. His companions (13:20; 27:17)

6 To understand a proverb and a
figure [of speech] *or* an enigma
with its interpretation,
And the words of the wise and
their riddles [that require
reflection].

7 The [reverent] fear of the LORD
[that is, worshiping Him
and regarding Him as truly
awesome] is the beginning
and the preeminent part of
knowledge [its starting point
and its essence];
But arrogant fools despise
[skillful and godly] wisdom and
instruction *and* self-discipline.
[Ps 111:10]

The Enticement of Sinners

8 My son, hear the instruction of
your father,
And do not reject the teaching of
your mother.
9 For they are a garland of grace on
your head,
And chains *and* ornaments [of
gold] around your neck.
10 My son, if sinners entice you,
Do not consent. [Ps 1:1; Eph 5:11]
11 If they say, "Come with us;
Let us lie in wait to *shed* blood,
Let us ambush the innocent
without cause;
12 Let us swallow them alive like
Sheol (the place of the dead),
Even whole, as those who go down
to the pit [of death];
13 We will find *and* take all kinds of
precious possessions,
We will fill our houses with
spoil;
14 Throw in your lot with us [they
insist];
We will all have one money bag
[in common],"
15 My son, do not walk on the road
with them;
Keep your foot [far] away from
their path,
16 For their feet run to evil,
And they hurry to shed
blood.
17 Indeed, it is useless to spread the
baited net
In the sight of any bird;
18 But [when these people set a trap
for others] they lie in wait for
their own blood;
They set an ambush for their
own lives [and rush to their
destruction].
19 So are the ways of everyone who
is greedy for gain;
Greed takes away the lives of
its possessors. [Prov 15:27;
1 Tim 6:10]

---

distinguish what is true, praiseworthy, and good from what is false, shameful, and bad (Ro 12:1 – 2).

1:7 *The [reverent] fear of the LORD.* This concept is the most basic ingredient in wisdom. Fools have rejected the fear of the Lord. The term "despise" is strongly negative. Not fearing God is the same as rejecting wisdom outright (Da 11:32; Jn 17:3).

1:8 *My son, hear.* The opening words of wisdom's instruction come as an appeal from parents to their son (a generic term for child) — a theme that continues throughout the book. Both the Old and New Testament have one central teaching for children to understand — obey your parents. The Fifth Commandment makes honoring parents the foundational teaching in human relationships. It is also the only Commandment that comes with a promise, "that your days [on the earth] may be prolonged" (Dt 5:16). Paul's teaching in Ephesians 6:1 echoes what we see here in Proverbs. Obeying parents is the right thing to do.

From obedience springs the ability to deal with all the other important issues of life. The child who has not learned to obey his parents, who are God's representatives in the family, will probably not learn to obey God.

Christ's obedience is the perfect illustration. He was obedient to God the Father even though that obedience resulted in His death (Php 2:6 – 8). Being obedient for Christ meant no qualifications or limitations on that obedience.

1:15 – 18 *My son, do not walk on the road with them.* The parents speak words of caution. One step on the precipitous path is a step toward destruction. Spreading a net in the sight of the bird one wishes to trap would be a fruitless task. Yet the fool is less sensible than the bird; he will watch the trap being set and get caught in it anyway.

1:19 *takes away the lives.* The study of wisdom is a matter of life and death.

6 Ps 78:2 **7** Job 28:28; Ps 111:10; Ecc 12:13 **8** Pr 4:1 **10** Ge 39:7 **11** Jer 5:26 **12** Ps 28:1 **15** Ps 1:1; Ps 119:101 **16** Isa 59:7 **19** 1Ti 6:10

Wisdom Warns

20 Wisdom shouts in the street,
She raises her voice in the markets;
21 She calls out at the head of the noisy streets [where large crowds gather];
At the entrance of the city gates she speaks her words:
22 "How long, O naive ones [you who are easily misled], will you love being simple-minded *and* undiscerning?
How long will scoffers [who ridicule and deride] delight in scoffing,
How long will fools [who obstinately mock truth] hate knowledge?
23 "If you will turn *and* pay attention to my rebuke,
Behold, I [Wisdom] will pour out my spirit on you;
I will make my words known to you. [Is 11:2; Eph 1:17–20]
24 "Because I called and you refused [to answer],
I stretched out my hand and no one has paid attention [to my offer]; [Is 65:11, 12; 66:4; Jer 7:13, 14; Zech 7:11–13]
25 And you treated all my counsel as nothing
And would not accept my reprimand,
26 I also will laugh at your disaster;
I will mock when your dread *and* panic come,
27 When your dread *and* panic come like a storm,
And your disaster comes like a whirlwind,
When anxiety and distress come upon you [as retribution].
28 "Then they will call upon me (Wisdom), but I will not answer;
They will seek me eagerly but they will not find me, [Job 27:9; 35:12, 13; Is 1:15, 16; Jer 11:11; Mic 3:4; James 4:3]
29 Because they hated knowledge
And did not choose the fear of the LORD [that is, obeying Him with reverence and awe-filled respect], [Prov 8:13]
30 They would not accept my counsel,
And they spurned all my rebuke.
31 "Therefore they shall eat of the fruit of their own [wicked] way
And be satiated with [the penalty of] their own devices.
32 "For the turning away of the naive will kill them,
And the careless ease of [self-righteous] fools will destroy them. [Is 32:6]
33 "But whoever listens to me (Wisdom) will live securely *and* in confident trust
And will be at ease, without fear *or* dread of evil."

The Pursuit of Wisdom Brings Security

2 MY SON, if you will receive my words
And treasure my commandments within you,
2 So that your ear is attentive to [skillful and godly] wisdom,

1:20–21 *Wisdom shouts.* The word *wisdom* is plural and intensive. This fact calls attention to the word and heightens its meaning.
1:22–27 *How long, O naive ones [you who are easily misled], will you love being simple-minded and undiscerning?* Wisdom addresses the *naive* ones. These are young people who have not yet made up their minds about life or the direction they will take. Wisdom ridicules those who reject her when they come to face the inevitable judgment of their foolishness (Ps 2:4). Yet wisdom also laughs with joy at God's work and has delight in the people of God (8:30–31).
1:28–33 *I will not answer.* When fools despise wisdom, they must face the results of their choice. Their hatred for wisdom arises out of refusal to fear God (v. 29). Fools bring about their own destruction. In contrast, those who listen to her will find security.
2:1–5 *My son.* These verses begin the second of the "my son" passages and tie the concepts of wisdom and the knowledge of God more closely

20 Jn 7:37 **23** Joel 2:28 **24** Isa 66:4; Jer 7:13; Zec 7:11 **25** Ps 107:11; Lk 7:30 **26** Ps 2:4 **27** Pr 10:24
28 Job 27:9; Isa 1:15; Jer 14:12; Eze 8:18; Mic 3:4; Zec 7:13; Jas 4:3 **29** Job 21:14; Ps 119:173 **30** Ps 81:11
31 Job 4:8; Isa 3:11; Jer 6:19 **33** Ps 25:12; 112:7 **CHAPTER 2** **1** Pr 4:21

And apply your heart to
understanding [seeking it
conscientiously and striving for
it eagerly];
3 Yes, if you cry out for insight,
And lift up your voice for
understanding;
4 If you seek skillful *and* godly
wisdom as you would silver
And search for her as you would
hidden treasures;
5 Then you will understand the
[reverent] fear of the LORD
[that is, worshiping Him
and regarding Him as truly
awesome]
And discover the knowledge of
God. [Prov 1:7]
6 For the LORD gives [skillful and
godly] wisdom;
From His mouth come knowledge
and understanding.
7 He stores away sound wisdom for
the righteous [those who are in
right standing with Him];
He is a shield to those who walk
in integrity [those of honorable
character and moral courage],
8 He guards the paths of justice;
And He preserves the way of His
saints (believers). [1 Sam 2:9;
Ps 66:8, 9]
9 Then you will understand
righteousness and justice [in
every circumstance]
And integrity and every good
path.
10 For [skillful and godly] wisdom
will enter your heart
And knowledge will be pleasant to
your soul.
11 Discretion will watch over you,
Understanding *and* discernment
will guard you,
12 To keep you from the way of evil
and the evil man,
From the man who speaks
perverse things;
13 From those who leave the paths of
uprightness
To walk in the ways of darkness;
14 Who find joy in doing evil
And delight in the perversity of
evil,
15 Whose paths are crooked,
And who are devious in their ways;
16 To keep you from the immoral
woman;
From the seductress with her
flattering words, [Prov 2:11]
17 Who leaves the companion
(husband) of her youth,
And forgets the covenant of her
God.
18 For her house leads down to death
And her paths lead to the dead;
19 None who go to her return again,
Nor do they regain the paths of
life—
20 So you will walk in the way
of good men [that is, those
of personal integrity, moral
courage and honorable
character],
And keep to the paths of the
righteous.
21 For the upright [those who are in
right standing with God] will
live in the land

---

together. Wisdom is near but not always easy to embrace.

2:5 – 8 *the [reverent] fear of the LORD . . . the knowledge of God.* When a person seeks wisdom, he or she finds it. Those who know God, fear or revere Him. ***sound wisdom.*** This is another word for wisdom that can also mean "abiding success" or "victory."

2:10 – 11 *wisdom will enter your heart.* This phrase stresses the internalization of wisdom. The proverbs do not merely provide knowledge; thy provide insight into practical living.

2:12 – 15 *the way of evil and the evil man.* Evil is directly contrasted with wisdom. It is characterized by perverse things such as lies, deceptions, and deviousness.

2:16 – 19 *the immoral woman.* Adultery was foreign and strange to the ideal of God's law. "Immoral" also implied prostitution, because of the ancient Middle Eastern fertility cults that included sexual practices in their worship rituals. The adulteress is described as a flatterer, and flattery is the method used by the adulteress, not only in trapping her victims, but in excusing her sin (30:20). She is unfaithful to her husband and prefers to forget the covenant of her God (2:17).

4 Pr 3:14; Mt 13:44 **6** 1Ki 3:9; Jas 1:5 **7** Ps 84:11 **8** 1Sa 2:9; Ps 66:9 **11** Pr 6:22 **13** Jn 3:19 **14** Jer 11:15; Ro 1:32 **15** Ps 125:5 **16** Pr 5:20; Pr 5:3 **17** See Mal 2:14,15 **18** Pr 7:27 **21** Ps 37:29

And those [of integrity] who are
blameless [in God's sight] will
remain in it;
22 But the wicked will be cut off from
the land
And the treacherous shall be
[forcibly] uprooted *and* removed
from it.

The Rewards of Wisdom

3 MY SON, do not forget my
teaching,
But let your heart keep my
commandments;
2 For length of days and years of life
[worth living]
And tranquility *and* prosperity
[the wholeness of life's blessings]
they will add to you.
3 Do not let mercy *and* kindness and
truth leave you [instead let these
qualities define you];
Bind them [securely] around your
neck,
Write them on the tablet of your
heart. [Col 3:9–12]
4 So find favor and high esteem
In the sight of God and man.
[Luke 2:52]
5 Trust in *and* rely confidently on
the LORD with all your heart
And do not rely on your own
insight *or* understanding.
6 In all your ways know *and*
acknowledge *and* recognize
Him,
And He will make your paths
straight *and* smooth [removing
obstacles that block your way].
7 Do not be wise in your own eyes;
Fear the LORD [with reverent
awe and obedience] and turn
[entirely] away from evil.
[Prov 8:13]
8 It will be health to your body
[your marrow, your nerves, your
sinews, your muscles—all your
inner parts]
And refreshment (physical well-
being) to your bones.
9 Honor the LORD with your wealth
And with the first fruits of all
your crops (income); [Deut 26:2;
Mal 3:10; Luke 14:13, 14]
10 Then your barns will be
abundantly filled
And your vats will overflow with
new wine. [Deut 28:8]
11 My son, do not reject *or* take
lightly the discipline of the LORD
[learn from your mistakes and
the testing that comes from His
correction through discipline];
Nor despise His rebuke, [Ps 94:12;
Heb 12:5, 6; Rev 3:19]
12 For those whom the LORD loves He
corrects,
Even as a father *corrects* the son
in whom he delights.

13 Happy [blessed, considered
fortunate, to be admired] is the
man who finds [skillful and
godly] wisdom,
And the man who gains
understanding *and* insight
[learning from God's word and
life's experiences],

3:3–4 *mercy and kindness and truth.* These words describe God's character (Ps 100:5). The apostle John used the Greek equivalent of these words, "grace and truth," to describe Jesus' character in John 1:14.
3:5–6 *Trust in and rely confidently on the LORD.* The verb "trust" is complemented by the verb "rely." Trusting in God is a conscious dependence on God, much like relying on a tree for support. The command to acknowledge Him means to observe Him and get to know Him in the process of living. These are the vital elements of faith that should fill every area of life.

3:9 *the first fruits of all your crops.* God expects that out of the blessings we receive we should readily give. One aspect of worship is giving. These verses should not be taken as a formula for getting rich. They point to what is the proper response to God's gifts to us, not a return we get for investing.
3:11–12 *the discipline of the LORD.* Discipline is the other side of God's grace. We should cherish God's correction in our lives, because God disciplines those he loves (Heb 2:7–10).
3:13–18 *Happy.* The Beatitudes of Jesus in the Sermon on the Mount (Mt 5:3–12) work much the

---

22 Job 18:17; Ps 37:28 **CHAPTER 3** **1** Dt 8:1 **2** Ps 119:165 **3** Ex 13:9; Dt 6:8; 2Co 3:3 **4** Ro 14:18 **5** Ps 37:3,5; Jer 9:23 **6** 1Ch 28:9; Jer 10:23 **7** Ro 12:16; Pr 16:6 **8** Job 21:24 **9** Ex 22:29 **10** Dt 28:8 **11** Job 5:17; Ps 94:12 **12** Dt 8:5 **13** Pr 8:34,35

14 For wisdom's profit is better than
the profit of silver,
And her gain is better than fine
gold.
15 She is more precious than rubies;
And nothing you can wish for
compares with her [in value].
[Job 28:12–18]
16 Long life is in her right hand;
In her left hand are riches and
honor. [Prov 8:12–21; 1 Tim 4:8]
17 Her ways are highways of
pleasantness *and* favor,
And all her paths are peace.
18 She is a tree of life to those who
take hold of her,
And happy [blessed, considered
fortunate, to be admired] is
everyone who holds her tightly.
19 The LORD by His wisdom has
founded the earth;
By His understanding He has
established the heavens.
[Col 1:16]
20 By His knowledge the deeps were
broken up
And the clouds drip with dew.
21 My son, let them not escape from
your sight,
But keep sound wisdom and
discretion,
22 And they will be life to your soul
(your inner self)
And a gracious adornment to your
neck (your outer self).
23 Then you will walk on your way
[of life] securely
And your foot will not stumble.
[Ps 91:11, 12; Prov 10:9]
24 When you lie down, you will not
be afraid;
When you lie down, your sleep
will be sweet.
25 Do not be afraid of sudden fear
Nor of the storm of the wicked
when it comes [since you will be
blameless];
26 For the LORD will be your
confidence, firm *and* strong,
And will keep your foot from
being caught [in a trap].
27 Do not withhold good from those
to whom it is due [its rightful
recipients],
When it is in your power to do it.
[Rom 13:7; Gal 6:10]
28 Do not say to your neighbor, "Go,
and come back,
And tomorrow I will give it,"
When you have it with you.
[Lev 19:13; Deut 24:15]
29 Do not devise evil against your
neighbor,
Who lives securely beside you.
30 Do not quarrel with a man without
cause,
If he has done you no harm.
[Rom 12:18]
31 Do not envy a man of violence
And do not choose any of his
ways. [Ps 37:1; 73:3; Prov 24:1]
32 For the devious are repulsive to the
LORD;
But His private counsel is with
the upright [those with spiritual
integrity and moral courage].
[Ps 25:14]
33 The curse of the LORD is on the
house of the wicked,
But He blesses the home of the
just *and* righteous. [Ps 37:22;
Zech 5:4; Mal 2:2]
34 Though He scoffs at the scoffers
and scorns the scorners,
Yet He gives His grace [His
undeserved favor] to the
humble [those who give up
self-importance]. [James 4:6;
1 Pet 5:5]
35 The wise will inherit honor *and*
glory,
But dishonor *and* shame is
conferred on fools. [Is 32:6]

---

way these verses do. God is pleased with people who discover that wisdom is a priceless treasure.

3:19 *by His wisdom has founded the earth.* One of the central themes in Proverbs is the association of wisdom with creation (8:1–36).

3:21 *let them not escape.* This verse encourages the son to keep faith with wisdom. The intent is much like that of the Shema (Dt 6:4–9).

14 Job 28:13; Ps 19:10 **15** Mt 13:44 **16** 1Ti 4:8 **17** Mt 11:29 **18** Ge 2:9 **19** Ps 104:24 **20** Ge 1:9; Dt 33:28; Job 36:28 **22** Pr 1:9 **23** Ps 37:24 **24** Lev 26:6; Ps 3:5 **25** Ps 91:5 **27** Ro 13:7; Gal 6:10 **28** Lev 19:13 **30** Ro 12:18 **31** Ps 37:1 **32** Ps 25:14 **33** Zec 5:3,4; Mal 2:2; Ps 1:3 **34** Jas 4:6; 1Pe 5:5

A Father's Instruction

4 HEAR, O children, the
instruction of a father,
And pay attention [and be willing
to learn] so that you may gain
understanding *and* intelligent
discernment.
2 For I give you good doctrine;
Do not turn away from my
instruction.
3 When I was a son with my father
(David),
Tender and the only son in the
sight of my mother (Bathsheba),
4 He taught me and said to me,
"Let your heart hold fast my
words;
Keep my commandments and live.
[1 Chr 28:9; Eph 6:4]
5 "Get [skillful and godly] wisdom!
Acquire understanding [actively
seek spiritual discernment,
mature comprehension, and
logical interpretation]!
Do not forget nor turn away from
the words of my mouth.
6 "Do not turn away from her
(Wisdom) and she will guard
and protect you;
Love her, and she will watch over
you.
7 "The beginning of wisdom is: Get
[skillful and godly] wisdom [it is
preeminent]!
And with all your acquiring, get
understanding [actively seek
spiritual discernment, mature
comprehension, and logical
interpretation]. [James 1:5]
8 "Prize wisdom [and exalt her], and
she will exalt you;
She will honor you if you embrace
her.
9 "She will place on your head a
garland of grace;
She will present you with a crown
of beauty *and* glory."
10 Hear, my son, and accept my
sayings,
And the years of your life will be
many.
11 I have instructed you in the way of
[skillful and godly] wisdom;
I have led you in upright paths.
12 When you walk, your steps will
not be impeded [for your path
will be clear and open];
And when you run, you will not
stumble.
13 Take hold of instruction; [actively
seek it, grip it firmly and] do not
let go.
Guard her, for she is your life.
14 Do not enter the path of the
wicked,
And do not go the way of evil men.
15 Avoid it, do not travel on it;
Turn away from it and pass on.
16 For the wicked cannot sleep unless
they do evil;
And they are deprived of sleep
unless they make someone
stumble *and* fall.
17 For they eat the bread of
wickedness
And drink the wine of violence.
18 But the path of the just (righteous)
is like the light of dawn,
That shines brighter and brighter
until [it reaches its full strength
and glory in] the perfect day.
[2 Sam 23:4; Matt 5:14; Phil 2:15]
19 The way of the wicked is like
[deep] darkness;
They do not know over what they
stumble. [John 12:35]

4:1 – 4 *I was a son with my father.* In Israel training in wisdom happened in the home. As his father had taught him, so the son now teaches his own sons, one generation instructing another. The call for parents to teach the things of God to their children is based on Deuteronomy 6:7.

4:5 – 7 *Get [skillful and godly] wisdom.* Verses 5 – 9 present an impassioned plea from the father to his sons to acquire wisdom whatever the cost. The presentation follows a pattern: statement, restatement, embellishment. By making generous use of creative restatement, the ideas come through strongly.

4:9 *garland of grace . . . crown of beauty and glory.* These phrases emphasize the supreme value of wisdom. The person who holds wisdom in highest esteem and embraces it will be exalted and honored.

CHAPTER 4 **1** Ps 34:11; Pr 1:8 **3** 1Ch 29:1 **4** 1Ch 28:9; Eph 6:4; Pr 7:2 **5** Pr 2:2,3 **6** 2Th 2:10 **7** Mt 13:44; Lk 10:42 **8** 1Sa 2:30 **9** Pr 1:9; 3:22 **10** Pr 3:2 **12** Ps 18:36; Ps 91:11,12 **14** Ps 1:1; Pr 1:10,15 **16** Ps 36:4; Isa 57:20 **18** Mt 5:14,45; Php 2:15; 2Sa 23:4 **19** 1Sa 2:9; Job 18:5,6; Isa 59:9,10; Jer 23:12; Jn 12:35

20 My son, pay attention to my words
and be willing to learn;
Open your ears to my sayings.
21 Do not let them escape from your sight;
Keep them in the center of your heart.
22 For they are life to those who find them,
And healing *and* health to all their flesh.
23 Watch over your heart with all diligence,
For from it *flow* the springs of life.
24 Put away from you a deceitful (lying, misleading) mouth,
And put devious lips far from you.
25 Let your eyes look directly ahead [toward the path of moral courage]
And let your gaze be fixed straight in front of you [toward the path of integrity].
26 Consider well *and* watch carefully the path of your feet,
And all your ways will be steadfast *and* sure.
27 Do not turn away to the right nor to the left [where evil may lurk];
Turn your foot from [the path of] evil.

Pitfalls of Immorality

5 MY SON, be attentive to my wisdom [godly wisdom learned by costly experience],
Incline your ear to my understanding; [1 Kin 4:29]
2 That you may exercise discrimination *and* discretion (good judgment),
And your lips may reserve knowledge *and* answer wisely [to temptation].
3 For the lips of an immoral woman drip honey [like a honeycomb]
And her speech is smoother than oil; [Ezek 20:30; Col 2:8–10; 2 Pet 2:14–17]
4 But in the end she is bitter like [the extract of] wormwood,
Sharp as a two-edged sword.
5 Her feet go down to death;
Her steps take hold of Sheol (the nether world, the place of the dead),
6 So that she does not think [seriously] about the path of life;
Her ways are aimless *and* unstable; you cannot know where her path leads.

7 Now then, my sons, listen to me
And do not depart from (forget) the words of my mouth.
8 Let your way [in life] be far from her,
And do not go near the door of her house [avoid even being near the places of temptation], [Prov 4:15; Rom 16:17; 1 Thess 5:19–22]
9 Or you will give your honor to others,
And your years to the cruel one,
10 And strangers will be filled with your strength
And your hard-earned wealth will go to the house of a foreigner [who does not know God];
11 And you will groan when your *life is* ending,
When your flesh and your body are consumed;

4:20 – 27 *Watch over your heart with all diligence.* This section demands constancy of heart and purpose, honesty in speech, steadiness of gaze, and a right goal in walk and life. Setting off on the path of wisdom is no casual thing.

5:1 – 6 *the lips of an immoral woman drip honey.* Chapter 5 returns to the theme of the immoral woman (2:16 – 19). This passage speaks strongly for marital fidelity against all pressure to the contrary.

5:5 *Her feet go down to death.* This verse warns us of the deadly effects of immorality. Fornication, adultery, and prostitution lead to personality decay, venereal disease, abortion, separation, and divorce.

5:8 – 10 *Let your way [in life] be far from her.* Some temptations should be avoided at all cost. A wise son knows this and will not go near an immoral woman. The apostle Paul's instruction to Timothy to flee youthful lusts (2Ti 2:22) teaches the same theme.

21 Pr 3:3,21; Pr 2:1 **22** Pr 3:8; 12:18 **27** Dt 5:32; 28:14; Jos 1:7; Isa 1:16; Ro 12:9 **CHAPTER 5** **2** Mal 2:7 **3** Pr 2:16; 6:24; Ps 55:21 **4** Ecc 7:26; Heb 4:12 **5** Pr 7:27

12 And you say, "How I hated
instruction *and* discipline,
And my heart despised correction
and reproof!
13 "I have not listened to the voice of
my teachers,
Nor have I inclined my ear to those
who instructed me.
14 "I was almost in total ruin
In the midst of the assembly and
congregation."

15 Drink water from your own
cistern [of a pure marriage
relationship]
And fresh running water from
your own well.
16 Should your springs (children)
be dispersed,
As streams of water in the
streets?
17 [Confine yourself to your own
wife.] Let *your children* be yours
alone,
And not *the children* of strangers
with you.
18 Let your fountain (wife) be
blessed [with the rewards
of fidelity],
And rejoice in the wife of your
youth. [Song 4:12, 15]
19 *Let her be as* a loving hind and
graceful doe,
Let her breasts refresh *and* satisfy
you at all times;
Always be exhilarated *and* delight
in her love.
20 Why should you, my son, be
exhilarated with an immoral
woman
And embrace the bosom of an
outsider (pagan)?
21 For the ways of man are
directly before the eyes of
the LORD,
And He carefully watches all of
his paths [all of his comings and
goings]. [2 Chr 16:9; Job 31:4;
34:21; Prov 15:3; Jer 16:17;
Hos 7:2; Heb 4:13]
22 The iniquities done by a wicked
man will trap him,
And he will be held with the cords
of his sin.
23 He will die for lack of instruction
(discipline),
And in the greatness of his
foolishness he will go astray *and*
be lost.

Parental Counsel

6 MY SON, if you have become
surety (guaranteed a debt or
obligation) for your neighbor,
If you have given your pledge
for [the debt of] a stranger *or*
another [outside your family],
2 If you have been snared with the
words of your lips,
If you have been trapped by the
speech of your mouth,
3 Do this now, my son, and
release yourself [from the
obligation];
Since you have come into the hand
of your neighbor,
Go humble yourself, and plead
with your neighbor [to pay his
debt and release you].
4 Give no [unnecessary] sleep to
your eyes,
Nor slumber to your eyelids;
5 Tear yourself away like a gazelle
from the hand of *the hunter*
And like a bird from the hand of
the fowler.

6 Go to the ant, O lazy one;
Observe her ways and be wise,
[Job 12:7]

5:15 *Drink waters from your own cistern.* This image is a clear call to marital fidelity.
5:18 *And rejoice in the wife of your youth.* We are encouraged to find mutual joy and pleasure in the marriage bed. It is in fact blessed by God.
6:1 *if you have become surety (guaranteed a debt or obligation) for your neighbor.* This phrase refers to responsibility for someone else's debt as in cosigning a loan. This does not mean we should never be generous, only that we should not promise what we cannot deliver.
6:6 *Go to the ant, O lazy one.* This passage is a warning about laziness. A lazy person is a captive to leisure. He can learn all he needs to know by studying the work habits of the ant.

12 Pr 1:29; Pr 1:25; 12:1 **18** Mal 2:14 **19** SS 2:9; 4:5 **20** Pr 2:16 **21** 2Ch 16:9; Job 31:4; Pr 15:3; Jer 16:17; Hos 7:2; Heb 4:13 **22** Ps 9:15 **23** Job 4:21; 36:12 **CHAPTER 6** **1** Pr 11:15 **4** Ps 132:4 **6** Job 12:7

7 Which, having no chief,
Overseer or ruler,
8 She prepares her food in the summer
And brings in her provisions [of food for the winter] in the harvest.
9 How long will you lie down, O lazy one?
When will you arise from your sleep [and learn self-discipline]? [Prov 24:33, 34]
10 "Yet a little sleep, a little slumber,
A little folding of the hands to lie down *and* rest"—
11 So your poverty will come like an *approaching* prowler who walks [slowly, but surely]
And your need [will come] like an armed man [making you helpless]. [Prov 10:4; 13:4; 20:4]

12 A worthless person, a wicked man,
Is one who walks with a perverse (corrupt, vulgar) mouth.
13 Who winks with his eyes [in mockery], who shuffles his feet [to signal],
Who points with his fingers [to give subversive instruction];
14 Who perversely in his heart plots trouble *and* evil continually;
Who spreads discord *and* strife.
15 Therefore [the crushing weight of] his disaster will come suddenly *upon him;*
Instantly he will be broken, and there will be no healing *or* remedy [because he has no heart for God].

16 These six things the LORD hates;
Indeed, seven are repulsive to Him:
17 A proud look [the attitude that makes one overestimate oneself and discount others], a lying tongue,
And hands that shed innocent blood, [Ps 120:2, 3]
18 A heart that creates wicked plans,
Feet that run swiftly to evil,
19 A false witness who breathes out lies [even half-truths],
And one who spreads discord (rumors) among brothers.

20 My son, be guided by your father's [God-given] commandment (instruction)
And do not reject the teaching of your mother; [Eph 6:1–3]
21 Bind them continually upon your heart (in your thoughts),
And tie them around your neck. [Prov 3:3; 7:3]
22 When you walk about, they (the godly teachings of your parents) will guide you;
When you sleep, they will keep watch over you;
And when you awake, they will talk to you.
23 For the commandment is a lamp, and the teaching [of the law] is light,
And reproofs (rebukes) for discipline are the way of life, [Ps 19:8; 119:105]
24 To keep you from the evil woman,
From [the flattery of] the smooth tongue of an immoral woman.

6:12 *a wicked man.* He is a troublemaker. Unlike the sluggard, whose only desire is to take a nap, the troublemaker cannot wait to cause more problems. He delights in creating dissension.

6:16 *Indeed, seven are repulsive to Him.* The use of numerical progression — six, indeed seven — in these proverbs is a rhetorical device that embellishes the poetry and serves as a memory aid. It gives the impression that there is more to be said about the topic. The word "repulsive" is the Bible's strongest expression of hatred for wickedness.

6:23 Illumination of God's Word — Illumination is the last of three important steps that God takes to communicate with us. The first step is revelation which occurred when God spoke to the authors of the Bible. The second step was inspiration, which is the process God used to guide them in correctly writing down His message. The third step provides understanding as men and women hear and see God's message. It is a divine process whereby God causes the written revelation to be understood by the human heart.

9 Pr 24:33 **11** Pr 10:4 **13** Job 15:12; Pr 10:10 **14** Mic 2:1; ver. 19 **15** Jer 19:11; 2Ch 36:16 **17** Ps 101:5; Ps 120:2,3; Isa 1:15 **18** Ge 6:5; Isa 59:7 **19** Ps 27:12; ver. 14 **20** Eph 6:1 **21** Pr 3:3 **22** Pr 3:23; Pr 2:11 **23** Ps 19:8 **24** Pr 2:16

25 Do not desire (lust after) her
beauty in your heart,
Nor let her capture you with her
eyelashes.
26 For on account of a prostitute one
is reduced to a piece of bread [to
be eaten up],
And the immoral woman hunts
[with a hook] the precious life
[of a man].
27 Can a man take fire to his chest
And his clothes not be burned?
28 Or can a man walk on hot coals
And his feet not be scorched?
29 So is the one who goes in to his
neighbor's wife;
Whoever touches her will not
be found innocent *or* go
unpunished.
30 People do not despise a thief if he
steals
To satisfy himself when he is
hungry;
31 But when he is found, he must
repay seven times [what he
stole];
He must give all the property of
his house [if necessary to meet
his fine].
32 But whoever commits adultery
with a woman lacks common
sense *and* sound judgment *and*
an understanding [of moral
principles];
He who would destroy his soul
does it.
33 Wounds and disgrace he will find,
And his reproach (blame) will not
be blotted out.
34 For jealousy enrages the
[wronged] husband;
He will not spare [the guilty one]
on the day of vengeance.
35 He will not accept any ransom
[offered to buy him off from
demanding full punishment];
Nor will he be satisfied though you
offer him many gifts (bribes).

The Wiles of the Prostitute

7 MY SON, keep my words
And treasure my commandments
within you [so they are readily
available to guide you].
2 Keep my commandments and live,
And keep my teaching *and* law as
the apple of your eye.
3 Bind them [securely] on your
fingers;
Write them on the tablet of your
heart.
4 Say to [skillful and godly] wisdom,
"You are my sister,"
And regard understanding *and*
intelligent insight as your
intimate friends;
5 That they may keep you from the
immoral woman,
From the foreigner [who does not
observe God's laws and] who
flatters with her [smooth] words.
6 For at the window of my house
I looked out through my lattice.
7 And among the naive [the
inexperienced and gullible],
I saw among the youths
A young man lacking [good]
sense,
8 Passing through the street near
her corner;
And he took the path to her house
9 In the twilight, in the evening;
In the black and dark night.
10 And there a woman met him,

Christians need this illumination because we are blinded by our fallen fleshly natures (1Co 2:14) and by Satan himself (2Co 4:3 – 4). The Holy Spirit is the one who illumines us (Jn 14:26). We see this illumination process at work in Acts 2 when over 3,000 people respond to Peter's message and become followers of Christ.

Christians also need this illumination on a day to day basis to help them fully grasp the marvelous message in God's Word. Paul tells us that the Holy Spirit will show these tremendous truths to us as we read the Scriptures (1Co 2:10; 2Co 4:6).

6:30 ***if he steals To satisfy himself . . . hungry.*** This passage is not condoning theft. It merely contrasts theft with adultery, which never makes sense. For ancient Israelites, marital fidelity was a mark of one's fidelity to God.

7:1 – 5 ***as the apple of your eye.*** People should guard wise words as instinctively as they protect the pupil of the eye.

---

25 Mt 5:28 **26** Pr 29:3; Ge 39:14; Eze 13:18 **31** Ex 22:1 **32** Pr 7:7 **CHAPTER 7** **1** Pr 2:1 **2** Lev 18:5; Pr 4:4; Dt 32:10 **3** Dt 6:8; 11:18; Pr 3:3; 6:21 **5** Pr 2:16; 5:3; 6:24 **7** Pr 6:32; 9:4,16 **9** Job 24:15

Dressed as a prostitute and sly *and* cunning of heart.
11 She was boisterous and rebellious;
She would not stay at home.
12 At times *she was* in the streets, at times in the market places,
Lurking *and* setting her ambush at every corner.
13 So she caught him and kissed him
And with a brazen *and* impudent face she said to him:
14 "I have peace offerings with me;
Today I have paid my vows.
15 "So I came out to meet you [that you might share with me the feast of my offering],
Diligently I sought your face and I have found you.
16 "I have spread my couch with coverings *and* cushions of tapestry,
With colored fine linen of Egypt.
17 "I have perfumed my bed
With myrrh, aloes, and cinnamon.
18 "Come, let us drink our fill of love until morning;
Let us console *and* delight ourselves with love.
19 "For my husband is not at home.
He has gone on a long journey;
20 He has taken a bag of money with him,
And he will come home on the appointed day."
21 With her many persuasions she caused him to yield;
With her flattering lips she seduced him.
22 Suddenly he went after her, as an ox goes to the slaughter [not knowing the outcome],
Or as one in stocks going to the correction [to be given] to a fool,
23 Until an arrow pierced his liver [with a mortal wound];
Like a bird fluttering straight into the net,
He did not know that it *would cost* him his life.

24 Now therefore, my sons, listen to me,
And pay attention to the words of my mouth.
25 Do not let your heart turn aside to her ways,
Do not stray into her [evil, immoral] paths.
26 For she has cast down many [mortally] wounded;
Indeed, all who were killed by her were strong. [Neh 13:26]
27 Her house is the way to Sheol,
Descending to the chambers of death. [1 Cor 6:9]

The Commendation of Wisdom

8 DOES NOT wisdom call,
And understanding lift up her voice?
2 On the top of the heights beside the way,
Where the paths meet, wisdom takes her stand;
3 Beside the gates, at the entrance to the city,
At the entrance of the doors, she cries out:
4 "To you, O men, I call,
And my voice is directed to the sons of men.
5 "O you naive *or* inexperienced [who are easily misled], understand prudence *and* seek astute common sense;

7:15 ***I came out to meet you.*** All the adulteress does is perverse. Here she presents an offering as a feast for the young man she plans to entrap. She overcomes her target's fear by assuring him that her husband will not come home and discover them together.

7:22 ***as one in stocks going to the correction.*** This passage uses several unflattering metaphors to describe how a young fool falls into immorality.

8:1 ***Does not wisdom call.*** Wisdom, in contrast to foolishness, wants to reach everyone and therefore broadcasts her message publicly, unlike the immoral woman, who uses privacy and deception to achieve her goals. Wisdom is open to all. Her location is at the place of decision, the place of authority, the place of beginnings. She speaks loudly, but only those who adjust their lives to God's truth actually enjoy the spoils of wisdom.

11 Pr 9:13; 1Ti 5:13; Titus 2:5 **16** Isa 19:9 **21** Pr 5:3; Ps 12:2 **23** Ecc 9:12 **26** Neh 13:26 **27** Pr 2:18; 5:5; 9:18
CHAPTER 8 **1** Pr 1:20; 9:3

And, O you [closed-minded, self-confident] fools, understand wisdom [seek the insight and self-discipline that leads to godly living]. [Is 32:6]
6 "Listen, for I will speak excellent *and* noble things;
And the opening of my lips *will reveal* right things.
7 "For my mouth will utter truth,
And wickedness is repulsive *and* loathsome to my lips.
8 "All the words of my mouth are in righteousness (upright, in right standing with God);
There is nothing contrary to truth or perverted (crooked) in them.
9 "They are all straightforward to him who understands [with an open and willing mind],
And right to those who find knowledge *and* live by it.
10 "Take my instruction rather than [seeking] silver,
And take knowledge rather than choicest gold,
11 "For wisdom is better than rubies;
And all desirable things cannot compare with her. [Job 28:15; Ps 19:10; 119:127]
12 "I, [godly] wisdom, reside with prudence [good judgment, moral courage and astute common sense],
And I find knowledge and discretion. [James 1:5]
13 "The [reverent] fear *and* worshipful awe of the LORD *includes* the hatred of evil;
Pride and arrogance and the evil way,
And the perverted mouth, I hate.
14 "Counsel is mine and sound wisdom;
I am understanding, power *and* strength are mine.
15 "By me kings reign
And rulers decide *and* decree justice. [Dan 2:21; Rom 13:1]
16 "By me princes rule, and nobles,
All who judge *and* govern rightly.
17 "I love those who love me;
And those who seek me early *and* diligently will find me. [1 Sam 2:30; Ps 91:14; John 14:21; James 1:5]
18 "Riches and honor are with me,
Enduring wealth and righteousness (right standing with God). [Prov 3:16; Matt 6:33]
19 "My fruit is better than gold, even pure gold,
And my yield is better than choicest silver.
20 "I, [Wisdom, continuously] walk in the way of righteousness,
In the midst of the paths of justice,
21 That I may cause those who love me to inherit wealth *and* true riches,
And that I may fill their treasuries.
22 "The LORD created *and* possessed me at the beginning of His way,
Before His works of old [were accomplished].
23 "From everlasting I was established *and* ordained,
From the beginning, before the earth existed, [I, godly wisdom, existed]. [John 1:1; 1 Cor 1:24]
24 "When there were no ocean depths I was born,
When there were no fountains *and* springs overflowing with water.
25 "Before the mountains were settled,
Before the hills, I was born; [Job 15:7, 8]
26 While He had not yet made the earth and the fields,
Or the first of the dust of the earth.
27 "When He established the heavens, I [Wisdom] was there;

8:13 *The [reverent] fear ... of the LORD includes the hatred of evil.* The offer of wisdom is held out only to those who fear God. Coming to wisdom requires coming to God, and coming to God means turning away from all that God hates — evil, pride, and arrogance.

8:15 *By me kings reign And rulers.* Power and authority require the use of wisdom.

6 Pr 22:20 **11** Job 28:15; Ps 19:10; 119:127; Pr 3:14,15; 4:5,7; 16:16 **13** Pr 16:6; Pr 6:17; Pr 4:24 **14** Ecc 7:19 **15** Da 2:21; Ro 13:1 **17** 1Sa 2:30; Ps 91:14; Jn 14:21; Jas 1:5 **18** Pr 3:16; Mt 6:33 **19** ver. 10; Pr 3:14 **22** Pr 3:19 **23** Ps 2:6 **25** Job 15:7,8

When He drew a circle upon the
face of the deep,
28 When He made firm the skies
above,
When the fountains and springs
of the deep became fixed *and*
strong,
29 When He set for the sea its
boundary
So that the waters would not
transgress [the boundaries set
by] His command,
When He marked out the
foundations of the earth—
[Job 38:10, 11; Ps 104:6–9; Jer 5:22]
30 Then I was beside Him, as a
master craftsman;
And I was daily His delight;
Rejoicing before Him always,
[Matt 3:17; John 1:2, 18]
31 Rejoicing in the world, His
inhabited earth,
And having my delight in the sons
of men. [Ps 16:3]

32 "Now therefore, O sons, listen to me,
For blessed [happy, prosperous, to
be admired] are they who keep
my ways. [Ps 119:1, 2; 128:1, 2;
Luke 11:28]
33 "Heed (pay attention to)
instruction and be wise,
And do not ignore *or* neglect it.
34 "Blessed [happy, prosperous, to be
admired] is the man who listens
to me,
Watching daily at my gates,
Waiting at my doorposts.
35 "For whoever finds me (Wisdom)
finds life
And obtains favor *and* grace from
the LORD.
36 "But he who fails to find me *or* sins
against me injures himself;
All those who hate me love *and*
court death."

Wisdom's Invitation

9 WISDOM HAS built her
[spacious and sufficient] house;
She has hewn out *and* set up her
seven pillars.
2 She has prepared her food, she has
mixed her wine;
She has also set her table.
[Matt 22:2–4]
3 She has sent out her maidens, she
calls
From the highest places of the city:
4 "Whoever is naive *or* inexperienced,
let him turn in here!"
As for him who lacks
understanding, she says,
5 "Come, eat my food
And drink the wine I have mixed
[and accept my gifts]. [Is 55:1;
John 6:27]
6 "Leave [behind] your foolishness
[and the foolish] and live,
And walk in the way of insight
and understanding."

7 He who corrects *and* instructs a
scoffer gets dishonor for himself,

8:30–31 *as a master craftsman.* With wisdom's skill, God created the universe. A proper study of the universe is a progressive study of God's wisdom. Her greatest joy comes in the finest of the work of God — the sons of men — that is, humankind.

9:1 *seven pillars.* The number seven represents completeness, as it often does in Semitic poetry. That is, it is not that there were precisely seven pillars so much as that the house of wisdom was solidly built and substantial in character.

9:2 *mixed her wine.* Wine was a staple in ancient Israel; but when a feast was special, a homemaker would add aromatic spices to the wine, enlivening the bouquet and improving the taste (SS 8:2). This idea sets up a contrast with the foolish woman. While wisdom is busy, attending to every detail like a gracious hostess, the foolish woman sits at the entrance of her house with very little to do (9:14).

9:4 *Whoever is naive or inexperienced.* Wisdom makes a point of inviting the naive, meaning those who have not yet made up their minds about their course in life. The person who comes to wisdom has nothing to lose but naiveté. Hebrews 5:14 speaks of a mature person as one who is able to eat and enjoy solid food, in contrast to the naive, who is able only to drink milk.

9:7 *He who corrects and instructs a scoffer.* This personality is thoroughly set against wisdom (1:22) and scoffs at the things of God (Ps 1:1). By contrast a wise man accepts correction and

29 Ge 1:9,10; Job 38:10; Jer 5:22; Job 38:4 **30** Jn 1:1,2; Mt 3:17; Col 1:13 **31** Ps 16:3 **32** Ps 119:1,2; Lk 11:28 **34** Pr 3:13,18 **35** Pr 12:2 **36** Pr 20:2 **CHAPTER 9** **1** Mt 16:18; Eph 2:20; 1Pe 2:5 **2** Mt 22:4; Pr 23:30 **3** Ro 10:15; Pr 8:1,2; ver. 14 **4** Ps 19:7; Pr 6:32 **5** SS 5:1; Isa 55:1; Jn 6:27

And he who rebukes a wicked
man gets insults for himself.
8 Do not correct a scoffer [who
foolishly ridicules and takes no
responsibility for his error] or he
will hate you;
Correct a wise man [who learns
from his error], and he will love
you. [Ps 141:5]
9 Give *instruction* to a wise man
and he will become even wiser;
Teach a righteous man and he will
increase his learning.
10 The [reverent] fear of the LORD
[that is, worshiping Him
and regarding Him as truly
awesome] is the beginning *and*
the preeminent part of wisdom
[its starting point and its
essence],
And the knowledge of the Holy
One is understanding *and*
spiritual insight.
11 For by me (wisdom from God)
your days will be multiplied,
And years of life shall be
increased.
12 If you are wise, you are wise for
yourself [for your own benefit];
If you scoff [thoughtlessly ridicule
and disdain], you alone will pay
the penalty.

13 The foolish woman is restless *and*
noisy;
She is naive *and* easily misled *and*
thoughtless, and knows nothing
at all [of eternal value].
14 She sits at the doorway of her
house,
On a seat by the high *and*
conspicuous places of the city,
15 Calling to those who pass by,
Who are making their paths
straight:
16 "Whoever is naive *or* inexperienced,
let him turn in here!"
And to him who lacks
understanding (common sense),
she says,
17 "Stolen waters (pleasures) are
sweet [because they are
forbidden];
And bread *eaten* in secret is
pleasant." [Prov 20:17]
18 But he does not know that the
spirits of the dead are there,
And that her guests are [already]
in the depths of Sheol (the
nether world, the place of the
dead).

Contrast of the Righteous and the Wicked

10 THE PROVERBS of Solomon:
A wise son makes a father glad,
But a foolish [stubborn] son [who
refuses to learn] is a grief to his
mother.
2 Treasures of wickedness *and* ill-
gotten gains do not profit,
But righteousness *and* moral
integrity in daily life rescues
from death.
3 The LORD will not allow the
righteous to hunger [God will
meet all his needs],
But He will reject *and* cast away
the craving of the wicked.
[Ps 34:9, 10; 37:25]
4 Poor is he who works with a
negligent *and* idle hand,

---

responds with gratitude to the one who points out his error.

9:13 – 18 *The foolish woman is restless and noisy.* This section is a parody of 9:1 – 6. Like personified wisdom, the woman of folly calls out an invitation. But she is brash, loud, undisciplined, and knows nothing (7:10 – 12). She cries out in the same words that wisdom has used, but she has no marvelous banquet for her guests, only shabby food, stolen and meager.

9:18 *the dead are there.* Fools cast away all restraint and express their freedom in direct defiance of heaven's moral law for the ordering of our conduct on earth. But they do not know that the end of such perverse behavior is death. The way of wisdom is to turn from such a disastrous course while there is time.

10:1 *The proverbs of Solomon.* This section focuses on the wise son in contrast with the foolish son. Son is used generically for son and daughter.

10:4 *negligent and idle hand.* Proverbs often links laziness with poverty, and hard work with riches.

8 Mt 7:6; Ps 141:5 **9** Mt 13:12 **10** Job 28:28; Pr 1:7 **11** Pr 3:2,16 **12** Job 35:6,7; Pr 16:26 **13** Pr 7:11 **14** ver. 3 **16** Pr 7:7,8 **17** Pr 20:17 **18** Pr 2:18 **CHAPTER 10** **1** Pr 15:20 **2** Ps 49:6; Lk 12:20; Da 4:27 **3** Ps 10:14 **4** Pr 19:15; Pr 13:4

But the hand of the diligent makes *him* rich.

[5]He who gathers during summer *and* takes advantage of his opportunities is a son who acts wisely,
But he who sleeps during harvest *and* ignores the moment of opportunity is a son who acts shamefully.

[6]Blessings are on the head of the righteous [the upright, those in right standing with God],
But the mouth of the wicked conceals violence.

[7]The memory of the righteous [person] is a [source of] blessing,
But the name of the wicked will [be forgotten and] rot [like a corpse]. [Ps 112:6; 9:5]

[8]The wise in heart [are willing to learn so they] will accept *and* obey commands (instruction),
But the babbling fool [who is arrogant and thinks himself wise] will come to ruin.

[9]He who walks in integrity *and* with moral character walks securely,
But he who takes a crooked way will be discovered *and* punished.

[10]He who [maliciously] winks the eye [of evil intent] causes trouble;
And the babbling fool [who is arrogant and thinks himself wise] will come to ruin.

[11]The mouth of the righteous is a fountain of life *and* his words of wisdom are a source of blessing,
But the mouth of the wicked conceals violence *and* evil.

[12]Hatred stirs up strife,
But love covers *and* overwhelms all transgressions [forgiving and overlooking another's faults].

[13]On the lips of the discerning, [skillful and godly] wisdom is found,
But discipline *and* the rod are for the back of the one who is without common sense *and* understanding.

[14]Wise men store up *and* treasure knowledge [in mind and heart],
But with the mouth of the foolish, ruin is at hand.

[15]The rich man's wealth is his fortress;
The ruin of the poor is their poverty. [Ps 52:7; 1 Tim 6:17]

[16]The wages of the righteous [the upright, those in right standing with God] is [a worthwhile, meaningful] life,
The income of the wicked, punishment. [Rom 6:21–23; 1 Tim 6:10]

[17]He who learns from instruction *and* correction is on the [right] path of life [and for others his example is a path toward wisdom and blessing],

---

10:7 *But the name of the wicked.* In biblical times a person's name was most significant. When a person's name was remembered by future generations for good, that person's life was believed to have been of great value. But when the memory of a name rotted away, it was as though that person had never lived.

10:9 *walks in integrity.* Many of the proverbs contrast two paths of life. This phrase means conforming to God's law as a course of life. Choosing crooked paths is willfully to disdain the guidance God so graciously provided.

10:12 *Hatred . . . love.* This verse describes interpersonal relationships, not salvation. When people respond in love to each other, they cover over the sins or offenses that would otherwise come between them.

10:13 *But discipline and the rod are for the back of the one.* Rod refers to punishment, in this case deserved. The phrase "lack of understanding" comes from the Hebrew idiom "lack heart." The one who "lacks heart" is contrasted with the one who is "wise in heart" (10:8).

10:14 – 15 *store up and treasure knowledge.* This set of verses contrasts the wise person's pursuit of knowledge with the empty talk of a fool. Wealth is like a fortress. In biblical times only walled cities had any defense against enemy armies.

10:16 – 17 *The wages of the righteous . . . is [a worthwhile, meaningful] life.* These verses present the doctrine of the two ways. The righteous are on the way of life but the wicked wander from it.

---

5 Pr 19:26 **6** ver. 11 **7** Ps 112:6; Ecc 8:10 **8** ver. 10 **9** Ps 23:4; Pr 28:18; Isa 33:15,16 **10** Pr 6:13; ver. 8
11 Ps 37:30; 107:42 **12** 1Co 13:7; 1Pe 4:8 **13** Pr 26:3 **14** Pr 18:7 **15** Job 31:24; 1Ti 6:17

But he who ignores *and* refuses
correction goes off course [and
for others his example is a path
toward sin and ruin].
18 He who hides hatred has lying
lips,
And he who spreads slander is a
fool. [Prov 26:24–26]
19 When there are many words,
transgression *and* offense are
unavoidable,
But he who controls his lips *and*
keeps thoughtful silence is wise.
20 The tongue of the righteous is like
precious silver (greatly valued);
The heart of the wicked is worth
little.
21 The lips of the righteous feed *and*
guide many,
But fools [who reject God and
His wisdom] die for lack of
understanding.
22 The blessing of the LORD brings
[true] riches,
And He adds no sorrow to it [for it
comes as a blessing from God].
23 Engaging in evil is like sport to the
fool [who refuses wisdom and
chases sin],
But to a man of understanding
[skillful and godly] wisdom
brings joy.
24 What the wicked fears will come
upon him,
But the desire of the righteous [for
the blessings of God] will be
granted.
25 When the whirlwind passes, the
wicked is no more,
But the righteous has an
everlasting foundation.
[Ps 125:1; Matt 7:24–27]
26 Like vinegar to the teeth and
smoke to the eyes,
So is the lazy one to those who
send him *to work.*
27 The [reverent] fear of the LORD
[worshiping, obeying, serving,
and trusting Him with awe-
filled respect] prolongs one's
life,
But the years of the wicked will be
shortened.
28 The hope of the righteous [those
of honorable character and
integrity] is joy,
But the expectation of the wicked
[those who oppose God and
ignore His wisdom] comes to
nothing.
29 The way of the LORD is a
stronghold to the upright,
But it is ruin to those who do evil.
30 The [consistently] righteous will
never be shaken,
But the wicked will not inhabit the
earth. [Ps 37:22; 125:1]
31 The mouth of the righteous
flows with [skillful and godly]
wisdom,
But the perverted tongue will be
cut out.
32 The lips of the righteous know
(speak) what is acceptable,
But the mouth of the wicked
knows (speaks) what is
perverted (twisted).

10:23 *Engaging in evil is like sport.* Sport here usually means "joyous laughter." Here the proverb uses the word in a completely negative sense. For the fool, wickedness is only a game. He makes up the rules as he goes along; for losing is only in getting caught. But a person who has understanding takes a longer-term perspective.

10:25 *But the righteous has an everlasting foundation.* The short-lived nature of the wicked is contrasted with the stability of the righteous. The foundation of righteousness is faith in God, much like the waters that nourish the tree of Psalm 1:3.

10:28 *hope . . . expectation.* The righteous have something to look forward to; the wicked do not.

10:29 *The way of the LORD is a stronghold to the upright.* Different people see the way of the Lord differently. Those who are innocent see it as a shelter from the storm. Those who practice iniquity see it only as a source of condemnation and wrath. The viewer's perspective makes all the difference.

10:31 – 32 *The mouth of the righteous flows with [skillful and godly] wisdom.* These verses form another pair of sentences about true and false speech. This repetition with variation indicates the significance of truth and falsehood.

18 Ps 15:3 **19** Ecc 5:3; Jas 3:2 **22** Ge 24:35; Ps 37:22 **23** Pr 15:21 **24** Job 15:21; Ps 145:19; Mt 5:6; 1Jn 5:14 **25** Ps 37:9,10; Ps 15:5; Mt 16:18 **27** Pr 9:11; Job 15:32 **28** Job 8:13 **29** Ps 1:6 **30** Ps 37:22 **31** Ps 37:30

Contrast the Upright and the Wicked

11 A FALSE balance *and*
dishonest business practices
are extremely offensive to the
LORD,
But an accurate scale is His
delight. [Lev 19:35, 36;
Prov 16:11]
2 When pride comes [boiling up
with an arrogant attitude of
self-importance], then come
dishonor *and* shame,
But with the humble [the teachable
who have been chiseled by
trial and who have learned to
walk humbly with God] there is
wisdom *and* soundness of mind.
3 The integrity *and* moral courage
of the upright will guide them,
But the crookedness of the
treacherous will destroy them.
4 Riches will not provide security
in the day of wrath *and*
judgment,
But righteousness rescues from
death. [Prov 10:2; Zeph 1:18]
5 The righteousness of the blameless
will smooth their way *and* keep
it straight,
But the wicked will fall by his own
wickedness.
6 The righteousness of the upright
will rescue them,
But the treacherous will be caught
by their own greed.
7 When the wicked man dies, his
expectation will perish;
And the hope of [godless] strong
men perishes.
8 The righteous is rescued from
trouble,
And the wicked takes his place.
9 With his mouth the godless man
destroys his neighbor,
But through knowledge *and*
discernment the righteous will
be rescued.
10 When it goes well for the
righteous, the city rejoices,
And when the wicked perish, there
are shouts of joy.
11 By the blessing [of the influence]
of the upright the city is exalted,
But by the mouth of the wicked it
is torn down.
12 He who despises his neighbor
lacks sense,
But a man of understanding keeps
silent.
13 He who goes about as a gossip
reveals secrets,
But he who is trustworthy *and*
faithful keeps a matter hidden.
14 Where there is no [wise,
intelligent] guidance, the people
fall [and go off course like a ship
without a helm],
But in the abundance of [wise and
godly] counselors there is victory.
15 He who puts up security *and*
guarantees a debt for an
outsider will surely suffer [for
his foolishness],
But he who hates (declines) being
a guarantor is secure [from its
penalties].

11:1 *A false balance and dishonest business practices are extremely offensive to the LORD.* Dealing fairly with one another is an outgrowth of the command to love one's neighbor as oneself (Lev 19:18), which in turn is an outgrowth of the central command given to Israel, to love God above all else (Dt 6:4–9). That is why dishonest scales are an abomination to God.

11:2 *When pride comes.* Many proverbs contrast the arrogant with the humble, as this one does. The Hebrew word for pride comes from a root that means "to boil up"; it refers to a raging arrogance or insolence.

11:10 *When it goes well for the righteous.* Truly righteous people bring justice to all the inhabitants of a city, and the city experiences true peace. Many of the psalm writers cried for vindication of the righteous and for a cessation of evil (Ps 69:22–28).

11:13 *a gossip reveals secrets.* A faithful friend conceals delicate matters that an unfaithful person reveals.

11:14 *in the abundance of [wise and godly] counselors.* In modern times, as in the past, leaders of nations need adequate counsel. We all need to seek advice from wise and trustworthy people.

CHAPTER 11 **1** Lev 19:35; Dt 25:13 **2** Pr 16:18 **3** Pr 13:6 **4** Eze 7:19; Zep 1:18; Ge 7:1 **6** Ecc 10:8 **7** Pr 10:28 **8** Pr 21:18 **10** Est 8:15 **11** Pr 29:8 **13** Lev 19:16; Pr 20:19 **14** 1Ki 12:1 **15** Pr 6:1

16 A gracious *and* good woman
attains honor,
And ruthless men attain riches
[but not respect].
17 The merciful *and* generous
man benefits his soul [for his
behavior returns to bless him],
But the cruel *and* callous man
does himself harm.
18 The wicked man earns deceptive
wages,
But he who sows righteousness
and lives his life with integrity
will have a true reward
[that is both permanent and
satisfying]. [Hos 10:12; Gal 6:8,
9; James 3:18]
19 He who is steadfast in
righteousness *attains* life,
But he who pursues evil *attains*
his own death.
20 The perverse in heart are repulsive
and shamefully vile to the LORD,
But those who are blameless *and*
above reproach in their walk are
His delight!
21 Assuredly, the evil man will not go
unpunished,
But the descendants of the
righteous will be freed.
22 As a ring of gold in a swine's snout,
So is a beautiful woman who is
without discretion [her lack of
character mocks her beauty].
23 The desire of the righteous brings
only good,
But the expectation of the wicked
brings wrath.
24 There is the one who [generously]
scatters [abroad], and yet
increases all the more;
And there is the one who
withholds what is justly due,
but it results only in want *and*
poverty.
25 The generous man [is a source
of blessing and] shall be
prosperous *and* enriched,
And he who waters will himself be
watered [reaping the generosity
he has sown]. [2 Cor 9:6–10]
26 The people curse him who holds
back grain [when the public
needs it],
But a blessing [from God and man]
is upon the head of him who
sells it.
27 He who diligently seeks good
seeks favor *and* grace,
But he who seeks evil, evil will
come to him.
28 He who leans on *and* trusts in *and*
is confident in his riches will
fall,
But the righteous [who trust in
God's provision] will flourish
like a *green* leaf.
29 He who troubles (mismanages) his
own house will inherit the wind
(nothing),
And the foolish will be a servant to
the wise-hearted.
30 The fruit of the [consistently]
righteous is a tree of life,
And he who is wise captures *and*
wins souls [for God—he gathers
them for eternity]. [Matt 4:19;
1 Cor 9:19; James 5:20]
31 If the righteous will be rewarded
on the earth [with godly
blessings],

11:17 *The merciful and generous man benefits his soul.* Throughout the Bible, God promises that good actions will return to you in benefits. Behavior that hurts others will hurt you as well.

11:19 *attains life.* Proverbs such as this remind us that the pursuit of righteousness is a matter of life and death.

11:22 *ring of gold.* A golden jewel would be ludicrous on a pig's snout. To the ancient Israelites, pigs were unclean and repellent. The immoral person is compared to such an animal, no matter what the outward appearance might be.

11:24 – 26 *There is the one who [generously] scatters.* These proverbs should shape our attitudes toward wealth: We should share it. Stinginess may lead to poverty. Generosity has the opposite effect. Selfishness is foolish because it only creates enemies and dishonors God.

11:31 *much more.* This proverb argues from a premise to a conclusion. Since the righteous will finally find their reward, it follows that the wicked, who are defiant toward God and in conflict with His works, will certainly receive judgment.

16 Pr 31:30 **17** Mt 5:7 **18** Hos 10:12 **21** Pr 16:5; Ps 112:2 **23** Ro 2:8,9 **24** Ps 112:9 **25** 2Co 9:6; Mt 5:7 **26** Am 8:5,6; Job 29:13 **27** Est 7:10; Ps 7:15,16 **28** Job 31:24; Mk 10:24; Lk 12:21; 1Ti 6:17; Ps 1:3; Jer 17:8 **29** Ecc 5:16 **30** Da 12:3; Jas 5:20 **31** Jer 25:29

How much more [will] the wicked
and the sinner [be repaid with
punishment]!

Contrast the Upright and the Wicked

12 WHOEVER LOVES
instruction *and* discipline loves
knowledge,
But he who hates reproof *and*
correction is stupid.
2 A good man will obtain favor from
the LORD,
But He will condemn a man who
devises evil.
3 A man will not be established by
wickedness,
But the root of the [consistently]
righteous will not be moved.
4 A virtuous *and* excellent wife
[worthy of honor] is the crown
of her husband,
But she who shames him [with her
foolishness] is like rottenness in
his bones. [Prov 31:23; 1 Cor 11:7]
5 The thoughts *and* purposes of the
[consistently] righteous are just
(honest, reliable),
But the counsels *and* schemes of
the wicked are deceitful.
6 The [malevolent] words of the
wicked lie in wait for [innocent]
blood [to slander],
But the mouth of the upright will
rescue *and* protect them.
7 The wicked are overthrown [by
their evil] and are no more,
But the house of the [consistently]
righteous will stand [securely].
8 A man will be commended
according to his insight *and*
sound judgment,
But the one who is of a perverse
mind will be despised.
9 Better is he who is lightly
esteemed and has a servant,
Than he who [boastfully] honors
himself [pretending to be what
he is not] and lacks bread.
10 A righteous man has kind regard
for the life of his animal,
But even the compassion of the
wicked is cruel. [Deut 25:4]
11 He who tills his land will have
plenty of bread,
But he who follows worthless
things lacks common sense *and*
good judgment.
12 The wicked desire the plunder of
evil men,
But the root of the righteous yields
richer fruit.
13 An evil man is [dangerously]
ensnared by the transgression of
his lips,
But the righteous will escape from
trouble.
14 A man will be satisfied with good
from the fruit of his words,
And the deeds of a man's hands
will return to him [as a harvest].
15 The way of the [arrogant] fool
[who rejects God's wisdom] is
right in his own eyes,
But a wise *and* prudent man is he
who listens to counsel. [Prov 3:7;
9:9; 21:2]
16 The [arrogant] fool's anger is
quickly known [because he lacks
self-control and common sense],
But a prudent man ignores an
insult.
17 He who speaks truth [when he
testifies] tells what is right,

12:1 *But he who hates reproof and correction is stupid.* Literally "stupid as a cow."
12:4 *A virtuous and excellent wife.* A husband should rejoice in such a woman because her noble character brings him honor.
12:5–6 *The thoughts and purposes of the [consistently] righteous.* A person's thoughts are the foundation of his or her words and deeds. The words of wicked persons can be like a deadly ambush.
12:9 *Better is he.* This verse contrasts a person who is a "nobody" but has a servant with a person who makes a great display but does not even have food on the table. Pretension destroys those who indulge in it.
12:16 *quickly known.* Careless words can make a fool out of us, so we are wise to think before we speak. Whereas the wise man restrains his anger and turns it away, the fool constantly loses his temper (29:11).

CHAPTER 12 **3** Pr 10:25 **4** 1Co 11:7; Pr 14:30 **6** Pr 1:11,18; Pr 14:3 **7** Ps 37:36 **8** 1Sa 25:17 **9** Pr 13:7 **10** Dt 25:4 **11** Ge 3:19; Pr 28:19; Pr 6:32 **13** Pr 18:7; 2Pe 2:9 **14** Pr 13:2; Isa 3:10,11 **15** Lk 18:11 **16** Pr 29:11 **17** Pr 14:5

But a false witness utters deceit [in
court].
18 There is one who speaks rashly
like the thrusts of a sword,
But the tongue of the wise brings
healing.
19 Truthful lips will be established
forever,
But a lying tongue is [credited]
only for a moment.
20 Deceit is in the heart of those who
devise evil,
But counselors of peace have joy.
21 No harm befalls the righteous,
But the wicked are filled with
trouble. [Job 5:19; Ps 91:3;
Prov 12:13; Is 46:4; Jer 1:8;
Dan 6:27; 2 Tim 4:18]
22 Lying lips are extremely
disgusting to the LORD,
But those who deal faithfully are
His delight. [Prov 6:17; 11:20;
Rev 22:15]
23 A shrewd man is reluctant to
display his knowledge [until the
proper time],
But the heart of [over-confident]
fools proclaims foolishness.
[Is 32:6]
24 The hand of the diligent will rule,
But the negligent *and* lazy will be
put to forced labor.
25 Anxiety in a man's heart weighs it
down,
But a good (encouraging)
word makes it glad. [Ps 50:4;
Prov 15:13]
26 The righteous man is a guide to
his neighbor,
But the way of the wicked leads
them astray.
27 The lazy man does not catch *and*
roast his prey,
But the precious possession of a
[wise] man is diligence [because
he recognizes opportunities and
seizes them].
28 In the way of righteousness is life,
And in its pathway there is no
death [but immortality—eternal
life]. [John 3:36; 4:36; 8:51; 11:26;
1 Cor 15:54; Gal 6:8]

Contrast the Upright and the Wicked

13 A WISE son heeds *and* accepts
[and is the result of] his father's
discipline *and* instruction,
But a scoffer does not listen to
reprimand *and* does not learn
from his errors.
2 From the fruit of his mouth a
[wise] man enjoys good,
But the desire of the treacherous is
for violence.
3 The one who guards his mouth
[thinking before he speaks]
protects his life;
The one who opens his lips wide
[and chatters without thinking]
comes to ruin.
4 The soul (appetite) of the lazy
person craves and gets nothing
[for lethargy overcomes
ambition],
But the soul (appetite) of the diligent
[who works willingly] is rich *and*
abundantly supplied. [Prov 10:4]
5 A righteous man hates lies,
But a wicked man is loathsome,
and he acts shamefully.

12:18 – 19 *But the tongue of the wise brings healing.* Many proverbs praise people who speak carefully and truthfully. Speech reflects a person's character. The words of a righteous person soothe the listener.
12:22 *Lying lips are extremely disgusting.* This phrase conveys extreme hatred.
12:25 *Anxiety in a man's heart weighs it down.* Anxiety loses some of its force in the face of a positive, encouraging word. Barnabas is an example of an encourager in the early church (Ac 4:36).
12:26 *The righteous man is a guide to his neighbor.* Our friends help to determine who we will become, and an excellent example inspires us to copy.
12:27 *The lazy man.* Lazy people do work, they just don't always finish what they start. The cure for their laziness is diligence — to follow through to the end.
13:5 *A righteous man hates lies.* The person who hates lying does not merely feel bad about it; he avoids it like the plague.

18 Ps 57:4; 64:3 **19** Pr 19:5,9 **22** Rev 22:15 **23** Pr 13:16 **24** Pr 10:4 **25** Pr 15:13; Isa 50:4 **CHAPTER 13**
1 Isa 28:15 **2** Pr 12:14 **3** Ps 39:1; Pr 21:23; Jas 3:2 **4** Pr 10:4

6 Righteousness (being in right
standing with God) guards the
one whose way is blameless,
But wickedness undermines *and*
overthrows the sinner.
7 There is one who pretends to be
rich, yet has nothing at all;
Another pretends to be poor, yet
has great wealth. [Prov 12:9;
Luke 12:20, 21]
8 The ransom for a man's life is his
wealth,
But the poor man does not even
have to listen to a rebuke *or*
threats [from the envious].
9 The light of the righteous [within
him—grows brighter and]
rejoices,
But the lamp of the wicked [is a
temporary light and] goes out.
10 Through pride *and* presumption
come nothing but strife,
But [skillful and godly] wisdom is
with those who welcome [well-
advised] counsel.
11 Wealth *obtained* by fraud dwindles,
But he who gathers gradually by
[honest] labor will increase [his
riches].
12 Hope deferred makes the heart
sick,
But when desire is fulfilled, it is a
tree of life.
13 Whoever despises the word
and counsel [of God] brings
destruction upon himself,
But he who [reverently] fears *and*
respects the commandment [of
God] will be rewarded.
14 The teaching of the wise is a
fountain *and* source of life,
So that one may avoid the snares
of death.
15 Good understanding wins favor
[from others],
But the way of the unfaithful is
hard [like barren, dry soil].
16 Every prudent *and* self-disciplined
man acts with knowledge,
But a [closed-minded] fool [who
refuses to learn] displays his
foolishness [for all to see].
17 A wicked messenger falls into
hardship,
But a faithful ambassador brings
healing.
18 Poverty and shame will come to
him who refuses instruction *and*
discipline,
But he who accepts *and* learns from
reproof *or* censure is honored.
19 Desire realized is sweet to the soul;
But it is detestable to fools to turn
away from evil [which they have
planned].
20 He who walks [as a companion]
with wise men will be wise,
But the companions of [conceited,
dull-witted] fools [are fools
themselves and] will experience
harm. [Is 32:6]
21 Adversity pursues sinners,

13:7 *rich, yet has nothing at all.* The paradox of greed causing poverty, and of generosity causing wealth, is a recurring theme in Scripture (Mt 6:19 – 21). The point is not how much money you have, but what you do with it.

13:9 *The light of the righteous [within him — grows brighter and] rejoices.* For an ancient Israelite, an oil lamp would be the only source of light at night. Without it, a person had no way of seeing the path in front of him.

13:10 *Through pride.* It is self-centeredness and having to push one's own ideas that bring quarrels. The wise know when to speak and when to keep still.

13:11 *Wealth obtained by fraud dwindles.* This proverb describes the natural long-term consequences of cheating. People who compromise their honesty to get rich merely postpone the inevitable need to earn their keep. The day comes when their cheating catches up with them, but by then their honest colleagues have become far better at obtaining wealth.

13:14 *fountain and source of life.* In an arid land such as ancient Judah, a fountain provided water for oneself and for one's flocks. It was a necessity — a source of life. A fountain is also a picture for salvation (Isa 12:1 – 3).

13:15 *Good understanding wins favor.* Favor with God and other people — a good reputation is highly desirable because it ensures that you won't be alone in life. A good reputation was the first qualification listed by the apostles for deacons in the early church (Acts 6:3).

13:20 *He who walks [as a companion] with wise men.* Our selection of friends (12:26) is

---

6 Pr 11:3,5,6 **7** Pr 12:9 **9** Job 18:5,6; 21:17; Pr 24:20 **11** Pr 10:2; 20:21 **12** ver. 19 **13** 2Ch 36:16 **14** Pr 10:11; 14:27; 16:22; 2Sa 22:6 **16** Pr 12:23; 15:2 **17** Pr 25:13 **18** Pr 15:5,31 **19** ver. 12 **21** Ps 32:10

But the [consistently] upright will
be rewarded with prosperity.
22 A good man leaves an inheritance
to his children's children,
And the wealth of the sinner is
stored up for [the hands of] the
righteous.
23 Abundant food is in the fallow
(uncultivated) ground of the poor,
But [without protection] it is swept
away by injustice.
24 He who withholds the rod [of
discipline] hates his son,
But he who loves him disciplines
and trains him diligently *and*
appropriately [with wisdom and
love]. [Prov 19:18; 22:15; 23:13;
29:15, 17; Eph 6:4]
25 The [consistently] righteous has
enough to satisfy his appetite,
But the stomach of the wicked is in
need [of bread].

Contrast the Upright and the Wicked

14 THE WISE woman builds her
house [on a foundation of godly
precepts, and her household
thrives],
But the foolish one [who lacks
spiritual insight] tears it
down with her own hands [by
ignoring godly principles].
2 He who walks in uprightness
[reverently] fears the LORD [and
obeys and worships Him with
profound respect],
But he who is devious in his ways
despises Him.
3 In the mouth of the [arrogant] fool
[who rejects God] is a rod for his
back,
But the lips of the wise [when they
speak with godly wisdom] will
protect them.
4 Where there are no oxen, the
manger is clean,
But much revenue [because of
good crops] comes by the
strength of the ox.
5 A faithful *and* trustworthy witness
will not lie,
But a false witness speaks lies.
6 A scoffer seeks wisdom and finds
none [for his ears are closed to
wisdom],
But knowledge is easy for one
who understands [because he is
willing to learn].
7 Leave the presence of a
[shortsighted] fool,
For you will not find knowledge *or*
hear godly wisdom from his lips.
8 The wisdom of the sensible is to
understand his way,
But the foolishness of
[shortsighted] fools is deceit.
9 Fools mock sin [but sin mocks the
fools],
But among the upright there is
good will *and* the favor *and*
blessing of God. [Prov 10:23]
10 The heart knows its own
bitterness,
And no stranger shares its joy.
11 The house of the wicked will be
overthrown,
But the tent of the upright will
thrive.
12 There is a way *which seems* right
to a man *and* appears straight
before him,
But its end is the way of death.

---

extremely important. Pressure from peers is much stronger than many people realize.
13:24 *hates . . . loves.* This is the first of several proverbs on parental discipline. A parent's loving discipline is modeled after God's loving correction (3:11 – 12).
14:1 *wise woman builds her house.* She develops a peaceful setting for family nurture.
14:2 *fears the LORD.* This phrase contrasts starkly with "despises Him." Love for uprightness will naturally coincide with love and respect for the most upright One of all, God Himself. Love for perversity will likewise result in hatred for Him. Fear of the Lord as the beginning of wisdom is the central theme of Proverbs (1:7).
14:4 *the manger is clean.* A farmer has to put up with some messes in the barn if he wants the help of an ox. This is not an excuse to be slovenly, but an encouragement to work hard.
14:12 *There is a way which seems right to a*

22 Job 27:17; Pr 28:8; Ecc 2:26 **23** Pr 12:11 **24** Pr 19:18; 22:15; 23:13; 29:15,17 **25** Ps 34:10; 37:3
CHAPTER 14 **2** Ro 2:4 **3** Pr 12:6 **5** ver. 25; Ex 20:16; 23:1; Pr 6:19; 12:17 **6** Pr 8:9; 17:24 **9** Pr 10:23
11 Job 8:15 **12** Pr 16:25; Ro 6:21

13 Even in laughter the heart may be
in pain,
And the end of joy may be grief.
14 The backslider in heart will have
his fill with his own [rotten]
ways,
But a good man will *be satisfied*
with his ways [the godly thought
and action which his heart
pursues and in which he delights].
15 The naive *or* inexperienced person
[is easily misled and] believes
every word he hears,
But the prudent man [is discreet
and astute and] considers well
where he is going.
16 A wise man suspects danger and
cautiously avoids evil,
But the fool is arrogant and careless.
17 A quick-tempered man acts
foolishly *and* without self-control,
And a man of wicked schemes is
hated.
18 The naive [are unsophisticated
and easy to exploit and] inherit
foolishness,
But the sensible [are thoughtful
and far-sighted and] are
crowned with knowledge.
19 The evil will bow down before the
good,
And the wicked [will bow down] at
the gates of the righteous.
20 The poor man is hated even by his
neighbor,
But those who love the rich are
many.
21 He who despises his neighbor sins
[against God and his fellow man],
But happy [blessed and favored by
God] is he who is gracious *and*
merciful to the poor.
22 Do they not go astray who devise
evil *and* wander from the way of
righteousness?
But kindness and truth will be to
those who devise good.
23 In all labor there is profit,
But mere talk leads only to
poverty.
24 The crown of the wise is their
wealth [of wisdom],
But the foolishness of [closed-
minded] fools is [nothing but]
folly.
25 A truthful witness saves
lives,
But he who speaks lies is
treacherous.
26 In the [reverent] fear of the LORD
there is strong confidence,
And His children will [always]
have a place of refuge.
27 The [reverent] fear of the LORD
[that leads to obedience and
worship] is a fountain of life,
So that one may avoid the snares
of death. [John 4:10, 14]
28 In a multitude of people is a
king's glory,
But in a lack of people is a
[pretentious] prince's ruin.
29 He who is slow to anger has great
understanding [and profits from
his self-control],
But he who is quick-tempered
exposes *and* exalts his
foolishness [for all to see].
[Prov 16:32; James 1:19]
30 A calm *and* peaceful *and* tranquil
heart is life *and* health to the
body,
But passion *and* envy are like
rottenness to the bones.
31 He who oppresses the poor taunts
and insults his Maker,
But he who is kind *and* merciful
and gracious to the needy
honors Him. [Prov 17:5;
Matt 25:40, 45]

---

man. Only when it is too late does the deluded person discover that he is on the crowded highway to death. The implication is not that he was tricked, but that he relied too heavily on his own "wisdom" rather than turning in humility to God.
14:19 *at the gates of the righteous.* In an ancient walled city, the gate area would normally be the weakest section of the wall. The city engineers of ancient Canaan developed complex structures to fortify this point. Controlling the gate of a city meant controlling the city.
14:31 *oppresses . . . honors.* The theme of "as you treat people, so you treat God" is central to Scripture (Ex 22:22 – 24; Mt 25:31 – 46).

13 Pr 5:4; Ecc 2:2 **14** Pr 1:31; 12:14 **16** Pr 22:3 **20** Pr 19:7 **21** Ps 41:1; 112:9 **25** ver. 5 **27** Pr 13:14 **29** Jas 1:19 **30** Ps 112:10; Pr 12:4 **31** Pr 17:5; Mt 25:40; Pr 22:2

32 The wicked is overthrown through
his wrongdoing,
But the righteous has hope *and*
confidence *and* a refuge [with
God] even in death.
33 Wisdom rests [silently] in the
heart of one who has
understanding,
But what is in the heart of
[shortsighted] fools is made
known. [Is 32:6]
34 Righteousness [moral and spiritual
integrity and virtuous character]
exalts a nation,
But sin is a disgrace to any
people.
35 The king's favor *and* good will
are toward a servant who acts
wisely *and* discreetly,
But his anger *and* wrath
are toward him who acts
shamefully. [Matt 24:45, 47]

Contrast the Upright and the Wicked

15 A SOFT *and* gentle *and*
thoughtful answer turns away
wrath,
But harsh *and* painful *and* careless
words stir up anger. [Prov 25:15]
2 The tongue of the wise speaks
knowledge that is pleasing *and*
acceptable,
But the [babbling] mouth of fools
spouts folly.
3 The eyes of the LORD are in every
place,
Watching the evil and the good [in
all their endeavors]. [Job 34:21;
Prov 5:21; Jer 16:17; 32:19;
Heb 4:13]
4 A soothing tongue [speaking
words that build up and
encourage] is a tree of life,
But a perversive tongue [speaking
words that overwhelm and
depress] crushes the spirit.
5 A [flippant, arrogant] fool rejects
his father's instruction *and*
correction,
But he who [is willing to learn and]
regards *and* keeps in mind a
reprimand acquires good sense.
6 Great *and* priceless treasure is in
the house of the [consistently]
righteous one [who seeks
godly instruction and grows in
wisdom],
But trouble is in the income of the
wicked one [who rejects the
laws of God].
7 The lips of the wise spread
knowledge [sifting it as chaff
from the grain];
But the hearts of [shortsighted]
fools are not so.
8 The sacrifice of the wicked
is hateful *and* exceedingly
offensive to the LORD,
But the prayer of the upright is
His delight! [Is 1:11; Jer 6:20;
Amos 5:22]
9 The way [of life] of the wicked
is hateful *and* exceedingly
offensive to the LORD,

14:32 *The wicked is overthrown through his wrongdoing.* Some of the proverbs describe deliverance from death itself (11:4). The teaching of life after death is not a major teaching in the Old Testament, but neither is it altogether neglected.
14:34 *Righteousness [moral and spiritual integrity and virtuous character] exalts a nation.* Although each individual is responsible for his or her actions, the effects extend to the whole community.
15:1 *A soft ... answer turns away wrath.* Often it is not so much what we say but the way we say it that prompts such varied responses as acceptance and anger. For Abigail's gentle words to David when he was angry, see 1 Samuel 25:12 – 34. Words can have either life-giving or death-producing results.
15:3 *The eyes of the LORD.* That they are in every place watching everything chills those who do evil and comforts those who submit to Him (Ecc 12:12).
15:6 *the house of the [consistently] righteous.* One house is a blessing and the other is ruinous; the reason for this lies in how the house was acquired and how it is being used. The house of the righteous contains great wealth because it is founded on wisdom and a proper response to God. On the other hand, the wicked never gain enough to suit them, and lose what they have because of their deceptive ways.

32 Job 13:15; Ps 23:4; 2Co 1:9; 2Ti 4:18 **33** Pr 12:16 **35** Mt 24:45 **CHAPTER 15** **1** Pr 25:15; 1Sa 25:10
2 Pr 12:23 **3** Job 34:21; Heb 4:13 **5** Pr 10:1; Pr 13:18 **8** Isa 1:11; Jer 6:20; Am 5:22 **9** Pr 21:21; 1Ti 6:11

CHARACTER TRAITS IN PROVERBS

TRAITS TO BE PROMOTED	
avoidance of strife	20:3
compassion for animals	12:10
contentment	13:25; 14:30; 15:27
diligence	6:6–13; 12:24,27; 13:4
faithful love	20:6
faithfulness	3:5–6; 5:15–17; 25:13; 28:20
generosity	21:26; 22:9
honesty	16:11; 24:26
humility	11:2; 16:19; 25:6–7; 29:23
integrity	11:3; 25:26; 28:18
kindness to others	11:16–17
kindness to enemies	25:21–22
leadership	30:19–31
loyalty	19:22
nobility	12:4; 31:10,29
patience	15:18; 16:32
peacefulness	16:7
praiseworthiness	27:21
righteousness	4:26–27; 11:5–6,30; 12:28; 13:6; 29:2
self-control	17:27; 25:28; 29:11
strength and honor	20:29
strength in adversity	24:10
teachableness	15:31
truthfulness	12:19,22; 23:23

TRAITS TO BE AVOIDED	
anger	29:22
antisocial behavior	18:1
beauty without discretion	11:22
blaming God	19:3
dishonesty	24:28
greed	28:25
hatred	29:27
hot temper	19:19; 29:22
immorality	6:20–35
inappropriate desire	27:7
injustice	22:16
jealousy	27:4
lack of mercy	21:13
laziness	6:6–11; 18:9; 19:15; 20:4; 24:30–34; 26:13–15
maliciousness	6:27
meddling	26:17; 30:10
pride	15:5; 16:18; 21:4,24; 29:23; 30:13
quarrelsomeness	26:21
self-conceit	26:12,16
self-deceit	28:11
self-glory	25:27
self-righteousness	30:12
social disruption	19:10
stubbornness	29:1
unfaithfulness	25:19
unneighborliness	3:27–30
vengeance	24:28–29
wickedness	21:10
wicked scheming	16:30

But He loves one who pursues
righteousness [personal
integrity, moral courage and
honorable character].
10 There is severe discipline for him
who turns from the way [of
righteousness];
And he who hates correction
will die.
11 Sheol (the nether world, the place
of the dead) and Abaddon
(the abyss, the place of eternal
punishment) *lie open* before the
LORD—
How much more the hearts *and*
inner motives of the children of
men. [Job 26:6; Ps 139:8; Rev 9:2;
20:1, 2]
12 A scoffer [unlike a wise man]
resents one who rebukes him
and tries to teach him;
Nor will he go to the wise [for
counsel and instruction].
13 A heart full of joy *and* goodness
makes a cheerful face,
But when a heart is full of sadness
the spirit is crushed. [Prov 17:22]
14 The mind of the intelligent *and*
discerning seeks knowledge *and*
eagerly inquires after it,
But the mouth of the [stubborn]
fool feeds on foolishness.
[Is 32:6]
15 All the days of the afflicted are bad,
But a glad heart has a continual
feast [regardless of the
circumstances].
16 Better is a little with the [reverent,
worshipful] fear of the LORD
Than great treasure and trouble
with it. [Ps 37:16; Prov 16:8;
1 Tim 6:6]
17 Better is a dinner of vegetables
and herbs where love is present
Than a fattened ox served with
hatred. [Prov 17:1]
18 A hot-tempered man stirs up strife,
But he who is slow to anger *and*
patient calms disputes.
19 The way of the lazy is like a hedge
of thorns [it pricks, lacerates,
and entangles him],
But the way [of life] of the upright
is smooth *and* open like a
highway.
20 A wise son makes a father glad,
But a foolish man despises his
mother.
21 Foolishness is joy to him who
is without heart *and* lacks
[intelligent, common] sense,
But a man of understanding walks
uprightly [making his course
straight]. [Eph 5:15]
22 Without consultation *and* wise
advice, plans are frustrated,
But with many counselors they are
established and succeed.

15:10 *severe discipline.* There is a consequence for those who forsake God's way. This discipline comes as a means of correction. Only the person who hates this correction will die.

15:11 *How much more the hearts.* This is a "how much more" proverb, which impresses on the reader the clarity with which the Lord sees people's hearts. The Hebrew word *sheol*, or "hell," connotes the fear of the unknown. The word actually means "the mysterious realm of death." Yet death is no mystery to the Lord. And if the mysterious realm of the dead is known to Him, then surely a person's heart is transparent to Him. This technique of arguing from the greater to the lesser appears in both Testaments.

15:12 *A scoffer [unlike a wise man] resents.* The scoffer (14:6) is used as a foil or comparison in Proverbs to expose more sharply the character of the wise. Whereas the sluggard is a comic figure in Proverbs, the scoffer is a villain. His basic problem is displayed in his response to correction. He does not learn from it nor does he seek it. The scoffer is adamant in his folly.

15:14 *The mind of the intelligent and discerning.* The person with an understanding heart, another description of the wise, is never satisfied with what he or she knows. The pursuit of wisdom and knowledge are lifelong occupations — never fully realized in this lifetime. But fools, not knowing the extent of their ignorance, continue to pursue folly.

15:18 *A hot-tempered man stirs up strife.* A hot-tempered person can stir up strife where there is none; but a person who has a slow fuse — who is slow to anger — soothes contention (15:1).

10 1Ki 22:8; Pr 5:12 **11** Job 26:6; Ps 139:8; 2Ch 6:30; Jn 2:24 **12** Am 5:10; 2Ti 4:3 **13** Pr 17:22; Pr 12:25 **15** Pr 17:22 **16** Ps 37:16; 1Ti 6:6 **17** Pr 17:1 **18** Pr 26:21 **19** Pr 22:5 **20** Pr 10:1 **21** Pr 10:23; Eph 5:15 **22** Pr 11:14

23 A man has joy in giving an
appropriate answer,
And how good *and* delightful
is a word spoken at the right
moment—how good it is!
24 The [chosen] path of life leads
upward for the wise,
That he may keep away from
Sheol (the nether world, the
place of the dead) below.
[Phil 3:20; Col 3:1, 2]
25 The LORD will tear down the house
of the proud *and* arrogant (self-righteous),
But He will establish *and* protect
the boundaries [of the land] of
the [godly] widow.
26 Evil plans *and* thoughts of the
wicked are exceedingly vile *and*
offensive to the LORD,
But pure words are pleasant words
to Him.
27 He who profits unlawfully brings
suffering to his own house,
But he who hates bribes [and does
not receive nor pay them] will
live. [Is 5:8; Jer 17:11]
28 The heart of the righteous thinks
carefully about how to answer
[in a wise and appropriate and
timely way],
But the [babbling] mouth of the
wicked pours out malevolent
things. [1 Pet 3:15]
29 The LORD is far from the wicked
[and distances Himself from
them],
But He hears the prayer of the
[consistently] righteous [that is,
those with spiritual integrity
and moral courage].
30 The light of the eyes rejoices the
hearts of others,
And good news puts fat on the
bones.
31 The ear that listens to *and* learns
from the life-giving rebuke
(reprimand, censure)
Will remain among the wise.
32 He who neglects *and* ignores
instruction *and* discipline
despises himself,
But he who learns from rebuke
acquires understanding [and
grows in wisdom].
33 The [reverent] fear of the LORD
[that is, worshiping Him
and regarding Him as truly
awesome] is the instruction for
wisdom [its starting point and
its essence];
And before honor comes humility.

Contrast the Upright and the Wicked

16 THE PLANS *and* reflections of
the heart belong to man,
But the [wise] answer of the
tongue is from the LORD.
2 All the ways of a man are clean
and innocent in his own eyes
[and he may see nothing wrong
with his actions],
But the LORD weighs *and*
examines the motives *and*
intents [of the heart and knows
the truth]. [1 Sam 16:7; Heb 4:12]
3 Commit your works to the LORD
[submit and trust them to Him],
And your plans will succeed [if
you respond to His will and
guidance].

15:25 ***The LORD will tear down the house of the proud.*** God will bring about justice in the end. To the haughty, God will give a dose of humility. But for the widow, a completely defenseless person in ancient times, God will provide protection.

15:32 ***despises himself.*** The natural instinct for self-preservation is dangerous when it is time to listen to a necessary rebuke.

15:33 ***The [reverent] fear of the LORD . . . instruction.*** Knowledge alone does not make a person wiser; the fear of the Lord must accompany it. The same is true of honor.

16:1–2 ***The plans and reflections of the heart.*** These verses contrast human limitations with the sovereignty of God. Man can plan, dream, and hope, but the final outcome is from the Lord. Rather than "resign ourselves to fate," we should trust in God.

16:3 ***Commit your works to the LORD.*** The verb "commit to" is from a word meaning "to roll." The idea is to "roll your cares onto the Lord."

23 Pr 25:11 **24** Php 3:20; Col 3:1,2 **25** Pr 12:7; Ps 68:5,6 **26** Pr 6:16,18; Ps 37:30 **27** Isa 5:8 **28** 1Pe 3:15 **29** Ps 10:1; 34:16; Ps 145:18 **31** ver. 5 **33** Pr 1:7; Pr 18:12 **CHAPTER 16** **1** Jer 10:23; Mt 10:19 **2** Pr 21:2; 1Sa 16:7 **3** Ps 37:5

[4]The LORD has made everything for
its own purpose,
Even the wicked [according to
their role] for the day of evil.
[5]Everyone who is proud *and*
arrogant in heart is disgusting
and exceedingly offensive to the
LORD;
Be assured he will not go
unpunished. [Prov 8:13; 11:20, 21]
[6]By mercy *and* lovingkindness
and truth [not superficial ritual]
wickedness is cleansed from
the heart,
And by the fear of the LORD one
avoids evil.
[7]When a man's ways please the
LORD,
He makes even his enemies to be
at peace with him.
[8]Better is a little with righteousness
Than great income [gained]
with injustice. [Ps 37:16;
Prov 15:16]
[9]A man's mind plans his way [as he
journeys through life],
But the LORD directs his steps
and establishes them. [Ps 37:23;
Prov 20:24; Jer 10:23]
[10]A divine decision [given by God]
is on the lips of the king [as His
representative];
His mouth should not be
unfaithful *or* unjust in judgment.
[Deut 17:18–20; 2 Sam 14:17–20;
1 Kin 3:9–12; Is 11:2]
[11]A just balance and [honest] scales
are the LORD's;
All the weights of the bag are His
concern [established by His
eternal principles].
[12]It is repulsive [to God and man] for
kings to behave wickedly,
For a throne is established on
righteousness (right standing
with God).
[13]Righteous lips are the delight of
kings,
And he who speaks right is loved.
[14]The wrath of a king is like a
messenger of death,
But a wise man will appease it.
[15]In the light of the king's face
is life,
And his favor is like a cloud
bringing the spring rain.
[16]How much better it is to get
wisdom than gold!
And to get understanding is to be
chosen above silver. [Prov 8:10, 19]
[17]The highway of the upright turns
away *and* departs from evil;
He who guards his way protects
his life (soul).

Trusting the Lord with our decisions frees us from preoccupation with our problems (3:5–6).

Dedication is the foundation of commitment. Without it the believer is unable to offer God anything else. Paul explains this dedication process in Romans 12:1–2. He emphasizes three things. First, it is our body which is to be dedicated as a living sacrifice to God. Second, we are to avoid being conformed to this world, but should strive to be transformed by the Word. Finally, by doing this we can discover God's perfect will for our lives.

After the dedication of our bodies, what are we to commit? We are to commit our salvation to God (2Ti 1:12). We are to commit our works (Pr 16:3). Then our goals in life are to be given to Him (Job 5:8; Ps 37:5). It is difficult but vital to commit our suffering experiences to God (1Pe 4:19). Our Lord Jesus did this very thing when He was on earth (1Pe 2:23). Finally, in the hour of death, we can with confidence commit our very souls to God (Ps 31:5). Paul the Apostle assures us that any and all such commitments to the Lord will be accepted and honored (1Co 15:58).

16:6 *By mercy and lovingkindness and truth.* These words can also be translated "by genuine piety." "Cleansed" probably alludes to a sacrificial offering, but not apart from a contrite heart.

16:10 *A divine decision.* This phrase refers to judicial decisions made by the king. Because the nation rested in the king's hands, his first responsibility was to obey God (King Josiah's reform of Israel, 2Ki 22). Even the king had to submit to the dictates of justice.

16:15 *life . . . his favor.* Successfully courting a powerful person's favor is like seeing rain clouds in a dry land. The phrase about the light of the face in this proverb helps us understand Aaron's benediction in Numbers 6:24–26.

16:17 *The highway of the upright.* This phrase is a metaphor for the way a person lives habitually. An *upright* person's highway or habit is to

4 Isa 43:7; Job 21:30 **5** Pr 8:13; Pr 11:21 **6** Da 4:27; Pr 14:16 **8** Ps 37:16 **9** Pr 19:21; Jer 10:23 **11** Lev 19:36
12 Pr 25:5 **13** Pr 14:35 **14** Pr 19:12 **15** Pr 19:12; Job 29:23 **16** Pr 8:11,19

18 Pride goes before destruction,
And a haughty spirit before a fall.
19 It is better to be humble in spirit with the lowly
Than to divide the spoil with the proud (haughty, arrogant).
20 He who pays attention to the word [of God] will find good,
And blessed (happy, prosperous, to be admired) is he who trusts [confidently] in the LORD.
21 The wise in heart will be called understanding,
And sweet speech increases persuasiveness *and* learning [in both speaker and listener].
22 Understanding (spiritual insight) is a [refreshing and boundless] wellspring of life to those who have it,
But to give instruction *and* correction to fools is foolishness.
23 The heart of the wise instructs his mouth [in wisdom]
And adds persuasiveness to his lips.
24 Pleasant words are like a honeycomb,
Sweet *and* delightful to the soul and healing to the body.
25 There is a way which seems right to a man *and* appears straight before him,
But its end is the way of death.
26 The appetite of a worker works for him,
For his hunger urges him on.
27 A worthless man devises *and* digs up evil,
And the words on his lips are like a scorching fire.
28 A perverse man spreads strife,
And one who gossips separates intimate friends. [Prov 17:9]
29 A violent *and* exceedingly covetous man entices his neighbor [to sin],
And leads him in a way that is not good.
30 He who [slyly] winks his eyes does so to plot perverse things;
And he who compresses his lips [as if in a secret signal] brings evil to pass.
31 The silver-haired head is a crown of splendor *and* glory;
It is found in the way of righteousness. [Prov 20:29]
32 He who is slow to anger is better *and* more honorable than the mighty [soldier],
And he who rules *and* controls his own spirit, than he who captures a city.
33 The lot is cast into the lap,
But its every decision is from the LORD.

Contrast the Upright and the Wicked

17 BETTER IS a dry morsel [of food served] with quietness *and* peace

---

depart from evil. He does not compromise; he consistently strives to do good.

16:24 *Pleasant words are like a honeycomb.* The Hebrew word for honeycomb is also used in Psalm 19:10 – 11 with regard to the Word of God. The Israelites saw honey as a healthy food as well as a sweetener. Any comparison to it would connote positive, healthful effects.

16:27 – 29 *worthless . . . perverse . . . violent and exceedingly covetous man.* These verses all begin in a similar way describing three different types of wicked people. The word "worthless" means a man of Belial; this person is a muckraker who uses bad information for evil purposes; he destroys people on purpose. The "perverse" person starts fights between friends. The "violent and exceedingly covetous man" uses his power of persuasion to recruit others to join in his attacks.

16:32 *better and more honorable than the mighty.* Even though one of the most favored persons in the ancient Middle East was the military hero, this proverb suggests that one who is "slow to anger" or who "rules and controls his own spirit" is a greater hero than a returning warrior.

16:33 *The lot is cast into the lap.* The use of lots in ancient Israel (16:10) could easily be confused with luck. But when a *lot* was cast as a means of determining God's will, the people knew it did not fall indiscriminately. God exercises sovereignty over human affairs (16:4).

17:1 *Better is a dry morsel.* This expression means "very little" especially in comparison to

---

20 Ps 34:8 **22** Pr 13:14 **25** Pr 14:12 **26** Ecc 6:7 **28** Pr 15:18; Pr 17:9 **29** Pr 1:10 **31** Pr 20:29 **32** Pr 19:11
CHAPTER 17 **1** Pr 15:17

Than a house full of feasting
[served] with strife *and*
contention.
2 A wise servant will rule over
the [unworthy] son who acts
shamefully *and* brings disgrace
[to the family]
And [the worthy servant] will
share in the inheritance among
the brothers.
3 The refining pot is for silver and
the furnace for gold,
But the LORD tests hearts. [Ps 26:2;
Prov 27:21; Jer 17:10; Mal 3:3]
4 An evildoer listens closely to
wicked lips;
And a liar pays attention to a
destructive *and* malicious tongue.
5 Whoever mocks the poor taunts
his Maker,
And he who rejoices at [another's]
disaster will not go unpunished.
[Job 31:29; Prov 14:31; Obad 12]
6 Grandchildren are the crown of
aged men,
And the glory of children is their
fathers [who live godly lives].
[Ps 127:3; 128:3]
7 Excellent speech does not benefit
a fool [who is spiritually blind],
Much less do lying lips *benefit* a
prince.
8 A bribe is like a bright, precious
stone in the eyes of its owner;
Wherever he turns, he prospers.
9 He who covers *and* forgives an
offense seeks love,
But he who repeats *or* gossips
about a matter separates
intimate friends.
10 A reprimand goes deeper into one
who has understanding *and* a
teachable spirit
Than a hundred lashes into a fool.
[Is 32:6]
11 A rebellious man seeks only evil;
Therefore a cruel messenger will
be sent against him.
12 Let a man meet a [ferocious] bear
robbed of her cubs
Rather than the [angry,
narcissistic] fool in his folly.
[Hos 13:8]
13 Whoever returns evil for good,
Evil will not depart from his
house. [Ps 109:4, 5; Jer 18:20]
14 The beginning of strife is like
letting out water [as from a
small break in a dam; first it
trickles and then it gushes];
Therefore abandon the quarrel
before it breaks out *and* tempers
explode.
15 He who justifies the wicked, and
he who condemns the righteous
Are both repulsive to the LORD.
[Ex 23:7; Prov 24:24; Is 5:23]
16 Why is there money in the hand of
a fool to buy wisdom,
When he has no common sense *or*
even a heart for it?
17 A friend loves at all times,
And a brother is born for
adversity.

---

feasting. But the feasting in this verse is tainted by contention. Feasting could also be part of a sacrifice to God, but even such a feast could be ruined by angry disputes between believers.

17:2 ***A wise servant.*** Reversals of fortune could happen if the wise servant was sufficiently skillful and the son and his brothers were undeserving. Much of Genesis describes the unexpected rise of a younger son over his older brother (Ge 25:23 – 34).

17:4 ***An evildoer listens closely to wicked lips.*** This proverb presents the "wicked doer" and the "liar" as a parody of the wise. As the righteous person listens with care to the instruction of a teacher, so the wicked person listens with care to the ruinous speech of the unrighteous.

17:7 ***Excellent speech.*** It is a contradiction in terms for a fool to speak well or for a prince to be a liar.

17:12 ***a [ferocious] bear robbed of her cubs.*** Nothing matches the rage of a mother bear who has been separated from her cubs; yet there is nothing in life more dangerous than the fool in the midst of his folly.

17:15 ***repulsive to the LORD.*** Since God is a God of justice, He detests those who pervert justice — both those who declare the innocent guilty and those who declare the guilty innocent.

2 Pr 10:5 **3** Jer 17:10 **5** Pr 14:31 **9** Pr 10:12; Pr 16:28 **12** Hos 13:8 **13** Ps 109:4,5; Jer 18:20 **14** Pr 20:3
15 Ex 23:7; Isa 5:23 **16** Pr 21:25,26 **17** Ru 1:16

18 A man lacking common sense gives a pledge
And becomes guarantor [for the debt of another] in the presence of his neighbor.
19 He who loves transgression loves strife *and* is quarrelsome;
He who [proudly] raises his gate seeks destruction [because of his arrogant pride].
20 He who has a crooked mind finds no good,
And he who is perverted in his language falls into evil. [James 3:8]
21 He who becomes the parent of a fool [who is spiritually blind] does so to his sorrow,
And the father of a fool [who is spiritually blind] has no joy.
22 A happy heart is good medicine *and* a joyful mind causes healing,
But a broken spirit dries up the bones. [Prov 12:25; 15:13, 15]
23 A wicked man receives a bribe from the [hidden] pocket
To pervert the ways of justice.
24 [Skillful and godly] wisdom is in the presence of a person of understanding [and he recognizes it],
But the eyes of a [thickheaded] fool are on the ends of the earth.
25 A foolish son is a grief *and* anguish to his father
And bitterness to her who gave birth to him.
26 It is also not good to fine the righteous,
Nor to strike the noble for their uprightness.
27 He who has knowledge restrains *and* is careful with his words,
And a man of understanding *and* wisdom has a cool spirit (self-control, an even temper). [James 1:19]
28 Even a [callous, arrogant] fool, when he keeps silent, is considered wise;
When he closes his lips he is regarded as sensible (prudent, discreet) *and* a man of understanding.

Contrast the Upright and the Wicked

18 HE WHO [willfully] separates himself [from God and man] seeks his own desire,
He quarrels against all sound wisdom.
2 A [closed-minded] fool does not delight in understanding,
But only in revealing his personal opinions [unwittingly displaying his self-indulgence and his stupidity].
3 When the wicked man comes [to the depth of evil], contempt [of all that is pure and good] also comes,
And with inner baseness (dishonor) comes outer shame (scorn).
4 The words of a man's mouth are like deep waters [copious and difficult to fathom];
The fountain of [mature, godly] wisdom is like a bubbling stream [sparkling, fresh, pure, and life-giving].
5 To show respect to the wicked person is not good,
Nor to push aside *and* deprive the righteous of justice.
6 A fool's lips bring contention *and* strife,
And his mouth invites a beating.
7 A fool's mouth is his ruin,
And his lips are the snare of his soul.
8 The words of a whisperer (gossip) are like dainty morsels [to be greedily eaten];

18:1 ***who [willfully] separates himself.*** When a person is seeking his own desires, he separates himself from wisdom. His selfishness puts him "at odds" with sound understanding.
18:2 ***A [close-minded] fool does not delight in understanding.*** A compulsive talker never listens, only pausing to plan what he will say next. Every speech confirms what a fool he is.
18:8 ***The words of a whisperer.*** These words are like delicious sweets. Although they are fun to eat,

18 Pr 6:1 **19** Pr 16:18 **20** Jas 3:8 **21** Pr 10:1 **22** Pr 12:25; Ps 22:15 **23** Ex 23:8 **24** Ecc 2:14 **25** Pr 10:1 **26** Pr 18:5 **27** Jas 1:19 **28** Job 13:5 **CHAPTER 18** **4** Pr 10:11; Jas 3:17 **5** Lev 19:15 **7** Pr 10:14 **8** Pr 12:18

They go down into the innermost
chambers of the body [to be
remembered and mused upon].
9 He who is careless in his work
Is a brother to him who destroys.
10 The name of the LORD is a strong
tower;
The righteous runs to it and is safe
and set on high [far above evil].
11 The rich man's wealth is his strong
city,
And like a high wall [of protection]
in his own imagination *and*
conceit.
12 Before disaster the heart of a man
is haughty *and* filled with self-
importance,
But humility comes before honor.
13 He who answers before he hears
[the facts]—
It is folly and shame to him.
[John 7:51]
14 The spirit of a man sustains him in
sickness,
But as for a broken spirit, who can
bear it?
15 The mind of the prudent [always]
acquires knowledge,
And the ear of the wise [always]
seeks knowledge.
16 A man's gift [given in love or
courtesy] makes room for him
And brings him before great
men. [Gen 32:20; 1 Sam 25:27;
Prov 17:8; 21:14]
17 The first one to plead his case
seems right,
Until another comes and cross-
examines him.
18 To cast lots puts an end to quarrels
And decides between powerful
contenders.
19 A brother offended *is harder to
win* over than a fortified city,
And contentions [separating
families] are like the bars of a
castle.
20 A man's stomach will be satisfied
with the fruit of his mouth;
He will be satisfied with the
consequence of his words.
21 Death and life are in the power of
the tongue,
And those who love it *and* indulge
it will eat its fruit *and* bear the
consequences of their words.
[Matt 12:37]
22 He who finds a [true and faithful]
wife finds a good thing
And obtains favor *and* approval
from the LORD. [Prov 19:14;
31:10]
23 The poor man pleads,
But the rich man answers roughly.
24 The man of *too many* friends
[chosen indiscriminately] will
be broken in pieces *and* come to
ruin,
But there is a [true, loving] friend
who [is reliable and] sticks
closer than a brother.

On Life and Conduct

19 BETTER IS a poor man who
walks in his integrity
Than a [rich] man who is
twisted in his speech and is a
[shortsighted] fool.
2 Also it is not good for a person to
be without knowledge,
And he who hurries with his
feet [acting impulsively and
proceeding without caution or
analyzing the consequences]
sins (misses the mark).

---

they ruin the person's health. Gossip is fun to listen to, but it damages the listener's innermost parts.

18:10–11 *The name of the LORD is a strong tower.* The phrase, *name of the Lord*, is a way of speaking of God's person. The righteous turn to God for security. Rich people, by contrast, tend to trust in their wealth.

18:12 *the heart of a man is haughty.* The Hebrew word for haughty, ordinarily negative, can also be used positively to mean courage and daring (2Ch 17:6). The path to "honor," which the proud so covet, is "humility."

18:14 *The spirit of a man sustains him in sickness.* This proverb affirms the value of coping skills. Sickness can be overcome, but there is no medicine for a *broken spirit*.

18:20 *stomach ... mouth.* Inner satisfaction comes from true and good speech.

18:22 *favor and approval from the LORD.* Problems in marriage arise from breakdowns

9 Pr 28:24 **10** 2Sa 22:3 **11** Pr 10:15 **12** Pr 16:18 **13** Jn 7:51 **16** Ge 32:20; 1Sa 25:27 **20** Pr 12:14
21 Mt 12:37 **22** Pr 31:10 **23** Jas 2:3 **24** Pr 17:17 **CHAPTER 19** **1** Pr 28:6

3 The foolishness of man
undermines his way [ruining
whatever he undertakes];
Then his heart is resentful *and*
rages against the LORD [for,
being a fool, he blames the LORD
instead of himself].
4 Wealth makes many friends,
But a poor man is separated from
his friend. [Prov 14:20]
5 A false witness will not go
unpunished,
And he who breathes out lies will
not escape. [Ex 23:1; Deut 19:16–
19; Prov 6:19; 21:28]
6 Many will seek the favor of a
generous *and* noble man,
And everyone is a friend to him
who gives gifts.
7 All the brothers of a poor man
hate him;
How much more do his friends
abandon him!
He pursues *them with* words, but
they are gone.
8 He who gains wisdom *and* good
sense loves (preserves) his own
soul;
He who keeps understanding will
find good *and* prosper.
9 A false witness will not go
unpunished,
And he who breathes lies will
perish.
10 Luxury is not fitting for a fool;
Much less for a slave to rule over
princes.
11 Good sense *and* discretion make a
man slow to anger,
And it is his honor *and* glory to
overlook a transgression *or*
an offense [without seeking
revenge and harboring
resentment].
12 The king's wrath *terrifies* like the
roaring of a lion,
But his favor is as [refreshing and
nourishing as] dew on the grass.
[Hos 14:5]
13 A foolish (ungodly) son is
destruction to his father,
And the contentions of a
[quarrelsome] wife are like a
constant dripping [of water].
14 House and wealth are the
inheritance from fathers,
But a wise, understanding,
and sensible wife is [a gift
and blessing] from the LORD.
[Prov 18:22]
15 Laziness casts one into a deep
sleep [unmindful of lost
opportunity],
And the idle person will suffer
hunger.
16 He who keeps *and* obeys the
commandment [of the LORD]
keeps (guards) his own life,
But he who is careless of his ways
and conduct will die. [Prov 13:13;
16:17; Luke 10:28; 11:28]
17 He who is gracious *and* lends a
hand to the poor lends to the
LORD,
And the LORD will repay him for
his good deed. [Prov 28:27;
Eccl 11:1; Matt 10:42; 25:40;
2 Cor 9:6–8; Heb 6:10]

---

in communication or mutual respect, not from some flaw in marriage itself (12:4).

19:4 *Wealth makes many friends.* This proverb speaks of the effects of wealth and poverty on friendship. It does not describe how friends ought to behave, but how many friends actually do. Like a faithful spouse, a faithful friend is priceless (14:20).

19:8 *He who keeps understanding will find good.* Ultimately to "find good" means to find the Lord in His Word (16:20).

19:10 *is not fitting.* This phrase might also be rendered "is not a pretty sight" (17:7). For the wrong people to rule is an outrage.

19:12 *roaring of a lion . . . dew on the grass.* These metaphors are especially fitting when a monarch has all power. His rage may be violent and unpredictable, his pleasure gracious and restorative. A good king will display rage and spread favor for the right reasons.

19:13 *A foolish (ungodly) son . . . the contentions of a [quarrelsome] wife.* The family exists as the basic unit of a godly society. Two threats against the family are pictured in this proverb. One is the wayward son. The second is an emotionally unstable wife.

3 Ps 37:7 **4** Pr 14:20 **5** Ex 23:1 **6** Pr 29:26; Pr 17:8 **7** Pr 14:20; Ps 38:11 **8** Pr 16:20 **9** ver. 5 **10** Pr 30:22 **11** Jas 1:19; Pr 16:32 **12** Pr 16:14; Hos 14:5 **13** Pr 10:1; Pr 21:9,19 **14** 2Co 12:14; Pr 18:22 **15** Pr 6:9; Pr 10:4 **16** Lk 10:28 **17** 2Co 9:6

18 Discipline *and* teach your son
while there is hope,
And do not [indulge your anger
or resentment by imposing
inappropriate punishment nor]
desire his destruction.
19 *A man of* great anger will bear the
penalty [for his quick temper
and lack of self-control];
For if you rescue him [and do
not let him learn from the
consequences of his action], you
will only have to rescue him
over and over again.
20 Listen to counsel, receive
instruction, *and* accept
correction,
That you may be wise in the time
to come.
21 Many plans are in a man's mind,
But it is the LORD's purpose for him
that will stand (be carried out).
[Job 23:13; Ps 33:10, 11; Is 14:26,
27; 46:10; Acts 5:39; Heb 6:17]
22 That which is desirable in a man is
his loyalty *and* unfailing love,
But it is better to be a poor man
than a [wealthy] liar.
23 The fear of the LORD *leads*
to life,
So that one may sleep satisfied,
untouched by evil. [Job 5:19;
Ps 91:3; Prov 12:13; Is 46:4;
Jer 1:8; Dan 6:27; 2 Tim 4:8]
24 The lazy man buries his hand in
the [food] dish,
But will not even bring it to his
mouth again.
25 Strike a scoffer [for refusing to
learn], and the naive may [be
warned and] become prudent;
Reprimand one who has
understanding *and* a teachable
spirit, and he will gain
knowledge *and* insight.
26 He who assaults his father and
chases away his mother
Is a son who brings shame and
disgrace. [1 Tim 5:8]
27 Cease listening, my son, to
instruction *and* discipline
And you will stray from the words
of knowledge.
28 A wicked *and* worthless witness
mocks justice,
And the mouth of the wicked
spreads iniquity.
29 Judgments are prepared for
scoffers,
And beatings for the backs of
[thickheaded] fools. [Is 32:6]

On Life and Conduct

20 WINE IS a mocker, strong
drink a riotous brawler;
And whoever is intoxicated by it is
not wise. [Prov 23:29, 30; Is 28:7;
Hos 4:11]
2 The terror of a king is like the
roaring of a lion;
Whoever provokes him to anger
forfeits his own life.
3 It is an honor for a man to keep
away from strife [by handling
situations with thoughtful
foresight],
But any fool will [start a] quarrel
[without regard for the
consequences].
4 The lazy man does not plow when
the winter [planting] season
arrives;

19:21 *Many plans are in a man's mind.* A wise person commits his or her plans to the Lord (16:3). A person whose plans oppose the Lord (as in Ps 2:1 – 3) may actually become God's enemy. But the person whose ways are from God will certainly succeed (16:1,9).
19:22 *man is his loyalty and unfailing love.* Unfailing love may also mean "beauty." Loyalty is beautiful, whereas deception is a disfigurement of character (3:14; 31:18).
19:26 – 27 *son.* The desire for a good son — or daughter — is the subject of a significant portion of Proverbs (ch. 1 – 9). A child who is abusive to his parents shames them and violates God's command (20:20; Ex 20:12; Dt 5:16). As an abusive son is shameful, so an obedient son is faithful.
20:1 *Wine is a mocker.* This chapter begins with a warning against the abuse of wine, or excessive drinking (see this theme more extensively in 23:29 – 35). A wise person takes the danger seriously.

18 Pr 13:24 **20** Ps 37:37 **21** Heb 6:17 **23** 1Ti 4:8 **24** Pr 15:19 **25** Dt 13:11; Pr 9:8 **26** Pr 17:2 **28** Job 15:16 **29** Pr 26:3 **CHAPTER 20** **1** Ge 9:21 **2** Pr 19:12; Pr 8:36 **3** Pr 17:14 **4** Pr 10:4; Pr 19:15

So he begs at the [next] harvest
and has nothing [to reap].
5 A plan (motive, wise counsel) in the heart of a man is like water in a deep well,
But a man of understanding draws it out. [Prov 18:4]
6 Many a man proclaims his own loyalty *and* goodness,
But who can find a faithful *and* trustworthy man?
7 The righteous man who walks in integrity *and* lives life in accord with his [godly] beliefs—
How blessed [happy and spiritually secure] are his children after him [who have his example to follow].
8 A [discerning] king who sits on the throne of judgment
Sifts all evil [like chaff] with his eyes [and cannot be easily fooled].
9 Who can say, "I have cleansed my heart,
I am pure from my sin?"
[1 Kin 8:46; 2 Chr 6:36; Job 9:30; 14:4; Ps 51:5; 1 John 1:8]
10 Differing weights [one for buying and another for selling] and differing measures,
Both of them are detestable *and* offensive to the LORD.
[Deut 25:13; Mic 6:10, 11]
11 Even a boy is known *and* distinguished by his acts,
Whether his conduct is pure and right.
12 The hearing ear and the seeing eye,
The [omnipotent] LORD has made both of them.
13 Do not love [excessive] sleep, or you will become poor;
Open your eyes [so that you can do your work] and you will be satisfied with bread.
14 "It is [almost] worthless, it is [almost] worthless," says the buyer [as he negotiates the price];
But when he goes his way, then he boasts [about his bargain].
15 There is gold, and an abundance of pearls,
But the lips of knowledge are a vessel of preciousness [the most precious of all]. [Job 28:12, 16–19; Prov 3:15; 8:11]
16 [The judge tells the creditor], "Take the clothes of one who is surety for a stranger;
And hold him in pledge [when he guarantees a loan] for foreigners." [Prov 27:13]
17 Food gained by deceit is sweet to a man,
But afterward his mouth will be filled with gravel [just as sin may be sweet at first, but later its consequences bring despair].
18 Plans are established by counsel;
So make war [only] with wise guidance.
19 He who goes about as a gossip reveals secrets;
Therefore do not associate with a gossip [who talks freely or flatters]. [Rom 16:17, 18]

20:5 *draws it out.* Motivation for behavior is complex. A gifted counselor is able to draw out from a person genuine feelings and motivations, just as someone draws water from a deep well.
20:9 *Who can say.* This proverb is a rhetorical question. Everyone sins, a theme that Paul addresses at length in Romans 3:10–23. Anyone who claims never to sin is a liar (1Jn 1:8–9). But those who confess their sin obtain forgiveness (Ro 4:7).
20:11 *by his acts.* A pattern established early in life may continue to mark a person for his or her lifetime. Even at a very early age, a person's moral character may be revealed.
20:13 *sleep.* While sleep is a gift from God, it can also be a matter of excess and laziness. Hard work is necessary to make a living; laziness leads only to poverty (6:6–9).
20:16 *Take the clothes.* Clothing could be taken as collateral for a debt (Dt 24:10–13). If someone assumes responsibility for the debt of an unknown stranger, he or she should be held accountable even to the point of taking his or her clothing as a pledge.
20:17 *But afterward.* The Scriptures do not say that there is no pleasure in sinning, only that the reward does not last (9:17–18).

---

6 Mt 6:2; Lk 18:8,11 **7** 2Co 1:12; Ps 37:26 **8** ver. 26 **9** 1Ki 8:46 **10** Dt 25:13 **11** Mt 7:16 **12** Ex 4:11
13 Ro 12:11 **15** Pr 3:15 **16** Pr 22:26 **17** Pr 9:17 **18** Pr 24:6; Lk 14:31 **19** Pr 11:13; Ro 16:18

20 Whoever curses his father or his mother,
His lamp [of life] will be extinguished in time of darkness.
21 An inheritance hastily gained [by greedy, unjust means] at the beginning
Will not be blessed in the end. [Prov 28:20; Hab 2:6]
22 Do not say, "I will repay evil";
Wait [expectantly] for the LORD, and He will rescue *and* save you. [Deut 32:35; 2 Sam 16:12; Rom 12:17–19; 1 Thess 5:15; 1 Pet 3:9]
23 Differing weights are detestable *and* offensive to the LORD,
And fraudulent scales are not good.
24 Man's steps are ordered *and* ordained by the LORD.
How then can a man [fully] understand his way?
25 It is a trap for a man to [speak a vow of consecration and] say rashly, "It is holy!"
And [not until] afterward consider [whether he can fulfill it].
26 A wise king sifts out the wicked [from among the good]
And drives the [threshing] wheel over them [to separate the chaff from the grain].
27 The spirit (conscience) of man is the lamp of the LORD,
Searching *and* examining all the innermost parts of his being. [1 Cor 2:11]
28 Loyalty *and* mercy, truth *and* faithfulness, protect the king,
And he upholds his throne by lovingkindness.
29 The glory of young men is their [physical] strength,
And the honor of aged men is their gray head [representing wisdom and experience].
30 Blows that wound cleanse away evil,
And strokes reach to the innermost parts.

On Life and Conduct

21 THE KING'S heart is like channels of water in the hand of the LORD;
He turns it whichever way He wishes. [Ex 10:1, 2; Ezra 6:22]
2 Every man's way is right in his own eyes,
But the LORD weighs *and* examines the hearts [of people and their motives]. [Prov 24:12; Luke 16:15]
3 To do righteousness and justice
Is more acceptable to the LORD than sacrifice [for wrongs repeatedly committed]. [1 Sam 15:22; Prov 15:8; Is 1:11; Hos 6:6; Mic 6:7, 8]

20:20 *Whoever curses.* This proverb is about breaking the Fifth Commandment, "Honor (respect, obey, care for) your father and your mother" (Ex 20:12). The term for "curses" is based on a word that means "to treat lightly, to regard as insignificant." The statement "His lamp [of life] will be extinguished in time of darkness," is a symbol of eternal damnation.

20:25 *It is holy.* Several proverbs warn against making rash promises about holy things, then withdrawing the promises later (Ecc 5:1–7). It is better never to vow than to vow and then change one's mind.

20:26 *A wise king sifts out the wicked.* This royal proverb presents discipline as a merciful act. To punish wickedness is entirely appropriate. When the wicked are separated and punished with the severity that their crimes demand, all of society benefits. Ideally, the king in Israel mirrored God's character.

20:30 *Blows that wound cleanse away evil.* Suffering cleanses. No one wants to be hurt, but God can bring good out of any evil and make us better through hardship.

21:1 *The king's heart is like channels of water.* A person can look at a river and think that it is following a random pattern, but the water is following the direction of God's hand. So is the king.

21:3 *To do righteousness and justice.* This proverb affirms, as do Psalm 40:6–8; Micah 6:8; and numerous other passages in the Bible, that righteous living is more important than sacrifice (1Sa 15:22).

20 Mt 15:4; Job 18:5,6 **21** Pr 28:20; Hab 2:6 **22** Ro 12:17; 2Sa 16:12 **23** ver. 10 **24** Ps 37:23 **25** Ecc 5:4,5 **26** Ps 101:8 **27** 1Co 2:11 **28** Ps 101:1 **29** Pr 16:31 **CHAPTER 21** **2** Pr 16:2; Pr 24:12; Lk 16:15 **3** 1Sa 15:22

4 Haughty *and* arrogant eyes and a
proud heart,
The lamp of the wicked [their self-
centered pride], is sin [in the
eyes of God].
5 The plans of the diligent lead
surely to abundance *and*
advantage,
But everyone who acts in haste
comes surely to poverty.
6 Acquiring treasures by a lying
tongue
Is a fleeting vapor, the seeking *and*
pursuit of death.
7 The violence of the wicked will
[return to them and] drag them
away [like fish caught in a net],
Because they refuse to act with
justice.
8 The way of the guilty is
[exceedingly] crooked,
But as for the pure, his conduct is
upright.
9 It is better to live in a corner of
the housetop [on the flat roof,
exposed to the weather]
Than in a house shared with
a quarrelsome (contentious)
woman.
10 The soul of the wicked desires evil
[like an addictive substance];
His neighbor finds no compassion
in his eyes. [James 2:16]
11 When the scoffer is punished, the
naive [observes the lesson and]
becomes wise;
But when the wise *and* teachable
person is instructed, he receives
knowledge. [Prov 19:25]
12 The righteous one keeps an eye on
the house of the wicked—
How the wicked are cast down to
ruin.
13 Whoever shuts his ears at the cry
of the poor
Will cry out himself and not be
answered. [Matt 18:30–34;
James 2:13]
14 A gift in secret subdues anger,
And a bribe [hidden] in the pocket,
strong wrath.
15 When justice is done, it is a joy
to the righteous (the upright,
the one in right standing
with God),
But to the evildoers it is disaster.
16 A man who wanders from the
way of understanding (godly
wisdom)
Will remain in the assembly of
the dead.
17 He who loves [only selfish]
pleasure *will become* a poor
man;
He who loves *and* is devoted to
wine and [olive] oil will not
become rich.
18 The wicked become a ransom for
the righteous,
And the treacherous in the place
of the upright [for they fall into
their own traps].
19 It is better to dwell in a desert land
Than with a contentious and
troublesome woman.
20 There is precious treasure and oil
in the house of the wise [who
prepare for the future],
But a short-sighted *and* foolish man
swallows it up *and* wastes it.
21 He who earnestly seeks
righteousness and loyalty

21:6 *Acquiring treasures by a lying tongue.* If you have to lie to gain your "treasure," you are ultimately choosing death to your dreams. There is no stability in anything gained by a lie.
21:9 *a corner of the housetop.* Ancient Israelite roofs were flat and could be used as a deck or terrace. On occasion people would build a temporary shelter on a part of the roof. Here, the harried husband finds he prefers to live on the housetop rather than below with the nagging words of his wife.
21:10 *The soul of the wicked desires evil.* Wicked persons typically refuse to think of anyone but themselves.
21:15 *When justice is done, it is a joy.* Justice is not a heavy obligation that weighs a person down. For the righteous, promoting justice is a joy.
21:16 *the assembly of the dead.* The term *dead* is a frightful one, meaning "depths" (9:18). Death in these verses may speak of physical death rather than spiritual death (as is the case in James 1).
21:21 *life, righteousness, and honor.* It is possible that these three ideas go together to mean "a more abundant life." The pursuit

4 Pr 6:17 **5** Pr 10:4 **6** 2Pe 2:3 **10** Jas 4:5 **11** Pr 19:25 **13** Mt 7:2 **20** Ps 112:3; Mt 25:3,4 **21** Mt 5:6

Finds life, righteousness, and
honor. [Prov 15:9; Matt 5:6]
22 A wise man scales the city [walls] of the mighty
And brings down the stronghold in which they trust.
23 He who guards his mouth and his tongue
Guards himself from troubles. [Prov 12:13; 13:3; 18:21; James 3:2]
24 "Proud," "Haughty," "Scoffer," are his names
Who acts with overbearing *and* insolent pride.
25 The desire of the lazy kills him,
For his hands refuse to labor;
26 He craves all the day long [and does no work],
But the righteous [willingly] gives and does not withhold [what he has]. [2 Cor 9:6–10]
27 The sacrifice of the wicked is detestable *and* offensive [to the LORD].
How much more [unacceptable and insulting can it be] when he brings it with evil intention?
28 A false witness will perish,
But a man who listens *to the truth* will speak forever *and* go unchallenged.
29 A wicked man puts on a bold face,
But as for the upright, he considers, directs, *and* establishes his way [with the confidence of integrity].
30 There is no [human] wisdom or understanding
Or counsel [that can prevail] against the LORD.
31 The horse is prepared for the day of battle,
But deliverance *and* victory belong to the LORD.

On Life and Conduct

22 A *GOOD* name [earned by honorable behavior, godly wisdom, moral courage, and personal integrity] is more desirable than great riches;
And favor is better than silver and gold.
2 The rich and poor have a common bond;
The LORD is the Maker of them all. [Job 31:15; Prov 14:31]
3 A prudent *and* far-sighted *person* sees the evil [of sin] and hides himself [from it],
But the naive continue on and are punished [by suffering the consequences of sin].
4 The reward of humility [that is, having a realistic view of one's importance] and the [reverent, worshipful] fear of the LORD
Is riches, honor, and life. [Prov 21:21]
5 Thorns and snares are in the way of the obstinate [for their lack of honor and their wrong-doing traps them];
He who guards himself [with godly wisdom] will be far from them *and* avoid the consequences they suffer.
6 Train up a child in the way he should go [teaching him to seek God's wisdom and will for his abilities and talents],

---

of righteousness is its own reward. But added rewards are found in fullness of life, achieving righteousness, and receiving honor. All these things are gifts from the Lord (15:9).

21:28 *A false witness will perish.* A large number of proverbs focus on bearing false witness (19:28). The problem with a false witness is that his lies pervert justice for others.

22:2 *The LORD is the Maker of them all.* This sentence repeats the theme of riches (v. 1). God makes both the rich and the poor. This means that those who favor the rich over the poor (Jas 2) have not only missed the point of creation, they have insulted the Creator (14:31).

22:4 *reward of humility . . . and the [reverent, worshipful] fear of the LORD.* The writer of this proverb makes humility synonymous with the fear of the Lord. True humility begins with a proper attitude toward God. In such a spirit of submission to God, true fear of God is exhibited.

22:6 *Train up a child.* This verse, like the other proverbs, contains a wise statement that is usually true. Who your child turns out to be is a reflection of your parenting. As God has taught elsewhere

---

22 Ecc 9:14 **23** Pr 12:13; Jas 3:2 **27** Jer 6:20 **30** Isa 8:9,10; Jer 9:23; Ac 5:39 **31** Ps 3:8 **CHAPTER 22** **1** Ecc 7:1 **6** Eph 6:4; 2Ti 3:15

Even when he is old he will
not depart from it. [Eph 6:4;
2 Tim 3:15]
7 The rich rules over the poor,
And the borrower is servant to the
lender.
8 He who sows injustice will reap [a
harvest of] trouble,
And the rod of his wrath [with
which he oppresses others] will
fail.
9 He who is generous will be blessed,
For he gives some of his food to
the poor. [2 Cor 9:6–10]
10 Drive out the scoffer, and
contention will go away;
Even strife and dishonor will cease.
11 He who loves purity of heart
And whose speech is gracious will
have the king as his friend.
12 The eyes of the LORD keep guard
over knowledge *and* the one
who has it,
But He overthrows the words of
the treacherous.
13 The lazy one [manufactures
excuses and] says, "There is a
lion outside!
I will be killed in the streets [if I go
out to work]!"
14 The mouth of an immoral
woman is a deep pit [deep and
inescapable];
He who is cursed by the LORD
[because of his adulterous sin]
will fall into it.
15 Foolishness is bound up in the
heart of a child;
The rod of discipline [correction
administered with godly
wisdom and lovingkindness]
will remove it far from him.
16 He who oppresses *or* exploits the
poor to get more for himself
Or who gives to the rich [to gain
influence and favor], will only
come to poverty.

17 Listen carefully and hear the
words of the wise,
And apply your mind to my
knowledge;
18 For it will be pleasant if you keep
them in mind [incorporating
them as guiding principles];
Let them be ready on your lips [to
guide and strengthen yourself
and others].
19 So that your trust *and* reliance
and confidence may be in
the LORD,
I have taught these things to you
today, even to you.
20 Have I not written to you excellent
things
In counsels and knowledge,

---

in His Word, parents are to teach their children the way of the Lord. Not only are they to teach it purposefully, but they are to do it constantly — when they talk and sit and walk and lie down and get up (Dt 6:7 – 8). If children see their parents speaking kindly, being forgiving and gracious, gentle and understanding, children will want these character attributes too. But even more important, if the parents teach that they depend upon God to build kindly habits in themselves, children will know that it is to the Lord that one turns to for help in every part of life. Training children undoubtedly involves everything from wiping feet and closing doors to saying "please" and "thank you" and "I am sorry." But the most important training that a child receives is the continual teaching and daily example of their parents' dependence on the Lord.

22:10 *the scoffer.* This kind of person should be expelled from the community because his influence is harmful to everyone. The wise know that the scoffer is not a laughing matter, because he is laughing at holy things, at God Himself.

22:12 *The eyes of the LORD.* God is the final arbiter of knowledge and justice. The eyes of human beings are simply not trustworthy.

22:13 *There is a lion outside.* This proverb about lazy people pokes fun at how the lazy invent all sorts of excuses for avoiding work and risk.

22:17 – 24:22 Proverbs Concerning Various Situations — Verse 17 marks a new section of Proverbs. Three elements distinguish this section: (1) the change from one-verse units to multiple-verse units; (2) section headings that are embedded in the text; and (3) the affinity of this section for ancient Egyptian wisdom texts.

22:17 – 21 *Listen carefully.* These introductory words call the reader to pay attention and to prepare to learn about and worship God. The advice emphasizes strongly that a person's trust must be in the Lord.

9 2Co 9:6 **10** Ps 101:5 **11** Ps 101:6 **13** Pr 26:13 **14** Pr 2:16; 5:3; 7:5; Ecc 7:26 **15** Pr 13:24

21 To let you know the certainty of
the words of truth,
That you may give a correct
answer to him who sent you?
[Luke 1:3, 4]

22 Do not rob the poor because he is
poor [and defenseless],
Nor crush the afflicted [by legal
proceedings] at the gate [where
the city court is held], [Ex 23:6;
Job 31:16, 21]
23 For the LORD will plead their
case
And take the life of those who rob
them. [Zech 7:10; Mal 3:5]

24 Do not even associate with a man
given to angry outbursts;
Or go [along] with a hot-tempered
man,
25 Or you will learn his
[undisciplined] ways
And get yourself trapped [in a
situation from which it is hard to
escape].

26 Do not be among those who give
pledges [involving themselves in
others' finances],
Or among those who become
guarantors for *others'* debts.
27 If you have nothing with which
to pay [another's debt when he
defaults],
Why should his creditor take your
bed from under you?

28 Do not move the ancient landmark
[at the boundary of the
property]
Which your fathers have set.
29 Do you see a man skillful *and*
experienced in his work?
He will stand [in honor] before
kings;
He will not stand before obscure
men.

On Life and Conduct

23 WHEN YOU sit down to dine
with a ruler,
Consider carefully what is [set]
before you;
2 For you will put a knife to your
throat
If you are a man of *great*
appetite.
3 Do not desire his delicacies,
For it is deceptive food [offered
to you with questionable
motives].

4 Do not weary yourself [with the
overwhelming desire] to gain
wealth;
Cease from your own
understanding of it. [Prov 28:20;
1 Tim 6:9, 10]
5 When you set your eyes on wealth,
it is [suddenly] gone.
For *wealth* certainly makes itself
wings
Like an eagle that flies to the
heavens.

6 Do not eat the bread of a selfish
man,
Or desire his delicacies;
7 For as he thinks in his heart, so
is he [in behavior—one who
manipulates].
He says to you, "Eat and drink,"
Yet his heart is not with you [but
it is begrudging the cost].
8 The morsel which you have eaten
you will vomit up,
And you will waste your
compliments.

9 Do not speak in the ears of
a fool,
For he will despise the [godly]
wisdom of your words. [Is 32:6]
10 Do not move the ancient landmark
[at the boundary of the property]

22:28 *Do not move the ancient landmark.* The ancient Israelites regarded respect for the posted landmark as more than a question of private property. They saw it as a basic part of civil life. People must feel a certain sense of public trust and fairness for society to function.

23:4–5 *Do not weary yourself [with the overwhelming desire] to gain wealth.* These verses call for moderation in work. Although the proverbs discourage laziness (22:13), they also discourage any overworking whose purpose is greater wealth.

21 Lk 1:3,4; 1Pe 3:15 **23** 1Sa 24:12; Ps 12:5 **26** Pr 11:15 **28** Dt 19:14 **CHAPTER 23** **4** 1Ti 6:9; Ro 12:16
6 Dt 15:9 **7** Ps 12:2 **9** Pr 9:8; Mt 7:6

And do not go into the fields of
the fatherless [to take what
is theirs], [Deut 19:14; 27:17;
Prov 22:28]
11 For their Redeemer is strong *and*
mighty;
He will plead their case against
you.
12 Apply your heart to discipline
And your ears to words of
knowledge.

13 Do not withhold discipline from
the child;
If you swat him with a *reed-like*
rod [applied with godly wisdom],
he will not die.
14 You shall swat him with the *reed-like* rod
And rescue his life from Sheol (the
nether world, the place of the
dead).

15 My son, if your heart is wise,
My heart will also be glad;
16 Yes, my heart will rejoice
When your lips speak right things.

17 Do not let your heart envy sinners
[who live godless lives and have
no hope of salvation],
But [continue to] live in the
[reverent, worshipful] fear of the
LORD day by day.
18 Surely there is a future [and a
reward],
And your hope *and* expectation
will not be cut off.
19 Listen, my son, and be wise,
And direct your heart in the way
[of the LORD].
20 Do not associate with heavy
drinkers of wine,
Or with gluttonous eaters of meat,
[Is 5:22; Luke 21:34; Rom 13:13;
Eph 5:18]
21 For the heavy drinker and the
glutton will come to poverty,
And the drowsiness [of
overindulgence] will clothe one
with rags.

22 Listen to your father, who sired
you,
And do not despise your mother
when she is old.
23 Buy truth, and do not sell it;
Get wisdom and instruction and
understanding.

24 The father of the righteous will
greatly rejoice,
And he who sires a wise child will
have joy in him.
25 Let your father and your mother
be glad,
And let her who gave birth to you
rejoice [in your wise and godly
choices].

26 My son, give me your heart
And let your eyes delight in my
ways,
27 For a prostitute is a deep pit,
And an immoral woman is a
narrow well.
28 She lurks *and* lies in wait like a
robber [who waits for prey],
And she increases the faithless
among men.

29 Who has woe? Who has sorrow?
Who has strife? Who has
complaining?
Who has wounds without cause?
Whose eyes are red *and* dim?

23:13 – 14 *If you swat him with a reed-like rod.* This language was designed to motivate overly permissive parents, who were afraid of damaging children with any kind of discipline, or of making rules and enforcing them. There is no call here for abuse. Loving discipline does not destroy rebellious children; it does them a big favor.

23:15 *if your heart is wise.* Wisdom is an outgrowth of a proper response to discipline. That wisdom in turn is immediately discernible to the father and brings joy that must be expressed.

23:21 *For the heavy drinker and the glutton.* These kinds of people have no self-control, and this fact plagues them. Hebrew culture gave a prominent place to eating and drinking, but it had little tolerance for drunkenness and gluttony.

23:29 – 35 *Who has woe?* Along with Isaiah's celebrated description of debauchery (Isa 19:11 – 15), this section is one of the sharpest attacks on drunkenness in the Bible (vv. 19 – 21). The satire is razor sharp and the imagery vivid.

11 Pr 22:23 **13** Pr 13:24 **17** Ps 37:1; Pr 28:14 **18** Ps 37:37 **20** Isa 5:22 **22** Pr 1:8; Eph 6:1,2 **23** Mt 13:44 **24** Pr 10:1 **27** Pr 22:14 **28** Pr 7:12; Ecc 7:26 **29** Isa 5:11,22; Ge 49:12

30 Those who linger long over wine,
Those who go to taste mixed wine. [Prov 20:1; Eph 5:18]
31 Do not look at wine when it is red,
When it sparkles in the glass,
When it goes down smoothly.
32 At the last it bites like a serpent
And stings like a viper.
33 Your [drunken] eyes will see strange things
And your mind will utter perverse things [untrue things, twisted things].
34 And you will be [as unsteady] as one who lies down in the middle of the sea,
And [as vulnerable to disaster] as one who lies down on the top of a ship's mast, *saying*,
35 "They struck me, but I was not hurt!
They beat me, but I did not feel it!
When will I wake up?
I will seek more wine."

Precepts and Warnings

24 DO NOT be envious of evil men,
Nor desire to be with them;
2 For their minds plot violence,
And their lips talk of trouble [for the innocent].
3 Through [skillful and godly] wisdom a house [a life, a home, a family] is built,
And by understanding it is established [on a sound and good foundation],
4 And by knowledge its rooms are filled
With all precious and pleasant riches.
5 A wise man is strong,
And a man of knowledge strengthens his power; [Prov 21:22; Eccl 9:16]
6 For by wise guidance you can wage your war,
And in an abundance of [wise] counselors there is victory *and* safety.
7 Wisdom is too exalted for a [hardened, arrogant] fool;
He does not open his mouth in the gate [where the city's rulers sit in judgment].
8 He who plans to do evil
Will be called a schemer *or* deviser of evil.
9 The devising of folly is sin,
And the scoffer is repulsive to men.
10 If you are slack (careless) in the day of distress,
Your strength is limited.
11 Rescue those who are being taken away to death,
And those who stagger to the slaughter, Oh hold them back [from their doom]!
12 If you [claim ignorance and] say, "See, we did not know this,"
Does He not consider it who weighs *and* examines the hearts *and* their motives?
And does He not know it who guards your life *and* keeps your soul?

24:6 The Will of God — Common sense tells us that God often works through circumstances and through wise counsel to reveal His will for us. A number of biblical examples illustrate this principle:

God directed Abraham to substitute a ram, whose horns had become entangled in a thicket, for the life of Isaac (Ge 22:13).

God arranged for Pharaoh's daughter to be bathing in the river Nile at the exact time the baby Moses floated by in an ark of bulrushes (Ex 2:1 – 10).

Paul's young nephew happened to overhear a plot to kill his uncle. He then reported it to the authorities who saved Paul's life (Ac 23:11 – 35).

In light of the above, the Christian should ask himself, "Is the Lord showing me something through these circumstances?" We can also take great comfort in Paul's reminder to the Romans that God causes all things to "work together [as a plan] for good for those who love God, to those who are called according to His plan and purpose" (Ro 8:28).

30 Eph 5:18; Ps 75:8 **35** Jer 5:3; Eph 4:19 **CHAPTER 24** **1** Ps 37:1; 73:3; Pr 3:31 **5** Pr 21:22 **6** Lk 14:31 **7** Ps 10:5 **8** Ro 1:30 **11** Ps 82:4; Isa 58:6,7; 1Jn 3:16 **12** Pr 21:2; Ps 62:12

And will He not repay [you and]
every man according to his
works?

13 My son, eat honey, because it is
good,
And the drippings of the
honeycomb are sweet to your
taste.
14 Know that [skillful and godly]
wisdom is [so very good] for
your life *and* soul;
If you find wisdom, then there will
be a future *and* a reward,
And your hope *and* expectation
will not be cut off.

15 Do not lie in wait, O wicked man,
against the dwelling of the
righteous;
Do not destroy his resting place;
16 For a righteous man falls seven
times, and rises again,
But the wicked stumble in *time of*
disaster *and* collapse. [Job 5:19;
Ps 34:19; 37:24; Mic 7:8]

17 Do not rejoice *and* gloat when your
enemy falls,
And do not let your heart be glad
[in self-righteousness] when he
stumbles,
18 Or the LORD will see your gloating
and be displeased,
And turn His anger away from
your enemy.

19 Do not get upset because of
evildoers,
Or be envious of the wicked,
20 For there will be no future for the
evil man;
The lamp of the wicked will be
put out.

21 My son, fear the LORD and the
king;
And do not associate with those
who are given to change
[of allegiance, and are
revolutionary],
22 For their tragedy will rise suddenly,
And who knows the punishment
that both [the LORD and
the king] will bring on the
rebellious?

23 These also are sayings of the wise:
To show partiality in judgment is
not good.
24 He who says to the wicked, "You
are righteous,"
Peoples will curse him, nations
will denounce him;
25 But to those [honorable judges]
who rebuke the *wicked,* it will
go well with them *and* they will
find delight,
And a good blessing will come
upon them.
26 He kisses the lips [and wins the
hearts of people]
Who gives a right *and*
straightforward answer.

27 Prepare your work outside
And get it ready for yourself in the
field;
Afterward build your house *and*
establish a home.

28 Do not be a witness against your
neighbor without cause,
And do not deceive with your lips
[speak neither lies nor half-
truths]. [Eph 4:25]
29 Do not say, "I will do to him as he
has done to me;
I will pay the man back for his
deed." [Prov 20:22; Matt 5:39, 44;
Rom 12:17, 19]

30 I went by the field of the lazy man,
And by the vineyard of the man
lacking understanding *and*
common sense;
31 And, behold, it was all overgrown
with thorns,
And nettles were covering its
surface,
And its stone wall was broken
down.

24:21 – 22 *fear the LORD and the king.* This proverb relates most fully to the Davidic kings, who were God's regents on earth; one way the ancient Israelites could show respect for God was to respect the king.

13 SS 5:1 **14** Ps 19:10 **16** Ps 34:19; Mic 7:8; Est 7:10; Am 5:2 **17** Job 31:29; Ob 12 **19** Ps 37:1 **21** Ro 13:7; 1Pe 2:17 **23** Lev 19:15; Dt 16:19 **24** Isa 5:23 **27** 1Ki 5:17 **28** Eph 4:25 **29** Mt 5:39 **31** Ge 3:18

[32]When I saw, I considered it well;
I looked and received instruction.
[33]"Yet a little sleep, a little slumber,
A little folding of the hands to rest
[and daydream],"
[34]Then your poverty will come as a robber,
And your want like an armed man.

Similitudes, Instructions

25 THESE ARE also the proverbs of Solomon, which the men of Hezekiah king of Judah copied: [1 Kin 4:32]

[2]It is the glory of God to conceal a matter,
But the glory of kings is to search out a matter. [Deut 29:29; Rom 11:33]
[3]As the heavens for height and the earth for depth,
So the hearts *and* minds of kings are unsearchable.
[4]Take away the dross from the silver,
And there comes out [the pure metal for] a vessel for the silversmith [to shape]. [2 Tim 2:21]
[5]Take away the wicked from before the king,
And his throne will be established in righteousness.
[6]Do not be boastfully ambitious *and* claim honor in the presence of the king,
And do not stand in the place of great men;
[7]For it is better that it be said to you, "Come up here,"
Than for you to be placed lower in the presence of the prince,
Whom your eyes have seen. [Luke 14:8–10]

[8]Do not rush out to argue *your* case [before magistrates or judges];
Otherwise what will you do in the end [when your case is lost and]
When your neighbor (opponent) humiliates you? [Prov 17:14; Matt 5:25]
[9]Argue your case with your neighbor himself [before you go to court];
And do not reveal another's secret, [Matt 18:15]
[10]Or he who hears it will shame you
And the rumor about you [and your action in court] will have no end.

[11]Like apples of gold in settings of silver
Is a word spoken at the right time. [Prov 15:23; Is 50:4]
[12]Like an earring of gold and an ornament of fine gold
Is a wise reprover to an ear that listens *and* learns.
[13]Like the cold of snow [brought from the mountains] in the time of harvest,
So is a faithful messenger to those who send him;
For he refreshes the life of his masters.
[14]Like clouds and wind without rain
Is a man who boasts falsely of gifts [he does not give]. [Jude 12]

25:1 *These are also the proverbs of Solomon.* After the first collection of proverbs from Solomon (10:1 – 22:16) and proverbs from foreign sources (22:17 – 24:22; 24:23 – 34) comes a collection of proverbs attributed to Solomon, but which were not compiled until the time of Hezekiah. The following observations can be made: (1) The wisdom tradition concerning Solomon was prodigious; (2) Israel's interest in wisdom was particularly centered in times of relative peace; (3) Hezekiah's involvement in this activity was a mark of the strength of his rule and the sense he had of restoring Solomon's glory.

25:6 *Do not be boastfully ambitious and claim honor.* Knowing your place is a recurring theme in the Bible. It is humiliating to be told to remove yourself from a seat of honor. Jesus spoke of the same need for deference (Lk 14:11).

25:7 *Whom your eyes have seen.* This phrase reflects the custom in the ancient world of never looking directly in the eyes of a superior until told to do so (Isa 6:5).

33 Pr 6:9 **CHAPTER 25** **1** 1Ki 4:32 **2** Ro 11:33; Job 29:16 **4** 2Ti 2:21 **5** Pr 20:8; Pr 16:12 **7** Lk 14:10
8 Mt 5:25 **9** Mt 5:25 **11** Pr 15:23 **13** Pr 13:17 **14** Pr 20:6; Jude 12

[15]By patience *and* a calm spirit a ruler may be persuaded,
And a soft *and* gentle tongue breaks the bone [of resistance]. [Gen 32:4; 1 Sam 25:24; Prov 15:1; 16:14]
[16]Have you found [pleasure sweet like] honey? Eat only as much as you need,
Otherwise, being filled excessively, you vomit it.
[17]Let your foot seldom be in your neighbor's house,
Or he will become tired of you and hate you.
[18]Like a club and a sword and a piercing arrow
Is a man who testifies falsely against his neighbor (acquaintance).
[19]Like a broken tooth or an unsteady foot
Is confidence in an unfaithful man in time of trouble.
[20]Like one who takes off a garment in cold weather, or like [a reactive, useless mixture of] vinegar on soda,
Is he who [thoughtlessly] sings [joyful] songs to a heavy heart. [Dan 6:18; Rom 12:15]
[21]If your enemy is hungry, give him bread to eat;
And if he is thirsty, give him water to drink; [Matt 5:44; Rom 12:20]
[22]For in doing so, you will heap coals of fire upon his head,
And the LORD will reward you.
[23]The north wind brings forth rain;
And a backbiting tongue, an angry countenance.
[24]It is better to live in a corner of the housetop [on the flat roof, exposed to the weather]
Than in a house shared with a quarrelsome (contentious) woman. [Prov 21:9]
[25]Like cold water to a thirsty soul,
So is good news from a distant land.
[26]Like a muddied fountain and a polluted spring
Is a righteous man who yields *and* compromises his integrity before the wicked.
[27]It is not good to eat much honey,
Nor is it glorious to seek one's own glory.
[28]Like a city that is broken down and without walls [leaving it unprotected]
Is a man who has no self-control over his spirit [and sets himself up for trouble]. [Prov 16:32]

Similitudes, Instructions

26 LIKE SNOW in summer and like rain in harvest,
So honor is not fitting for a [shortsighted] fool. [Is 32:6]
[2]Like the sparrow in her wandering, like the swallow in her flying,
So the curse without cause does not come *and* alight [on the undeserving]. [Num 23:8]
[3]A whip for the horse, a bridle for the donkey,
And a rod for the backs of fools [who refuse to learn].
[4]Do not answer [nor pretend to agree with the frivolous comments of] a [closed-minded] fool according to his folly,

---

25:15 *By patience and a calm spirit a ruler may be persuaded.* In this passage the general rule that a gentle answer turns away wrath is applied to a particular and most difficult situation.
25:21 – 22 *coals of fire.* The words of Jesus in Matthew 5:43 – 48 have direct ties to these verses. They speak of God's judgment (Ps 120:4; 140:10); the idea is that an act of kindness to your enemy may cause him or her to feel ashamed. This is just one way to overcome evil with good (Ro 12:20).

26:4 – 5 *according to his folly.* Some people have called the two proverbs here contradictory, but that is not necessarily true. The phrase appears twice as a play on words with two shades of meaning. On the one hand, it means "avoid the temptation to stoop to his level"; that is do not use his methods, "Otherwise you . . . will be like him." On the other hand, it means "avoid the temptation to ignore him altogether"; that is, respond in some way, or else he will become wise in his own eyes and his folly will get worse.

15 Pr 15:1 **16** ver. 27 **18** Ps 57:4 **20** Da 6:18 **21** Mt 5:44 **22** 2Sa 16:12 **23** Job 37:22; Ps 101:5 **24** Pr 19:13 **27** ver. 16; Pr 27:2 **28** Pr 16:32 **CHAPTER 26** **1** 1Sa 12:17 **2** Dt 23:5 **3** Ps 32:9

Otherwise you, even you, will be
like him.
5 Answer [and correct the erroneous
concepts of] a fool according to
his folly,
Otherwise he will be wise in his
own eyes [if he thinks you agree
with him]. [Matt 16:1–4; 21:24–27]
6 He who sends a message by the
hand of a fool
Cuts off *his own* feet (sabotages
himself) and drinks the violence
[it brings on himself as a
consequence]. [Prov 13:17]
7 Like the legs which are useless to
the lame,
So is a proverb in the mouth of a
fool [who cannot learn from its
wisdom].
8 Like one who [absurdly] binds
a stone in a sling [making it
impossible to throw],
So is he who [absurdly] gives
honor to a fool.
9 Like a thorn that goes [without
being felt] into the hand of a
drunken man,
So is a proverb in the mouth of a
fool [who remains unaffected by
its wisdom].
10 Like a [careless] archer who
[shoots arrows wildly and]
wounds everyone,
So is he who hires a fool or those
who [by chance just] pass by.
11 Like a dog that returns to his
vomit
Is a fool who repeats his foolishness.
12 Do you see a man [who is
unteachable and] wise in his
own eyes *and* full of self-
conceit?
There is more hope for a fool than
for him. [Prov 29:20; Luke 18:11;
Rom 12:16; Rev 3:17]
13 The lazy person [who is self-
indulgent and relies on lame
excuses] says, "There is a lion in
the road!
A lion is in the open square [and
if I go outside to work I will be
killed]!" [Prov 22:13]
14 As the door turns on its hinges,
So does the lazy person on his bed
[never getting out of it].
15 The lazy person buries his hand
in the dish [losing opportunity
after opportunity];
It wearies him to bring it back to
his mouth. [Prov 19:24]
16 The lazy person is wiser in his
own eyes
Than seven [sensible] men who
can give a discreet answer.
17 Like one who grabs a dog by the
ears [and is likely to be bitten]
Is he who, passing by, stops to
meddle with a dispute that is
none of his business.
18 Like a madman who throws
Firebrands, arrows, and death,
19 So is the man who deceives his
neighbor (acquaintance, friend)
And then says, "Was I not joking?"
[Eph 5:4]
20 For lack of wood the fire goes out,
And where there is no whisperer
[who gossips], contention quiets
down.
21 Like charcoal to hot embers and
wood to fire,
So is a contentious man to kindle
strife. [Prov 15:18; 29:22]
22 The words of a whisperer (gossip)
are like dainty morsels [to be
greedily eaten];
They go down into the innermost
chambers of the body [to be
remembered and mused upon].
[Prov 18:8]
23 Like a [common] clay vessel
covered with the silver dross
[making it appear silver when it
has no real value]
Are burning lips [murmuring
manipulative words] and a
wicked heart.
24 He who hates, disguises it with his
lips,

26:23 clay vessel covered with the silver dross. The meaning of this proverb is similar to Jesus' remarks to His enemies that they were like whitewashed tombs (Mt 23:27). No amount of painting on the outside changes the value of the rotten interior.

26:24–26 revealed openly before the assembly. A person who hates says one thing

5 Mt 16:1-4 **11** 2Pe 2:22; Ex 8:15 **12** Rev 3:17 **19** Eph 5:4 **21** Pr 15:18

But he stores up deceit in his heart.
[25]When he speaks graciously *and* kindly [to conceal his malice], do not trust him,
For seven abominations are in his heart.
[26]*Though his* hatred covers itself with guile *and* deceit,
His malevolence will be revealed openly before the assembly.
[27]Whoever digs a pit [for another man's feet] will fall into it,
And he who rolls a stone [up a hill to do mischief], it will come back on him. [Ps 7:15, 16; 9:15; 10:2; 57:6; Prov 28:10; Eccl 10:8]
[28]A lying tongue hates those it wounds *and* crushes,
And a flattering mouth works ruin.

Warnings and Instructions

27 DO NOT boast about tomorrow,
For you do not know what a day may bring. [Luke 12:19, 20; James 4:13]
[2]Let another praise you, and not your own mouth;
A stranger, and not your own lips.
[3]Stone is heavy and the sand weighty,
But a fool's [unreasonable] wrath is heavier *and* more burdensome than both of them.
[4]Wrath is cruel and anger is an overwhelming flood,
But who is able to endure *and* stand before [the sin of] jealousy?
[5]Better is an open reprimand [of loving correction]
Than love that is hidden. [Prov 28:23; Gal 2:14]
[6]Faithful are the wounds of a friend [who corrects out of love and concern],
But the kisses of an enemy are deceitful [because they serve his hidden agenda].
[7]He who is satisfied loathes honey,
But to the hungry soul any bitter thing is sweet.
[8]Like a bird that wanders from her nest [with its comfort and safety],
So is a man who wanders from his home.
[9]Oil and perfume make the heart glad;
So does the sweetness of a friend's counsel that comes from the heart.
[10]Do not abandon your own friend and your father's friend,
And do not go to your brother's house in the day of your disaster.
Better is a neighbor who is near than a brother who is far away.
[11]My son, be wise, and make my heart glad,
That I may reply to him who reproaches (reprimands, criticizes) me. [Prov 10:1; 23:15, 24]
[12]A prudent man sees evil and hides himself *and* avoids it,
But the naive [who are easily misled] continue on and are punished [by suffering the consequences of sin]. [Prov 22:3]
[13][The judge tells the creditor,] "Take the garment of one who is surety (guarantees a loan) for a stranger;
And hold him in pledge when he is surety for an immoral woman [for it is unlikely the debt will be repaid]." [Prov 20:16]
[14]He who blesses his neighbor with a loud voice early in the morning,
It will be counted as a curse to him [for it will either be annoying or his purpose will be suspect].
[15]A constant dripping on a day of steady rain
And a contentious (quarrelsome) woman are alike; [Prov 19:13]

---

but stores up anger within. He may find that his hatred hurts him, when in his life there is so much falsehood that no one believes him no matter how gracious and truthful he might be at times.

27:7 to the hungry soul. Those who are full do not appreciate what they have, while to those who are hungry, anything tastes good.

25 Ps 28:3 **27** Ps 7:15 **CHAPTER 27** **10** Pr 17:17 **11** Ps 127:5

16 Whoever attempts to restrain her
[criticism] might as well try to
stop the wind,
And grasps oil with his right hand.
17 As iron sharpens iron,
So one man sharpens [and
influences] another [through
discussion].
18 He who tends the fig tree will eat
its fruit,
And he who faithfully protects
and cares for his master will be
honored. [1 Cor 9:7, 13]
19 As in water face *reflects* face,
So the heart of man reflects man.
20 Sheol (the place of the dead) and
Abaddon (the underworld) are
never satisfied;
Nor are the eyes of man ever
satisfied. [Prov 30:16; Hab 2:5]
21 The refining pot is for silver and
the furnace for gold [to separate
the impurities of the metal],
And each is tested by the praise
given to him [and his response
to it, whether humble or
proud].
22 Even though you pound a
[hardened, arrogant] fool [who
rejects wisdom] in a mortar with
a pestle like grain,
Yet his foolishness will not leave
him.
23 Be diligent to know the condition
of your flocks,
And pay attention to your herds;
24 For riches are not forever,
Nor does a crown *endure* to all
generations.
25 When the grass is gone, the new
growth is seen,
And herbs of the mountain are
gathered in,
26 The lambs will *supply wool* for
your clothing,
And the goats will bring the price
of a field.
27 And *there will be* enough goats'
milk for your food,
For the food of your household,
And for the maintenance of your
maids.

Warnings and Instructions

28 THE WICKED flee when no
one pursues them,
But the righteous are as bold as a
lion. [Lev 26:17, 36; Ps 53:5]
2 When a land does wrong, it has
many princes,
But when the ruler is a man of
understanding and knowledge,
its stability endures.
3 A poor man who oppresses *and*
exploits the lowly
Is like a sweeping rain which
leaves no food. [Matt 18:28]
4 Those who set aside the law
[of God and man] praise the
wicked,
But those who keep the law [of
God and man] struggle with
them. [Prov 29:18]
5 Evil men do not understand
justice,
But they who long for *and*
seek the LORD understand it
fully. [John 7:17; 1 Cor 2:15;
1 John 2:20, 27]
6 Better is the poor who walks in his
integrity
Than he who is crooked *and*
two-faced though he is rich.
[Prov 19:1]
7 He who keeps the law [of God and
man] is a wise *and* discerning
son,

27:17 *iron sharpens iron.* This may also be translated as applying to the will; "let iron sharpen iron, and so let a person sharpen his friend." The idea is that people grow from interaction with one another.

28:4 – 5 *Those who set aside the law.* When a person abandons God's law, he or she loses all sense of right and praise the wicked (Ro 1:28 – 32). Since true justice is from God, the ungodly have trouble understanding it. This is why the fear of the Lord is the beginning of wisdom (1:7).

28:7 *a companion of gluttons.* One way of breaking God's law is to be a companion of the gluttonous (23:20 – 21). This is why Jesus' enemies charged Him with associating with gluttons and winebibbers. Such accusations were attacks on His faithfulness to God (Mt 11:19).

18 1Co 9:7 **20** Hab 2:5; Ecc 1:8 **21** Pr 17:3 **22** Jer 5:3 **25** Ps 104:14 **CHAPTER 28** **1** Ps 53:5 **3** Mt 18:28 **4** Ro 1:32; 1Ki 18:18 **5** Ps 92:6; Jn 7:17 **6** Pr 19:1 **7** Pr 29:3

But he who is a companion of
gluttons humiliates his father
[and himself].
8 He who increases his wealth by
interest and usury (excessive
interest)
Gathers it for him who is gracious
to the poor. [Job 27:16, 17;
Prov 13:22; Eccl 2:26]
9 He who turns his ear away from
listening to the law [of God and
man],
Even his prayer is repulsive [to
God]. [Ps 66:18; 109:7; Prov 15:8;
Zech 7:11]
10 He who leads the upright astray on
an evil path
Will himself fall into his own pit,
But the blameless will inherit good.
11 The rich man [who is conceited
and relies on his wealth instead
of God] is wise in his own eyes,
But the poor man who has
understanding [because he
relies on God] is able to see
through him.
12 When the righteous triumph, there
is great glory *and* celebration;
But when the wicked rise
[to prominence], men hide
themselves.
13 He who conceals his
transgressions will not prosper,
But whoever confesses and turns
away from his sins will find
compassion *and* mercy. [Ps 32:3,
5; 1 John 1:8–10]
14 Blessed *and* favored by God is
the man who fears [sin and its
consequence] at all times,
But he who hardens his heart [and
is determined to sin] will fall
into disaster.
15 Like a roaring lion and a charging
bear
Is a wicked ruler over a poor people.
16 A leader who is a great oppressor
lacks understanding *and*
common sense [and his
wickedness shortens his days],
But he who hates unjust gain will
[be blessed and] prolong his days.
17 A man who is burdened with the
guilt of human blood (murder)
Will be a fugitive until death; let
no one support him *or* give him
refuge.
18 He who walks blamelessly *and*
uprightly will be kept safe,
But he who is crooked (perverse)
will suddenly fall.
19 He who cultivates his land will
have plenty of bread,
But he who follows worthless
people *and* frivolous pursuits
will have plenty of poverty.
20 A faithful (right-minded) man will
abound with blessings,
But he who hurries to be rich will
not go unpunished. [Prov 13:11;
20:21; 23:4; 1 Tim 6:9]
21 To have regard for one person over
another *and* to show favoritism
is not good,
Because for a piece of bread a man
will transgress.
22 He who has an evil *and* envious
eye hurries to be rich
And does not know that poverty
will come upon him. [Prov 21:5;
28:20]
23 He who [appropriately]
reprimands a [wise] man will
afterward find more favor
Than he who flatters with the
tongue.
24 He who robs his father or his
mother
And says, "This is no sin,"
Is [not only a thief but also] the
companion of a man who
destroys.

28:8 *interest and usury.* Profit gained by charging interest or high "profit margins" is unjust. God will help the poor eventually at their exploiters expense.

28:14 *Blessed and favored by God is the man.* This is a repeat of Psalm 1:1 about a person who is in awe of God. The person who never thinks of God faces calamity.

28:23 *He who [appropriately] reprimands a [wise] man.* Constructive criticism has more value than flattery, which aims only to win people's affection.

8 Pr 13:22 **9** Ps 66:18 **10** Pr 26:27; Mt 6:33 **12** Pr 11:10 **13** Ps 32:3,5 **14** Ps 16:8; Ro 2:5 **15** 1Pe 5:8; Mt 2:16 **17** Ge 9:6 **18** Pr 10:9,25; ver. 6 **19** Pr 12:11 **20** 1Ti 6:9 **21** Pr 18:5; Eze 13:19 **22** ver. 20 **23** Pr 27:5,6 **24** Pr 18:9

[25] An arrogant *and* greedy man stirs
up strife,
But he who trusts in the LORD will
be blessed *and* prosper.
[26] He who trusts confidently
in his own heart is a [dull,
thickheaded] fool,
But he who walks in [skillful and
godly] wisdom will be rescued.
[James 1:5]
[27] He who gives to the poor will
never want,
But he who shuts his eyes [from
their need] will have many curses.
[Deut 15:7; Prov 19:17; 22:9]
[28] When the wicked rise [to power],
men hide themselves;
But when the wicked perish, the
[consistently] righteous increase
and become great. [Prov 28:12]

Warnings and Instructions

29 HE WHO hardens his neck
and refuses instruction after
being often reproved (corrected,
criticized),
Will suddenly be broken beyond
repair.
[2] When the righteous are in
authority *and* become great, the
people rejoice;
But when the wicked man rules,
the people groan *and* sigh.
[3] A man who loves [skillful and
godly] wisdom makes his father
joyful,
But he who associates with
prostitutes wastes his wealth.
[4] The king establishes (stabilizes)
the land by justice,
But a man who takes bribes
overthrows it.
[5] A man who flatters his neighbor
[with smooth words intending to
do harm]
Is spreading a net for his own feet.
[6] By his wicked plan an evil man is
trapped,
But the righteous man sings and
rejoices [for his plan brings good
things to him].
[7] The righteous man cares for the
rights of the poor,
But the wicked man has no
interest in such knowledge.
[Job 29:16; 31:13; Ps 41:1]
[8] Scoffers set a city afire [by stirring
up trouble],
But wise men turn away anger
[and restore order with their
good judgment].
[9] If a wise man has a controversy
with a foolish *and* arrogant man,
The foolish man [ignores logic
and fairness and] only rages or
laughs, and there is no peace
(rest, agreement).
[10] The bloodthirsty hate the
blameless [because of his
integrity],
But the upright are concerned for
his life. [Gen 4:5, 8; 1 John 3:12]
[11] A [shortsighted] fool always loses
his temper *and* displays his
anger,
But a wise man [uses self-control
and] holds it back.
[12] If a ruler pays attention to lies [and
encourages corruption],
All his officials *will become* wicked.
[13] The poor man and the oppressor
have this in common:
The LORD gives light to the eyes of
both. [Prov 22:2]
[14] If a king faithfully *and* truthfully
judges the poor,
His throne shall be established
forever.
[15] The rod and reproof (godly
instruction) give wisdom,

28:25 – 26 *An arrogant and greedy man.* One of the main causes of strife is pride; trust in God leads to blessing.
29:5 *spreading a net.* Flattery is a lie. If you flatter your neighbor you are making a trap of some kind for him. God never lies. He always tells the truth and so should we.
29:13 *The poor man and the oppressor.* God is responsible for giving life to both. Jesus attested that God causes rain to fall on the just and the unjust (Mt 5:45).

25 Pr 13:10; 1Ti 6:6 **27** Dt 15:7 **28** ver. 12; Job 24:4 **CHAPTER 29** **1** 2Ch 36:16 **2** Est 8:15; Est 3:15 **3** Pr 10:1; Lk 15:13 **7** Job 29:16; Ps 41:1 **8** Pr 11:11; Eze 22:30 **9** Mt 11:17 **10** 1Jn 3:12 **11** Pr 12:16 **13** Mt 5:45 **14** Pr 20:28 **15** Pr 17:21,25

But a child who gets his own way
brings shame to his mother.
16 When the wicked are in authority,
transgression increases,
But the righteous will see the
downfall of the wicked.
17 Correct your son, and he will give
you comfort;
Yes, he will delight your soul.
18 Where there is no vision [no
revelation of God and His word],
the people are unrestrained;
But happy *and* blessed is he
who keeps the law [of God].
[1 Sam 3:1; Amos 8:11, 12]
19 A servant will not be corrected by
words *alone;*
For though he understands, he will
not respond [nor pay attention].
20 Do you see a [conceited] man who
speaks quickly [offering his
opinions or answering without
thinking]?
There is more hope for a
[thickheaded] fool than
for him.
21 He who pampers his slave from
childhood
Will find him to be a son in the end.
22 An angry man stirs up strife,
And a hot-tempered *and*
undisciplined man commits
many transgressions.
23 A man's pride *and* sense of self-
importance will bring him down,
But he who has a humble spirit will
obtain honor. [Prov 15:33; 18:12;
Is 66:2; Dan 4:30; Matt 23:12;
James 4:6, 10; 1 Pet 5:5]
24 Whoever is partner with a thief
hates his own life;
He hears the curse [when
swearing an oath to testify], but
discloses nothing [and commits
perjury by omission].
25 The fear of man brings a snare,
But whoever trusts in *and* puts his
confidence in the LORD will be
exalted *and* safe.
26 Many seek the ruler's favor,
But justice for man comes from the
LORD.
27 An unjust man is repulsive to the
righteous,
And he who is upright in the way
[of the LORD] is repulsive to the
wicked.

The Words of Agur

30 THE WORDS of Agur the son
of Jakeh, the oracle:
The man says to Ithiel, to Ithiel and
to Ucal:
2 Surely I am more brutish *and*
stupid than any man,
And I do not have the
understanding of a man [for I do
not know what I do not know].
3 I have not learned [skillful and
godly] wisdom,
Nor do I have knowledge of the
Holy One [who is the source of
wisdom].
4 Who has ascended into heaven
and descended?
Who has gathered the wind in His
fists?

29:18 *Where there is no vision.* The Hebrew word for vision speaks of a revelatory word from God. Without God's revelation of the law, the people flounder. True happiness is discovered within the constraints of revelation, in the counsel of the Savior.
29:23 *A man's pride and sense of self-importance will bring him down.* Pride, inordinate self-esteem, causes others to lose respect for the conceited egotist. In contrast to this, humility draws honor from others. However, pride takes many forms and is not always the adornment of just the conceited egotist.
29:26 *But justice for man comes from the LORD.* God controls human affairs. Therefore it makes more sense to seek the Lord first before stooping to seek the favor of human rulers.
30:1 *The words of Agur.* This verse starts an entirely new section of Proverbs. Like Lemuel (31:1 – 9), Agur was a non-Hebrew contributor to the Book of Proverbs. He came to faith in the God of Israel in a foreign land.
30:4 *What is His name.* This verse gives the riddle that perplexed Agur. The questions all culminate in the last two lines. The Old Testament would answer that "His name" is the Lord God, but did not have a name for His Son. This riddle

16 Ps 37:36 **17** Pr 19:18 **18** 1Sa 3:1; Am 8:11; Jn 13:17 **20** Pr 26:12 **22** Pr 26:21 **23** Job 22:29; Isa 66:2; Da 4:30; Mt 23:12 **24** Lev 5:1 **25** Ge 12:12 **26** Ps 20:9 **CHAPTER 30** **2** Ps 73:22 **4** Jn 3:13; Job 38:4; Ps 104:3; Isa 40:12

Who has bound the waters in His
garment?
Who has established all the ends
of the earth?
What is His name, and what is His
Son's name?
Certainly you know! [John 3:13;
Rev 19:12]

5 Every word of God is tested *and*
refined [like silver];
He is a shield to those who
trust *and* take refuge in Him.
[Ps 18:30; 84:11; 115:9–11]
6 Do not add to His words,
Or He will reprove you, and you
will be found a liar.

7 Two things I have asked of You;
Do not deny them to me before
I die:
8 Keep deception and lies far
from me;
Give me neither poverty nor
riches;
Feed me with the food that is my
portion,
9 So that I will not be full and deny
You and say, "Who is the LORD?"
Or that I will not be poor and steal,
And so profane the name of my
God. [Deut 8:12, 14, 17; Neh 9:25,
26; Job 31:24; Hos 13:6]

10 Do not slander *or* malign a servant
before his master [stay out of
another's personal life],
Or he will curse you [for your
interference], and you will be
found guilty.

11 There is a generation (class of
people) that curses its father
And does not bless its mother.
12 There is a generation (class of
people) that is pure in its own
eyes,
Yet is not washed from its
filthiness.
13 There is a generation (class of
people)—oh, how lofty are their
eyes!
And their eyelids are raised *in
arrogance*.
14 There is a generation (class of
people) whose teeth are like
swords
And whose jaw teeth are like
knives,
To devour the afflicted from the
earth
And the needy from among men.

15 The leech has two daughters,
"Give, give!"
There are three things that are
never satisfied,
Four that do not say, "It is enough":
16 Sheol, and the barren womb,
Earth that is never satisfied with
water,
And fire that never says, "It is
enough."
17 The eye that mocks a father
And scorns a mother,
The ravens of the valley will pick
it out,
And the young vultures will devour
it. [Lev 20:9; Prov 20:20; 23:22]

18 There are three things which
are too astounding *and*
unexpectedly wonderful for me,
Four which I do not understand:
19 The way of an eagle in the air,
The way of a serpent on a rock,
The way of a ship in the middle of
the sea,
And the way of a man with a
maid.
20 This is the way of an adulterous
woman:
She eats and wipes her mouth
And says, "I have done no wrong."

21 Under three things the earth is
disquieted *and* quakes,
And under four it cannot bear up:

---

was to remain unsolved until Jesus answered it for Nicodemus (Jn 3:13). These verses form one of the most straightforward messianic texts in the Bible.
30:19 ***maid.*** This term could also read virgin or young woman in this context.

30:20 ***This is the way.*** This verse contrasts with the way of verse 19; this way is awful whereas the former is wonderful. The *adulterous woman* regards her illicit sexual relations without remorse.

5 Ps 12:6; Ps 18:30 **6** Dt 4:2; Rev 22:18 **8** Mt 6:11 **9** Dt 8:12 **12** Lk 18:11 **13** Ps 131:1; Pr 6:17 **14** Job 29:17; Ps 52:2; Ps 14:4; Am 8:4 **16** Pr 27:20; Hab 2:5 **17** Ge 9:22; Lev 20:9; Pr 20:20; 23:22

22 Under a servant when he reigns,
Under a [spiritually blind] fool
when he is filled with food,
23 Under an unloved woman when
she gets married,
And *under* a maidservant when
she supplants her mistress.

24 There are four things that are
small on the earth,
But they are exceedingly wise:
25 The ants are not a strong people,
Yet they prepare their food in the
summer; [Prov 6:6]
26 The shephanim are not a mighty
folk,
Yet they make their houses in the
rocks; [Ps 104:18]
27 The locusts have no king,
Yet all of them go out in
groups;
28 You may grasp the lizard with
your hands,
Yet it is in kings' palaces.

29 There are three things which are
stately in step,
Even four which are stately in
their stride:
30 The lion, which is mighty among
beasts
And does not turn back before
any;
31 The strutting rooster, the male
goat also,
And the king *when his* army is
with him.

32 If you have foolishly exalted
yourself,
Or if you have plotted *evil, put
your* hand on your mouth.
[Job 21:5; 40:4]
33 Surely the churning of milk
produces butter,
And wringing the nose produces
blood;
So the churning of anger produces
strife.

The Words of Lemuel

31 THE WORDS of King Lemuel,
the oracle, which his mother
taught him:

2 What, O my son?
And what, O son of my womb?
And what [shall I advise you],
O son of my vows?
3 Do not give your [generative]
strength to women [neither
foreign wives in marriages of
alliances, nor concubines],
Nor your ways to that which
destroys kings.
4 It is not for kings, O Lemuel,
It is not for kings to drink wine,
Or for rulers to desire strong
drink, [Eccl 10:17; Hos 4:11]
5 Otherwise they drink and forget
the law *and* its decrees,
And pervert the rights *and* justice
of all the afflicted.
6 Give strong drink [as medicine]
to him who is ready to pass
away,
And wine to him whose life is
bitter.
7 Let him drink and forget his
poverty
And no longer remember his
trouble.
8 Open your mouth for the mute,
For the rights of all who are
unfortunate *and* defenseless;
[1 Sam 19:4; Esth 4:16;
Job 29:15, 16]
9 Open your mouth, judge
righteously,

30:24–28 *four things that are small on the earth.* This numerical proverb speaks of four creatures that are small in size but amazing in behavior. Each of these small creatures has a behavioral trait from which wise people can learn.
30:32–33 *put your hand on your mouth.* This phrase means "stop it." The idea is if you are in the middle of making trouble and suddenly realize your foolishness, stop right then before things get worse.
31:1 *The words of King Lemuel.* This verse begins a new section of material from a non-Israelite source.
31:4–5 *Otherwise they drink and forget the law.* In this passage the consumption of strong drink is linked to injustice.

22 Pr 19:10; Ecc 10:7 **25** Pr 6:6 **26** Ps 104:18 **32** Job 21:5; 40:4; Mic 7:16 **CHAPTER 31** **2** Isa 49:15 **3** Pr 5:9; Dt 17:17; Neh 13:26; Pr 7:26; Hos 4:11 **4** Ecc 10:17 **5** Hos 4:11 **6** Ps 104:15 **8** See Job 29:15,16 **9** Lev 19:15; Dt 1:16; Job 29:12; Isa 1:17; Jer 22:16

And administer justice for the
afflicted and needy. [Lev 19:15;
Deut 1:16; Job 29:12; Is 1:17;
Jer 22:16]

Description of a Worthy Woman

10 An excellent woman [one who is
spiritual, capable, intelligent,
and virtuous], who is he who
can find her?
Her value is more precious
than jewels *and* her worth
is far above rubies *or* pearls.
[Prov 12:4; 18:22; 19:14]
11 The heart of her husband trusts in
her [with secure confidence],
And he will have no lack of gain.
12 She comforts, encourages, *and*
does him only good and
not evil
All the days of her life.
13 She looks for wool and flax
And works with willing hands in
delight.
14 She is like the merchant ships
[abounding with treasure];
She brings her [household's] food
from far away.
15 She rises also while it is still night
And gives food to her household
And assigns tasks to her maids.
[Job 23:12]
16 She considers a field before she
buys *or* accepts it [expanding
her business prudently];
With her profits she plants fruitful
vines in her vineyard.
17 She equips herself with strength
[spiritual, mental, and physical
fitness for her God-given task]
And makes her arms strong.
18 She sees that her gain is good;
Her lamp does not go out, but
it burns continually through
the night [she is prepared for
whatever lies ahead].
19 She stretches out her hands to the
distaff,
And her hands hold the spindle
[as she spins wool into thread
for clothing].
20 She opens *and* extends her hand
to the poor,
And she reaches out her filled
hands to the needy.
21 She does not fear the snow for her
household,
For all in her household are clothed
in [expensive] scarlet [wool].
[Josh 2:18, 19; Heb 9:19–22]
22 She makes for herself coverlets,
cushions, *and* rugs of tapestry.
Her clothing is linen, pure *and*
fine, and purple [wool]. [Is 61:10;
1 Tim 2:9; Rev 3:5; 19:8, 14]
23 Her husband is known in the
[city's] gates,
When he sits among the elders of
the land. [Prov 12:4]
24 She makes [fine] linen garments
and sells them;
And supplies sashes to the
merchants.
25 Strength and dignity are her
clothing *and* her position is
strong and secure;
And she smiles at the future
[knowing that she and her
family are prepared].
26 She opens her mouth in [skillful
and godly] wisdom,
And the teaching of kindness is on
her tongue [giving counsel and
instruction].
27 She looks well to how things go in
her household,

31:10 ***An excellent woman.*** Proverbs 31:10 – 31 is an acrostic poem; each verse begins with a successive letter to the Hebrew alphabet. As the Book of Proverbs begins with a Prologue (1:1 – 7), which gives the goals of wisdom in general terms, so now it concludes with this Epilogue, which presents them in a case study.

31:20 – 22 ***to the poor.*** The excellent woman works not to get rich, but to give to the poor. She can be concerned for others because she has provided for her own family.

31:26 ***the teaching of kindness is on her tongue.*** This attribute of kindness in a woman is valued far above physical charm in God's sight. Peter describes real beauty as a product of the heart and not the combination of certain physical features (1Pe 3:1 – 5).

10 Pr 12:4; 18:22; 19:14 **15** Ro 12:11; Lk 12:42 **20** Eph 4:28; Heb 13:16 **23** Pr 12:4

And does not eat the bread of
idleness. [1 Tim 5:14; Titus 2:5]
28 Her children rise up and call her
blessed (happy, prosperous, to
be admired);
Her husband also, and he praises
her, *saying*,
29 "Many daughters have done nobly,
and well [with the strength of
character that is steadfast in
goodness],
But you excel them all."
30 Charm *and* grace are deceptive,
and [superficial] beauty is vain,
But a woman who fears the LORD
[reverently worshiping, obeying,
serving, and trusting Him with
awe-filled respect], she shall be
praised.
31 Give her of the product of her
hands,
And let her own works praise
her in the gates [of the city].
[Phil 4:8]

31:30–31 ***Charm and grace.*** Charm and grace, like beauty, can deceive us about the true nature of someone's character. But if a woman fears the Lord, that is trustworthy and more worthy of praise than physical comeliness.

ECCLESIASTES

▸ **AUTHOR:** The author calls himself "the son of David, king in Jerusalem" in 1:1. Solomonic authorship is the standard Christian position, although some scholars, along with the Talmud, believe the work was later edited during the time of Hezekiah or possibly Ezra. The proverbs in this book are similar to those in the Book of Proverbs (Ecc 7; 10). According to 12:9, Qoheleth collected and arranged many proverbs, perhaps referring to the two Solomonic collections in Proverbs.

▸ **TIMES:** c. 935 BC ▸ **KEY VERSE:** Ecc 2:24

▸ **THEME:** Ecclesiastes is a Greek word that is usually translated "the preacher" or "the teacher." The book was likely written late in Solomon's life, when he could see that the glorious era of his kingdom was beginning to decline. He had it all, power, prestige, pleasure, but none of that provides ultimate satisfaction. That fulfillment comes only through a relationship with God and obedience to His word. It is important to note that the arguments of the book are more thematic than linear. The same topics are addressed in different ways at different points within the work.

The Futility of All Endeavors

1 THE WORDS of the Preacher, the son of David, king in Jerusalem.

2 "Vanity of vanities," says the
Preacher.
"Vanity of vanities! All [that is
done without God's guidance] is
vanity [futile, meaningless—a
wisp of smoke, a vapor that
vanishes, merely chasing the
wind]." [Rom 8:20]

3 What advantage does man have
from all his work
Which he does under the sun
(while earthbound)?

4 One generation goes and another
generation comes,
But the earth remains forever.
[Ps 119:90]

5 Also, the sun rises and the
sun sets;
And hurries to the place where it
rises again.

1:1 ***the Preacher.*** This word denotes a function or a profession. It literally means "one who assembles or gathers people together." Thus the word refers to Solomon as a person who convened an assembly of the wise in order to explore in a formal manner the meaning of life.

1:2 ***Vanity of vanities.*** This phrase translates the Hebrew superlative, familiar from such phrases as "Song of Songs" and "holy of holies." Here it might express "the ultimate absurdity" or "utter emptiness." The word vanity means "breath" or "vapor" and thus speaks of life as "quickly passing." Life is like a vapor; indeed, it is like the thinnest of vapors. Wherever we read the word *vanity* in Ecclesiastes, we should think not of what is "meaningless," but of what is "quickly passing" (v. 14; 6:12). This is one of the key terms in the Book of Ecclesiastes, for it is found 38 times here, but only 34 times throughout the rest of the Old Testament. The teaching of the Preacher is to realize that life is a fleeting thing that needs to be savored and enjoyed as a gift from God.

1:4 ***One generation.*** This term suggests both the human actors and the natural phenomena as well.

CHAPTER 1 **1** ver. 12; Ecc 7:27; 12:8-10 **2** Ps 39:5,6; 62:9; 144:4; Ecc 12:8; Ro 8:20 **3** Ecc 2:22 **4** Ps 104:5; 119:90 **5** Ps 19:4-6

6 The wind blows toward the south,
Then circles toward the north;
The wind circles *and* swirls
endlessly,
And on its circular course the
wind returns. [John 3:8]
7 All the rivers flow into the sea,
Yet the sea is not full.
To the place where the rivers flow,
There they flow again.
8 All things are wearisome *and* all
words are frail;
Man cannot express it.
The eye is not satisfied with seeing,
Nor is the ear filled with hearing.
[Prov 27:20]
9 That which has been is that which
will be [again],
And that which has been done is
that which will be done again.
So there is nothing new under the
sun.
10 Is there anything of which it can
be said,
"See this, it is new"?
It has already existed for [the
vast] ages [of time recorded or
unrecorded]
Which were before us.
11 There is no remembrance of
earlier things,
Nor also of the later things that are
to come;
There will be for them no
remembrance
By generations who will come
after them.

The Futility of Wisdom

12 I, the Preacher, have been king
over Israel in Jerusalem.
13 And I set my mind to seek and ex-
plore by [man's] wisdom all [human
activity] that has been done under
heaven. It is a miserable business *and*
a burdensome task which God has
given the sons of men with which to
be busy *and* distressed.
14 I have seen all the works which
have been done under the sun, and
behold, all is vanity, a futile grasping
and chasing after the wind.
15 What is crooked cannot be
straightened and what is defective *and*
lacking cannot be counted.
16 I spoke with my heart, saying, "Be-
hold, I have acquired great [human] wis-
dom *and* experience, more than all who
were over Jerusalem before me; and my
mind has observed a wealth of [moral]
wisdom and [scientific] knowledge."
17 And I set my mind to know [practi-
cal] wisdom and to discern [the charac-
ter of] madness and folly [in which men
seem to find satisfaction]; I realized
that this too is a futile grasping *and*
chasing after the wind. [1 Thess 5:21]
18 For in much [human] wisdom there
is much displeasure *and* exaspera-
tion; increasing knowledge increases
sorrow.

The Futility of Pleasure and Possessions

2 I SAID to myself, "Come now, I
will test you with pleasure *and*
gratification; so enjoy yourself *and*
have a good time." But behold, this too
was vanity (futility, meaninglessness).
[Luke 12:19, 20]
2 I said of laughter, "It is madness," and
of pleasure, "What does it accomplish?"

With the verb "goes" we have the first of a series of antitheses in Ecclesiastes. ***the earth remains forever.*** Only God is eternal and everlasting in the fullest sense. But compared to the lives of humankind, the earth abides with little change. **1:13 *under heaven.*** This is a synonymous expression for "under the sun" (vv. 3,9); it refers to life as it is lived by people on earth. **1:14 *futile grasping and chasing after the wind.*** This phrase does not occur in the Hebrew Bible outside of Ecclesiastes. Seven of its nine occurrences (v. 14; 2:11,17,26; 4:4,6; 6:9) follow "vanity" statements. The phrase explains the nature of life according to the Preacher. Life is real, but quickly passing; any attempt to slow it is futile. **2:1 *Come now, I will test you with pleasure and gratification.*** The Preacher uses a literary device of conversing with himself as a way of describing his thought processes. ***have a good time.*** A new test is proposed, following the test of wisdom. It is the test of "joy." **2:2 *It is madness.*** Solomon labels the lighter

6 Jn 3:8 **7** Ps 104:8,9; Jer 5:22 **8** Pr 27:20 **9** Ecc 3:15 **12** ver. 1 **13** Ge 3:19; Ecc 3:10 **15** Ecc 7:13 **16** 1Ki 3:12,13 **17** Ecc 2:3,12 **18** Ecc 12:12 **CHAPTER 2** **1** Lk 12:19; Ecc 1:2

3 I explored with my mind how to gratify myself with wine while [at the same time] having my mind remain steady *and* guide me wisely; and how to take control of foolishness, until I could see what was good for the sons of men to do under heaven all the days of their lives.

4 I made great works: I built houses for myself; I planted vineyards for myself;

5 I made gardens and orchards for myself and I planted in them all kinds of fruit trees;

6 I made pools of water for myself from which to water the forest *and* make the trees bud.

7 I bought male and female slaves and had slaves born in my house. I also possessed herds and flocks larger than any who preceded me in Jerusalem.

8 Also, I collected for myself silver and gold and the treasure of kings and provinces. I provided for myself male singers and female singers, and the delights *and* pleasures of men—many concubines. [1 Kin 9:28; 10:10, 14, 21]

9 So I became great and excelled more than all who preceded me in Jerusalem. My wisdom also remained with me.

10 Whatever my eyes looked at with desire I did not refuse them. I did not withhold from my heart any pleasure, for my heart was pleased because of all my labor; and this was my reward for all my labor.

11 Then I considered all which my hands had done and labored to do, and behold, all was vanity and chasing after the wind and there was no profit (nothing of lasting value) under the sun. [Matt 16:26]

Wisdom Excels Folly

12 So I turned to consider [secular] wisdom, madness, and folly; for what will the man do who succeeds the king? Nothing *except* what has already been done.

13 Then I saw that [even secular] wisdom [that brings sorrow] is better than [the pleasures of] folly *and* self-indulgence as light excels darkness.

14 The wise man's eyes are in his head, but the fool walks in darkness; and yet I know that [in the end] one fate happens to them both. [Prov 17:24]

15 Then I said to myself, "As it happens to the fool, so death will also happen to me. What use is it then for me to be extremely wise?" Then I said in my heart, "This too is vanity (meaningless)."

16 For there is no [more] lasting remembrance of the wise man than of the fool, since in the days to come all will be long forgotten. And how does the wise man die? Even as the fool!

17 So I hated life, for the work which had been done under the sun caused me only great sorrow; because all is futility and chasing after the wind.

The Futility of Labor

18 So I hated all the fruit (gain) of my labor for which I had labored under the sun, because I must leave it to the man who will succeed me. [Ps 49:10]

19 And who knows whether he will be a wise man or a fool? Yet he will have control over all the fruit of my labor for which I have labored by acting wisely under the sun. This too is vanity (futility, self-conceit).

20 So I turned aside and let my heart despair over all the fruit of my labor for which I had labored under the sun.

---

side of pleasure and joy as sheer madness, but even the weightier aspects of laughter cause Solomon to ask if anything substantial is really achieved. As Solomon writes in Proverbs 14:13, "Even in laughter the heart may be in pain, and the end of joy may be grief."

2:10 *my eyes looked at with desire.* Solomon had limitless ability to fulfill any and all of his desires.

2:11 *behold, all was vanity.* At the end of his grand quest for possessions and experiences, Solomon concluded that it was "vanity" or a "vapor," a striving after the wind. That is, even with all he had done and experienced, there was still a sense that nothing lasting or enduring had been achieved.

2:17 *So I hated life.* Such hatred of life is astonishing since the one who finds wisdom also finds life, according to Proverbs 3:16. But the Preacher's dissatisfaction was related to the quickly passing nature of everything (1:2), including the good things.

3 Ecc 1:17 **8** 1Ki 9:28; 10:10,14,21 **10** Ecc 3:22; 5:18; 9:9 **11** Ecc 1:3,14 **12** Ecc 1:17; 7:25 **14** Pr 17:24; Ecc 8:1; Ps 49:10; Ecc 9:2,3,11 **18** Ps 49:10

21 For there is a man who has labored with wisdom and knowledge and skill, yet gives his legacy to one who has not labored for it. This too is vanity and a great evil.

22 For what does a man get from all his labor and from the striving *and* sorrow of his heart with which he labors under the sun?

23 For all his days his work is painful and sorrowful; even at night his mind does not rest. This too is vanity (worthless).

24 There is nothing better for a man than to eat and drink and assure himself that there is good in his labor. Even this, I have seen, is from the hand of God.

25 For who can eat and who can have enjoyment without Him?

26 For to the person who pleases Him God gives wisdom, knowledge, and joy; but to the sinner He gives the work of gathering and collecting so that he may give to one who pleases God. This too is vanity and chasing after the wind.

A Time for Everything

3 THERE IS a season (a time appointed) for everything and a time for every delight *and* event *or* purpose under heaven—

2 A time to be born and a time to die;
A time to plant and a time
to uproot what is planted.
[Heb 9:27]
3 A time to kill and a time to heal;
A time to tear down and a time to
build up.
4 A time to weep and a time to
laugh;
A time to mourn and a time to
dance.
5 A time to throw away stones and a
time to gather stones;
A time to embrace and a time to
refrain from embracing.
6 A time to search and a time to give
up as lost;
A time to keep and a time to throw
away.
7 A time to tear apart and a time to
sew together;
A time to keep silent and a time to
speak. [Amos 5:13]
8 A time to love and a time to hate;
A time for war and a time for
peace. [Luke 14:26]

9 What profit is there for the worker from that in which he labors?

10 I have seen the task which God has given to the sons of men with which to occupy themselves.

2:21 *This too is vanity and a great evil.* The term *evil* often has a sense of moral evil; here, however it may mean "calamity" or "ruin." There is a sense of sadness that runs through this section. Nothing that we gain in this life can be carried on into the life to come.

2:24 *eat and drink.* The Preacher concludes that all good is located only in God. This phrase marks one of the central affirmations of the book (3:12; 3:22; 8:15; 9:7); in the midst of a world of trouble, a believer is able to seize the moment in joy from God. Only God supplies the key to the meaning of life. Without Him, genuine meaning, satisfaction, and enjoyment in life are ultimately elusive.

2:26 *God gives wisdom, knowledge, and joy.* One of the words used most frequently in Ecclesiastes to describe God's relationship to individuals is a verb "to give." It appears 11 times with God as the subject. Joy is God's gift to the man who is good in His sight. God has designed us so that true joy is possible only through Him.

3:1 – 15 *There is a season (a time appointed) for everything.* Some regard the Book of Ecclesiastes as describing life apart from God. But clearly this text describes life that is lived in relationship with God. Through these words, the Preacher is not saying that everything has an opportune time according to which one should choose one action or the other. Rather, he teaches that all events are in the hand of God, who makes everything happen in the time He judges appropriate.

3:5 *A time to throw away stones.* In times of peace, stones were cleared from the fields allowing for cultivation. In wartime, the rocks were thrown on the fields to make them unusable (2Ki 3:19,25).

3:7 *A time to tear apart and a time to sew together.* When bad news came, it was customary to rip one's garments to show grief (2Sa 13:31). When the problem passed, it was just as well to sew the garment back together.

3:9 *What profit is there.* This is the same question posed in 1:3. The answer here is that all of life

22 Ecc 1:3; 3:9 **23** Job 5:7; 14:1 **24** Ecc 3:12,13,22; 5:18; 8:15 **26** Job 27:16,17; Pr 28:8 **CHAPTER 3 1** ver. 17; Ecc 8:6 **2** Heb 9:27 **5** Joel 2:16; 1Co 7:5 **7** Am 5:13 **8** Lk 14:26 **9** Ecc 1:3 **10** Ecc 1:13

God Set Eternity in the Heart of Man

11 He has made everything beautiful *and* appropriate in its time. He has also planted eternity [a sense of divine purpose] in the human heart [a mysterious longing which nothing under the sun can satisfy, except God]—yet man cannot find out (comprehend, grasp) what God has done (His overall plan) from the beginning to the end.

12 I know that there is nothing better for them than to rejoice and to do good as long as they live;

13 and also that every man should eat and drink and see *and* enjoy the good of all his labor—it is the gift of God.

14 I know that whatever God does, it endures forever; nothing can be added to it nor can anything be taken from it, for God does it so that men will fear *and* worship Him [with awe-filled reverence, knowing that He is God]. [Ps 19:9; James 1:17]

15 That which is has already been, and that which will be has already been, for God seeks what has passed by [so that history repeats itself].

16 Moreover, I have seen under the sun that in the place of justice there is wickedness, and in the place of righteousness there is wickedness.

17 I said to myself, "God will judge both the righteous and the wicked," for there is a time [appointed] for every matter and for every deed.

18 I said to myself regarding the sons of men, "God is surely testing them in order for them to see that [by themselves, without God] they are [only] animals."

19 For the [earthly] fate of the sons of men and the fate of animals is the same. As one dies, so dies the other; indeed, they all have the same breath and there is no preeminence *or* advantage for man [in and of himself] over an animal, for all is vanity.

20 All go to the same place. All came from the dust and all return to the dust.

21 Who knows if the spirit of man ascends upward and the spirit of the animal descends downward to the earth?

22 So I have seen that there is nothing better than that a man should be happy in his own works *and* activities, for that is his portion (share). For who will bring him [back] to see what will happen after he is gone?

The Evils of Oppression

4 THEN I looked again *and* considered all the acts of oppression that were being practiced under the sun. And behold *I saw* the tears of the oppressed and they had no one to comfort them; and on the side of their

---

unfolds at the appointment of God. All the toiling of man cannot change the time, circumstances, and control of events that God has reserved for Himself.

3:11 ***planted eternity [a sense of divine purpose] in the human heart.*** This phrase refers to a deep-seated, compulsive drive to transcend our mortality by knowing the meaning and destiny of the world. Because we are made in the image of God, we have an inborn inquisitiveness about eternal realities. We can find peace only when we come to know our eternal Creator. Even then, we know God only in part (1Co 13:12).

3:12–13 ***nothing better ... to rejoice.*** As in 2:24, the advice of the Preacher is to seize the day in the joy of God. Biblical faith is a call for joy, even when we live in a wicked world and under terrible stress; this is because we find true joy in the living God.

3:16–17 ***I have seen ... the place of justice there is wickedness.*** It was outrageous that in the very establishments where people should expect justice, they could find only wickedness. The Preacher warns the wicked judges that God, the final Judge, will come to rectify all wrong doing and bring true justice.

3:20 ***All go to the same place.*** Both humans and beasts die and go to the grave. But this is not the end for human beings—they will face eternal life or death. People and animals differ; their bodies go back to the dust from which they came, but the human spirit is immortal.

4:1 ***they had no one to comfort them.*** So much pain can come to the downtrodden that they may even despair of life (1Ki 19:4). Only when the oppressed go into the house of God will they gain perspective (5:1–6; Ps 73:17).

11 Ecc 8:17; Ro 11:33 **13** Ecc 2:24 **14** Jas 1:17 **15** Ecc 1:9 **16** Ecc 5:8 **17** Ro 2:6-8; 2Co 5:10; 2Th 1:6; ver. 1 **19** Ps 49:12,20; 73:22; Ecc 2:16 **20** Ge 3:19 **21** Ecc 12:7 **22** ver. 12; Ecc 2:24; 5:18; 11:9; Ecc 2:10; Ecc 6:12; 8:7; 10:14 **CHAPTER 4** **1** Ecc 3:16; 5:8

oppressors was power, but they had no one to comfort them.

[2]So I congratulated *and* thought more fortunate are those who are already dead than the living who are still living.

[3]But better off than either of them is the one who has not yet been born, who has not seen the evil deeds that are done under the sun.

[4]I have seen that every [effort in] labor and every skill in work *comes from* man's rivalry with his neighbor. This too is vanity (futility, false pride) and chasing after the wind.

[5]The fool folds his hands [together] and consumes his own flesh [destroying himself by idleness and apathy].

[6]One hand full of rest *and* patience is better than two fists full of labor and chasing after the wind.

[7]Then I looked again at vanity under the sun [in one of its peculiar forms].

[8]There was a certain man—without a dependent, having neither a child nor a brother, yet there was no end to all his labor. Indeed, his eyes were not satisfied with riches *and he never asked,* "For whom do I labor and deprive myself of pleasure?" This too is vanity (a wisp of smoke, self-conceit); yes, it is a painful effort *and* an unhappy task. [Prov 27:20; 1 John 2:16]

[9]Two are better than one because they have a more satisfying return for their labor;

[10]for if either of them falls, the one will lift up his companion. But woe to him who is alone when he falls and does not have another to lift him up.

[11]Again, if two lie down together, then they keep warm; but how can one be warm *alone?*

[12]And though one can overpower him who is alone, two can resist him. A cord of three *strands* is not quickly broken.

[13]A poor yet wise youth is better than an old and foolish king who no longer knows how to receive instruction *and* counsel (friendly reproof, warning)—

[14]for the poor youth has [used his wisdom and] come out of prison to become king, even though he was born poor in his kingdom.

[15]I have seen all the living under the sun join with the second youth (the king's acknowledged successor) who replaces him.

[16]There is no end to all the people; to all who were before them. Yet those who come later will not be happy with him. Surely this also is vanity (emptiness) and chasing after the wind.

Your Attitude Toward God

5 GUARD YOUR steps *and* focus on what you are doing as you go to the house of God and draw near to listen rather than to offer the [careless or irreverent] sacrifice of fools; for they are too ignorant to know they are doing evil. [Gen 35:1–4; Ex 3:5]

[2]Do not be hasty with your mouth [speaking careless words or vows] or impulsive in thought to bring up a matter before God. For God is in heaven and you are on earth; therefore let your words be few.

[3]For the dream comes through much effort, and the voice of the fool through many words.

4:3 *who has not yet been born.* So powerfully wrong and so lonely is the suffering of the oppressed, that Solomon, with a good deal of poetic license similar to Job 3:3 – 10, argues that nonexistence could be preferred over existence.

4:8 *his eyes were not satisfied.* Man is in love with what is vanishing. The antidote for covetousness is to replace sinful desire for increase in wealth, with a strong passion for doing the will of God (1Jn 2:17).

4:9 – 12 *Two are better than one.* Throughout this section there is an emphasis on the obvious benefits of companions. The intimacy and sharing of life brings relief for the problem of isolation and loneliness. A companion can offer assistance, comfort, and defense — a threefold chord.

5:1 *Guard your steps.* This means behave yourself. The idea of righteous behavior is rephrased at the end of the section in the words: "fear God" (5:7).

2 Job 3:17 **3** Job 3:11,16,21; Ecc 6:3 **5** Pr 6:10; 24:33 **6** Pr 15:16,17; 16:8 **8** Pr 27:20; 1Jn 2:16; Ps 39:6
CHAPTER 5 **1** See Ex 3:5; Isa 1:12; 1Sa 15:22; Ps 50:8; Pr 15:8; 21:27; Hos 6:6 **2** Pr 10:19; Mt 6:7 **3** Pr 10:19

4 When you make a vow *or* a pledge
to God, do not put off paying it; for
God takes no pleasure in fools [who
thoughtlessly mock Him]. Pay what
you vow. [Ps 50:14; 66:13, 14; 76:11]
5 It is better that you should not vow
than that you should vow and not pay.
[Prov 20:25; Acts 5:4]
6 Do not allow your speech to cause
you to sin, and do not say before the
messenger (priest) *of God* that it was
a mistake. Why should God be angry
because of your voice (words) and de-
stroy the work of your hands? [Mal 2:7]
7 For in a multitude of dreams and
in a flood of words there is worthless-
ness. Rather [reverently] fear God [and
worship Him with awe-filled respect,
knowing who He is].
8 If you see the oppression of the poor
and the denial of justice and righteous-
ness in the province, do not be shocked
at the sight [of corruption]; for a higher
official watches over another official,
and there are higher ones over them
[looking out for one another].
9 After all, a king who cultivates the
field is an advantage to the land.

The Folly of Riches

10 He who loves money will not be
satisfied with money, nor he who loves
abundance *with its* gain. This too is
vanity (emptiness).
11 When good things increase, those
who consume them increase. So what
advantage is there to their owners ex-
cept to see them with their eyes?
12 The sleep of a working man is
sweet, whether he eats little or much;
but the full stomach (greed) of the rich
[who hungers for even more] will not
let him sleep.
13 There is a grievous evil which I
have seen under the sun: riches being
kept *and* hoarded by their owner to his
own misery.
14 For when those riches are lost in
bad investments and he becomes the
father of a son, then there is nothing in
his hand [for the support of the child].
15 As he came naked from his moth-
er's womb, so he will return as he
came; and he will take away nothing
from all his labor that he can carry in
his hand. [Job 1:21; 1 Tim 6:7]
16 This also is a grievous evil—
exactly as he was born, so he shall
die. So what advantage has he who
labors for the wind? [1 Tim 6:6]
17 All of his life he also eats in dark-
ness [cheerlessly, without sweetness
and light], with great frustration, sick-
ness, and anger.
18 Behold, here is what I have seen to
be good and fitting: to eat and drink,
and to find enjoyment in all the la-
bor in which he labors under the sun
during the few days of his life which
God gives him—for this is his [allotted]
reward. [1 Tim 6:17]
19 Also, every man to whom God has
given riches and possessions, He has
also given the power *and* ability to
enjoy them and to receive [this as] his
[allotted] portion and to rejoice in his
labor—this is the gift of God [to him].
20 For he will not often consider the
[troubled] days of his life, because God
keeps him occupied *and* focused on the
joy of his heart [and the tranquility of
God indwells him].

5:4 – 5 *When you make a vow or a pledge to God.* One should not attempt to bribe God with a hasty vow. The first part of this verse is almost identical to Deuteronomy 23:21. See the later example of the lie of Ananias and Sapphira (Ac 5:1 – 11).
5:7 *fear God.* This is a central theme of the Book of Ecclesiastes. It does not mean to be afraid of God (Ex 20:2). It means to have reverence, awe, and wonder in response to His glory.
5:10 *will not be satisfied.* Desire always outruns possessions, no matter how vast acquisitions may grow.
5:15 *As he came naked.* The maxim that "you can't take it with you" is affirmed here (2:21).
5:19 *this is the gift of God.* God has separated the gift of enjoying something from the gift of the object itself so that we might be driven back to the Giver.

4 Nu 30:2; Dt 23:21 **5** Pr 20:25; Ac 5:4 **6** 1Co 11:10 **7** Ecc 12:13 **8** Ecc 3:16; Ps 12:5; 58:11; 82:1 **13** Ecc 6:1 **15** Job 1:21; Ps 49:17; 1Ti 6:7 **16** Ecc 1:3; Pr 11:29 **17** Ps 127:2 **18** Ecc 2:24; 3:12,13; 9:7; 11:9; 1Ti 6:17; Ecc 2:10; 3:22 **19** Ecc 2:24; 3:13

The Futility of Life

6 THERE IS an evil which I have seen under the sun, and it weighs heavily on men:

2 a man to whom God has given riches and wealth and honor, so that he lacks nothing of all that he desires, yet God has not given him the power *or* capacity to enjoy them [all those things which are gifts from God], but a stranger [in whom he has no interest succeeds him and] enjoys them. This is vanity and it is a [cause of] great distress. [Luke 12:20]

3 If a man fathers a hundred *children* and lives many years, however many they may be, but his soul is not satisfied with good things and he is not respected *and* is not given a *proper* burial [he is not laid to rest in the sepulcher of his fathers], then I say, "Better the miscarriage than he, [Job 3:16]

4 for the miscarriage comes in futility (in vain) and passes into obscurity; and its name is covered in obscurity.

5 "It has not seen the sun nor had any knowledge; yet it has more rest *and* is better off than he.

6 "Even if the *other* man lives a thousand years twice over and yet has seen no good *and* experienced no enjoyment—do not both go to one place [the grave]?"

7 All the labor of man is for his mouth [for self-preservation and enjoyment], and yet the desire [of his soul] is not satisfied. [Prov 16:26]

8 For what advantage has the wise man over the fool [for being worldly-wise is not the secret to happiness]? What *advantage* has the poor man who has learned how to walk [publicly] among the living [with men's eyes on him; for being poor is not the secret to happiness either]?

9 What the eyes see [enjoying what is available] is better than [craving] what the soul desires. This too is futility and chasing after the wind.

10 Whatever exists has already been named [long ago], and it is known what [a frail being] man is; for he cannot dispute with Him who is mightier than he.

11 For there are many other words that increase futility. What then is the advantage for a man?

12 For who [limited by human wisdom] knows what is good for man during his lifetime, during the few days of his futile life? He spends them like a shadow [staying busy, but achieving nothing of lasting value]. For who can tell a man what will happen after him [to his work, his treasure, his plans] under the sun [after his life is over]?

Wisdom and Folly Contrasted

7 A GOOD name is better than
precious perfume,
And the day of one's death better
than the day of one's birth.
2 It is better to go to the house of
mourning
Than to go to the house of feasting,
For that [day of death] is the end of
every man,
And the living will take it to
heart *and* solemnly ponder its
meaning.

6:2 *God has not given him the power.* Prosperity without the divine gift of enjoyment amounts to nothing (5:19).
6:6 *do not both go to one place.* That *one place* is the grave (3:20). If a long life terminates in death with no prospect of anything else, will that life have been worthwhile? Long life without knowing God and without the power to enjoy it is indeed frustrating and useless.
6:12 *like a shadow.* This phrase is a confirmation of the meaning of the Hebrew word translated vanity. Life passes away quickly, like a vapor. ***what will happen after him.*** The implied answer is that only God knows what will happen to us after death. Rather than imply that nothing exists beyond the grave, this book teaches that each person's life will be reviewed by God after death.
7:2–4 *house of mourning.* We may learn more about the meaning of life in the *house of mourning* than in the *house of pleasure*.

CHAPTER 6 1 Ecc 5:13 2 Job 21:10; Ps 17:14; 73:7; Lk 12:20 3 2Ki 9:35; Isa 14:19,20; Jer 22:19; Job 3:16; Ps 58:8; Ecc 4:3 7 Pr 16:26 10 Job 9:32; Isa 45:9; Jer 49:19 12 Ps 102:11; 144:4; Jas 4:14; Ps 39:6; Ecc 8:7
CHAPTER 7 1 Pr 22:1

3 Sorrow is better than laughter,
For when a face is sad (deep in
thought) the heart may be
happy [because it is growing in
wisdom]. [2 Cor 7:10]
4 The heart of the wise [learns when
it] is in the house of mourning,
But the heart of fools is [senseless]
in the house of pleasure.
5 It is better to listen to the rebuke
of the wise man *and* pursue
wisdom
Than for one to listen to the song
of fools *and* pursue stupidity.
6 For like the crackling of [burning]
thorn bushes under a pot,
So is the laughter of the fool;
And this too is vanity (futility).
7 For oppression makes a wise man
foolish,
And a bribe corrupts the [good
judgment of the] heart.
8 The end of a matter is better than
its beginning;
Patience of spirit is better than
haughtiness of spirit (pride).
9 Do not be eager in your heart to be
angry,
For anger dwells in the heart of
fools. [James 1:19, 20]
10 Do not say, "Why were the old
days better than these?"
For it is not from wisdom that you
ask about this.
11 Wisdom along with an inheritance
is good
And an [excellent] advantage for
those who see the sun.
12 For wisdom is a protection *even as*
money is a protection,
But the [excellent] advantage
of knowledge is that wisdom
shields *and* preserves the lives
of its possessors.
13 Consider the work of God:
Who can make straight what He
has bent?
14 In the day of prosperity be joyful,
But in the day of adversity
consider that
God has made the one as well as
the other,
So that man will not find out
anything *that will be* after him.

15 I have seen everything during my
[fleeting] days of futility; there is a
righteous man who perishes in [spite
of] his righteousness, and there is a
wicked man who lives a long *life* in
[spite of] his wickedness.
16 Do not be excessively righteous
[like those given to self-conceit], and
do not be overly wise (pretentious)—
why should you bring yourself to ruin?
17 Do not be excessively *or* willful-
ly wicked and do not be a fool. Why
should you die before your time?
18 It is good that you take hold of one
thing (righteousness) and also not let
go of the other (wisdom); for the one
who fears *and* worships God [with
awe-filled reverence] will come forth
with both of them.
19 Wisdom strengthens the wise man
more than ten rulers who are in a city.
[Ps 127:1; 2 Tim 3:15]

7:9 *For anger dwells in the heart of fools.* Anger is a destructive flood, working all kinds of havoc in our lives. It often leads to protracted and bitter strife (Pr 30:33). It disrupts and disunites families (1Sa 20:30) and may lead to murder (Ge 4:4 – 5; 49:6).

7:13 *straight what He has bent.* The bent that needs straightening is the presence of afflictions and adversities in life. Both prosperity and adversity come from the hand of God. For prosperity give thanks, but in adversity reflect on the goodness and the comprehensiveness of the plan of God.

7:15 *there is a righteous man.* There are inequities in life that will always be a mystery (3:16 – 4:3; 8:14).

7:16 – 18 *Do not be excessively righteous.* Few verses in Ecclesiastes are more susceptible to incorrect interpretation than these. This one is not the so-called golden mean that advises: "Don't be too holy and don't be too wicked; sin to a moderate degree." The Preacher was warning instead about pseudo-religiosity and showy forms of worship as well as self-righteousness and judgmental legalism.

3 2Co 7:10 **5** Ps 141:5; Pr 15:31 **6** Ecc 2:2 **7** Ex 23:8; Dt 16:19 **8** Pr 14:29 **9** Pr 14:17; Jas 1:19 **11** Ecc 11:7 **13** Job 12:14; Ecc 1:15 **14** Dt 28:47 **15** Ecc 8:14 **16** Pr 25:16; Ro 12:3 **17** Job 15:32; Ps 55:23 **19** Pr 21:22; Ecc 9:16,18

20 Indeed, there is not a righteous
man on earth who *always* does good
and who never sins. [Is 53:6; Rom 3:23]
21 Also, do not take seriously every-
thing that is said, so that you will not
hear your servant cursing you,
22 for you also know that you too have
cursed others many times.
23 I have tested all this with wisdom.
I said, "I will be wise [independently of
God]," but true wisdom was far from me.
24 Whatever has been is far off, deep-
ly remote and exceedingly mysterious.
Who can discover it [for it is beyond
the grasp of man]? [Job 28:12–28;
1 Cor 2:9–16]
25 I turned around *and* directed my
heart to know, to investigate and to
seek [skillful and godly] wisdom and
the reason for things, and to know that
wickedness is folly and that foolish-
ness is madness [leading to stupidity
and recklessness].
26 And I discovered that [of all irratio-
nal sins none has been so destructive
in beguiling one away from God as
immoral women for] more bitter than
death is the woman whose heart is
[composed of] snares and nets, and
whose hands are chains. Whoever
pleases God will escape from her, but
the sinner will be taken captive by
her [evil].
27 "Behold, I have discovered this,"
says the Preacher, "while *adding* one
thing to another to find an explanation,
28 which I am still seeking but have
not found. I have found one man
among a thousand [who pleases God],
but I have not found [such] a woman
among all these [a thousand in my
harem]. [1 Kin 11:3]
29 "Behold, I have found only this [as
a reason]: God made man upright *and*
uncorrupted, but they [both men and
women] have sought out many devices
[for evil]."

Obey Rulers

8 WHO IS like the wise man?
And who knows the
interpretation of a matter?
A man's wisdom illumines his face,
And causes his stern face to beam.

2 I counsel you to keep the command
of the king because of the oath before
God [by which you swore loyalty to
him]. [2 Sam 21:7]
3 Do not be in a hurry to get out of his
presence. Do not join in a malevolent
matter, for the king will do whatever
he pleases.

4 For the word of a king is
authoritative *and* powerful,
And who will say to him, "What
are you doing?"
5 Whoever keeps *and* observes a
royal command will experience
neither trouble *nor* misery;
For a wise heart will know the
proper time and [appropriate]
procedure.
6 For there is a proper time and
[appropriate] procedure for
every delight,
Though mankind's misery *and*
trouble lies heavily upon him
[who rebels against the king].

7:20 Individual Sin — The depravity of man is the one Christian doctrine that is verifiable. In Romans 3:23, Paul echoes this when he says, "all have sinned and continually fall short of the glory of God." All we have to do is watch the news or pick up a paper and we are forced to deal with this reality. Each individual man, woman, and child needs the righteousness of God. Without God's righteousness no one can ever enter or stand in God's presence. We all need new life in Christ because we are all sinners.

7:24 Who can discover it. The theme of wisdom's inaccessibility also appears in Job 28. The answer to this search for wisdom is that God can find wisdom (Job 28:23 – 28).

7:29 God made man upright and uncorrupted. God created men to do right. They have preferred to search out their own path.

8:1 man's wisdom illumines his face, And causes his stern face to beam. This idiom is an image of a person who is stable. Out of the depths of experience and understanding, that person is able to enjoy life and build up others.

20 1Ki 8:46; 2Ch 6:36; Pr 20:9; 1Jn 1:8 **23** Ro 1:22 **24** Job 28:12; 1Ti 6:16; Ro 11:33 **25** Ecc 1:17 **26** Pr 5:3,4 **27** Ecc 1:1,2 **28** Job 33:23; Ps 12:1 **29** Ge 1:27; Ge 3:6,7 **CHAPTER 8** **1** Pr 4:8,9; Ac 6:15; Dt 28:50 **2** 1Ch 29:24; Eze 17:18 **3** Ecc 10:4 **4** Job 34:18 **6** Ecc 3:1

7 For no one knows what will
happen;
So who can tell him how *and* when
it will happen?
8 There is no man who has power
and authority over the wind to
restrain the wind,
Nor does he have authority over
the day of death;
There is no discharge [from
service] during time of war,
And evil will not rescue those who
[actively seek to] practice it.

9 All this I have seen while applying my mind to every deed that is done under the sun. There is a time in which one man has exercised power over others to their detriment.

10 So then, I have seen the wicked buried, those who used to go in and out of the holy place [but did not thereby escape their doom], and they are [praised in spite of their evil and] soon forgotten in the city where they did such things. This too is futility (vanity, emptiness).

11 Because the sentence against an evil act is not executed quickly, the hearts of the sons of men are fully set to do evil.

12 Though a sinner does evil a hundred *times* and his life [seemingly] is prolonged [in spite of his wickedness], still I know that it will be well with those who [reverently] fear God, who fear *and* worship Him openly [realizing His omnipresence and His power]. [Ps 37:11, 18, 19; Is 3:10, 11; Matt 25:34]

13 But it will not be well for the evil man, nor will he lengthen his days like a shadow, because he does not fear God. [Matt 25:41]

14 There is a meaningless *and* futile thing which is done on the earth: that is, there are righteous men whose gain is as though they were evil, and evil men whose gain is as though they were righteous. I say that this too is futility (meaningless, vain).

15 Then I commended pleasure *and* enjoyment, because a man [without God] has no better thing under the sun than to eat and to drink and to be merry, for this will stand by him in his toil through the days of his life which God has given him under the sun.

16 When I applied my mind to know wisdom and to see the activities [of mankind] that take place upon the earth—how some men seem to sleep neither day nor night—

17 and I saw all the work of God, I *concluded* that man cannot discover the work that is done under the sun. Even though man may labor in seeking, he will not discover; and [more than that], though a wise man thinks *and* claims he knows, he will not be able to find it out. [Deut 29:29; Rom 11:33]

Men Are in the Hand of God

9 FOR I have taken all this to heart, exploring *and* examining it all, how the righteous (those in right standing with God) and the wise and their deeds are in the hands of God. No man knows whether it will be love or hatred; anything awaits him.

2 It is the same for all. There is one fate for the righteous and for the

---

8:8 *no man who has power and authority over the wind to restrain the wind.* The word for *wind* is also translated *spirit*. In this context it could mean "life force" (3:19). God is in charge.

8:15 *no better thing under the sun than to eat and to drink and to be merry.* In contrast to the search for the meaning of all things is the contentment that a wise, loving God gives to those who will receive His gifts. Here is one of the central themes of Ecclesiastes. The Preacher marks the end of the third major section of his book with this refrain. The wicked person (the fool) decides that the best thing to do is "to eat and to drink and to be merry" with no thought given to the living God. But the righteous person (the wise) can enjoy life while thinking of God and His good gifts.

9:1 *love or hatred.* Sometimes in Hebrew two opposites together are a way of saying "everything." Love and hate are best viewed as words for God's favor and disfavor.

7 Pr 24:22; Ecc 6:12; 9:12; 10:14 **8** Ps 49:6,7 **11** Ps 10:6; 50:21; Isa 26:10 **12** Isa 65:20; Ro 2:5; Ps 37:11,18,19; Pr 1:32,33; Isa 3:10,11; Mt 25:34,41 **14** Ps 73:14; Ecc 2:14; 7:15; 9:1-3 **15** Ecc 2:24; 3:12,22; 5:18; 9:7 **17** Job 5:9; Ecc 3:11; Ro 11:33 **CHAPTER 9** **1** Ecc 8:14 **2** Job 21:7; Ps 73:3,12,13; Mal 3:15

wicked; for the good, for the clean and for the unclean; for the man who offers sacrifices and for the one who does not sacrifice. As the good man is, so is the sinner; as he who swears *an oath* is, so is he who is afraid to swear *an oath.*
[3]This evil is in all that is done under the sun, that one fate comes to all. Also, the hearts of the sons of men are full of evil, and madness is in their hearts while they live, and afterwards they go to the dead.
[4][There is no exemption,] but whoever is joined with all the living, has hope; surely a live dog is better than a dead lion.
[5]For the living know that they will die; but the dead know nothing, and they no longer have a reward [here], for the memory of them is forgotten.
[6]Indeed their love, their hatred and their zeal have already perished, and they will no longer have a share [in this age] in anything that is done under the sun.
[7]Go *your way,* eat your bread with joy and drink your wine with a cheerful heart [if you are righteous, wise, and in the hands of God]; for God has already approved *and* accepted your works.
[8]Let your clothes always be white [with purity], and do not let the oil [of gladness] be lacking on your head.
[9]Live joyfully with the wife whom you love all the days of your fleeting life which He has given you under the sun—all the days of vanity *and* futility. For this is your reward in life and in your work in which you have labored under the sun.

Whatever Your Hand Finds to Do

[10]Whatever your hand finds to do, do it with all your might; for there is no activity or planning or knowledge or wisdom in Sheol (the nether world, the place of the dead) where you are going.
[11]I again saw under the sun that the race is not to the swift and the battle is not to the strong, and neither is bread to the wise nor riches to those of intelligence *and* understanding nor favor to men of ability; but time and chance overtake them all. [Ps 33:16–19; Rom 9:16]
[12]For man also does not know his time [of death]; like fish caught in a treacherous net, and birds caught in the snare, so the sons of men are ensnared in an evil time when a dark cloud suddenly falls on them.
[13]This [illustration of] wisdom I have also seen under the sun, and great it was to me:
[14]There was a little city with few men in it and a great king came against it and besieged it and built great battlements against it.
[15]But there was found in it a poor wise man, and by his wisdom he rescued the city. Yet no man [seriously] remembered that poor man.
[16]But I say that wisdom is better than strength, though the poor man's wisdom is despised and his words are not heeded.
[17]The words of wise men heard in quietness are *better* than the shouting of one who rules among fools.
[18]Wisdom is better than weapons of war, but one sinner destroys much good.

9:5 *the dead know nothing.* This is not a flat denial of any hope beyond the grave. The point of view is limited to what can be known strictly from the human point of view, "under the sun."
9:8 *Let your clothes always be white.* It was difficult in ancient times to keep white clothing clean (see analogy in Isa 1:18). White clothing and ointments—oil—were symbols of joy and purity.
9:11 *not to the swift . . . to the strong . . . wise . . . understanding . . . men of ability.* We would like to think that the best always win, that the deserving are always rewarded. But our experience shows that these expectations are not always realized. These five assets were enjoyed by individuals. But while some planned and counted on their assets, God in the end determined their lot.
9:14–18 *There was a little city.* Here is a parable about how an unstoppable military operation against a small city was prevented by the wisdom of one poor but wise man. The conclusion is that wisdom is preferable to strength, and should be heeded.

5 Job 14:21; Isa 63:16; Job 7:8-10; Isa 26:14 **7** Ecc 8:15 **9** Ecc 2:10,24; 3:13,22; 5:18 **11** Am 2:14,15; Jer 9:23 **12** Ecc 8:7; Pr 29:6; Lk 12:20,39; 17:26; 1Th 5:3 **14** See 2Sa 20:16-22 **16** ver. 18; Pr 21:22; 24:5; Ecc 7:19; Mk 6:2 **18** ver. 16; Jos 7:1

A Little Foolishness

10 DEAD FLIES make the oil of the perfumer give off a foul odor; so a little foolishness [in one who is esteemed] outweighs wisdom and honor.
[2]A wise man's heart *turns him* toward the right [which is the way of blessing], but a fool's heart *turns him* toward the left [which is the way of condemnation]. [Matt 25:31–41]
[3]Even when a fool walks along the road, his [common] sense *and* good judgment fail him and he demonstrates to everyone that he is a fool.
[4]If the temper of the ruler rises against you, do not leave your post [showing resistance], because composure *and* calmness prevent great offenses.
[5]There is an evil I have seen under the sun, like an error which proceeds from the ruler—
[6]folly is set in many exalted places *and* in great dignity while the rich sit in humble places.
[7]I have seen slaves *riding* on horses and princes walking like slaves on the ground.
[8]He who digs a pit [for others] may fall into it, and a serpent may bite him who breaks through a [stone] wall. [Ps 57:6]
[9]He who quarries stones may be hurt with them, and he who splits logs may be endangered by them. [Prov 26:27]
[10]If the axe is dull and he does not sharpen its edge, then he must exert more strength; but wisdom [to sharpen the axe] helps him succeed [with less effort].
[11]If the serpent bites before being charmed, then there is no profit for the charmer.
[12]The words of a wise man's mouth are gracious *and* win him favor, but the lips of a fool consume him;
[13]the beginning of his talking is foolishness and the end of his talk is wicked madness.
[14]Yet the fool multiplies words, though no man knows what will happen, and who can tell him what will come after he is gone?
[15]The labor of a fool so wearies him [because he is ignorant] that he does not even know how to go to a city.
[16]Woe to you, O land, when your king is a child and when your [incompetent] officials *and* princes feast in the morning.
[17]Blessed [prosperous and admired] are you, O land, when your king is a man of noble birth, and your princes *and* officials feast at the proper time—for strength and not for drunkenness. [Is 32:8]
[18]Through laziness the rafters [of state affairs] decay *and* the roof sags, and through idleness [the roof of] the house leaks.
[19]*The officials* make a feast for enjoyment [instead of repairing what is broken], and serve wine to make life merry, and money is the answer to everything.
[20]Moreover, do not curse the king, even in your bedroom, and in your sleeping rooms do not curse the rich, for a bird of the air will carry the sound and a winged creature will make the matter known. [Ex 22:28]

10:1 ***Dead flies make the oil of the perfumer . . . foul odor.*** Just as one fly can ruin a whole batch of ointment, so an ounce of folly will spoil a pound of wisdom.
10:2 ***A wise man's heart turns him toward the right.*** In ancient thought, the right hand was the place of honor and favor, while the left hand was the reverse.
10:10 ***If the axe is dull.*** The wise person will sharpen the axe. A person of limited training will have to work harder, as though with a dull axe, than someone wiser whose tools are maintained.
10:17 ***Blessed [prosperous and admired] are you, O land.*** Useful nobility expresses itself in a sense of responsibility and deference to social order. This verse is an argument for propriety.

CHAPTER 10 **3** Pr 13:16; 18:2 **4** Ecc 8:3; 1Sa 25:24; Pr 25:15 **6** Est 3:1 **7** Pr 19:10; 30:22 **8** Ps 7:15; Pr 26:27 **11** Ps 58:4,5; Jer 8:17 **12** Pr 10:14,32 **14** Pr 15:2; Ecc 3:22; 8:7 **16** Isa 3:4,5; 5:11 **17** Pr 31:4 **19** Ps 104:15 **20** Ex 22:28; Ac 23:5

Cast Your Bread on the Waters

11 CAST YOUR bread on the surface of the waters, [be diligently active, make thoughtful decisions], for you will find it after many days.

[2]Give a portion to seven, or even [divide it] to eight, for you do not know what misfortune may occur on the earth.

[3]If the clouds are full [of rain], they empty themselves on the earth; and if a tree falls toward the south or toward the north, in the place where the tree falls, there it lies.

[4]He who watches the wind [waiting for all conditions to be perfect] will not sow [seed], and he who looks at the clouds will not reap [a harvest].

[5]Just as you do not know the way *and* path of the wind or how the bones *are formed* in the womb of a pregnant woman, even so you do not know the activity of God who makes all things.

[6]Sow your seed in the morning and do not be idle with your hands in the evening, for you do not know whether morning or evening planting will succeed, whether this or that, or whether both alike will be good.

[7]The light is sweet *and* pleasant, and it is good for the eyes to see the sun.

[8]Yes, if a man should live many years, let him rejoice in them all; yet let him remember the days of darkness, for they will be many. All that is to come will be futility.

[9]Rejoice, young man, in your childhood, and let your heart be pleasant in the days of your young manhood. And walk in the ways of your heart and in the desires of your eyes, but know that God will bring you into judgment for all these things.

[10]Therefore, remove sorrow and anger from your heart and put away pain from your body, for childhood and the prime of life are fleeting. [2 Cor 7:1; 2 Tim 2:22]

Remember God in Your Youth

12 REMEMBER [thoughtfully] also your Creator in the days of your youth [for you are not your own, but His], before the evil days come or the years draw near when you will say [of physical pleasures], "I have no enjoyment *and* delight in them"; [2 Sam 19:35]

[2]before the sun and the light, and the moon and the stars are darkened [by impaired vision], and the clouds [of depression] return after the rain [of tears];

[3]in the day when the keepers of the house (hands, arms) tremble, and the strong men (feet, knees) bow themselves, and the grinders (molar teeth) cease because they are few, and those (eyes) who look through the windows grow dim;

[4]when the doors (lips) are shut in the streets and the sound of the grinding

---

11:1 *Cast your bread on the surface of the waters.* Verses 1 – 6 emphasize the element of risk and uncertainty in commercial and agricultural enterprises. Thus if the preceding proverbs in chapter 10 deal with royalty and leaders, these in verses 1 – 6 deal with common people. Men and women must venture forth judiciously if they are ever to realize a gain, even though there is always a certain amount of risk.

11:2 *to seven, or even [divide it] to eight.* This urges us to be generous to as many as possible — and then some.

11:4 *will not sow . . . will not reap.* The person who is so cautious that he must wait for the ideal time before he makes a move is doomed to fail.

11:9 *walk in the ways of your heart.* This verse is not an invitation to live sinfully in sensual pleasure (as Nu 15:39 describes). Instead, it urges young people to enjoy themselves completely while not forgetting that God will review the quality of their life (3:17; 12:14).

12:1 – 8 *Remember [thoughtfully] also your Creator.* Most interpreters have argued that this poem is an allegory of old age.

12:2 *before the sun and the light, and the moon and the stars are darkened.* The person is losing his sight.

12:4 *sound of the grinding [of the teeth] is low.* A depiction of toothless old age when eating only soft foods makes little or no noise.

CHAPTER 11 **1** See Isa 32:20; Dt 15:10; Pr 19:17; Mt 10:42 **2** Ps 112:9; 1Ti 6:18; Mic 5:5; Eph 5:16 **5** Jn 3:8; Ps 139:14 **7** Ecc 7:11 **9** Nu 15:39; Ecc 12:14 **10** 2Co 7:1; Ps 39:5 **CHAPTER 12** **1** La 3:27; 2Sa 19:35 **4** 2Sa 19:35

[of the teeth] is low, and one rises at the
sound of a bird *and* the crowing of a
rooster, and all the daughters of music
(voice, ears) sing softly.
5 Furthermore, they are afraid of a
high place and of dangers on the road;
the almond tree (hair) blossoms [white],
and the grasshopper (a little thing) is a
burden, and the caperberry (desire, ap-
petite) fails. For man goes to his eternal
home and the mourners go about the
streets *and* market places. [Job 17:13]
6 *Earnestly remember your Creator*
before the silver cord [of life] is broken,
or the golden bowl is crushed, or the
pitcher at the fountain is shattered and
the wheel at the cistern is crushed;
7 then the dust [out of which God
made man's body] will return to the
earth as it was, and the spirit will re-
turn to God who gave it.
8 "Vanity of vanities," says the
Preacher. "All [that is done without
God's guidance] is vanity (futility)."
[Eccl 1:2; Rom 8:20]

Purpose of the Preacher

9 Furthermore, because the Preach-
er was wise, he still taught the peo-
ple knowledge; and he pondered and
searched out and arranged many
proverbs.
10 The Preacher sought to find de-
lightful words, even to write correctly
words of truth.
11 The words of the wise are like
[prodding] goads, and *these* collected
sayings are [firmly fixed in the mind]
like well-driven nails; they are given
by one Shepherd. [Ezek 37:24]
12 But beyond this my son, [about
going further than the words given by
one Shepherd], be warned: the writing
of many books is endless [so do not
believe everything you read], and ex-
cessive study *and* devotion *to books* is
wearying to the body.
13 When all has been heard, the end
of the matter is: fear God [worship Him
with awe-filled reverence, knowing
that He is almighty God] and keep
His commandments, for this applies
to every person.
14 For God will bring every act to
judgment, every hidden *and* secret
thing, whether it is good or evil.
[Matt 12:36; Acts 17:30, 31; Rom 2:16;
1 Cor 4:5]

12:6 *the wheel at the cistern is crushed.* The system of veins and arteries radiating out from the heart might have appeared to the ancients like the spokes on a wheel.

12:11 *The words of the wise are like [prodding] goads.* Just as an ox goad prods an animal in the right direction, so will the words of this book, when they are properly understood. ***well-driven nails.*** The nails or "pegs" referred to here are the same as in 2 Chronicles 3:9 and Jeremiah 10:4. These are hooks in tents where families hung the clothes and pots needed for everyday life. Here they refer to mental hooks giving stability and perspective to life.

12:13 *keep His commandments.* The commandments of the law are in view here. Jesus summed them up as to "love the Lord your God" and "your neighbor as yourself" (Mt 22:34–40). We are whole or complete only when we fear God and obey His commandments. What profit is there in living? If we follow what this book has said, we will have a relationship with God and find life in Him.

5 Job 17:13; Jer 9:17 **7** Ge 3:19; Ecc 3:21; Nu 16:22; Job 34:14; Zec 12:1 **8** Ps 62:9 **9** 1Ki 4:32 **12** Ecc 1:18 **13** Dt 10:12 **14** Mt 12:36

THE SONG OF SOLOMON

▸ **AUTHOR:** According to 1 Kings 4:32, Solomon wrote 1,005 songs, but this eulogy of love stood out among them as the "song of songs." Tradition strongly favors Solomon as the author of this book. Solomon is specifically mentioned seven times, and he is identified as the groom. There is also evidence in the book of incredible royal luxury and expensive imported goods, things that characterized Solomon's reign.

▸ **TIMES:** c. 965 BC ▸ **KEY VERSE:** SS 7:10

▸ **THEME:** Song of Solomon, or Song of Songs as it is sometimes known, is a one of kind love poem that concentrates on elements of the physical attraction between the sexes. It is possible that the Shulammite maiden was Abishag, who attended to David in his last days. Like Jesus' presence at a wedding, Song of Songs is an indication of God's blessing on the physical union of man and woman. God created us for each other, and we should delight in physical intimacy within the context of marriage that God has sanctioned for us.

The Young Shulammite Bride and Jerusalem's Daughters

1 THE SONG of Songs [the best of songs], which is Solomon's. [1 Kin 4:32]

(The Shulammite Bride)

2 "May he kiss me with the kisses of
his mouth!" [Solomon arrives,
she turns to him, saying,]
"For your love is better than wine.
3 "The aroma of your oils is fragrant
and pleasing;
Your name is perfume poured out;
Therefore the maidens love you.
4 "Draw me away with you *and* let
us run *together!*
Let the king bring me into his
chambers."

(The Chorus)

"We will rejoice and be glad in
you;
We will remember *and* extol your
love more [sweet and fragrant]
than wine.
Rightly do they love you."

(The Shulammite Bride)

5 "I am deeply tanned but lovely,
O daughters of Jerusalem,

1:1 *Song of Songs.* Like the superlative expressions "holy of holies" or "King of kings," *song of songs* means "the loveliest of songs." There are two principal speakers in this book, the woman (the Shulammite) and the man (Solomon).
1:2 *For your love is better than wine.* The Hebrew noun used here means sexual love, as it clearly does in Ezekiel 16:8. This is the Hebrew word that most approximates the Greek word *eros.* In the Song of Solomon, this plural word (a mark of intensity) speaks of divinely blessed lovemaking.
1:3 *aroma of your oils is fragrant and pleasing.* It was customary in biblical times to rub the body with fragrant oils after a bath in preparation for a festive occasion (Ru 3:3).
1:5 *I am deeply tanned but lovely.* The Shulammite compares her dark coloring acquired from long hours working in the vineyards (v. 6)

CHAPTER 1 **1** 1Ki 4:32 **2** SS 4:10 **4** Hos 11:4; Jn 6:44; 12:32; Php 3:12-14; Ps 45:14,15; Jn 14:2; Eph 2:6

[I am dark] like the tents of [the Bedouins of] Kedar,
Like the [beautiful] curtains of Solomon.
6 "Do not gaze at me because I am deeply tanned,
[I have worked in] the sun; it has left its mark on me.
My mother's sons were angry with me;
They made me keeper of the vineyards,
But my own vineyard (my complexion) I have not kept."
7 "Tell me, O you whom my soul loves,
Where do you pasture *your flock,*
Where do you make it lie down at noon?
For why should I be like one who is veiled
Beside the flocks of your companions?" [Ps 23:1, 2]

Solomon, the Lover, Speaks

(The Bridegroom)

8 "If you do not know [where your lover is],
O you fairest among women,
Run along, follow the tracks of the flock,
And pasture your young goats
By the tents of the shepherds.

9 "To me, my love, you are like
My [favorite] mare among the chariots of Pharaoh.
10 "Your cheeks are lovely with ornaments,
Your neck with strings of jewels."

(The Chorus)

11 "We will make for you chains *and* ornaments of gold,
[Studded] with beads of silver."

(The Shulammite Bride)

12 "While the king was at his table,
My perfume (Solomon) sent forth [his] fragrance [surrounding me].
13 "My beloved is to me like a pouch of myrrh
Which lies all night between my breasts.
14 "My beloved is to me a cluster of henna flowers
In the [fragrant] vineyards of Engedi."

(The Bridegroom)

15 "Behold, how beautiful you are, my darling,
Behold, how beautiful you are!
Your eyes are dove's eyes."

(The Shulammite Bride)

16 "Behold, how fair *and* handsome you are, my beloved;
And so delightful!
Our arbor is green *and* luxuriant.
17 "The beams of our houses are cedars,
Our rafters *and* panels are cypresses.

---

with the lighter complexion of the city maidens. The point here is her class and station in life. Unlike the young women of the court in Jerusalem who had been raised in comfort and conditions of ease, this woman had worked as a field hand in the sun. She knows her beauty is not diminished by her more rugged manner of living.

1:7 *O you whom my soul loves.* Here the woman mentally addresses Solomon, her husband. She pictures him as the shepherd of Israel.

1:8 *Run along, follow the tracks of the flock.* It would be better if she returned to the borders of Lebanon and the life of the farm rather than live alone and anxious in Solomon's palace. The point of this verse is that one should always count the cost of marriage to a particular person before the marriage.

1:13 *My beloved is to me like a pouch of myrrh.* This verse refers to an oriental custom for a woman to wear a small bag of myrrh, a perfumed ointment, around her neck at night. All the next day a lovely fragrance would linger about her.

1:17 *The beams of our houses are cedars.* As the Shulammite lies on their wedding bed (v. 16), she observes the marvelous cedar beams above her head. The opulence of Solomon's personal and public buildings in Jerusalem is well documented (1Ki 7:1 – 12).

8 SS 5:9 **9** SS 2:2,10,13; 4:1,7; Jn 15:14; 2Ch 1:16 **10** Eze 16:11 **15** SS 4:1; 5:12

The Bride's Admiration

2 "I AM the rose [of the plain] of
Sharon,
The lily of the valleys [that grows
in deep places]."

(The Bridegroom)

2 "Like the lily among the thorns,
So are you, my darling, among the
maidens."

(The Shulammite Bride)

3 "Like an apple tree [rare and
welcome] among the trees of
the forest,
So is my beloved among the
young men!
In his shade I took great delight
and sat down,
And his fruit was sweet *and*
delicious to my palate.
4 "He has brought me to his
banqueting place,
And his banner over me is love
[waving overhead to protect and
comfort me].
5 "Sustain me with raisin cakes,
Refresh me with apples,
Because I am sick with love.
6 "Let his left hand be under my
head
And his right hand embrace me."
[Deut 33:27; Matt 28:20]

(The Bridegroom)

7 "I command that you take an oath,
O daughters of Jerusalem,
By the gazelles or by the does of
the field [which run free],
That you do not rouse nor awaken
my love
Until she pleases."

(The Shulammite Bride)

8 "Listen! My beloved!
Behold, he comes,
Climbing on the mountains,
Leaping *and* running on the hills!
[John 10:27]
9 "My beloved is like a gazelle or a
young stag.
Behold, he is standing behind our
wall,
He is looking through the
windows,
He is gazing through the lattice.
10 "My beloved speaks and says
to me,
'Arise, my love, my fair one,
And come away.
11 'For behold, the winter is past,
The rain is over and gone.
12 'The flowers appear on the earth
once again;
The time for singing has come,
And the voice of the turtledove
is heard in our land.
13 'The fig tree has budded *and*
ripens her figs,
And the vines are in blossom
and give forth their
fragrance.
Arise, my love, my fair one,
And come away [to climb the
rocky steps of the hillside].' "

(The Bridegroom)

14 "O my dove, [here] in the clefts in
the rock,
In the sheltered *and* secret place
of the steep pathway,
Let me see your face,
Let me hear your voice;
For your voice is sweet,
And your face is lovely."

2:3 *Like an apple tree.* Raisin cakes (v. 5) and apples are symbols for sexual passion in ancient love songs.
2:4 *to his banqueting place.* The literal meaning of the phrase is "the house of wine," used because of the role that wine plays not only in feasting, but especially in weddings in biblical cultures (1:2). In the Bible, wine is a symbol of joy (Ps 104:15).
2:8 *Leaping and running on the hills.* This is the young bride's imaginative way of recalling the joy she experienced at her husband's arrival.
2:11 – 13 *the winter is past.* By this Solomon means that the time of joy has come; it is the summer of their love. Solomon may have come at a time of great beauty in the fields and forests where the young woman lived; he uses the beauty of creation to describe the ripeness of time for their love.

CHAPTER 2 **3** Rev 22:1,2 **6** SS 8:3 **7** SS 3:5; 8:4 **9** ver. 17 **10** ver. 13 **13** ver. 10 **14** SS 8:13

(The Chorus)

15 "Catch the foxes for us,
The little foxes that spoil *and* ruin the vineyards [of love],
While our vineyards are in blossom."

(The Shulammite Bride)

16 "My beloved is mine and I am his;
He pastures *his flock* among the lilies. [Matt 10:32; Acts 4:12]
17 "Until the cool of the day when the shadows flee away,
Return quickly, my beloved, and be like a gazelle
Or a young stag on the mountains of Bether [which separate us]."

The Bride's Troubled Dream

(The Shulammite Bride)

3 "ON MY bed night after night [I dreamed that] I sought the one
Whom my soul loves;
I sought him but did not find him. [Is 26:9]
2 "*I said* 'So I must arise now and go out into the city;
Into the streets and into the squares [places I do not know]
I must seek him whom my soul loves.'
I sought him but I did not find him.
3 "The watchmen who go around the city found me,
And I said, 'Have you seen him whom my soul loves?'
4 "Scarcely had I passed them
When I found him whom my soul loves.
I held on to him and would not let him go
Until I had brought him to my mother's house,
And into the chamber of her who conceived me." [Rom 8:35; 1 Pet 2:25]

(The Bridegroom)

5 "I command that you take an oath, O daughters of Jerusalem,
By the gazelles or by the does of the field,
That you do not rouse nor awaken my love
Until she pleases."

Solomon's Wedding Day

(The Shulammite Bride)

6 "What is this coming up from the wilderness
Like [stately] pillars of smoke
Perfumed with myrrh and frankincense,
With all the fragrant powders of the merchant?"

(The Chorus)

7 "Behold, it is the couch (palanquin) of Solomon;
Sixty mighty men around it,
Of the mighty men of Israel.
8 "All of them handle the sword,
All expert in war;
Each man has his sword at his thigh,
Guarding against the terrors of the night.
9 "King Solomon has made for himself a palanquin
From the [cedar] wood of Lebanon.

2:15 *Catch the foxes.* The Shulammite's brothers called on Solomon to catch them the foxes. Many times they had seen little foxes creep into the vineyards they tended and destroy the roots by gnawing on them.
3:1 *On my bed.* This is a dream that took place before they were married. The young woman was becoming concerned about what she would be getting into in the royal marriage.
3:3 *Have you seen him.* Her frantic search for her beloved is initially unsuccessful.
3:4 *whom my soul loves.* At last she finds him and in her dream takes him to her mother's house. The worry of his absence is intolerable to her; she wants him to move back with her to her familiar home and lifestyle.
3:7 *Behold, it is the couch.* This was a sedan chair with poles projecting from the front and back so that a person could be carried by several bearers (vv. 9 – 10). The Shulammite was being carried to the wedding and to her groom on Solomon's own couch.

15 Ps 80:13; Eze 13:4; Lk 13:32 **16** SS 6:3 **17** SS 4:6; ver. 9; SS 8:14 **CHAPTER 3** **1** Isa 26:9 **3** SS 5:7 **5** SS 2:7; 8:4 **6** SS 8:5

10 "He made its posts of silver,
Its back of gold,
Its seat of purple cloth,
The interior lovingly *and* intricately wrought
By the daughters of Jerusalem.
11 "Go forth, O daughters of Zion,
And gaze on King Solomon wearing the crown
With which his mother [Bathsheba] has crowned him
On the day of his wedding,
On the day of his gladness of heart."

Solomon's Love Expressed

(The Bridegroom)

4 "HOW FAIR *and* beautiful you are, my darling,
How very beautiful!
Your eyes behind your veil are like those of a dove;
Your hair is like [the shimmering black fleece of] a flock of [Arabian] goats
That have descended from Mount Gilead [beyond the Jordan].
2 "Your teeth are like a flock of *newly* shorn ewes
Which have come up from washing,
All of which bear twins,
And not one among them has lost her young.
3 "Your lips are like a ribbon of scarlet,
And your mouth is lovely.
Your temples are like a slice of the pomegranate
Behind your veil.
4 "Your neck is like the tower of David,
Built with rows of [glistening] stones,
Whereon hang a thousand shields,
All of them shields of warriors.
5 "Your two breasts are like two fawns,
Twins of a gazelle
Which feed among the lilies.
6 "Until the day breaks
And the shadows flee away,
[In my thoughts] I will go my way to the mountain of myrrh
And to the hill of frankincense.

7 "O my love, you are altogether beautiful *and* fair.
There is no flaw *nor* blemish in you! [John 14:18; Eph 5:27]
8 "*Come away* with me from Lebanon, my [promised] bride,
May you come with me from Lebanon.
Journey down from the top of Amana,
From the summit of Senir and Hermon,
From the dens of lions,
From the mountains of leopards. [2 Cor 11:2, 3]
9 "You have ravished my heart *and* given me courage, my sister, my [promised] bride;
You have ravished my heart *and* given me courage with a single *glance* of your eyes,
With one jewel of your necklace.
10 "How beautiful is your love, my sister, my [promised] bride!
How much better is your love than wine,
And the fragrance of your oils
Than all *kinds* of balsam *and* spices. [John 15:9; Rom 8:35]
11 "Your lips, my [promised] bride, drip honey [as the honeycomb];

4:1 *How fair and beautiful.* Solomon lavishly praises his bride's great beauty. He uses verbal symbols of loveliness to paint a picture of the breathtaking charm of the Shulammite. Dove's eyes are a picture of purity, innocence, and beauty. The king compared the movement of her flowing hair to the graceful movement of a flock of goats in their descent down from Mount Gilead.

4:2–5 *teeth . . . lips . . . neck . . . breasts.* The king rhapsodizes of the perfection of her physical features. Her beauty is exquisite.

4:9 *my sister, my [promised] bride.* This strange pairing of words was based on the idea that in marriage a couple became "related." The woman was dignified as a member of the king's family.

4:11 *lips . . . Honey and milk.* The sweetness of his bride's kisses are like food to him (5:1; compare 1:2).

CHAPTER 4 **1** SS 1:15; 5:12; SS 6:5 **2** SS 6:6 **3** SS 6:7 **4** SS 7:4; Neh 3:19 **5** See Pr 5:19; SS 7:3 **6** SS 2:17 **7** Eph 5:27 **8** Dt 3:9 **10** SS 1:2 **11** Pr 24:13,14; SS 5:1; Ge 27:27; Hos 14:6,7

Honey and milk are under your
tongue,
And the fragrance of your
garments is like the fragrance
of Lebanon.
12 "A garden enclosed is my sister,
my [promised] bride—
A rock garden locked, a spring
sealed up.
13 "Your shoots are an orchard of
pomegranates,
[A paradise] with precious fruits,
henna with fragrant plants,
[John 15:5; Eph 5:9]
14 Fragrant plants and saffron,
calamus and cinnamon,
With all trees of frankincense,
Myrrh and aloes, along with all
the finest spices.
15 "*You are* a fountain in a garden,
A well of fresh *and* living water,
And streams *flowing* from
Lebanon." [John 4:10; 7:37, 38]

(The Shulammite Bride)

16 "Awake, O north *wind*,
And come, south *wind* [blow softly
upon my garden];
Make my garden breathe out
fragrance, [for the one in whom
my soul delights],
Let its spices flow forth.
Let my beloved come into his
garden
And eat its choicest fruits."

The Torment of Separation

(The Bridegroom)

5 "I HAVE come into my garden,
my sister, my [promised]
bride;
I have gathered my myrrh along
with my balsam *and* spice [from
your sweet words].
I have eaten my honeycomb with
my honey;
I have drunk my wine with my
milk.
Eat, friends;
Drink and drink deeply, O lovers."
[John 16:33]

(The Shulammite Bride)

2 "I was asleep, but my heart was
awake.
A voice [in my dream]! My beloved
was knocking:
'Open to me, my sister, my darling,
My dove, my perfect one!
For my head is drenched with the
[heavy night] dew;
My hair [is covered] with the
dampness of the night.'
[Job 11:13–15]
3 "I had taken off my dress,
How can I put it on *again*?
I had washed my feet,
How could I get them dirty *again*?
[Is 32:9; Heb 3:15]
4 "My beloved extended his hand
through the opening [of the
door],
And my feelings were aroused for
him.
5 "I arose to open for my beloved;
And my hands dripped with
myrrh,
And my fingers with liquid [sweet-
scented] myrrh,
On the handles of the bolt.
6 "I opened for my beloved,
But my beloved had turned away
and was gone.

4:12 *A garden enclosed . . . a spring sealed up.* Solomon evokes thoughts of refreshment and delight. His use of the words "locked" and "sealed" indicate, in a poetic manner, his wife's virginity on their wedding night. This was the treasure she brought to him, and which she charged the other young women in the court to maintain for their wedding nights as well (2:7).
4:16 *Let my beloved come into his garden.* The bride is now ready to accept her lover for the first time to her "garden." She calls on the wind to blow through. That is, she is ready to make love to her husband for the first time.
5:1 *I have drunk my wine with my milk.* At the conclusion of their lovemaking, the groom speaks of his complete satisfaction in his beautiful bride.
5:2 – 7 *I was asleep.* These words begin a section (vv. 2 – 8) that most likely is another dream sequence (3:1 – 5). The bride dreams that her lover is coming to her, but she has already washed, removed her robe, and gotten into bed (v. 3). She finally goes to the door to let him in, but he

15 Jn 4:10; 7:38 **16** SS 5:1 **CHAPTER 5** **1** SS 4:11,16; Lk 15:7,10 **2** Rev 3:20 **6** SS 3:1

My heart went out *to him* when he
spoke.
I searched for him, but I could not
find him;
I called him, but he did not answer
me.
7 "The watchmen who make the
rounds in the city found me.
They struck me, they wounded me;
The guardsmen of the walls took
my shawl from me.
8 "I command that you take an oath,
O daughters of Jerusalem,
If you find my beloved,
As to what you tell him—
[Say that] I am sick from love
[sick from being without him]."
[Ps 63:1]

(The Chorus)

9 "What is your beloved more than
another beloved,
O most beautiful among
women?
What is your beloved more than
another beloved,
That you should so command us
to take an oath?" [John 10:26]

Admiration by the Bride

(The Shulammite Bride)

10 "My beloved is exquisitely
handsome and ruddy,
Outstanding among ten thousand.
[Ps 45:2; John 1:14]
11 "His head is *like* [precious] gold,
pure gold;
His hair is [curly] *like* clusters of
dates
And black as a raven.
12 "His eyes are like doves
Beside streams of water,
Bathed in milk
And reposed in their setting.
13 "His cheeks are like a bed of
balsam,
Banks of sweet, fragrant herbs.
His lips are lilies
Dripping *sweet-scented* myrrh.
14 "His hands are rods of gold
Set with beryl;
His abdomen is a figure of carved
ivory
Inlaid with sapphires.
15 "His legs are [strong and steady]
pillars of alabaster
Set upon pedestals of fine gold.
His appearance is like Lebanon,
Stately *and* choice as the cedars.
16 "His mouth is *full of* sweetness;
Yes, he is altogether lovely *and*
desirable.
This is my beloved and this is my
friend,
O daughters of Jerusalem."
[Ps 92:15; Col 1:15]

Mutual Delight in Each Other

(The Chorus)

6 "WHERE HAS your beloved
gone,
O most beautiful among women?
Where is your beloved hiding
himself,
That we may seek him with you?"

(The Shulammite Bride)

2 "My beloved has gone down to his
garden,
To the beds of balsam,
To feed *his flock* in the gardens
And gather lilies.
3 "I am my beloved's and my
beloved is mine,
He who feeds *his flock* among the
lilies."

---

is gone. Her sorrow at this drives her into the city to search for him.

5:8–9 *O daughters of Jerusalem.* She asks for help in her search, but the daughters question what is so special about the one for whom she seeks.

6:1 *That we may seek him with you.* The chorus members now join in the search. In the dream sequence, we suspect that the chorus is well aware of his location. It is only the bride who needs to discover his whereabouts.

6:3 *I am my beloved's and my beloved is mine.* These words are an inversion of the words of 2:16; compare also 7:10. ***He who feeds his flock among the lilies.*** With these words the bride comes to terms with the reality that, as much as she and the king are in love, he still has other responsibilities and so does she. His work as king makes him the shepherd of his people, yet his love for her does not necessarily diminish because of his devotion to his work.

7 SS 3:3 **9** SS 1:8 **12** SS 1:15; 4:1 **CHAPTER 6** **1** SS 1:8 **3** SS 2:16; 7:10

(The Bridegroom)

4 "You are as beautiful as Tirzah,
my darling,
As lovely as Jerusalem,
As majestic as an army with
banners!
5 "Turn your [flashing] eyes away
from me,
For they have confused *and*
overcome me;
Your hair is like [the shimmering
black fleece of] a flock of
[Arabian] goats
That have descended from Mount
Gilead.
6 "Your teeth are like a flock of ewes
Which have come up from their
washing,
All of which bear twins,
And not one among them has lost
her young.
7 "Your temples are like a slice of
the pomegranate
Behind your veil.
8 "There are sixty queens and
eighty concubines,
And maidens without number;
9 But my dove, my perfect one,
stands alone [above them all];
She is her mother's only *daughter;*
She is the pure *child* of the one
who bore her.
The maidens saw her and called
her blessed *and* happy,
The queens and the concubines
also, and they praised her,
saying, [Col 2:8, 9]

10 'Who is this that looks down like
the dawn,
Fair *and* beautiful as the full
moon,
Clear *and* pure as the sun,
As majestic as an army with
banners?'
11 "I went down to the orchard of nut
trees
To see the flowers of the valley,
To see whether the grapevine had
budded
And the pomegranates were in
flower.
12 "Before I was aware [of what was
happening], my desire had
brought me
Into the area of the princes of my
people [the king's retinue]."

(The Chorus)

13 "Return, return, O Shulammite;
Return, return, that we may gaze
at you."

(The Bridegroom)

"**W**hy should you gaze at the
Shulammite,
As at the dance of the two armies?

Admiration by the Bridegroom

7 "HOW BEAUTIFUL are your feet
in sandals,
O prince's daughter!
The curves of your hips are like
jewels,
The work of the hands of an artist.
2 "Your navel is a round goblet
Which never lacks mixed wine.
Your belly is like a heap of wheat
Surrounded with lilies.
3 "Your two breasts are like two
fawns,
The twins of a gazelle.
4 "Your neck is like a tower of ivory,
Your eyes the [sparkling] pools of
Heshbon
By the gate of Bath-rabbim.
Your nose is like the tower of
Lebanon
Which looks toward Damascus.
5 "Your head crowns you like Mount
Carmel,
And the flowing hair of your head
like purple threads;
I, the king, am held captive by
your tresses.

6:8 – 9 *sixty . . . eighty.* This use of numbers is a rhetorical device to emphasize that the bride alone is Solomon's love.
6:13 *Return, return, O Shulammite.* The chorus calls the bride back from her daydreams and reminds her that she is Solomon's queen.
7:1 *The curves of your hips.* The Hebrew wording suggests not only her form but also the fluid motion of her dance (6:13).

4 ver. 10 **5** SS 4:1 **6** SS 4:2 **7** SS 4:3 **10** ver. 4 **11** SS 7:12 **CHAPTER 7** **1** Ps 45:13 **3** SS 4:5 **4** SS 4:4

6 "How beautiful and how delightful
you are,
My love, with all your delights!
7 "Your stature is like that of a palm
tree
And your breasts *like its* clusters
[of dates].
8 "I said, 'I will climb the palm
tree;
I will grasp its branches.
Let your breasts be like clusters of
the grapevine,
And the fragrance of your breath
like apples,
9 'And your kisses like the best
wine!' "

(The Shulammite Bride)

"It goes *down* smoothly *and*
sweetly for my beloved,
Gliding gently over his lips while
he sleeps.

The Union of Love

10 "I am my beloved's,
And his desire is for me.
[John 10:28]
11 "Come, my beloved, let us go out
into the country,
Let us spend the night in the
villages. [Luke 14:33]
12 "Let us go out early to the
vineyards;
Let us see whether the vine has
budded
And its blossoms have opened,
And whether the pomegranates
have flowered.
There I will give you my love.
13 "The mandrakes give forth
fragrance,
And over our doors are all [kinds
of] choice *fruits,*
Both new and old,
Which I have saved up for you, my
beloved.

The Lovers Speak

8 "OH, THAT you were like a
brother to me,
Who nursed at the breasts of my
mother.
If I found you out of doors, I would
kiss you;
No one would blame me *or* despise
me, either. [Ps 143:6]
2 "I would lead you and bring you
Into the house of my mother, who
used to instruct me;
I would give you spiced wine
to drink from the juice of my
pomegranates.
3 "Let his left hand be under my head
And his right hand embrace me."
[Ex 19:4; Deut 33:27]

(The Bridegroom)

4 "I command you to take an oath,
O daughters of Jerusalem,
That you do not rouse nor awaken
my love
Until she pleases."

(The Chorus)

5 "Who is this coming up from the
wilderness
Leaning upon her beloved?"

(The Shulammite Bride)

"Under the apple tree I awakened
you [to my love];
There your mother was in labor
with you,
There she was in labor and gave
you birth.

6 "Put me like a seal on your heart,
Like a seal on your arm;

7:7 – 8 *like that of a palm tree.* This is a sexual image that has its basis in the pollination of palm trees. To fertilize a female palm tree, the gardener climbs the male tree and takes some of its flowers. Then he climbs the female tree and ties the pollen-bearing flowers among its branches.

7:13 *The mandrakes.* The yellow fruit of the mandrake was small, sweet-tasting, and fragrant. It was considered a love potion (Ge 30:16).

8:3 *left . . . right.* The repetition of 2:6 – 7 punctuates both the joy of sexual intimacy with marriage and the warnings against sexual activity before marriage.

8:6 *like a seal.* This is a symbol of possession or ownership. The Shulammite wants the king

10 SS 2:16; 6:3; Ps 45:11 **12** SS 6:11 **13** Ge 30:14; Mt 13:52 **CHAPTER 8** **2** Pr 9:2 **3** SS 2:6 **4** SS 2:7; 3:5 **5** SS 3:6 **6** Isa 49:16; Jer 22:24; Hag 2:23

For love is as strong as
death,
Jealousy is as severe *and* cruel
as Sheol (the place of the
dead).
Its flashes are flashes of fire,
[A most vehement flame] the
very flame of the LORD!
[Deut 4:24; Is 49:16;
1 Cor 10:22]
7 "Many waters cannot quench
love,
Nor can rivers drown it.
If a man would offer all the riches
of his house for love,
It would be utterly scorned *and*
despised."

(The Chorus)

8 "We have a little sister
And she has no breasts.
What shall we do for our sister
On the day when she is spoken for
[in marriage]?
9 "If she is a wall (discreet,
womanly),
We will build on her a turret
(dowry) of silver;
But if she is a door (bold,
flirtatious),
We will enclose her with planks
of cedar."

(The Shulammite Bride)

10 "I was a wall, and my breasts were
like the towers.
Then I became in the king's eyes
As one [to be respected and
allowed] to find peace.
11 "Solomon had a vineyard at Baal-
hamon;
He entrusted the vineyard to
caretakers;
Each one was to bring him a
thousand *shekels* of silver for
its fruit.
12 "My very own vineyard is at my
disposal;
The thousand [shekels of silver]
are for you, O Solomon,
And two hundred are for those
who tend the fruit."

(The Bridegroom)

13 "O you who sit in the gardens,
My companions are listening for
your voice—
Let me hear it."

(The Shulammite Bride)

14 "Hurry, my beloved *and* come
quickly,
Like a gazelle or a young stag
[taking me home]
On the mountains of spices."

---

to feel a total ownership of her in his heart. She is committed only to him; and she wants him to be completely committed to her. As long as she resides in his heart, she feels secure.

8:7 *quench ... scorned and despised.* The point of this verse is that true love cannot be destroyed or purchased.

8:10 *I was a wall ... towers.* The woman explains that she has been virtuous in youth and that she will remain faithful in her adulthood.

8:14 *mountains of spices.* That is, she wants him to return to her loving embrace (1:13).

7 Pr 6:35 **8** Eze 23:33 **11** Mt 21:33 **13** SS 2:14 **14** See Rev 22:17,20; SS 2:17

THE BOOK OF

ISAIAH

▸ **AUTHOR:** Although there is much argument regarding the unity of the work, most scholars acknowledge Isaiah as the author of this book. He was from a distinguished Jewish family and his education is evident in his impressive vocabulary and style. The New Testament writers, John, Paul, Matthew, and Luke as well as Jesus himself all quote from the Book of Isaiah and credit him with its authorship. This great poet was uncompromising, sincere, and compassionate. Isaiah maintained close contact with the royal court, but his exhortations against alliances with foreign powers were not always well received.

▸ **TIMES:** c. 740 – 680 BC ▸ **KEY VERSES:** Isa 9:6 – 7

▸ **THEME:** Because of the length of the book and Isaiah's interactions with the politics of the time, we probably get a better picture of Isaiah's ministry than we do of any of the other prophets. It also contains more of the well-known, classic prophecy texts than any other book. One commentator calls Isaiah the "Romans" of the Old Testament, as in Isaiah we get a broad perspective on how and why God is working in history. Both God's holiness and grace come clearly into perspective through a careful study of this book.

Rebellion of God's People

1 THE VISION of [the prophet] Isaiah the son of Amoz concerning [the kingdom of] Judah and [its capital] Jerusalem, which he saw [as revealed by God] during the reigns of Uzziah, Jotham, Ahaz, and Hezekiah, kings of Judah.

2 Hear, O heavens, and listen,
O earth;
For the LORD has spoken:
"I have reared and brought up
sons,
But they have rebelled against Me
and have broken away.
3 "The ox [instinctively] knows its
owner,
And the donkey its master's
feeding trough,
But Israel does not know [Me as
LORD],
My people do not understand."
4 Ah, sinful nation,
A people loaded down with
wickedness [with sin, with
injustice, with wrongdoing],
Offspring of evildoers,

1:1 ***Isaiah the son of Amoz.*** God sent His message through Isaiah to Judah, the people of the Southern Kingdom — specifically to their magistrates, priests, and prophets in Jerusalem. The nation had been divided into two parts: Judah (the Southern Kingdom) and Israel (the Northern Kingdom). While Isaiah's message was primarily for the Southern Kingdom, it was also for the Northern Kingdom. The entire nation was heading down a path of sin and idolatry that would end in destruction. Isaiah lived to see the nation of Assyria take the Northern Kingdom into captivity in 722 BC. The record of Isaiah's visions contains the revelations that God gave during the reigns of Uzziah (792 – 740 BC), Jotham (752 – 736 BC), Ahaz (736 – 720 BC), and Hezekiah (729 – 699 BC). God never changes, and this revelation is still relevant for His people today.

CHAPTER 1 **1** Nu 12:6 **2** Jer 2:12 **3** Jer 8:7; Jer 9:3,6 **4** Mt 3:7

Sons who behave corruptly!
They have abandoned (rejected) the LORD,
They have despised the Holy One of Israel [provoking Him to anger],
They have turned away from Him.

5 Why should you be stricken *and* punished again [since no change results from it]?
You [only] continue to rebel.
The whole head is sick
And the whole heart is faint *and* sick.
6 From the sole of the foot even to the head
There is nothing healthy in the nation's body,
Only bruises, welts, and raw wounds,
Not pressed out or bandaged,
Nor softened with oil [as a remedy].

7 Your land lies desolate [because of your disobedience],
Your cities are burned with fire,
Your fields—strangers are devouring them in your very presence;
It is desolate, as overthrown by strangers.
8 The Daughter of Zion (Jerusalem) is left like a [deserted] shelter in a vineyard,
Like a watchman's hut in a cucumber field, like a besieged city [isolated, surrounded by devastation].
9 If the LORD of hosts
Had not left us a few survivors,
We would be like Sodom,
We would be like Gomorrah. [Gen 19:24, 25; Rom 9:29]

God Has Had Enough

10 Hear the word of the LORD [rulers of Jerusalem],
You rulers of [another] Sodom,
Listen to the law *and* instruction of our God,
You people of [another] Gomorrah.
11 "What are your multiplied sacrifices to Me [without your repentance]?"
Says the LORD.
"I have had enough of [your] burnt offerings of rams
And the fat of well-fed cattle [without your obedience];
And I take no pleasure in the blood of bulls or lambs or goats [offered without repentance].
12 "When you come to appear before Me,
Who requires this of you, this trampling of My [temple] courts [by your sinful feet]?
13 "Do not bring worthless offerings again,
[Your] incense is repulsive to Me;
[Your] New Moon and Sabbath [observances], the calling of assemblies—
I cannot endure wickedness [your sin, your injustice, your wrongdoing] and [the squalor of] the festive assembly.
14 "I hate [the hypocrisy of] your New Moon festivals and your appointed feasts.
They have become a burden to Me;
I am weary of bearing them.
15 "So when you spread out your hands [in prayer, pleading for My help],
I will hide My eyes from you;
Yes, even though you offer many prayers,
I will not be listening.
Your hands are full of blood!
16 "Wash yourselves, make yourselves clean;
Get your evil deeds out of My sight.
Stop doing evil,

1:9 *LORD of hosts.* Isaiah describes God as ruler over all powers in heaven and earth through His command of His angelic armies. ***a few survivors.*** Though God punished His sinful people, he always preserved a remnant, or survivor (Ge 22:16–17; Ex 34:6–7; Mic 7:19–20; Ro 9:29; 11:15). ***Sodom ... Gomorrah.*** These two cities were regarded as the epitome of sinfulness. It was a scathing condemnation to say that Jerusalem had become like those cities.

5 Isa 9:13 **7** Dt 28:51 **8** Job 27:18; Jer 4:17 **9** La 3:22; Ge 19:24 **10** Dt 32:32 **11** 1Sa 15:22 **12** Ex 23:17 **13** Mt 15:9; Joel 1:14 **14** Nu 28:11; La 2:6; Isa 43:24 **15** Pr 1:28; Mic 3:4; Ps 66:18 **16** Jer 4:14; Ro 12:9

17 Learn to do good.
Seek justice,
Rebuke the ruthless,
Defend the fatherless,
Plead for the [rights of the] widow
[in court].

"Let Us Reason"

18 "Come now, and let us reason
together,"
Says the LORD.
"Though your sins are like scarlet,
They shall be as white as snow;
Though they are red like crimson,
They shall be like wool.
19 "If you are willing and obedient,
You shall eat the best of the land;
20 But if you refuse and rebel,
You shall be devoured by the
sword."
For the mouth of the LORD has
spoken.

Zion Corrupted, to Be Redeemed

21 How the faithful city has become
a prostitute [idolatrous,
despicable],
She who was full of justice!
Right standing with God once
lodged in her,
But now murderers.
22 Your silver has turned to lead,
Your wine is diluted with water.
23 Your rulers are rebels
And companions of thieves;
Everyone loves bribes
And chases after gifts.
They do not defend the fatherless,
Nor does the widow's cause come
before them [instead they delay
or turn a deaf ear].

24 Therefore the Lord GOD of hosts,
The Mighty One of Israel, declares:
"Ah, I will be freed of My
adversaries
And avenge Myself on My enemies.
25 "And I will turn My hand against
you,
And will [thoroughly] purge away
your dross as with lye
And remove all your tin (impurity).
26 "Then I will restore your judges as
at the first,
And your counselors as at the
beginning;
Afterward you will be called the
city of righteousness,
The faithful city."

27 Zion will be redeemed with justice
And her repentant ones with
righteousness.
28 But rebels and sinners will be
crushed *and* destroyed together,

1:18–20 The Message of the Prophets—These verses contain the essence of the prophet's message to Israel, which is also meant for us today. We need to recognize the reality of our condition. We are a stiffnecked and rebellious people, who would rather do what we want, when we want. Even today, we want the benefits of God's grace without accepting any accountability to God.

Just as in the days of Isaiah, God's people attempt to replace obedience with ceremony. We ignore God's commands to care for the destitute, and we lose sight of God's requirements for justice and righteousness. Each of us stands before God dirty and bloody, saying we are still His people, when we are clearly not ready to fellowship with a holy God. We need to be cleaned up first.

Our God is a redeeming God who knows how to deal with sin. Although there is no rebellion that goes beyond His reach, the remedy has to be His. The first step in obedience is repentance—turning away from the direction we are going in order to see God.

1:18 *reason together.* This term means "to come to a legal decision." It is not an invitation to negotiate or compromise. The people were to come to an agreement with God concerning the enormous gravity of their sin. God was not declaring His people innocent of wickedness, but He was prepared to pardon their sins if they would repent and turn to Him.

1:20 *has spoken.* The verb "has spoken" indicates finality (contrast the verb "says" in v. 18). God had graciously extended His offer of mercy over a significant period of time, but this was the only offer that He made. They could not "cut another deal" with Him (40:5; 55:11).

1:27 *redeemed.* The Hebrew word for "redeemed" means "ransomed" or "freed" from

---

18 Isa 43:26; Ps 51:7; Rev 7:14 **20** Titus 1:2 **21** Jer 2:20 **22** Jer 6:28 **23** Hos 9:15; Pr 29:24; Jer 22:17; Eze 22:12; Jer 5:28; Zec 7:10 **24** Dt 28:63 **25** Mal 3:3 **26** Jer 33:7; Zec 8:3 **28** Job 31:3

And those who abandon (turn away from) the LORD will be consumed (perish).
29 For you will be ashamed [of the degradation] of the oaks in which you took [idolatrous] pleasure,
And you will be ashamed of the gardens [of passion] which you have chosen [for pagan worship].
30 For you will be like an oak whose leaf withers *and* dies
And like a garden that has no water.
31 The strong man will become tinder,
And his work a spark.
So both will burn together
And there will be none to quench them.

God's Universal Reign

2 THE WORD [from God] which Isaiah son of Amoz saw [in a vision] concerning [the nation of] Judah and [its capital city] Jerusalem.

2 Now it will come to pass that
In the last days
The mountain of the house of the LORD
Will be [firmly] established as the highest of the mountains,
And will be exalted above the hills;
And all the nations will stream to it.
3 And many peoples shall come and say,
"Come, let us go up to the mountain of the LORD,
To the house (temple) of the God of Jacob;
That He may teach us His ways
And that we may walk in His paths."
For the law will go out from Zion
And the word of the LORD from Jerusalem.
4 And He will judge between the nations,
And will mediate [disputes] for many peoples;
And they will beat their swords into plowshares and their spears into pruning hooks.
Nation will not lift up the sword against nation,
And never again will they learn war. [Mic 4:1–3]

5 O house of Jacob, come, let us walk in the light of the LORD.
6 Most certainly [LORD] You have abandoned your people, the house of Jacob,
Because they are filled *with influences* from the east,

---

another's ownership through the payment of a price. ***repentant ones.*** Zion's penitents, those who turned their backs on idolatry and injustice, found freedom from sin and judgment.

1:29 *oaks . . . gardens.* The oak, or terebinth, was a sacred tree, and the gardens with sacred groves for fertility rites were part of idol worship, which the people had chosen instead of worshiping only the Living God.

2:2 *In the last days.* The last days refer to the conditions in Christ's (the Messiah's) future kingdom. At the time of the writing of the Book of Isaiah, no one had a clear idea of what the coming of the Messiah would mean. They believed that, under His rule, earthly kingdoms and authorities would vanish, and everything would at last be the way God originally planned before the fall (Ge 3:1 – 22). But they did not yet have an understanding of Christ dying on the cross for the sins of the whole world, or of the church age. Isaiah was looking forward to what Christians are still looking forward to — what we call the second coming, or return of Christ (Ac 1:11; Rev 21 – 22).

2:4 *never again will they learn war.* The Old Testament term for "peace" meant soundness or completeness. Just as man can never be truly at peace apart from his Creator, so a nation of sinful humanity cannot truly achieve peace apart from God. Men or nations will be rebellious, self-centered, and at odds with each other unless their harmony with God is restored. This can only happen when, person by person, peace is provided by the Prince of Peace, Jesus Christ. To look forward to the day when there will be this peace for the whole world is to understand the magnitude of God's promise in this passage.

2:6 *You have abandoned.* This was a present condition — but not a permanent

---

29 Isa 57:5; Isa 65:3 **31** Eze 32:21; Isa 43:17 **CHAPTER 2** **2** Mic 4:1; Ge 49:1; Jer 23:20; Ps 68:15; Ps 72:8
3 Jer 50:5; Zec 8:21; Lk 24:47 **4** Ps 46:9; Ps 72:3,7 **5** Eph 5:8 **6** Nu 23:7; Dt 18:14; Ps 106:35; Jer 10:2

And they are soothsayers [who
foretell] like the Philistines;
Also they strike *bargains* with the
children of foreigners (pagans).
[Deut 18:9–12]
7 Their land has also been filled
with silver and gold
And there is no end to their
treasures;
Their land has also been filled
with horses
And there is no end to their
chariots. [Deut 17:14–17]
8 Their land has also been filled
with idols;
They worship the work of their
hands,
That which their own fingers have
made.
9 So the *common* man has been
humbled [before idols]
And the man *of importance* has
been degraded,
Therefore do not forgive them
[O LORD].
10 Go among the rocks and hide in
the dust
From the terror of the LORD and
from the splendor of His majesty.
11 The proud look of man will be
degraded
And the arrogance of men will be
humbled,
And the LORD alone will be exalted
in that day.

A Day of Reckoning Coming

12 For the LORD of hosts will have a
day *of reckoning*
Against all who are proud and
arrogant
And against all who are lifted up,
That they may be degraded.
[Zeph 2:3; Mal 4:1]
13 And the wrath of God will
be against all the cedars of
Lebanon [west of the Jordan]
that are high and lifted up,
Against all the oaks of Bashan
[east of the Jordan],
14 Against all the high mountains,
Against all the hills that are lifted
up,
15 Against every high tower,
Against every fortified wall,
16 Against all the ships of Tarshish
And against all the beautiful craft.
17 Then the pride of man will be
humbled
And the arrogance of men will be
degraded;
The LORD alone shall be exalted in
that day,
18 And the idols will completely
vanish (be abolished).
19 They [the stricken, deprived of all
in which they had trusted] will
go into the caves of the rocks
And into the holes of the ground
[fleeing]
From the terror *and* dread of the
LORD
And from the splendor of His
majesty,
When He arises to terrify the
earth. [Luke 23:30]
20 In that day men will throw away to
the moles and to the bats
Their idols of silver and their idols
of gold,
Which they made for themselves
[as objects] to worship,

condition — for the Israelites. God's covenant with Israel had always been based on their obedience, and the Israelites (or house of Jacob) were finally going to experience the results of their disobedience (Dt 27 – 30). ***filled with influences from the east . . . soothsayers.*** Copying other religions and participating in the occult practices of peoples of Canaan were strictly forbidden (Dt 18:9 – 14). Whoever did these things was detestable to the Lord.

2:7 ***filled with silver and gold . . . filled with horses.*** The king was not to multiply horses, wives, or gold and silver for himself, for this would cause his heart to turn away from the Lord (Dt 17:14 – 17).

2:8 ***filled with idols.*** Idolatry was forbidden in the Ten Commandments (Ex 20:4; Dt 13), and it was a flagrant rebellion against the Lord who had rescued them from the land of Egypt and redeemed them from slavery. It was a seduction to unfaithfulness and was to be punished with death.

2:19 ***the caves of the rocks . . . From the terror and dread of the LORD.*** Men will want to

7 Dt 17:16 **8** Jer 2:28 **10** Rev 6:15 **11** Isa 5:15; Hos 2:16; Zec 9:16 **13** Isa 14:8; Eze 31:3; Zec 11:1 **14** Isa 30:25 **16** 1Ki 10:22 **17** ver. 11; ver. 11 **19** Hos 10:8; Rev 9:6; 2Th 1:9; Hag 2:6,21

21 To go into the caverns of the
rocks and into the clefts of the
[ragged] cliffs [as they flee]
From the terror *and* dread of the
LORD and the splendor of His
majesty,
When He arises to terrify the
earth.
22 Stop regarding man, whose breath
[of life] is in his nostrils [for so
little time];
For why should he be esteemed?

God Will Remove the Leaders

3 LISTEN CAREFULLY, the Lord
GOD of hosts is removing from
Jerusalem and from Judah
Both supply and support, the
whole supply of bread
And the whole supply of water;
2 The brave man and the warrior
[He is also removing],
The judge and the prophet,
The diviner and the elder,
3 The captain of fifty and the man
of honor,
The counselor and the expert
artisan,
And the skillful enchanter.
4 And I will make *mere* boys their
princes,
And capricious (impulsive,
unpredictable) children will rule
over them.
5 And the people will be oppressed,
Each one by another, and each one
by his neighbor;
The boy will be arrogant *and*
insolent toward the elder
And the vulgar (common) toward
the honorable [person of rank].
6 When a man takes hold of his
brother in the house of his
father, *saying,*
"You have a robe, you shall be our
judge *and* ruler,
And this pile of ruins will be under
your control,"
7 He will protest on that day, saying,
"I will not be a governor;
For in my house there is neither
bread nor clothing;
You should not make me a judge
and ruler of the people."
8 For Jerusalem has stumbled and
Judah has fallen,
Because their words and their
actions are against the LORD,
To rebel against His glorious
presence *and* defiantly provoke
Him.
9 Their partiality testifies against
them,
They display their sin like Sodom;
They do not even hide it.
Woe (judgment is coming) to them!
For they have brought evil on
themselves [as a reward].
10 Say to the righteous that *it will go*
well with them,
For they will eat the fruit of their
[righteous] actions.
11 Woe (judgment is coming) to the
wicked! *It shall go* badly *with
him,*
For what his hand has done shall
be done to him.
12 O My people! Children are their
oppressors,
And women rule over them.
O My people! Your leaders lead
you astray

---

hide from the Lord whom they have not been willing to obey (Rev 6:15 – 17).

3:4 *boys . . . children.* The rulers would be incompetent and inexperienced.

3:8 *against the LORD.* Prior to entering Canaan, Moses had the blessings and the curses of the law of God recited to the people, warning of the serious consequences of unbelief. Unfaithfulness would result in captivity, worldwide dispersion, and aimless wandering among the Gentile nations (Dt 28). Joshua gave the same warning after bringing them into the land (Jos 24). Both warnings went unheeded. From a historical perspective, it is easy to be appalled at the people's heedlessness. They ignored specific and direct commands, apparently knowing well that they were courting disaster. But, if we as believers examine ourselves carefully, we might be appalled at our own unfaithfulness in certain areas. God's directives are always there for a reason, and unfaithfulness, even in little things, causes a rift in our relationship with God.

21 ver. 19; ver. 10,19 **22** Ps 146:3; Job 27:3 **CHAPTER 3** **1** Jer 37:21; Lev 26:26 **2** 2Ki 24:14 **4** Ecc 10:16 **8** Mic 3:12 **9** Ge 13:13 **10** Ecc 8:12; Ps 128:2 **11** Ps 11:6 **12** ver. 4; Isa 9:16

And confuse (destroy, swallow up)
the direction of your paths.

God Will Judge

13 The LORD rises to contend,
And stands to judge the people.
14 The LORD enters into judgment
with the elders of His people and
their princes,
"For it is you who have devoured
the vineyard [with your
oppression, you have robbed the
people and ruined the country];
The plunder of the poor is in your
houses.
15 "What do you mean by crushing
My people
And grinding the face of the
poor?"
Declares the Lord GOD of hosts.

Judah's Women Denounced

16 Moreover, the LORD said, "Because
the daughters of Zion are proud
And walk with outstretched
necks and seductive (flirtatious,
alluring) eyes,
And trip along with mincing steps
and an affected gait
And walk with jingling anklets on
their feet,
17 Therefore the Lord will afflict
the crown of the head of the
daughters of Zion with scabs
[making them bald],
And the LORD will expose their
foreheads (send them into
captivity)."

18 In that day the Lord will take away
the beauty of their anklets, [braided]
caps, crescent [head] ornaments,
19 dangling earrings, bracelets, and
the hanging veils *and* scarves,
20 head wraps (turbans), [short, jin-
gling] ankle chains, sashes, perfume
boxes, amulets (charms),
21 signet [finger] rings, nose rings,
22 festival robes, outer tunics, shawls,
handbags,
23 hand mirrors, [fine linen] under-
garments, headbands, and veils [cov-
ering the entire body].

24 Now it will come to pass that
instead of the sweet fragrance of
spices there will be [the stench
of] rottenness;
Instead of a belt, a rope;
Instead of well-set hair, baldness;
Instead of fine clothes, a robe of
sackcloth;
And branding [of captives by
the scorching heat] instead of
beauty.
25 Your men will fall by the sword
And your mighty men in battle.
26 And Jerusalem's gates will lament
(cry out in grief) and mourn [as
those who wail for the dead];
And she, being ruined *and*
desolate, will sit upon the
ground.

A Remnant Prepared

4 AND IN that day seven women will
take hold of one man, saying, "We
will eat our own food and wear [and
provide] our own clothes; only let us
be called by your name; take away our
shame [of being unmarried]."
2 In that day the Branch of the LORD
will be splendid and glorious, and the
fruit of the land will be excellent and
lovely to those of Israel who have sur-
vived. [Jer 23:5; 33:15; Zech 3:8; 6:12]
3 It will come to pass that he who is
left in Zion and remains in Jerusalem

3:16 *daughters of Zion.* The plural "daughters" suggests the women of the city as well as a personification of Jerusalem. The list of finery (vv. 18 – 23), whether applied figuratively to the city of Jerusalem or to specific women, indicated a preoccupation with frivolity and wealth.
4:1 *take away our shame.* It was considered a sign of inadequacy to have no children.

4:2 *In that day.* Isaiah is speaking of the future revelation of the glory of the Lord on earth (2:2 – 4). ***the Branch of the LORD.*** Jesus Christ is the fruitful Branch (Jer 23:5; Zec 3:8). The reign of Jesus, the King of Creation, will be marked by plenty. The earth will be released from its curse, producing all that God intended it to produce in the beginning.

13 Mic 6:2 **14** Mt 21:33 **15** Mic 3:2,3 **17** Dt 28:27; Jer 13:22 **18** Jdg 8:21 **24** Isa 22:12 **26** Jer 14:2; La 2:10
CHAPTER 4 **1** Isa 2:11,17; 2Th 3:12; Lk 1:25 **2** Jer 23:5 **3** Isa 60:21; Php 4:3

will be called holy (set apart for God)—everyone who is recorded for [eternal] life in Jerusalem. [Joel 3:17; Phil 4:3]

4 When the Lord has washed away the [moral] filth of the daughters of Zion and has cleansed the bloodstains of Jerusalem from her midst, by the spirit of judgment and by the spirit of burning,

5 then the LORD will create over the entire site of Mount Zion and over her assemblies, a cloud by day, smoke, and the brightness of a flaming fire by night; for over all the glory *and* brilliance will be a canopy [a defense, a covering of His divine love and protection].

6 And there will be a pavilion for shade from the heat by day, and a refuge and a shelter from the storm and the rain.

Parable of the Vineyard

5 NOW LET me sing for my greatly
Beloved [LORD]
A song of my Beloved about His
vineyard (His chosen people).
My greatly Beloved had a
vineyard on a very fertile slope
(the promised land, Canaan).
[Song 6:3; Matt 21:33–40]
2 He dug it all around and cleared
away its stones,
And planted it with the choicest
vine (the people of Judah).
And He built a tower in the center
of it;
And also hewed out a wine vat in it.
Then He expected it to produce
[the choicest] grapes,
But it produced *only* worthless
ones.
3 "And now, *says the* LORD,
O inhabitants of Jerusalem and
men of Judah,
Judge between Me and My
vineyard (My people).
4 "What more could have been done
for My vineyard that I have not
done in it?
When I expected it to produce
good grapes, why did it yield
worthless ones?
5 "So now let me tell you what I am
going to do to My vineyard:
I will take away its thorn-hedge,
and it will be burned up;
I will break down its stone wall
and it will be trampled down [by
enemies].
6 "I will turn it into a wasteland;
It will not be pruned or cultivated,
But briars and thorns will come up.
I will also command the clouds not
to rain on it."
7 For the vineyard of the LORD of
hosts is the house (nation) of
Israel
And the men of Judah are His
delightful planting [which He
loves].
So He looked for justice, but in
fact, [He saw] bloodshed *and*
lawlessness;
[He looked] for righteousness,
but in fact, [He heard] a cry of
distress *and* oppression.

Woes for the Wicked

8 Woe (judgment is coming) to those
who join house to house and join
field to field [to increase their
holdings by depriving others],
Until there is no more room [for
others],
So that you have to live alone in
the midst of the land!
9 In my ears the LORD of hosts *said*,
"Be assured that many houses
will become desolate,

5:4 *What more could have been done for My vineyard.* This is a rhetorical question. There was nothing more that God could or should have done to bring forth good fruit from His vineyard. The failure was on the part of the people, not God (Jn 15:1).
5:6 *briars and thorns.* Briars and thorns symbolize the anarchy that will take over the land after the exile (3:4 – 5). ***not to rain.*** As God promised in His covenant on Mount Sinai, sufficient rainfall would come to the people who were faithful to His commands, but the rain would be withheld if the people were rebellious (Dt 28:12,23 – 24).

4 Mal 3:2,3 **5** Ex 13:21; Zec 2:5 **6** Isa 25:4 **CHAPTER 5** **1** Ps 80:8; Jer 2:21; Mt 21:33; Mk 12:1 **2** Dt 32:6 **3** Ro 3:4 **5** Ps 80:12 **8** Mic 2:2 **9** Isa 22:14

Even great and beautiful ones will
be unoccupied.
10 "For ten acres of vineyard will
yield [only] one bath *of wine*,
And a homer (six bushels) of seed
will produce [only] one ephah of
grain."
11 Woe (judgment is coming) to those
who rise early in the morning to
pursue intoxicating drink,
Who stay up late in the night till
wine inflames them!
12 They have lyre and harp,
tambourine and flute, and wine
at their feasts;
But they do not regard *nor* even
pay attention to the deeds of the
LORD,
Nor do they consider the work of
His hands.
13 Therefore My people go into exile
because they lack knowledge
[of God];
And their honorable men are
famished,
And their common people are
parched with thirst.
14 Therefore Sheol (the realm of the
dead) has increased its appetite
and opened its mouth beyond
measure;
And Jerusalem's splendor, her
multitude, her [boisterous]
uproar and her [drunken]
revelers descend *into it*.
15 So the *common* man will be
bowed down and the man of
importance degraded,
And the eyes of the proud
(arrogant) will be degraded.
16 But the LORD of hosts will be
exalted in justice,
And God, the Holy One, will show
Himself holy in righteousness
[through His righteous
judgments].
17 Then the lambs will graze [among
the ruins] as in their own
pasture,
And strangers will eat in the
desolate places of the [exiled]
wealthy.
18 Woe (judgment is coming) to those
who drag along wickedness
with cords of falsehood,
And sin as if with cart ropes
[towing their own punishment];
19 Who say, "Let Him move speedily,
let Him expedite His work [His
promised vengeance], so that we
may see it;
And let the purpose of the Holy
One of Israel approach
And come to pass, so that we may
know it!"
20 Woe (judgment is coming) to those
who call evil good, and good
evil;
Who substitute darkness for light
and light for darkness;
Who substitute bitter for sweet
and sweet for bitter!
21 Woe (judgment is coming) to those
who are wise in their own eyes
And clever *and* shrewd in their
own sight!
22 Woe (judgment is coming) to those
who are heroes at drinking wine
And men of strength in mixing
intoxicating drinks,
23 Who justify the wicked *and* acquit
the guilty for a bribe,
And take away the rights of those
who are in the right!

5:14 *Sheol.* This word is used for the grave or the place where the body goes after death. Its meaning is not precise, but this word is sometimes translated "hell" where the context considers the "grave" in a negative sense.

5:18 *falsehood.* A falsehood is a lie. Those who "drag along wickedness with cords of falsehood" are those who are dragging sin behind them with ropes of lies. Essentially, these lies are the various ways people have of justifying sin. They are not ashamed of their sin, but are quite openly attached to it, carrying it wherever they go. Of course, the big lie is the lie that sin does not matter, that judgment will not come. The truth is that the fruits of sin always catch up with us, and, unless we make peace with God through Christ, the judgment for sin will follow.

10 Eze 45:11 **11** Pr 23:29 **12** Am 6:5; Job 34:27; Ps 28:5 **13** Hos 4:6 **15** Isa 2:9,11 **17** Isa 10:16 **19** Jer 17:15; Am 5:18 **21** Ro 1:22 **23** Pr 17:15

24 Therefore, as the tongue of fire
consumes the stubble [from
straw]
And the dry grass collapses into
the flame,
So their root will become like rot
and their blossom blow away
like fine dust;
Because they have rejected the law
of the LORD of hosts
And despised *and* discarded the
word of the Holy One of Israel.
25 Therefore the anger of the LORD
has burned against His people,
And He has stretched out His hand
against them and has struck
them down.
And the mountains trembled, and
their dead bodies lay like rubbish
in the middle of the streets.
In *spite* of all this God's anger is
not turned away,
But His hand is still stretched out
[in judgment].
26 He will lift up a flag to [call] the
distant nations [to bring His
judgment on Judah],
And will whistle for them from the
ends of the earth;
And indeed, they will come with
great speed swiftly.
27 No one among them is weary or
stumbles,
No one slumbers or sleeps;
Nor is the belt at their waist
undone [as if unprepared for
action],
Nor is the strap of their sandal
broken.
28 Their arrows are sharp and all
their bows are strung *and* bent;
Their horses' hoofs seem like flint
and their *chariot* wheels like a
whirlwind.
29 Their roaring is like a lioness, they
roar like young lions;
They growl and seize their prey
And carry it off and there is no
one to save it.
30 And in that day they will roar
against them (Judah) like the
roaring of the sea.
And if one looks to the land, in
fact, there is darkness and
distress;
Even the light will be darkened by
its clouds.

Isaiah's Vision

6 IN THE year that King Uzziah died,
I saw [in a vision] the Lord sitting
on a throne, high and exalted, with the
train of His royal robe filling the [most
holy part of the] temple. [John 12:41]
2 Above Him seraphim (heavenly be-
ings) stood; each one had six wings:
with two *wings* he covered his face,
with two *wings* he covered his feet,
and with two *wings* he flew.
3 And one called out to another, saying,

"Holy, Holy, Holy is the LORD of
hosts;
The whole earth is filled with His
glory."

6:1 *King Uzziah died.* King Uzziah died in 740 BC, signaling the end of an age. He is described as a good king (2Ch 26:1–15), but in his pride he was unfaithful to God (2Ch 26:16–23), and he died a leper. He was succeeded by his son Jotham, who did right, and then by wicked Ahaz (7:1). The relative prosperity of the first half of the eighth century was replaced by the Syro-Ephraimite wars and the Assyrian campaigns into Israel.
6:3 *Holy, Holy, Holy.* To say the word "holy" twice in Hebrew is to describe someone as "most holy." To say the word three times intensifies the idea to the highest level. ***The whole earth is filled with His glory.*** We know that the glory of God transcends the universe, yet this phrase emphasizes God's closeness to His creation — His involvement with the earth and its people.

We know that our greatest failing is not only realizing who God is but what His character is like. This is particularly true in the case of God's holiness. To be holy means "to be set apart." God is set apart from the power, practice, and presence of sin, and is set apart to absolute righteousness and goodness. There is no sin in God and God can have nothing to do with sin. If we are to approach God, we must do so on God's terms. We must be made holy by God's action in Christ.

Most of our lives are so caught up in the mundane that we don't understand and experience God's holiness as we should. There is little

24 Ex 15:7; Job 18:16 **25** 2Ki 22:13; Jer 4:24; Isa 9:12,17 **26** Isa 11:12; Isa 7:18; Mal 1:11; Joel 2:7 **27** Da 5:6 **28** Jer 5:16 **30** Isa 8:22 **CHAPTER 6** **1** Jn 12:41 **2** Eze 1:11 **3** Rev 4:8; Ps 72:19

[4]And the foundations of the thresholds trembled at the voice of him who called out, and the temple was filling with smoke.

[5]Then I said,

"Woe is me! For I am ruined,
Because I am a man of
[ceremonially] unclean lips,
And I live among a people of
unclean lips;
For my eyes have seen the King,
the LORD of hosts."

[6]Then one of the seraphim flew to me with a burning coal in his hand, which he had taken from the altar with tongs.

[7]He touched my mouth *with it* and said, "Listen carefully, this has touched your lips; your wickedness [your sin, your injustice, your wrongdoing] is taken away and your sin atoned for *and* forgiven."

Isaiah's Commission

[8]Then I heard the voice of the Lord, saying, "Whom shall I send, and who will go for Us?" Then I said, "Here am I. Send me!"

[9]And He said, "Go, and tell this people:

'Keep on listening, but do not
understand;
Keep on looking, but do not
comprehend.'
10 "Make the heart of this people
insensitive,
Their ears dull,
And their eyes dim,
Otherwise they might see with
their eyes,
Hear with their ears,
Understand with their hearts,
And return and be healed."

[11]Then I said, "Lord, how long?" And He answered,

"Until cities are devastated and
without inhabitant,
And houses are without people
And the land is utterly desolate,
12 The LORD has removed [His]
people far away,
And there are many deserted
places in the midst of the
land.
13 "And though a tenth [of the
people] remain in the land,
It will again be *subject* to
destruction [consumed and
burned],
Like a massive terebinth tree or
like an oak
Whose stump remains when it is
chopped down.
The holy seed [the elect remnant]
is its stump [the substance of
Israel]."

War against Jerusalem

7 NOW IT came to pass in the days of Ahaz the son of Jotham, the son of Uzziah, king of Judah, that Rezin king

---

appreciation or understanding of the sacred "otherness" of God. We have too often reduced Him to only friend and advisor. We do so at our own peril; for it is that sacred "otherness" that brings us to our knees. That is where the relationship needs to begin. Isaiah received God's call in that position. He recognized God's holiness and his own uncleanness and the need for God to purify him before he would be fit to serve as a prophet.

The experience of coming to understand God's holiness is simultaneously humbling, challenging, and exhilarating. We touch the fullness of our potential as we are touched and purified by God in Christ's sacrifice for us.

6:6 *burning coal . . . from the altar.* Brought face to face with the holiness of the Lord, Isaiah was stunned by his own uncleanness. Without taking any action on his own, Isaiah was offered forgiveness and cleansing. This was a unique event, especially for Isaiah, but not the last time that the Lord reached out to man to offer forgiveness and cleansing. Salvation through Christ is a gift, not received through works (Eph 2:8 – 9).

6:10 *heart . . . insensitive.* Isaiah's call was to a very discouraging ministry. They were "padded" with self-satisfaction so they could not feel the prick of the Lord's words. The more Isaiah proclaimed the Word of God, the less response he received from the people. In truth, the call of God was for faithfulness to God, to His word, and to the call itself.

6:13 *tenth.* A "tenth" is one of Isaiah's expressions for the "remnant."

7:1 *it came to pass.* The next five chapters contain a series of prophecies related specifically to

6 Rev 8:3 **7** Jer 1:9 **8** Ge 1:26 **10** Ps 119:70; Jer 5:21 **11** Mic 3:12 **12** 2Ki 25:21 **13** Ezr 9:2

of Aram (Syria) and Pekah the son of Remaliah, king of Israel, went up to Jerusalem to wage war against it, but they could not conquer it.
2When the house of David (Judah) was told, "Aram is allied with Ephraim (Israel)," the hearts of Ahaz and his people trembled as the trees of the forest tremble in the wind.
3Then the LORD said to Isaiah, "Go out to meet Ahaz [king of Judah], you and your son Shear-jashub, at the end of the aqueduct of the Upper Pool, on the highway to the Fuller's Field;
4and say to him, 'Take care and be calm, do not fear and be weak-hearted because of these two stumps of smoldering logs, on account of the fierce anger of [King] Rezin and Aram and of the son of Remaliah (Pekah, usurper of the throne of Israel).
5'Because Aram, *along with* Ephraim (Israel) and the son of Remaliah, have planned evil against you (Judah), saying,
6"Let us go up against Judah and terrorize it; and let us breach its wall *and* tear it apart [each of us taking a portion] and set up the son of Tabeel over it as its [puppet] king,"
7for this is what the Lord GOD says, "It shall not stand nor shall it happen.
8"For the head (capital) of Aram is Damascus and the head of Damascus is [King] Rezin (now within sixty-five years Ephraim will be broken to pieces and will no longer be a people).
9"And the head (capital) of Ephraim is Samaria, and the head of Samaria is Remaliah's son [King Pekah]. If you will not believe [and trust in God and His message], be assured that you will not be established." ' "

The Child Immanuel

10Then the LORD spoke again to [King] Ahaz, saying,
11"Ask a sign for yourself from the LORD your God [one that will convince you that God has spoken and will keep His word]; make your request as deep as Sheol or as high as heaven."
12But Ahaz said, "I will not ask, nor will I test the LORD!"
13Then Isaiah said, "Hear then, O house of David! Is it too small a thing for you to try the patience of men, but will you try the patience of my God as well?
14"Therefore the Lord Himself will give you a sign: Listen carefully, the virgin will conceive and give birth to a son, and she will call his name Immanuel (God with us). [Is 9:6; Jer 31:22; Mic 5:3–5; Matt 1:22, 23]
15"He will eat curds and honey when he knows *enough* to refuse evil and choose good.

---

the Syro-Ephraimite wars — the invasion of Judah by Rezin and Pekah (2Ki 16). These prophecies aimed to call Judah back to faith in God.
7:2 *house of David.* The king was descended from David and was referred to as "from the house of David." ***Ephraim.*** The word Ephraim represents the Northern Kingdom of Israel.
7:3 *Shear-jashub.* The name of Isaiah's son meant "a remnant will return." This name referred to a coming exile and the salvation of the remaining faithful, although all of those events occurred long after Isaiah's lifetime.
7:4 *son of Remaliah.* The son of Remaliah is Pekah, king of Israel.
7:6 *son of Tabeel.* Tabeel means "good for nothing." Syria and Israel wanted to place an incompetent puppet king over Judah.
7:12 *not ask, nor will I test.* In the mouth of the wicked Ahaz, these words rang hollow. Ahaz was continually testing the Lord's patience by his disobedience.
7:14 *Immanuel.* The Christian church traditionally has seen this verse as a prophecy of the Christ child, in whose incarnation God became present in physical form with mankind. The name "Immanuel" means "God with us." Christ, as a descendant of the house of David, fulfills the requirements of the sign and reinforces Isaiah's message that the nation's destiny does not rest with a foreign people, but with the God of Sinai.
7:15 *curds and honey.* Curds, or "butter," and honey contrast with "bread and wine" from cultivated lands and symbolically represent the Judean's simple diet after the Assyrian invasion. Thus, the Child, similar to Isaiah's son Shear-jashub (v. 3), would be identified with the remnant.

CHAPTER 7 **7** Isa 8:10 **8** 2Sa 8:6 **9** 2Ch 20:20 **11** Mt 12:38 **14** Mt 1:23; Isa 9:6; Isa 8:8

[16]"For before the child will know *enough* to refuse evil and choose good, the land (Canaan) whose two kings you dread will be deserted [both Ephraim and Aram]. [Is 7:2]

Trials to Come for Judah

[17]"The LORD will bring on you, on your people, and on your father's house such days as have not come since the day that Ephraim (the ten northern tribes) separated from Judah—[He will call for] the king of Assyria."

[18]In that day the LORD will whistle for the fly that is in the mouth of the rivers *and* canals of Egypt and for the bee that is in the land of Assyria.

[19]These [armies, like flies and bees] will all come and settle on the steep *and* rugged ravines and in the clefts of the rocks, and on all the thorn bushes and in all the watering places.

[20]In that day [when foreign armies swarm the land] the Lord will shave with a razor, hired from the regions beyond the Euphrates (*that is*, with the king of Assyria), [that razor will shave] the head and the hair of the legs; and it will also remove the beard [leaving Judah stripped, shamed and scorned]. [2 Kin 16:7, 8; 18:13–16]

[21]Now in that day [because of the poverty caused by the invaders] a man will keep alive only a young milk cow and two sheep;

[22]and because of the abundance of milk produced he will eat curds, for everyone that is left in the land will eat [only] curds and [wild] honey.

[23]And it will come to pass in that day, in every place where there used to be a thousand vines, *worth* a thousand silver *shekels*, there will be briars and thorns.

[24]People will come there [to hunt] with arrows and with bows because all the land will be briars and thorns.

[25]As for all the hills which used to be cultivated with the pick *and* the hoe, you will no longer go there for fear of briars and thorns; but they will become a place where oxen are pastured and where sheep tread.

Damascus and Samaria Fall

8 THEN THE LORD said to me, "Take for yourself a large tablet [for public display] and write on it in ordinary characters: *Belonging* to Maher-shalal-hash-baz.

[2]"And I will get faithful witnesses to attest [to this prophecy] for me, Uriah the priest and Zechariah the son of Jeberechiah."

[3]So I approached [my wife] the prophetess, and she conceived and gave birth to a son. Then the LORD said to me, "Name him Maher-shalal-hash-baz [to remind the people of the prophecy];

[4]for before the boy knows how to say, 'My father' or 'My mother,' the

---

7:16 *For before.* Similar prophecies were spoken of the child's birth and Isaiah's other son, Maher-shalal-hash-baz (8:3). Israel and Syria would be destroyed before the child and Isaiah's son would reach maturity (see 8:4, where Syria is referred to as Damascus and Israel as Samaria). It is not uncommon for biblical prophecies to have one level of fulfillment in the immediate future and a final fulfillment many years later in the person and work of the Savior, Jesus. Thus, the birth of Isaiah's son could have been a sign to King Ahaz. However, this would have been an early fulfillment, not the ultimate fulfillment. It was the coming of Jesus, God's only Son, which was the complete fulfillment.
7:20 *shave with a razor.* This was a symbol of humiliation.

8:2 *Zechariah the son of Jeberechiah.* This was not the Zechariah who wrote the Book of Zechariah.
8:3 *the prophetess.* Isaiah's wife was a prophetess in her own right. It is possible that this was a new wife, following the death of the mother of Shear-jashub (7:3). ***Maher-shalal-hash-baz.*** The child's name means "Speed the Spoil, Hasten the Booty."
8:4 *spoil of Samaria . . . king of Assyria.* This was a specific prediction of the fall of Samaria to the Assyrians in 722 BC. This prophecy must have been written shortly before that time, as the fulfillment would come before the new child would be able to speak.

16 See Isa 8:4; 2Ki 15:30 **17** 2Ch 28:19; 1Ki 12:16 **18** Isa 5:26 **19** Jer 16:16 **20** 2Ki 16:7 **23** Isa 5:6
CHAPTER 8 **1** Hab 2:2 **2** 2Ki 16:10 **4** Isa 7:16; 2Ki 15:29

riches of Damascus (Aram's capital) and the spoil of Samaria (Israel's capital) will be carried away by the king of Assyria."

5 Again the LORD spoke to me, saying,

6 "Because these people (Judah)
have refused the gently flowing
waters of Shiloah
And rejoice in Rezin [the king
of Aram] and Remaliah's son
[Pekah the king of Israel],
7 Now therefore, listen carefully, the
Lord is about to bring on them
the waters of the [Euphrates]
River, strong and abundant—
The king of Assyria and all his
glory;
And it will rise over all its
channels *and* canals and go far
beyond its banks. [Is 7:17]
8 "Then it will sweep on into Judah;
it will overflow and pass
through [the hills],
Reaching even to the neck [of
which Jerusalem is the head],
And its outstretched wings (the
armies of Assyria) will fill the
width of Your land, O Immanuel.
[Num 14:9; Ps 46:7]

A Believing Remnant

9 "Be broken [in pieces], O peoples,
and be shattered!
Listen, all you [our enemies from
the] far countries.
Prepare yourselves [for war], and
be shattered;
Prepare yourselves [for war], and
be shattered.
10 "Take counsel together [against
Judah], but it will come to
nothing;
Speak the word, but it will not
stand,
For God is with us (Immanuel)."

11 For in this way the LORD spoke to me with His strong hand [upon me] and instructed me not to walk in the way of this people [behaving as they do], saying,

12 "You are not to say, 'It is a
conspiracy!'
In regard to all that this people call
a conspiracy,
And you are not to fear what they
fear nor be in dread of it.
13 "It is the LORD of hosts whom
you are to regard as holy *and*
awesome.
He shall be your [source of] fear,
He shall be your [source of] dread
[not man].
14 "Then He shall be a sanctuary [a
sacred, indestructible shelter for
those who fear and trust Him];
But to both the houses of Israel
[both the northern and southern
kingdoms—Israel and Judah,
He will be] a stone on which to
stumble and a rock on which to
trip,
A trap and a snare for the
inhabitants of Jerusalem.
[Is 28:6; Rom 9:33; 1 Pet 2:6–8]
15 "Many [among them] will stumble
over them;
Then they will fall and be broken,
They will even be snared and
trapped."

16 Bind up the testimony, seal the law *and* the teaching among my (Isaiah's) disciples.

17 And I will wait for the LORD who

8:8 *O Immanuel.* Isaiah bestowed on Judah the name of the promised Child, Immanuel, which means "God with us" (7:14), because it would be preserved only because God was with that nation.
8:14 *a stone on which to stumble and a rock on which to trip.* God is a stone of stumbling for unbelievers (Ps 118:22; Lk 20:17–18; Ro 9:33; 1Pe 2:6–8).

8:16 *testimony ... law.* The testimony refers to a legal transaction. The law refers to God's instruction revealed through Isaiah. Isaiah's disciples put his prophecies in the form of a legal transaction, probably to prove their authenticity when they were fulfilled (see vv. 1–2; compare Jer 28:9; 32:12–14).

6 Jn 9:7; Isa 7:1,2 **8** Isa 30:28; Isa 7:14 **9** Joel 3:9 **10** Job 5:12; Isa 7:7; Isa 7:14; Ro 8:31 **12** Isa 7:2; 1Pe 3:14 **13** Nu 20:12; Ps 76:7; Lk 12:5 **14** Eze 11:16; Lk 2:34; Ro 9:33; 1Pe 2:8 **15** Mt 21:44; Lk 20:18; Ro 11:25 **17** Isa 54:8; Hab 2:3; Lk 2:25

is hiding His face from the house of
Jacob; and I will look eagerly for Him.
18 Listen carefully, I and the children
whom the LORD has given me are for
signs and wonders [that will occur]
in Israel from the LORD of hosts, who
dwells on Mount Zion.
19 When the people [instead of trust-
ing God] say to you, "Consult the me-
diums [who try to talk to the dead] and
the soothsayers who chirp *and* whis-
per and mutter," should not a people
consult their God? *Should they consult*
the dead on behalf of the living?
20 [Direct those people] to the law
and to the testimony! If their teachings
are not in accord with this word, it is
because they have no dawn.
21 They [who consult mediums and
soothsayers] will pass through the
land deeply distressed and hungry, and
when they are hungry, they will be-
come enraged and will curse their king
and their God as they look upward.
22 Then they will look to the earth,
they will see only distress and dark-
ness, the gloom of anguish; and *they
will be* driven away into darkness *and*
overwhelming night.

Birth and Reign of the Prince of Peace

9 BUT THERE will be no *more* gloom
for her who was in anguish [for
with judgment comes the promise of
salvation]. In earlier times He treated
the land of Zebulun and the land of
Naphtali with contempt, but later on
He will make them honored [by the
presence of the Messiah], by the way
of the sea, on the other side of Jordan,
Galilee of the Gentiles.

2 The people who walk in [spiritual]
darkness
Will see a great Light;
Those who live in the dark land,
The Light will shine on them.
[Is 42:6; Matt 4:15, 16]
3 You [O God] will increase the
nation,
You will multiply their joy;
They will rejoice before You
Like the joy *and* jubilation of the
harvest,
As men rejoice when they divide
the spoil [of victory].
4 For You will break the yoke of
Israel's burden and the staff
(goad) on their shoulders,
The rod of their oppressor, as at
the battle of Midian. [Judg 7:8–
22]
5 For every boot of the marching
warrior in the *battle* tumult,
And [every soldier's] garment
rolled in blood, will be *used* for
burning, fuel for the fire.
6 For to us a Child shall be born, to
us a Son shall be given;

8:18 *children.* Isaiah's name means "Jehovah has saved," and his two sons' names speak of the impending judgment of God (7:3; 8:3). They were symbols of God's intentions for the nation.
8:19 *Consult the mediums [who try to talk to the dead] and the soothsayers.* This indicates that the people were involved in necromancy, the practice of conjuring up the spirits of the dead in order to influence events. This practice, as well as the use of any mediums or spiritists, was strictly forbidden (Dt 18:9–14).
9:1 *with contempt.* The ancient tribal allotments of Zebulun and Naphtali (Jos 19:10–16,32–39), which included Galilee, were the first to feel the brunt of the Assyrian invasions (2Ki 15:29). ***the way of the sea, on the other side of Jordan, Galilee of the Gentiles.*** These three phrases indicate administrative districts of the Assyrian conqueror Tiglath-Pileser III as a result of the three campaigns he waged in the west around 733 BC. The city of Capernaum is "by the way of the sea" (Galilee) in the region of Zebulun and Naphtali. This is where Jesus began his ministry, in fulfillment of the prophecy of Isaiah 9:1–2 (Mt 4:15–16).
9:2 *Will see a great Light.* The light stands for God's blessings, presence, and revelation, fulfilled in Jesus who came in the flesh (Mt 4:15–16). The coming of Jesus revealed the mercy and grace of God in the same way that the rising sun reveals the nature of the land it shines upon. All history is labeled from that definitive moment: before the Light, or after the Light (Jn 1:9).
9:6–7 *a Child.* In this triumphant song Isaiah rejoices as though the promised Child of the

18 Heb 2:13; Ps 71:7; Zec 3:8 **19** 1Sa 28:8; Isa 29:4; Ps 106:28 **20** Lk 16:29; Mic 3:6 **21** Rev 16:11 **22** Isa 5:30; Isa 9:1 **CHAPTER 9** **1** Isa 8:22; 2Ki 15:29; 2Ch 16:4; Lev 26:24; 2Ki 17:5; 1Ch 5:26 **2** Mt 4:16; Eph 5:8,14 **3** Jdg 5:30 **4** Isa 10:5; Jdg 7:22; Ps 83:9 **5** Isa 66:15 **6** Isa 7:14; Lk 2:11; Jn 3:16; Mt 28:18; 1Co 15:25; Jdg 13:18; Titus 2:13; Eph 2:14

And the government shall be upon
His shoulder,
And His name shall be called
Wonderful Counselor, Mighty
God,
Everlasting Father, Prince
of Peace. [Is 25:1; 40:9–11;
Matt 28:18; Luke 2:11]
7 There shall be no end to the
increase of His government and
of peace,
[He shall rule] on the throne of
David and over his kingdom,
To establish it and to uphold it with
justice and righteousness
From that time forward and
forevermore.
The zeal of the LORD of hosts will
accomplish this. [Dan 2:44;
1 Cor 15:25–28; Heb 1:8]

God's Anger with Israel's Arrogance

8 The Lord sends a word (message)
against Jacob,
And it falls on Israel [the ten
northern tribes, the kingdom
of Ephraim].
9 And all the people know it,

---

house of David has already been born. The Child's birthright involves authority and rule, while His character is depicted with descriptive names. As "Wonderful Counselor," He represents the sum of wisdom and knowledge, and His divinity is established clearly by the title "Mighty God." The Fatherhood of the Messiah is eternal, which again demonstrates His identity with God (Jo10:30). Finally, as the "Prince of Peace" He brings peace into the world by His atoning death on the cross, paying the price of human sin and reconciling us to God. The line of David will be the human line for the source of these blessings (2Sa 7:8 – 16; Lk 1:32 – 33), and the divine nature of the Messiah will guarantee their permanence.

9:7 The Son of God — In Luke 24:25 – 27 Jesus goes to great lengths to help two of his disciples understand what the Jewish Scriptures (the Old Testament) said about Him. Throughout the Old Testament there are numerous passages that point towards Jesus Christ in several ways. This prophecy in Isaiah is one of the most important of these passages. Here He is spoken of as a son before He became a man (See also Gal 4:4). Micah prophesies His birth, but also states that His "goings forth (appearances) are from long ago, from ancient days" (Mic 5:2). John says that He existed "in the beginning" before anything was created (Jn 1:1 – 3).

Even before He was born of Mary, He appeared to men in the Old Testament as the "angel of the Lord." It is clear that this angel is no ordinary angel because He is identified as God (Ex 3:2). He pardons sin (Ex 23:20 – 21), and He is worshiped (Jos 5:13 – 15). While these passages do not say that this member of the Godhead was the preincarnate Christ, we may conclude that they are the same person since their work is the same.

While Christ occasionally appeared to men in the Old Testament, He took on a physical, human body when He was conceived in Mary's womb. This incomparable event of God's becoming man in Jesus Christ is called the incarnation. This miracle was prophesied hundreds of years previously (7:14) and was fulfilled historically when Christ was born (Lk 2:7). Thus Christ, the sinless God-man, was qualified to become our Redeemer (2Co 5:21).

As a man, Christ experienced the normal physical, mental, social, and spiritual growth as others did (Lk 2:52). He suffered pain, hunger, thirst, fatigue, temptation, pleasure, rest, and even lack of knowledge (Mk 13:32). Because of His complete humanity He can be sympathetic and compassionate toward us (Heb 4:15).

While Christ was fully man He was also fully God, as these facts indicate: He is called God (Jn 1:1; Heb 1:8); He did works that only God could do, such as forgive sins (Mk 2:7) and create (Col 1:16); He had attributes that only God could have, such as truth (Jn 14:6) and omniscience (Jn 2:24 – 25); and He claimed equality with God (Jn 10:30).

The question may be raised as to whether Christ lost anything of deity when He became a man (Php 2:6 – 8). While there is an inscrutable mystery involved in this unparalleled act of condescension, one can be certain that He lost none of God's attributes, because He was still God (Jn 20:28). He is fully God and fully man united in one person forever. Even now, at the right hand of God, He is the God-man (1Ti 2:5). The great condescension of the Son of God in becoming a man, serves eternally as a perfect model of humility and self-giving love (Php 2:8).

9:8 *word (message) against Jacob.* The message was a judgment against the Northern Kingdom. The Lord would destroy it and its capital, Samaria.

---

7 Da 2:44; Lk 1:32; Isa 37:32

That is, Ephraim and the inhabitants of Samaria [its capital],
Who say in pride and arrogance of heart:
10 "The bricks have fallen down,
But we will rebuild [all the better] with ashlar (hewed stones);
The sycamores have been cut down,
But we will replace them with [expensive] cedars."
11 Therefore the LORD raises against Ephraim adversaries from Rezin [king of Aram]
And spurs their enemies on,
12 The Arameans on the east and the Philistines on the west;
And they devour Israel with gaping jaws.
In *spite of* all this, God's anger does not turn away
But His hand is still stretched out [in judgment].

13 Yet the people do not turn back [in repentance] to Him who struck them,
Nor do they seek the LORD of hosts [as their most essential need].
14 Therefore the LORD cuts off head and tail [the highest and the lowest] from Israel,
Both [the high] palm branch and [the low] bulrush in one day.
15 The elderly and honorable man, he is the head;
And the prophet who teaches lies, he is the tail.
16 For those who lead this people are causing *them* to go astray;
And those who are led [astray] by them are swallowed up.
17 Therefore the Lord does not rejoice over their young men,
Nor does He have compassion on their fatherless or their widows;
For every one of them is godless and an evildoer,
And every mouth is speaking foolishness.
In *spite of* all this, God's anger does not turn away
But His hand is still stretched out [in judgment].

18 For wickedness burns like a fire;
It consumes briars and thorns,
It even sets the forest thickets ablaze;
And it swirls upward in a column of smoke.
19 By the wrath of the LORD of hosts the land is burned up,
And the people are like fuel for the fire;
No man spares his brother.
20 They slice off [in discord] *what is* on the right hand but are *still* hungry,
And they eat *what is* on the left hand but they are not satisfied;
Each eats the flesh of his own arm.
21 [The tribe of] Manasseh *devours* [the tribe of his brother] Ephraim, and Ephraim Manasseh,
And together they are against Judah (the southern kingdom, the house of David).
In *spite of* all this, God's anger does not turn away
But His hand is still stretched out [in judgment].

Assyria Is God's Instrument

10 WOE (JUDGMENT is coming) to those [judges] who issue evil statutes,
And to those [magistrates] who constantly record unjust *and* oppressive decisions,
2 So as to deprive the needy of justice
And rob the poor of My people of rightful claims,
So that widows may be their spoil

10:1 *Woe.* Woe is a chilling word when spoken by God (5:8 – 23; 10:5). The leaders who make laws that affect a community for good or evil bear a fearful responsibility before God, whether they acknowledge it or not.

12 Jer 4:8 **13** Jer 5:3 **14** Rev 18:8 **16** Isa 3:12 **17** Ps 147:10; Isa 5:25 **18** Mal 4:1 **19** Isa 8:22; Mic 7:2,6 **20** Lev 26:26; Jer 19:9 **21** ver. 12,17 **CHAPTER 10** **1** Ps 58:2

And that they may plunder the
fatherless.
3 Now what will you do in the day of
[God's] punishment,
And in the storm of devastation
which will come from far away?
To whom will you flee for help?
And where will you leave your
wealth [for safekeeping]?
4 Nothing *remains* but to crouch
among the captives
Or fall [dead] among the slain [on
the battlefield].
In *spite of* all this, God's anger
does not turn away,
But His hand is still stretched out
[in judgment].

5 Woe to Assyria, the rod of My
anger [against Israel],
The staff in whose hand is My
indignation *and* fury [against
Israel's disobedience]!
6 I send Assyria against a godless
nation
And commission it against the
people of My wrath
To take the spoil and to seize the
plunder,
And to trample them down like
mud in the streets.
7 Yet it is not Assyria's intention [to
do My will],
Nor does it plan so in its heart,
But instead it is its purpose to
destroy
And to cut off many nations.
8 For Assyria says, "Are not my
princes all kings?
9 "Is not Calno [conquered] like
Carchemish [on the Euphrates]?
Is not Hamath [subdued] like
Arpad [her neighbor]?
Is not Samaria [in Israel] like
Damascus [in Aram]?
10 "As my hand has reached to the
kingdoms of the idols,
Whose carved images were
greater *and* more feared than
those of Jerusalem and Samaria,
11 Shall I not do to Jerusalem and her
images
Just as I have done to Samaria and
her idols?" [declares Assyria].

12 So when the Lord has completed
all His work [of judgment] on Mount
Zion and on Jerusalem, *He will say,* "I
will punish the fruit [the thoughts, the
declarations, and the actions] of the
arrogant heart of the king of Assyria
and the haughtiness of his pride."
13 For the Assyrian king has said,

"I have done this by the power
of my [own] hand and by my
wisdom,
For I have understanding *and* skill.
I have removed the boundaries of
the peoples
And have plundered their
treasures;
Like a bull I have brought down
those who sat on thrones.
14 "My hand has found the wealth of
the people like a nest,
And as one gathers eggs that are
abandoned, so I have gathered
all the earth;
And there was not one that
flapped its wing, or that opened
its beak and chirped."
15 Is the axe able to lift itself over the
one who chops with it?
Is the saw able to magnify itself
over the one who wields it?

10:3 *from far away.* The Assyrians were the devastation that came from afar.
10:5 *Woe to Assyria.* Though God uses sinners as instruments of His will (7:17; 13:5), they will still be held accountable for their own wickedness. In this, God shows that He is just in all His ways (Hab 1 – 3).
10:6 *a godless nation.* The godless nation is Judah (vv. 11 – 12).
10:9 *Calno . . . Damascus.* This is a list of cities that had already fallen to Assyria.
10:10 *idols . . . images.* The Assyrians had conquered the nations who had false gods. Surely, they believed, they would also have an easy time against "Jerusalem and her images." Only the Living God was to be worshiped by the Israelites, but they had repeatedly broken that command (Ex 20:4 – 6; Jdg 2:19).
10:15 *Is the axe able to lift itself.* The axe was the Assyrian army. They were an instrument in the hands of God.

3 Job 31:14; Hos 9:7 **4** Isa 5:25 **5** Jer 51:20 **6** Isa 9:17; Jer 34:22 **7** Ge 50:20 **8** 2Ki 19:10 **9** Am 6:2; 2Ch 35:20; 2Ki 16:9 **12** 2Ki 19:31; Jer 50:18 **13** Isa 37:24 **14** Job 31:25 **15** Jer 51:20

That would be like a club moving
those who lift it,
Or like a staff raising *him who* is
not [made of] wood [like itself]!
16 Therefore the Lord, the GOD of
hosts, will send a wasting
disease among the stout
warriors of Assyria;
And under his glory a fire will be
kindled like a burning flame.
17 And the Light of Israel will
become a fire and His Holy One
a flame,
And it will burn and devour
Assyria's thorns and briars in
a single day. [2 Kin 19:35–37;
Is 31:8, 9; 37:36]
18 The Lord will consume the glory of
Assyria's forest and of its fruitful
garden, both soul and body,
And it will be as when a sick man
wastes away.
19 And the remaining trees of
Assyria's forest will be so few in
number
That a child could write them
down.

A Remnant Will Return

20 Now in that day the remnant of
Israel, and those of the house of Jacob
who have escaped, will never again
rely on the one who struck them, but
will truly rely on the LORD, the Holy
One of Israel.

21 A remnant will return, a remnant
of Jacob, to the mighty God.
22 For though your people, O Israel,
may be as the sand of the sea,
Only a remnant within them will
return;
The destruction is determined
[it is decided and destined for
completion], overflowing with
justice (righteous punishment).
[Rom 9:27, 28]

23 For the Lord, the GOD of hosts, will ex-
ecute a complete destruction, one that
is decreed, in the midst of all the land.
24 Therefore, the Lord GOD of hosts
says this, "O My people who dwell in
Zion, do not be afraid of the Assyrian
who strikes you with a rod and lifts up
his staff against you, as [the king of]
Egypt did. [Ex 5]
25 "For yet a very little while and My
indignation [against you] will be ful-
filled and My anger *will be directed* to-
ward the destruction of the Assyrian."
26 The LORD of hosts will brandish a
whip against them like the slaughter
of Midian at the rock of Oreb; and His
staff will be over the [Red] Sea and He
will lift it up the way *He did* in [the flight
from] Egypt. [Ex 14:26–31; Judg 7:24, 25]
27 So it will be in that day, that the
burden of the Assyrian will be re-
moved from your shoulders and his
yoke from your neck. The yoke will be
broken because of the fat. [Deut 32:15]

28 The Assyrian has come against
Aiath [in Judah],
He has passed through Migron
[with his army];
At Michmash he stored his
equipment.
29 They have gone through the pass,
saying,
"Geba will be our lodging place for
the night."
Ramah trembles, and Gibeah [the
city] of Saul has fled.

10:16 *stout warriors.* The stout warriors who come under judgment are the Assyrians.

10:20 *remnant.* The Hebrew word used here for "remnant" is different than the word used in 1:9. The difference may be considered slight; it is the difference between those who were left, or remained (10:20,22), and those who survived (1:9).

10:22 *as the sand of the sea, Only a remnant.* Most of the people of the Northern Kingdom were carried off into captivity. But some Israelites made their way to Judah and became part of the Southern Kingdom. These people and their descendants would act as a remnant by preserving the names of the northern tribes among the people of God.

10:28 – 32 *Aiath . . . Jerusalem.* These verses depict Isaiah's vision of the king of Assyria's relentless march south over difficult terrain from Aiath (or Ai), which was ten miles north of Jerusalem on a point overlooking the city. The cities as listed in these verses are closer and closer to the capital at Jerusalem.

17 Isa 9:18 **18** 2Ki 19:23 **20** 2Ki 16:7 **22** Ro 9:27; Isa 6:13 **23** Da 9:27; Ro 9:28 **24** Isa 37:6; Ex 14
25 Da 11:36 **26** 2Ki 19:35; Isa 9:4; Ex 14:26 **27** Ps 105:15; 1Jn 2:20 **29** 1Sa 13:23; 11:4

[30] Cry aloud with your voice [in consternation], O Daughter of Gallim!
Pay attention, Laishah! Answer her, Anathoth!
[31] Madmenah has fled;
The inhabitants of Gebim have fled [with their belongings] to safety.
[32] Yet today the Assyrian will halt at Nob [the city of priests];
He shakes his fist at the mountain of the Daughter of Zion, at the hill of Jerusalem.

[33] Listen carefully, the Lord, the GOD of hosts, will lop off the [beautiful] boughs with terrifying force;
The tall in stature will be cut down
And the lofty will be abased *and* humiliated.
[34] He will cut down the thickets of the forest with an iron *axe*,
And Lebanon (the Assyrian) will fall by the Mighty One. [Gen 49:24; Is 9:6]

Righteous Reign of the Branch

11 THEN A Shoot (the Messiah) will spring from the stock of Jesse [David's father],
And a Branch from his roots will bear fruit. [Is 4:2; Matt 2:23; Rev 5:5; 22:16]
[2] And the Spirit of the LORD will rest on Him—
The Spirit of wisdom and understanding,
The Spirit of counsel and strength,
The Spirit of knowledge and of the [reverential and obedient] fear of the LORD—
[3] And He will delight in the fear of the LORD,
And He will not judge by what His eyes see,
Nor make decisions by what His ears hear;
[4] But with righteousness *and* justice He will judge the poor,
And decide with fairness for the downtrodden of the earth;
And He shall strike the earth with the rod of His mouth,
And with the breath of His lips He shall slay the wicked.
[5] And righteousness will be the belt around His loins,
And faithfulness the belt around His waist.

[6] And the wolf will dwell with the lamb,
And the leopard will lie down with the young goat,
And the calf and the young lion and the fatted steer together;
And a little child will lead them.

10:32 ***He.*** "He" refers to Assyria, the enemy. **10:33–34** ***boughs...thickets.*** The boughs and the thickets are the Assyrian leaders and the Assyrian army. The point is that God will bring judgment on the instruments He used to judge Israel. **11:1** ***a Shoot (the Messiah) will spring from the stock of Jesse.*** Jesse was King David's father (1Sa 16:10–13). As David inaugurated a kingdom of righteousness and peace, the new David—the "rod" or "root" (53:2) from David's line—will establish an incomparably greater kingdom. The words "rod" and "root" are messianic terms. They are figurative words for the great descendant of the household of David, the Seed of the woman promised in Genesis 3:15, Jesus Christ Himself (Mt 1:17). **11:2** ***Spirit.*** As in the case of David (1Sa 16:13), the Messiah would be empowered by the Holy Spirit (4:4; 42:1; 48:16; 59:21; 61:1; Lk 3:22), who was the Agent for establishing God's kingdom (Ge 1:1–2; Jdg 3:10; 6:34; 1Sa 10:6). ***wisdom and understanding.*** The Messiah will be the ideal king. He will embody the administrative skill to govern with righteousness and justice far more than even Solomon (1Ki 3:9), who asked for those gifts when he became king. ***counsel.*** The Holy Spirit's "counsel" is not advice, but authoritative plans and decisions. ***fear of the LORD.*** The Messiah would demonstrate in all His life the correct response to God; He would honor and obey Him (Ex 20:20). **11:4** ***judge.*** In this context, judge does not mean to bring people to account, but to act on their behalf. As the Judge of His people, God sentences the wicked and offers protection and defense for the innocent and oppressed. ***rod of His mouth...breath of His lips.*** This concept is repeated in Revelation 19:15, when the Lord Jesus returns with power and great glory. **11:6–9** ***wolf will dwell with the lamb...will***

30 1Sa 25:44; Jdg 18:7 **31** Jos 15:31 **32** 1Sa 21:1; Neh 11:32; Isa 13:2; Isa 37:22 **33** Am 2:9 **CHAPTER 11**
1 Zec 6:12; Rev 5:5; Ac 13:23; Isa 4:2 **2** Isa 61:1; Jn 1:32 **4** Rev 19:11; Job 4:9; Mal 4:6; 2Th 2:8 **6** Hos 2:18

[7] And the cow and the bear will
graze [together],
Their young will lie down together,
And the lion shall eat straw like
the ox.
[8] And the nursing child will [safely]
play over the hole of the cobra,
And the weaned child will put his
hand on the viper's den [and not
be hurt].
[9] They will not hurt or destroy in all
My holy mountain,
For the earth will be full of the
knowledge of the LORD
As the waters cover the sea.

[10] Then in that day
The nations will make
supplications to the Root of
Jesse
Who will stand as a signal for the
peoples;
And His resting place will be
glorious. [John 12:32]

The Restored Remnant

[11] Then it will happen on that day
that the Lord
Will again acquire with His hand
a second time
The remnant of His people, who
will remain,
From Assyria, from [Lower]
Egypt, from Pathros, from
Cush (Ethiopia), from Elam [in
Persia], from Shinar [Babylonia],
from Hamath [in Aram],
And from the coastlands
bordering the [Mediterranean]
Sea. [Jer 23:5–8]
[12] And He will lift up a signal for the
nations
And assemble the outcasts of
Israel,
And will gather the dispersed of
Judah
From the four corners of the earth.
[13] Then the jealousy of Ephraim will
depart,
And those who harass Judah will
be cut off;
Ephraim will not be jealous of
Judah,
And Judah will not harass
Ephraim.
[14] Ephraim and Judah will [unite and]
swoop down on the slopes of the
Philistines toward the west;
Together they will plunder the
sons (Arabs) of the east.
They will possess Edom and Moab,
And the sons of Ammon will be
subject to them.
[15] And the LORD will utterly destroy
The tongue of the Sea of Egypt;
And with His scorching wind
He will wave His hand over the
River;
He will strike *and* divide it into
seven channels
And make [it possible for] people
[to] walk over in sandals.
[16] And there will be a highway from
Assyria
For the remnant of His people who
will be left,
Just as there was for Israel
In the day when they came up out
of the land of Egypt.

Thanksgiving Expressed

12 AND ON that day you will say,
"I will give thanks to You,
O LORD;
For though You were angry with me,
Your anger has turned away,
And You comfort me.

not hurt or destroy. This picture of cruel beasts regenerated with a new nature that makes them protect their natural prey portrays a reign of peace and security. This can only be realized in the return of the Messiah to establish the kingdom of God (65:17–25; Rev 21:1–8).
11:10 *the peoples.* The revelation of the Messiah is for people of all nations.
11:11 *a second time.* The "second time" may refer to the remnant coming back to the land in 538 BC, in contrast to the first exodus from Egypt. Beyond that, it could also refer to the remnant's coming to Christ in the present age (Ro 11:5) or to its future return to Christ (Ro 11:11–27; Rev 7:4–8).
12:1 *on that day.* The day refers to the day that the Lord rescues His people, whether it was the return of the remnant or the future return of Christ as portrayed in the Book of Revelation.

9 Job 5:23; Hab 2:14 **10** Isa 2:11; Ro 15:10,12 **11** Zec 10:10 **12** Jn 7:35 **13** Jer 3:18; Eze 37:16,17,22 **14** Da 11:41 **15** Zec 10:11; Rev 16:12 **16** Isa 19:23; Ex 14:29 **CHAPTER 12** **1** Isa 2:11

[2]"Behold, God, my salvation!
I will trust and not be afraid,
For the LORD GOD is my strength
and song;
Yes, He has become my salvation."
[3]Therefore with joy you will draw
water
From the springs of salvation.
[4]And in that day you will say,
"Give thanks to the LORD, call on
His name [in prayer].
Make His deeds known among the
peoples [of the earth];
Proclaim [to them] that His name
is exalted!"
[5]Sing praises to the LORD, for He
has done excellent *and* glorious
things;
Let this be known throughout the
earth.
[6]Rejoice and shout for joy,
O inhabitant of Zion,
For great in your midst is the Holy
One of Israel.

Prophecies about Babylon

13 THE [MOURNFUL, inspired] oracle (a burden to be carried) concerning Babylon which Isaiah the son of Amoz saw [in a prophetic vision]:

[2]Lift up a signal banner on the bare
mountain,
Summon them [the Medes and
Persians] with a loud voice,
Wave the [beckoning] hand so that
they may enter the doorways of
the [Babylonian] nobles.
[3]I [the LORD] have commanded My
consecrated ones,
I have even called My great
warriors,
My proudly exulting ones [the
Medes and the Persians who
triumph for My honor]—
To *execute* My anger.
[4]A sound of tumult on the
mountains,
Like that of many people!
A sound of the uproar of the
kingdoms,
Of nations gathered together!
The LORD of hosts is mustering an
army for battle.
[5]They are coming from a distant
country,
From the end of heaven [the
farthest horizon]—
The LORD and the weapons of His
indignation—
To destroy the whole land.
[Ps 19:4–6; Is 5:26]

Judgment on the Day of the LORD

[6]Wail, for the day of the LORD is at
hand!
It will come as destruction from
the Almighty (All Sufficient
One—Invincible God)! [Gen 17:1]

12:2 *my strength and song.* This psalm of redemption is based on the first psalm of redemption in Exodus (Ex 15:2; Ps 118:14).
12:3 *springs of salvation.* In an arid land, the provision of wells and springs was regarded as a divine gift. Hebrew poets often associate water with salvation (Ex 17:1–7).
13:1 *oracle . . . which Isaiah . . . saw.* The Book of Isaiah takes a major turn at chapter 13, which continues through chapter 27. The focus in this extended section is first on the Lord's judgments against the nations, through chapter 23, followed by an end-time prophecy in chapters 24–27. ***Babylon.*** Babylon was the crown jewel of the Assyrian Empire. This burden may refer to its destruction around 689 BC when Sennacherib quelled a rebellion there. Yet the Lord's overthrow of Babylon, the "glory of kingdoms" (v. 19), symbolizes His triumph over the world (v. 11). Babylon is the epitome of religion and culture in the ancient Middle East. Thus the burden is indirectly against all nations, especially Assyria (14:24–27). Peter uses the term Babylon symbolically in the New Testament (1Pe 5:13), as does John (Rev 14:8; 18:2,10–21).
13:6 *the day of the Lord.* This designated "day" refers to a time of unusual activity of God in the lives of people, for judgment or for mercy. ***is at hand.*** The basic idea of this term is not that of approaching a fixed date, but that the day of the Lord is about to burst into one's world. The day of the Lord is imminent—able to happen at any time—not because people have almost reached it as a destination, but because it may burst in upon people without further warning.

2 Ps 83:18; Ex 15:2; Ps 118:14 **3** Jn 4:10 **4** 1Ch 16:8; Ps 105:1; Ps 145:4-6; Ps 34:3 **5** Ex 15:1; Ps 98:1 **6** Zep 3:14; Ps 89:18 **CHAPTER 13** **1** Jer 50; 51 **2** Isa 18:3; Jer 51:25; Isa 10:32 **3** Joel 3:11; Ps 149:2 **6** Zep 1:7; Rev 6:17; Job 31:23; Joel 1:15

7 Therefore all hands will fall limp,
And every man's heart will melt.
8 They [of Babylon] will be shocked *and* terrified,
Pains and anguish will grip them;
They will be in pain like a woman in childbirth.
They will stare aghast *and* horrified at one another,
Their faces aflame [from the effects of the unprecedented warfare].
9 Listen carefully, the day of the LORD is coming,
Cruel, with wrath and raging anger,
To make the land a horror [of devastation];
And He shall exterminate its sinners from it. [Is 2:10–22; Rev 19:11–21]
10 For the stars of heaven and their constellations
Will not flash with their light;
The sun will be dark when it rises,
And the moon will not shed its light.
11 In this way I will punish the world for its evil
And the wicked for their wickedness [their sin, their injustice, their wrongdoing];
I will also put an end to the arrogance of the proud
And will abase the arrogance of the tyrant.
12 I will make mortal man more rare than fine gold,
And mankind [scarcer] than the pure gold of Ophir.
13 Therefore I will make the heavens tremble;
And the earth will be shaken from its place
At the wrath of the LORD of hosts
In the day of His burning anger.
14 And like the hunted gazelle,
Or like sheep that no man gathers,
Each [foreign resident] will turn [and go back] to his own people,
And each one flee to his own land.
15 Anyone who is found will be pierced through,
And anyone who is captured will fall by the sword.
16 Their children also will be smashed to pieces
Before their eyes;
Their houses will be looted
And their wives ravished.

Babylon Will Fall to the Medes

17 Listen carefully, I will put the Medes [in motion] against them,
Who have no regard for silver and do not delight in gold [and therefore cannot be bribed].
18 Their bows will cut down the young men [of Babylon];
They will take no pity on the fruit of the womb,
Their eyes will not look with compassion on the children.
19 And Babylon, the glory of kingdoms, the beauty of the Chaldeans' pride,
Will be like Sodom and Gomorrah when God overthrew them.
20 Babylon will never be inhabited or lived in from generation to generation;
Nor will the Arab pitch his tent there,
Nor will the shepherds let *their sheep* lie down there.
21 But desert creatures will lie down there,
And their houses will be full of owls;
Ostriches also will live there, and wild goats will dance there.
22 Hyenas will howl in their castles,
And jackals in their luxurious palaces.
Babylon's time has nearly come,
And her days will not be prolonged.

13:21–22 *owls . . . jackals.* With the exception of the goat, all of the animals mentioned in these verses are unclean. This image created a clear message to the people of Israel of a place that was desolate and unfit to inhabit.

8 Ps 48:6 **9** Mal 4:1; Ps 104:35; Pr 2:22 **10** Eze 32:7; Joel 2:31; Mt 24:29; Mk 13:24 **11** Isa 2:17 **13** Hag 2:6; Ps 110:5; La 1:12 **14** Jer 50:16 **16** Ps 137:9; Na 3:10; Zec 14:2 **17** Jer 51:11; Da 5:28 **19** Isa 14:4; Ge 19:24; Dt 29:23; Jer 50:40 **20** Jer 50:3 **21** Isa 34:11 **22** Jer 51:33

Israel's Taunt

14 FOR THE LORD will have compassion on Jacob (the captives in Babylon) and will again choose Israel, and will settle them in their own land. Foreigners (Gentiles) will join them [as proselytes] and will attach themselves to the house of Jacob (Israel). [Esth 8:17]

2 The peoples will take them along and bring them to their own place (Judea), and the house of Israel will possess them as an inheritance in the land of the LORD as male and female servants; and they will take captive those whose captives they have been, and they will rule over their [former] oppressors. [Ezra 1]

3 And it will be in the day when the LORD gives you rest from your pain and turmoil and from the harsh service in which you have been enslaved,
4 that you will take up this taunt against the king of Babylon, and say,

"How the oppressor has ceased
[his insolence],
And how the fury has ceased!
5 "The LORD has broken the staff of
the wicked,
The scepter of the [tyrant] rulers
6 Which used to strike the peoples
in anger with incessant blows,
Which subdued *and* ruled
the nations in wrath with
unrelenting persecution.
7 "The whole earth is at rest and is
quiet;
They break into shouts of joy.
8 "Even the cypress trees rejoice
over you [kings of Babylon],
even the cedars of Lebanon,
saying,
'Since you were laid low, no
woodcutter comes up against
us.'
9 "Sheol below is excited about you
to meet you when you come [you
tyrant of Babylon];
It stirs up the spirits of the dead [to
greet you], all the leaders of the
earth;
It raises all the kings of the
nations from their thrones [in
astonishment at your fall].
10 "All of them will respond
[tauntingly] and say to you,
'You have become as weak as we
are.
You have become like us.
11 'Your pomp and magnificence
have been brought down to
Sheol,
Along with the music of your
harps;
The maggots [which prey on the
dead] are spread out under you
[as a bed]
And worms are your covering
[Babylonian rulers].'
12 "How you have fallen from heaven,
O star of the morning [light-
bringer], son of the dawn!
You have been cut down to the
ground,

14:4 *Babylon.* Babylon is often used in Scripture for Satan's kingdom. This passage can be read with a double point of view. One, as if it were talking about an unnamed political king; and two, as a reference to and description of Satan's career. Both views are sobering and worth taking note of.

14:8 *the cypress trees rejoice.* The trees will no longer be cut down to construct machines of war.

14:9 *Sheol below is excited.* The commotion in the "grave" when the king of Babylon (or Satan; see Rev 20:1 – 3) arrives contrasts sharply with the rest on earth when he is gone (v. 7).

14:12 *fallen from heaven.* This is a figure of speech meaning cast down from an exalted political position. Jesus said, "And you, Capernaum, will not be exalted to heaven, will you? You will descend to Hades (the realm of the dead)" (Lk 10:15); and, apparently with the same meaning, "I watched Satan fall from heaven like [a flash of] lightning" (Lk 10:18). The "son of the morning," called Lucifer or Day Star in Hebrew, is the planet Venus. The poetic language of this verse describes the aspiration of this brightest star to climb to the zenith of the heavens and its extinction before the rising sun. This is an apt summary of the failed goal of Satan (or the king of Babylon, v. 4), who wanted to grasp universal and eternal domination (Eze 28:14 – 16; Rev 12:12 – 13; 20:2).

CHAPTER 14 **1** Ps 102:13; Zec 1:17; Isa 60:4,5,10 **2** Isa 49:22; 60:9; 66:20; Isa 60:14 **4** Isa 13:19; Hab 2:6; Rev 18:16 **5** Ps 125:3 **8** Isa 55:12; Eze 31:16 **9** Eze 32:21 **12** Isa 34:4

You who have weakened the
nations [king of Babylon]!
13 "But you said in your heart,
'I will ascend to heaven;
I will raise my throne above the
stars of God;
I will sit on the mount of
assembly
In the remote parts of the north.
14 'I will ascend above the heights of
the clouds;
I will make myself like the Most
High.'
15 "But [in fact] you will be brought
down to Sheol,
To the remote recesses of the pit
(the region of the dead).
16 "Those who see you will gaze at
you,
They will consider you, *saying*,
'Is this the man who made the
earth tremble,
Who shook kingdoms,
17 Who made the world like a
wilderness
And overthrew its cities,
Who did not permit his prisoners
to return home?'
18 "All the kings of the nations, all of
them lie [dead] in glorious
array,
Each one in his own sepulcher.
19 "But you [king of Babylon] have
been cast out of your tomb
(denied burial)
Like a rejected branch,
Clothed with the slain who are
pierced by the sword,
Who go down to the stones of the
pit [into which carcasses are
thrown],
Like a dead body trampled
[underfoot].
20 "You will not be united with them
in burial,
Because you have destroyed your
land,
You have slain your people.
May the descendants of evildoers
never be named!
21 "Prepare a slaughtering place for
his sons
Because of the wickedness
[the sin, the injustice, the
wrongdoing] of their fathers.
They must not rise and take
possession of the earth,
And fill the face of the world with
cities."

22 "I will rise up against them," says the
LORD of hosts, "and will cut off from
Babylon name and survivors, and son
and grandson," declares the LORD.
23 "I will also make Babylon a posses-
sion of the hedgehog and of swamps
of water, and I will sweep it away with
the broom of destruction," declares the
LORD of hosts.

Judgment on Assyria

24 The LORD of hosts has sworn [an
oath], saying, "Just as I have intended,
so it has certainly happened, and just
as I have planned, so it will stand—
25 to break the Assyrian in My land,
and on My mountains I will trample
him underfoot. Then the Assyrian's
yoke will be removed from them (the
people of Judah) and his burden re-
moved from their shoulder.
26 "This is the plan [of God] decided
for the whole earth [regarded as con-
quered and put under tribute by Assyr-
ia]; and this is the hand [of God] that
is stretched out over all the nations.
27 "For the LORD of hosts has decided
and planned, and who can annul it?
His hand is stretched out, and who can
turn it back?"

14:14 *I will make myself like the Most High*. This is the most outrageous of the arrogant desires of Satan (or of this unnamed king). He wanted to surpass the Most High, a term for the Lord that is often used in connection with the nations of the world (Ps 87:5; 91:1; 92:1). This statement strongly speaks of Satan (v. 12), who purposes to work against God in every possible way. Satan's sin is centered in pride, the desire to be in submission to no one, not even God (1Ti 3:6). Ezekiel saw Satan's work in the king of Tyre (Eze 28), and Isaiah sees the parallel between the character and goals of Satan and this unnamed Babylonian king.

13 Mt 11:23; Da 8:10; Ps 48:2 **14** Isa 47:8; 2Th 2:4 **15** Mt 11:23 **20** Job 18:19; Ps 21:10; 37:28; 109:13 **21** Ex 20:5; Mt 23:35 **22** Pr 10:7; Jer 51:62; 1Ki 14:10; Job 18:19 **23** Isa 34:11; Zep 2:14 **25** Isa 10:27 **27** 2Ch 20:6; Job 9:12; 23:13; Ps 33:11; Pr 19:21; 21:30; Isa 43:13; Da 4:31,35

Judgment on Philistia

[28]In the year that King Ahaz [of Judah] died this [mournful, inspired] oracle (a burden to be carried) came:

29 "Do not rejoice, O Philistia, any of you,
Because the rod [of Judah] that struck you is broken;
For out of the serpent's root will come a viper [King Hezekiah of Judah],
And its offspring will be a flying serpent. [2 Kin 18:1, 3, 8]
30 "The firstborn of the helpless [of Judah] will feed [on My meadows],
And the needy will lie down in safety;
But I will kill your root with famine,
And your survivors will be put to death.
31 "Howl, O gate; cry, O city!
Melt away, O Philistia, all of you;
For smoke comes out of the north,
And there is no straggler in his ranks *and* no one stands detached [in Hezekiah's battalions].
32 "Then what answer will one give the messengers of the [Philistine] nation?
That the LORD has founded Zion,
And the afflicted of His people will seek *and* find refuge in it."

Judgment on Moab

15 THE [MOURNFUL, inspired] oracle (a burden to be carried) concerning Moab:

Because in a night Ar of Moab is devastated and ruined;
Because in a night Kir of Moab is devastated and ruined.
2 They have gone up to the temple and to Dibon, to the high places to weep.
Moab wails over Nebo and over Medeba;
Everyone's head is shaved, and every beard is cut off [in mourning]. [Jer 48:37]
3 In their streets they have wrapped themselves with sackcloth;
On their [flat] housetops and in their open squares
Everyone is wailing, dissolved in tears.
4 Heshbon and Elealeh [cities claimed by Moab] cry out;
Their voice is heard as far as Jahaz.
Therefore the armed men of Moab cry out;
Moab's soul trembles within him.
5 My heart cries out for Moab;
His fugitives are [fleeing] as far as Zoar and Eglath-shelishiyah.
For they go up the ascent of Luhith weeping;
For on the road to Horonaim they raise a cry of distress over their destruction. [Jer 48:5]
6 For the waters of Nimrim are desolate.
Indeed the grass is withered, the new growth dies;
There is no green thing.
7 Therefore the abundance *which* they have acquired and stored away
They carry off over the Brook of the Willows.
8 For the cry of distress has echoed around the territory of Moab;

14:28 *Ahaz.* King Ahaz died in 720 BC.
14:29 *rod.* The rod is probably a metaphor for the Assyrian king (10:5).
14:31 *gate.* The gate of a walled city was its weakest point. When the gate fell, the city could be taken. ***out of the north.*** The Assyrian army would come from the north.
15:1 *Moab.* For the origin of the people of Moab, see the story of Lot and his daughters in Genesis 19:30 – 38 (also Nu 22 – 25; Dt 1:5).
15:2 *high places.* High places were sites of pagan worship (16:12).
15:5 *heart cries out.* Isaiah does not rejoice in the downfall of Moab. He knew that the judgment from God was righteous, and he remembered that Moab had been a treacherous enemy to his nation, yet his heart cried out in pity. It is the mark of God's people that they do not rejoice in the downfall of the wicked, even though they may be glad to be free from oppression.

28 2Ki 16:20 **29** 2Ch 26:6; 2Ki 18:8 **32** Ps 87:1,5; Zec 11:11 **CHAPTER 15** **1** Jer 48:1; Nu 21:28 **2** Lev 21:5 **5** Jer 48:31; Jer 48:5 **6** Nu 32:36

The wailing *goes* as far as Eglaim
and the mournful cry to Beer-elim.
9 For the waters of Dimon are full of blood;
Yet I will bring even more *woes* on Dimon—
A lion upon those of Moab who escape and upon the remnant of the land.

Prophecy of Moab's Devastation

16 SEND LAMBS to the ruler of the land [you Moabites],
From Sela [that is, Petra in Edom] through the wilderness to the mountain of the Daughter of Zion (Jerusalem). [2 Kin 3:4, 5]
2 For like wandering birds or scattered nestlings,
The daughters of Moab will be at the fords of the [river] Arnon.
3 [Say to the ruler] "Give us advice, make a decision [for Moab, king of Judah];
Cast your shadow [over us] like night in the midst of noon;
Hide the outcasts, do not betray the fugitive [to his pursuer].
4 "Let our outcasts of Moab live among you;
Be a [sheltered] hiding place to them from the destroyer."
For the extortioner has come to an end, destruction has ceased,
Oppressors [who trample men] have completely *disappeared* from the land,
5 A throne will be established in lovingkindness,
And One will sit on it in faithfulness in the tent (dynasty, family) of David;
Judging *and* seeking justice
And being prompt to do righteousness. [Ps 96:13; Jer 48:47]
6 We have heard of the pride of Moab, an excessive pride—
Even of his arrogance, his conceit, his rage,
His untruthful boasting.
7 Therefore Moab will wail for Moab; everyone will wail.
You will mourn for the raisin cakes of Kir-hareseth,
As those who are utterly stricken *and* discouraged.
8 For the fields of Heshbon have languished *and* withered, and the vines of Sibmah *as well;*
The lords of the nations have trampled down [Moab's] choice vine branches,
Which reached as far as Jazer and wandered into the wilderness;
Its tendrils stretched out, they passed over [the shores of] the [Dead] Sea.
9 Therefore I (Isaiah) will weep bitterly for Jazer, for the vines of Sibmah.
I will drench you with my tears, O Heshbon and Elealeh;
For the war-cry [of the enemy] has fallen on your summer fruits and your harvest.

15:9 *Dimon.* The term Dimon sounds like "blood" in Hebrew. ***lion.*** Fleeing from one tragedy after another in their flight southward, the refugees turned to Judah in the west for asylum (16:1 – 5). A remnant would survive in Moab, as would be the case with Israel (1:9; 6:13; 10:20; 11:16) — but not with Assyria (14:22) and Philistia (14:30).

16:5 *A throne will be established.* Moab's salvation ultimately lies in the coming one, Jesus the Messiah, whose throne will be established (9:1 – 7; 11:1 – 5; Am 9:11 – 12; Ac 15:16 – 17).

16:6 *pride.* In the end, it was the pride and the haughtiness and the wrath of Moab that brought the nation into judgment. The pride of Moab is not the honest pride in a difficult task well done, but the pride of a haughty, disdainful people who considered themselves above remonstrance. The third element of Moab's downfall, wrath, is closely linked with pride. A people who consider themselves the center of interest and importance lose their natural inhibition. They feel free to indulge in wrath because they are convinced that whatever they do is right.

16:8 *vine.* The vine refers to Moab.

16:9 *Heshbon and Elealeh.* These cities were among the principal settlements in ancient Moab (15:4).

---

9 2Ki 17:25 **CHAPTER 16** **1** 2Ki 3:4; 14:7 **2** Nu 21:13 **5** Lk 1:33; Ps 72:2 **6** Jer 48:29; Isa 28:15 **7** Jer 48:20; 2Ki 3:25 **8** Isa 24:7; ver. 9 **9** Isa 15:4

10 Gladness and joy are taken away
from the fruitful field;
In the vineyards there will be no
singing or joyful sound;
No treader treads out wine in the
presses,
For I (God) put an end to the joyful
shouting.
11 Therefore my heart sounds like a
harp [in mournful compassion]
for Moab,
And my inner being *mourns* for
Kir-hareseth.
12 So it will come to pass when Moab
presents himself,
When he wearies himself
[worshiping] on his high place
[of idolatry]
And comes to his sanctuary
[of Chemosh, god of Moab] to
pray,
That he will not prevail. [Jer 48:13]

13 This is the word which the LORD
spoke earlier concerning Moab [when
Moab's pride and resistance to God
were first known].
14 But now the LORD speaks, saying,
"Within three years, as the years of
a hired man [who will not serve lon-
ger than the agreed time], the glory of
Moab will be degraded along with all
the great population, and the remnant
[that survives] will be very small and
of no account."

Prophecy about Damascus

17 THE [MOURNFUL, inspired] or-
acle (a burden to be carried) con-
cerning Damascus [capital of Aram
(Syria), and Israel's defense against
Assyria].
"Listen carefully, Damascus will
cease to be a city
And will become a fallen ruin.
2 "The cities of Aroer [east of the
Jordan] are deserted;
They will be [only a refuge] for
flocks to lie down in,
And there will be no one to make
them afraid.
3 "The fortified city will disappear
from Ephraim,
And the kingdom from Damascus
And the remnant of Aram (Syria);
They will be like the [departed]
glory of [her ally] the children of
Israel,"
Declares the LORD of hosts.

4 "Now in that day the [former]
glory of Jacob [Israel—his
might, his population, his
prosperity] will fade,
And the fatness of his flesh will
become lean.
5 "And it will be like the reaper
gathering the standing grain,
As his arm harvests the ears of
grain;
Yes, it will be like one gleaning
ears of grain
In the [fertile] Valley of Rephaim.
6 "Yet gleanings will be left in the
land [of Israel] like the shaking
of the olive tree,
Two or three olives on the topmost
branch,
Four or five on the [outermost]
branches of the fruitful tree,"
Declares the LORD, the God of
Israel.
7 In that day man will have regard
for his Maker,

16:12 *high place ... sanctuary.* As long as people worship false gods, they will be doomed to pain, judgment, and recurring trouble (15:2–4). Even when the people weary of the false gods and try to pray to the one true God, they will not be able to communicate with Him because they have not repented and renounced the false gods.
16:14 *Within three years.* A former prophecy against Moab (15:2) would be realized within three years, perhaps referring to the quelling of a rebellion against Sargon in 715 BC. However, a remnant would remain (15:9). Moab had far more hope for salvation than did either Babylon or Philistia.
17:3 *fortified city.* This city may be Samaria, the capital city. ***Ephraim.*** Ephraim designates northern Israel.
17:5 *Rephaim.* The word "Rephaim" is the Hebrew word for "shades" or "ghosts." The "Valley of Rephaim" is the valley of Death.
17:6 *left.* A remnant would be left (10:20) even though it would be pitifully small.

10 Isa 24:8; Jer 48:33 **11** Jer 48:36 **12** Isa 15:2 **14** Isa 21:16 **CHAPTER 17** **1** Jer 49:23; Am 1:3; Zec 9:1
2 Jer 7:33 **3** Isa 7:16; 8:4 **4** Isa 10:16 **5** Jer 51:33 **6** Isa 24:13 **7** Mic 7:7

And his eyes will regard the Holy
One of Israel [with awe-inspired
reverence].
8 And he will not have regard for
the [idolatrous] altars, the work
of his hands,
Nor will he look to that which his
fingers have made,
Neither the Asherim (symbols of
the goddess Asherah) nor the
incense altars.
9 In that day the strong cities of
Aram and Israel will be like
deserted places in the forest,
Or like branches which they
abandoned before the children
of Israel;
And the land will be a desolation.
10 Because you [Judah] have
forgotten the God of your
salvation
And have not remembered the
Rock of your Stronghold—
Therefore you plant lovely plants
And set the grounds with vine
slips of a strange *god*,
11 In the day that you plant it you
carefully fence it in,
And in the morning you bring
your seed to blossom;
Yet [promising as it is] the harvest
will be a heap [of ruins that
passes away]
In the day of sickness and
incurable pain.
12 Oh, the uproar of many peoples
Who roar like the roaring of the
seas,
And the noise of nations
Who roar like the rumbling of
mighty waters!
13 The nations roar on like the
roaring of many waters,
But God will rebuke them and
they will flee far away,
And be chased like chaff on the
mountains before the wind,
Or like whirling dust before the
storm.
14 At evening time, now look, sudden
terror!
Before morning the Assyrians are
no more.
This is the portion (fate) of those
who plunder us,
And the lot of those who pillage
us.

Message to Ethiopia

18 WOE (JUDGMENT is coming)
to the land of whirring wings
Which is beyond the rivers of Cush
(Ethiopia),
2 Which sends ambassadors by the
sea,
Even in vessels of papyrus on the
surface of the waters.
Go, swift messengers, to a nation
[of people] tall and smooth
(clean shaven),
To a people feared far and wide,
A powerful and oppressive nation
Whose land the rivers divide.
3 All you inhabitants of the world,
you who dwell on the earth,

17:10 *forgotten.* Forgetting God is letting the truth of God fade by ignoring Him. In the end, such neglect is unbelief, refusing to believe in God and refusing to believe His Word. The safe caring place, the Refuge from storms, is forgotten. God becomes like a friend whom you never visit any more or think much about and finally do not remember at all. This slippery slope takes us far from the Rock of our refuge, the God of our Salvation.

17:11 *bring your seed to blossom.* This phrase may allude to the ancient practice of force-blooming potted plants and allowing them *to die.* Pagans believed that this reenactment of the life cycle would secure fertile fields. But even after performing this rite, the harvest would be in ruin. Just as the choice vines of the Lord's vineyard disappointed Him (5:1–7), so His errant people would find their harvest hopes shattered.

17:12 *many peoples.* The many peoples are the nations that plunder Israel (v. 14).

17:14 *Before morning.* Sennacherib's army would be destroyed between evening time and morning (37:36–38). ***us.*** Isaiah identified himself with his plundered people.

18:1 *Cush.* Also called Ethiopia in the Bible, Cush was at the southern end of Isaiah's world. A Cushite dynasty took over Egypt in 715 BC and probably sent ambassadors to Jerusalem.

10 Ps 68:19 **12** Jer 6:23 **13** Ps 9:5; Ps 88:13; Hos 13:3 **CHAPTER 18** **1** Isa 20:4,5; Eze 30:4,5,9; Zep 2:12; 3:10 **2** ver. 7 **3** Isa 5:26

When a banner is raised on the
mountains, you will see it!
When a trumpet is blown, you will
hear it!

4For this is what the LORD has said to me,

"I will be quiet and I will look on
from My dwelling place,
Like shimmering heat above the
sunshine,
Like a cloud of dew in the heat of
harvest."
5For before the harvest, when the
blossom is over
And the flower becomes a
ripening grape,
He will cut off the sprigs [without
buds] with pruning knives,
And [He will] remove and cut
away the spreading branches.
6They (warriors) will be left
together for the mountain birds
of prey,
And for the beasts of the earth;
And the birds of prey will [spend
the] summer *feeding* on them,
And all the beasts of the earth will
spend harvest time on them.
7At that time a gift of homage will
be brought to the LORD of
hosts
From a people tall and smooth
(clean shaven),
From a people feared far and wide,
A powerful and oppressive
nation,
Whose land the rivers divide—
To the place [of worship] of the
name of the LORD of hosts, to
Mount Zion [in Jerusalem].
[Deut 12:5; 2 Chr 32:23; Is 16:1;
45:14; Zeph 3:10]

Message to Egypt

19 THE [MOURNFUL, inspired] oracle (a burden to be carried) concerning Egypt:

Listen carefully, the LORD is riding
on a swift cloud and is about to
come to Egypt;
The idols of Egypt will tremble at
His presence,
And the heart of the Egyptians
will melt within them.
2"So I will provoke Egyptians
against Egyptians;
And they will fight, each one
against his brother and each one
against his neighbor,
City against city, kingdom against
kingdom.
3"Then the spirit of the Egyptians
will become exhausted within
them *and* emptied out;
And I will confuse their strategy,
So that they will consult the idols
and the spirits of the dead,
And mediums and soothsayers.
4"And I will hand over the
Egyptians to a hard *and* cruel
master,
And a mighty king will rule over
them," declares the Lord GOD of
hosts.

5The waters from the sea will dry up,
And the river will be parched and
dry.
6The canals will become foul-
smelling,
The streams of Egypt will thin out
and dry up,
The reeds and the rushes will rot
away.
7The meadows by the Nile, by the
edge of the Nile,

18:5 *before the harvest ... cut off.* This is another example of a bad harvest (17:10–11).
18:7 *place [of worship] of the name.* Note how closely the Lord identifies with Mount Zion. This was the one place for the true worship of God.
19:2 *Egyptians against Egyptians.* The political anarchy of the Egyptians has religious roots: their many gods failed them.
19:3 *spirit of the Egyptians.* The principal key for understanding the world of ancient Egypt is the concept of order, or *ma'at.* When the spirit of the Egyptians was demoralized, they lost their sense of order and purpose. This would completely confuse and disarm any aggression and would cause economic and political upheaval.

7 See Ps 68:31; 72:10; Isa 16:1; Zep 3:10; Mal 1:11 **CHAPTER 19** **1** Jer 46:13; Eze 29; 30; Ps 18:10; 104:3; Ex 12:12; Jer 43:12 **2** Jdg 7:22; 1Sa 14:16,20; 2Ch 20:23 **3** Isa 8:19; 47:12 **4** Isa 20:4; Jer 46:26; Eze 29:19 **5** Jer 51:36; Eze 30:12 **6** 2Ki 19:24

And all the sown fields of the Nile
Will become dry, be blown away,
and be no more.
8 The fishermen will lament (cry out
in grief),
And all those who cast a hook into
the Nile will mourn,
And those who spread nets upon
the waters will languish.
9 Moreover, those who make linen
from combed flax
And those who weave white cloth
will be ashamed.
10 [Those who are] the pillars *and*
foundations *of Egypt* will be
crushed;
And all those who work for wages
will be grieved in soul.
11 The princes of Zoan are complete
fools;
The counsel of the Pharaoh's wisest
advisors has become stupid.
How can you say to Pharaoh,
"I am a son of the wise, a son of
ancient kings?"
12 Where then are your wise men?
Please let them tell you,
And let them understand what the
LORD of hosts
Has purposed against Egypt [if
they can].
13 The princes of Zoan have acted
like fools,
The princes of Memphis are deluded
[and entertain false hope];
Those who are the cornerstone of
her tribes
Have led Egypt astray.
14 The LORD has mixed a spirit of
distortion within her;
Her leaders have caused Egypt to
stagger in all that she does,
As a drunken man staggers in his
vomit.
15 There will be no work for Egypt
Which head or tail, [high] palm
branch or [low] bulrush, may do.

16 In that day the Egyptians will be-
come like [helpless] women, and they
will tremble and be frightened because
of the waving of the hand of the LORD
of hosts, which He is going to wave
over them.
17 The land of Judah [Assyria's ally]
will become a terror to the Egyptians;
everyone to whom Judah is mentioned
will be in dread of it, because of the
purpose of the LORD of hosts which He
is planning against Egypt.
18 In that day five cities in the land
of Egypt will speak the language of
[the Hebrews of] Canaan and swear
allegiance to the LORD of hosts. One
[of them] will be called the City of De-
struction.
19 In that day there will be an altar
to the LORD in the midst of the land of
Egypt, and a memorial stone to the
LORD near its border.
20 It will become a sign and a wit-
ness to the LORD of hosts in the land of
Egypt; for they will cry to the LORD be-
cause of oppressors, and He will send
them a Savior, a [Great] Defender, and
He will rescue them. [Judg 2:18; 3:9, 15]
21 And so the LORD will make Himself
known to Egypt, and the Egyptians
will know [heed, honor, and cherish]
the LORD in that day. They will even
worship with sacrifices [of animals]
and offerings [of produce]; they will
make a vow to the LORD and fulfill it.
22 The LORD will strike Egypt, strik-
ing but healing it; so they will return to
the LORD, and He will respond to them
and heal them.
23 In that day there will be a high-
way from Egypt to Assyria, and the
Assyrians will come into Egypt and

19:13 *Memphis.* Memphis was Egypt's ancient capital.

19:19 – 21 Worship — The prophets spoke of the future when the Gentile nations would come to know God and worship Him. Egypt is one of these nations for which there is a future mercy. The Egyptians will swear allegiance to the true God, institute extensive public worship of God, and become equal partners in the community of believers. This is a remarkable promise from our God, and one that is worth remembering in troubling political times.

9 1Ki 10:28; Pr 7:16 **11** Nu 13:22 **12** 1Co 1:20 **13** Jer 2:16 **14** 1Ki 22:22; Isa 29:10 **15** Isa 9:14 **16** Jer 51:30; Na 3:13; Isa 11:15 **18** Zep 3:9 **19** Ge 28:18; Ex 24:4; Jos 22:10,26,27 **20** Jos 4:20; 22:27 **21** Mal 1:11 **23** Isa 11:16

the Egyptians into Assyria; and the Egyptians will worship *and* serve [the LORD] with the Assyrians.
[24]In that day Israel will be the third *party* with Egypt and with Assyria [in a Messianic league], a blessing in the midst of the earth,
[25]whom the LORD of hosts has blessed, saying, "Blessed is Egypt My people, and Assyria the work of My hands, and Israel My heritage."

Prophecy about Egypt and Cush (Ancient Ethiopia)

20 IN THE year that the Tartan [the Assyrian commander in chief] came to Ashdod [in Philistia], when Sargon king of Assyria sent him and he fought against Ashdod and captured it,
[2]at that time the LORD spoke through Isaiah the son of Amoz, saying, "Go, untie the sackcloth from your hips and take your sandals off your feet." And he did so, walking around stripped [to his loincloth] and barefoot. [Mic 1:8]
[3]And the LORD said, "Even as My servant Isaiah has walked stripped and barefoot for three years as a sign and forewarning concerning Egypt and Cush (Ethiopia),
[4]in the same way the king of Assyria will lead away the Egyptian captives and the Cushite exiles, young and old, stripped and barefoot, even with buttocks uncovered—to the shame of Egypt.
[5]"Then they will be dismayed and ashamed because of Cush their hope and Egypt their boast.
[6]"So the inhabitants of this coastland [the Israelites and their neighbors] will say in that day, 'Look what has happened to those in whom we hoped *and* trusted and to whom we fled for help to be spared from the king of Assyria! But we, how will we escape [captivity and exile]?' "

God Commands That Babylon Be Taken

21 THE [MOURNFUL, inspired] oracle (a burden to be carried) concerning the Desert of the Sea (the seasonally flooded plains just south of Babylon):

As windstorms in the Negev (the
South) sweep through,
So it (God's judgment) comes from
the desert, from [the hostile
armies of] a terrifying land.
[2]A harsh vision has been shown
to me;
The treacherous one deals
treacherously, and the destroyer
destroys.
Go up, Elam! Lay siege, Media!
All the groaning [caused by
Babylon's ruthless oppressions]
I [the LORD] have brought to an
end. [Is 11:11; 13:17]
[3]Therefore [continues Isaiah]
my loins are filled with
anguish;
Pains have seized me like the
pains of a woman in
childbirth;
I am so bent *and* bewildered that
I cannot hear, I am so terrified
that I cannot see.

19:25 *My people . . . the work of My hands.* Historically, Egypt and Assyria were enemies. When they change and turn to the Lord (symbolic of all converted Gentiles), they will be healed (v. 22) and blessed by God.
20:2 *sackcloth.* Isaiah replaced the garb of spiritual mourning with the signs of being exiled into captivity.
20:3 *three years.* Three years means "involving three years," a minimum of 14 months, but possibly more.
20:6 *inhabitants of this coastland.* Coastland in this context could mean coast, country, or island. It probably refers to the nations, including Judah, bordering on the eastern shore of the Mediterranean Sea, who looked to Egypt to save them from Assyria.
21:2 *Elam . . . Media.* Elam, a major part of Persia, and Media were allied in 700 BC. Perhaps as a part of the Assyrian army (5:26), they helped to bring about the fall of Babylon in 689 BC, since they certainly did so in 539 BC (11:11; 13:17).

25 Ps 100:3; Isa 29:23; Hos 2:23; Eph 2:10 **CHAPTER 20** **1** 2Ki 18:17 **2** Zec 13:4; 1Sa 19:24; Mic 1:8,11 **3** Isa 8:18 **4** 2Sa 10:4; Isa 3:17; Jer 13:22; Mic 1:11 **5** 2Ki 18:21 **CHAPTER 21** **1** Zec 9:14 **2** Isa 33:1; Isa 13:17; Jer 49:34 **3** Isa 15:5; 16:11; Isa 13:8

[4]My mind reels, horror overwhelms
me;
The twilight I longed for has been
turned into fear *and* trembling
for me. [Dan 5:1–4]
[5]They set the table [for the doomed
banquet], they spread out the
cloth, they eat, they drink;
"Rise up, captains [of Belshazzar's
court], oil your shields [for battle,
for your enemy is at the
gates]!"
[6]This is what the Lord says to me,

"Go, station the lookout, let him
report what he sees.
[7]"When he sees a chariot,
horsemen in pairs,
A train of donkeys and a train of
camels,
Let him pay attention *and* listen
closely, very closely."

[8]And the lookout called *like* a lion,

"O Lord, I stand continually on the
watchtower by day,
And I am stationed every night at
my guard post.
[9]"Now look! Here comes a troop of
riders, horsemen in pairs."
And one said, "Fallen, fallen is
Babylon;
And all the carved images of her
gods are shattered on the
ground."
[10]O my threshed *people* [Judah, who
must be judged and trampled
down by Babylon], my afflicted
of the threshing floor.
What I have heard from the LORD
of hosts,
The God of Israel, I have [joyfully]
announced to you [that Babylon
is to fall].

Oracles about Edom and Arabia

[11]The [mournful, inspired] oracle
(a burden to be carried) concerning
Dumah (Edom):

Someone keeps calling to me from
Seir (Edom),
"Watchman, what is left of the
night [of Assyrian oppression]?
Watchman, what is left of
the night? [How long until
morning?]"
[12]The watchman says,
"The morning comes [only briefly],
but also [comes] the night [of
Babylonian oppression].
If you would ask [of me then], ask
[again, if Edom really wishes to
know];
Come back again."

[13]The [mournful, inspired] oracle
(a burden to be carried) concerning
Arabia:

In the thickets of Arabia you must
spend the night,
Caravans of Dedanites.
[14]Bring water for the thirsty
[Dedanites],
O inhabitants of the land of Tema
[in Arabia];
Meet the fugitive with bread.
[15]For they have fled from the
swords,
From the drawn sword, from the
bent bow
And from the press of battle *and*
grief of war.

[16]For the Lord has said this to me,
"Within a year, according to the years
of a hired man [who will work no lon-
ger than was agreed], all the splendor
of [the tribe of] Kedar will end;

21:4 *mind reels.* Isaiah saw that even a longed-for event can have terrible consequences in its wake. The judgment of God on Babylon would not be easy to witness.
21:7 *donkeys . . . camels.* The Persians, who overthrew Babylon in 539 BC, used donkeys and camels in their army.
21:11 *Watchman.* The watchman was the night patrol who kept watch on the city. The metaphor refers to the prophet Isaiah, who, as a guard on the walls, could see the dawn — the light of salvation — in the east before the others.
21:13 *Caravans of Dedanites.* The Dedanites may refer to the refugees (v. 15) from Dedan, which was about 90 miles southeast of Tema (v. 14).

4 Dt 28:67 **5** Da 5:5 **7** ver. 9 **8** Hab 2:1 **9** Jer 51:8; Rev 14:8; 18:2; Isa 46:1; Jer 50:2; 51:44 **10** Jer 51:33
11 1Ch 1:30; Jer 49:7,8; Eze 35:2; Ob 1 **13** Jer 49:28; 1Ch 1:9 **16** Isa 16:14; Ps 120:5; Isa 60:7

[17]and the remainder of the number of archers, the mighty men of the sons of Kedar, will be few; for the LORD, the God of Israel, has spoken."

The Valley of Vision

22 THE [MOURNFUL, inspired] oracle (a burden to be carried) concerning the Valley of Vision:

What is the matter with you now,
that you have all gone up to the housetops,
[2]You [Jerusalem] who were full of noise,
A tumultuous city, a joyous *and* exuberant city;
Your slain were not slain [in a glorious death] with the sword,
Nor did they die in battle.
[3]All your leaders have fled together [with your king],
And have been captured without the bow [which they had thrown away];
All of you who were found were taken captive together,
Though they had fled far away.
[4]Therefore I say, "Look away from me;
Let me weep bitterly.
Do not try to comfort me over the destruction of the daughter of my people."
[5]For the Lord GOD of hosts has a day of panic *and* of tumult, of trampling, of confusion
In the Valley of Vision,
A [day of] breaking down walls
And a crying [for help] to the mountain.
[6]Elam took up the quiver
With the chariots, infantry and horsemen;
And Kir uncovered the shield.
[7]And it came to pass that your choicest valleys were full of chariots,
And the horsemen took their fixed positions [in an offensive array] at the gate [of Jerusalem]. [2 Chr 32; Is 36]
[8]Then God removed the [protective] covering of Judah;
And in that day you looked to the weapons of the House of the Forest (Solomon's armory). [1 Kin 7:2; 10:17, 21]
[9]You saw that the breaches
In the wall of the City of David [the citadel of Zion] were many;
You collected [within the city's walls] the waters of the Lower Pool (Siloam).
[10]Then you counted the houses of Jerusalem
And you tore down the houses [to get materials] to fortify the city wall [by extending it].
[11]You also made a reservoir between the two walls
For the waters of the Old Pool,
But you did not look to its Maker,
Nor did you recognize Him who planned it long ago.
[12]Therefore in that day the Lord GOD of hosts called you to weeping, to mourning,
To shaving the head and to wearing sackcloth [in humiliation].
[13]Instead, there is joy and jubilation,
Killing of oxen and slaughtering of sheep,
Eating meat and drinking wine, *saying,*
"Let us eat and drink, for tomorrow we may die."
[14]But the LORD of hosts revealed Himself in my ears,
"This sin absolutely will not be forgiven you
Until you die," says the Lord GOD of hosts.

22:11 *reservoir between the two walls.* The defense of the city depended upon the availability of water within its walls. Hezekiah addressed this need by digging a tunnel beneath the city, connecting the lower pool in Jerusalem's southwestern valley with the old pool, the source of water in the eastern valley.

CHAPTER 22 **2** Isa 32:13 **4** Jer 4:19 **5** Isa 37:3; La 1:5 **6** Jer 49:35; Isa 15:1 **8** 1Ki 7:2; 10:17 **9** 2Ki 20:20; 2Ch 32:4 **11** Neh 3:16 **12** Joel 1:13; See Ezr 9:3; Isa 15:2; Mic 1:16 **13** Isa 56:12; 1Co 15:32 **14** Isa 5:9; 1Sa 3:14; Eze 24:13

15 For the Lord GOD of hosts says
this, "Go to this [contemptible]
steward,
To Shebna, who is in charge of the
royal household [but is building
himself a tomb worthy of a king,
and say to him],
16 'What business do you have here?
And whom do you have here,
That you have hewn out a tomb
here for yourself,
You who hew a sepulcher on the
height,
You who carve a resting place for
yourself in the rock?
17 'Listen carefully, the LORD is about
to hurl you away violently,
O man;
And He is about to grasp you
firmly
18 And roll you up tightly like a ball
And toss you into a vast country;
There you will die
And there your splendid chariots
will be,
You shame of your master's house.'
19 "I will depose you from your
office,
And you will be pulled down from
your position [of importance].
20 "Then it will come to pass in that
day
That I will summon My servant
Eliakim the son of Hilkiah.
21 "And I will clothe him with your
tunic [of distinction]
And tie your sash securely around
him.
I will entrust him with your
authority;
He will become a father to the
inhabitants of Jerusalem and to
the house of Judah.
22 "Then I will set on his shoulder the
key of the house of David;
When he opens no one will shut,
When he shuts no one will open.
23 "I will drive him *like* a peg in a
firm place,
And he will become a throne of
honor *and* glory to his father's
house.

24 "So they will hang on him all the
honor *and* glory [the complete respon-
sibility] of his father's house, offspring
and issue [of the family, high and low],
all the least of the articles, from the
bowls to all the jars.
25 "In that day," declares the LORD of
hosts, "the peg (Eliakim) that was driv-
en into the firm place will give way; it
will even break off and fall, and the
burden hanging on it will be cut off,
for the LORD has spoken."

The Fall of Tyre

23 THE [MOURNFUL, inspired]
oracle (a burden to be carried)
concerning Tyre:

Wail, O ships of Tarshish,
For *Tyre* is destroyed, without
house, without harbor;
It is reported to them from the land
of Cyprus (Kittim).
2 Be silent, you inhabitants of the
coastland,
You merchants of Sidon;
Your messengers crossed the sea
3 And *they were* on great waters.
The grain of the Shihor, the
harvest of the Nile River, was
Tyre's revenue;
And she was the market of
nations.
4 Be ashamed, O Sidon [mother-
city of Tyre, now like a widow
bereaved of her children];
For the sea speaks, the stronghold
of the sea, saying,
"I have neither labored nor given
birth [to children];
I have neither brought up young
men nor reared virgins."
5 When the report *reaches* Egypt,
They will be in agony at the report
about Tyre.

22:25 peg . . . be cut off. Even the firmly reliable Eliakim could not sustain the burden of government. Only Immanuel could do that (9:6–7).

23:1 *Tyre.* Tyre was besieged several times over a period of about 400 years before it was finally laid waste by Alexander the Great in 332 BC.

15 2Ki 18:37; Isa 36:3 **16** See 2Sa 18:18; Mt 27:60 **17** Est 7:8 **20** 2Ki 18:18 **22** Job 12:14 **23** Ezr 9:8
CHAPTER 23 **1** Jer 25:22; 47:4; Eze 26; 27; 28; Am 1:9; Zec 9:2,4; ver. 12 **3** Eze 27:3 **5** Isa 19:16

[6]Cross over to Tarshish [to seek
safety as exiles];
Wail, O inhabitants of the
coastland [of Tyre].
[7]Is this your jubilant *city*,
Whose origin dates back to
antiquity,
Whose feet used to carry her [far
away] to colonize distant places?
[8]Who has planned this against
Tyre, the bestower of crowns,
Whose merchants were princes,
whose traders were the honored
of the earth?
[9]The LORD of hosts has planned it,
to defile the pride of all beauty,
To bring into contempt *and*
humiliation all the honored of
the earth.
[10]Overflow your land like
[the overflow of] the Nile,
O Daughter of Tarshish;
There is no more restraint [on you
to make you pay tribute to Tyre].
[11]He has stretched out His hand over
the sea,
He has shaken the kingdoms;
The LORD has given a command
concerning Canaan to destroy
her strongholds *and* her
fortresses [like Tyre and Sidon].
[12]He has said, "You shall never
again exult [in triumph],
O crushed Virgin Daughter of
Sidon.
Arise, cross over to Cyprus; even
there you will find no rest."

[13]Now look at the land of the Chal-
deans (Babylonia)—this is the people
which was not; the Assyrians allocated
Tyre for desert creatures—they set up
their siege towers, they stripped its
palaces, they made it a ruin.

[14]Wail, O ships of Tarshish,
For your stronghold [of Tyre] is
destroyed.

[15]Now in that day Tyre will be forgot-
ten for seventy years, like the days of
one king. At the end of seventy years
it will happen to Tyre as in the prosti-
tute's song:

[16]Take a harp, walk around the city,
O forgotten prostitute;
Play the strings skillfully, sing
many songs,
That you may be remembered.

[17]It will come to pass at the end of sev-
enty years that the LORD will remem-
ber Tyre. Then she will return to her
prostitute's wages and will play the
[role of a] prostitute [by trading] with
all the kingdoms on the face of the
earth.
[18]But her commercial gain and her
prostitute's wages will be dedicated
to the LORD; it will not be treasured
or stored up, but her commercial gain
will become sufficient food and stately
clothing for those who dwell (minister)
in the presence of the LORD.

Judgment on the Earth

24 BEHOLD, THE LORD lays waste
to the earth, devastates it, twists
and distorts its face and scatters its
inhabitants.
[2]And the people will be like the
priest, the servant like his master, the
maid like her mistress, the buyer like
the seller, the lender like the borrower,
the creditor like the debtor [as God's

23:6 *Tarshish.* Tarshish is Tartessus in Spain and represents the most distant place to the ancient Israelites.
23:15 *seventy years.* Seventy years symbolizes a full measure of time, a lifetime.
23:18 *her prostitute's wages . . . dedicated to the LORD.* This was not a violation of God's command (Dt 23:18) which forbade bringing a harlot's pay (v. 17) to the temple. Tyre's destruction was part of the Lord's war against the unrighteous. The spoils would belong to Him as the Victor (Dt 2:35; Jos 6:17,19).
24:1 – 27:12 *Behold, the LORD.* The section describing the Lord's "burdens" against particular nations (chs. 13 – 23) is now placed in a larger framework that shows God's triumph over the entire earth for His elect. Chapter 24 focuses on God's overthrow of the corrupted earth; chapter 25 focuses on the responsive praise to His actions. Chapters 26 and 27 focus on God's efforts for His people.

7 Isa 22:2 **8** See Eze 28:2,12 **12** Rev 18:22; ver. 1 **13** Ps 72:9 **17** Rev 17:2 **18** Zec 14:20,21
CHAPTER 24 **2** Hos 4:9; Eze 7:12,13

impartial judgment of sin comes on all].

[3]The earth will be completely laid waste and utterly pillaged, for the LORD has spoken this word.

[4]The earth dries up and crumbles away, the world dries out and crumbles away, the exalted of the people of the earth fade away.

[5]The earth also is polluted by its inhabitants, because they have transgressed laws, violated statutes, and broken the everlasting covenant. [Gen 9:1–17; Deut 29:20]

[6]Therefore, a curse devours the earth, and those who live on it suffer the punishment of their guilt. Therefore, the inhabitants of the earth are burned [under the curse of God's wrath], and few people are left. [Rom 1:20]

[7]The new wine mourns,
The vine decays;
All the merry-hearted sigh *and* groan.
[8]The mirth of the timbrels (tambourines) ceases,
The noise of those who rejoice ends,
The joy of the harp ceases.
[9]They do not drink wine with a song;
Strong drink is bitter to those who drink it.
[10]The city of chaos is broken down;
Every house is shut up so that no one may enter.
[11]There is an outcry in the streets concerning the wine;
All jubilation is darkened,
The joy of the earth is banished.
[12]Horrible desolation is left in the city,
And the gate is battered into ruins.
[13]For so it will be in the midst of the earth among the peoples,
As the shaking of an olive tree,
As the gleanings when the grape harvest is over [and only a little of the fruit remains].
[14]They [who have escaped and remain] raise their voices, they shout for joy;
They rejoice from the [Mediterranean] Sea in the majesty of the LORD.
[15]Therefore honor *and* glorify the LORD in the east [in the region of light],
The name of the LORD, the God of Israel [honor His name],
In the coastlands *and* islands of the [Mediterranean] Sea.
[16]From the ends of the earth we hear songs, "Glory *and* honor to the Righteous One,"
But I say, "I waste away, I waste away. Woe to me!
The treacherous deal treacherously,
Indeed, the treacherous deal very treacherously."
[17]Terror and pit [of destruction] and snare
Confront you, O inhabitant of the earth.
[18]Then it will be that he who flees at the sound of terror will fall into the pit,
And he who comes up out of the pit will be caught in the snare;

24:4 *The earth dries up.* For a similar idea, see Romans 8:22.

24:5 *laws . . . statutes . . . covenant.* The usual language concerning a breach of the covenant is applied more generally to the wicked nations. Perhaps these words speak of that innate sense of right and wrong — the conscience — that God has given to all mankind, but which everyone violates (Ac 24:16; Ro 1:18 – 32).

24:14 – 16 *raise their voices.* Isaiah cannot join in the chorus of praise, because he, like Daniel (Da 7:28; 8:27), was too overwhelmed by the tragedy that was to come. It is impossible to tell whether the people who praised the Lord were faithful followers who had been oppressed by the treacherous leaders, or whether those who praised were the unfaithful leaders who were beginning to remember the Lord. There comes a time when the Lord does not wait any more, but He carries out the promised punishment for sinful behavior. Those who have trusted in Him will always find their souls secure, but that does not mean that they will not see dreadful sights or perhaps even be martyred for their faith.

5 Ge 3:17; Nu 35:33 **6** Mal 4:6 **7** Isa 16:8,9; Joel 1:10,12 **8** Jer 7:34; 16:9; 25:10; Eze 26:13; Hos 2:11; Rev 18:22 **13** Isa 17:5,6 **15** Mal 1:11 **16** Jer 5:11 **17** See Jer 48:43,44 **18** Ge 7:11; Ps 18:7

For the windows of heaven are opened, and the foundations of the earth tremble.
19 The earth is broken completely apart,
The earth is split apart,
The earth is shaken violently.
20 The earth reels back and forth like a drunkard
And sways like a shack;
Its transgression lies heavily upon it,
And it will fall and not rise again.
21 So it will happen in that day
That the LORD will visit *and* punish the host (fallen angels) of heaven on high,
And the kings of the earth on the earth. [1 Cor 15:25; Eph 3:10; 6:12]
22 They will be gathered together
As prisoners [are gathered] in a dungeon;
They will be shut up in prison,
And after many days they will be visited *and* punished. [Zech 9:11, 12; 2 Pet 2:4; Jude 6]
23 Then the full moon will be embarrassed and the sun ashamed,
For the LORD of hosts will reign on Mount Zion and in Jerusalem,
And *His* glory *and* brilliance will shine before His elders.

Song of Praise for God's Favor

25 O LORD, You are my God;
I will exalt You, I will praise *and* give thanks to Your name;
For You have done miraculous things,
Plans *formed* long, long ago, [fulfilled] with perfect faithfulness.
2 For You have made a city into a heap [of trash],
A fortified city into a ruin;
A palace of foreigners is no longer a city,
It will never be rebuilt.
3 Therefore a strong people will honor You;
Cities of terrible *and* violent nations will fear You.
4 For You have been a stronghold for the helpless,
A stronghold for the poor in his distress,
A shelter from the storm, a shade from the heat;
For the breath of tyrants
Is like a rainstorm *against* a wall.
5 Like heat in a dry land, You will subdue the noise of foreigners [rejoicing over their enemies];
Like heat in the shadow of a cloud, the song of the tyrants is silenced.

6 On this mountain [Zion] the LORD of hosts will prepare a lavish banquet for all peoples [to welcome His reign on earth],
A banquet of aged wines—choice pieces [flavored] with marrow,
Of refined, aged wines.
7 And on this mountain He will destroy the covering that is [cast] over all peoples,
And the veil [of death] that is woven *and* spread over all the nations.
8 He will swallow up death [and abolish it] for all time.
And the Lord GOD will wipe away tears from all faces,
And He will take away the disgrace of His people from all the earth;
For the LORD has spoken.
[1 Cor 15:26, 54; 2 Tim 1:10]

24:21 *that day.* "That day" is the day that the Lord will finally judge the whole world (Rev 20:11–15).

25:5 *tyrants.* The use of the term "tyrants" two times in verses 3–5 emphasizes divine judgment on the nations represented.

25:8 *wipe away tears.* When the first earth passes away and the tabernacle of God is among men, finally the whole creation will be as it should be, and God will tenderly wipe away the tears of his people (Rev 7:17; 21:4).

19 Jer 4:23 **20** Isa 19:14 **21** Ps 76:12 **23** Isa 13:10; 60:19; Eze 32:7; Joel 2:31; 3:15; Rev 19:4,6; Heb 12:22
CHAPTER 25 **1** Ex 15:2; Ps 98:1; Nu 23:19 **2** Isa 21:9; 23:13; Jer 51:37 **3** Rev 11:13 **4** Isa 4:6 **6** Isa 2:2,3; Pr 9:2; Mt 22:4; Da 7:14; Mt 8:11 **7** 2Co 3:15; Eph 4:18 **8** Hos 13:14; 1Co 15:54; Rev 7:17; 21:4

9 It will be said in that day,
"Indeed, this is our God for whom
we have waited that He would
save us.
This is the LORD for whom we have
waited;
Let us shout for joy and rejoice in
His salvation."
10 For the hand of the LORD will rest
on this mountain [Zion],
And Moab will be trampled down
in his place
As straw is trampled down in the
[filthy] water of a manure pile.
11 And Moab will spread out his
hands in the middle of the filth
As a swimmer spreads out *his
hands* to swim,
But *the Lord* will humiliate his
pride in spite of the [skillful]
movements of his hands.
12 The high fortifications of your
walls He will bring down,
Lay low, and cast to the ground, to
the dust.

Song of Trust in God's Protection

26 IN THAT day this song will be
sung in the land of Judah:
"We have a strong city;
He sets up salvation as walls and
ramparts.
2 "Open the gates, that the righteous
nation may enter,
The one that remains faithful *and*
trustworthy.
3 "You will keep in perfect *and*
constant peace *the one* whose
mind is steadfast [that is,
committed and focused on
You—in both inclination and
character],
Because he trusts *and* takes refuge
in You [with hope and confident
expectation].
4 "Trust [confidently] in the LORD
forever [He is your fortress, your
shield, your banner],
For the LORD GOD is an everlasting
Rock [the Rock of Ages].
5 "For He has thrown down the
[arrogant] ones who dwell on
high, the lofty *and* inaccessible
city;
He lays it low, He lays it low to the
ground, He hurls it to the dust.
6 "The foot will trample it,
Even the feet of the suffering, and
the steps of the helpless."

7 The way of the righteous [those in
right-standing with God—living
in moral and spiritual integrity]
is smooth *and* level;
O Upright One, make a level path
for the just *and* righteous.
8 Indeed, in the path of Your
judgments, O LORD,
We have waited expectantly for
You;
Your name, even Your memory, is
the desire *and* deep longing of
our souls.
9 In the night my soul longs for You
[O LORD],
Indeed, my spirit within me seeks
You diligently;
For [only] when Your judgments
are experienced on the earth
Will the inhabitants of the world
learn righteousness.
10 *Though* the wicked is shown
compassion *and* favor,
He does not learn righteousness;
In the land of uprightness he deals
unjustly,
And refuses to see the majesty of
the LORD.
11 *Though* Your hand is lifted up [to
strike], O LORD, the wicked do
not see it.

26:3 *peace.* The result of a settled faith in God is "perfect peace." Faith in God is the only thing that brings inner peace to man. One must come to the point of recognizing his own utter sinfulness and his deep need of a redeemer before he can find peace. Only when one is at peace with God can he have peace with others. Only a mind settled in God can tolerate the changing circumstances of life.

26:8 *waited.* Waiting for — or on — the Lord is a waiting with expectation. Perhaps one could describe it as the difference between waiting for

9 Ge 49:18; Titus 2:13; Ps 20:5 **12** Isa 26:5 **CHAPTER 26** **1** Isa 2:11; Isa 60:18 **2** Ps 118:19,20 **4** Isa 45:17 **5** Isa 25:12; 32:19 **7** Ps 37:23 **8** Isa 64:5 **9** Ps 63:6; SS 3:1 **10** Ecc 8:12; Rom 2:4; Ps 143:10 **11** Job 34:27; Ps 28:5; Isa 5:12

Let them see Your zeal for *Your* people and be put to shame;
Indeed, let the fire reserved for Your enemies consume them.
12 LORD, You will establish peace for us,
Since You have also performed for us all that we have done.
13 O LORD our God, other masters besides You have ruled over us;
But through You alone we confess Your name.
14 The [wicked] dead will not live [again], the spirits of the dead will not rise *and* return;
Therefore You have punished and destroyed them,
And You have wiped out every memory of them [every trace of them].
15 You have increased the nation, O LORD;
You have increased the nation, You are glorified;
You have extended all the borders of the land.
16 O LORD, they sought You in distress;
They managed only a prayerful whisper
When Your discipline was upon them.
17 As a woman with child approaches *the time* to give birth,
She is in pain *and* struggles and cries out in her labor,
So we were before You, O LORD.
18 We have been with child, we have twisted *and* struggled *in labor;*
We gave birth, as it seems, *only* to wind.
We could not accomplish salvation for the earth,
Nor were inhabitants of the world born.
19 Your dead will live;
Their dead bodies will rise.
You who lie in the dust, awake and shout for joy!
For your dew is a dew of [celestial] light [heavenly, supernatural],
And the earth will give birth to the spirits of the dead. [Ezek 37:11, 12]

20 Come, my people, enter your chambers
And shut your doors behind you;
Hide for a little while
Until the [LORD's] wrath is past.
21 Listen carefully, the LORD is about to come out of His [heavenly] place
To punish the inhabitants of the earth for their wickedness [their sin, their injustice, their wrongdoing];
The earth will reveal the [innocent] blood shed upon her
And will no longer cover her slain.

The Deliverance of Israel

27 IN THAT day the Lord will punish Leviathan the fleeing serpent
With His fierce and great and mighty sword [rescuing Israel from her enemy],
Even Leviathan the twisted serpent;
And He will kill the dragon who *lives* in the sea.

---

the arrival of an airplane with a loved one arriving, and the waiting one does at a traffic light. (For a similar idea, see 40:31.)
26:18 *gave birth . . . only to wind.* Even the faithful followers of the Lord cannot bring new life to the earth. Only God can regenerate the world and its inhabitants. The new life can come only through Jesus Christ, whose coming was still in the future at the time of Isaiah's writing.
26:21 *The earth will reveal the [innocent] blood.* In that day of judgment, there will be no unsolved murders, no injustice that is unrevealed.
27:1 *punish.* The punishment in this verse links it with 26:21; this verse is the climax of the preceding section. ***Leviathan.*** This creature was used to poetically describe various evil forces over which God has ultimate control and victory (Job 3:8; Ps 74:14). Eventually the Leviathan (Job 41:1) became a symbol for Satan, who is "the dragon, that old serpent" (Rev 20:2).

13 2Ch 12:8 **16** Hos 5:15 **17** Isa 13:8; Jn 16:21 **18** Ps 17:14 **19** Eze 37:1; Da 12:2 **20** Ex 12:22,23; Ps 30:5; Isa 54:7,8; 2Co 4:17 **21** Mic 1:3; Jude 14 **CHAPTER 27** **1** Ps 74:13,14; Isa 51:9; Eze 29:3; 32:2

2 In that day [it will be said of the
redeemed nation of Israel],
"A vineyard of wine, sing in praise
of it!
3 "I, the LORD, am its Keeper;
I water it every moment.
So that no one will harm it,
I guard it night and day.
4 "I have no wrath.
Should anyone give Me briars *and*
thorns in battle,
I would step on them, I would set
them all on fire.
5 "Or let him (Israel) cling to
My strength *and* rely on My
protection [My stronghold],
Let him make peace with Me,
Let him make peace with Me."
6 In the generations to come Jacob
will take root;
Israel will blossom and sprout,
And they will fill the surface of
the world with fruit. [Hos 14:1–6;
Rom 11:12]

7 Like the striking by Him who
has struck them, has He struck
them?
Or like the slaughter of His slain,
have they been slain?
8 You contended with them by exile,
by driving them away [from
Canaan];
He has expelled them with His
fierce wind on the day of the
east wind.
9 Therefore through this the
wickedness [the sin, the
injustice, the wrongdoing] of
Jacob (Israel) will be atoned for
and forgiven;
And this will be the full price [that
God requires] for taking away
his sin:
When Israel makes all the stones
of the [pagan] altars like
crushed chalk stones;
When the Asherim and the
incense altars will not
stand.
10 For the fortified city is isolated,
A settlement deserted and
abandoned like the desert;
There the calf will graze,
And there it will lie down and
feed on its branches.
11 When its branches are dry, they
are broken off;
The women come and make a fire
with them.
For they are not a people of
understanding,
Therefore He who made them
will not have compassion on
them,
And He who created them will not
be gracious to them.

12 In that day the LORD will thresh
[out His grain] from the flowing stream
of the River [Euphrates] to the Brook
of Egypt, and you will be gathered up
one by one, O sons of Israel.
13 It will come to pass in that day
that a great trumpet will be blown,
and those who were lost *and* perish-
ing in the land of Assyria and who
were scattered in the land of Egypt will
come and worship the LORD on the holy
mountain at Jerusalem. [Zech 14:16;
Matt 24:31; Rev 11:15]

27:2 *vineyard.* The vineyard is Israel (5:7; 27:6). The language of the vineyard is used frequently in Scripture. The good vines are planted or cared for by God and His servants. They are supposed to bear good fruit and be worthy of the care of the Master. Sometimes the fruit is bad, sometimes the servants are unfaithful, but the vines always belong to God (Mt 21:33–46; Mk 12:1–12; Lk 20:9–19).

27:3 *I, the LORD, am its Keeper ... water.* The "keeper" of the vineyard contrasts with the one who will lay waste, and watering it "every moment" contrasts with no "rain" (5:6).

27:12 *thresh ... gathered.* Beating and gathering are threshing terms where the grain is separated from the chaff. The grain is saved or "gathered," and the chaff is thrown away. Threshing can be accomplished by beating the grain heads with flails or driving a cart over the grain to separate the grain from the stalks and husks. The grain is then gathered in baskets and tossed in the air, where the wind blows away the chaff and bits of straw, and the ripe grain falls back down into the basket.

2 Isa 5:1; Ps 80:8; Jer 2:21 **3** Ps 121:4,5 **4** 2Sa 23:6; Isa 9:18 **5** Isa 25:4; Job 22:21 **6** Isa 37:31; Hos 14:5,6 **8** Job 23:6; Ps 6:1; Jer 10:24; 30:11; 46:28; 1Co 10:13; Ps 78:38 **10** See Isa 17:2; 32:14 **11** Dt 32:28; Isa 1:3; Jer 8:7; Dt 32:18; Isa 43:1,7; 44:2,21,24 **13** Isa 2:11; Mt 24:31; Rev 11:15

Ephraim's Captivity Predicted

28 WOE (JUDGMENT is coming) to [Samaria] the splendid crown of the drunkards of Ephraim,
And to the fading flower of its glorious beauty,
Which is at the head of the rich valley
Of those who are overcome with wine!
2 Listen carefully, the Lord has a strong and mighty *agent* [the Assyrian];
Like a tempest of hail, a disastrous storm,
Like a tempest of mighty overflowing waters,
He has cast it down to the earth with *His* hand.
3 The splendid crown of the drunkards of Ephraim is trampled by [the foreigners'] feet.
4 And the fading flower of its glorious beauty,
Which is at the head of the rich valley,
Will be like the early fig before the summer,
Which one sees,
And as soon as it is in his hand
He [greedily] swallows it [and so will the Assyrians rapidly devour Samaria, Israel's capital].
5 In that day the LORD of hosts will become a magnificent crown
And a glorious diadem to the [converted] remnant of His people,
6 A spirit of justice for him who sits in judgment [administering the law],
A strength to those who drive back the battle at the gate.
7 But even these reel with wine and stagger from strong drink:
The priest and the prophet reel with strong drink;
They are confused by wine, they stagger from strong drink;
They reel while seeing visions,
They stagger *when pronouncing* judgment.
8 For all the tables are full of filthy vomit, so that there is no place [that is clean.]

9 *They say* "To whom would He teach knowledge?
And to whom would He explain the message?
Those *just* weaned from milk?
Those *just* taken from the breast?
10 "For *He says,*
'Precept upon precept, precept upon precept,
Rule upon rule, rule upon rule,
Here a little, there a little.' "
11 Indeed, the LORD will teach this people [in a more humiliating way]
By [men with] stammering lips and a foreign tongue,
12 He who said to them, "This is the place of quiet, give rest to the weary,"
And, "This is the resting place," yet they would not listen.
13 Therefore the word of the LORD to them will be [merely monotonous repetitions]:
"Precept upon precept, precept upon precept,
Rule upon rule, rule upon rule,

28:1 *crown of the drunkards.* The crown on Ephraim's drunkards is part of a word picture (v. 3) contrasting the debasing actions of a drunkard with the crown of flowers, which was customary to wear at feasts. The incongruity of this image parallels God's view of the debauchery of the Israelites in the beautiful land He had given them.
28:5 *glorious diadem.* The crown of the Lord of Hosts, which is Himself, sits in true beauty on the remnant of His people. Unlike the fading beauty of the crown of flowers, the glorious crown will be a lasting beauty.
28:9 *Those just weaned.* A child was weaned between the ages of three and five, the time for elementary moral education, which is described in verse 10.
28:13 *stumble backward, and be broken, ensnared.* In keeping with their drunken habits, the people would not be able to hear the teaching of the Lord.

CHAPTER 28 **1** ver. 3; ver. 4 **2** Isa 30:30; Eze 13:11 **3** ver. 1 **4** ver. 1 **7** Pr 20:1; Hos 4:11; Isa 56:10,12 **9** Jer 6:10 **11** 1Co 14:21

Here a little, there a little."
That they may go and stumble
backward, and be broken,
ensnared, and taken captive.

Judah Is Warned

14 Therefore, hear the word of the
Lord, you arrogant men
Who rule this people who are in
Jerusalem!
15 Because you have said, "We have
made a covenant with death,
And with Sheol (the place of
the dead) we have made an
agreement,
When the overwhelming scourge
passes by, it will not reach us,
For we have made lies our
refuge and we have concealed
ourselves in deception."
16 Therefore the Lord God says this,

"Listen carefully, I am laying in
Zion a Stone, a tested Stone,
A precious Cornerstone for the
[secure] foundation, firmly placed.
He who believes [who trusts in,
relies on, and adheres to that
Stone] will not be disturbed
or give way [in sudden panic].
[Ps 118:22; Matt 21:42; Acts 4:11;
Rom 9:33; Eph 2:20; 1 Pet 2:4–6]
17 "I will make justice the measuring
line
And righteousness the mason's
level;
Then hail will sweep away the
refuge of lies
And waters will flood over the
secret [hiding] place.
18 "Your covenant with death will be
annulled,
And your agreement with Sheol
(the place of the dead) will not
stand;
When the overwhelming scourge
passes through,
Then you will become its
trampling ground.
19 "As often as it passes through, it
will seize you;
For morning after morning it will
pass through, by day and by
night,
And it will be sheer terror to
understand what it means."
20 For the bed is too short to stretch
out on,
And the blanket is too narrow
to wrap around oneself [and
likewise all their preparations
are inadequate].
21 For the Lord will rise up as at
Mount Perazim,
He will be stirred up as in the
Valley of Gibeon,
To do His work, His unusual *and*
incredible work,
And to accomplish His work,
His extraordinary work.
[2 Sam 5:20; 1 Chr 14:16]
22 Now do not carry on as scoffers,
Or the bands which bind you will
be made stronger;
For I have heard from the Lord
God of hosts [a decree]
Of decisive destruction on all the
earth.
23 Listen and hear my voice;
Listen carefully and hear my
words.
24 Does the farmer plow all day to
plant seed?
Does he *continually* dig furrows
and harrow his ground [after it
is prepared]?
25 When he has leveled its surface,
Does he not sow [the seed of] dill
and scatter cumin,
And plant wheat in rows,

28:14 *arrogant*. The arrogant, or scoffers, are worse than "fools." Beyond choosing what is bad, they despise what is good (Ps 1:1).
28:16 *precious Cornerstone*. The apostles identified the cornerstone as Jesus Christ (1Pe 2:4–6).
28:20 *bed . . . blanket*. The word picture of the short bed and inadequate blanket is an illustration of the inadequacy of any security that is not based on a relationship with the Living God as He has outlined it in Scripture.

15 Am 2:4 **16** Ge 49:24; Ps 118:22; Mt 21:42; Ac 4:11; Ro 9:33; 10:11; Eph 2:20; 1Pe 2:6-8 **17** ver. 15 **21** 2Sa 5:20; 1Ch 14:11; Jos 10:10,12; 2Sa 5:25; 1Ch 14:16; La 3:33 **22** Isa 10:22; Dan 9:27

And barley in its [intended] place
and rye within its border?
26 For his God instructs [him
correctly] and teaches him
properly.
27 For dill is not threshed with a
sharp threshing sledge,
Nor is a cartwheel rolled over
cumin;
But dill is beaten out with a staff,
and cumin with a rod.
28 Bread *grain* is crushed fine,
Indeed, the farmer does not
continue to thresh it forever.
Because the wheel of his cart and
his horses *eventually* damage it,
He does not thresh it longer.
29 This also comes from the LORD of
hosts,
Who has made His counsel
wonderful and His wisdom
great.

Jerusalem Is Warned

29 WOE (JUDGMENT is coming)
to Ariel, to Ariel, the city
where David [once] camped!
Add yet another year; let the feasts
run their course [but only one
year more].
2 Then I will harass Ariel,
And she will be a *city of* mourning
and lamenting (crying out in
grief)
Yet she will be like an Ariel [an
altar hearth] to Me.
3 I will camp against you and
encircle you,
And I will hem you in with siege
works,
And I will raise fortifications
against you.
4 Then you [Jerusalem] will be
brought low,
You will speak from the earth,
And from the dust where you lie
face down
Your muffled words *will come.*
Your voice will also be like that of
a spirit from the earth [like one
produced by a medium],
And your speech will whisper *and*
squeak from the dust.
5 But the multitude of your enemies
[that assault you] will become
like fine dust,
And the multitude of the tyrants
like the chaff which blows away;
And it will happen in an instant,
suddenly [that your enemy is
destroyed].
6 You will be punished by the LORD
of hosts with thunder and
earthquake and great noise,
With whirlwind and tempest and
the flame of a consuming fire.
7 And the multitude of all the
nations that fight against Ariel
(Jerusalem),
Even all who fight against her and
her stronghold, and who distress
her,
Will be like a dream, a vision of
the night.
8 It will be as when a hungry man
dreams
That he is eating,
But when he awakens, his hunger
is not satisfied;

28:27 ***dill . . . threshing sledge.*** Dill cannot be threshed with a sledge. The cart and sledge are too large for such a fine seed as dill and cumin (27:12).
28:29 ***made His counsel wonderful.*** The wisdom that the farmer uses to tend his crops comes from God, the source of all good counsel.
29:1 ***Ariel.*** Ariel probably means "altar" (Eze 43:15 – 16). The destruction and bloodshed in Jerusalem would make the city appear like an altar. The repetition of the term *Ariel* indicates the Lord's sorrow over the state to which His city had fallen. ***where David [once] camped.*** David made Jerusalem his capital and planned the temple that Solomon later built in that city. These words show God's continuing love for His servant David.
29:7 ***like a dream.*** No city has suffered desolation and later been rebuilt like Jerusalem. One final time the fires of God's wrath will be allowed to burn on the City of Peace. God's eternal purpose will bring the city to its knees. Judgment is God's unwilling work. He never allows the fires of discipline to punish His own for no reason. When His disciplines have accomplished His task, peace is sure to follow.

29 Ps 92:5; Jer 32:19 **CHAPTER 29** **1** Eze 43:15,16; 2Sa 5:9 **4** Isa 8:19 **5** Isa 25:5; Job 21:18; Isa 17:13; Isa 30:13 **6** Isa 28:2; 30:30 **7** Isa 37:36; Job 20:8 **8** Ps 73:20

Or as when a thirsty man dreams
That he is drinking,
But when he awakens, in fact, he
is faint
And his thirst is not quenched.
So will the multitude of all the
nations be
Who fight against Mount Zion.

9 Stop *and* take some time and
wonder [at this prophecy],
Blind yourselves and be blinded [at
its fulfillment by your spiritual
incompetence].
They are drunk, but not from wine;
They stagger, but not from strong
drink.
10 For the LORD has poured over you
a spirit of deep sleep.
He has closed your eyes, [you who
are] the prophets;
And He has covered your heads,
[you who are] the seers.

11 The entire vision [of all these
things] will be to you like the words of
a scroll that is sealed, which they give
to one who can read, saying, "Read
this, please," he shall say, "I cannot,
for it is sealed."
12 Then the book will be given to the
one who cannot read, saying, "Read
this, please." And he will say, "I cannot
read."
13 Then the Lord said,

"Because this nation approaches
[Me only] with their words
And honors Me [only] with their
lip service,
But they remove their hearts far
from Me,
And their reverence for Me is
a tradition that is learned *by
rote* [without any regard for its
meaning],
14 Therefore, listen carefully, I
will again do marvelous *and*
amazing things with this people,
wonderful and astonishing
things;
And the wisdom of their wise men
will perish,
And the understanding of their
discerning men will be hidden."
15 Woe (judgment is coming) to those
who [try to] deeply hide their
plans from the LORD,
Whose deeds are *done* in a dark
place,
And who say, "Who sees us?" or
"Who knows us?"
16 You turn *things* upside down [with
your perversity]!
Shall the potter be considered
equal with the clay,
That the thing that is made would
say to its maker, "He did not
make me";
Or the thing that is formed say to
him who formed it, "He has no
understanding"?

Blessing after Discipline

17 Is it not yet a very little while
Until Lebanon will be turned into
a fertile field,
And the fertile field regarded as a
forest?
18 On that day the deaf will hear the
words of a book,
And out of *their* gloom and
darkness the eyes of the blind
will see [the words of the book].
19 The afflicted also will increase
their joy in the LORD,
And the needy of mankind will
rejoice *and* celebrate in the Holy
One of Israel.

29:17 *Lebanon . . . fertile field.* This is a statement of sharp changes. Lebanon was a land of forests. As valuable as a fertile field was, a forest was even more valuable in Israel and Judah, which did not have large stands of trees suitable for lumber. It would indicate some major economic and physical changes for Lebanon to become a field and for a fertile field to be as valuable as a forest.
29:19 *needy . . . rejoice.* God always notices the poor and commands His people to do likewise. The poor and the humble are particularly vulnerable to exploitation, and God in His justice does not forget this when He is dealing with disobedient leaders.

9 See Isa 28:7,8; Isa 51:21 **10** Ro 11:8; Ps 69:23; Isa 6:10; 1Sa 9:9 **11** Isa 8:16; Da 12:4; Rev 5:1-5,9 **13** Eze 33:31; Mt 15:8,9; Mk 7:6,7; Col 2:22 **14** Hab 1:5; Jer 49:7; Ob 8; 1Co 1:19 **15** Isa 30:1; Ps 94:7 **16** Isa 45:9; Ro 9:20 **17** Isa 32:15 **18** Isa 35:5 **19** Isa 61:1; Jas 2:5

20 For the tyrant will come to an end
and the scorner will be finished,
Indeed all who are intent on doing
evil will be cut off—
21 Those who cause a person to be
condemned with a [false] word,
And lay a trap for him who
upholds justice at the [city] gate,
And defraud the one in the right
with meaningless arguments.

22 Therefore, the LORD, who redeemed
Abraham [from paganism] says this,
concerning the house of Jacob (Israel):

"Jacob will not be ashamed, nor
will his face turn pale [with
disappointment because of his
children's degenerate behavior];
23 For when he sees his children, the
work of My hands, in his midst,
They will sanctify My Name;
They will sanctify the Holy One of
Jacob
And will stand in awe *and* reverent
fear of the God of Israel.
24 "Those who err in mind will know
the truth,
And those who criticize *and*
murmur discontentedly will
accept instruction.

Judah Warned against Egyptian Alliance

30 "WOE (JUDGMENT is
coming) to the rebellious
children," declares the LORD,
"Who carry out a plan, but not
Mine,
And make an alliance [by pouring
out a libation], but not of My
Spirit,
In order to add sin to sin;
2 Who proceed down to Egypt
Without consulting Me,
To take refuge in the stronghold of
Pharaoh
And to take shelter in the shadow
of Egypt!
3 "Therefore the safety *and*
protection of Pharaoh will be
your shame
And the refuge in the shadow of
Egypt, your humiliation *and*
disgrace.
4 "For his princes are at Zoan
And his ambassadors arrive at
Hanes [in Egypt].
5 "All will be ashamed because of
a people (the Egyptians) who
cannot benefit them,
Who are not a help or benefit, but
a shame and also a disgrace."

6 A [mournful, inspired] oracle (a
burden to be carried) concerning the
beasts of the Negev (the South):

Through a land of trouble and
anguish,
From where *come* lioness and lion,
viper and [fiery] flying serpent,
They carry their riches on the
shoulders of young donkeys
And their treasures on the humps
of camels,
To a people (Egyptians) who
cannot benefit them.
7 For Egypt's help is worthless and
good for nothing.
Therefore, I have called her
"Rahab Who Has Been
Exterminated."
8 Now, go, write it on a tablet before
them
And inscribe it on a scroll,
So that it may serve in the time to
come
As a witness [against them]
forevermore.

29:21 *with a [false] word ... lay a trap ... meaningless arguments.* The central issue in this passage is justice. The evil ones miscarry justice with "a word" or false testimony, "trap" through legal technicalities, and win cases with empty words or lies and clever arguments that obscure true justice.

30:1 *Woe.* This is the fourth woe. The rebellious children are Hezekiah's advisers. To the sin of injustice, they add the sin of devising plans independently of God.

30:4 *Zoan ... Hanes.* Zoan, which was in the Delta, was the capital of Egypt at this time (19:11 – 13). Hanes was 50 miles south of Cairo.

20 Isa 28:14,22; Mic 2:1 **21** Am 5:10,12; Pr 28:21 **22** Jos 24:3 **23** Isa 19:25; 45:11; 60:21; Eph 2:10 **24** Isa 28:7
CHAPTER 30 **1** Isa 29:15; Dt 29:19 **2** Isa 31:1; Nu 27:21; Jos 9:14; 1Ki 22:7; Jer 21:2; 42:2,20 **3** Isa 20:5; Jer 37:5,7
4 Isa 19:11 **5** Jer 2:36 **6** Isa 57:9; Hos 8:9; 12:1; Dt 8:15 **7** Jer 37:7; ver. 15 **8** Hab 2:2

9 For this is a rebellious people,
lying sons,
Sons who refuse to listen to
The law *and* instruction of the
LORD;
10 Who say to the seers, "You must
not see *visions from God*";
And to the prophets, "You must
not prophesy to us what is right!
Speak to us pleasant things *and*
smooth words,
Prophesy [deceitful] illusions [that
we will enjoy].
11 "Get out of the [true] way, turn
aside from the path [of God],
Stop bothering us with the Holy
One of Israel."

12 Therefore, the Holy One of Israel says
this,

"Because you have refused *and*
rejected this word [of Mine]
And have put your trust in
oppression and guile, and have
relied on them,
13 Therefore this wickedness
[this sin, this injustice, this
wrongdoing] will be to you
Like a crack [in a wall] about to
fall,
A bulge in a high wall,
Whose collapse comes suddenly in
an instant,
14 "Whose collapse is like the
smashing of a potter's jar,
Crushed so savagely
that there cannot be found among
its pieces a potsherd [large
enough]
To take [coals of] fire from a
fireplace,
Or to scoop water from a cistern."

15 For the Lord GOD, the Holy One of
Israel has said this,

"In returning [to Me] and rest you
shall be saved,
In quietness and confident trust is
your strength."
But you were not willing,
16 And you said, "No! We will flee on
horses!"
Therefore you will flee [from your
enemies]!
And [you said], "We will ride on
swift horses!"
Therefore those who pursue you
shall be swift.
17 A thousand *of you will flee* at the
threat of one *man;*
You will flee at the threat of five,
Until you are left like a flag on the
top of a mountain,
And like a signal on a hill.

God Is Gracious and Just

18 Therefore the LORD waits
[expectantly] *and* longs to be
gracious to you,
And therefore He waits on high to
have compassion on you.
For the LORD is a God of justice;
Blessed (happy, fortunate) are
all those who long for Him
[since He will never fail them].
[John 14:3, 27; 2 Cor 12:9;
Heb 12:2; 1 John 3:16; Rev 3:5]

19 O people in Zion, inhabitant in Je-
rusalem, you will weep no longer. He
will most certainly be gracious to you
at the sound of your cry for help; when
He hears it, He will answer you.
20 Though the Lord gives you the
bread of adversity and the water of
oppression, yet your Teacher will no

30:15 *confident trust.* A quiet, patient trust in God provides more strength for a follower of God than any alliance with any other person or system. When danger threatens, it is difficult not to look for ways to use one's own strength. It is also difficult to maintain inward composure and not trust in external sources of help. Even if we cannot imagine how we can be helped, if we are trusting God, we can have confidence and therefore have peace that He will not forsake us in our hour of need. God may use our strength or the help of others, but, when we turn to God first, we can learn which resources, if any, are the ones He wants us to use. When God is first, then our decisions are wise.

9 Dt 32:20; Isa 1:4 **10** Jer 11:21; Am 2:12; Mic 2:6; 1Ki 22:13; Mic 2:11 **13** Ps 62:3; Isa 29:5 **14** Ps 2:9; Jer 19:11 **15** Isa 7:4; Mt 23:37 **17** Lev 26:8; Dt 28:25; Jos 23:10 **18** Ps 2:12; 34:8; Pr 16:20; Jer 17:7 **19** Isa 65:9 **20** 1Ki 22:27; Ps 127:2; Ps 74:9; Am 8:11

longer hide Himself, but your eyes will [constantly] see your Teacher.

21 Your ears will hear a word behind you, "This is the way, walk in it," whenever you turn to the right or to the left.

22 And you will defile your carved images overlaid with silver, and your cast images plated with gold. You will scatter them like a bloodstained *cloth*, and will say to them, "Be gone!"

23 Then He will give you rain for the seed with which you sow the ground, and bread [grain] from the produce of the ground, and it will be rich and plentiful. In that day your livestock will graze in large *and* roomy pastures.

24 Also the oxen and the young donkeys that work the ground will eat salted fodder, which has been winnowed with shovel and pitchfork.

25 On every lofty mountain and on every high hill there will be streams of water on the day of the great slaughter (the day of the LORD), when the towers fall [and all His enemies are destroyed].

26 The light of the full moon will be like the light of the sun, and the light of the sun will be seven times *brighter*, like the light of seven days [concentrated in one], in the day the LORD binds up the fracture of His people and heals the wound He has inflicted [because of their sins].

27 Now look, the name of the LORD
comes from far away,
Burning with His anger, and
heavy with smoke;
His lips are full of indignation,
And His tongue is like a
consuming fire.

28 His breath is like an overflowing
river,
Which reaches to the neck,
To sift the nations back and forth
in a sieve [of disaster],
And *to put* in the jaws of the
peoples the bridle which leads
to ruin.

29 You will have a song as in the
night when a holy feast is kept,
And joy of heart as when one
marches [in procession] with a
flute,
To go to the [temple on the]
mountain of the LORD, to the
Rock of Israel.

30 And the LORD will make His
majestic voice heard,
And show the descending of His
arm [striking] in [His] fierce
anger,
And in the flame of a devouring
fire,
In the crashing sound *of heavy*
rain, cloudburst, and hailstones.

31 For at the voice of the LORD the
Assyrians will be terrified,
When He strikes [them] with the
rod.

32 And every blow of the rod of
punishment,
Which the LORD will lay on them,
Will be to *the music of Israel's*
tambourines and lyres;
And in battles, brandishing
weapons, He will fight Assyria.

33 For Topheth [in Hinnom] has long
been ready;
Indeed, it has been prepared for
the [Assyrian] king.
He has made it deep and wide,
A pit of fire with plenty of wood;

30:23 – 24 ***give you rain.*** The promises that were part of the original Mosaic covenant were in force again. Blessing would extend from field to flock (Dt 28:11 – 12).

30:30 ***descending of His arm.*** The strong arm of God had delivered the Israelites from Egypt. Now His arm would descend in judgment (Ex 6:6).

30:33 ***Topheth.*** Topheth was a place where Judah made human sacrifices to the heathen god Molech. The prophet uses it as a picture of God's vengeance on the wicked. He is not picturing temporal punishment, but everlasting destruction. This punishment will be in a place that is "deep" or inescapable. Then Isaiah draws the picture of the punishment by fire in hell. Some claim that the fire is symbolic, but it should be remembered that the reality is always greater than the symbol. The bliss of the righteous cannot be fully comprehended, and neither can the terror that awaits the wicked.

21 Jos 1:7 **22** 2Ch 31:1; Isa 31:7; Hos 14:8 **23** Mt 6:33; 1Ti 4:8 **25** Isa 2:14,15 **26** Isa 60:19,20 **28** Isa 11:4; Isa 8:8; Isa 37:29 **29** Isa 2:3 **30** Isa 29:6; Isa 28:2 **31** Isa 37:36; Isa 10:5,24 **32** Isa 11:15 **33** Jer 7:31

The breath of the LORD, like a river
of brimstone (blazing sulfur),
kindles *and* fans it. [Jer 7:31, 32;
Matt 5:22; 25:41]

Look Not to Egypt but to God

31 WOE (JUDGMENT is coming)
to those who go down to Egypt
for help,
Who rely on horses
And trust in chariots because they
are many,
And in horsemen because they are
very strong,
But they do not look to the Holy
One of Israel, nor seek *and*
consult the LORD!
2 Yet He is also wise and will bring
disaster,
And does not retract His words,
But will arise against the house of
evildoers
And against the helpers of those
who do evil.
3 Now the Egyptians are men and
not God,
And their horses are flesh and not
spirit;
And the LORD will stretch out His
hand,
And he (Egypt) who helps will
stumble,
And he (Judah) who is helped will
fall,
And all of them will perish
together.

4 For so the LORD says to me,

"As the lion or the young lion
growls over his prey,
And though a large group of
shepherds is called out against
him
He will not be terrified at their
voice nor cringe at their noise,
So the LORD of hosts will come
down to wage war on Mount
Zion and on its hill."
5 Like flying birds, so will the LORD
of hosts protect Jerusalem;
He will protect and save it,
He will pass over and rescue it.

6 Return to Him from whom you
have so deeply defected, O sons of
Israel.
7 For in that day every man will reject
and throw away his idols of silver and
his idols of gold [in disgust], which
your own hands have sinfully made
for you.

8 Then the Assyrian will fall by a
sword not of man,
And a sword not of man will
devour him.
And he will flee from the sword [of
God],
And his young men will become
forced labor.
9 "His rock [his stronghold] will
pass away because of panic,
And his princes will be terrified
at the [sight of the battle]
standard,"
Declares the LORD, whose fire is
in Zion and whose furnace is in
Jerusalem.

The Glorious Future

32 BEHOLD, A King will reign in
righteousness,
And princes will rule with justice.
2 Each [one of them] will be like a
hiding place from the wind
And a shelter from the storm,
Like streams of water in a dry land,

31:1 ***Woe.*** The fifth woe reaffirms the fourth woe (30:1–33). It, too, was addressed to those who replace faith in the Lord with reliance on Egypt. **31:2** ***house of evildoers ... helpers.*** This "house" refers to Judah, and their "helpers" refer to Egypt. **31:7** ***that day.*** "That day" refers to the day when God will judge the rebellious (24:21; 26:1). God had judged nations from time to time over the ages (Canaan, Egypt, Babylon, Israel, etc.), but the final day of judgment when everything will be made new is still in the future (Rev 20:11–15). **32:1** ***Behold.*** The fifth woe concludes with a prophecy about leadership and its effects. ***a King will reign in righteousness.*** The prophecy concerning this king is fulfilled in the Lord Jesus Christ (7:14; 9:1–7; 11:1–5; 28:16; Jn 10:11). ***princes.*** The princes are Jesus' shepherds (1Pe 5:2–4).

CHAPTER 31 **1** Isa 30:2; Ps 20:7; Da 9:13 **2** Nu 23:19 **4** Am 3:8 **5** Dt 32:11 **7** Isa 2:20; 1Ki 12:30 **8** 2Ki 19:35,36 **9** Isa 37:37 **CHAPTER 32** **1** Ps 45:1 **2** Isa 4:6

Like the shade of a huge rock in
a parched *and* weary land [to
those who turn to them].
[3]Then the eyes of those who see
will not be blinded,
And the ears of those who hear
will listen attentively.
[4]The heart (mind) of those who
act impulsively will discern the
truth,
And the tongue of the stammerers
will hurry to speak clearly.
[5]The fool (the good-for-nothing)
will no longer be called noble,
Nor the rogue said to be generous.
[6]For the fool speaks nonsense,
And his heart (mind) plans
wickedness:
To practice ungodliness and to
speak error concerning the
LORD,
To keep the craving of the hungry
unsatisfied
And to deprive the thirsty of drink.
[7]As for the rogue, his weapons are
evil;
He conceives wicked plans
To ruin the poor with lies,
Even when the plea of the needy
one is just *and* right.
[8]But the noble man conceives noble
and magnificent things;
And he stands by what is noble
and magnificent.

[9]Rise up, you women who are
carefree,
And hear my voice,
You confident *and* unsuspecting
daughters!
Listen to what I am saying.
[10]In little more than a year
You will tremble [with anxiety],
you unsuspecting *and*
complacent women;
For the vintage has ended,
And the harvest will not come.
[11]Tremble, you women who are
carefree;
Tremble with fear, you complacent
ones!
Strip, undress and wear *sackcloth*
on your waist [in grief],
[12]Beat your breasts [in mourning]
for the beautiful fields, for the
fruitful vine,
[13]For the land of my people growing
over with thorns and briars—
Yes, [mourn] for all the houses of
joy in the joyous city.
[14]For the palace has been
abandoned, the populated city
deserted;
The hill [of the city] and the
watchtower have become caves
[for wild animals] forever,
A delight for wild donkeys, a
pasture for flocks,
[15]Until the Spirit is poured out upon
us from on high,
And the wilderness becomes a
fertile field,
And the fertile field is valued as a
forest. [Ps 104:30; Ezek 36:26, 27;
39:29; Zech 12:10]
[16]Then justice will dwell in the
wilderness,
And righteousness will live in the
fertile field.
[17]And the effect of righteousness
will be peace,
And the result of righteousness
will be quietness and confident
trust forever.
[18]Then my people will live in a
peaceful surrounding,
And in secure dwellings and in
undisturbed resting places.
[19]But it will hail, when the forest
comes down,
And the [capital] city will fall in
utter humiliation.
[20]Blessed (happy, fortunate) are you
who cast your seed upon all
waters [when the river overflows
its banks and irrigates the land],
You who allow the ox and the
donkey to roam freely.

32:9 – 11 *carefree.* The word "carefree" has connotations of "trust," as one who has taken refuge, or who is secure and without care. These women were complacent, but it was a false security.

sackcloth. Mourning women removed their clothing and wore sackcloth around their waists (Ge 37:34).

3 Isa 29:18 **9** Am 6:1 **13** Hos 9:6; Isa 22:2 **14** Isa 27:10 **15** Joel 2:28; Isa 29:17 **17** Jas 3:18 **19** Isa 30:30; Zec 11:2 **20** Isa 30:24

The Judgment of God

33 WOE (JUDGMENT is coming) to you, O destroyer,
You who were not destroyed,
And he who is treacherous,
while *others* did not deal
treacherously with him.
As soon as you finish destroying,
you will be destroyed;
As soon as you stop dealing
treacherously, *others* will deal
treacherously with you.
2 O LORD, be gracious to us; we have
waited [expectantly] for You.
Be the arm of Your servants every
morning [that is, their strength
and their defense],
Our salvation also in the time of
trouble.
3 At the sound of the tumult, the
peoples flee;
At the lifting up of Yourself
nations scatter.
4 Your spoil [of Israel's foe] is
gathered [by the people of
Jerusalem] as the caterpillar
gathers;
As locusts swarming so people
swarm on it.
5 The LORD is exalted, for He dwells
on high;
He has filled Zion with justice and
righteousness.
6 And He will be the security *and*
stability of your times,
A treasure of salvation, wisdom
and knowledge;
The fear of the LORD is your
treasure.
7 Now look, their brave men shout
outside;
The ambassadors [seeking a
treaty] of peace weep bitterly.
8 The highways are deserted, the
traveler has ceased [to appear].
The enemy has broken the
covenant, he has rejected the
cities,
He has no regard for [any] man.
9 The land mourns and dries out,
Lebanon is shamed and [its lush
foliage] withers;
Sharon is like a desert plain,
And Bashan and [Mount] Carmel
shake off *their leaves*.
10 "Now I will arise," says the LORD.
"Now I will be exalted; now I will
be lifted up.
11 "You have conceived dried grass,
you will give birth to stubble;
My breath is a fire that will
consume you.
12 "The peoples will be burned to lime,
Like thorns cut down which are
burned in the fire.

13 "You who are far away, hear what
I have done;
And you who are near,
acknowledge My might."
14 The sinners in Zion are terrified;
Trembling has seized the godless.
[They cry] "Who among us can
live with the consuming fire?
Who among us can live with
everlasting burning?"
15 He who walks righteously and
speaks with integrity,
Who rejects gain from fraud *and*
from oppression,
Who shakes his hand free from
the taking of bribes,
Who stops his ears from hearing
about bloodshed
And shuts his eyes to avoid
looking upon evil;

33:1 *Woe.* The sixth woe differs from the others in that it is addressed to Assyria, not to Judah. By focusing exclusively on Assyria's defeat and Judah's salvation, the prophecy magnifies Judah's exalted King.
33:3 *lifting up of Yourself.* This passage refers to an exaltation of the heavenly King (vv. 5,10) as He rises to demonstrate His glory and vindicate His justice.
33:4 *spoil.* The plunder, or "spoil," of God's war with His enemies belongs to the Lord, the true Victor (23:18; 34:2).
33:9 *Sharon ... Bashan.* Sharon was on the western coastal plain, and Bashan was on the east side of the Jordan.
33:15 *walks righteously.* For a similar description of the person who can approach the Holy One, see Psalm 1:1–2; 15:2; Galatians 5:22–25; and Ephesians 5:1–2.

CHAPTER 33 **1** Isa 21:2; Hab 2:8; Rev 13:10 **2** Isa 25:9 **5** Ps 97:9 **7** 2Ki 18:18,37 **8** Jdg 5:6; 2Ki 18:14-17 **9** Isa 24:4 **10** Ps 12:5 **11** Ps 7:14; Isa 59:4 **12** Isa 9:18 **13** Isa 49:1 **15** Ps 15:2; 24:4; 119:37

16 He will dwell on the heights,
His place of defense will be the
fortress of rocks,
His bread will be given him;
His water will be permanent.

17 Your eyes will see the King in His
beauty;
They will see a far-distant land.
18 Your mind will meditate on the
terror [asking]:
"Where is he who counts?
Where is he who weighs [the
tribute]?
Where is he who counts the
towers?"
19 You will no longer see the fierce
and insolent people,
A people of unintelligible speech
which no one comprehends,
Of a strange *and* stammering
tongue which no one
understands.
20 Look upon Zion, the city of
our appointed feasts *and*
observances;
Your eyes will see Jerusalem, a
undisturbed settlement,
A tent which will not be taken
down;
Not one of its stakes will ever be
pulled up,
Nor any of its ropes be severed.
21 But there the mighty *and*
magnificent LORD will be for us
A place of broad rivers and
streams,
Where no oar-driven boat will go,
And on which no mighty *and*
stately ship will pass.
22 For the LORD is our Judge,
The LORD is our Ruler,
The LORD is our King;
He will save us. [Is 2:3, 4; 11:4; 32:1;
James 4:12]
23 Your ship's ropes (tackle) hang
loose;
They cannot hold the base of their
mast firmly,
Nor spread out the sail.
Then an abundance of spoil and
plunder will be divided;
Even the lame will take the
plunder.
24 And no inhabitant [of Zion] will
say, "I am sick";
The people who dwell there will
be forgiven their wickedness
[their sin, their injustice, their
wrongdoing].

God's Wrath against Nations

34 COME NEAR, you nations, to
hear; and listen, O peoples!
Let the earth and all that is in it
hear, and the world and all that
comes forth from it.
2 For the LORD is angry at all the
nations,
And *His* wrath is against all their
armies;
He has utterly doomed them,
He has given them over to
slaughter.
3 So their slain will be thrown out,
And the stench of their corpses
will rise,
And the mountains will flow with
their blood.
4 All the host of heaven will be
dissolved,

33:17 ***far-distant land.*** The prophet's land was continually threatened by the Assyrian army. But, in prophetic vision, Isaiah saw a little picture of the beauty of heaven. In the mind of the believer, the trials of the present fade into insignificance if he only contemplates that glorious time when he will dwell in the presence of his King.
33:18 ***he who counts.*** The scribe who counted was the one who took tribute (2Ki 18:14).
33:19 ***people of unintelligible speech.*** For a similar idea concerning Israel's enemies, see Deuteronomy 28:49.
33:22 ***the LORD is our Ruler.*** The Ruler is associated with other acts of mercy (Dt 6:1 – 3; Jn 1:14 – 18); the giving of the law was God's way to point out the correct path for the Israelites to follow. His commitment to set our feet on the right path is one of His acts of mercy.
34:4 ***host of heaven.*** The host of heaven here refers to pagan deities (24:21; 2Ki 17:16). ***skies will be rolled up like a scroll.*** The old cosmos will give way to the new (51:6; Mt 24:29; Rev 6:13 – 14; 21:1).

18 1Co 1:20 **19** 2Ki 19:32; Dt 28:49,50; Jer 5:15 **20** Ps 48:12; Ps 46:5; 125:1,2; Isa 37:33; Isa 54:2 **22** Jas 4:12; Ps 89:18 **24** Jer 50:20 **CHAPTER 34** **1** Ps 49:1; Dt 32:1 **3** Joel 2:20 **4** Ps 102:26; Eze 32:7,8; Joel 2:31; Mt 24:29; 2Pe 3:10; Isa 14:12; Rev 6:13

And the skies will be rolled up like
a scroll;
All their hosts [the stars and the
planets] will also wither away
As a leaf withers from the vine,
And as a *fig* withers from the fig
tree. [Rev 6:13, 14]
5 For My sword is satiated [with
blood] in heaven;
Indeed, it will come down for
judgment on Edom
And on the people whom I have
doomed for destruction. [Obad
8–21]
6 The sword of the LORD is filled
with blood [from sacrifices],
It drips with fat, with the blood of
lambs and goats,
With the fat of the kidneys of
rams.
For the LORD has a sacrifice in
Bozrah (Edom's capital city)
And a great slaughter in the land
of Edom.
7 Wild oxen will also fall with
them
And the young bulls with the
strong bulls;
And their land will be soaked with
blood,
And their dust made greasy with
fat.
8 For the LORD has a day of
vengeance,
A year of retribution for the cause
of Zion.
9 The streams [of Edom] will be
turned into pitch,
And its dust into brimstone,
And its land will become burning
pitch.
10 The burning will not be quenched
night or day;
Its smoke will go up forever.
From generation to generation it
will lie in ruins;
No one will ever again pass
through it. [Rev 19:3]
11 But the pelican and the porcupine
will take possession of it;
The owl and the raven will dwell
in it.
And He will stretch over it (Edom)
the measuring line of desolation
And the plumb line of emptiness.
12 Its nobles—there is no one there
Whom they may proclaim king—
And all its princes will be
nothing.
13 Thorns will come up in its fortified
palaces,
Nettles and brambles in its
fortified cities;
It will be a haunt for jackals,
An abode for ostriches.
14 The creatures of the desert will
encounter jackals
And the hairy goat will call to its
kind;
Indeed, Lilith (night demon) will
settle there
And find herself a place of rest.
15 There the arrow snake will make
her nest and lay her eggs,
And hatch them and gather *her
young* under her protection;
Indeed, the birds of prey will be
gathered there [to breed],
Every one with its own kind.

16 Seek from the book of the LORD,
and read:

Not one of these [creatures] will be
missing;
None will lack its mate.
For His mouth has commanded,
And His Spirit has gathered
them.
17 The LORD has cast the lot for
them,
And His hand has divided *and*
apportioned Edom to the wild
beasts by measuring-line.
They will possess it forever;
From generation to generation
they will dwell in it.

34:8 *vengeance.* The Lord has promised that He will one day right the wrongs suffered by His followers, but that vengeance is His, and His alone (Dt 32:35; Ro 12:19).

34:9 *brimstone . . . burning pitch.* Brimstone and burning pitch may be allusions to Sodom and Gomorrah (30:33; Ge 19:24; Eze 38:22).

5 Jer 46:10; Jer 49:7; Mal 1:4 **6** Zep 1:7 **8** Isa 63:4 **9** Dt 29:23 **10** Rev 14:11; 18:18; 19:3; Mal 1:4 **11** Isa 14:23; Zep 2:14; Rev 18:2; 2Ki 21:13; La 2:8 **13** Isa 32:13; Hos 9:6; Isa 13:21 **16** Mal 3:16

Zion's Joyful Future

35 THE WILDERNESS and the dry land will be glad;
The Arabah (desert) will shout in exultation and blossom
Like the autumn crocus.
2 It will blossom abundantly
And rejoice with joy and singing.
The glory of Lebanon will be given to it,
The majesty of [Mount] Carmel and [the plain] of Sharon.
They will see the glory of the LORD,
The majesty *and* splendor of our God.
3 Encourage the exhausted, and make staggering knees firm. [Heb 12:12]
4 Say to those with an anxious *and* panic-stricken heart,
"Be strong, fear not!
Indeed, your God will come with vengeance [for the ungodly];
The retribution of God will come,
But He will save you."
5 Then the eyes of the blind will be opened
And the ears of the deaf will be unstopped.
6 Then the lame will leap like a deer,
And the tongue of the mute will shout for joy.
For waters will break forth in the wilderness
And streams in the desert. [Matt 11:5]
7 And the burning sand (mirage) will become a pool [of water]
And the thirsty ground springs of water;
In the haunt of jackals, where they lay resting,
Grass becomes reeds and rushes.
8 A highway will be there, and a roadway;
And it will be called the Holy Way.
The unclean will not travel on it,
But it will be for those who walk on the way [the redeemed];
And fools will not wander *on it.*
9 No lion will be there,
Nor will any predatory animal come up on it;
They will not be found there.
But the redeemed will walk *there.*
10 And the ransomed of the LORD will return
And come to Zion with shouts of jubilation,
And everlasting joy will be upon their heads;
They will find joy and gladness,
And sorrow and sighing will flee away.

35:1–2 *rejoice.* Isaiah 35 stands in contrast to Isaiah 34. This chapter opens with the lilt of joy. The Arabah, or desert plain, shall blossom and break into bloom. Centuries before, Moses had warned of a day when the rain of this land would become "powder and dust" (Dt 28:24). That day came because Israel was disobedient to God. But, at the second coming of Christ (Rev 20:1–6), Israel will be restored spiritually, and with spiritual restoration comes physical blessing. When judgment is removed, great blessing follows. Restoration follows repentance, and restoration is accompanied by joy.

35:3 *Encourage the exhausted.* This phrase is cited in Hebrews 12:12 (Jos 1:6–7,9,18). We can reassure ourselves with the knowledge that our Savior is coming. In that day, justice will be restored.

35:5–6 *eyes... ears... lame... tongue.* This prophecy of healings was fulfilled by Jesus (Mt 12:22; Lk 4:18; 7:22), and it was this passage in Isaiah that Jesus referred to when He answered John the Baptist's disciples who asked if He was the Expected One. The reply was somewhat cryptic, but it was something that John would understand in prison, without requiring Jesus to expose Himself before it was time (Mt 11:27; Lk 7:22).

35:10 *ransomed.* Someone who is ransomed is someone who has had a price paid to set him free from captivity. This promise looked forward to the return of the political captives and, in a much fuller sense, to the salvation through Jesus Christ, who gave "His life as a ransom for many" (Mt 20:28; Mk 10:45; 1Ti 2:6).

CHAPTER 35 **1** Isa 55:12 **2** Isa 32:15 **3** Job 4:3,4; Heb 12:12 **5** Isa 29:18; Mt 9:27; 11:5; Jn 9:6,7; Mt 11:5 **6** Mt 11:5; 15:30; Jn 5:8,9; Ac 8:7; Isa 32:4; Mt 9:32; 12:22; Isa 41:18; Jn 7:38 **7** Isa 34:13 **8** Isa 52:1; Rev 21:27 **9** Lev 26:6; Isa 11:9; Eze 34:25 **10** Isa 51:11; Isa 25:8; Rev 7:17; 21:4

Sennacherib Invades Judah

36 NOW IN the fourteenth year of King Hezekiah, Sennacherib king of Assyria came up against all the fortified cities of Judah and conquered them. [2 Kin 18:13, 17–37; 2 Chr 32:9–19]

2And the king of Assyria sent the Rabshakeh [his military commander] from Lachish [the Judean fortress commanding the road from Egypt] to King Hezekiah at Jerusalem with a large army. And he stood by the canal of the Upper Pool on the highway to the Fuller's Field.

3Then Eliakim the son of Hilkiah, who was in charge of the [royal] household, and Shebna the scribe, and Joah the son of Asaph, the recording historian, came out to [meet] him.

4Then the Rabshakeh said to them, "Say to Hezekiah, 'This is what the great king, the king of Assyria says, "What is [the reason for] this confidence that you have?

5"I say, 'Your plan and strength for the war are only empty words.' Now in whom do you trust *and* on whom do you rely, that you have rebelled against me? [2 Kin 18:7]

6"Listen carefully, you rely on the staff of this broken reed, Egypt, which will pierce the hand of any man who leans on it. So is Pharaoh king of Egypt to all who rely on him.

7"But if you say to me, 'We trust in *and* rely on the LORD our God,' is it not He whose high places and whose altars Hezekiah has taken away, saying to Judah and to Jerusalem, 'You shall worship before this altar'? [2 Kin 18:4, 5]

8"So now, exchange pledges with my master the king of Assyria and I will give you two thousand horses, if you are able on your part to put riders on them.

9"How then can you repulse [the attack of] a single commander of the least of my master's servants, and rely on Egypt for chariots and for horsemen?

10"Moreover, is it without the LORD that I have now come up against this land to destroy it? The LORD said to me, 'Go up against this land and destroy it.' " ' "

11Then Eliakim and Shebna and Joah said to the Rabshakeh, "Please, speak to your servants in Aramaic, because we understand it; and do not speak to us in Judean (Hebrew) in the hearing of the people who are [stationed] on the wall."

12But the Rabshakeh said, "Has my master sent me to speak these words *only* to your master and to you, and not to the men sitting on the wall, *doomed* to eat their own dung and drink their own urine with you?"

13Then the Rabshakeh stood and called out with a loud voice in Judean (Hebrew): "Hear the words of the great king, the king of Assyria.

14"This is what the king says, 'Do not let Hezekiah deceive you, for he will not be able to rescue you;

15nor let Hezekiah make you trust in the LORD, saying, "The LORD will most certainly rescue us; this city will not be given into the hand of the king of Assyria."

16'Do not listen to Hezekiah,' for this is what the king of Assyria says, 'Make peace with me and come out to me, and each one of you will eat from his own vine and each from his own fig tree

---

36:1 *fourteenth year.* The fourteenth year of King Hezekiah's sole reign was 701 BC. ***all.*** In his annals, Sennacherib mentions 46 cities that he attacked.
36:2 *Rabshakeh.* This was probably the title of one of Sennacharib's officials (2Ki 18:17).
36:7 *taken away.* Hezekiah had destroyed the idolatrous high places and altars that his father Ahaz had built (2Ki 18:1 – 5; 2Ch 31:1 – 3).
36:8 *riders.* Micah referred to Jerusalem's soldiers as merely "troops" (Mic 5:1) compared to the enormous international army of Assyria.
36:10 *the LORD said to me.* Ancient Middle Eastern conquerors liked to claim that the gods of their defeated enemies had joined their side (2Ch 35:21). These words about the Lord were no more than a boast.
36:11 *Aramaic.* Aramaic was the language of international diplomacy.

CHAPTER 36 **1** 2Ki 18:13,17; 2Ch 32:1 **4** 2Ki 18:19 **6** Eze 29:6,7 **16** Zec 3:10

and each [one of you] drink from the
water of his own cistern,
[17]until I come and take you away to
a land like your own land, a land of
grain and new wine, a land of bread
and vineyards.
[18]'*Beware* that Hezekiah does not
mislead you by saying, "The LORD will
rescue us." Has any one of the gods
of the nations [ever] rescued his land
from the hand of the king of Assyria?
[19]'Where are the gods of Hamath
and Arpad [in Aram]? Where are the
gods of Sepharvaim? And when have
they rescued Samaria from my hand?
[20]'Who among all the gods of these
lands have rescued their land from my
hand, that [you should think that] the
LORD would rescue Jerusalem from
my hand?' "
[21]But they kept silent and did not
say a word to him in reply, for King
Hezekiah's command was, "Do not
answer him."
[22]Then Eliakim the son of Hilkiah,
who was in charge of the household,
and Shebna the scribe and Joah the
son of Asaph, the recording historian,
came to Hezekiah with their clothes
torn [in grief], and told him the words
of the Rabshakeh [the Assyrian commander].

Hezekiah Seeks Isaiah's Help

37 AND WHEN King Hezekiah
heard this, he tore his clothes
and covered himself with sackcloth
and went into the house of the LORD.
[2 Kin 19:1–13]
[2]Then he sent Eliakim, who was in
charge of the [royal] household, and
Shebna the scribe, and the elders of
the priests, covered with sackcloth, to
Isaiah the prophet, the son of Amoz.
[3]They said to him, "This is what
Hezekiah says, 'This day is a day of
distress, rebuke and disgrace; for children have come to birth, and there is
no strength to deliver them.
[4]'It may be that the LORD your God
will hear the words of the Rabshakeh
[the commander], whom his master the
king of Assyria has sent to taunt *and*
defy the living God, and will avenge
the words which the LORD your God
has heard. Therefore, offer a prayer
for the remnant [of His people] that
is left.' "
[5]So the servants of King Hezekiah
came to Isaiah.
[6]Isaiah said to them, "You shall say
the following to your master: 'This is
what the LORD says, "Do not be afraid
because of the words that you have
heard, with which the servants of the
king of Assyria have blasphemed Me.
[7]"Listen carefully, I will put a spirit
in him so that he will hear a rumor
and return to his own land. And I will
make him fall by the sword in his own
land." ' "
[8]So the Rabshakeh returned and
found the king of Assyria fighting
against Libnah [a fortified city of Judah], for he had heard that the king
had left Lachish.
[9]And Sennacherib king of Assyria,
heard *them* say concerning Tirhakah
king of Cush (Ethiopia), "He has come
out to fight against you." And when he
heard it, he sent messengers to Hezekiah, saying,
[10]"You shall say to Hezekiah king of
Judah, 'Do not let your God in whom

36:19 *have they rescued Samaria.* Like the Assyrian king (10:11), Rabshakeh assumed that different gods were worshiped in Samaria than in Jerusalem.
36:22 *Shebna.* Isaiah had earlier condemned Shebna for presumption (22:15 – 23). Apparently that was a warning which was heeded, for his attitude was of mourning, repentance, and humility at this time.
37:6 *Do not be afraid.* The Lord commonly reassured His servants with these words (7:4; 35:4; Ge 15:1; Jos 1:9). We have no reason to fear if our trust is in the all-powerful God (Heb 13:6).
37:10 *You shall say.* Blasphemous and malicious designs against God and His people should motivate us to rely completely on the Lord and earnestly seek His strength. The response of God's people to blasphemers must never be incited by personal feelings, but by the desire that "all the kingdoms of the earth may know and fully realize that You alone, LORD, are God" (37:20).

CHAPTER 37 **1** 2Ki 19:1

you trust deceive you, saying, "Jerusalem will not be given into the hand of the king of Assyria."

[11]'Listen carefully, you have heard what the kings of Assyria have done to all lands, utterly destroying them. So will you be rescued?

[12]'Did the gods of the nations which my fathers destroyed rescue them—Gozan, Haran [of Mesopotamia], Rezeph, and the sons of Eden who were in Telassar?

[13]'Where is the king of Hamath, the king of Arpad [of northern Syria], the king of the city of Sepharvaim, [the king of] Hena, or [the king of] Ivvah?' "

Hezekiah's Prayer in the Temple

[14]Then Hezekiah took the letter from the hand of the messengers and read it, and he went up to the house of the LORD and spread it out before the LORD. [2 Kin 19:14–19]

[15]And Hezekiah prayed to the LORD saying,

[16]"O LORD of hosts, God of Israel, who is enthroned *above* the cherubim, You are the God, You alone, of all the kingdoms of the earth. You have made heaven and earth.

[17]"Incline Your ear, O LORD, and hear; open Your eyes, O LORD, and see; and hear all the words of Sennacherib that he has sent to taunt *and* defy the living God.

[18]"It is true, O LORD, that the kings of Assyria have laid waste all the countries and their lands,

[19]and have cast the gods [of those peoples] into the fire, for they were not gods but the work of men's hands, wood and stone. Therefore they have destroyed them.

[20]"Now, O LORD our God, save us from his hand so that all the kingdoms of the earth may know *and* fully realize that You alone, LORD, are God."

God Answers through Isaiah

[21]Then Isaiah son of Amoz sent *word* to Hezekiah, saying, "For the LORD, the God of Israel says this, 'Because you have prayed to Me about Sennacherib king of Assyria, [2 Kin 19:20–37; 2 Chr 32:20, 21]

[22]this is the word that the LORD has spoken against him:

"She has shown contempt for you
and mocked you,
The Virgin Daughter of Zion
(Jerusalem);
She has shaken her head behind
you,
The Daughter of Jerusalem!

[23]"Whom have you taunted and
blasphemed?
And against whom have you
raised your voice
And haughtily lifted up your eyes?
Against the Holy One of Israel!

[24]"Through your servants you have
taunted *and* defied the Lord,
And you have said, 'With my
many chariots I have gone up to
the heights of the mountains,
To the remotest parts of Lebanon.
I cut down its tallest cedars and its
choicest cypress trees;
And I will go to its remotest height,
its most luxuriant *and* thickest
forest.

[25]'I dug *wells* and drank [foreign]
waters,
And with the sole of my feet I
dried up
All the canals [of the Nile] of
Egypt.'

[26]"Have you not heard [says the God
of Israel]
That I did it long ago,
That I planned it in ancient times?

37:21 ***the LORD, the God of Israel says this.*** Hezekiah's plea for help against the Assyrian menace brought a word from the Lord. Hezekiah was assured that the Lord was in absolute charge, even to the extent that the Assyrian king's activities were brought about through God's own plan (37:26). Sennacherib's forces fell before the mighty power of the angel of the Lord (37:36), as a witness to the truth of the Word of God that the king's heart is turned by the hand of the Lord (Pr 21:1).

13 Jer 49:23 **17** Da 9:18

Now I have brought it to pass,
That you [king of Assyria] would
[be My instrument to] turn
fortified cities into ruinous
heaps.
27 "Therefore their inhabitants had
little power,
They were terrorized and
shamed;
They were like the grass of the
field and the green vegetation,
Like grass on the housetops *and*
like a field [of grain] scorched
before it is grown.
28 "But I know your sitting down
And your going out and your
coming in [every detail of your
life],
And your raging against Me.
29 "Because your raging against Me
And your arrogance has come up
to My ears,
I will put My hook in your nose
And My bridle in your mouth,
And I will turn you back by the
way you came.

30 "This shall be the sign [of these
things] to you [Hezekiah]: you are to
eat this year what grows of itself, and
in the second year that which springs
from the same, and in the third year
you are to sow and harvest, and plant
vineyards and eat their fruit.
31 "The surviving remnant of the
house of Judah will again take root
downward and bear fruit upward.
32 "For out of Jerusalem will come a
remnant and from Mount Zion a band
of survivors. The zeal of the LORD of
hosts will do this." '
33 "Therefore, the LORD says this con-
cerning the king of Assyria, 'He will
not come into this city or shoot an ar-
row there, or come before it with shield,
or raise an assault ramp against it.
34 'By the way that he came, by the
same way he will return, and he will
not come into this city,' declares the
LORD.
35 'For I will defend this city to save
it, for My own sake and for the sake of
My servant David.' "

Assyrians Destroyed

36 And the angel of the LORD went out
and struck 185,000 in the camp of the
Assyrians; and when the [surviving]
men got up early the next morning,
they saw all the dead. [2 Kin 19:35]
37 So Sennacherib king of Assyria
departed and returned and lived at
Nineveh.
38 It came to pass as he was worship-
ing in the house of Nisroch his god,
that Adrammelech and Sharezer his
sons killed him with the sword; and
they escaped into the land of Ararat
[in Armenia]. And Esarhaddon his son
became king in his place.

Hezekiah Healed

38 IN THOSE days Hezekiah [king
of Judah] became sick and was
at the point of death. And Isaiah the
prophet, the son of Amoz, came to him
and said, "For the LORD says this, 'Set
your house in order *and* prepare a will,
for you shall die; you will not live.' "
[2 Kin 20:1–11; 2 Chr 32:24–26]
2 Then Hezekiah turned his face to
the wall and prayed to the LORD,
3 and said, "Please, O LORD, just re-
member how I have walked before You
in faithfulness *and* truth, and with a
whole heart [absolutely devoted to You],
and have done what is good in Your
sight." And Hezekiah wept greatly.
4 Then the word of the LORD came to
Isaiah, saying,
5 "Go and say to Hezekiah, 'For the
LORD, the God of David your father
says this, "I have heard your prayer, I

37:29 *My hook in your nose.* The Assyrians dragged prisoners away with a hook in the nose. The Lord's judgment was coming, and soon the Assyrians would experience being pulled away where they did not want to go.
37:36 *angel of the LORD . . . struck.* This verse is the fulfillment of God's promise to take vengeance on those who trouble His people (34:8).
37:38 *Esarhaddon.* Esarhaddon began his reign in 681 BC.
38:5 *add fifteen years to your life.* Hezekiah had no male heir at the time of his illness.

29 Isa 30:28; Eze 38:4 **32** 2Ki 19:31; Isa 9:7 **35** 2Ki 20:6; Isa 38:6 **36** 2Ki 19:35 **CHAPTER 38** **1** 2Ki 20:1; 2Ch 32:24; 2Sa 17:23 **3** Neh 13:14

have seen your tears; listen carefully, I will add fifteen years to your life.
[6]"I will rescue you and this city from the hand of the king of Assyria; and I will defend this city [Jerusalem]." '
[7]"This shall be the sign to you from the LORD, that the LORD will do this thing that He has spoken:
[8]"Listen carefully, I will turn the shadow on the stairway [denoting the time of day] ten steps backward, *the shadow* on the stairway (sundial) of Ahaz." And the sunlight went ten steps backward on the stairway where it had [previously] gone down.
[9]*This is the* writing of Hezekiah king of Judah after he had been sick and had recovered from his illness:

[10]I said, "In mid-life
I am to go through the gates of
Sheol (the place of the dead),
I am to be summoned, *deprived of*
the remainder of my years."
[11]I said, "I will not see the LORD
The LORD in the land of the living;
I will no longer see man among
the inhabitants of the world.
[12]"My dwelling (body) is pulled up
and removed from me like a
shepherd's tent;
I have rolled up my life as a
weaver [rolls up the finished
web].
He cuts me free from the warp [of
the loom];
From day to night You bring me to
an end.
[13]"I lay down until morning.
Like a lion, so He breaks all my
bones;
From day until night You bring me
to an end.
[14]"Like a swallow, like a crane, so I
chirp;
I coo like a dove.
My eyes look wistfully upward;
O Lord, I am oppressed, take my
side *and* be my security.
[15]"What shall I say?
For He has spoken to me, and He
Himself has done it;
I will wander aimlessly all my
years because of the bitterness
of my soul.
[16]"O Lord, by *these* things men live,
And in all these is the life of my
spirit;
Restore me to health and let me
live!
[17]"Indeed, it was for my own well-
being that I had such
bitterness;
But You have loved back my life
from the pit of nothingness
(destruction),
For You have cast all my sins
behind Your back.
[18]"For Sheol cannot praise *or* thank
You,
Death cannot praise You *and*
rejoice in You;
Those who go down to the
pit cannot hope for Your
faithfulness.
[19]"It is the living who give praise
and thanks to You, as I do today;
A father tells his sons about Your
faithfulness.
[20]"The LORD is ready to save me;
Therefore we will play my songs
on stringed instruments
All the days of our lives at the
house of the LORD."

[21]Now Isaiah had said, "Have them take a cake of figs and rub it [as an ointment] on the inflamed spot, that he may recover."
[22]Hezekiah also had said, "What is the sign that I will go up to the house of the LORD?"

Manasseh, the successor to his throne, was 12 when Hezekiah died (2Ki 20:21 – 21:1).
38:9 *writing of Hezekiah.* Scriptures attest to King Hezekiah's interest in devotional literature. Apparently, he instructed his scribes to compile some of the proverbs of Solomon (Pr 25:1). He ordered the Levites to worship God with the psalms of David and Asaph (2Ch 29:30), and the song of praise (vv. 10 – 20) has some similarities with those psalms.
38:22 *sign.* Depending on one's attitude, the request for a sign may express either unbelief

6 Isa 37:35 **7** 2Ki 20:8; Isa 7:11 **11** Ps 27:13; 116:9 **12** Job 7:6 **14** Isa 59:11 **15** Job 7:11 **18** Ps 6:5; 30:9; 88:11; 115:17; Ecc 9:10 **19** Dt 4:9; 6:7; Ps 78:3,4 **21** 2Ki 20:7 **22** 2Ki 20:8

Hezekiah Shows His Treasures

39 AT THAT time Merodach-
baladan son of Baladan, king
of Babylon, sent [messengers with]
letters and a present to Hezekiah, for
he had heard that he had been sick and
had recovered. [2 Kin 20:12–19]
2 Hezekiah was pleased and showed
them his treasure house—the silver,
the gold, the spices, the precious oil,
his entire armory and everything that
was found in his treasuries. There was
nothing in his house nor in all his area
of dominion that Hezekiah did not
show them.
3 Then Isaiah the prophet came to
King Hezekiah and asked, "What did
these men say? From where have they
come to you?" And Hezekiah said,
"They came to me from a far country,
from Babylon."
4 Then Isaiah said, "What have they
seen in your house?" And Hezekiah
answered, "They have seen everything
that is in my house; there is nothing
among my treasures that I have not
shown them."
5 Then Isaiah said to Hezekiah,
"Hear the word of the LORD of hosts,
6 'Listen carefully, the days are com-
ing when everything that is in your
house and everything that your prede-
cessors have stored up until this day
will be carried to Babylon; nothing will
be left,' says the LORD.
7 'And some of your own sons (de-
scendants) who will come from you,
whom you will father, will be taken
away, and they will become officials
in the palace of the king of Babylon.' "
8 Then said Hezekiah to Isaiah, "The
word of the LORD which you have spo-
ken is good." For he thought, "There
will be peace and faithfulness [to God's
promises to us] in my days."

The Greatness of God

40 "COMFORT, O comfort My
people," says your God.
2 "Speak tenderly to Jerusalem,
And call out to her, that her time of
compulsory service in warfare
is finished,
That her wickedness has
been taken away [since her
punishment is sufficient],
That she has received from the
LORD's hand

(Mt 12:39; Jn 6:30) or faith (v. 7). The healing of a boil would be the sign that the Lord would save Hezekiah (vv. 20–21).

39:1 ***recovered.*** The miracle of the sundial (38:8) would have held special interest for the astronomy-minded Babylonians (2Ch 32:31).

39:2 ***showed them his treasure house.*** Hezekiah was flattered to receive the attention of the Babylonian delegation and wanted to show how important he was.

40:1–55:13 ***Comfort.*** This section is addressed to the Babylonian exiles in a prophetic manner. This book of comfort, written about 150 years before the time of Cyrus, promised the exiles from Judah that they would return to Jerusalem (40:1–2). The restoration after the exile pointed to the coming of the Lord's kingdom. In Isaiah's prophecy, this first taste of salvation merges with predictions of the full salvation that Jesus Christ would bring.

40:2–5 Preparing the Way — Biblical scholars think this passage was originally intended to encourage the Israelite exiles, which were looking forward to their return to Israel. The obstacles to getting back home included both a release from slavery and a journey of hundreds of miles on foot through hostile territory. There was also much to be apprehensive about when they arrived home. How were they ever going to be able to rebuild their communities when they were virtually penniless and without resources?

Experts also see this passage as being one of the key messianic prophecies. The image of verses 3–4 is that of the ancient Near Eastern practice of "rolling out the red carpet" for a visiting monarch. Mark makes use of these verses to describe the ministry of John the Baptist, as the prophet urges people to prepare for the coming of the Messiah.

Both applications point to the same concepts. God is saying, "Trust Me, I will make it right. I will make a way through the obstacles. No matter how large the obstacles, I will overcome them." We should see these as some of the strongest words of comfort in the Bible.

40:2 ***Jerusalem.*** In this case, Jerusalem represents the exiles. ***warfare.*** Warfare refers to Israel's hard service in Babylon.

CHAPTER 39 **1** 2Ki 20:12 **2** 2Ch 32:31 **6** Jer 20:5 **8** 1Sa 3:18 **CHAPTER 40** **2** Isa 61:7

Double [punishment] for all her
sins."
3 A voice of one is calling out,
"Clear the way for the LORD in
the wilderness [remove the
obstacles];
Make straight *and* smooth in the
desert a highway for our God.
[Mark 1:3]
4 "Every valley shall be raised,
And every mountain and hill be
made low;
And let the rough ground become
a plain,
And the rugged places a broad
valley.
5 "And the glory *and* majesty *and*
splendor of the LORD will be
revealed,
And all humanity shall see it
together;
For the mouth of the LORD has
spoken it." [Luke 3:5, 6]
6 A voice says, "Call out [prophesy]."
Then he answered, "What shall I
call out?"
[The voice answered:] All
humanity is [as frail as] grass,
and all that makes it attractive
[its charm, its loveliness] is
[momentary] like the flower of
the field.
7 The grass withers, the flower
fades,
When the breath of the LORD
blows upon it;
Most certainly [all] the people are
[like] grass.
8 The grass withers, the flower
fades,
But the word of our God stands
forever. [James 1:10, 11;
1 Pet 1:24, 25]
9 O Zion, herald of good news,
Get up on a high mountain.
O Jerusalem, herald of good news,
Lift up your voice with strength,
Lift it up, do not fear;
Say to the cities of Judah,
"Here is your God!" [Acts 10:36;
Rom 10:15]
10 Listen carefully, the Lord GOD will
come with might,
And His arm will rule for Him.
Most certainly His reward is with
Him,
And His restitution accompanies
Him. [Rev 22:7, 12]
11 He will protect His flock like a
shepherd,
He will gather the lambs in His
arm,
He will carry them in His bosom;
He will gently *and* carefully lead
those nursing their young.

12 Who has measured the waters in
the hollow of His hand,

40:3 ***voice of one is calling out.*** John referred to this passage to explain who he was (Jn 1:23) as the forerunner of Christ.

40:5 ***glory . . . will be revealed.*** The glory of the Lord is revealed in the restoration of the captives, but in a fuller sense it is revealed in the coming of the Lord Jesus Christ (Lk 2:29 – 32; Jn 1:14).

40:9 ***good news.*** Good news from God to man can always be properly described as "gospel." Here, the glad tidings are that the God who once delivered His captive people from bondage in Egypt is again at hand to rescue and protect His beleaguered Israelites. The assurance that God is with us (7:14; Jn 1:14) to save is at the heart of the Christian gospel (1Co 15:3 – 4), and it is always "good news," even when it is something we have heard before.

40:12 – 31 God's Sovereignty Over the Nations — God controls the destinies of rulers and politicians and public figures, no matter how much power they think they have. When times are rough, we wonder if God is really in charge. We wonder why He lets us get moved around by so many economic and political forces beyond our control. We sometimes wonder if He really even cares about what is going on in the world or our lives. If He really is in charge, does He know what He is doing?

The testimony of Isaiah is a resounding Yes! Nations may rise and fall. Rulers may come and go. God remains both Starter and Finisher. The circumstances that surround us are temporary conditions in the scheme of eternity. As God sustains the stars in heaven and the whole universe, He sustains our lives. We may not be able to say that easily every day, but if we keep coming back to Him, He will not disappoint us.

40:12 ***span.*** A span is the width of an outstretched hand. This verse dramatically imposes images of the grandeur of God.

---

3 Mt 3:3; Mal 3:1; Ps 68:4 **4** Isa 45:2 **6** Job 14:2 **8** Jn 12:34 **10** Isa 59:16; Isa 62:11 **11** Eze 34:23; Jn 10:11; Heb 13:20; 1Pe 2:25 **12** Pr 30:4

And marked off the heavens with a span [of the hand],
And calculated the dust of the earth with a measure,
And weighed the mountains in a balance
And the hills in a pair of scales?
13 Who has directed the Spirit of the LORD,
Or has taught Him as His counselor? [Rom 11:34]
14 With whom did He consult and *who* enlightened Him?
Who taught Him the path of justice and taught Him knowledge
And informed Him of the way of understanding?
15 In fact, the nations are like a drop from a bucket,
And are regarded as a speck of dust on the scales;
Now look, He lifts up the islands like fine dust.
16 And [the forests of] Lebanon cannot supply sufficient *fuel* to start a fire,
Nor are its wild beasts enough for a burnt offering [worthy of the LORD].
17 All the nations are as nothing before Him,
They are regarded by Him as less than nothing and meaningless.

18 To whom then will you liken God?
Or with what likeness will you compare Him? [Acts 17:29]
19 *As for* the cast image (idol), a metalworker casts it,
A goldsmith overlays it with gold
And a silversmith *casts its* silver chains.
20 He who is too impoverished for *such* an offering [to give to his god]
Chooses a tree that will not rot;
He seeks out for himself a skillful craftsman
To [carve and] set up an idol that will not totter.

21 Do you [who worship idols] not know? Have you not heard?
Has it not been told to you from the beginning?
Have you not understood from the foundations of the earth [the omnipotence of God and the stupidity of bowing to idols]? [Rom 1:20, 21]
22 It is He who sits above the circle of the earth,
And its inhabitants are like grasshoppers;
[It is He] who stretches out the heavens like a veil
And spreads them out like a tent to dwell in.
23 It is He who reduces dignitaries to nothing,
Who makes the judges (rulers) of the earth meaningless (useless).
24 Scarcely have they been planted,
Scarcely have they been sown,
Scarcely has their stock taken root in the earth,
But He merely blows on them, and they wither,
And a strong wind carries them away like stubble.
25 "To whom then will you compare Me
That I would be his equal?" says the Holy One.
26 Lift up your eyes on high
And see who has created these *heavenly bodies*,
The One who brings out their host by number,

40:15 *nations are like a drop from a bucket.* Wicked nations have no power to thwart the purposes of God (Ps 2:1 – 6).
40:19 – 20 *cast image.* Many idols were made with wood, then overlaid with gold. The poor had to choose the best wood available and hope it was good enough. But of what value is the prayer of a poor man to a plain idol? What is the value of the rich to one covered with gold? To both questions, the answer is "none."
40:26 *who has created these heavenly bodies.* The Babylonian gods were identified with the heavenly bodies. These words would have been comforting and encouraging to the Israelites who had learned to say no to Babylon and yes to the Lord.

13 Job 21:22; 1Co 2:16 **17** Da 4:35; Ps 62:9 **18** Isa 46:5; Ac 17:29 **19** Isa 41:6,7; 44:12; Jer 10:3 **20** Isa 41:7; Jer 10:4 **21** Ps 19:1; Ac 14:17; Ro 1:19 **22** Job 9:8; Ps 104:2; Isa 42:5; 51:13; Jer 10:12 **23** Job 12:21; Ps 107:40 **25** ver. 18 **26** Ps 147:4

He calls them all by name;
Because of the greatness of His might and the strength of His power,
Not one is missing.

27 Why, O Jacob, do you say, and declare, O Israel,
"My way is hidden from the LORD,
And the justice due me escapes the notice of my God"?
28 Do you not know? Have you not heard?
The Everlasting God, the LORD, the Creator of the ends of the earth
Does not become tired or grow weary;
There is no searching of His understanding.
29 He gives strength to the weary,
And to him who has no might He increases power. [2 Cor 12:9]
30 Even youths grow weary and tired,
And vigorous young men stumble badly,
31 But those who wait for the LORD [who expect, look for, and hope in Him]
Will gain new strength *and* renew their power;
They will lift up their wings [and rise up close to God] like eagles [rising toward the sun];
They will run and not become weary,
They will walk and not grow tired. [Heb 12:1–3]

Israel Encouraged

41 "LISTEN TO me in silence, you islands *and* coastlands,
And let the nations gain their strength;
Let them come near, then let them speak;
Let us come together for judgment [and decide the issue between us concerning the enemy from the east].
2 "Who has stirred up *and* put into action one from the east [the king of Persia, Cyrus the Great]
Whom He calls in righteousness to His service *and* whom victory meets at every step?
The LORD turns nations over to him
And subdues kings.
He makes them like dust with his sword,
Like wind-driven chaff with his bow. [Ezra 1:2]
3 "He (Cyrus) pursues them and passes along safely,
By a way his feet had not traveled before.
4 "Who has performed and done this,
Calling forth [and guiding the destinies of] the generations [of the nations] from the beginning?
'I, the LORD—the first, and with the last [existing before history began, the ever-present, unchanging God]—I am He.' "

5 The islands *and* coastlands have seen and they fear;
The ends of the earth tremble;
They have drawn near and have come.
6 They each help his neighbor
And say to his brother [as he fashions his idols], "Be of good courage!"
7 So the craftsman encourages the goldsmith,
And he who smooths *metal* with the smith's hammer *encourages* him who beats the anvil,

40:27 *justice due me escapes the notice of my God.* The captives in their weariness may have complained that they were forgotten by God.
40:31 *wait.* To "wait" for the Lord entails confident expectation and active hope, never passive resignation.
41:2 *one from the east.* This refers to Cyrus, king of Persia (559 – 530 BC; see 46:11).
41:4 *first . . . last.* The Lord also refers to Himself as the first and last in Revelation 22:13, when He is speaking to the apostle John of the things that will happen at the end of the age. This description speaks of His sovereignty over all time.

28 Ps 147:5; Ro 11:33 **31** Ps 103:5 **CHAPTER 41** **1** Zec 2:13 **2** Isa 46:11; Ge 14:14; Isa 45:1 **4** ver. 26; Isa 44:6; Rev 1:17; 22:13 **6** Isa 40:19 **7** Isa 40:19,20

Saying of the soldering (welding),
"That is good";
And he fastens the idol with
nails,
So that it will not totter *nor* be
moved.
8 "But you, Israel, My servant,
Jacob whom I have chosen,
The offspring of Abraham My
friend, [Heb 2:16; James 2:23]
9 You whom I [the LORD] have taken
from the ends of the earth,
And called from its remotest
parts
And said to you, 'You are My
servant,
I have chosen you and have not
rejected you [even though you
are exiled].
10 'Do not fear [anything], for I am
with you;
Do not be afraid, for I am your
God.
I will strengthen you, be assured I
will help you;
I will certainly take hold of you
with My righteous right hand
[a hand of justice, of power,
of victory, of salvation].'
[Acts 18:10]
11 "Indeed, all those who are angry
with you will be put to shame
and humiliated;
Those who strive against you will
be as nothing and will perish.
12 "You shall search for those who
quarrel with you, but will not
find them;
They who war against you will be
as nothing, as nothing at all.
13 "For I the LORD your God keep
hold of your right hand; [I am
the Lord],
Who says to you, 'Do not fear, I
will help you.'
14 "Do not fear, you worm Jacob, you
men of Israel;
I will help you," declares the LORD,
"and your Redeemer is the Holy
One of Israel.
15 "In fact, I have made of you a new,
sharp threshing implement with
sharp edges;
You will thresh the mountains and
crush them,
And make the hills like chaff.
16 "You will winnow them, and the
wind will carry them away,
And a high wind will scatter
them;
But you will rejoice in the LORD,
You will glory in the Holy One of
Israel.

17 "The poor and needy are seeking
water, but there is none;
Their tongues are parched with
thirst.
I, the LORD, will answer them
Myself;
I, the God of Israel, will not neglect
them.
18 "I will open rivers on the barren
heights
And springs in the midst of the
valleys;
I will make the wilderness a reed-
pool of water
And the dry land springs of
water.
19 "I will put the cedar in the
wilderness,
The acacia, the myrtle and the
olive tree;
I will place the juniper in the
desert
Together with the box tree and the
cypress,
20 So that they may see and know,
And consider and understand
together,
That the hand of the LORD has
done this,
That the Holy One of Israel has
created it.

41:14 *Redeemer.* For Israel, the redeemer was the family protector of distressed relatives, who could avenge murder (Nu 35:19) and redeem indentured slaves (Lev 25:47 – 49). When the Lord is called the Redeemer, the title highlights His zeal to defend, protect, and purchase back His people (49:26).
41:16 *winnow them.* As threshed grain is tossed in the air or "winnowed" to separate the chaff, so the victorious people of God would be able to "blow away" their enemies.

8 Dt 7:6; 10:15; Ps 135:4; Isa 43:1; 2Ch 20:7; Jas 2:23 **10** ver. 13,14; Isa 43:5; Dt 31:6 **11** Ex 23:22; Isa 45:24; 60:12; Zec 12:3 **15** Mic 4:13; 2Co 10:4 **16** Jer 51:2; Isa 45:25 **18** Isa 35:6,7; 43:19; 44:3; Ps 107:35 **20** Job 12:9

21 "Present your case [for idols made
by men's hands]," says the LORD.
"Produce your evidence [of
divinity],"
Says the king of Jacob.
22 Let them bring forward [their
evidence] and tell us what is
going to happen.
Regarding the former events, tell
what they were,
That we may consider them and
know their outcome;
Or announce to us the things that
are going to come.
23 Tell us the things that are to come
afterward,
That we may know that you are
gods;
Indeed, you should do *something*
good or do evil, that we may be
afraid and fear [you] together [as
we observe the miracle].
24 Hear this! You [idols] are less than
nothing,
And your work is worthless;
The worshiper who chooses you
[as a god] is repulsive. [1 Cor 8:4]

25 "I have stirred up *and* put into
action one from the north [the
king of Persia, Cyrus the Great],
and he has come;
From the rising of the sun he will
call on My Name [in prayer].
And he will trample on [the
Babylonian] officials as on
mortar,
Even as a potter treads clay."
[2 Chr 36:23; Ezra 1:1–3]
26 Who [among the idols] has
declared this from the
beginning, so that we could
know?
Or from earlier times, so
that we could say, "*He is*
[unquestionably] right!"?
In fact, there was no one who
declared it,
Indeed, there was no one who
proclaimed it;
There was no one at all who heard
you speak [for you pagan gods
are speechless].
27 "I was first to say to Zion, 'Listen
carefully, here they are [the
Jews who will be restored to
their own land].'
And to Jerusalem, 'I will provide a
messenger (Isaiah) to bring the
good news [that Cyrus will be
stirred up *and* put into action to
save them].' [Is 40:9; 52:7]
28 "But when I look [on the pagan
prophets and priests], there is
no one [who could predict these
events],
And there is no counselor among
them,
Who, if I ask, can give an answer.
29 "In fact, all of these [pagan
prophets and priests] are false;
Their works are worthless,
Their cast images are [merely]
wind and emptiness.

God's Promise concerning His Servant

42 "BEHOLD, MY Servant, whom
I uphold;
My Chosen One *in whom* My soul
delights.
I have put My Spirit upon Him;
He will bring forth justice to the
nations. [Matt 3:16, 17]

41:21 *Present your case.* The Lord is addressing the idols in this passage. He is pointing out that only the Lord can tell the past or the future; He challenges the idols to prove themselves, but they cannot.
41:24 *repulsive.* If the Lord regards idol worshipers as repulsive, we should too.
41:25 *from the north.* The conquest of Media by Cyrus (550 BC) made him master of the territories north of Babylon. Cyrus did not personally know God (45:4), but he nevertheless called on God's name when he released the exiles (2Ch 36:23; Ezr 1:1 – 4).
42:1 *My Servant.* The Lord formally presents His servant. This title is identified with Jesus Christ in the New Testament. This is the beginning of the first song of the Suffering Servant (vv. 1 – 13).

22 Isa 45:21 **23** Isa 42:9; 44:7,8; 45:3; Jn 13:19; Jer 10:5 **24** Ps 115:8; Isa 44:9; 1Co 8:4 **25** Ezr 1:2; ver. 2 **26** Isa 43:9 **27** ver. 4; Isa 40:9 **28** Isa 63:5 **29** ver. 24 **CHAPTER 42 1** Isa 43:10; 49:3,6; Mt 12:18; Php 2:7; Mt 3:17; 17:5; Eph 1:6; Isa 11:2; Jn 3:34

2 "He will not call out or shout
aloud,
Nor make His voice heard in the
street.
3 "A broken reed He will not break
[off]
And a dimly burning wick He
will not extinguish [He will not
harm those who are weak and
suffering];
He will faithfully bring forth
justice. [Matt 12:17–21]
4 "He will not be disheartened or
crushed [in spirit];
[He will persevere] until He has
established justice on the earth;
And the coastlands will wait
expectantly for His law."
[Rom 8:22–25]

5 This is what God the LORD says,

He who created the heavens and
stretched them out,
Who spread out the earth and its
produce,
Who gives breath to the people
on it
And spirit to those who walk on it,
6 "I am the LORD, I have called You
(the Messiah) in righteousness
[for a righteous purpose],
I will also take You by the hand
and keep watch over You,
And I will appoint You as a
covenant to the people [Israel],
As a light to the nations (Gentiles),
7 To open the eyes of the blind,
To bring out prisoners from the
dungeon
And those who sit in darkness
from the prison. [Matt 12:18–21]
8 "I am the LORD, that is My Name;
My glory I will not give to another,
Nor My praise to carved idols.
9 "Indeed, the former things have
come to pass,
Now I declare new things;
Before they spring forth I proclaim
them to you."
10 Sing to the LORD a new song,
Sing His praise from the end of the
earth!
You who go down to the sea, and
all that is in it,
You islands *and* coastlands, and
those who inhabit them [sing
His praise]!
11 Let the wilderness and its cities lift
up *their voices,*
The villages where Kedar lives.
Let the inhabitants of Sela shout
for joy,
Let them shout joyfully from the
tops of the mountains.
12 Let them give glory to the LORD
And declare His praise in the
islands *and* coastlands.
13 The LORD will go forth like a
warrior,
He will stir up *His* zeal like a man
of war;
He will shout out, yes, He will
raise a war cry.
He will prevail [mightily] against
His enemies.

The Blindness of the People

14 "I [the LORD] have been silent for a
long time,
I have been still and restrained
Myself.
Now I will moan like a woman in
labor,
I will both gasp and pant.
15 "I will lay waste the mountains
and hills
And wither all their vegetation;
I will turn the rivers into
coastlands
And dry up the ponds.
16 "I will lead the blind by a way they
do not know;

42:3 *broken reed ... dimly burning wick.* The Servant will restore that which is broken; He will not break or snuff out the needy.
42:6 *covenant.* The Servant will institute a new covenant binding Israel to the Lord (49:8). The prophets refer to this new covenant as a "covenant of peace" (54:10; Eze 34:25); an "everlasting covenant" (which is also associated with the Davidic covenant, 55:3); a "new covenant" (Jer 31:31 – 34); and most often simply as covenant. ***people.*** The "people" refers to the Gentiles.

4 Ge 49:10 **5** Isa 44:24; Zec 12:1; Ac 17:25 **6** Isa 43:1; Isa 49:8; Isa 49:6; Lk 2:32; Ac 13:47 **7** Isa 35:5; Isa 61:1; Lk 4:18; 2Ti 2:26; Heb 2:14; Isa 9:2 **8** Isa 48:11 **10** Ps 33:3; 40:3; 98:1; Ps 107:23 **13** Isa 31:4

I will guide them in paths that they do not know.
I will make darkness into light before them
And rugged places into plains.
These things I will do [for them],
And I will not leave them abandoned *or* undone."
17 Those who trust in carved idols will be turned back,
And utterly put to shame,
Who say to cast images,
"You are our gods."

18 Hear, you deaf!
And look, you blind, that you may see.
19 Who is blind but My servant [Israel],
Or deaf like My messenger whom I send?
Who is blind like the one who is at peace *with Me* [in a covenant relationship],
Or so blind as the servant of the LORD?
20 You have seen many things, but you do not observe them;
Your ears are open, but no one hears.
21 The LORD was pleased for His righteousness' sake
To make the law great and prove to be glorious.
22 But this is a people despoiled and plundered;
All of them are trapped in holes,
Or are hidden away in prisons.
They have become a prey with no one to rescue them,
And a spoil, with no one to say,
"Give them back!" [Luke 19:41–44]
23 Who among you will listen to this?
Who will listen and pay attention in the time to come?
24 Who gave up Jacob [the kingdom of Judah] for spoil, and [the kingdom of] Israel to the plunderers?
Was it not the LORD, He against whom we [of Judah] have sinned,
And in whose ways they [of Israel] were unwilling to walk,
And whose law *and* teaching they did not obey?
25 Therefore He poured out on Israel the heat of His anger
And the fierceness of battle;
And engulfed him in fire,
Yet he did not recognize [the lesson of repentance which the Assyrian conquest was intended to teach];
It burned him, but he did not take it to heart.

Israel Redeemed

43 BUT NOW, this is what the LORD, your Creator says, O Jacob,
And He who formed you, O Israel,
"Do not fear, for I have redeemed you [from captivity];
I have called you by name; you are Mine!
2 "When you pass through the waters, I will be with you;
And through the rivers, they will not overwhelm you.
When you walk through fire, you will not be scorched,
Nor will the flame burn you.

42:17 *carved idols.* Why is idolatry so terrible in God's sight? Several reasons may be given. It displays a total ignorance of the true nature and being of the Creator. He is invisible, eternal, all-knowing, and all-present Spirit, without limitations. Idolatry usually reduces the concept of God to an ugly metal or wooden object, which is almost always perceived as evil and bloodthirsty, selfish and capricious. Finally, idolatry provides absolutely no indication of those characteristics closest to God's heart — His love, mercy, grace, and holiness.

42:18 – 25 *Hear, you deaf.* This prophecy, justifying the exile as punishment, consists of two parts. First, the Lord addresses the fact that the people did not listen to Him.

42:24 *sinned.* The second part of the prophecy addresses the sin of the exiles, which was the reason for the punishment.

43:1 *this is what the LORD, your Creator says.* This statement emphasizes the authority of the words that will follow.

17 Ps 97:7; Isa 1:29; 44:11; 45:16 **19** Isa 43:8; Eze 12:2; See Jn 9:39,41 **20** Ro 2:21 **25** 2Ki 25:9; Hos 7:9
CHAPTER 43 **1** ver. 7,21; Isa 44:2,21; Isa 44:6; Isa 42:6; 45:4 **2** Ps 66:12; 91:3; Dt 31:6; Da 3:25

3 "For I am the LORD your God,
The Holy One of Israel, your Savior;
I have given Egypt [to the Babylonians] as your ransom,
Cush (ancient Ethiopia) and Seba [its province] in exchange for you.
4 "Because you are precious in My sight,
You are honored and I love you,
I will give *other* men in return for you and *other* peoples in exchange for your life.
5 "Do not fear, for I am with you;
I will bring your offspring from the east [where they are scattered],
And gather you from the west. [Acts 18:10]
6 "I will say to the north, 'Give them up!'
And to the south, 'Do not hold them back.'
Bring My sons from far way
And My daughters from the ends of the earth,
7 Everyone who is called by My Name,
Whom I have created for My glory,
Whom I have formed, even whom I have made."

Israel Is God's Witness

8 Bring out the people who are blind, even though they have eyes,
And the deaf, even though they have ears.
9 All the nations have gathered together
So that the peoples may be assembled.
Who among them (the idolaters) can predict this [that Judah would return from captivity]
And proclaim to us the former events?
Let them provide their witnesses so that they may be justified,
Or let them hear and say [in acknowledgement], "It is the truth." [Ps 123:3, 4]
10 "You are My witnesses," declares the LORD,
"And My servant whom I have chosen,
That you may know and believe Me
And understand that I am He.
Before Me there was no God formed,
And there will be none after Me.
11 "I, [only] I, am the LORD,
And there is no Savior besides Me.
12 "I have declared [the future] and saved [the nation] and proclaimed [that I am God],
And there was no strange (alien) *god* among you;
Therefore you are My witnesses [among the pagans]," declares the LORD,
"That I am God.
13 "Even from eternity I am He,
And there is no one who can rescue from My hand;
I act, and who can revoke *or* reverse it?"

Babylon to Be Destroyed

14 This is what the LORD your Redeemer, the Holy One of Israel says,

"For your sake I have sent [one] to Babylon,
And I will bring down all of them as fugitives,
Even the Chaldeans [who reign in Babylon], into the ships over which they rejoiced.
15 "I am the LORD, your Holy One,
The Creator of Israel, your King."

16 This is what the LORD says,

He who makes a way through the sea

43:14 ***This is what the LORD . . . says.*** The same phrase (v. 1) is used to emphasize the ultimate source of this prophecy, God Himself. ***Redeemer.*** The Lord is described as Redeemer because He zealously defends, protects, and purchases back His people (41:14).

3 Pr 11:8; 21:18 **5** Isa 41:10; 44:2; Jer 30:10; 46:27,28 **7** Isa 63:19; Jas 2:7; Ps 100:3; Isa 29:23; Jn 3:3,5; 2Co 5:17; Eph 2:10; ver. 1 **8** Isa 6:9; 42:19; Eze 12:2 **9** Isa 41:21,22,26 **10** Isa 44:8; Isa 55:4; Isa 44:6 **11** Isa 45:21; Hos 13:4 **12** Dt 32:16; Ps 81:9; Isa 44:8 **13** Ps 90:2; Jn 8:58; Job 9:12; Isa 14:27 **16** Ex 14:16; Ps 77:19; Isa 51:10; Jos 3:13

And a path through the mighty
waters,
17 He who brings out the chariot and
the horse,
The army and the mighty *warrior*,
(They will lie down together, they
will not rise again;
They have been extinguished, they
have been put out like a *lamp's*
wick):
18 "Do not remember the former
things,
Or ponder the things of the past.
19 "Listen carefully, I am about to do
a new thing,
Now it will spring forth;
Will you not be aware of it?
I will even put a road in the
wilderness,
Rivers in the desert.
20 "The beasts of the field will honor
Me,
Jackals and ostriches,
Because I have given waters in the
wilderness
And rivers in the desert,
To give drink to My people, My
chosen. [Is 41:17, 18; 48:21]
21 "The people whom I formed for
Myself
Will make known My praise.

The Shortcomings of Israel

22 "Yet you have not called on Me [in
prayer and worship], O Jacob;
But you have grown weary of Me,
O Israel.
23 "You have not brought Me your
sheep *or* goats for your burnt
offerings,
Nor honored Me with your
sacrifices.
I have not burdened you with
offerings,
Nor wearied you with [demands
for offerings of] incense.
24 "You have not bought Me sweet
cane with money,
Nor have you filled Me with the fat
of your sacrifices;
But you have burdened Me with
your sins,
You have wearied Me with your
wickedness.
25 "I, *only* I, am He who wipes out
your transgressions for My own
sake,
And I will not remember your sins.
26 "Remind Me [of your merits with
a thorough report], let us plead
and argue our case together;
State your *position*, that you may
be proved right.
27 "Your first father [Jacob] sinned,
And your spokesmen [the priests
and the prophets—your
mediators] have transgressed
against Me.
28 "So I will profane the officials of
the sanctuary,
And I will consign Jacob to
destruction and [I will subject]
Israel to defamation *and* abuse.

The Blessings of Israel

44 "BUT NOW listen, O Jacob,
My servant,
And Israel, whom I have chosen:
2 This is what the LORD who made
you
And formed you from the womb,
who will help you says,
'Fear not, O Jacob My servant;
And Jeshurun (Israel, the upright
one) whom I have chosen.
[Deut 32:15; 33:5, 26]
3 'For I will pour out water on him
who is thirsty,
And streams on the dry ground;
I will pour out My Spirit on your
offspring

43:22 *Yet you.* After the splendid and glorious declarations of His faithfulness, the Lord addresses the unfaithfulness of His people.
43:25 *for My own sake.* The Lord chooses to save and forgive. This arises out of His own character (37:35; 42:21; 48:9,11).
44:2 *Jeshurun.* Jeshurun, meaning "upright one," is a poetic word for the nation of Israel (Dt 32:15).

17 Ex 14:4-9,25 **18** Jer 16:14 **19** 2Co 5:17; Rev 21:5; Ex 17:6; Nu 20:11; Dt 8:15; Ps 78:16 **20** Isa 48:21 **21** Ps 102:18; Eph 1:5,6 **22** Mal 1:13 **23** Am 5:25 **24** Isa 1:14; Mal 2:17 **25** Isa 44:22; Jer 50:20; Ac 3:19; Eze 36:22; Isa 1:18; Jer 31:34 **28** Isa 47:6; La 2:2,6; Ps 79:4; Jer 24:9; Da 9:11; Zec 8:13 **CHAPTER 44** **1** ver. 21; Jer 30:10; 46:27,28 **2** Isa 43:1,7; Dt 32:15 **3** Isa 35:7; Joel 2:28; Jn 7:38; Ac 2:18

And My blessing on your
descendants; [Is 32:15; 35:6, 7; Joel 2:28; John 7:37–39]
4 And they will spring up among the grass
Like willows by the streams of water.'
5 "One will say, 'I am the LORD's';
And another will name himself after Jacob;
And another will write on his hand, 'I am the LORD's,'
And be called by the [honorable] name of Israel.

6 "For the LORD, the King of Israel
and his Redeemer, the LORD of hosts
says this,
'I am the First and I am the Last;
And there is no God besides Me. [Rev 1:17; 2:8; 22:13]
7 'Who is like Me? Let him proclaim it and declare it;
Yes, let him confront Me,
Since I established the people of antiquity.
And let them [those supposed gods] tell those people [who foolishly follow them] the things to come
And the events that are going to take place.
8 'Do not tremble nor be afraid [of the violent upheavals to come];
Have I not long ago proclaimed it to you and declared it?
And you are My witnesses.
Is there a God besides Me?
There is no *other* Rock;
I know of none.' "

The Folly of Idolatry

9 All who make carved idols are
nothing. Their precious objects are
worthless [to them], and their own witnesses (worshipers) fail to see or know, so that they will be put to shame.
10 Who has made a god or cast an idol
which is profitable for nothing?
11 In fact, all his companions will be
put to shame, for the craftsmen themselves are mere men. Let them all assemble, let them stand up, let them be terrified, let them together be put to shame.
12 The ironsmith shapes iron *and*
uses a chisel and works it over the coals. He forms the [idol's] core with hammers and works it with his strong arm. He also becomes hungry and his strength fails; he drinks no water and grows tired.
13 The carpenter stretches out a mea-
suring line, he marks out the shape [of the idol] with red chalk; he works it with planes and outlines it with the compass; and he makes it like the form of a man, like the beauty of man, that it may sit in a house.
14 He cuts cedars for himself, and
takes a cypress or an oak and lets it grow strong for himself among the trees of the forest. He plants a fir, and the rain nourishes it.
15 Then it becomes *fuel* for a man
to burn, so he takes one of them and warms himself; he also kindles a fire to bake bread. He also makes a god [from the same wood] and worships it. He makes it into a carved idol [with his own hands] and falls down and worships it!
16 He burns half of the wood in the
fire; over this half he [cooks and] eats meat, he roasts meat and is satisfied. Also he warms himself and says, "Aha! I am warm, I have seen the fire."
17 But from what is left of the wood

44:6 *King of Israel.* For background, read Psalm 99, which begins by declaring, "The LORD reigns."
44:8 *you are My witnesses.* The people of Israel had already witnessed great miracles on their behalf (43:10).
44:9 – 20 *All who make carved idols.* This passage skillfully displays the utter absurdity of trusting in idols. Idolatry is a source of shame (v. 11), and it is caused by a deceived heart (v. 20). This is a passage to remember and to come back to, for idolatry was a continual snare to the Israelites. We need to remember in our modern age that we are not immune to this sin; it is the Second Commandment, the reminder that nothing must come between us and our relationship to God.

6 Isa 41:4; Rev 1:8,17; 22:13 **7** Isa 41:4,22 **8** Isa 41:22; Isa 43:10; Dt 4:35; 32:39; 1Sa 2:2; 2Sa 22:32 **9** Isa 41:24; Ps 115:4 **10** Jer 10:5; Hab 2:18 **11** Ps 97:7; Isa 1:29; 42:17 **12** Isa 40:19; Jer 10:3

he makes a god, his carved idol. He falls down before it, he worships it and prays to it and says, "Save me, for you are my god."
18 They do not know, nor do they understand, for God has muddied their eyes so that they cannot see, and their hearts (minds) *as well* so that they cannot understand.
19 No one remembers, nor has knowledge and understanding [enough] to say [to himself], "I have burned half of this log in the fire, and also baked bread on its coals and have roasted meat and eaten it. Then I make the rest of it into an repulsive thing [to God]; I bow down [to worship] before a block of wood!"
20 That kind of man (the idolater) feeds on ashes [and is satisfied with ashes]! A deceived mind has led him astray, so that he cannot save himself, or ask, "Is this thing [that I am holding] in my right hand not a lie?"

God Forgives and Redeems

21 "Remember [the foolishness of] these things, O Jacob
And Israel, for you are My servant!
I formed you, you are My servant;
O Israel, you will not be forgotten by Me.
22 "I have wiped out your transgressions like a thick cloud
And your sins like a heavy mist.
Return to Me, for I have redeemed you."
23 Shout for joy, O heavens, for the LORD has done it!
Shout in triumph, you depths of the earth;
Break forth into jubilant rejoicing, you mountains,
O forest, and every tree in it!
For the LORD has redeemed Jacob,
And He shows His glory in Israel.

24 For the LORD, your Redeemer, and He who formed you from the womb says this,

"I am the LORD, Maker of all things,
Who alone stretches out the heavens,
Who spreads out the earth by Myself,
25 Frustrating the signs *and* confounding the omens of boasters (false prophets),
Making fools out of fortune-tellers,
Counteracting the wise
And making their knowledge ridiculous, [1 Cor 1:20]
26 Confirming the word of His servant
And carrying out the plan of His messengers.
It is I who says of Jerusalem, 'She shall [again] be inhabited!'
And of the cities of Judah, 'They shall [again] be built.'
And I will raise up *and* restore her ruins.
27 "*It is I* who says to the deep, 'Be dried up!'
And I will make your rivers dry.
28 "*It is I* who says of Cyrus, 'He is My shepherd (ruler),
And he will carry out all that I desire—'
Saying of Jerusalem, 'She shall [again] be built,'

44:22 *wiped out.* The idea of total forgiveness of sins is also found in 40:2 and 43:25.
44:23 *shows His glory.* When He saves, the Lord demonstrates to the world His mercy and His power and His glory.
44:24 *the LORD . . . says this.* Because the Lord says it, it will come to pass.
44:25 *fortune-tellers.* This term refers to people who attempt to foretell the future through occult practices. They are often mentioned along with other practitioners of the occult — all of whom were forbidden in Israel (Dt 18:10 – 22). Fortune-tellers brought trouble on themselves, and on their nations as well (Dt 18:10; 2Ki 17:17 – 18; Mic 3:6 – 7).
44:28 *Cyrus.* Here, Isaiah mentions by name the king of Persia who would allow the Israelites to return to Jerusalem in 538 BC (Ezr 1:1 – 4). He was a chosen servant of God, even though he was not an Israelite. Isaiah's prophecy was made more than 150 years before it was fulfilled.

18 Isa 45:20; 2Th 2:11 **19** Isa 46:8 **20** Hos 4:12; Ro 1:21; 2Th 2:11 **21** ver. 1,2 **22** Isa 43:25; Isa 43:1; 1Co 6:20; 1Pe 1:18 **23** Ps 69:34; Isa 42:10; 49:13; Jer 51:48; Rev 18:20 **24** Isa 43:14; Isa 43:1; Job 9:8 **25** Isa 47:13; Jer 50:36; 1Co 1:20 **26** Zec 1:6 **27** Jer 50:38; 51:32,36 **28** 2Ch 36:22; Ezr 1:1; Isa 45:13

And of the temple, 'Your
foundation shall [again] be
laid.' "

God Uses Cyrus

45 THIS IS what the LORD says to
His anointed, to Cyrus [king of
Persia],
Whose right hand I have held
To subdue nations before him,
And I will ungird the loins of
kings [disarming them];
To open doors before him so that
gates will not be shut:
2 "I will go before you and level the
mountains;
I will shatter the doors of bronze
and cut through the bars of iron.
3 "I will give you the treasures
of darkness [the hoarded
treasures]
And the hidden riches of secret
places,
So that you may know that it is I,
The LORD, the God of Israel, who
calls you (Cyrus the Great) by
your name.
4 "For the sake of Jacob My servant,
And of Israel My chosen,
I have also called you by your name;
I have given you an honorable
name
Though you have not known Me.
5 "I am the LORD, and there is no one
else;
There is no God except Me.
I will embrace *and* arm you,
though you have not
known Me,
6 That people may know from the
rising to the setting of the sun
[the world over]
That there is no one except Me.
I am the LORD, and there is no
other,
7 The One forming light and
creating darkness,
Causing peace and creating
disaster;
I am the LORD who does all these
things.

God's Supreme Power

8 "Rain down, O heavens, from
above,
Let the clouds pour down
righteousness [all the blessings
of God];
Let the earth open up, let salvation
bear fruit,
And righteousness spring up
with it;
I, the LORD, have created it.
9 "Woe (judgment is coming) to him
who quarrels with his Maker—

45:3 *treasures of darkness.* These treasures are an allusion to the fabled wealth of Sardis captured by Cyrus in 546 BC. ***who calls you (Cyrus the Great) by your name.*** The Lord specifically named Cyrus and appointed his work before he became king, and even before he was born. Isaiah was ministering from approximately 740 to 701 BC, which was at least 150 years before Cyrus became prominent. The Lord picked out Cyrus, but He picked out each of us too, to do good works which He had planned beforehand for us to do (Eph 2:10).

45:8 *have created it.* In the Middle East, pagan people commonly believed that the fertility of the earth and maintenance of the social order depended on the king's right relationship with a deity. Isaiah was proclaiming the Lord's clear statement that it is the Lord alone who made the earth and blesses it with rain and with righteousness.

45:9 *broken pieces.* The ultimate act of insanity committed by the human soul is unfaithfulness. As the prophet Isaiah shows, how inconceivable and ridiculous it would be for a simple piece of pottery to lash out at the craftsman. And yet, that was what Israel had consistently done from the exodus of Egypt to the destruction of the second temple by Titus in 70 AD Jonah was a classic example of unfaithfulness. In the Book of Jonah, all nature spontaneously obeyed its Creator. The ocean churned, the fish appeared, the gourd grew, the worm ate, and the east wind blew at the command of God. The only object in that narrative that dared disobey was Jonah the prophet. What law of logic would allow a finite and sinful creature to brazenly speak out against the infinite and sovereign Creator of all things? (Compare Romans 9:20.)

CHAPTER 45 **1** Isa 41:13; Da 5:30 **2** Isa 40:4; Ps 107:16 **3** Isa 41:23; Ex 33:12 **4** Isa 44:1 **5** Dt 4:35; 32:39; Isa 44:8; ver. 14,18; Ps 18:32 **6** Ps 102:15; Mal 1:11 **7** Am 3:6 **8** Ps 85:11 **9** Isa 64:8; Isa 29:16; Jer 18:6; Ro 9:20

A [worthless] piece of broken
pottery among other broken
pieces [equally worthless]!
Shall the clay say to the potter,
'What are you doing?'
Or does the thing say, 'He has no
hands'? [Rom 9:20]
10 "Woe (judgment is coming) to him
who says to a father, 'What are
you fathering?'
Or to a woman, 'With what are
you in labor?' "

11 For the LORD, the Holy One of Is-
rael, and its Maker says this,

"Ask Me about the things to come
concerning My sons,
And give Me orders concerning
the work of My hands.
12 "I made the earth and created man
upon it.
My hands, stretched out the
heavens,
And I commanded all their host.
13 "I have stirred up Cyrus *and* put
him into action in righteousness
[to accomplish My purpose]
And I will make all his ways
smooth;
He will build My city and let My
exiles go,
Without any payment or reward,"
says the LORD of hosts.

14 For this is what the LORD says,

"The products of Egypt and the
merchandise of Cush (ancient
Ethiopia)
And the Sabeans, men of
stature,
Will come over to you and they
will be yours;
They will walk behind you, in
chains [of subjection to you] they
will come over,
And they will bow down before
you;
They will make supplication to
you, [humbly and earnestly]
saying,
'Most certainly God is with you,
and there is no other,
No other God [besides Him].' "
[1 Cor 14:25]
15 Truly, You are a God who hides
Himself,
O God of Israel, Savior!
16 They will be put to shame and also
humiliated, all of them;
They who make idols will go away
together in humiliation.
17 Israel has been saved by the LORD
With an everlasting salvation;
You will not be put to shame or
humiliated
for all eternity. [Heb 5:9]

18 For the LORD, who created the
heavens (He is God, who formed the
earth and made it; He established it
and did not create it to be a wasteland,
but formed it to be inhabited) says this,

"I am the LORD, and there is no
one else.
19 "I have not spoken in secret,
In a corner of a land of darkness;
I did not say to the descendants of
Jacob,
'Seek Me in vain [with no benefit
for yourselves].'
I, the LORD, speak righteousness
[the truth—trustworthy, a
straightforward correlation
between deeds and words],
Declaring things that are upright.
[John 18:20]
20 "Assemble yourselves and come;
Come together, you survivors of
the nations!
They are ignorant,
Who carry around their wooden
idols [in religious processions or
into battle]

45:14 *Will come over to you and they will be yours.* The "you" and "yours" are both feminine singular, referring to the Daughter of Zion.
45:19 *in secret . . . darkness.* The diviners pronounced their mysterious and ambiguous oracles in secret and dark places. The Lord's prophets proclaimed the truth openly to all who would listen.

11 Jer 31:9; Isa 29:23 **12** Isa 42:5; Ge 1:26; 2:1 **13** Isa 41:2; 2Ch 36:22; Ro 3:24 **14** Ps 68:31; Zec 8:22; Ps 149:8; 1Co 14:25; ver. 5 **15** Ps 44:24; Isa 57:17 **16** Isa 44:11 **17** Isa 26:4 **18** Isa 42:5; ver. 5 **19** Dt 30:11; Ps 19:8 **20** Isa 46:7

And keep on praying to a god that
cannot save them.
21 "Declare and present *your defense of idols;*
Indeed, let them consult together.
Who announced this [rise of Cyrus and his conquests] long before *it happened?*
Who declared it long ago?
Was it not I, the LORD?
And there is no other God besides Me,
A [consistently and uncompromisingly] just *and* righteous God and a Savior;
There is none except Me.
22 "Turn to Me and be saved, all the ends of the earth;
For I am God, and there is no other.
23 "I have sworn [an oath] by Myself,
The word is gone out of My mouth in righteousness
And shall not return,
That to Me every knee shall bow, every tongue shall swear [allegiance]. [Rom 14:11; Phil 2:10, 11; Heb 6:13]
24 "It shall be said of Me, 'Only in the LORD are righteousness and strength.'
To Him people will come,
And all who were angry at Him will be put to shame. [1 Cor 1:30, 31]
25 "In the LORD all the offspring of Israel
Will be justified (declared free of guilt) and will glory [in God]."

Babylon's Idols and the True God

46 BEL HAS bowed down, Nebo stoops over;
Their idols are on the beasts [of burden] and on the cattle.
Your burdens [of idols] are loaded [on them],
Burdens on the weary *animals.*
2 They stooped over, they have bowed down together;
They could not rescue the burden [of their own idols],
But have themselves gone into captivity.

3 "Listen to Me," [says the LORD], "O house of Jacob,
And all the remnant of the house of Israel,
You who have been carried *by Me* from your birth
And have been carried [in My arms] from the womb,
4 Even to *your* old age I am He,
And even to *your* advanced old age I will carry you!
I have made *you,* and I will carry *you;*
Be assured I will carry *you* and I will save *you.*

5 "To whom would you liken Me
And make Me equal and compare Me,
That we may be alike? [Is 40:18–20]
6 "Those who lavish gold from the bag
And weigh out silver on the scales

45:23 ***I have sworn [an oath] by Myself.*** The Lord's promise to Abraham was sworn by Himself (Ge 22:16; Heb 6:13), and whatever God promises will come to pass, for He cannot lie. The certainty of the Word of the Lord is emphasized strongly in the Book of Isaiah (40:8). ***to Me every knee shall bow.*** This promise will be fulfilled in Jesus Christ (Ro 14:11; 1Co 15:24–25; Php 2:10–11).
45:24–25 ***justified.*** God breaks the stranglehold of nations to secure the release of His people from captivity. In the same way, God also breaks the stranglehold of sin to release his people from spiritual bondage. He does so by pouring forth righteousness through the atoning sacrifice of Jesus Christ on the cross. This is the centerpiece of God's salvation, which is worldwide in its scope. It is the only ground for acceptance by God, the only foundation for fellowship with God, and the only platform of service to God. Those who embrace it find that they are released from sin's guilt and that they are also given strength to have victory over sin. No wonder this all evokes jubilant praise!
46:1 ***Bel . . . Nebo.*** Bel, meaning "Lord," was a title of Marduk, Babylon's chief deity. Nebo, Marduk's son, was the god of fate, writing, and wisdom.

21 Isa 41:22; 43:9; Isa 44:8 **22** Ps 22:27; 65:5 **23** Heb 6:13; Php 2:10; Ps 63:11 **24** Jer 23:5; 1Co 1:30; Isa 41:11 **25** ver. 17; 1Co 1:31 **CHAPTER 46** **1** Isa 21:9; Jer 50:2; Jer 10:5 **2** Jer 48:7 **3** Dt 32:11; Ps 71:6 **4** Mal 3:6; Ps 48:14 **5** Isa 40:18 **6** Isa 40:19; 41:6; Jer 10:3

Hire a goldsmith, and he makes it
into a god;
They bow down, indeed they
worship it.
7 "They lift it on their shoulders [in
religious processions or into
battle] and carry it;
They set it in its place and *there* it
remains standing.
It cannot move from its place.
Even if one cries to it [for help], the
idol cannot answer;
It cannot save him from his distress.
8 "Remember this, and take courage;
Take it to heart, you rebellious *and*
disloyal people.
9 "Remember [carefully] the former
things [which I did] from ages
past;
For I am God, and there is no one
else;
I am God, and there is no one
like Me,
10 Declaring the end *and* the result
from the beginning,
And from ancient times the things
which have not [yet] been done,
Saying, 'My purpose will be
established,
And I will do all that pleases Me
and fulfills My purpose,'
11 Calling a bird of prey from the east,
From a far country, the man
(Cyrus) of My purpose.
Truly I have spoken; truly I will
bring it to pass.
I have planned it, *be assured* I will
do it.
12 "Listen to Me, you stiff-necked
people,
You who are far from righteousness
(right standing with God).
13 "I bring near My righteousness [in
the salvation of Israel], it is not
far away;
And My salvation will not delay.
And I will grant salvation in Zion,
And My glory for Israel.

Lament for Babylon

47 "COME DOWN and sit in the
dust,
O virgin daughter of Babylon;
Sit on the ground [in abject
humiliation]; there is no throne
for you,
O daughter of the Chaldeans,
For you will no longer be called
tender and delicate.
2 "Take millstones [as a female slave
does] and grind meal;
Remove your veil, strip off the
skirt,
Uncover the leg, cross the rivers [at
the command of your captors].
3 "Your nakedness will be
uncovered,
Your shame will also be exposed;
I will take vengeance and will
spare no man."
4 Our Redeemer [will do all this], the
LORD of hosts is His name,
The Holy One of Israel.
5 "Sit in silence, and go into
darkness,
O daughter of the Chaldeans;
For you will no longer be called
The queen of kingdoms.
6 "I was angry with My people,
I profaned [Judah] My inheritance
And gave them into your hand
[Babylon].
You showed them no mercy;
You made your yoke very heavy
on the aged.

46:11 *bird of prey from the east.* The ravenous bird refers to Cyrus (41:2) and to the speed and power of his conquests.
47:2 *grind meal.* Grinding meal was usually a job for female slaves (Ex 11:5). ***Uncover the leg.*** This phrase suggests doing menial labor with overtones of the shame of indecent exposure. A woman who was doing heavy labor may have needed more freedom of movement than was possible without shortening her skirts.
47:3 *nakedness.* Nakedness indicates disgrace, impropriety, lack of dignity, and vulnerability (Ge 9:22–23).
47:6 *You showed them no mercy.* Babylon's cruel abuse of Israel when the Lord had given them into Babylon's "hand" would be avenged,

7 Jer 10:5; Isa 45:20 **8** Isa 44:19 **9** Dt 32:7; Isa 45:5,21 **10** Isa 45:21; Ps 33:11; Pr 19:21; Ac 5:39; Heb 6:17 **11** Isa 41:2,25; Isa 44:28; Nu 23:19 **12** Ps 76:5; Ro 10:3 **13** Ro 1:17; Hab 2:3; Isa 62:11 **CHAPTER 47** **1** Jer 48:18; Isa 3:26 **2** Ex 11:5; Jdg 16:21; Mt 24:41 **3** Isa 3:17; 20:4; Jer 13:22; Na 3:5; Ro 12:19 **4** Jer 50:34 **5** 1Sa 2:9; Da 2:37 **6** See 2Sa 24:14; 2Ch 28:9; Zec 1:15; Isa 43:28; Dt 28:50

7 "And you said, 'I shall be a queen
forevermore.'
You did not consider these things,
Nor did you [seriously] remember
the [ultimate] outcome of such
conduct.

8 "Now, then, hear this, you who live
a luxuriant life,
You who dwell safely *and* securely,
Who say in your heart (mind),
'I am [the queen], and there is no
one besides me.
I shall not sit as a widow,
Nor know the loss of children.'
9 "But these two things shall come
to you abruptly, in one day:
Loss of children and widowhood.
They will come on you in full
measure
In spite of your many [claims of
power through your] sorceries,
In spite of the great power of your
enchantments. [Rev 18:7, 8]
10 "For you [Babylon] have trusted
and felt confident in your
wickedness; you have said,
'No one sees me.'
Your wisdom and your knowledge
have led you astray,
And you have said in your heart
(mind),
'I am, and there is no one besides
me.'
11 "Therefore disaster will come on
you;
You will not know how to make it
disappear [with your magic].
And disaster will fall on you
For which you cannot atone [with
all your offerings to your gods];
And destruction about which you
do not know
Will come on you suddenly.
12 "Persist, then, [Babylon] in your
enchantments
And your many sorceries
With which you have labored from
your youth;
Perhaps you will be able to profit
[from them],
Perhaps you may prevail *and*
cause trembling.
13 "You are wearied by your many
counsels.
Just let the astrologers,
The stargazers,
Those who predict by the new
moons [each month]
Stand up and save you from the
things that will come upon you
[Babylon].
14 "In fact, they are like stubble;
Fire burns them.
They cannot save themselves from
the power of the flame [much
less save the nation],
There is no blazing coal for
warming
Nor fire before which to sit!
15 "This is how they have become
to you, those [astrologers and
sorcerers] with whom you have
labored,
Those who have done business
with you from your youth;
Each has wandered in his own way.
There is no one to save you.

Israel's Obstinacy

48 "HEAR THIS, O house of
Jacob, you who are called by
the name of Israel
And who come from the seed of
Judah,
You who swear [allegiance] by the
name of the LORD
And invoke the God of Israel,
But not in truth (sincerity) nor in
righteousness [with moral and
spiritual integrity].

---

as in the case of the Assyrians (10:1–19; 49:25). When God chooses to punish, He is never pleased with a bystander who cheers over the downfall of another.

47:10 *trusted and felt confident in your wickedness.* The selfish pride of the wicked is based in part on believing that there is not an all-knowing, all-seeing God in the universe.

47:12 *Persist.* The admonition to "persist" is facetious. The sorcerers and astrologers have nothing real to offer a person or nation that is having trouble.

---

7 Rev 18:7; Isa 46:8; Dt 32:29 **8** Zep 2:15; Rev 18:7 **9** Isa 51:19; 1Th 5:3; Na 3:4 **10** Ps 52:7; Isa 29:15; Eze 8:12; ver. 8 **11** 1Th 5:3 **13** Isa 57:10; Da 2:2 **14** Na 1:10; Mal 4:1 **15** Rev 18:11 **CHAPTER 48 1** Ps 68:26; Dt 6:13; Zep 1:5; Jer 4:2

2 "For they call themselves [citizens
of Jerusalem] after the holy city
And depend on the God of Israel;
The LORD of hosts is His name.
3 "I have declared the former things
[which happened to Israel] in
times past;
They went forth from My mouth
and I proclaimed them;
Suddenly I acted, and they came
to pass.
4 "Because I know that you are
obstinate,
And your neck is an iron tendon
And your brow is bronze [both
unyielding],
5 I have declared them to you long
ago;
Before they came to pass I
announced them to you,
So that you could not say, 'My idol
has done them,
And my carved image and my
cast image have commanded
them.'
6 "You have heard [these things
foretold]; look at all this [that
has been fulfilled].
And you, will you not declare it?
I proclaim to you [specific] new
things from this time,
Even hidden things which you
have not known.
7 "They are created now [called into
being by the prophetic word]
and not long ago;
And before today you have not
heard of them,
So that you will not say, 'Oh yes!
I knew them.'
8 "You have not heard, you have not
known;
Even from long ago your ear has
not been open.
For I [the LORD] knew that
you [Israel] would act very
treacherously;
You have been called a
transgressor *and* a rebel from
birth.
9 "For the sake of My Name I refrain
from My wrath,
And *for* My praise I restrain
Myself from you,
So that I do not cut you off.
10 "Indeed, I have refined you, but not
as silver;
I have tested *and* chosen you in the
furnace of affliction.
11 "For My own sake, for My own
sake, I will do it [I refrain and do
not completely destroy you];
For how can *My Name* be defiled
and profaned [as it would if My
chosen people were completely
destroyed]?
And I will not give My glory to
another [by permitting the
worshipers of idols to triumph
over you].

End of Captivity Promised

12 "Listen to Me, O Jacob, and Israel,
whom I called;
I am He, I am the First, I am the
Last. [Is 41:4]
13 "My hand founded *and* established
the earth,
And My right hand spread out the
heavens;
When I call to them, they stand
together [in obedience to carry
out My decrees].
14 "Assemble, all of you, and
listen!
Who among them [the idols and
Chaldean astrologers] has
declared these things?

48:5 *declared them to you.* God told His people of events that would come to pass in the future so that they would know that it was He, and He alone, who controlled history.
48:6 *new things . . . hidden things.* God did not tell His people all that the future would unfold. He knew that, if they had possessed such knowledge, they would have misused that knowledge to the detriment of God's plan and themselves.
48:11 *For My own sake.* God's acts of mercy are His own initiative, springing from the depths of His mercy (37:35; 42:21; 43:25).
48:12 *Listen to Me.* This section (vv. 12 – 22) is directed to all Israel and encourages the unrighteous to participate in the Lord's redemption of the nation from Babylon.

2 Isa 52:1; Mic 3:11; Ro 2:17 **3** Isa 44:7,8; Jos 21:45 **4** Ex 32:9; Dt 31:27 **5** ver. 3 **8** Ps 58:3 **9** Ps 79:9; 106:8; Eze 20:9; Ps 78:38 **10** Ps 66:10 **11** ver. 9; Dt 32:26; Eze 20:9; Isa 42:8 **12** Dt 32:39; Isa 44:6; Rev 22:13 **13** Ps 102:25; Isa 40:26 **14** Isa 45:1; Isa 44:28

The LORD loves him (Cyrus
of Persia); he will do His
pleasure *and* purpose against
Babylon,
And his arm *will be against*
the Chaldeans [who reign in
Babylon].
15 "I, even I, have spoken; indeed, I
have called Cyrus;
I have brought him, and will make
his way successful.
16 "Come near to Me, listen to this:
From the beginning I have not
spoken in secret,
From the time that it happened, I
was there.
And now the Lord GOD has sent
Me, and His [Holy] Spirit."

17 This is what the LORD, your Redeemer, the Holy One of Israel says,

"I am the LORD your God, who
teaches you to profit (benefit),
Who leads you in the way that you
should go.
18 "Oh, that you had paid attention to
My commandments!
Then your peace *and* prosperity
would have been like a [flowing]
river,
And your righteousness [the
holiness and purity of the
nation] like the [abundant]
waves of the sea.
19 "Your offspring would have been
like the sand,
And your descendants [in number]
like the grains of sand;
Their name would never be cut off
or destroyed from My presence."
[Gen 13:16; Jer 33:22; Luke 19:42]
20 Get out of Babylon! Flee from the
Chaldeans [who reign there]!
Declare with a voice of jubilation,
proclaim this,
Send it out to the end of the earth;
Say, "The LORD has redeemed His
servant Jacob."
21 They did not thirst when He led
them through the deserts.
He made the waters flow out of the
rock for them;
He split the rock and the waters
flowed.
22 "There is no peace for the wicked,"
says the LORD.

Salvation Reaches to the End of the Earth

49 LISTEN TO Me, O islands *and*
coastlands,
And pay attention, you peoples
from far away.
The LORD has called Me from the
womb;
From the body of My mother He
has named Me.
2 He has made My mouth like a
sharp sword,
In the shadow of His hand He has
kept Me hidden;
And He has made Me a sharpened
arrow,
In His quiver He has hidden Me.
3 And [the LORD] said to Me, "You
are My Servant, Israel,

48:16 *His [Holy] Spirit.* One of the works of the Holy Spirit is to empower believers and their message. Isaiah recognized this task of the Spirit of God. The prophet had delivered unbelievable prophecies in a time when Assyria reigned supreme, speaking of a day when Babylon would replace the Assyrians. He even named the Persian King Cyrus, who would rescue Judah from Babylon. Knowing that these things were hard to believe, he urged the people to listen. He appealed to them on the basis that the Lord had sent him "and his Spirit." Isaiah's message was not simply the message of a man, but the Word of the Holy Spirit, the teacher and director of God's messengers.

48:20 *Declare.* By putting the command "declare" in the present tense, the future salvation is brought vividly into the present.

49:1 – 13 *Listen.* This second song of the Suffering Servant (42:1 – 13) consists of two parts: the Servant's soliloquy (1 – 6) and the Lord's oracles to Him (7 – 9). The song is followed by Isaiah's elaboration (9 – 12), and it concludes with a hymn of praise.

49:2 *mouth like a sharp sword.* The truth is "sharp." It cuts through lies and deception like a sharp sword (Eph 6:17; Heb 4:12; Rev 1:16; 19:15).

15 Isa 45:1,2 **16** Isa 45:19; Zec 2:8 **17** Isa 43:14; Ps 32:8 **18** Dt 32:29; Ps 81:13; Ps 119:165 **19** Ge 22:17; Hos 1:10 **20** Jer 50:8; Ex 19:4-6 **21** Isa 41:17,18; Ex 17:6; Ps 105:41 **22** Isa 57:21 **CHAPTER 49** **1** Isa 41:1; Jer 1:5; Mt 1:20; Jn 10:36 **2** Isa 11:4; Hos 6:5; Rev 1:16; Isa 51:16; Ps 45:5 **3** Isa 42:1; Zec 3:8; Jn 15:8; Eph 1:6

In Whom I will show My glory."
[Gen 32:28; Deut 7:6; 26:18, 19; Eph 1:4–6]
4 Then I said, "I have labored in vain,
I have spent My strength for nothing and vanity (pride, uselessness);
However My justice is with the LORD,
And My reward is with My God."

5 And now says the LORD, who formed Me from the womb to be His Servant,
To bring Jacob back to Him and that Israel might be gathered to Him,
—For I am honored in the eyes of the LORD,
And My God is My strength—
6 He says, "It is too trivial a thing that You should be My Servant
To raise up the tribes of Jacob and to restore the survivors of Israel;
I will also make You a light to the nations
That My salvation may reach to the end of the earth."
7 This is what the LORD, the Redeemer of Israel, Israel's Holy One says,
To the thoroughly despised One,
To the One hated by the nation
To the Servant of rulers,
"Kings will see and arise,
Princes shall also bow down,
Because of the LORD who is faithful, the Holy One of Israel who has chosen You."
8 This is what the LORD says,
"In a favorable time I have answered You,
And in a day of salvation I have helped You;
And I will keep watch over You and give You for a covenant of the people,
To restore the land [from its present state of ruin] and to apportion *and* give as inheritances the deserted hereditary lands, [2 Cor 6:2]
9 Saying to those who are bound *and* captured, 'Go forth,'
And to those who are in [spiritual] darkness, 'Show yourselves [come into the light of the Savior].'
They will feed along the roads [on which they travel],
And their pastures will be on all the bare heights.
10 "They will not hunger or thirst,
Nor will the scorching heat or sun strike them down;
For He who has compassion on them will lead them,
And He will guide them to springs of water. [Rev 7:16, 17]
11 "And I will make all My mountains a roadway,
And My highways will be raised.
12 "In fact, these will come from far away;
And, lo, these *shall come* from the north and from the west,
And these from the land of Aswan (southern Egypt)."
13 Shout for joy, O heavens, and rejoice, O earth,
And break forth into singing, O mountains!
For the LORD has comforted His people
And will have compassion on His afflicted.

Promise to Zion

14 But Zion (Jerusalem in captivity) said, "The LORD has abandoned me,
And my Lord has forgotten me."

49:5 *bring Jacob back.* The political mission of Cyrus to bring Jacob back from Babylon (44:28; 45:13) foreshadows the spiritually redemptive mission of the Servant to free His people from their captivity to sin (42:7).
49:6 *to the nations.* The "nations" refers to those who are not Israel.
49:9 *Go forth.* This is an allusion to Isaiah's command for the exiles to leave Babylon (48:20).
49:14 *has abandoned me.* The complaint that the Lord had forsaken Zion resembles that in 40:27 – 31. The Lord disciplined the Israelites briefly because of their sin (54:7; La 5:20 – 22), but the things that Isaiah was saying about captivity

4 Eze 3:19 **5** ver. 1; Mt 23:37 **6** Lk 2:32 **7** Mt 26:67; Ps 72:10 **8** Ps 69:13; 2Co 6:2; Isa 42:6 **9** Zec 9:12 **10** Rev 7:16; Ps 121:6; 23:2 **11** Isa 40:4 **12** Isa 43:5,6 **13** Isa 44:23 **14** Isa 40:27

15 [The LORD answered] "Can a
woman forget her nursing child
And have no compassion on the
son of her womb?
Even these may forget, but I will
not forget you.
16 "Indeed, I have inscribed [a picture
of] you on the palms *of My*
hands;
Your city walls [Zion] are
continually before Me.
17 "Your builders hurry;
Your destroyers and devastators
Will go away from you.
18 "Lift up your eyes and look around
[at the returning exiles];
All these gather together and they
come to you [to rebuild you].
As I live," declares the LORD,
"You [Zion] will indeed clothe
yourself with all of them as
jewels and tie them on as a bride.
19 "For your ruins and desolate
places and your land [once the
scene] of destruction—
Certainly now [in the coming
years] will be too cramped for
the inhabitants,
And those who *once* engulfed you
will be far away.
20 "The children of your bereavement
[those born in captivity] will yet
say in your ears,
'The place is too cramped for me';
Make room for me that I may live
here.
21 "Then [Zion], you will say in your
heart,
'Who has borne me these *children,*
Since I have been bereaved of my
children
And am barren, an exile and a
wanderer?
And who has reared these?
Indeed, I was left alone;
From where then did these
children come?' "

22 This is what the Lord GOD says,

"Listen carefully, I will lift up My
hand to the [Gentile] nations
And set up My banner to the
peoples;
And they will bring your sons in
the fold of their garments,
And your daughters will be
carried on their shoulders.
23 "Kings will be your attendants,
And their princesses your nurses.
They will bow down to you with
their faces to the earth
And lick the dust of your feet;
And you shall know [with an
understanding based on
personal experience] that I am
the LORD;
For they shall not be put to shame
who wait *and* hope expectantly
for Me.
24 "Can the spoils of war be taken
from the mighty man,
Or the captives of a tyrant be
rescued?"

25 Indeed, this is what the LORD says,

"Even the captives of the mighty
man will be taken away,

---

were still in the future. A message such as this would be good to remember in the days of captivity when it seemed that they were waiting a long time for the Lord to rescue them.

49:15 ***Can a woman forget.*** In the strongest of human ties, the tenderness of the mother for her precious and dependent child, the Lord draws a parallel picture of Himself. Even if the mother could forget, the Lord will never forget. Human parents often fail, but the Lord is the parent who never forgets how much His child needs Him.

49:20 ***too cramped.*** The complaint that the place is too small is in fact a cause for rejoicing (54:1 – 3; Zec 2:4 – 5), because it means that the Lord would cause His people to grow. This prophecy points to the return of the exiles to Jerusalem, for under Ezra and Nehemiah the exiles built a relatively small city (Ezr 2; Neh 7). Some view the ultimate fulfillment of this prophecy to be the gathering of the Lord's people at the coming of Jesus' kingdom.

49:22 ***lift up My hand to the [Gentile] nations.*** The return of the Israelites from all the nations, not only from Babylon, shows that the future salvation of all Israel is in view (Ro 11:26).

15 Ps 103:13; Mal 3:17; Mt 7:11; Ro 11:29 **16** Ex 13:9; SS 8:6 **17** ver. 19 **18** Isa 60:4; Pr 17:6 **19** Isa 54:1,2; Zec 10:10 **20** Isa 60:4; Mt 3:9; Ro 11:11 **22** Isa 60:4 **23** Ps 72:11; Isa 52:15; 60:16; Ps 72:9; Mic 7:17; Ps 34:22; Ro 5:5; 9:33 **24** Mt 12:29; Lk 11:21,22

And the tyrant's spoils of war will be rescued;
For I will contend with your opponent,
And I will save your children.
26 "I will make those who oppress you consume their own flesh [in mutually destructive wars]
And they will become drunk with their own blood as with sweet wine;
And all mankind will know [with a knowledge grounded in personal experience] that I, the LORD, am your Savior
And your Redeemer, the Mighty One of Jacob."

God Helps His Servant

50 THE LORD declares this;
"Where is the certificate of divorce
By which I have sent your mother away, [O Israel]?
Or to which one of My creditors did I sell you [as slaves]?
In fact, You were sold for your wickedness [your sin, your injustice, your wrongdoing],
And for your transgressions your mother was sent away.
2 "Why, when I came, was there no man [to greet Me]?
When I called, why was there no one to answer?
Is My hand really so short that it cannot redeem [My servants]?
Or have I no power to rescue?
Listen carefully, with My rebuke I dry up the sea,
I make the rivers into a desert;
Their fish stink because there is no water
And die of thirst.
3 "I clothe the heavens with the blackness [of storm clouds]
And make sackcloth [of mourning] their clothing."

4 The Lord GOD has given Me [His Servant] the tongue of disciples [as One who is taught],
That I may know how to sustain the weary with a word.
He awakens *Me* morning by morning,
He awakens My ear to listen as a disciple [as One who is taught].
5 The Lord GOD has opened My ear,
And I have not been rebellious
Nor have I turned back.
6 I turned My back to those who strike *Me*,
And My cheeks to those who pluck out the beard;
I did not hide My face from insults and spitting. [Matt 26:67; 27:30; John 19:1]
7 For the Lord GOD helps Me,

50:1 ***divorce.*** The Lord had put away Israel as a husband might put away a wife, but it was for only a short period of exile (54:5 – 7; 62:4) and not permanently. Permanent exile would have required a certificate of divorce (Dt 24:1 – 4). If the Lord had issued one, He could not have taken Israel back (Jer 3:1,8). No prophet suggested that God had completely broken His covenant; rather, they predicted God's faithfulness to a remnant who would return (Mic 4:9 – 10). ***creditors.*** If the Lord had sold Israel to creditors (Ex 21:7; 2Ki 4:1; Neh 5:5), He would not have any authority over its destiny. But the Israelites sold themselves because of their own iniquities (42:23 – 25). Therefore God as their Redeemer could buy them back (41:14; 52:3). ***your mother.*** The mother is Jerusalem — more specifically, the inhabitants of the preceding generation that had gone into exile.
50:2 ***I came.*** God came to Israel at the time of the exile through the prophets whom He sent. Later God came to this earth through His Servant and Son, Jesus (41:9).
50:4 ***given Me [His Servant] the tongue of disciples.*** The third Servant song consists of a reflection by the Servant (4 – 9) and the prophet's address to the believing and unbelieving Israel (10 – 11).
50:6 ***insults and spitting.*** This prophecy was fulfilled in the suffering of Jesus Christ (Mt 27:30).
50:7 ***face like flint.*** Setting one's face like a flint indicates determination in the face of opposition (Eze 3:8 – 9; Lk 9:51).

26 Isa 9:20; Rev 14:20; 16:6; Ps 9:16; Isa 60:16 **CHAPTER 50** **1** Dt 24:1; Jer 3:8; Hos 2:2; 2Ki 4:1; Mt 18:25; Isa 52:3 **2** Pr 1:24; Isa 65:12; Jer 35:15; Nu 11:23; Ps 106:9; Na 1:4; Ex 14:21; Jos 3:16; Ex 7:18 **3** Ex 10:21; Rev 6:12 **4** Ex 4:11; Mt 11:28 **5** Ps 40:6-8; Mt 26:39; Jn 14:31; Heb 10:5 **6** Mt 26:67; La 3:30 **7** Eze 3:8,9

Therefore, I have not been
ashamed *or* humiliated.
Therefore, I have made My face
like flint,
And I know that I shall not be put
to shame. [Luke 9:51; Is 52:13;
53:10–12]
8 He who declares Me in the right is
near;
Who will [dare to] contend with
Me?
Let us stand up to each other;
Who is My adversary?
Let him approach Me. [Rom 8:33–
35; 1 Tim 3:16]
9 In fact, the Lord GOD helps Me;
Who is he who condemns Me [as
guilty]?
Indeed, they will all wear out like
a garment;
The moth will eat them. [Heb 1:11,
12]
10 Who is among you who fears the
LORD,
Who obeys the voice of His
Servant,
Yet who walks in darkness and
has no light?
Let him trust *and* be confident in
the name of the LORD and let
him rely on his God.
11 Listen carefully, all you who
kindle your own fire [devising
your own man-made plan of
salvation],
Who surround yourselves with
torches,
Walk by the light of your [self-
made] fire
And among the torches that you
have set ablaze.
But this you will have from My
hand:
You will lie down in [a place of]
torment. [Is 66:24]

Israel Exhorted

51 "LISTEN TO Me, you who
pursue righteousness (right
standing with God),
Who seek *and* inquire of the LORD:
Look to the rock from which you
were cut
And to the excavation of the
quarry from which you were
dug.
2 "Look to Abraham your father
And to Sarah who gave birth to
you in pain;
For I called him when *he was but*
one,
Then I blessed him and made him
many."
3 For the LORD will comfort Zion [in
her captivity];
He will comfort all her ruins.
And He will make her wilderness
like Eden,
And her desert like the garden of
the LORD;
Joy and gladness will be found in
her,
Thanksgiving and the voice of a
melody.
4 "Listen carefully to Me [says the
LORD], O My people,
And hear Me, O My nation;

50:8 *declares Me in the right.* God's Servant fully anticipates vindication before the bar of God's justice. He was told to obey God perfectly, and He did. He was sent to suffer sacrificially, and He did. No prosecutor has a case against Him. In a stupendous development, God discloses that the sinners who identify themselves with the Servant may expect the same, although they are not righteous. Sin does carry the death penalty, but identification with the Servant brings exchange and substitution, in which the Servant takes the sinners' place. This makes the justification of sinners both possible and just. Their sins are transferred to Him, and He dies in their place. His shed blood removes their guilt, and they will be declared not guilty. His perfection makes them righteous, and they will be declared righteous. Every accuser will be silenced. Every attempt to have them convicted will be thrown out of court. God is just when He justifies those who belong to the Servant Savior (Ro 8:31 – 34).

50:11 *kindle your own fire.* Those who kindle a fire instead of the Light from God are those who are self-reliant. When the Light comes into the world, some will choose darkness (Jn 3:17 – 18).

8 Ro 8:32 **9** Job 13:28; Ps 102:26; Isa 51:6; Isa 51:8 **10** Ps 23:4; 2Ch 20:20; Ps 20:7 **11** Jn 9:39; Ps 16:4
CHAPTER 51 **1** Ro 9:30-32 **2** Ro 4:1; Heb 11:11; Ge 12:1; Ge 24:35 **3** ver. 12; Isa 52:9; Ge 13:10; Joel 2:3
4 Isa 2:3; Isa 42:6

For a [divine] law will go forth
from Me,
And I will quickly *establish* My
justice as a light to the peoples.
5 "My righteousness (justice) is near,
My salvation has gone forth,
And My arms will judge the
peoples;
The islands *and* coastlands will
wait for Me,
And they will wait with hope *and*
confident expectation for My
arm.
6 "Lift up your eyes to the heavens,
Then look to the earth beneath;
For the heavens will be torn to
pieces *and* vanish like smoke,
And the earth will wear out like a
garment
And its inhabitants will die in like
manner.
But My salvation will be forever,
And My righteousness (justice)
[and faithfully fulfilled promise]
will not be broken. [Matt 24:35;
Heb 1:11; 2 Pet 3:10]
7 "Listen to Me, you who know
righteousness (right standing
with God),
The people in whose heart is My
law *and* instruction;
Do not fear the reproach *and*
taunting of man,
Nor be distressed at their reviling.
8 "For the moth will eat them like a
garment,
And the worm will eat them like
wool.
But My righteousness *and* justice
[faithfully promised] will exist
forever,
And My salvation to all generations."

9 Awake, awake, put on strength
and might, O arm of the LORD;
Awake as in the ancient days, as in
the generations of long ago.
Was it not You who cut Rahab
(Egypt) in pieces,
Who pierced the dragon [of
Egypt]? [Is 30:7]
10 Was it not You who dried up the
[Red] Sea,
The waters of the great deep,
Who made the depths of the sea a
pathway
For the redeemed to cross over?
11 So the redeemed of the LORD will
return
And come with joyful shouting to
Zion;
Everlasting joy will be on their
heads.
They will obtain gladness and joy,
And sorrow and sighing will flee
away. [Rev 7:17; 21:1, 4]

12 "I, even I, am He who comforts
you.
Who are you that you are afraid of
man who dies
And of a son of man who is made
[as destructible] as grass,
13 That you have forgotten the LORD
your Maker,
Who stretched out the heavens
And laid the foundations of the
earth,
That you continually tremble with
fear all day long because of the
rage of the oppressor,
As he takes aim to destroy?
And where is the rage of the
oppressor?

14 The [captive] exile will soon be set
free, and will not die in the dungeon,
nor will his food be lacking.
15 "For I am the LORD your God, who
stirs up the sea so that its waves roar—
the LORD of hosts is His name.
16 "I have put My words in your
mouth and have covered you with the
shadow of My hand, to establish the
[renewed] heavens and lay the foun-
dations of the [renewed] earth, and to
say to Zion (Jerusalem), 'You are My
people.' " [Is 65:17; 66:22; Rev 21:1]

51:14 *exile . . . in the dungeon.* The exile refers to those who were captive in Babylon. The meaning also extends to all who experience the darkness of sin and alienation from God (48:20; 49:9).

5 Isa 46:13; Ro 1:16; Ps 67:4; Isa 60:9; Ro 1:16 **6** Isa 40:26; Ps 102:26; Mt 24:35; 2Pe 3:10; Isa 50:9 **7** ver. 1; Ps 37:31; Mt 10:28; Ac 5:41 **8** Isa 50:9 **9** Ps 44:23; 93:1; 44:1; Job 26:12; Ps 87:4; 89:10; Ps 74:13; Eze 29:3 **10** Ex 14:21; Isa 43:16 **11** Isa 35:10 **12** 2Co 1:3; Ps 118:6; 1Pe 1:24 **13** Ps 104:2; Job 20:7 **14** Zec 9:11 **15** Job 26:12; Ps 74:13; Jer 31:35 **16** Dt 18:18; Isa 59:21; Jn 3:34; Isa 49:2; Isa 65:17

[17]Wake yourself up! Wake yourself
up! Stand up, O Jerusalem,
You who have drunk at the hand
of the LORD the cup of His
wrath,
You who have drunk the cup of
staggering *and* intoxication
to the dregs [leaving only
sediment].
[18]There is no one to guide her
among all the sons she has
borne,
Nor is there anyone to take her by
the hand among all the sons she
has reared.
[19]These two *tragedies* have befallen
you;
Who will show sympathy for you
and mourn with you?
The desolation and destruction [on
the land and city], famine and
sword [on the inhabitants];
How shall I comfort you?
[20]Your sons have fainted;
They lie *helpless* at the head of
every street,
Like an antelope in a net,
Full [from drinking] of the wrath
of the LORD,
The rebuke of your God.

[21]Therefore, now hear this, you who
are afflicted,
Who are drunk, but not with wine
[but overwhelmed by the wrath
of God].
[22]So says your Lord, the LORD, *who*
is also your God
Who pleads the cause of His
people,
"Listen carefully, I have taken
from your hand the cup of
staggering *and* intoxication,
The cup of My wrath;
You shall never drink it again.
[23]"I will put it into the hands of your
tormentors,
Who have said to you, 'Lie down
so that we may walk over you.'
You have even made your back
like the ground
And like the street for those who
walk over it."

Cheer for Downtrodden Zion

52 AWAKE, AWAKE,
Put on your strength, O Zion;
Put on your beautiful garments,
O Jerusalem, the holy city;
For the uncircumcised and the
unclean
Will no longer come into you.
[Rev 21:27]
[2]Shake yourself from the dust,
arise,
O captive Jerusalem;
Rid yourself of the chains around
your neck,
O captive Daughter of Zion.

[3]For the LORD says this, "You were
sold for nothing and you will be re-
deemed, but not with money."
[4]For the Lord GOD says this, "My
people went down at the first into
Egypt to live there; and [many years
later Sennacherib] the Assyrian op-
pressed them without cause.
[5]"But now, what do I have here," de-
clares the LORD, "seeing that My people
have been taken away without reason?
Those who rule over them howl [with
taunting and mockery of salvation],"
declares the LORD, "and My name is
continually blasphemed all day long.
[Rom 2:24]
[6]"Therefore My people shall know
My Name *and* what it means. There-
fore in that day I am the One who is
speaking, 'Here I am.' " [Ex 3:13, 14]

51:19 *These two tragedies.* The two tragedies are the desolation of the land and the destruction of the people.
51:21 *drunk, but not with wine.* The cause of drunkenness was not wine, but the "cup of trembling" (v. 22), the terror of God's judgment.
52:6 *shall know My Name.* The people are the redeemed exiles, as well as the people who believe in and follow the Servant (Messiah). Isaiah was speaking of a time beyond his own time, to people who were not yet born (1Pe 1:10 – 12). Jesus speaks strongly of this concept when He says, I "know [without any doubt those who are] My own and my own know Me" (Jn 10:11 – 18).

17 Isa 52:1; Job 21:20; Jer 25:15; See Dt 28:28,34; Ps 60:3; Eze 23:32-34 **19** Isa 47:9; Am 7:2 **20** La 2:11
21 See ver. 17; La 3:15 **22** Jer 50:34 **23** Jer 25:17; Zec 12:2; Ps 66:11 **CHAPTER 52** **1** Isa 51:9,17; Neh 11:1;
Mt 4:5; Rev 21:2; Na 1:15; Rev 21:27 **2** Isa 3:26; Zec 2:7 **3** Ps 44:12 **4** Ge 46:6 **5** Eze 36:20

7 How beautiful *and* delightful on
the mountains
Are the feet of him who brings
good news,
Who announces peace,
Who brings good news of good
[things],
Who announces salvation,
Who says to Zion, "Your God
reigns!" [Acts 10:36; Rom 10:15;
Eph 6:14–16]
8 Listen! Your watchmen lift up their
voices,
Together they shout for joy;
For they will see face to face
The return of the LORD to Zion.
9 Break forth, shout joyfully
together,
You ruins of Jerusalem;
For the LORD has comforted His
people,
He has redeemed Jerusalem.
10 The LORD has bared His holy arm
(His infinite power)
Before the eyes of all the nations
[revealing Himself as the One by
Whom Israel is redeemed from
captivity],
That all the ends of the earth may
see
The salvation of our God.
[Luke 2:29–32; 3:6]

11 Depart, depart, go out from there
(the lands of exile),
Touch no unclean thing;
Go out of the midst of her
(Babylon), purify yourselves,
You who carry the articles of the
LORD [on your journey from
there]. [2 Cor 6:16, 17]
12 For you will not go out in a hurry
[as when you left Egypt],
Nor will you go in flight [fleeing,
as you did from the
Egyptians];
For the LORD will go before
you,
And the God of Israel will be your
rear guard.

The Exalted Servant

13 Indeed, My Servant (the Messiah)
will act wisely *and* prosper;
He will be raised and lifted up and
greatly exalted.
14 Just as many were astonished *and*
appalled at you, *My people,*
So His appearance was marred
more than any man
And His form [marred] more than
the sons of men.
15 So He will sprinkle many nations
[with His blood, providing
salvation],
Kings will shut their mouths
because of Him;
For what they had not been told
they will see,
And what they had not heard they
will understand. [Rom 15:21]

The Suffering Servant

53 WHO HAS believed
[confidently trusted in, relied
on, and adhered to] our message
[of salvation]? [Is 52:7, 10]
And to whom [if not us] has
the arm *and* infinite power
of the LORD been revealed?
[John 12:38–41; Rom 10:16]

52:12 *go before you . . . rear guard.* This is an allusion to the pillar of cloud and fire that protected Israel in its flight from Egypt (Ex 13:21 – 22; 14:19 – 20).
52:13 – 53:12 *Indeed.* The fourth of the Servant songs, which form the central unit of chapters 40 – 66, begins with the praise of the Father for the work of the Servant.
52:14 *appearance was marred.* This speaks of the physical punishment that the Servant, Jesus Christ, endured when he was bearing the sins of the world on the cross. He was cruelly beaten, even before He was crucified (Mt 27:27 – 31; Mk 15:16 – 20; Jn 19:1 – 3).
52:15 *shut their mouths.* The kings are silent in stunned respect.
53:1 – 12 The Suffering Servant — Along with Psalm 22, this Scripture is understood to be one of the key prophetic Old Testament passages pointing to the saving work of Christ. This passage presents the whole idea of the "Suffering Servant," which is one of the central concepts of Isaiah, and for many, Judaism. Christ's fulfillment of this passage in His passion is remarkable. The

7 Ro 10:15; Ps 93:1 **10** Ps 98:2,3; Lk 3:6 **11** Isa 48:20; Lev 22:2 **12** Ex 12:33; Mic 2:13; Ex 14:19 **13** Isa 42:1; Php 2:9 **14** Ps 22:6,7 **15** Eze 36:25; Eph 3:5,9 **CHAPTER 53** **1** Jn 12:38; Ro 10:16

2 For He [the Servant of God] grew
up before Him like a tender
shoot (plant),
And like a root out of dry ground;
He has no *stately* form or *majestic*
splendor
That we would look at Him,
Nor [handsome] appearance that
we would be attracted to Him.
3 He was despised and rejected by
men,
A Man of sorrows *and* pain and
acquainted with grief;
And like One from whom men
hide their faces
He was despised, and we did not
appreciate His worth *or* esteem
Him.

4 But [in fact] He has borne our
griefs,
And He has carried our sorrows
and pains;
Yet we [ignorantly] assumed that
He was stricken,
Struck down by God and degraded
and humiliated [by Him].
[Matt 8:17]
5 But He was wounded for our
transgressions,
He was crushed for our
wickedness [our sin, our
injustice, our wrongdoing];
The punishment [required] for our
well-being *fell* on Him,
And by His stripes (wounds) we
are healed.
6 All of us like sheep have gone
astray,
We have turned, each one, to his
own way;
But the LORD has caused the
wickedness of us all [our sin, our
injustice, our wrongdoing]
To fall on Him [instead of us].
[1 Pet 2:24, 25]

QUOTATIONS FROM AND REFERENCES TO ISAIAH 53 IN THE NEW TESTAMENT

ISAIAH 53	NEW TESTAMENT
53:1–12	Lk 24:27,46; 1Pe 1:11
53:1	Jn 12:38; Ro 10:16
53:2	Mt 2:23
53:3	Mk 9:12
53:4	Mt 8:17; 1Pe 2:24
53:4–5	Ro 4:25
53:5	Mt 26:67; 1Pe 2:24
53:5–6	Ac 10:43
53:6	1Pe 2:25
53:6–7	Jn 1:29
53:7	Mt 26:63; 27:12,14; Mk 14:60–61; 15:4–5; 1Co 5:7; 1Pe 2:23; Rev 5:6,12; 13:8
53:7–8 lxx	Ac 8:32–33
53:8–9	1Co 15:3
53:9	Mt 26:24; 1Pe 2:22; 1Jn 3:5; Rev 14:5
53:11	Ro 5:19
53:12	Mt 27:38; Lk 22:37; 23:33–34; Heb 9:28; 1Pe 2:24

New Testament writers point often to Isaiah 53 and how Christ fulfilled this prophecy (Mt 8:17; Lk 23:8–9; Jn 12:38; Ro 10:16; 1Pe 2:25). It is also the Scripture that Philip explained to the Ethiopian eunuch in Acts 8:32–33.

In the Old Testament sacrificial system people offered animals to atone for sin (Lev 16). The Bible presents Christ as the ultimate sacrifice that died once and for all for the sins of the world (Heb 8–10). Our sins are forgiven and we become righteous through Christ's great work on the cross (2Co 5:21).

53:2 *no stately form or majestic splendor.* There was nothing in the Promised Servant's appearance to mark His special calling.

53:3 *despised and rejected.* The Servant was not received joyfully by the people who needed Him so much (Mk 9:12). ***Man of sorrows.*** This phrase does not indicate that the Servant would be dour, but that He knew better than anyone the havoc that sin brings into human life, and, as the kindest of friends, He was sorry for the pain of His people.

53:4 *borne our griefs.* The Savior Jesus came to suffer and die for the sins of others (Mt 8:17; Heb 9:28; 1Pe 2:24). Griefs, pain and sorrows, and sickness refer to the consequences of sin.

3 Ps 22:6; Heb 4:15; Jn 1:10 **4** Mt 8:17; Heb 9:28 **5** Ro 4:25; 1Pe 2:24

7 He was oppressed and He was afflicted,
Yet He did not open His mouth [to complain or defend Himself];
Like a lamb that is led to the slaughter,
And like a sheep that is silent before her shearers,
So He did not open His mouth.
8 After oppression and judgment He was taken away;
And as for His generation [His contemporaries], who [among them] concerned himself *with the fact*
That He was cut off from the land of the living [by His death]
For the transgression of my people, to whom the stroke [of death] *was due*?
9 His grave was assigned with the wicked,
But He was with a rich man in His death,
Because He had done no violence,
Nor was there any deceit in His mouth. [Matt 27:57–60; 1 Pet 2:22, 23]

10 Yet the LORD was willing
To crush Him, causing Him to suffer;
If He would give Himself as a guilt offering [an atonement for sin],
He shall see *His* [spiritual] offspring,
He shall prolong *His* days,
And the will (good pleasure) of the LORD shall succeed *and* prosper in His hand.
11 As a result of the anguish of His soul,
He shall see it and be satisfied;
By His knowledge [of what He has accomplished] the Righteous One,
My Servant, shall justify the many [making them righteous—upright before God, in right standing with Him],
For He shall bear [the responsibility for] their sins.
12 Therefore, I will divide *and* give Him a portion with the great [kings and rulers],
And He shall divide the spoils with the mighty,
Because He [willingly] poured out His life to death,
And was counted among the transgressors;
Yet He Himself bore *and* took away the sin of many,
And interceded [with the Father] for the transgressors. [Luke 22:37]

The Fertility of Zion

54 "SHOUT FOR joy, O barren one, she who has not given birth;
Break forth into joyful shouting and rejoice, she who has not gone into labor [with child]!
For the [spiritual] sons of the desolate one *will be* more numerous
Than the sons of the married woman," says the LORD. [Gal 4:27]
2 "Enlarge the site of your tent [to make room for more children];

53:7 *He did not open His mouth.* Jesus did not open His mouth to defend Himself or to answer the false charges made against Him (Mt 26:63; Mk 14:61; Lk 23:9; Jn 19:9).
53:10 *the LORD was willing To crush Him.* The Old Testament pointed to the doctrine of the atonement long before Jesus died for our sins (1Co 15:3). In fact, the atonement was part of God's eternal plan (Eph 1:4–7). The Father was pleased that His Son should die because it would cover up the sins of many and reconcile them to Himself. ***guilt offering.*** The guilt offering, or "trespass offering," was the sacrifice of a ram to secure the Lord's atonement for sin (Lev 5:6–7,15; 7:1; 14:12; 19:21). Here, the prophet Isaiah describes the Servant Jesus as a guilt offering. ***His [spiritual] offspring.*** If the Spirit of God dwells in us (Ro 8:9–11), and if we are led by the Spirit, then we are sons of God—His offspring (Ro 8:14).
54:1 *has not gone into labor.* The Israelites received a liberation (through the promised Cyrus for the Babylonian exiles, or through the Messiah, in the fullest sense) that they did not work for—it was God's idea.

7 Mt 26:63; Ac 8:32 **8** Da 9:26 **9** Mt 27:57; 1Jn 3:5 **10** 2Co 5:21 **11** 1Jn 2:1; Isa 42:1; Rom 5:18 **12** Ps 2:8; Col 2:15; Lk 22:37; Lk 23:34 **CHAPTER 54** **1** Gal 4:27; 1Sa 2:5 **2** Isa 49:19,20

Stretch out the curtains of your
dwellings, do not spare them;
Lengthen your tent ropes
And make your pegs (stakes) firm
[in the ground].
3 "For you will spread out to the
right and to the left;
And your descendants will take
possession of nations
And will inhabit deserted cities.

4 "Do not fear, for you will not be
put to shame,
And do not feel humiliated *or*
ashamed, for you will not be
disgraced.
For you will forget the shame of
your youth,
And you will no longer remember
the disgrace of your widowhood.
5 "For your husband is your Maker,
The LORD of hosts is His name;
And your Redeemer is the Holy
One of Israel,
Who is called the God of the whole
earth.
6 "For the LORD has called you,
Like a wife who has been
abandoned, grieved in spirit,
And like a wife [married] in
her youth when she is [later]
rejected *and* scorned,"
Says your God.
7 "For a brief moment I abandoned
you,
But with great compassion *and*
mercy I will gather you [to
Myself again].
8 "In an outburst of wrath
I hid My face from you for a
moment,
But with everlasting kindness I
will have compassion on you,"
Says the LORD your Redeemer.
9 "For this is *like* the waters of Noah
to Me,
As I swore [an oath] that the
waters of Noah
Would not flood the earth again;
In the same way I have sworn that
I will not be angry with you
Nor will I rebuke you.
10 "For the mountains may be
removed and the hills may shake,
But My lovingkindness will not be
removed from you,
Nor will My covenant of peace be
shaken,"
Says the LORD who has
compassion on you.

11 "O you afflicted [city], storm-
tossed, and not comforted,
Listen carefully, I will set your
[precious] stones in mortar,
And lay your foundations with
sapphires.
12 "And I will make your battlements
of rubies,
And your gates of [shining] beryl
stones,
And all your [barrier] walls of
precious stones. [Rev 21:19–21]
13 "And all your [spiritual] sons will
be disciples [of the LORD],
And great will be the well-being of
your sons. [John 6:45]
14 "You will be firmly established in
righteousness:
You will be far from [even the
thought of] oppression, for you
will not fear,
And from terror, for it will not
come near you.
15 "If anyone fiercely attacks you it
will not be from Me.
Whoever attacks you will fall
because of you.
16 "Listen carefully, I have created
the smith who blows on the fire
of coals
And who produces a weapon for
its purpose;

54:4 *widowhood.* The widowhood was the time without the working presence of God in the lives of the people of God, the time of exile. In the fullest sense, every sinner is a "widow" without God, who has the role of protector and provider.

54:11 *foundations with sapphires.* For a more detailed description of the New Jerusalem, see Revelation 21:18 – 21. It will be a city of stunning beauty and grand proportions.

3 Isa 55:5 **5** Jer 3:14; Lk 1:32; Zec 14:9; Ro 3:29 **6** Isa 62:4 **7** Ps 30:5; Isa 26:20; 60:10; 2Co 4:17 **8** Isa 55:3; Jer 31:3 **9** Ge 8:21 **10** Ps 46:2; Isa 51:6; Mt 5:18; Ps 89:33 **11** 1Ch 29:2; Rev 21:18 **13** Isa 11:9; Jer 31:34; Jn 6:45; 1Co 2:10; 1Th 4:9; 1Jn 2:20; Ps 119:165

And I have created the destroyer to inflict ruin.
17 "No weapon that is formed against you will succeed;
And every tongue that rises against you in judgment you will condemn.
This [peace, righteousness, security, and triumph over opposition] is the heritage of the servants of the LORD,
And *this is* their vindication from Me," says the LORD.

The Free Offer of Mercy

55 "EVERYONE WHO thirsts, come to the waters;
And you who have no money come, buy grain and eat.
Come, buy wine and milk
Without money and without cost [simply accept it as a gift from God]. [Rev 21:6, 7; 22:17]
2 "Why do you spend money for that which is not bread,
And your earnings for what does not satisfy?
Listen carefully to Me, and eat what is good,
And let your soul delight in abundance. [Jer 31:12–14]
3 "Incline your ear [to listen] and come to Me;
Hear, so that your soul may live;
And I will make an everlasting covenant with you,
According to the faithful mercies [promised and] shown to David. [2 Sam 7:8–16; Acts 13:34; Heb 13:20]
4 "Listen carefully, I have appointed him [David, representing the Messiah] to be a witness to the nations [regarding salvation],
A leader and commander to the peoples.
5 "In fact, you [Israel] will call a nation that you do not know,
And a nation that does not know you will run to you,
Because of the LORD your God, even the Holy One of Israel;
For He has glorified you."
6 Seek the LORD while He may be found;
Call on Him [for salvation] while He is near.
7 Let the wicked leave (behind) his way
And the unrighteous man his thoughts;
And let him return to the LORD,
And He will have compassion (mercy) on him,
And to our God,
For He will abundantly pardon.
8 "For My thoughts are not your thoughts,
Nor are your ways My ways," declares the LORD.
9 "For as the heavens are higher than the earth,

54:17 *the servants of the LORD.* Throughout the rest of Isaiah, the word "servants" refers to all saints, Jews and Gentiles (56:6 – 8; 63:17; 65:8 – 9,13 – 15; 66:14), the offspring of the Servant (Jesus).

55:4 *witness.* God's fulfillment of the promises to the house of David, climaxing in the resurrection of Christ, serves as a witness to the nations (43:10,12; 44:8). It shows that He has fulfilled His prophecies and promises, and that He is who He says He is: the King of the universe.

55:6 *while He may be found.* Solomon warned his readers to remember their Creator in the days of their youth, when the evil days have not yet come (Ecc 12:1). The writer to the Hebrews admonishes his readers, "Today, if you will hear His voice, do not harden your hearts" (Ps 95:7 – 8; Heb 4:7). Responding to the call of God is not something to be put off. Hardened hearts become a habit, or evil days may impair our ability to think clearly. If the Lord is calling, respond to Him. We do not know how long we have to live. No one knows whether "this night" his soul may be required (Lk 12:20).

55:9 *higher.* The gulf existing between human and divine nature is expressed here in graphic terms. God functions at the level of pure holiness, and He is motivated by complete love and service to others. The corruption of human nature

---

17 Isa 45:24,25 **CHAPTER 55** **1** Jn 4:14; Mt 13:44; Rev 3:18 **3** Mt 11:28; Isa 54:8; 61:8; Jer 32:40; 2Sa 7:8; Ps 89:28; Ac 13:34 **4** Jn 18:37; Rev 1:5; Jer 30:9; Eze 34:23; Da 9:25; Hos 3:5 **5** Isa 52:15; Eph 2:11; Isa 60:5; Isa 60:9 **6** Ps 32:6; Mt 5:25; 25:11; Jn 7:34; 8:21; 2Co 6:1; Heb 3:13 **7** Isa 1:16; Zec 8:17; Ps 130:7; Jer 3:12 **8** 2Sa 7:19 **9** Ps 103:11

So are My ways higher than your
ways
And My thoughts *higher* than your
thoughts.
10 "For as the rain and snow come
down from heaven,
And do not return there without
watering the earth,
Making it bear and sprout,
And providing seed to the
sower and bread to the eater,
[2 Cor 9:10]
11 So will My word be which goes out
of My mouth;
It will not return to Me void
(useless, without result),
Without accomplishing what I
desire,
And without succeeding *in the
matter* for which I sent it.
12 "For you will go out [from exile]
with joy
And be led forth [by the LORD
Himself] with peace;
The mountains and the hills will
break forth into shouts of joy
before you,
And all the trees of the field will
clap their hands.
13 "Instead of the thorn bush the
cypress tree will grow,
And instead of the nettle the
myrtle tree will grow;
And it will be a memorial to the
LORD,
For an everlasting sign [of His
mercy] which will not be cut off."

Rewards for Obedience to God

56 THIS IS what the LORD says,
"Maintain justice and do
righteousness,
For My salvation is soon to come,
And My righteousness *and*
justice *is soon* to be revealed.
[Is 62:1, 11; Matt 3:2; Luke 21:31;
Rom 13:11, 12]
2 "Blessed (happy, fortunate) is the
man who does this,
And the son of man who takes
hold of it,
Who keeps the Sabbath without
profaning it,
And keeps his hand from doing
any evil."
3 Do not let the foreigner who has
joined himself to the LORD
say,
"The LORD will most certainly
separate me from His people."
And do not let the eunuch say,
"Look, I am a dry tree."

4 This is what the LORD says,
"To the eunuchs who keep My
Sabbaths
And choose what pleases Me,
And hold firmly to My covenant,
5 To them I will give in My
house and within My walls a
memorial,
And a name better than that of
sons and daughters;
I will give them an everlasting
name which will not be cut off.

6 "Also the foreigners who join
themselves to the LORD,
To minister to Him, and to love the
name of the LORD,
To be His servants, everyone who
keeps the Sabbath without
profaning it
And holds fast to My covenant [by
conscientious obedience];
7 All these I will bring to My holy
mountain

---

by sin introduces carnal elements that are totally unknown to the nature of God, and by contrast are base both in character and execution. It is only when we are born again that we can understand the things of the Spirit, the ways of God (Jn 3:9–21).

56:3 *foreigner.* In speaking of the foreigner who joined himself to the Lord, Isaiah was not speaking of the foreign wives that the returning exiles would have married (Ezr 9:1–4). Those foreign wives were considered a corrupting influence because they had not become followers of the Living God. The foreigners that Isaiah was prophesying about would be converted to worship the true Lord (44:5).

56:5 *not be cut off.* This phrase is an idiom for preserving one's name through one's offspring. The phrase links this passage with 55:13.

10 Dt 32:2 **11** Isa 54:9 **12** Isa 35:10; Ps 98:8; 1Ch 16:33 **13** Isa 41:19; Mic 7:4; Jer 13:11 **CHAPTER 56 1** Mt 4:17 **2** Isa 58:13 **3** Ac 8:27 **5** 1Ti 3:15; 1Jn 3:1 **7** Isa 2:2; Ro 12:1; Heb 13:15; 1Pe 2:5; Mt 21:13; Mal 1:11

And make them joyful in My
house of prayer.
Their burnt offerings and their
sacrifices will be accepted on
My altar;
For My house will be called a house
of prayer for all the peoples."
8 The Lord God, who gathers the
dispersed of Israel, declares:
"I will gather yet *others* to them
(Israel), to those [already]
gathered."

9 All you beasts of the field,
All you beasts (hostile nations) in
the forest,
Come to eat.
10 Israel's watchmen are blind,
They are all without knowledge.
They are all mute dogs, they
cannot bark;
Panting, lying down, they love to
slumber.
11 And the dogs are greedy; they
never have enough.
They are shepherds who have no
understanding;
They have all turned to their own
way,
Each one to his unlawful gain,
without exception.
12 "Come," [they say,] "let us get
wine, and let us fill ourselves
with strong drink;
And tomorrow will be like today,
very great indeed."

Evil Leaders Rebuked

57 THE RIGHTEOUS man
perishes [at the hand of evil],
and no one takes it to heart;
Faithful *and* devout men are taken
away, while no one understands
That the righteous person is
taken away [to be spared] from
disaster *and* evil.
2 He enters into peace [through
death];
They rest in their beds (graves),
Each one who walked uprightly
[following God's will, living with
integrity].
3 "But come here, you sons of a
sorceress [raised in deception
and superstition],
Offspring of an adulterer and a
prostitute.
4 "Of whom do you make fun?
Against whom do you open wide
your mouth
And stick out your tongue?
Are you not children of rebellion
(sin),
Offspring of deceit,
5 Who inflame yourselves [with lust
in pagan rites] among the oaks
(terebinth trees),
Under every green *and* leafy tree,
Who slaughter the children [in
sacrifice] in the ravines
Under the clefts of the rocks?
6 "Among the smooth *stones* of the
ravine
Is your portion, they (the idols) are
your lot;
Even to them you have poured out
a drink offering,
You have offered a grain offering.
Should I be quiet concerning
these things [leaving them
unpunished—bearing them with
patience]?
7 "Upon a high and lofty mountain
You have [openly and shamelessly]
made your [idolatrous and
adulterous] bed;
Even there you went up to offer
sacrifice [to idols, in spiritual
unfaithfulness to Me].
8 "Behind the door and the doorpost
You have set up your [pagan]
symbol;

56:9 *beasts.* The unclean, ravenous beasts summoned to attack the ungodly community are hostile nations (Jer 12:8 – 9; Eze 34:5,8).
56:11 *dogs.* The dog was not highly regarded in biblical culture, and to the Jews they were unclean. In Deuteronomy 23:18, a "dog" is discussed in the context of a prostitute.
57:5 *slaughter the children.* Killing the children was associated with the worship of Molech and with demon worship (30:33; 2Ki 23:10; Ps 106:37 – 38; Jer 7:31).

8 Isa 11:12; Jn 10:16 **9** Jer 12:9 **10** Mt 15:14; Php 3:2 **11** Mic 3:11; Eze 34:2 **12** Ps 10:6; Pr 23:35; Lk 12:19
CHAPTER 57 **1** Ps 12:1; 1Ki 14:13 **2** 2Ch 16:14 **3** Mt 16:4 **5** 2Ki 16:4; Lev 18:21; 2Ki 16:3; Jer 7:31; Eze 16:20
7 Eze 16:16; Eze 23:41 **8** Eze 16:26

Indeed, far removed from Me, you
have uncovered yourself,
And have gone up and made your
bed wide.
And you have made a [new]
agreement for yourself with the
adulterers,
You have loved their bed,
You have looked [with passion] on
their manhood. [Deut 6:5, 6, 9;
11:18, 20]
9 "You have gone to the king [of a
pagan land] with oil
And increased your perfumes;
You have sent your messengers a
great distance
And made *them* go down to Sheol
(the realm of the dead).
10 "You were wearied by the length
of your road,
Yet you did not say, 'It is no use.'
You found renewed strength,
Therefore you did not grow
weak.
11 "About whom were you worried
and fearful
That you lied and did not
remember Me,
Nor give Me a thought?
Was I not silent even for a long
time
And [as a result] you do not fear
Me?
12 "I will declare your [hypocritical]
righteousness and your deeds,
But they will not benefit you.
13 "When you cry out [for help], let
your [ridiculous] collection *of
idols* save you.
But the wind will carry them all
away,
A [mere] breath will take them.
But he who takes refuge in Me will
possess the land [Judea]
And will inherit My holy
mountain." [Ps 37:9, 11; 69:35, 36;
Is 49:8; Matt 5:5; Heb 12:22]
14 And it will be said,
"Build up, build up, clear the way.
Remove the stumbling block out of
the way [of the spiritual return]
of My people."
15 For the high and exalted One
He who inhabits eternity, Whose
name is Holy says this,
"I dwell on the high and holy
place,
But *also* with the contrite and
humble in spirit
In order to revive the spirit of the
humble
And to revive the heart of the
contrite [overcome with sorrow
for sin]. [Matt 5:3]
16 "For I will not contend forever,
Nor will I always be angry;
For [if I did stay angry] the spirit
[of man] would grow weak
before Me,
And the breath *of those whom* I
have created.
17 "Because of the wickedness of his
unjust gain I was angry and
struck him;
I hid *My face* and was angry,
And he went on turning away *and*
backsliding, in the way of his
[own willful] heart.
18 "I have seen his [willful] ways, but
I will heal him;
I will lead him [also] and will
restore comfort to him and
to those who mourn for him,
[Is 61:1, 2; 66:10]
19 As I create the praise of his lips,
Peace, peace, to him who is far
away [both Jew and Gentile]
and to him who is near!"

57:12 *your [hypocritical] righteousness.* This phrase is stated in sarcasm or irony. The people had found a counterfeit life in idolatry and immorality that would only lead to death.
57:14 *Build up.* This verse is based on 40:1–4. The phrase "build up" resembles "every valley shall be raised."

57:16 *will not contend forever.* God was addressing the human failure to keep His good laws, but humans will always fail. God knew this, so He created a way of salvation, a way to heal the problem of sin (v. 18). He knew that they needed to be radically rescued, for the law was powerless to save them (Ro 2–8).

9 Hos 7:11 **10** Jer 2:25 **11** Isa 51:12; Ps 50:21 **14** Isa 40:3 **15** Job 6:10; Lk 1:49; Zec 2:13; Ps 34:18; 51:17; Ps 147:3; Isa 61:1 **16** Ps 85:5; 103:9; Mic 7:18; Nu 16:22; Job 34:14; Heb 12:9 **17** Jer 6:13; Isa 8:17; 45:15; Isa 9:13 **18** Jer 3:22; Isa 61:2 **19** Heb 13:15; Ac 2:39; Eph 2:17

Says the LORD;
"And I will heal him [making his lips blossom anew with thankful praise]." [Acts 2:39; Eph 2:13–17, 18; Heb 13:15]
20 But the wicked are like the tossing sea,
For it cannot be quiet,
And its waters toss up mire and mud.
21 "There is no peace," says my God, "for the wicked."

Observances of Fasts

58 "CRY ALOUD, do not hold back;
Lift up your voice like a trumpet,
And declare to My people their transgression
And to the house of Jacob their sins.
2 "Yet they seek Me day by day and delight [superficially] to know My ways,
As [if they were in reality] a nation that has done righteousness
And has not abandoned (turned away from) the ordinance of their God.
They ask of Me righteous judgments,
They delight in the nearness of God.
3 'Why have we fasted,' *they say,* 'and You do not see it?
Why have we humbled ourselves and You do not notice?'
Hear this [O Israel], on the day of your fast [when you should be grieving for your sins] you find *something you* desire [to do],
And you force your hired servants to work [instead of stopping all work, as the law teaches]. [Lev 16:29]
4 "The facts are that you fast *only* for strife and brawling and to strike with the fist of wickedness.
You do not fast as *you do* today to make your voice heard on high.
5 "Is a fast such as this what I have chosen, a day for a man to humble himself [with sorrow in his soul]?
Is it *only* to bow down his head like a reed
And to make sackcloth and ashes as a bed [pretending to have a repentant heart]?
Do you call this a fast and a day pleasing to the LORD?
6 "[Rather] is this not the fast which I choose,
To undo the bonds of wickedness,
To tear to pieces the ropes of the yoke,
To let the oppressed go free
And break apart every [enslaving] yoke? [Acts 8:23]
7 "Is it not to divide your bread with the hungry
And bring the homeless poor into the house;
When you see the naked, that you cover him,
And not to hide yourself from [the needs of] your own flesh *and* blood?
8 "Then your light will break out like the dawn,
And your healing (restoration, new life) will quickly spring forth;
Your righteousness will go before you [leading you to peace and prosperity],
The glory of the LORD will be your rear guard. [Ex 14:19, 20; Is 52:12]

58:2 *delight [superficially] to know My ways . . . delight in the nearness of God.* Unfortunately, one can really enjoy all the religious ritual without really wanting to know God. God can always tell the difference between the heart that is turned toward Him and the heart that is devoted to religious form.

58:6 *To undo . . . To tear . . . free.* Love is right at the top of the list in relating to God and to other people (1Jn 4:7 – 21). Once again, the Lord is defining true religion. It is always horizontal (directed toward other people) as well as vertical (directed toward God). If we love God, we will be just and merciful to other people (Mic 6:8; Jas 1:26 – 27).

20 Job 15:20; Pr 4:16 **21** Isa 48:22 **CHAPTER 58** **3** Mal 3:14; Lev 16:29; 23:27 **4** 1Ki 21:9 **5** Zec 7:5; Lev 16:29; Est 4:3; Job 2:8; Da 9:3 **6** Neh 5:10; Jer 34:9 **7** Eze 18:7; Mt 25:35; Job 31:19; Ge 29:14; Neh 5:5 **8** Job 11:17; Ex 14:19; Isa 52:12

9 "Then you will call, and the LORD
will answer;
You will cry for help, and He will
say, 'Here I am.'
If you take away from your midst
the yoke [of oppression],
The finger pointed in scorn [toward
the oppressed or the godly], and
[every form of] wicked (sinful,
unjust) speech, [Ex 3:14]
10 And if you offer yourself to [assist]
the hungry
And satisfy the need of the afflicted,
Then your light will rise in
darkness
And your gloom *will become* like
midday.
11 "And the LORD will continually
guide you,
And satisfy your soul in scorched
and dry places,
And give strength to your bones;
And you will be like a watered
garden,
And like a spring of water whose
waters do not fail.
12 "And your people will rebuild the
ancient ruins;
You will raise up *and* restore
the age-old foundations [of
buildings that have been laid
waste];
You will be called Repairer of the
Breach,
Restorer of Streets with Dwellings.

Keeping the Sabbath

13 "If you turn back your foot from
[unnecessary travel on] the
Sabbath,
From doing your own pleasure on
My holy day,
And call the Sabbath a [spiritual]
delight, and the holy day of the
LORD honorable,
And honor it, not going your own
way
Or engaging in your own
pleasure
Or speaking your own [idle]
words,
14 Then you will take pleasure in the
LORD,
And I will make you ride on the
high places of the earth,
And I will feed you with the
[promised] heritage of Jacob
your father;
For the mouth of the LORD has
spoken." [Gen 27:28, 29; 28:13–15]

Separation from God

59 BEHOLD, THE LORD's hand is
not so short
That it cannot save,
Nor His ear so impaired
That it cannot hear.
2 But your wickedness has
separated you from your God,
And your sins have hidden *His*
face from you so that He does
not hear.
3 For your hands are defiled with
blood
And your fingers with wickedness
[with sin, with injustice, with
wrongdoing];
Your lips have spoken lies,
Your tongue mutters
wickedness.

59:2 The Effects of Sin — Sin, regardless of how serious, always has an effect — separation. Sin separates one from God. This separation from God is death. Adam was told that if he ate of the tree of the knowledge of good and evil he would die (Ge 3:3). Adam ate of the tree anyway and immediately died spiritually — his soul was separated from God — and he then began to die physically. The entrance of sin into the world brought with it death (Ro 5:12; 6:23). That man is a sinner is proven by the fact that he dies — where there is death, there is sin. Sin's penalty, death, can be remedied by life — union with God. This is achieved by belief in Jesus, who died to pay the penalty of man's sin (Ro 5:21). For one who believes in Jesus, the penalty of sin is broken. He will die physically but physical death for him is only the doorway into the presence of God.

Sin has an effect upon the believer, for it mars his fellowship with God. Sin in the believer's life is a terrible thing and is not to be tolerated. While it is probable that the believer will sin, it is never necessary for him to do so (1Jn 2:1).

9 Ps 12:2 **12** Isa 61:4 **13** Isa 56:2 **14** Job 22:26; Dt 32:13; 33:29; Isa 1:20; 40:5; Mic 4:4 **CHAPTER 59** **1** Nu 11:23; Isa 50:2 **3** Isa 1:15

4 No one sues righteously [but for
the sake of doing injury to
others—to take some undue
advantage], and no one pleads
[his case] in truth; [but rather]
They trust in empty *arguments*
and speak lies;
They conceive trouble and bring
forth injustice.
5 They hatch vipers' eggs and weave
the spider's webs;
He who eats of their eggs dies,
And *from an egg* which is crushed
a viper breaks out.
6 Their webs will not serve as
clothing,
Nor will they cover themselves
with what they make;
Their works are works of
wickedness [of sin, of injustice,
of wrongdoing],
And the act of violence is in their
hands.
7 Their feet run to evil,
And they rush to shed innocent
blood.
Their thoughts are thoughts of
wickedness [of sin, of injustice,
of wrongdoing];
Devastation and destruction are in
their highways.
8 They do not know the way of
peace,
And there is no justice in their
tracks.
They have made them into
crooked paths;
Whoever walks on them does not
know peace. [Rom 3:15–18]

A Confession of Wickedness

9 Therefore justice is far from us,
And righteousness does not
overtake us.
We [expectantly] hope for light,
but only see darkness;
We hope for gleam of light, *but* we
walk in darkness *and* gloom.
10 We grope for a wall like the blind,
We grope like those who have no
eyes.
We stumble at midday as in the
twilight;
Among those who are healthy *we
are* like dead men.
11 We all groan *and* growl like bears,
And coo sadly like doves;
We hope for justice, but there is
none,
For salvation, but it is far from us.
12 For our transgressions are
multiplied before You [O LORD],
And our sins testify against us;
For our transgressions are with us,
And we know *and* recognize
our wickedness [our sin, our
injustice, our wrongdoing]:
13 Rebelling against and denying the
LORD,
Turning away from [following] our
God,
Speaking oppression and revolt,
Conceiving and muttering from
the heart lying words.
14 Justice is pushed back,
And righteous behavior stands far
away;
For truth has fallen in the city
square,
And integrity cannot enter.
15 Yes, truth is missing;
And he who turns away from evil
makes himself a prey.

Now the LORD saw it,
And it displeased Him that there
was no justice.
16 He saw that there was no man,
And was amazed that there was
no one to intercede [on behalf of
truth and right];
Therefore His own arm brought
salvation to Him,

59:5 ***vipers' eggs.*** The viper is a poisonous snake (Ac 28:3–6).
59:7–8 ***feet run to evil.*** This passage is cited in Romans 3:15–17 to document the universal aspect of sin.
59:9 ***Therefore.*** "Therefore" links Israel's repentance with the prophet's reprimand. With the pronoun "us," Isaiah identified himself with his people's sins (Eze 9:6–7; Da 9:5).
59:16 ***no man.*** God's salvation does not depend on humans (Eze 22:30).

4 Job 15:35; Ps 7:14 **6** Job 8:14 **7** Pr 1:16; Ro 3:15 **8** Ps 125:5; Pr 2:15 **9** Jer 8:15 **10** Dt 28:29; Job 5:14; Am 8:9 **11** Isa 38:14; Eze 7:16 **13** Mt 12:34 **16** Eze 22:30; Mk 6:6; Ps 98:1; Isa 63:5

And His own righteousness
sustained Him. [Is 53:11; Col 2:9;
1 John 2:1, 2]
17 For He [the LORD] put on
righteousness like a coat of
armor,
And salvation like a helmet on His
head;
He put on garments of vengeance
for clothing
And covered Himself with zeal
[and great love for His people]
as a cloak. [Eph 6:14, 17;
1 Thess 5:8]
18 As their deeds deserve, so He will
repay:
Wrath to His adversaries,
retribution to His enemies;
To the islands *and* coastlands He
will repay.
19 So they will fear the name of the
LORD from the west
And His glory from the rising of
the sun.
For He will come in like a narrow,
rushing stream
Which the breath of the LORD
drives [overwhelming the
enemy]. [Matt 8:11; Luke 13:29]
20 "A Redeemer (Messiah) will come
to Zion,
And to those in Jacob (Israel) who
turn from transgression (sin),"
declares the LORD.

21 "As for Me, this is My covenant
with them," says the LORD: "My Spirit
which is upon you [writing the law
of God on the heart], and My words
which I have put in your mouth shall
not depart from your mouth, nor from
the mouths of your [true, spiritual]
children, nor from the mouth of your
children's children," says the LORD,
"from now and forever." [Jer 31:33;
Rom 11:26, 27; Gal 3:29; Heb 12:22–24]

A Glorified Zion

60 "ARISE [from spiritual
depression to a new life], shine
[be radiant with the glory *and*
brilliance of the LORD]; for your
light has come,

59:17 *righteousness like a coat of armor.* This idea of the righteous warrior is repeated in Ephesians 6:13 – 17. Right standing with God is our protection, as surely as the warrior depends on the heavy body shield over his heart to protect him from the arrows of the enemy.
59:20 *A Redeemer (Messiah) will come.* The Redeemer comes in the person of Jesus Christ.
59:21 *My Spirit.* God promised that His Spirit and His Word would never be lost to His people. The covenant that He made with them affirms that the Word is firm and unshakable. It may not be performed immediately, but the hearers can be assured of its truth. He also promised that He would always be present with His people through the Spirit. This is a promise that continues to be comforting to the people of God, and it must have brought particular comfort to the people who lived in the "silent" years between the preaching of Malachi and the coming of John the Baptist.
59:21 Inspiration of God's Word — The word *inspiration* occurs only once in the New Testament in 2 Timothy 3:16. Paul says there "All Scripture is God-breathed [given by divine inspiration]." God takes the initiative in communicating with us. Divine inspiration logically follows divine revelation. In revelation God speaks to man's ear, while by inspiration He guides the pen to ensure that the imparted message is correctly written down. God's intent is to give His people a right understanding of His revelation and a permanent record of His dealings with mankind. The authority of the Bible is from God Himself.

Bible authors understood that their writings were being guided by the Spirit of God, even as they wrote them. Peter said this was true of Old Testament authors (2Pe 1:20 – 21). He then stated his own letters were inspired by God (2Pe 3:1 – 2). Finally, he pointed out this was also true concerning Paul's writings (2Pe 3:15).

This means that the Bible is more than just the wise insights of men who desired to follow God. God worked in the thinking of the biblical writers so the message they wrote was also God's message. While the writings certainly display the individual characteristics of all of the different authors, there is also an overall divine influence that uniquely unifies the Bible as no other book.
60:1 *Arise [from spiritual depression to a new life], shine.* This command is directed to Zion (v. 14), who is both the recipient of God's light and the reflector of it. It is difficult to imagine the world without the knowledge of Christ, yet each believer who remembers his life before

17 Eph 6:14,17; 1Th 5:8 **18** Isa 63:6 **19** Ps 113:3; Mal 1:11; Rev 12:15 **20** Ro 11:26 **21** Heb 8:10; 10:16
CHAPTER 60 **1** Eph 5:14; Mal 4:2

And the glory *and* brilliance of
the LORD has risen upon you.
[Zech 8:23]
2 "For in fact, darkness will cover
the earth
And deep darkness *will cover* the
peoples;
But the LORD will rise upon you
[Jerusalem]
And His glory *and* brilliance will
be seen on you. [Is 60:19–22;
Mal 4:2; Rev 21:2, 3]
3 "Nations will come to your light,
And kings to the brightness of
your rising. [Is 2:2, 3; Jer 3:17]
4 "Lift up your eyes around you and
see;
They all gather together, they
come to you.
Your sons will come from far
away,
And your daughters will be looked
after at *their* side.
5 "Then you will see and be radiant,
And your heart will tremble [with
joy] and rejoice
Because the abundant wealth of
the seas will be brought to you,
The wealth of the nations will
come to you. [Ps 119:32]
6 "A multitude of camels [from the
eastern trading tribes] will cover
you [Jerusalem],
The young camels of Midian and
Ephah;
All those from Sheba [who once
came to trade] will come
Bringing gold and frankincense
And proclaiming the praises of the
LORD. [Matt 2:11]
7 "All the flocks of Kedar will be
gathered to you [as the eastern
pastoral tribes join the trading
tribes],
The rams of Nebaioth will serve
you;
They will go up with acceptance
[as sacrifices] on My altar,
And I will glorify the house of My
honor *and* splendor.
8 "Who are these who fly like a
cloud
And like doves to their windows?
9 "The islands *and* coastlands will
confidently wait for Me;
And the ships of Tarshish *will
come* first,
To bring your sons from far away,
Their silver and gold with them,
For the name of the LORD your
God,
For the Holy One of Israel because
He has glorified you.

10 "Foreigners will build up your
walls,
And their kings will serve you;
For in My [righteous] wrath I
struck you,
But in My favor *and* grace I have
had compassion on you.
11 "Your gates will be open
continually;
They shall not be shut day or
night,

---

he was born again can testify to the power of the light of the gospel. It is a great joy to come from the darkness of sin and doubt to the light of forgiveness and knowledge of Jesus Christ. What a joyful command, to "shine" for the Savior.

60:9 *ships of Tarshish*. The reference to the ships of Tarshish alludes to the wealth of King Solomon (2:16; 1Ki 10:22).

61:10 Christ's Righteousness — One of the most awesome requirements made upon men and women by God is that they be righteous, that is, conform to His ethical and moral standards (Ps 15:2; Mic 6:8). Since God is holy He cannot allow sinners into His presence (Isa 6:3–5). We sinners cannot save ourselves or make ourselves righteous. Only God's intervention can save us and make us righteous. God sent Christ, who never sinned, to die for our sins and thus satisfy His own wrath towards us and our sin. God, at the cross, treated Christ as though He had committed our sins even though He was righteous. On the other hand, when we believe in Christ, He treats us as though we were as righteous as Himself (2Co 5:21). It is as if God deposits in our spiritual account the very worth of Christ, much as though He were a banker adding an inexhaustible deposit to our bank account.

3 Isa 49:6,23; Rev 21:24 **4** Isa 49:18; Isa 49:20-22; 66:12 **5** Ro 11:25 **6** Ge 25:4; Ps 72:10; Isa 61:6; Mt 2:11 **7** Ge 25:13; Hag 2:7,9 **9** Ps 72:10; Isa 51:5; Gal 4:26; Ps 68:30; Zec 14:14; Jer 3:17; Isa 55:5 **10** Zec 6:15; Isa 49:23; Rev 21:24; Isa 57:17; Isa 54:7,8 **11** Rev 21:25

So that people may bring to you
the wealth of the nations—
With their kings led in procession.
[Rev 21:24–27]
12 "For the nation or the kingdom
which will not serve you
[Jerusalem] shall perish,
And the nations [that refuse
to serve] shall be utterly
ruined.
13 "The glory of Lebanon will come
to you,
The cypress, the juniper, and the
cedar together,
To beautify the place of My
sanctuary;
And I will honor *and* make the
place of My feet glorious.
14 "The sons of those who oppressed
you will come bowing down to
you [in submission],
And all those who despised you
and treated you disrespectfully
will bow down at the soles of
your feet,
And they will call you the City
of the LORD,
The Zion of the Holy One of Israel.
[Rev 3:9]

15 "Whereas you [Jerusalem] have
been abandoned and hated
With no one passing through,
I will make you an object of pride
forever,
A joy from generation to
generation.
16 "You will suck the milk of the
[Gentile] nations
And suck the breast (abundance)
of kings;
Then you will recognize *and*
know that I, the LORD, am your
Savior
And your Redeemer, the Mighty
One of Jacob.
17 "Instead of bronze I will bring
gold,
And instead of iron I will bring
silver,
And instead of wood, bronze,
And instead of stones, iron.
And [instead of the tyranny of the
present] I will appoint peace as
your officers,
And righteousness your rulers.
18 "Violence will not be heard again
in your land,
Nor devastation or destruction
within your borders;
But you will call your walls
Salvation, and your gates Praise
[to God].
19 "The sun will no longer be your
light by day,
Nor shall the bright glow of the
moon give light to you,
But the LORD will be an everlasting
light for you;
And your God will be your glory
and splendor. [Jer 9:23, 24;
Rev 21:23]
20 "Your sun will no longer set,
Nor will your moon wane;
For the LORD will be your
everlasting light,
And the days of your mourning
will be over.
21 "Then all your people will be
[uncompromisingly and
consistently] righteous;
They will possess the land
forever,
The branch of My planting,
The work of My hands,
That I may be glorified.
22 "The smallest one will become a
thousand (a clan),
And the least one a mighty nation.
I, the LORD, will quicken it in its
[appointed] time."

60:12 ***not serve you [Jerusalem] shall perish.*** The nation and kingdom that does not serve Zion, where Christ now reigns (Ac 2:29–36), shall perish (Jn 3:18; Heb 2:3; 9:27; 10:27).
60:18 ***Salvation . . . Praise.*** Judging from the figurative language in verses 15–22, especially verse 17, God's Salvation and Israel's praise will be the city's defense (Zec 2:4–5).
60:19–20 ***no longer.*** These verses form the basis for the description of the New Jerusalem in the new heaven and earth (Rev 21:1,23; 22:5).

12 Zec 14:17; Mt 21:44 **13** Isa 35:2; 1Ch 28:2; Ps 132:7 **14** Isa 49:23; Rev 3:9; Heb 12:22; Rev 14:1 **16** Isa 49:23; 61:6; Isa 43:3 **18** Isa 26:1 **19** Rev 21:23; Zec 2:5 **20** Am 8:9 **21** Isa 52:1; Rev 21:27; Ps 37:11; Mt 5:5; Isa 61:3; Mt 15:13; Jn 15:2; Isa 29:23; Eph 2:10 **22** Mt 13:31

Exaltation of the Afflicted

61 THE SPIRIT of the Lord GOD is upon me,
Because the LORD has anointed *and* commissioned me
To bring good news to the humble *and* afflicted;
He has sent me to bind up [the wounds of] the brokenhearted,
To proclaim release [from confinement and condemnation] to the [physical and spiritual] captives
And freedom to prisoners,
[Rom 10:15]
2 To proclaim the favorable year of the LORD,
And the day of vengeance *and* retribution of our God,
To comfort all who mourn,
[Matt 11:2–6; Luke 4:18, 19; 7:22]
3 To grant to those who mourn in Zion *the following:*
To give them a turban instead of dust [on their heads, a sign of mourning],
The oil of joy instead of mourning,
The garment [expressive] of praise instead of a disheartened spirit.
So they will be called the trees of righteousness [strong and magnificent, distinguished for integrity, justice, and right standing with God],
The planting of the LORD, that He may be glorified.

4 Then they will rebuild the ancient ruins,
They will raise up *and* restore the former desolations;
And they will renew the ruined cities,
The desolations (deserted settlements) of many generations.
5 Strangers will stand and feed your flocks,
And foreigners will be your farmers and your vinedressers.
6 But you shall be called the priests of the LORD;
People will speak of you as the ministers of our God.
You will eat the wealth of nations,
And you will boast of their riches.
[Ex 19:6; 1 Pet 2:5; Rev 1:6; 5:10; 20:6]
7 Instead of your [former] shame *you will have* a double *portion;*
And *instead of* humiliation your people will shout for joy over their portion.
Therefore in their land they will possess double [what they had forfeited];
Everlasting joy will be theirs.
8 For I, the LORD, love justice;
I hate robbery with a burnt offering.
And I will faithfully reward them,
And make an everlasting covenant with them.
9 Then their offspring will be known among the nations,
And their descendants among the peoples.
All who see them [in their prosperity] will recognize *and* acknowledge them
That they are the people whom the LORD has blessed.

10 I will rejoice greatly in the LORD,
My soul will exult in my God;
For He has clothed me with garments of salvation,
He has covered me with a robe of righteousness,
As a bridegroom puts on a turban,
And as a bride adorns herself with her jewels.

61:1 *me.* The "me" featured so prominently here is the same as the Servant in 42:1; 49:1; 50:4; 52:13. The Servant is the Messiah, the Lord Jesus Christ. This verse is the passage from Isaiah that Jesus read in the synagogue at the beginning of His ministry (Lk 4:16 – 21). When He finished reading it, He said, "Today this Scripture has been fulfilled in your hearing and in your presence."

61:2 *day of vengeance.* The day of God's vengeance is yet to come. This is the "day" that the Book of Revelation is talking about (Rev 11:14 – 19).

CHAPTER 61 **1** Lk 4:18; Jn 1:32; 3:34; Ps 45:7; Ps 147:3; Isa 57:15; Isa 42:7; Jer 34:8 **2** Lev 25:9; Isa 34:8; Mal 4:1,3; 2Th 1:7; Isa 57:18; Mt 5:4 **3** Ps 30:11; Isa 60:21; Jn 15:8 **4** Isa 49:8; Eze 36:33 **5** Eph 2:12 **6** Ex 19:6; Isa 60:17; 1Pe 2:5; Rev 1:6; 5:10; Isa 60:5 **7** Isa 40:2; Zec 9:12 **8** Ps 11:7; Isa 1:11,13; Isa 55:3 **9** Isa 65:23 **10** Hab 3:18; Ps 132:9,16; Isa 49:18; Rev 21:2

[11]For as the earth brings forth its
sprouts,
And as a garden causes what is
sown in it to spring up,
So the Lord GOD will [most
certainly] cause righteousness
and justice and praise
To spring up before all the nations
[through the power of His word].

Zion's Glory and New Name

62 FOR ZION'S sake I (Isaiah)
will not be silent,
And for Jerusalem's sake I will not
keep quiet,
Until her righteousness *and*
vindication go forth as
brightness,
And her salvation goes forth like a
burning torch.
[2]The nations will see your
righteousness *and* vindication
[by God],
And all kings [will see] your glory;
And you will be called by a new
name
Which the mouth of the LORD will
designate. [Rev 2:17]
[3]You will also be [considered] a
crown of glory *and* splendor in
the hand of the LORD,
And a royal diadem [exceedingly
beautiful] in the hand of your
God.
[4]It will no longer be said of you
[Judah], "Azubah (Abandoned),"
Nor will it any longer be said
of your land, "Shemamah
(Desolate)";
But you will be called, "Hephzibah
(My Delight is in Her),"
And your land, "Married";
For the LORD delights in you,
And *to Him* your land will be
married [owned and protected
by the LORD].
[5]For as a young man marries a
virgin [O Jerusalem],
So your sons will marry you;
And as the bridegroom rejoices
over the bride,
So your God will rejoice over you.

[6]On your walls, O Jerusalem, I
have appointed *and* stationed
watchmen (prophets),
Who will never keep silent day or
night;
You who profess the LORD, take no
rest for yourselves,
[7]And give Him no rest [from your
prayers] until He establishes
Jerusalem
And makes her a praise on the
earth.
[8]The LORD has sworn [an oath]
by His right hand and by His
mighty arm,
"I will never again give your grain
as food for your enemies,
Nor will [the invading] foreigners
drink your new wine for which
you have labored."
[9]But they who have harvested it
will eat it and praise the LORD,
And they who have gathered
it will drink it [at the feasts
celebrated] in the courtyards of
My sanctuary.

[10]Go through, go through the gates,
Clear the way for the people;
Build up, build up the highway,
Remove the stones, lift up a
banner over the peoples.

62:2 *a new name.* A new name, like new clothing, signified a new status (Ge 17:5,15; 32:28; Rev 2:17).
62:4 *Hephzibah . . . "Married."* The name "Hephzibah" means "my delight is in her" — in this case, it is the Lord's delight. Both of these names are symbolic, pointing to a time when Israel's relationship with the Lord is restored.
62:6 *You who profess the LORD.* The "watchmen," or prophets, were intercessors. They prayed that the Lord's promises would be fulfilled.
62:8 *The LORD has sworn.* When God made the promise to Abraham (Heb 6:13), He swore by Himself; so here He again swears in His own name. There is no greater name than the name of the Lord, and He cannot lie — this is the surest promise man can receive.

11 Ps 72:3; 85:11; Isa 60:18; 62:7 **CHAPTER 62** **2** Isa 60:3; See ver. 4,12 **3** Zec 9:16 **4** Hos 1:10; Isa 49:14; 54:6,7; Isa 54:1 **5** Isa 65:19 **7** Isa 61:11; Zep 3:20 **8** Dt 28:31; Jer 5:17 **9** See Dt 12:12; 14:23,26; 16:11,14 **10** Isa 40:3; 57:14; Isa 11:12

11 Listen carefully, the LORD has
proclaimed to the end of the
earth,
Say to the Daughter of Zion, "Look
now, your salvation is coming
[in the LORD];
Indeed, His reward is with Him,
and His restitution accompanies
Him." [Is 40:10]
12 And they will call them "The Holy
People,
The Redeemed of the LORD";
And you will be called "Sought
Out, A City Not Deserted."

God's Vengeance on the Nations

63 WHO IS this who comes from
Edom,
With crimson-stained garments
from Bozrah [in Edom],
This One (the Messiah) who is
majestic in His apparel,
Marching in the greatness of His
might?
"It is I, [the One] who speaks in
righteousness [proclaiming
vindication], mighty to save."
2 Why is Your apparel red,
And Your garments like the one
who treads in the wine press?
3 "I have trodden the wine trough
alone,
And of the peoples there was no
one with Me.
I also trod them in My anger
And trampled them in My wrath;
And their lifeblood is sprinkled on
My garments,
And I stained all My clothes.
4 "For the day of vengeance [against
ungodliness] was in My heart,
And My year of redemption [of
those who put their trust in
Me—the year of My redeemed]
has come.
5 "I looked, but there was no one to
help,
And I was amazed *and* appalled
that there was no one to uphold
[truth and right].
So My own arm brought salvation
to Me,
And My wrath sustained Me.
6 "I trampled the peoples in My anger
And made them drunk with [the
cup of] My wrath,
And I spilled their lifeblood on the
earth."

God's Ancient Mercies Recalled

7 I will tell of the lovingkindnesses
of the LORD, and the
praiseworthy deeds of the LORD,
According to all that the LORD has
done for us,
And *His* great goodness toward
the house of Israel,
Which He has shown them
according to His compassion
And according to the abundance
of His lovingkindnesses.
8 For He said, "Be assured, they are
My people,
Sons who will not be faithless."
So He became their Savior [in all
their distresses].
9 In all their distress He was
distressed,
And the angel of His presence
saved them,
In His love and in His compassion
He redeemed them;
And He lifted them up and
carried them all the days of
old. [Ex 23:20–23; 33:14, 15;
Deut 1:31; 32:10–12]
10 But they rebelled
And grieved His Holy Spirit;
Therefore He changed into their
enemy,
And He fought against them.
11 Then His people remembered the
days of old, of Moses [and they
said],

63:1 *Edom.* Edom epitomized Israel's enemies (Ps 137:7; La 4:21 – 22; Eze 25:12; 35:1 – 5; Ob 13 – 14). It was famous for its winemaking (v. 3). ***Bozrah.*** Bozrah was the chief town of Edom.

63:3 *I.* The pronoun "I" refers to Christ in Revelation 19:5.

63:11 *put His Holy Spirit in their midst.* This refers to the presence of the Holy Spirit

---

11 Zec 9:9; Mt 21:5; Jn 12:15; Isa 40:10; Rev 22:12 **12** ver. 4 **CHAPTER 63** **2** Rev 19:13 **3** La 1:15; Rev 14:19,20; 19:15 **4** Isa 34:8; 61:2 **5** Isa 41:28; 59:16; Jn 16:32; Ps 98:1; Isa 59:16 **9** Jdg 10:16; Ac 9:4; Ex 14:19; Ac 12:11; Dt 7:7; Ex 19:4 **10** Ex 15:24; Ps 95:9; 78:40; Ac 7:51; Ex 23:21 **11** Ex 14:30; Nu 11:17

Where is He who brought our
fathers up out of the [Red] Sea,
with the shepherds of His flock
[Moses and Aaron]?
Where is He who put His Holy
Spirit in their midst,
12 Who caused His glorious arm *and*
infinite power to go at the right
hand of Moses,
Dividing the waters before them to
make for Himself an everlasting
name,
13 Who led them through the depths
[of the Red Sea],
Like a horse in the wilderness, [so
that] they did not stumble?
14 Like the cattle that go down into
the valley [to find better pasture
and rest],
The Spirit of the LORD gave them
rest.
So You led Your people [O LORD]
To make for Yourself a beautiful
and glorious name [preparing
the way for the acknowledgment
of Your name by all nations].

"You Are Our Father"

15 Look down from heaven and see
from Your lofty dwelling place,
holy and glorious.
Where are Your zeal and Your
mighty acts [Your miracles
which you did for Your people]?
The stirring of Your heart and
Your compassion are restrained
and withheld from me.
16 For [most certainly] You are our
Father, even though Abraham
[our ancestor] does not know us
And Israel does not acknowledge
us.
You, O LORD, are [still] our Father,
Our Redeemer from everlasting is
Your name.
17 O LORD, why do You cause us to
stray from Your ways
And harden our heart from
fearing You [with reverence and
awe]?
Return for Your servants' sake, the
tribes of Your heritage.
18 Your holy people possessed Your
sanctuary for [only] a little while;
Our adversaries have trampled it
down.
19 We have become *like* those over
whom You have never ruled,
Like those who were not called by
Your name.

Prayer for Mercy and Help

64 OH, THAT You would tear
open the heavens and come
down,
That the mountains might quake
at Your presence—
2 As [sure as] fire kindles the
brushwood, as fire causes water
to boil—
To make Your name known to
Your adversaries,
That the nations may tremble at
Your presence!
3 When You did awesome *and*
amazing things which we did
not expect,
You came down [at Sinai]; the
mountains quaked at Your
presence.
4 For from days of old no one has
heard, nor has ear perceived,
Nor has the eye seen a God
besides You,
Who works *and* acts in behalf of
the one who [gladly] waits for
Him.
5 You meet him who rejoices in
doing that which is morally
right,

---

on Moses and his helpers in the desert (Nu 11:17,25).

63:12 ***glorious arm.*** This verse refers to God dividing the Red Sea (Ex 15:6; 14:16,21; Ps 78:13). Isaiah is reminding his hearers of the mighty acts that God did in the past, as well as the things that He has promised to do in the future. Such perspective is often helpful when one is bearing difficult times in the present.

64:4 ***Nor has the eye seen.*** Paul cites this verse with some changes in 1 Corinthians 2:9.

12 Ex 15:6; Jos 3:16 **13** Ps 106:9 **14** 2Sa 7:23 **15** Dt 26:15; Ps 80:14; Ps 33:14; Jer 31:20; Hos 11:8 **16** Dt 32:6; Job 14:21 **17** Ps 119:10; Jn 12:40; Ps 90:13 **18** Dt 7:6; Ps 74:7 **CHAPTER 64** **1** Ps 144:5; Mic 1:4 **3** Ex 34:10; Ps 68:8 **4** Ps 31:19; 1Co 2:9 **5** Ac 10:35; Isa 26:8; Mal 3:6

Who remembers You in Your ways.
Indeed, You were angry, for we sinned;
We have long *continued* in our sins [prolonging Your anger].
And shall we be saved [under such circumstances]?
6 For we all have become like one who is [ceremonially] unclean [like a leper],
And all our deeds of righteousness are like filthy rags;
We all wither *and* decay like a leaf,
And our wickedness [our sin, our injustice, our wrongdoing], like the wind, takes us away [carrying us far from God's favor, toward destruction]. [Lev 13:45, 46]
7 There is no one who calls on Your name,
Who awakens *and* causes himself to take hold of You;
For You have hidden Your face from us
And have handed us over to the [consuming and destructive] power of our wickedness [our sin, our injustice, our wrongdoing]. [Rom 1:21–24]

8 Yet, O LORD, You are our Father;
We are the clay, and You our Potter,
And we all are the work of Your hand.
9 Do not be angry beyond measure, O LORD,
Do not remember our wickedness [our sin, our injustice, our wrongdoing] forever.
Now look, consider, for we are all Your people.
10 Your holy cities have become a wilderness,
Zion has become a wilderness,
Jerusalem a desolation.
11 Our holy and beautiful house [the temple built by Solomon],
Where our fathers praised You,
Has been burned by fire;
And all our precious objects are in ruins.
12 Considering these [tragedies], will You restrain Yourself, O LORD [and not help us]?
Will You keep silent and humiliate *and* oppress us beyond measure?

A Rebellious People

65 "I LET Myself be sought by those who did not ask *for Me;*
I let Myself be found by those who did not seek Me.
I said, 'Here am I, here am I,'
To the nation [Israel] which did not call on My Name. [Ex 3:14; Is 58:9]
2 "I have spread out My hands all the day long to a rebellious *and* stubborn people,
Who walk in the way that is not good, [following] after their own thoughts *and* intentions,
3 The people who continually provoke Me to My face,
Sacrificing [to idols] in gardens and making offerings with incense on bricks [instead of at the designated altar];
4 Who sit among the graves [trying to conjure up evil spirits] and spend the night in the secret places [where spirits are thought to dwell];
Who eat swine's flesh,
And their pots *hold* the broth of unclean meat;
5 Who say, 'Keep to yourself, do not come near me,
For I am too holy for you [and you might defile me]!'
These [people] are smoke in My nostrils,

64:10 *wilderness . . . desolation.* The prophetic picture of devastation of the land is probably referring to the time of the Babylonian invasion.

65:1 *those who did not ask for Me.* Paul saw his ministry to the Gentiles as a fulfillment of this promise (Ro 10:20 – 21).

6 Php 3:9; Ps 90:5,6 **8** Isa 63:16; Isa 29:16; Eph 2:10 **9** Ps 74:1,2; 79:13 **10** Ps 79:1 **11** Ps 74:7; Eze 24:21 **12** Isa 42:14; Ps 83:1 **CHAPTER 65** **1** Ro 9:24; Eph 2:12; Isa 63:19 **2** Ro 10:21 **3** Dt 32:21; Isa 1:29; Lev 17:5 **4** Dt 18:11; Isa 66:17 **5** Mt 9:11; Lk 18:11; Jude 19

A fire that burns all the day.
6 "Indeed, it is written before Me,
I will not keep silent, but I will repay;
I will even repay it [directly] into their arms,
7 Both your own wickedness and the wickedness of your fathers,"
says the LORD.
"Since they *too* have made offerings with incense on the mountains
And scorned *and* taunted Me on the hills,
I therefore will measure [punishment for] their former work [directly] into their arms."

8 This is what the LORD says,

"As the new wine is found in the cluster,
And one says, 'Do not destroy it, for there is a blessing *and* benefit in it,'
So I will do for the sake of My servants
In order not to destroy all of them.
9 "I will bring forth descendants from Jacob,
And an heir of My mountains from Judah;
Even My chosen ones shall inherit it,
And My servants will live there.
10 "And [the plain of] Sharon will be a place for flocks to graze,
And the Valley of Achor a resting place for herds,
For My people who seek Me [who long for Me and require My presence in their lives].
11 "But you who abandon (turn away from) the LORD,
Who forget *and* ignore My holy mountain (Zion),
Who set a table for Gad [the Babylonian god of fortune],
And who fill a jug of mixed wine for Meni [the god of fate],
12 I will destine you for the sword, [says the LORD],
And all of you will bow down to the slaughter,
Because when I called, you did not answer;
When I spoke, you did not listen *or* obey.
But you did [what was] evil in My sight
And chose that in which I did not delight."

13 Therefore, the Lord GOD says this,

"Listen carefully, My servants will eat, but you will be hungry;
Indeed, My servants will drink, but you will be thirsty;
Indeed, My servants will rejoice, but you will be put to shame.
14 "Indeed, My servants will shout for joy from a happy heart,
But you will cry out with a heavy heart,
And you shall wail *and* howl from a broken spirit.
15 "And you will leave your name behind to My chosen ones [who will use it] as a curse,
And the Lord GOD will put you to death,
But He will call His servants by another name [a much greater name, just as the name Israel was greater than the name Jacob]. [Gen 32:28; Jer 29:22]
16 "Because he who blesses himself on the earth
Will bless himself by the God of truth *and* faithfulness;
And he who swears [an oath] on the earth
Will swear by the God of truth *and* faithfulness;
Because the former troubles are forgotten,
And because they are hidden from My sight. [2 Cor 1:20; Rev 3:14]

65:10 *Sharon ... Valley of Achor.* Sharon, on the coastal plain in the west, and the valley of Achor, near Jericho in the east, represent the whole land.

6 Dt 32:34; Mal 3:16; Ps 50:3; Ps 79:12; Jer 16:18; Eze 11:21 **7** Ex 20:5; Eze 18:6; Eze 20:27 **8** Joel 2:14 **9** Mt 24:22 **10** Isa 33:9; Jos 7:24; Hos 2:15 **11** Isa 56:7; Eze 23:41; 1Co 10:21 **12** 2Ch 36:15,16; Pr 1:24; Jer 7:13 **14** Mt 8:12; Lk 13:28 **15** Jer 29:22; Zec 8:13; ver. 9,22; Ac 11:26 **16** Ps 72:17; Jer 4:2; Dt 6:13; Zep 1:5

New Heavens and a New Earth

17 "Behold, I am creating new heavens and a new earth;
And the former things [of life] will not be remembered or come to mind. [Is 66:22; 2 Pet 3:13; Rev 21:1]
18 "But be glad and rejoice forever over what I create;
Behold, I am creating Jerusalem to be a *source of* rejoicing
And her people a joy.
19 "I will also rejoice in Jerusalem and be glad in My people;
And there will no longer be heard in her
The voice of weeping and the sound of crying.
20 "No longer shall there be in it an infant *who lives only a few* days,
Or an old man who does not finish his days;
For the youth who dies at the age of a hundred,
And the one who does not reach the age of a hundred
Will be *thought of as* accursed.
21 "They will build houses and live *in them;*
They will plant vineyards and eat the fruit.
22 "They will not build and another occupy;
They will not plant and another eat [the fruit].
For as the lifetime of a tree, *so will be* the days of My people,
And My chosen [people] will fully enjoy [and long make use of] the work of their hands.
23 "They will not labor in vain,
Or bear *children* for disaster;
For they are the descendants of those blessed by the LORD,
And their offspring with them.

24 "It shall also come to pass that before
they call, I will answer; and while they
are still speaking, I will hear. [Is 30:19;
58:9; Matt 6:8]
25 "The wolf and the lamb will graze
together, and the lion will eat straw
like the ox [there will no longer be
predator and prey]; and dust will be the
serpent's food. They will do no evil or
harm in all My holy mountain (Zion),"
says the LORD.

Heaven Is God's Throne

66 THIS IS what the LORD says,
"Heaven is My throne and the earth is My footstool.
Where, then, is a house that you could build for Me?
And where will My resting place be? [Acts 17:24]
2 "For all these things My hand has made,
So all these things came into being [by and for Me]," declares the LORD.
"But to this one I will look [graciously],
To him who is humble and contrite in spirit, and who [reverently] trembles at My word *and* honors My commands. [John 4:24]

65:17 *new heavens and a new earth.* As God fashioned the existing heavens and earth, so He will fashion a new cosmos that will be ready for His presence and for the enjoyment of His people (Rev 21:4).
65:20 *youth who dies at the age of a hundred.* In the coming kingdom the life spans will be much greater. People will not be affected by disease and aging in the same way as in our present age. This time probably refers to the millennial kingdom (Rev 20:1–6).
65:25 *wolf ... lamb.* This picture is also presented in 11:6–9. It is a picture of regenerated nature that will occur in the new heavens and new earth.
66:1 *Where, then, is a house.* No place on earth can accommodate the transcendent God. Even the temple built by Solomon, which was filled with the glory of the Lord (1Ki 8:11), did not really contain the Lord. He called it a "house for My Name" (1Ki 8:18).

17 2Pe 3:13; Rev 21:1 **19** Isa 62:5; Isa 35:10; Rev 7:17 **20** Ecc 8:12 **22** Ps 92:12; ver. 9,15 **23** Hos 9:12; Isa 61:9 **24** Da 9:21 **25** Isa 11:6; Ge 3:14 **CHAPTER 66 1** 1Ki 8:27; 2Ch 6:18; Mt 5:34; Ac 17:24 **2** Isa 57:15; 61:1; Ps 34:18; 51:17; ver. 5; Ezr 9:4; 10:3; Pr 28:14

Hypocrisy Rebuked

3 "He who kills an ox [for pagan
sacrifice] is [as guilty] as one
who kills a man;
He who sacrifices a lamb, as one
who breaks a dog's neck;
He who offers a grain offering, *as
one who offers* swine's blood;
He who offers incense, as one who
blesses an idol.
Such people have chosen their
own ways,
And their soul delights in their
repulsive acts;
4 So I will choose their punishments,
And will bring the things they
dread upon them
Because I called, but no one
answered;
I spoke, but they did not listen *or*
obey.
But they did evil in My sight
And chose that in which I did not
delight."
5 Hear the word of the LORD, you
who tremble [with awe-filled
reverence] at His word:
"Your brothers who hate you, who
exclude you for My Name's sake,
Have said, 'Let the LORD be
glorified, that we may see your
joy.'
But they will be put to shame.
6 "The sound of an uproar from the
city! A voice from the temple!
The voice of the LORD, providing
retribution to His enemies.
7 "Before she (Zion) was in labor,
she gave birth;
Before her labor pain came, she
gave birth to a boy.
8 "Who has heard of such a thing?
Who has seen such things?
Can a land be born in one day?
Or can a nation be brought forth in
a moment?
As soon as Zion was in labor, she
also brought forth her sons.
9 "Shall I bring to the moment of
birth and not give delivery?"
says the LORD.
"Or shall I who gives delivery shut
the womb?" says your God.

Joy in Jerusalem's Future

10 "Rejoice with Jerusalem and be
glad for her, all you who love
her;
Rejoice greatly with her, all you
who mourn over her,
11 That you may nurse and be
satisfied with her comforting
breasts,
That you may drink deeply and
be delighted with her bountiful
bosom."
12 For the LORD says this, "Behold, I
extend peace to her (Jerusalem)
like a river,
And the glory of the nations like
an overflowing stream;
And you will be nursed, you
will be carried on *her* hip and
[playfully] rocked on *her* knees.
13 "As one whom his mother
comforts, so I will comfort you;
And you will be comforted in
Jerusalem."
14 When you see this, your heart will
rejoice;
Your bones will flourish like new
grass.
And the [powerful] hand of the
LORD will be revealed to His
servants,
But His indignation will be toward
His enemies.
15 For indeed, the LORD will come in
fire
And His chariots will be like the
stormy wind,
To render His anger with rage,

66:3 ***as one who kills a man.*** This may refer to child sacrifice (57:5). ***one who breaks a dog's neck ... offers swine's blood.*** The dog and the pig were both unclean animals; this may refer to a pagan practice.

66:6 ***sound of an uproar from the city ... voice from the temple ... enemies.*** Isaiah heard the sound of noise from the city and the temple, the Lord giving His enemies what they deserved. This prophecy may find its fulfillment at the Lord's second coming (66:17; 2Th 1:7 – 10).

3 Isa 1:11; Dt 23:18 **4** Pr 1:24; Isa 65:12; Jer 7:13 **5** ver. 2; Isa 5:19; 2Th 1:10; Titus 2:13 **12** Isa 48:18; 60:5,16; Isa 49:22; 60:4 **14** See Eze 37:1 **15** Isa 9:5

And His rebuke with flames of
fire.
16 For the LORD will execute
judgment by fire
And by His sword on all
mankind,
And those slain by the LORD will
be many.
17 "Those who [vainly attempt to]
sanctify and cleanse themselves
to go to the gardens [to sacrifice
to idols],
Following after one in the center,
Who eat swine's flesh, detestable
things and mice,
Will come to an end together," says
the LORD.

18 "For I know their works and their
thoughts. *The time* is coming to gather
all nations and languages, and they
will come and see My glory.
19 "I will set up a [miraculous] sign
among them, and from them I will
send survivors to the nations: Tar-
shish, Pul (Put), Lud, Meshech, Tubal
and Javan, to the distant islands *and*
coastlands that have not heard of My
fame nor seen My glory. And they will
declare *and* proclaim My glory among
the nations.
20 "Then they shall bring all your
countrymen (children of Israel) from
all the nations as a grain offering to the
LORD—on horses, in chariots, in litters,
on mules and on camels—to My holy
mountain Jerusalem," says the LORD,
"just as the sons of Israel bring their
grain offering in a clean vessel to the
house of the LORD.
21 "I will also take some of them as
priests and Levites," says the LORD.

22 "For just as the new heavens and
the new earth
Which I make will remain *and*
endure before Me," declares the
LORD,
"So your offspring and your name
will remain *and* endure.
23 "And it shall be that from New
Moon to New Moon
And from Sabbath to Sabbath,
All mankind will come to bow
down *and* worship before Me,"
says the LORD.
24 "Then they will go forth and look
Upon the dead bodies of the
[rebellious] men
Who have transgressed against
Me;
For their worm (maggot) will not
die,
And their fire will not go out;
And they will be an abhorrence to
all mankind."

66:16 ***fire . . . sword.*** The Divine Warrior comes with fire and sword (Lk 21:24; Rev 19:11 – 15). The word picture promises judgment and punishment.

66:23 ***All mankind will come to bow down and worship before Me.*** In the end, every person will bow to the Lord, whether they were followers of God or not. This idea is repeated in more detail in Romans 14:11, 1 Corinthians 15:24 – 25, Philippians 2:10, and Revelation 15:4.

66:24 ***their fire will not go out.*** This verse is cited by Jesus in Mark 9:44,46,48. The imagery is drawn from the valley of Hinnom that was Jerusalem's garbage dump, where unclean corpses decomposed and were burned. The final eternal punishment is the lake of fire (Rev 20:1 – 15). Although the Book of Isaiah depicts God's coming salvation, it closes with a strong statement of the judgment of the wicked.

16 Isa 27:1 **17** Isa 65:3,4 **19** Lk 2:34; Mal 1:11 **20** Ro 15:16 **21** Ex 19:6; Isa 61:6; 1Pe 2:9; Rev 1:6 **23** Zec 14:16; Ps 65:2 **24** ver. 16; Mk 9:44,46,48

THE BOOK OF

JEREMIAH

▸ **AUTHOR:** Jeremiah was the son of Hilkiah the priest and lived just over two miles north of Jerusalem. The book clearly states that Jeremiah is its author, and that he dictated all his prophecies to his secretary Baruch. A first copy of the work was destroyed by the king, after which Jeremiah produced a more complete edition (36 – 38). The only segment of this book not credited to Jeremiah is chapter 52. This supplement is almost identical to 2 Kings 24:18 – 25:30, and may have been added by Baruch. Daniel alludes to Jeremiah's prophecy of the seventy year captivity (25:11 – 14; 29:10; Da 9:2), and Jeremiah's authorship is also confirmed by Ecclesiasticus, Josephus, and the Talmud.

▸ **TIMES:** c. 627 – 580 BC ▸ **KEY VERSES:** Jer 7:23 – 24

▸ **THEME:** In the Book of Jeremiah we get an intimate picture of this prophet's life and thoughts. He was constantly rejected for speaking God's message, often lamenting to God. For this fact he is often called the weeping prophet. His ministry begins in 527 BC, during the reign of King Josiah, who brought about reform after finding the Book of Deuteronomy in the temple. By that time Judah was a weak kingdom that was subject to the major political forces of the day, which were Egypt and Babylon. While Josiah's reform was certainly a step in the right direction, many of the people didn't follow through on the implications of what the law taught. Jeremiah demonstrated God's perspective on the political upheaval going on throughout Judah in his day.

Jeremiah's Call and Commission

1 THE WORDS of Jeremiah the son of
Hilkiah, [one] of the priests who were
in Anathoth in the land of Benjamin,
2 to whom the word of the LORD came
during the thirteenth year (627 B.C.) of
the reign of Josiah the son of Amon,
king of Judah.
3 It came [to Jeremiah] also in the
days of Jehoiakim the son of Josiah,
king of Judah, [continuing] until the
end of the eleventh year of Zedekiah
the son of Josiah, king of Judah, [and
continuing] until the exile of [the peo-
ple of] Jerusalem in the fifth month
(July-August, 586 B.C.). [2 Kin 25:8–11]
4 Now the word of the LORD came to
me, saying,

5 "Before I formed you in the womb
I knew you [and approved of you
as My chosen instrument],
And before you were born I
consecrated you [to Myself as
My own];
I have appointed you as a prophet
to the nations." [Ex 33:12; Is 49:1, 5; Rom 8:29]

1:1 *Jeremiah.* The name probably means either "the Lord exalts" or "the Lord establishes."
1:4 *Now the word of the LORD came to me, saying.* This was a standard way of introducing a divine oracle at the beginning of a prophetic book. Jeremiah did not speak out of his own imagination. He spoke as God revealed His word and will.
1:5 *Before I formed you in the womb I knew you.* Jeremiah was keenly aware that the call of God in his life had been determined by God from

CHAPTER 1 **1** Jos 21:18; 1Ch 6:60; Jer 32:7,8 **2** Jer 25:3 **3** Jer 39:2; Jer 52:12; 2Ki 25:8 **5** Isa 49:1,5; Ex 33:12; Lk 1:15; Gal 1:15

CHRONOLOGY OF JEREMIAH

DATE	EVENT
686	Manasseh assumes sole kingship
648	Birth of Josiah
642	Amon succeeds Manasseh as king
640	Josiah succeeds Amon
633	Josiah seeks after God (2Ch 34:3) Cyaxares becomes king of Media
628	Josiah begins reforms
626	Jeremiah called to be a prophet Nabopolassar becomes king of Babylonia
621	Book of the Law found in the temple
612	Nineveh destroyed
609	Josiah slain at Megiddo Jehoahaz rules three months Jehoiakim enthroned in Jerusalem
605	Babylonia defeats Egypt at Carchemish Hostages and vessels taken to Babylon Nebuchadnezzar becomes king of Babylonia
604	Nebuchadnezzar returns to Judah to receive tribute
601	Nebuchadnezzar defeated near Egypt
598	Jehoiakim's reign ends Jehoiachin rules Dec. 9, 598, to Mar. 16, 597
597	Jehoiachin deported Apr. 22 Zedekiah becomes king in Judah
588	Siege of Jerusalem begins Jan. 15
587	Jeremiah imprisoned (Jer 32:1–2)
586	July 18, Zedekiah flees (Jer 39:4) Aug. 14, destruction begins (2Ki 25:8–10) Oct. 7, Gedaliah slain; Jews migrate to Egypt.

Adapted from *The Zondervan Encyclopedia of the Bible*: Vol. 3 by MOISÉS SILVA. Copyright © 2009 by Zondervan, p. 500–501.

6 Then I said, "Ah, Lord GOD!
Behold, I do not know how to speak,
For I am [only] a young man."
[Ex 4:10; 6:12, 30; 1 Kin 3:7]
7 But the LORD said to me,
"Do not say, 'I am [only] a young man,'
Because everywhere I send you, you shall go,
And whatever I command you, you shall speak.
8 "Do not be afraid of them [or their hostile faces],
For I am with you [always] to protect you *and* deliver you,"
says the LORD.
9 Then the LORD stretched out His hand
and touched my mouth, and the LORD
said to me,
"Behold (hear Me), I have put My words in your mouth.
10 "See, I have appointed you this day over the nations and over the kingdoms,
To uproot and break down,
To destroy and to overthrow,
To build and to plant."

The Almond Branch and Boiling Pot

11 The word of the LORD came to me,
saying, "Jeremiah, what do you see?"
And I said, "I see the branch of an
almond tree."
12 Then the LORD said to me, "You
have seen well, for I am [actively]
watching over My word to fulfill it."

---

before his conception. As God's word became a reality in his life, the prophet understood that God knew him and had called him to proclaim a critical message at a crucial point in the history of the nation. The word "knew" refers to an intimate knowledge that comes from relationship and personal commitment.

1:8 *For I am with you [always] to protect you and deliver you.* Twice in his call (v. 19), God reassured Jeremiah of His presence and protection. In moments of personal crisis, Jeremiah prays these words back to God (20:11).

1:9 *I have put My words in your mouth.* This verse gives us an understanding of the dual nature of Scripture. The message is the Lord's; its expression is accomplished through His servants the prophets (Heb 1:1).

1:10 *I have appointed you this day over the nations.* The nations were instruments in God's purpose of revealing Himself. The Lord would use Babylon to punish Judah, and then He would use the Persians to punish Babylon.

1:11 *I see the branch of an almond tree.* God confirmed His call to Jeremiah with two visions. The first vision involved an almond tree, which blossoms when other trees are still dormant. The

6 Ex 4:10; 6:12,30 **7** Nu 22:20,38; Mt 28:20 **8** Eze 2:6; 3:9; Ex 3:12; Dt 31:6; Jos 1:5; Jer 15:20; Ac 26:17; Heb 13:6 **9** Isa 6:7; Isa 51:16; Jer 5:14 **10** 1Ki 19:17; Jer 18:7; 2Co 10:4

13The word of the LORD came to me
a second time, saying, "What do you
see?" And I said, "I see a boiling pot,
tilting away from the north [its mouth
about to pour out on the south, on Ju-
dea]."
14Then the LORD said to me, "Out of
the north the evil [which the prophets
foretold as the result of national sin]
will reveal itself *and* spill out on all
the people of the land.
15"For, behold, I will call all the tribes
of the kingdoms of the north," says the
LORD; "and they will come and each
one will set his throne at the entrance
of the gates of Jerusalem, and against
all its surrounding walls, and against
all the cities of Judah [as My judicial
act, the consequence of Judah's delib-
erate disobedience].
16"I will speak My judgments against
them for all the wickedness of those
who have abandoned (rejected) Me,
offered sacrifices *or* burned incense to
other gods, and worshiped the [idola-
trous] works of their own hands.
17"But you [Jeremiah], gird up your
loins [in preparation]! Get up and tell
them all which I command you. Do not
be distraught *and* break down at the
sight of their [hostile] faces, or I will
bewilder you before them *and* allow
you to be overcome.
18"Now behold, I have made you to-
day like a fortified city and like an iron
pillar and like bronze walls against
the whole land—against the [succes-
sive] kings of Judah, against its lead-
ers, against its priests, and against
the people of the land [giving you di-
vine strength which no hostile power
can overcome]. [Is 50:7; 54:17; Jer 6:27;
15:20; Luke 21:15; Acts 6:10]
19"They will fight against you, but
they will not [ultimately] prevail over
you, for I am with you [always] to
protect you *and* deliver you," says the
LORD.

Judah's Apostasy

2 NOW THE word of the LORD came
to me saying,
2"Go and proclaim in the ears of Je-
rusalem, saying, 'Thus says the LORD,

"I remember [earnestly] the
lovingkindness *and* devotion of
your youth,
Your time of betrothal [like that of
a bride during the early years in
Egypt and again at Sinai],
When you followed Me in the
wilderness,
Through a land not sown.
3"Israel was holy [something set
apart from ordinary purposes,
consecrated] to the LORD,
The first fruits of His harvest [in
which no outsider was allowed
to share].
All who ate of it [injuring Israel]
became guilty;
Evil came on them," says the
LORD.' "

4Hear the word of the LORD, O house
of Jacob, and all the families of the
house of Israel.
5Thus says the LORD,

---

almond tree served as a harbinger of spring, as though it "watched over" the beginning of the season. In a similar fashion, God was "watching over" His word, ready to bring judgment on Israel.

1:13 ***I see a boiling pot, tilting away from the north.*** This is the second vision God used to confirm Jeremiah's call. Judgment was coming from the north.

1:17 ***But you [Jeremiah], gird up your loins.*** This means tuck your robe into your belt so you can run, or prepare yourself (1Sa 2:4).

1:18 ***I have made you today like a fortified city.*** This military language indicates that God would fight for Jeremiah. His defense system could not be battered down or tunneled under by men and armies.

2:1–3 ***Your time of betrothal.*** Chapter 2 is presented in the form of a covenant lawsuit, an indictment brought by God against His people. Jeremiah challenged the people of Judah to remember God.

2:5 ***walked after emptiness and futility and became empty.*** People who serve idols, which are as vapor, become like that vapor themselves.

---

13 Eze 11:3; 24:3 **14** Jer 6:1 **15** Jer 6:22; Jer 39:3 **16** Dt 28:20; Jer 17:13 **17** 2Ki 4:29; Job 38:3; Lk 12:35; 1Pe 1:13; Ex 3:12; Eze 2:6 **18** Isa 50:7; Jer 6:27; 15:20 **19** ver. 8 **CHAPTER 2** **2** Eze 16:8,22,60; 23:3,8; Hos 2:15; Dt 2:7 **3** Ex 19:5,6; Jas 1:18; Rev 14:4; Jer 12:14; See Jer 50:7 **5** Isa 5:4; Mic 6:3; 2Ki 17:15; Jnh 2:8

"What injustice *or* unrighteousness
did your fathers find in Me,
That they have wandered far from
Me
And [habitually] walked after
emptiness *and* futility and
became empty?
6 "They did not say, 'Where is the
LORD
Who brought us up from the land
of Egypt,
Who led us through the wilderness,
Through a land of deserts and of
pits,
Through a land of drought and
of the deep darkness [of the
shadow of death],
Through a land that no man
passed through
And where no man lived?'
7 "I brought you into a plentiful land
To eat its fruit and [enjoy] its good
things.
But you came and defiled My land
And you made My inheritance
repulsive.
8 "[Even] the priests did not say,
'Where is the LORD?'
And those who deal with the law
[given to Moses] did not know Me.
The rulers *and* shepherds also
transgressed against Me,
And the prophets prophesied by
[the authority and in the name
of] Baal
And walked after [idolatrous]
things that did not benefit
[them].

9 "Therefore I will still contend
(struggle) with you [by bringing
judgment on you]," says the LORD,
"And I will contend with your
children's children."

10 "For cross over to the coasts of
Kittim (Cyprus) [to the west] and
see,
Send also to Kedar (Arabia) [to the
east] and carefully observe *and*
consider
And see whether there has been
such [a thing] as this!
11 "Has a nation [ever] changed gods
Even though they were not gods
[but merely man-made objects]?
But My people have exchanged
their Glory (the true God)
For that [man-made idol] which
does not benefit [them].
12 "Be appalled, O heavens, at this;
Be shocked *and* shudder with
horror [at the behavior of the
people]," says the LORD.
13 "For My people have committed
two evils:
They have abandoned (rejected) Me,
The fountain of living water,
And they have carved out their
own cisterns,
Broken cisterns
That cannot hold water.

14 "Is Israel a servant? Is he a slave
by birth?
Why has he become a captive *and*
a prey?
15 "The young lions have roared at
him,
They have made their voices heard
and roared loudly.
And they have made his land a
waste;
His cities have been destroyed
and are burned ruins, without
inhabitant.
16 "Moreover, the men of Memphis
and Tahpanhes [as powerful
enemies]

2:8 *priests ... rulers and shepherds ... prophets.* Those who should have known God most intimately did not know Him at all. The rulers transgressed against God and His covenant. The prophets prophesied in the name of Baal rather than God.
2:13 *carved out their own cisterns, Broken cisterns.* The people could have chosen a "fountain of living waters." Instead they chose broken cisterns that would have been useless for sustaining life.
2:15 *The young lions.* Assyria laid waste to Israel and Judah during several invasions between 734 and 701 BC.
2:16 *the men of Memphis and Tahpanhes.* Egypt forced Judah into a vassal relationship.

6 Isa 63:9; Dt 8:15 **7** Nu 13:27; 35:33 **8** Ro 2:20; Jer 23:13 **9** Eze 20:35,36; Mic 6:2 **11** Mic 4:5; Ps 115:4; Isa 37:19; Ps 106:20; Ro 1:23 **13** Ps 36:9; Jn 4:14 **14** Ex 4:22 **15** Isa 1:7 **16** Jer 43:7-9

Have shaved the crown of your
head [to degrade you].
17 "Have you not brought this on
yourself
By abandoning (rejecting) the
LORD your God
When He led you in the way?
18 "Now what are you doing by going
to Egypt [in search of an ally],
To drink the [muddy] waters of the
Nile?
Or what are you doing by going to
Assyria [in search of an ally],
To drink the [muddy] waters of the
Euphrates?
19 "Your own wickedness will
discipline you,
And your desertion of the faith
will punish you.
Know therefore that it is an evil
and bitter thing
For you to abandon (reject) the
LORD your God,
And for you to be indifferent to Me
and dismiss the [reverent] fear
of Me," says the Lord GOD of
hosts.
20 "For long ago you broke your yoke
[in deliberate disobedience]
And tore off your bonds [of the law
that I gave you];
You said, 'I will not serve *and* obey
You!'
For on every high hill
And under every green tree
You have lain down [in idolatrous
worship] like a [compliant]
prostitute.
21 "Yet I had planted you [O house of
Israel as] a choice vine,
A completely faithful seed.
How then have you turned against
Me
Into degenerate shoots of a foreign
and wild vine [alien to Me]?
22 "For though you wash yourself
with lye
And use much soap,
The stain of your guilt is [still]
before Me [and you are soiled
and dirty]," says the Lord GOD.
23 "How can you say, 'I am not
defiled,
I have not gone after [man-made
gods like] the Baals'?
Look at your way in the valley;
Know [without any doubt] what
you have done!
You are a swift *and* restless young
[female] camel [in the heat of her
passion] running here and there,
24 Or [you have the untamed and
reckless nature of] a wild
donkey accustomed to the
wilderness,
That sniffs the wind in her passion
[for the scent of a mate].
In her mating season who can
restrain her?
No males seeking her need to
weary themselves;
In her month they will find her
[looking for them].
25 "[Cease your mad running after
idols to]
Keep your feet from becoming
bare
And your throat from becoming
dry;
But you said, 'It is hopeless!
For I have loved strangers *and*
foreign gods,
And I will walk after them.'
26 "As the thief is shamed when he is
caught,
So the house of Israel is shamed—
They, their kings, their leaders,
Their priests, and their prophets—
27 Who say to a tree, 'You are my
father,'
And to a stone, 'You gave me birth.'
For they have turned their backs
to Me,
And not their faces;

2:19 *desertion of the faith.* Israel had turned in every direction for help except to the true source of safety and security.

2:23–25 *You are a swift and restless young [female] camel.* The image is that of a camel who is in heat, vividly portraying Israel's lust for foreign gods.

17 Jer 4:18; Dt 32:10 **18** Isa 30:1,2; Jos 13:3 **20** Jdg 10:16; Dt 12:2; Ex 34:15 **21** Ex 15:17; Isa 5:4 **23** Pr 30:12 **25** Jer 3:13 **27** Isa 26:16

But in the time of their trouble
they will say,
'Arise [O LORD] and save us.'
28 "But where are your gods
Which you made for yourself?
Let them get up, if they can save
you
In the time of your trouble!
For [as many as] the number of
your cities
Are your gods, O Judah. [Why do
not your many man-made idols
run to help you?]

29 "Why do you complain *and*
contend with Me?
You have all rebelled
(transgressed) against Me," says
the LORD.
30 "In vain I have punished your
people [with the consequences
of their disobedience];
They received no insight from
correction [and refused to
change].
Your [own] sword has devoured
your prophets
Like a destroying lion.
31 "O generation [that you are],
consider *and* regard carefully
the word of the LORD.
Have I been a wilderness to Israel
[like a land without food],
A land of thick *and* deep darkness
[like a path without light]?
Why do My people say, 'We [have
broken loose and we] are *free to*
roam [at will];
We will no longer come to You'?
32 "Can a virgin forget [to wear] her
ornaments,
Or a bride her attire [that identifies
her as a married woman]?
Yet My people have forgotten Me
Days without number.
33 "How well you prepare your path
To seek *and* obtain [adulterous]
love!
Even the most wicked of women
Have learned [indecent] ways from
you.
34 "Also on your skirts is found
The lifeblood of the innocent poor;
You did not find them breaking in
[a house].
But in spite of all these things
[your disobedience, your
love of idolatry, your lack of
compassion]—
35 Yet you keep saying, 'I am innocent;
Surely His anger has turned away
from me.'
Behold (listen very carefully), I
will bring you to judgment *and*
will plead my case against you
Because you say, 'I have not
sinned.'
36 "Why do you go around *and*
wander so much
Changing your way?
Also, you will be shamed by Egypt
As you were shamed by Assyria.
37 "From Egypt also you will come
away [as captives]
With your hands on your head;
For the LORD has rejected those in
whom you trust (confide),
And you will not be successful
with them."

The Polluted Land

3 THAT IS to say, "If a man
divorces his wife
And she goes [away] from him
And becomes another man's [wife],

2:32 *Yet My people have forgotten Me.* In the ancient world, those women who were not slaves normally possessed a variety of rings, bracelets, and ornaments made from gold, silver, or bronze. Many of these were exquisite in appearance and were frequently inlaid with semiprecious stones. Ornaments of this kind were commonly part of the wedding finery of a bride. The nation Israel, however, which was God's bride, had behaved in a completely unnatural fashion by presuming to forget the God to whom the people were so intimately bound by the Sinai covenant. In forgetting their God for so long a time they had actually rejected Him and His claims upon them, a prospect which Jeremiah found almost impossible to believe.

3:1 *If a man divorces his wife.* Deuteronomy 24:1–4 forbids a man to remarry his divorced

28 Jdg 10:14; Isa 45:20; Jer 11:13 **30** Isa 9:13; Ac 7:52 **31** Dt 32:15 **32** Ps 106:21 **34** Ps 106:38 **35** ver. 23,29; ver. 9; Pr 28:13 **36** Hos 12:1; Isa 30:3; 2Ch 28:16 **37** 2Sa 13:19 **CHAPTER 3** **1** Dt 24:4; Jer 2:7; Jer 2:20; Eze 16:26; Zec 1:3

Will he return to her again? [Of
course not!]
Will not that land [where such a
thing happened] be completely
desecrated?
But you [rebelled against Me and
you] are a prostitute with many
lovers;
Yet you turn to Me." says the LORD.
2 "Lift up your eyes to the barren
heights and see;
Where have you not been violated?
You sat by the road waiting
[eagerly] for them [those man-
made gods]
Like an Arab [tribesman who
waits to attack] in the desert,
And you have desecrated the
land
With your [vile] prostitution and
your wickedness (disobedience
to God).
3 "Therefore the showers have been
withheld,
And there has been no spring
rain.
Yet you have the forehead
(appearance) of a prostitute;
You refuse to be ashamed.
4 "Will you not just now call out to
Me,
'My Father, you were the guide
and companion of my youth?
5 'Will He be angry forever?
Will He be indignant to the end?'
Behold, you have spoken,
And you have done all the evil
things [you could],
And you have had your way
and have carried out your
wickedness."

Faithless Israel

6 Moreover, the LORD said to me in
the days of Josiah the king [of Judah],
"Have you seen what that faithless
Israel has done—how she went up on
every high hill and under every green
tree, and there she was a prostitute?
7 "I thought, 'After she has done all
these things she will return to Me'; but
she did not return, and her treacherous
(faithless) sister Judah saw it.
8 "And I saw [that even though Ju-
dah knew] that for all the acts of adul-
tery (idolatry) of faithless Israel, I [the
LORD] had sent her away and given her
a certificate of divorce, yet her treach-
erous sister Judah was not afraid; but
she went and was a prostitute also
[following after idols].
9 "Because of the thoughtlessness of
Israel's prostitution [her immorality
mattered little to her], she desecrated
the land and committed adultery with
[idols of] stones and trees.
10 "Yet in spite of all this her treach-
erous sister Judah did not return to
Me with her whole heart, but rath-
er in [blatant] deception [she mere-
ly pretended obedience to King Jo-
siah's reforms]," declares the LORD.
[2 Chr 34:33; Hos 7:13, 14]

God Invites Repentance

11 And the LORD said to me, "Faithless
Israel has proved herself less guilty
than treacherous Judah [a land of ren-
egades].
12 "Go and proclaim these words to-
ward the north [where the ten tribes
have been taken as captives] and say,

---

wife if she has remarried and been divorced in the meantime. The implication is that the woman has been defiled by the second marriage. After forsaking God, Israel had taken many other lovers, that is, the nation worshiped many other gods. Yet the Lord in His mercy still extended His loving hand to His unfaithful bride.

3:3 *showers . . . spring rain.* There were two types of rain that fell in Israel in the spring from March to early April. These were vital for the fields and crops.

3:6 *in the days of Josiah the king.* The reign of Josiah (640 – 609 BC) followed the idolatrous reigns of Manasseh (697 – 642 BC) and Amon (642 – 640 BC).

3:8 *the acts of adultery (idolatry) of faithless Israel.* Because of Israel's adultery, the Lord presented her with a certificate of divorce based on Dt 24:1 – 4. As a consequence, in 722 BC Israel was taken captive by Assyria, and Samaria was destroyed. Judah looked on but did not learn from Israel's example.

2 Dt 12:2; Pr 23:28; Jer 2:7 **3** Lev 26:19; Zep 3:5 **4** Pr 2:17; Hos 2:15 **5** Ps 103:9; Isa 57:16 **6** Jer 7:24; Jer 2:20 **7** 2Ki 17:13; Eze 16:46 **8** Eze 23:9; 2Ki 17:6; Eze 23:11 **9** Jer 2:7; Jer 2:27 **10** Hos 7:14 **11** Eze 16:51 **12** 2Ki 17:6; Ps 86:15

'Return, faithless Israel,' says the
LORD;
'I will not look on you in anger.
For I am gracious *and* merciful,'
says the LORD;
'I will not be angry forever.
13 'Only understand fully *and*
acknowledge your wickedness
and guilt,
That you have rebelled
(transgressed) against the LORD
your God
And have scattered your favors
among strangers under every
green tree,
And you have not obeyed My
voice,' says the LORD.
14 'Return, O faithless children [of
the twelve tribes],' says the
LORD,
'For I am a master *and* husband to
you,
And I will take you [not as a
nation, but individually]—one
from a city and two from a
[tribal] family—
And I will bring you to Zion.'
[Luke 15:20–22]

15 "Then [in the final time] I will give
you [spiritual] shepherds after My own
heart, who will feed you with knowl-
edge and [true] understanding.
16 "It will be in those days when you
have [repented and] multiplied and
increased in the land," says the LORD,
"they will no longer say, 'The ark of
the covenant of the LORD.' It will not
come to mind, nor will they [seriously]
remember it, nor will they miss it, nor
will it be made again [for instead of the
ark, which symbolized My presence,
I will be present]. [Is 65:17; Rev 21:3,
22, 23]
17 "At that time they will call Jeru-
salem 'The Throne of the LORD,' and
all the nations will be gathered to it,
to Jerusalem, for the name (renown)
of the LORD; and they will not walk
anymore after the stubbornness of
their [own] evil heart.
18 "In those days the house of Judah
will walk with the house of Israel, and
they will come together from the land
of the north to the land that I gave your
fathers as an inheritance.
19 "Then I said,

'How [gloriously and honorably]
I would set you among My
children
And give you a pleasant land—a
wonderful heritage,
The most beautiful inheritance of
the nations!'
And I said, 'You shall call Me, My
Father
And not turn away from following
Me.'
20 "Surely, as a wife treacherously
(unfaithfully) leaves her
husband,
So you have dealt treacherously
with Me,
O house of Israel," says the LORD.
21 A voice is heard on the barren
heights,
The weeping and pleading of the
children of Israel,
Because they have lost their way,
They have [deliberately] forgotten
the LORD their God.
22 "Return, O faithless sons," [says
the LORD],
"I will heal your unfaithfulness."
[They answer] "Behold, we come
to You,

3:15 *I will give you [spiritual] shepherds.* Throughout the Bible God provides shepherds for His people to watch over them, guide them, care for them, and lead them. From Moses in the Old Testament to Jesus in the New, God provides faithful, devoted leaders after His own heart.
3:16 *when you have [repented and] multiplied and increased.* God ordained that His shepherds would lead Israel through a time of blessing, increase in numbers, and material prosperity.
3:19 *And give you a pleasant land.* The possession of the land was always dependent on the covenant faithfulness of Israel to their God. The Lord's desire has always been to bless His people.

13 Dt 30:1; Eze 16:15; Jer 2:25; Dt 12:2 **14** Hos 2:19; Ro 11:5 **15** Eze 34:23; Eph 4:11; Ac 20:28 **16** Isa 65:17 **17** Isa 60:9; Jer 11:8 **18** Isa 11:13; Hos 1:11; Jer 31:8; Am 9:15 **19** Ps 106:24; Isa 63:16 **20** Isa 48:8 **21** Isa 15:2 **22** ver. 14; Hos 14:1; Hos 6:1; 14:4 **23** Ps 121:1,2; Ps 3:8

For You are the LORD our God.
23 "Truly, [the hope of salvation
from] the hill [where idols are
worshiped] is a deception,
A tumult *and* noisy multitude on
the mountains;
Truly in the LORD our God
Is the salvation of Israel.

24 "But the shameful act [of idolatry]
has consumed the labor of our fathers
since our youth—their flocks and their
herds, their sons and their daughters.
25 "Let us lie down in our shame, and
let our dishonor *and* humiliation cover
us; for we have sinned against the LORD
our God, we and our fathers; from our
youth even to this day we have not
obeyed the voice of the LORD our God."

Judah Threatened with Invasion

4 "IF YOU will return, O Israel,"
says the LORD,
"If you will return to Me,
And if you will put away your
detestable things *and* remove
your man-made gods from My
sight,
And not stray *or* waver,
2 And if you swear [your oaths], 'As
the LORD lives,'
In truth, in justice, and in
righteousness,
Then the nations will bless
themselves in Him,
And in Him they will glory."

3 For this is what the LORD says to the
men of Judah and to Jerusalem,

"Plow your uncultivated ground
[for a season],
And do not sow among thorns.
4 "Circumcise (dedicate, sanctify)
yourselves to the LORD
And remove the foreskin [sins] of
your heart,
Men of Judah and inhabitants of
Jerusalem,
Or else My wrath will go forth like
fire [consuming all that gets in
its way]
And burn and there will be no one
to quench it,
Because of the evil of your acts."
5 Declare in Judah and proclaim in
Jerusalem, and say,
"Blow the trumpet in the land;
Cry aloud and say,
'Assemble yourselves, and let us go
Into the fortified cities.'
6 "Raise a banner toward Zion [to
mark the way for those seeking
safety inside Jerusalem's walls]!
Seek refuge, do not stand
[immobile],
For I am bringing evil from the
north (the army of Babylon),
And great destruction.
7 "A lion has left his lair,
And a destroyer of nations is on
his way.

3:23 *tumult and noisy multitude on the mountains.* The mountains were centers of idol worship and thus were strongholds of falsehood. True salvation or deliverance could be found only in the true God of Israel.

4:2 *As the LORD lives.* This phrase was regularly used in oaths. When spoken by those faithful to the covenant, it should have been a sign of truth, judgment, and righteousness.

Failure to be willing to owe God their faithfulness and worship brought terrible consequences to Israel, the Northern Kingdom, and then to Judah and resulted in failure of the nations to be converted as well. Because Israel would not give glory to God, the rest of the world could not.

4:4 *Circumcise (dedicate, sanctify) yourselves to the LORD.* Circumcision was a sign of the covenant relationship between Israel and God (Ge 17:10 – 14). The intent of God was always that the outward symbol should be a sign of a reality of total devotion to Him (Dt 10:12 – 21).

4:5 *Blow the trumpet in the land.* Jeremiah announced the judgment of Judah and Jerusalem with the alarming sound of a trumpet, literally a shofar made of a ram's horn. This was the instrument used to sound the alarm when an enemy attacked a city.

4:7 *left his lair.* Destruction would come as a terrible surprise, like a lion hiding and then pouncing on its prey. The desolation of the land and the deportation of the people would be the result.

24 Jer 11:13; Hos 9:10 **25** Ezr 9:7; Jer 22:21 **CHAPTER 4** **1** Jer 3:1,22; Joel 2:12 **2** Dt 10:20; Isa 45:23; 65:16; See Jer 5:2; Isa 48:1; Zec 8:8; Ge 22:18; Ps 72:17; Gal 3:8; 1Co 1:31 **3** Hos 10:12; Mt 13:7 **4** Dt 10:16; Jer 9:26; Ro 2:28 **5** Jer 8:14 **6** Jer 1:13-15; 6:1,22 **7** 2Ki 24:1; Jer 5:6; Da 7:4; Jer 25:9; Isa 1:7

He has gone out from his place
To desolate your land;
Your cities will be in ruins
Without an inhabitant.
8 "For this reason, put on sackcloth
[for mourning],
Lament (mourn with expressions
of grief for the dead) and wail,
For the fierce anger of the LORD
Has not turned back from us."

9 "It shall come about in that day," says
the LORD, "that the heart *and* courage
of the king will fail (be paralyzed), and
also the heart of the princes; the priests
will be appalled and the prophets will
be astounded *and* horrified."
10 Then I said, "Alas, Lord GOD! Sure-
ly You have completely deceived *and*
misled this people and Jerusalem, [for
the prophets represented You as] say-
ing [to Your people], 'You will have
peace,' but [in fact] a sword reaches to
their throat."
11 In that time it will be said to this
people and to Jerusalem, "A scorching
wind from the barren heights in the
wilderness [comes at My command]
against the daughter of My people—
not [a wind] to winnow and not to
cleanse [from chaff, as when thresh-
ing, but]
12 a wind too strong *and* full for this
comes at My word. Now I will also
speak judgment against My people."

13 "Behold, the enemy comes up like
clouds,
His chariots like the whirlwind;
His horses are swifter than eagles.
Woe (judgment is coming) to us,
for we are ruined!"
14 O Jerusalem, wash your heart
from wickedness,
That you may be saved.
How long will your wicked *and*
immoral thoughts
Lodge within you?
15 For a voice declares from Dan [far
in the north],
And proclaims evil from Mount
Ephraim.
16 "Warn the [neighboring] nations
now [that our enemy is coming]!
Announce to Jerusalem,
'Besiegers are coming from a far
country,
And they lift their voices *and* shout
against the cities of Judah.
17 'Like watchmen of a field they are
against her on all sides,
Because she has rebelled against
Me,' says the LORD.
18 "Your ways and your deeds
Have brought these things on you.
This is your tragedy *and* doom;
how bitter,
How it has touched your heart!"

Lament over Judah's Devastation

19 My soul, my soul! I writhe in
anguish *and* pain! Oh, the walls
of my heart!
My heart is pounding *and*
throbbing within me;
I cannot be silent,
For you have heard, O my soul,
The sound of the trumpet,
The alarm of war.
20 News of one [terrible] disaster
comes close after another,
For the whole land is devastated;

4:8 *For this reason, put on sackcloth.* This material was a rough-textured fabric that was worn as a sign of mourning or distress (6:21).
4:13 *Behold, the enemy comes up like clouds.* Judah had become the foe of God, and He would use the nation's international foes to discipline the nation. The imagery of clouds and chariots like a whirlwind portrays the thoroughness and swiftness of God's judgment.
4:15 *Dan . . . Mount Ephraim.* Dan was the most northern tribe of Israel. Ephraim was the southernmost region of the Northern Kingdom of Israel. The message is that just as Israel had been subjugated, Judah was also in danger.
4:19 *My soul, my soul.* Soul here means *bowels* or *belly*, a reference to the internal organs. In ancient Middle Eastern thought, the internal organs were the seat of emotions and feelings. The phrase describes Jeremiah's anguish over the destruction of Jerusalem.

8 Isa 22:12 **10** Eze 14:9; 2Th 2:11; Jer 14:13 **11** Jer 51:1; Eze 17:10; Hos 13:15 **12** Jer 1:16 **13** Isa 5:28; Dt 28:49; La 4:19; Hos 8:1; Hab 1:8 **14** Isa 1:16; Jas 4:8 **15** Jer 8:16 **17** 2Ki 25:1 **18** Ps 107:17; Isa 50:1; Jer 2:17,19 **19** Isa 15:5; 16:11; 21:3; See Lk 19:42 **20** Ps 42:7; Eze 7:26; Jer 10:20

Suddenly my tents are spoiled *and* destroyed,
My [tent] curtains [ruined] in a moment.
21 How long [O LORD] must I see the banner [marking the way for flight]
And hear the sound of the trumpet [urging the people to run for safety]?
22 "For My people are stupid *and* foolish," [says the LORD to Jeremiah];
"They do not know Me;
They are foolish children
And have no understanding.
They are shrewd [enough] to do evil,
But they do not know [how] to do good."

23 I looked at the earth [in my vision], and behold, it was [as at the time of creation] formless and void;
And to the heavens, and they had no light.
24 I looked at the mountains, and behold, they were trembling,
And all the hills moved back and forth.
25 I looked, and behold, there was no man,
And all the birds of the air had fled.
26 I looked, and behold, the fertile land was a wilderness,
And all its cities were pulled down
Before the [presence of the] LORD, before His fierce anger.

27 Therefore says the LORD,
"The whole land shall be a desolation,
Yet I will not cause total destruction. [Jer 5:10, 18; 30:11; 46:28]
28 "For this reason the earth shall mourn
And the heavens above shall become dark,
Because I have spoken, I have decided,
And I will not change my mind (relent), nor will I turn back from it."
29 Every city runs away at the sound of the horsemen and archers.
They go into the thickets and climb among the rocks;
Every city is deserted,
And no man lives in them.
30 And you, O desolate one, what will you do?
Though you clothe yourself in scarlet,
Though you adorn *yourself with* ornaments of gold,
Though you enlarge your eyes with paint,
You make yourself beautiful in vain.
Your lovers (allies) despise you;
They seek your life.
31 For I heard a cry like a woman in labor,
The anguish as of one giving birth to her first child,
The cry of the Daughter of Zion (Jerusalem), who gasps for breath,
Who stretches out her hands, saying,
"Woe is me [my judgment comes]!
I faint [in fear] before the murderers."

4:23 *it was [as at the time of creation] formless and void.* This Hebrew phrase is the same one used in Genesis 1:2 to describe the chaos before the ordering of the cosmos. ***no light.*** The prophets spoke of darkness as part of God's judgment on the world. Here the lack of light describes the disastrous effects of sin on creation, particularly on the land of Judah.
4:24 *they were trembling.* The symbols of stability and of strength would be shaken as by an earthquake. Birds would disappear as Hosea had proclaimed (Hos 4:3). In Genesis 1, the creation of the birds of the heavens depicts the fulfillment of the creative process. In Jeremiah and Hosea, the removal of the birds symbolizes the reversal of creation.
4:28 *the heavens above shall become dark.* The dark skies are associated with God's judgment.

22 Ro 16:19 **23** Isa 24:19; Ge 1:2 **24** Isa 5:25; Eze 38:20 **25** Zep 1:3 **27** Jer 5:10,18; 30:11; 46:28 **28** Hos 4:3; Isa 5:30; 50:3; Nu 23:19; Jer 7:16 **30** 2Ki 9:30; Jer 22:20,22 **31** Isa 1:15; La 1:17

Jerusalem's Godlessness

5 "ROAM BACK and forth through
the streets of Jerusalem,
And look now and take note.
And look in her open squares
To see if you can find a man [as
Abraham sought in Sodom],
One who is just, who [has integrity
and moral courage and] seeks
truth (faithfulness);
Then I will pardon Jerusalem—
[for the sake of one
uncompromisingly righteous
person]. [Gen 18:22–32]
2 "And though they say, 'As the LORD
lives,'
Surely they swear [their oaths]
falsely."
3 O LORD, do not Your eyes look for
truth?
You [have seen their faithless
heart and] have stricken
them,
But they did not weaken;
You have consumed them,
But they refused to take correction
or instruction.
They have made their faces harder
than rock;
They have refused to repent *and*
return to You.
4 Then I said, "[Surely] these are
only the poor (uneducated);
They are [sinfully] foolish
and have no [spiritual]
understanding,
For they do not know the way of
the LORD
Or the ordinance of their God [and
the requirements of His just and
righteous law].
5 "I will go to the great [men]
And speak to them,
For they [must] know the way of
the LORD,
The ordinance of their God."
But [I found the reverse to be
true, that] they too had all alike
broken the yoke [of God's law]
And had burst the bonds [of
obedience to Him].
6 Therefore a lion from the forest
will kill them,
A wolf of the deserts will destroy
them,
A leopard is watching their cities.
Everyone who goes out of them
shall be torn in pieces,
Because their transgressions are
many,
Their desertions of faith are
countless.
7 "Why should I [overlook these
offenses and] forgive you?
Your children have abandoned
(rejected) Me
And sworn [their oaths] by those
who are not gods.
When I had fed them until they
were full [and bound them to Me
by a promise],
They committed [spiritual] adultery,
Assembling in troops at the houses
of prostitutes (idols).
8 "They were like well-fed, lusty
stallions,

5:1 *if you can find a man [as Abraham sought in Sodom], One who is just.* Similar to Abraham's plea that Sodom be saved on account of the few faithful people among its inhabitants (Ge 18:16 – 33), so Jeremiah summoned the people to search the city of Jerusalem for one just and righteous person.

5:3 *But they refused to take correction or instruction.* The Hebrew term translated *correction* means "chastisement" or "discipline." In the Prophets, it generally refers to God's attempt to teach His children faithfulness by means of discipline or punishment (7:28). But despite the words of Jeremiah and other prophets, Israel refused "correction" and continued down the path of self-destruction.

5:5 *broken the yoke.* Jeremiah paints a picture of Judah as oxen that are wandering aimlessly through the field, guided by their own desires. They are exposed to the elements and the wild animals of the forest and desert.

5:7 *They committed [spiritual] adultery.* The prophets generally refer to cultic prostitution as adultery. Such immoral behavior violated covenant law (Ex 20:14) and set in motion the curses of the covenant.

CHAPTER 5 **1** Eze 22:30; Ge 18:23; Ge 18:26 **2** Titus 1:16; Jer 4:2; Jer 7:9 **3** 2Ch 16:9; Isa 1:5; 9:13; Jer 2:30; Jer 7:28; Zep 3:2 **4** Jer 8:7 **5** Mic 3:1; Ps 2:3 **6** Jer 4:7; Ps 104:20; Hab 1:8; Zep 3:3; Hos 13:7 **7** Jos 23:7; Zep 1:5; Dt 32:21; Gal 4:8; Dt 32:15 **8** Eze 22:11

Each one neighing after his neighbor's wife.
9 "Shall I not punish them [for these things]?" says the LORD;
"Shall I not avenge Myself
On a nation such as this?"

10 "Go up through the rows of Jerusalem's vineyards and destroy [them],
But do not completely destroy *everything*.
Strip away her branches *and* the tendrils [of her vines],
For they are not the LORD's.
11 "For the house of Israel and the house of Judah
Have dealt very treacherously (faithlessly) with Me," declares the LORD.
12 They have lied about *and* denied the LORD
By saying, "It is not He [who speaks through His prophets];
Misfortune *and* evil shall not come on us,
Nor will we see war or famine.
13 "The prophets are like the wind [their prophecy will not come to pass],
And the word [of God] is not in them.
In this manner it will be done to them [as they prophesied, not to us]."

Judgment Proclaimed

14 Therefore, thus says the LORD God of hosts,
"Because you [people] have spoken this word,
Behold, I am making My words a fire in your mouth [Jeremiah]
And this people wood, and My words will consume them.
15 "Behold, I am bringing a nation against you from far away,
O house of Israel," says the LORD.
"It is a mighty *and* enduring nation,
It is an ancient nation,
A nation whose language you do not know,
Whose words you do not comprehend.
16 "Their quiver is [filled with the dead] like an open grave;
They are all mighty men [heroes of their nation].
17 "They will consume your harvest and [eat up] your bread;
They will consume your sons and your daughters;
They will consume your flocks and your herds;
They will consume your vines and your fig trees.
With the sword they will break down *and* demolish your fortified cities in which you trust.

18 "But even in those days," says the
LORD, "I will not totally destroy you.
19 "It will come about when your peo-
ple say, 'Why has the LORD our God
done all these things to us?' then you
shall answer them, 'As you have aban-
doned (rejected) Me,' [says the LORD,]
'and have served strange *and* foreign
gods in your land, so you will serve
strangers in a land that is not yours.'

20 "Declare this in the house of Jacob
And proclaim it in Judah, saying:

5:9 *Shall I not punish them [for these things]?* The Hebrew word translated *punish* (9:9), literally meaning "to visit," can be used of the visitation of God in mercy (Ps 65:9) or in wrath. Here it clearly refers to wrath.
5:13 *The prophets are like the wind.* False prophets like Hananiah (28:11) had foretold a time of peace and deliverance from the domination and destructiveness of their enemies. But their word was like an empty breeze. The very sword they denied would seal their fate.
5:17 *They will consume.* The word consume is used four times in this verse to paint an image of the enemy as consuming field, flock, and fortifications.
5:20 *house of Jacob.* Even after the Northern Kingdom had been destroyed, the prophets still spoke of Israel. There was not a complete

9 ver. 29; Jer 9:9; Jer 44:22 **10** Jer 39:8; ver. 18; Jer 4:27 **11** Jer 3:20 **12** 2Ch 36:16; Jer 4:10; Isa 28:15; Jer 14:13 **14** Jer 1:9 **15** Dt 28:49; Isa 5:26; Jer 1:15; 6:22; Isa 39:3; Jer 4:16 **17** Lev 26:16; Dt 28:31,33 **18** Jer 4:27 **19** Dt 29:24; 1Ki 9:8,9; Jer 13:22; 16:10; Jer 2:13; Dt 28:48

21 'Now hear this, O foolish people
without heart,
Who have eyes but do not see,
Who have ears but do not hear.
[Is 6:9, 10; Matt 13:10–15;
Mark 8:17, 18]
22 'Do you not fear Me?' says the
LORD.
'Do you not tremble [in awe] in My
presence?
For I have placed the sand as a
boundary for the sea,
An eternal decree *and* a perpetual
barrier beyond which it cannot
pass.
Though the waves [of the sea]
toss *and* break, yet they cannot
prevail [against the sand
ordained to hold them back];
Though the waves *and* the billows
roar, yet they cannot cross over
[the barrier].
[Is not such a God to be feared?]
23 'But this people has a stubborn
heart and a rebellious will [that
draws them away from Me];
They have turned away and have
gone [into idolatry].
24 'They do not say in their heart,
"Let us now fear *and* worship the
LORD our God [with profound
awe and reverence],
Who gives rain in its season,
Both the autumn and the spring
rain,
Who keeps for us
The appointed weeks of the
harvest."
25 'Your wickedness has turned these
[blessings] away,
And your sins have withheld good
[harvests] from you.
26 'For wicked men are found among
My people,
They watch like fowlers who lie in
wait;
They set a trap,
They catch men.
27 'As a cage is full of birds,
So are their houses full of deceit
and treachery;
Therefore they have become
influential and rich.
28 'They are fat and they are sleek
(prosperous),
They excel in acts of wickedness;
They do not plead the cause,
The cause of the orphan, so that
they [the wicked] may prosper,
And they do not defend the rights
of the poor.
29 'Shall I not punish them [for these
things]?' says the LORD.
'Shall I not avenge Myself
On such a nation as this?'

30 "An appalling and horrible thing
[bringing desolation and
destruction]
Has come to pass in the land:
31 The prophets prophesy falsely,
And the priests rule on their own
authority;
And My people love [to have] it so!
But what will you do when the end
comes?

Destruction of Jerusalem Impending

6 "RUN FOR safety, you children of
Benjamin,
Out of the midst of Jerusalem!
And blow a trumpet in Tekoa [in
Judah]
And raise a signal-fire in Beth-
haccherem [near Jerusalem];
For evil is looking down [with eager
anticipation] from the north,

---

destruction of the northern tribes, as is commonly thought.
5:26–28 ***wicked men.*** Those responsible for the welfare of the whole populace had abused their positions by exploiting the lesser elements of Israelite society. The picture presented is one of birds, or the poor, being ensnared by great men who were building wealth at the expense of orphans and the needy (Dt 10:18).
5:31 ***prophets ... priests.*** The deterioration of the leadership of the land reached the very people who were supposed to be the mainstays of righteousness among the people. Both offices had succumbed to the temptation of abusing

21 Isa 6:9; Eze 12:2; Mt 13:14; Jn 12:40; Ac 28:26; Ro 11:8 **22** Rev 15:4; Job 26:10; Pr 8:29 **24** Ps 147:8; Ac 14:17; Joel 2:23; Ge 8:22 **25** Jer 3:3 **26** Pr 1:11; Hab 1:15 **28** Dt 32:15; Isa 1:23; Zec 7:10; Job 12:6; Ps 73:12 **29** Mal 3:5 **30** Hos 6:10 **31** Jer 14:14; 23:25,26; Eze 13:6; Mic 2:11 **CHAPTER 6** **1** Neh 3:14; Jer 4:6

And great destruction.
2 "I will destroy the Daughter of
Zion (Jerusalem), the lovely and
delicate one [so like a luxurious
pasture].
3 "Shepherds with their flocks will
come against her;
They will pitch their tents all
around her;
They will pasture, each one in
his place [eating up all her rich
grasses].
4 "[They shout], 'Prepare for war
against her;
Arise, let us [take her by surprise
and] attack her at noon.
But alas, the daylight pales,
The evening shadows grow long.
5 'Arise, let us [awaken to] attack her
at night
And destroy her [fortified]
palaces!' "

6 For the LORD of hosts has said,

"Cut down her trees
And build a siege [mound] against
Jerusalem.
This is the city which must be
punished;
There is nothing but oppression
inside her [walls].
7 "As a fountain springs up *and*
pours out its fresh waters,
So she [continually] pours out her
fresh wickedness.
Violence and destruction are
heard inside her [walls];
Sickness and wounds are always
before Me.
8 "Be wise *and* be warned,
O Jerusalem,
Or I will be alienated from you,
And make you a desolation,
An uninhabited land."

9 Thus says the LORD of hosts,
"They will thoroughly gather like
[fruit on] a vine what is left of
Israel;
Pass your hand [over the vine]
again *and* again [Babylon, tool
of destruction] like a grape
gatherer,
Over the branches [stripping the
tendrils off the vine]."
10 To whom shall I (Jeremiah) speak
and give warning
That they may hear?
Behold, their ears are closed
[absolutely deaf to God]
And they cannot listen.
Behold, the word of the LORD has
become a reprimand *and* an
object of scorn to them;
They have no delight in it. [Acts 7:1]
11 But I am full of the wrath
(judgment) of the LORD;
I am tired of restraining it.
"[I will] pour it out on the children
in the street
And on the young men gathered
together;
For both the husband and wife
shall be taken,
The aged and the very old [though
full of days they are not exempt
from judgment].
12 "Their houses shall be turned over
to others,

---

their power, rejecting their responsible roles as messengers and servants of God.

6:4–5 *Prepare for war against her.* Prepare can also be translated "make holy." It refers to ritual sanctification performed in preparation for battle. The words are overheard in the camps of the enemies who are about to come against Jerusalem. Sorcerers and diviners were called upon to perform sacrifices to determine the will of the gods and assure a successful outcome in battle.

6:6 *Cut down her trees And build a siege [mound].* A siege mound was a ramp of wood, stone, and sand that sloped toward the wall of a city. Armored siege machines could go up the ramp and attack the city walls.

6:7 *Violence and destruction.* Jerusalem had once been a city that had peace, justice, and righteousness. Under the siege of the Babylonians in 588–586 BC conditions were unspeakable (see the Book of Lamentations).

6:11 *I am full of the wrath (judgment) of the LORD.* Jeremiah's own emotions reveal his identification with God's feelings about Judah. The prophet was both angry and weary with the entire nation, both young and old.

3 2Ki 25:1 **4** Joel 3:9; Jer 15:8 **7** Isa 57:20; Ps 55:9; Jer 20:8; Eze 7:11 **8** Hos 9:12 **10** Ac 7:51; See Ex 6:12; Jer 20:8 **11** Jer 20:9; Jer 9:21 **12** Dt 28:30; Jer 8:10

Their fields and their wives
together;
For I will stretch out My hand
Against the inhabitants of the
land," says the LORD.
13 "For from the least of them even to
the greatest of them,
Everyone is greedy for [unfair]
gain;
And from the prophet even to the
priest
Everyone deals deceitfully.
14 "They have treated superficially
the [bloody] broken wound of
My people,
Saying, 'Peace, peace,'
When there is no peace.
15 "Were they ashamed because they
had committed disgusting *and*
vile things?
No, they were not at all ashamed;
They did not even know how to
blush [at their idolatry].
Therefore they will fall among
those who fall;
At the time that I punish them
They will be overthrown," says the
LORD.

16 Thus says the LORD,
"Stand by the roads and look; ask
for the ancient paths,
Where the good way is; then walk
in it,
And you will find rest for your souls.
But they said, 'We will not walk in
it!' [Matt 11:29]
17 "I have set watchmen (prophets)
over you,
Saying, 'Listen *and* pay attention
to the [warning] sound of the
trumpet!'
But they said, 'We will not listen.'
18 "Therefore hear, O [Gentile]
nations,
And see, O congregation, what
[vengeful act] is to be done to
them.
19 "Hear, O earth: behold, I am
bringing disaster on this people,
The fruit of their schemes,
Because they have not listened *and*
paid attention to My words,
And as for My law, they have
rejected it also.
20 "For what purpose does
frankincense come to Me from
Sheba
And the sweet cane from a distant
land?
Your burnt offerings are not
acceptable
And your sacrifices are not sweet
and pleasing to Me."

21 Therefore, thus says the LORD,
"Behold, I am laying stumbling
blocks before this people.
The fathers and the sons together
Will stumble against them;
The neighbor and his friend will
perish."

The Enemy from the North

22 Thus says the LORD,
"Behold, a people is coming from
the north country,
And a great nation shall be stirred
up *and* put into action from the
remote parts of the earth.
23 "They seize bow and spear;
They are cruel *and* inhuman and
have no mercy.

6:13 *Everyone is greedy for [unfair] gain.* The accusation of covetousness suggests monetary gain by means of deception and fraud. Even those called to guide the nation in its covenant relationship had defrauded God and man.

6:15 *They did not even know how to blush.* The people had lost all sense of what was right before God.

6:16–17 *ancient paths.* This phrase probably refers to the Sinai covenant and the Book of Deuteronomy, as Jeremiah called the people back to former days of steadfast devotion.

6:20 *Your burnt offerings are not acceptable.* There is a common misconception that in the Old Testament, prior to the cross, God was primarily interested in outward and formal religious rites, such as circumcision, Sabbath-day observance, and animal sacrifices. Nothing could be more removed from the truth. In both Testaments, God is basically concerned with the attitudes of the heart (Dt 10:6).

13 Isa 56:11; Jer 8:10; Mic 3:5,11 **14** Jer 8:11; Eze 13:10; Jer 4:10; 23:17 **15** Jer 3:3 **16** Isa 8:20; Jer 18:15; Mal 4:4; Lk 16:29; Mt 11:29 **17** Isa 21:11; 58:1; Jer 25:4; Eze 3:17; Hab 2:1 **19** Isa 1:2; Pr 1:31 **20** Ps 40:6; 50:7-9; Isa 1:11; 66:3; Am 5:21; Mic 6:6; Isa 60:6; Jer 7:21 **22** Jer 1:15; 10:22 **23** Isa 5:30

Their voice sounds like the roaring
sea;
They ride [in formation] on horses,
Arrayed as a man for battle
Against you, O Daughter of Zion
(Jerusalem)!"
24 We have heard the report of it;
Our hands become limp *and*
helpless.
Anguish has gripped us,
Pain like that of a woman in
childbirth.
25 Do not go out into the field
Nor walk on the road,
For the enemy is armed with the
sword;
Terror is on every side.
26 O daughter of my people [says
Jeremiah],
Clothe yourself in sackcloth and
wallow in ashes;
Mourn [aloud] as for an only son,
A most bitter cry [of sorrow and
regret],
For suddenly the destroyer will
come upon us [on both prophet
and people].
27 "I [the LORD] have set you as an
assayer [O Jeremiah] and as a
tester [of the ore] of My people,
That you may know and analyze
their acts."
28 They are all the worst [kind] of
[stiff-necked, godless] rebels,
Going around spreading slander.
They are [not gold and silver ore,
but] bronze and iron;
They are all corrupt.
29 The bellows blow fiercely,
The lead is consumed by the fire;
In vain they continue refining,
But the wicked are not separated
and removed.
30 They call them rejected silver
[only dross, without value],
Because the LORD has rejected
them.

Message at the Temple Gate

7 THE WORD that came to Jeremiah
from the LORD, saying,
2 "Stand in the gate of the LORD's
house and proclaim there this word
and say, 'Hear the word of the LORD, all
you of Judah who enter by these gates
to worship the LORD.' "
3 Thus says the LORD of hosts, the
God of Israel, "Change your ways and
your behavior, and I will let you live in
this place.
4 "Do not trust in the deceptive *and*
lying words [of the false prophets who
claim that Jerusalem will be protected
by God because of the temple], saying,
'This is the temple of the LORD, the tem-
ple of the LORD, the temple of the LORD.'
5 "For if you thoroughly change your
ways and your behavior, if you thor-
oughly *and* honestly practice justice
between a man and his neighbor,
6 if you do not oppress the transient
and the foreigner, the orphan, or the
widow, and do not shed innocent blood

6:26 *and wallow in ashes.* This action symbolically expressed sorrow and despair.
6:27 *I [the LORD] have set you as an assayer.* Jeremiah would act as the nation's assayer, the one who tests or evaluates quality or purity.
6:29–30 *In vain they continue refining.* Jeremiah assesses Judah as a refiner purifies silver, using lead to remove impurities (9:7). The lead is consumed, so the dross in the silver ore cannot be purged. This results in the refiner discarding the ore because it is so impure that the smelting process is not worth the energy it takes. Similarly God rejects those whose wickedness cannot be refined.
7:2 *Stand in the gate.* The parallel in 26:2 suggests the proclamation was made in the outer court of the temple, where Jeremiah would have been guaranteed a large audience.
7:4 *Do not trust in the deceptive and lying words.* Trust conveys the sense of security and confidence that the people had in their holy place. They believed that since God had chosen Jerusalem as His dwelling, had promised that a Davidic king would remain on the throne forever, and had delivered the city from attack in the days of Hezekiah and Isaiah, He would never allow the city or the temple to be destroyed. ***the temple of the LORD.*** The Israelites believed that the building guaranteed their security whether or not they obeyed the provisions of the covenant. This false hope was a lie (3:23; 7:9).

24 Jer 4:31; 13:21; 49:24; 50:43 **26** Jer 4:8; Jer 25:34; Mic 1:10; Zec 12:10 **27** Jer 1:18; 15:20 **28** Jer 5:23; Jer 9:4; Eze 22:18 **30** Isa 1:22 **CHAPTER 7** **2** Jer 26:2 **3** Jer 18:11; 26:13 **4** Mic 3:11 **5** Jer 22:3 **6** Dt 6:14,15; 8:19; Jer 13:10

[by oppression and by unjust judicial
murders] in Jerusalem, nor follow after
other gods to your own ruin,
7 then I will let you live in this place,
in the land that I gave to your fathers
[to live in] forever and ever.
8 "Behold, you are trusting in decep-
tive *and* useless words that bring no
benefit.
9 "Will you steal, murder, commit
adultery, swear [oaths] falsely, offer
sacrifices *or* burn incense to Baal, and
follow after other gods that you have
not known,
10 and [then dare to] come and stand
before Me in this house, which is called
by My Name, and say, 'We are pro-
tected *and* set free [by this act of reli-
gious ritual]!'—only to go on with this
wickedness *and* these disgusting and
loathsome things?
11 "Has this house, which is called by
My Name, become a den of robbers
in your eyes [a place of retreat for you
between acts of violence]? Behold, I
Myself have seen it," says the LORD.
12 "But go now to My place which
was in Shiloh [in Ephraim], where I
first set My Name, and see what I did
to it because of the wickedness of My
people Israel. [1 Sam 4:10–18]
13 "And now, because you have done
all these things," says the LORD, "and I
spoke [persistently] to you, even rising
up early and speaking, but you did not
listen, and I called you but you did not
answer,
14 therefore, I will do to this house
(the temple) which is called by My
Name, in which you trust, and to the
place which I gave you and your fa-
thers, just as I did to Shiloh.
15 "I will cast you out of My sight,
as I have cast out all your brothers
(relatives through Jacob), all the de-
scendants of Ephraim.
16 "Therefore, do not pray for this
people [of Judah] or lift up a cry or
entreaty for them or make intercession
to Me, for I do not hear you.
17 "Do you not see what they are do-
ing in the cities of Judah and in the
streets of Jerusalem?
18 "The children gather wood, the
fathers kindle the fire, and the women
knead the dough to make cakes for the
queen of heaven; and they pour out
drink offerings to other gods that they
may offend *and* provoke Me to anger.
19 "Do they offend *and* provoke Me
to anger?" says the LORD. "Is it not
themselves [they offend], to their own
shame?"
20 Therefore thus says the Lord GOD,
"Behold, My anger and My wrath will
be poured out on this place, on man
and beast, on the trees of the field
and the fruit of the ground; and it
will burn and [the fire will] not be
quenched."

7:10 *stand before Me.* This means "to place (oneself) in submissive service to someone." Entering the temple of God in such a manner, while worshiping other gods, was incomprehensible. Furthermore, for the people to think that they were secure enough to perform perverted abominations was the ultimate hypocrisy.

7:11 *den of robbers.* Like thieves hiding in a cave for safety, Judah attempted to hide behind the sanctuary of the temple for protection from the divine hand of judgment. But the Lord had seen the hypocrisy of Israel's ways. Jesus quoted this verse when He cleansed the second temple (Mt 21:13).

7:16 *do not pray for this people.* God's instruction to Jeremiah indicates the extreme depravity of Jerusalem's inhabitants (11:14; 14:11). No manner of intercession was to be made on behalf of Judah. God would not hear Jeremiah's appeals.

7:18 *the queen of heaven.* This is a reference to the goddess Ishtar, who was worshiped in open-air cultic centers throughout the eastern Mediterranean region and Mesopotamia. Worship of Ishtar involved the preparation of special cakes that bore the goddess's image, as well as drink offerings (44:19). The family cooperation in the idolatrous worship of Ishtar stood in direct opposition to the covenant demands that a father instruct his children in the ways of the Lord (Dt 6:4–9).

---

7 Dt 4:40; Jer 3:18 **8** ver. 4; Jer 5:31; 14:13,14 **9** 1Ki 18:21; Hos 4:1,2; Zep 1:5; Ex 20:3 **10** Eze 23:39; ver. 11,14; Jer 32:34; 34:15 **11** Isa 56:7; Mt 21:13; Mk 11:17; Lk 19:46 **12** Jos 18:1; Jdg 18:31; Dt 12:11; 1Sa 4:10; Ps 78:60; Jer 26:6 **13** 2Ch 36:15; Jer 11:7; Pr 1:24; Isa 65:12; 66:4 **14** 1Sa 4:10; Ps 78:60 **15** 2Ki 17:23; Ps 78:67 **16** Ex 32:10; Jer 15:1 **18** Jer 44:17; Jer 19:13 **19** Dt 32:16,21

[21]Thus says the LORD of hosts, the God of Israel, "Add your burnt offerings to your sacrifices and eat the meat.

[22]"For in the day that I brought them out of the land of Egypt, I did not speak to your fathers or command them concerning burnt offerings or sacrifices.

[23]"But this thing I did command them: 'Listen to *and* obey My voice, and I will be your God, and you shall be My people; and you will walk in all the way which I command you, so that it may be well with you.'

[24]"But they did not obey Me or bend their ear [to hear Me], but followed the counsels and the stubbornness of their [own] evil heart (mind), and [they turned and] went backward instead of forward.

[25]"Since the day that your fathers came out of the land of Egypt until this day, I have [persistently] sent you all My servants the prophets, sending them daily, early [and late].

[26]"Yet they did not listen to Me *and* obey Me or bend their ear [to hear Me], but stiffened their neck; they did more evil *and* behaved worse than their fathers.

[27]"You shall speak all these words to them, but they will not listen to you; and you shall [also] call to them, but they will not answer you.

[28]"You shall say to them, 'This is the nation that did not obey the voice of the LORD their God or accept correction *and* warning; truth *and* faithfulness have perished and have completely vanished from their mouths.

[29]'Cut off your hair [your crown,
O Jerusalem] and throw it away,
And take up a mournful cry on the barren heights,
For the LORD has rejected and abandoned
The generation of His wrath.'

[30]"For the children of Judah have done evil in My sight," says the LORD; "they have set their disgusting *and* shamefully vile things in the house which is called by My Name, to defile it.

[31]"They have built the high places of Topheth, which is in the Valley of Ben-hinnom (son of Hinnom), to burn their sons and their daughters in the fire [to honor Molech, the fire god]—which I did not command, nor did it come into My heart (mind). [Lev 18:21; Josh 15:8; 2 Kin 16:2, 3; 21:1, 6; Is 30:33]

[32]"Therefore, behold, the days are coming," declares the LORD, "when it will no longer be called Topheth or the Valley of Ben-hinnom, but the Valley of the Slaughter, for [in bloody warfare] they will bury [the dead] in Topheth until there is no more room. [Jer 19:6]

[33]"And the dead bodies of this people will be food for the birds of the air and for the beasts of the earth and no one will frighten them away.

7:21 ***Add your burnt offerings to your sacrifices.*** Because the people had missed the true meaning of the Lord's worship, they could multiply their offerings as much as they liked and it would do them no good. The Lord cared for none of their sacrifices. To Him they were simply meat.

7:23 ***that it may be well with you.*** God required that His people obey His voice. Obedience would bring blessing. When the prophets lashed out against sacrifice, it was not against the sacrificial system as God had established it, but against the corruption of that system as the people practiced it. The same thing is found in the New Testament passages that seemingly speak against the law. Both the New Testament writers and the Hebrew prophets denounce the abuses of divine systems in human hands.

7:26 ***bend their ear [to hear Me], but stiffened their neck.*** These phrases suggest a cold rebuff to the will and work of God. Jeremiah, like Isaiah before him (Isa 6:9,10), was told that the people would not respond to his message.

7:29 ***Cut off your hair.*** This practice was a way of expressing mourning and grief. The act may also have symbolized that Judah had rejected the covenant relationship just as if they had broken a Nazirite vow, a sign of personal devotion that required the hair not to be cut (Nu 6:1 – 21).

7:33 ***dead bodies of this people.*** Unburied corpses left to the elements and animals were

21 Isa 1:11; Am 5:21; Hos 8:13 **22** 1Sa 15:22; Ps 51:16; Hos 6:6 **23** Ex 15:26; Dt 6:3; Ex 19:5; Lev 26:12 **24** Ps 81:11; Ps 81:12; Jer 32:33 **25** 2Ch 36:15; ver. 13 **26** Jer 11:8; Neh 9:17; Jer 16:12 **27** Eze 2:7 **28** Jer 5:3; Jer 9:3 **29** Job 1:20; Isa 15:2; Mic 1:16 **30** 2Ki 21:4; 2Ch 33:4; Eze 7:20; Da 9:27 **31** 2Ki 23:10; Ps 106:38; Dt 17:3 **32** Jer 19:6; 2Ki 23:10; Jer 19:11 **33** Dt 28:26

34 “Then I will cause the voices of joy and gladness, and the voices of the bridegroom and the bride to vanish from the cities of Judah and from the streets of Jerusalem; for the land will become a ruin—a wasteland.

The Sin and Treachery of Judah

8 “AT THAT time,” says the LORD, “they [the Babylonian army] will bring out from their graves the bones of the kings of Judah, the bones of its princes, the bones of the priests, the bones of the prophets, and the bones of the inhabitants of Jerusalem.

2 “They will [carelessly scatter and] spread them out before the sun and the moon and all the host of heaven, which the dead have loved and which they have served, and which they have walked after and which they have sought, and which they have worshiped. They will not be gathered or be buried; they will be like dung on the face of the earth.

3 “And death will be chosen rather than life by all the remnant of those who remain of this evil family (nation), who remain in all the places to which I have driven them,” says the LORD of hosts.

4 “Moreover [Jeremiah], you shall say to them, ‘Thus says the LORD,

“Do men fall and not rise up
again?
Does one turn away [from God]
and not repent *and* return [to
Him]?
5 “Why then has this people of
Jerusalem
Turned away with a perpetual
turning away [from Me]?
They hold tightly to deceit
(idolatry);
They refuse to repent *and* return
[to God].
6 “I have listened and heard,
But they have spoken what is not
right;
No man repented of his
wickedness,
Saying, ‘What have I done?’
Everyone turns to his [individual]
course,
As the horse rushes like a torrent
into battle.
7 “Even the stork in the sky
Knows her seasons [of migration],
And the turtledove, the swallow
and the crane
Observe the time of their return.
But My people do not know
The law of the LORD.

8 “How can you say, ‘We are wise,
And the law of the LORD is with
us [and we are learned in its
language and teachings]’?
Behold, [the truth is that] the lying
pen of the scribes
Has made the law into a lie
[a mere code of ceremonial
observances]. [Mark 7:13]
9 “The wise men are shamed,
They are dismayed and caught.
Behold, they have [manipulated
and] rejected the [truth in the]
word of the LORD,
And what kind of wisdom *and*
insight do they have?
10 “Therefore I will give their wives
to others
And their fields to new owners;
Because from the least even to the
greatest
Everyone is greedy for [unjust]
gain;
From the prophet even to the priest
Everyone practices deceit *and*
deals in corruption.

---

regarded as a horrible desecration in the ancient Middle East.

8:1–3 *the sun and the moon and all the host of heaven.* The gods and goddesses to whom Jerusalem looked for deliverance would stand over the people's desecrated corpses, which are pictured here as dung. Those who survived the siege and attack as exiles and slaves would prefer death over life.

8:7 *seasons.* Whereas the birds follow their instincts to migrate, the people of Israel refused to follow God's promptings to obey His covenant. Note that God still refers to the people of Judah

34 Isa 24:7,8; Eze 26:13; Hos 2:11; Rev 18:23; Lev 26:33 **CHAPTER 8** **2** 2Ki 23:5; Eze 8:16; Jer 22:19 **3** Job 3:21; 7:15,16; Rev 9:6 **5** Jer 7:24; Jer 9:6; Jer 5:3 **6** 2Pe 3:9 **7** Isa 1:3; SS 2:12; Jer 5:4,5 **8** Ro 2:17 **9** Jer 6:15 **10** Zep 1:13

11 "For they have treated the
brokenness of the daughter of
My people superficially,
Saying, 'Peace, peace,'
When there is no peace.
12 "Were they ashamed because of
the extremely disgusting *and*
shamefully vile things they had
done?
They were not at all ashamed,
And they did not know how to
blush.
Therefore, they shall fall among
those who fall;
At the time of their punishment
they shall be overthrown,"
Says the LORD. [Jer 6:12–15]

13 "I will gather *and* snatch them
away [utterly consuming them],"
says the LORD.
"There will be no grapes on the
vine,
Nor figs on the fig tree,
And even the leaf will wither;
And the things that I have given
them will pass away [by the
hand of those whom I have
appointed]." ' " [Matt 21:18, 19]
14 Why are we sitting still [the people
wonder]?
Assemble yourselves, and let us
enter the fortified cities
And let us die there,
For the LORD our God has decreed
our ruin
And given us bitter *and* poisonous
water to drink,
Because we have sinned against
the LORD.
15 We waited for peace *and* salvation,
but no good came,
And for a time of healing, but
behold, terror!
16 The snorting of [Nebuchadnezzar's]
horses is heard from Dan [on
Palestine's northern border].
At the sound of the neighing of his
strong stallions
The whole land quakes;
For they come and devour the land
and all that is in it,
The city and those who live in it.
17 "For behold, I am sending serpents
among you,
Vipers which cannot be charmed,
And they will bite you," says the
LORD.

18 Oh, that I (Jeremiah) could find
comfort from my sorrow [for my
grief is beyond healing],
My heart is sick *and* faint *within
me!*
19 Behold, [hear the sound of] the
cry of the daughter of my
people from the distant land [of
Babylon]:
"Is not the LORD in Zion? Is not her
King within her?"
[But the LORD answers] "Why have
they provoked Me to anger with
their carved images and with
foreign idols?"
20 "The harvest is past, the summer
has ended *and* the gathering of
fruit is over,
But we are not saved," [comes the
voice of the people again].
21 For the brokenness of the daughter
of my people I (Jeremiah) am
broken;
I mourn, anxiety has gripped me.
22 Is there no balm in Gilead?
Is there no physician there?
Why then has not the [spiritual]
health of the daughter of my
people been restored?

---

as "my people" even though they continued to rebel against Him.

8:17 *I am sending serpents among you.* Judgment by means of poisonous snakes is described in Numbers 21:6.

8:20 *harvest is past, the summer has ended.* This proverb reflects the sense of helplessness in the early fall. The harvest was meager and the oppression persisted. Even Jeremiah was deeply hurt — this translates a Hebrew word derived from the verb meaning "to break," "to shatter"; in other words, the prophet's spirit was broken over the fate of his people.

8:22 *Is there no balm in Gilead?* The region of Gilead was known for its balsam ointment (Ge 37:25). There is no healing, physical or spiritual, for a people intent on rebelling against God.

11 Jer 6:14; Eze 13:10 **12** Jer 3:3 **13** Joel 1:7; Mt 21:19 **14** Jer 4:5; Jer 9:15 **15** Jer 14:19 **16** Jer 4:15; Jer 47:3 **17** Ps 58:4,5 **19** Isa 39:3 **21** Jer 9:1; Joel 2:6 **22** Jer 46:11

A Lament over Zion

9 OH THAT my head were waters
And my eyes a fountain of tears,
That I might weep day and night
For the slain of the daughter of my people!
2 Oh that I had in the wilderness
A lodging place (a mere shelter) for wayfaring men,
That I might leave my people
And go away from them!
For they are all adulterers [worshiping idols instead of the LORD],
[They are] an assembly of treacherous men [of weak character, men without integrity].
3 "They bend their tongue like their bow;
[Their] lies and not truth prevail *and* grow strong in the land;
For they proceed from evil to evil,
And they do not know *and* understand *and* acknowledge Me," says the LORD.
4 "Let everyone beware of his neighbor
And do not trust any brother.
For every brother is a supplanter [like Jacob, a deceiver, ready to grab his brother's heel],
And every neighbor goes around as a slanderer. [Gen 25:26]
5 "Everyone deceives *and* mocks his neighbor
And does not speak the truth.
They have taught their tongue to speak lies;
They exhaust themselves with sin *and* cruelty.
6 "Your dwelling is in the midst of deceit [oppression upon oppression and deceit upon deceit];
Through deceit they refuse to know (understand) Me," says the LORD.

7 Therefore thus says the LORD of hosts,

"Behold, I will refine them [through suffering] and test them;
For how else should I deal with the daughter of My people?
8 "Their tongue is a murderous arrow;
It speaks deceit;
With his mouth one speaks peace to his neighbor,
But in his heart he lays traps *and* waits in ambush for him.
9 "Shall I not punish them for these things?" says the LORD.
"Shall I not avenge Myself
On such a nation as this?

10 "I will take up a weeping and wailing for the mountains,
And a [funeral] dirge for the pastures of the wilderness,
Because they are burned up *and* desolated so that no one passes through [them];
Nor can anyone hear the lowing of cattle.
Both the birds of the air and the beasts have fled; they are gone.
11 "I will make Jerusalem a heap of ruins,
A haunt *and* dwelling place of jackals;

9:1 *my eyes a fountain of tears.* Jeremiah, who is known as the "weeping prophet," identified personally with the suffering of his people. Here he expresses his desire for a reserve of tears that would flow without stopping.

9:3 *They bend their tongue like their bow.* Once falseness takes hold in a community or nation, it seems to pervade every area of life. Such a condition is what Jeremiah describes here. There was falsity in every relation. There was a lack of fidelity and trust.

9:4 *Let everyone beware of his neighbor.* The personal affairs of the people were characterized by deceit, slander, and mistrust. Ethical standards had collapsed.

9:8 *Their tongue is a murderous arrow.* Jeremiah returns to the imagery of bow and arrow to depict Judah's deceit (v. 3). The picture is of a person speaking peaceably to his neighbor while lying in wait to ambush him.

CHAPTER 9 **1** Isa 22:4 **2** Jer 5:7,8 **3** Ps 64:3; 1Sa 2:12 **4** Mic 7:5,6; Jer 6:28 **7** Isa 1:25; Hos 11:8 **8** Ps 12:2; 55:21 **9** Jer 5:9,29 **10** Hos 4:3; Jer 4:25 **11** Isa 25:2; 13:22; 34:13

And I will make the cities of
Judah a desolation, without
inhabitant."

12Who is the wise man who may
understand this [without any doubt]?
To whom has the mouth of the LORD
spoken, so that he may declare it?
Why is the land ruined, laid waste
like a wilderness, so that no one passes
through?
13The LORD said, "Because they have
turned away from My law which I set
before them, and have not listened to
and obeyed My voice nor walked in
accordance with it,
14but have walked stubbornly after
their [own] heart and after the Baals,
as their fathers taught them,"
15therefore thus says the LORD of
hosts, the God of Israel, "behold, I will
feed them, this people, with worm-
wood and give them bitter *and* poison-
ous water to drink.
16"I will [also] scatter them among
nations that neither they nor their fa-
thers have known, and I will send the
sword after them until I have annihi-
lated them."
17Thus says the LORD of hosts,

"Consider and call for the
mourning women to come;
Send for the wailing women to
come.
18"Let them hurry and take up a
wailing for us,
That our eyes may shed tears
And our eyelids flow with water.
19"For a sound of wailing is heard
[coming] from Zion:
'How we are ruined!
We are greatly perplexed *and*
utterly shamed,
Because we have left the land,
Because they have torn down our
dwellings.' "
20Now hear the word of the LORD,
O you women,
And let your ear hear the word of
His mouth;
Teach your daughters a song of
mourning,
And each one [teach] her neighbor
a dirge.
21For death has come up through
our windows;
It has entered our palaces,
Cutting off the children from the
streets
And the young men from the town
squares.
22Speak, "Thus says the LORD,
'The dead bodies of men will fall
like dung on the open field,
And like sheaves [of grain] behind
the reaper,
And no one will gather them.' "
[Jer 8:2]

23Thus says the LORD, "Let not the
one who is wise *and* skillful boast
in his insight; let not the one who is
mighty *and* powerful boast in his
strength; let not the one who is rich
boast in his [temporal satisfactions
and earthly] abundance;
24but let the one who boasts boast in
this, that he understands and knows
Me [and acknowledges Me and honors
Me as God and recognizes without
any doubt], that I am the LORD who
practices lovingkindness, justice and
righteousness on the earth, for in

9:13 *have not listened to and obeyed.* The word "obey," which comes from the Hebrew word meaning "to hear," implies an active response to the hearing of God's Word. Instead of walking according to God's law, the people walked according to the dictates or stubbornness of their own hearts.
9:18 *Let them hurry.* There is urgency in summoning the skilled mourners to lead the people in tearful lament over the imminent destruction of Judah.
9:21 *death has come.* The Canaanite god of death, Mot, was believed to enter a household through an open window to bring adversity, destruction, and death.
9:24 *lovingkindness, justice and righteousness on the earth.* True knowledge of God resulting from an intimate relationship with Him will be demonstrated in a person's character. God demands these attributes of his followers.

12 Hos 14:9 **14** Jer 7:24; Gal 1:14 **15** Ps 80:5; Jer 8:14; La 3:19 **16** Lev 26:33; Dt 28:64; Lev 26:33; Jer 44:27; Eze 5:2 **17** 2Ch 35:25; Job 3:8; Ecc 12:5; Am 5:16; Mt 9:23 **18** Jer 14:17 **19** Lev 18:28 **21** Jer 6:11 **22** Jer 8:2 **23** Ecc 9:11 **24** 1Co 1:31; 2Co 10:17; Mic 7:18

these things I delight," says the LORD.
[1 Cor 1:31; 2 Cor 10:17]
25 "Behold, the days are coming,"
says the LORD, "when I will punish
all who are circumcised [physically]
and yet uncircumcised [spiritually]—
[Rom 2:25–29]
26 Egypt and Judah, and Edom and
the sons of Ammon, and Moab and
all those who live in the desert who
clip off the hair on their temples; for
all these nations are uncircumcised
(sinful, impure), and all the house of
Israel are uncircumcised in heart."

A Satire on Idolatry

10 HEAR THE word which the LORD speaks to you, O house of Israel.

2 Thus says the LORD,

"Do not learn the way of the [pagan] nations,
And do not be terrified *and* distressed by the signs of the heavens
Although the pagans are terrified by them;
3 For the customs *and* decrees of the peoples are [mere] delusion [exercises in futility];
It is only wood which one cuts from the forest [to make a god],
The work of the hands of the craftsman with the axe *or* cutting tool.
4 "They adorn the idol with silver and with gold;
They fasten it with hammers and nails
So that it will not fall apart.
5 "They are like scarecrows in a cucumber field;
They cannot speak;
They have to be carried,
Because they cannot walk!
Do not be afraid of them,
For they can do no harm *or* evil,
Nor can they do any good."
6 There is none like You, O LORD;
You are great, and great is Your mighty *and* powerful name.
7 Who would not fear You, O King of the nations?
For it is appropriate *and* it is Your due!
For among all the wise men of the nations
And in all their kingdoms,
There is none like You.
8 But they are altogether irrational *and* stupid and foolish
In their discipline of delusion—their idol is [only] wood [it is ridiculous, empty and worthless]!
9 Silver *that has been* beaten [into plates] is brought from Tarshish,
And gold from Uphaz,
The work of the craftsman and of the hand of the goldsmith;
Violet and purple are their clothing;
They are all the work of skilled men.
10 But the LORD is the true God *and* the God who is Truth;
He is the living God and the everlasting King.

10:2 *the way of the [pagan] nations.* The Gentiles worshiped natural phenomena by means of handmade icons and symbolic imagery. ***the signs of the heavens.*** These were astral deities (8:1 – 3) worshiped in the days of Manasseh and reinstituted following the death of Josiah and the collapse of his reforms.

10:6 – 7 *There is none like You, O LORD.* This phrase expresses one of the great teachings of the prophets — the incomparability of God. God is not simply better than other gods; He alone is the living God.

10:9 *They are all the work of skilled men.* No matter how skilled the idol makers were, the fabricated icons were lifeless, deteriorating, false gods who were no more powerful or wise than their makers.

10:10 *the LORD is the true God.* Jeremiah speaks of Israel's God not only as living, but also as being the true God and the nation's everlasting King. He thus governs His covenant people by principles of truth, and with a power that far surpasses the might of earthly kings. Whereas pagan gods cannot alter the course of nature in the slightest

25 Ro 2:8,9 **26** Jer 25:23; Lev 26:41; Eze 44:7; Ro 2:28 **CHAPTER 10** **2** Lev 18:3 **3** Isa 40:19; 45:20 **4** Isa 41:7 **5** Ps 115:5; Hab 2:19; 1Co 12:2; Ps 115:7; Isa 46:1,7; Isa 41:23 **6** Ex 15:11; Ps 86:8,10 **7** Rev 15:4; Ps 89:6 **8** Ps 115:8; Hab 2:18 **9** Da 10:5; Ps 115:4 **10** 1Ti 6:17; Ps 10:16

The earth quakes *and* shudders at
His wrath,
And the nations are not able to
endure His indignation.

11 In this manner you shall say to
them, "The gods that did not make
the heavens and the earth will perish
from the earth and from under the
heavens."

12 God made the earth by His power;
He established the world by His
wisdom
And by His understanding *and*
skill He has stretched out the
heavens.
13 When He utters His voice, *there*
is a tumult of waters in the
heavens,
And He causes the clouds *and* the
mist to ascend from the end of
the earth;
He makes lightning for the rain,
And brings out the wind from
His treasuries *and* from His
storehouses.
14 Every man has become [like a
brute] irrational *and* stupid,
without knowledge [of God];
Every goldsmith is shamed by his
carved idols;
For his molten images are frauds
and lies,
And there is no breath in them.
15 They are worthless *and* devoid of
promise, a work of delusion *and*
mockery;
In their time of [trial and]
punishment they will perish
[without hope].
16 The Portion of Jacob [the true God
on whom Israel has a claim] is
not like these;
For He is the Designer *and* Maker
of all things,
And Israel is the tribe of His
inheritance [and He will not fail
them]—
The LORD of hosts is His name.

17 Gather up your bundle [of goods]
from the ground,
You who live under siege.

18 For thus says the LORD;

"Behold, I am slinging out at this
time the people of this land,
And will cause them [great]
distress,
That they may find it [to be as I
have said]."

19 "Woe to me because of my
[spiritual] brokenness!" [says
Jeremiah, speaking for the
nation.]
"My wound is incurable."
But I said, "Surely this sickness
and suffering *and* grief are mine,
And I must bear it."
20 My tent is destroyed,
And all my [tent] cords are broken;
My children have been taken from
me [as captives] and are no
more.
There is no one to stretch out my
tent again
And to set up my [tent] curtains.
21 For the shepherds [of the people]
have become [like brutes,]
irrational *and* stupid,

---

degree, even though their worshipers believed very much to the contrary, the God of Sinai is the Creator of nature. He can punish the wicked by storm, flood, earthquake, or pestilence, and strike terror into the hearts of all those who oppose Him.
10:12 ***God made the earth.*** Jeremiah emphasizes the creative power of God, drawing on the imagery of Job 38 and Psalm 8. Jeremiah was reminding the people of Judah that their God not only created the universe but also governs its ongoing life.

10:17 ***Gather up your bundle [of goods] from the ground.*** The Assyrian stone reliefs of Shalmaneser III depict captives transporting household goods on their heads as they go into exile in the eastern reaches of the empire. Soon, this would be the fate of the people of Judah.
10:19 ***Woe to me.*** Jeremiah personally identified with Judah and the destruction of Jerusalem. The injuries inflicted upon Judah were severe.

11 Ps 96:5; Zec 13:2 **12** Ge 1:1,6; Ps 136:5; Ps 93:1; Job 9:8; Ps 104:2; Isa 40:22 **13** Job 38:34; Ps 135:7
14 Jer 51:17; Pr 30:2; Isa 42:17; 44:11; Hab 2:18 **16** La 3:24; Dt 32:9; Isa 47:4; 54:5 **17** Jer 6:1; Eze 12:3
18 1Sa 25:29; Eze 6:10 **19** Jer 8:21; Ps 77:10; Mic 7:9 **20** Jer 4:20

And have not searched for the
LORD *or* asked about Him *or*
realized their need for Him;
Therefore they have not been wise
and have not prospered,
And all their flocks are scattered.
22 The sound of a report! Behold, [the
invader] comes—
A great commotion from
the country of the north
(Babylonia)—
To make the cities of Judah
A desolation, a haunt *and* dwelling
place of jackals.

23 O LORD, I know that the path of
[life of] a man is not in himself;
It is not within [the limited ability
of] man [even one at his best] to
choose *and* direct his steps [in
life]. [Ps 37:23; Prov 20:24]
24 O LORD, correct me [along with
Your people], but with mercy
and in just measure—
Not in Your anger, or You will
crush me *and* bring me to
nothing.
25 Pour out Your wrath on the
nations that do not know *nor*
recognize You
And on the families that do not
call Your name.
For they have devoured Jacob;
They have devoured him and
consumed him
And made his land a desolate waste.

The Broken Covenant

11 THE WORD that came to Jeremiah from the LORD,
2 "Hear the words of this [solemn]
covenant, and speak to the men of Ju-
dah and to the people of Jerusalem.
3 "Say to them, 'Thus says the LORD,
the God of Israel, "Cursed is the man
who does not heed the words of this
covenant
4 which I commanded your fathers at
the time that I brought them out of the
land of Egypt, from the iron furnace,
saying, 'Listen to My voice and do ac-
cording to all that I command you. So
you shall be My people, and I will be
your God,'
5 that I may complete the oath which
I swore to your fathers, to give them
a land [of plenty] flowing with milk
and honey, as it is this day." ' " Then I
answered, "Amen (so be it), O LORD."
6 And the LORD said to me, "Proclaim
all these words in the cities of Judah
and in the streets of Jerusalem: 'Hear
the words of this [solemn] covenant
and do them.
7 'For I solemnly warned your fathers
at the time that I brought them up from
the land of Egypt, even to this day,
warning them persistently, saying,
"Obey My voice."
8 'Yet they did not obey or incline
their ear [to listen to Me], but every-
one walked in the stubborn way of his
[own] evil heart. Therefore I brought on
them all [the suffering threatened in] the
words of this covenant, which I com-
manded them to do, but they did not.' "
9 Then the LORD said to me, "A con-
spiracy has been found among the
men of Judah and among the people
of Jerusalem.
10 "They have returned to the wick-
edness of their ancestors who refused
to hear My words; they have followed
other gods [in order] to serve them. The
house of Israel and the house of Judah

11:2 *Hear the words of this [solemn] covenant.* Jeremiah's message from the Lord here is strongly associated with the Book of Deuteronomy. The term "words" is the Hebrew name of the Book of Deuteronomy; it is also used to refer to the terms of the covenant. A covenant is a legal treaty or relationship between individuals, between nations, or — in the case of Israel — between a nation and its God. The covenant specified rights, obligations, and responsibilities of the parties entering into the agreement.

11:4 *iron furnace.* This terminology comes directly from Deuteronomy 4:20, which is set in a context of a warning against worshiping idols.

11:5 *that I may complete the oath.* The blessing of land, as promised to Abraham, was dependent upon the covenant loyalty of the people.

---

22 Jer 5:15; Jer 9:11 **23** Pr 16:1 **24** Jer 30:11 **25** Ps 79:6; Job 18:21; Jer 8:16 **CHAPTER 11** **3** Dt 27:26 **4** Dt 4:20; Lev 26:12; Jer 7:23 **5** Dt 7:12; Ps 105:9 **6** Ro 2:13; Jas 1:22 **7** Jer 35:15 **8** Jer 7:26; Jer 9:14 **9** Eze 22:25 **10** Eze 20:18

have broken My [solemn] covenant which I made with their fathers."

11 Therefore thus says the LORD, "Behold I am bringing disaster *and* suffering on them which they will not be able to escape; though they cry to Me, I will not listen to them.

12 "Then the cities of Judah and the people of Jerusalem will go and cry to the [man-made] gods to whom they burn incense, but they cannot save them in the time of their disaster.

13 "For [as many as] the number of your cities are your gods, O Judah; and [as many as] the number of the streets of Jerusalem are the altars you have set up to the shameful thing, altars to burn incense to Baal.

14 "Therefore do not pray for this people, nor lift up a cry or prayer for them, for I shall not listen when they cry to Me in the time of their disaster.

15 "What right has My beloved [to be] in My house
When she has done many vile things *and* acted treacherously [over and over again]?
Can vows *and* the meat of your sacrifices remove your wickedness from you *and* cancel the consequences of your sin,
So that you can [escape your judgment and] rejoice?"
16 The LORD [acknowledged you once as worthy and] called your name,
"A green olive tree, fair *and* beautiful in fruit and form";
But with the roar of a great tempest
He has set fire to it,
And its branches are worthless.
[Ps 52:8; Jer 21:14]

17 For the LORD of hosts, who planted you, has pronounced evil *and* horror against you because of the evil of the house of Israel and of the house of Judah, which they have done to provoke Me [to anger] by offering sacrifices *and* burning incense to Baal.

Plots against Jeremiah

18 Then the LORD gave me knowledge [of their plot], and I knew it;
So You [O LORD] revealed their deeds to me.
19 But I was like a gentle *and* tame lamb brought to the slaughter;
And I did not know that they had devised plots *and* schemes against me, saying,
"Let us destroy the tree with its fruit;
Let us cut him off from the land of the living,
That his name be remembered no longer."
20 But, O LORD of hosts, who judges righteously,
Who tests the feelings and the heart (mind),
Let me see Your vengeance on them,
For to You I have committed my cause.

21 Therefore thus says the LORD regarding the men of Anathoth, who seek your life, saying, "Do not prophesy in

---

11:11 ***I am bringing disaster and suffering on them.*** Because the heart of the nation was evil, God would bring disaster upon the people. God's justice is inescapable when sin is intrinsic to one's character. Even if the people were to cry out in distress, God would not listen.
11:17 ***planted.*** This term recalls the theme of Jeremiah 2:21, the idea that God had established Israel as His choicest vine. However, here the context is the impending doom that would result from the evil done by the Lord's people.
11:20 ***Let me see Your vengeance on them.*** Jeremiah appealed for vindication to God as the one true righteous judge. "Heart" refers to the seat of intellect and will. "Vengeance" describes God's fury and anger against sin that demands punishment.
11:21 – 23 ***the men of Anathoth.*** These men insisted that Jeremiah not prophesy in the name of the Lord. If Jeremiah had yielded to their demand, he would have repudiated his calling, his person, and his God. The threat of death to Jeremiah was answered by punishment of the young men as well as their children. The prediction of death by famine was fulfilled when the city was besieged by the Babylonians in the days of Zedekiah.

11 Ps 18:41; Pr 1:28 **12** Dt 32:37 **13** Jer 2:28 **14** Ex 32:10 **15** Ps 50:16; Eze 16:25; Titus 1:15; Pr 2:14
16 Ps 52:8 **17** Isa 5:2 **19** Ps 83:4; 27:13 **20** 1Ch 28:9; Ps 7:9 **21** Jer 12:5,6; Mic 2:6

the name of the LORD, so that you will not die by our hand."
[22]Therefore, thus says the LORD of hosts, "Behold, I am about to punish them. Their young men will die by the sword, their sons and their daughters will die by famine;
[23]and there will be no remnant [of the conspirators] left, for I will bring disaster *and* horror on the men of Anathoth in the year of their punishment."

Jeremiah's Prayer

12 YOU, O LORD are
[uncompromisingly] righteous
and consistently just when I
plead my case with You;
Yet let me discuss issues of justice
with You:
Why has the way of the wicked
prospered?
Why are those who deal in
treachery (deceit) at ease *and*
thriving?
[2]You have planted them, they have
also taken root;
They grow, they have even
produced fruit.
You are honored by their
[hypocritical] lips
But [You are] far from their heart
and mind.
[3]But You, O LORD, know me [and
understand my devotion to You];
You see me;
And You examine *the attitude of*
my heart toward You.
Drag out the faithless like sheep
for the slaughter [O LORD]
And set them apart for the day of
slaughter.
[4]How long must the land mourn
And the grass of the countryside
wither?
Because of the wickedness *and*
hypocrisy of those who live in it,
The beasts and the birds are
consumed *and* are swept away
[by the drought],
Because men [mocking me] have
said, "He will not [live long
enough to] see [what happens at]
our final end."
[5][The LORD rebukes Jeremiah for
his impatience, saying] "If you
have raced with men on foot and
they have tired you out,
Then how can you compete with
horses?
If you fall down in a land of peace
[where you feel secure],
Then how will you do [among the
lions] in the [flooded] thicket
beside the Jordan?
[6]"For even your [tribal] brothers
and the household of your
father,
Even they have dealt treacherously
(unfaithfully) with you;
Indeed they are [like a pack of
hounds] howling after you.
Do not believe them, although
they may say kind words *and*
promise you good things."

God's Answer

[7]"I have abandoned My house,
I have given up My [precious]
inheritance (Judah);
I have given the [dearly] beloved of
My life

12:4 ***How long must the land mourn.*** Jeremiah's question related to God's delay of judgment on the people of the land. "Land mourn … grass of the countryside wither … beasts and the birds are consumed" are phrases that are recurring themes in Jeremiah and other prophetic texts (4:28; 40:7; Zep 1:3). In spite of past chastisement, the people believed that God would not bring their country to an end.
12:5 – 6 ***If you have raced with men on foot.*** God's response to Jeremiah's question (v. 4) comes in the form of two metaphorical questions. The first metaphor of foot racing was designed to teach Jeremiah that the obstacles he faced in his hometown were meager compared to those he would encounter before the kings of Judah and Babylon (the horses). ***land of peace.*** This second metaphor was designed to remind the prophet of the impending turmoil he would have to endure in proclaiming the message of judgment to an unrepentant leadership. The relatively peaceful setting of Anathoth, with its minor opposition from treacherous family members, served to prepare Jeremiah to struggle against greater antagonists.

23 Jer 23:12 **CHAPTER 12** **1** Ps 51:4; Mal 3:15 **2** Mt 15:8 **3** Ps 17:3; Jer 11:20; Jas 5:5 **4** Hos 4:3; Ps 107:34; Jer 9:10 **5** Jos 3:15; 1Ch 12:15 **6** Jer 9:4; Pr 26:25

Into the hands of her enemies.
8 "My inheritance has become to Me
Like a lion in the forest;
She has raised her voice *and* roared against Me;
So I have come to [treat her as if I] hate her.
9 "Is My inheritance like a speckled bird of prey to Me [unlike the others]?
Are the birds of prey (enemies) surrounding her on every side?
Go, gather all the [wild] beasts of the field;
Bring them to devour [her]!
10 "Many shepherds (invaders) have destroyed My vineyard (Judah),
They have trampled My field underfoot;
They have made My pleasant field
A desolate wilderness.
11 "They have made it a wasteland,
Desolate, it mourns before Me;
The whole land has been made a wasteland,
Because no man takes it to heart.
12 "Destroyers have come
On all the caravan roads in the desert,
For the sword of the LORD (Babylon) is devouring
From one end of the land even to the other;
No one has peace *or* a way of escape.
13 "They have planted wheat but have reaped thorns;
They have exhausted themselves but without profit.
So be ashamed of your harvest
Because of the fierce *and* raging anger of the LORD."

14 Thus says the LORD regarding all
My evil neighbors (Gentile nations)
who strike at the inheritance which
I have granted to My people Israel,
"Behold, I will uproot them from their
land and I will uproot the house of
Judah from among them.
15 "And it shall come about that after
I have uprooted them, I will return *and*
have compassion on them; and I will
bring them back again, each one to his
inheritance and each one to his land.
16 "And if these [neighboring nations]
will diligently learn the ways of My
people, to swear by My Name, say-
ing, 'As the LORD lives'—even as they
taught My people to swear by Baal,
then they will be built up among My
people.
17 "But if [any nation] will not listen
and obey, I will [completely] uproot and
destroy that nation, says the LORD."

The Ruined Waistband

13 THUS THE LORD said to me, "Go
and buy yourself a linen waist-
band and put it on your loins, but do
not put it in water."
2 So I bought the waistband accord-
ing to the word of the LORD and put it
on my loins.
3 Then the word of the LORD came to
me a second time, saying,
4 "Get up and take the waistband that
you have bought, which is [wrapped]

12:10 – 11 *Many shepherds.* This phrase refers to the foreign kings who had come as agents of God to judge Judah. The repetition of the word "desolate" describes the complete devastation of Judah (Isa 6:11). Because of sin, the land that once saw God's bounteous blessing would experience His devastating judgment.

12:15 *after I have uprooted them.* This verse offers a glimmer of hope in the middle of a prophecy of judgment. In the midst of His judgment, God would remember His covenant with Abraham. Eventually He would return and have compassion on His people.

12:16 *swear by My Name.* Only the everlasting love of God provides an answer to what God will do in a life that turns from an oath to a false god to an oath to serve the Lord. What unfathomable blessing can be ours from a God like this when we pledge our allegiance to Him. He asks our allegiance, and He asks us to truly learn the ways that He has established for His people.

13:1 – 5 *linen waistband.* This was an article of clothing that was like a short skirt or kilt worn by men. Jeremiah was not supposed to wash it.

9 Isa 56:9 **10** Jer 6:3; Isa 5:1,5; 63:18 **11** ver. 4; Isa 42:25 **13** Lev 26:16; Dt 28:38; Mic 6:15; Hag 1:6 **14** Zec 2:8; Dt 30:3; Jer 32:37 **15** Eze 28:25; Am 9:14 **16** Jer 4:2; Eph 2:20,21; 1Pe 2:5 **17** Isa 60:12

around your loins, and go to the [river]
Euphrates and hide it there in a crevice
of the rock."
5 So I went and hid it by the Euphrates, as the LORD had commanded me.
6 And after many days the LORD said
to me, "Get up, go to the Euphrates and
get the waistband which I commanded
you to hide there."
7 Then I went to the Euphrates and
dug, and I took the waistband from the
place where I had hidden it. And behold, the waistband was decayed *and*
ruined; it was completely worthless.
8 Then the word of the LORD came to
me, saying,
9 "Thus says the LORD, 'In this same
way I shall destroy the pride of Judah
and the great pride of Jerusalem.
10 'These wicked *and* malevolent people, who refuse to listen to My words,
who walk in the stubborn way of their
heart and have followed other gods
[which are nothing—just man-made
carvings] to serve them and to worship
them, let them be just like this waistband which is completely worthless.
11 'For as the waistband clings to the
body of a man, so I caused the whole
house of Israel and the whole house of
Judah to cling to Me,' says the LORD,
'that they might be for Me a people, a
name, a praise, and a glory; but they
did not listen *and* obey.'

Captivity Threatened

12 "Therefore you are to speak this
word to them, 'Thus says the LORD,
the God of Israel, "Every jar should be
filled with wine." ' The people will say
to you, 'Do we not already know that
every jar should be filled with wine?'
13 "Then say to them, 'Thus says the
LORD, "Behold, I am about to fill with
drunkenness all the people of this
land, even the kings who sit on David's
throne, the priests, the prophets and all
the people of Jerusalem.
14 "I will smash them one against another, both the fathers and the sons together," says the LORD. "I shall destroy
them [nothing will restrain Me]; I will
not show pity nor be sorry nor have
compassion." ' "

15 Listen and pay close attention,
do not be haughty *and*
overconfident,
For the LORD has spoken [says
Jeremiah].
16 Give glory to the LORD your God,
Before He brings darkness
And before your feet stumble
On the dark *and* shadowy
mountains,
And while you are longing for
light
He turns it into the shadow of
death,
And makes it into thick darkness.
17 But if you will not listen *and* obey,
My soul will weep in secret for
your pride;
My eyes will weep bitterly
And flow with tears,
Because the LORD's flock has been
taken captive.
18 Say to the king and the queen
mother,
"Humble yourselves *and* take a
lowly seat,
For your beautiful crown [the
crown of your glory]
Has come down from your head."
19 The cities of the South (the Negev)
have been closed up,

13:6 – 7 *it was completely worthless.* Because Jeremiah's girdle was dirty and then was exposed to the elements, it was ruined and useless.

13:8 – 11 *who refuse to listen to My words, who walk in the stubborn way of their heart and have followed other gods.* As Jeremiah's waistband was ruined, so Judah's pride would be reduced to ruin. Pride describes the self-exalting conduct that characterized Israel in its love for idols. This pride is explained in a triplet of verbal phrases.

13:14 *I will smash them one against another.* The wine jars of God's wrath would be smashed and broken together, a picture of a devastated nation.

13:16 *Give glory to the LORD your God.* This means exalt and worship Him. The verse warns of the consequences of failing to glorify God. Four Hebrew synonyms for darkness are found in this verse, deepening the impression of divine displeasure meted out against God's people.

CHAPTER 13 **9** Lev 26:19 **10** Jer 9:14; 11:8; 16:12 **11** Ex 19:5; Jer 33:9 **13** Isa 51:17,21; 63:6; Jer 25:27; 51:7 **14** Ps 2:9 **16** Isa 5:30; 8:22; Am 8:9; Isa 59:9; Ps 44:19 **17** Jer 9:1; 14:17; La 1:2,16; 2:18 **18** 2Ki 24:12; Jer 22:26

And there is no one to open them;
All Judah has been carried into exile,
Completely carried away into exile.

20 "Lift up your eyes and see
Those coming from the north.
Where is the flock that was given to you [to shepherd],
Your beautiful flock?
21 "What will you say [O Jerusalem] when the LORD appoints [foreign nations to rule] over you—
Those former friends and allies whom you have encouraged [to be your companions]—
Will not pain seize you
Like [that of] a woman in childbirth?
22 "And if you [wonder and] say in your heart,
'Why have these things happened to me?'
It is because of the greatness *and* nature of your sin
That your skirts have been pulled away [subjecting you to public disgrace]
And [like a barefoot slave] your heels have been wounded.
23 "Can the Ethiopian change his skin
Or the leopard his spots?
Then you also can do good
Who are accustomed to evil *and* even trained to do it.
24 "Therefore I will scatter you like drifting straw
[Driven away] by the desert wind.
25 "This is your destiny, the portion [of judgment] measured to you
From Me," says the LORD,
"Because you have forgotten Me
And trusted in [pagan] lies [the counterfeit gods, and the pretense of alliance]."
26 "So I Myself will throw your skirts up over your face,
That your shame may be exposed [publicly].
27 "I have seen your vile *and* detestable acts,
Even your adulteries and your *lustful* neighings [after idols],
And the lewdness of your prostitution
On the hills in the fields.
Woe (judgment is coming) to you, O Jerusalem!
How long will you remain unclean [by ignoring My precepts]?"

Drought and a Prayer for Mercy

14 THE WORD of the LORD that came to Jeremiah concerning the drought:

2 "Judah mourns
And her gates languish;
Her people sit on the ground in mourning *clothes*
And the cry of Jerusalem has gone up.
3 "Their nobles have sent their servants for water;
They have come to the cisterns and found no water.
They have returned with empty vessels;
They have been shamed and humiliated,
And they cover their heads.
4 "The ground is cracked
Because there has been no rain on the land;
The farmers are distressed,

13:20 *Those coming from the north.* This phrase refers to Babylon.
13:23 *Can the Ethiopian change his skin.* The negative rhetorical question confirmed Judah's inability to change its own ways. The nation had reinforced its habit of doing evil (4:22) for so long that it did not know how to do good.
13:26 – 27 *your skirts up over your face.* This phrase meant public exposure (v. 22). Since Judah had lustfully sought adulterous relationships with foreign gods and goddesses, God would expose and bring to shame its actions.
14:2 *mourns.* This is a general word for grief over the dead. It describes the dark gloom of weeping and wailing.

20 Jer 6:22 **21** Jer 6:24 **22** Jer 16:10; Isa 3:17; 47:2,3; Eze 16:37-39; Na 3:5 **24** Ps 1:4; Hos 13:3 **25** Job 20:29; Ps 11:6; Jer 10:14 **26** La 1:8; Eze 16:37; Hos 2:10 **27** Jer 5:8; Isa 65:7; Jer 2:20 **CHAPTER 14 2** Isa 3:26; Jer 8:21; 1Sa 5:12 **3** Ps 40:14; 2Sa 15:30

And they have covered their heads
[in shame].
5 "The doe in the field has given
birth only to abandon *her young*
Because there is no grass.
6 "And the wild donkeys stand on
the barren heights;
They pant for air like jackals,
Their eyesight fails
Because there is no grass.
7 "O LORD, though our many sins
testify against us" [prays
Jeremiah],
"Act now [for us and] for Your
name's sake [so that the faithless
may witness Your faithfulness]!
For our backslidings are countless;
We have sinned against You.
8 "O Hope of Israel,
Her Savior in time of distress *and*
trouble,
Why should You be like a
sojourner (temporary resident)
in the land
Or like a traveler who turns aside
and spreads his tent to linger
[only] for a night?
9 "Why should You be [hesitant and
inactive] like a man astounded
and perplexed,
Like a mighty man unable to save?
Yet You, O LORD, are among us,
And we are called by Your name;
Do not leave us!"

10 Thus says the LORD to this peo-
ple [Judah], "In the manner *and* to
the degree [already pointed out] they
have loved to wander; they have not
restrained their feet. Therefore the
LORD does not accept them; He will
now remember [in detail] their wick-
edness and punish them for their sins."
11 So the LORD said to me, "Do not
pray for good things for this people.
12 "Though they fast, I will not hear
their cry; and though they offer burnt
offerings and grain offerings, I will not
accept them [because they are done
as obligations, and not as acts of lov-
ing obedience]. Instead I will consume
them by the sword, by famine, and by
pestilence."

False Prophets

13 But I said, "Alas, Lord GOD! Behold,
the [false] prophets are telling them,
'You will not see the sword nor will
you have famine, but I [the LORD] will
give you lasting peace in this place.' "
14 Then the LORD said to me, "The
[counterfeit] prophets are prophesying
lies in My Name. I have neither sent
them nor authorized them nor spoken
to them. They are prophesying to you
made-up visions [pretending to call
forth responses from handmade gods],
a worthless divination and the deceit
of their own mind.
15 "Therefore, thus says the LORD con-
cerning the [false] prophets who are
prophesying in My Name, although
I did not send them—yet they keep
saying, 'Sword and famine shall not
be in this land': by sword and famine
those prophets shall meet their end
and be consumed.
16 "And the people to whom they are
prophesying will be thrown out into
the streets of Jerusalem, victims of
famine and sword; and they will have

14:8 *Hope . . . Savior.* Jeremiah pleaded with God on the basis of God's name and character. Instead of having an intimate relationship with Judah, God had become like a stranger or a traveler in the land, because the people worshiped other gods.

14:10 *they have loved to wander.* "Loved" describes voluntary desire. "Wander" describes a repetitive back and forth movement — in this case, of seeking every possible occasion for sin. Because no one displayed any restraint from sin, God could not violate His holy character and accept the people of Judah.

14:13 *I [the Lord] will give you lasting peace.* Jeremiah complained to the Lord about false prophets who were proclaiming a message of peace instead of war and pestilence. These pretentious prophets presumed upon God's mercy and promise of deliverance as demonstrated in the days of Hezekiah and Isaiah, when Jerusalem was miraculously rescued from the siege of Sennacherib's army.

6 Jer 2:24 **7** Ps 25:11 **8** Jer 17:13 **9** Isa 59:1; Ex 29:45; Lev 26:11 **10** See Jer 2:23-25; Hos 8:13 **11** Ex 32:10 **12** Pr 1:28; Isa 1:15; Eze 8:18; Zec 7:13; Jer 6:20; Jer 9:16 **13** Jer 4:10 **14** Jer 27:10; Jer 29:8,9 **15** Jer 5:12 **16** Ps 79:3

no one to bury them—neither them, nor
their wives, nor their sons, nor their
daughters. For I will pour out their
[own] wickedness on them [and not
only on the imposters posing as proph-
ets, for the people could not have been
deceived without their own consent].

17 "Therefore [Jeremiah] you will say
this word to them,
'Let my eyes flow with tears night
and day,
And let them never cease;
For the virgin daughter of my
people has been crushed with a
great blow,
With a very serious *and* severely
infected wound.
18 'If I go out into the field,
Then I gaze on those slaughtered
with the sword!
And if I enter the city,
Then I gaze on [those tormented
with] the diseases of famine!
For both prophet and priest [who
should have guided the people]
Go about [bewildered and exiled]
in a land (Babylon) that they do
not know *or* understand.' "

19 Have You [O LORD] completely
rejected Judah?
Do You loathe Zion?
Why have You stricken us so that
there is no healing for us?
We looked for peace *and*
completeness, but nothing good
came;
And [we hoped] for a time of
healing, but behold, terror!
20 We know *and* acknowledge,
O LORD,
Our wickedness and the iniquity
of our fathers; for we have
sinned against You.
21 Do not treat us with contempt
and condemn us, for Your own
name's sake;
Do not disgrace Your glorious
throne;
Remember [with consideration]
and do not break Your [solemn]
covenant with us.
22 Are there any among the idols of
the nations who can send rain?
Or can the heavens [of their own
will] give showers?
Is it not You, O LORD our God?
Therefore we will wait *and* hope
[confidently] in You,
For You are the one who has made
all these things [the heavens and
the rain].

Judgment Must Come

15 THEN THE LORD said to me,
"Even though Moses and Samuel
were to stand before Me [interceding
for them], My heart would still not be
[turned with favor] toward this peo-
ple [Judah]. Send them away from My
presence *and* out of My sight and let
them go!
2 "And it shall be that when they say
to you, 'Where should we go?' then tell
them, 'Thus says the LORD:

"Those [destined] for death, to
death;
Those for the sword, to the sword;
Those for famine, to famine;
Those for captivity, to captivity." '

3 "I will appoint four kinds of destroy-
ers over them," says the LORD, "the
sword to slay, the dogs to tear *and* drag
away, and the birds of the air and the
beasts of the earth to devour and to
destroy.

14:21–22 *for Your own name's sake.* The people's plea for God's mercy was based on His character. Entreaties based on divine character and attributes are common in the Psalms. At stake was God's reputation and the blessing that would come to the people, but here the obligations of the people to the Lord are disregarded.
15:2 *death ... the sword ... famine ... captivity.* These all would be the outcome of God's judgment. He would use foreign armies as instruments of judgment (14:11–12).
15:3–4 *I will appoint four kinds of destroyers over them.* The judgment of Judah is described. The imagery of dogs, birds, and beasts devouring human flesh vividly illustrates not only death, but desecration. The basis for this desecration is the defilement of Jerusalem that took place during the reign of Manasseh, when

17 Jer 9:1; Jer 8:21 **18** Eze 7:15 **19** La 5:22; Jer 15:18; Jer 8:15 **20** Ps 106:6; Da 9:8 **21** Ps 106:45 **22** Zec 10:1; Dt 32:21; Ps 135:7 **CHAPTER 15** **1** Eze 14:14; Ex 32:11; Ps 99:6; 1Sa 7:9 **2** Eze 5:2; Zec 11:9 **3** Lev 26:16; Dt 28:26

4"I will make them an object of horror to all nations of the earth because of Manasseh [the despicable] son of Hezekiah, king of Judah, for the [evil and detestable] things which he did in Jerusalem. [2 Kin 21:1–18]

5"For who will have pity on you,
O Jerusalem,
Or who will mourn for you,
Or who will turn aside to ask
about your welfare?
6"You have abandoned (rejected)
Me," says the LORD.
"You keep going backward.
Therefore I shall stretch out My
hand against you and destroy
you;
I am tired of delaying [your
punishment]!
7"I will winnow (sort, separate)
them with a winnowing fork
At the gates of the land;
I will deprive them of children, I
will destroy My people;
They did not repent *and* turn from
their [evil] ways.
8"I will make their widows more
numerous before Me
Than the sand of the seas;
I will bring against them, against
the mother of the young men,
A destroyer at noonday;
I will suddenly cause anguish and
terror
To fall on her.
9"She who has borne seven [sons]
languishes;
She has breathed out her soul.
Her sun has set while it was still
day;
She has been shamed and
humiliated.
So I will hand over [the rest of] the
survivors to the sword
Before their enemies," says the
LORD.

10Woe to me, my mother, that you
have given birth to me
To be a man of strife and a man of
contention to all the earth!
I have not loaned, nor have men
lent money to me,
Yet everyone curses me.
[Jer 1:18, 19]
11The LORD said, "Surely [it will
go well for Judah's obedient
remnant for] I will set you free
for good *purposes;*
Surely [Jeremiah] I will [intercede
for you with the enemy and I
will] cause the enemy to plead
with you [for help]
In a time of disaster and a time of
distress. [Jer 21:1, 2; 37:3; 42:2;
Rom 8:28]
12"Can anyone crush iron,
The iron from the north, or
bronze?
13"Your [nation's] riches and your
treasures
I will give as plunder without price
[to the Babylonians],
Because of all your sins
And within all your territories.
14"Then I will make your enemies
bring [you along with] your
possessions
Into a land which you do not know
[for there you will serve your
conquerors];
For a fire has been kindled in My
anger,
Which will burn upon you."

---

idolatry reigned in the temple courts and children were sacrificed to Molech (7:31).

15:7–8 *I will winnow (sort, separate) them with a winnowing fork.* Like wheat chaff that is scattered by the winnowing fork and the wind, the people of Judah would be dispersed. The population would be decimated. The further ravaging of the land is revealed in the numerous widows who would be left in the wake of the death of the men of Judah.

15:9 *She who has borne seven.* The blessing of seven sons was the ultimate hope for ancient mothers and fathers. But the utmost horror was to lose all seven in death, resulting in the loss of an heir.

15:10 *everyone curses me.* To curse someone in ancient Israel was to invoke condemnation on that person with a prescribed formula.

4 Dt 28:25; 2Ki 24:3,4 **6** Jer 2:13; Jer 7:24; Hos 13:14 **9** 1Sa 2:5; Am 8:9 **10** Job 3:1 **11** Jer 40:4,5 **13** Ps 44:12 **14** Jer 16:13; Dt 32:22

Jeremiah's Prayer and God's Answer

15 O LORD, You know *and* understand;
Remember me [thoughtfully], take notice of me,
take vengeance for me on my persecutors.
Do not, in view of Your patience, take me away;
Know that for Your sake I endure [continual] rebuke *and* dishonor.
16 Your words were found and I ate them,
And Your words became a joy to me and the delight of my heart;
For I have been called by Your name,
O LORD God of hosts.
17 I did not sit with the group of those who celebrate,
Nor did I rejoice;
I sat alone because Your [powerful] hand was *upon me,*
For You had filled me with indignation [at their sin].
18 Why has my pain been perpetual
And my wound incurable, refusing to be healed?
Will you indeed be to me like a deceptive *brook*
With water that is unreliable?
19 Therefore, thus says the LORD [to Jeremiah],
"If you repent [and give up this mistaken attitude of despair and self-pity], then I will restore you [to a state of inner peace]
So that you may stand before Me [as My obedient representative];
And if you separate the precious from the worthless [examining yourself and cleansing your heart from unwarranted doubt concerning My faithfulness],
You will become My spokesman.
Let the people turn to you [and learn to value My values]—
But you, you must not turn to them [with regard for their idolatry and wickedness].
20 "And I will make you to this people
A fortified wall of bronze;
They will fight against you,
But they will not prevail over you,
For I am with you [always] to save you
And protect you," says the LORD.
21 "So I will rescue you out of the hand of the wicked,
And I will redeem you from the [grasping] palm of the terrible *and* ruthless [tyrant]."

Distresses Foretold

16 THE WORD of the LORD also came to me, saying,
2 "You shall not take a wife or have
sons and daughters in this place (Je-
rusalem)."
3 For thus says the LORD concerning
the sons and daughters who are born
in this place, and concerning the moth-
ers who give birth to them, and the
fathers who father them in this land:
4 "They will die of deadly diseases.
They will not be mourned or buried;
they will be like dung on the surface
of the ground and come to an end by
sword and famine, and their dead bod-
ies will be food for the birds of the air
and for the beasts of the earth."

15:16 *Your words were found and I ate them.* Eating the words of the Lord means to internalize them and allow their meaning to become a reality in one's life.
15:17 *I did not sit with the group of those who celebrate.* Jeremiah's isolation was the result of his obedience to the word and calling of God.
15:18 *With water that is unreliable.* This simile is a vivid picture of the arid regions in the Middle East, where water is at a premium.
16:1–2 *You shall not take a wife.* In the case of Jeremiah, the prohibition against marriage was both a sign to the nation and a blight against his name among the people. Celibacy was abnormal; large families were indicative of God's blessing upon a household. Jeremiah faced life with God as his sole comfort and support.

15 Jer 12:3; Jer 20:12; Ps 69:7 **16** Eze 3:1,3; Rev 10:9; Job 23:12; Ps 119:72 **17** Ps 26:4,5 **18** Jer 30:15; Jer 1:18,19 **19** Zec 3:7; ver. 1; Eze 22:26 **20** Jer 20:11 **CHAPTER 16** **4** Jer 15:2; Jer 22:18; 25:33; Ps 83:10; Jer 8:2; 9:22; Ps 79:2; Jer 7:33; 34:20

[5]For thus says the LORD, "Do not
enter a house of mourning, nor go to
lament (express grief) or bemoan [the
dead], for I have taken My peace away
from this people," says the LORD, "even
My lovingkindness and compassion.
[6]"Both great men and small will die
in this land; they will not be buried, nor
will they be lamented (mourned over
with expressions of grief in death), nor
will anyone cut himself or shave his
head for them [in mourning].
[7]"*People* will not offer food to the
mourners, to comfort anyone [as they
grieve] for the dead, nor give them a
cup of consolation to drink for any-
one's father or mother.
[8]"And you [Jeremiah] shall not go
into a house of feasting to sit with them
to eat and drink."
[9]For thus says the LORD of hosts, the
God of Israel, "Behold, I will remove
from this place, before your very eyes
and in your time, the sound of joy and
the shout of gladness, the voice of the
bridegroom and the voice of the bride.
[10]"Now when you tell these people
all these words and they ask you, 'Why
has the LORD decreed all this great
tragedy against us? And what is our
iniquity, what is the sin which we have
committed against the LORD our God?'
[11]"Then you are to say to them, 'It is
because your fathers have abandoned
(rejected) Me,' says the LORD, 'and
have walked after other gods and have
served them and bowed down to the
handmade idols and have abandoned
(rejected) Me and have not kept My law,
[12]and because you have done worse
[things] than your fathers. Just look,
every one of you walks in the stub-
bornness of his own evil heart, so that
you do not listen [obediently] to Me.
[13]'Therefore I will hurl you out of this
land [of Judah] into the land [of the Bab-
ylonians] which neither you nor your
fathers have known, and there you will
serve other gods day and night, for I
will show you no compassion.'

God Will Restore Them

[14]"Therefore behold, the days are
coming," says the LORD, "when it will
no longer be said, 'As the LORD lives,
who brought up the sons of Israel out
of the land of Egypt,'
[15]but, 'As the LORD lives, who brought
up the sons of Israel from the land of
the north and from all the countries to
which He had driven them.' And I will
bring them back to their land which I
gave to their fathers.
[16]"Behold (listen carefully), I will
send for many fishermen," says the
LORD, "and they will fish for them; and
afterward I will send for many hunters,
and they will hunt them from every
mountain and from every hill and out
of the clefts of the rocks.
[17]"For My eyes are on all their ways;
they are not hidden from My face, nor
is their wickedness concealed from
My eyes.
[18]"I will first doubly repay *and* pun-
ish them for their wickedness and their
sin [before I return them to their land],
because they have profaned My land;
they have filled My inheritance with
the carcasses of their detestable idols
and with their abominations."

[19][Then said Jeremiah] "O LORD, my
Strength and my Stronghold,

16:10 *Why has the LORD decreed.* The trio of questions posed by the people indicates their lack of understanding of God's word. The people of Judah had missed the purpose for which they were chosen, to manifest to the world the nature and character of God by living as the people of God.

16:16 *many fishermen ... many hunters.* These words refer to the Babylonian armies that would scour the land for Judah's rebels. Hunting and fishing imagery as a metaphor for deportation is also found in Ezekiel 12:3 and Amos 4:2.

16:19 – 20 *Strength ... Stronghold ... Refuge.* Jeremiah knew that his only place of safety was in God. The scope of Jeremiah's hope is universal. The Gentiles, among whom the people of Judah would be exiled, would come to the God of Israel in fulfillment of the promise of Genesis 12:1 – 3.

5 Eze 24:17,22,23 **6** Jer 22:18; Lev 19:28; Dt 14:1; Jer 41:5; 47:5; Isa 22:12; Jer 7:29 **7** Pr 31:6 **9** Isa 24:7,8; Eze 26:13; Hos 2:11; Rev 18:23 **10** Dt 29:24; Jer 5:19 **11** Dt 29:25; Jer 22:9 **12** Jer 7:26; Jer 13:10 **13** Dt 4:26; 28:36,63; Jer 15:14 **14** Isa 43:18; Jer 23:7,8 **15** Jer 24:6; 30:3; 32:37 **16** Am 4:2; Hab 1:15 **17** Job 34:21; Pr 5:21; 15:3; Jer 32:19 **18** Isa 40:2; Jer 17:18; Eze 43:7 **19** Ps 18:2; Jer 17:17; Isa 44:10; Jer 10:5

And my Refuge in the day of
distress *and* need,
The nations will come to You
From the ends of the earth and
say,
'Our fathers have inherited
nothing but lies *and* illusion,
[Worthless] things in which there
is no benefit!'
20 "Can a man make gods for
himself?
Such [things] are not gods!
21 "Therefore," [says the LORD]
"behold, I will make them
know—
This time I will make them know
My power and My might;
And they will know *and* recognize
[without any doubt] that My
Name is the LORD."

The Deceitful Heart

17 THE SIN of Judah is written
down with an iron stylus;
With a diamond point it is
engraved upon the tablet of their
heart
And on the horns of their altars.
2 As they remember their children,
So they *remember* [in detail]
their [pagan] altars and their
Asherim
Beside green trees on the high
hills.
3 O [Jerusalem] My mountain in the
countryside,
I will give [to the Babylonians,
as the cost of your sin] your
wealth and all your treasures as
plunder,
And throughout your territory,
your high places of sin.
4 And you will, through your own
fault, let go of your [grip on
your] inheritance
That I gave you;
And I will make you serve your
enemies
In a land which you do not know;
For you have kindled a fire in My
anger
Which will burn forever.
5 Thus says the LORD,
"Cursed is the man who trusts in
and relies on mankind,
Making [weak, faulty human]
flesh his strength,
And whose mind *and* heart turn
away from the LORD.
6 "For he will be like a shrub in the
[parched] desert;
And shall not see prosperity when
it comes,
But shall live in the rocky places of
the wilderness,
In an uninhabited salt land.
7 "Blessed [with spiritual security] is
the man who believes *and* trusts
in *and* relies on the LORD
And whose hope *and* confident
expectation is the LORD.
8 "For he will be [nourished] like a
tree planted by the waters,
That spreads out its roots by the
river;
And will not fear the heat when it
comes;
But its leaves will be green *and*
moist.
And it will not be anxious *and*
concerned in a year of
drought
Nor stop bearing fruit.

17:3 *your high places of sin.* Jerusalem and the other cities of Judah were demolished and plundered by the Babylonians. The remaining treasures of the temple of God were carried by Nebuchadnezzar's army to Babylon. Even the idolatrous cultic centers were destroyed (15:13–14).

17:4 *let go of your [grip on your] inheritance.* This phrase, when used in the context of land, usually refers to letting the land lie fallow during the sabbatical year (Ex 23:10–11). Judah's captivity would provide rest for the land from the idolatrous activities of its people.

17:5 *Cursed is the man.* One cannot trust in both God and humankind.

17:7 *Blessed [with spiritual security] is the man who believes . . . on the LORD.* The basic element in a life of faith is stability. Man depending upon his own strength is unstable. But faith in God brings stability.

20 Isa 37:19; Jer 2:11; Gal 4:8 **21** Ex 15:3; Jer 33:2; Am 5:8 **CHAPTER 17** **1** Job 19:24; Pr 3:3; 2Co 3:3 **2** Jdg 3:7; 2Ch 24:18; 33:3,19; Jer 2:20 **4** Jer 16:13; Jer 15:14 **5** Isa 30:1,2; 31:1; See Isa 31:3 **6** Jer 48:6; Job 20:17; Dt 29:23 **7** Ps 2:12; 34:8; Pr 16:20; Isa 30:18 **8** Job 8:16; Ps 1:3

9 "The heart is deceitful above all things
And it is extremely sick;
Who can understand it fully
and know its secret motives?
[Matt 13:15–17; Mark 7:21–23; Eph 4:20–24]
10 "I, the LORD, search *and* examine the mind,
I test the heart,
To give to each man according to his ways,
According to the results of his deeds.
11 "Like the partridge that hatches eggs which she has not laid,
So is he who makes a fortune in ways that are unjust.
It will be lost to him before his days are over,
And in the end he will be [nothing but] a fool."

12 A glorious throne, set on high from the beginning,
Is the place of our sanctuary (the temple).
13 O LORD, the hope of Israel,
All who abandon You will be shamed.
Those who turn away on earth will be written down,
Because they have abandoned the LORD, the fountain of living waters.
14 Heal me, O LORD, and I will be healed;
Save me and I will be saved,
For You are my praise.
15 Behold, they keep saying to me,
"Where is the word of the LORD [that is, the disaster that you prophesied]?
Let it come now!"
16 But as for me, I have not tried to escape from being a shepherd [walking] after You,
Nor have I longed for the woeful day [of judgment];
You know that, whatever I said
Was [spoken] in Your presence *and* was from You.
17 Do not be a terror to me;
You are my refuge *and* my hope in the day of disaster.
18 Let those who persecute me be shamed, but as for me, protect me from shame;
Let them lose courage, but let me be undaunted.
Bring on them a day of tragedy,
And destroy them with double destruction!

The Sabbath Must Be Kept

19 Thus the LORD said to me, "Go and
stand in the public gate, through which
the kings of Judah come in and go
out, and [stand] also in all the gates of
Jerusalem;
20 and say to them, 'Listen to the word
of the LORD, kings of Judah, and all
Judah, and all the people of Jerusalem
who enter through these gates.
21 'Thus says the LORD, "Pay attention
for your own good, [and for the sake of

17:11 *Like the partridge that hatches eggs which she has not laid.* The teaching of Jeremiah 17:1 – 10 is supported by a proverb based on the common belief that the partridge hatched eggs other than its own. When the young birds recognized that the partridge was not their mother, they would leave her. Similarly, a man who unjustly gains wealth will be abandoned by the wealth and then be known as a fool.

17:12 – 13 *A glorious throne, set on high.* This phrase refers to the temple in Jerusalem and the ark of the covenant, the symbol of God's presence and sovereignty over the nations.

17:17 *Do not be a terror to me.* This refers to physical, emotional, or mental horror.

17:18 *Let those who persecute me be shamed.* Jeremiah called for his persecutors to be ashamed and dismayed, to be dishonored and demoralized. The prophet also called upon the Lord to confirm the message of judgment in the day of doom and double destruction.

17:21 – 22 *Pay attention for your own good.* This same phrasing is used in Deuteronomy 4:15 in a warning against idolatry. The sanctity of the Sabbath was a most serious matter. The Sabbath stood as a sign of creation and the covenant relationship between God and Israel.

10 1Sa 16:7; 1Ch 28:9; Ps 7:9; 139:23,24; Pr 17:3; Jer 20:12; Ro 8:27; Rev 2:23; Ps 62:12; Jer 32:19; Ro 2:6 **11** Ps 55:23; Lk 12:20 **13** Jer 14:8; Ps 73:27; Isa 1:28; See Lk 10:20; Jer 2:13 **14** Dt 10:21; Ps 109:1; 148:14 **15** Isa 5:19; Eze 12:22; Am 5:18; 2Pe 3:4 **16** Jer 1:4 **17** Jer 16:19 **18** Ps 35:4; 70:2; Ps 25:2; Jer 11:20 **20** Jer 19:3 **21** Nu 15:32; Neh 13:19

your future] do not carry any load on the Sabbath day or bring anything in through the gates of Jerusalem.

22“You shall not carry a load out of your houses on the Sabbath day nor do any work, but keep the Sabbath day holy [by setting it apart as a day of worship], as I commanded your fathers.

23“Yet they would not listen *and* obey *and* control their behavior; but they were stiff-necked in order not to hear and take instruction.

24“But it will come about, if you listen diligently to Me,” says the LORD, “to bring no load in through the gates of this city on the Sabbath day, but keep the Sabbath day holy by doing no work on it,

25then kings and princes who will sit on the throne of David will enter through the gates of this city, riding in chariots and on horses—the kings and their princes, the men of Judah and the inhabitants of Jerusalem; and this city will be inhabited *and* endure throughout the ages.

26“People will come from the cities of Judah and the places all around Jerusalem, from the land of Benjamin, from the lowland, from the hill country and from the South (the Negev), bringing burnt offerings and sacrifices, grain offerings and incense, and bringing sacrifices of thanksgiving to the house of the LORD.

27“But if you will not listen to Me and keep the Sabbath day holy by not carrying a load as you come in the gates of Jerusalem on the Sabbath day, then I will kindle a fire in her gates that cannot be extinguished, and it will devour the palaces of Jerusalem.” ’ ”

The Potter and the Clay

18 THE WORD which came to Jeremiah from the LORD:

2“Arise and go down to the potter’s house, and there I will make you hear My words.”

3Then I went down to the potter’s house, and saw that he was working at the wheel.

4But the vessel that he was making from clay was spoiled by the potter’s hand; so he made it over, reworking it and making it into another pot that seemed good to him.

5Then the word of the LORD came to me:

6“O house of Israel, can I not do with you as this potter does?” says the LORD. “Look carefully, as the clay is in the potter’s hand, so are you in My hand, O house of Israel.

7“At one moment I might [suddenly] speak concerning a nation or kingdom, that I will uproot and break down and destroy;

8if that nation against which I have spoken turns from its evil, I will relent *and* reverse My decision concerning the devastation that I intended to do.

9“Or at another time I might [suddenly] speak about a nation or kingdom that I will build up or establish;

10and if they do evil in My sight by not obeying My voice, then I will reverse My decision concerning the good with which I had promised to bless them.

11“Now then, say to the men of Judah and to the citizens of Jerusalem, ‘Thus says the LORD, “Behold, I am shaping a disaster and working out a plan against you. Turn back, each of you from his evil way; correct your habits and change your actions for the better.” ’

12“But they will say, ‘That is hopeless! For we are going to follow our own plans, and each of us will act in accordance with the stubbornness of his evil heart.’

13“Therefore thus says the LORD,
‘Ask now among the nations,

18:4–6 *was spoiled by the potter’s hand.* The potter’s vessel was spoiled and thus unsuitable for its intended purpose. The potter’s remolding of the clay into an acceptable and unblemished work symbolized God’s action in reforming Israel. The people had become marred and defiled and had to be reformed into a vessel fit to be identified with the Lord.

22 Ex 20:8; 31:13; Eze 20:12 **23** Jer 7:24,26 **25** Jer 22:4 **26** Jer 33:13; Zec 7:7; Ps 107:22; 116:17 **27** Jer 21:14; La 4:11; Am 1:4,7,10,12; 2Ki 25:9; Jer 52:13 **CHAPTER 18** **6** Isa 45:9; Ro 9:20; Isa 64:8 **7** Jer 1:10 **8** Eze 18:21; 33:11; Jer 26:3; Jnh 3:10 **11** 2Ki 17:13; Jer 7:3 **12** Jer 2:25 **13** Jer 2:10; 1Co 5:1; Jer 5:30

Who has heard of such things?
The virgin Israel
Has done a very vile *and* horrible thing.
14 'Will the snow of [Mount] Lebanon melt *and* vanish from its rocks [which tower above Israel]?
Will the cold, rushing waters of foreign *lands* [that flow down from the distant land] be dried up?
15 'Yet My people have forgotten Me;
They burn incense to worthless gods,
They have stumbled from their ways
From the ancient roads,
To walk in pathways,
Not on a highway,
16 Making their land a desolation *and* a horror,
A thing to be hissed at perpetually;
Everyone who passes by will be astounded
And shake his head [in scorn].
17 'I will scatter them like an east wind
Before the enemy;
I will show them My back and not My face
In the day of their disaster [says the LORD].' "

18 Then [my enemies] said, "Come
and let us work out schemes against
Jeremiah. Surely the law is not going
to be lost to the priest [as Jeremiah
predicts], nor the counsel from the
wise, nor the word from the prophet.
Come and let us strike him with our
tongue [by making charges against
him before the king], and let us ignore
anything he says."

19 Pay attention to me, O LORD [and intercede];
Listen to what my adversaries are saying [and are plotting against me]—
20 Should good be repaid with evil?
Yet they have dug a pit for me.
Remember [with compassion] that I stood before You
To speak good on their behalf,
To turn Your anger away from them.
21 Therefore, give their children over to the famine;
Give them over to the power of the sword.
And let their wives become childless and widowed;
Let their men meet death [by virulent disease],
Their young men be struck down by the sword in battle.
22 Let an outcry be heard from their houses
When You suddenly bring [a troop of] raiders upon them,
For they have dug a pit to capture me
And have hidden snares for my feet.
23 Yet You, O LORD, know
All their deadly plotting against me;
Do not forgive their wickedness
Or blot out their sin from Your sight.
But let them be overthrown before You;
Deal with them in the time of Your anger.

18:13 – 14 *Who has heard of such things?* Negative rhetorical questions show the absurdity of Israel's rebellion. ***snow of [Mount] Lebanon.*** This describes the Mount Hermon watershed that erupts in numerous springs, providing most of the water for the Jordan River. God's blessing was often demonstrated in the provision of water from rocks in arid regions (Ex 17:6).
18:15 *burn incense to worthless gods.* Foreign deities such as Baal and Asherah were represented by empty and ineffective cultic figurines.
18:17 *like an east wind.* This line refers to the scorching late-spring scirocco wind from the northern Arabian desert.
18:19 – 20 *Yet they have dug a pit for me.* Jeremiah reminded the Lord how he had interceded for the people and had asked God to turn away His wrath and judgment. But instead of showing their appreciation for Jeremiah's intervention, the people prepared his grave.

15 Jer 2:13,32; Jer 6:16 **16** Jer 19:8; 1Ki 9:8; La 2:15; Mic 6:16 **17** Jer 13:24; Ps 48:7; See Jer 2:27 **18** Jer 11:19; Lev 10:11; Mal 2:7; Jn 7:48 **20** Ps 109:4; ver. 22; Ps 35:7 **21** Ps 109:9 **22** ver. 20 **23** Ps 35:4; 109:14; Jer 11:20

The Broken Jar

19 THUS SAYS the LORD, "Go and buy a potter's earthenware jar, and take some of the elders of the people and some of the senior priests

2 and go out to the Valley of Ben-hinnom (son of Hinnom), which is near the entrance of the Potsherd Gate; and proclaim there the words that I tell you,

3 and say, 'Hear the word of the LORD, O kings of Judah and inhabitants of Jerusalem. Thus says the Lord of hosts, the God of Israel, "Behold (listen carefully), I am going to bring such disaster on this place that the ears of everyone who hears about it will tingle [in shock].

4 "Because the people [of Jerusalem] have abandoned (rejected) Me and have made this an alien *and* profaned place by burning sacrifices *and* incense in it to other gods, that neither they nor their fathers nor the kings of Judah ever knew, and because they have filled this place with the blood of the innocent

5 and have built the high places of Baal to burn their sons in the fire as burnt offerings to Baal, which I never commanded or spoke of, nor did it ever enter My mind (heart);

6 therefore, listen very closely, the days are coming," says the LORD, "when this place shall no longer be called Topheth or the Valley of Ben-hinnom, but the Valley of Slaughter. [Jer 7:31–32]

7 "I will pour out *and* nullify the counsel (plans) of [the men of] Judah and Jerusalem in this place, and I will make their people fall by the sword before their enemies and by the hand of those who seek their lives; and I will give their dead bodies as food for the birds of the air and for the beasts of the earth.

8 "I will make this city a desolation and an *object of* hissing; everyone who passes by it will be amazed and will hiss [in scorn] because of all its plagues *and* disasters.

9 "And I will make them eat the flesh of their sons and their daughters, and each one will eat one another's flesh during the siege and distress brought by their enemies and those who seek their lives." '

10 "Then you are to break the jar in the sight of the men who accompany you,

11 and say to them, 'Thus says the LORD of hosts, "This is the way I will break this people and this city as one breaks a potter's vessel, so that it cannot be mended. They will bury [corpses] in Topheth until there is no more room left [in that place] to bury [the dead].

12 "This I will do to this place," says the LORD, "and to its inhabitants; and I will even make this city like Topheth.

13 "The houses of Jerusalem and the houses of the kings of Judah will be defiled like this place, Topheth, all the houses on whose rooftops incense has been burned to all the host of heaven (sun, moon, stars), and where drink offerings have been poured out to other gods." ' " [Acts 7:42, 43]

14 Then Jeremiah came from Topheth, where the LORD had sent him

---

19:3 ***Hear the word of the LORD.*** This key word of the Deuteronomic code (Dt 6:4) calls for a decision regarding the content of the message. ***the ears . . . will tingle.*** This expression is used to refer to a harsh, ringing judgment announcement (1Sa 3:11).

19:4–5 ***the blood of the innocent.*** This phrase refers to the murderous act of child sacrifice (7:31). Human sacrifice was known among the Phoenicians, Moabites, and Canaanites. This abominable practice, performed in the name of religious worship, was explicitly forbidden in the covenant (Dt 12:31).

19:9 ***I will make them eat the flesh of their sons.*** The gruesome practice of cannibalism appears, recalling the words of Deuteronomy 28:53. After years of siege resulting in severe famine, the people would resort to eating human flesh in order to survive. This prophecy was literally fulfilled in 586 BC when Nebuchadnezzar

CHAPTER 19 **2** Jos 15:8; 2Ki 23:10 **3** Jer 17:20; 1Sa 3:11; 2Ki 21:12 **4** Dt 28:20; Isa 65:11; 2Ki 21:16; Jer 2:34 **5** Jer 7:31; 32:35; Lev 18:21 **6** Jos 15:8 **7** Lev 26:17; Dt 28:25; Ps 79:2; Jer 7:33; 16:4; 34:20 **8** Jer 18:16; 49:13; 50:13 **9** Lev 26:29; Dt 28:53; Isa 9:20; La 4:10 **10** Jer 51:63,64 **11** Ps 2:9; Isa 30:14; La 4:2; Jer 7:32 **13** 2Ki 23:10,12; Jer 32:29; Zep 1:5; Jer 7:18 **14** See 2Ch 20:5

to prophesy; and he stood in the court
of the LORD's house and said to all the
people:
15 "Thus says the LORD of hosts, the
God of Israel, 'Behold, I am going to
bring on this city and on all its towns,
all the devastation that I have declared
against it, because they have become
stiff-necked and refused to hear *and*
obey My words.' "

Pashhur Persecutes Jeremiah

20 NOW PASHHUR the son of Im-
mer, the priest, who was [also]
chief officer in the house of the LORD,
heard Jeremiah prophesying these
things.
2 Then Pashhur beat Jeremiah the
prophet and put him in the stocks that
were at the upper Benjamin Gate by
the house of the LORD. [Jer 1:19; 15:15]
3 And the next day Pashhur brought
Jeremiah out of the stocks. Then Jere-
miah said to him, "The LORD does not
call your name Pashhur, but Magor-
missabib (terror on every side).
4 "For thus says the LORD, 'Behold,
I will make you a terror to yourself
and to all your friends; they will fall
by the sword of their enemies while
you look on. And I will give all Judah
into the hand of the king of Babylon;
he will carry them away to Babylon as
captives and will slaughter them with
the sword.
5 'Moreover, I will hand over all the
riches of this city, all the result of its
labor, all its precious things; even all
the treasures of the kings of Judah I
will hand over to their enemies, and
they will plunder them, and take them
away and carry them to Babylon.
6 'And you, Pashhur, and all who live
in your house will go into captivity;
you will go to Babylon, and there you
will die and be buried, you and all
your friends to whom you have falsely
prophesied.' "

Jeremiah's Complaint

7 [Jeremiah said,] O LORD, You
have persuaded me and I was
deceived;
You are stronger than I and You
have prevailed.
I am a laughingstock all day long;
Everyone mocks me.
8 For whenever I speak, I must shout
out;
I shout violence and destruction,
Because the word of the LORD has
become to me
A reprimand and a mockery *and*
has brought me insult all day
long.
9 If I say, "I will not remember Him
Or speak His name anymore,"
Then my heart becomes a burning
fire
Shut up in my bones.
And I am weary of enduring *and*
holding it in;

---

invaded Judah, and again in AD 70 when Titus destroyed Jerusalem.

20:1 ***Pashur . . . chief officer.*** A person in this position had to be a priest. He had oversight of the temple, the temple guards, entry into the courts, and so on. Jeremiah's proclamations against the city and the temple were of grave concern to Pashur because of the threat to the continuation of the cult in which he was involved.

20:2 ***upper Benjamin Gate.*** This portal provided access into the temple courtyards from the north, the direction of Benjamin's territory.

20:3–4 ***Magor-missabib.*** This means "terror on every side." As Pashur had been a terror to Jeremiah, so he would become a terror to himself, his family, and his associates.

20:6 ***Pashur, and all who live in your house.*** Pashur's whole family and his close associates, who had opposed Jeremiah, would be deported to Babylon because Pashur had prophesied lies. Pashur apparently had announced that Jerusalem would not suffer destruction.

20:7 ***You have persuaded me and I was deceived.*** A play on words is intended by using two forms of the same word, which means "to entice." Jeremiah claimed that the Lord had seduced him and that he had succumbed to the temptation.

20:8 ***the word of the LORD has become to me A reprimand and a mockery.*** Jeremiah had faithfully proclaimed the Lord's word of judgment and destruction, but the prophecy had not been fulfilled, thus opening the prophet up to criticism.

15 Jer 7:26; 17:23 **CHAPTER 20** **1** 1Ch 24:14 **5** 2Ki 20:17; 24:12-16; 25:13; Jer 3:24 **6** Jer 14:13,14; 28:15; 29:21 **7** Jer 1:6,7; La 3:14 **8** Jer 6:7 **9** Job 32:18,19; Ps 39:3; Job 32:18; Ac 18:5

I cannot endure it [nor contain it
any longer].
10 For I have heard the whispering
and defaming words of many,
"Terror on every side!
Denounce him! Let us denounce
him!"
All my familiar *and* trusted
friends,
[Those who are] watching for my
fall, say,
"Perhaps he will be persuaded *and*
deceived; then we will overcome
him,
And take our revenge on him."
11 But the LORD is with me as a dread
champion [one to be greatly
feared];
Therefore my persecutors will
stumble and not overcome [me].
They will be completely shamed,
for they have not acted wisely
and have failed [in their
schemes];
Their eternal dishonor will never
be forgotten.
12 But, O LORD of hosts, You who
examine the righteous,
Who see the heart and the mind,
Let me see Your vengeance on
them;
For to You I have committed my
cause.
13 Sing to the LORD! Praise the LORD!
For He has rescued the life of the
needy one
From the hand of evildoers.

14 Cursed be the day on which I was
born;
Do not bless the day on which my
mother gave birth to me!
15 Cursed be the man who brought
the news
To my father, saying,
"A son has been born to you!"
Making him very glad.
16 And let that man be like the cities
Which the LORD overthrew
without regret.
Let him hear an outcry in the
morning
And a shout of alarm at noon;
17 Because he did not kill me before
my birth,
So that my mother might have
been my grave,
And her womb always pregnant.
18 Why did I come out of the womb
To see trouble and sorrow,
So that my days have been filled
with shame?

Jeremiah's Message for Zedekiah

21 THE WORD which came to Jere-
miah from the LORD when King
Zedekiah sent to him Pashhur the son
of Malchijah, and Zephaniah the priest
the son of Maaseiah, saying,
2 "Please inquire of the LORD for us,
because Nebuchadnezzar king of Bab-
ylon is making war against us. Perhaps
the LORD will deal [favorably] with us
according to all His wonderful works
and force him to withdraw from us."
3 Then Jeremiah said to them, "Say
this to Zedekiah:
4 'Thus says the LORD, the God of Is-
rael, "Behold, I will turn back *and* dull
the edge of the weapons of war that are
in your hands, [those] with which you
fight against the king of Babylon and
the Chaldeans who are besieging you
outside the walls; and I will bring them
into the center of this city (Jerusalem).
5 "I Myself will fight against you

20:11 *the LORD is with me.* In order for a prophet to endure the pain and suffering that goes with the job, he needs to be aware of God's presence, power and approval.
20:12 *who examine the righteous.* God tests (6:27; 17:10) and judges the righteous, those who walk uprightly in His ways and truth.
20:14–15 *Cursed be the day.* In ancient Israel, to curse God or one's parents was an offense punishable by death. Jeremiah avoided committing a capital offense by cursing his conception and birth, and hence his call from God.
21:2 *inquire of the LORD.* This phrase means to seek His will.
21:5 *with an outstretched hand.* Because the people of Judah had become God's enemies, God

10 Ps 31:13; Job 19:19; Ps 41:9; 55:13,14; Lk 11:53,54 **11** Jer 15:20; 17:18; Jer 23:40 **12** Jer 11:20; 17:10; Ps 54:7; 59:10 **13** Ps 35:9,10; 109:30,31 **14** Job 3:3; Jer 15:10 **16** Ge 19:25; Jer 18:22 **17** Job 3:10,11 **18** Job 3:20; La 3:1 **CHAPTER 21** **1** Jer 38:1; 2Ki 25:18; Jer 29:25; 37:3 **2** Jer 37:3,7 **4** Isa 13:4 **5** Ex 6:6

with an outstretched hand and with a strong arm in anger, in fury, and in great indignation *and* wrath.

6 "I will also strike the inhabitants of this city, both man and beast; they will die of a great virulent disease.

7 "Then afterward," says the LORD, "I will hand over Zedekiah king of Judah and his servants and the people in this city who survive the virulent disease, the sword, and the famine, to Nebuchadnezzar king of Babylon, and into the hand of their enemy, into the hand of those who seek their lives. And he will strike them with the edge of the sword; he will not spare them nor have mercy and compassion on them." '

8 "And to this people you (Jeremiah) shall also say, 'Thus says the LORD, "Behold, I set before you the way of life and the way of death.

9 "He who remains in this city [of Jerusalem] will die by the sword and by famine and by virulent disease. But he who goes outside and surrenders to the Chaldeans who are besieging you will live, and his life will be like a prize of war to him.

10 "For I have set My face against this city to do harm and not good," says the LORD. "It shall be given into the hand of the king of Babylon and he will burn it with fire." '

11 "And concerning the royal house of the king of Judah [you shall say], 'Hear the word of the LORD,

12 O house of David, thus says the LORD:

"Administer justice in the morning,
And rescue the one who has been
robbed from the hand of his
oppressor,
That My wrath will not roar up
like fire
And burn so [hotly] that none can
extinguish it,
Because of the evil of their deeds.

13 "Understand this, I am against
you, O inhabitant of the valley,
O rock of the plain," says the
LORD—
"You who say, 'Who will come
down against us?
Or who will enter into our
dwelling places?'
14 "But I will punish you in
accordance with the
[appropriate] consequences
of your decisions *and* your
actions," says the LORD.
"I will kindle a fire in your forest,
And it will devour all that is
around you." ' "

Warning of Jerusalem's Fall

22 THUS SAYS the LORD, "Go down to the house of the king of Judah and speak this word there:

2 'Hear the word of the LORD, O king of Judah, you who sit on the throne of

---

would fight against them. The divine instruments by which Israel had gained freedom from Egypt (Ex 15:6; Dt 6:21) and deliverance from their enemies would be used against them.

21:8 – 9 ***way of life and the way of death.*** Death would come to those who attempted to survive the siege of Jerusalem; life was possible through surrender to the Chaldeans (Babylonians).

21:10 ***For I have set My face.*** This phrase describes the fixed intention of God, which in this context was against Jerusalem. The result would be adversity rather than good.

21:13 ***come down against us.*** Attacking armies generally approached Jerusalem from the north along an elevated ridge.

22:1 ***Go . . . king of Judah . . . speak this word there.*** This is the first of three messages directed at specific kings of Judah. Shallum, the fourth son of Josiah, was placed on the throne by the people of Judah, but he was dethroned after three months by Pharaoh-necho. Shallum was imprisoned and taken captive to Egypt (2Ch 36:1 – 4). Eliakim (Jehoiakim), Shallum's brother, was placed on the throne as an Egyptian vassal. Necho maintained control of Palestine until Nebuchadnezzar defeated Egypt at the Battle of Carchemish in 605 BC. Shallum died without returning from Egypt, in fulfillment of Jeremiah's prophecy.

22:2 ***who sit on the throne of David.*** Jeremiah's prophecy was addressed to three groups: the kings who are of David's lineage, the kings' servants, and "your people who enter by these

---

7 Jer 37:17; 39:5; 52:9; Dt 28:50; 2Ch 36:17 **8** Dt 30:19 **9** Jer 38:2,17,18; Jer 39:18; 45:5 **10** Lev 17:10; Jer 44:11; Am 9:4; Jer 38:3; Jer 34:2,22; 37:10; 38:18,23; 52:13 **12** Jer 22:3; Zec 7:9; Ps 101:8 **13** Eze 13:8; Jer 49:4 **14** Pr 1:31; Isa 3:10,11; 2Ch 36:19; Jer 52:13 **CHAPTER 22** **2** Jer 17:20

David—you and your servants and
your people who enter by these gates.
3 ‘Thus says the LORD, “Execute jus-
tice and righteousness, and rescue
the one who has been robbed from
the hand of his oppressor. And do no
wrong; do no violence to the stranger,
the fatherless, or the widow, nor shed
innocent blood in this place.
4 “For if you will indeed obey this
word, then kings will enter through the
gates of this palace, sitting in David’s
place on his throne, riding in chariots
and on horses, *even the king* himself
and his servants and his people.
5 “But if you will not hear *and* obey
these words, I swear [an oath] by My-
self,” says the LORD, “that this house
will become a desolation.” ’ ”
6 For thus says the LORD in regard to
the house of the king of Judah:

“You are [as valuable] to Me as
  [the green pastures of] Gilead
  [east of the Jordan]
Or as the [plentiful] summit of
  Lebanon [west of the Jordan],
Yet most certainly [if you will not
  listen to Me] I will make you a
  wilderness,
And uninhabited cities.
7 “For I will prepare *and* appoint
  destroyers [to execute My
  judgments] against you,
Each with his weapons;
And they will cut down your
  [palaces built of] choicest cedars
And throw them in the fire.

8 “Many nations will pass by this
city; and each man will say to another,
‘Why has the LORD done this to this
great city?’
9 “Then they will answer, ‘Because
the people ignored *and* abandoned
the [solemn] covenant with the LORD
their God and worshiped other gods
and served them.’ ”

10 Do not weep for the dead or mourn
  for him;
But weep bitterly for the one who
  goes away [into exile],
For he will never return
And see his native country [again].

11 For thus says the LORD in regard
to Shallum (Jehoahaz) the [third] son
of Josiah, king of Judah, who reigned
instead of Josiah his father and who
went from this place, “Shallum will
not return here anymore;
12 he will die in the place where they
led him captive and not see this land
again.

Messages about the Kings

13 “Woe (judgment is coming) to him
  who builds his house by [acts of]
  unrighteousness
And his upper chambers by
  injustice,
Who uses his neighbor’s service
  without pay
And does not give him wages [for
  his work],
14 Who says, ‘I will build myself a
  spacious house
With large upper rooms,
And cut out its [wide] windows,

---

gates.” The last phrase may refer to the citizens in general or to personnel who regularly entered the palace gates.

22:3 *Execute justice and righteousness.* For all practical purposes these two terms are synonymous. One could not have one without the other.

22:6–7 *Gilead ... Lebanon.* The territories were sources for timber for the royal palaces. These luxurious residences would be reduced to deserted wilderness and set ablaze if the kings disobeyed the covenant.

22:9 *worshiped other gods.* The pagan nations would recognize that the destruction of Jerusalem was the result of Judah’s violation of its covenant with God. The people of Judah had exchanged their God for alien deities, whom they worshiped and served.

22:13 *Who uses his neighbor’s service without pay.* The king was supposed to be the guardian of his people, but Jehoiakim enslaved his fellow Israelites to build his self-aggrandizing palaces.

3 Jer 21:12 **4** Jer 17:25 **5** Heb 6:13,17 **7** Isa 37:24; Jer 21:14 **8** Dt 29:24,25; 1Ki 9:8,9 **9** 2Ki 22:17; 2Ch 34:25 **10** 2Ki 22:20; ver. 11 **11** See 1Ch 3:15, with 2Ki 23:30; 2Ki 23:34 **13** ver. 18; 2Ki 23:35; Lev 19:13; Dt 24:14,15; Mic 3:10; Hab 2:9; Jas 5:4

And panel it with cedar and paint
it vermilion.'
15 "Do you think that you become
a king because you have much
more cedar [in your palace than
Solomon]?
Did not your father [Josiah], as he
ate and drank,
Do just and righteous acts [being
upright and in right standing
with God]?
Then all was well with him.
16 "He defended the cause of the
afflicted and needy;
Then all was well.
Is that not what it means to know
Me?"
Says the LORD.
17 "But your eyes and your heart
Are only intent on your own
dishonest gain,
On shedding innocent blood,
On oppression and extortion *and*
violence."

18 Therefore thus says the LORD in
regard to Jehoiakim the [second] son
of Josiah, king of Judah,

"The relatives will not lament
(mourn over with expressions of
grief) for him:
'Alas, my brother!' or, 'Alas, sister,'
[how great our loss]!
The subjects will not lament for
him:
'Alas, master!' or 'Alas, majesty
[how great was his glory]!'
19 "He shall be buried with the burial
of a donkey—
Dragged off and thrown out
beyond the gates of Jerusalem.
20 "Go up [north] to Lebanon and cry
out,
And raise your voice in [the hills
of] Bashan [across the Jordan];
Cry out also from Abarim,
For all your lovers (allies) have
been destroyed. [Jer 27:6, 7]
21 "I spoke to you in your [times of]
prosperity,
But you said, 'I will not listen!'
This has been your attitude *and*
practice from your youth;
You have not obeyed My voice.
22 "The wind [of adversity] will carry
away all your shepherds (rulers,
statesmen),
And your lovers (allies) will go into
exile.
Surely then you will be ashamed
and humiliated *and* disgraced
Because of all your wickedness.
23 "O inhabitant of [Jerusalem, whose
palaces are made from the
cedars of] Lebanon,
You who nest in the cedars,
How you will groan *and* how
miserable you will be when
pains come on you,
Pain like a woman in childbirth!
[1 Kin 7:2]

24 "As I live," says the LORD, "though
Coniah the son of Jehoiakim king of
Judah were the signet [ring] on My
right hand, yet would I pull you (Co-
niah) off.
25 "And I will place you in the hand of
those who seek your life and in the hand
of those whom you fear, even into the
hand of Nebuchadnezzar king of Bab-
ylon and into the hand of the Chaldeans.
26 "I will hurl you and the mother who
gave you birth into another country
where you were not born, and there
you will die.

22:18 – 19 *He shall be buried with the burial of a donkey.* A king of such despicable character as Jehoiakim deserved no lament. Instead of proper funeral rights due a king, Jehoiakim would receive an ignoble burial, like an animal, alone and unlamented.

22:22 – 23 *The wind [of adversity] will carry away all your shepherds.* The winds of adversity and invasion would carry off Judah's leaders and allies alike. The nation would be ashamed that it had entered into such futile associations.

22:24 – 27 *Coniah.* This was another name for Jehoiachin. He succeeded his father in 598 BC under the threat of siege from Babylon as a result of Jehoiakim's rebellion. Jehoiachin reigned for three months until he and his family were exiled to Babylon by Nebuchadnezzar (2Ki 24:6 – 16). Eventually Jehoiachin was released from prison after the death of Nebuchadnezzar.

15 Ps 128:2; Isa 3:10 **17** Eze 19:6 **18** Jer 16:4,6; See 1Ki 13:30; Fulfilled **19** 2Ch 36:6; Jer 36:30 **21** Jer 3:25; 7:23 **22** Jer 23:1 **23** Jer 6:24 **24** See 2Ki 24:6,8; 1Ch 3:16; Jer 37:1; SS 8:6; Hag 2:23 **25** Jer 34:20 **26** 2Ki 24:15; 2Ch 36:10

27"But as for the land to which they long to return, they will not return to it.

28"Is this man [King] Coniah a
despised, broken jar?
Is he a vessel in which no one
takes pleasure?
Why are he and his [royal]
descendants hurled out
And cast into a land which they do
not know *or* understand?
29"O land, land, land,
Hear the word of the LORD!

30"Thus says the LORD,

'Write this man [Coniah] down as
childless,
A man who will not prosper
(succeed) in his lifetime;
For not one of his descendants will
succeed
In sitting on the throne of David
Or ruling again in Judah.' "

The Coming Messiah: the Righteous Branch

23 "WOE TO the shepherds (civil
leaders, rulers) who are destroy-
ing and scattering the sheep of My
pasture!" says the LORD.
2Therefore thus says the LORD, the
God of Israel, in regard to the shep-
herds who care for *and* feed My people:
"You have scattered My flock and driv-
en them away, and have not attended
to them; hear this, I am about to visit
and attend to you for the evil of your
deeds," says the LORD.
3"Then I will gather the remnant
of My flock out of all the countries to
which I have driven them and bring
them back to their folds *and* pastures;
and they will be fruitful and multiply.
4"I will set up shepherds over them
who will feed them. And they will not
be afraid any longer, nor be terrified,
nor will any be missing," says the LORD.

5"Behold (listen closely), the days
are coming," says the LORD,
"When I will raise up for David a
righteous Branch;
And He will reign as King and act
wisely
And will do [those things that
accomplish] justice and
righteousness in the land.
6"In His days Judah will be saved,
And Israel will dwell safely;
Now this is His name by which He
will be called;
'The LORD Our Righteousness.'
[Matt 1:21–23; Rom 3:22]

7"Therefore behold, the days are
coming," says the LORD, "when they
will no longer say, 'As the LORD lives,
who brought up the children of Israel
from the land of Egypt,'
8but [they will say], 'As the LORD
lives, who brought up and led back
the descendants of the house of Israel
from the north country and from all
the countries to which I had driven
them.' Then they will live in their own
land." [Jer 16:14, 15]

False Prophets Denounced

9Concerning the prophets:
My heart [says Jeremiah] is
broken within me,

23:3 *I will gather the remnant.* The kings of Israel had caused the dispersion of the nation; but the Lord would mercifully bring about the restoration of the remnant. This concept was a popular one with many of the prophets. (Isa 1:9; 10:20 – 23). The blessing of restoration and prosperity as a consequence of repentance is outlined in Deuteronomy 30:1 – 10.
23:5 *a righteous Branch.* Beginning with Isaiah 4:2 this term is used of the promised Messiah (33:15); Zec 3:8). This great king will reign with justice and righteousness. This ideal was founded on God's promise to David (2Sa 7:16).
23:7 – 8 *the days are coming.* The future restoration of Israel would exceed anything in the past; it would surpass even the first exodus, the deliverance from Egypt.
23:9 – 10 *My heart [says Jeremiah] is broken within me.* Jeremiah's dismay over the false prophets weakened him mentally and physically,

28 Ps 31:12; Jer 48:38; Hos 8:8 **29** Dt 32:1; Isa 1:2; 34:1; Mic 1:2 **30** See 1Ch 3:16,17; Mt 1:12; Jer 36:30
CHAPTER 23 **1** Jer 10:21; 22:22; Eze 34:2 **2** Ex 32:34 **3** Jer 32:37; Eze 34:13 **4** Jer 3:15; Eze 34:23 **5** Isa 4:2; 11:1; 40:10,11; Jer 33:14; Da 9:24; Zec 6:12; Jn 1:45; Ps 72:2; Isa 9:7; 32:1,18 **6** Dt 33:28; Zec 14:11; Jer 32:37; Jer 33:16; 1Co 1:30 **7** Jer 16:14 **8** Isa 43:5,6 **9** See Hab 3:16

All my bones shake;
I have become like a drunken
man,
A man whom wine has overcome,
Because of the LORD
And because of His holy words
[declared against unfaithful
leaders].
10 For the land is full of adulterers
(unfaithful to God);
The land mourns because of the
curse [of God upon it].
The pastures of the wilderness
have dried up.
The course of action [of the false
prophets] is evil *and* they rush
into wickedness;
And their power is not right.
11 "For both [false] prophet and priest
are ungodly (profane, polluted);
Even in My house I have found
their wickedness," says the
LORD.
12 "Therefore their way will be to
them like slippery paths
In the dark; they will be pushed
and fall into them;
For I will bring disaster on them,
In the year of their punishment,"
says the LORD.
13 "And I have seen a foolish *and* an
offensive thing in the prophets
of Samaria:
They prophesied by Baal and
caused My people Israel to go
astray.
14 "Also I have seen a horrible thing
in the prophets of Jerusalem:
They commit adultery and walk in
lies;
They encourage *and* strengthen
the hands of evildoers,
So that no one has turned back
from his wickedness.
All of them have become like
Sodom to Me,
And her inhabitants like
Gomorrah.

15 "Therefore thus says the LORD of
hosts in regard to the prophets,

'Behold, I am going to feed them
[the bitterness of] wormwood
And make them drink the
poisonous water [of gall],
For from the [counterfeit] prophets
of Jerusalem
Profaneness *and* ungodliness have
spread into all the land.' "

16 Thus says the LORD of hosts,
"Do not listen to the words of the
[false] prophets who prophesy
to you.
They are teaching you worthless
things *and* are leading you into
futility;
They speak a vision of their own
mind *and* imagination
And not [truth] from the mouth of
the LORD.
17 "They are continually saying to
those who despise Me [and My
word],
'The Lord has said, "You will have
peace" ';
And they say to everyone who
walks after the stubbornness of
his own heart,
'No evil will come on you.'
18 "But who [among them] has stood
in the council of the LORD,
That he would perceive and hear
His word?
Who has marked His word
[noticing and observing and
paying attention to it] and has
[actually] heard it?

---

so much so that he felt drunken from the inner turmoil.

23:15 *I am going to feed them [the bitterness of] wormwood.* This word refers to bitterness and death by poison. According to Deuteronomy 18:20, the consequence of false prophecy was death.

23:16 *a vision of their own mind and imagination.* Visions were commonly understood to be a means of receiving a message from God (or the gods). The term *vision* used here and in Jeremiah 14:14 is also found in Daniel 1:17 and 8:1; plus it is used in other prophetic books to describe a divine revelation (Isa 1:1; Mic 3:6).

10 Jer 9:2; Hos 4:2,3; Jer 9:10 **11** Zep 3:4; Jer 7:30; Eze 8:11; 23:39 **12** Ps 35:6; Pr 4:19; Jer 13:16; Jer 11:23 **13** Jer 2:8; Isa 9:16 **14** Jer 29:23; ver. 26; Eze 13:22; Isa 1:9,10 **15** Jer 9:15 **16** Jer 14:14 **17** Jer 8:11; Eze 13:10; Zec 10:2; Mic 3:11 **18** Job 15:8; 1Co 2:16

19 "Behold, the tempest of the LORD
has gone forth in wrath,
A whirling tempest;
It will whirl *and* burst on the heads
of the wicked.
20 "The anger of the LORD will not
turn back
Until He has set in motion and
accomplished the thoughts *and*
intentions of His heart;
In the last days you will clearly
understand it.
21 "I did not send [these counterfeit]
prophets,
Yet they ran;
I did not speak to them,
Yet they prophesied.
22 "But if they had stood in My council,
Then they would have caused My
people to hear My words,
Then they would have turned My
people from their evil way
And from the evil of their
decisions *and* deeds.
23 "Am I a God who is at hand," says
the LORD,
"And not a God far away?"
24 "Can anyone hide himself in secret
places
So that I cannot see him?" says the
LORD.
"Do I not fill heaven and earth?"
says the LORD.

25 "I have heard what the prophets
have said who prophesy lies in My
Name, saying, 'I have dreamed, I have
dreamed [visions when on my bed at
night].'
26 "How long [shall this state of af-
fairs continue]? Is there anything in
the hearts of the prophets who proph-
esy falsehood, even these prophets of
the deception of their own heart,
27 who think that they can make My
people forget My Name by their [con-
trived] dreams which each one tells
another, just as their fathers forgot My
Name because of Baal?
28 "The prophet who has a dream
may tell his dream; but he who has My
word, let him speak My word faithfully.
What has straw in common with wheat
[for nourishment]?" says the LORD.
29 "Is not My word like fire [that con-
sumes all that cannot endure the test]?"
says the LORD, "and like a hammer
that breaks the [most stubborn] rock
[in pieces]?
30 "Therefore behold (hear this), I
am against the [counterfeit] proph-
ets," says the LORD, "[I am descend-
ing on them with punishment, these
prophets] who steal My words from
one another [imitating the words of
the true prophets].
31 "Hear this, I am against the proph-
ets," says the LORD, "who use their
[own deceitful] tongues and say, 'Thus
says *the Lord*.'
32 "Hear this, I am against those who
have prophesied false *and* made-up
dreams," says the LORD, "and have told
them and have made My people err *and*
go astray by their lies and by their reck-
less boasting; yet I did not send them
or command them nor do they benefit
and enhance [the life of] these people
in the slightest way," says the LORD.
33 "Now when this people or a proph-
et or a priest asks you [in jest], 'What
is the oracle of the LORD [the burden
to be lifted up and carried]?' Then
you shall say to them, 'What oracle
[besides the one that declares you
people to be the burden]!' The LORD
says, 'I will unburden Myself *and* I
will abandon you.'

23:19 *the tempest of the LORD.* This is a symbol of God's judgment (Isaa 29:6).

23:21 – 22 *I did not send [these counterfeit] prophets.* A true prophet must be sent by God with a word from God. A true prophet of God calls people to repentance of sin or evil and to renewed faith.

23:26 *the deception of their own heart.* The character of the false prophets was based on lies and deceit. Their deception was apparent because their goal was to draw the people into idolatry with their fanciful dreams, leading people to forget God and follow Baal (2:8).

23:28 – 29 *What has straw in common with wheat.* This poetic interlude compares dream and word. A dream is fleeting, like chaff in the wind. God's word has the force of fire and a hammer.

19 Jer 25:32; 30:23 **20** Jer 30:24; Ge 49:1 **21** Jer 14:14 **22** ver. 18; Jer 25:5 **24** Ps 139:7; Am 9:2,3; 1Ki 8:27; Ps 139:7 **27** Jdg 3:7 **30** Dt 18:20; Jer 14:14,15 **32** Zep 3:4 **33** Mal 1:1; ver. 39

34 “And as for the prophet, the priest, or [any of] the people, whoever says, ‘The oracle of the LORD,’ [as if he knows God’s will], I will punish that man and his household.

35 “[For the future, in speaking of the words of the LORD] thus each of you shall say to his neighbor and to his brother, ‘What has the LORD answered?’ or, ‘What has the LORD spoken?’

36 “For you will no longer remember the oracle of the LORD, because every man’s own word will become the oracle, [for as they mockingly call all prophecies oracles, whether good or bad, so will it prove to be to them; God will take them at their own word]; and you have perverted the words [not of a lifeless idol, but] of the living God, the LORD of hosts, our God.

37 “Thus you will [reverently] say to the prophet, ‘What has the LORD answered you?’ and, ‘What has the LORD spoken?’

38 “For if you say, ‘The oracle of the LORD!’ surely thus says the LORD, ‘Because you said this word, “The oracle of the LORD!” when I have also sent to you, saying, “You shall not say, ‘The oracle of the LORD!’ ” ’

39 “Therefore behold, I, even I, will assuredly forget you and send you away from My presence, you and the city (Jerusalem) which I gave to you and to your fathers.

40 “And I will bring an everlasting disgrace on you and a perpetual humiliation (shame) which will not be forgotten.”

Baskets of Figs and the Returnees

24 AFTER NEBUCHADNEZZAR king of Babylon had taken Jeconiah [who was also called Coniah and Jehoiachin] the son of Jehoiakim, king of Judah, and the princes of Judah [along] with the craftsmen and smiths into exile from Jerusalem to Babylon, the LORD showed me [in a vision] two baskets of figs set before the temple of the LORD.

2 One basket had very good figs, like the figs that are the first to ripen; but the other basket had very bad figs, so rotten that they could not be eaten.

3 Then the LORD said to me, “What do you see, Jeremiah?” And I said, “Figs, the good figs, very good; and the bad *figs,* very bad, so rotten that they cannot be eaten.”

4 Again the word of the LORD came to me, saying,

5 “Thus says the LORD, the God of Israel, ‘Like these good figs, so I will regard as good the captives of Judah, whom I have sent from this place into the land of the Chaldeans.

6 ‘For I will set My eyes on them for good, and I will bring them again to this land; and I will build them up and not overwhelm them, and I will plant them and not uproot them.

7 ‘I will give them a heart to know Me, [understanding fully] that I am the LORD; and they will be My people, and I will be their God, for they will return to Me with their whole heart.

8 ‘And as for the bad figs, which are so rotten that they cannot be eaten,’ surely thus says the LORD, ‘so I will abandon Zedekiah king of Judah and his princes, and the remnant of Jerusalem who remain in this land and those who live in the land of Egypt.

9 ‘I will make them a focus of ridicule *and* disappointment [tossed back and forth] among all the kingdoms of the earth, a [notorious] disgrace, a byword, a taunt and a curse in all places where I will scatter them.

10 ‘I will send the sword, famine and virulent disease among them until they

---

23:38 – 40 *The oracle of the LORD.* False prophets could not speak an oracle. The disgrace that resulted from the false prophets would last for an extended period of time: Its memory would endure forever (20:11).

24:4 – 7 *Like these good figs.* These are identified with the deported exiles, including Jeconiah’s royal household, whom God set apart. God would bring back the captives, establish them in the land, and multiply their crops.

39 Hos 4:6; ver. 33 **40** Jer 20:11 **CHAPTER 24** **1** Am 7:1,4; 8:1; 2Ki 24:12; 2Ch 36:10; See Jer 22:24; 29:2
6 Jer 12:15; 29:10; Jer 32:41; 33:7; 42:10 **7** Dt 30:6; Jer 32:39; Eze 11:19; 36:26,27; Jer 30:22; 31:33; 32:38; Jer 29:13
8 Jer 29:17; See Jer 43; 44 **9** Dt 28:25,37; 1Ki 9:7; 2Ch 7:20; Jer 15:4; 29:18; 34:17; Ps 44:13,14

are consumed from the land which I gave to them and to their fathers.' "

Prophecy of the Captivity

25 THE WORD that came to Jeremiah in regard to all the people of Judah in the fourth year of the reign of Jehoiakim the son of Josiah, king of Judah (that was the first year of the reign of Nebuchadnezzar king of Babylon),

2 which Jeremiah the prophet spoke to all the people of Judah and to all the inhabitants of Jerusalem, saying,

3 "For these twenty-three years—from the thirteenth year of Josiah the son of Amon, king of Judah, even to this day—the word of the LORD has come to me and I have spoken to you over and over again, but you have not listened.

4 "Although the LORD has persistently sent to you all His servants the prophets, you have not listened nor [even] inclined your ear to hear [His message],

5 saying, 'Turn now everyone from his evil way and the evil of your actions [that you may not forfeit the right to] live in the land that the LORD has given to you and your forefathers forever and ever;

6 and do not go after other gods to serve them and to worship them, and do not provoke Me to anger with the work of your hands, and I will do you no harm.'

7 "Yet you have not listened to Me," says the LORD, "so that you have provoked Me to anger with the work (idols) of your hands to your own harm.

8 "Therefore thus says the LORD of hosts, 'Because you have not obeyed My words,

9 behold (hear this), I will send for all the families of the north,' says the LORD, 'and *I will send* for Nebuchadnezzar king of Babylon, My servant [to enact My plan], and I will bring them against this land and against its inhabitants and against all these surrounding nations; and I will utterly destroy them and make them a horror and a hissing [that is, an object of warning and ridicule] and an everlasting desolation.

10 'Moreover, I will take from them the voice of joy and the voice of gladness, the voice of the bridegroom and the voice of the bride, the sound of the millstones [grinding meal] and the light of the lamp [to light the night]. [Jer 7:34]

11 'This whole land will be a waste and a horror, and these nations will serve the king of Babylon seventy years. [2 Chr 36:20–23; Jer 4:27; 12:11, 12; Dan 9:2]

Babylon Will Be Judged

12 'Then when seventy years are completed, I will punish the king of Babylon and that nation, the land of the Chaldeans (Babylonia),' says the LORD, 'for their wickedness, and will make the land [of the Chaldeans] a perpetual waste. [Jer 29:10]

13 'I will bring on that land all My words which I have pronounced against it, all that is written in this book which Jeremiah has prophesied against all the nations.

14 '(For many nations and great kings will make slaves of them, even the Chaldeans [who enslaved other nations]; and I will repay [all of] them according to their deeds and according to the work of their [own] hands.)' "

15 For thus says the LORD, the God of Israel, to me, "Take this cup of the wine of wrath from My hand and cause all the nations to whom I send you to drink it.

25:3 *I have spoken to you over and over again.* This phrase describes Jeremiah's diligence and persistence.

25:9 *Nebuchadnezzar ... My servant.* This expression does not imply that the Babylonian monarch worshiped Israel's God, but simply that he was used by God to fulfill His purposes (as in the case of Cyrus, who is called the Lord's "anointed" in Isa 45:1).

CHAPTER 25 **1** ch 36:1 **3** Jer 1:2; Jer 7:13; 11:7,8,10 **4** Jer 7:13,25 **5** Jer 18:11; Jnh 3:8 **7** Dt 32:21 **9** Jer 1:15; Jer 27:6; Isa 45:1; Jer 18:16 **10** Isa 24:7; Hos 2:11; Rev 18:23; Ecc 12:4 **12** 2Ch 36:21,22; Ezr 1:1; Da 9:2; Isa 21:1; Jer 50:3 **14** Jer 50:9; 51:27,28; Jer 27:7; Jer 50:29; 51:6,24 **15** Job 21:20; Ps 75:8; Isa 51:17; Rev 14:10

16 “They will drink and stagger and go mad because of the sword that I will send among them.”

17 Then I (Jeremiah) took the cup from the LORD’s hand and made all the nations to whom the LORD had sent me drink it:

18 Jerusalem and the cities of Judah [being most guilty because their privileges were greatest], its kings and princes, to make them a horror, a ruin, a hissing and a curse, as it is to this day; [1 Pet 4:17]

19 Pharaoh king of Egypt, his servants, his princes, all his people,

20 and all the foreign (mixed) population, all the kings of the land of Uz, and all the kings of the land of the Philistines (and [their cities of] Ashkelon, Gaza, Ekron, and the remnant of Ashdod);

21 Edom, Moab, and the children of Ammon;

22 all the kings of Tyre, all the kings of Sidon, and the kings of the islands *and* the coastlands across the [Mediterranean] Sea;

23 Dedan, Tema, Buz [the neighboring tribes north of Arabia], and all who clip off the side-growth *of their hair;* [Lev 19:27; Jer 9:26]

24 all the kings of Arabia and all the kings of the foreign population who live in the desert;

25 all the kings of Zimri, all the kings of Elam (Persia), and all the kings of Media;

26 all the kings of the north, far and near, one after another—and all the kingdoms of the world which are on the face of the earth. And the king of Sheshach (Babylon) shall drink after them.

27 “Then you shall say to them, ‘Thus says the LORD of hosts, the God of Israel, “Drink, be drunk, vomit, and fall to rise no more because of the sword which I will send among you.” ’

28 “And if they refuse to take the cup from your hand to drink, then you will say to them, ‘Thus says the LORD of hosts, “You shall surely drink!

29 “For behold, I am beginning to work disaster in the city which is called by My Name, and shall you go unpunished? You will not be exempt from punishment, for I am calling for a sword against all the inhabitants of the earth,” says the LORD of hosts.’ [Jer 7:10]

30 “Therefore prophesy all these words against them and say to them:

‘The LORD will roar from on high
And utter His voice from His holy
dwelling;
He will roar mightily against His
fold *and* pasture.
He will jubilantly shout like those
who tread *the grapes* [in the
wine press],
Against all the inhabitants of the
earth.
31 ‘A noise has come to the end of the
earth,
For the LORD has a controversy
with *and* an indictment against
the nations.

25:16 *drink and stagger and go mad.* This triad sequence depicts the judgment process by which the sword of the Lord subdues those opposed to Him. The state of drunkenness was condemned in the Old Testament: to drink the cup and stagger was to display one’s guilt (Nu 5:19–28).

25:18 *to make them a horror, a ruin, a hissing and a curse.* The list of nations that would be made to drink from the cup of the Lord’s judgment begins with Judah and Jerusalem, which would be made a source of derision (19:8).

25:27–28 *Drink, be drunk, vomit.* These terms for progressive inebriation emphasize the extent of judgment that would flow from God’s cup of wrath. Those who refused the cup would be forced to drink.

25:30 *The LORD will roar from on high.* Generally this phrase refers to God’s abode on Mount Zion (Joel 3:16; Am 1:2).

25:31 *A noise has come.* This noise refers to a thunderous judgment resulting from God’s “covenant lawsuit” against the nations. Though they had not received the law like Judah and Israel, the Gentiles would be judged because they were “wicked.” The word “wicked” refers to the guilt associated with the breach of ethical standards, including violating the poor and needy and abusing the oppressed.

16 Jer 51:7; Eze 23:34; Na 3:11 **18** ver. 9,11; Jer 24:9 **20** Job 1:1; Isa 20:1 **21** Jer 49:7 **22** Jer 47:4; Jer 49:23 **23** Jer 49:8 **24** Eze 30:5 **26** Jer 50:9 **27** Hab 2:16; Isa 63:6 **29** Eze 9:6; Lk 23:31; 1Pe 4:17; Da 9:18; Eze 38:21 **30** Isa 42:13; Joel 3:16; Am 1:2; Ps 11:4; 1Ki 9:3; Ps 132:14; Isa 16:9; Jer 48:33 **31** Hos 4:1; Mic 6:2; Isa 66:16; Joel 3:2

He is entering into judgment with
all mankind;
As for the wicked, He has given
them to the sword,' says the
LORD."

32 Thus says the LORD of hosts,
"Behold, evil is going forth
From nation to nation,
And a great whirling tempest is
rising
From the remotest part of the
earth.

33 "And those slain by the LORD on
that day will be from one end of the
earth to the other end of the earth.
They will not be lamented (mourned
over with expressions of grief) or gath-
ered or buried; they will be like dung
on the ground. [Jer 8:2; 16:4]

34 "Wail, you shepherds, and cry;
And roll in ashes, you masters of
the flock.
For the days of your slaughter and
of your dispersions have come
in full,
And you will fall *and* be broken
into pieces like a choice vessel.
35 "The shepherds will have no way
to flee,
Nor the masters of the flock any
[way of] escape.
36 "A voice! The cry of the shepherds
And the wailing of the masters of
the flock!
For the LORD is destroying their
pasture,
37 "And the peaceful folds are
devastated *and* made silent
Because of the fierce anger of the
LORD.
38 "He has left His lair like the lion;
For their land has become a horror
Because of the fierceness of the
oppressor
And because of the LORD's fierce
anger."

Cities of Judah Warned

26 IN THE beginning of the reign
of Jehoiakim the son of Josiah,
king of Judah, this word came from
the LORD, saying,
2 "Thus says the LORD, 'Stand in the
court of the LORD's house [Jeremiah],
and speak to all [the people of] the cit-
ies of Judah who have come to worship
in the LORD's house all the words that
I have commanded you to speak to
them. Do not omit a word!
3 'It may be that they will listen and
everyone will turn from his wicked-
ness, so that I may relent *and* reverse
[My decision concerning] the disaster
which I am planning to do to them
because of their malevolent deeds.'
4 "And you will say to them, 'Thus
says the LORD, "If you will not listen
to Me and obey My law which I have
set before you,
5 and listen *and* follow [carefully]
the words of My servants the proph-
ets, whom I have been sending to you
repeatedly—though you have not lis-
tened—
6 then I will make this house [the tem-
ple] like Shiloh, and I will make this
city [subject to] the curse of all nations
of the earth [because it will be so vile
in their sight]." ' " [1 Sam 4; Jer 7:12]

A Plot to Murder Jeremiah

7 The priests and the [false] proph-
ets and all the people heard Jeremiah

25:37 ***Because of the fierce anger of the LORD.*** Human anger is an emotion. God's anger is an aspect of the righteous administration of His laws — natural, moral, and spiritual.
26:2 ***Do not omit a word.*** Jeremiah was told to speak unsparingly with unwavering boldness.
26:3 ***It may be that they will listen.*** The introduction to the judgment oracle is expressed in conditional terms. If the people repented of evil, the Lord would relent from the calamity He was threatening to bring on them.
26:6 ***then I will make this house [the temple] like Shiloh.*** This city was not far from Jerusalem. The people could see the effects of its destruction by the Philistines in 1050 BC, a destruction that overtook it even though it was the first resting place of the ark of the covenant. Jeremiah uses Shiloh as an illustration of the coming judgment

32 Jer 23:19; 30:23 **33** Isa 66:16; Jer 16:4,6; Ps 79:3; Jer 8:2; Rev 11:9 **34** Jer 4:8; 6:26 **CHAPTER 26** **2** Jer 19:14; Eze 3:10; Mt 28:20; Ac 20:27 **3** Jer 36:3; Jer 18:8; Jnh 3:8,9 **4** Lev 26:14; Dt 28:15 **5** Jer 7:13,25; 11:7; 25:3,4 **6** 1Sa 4:10,11; Ps 78:60; Jer 7:12,14; Isa 65:15; Jer 24:9

speaking these words in the house of
the LORD.
[8]Now when Jeremiah finished pro-
claiming everything that the LORD
had commanded him to speak to all
the people, the priests and the [false]
prophets and all the people seized him,
saying, "You must die!
[9]"Why have you prophesied in the
name of the LORD saying, 'This house
will be like Shiloh [after the ark of the
LORD had been taken by our enemies]
and this city [Jerusalem] will be deso-
late, without inhabitant'?" And all the
people were gathered around Jeremiah
in the [outer area of the] house of the
LORD.
[10]When the princes (court officials)
of Judah heard these things, they came
up from the king's house to the house
of the LORD and sat in the entrance of
the New Gate of the house of the LORD.
[11]Then the priests and the [false]
prophets said to the princes and to all
the people, "This man is deserving of
death, for he has prophesied against
this city as you have heard with your
own ears."
[12]Then Jeremiah spoke to all the
princes and to all the people, saying,
"The LORD sent me to prophesy against
this house and against this city all the
words that you have heard.
[13]"Therefore, now change your ways
and your deeds and obey the voice
of the LORD your God; then the LORD
will relent *and* reverse His decision
concerning the misfortune which He
has pronounced against you.
[14]"As for me, behold, I am in your
hands; do with me as seems good and
suitable to you.
[15]"But know for certain that if you
put me to death, you will bring inno-
cent blood on yourselves and on this
city and on its inhabitants, for in truth
the LORD has sent me to you to speak
all these words in your hearing."

Jeremiah Is Spared

[16]Then the princes and all the people
said to the priests and to the [false]
prophets, "This man is not deserving
of death, for he has spoken to us in the
name of the LORD our God."
[17]Then some of the elders of the land
stood up and spoke to all the assembly
of the people, saying,
[18]"Micah of Moresheth prophesied
in the days of Hezekiah king of Judah;
and he spoke to all the people of Judah,
saying, 'Thus says the LORD of hosts,

"Zion will be plowed like a field,
And Jerusalem will become [heaps
of] ruins,
And the mountain of the house
[of the LORD—Mount Moriah,
on which stands the temple,
shall become covered not with
buildings, but] like a densely
wooded height." ' [Mic 3:12]

[19]"Did Hezekiah king of Judah and all
Judah put Micah to death? Did he not
[reverently] fear the LORD and entreat
the favor of the LORD? And did not the
LORD relent *and* reverse His decision
concerning the misfortune which He
had pronounced against them? But
[here] we are [thinking of] committing
a great evil against ourselves."
[20]And there was also a man who
prophesied in the name of the LORD,
Uriah the son of Shemaiah of Kiriath-
jearim, who prophesied against this
city and against this land in words
similar to all those of Jeremiah.

---

of Jerusalem even though the temple of God had been built there.

26:13 ***obey the voice of the LORD your God.*** Jeremiah gives the Lord's assurance that if we, like Judah, turn to obey Him, our future will be changed from punishment to blessing.

26:15 ***if you put me to death.*** Jeremiah defended himself and pointed to the potential sin of shedding innocent blood. He had already accused the leaders of Jerusalem of child sacrifices in the Hinnom valley (2:34; 19:4).

26:18 ***Micah of Moresheth.*** In the reign of Hezekiah, Micah had announced the impending destruction of Jerusalem by the Assyrians (Mic 3:12). Yet because of the repentance of Hezekiah and the inhabitants, the city was spared from the onslaught of the Assyrian army under Sennacherib (701 BC).

11 Jer 38:4 **13** Jer 7:3; ver. 3,19 **14** Jer 38:5 **17** See Ac 5:34 **18** Mic 1:1; Mic 3:12 **19** 2Ch 32:26; Ex 32:14; 2Sa 24:16; Ac 5:39

21 And when Jehoiakim the king,
with all his mighty men and all the
princes, heard his words, the king
sought to put Uriah to death; but when
Uriah heard of it, he was afraid and
fled and escaped to Egypt.
22 Then Jehoiakim the king sent men
to Egypt: Elnathan the son of Ach-
bor and certain [other] men with him
[went] to Egypt.
23 And they brought Uriah [God's
spokesman] from Egypt and led him to
King Jehoiakim, who executed him with
a sword and threw his dead body among
the graves of the common people.
24 But the hand of Ahikam the son of
Shaphan was with Jeremiah, so that
he was not given into the hands of the
people to put him to death.

The Nations to Submit to Nebuchadnezzar

27 IN THE beginning of the reign of
Zedekiah the son of Josiah, king
of Judah, this word came to Jeremiah
from the LORD:
2 Thus says the LORD to me, "Make
for yourself bonds and yokes and put
them on your neck,
3 and send word to the king of Edom,
to the king of Moab, to the king of the
sons of Ammon, to the king of Tyre,
and to the king of Sidon by the mes-
sengers who come to Jerusalem to Zed-
ekiah king of Judah.
4 "Command them to go to their mas-
ters, saying, 'Thus says the LORD of
hosts, the God of Israel, you shall say
this to your masters:
5 "I have made the earth, the men and
the animals that are on the face of the
earth by My great power and by My
outstretched arm, and I will give it to
whomever pleases Me.
6 "Now I have given all these lands
into the hand of Nebuchadnezzar king
of Babylon, My servant *and* instru-
ment, and I have also given the wild
animals of the field to serve him.
7 "All nations shall serve him and
his son and his grandson until the [ap-
pointed] time [of punishment] for his
own land comes; then many nations
and great kings shall make him their
servant.
8 "But any nation or kingdom that
will not serve this same Nebuchad-
nezzar king of Babylon and put its
neck under the yoke of the king of
Babylon, that nation I will punish,"
says the LORD, "with the sword, with
famine and with pestilence (virulent
disease), until I have destroyed it by
Nebuchadnezzar's hand.
9 "And as for you, do not listen to
your [counterfeit] prophets, your divin-
ers, your dreams *and* dreamers, your
soothsayers or your sorcerers, who say
to you, 'You will not serve the king of
Babylon.'

26:24 ***Ahikam the son of Shaphan.*** This man, along with his father, served as a scribe under Josiah when the Book of the Law was found in the temple (2Ki 22:8 – 14). Ahikam's brother Gemariah also opposed Jehoiakim's burning of Jeremiah's scroll (36:25). This faithful family was supportive of Jeremiah and was instrumental in saving his life.

27:2 – 3 ***bonds and yokes.*** These are wooden bars or beams that attach to a pair of oxen with leather bands. The symbolic act of wearing the yoke would communicate bondage, restraint, and enslavement.

27:7 ***All nations shall serve him and his son and his grandson.*** Following the death of Nebuchadnezzar in 562 BC, his heirs and successors retained control of Babylon for only 24 years. Babylon fell without a battle to Cyrus and the Persian armies in 539 BC, and later to Alexander the Great of Greece.

27:9 – 10 ***do not listen.*** The way kings summoned various prophet-diviners to give them direction is well known from the Book of Daniel (Da 2:2; 5:7). Besides prophets, there were diviners, like Balaam (Nu 22 – 24), who were prohibited from practicing their craft in Israel (Dt 18:9 – 14). The collective effort of these diviners to determine the fate of their nations failed. Like the false prophets of Judah, they heralded a message of rebellion and resistance against Babylon. Only Jeremiah stood for the truth. The Lord would punish Judah through Nebuchadnezzar.

24 2Ki 22:12,14; Jer 39:14 **CHAPTER 27** **1** See ver. 3,12,20; Jer 28:1 **2** Jer 28:10,12; Eze 4:1; 12:3; 24:3 **5** Ps 115:15; 146:6; Isa 45:12; Ps 115:16; Da 4:17,25,32 **6** Jer 28:14; Jer 25:9; 43:10; Eze 29:18,20; Jer 28:14; Da 2:38 **7** 2Ch 36:20; Jer 25:12; 50:27; Da 5:26; Jer 25:14

10“For they prophesy a lie to you
which will cause you to be removed
far from your land; and I will drive you
out and you will perish.
11“But the nation which will bow its
neck under the yoke of the king of Bab-
ylon and serve him, that nation I will
let remain on its own land,” says the
LORD, “to cultivate it and live in it.” ’ ”
12I spoke to Zedekiah king of Judah
in the same way, saying, “Bring your
necks under the yoke of the king of
Babylon and serve him and his people,
and live!
13“Why will you die, you and your
people, by the sword, by famine and
by virulent disease, as the LORD has
spoken to any nation which will not
serve the king of Babylon?
14“Do not listen to *and* believe the
words of the [false] prophets who are
saying to you, ‘You will not serve the
king of Babylon,’ for they prophesy a
lie to you;
15for I have not sent them,” says the
LORD, “but they are prophesying false-
ly in My Name, in order that I may
drive you out and that you may perish,
you [together] with the [false] prophets
who prophesy to you.”
16Then I said to the priests and to all
these people, saying, “Thus says the
LORD: Do not listen to the words of your
[false] prophets who are prophesying
to you, saying, ‘Behold, the articles of
the LORD’s house will now shortly be
brought back from Babylon’; for they
are prophesying a lie to you.
17“Do not listen to them; serve the
king of Babylon, and live! Why should
this city become a ruin?
18“But if they are [true] prophets, and
if the word of the LORD is [really spo-
ken] by them, let them now entreat the
LORD of hosts that the articles which
are [still] left in the house of the LORD,
in the house of the king of Judah and
in Jerusalem may not go to Babylon.
19“For thus says the LORD of hosts
concerning the [bronze] pillars, the
[bronze] Sea, the [bronze] bases [of the
ten basins in Solomon’s temple used
for washing sacrificial animals], and
the rest of the articles that are left in
this city (Jerusalem), [1 Kin 7:23–37;
2 Chr 4:6; Jer 52:17]
20which Nebuchadnezzar king of
Babylon did not take when he carried
Jeconiah the son of Jehoiakim, king
of Judah, into exile from Jerusalem to
Babylon, along with all the nobles of
Judah and Jerusalem.
21“Yes, thus says the LORD of hosts,
the God of Israel, concerning the arti-
cles which remain in the house of the
LORD, in the house of the king of Judah
and in Jerusalem,
22‘They will be carried to Babylon
and they will be there until the day
that I visit them [with My favor],’ says
the LORD. ‘Then I will bring them back
and restore them to this place.’ ”

Hananiah’s False Prophecy

28 IN THE same year, in the be-
ginning of the reign of Zede-
kiah king of Judah, in the fourth year
and the fifth month, the [false] prophet
Hananiah the son of Azzur, who was
from Gibeon [one of the priests’ cities],
spoke [without godly authority] to me
in the house of the LORD in the pres-

27:21–22 *concerning the articles.* Jeremiah’s message from the Lord is presented in detail. The remaining articles in the temple, as well as in the king’s palace, would be carried to Babylon until the Lord restored His people. In the midst of a prophetic message against the false prophets, Jeremiah spoke a message of hope and restoration. Destruction was imminent, but God does not forget His people. He would restore the righteous remnant.

28:1–4 *Hananiah the son of Azzur.* This prophet believed that God’s message for Judah was one of imminent deliverance — within two years — from servitude to the king of Babylon. Hananiah also prophesied the return of the holy vessels taken by Nebuchadnezzar from the temple. Furthermore, Hananiah espoused the popular belief that the kingship of Zedekiah was illegitimate and that God would restore Jeconiah (Jehoiachin) to the throne in Jerusalem.

10 ver. 14 **12** Jer 28:1; 38:17 **13** Eze 18:31 **14** Jer 14:14; 23:21; 29:8,9 **16** 2Ch 36:7,10; Jer 28:3; Da 1:2 **19** 2Ki 25:13; Jer 52:17,20,21 **20** 2Ki 24:14,15; Jer 24:1 **22** 2Ki 25:13; 2Ch 36:18; 2Ch 36:21; Jer 29:10; 32:5; Ezr 1:7; 7:19 **CHAPTER 28** **1** Jer 27:1

ence of the priests and all the people,
saying:
2 “Thus says the LORD of hosts, the
God of Israel, ‘I have broken the yoke
of the king of Babylon.
3 ‘Within two years I am going to
bring back to this place all the arti-
cles of the LORD’s house, which Nebu-
chadnezzar king of Babylon took away
from this place and carried to Babylon.
4 ‘And I will also bring back to this
place Jeconiah the son of Jehoiakim,
king of Judah, along with all the exiles
from Judah who went to Babylon,’ says
the LORD, ‘for I will break the yoke of
the king of Babylon.’ ” [Jer 22:10, 24–
27; 52:34]
5 Then the prophet Jeremiah spoke to
the prophet Hananiah in the presence
of the priests and all the people who
stood in the house of the LORD,
6 and the prophet Jeremiah said,
“Amen! May the LORD do so; may the
LORD confirm *and* fulfill your words
which you have prophesied to bring
back the articles of the LORD’s house
and all the captives, from Babylon to
this place.
7 “Nevertheless, listen now to this
word which I am about to speak in
your hearing and in the hearing of all
the people!
8 “The prophets who were before me
and before you from ancient times
prophesied against many lands and
against great kingdoms, of war and of
disaster and of virulent disease.
9 “But as for the prophet who [on the
contrary] prophesies of peace, when
that prophet’s word comes to pass,
[only] then will it be known that the
LORD has truly sent him.”
10 Then Hananiah the [false] prophet
took the yoke off the neck of the proph-
et Jeremiah and smashed it.
11 Hananiah spoke in the presence of
all the people, saying, “Thus says the
LORD, ‘Even so within two full years I
will break the yoke of Nebuchadnez-
zar king of Babylon from the neck of
all the nations.’ ” Then the prophet
Jeremiah went his way.
12 The word of the LORD came to Jere-
miah [some time] after Hananiah the
prophet had broken the yoke off the
neck of the prophet Jeremiah, saying,
13 “Go and tell Hananiah, ‘The LORD
says this, “You have broken yokes of
wood, but you have made in their place
bars of iron.”
14 ‘For thus says the LORD of hosts, the
God of Israel, “I have put the iron yoke
[of servitude] on the neck of all these
nations, that they may serve Nebuchad-
nezzar king of Babylon; and they will
serve him. And I have even given him
the beasts of the field.” ’ ” [Jer 27:6, 7]
15 Then the prophet Jeremiah said to
Hananiah the prophet, “Listen now,
Hananiah, the LORD has not sent you,
and you have made this people trust
in a lie.
16 “Therefore thus says the LORD,
‘Behold, I am about to send you away
from the face of the earth. This year
you will die, because you have spoken
and counseled rebellion against the
LORD.’ ”
17 So Hananiah the [false] prophet
died [two months later], the same year,
in the seventh month.

Message to the Exiles

29 NOW THESE are the words of
the letter which Jeremiah the
prophet sent from Jerusalem to the
rest of the elders in exile and to the
priests, the prophets and all the people
whom Nebuchadnezzar had taken into
captivity from Jerusalem to Babylon.
2 (This was after King Jeconiah
and the queen mother, the eunuchs,

28:7 – 9 *of war and of disaster and of virulent disease.* Hananiah’s message of peace and prosperity ran contrary to the long tradition of the genuine Hebrew prophets. Amos, Hosea, Micah, Joel, and Nahum spoke words of judgment and destruction against the great kingdoms like Assyria and Egypt.

28:15 – 16 *you have made this people trust in a lie.* Hananiah had not been sent by God, but he had led the people astray with a lie. As a result, Hananiah would die that very year.

29:2 *This was after.* This parenthetical passage provides background from 2 Kings 24:12 – 16

---

2 Jer 27:12 **3** Jer 27:16 **6** 1Ki 1:36 **9** Dt 18:22 **10** Jer 27:2 **11** Jer 27:7 **14** Dt 28:48; Jer 27:7; Jer 27:6 **15** Jer 29:31; Eze 13:22 **16** Dt 13:5; Jer 29:32 **CHAPTER 29** **2** 2Ki 24:12; Jer 22:26; 28:4

the princes (court officials) of Judah and Jerusalem, the craftsmen and the smiths had departed from Jerusalem.)

[3]*The letter was* hand-carried by Elasah the son of Shaphan and Gemariah the son of Hilkiah, whom Zedekiah king of Judah sent to Babylon to Nebuchadnezzar king of Babylon, saying,

[4]"So says the LORD of hosts, the God of Israel, to all the captives whom I have sent into exile from Jerusalem to Babylon,

[5]'Build houses and live *in them;* plant gardens and eat their fruit.

[6]'Take wives and have sons and daughters; take wives for your sons and give your daughters in marriage, that they may bear sons and daughters; multiply there and do not decrease [in number].

[7]'Seek peace *and* well-being for the city where I have sent you into exile, and pray to the LORD on its behalf; for in its peace (well-being) you will have peace.'

[8]"For thus says the LORD of hosts, the God of Israel, 'Do not let your [false] prophets who are among you and your diviners deceive you; pay no attention *and* attach no significance to the dreams which they dream *or* to yours,

[9]for they prophesy falsely to you in My Name. I have not sent them,' says the LORD.

[10]"For thus says the LORD, 'When seventy years [of exile] have been completed for Babylon, I will visit (inspect) you and keep My good promise to you, to bring you back to this place.

[11]'For I know the plans *and* thoughts that I have for you,' says the LORD, 'plans for peace *and* well-being and not for disaster to give you a future and a hope.

[12]'Then you will call on Me and you will come and pray to Me, and I will hear [your voice] *and* I will listen to you.

[13]'Then [with a deep longing] you will seek Me *and* require Me [as a vital necessity] and [you will] find Me when you search for Me with all your heart. [Deut 4:29, 30]

[14]'I will be found by you,' says the LORD, 'and I will restore your fortunes and I will [free you and] gather you

---

concerning the deportation of Jeconiah (Jehoiachin) to Babylon in 597 BC. This method of eliminating leaders and leaving the peasant population to pay taxes to the kingdom was learned from the Assyrians and was designed to reduce the likelihood of rebellion.

29:4 ***to all the captives whom I have sent into exile.*** Jeremiah reminded the exiled community that ultimately it was God, not Nebuchadnezzar, who had caused them to be taken to Babylon.

29:10 ***When seventy years [of exile] have been completed.*** The concept of seventy years of Babylonian captivity is reiterated from Jeremiah 25:12. The number 70 symbolizes completion and fulfillment of God's sovereign plans for creation and human history. The completion of the years of the kingdom of Babylon would also be the completion of Judah's exile.

29:11 A Future and a Hope — This text comes from a letter from Jeremiah to the exiles from Judah who were living in Babylon (Jer 29:4–9). The exiles must have had a lot of questions about their situation before they heard from Jeremiah. Had God abandoned them forever? How could they serve God properly while under the domination of the nation of Babylon? When would the exile end? Would they ever see Jerusalem again? What was the plan?

The answer that Jeremiah wrote to them probably wasn't satisfactory for all. They still would have had questions. Many would have wanted more specific answers. They would have wanted to know how long they would be in Babylon. They would have asked if they could do anything to hasten their return. These are not unlike the questions we ask of God on a daily basis.

Perhaps the best way to describe the content of Jeremiah's letter is to say that he is pointing to the fact that all the specifics are wrapped up in their relationship with God. The promises are ultimate promises. If we seek Him, we will find Him. God Himself is our hope. Shouldn't knowing this give us all the direction we need? Isn't this what our faith is all about? On the basis of knowing what God has done and what he has promised to do, we will move ahead in trust. We may not see the path clearly, but we know He does lead and He is leading us.

29:14 ***I will be found by you.*** Those who seek God with a whole heart will find Him and experience His renewal. ***I will bring you back to the***

5 ver. 28 **7** Ezr 6:10; 1Ti 2:2 **8** Jer 14:14; 23:21; 27:14,15; Eph 5:6 **9** ver. 31 **10** 2Ch 36:21,22; Ezr 1:1; Jer 25:12; 27:22; Da 9:2 **12** Da 9:3 **13** Lev 26:39,40; Dt 30:1; Jer 24:7 **14** Dt 4:7; Ps 32:6; 46:1; Isa 55:6; Jer 23:3,8; 30:3; 32:37

from all the nations and from all the
places where I have driven you,' says
the LORD, 'and I will bring you back to
the place from where I sent you into
exile.'
15 "Because you [who have remained
in Jerusalem] have said, 'The LORD has
raised up prophets for us in Babylon,'
16 thus says the LORD concerning the
king who sits on the throne of David,
and concerning all the people who
live in this city, your brothers (fellow
people of Judah) who did not go with
you into captivity—
17 thus says the LORD of hosts, 'Behold
(listen very carefully), I am sending the
sword, famine, and virulent disease
(pestilence) on them, and I will make
them like rotten figs that are so bad
they cannot be eaten.
18 'I will pursue them with the sword,
with famine and with virulent disease;
and I will make them a terror (warning)
to all the kingdoms of the earth,
to be a curse, a horror, a hissing, and
a disgrace among all the nations to
which I have driven them,
19 because they have not listened to
and honored My words,' says the LORD,
'which I sent to them again and again
by My servants the prophets. Moreover,
you [exiles] did not listen [either],'
says the LORD. [Ezek 2:5, 7]
20 "Hear, therefore, the word of the
LORD, all you exiles whom I have sent
away from Jerusalem to Babylon.
21 "Thus says the LORD of hosts, the
God of Israel, concerning Ahab the
son of Kolaiah and concerning Zedekiah
the son of Maaseiah, who are
prophesying lies to you in My Name,
'Behold, I will hand them over to Nebuchadnezzar
king of Babylon, and
he will slaughter them before your
eyes [yes, all the false prophets in
Babylon whom you follow shall die]!
[Jer 29:15]
22 'Because of them, this curse shall
be taken up *and* used by all the exiles
from Judah who are in Babylon, saying,
"May the LORD make you like Zedekiah
and like Ahab, whom the king
of Babylon roasted in the fire,
23 because they have acted foolishly
in Israel and have committed adultery
with their neighbors' wives and in My
Name have spoken false *and* concocted
words, which I did not command
them. I am He who knows and I am a
witness,' says the LORD.' "
24 Also you shall speak to Shemaiah
of Nehelam [among the exiles in Babylon],
saying,
25 "Thus says the LORD of hosts, the
God of Israel, 'Because you have sent
letters in your own name to all the
people who are in Jerusalem, and to
Zephaniah the son of Maaseiah, the
priest, and to all the priests, saying,
26 "The LORD has made you [Zephaniah]
priest instead of Jehoiada the
[deputy] priest, to be the overseer in
the house of the LORD over every madman
who prophesies, to put him in the
stocks and in the iron collar,
27 now therefore [continued the letter
from Shemaiah in Babylon to Zephaniah
in Jerusalem], why have you not
rebuked Jeremiah of Anathoth, who
prophesies to you?
28 "For he has sent *word* to us in Babylon,
saying, *'This captivity* [of yours]
will be long; build houses and live *in
them* and plant gardens and eat their
fruit.' " ' "
29 Zephaniah the priest read this letter
to Jeremiah the prophet.
30 Then came the word of the LORD
to Jeremiah, saying,
31 "Send [this message] to all the

---

place. God was the captor, and He would restore His people from captivity.

29:21 ***Ahab the son of Kolaiah and concerning Zedekiah the son of Maaseiah.*** These two were the prophets spoken of in Jeremiah 29:15. They were accused by Jeremiah of a deplorable crime; prophesying the imminent collapse of Babylon and the restoration of the captives to Jerusalem. Such false prophecy urging rebellion against God was a capital offense (Dt 14:5 – 10). The prophetic punishment of Ahab and Zedekiah was death by command of Nebuchadnezzar.

17 Jer 24:8 **18** Dt 28:25; 2Ch 29:8; Jer 15:4; 24:9; 34:17; Jer 26:6; 42:18 **19** Jer 25:4; 32:33 **22** See Ge 48:20; Isa 65:15; Da 3:6 **23** Jer 23:14 **25** 2Ki 25:18; Jer 21:1 **26** Jer 20:1; 2Ki 9:11; Ac 26:24; Jer 20:2 **28** ver. 5 **31** Jer 28:15

exiles, saying, 'Thus says the LORD
concerning Shemaiah of Nehelam,
"Because Shemaiah has prophesied
to you, although I did not send him,
and he has made you trust in a lie,"
32 therefore thus says the LORD, "Be-
hold, I am about to punish Shemaiah of
Nehelam and his descendants. He will
not have anyone [born] to live among
this people, nor will he see the good that
I am about to do to My people," says
the LORD, "because he has spoken *and*
preached rebellion against the LORD." ' "

Freedom from Captivity Promised

30 THE WORD which came to Jeremiah from the LORD:
2 "Thus says the LORD God of Israel,
'Write in a book all the words which I
have spoken to you.
3 'For behold (hear this), the days are
coming,' says the LORD, 'when I will
restore the fortunes of My people Is-
rael and Judah,' says the LORD, 'and I
will return them to the land that I gave
to their forefathers and they will take
possession of it.' "
4 Now these are the words the LORD
spoke concerning Israel and Judah:
5 "Thus says the LORD,

'We have heard a terrified voice
Of panic *and* dread, and there is
no peace.
6 'Ask now, and see
Whether a man can give birth [to
a child].
Why then do I see every man
With his hands on his loins, as a
woman in labor?
Why have all faces turned pale?
7 'Alas! for that day is great,
There is none like it;
It is the time of Jacob's [unequaled]
trouble,
But he will be saved from it.
[Matt 24:29, 30; Rev 7:14]

8 'It shall come about on that day,'
says the LORD of hosts, 'that I will break
the yoke off your neck and I will tear
off your bonds *and* force apart your
shackles; and strangers will no longer
make slaves of the people [of Israel].
9 'But they shall serve the LORD their
God and [the descendant of] David
their King, whom I will raise up for
them. [Jer 23:5]

10 'Fear not, O Jacob My servant,'
says the LORD,
'Nor be dismayed *or* downcast,
O Israel;
For behold, I will save you from a
distant land [of exile]
And your descendants from the
land of their captivity.
Jacob will return and will be quiet
and at ease,
And no one will make him afraid.
11 'For I am with you,' says the LORD,
'to save you;
For I will destroy completely
all the nations where I have
scattered you,
But I will not destroy you
completely.
But I will judge *and* discipline you
fairly
And will by no means regard
you as guiltless *and* leave you
unpunished.'

12 "For thus says the LORD,
'Your wound is incurable
And your injury is beyond healing.

30:2 *Write in a book all the words.* The oracles of Jeremiah were recorded by the scribe Baruch (ch. 36). "Book" refers to any type of writing medium, from a clay tablet to a parchment scroll. Jeremiah's oracles were recorded on a scroll (36:2).
30:6 *hands on his loins.* This phrase symbolizes the agony of God's people who had become like defenseless pregnant women in the midst of delivery before their enemies (4:31; 6:24).
30:8 *It shall come about on that day.* The day of the Lord was an ordained time of horror and distress for Israel and Judah, out of which the Lord would save them. Jeremiah expressed the hope of release from the bondage of the yoke of Babylon according to the Lord's timing (25:12) and not that of men (28:11).
30:12 *Your wound is incurable.* God's hand of judgment had brought serious harm to the nation, a mortal wound unless God intervened.
30:13 *No [device to close and allow the]*

32 Jer 28:16 **CHAPTER 30** **3** ver. 18; Jer 32:44; Eze 39:25; Am 9:14,15; Jer 16:15 **6** Jer 4:31; 6:24 **7** Joel 2:11,31; Am 5:18; Zep 1:14; Da 12:1 **9** Isa 55:3,4; Eze 34:23; 37:24; Hos 3:5; Lk 1:69; Ac 2:30; 13:23 **10** Isa 41:13; 43:5; 44:2; Jer 46:27,28; Jer 3:18 **11** Am 9:8; Jer 4:27; Ps 6:1; Isa 27:8; Jer 10:24; 46:28 **12** 2Ch 36:16; Jer 15:18

13 'There is no one to plead your
cause;
No [device to close and allow the]
healing of your wound,
No recovery for you.
14 'All your lovers (allies) have
forgotten you;
They do not seek *and* long for
you.
For I have injured you with the
wound of an enemy,
With the punishment of a cruel
and merciless foe,
Because your guilt is great
And your sins are glaring *and*
innumerable.
15 'Why do you cry out over your
injury [since it is the natural
result of your sin]?
Your pain is incurable (deadly).
Because your guilt is great
And your sins are glaring *and*
innumerable,
I have done these things to you.
16 'Therefore all who devour you will
be devoured;
And all your adversaries, every
one of them, will go into
captivity.
And they who plunder you will
become plunder,
And all who prey upon you I will
give for prey.
17 'For I will restore health to you
And I will heal your wounds,' says
the LORD,
'Because they have called you an
outcast, saying:
"This is Zion; no one seeks her *and*
no one cares for her." '

Restoration of Jacob

18 "Thus says the LORD,
'Behold (hear this), I will restore
the fortunes of the tents of
Jacob
And have mercy on his dwelling
places;
The city will be rebuilt on its [old,
mound-like] ruin,
And the palace will stand on its
rightful place.
19 'From them (city, palace) will come
[songs of] thanksgiving
And the voices of those who dance
and celebrate.
And I will multiply them and
they will not be diminished [in
number];
I will also honor them and they
will not be insignificant.
20 'Their children too will be as in
former times,
And their congregation will be
established before Me;
And I will punish all their
oppressors.
21 'Their prince will be one of them,
And their ruler will come forward
from among them.
I will bring him near and he shall
approach Me,
For who is he who would have the
boldness *and* would dare [on his
own initiative] to risk his life to
approach Me?' says the LORD.
22 'Then you shall be My people,
And I will be your God.' " [Jer 7:23]
23 Behold, the tempest of the LORD!
Wrath has gone forth,

healing of your wound. This refers to the growth of new skin over an open wound.
30:14 *All your lovers (allies) have forgotten you.* Israel's lovers were the surrounding nations like Assyria, Egypt, Phoenicia, Ammon, and Edom, with whom it had made political and religious alliances. These nations had quickly forgotten Judah; they shrank back or were defeated by Nebuchadnezzar.
30:17 *For I will restore health to you.* Restoration and healing of Israel came in two forms: retribution against its enemies and healing of its wounds.
30:18 *tents of Jacob . . . dwelling places . . . city . . . palace.* These phrases emphasize God's work in rebuilding the homes and cities of His returning exiles, from the peasant population to the administration.
30:21 *Their prince will be one of them.* Israel's leaders would no longer be appointed by foreign kings, and foreign rulers would not preside over Israel's lands.

13 Jer 8:22 **14** La 1:2; Job 13:24; 16:9; 19:11; Job 30:21; Jer 5:6 **15** Jer 15:18 **16** Ex 23:22; Isa 33:1; 41:11; Jer 10:25 **17** Jer 33:6 **18** ver. 3; Jer 33:7,11; Ps 102:13 **19** Isa 51:11; Zec 10:8 **20** Isa 1:26 **21** Ge 49:10; Nu 16:5 **22** Jer 31:1,33 **23** Jer 23:19; 25:32

A sweeping *and* gathering tempest;
It will burst on the head of the
wicked.
24 The fierce (righteous) anger of the
LORD will not turn back
Until He has fulfilled and until He
has accomplished
The intent of His heart (mind);
In the latter days you will
understand this.

Israel's Mourning Turned to Joy

31 "AT THAT time," says the
LORD, "I will be the God of all
the families of Israel, and they
shall be My people."
2 Thus says the LORD,
"The people who survived the
sword
Found grace in the wilderness [of
exile]—
Israel (the Northern Kingdom),
when it went to find its rest."
3 The LORD appeared to me (Israel)
from ages past, *saying*,
"I have loved you with an
everlasting love;
Therefore with lovingkindness I
have drawn you *and* continued
My faithfulness to you.
[Deut 7:8]
4 "Again I will build you and you
will be rebuilt,
O Virgin Israel!
You will again be adorned with
your tambourines *and* timbrels
And go out to the dances of
those who celebrate. [Is 37:22;
Jer 18:13]
5 "Again you will plant vineyards
On the mountains of Samaria;
The planters will plant
And enjoy the [abundant] fruit [in
peace].
6 "For there will be a day when the
watchmen
On the hills of Ephraim cry out,
'Arise, and let us go up to Zion,
To the LORD our God.' "
7 For thus says the LORD,
"Sing aloud with gladness for
Jacob,
And shout for the first *and*
foremost of the nations [the
chosen people, Israel];
Proclaim, give praise and say,
'O LORD save Your people,
The remnant of Israel!'
8 "Behold, I am bringing them from
the north country,
And I will gather them from the
remote parts of the earth,
Among them [will be] the blind
and the lame,
The woman with child and she
who labors in childbirth,
together;
A great company, they will return
here [to Jerusalem].
9 "They will come with weeping [in
repentance and for joy],
And by [their] prayer [for the
future] I will lead them;
I will make them walk by streams
of waters,
On a straight path in which they
will not stumble,

31:3 ***everlasting love . . . lovingkindness.*** These strong words are in parallel and point toward a love characterized by loyalty, a king of covenant love. Out of His faithfulness to the covenants God established with Abraham and Moses, and out of His great love, God established the nation Israel for His glory and for hers. The Lord would also deliver His people from captivity and reestablish them by His love.

31:4 ***O Virgin Israel.*** Earlier in Jeremiah, this expression was used sadly in depicting the departure of Israel from faith in God (2:32; 14:17). Here the image is reversed. Israel is rebuilt in the manner of her former betrothal (2:2), having become again a virgin bride to God. ***go out to the dances of those who celebrate.*** A joyful celebration of marriage and festival throughout villages is in view here (v. 13).

31:6 ***watchmen.*** This time the watchman's purpose is not to warn the people about oncoming armies but to call them to come with joy to the holy city.

31:9 ***I am a Father to Israel.*** This text is one of the few cases in the Old Testament where the fatherhood of God is portrayed directly (Dt 32:6; Isa 63:16). Israel was familiar with the idea

24 Ge 49:1 **CHAPTER 31** **1** Jer 30:24; Jer 30:22 **2** Nu 10:33; Dt 1:33; Ps 95:11; Isa 63:14 **3** Mal 1:2; Ro 11:28; Hos 11:4 **4** Jer 33:7; Ex 15:20; Jdg 11:34; Ps 149:3 **5** Isa 65:21; Am 9:14 **6** Isa 2:3; Mic 4:2 **7** Isa 12:5,6 **8** Jer 3:12,18; 23:8; Eze 20:34,41; 34:13 **9** Jer 50:4; Isa 35:8; 43:19; 49:10,11; Ex 4:22

For I am a Father to Israel,
And Ephraim (Israel) is My firstborn."

[10] Hear the word of the LORD, O you nations,
And declare it in the isles *and* coastlands far away,
And say, "He who scattered Israel will gather him
And will keep him as a shepherd keeps his flock."
[11] For the LORD has ransomed Jacob
And has redeemed him from the hand of him who was stronger than he.
[12] "They will come and sing aloud *and* shout for joy on the height of Zion,
And will be radiant [with joy] over the goodness of the LORD—
For the grain, for the new wine, for the oil,
And for the young of the flock and the herd.
And their life will be like a watered garden,
And they shall never sorrow *or* languish again.
[13] "Then the virgin will rejoice in the dance,
And the young men and old, together,
For I will turn their mourning into joy
And will comfort them and make them rejoice after their sorrow.
[14] "I will fully satisfy the soul of the priests with abundance,
And My people will be satisfied with My goodness," says the LORD.

[15] Thus says the LORD,
"A voice is heard in Ramah,
Lamentation (songs of mourning) and bitter weeping.
Rachel (Israel) is weeping for her children;
She refuses to be comforted for her children,
Because they are gone." [Matt 2:18]

[16] Thus says the LORD,

"Restrain your voice from weeping
And your eyes from tears,
For your work will be rewarded," says the LORD;
"And your children will return from the enemy's land.
[17] "There is [confident] hope for your future," says the LORD;
"Your children will come back to their own country.
[18] "I have surely heard Ephraim (Israel) moaning *and* grieving,
'You have chastised me, and I was chastised,
Like a bull unaccustomed to the yoke *or* an untrained calf;
Bring me back that I may be restored,
For You are the LORD my God.
[19] 'After I turned away [from You], I repented;
After I was instructed, I struck my thigh [in remorse];
I was ashamed and even humiliated
Because I carried the disgrace of my youth [as a nation].'
[20] "Is Ephraim My dear son?
Is he a darling *and* beloved child?
For as often as I have spoken against him,
I certainly still remember him.
Therefore My affection is renewed *and* My heart longs for him;

---

of God as Father, but it was not until the teaching of Jesus that the phrase took on the importance that we understand it to have in our lives today.
31:12 *the goodness of the LORD.* The blessings of the goodness of the Lord are bountiful crops, flocks, and vineyards (Ps 65).
31:14 *I will fully satisfy the soul of the priests with abundance.* The theme of joy is summarized in God's intention to fill the priests and the people with abundance. Jeremiah gave the people hope and comfort in facing the poverty and oppression of exile and captivity.
31:19 *I struck my thigh.* This indicates an outward demonstration of remorse over sin and change of life (Eze 21:12).

10 Isa 40:11; Eze 34:12-14 **11** Isa 44:23; 48:20; Isa 49:24 **12** Eze 17:23; Hos 3:5; Isa 58:11; Isa 35:10; 65:19; Rev 21:4 **15** Mt 2:17,18; Jos 18:25; Ge 42:13 **16** ver. 4,5; Ezr 1:5; Hos 1:11 **18** La 5:21 **19** Dt 30:2 **20** Dt 32:36; Isa 63:15; Hos 11:8; Isa 57:18; Hos 14:4

I will surely have mercy on him,"
says the LORD.

21 "Place for yourself road signs
[toward Canaan],
Make for yourself guideposts;
Turn your thought *and* attention to
the highway,
To the way by which you went
[into exile].
Retrace your steps, O virgin of Israel,
Return to these your cities.
22 "How long will you hesitate [to
return],
O you faithless *and* renegade
daughter?
For the LORD has created a new
thing in the land [of Israel]:
A woman will encompass (tenderly
love) a man."

23 Thus says the LORD of hosts, the
God of Israel, "Once more they will
speak these words in the land of Judah
(the Southern Kingdom) and in her
cities when I restore their fortunes *and*
release them from exile,

'The LORD bless you, O habitation
of justice *and* righteousness,
O holy mountain!'

24 "And [the people of] Judah and all
its cities will live there together—the
farmer and they who wander about
with flocks.
25 "For I [fully] satisfy the weary soul,
and I replenish every languishing *and*
sorrowful person."
26 At this I (Jeremiah) awoke and
looked, and my [trancelike] sleep was
sweet [in the assurance it gave] to me.

A New Covenant

27 "Behold (listen carefully), the days
are coming," says the LORD, "when I
will sow the house of Israel and the
house of Judah with the seed of man
and with the seed of beast.
28 "It will be that as I have watched
over them to uproot and to break down,
to overthrow, destroy, and afflict with
disaster, so I will watch over them to
build and to plant [with good]," says
the LORD.

29 "In those days they will not say
again,
'The fathers have eaten sour
grapes,
And the children's teeth are set on
edge.' [Ezek 18:2]

30 "But everyone will die [only] for his
own wickedness; every man who eats
sour grapes—his [own] teeth shall be
set on edge.
31 "Behold, the days are coming,"
says the LORD, "when I will make a
new covenant with the house of Israel
(the Northern Kingdom) and with the

31:21 ***road signs . . . guideposts.*** These would point out the way to the people's homeland. More importantly, Israel was instructed to set its heart toward the way that is the path of faith in its God.
31:27 ***I will sow the house of Israel.*** God would plant and multiply the seed of man and animal in the land of Judah.
31:28 ***to build and to plant.*** These are the same terms used in Jeremiah's call (1:10).
31:31 – 34 The New Covenant — The New Covenant is called "new" in contrast to the covenant with Moses which is called "old" (Jer 31:32; Heb 8:6 – 13) because it actually accomplishes what the Mosaic Covenant could only point to, that is, the child of God living in a manner that is consistent with the character of God. Four provisions are made in this covenant: (1) **Regeneration** — God will put His law in their inward parts and write it in their hearts (31:33), (2) **A national restoration** — Yahweh will be their God and the nation will be His people (31:33), (3) **Personal ministry of the Holy Spirit** — they will all be taught individually by God (31:34), and (4) **Full justification** — their sins will be forgiven and completely removed (31:34). The New Covenant is made sure by the blood that Jesus shed on Calvary's cross. The blood that guarantees to Israel its New Covenant also provides for the forgiveness of sins for the believers who comprise the church. Jesus' payment for sin is more than adequate to pay for the sins of all who will believe in Him.

---

21 Jer 50:5 **22** Jer 2:18,23,36; Jer 3:6,8, 11,12,14,22 **23** Ps 122:5-8; Isa 1:26; Zec 8:3 **24** Jer 33:12 **27** Eze 36:9-11 **28** Jer 44:27; Jer 1:10; 18:7; Jer 24:6 **29** Eze 18:2,3 **30** Gal 6:5,7 **31** Jer 32:40; 33:14; Eze 37:26; Heb 8:8-12; 10:16,17

house of Judah (the Southern Kingdom), [Luke 22:20; 1 Cor 11:25]
32not like the covenant which I made with their fathers in the day when I took them by the hand to bring them out of the land of Egypt, My covenant which they broke, although I was a husband to them," says the LORD.
33"But this is the covenant which I will make with the house of Israel after those days," says the LORD, "I will put My law within them, and I will write it on their hearts; and I will be their God, and they will be My people.
34"And each man will no longer teach his neighbor and his brother, saying, 'Know the LORD,' for they will all know Me [through personal experience], from the least of them to the greatest," says the LORD. "For I will forgive their wickedness, and I will no longer remember their sin." [Heb 8:8–12; 10:16, 17]

35Thus says the LORD,
Who gives the sun for light by day
And the fixed order of the moon
and of the stars for light by night,
Who stirs up the sea's roaring
billows *or* stills the waves when
they roar;
The LORD of hosts is His name:
36"If this fixed order departs
From before Me," says the LORD,
"Then the descendants of Israel
also will cease
From being a nation before Me
forever."

37Thus says the LORD,

"If the heavens above can be
measured
And the foundations of the earth
searched out below,
Then I will also cast off *and*
abandon all the descendants of
Israel
For all that they have done," says
the LORD.

38"Behold, the days are coming,"
says the LORD, "when the city [of Jerusalem] will be rebuilt for the LORD from the Tower of Hananel to the Corner Gate.
39"The measuring line will go out
farther straight ahead to the hill Gareb; then it will turn to Goah.
40"And the whole valley (Hinnom)
of the dead bodies and [the hill] of the ashes [long dumped there from the temple sacrifices], and all the

31:32 *the covenant which I made with their fathers.* The old covenant demanded adherence to stipulations (Ex 19:1 – 23:33) which the people were unable to keep. Above all other commandments, the people were commanded to love and serve God and abandon all others (Dt 6:4 – 5). This they did not do. From the wilderness period (Ex 32:1 – 10; Nu 25:1 – 9) until the days of Manasseh, the history of Israel was permeated with idolatrous activity, only occasionally broken by periods of true faithfulness to God. The people seemed incapable of acting in sustained obedience to the covenant. ***husband.*** As Hosea was to Gomer, the Lord had been a faithful and devoted husband to Israel.

31:33 *the covenant which I will make.* The new covenant would be initiated by God Himself, assuring its effectiveness. ***after those days.*** This expression looks forward to the time of fulfillment of the new covenant, which found fruition in the life, death, and resurrection of Jesus Christ.

31:34 *each man will no longer teach.* No longer would intermediaries like priests or prophets be needed to show the people how to know the Lord. Knowledge of God is a major theme of Jeremiah (2:8; 4:22; 5:4; 8:7). This knowledge is an intimate relationship with God evidenced by faith, obedience, and devotion.

31:36 – 37 *If this fixed order departs.* The foundation of the new covenant is as sure as the God who maintains creation. At the peak of Judah's apostasy, shortly before the destruction of the nation by Babylon in divine judgment, the Lord emphatically reaffirmed His covenant relationship with the Jewish people in such strong terms that the promise was unbreakable, even by Him. When we observe the sun, moon, or stars in the sky, we should remember God's promise to the Jewish people, even as God does.

32 Dt 1:31 **33** Jer 32:40; Ps 40:8; Eze 11:19; 36:26,27; Jer 24:7; 30:22; 32:38 **34** Isa 54:13; Jn 6:45; 1Co 2:10; 1Jn 2:20; Jer 33:8; 50:20; Mic 7:18; Ac 10:43; 13:39; Ro 11:27 **35** Ge 1:16; Ps 72:5,17; 89:2,36; 119:91; Isa 51:15; Jer 10:16 **36** Ps 148:6; Isa 54:9,10; Jer 33:20 **37** Jer 33:22 **38** Neh 3:1; Zec 14:10 **39** Eze 40:8; Zec 2:1 **40** 2Ch 23:15; Neh 3:28; Joel 3:17

fields as far as the brook Kidron, to the corner of the Horse Gate toward the east, shall be holy to the LORD. It (the city) will not be uprooted or overthrown anymore to the end of the age." [Zech 14:10, 11]

Jeremiah Imprisoned

32 THE WORD that came to Jeremiah from the LORD in the tenth year of Zedekiah king of Judah, which was the eighteenth year of Nebuchadnezzar.
2 Now at that time the army of the king of Babylon was besieging Jerusalem, and Jeremiah the prophet was shut up in the court of the guard, which was in the house of the king of Judah.
3 For Zedekiah [the last] king of Judah had locked him up, saying, "Why do you prophesy [disaster] and say, 'Thus says the LORD, "Behold, I am giving this city into the hand of the king of Babylon, and he shall take it;
4 and Zedekiah king of Judah will not escape from the hand of the Chaldeans, but he will surely be given into the hand of the king of Babylon, and he will speak with him face to face and see him eye to eye;
5 and he will lead Zedekiah to Babylon, and he will be there until I visit him [for evaluation and judgment]," says the LORD. "If you fight against the Chaldeans, you will not succeed" '?" [Jer 21:3–7; 34:2–5; 37:17; 52:7–14]
6 And Jeremiah [answered King Zedekiah and] said, "The word of the LORD came to me, saying,
7 'Behold (listen carefully), Hanamel the son of Shallum your uncle is coming to you, saying, "Buy my field that is in Anathoth, for you have the right of redemption to buy it [in accordance with the law]." '
8 "Then Hanamel my uncle's son came to me in the court of the guard in accordance with the word of the LORD, and he said to me, 'Please buy my field that is at Anathoth, which is in the land of Benjamin, for you have the right of inheritance and the redemption is yours; buy it for yourself.' Then I knew that this was the word of the LORD.
9 "I bought the field that was at Anathoth from Hanamel my uncle's son, and weighed out the money for him, seventeen shekels of silver.
10 "I signed the deed and sealed it, and called in witnesses, and weighed out the money on the scales.
11 "So I took the deeds of the purchase, both the sealed *copy containing* the terms and conditions, and the unsealed copy;
12 and I gave the purchase deed to Baruch the son of Neriah, the son of Mahseiah, in the sight of Hanamel my uncle's son and in sight of the witnesses who signed the purchase deed, in the presence of all the Jews who were sitting in the court of the guard.
13 "And I commanded Baruch in their presence, saying,
14 'Thus says the LORD of hosts, the God of Israel, "Take these deeds, both this purchase deed which is sealed and this unsealed deed, and put them in an earthen jar, that they may last a long time."
15 'For thus says the LORD of hosts, the God of Israel, "Houses and fields and vineyards will again be purchased in this land." '

Jeremiah Prays and God Explains

16 "Now when I had delivered the purchase deed to Baruch the son of Neriah, I prayed to the LORD, saying,

---

32:6 – 8 ***that is in Anathoth.*** The Lord instructed Jeremiah to purchase a field in his hometown three miles north of Jerusalem.
32:13 – 15 ***earthen jar.*** Examples of storage jars that served as safety-deposit vessels have been excavated in Judah. The Dead Sea Scrolls were also stored in ceramic vessels, aiding their preservation for almost two thousand years. The illustrated message of the purchase was assurance and confirmation that restoration of the land was certain.

CHAPTER 32 **1** 2Ki 25:1; Jer 39:1 **2** Neh 3:25; Jer 33:1; 37:21; 39:14 **3** Jer 34:2 **4** Jer 34:3; 38:18,23; 39:5; 52:9 **5** Jer 27:22; Jer 21:4; 33:5 **7** Lev 25:24,25,32; Ru 4:4 **9** Ge 23:16; Zec 11:12 **12** Jer 36:4; See Isa 8:2 **15** ver. 37,43

17 ‘Ah Lord God! Behold, You have made the heavens and the earth by Your great power and by Your outstretched arm! There is nothing too difficult *or* too wonderful for You—

18 You who show lovingkindness to thousands, but repay the wickedness (sin, guilt) of the fathers into the bosom of their children after them [that is, calling the children to account for the sins of their fathers], O great and mighty God; the Lord of hosts is His name;

19 great [are You] in counsel and mighty in deed, whose eyes are open to all the ways of the sons of men, to reward *or* repay each one according to his ways and according to the fruit of his deeds;

20 who set signs and wonders in the land of Egypt, and even to this day [continues to do so] both in Israel and among mankind; and You have made a name for Yourself, as at this day.

21 ‘You brought Your people Israel out of the land of Egypt with signs and wonders, with a strong hand and with an outstretched arm and with great terror;

22 and gave them this land, which You swore to their forefathers to give them, a land [of plenty] flowing with milk and honey.

23 ‘They entered and took possession of it, but they did not obey Your voice or walk in Your law; they have done nothing of all that You commanded them to do. Therefore You have caused all this disaster *and* suffering to come upon them.

24 ‘See the siege ramps [of mounded earth that the enemy has built against the walls]; they have come up to the city to capture it. And the city is given into the hand of the Chaldeans [of Babylon] who fight against it, because of the sword, the famine and the virulent disease [that have overcome the people]. What You have spoken has come to pass, and behold, You see it.

25 ‘Yet, O Lord God, You said to me, “Buy the field with money and get witnesses,” even though the city is given into the hands of the Chaldeans.’ ”

26 Then came the word of the Lord to Jeremiah, saying,

27 “Behold, I am the Lord, the God of all flesh; is there anything too difficult for Me?”

28 Therefore thus says the Lord, “Behold, I am about to give this city into the hand of the Chaldeans and into the hand of Nebuchadnezzar king of Babylon, and he will take it.

29 “The Chaldeans who are fighting against this city will come in and set this city on fire and burn it, along with the houses on whose roofs incense has been offered to Baal and drink offerings have been poured out to other gods to provoke Me to anger. [Jer 19:13]

30 “For the children of Israel and the children of Judah have done only evil in My sight from their youth; for the children of Israel have been provoking Me to anger by the [idols that are the] work of their hands,” says the Lord.

31 “From the day that they built it [during the reign of Solomon], even to this day, this city has been such *a provocation of* My anger and My wrath, that I must remove it from My sight, [1 Kin 11:1–13]

32 because of all the evil of the children of Israel and of the children of Judah which they have done to provoke Me to anger—they, their kings, their princes, their priests, their prophets, the men of Judah and the inhabitants of Jerusalem.

32:20 – 21 *signs and wonders in the land of Egypt.* The great historical demonstration of God’s loyal love was the exodus of Israel from Egypt. The miracles that accompanied the exodus made God known among the nations such as Moab (Nu 22 – 24).

32:27 *the God of all flesh.* God was Lord over Israel and Judah, and Lord over the nations (27:11), including mighty Babylon (25:15 – 26).

17 2Ki 19:15; ver. 27; Ge 18:14; Lk 1:37 **18** Ex 20:6; 34:7; Dt 5:9,10; Isa 9:6; Jer 10:16 **19** Isa 28:29; Job 34:21; Ps 33:13; Pr 5:21; Jer 16:17; Jer 17:10 **20** Ex 9:16; 1Ch 17:21; Isa 63:12; Da 9:15 **21** Ex 6:6; 2Sa 7:23; 1Ch 17:21; Ps 136:11,12 **22** Ex 3:8,17; Jer 11:5 **23** Neh 9:26; Jer 11:8; Da 9:10-14 **24** ver. 25,36; Jer 14:12 **25** ver. 24 **27** Nu 16:22; ver. 17 **28** ver. 3 **29** Jer 21:10; 37:8,10; 52:13; Jer 19:13 **30** Jer 2:7; 3:25; 7:22-26; Eze 20:28 **31** 2Ki 24:3 **32** Isa 1:4,6; Da 9:8

33“They have turned their back to Me and not their face; though I taught them repeatedly, yet they would not listen and receive instruction.

34“But they put their detestable things (idols) in the house which is called by My Name, to defile it.

35“They built the high places [for worship] of Baal in the Valley of Ben-hinnom (son of Hinnom) to make their sons and their daughters pass through *the fire* to [worship and honor] Molech—which I had not commanded them nor had it entered My mind that they should do this repulsive thing, to cause Judah to sin. [Jer 7:30, 31]

36“Now therefore thus says the LORD God of Israel concerning this city of which you say, ‘It is given into the hand of the king of Babylon by sword and by famine and by virulent disease.’

37“Behold, I will gather them out of all countries to which I have driven them in My anger, in My wrath and in great indignation; and I will bring them back to this place and make them live in safety.

38“They will be My people, and I will be their God;

39and I will give them one heart and one way, that they may [reverently] fear Me forever, for their own good and for the good of their children after them.

40“I will make an everlasting covenant with them that I will do them good and not turn away from them; and I will put in their heart a fear *and* reverential awe of Me, so that they will not turn away from Me. [Jer 31:31–34]

41“I will rejoice over them to do them good, and I will faithfully plant them in this land with all My heart and with all My soul.

42“For thus says the LORD, ‘Just as I have brought all this great disaster on this people, so I am going to bring on them all the good that I am promising them.

43‘Fields will be bought in this land of which you say, “It is desolate, without man or animal; it is given into the hands of the Chaldeans.”

44‘People will buy fields for money, sign deeds, seal them, and call in witnesses in the land of Benjamin, in the places around Jerusalem, in the cities of Judah, in the cities of the hill country, in the cities of the lowland, and in the cities of the South (the Negev); for I will restore their fortunes *and* release them from exile,’ says the LORD.”

Restoration Promised

33 THEN THE word of the LORD came to Jeremiah the second time, while he was still confined in the court of the guard, saying,

2“Thus says the LORD who made *the earth*, the LORD who formed it to establish it—the LORD is His name,

3‘Call to Me and I will answer you, and tell you [and even show you] great and mighty things, [things which have been confined and hidden], which you do not know *and* understand *and* cannot distinguish.’

4“For thus says the LORD, the God of Israel, concerning the houses of this city and the houses of the kings of

---

32:39 *one heart and one way.* Because the Lord had written on the heart of the people a new covenant (31:33), no longer would they worship other deities and turn to foreign nations for help. The word “way” is often used in Jeremiah to denote the character of a person’s life, whether evil (4:18) or good (7:23).

32:40 *everlasting covenant.* This expression is also found in Isaiah 55:3; Ezekiel 16:60; 37:26. In Ezekiel it is equated with a covenant of peace that God will establish with His people. This covenant will be everlasting, unlike the Sinai covenant which had been broken and ignored for so long.

33:1 *while he was still confined.* A chronological tie is made to 32:2 (588 BC). Jeremiah had been placed under palace court guard because of what his enemies regarded as “seditious speeches,” announcing the fall of Jerusalem and giving advice to Zedekiah to surrender to Nebuchadnezzar.

---

33 Jer 2:27; 7:13,24 **34** Jer 23:11; Eze 8:5,6 **35** Jer 7:31; 19:5; Lev 18:21; 1Ki 11:33; Jer 7:31 **36** ver. 24 **37** Dt 30:3; Jer 23:3; 29:14; Eze 37:21; Jer 33:16 **38** Jer 24:7; 30:22; 31:33 **39** Jer 24:7; Eze 11:19 **40** Isa 55:3; Jer 31:31; Jer 31:33 **41** Dt 30:9; Zep 3:17; Jer 24:6; 31:28; Am 9:15 **42** Jer 31:28 **43** ver. 15; Jer 33:10 **44** Jer 17:26; Jer 33:7,11 **CHAPTER 33** **1** Jer 32:2,3 **2** Isa 37:26; Ex 15:3; Am 5:8; 9:6 **3** Ps 91:15; Jer 29:12 **4** Jer 32:24

Judah which are torn down *to make a defense* against the siege ramps and against the sword, [Is 22:10; Jer 6:6]
5 'While they (the besieged Jews) are coming to fight against the Chaldeans and to fill the houses with the dead bodies of men whom I have slain in My anger and in My wrath, for I have hidden My face [in disgust] from this city because of all their wickedness.
6 'Behold, [in the restored Jerusalem] I will bring to it health and healing, and I will heal them; and I will reveal to them an abundance of peace (prosperity, security, stability) and truth.
7 'I will restore the fortunes of Judah and the fortunes of Israel and will rebuild them as they were at first.
8 'I will cleanse them from all their wickedness (guilt) by which they have sinned against Me, and I will pardon (forgive) all their sins by which they rebelled against Me.
9 'Jerusalem will be to Me a name of joy, praise and glory before all the nations of the earth which will hear of all the good that I do for it, and they shall fear and tremble because of all the good and all the peace (prosperity, security, stability) that I provide for it.'
10 "Thus says the LORD, 'Yet again there will be heard in this place of which you say, "It is a [desolate] waste, without man and without animal"—even in the cities of Judah and in the streets of Jerusalem that are desolate, without man and without inhabitant and without animal—
11 the [sound of the] voice of joy and the voice of gladness, the voice of the bridegroom and the voice of the bride, the [song-filled] voice of those who say,

"Give praise *and* thanks to the
LORD of hosts,
For the LORD is good;
For His [steadfast] lovingkindness
(mercy) endures forever";

and of those who bring a thank offering into the house of the LORD. For I will restore the fortunes of the land as they were at first,' says the LORD.
12 "Thus says the LORD of hosts, 'There will again be in this desolate place—[a place] without man or animal—and in all its cities, pastures for shepherds who rest their flocks.
13 'In the cities of the hill country, in the cities of the lowland, in the cities of the South (the Negev), in the land of Benjamin, in the places around Jerusalem and in the cities of Judah, the flocks will again pass under the hand of the one who counts them,' says the LORD.

The Davidic Kingdom

14 'Behold, the days are coming,' says the LORD, 'when I will fulfill the good word *and* promise which I have made regarding the house of Israel and the house of Judah.
15 'In those days and at that time I will cause a righteous Branch of David to spring forth; and He (the Messiah) shall execute justice and righteousness on the earth. [Is 4:2; Jer 23:5; Zech 3:8; 6:12]
16 'In those days Judah will be saved and [the people of] Jerusalem will live in safety; and this is *the name* by which she will be called: the LORD Our Righteousness (Justice).'
17 "For thus says the LORD, 'David shall never lack a man (descendant) to sit on the throne of the house of Israel;

33:8 *cleanse ... pardon.* Forgiveness is described with these two terms. The word "cleanse" describes ritual purification of what is physically or spiritually unclean or defiled, like Israel and Judah (2:23; 7:30). "Pardon" means "to forgive," and in the Old Testament is used only with God as the subject as He forgives man. This fact helps us understand the reaction of the scribes when they heard Jesus forgiving sins (Mk 2:7).

33:13 *flocks will again pass under.* The term "flocks" is used to depict the Israelites as they returned from captivity into the fold of the holy city of Jerusalem.

33:16 *will live in safety.* Following the devastation of the Babylonian onslaught, Jerusalem would exist under divine protection.

33:17 *David shall never lack.* The Davidic covenant of divine succession is reiterated

5 Jer 32:5 **6** Jer 30:17 **7** Jer 30:3; 32:44; Isa 1:26; Jer 24:6; 30:20; 31:4,28; 42:10 **8** Eze 36:25; Zec 13:1; Heb 9:13,14; Jer 31:34; Mic 7:18 **9** Isa 62:7; Jer 13:11; Isa 60:5 **10** Jer 32:43 **11** Jer 7:34; 16:9; 25:10; Rev 18:23; 1Ch 16:8; 2Ch 5:13; Ezr 3:11; Ps 136:1; Isa 12:4; Lev 7:12; Ps 107:22; 116:17; ver. 7 **12** Isa 65:10; Jer 31:24; 50:19 **13** Jer 17:26; 32:44; Lev 27:32 **14** Jer 23:5; 31:27,31; Jer 29:10 **15** Isa 4:2; 11:1; Jer 23:5 **17** 2Sa 7:16; 1Ki 2:4; Ps 89:29; Lk 1:32

18 and the Levitical priests shall never
lack a man (descendant) to offer burnt
offerings before Me and to burn grain
offerings and to prepare sacrifices all
day long.' "
19 The word of the LORD came to Jere-
miah, saying,
20 "Thus says the LORD, 'If you can
break My covenant for the day and
My covenant for the night, so that day
and night do not take place at their
appointed times,
21 then My covenant may also be bro-
ken with David My servant so that he
will not have a son to reign on his throne,
and [My covenant may also be broken]
with the Levitical priests, My ministers.
22 'As the host of [the stars of] heaven
cannot be counted and the sand of the
sea cannot be measured, so I will multi-
ply the descendants of David My servant
and the Levites who minister to Me.' "
23 And the word of the LORD came to
Jeremiah, saying,
24 "Have you not noticed what this
people have spoken, saying, 'The two
families [Israel the northern kingdom,
and Judah the southern kingdom]
which the LORD chose, He has reject-
ed'? Thus they despise My [chosen]
people, no longer are they [considered]
as a nation in their sight.
25 "Thus says the LORD, 'If My cov-
enant with day and night does not
stand, and if I have not established
the fixed patterns of heaven and earth,
[the whole order of nature,]
26 then I would [also] reject the de-
scendants of Jacob and David My
servant, not taking from his descen-
dants rulers over the descendants of
Abraham, Isaac, and Jacob. But I will
restore their fortunes, and will have
mercy on them.' " [Gen 49:10]

A Prophecy against Zedekiah

34 THE WORD that came to Jere-
miah from the LORD when Nebu-
chadnezzar king of Babylon and all his
army, with all the kingdoms of the earth
that were under his sovereignty and
all the peoples, were fighting against
Jerusalem and against all of its cities:
2 "Thus says the LORD God of Israel,
'Go and speak to Zedekiah king of
Judah and tell him: "Thus says the
LORD, 'Behold, I am giving this city into
the hand of the king of Babylon, and
he will set it on fire *and* burn it down.
3 'You will not escape from his hand,
for you will definitely be captured and
handed over to him; you will see the
king of Babylon eye to eye, and he will
speak with you face to face; and you
will go to Babylon.' " '
4 "Yet hear the word of the LORD,
O Zedekiah king of Judah! Thus says
the LORD concerning you, 'You will not
die by the sword.
5 'You will die in peace; and as *spices*
were burned for [the memory and hon-
or of] your fathers, the former kings
who reigned before you, so shall a [cer-
emonial] burning be made for you; and
people will lament (grieve) for you,
saying, "Alas, lord (master)!" ' For I
have spoken the word," says the LORD.
6 Then Jeremiah the prophet spoke
all these words to Zedekiah king of
Judah in Jerusalem
7 when the army of the king of Bab-
ylon was fighting against Jerusalem
and against all the remaining cities of
Judah, against Lachish and Azekah,

(2Sa 7:12 – 16). The Levitical priesthood would likewise be heirs to a divine succession in overseeing the sacrificial system in the Jerusalem temple. Jesus, as Priest and King, fulfills both offices in the New Covenant.

34:3 *You will not escape from his hand.* Though Zedekiah attempted to flee to Jericho, Nebuchadnezzar's forces captured and brought him to Riblah for a face to face meeting with Nebuchadnezzar (32:3,4).

34:5 *You will die in peace.* Jeremiah proclaimed the destruction of Jerusalem and the death of its inhabitants by sword, pestilence, and famine. The particular implications for Zedekiah are outlined here. He would not be executed by the sword. According to 2 Kings 25:6 – 7, his sons

18 Ro 12:1; 15:16; 1Pe 2:5,9; Rev 1:6 **20** ver. 25; Ps 89:37; Isa 54:9; Jer 31:36 **21** Ps 89:34 **22** Ge 15:5 **24** ver. 21,22 **25** ver. 20; Ge 8:22; Ps 74:16; 104:19; Jer 31:35,36 **26** Jer 31:37; ver. 7,11; Ezr 2:1 **CHAPTER 34** **1** 2Ki 25:1; Jer 39:1; 52:4; Jer 1:15 **2** Jer 21:10; 32:3,28; ver. 22; Jer 32:29 **3** Jer 32:4 **5** 2Ch 16:14; 21:19; Da 2:46; See Jer 22:18 **7** 2Ki 18:13; 19:8; 2Ch 11:5,9

for these were the [only] fortified cities
among the cities of Judah.
8 The word came to Jeremiah from
the LORD after King Zedekiah had
made a covenant (solemn pledge)
with all the [Hebrew] people who were
[slaves] in Jerusalem to proclaim lib-
erty to them:
9 that every man should let his He-
brew slaves, male and female, go free,
so that no one should make a slave of
a Jew, his brother.
10 So all the princes and all the peo-
ple who had entered into the covenant
agreed that everyone would let his
male servant and his female servant go
free, and that no one would keep them
in bondage any longer; they obeyed,
and set *them free.*
11 But afterward they backed out [of
the covenant] and made the male ser-
vants and the female servants whom
they had set free return [to them], and
brought the male servants and the fe-
male servants again into servitude.
12 Therefore the word of the LORD
came to Jeremiah from the LORD,
saying,
13 "Thus says the LORD, the God of
Israel, 'I made a covenant (solemn
pledge) with your forefathers in the
day that I brought them out of the land
of Egypt, out of the house of bondage,
saying,
14 "At the end of seven years each of
you shall set free his Hebrew brother
who has sold himself [into servitude]
or who has been sold to you and has
served you six years, you shall release
him from [serving] you; but your fore-
fathers did not listen [submissively] to
Me or obey Me. [Deut 15:12]
15 "So then you recently turned *and*
repented, doing what was right in My
sight, each man proclaiming release
[from servitude] to his countryman
[who was his bond servant]; and you
had made a covenant before Me in the
house which is called by My Name.
16 "Yet you backed out [of the cov-
enant] and profaned My Name, and
each man took back his servants, male
and female, whom had been set free in
accordance with their desire, and you
brought them into servitude [again] to
be your male servants and your female
servants." '
17 "Therefore says the LORD, 'You
have not obeyed Me; you have not pro-
claimed liberty to your brother and
your countryman. Behold (listen very
carefully), I am proclaiming liberty to
you—[liberty to be put] to the sword,
[liberty] to [be ravaged by] the virulent
disease, and [liberty] to [be decimated
by] famine,' says the LORD; 'and I will
make you a horror *and* a warning to
all the kingdoms of the earth.
18 'The men who have violated My
covenant, who have not kept the terms

---

were killed before his eyes and then his eyes were put out before being taken to Babylon.

34:8 Zedekiah had made a covenant (solemn pledge) with all the [Hebrew] people. A legal agreement was made between Zedekiah and the people of Jerusalem during the Babylonian siege to release from bondage all Hebrew slaves.

34:12–14 Thus says the LORD. Jeremiah, a faithful steward of the word of God, began his attack against Judah's leaders by recounting the teaching of the law on the matter of emancipating slaves (Ex 21:2–6; Dt 15:12–15). He reminded the people that their forefathers were slaves in Egypt, and that God had freed them from slavery and oppression.

34:16 Yet you backed out [of the covenant] and profaned My Name. When the princes of Judah emancipated their Hebrew slaves, it demonstrated their covenant faithfulness and devotion to God (v. 10). But when the righteous decision was reversed (v. 11), the name of God was profaned. The name of God sums up and represents His attributes, character, and work. That name had been defiled by the breach of covenant in the same way that the people had defiled the land with their idolatry (16:18).

34:18–19 they split the [sacrificial] calf in half. The covenant ceremony is outlined. The main ritual of the two-party covenant began with cutting the sacrificial animal in half, after which the two participants would walk together between the parts (Ge 15). The divided animal portrayed the potential fate of one who broke the covenant stipulations.

8 ver. 14; Ex 21:2; Lev 25:10 **9** Neh 5:11; Lev 25:39-46 **11** See ver. 21; Jer 37:5 **14** Ex 21:2; 23:10; Dt 15:12
15 2Ki 23:3; Neh 10:29; Jer 7:10 **16** Ex 20:7; Lev 19:12 **17** Mt 7:2; Gal 6:7; Jas 2:13; Jer 32:24,36; Dt 28:25,64; Jer 29:18 **18** See Ge 15:10,17

of the solemn pledge which they made before Me when they split the [sacrificial] calf in half, and then afterwards walked between its separated pieces [sealing their pledge to Me by placing a curse on themselves should they violate the covenant—those men I will make like the calf]! [Gen 15:9, 10, 17]

19‘The princes of Judah, the princes of Jerusalem, the high officials, the priests, and all the people of the land who passed between the parts of the calf,

20I will give into the hand of their enemies and into the hand of those who seek their lives. And [like the body of the calf] their dead bodies will be food for the birds of the sky and the beasts of the earth.

21‘Zedekiah king of Judah and his princes I will place into the hand of their enemies and into the hand of those who seek their life, and into the hand of the army of the king of Babylon which has withdrawn from you.

22‘Behold, I am going to command [the Chaldeans who rule Babylon],’ says the LORD, ‘and I will bring them back to this city; and they will fight against it and take it and set it on fire. I will make the cities of Judah a desolation without inhabitant.’ ”

The Rechabites’ Obedience

35 THE WORD that came to Jeremiah from the LORD in the days of Jehoiakim the son of Josiah, king of Judah:

2“Go to the house of the Rechabites and speak to them, and bring them into the house of the LORD, into one of the [side] chambers; then give them [who are pledged not to drink wine] some wine to drink.”

3So I took Jaazaniah the son of Jeremiah, the son of Habazziniah, and his brothers and all his sons and the whole house of the Rechabites,

4and I brought them into the house of the LORD, into the chamber of the sons of Hanan the son of Igdaliah, the man of God, which was near the chamber of the princes, above the chamber of Maaseiah the son of Shallum the doorkeeper.

5Then I set before the men of the house of the Rechabites pitchers full of wine, and cups, and I said to them, “Drink wine.”

6But they said, “We will not drink wine, for Jonadab the son of Rechab, our father, commanded us: ‘You shall not drink wine, neither you nor your sons, forever.

7‘Nor shall you build a house or sow seed or plant a vineyard or own one; but you shall live in tents all your days, that you may live many days in the land where you are sojourners (temporary residents).’

8“We have obeyed the words of Jonadab the son of Rechab, our father, in all that he commanded us, in all our days we have never drunk wine, nor have our wives, our sons, or our daughters,

9nor have we built ourselves houses to live in; nor do we have vineyards or fields or seed.

10“We have lived only in tents, and have obeyed and done [everything] according to all that Jonadab our father commanded us.

11“But when Nebuchadnezzar king of Babylon came up against the land, we said, ‘Come and let us go to Jerusalem for fear of the army of the Chaldeans [who rule Babylon] and for fear of the army of the Arameans.’ So we have lived in Jerusalem.”

Judah Rebuked

12Then came the word of the LORD to Jeremiah, saying,

13“Thus says the LORD of hosts, the

35:2 *the house of the Rechabites.* This clan was a tightly knit group of descendants of the Kenites (Jdg 1:16; 1Ch 2:55). They lived as nomads, rejecting all forms of urban and agrarian life. They refused to drink wine or strong drink and would not cultivate vineyards. They also would not plant any other crops. They were invited by Jeremiah into one of the chambers surrounding the courtyard of the temple of God for a symbolic demonstration.

35:13 – 16 *obeyed their father’s command.* The Rechabites held to the teaching of their

20 Jer 7:33; 16:4; 19:7 **21** See Jer 37:5,11 **22** Jer 37:8,10; Jer 38:3; 39:1,2,8; 52:7,13; Jer 9:11; 44:2,6 **CHAPTER 35** **2** 2Ki 10:15; 1Ch 2:55; 1Ki 6:5 **4** 2Ki 12:9; 25:18; 1Ch 9:18,19 **6** 2Ki 10:15 **7** Ex 20:12; Eph 6:2,3 **13** Jer 32:33

God of Israel, 'Go and say to the men
of Judah and the inhabitants of Jerusa-
lem, "Will you not receive instruction
by listening to My words *and* honoring
them?" says the LORD.
[14]"The command which Jonadab the
son of Rechab gave to his sons not to
drink wine has been observed [as a
custom for more than two hundred
years]. To this day they do not drink
wine, for they have obeyed their fa-
ther's command. But I have repeat-
edly spoken to you, yet you have not
listened to Me.
[15]"I have also sent to you all My ser-
vants the prophets, sending them re-
peatedly, saying, 'Let every one of you
turn now from his evil way and alter
your behavior, and do not follow other
gods to worship *and* serve them; and
then you will live in the land which I
have given to you and to your forefa-
thers. But you have not submitted or
listened to Me.
[16]'Indeed, the sons of Jonadab the
son of Rechab have observed the com-
mand of their father which he gave
them, but this people has not listened
to Me.' " '
[17]"Therefore thus says the LORD God
of hosts, the God of Israel, 'Behold
(hear this), I am bringing on Judah
and all the inhabitants of Jerusalem
all the disaster that I have pronounced
against them, because I have spoken to
them, but they have not listened, and I
have called to them, but they have not
answered.' "
[18]Then Jeremiah said to the house of
the Rechabites, "Thus says the LORD of
hosts, the God of Israel, 'Because you
have obeyed the command of Jona-
dab your father and have kept all his
commands and have done according
to all that he commanded you,
[19]therefore thus says the LORD of
hosts, the God of Israel, "Jonadab the
son of Rechab shall never fail to have
a man (descendant) to stand before Me
always." ' "

Jeremiah's Scroll Read in the Temple

36 IN THE fourth year of Jehoia-
kim the son of Josiah, king of
Judah, this word came to Jeremiah
from the LORD, saying,
[2]"Take a scroll [of parchment] and
write on it all the words which I have
spoken to you concerning Israel and
Judah, and all the nations, from the
day I [first] spoke to you in the days of
[King] Josiah until this day.
[3]"It may be that the house of Judah
will hear all the disaster which I plan
to bring on them, so that each one will
turn from his evil way, that I may for-
give their wickedness and their sin."
[Jer 18:7–10; 26:3]
[4]Then Jeremiah called Baruch the
son of Neriah, and Baruch wrote on the
scroll of the book all the words which
Jeremiah dictated, [words] which the
LORD had spoken to him.
[5]Jeremiah commanded Baruch,
saying, "I am [in hiding, virtually] re-
strained; I cannot go into the house of
the LORD.
[6]"So you go to the LORD's house on a
day of fasting and read from the scroll
the words of the LORD to the people
which you have written as I dictated.
And also you shall read them to all
the people of Judah who come from
their cities.
[7]"It may be that their supplication
[for mercy] will come before the LORD,
and everyone will turn from his evil
way, for great is the anger and the

---

forefather, while the Israelites continually re-
belled against the teaching of God.

36:2 *Take a scroll [of parchment] and write on it.* The usual material for a scroll was parch-
ment (a kind of leather), though Egyptian papyrus
was also available. The contents of the scroll were
the oracles dating from the days of Josiah, at the
advent of Jeremiah's ministry (626 BC).

36:6 *go . . . and read from the scroll.* This scroll
was to be read on a day of fasting, a time set aside
by official declaration of the king or priests (v. 9)
in a period of national crisis.

14 2Ch 36:15; Jer 7:13; 25:3 **15** Jer 18:11; 25:5,6 **17** Pr 1:24; Isa 65:12; 66:4; Jer 7:13 **19** Jer 15:19
CHAPTER 36 **2** Isa 8:1; Eze 2:9; Zec 5:1; Jer 30:2; Jer 25:15; Jer 25:3 **3** ver. 7; Jer 26:3; Jer 18:8; Jnh 3:8
4 Jer 32:12; See Jer 45:1 **6** Lev 16:29; 23:27-32; Ac 27:9 **7** ver. 3

wrath that the LORD has pronounced
against this people."
8 Baruch the son of Neriah did every-
thing that Jeremiah the prophet com-
manded him, reading from [Jeremiah's
scroll] the words of the LORD in the
LORD's house.
9 Now in the fifth year of Jehoiakim
the son of Josiah, king of Judah, in the
ninth month, a fast was proclaimed
before the LORD for all the people in
Jerusalem and all the people who came
to Jerusalem from the cities of Judah.
10 Then Baruch read to all the people
the words of Jeremiah from the scroll
of the book in the house of the LORD,
in the chamber of Gemariah the son
of Shaphan the scribe, in the upper
court, at the entry of the New Gate of
the LORD's house.
11 When Micaiah the son of Gemari-
ah, the son of Shaphan, had heard all
the words of the LORD from the scroll,
12 he went down to the king's house,
into the scribe's chamber; and behold,
all the princes were sitting there: Elish-
ama the scribe, Delaiah the son of She-
maiah, Elnathan the son of Achbor,
Gemariah the son of Shaphan, Zede-
kiah the son of Hananiah, and all the
[other] princes.
13 Then Micaiah declared to them
all the words that he had heard when
Baruch read from the scroll to all the
people.
14 Therefore all the princes sent Je-
hudi the son of Nethaniah, the son of
Shelemiah, the son of Cushi, to Baruch,
saying, "Take in your hand the scroll
from which you have read to the people
and come [to us]." So Baruch the son
of Neriah took the scroll in his hand
and went to them.
15 And they said to him, "Sit down
now and read it to us." So Baruch read
it to them.
16 Now when they had heard all the
words, they turned one to another in
fear and said to Baruch, "We must
surely report all these words to the
king."
17 And they asked Baruch, "Tell
us now, how did you write all these
words? At his (Jeremiah's) dictation?"
18 Then Baruch answered them, "He
dictated all these words to me, and I
wrote them with ink on the scroll."
19 Then the princes said to Baruch,
"Go and hide, you and Jeremiah, and
do not let anyone know where you
are."

The Scroll Is Burned

20 Then they went into the court to
the king, but they [first] put the scroll
in the chamber of Elishama the scribe;
then they reported all the words to the
king.
21 So the king sent Jehudi to get the
scroll, and he took it out of the cham-
ber of Elishama the scribe. And Jehudi
read it to the king and all the princes
who stood beside the king.
22 Now it was the ninth month, and
the king was sitting in the winter
house, with *a fire* burning there in
the brazier before him.
23 And after Jehudi had read three
or four columns [of the scroll], *King
Jehoiakim* would cut off *that portion*
with a scribe's knife and throw it into
the fire that was in the brazier, until
the [entire] scroll was consumed by
the fire.
24 Yet the king and all his servants
who heard all these words were not
afraid, nor did they tear their clothes.
25 Even though Elnathan and Delaiah
and Gemariah pleaded with the king
not to burn the scroll, he would not
listen to them.
26 And the king commanded Je-
rahmeel the king's son, Seraiah the
son of Azriel, and Shelemiah the son of

36:8 *Baruch . . . did everything that Jeremiah the prophet commanded him.* As a faithful disciple, Baruch read from the book of God's words in the temple of the Lord. This act closely parallels the reading of the Book of the Law in the temple after it was discovered there under Josiah.

36:20 – 24 *cut off that portion with a scribe's knife.* Jehoiakim showed no signs of fear or lamentation, unlike Josiah when the Book of the Law was read in his hearing (2Ki 22:11 – 13). Instead he cuts the scroll up and throws it into a fire.

10 Jer 26:10 **22** See Am 3:15 **24** 2Ki 22:11; Isa 36:22; 37:1

Abdeel to seize Baruch the scribe and
Jeremiah the prophet, but the LORD
hid them.

The Scroll Is Replaced

27Then the word of the LORD came
to Jeremiah after the king had burned
the scroll containing the words which
Baruch had written at the dictation of
Jeremiah:
28"Take another scroll and write on
it all the former words that were on the
first scroll which Jehoiakim the king
of Judah burned.
29"And concerning Jehoiakim king
of Judah you shall say, 'Thus says the
LORD, "You have burned this scroll,
saying, 'Why have you written on it
that the king of Babylon will certainly
come and destroy this land, and will
cut off man and beast from it?' "
30'Therefore thus says the LORD con-
cerning Jehoiakim king of Judah, "He
shall have no heir to sit on the throne
of David, and his dead body shall be
thrown out to the heat of the day and
to the frost of the night.
31"I will also punish him and his de-
scendants and his servants for their
wickedness, and I will bring on them
and the inhabitants of Jerusalem and
the men of Judah all the destruction
that I have declared against them—but
they would not listen." ' "
32Then Jeremiah took another scroll
and gave it to Baruch the scribe, the
son of Neriah, who wrote on it at the
dictation of Jeremiah all the words of
the scroll which Jehoiakim king of Ju-
dah had burned in the fire; and many
similar words were added to them.

Jeremiah Warns against Trust in Pharaoh

37 NOW NEBUCHADNEZZAR
king of Babylon made Zedekiah
the son of Josiah king in the land of
Judah so he reigned as king instead
of Coniah (also called Jeconiah and
Jehoiachin) the son of Jehoiakim.
2But neither he nor his servants nor
the people of the land listened to the
words of the LORD which He spoke
through the prophet Jeremiah.
3Yet King Zedekiah sent Jehucal the
son of Shelemiah [along] with Zepha-
niah the son of Maaseiah, the priest, to
the prophet Jeremiah, saying, "Please
pray [now] to the LORD our God for us."
4Now Jeremiah was coming and go-
ing among the people, for they had not
[yet] put him in prison.
5Meanwhile, Pharaoh's army had set
out from Egypt; and when the Chal-
deans who were besieging Jerusalem
heard the news about them, they with-
drew from Jerusalem.
6Then the word of the LORD came to
the prophet Jeremiah:
7"Thus says the LORD, the God of
Israel, 'This is what you are to say to
the king of Judah, who sent you to Me
to inquire of Me: "Behold, Pharaoh's
army, which has come out to help you,
will return to Egypt, to their own land.
8"And the Chaldeans [of Babylon]

36:29–31 ***Jehoiakim king of Judah.*** Indictment and judgment against Jehoiakim is pronounced. The indictment was declared because he destroyed the scroll of the Word of the Lord. First, the Davidic lineage would not continue through him. His son would rule for only three months before Nebuchadnezzar deported Jehoiachin to Babylon, where he died. Second, the king's body would be treated disgracefully after his death. As the king had cast the scroll into the fire, so his body would be cast from the royal palace. Third, the royal household would experience the destructive judgment that had been proclaimed in the words of the original scroll.

37:2 ***neither he nor his servants nor the people of the land listened.*** It is eminently possible and easy to reject God's message. As Zedekiah and all the people did, so can we deliberately refuse to heed the Lord, even when events have shown the truth of His message.

37:5 ***Pharaoh's army had set out from Egypt.*** In late spring or early summer 588 BC, Pharaoh Hophra led the Egyptian army into southern Palestine. The Babylonian forces withdrew their siege of Jerusalem to confront the Egyptians. Zedekiah hoped the Babylonians would be defeated, but his hopes proved to be in vain.

30 Jer 22:30; Jer 22:19 **CHAPTER 37** **1** 2Ki 24:17; 2Ch 36:10; Jer 22:24 **2** 2Ch 36:12,14 **3** Jer 21:1,2; 29:25; 52:24 **5** See 2Ki 24:7; Eze 17:15; ver. 11; Jer 34:21 **7** Jer 21:2 **8** Jer 34:22

will come again and fight against this
city, and they will capture it and set it
on fire." '
9 "Thus says the LORD, 'Do not de-
ceive yourselves, saying, "The Chal-
deans will certainly stay away from
us," for they will not stay away.
10 'For even if you had defeated the
whole army of the Chaldeans who
fight against you, and there remained
only the wounded men among them,
yet they would rise up, every man con-
fined in his tent, and burn down this
city with fire.' "

Jeremiah Imprisoned

11 Now it happened when the army of
the Chaldeans departed from Jerusa-
lem for fear of Pharaoh's [approaching]
army,
12 that Jeremiah left Jerusalem
[during the withdrawal of the Chal-
dean invaders] to go to [Anathoth, his
hometown, in] the land of Benjamin to
take possession of [the title to] the land
[which he had purchased] there among
the people. [Jer 32:6–12]
13 When he was at the Gate of Ben-
jamin, a captain of the guard whose
name was Irijah, the son of Shelemiah
the son of Hananiah was there; and
he seized *and* arrested Jeremiah the
prophet, saying, "You are deserting
to join the Chaldeans [of Babylon]!"
14 But Jeremiah said, "That is a lie!
I am not deserting to join the Chal-
deans." But the guard would not lis-
ten to him. So Irijah took Jeremiah
and brought him to the princes (court
officials).
15 The princes were enraged with
Jeremiah and beat him and put him
in prison in the house of Jonathan the
scribe—for they had made that the
prison.
16 When Jeremiah had come into the
vaulted cell in the dungeon and had
remained there many days,
17 Zedekiah the king sent and
brought him out; and in his palace
the king secretly asked him, "Is there
any word from the LORD?" And Jere-
miah said, "There is!" Then he said,
"You will be handed over to the king
of Babylon."
18 Moreover, Jeremiah said to King
Zedekiah, "In what way have I sinned
against you, or against your servants,
or against this people, that you have
put me in prison?
19 "Where then are your prophets
who prophesied to you, saying, 'The
king of Babylon will not come against
you or against this land?'
20 "Therefore now, please listen, O my
lord the king; please let my petition
come before you *and* be acceptable and
do not make me return to the house
of Jonathan the scribe, that I may not
die there."
21 Then King Zedekiah commanded,
and they committed Jeremiah to the
court of the guardhouse, and a [round]
loaf of bread from the bakers' street
was given to him daily, until all the
bread in the city was gone. So Jere-
miah remained [imprisoned] in the
court of the guardhouse.

Jeremiah Thrown into the Cistern

38 NOW SHEPHATIAH the son of
Mattan, and Gedaliah the son of
Pashhur, and Jucal (also called Jehu-

37:9 *Do not deceive yourselves.* To think that the brief respite caused by the Egyptian appearance in the southern coastal plain was proof of imminent deliverance, as the false prophets declared, was an exercise in self-deception and futile imagination.
37:14 – 16 *I am not deserting to join the Chaldeans.* Jeremiah denied the accusation of defection but to no avail. Irijah arrested the prophet and arraigned him before the court of princes. Prison space was lacking in Jerusalem due to the crowded conditions of the siege, so a prison had to be devised.
37:17 – 19 *Zedekiah the king sent and brought him out.* Fearing possible exposure and opposition from his courtiers, Zedekiah secretly summoned Jeremiah and asked of him a word from the Lord. He seems to have earnestly desired a word from God but could not come to grips with the reality and respond appropriately. Jeremiah appealed to Zedekiah's sense of

10 Jer 21:4,5 **11** ver. 5 **15** Jer 38:26 **16** Jer 38:6 **21** Jer 32:2; 38:13,28; Jer 38:9; 52:6 **CHAPTER 38** **1** Jer 37:3; Jer 21:1; Jer 21:8

cal) the son of Shelemiah, and Pashhur the son of Malchijah heard the words that Jeremiah was speaking to all the people, saying,
2"So says the LORD, 'He who remains in this city will die by the sword, by famine, and by virulent disease (pestilence), but he who goes out to the Chaldeans [of Babylon] will live and have his [own] life as a reward and stay alive.' [Jer 21:9]
3"Thus says the LORD, 'This city will certainly be given into the hand of the army of the king of Babylon and he will take it.' "

4Therefore the princes (court officials) said to the king, "Please [we implore you] let this man [Jeremiah] be put to death; for [speaking] in this way he discourages *and* weakens [the will of] the soldiers who remain in this city and he discourages *and* weakens [the will of] all the people by speaking such words to them; for this man is not seeking the well-being of these people, but rather their harm."
5Then King Zedekiah [fearing the princes] said, "Listen, he is in your hand; for the king is in no position to do anything against you."
6So they took Jeremiah and threw him into the cistern of Malchijah the king's son, which was in the court of the guardhouse; and they let Jeremiah down [into the cistern] with ropes. Now there was no water in the cistern but only mud, and Jeremiah sank in the mud.
7Now Ebed-melech the Ethiopian (Cushite), one of the eunuchs who was in the king's palace, heard that they had put Jeremiah in the cistern, and while the king was sitting in the Gate of Benjamin,
8Ebed-melech went out of the king's palace and spoke to the king, saying,
9"My lord the king, these men have acted wickedly in all that they have done to Jeremiah the prophet whom they have thrown into the cistern; and he will die [of hunger] where he is because of the famine, for there is no more bread in the city."
10Then the king commanded Ebed-melech the Ethiopian, saying, "Take thirty men from here with you and lift Jeremiah the prophet out of the cistern before he dies."
11So Ebed-melech took the men with him and went into the palace of the king to *a place* under the storeroom and took from there old rags and worn-out clothes and let them down by ropes into the cistern to Jeremiah.
12Then Ebed-melech the Ethiopian said to Jeremiah, "Now put these old rags and worn-out clothes under your armpits, then place the ropes under the padding"; and Jeremiah did so.
13So they pulled Jeremiah up with the ropes and took him up out of the cistern; and Jeremiah remained in the court of the guardhouse.
14Then King Zedekiah sent and had Jeremiah the prophet brought to him at the third entrance that is in the house of the LORD. And the king said to Jeremiah, "I am going to ask you something; hide nothing from me."
15Then Jeremiah said to Zedekiah, "If I tell you, will you not certainly put me to death? Even if I do give you advice, you will not listen to me."
16But King Zedekiah swore secretly to Jeremiah, "As the LORD lives, who made our lives, be assured that I will not put you to death or put you into the hand of these men who are seeking your life."

---

justice and decency and asked to be released from prison. Zedekiah consented.

38:2 – 3 *He who remains in this city.* Verse 2 is almost an exact duplicate of 21:9. Jeremiah said the choice was between life under the Babylonians and death among the ruins of Jerusalem. Such a statement was treasonous, as was the statement that Jerusalem must fall.

38:7 *Ebed-melech.* This man took special care to obtain rags for Jeremiah to cushion his armpits, preventing the ropes from cutting his skin. A foreigner, a once despised Cushite (from Egypt), cared more for the prophet of God than did the king and the princes of Jeremiah's own people.

2 Jer 21:9 **3** Jer 21:10; 32:3 **4** See Jer 26:11 **6** Jer 37:21 **7** Jer 39:16 **13** ver. 6; Jer 37:21 **16** Isa 57:16

Interview with Zedekiah

17 Then Jeremiah said to Zedekiah, "Thus says the LORD God of hosts, the God of Israel, 'If you will go out *and* surrender to the officers of the king of Babylon, then you will live and this city will not be burned with fire; and you and your household will live.

18 'But if you will not go out to the officers of the king of Babylon, then this city will be given into the hand of the Chaldeans [of Babylon] and they will set it on fire; and you yourself will not escape from their hand.' "

19 Then King Zedekiah said to Jeremiah, "I am afraid of the Jews [my former subjects] who have deserted to join the Chaldeans, for the enemy may put me into their hand and they will mock me *and* abuse me."

20 But Jeremiah said, "They will not hand you over [to them]. Please obey [the voice of] the LORD [who speaks to you through me] in what I am saying to you. Then it will go well with you and you will live.

21 "But if you keep refusing to go out *and* surrender to them, this is the word [and the vision] which the LORD has shown me:

22 'Then behold, all the women who are left in the palace of the king of Judah will be brought out to the officers of the king of Babylon and those women will say [to you, King Zedekiah],

"Your close friends
Have prevailed against your better
judgment *and* have overpowered
and deceived you;
While your feet were sunk in the
mire [of trouble],
They turned back."

23 'Also, all your wives and your children will be brought out to the Chaldeans; and you yourself will not escape from their hand, but you will be seized by the king of Babylon, and this city [Jerusalem] will be burned down with fire.' "

24 Then Zedekiah said to Jeremiah, "Let no man know about this conversation and you will not die.

25 "But if the princes (court officials) hear that I have talked with you, and they come to you and say, 'Tell us now what you said to the king and what he said to you; do not hide it from us and we will not execute you,'

26 then you are to say to them, 'I was presenting my [humble] petition *and* plea to the king so that he would not send me back to Jonathan's house to die there.' "

27 Then all the princes (court officials) came to Jeremiah and asked him [just what King Zedekiah had anticipated they would ask], and he reported to them in accordance with all that the king had commanded. So they stopped questioning him, since the conversation [with the king] had not been overheard.

28 So Jeremiah remained in the court of the guardhouse until the day that Jerusalem was captured [by the Chaldeans of Babylon].

Jerusalem Captured

39 NOW REGARDING the capture of Jerusalem: In the ninth year of [the reign of] Zedekiah king of Judah, in the tenth month, Nebuchadnezzar king of Babylon and all his army came against Jerusalem and besieged it; [Jer 52:4–27]

38:17 *Then Jeremiah said to Zedekiah.* Jeremiah repeated to the king the message recorded in Jeremiah 38:2 – 3. Surrender would spare the life of the king, and the city's failure to surrender would bring death and destruction.

38:20 – 23 *Then it will go well with you.* Jeremiah tried to settle Zedekiah's fears and to resolve his moral and ethical dilemma by reassuring him that surrender would result in his personal safety. But if the king refused to surrender to Nebuchadnezzar, the word of judgment would fall. Women and children would be handed over to Nebuchadnezzar and Jerusalem would be destroyed.

39:1 *king of Babylon and all his army came against Jerusalem and besieged it.* The Babylonian siege began in December 589 BC and ended about 30 months later when the walls of Jerusalem were breached.

17 2Ki 24:12; Jer 39:3 **18** ver. 23; Jer 32:4; 34:3 **19** 1Sa 31:4 **23** Jer 39:6; 41:10 **26** Jer 37:20; Jer 37:15 **28** Jer 37:21; 39:14 **CHAPTER 39** **1** 2Ki 25:1-4

2 and in the eleventh year of Zede-
kiah, in the fourth month, on the ninth
day of the month, they breached the
wall *and* broke into the city.
3 Then all the officials of the king of
Babylon came in and sat in the Middle
Gate [establishing both military con-
trol of the city and their authority to
judge the captives]: Nergal-sar-ezer,
Samgar-nebu, Sar-sekim the Rab-saris
(chief of the eunuchs), and Nergal-sar-
ezer the Rab-mag (chief of the magi-
cians), with all the rest of the officials
of the king of Babylon.
4 When Zedekiah the king of Judah
and all the men of war saw them, they
fled and escaped from the city at night
by way of the king's garden, through
the gate between the two walls; and
the king went out toward the Arabah
(Jordan Valley).
5 But the Chaldean (Babylonian) army
pursued them and overtook Zedekiah
in the plains of Jericho. When they had
seized him, they brought him up to Neb-
uchadnezzar king of Babylon at Rib-
lah in the [Aramean] land of Hamath,
where he passed sentence on him.
6 Then at Riblah the king of Babylon
killed the sons of Zedekiah before his
eyes; the king of Babylon also killed
all the nobles of Judah.
7 Moreover, he blinded Zedekiah and
bound him with bronze shackles to
take him to Babylon. [Ezek 12:13]
8 The Chaldeans also burned down
the king's palace and the houses of the
people, and they broke down the walls
of Jerusalem.
9 Then Nebuzaradan the [chief ex-
ecutioner and] captain of the body-
guard took the rest of the people who
remained in the city, along with those
who had deserted *and* surrendered
to him, and the rest of the [so-called
better class of] people who were left
and carried them into exile in Babylon.
10 But Nebuzaradan the [Babylonian]
captain of the bodyguard left behind
in the land of Judah some of the poor
people who had nothing, and gave
them vineyards and fields at that time.

Jeremiah Spared

11 Now Nebuchadnezzar king of Bab-
ylon gave orders concerning Jeremiah
through Nebuzaradan the captain of
the bodyguard, saying,
12 "Take him and look after him; do
nothing to harm him, but rather deal
with him just as he asks of you."
13 So Nebuzaradan the captain of
the bodyguard sent *word,* along with
Nebushazban the Rab-saris (chief of
the high officials), and Nergal-sar-ezer
the Rab-mag (chief of the magicians),
and all the leading officers of the king
of Babylon;
14 they even sent and took Jeremiah
out of the court of the guardhouse and
entrusted him to Gedaliah [a promi-
nent citizen], the son of Ahikam [who
had once saved Jeremiah's life], the son
of Shaphan, to take him home [with
him to Mizpah]. So Jeremiah [was re-
leased and] lived among the people.
[Jer 26:24]
15 Now the word of the LORD had
come to Jeremiah while he was [still]
confined in the court of the guard-
house, saying,
16 "Go and speak to Ebed-melech the
Ethiopian, saying, 'Thus says the LORD
of hosts, the God of Israel, "Behold, I
am about to bring My words [of judg-
ment] against this city through disas-
ter and not for good; and they will take
place before you on that day.

39:3 – 7 *all the officials of the king of Babylon.* When Zedekiah saw the Babylonian officers enter the gate on the north side of Jerusalem, he and his men left at night through another gate on the south side of the city. They were captured near Jericho and taken to Riblah to meet Nebuchadnezzar.
39:8 – 10 *The Chaldeans also burned.* In addition to the royal palace and homes of the inhabitants, Jeremiah 52:13 includes the "house of the LORD" among the buildings burned in Jerusalem. ***the poor people.*** Typically the Babylonians deported the upper classes, such as court officials, merchants, artisans, and craftsmen, and left behind peasants to work the fields.

3 Jer 38:17 **4** 2Ki 25:4; Jer 52:7 **5** Jer 32:4; 38:18,23; 2Ki 23:33 **7** Eze 12:13 **8** 2Ki 25:9; Jer 38:18; 52:13
9 2Ki 25:11 **14** Jer 38:28; Jer 40:5; Jer 26:24 **16** Jer 38:7,12; Da 9:12

17“But I will protect you [Ebed-melech]
on that day,” says the LORD, “and you
will not be handed over to the men of
whom you are afraid. [Jer 38:7–13]
18“For I will certainly rescue you; and
you will not fall by the sword, but you
will have your [own] life as a reward
of battle, because you have placed your
trust in Me,” says the LORD.’ ”

Jeremiah Remains in Judah

40 THE WORD which came to Jere-
miah from the LORD after Nebu-
zaradan the captain of the bodyguard
had released him from Ramah, when
he had taken him bound in chains
among all the captives of Jerusalem
and Judah who were being taken as
exiles to Babylon.
2And the captain of the bodyguard
had taken Jeremiah and said to him,
“The LORD your God promised this
disaster on this place.
3“Now the LORD has brought it about
and has done just as He promised.
Because you [people of Judah] have
sinned against the LORD and did not
listen to *and* honor His voice, therefore
this thing has happened to you.
4“But now, listen carefully, [because
of your innocence] I am freeing you to-
day from the chains which are on your
hands. If you would prefer to come
with me to Babylon, come, and I will
look after you [carefully]; but if you
would prefer not to come with me to
Babylon, then do not do so. Look, all
the land is before you; go wherever it
seems good and right (convenient) for
you to go.”
5While Jeremiah was still hesitating,
the captain of the bodyguard said, “Go
on back then to Gedaliah the son of
Ahikam, the son of Shaphan, whom
the king of Babylon has appointed
[governor] over the cities of Judah,
and stay with him among the people;
or else go wherever it seems right for
you to go.” So the captain of the body-
guard gave him an allowance of food
and a gift and let him go.
6Then Jeremiah went to Gedaliah
the son of Ahikam at Mizpah and
stayed with him among the people
who were left in the land.
7Now when all the commanders of
the forces that were [scattered] in the
open country [of Judah] and their men
heard that the king of Babylon had
made Gedaliah the son of Ahikam
governor in the land [of Judah] and had
put him in charge of the men, women,
and children, those of the poorest of
the land who had not been exiled to
Babylon,
8they went to Gedaliah at Mizpah—
Ishmael the son of Nethaniah, Joha-
nan and Jonathan the sons of Kareah,
Seraiah the son of Tanhumeth, the
sons of Ephai the Netophathite, and
Jezaniah the son of the Maacathite,
they and their men.
9Then Gedaliah the son of Ahikam,
the son of Shaphan, swore to them and
their men, saying, “Do not be afraid to
serve the Chaldeans; stay in this land
and serve the king of Babylon, that it
may go well with you.
10“As for me, I am going to stay at
Mizpah to stand [for you] before the

39:18 *you will have your [own] life as a reward of battle ... your trust in Me.* Ebed-melech experienced the power and grace of God in the deliverance of his life simply because he exercised faith.

40:2 – 3 *the Lord has brought it about and has done just as He promised.* Prophets whose words were deemed verified were generally treated well by peoples of the ancient Middle East.

40:4 – 5 *I am freeing you today from the chains.* Jeremiah was released from bondage and given three options: (1) to go with Nebuzaradan to Babylon and enjoy special treatment and protection there; (2) to remain in the care of Gedaliah, the district governor at Mizpah; (3) to live in the land as he chose.

40:7 – 10 *the commanders of the forces.* This phrase refers to the surviving Jewish commanders of the armies in the towns throughout Judah who had fled into the rugged hill country. Among the list of escaped leaders was Ishmael, a member of the royal family and a court officer (41:1).

18 Jer 21:9; 45:5; 1Ch 5:20; Ps 37:40 **CHAPTER 40** **1** Jer 39:14 **2** Jer 50:7 **3** Dt 29:24,25; Da 9:11 **4** Jer 39:12; Ge 20:15 **5** See Jer 41:10 **6** Jer 39:14; Jdg 20:1 **7** 2Ki 25:23; Jer 39:10 **8** Jer 41:1

Chaldeans who come to us [ministering to them and looking after the king's interests]; but as for you, gather in wine, summer fruit and oil and store them in your utensils [designed for such purposes], and live in your cities that you have taken over."
11Likewise, when all the Jews who were in Moab and among the people of Ammon and in Edom and who were in all the [other] countries heard that the king of Babylon had left a remnant [of the people] in Judah and had appointed Gedaliah the son of Ahikam, the son of Shaphan over them [as governor],
12then all the Jews returned from all the places to which they had been driven and came back to the land of Judah, to Gedaliah at Mizpah, and gathered a great abundance of wine and summer fruits.
13Moreover, Johanan the son of Kareah and all the commanders of the forces that were [scattered] in the open country came to Gedaliah at Mizpah
14and said to him, "Do you know that Baalis the king of the Ammonites has sent Ishmael the son of Nethaniah to take your life?" But Gedaliah the son of Ahikam did not believe them.
15Then Johanan the son of Kareah spoke secretly to Gedaliah in Mizpah, saying, "Let me go and kill Ishmael the son of Nethaniah, and not a man will know [who is responsible]. Why should he kill you and cause all the Jews who are gathered near you to be scattered and the remnant of Judah to perish?"
16But Gedaliah the son of Ahikam said to Johanan the son of Kareah, "Do not do this thing, for you are lying about Ishmael."

Gedaliah Is Murdered

41 NOW IN the seventh month Ishmael the son of Nethaniah, the son of Elishama, of the royal family [of David] and one of the princes of the king, came [at the instigation of the Ammonites] with ten men to Gedaliah the son of Ahikam in Mizpah. As they were eating a meal together there in Mizpah,
2Ishmael the son of Nethaniah and the ten men who were with him got up and struck down Gedaliah the son of Ahikam, the son of Shaphan, with the sword and killed the one whom the king of Babylon had appointed [governor] over the land. [2 Kin 25:25]
3Ishmael also killed all the Jews who were [at the banquet] with Gedaliah at Mizpah, in addition to the Chaldean soldiers who were there.
4Now it happened on the second day after the killing of Gedaliah, before anyone knew about it,
5that eighty men came from Shechem, from Shiloh, and from Samaria with their beards shaved off and their clothes torn and their bodies cut, carrying in their hands grain offerings and incense to present at the [site of the] house of the Lord [in Jerusalem].
6Then Ishmael the son of Nethaniah went out from Mizpah to meet them, weeping [false tears] as he went. As he met them, he said to them, "Come to Gedaliah the son of Ahikam!"
7Yet when they came into the city, Ishmael the son of Nethaniah and the men who were with him slaughtered them *and threw them* into the cistern (underground water reservoir).
8But ten men who were among them said to Ishmael, "Do not kill us! We have stores of wheat and barley and oil and honey hidden in the field." So he stopped and did not kill them along with their companions.
9Now the cistern into which Ishmael had thrown all the corpses of the men whom he had killed along with Gedaliah was the one which King

40:11 – 12 *the Jews*. Those who had escaped the Babylonian onslaught into neighboring states returned home and began working the fields, vineyards, and orchards.
40:13 – 16 *Johanan*. This man led a group of leaders to Gedaliah to warn him of a plot by Ishmael. He even asked for permission to kill the plotter, Ishmael. Unfortunately, Gedaliah was far too trusting of Ishmael and didn't take the warning seriously enough.

14 See Jer 41:10 **CHAPTER 41** **1** 2Ki 25:25; Jer 40:6,8 **2** 2Ki 25:25 **5** Lev 19:27,28; Dt 14:1; Isa 15:2; See 1Sa 1:7; 2Ki 25:9 **9** 1Ki 15:22; 2Ch 16:6

Asa [of Judah] had made [about three hundred years earlier] on account of King Baasha of Israel [believing that Baasha would lay siege to Mizpah]. Ishmael the son of Nethaniah filled it with [the bodies of] those who were killed.

[10]Then Ishmael took captive all the rest of the people who were in Mizpah—even the king's daughters (ladies of the court) and all the people who remained in Mizpah, whom Nebuzaradan the captain of the bodyguard had put under the charge of Gedaliah the son of Ahikam. Ishmael the son of Nethaniah took them captive and crossed over [the Jordan] to [meet his allies] the Ammonites.

Johanan Rescues the People

[11]But when Johanan the son of Kareah and all the commanders of the forces that were with him heard of the murderous behavior of Ishmael the son of Nethaniah,

[12]they took all their men and went to fight with Ishmael the son of Nethaniah and found him by the great pool in Gibeon.

[13]Now when all the [captive] people who were with Ishmael saw Johanan the son of Kareah and all the commanders of the forces that were with him, they were glad.

[14]So all the people whom Ishmael had taken captive from Mizpah turned around and came back, and joined Johanan the son of Kareah.

[15]But Ishmael the son of Nethaniah escaped from Johanan with eight men and went to join the Ammonites.

[16]Then Johanan the son of Kareah and all the commanders of the forces that were with him took from Mizpah all the people whom he had rescued from Ishmael the son of Nethaniah, after Ishmael had killed Gedaliah the son of Ahikam: the soldiers, the women, the children, and the high officials whom Johanan had brought back from Gibeon.

[17]And they went and stayed in Geruth [the lodging place of] Chimham, which is near Bethlehem, intending to go to Egypt

[18]because of the Chaldeans; for they were afraid of them because Ishmael the son of Nethaniah had killed Gedaliah the son of Ahikam, whom the king of Babylon had appointed [governor] over the land [and whose death the king might avenge].

Warning against Going to Egypt

42 THEN ALL the commanders of the forces, and Johanan the son of Kareah and Jezaniah (Azariah) the son of Hoshaiah, and all the people from the least to the greatest approached

[2]and said to Jeremiah the prophet, "Please let our petition be presented before you, and pray to the LORD your God for us, *that is,* for all this remnant [of the people of Judah]; for we were once many, but now [only] a few of us are left, as you see with your own eyes, [so please pray]

[3]that the LORD your God may show us the way in which we should walk and the thing that we should do."

[4]Then Jeremiah the prophet said to them, "I have heard you. Now hear me, I will pray to the LORD your God in accordance with your words; and I will declare to you whatever message the LORD answers; I will keep nothing back from you."

[5]Then they said to Jeremiah, "May

41:11 – 12 *they took all their men.* After Ishmael assassinates Gedaliah, Johanan gathered forces to fight Ishmael's army at Gibeon. Then he started for Egypt and safety.

42:1 – 3 *said to Jeremiah.* The people asked Jeremiah to intercede with the Lord on their behalf.

42:4 – 6 *I will pray.* Jeremiah cautiously agreed to pray to God. He asked the people to agree to abide by the answer he received. The people responded with an oath of obedience, calling upon the Lord as witness.

10 Jer 43:6; Jer 40:7; Jer 40:14 **11** Jer 40:7,8,13 **12** 2Sa 2:13 **17** 2Sa 19:37,38 **18** Jer 40:5 **CHAPTER 42** **1** Jer 40:8,13; 41:11 **2** 1Sa 7:8; 12:19; Isa 37:4; Jas 5:16; Lev 26:22 **3** Ezr 8:21 **4** 1Ki 22:14; 1Sa 3:18; Ac 20:20 **5** Ge 31:50

the LORD be a true and faithful witness against us if we fail to act in accordance with all the things that the LORD your God sends you to tell us.

6 “Whether it is pleasant or unpleasant, we will listen to *and* honor the voice of the LORD our God to whom we are sending you, so that it may go well with us when we listen to the voice of the LORD our God.”

7 Now after ten days [of prayer] had passed the word of the LORD came to Jeremiah.

8 Then he called for Johanan the son of Kareah and all the commanders of the forces that were with him and all the people from the least to the greatest,

9 and said to them, “Thus says the LORD, the God of Israel, to whom you sent me to present your petition before Him:

10 ‘If you will indeed remain in this land, then I will build you up and not tear you down, and I will plant you and not uproot you; for I will relent *and* be satisfied concerning the disaster that I have inflicted on you [as discipline, and I will replace judgment with compassion]. [Jer 31:4, 28]

11 ‘Do not be afraid of the king of Babylon, whom you now fear [as if he were deity]; do not be afraid of him,’ says the LORD, ‘for [he is a mere man, but I am the living, omniscient God and] I am with you [always] to protect you and to deliver you from his hand.

12 ‘And I will show you compassion, so that he will have compassion on you and restore you to your own land.

13 ‘But if you are going to say, “We will not stay in this land,” and [in so doing] do not listen to the voice of the LORD your God,

14 saying, “No, but we will go to the land of Egypt, where we will not see war or hear the sound of the [warrior’s] trumpet or hunger for bread, and we will stay there,”

15 then in that case listen to the word of the LORD, O remnant of Judah. Thus says the LORD of hosts, the God of Israel, “If you are really determined to go to Egypt and to reside there [temporarily],

16 then the sword, of which you are afraid, will overtake you there in the land of Egypt; and the famine of which you are afraid will follow closely after you in Egypt, and you will die there.

17 ‘So all the men who set their mind to go to Egypt to reside there [temporarily] will die by the sword, by famine and by virulent disease; none of them will remain or survive the disaster that I am going to bring on them.” ’ ”

18 For thus says the LORD of hosts, the God of Israel, “As My anger and My wrath have been poured out on the inhabitants of Jerusalem, so My wrath will be poured out on you when you enter Egypt. You will become detested, an object of horror, a curse and a people scorned; and you will no longer see this place.”

19 The LORD has spoken to you, O remnant of Judah, “Do not go into Egypt!” Know with certainty that I [Jeremiah] have warned you *and* testified to you this day

20 that you have deceived yourselves; for you sent me to the LORD your God, saying, “Pray for us to the LORD our God; and whatever the LORD our God says, declare it to us and we will do it.”

21 And so I have told you today, but you have not listened to the voice of the LORD your God, in anything that He has sent me to tell you.

22 Now therefore know for certain that you will die by the sword, by famine, and by virulent disease in the land [of Egypt] where you wish to reside [temporarily].

42:15 *really determined.* This expression indicates the fixed intentions of the people. The announcement of judgment against the disobedient evacuees echoes Jeremiah’s earlier pronouncements against Judah. The very thing they were trying to escape from would meet them in Egypt.

6 Dt 6:3; Jer 7:23 **10** Jer 24:6; 31:28; 33:7; Dt 32:36; Jer 18:8 **11** Isa 43:5; Ro 8:31 **12** Ps 106:45,46 **13** Jer 44:16 **15** Dt 17:16; Jer 44:12-14; Lk 9:51 **17** ver. 22; Jer 24:10; See Jer 44:14,28 **18** Jer 7:20; Jer 18:16; 24:9; 26:6; 29:18,22; 44:12; Zec 8:13 **19** Dt 17:16 **22** ver. 17; Eze 6:11

In Egypt Jeremiah Warns of Judgment

43 NOW IT happened when Jeremiah, whom the LORD their God had sent, had finished telling all the people all the words of the LORD their God—that is, all these words—

2 Azariah the son of Hoshaiah and Johanan the son of Kareah and all the proud *and* insolent men said to Jeremiah, "You are not telling the truth! The LORD our God has not sent you to say, 'Do not go into Egypt to live there.'

3 "But Baruch the son of Neriah is inciting you against us to hand us over to the Chaldeans, so they may [either] put us to death or exile us to Babylon."

4 So Johanan the son of Kareah and all the commanders of the forces and all the people disobeyed the voice of the LORD [which told them] to stay in the land of Judah.

5 But Johanan the son of Kareah and all the commanders of the forces took all the remnant of Judah who had returned to live in the land of Judah from all the nations to which they had been driven—

6 the men, women, and children, the king's daughters (ladies of the court), and every person whom Nebuzaradan the captain of the bodyguard had left with Gedaliah the son of Ahikam, the son of Shaphan; he also took Jeremiah the prophet and Baruch the son of Neriah.

7 So they entered the land of Egypt (for they did not obey the voice of the LORD) and they went in as far as Tahpanhes.

8 Then came the word of the LORD to Jeremiah in Tahpanhes, saying,

9 "Take some large stones in your hands and hide them in the mortar in the brickwork [of the terrace] which is at the entrance of Pharaoh's house in Tahpanhes, in the sight of some of the *men of* Judah;

10 and say to them, 'Thus says the LORD of hosts, the God of Israel, "Behold, I am going to send and get Nebuchadnezzar the king of Babylon, My servant, and I am going to set his throne over these stones that I have hidden; and his [majestic, royal] canopy will be spread over them. [Ezek 29:19, 20]

11 "He will also come and strike the land of Egypt, giving those who are [destined] for death, to death, and those who are [destined] for captivity, to captivity, and those who are [destined] for the sword, to the sword.

12 "And [through him] I will set fire to the temples of the gods of Egypt, and he will burn them and take them (Egyptian idols) captive. He will wrap himself with the land of Egypt as a shepherd wraps himself with his garment, and he will go away from there safely.

13 "Nebuchadnezzar will also break the images *and* shatter the obelisks of Heliopolis in the land of Egypt; and he will burn down the temples of the gods of Egypt." ' "

Conquest of Egypt Predicted

44 THE WORD that came to Jeremiah concerning all the Jews who were living in the land of Egypt—at Migdol, at Tahpanhes, at Memphis, and in the land of Pathros, saying,

2 "Thus says the LORD of hosts, the God of Israel, 'You have seen all the disaster that I have brought on Jerusalem and on all the cities of Judah; and see, this day they are desolated and no one lives in them

3 because of the wickedness which they committed, provoking Me to anger by continuing to burn sacrifices *and* incense to serve other gods that they had not known, *neither* they, nor you, nor your fathers.

4 'Yet I sent to you all My servants the prophets, again and again, saying,

---

43:4–7 ***all the people disobeyed.*** Johanan led the migration to Egypt, against the direction of the Lord through Jeremiah.

43:10 ***these stones.*** These symbolized the strong foundation of Nebuchadnezzar's empire, the point from which he would spread his canopy.

CHAPTER 43 **2** Jer 42:1 **5** Jer 40:11,12 **6** Jer 41:10; Jer 39:10; 40:7 **7** Jer 2:16; 44:1 **10** Jer 25:9; 27:6; See Eze 29:18,20 **11** Jer 44:13; 46:13; Jer 15:2; Zec 11:9 **12** Jer 46:25 **CHAPTER 44** **1** Ex 14:2; Jer 46:14; Jer 43:7; Isa 19:13 **2** Jer 9:11; 34:22 **3** Jer 19:4; Dt 13:6; 32:17 **4** 2Ch 36:15; Jer 7:25; 25:4; 26:5; 29:19

"Oh, do not do this shamefully vile
thing which I hate."
5'But they did not listen or turn [obe-
diently] from their wickedness, and
stop burning sacrifices *and* incense
to other gods.
6'Therefore My wrath and My an-
ger were poured out and burned in
the cities of Judah and in the streets
of Jerusalem; so they have become a
ruin and a desolation, as it is this day.
7'Therefore now thus says the LORD
God of hosts, the God of Israel, "Why
did you commit this great evil against
yourselves [bringing disaster] that will
cut off from you man and woman,
child and infant, out of Judah, leaving
yourselves without a remnant?
8"Why do you [deliberately] provoke
Me to anger with the works (idols) of
your hands, burning sacrifices *and*
incense to [make-believe] gods in the
land of Egypt, where you [of your own
accord] have come to live [as tempo-
rary residents], that you might be cut
off and become a curse and a disgrace
[an object of taunts] among all the na-
tions of the earth?
9"Have you forgotten the wicked-
ness of your fathers, the wickedness of
the kings of Judah, the wickedness of
their wives [who served their foreign
gods], your own wickedness, and the
wickedness of your wives [who imitat-
ed the sin of the queens], which they
committed in the land of Judah and in
the streets of Jerusalem?
10"They have not become apologetic
[for their guilt and sin] even to this
day; they have not feared [Me with
reverence] nor walked in My law or
My statutes, which I have set before
you and before your fathers." ' [Jer 6:15;
26:4–6; 44:23]
11"Therefore thus says the LORD of
hosts, the God of Israel, 'Behold, I am
going to set My face against you for
woe—even to cut off (destroy) all Ju-
dah [from the land].
12'And I will take the remnant of Ju-
dah who have decided to go into the
land of Egypt to live there [instead
of surrendering to the Chaldeans as
directed], and they will all fall and die
in the land of Egypt; they will fall by
the sword or perish by famine. From
the least to the greatest, they will die
by the sword or by famine; and they
will become detestable, an object of
horror, a curse, and a disgrace.
13'For I will punish all the inhabi-
tants of the land of Egypt, as I have
punished Jerusalem, with the sword,
with famine, and with virulent disease;
14so none of the survivors from the
remnant of Judah who have entered
the land of Egypt to live there will
survive, even though they lift up their
souls in longing to return to the land of
Judah, [the place] to which they long to
return to live; none will return except
a few refugees.' "
15Then all the men who knew that
their wives were burning sacrifices
to other gods, and all the women who
were standing by, a large group, in-
cluding all the people who were liv-
ing in Pathros in the land of Egypt,
answered Jeremiah, saying,
16"As for the word (message) that you
have spoken to us in the name of the
LORD, we are not going to listen to you.
17"But rather we will certainly per-
form every word of the vows we have
made: to burn sacrifices to the queen of
heaven (Ishtar) and to pour out drink
offerings to her, just as we ourselves
and our forefathers, our kings and our
princes did in the cities of Judah and
in the streets of Jerusalem; for [then]
we had plenty of food and were pros-
perous and saw no misfortune.

44:8 *provoke*. This term indicates willful, stubborn rebellion against God, which roused His anger.
44:10 *They have not become apologetic*. The present generation of Jews had learned nothing from the past failures of the nation. The people were not broken in heart, only more stubborn.
44:13 *I will punish all the inhabitants of the land of Egypt*. The Jews in Egypt would suffer the same judgment as those in Jerusalem. Only a small remnant would survive to tell their story.

7 Nu 16:38; Jer 7:19 **8** Jer 25:6,7; ver. 12; Jer 42:18 **10** Pr 28:14 **11** Lev 17:10; 20:5,6; Jer 21:10; Am 9:4 **12** Jer 42:15-17,22; Jer 42:18 **13** Jer 43:11 **14** ver. 28 **16** Jer 6:16 **17** See ver. 25; Nu 30:12; Dt 23:23; Jdg 11:36; Jer 7:18

18 "But since we stopped burning sacrifices to the queen of heaven and pouring out drink offerings to her, we have lacked everything and have been consumed by the sword and by famine."

19 *And said the wives,* "When we were burning sacrifices to the queen of heaven and were pouring out drink offerings to her, was it without [the knowledge and approval of] our husbands that we made cakes [in the shape of a star] to represent her and pour out drink offerings to her?"

Tragedy for the Jews

20 Then Jeremiah said to all the people, to the men and to the women and to all the people who had given him that answer,

21 "The smoking sacrifices (incense) that you burned in the cities of Judah and in the streets of Jerusalem—you and your forefathers, your kings and your princes, and the people of the land—did not the LORD remember [in detail your idolatry] and did it not all come into His mind?

22 "The LORD could no longer endure it, because of the evil of your acts and the repulsive acts which you have committed; because of them your land has become a ruin, an object of horror and a curse, without inhabitant, as it is this day.

23 "Because you have burned sacrifices [to idols] and because you have sinned against the LORD and have not obeyed the voice of the LORD or walked in His law and in His statutes and in His testimonies, therefore this tragedy has fallen on you, as it has this day."

24 Then Jeremiah said to all the people, including all the women, "Hear the word of the LORD, all [you of] Judah who are in the land of Egypt,

25 thus says the LORD of hosts, the God of Israel, as follows: 'You and your wives have both declared with your mouth and fulfilled it with your hand, saying, "We will certainly perform our vows that we have vowed, to burn sacrifices to the queen of heaven (Ishtar) and to pour out drink offerings to her." Surely then confirm your vows and go ahead and perform your vows! [If you intend to defy all My warnings, proceed!]'

26 "Therefore hear the word of the LORD, all [you people of] Judah who are living in the land of Egypt, 'Behold, I have sworn [an oath] by My great Name,' says the LORD, 'that My Name shall never again be invoked by the mouth of any man of Judah in all the land of Egypt, saying, "As the Lord GOD lives."

27 'Behold, I am watching over them for harm and not for good; and all the men of Judah who are in the land of Egypt shall be consumed by the sword and by famine until they are all destroyed.

28 'Yet a small number [of My choosing] who escape the sword will return from the land of Egypt to the land of Judah; and all the remnant of Judah who have gone to the land of Egypt to reside there will know whose words will stand, Mine or theirs.

29 'And this will be the sign to you,' says the LORD, 'that I am going to punish you in this place, so that you may

---

44:18 *queen of heaven.* The people reasoned that when they stopped worshiping the queen of heaven in the days of Josiah's reform, their king was killed and their land was overrun and destroyed.
44:24 *including all the women.* The focus here is on the stubbornness of the women who persisted in their idolatry. Nothing could make them abandon their vows to worship Ishtar.
44:26–27 *by My great Name.* The name of God reveals His quality and character in dealing with humankind.
44:28 *all the remnant of Judah.* A small remnant would survive and see the fulfillment of God's word as revealed through Jeremiah. Their own hopes of prosperity in Egypt would vanish, and the sign of God's work against them would be the fall of Pharaoh Hophra of Egypt. In 570 BC, Hophra was overthrown in a military coup by his own general, Amasis. Three years later he was executed in fulfillment of Jeremiah's prophecy.

19 Jer 7:18 **22** Jer 25:11,18,38; ver. 6 **23** Da 9:11,12 **24** ver. 15; Jer 43:7 **25** ver. 15 **26** Ge 22:16; Eze 20:39 **27** Jer 1:10; 31:28; Eze 7:6; ver. 12 **28** ver. 14; Isa 27:13; ver. 17,25,26

know that My words will surely stand
against you for harm.'
30"Thus says the LORD, 'Behold, I will
give Pharaoh Hophra king of Egypt
into the hand of his enemies and into
the hand of those who seek his life, just
as I gave Zedekiah king of Judah into
the hand of Nebuchadnezzar king of
Babylon, who was his enemy and was
seeking his life.' "

Message to Baruch

45 THE WORD that Jeremiah the
prophet spoke to Baruch the son
of Neriah, when he had written these
words in a book at the dictation of
Jeremiah, in the fourth year of Jehoi-
akim the son of Josiah, king of Judah,
saying,
2"Thus says the LORD, the God of
Israel, to you, O Baruch:
3'You said, "Woe is me! For the LORD
has added sorrow to my pain; I am
weary with my groaning *and* sighing
and I find no rest." '
4"Say this to him, 'The LORD speaks
in this way, "Behold, what I have built
I will break down, and that which I
have planted I will uproot, that is, the
whole land."
5'And do you seek great things for
yourself? Do not seek them; for behold,
I will bring disaster on all flesh,' says
the LORD, 'but I will give your life to
you [as your only reward and] as a
prize of war wherever you go.' "

Defeat of Pharaoh Foretold

46 THE WORD of the LORD that
came to Jeremiah the prophet
concerning the [Gentile] nations.
2Concerning Egypt, against the
army of Pharaoh Neco king of Egypt,
which was by the river Euphrates at
Carchemish, which Nebuchadnezzar
king of Babylon defeated [decisively]
in the fourth year of Jehoiakim son of
Josiah, king of Judah: [Is 19–20; Ezek
29–32; Zech 14:18, 19]

3"Line up the buckler (small shield)
and [large] shield,
And advance for battle!
4"Harness the horses,
And mount, you riders!
Take your stand with your
helmets!
Polish the spears,
Put on the coats of mail!
5"Why have I seen it?
They are terrified
And have turned back,
And their warriors are beaten
down.
They take flight in haste
Without looking back;
Terror is on every side!"
Says the LORD. [Ps 31:13; Jer 6:25;
20:3, 10; 49:29]
6Do not let the swift man run,
Nor the mighty man escape;
In the north by the river Euphrates
They have stumbled and fallen.
7Who is this that rises up like the
Nile [River],
Like the rivers [in the delta of
Egypt] whose waters surge
about?
8Egypt rises like the Nile,
Even like the rivers whose waters
surge about.
And He has said, "I will rise, I will
cover that land;
I will certainly destroy the city
and its inhabitants."
9Charge, you horses,
And drive like madmen, you
chariots!
Let the warriors go forward:

45:2–3 *to you, O Baruch.* Jeremiah addressed Baruch in light of the scribe's sorrow. Baruch lamented his plight in the same manner that Jeremiah had done (15:10). He also suffered mental anguish and personal rejection from his people due to his association with Jeremiah (36:15–19).
46:1 *concerning the [Gentile] nations.* This verse introduces a collection of oracles. The text moves generally from the west — Egypt — to the east — Elam and Babylon. Scattered throughout the oracles are brief messages of the restoration of Israel and Judah. The main message of these oracles is the sovereignty of God over all the nations of the earth.

30 Jer 46:25,26; Eze 29:3; 30:21; Jer 39:5 **CHAPTER 45** **1** Jer 36:1,4,32 **4** Isa 5:5 **5** Jer 25:26; Jer 21:9; 38:2; 39:18 **CHAPTER 46** **1** Jer 25:15 **2** 2Ki 23:29; 2Ch 35:20; Fulfilled presently **3** Jer 51:11,12; Na 2:1; 3:14 **5** Jer 49:29 **6** Da 11:19 **7** Isa 8:7,8; Jer 47:2 **9** Isa 66:19

Ethiopia and Put (Libya) who
handle the shield,
And the Lydians who handle and
bend the bow.
10 For that day belongs to the Lord
GOD of hosts,
A day of vengeance, that He
may avenge Himself on His
adversaries.
And the sword will devour and be
satiated
And drink its fill of their blood;
For the Lord GOD of hosts has a
sacrifice [like that of a great sin
offering]
In the north country by the river
Euphrates.
11 Go up to Gilead and obtain
[healing] balm,
O Virgin Daughter of Egypt!
In vain you use many medicines;
For you there is no healing *or*
remedy.
12 The nations have heard of your
disgrace *and* shame,
And your cry [of distress] has
filled the earth.
For warrior has stumbled against
warrior,
And both of them have fallen
together.

13 The word that the LORD spoke to
Jeremiah the prophet concerning the
coming of Nebuchadnezzar king of
Babylon to strike the land of Egypt:

14 "Declare in Egypt and proclaim in
Migdol,
And proclaim in Memphis and in
Tahpanhes;
Say, 'Take your stand and get
yourself ready,
For the sword has devoured those
around you.'
15 "Why have your strong ones been
cut down?
They do not stand because the
LORD drove them away.
16 "He will make many stumble *and*
fall;
Yes, they have fallen one on
another.
Then they said, 'Arise, and let us
go back
To our own people and to the land
of our birth,
Away from the sword of the
oppressor.'
17 "They cried there, 'Pharaoh king
of Egypt is destroyed *and* is
merely a loud noise;
He has let the appointed time [of
opportunity] pass by!'
18 "As I live," says the King,
Whose name is the LORD of hosts,
"Surely like Tabor among the
mountains
Or like Carmel by the sea,
So shall he [the great king of
Babylon] come.
19 "O you daughter who dwells in
Egypt *and* you who dwell with
her,
Prepare yourselves [with all you
will need] to go into exile,
For Memphis will become desolate;
It will even be burned down and
without inhabitant.
20 "Egypt is a very pretty heifer,
But a horsefly (Babylonia) is
coming [against her] out of the
north!
21 "Also her mercenaries in her army
Are like fattened calves,
For they too have turned back and
have fled together;
They did not stand [their ground],

46:10–12 ***day belongs to the Lord GOD of hosts.*** This time the day is a day of vengeance in which Egypt is punished for the death of Josiah. The imagery of a devouring sword is also found in Jeremiah 2:30. Egypt's demise is pictured as a sacrificial feast. As there was no healing balm for sinful Judah, so now Egypt was mortally wounded, stumbling to its death.

46:15–17 ***Why have your strong ones been cut down?*** The fall of the gods before God in judgment is a prominent theme in the oracles against the nations (v. 25).

46:18 ***King . . . LORD of hosts.*** The term "hosts" can also be translated "armies." God is the true and sovereign King over all the armies of heaven and earth.

10 Isa 13:6; Joel 1:15; Dt 32:42; Isa 34:6; Isa 34:6; Zep 1:7; See Eze 39:17 **11** Jer 8:22; Isa 47:1; Eze 30:21 **13** Isa 19:1; Eze 29; 30; 32 **14** ver. 3,4; ver. 10 **16** Lev 26:37 **18** Isa 47:4; Jer 48:15 **19** Jer 48:18; Isa 20:4 **20** Hos 10:11; Jer 1:14 **21** Ps 37:13; Jer 50:27

Because the day of their disaster
has come upon them,
The time of their punishment.
22 "The sound [of Egypt fleeing from
the enemy] is like [the rustling
of] an escaping serpent,
For her foes advance with a
mighty army
And come against her like
woodcutters with axes.
23 "They have cut down her forest,"
says the LORD;
"Certainly it will no longer be
found,
Because they (the invaders) are
more numerous than locusts
And cannot be counted.
24 "The Daughter of Egypt has been
shamed,
Given over to the power of
the people of the north [the
Chaldeans of Babylonia]."

25 The LORD of hosts, the God of Is-
rael, says, "Behold, I am going to pun-
ish Amon [chief god of the sacred city]
of Thebes [the capital of Upper Egypt],
and Pharaoh, and Egypt along with
her gods and her kings—even Pharaoh
and those who put their trust in him
[as a shield against Babylon].
26 "I will put them into the hand of
those who seek their lives, and into the
hand of Nebuchadnezzar king of Bab-
ylon and into the hand of his servants.
Afterward Egypt will be inhabited as
in the days of old," says the LORD.

27 "But as for you, do not fear, O My
servant Jacob,
Nor be dismayed, O Israel!
For behold, I will save you from
[your captivity in] a distant *land*,
And your descendants from the
land of their exile;
And Jacob will return and be quiet
and secure,
And no one will make him afraid.
28 "Do not fear, O Jacob My servant,"
says the LORD,
"For I am with you.
For I will make a full *and* complete
end of all the nations
To which I have driven you;
Yet I will not make a full end of
you.
But I will discipline *and* correct
you appropriately
And by no means will I declare
you guiltless *or* leave you
unpunished."

Prophecy against Philistia

47 THE WORD of the LORD that
came to Jeremiah the proph-
et concerning the Philistines before
Pharaoh attacked *and* conquered [the
Philistine city of] Gaza. [Is 14:29–31;
Ezek 25:15–17; Amos 1:6–8; Zeph 2:4–7;
Zech 9:5–7]
2 Thus says the LORD:

"Behold, waters are going to rise
out of the north (Babylonia)
And become an overflowing
stream
And overflow the land and all that
is in it,
The city and those who live in it.
Then the people will cry out,
And all the inhabitants of the land
[of Philistia] will wail.
3 "Because of the noise of the
stamping of the hoofs of the
war-horses [of the Babylonian
king],
The rattling of his chariots, and
the rumbling of his wheels,
The fathers have not looked *and*
turned back for their children,
So weak are their hands [with
terror]
4 Because of the day that is coming
To destroy all the Philistines
And to cut off from Tyre and Sidon

46:25 – 26 *with her gods and her kings.* The gods and goddesses of Egypt were punished in the defeat of the people who worshiped them.
47:3 *weak are their hands.* This phrase means lacking courage. It describes the paralyzing terror felt by parents as they abandon their children in flight.

22 Isa 29:4 **23** Isa 10:34; Jdg 6:5 **24** Jer 1:15 **25** Eze 30:14; Jer 43:12 **26** Eze 32:11; Eze 29:11, 13,14 **27** Isa 41:13 **28** Jer 10:24 **CHAPTER 47** **1** Zep 2:4; Am 1:6 **2** Isa 8:7; Jer 1:14 **3** Jer 8:16 **4** Jer 25:22; Eze 25:16; Ge 10:14

Every ally who remains.
For the LORD is going to destroy
the Philistines,
The remnant [still surviving]
of the coastland of Caphtor.
[Amos 9:7]
5 "Baldness [as a sign of mourning]
will come on Gaza;
Ashkelon will be cut off *and* ruined.
O remnant of their valley,
How long will you gash yourselves
[as a sign of mourning]?
6 "O you sword of the LORD,
How long will it be before you are
quiet?
Put yourself into your sheath;
Rest and be still.
7 "How can His sword be quiet
When the LORD has given it an
order?
Against Ashkelon and against the
[whole Philistine] seashore
There He has assigned it."

Prophecy against Moab

48 CONCERNING MOAB.
Thus says the LORD of hosts, the
God of Israel,
"Woe (judgment is coming) to [the
city of] Nebo, for it has been
destroyed!
Kiriathaim has been shamed, it
has been captured;
Misgab [the high fortress] has
been shamed, broken down
and crushed. [Is 15–16; 25:10–
12; Ezek 25:8–11; Amos 2:1–3;
Zeph 2:8–11]
2 "The glory of Moab is no more;
In Heshbon they planned evil
against her,
Saying, 'Come, let us cut her off
from being a nation!'
You also, O [city of] Madmen, shall
be silenced;
The sword will pursue you.
3 "The sound of an outcry from
Horonaim,
'Desolation and great destruction!'
4 "Moab is destroyed;
Her little ones have called out a
cry *of distress* [to be heard as
far as Zoar].
5 "For the Ascent of Luhith
Will be climbed by [successive
groups of] fugitives with
continual weeping;
For on the descent of Horonaim
They have heard the distress of the
cry of destruction.
6 "Run! Save your lives,
That you may be like a juniper in
the wilderness.
7 "For because you have trusted in
your works [your hand-made
idols] and in your treasures
[instead of in God],
Even you yourself will be captured;
And Chemosh [your disgusting
god cannot rescue you, but] will
go away into exile [along with
the fugitives]
Together with his priests and his
princes.
8 "And the destroyer will come upon
every city;
No city will escape.
The [Jordan] valley also will be
ruined
And the plain will be devastated,
As the LORD has said.
9 "Give a gravestone to Moab,
For she will fall into ruins;
Her cities (pastures, farms) will be
desolate,
Without anyone to live in them.
10 "Cursed is the one who does the
work of the LORD negligently,
And cursed is the one who
restrains his sword from blood
[in executing the judgment of
the LORD].

47:6–7 *sword of the LORD.* This image is used often to portray divine judgment (12:2; 46:10,14,16).
48:6–8 *the wilderness.* This tree ekes out its stunted growth in the wilderness, hiding in crevasses of rock. ***exile.*** Taking a deity captive was a well-known Middle Eastern custom. The national statue of the patron deity was seized, and it was believed that the captured god could no longer protect its people.

5 Mic 1:16; Jer 25:20 **6** Eze 21:3 **7** Eze 14:17; Mic 6:9 **CHAPTER 48** **1** Isa 15; 16; Nu 32:37 **2** Isa 16:14; Isa 15:4 **5** Isa 15:5 **6** Jer 17:6 **7** Nu 21:29; Jdg 11:24; Isa 46:1,2; Jer 49:3 **8** Jer 6:26 **9** Ps 55:6 **10** Jdg 5:23; 1Sa 15:3; 1Ki 20:42

[11]"Moab has been at ease from his
youth;
He has also been undisturbed, and
settled like wine on his dregs,
And he has not been emptied from
one vessel to another,
Nor has he gone into exile.
Therefore his flavor remains in
him,
And his scent has not changed.

[12]"Therefore behold, the days are com-
ing," says the LORD, "when I will send
to Moab those who will tip him over
and who will empty his vessels and
break his [earthenware] jars in pieces.
[13]"And Moab shall be ashamed of
Chemosh [his worthless, disgust-
ing god], as the house of Israel was
ashamed of Bethel, their [misplaced]
confidence. [1 Kin 12:28, 29]

[14]"How can you say, 'We are great
warriors
And valiant men in war?'
[15]"Moab has been made desolate
and his cities have gone up [in
smoke and flame];
And his chosen young men have
gone down to the slaughter,"
Says the King, whose name is the
LORD of hosts.
[16]"The destruction of Moab will
come soon,
And his disaster hurries quickly.
[17]"Show sympathy for him, all you
[nations] who are around him,
And all you [distant nations] who
know his name;
Say, 'How has the mighty scepter
[of national power] been broken,
And the splendid staff [of glory]!'
[18]"Come down from your glory,
O Daughter living in Dibon,
And sit on the parched ground
[among the thirsty]!
For the destroyer of Moab has
advanced against you;
He has destroyed your
strongholds.
[19]"O inhabitant of Aroer,
Stand by the road and keep
watch!
Ask [of] him who flees and [ask of]
her who escapes,
Saying, 'What has happened?'
[20]"Moab is shamed, for she has been
broken down *and* shattered.
Wail and cry out!
Tell by [the banks of] the Arnon
That Moab has been destroyed.

[21]"Judgment has come on [the land
of] the plain—upon Holon, Jahzah,
and against Mephaath,
[22]against Dibon, Nebo, and Beth-
diblathaim,
[23]against Kiriathaim, Beth-gamul,
and Beth-meon,
[24]against Kerioth, Bozrah and all the
cities of the land of Moab, far and near.
[25]"The horn (strength) of Moab has
been cut off and his arm [of authority]
is shattered," says the LORD.
[26]"Make him drunk, for he has be-
come arrogant *and* magnified himself
against the LORD [by denying Reuben's
occupation of the land the LORD had
assigned him]. Moab also will wallow
in his vomit, and he too shall become
a laughingstock. [Num 22:1–7]
[27]"For was not Israel a laughingstock
to you? Was he caught among thieves?
For whenever you speak of him you
shake *your head in scorn.*

[28]"You inhabitants of Moab,
Leave the cities and live among
the rocks,
And be like the dove that makes
her nest
In the walls of the yawning ravine.

48:17 *Show sympathy for him, all you [nations] who are around him.* A note of sarcasm is communicated. The nations around Moab, like Judah, who was attacked by Moab's mercenaries, were called upon to lament Moab's destruction.
48:18 *Come down from your glory.* The haughty Moab was shamed by the destruction of its fortresses.
48:26–29 *Make him drunk.* Judgment is portrayed in the form of drunkenness to the point of vomiting, the result of Moab's mockery of Israel (25:15–29).

11 Zep 1:12 **13** 1Ki 11:7; Hos 10:6; 1Ki 12:29 **14** Isa 16:6 **15** ver. 8,9,18; Jer 50:27; Jer 46:18 **17** Isa 9:4; 14:4,5 **18** Isa 47:1; Nu 21:30; Isa 15:2; ver. 8 **19** Dt 2:36; 1Sa 4:13 **20** Isa 16:7; Nu 21:13 **21** ver. 8 **24** Am 2:2 **25** Ps 75:10; Eze 30:21 **26** Jer 25:15 **27** Zep 2:8; Jer 2:26 **28** Ps 55:6,7; SS 2:14

29 "We have heard of the [giddy]
pride of Moab, the extremely
proud one—
His haughtiness, his arrogance,
his conceit, and his self-
exaltation.
30 "I know his [insolent] wrath," says
the LORD,
"But it is futile;
His idle boasts [in his deeds] have
accomplished nothing.
31 "Therefore I will wail over Moab,
And I will cry out for all Moab.
I will sigh *and* mourn over the
men of Kir-heres (Kir-hareseth).
[Is 15:1; 16:7, 11]
32 "O vines of Sibmah, I will weep for
you
More than the weeping of Jazer
[over its ruins and wasted
vineyards].
Your tendrils [of influence]
stretched across the sea,
Reaching [even] to the sea of
Jazer.
The destroyer has fallen
On your summer fruits and your
[season's] crop of grapes.
33 "So joy and gladness are taken
away
From the fruitful field and from
the land of Moab.
And I have made the wine cease
from the wine presses;
No one treads *the grapes* with
shouting.
Their shouting is not joyful
shouting [but is instead, a battle
cry].

34 "From the outcry at Heshbon even
to Elealeh, even to Jahaz they have
raised their voice, from Zoar even to
Horonaim and Eglath-shelishiyah; for
even the waters of Nimrim will become
desolations.

35 "Moreover, I will cause to cease in
Moab," says the LORD, "the one who
ascends *and* offers sacrifice in the high
place and the one who burns incense
to his gods.
36 "Therefore My heart moans *and*
sighs for Moab like flutes, and My
heart moans *and* sighs like flutes for
the men of Kir-heres (Kir-hareseth);
therefore [the remnant of] the abun-
dant riches they gained has perished.
37 "For every head is [shaven] bald
and every beard cut off; there are cuts
(slashes) on all the hands and sack-
cloth on the loins [all expressions of
mourning]. [Is 15:2, 3]
38 "On all the housetops of Moab and
in its streets there is lamentation (ex-
pressions of grief for the dead) every-
where, for I have broken Moab like a
vessel in which there is no pleasure,"
says the LORD.
39 "How it is broken down! How they
have wailed! How Moab has turned his
back in shame! So Moab will become
a laughingstock and a [horrifying]
terror to all who are around him."
40 For thus says the LORD:

"Behold, one (Nebuchadnezzar of
Babylon) will fly swiftly like an
eagle
And spread out his wings against
Moab. [Ezek 17:3]
41 "Kerioth [and the cities] has been
taken
And the strongholds seized;
And the hearts of the warriors of
Moab in that day
Shall be like the heart of a woman
in childbirth.
42 "Moab will be destroyed from
being a nation (people)
Because he has become arrogant
and magnified himself against
the LORD.

48:33 ***joy and gladness are taken away.*** The joy once heard echoing from the vineyards and winepresses had vanished before the horrifying sound of horses' hoofbeats and clashing weapons. **48:40–44** ***will fly swiftly like an eagle.*** The imagery is that of Babylon spreading its ravaging armies over Moab like an eagle spreading its wings. ***he has become arrogant and magnified himself.*** Moab's chief sin was pride, considering itself greater than the God of Israel. Its pride would be turned to fear and terror, and then the nation would be taken captive.

29 Isa 16:6 **30** Isa 16:6; Jer 50:36 **31** Isa 15:5 **32** Isa 16:8,9 **33** Isa 16:10; Joel 1:12 **34** Isa 15:4-6 **35** Isa 15:2; 16:12 **36** Isa 15:5; 16:11; 15:7 **37** Isa 15:2,3; Ge 37:34 **38** Jer 22:28 **40** Dt 28:49; Hab 1:8; Isa 8:8 **41** ver. 24; Isa 13:8; 21:3; Mic 4:9 **42** Ps 83:4

43 "Terror and pit and snare are
before you,
O inhabitant of Moab," says the
Lord. [Is 24:7]
44 "The one who flees from the terror
Will fall into the pit,
And the one who gets up out of the
pit
Will be taken *and* caught in the
trap;
For I shall bring upon it, even upon
Moab,
The year of their punishment,"
says the Lord.

45 "In the shadow of Heshbon
The fugitives stand powerless
[helpless and without
strength],
For a fire has gone out from
Heshbon,
A flame from the midst of Sihon;
It has destroyed the forehead of
Moab
And the crowns of the heads of
[the arrogant Moabites] the ones
in tumult.
46 "Woe (judgment is coming) to you,
O Moab!
The people of [the pagan god
called] Chemosh have perished;
For your sons have been taken
away captive
And your daughters into captivity.
47 "Yet I will return the captives *and*
restore the fortunes of Moab
In the latter days," says the Lord.

Thus far is the judgment on Moab.

Prophecy against Ammon

49 CONCERNING THE sons (descendants) of Ammon.

Thus says the Lord:
"Does Israel have no sons
[to reclaim Gad from the
Ammonites]?
Has he no heir?
Why then has Malcam taken
possession of Gad
And [why do] his people live in the
cities [of Gad]?
2 "Therefore behold, the days are
coming," says the Lord,
"When I will cause an alarm of
war to be heard
Against Rabbah of the
Ammonites;
And it [along with the high ground
on which it stands] will become
a desolate heap,
And its villages will be set on fire.
Then will Israel take possession of
his possessors,"
Says the Lord. [Ezek 21:28–
32; 25:1–7, 11; Amos 1:13–15;
Zeph 2:8–11]
3 "Wail, O Heshbon, for Ai [in
Ammon] has been destroyed!
Cry out, O daughters of Rabbah!
Wrap yourselves with sackcloth
and lament (cry out in grief),
And rush back and forth inside the
enclosures;
For Malcam [your powerless god]
will go into exile
Together with his priests and his
princes.
4 "Why do you boast of your
valleys?
Your valley is flowing away,
[O Ammon] rebellious *and*
faithless daughter
Who trusts in her treasures,
saying,
'Who will come against me?'
5 "Behold, I am going to bring terror
on you,"
Says the Lord God of hosts,
"From all who are around you;
And each of you will be driven out
headlong,
And there will be no one to gather
the fugitives together.
6 "But afterward I will reverse
The captivity of the children
of Ammon *and* restore their
fortunes,"
Says the Lord.

49:1 – 2 *Malcam.* This was the patron deity of the Ammonites and is pictured here as taking possession of the land formerly belonging to the Gadites, a process that began in the days of the judges.

---

43 Isa 24:17 **44** Jer 11:23 **45** Nu 21:28; Nu 24:17 **46** Nu 21:29 **47** Jer 49:6 **CHAPTER 49** **1** Eze 21:28; 25:2; Am 1:13; Zep 2:8,9; Am 1:13 **2** Eze 25:5; Am 1:14 **3** Isa 32:11; Jer 48:7 **4** Jer 3:14; Jer 21:13 **6** ver. 39; Jer 48:47

Prophecy against Edom

7 Concerning Edom.
Thus says the LORD of hosts,
"Is there no longer any wisdom in Teman?
Has good counsel vanished from the intelligent *and* prudent?
Has their wisdom decayed? [Is 34; 63:1–6; Ezek 25:12–14; 35; Amos 1:11, 12; Obad 1–16; Mal 1:2–5]
8 "Flee, turn back, dwell in the depths [of the desert to escape the judgment of Edom],
O inhabitants of Dedan,
For I will bring the destruction of Esau (Edom) upon him
When I inspect *and* punish him.
9 "If grape gatherers came to you,
Would they not leave some ungleaned grapes [on the vines]?
If thieves came by night,
Would they not destroy [only] what is enough [for them]?
10 "But I have stripped Esau (Edom) bare;
I have uncovered his hiding places
And he cannot hide himself.
His descendants have been destroyed along with his brothers (relatives) and his neighbors;
And he is no more.
11 "Leave your orphans behind; I will [do what is needed to] keep them alive.
And let [those who are] your widows trust *and* confide in Me."

12 For thus says the LORD, "Behold,
those (Israel) who were not sentenced
to drink the cup [of wrath] shall cer-
tainly drink it, and are you to remain
unpunished? You will not be acquitted
and go unpunished, but you will cer-
tainly drink [from the cup of wrath and
judgment]. [Jer 25:28, 29]
13 "For I have sworn [an oath] by My-
self," says the LORD, "that Bozrah will
become an object of horror, a reproach,
a ruin, and a curse; and all its cities
will become perpetual ruins."

14 I have heard a report from the LORD,
And a messenger has been sent to the nations, saying,
"Gather together and come against her,
And rise up for the battle."
15 "For behold, [Edom] I have made you small among the nations
And despised among men. [Ezek 35:9]
16 "As for Your terror,
The pride *and* arrogance of your heart have deceived you,
O you who live in the clefts of the rock (Sela also called Petra),
Who hold *and* occupy the height of the hill.
Though you make your nest as high as the eagle's,
I will bring you down from there," says the LORD.

17 "Edom will become an object of
horror; everyone who goes by it will be
astonished and shall hiss [scornfully]
at all its plagues *and* disasters.
18 "As [it was] in the overthrow of
Sodom and Gomorrah with their
neighboring cities," says the LORD, "no
man will live there, nor will a son of
man dwell in it.
19 "See, one will come like a lion from
the thicket of the Jordan against the
enduring habitation [of Edom] *and* its
watered pastures; for in an instant I
will make him (Edom) run from his
land. I will appoint over him the one

49:9–11 *grape gatherers.* This imagery is derived from 6:9, but there was no real remnant left in Edom. The nation had been totally ravaged and stripped bare, with only women and children left alive to work the land.
49:17–19 *an object of horror.* Like Israel, Judah, Egypt, Moab, and Ammon, Edom would be destroyed and would become an object of derision. Like the lion that emerges from the thickets along the lower Jordan and seizes its prey, God would attack the Edomites through His appointed instrument.

7 Eze 25:12; Ob 8; Isa 19:11 **8** ver. 30; Jer 25:23 **9** Ob 5 **10** Mal 1:3; Isa 17:14 **12** Jer 25:29; Ob 16 **13** Ge 22:16; Isa 45:23; Am 6:8; Isa 34:6; 63:1 **14** Ob 1-3 **16** Ob 4; Job 39:27; Am 9:2 **17** Jer 18:16; 50:13 **18** Ge 19:25; Dt 29:23; Jer 50:40 **19** Jer 50:44; Jer 12:5; Ex 15:11; Job 41:10

whom I choose. For who is like Me,
and who will summon Me [into court]
and prosecute Me [for this]? Who is
the [earthly] shepherd who can stand
[defiantly] before Me?"
20 Therefore hear the plan of the LORD
which He has devised against Edom,
and [hear] what He has purposed
against the inhabitants of Teman: sure-
ly they will be dragged away, even the
little ones of the flock; surely He will
make their dwelling place desolate
because of them.
21 The earth has quaked at the noise
of their downfall. There is an outcry!
The sound of its noise has been heard
at the Red Sea.
22 Behold, He will mount up and fly
swiftly like an eagle and spread His
wings against [the city of] Bozrah;
and in that day the heart of the mighty
warriors of Edom will be like the heart
of a woman in childbirth. [Jer 48:41]

Prophecy against Damascus

23 Concerning Damascus [in Syria].

"Hamath and Arpad are perplexed
and shamed,
For they have heard bad news;
They are disheartened;
Troubled *and* anxious like a
[storm-tossed] sea
Which cannot be calmed.
24 "Damascus has become helpless;
She has turned away to flee,
Terror (panic) has seized her;
Anguish and distress have gripped
her
Like a woman in childbirth.
25 "Why has the renowned city not
been deserted,
The city of My joy!
26 "Therefore, her young men will
fall in her streets,
And all her men of war will be
destroyed in that day," says
the LORD of hosts. [Is 17:1–3;
Amos 1:3–5; Zech 9:1]
27 "I will set fire to the wall of
Damascus,
And it will consume the palaces of
Ben-hadad."

Prophecy against Kedar and Hazor

28 Concerning Kedar and concerning
the kingdoms of Hazor, which Nebu-
chadnezzar king of Babylon defeated.
Thus says the LORD,

"Arise, go up against Kedar
And destroy the men of the east.
29 "They (the Babylonians) will take
away their tents and their flocks;
They will carry off for themselves
Their tent curtains, all their goods
and their camels,
And they will call out to one
another, 'Terror on every side!'
[Ps 31:13; Jer 6:25; 20:3, 10; 46:5]
30 "Flee, run far away! Dwell in the
depths [of the desert],
O inhabitants of Hazor," says the
LORD,
"For Nebuchadnezzar king of
Babylon has planned a course of
action against you
And devised a scheme against you.
31 "Arise [Nebuchadnezzar], go up
against a nation which is at
ease,
Which lives securely," says the
LORD,
"A nation which has neither gates
nor bars;
They dwell apart *and* alone.
32 "Their camels will become
plunder,
And their herds of cattle a spoil;
And I will scatter to all the [four]
winds those who cut the corners
of their hair [as evidence of their
idolatry],
And I will bring their disaster
from every side," says the LORD.
[Lev 19:27]

49:30–33 Hazor will become a haunt and dwelling place of jackals. Nebuchadnezzar's destructive army would attack the tent villages of Kedar and Hazor. The oases would be left to the jackals for habitation (9:11; 10:22). The Bedouin peoples would be scattered afar, as if by the hot desert winds.

---

20 Jer 50:45 **21** Jer 50:46 **22** Jer 48:40,41 **23** Isa 17:1; 37:13; Am 1:3; Zec 9:1,2; Isa 57:20 **24** Isa 13:8; Jer 4:31; 6:24; 48:41 **25** Jer 33:9 **26** Jer 50:30 **27** Am 1:4 **28** Isa 21:13; Jdg 6:3; Job 1:3 **29** Ps 120:5; Jer 46:5 **30** ver. 8 **31** Eze 38:11; Nu 23:9; Dt 33:28; Mic 7:14

33 "Hazor will become a haunt *and* dwelling place of jackals,
A desolation forever;
No one will live there,
Nor will a son of man reside in it."

Prophecy against Elam

34 The word of the LORD that came to Jeremiah the prophet concerning Elam, in the beginning of the reign of Zedekiah king of Judah, saying:

35 "Thus says the LORD of hosts,
'Behold (listen carefully), I am going to break the bow of Elam,
The finest [weapon] of their strength.
36 'And I will bring upon Elam the four winds
From the four corners of heaven;
And I will scatter them toward all those winds,
And there will be no nation
To which the outcasts of Elam will not go.
37 'So I will cause Elam to be shattered (dismayed) before their enemies
And before those who seek their lives;
And I will bring disaster on them,
Even My fierce anger,' says the LORD.
'And I will send the sword after them
Until I have consumed them.
38 'Then I will set My throne [of judgment] in Elam
And I will destroy from there the king and princes,'
Says the LORD. [Neh 1:1; Esth 1:2; Dan 8:1, 2]
39 'But it will be in the last days (the end of days)
That I will reverse the captivity *and* restore the fortunes of Elam,' "
Says the LORD.

Prophecy against Babylon

50 THE WORD that the LORD spoke concerning Babylon and concerning the land of the Chaldeans through Jeremiah the prophet: [Is 13:1–14:23; 47; Hab 1:1, 2]

2 "Declare among the nations.
Lift up a signal [to spread the news]—publish *and* proclaim it,
Do not conceal it; say,
'Babylon has been taken,
Bel [the patron god] has been shamed, Marduk (Bel) has been shattered.
Babylon's images have been shamed, her [worthless] idols have been thrown down.'

3 "For out of the north a nation (Media)
has come against her which will make
her land desolate, and no one will live
there. They have fled, they have gone
away—both man and animal.
4 "In those days and at that time,"
says the LORD, "the children of Israel
will come, they and the children of Judah together; they will come up weeping [in repentance] as they come and
seek the LORD their God [inquiring for
and of Him].
5 "They will ask the way to Zion, with
their faces in that direction, saying,
'Come, let us join ourselves to the LORD
in an everlasting covenant that will not
be forgotten.'

6 "My people have become lost sheep;
Their shepherds have led them astray.

49:34–36 *break the bow.* The Elamites were famous for their skilled archers (Isa 22:6), who became an important part of the Persian army under Cyrus. ***four winds.*** This expression indicates the military might that the Lord musters against His enemies (Eze 37:9).
50:2–3 *Bel [the patron god] has been shamed.* Bel was a title like Baal, meaning "Lord," another name for Babylon's patron deity, Marduk. The oracle begins with a defamation of the gods of Babylon. The term translated "images" means animal droppings. The Hebrew prophets are openly contemptuous of idols and speak of them with ridicule.

33 Jer 9:11; 10:22; Mal 1:3; ver. 18 **34** Jer 25:25 **35** Isa 22:6 **36** ver. 32 **37** Jer 9:16 **38** Jer 43:10 **39** Jer 48:47 **CHAPTER 50** **1** Isa 13:1; 47:1 **2** Isa 46:1; Jer 51:44; See Jer 43:12,13 **3** Jer 51:48; Isa 13:17,18,20 **4** Hos 1:11; Ezr 3:12; Jer 31:9; Zec 12:10; Hos 3:5 **5** Jer 31:31 **6** Isa 53:6; 1Pe 2:25; Jer 2:20; 3:6,23

They have made them turn aside
[to the seductive places of
idolatry] on the mountains.
They have gone along [from one
sin to another] from mountain
to hill;
They have forgotten their [own]
resting place. [Is 53:6; 1 Pet 2:25]
7 "All who found them have
devoured them;
And their adversaries have said,
'We are not guilty,
Because they have sinned against
the LORD [and are no longer holy
to Him], their [true] habitation of
righteousness *and* justice,
Even the LORD, the [confident]
hope of their fathers.'
8 "Wander away from the midst of
Babylon
And go out of the land of the
Chaldeans;
Be like the male goats [who serve
as leaders] at the head of the
flocks. [Jer 51:6, 9, 45; 2 Cor 6:17;
Rev 18:4]
9 "For behold, I will stir up and
bring up against Babylon
An assembly of great nations from
the north country.
They will equip themselves *and* set
up the battle lines against her;
From there she will be taken
captive.
Their arrows will be like an expert
warrior
Who will not return empty-
handed.
10 "Chaldea will become plunder;
All who plunder her will be
satisfied," says the LORD.

11 "Though you are glad, though you
rejoice,
O you who plunder My heritage,
Though you are wanton *and* skip
about like a heifer in the grass
And neigh like stallions,
12 Your mother [Babylon] shall be
greatly shamed;
She who gave you birth will be
ashamed.
Behold, *she will be* the least of the
nations,
A wilderness, a parched land and
a desert.
13 "Because of the wrath of the LORD
she will not be inhabited
But she will be completely
desolate;
Everyone who goes by Babylon
will be appalled
And will hiss (mock) at all her
wounds *and* plagues.
14 "Set yourselves in battle formation
against Babylon on every side,
All you archers.
Shoot at her! Do not spare the
arrows,
For she has sinned against the
LORD.
15 "Raise the battle cry against her
on every side!
She has given her hand
[in agreement] *and* has
surrendered; her pillars have
fallen,
Her walls have been torn down.
For this is the vengeance of the
LORD:
Take vengeance on her;
As she has done [to others], do to
her.
16 "Cut off the sower from Babylon
And the one who handles the
sickle at the time of harvest.
For fear of the sword of the
oppressor
Everyone will return to his own
people
And everyone will flee to his own
land.

17 "Israel is a hunted *and* scattered
flock [driven here and there as prey];
the lions have chased *them away.*

50:11–13 *O you who plunder My heritage.* Babylon's plunder would be its punishment for gloating over Judah's demise and the abuse of God's heritage. Babylon would be "a wilderness." Defamation, drought, dehabitation, desolation, and derision was Babylon's destiny (18:16; 19:8; 49:17).

7 Ps 79:7; Jer 40:2,3; Zec 11:5; See Jer 2:3; Da 9:16; Ps 90:1; 91:1; Ps 22:4 **8** Isa 48:20; Jer 51:6,45; Zec 2:6,7; Rev 18:4 **9** Jer 15:14; 51:27; 2Sa 1:22 **10** Rev 17:16 **11** Isa 47:6; Hos 10:11 **13** Jer 25:12; Jer 49:17 **14** Jer 51:2; ver. 29 **15** 1Ch 29:24; 2Ch 30:8; La 5:6; Eze 17:18; Jer 51:58; Jer 51:6,11 **16** Isa 13:14 **17** ver. 6; Jer 2:15; 2Ki 17:6; 2Ki 24:10,14

First the king of Assyria devoured
him, and now at last Nebuchadnezzar
king of Babylon has broken (gnawed)
his bones.
18"Therefore thus says the LORD of
hosts, the God of Israel, 'Behold, I will
visit (inspect, examine) *and* punish
the king of Babylon and his land, just
as I visited *and* punished the king of
Assyria.
19'And I will bring Israel [home]
again to his pasture and he will graze
on [the most fertile lands of] Carmel
[in the west] and Bashan [in the east],
and his soul will be satisfied on the
hills of Ephraim and Gilead.
20'In those days and at that time,'
says the LORD, 'a search will be made
for the wickedness of Israel, but there
will be none and for the sins of Judah, but none will be found, for I will
pardon those whom I leave as a remnant.' [Is 1:9; 43:25; Jer 31:34; 33:8;
Rom 9:27]

21"Go against [Babylon] the land of
Merathaim (Double Rebellion),
Go up against it and against the
people of Pekod (Punishment).
Kill and utterly destroy them,"
says the LORD,
"And do everything that I have
commanded you."
22"The noise of battle is in the land,
And [the noise of] great
destruction.
23"How the hammer of the whole
earth
Is crushed and broken!
How Babylon has become
A horror [of desolation] among the
nations!
24"I set a trap for you and you also
were caught, O Babylon,
And you did not know it;
You have been found and also
seized
Because you have struggled
against the LORD."
25The LORD has opened His armory
And has brought out [the nations
who unknowingly are] the
weapons of His indignation
(wrath),
For it is a work of the Lord GOD of
hosts
In the land of the Chaldeans.
26Come against her from the
farthest border.
Open her storehouses;
Pile it up like heaps of rubbish.
Burn *and* destroy her completely;
Let nothing be left of her.
27Kill all her young bulls [her
strength—her young men];
Let them go down to the
slaughter!
Woe (judgment is coming) to the
Chaldeans, for their day has
come,
The time of their punishment.
28Listen to the voice of the refugees
who flee and escape from the
land of Babylon,
Proclaiming in Zion the vengeance
of the LORD our God,
The vengeance [of the LORD
against the Chaldeans] for
[plundering and destroying] His
temple.
29"Call together many [archers]
against Babylon,
All those who bend the bow.
Encamp against her on every side;
Let no one from there escape.
Repay her according to her
actions;
Just as she has done, do to her.
For she has been proudly defiant
and presumptuous against the
LORD,
Against the Holy One of Israel.
30"Therefore her young men will fall
in her streets,
And all her soldiers will be
destroyed on that day," says the
LORD.

50:21–28 *utterly destroy them.* The tables would be turned on Babylon. The Lord God had launched His vengeful weapons upon the city through His anointed servant Cyrus (2Ch 36:22,23; Isa 45:1).

19 Isa 65:10; Jer 33:12; Eze 34:13 **20** Jer 31:34; Isa 1:9 **21** Eze 23:23; See 2Sa 16:11; 2Ki 18:25; 2Ch 36:23; Isa 10:6; 44:28; 48:14 **22** Jer 51:54 **23** Isa 14:6; Jer 51:20 **24** Jer 51:8,31; Da 5:30 **25** Isa 13:5 **27** Ps 22:12; Isa 34:7; Jer 46:21; Jer 48:44 **28** Jer 51:10 **29** ver. 14; ver. 15; Jer 51:56; Rev 18:6; Isa 47:10 **30** Jer 49:26; 51:4

31 "Behold, I am against you,
[O Babylon, you] arrogant one, [you who are pride and presumption personified],"
Says the Lord God of hosts,
"For your day has come,
The time when I will punish you.
32 "The arrogant (proud) one will stumble and fall
With no one to raise him up;
And I will set fire to his cities
And it will devour all who are around him."

33 Thus says the Lord of hosts,
"The children of Israel are oppressed,
And the children of Judah as well;
And all who took them captive have held them tightly,
They have refused to let them go.
34 "Their Redeemer is strong; the Lord of hosts is His name.
He will most certainly plead their case *and* defend their cause
So that He may bring rest to their land,
But turmoil to the inhabitants of Babylon.
35 "A sword against the Chaldeans," says the Lord,
"And against the inhabitants of Babylon
And against her princes (officials, civic rulers) and against her wise men (astrologers, religious rulers)!
36 "A sword against the oracle priests (the babbling liars), and they will become fools!
A sword against her mighty warriors, and they will be shattered *and* destroyed!
37 "A sword against their horses and against their chariots
And against all the foreign troops that are in her midst,
And they will become [as weak and defenseless as] women!
A sword against her treasures, and they will be plundered!
38 "A drought on her waters, and they will dry up!
For it is a land of [worthless] idols,
And they are mad over fearsome idols [those objects of terror in which they foolishly trust].
39 "Therefore wild beasts of the desert will live there [in Babylon] with the jackals;
The ostriches also will live there,
And it will never again be inhabited [with people]
Or lived in from generation to generation. [Is 13:20–22]
40 "As when God overthrew Sodom
And Gomorrah and their neighboring cities," says the Lord,
"So no man will live there;
Nor shall any son of man live there." [Jer 49:18]

41 "Behold, a people is coming from the north,
And a great nation and many kings
Will be stirring from the remote parts of the earth.
42 "They seize their bow and spear;
They are cruel and have no compassion.
They sound like the roaring of the sea;
They ride on horses,
Every man equipped like a man [ready] for the battle
Against you, O Daughter of Babylon.
43 "The king of Babylon has heard the report about them,
And his hands fall limp *and* helpless;
Anguish has seized him,
And agony like that of a woman in childbirth.

50:34 *Their Redeemer is strong.* One who secured the freedom of a kinsman, protecting family rights, was called a kinsmen redeemer. Here God, the Redeemer of Israel (Isa 47:4), offers to obtain the legal freedom of His people from captivity.

31 ver. 27 **32** Jer 21:14 **34** Rev 18:8; Isa 47:4 **35** Da 5:30; Isa 47:13 **36** Isa 44:25; Jer 48:30 **37** Jer 25:20; Eze 30:5; Jer 51:30; Na 3:13 **38** Isa 44:27; Jer 51:36; Rev 16:12; ver. 2 **39** Isa 13:21,22; 34:14; Jer 51:37; Rev 18:2; Isa 13:20; Jer 25:12 **40** Ge 19:25; Isa 13:19; Jer 51:26 **41** ver. 9; Jer 6:22; 25:14; 51:27; Rev 17:16 **42** Jer 6:23; Isa 13:18; 5:30

44 "See, one will come up like a lion
from the thicket of the Jordan against
the enduring habitation [of Babylon]
and its watered pastures; for in an in-
stant I will make Babylon run from his
land. I will appoint over Babylon the
one whom I choose. For who is like Me,
and who will summon Me [into court]
and prosecute Me [for this]? Who is
the [earthly] shepherd who can stand
[defiantly] before Me?" [Jer 49:19]

45 Therefore hear the plan of the LORD
which He has devised against Bab-
ylon, and hear what He has purposed
against [the inhabitants of the land
of] the Chaldeans: surely they will be
dragged away, [even] the little ones of
the flock; surely He will make their
habitation desolate because of them.

46 At the shout, "Babylon has been
seized!" the earth quakes, and an out-
cry is heard among the nations.

Babylon Judged for Sins against Israel

51 THUS SAYS the LORD:
"Behold, I am going to stir up *and*
put into action [a fury] against
Babylon
And against the [rebellious] people
of Leb-kamai (Chaldea)
A destroying wind *and* hostile
spirit;
2 "And I will send foreigners to
Babylon that they may winnow
her
And may devastate *and* empty her
land;
For in the day of destruction
They will be against her on every
side.
3 "Do not let him (the Chaldean
defender) who bends his bow
bend it,
Nor let him rise up in his coat of
armor.
So do not spare her young men;
Devote her entire army to
destruction.
4 "They shall fall down dead in the
land of the Chaldeans,
And wounded in her streets."
5 For neither Israel nor Judah has
been abandoned
By his God, the LORD of hosts,
Though their land is full of sin *and*
guilt
Before the Holy One of Israel.
6 Flee out of Babylon,
Let every one of you save his life!
Do not be destroyed in her
punishment,
For this is the time of the LORD's
vengeance;
He is going to pay her what
she has earned. [Jer 50:28;
2 Cor 6:17; Rev 18:4]
7 Babylon has been a golden cup in
the LORD's hand,
Intoxicating all the earth.
The nations drank her wine;
Therefore the nations have gone
mad. [Rev 14:8; 17:4]
8 Babylon has suddenly fallen and is
shattered!
Wail for her [if you care to]!
Get balm for her [incurable]
pain;
Perhaps she may be healed.
[Jer 25:15; Rev 14:8–10; 16:19;
18:2, 3]
9 We would have healed Babylon,
but she was not to be healed.
Abandon her and let each [captive]
return to his own country,
For her guilt *and* judgment have
reached to heaven
And are lifted up to the very skies.
[Gen 18:20, 21]

51:6 – 10 *Babylon has been a golden cup.* The imagery of Babylon's cup of fury from 25:15 – 19 is reversed. Here Babylon's cup is broken by the Lord. ***Get balm.*** As in the case of Judah (8:22), decadent Babylon was beyond healing and had to be abandoned. The destruction of Babylon was the vindication of the justice of God. Jeremiah's prediction (25:12 – 14) would be realized: Israel would be made righteous through God's work.

44 Jer 49:19; Job 41:10; Jer 49:19 **45** Isa 14:24; Jer 51:11 **46** Rev 18:9 **CHAPTER 51** **1** 2Ki 19:7; Jer 4:11 **2** Jer 15:7; Jer 50:14 **3** Jer 50:14,21 **4** Jer 49:26; 50:30,37 **6** Jer 50:8; Rev 18:4; Jer 50:15; Jer 25:14 **7** Rev 17:4; 14:8; Jer 25:16 **8** Isa 21:9; Rev 14:8; 18:2; Jer 48:20; Rev 18:9,11,19; Jer 46:11 **9** Isa 13:14; Jer 50:16; Rev 18:5

10 The LORD has brought about our
vindication *and* has revealed the
righteousness of our cause;
Come and let us proclaim in Zion
The work of the LORD our God!

11 Sharpen the arrows, take up the
shields [and cover yourselves]!
The LORD has stirred up the spirit
of the kings of the Medes,
Because His purpose concerning
Babylon is to destroy it;
For that is the vengeance of the
LORD, vengeance [on Babylon]
for [plundering and destroying]
His temple.
12 Set up a signal on the walls of
Babylon [to spread the news];
Post a strong blockade,
Station the guards,
Prepare the men for ambush!
For the LORD has both purposed
and done
That which He spoke against the
people of Babylon.
13 [O Babylon] you who live by many
waters,
Rich in treasures,
Your end has come,
And the line measuring your life is
cut. [Rev 17:1–6]
14 The LORD of hosts has sworn [an
oath] by Himself, saying,
"Surely I will fill you with men, as
with [a swarm of] locusts [who
strip the land clean],
And they will lift up a song *and*
shout of victory over you."

15 He made the earth by His power;
He established the world by His
wisdom
And stretched out the heavens by
His understanding.
16 When He utters His voice, *there
is* a tumult of waters in the
heavens,
And He causes the clouds to
ascend from the ends of the
earth.
He makes lightnings for the rain
And brings out the wind from His
storehouses.
17 Every man has become stupid *and*
brutelike, without knowledge [of
God];
Every goldsmith is shamed by the
cast images he has made;
For his molten idols are a lie,
And there is no breath [of life] *or*
spirit in them.
18 They are worthless (empty, false,
futile), a work of delusion *and*
worthy of derision;
In the time of their inspection *and*
punishment they will perish.
19 The Portion of Jacob [the true
God of Israel] is not like these
[handmade gods];
For He is the Maker of all *and* the
One who formed *and* fashioned
all things,
And Israel is the tribe of His
inheritance—
The LORD of hosts is His name.
[Jer 10:12–16]
20 "You [Cyrus of Persia, soon to
conquer Babylon] are My battle-
axe and weapon of war—
For with you I shatter nations,
With you I destroy kingdoms.
21 "With you I shatter the horse and
his rider,
With you I shatter the chariot and
its driver,
22 With you I shatter man and
woman,
With you I shatter old man and
youth,
With you I shatter young man and
virgin,
23 With you I shatter the shepherd
and his flock,
With you I shatter the farmer and
his yoke of oxen,
And with you I shatter governors
and commanders.

24 "And I will [completely] repay Bab-
ylon and all the people of Chaldea

51:20–26 ***You . . . are My battle-axe.*** Babylon had been God's implement for judgment against the nations, and Judah in particular.

10 Ps 37:6; Jer 50:28 **11** Jer 46:4; ver. 28; Isa 13:17; Jer 50:45; Jer 50:28 **12** Na 2:1; 3:14 **13** Rev 17:1,15 **14** Jer 49:13; Am 6:8; Na 3:15; Jer 50:15 **15** Ge 1:1,6; Jer 10:12; Job 9:8; Ps 104:2; Isa 40:22 **16** Ps 135:7 **17** Jer 10:14; Jer 50:2 **18** Jer 10:15 **19** Jer 10:16 **20** Isa 10:5,15; Jer 50:23 **22** 2Ch 36:17 **24** Jer 50:15

for all the evil that they have done in
Zion—before your very eyes [I will do
it]," says the LORD.

25 "Behold, I am against you,
O destroying mountain [conqueror of nations],
Who destroys the whole earth,"
declares the LORD,
"I will stretch out My hand against you,
And roll you down from the [rugged] cliffs,
And will make you a burnt mountain (extinct volcano).
26 "They will not take from you [even] a stone for a cornerstone
Nor any rock for a foundation,
But you will be desolate forever,"
says the LORD.

27 Lift up a signal in the land [to spread the news]!
Blow the trumpet among the nations!
Dedicate the nations [for war] against her;
Call against her the kingdoms of Ararat, Minni, and Ashkenaz.
Appoint a marshal against her;
Cause the horses to come up like bristly locusts [with their wings not yet released from their cases].
28 Prepare *and* dedicate the nations for war against her—
The kings of Media,
With their governors and commanders,
And every land of their dominion.
29 The land trembles and writhes [in pain and sorrow],
For the purposes of the LORD against Babylon stand,
To make the land of Babylon
A desolation without inhabitants.
30 The mighty warriors of Babylon have ceased to fight;
They remain in their strongholds.
Their strength *and* power have failed;
They are becoming [weak and helpless] like women.
Their dwelling places are set on fire;
The bars on her *gates* are broken.
31 One courier runs to meet another,
And one messenger to meet another,
To tell the king of Babylon
That his city has been captured from end to end;
32 And that the fords [across the Euphrates] have been blocked *and* [the ferries] seized,
And they have set the [great] marshes on fire,
And the men of war are terrified.

33 For thus says the LORD of hosts, the
God of Israel:

"The Daughter of Babylon is like a threshing floor
At the time it is being trampled *and* prepared;
Yet in a little while the time of harvest will come for her."
34 "Nebuchadnezzar king of Babylon has devoured me, he has crushed me,
He has set me down like an empty vessel.
Like a monster he has swallowed me up,
He has filled his belly with my delicacies;
He has spit me out *and* washed me away.
35 "May the violence done to me and to my flesh *and* blood be upon Babylon,"
The inhabitant of Zion will say;
And, "May my blood be upon the inhabitants of Chaldea,"
Jerusalem will say.

51:29 – 32 *The mighty warriors of Babylon have ceased to fight.* The Nabonidus *Chronicle*, an ancient text describing the fall of Babylon, reports that "Cyrus entered Babylon without a battle." By the time Cyrus reached Babylon, he had conquered all of Babylonia except for the capital city, cutting off roads and supply routes.

25 Isa 13:2; Zec 4:7; Rev 8:8 **26** Jer 50:40 **27** Isa 13:2; Jer 25:14; Jer 50:41 **28** ver. 11 **29** ver. 43; Jer 50:13 **30** Isa 19:16; Jer 48:41; 50:37; La 2:9; Am 1:5; Na 3:13 **31** Jer 50:24 **32** Jer 50:38 **33** Isa 21:10; Am 1:3; Mic 4:13; Isa 41:15; Hab 3:12; Isa 17:5; Hos 6:11; Joel 3:13; Rev 14:15 **34** Jer 50:17

[36]Therefore thus says the LORD,

"Behold, I will plead your case
And take full vengeance for you;
I will dry up her sea *and* great
reservoir
And make her fountain dry.
[37]"Babylon will become a heap [of
ruins], a haunt *and* dwelling
place of jackals,
An object of horror (an
astonishing desolation)
and a hissing [of scorn
and amazement], without
inhabitants.
[38]"They (the Chaldean lords) will be
roaring together [before their
sudden capture] like young lions
[roaring over their prey],
They (the princes) will be growling
like lions' cubs.
[39]"When they are inflamed [with
wine and lust during their
drinking bouts], I will prepare
them a feast [of My wrath]
And make them drunk, that they
may rejoice
And may sleep a perpetual sleep
And not wake up," declares the
LORD.
[40]"I will bring them down like lambs
to the slaughter,
Like rams together with male
goats.
[41]"How Sheshak (Babylon) has been
captured,
And the praise of the whole earth
been seized!
How Babylon has become an
astonishing desolation *and*
an object of horror among the
nations!
[42]"The sea has come up over
Babylon;
She has been engulfed with its
tumultuous waves.
[43]"Her cities have become an
astonishing desolation *and* an
object of horror,
A parched land and a desert,
A land in which no one lives,
And through which no son of man
passes.
[44]"I will punish *and* judge Bel [the
handmade god] in Babylon
And take out of his mouth what
he has swallowed up [the stolen
sacred articles and the captives
of Judah and elsewhere].
The nations will no longer flow to
him.
Yes, the wall of Babylon has fallen
down!
[45]"Come out of her midst, My
people,
And each of you [escape and] save
yourself
From the fierce anger of the LORD.
[Jer 50:8; 2 Cor 6:17; Rev 18:4]
[46]"Now *beware* so that you do not
lose heart,
And so that you are not afraid at
the rumor that will be heard in
the land—
For the rumor shall come one year,
And after that another rumor in
another year,
And violence *shall be* in the land,
Ruler against ruler—
[47]"Therefore behold (listen
carefully), the days are coming
When I will judge *and* punish the
idols of Babylon;
Her whole land will be perplexed
and shamed,
And all her slain will fall in her
midst.
[48]"Then heaven and earth and all
that is in them
Will shout *and* sing for joy over
Babylon,

51:47–48 *the days are coming.* This expression usually introduces a message of divine intervention into history. ***I will judge and punish the idols of Babylon.*** The city was known for its thousands of idols of its numerous gods and goddesses. As the king claimed to conquer nations in the name of his patron deity, so the gods of the defeated would be punished along with their worshipers. The devastation of decadent Babylon would be no cause for mourning among the nations. Instead, the nations would sing joyfully of Babylon's fall.

36 Jer 50:34; Jer 50:38 **37** Isa 13:22; Jer 50:39; Rev 18:2; Jer 25:9,18 **39** ver. 57 **41** Jer 25:26; Isa 13:19 **42** See Isa 8:7 **43** ver. 29; Jer 50:39 **44** Isa 46:1; ver. 58 **45** ver. 6; Jer 50:8; Rev 18:4 **46** 2Ki 19:7 **47** ver. 52 **48** Isa 44:23; Jer 50:3,41

For the destroyers will come
against her from the north,"
Says the LORD. [Is 44:23; Jer 51:11;
Rev 12:12; 18:20]
49 Indeed Babylon is to fall for the
slain of Israel,
As also for Babylon the slain of all
the earth have fallen.
50 You who have escaped the sword,
Go away! Do not stay!
Remember the LORD from far
away,
And let [desolate] Jerusalem come
into your mind.
51 We are perplexed *and* ashamed,
for we have heard reproach;
Disgrace has covered our faces,
For foreigners [from Babylon] have
come
Into the [most] sacred parts of the
sanctuary of the LORD [even
those places forbidden to all but
the appointed priest].
52 "Therefore behold, the days are
coming," says the LORD,
"When I will judge *and* punish the
idols [of Babylon],
And throughout her land the
mortally wounded will groan."
53 "Though Babylon should ascend to
the heavens,
And though she should fortify her
lofty stronghold,
Yet destroyers will come on her
from Me," says the LORD.
54 The sound of an outcry [comes]
from Babylon,
And [the sound] of great
destruction from the land of the
Chaldeans!
55 For the LORD is going to destroy
Babylon *and* make her a ruin,
And He will still her great voice
[that hums with city life].
And the waves [of her conquerors]
roar like great waters,
The noise of their voices is raised
up [like the marching of an
army].
56 For the destroyer is coming
against her, against Babylon;
And her mighty warriors will be
captured,
Their bows are shattered;
For the LORD is a God of [just]
restitution;
He will fully repay.
57 "I will make her princes and her
wise men drunk,
Her governors and her
commanders and her mighty
warriors;
They will sleep a perpetual sleep
and not wake up,"
Says the King—the LORD of hosts
is His name.

58 Thus says the LORD of hosts,
"The broad wall of Babylon will be
completely overthrown *and* the
foundations razed
And her high gates will be set on
fire;
The peoples will labor in vain,
And the nations become exhausted
[only] for fire [that will destroy
their work]." [Hab 2:13]

59 The message which Jeremiah the
prophet commanded Seraiah the son
of Neriah, the grandson of Mahseiah,
when he went with Zedekiah the king
of Judah to Babylon in the fourth year
of his reign. Now this Seraiah was
chief chamberlain *or* quartermaster
[and brother of Baruch].
60 So Jeremiah wrote in a single
scroll all the disaster which would
come on Babylon, [that is] all these
words which have been written con-
cerning Babylon.
61 Then Jeremiah said to Seraiah,
"When you come to Babylon, see to it
that you read all these words aloud,
62 and say, 'You, O LORD, have prom-
ised concerning this place to cut it off
and destroy it, so that there shall be
nothing living in it, neither man nor
animal, but it will be perpetually des-
olate.'
63 "And as soon as you finish read-
ing this scroll, you shall tie a stone to
it and throw it into the middle of the
Euphrates.
64 "Then say, 'In the same way Bab-
ylon will sink down and not rise be-
cause of the disaster that I will bring

50 Jer 44:28 **51** Ps 44:15; 79:4 **52** ver. 47 **53** Jer 49:16; Am 9:2; Ob 4 **54** Jer 50:22 **56** ver. 24; Ps 94:1; Jer 50:29 **57** ver. 39; Jer 46:18; 48:15 **58** ver. 44; Hab 2:13 **62** ver. 29; Jer 50:3,39 **63** See Rev 18:21 **64** ver. 58

on her; and the Babylonians will be-
come [hopelessly] exhausted.' " Thus
the words of Jeremiah are completed.
[Rev 18:21]

The Fall of Jerusalem

52 ZEDEKIAH WAS twenty-one
years old when he became king,
and he reigned eleven years in Jeru-
salem; and his mother's name was
Hamutal the daughter of Jeremiah of
Libnah. [2 Kin 24:18–25:21]
2 He did that which was evil in the
sight of the LORD like all that Jehoia-
kim had done.
3 For all this came about in Jerusalem
and Judah because of the anger of the
LORD, and [in the end] He cast them
from His presence. And Zedekiah re-
belled against the king of Babylon.
4 Now it came about in the ninth year
of his reign, in the tenth month, on
the tenth day, Nebuchadnezzar king
of Babylon came, he and all his army,
against Jerusalem; and they camped
against it and built moveable tow-
ers *and* siege mounds all around it.
[Jer 39:1–10]
5 So the city was besieged until
the eleventh year of King Zedekiah.
[2 Chr 36:11–13]
6 In the fourth month, on the ninth
day of the month, the famine was so
severe in the city that there was no
food for the people of the land.
7 Then the city was broken into, and
all the soldiers fled. They left the city
at night [as Ezekiel prophesied] pass-
ing through the gate between the two
walls by the king's garden, though the
Chaldeans were all around the city.
They fled by way of the Arabah (the
Jordan Valley). [Ezek 12:12]
8 But the army of the Chaldeans pur-
sued the king and overtook Zedekiah
in the plains of Jericho; and his entire
army was scattered from him.
9 Then they seized the king and
brought him to the king of Babylon
at Riblah in the [Syrian] land of Ha-
math [on the northern border of Israel],
where he pronounced sentence on him.
10 The king of Babylon killed the sons
of Zedekiah before his eyes; he also
killed all the princes of Judah at Rib-
lah.
11 Then the king of Babylon blind-
ed Zedekiah, bound him with bronze
shackles and took him to Babylon and
there he put him in prison [in a mill]
until the day of his death. [Ezek 12:13]
12 Now in the fifth month, on the
tenth day, which was the nineteenth
year of Nebuchadnezzar king of Bab-
ylon, Nebuzaradan captain of the
guard, who served the king of Bab-
ylon, came to Jerusalem.
13 He burned down the house of the
LORD and the king's palace and all the
houses of Jerusalem; every great house
or important structure he set on fire.
14 So all the army of the Chaldeans
who were with the captain of the guard
broke down all the walls around Je-
rusalem.
15 Then Nebuzaradan the captain of
the guard took away into exile some
of the poorest of the people, those
who were left in the city [at the time it
was captured], along with those who
deserted to join the king of Babylon
[during the siege] and the rest of the
artisans.
16 But Nebuzaradan the captain of
the guard left some of the poorest of
the land to be vinedressers and farm-
ers.
17 Now the Chaldeans broke into
pieces the pillars of bronze which be-
longed to the house of the LORD, and
the bronze pedestals [which supported
the ten basins] and the [enormous]
bronze Sea, which were in the house
of the LORD, and carried all the bronze
to Babylon.
18 They also took away the pots [for

52:13–16 *He burned down the house of the LORD.* The entire city of Jerusalem was burned, from the temple to the royal palace to the houses. The city walls were demolished. Leading citizens and some of the poor were deported under Nebuzaradan's command, leaving only a remnant of peasant farmers to work the fields, vineyards, and orchards.

CHAPTER 52 **1** 2Ki 24:18 **4** 2Ki 25:1-27; Jer 39:1; Zec 8:19 **9** Jer 32:4 **10** Eze 12:13 **12** Zec 7:5; 8:19; See ver. 29; Jer 39:9 **15** Jer 39:9 **17** Jer 27:19; See 1Ki 7:15,23,27,50 **18** Ex 27:3; 2Ki 25:14-16

carrying away ashes] and the shovels
and the snuffers and the bowls and the
spoons and all the bronze articles used
in the *temple* service.
[19]The captain of the guard also took
away the [small] bowls and the fire-
pans and the basins and the pots and
the lampstands and the incense cups
and the bowls for the drink offerings—
whatever was made of fine gold and
whatever was made of fine silver.
[20]The two pillars, the one [enormous]
Sea (basin), and the twelve bronze
bulls under the Sea, and the stands,
which King Solomon had made for
the house of the LORD—the bronze of
all these things was beyond weighing.
[21]Concerning the pillars, the height
of each pillar was eighteen cubits
(twenty-seven feet), and a line [an or-
namental molding] of twelve cubits
(eighteen feet) went around its circum-
ference; it was four fingers thick, and
[the pillar was] hollow.
[22]A capital of bronze was on [top of]
it. The height of each capital was five
cubits (seven and one-half feet), with a
lattice-work and pomegranates around
it, all of bronze. The second pillar also,
with its pomegranates, was similar to
these.
[23]There were ninety-six pomegran-
ates on the sides; and a hundred pome-
granates were on the lattice-work all
around.
[24]Then the captain of the guard took
[as prisoners] Seraiah the chief priest
and Zephaniah the second priest and
the three doorkeepers.
[25]He also took out of the city one of-
ficial who was overseer of the soldiers,
and seven of the king's advisers who
were found in the city, and the scribe
of the commander of the army who
mustered the people of the land, and
sixty men who were still in the city.
[26]Nebuzaradan the captain of the
guard took them and brought them to
the king of Babylon at Riblah.
[27]Then the king of Babylon struck
them down and put them to death at
Riblah in the land of Hamath. So Ju-
dah was led away into exile from its
own land.
[28]This is the number of people whom
Nebuchadnezzar took captive *and* ex-
iled: in the seventh year, 3,023 Jews;
[29]in the eighteenth year of Nebu-
chadnezzar, [he took captive] 832 per-
sons from Jerusalem;
[30]in the twenty-third year of Nebu-
chadnezzar, Nebuzaradan the captain
of the [Babylonian] guard took captive
745 Jewish people; there were 4,600
persons in all.
[31]Now it came about in the thirty-
seventh year of the exile of Jehoia-
chin [also called Coniah and Jeconiah]
king of Judah, in the twelfth month,
on the twenty-fifth of the month, Evil-
merodach king of Babylon, in the first
year of his reign, showed favor to Je-
hoiachin king of Judah and brought
him out of prison. [2 Kin 25:27–30]
[32]He spoke kindly to him and gave
him a throne above the thrones of the
kings who were [captives] with him
in Babylon.
[33]Jehoiachin changed his prison
clothes, and he dined regularly at the
king's table all the days of his life.
[34]And his allowance, a regular al-
lowance was given to him by the king
of Babylon, a daily portion [according
to his needs] until the day of his death,
all the days of his life.

52:31 – 34 *Evil-merodach.* Nebuchadnezzar's son became king next but only reigned for two years. Jehoiachin was released from prison during his reign and pardoned. He was provided with food and given a seat of honor in Babylon. This restoration was symbolic of the future restoration of Israel and Judah to their homeland.

20 1Ki 7:47 **21** 1Ki 7:15; 2Ki 25:17; 2Ch 3:15 **23** See 1Ki 7:20 **24** 2Ki 25:18; Jer 21:1; 29:5 **28** 2Ki 24:2; See 2Ki 24:12; See 2Ki 24:14 **29** See ver. 12; Jer 39:9 **31** 2Ki 25:27-30; Ge 40:13,20 **33** 2Sa 9:13

THE LAMENTATIONS OF JEREMIAH

▸ **AUTHOR:** The universal consensus of early Jewish and Christian tradition attributes this book to Jeremiah. Even though the author is unnamed in the book, the superscription to Lamentations in the Septuagint states: "And it came to pass, after Israel had been carried away captive, and Jerusalem had become desolate, that Jeremiah sat weeping, and lamented with this lamentation over Jerusalem saying…." The Talmud, as well as many other ancient sources, also supports this position.

▸ **TIMES:** c. 586 BC ▸ **KEY VERSES:** Lam 3:22 – 23

▸ **THEME:** A lament is a vehicle for working through sorrow. While grief is expressed in words, its resolution is in God and the hope He gives for the future. In a way, the lamentation process is one of coming to grips with all that God wants us to see about our present circumstances. For the people of Judah to lose a country meant not only the loss of the homeland, but the loss of God's presence and power to sustain the people in that land. It is hard for people who have never experienced such loss to understand the depth of grief expressed in this book.

The Sorrows of Zion

1 HOW SOLITARY *and* lonely sits the city [Jerusalem]
That was [once] full of people!
How like a widow she has become.
She who was great among the nations!
The princess among the provinces,
Has become a forced laborer!
2 She weeps bitterly in the night
And her tears are [constantly] on her cheeks;
Among all her lovers (political allies)
She has no one to comfort her.
All her friends have dealt treacherously with her;
They have become her enemies. [Jer 3:1; 4:30]
3 Judah has gone into exile under affliction
And under harsh servitude;
She dwells among the [pagan] nations,
But she has found no rest;
All her pursuers have overtaken her
In the midst of [her] distress.
4 The roads to Zion are in mourning
Because no one comes to the appointed feasts.

1:1 ***How.*** This exclamatory word is used frequently in laments and funeral songs. It expresses astonishment, sorrow, and dismay (2:1; 4:1).
1:2 ***Among all her lovers.*** Verse 19 describes Judah's sin of turning away from God and toward the gods of Canaan (Jer 3:1 – 6). Also, the sins of Judah often involved the sexual forms of pagan worship that characterized the Canaanite people.
1:4 ***The roads to Zion are in mourning.*** When the temple was built, Zion was used to describe the hill on which the temple was located. Later, the name came to stand for the whole city. The

CHAPTER 1 **1** Isa 47:7,8 **2** Jer 13:17; Job 7:3 **3** La 2:9

All her gates are desolate;
Her priests are groaning,
Her virgins are grieved *and* suffering,
And she suffers bitterly.
5 Her adversaries have become her masters,
Her enemies prosper;
For the LORD has caused her grief
Because of the multitude of her transgressions;
Her young children have gone
Into captivity before the enemy.
[Jer 30:14, 15; 52:28; Dan 9:7–14]
6 All her beauty *and* majesty
Have departed from the Daughter of Zion (Jerusalem).
Her princes have become like deer
That have found no pasture;
They have fled without strength
Before the pursuer.
7 In the days of her affliction and homelessness
Jerusalem remembers all her precious things
That she had from the days of old,
When her people fell into the hand of the adversary,
And no one helped her,
The enemy saw her,
They mocked at her downfall.
8 Jerusalem sinned greatly;
Therefore she has become an unclean thing [and has been removed].
All who honored her [now] despise her
Because they have seen her nakedness;
Even she herself groans and turns [her face] away.
9 Her (ceremonial) uncleanness was on her skirts;
She did not [seriously] consider her future.
Therefore she has come down [from throne to slavery] in an astonishing manner;
She has no comforter.
"O LORD" [cries Jerusalem], "look at my affliction,
For the enemy has magnified himself [in triumph]!"
10 The adversary has spread out his hand
Over all her precious *and* desirable things;
For she has seen the [Gentile] nations enter her sanctuary (the Jerusalem temple)—
The ones whom You commanded
That they should not enter into Your congregation [not even in the outer courts]. [Deut 23:3; Jer 51:51; Ezek 44:7, 9]
11 All her people groan, seeking bread;
They have exchanged their desirable *and* precious things for food
To restore their lives.
"See, O LORD, and consider
How despised *and* repulsive I have become!"
12 "Is it nothing to you, all you who pass this way?
Look and see if there is any pain like my pain
Which was severely dealt out to me,
Which the LORD has inflicted [on me] on the day of His fierce anger.
13 "From on high He sent fire into my bones,
And it prevailed *over them.*

---

roads "mourned" because there would no longer be throngs of pilgrims traveling to Jerusalem to worship at the temple.

1:5 ***Her young children have gone Into captivity.*** God had warned Israel in Leviticus 26:41 that captivity in a foreign land would be the result of continued sinning.

1:7 ***In the days of her affliction and homelessness.*** The emphasis is on Jerusalem's utter helplessness as her enemies ridiculed her homelessness (v. 21).

1:10 ***the [Gentile] nations enter her sanctuary.*** Since God's people had not preserved the sanctuary of their hearts from pollution, they had no reason to be amazed when their enemies desecrated the earthly sanctuary. As a rule, Gentiles were forbidden to enter the congregation of the Lord.

1:13 ***He sent fire into my bones.*** Jerusalem's

---

5 Dt 28:43; Jer 30:14; Da 9:7; Jer 52:28 **8** 1Ki 8:46; Jer 13:22; Eze 16:37; Hos 2:10 **9** Dt 32:29; Isa 47:7; ver. 2,17,21 **10** ver. 7; Jer 51:51; Dt 23:3; Neh 13:1 **11** Jer 38:9; 52:6 **12** Da 9:12 **13** Eze 12:13

He has spread a net for my feet;
He has turned me back.
He has made me desolate *and*
hopelessly miserable,
Faint all the day long.
14 "The yoke of my transgressions is
bound;
By His hand they are knit *and*
woven together.
They have come upon my neck.
He has made my strength fail;
The Lord has put me into the
hand
Of *those against whom* I cannot
stand. [Deut 28:48]
15 "The Lord has rejected all the
strong men
In my midst;
He has proclaimed an established
time against me
To crush my young men.
The Lord has trampled down as in
a wine press
The Virgin Daughter of Judah.
16 "I weep for these things;
My eyes overflow with tears,
Because a comforter,
One who could restore my soul, is
far away from me.
My children are desolate *and*
perishing,
For the enemy has prevailed."
[Lam 1:21]
17 Zion stretches out her hands,
But there is no comforter for her.
The LORD has commanded
concerning Jacob
That his neighbors should be his
enemies;
Jerusalem has become a filthy
thing [an object of contempt]
among them.
18 "The LORD is righteous *and* just;
For I have rebelled against His
commandment (His word).
Hear now, all you peoples,
And look at my pain;
My virgins and my young men
Have gone into captivity.
19 "I [Jerusalem] called to my lovers
(political allies), but they
deceived me.
My priests and my elders perished
in the city
While they looked for food to
restore their strength.
20 "See, O LORD, how distressed I am!
My spirit is deeply disturbed;
My heart is overturned within me
and cannot rest,
For I have been very rebellious.
In the street the sword kills *and*
bereaves;
In the house there is [famine,
disease and] death!
21 "People have heard that I groan,
That I have no comforter [in You].
All my enemies have heard of my
desperation;
They are delighted [O LORD] that
You have done it.
Oh, that You would bring the day
[of judgment] which You have
proclaimed
So that they will become like me.
[Is 14:5, 6; Jer 30:16]
22 "Let all their wickedness come
before You;

---

suffering is portrayed, using several metaphors: (1) fire from heaven, (2) a hunter's net spread to trap animals, (3) an animal yoke fastened about the head of a person, and (4) the crushing of grapes in a winepress. The purpose of Jerusalem's suffering was to bring about a turning or repentance.

1:15 *The Virgin Daughter of Judah.* Jerusalem (Judah) was supposed to be the chaste bride of God. Instead, she had become a polluted harlot because her people worshiped other gods than the God with whom they covenanted.

1:16 *comforter.* The real comforter of Judah is God. But because of Judah's sin, God would not come to their assistance.

1:21 *All my enemies.* Those who previously had been friends of Judah (v. 2) became Judah's enemies. ***bring the day.*** Several times the "day" of God's wrath is mentioned in the Book of Lamentations (2:1,21 – 22). The term is used to refer not only to the time of Jerusalem's fall in the past, but also to a future day when God would rectify all of the wrongs that the nations had committed against Israel and God.

14 Dt 28:48 **15** Isa 63:3; Rev 14:19 **16** Jer 13:17; La 2:18; ver. 2,9 **17** Jer 4:31; ver. 2,9 **18** Neh 9:33; Da 9:7,14; 1Sa 12:14 **19** ver. 2; Jer 30:14; ver. 11 **20** Job 30:27; Isa 16:11; Jer 4:19; Hos 11:8; Dt 32:25; Eze 7:15 **21** ver. 2; Isa 13; Jer 46 **22** Ps 109:15; La 5:17

And deal with them as You have
dealt with me
Because of all my transgressions;
For my groans are many and my
heart is faint."

God's Anger over Israel

2 HOW THE Lord has covered the
Daughter of Zion (Jerusalem)
With a cloud in His anger!
He has cast down from heaven to
the earth
The glory *and* splendor of Israel
And has not remembered His
footstool
In the day of His anger.
2 The Lord has swallowed up; He
has not spared
All the country places of Jacob.
In His wrath He has thrown down
The strongholds of the Daughter of
Judah (Jerusalem).
He has brought them down to the
ground [in disgrace];
He has debased the kingdom and
its princes.
3 In fierce anger He has cut off *and*
destroyed
Every horn of Israel.
He has withdrawn His right hand
From the presence of the enemy.
And He has burned in Jacob like a
flaming fire
Consuming all around.
4 He has bent His bow like an
enemy;
He has set His right hand like an
adversary
And slain all that were delightful
and pleasing to the eye;
In the tent of the Daughter of Zion
He has poured out His wrath like
fire.
5 The Lord has become like an
enemy;
He has swallowed up Israel.
He has swallowed up all its
palaces;
He has destroyed its strongholds
And multiplied in the Daughter of
Judah
Mourning and lamentation
(expressions of grief).
6 And He has violently broken down
His temple like a [fragile] garden
hedge;
He has destroyed His appointed
meeting place.
The LORD has caused the
appointed feast and Sabbath
To be forgotten in Zion
And has despised *and* rejected the
king and the priest
In the indignation of His anger.
7 The Lord has rejected His altar;
He has abandoned His sanctuary.
He has given into the hand of the
enemy
The walls of her palaces;
They have made a noise in the
house of the LORD
As on a day of an appointed feast.
8 The LORD determined to lay in
ruins
The [city] wall of the Daughter of
Zion.
He has stretched out a line,
He has not stopped His hand from
destroying.
He has caused the rampart and the
wall to lament (mourn in grief);
They have languished together.
9 Her gates have sunk into the
ground;
He has destroyed and broken her
bars.
Her king and her princes are
[exiled] among the nations;
The law is no more.

2:1 *His anger.* This word is a firm expression of God's displeasure with wickedness and sin. Yet God's anger never shuts us off from His compassion (Ps 77:9).
2:3 *withdrawn His right hand.* Usually the right hand of God is understood as the instrument of help for God's people stretched out against their enemies (Ex 15:6; Ps 20:6). Here God's hand is withdrawn from the enemies, leaving the people of God at their mercy.
2:9 *The law is no more.* These words do not suggest the end of the law, but rather the ceasing of the work of the law in the lives of the people for their blessing (Dt 6:1 – 3).

CHAPTER 2 **1** Mt 11:23; 2Sa 1:19; 1Ch 28:2; Ps 99:5 **2** Ps 89:39 **3** Ps 74:11; Ps 89:46 **4** Isa 63:10; Eze 24:25 **5** Jer 30:14; 2Ki 25:9; Jer 52:13 **6** Ps 80:12; 89:40; Isa 5:5; Isa 1:8; La 1:4 **7** Ps 74:4 **8** 2Ki 21:13; Isa 34:11 **9** Jer 51:30; Dt 28:36; 2Ki 24:15; 2Ch 15:3; Ps 74:9; Eze 7:26

Also, her prophets no longer find
Vision from the Lord.
10 The elders of the Daughter of Zion
Sit on the ground keeping silent;
They have thrown dust on their
heads,
They have covered themselves
with sackcloth.
The virgins of Jerusalem
Have bowed their heads to the
ground.
11 My eyes fail because of tears
[mourns Jeremiah],
My spirit is deeply disturbed;
My heart is poured out on the
earth [in grief]
Because of the destruction of
the daughter of my people
[Jerusalem],
When little ones and infants faint
In the streets of the city.
12 They cry to their mothers,
"Where is grain and wine?"
As they faint like a wounded man
In the streets of the city,
As their life [slips away and] is
poured out
In their mothers' arms.
13 How shall I console you?
To what shall I compare you,
O Daughter of Jerusalem?
With what shall I compare you, so
that I may comfort you,
O Virgin Daughter of Zion?
For your ruin is as vast as the sea;
Who can heal you? [Lam 1:12;
Dan 9:12]
14 Your prophets have seen
(imagined) for you
False and foolish *visions;*
And they have not exposed your
wickedness
To restore you from captivity [by
teaching you to repent],
But they have seen (imagined)
and declared to you false and
misleading oracles.
15 All who pass along the way
Clap their hands *in derision* at you;
They scoff and shake their heads
At the Daughter of Jerusalem,
saying,
"Is this the city that was called
'The perfection of beauty,
The joy of all the earth'?"
16 All your enemies
Have opened their mouths wide
against you;
They [scornfully] hiss and gnash
their teeth.
They say, "We have swallowed her
up!
Certainly this is the day for which
we waited;
We have reached it, we have seen
it!"
17 The Lord has done what He
planned;
He has accomplished His word
Which He commanded from days
of old.
He has demolished without sparing,
And He has caused the enemy to
rejoice over you;
He has exalted the power of
your enemies. [Lev 26:14–39;
Deut 28:15–68]
18 Their hearts cried out to the Lord.
"O wall of the Daughter of Zion,
Let your tears run down like a
river day and night;
Give yourself no relief,
Let your eyes have no rest.
19 "Arise, cry aloud in the night,

2:10 ***They have thrown dust on their heads.*** This custom was a common sign of mourning in Israel and in other countries of the ancient world. ***virgins of Jerusalem.*** Their sadness was increased by the knowledge that this was not a time for marriage and family. Even though their lives had been spared, they had lost their futures. **2:15** ***shake their heads.*** This was a common expression of derision (Ps 22:7; 109:25; Jer 19:8). Losing face in the ancient Middle East was a terrible evil.
2:18 ***O wall.*** The wall of the people's hearts was more impenetrable than the wall of the city of Jerusalem (2:7–8).
2:19 ***Arise.*** The call is for people to awaken and scream for mercy from the Lord. ***Lift up your hands.*** This refers to a posture of prayer (1:17; Ps 134:2).

10 Job 2:13; Isa 3:26; Job 2:12; Isa 15:3 **11** La 3:48; La 1:20; Job 16:13; Ps 22:14; La 4:4 **13** La 1:12; Da 9:12
14 Jer 2:8; Eze 13:2; Isa 58:1 **15** Eze 25:6; 2Ki 19:21; Ps 44:14; Ps 48:2 **16** Job 16:9; La 3:46; Ps 56:2; Ps 35:21
17 Lev 26:16; Dt 28:15; Ps 38:16 **18** Jer 14:17 **19** Ps 119:147; 62:8; Isa 51:20; Na 3:10

At the beginning of the night
watches;
Pour out your heart like water
Before the presence of the Lord;
Lift up your hands to Him
For the life of your little ones
Who are faint from hunger
At the head of every street." [Ps 62:8]
20 See, O LORD, and look!
With whom have You dealt this
way?
Should women eat their offspring,
The little ones *who were born*
healthy and beautiful?
Should priest and prophet be
killed
In the sanctuary of the Lord?
21 The young and the old
Lie on the ground in the streets;
My virgins and my young men
Have fallen by the sword.
You have killed them in the day of
Your anger,
You have slaughtered, not sparing.
22 You [LORD] called as in the day of
an appointed feast
My terrors (dangers) on every side;
And there was no one who
escaped or survived
In the day of the LORD's anger.
Those I have cared for and
brought up with tenderness,
My enemy annihilated them.

Jeremiah Shares Israel's Affliction

3 I AM [Jeremiah] the man who
has seen affliction
Because of the rod of His wrath.
2 He has led me and made me walk
In darkness and not in light.
3 Surely He has turned His hand
against me
Repeatedly all the day.
4 He has caused my flesh and my
skin to waste away;
He has shattered my bones.
5 He has besieged and surrounded
me with bitterness and hardship.
6 He has made me live in dark
places
Like those who have long been
dead.
7 He walled me in so that I cannot
get out;
He has weighted down my chain.
8 Even when I cry out and shout for
help,
He shuts out my prayer.
9 He has blocked my ways with cut
stone;
He has made my paths crooked.
10 He is to me like a bear lying in
wait,
And like a lion [hiding] in secret
places.
11 He has turned aside my ways and
torn me in pieces;
He has made me desolate.
12 He has bent His bow
And set me as a target for the
arrow.
13 He has caused the arrows of His
quiver
To enter my inner parts.
14 I have become the [object of]
ridicule to all my people,
And [the subject of] their *mocking*
song all the day.
15 He has filled me with bitterness;
He has made me drunk with
wormwood (bitterness).
16 He has broken my teeth with
gravel;
He has [covered me with ashes
and] made me cower in the dust.

2:20 *Should women eat their offspring.* So desperate were the scenes of starvation in Jerusalem that women actually fought over whose deceased child would be eaten next.
3:4 *my flesh and my skin to waste away.* This imagery suggests the ebbing and wasting away of Jeremiah's life and that of the nation.
3:9 *He has blocked my ways with cut stone.* A common practice of the Assyrians was to wall up prisoners in extremely confined places and leave them to die.
3:15 *drunk with wormwood.* This was a bitter herb used to flavor some drinks.
3:16 *He has broken my teeth with gravel.* he people had sensed that they were so associated with dust and sackcloth — symbols of

20 Lev 26:29; Dt 28:53; Jer 19:9; La 4:10; La 4:13,16 **21** 2Ch 36:17; La 3:43 **22** Ps 31:13; Jer 6:25; 46:5; Hos 9:12
CHAPTER 3 **4** Job 16:8; Ps 51:8; Isa 38:13 **6** Ps 88:5,6 **7** Hos 2:6 **8** Job 30:20 **10** Isa 38:13; Hos 5:14
11 Hos 6:1 **12** Job 7:20; Ps 38:2 **13** Job 6:4 **14** Jer 20:7; Job 30:9; Ps 69:12 **15** Jer 9:15 **16** Pr 20:17

[17]My soul has been cast far away
from peace;
I have forgotten happiness.
[18]So I say, "My strength has
perished
And so has my hope *and*
expectation from the LORD."

Hope of Relief in God's Mercy

[19]Remember [O LORD] my
affliction and my wandering,
the wormwood and the gall
(bitterness).
[20]My soul *continually* remembers
them
And is bowed down within me.
[21]But this I call to mind,
Therefore I have hope.
[22]It is because of the LORD's
lovingkindnesses that we are
not consumed,
Because His [tender] compassions
never fail. [Mal 3:6]
[23]They are new every morning;
Great *and* beyond measure is Your
faithfulness. [Is 33:2]
[24]"The LORD is my portion *and* my
inheritance," says my soul;
"Therefore I have hope in Him
and wait expectantly for Him."
[Num 18:20]
[25]The LORD is good to those who
wait [confidently] for Him,
To those who seek Him [on the
authority of God's word].
[26]It is good that one waits quietly
For the salvation of the LORD.
[27]It is good for a man that he should
bear
The yoke [of godly discipline] in
his youth.
[28]Let him sit alone [in hope] and
keep quiet,
Because God has laid it on him [for
his benefit]. [Rom 8:28]
[29]Let him put his mouth in the
dust [in recognition of his
unworthiness];
There may yet be hope. [Mic 7:17]
[30]Let him give his cheek to the one
who strikes him;
Let him be filled with reproach.
[31]For the Lord will not reject forever,
[Ps 94:14]
[32]For if He causes grief,
Then He will have compassion
According to His abundant
lovingkindness *and* tender
mercy.
[33]For He does not afflict willingly
and from His heart
Or grieve the children of men.
[Ezek 18:23, 32; Hos 11:8;
Heb 12:5–10; 2 Pet 3:9]
[34]To trample *and* crush under His
feet
All the prisoners of the land,
[35]To deprive a man of justice
In the presence of the Most High,
[36]To defraud a man in his lawsuit—
The Lord does not approve of
these things.
[37]Who is there who speaks and it
comes to pass,
Unless the Lord has authorized
and commanded it?
[38]Is it not from the mouth of the
Most High
That both adversity (misfortune)
and good (prosperity, happiness)
proceed?

---

mourning—that it was as though they fed on dirt. The dust became gravel which broke the people's teeth.

3:22 ***Because His [tender] compassions never fail.*** This verse seems to contradict all that had been written up to this point (2:1–5). Yet the very fact that there was a prophet left to write these words and a remnant left to read them showed that not every person in Jerusalem had been consumed.

3:23 ***Great and beyond measure is Your faithfulness.*** Here is the heart of the Book of Lamentations. The comforting, compassionate character of God dominates the wreckage of every other institution and office. God remains "abounding in lovingkindness and truth" in every situation (Ex 34:6; Jn 1:14).

3:29 ***put his mouth in the dust.*** This expression is a figure of speech for conquest. The phrase pictures a captive lying face down with the conqueror's foot on his back.

18 Ps 31:22 **19** Jer 9:15 **22** Mal 3:6 **23** Isa 33:2 **24** Ps 16:5 **25** Isa 30:18; Mic 7:7 **26** Ps 37:7 **27** Ps 94:12 **28** Jer 15:17 **29** Job 42:6 **30** Isa 50:6; Mt 5:39 **31** Ps 94:14 **33** Eze 33:11 **36** Hab 1:13 **37** Ps 33:9 **38** Job 2:10; Am 3:6

39 Why should any living mortal, or
any man,
Complain [of punishment] in view
of his sins?
40 Let us test and examine our ways,
And let us return to the LORD.
41 Let us lift up our hearts and our
hands [in prayer]
Toward God in heaven;
42 We have transgressed and
rebelled,
You have not pardoned.
43 You have covered *Yourself* with
anger
And pursued us;
You have slain [without pity] and
have not spared.
44 You have covered Yourself with a
cloud
So that no prayer can pass
through.
45 You have made us scum and refuse
Among the peoples (Gentile
nations).
46 All our enemies have gaped at us.
47 Panic and pitfall (traps, danger)
have come on us,
Devastation and destruction.
48 My eyes overflow with streams of
tears
Because of the destruction of
the daughter of my people
(Jerusalem).
49 My eyes overflow unceasingly,
Without stopping,
50 Until the LORD looks down
And sees from heaven.
51 My eyes [see things that] bring
pain to my soul
Because of all the daughters of my
city.
52 Without cause my enemies
Hunted me down like a bird;
53 They silenced me in the pit
And placed a stone over me.
[Jer 38]
54 The waters ran down on my head;
I said, "I am cut off (destroyed)!"
55 I called on Your name, O LORD,
Out of the lowest pit. [Jer 38:6]
56 You have heard my voice,
"Do not hide Your ear from my
prayer for relief,
From my cry for help."
57 You drew near on the day I called
to You;
You said, "Do not fear." [James 4:8]
58 O Lord, You have pleaded my
soul's cause [You have guided
my way and protected me];
You have rescued *and* redeemed
my life.
59 O LORD, You have seen the wrong
[done to me];
Judge my case.
60 You have seen all their vengeance,
All their schemes against me.
61 You have heard their reproach,
O LORD,
And all their schemes against me.
62 The lips and whispering of my
assailants
Are against me all day long.
63 Look at their sitting and their
rising [their actions and secret
counsels];
I am their mocking song [the
subject of their ridicule].
[Ps 139:2; Is 37:28]
64 You will repay them, O LORD,
According to the work of their
hands.
65 You will harden their hearts;
Your curse will be upon them.
66 You will pursue them in anger and
destroy them
From under the heavens of the LORD.

3:44 *with a cloud.* So long as sin festered, God's wrath was a cloud or veil through which no prayer could penetrate — including the prayers of the people and the prayers of Jeremiah.

3:52 – 54 *silenced me in the pit.* Jeremiah speaks not only of his own experience of being cast into a pit (Jer 38:4 – 6), but also of his pain and grief over the wretched condition of his fellow countrymen. The pit is a metaphor for the grave or extreme danger (Ps 28:1; 40:2).

3:64 – 66 *You will repay them.* The request for divine vindication is an expression of a longing for God's righteousness and the success of His kingdom and His truth.

39 Pr 19:3; Mic 7:9 **41** Ps 86:4 **42** Da 9:5 **44** ver. 8 **45** 1Co 4:13 **46** La 2:16 **47** Isa 24:17; 51:19 **48** Jer 4:19 **49** Ps 77:2 **50** Isa 63:15 **52** Ps 35:7 **53** Jer 37:16; Da 6:17 **54** Ps 69:2; Isa 38:10 **55** Ps 130:1 **56** Ps 3:4 **57** Jas 4:8 **58** Ps 35:1; Jer 51:36; Ps 71:23 **59** Ps 9:4 **60** Jer 11:19 **63** Ps 139:2 **64** Ps 28:4; Jer 11:20 **66** Dt 25:19; Jer 10:11; Ps 8:3

Distress of the Siege Described

4 HOW DARK *and* dim the gold
has become,
How the pure gold has changed!
The sacred stones [of the temple]
are poured out *and* scattered
At the head of every street.
2 The [noble and] precious sons of
Zion,
[Once] worth their weight in fine
gold,
How they are regarded [merely] as
earthen jars,
The work of a potter's hands!
[Is 30:14; Jer 19:11; 2 Cor 4:7]
3 Even the jackals offer the breast,
They nurse their young;
But the daughter of my people has
become cruel
Like ostriches in the wilderness
[that desert their young].
4 The tongue of the infant clings
To the roof of its mouth because of
thirst;
The little ones ask for food,
But no one gives it to them.
5 Those who feasted on delicacies
Are perishing in the streets;
Those reared in purple [as nobles]
Embrace ash heaps.
6 For the [punishment of the]
wickedness of the daughter of
my people [Jerusalem]
Is greater than the [punishment for
the] sin of Sodom,
Which was overthrown in a
moment,
And no hands were turned toward
her [to offer help]. [Gen 19:25]
7 Her princes were purer than snow,
They were whiter than milk [in
appearance];
They were more ruddy in body
than rubies,
Their polishing was like lapis
lazuli (sapphire).
8 Their appearance is [now] blacker
than soot [because of the
prolonged famine];
They are not recognized in the
streets;
Their skin clings to their bones;
It is withered, and it has become
[dry] like wood.
9 Those killed with the sword
Are more fortunate than those
killed with hunger;
For the hungry pine *and* ebb away,
For the lack of the fruits of the
field.
10 The hands of compassionate
women
Boiled their own children;
They became food for them
Because of the destruction of the
daughter of my people [Judah].
11 The LORD has fulfilled His wrath;
He has poured out His fierce anger
And has kindled a fire in Zion
That has consumed her
foundations.
12 The kings of the earth did not
believe,
Nor did any of the inhabitants of
the earth,
That the adversary (oppressor)
and enemy
Could enter the gates of Jerusalem.
13 Because of the sins of her
[counterfeit] prophets
And the wickedness of her
[unfaithful] priests,
Who have shed in her midst
The blood of the just *and*
righteous;
14 They wandered, blind, in the
streets;
They were defiled with blood
So that no one could touch their
garments.
15 People cried to them, "Go away!
Unclean!

4:1 – 2 *sacred stones [of the temple] are poured out.* The Babylonian army looted the temple and overturned all its huge stones.
4:4 *The tongue of the infant.* The theme of thirsting and starving children is revisited (2:11 – 13).

4:10 *compassionate women Boiled their own children.* This verse describes the horrible effects of the long siege that were alluded to in 2:20. This unimaginable horror could only have occurred in the most inhumane conditions of human suffering.

CHAPTER 4 **1** La 2:19 **2** Isa 30:14; Jer 19:11 **3** Job 39:14 **4** Ps 22:15; See La 2:11,12 **5** Job 24:8 **6** Ge 19:25 **8** La 5:10; Joel 2:6; Na 2:10; Ps 102:5 **10** La 2:20; Isa 49:15; Dt 28:57 **11** Jer 7:20; Dt 32:22 **13** Jer 6:13; Eze 22:26; Mt 23:31 **14** Jer 2:34; Nu 19:16 **15** Lev 13:45

Depart! Depart! Do not touch!"
So they fled, then they wandered
[as fugitives];
People among the nations said,
"They shall not stay here any
longer *with us*."
16 The presence of the LORD scattered
them [among the nations];
He will not continue to look after
them.
They did not honor the priests;
They did not favor the elders.
17 [And as for us,] yet our eyes failed,
Looking in vain for help.
Watching [from the towers] we
watched
For a nation that could not save.
[Ezek 29:16]
18 The enemy hunted our steps,
So that we could not walk in our
streets;
Our end drew near,
Our days were finished
For our end had come.
19 Our pursuers were swifter
Than the eagles of the sky;
They pursued us on the mountains,
They waited in ambush for us in
the wilderness.
20 The breath of our nostrils, the
anointed of the LORD [our king],
Was captured in their snares,
He of whom we had said, "Under
his shadow
We shall live among the nations."
21 Rejoice and be glad, O Daughter of
Edom,
Who lives in the land of Uz.
But the cup [of the wine of God's
wrath] will pass to you as well;
You will become drunk and make
yourself naked. [Jer 25:17]
22 *The punishment* of your sin has
been completed, O Daughter of
Zion;
The LORD will no longer send you
into exile.
But He will punish your sin,
O Daughter of Edom;
He will expose your sins. [Ps 137:7]

A Prayer for Mercy

5 O LORD, remember what has
come upon us;
Look, and see our reproach
(national disgrace)!
2 Our inheritance has been turned
over to strangers,
Our houses to foreigners.
3 We have become orphans without
a father;
Our mothers are like widows.
4 We have to pay for our drinking
water;
Our wood comes to us at a price.
5 Our pursuers are at our necks;
We are worn out, there is no rest
for us.
6 We have given the hand [as
a pledge of fidelity and
submission] to Egypt and
Assyria to get enough bread.
7 Our fathers sinned, and are no
more;
It is we who have carried their
sin. [Is 65:7; Jer 16:11, 12; 31:29;
Ezek 18:2–4]
8 Servants rule over us;
There is no one to rescue us out of
their hand. [Neh 5:15]
9 We get our bread at the risk of our
lives
Because of the sword [of the
Arabs] in the wilderness [who
may attack if we go out to
harvest the crop].
10 Our skin is as hot as [the heat of]
an oven
Because of the burning heat of [the
fever of] famine.

5:2–3 *Our inheritance.* The promised land had been a gift from the Lord to Abraham. This inheritance was a kind of "down payment" on the future reign of God that would include the restoration of His people to that land. God demonstrated that He owned all nations and that Israel was to be His instrument for blessing all the nations on the earth. Yet in their present condition, the people of Israel seemed to be the most helpless of all peoples.

5:10 *Our skin is as hot as [the heat of] an oven.* Disease would have been rampant during the siege.

16 La 5:12 **17** 2Ki 24:7; Isa 20:5; Jer 37:7 **18** 2Ki 25:4; Ezek 7:2,3 **19** Dt 28:49 **20** Ge 2:7; Jer 52:9; Eze 12:13 **21** Jer 25:15; Ob 10 **22** Isa 40:2; Ps 137:7 **CHAPTER 5** **1** Ps 89:50; Ps 79:4; La 2:15 **2** Ps 79:1 **5** Jer 28:14 **6** Ge 24:2; Hos 12:1 **7** Jer 31:29

[11]They ravished the women in Zion,
The virgins in the cities of Judah.
[12]Princes were hung by their hands;
Elders were not respected.
[13]Young men worked at the grinding mill,
And boys fell [staggering] under loads of wood.
[14]Elders are gone from the gate;
Young men from their music.
[15]The joy of our hearts has ended;
Our dancing has been turned into mourning.
[16]The crown has fallen from our head [our honor is covered with dust]!
Woe to us, for we have sinned!
[17]Because of this our heart is faint,
Because of these things our eyes are dim.
[18]As for Mount Zion, which lies desolate,
Foxes *and* the jackals prowl over it.

[19]But You, O LORD, reign forever;
Your throne endures from generation to [all] generations.
[20]Why do You forget us forever?
Why do You forsake us so long?
[21]Return us to You, O LORD, so that we may be restored;
Renew our days as of old,
[22]Unless You have utterly rejected us
And are exceedingly angry with us.

5:16 ***The crown has fallen from our head.*** This phrase expresses the loss of Judah's position of honor.

5:17 ***our heart is faint . . . our eyes are dim.*** The normal zest for life was gone. Death would be better than a horrible existence during the siege of Jerusalem.

5:18 ***Foxes and the jackals prowl over it.*** The idea of wild animals roaming the holy city where the people of God once came in glad worship was the final indignity.

5:19 ***You, O LORD, reign forever.*** God's eternal rule and reign are a hope and support during the bleakest moments of suffering and despair (Ps 80:1; 103:19).

16 Ps 89:39 **17** Ps 6:7 **19** Ps 9:7; Ps 45:6 **20** Ps 13:1

THE BOOK OF

EZEKIEL

▸ **AUTHOR:** There is strong evidence in favor of Ezekiel's authorship of this book. The first person singular is used throughout the book, indicating that it is the work of one person. This person is actually identified in 1:3 and 24:24 as Ezekiel. The unity and integrity of Ezekiel's prophetic record are supported and the style, language, and thematic development are consistent throughout the book. Like Jeremiah, Ezekiel was a priest who was called to be a prophet of the Lord. Ezekiel was privileged to receive a number of visions of the power and plan of God, and he was careful and artistic in his written presentation.

▸ **TIMES:** c. 592 – 570 BC ▸ **KEY VERSES:** Eze 36:33 – 35

▸ **THEME:** Ezekiel was an exilic prophet, meaning he prophesied to the exiles in Babylon. He was one of the 10,000 taken there by Nebuchadnezzar in 597 BC (2Ki 24:14). The book contains a series of prophetic messages, which represents a lifetime of ministry to the exiles in Babylon. Ezekiel sees himself as a watchman or lookout, compelled to warn people of coming danger and of the need for personal responsibility to an awesome, all-seeing, all-knowing God. The last half of the book is more concerned with encouraging the people to hope for God's promise of restoration back to the land of Israel. The restoration of the temple is a key element of chapters 40 – 48.

The Vision of Four Figures

1 NOW IT came about [when I was] in my thirtieth year [of life], on the fifth day of the fourth month, while I was among the exiles beside the River Chebar [in Babylonia], the heavens were opened and I saw visions of God.
2(On the fifth of the month, which was in the fifth year of King Jehoiachin's captivity, [2 Kin 24:12–14]
3the word of the LORD came expressly to Ezekiel the priest, the son of Buzi, in the land of the Chaldeans by the River Chebar; and the hand of the LORD came upon him there.) [1 Kin 18:46; 2 Kin 3:15]
4As I looked, I saw a stormy wind coming out of the north, a great cloud

---

1:1 ***in my thirtieth year.*** This most likely refers to Ezekiel's age. He was preparing to become a priest when the Babylonians attacked Judah in 597 BC. ***I saw visions of God.*** As with all the true prophets of ancient Israel, the visitation of God was at His initiative, calling certain people to special responsibilities. The word "vision" is derived from the common Hebrew verb meaning "to see," rather than from the specific verb used for prophetic vision as in Isaiah 1.
1:3 ***the word of the LORD.*** Ezekiel uses this introductory phrase 50 times in this book. It always introduces a divine message and sometimes a new section. ***Ezekiel.*** The name comes from the verb meaning "to seize, to hold fast," coupled with the term meaning "God." Thus Ezekiel's name indicates that he was a man whom God had seized.
1:4 ***stormy wind . . . great cloud . . . fire flashing continually.*** Compare the descriptions of divine appearance in Exodus 19:16 – 20; Psalm 18:7 – 15; and Micah 1:2 – 4.

CHAPTER 1 **1** Eze 3:15,23; Mt 3:16; Ac 7:56; Eze 8:3 **2** 2Ki 24:12 **3** 1Ki 18:46; Eze 3:14 **4** Jer 23:19; 25:32; Jer 1:14

DATES IN EZEKIEL

REFERENCE	YEAR	MONTH	DAY	MODERN RECKONING	EVENT
1. 1:1	30	4	5	July 31, 593 BC	Inaugural vision
1:2	5	—	5		
3:16	"At the end of seven days"				
2. 8:1	6	6	5	Sept. 17, 592	Transport to Jerusalem
3. 20:1–2	7	5	10	Aug. 14, 591	Negative view of Israel's history
4. 24:1	9	10	10	Jan. 15, 588	Beginning of siege (see also 2Ki 25:1)
5. 26:1	11	—	1	Apr. 23, 587 to Apr. 13, 586	Prophecy against Tyre (see note on 26:1)
6. 29:1	10	10	12	Jan. 7, 587	Prophecy against Egypt
7. 29:17	27	1	1	Apr. 26, 571	Egypt in exchange for Tyre
8. 30:20	11	1	7	Apr. 29, 587	Prophecy against Pharaoh
9. 31:1	11	3	1	June 21, 587	Prophecy against Pharaoh
10. 32:1	12	12	1	Mar. 3, 585	Lament over Pharaoh
11. 32:17	12	—	15	Apr. 13, 586 to Apr. 1, 585	Egypt dead
12. 33:21	12	10	5	Jan. 8, 585	Arrival of first fugitive
13. 40:1	25	1	10	Apr. 28, 573	Vision of the future
40:1	"fourteenth year after the fall of the city"				

with fire flashing continually from it;
and a brightness was around it, and
in its core [there was] something like
glowing [amber-colored] metal in the
midst of the fire.
5Within it there were figures resem-
bling four living beings. And this was
their appearance: they had human form.
6Each one had four faces and four
wings.
7Their legs were straight and the
soles of their feet were like a calf's
hoof, and they sparkled *and* gleamed
like shiny bronze.
8Under their wings on their four
sides they had human hands. As for
the faces and wings of the four of them,
9their wings touched one another;
their faces did not turn when they
moved, each went straight forward.
10Regarding the form *and* appear-
ance of their faces: they [each] had
the face of a man [in front], and each
had the face of a lion on the right side,
and the face of an ox on the left side;
all four also had the face of an eagle
[at the back of their heads]. [Rev 4:7]
11Such were their faces. Their wings
were stretched out upward; two [wings]
of each one were touching another [the
wings of the beings on either side of
it], and [the remaining] two [wings of
each being] were covering their bodies.
12And each went straight forward;

1:5 ***four living beings.*** These creatures are *related to the cherubim*—celestial beings associated with God's holiness and glory, and sometimes poetically with storm winds upon which God travels (Ps 18:10). There are two basic approaches to understanding them: as a highly symbolic representation of deity, or as highly symbolic representations of angelic beings who serve in God's presence. Probably they are angels, since God Himself is not revealed until the end of the section (v. 26).

1:10 ***man ... lion ... ox ... eagle.*** Composite fantastic figures in these classic combinations have been found in Mesopotamian and Egyptian iconography. The idealized strengths of each figure were thus presumed to reside in these living beings.

5 Rev 4:6; Eze 10:8; Eze 10:14 **7** Da 10:6; Rev 1:15 **8** Eze 10:8 **9** ver. 11; ver. 12 **10** Rev 4:7; Nu 2:10; Nu 2:3; Nu 2:18; Nu 2:25 **11** Isa 6:2 **12** Eze 10:22; ver. 20

wherever the spirit was about to go, they would go, without turning as they went.

13 Among the living beings there was something that looked like burning coals of fire, like torches moving back and forth among the living beings. The fire was bright, and lightning was flashing from the fire.

14 And the living beings moved rapidly back and forth like flashes of lightning.

15 Now as I looked at the living beings, I saw one wheel on the ground beside the living beings, for each of the four of them.

16 Regarding the appearance of the wheels and their construction: they gleamed like chrysolite (beryl, olivine); and the four were made alike. Their appearance and construction were a wheel [set at a right angle] within a wheel.

17 Whenever they moved, they went in any [one] of their four directions without turning as they moved.

18 Regarding their rims: they were so high that they were awesome *and* dreadful, and the rims of all four of them were full of eyes all around.

19 Whenever the living beings moved, the wheels moved with them; and when the living beings rose from the earth, the wheels rose also.

20 Wherever the spirit went, the beings went in that direction. And the wheels rose along with them; for the spirit *or* life of the living beings was in the wheels.

21 Whenever those went, these went; and whenever those came to a stop, these came to a stop; and whenever those rose from the earth, the wheels rose close beside them, for the spirit of the living beings was in the wheels.

Vision of Divine Glory

22 Now stretched over the heads of the living beings *there was* something like an expanse, looking like the terrible *and* awesome shimmer of icy crystal.

23 Under the expanse their wings *were stretched out* straight, one toward another. Every living being had two wings which covered its body on one side and on the other side.

24 As they moved, I also heard the sound of their wings like the sound of great [rushing] waters, like the voice of the Almighty, the sound of tumult like the noise of an army camp. Whenever they came to a stop, they lowered their wings.

25 And there was a voice above the expanse that was over their heads; whenever they stopped, they lowered their wings.

26 Now above the expanse that was over their heads there was something resembling a throne, it appeared like [it was made of] sapphire *or* lapis lazuli; and [seated] on that which looked like a throne, high up, was a figure with the appearance of a man. [Phil 2:5–8]

27 Now upward, from that which appeared to be His waist, I saw something like glowing metal that looked like it was filled with fire all around it; and downward, from that which

---

1:18 *rims . . . full of eyes.* The wheels had an exquisite beauty and an animate intelligence.

1:19 – 21 *spirit . . . in the wheels.* The prophet stresses the association of the wheels with the living beings, as well as the beings' ability to travel where they wished. It appears that the wheels represented the flexibility and mobility of the living beings. This is a pictorial representation of God's omnipresence.

1:24 *Almighty.* This is the divine name *Shaddai*, most likely based on a word meaning "mountain," to suggest God's omnipotence and majesty (10:5).

1:26 *throne.* While Isaiah describes the elevation of the Lord's throne (Isa 6:1), Ezekiel focuses on its beauty.

1:27 – 28 *glory and brilliance of the LORD.* The "glory" indicates the wonder, majesty, and worthiness of the living God. Amid the wheels,

---

13 Rev 4:5 **14** Mt 24:27 **15** Eze 10:9 **16** Eze 10:9,10; Da 10:6 **17** ver. 12 **18** Eze 10:12; Zec 4:10 **19** Eze 10:16,17 **20** ver. 12; Eze 10:17 **21** ver. 19,20; Eze 10:17 **22** Eze 10:1 **24** Eze 10:5; Eze 43:2; Da 10:6; Rev 1:15; Job 37:4,5; Ps 29:3,4; 68:33 **26** Eze 10:1; Ex 24:10 **27** Eze 8:2

appeared to be His waist, I saw something like fire; and *there was* a brightness *and* a remarkable radiance [like a halo] around Him.

28 As the appearance of the rainbow in the clouds on a rainy day, so was the appearance of the surrounding radiance. This was the appearance of the likeness of the glory *and* brilliance of the LORD. And when I saw it, I fell face downward and I heard a voice of One speaking. [Rev 4:3]

The Prophet's Call

2 THEN HE said to me, "Son of man, stand on your feet and I will speak to you."

2 Then as He spoke to me the Spirit entered me and set me on my feet; and I heard Him speaking to me.

3 And He said to me, "I am sending you, son of man, to the children of Israel, to a rebellious people [in both the north and the south] that have rebelled against Me; they and their fathers have sinned *and* revolted against Me to this very day.

4 "I am sending you to them who are stubborn and obstinate children, and you shall say to them, 'Thus says the Lord GOD.'

5 "As for them, whether they listen or refuse [to listen]—for they are a rebellious house—yet they will know *and* be fully aware of the fact that there has been a prophet among them.

6 "And you, son of man, neither fear them nor fear their words; though briars and thorns are all around you and you sit among scorpions, neither fear their words nor be dismayed at their presence, for they are a rebellious house.

7 "But you shall speak My words to them whether they will listen or refuse [to listen], for they are [most] rebellious.

8 "As for you, son of man, listen to what I say to you; do not be rebellious like that rebellious house; open your mouth and eat what I am giving you."

9 Then I looked, and I saw a hand stretched out toward me; and behold, a scroll of a book was in it.

10 And He spread it before me, and it was written on the front and on the back, and written on it were [words of] lamentation (funeral songs) and mourning and woe.

---

the beings, the colors, and the dazzling light was a figure who appeared like a man (v. 26). Compare the vision of Daniel who saw One "like a Son of Man" (Da 7:13). ***I fell face downward.*** The prophet's response was to fall down in worship and submission. All believers should recognize God's great glory and fall down in humble submission before Him (Php 2:10 – 11).

2:1 *Son of man.* Ezekiel uses this phrase more than 90 times to refer to himself. It emphasizes his humanity in his God-given role as a spokesman for God. The meaning of the phrase is "human one." In the Old Testament, only Daniel 7:13 and 8:17 also employ this phrase. In the New Testament, "Son of man" is used frequently by Jesus for Himself. With this phrase Jesus was calling Himself "the Human One"—the long-awaited Messiah who came as God in the flesh (Lk 21:27; Jn 1:14; 2Jn 7).

2:2 *the Spirit entered me.* This reference to the indwelling of the Holy Spirit in God's prophet is of great importance. The visions and messages of Ezekiel were revelations from the living God.

2:5 *they are a rebellious house.* God told Ezekiel to take His Word to the sons of Israel. These people were to hear what the Lord Himself was to say to them. Listening or not listening, belief or unbelief, would not change what was spoken. Our belief or unbelief has no effect on what God tells us or what the Bible says. His word remains true. By its very nature, it is worthy of belief.

2:6 *briers . . . thorns . . . scorpions.* These images vividly portray the nature of the rebellious opponents of Ezekiel's warnings. God told Ezekiel not to allow fear to hinder his message, whether or not the message was wanted (v. 7).

2:10 *lamentation (funeral songs) and mourning and woe.* The unusual feature of writing on both sides of a scroll indicates the magnitude of the nation's transgressions and its need for words of grief (Zec 5:3; Rev 5:1). Although Ezekiel would later bring words of comfort and consolation (chs. 33 – 48), his first prophecies from God contained only sorrow and sadness.

28 Rev 4:3; 10:1; Eze 3:23; 8:4; Eze 3:23; Da 8:17; Ac 9:4; Rev 1:17 **CHAPTER 2 1** Da 10:11 **2** Eze 3:24 **3** Jer 3:25; Eze 20:18,21,30 **4** Eze 3:7 **5** Eze 3:11,26,27; Eze 33:33 **6** Jer 1:8,17; Lk 12:4; Isa 9:18; Jer 6:28; Mic 7:4; Eze 3:9; 1Pe 3:14; Eze 3:9,26,27 **7** Jer 1:7,17; ver. 5 **8** Rev 10:9 **9** Jer 1:9; Eze 8:3; Eze 3:1

Ezekiel's Commission

3 HE SAID to me, "Son of man, eat what you find [in this book]; eat this scroll, then go, speak to the house of Israel."

2 So I opened my mouth, and He fed me the scroll.

3 He said to me, "Son of man, eat this scroll that I am giving you and fill your stomach with it." So I ate it, and it was as sweet as honey in my mouth.

4 Then He said to me, "Son of man, go to the house of Israel and speak My words to them.

5 "For you are not being sent to a people of unintelligible speech or difficult language, but to the house of Israel,

6 not to many peoples of unintelligible speech or difficult language, whose words you cannot understand. But I have sent you to them who should listen to you *and* pay attention to My message;

7 yet the house of Israel will not be willing to listen to you *and* obey you, since they are not willing to listen to Me *and* obey Me, for the entire house of Israel is stubborn and obstinate.

8 "Behold, I have made your face as hard as their faces and your forehead as hard as their foreheads.

9 "I have made your forehead like emery (diamond), harder than flint. Do not be afraid of them or be dismayed before them, though they are a rebellious house." [Is 50:7; Jer 1:18; 15:20; Mic 3:8]

10 Moreover, He said to me, "Son of man, receive into your heart all My words which I will speak to you and hear with your ears (listen closely).

11 "Go to the [Jewish] exiles [in Babylon], to the children of your people, and speak to them, whether they listen or not, and tell them, 'Thus says the Lord GOD.' "

12 Then the Spirit lifted me up, and I heard a great rushing sound behind me, "Blessed be the glory of the LORD in His place [above the expanse]."

13 And then I *heard* the sound of the wings of the living beings as they touched one another and [I heard] the sound of the wheels beside them, a great rushing sound.

14 So the Spirit lifted me up and took me away, and I went embittered [by the sins of Israel] in the rage of my spirit; and the hand of the LORD was strong on me.

15 Then I came to the exiles who lived beside the River Chebar at Tel Abib. I sat there for seven days [in the place] where they were living, overwhelmed with astonishment [by my vision and the work before me].

16 At the end of seven days the word of the LORD came to me, saying,

17 "Son of man, I have appointed you as a watchman to the house of Israel; whenever you hear a word from My mouth, warn them from Me. [Is 52:8; 56:10; 62:6; Jer 6:17]

18 "When I say to the wicked, 'You will certainly die,' and you do not warn him or speak out to tell him to turn from his wicked way to save his life, that same evil man will die in his sin, but you will be responsible for his blood.

19 "However, if you have warned the wicked and he does not turn from his

---

3:1 – 3 ***eat this scroll.*** The symbolic act of eating the scroll demonstrated that Ezekiel internalized the message in preparation for speaking to the people.

3:8 – 9 ***I have made your face as hard as their faces.*** There may have been an intentional pun on Ezekiel's name, which means "strongly seized by God" (1:3) or "God strengthens." Double meanings in biblical names are common.

3:14 ***I went embittered [by the sins of Israel] in the rage of my spirit.*** Ezekiel's human perspective caused him to focus on the distasteful calling of delivering a message that would not be well received. The prophet was angry and appalled. But God was present to help him deal with these feelings and then move him on to live and work among the captives.

3:17 ***a watchman.*** He stood on the city wall guarding against any external or internal threat. He would sound an alarm upon sighting

---

CHAPTER 3 **1** Eze 2:8,9 **3** Rev 10:9; See Jer 15:16; Ps 19:10; 119:103 **6** Mt 11:21 **7** Jn 15:20; Eze 2:4 **9** Isa 50:7; Jer 1:18; Mic 3:8; Jer 1:8,17; Eze 2:6 **11** Eze 2:5,7 **12** Eze 8:3; 1Ki 18:12; Ac 8:39 **14** ver. 12; Eze 8:3; 2Ki 3:15; Eze 1:3; 8:1 **15** Job 2:13; Ps 137:1 **17** Eze 33:7-9; Isa 52:8; 56:10; Jer 6:17 **18** Eze 33:6; Jn 8:21 **19** Isa 49:4,5; Ac 20:26

wickedness or from his wicked way, he
will die in his sin; but you have freed
yourself [from responsibility].
20“Again, when a righteous man
turns from his righteousness (right
standing with God) and sins, and I
place an obstacle before him, he will
die; since you have not warned him,
he will die in his sin, and the righteous
deeds which he has done will not be
remembered; but you will be respon-
sible for his blood.
21“However, if you have warned the
righteous man not to sin and he does
not sin, he will surely live because he
took warning; also you have freed
yourself [from responsibility].”
22The hand of the LORD was on me
there, and He said to me, “Arise, go out
to the plain, and I will speak to you.”
23So I got up and went out to the
plain; and behold, the glory *and* bril-
liance of the LORD was standing there,
like the glory I had seen by the River
Chebar, and I fell face downward.
24Then the Spirit entered me and
made me stand on my feet; He spoke
and said to me, “Go, shut yourself up
in your house.
25“As for you, son of man, they will
put ropes on you and bind you with
them so that you cannot go out among
them.
26“And I will make your tongue stick
to the roof of your mouth so that you
cannot talk and you cannot be a man
who rebukes the people, for they are
a rebellious house.
27“But when I speak with you, I will
open your mouth and you will say to
them, ‘Thus says the Lord GOD.’ He
who hears, let him hear; and he who
refuses [to hear], let him refuse; for
they are a rebellious house.

Siege of Jerusalem Predicted

4 “NOW YOU, son of man, take a
brick, place it before you and in-
scribe on it [a diagram of] the city of
Jerusalem.
2“Then lay siege against it, build a
siege wall, raise a ramp against it; set
up [enemy] camps and place battering
rams all around it.
3“Further, take an iron plate and
place it as an iron wall between you
and the city, and set your face toward
it so that it is under siege, and besiege
it. This is a sign to the house of Israel.
4“Then lie down on your left side
(toward the north) to bear [symboli-
cally] the wickedness *and* punishment

impending danger (2Sa 18:24). God made Ezekiel a spiritual watchman over His people.

3:20 *when a righteous man turns from his righteousness . . . and sins.* The prophet's responsibility was to warn, if he saw apostasy taking place. If he did not, he became culpable too. Even for the most devoted and the most saintly, righteousness can become something to spurn and iniquity can become something to embrace. God says that repudiation of righteousness leads to death.

3:26 *cannot be a man who rebukes the people.* This phrase qualified what was meant by Ezekiel's being mute. The idea may be better stated as "not be a legal mediator." During his "mute" period, Ezekiel would not be allowed to speak as a mediator on behalf of the people before God, their Judge.

3:27 *He who hears, let him hear.* Jesus used this warning often in His teaching (Mk 4:23). The phrasing emphasizes individual responsibility and readiness to accept the divine message.

4:1 *take a brick.* The brick would have been soft enough to inscribe with a stylus.

4:2 *lay siege.* The city of Jerusalem would come under siege, meaning that the Babylonians would surround the city and cut off its outside supplies. The purpose was to starve its inhabitants into submission. By his symbolic drawing, Ezekiel may have been commanded to do what other "prophets" of the nations might do. That is, the hired "prophets" of pagan nations might use such a drawing as a device for invoking the gods to bring about the event graphically described. In Ezekiel's case, the drawing was the opposite of what the people wanted. As they sat in captivity, the worst news would have been that the holy city had been destroyed.

4:3 *an iron plate.* This was a plate that Ezekiel possessed as a priest; it was for baking grain for the cereal offerings (Lev 2:5; 6:21). Here its purpose was to represent a wall between Ezekiel and the city.

20 Eze 18:24; 33:12,13 **22** Eze 1:3; Eze 8:4 **23** Eze 1:28; Eze 1:1; Eze 1:28 **24** Eze 2:2 **25** Eze 4:8 **26** Eze 24:27; Lk 1:20; Eze 2:5-7 **27** Eze 24:27; 33:22; ver. 11 **CHAPTER 4** **3** Eze 12:6,11; 24:24,27

of the house of Israel. You shall bear their wickedness *and* punishment for the number of days that you lie on your side.

5 “For I have assigned you the years of their wickedness *and* punishment, according to the number of the days, three hundred and ninety days [representing three hundred and ninety years]; in this way you shall bear [symbolically] the wickedness *and* punishment of the house of Israel.

6 “When you have completed these [days for Israel], lie down again, but on your right side (toward the south), and you shall bear the wickedness *and* punishment of the house of Judah forty days. I have assigned you one day for each year.

7 “Then you shall set your face toward the siege of Jerusalem with your arm bared and prophesy against it.

8 “Now behold, I will put ropes on you so that you cannot turn from one side to the other until you have completed the days of your siege.

Defiled Bread

9 “But as for you, take wheat, barley, beans, lentils, millet, and spelt, and put them into one vessel and make them into bread for yourself. You shall eat it according to the number of the days that you lie on your side, three hundred and ninety days.

10 “The food you eat each day *shall be* [measured] by weight, twenty shekels, to be eaten daily at a set time.

11 “You shall drink water by measure also, the sixth part of a hin; you shall drink daily at a set time.

12 “You shall eat your food as barley cakes, having baked it in their sight over human dung.”

13 Then the LORD said, “Thus the children of Israel will eat their bread unclean *and* defiled among the nations where I will banish them.” [Hos 9:3]

14 But I said, “Ah, Lord GOD! Behold (hear me), I have never been defiled; for from my youth until now I have never eaten what died on its own or was torn by beasts, nor has any unclean meat ever entered my mouth.” [Acts 10:14]

15 Then He said to me, “See, I will let you use cow’s dung instead of human dung over which you shall prepare your food.”

16 Moreover, He said to me, “Son of man, behold (listen carefully), I am going to break the staff of bread [that supports life] in Jerusalem; and they shall eat bread [rationed] by weight and [eat it] with anxiety *and* fear, and drink water by measure and [drink it] in horror [of the impending starvation], [Lev 26:26; Ps 105:16; Is 3:1]

17 because bread and water will be scarce; and they will look at one another in dismay and waste away [in punishment] for their wickedness.

Jerusalem’s Desolation Foretold

5 “AND YOU [Ezekiel], son of man, take a sharp sword and use it as a barber’s razor and shave your head

---

4:7 ***set your face toward the siege.*** As horrible as it was, the siege ultimately showed God’s faithfulness to His covenant established in the days of Moses — that idolatry and disobedience would bring curses, which would include being conquered, captured, and removed from the land (Dt 28:15 – 68).

4:8 ***put ropes on you.*** Ezekiel was bound while lying on either side for the entire 430 days, but the activities described in Ezekiel 4:9 – 17 show that his lying down and being tied up occurred only during parts of each day.

4:17 ***waste away [in punishment] for their wickedness.*** The people had broken their covenant with God, and He had no choice but to bring upon them the promised consequences of their disobedience (Lev 26:14 – 29).

5:1 ***a barber’s razor and shave your head and your beard.*** Shaving the head was an act showing shame or disgrace in Hebrew culture (7:18). It also represented a type of pagan mourning forbidden by the law (27:31). Shaving the head was a mark of defilement, making a priest like Ezekiel ritually unclean, and so unable to

---

5 Nu 14:34 **8** Eze 3:25 **13** Hos 9:3 **14** Ac 10:14; Ex 22:31; Lev 11:40; 17:15; Dt 14:3; Isa 65:4 **16** Lev 26:26; Ps 105:16; Isa 3:1; Eze 5:16; 14:13; ver. 10; Eze 12:19; ver. 11 **17** Lev 26:39; Eze 24:23 **CHAPTER 5** **1** See Lev 21:5; Isa 7:20; Eze 44:20

and your beard. Then take scales for
weighing and divide the hair [into
three parts].
2“You shall burn one third with fire
in the center of the city, when the days
of the siege are completed. Then you
shall take one third and strike it with
the sword all around the city, and one
third you shall scatter to the wind; and
I will unsheathe a sword behind them.
3“Also take some of them and bind
them in the edges of your robes.
4“Again take some hair and throw
them into the fire and burn them in the
fire; from it a fire will spread to all the
house of Israel.
5“Thus says the Lord GOD, ‘This is
Jerusalem; I have set her in the cen-
ter of the nations, and countries are
around her.
6‘And she has rebelled against My
ordinances more wickedly than the
[pagan] nations and against My stat-
utes more than the countries that are
around her; for Israel has rejected My
ordinances and has not walked in My
statutes.’ [Rom 2:14, 15]
7“Therefore, thus says the Lord GOD,
‘Because you have more turmoil than
the nations which surround you and
have not walked in My statutes, nor
kept My ordinances, nor observed
the ordinances of the nations which
surround you,’ [Deut 7:2–6; Josh 23:7;
Judg 2:2]
8therefore, thus says the Lord GOD,
‘Behold, I, I Myself, am against you,
and I will execute judgments among
you in the sight of the nations.
9‘And because of all your abomina-
tions, I will do among you that which
I have not done, and the like of which
I will not do again. [Lam 4:6; Dan 9:12;
Amos 3:2]
10‘Therefore, fathers will eat their
sons among you, and sons will eat
their fathers; and I will execute judg-
ments on you and I will scatter to all the
winds the remnant of you. [Lev 26:33;
Deut 28:64; Ezek 12:14; Zech 2:6]
11‘So, as I live,’ says the Lord GOD,
‘surely, because you have defiled My
sanctuary with all your detestable
idols and with all your abominations,
therefore I will also diminish you *and*
withdraw, and My eye will have no pity
and I will not spare [you].
12‘One third of you will die of viru-
lent disease or be consumed by famine
among you; one third will fall by the
sword around you; and one third I will
scatter to all the winds, and I will un-
sheathe a sword behind them.
13‘Thus My anger will come to an
end and I will satisfy My wrath on
them, and I will be appeased; then
they will know [without any doubt]
that I the LORD have spoken in My zeal
when I have spent My wrath on them.
[Ezek 36:6; 38:19]
14‘Moreover, I will make you a des-
olation and a disgrace among the na-
tions which surround you and in the
sight of all who pass by. [Lev 26:31,
32; Neh 2:17]
15‘So it will be a disgrace, a taunt,
a warning and an object of horror to
the [pagan] nations who surround you

---

perform his duties in the temple (Lev 21:5). This message was telling the people that they were about to be humiliated and defiled.

5:2 *one third . . . one third . . . one third.* Each citizen of Jerusalem would suffer one of the three fates depicted by each of the three mounds of hair: (1) some would be burned along with the city or would die from plague, famine, or other siege conditions (5:12; 2Ki 25:9); (2) some would be murdered by the sword during the attack (5:12; 2Ki 25:18 – 21); and (3) some would be scattered in the wind — referring to the exile (5:12; 2Ki 25:11 – 17).

5:9 – 17 *I will do among you that which I have not done.* The elements in God's judgment on the people for their sins can be enumerated in this way: (1) a judgment that will be worse in extent that ever before; (2) a terrible famine that will lead to cannibalism; (3) pestilence, meaning plagues and diseases associated with famine; (4) violent death by sword or wild beasts; and (5) the scattering and killing of a remnant. These

2 ver. 12; Eze 4:1; Eze 4:8,9 **3** Jer 40:6; 52:16 **4** Jer 41:1,2; 44:14 **7** Jer 2:10,11; Eze 16:47 **9** La 4:6; Da 9:12; Am 3:2 **10** Lev 26:29; Dt 28:53; 2Ki 6:29; Jer 19:9; La 2:20; 4:10; Lev 26:33; Dt 28:64; Eze 12:14; Zec 2:6 **11** 2Ch 36:14; Eze 7:20; Eze 11:21; Eze 7:4,9 **12** Jer 15:2; 21:9; Eze 6:12; Jer 9:16; ver. 2; Lev 26:33; Eze 12:14 **13** La 4:11; Eze 6:12; 7:8; Eze 21:17; Dt 32:36; Isa 1:24; Eze 36:6; 38:19 **14** Lev 26:31; Neh 2:17 **15** Dt 28:37; 1Ki 9:7; Ps 79:4; Jer 24:9; La 2:15; Eze 25:17

when I execute judgments against you
in anger and in wrath and in raging
reprimands—I, the LORD, have spoken.
[Deut 28:37; Ps 79:4; Jer 24:9]
16‘When I send against them the
deadly arrows of hunger which were
for the destruction of those whom I
will send to destroy you, then I will in-
crease the famine upon you and break
your staff of bread.
17‘Further, I will send against you
hunger and wild beasts, and they
will bereave you of children; virulent
disease and bloodshed also will pass
through you, and I will bring the sword
on you. I, the LORD, have spoken.’ ”

Idolatrous Worship Denounced

6 AND THE word of the LORD came
to me, saying,
2“Son of man, set your face against
the mountains of Israel and prophesy
against them,
3and say, ‘You mountains of Israel,
hear the word of the Lord GOD! Thus
says the Lord GOD to the mountains and
the hills, to the ravines and the valleys:
“Behold, I Myself am going to bring a
sword on you, and I will destroy your
high places [of idolatrous worship],
4and your altars will become desert-
ed and your pillars for sun-worship
will be smashed in pieces; and I will
throw down your slain in front of your
idols [that cannot bring them back to
life]. [Lev 26:30]
5“I will also lay the dead bodies of
the children of Israel in front of their
[Canaanite] idols; and I will scatter
your bones all around your altars.
6“Everywhere you live, the cities will
become waste and the high places will
become deserted, so that your altars
may bear their guilt *and* become de-
serted, your idols may be broken and
destroyed, your incense altars [for sun-
worship] may be cut down, and your
works may be blotted out.
7“The slain will fall among you, then
you shall know [without any doubt]
that I am the LORD.
8“Yet I will leave some of you alive [a
remnant], for you will have some who
escaped the sword among the nations
when you are scattered throughout
the countries.
9“Then those of you who escape will
remember Me among the nations to
which they will be exiled, how I have
been broken by their lewdness *and*
their adulterous hearts which have
turned away from Me, and by their
eyes which lust after their idols; and
they will loathe themselves for the
evils which they have committed, for
all their repulsive acts.
10“Then they will know [without any
doubt] that I am the LORD; I have not
said in vain that I would bring this
disaster [as punishment] on them.” ’
11“Thus says the Lord GOD, ‘Strike
with your fist, stamp with your foot
and say, “Alas, because of all the evil
atrocities of the house of Israel, which
will fall by sword, by famine, and by
virulent disease!
12“He who is far away will die of the
virulent disease, and he who is near will
fall by the sword, and he who remains
and is besieged will die by the famine.
Thus I will spend My wrath on them.
13“Then you will know [without any

---

punishments would come as the result of the people's idolatry.

6:2–3 *high places.* These were originally elevated locations for worship of the god Baal and other deities of the Canaanite pantheon. The term "high place" could be used of any location, whether hilltop or valley. Before entering the promised land, the Hebrews had been commanded to abolish all the high places where idols were worshiped (Nu 33:52).

6:4–6 *I will throw down your slain . . . lay the dead bodies . . . scatter your bones.* These phrases refer to God's judgment. Dead people lying unburied and bones scattered around signify the ultimate defilement of the land. God would bring this upon them because they had defiled and desecrated themselves by worshiping in the pagan high places.

6:13 *Then you will know [without any doubt] that I am the LORD.* As in verses 7 and 10, the

16 Dt 32:23; Lev 26:26; Eze 4:16; 14:13 **17** Lev 26:22; Dt 32:24; Eze 14:21; 33:27; 34:25; Eze 38:22 **CHAPTER 6**
2 Eze 20:46; 21:2; 25:2; Eze 36:1 **3** Lev 26:30 **4** Lev 26:30 **7** ver. 13; Eze 7:4,9 **8** Jer 44:28; Eze 5:2,12; 12:16;
14:22 **9** Ps 78:40; Isa 7:13; 43:24; Nu 15:39; Eze 20:7,24; Lev 26:39; Job 42:6; Eze 20:43; 36:31 **11** Eze 21:14;
Eze 5:12 **12** Eze 5:13 **13** ver. 7; Jer 2:20; Hos 4:13; Isa 57:5

doubt] that I am the LORD, when their slain are among their idols around their altars, on every high hill, on all the tops of the mountains, under every leafy tree and under every oak with thick branches, the places where they offered sweet incense *and* a soothing aroma to all their idols.

14 “And I will stretch out My hand against them and make the land a more desolate waste than the wilderness toward Diblah [the Moabite city], throughout all the places where they live; and they will know [without any doubt] that I am the LORD.” ’ ”

Punishment for Wickedness Foretold

7 MOREOVER, THE word of the LORD came to me, saying,

2 “Also, son of man, thus says the Lord GOD to the land of Israel, ‘An end! The end is coming on the four corners of the land. [Ezek 11:13; Amos 8:2]

3 ‘Now the end is upon you, and I will send My anger against you and will judge you in accordance with your ways and I will bring [retribution for] all your abominations upon you.

4 ‘For My eye will have no pity on you, nor will I spare you, but I will repay you for your evil ways, while your abominations are among you; and you will know (recognize, understand) [without any doubt] that I am the LORD.’

5 “Thus says the Lord GOD, ‘A disaster is coming, [one so destructive and injurious, so sudden and violent, that it stands alone,] a unique disaster, look it is coming!

6 ‘An end is coming; the end has come! It has awakened against you. Look, it has come!

7 ‘Your doom has come to you, O inhabitant of the land; the time has come, the day is near—tumult rather than joyful shouting on the mountains.

8 ‘Now I will soon pour out My wrath on you and spend My anger against you, and I will judge you in accordance with your ways and will repay you [with punishment] for all your outrageous acts.

9 ‘My eye will show no pity nor will I spare [you]. I will repay you in accordance with your ways, while your abominations are in your midst; then you will know *and* understand that it is I, the LORD, who strikes you.

10 ‘Behold, the day! Behold, it is coming! Your doom has gone forth, the rod has blossomed, arrogance has sprouted.

11 ‘Violence has grown into a rod of wickedness; none of them (Israel) *will remain,* none of their people, none of their wealth, nor anything eminent among them.

12 ‘The time has come, the day has arrived. Let not the buyer rejoice nor the seller mourn, for wrath is against all their multitude [of people].

Lord states the purpose of the coming destruction of His city and many of its people. The use of God’s personal name further emphasizes the intent to bring His people back to a personal, intimate relationship with Himself.

6:13 God’s Desire for Exclusiveness — God’s point throughout the Book of Ezekiel is the same; His relationship with us is exclusive. He doesn’t share that primary God-man relationship with anybody else or anything. As a model for exclusiveness, Ezekiel uses the marriage relationship. Exclusiveness is the boundary that provides the shape to that relationship. It is the same with our relationship with God. When we violate God’s desire for exclusiveness, we ruin our relationship with Him. God designed us for Himself alone. If we have anything less than an exclusive relationship with Him, we become less than what we were created to be.

7:2–3 *The end.* Three uses of this key word stressed that the fulfillment of the prophecy was at hand.

7:10 *the rod has blossomed.* The flowering of the rod indicates that the time to bring judgment was ripe. These words describe one whose time had come, a person marked by arrogance. In this case, it pictures the chosen instrument of God (Nu 17:5) with whom He would discipline Jerusalem and Judah — namely Nebuchadnezzar, king of Babylon and the characteristic representative of the arrogant and evil Babylonians.

7:12 *Let not the buyer rejoice.* The fact of coming judgment was so certain, and its effects would be so lasting and devastating, that transactions

14 Isa 5:25; Nu 33:46; Jer 48:22 **CHAPTER 7** **2** Am 8:2; Mt 24:6,13,14 **4** Eze 5:11; Eze 12:20 **7** ver. 10; Zep 1:14,15 **8** Eze 20:8,21 **10** ver. 7 **11** Jer 6:7; 16:5,6; Eze 24:16,22

13 'For the seller will not regain *and* return to what he sold, even were they yet alive; for the vision [of punishment] regarding all the multitude [of people] will not be turned back, nor will any one of them sustain his life because of his sin.

14 'They have blown the trumpet and have made everything ready, but no one is going to the battle, for My wrath is against all their multitude [of people].

15 'The sword is outside and virulent disease and famine are within. He who is in the field will die by the sword, and famine and disease will devour those in the city.

16 'Even when their survivors escape, they will be on the mountains like doves of the valleys, all of them moaning, each over his [punishment for] sin.

17 'All hands will hang limp and all knees will be as weak as water. [Is 13:7; Jer 6:24; Ezek 21:7]

18 'They will also cover themselves with sackcloth; horror will overwhelm them, and shame *will be* on all faces and baldness on all their heads [as evidence of grief].

19 'They will fling their silver into the streets and their gold will be [discarded] like something unclean; their silver and their gold shall not be able to save them in the day of the wrath of the LORD. These [things] cannot satisfy their soul nor fill their stomachs, for they have become their stumbling block *and* source of sin. [Prov 11:4; Zeph 1:18]

The Temple Profaned

20 'As for the beauty of [gold for] ornaments, they turned it to pride and from it made the images of their repulsive things (idols) and of their vile things. Therefore I will make it an unclean thing to them.

21 'I will give it into the hands of strangers (Babylonians) as plunder and to the wicked of the earth as spoil, and they shall profane it.

22 'I will also turn My face away from them, and they will desecrate My secret treasure (the Jerusalem temple); and robbers will enter [irreverently] into it (the Holy of Holies) and violate it.

23 'Prepare the chain [for imprisonment], for the land is full of bloody crimes [murders committed under the pretense of civil justice] and the city is full of violence.

24 'Therefore, I will bring the worst of the [Gentile] nations, and they will take possession of their houses [those of the people of Judah]; I will also silence their pride, and their holy places will be profaned.

25 'When anguish comes, they [of Judah] shall seek peace, but there will be none.

26 'Disaster will come upon disaster and rumor will be *heaped* on rumor; they will seek a vision from a prophet, but the law *and* guidance will be lost from the priest and [wise] counsel [will cease] from the elders. [Ps 74:9; Lam 2:9]

27 'The king [of Judah] will mourn and the prince (Zedekiah) will be clothed with [garments of] despair *and* anguish, and the hands of the people of the land shall tremble [in terror]. I will deal with them in accordance with their conduct, and by their judgments I will judge them. And they will know [without any doubt] that I am the LORD.' "

Vision of Repulsive Acts in Jerusalem

8 IT CAME about in the sixth year [of the captivity of King Jehoiachin], on the fifth day of the sixth month, as I sat in my house [near Babylon] with the el-

---

of buying and selling would be concluded improperly or not at all.

7:16–19 *Even when their survivors escape.* Those left alive would hide in the hills and be characterized by four things: (1) mourning—displaying their humiliation over sin by wearing sackcloth and shaving their heads (Isa 15:2); (2) weakness; (3) horror; and (4) disgust and disillusionment over wealth.

7:20 *the beauty of [gold for] ornaments.* The people had sinned horribly when they crafted idols out of the temple treasures and then worshiped what their hands had made (Ro 1:25).

---

15 Dt 32:25; La 1:20 **17** Isa 13:7; Jer 6:24 **18** Isa 3:24; Am 8:10 **19** Pr 11:4; Zep 1:18 **20** Jer 7:30 **23** 2Ki 21:16
26 Dt 32:23; Jer 4:20; Ps 74:9; Eze 20:1,3 **CHAPTER 8** **1** Eze 14:1; 20:1; 33:31; Eze 1:3; 3:22

ders of Judah sitting before me, that the hand of the Lord GOD fell on me there.

2 Then I looked, and behold, a likeness [of a man] with the appearance of fire; from His loins downward He was like fire, and from His loins upward He had the appearance of brightness, like gleaming metal (bronze).

3 He stretched out the form of a hand and took me by a lock of hair on my head; and the Spirit lifted me up between earth and heaven and brought me in the visions of God to Jerusalem, to the entrance of the north gate of the inner *courtyard,* where the seat of the idol (image) of jealousy, which provokes to jealousy, was *located.* [2 Kin 16:10–16; 21:4, 5]

4 And behold, the glory *and* brilliance of the God of Israel [who had loved and chosen them] was there, like the vision which I saw in the plain. [Ezek 1:28; 3:22, 23]

5 Then He said to me, "Son of man, now raise your eyes toward the north." So I looked toward the north, and behold, to the north of the altar gate was this idol (image) of jealousy at the entrance.

6 Furthermore, He said to me, "Son of man, do you see what they are doing, the great repulsive acts which the house of Israel is committing here, to drive Me far away from My sanctuary? But you will again see greater repulsive acts."

7 Then He brought me to the entrance of the courtyard; and when I looked, behold, [there was] a hole in the wall.

8 He said to me, "Son of man, now dig into the wall." And when I had dug into the wall, behold, there was an entrance.

9 And He said to me, "Go in and see the wicked, repulsive acts that they are committing here."

10 So I entered and looked, and saw every kind of creeping things and beasts and loathsome things, and all the idols of the house of Israel, carved all around on the wall.

11 Standing before these [images] were seventy elders of the house of Israel, and among them stood Jaazaniah the son of Shaphan [the scribe], each man with his censer in his hand and a thick *and* fragrant cloud of incense was rising [as they prayed to these gods].

12 Then He said to me, "Son of man, do you see what the elders of the house of Israel do in the dark, each man in his [secret] room of carved images? For they say, 'The LORD does not see us; the LORD has abandoned the land.' "

13 He also said to me, "Yet again you will see even greater repulsive acts which they are committing."

14 Then He brought me to the entrance of the north gate of the LORD's house; and behold, women were sitting there weeping for Tammuz.

15 He said to me, "Do you see this, son of man? Yet you will see still greater repulsive acts than these [that they are committing]."

16 So He brought me to the inner court of the LORD's house. And behold, at the entrance to the temple of the LORD, between the porch (vestibule, portico) and the [bronze] altar, were about twenty-five men with their backs to the temple of the LORD and their faces toward the east; and they were bowing down toward the east *and* worshiping the sun.

8:5 – 6 *to drive Me far away from My sanctuary.* The people thought that just because the temple stood among them, whatever wrong they might do could not bring ultimate disaster. They thought the temple guaranteed their security. They did not realize that their evil had actually caused God to leave His temple, which would then no longer be their protection.

8:11 *seventy elders.* These men were the nation's leaders (Nu 11:16 – 25).

8:13 – 14 *Tammuz.* This was a fertility god. The women were crying out to the idol because they had no children or because the crops were failing. In the sixth month, August-September, Tammuz was thought to "die" with the scorched land. Worshipers would wail over his death and cry for his resurgence.

2 Eze 1:26,27; Eze 1:4 **3** Da 5:5; Eze 3:14; Eze 11:1,24; 40:2; Jer 7:30; 32:34; Eze 5:11; Dt 32:16,21 **4** Eze 1:28; 3:22,23 **12** Eze 9:9 **16** Joel 2:17; Eze 11:1; Jer 2:27; 32:33; Dt 4:19; 2Ki 23:5,11; Job 31:26; Jer 44:17

17 He said to me, “Do you see this, son
of man? Is it too slight a thing for the
house of Judah to commit the repulsive
acts which they have committed here,
that they have filled the land with vi-
olence and repeatedly provoked Me to
anger? And behold, they are putting
the branch to their nose.
18 “Therefore, I indeed will deal in
wrath. My eye will have no pity nor
will I spare [them]; and though they
cry loudly in My ears, yet I will not
listen to them.” [Prov 1:28; Is 1:15;
Jer 11:11; 14:12; Mic 3:4; Zech 7:13]

The Vision of Slaughter

9 THEN [in my vision] I heard Him
cry out with a thunderous voice,
saying, “Approach now, executioners
of the city, each with his weapon of
destruction in his hand.”
2 Behold, six men [angelic beings]
came from the direction of the Upper
Gate, which faces north, each with
his battle-axe in his hand; and among
them was a certain man clothed in
linen, with a scribe’s writing case at
his side. They entered and stood beside
the bronze altar.
3 Then the [Shekinah] glory *and* bril-
liance of the God of Israel (the cloud)
went up from the cherubim on which it
had rested, to [stand above] the thresh-
old of the [LORD’s] temple. And the
LORD called to the man clothed with
linen, who had the scribe’s writing
case at his side.
4 The LORD said to him, “Go through
the midst of the city, throughout all
of Jerusalem, and put a mark on the
foreheads of the men who sigh [in dis-
tress] and grieve over all the repulsive
acts which are being committed in it.”
5 But to the others I heard Him say,
“Follow him [the man with the scribe’s
writing case] throughout the city and
strike; do not let your eyes have pity
and do not spare [anyone].
6 “Utterly slay old men, young men,
maidens, little children, and women;
but do not touch *or* go near anyone on
whom is the mark. Begin at My sanc-
tuary.” So they began with the old men
who were in front of the temple [who
did not have the LORD’s mark on their
foreheads]. [1 Pet 4:17]
7 And He said to the executioners,
“Defile the temple and fill its court-
yards with the dead. Go out!” So they
went out and struck down *the people*
in the city.
8 As they were executing them and
I *alone* was left, I fell face downward
and cried out, “Alas, Lord GOD! Will
You destroy all that is left of Israel [the
whole remnant] by pouring out Your
wrath *and* indignation on Jerusalem?”
9 Then He said to me, “The wick-
edness (guilt) of the house of Israel
and Judah is extremely great; the land
is full of blood and the city is full of
perversion *and* injustice; for they say,
‘The LORD has abandoned the land; the
LORD does not see [what we are doing].’
10 “But as for Me, My eye will have no
pity, nor will I spare, but I will bring
their [wicked] conduct upon their
[own] heads.”

8:17 – 18 *they are putting the branch to their nose.* This action is not mentioned elsewhere. In the context it appears to be (1) a ritualistic gesture used in idol worship, or (2) an action indicative of the extensive violence which was occurring in Judah as a result of idolatry.

9:5 – 6 *Follow him ... throughout the city.* The universality of this judgment is shocking to us; but this is in line with divine judgments from the time of the flood in Genesis to the final judgment described in Revelation.

9:6 – 7 *My sanctuary.* The corrupt spiritual leaders had been practicing idolatry and immorality in the temple itself (8:3 – 16). Judgment would begin with them because they had led the nation astray.

9:9 *wickedness . . . blood . . . perversion and injustice.* These three reasons are given as the offenses that deserve this terrible outpouring of God’s wrath. The people and especially rich rulers willfully chose to believe that God did not see or care what injustices went on.

17 Eze 9:9 **18** Eze 5:13; 16:42; 24:13; Eze 5:11; 7:4,9; 9:5,10; Pr 1:28; Isa 1:15; Jer 11:11; 14:12; Mic 3:4; Zec 7:13
CHAPTER 9 **2** Lev 16:4; Eze 10:2,6,7; Rev 15:6 **3** See Eze 3:23; 8:4; 10:4,18; 11:22,23 **4** Ex 12:7; Rev 7:3; 9:4; 13:16,17; 20:4; Ps 119:53,136; Jer 13:17; 2Co 12:21; 2Pe 2:8 **5** ver. 10; Eze 5:11 **6** 2Ch 36:17; Rev 9:4; Jer 25:29; 1Pe 4:17; Eze 8:11,12,16 **8** Nu 14:5; 16:4,22,45; Jos 7:6; Eze 11:13 **9** 2Ki 21:16; Eze 8:17; Eze 8:12; Ps 10:11; Isa 29:15 **10** Eze 5:11; 7:4; 8:18; Eze 11:21

11 Then behold, the man clothed in linen, who had the scribe's writing case at his side, reported, "I have done just as You have commanded me."

Vision of God's Glory Departing from the Temple

10 THEN I looked, and behold, in the expanse (firmament) that was over the heads of the cherubim there appeared something [glorious and brilliant] above them looking like a [huge] sapphire stone, formed to resemble a throne.

2 And the LORD spoke to the man (seventh angel) clothed in linen and said, "Go between the whirling wheels under the cherubim; fill your hands with coals of fire from between the cherubim and scatter them over the city." And he entered as I watched. [Rev 8:5]

3 Now the cherubim were standing on the right side of the temple when the man entered; and a cloud [the Shekinah glory of God] filled the inner courtyard.

4 Then the glory *and* brilliance of the LORD moved upward from the cherubim to [rest over] the threshold of the temple; and the temple was filled with the cloud and the courtyard was filled with the brightness of the LORD's glory. [1 Kin 8:10, 11; Ezek 43:5]

5 And the sound of the wings of the cherubim was heard [even] as far as the outer courtyard, like the voice of God Almighty when He speaks. [Ps 29:3, 4]

6 It came about when He commanded the man clothed in linen, saying, "Take fire from between the whirling wheels, from between the cherubim," the man entered and stood beside a wheel.

7 Then a cherub stretched out his hand from between the cherubim to the fire that was between [the four of] them, and took some [of it] and put it into the hands of the man clothed in linen, who took it and departed.

8 Beneath their wings the cherubim seemed to have [something in] the form of a man's hand.

9 Then I looked and behold, [there were] four wheels beside the cherubim, one wheel beside one cherub and another wheel beside each other cherub; and the appearance of the wheels was like a sparkling Tarshish stone (beryl).

10 As for their appearance, all four looked alike, as if one wheel were within another wheel.

11 When they moved, they went in any of their four directions without turning as they went; but they followed in the direction which they faced, without turning as they went.

12 Their whole body, their backs, their hands, their wings, and the wheels were full of eyes all around, even the wheels belonging to all four of them.

13 Regarding the wheels [attached to them], I heard them called, "the whirling (rolling, revolving) wheels."

14 And each one had four faces: the first face was the face of the cherub, the second the face of a man, the third the face of a lion, and the fourth the face of an eagle.

15 Then the cherubim rose upward. They are the [same four] living beings [regarded as one] that I saw by the River Chebar [in Babylonia]. [Ezek 1:5]

16 Now when the cherubim moved, the wheels would go beside them; and when the cherubim lifted up their wings to rise from the earth, the wheels would remain beside them.

17 When the cherubim stood still, the

10:3 – 5 a cloud [the Shekinah glory of God] filled the inner courtyard. The cloud represented God's glory (as in 1:4), which was seen moving from the inner court to the threshold of the temple. From there it filled the temple.

10:9 – 17 the first face was the face of the cherub. Whereas one of the four faces in 1:10 is a bull, here it is a cherub. These are ancient sculptures with animal bodies and wings but human faces. The difference of the faces between 1:10 and 10:14 should not be called an error; it is possible that the images that Ezekiel saw were changing from time to time.

CHAPTER 10 **1** Eze 1:2,26 **2** Eze 9:2,3; Eze 1:13; See Rev 8:5 **4** See ver. 18; Eze 1:28; 9:3; 1Ki 8:10; Eze 43:5 **5** Eze 1:24; Ps 29:3 **8** ver. 21 **9** Eze 1:15; Eze 1:16 **11** Eze 1:17 **14** Eze 1:6,10 **15** Eze 1:5 **16** Eze 1:19 **17** Eze 1:12,20,21

wheels would stand still; and when
they rose upward, the wheels would
rise with them, for the spirit of the
living beings was in these [wheels].
[Ezek 1:21]
18Then the [Shekinah] glory of the
LORD departed from the threshold of the
temple and rested over the cherubim.
19As I looked at them, the cheru-
bim lifted up their wings and rose up
from the earth, they departed with the
wheels beside them; and they stood
still at the entrance of the east gate of
the house of the LORD, and the glory
and brilliance of the God of Israel hov-
ered over them.
20These are the living beings that I
saw beneath the God of Israel by the
River Chebar; and I knew that they
were cherubim.
21Each one had four faces and each
one had four wings, and beneath their
wings was the form of human hands.
22As for the likeness of their faces,
they were the same faces whose ap-
pearance I had seen by the River Che-
bar. Each one went straight forward.

Evil Rulers to Be Judged

11 MOREOVER, THE Spirit lifted
me up and brought me to the gate
of the LORD's house, which faced east-
ward. And behold, at the entrance of
the gate *there were* twenty-five men;
and I saw among them Jaazaniah the
son of Azzur and Pelatiah the son of
Benaiah, princes of the people.
2Then the Spirit said to me, "Son of
man, these are the men who devise
evil and give wicked advice in this city,
3who say, 'Is not *the time* near to
build houses? This *city* is [secure just
like] the pot and we are the meat [in it].'
4"Therefore, prophesy against them;
prophesy, son of man!"
5Then the Spirit of the LORD fell
upon me, and He said to me, "Say,
'Thus says the LORD, "This is what
you think, house of Israel, for I know
your thoughts.
6"You have multiplied your slain in
this city, and you have filled its streets
with the corpses [of righteous men]."
7'Therefore, thus says the Lord GOD,
"Your dead whom you have laid in the
midst of your city are the meat and this
city is the pot; but I shall force you out
of [the security of] it.
8"You have feared the sword; so I
will bring a sword upon you," says the
Lord GOD.
9"And I will bring you out of the
midst of the city and hand you over
to strangers and execute judgment
against you.
10"You will fall by the sword; I will
judge *and* punish you [in front of your
neighbors] at the border of [the land of]
Israel; and you will know [without any
doubt] that I am the LORD.
11"This *city* will not be a pot for you,
nor will you be meat [safe] in it, but I
will judge you at the border of Israel.
12"And you will know [without any
doubt] that I am the LORD; for you have
not walked in My statutes nor have you
executed My ordinances, but you have
acted in accordance with the ordinanc-
es of the nations around you." ' "
13Now it came about while I was
prophesying, that Pelatiah the son of
Benaiah died. Then I fell face down-

10:20–22 *and I knew that they were cherubim.* They sometimes serve as guardians (Ge 3:24). They are associated with God's throne and presence (the mercy seat on the ark, Ex 25:18–22; 1Ch 13:6). They are also associated with God's chariot-like throne (v. 1; 1:20–26; Ps 18:10).

11:3 *Is not the time near to build houses?* These officials were proclaiming that the inhabitants of Jerusalem were as secure behind the city's walls as meat was safe in its cooking pot. There was no impending doom, they said; therefore, new construction projects were encouraged.

11:13 *Alas, Lord GOD.* Ezekiel's reaction showed that Pelatiah, one of the corrupt city leaders (v. 1), was struck dead by God as undeniable proof that the prophet's message would come true. Ezekiel himself was awestruck and asked if this meant that God would not after all preserve a remnant.

---

18 ver. 4; Hos 9:12 **19** Eze 11:22 **20** ver. 15; Eze 1:22; Eze 1:1 **21** Eze 1:6 **22** Eze 1:10; Eze 1:12 **CHAPTER 11**
1 ver. 24; Eze 3:12,14; Eze 10:19; See Eze 8:16 **3** Eze 12:22,27; 2Pe 3:4; See Jer 1:13; Eze 24:3 **5** Eze 2:2; 3:24
6 Eze 7:23 **7** Eze 24:3,6; Mic 3:3; ver. 9 **9** Eze 5:8 **10** 2Ki 25:19-21; Jer 39:6; 52:10; 1Ki 8:65; 2Ki 14:25; Ps 9:16;
Eze 6:7; 13:9,14,21,23 **11** See ver. 3 **12** ver. 10; Lev 18:3,24; Dt 12:30,31; Eze 8:10,14,16 **13** Ac 5:5; Eze 9:8

ward and cried out loudly, "Alas, Lord
GOD! Will You bring the remnant of
Israel to a complete end?"

Promise of Restoration

14 Then the word of the LORD came
to me, saying,
15 "Son of man, your brothers, your
relatives, your fellow exiles and the
whole house of Israel, all of them, are
those to whom the [present] inhabi-
tants of Jerusalem have said, 'Go far
away from the LORD; this land has been
given to us as a possession.'
16 "Therefore say, 'Thus says the Lord
GOD, "Though I had removed Israel far
away among the nations and though
I had scattered them among the coun-
tries, yet I have been a sanctuary for
them for a little while in the countries
to which they had gone." '
17 "Therefore say, 'Thus says the Lord
GOD, "I will gather you from the peo-
ples and assemble you out of the coun-
tries where you have been scattered,
and I will give [back] to you the land
of Israel." '
18 "When they return there, they will
remove from it all [traces of] its detest-
able things and all its repulsive things
(remnants of paganism).
19 "And I will give them one heart [a
new heart], and put a new spirit within
them. I will take from them the heart
of stone, and will give them a heart of
flesh [that is responsive to My touch],
[Ezek 18:31; 36:26; 2 Cor 3:3]
20 that they may walk in My statutes
and keep My ordinances and do them.
Then they shall be My people, and I
will be their God.
21 "But as for those whose heart longs
for *and* follows after their detestable
things and their repulsive things [asso-
ciated with idolatry], on their own head
I will repay [them in full for] their [vile]
conduct," says the Lord GOD.
22 Then the cherubim lifted up their
wings with the wheels beside them,
and the [Shekinah] glory of the God
of Israel hovered over them.
23 Then the glory *and* brilliance of
the LORD went up from the midst of the
city and paused over the mountain, [the
Mount of Olives] which is east of the city.
24 And the Spirit lifted me up and
brought me in a vision by the Spirit of
God to the exiles in Chaldea (Babylo-
nia). Then the vision that I had seen
left me.
25 Then I told the exiles everything
that the LORD had shown me.

Ezekiel Prepares for Exile

12 THE WORD of the LORD also
came to me, saying,
2 "Son of man, you live among a re-
bellious house, who have eyes to see
but do not see, who have ears to hear
but do not hear; for they are a rebel-
lious people. [Mark 8:18]
3 "Therefore, son of man, prepare
your belongings for exile, and move

11:15 *your fellow exiles.* The people in Jerusalem (representative of Judah) regarded the exiles as sinners because they had been deported to Babylon. **11:16 *yet I have been a sanctuary for them.*** God explained to Ezekiel that the Hebrews taken captive and spread among foreign lands were actually the remnant whom God was protecting. God Himself would continue as their sanctuary—a word in Hebrew that literally means a "holy place." **11:18–20 *they will remove from it all [traces of] its detestable things.*** When the remnant returned to the land, they would abolish idolatry. At that time God would establish a new covenant with them (Jer 31:31–34). Then God would pour out His Spirit (36:26–27; Joel 2:28–29) so that His people would become united in purpose and empowered to maintain their righteousness. They would finally and truly become His people (Ex 6:6–8). **11:23 *the glory and brilliance of the LORD went up.*** The Hebrew term for "glory" literally means of "weight" or "significance" and refers to the wonder and majesty of the living God. **11:24–25 *And the Spirit lifted me up.*** Ezekiel's visions are not merely dreams; they were inspired by God Himself and thus were prophetic. ***Chaldea.*** This is an alternative term for Babylon. **12:3–7 *prepare your belongings for exile, and move.*** Ezekiel's next visual demonstration

---

16 Ps 90:1; 91:9; Isa 8:14 **17** Jer 24:5; Eze 38:25; 34:13 **18** Eze 37:23 **19** Jer 32:39; Eze 36:26; See Zep 3:9; Ps 51:10; Jer 31:33; Eze 18:31; Zec 7:12 **20** Ps 105:45; Jer 24:7; Eze 14:11; 36:28; 37:27 **21** Eze 9:10; 22:31 **22** Eze 1:19; 10:19 **23** Eze 8:4; 9:3; 10:4,18; 43:4; See Zec 14:4; Eze 43:2 **24** Eze 8:3 **CHAPTER 12** **2** Eze 2:3,6-8; 3:26,27; Isa 6:9; 42:20; Jer 5:21; Mt 13:13,14; Eze 2:5

into exile during the day when they
will see you; even go into exile from
your place to another place as they
watch. Perhaps they will understand
even though they are a rebellious peo-
ple.
4"Bring your provisions *and* sup-
plies out during the day as they watch,
as provisions *and* supplies for [going
into] exile. Then you shall go out at
evening as they watch, as those going
into exile.
5"Dig through the wall as they watch
and go out through the hole.
6"As they look on, load *the provi-
sions and supplies* on your shoulder
and carry it out in the dark. You shall
cover your face so that you cannot see
the land, for I have set you as a sign to
the house of Israel."
7I did as I had been commanded. I
brought out my provisions *and* sup-
plies during the day, like the provisions
and supplies of an exile, and in the
evening I dug through the wall with
my hands. I brought out *my provisions
and supplies* in the dark, carrying it on
my shoulder as they watched.
8In the morning the word of the
LORD came to me, saying,
9"Son of man, has not the house of
Israel, the rebellious house, asked you,
'What you are doing?'
10"Say to them, 'Thus says the Lord
GOD, "This oracle (a burden to be car-
ried) concerns the prince (Zedekiah)
in Jerusalem as well as all the house
of Israel who are there." '
11"Say, 'I am a sign to you. As I have
done, so it will be done to them; they
will go into exile, into captivity.'
12"The prince who is among them
will load *his provisions and supplies*
on his shoulder in the dark and go out.
They will dig a hole through the wall
to go out. He will cover his face so that
he cannot see the land with his eyes.
13"I will also spread My net over him,
and he will be caught in My snare. And
I will bring him to Babylon, to the land
of the Chaldeans; yet he will not see it,
though he will die there. [2 Kin 25:1–7;
Jer 39:5; 52:7–11]
14"I will scatter to every wind all who
are around him, his helpers and all his
troops; and I will draw out a sword
after them.
15"So they will know *and* understand
fully that I am the LORD when I scatter
them among the nations and disperse
them among the [pagan] countries.
16"But I will leave a few [survivors]
who will escape the sword, the famine,
and the virulent disease, that they may
confess all their repulsive (idolatrous)
acts among the nations where they go,
and may know [without any doubt]
that I am the LORD."
17Moreover, the word of the LORD
came to me, saying,
18"Son of man, eat your bread with
anxiety, and drink your water with
trembling and with fear.
19"Then say to the people of the
land, 'Thus says the Lord GOD con-
cerning the inhabitants of Jerusalem

---

warned the captives already in Babylon that they should not expect a quick return to Jerusalem. He had already shown that the city would soon fall (chs. 4 – 5) and those not killed would be led into exile. These exiles should have understood Ezekiel's meaning.

12:11 – 14 *they will go into exile, into captivity.* Speaking in 592 BC, Ezekiel predicted the deportation of Jerusalem's population to Babylon six years later and prophesied exactly what would happen to their leader Zedekiah. The king would attempt to escape by night, secretly and in disguise; but he would be caught and blinded by the Babylonians, then carried off to Babylon where he would later die.

12:15 – 16 *So they will know and understand fully that I am the LORD.* The defeat of God's people would not indicate the Lord's lack of strength, but the serious consequences of sin against Him. Yet He would demonstrate that His purpose had always been to restore His people to Himself (Heb 12:1 – 11). Through the difficult experience, His people would learn that their God was both holy and loving. Sin offended Him, but He still would reach out to restore the sinner.

---

6 ver. 11; Isa 8:18; Eze 4:3; 24:24 **9** Eze 2:5; Eze 17:12; 24:19 **10** Mal 1:1 **11** ver. 6; 2Ki 25:4,5,7 **12** Jer 39:4 **13** Job 19:6; Jer 52:9; La 1:13; Eze 17:20; 2Ki 25:7; Jer 52:11; Eze 17:16 **14** 2Ki 25:4; Eze 5:10; Eze 5:2,12 **15** ver. 16,20; Ps 9:16; Eze 6:7,14; 11:10 **16** Eze 6:8-10 **18** Eze 4:16 **19** Zec 7:14; Ps 107:34

in the land of Israel, “They will eat
their bread with anxiety and drink
their water with horror, because their
land will be stripped *and* looted of its
fullness because of the violence of all
those who live in it.
20“The cities that are inhabited will
be in ruins and the land will be desert-
ed; and you will know [without any
doubt] that I am the LORD.” ’ ”
21Then the word of the LORD came
to me, saying,
22“Son of man, what is this prov-
erb that you have in the land of Israel,
saying, ‘The days are long and every
vision fails’?
23“Therefore tell them, ‘Thus says
the Lord GOD, “I will put an end to
this proverb, and they will no longer
use it as a proverb in Israel.” But say to
them, “The days draw near as well as
the fulfillment of every vision.
24“For there will no longer be any
false *and* empty vision or flattering
divination within the house of Israel.
25“For I the LORD will speak, and
whatever word I speak will be accom-
plished. It will no longer be delayed,
for in your days, O rebellious house,
I will speak the word and I will fulfill
it,” says the Lord GOD.’ ”
26Again the word of the LORD came
to me, saying,
27“Son of man, behold, the house of
Israel is saying, ‘The vision that Ezek-
iel sees is for many years *from now*,
and he prophesies of the times that
are far off.’
28“Therefore say to them, ‘Thus says
the Lord GOD, “None of My words will
be delayed any longer. Whatever word
I speak will be fulfilled completely,” ’ ”
says the Lord GOD.

False Prophets Condemned

13 AND THE word of the LORD
came to me saying,
2“Son of man, prophesy against the
prophets of Israel who prophesy, and
say to those who prophesy from their
own inspiration, ‘Hear the word of
the LORD!
3‘Thus says the Lord GOD, “Woe
(judgment is coming) to the foolish
prophets who are following their own
spirit [claiming to have seen things]
but have [in fact] seen nothing.
4“O Israel, your prophets have been
like foxes among the ruins.
5“You have not gone up into the gaps
or breaches, nor built the wall around
the house of Israel that it might stand
in the battle on the day of the LORD.
6“They have seen falsehood and ly-
ing divination, saying, ‘The LORD says,’
but the LORD has not sent them. Yet
they hope *and* make men to hope for
the confirmation of their word.
7“Did you not see (make up) a false
vision and speak a lying divination
when you said, ‘The LORD declares,’
but it is not I who have spoken?” ’ ”

12:22 *The days are long and every vision fails.* This proverb among the exiles indicates how hardened they were to Ezekiel’s prophecies. Although already captive, the people were cynical and apathetic, mistakenly thinking that a delay in judgment meant no judgment, at least in their lifetime (vv. 25,27 – 28; 2Pe 3:3 – 4).

12:23 – 25 *The days draw near as well as the fulfillment of every vision.* This proverb would replace the old one (v. 22), and false prophets opposing Ezekiel would cease to speak. The exiles would live to see the judgment on Jerusalem fulfilled.

13:2 – 4 *foxes among the ruins.* In the immediate context (v. 5), the foxes are pictured roaming amid the rubble of ruined city walls. The prophets were fools because they confused their own thoughts with God’s. They were like foxes among the ruins because they scavenged for themselves while causing, ignoring, and profiting from the human wreckage surrounding them.

13:5 *the day of the LORD.* This phrase refers to times when God triumphs (7:19; 30:3). It is particularly used by the prophets to describe those periods in which God is unusually active in the affairs of His people, either for deliverance or for judgment (Joel 2:1; Zep 1:7). In that day, God will actively bring about His purposes for the world; He will rescue the righteous and judge evildoers.

22 ver. 27; Eze 11:3; Am 6:3; 2Pe 3:4 **23** Joel 2:1; Zep 1:14 **24** Eze 13:23; La 2:14 **25** ver. 28; Isa 55:11; Da 9:12; Lk 21:33 **27** ver. 22 **28** ver. 23,25 **CHAPTER 13** **2** ver. 17; Jer 14:14; 23:16,26 **4** SS 2:15 **5** Ps 106:23,30; Eze 22:30 **6** ver. 23; Eze 12:24; 22:28

8"Therefore, thus says the Lord GOD,
"Because you have spoken empty *and*
delusive words and have seen lies,
therefore behold, I am against you,"
says the Lord GOD.
9"So My hand will be against the
[counterfeit] prophets who see (make
up) empty *and* delusive visions and
who give lying prophecies. They will
have no place in the [secret] council of
My people, nor will they be recorded
in the register of the house of Israel,
nor will they enter into the land of Is-
rael, that you may know [without any
doubt] that I am the Lord GOD.
10"It is definitely because they have
seduced My people, saying, 'Peace,'
when there is no peace, and because
when one builds a [flimsy] wall, be-
hold, these [lying] prophets plaster it
over with whitewash;
11so tell those who plaster it with
whitewash, that it will fall! A flooding
rain [of judgment] will come, and you,
O [great] hailstones, will fall; and a
violent wind will tear the wall apart.
12"Behold, when the wall has fall-
en, will you not be asked, 'Where is
the coating with which you [prophets]
plastered it?' "
13Therefore, thus says the Lord GOD,
"I will make a violent wind break out
in My wrath, and there will be in My
anger an overwhelming rain and
great hailstones to destroy [that wall]
in wrath.
14"So I will tear down the wall which
you have plastered with whitewash
and bring it down to the ground, so
that its foundations will be exposed;
when it falls, you will perish in its
midst. And you shall know *and* under-
stand fully that I am the LORD.
15"Thus I will expend My wrath on
the wall and on those who have plas-
tered it with whitewash and I will say
to you, 'The wall is gone and its plas-
terers are gone,
16*along with* the [false] prophets of
Israel who prophesy [deceitfully] to Je-
rusalem, and who see [false] visions of
peace for her when there is no peace,'
says the Lord GOD.
17"Now you, son of man, set your
face against the daughters of your peo-
ple who are prophesying out of [the
wishful thinking of] their own mind
(inspiration). Prophesy against them
18and say, 'Thus says the Lord GOD,
"Woe to the women who fasten *magic*
(protective) charms on all wrists and
make veils for the heads of those of
every stature to capture [human] lives!
Will you capture the lives of My people
but keep your own?
19"You have profaned Me among
My people [in payment] for handfuls
of barley and for pieces of bread, kill-
ing people who should not die and
giving [a guarantee of] life to those
who should not live, because of your
lies to My people who pay attention
to lies." ' "
20Therefore, thus says the Lord GOD,
"Behold, I am against your *magic*
bands [and veils] by which you hunt
[human] lives as birds and I will tear
them from your arms; and I will let the
lives you hunt go free, even those lives
whom you hunt as birds.
21"I will also tear off your [pagan]
veils and rescue My people from your
hands, and they will no longer be in
your grip to be hunted *and* trapped.
Then you will know [without any
doubt] that I am the LORD.

13:10–16 *you will perish in its midst.* The false prophets would experience God's wrath — just as the walls of Jerusalem which were being constructed at that time would be destroyed. Jerusalem would be conquered and captured for the sins of its inhabitants. The preaching of a false peace had prompted people to build for a "certain" future, but only the opposite was certain. The false prophets had deceived the people with false hopes of comfort and prosperity (v. 10). Their deception placed them not only at odds with God's truth, but also with God Himself. Their destruction was certain.

13:17–19 *set your face against the daughters of your people.* The Hebrew women who were false prophetesses were confusing their own ideas with God's and casting magic death spells through sorcery or witchcraft (Lev 19:26).

---

9 Ezr 2:59,62; Neh 7:5; Ps 69:28; Eze 20:38; Eze 11:10,12 **10** Jer 6:14; 8:11; Eze 22:28 **11** Eze 38:22 **14** ver. 9, 21,23; Eze 14:8 **16** Jer 6:14; 28:9 **17** Eze 20:46; 21:2; ver. 2 **18** 2Pe 2:14 **19** See Pr 28:21; Mic 3:5 **21** ver. 9

22“Because you disheartened the
righteous with falsehood when I did
not cause him grief, but have encour-
aged the wicked not to turn from his
wicked way and preserve his life,
23therefore, you women will no lon-
ger see false visions or practice divina-
tions, and I will rescue My people from
your hand. Then you will know [with-
out any doubt] that I am the LORD.”

Idolatrous Elders Condemned

14 THEN CERTAIN of the elders
of Israel came to me [seeking an
oracle from God] and sat down before
me.
2And the word of the LORD came to
me, saying,
3“Son of man, these men have set
up [and honored] their idols in their
hearts and have put right before their
faces the [vile] stumbling block of their
wickedness *and* guilt; should I [permit
Myself to] be consulted by them at all?
4“Therefore speak to them and say to
them, ‘Thus says the Lord GOD, “Any
man of the house of Israel who takes
his idols [of rebellion] into his heart,
and puts the [vile] stumbling block of
his wickedness *and* guilt [images of
silver and gold] before his face, and yet
comes to the prophet [to ask of him], I
the LORD will answer him, [but I will
answer him] in accordance with the
number of his idols,
5in order that I may take hold of the
heart (mind) of the house of Israel who
are all estranged from Me because of
their idols.” ’
6“Therefore say to the house of Is-
rael, ‘Thus says the Lord GOD, “Repent
and turn away from your idols and
turn your faces away from all your
disgusting *and* vile acts.
7“For anyone of the house of Israel or
among the strangers who immigrate to
Israel who separates himself from Me,
taking his idols into his heart, and puts
right before his face the [vile] stum-
bling block of his wickedness *and*
guilt, and [then] comes to the prophet
to ask of Me for himself, I the LORD will
answer him Myself.
8“I will set My face against that man
[that hypocrite] and will make him a
sign and a proverb, and I will cut him
off from among My people; and you
will know [without any doubt] that I
am the LORD.
9“But if the prophet [who speaks
without My authority] is enticed to
speak a word [of his own], it is I the
LORD who have caused that prophet
[to speak falsely to please the inquirer,
thus allowing himself to be a party to
the inquirer’s sin], and I will stretch out
My hand against him and destroy him
from among My people Israel.
10“They [both] will bear *the punish-
ment* of their wickedness; the sin of the
[counterfeit] prophet will be the same
as the sin of the [hypocritical] inquirer,
11so that the house of Israel may no
longer drift away from Me and no lon-
ger defile themselves with all their
transgressions, but they will be My
people, and I will be their God,” ’ says
the Lord GOD.”

14:1 – 3 *certain of the elders of Israel.* God revealed to Ezekiel that this group consisted of double-minded men (1Ki 18:21; Mt 6:24; Jas 1:5 – 8). Outwardly, they came to seek a word from God through His true prophet Ezekiel, but in their hearts they harbored loyalties to other gods.

14:5 *take hold of the heart (mind) of the house of Israel.* These words announce God’s restorative purpose (Pr 3:12; Rev 3:19) in allowing sin to run its course.

14:8 *I will cut him off from among My people.* The unrepentant idolater would be separated not only from God, but also from God’s people (13:9). This experience would be a strong visual warning and an international example — proverb — of God’s absolute honoring of His promise to punish disobedience with cursing (Lev 20:1 – 7).

14:9 – 11 *They [both] will bear the punishment of their wickedness.* The relationship between God’s sovereignty and human responsibility is implicit in these verses. God allows false preaching for His own inscrutable purposes, but the preacher is held accountable for the content of the message. These were Israelite false prophets who deliberately ignored the truth and mixed it with falsehood.

22 Jer 23:14 **23** ver. 6; Eze 12:24; Mic 3:6 **CHAPTER 14 1** Eze 8:1; 20:1; 33:31 **3** ver. 4,7; Eze 7:19; 2Ki 3:13 **8** Lev 17:10; 20:3,5,6; Jer 44:11; Eze 15:7; Nu 26:10; Dt 28:37; Eze 5:15; Eze 6:7 **9** 1Ki 22:23; Job 12:16; Jer 4:10; 2Th 2:11 **11** 2Pe 2:15; Eze 11:20; 37:27

The City Will Not Be Spared

12 The word of the LORD came [again] to me, saying,

13 “Son of man, if a land sins against Me by committing unfaithfulness, and I stretch out My hand against it and destroy its source of bread and send famine on it and cut off from it both man and animal,

14 even if these three men, Noah, Daniel, and Job were in that land, by their own righteousness (right standing with God) they could only save (deliver) themselves,” says the Lord GOD.

15 “If I were to cause predatory beasts to pass through the land and they ravaged it *and* depopulated it of children, and it became desolate so that no one would pass through because of the predators,

16 *though* these three men were in the land, as I live,” says the Lord GOD, “they could not save either their sons or their daughters. They alone would be saved, but the land would be desolate (ruined, deserted).

17 “Or if I were to bring a sword on that land and say, ‘Let a sword go through the land and cut off man and animal from it,’

18 even *though* these three men were in the land, as I live,” says the Lord GOD, “they could not save either their sons or their daughters, but they alone would be saved.

19 “Or if I should send a virulent disease into that land and pour out My wrath in blood on it to cut off man and animal from it,

20 even though Noah, Daniel, and Job were in the land, as I live,” says the Lord GOD, “they could not save either their son or their daughter; they would save only themselves by their righteousness [that is, their right-standing with God—their moral and spiritual integrity].”

21 For thus says the Lord GOD, “How much more when I send My four severe judgments against Jerusalem—sword, famine, predatory beasts, and virulent disease—to cut off man and animal from it! [Lev 26:21–33]

22 “Yet, behold, survivors will be left in it [escaping the judgments], both sons and daughters. Listen carefully, they are going to come out to you [in Babylon] and you will see their [wicked] conduct and [despicable] actions; then you will be at peace in regard to the disaster which I have brought against Jerusalem for everything which I have brought on it [has been deserved].

23 “Then they will reassure you [in regard to the appropriateness of the judgments] when you see their [heinous] conduct and actions, for you will know that I have not done without cause whatever I did to it,” declares the Lord GOD.

Jerusalem like a Useless Vine

15 AND THE word of the LORD came to me, saying,

2 “Son of man, how is the wood of the grapevine (Israel) better than any wood of a branch which is among the trees of the forest? [Ps 80:8–13; Jer 2:21]

3 “Can wood be taken from it to make any object? Or can men take a peg from it on which to hang any vessel?

4 “If it has been thrown into the fire for fuel, and the fire has consumed both of its ends and the middle section has been charred, is it suitable *or* useful for anything?

5 “Notice this, even when it was complete, it was not useful *and* was not made into anything. How much less, after the fire has burned [part of] it and [the remainder of] it is charred, can it still be made into anything?

6 “Therefore, thus says the Lord GOD, ‘Like the wood of the grapevine among the trees of the forest, which I have

---

15:6 *the grapevine among the trees of the forest.* Unlike an olive tree whose wood is also useful, the grapevine has only one use, to bear grapes.

13 Lev 26:26; Isa 3:1; Eze 4:16; 5:16 **14** ver. 16,18,20; Jer 15:1; See Jer 7:16; 11:14; 14:11; Pr 11:4 **15** Lev 26:22; Eze 5:17 **16** ver. 14,18,20 **17** Lev 26:25; Eze 5:12; 21:3,4; 29:8; 38:21; Eze 25:13; Zep 1:3 **18** ver. 14 **19** 2Sa 24:15; Eze 38:22; Eze 7:8 **20** ver. 14 **21** Eze 5:17; 33:27 **22** Eze 6:8; Eze 20:43 **23** Jer 22:8,9
CHAPTER 15 **4** Jn 15:6

given to the fire for fuel, so have I given
up the people of Jerusalem;
7 and I set My face against them.
Though they have come out of the fire,
yet the fire will consume them. Then
you will know [without any doubt]
that I am the LORD, when I set My face
against them.
8 'I will make the land desolate (ruined, deserted), because they have
acted unfaithfully [through their idolatry],' says the Lord GOD."

God's Grace to Unfaithful Jerusalem

16 AGAIN THE word of the LORD
came to me, saying,
2 "Son of man, make Jerusalem
understand [the heinous and vile nature of] her repulsive (idolatrous) acts
3 and say, 'Thus says the Lord GOD to
Jerusalem (all of Israel), "Your [spiritual] origin and your birth are from the
land of the Canaanite; your [spiritual]
father was an Amorite and your [spiritual] mother a Hittite. [Ezek 16:45;
John 8:44]
4 "And as for your birth, on the day
you were born your navel cord was not
cut, nor were you washed with water
for cleansing, nor were you rubbed
with salt or even wrapped in cloths.
5 "No eye looked with pity on you
to do any of these things for you, to
have compassion on you; but you were
thrown out in the open field, for you
were loathed on the day that you were
born.
6 "When I passed by you and saw you
squirming in your [newborn] blood,
I said to you while you were there in
your blood, 'Live!' Yes, I said to you
while you were there in your blood,
'Live!'
7 "I made you (Israel) multiply like
plants [which grow] in the field, and
you grew up and became tall and you
reached the age for [wearing] fine jewelry; your breasts were formed and
your hair had grown, yet you were
naked and bare.
8 "Then I passed by you [again] and
looked on you; behold, you were maturing *and* at the time for love, and I
spread My skirt over you and covered
your nakedness. Yes, I swore [an oath]
to you and entered into a covenant
with you," says the Lord GOD, "and you
became Mine."
9 "Then I washed you with water; yes,

15:6 – 8 *the fire will consume them.* God had designed the people of Israel for a particular purpose, to bring glory to His name by living faithfully to His covenant and by bringing the nations to the knowledge of the Lord. Instead, Israel had become like the pagan nations around them.

16:2 *make Jerusalem understand [the heinous and vile nature of] her repulsive (idolatrous) acts.* What follows is an animated development of the dreary story, designed to teach errant Jerusalem the real nature of her character in the eyes of God. The word "abominations" describes that which makes one physically ill.

16:3 *your [spiritual] father was an Amorite and your [spiritual] mother a Hittite.* These shocking words refer to the cultural and moral origins of Jerusalem. Ancient Canaan was inhabited by Semitic and non-Semitic peoples. The Amorites and Hittites are associated in Scripture with the southern hill country, where Jerusalem is (Nu 13:29). The point is that non-Israelites founded this city. Jebusites controlled it when the Israelites entered the land under Joshua (Jos 15:8). Israel did not obtain full control of the city until David conquered it (2Sa 5:6 – 7). In other words, Israel was not as pure as it thought it was.

16:4 *nor were you rubbed with salt.* God reminds Jerusalem that He had rescued them from being like an abandoned newborn child — unwashed, unsanitary, and exposed to the elements to die. God alone has given her glory.

16:6 *while you were there in your blood, 'Live!'* Ezekiel warned the Jews remaining in Jerusalem to repent, reminding them that not merely their existence, but their living relation to God, was dependent upon His free grace. God alone is the Author of eternal life, just as He is Creator of all life (Jn 5:24).

16:7 – 9 *your breasts were formed.* The city is compared to a young woman, mature and lovely. Yet it was naked and bare until God covered it with a relationship of covenantal love. This began when David moved the ark of the covenant there and God established the covenant with David (2Sa 6:1 – 7:17).

---

7 Lev 17:10; Eze 14:8; Isa 24:18; Eze 7:4 **CHAPTER 16** **2** Eze 20:4; 22:2 **3** Eze 21:30; ver. 45 **4** Hos 2:3 **7** Ex 1:7
8 Ru 3:9; Ex 19:5; Jer 2:2

I [thoroughly] washed away from you the [clinging] blood and anointed you with oil.

[10]"I also clothed you with embroidered cloth and put sandals of porpoise skin on your feet; and I wrapped you with fine linen and covered you with silk.

[11]"I adorned you with ornaments and I put bracelets on your wrists and a necklace around your neck.

[12]"I also put a ring in your nostril and earrings in your ears and a beautiful crown on your head.

[13]"Thus you were adorned with gold and silver, and your dress was [made] of fine linen and silk and embroidered cloth. You ate fine flour and honey and oil; so you were extremely beautiful and you advanced *and* prospered into royalty.

[14]"Then your fame went out among the nations on account of your beauty, for it was perfect because of My majesty *and* splendor which I bestowed on you," says the Lord God.

[15]"But you trusted in *and* relied on your beauty and prostituted yourself [in idolatry and its debauched rituals] because of your fame, and you poured out your immoralities on every [willing] passer-by and your beauty was his [as you worshiped the idols of the Gentile nations].

[16]"You took some of your clothes and made for yourself [decorated] high places *and* shrines of various colors and prostituted yourself on them—things which should never have come about and taken place.

[17]"You also took your beautiful jewels *and* beautiful vessels made of My gold and My silver, which I had given you, and made for yourself images of men so that you could prostitute yourself with them;

[18]and you took your embroidered clothing and covered them, and offered My oil and My incense before them.

[19]"Also My bread which I gave you, [made from the] fine flour and oil and honey with which I fed you, you even offered it before idols [no better than cow dung] as a sweet *and* soothing aroma; so it happened," says the Lord God.

[20]"Moreover, you took your sons and your daughters whom you had borne to Me, and you destroyed them as sacrifices [to your man-made gods]. Were your gross immoralities so small a matter?

[21]"You slaughtered My children and offered them up to [worthless] idols, forcing them to pass through the [hideousness of the] fire.

[22]"And in all your repulsive acts and prostitutions (idolatrous immoralities) you did not [pause to] remember the days of your youth, when you were naked and bare, squirming in your [newborn] blood.

[23]"Then it came about after all your wickedness ('Woe, woe to you!' says the Lord God),

[24]that you built yourself an altar for prostitution and made yourself a high place [for ritual prostitution] in every square [of Jerusalem].

[25]"At the beginning of every street you built your high place and made your beauty repulsive; and you offered your body to every passer-by and multiplied your obscene immorality.

[26]"You also prostituted yourself with the Egyptians, your lustful neighbors [by embracing their pagan rituals], and you multiplied your obscene immorality to provoke Me to anger.

[27]"Behold now [listen very carefully], I have stretched out My hand against you, reduced your portion, and handed

16:15 *you trusted in and relied on your beauty.* These words indict God's people for forgetting that their fame and fortune were God's gifts and not their own doing (v. 14). They relied on themselves and their gifts instead of on God. They came to believe that their material wealth and health as a nation absolutely demonstrated God's approval of their spiritual life, even though they were becoming spiritually corrupt.

16:27 – 29 *You prostituted yourself.* Jerusalem's kings had sought political alliances with Assyria (2Ki 15:17 – 20) and Babylon (2Ki 20:12 – 19)

11 Ge 24:22; Pr 1:9 **13** Dt 32:13,14; Ps 48:2 **14** La 2:15 **15** Dt 32:15; Jer 7:4; Mic 3:11; Isa 1:21; 57:8; Jer 2:20; 3:2,6,20; Eze 23:3,8 **16** 2Ki 23:7; Eze 7:20; Hos 2:8 **19** Hos 2:8 **20** 2Ki 16:3; Ps 106:37; Isa 57:5; Jer 7:31; Eze 20:26 **22** ver. 43,60; Jer 2:2; Hos 11:1; ver. 4,5,6 **24** ver. 31; Isa 57:5,7; Jer 2:20; 3:2 **25** Pr 9:14 **26** Eze 8:10,14 **27** ver. 57; 2Ch 28:18

you over to the desire of those who hate
you, the daughters of the Philistines,
who are ashamed of your infamous
behavior.
28"You prostituted yourself with the
Assyrians because you were not sat-
isfied; you prostituted yourself with
them and still were not satisfied.
29"Moreover, you increased your
obscene immorality with the land of
tradesmen, Chaldea (Babylonia), and
yet even with this you were not satis-
fied." ' "
30"How weakened by longing *and*
lust is your heart (mind)," says the Lord
GOD, "while you do all these things, the
actions of a bold *and* brazen prostitute.
31"When you built your shrine altar
for prostitution at the beginning of
every street and made your high place
in every public square, you were not
like a prostitute because you refused
payment.
32"You adulterous wife, who wel-
comes *and* receives strangers instead
of her husband!
33"Men give gifts to all prostitutes,
but you give your gifts to all your lov-
ers, bribing the pagan nations to come
to you [as allies] from every direction
for your obscene immoralities.
34"And you are different from other
[unfaithful] women in your promiscu-
ity, in that no one follows you to lure
you into prostitution, and because you
give money and no money is given you;
in this way you are different."
35Therefore, O prostitute [Israel],
hear the word of the LORD.
36Thus says the Lord GOD, "Because
your lewdness was poured out and
your nakedness uncovered through
your obscene immoralities with your
lovers (pagan allies), and with all your
[repulsive] idols, and because of the
blood of your sons that you gave to
them,
37therefore, listen, I will gather all
your lovers (pagan allies) with whom
you took pleasure, and all those whom
you loved with all those whom you
hated; I will even gather them against
you from every direction and will ex-
pose your nakedness to them that they
may see all your nakedness [making
you, Israel, an object of loathing and
of mockery, a spectacle among the
nations].
38"And I [the Lord GOD] will judge
you like women who commit adultery
or shed blood are judged; and I will
bring on you the blood of wrath and
jealousy. [Num 5:18]
39"I will also hand you over to your
lovers, and they will tear down your
shrines, demolish your high places,
strip you of your clothing, take away
your jewels, and they will leave you
naked and bare.
40"They will also incite a crowd
against you and they will stone you
and slaughter you with their swords.
41"They will burn down your hous-
es with fire and execute judgments
on you in the sight of many women
(Gentile nations). Then I will make you
cease your prostitution, and you will
no longer hire your lovers.
42"So I will calm My wrath toward
you and My jealousy [resulting from
being denied what is rightfully and
uniquely mine] will turn away from
you; I will be pacified and no longer
angry.
43"Because you have not remem-
bered the days of your youth but have

---

instead of relying on their God for security. Probably a part of the treaty-making ceremonies was to worship the other nation's god. For Israel to do this would be a violation of the First Commandment.

16:36 *your lewdness was poured out.* Jerusalem was filthy spiritually because the city had soiled itself by worshiping foreign idols and practicing infanticide (vv. 20–21; Dt 12:29–32).

16:41 *I will make you cease your prostitution.* During the captivity, Israel would abandon idolatry and polytheism, as Ezekiel predicted. God's anger over the people's sin would be satisfied.

---

29 Eze 23:14 **31** ver. 24,39 **33** Isa 30:6; Hos 8:9 **36** ver. 20; Jer 2:34 **37** Jer 13:22,26; La 1:8; Eze 23:9,10,22,29; Hos 2:10; 8:10; Na 3:5 **38** Lev 20:10; Dt 22:22; Eze 23:45; See ver. 20,36; Ge 9:6; Ex 21:12 **39** ver. 24,31; Eze 23:26; Hos 2:3 **40** Eze 23:46; Jn 8:5,7 **41** Dt 13:16; 2Ki 25:9; Jer 39:8; 52:13; Eze 5:8; 23:10,48; Eze 23:27 **42** Eze 5:13 **43** ver. 22; Ps 78:42; Eze 9:10; 11:21; 22:31

enraged Me with all these things, therefore, I in turn will bring your conduct down on your own head," says the Lord God, "so that you will not commit this lewdness on top of all your other repulsive acts.

44 "Behold, everyone who uses proverbs will use this proverb against you: 'Like mother, like daughter.'

45 "You are the daughter of your mother, who loathed her husband and her children. You are the sister of your sisters, who loathed their husbands and their children. Your [spiritual] mother was a Hittite and your [spiritual] father an Amorite.

46 "Now your older sister is Samaria, she with her daughters (outlying cities) who live north of you; and your younger sister is Sodom, she with her daughters who live south of you.

47 "Yet you have not merely walked in their ways or behaved in accordance with their pagan practices; but, as if that were too little, you [soon] acted more corruptly in all your ways than they. [Matt 11:20–24]

48 "As I live," says the Lord God, "Sodom, your sister and her daughters have not done as you and your daughters have done.

49 "Behold, this was the sin of your sister Sodom: she and her daughters (outlying cities) had arrogance, abundant food, and careless ease, but she did not help the poor and needy.

50 "They were haughty and committed repulsive acts before Me; therefore I removed them when I saw it. [Gen 13:13; 18:20; 19:5]

51 "Furthermore, Samaria did not commit half of your sins, but you have greatly increased your repulsive acts more than they. So you have made your [wicked] sisters [Samaria and Sodom] appear righteous *and* justified by [comparison to] all the disgusting things which you have done.

52 "Also bear your disgrace [as punishment], having made judgment favorable for your sisters, for [you virtually absolved them] because of your sins in which you behaved more repulsively than they; they are more in the right than you. Yes, be ashamed and bear your disgrace, for you made your [pagan] sisters seem righteous.

53 "Nevertheless, I will restore them [again] from their captivity, the captivity of Sodom and her daughters (outlying cities), the captivity of Samaria and her daughters, and along with them [I will restore you from] your own captivity [in the day of the Lord God], [Is 1:9]

54 so that you [Judah] will bear your humiliation *and* disgrace, and be [thoroughly] ashamed for all [the wickedness] that you have done to console *and* comfort them.

55 "Your sisters, Sodom and her daughters and Samaria and her daughters will return to their former state; and you and your daughters will return to your former state.

56 "For [the name of] your sister Sodom was not mentioned by you [except as a byword] in the day of your pride [when David ruled],

57 before your [own] wickedness was uncovered. Now you have become an object of reproach *and* a byword for the daughters of Aram *and* of Edom and all who are around her, and for the daughters of the Philistines—those surrounding you who despise you.

58 "You have borne [the penalty of] your lewdness and your repulsive acts," says the Lord.

59 Yes, thus says the Lord God, "I will also deal with you as you have done,

16:44–47 *Samaria . . . Sodom.* Along with Jerusalem, these three are presented as sisters in the religiously and morally corrupt cultures in Canaan. Ezekiel even makes the point that Jerusalem had become more corrupt than the other two.

16:53–59 *you who have despised the oath by breaking the covenant.* The punishment of the exile and captivity was appropriate. The clear promise of the covenant was that blessings and curses were dependent upon Israel's obedience or disobedience (Ex 24; Lev 26; Dt 28–29).

45 ver. 3 **46** Dt 32:32; Isa 1:10 **47** ver. 48,51; 2Ki 21:9; Eze 5:6,7 **48** Mt 10:15; 11:24 **49** Ge 13:10 **50** Ge 13:13; 18:20; 19:5; Ge 19:24 **51** Jer 3:11; Mt 12:41 **53** See Isa 1:9; ver. 60; Jer 20:16 **54** Eze 14:22 **57** 2Ki 16:5; 2Ch 28:18; Isa 7:1; 14:28; ver. 27 **58** Eze 23:49 **59** Eze 17:13; Dt 29:12

you who have despised the oath by
breaking the covenant.

The Covenant Remembered

60"Nevertheless, I will remember
[with compassion] My covenant with
you in the days of your youth, and I
will establish an everlasting covenant
with you. [Ps 106:45]
61"Then you will remember your
ways and be ashamed when you re-
ceive your sisters, both your older and
your younger; I will give them to you
as daughters, but not because of your
covenant [with Me]. [John 10:16]
62"And I will establish My covenant
with you, and you will know [with-
out any doubt] that I am the LORD,
[Hos 2:19, 20]
63so that you may remember [in detail]
and be ashamed and never open your
mouth again because of your humili-
ation, when I have forgiven you for all
that you have done," says the Lord GOD.

Parable of Two Eagles and a Vine

17 NOW THE word of the LORD
came to me, saying,
2"Son of man, ask a riddle and tell a
parable to the house of Israel,
3saying, 'Thus says the Lord GOD,
"A great eagle (Nebuchadnezzar) with
great wings, long pinions and a rich
plumage of many colors came to Leb-
anon (Jerusalem) and took away the
top of the cedar (Judah).
4"He broke off the topmost of its
young twigs (young King Jehoiachin)
and carried it to a land of traders (Bab-
ylonia); he set it in a city of merchants
(Babylon).
5"He also took some of the seed of
the land (Zedekiah, of the royal family)
and planted it in fertile soil *and* a fruit-
ful field; he placed it beside abundant
waters and set it like a willow tree.
6"Then it sprouted *and* grew and
became a low, spreading vine whose
branches turned [in submission] to-
ward him, but its roots remained under
it. So it became a vine and yielded
shoots and sent out branches.
7"There was [also] another great ea-
gle with great wings and many feath-
ers; and behold, this vine (Zedekiah)
bent its roots toward him and sent out
its branches toward him, away from
the beds where it was planted, for him
to water.
8"It was planted in good soil where
water was plentiful for it to produce
leaves *and* branches and to bear fruit,
so that it might become a splendid
vine." '

16:60 – 63 *Nevertheless, I will remember.* Despite Jerusalem's disobedience to the Mosaic covenant and the resulting punishment, the covenant with Abraham — *My covenant* — would still be honored. Fulfillment of the covenant with Abraham did not depend on the people's faithfulness; God had made the promise and He would keep it (Ge 15; 17:7 – 8; Lev 26:40 – 45; Ps 145:13). The everlasting covenant had been made with Abraham before the Hebrew nation even existed. This covenant would be remembered and reestablished with the exiled Judeans. At that time, God's people would be ashamed by the contrast *between their faithlessness and* God's faithfulness and the fact that they were being exalted over those who were less sinful — Sodom and Samaria. The people of these other sinful nations would also inherit land, but only by God's grace, because no such covenant was made with them.

17:2 – 10 *ask a riddle and tell a parable.* Both of these words can be used to refer to an allegory. The "parable" primarily refers to a comparison between two things. A "riddle" was sometimes used as a political contest of mental competition between kings, in which the loser would submit to the winner and be killed. The details of the allegory: *great eagle* is the king of Babylon (v. 12); *Lebanon* symbolizes Canaan, of which Jerusalem (v. 12) is the major city; *the top of the cedar* is the king of Jerusalem and Judah (v. 12); *the topmost of its young twigs* refers to the nobility of Judah; the *city of merchants* is Babylon; *the seed* is a member of the royal family (v. 13); the *fruitful field* is the land where this royal offspring would rule (vv. 13 – 14); *another great eagle* is the king of Egypt (v. 15); and the *vine* is the remnant and ruler left in Judah. This remnant failed to prosper because they made a treaty with the Egyptian Pharaoh. As a result, even the remnant was slain and scattered by Babylon's army (vv. 15 – 21).

60 Ps 106:45; Jer 32:40; 50:5 **61** Eze 20:43; 36:31; Isa 54:1; 60:4; Gal 4:26; Jer 31:31 **62** Hos 2:19 **63** Rom 3:19
CHAPTER 17 **3** See ver. 12; 2Ki 24:12 **5** Dt 8:7; Isa 44:4 **6** ver. 14 **7** ver. 15

9“Thus says the Lord GOD, ‘Ask,
“Will it thrive? Will he (Nebuchad-
nezzar) not uproot it and strip off its
fruit so that all its sprouting leaves will
wither? It will not take a strong arm
or many people to uproot it [ending Is-
rael’s national existence]. [2 Kin 25:1–7]
10“Though it is planted, will it thrive
and grow? Will it not completely with-
er when the east wind touches it? It will
wither in the beds where it grew.” ’ ”
[Hos 13:9–12, 15]

Zedekiah’s Rebellion

11Moreover, the word of the LORD
came to me, saying,
12“Say now to the rebellious house,
‘Do you not know (realize) what these
things *mean?*’ Tell them, ‘Hear this, the
king of Babylon came to Jerusalem
and took its king [Jehoiachin] and its
princes and brought them with him to
Babylon. [2 Kin 24:11–16]
13‘And he took a member of the royal
family [the king’s uncle, Zedekiah] and
made a covenant with him, putting him
under oath. He also took the important
leaders of the land, [2 Kin 24:17]
14so that the kingdom would be in
subjection, unable to restore itself *and*
rise again, but that by keeping his cov-
enant it might continue.
15‘But Zedekiah rebelled against Neb-
uchadnezzar by sending his ambassa-
dors to Egypt so that they might give
him horses and many troops. Will he
succeed? Will he who does such things
escape? Can he indeed break the cov-
enant [with Babylon] and [still] escape?
16‘As I live,’ says the Lord GOD, ‘sure-
ly in the country of the king (Nebu-
chadnezzar) who made Zedekiah [the
vassal] king, whose oath he despised
and whose covenant he broke, in Bab-
ylon Zedekiah shall die.
17‘Pharaoh with his mighty army
and great company will not help him in
the war, when they (the Babylonians)
put up ramps and build siege walls to
destroy many lives.
18‘Now Zedekiah dishonored the
oath by breaking the covenant, and
behold, he gave his hand *and* pledged
his allegiance, yet did all these things;
he shall not escape.’ ”
19Therefore, thus says the Lord GOD,
“As I live, I will bring down on his own
head My oath [made on My behalf by
Nebuchadnezzar] which Zedekiah dis-
honored and My covenant which he
broke.
20“I will spread My net over him, and
he will be caught in My snare; and I
will bring him to Babylon and will
enter into judgment with him there for
his treason which he has committed
against Me.
21“All the choice men [from Judah]
in all his troops will fall by the sword,
and those that survive will be scat-
tered to every wind; and you will know
[without any doubt] that I the LORD
have spoken.”
22Thus says the Lord GOD, “I Myself
will take *a twig* from the lofty top of
the cedar and will set it out; I will crop
off from the topmost of its young twigs
a tender one and I will plant it on a
high and lofty mountain. [Is 11:1, 10;
53:2; Jer 23:5; Zech 3:8]
23“I will plant it on the mountain
heights of Israel, that it may grow

17:11 – 21 *Say now to the rebellious house.* Since Ezekiel had preached earlier about Jerusalem’s past abominations (ch. 16), the people were likely charging God with unfairness in punishing the present population. Ezekiel points out that present and past sins make God’s actions just and fair. In this section, the Lord explains His grounds for using Babylon to judge Judah.

17:22 *I Myself will take.* The Hebrew is emphatic: “I myself will take.” In contrast to human kings, God declared that He personally would pick out, plant, and make prominent “a tender one,” that is a twig or a sprig. Cedar branches are symbolic of rulers on the Davidic throne (17:3 – 4,12 – 13) and elsewhere of a line of David’s descendants prophesied to produce the Messiah (2Sa 7:16; Isa 11:1 – 5; Jer 22:24 – 30; Zec 6:9 – 13; Mt 1:1 – 17).

17:23 – 24 *make the dry tree flourish.* What was accomplished in the restoration under Zerubbabel was a fulfillment of this promise.

9 2Ki 25:7 **10** Eze 19:12; Hos 13:15 **12** Eze 2:5; 12:9; ver. 3; 2Ki 24:11-16 **13** 2Ki 24:17; 2Ch 36:13 **14** ver. 6; Eze 29:14 **15** 2Ki 24:20; 2Ch 36:13; Dt 17:16; Isa 31:1,3; 36:6,9; ver. 9 **16** Jer 32:5; 34:3; Eze 12:13 **17** Jer 37:7; Jer 52:4 **18** 1Ch 29:24; La 5:6 **20** Eze 12:13; Eze 20:36 **21** Eze 12:14 **22** Isa 11:1; Jer 23:5; Zec 3:8; Isa 53:2; Ps 2:6 **23** Isa 2:2,3; See Eze 31:6; Da 4:12

boughs and bear fruit and be a noble *and* stately cedar. And birds of every kind will live under it; they will nest [securely] in the shade of its branches.

24 “All the trees of the field will know that I the LORD bring down the tall tree, exalt the low tree, dry up the green tree, and make the dry tree flourish. I am the LORD; I have spoken, and I will fulfill it.”

God Deals Justly with Individuals

18 THE WORD of the LORD came to me again, saying,

2 “What do you mean by using this proverb concerning the land of Israel,

‘The fathers eat sour grapes [they sin],
But the children’s teeth are set on edge’?

3 “As I live,” says the Lord GOD, “you are certainly not going to use this proverb [as an excuse] in Israel anymore.

4 “Behold (pay close attention), all souls are Mine; the soul of the father as well as the soul of the son is Mine. The soul who sins will die. [Rom 6:23]

5 “But if a man is righteous (keeps the law) and practices justice and righteousness,

6 and does not eat [at the pagan shrines] on the mountains or raise his eyes to the idols of the house of Israel, or defile his neighbor’s wife or approach a woman during her [monthly] time of impurity—

7 if a man does not oppress anyone, but restores to the debtor his pledge, does not commit robbery, but gives his bread to the hungry and covers the naked with clothing,

8 if he does not charge interest or take *a percentage of* increase [on what he lends in compassion], if he keeps his hand from sin and executes true justice between man and man,

9 if he walks in My statutes and [keeps] My ordinances so as to act with integrity; [then] he is [truly] righteous and shall certainly live,” says the Lord GOD. [Ezek 20:11; Amos 5:4]

10 “If he is the father of a violent son who sheds blood, and who does any of these things to a brother

11 (though the father did not do any of these things), that is, the son even eats [the food set before idols] at the mountain *shrines*, and defiles his neighbor’s wife,

12 oppresses the poor and needy, commits robbery, does not restore [to the debtor] his pledge, but raises his eyes to the idols, and commits repulsive acts,

13 and charges interest and takes [a percentage of] increase on what he has loaned; will he then live? He will not live! He has done all these disgusting things, he shall surely be put to death; his blood will be on his own head.

14 “Now behold, if this [wicked] man has a son who has observed all the sins which his father committed, and considers [thoughtfully what he has observed] and does not do like his father:

But as is often the case, in biblical prophecy, the greater fulfillment is still to come in the reign of the Savior King.

18:2–3 ***set on edge.*** The Hebrew word that is rendered here is literally “made dull” but can refer to a sour sensation. The main idea of the proverb is that children are affected by their parents’ behavioral choices just as eating sour grapes produces a bitter taste. However, the people were interpreting and applying this proverb incorrectly; therefore, God said they should not use it any longer.

18:4 ***The soul who sins will die.*** In this verse, the physical, earthly consequences of sinful behavior are being addressed (3:16–21; 33:12–20; Dt 30:15–20).

18:6 ***approach a woman during her [monthly] time of impurity.*** In ancient Israel, intimacy during the woman’s menstrual period was prohibited. The Old Testament does not explain the reason for this, but it may be tied to the special role of blood for the atoning of sin (Lev 15:19–33).

---

24 Lk 1:52; Eze 22:14 **CHAPTER 18** **2** Jer 31:29; La 5:7 **4** Ro 6:23 **6** Eze 22:9; Lev 18:20; 20:10; Lev 18:19; 20:18 **7** Ex 22:21; Lev 19:15; 25:14; Ex 22:26; Dt 24:12; Dt 15:7; Isa 58:7; Mt 25:35 **8** Ex 22:25; Lev 25:36; Dt 23:19; Neh 5:7; Ps 15:5; Dt 1:16; Zec 8:16 **9** Eze 20:11; Am 5:4 **10** Ge 9:6; Ex 21:12; Nu 35:31 **12** Eze 8:6,17 **13** Lev 20:9,11-13, 16,27; Eze 3:18; Ac 18:6

15 "He does not eat [food set before idols] at the mountain *shrines* or raise his eyes to the idols of the house of Israel, or defile his neighbor's wife,

16 or oppress anyone, or take anything in pledge, or commit robbery, but he gives his bread to the hungry and covers the naked with clothing,

17 he keeps his hand from [oppressing] the poor, does not receive interest or increase [from the needy], but executes My ordinances and walks in My statutes; he shall not die for the sin (guilt) of his father; he shall certainly live.

18 "As for his father, because he practiced extortion, robbed his brother, and did that which is not good among his people, behold, he shall die for his sin.

19 "Yet do you say, 'Why should the son not bear the punishment for the father's sin?' When the son has practiced justice and righteousness and has kept all My statutes and has done them, he shall certainly live.

20 "The person who sins [is the one that] will die. The son will not bear the punishment for the sin of the father, nor will the father bear the punishment for the sin of the son; the righteousness of the righteous shall be on himself, and the wickedness of the wicked shall be on himself.

21 "But if the wicked man turns [away] from all his sins which he has committed and keeps all My statutes and practices justice and righteousness, he shall certainly live; he shall not die.

22 "All of his transgressions which he has committed will not be remembered against him; because of his righteousness which he has practiced [for his moral and spiritual integrity in every area and relationship], he will live.

23 "Do I take any pleasure in the death of the wicked," says the Lord God, "rather than that he should turn [away] from his [malevolent] acts and live?

24 "But when the righteous man turns away from his righteousness and commits sin and acts in accordance with all the repulsive things that the wicked man does, will he live? All of his righteous deeds which he has done will not be remembered because of the treachery that he has committed and for his sin which he has committed; for them he shall die.

25 "Yet you say, 'The way of the Lord is not right.' Hear now, O house of Israel! Is My way not right? Is it not your ways that are not right?

26 "When a righteous man turns away from his righteousness, and commits sin and dies because of it, it is for his sin which he has committed that he dies.

27 "Again, when a wicked man turns away from his wickedness which he has committed and practices justice and righteousness, he will save his life.

28 "Because he considered and turned away from all the transgressions which he had committed, he shall certainly live; he shall not die.

29 "Yet the house of Israel says, 'The way of the Lord is not right!' O house of Israel, are My ways not right? Is it not your ways that are not right?

30 "Therefore I will judge you, O house of Israel, each one in accordance with his conduct," says the Lord God. "Repent (change your way of thinking) and turn away from all your transgressions, so that sin may not become a stumbling block to you. [Matt 3:2; Rev 2:5]

31 "Cast away from you all your transgressions which you have committed [against Me], and make yourselves a new heart and a new spirit! For

18:19–32 *Why should the son not bear the punishment for the father's sin?* In this passage, Ezekiel further clarifies his teaching on individual responsibility for sin by answering certain questions that reflect what his audience might be thinking in response to his previous message. God's response to their questions through Ezekiel is, in part, also composed of questions.

15 ver. 6 **18** Eze 3:18 **19** Ex 20:5; Dt 5:9; 2Ki 23:26; 24:3,4 **20** ver. 4; Dt 24:16; 2Ki 14:6; 2Ch 25:4; Jer 31:29,30; Isa 3:10,11; Ro 2:9 **21** ver. 27; Eze 33:12,19 **22** Eze 33:16 **23** ver. 32; Eze 33:11; 1Ti 2:4; 2Pe 3:9 **24** Eze 3:20; 33:12,13,18; 2Pe 2:20 **25** ver. 29; Eze 33:17,20 **26** ver. 24 **27** ver. 21 **28** ver. 14 **29** ver. 25 **30** Eze 7:3; 33:20; Mt 3:2; Rev 2:5 **31** Eph 4:22,23; Jer 32:39; Eze 11:19; 36:26

why should you die, O house of Israel?
[Eph 4:22, 23]
32 "For I have no pleasure in the death
of anyone who dies," says the Lord
God. "Therefore, repent and live!"

Dirge for the Princes of Israel

19 "AS FOR you, take up a dirge
(funeral poem to be sung) for the
princes of Israel
2 and say,

'What was your mother
[Jerusalem and Judah]?
A lioness among lions!
She lay down among young lions,
She reared her cubs.
3 'When she [the royal mother-city]
brought up [Jehoahaz] one of
her cubs,
He became a [young] lion,
And he learned to catch *and* tear
the prey;
He devoured men. [2 Kin 23:30, 32]
4 'The nations heard about him;
He was captured in their pit,
And they brought him with hooks
To the land of Egypt. [2 Chr 36:1, 4]
5 'When she saw, as she waited,
That her hope was lost,
She took another of her cubs
And made him a young lion.
[2 Kin 23:34; 24:1, 6]
6 'And he moved among the lions;
He became a young lion,
He learned to tear the prey;
He devoured men.
7 'He destroyed their palaces
And he flattened their cities;
And the land and all who were in
it were appalled
By the sound of his roaring.
8 'Then the nations set against him
(the king)
On every side from the provinces,
And they spread their net over him;
He was captured in their pit.
[2 Kin 24:8–15]
9 'They put him in a cage with
hooks *and* chains
And brought him to the king of
Babylon;
They brought him in hunting
nets
So that his voice would be heard
no more
On the mountains of Israel.
10 'Your mother [Jerusalem] was like
a vine in your vineyard,
Planted by the waters;
It was fruitful and full of branches
Because of abundant water.
[2 Kin 24:17; Ezek 17:7]
11 'And it had strong branches for the
scepters of rulers,
And its height was raised above
the thick branches *and* into the
clouds
So that it was seen [easily] in
its height with the mass of its
branches.
12 'But the vine was uprooted
in [godly] wrath [by His
representative]
And it was thrown down to the
ground;
The east wind dried up its fruit.
Its strong branch was broken off
So that it withered;
The fire [of God's judgment]
consumed it.
13 'And now it is transplanted in the
wilderness,
In a dry and thirsty land [of
Babylon].
14 'And the fire [of Zedekiah's
rebellion] has gone out from its
branch;
It has consumed the vine's shoots
and fruit,
So that it has in it no [longer a]
strong branch
As a scepter to rule.' "

19:2 – 10 *lioness ... vine in your vineyard.* Most likely both of these terms represented the nation of Israel since each was a "mother" of kings — the "cubs" and the "branches." The vine and lion images are common symbols for Hebrew royalty and nationality (15:1 – 6; 17:1 – 10; Ge 49:9).

19:13 *In a dry and thirsty land.* To anyone who loved the covenantal promises focused on God's worship in Jerusalem, any alternative to Jerusalem was akin to living in the desert.

32 ver. 23; La 3:33; Eze 33:11; 2Pe 3:9 **CHAPTER 19** **1** Eze 26:17; 27:2 **3** ver. 6; 2Ki 23:31,32 **4** 2Ki 23:33; 2Ch 36:4; Jer 22:11,12 **5** 2Ki 23:34 **6** Jer 22:13-17; ver. 3 **8** 2Ki 24:2; ver. 4 **9** 2Ch 36:6; Jer 22:18; Eze 6:2 **10** Eze 17:6; Dt 8:7-9 **11** Eze 31:3; Da 4:11 **12** Eze 17:10; Hos 13:15 **14** Jdg 9:15; 2Ki 24:20; Eze 17:18; La 4:20

This is a dirge (funeral poem to be sung), and has become a dirge.

God's Dealings with Israel Rehearsed

20 IN THE seventh year, in the fifth *month,* on the tenth of the month [after the beginning of the exile in Babylon], certain of the elders of Israel came to inquire of the LORD and sat down before me. [Jer 25:11; 29:10]

2 Then came the word of the LORD to me, saying,

3 "Son of man, speak to the elders of Israel and say to them, 'Thus says the Lord GOD, "Have you come to inquire of Me? As I live," says the Lord GOD, "I will not be inquired of by you." '

4 "Will you judge them, son of man, will you judge them? Then make them know [accurately] *and* understand fully the repulsive acts of their fathers; [Matt 23:29–33; Acts 7:51, 52]

5 and say to them, 'Thus says the Lord GOD, "On the day when I chose Israel and lifted up My hand *and* swore to the descendants of the house of Jacob and made Myself known to them in the land of Egypt, when I swore to them, saying, I am the LORD your God,

6 on that day I swore to them to bring them out of the land of Egypt into a land that I had selected for them, [plentiful and] flowing with milk and honey, [a land] which is an ornament *and* a glory to all lands.

7 "Then I said to them, 'Let every man throw away the detestable things on which he feasts his eyes, and do not defile yourselves with the idols of Egypt; I am the LORD your God.'

8 "But they rebelled against Me and were not willing to listen to Me; they did not throw away the detestable things on which they feasted their eyes, nor did they give up the idols of Egypt.

"Then I decided to pour out My wrath on them and finish My anger against them in the land of Egypt.

9 "But I acted for My Name's sake, that it would not be profaned in the sight of the [pagan] nations among whom they lived, in whose sight I made Myself known to them by bringing them out of the land of Egypt.

10 "So I made them leave the land of Egypt and brought them into the wilderness.

11 "I gave them My statutes and explained My ordinances to them, which, if a man keeps, he will live.

12 "Also I gave them My Sabbaths to be a sign between Me and them, that they might know [without any doubt] that I am the LORD who sanctifies them (separates and sets them apart).

13 "But the house of Israel rebelled against Me in the wilderness. They

---

20:2 – 4 *I will not be inquired of by you.* God explains to Ezekiel that the elders of Israel had forfeited any right to inquire of Him due to the abominations of their fathers. All the people are responsible for their own sins, and this does not mean that these Hebrews were paying for sins their ancestors had committed. Instead, the present generation of Hebrews in exile had clearly shown their failure to learn practical lessons from history, and thus had condemned themselves to repeat many mistakes. These leaders came to God with questions, but the questions were foolish and demonstrated the people's sinfulness. God gives a remedial review of their past.

20:11 *if a man keeps, he will live.* Following their exodus from slavery in Egypt, God began to sanctify the Israelites by revealing to them a code of law and entering a covenant relationship with them on a Creator-creature basis. This does not teach that eternal salvation can be earned by good works, but that the quality of the believer's physical and spiritual life on earth are related to his or her obedience to the living God.

20:12 *I gave them My Sabbaths.* This is an important verse for understanding the Sabbath (Ex 20:8 – 11; Dt 5:12 – 15). Sabbath means "rest." That is, the Sabbath was a day to cease all ordinary work or labor, as clearly emphasized in Exodus 20:8 – 11. The Sabbath was to serve as a sign of God's covenantal relationship with His people, Israel.

CHAPTER 20 **1** Eze 8:1 **3** Eze 14:3 **4** Eze 22:2; Eze 16:2 **5** Ex 6:7; Dt 7:6; Ex 3:8; 4:31; Dt 4:34; Ex 20:2 **6** Ex 3:8,17; Dt 8:7-9; Jer 32:22; ver. 15; Ps 48:2; Da 8:9; Zec 7:14 **7** Eze 18:31; 2Ch 15:8; Lev 18:3; Dt 29:16; Jos 24:14 **8** Eze 7:8 **9** Nu 14:13; Eze 36:21,22 **10** Ex 13:18 **11** Dt 4:8; Neh 9:13; Ps 147:19; Lev 18:5; Ro 10:5; Gal 3:12 **12** Ex 20:8; Dt 5:12; Neh 9:14 **13** Nu 14:22; Ps 78:40; 95:8-10; Pr 1:25; Ex 16:27; Nu 14:29; Ps 106:23

did not walk in My statutes and they despised *and* rejected My ordinances, which, if a man keeps, he will live; and they greatly profaned My Sabbaths. Then I decided to pour out My wrath on them in the wilderness, to annihilate them.

14 “But I acted for My Name’s sake, that it would not be profaned in the sight of the [pagan] nations in whose sight I had brought them out [of slavery].

15 “I also swore to them in the wilderness that I would not bring them into the land which I had given them, [a land of plenty] flowing with milk and honey, which is the ornament *and* glory of all lands,

16 because they rejected My ordinances, and as for My statutes, they did not walk in them; they even profaned My Sabbaths, for their heart continually went after their [worthless] idols.

17 “Yet My eye [looked on them with compassion and] spared them instead of destroying them, and I did not annihilate them in the wilderness.

18 “But I said to their children in the wilderness, ‘Do not walk in the statutes of your fathers nor observe their ordinances nor defile yourselves with their idols.

19 ‘I am the LORD your God; walk in My statutes and keep My ordinances and observe them.

20 ‘Sanctify My Sabbaths *and* keep them holy; and they shall be a sign between Me and you, that you may know [without any doubt] that I am the LORD your God.’

21 “Yet the children rebelled against Me; they did not walk in My statutes, nor were they careful to observe My ordinances, which, if a man keeps, he will live; they profaned My Sabbaths. Then I decided to pour out My wrath on them and finish My anger against them in the wilderness.

22 “Yet I withdrew My hand and acted for My Name’s sake, that it would not be profaned in the sight of the [pagan] nations in whose sight I had brought them out [of slavery].

23 “Moreover, I swore to them in the wilderness that I would scatter them among the [Gentile] nations and disperse them among the countries,

24 because they had not observed My ordinances, but had [dishonored and] rejected My statutes and had profaned My Sabbaths, and set their eyes on the [man-made] idols of their fathers.

25 “[Therefore] I also gave them statutes that were not good and ordinances by which they could not live; [Ps 81:12; Is 66:4; Rom 1:21–25, 28]

26 and I pronounced them unclean because of their offerings [to their idols], in that they made all their firstborn pass through *the fire* [as pagan sacrifices], so that I might make them desolate, in order that they might know [without any doubt] that I am the LORD.” ’ [Lev 20:2–5]

27 “Therefore, son of man, speak to the house of Israel and say to them, ‘Thus says the Lord GOD, “Again in this your fathers have blasphemed Me, in that they acted faithlessly *and* treacherously against Me.

28 “For when I had brought them into the land which I swore to give to them, they saw every high hill and every dark *and* leafy tree [as a place for idol worship], and there they offered their sacrifices and there they presented their offering that provoked My anger; there also they made their sweet-smelling aroma and there poured out their drink offerings.

29 “Then I said to them, ‘What is the high place to which you go?’ So the name of it is called Bamah (High Place) to this day.” ’

30 “Therefore, say to the house of

20:20 *Sanctify My Sabbaths*. This word means “to treat as holy,” “to observe as distinct,” and “to consecrate.” God commands that His Sabbaths be continually maintained by His people as sacred — distinct and separate from ordinary days.

---

14 ver. 9,22 **15** Nu 14:28; Ps 95:11; 106:26; ver. 6 **16** ver. 13,24; Nu 15:39; Ps 78:37; Am 5:25; Ac 7:42 **17** Ps 78:38 **19** Dt 5:32; chs. 6,7,8,10,11,12 **20** Jer 17:22 **21** Nu 25:1; Dt 9:23; ver. 11,13; ver. 8,13 **22** ver. 17; ver. 9,14 **23** Lev 26:33; Dt 28:64; Ps 106:27; Jer 15:4 **24** ver. 13,16; See Eze 6:9 **25** See Ps 81:12; Ro 1:24; 2Th 2:11 **26** 2Ki 17:17; 21:6; 2Ch 28:3; 33:6; Jer 32:35; Eze 16:20; Eze 6:7 **27** Ro 2:24 **28** Isa 57:5; Eze 6:13; Eze 16:19

Israel, ‘Thus says the Lord GOD, “Will you [exiles] defile yourselves in the same manner as your fathers? And will you prostitute yourselves before their loathsome *and* heinous things?

31“When you offer your gifts, when you make your sons pass through the fire, you are defiling yourselves with all your idols to this day. And shall I be asked by you [for an oracle], O house of Israel? As I live,” says the Lord GOD, “I will not be inquired of by you.

32“What comes into your mind will never happen, when you say, ‘We will be like the [pagan] nations, like the tribes of the [Gentile] countries, serving [idols made of] wood and stone.’

God Will Restore Israel to Her Land

33“As I live,” says the Lord GOD, “most certainly with a mighty hand and an outstretched arm and with wrath poured out, I shall be King over you.

34“I will bring you out from the peoples and will gather you from the countries in which you are scattered, with a mighty hand and with an outstretched arm, and with wrath poured out;

35and I will bring you into the wilderness of the peoples, and there I will enter into judgment with you *and* contend with you face to face.

36“As I entered into judgment with your fathers in the wilderness of the land of Egypt, so I will enter into judgment *and* contend with you,” says the Lord GOD. [Num 11; Ps 106:15; 1 Cor 10:5–10]

37“I will make you pass under the rod [as the shepherd does with his sheep when he counts them, and I will count you as Mine and constrain you] and bring you into the bond of the covenant [to which you are permanently bound]. [Lev 27:32]

38“And I will separate from you the rebels and those who transgress against Me; I will bring them out of the land where they temporarily live, but they will not enter the land of Israel. Thus you will know [without any doubt] that I am the LORD. [Heb 4:2, 3]

39“As for you, O house of Israel,” thus says the Lord GOD, “Go, let everyone serve his idols; but later you shall most certainly listen to Me, and you shall no longer profane My holy name with your gifts and with your idols.

40“For on My holy mountain, on the high mountain of Israel (Zion),” says the Lord GOD, “there the whole house of Israel, all of them in the land, shall serve Me. There I will [graciously] accept them, and there I will seek (require) your offerings and the choicest of your gifts, with all your holy *and* sacred things.

41“I will accept you [graciously] as a pleasant *and* soothing aroma when I bring you out from the peoples and gather you from the lands in which you have been scattered; and I will prove Myself holy *and* manifest My holiness among you in the sight of the nations. [Eph 5:2; Phil 4:18]

42“And you will know [without any doubt] that I am the LORD, when I bring

---

20:32 *We will be like the [pagan] nations.* Chosen to be a nation separate from sin and secular ways — a special instrument to reveal God’s glory — Israel’s consistent tendency was to identify with the neighboring ungodly nations and to take on their idolatrous ways (Ex 19:5).

20:33 – 36 *I will bring you out from the peoples.* The judgment of captivity in Babylon had begun in the deportations of 605 and 597 BC and would be continued with Jerusalem’s fall in 586 BC. However, God also promised to restore Judah and to judge her enemies with fury (Dt 4:34). This refers to the Persian conquest of Babylon in 539 BC and to the three returns of the Jews to their land and the rebuilding of their homeland (538 — 330 BC), yet Israel would again be taken captive and made to wander throughout the nations during the Roman occupation.

20:37 *I will make you pass under the rod.* This is the way a shepherd counts and controls his sheep (Lev 27:32; Jer 33:13).

20:39 *Go, let everyone serve his idols.* This is an ironic command; the rest of the verse indicates that God was giving the stubborn people over to what they had decided. God grants each one a destiny consistent with his or her decisions.

---

31 ver. 26 **32** Eze 11:5 **33** Jer 21:5 **35** Jer 2:9,35; Eze 17:20 **36** Nu 14:21-23,28 **37** Lev 27:32; Jer 33:13 **38** Eze 34:17; Mt 25:32; Jer 44:14 **39** Jdg 10:14; Ps 81:12; Am 4:4; Isa 1:13; Eze 23:38 **40** Isa 2:2,3; Eze 17:23; Mic 4:1; Isa 56:7; 60:7; Zec 8:20; Mal 3:4; Ro 12:1 **41** Eph 5:2; Php 4:18 **42** ver. 38,44; Eze 36:23; 38:23; Eze 11:17; 34:13; 36:24

you into the land of Israel, into the land
which I swore to give to your fathers.
43"There you will remember your
ways and all your deeds with which
you have defiled yourselves; and you
will loathe yourselves in your own
sight because of all your evil deeds
which you have done.
44"And you will know [without any
doubt] that I am the LORD when I have
dealt with you for My Name's sake, not
in accordance with your evil ways nor
with your corrupt conduct, O house of
Israel," says the Lord GOD.' "
45Now the word of the LORD came
to me, saying,
46"Son of man, set your face toward
Teman, and speak out against the
south and prophesy against the forest
land of the Negev (the South),
47and say to the forest of the Negev,
'Hear the word of the LORD: thus says
the Lord GOD, "Behold, I am about to
kindle a fire in you, and it will devour
every one of your green trees, as well
as every one of your dry trees. The
blazing flame will not be quenched
and the whole surface from the south
to the north will be burned by it.
48"All flesh will see that I the
LORD have kindled it; it will not be
quenched." ' "
49Then I said, "Ah, Lord GOD! They
are saying of me, 'Is he not [just]
speaking in parables *and* making al-
legories?' "

Parable of the Sword of the LORD

21 AND THE word of the LORD
came to me, saying,
2"Son of man, set your face toward
Jerusalem, and direct your [prophetic]
word against the sanctuaries; prophe-
sy against the land of Israel
3and say to the land of Israel, 'Thus
says the LORD, "Behold, I am against
you and will draw My sword out of its
sheath and I will cut off from you both
the righteous and the wicked.
4"Because I will cut off from you both
the righteous and the wicked, there-
fore My sword will go from its sheath
against all flesh from south to north,
5and all living will know [without
any doubt] that I the LORD have drawn
My sword out of its sheath; it will not
be sheathed again." '
6"As for you, son of man, groan with
breaking heart and bitter grief, groan
in their sight.
7"And when they say to you, 'Why do
you sigh *and* groan?' you shall answer,
'Because of the news that is coming;
and every heart will melt and all hands
will be frail, and every spirit will faint
and all knees will be weak as water.
Behold, it comes and it will happen,'
says the Lord GOD."
8Again the word of the LORD came
to me, saying,
9"Son of man, prophesy and say,
'Thus says the LORD.' Say,

'A sword, a sword [from Babylon]
is sharpened
And also polished!
10'It is sharpened to make a
slaughter,
Polished to flash *and* glimmer like
lightning!'

Shall we then rejoice [when such a di-
saster approaches]? But it rejects *and*
views with contempt the scepter of My
son [Judah]. [Gen 49:9, 10; 2 Sam 7:23]
11"The sword [of Babylon] is ready to
be polished so that it may be handled
and put to use; the sword is sharpened
and polished to be put in the hand of
the slayer (Nebuchadnezzar).

20:44 ***And you will know [without any doubt] that I am the LORD.*** The promise of this verse is that the Lord will gather the nation of Israel from places where they have been dispersed and that they will repent because of the evil things they have done.

20:46–47 ***the forest land of the Negev.*** This refers to the land of Judah—the Southern Kingdom—which had more trees then than now.

21:6 ***groan with breaking heart.*** This phrase translates words that literally mean "breaking of the loins," suggesting intense emotional upheaval.

43 Eze 16:61; Lev 26:39; Eze 6:9; Hos 5:15 **44** ver. 38; Eze 24:24; Eze 36:22 **46** Eze 21:2 **47** Jer 21:14; Lk 23:31; Eze 21:4 **CHAPTER 21** **2** Eze 20:46; Am 7:16 **3** Job 9:22 **4** Eze 20:47 **5** Isa 45:23; 55:11 **6** Isa 22:4 **7** Eze 7:17 **9** ver. 15,28; Dt 32:41 **11** ver. 19

[12]"Cry out and wail, son of man, for it is against My people; it is against all the princes of Israel. They are thrown to the sword along with My [terrified] people. Therefore strike your thigh *and* strike your chest [in grief].

[13]"For this sword has been tested [on others]; and what if it views with contempt the scepter [of Judah]? The scepter shall be no more [but shall be swept away]," says the Lord God.

[14]"Therefore, son of man, prophesy and strike your hands together; and let the sword be doubled the third time [in intensity], the sword for the slain. It is the sword for the great slaughter which surrounds them [so that no one can escape, even by hiding in their inner rooms],

[15]so that hearts may melt, and many will fall at their gates. I have given the glittering sword. Ah! It is made [to flash] like lightning; it is pointed *and* sharpened for slaughter.

[16]"Turn O sword and cut right or cut left, whichever way your thirst for blood *and* your edge direct you.

[17]"I will also strike My hands together, and I will cause My wrath to rest. I the Lord have spoken."

The Instrument of God's Judgment

[18]The word of the Lord came to me, saying,

[19]"As for you, son of man, mark out two ways for the sword of the king of Babylon to come, both starting from the same land. And make a signpost; place it at the head of the way to the city.

[20]"You shall point out a way for the [Babylonian] sword to come to Rabbah [the capital] of the sons of Ammon, and to Judah into fortified Jerusalem.

[21]"For the king of Babylon stands at the parting of the way, at the fork of the two ways, to use divination. He shakes the arrows, he consults the teraphim (household idols), he looks at the liver [of an animal for an omen].

[22]"In his right hand is the lot marked for Jerusalem: to set battering rams, to open the mouth calling for destruction, to lift up the voice with a war cry, to set battering rams against the gates, to put up assault ramps, and to build siege walls.

[23]"It will seem like a false divination in their eyes, those who have sworn solemn oaths [of allegiance to Nebuchadnezzar]. But he will remind them of their guilt [by rebelling and violating their oath], that they may be caught. [2 Chr 36:10, 13; Ezek 17:15, 18–21]

[24]"Therefore, thus says the Lord God, 'Because you have caused your guilt to be remembered, in that your rebellion is uncovered, so that your sins appear in everything that you do—because you have come to mind, you will be seized with the hand [of the enemy].

[25]'And you, O dishonored and wicked one [Zedekiah], the prince of Israel, whose day has come, whose time of final punishment is here,'

[26]thus says the Lord God, 'Remove the turban and take off the crown; things shall not remain as they have been. Exalt that which is low and abase the high.

21:12 ***Cry out and wail . . . strike your thigh.*** Ezekiel was told to add verbal groans and a physical gesture to his musical message. In that culture, these actions displayed great grief and sorrow (Jer 31:19).

21:14 – 17 ***let the sword be doubled the third time.*** This was a numeric device (Pr 6:16) used here to emphasize the extent and effectiveness of the sword's employment against Judah.

21:19 – 20 ***point out a way.*** Ezekiel was to place a signpost at a fork in the road leading to the capital cities of Ammon and Judah.

21:21 ***shakes the arrows.*** There was a method of casting lots using arrows inscribed with names. They were shaken about in the quiver and then dropped to the ground like throwing dice. ***looks at the liver.*** Sheep livers from sacrificed animals were studied. The shades and shapes of various sections of the organ were the basis for a positive or negative prediction.

21:26 – 27 ***turban . . . crown.*** These stand for the priesthood and kingship. Both would be removed from Judah.

---

12 Jer 31:19 **13** Job 9:23; 2Co 8:2; ver. 27 **14** Nu 24:10; 1Ki 20:30 **15** ver. 10,28 **16** Eze 14:17 **17** ver. 14; Eze 22:13; Eze 5:13 **20** Jer 49:2; Am 1:14 **22** Jer 51:14; Eze 4:2 **23** Eze 17:13 **25** Jer 52:2; ver. 29 **26** Lk 1:52

[27]'A ruin, a ruin, I will make it a ruin!
It shall no longer exist until He comes
whose right it is [to reign], and I will
give it *to Him.*' [Gen 49:10; Is 9:6, 7;
11:1–4; Dan 7:14; Luke 1:31–33]
[28]"And you, son of man, prophe-
sy and say, 'Thus says the Lord GOD
concerning the sons of Ammon and
concerning their reproach (disgrace),'
and say: 'A sword, a sword is drawn
for the slaughter; it is sharpened *and*
polished to put an end [to everything],
and to flash like lightning,
[29]while they (Ammonite prophets)
see false visions [of peace] for you,
while they divine lies [of escape] for
you—to place you [of Ammon] on the
headless bodies of the wicked who are
slain, whose day has come, whose time
of the final punishment is here.
[30]'Return the sword to its sheath. In
the place where you were created, in
the land of your origin (birth), I will
judge you.
[31]'I will pour out My indignation on
you [sons of Ammon]; I will blow on
you with the fire of My wrath, and I
will place you in the hand of brutal
men, skilled in destruction.
[32]'You will be fuel for the fire; your
blood will be in the midst of the land.
You will not be remembered, for I
the LORD have spoken.' " [Jer 49:1–6;
Ezek 25:1–7; Amos 1:13–15; Zeph 2:8–11]

The Sins of Israel

22 THEN THE word of the LORD
came to me, saying,
[2]"And you, son of man [Ezekiel], will
you judge, will you judge the city of
bloodshed? Then make her recognize
all her repulsive acts.
[3]"You shall say, 'Thus says the Lord
GOD, "A city that sheds blood in her
midst, so that her time [of doom] will
come, and makes idols to defile her,
contrary to her *interest!*
[4]"You have become guilty by the
blood which you have shed, and you
are defiled by the idols which you have
made. Thus you have caused your day
[of judgment and punishment] to ap-
proach and have arrived at [the com-
pletion of] your years; therefore, I have
made you an object of scorn to the [pa-
gan] nations and a thing to be mocked
by all countries.
[5]"Those who are near and those
who are far from you will mock you,
you [infamous one] of ill repute, full
of turmoil.
[6]"Behold, the princes of Israel, every
one according to his power, have been
intending to shed blood in you.
[7]"In you they have treated father and
mother lightly. They have oppressed
the stranger among you; and in your
presence they have wronged the fa-
therless and the widow.
[8]"You have despised *and* scorned
My sacred things and have profaned
My Sabbaths.
[9]"In you are men who slander for the
purpose of shedding blood, and in your
presence they have eaten [food offered
to idols] at the mountain shrines; in

21:28 *concerning the sons of Ammon.* The Ammonites joined other nations east of the Jordan in raiding Judean territory, in return for protection from Nebuchadnezzar. Later, during the reign of Zedekiah, Ammon, Moab, Edom, and others conspired against Babylon, but with false hopes of help from Egypt (Jer 27:3 – 11).

22:1 – 5 *you have caused your day [of judgment and punishment] to approach.* The city was ripe for judgment. When such hypocrisy is exposed and punishment is executed before the world, God's people become lasting objects of ridicule.

22:6 – 12 *the princes of Israel.* Jerusalem's princes had shed the blood of innocent people (7:27; 11:1; 12:10; 19:1; 21:13). These evil leaders had been (1) taking advantage of parents and the weak; (2) rejecting God and His covenant, leading to ungodliness and inhumanity; (3) murdering the innocent by slandering them; (4) preferring idolatrous religion and its immoral rituals; (5) engaging in sexual immorality with neighbors, family, and relatives; and (6) loving money and using it to get ahead of fellow citizens.

27 Ge 49:10; Lk 1:32 **28** Eze 25:2,3 **29** Eze 12:24; Job 18:20; Ps 37:13 **30** Jer 47:6,7; Ge 15:14; Eze 16:3 **31** Eze 7:8; Eze 22:20 **32** Eze 25:10 **CHAPTER 22** **2** Eze 20:4; Na 3:1 **4** 2Ki 21:16; Dt 28:37; Da 9:16 **6** Isa 1:23 **7** Dt 27:16; Ex 22:21 **8** Lev 19:30 **9** Lev 19:16; Eze 18:6,11

your midst they have committed acts of lewdness.

10 “In you men have uncovered their fathers’ nakedness [the nakedness of mother or stepmother]; in you they have violated women who are [set apart as ceremonially] unclean during their menstrual impurity [or after childbirth].

11 “In you one has committed a shameful act with his neighbor’s wife, another has lewdly defiled his daughter-in-law, and another has violated his sister, his father’s daughter.

12 “In you they have accepted bribes to shed blood; you have taken [forbidden] interest and [a percentage of] profits, and you have injured your neighbors for gain by oppression *and* extortion, and you have forgotten Me,” says the Lord GOD.

13 “Behold, therefore, I strike My hands [together] at your dishonest gain which you have acquired and at the bloodshed which is among you.

14 “Can your heart (courage) endure, or can your hands be strong in the days that I will deal with you? I the LORD have spoken, and will act.

15 “I will scatter you among the nations and disperse you through the countries, and I will destroy your filthiness.

16 “You will defile yourself in the sight of the [Gentile] nations, and you will know [without any doubt] that I am the LORD.” ’ ”

17 And the word of the LORD came to me, saying,

18 “Son of man, the house of Israel has become dross (metallic waste) to Me. All of them are (useless) bronze, tin, iron, and lead in the furnace; they are the dross of silver.

19 “Therefore, thus says the Lord GOD, ‘Because you have all become dross, therefore, behold, I will gather you [O Israel] into the midst of Jerusalem.

20 ‘As they gather silver and bronze and iron and lead and tin into the furnace to blow fire on it in order to melt it, so I will gather you in My anger and in My wrath, and I will put you there and melt you.

21 ‘I will gather you and blow on you with the fire of My wrath, and you will be melted in the midst of it.

22 ‘As silver is melted in the furnace, so will you be melted in the midst of it; and you will know [without any doubt] that I the LORD have poured out My wrath on you [O Israel].’ ”

23 And the word of the LORD came to me, saying,

24 “Son of man, say to her, ‘You [Israel] are a land that is not pronounced clean or rained on in the day of indignation.’

25 “There is a conspiracy of her [false] prophets in her midst, like a roaring lion tearing the prey. They have devoured [human] life; they have taken [in their greed] treasure and precious things; they have made many widows among her.

26 “Her priests have done violence to My law and have profaned My holy things. They have made no distinction between the holy (sacred) and the profane (secular), they have not taught [people] the difference between the unclean and the clean; and they hide their eyes from My Sabbaths, and I am profaned among them.

27 “Her princes within her are like wolves tearing *and* devouring the prey, shedding blood and destroying lives in order to get dishonest gain.

28 “Her prophets have smeared whitewash for them, seeing false visions and divining lies for them, saying, ‘Thus says the Lord GOD’—when the LORD has not spoken.

29 “The people of the land have prac-

22:26 ***Her priests.*** Those who were supposed to be leaders were not examples of separation from worldly ways (Ex 19:6). Some at least were motivated by monetary gain (Mic 3:11).

22:28 ***have smeared whitewash for them.*** The false prophets were involved in “whitewashing” the sins of the nation’s leaders.

10 Lev 18:7,8; 18:19 **11** Lev 18:20; Lev 18:15; Lev 18:9 **12** Ex 23:8; Dt 16:19; Ex 22:25; Jer 3:21 **13** Eze 21:17 **14** Eze 21:7; Eze 17:24 **15** Dt 4:27; Eze 23:27 **16** Ps 9:16 **18** Ps 119:119; Isa 1:22; Jer 6:28 **22** Eze 20:8,33 **25** Hos 6:9; Mt 23:14; Mic 3:11 **26** Mal 2:8; 1Sa 2:29; Lev 10:10 **27** Isa 1:23; Eze 22:6 **28** Eze 13:6,7,10 **29** Ex 23:9; Lev 19:33

ticed oppression *and* extortion and have committed robbery; they have wronged the poor and needy and they have oppressed the stranger without justice.

30 "I searched for a man among them who would build up the wall and stand in the gap before Me for [the sake of] the land, that I would not destroy it, but I found no one [not even one].

31 "Therefore I have poured out My indignation on them; I have consumed them with the fire of My wrath; I have repaid their way [by bringing it] upon their own heads," says the Lord GOD.

Oholah and Oholibah's Sin and Its Consequences

23 THE WORD of the LORD came to me again, saying,

2 "Son of man, there were two women (Israel and Judah), the daughters of one mother (the united kingdom);

3 and they prostituted themselves in Egypt. From their youth they were grossly immoral; in that place their breasts were embraced and their virgin bosom was grasped.

4 "Their names were Oholah the elder and Oholibah her sister, and they became Mine and they gave birth to sons and daughters. And as for [the identity of] their names, Oholah is Samaria (capital city of Israel) and Oholibah is Jerusalem (capital city of Judah).

5 "Oholah played the prostitute while she was Mine; and she adored *and* lusted after her lovers (allies), the Assyrians, her neighbors,

6 who were clothed in purple, governors and officials, all of them attractive young men, horsemen riding on horses.

7 "She bestowed [freely] her immoralities on them, the choicest men of Assyria, all of them; and with all whom she adored *and* lusted after, she defiled herself with their idols.

8 "She did not give up the acts of prostitution that originated *during her time in* Egypt; for in her youth men had lain with her, and they handled her virgin bosom and poured out their depravity on her.

9 "Therefore, I placed her in the hand of her lovers (allies), into the hand of the Assyrians whom she adored.

10 "They uncovered her nakedness; they took her sons and her daughters and they killed her with the sword. So she became notorious among women, and they executed judgments on her.

11 "Now her sister Oholibah saw this, yet she was more corrupt in her lust than she, and her acts of prostitution were more [wanton] than the immoralities of her sister.

12 "She lusted after the Assyrians— governors and officials, her neighbors, magnificently clothed, horsemen riding on horses, all of them desirable young men.

13 "I saw that she had defiled herself; they both *behaved* the same way.

14 "But Oholibah carried her depravity further, for she saw men pictured on the wall, the images of the Chaldeans (Babylonians) sketched *and* portrayed in vermilion (bright red pigment),

15 girded with belts on their loins, with flowing turbans on their heads, all of them looking like officers, like the Babylonian men whose native land was Chaldea.

16 "When she saw [the sketches of] them, she lusted after them and sent messengers to them in Chaldea.

22:30 *searched for a man among them.* God could not find a spiritual leader to guide the people in godliness.

23:4 *Oholah.* In Hebrew, Oholah means "her own tabernacle" and ***Oholibah*** means "My tabernacle is in her." These seem to refer to God's sanctuaries in each land or, in a distinct usage, to the tent shrines for Canaanite idols as opposed to God's true temple.

23:9 – 10 *They uncovered her nakedness.* This means to be stripped bare and so put to great shame. Ezekiel is reminding his audience of how God already had judged Samaria through Assyrian conquest and captivity in 722 BC (2Ki 17:5 – 41).

23:14 *she saw men pictured on the wall.* These lines tell how Judean envoys to Babylon became enamored of Babylonian rulers and their power through pictures (Jer 22:14) on their palace and temple walls.

30 Jer 5:1; Eze 13:5; Ps 106:23 **31** ver. 22; Eze 9:10 **CHAPTER 23** **2** Jer 3:7,8 **3** Lev 17:7; Jos 24:14; Eze 16:22 **4** Eze 16:8,20 **5** Hos 8:9 **8** ver. 3 **9** 2Ki 17:3 **11** Jer 3:8; Jer 3:11 **12** 2Ki 16:7; ver. 6,23 **16** 2Ki 24:1

17“The Babylonians came to her to the bed of love and they defiled her with their evil desire; and when she had been defiled by them, she (Jerusalem) broke the relationship *and* pushed them away from her in disgust.

18“So she flaunted her acts of prostitution and exposed her nakedness; then I became disgusted with her [and turned away], as I had become disgusted with her sister [and turned away].

19“Yet she multiplied her depravities, remembering the days of her youth, when she was actively immoral in the land of Egypt.

20“For she lusted after her lovers [there], whose flesh is like the flesh of donkeys and whose issue is like the issue of horses.

21“Thus you longed for the lewdness *and* vulgarity of your youth, when the Egyptians handled your bosom on account of the breasts of your youth.

22“Therefore, O Oholibah, thus says the Lord God, ‘Behold, I will stir up your lovers (allies) against you, from whom you turned away in disgust, and I will bring them against you from every side:

23the Babylonians and all the Chaldeans, Pekod and Shoa and Koa, and all the Assyrians with them, desirable young men, governors and officials all of them, princes, officers and men of renown, all of them riding on horses.

24‘They will come against you with weapons, chariots, and wagons, and with a company of people (infantry) who will array themselves against you on every side with large shield and small, and helmet; and I will commit the judgment *and* the punishment to them, and they will judge *and* punish you in accordance with their [pagan] customs.

25‘I will set My jealous indignation against you [demanding what is rightfully and uniquely mine], and they will deal with you in fury. They will remove your nose and your ears, and your survivors will fall by the sword. They will take your sons and your daughters; and the survivors will be devoured by the fire.

26‘They will also strip you (Judah) of your clothes and take away your beautiful jewels.

27‘Thus I will put an end to your lewdness and your prostitution *brought* from the land of Egypt, so that you will not lift up your eyes to them or remember Egypt [with longing] anymore.’

28“For thus says the Lord God, ‘Behold, I will place you into the hands of those whom you hate, into the hands of those from whom you turned away in disgust.

29‘They will deal with you in hatred, take all your property, and leave you naked and bare. And the nakedness of your depravity will be uncovered, both your lewdness and your obscene practices.

30‘These things will be done to you because you have prostituted yourself with the [Gentile] nations, because you have defiled yourself with their idols.

31‘You have walked in the way of your sister (Samaria); therefore I will give her cup [of judgment] into your hand.’

32“Thus says the Lord God,

‘You will drink your sister’s cup,
Which is deep and wide [and filled
to the brim].
You shall be laughed at and derided;
It contains much [too much to
endure].

33‘You shall be filled with
drunkenness and sorrow,
With the cup of horror and
desolation,

23:17–18 ***she had been defiled by them.*** This is an allusion to Judah’s turning in disappointment and disgust from relying on Babylon to relying on Egypt (2Ki 23:28–24:1). God’s alienation from Jerusalem is an allusion to the city’s coming defeat by Nebuchadnezzar.

23:24 ***large shield.*** This large shield was rectangular in shape.

23:32–34 ***You will drink your sister’s cup.*** The cup is often symbolic of God’s judgment (Ps 75:7–8; Jer 25:15–29). The phrase portrays how completely Judah would drink the cup of

17 ver. 22,28 **18** Jer 6:8 **19** ver. 3 **22** ver. 28; Eze 16:37 **23** Jer 50:21; ver. 12 **26** Eze 16:39 **27** Eze 16:41; 22:15; ver. 3,19 **28** Eze 16:37; ver. 17 **29** ver. 26; Eze 16:39 **30** Eze 6:9 **31** Jer 25:15 **32** Eze 22:4,5

With the cup of your sister
Samaria.
34 'You will drink it and drain it,
Then you will gnaw its fragments
And tear your breasts;

for I have spoken,' says the Lord GOD.
35 "Therefore, thus says the Lord
GOD, 'Because you have forgotten Me
and cast Me behind your back, there-
fore bear now [the consequences of]
your lewdness and prostitution.' "
36 Moreover, the LORD said to me,
"Son of man, will you judge Oholah
(Samaria, capital of Israel) and Ohol-
ibah (Jerusalem, capital of Judah)?
Then inform them of their atrocities
[the detestable and vile things they do].
37 "For they have committed adultery,
and blood is on their hands. They have
committed adultery [against Me] with
their idols and have even forced their
sons, whom they bore to Me, to pass
through the fire as [an offering of] food
to them (idols).
38 "Moreover, they have done this to
Me: they have defiled My sanctuary on
the same day [of their idolatries] and
have profaned My Sabbaths.
39 "For when they had killed their
children [as offerings] to their idols,
then they came the same day to My
sanctuary to profane it [by daring to
offer a sacrifice there also]. And be-
hold, this they did within My house.
40 "Furthermore, you have even sent
a messenger for men to come from far
away; and behold, they came—those
for whom you bathed, painted your
eyes, and decorated yourself with or-
naments;
41 and you sat on a splendid couch
with a table arranged before it on
which you had set My incense and
My oil.
42 "The sound of a carefree crowd
was with her; and drunkards were
brought from the wilderness with men
of a common sort, who put bracelets on
the hands of the women (both sisters)
and beautiful crowns on their heads.
43 "Then I said concerning the one
(Oholah) worn out by adulteries, 'Will
they now commit adultery with her
when she is like this?'
44 "But they committed adultery with
her as they would with a prostitute. So
they went in to Oholah (Israel) and to
Oholibah (Judah), the lewd women.
45 "And they, righteous men, will
judge *and* condemn them with the
judgment (punishment) of adulteresses
and with the judgment of women who
shed blood, because they are adulter-
esses and blood is on their hands.
46 "For thus says the Lord GOD, 'Bring
up a horde (mob) against them and
hand them over to terror and plunder.
47 'And the horde will stone them with
stones and cut them down with their
swords; they will kill their sons and
their daughters and burn down their
houses with fire.
48 'Thus I will make lewdness cease
from the land, that all women may be
admonished *and* taught not to commit
immoral acts as you have done.
49 'Thus your lewdness will be repaid
to you, and you will suffer the penalty
for your [sinful] idolatry; and you will
know [without any doubt] that I am
the Lord GOD.' "

Parable of the Boiling Pot

24 AGAIN IN the ninth year [of
King Jehoiachin's captivity by
Nebuchadnezzar of Babylon], in the
tenth month, on the tenth [day] of the
month, the word of the LORD came to
me, saying,
2 "Son of man, record the name of the
day, this very day. The king of Bab-
ylon has laid siege to Jerusalem this
very day.

---

wrath, breaking what was already broken. ***tear your breasts.*** This image gives a picture of the resultant agony and anguish.

24:1 – 2 *record the name of the day.* This would be a bitter reminder of God's trustworthiness to do what He promised through the prophets.

---

34 Ps 75:8; Isa 51:17 **35** Jer 2:32; 3:21; 13:25; Eze 22:12; 1Ki 14:9; Neh 9:26 **36** Eze 20:4; 22:2; Isa 58:1 **37** ver. 45; Eze 16:38; Eze 16:20, 21,36,45; 20:26,31 **38** Eze 22:8 **39** 2Ki 21:4 **40** Isa 57:9; Ru 3:3; 2Ki 9:30; Jer 4:30 **41** Est 1:6; Isa 57:7; Am 2:8; 6:4; Pr 7:17; Eze 16:18,19; Hos 2:8 **45** Eze 16:38; ver. 37 **46** Eze 16:40 **47** Eze 16:40; 2Ch 36:17,19; Eze 24:21 **48** Eze 22:15; Dt 13:11; 2Pe 2:6 **49** ver. 35; Eze 20:38,42,44; 25:5
CHAPTER 24 **2** 2Ki 25:1; Jer 39:1; 52:4

3"Speak a parable against the rebellious house [of Judah] and say to them, 'Thus says the Lord GOD,

"Put on a pot; put it on and also
pour water into it;
4"Put in it the pieces [of meat],
Every good piece (the people of
Jerusalem), the thigh and the
shoulder;
Fill it with choice bones.
5"Take the choicest of the flock,
And also pile wood under the pot.
Make it boil vigorously
And boil its bones in the pot."

6'Therefore, thus says the Lord GOD,
"Woe (judgment is coming) to the
bloody city,
To the pot in which there is rust
And whose rust has not gone out
of it!
Take out of it piece by piece,
Without making any choice.
7"For her blood [that she has shed]
remains in her midst;
She put it on the bare rock;
She did not pour it on the ground
To cover it with dust.
8"That it may cause wrath to come
up to take vengeance,
I have put her blood [guilt for her
children sacrificed to Molech] on
the bare rock,
That it may not be covered."

9'Therefore, thus says the Lord GOD,

"Woe to the bloody city!
I will also make the pile [of wood]
high.
10"Heap on wood, kindle the fire,
Boil the meat well [done]
And mix in the spices,
And let the bones be burned.
11"Then set the empty pot
(Jerusalem) back on the coals
So that it may be hot
And its bronze may glow
And its filthiness may be melted
And its rust (scum) may be
consumed.
12"She has wearied Me with toil,
Yet her great rust has not left her;
Her thick rust *and* filth will not be
burned away by fire [no matter
how hot the flame].
13"In your filthiness are lewdness
and outrage.
Therefore I *would* have cleansed
you,
Yet you were not [willing to be]
cleansed,
You will not be cleansed from your
filthiness again
Until I have satisfied My wrath
against you.

14"I the LORD have spoken; it is coming
and I will act. I will not relent, and I
will not have compassion and I will
not be sorry; in accordance with your
ways and in accordance with your
deeds I will judge *and* punish you,"
says the Lord GOD.' "

Death of Ezekiel's Wife Is a Sign

15Also the word of the LORD came to
me, saying,
16"Son of man, listen carefully, I am
about to take away from you the desire
of your eyes [your wife] with a single
stroke. Yet you shall not mourn and

24:5 *flock.* The flock was symbolic of God's chosen people (ch. 34). ***bones.*** Bones were sometimes used as fuel for fire.

24:6 *Without making any choice.* God does not play favorites; His judgment would fall equally on all inhabitants of the city, for they all had sinned.

24:16 *you shall not mourn and you shall not weep.* This command of God may be one of the hardest ever given to one of His servants. The picture of Ezekiel's wife dying and Ezekiel not being allowed to grieve illustrated God's pain over the death of His wife — Jerusalem — and His inability to mourn because the nation deserved the punishment. Ezekiel was called by God to "be a sign to the exiles" by demonstrating what they should do in response to the "death" of their desire and delight — their nation and its capital city. What Ezekiel was commanded to accept and do illustrated the degree of personal sacrifice and separation from ordinary life that the prophetic ministry often required. A long period of mourning was normal in the ancient Middle East.

3 Eze 17:12; See Jer 1:13; Eze 11:3 **6** Eze 22:3; See 2Sa 8:2; Joel 3:3; Ob 11; Na 3:10 **7** Lev 17:13; Dt 12:16 **8** Mt 7:2 **9** ver. 6; Hab 2:12 **11** Eze 22:15 **13** Eze 8:18 **14** 1Sa 15:29; Eze 5:11

you shall not weep, and your tears
shall not flow.
17“Sigh *and* groan in silence; do not
mourn for the dead. Bind on your tur-
ban and put your sandals on your feet,
and do not cover your mustache or eat
the bread of [mourners furnished by
other] men.”
18So I spoke to the people in the
morning, and in the evening my wife
died. And the next morning I did as I
was commanded.
19The people said to me, “These
things that you are doing—tell us, what
do they mean for us?”
20Then I answered them, “The word
of the LORD came to me, saying,
21‘Speak to the house of Israel, “Thus
says the Lord GOD, ‘Behold, I will pro-
fane My sanctuary, the pride of your
strength, the desire of your eyes, and
the delight of your soul; and your sons
and your daughters whom you have
left behind [in Jerusalem] will fall by
the sword.
22‘You will do as I [Ezekiel] have
done; you shall not cover your mus-
tache nor eat the bread of [mourning
brought to you by other] men.
23‘Your turbans will be on your
heads and your sandals on your feet.
You will not mourn or weep, but you
will rot away in your sins and you will
groan to one another. [Lev 26:39]
24‘So Ezekiel will be a sign to you; in
accordance with all that he has done
you will do. And when this [destruc-
tion of the temple] comes, then you will
know [without any doubt] that I am the
Lord GOD.’ ”
25‘As for you, son of man, on the day
when I take their strength *and* their
stronghold from them, their joy and
their glory, the desire of their eyes and
their heart’s [chief] delight (the temple),
and I also take their sons and their
daughters,
26that on that day a survivor will
come to you to let you hear [of the
destruction of Jerusalem] with your
[own] ears.
27‘On that day your mouth will be
opened to him who escaped, and you
will speak and no longer be mute. In
this way you shall be a sign to them,
and they will know [without any doubt]
that I am the LORD.’ ”

Judgment on Gentile Nations—Ammon

25 THE WORD of the LORD came
to me again, saying,
2“Son of man, set your face toward
the Ammonites and prophesy against
them.
3“And say to the Ammonites, ‘Hear
the word of the Lord GOD, for thus
says the Lord GOD, “Because you said,
‘Aha!’ against My sanctuary when it
was profaned and against the land of
Israel when it was made desolate and
against the house of Judah when they
went into exile,
4therefore, behold, I am going to
give you to the people of the East as
a possession, and they will set their
encampments among you and make
their dwellings among you; they will
eat your fruit and drink your milk.
5“I will make Rabbah [your chief
city] a pasture for camels and [the

24:21 *the delight of your soul.* The Judeans had the wrong kind of pride about the temple. Instead of the temple being a place of worship and the house of God, the Judeans took pride in the building as a sign of their importance.

24:22–24 *sign.* When Jerusalem fell, God would prove Himself as trustworthy and righteous, and Ezekiel as His true prophet (v. 27). ***you will know [without any doubt] that I am the Lord GOD.*** The trials that the Israelites were going through would prompt them to depend on the Lord and know that He is holy.

25:2 *set your face toward the Ammonites.* This country corresponds roughly to the present-day country of Jordan with its capital Amman.

25:4 *people of the East.* This is another title for the Babylonians (21:31). Ancient historical records mention Ammon’s subjugation by Nebuchadnezzar five years after the fall of Jerusalem.

17 Jer 16:5; See Lev 10:6; 21:10; 2Sa 15:30; Mic 3:7 **19** Eze 12:9; 37:18 **21** Jer 7:14; Eze 7:20; Eze 23:47 **22** ver. 17; Jer 16:6,7 **23** Job 27:15; Ps 78:64; Lev 26:39 **24** Isa 20:3; Eze 4:3; 12:6,11; Jer 17:15; Jn 13:19; 14:29; Eze 6:7; 25:5 **25** ver. 21 **26** Eze 33:21 **27** Eze 3:26 **CHAPTER 25** **2** Eze 35:2; Jer 49:1; Eze 21:28; Zep 2:9 **3** Pr 17:5; Eze 26:2 **5** Eze 21:20; Isa 17:2; Eze 24:24

cities of] the Ammonites a resting place for flocks [of sheep]. And you will know [without any doubt] that I am the LORD."

[6]"For thus says the Lord GOD, "Because you have clapped your hands and stamped your feet and rejoiced with all the contempt, *and* malice, *and* spite of your soul against the land of Israel,

[7]therefore, behold, I have stretched out My hand against you and will hand you over as prey *and* spoil to the nations. And I will cut you off from the peoples and will cause you to perish from the countries; I will destroy you. Then you shall know [without any doubt] that I am the LORD." [Jer 49:1–6; Ezek 21:28–32; Amos 1:13–15; Zeph 2:8–11]

Moab

[8]"Thus says the Lord GOD, "Because Moab and Seir (Edom) say, 'Behold, the house of Judah is like all the [pagan] nations,'

[9]therefore, behold, I will deprive the flank of Moab of its cities which are on its frontiers, the glory of the land, Beth-jeshimoth, Baal-meon and Kiriathaim.

[10]"I will give it, along with the children of Ammon, to the people of the East as a possession, so that the children of Ammon will not be remembered among the nations [any longer].

[11]"Thus I will execute judgment *and* punishment on Moab, and they will know [without any doubt] that I am the LORD." [Is 15, 16; Jer 48; Amos 2:1–3; Zeph 2:8–11]

Edom

[12]"Thus says the Lord GOD, "Because Edom has acted against the house of Judah by taking vengeance, and has greatly offended *and* has incurred grievous guilt by taking revenge on them,"

[13]therefore thus says the Lord GOD, "I will also stretch out My hand against Edom and I will cut off *and* destroy man and beast. I will make it desolate; from Teman even to Dedan they will fall by the sword.

[14]"I will take My vengeance on Edom by the hand of My people Israel. Therefore, they will act in Edom in accordance with My anger and My wrath, and they will know *and* experience My vengeance," says the Lord GOD. [Is 34; Ezek 35; Amos 1:11, 12; Obad]

Philistia

[15]"Thus says the Lord GOD, "Because the Philistines have acted revengefully and have taken vengeance [contemptuously] with malice in their hearts to destroy with everlasting hostility *and* hatred,"

[16]therefore thus says the Lord GOD, "Behold, I will stretch out My hand against the Philistines, and I will cut off the Cherethites and destroy the remnant of the seacoast.

[17]"I will execute great vengeance on them with wrathful rebukes *and* chastisements and they will know [without any doubt] that I am the LORD when I lay My vengeance on them." ' " [Is 14:29–31; Jer 47; Amos 1:6–8; Zeph 2:4–7; Zech 9:5–7]

Judgment on Tyre

26 NOW IN the eleventh year, on the first [day] of the month [after the capture of King Jehoiachin], the word of the LORD came to me, saying,

---

Arab invaders came to dominate the territory, and Persian control began about 530 BC.

25:8 – 12 *Moab and Seir.* Moab was south of Ammon and east of the Dead Sea. Seir (Edom) was located south of Moab. They were the descendants of Esau.

25:15 *Philistines.* The Philistines were along the Mediterranean coast in southwest Palestine.

25:16 *Cherethites.* This term was used here as a substitute term for some or all of the Philistines who had migrated from Crete. Their remote ancestors were Aegeans.

26:2 *Tyre.* Tyre was a major seaport and the leading city in Phoenicia (present-day Lebanon). ***has said.*** The past tense could refer to an event that had not yet taken place, using a Hebrew

---

6 Job 27:23; La 2:15; Zep 2:15; Eze 36:5 **7** Eze 35:3 **8** Isa 15; 16; Jer 48:1; Am 2:1; Eze 35:2,5 **10** ver. 4; Eze 21:32 **12** 2Ch 28:17; Ps 137:7; Jer 49:7,8; Am 1:11; Ob 10 **14** Isa 11:14 **15** Jer 25:20; Am 1:6; 2Ch 28:18 **16** Zep 2:4; 1Sa 30:14; Jer 47:4 **17** Eze 5:15; Ps 9:16

2"Son of man, because Tyre has said
against Jerusalem, 'Aha! The gateway
of the people is broken; she is open to
me. I will be filled, *now that* she is a
desolate waste,'
3therefore, thus says the Lord GOD,
'Behold, I am against you, O Tyre, and
I will cause many nations to come up
against you, as the sea makes its waves
crest.
4'They will destroy the walls of Tyre
and break down her towers; and I will
scrape her dust *and* debris from her
and make her as bare as [the top of]
a rock.
5'Her island in the midst of the sea
will become a dry place to spread nets,
for I have spoken,' says the Lord GOD,
'and she will become a prey *and* a spoil
for the nations.
6'Also Tyre's daughters (towns, vil-
lages) on the mainland will be killed by
the sword, and they will know [without
any doubt] that I am the LORD.' "
7For thus says the Lord GOD, "Be-
hold, I will bring upon Tyre from the
north Nebuchadnezzar the king of
Babylon, king of kings, with horses
and chariots and with horsemen and
a great army.
8"He will kill your daughters on the
mainland with the sword, and he shall
make siege walls against you and build
a siege ramp against you and raise [a
roof of] large shields [as a defense]
against you.
9"He will direct the [shocking] blow
of his battering rams against your
walls, and he will tear down your tow-
ers with his crowbars.
10"Because of the great number of
his horses, their dust will cover you;
your walls [O Tyre] will shake from
the noise of the horsemen and the wag-
ons and the chariots when he enters
your gates as men enter a city that is
breached.
11"With the hoofs of his horses Neb-
uchadnezzar will trample all your
streets; with the sword he will kill
your people, and your strong pillars
(obelisks) will fall to the ground.
12"Also they will take your riches
as spoil and plunder your merchan-
dise, and tear down your walls and
your pleasant houses, and throw your
stones and your timber and the debris
[from your city] out in the water.
13"So I will silence your songs, and
the sound of your lyres will no longer
be heard.
14"I will make you [Tyre] a bare rock;
you will be a dry place on which to
spread nets. You will never be rebuilt,
for I the LORD have spoken," says the
Lord GOD.
15Thus says the Lord GOD to Tyre,
"Shall not the coastlands shake at the
sound of your fall when the wounded
groan, when the slaughter occurs in
your midst?
16"Then all the princes of the sea will
go down from their thrones and re-
move their robes and take off their em-
broidered garments. They will clothe
themselves with trembling; they will
sit on the ground, tremble again and
again, and be appalled at you.
17"They will take up a dirge (funeral
poem to be sung) for you and say to
you,

'How you have perished *and*
vanished, O renowned city,
From the seas, O renowned city,
Which was mighty on the sea,
She and her inhabitants,
Who imposed her terror
On all who lived there!
18'Now the coastlands will tremble
On the day of your fall;

---

idiom which describes a future event so certain that it can be expressed as having already been accomplished (Isa 9:6; 52:13 – 53:12).

26:7 – 14 *I will make you [Tyre] a bare rock.* This prophecy of Tyre's fate had two steps. First the Babylonian army under Nebuchadnezzar laid siege to it, and Persia defeated it in about 525 BC. Then in 322 BC Alexander the Great defeated it again when his army built a causeway a half a mile long between the shore and the city on its island. He tore down defensive walls to build the causeway.

CHAPTER 26 **2** Isa 23; Jer 25:22; Am 1:9; Zec 9:2; Eze 25:3 **4** ver. 14 **5** Eze 27:32 **6** Eze 25:5 **7** Ezr 7:12; Da 2:37 **8** Eze 21:22 **13** Isa 14:11; 24:8; Jer 7:34; 25:10; Isa 23:16; Eze 28:13; Rev 18:22 **14** ver. 4,5 **15** ver. 18; Jer 49:21; Eze 27:28 **16** Isa 23:8; Jnh 3:6; Job 2:13; Eze 32:10; Eze 27:35 **17** Eze 27:32; Rev 18:9; Isa 23:4 **18** ver. 15

Yes, the coastlands which are by
the sea
Will be terrified at your
departure.' "

19 For thus says the Lord GOD, "When
I make you a desolate city, like the
cities which are not inhabited, when I
bring up the deep over you and great
waters cover you,
20 then I will bring you down with
those who descend into the pit (the
place of the dead), to the people of old,
and I will make you [Tyre] live in the
depths of the earth, like the ancient
ruins, with those who go down to the
pit, so that you will not be inhabited;
but I will set glory *and* splendor in the
land of the living.
21 "I will bring terrors on you and
you will be no more. Though you will
be sought, yet you will never be found
again," says the Lord GOD.

Dirge for Tyre

27 THE WORD of the LORD came
to me again, saying,
2 "Now you, son of man, take up a
dirge (funeral poem to be sung) for Tyre,
3 and say to Tyre, who lives at the
entrance to the sea, merchant of the
peoples to many coastlands, 'Thus
says the Lord GOD,

"O Tyre, you have said, 'I am
perfect in beauty.'
4 "Your borders are in the heart of
the seas;
Your builders have perfected your
beauty.
5 "They have made all your planks
of fir trees from Senir;
They have taken a cedar from
Lebanon to make a mast for you.
6 "Of the oaks of Bashan they have
made your oars;
They have made your deck of
boxwood from the coastlands of
Cyprus, inlaid with ivory.
7 "Your sail was of fine embroidered
linen from Egypt
So that it became your
distinguishing mark (insignia);
Your [ship's] awning [which
covered you] was blue and
purple from the coasts of
Elishah [of Asia Minor].
8 "The inhabitants of Sidon and
[the island] of Arvad were your
oarsmen;
Your skilled *and* wise men, O Tyre,
were with you; they were your
pilots.
9 "The elders of Gebal and its skilled
and wise men were with you,
repairing your leaks;
All the ships of the sea with their
mariners were with you to deal
in your merchandise.

10 "Persia and Lud and Put (Libya)
were in your army as your men of war.
They hung the shield and the helmet
on you; they gave you splendor.
11 "The men of Arvad with your army
were upon your walls, all around, and
the Gammadim (men of valor) were in
your towers. They hung their shields
on your walls, all around; they perfect-
ed your beauty.
12 "Tarshish [in Spain] was your cus-
tomer *and* traded with you because
of the abundance of your riches of all
kinds; with silver, iron, tin, and lead
they paid for your wares.
13 "Javan (Greece), Tubal and
Meshech (Asia Minor) traded with you;

27:1 – 25 *take up a dirge (funeral poem to be sung) for Tyre.* Prosperity often leads to pride, which results in the abandonment of God (Dt 18:11 – 14). Jerusalem and Tyre both claimed to be unique, the former because of her exclusive claim to true religion and the latter because of the exclusive emphasis on material gain. Yet the wealth of Tyre vanished quickly.

27:6 *Bashan.* This was the broad and fertile plateau east of the Sea of Galilee and the upper Jordan.

27:8 *Sidon.* Sidon was a Phoenician seaport about 30 miles north of Tyre. The two cities were rivals but Tyre tended to dominate.

27:10 – 11 *Lud and Put.* These places were thought to be in western Asia Minor and Africa.

27:13 *Javan (Greece), Tubal and Meshech.* Javan is Greece. Tubal and Meshech are thought to have been in eastern Asia Minor or modern Turkey.

20 Eze 32:18,23 **21** Eze 28:19; Ps 37:36 **CHAPTER 27** **2** Eze 26:17 **3** Eze 28:2; Isa 23:3; Eze 28:12 **5** Dt 3:9 **6** Jer 2:10 **9** 1Ki 5:18; Ps 83:7 **11** ver. 3 **12** Ge 10:4; 2Ch 20:36 **13** Ge 10:2; Rev 18:13

with the lives of men [taken as slaves]
and vessels of bronze they paid for
your merchandise.
14"Those from Beth-togarmah (Ar-
menia) traded for your wares with
[chariot] horses, war horses, and
mules.
15"The men of Dedan were your
traders. Many coastlands were your
markets; ivory tusks and ebony they
brought to you in payment *or* as gifts.
16"Aram traded with you because of
the abundance of the goods you made.
They paid for your merchandise with
emeralds, purple, embroidered work,
fine linen, coral, and rubies.
17"Judah and the land of Israel, they
were your traders; with the wheat of
Minnith [in Ammon], cakes, honey,
oil, and balm they paid for your goods.
18"Damascus traded with you be-
cause of the abundance of your hand-
iworks and the immense wealth of
every kind, with the wine of Helbon
[Aleppo] and the white wool [of Sachar
in Syria].
19"Vedan and Javan traded with
yarn from Uzal [in Arabia] for your
wares; wrought iron, cassia, and sweet
cane were among your merchandise.
20"Dedan traded with you in saddle
blankets for riding.
21"Arabia and all the princes of Ke-
dar, they were your customers for
lambs, rams, and goats [favored by
you]; for these they were your cus-
tomers.
22"The merchants of Sheba and
Raamah [in Arabia], they traded with
you; they paid for your wares with the
choicest of all kinds of spices and all
kinds of precious stones and gold.
23"Haran and Canneh and Eden [in
Mesopotamia], the merchants of Sheba
[on the Euphrates], Asshur and Chil-
mad traded with you.
24"They traded with you in choice
fabrics *and* garments, in clothes of blue
or violet and embroidered work, and
in [treasures of] multi-colored damask
and knotted carpets bound with tightly
wound cords, *which were* among your
merchandise.
25"The ships of Tarshish were the
caravans for your merchandise,

And you [Tyre] were replenished
and very glorious [heavily laden
with an imposing fleet]
In the heart of the seas.
26"Your rowers have brought you
Into great *and* deep waters;
The east wind has broken *and*
shipwrecked you
In the heart of the seas.
27"Your riches, your wares, your
merchandise
Your oarsmen and your pilots,
Your caulkers, your dealers in
merchandise,
And all your men of war who are
with you,
With all your company that is in
your midst,
Will sink in the heart of the seas
On the day of your ruin.
28"The pasture lands *and* the
countryside will shake
At the [piercing] sound of the
[hopeless, wailing] cry of your
pilots.
29"All who handle the oar,
The mariners and all the pilots of
the sea

27:14 *Beth-togarmah.* This phrase may refer to the people of Armenia in eastern Asia Minor (38:6).
27:15 *Dedan.* This may have been "Redan" or Rhodes which was a major trading center in the southern Aegean Sea.
27:17 *balm.* Balm was an aromatic resin or other gummy substance that may have had medicinal value (Jer 8:22).
27:19 *cassia.* Cassia was either a type of cinnamon tree or a plant from which perfume and incense were made. ***sweet cane.*** This refers to an oil-producing reed found in swamps.
27:21 *Kedar.* Kedar was a nomadic tribe in Arabia.
27:22 *Sheba and Raamah.* These places were located near Arabia (Ge 10:6–7).
27:23 *Canneh and Eden . . . Chilmad.* These three places were probably in Mesopotamia, most likely south of Haran.

14 Eze 38:6 **15** Ge 10:7 **17** Jdg 11:33; Jer 8:22 **20** Ge 25:3 **21** Ge 25:13; Isa 60:7 **22** Ge 10:7; 1Ki 10:1,2; Ps 72:10; Isa 60:6 **23** Ge 11:31; 2Ki 19:12; Ge 25:3 **25** Ps 48:7; Isa 2:16; ver. 4 **26** Ps 48:7 **27** Pr 11:4 **28** Eze 26:15 **29** Rev 18:17

Will come down from their ships;
They will stand on the shore,
30 And they will make their voice heard [as they wail loudly] over you
And they will cry bitterly.
They will throw dust on their heads;
They will wallow in ashes.
31 "And they will make themselves [completely] bald for you
And wrap themselves in sackcloth;
And in bitterness of soul they will weep for you
With bitter mourning *and* wailing.
32 "In their wailing they will take up a dirge (funeral poem to be sung) for you
And sing a dirge for you:
'Who is like Tyre,
Like her who is silent [destroyed] in the midst of the sea?
33 'When your wares went out to the sea,
You met the desire, *and* the demand, *and* the necessities of many people;
You enriched the kings of the earth
With your abundant wealth and merchandise.
34 'Now you are shattered by the seas
In the depths of the waters;
Your merchandise and all your crew
Have gone down with you.
35 'All the inhabitants of the coastlands
Are aghast *and* appalled at you,
And their kings are horribly frightened *and* shudder;
Their faces twitch *and* pale.
36 'The merchants among the people hiss at you [with malicious joy];
You have become a horror *and* a source of terrors.
You will cease to be forever.' " ' "

Tyre's King Overthrown

28 THE WORD of the LORD came again to me, saying,
2 "Son of man, say to the prince of
Tyre, 'Thus says the Lord GOD,

"Because your heart is lifted up
And you have said *and* thought, 'I am a god,
I sit in the seat of the gods
In the heart of the seas';
Yet you are [only] a man [weak, feeble, made of earth] and not God,
Though you [imagine yourself to be more than mortal and] think your mind is as [wise as] the mind of God—
3 Behold, you are [imagining yourself] wiser than Daniel;
There is no secret [you think] that is hidden from you;
4 With your [own] wisdom and with your [own] understanding
You have acquired your riches *and* power
And have brought gold and silver into your treasuries;
5 By your great wisdom and by your trade
You have increased your riches *and* power,
And your heart is proud *and* arrogant because of your wealth;
6 Therefore thus says the Lord GOD,
'Because you have imagined your mind [to be]
Like the mind of God [having thoughts and plans like God Himself], [Obad 3]
7 Therefore, behold, I will bring strangers (Babylonians) upon you,
The most ruthless *and* violent of the nations.

28:2 ***Because your heart is lifted up.*** Ezekiel rebuked the king of Tyre for imagining that by his wisdom he had acquired his riches of silver and gold. He had filled the city with violence because of the abundance and unrighteousness of his trade. God would therefore bring a ruthless nation against him.

30 Job 2:12; Rev 18:19; Est 4:1,3; Jer 6:26 **31** Jer 16:6 **32** Eze 26:17; Rev 18:18 **33** Rev 18:19 **34** Eze 26:19; ver. 27 **35** Eze 26:15 **36** Jer 18:16; Eze 26:21 **CHAPTER 28** **2** ver. 9; Eze 27:3,4; Isa 31:3 **3** Zec 9:2 **5** Ps 62:10; Zec 9:3 **7** Eze 30:11; 31:12; 32:12

And they will draw their swords
Against the beauty of your wisdom [O Tyre]
And defile your splendor.
8 'They will bring you down to the pit [of destruction],
And you will die the death of all those who die
In the heart of the seas.
9 'Will you still say, "I am a god,"
In the presence of him who kills you?
But you are [only] a man [made of earth] and not God,
In the hands of those who wound *and* profane you.
10 'You will die the death of the uncircumcised [barbarian]
By the hand of strangers,
For I have spoken!' says the Lord GOD." ' "

11 Again the word of the LORD came
to me, saying,
12 "Son of man, take up a dirge (funeral poem to be sung) for the king of Tyre and say to him, 'Thus says the Lord GOD,

"You had the full measure of perfection *and* the finishing touch [of completeness],
Full of wisdom and perfect in beauty.
13 "You were in Eden, the garden of God;
Every precious stone was your covering:
The ruby, the topaz, and the diamond;
The beryl, the onyx, and the jasper;
The lapis lazuli, the turquoise, and the emerald;
And the gold, the workmanship of your settings and your sockets,
Was in you.
They were prepared
On the day that you were created.
[Gen 3:14, 15; Is 14:12–15; Matt 16:23]
14 "You were the anointed cherub who covers *and* protects,
And I placed you there.
You were on the holy mountain of God;
You walked in the midst of the stones of fire [sparkling jewels].
[Ex 24:10]
15 "You were blameless in your ways
From the day you were created
Until unrighteousness *and* evil were found in you.
16 "Through the abundance of your commerce
You were internally filled with lawlessness *and* violence,
And you sinned;
Therefore I have cast you out as a profane *and* unholy thing
From the mountain of God.
And I have destroyed you,
O covering cherub,
From the midst of the stones of fire.
17 "Your heart was proud *and* arrogant because of your beauty;
You destroyed your wisdom for the sake of your splendor.

28:10 ***the death of the uncircumcised.*** This term denotes a disgraceful death (31:18).
28:12 ***king of Tyre.*** The lamentation is for the king of Tyre because he is exhibiting the character and attitudes of Satan. ***You had the full measure.*** In effect, the king affixed the official seal of his signet ring to the plans that made Tyre one of the leading centers of commerce in that day.
28:14 ***cherub.*** Satan was a created being (v. 13). He does not have the characteristics of God. He belonged to the order of angels called Cherubim. ***the holy mountain of God.*** The focus here seems to be on the king of Tyre's attempt to enter into the council of the gods. So instead of the verse referring to the king's presence in Jerusalem, it could refer more logically to a Phoenician ritual, the celebration of their patron god Melqart's fiery resurrection. This king wanted to imitate Melqart.
28:15 ***blameless.*** Satan was not created evil. ***unrighteousness and evil.*** The Bible does not say where this iniquity came from, but his sin was pride (1Ti 3:6).
28:16 – 19 ***the abundance of your commerce.*** The expression is most easily and appropriately applied to the human king who was the driving force behind the development of Tyre's commercial empire.
28:17 ***because of your beauty.*** This was part

9 ver. 2 **10** Eze 31:18; 32:19,21, 25,27 **12** Eze 27:2; ver. 3; Eze 27:3 **13** Eze 31:8,9; Eze 26:13 **14** ver. 16; See Ex 25:20; Eze 20:40 **16** ver. 14 **17** ver. 2,5

I cast you to the ground;
I lay you before kings,
That they might look at you.
18 "You profaned your sanctuaries
By the great quantity of your sins
and the enormity of your guilt,
By the unrighteousness of your
trade.
Therefore I have brought forth a
fire from your midst;
It has consumed you,
And I have reduced you to ashes
on the earth
In the sight of all who look at you.
19 "All the peoples (nations) who
knew you
Are appalled at you;
You have come to a horrible *and*
terrifying end
And will forever cease to be." ' "
[Is 23; Joel 3:4–8; Amos 1:9, 10;
Zech 9:3, 4]

Judgment of Sidon

20 Again the word of the LORD came
to me, saying,
21 "Son of man, set your face toward
Sidon, and prophesy against her
22 and say, 'Thus says the Lord GOD,

"Behold, I am against you, O Sidon,
And I will show My glory *and* be
glorified in your midst.
Then they will know [by personal
experience] that I am the LORD
when I bring judgment *and*
punishment on her,
And I will manifest My holiness in
her.
23 "For I will send virulent disease to
her
And blood into her streets,
And the wounded will fall in her
midst
By the sword upon her from every
side,
And they shall know [without any
doubt] that I am the LORD.

24 "And there will no longer be a briar
or a painful thorn to prick the house
of Israel from all those around them
who treated them with contempt; then
they will know [with clarity] that I am
the Lord GOD."

Israel Regathered

25 'Thus says the Lord GOD, "When I
gather the house of Israel from the na-
tions among whom they are scattered,
and I manifest my Holiness in them in
the sight of the nations, then they will
live in their own land which I gave to
My servant Jacob.
26 "They shall live in it securely; and
they will build houses, plant vineyards
and live securely when I execute judg-
ment on all those around them who
despise them. Then they will know
[with clarity and confidence] that I am
the LORD their God." ' "

Judgment of Egypt

29 IN THE tenth year [of the cap-
tivity of King Jehoiachin by the
king of Babylon], in the tenth *month*,
on the twelfth of the month, the word
of the LORD came to me, saying,
2 "Son of man, set your face toward
Pharaoh king of Egypt, and prophesy
against him and against all Egypt.
3 "Speak and say, 'Thus says the Lord
GOD,

"Behold, I am against you,
Pharaoh king of Egypt,
The great monster that lies in the
midst of his rivers,

---

of the sin of pride, which made Satan want to be like the Most High (Isa 14:13 – 14). ***cast you to the ground.*** Jesus said that He saw Satan fall (Lk 10:18).
28:24 ***briar or a painful thorn.*** These words refer to the nations around Israel who had been enemies and evil influences. When the judgments were executed fully, these nations would no longer be able to harass and oppress Israel.
29:3 ***The great monster.*** The Pharaoh is pictured here as a crocodile. Pharaoh's arrogant pride is described by his words about the Nile River, "I have made it for myself."

19 Eze 26:21; 27:36 **21** Eze 6:2; 25:2; 29:2; Isa 23:4,12; Jer 25:22; 27:3; Eze 32:30 **22** Ex 14:4,17; Eze 39:13; Ps 9:16; ver. 25; Eze 20:41; 36:23 **23** Eze 38:22 **24** Nu 33:55; Jos 23:13 **25** Isa 11:12; Eze 11:17; 20:41; 34:13; 37:21; ver. 22 **26** Jer 23:6; Eze 36:28; Isa 65:21; Am 9:14; Jer 31:5 **CHAPTER 29** **2** Eze 28:21; Isa 19:1; Jer 25:19; 46:2,25 **3** ver. 10; Jer 44:30; Eze 28:22; Ps 74:13,14; Isa 27:1; 51:9; Eze 32:2; See Eze 28:2

[Boastfully] declaring, 'My Nile is
my own, and I have made it for
myself.'
4 "I will put hooks in your jaws
And [I will] make the fish of your
rivers stick to your scales.
And I will pull you up from the
midst of your rivers,
And all the fish of your rivers will
stick to your scales.
5 "I will abandon you to the
wilderness, you and all the fish
of your rivers;
You will fall on the open field; and
you will not be gathered up or
buried.
I have given you as food to the
[wild] animals of the earth and
the birds of the sky.
6 "And all the inhabitants of Egypt
will know [without any doubt]
that I am the LORD,
Because they have been [only] a
staff made of [fragile] reeds to
the house of Israel.
7 "When they (Israel) grasped you
(Egypt) by the hand,
You broke and tore apart their
hands;
When they leaned on you,
You broke and strained their
backs."

8 'Therefore thus says the Lord GOD,
"Behold, I am going to bring a sword
on you and cut off (destroy) both man
and animal,
9 and the land of Egypt will be a des-
olation and a wasteland. And they will
know [without any doubt] that I am
the LORD.
"**B**ecause you said, 'The Nile is mine
and I have made it,'
10 behold (hear this), therefore, I am
against you and against your rivers
(the Nile, its tributaries), and I will
make the land of Egypt a complete
waste and a desolation, from [north-
ern] Migdol to [southern] Syene, even
as far as the border of Ethiopia (Cush).
11 "No man's foot will pass through
it, no animal's foot will pass through
it, and it will not be inhabited for forty
years.
12 "So I will make the land of Egypt
a desolation [plundered and ruined]
among desolated lands; and her cities,
among cities that are laid waste, will
be desolate forty years. I will scat-
ter the Egyptians among the nations
and [I will] disperse them through the
lands."
13 'For thus says the Lord GOD, "At the
end of forty years I will gather the Egyp-
tians from the nations among whom
they were scattered. [Jer 46:25, 26]
14 "I will reverse the fortunes of Egypt
[as I will that of Israel] and cause them
to return to the land of Pathros, the
land of their origin, and there they will
be a lowly kingdom.
15 "It will be the lowliest of the king-
doms, and it will never again exalt
itself above the nations; I will diminish
the Egyptians so they will never again
rule over the nations.
16 "And Egypt will never again have
the confidence of the house of Israel;
their wickedness will be remembered
whenever Israel looks toward them [for
help]. Then they will know [without
any doubt] that I am the Lord GOD." ' "
17 In the twenty-seventh year [after
King Jehoiachin was taken to Babylon],

29:4 – 5 *I will put hooks in your jaws.* Whereas verse 3 explains why Pharaoh would be punished, these verses explain how the punishment would be accomplished. The imagery pictures a crocodile being caught, carried out of the water onto land, and left as carrion.

29:8 *sword.* Here is another reference to the Babylonian army under Nebuchadnezzar, the predicted human instrument of God's coming wrath (21:1 – 7; 9 – 11,19 – 20).

29:10 *to [southern] Syene, even as far as the border of Ethiopia.* This phrase refers to places most likely near the northern and southern boundaries of ancient Egypt, indicating the totality of the land (Jdg 20:1). The desolation would extend to the land south of Egypt — ancient Nubia, which is modern Sudan.

29:14 – 15 *land of Pathros.* This was southern Egypt. It would thereafter never again dominate other nations.

4 Isa 37:29; Eze 38:4 **5** Jer 8:2; 16:4; 25:33; Jer 7:33; 34:20 **6** 2Ki 18:21; Isa 36:6 **7** Jer 37:5,7,11; Eze 17:17 **8** Eze 14:17; 32:11-13 **10** Eze 30:6,12 **11** Eze 32:13 **12** Eze 30:7,26 **13** Isa 19:23; Jer 46:26 **14** Eze 17:6,14 **16** Isa 30:2,3; 36:4,6

in the first *month,* on the first of the month, the word of the LORD came to me, saying,

18 “Son of man, Nebuchadnezzar king of Babylon made his army work hard [at My command] against Tyre; every [soldier’s] head became bald and every shoulder was worn *and* peeled [from carrying loads of dirt and stones for siege works]. Yet he had no wages from Tyre [in proportion to the time and labor expended during the siege], either for himself or his army, for the work that he had done against it [for Me].”

19 Therefore thus says the Lord GOD, “Behold, I will give the land of Egypt to Nebuchadnezzar king of Babylon. And he will carry off her wealth and capture her spoil and seize her plunder; and it shall be the wages for his army.

20 “I have given him the land of Egypt for the hard work which he did [against Tyre], because they did it for Me,” says the Lord GOD.

21 “In that day I will make a horn sprout for the house of Israel, and I will open your mouth among them, and they will know [without any doubt] that I am the LORD [when I renew their strength].”

Dirge for Egypt

30 THE WORD of the LORD came again to me, saying,

2 “Son of man, prophesy and say, ‘Thus says the Lord GOD,

“Wail, ‘Alas for the day!’
3 “For the day is near,
Even the day of the LORD is near,
It will be a cloudy day;
A time *of doom* for the nations.
4 “A sword will come upon Egypt,
And anguish *and* trembling will
be in Ethiopia (Cush),
When the slain fall in Egypt
And they [of Babylon] carry away
her great mass of people *and* her
riches
And her foundations are torn
down.

5 “Ethiopia (Cush), Put, Lud, all Arabia, Libya (Cub) and the people of the land of the covenant [the Jews who had taken refuge in Egypt] will fall with the Egyptians by the sword.”

6 ‘Thus says the LORD,
“Those who uphold *and* support
Egypt will fall
And the pride of her power will
come down;
From Migdol [in the north] to
Syene [in the south]
They will fall within her by the
sword,”
Says the Lord GOD.
7 “And they will be desolate
In the midst of countries that are
desolated;
And her cities will be
Among cities that are devastated
[by plunder and slavery].
8 “And they will know [without any
doubt] that I am the LORD,
When I have set a fire in Egypt
And all her helpers are shattered
and destroyed.

9 “On that day [swift] messengers will go from Me in ships to frighten the careless *and* unsuspecting Ethiopians, and there will be anguish *and* trembling in them as in the day of [judgment for] Egypt; for behold, it is coming!”

10 ‘Thus says the Lord GOD,

“I will also make the great people
of Egypt cease

29:18 *every [soldier’s] head became bald.* The siege of Tyre was protracted, lasting about 13 years.

29:21 *In that day.* This refers to the day when Egypt would fall to Babylon, and a prophecy about the Messiah should not be read into this text.

30:5 *Ethiopia.* This is the Hebrew Cush, and refers to the area south of Egypt toward modern Ethiopia.

30:9 *day of [judgment for] Egypt.* This was the day that Egypt and her allies would be conquered. It was part of a larger period of God’s judgment on the nations outside Israel by means of Babylon; in fact, Ezekiel describes the Babylonians as “messengers” sent from God Himself.

18 Jer 27:6; Eze 26:7,8 **20** Jer 25:9 **21** Ps 132:17; Eze 24:27 **CHAPTER 30** **2** Isa 13:6 **3** Eze 7:7,12; Joel 2:1; Zep 1:7 **4** Eze 29:19; Jer 50:15 **5** Jer 25:20,24 **6** Eze 29:10 **7** Eze 29:12 **9** Isa 18:1,2 **10** Eze 29:19

By the hand of Nebuchadnezzar
king of Babylon.
11 "He and his people with him,
The most violent *and* ruthless of
the nations,
Will be brought in to destroy the
land,
And they will draw their swords
against Egypt
And fill the land with the slain.
12 "And I will make the rivers [of the
Nile delta] dry
And sell the land into the hands of
evil men;
I will make the land desolate
And all that is in it,
By the hand of strangers. I the
LORD have spoken."

13 'Thus says the Lord GOD,
"I will also destroy the idols
And I will put an end to the images
in Memphis;
There will no longer be a prince of
the land of Egypt.
And I will put fear in the land of
Egypt.
14 "I will make Pathros desolate,
Set fire to Zoan
And execute judgments *and*
punishments on Thebes.
15 "I will pour out My wrath on
Pelusium,
The stronghold of Egypt,
And I will cut off (destroy) the
population of Thebes.
16 "I will set fire to Egypt;
Pelusium will writhe in [great]
anguish,
Thebes shall be torn open
And Memphis shall be in daily
distress.
17 "The young men of On (Aven) and
of Pi-beseth
Will fall by the sword,
And the women [and children] will
go into captivity.
18 "In Tehaphnehes the day will be
dark
When I break the yoke bars *and*
dominion of Egypt there.
Then the pride of her power will
come to an end;
A cloud [of disasters] will cover
her,
And her daughters will go into
captivity.
19 "In this way I will bring judgment
and punishment on Egypt.
Then they shall know [without any
doubt] that I am the LORD." ' "

Victory for Babylon

20 In the eleventh year [after King
Jehoiachin was taken to Babylon], in
the first *month,* on the seventh of the
month, the word of the LORD came to
me, saying,
21 "Son of man, I have broken the
arm of Pharaoh king of Egypt; and
behold, it has not been bound up to
heal or wrapped with a bandage, so
that it may be strong to hold *and* wield
the sword.
22 "Therefore thus says the Lord GOD,
'Behold, I am against Pharaoh king of
Egypt and will break his arms, both
the strong one and the broken, and I
will make the sword fall from his hand.
23 'I will scatter the Egyptians among
the nations and will disperse them
throughout the lands.
24 'I will strengthen the arms of the
king of Babylon and put My sword in
his hand; but I will break Pharaoh's
arms and he will groan before him
(Nebuchadnezzar) with the groanings
of a [mortally] wounded man.
25 'But I will strengthen *and* hold up
the arms of the king of Babylon and
the arms of Pharaoh will fall down.
Then the people [of Egypt] will know
that I am the LORD, when I put My
sword into the hand of the king of Bab-
ylon and he stretches it out against the
land of Egypt.

30:13 – 19 ***Memphis.*** Ancient Memphis was a significant city in Egypt. It was capital of the Old Kingdom in the third century BC.
30:21 ***I have broken the arm of Pharaoh.*** The prophecy refers to Pharaoh Hophra's unsuccessful attempt to relieve the siege of Jerusalem just a few months earlier (29:2,6 – 7). God used Nebuchadnezzar to defeat the Egyptian army.

11 Eze 28:7 **12** Isa 19:5,6; 19:4 **13** Isa 19:1; Jer 43:12; 46:25; Zec 13:2; Zec 10:11; Isa 19:16 **14** Eze 29:14; Ps 78:12,43; Na 3:8-10 **15** Jer 46:25 **16** ver. 8 **18** Jer 2:16 **21** Jer 48:25; Jer 46:11 **22** Ps 37:17 **23** ver. 26; Eze 29:12 **25** Ps 9:16

[26]'When I scatter the Egyptians among the nations and disperse them through the lands, then they will know [without any doubt] that I am the LORD.'"

Pharaoh Warned of Assyria's Fate

31 IN THE eleventh year [after King Jehoiachin was taken captive to Babylon], in the third *month,* on the first of the month, the word of the LORD came to me, saying,

[2]"Son of man, say to Pharaoh king of Egypt and to his hordes,

'Whom are you like in your
greatness?
[3]'Behold (listen carefully), Assyria
was a cedar in Lebanon
With beautiful branches and with
forest shade,
And of high stature,
With its top among the clouds.
[4]'The waters nourished it, the deep
[underground waters] made it
grow tall.
Its rivers ran all around the place
where it was planted,
Sending out its streams to all the
trees (other nations) of the field.
[5]'Therefore it towered higher than
all the trees of the forest
And its boughs multiplied and its
branches grew long;
Because there was so much water
they spread outward.
[6]'All the birds of the sky made their
nests in its twigs,
And under its branches all the
animals of the field gave birth
[to their young],
And all of the great nations lived
under its shadow.
[7]'So it was beautiful in its
greatness, in the length of its
branches;
For its roots extended [downward]
to great waters.
[8]'The cedars in the garden of God
could not hide *or* rival it;
The cypress trees did not have
boughs like it,
And the plane trees did not have
branches like it.
No tree in the garden of God was
like it in its beauty.
[9]'I made it beautiful with the great
mass of its branches,
So that all the trees of Eden which
were in the garden of God were
jealous of it (Assyria).

[10]'Therefore thus says the Lord GOD, "Because it is high in stature and has set its top among the thick boughs *and* the clouds, and its heart is proud of its height, [2 Kin 18:31–35]
[11]I will hand it over to a mighty one *and* a mighty one of the nations; he will most certainly deal with it. I have driven it away in accordance with its wickedness.
[12]"Alien tyrants of the nations have cut it down and left it; its foliage has fallen on the mountains and in all the valleys and its branches have been broken in all the ravines of the land. And all the nations of the earth have come from under its shade and have left it.
[13]"All the birds of the sky will nest in its ruins, and all the animals of the field will rest on its *fallen* branches
[14]so that none of the trees by the waters may exalt themselves because of their height, nor set their top among the clouds, nor their well-watered mighty ones stand [arrogantly] in their height. For they have all been handed over to death, to the earth beneath, among the sons of men, with those who go down to the pit (the grave)."
[15]'Thus says the Lord GOD, "On the

31:4 ***The waters nourished it.*** These waters were the Tigris and Euphrates rivers. They were important for agricultural fertility and fostered the development of great cities along trade routes.
31:10 – 14 ***I will hand it over to a mighty one and a mighty one of the nations.*** The meaning is that Assyria had been cut down by Babylon. The picturesque conclusion to this second message of chapter 31 indicates that all the other nations that observe Assyria's ruin would share its destiny of death.

26 ver. 23; Eze 29:12 **CHAPTER 31** **2** ver. 18 **3** Da 4:10 **4** Jer 51:36 **5** Da 4:11 **6** Eze 17:23; Da 4:12 **8** Ge 2:8; 13:10; Eze 28:13 **10** Da 5:20 **12** Eze 28:7; Eze 32:5; 35:8 **13** Isa 18:6; Eze 32:4 **14** Ps 82:7; Eze 32:18

day when Assyria went down to Sheol
(the place of the dead) I caused mourn-
ing; I closed the deep [subterranean
waters] over it and restrained its rivers.
And the many waters [that contributed
to its prosperity] were held back; and I
made [the heart of] Lebanon mourn for
it, and all the trees of the field wilted
away because of it.
16"I made the nations quake at the
sound of its fall when I cast it down to
Sheol with those who descend into the
pit; and all the well-watered trees of
Eden, the choicest and the best of Leb-
anon, will be comforted in the earth
beneath [at Assyria's downfall].
17"They also went down to Sheol with
it to those who were slain by the sword;
those who were its strength lived under
its shade among the nations.
18"Which among the trees of Eden
do you equal in glory and in great-
ness [O Egypt]? Yet you [also] will be
brought down with the trees of Eden to
the earth beneath (nether world). You
will lie among the uncircumcised (the
barbaric, the boorish, the crude) with
those who were slain by the sword.
This is *how it shall be* with Pharaoh
and all his hordes!" ' says the Lord
GOD." [Ezek 28:10; 32:19]

Dirge for Pharaoh and Egypt

32 IN THE twelfth year [after King
Jehoiachin of Judah was taken
into exile by the king of Babylon], in
the twelfth month, on the first of the
month, the word of the LORD came to
me, saying,
2"Son of man, take up a dirge (fu-
neral poem to be sung) over Pharaoh
king of Egypt and say to him,

'You have compared yourself to a
young lion among the nations,
But you are like a monster in the
seas;
You burst into your rivers
And disturbed *and* muddied the
waters with your feet
And fouled their rivers [the source
of their prosperity].' "

3Thus says the Lord GOD,

"I will spread out My net over you
With a company of many nations,
And they will bring you up in My
net.
4"Then I will leave you (Egypt) on
the land;
I will hurl you on the open field.
And I will make all the birds of the
sky dwell on you,
And I will satisfy the animals of
all the earth with you.
5"And I will scatter your flesh on
the mountains
And fill the valleys with your
debris [your corpses and their
worms].
6"I will also water the land with
your flowing blood
As far as the mountains,
And the ravines will be full of you.
7"And when I extinguish you,
I will cover the heavens [of Egypt]
and darken their stars;
I will cover the sun with a cloud
And the moon will not give its
light.
8"All the bright lights in the heavens
I will darken over you
And I will place darkness on your
land,"
Says the Lord GOD.

9"I will also put fear into the hearts
of many peoples when I bring your
destruction [and captivity] among the
nations, into countries which you have
not known.
10"I will make many peoples ap-
palled at you [at your judgment and
your defeat], and their kings will be
horribly afraid of you when I brandish
My sword [of judgment] before them;
they will tremble *and* shudder every

31:18 ***Pharaoh and all his hordes.*** If Assyria, the greatest nation, had fallen to the Babylonians, surely a nation less great (Egypt) would also fall.

32:2 ***lion . . . monster in the seas.*** These words depict Egypt as proud and powerful.

16 Eze 26:15; Isa 14:15; Isa 14:8; Eze 32:31 **17** La 4:20 **18** ver. 2; Eze 32:19; Eze 28:10; 32:19,21,24
CHAPTER 32 **2** ver. 16; Eze 27:2; Eze 19:3,6; 38:13; Eze 29:3; Eze 34:18 **3** Eze 12:13; 17:20; Hos 7:12
4 Eze 29:5; Eze 31:13 **5** Eze 31:12 **7** Isa 13:10; Joel 2:31; 3:15; Am 8:9; Mt 24:29; Rev 6:12,13 **10** Eze 26:16

moment, every man for his own life, on the day of your downfall."

11 For thus says the Lord GOD, "The sword of the king of Babylon will come on you.

12 "I will make your horde [of people] fall by the swords of the mighty—all of them are tyrants among the nations,

And they will devastate the pride
and presumption of Egypt,
And all its hordes will be
destroyed.
13 "I will also destroy all its cattle
from beside its great waters;
And the foot of man will not
muddy them anymore
Nor will the hoofs of the animals
muddy them.
14 "Then I will make their waters
quiet *and* clear;
I will make their rivers run [slowly
and smoothly] like oil,"
Says the Lord GOD.
15 "When I make the land of Egypt
desolate,
And the country is stripped *and*
deprived of all that which filled it,
When I strike all those who live
in it,
Then they will know [without any
doubt] that I am the LORD.

16 "This is the dirge (funeral poem to be sung) and they shall sing it [for her]. The daughters of the nations shall sing it; for Egypt and for all her hordes they shall sing it," says the Lord GOD.

17 In the twelfth year [after King Jehoiachin of Judah was taken into exile], on the fifteenth of the month, the word of the LORD came to me, saying,

18 "Son of man, wail over the hordes of Egypt and cast them down, both her and the daughters of the powerful *and* majestic nations, to the nether world (the place of the dead), with those who go down to the pit;

19 'Whom [among them] do you
surpass in beauty?
Go down and make your bed with
the uncircumcised (the barbaric,
the boorish, the crude).'

20 "They will fall among those who are slain by the sword. She (Egypt) is handed over to the sword; they have drawn her and all her hordes away [to judgment].

21 "The strong among the mighty rulers will say of him (Pharaoh) and his allies from the midst of Sheol, 'They have gone down [defeated]; they lie still, the uncircumcised, slain by the sword.'

22 "Assyria is there with all her warriors; their graves are all around her. All of them are slain, fallen by the sword,

23 whose graves are set in the remotest parts of the pit and her army is all around her grave. All of them are slain, fallen by the sword, who spread terror in the land of the living.

24 "Elam [a conquest of Assyria] is there and all her hordes around her grave; all of them slain, fallen by the sword, who have gone down uncircumcised to the lower parts of the earth, who made their terror spread in the land of the living and bore their shame *and* defeat with those who went down to the pit.

25 "They have made a bed for her among the slain with all her hordes. Her graves are around it; they are all uncircumcised (barbaric, boorish, crude), slain by the sword (for their terror had been spread in the land of the living), and they bore their disgrace with those who go down to the pit; they were laid among the slain.

26 "Meshech, Tubal, and all their hordes are there; their graves surround them. All of them uncircumcised, slain by the sword, for they spread their terror in the land of the living.

32:14 *rivers run [slowly and smoothly] like oil.* This phrase is not used anywhere else in the Bible. It pictures the time following massive killing when the Nile and its tributaries would experience a "deadly" calm.

32:24 *Elam [a conquest of Assyria] is there.* Elam was east and southeast of Assyria in what is now Iran. The people of Elam were descended from one of the sons of Shem (Ge 10:22; 1Ch 1:17).

11 Jer 46:26; Eze 30:4 **12** Eze 28:7; Eze 29:19 **13** Eze 29:11 **15** Ex 7:5; 14:4,18; Ps 9:16; Eze 6:7 **16** ver. 2; 2Sa 1:17; 2Ch 35:25; Eze 26:17 **18** Eze 26:20; 31:14 **19** Eze 31:2,18; ver. 21,24; Eze 28:10 **21** ver. 27; Isa 1:31; 14:9,10; ver. 19,25 **23** Isa 14:15; ver. 24-27,32 **24** Jer 49:34; ver. 21; ver. 23 **26** Ge 10:2; Eze 27:13; ver. 19,20

27“Nor do they lie beside the fallen
heroes of the uncircumcised, who went
down to Sheol with their weapons of
war, whose swords were laid [with
honors] under their heads. The pun-
ishment for their sins rested on their
bones, for the terror of these heroes
was once in the land of the living.
28“But you will be broken in the
midst of the uncircumcised and you
will lie [without honors] with those
who are slain by the sword.
29“Edom is there also, her kings and
all her princes, who for all their power
and strength are laid with those who
were slain by the sword; they will lie
[in shame and defeat] with the uncir-
cumcised and with those who go down
to the pit.
30“The princes of the north are there
also, all of them, and all the Sidonians,
who in spite of the terror resulting
from their power, have gone down in
shame with the slain. So they lay down
uncircumcised with those slain by the
sword and bore their disgrace with
those who go down to the pit.
31“Pharaoh will see them, and he will
be comforted for all his hordes slain by
the sword—Pharaoh and all his army,”
says the Lord GOD.
32“Though I instilled a terror of him
in the land of the living, yet he will be
made to lie down among the uncir-
cumcised along with those slain by
the sword, even Pharaoh and all his
hordes,” says the Lord GOD. [Is 19; Jer
46; Zech 14:18, 19]

The Watchman’s Duty

33 AND THE word of the LORD
came to me, saying,
2“Son of man, speak to the sons of
your people [who are exiled in Bab-
ylon] and say to them, ‘If I bring a
sword on a land, and the people of the
land take one man from among them
and make him their watchman,
3and he sees the sword coming on
the land, and he blows the trumpet and
warns the people,
4then whoever hears the sound of the
trumpet and does not take warning,
and a sword comes and takes him away,
his blood will be on his [own] head.
5‘He heard the sound of the trumpet
but did not take warning; his blood
shall be on himself. But if he had taken
warning, he would have saved his life.
6‘But if the watchman sees the sword
coming and does not blow the trumpet
and the people are not warned, and
the sword comes and takes any one of
them, he is taken away because of his
corruption *and* sin; but I will require
his blood from the watchman’s hand.’
7“Now as for you, son of man, I have
made you a watchman for the house
of Israel; so you shall hear a message
from My mouth and give them a warn-
ing from Me.
8“When I say to the wicked, ‘O wick-
ed man, you will certainly die,’ and
you do not speak to warn the wicked
from his way, that wicked man will die
because of his sin; but I will require his
blood from your hand.
9“But if you on your part warn the
wicked man to turn from his [evil] way
and he does not turn from his [evil]
way, he will die in his sin; but you have
saved your life.
10“Now as for you, son of man, say
to the house of Israel, ‘Thus you have
said, “Truly our transgressions and
our sins are on us, and we are rotting
away because of them; how then can
we live?” ’
11“Say to them, ‘As I live,’ says the
Lord GOD, ‘I take no pleasure in the
death of the wicked, but rather that

32:30 *princes of the north.* This is a reference to lands that are north of Israel like Tyre and Sidon.

32:31 *Pharaoh will see.* Now the message (vv. 17–32) comes full circle. The point is that Egypt and Pharaoh will die like the other nations at the hand of the living God who judges every nation with justice.

33:2 *the sons of your people.* This phrase refers to fellow Israelites in exile with Ezekiel, now including the people of Judah deported to Babylon after Nebuchadnezzar.

27 ver. 21; Isa 14:18,19 **29** Eze 25:12 **30** Eze 38:6,15; 39:2; Eze 28:21 **31** Eze 31:16 **CHAPTER 33** **2** Eze 3:11; Eze 14:17; ver. 7; 2Sa 18:24,25; 2Ki 9:17; Hos 9:8 **4** Eze 18:13 **6** ver. 8 **7** Eze 3:17 **10** Eze 24:23; Isa 49:14 **11** 2Sa 14:14; 2Pe 3:9; Eze 18:31

the wicked turn from his way and live. Turn back (change your way of thinking), turn back [in repentance] from your evil ways! For why should you die, O house of Israel?'

12 "And you, son of man, say to the sons of your people, 'The righteousness of the righteous man will not save him in the day of his transgression; and as for the wickedness of the wicked, he will not stagger because of it in the day that he turns from his wickedness, whereas a righteous man will not be able to live because of his [previous acts of] righteousness on the day when he commits sin.'

13 "When I say to the righteous that he will most certainly live, and he trusts in his [previous acts of] righteousness [to save him] and commits injustice, none of his righteous deeds will be remembered; but he will die for his injustice that he committed.

14 "But when I say to the wicked, 'You will certainly die,' and he turns from his sin and practices that which is just (fair) and right—

15 if a wicked man returns [what he took as] a pledge, pays back what he had taken by robbery, walks in the statutes which ensure life, without committing injustice, he will certainly live; he will not die.

16 "None of his sins that he has committed will be remembered against him. He has practiced that which is just (fair) and right; he will most certainly live.

17 "Yet your people [who are in exile in Babylon] say, 'The way of the Lord is not right;' but as for them, it is their own way that is not right.

18 "When the righteous turns back from his righteousness and commits injustice, he will also die because of it.

19 "But when a wicked man turns back from his wickedness and practices what is just (fair) and right, he will live because of it.

20 "Yet you say, 'The way of the Lord is not right.' O house of Israel, I will judge you, every one [of you] in accordance with his own ways!"

Word of Jerusalem's Capture

21 In the twelfth year of our exile [in Babylon], on the fifth of the tenth month, a survivor from Jerusalem came to me, saying, "The city has been captured."

22 Now the hand of the LORD had been upon me in the evening, before the survivor came. And He opened my mouth at the time he came to me in the morning; so my mouth was opened [in readiness] and I was no longer mute.

23 Then the word of the LORD came to me, saying,

24 "Son of man, those [back in Palestine] who inhabit these ruins in the land of Israel are saying, 'Abraham was [only] one man and he took possession of the land, but we are many; the land has [most certainly] been given to us [to possess] as property.'

25 "Therefore say to them, 'Thus says the Lord GOD, "You eat meat with the blood *in it* and raise your eyes to your idols and shed blood. Should you take possession of the land? [Gen 9:4; Lev 3:17; 7:27; Acts 15:28, 29]

26 "You rely on your sword [as your security]; you commit outrageous *and* disgraceful acts and each of you defiles his neighbor's wife. Should you then take possession of the land?" '

33:12 – 20 *I will judge you, every one [of you] in accordance with his own ways.* God presents His rationale in these verses for deciding who would be rewarded with life and who would suffer death; He would save those who repent and turn to Him, but would condemn those who trust in themselves and do evil. After presenting His rationale, God declares that His judgment is just and fair — certainly more just than the practices of the Israelites.

33:25 – 26 *Should you take possession of the land?* Ezekiel confronted his people with specific examples of their past and present refusal to obey God's revealed will for their lives (18:6,10; 22:11; Ex 20:4 – 5,13; Lev 7:26 – 27; 17:10 – 14; Dt 12:16,23). Was it not then reasonable

12 Eze 3:20; 18:24,26; 2Ch 7:14 **13** Eze 3:20; 18:24 **14** Eze 3:18,19; 18:27 **15** Eze 18:7; Ex 22:1,4; Lev 6:2,4,5; Lev 18:5; Eze 20:11,13,21 **16** Eze 18:22 **17** ver. 20; Eze 18:25,29 **18** Eze 18:26 **20** ver. 17; Eze 18:25 **21** Eze 1:2; Eze 24:26; 2Ki 25:4 **22** Eze 1:3; Eze 24:27 **24** Eze 34:2; ver. 27; Eze 36:4; Isa 51:2; Ac 7:5; Mic 3:11; Mt 3:9; Jn 8:39 **25** Ge 9:4; Lev 3:17; 7:26; 17:10; 19:26; Dt 12:16; Eze 18:6; Eze 22:6,9 **26** Eze 18:6; 22:11

27 “You shall say this to them, ‘Thus says the Lord God, “As I live, those who are in the ruins certainly will fall by the sword, and I will give whoever is in the open field to the [predatory] animals to be devoured, and those who are in strongholds and in caves will die of virulent diseases.

28 “And I will make the land [of Israel] a desolation and a ruin, and her pride in her power will be brought to an end; and the mountains of Israel will be so deserted that no one will pass through.

29 “Then they will know [without any doubt] that I am the Lord, when I make the land a desolation and a ruin because of all the atrocities which they have committed.” ’

30 “But as for you, son of man, your people who talk about you by the walls and in the doorways of the houses say one to another, every one to his brother, ‘Come now and hear what the message is that comes from the Lord.’

31 “They come to you as people come, and they sit before you as My people, and they hear your words, but they do not practice them; for with their mouth they *express* loving devotion, but their heart goes after their (unlawful) gain.

32 “Behold, you are to them like a love song by one who has a pleasant voice and plays well on a stringed instrument [merely to entertain them]; for they hear your words but do not practice them.

33 “So when it comes to pass—as it most certainly will—then they will know [without any doubt] that a prophet has been among them.”

Prophecy against the Shepherds of Israel

34 AND THE word of the Lord came to me, saying,

2 “Son of man, prophesy against the shepherds of Israel. Prophesy and say to them, the [spiritual] shepherds, ‘Thus says the Lord God, “Woe (judgment is coming) to the [spiritual] shepherds of Israel who have been feeding themselves! Should not the shepherds feed the flock?

3 “You eat the fat [the choicest of meat], and clothe yourselves with the wool, you slaughter the best of the livestock, but you do not feed the flock.

4 “You have not strengthened those who are weak, you have not healed the sick, you have not bandaged the crippled, you have not brought back those gone astray, you have not looked for the lost; but you have ruled them with force and violence.

5 “They were scattered because there was no shepherd, and when they were scattered they became food for all the predators of the field.

6 “My flock wandered through all the mountains and on every high hill; My flock was scattered over all the face of the earth and no one searched or sought them.” ’ ” [Matt 9:36]

7 Therefore, you [spiritual] shepherds, hear the word of the Lord:

8 “As I live,” says the Lord God, “certainly because My flock has become prey, My flock has even become food for every predator of the field for lack of a shepherd, and My shepherds did not search for My flock, but *rather* the

---

that God would punish the present generation by removing them from the land, at least temporarily? The writer of Hebrews, after using the example of Israel’s failure to enter the land, admonished the church in a similar way (Heb 4:1).

33:30 – 33 *they hear your words, but they do not practice them.* This section contrasts the actions and attitudes of the exiles with the life of God’s prophet Ezekiel. The exiles had claimed to go to the prophet to receive God’s revelation, but their behavior was inconsistent with their stated beliefs. Their true desire was for entertainment, not for divine enlightenment. If the fall of Jerusalem failed to awaken them spiritually, nothing would. Yet it certainly would open their eyes to the divine truth of Ezekiel’s preaching. In these verses then, God also comforted and consoled Ezekiel.

34:7 – 10 *did not feed My flock.* The crimes of Israel’s leaders come under review before their punishment is pronounced.

---

27 ver. 24; Eze 39:4; Jdg 6:2; 1Sa 13:6 **28** Jer 44:2,6,22; Eze 36:34,35; Eze 7:24; 24:21; 30:6,7; Eze 6:2,3,6 **30** Isa 29:13 **31** Eze 14:1; 20:1; Eze 8:1; Ps 78:36,37; Isa 29:13; Mt 13:22 **33** 1Sa 3:20; Eze 2:5 **CHAPTER 34** **2** Jer 23:1; Zec 11:17 **3** Isa 56:11; Zec 11:16 **4** Zec 11:16; Lk 15:4; 1Pe 5:3 **5** Eze 33:21; 1Ki 22:17; Mt 9:36; Isa 56:9; Jer 12:9 **8** ver. 2,5,6,10

shepherds fed themselves and did not feed My flock;

9therefore, you [spiritual] shepherds, hear the word of the LORD:

10‘Thus says the Lord GOD, “Behold, I am against the shepherds, and I will demand My flock from them and make them stop tending the flock, so that the shepherds cannot feed themselves anymore. I will rescue My flock from their mouth, so that they will not be food for them.” ’ ”

The Restoration of Israel

11For thus says the Lord GOD, “Behold, I Myself will search for My flock and seek them out.

12“As a shepherd cares for his sheep on the day that he is among his scattered flock, so I will care for My sheep; and I will rescue them from all the places to which they were scattered on a cloudy and gloomy day.

13“I will bring them out from the nations and gather them from the countries and bring them to their own land; and I will feed them on the mountains of Israel, by the streams, and in all the inhabited places of the land.

14“I will feed them in a good pasture, and their grazing ground will be on the mountain heights of Israel. There they will lie down on good grazing ground and feed in rich pasture on the mountains of Israel.

15“I will feed My flock and I will let them lie down [to rest],” says the Lord GOD.

16“I will seek the lost, bring back the scattered, bandage the crippled, and strengthen the weak *and* the sick; but I will destroy the fat and the strong [who have become hard-hearted and perverse]. I will feed them with judgment *and* punishment. [Luke 19:10]

17“And as for you, My flock, thus says the Lord GOD, ‘Behold, I judge between one sheep and another, between the rams and the male goats [between the righteous and the unrighteous].

18‘Is it too little a thing for you that you [unrighteous ones who are well-fed] feed in the best pasture, yet you must trample down with your feet [of wickedness] the rest of your pastures? Or that you drink clear [still] water, yet you must muddy with your feet [of wickedness] the rest [of the water]?

19‘As for My flock (the righteous), they must feed on what you trample with your feet and drink what you muddy with your feet!’ ”

20Therefore thus says the Lord GOD to them, “Behold, I Myself will judge between the [well-fed] fat sheep and the lean sheep.

21“Because you push with side and shoulder, and gore with your horns all those that have become weak *and* sick until you have scattered them away,

22therefore, I will rescue My flock, and they shall no longer be prey; and I will judge between one sheep [ungodly] and another [godly].

23“Then I will appoint over them one shepherd and he will feed them, [a ruler like] My servant David; he will feed them and be their shepherd. [Ezek 37:24; John 10:14–18]

24“And I the LORD will be their God, and My servant David will be a prince among them; I the LORD have spoken.

25“I will make a covenant of peace with them and will eliminate the predatory animals from the land so that they may live securely in the wilder-

34:11 – 16 ***a cloudy and gloomy day.*** This was the day Jerusalem fell (30:1 – 5). It may also speak of the future day of deliverance when God will seek out His sheep. Israel, though guilty and misguided, would eventually be rescued by the divine Good Shepherd and restored to the promised land (chs. 33 – 39).

34:23 – 24 ***I will appoint . . . he will feed.*** The change from the pronoun *I* to *he* in this verse indicates that God would continue operating as the Chief Shepherd through this chosen future ruler from the Davidic line. He is the Messiah — God's only Son and His servant.

34:25 – 31 ***covenant of peace.*** These exiles were encouraged through these promises (37:26 – 28; 38:11 – 13; 39:25 – 29; Isa 54:10):

10 Eze 3:18; Heb 13:17; ver. 2,8 **12** Eze 30:3 **13** Isa 65:9,10; Jer 23:3 **14** Ps 23:2; Jer 33:12 **16** Isa 40:11; Mic 4:6; Mt 18:11; Lk 5:32; Isa 10:16; Am 4:1; Jer 10:24 **17** Eze 20:37; Mt 25:32 **20** ver. 17 **23** Isa 40:11; Jn 10:11; Heb 13:20; 1Pe 2:25; Jer 30:9; Hos 3:5 **24** Ex 29:45; Eze 37:22 **25** Eze 37:26; Lev 26:6; Isa 11:6-9; Hos 2:18; Jer 23:6

ness and sleep [safely] in the woods. [Ps 127:2; Is 11:6–9; John 14:27; 16:33]
26"I will make them and the plac-
es around My hill (Jerusalem, Zion) a blessing. And I will make showers come down in their season; there will be [abundant] showers of blessing (divine favor).
27"Also the tree of the field will yield
its fruit and the earth will yield its produce; and My people will be secure on their land. Then they will know [with confidence] that I am the LORD, when I have broken the bars of their yoke and have rescued them from the hand of those who made them slaves.
28"They will no longer be prey to
the nations, and the predators of the earth will not devour them; but they will live safely, and no one will make them afraid [in the day of the Messiah's reign]. [Is 60:21; 61:3]
29"I will prepare for them a place re-
nowned for planting [crops], and they will not again be victims of famine in the land, and they will not endure the insults of the nations any longer.
30"Then they will know [with assur-
ance] that I the LORD their God, am with them and that they, the house of Israel, are My people," says the Lord GOD.
31"As for you, My flock, the flock of
My pasture, you are men, and I am your God," says the Lord GOD.

Prophecy against Mount Seir

35 MOREOVER, THE word of the LORD came to me, saying,
2"Son of man, set your face against
Mount Seir (Edom), and prophesy against it
3and say to it, 'Thus says the Lord
GOD,

"Behold, Mount Seir, I am against
you,
And I will stretch out My hand
against you
And make you completely
desolate.
4"I will destroy your cities
And you will become a wasteland.
Then you shall know [without any
doubt] that I am the LORD.

5"Because you [descendants of Esau]
have had an everlasting hatred [for Jacob (Israel)] and you handed over the sons of Israel to the power of the sword at the time of their tragedy, at the time of their final punishment [the Babylonian conquest], [Ezek 25:12–14; 36:5]
6therefore, as I live," says the Lord
GOD, "I will hand you over to bloodshed, and bloodshed will pursue you since you have not hated bloodshed, bloodshed will pursue you.
7"I will make Mount Seir (Edom) a
ruin and a desolate wasteland and I will cut off from it the one who passes through it and the one who returns.
8"I will fill its mountains with its
slain; those killed by the sword will fall on your hills, and in your valleys, and in all your ravines.
9"I will make you an everlasting des-
olation and your cities will not be inhabited. Then you will know [without any doubt] that I am the LORD.
10"Because you [descendants of
Esau] have said, 'These two nations [Israel and Judah] and these two lands shall be mine, and we will take possession of them,' although the LORD was there,
11therefore, as I live," says the Lord
GOD, "I will deal with you in accordance with the anger and envy you

---

(1) security from foreign aggressor nations; (2) showers of blessing, meaning productivity and prosperity; and (3) the certainty that the Lord is Israel's God and desires reunion with His people and a lasting relationship built on a new covenant (Jer 31:31 – 34; Heb 8:6).

35:6 – 9 *I will make you an everlasting desolation.* Having stated why Edom deserved judgment, Ezekiel explained how the nation would be punished. The punishment would include widespread death and unrelieved destruction (Isa 34:6 – 8; 63:1 – 6; Jer 49:7 – 13).

26 Isa 56:7; Ge 12:2; Isa 19:24; Zec 8:13; Lev 26:4; Ps 68:9 **27** Lev 26:4; Ps 85:12; Isa 4:2; Jer 2:20; Jer 25:14 **28** Jer 30:10 **29** Isa 11:1; Eze 36:3,6 **30** ver. 24 **31** Ps 100:3; Jn 10:11 **CHAPTER 35** **2** Dt 2:5; Am 1:11 **3** Eze 6:14 **5** Eze 25:12; Ps 137:7; Da 9:24 **6** Ps 109:17 **7** Jdg 5:6 **9** Jer 49:17; Eze 36:11 **10** Ps 83:4,12; Ps 48:1,3; Eze 48:35 **11** Mt 7:2; Jas 2:13

showed because of your hatred for
them; and I will make Myself known
among them [as Judge] when I judge
and punish you.
12 “Then you will know [without any
doubt] that I am the LORD, and that I
have heard all your scornful speeches
which you have spoken against the
mountains of Israel, saying, ‘They have
been made a wasteland; they have
been given to us as food.’
13 “So you have boasted *and* spoken
arrogantly against Me, and have mul-
tiplied your words against Me; I have
heard it.”
14 ‘Thus says the Lord GOD, “While
the whole earth rejoices, I will make
you a wasteland.
15 “As you rejoiced over the inheri-
tance of the house of Israel because it
was desolate, so I will do to you; you
will be a desolate waste, O Mount Seir,
and all Edom, all of it. Then they will
know [without any doubt] that I am
the LORD.” ’

The Mountains of Israel to Be Blessed

36 “AND YOU, son of man, prophe-
sy to the mountains of Israel and
say, ‘You mountains of Israel, hear the
word of the LORD.
2 ‘Thus says the Lord GOD, “Because
the enemy has said of you, ‘Aha!’ and,
‘The ancient heights have become our
property,’
3 therefore prophesy and say, ‘Thus
says the Lord GOD, “For good reason
they have made you a desolation, and
they crushed you from every side so
that you would become a possession
of the rest of the nations and you have
become the talk and the whispering of
the people.” ’ ”
4 ‘Therefore, O mountains of Israel,
hear the word of the Lord GOD. Thus
says the Lord GOD to the mountains
and to the hills, to the ravines and to
the valleys, to the desolate ruins and to
the deserted cities which have become
prey and a mockery to the rest of the
nations which surround you,
5 therefore thus says the Lord GOD,
“Most certainly in the fire of My jeal-
ousy (love for that which is Mine) I
have spoken against the rest of the
nations and against all Edom, who
appropriated My land for themselves
as a possession with wholehearted joy
and with uttermost contempt, so that
they might empty it out [and possess
it] as prey.”
6 ‘Therefore prophesy concerning the
land of Israel and say to the mountains
and to the hills, to the ravines and to
the valleys, “Thus says the Lord GOD,
‘Behold, I have spoken in My jealousy
(love for that which is Mine) and in
My wrath because you have endured
the [shameful] insults of the nations.’
7 “Therefore thus says the Lord GOD,
‘I have lifted up My hand *and* sworn
[an oath] that the nations that are
around you will themselves endure
their [shameful] insults.
8 ‘But you, O mountains of Israel, will
put out your branches and bear your
fruit to My people Israel; for they will
soon come [home].
9 ‘For, behold, I am for you, and I will
turn to you [in favor], and you shall be
cultivated and sown.
10 ‘I will multiply people on you, all
the house of Israel, [indeed] all of it; the
cities shall be inhabited and the ruins
will be rebuilt.
11 ‘I will multiply on you man and
animal; and they will increase and
be fruitful. And I will cause you to be
inhabited as you were formerly, and I
will do better [things] for you than at
your beginning. Then you will know
[with great confidence] that I am the
LORD.

36:1–7 *The ancient heights.* This was a term for Israel because the hill country was central to the country's geography. God is glorified and the exiles comforted by the following: (1) exposing the crimes of the enemies of His nation; (2) exonerating His land from false charges; and (3) executing judgment and justice against the foreign nations.

---

12 Ps 9:16 **13** 1Sa 2:3 **14** Isa 65:13 **15** Ob 12,15 **CHAPTER 36** **1** Eze 6:2,3 **2** Eze 25:3; Dt 32:13; Eze 35:10 **3** Dt 28:37 **4** Eze 34:28; Ps 79:4 **5** Dt 4:24; Eze 38:19; Eze 35:10,12 **6** ver. 15; Ps 123:3,4; Eze 34:29 **7** Eze 20:5 **10** ver. 33; Isa 58:12; 61:4; Am 9:14 **11** Jer 31:27; 33:12; Eze 35:9; 37:6,13

12'Yes, [O mountains of Israel] I will
cause men—My people Israel—to walk
on you and take possession of you,
so that you will become their inher-
itance and never again bereave them
of children.'
13"Thus says the Lord GOD, 'Because
they say to you, "You [O land] are a
devourer of people and have bereaved
your nation of children,"
14therefore you will no longer devour
people, and no longer bereave your
nation of children,' says the Lord GOD.
15"I will not let you hear insults from
the nations anymore, nor will you bear
disgrace from the peoples any longer,
nor will you cause your nation to stum-
ble [through idolatry] any longer," says
the Lord GOD.' "
16Moreover, the word of the LORD
came to me, saying,
17"Son of man, when the house of
Israel was living in their own land,
they defiled it by their [own] behav-
ior and by their [idolatrous] actions.
Their conduct before Me was like the
uncleanness of a woman during her
[physical] impurity.
18"So I poured out My wrath on them
for the blood which they had shed on
the land and because they had defiled
it with their idols.
19"Also I scattered them among
the nations and they were dispersed
throughout the countries. I judged *and*
punished them in accordance with
their conduct and their [idolatrous]
behavior.
20"When they came to the nations
wherever they went, they profaned My
holy name, because it was said of them,
'These are the people of the LORD; yet
they have come out of His land.'
21"But I had concern for My holy
name, which the house of Israel had
profaned among the nations where
they went.

Israel to Be Renewed for His Name's Sake

22"Therefore say to the house of Is-
rael, 'Thus says the Lord GOD, "It is not
for your sake, O house of Israel, that I
am about to act, but for My holy name,
which you have profaned among the
nations where you went.
23"I will vindicate the holiness of My
great name which has been profaned
among the nations, which you have
profaned among them. Then the na-
tions will know [without any doubt]
that I am the LORD," says the Lord GOD,
"when I prove Myself holy among you
in their sight.
24"For I will take you from the na-
tions and gather you from all the coun-
tries and bring you into your own land.
25"Then I will sprinkle clean water
on you, and you will be clean; I will
cleanse you from all your uncleanness
and from all your idols.
26"Moreover, I will give you a new
heart and put a new spirit within you,
and I will remove the heart of stone from
your flesh and give you a heart of flesh.
27"I will put my Spirit within you
and cause you to walk in My statutes,

36:12 *My people Israel.* Despite all their sinfulness, which the book has taken enormous pains to detail and describe, the nation was still referred to as the people of God. They would finally and forever take possession of their land, symbolized by the mountains and the central hills of Palestine, which are personified as "you" in this verse.
36:19 *I judged and punished them in accordance with their conduct and their [idolatrous] behavior.* Israel had been hypocritical and unholy; they had not separated themselves or made themselves distinct from the pagan world around them (v. 18). God had given His people the promised land as a place where they could show the world the difference it makes to follow the true God (Dt 7:1 – 11). They failed to follow God, so He forced them out of the land. Through either their obedience or their disobedience, God would demonstrate to the watching world His personality, power, and plans.
36:25 *sprinkle clean water on you.* This symbolized cleansing from sin.
36:27 *I will put my Spirit within you.* The regenerating and empowering work of the Holy Spirit on individuals would not only restore the

12 Ob 17; See Jer 15:7 **13** Nu 13:32 **15** Eze 34:29 **17** Lev 18:25,27,28; Jer 2:7; Lev 15:19 **18** Eze 16:36,38; 23:37 **19** Eze 7:3; 18:30; 39:24 **20** Isa 52:5; Ro 2:24 **21** Eze 20:9,14 **22** Ps 106:8 **23** Eze 20:41; 28:22 **24** Eze 34:13; 37:21 **25** Isa 52:15; Heb 10:22; Jer 33:8 **26** Jer 32:39; Eze 11:19 **27** Eze 11:19; 37:14

and you will keep My ordinances and do them.

28“You will live in the land that I gave to your fathers; and you will be My people, and I will be your God.

29“I will also save you from all your uncleanness, and I will call for the grain and make it abundant, and I will not bring famine on you.

30“I will multiply the fruit of the tree and the produce of the field, so that you will not suffer again the disgrace of famine among the nations.

31“Then you will remember [clearly] your [own] evil ways and your deeds that were not good, and you will loathe yourselves in your own sight for your sins and for your outrageous atrocities.

32“I am not doing this for your sake,” says the Lord God. “Let that be known to you. Be ashamed and humiliated for your [wicked] ways, O house of Israel!”

33‘Thus says the Lord God, “On the day that I cleanse you from all your sins I will also cause the cities [of Israel] to be inhabited, and the ruins will be rebuilt.

34“The desolate land will be cultivated instead of being a desolation in the sight of everyone who passes by.

35“Then they will say, ‘This land that was deserted *and* desolate has become like the garden of Eden; and the waste, desolate, and ruined cities are fortified and inhabited.’

36“Then the nations that are left around you will know that I the LORD have rebuilt the ruined places and planted that which was desolate. I the LORD have spoken, and will do it.”

37‘Thus says the Lord God, “This too I will let the house of Israel ask Me to do for them: I will increase their people like a flock.

38“Like the flock for sacrifices, like the flock at Jerusalem during her appointed feasts, so will the desolate cities be filled with flocks of people. Then they will know [with confident assurance] that I am the LORD.” ’ ”

Vision of the Valley of Dry Bones

37 THE HAND of the LORD was upon me, and He brought me out in the Spirit of the LORD and set me down in the middle of the valley; and it was full of bones.

2He caused me to pass all around them, and behold, *there were* very many [human bones] in the open valley; and lo, *they were* very dry.

3And He said to me, “Son of man, can these bones live?” And I answered, “O Lord God, You know.” [1 Cor 15:35]

4Again He said to me, “Prophesy to these bones and say to them, ‘O dry bones, hear the word of the LORD.’ [John 5:28]

5“Thus says the Lord God to these bones, ‘Behold, I will make breath enter you so that you may come to life.

6‘I will put sinews on you, make flesh grow back on you, cover you with skin, and I will put breath in you so that you

---

people physically to the land, but would restore them spiritually, by giving them a new heart and new spirit to help them follow Him and do His will (11:19 – 20; 18:31; 37:14; Jer 31:31 – 34; Joel 2:28 – 29; Ro 7:7 – 8:11).

36:28 – 30 *you will be My people.* The purpose of the Mosaic covenant would finally be realized (Dt 26:16 – 19; 29:13; 30:8). The Israelites would become a people dedicated to God’s ways.

36:31 – 32 *I am not doing this for your sake.* The restoration from the exile would recover God’s glorious reputation among the nations and erase the guilt of the Israelites’ sin. This is all a product of God’s favor on the Israelites — even though they had done nothing to merit such mercy.

37:4 *Prophesy to these bones.* Ezekiel’s prophecies had often been directed to people as deaf as these old, dry bones.

37:5 *breath.* This word is translated as wind or spirit in other places. The breath sent by God into the lifeless bodies symbolizes the Holy Spirit who brings renewal, regeneration, and rebirth (Jn 3:5 – 8; 6:44; 7:37 – 39; Ro 8:9 – 11).

37:6 *you may come alive.* This passage is not about resurrection from physical death, but

28 Eze 28:25; 37:25; Jer 30:22; Eze 11:20; 37:27 **29** Mt 1:21; Ro 11:26; See Ps 105:16; Eze 34:29 **30** Eze 34:27 **31** Eze 16:61,63; Lev 26:39; Eze 6:9; 20:43 **32** ver. 22; Dt 9:5 **33** ver. 10 **35** Isa 51:3; Eze 28:13; Joel 2:3 **36** Eze 17:24; 22:14; 37:14 **37** See Eze 14:3; 20:3,31; ver. 10 **CHAPTER 37** **1** Eze 1:3; Eze 3:14; 8:3; 11:24; Lk 4:1 **3** Dt 32:39; 1Sa 2:6; Jn 5:21; Ro 4:17; 2Co 1:9 **5** ver. 9; Ps 104:30 **6** Eze 6:7; 35:12; Joel 2:27; 3:17

may come alive; and you will know
that I am the LORD.' "
7So I prophesied as I was command-
ed; and as I prophesied, there was a
[thundering] noise, and behold, a rat-
tling; and the bones came together,
bone to its bone.
8And I looked, and behold, there
were sinews on the bones, and flesh
grew and skin covered them; but there
was no breath in them.
9Then He said to me, "Prophesy
to the breath, son of man, and say to
the breath, 'Thus says the Lord GOD,
"Come from the four winds, O breath,
and breathe on these slain, that they
may live." ' "
10So I prophesied as He commanded
me, and the breath came into them,
and they came to life and stood up on
their feet, an exceedingly great army.
[Rev 11:11]

The Vision Explained

11Then He said to me, "Son of man,
these bones are the whole house of Is-
rael. Behold, they say, 'Our bones are
dried up and our hope is lost. We are
completely cut off.'
12"Therefore prophesy and say to
them, 'Thus says the Lord GOD, "Be-
hold, I will open your graves and make
you come up out of your graves, My
people; and I will bring you [back
home] to the land of Israel. [Hos 13:14]
13"Then you will know [with con-
fidence] that I am the LORD, when I
have opened your graves and made
you come up out of your graves, My
people.
14"I will put My Spirit in you and
you will come to life, and I will place
you in your own land. Then you will
know that I the LORD have spoken, and
fulfilled it," says the LORD.' "

Reunion of Judah and Israel

15The word of the LORD came again
to me, saying,
16"And you, son of man, take a stick
and write on it, 'For Judah and for the
children of Israel, his companions';
then take another stick and write on it,
'For Joseph, the stick of Ephraim and
all the house of Israel, his companions.'
17Then join them together into one
stick, so that they may become one in
your hand.
18"When your people say to you,
'Will you not tell us what you mean
by these?'
19say to them, 'Thus says the Lord
GOD, "Behold, I am going to take the
stick of Joseph, which is in the hand of
Ephraim, and the tribes of Israel, his
companions; and I will join the stick of
Judah with it and make them one stick,
and they will be one in My hand." '
20"The sticks on which you write
shall be in your hand before their eyes.
21"Say to them, 'Thus says the Lord
GOD, "Behold, I am going to take the
children of Israel from among the na-
tions where they have gone, and I will
gather them from every side and bring
them into their own land;
22and I will make them one nation
in the land, on the mountains of Israel;
and one king will be king over all of
them; and they will no longer be two

---

rebirth from spiritual death brought about by divine power. Psalm 87 is another text that speaks of spiritual rebirth. The point of Jesus' words to Nicodemus in John 3 was that he should have known and understood the concept of a second birth.

37:10 *an exceedingly great army.* The dead bones in the valley (vv. 1 – 2) must have looked like the aftermath of a horrible military defeat in which there were no survivors even to bury the dead.

37:11 – 14 *these bones*. The bones symbolize the whole house of Israel. This identification picks up on imagery already used: (1) those identified as dry or spiritually dead; (2) those identified as despondent and dejected, with no apparent hope of being "resurrected" as the people of the living God; and (3) those described as disassembled and dispersed before being rejoined and rebuilt. The major thrust of this passage is the coming spiritual rebirth of God's chosen people through the agency of His Spirit.

9 ver. 5; Ps 104:30 **10** Rev 11:11 **11** Ps 141:7; Isa 49:14 **12** Isa 26:19; Hos 13:14; ver. 25; Eze 36:24 **14** Eze 36:27 **16** See Nu 17:2; 2Ch 11:12,13,16; 15:9; 30:11,18 **17** See ver. 22,24 **18** Eze 12:9; 24:19 **19** Zec 10:6; ver. 16,17 **20** Eze 12:3 **21** Eze 36:24 **22** Isa 11:13; Jer 3:18; Hos 1:11; Eze 34:23; Jn 10:16

nations, and will no longer be divided
into two kingdoms. [Jer 50:4]
23 “They will no longer defile them-
selves with their idols, or with their
detestable things, or with any of their
transgressions; but I will save them
from all their transgressions in which
they have sinned, and I will cleanse
them. So they will be My people, and
I will be their God.

The Davidic Kingdom

24 “My servant David will be king
over them, and they all will have one
shepherd. They will also walk in My
ordinances and keep My statutes and
observe them.
25 “They will live in the land where
your fathers lived, [the land] that I gave
to My servant Jacob, and they will
live there, they and their children and
their children's children, forever; and
My servant David will be their leader
forever. [Is 60:21; Joel 3:20; Amos 9:15]
26 “I will make a covenant of peace
with them; it will be an everlasting
covenant with them. And I will place
them and multiply them, and will put
My sanctuary in their midst forever.
27 “My dwelling place also will be
with them; and I will be their God, and
they will be My people.
28 “Then the nations will know [with-
out any doubt] that I am the LORD who
sets apart *and* sanctifies Israel [for holy
use], when My sanctuary is in their
midst forever.” ’ ”

Prophecy about Gog and Future Invasion of Israel

38 AND THE word of the LORD
came to me, saying,
2 “Son of man, set your face against
Gog of the land of Magog, the chief rul-
er of Meshech and Tubal, and prophesy
against him,
3 and say, ‘Thus says the Lord GOD,
“Behold, I am against you, O Gog, chief
ruler of Meshech and Tubal.
4 “I will turn you around and put
hooks into your jaws, and I will bring
you out, and all your army, horses and
horsemen, all of them magnificently
clothed in full armor, a great horde
with buckler (small shield) and [large]
shield, all of them wielding swords;
5 Persia (Iran), Cush (Ethiopia), and
Put (Libya, N. Africa) with them, all of
them with shield and helmet;
6 Gomer and all its troops; Beth-
togarmah from the remote parts of
the north and all its troops—many
peoples with you.
7 “You [Gog] be prepared; prepare
yourself, you and all your hordes that
are assembled around you, and be a
guard *and* a lookout for them.
8 “After many days you will be sum-
moned [for service]; in the latter years
you shall come into the land that is re-

37:24 – 25 *My servant David.* This title refers to the Messiah and King who would come from David's line to save Israel (2Sa 7:8 – 16).
37:26 – 28 *My sanctuary in their midst.* The sanctuary or holy place of the living God is His dwelling place among His people (Zep 3:15 – 18). ***My sanctuary.*** This is a synonym for tabernacle. Both can be used of God's dwelling in the midst of His people in the wilderness. Here they point to the future dwelling of the living God in the midst of His people forevermore.
38:2 *Son of man.* This is a title for Ezekiel emphasizing his humanity, even though his message was from God. The proper names in this prophecy do not have to be specifically identified for an understanding of the main message.
38:3 *Gog.* This leader or king only appears in Scripture here and in Revelation 20:8. Several ideas about his identity have been suggested but none are completely convincing.
38:8 *After many days . . . in the latter years.* The first phrase usually denotes an indefinite time period, sometimes extending into the distant future or the end times (Da 8:26). The second phrase frequently points to messianic times or to the times when Israel is regathered. From Ezekiel's viewpoint, he was predicting a time in the very distant future — the end times. Unless the passage refers to spiritual warfare, the invasion of Israel and the subsequent time of confident and carefree peace are still future events. ***they are living securely.*** This phrase indicates that

23 Eze 36:25; Eze 36:28 **24** Isa 40:11; Jer 23:5; Lk 1:32; Jn 10:16; Eze 36:27 **25** Eze 36:28; Isa 60:21; Joel 3:20; Am 9:15; Jn 12:34 **26** Ps 89:3; Isa 55:3; Jer 32:40; Eze 36:10; 2Co 6:16 **27** Lev 26:11; Jn 1:14; Eze 11:20 **28** Eze 36:23; Eze 20:12 **CHAPTER 38** **2** Eze 39:1; Eze 35:2,3; Rev 20:8; Eze 32:26 **4** 2Ki 19:28; Eze 29:4; Eze 23:12 **6** Ge 10:2; Eze 27:14 **7** Isa 8:9,10; Jer 46:3,4 **8** ver. 16; Dt 4:30; Isa 29:6; Eze 34:13; Eze 36:1,4; Jer 23:6

stored from [the ravages of] the sword,
where people have been gathered out
of many nations to the mountains of
Israel, which had been a continual
wasteland; but its people were brought
out of the nations, and they are living
securely, all of them. [Is 24:22]
9 “You will go up [against them], you
will come like a storm; you shall be
like a cloud covering the land, you
and all your troops, and many peoples
with you.”
10 ‘Thus says the Lord GOD, “It will
come about on that day that thoughts
will come into your mind, and you will
devise an evil plan,
11 and you will say, ‘I will go up
against an open country; I will come
against those who are at rest *and*
peaceful, who live securely, all of them
living without walls and having nei-
ther bars nor gates,
12 to take spoil and seize plunder,
to turn your hand against the ruins
which are now inhabited, and against
the people who are gathered from the
nations, who have acquired cattle and
goods, who live at the center of the
world [Israel].’
13 “Sheba and Dedan and the mer-
chants of Tarshish (southern Spain),
with all its young lions (villages) will
say to you, ‘Have you come to take
spoil? Have you assembled your hordes
[of fighting men] to seize plunder, to
carry away silver and gold, to take
away cattle and goods, to take great
spoil?’ ” ’
14 “Therefore, son of man, prophesy
and say to Gog, ‘Thus says the Lord
GOD, “On that day when My people Is-
rael live securely, will you not become
aware of it [and become active]?
15 “You will come from your place in
the remote parts of the north, you and
many nations with you, all of them
riding horses, a great horde, and a
mighty army;
16 and you will go up against My peo-
ple Israel like a cloud to cover the land.
In the last days it will come about that
I will bring you against My land, so
that the nations may know Me when I
show Myself holy through you before
their eyes, O Gog.”
17 ‘Thus says the Lord GOD, “Are you
the one of whom I spoke in former days
through My servants, the prophets of
Israel, who prophesied in those days
for many years that I would bring you
(Gog) against them?
18 “It will come about on that day,
when Gog comes against the land of
Israel,” says the Lord GOD, “that My
wrath will rise and show on My face.
19 “In My zeal and in My blazing rage
I declare that on that day there will
most certainly be a great earthquake
in the land of Israel,
20 so that the fishes of the sea, the
birds of the sky, the animals of the
field, all the creatures that crawl on
the earth, and all the men that are on
the face of the earth will tremble *and*
shake at My presence; the mountains
will crumble, the steep places will fall,
and every wall will fall to the ground.
21 “I will call for a sword against Gog
throughout all My mountains,” says
the Lord GOD. “Every man’s (invading
soldier’s) sword will be against his
brother (ally) [in panic and confusion].
22 “With pestilence and with bloodshed
I will enter into judgment with Gog; and
I will rain on him torrents of rain with
[great] hailstones, fire and brimstone
on his hordes and on the many nations
that are with him. [Ps 11:6]
23 “Thus I shall magnify Myself *and*
demonstrate My greatness and sancti-
fy Myself, and I will be recognized *and*
will make Myself known in the sight of

---

the Israel of this passage is secure; the nation is not safe from attack, but it is safe from defeat.
38:18–23 My wrath will rise and show on My face. These verses speak of God defending His nation against Gog and his army with supernatural and earthshaking methods. Unusually strong language concerning the wrath of God is found in these verses.

---

9 Isa 28:2; Jer 4:13 **11** Jer 49:31; ver. 8 **12** ver. 8 **13** Eze 27:12,15,22; Eze 19:3,5 **14** Isa 4:1; ver. 8 **15** Eze 39:2; ver. 6 **16** ver. 9; ver. 8 **19** Eze 36:5,6; Ps 89:46; Hag 2:6,7; Rev 16:18 **20** Hos 4:3; Jer 4:24 **21** Ps 105:16; Eze 14:17; Jdg 7:22; 1Sa 14:20 **22** Isa 66:16; Jer 25:31; Eze 5:17; Ps 11:6; Isa 30:30; Rev 16:21 **23** Eze 36:23; Eze 37:28

many nations; they will know [without
any doubt] that I am the LORD." '

Prophecy against Gog—Invaders Destroyed

39 "AND YOU, son of man, proph-
esy against Gog, 'Thus says the
Lord GOD, "Behold, I am against you,
O Gog, chief prince (ruler) of Meshech
and Tubal;
2 and I will turn you around and lead
you along, and bring you up from the
remotest parts of the north, and I will
bring you against the mountains of
Israel.
3 "I will strike your bow from your
left hand and make your arrows to fall
out of your right hand.
4 "You will fall [dead] on the moun-
tains of Israel, you and all your troops
and the nations who are with you. I
will give you to every kind of predatory
bird and animal of the field as food.
5 "You will fall in the open field, for I
have spoken," says the Lord GOD.
6 "I will also send fire on Magog and
on those who live securely in the coast-
lands; and they will know [without any
doubt] that I am the LORD.
7 "I will make My holy name known
in the midst of My people Israel, and
I will not let them profane My holy
name anymore; and the nations will
know that I am the LORD, the Holy
One of Israel.
8 "Behold, it is coming and it will be
done," says the Lord GOD. "That is the
day of which I have spoken.
9 "And [when you, Gog, no longer
exist] those who live in the cities of
Israel will go out and make fires with
the weapons and burn them, both the
[large] shields and the bucklers (small
shields), the bows and the arrows, the
war clubs and the spears; and for seven
years they will burn them.
10 "They will not take any wood
from the field or cut down *and* gather
[any] firewood from the forests, be-
cause they will make their fires using
the weapons. And they will take the
spoil from those who despoiled them
and seize the plunder of those who
plundered them," says the Lord GOD.
11 "And on that day I will give Gog
a place for burial there in Israel, the
valley of those who pass through east
of the sea, and it will block the way
of those who would pass through. So
they will bury Gog there with all his
hordes, and they will call it the Valley
of Hamon-gog (the multitude of Gog).
12 "For seven months the house of
Israel will be burying them in order
to cleanse the land.
13 "Yes, all the people of the land will
bury them; and it will be to their re-
nown on the day that I appear in My
glory *and* brilliance," says the Lord
GOD.
14 "They will elect men who will
constantly go through the land, [men
commissioned] to bury those who were
passing through, those bodies that lie
unburied on the surface of the ground,
in order to cleanse it. At the end of
seven months they will do a search.
15 "As those who pass through the
land pass through and anyone sees a
human bone, he will set up a marker
beside it, until the buriers have buried
it in the Valley of Hamon-gog.
16 "And even the name of the city will
be Hamonah. In this manner they shall
cleanse the land." '
17 "As for you, son of man, thus says
the Lord GOD, 'Say to every kind of
bird and to every animal of the field,

39:6 *I will also send fire.* Often fire from the Lord has the form of lightning bolts (1Ki 18:38).
39:12 *cleanse the land.* The law of Moses prescribed the sacrifice of a heifer to cleanse the land if a murdered person was found in a region (Dt 21:1–9).
39:17–20 *Say to every kind of bird.* A poem or song is addressed to the scavenging birds and beasts who come to the multitude of dead bodies (vv. 14–16). Whether figurative or not, the passage powerfully pictures God's sovereign control over the complete conquest of Israel's future and most ferocious enemies (Rev 19:11–21). The meal would be a divinely prepared sacrifice served at God's table.

CHAPTER 39 **1** Eze 38:2,3 **2** Eze 38:15 **4** Eze 38:21; Eze 33:27 **6** Am 1:4; Ps 72:10 **7** ver. 22; Lev 18:21; Eze 38:16 **8** Rev 16:17; 21:6; Eze 38:17 **10** Isa 14:2 **12** Dt 21:23 **13** Eze 28:22 **14** ver. 12 **16** ver. 12 **17** Rev 19:7; Isa 18:6; Zep 1:7; ver. 4

“Assemble and come, gather from
every side to My sacrifice that I am
slaughtering for you, as a great sacri-
ficial feast on the mountains of Israel,
and you will eat flesh and drink blood.
18“You will eat the flesh of mighty
men and drink the blood of the princ-
es of the earth, *as though they were*
rams, lambs, goats, and bulls, all of
them fatlings of Bashan [east of the
Jordan].
19“So you will eat fat until you are
filled and drink blood till you are
drunk, at the sacrificial feast which I
have prepared for you.
20“You will eat your fill at My table
with horses and riders, with mighty
men, and with all the men of war,” says
the Lord God.
21“And I will bring [and manifest]
My glory among the nations; and all
the nations will see My judgment *and*
justice [in the punishment] which I
have executed and My hand which I
have laid on them.
22“So the house of Israel will know
[with absolute confidence] that I am the
LORD their God from that day forward.
23“And the nations will know [with-
out any doubt] that the house of Israel
went into exile for their great sin, be-
cause they acted treacherously against
Me; and I hid My face (favor, blessing)
from them. So I gave them into the
hand of their enemies, and they all fell
[into captivity or were killed] by [the
power of] the sword. [Deut 31:17]
24“I dealt with them in accordance
with their uncleanness and their trans-
gressions, and I hid My face from
them.” ’ ”

Israel Restored

25Therefore thus says the Lord God,
“Now I will restore the fortunes of Ja-
cob (Israel) and have mercy on the
whole house of Israel; and I will be
jealous for My holy name [demanding
what is rightfully and uniquely mine].
26“They will forget their disgrace
and all their treachery (unfaithfulness)
which they perpetuated against Me,
when they live securely in their own
land and there is no one who makes
them afraid.
27“When I bring them back from the
nations and gather them out of their
enemies’ lands, then I shall show My-
self holy [and My justice and holiness
will be vindicated] through them in the
sight of many nations.
28“Then they will know [without any
doubt] that I am the LORD their God be-
cause I made them go into exile among
the nations, and then gathered them to
their own land. I will leave none of them
there [among the nations] any longer.
29“I will not hide My face from them
any longer, because I will have poured
out My Spirit on the house of Israel,”
says the Lord God.

Vision of the Man with a Measuring Rod

40 IN THE twenty-fifth year of our
exile [in Babylon], in the begin-
ning of the year, on the tenth [day] of
the month, in the fourteenth year after
the city [of Jerusalem] was taken, on
that [very] same day the hand of the
LORD was upon me and He brought
me there.

39:21 – 22 *My glory among the nations.* The universal knowledge of the living God of Israel will be based finally on the outcome of the battle described in chapters 38 and 39. Ezekiel followed the great theme of biblical theology begun in Genesis 12:3 that the ultimate purpose of God in His choice of Abraham and Sarah was to make His blessings known to all the families of the earth. God will demonstrate His glory both among the nations and among His chosen people Israel.

40:1 *In the twenty-fifth year of our exile.* The actual date would have been about 573 BC. This final vision of the temple in the book is one of God returning to dwell in the midst of His people who are now restored in their homeland. These are difficult chapters to interpret because of how easy it is to get bogged down in the architectural details. The writing is apocalyptic in style and expresses in symbolic manner how God would restore Israel in the future.

18 Rev 19:18; Dt 32:14; Ps 22:12 **20** Ps 76:6; Eze 38:4; Rev 19:18 **21** Eze 38:16,23; Ex 7:4 **22** ver. 7,28 **23** Eze 36:18-20,23; Dt 31:17; Isa 59:2; Lev 26:25 **24** Eze 36:19 **25** Jer 30:3,18; Eze 34:13; 36:24; Eze 20:40; Hos 1:11 **26** Da 9:16; Lev 26:5,6 **27** Eze 28:25,26; Eze 36:23,24; 38:16 **28** ver. 22; Eze 34:30 **29** Isa 54:8; Joel 2:28; Zec 12:10; Ac 2:17 **CHAPTER 40** **1** Eze 33:21; Eze 1:3

2 In the visions of God He brought me
to the land of Israel and set me down
on a very high mountain, on the south
side of which *there was* what seemed
to be a structure of a city.
3 So He brought me there; and behold,
there was a man [an angel] whose ap-
pearance was like bronze, with a line of
flax and a measuring rod in his hand;
and he was standing in the gateway.
4 The man said to me, "Son of man,
look with your eyes and hear with your
ears and set your heart on all that I
am going to show you; for you have
been brought here that I may show it
to you. Declare to the house of Israel
all that you see."

Measurements Relating to the Temple

5 And behold, there was a wall all
around the outside [area] of the temple
(house) [of the LORD], and in the man's
hand a measuring rod six cubits long
(10.2 ft.), each cubit being longer than
the standard one by a hand width. So
he measured the thickness of the wall,
one rod; and the height, one rod.
6 Then he went to the gate which
faced the east and went up its [seven]
steps and measured the threshold of
the gate, one rod in width; and the
other threshold [of the gate inside the
thick wall] was one rod in width.
7 The guardroom was one rod long
and one rod wide, and [the space] be-
tween the guardrooms was five cubits.
And the threshold of the gate by the
porch (portico) of the gate facing in-
ward was one rod.
8 He also measured the porch of the
gate facing inward [toward the temple
of the LORD], one rod.
9 Then he measured the porch of the
gate, eight cubits, and its side pillars,
two cubits. The porch of the gate faced
inward [toward the temple of the LORD].
10 There were three guardrooms on
each side of the gate toward the east; the
three were the same size, and the side
pillars on each side measured the same.
11 And he measured the width of the
gateway, ten cubits, and the length of
the gate, thirteen cubits.
12 On each side a border (barrier
wall) one cubit wide stood in front of
the guardrooms on each side; and the
guardrooms were six cubits *square*
on each side.
13 He measured the gate from the
roof of one guardroom to the roof of
the other, a width of twenty-five cubits
from one door to the opposite door.
14 He made [the measurement of] the
side pillars sixty cubits *high;* the gate
extended all around to the side pillar
of the courtyard.
15 From the front of the entrance gate
[on the outside] to the front of the inner
porch (portico) of the gate [the dis-
tance] was fifty cubits.
16 *There were* shuttered windows
looking toward the guardrooms, and
toward their side pillars within the
gate all around, and likewise for the
porches. And windows were all around
inside; and palm tree decorations were
on each side pillar.
17 Then he brought me into the out-
er courtyard, and behold, *there were*
chambers and a pavement made for the
courtyard all around; thirty chambers
faced the pavement.
18 The pavement (*that is,* the low-
er pavement) was by the side of the
gates, corresponding to the length of
the gates.

40:3 – 5 *a line of flax and a measuring rod in his hand.* This man with a measuring rod is a kind of angelic architect who serves as both a guide and an interpreter for Ezekiel. *Declare to the house of Israel all that you see.* The details of the temple would have been of great importance and enormous interest to the exiles because the temple was the focal point of all of their worship.

40:7 *cubits . . . rod.* A cubit was about 18 inches long. A measuring rod was six cubits or ten and one-half feet in length.

40:16 *palm tree decorations.* These were common decorations that were also found in Solomon's temple (1Ki 6:29 – 35).

2 Eze 8:3; Rev 21:10 **3** Eze 1:7; Da 10:6; Eze 47:3; Rev 11:1; 21:15 **4** Eze 44:5; Eze 43:10 **5** Eze 42:20 **16** 1Ki 6:4 **17** Rev 11:2; 1Ki 6:5; Eze 45:5

EZEKIEL'S TEMPLE

Ezekiel uses a long or "royal" cubit, about 21 inches or 53 centimeters ("cubit and a handbreadth," Eze 40:5) as opposed to the standard Hebrew cubit of about 18 inches or 46 centimeters.

Scripture describes a floor plan but provides few height dimensions. This artwork shows an upward projection of the temple over the floor plan. This temple existed only in a vision of Ezekiel (Eze 40:2) and was never actually built as were the temples of Solomon, Zerubbabel and Herod, but some premillennial interpreters believe that it will be built in the future.

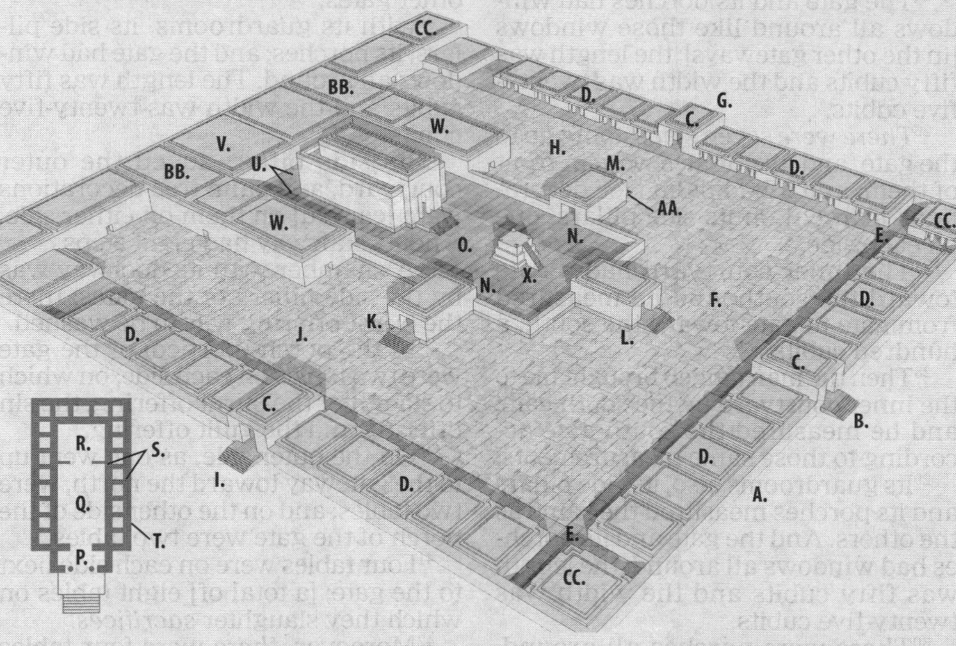

A. Wall (40:5,16–20)	**H.** North inner court (40:23)	**O.** Court (40:47)	**V.** West building (41:12)
B. East gate (40:6–14,16)	**I.** South gate (40:24–26)	**P.** Temple portico (40:48–49)	**W.** Priests' rooms (42:1–10)
C. Portico (40:8)	**J.** South inner court (40:27)	**Q.** Outer sanctuary (41:1–2)	**X.** Altar (43:13–17)
D. Outer court (40:17)	**K.** Gateway (40:28–31)	**R.** Most Holy Place (41:3–4)	**AA.** Rooms for preparing sacrifices (40:39–43)
E. Pavement (40:17)	**L.** Gateway (40:32–34)	**S.** Temple walls (41:5–7,9,11)	
F. East inner court (40:19)	**M.** Gateway (40:35–38)	**T.** Base (41:8)	**BB.** Ovens (46:19–20)
G. North gate (40:20–22)	**N.** Priests' rooms (40:44–45)	**U.** Open area (41:10)	**CC.** Kitchens (46:21–24)

[19]Then he measured the width from
the front of the lower gate to the front
of the exterior of the inner court, a
hundred cubits [both] on the east and
on the north.
[20]And as for the gate of the outer
courtyard which faced the north he
measured [both] its length and its
width.
[21]Its guardrooms, three on each side,
and its side pillars and its porches had
the same measurement as the first
gate. Its length was fifty cubits and the
width was twenty-five cubits.
[22]Its windows and its porches and
its palm tree decorations had the same
measurements as the gate that faced
toward the east. It was reached by go-
ing up seven steps, and its porch was
in front of them.
[23]The inner courtyard had a gate op-
posite the gate on the north as well as

40:22 ***It was reached by going up seven steps.*** This would indicate that the temple area is a huge raised area, built up above the level of the surrounding land.

the gate on the east; and he measured
a hundred cubits from gate to gate.
24 Then he led me toward the south,
and behold, there was a gate toward
the south; and he measured its side
pillars and its porches, and they mea-
sured the same as the others.
25 The gate and its porches had win-
dows all around like those windows
[in the other gateways]; the length was
fifty cubits and the width was twenty-
five cubits.
26 *There were* seven steps going up to
the gate, and its porches were in front
of them; and it had palm tree decora-
tions [carved] on its side pillars, one
on each side.
27 The inner courtyard had a gate
toward the south; and he measured
from gate to gate toward the south, a
hundred cubits.
28 Then the man (angel) brought me to
the inner courtyard by the south gate;
and he measured the south gate ac-
cording to those same measurements.
29 Its guardrooms also, its side pillars
and its porches measured the same as
the others. And the gate and its porch-
es had windows all around; the length
was fifty cubits and the width was
twenty-five cubits.
30 *There were* porches all around,
twenty-five cubits long and five cubits
wide.
31 Its porches faced the outer court-
yard; and palm tree decorations were
[carved] on its side pillars, and its stair-
way had eight steps.
32 He brought me into the inner court-
yard toward the east, and he measured
the gate; it measured the same as the
others.
33 Its guardrooms also, its side pillars
and its porches measured the same as
the others. The gate and its porches
had windows all around; it was fif-
ty cubits long and twenty-five cubits
wide.
34 Its porches faced the outer court-
yard; and palm tree decorations were
[carved] on either side of its side pil-
lars, and its stairway had eight steps.
35 Then he brought me to the north
gate and he measured it; the measure-
ments were the same as those of the
other gates,
36 with its guardrooms, its side pil-
lars, its porches; and the gate had win-
dows all around. The length was fifty
cubits and the width was twenty-five
cubits.
37 Its side pillars faced the outer
courtyard, and palm tree decorations
were [carved] on them on either side.
And its stairway had eight steps.
38 A chamber with its doorway was
by the side pillars of the gates; there
the burnt offering was to be washed.
39 In the porch (portico) of the gate
were two tables on each side, on which
to slaughter the burnt offering, the sin
offering and the guilt offering.
40 On the outer side, as one went up
to the gateway toward the north, were
two tables; and on the other side of the
porch of the gate were two tables.
41 Four tables were on each side next
to the gate; [a total of] eight tables on
which they slaughter *sacrifices.*
42 Moreover, *there were* four tables
of hewn stone (ashlar) for the burnt
offering, a cubit and a half long, a cubit
and a half wide, and one cubit high, on
which they lay the instruments with
which they slaughter the burnt offer-
ing and the sacrifice.
43 The double hooks, one hand width
in length were installed in the house all
around. The meat of the offering was
[to be placed] on the tables.
44 From the outside to the inner gate
were chambers for the singers in the
inner courtyard, *one of* which was
beside the north gate, with its front
toward the south, and one beside the
south gate facing toward the north.

40:38 – 43 *Four tables were on each side . . . on which they slaughter sacrifices.* Ezekiel observes a room where the animals are slaughtered and washed for sacrificial offerings. These sacrifices point to the ultimate sacrifice; the sacrifice of God's only Son on the cross once for all (Heb 7:20 – 28; 9:25 – 30).

40:44 – 47 *chamber . . . for the priests*. The guide explains that the chamber on the north side is for the priests who run the day-to-day

30 See ver. 21,25,33,36 **39** Lev 4:2,3; Lev 5:6; 6:6; 7:1 **44** 1Ch 6:31

45He [who was guiding me] said to me, "This is the chamber which faces toward the south; it is for the priests who have the responsibility *and* take care of the temple;

46but the chamber which faces toward the north is for the priests who have the responsibility *and* take care of the altar. These are the sons of Zadok, who [alone] from the sons of Levi come near to the LORD to minister to Him."

47He measured the courtyard, a hundred cubits long and a hundred cubits wide, a *perfect* square; and the altar was in front of the temple.

48Then he brought me to the porch of the temple, and he measured each side pillar of the porch, five cubits on each side; and the width of the gate was three cubits on each side.

49The length of the porch was twenty cubits and the width eleven cubits; and at the stairway by which it was ascended, there were [two] columns beside the side pillars, one on each side [of the entrance].

The Inner Temple

41 THEN HE (the angel) brought me to the nave (outer sanctuary) and measured the side pillars; six cubits wide on each side was the width of the side pillar.

2The width of the entrance was ten cubits and the sides of the entrance were five cubits on each side; and he measured its length, forty cubits, and its width, twenty cubits.

3Then he went inside [the inner sanctuary] and measured each side pillar of the doorway, two cubits, and the doorway, six cubits [high], and the width of the doorway, seven cubits. [Heb 9:6, 7; 10:19–25]

4He measured the length [of the interior of the inner sanctuary], twenty cubits, and the width, twenty cubits, opposite the nave (outer sanctuary); and he said to me, "This is the Most Holy Place."

5Then he measured the wall of the temple, six cubits [thick, to accommodate side chambers]; and the width of every side chamber, four cubits, all around the temple on every side.

6The side chambers were three stories [high], one above another, and thirty chambers in each story; and the side chambers extended to the wall which stood on their inward side all around, so that they would be attached, but not attached to the wall of the temple *itself*.

7The side chambers became wider at each successive level as they encompassed the temple. Because the structure surrounding the temple went higher by stages on all sides of the temple, for that reason the width of the temple *increased* as it went higher; and thus one went up from the lowest *story* to the highest one by way of the second *story*.

8I also saw that the temple (house) had a raised platform all around it; the foundations of the side chambers *measured* a full rod of six long cubits *in height*.

9The thickness of the outer wall of the side chambers was five cubits. But the free space between the side chambers belonging to the temple

10and the *outer* chambers was a width of twenty cubits all around the temple on every side.

11The doorways of the side chambers toward the free space were one doorway toward the north and another doorway toward the south; and the width of the free space was five cubits all around.

12The building that was in front of the separate area on the side toward

---

operations of the temple. The chamber on the south side is for the priests who perform the sacrifices.

41:1–4 *Then he (the angel) brought me to the nave.* The basic temple has three areas: the outer area, the holy place or "nave," and the inner area or the "most holy place." The innermost room is the focal point of the whole structure. Only the High Priest could enter it and then only once a year on the Day of Atonement.

45 Lev 8:35; Nu 3:27,28,32, 38; 18:5; 1Ch 9:23; 2Ch 13:11; Ps 134:1 **46** Nu 18:5; Eze 44:15; 1Ki 2:35; Eze 43:19; 44:15,16 **49** 1Ki 6:3; 1Ki 7:21 **CHAPTER 41** **4** 1Ki 6:20; 2Ch 3:8 **6** 1Ki 6:5,6 **7** 1Ki 6:8 **8** Eze 40:5

the west was seventy cubits wide; and
the wall of the building was five cubits
thick all around, and its length was
ninety cubits.
[13]Then he measured the temple, a
hundred cubits long; the separate area
and the building with its walls were
also a hundred cubits long.
[14]Also the width of the front of the
temple and the separate areas along
the east *side totaled* a hundred cubits.
[15]He (the angel) measured the length
of the building along the front of the
separate area behind it, with a gallery
on each side, a hundred cubits; he also
measured the inner sanctuary and the
porches (porticoes) of the courtyard.
[16]The thresholds, the latticed win-
dows, and the galleries all around their
three stories, opposite the threshold,
were paneled with wood all around,
and from the ground to the windows
(but the windows were covered),
[17]over the entrance, and to the inner
room, and on the outside, and on all the
wall all around inside and outside, by
measurement.
[18]It was carved with [figures of]
cherubim and palm trees; so that a
palm decoration was between cherub
and cherub, and every cherub had two
faces,
[19]so that the face of a man was to-
ward the palm decoration on the one
side, and the face of a young lion to-
ward the palm decoration on the other
side. It was carved [this way] on the
entire house (temple) all around.
[20]From the floor to [the space] above
the entrance cherubim and palm dec-
orations were carved, and also on the
wall of the nave [the Holy Place].
[21]The doorposts of the nave were
square; as for the front of the sanctu-
ary, the appearance of one doorpost
was like that of the other.
[22]The altar was of wood, three cubits
high and two cubits long; and its cor-
ners, its base, and its sides were wood.
And he said to me, "This is the table
that is before the LORD."
[23]The nave (Holy Place) and the
sanctuary (Holy of Holies) each had
a double door.
[24]Each of the doors had two leaves,
two swinging (folding) leaves; two
leaves for the one door and two leaves
for the other.
[25]And there were carved on them, on
the doors of the nave, cherubim and
palm decorations like those carved on
the walls; and *there was* a threshold of
wood on the front of the porch outside.
[26]*There were* latticed windows and
palm decorations on one side and on
the other, on the sides of the porch.
Thus were the side chambers and the
thresholds of the house.

Chambers of the Temple

42 THEN HE (the angel) brought
me out into the outer courtyard,
toward the north; and he led me to the
[attached] chamber which was oppo-
site the separate area and opposite the
building to the north.
[2]Along the length, one hundred cu-
bits, was the north door; and the width
was fifty cubits.
[3]Opposite the twenty *cubits* which

41:13 – 15 *Then he measured the temple.* Ezekiel would have found pleasure in the symmetrical precision of the temple. It would have meant that it all fit together perfectly. There was nothing that was out of place. This may represent the order and harmony in God's future kingdom.

41:22 *This is the table that is before the LORD.* This is a reference to the table that held the shewbread or bread of the Presence (Ex 25:23 – 30), a reminder that man lives his whole life constantly in the divine presence. When God is not present to bless His people, their worship is unacceptable, because such worship will inevitably be merely formal and devoid of blessing. When God is present with His people in worship, they are then enabled to worship.

42:1 – 14 *Then he (the angel) brought me out into the outer courtyard.* At this point the text has given us many details of the physical descriptions of the temple. No references have been made to God's spiritual presence. Ezekiel has set the scene for the return of the Lord to His temple and city.

---

16 ver. 26; Eze 40:16 **18** 1Ki 6:29 **19** See Eze 1:10 **22** Ex 30:1; Eze 44:16; Mal 1:7,12; Ex 30:8 **23** 1Ki 6:31-35 **26** ver. 16; Eze 40:16 **CHAPTER 42** **1** Eze 41:12,15 **3** Eze 41:16

belonged to the inner courtyard, and
opposite the pavement which belonged
to the outer courtyard, was gallery
(balcony) corresponding to gallery in
three stories.
4In front of the [attached] chambers
was an inner walkway ten cubits wide
and one *hundred* cubits long; and their
entrances were on the north.
5Now the upper chambers were
smaller because the galleries took
away more *space* from them than from
the chambers on the lower and middle
stories of the building;
6for they were in three stories and
did not have pillars like the pillars of
the [outer] courtyards; therefore *the
upper chambers* were set back from
the ground more than the lower and
the middle ones.
7And the outer wall, by the side of
the chambers, toward the outer court-
yard facing the chambers, was fifty
cubits long.
8For the length of the chambers
which were in the outer courtyard was
fifty cubits, while *the length of* those
facing the temple was a hundred cubits.
9Below these chambers was the en-
trance on the east side, as one enters
them from the outer courtyard.
10In the width of the wall of the
courtyard toward the east, facing the
separate area and facing the building,
were chambers;
11and a passage in front of them was
like the appearance of the [attached]
chambers on the north, *and* they had
the same length and width, and all
their exits were like both their ar-
rangements and their entrances.
12And like the entrances of the
chambers that were toward the south
there was an entrance at the head of
the walkway, the walkway in front of
the dividing wall toward the east, as
one enters them.
13Then he (the angel) said to me,
"The north chambers and the south
chambers, which are opposite the
separate area, are the holy chambers
where the priests who are close to the
LORD shall eat the most holy *offerings*.
There they shall place the most holy
things—the grain offering, the sin of-
fering, and the guilt offering—for the
place is holy.
14"When the priests enter [the Holy
Place], they shall not go out from the
sanctuary into the outer court unless
they lay there their garments in which
they minister, for these are holy (set
apart). They shall put on other gar-
ments before they approach that which
is for the people."
15Now when he had finished mea-
suring the inner temple, he brought
me out toward the gate which faced
east and measured the outer area all
around.
16He measured the east side with the
measuring rod, five hundred rods by
the measuring rod.
17He measured the north side, five
hundred rods by the measuring rod.
18He measured the south side, five
hundred rods by the measuring rod.
19He turned about to the west side
and measured five hundred rods by
the measuring rod.
20He measured it on the four sides; it
had a wall all around, the length five
hundred and the width five hundred,
to make a separation between that
which was holy [the temple proper]
and that which was common [the outer
area].

Vision of the Glory of God Filling the Temple

43 THEN HE (the angel) led me
to the gate, the gate that faces
toward the east.

42:13 – 14 *the holy chambers where the priests who are close to the LORD shall eat.* This chapter focuses on the buildings designed for the use of the priests. They were used for storage, changing, and eating.

42:15 – 20 *he brought me out.* After seeing the inside of the temple area, the guide takes Ezekiel to see the surrounding grounds.

11 ver. 4 **13** Lev 6:16,26; 24:9; Lev 2:3,10; 6:14,17,25,29 **14** Eze 44:19 **20** Eze 40:5; Eze 45:2
CHAPTER 43 **1** Eze 10:19; 46:1

2 And behold, the glory *and* brilliance of the God of Israel was coming from the way of the east; and His voice was like the sound of many waters, and the earth shone with His glory. [Rev 1:15; 14:2]

3 And it was like the appearance of the vision which I saw, like the vision I saw when He came to destroy the city. And the visions were like the vision I saw beside the River Chebar [near Babylon]; and I fell face downward. [Ezek 1:4; 3:23; 10:15, 22]

4 And the glory *and* brilliance of the LORD entered the temple by way of the gate facing toward the east.

5 Then the Spirit lifted me up and brought me into the inner courtyard; and behold, the glory *and* brilliance of the LORD filled the temple.

6 And I heard One speaking to me from the temple, while a man was standing beside me.

7 And He [the LORD] said to me, "Son of man, *this is* the place of My throne and the place of the soles of My feet, where I will dwell in the midst of the sons (descendants) of Israel forever. And the house of Israel will not again defile My holy name, neither they nor their kings, by their [idolatrous] prostitution and by the corpses *and* monuments of their kings in their graves,

8 by setting their threshold by My threshold and their doorpost beside My doorpost, with [only] the wall between Me and them. They have defiled *and* desecrated My holy name by the vile atrocities which they have committed. So I have consumed them in My anger.

9 "Now let them put far away from Me their [idolatrous] prostitution and the corpses *and* monuments of their kings, and I will dwell in their midst forever.

10 "As for you, son of man, describe the temple to the house of Israel, so that they will be ashamed of their sins; and let them measure its plan [in detail].

11 "If they are ashamed of all that they have done, make known to them the design of the temple (house), its layout, its exits, its entrances, all its designs, all its statutes, and all its laws. And write it down in their sight, so that they may keep its whole design and all its statutes and do them.

12 "This is the law of the temple: Its entire area all around on the top of the mountain (Mount Moriah) *shall be* most holy. Behold, this is the law of the temple.

The Altar of Sacrifice

13 "And these are the measurements of the altar [of burnt offering] in cubits (the cubit being a [long] cubit [the length of a forearm] and a hand width): the base *shall be* a cubit [long] and a cubit wide, with its border on its edge all around it of a span [in width]. And this *shall be the height of* the base of the altar.

14 "From the base on the ground to the lower ledge *shall be* two cubits and the width one cubit; and from the smaller ledge to the larger ledge *shall be* four cubits and the width one cubit.

15 "The altar hearth *shall be* four cubits high, and from the altar hearth shall extend upwards four horns [one from each corner, each one cubit high].

16 "Now the altar hearth *shall be*

43:2 *the glory and brilliance of the God of Israel was coming.* Nineteen years before, Ezekiel had a vision of the Lord leaving His temple (10:18 – 22; 11:22 – 24). Now he gets a chance to see His return. Ezekiel's response is one of being overwhelmed with awe.

43:3 *the River Chebar.* This was where the Jewish exiles were located in Babylonia.

43:7 – 12 *I will dwell in the midst of the sons (descendants) of Israel forever.* When God left Jerusalem, it rapidly moved towards destruction. Here, when God returned, everything was rebuilt as a permanent dwelling. The Lord stipulated that Israel was not to defile God's holiness as it had done in the past.

2 Eze 11:23; Eze 1:24; Rev 1:15; 14:2; Eze 10:4; Rev 18:1 **3** Eze 1:4,28; Jer 1:10; Eze 3:23 **4** Eze 10:19 **5** Eze 3:12,14; 8:3; 1Ki 8:10,11 **6** Eze 40:3 **7** Ps 99:1; 1Ch 28:2; Ps 99:5; Ex 29:45; Ps 68:16; 132:14; Joel 3:17; Jn 1:14; 2Co 6:16; Eze 39:7; Lev 26:30; Jer 16:18 **8** See 2Ki 16:14; 21:4,5,7; Eze 8:3; 23:39; 44:7 **9** ver. 7; ver. 7 **10** Eze 40:4 **12** Eze 40:2 **13** Eze 41:8

twelve *cubits* long by twelve wide, square in its four sides.

17 “The ledge *shall be* fourteen *cubits* long by fourteen wide on its four sides, and the border around it *shall be* half a cubit; and its base *shall be* a cubit all around, and its steps shall face the east.” [Ex 20:26]

The Offerings

18 And He [the LORD] said to me, “Son of man, thus says the Lord GOD, ‘These are the statutes *and* regulations for [the use of] the altar on the day that it is built, to offer burnt offerings on it and to sprinkle blood on it.

19 ‘You shall give to the priests, the Levites who are from the descendants of Zadok, who are close to Me to minister to Me,’ says the Lord GOD, ‘a young bull for a sin offering [as a memorial to Christ’s sacrifice].

20 ‘And you shall take some of its blood and put it on the four horns [of the altar of burnt offering] and on the four corners of the ledge and on the border all around; thus you shall cleanse it (from sin) and make atonement for it.

21 ‘You shall also take the bull for the sin offering, and it shall be burned in the appointed place of the temple, outside the sanctuary. [Heb 13:11]

22 ‘On the second day you shall offer a male goat without blemish for a sin offering, and they shall cleanse the altar as they cleansed it with the bull.

23 ‘When you have finished cleansing it, you shall offer a young bull without blemish and a ram from the flock without blemish.

24 ‘You shall present them before the LORD, and the priests shall throw salt on them, and they shall offer them up as a burnt offering to the LORD.

25 ‘For seven days you shall prepare daily a goat for a sin offering; also a young bull and a ram from the flock, without blemish, shall be prepared.

26 ‘For seven days they shall make atonement for the altar and purify it; so the priests shall consecrate it [to receive offerings]. [Ex 29:37]

27 ‘When they have completed these days, on the eighth day and from then onward, the priests shall offer your burnt offerings on the altar, and your peace offerings; and I will accept you,’ says the Lord GOD.” [Rom 12:1; 1 Pet 2:5]

Gate for the Prince

44 THEN HE brought me back by the way of the outer gate of the sanctuary, which faces the east; and it was shut.

2 Then the LORD said to me, “This gate shall be shut; it shall not be opened, and no one shall enter by it, for the LORD, the God of Israel, has entered by it; therefore it shall be shut.

3 “As for the prince, he shall sit in it as prince to eat bread before the LORD; he shall enter by way of the porch (portico) of the gate and shall go out the same way.”

4 Then He brought me by way of the north gate to the front of the house; I looked, and behold, the glory *and* brilliance of the LORD filled the house of the LORD, and I fell face downward. [Rev 15:8]

43:20–23 *make atonement ... sin offering.* These suggest purification and cleansing from sin. Because of the sinlessness — without blemish — of the sacrifice, the people for whom the sacrifice is made are declared acceptable before God (v. 27; Ex 29:14; Lev 3; 4:12).

44:1–3 *This gate shall be shut.* Today this is known as the “Golden Gate” and dates from several centuries after Christ. It is walled shut today in accordance with an Islamic tradition.

44:4–9 *I looked, and behold, the glory and brilliance of the LORD filled the house of the LORD, and I fell face downward.* Ezekiel experiences another awe-inspiring vision of God’s glory leading him to bow in worship (1:28–2:1). God demands that His renewed people follow His regulations exactly. He emphasizes the necessity of holiness and righteousness, especially in light of Israel’s past.

17 See Ex 20:26 **18** Lev 1:5 **19** Eze 44:15; Ex 29:10; Lev 8:14; Eze 45:18 **21** Ex 29:14; Heb 13:11 **24** Lev 2:13 **25** Ex 29:35; Lev 8:33 **27** Lev 9:1; Eze 20:40,41; Ro 12:1; 1Pe 2:5 **CHAPTER 44** **1** Eze 43:1 **2** Eze 43:4 **3** Ge 31:54; 1Co 10:18; Eze 46:2,8 **4** Eze 3:23; Eze 1:28

5 The LORD said to me, “Son of man, pay careful attention, see with your eyes and hear with your ears all that I say to you concerning all the statutes of the house of the LORD and all its laws; and pay careful attention to the entering of the house [by people], with all the departures *from* the sanctuary [of people, those who are allowed to enter the temple and all those who are excluded from the sanctuary].

6 “You shall say to the rebellious ones, to the house of Israel, ‘Thus says the Lord GOD, “Enough of all your repulsive acts, O house of Israel!

7 “In that you brought in foreigners, uncircumcised in heart and uncircumcised in flesh, to be in My sanctuary to pollute *and* profane it—My house—when you offered My bread, the fat, and the blood; and they made My covenant void—*this* in addition to all your *other* repulsive acts.

8 “And you have not kept charge of My holy things yourselves, but you have chosen *foreigners* [to please yourselves] and have set them in charge of My sanctuary.”

9 ‘Thus says the Lord GOD, “No foreigner uncircumcised in heart and flesh, of all the foreigners who are among the sons of Israel, shall enter My sanctuary.

10 “But the Levites who went far away from Me when Israel went astray, who went astray from Me after their idols, they shall bear *the punishment for* their sin *and* guilt.

11 “Yet they shall minister in My sanctuary, having oversight [as guards] at the gates of the temple and ministering in the temple. They shall slaughter the burnt offering and the sacrifice for the people, and they shall stand before them to minister to them.

12 “Because the priests ministered to them before their idols and became a stumbling block of sin to the house of Israel, therefore I have lifted up My hand *and* have sworn [an oath] against them,” says the Lord GOD, “that they shall bear *the punishment for* their sin *and* guilt.

13 “And they shall not come near to Me to serve as priests to Me, nor come near to any of My holy things, to the things that are most holy; but they shall bear their shame *and* their disgrace and [the consequences of] their repulsive acts which they have committed.

14 “Yet I will appoint them as caretakers of the temple, for all its service and for all that shall be done in it.

Ordinances for the Levites

15 “But the Levitical priests, the sons of Zadok, who performed the duty of My sanctuary when the children (descendants) of Israel went astray from Me, shall come near to Me to minister to Me; and they shall stand before Me to offer to Me the fat and the blood,” declares the Lord GOD.

16 “They shall enter into My sanctuary; and they shall come near to My table to minister to Me and they shall perform [the priestly] duty to me.

17 “It shall be that when they enter the gates of the inner courtyard, they shall be clothed in linen garments; no wool shall be on them while they minister at the gates of the inner courtyard and within the temple (house).

18 “They shall have linen turbans on their heads and linen undergarments on their loins; they shall not dress themselves with *anything which makes them* sweat.

19 “When they go out into the outer

44:11–14 *Yet they shall minister in My sanctuary.* God explains to Ezekiel why the Levites would be limited to certain types of temple ministry. The Levites (with the exception of the sons of Zadok; v. 15) could not be priests but could be ministers (servants or attendants). They could not serve in the inner court or temple, where the holy things are located; but they could oversee the general operation of the temple complex.

5 Eze 40:4 **6** Eze 2:5; Eze 45:9; 1Pe 4:3 **7** ver. 9; Eze 43:8; Ac 21:28; Lev 22:25; Lev 26:41; Ac 7:51; Lev 21:17; Lev 3:16 **8** Lev 22:2 **9** ver. 7 **10** 2Ki 23:8; Eze 48:11 **11** 1Ch 26:1; 2Ch 29:34; Nu 16:9 **12** Isa 9:16; Mal 2:8; Ps 106:26 **13** Nu 18:3; 2Ki 23:9; Eze 32:30 **14** Nu 18:4; 1Ch 23:28 **15** Eze 40:46; 1Sa 2:35; ver. 10; Dt 10:8; ver. 7 **16** Eze 41:22 **17** Ex 28:39 **18** Ex 28:40; 39:28 **19** Eze 42:14; Eze 46:20; Ex 30:29; Lev 6:27; Mt 23:17

court, into the outer courtyard to the people, they shall take off the garments in which they have been ministering and leave them in the holy chambers; then they shall put on other clothing so that they will not transmit holiness to the people with their [ceremonial] garments.
[20]"Also they shall not shave their heads, yet they shall not allow their hair to grow long; they shall only cut short *or* trim their hair.
[21]"Nor shall any priest drink wine when he enters the inner courtyard.
[22]"And they shall not marry a widow or a divorced woman; but they shall marry virgins of the descendants of the house of Israel, or a widow who was previously married to a priest.
[23]"The priests shall teach My people *the difference* between the holy and the common, and teach them to distinguish between the (ceremonially) unclean and the clean.
[24]"In a controversy they shall take their stand to act as judges; they shall judge it in accordance with My ordinances. They shall also keep My laws and My statutes in all My appointed feasts and sanctify My Sabbaths.
[25]"They shall not go to a dead person to defile *themselves;* except for father or for mother, for son or for daughter, for brother or for sister who has had no husband; they may defile themselves. [Lev 21:1, 2]
[26]"After he is cleansed [from the defilement of a corpse], seven days more shall elapse for him [before returning to the temple].
[27]"On the day that he goes into the sanctuary, into the inner courtyard to minister in the sanctuary, he shall offer his sin offering," says the Lord GOD.
[28]"It [their ministry to Me] shall be as an inheritance to them, for I am their inheritance; and you shall give them no property (land) in Israel, for I am their possession. [Josh 13:14, 33]
[29]"They shall eat the grain offering, the sin offering and the guilt offering; and every devoted thing (offering) in Israel [dedicated by a solemn vow to God] shall be theirs.
[30]"The first of all the first fruits of every kind, and every contribution *and* offering of every kind, from all your contributions *and* offerings, shall belong to the priests. You shall also give to the priest the first of your coarse meal *and* bread dough, so that a blessing may rest on your house.
[31]"The priests shall not eat any bird or animal that has died a natural death or has been torn to pieces.

The LORD's Portion of the Land

45 "MOREOVER, WHEN you divide the land by lot for inheritance, you shall [set apart and] offer an allotment (contribution) to the LORD, a holy portion of the land [to be used for sacred purposes]. The length shall be 25,000 *cubits,* and the width shall be 20,000 *cubits.* It shall be holy (set apart for sacred use) within its every area. [Ezek 48:9, 12, 13]
[2]"Of this there shall be a square plot five hundred by five hundred *cubits* in perimeter for the holy place, and fifty cubits for the open space around it.

44:23 *The priests shall teach My people the difference between the holy and the common.* These verses speak of holiness in conduct. These regulations continued practices already prescribed in the law of Moses (Lev 10:6,9; 21:1 – 7,10,14). Their aim was to help the priests avoid conformity to the immoral and idolatrous religious rituals and conduct among the pagan nations. The priests, then and in the future, have the responsibility of modeling and maintaining the highest standards of morality, self-control, self-denial, discipline, and obedience to God's will.

44:28 *I am their inheritance.* God was to be the priests' inheritance in all respects; they were not to inherit land or cities.

45:1 – 5 *the holy portion of the land.* A distinct or holy section was to be allocated for God. This area would be divided into two equal sections. One would be the portion for the Zadokites. In the center of this part of the holy district is the holy square-mile environs for the temple. The

20 Lev 21:5 **21** Lev 10:9 **22** Lev 21:7 **23** Eze 22:26; Mal 2:7 **24** Dt 17:8; 2Ch 19:8; See Eze 22:26 **26** Nu 6:10; 19:11 **27** ver. 17; Lev 4:3 **28** Nu 18:20; Dt 10:9; 18:1,2; Jos 13:14 **29** Lev 7:6; Lev 27:21,28 compared with Nu 18:14 **30** Ex 13:2; 22:29; 23:19; Nu 3:13; 18:12; Nu 15:20; Neh 10:37; Pr 3:9; Mal 3:10 **31** Ex 22:31; Lev 22:8
CHAPTER 45 **1** Eze 47:22; Eze 48:8

3"And in this area you shall measure
off a portion 25,000 *cubits* in length
and 10,000 *cubits* in width. And in it
shall be the sanctuary which is most
holy.
4"It shall be the holy portion of the
land; it shall be for the priests, the min-
isters of the sanctuary, who come near
to minister to the LORD, and it shall be a
place for their houses and a holy place
for the sanctuary.
5"And *another portion of land* 25,000
cubits long and 10,000 cubits wide
shall be for the Levites, the ministers
of the temple (house), and they shall
possess it as a place in which to live.
6"You shall give the city possession
of *an area* 5,000 *cubits* wide and 25,000
cubits long, alongside the portion set
aside as a holy section. It shall belong
to the whole house of Israel.

Portion for the Prince

7"The prince shall have *land* on either side of the portion set aside as a holy section and the property of the city, adjacent to the holy section and the property of the city, on the west side toward the west and on the east side toward the east, and in length comparable to one of the portions, from the west border to the east border.
8"This shall be his land for a pos-
session in Israel; so My princes shall
no longer oppress My people, but
they shall give *the rest of* the land to
the house of Israel according to their
tribes."
9"Thus says the Lord GOD, "Enough,
O princes of Israel! Put away violence
and destruction, and practice justice
and righteousness. Stop your forceful
seizure of property from My people,"
says the Lord GOD.
10"You shall have just balances *and*
weights [on your scales and just mea-
sures], a just ephah [dry volume mea-
sure] and a just bath [liquid measure].
11"The ephah and the bath [mea-
sures] shall be the same quantity, the
bath containing one tenth of a homer
and the ephah one tenth of a homer;
their standard [measure] shall be ac-
cording to the homer.
12"The shekel shall be twenty gerahs;
twenty shekels, twenty-five shekels,
and fifteen shekels [added together,
a total of sixty] shall be your maneh
(mina).
13"This is the offering that you shall
offer: a sixth of an ephah from a homer
of wheat; a sixth of an ephah from a
homer of barley;
14and the prescribed portion of oil,
(*namely,* the bath of oil), a tenth part
of a bath [of oil] from *each* kor (*which*
is ten baths or a homer, for ten baths
make a homer);
15and [you shall offer] one sheep out
of every flock of two hundred from the
watering places of Israel—for a grain
offering, for a burnt offering, and for
peace offerings to make atonement
for [those who brought] them," says
the Lord GOD.
16"All the people of the land shall
give to this offering for the prince in
Israel.
17"It shall be the prince's *responsibil-
ity to provide* the burnt offerings, the
grain offerings, and the drink offer-
ings at the feasts, on the New Moons
and on the Sabbaths, at all the appoint-
ed feasts of the house of Israel. He shall

---

other half of the holy district would be the portion given to the Levites. All this is holy; God owns it.

45:6 ***the city.*** Most likely the city is Jerusalem.

45:7 – 8 ***My princes.*** Their identity is unknown (44:3), but his allotted area is on both sides of the holy district. The prince and God's princes of the Messianic Period — in contrast to previous leaders of Israel (11:1 – 13; 14:1 – 11,20 – 22; 34:1 – 10) — will not be greedy for riches and real estate but will give the land that remains to the people.

45:10 – 11 ***Ye shall have just balances.*** The merchants were exhorted to use accurate measures. They must not cheat anymore when weighing produce (Lev 19:35; Am 8:5; Mic 6:10 – 12). God called for an end to dishonesty and deceit; a time is coming when all such scheming will end (37:15 – 28).

3 Eze 48:10 **4** ver. 1; Eze 48:10 **5** Eze 48:13; See Eze 40:17 **6** Eze 48:15 **7** Eze 48:21 **8** See Jer 22:17; Eze 22:27; 46:18 **9** Eze 44:6; Jer 22:3 **10** Lev 19:35,36; Pr 11:1 **12** Ex 30:13; Lev 27:25; Nu 3:47 **15** Lev 1:4 **18** Lev 16:16

prepare *and* provide the sin offering,
the grain offering, the burnt offering
and the peace offerings, to make atone-
ment for the house of Israel."
18 'Thus says the Lord GOD, "In the
first *month,* on the first of the month,
you shall take a young bull without
blemish and cleanse the sanctuary
(from sin).
19 "The priest shall take some of the
blood of the sin offering and put it on
the door posts of the temple, on the
four corners of the ledge of the altar,
and on the posts of the gate of the inner
courtyard.
20 "You shall do this on the seventh
[day] of the month for everyone who
goes astray [and sins through error or
ignorance] and for him who is naive;
so shall you make atonement for the
temple (house).
21 "In the first *month,* on the four-
teenth day of the month, you shall have
the Passover, a feast of seven days;
unleavened bread shall be eaten.
22 "On that day the prince shall pro-
vide for himself and for all the people
of the land a bull for a sin offering.
23 "And for the seven days of the feast
he shall provide as a burnt offering to
the LORD seven bulls and seven rams
without blemish on every day for the
seven days, and a male goat daily for
a sin offering.
24 "He shall provide as a grain offer-
ing [to be offered] with each bull an
ephah [of grain], an ephah with each
ram, and a hin of oil with each ephah
[of grain].
25 "In the seventh *month,* on the fif-
teenth day of the month at the feast,
he shall provide [offerings] like these
for the seven days, as the sin offering,
the burnt offering, the grain offering,
and the oil."

The Prince's Offerings

46 'THUS SAYS the Lord GOD,
"The gate of the inner courtyard
that faces east shall be shut during
the six working days, but it shall be
opened on the Sabbath day and opened
on the day of the New Moon.
2 "The prince shall enter by the porch
(portico) of the gate from outside and
stand by the post of the gate. The
priests shall prepare *and* provide his
burnt offering and his peace offerings,
and he shall worship at the threshold
of the gate and then go out; but the gate
shall not be shut until evening.
3 "The people of the land shall also
worship at the entrance of that gate
before the LORD on the Sabbaths and
on the New Moons.
4 "The burnt offering which the
prince shall offer to the LORD on the
Sabbath day shall be six lambs without
blemish and a ram without blemish.
5 "The grain offering shall be an
ephah with the ram, and the grain
offering with the lambs as much as
he is able to give, and a hin of oil with
an ephah.
6 "On the day of the New Moon *he
shall offer* a young bull without blem-
ish, also six lambs and a ram, without
blemish.
7 "And he shall provide a grain of-
fering, an ephah with the bull and
an ephah with the ram, and with the
lambs as much as he is able, and a hin
of oil with an ephah.

45:18 *In the first month, on the first of the month.* This is an annual day of purifying the temple sanctuary. In the light of Jesus' death on the cross, the actions of the prince symbolize and emphasize that God has made atonement for all through the sacrifice of the Messiah. The prince represents the people in these actions of worship.

45:21 *you shall have the Passover, a feast of seven days.* In this passage the Feasts of Passover and Tabernacles are observed (Ex 12:1 – 14; Lev 23:5 – 8,33 – 43; Nu 28:16 – 25). The dates are in relation to the Levitical calendar, the Jewish religious year. The procedures as well are very similar to those of the Mosaic system. These feasts commemorate God's faithfulness to His promises.

46:1 – 8 *The prince shall enter.* What the rituals signified under the law was fulfilled by the Messiah. At the time of this prince, certain

19 Eze 43:20 **20** Lev 4:27 **21** Ex 12:18; Lev 23:5,6; Nu 9:2,3; 28:16,17; Dt 16:1 **22** Lev 4:14 **23** Lev 23:8; See Nu 28:15,22,30; 29:5,11,16,19 **24** Eze 46:5,7 **25** Lev 23:34; Nu 29:12; Dt 16:13 **CHAPTER 46** **2** ver. 8; Eze 44:3 **4** Eze 45:17 **5** ver. 7,11; Eze 45:24

8 “When the prince enters, he shall enter by way of the porch of the gate and go out by the same way.

9 “But when the people of the land come before the LORD at the appointed feasts, he who enters by way of the north gate to worship shall go out by way of the south gate. And he who enters by way of the south gate shall go out by way of the north gate. No one shall return by way of the gate through which he entered, but shall go out straight ahead [through the opposite gate]. [Phil 3:13]

10 “When they go in, the prince shall go in among them; and when they go out, he shall go out.

11 “At the feasts and the appointed festivals the grain offering shall be an ephah with a bull and an ephah with a ram, and with the lambs as much as one is able to give, and a hin of oil with an ephah.

12 “When the prince provides a freewill offering, a burnt offering, or peace offerings voluntarily to the LORD, the gate that faces east shall be opened for him, and he shall provide his burnt offering and his peace offerings as he does on the Sabbath day. Then he shall go out, and after he goes out the gate shall be shut.

13 “And you [priests] shall provide a lamb a year old without blemish as a burnt offering to the LORD each day; morning by morning you shall provide it.

14 “Also you shall provide a grain offering with it morning by morning, one-sixth of an ephah with one-third of a hin of oil to sprinkle on the finely-milled flour. This is a perpetual ordinance for a continual grain offering to the LORD.

15 “Thus they shall provide the lamb, the grain offering and the oil every morning as a continual burnt offering.”

16 ‘Thus says the Lord GOD, “If the prince gives a gift to any of his sons from his inheritance, it shall belong to his sons [permanently]; it is their possession by inheritance.

17 “But if he gives a gift from his inheritance to one of his servants, then it shall be his until the year of liberty [the Year of Jubilee]; after that it shall be returned to the prince. His inheritance *shall be* only his sons’ [permanently]; it shall belong to them.

18 “Moreover, the prince shall not take from the people’s inheritance by oppression *and* by evicting them from their property; he shall give his sons an inheritance from his own possession, so that My people will not be scattered, anyone from his possession.” ’ ”

The Boiling Places

19 Then he [my guide] brought me through the entrance, which was at the side of the gate, into the holy chambers for the priests, which faced the north; and behold, a place was there at their extreme westward end.

20 He said to me, “This is the place where the priests shall boil (cook) the guilt offering and the sin offering, and where they shall bake the grain offering, so that they do not bring them out into the outer courtyard to transmit holiness to the people.”

21 Then he brought me out into the outer courtyard and led me across to the four corners of the courtyard; and behold, in every corner of the courtyard *there was a small* courtyard.

22 In the four corners of the courtyard *there were* enclosed courtyards, forty *cubits* long and thirty wide; these four in the corners were the same size.

---

promises were being fulfilled and the covenants consummated in the Messianic Age (40:6 – 16,28 – 37; 43:18 – 27; Ex 20:8 – 11).

46:9 *No one shall return by way of the gate through which he entered.* The prescribed protocol was probably to ensure an orderly procession and service. Such regulations would be needed on the special feast days due to the participation of large numbers of people.

46:14 *a perpetual ordinance.* This is a change from the provisions in the law (Nu 28:5). God’s people cannot be reminded too often of God’s provisions for them; nor can they thank Him too much or too frequently.

8 ver. 2 **9** Ex 23:14-17; Dt 16:16 **11** ver. 5 **12** ver. 2; Eze 44:3 **13** Ex 29:38; Nu 28:3 **17** Lev 25:10 **18** Eze 45:8 **20** 2Ch 35:13; Lev 2:4,5,7; Eze 44:19

23 *There was* a row *of masonry* all
around inside them, around [each of]
the four courtyards, and it was made
with cooking hearths under the rows
all around.
24 Then he said to me, "These are
the kitchens of the cooks, where the
ministers (Levites) of the temple shall
boil (cook) the sacrifices of the people."

Water from the Temple

47 THEN HE [my guide] brought
me back to the door of the house
[the temple of the LORD]; and behold,
water was flowing from under the
threshold of the house (temple) toward
the east, for the front of the temple was
facing east. And the water was flowing
down from under, from the right side
of the house, from south of the altar.
2 Then he brought me out by way
of the north gate and led me around
on the outside to the outer gate by the
way of *the gate* that faces east. And
behold, water was spurting out from
the south side [of the gate]. [Zech 14:8;
Rev 22:1, 2]
3 When the man went out toward the
east with a measuring line in his hand,
he measured a thousand cubits, and he
led me through the water, water that
was ankle-deep.
4 Again he measured a thousand [cu-
bits] and led me through the water,
water that was knee-deep. Again he
measured a thousand [cubits] and led
me through *the water,* water *reaching*
the hips.
5 Again he measured a thousand [cu-
bits]; *and it was* a river that I could not
pass through, for the water had risen,
enough water to swim in, a river that
could not be crossed [by wading].
6 And he said to me, "Son of man,
have you seen this?" Then he brought
me back to the bank of the river.
7 Now when I had returned, behold,
on the bank of the river were very
many trees on the one side and on the
other.
8 Then he said to me, "These waters
go out toward the eastern region and
go down into the Arabah (the Jordan
Valley); then they go toward the sea,
being made to flow into the sea, and
the waters *of the Dead Sea* shall be
healed *and* become fresh.
9 "It will come about that every living
creature which swarms in every place
where the river goes, will live. And
there will be a very great number of
fish, because these waters go there so
that the waters of the sea are healed
and become fresh; so everything will
live wherever the river goes.
10 "And it will come about that fisher-
men will stand beside it [at the banks
of the Dead Sea]; from Engedi to
Eneglaim there will be dry places to
spread nets. Their fish will be of very
many kinds, like the fish of the Great
[Mediterranean] Sea.
11 "But its swamps and marshes will
not become fresh [and wholesome for
animal life]; they will [as the river sub-
sides] be left encrusted with salt.
12 "By the river on its bank, on one
side and on the other, will grow all
kinds of trees for food. Their leaves
will not wither and their fruit will not
fail. They shall bear every month be-
cause their water flows from the sanc-
tuary, and their fruit will be for food
and their leaves for healing." [Rev 22:2]

Boundaries and Division of the Land

13 Thus says the Lord GOD, "This
shall be the boundary by which you
shall divide the land as an inheritance
among the twelve tribes of Israel; Jo-
seph *shall have* two portions.

46:24 *These are the kitchens of the cooks.* These were kitchen areas for the people to boil their sacrifices. The temple was a place for sacrificing, cooking, and eating. To combine the two elements is healthy for spiritual fellowship.

47:7–12 *their water flows from the sanctuary.* The living water that God will provide has immeasurable power to renew, restore, and resurrect life. The water is a river of healing and the source of abundant life for everything and everyone.

24 See ver. 20 **CHAPTER 47** **1** Joel 3:18; Zec 13:1; 14:8; Rev 22:1 **3** Eze 40:3 **7** ver. 12; Rev 22:2 **10** Nu 34:3; Jos 23:4; Eze 48:28 **12** ver. 7; Job 8:16; Ps 1:3; Jer 17:8; Rev 22:2 **13** Ge 48:5; 1Ch 5:1; Eze 48:4,5

14 “You shall divide it as an inheri-
tance, each one equally with the other.
I lifted up My hand *and* swore to give
it to your fathers, and this land shall
fall to you as an inheritance.
15 “And this shall be the boundary
of the land on the north side: from the
Great [Mediterranean] Sea by way of
Hethlon to the entrance of Zedad,
16 Hamath, Berothah, Sibraim, which
is between the border of Damascus
and the border of Hamath; [as far as]
Hazer-hatticon, which is on the border
of Hauran.
17 “So the boundary will extend from
the [Mediterranean] Sea to Hazar-
enan at the border of Damascus, and
on the north, northward, is the border
of Hamath. This is the north side.
18 “The east side, from between Hau-
ran, Damascus, Gilead, and the land
of Israel, *shall be* the Jordan; from the
north border to the eastern sea you
shall measure. This is the east side.
19 “The south side, southward, from
Tamar [near the Dead Sea] *shall ex-
tend* as far as the waters of Meribath-
kadesh, to the Brook of Egypt and to
the Great [Mediterranean] Sea. This is
the south side toward the south.
20 “The west side *shall be* the Great
[Mediterranean] Sea, from the *south*
border to a point opposite Lebo-
hamath [north of Mount Hermon]. This
is the west side.
21 “So you shall divide this land
among yourselves according to the
tribes of Israel.
22 “You shall divide it by lot as an
inheritance among yourselves and
among the foreigners who stay among
you, who give birth to sons among you.
They shall be to you as the native-born
[in the country] among the children
(descendants) of Israel; they shall be al-
lotted an inheritance with you among
the tribes of Israel.
23 “In whatever tribe the foreigner
resides, there shall you give him his
inheritance,” says the Lord GOD.

Division of the Land

48 “NOW THESE are the names of
the tribes: from the north end,
beside the way of Hethlon to Lebo-
hamath, as far as Hazar-enan, which
is on the northern border of Damascus,
beside Hamath, and running from the
east to the west, Dan, one *portion*.
2 “Beside the border of Dan, from
the east side to the west side, Asher,
one *portion*.
3 “Beside the border of Asher, from
the east side to the west side, Naphtali,
one *portion*.
4 “Beside the border of Naphtali, from
the east side to the west side, Manas-
seh, one *portion*.
5 “Beside the border of Manasseh,
from the east side to the west side,
Ephraim, one *portion*.
6 “Beside the border of Ephraim,
from the east side to the west side,
Reuben, one *portion*.
7 “Beside the border of Reuben, from
the east side to the west side, Judah,
one *portion*.
8 “And beside the border of Judah,
from the east side to the west side,
shall be the allotment *and* contribu-
tion of land which you shall set apart
and offer, 25,000 *cubits* in width, and
in length like one of the [tribal] por-
tions, from the east side to the west
side; and the sanctuary shall be in the
midst of it.

47:14 *You shall divide it as an inheritance, each one equally with the other.* Equality of inheritance is stressed. The unilateral and unconditional nature of the Abrahamic covenant is suggested; this inheritance is a free gift of God's grace which God's people did and could do nothing to deserve.

47:21 – 23 *and among the foreigners.* Non-Israelites who married and settled within the Jewish communities were to be accepted as native Israelites, qualified to share in the territorial inheritance of whatever tribe they joined (Lev 19:34).

48:1 *Now these are the names.* The land would be divided into thirteen parts. The division makes it clear that all who believe have a place.

14 Ge 12:7; 13:15; 15:7; 17:8; 26:3; 28:13; Eze 20:5,6,28,42; Eze 48:29 **15** Eze 48:1; Nu 34:8 **16** Nu 34:8; 2Sa 8:8 **17** Nu 34:9; Eze 48:1 **19** Nu 20:13; Dt 32:51; Ps 81:7; Eze 48:28 **22** See Eph 3:6; Rev 7:9,10; Ro 10:12; Gal 3:28; Col 3:11 **CHAPTER 48** **1** Eze 47:15 **8** Eze 45:1-6

9 “The allotment [of land] that you shall set apart *and* offer to the LORD *shall be* 25,000 *cubits* in length and 10,000 in width.

Portion for the Priests

10 “The holy allotment shall be for these, *namely* for the priests, toward the north 25,000 *cubits in length,* and toward the west 10,000 in width, and toward the east 10,000 in width, and toward the south 25,000 in length; and the sanctuary of the LORD shall be in the midst of it.

11 “*It shall be* for the priests who are sanctified of the sons of Zadok, who have kept My charge, and who did not go astray when the children (descendants) of Israel went astray as the [other] Levites did.

12 “And this [land offering] shall be an allotment to them from the allotment of the land, a most holy portion beside the border of the [other] Levites.

13 “Alongside the border of the priests, the [other] Levites *shall have* 25,000 *cubits* in length and 10,000 in width. The whole length *shall be* 25,000 *cubits* and the width 10,000.

14 “And they shall not sell any of it or exchange it, or allow this choice *portion* of land to pass *to others;* for it is holy to the LORD.

15 “The remaining [strip of] 5,000 *cubits* in width and 25,000 in length shall be for the city's common (secular) use, for a place in which to live and for open country. The city shall be in the midst of it.

16 “These *shall be* the measurements of it: the north side 4,500 *cubits,* the south side 4,500, the east side 4,500, and the west side 4,500. [Rev 21:16]

17 “The city shall have open country: toward the north 250 *cubits,* and toward the south 250, toward the east 250, *and* toward the west 250.

18 “The remainder of the length alongside the holy allotment shall be 10,000 *cubits* to the east and 10,000 to the west; and it shall be beside the holy allotment. The produce from it shall be food for the workers of the city.

19 “The workers of the city, from all the tribes of Israel shall cultivate it.

20 “The whole allotment *shall be* 25,000 by 25,000 *cubits;* you shall set apart the holy allotment, a square, with the property of the city.

Portion for the Prince

21 “The remainder, on both sides of the holy allotment and of the property possessed by the city, *shall belong* to the prince. In front of the 25,000 *cubits* of the allotment toward the east border and westward in front of the 25,000 toward the west border, alongside the [tribal] portions, *it shall be* for the prince. The holy allotment with the sanctuary of the temple shall be in the midst of it.

22 “Exclusive of the property of the Levites and of the property of the city, which are in the middle of that which belongs to the prince, *everything* between the border of Judah and the border of Benjamin shall be for the prince.

Portion for Other Tribes

23 “As for the rest of the tribes: from the east side to the west side, Benjamin, one *portion.*

24 “Beside the border of Benjamin, from the east side to the west side, Simeon, one *portion.*

25 “Beside the border of Simeon, from the east side to the west side, Issachar, one *portion.*

26 “Beside the border of Issachar, from the east side to the west side, Zebulun, one *portion.*

27 “Beside the border of Zebulun, from the east side to the west side, Gad, one *portion.*

28 “And beside the border of Gad, at the south side, southward, the border shall extend from Tamar to the waters of Meribath-kadesh, to the Brook [of Egypt], to the Great [Mediterranean] Sea.

29 “This is the land which you shall divide by lot among the tribes of Israel as their inheritance, and these are their *several* portions,” says the Lord GOD.

11 Eze 44:10,15 **14** Ex 22:29; Lev 27:10,28,33 **15** Eze 45:6; Eze 42:20 **19** Eze 45:6 **21** Eze 45:7; ver. 8,10 **28** Eze 47:19 **29** Eze 47:14,21,22

The City Gates

30"These are the exits of the city: on the north side, [which is to extend] 4,500 *cubits* by measurement,
31there shall also be gates of the city, *named* after the names of the tribes of Israel, three gates toward the north: one gate of Reuben, one gate of Judah, one gate of Levi.
32"On the east side, 4,500 *cubits,* also three gates: one gate of Joseph, one gate of Benjamin, one gate of Dan.
33"On the south side, 4,500 *cubits,* by measurement, also three gates: one gate of Simeon, one gate of Issachar, one gate of Zebulun.
34"On the west side, 4,500 *cubits,* three gates: one gate of Gad, one gate of Asher, one gate of Naphtali.
35"The distance around the city shall be 18,000 (4 x 4,500) *cubits;* and the name of the city from that day [and ever after] *shall be,* 'The LORD is There.' " [Rev 21:12, 13, 16]

48:31 *named after the names of the tribes of Israel.* The gates are named after the original twelve tribes (Rev 21:12 – 13). The gate for Joseph represents the two tribes of Manasseh and Ephraim.

48:35 *The LORD is There.* This return of the Lord and the regathering of His people is predicted by Ezekiel in 11:17; 20:33 – 44; 37:15 – 28 and 39:21 – 29. The Lord was forced to depart from the city and the temple because of the wickedness of the Israelites (8:6; 10:18). But here, Ezekiel foresees the return of God in all His glory to His people, His temple, and His land. This was a powerful message in its context. Ezekiel and his immediate audience were far away from their homeland. This vision of the coming restoration would have inspired much hope in the faithful.

31 Rev 21:12 **35** Jer 33:16; Jer 3:17; Joel 3:21; Zec 2:10; Rev 21:3; 22:3

THE BOOK OF

DANIEL

▸ **AUTHOR:** Daniel's life and ministry bridge the entire seventy-year period of Babylonian captivity. This claims Daniel as author, and it uses the first person from 7:2 onward. The Jewish Talmud supports this claim, and Christ attributed a quote from 9:27 to "the prophet Daniel" (Mt 24:15). Daniel's wisdom and divinely given interpretive abilities brought him into a position of prominence, especially in the courts of Nebuchadnezzar and Darius.

▸ **TIMES:** c. 605 – 536 BC ▸ **KEY VERSES:** Da 2:20 – 22

▸ **THEME:** Daniel is one of very few heroes in the Bible whose record is flawless. He is an example of how to live and work as a believer in a hostile environment; a man of action while at the same time fully aware of his dependence on God. The important prophecies in Daniel have inspired many interpretations over the years. Many have attempted to identify the various elements of the prophecies and apply them to contemporary figures.

The Choice Young Men

1 IN THE third year of the reign of
Jehoiakim king of Judah, Nebuchadnezzar king of Babylon came to
Jerusalem and besieged it.
2 The Lord gave Jehoiakim king of
Judah into his hand, along with some
of the articles of the house of God;
and he brought them into the land of
Shinar, to the house of his god, and
brought the articles into the treasury
of his god. [2 Chr 36:5–7; Jer 27:19, 20;
Dan 5:1–3]
3 And the [Babylonian] king told
Ashpenaz, the chief of his officials,
to bring in some of the sons of Israel,
including some from the royal family
and from the nobles, [2 Kin 20:17, 18]
4 young men without blemish and
handsome in appearance, skillful
in all wisdom, endowed with intelligence *and* discernment, and quick
to understand, competent to stand [in
the presence of the king] *and* able to
serve in the king's palace. He also
ordered Ashpenaz to teach them
the literature and language of the
Chaldeans.

1:1 *Jehoiakim king of Judah.* Jehoiakim was an evil king who sided first with the Egyptians and then with the Babylonians, until he finally decided to rebel. His independence was short-lived, however, and he remained under Babylonian domination until his death (2Ki 23:34 – 24:6).
1:2 *the treasury of his god.* These articles taken from the temple appear later, on the night of Belshazzar's feast (ch. 5). Eventually they were returned to Zerubbabel, who brought them back to Israel (Ezr 1:7).
1:3 *chief of his officials.* A term which became synonymous with "official." In ancient Middle Eastern monarchies, royal harems were typically superintended by men who had been emasculated and were considered reliable to serve in that capacity. A eunuch was often regarded as a privileged official. Some have speculated that Daniel and his friends were eunuchs, but there is no specific statement in the book to this effect.
1:4 *literature and language.* The language of most of Mesopotamia was Akkadian, which was written in cuneiform script. Over the centuries the Babylonians and Assyrians produced

CHAPTER 1 **1** 2Ki 24:1; 2Ch 36:6 **2** Jer 27:19; Ge 10:10; Zec 5:11; 2Ch 36:7 **4** See Lev 24:19,20; Ac 7:22

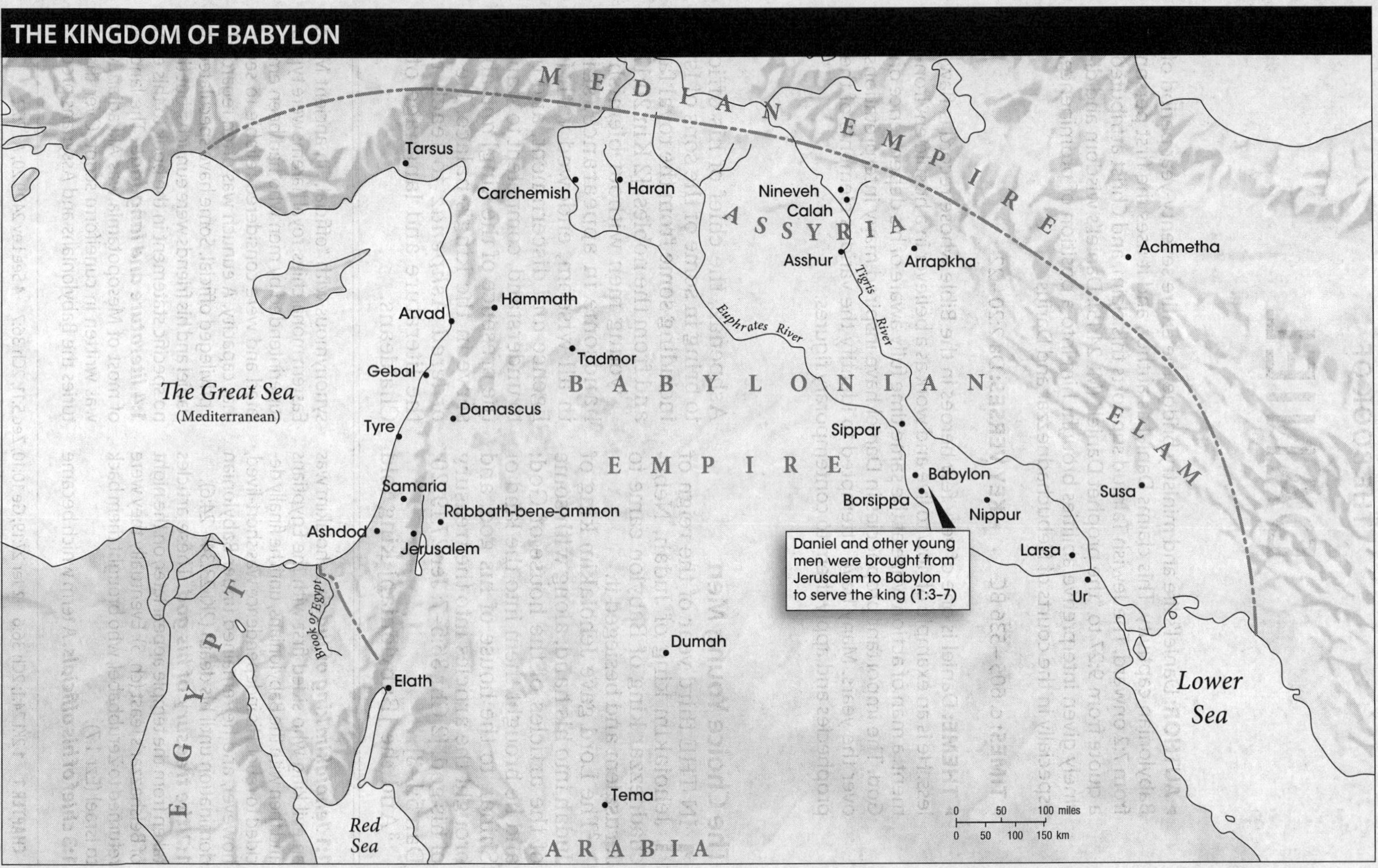
THE KINGDOM OF BABYLON
M E D I A N   E M P I R E
A S S Y R I A
B A B Y L O N I A N
E M P I R E
E L A M
A R A B I A
E G Y P T
The Great Sea
(Mediterranean)
Lower Sea
Red Sea
Brook of Egypt
Euphrates River
Tigris River
Tarsus
Carchemish
Haran
Nineveh
Calah
Asshur
Arrapkha
Achmetha
Hammath
Arvad
Tadmor
Gebal
Damascus
Tyre
Sippar
Babylon
Borsippa
Nippur
Susa
Samaria
Rabbath-bene-ammon
Ashdod
Jerusalem
Larsa
Ur
Dumah
Elath
Tema
Daniel and other young men were brought from Jerusalem to Babylon to serve the king (1:3–7)
0 50 100 miles
0 50 100 150 km

5 The king assigned a daily ration for
them from his finest food and from the
wine which he drank. They were to be
educated *and* nourished this way for
three years so that at the end of that
time they were [prepared] to enter the
king's service.
6 Among them from the sons of Ju-
dah were: Daniel, Hananiah, Mishael,
and Azariah.
7 The commander of the officials
gave them [Babylonian] names: Daniel
he named Belteshazzar, Hananiah *he
named* Shadrach, Mishael *he named*
Meshach, and Azariah *he named*
Abed-nego.

Daniel's Resolve

8 But Daniel made up his mind that
he would not defile (taint, dishonor)
himself with the king's finest food or
with the wine which the king drank;
so he asked the commander of the offi-
cials that he might [be excused so that
he would] not defile himself. [Num 6:1–
4; 1 Cor 10:21]
9 Now God granted Daniel favor and
compassion in the sight of the com-
mander of the officials,
10 and the commander of the officials
said to Daniel, "I am afraid of my lord
the king, who has prearranged your
food and your drink; for why should he
see your faces looking more haggard
than the young men who are your own
age? Then you would make me forfeit
my head to the king."
11 But Daniel said to the overseer
whom the commander of the officials
had appointed over Daniel, Hananiah,
Mishael, and Azariah,
12 "Please, test your servants for ten
days, and let us be given some vegeta-
bles to eat and water to drink.
13 "Then let our appearance and the
appearance of the young men who
eat the king's finest food be observed
and compared by you, and deal with
your servants in accordance with what
you see."
14 So the man listened to them in this
matter and tested them for ten days.
15 At the end of ten days it seemed
that they were looking better and
healthier than all the young men who
ate the king's finest food.
16 So the overseer continued to with-
hold their fine food and the wine they
were to drink, and kept giving them
vegetables.
17 As for these four young men, God
gave them knowledge and skill in all
kinds of literature and wisdom; Daniel
also understood all *kinds of* visions
and dreams. [Luke 21:15; James 1:5–7]
18 At the end of the time set by the
king to bring all the young men in
[before him], the commander of the
officials presented them to Nebuchad-
nezzar.
19 The king spoke with them, and
among them all not one was found
like Daniel, Hananiah, Mishael, and
Azariah; so they were [selected and]
assigned to stand before the king *and*
enter his personal service.
20 In every matter of wisdom and
understanding about which the king

---

a massive body of literature of all types. Though Aramaic had begun to replace Akkadian by the time of Nebuchadnezzar, scholars continued to study and write literature in their classical tongue. ***Chaldeans.*** This name was commonly applied to Babylonians in general, and also to the guild of astrologers, diviners, and other practitioners of wisdom to which Daniel was being introduced (1:17; 2:2; 3:8).

1:7 *names.* Daniel means "God is my Judge"; Belteshazzar means "Lady protect the king," referring to the goddess Sarpanitu, wife of the god Marduk. Hananiah means "The Lord is gracious"; Shadrach means "I am fearful of the God." Mishael means "Who is what God is?"; Meshach means "I am of little account." Azariah means "The Lord has helped me"; Abed-nego means "Servant of [the god] Nebo."

1:8 *defile (taint, dishonor) himself.* The issue here was not the richness of the food or the alcohol. The king's table no doubt included unclean meats and food which had not been prepared according to the law. In addition, both meat and wines may well have already been offered to idols.

5 ver. 19; Ge 41:46; 1Ki 10:8 **7** Ge 41:45; 2Ki 24:17; Da 4:8; 5:12 **8** Dt 32:38; Eze 4:13; Hos 9:3 **9** See Ge 39:21; Ps 106:46; Pr 16:7 **17** 1Ki 3:12; Jas 1:5,17; Ac 7:22; Nu 12:6; 2Ch 26:5; Da 5:11,12,14; 10:1 **19** ver. 5; Ge 41:46 **20** 1Ki 10:1

consulted them, he found them ten times better than all the [learned] magicians and enchanters (Magi) in his whole realm.

21 And Daniel remained there until the first year of [the reign of] King Cyrus [over Babylon; now this was at the end of the seventy-year exile of Judah (the Southern Kingdom) in Babylonia, as foretold by Jeremiah]. [Ezra 1:1–3; Jer 25:11, 12; 29:10]

The King's Forgotten Dream

2 IN THE second year (604 B.C.) of the reign of Nebuchadnezzar, Nebuchadnezzar had dreams which troubled *and* disturbed his spirit and [interfered with] his ability to sleep.

2 Then the king gave a command to call the magicians, the enchanters, the sorcerers, and the Chaldeans to tell the king his dreams. So they came in and stood before the king.

3 The king said to them, "I had a dream, and my spirit is troubled *and* anxious to know the [content and meaning of the] dream."

4 Then the Chaldeans said to the king in Aramaic, "O king, live forever! Tell the dream to your servants, and we will declare the interpretation."

5 The king replied to the Chaldeans, "My command is firm *and* unchangeable: if you do not reveal to me the [content of the] dream along with its interpretation, you shall be cut into pieces and your houses shall be made a heap of rubbish.

6 "But if you tell [me] the [content of the] dream along with its interpretation, you shall receive from me gifts and rewards and great honor. So tell me the dream and its interpretation."

7 They answered again, "Let the king tell the dream to his servants, and we will explain its interpretation [to you]."

8 The king replied, "I know for certain that you are bargaining for time, because you have seen that my command [to you] is firm *and* irrevocable.

9 "If you will not reveal to me the [content of the] dream, there is but one sentence for you; for you have [already] prepared lying and corrupt words [and you have agreed together] to speak [them] before me [hoping to delay your execution] until the situation is changed. Therefore, tell me the dream [first], and then I will know [with confidence] that you can give me its interpretation."

10 The Chaldeans answered the king and said, "There is not a man on earth who can tell the king this matter, for no king, lord or ruler has ever asked such a thing as this of any magician or enchanter or Chaldean.

11 "Furthermore, what the king demands is an unusual *and* difficult thing indeed! No one except the gods can reveal it to the king, and their dwelling is not with [mortal] flesh."

12 Because of this the king was indignant and extremely furious and gave a command to destroy all the wise men of Babylon.

13 So the decree went out that the wise men were to be killed; and they looked for Daniel and his companions to put them to death.

14 Then Daniel replied with discretion and wisdom to Arioch, the captain of the king's bodyguard, who had gone out to execute the wise men of Babylon;

15 he said to Arioch, the king's captain, "Why is the decree from the king so harsh *and* urgent?" Then Arioch explained the matter to Daniel.

2:2 *magicians.* The word translated "magicians" refers to those who use a pen — most likely, those learned in the sacred writings of the Babylonians.
2:4 *in Aramaic.* Daniel 2:4b – 7:28 is written in Aramaic, the common language of the day.
2:8 *bargaining for time.* Nebuchadnezzar obviously did not have any faith in the integrity of his wise men or in the reality of their wisdom. He wanted to know for sure that the interpretation of his dream was a supernatural revelation, not just a clever story to please a king.
2:11 *except the gods.* The wise men were forced to acknowledge their own limitations. As far as they knew, they were doomed because the gods who had the answers did not speak with men.

21 Da 6:28; 10:1 **CHAPTER 2** **1** Ge 41:8; Da 4:5; Est 6:1; Da 6:18 **2** Ge 41:8; Ex 7:11; Da 5:7 **4** 1Ki 1:31; Da 3:9; 5:10; 6:6,21 **5** 2Ki 10:27; Ezr 6:11; Da 3:29 **6** Da 5:16 **11** Da 5:11

[16]So Daniel went in and asked the
king to appoint a date *and* give him
time, so that he might reveal to the
king the interpretation *of the dream*.
[17]Then Daniel returned to his house
and discussed the matter with Hana-
niah, Mishael, and Azariah, his com-
panions,
[18]in order that they might seek com-
passion from the God of heaven regard-
ing this secret, so that Daniel and his
companions would not be executed with
the rest of the wise men of Babylon.

The Secret Is Revealed to Daniel

[19]Then the secret was revealed to
Daniel in a vision of the night, and
Daniel blessed the God of heaven.
[20]Daniel answered,

"Blessed be the name of God
forever and ever,
For wisdom and power belong to
Him.
[21]"It is He who changes the times
and the seasons;
He removes kings and establishes
kings.
He gives wisdom to the wise
And [greater] knowledge to those
who have understanding!
[Dan 4:35]
[22]"It is He who reveals the profound
and hidden things;
He knows what is in the darkness,
And the light dwells with Him.
[Job 15:8; Ps 25:14; Matt 6:6]
[23]"I thank You and praise You,
O God of my fathers,
For You have given me wisdom
and power;
Even now You have made known
to me what we requested of You,
For You have made known to
us [the solution to] the king's
matter."

[24]So Daniel went to Arioch, whom
the king had appointed to destroy the
wise men of Babylon; he went and said
this to him: "Do not execute the wise
men of Babylon! Bring me before the
king, and I will reveal to the king the
interpretation [of his dream]."
[25]Then Arioch hurriedly brought
Daniel before the king and said this to
him: "I have found a man among the
exiles of Judah who can explain to the
king the interpretation [of the dream]."
[26]The king said to Daniel, whose
[Babylonian] name was Belteshazzar,
"Are you able to reveal to me the [con-
tent of the] dream which I have seen
and its interpretation?"
[27]Daniel answered the king and said,
"Regarding the mystery about which
the king has inquired, neither the wise
men, enchanters, magicians, nor as-
trologers are able to answer the king,
[28]but there is a God in heaven who
reveals secrets, and He has shown
King Nebuchadnezzar what will take
place in the latter days (end of days).
This was your dream and the vision
[that appeared] in your mind while
on your bed.
[29]"As for you, O king, as you were
lying on your bed thoughts came into
your mind about what will take place
in the future; and He who reveals se-
crets has shown you what will occur.
[30]"But as for me, this secret has not
been revealed to me because my wis-
dom is greater than that of any other
living man, but in order to make the
interpretation known to the king, and
so that you may understand [fully] the
thoughts of your mind.

2:18 *that they might seek compassion from the God of heaven.* Daniel and his friends knew the same thing that the other wise men did: only God could possibly reveal the king's dream. But, unlike the other wise men, they knew that their God would answer when they called on Him.

2:28 *the latter days.* This is an expression used frequently for the end times when God will intervene in human history to establish His eternal kingdom (Isa 2:2; Hos 3:5; Mic 4:1 – 3).

18 Mt 18:19 **19** Nu 12:6; Job 33:15 **20** Ps 113:2; Jer 32:19 **21** Est 1:13; Job 12:18; Ps 75:6,7; Jer 27:5; Jas 1:5 **22** Job 12:22; Ps 25:14; Ps 139:11; Heb 4:13; Da 5:11,14 **23** ver. 18 **28** Ge 40:8; Am 4:13; Ge 49:1 **29** ver. 22,28 **30** Ac 3:12; ver. 47

The King's Dream

31 "You, O king, were looking, and
behold, [there was] a single great stat-
ue; this image, which was large and of
unsurpassed splendor, stood before
you, and its appearance was awesome
and terrifying.
32 "As for this statue, its head *was*
made of fine gold, its breast and its
arms of silver, its belly and its thighs
of bronze,
33 its legs of iron, its feet partly of iron
and partly of clay [pottery].
34 "As you were looking, a stone was
cut out without [human] hands, and it
struck the statue on its feet of iron and
clay and crushed them. [1 Pet 2:3–8]
35 "Then the iron, the clay, the bronze,
the silver, and the gold were crushed
together and became like the chaff
from the summer threshing floors;
and the wind carried them away so
that not a trace of them could be found.
And the stone that struck the statue
became a great mountain and filled
the whole earth.

The Interpretation—Babylon the First Kingdom

36 "This was the dream; now we will
tell the king its interpretation.
37 "You, O king, are the king of
[earthly] kings, to whom the God of
heaven has given the kingdom, the
power, the strength and the glory;
[Jer 25:9; 27:6; 28:14]
38 and wherever the sons of men
dwell, and the beasts of the field, and
the birds of the heavens, He has given
them into your hand and has made
you ruler over them all. You [king of
Babylon] are the head of gold.

Medo-Persia and Greece

39 "After you will arise another king-
dom (Medo-Persia) inferior to you,
and then a third kingdom of bronze
(Greece under Alexander the Great),
which will rule over all the earth.

Rome

40 "Then a fourth kingdom (Rome)
will be strong as iron, for iron breaks
to pieces and shatters all things; and
like iron which crushes things in piec-
es, it will break and crush all these
[others]. [Dan 7:7, 23]
41 "And as you saw the feet and toes,
partly of potter's clay and partly of
iron, it will be a divided kingdom; but
there will be in it some of the durability
and strength of iron, just as you saw
the iron mixed with common clay.
42 "As the [ten] toes of the feet were

2:31 *a single great statue.* The image that Nebuchadnezzar saw represented four kingdoms that would rule over all the earth.

2:37 *to whom the God of heaven has given the kingdom.* The rulers of the nations of the world may not recognize God's authority, but that does not alter the fact that they have their positions only through His permission.

2:38 *head of gold.* The first worldwide empire, the head of gold, was Babylon.

2:39 *another kingdom (Medo-Persia) inferior to you.* The second empire, the chest and arms of silver, was Medo-Persia. Just as silver is inferior to gold, Medo-Persia was inferior to Babylon, not in size but in its effectiveness in governing its people. ***third kingdom of bronze.*** The third kingdom would be the Greek Empire.

2:40 *a fourth kingdom (Rome) will be strong as iron.* The fourth kingdom, the legs of iron, is the only one not specifically identified within the Book of Daniel. Rome is the most likely choice, for it succeeded Greece, and was certainly a very strong empire.

2:41 – 45 *it will be a divided kingdom.* Some believe that this is a reference to the Roman Empire's decline, when the kingdom was divided and the fabric of the empire was weakening in the early centuries after Christ. In this case the "kingdom that will never be destroyed" (obviously the kingdom of God) is a spiritual kingdom introduced by Christ at His first coming, and the mountain that grew from the rock would be a reference to the spread of Christianity, which eventually was named the state religion of the Roman Empire.

Others believe that verses 41 – 45 point to future events that have not yet been fulfilled. When this vision is compared with the four beasts of chapter 7, it seems clear that the fourth kingdom is yet to come. It is theorized that the kingdom

---

32 See ver. 38 **34** Zec 4:6; 2Co 5:1; Heb 9:24 **35** Hos 13:3; Ps 37:10,36; Isa 2:2,3; Ps 80:9 **37** Ezr 7:12; Isa 47:5; Jer 27:6,7; Eze 26:7; Hos 8:10; Ezr 1:2 **38** Da 4:21,22; Jer 27:6; ver. 32 **39** Da 5:28,31; ver. 32 **40** Da 7:7,23

partly of iron and partly of clay, so some of the kingdom will be strong, and *another* part of it will be brittle.
[43]"And as you saw the iron mixed with common clay, so they will combine with one another in the seed of men; but they will not merge [for such diverse things or ideologies cannot unite], even as iron does not mix with clay.

The Divine Kingdom

[44]"In the days of those [final ten] kings the God of heaven will set up a kingdom that will never be destroyed, nor will its sovereignty be left for another people; but it will crush and put an end to all these kingdoms, and it will stand forever. [Dan 7:14–17; Luke 1:31–33; Rev 11:15]
[45]"Just as you saw that a stone was cut out of the mountain without hands and that it crushed the iron, the bronze, the clay, the silver and the gold, the great God has revealed to the king what will take place in the future; so the dream is true and its interpretation is trustworthy."

Daniel Promoted

[46]Then King Nebuchadnezzar fell face downward and paid respect to Daniel [as a great prophet of the highest God], and gave orders for an offering and fragrant incense to be presented to him [in honor of his God].
[47]The king answered Daniel and said, "Most certainly your God is the God of gods and the Lord of kings and a revealer of mysteries, since you have been able to reveal this mystery!" [Prov 3:32; Rev 19:16]
[48]Then the king promoted Daniel [to an exalted position] and gave him many great gifts, and he made him ruler over the entire province of Babylon and chief governor over all the wise men of Babylon.
[49]And Daniel made a request of the king, and he appointed Shadrach, Meshach, and Abed-nego over the affairs of the province of Babylon, while Daniel was at the court of the king.

The King's Golden Image

3 NEBUCHADNEZZAR THE king made a gold [-plated] image, whose height [including the pedestal] was sixty cubits (ninety feet) and its width six cubits (nine feet). He set it up on the plain of Dura in the province of Babylon.
[2]Then Nebuchadnezzar the king sent *word* to assemble the satraps, the prefects and the governors, the counselors, the treasurers, the judges, the magistrates *and* lawyers and all the chief officials of the provinces to come to the dedication of the image that King Nebuchadnezzar had set up.
[3]Then the satraps, the prefects, the governors, the counselors, the treasurers, the judges, the magistrates *and* lawyers, and all the chief officials of the provinces gathered together for the dedication of the image that King Nebuchadnezzar had set up; and they stood before it.
[4]Then the herald loudly proclaimed, "You are commanded, O peoples, nations, and *speakers of every* language,
[5]that at the moment you hear the sound of the horn, pipe, lyre, trigon (four-stringed harp), dulcimer, bagpipe, and all kinds of music, you are to fall down and worship the golden image that King Nebuchadnezzar has set up.

---

of iron does actually refer to the Roman Empire, which will be revived in some form in the last days, perhaps as a ten-nation confederacy (the ten toes, or the ten horns of the beast of chapter 7). In this case, the "kingdom that will never be destroyed" is a literal kingdom to be established by Jesus Christ at the second coming, at which time He will destroy the kingdoms of the world (Rev 19:15).

3:1 *cubits.* A cubit in Israel was approximately 18 inches; in Babylon it was about 20 inches. Nebuchadnezzar's image was 90 to 100 feet tall. The odd proportions of this figure (a normal human height-to-width ratio is about 4:1 rather than 10:1) may indicate that the height includes a base or pedestal.

3:2 *satraps.* Satraps were the chief officials of the provinces of the empire.

44 ver. 28; Da 4:3,34; 6:26; 7:14,27; Mic 4:7; Lk 1:32,33; Ps 2:9; Isa 60:12; 1Co 15:24 **45** ver. 35; Isa 28:16 **46** See Ac 10:25; 14:13; 28:6; Ezr 6:10 **48** ver. 6; Da 4:9; 5:11 **49** Da 3:12; Est 2:19,21; 3:2 **CHAPTER 3** **4** Da 4:1; 6:25

[6]"Whoever does not fall down and worship shall immediately be thrown into the midst of a furnace of blazing fire."
[7]So when the people heard the sound of the horn, pipe, lyre, trigon, dulcimer, bagpipe and all kinds of music, all the peoples, nations, and *speakers of every* language fell down and worshiped the golden image that Nebuchadnezzar the king had set up.

Worship of the Image Refused

[8]At that time certain Chaldeans came forward and brought [malicious] accusations against the Jews.
[9]They said to King Nebuchadnezzar, "O king, live forever!
[10]"You, O king, have made a decree that everyone who hears the sound of the horn, pipe, lyre, trigon, harp, dulcimer, bagpipe, and all kinds of music is to fall down and worship the golden image.
[11]"Whoever does not fall down and worship shall be thrown into the midst of a furnace of blazing fire.
[12]"There are certain Jews whom you have appointed over the administration of the province of Babylon, *namely* Shadrach, Meshach, and Abed-nego. These men, O king, pay no attention to you; they do not serve your gods or worship the golden image which you have set up."
[13]Then Nebuchadnezzar in a furious rage gave a command to bring Shadrach, Meshach, and Abed-nego; and these men were brought before the king.
[14]Nebuchadnezzar said to them, "Is it true, Shadrach, Meshach, and Abed-nego, that you do not serve my gods or worship the golden image which I have set up?
[15]"Now if you are ready, when you hear the sound of the horn, pipe, lyre, trigon, harp, dulcimer, and all kinds of music, to fall down and worship the image which I have made, very good. But if you do not worship, you shall be thrown at once into the midst of a furnace of blazing fire; and what god is there who can rescue you out of my hands?"
[16]Shadrach, Meshach, and Abed-nego answered the king, "O Nebuchadnezzar, we do not need to answer you on this point.
[17]"If it be so, our God whom we serve is able to rescue us from the furnace of blazing fire, and He will rescue us from your hand, O king.
[18]"But even if *He does* not, let it be known to you, O king, that we are not going to serve your gods or worship the golden image that you have set up!" [Job 13:15; Acts 4:19, 20]

Daniel's Friends Protected

[19]Then Nebuchadnezzar was filled with fury, and his facial expression changed toward Shadrach, Meshach, and Abed-nego. Then he gave a command that the furnace was to be heated seven times hotter than usual.
[20]He commanded certain strong men in his army to tie up Shadrach, Meshach, and Abed-nego and to throw them into the furnace of blazing fire.
[21]Then these [three] men were tied up in their trousers, their coats, their turbans, and their other clothes, and were thrown into the midst of the furnace of blazing fire.
[22]Because the king's command was urgent and the furnace was extremely hot, the flame of the fire killed the men who carried up Shadrach, Meshach, and Abed-nego.
[23]But these three men, Shadrach, Meshach, and Abed-nego, fell into the midst of the furnace of blazing fire *still* tied up.

3:18 *But even if He does not.* The faithful men knew that God could deliver them (v. 17), yet they were also aware that God could have chosen not to do so. Faith in God may not translate into victory in every circumstance (Heb 11:32 – 39). To these men the outcome was irrelevant, for what was at stake was not God's ability or their own lives, but their faith and obedience to serve Him regardless of the cost.

6 Jer 29:22; Rev 13:15 **8** Da 6:12 **9** Da 2:4; 5:10; 6:6,21 **12** Da 2:49 **15** As Ex 32:32; Lk 13:9; Ex 5:2; 2Ki 18:35 **16** Mt 10:19

[24]Then Nebuchadnezzar the king [looked and] was astounded, and he jumped up and said to his counselors, "Did we not throw three men who were tied up into the midst of the fire?" They replied to the king, "Certainly, O king."
[25]He answered, "Look! I see four men untied, walking around in the midst of the fire, and they are not hurt! And the appearance of the fourth is like a son of the gods!" [Phil 2:5–8]
[26]Then Nebuchadnezzar approached the door of the blazing furnace and said, "Shadrach, Meshach, and Abed-nego, servants of the Most High God, come out [of there]! Come here!" Then Shadrach, Meshach, and Abed-nego came out of the midst of the fire.
[27]The satraps, the prefects, the governors and the king's counselors gathered around them and saw that in regard to these men the fire had no effect on their bodies—their hair was not singed, their clothes were not scorched *or* damaged, even the smell of smoke was not on them.
[28]Nebuchadnezzar responded and said, "Blessed be the God of Shadrach, Meshach, and Abed-nego, who has sent His angel and rescued His servants who believed in, trusted in, *and* relied on Him! They violated the king's command and surrendered their bodies rather than serve or worship any god except their own God.
[29]"Therefore I make a decree that any people, nation, or language that speaks anything offensive against the God of Shadrach, Meshach, and Abed-nego shall be cut into pieces and their houses be made a heap of rubbish, for there is no other god who is able to save in this way!"
[30]Then the king caused Shadrach, Meshach, and Abed-nego to prosper in the province of Babylon.

The King Acknowledges God

4 NEBUCHADNEZZAR THE king, to all the peoples, nations, and *speakers of every* language that live in all the earth: "May your peace abound!
[2]"It has seemed good to me to declare the signs and wonders which the Most High God has done for me.

[3]"How great are His signs
And how mighty are His wonders!
His kingdom is an everlasting
kingdom
And His dominion is from
generation to generation.
[Dan 7:13, 14; Luke 1:31–33]

The Vision of a Great Tree

[4]"I, Nebuchadnezzar, was at rest in my house and prospering in my palace.
[5]"I saw a dream and it made me afraid; and the fantasies *and* thoughts and the visions [that appeared] in my mind *as I lay* on my bed kept alarming me.
[6]"So I gave orders to bring in before me all the wise men of Babylon, so that they might make known to me the interpretation of the dream.
[7]"Then the magicians, the enchanters (Magi), the Chaldeans [who were the master astrologers] and the diviners came in, and I told them the dream, but they could not interpret it *and* make known its meaning to me.
[8]"But at last Daniel came in before me, whose name is Belteshazzar, after the name of my god, and in whom is

3:25 *I see four men untied.* The fourth man walking with the three friends in the furnace may have been an angel. Many believe that this was an appearance of the pre-incarnate Christ.
3:28 *Blessed be the God of Shadrach, Meshach, and Abed-nego.* Pagan cultures did not deny the existence of other gods, even those of other peoples. Nebuchadnezzar was impressed with the God of Israel, but that did not mean that he recognized that God is the only true god.

4:1 *Nebuchadnezzar the king.* These verses are a royal proclamation by Nebuchadnezzar concerning the God of Israel, in which the king celebrated what God had done for him and extolled His power and dominion.
4:8 *my god.* This refers to Marduk. Nebuchadnezzar was still a pagan, but he also recognized that Daniel had the spirit of his God, and that Daniel's God was different from other gods.

25 Isa 43:2; ver. 28; Job 1:6; 38:7; Ps 34:7 **27** Heb 11:34 **28** Ps 34:7,8; Jer 17:7; Da 6:22,23 **29** Da 6:26; Da 2:5; Da 6:27 **CHAPTER 4** **1** Da 3:4; 6:25 **2** Da 3:26 **3** Da 6:27; ver. 34; Da 2:44; 6:26 **5** Da 2:28,29; Da 2:1 **7** Da 2:2 **8** Da 1:7; ver. 18; Isa 63:11; Da 2:11; 5:11,14

a spirit of the holy gods; and I told the
dream to him, *saying*,
9 'O Belteshazzar, chief of the magi-
cians, because I know that a spirit of
the holy gods is in you and no mystery
baffles *or* troubles you, tell me the vi-
sions of my dream which I have seen,
along with its interpretation.
10 'The visions that passed through
my mind as I lay on my bed were these:
I was looking, and behold, *there was*
a tree in the middle of the earth, and
its height was great.

11 'The tree grew large and became
strong
And its height reached to heaven,
And it was visible to the end of the
earth.
12 'Its leaves were beautiful and its
fruit abundant,
And in it was food for all.
The beasts of the field found shade
under it,
And the birds of the sky nested in
its branches,
And all living creatures fed
themselves from it.

13 'And behold, I saw in the visions of
my mind *as I lay* on my bed, an *angelic*
watcher, a holy one, descended from
heaven.

14 'He shouted aloud and said this:
"Cut down the tree and cut off its
branches;
Shake off its leaves and scatter its
fruit;
Let the living creatures run from
under it
And the birds fly from its
branches.
15 "Nevertheless leave the stump
with its roots in the ground,
Bound with a band of iron and
bronze
In the new grass of the field;
And let him be wet with the dew of
heaven,
And let him feed with the animals
in the grass of the earth.
16 "Let his mind *and* nature be
changed from a man's
And let an animal's mind *and*
nature be given to him,
And let seven periods of time pass
over him.
17 "This sentence is by the decree of
the *angelic* watchers
And the decision is a command of
the holy ones,
So that the living may know
[without any doubt]
That the Most High [God] rules
over the kingdom of mankind
And He bestows it on whomever
He desires
And sets over it the humblest *and*
lowliest of men." [Dan 2:21; 5:21]

18 'This is the dream which I, King Neb-
uchadnezzar, have seen. Now you, Bel-
teshazzar, explain its meaning, since
none of the wise men of my kingdom
are able to reveal its interpretation to
me; but you are able, for a spirit of the
holy gods is in you.'

Daniel Interprets the Vision

19 "Then Daniel, whose [Babylonian]
name was Belteshazzar, was appalled
and speechless for a while [because
he was deeply concerned about the
destiny of the king], and his thoughts
alarmed him. The king said, 'Belte-
shazzar, do not let the dream or its
interpretation frighten you.' Belteshaz-
zar answered, 'My lord, may the dream

4:9 *chief of the magicians.* Daniel's position as head magician did not mean that he practiced sorcery or witchcraft, a thing clearly forbidden by the law (Dt 18:10 – 11). In the pluralistic Babylonian society, Daniel's relationship with the God of Israel would automatically have been categorized as another form of magic, or astrology, or divination, the "wisdom" of the day. He received the honor and position of one who has favor with the gods.

4:16 *seven periods of time.* These times could refer to years, months, weeks, days, or hours. Most take them as years, as elsewhere in the book (7:25).

9 Da 2:48; 5:11 **10** ver. 20; Eze 31:3 **12** Eze 17:23; 31:6; See La 4:20 **13** ver. 17,23; Dt 33:2; Da 8:13; Zec 14:5; Jude 14 **14** Mt 3:10; Eze 31:12 **16** Da 11:13; 12:7 **17** Ps 9:16; ver. 25,32; Da 2:21; 5:21 **18** Ge 41:8,15; Da 5:8,15; ver. 8 **19** ver. 8; See 2Sa 18:32; Jer 29:7

be [meant] for those who hate you and
its message for your enemies!
20 'The tree that you saw, which be-
came great and grew strong, whose
height reached to heaven and which
was visible to all the earth,
21 whose foliage was beautiful and
its fruit abundant, and on which was
food for all, under which the beasts of
the field lived, and in whose branches
the birds of the sky nested—
22 it is you, O king, who have become
great and grown strong; your great-
ness has increased and it reaches to
heaven, and your dominion [reaches]
to the ends of the earth.
23 'In that the king saw an *angelic*
watcher, a holy one, descending from
heaven and saying, "Cut the tree down
and destroy it; but leave the stump with
its roots in the earth, but with a band
of iron and bronze *around it* in the new
grass of the field, and let him be wet
with the dew of heaven, and let him
feed with the beasts of the field until
seven periods of time pass over him,"
24 this is the interpretation, O king: It
is the decree of the Most High [God],
which has come upon my lord the king:
25 that you shall be driven from man-
kind and your dwelling place shall be
with the beasts of the field; and that
you be given grass to eat like the cattle
and be wet with the dew of heaven;
and seven periods of time shall pass
over you, until you know [without any
doubt] that the Most High [God] rules
over the kingdom of mankind and He
bestows it to whomever He desires.
26 'And in that it was commanded to
leave the stump with the roots of the
tree [in the earth], your kingdom shall
be restored to you after you recognize
(understand fully) that Heaven rules.
27 'Therefore, O king, let my advice
to you be [considered and found] ac-
ceptable; break away now from your
sins *and* exhibit your repentance by
doing what is right, and from your
wickedness by showing mercy to the
poor, so that [if you repent] there may
possibly be a continuance of your pros-
perity *and* tranquility *and* a healing of
your error.'

The Vision Fulfilled

28 "All this happened to Nebuchad-
nezzar the king.
29 "Twelve months later he was walk-
ing on the upper level of the royal pal-
ace of Babylon.
30 "The king said thoughtfully, 'Is not
this the great Babylon which I myself
have built as the royal residence *and*
seat of government by the might of my
power and for the honor *and* glory of
my majesty?'
31 "While the words were still in the
king's mouth, a voice came [as if fall-
ing] from heaven, *saying*, 'O King Neb-
uchadnezzar, to you it is declared: "The
kingdom has been removed from you,
32 and you will be driven away from
mankind, and your dwelling place will
be with the animals of the field. You
will be given grass to eat like the cattle,
and seven periods of time will pass
over you until you know [without any
doubt] that the Most High God rules
over the kingdom of mankind and He
bestows it on whomever He desires." '
33 "Immediately the word concerning
Nebuchadnezzar was fulfilled. He was
driven away from mankind and began
eating grass like cattle, and his body
was wet with the dew of heaven until
his hair had grown like eagles' *feath-
ers* and his nails were like birds' *claws*.
34 "But at the end of the days [that
is, at the seven periods of time], I,

4:20 *tree*. In the Old Testament, a tree is a common symbol for a ruler (Jdg 9:7 – 15; Eze 31:2 – 14; Zec 11:1 – 2).

4:23 *angelic watcher*. The term "watcher" means "waking one," one who is constantly alert. The parallel "holy one" suggests that the watcher is either the Lord Himself or one of His angels (3:28; 6:22; 8:16; 10:13).

4:32 *until you know [without any doubt] that the Most High God rules*. Nebuchadnezzar would become insane, yet in his animal-like state he would learn more of God than he ever had

20 ver. 10,11,12 **22** Da 2:38; Jer 27:6-8 **23** ver. 13; Da 5:21 **25** ver. 32; Da 5:21; Ps 106:20; ver. 17,32; Ps 83:18; Jer 27:5 **26** Mt 21:25; Lk 15:18 **27** 1Pe 4:8; Ps 41:1; 1Ki 21:29 **30** Pr 16:18; Da 5:20 **31** Da 5:5; Lk 12:20; ver. 24 **32** ver. 25 **34** ver. 26; Da 12:7; Rev 4:10; Ps 10:16; Da 2:44; Mic 4:7; Lk 1:33

Nebuchadnezzar, raised my eyes toward heaven, and my understanding *and* reason returned to me; and I blessed the Most High [God] and I praised and honored *and* glorified Him who lives forever,

For His dominion is an everlasting
  dominion;
And His kingdom *endures* from
  generation to generation.
35 "All the inhabitants of the earth
  are regarded as nothing.
But He does according to His will
  in the host of heaven
And among the inhabitants of the
  earth;
And no one can hold back His
  hand
Or say to Him, 'What have You
  done?'

36 "Now at the same time my reason returned to me; and for the glory of my kingdom, my majesty and splendor were returned to me, and my counselors and my nobles began seeking me out; so I was re-established in my kingdom, and still more greatness [than before] was added to me.

37 "Now I, Nebuchadnezzar, praise and exalt and honor the King of heaven, for all His works are true *and* faithful and His ways are just, and He is able to humiliate *and* humble those who walk in [self-centered, self-righteous] pride."

Belshazzar's Feast

5 BELSHAZZAR THE king [who was a descendant of Nebuchadnezzar] gave a great feast for a thousand of his nobles, and he was drinking his wine in the presence of the thousand [guests].

2 Belshazzar, as he tasted the wine, gave a command to bring in the gold and silver vessels which his father Nebuchadnezzar had taken out of the temple which was in Jerusalem, so that the king and his nobles, his wives and his concubines might drink from them.

3 Then they brought in the gold *and* silver vessels that had been taken out of the temple, the house of God which was in Jerusalem; and the king and his nobles, his wives and his concubines drank from them.

4 They drank the wine and praised the gods of gold and silver, of bronze, iron, wood and stone.

5 Suddenly the fingers of a man's hand appeared and began writing opposite the lampstand on [a well-lit area of] the plaster of the wall of the king's palace, and the king saw the part of the hand that did the writing.

6 Then the king's face grew pale, and his thoughts alarmed him; the joints *and* muscles of his hips *and* back weakened and his knees began knocking together.

7 The king called aloud to bring in the enchanters (Magi), the Chaldeans [who were master astrologers] and the diviners. The king said to the wise men of Babylon, "Whoever can read this writing and explain its interpretation to me shall be clothed with purple and have a chain of gold put around his neck, and have authority as the third *ruler* in the kingdom."

8 Then all the king's wise men came

---

before. The chastisement of God is always for a holy and helpful purpose, if we will accept it.

5:1 *Belshazzar the king.* Belshazzar is called the king and the son of Nebuchadnezzar. Other ancient records, however, seem to dispute both facts. These records indicate that Belshazzar was the son of Nabonidus, the last king of Babylon. It is possible that Belshazzar was the grandson of Nebuchadnezzar. In ancient writings, the term *father* is often used to indicate ancestry rather than immediate family (2Ki 14:3). Belshazzar may have served as vice-regent while his father was still living (Nabonidus seems to have spent a number of the years of his reign in Arabia). Thus, he would have been acting as king, even if he was not officially king. Note that Darius the Mede was also called king, even though he served Cyrus (5:31; 6:6).

5:7 *third ruler.* Assuming that Belshazzar was acting as regent for his father Nabonidus, the "third ruler" would have been next in line for the throne.

35 Isa 40:15; Ps 115:3; 135:6; Job 34:29; Job 9:12; Isa 45:9; Ro 9:20 **36** ver. 26; Job 42:12; Pr 22:4; Mt 6:33 **37** Ps 33:4; Rev 15:3; Ex 18:11; Da 5:20 **CHAPTER 5** **1** Est 1:3 **2** Da 1:2; Jer 52:19 **4** Rev 9:20 **5** Da 4:31 **6** Na 2:10 **7** Da 4:6; Isa 47:13; Da 6:2 **8** Da 2:27

in, but they could not read the writing
or reveal to the king its interpretation.
[9]Then King Belshazzar was greatly
perplexed, his face became even paler,
and his nobles were bewildered *and*
alarmed.
[10]Now the queen [mother], overhear-
ing the [excited] words of the king
and his nobles, came into the banquet
area. The queen [mother] spoke and
said, "O king, live forever! Do not be
alarmed at your thoughts or let your
face be changed.
[11]"There is a man in your kingdom in
whom is a spirit of the holy gods; and
in the days of your father, illumina-
tion, understanding and wisdom like
the wisdom of the gods were found
in him. And King Nebuchadnezzar,
your father—your father the king, ap-
pointed him chief of the magicians,
enchanters, Chaldeans and diviners.
[12]"It was because an extraordinary
spirit, knowledge and insight, the abil-
ity to interpret dreams, clarify rid-
dles, and solve complex problems were
found in this Daniel, whom the king
named Belteshazzar. Now let Daniel
be called and he will give the inter-
pretation."

Daniel Interprets Handwriting on the Wall

[13]Then Daniel was brought in before
the king. And the king said to Daniel,
"Are you that Daniel who is one of the
sons of the exiles of Judah, whom my
father the king brought from Judah?
[14]"I have heard of you, that a spirit
of the gods is in you, and that illu-
mination, insight, and extraordinary
wisdom have been found in you.
[15]"Now the wise men and the en-
chanters, were brought in before me
so that they might read this writing
and reveal its meaning to me, but they
could not give the interpretation of the
message.
[16]"But I personally have heard about
you, that you are able to make interpre-
tations and solve complex problems.
Now if you are able to read the writing
and reveal its interpretation to me, you
shall be clothed with purple and have
a chain of gold put around your neck,
and you shall have authority as the
third *ruler* in the kingdom."
[17]Then Daniel answered and said
before the king, "Keep your gifts for
yourself and give your rewards to
someone else; however, I will read the
writing to the king and reveal the in-
terpretation to him.
[18]"O king, the Most High God gave
Nebuchadnezzar your father a king-
dom and greatness and glory and
majesty;
[19]and because of the greatness
that He gave him, all the peoples, na-
tions, and *speakers of every* language
trembled and feared him. Whomever
he wished he killed, and whomever
he wished he kept alive; whomever he
wished he promoted and whomever
he wished he humbled.
[20]"But when his heart was lifted up
and his spirit became so proud that he
behaved arrogantly, he was deposed
from his royal throne and his glory
was taken away from him.
[21]"He was also driven from man-
kind, and his mind was made like that
of an animal, and his dwelling place
was with the wild donkeys. He was
given grass to eat like cattle, and his
body was wet with the dew of heaven
until he came to know [without any
doubt] that the Most High God rules
over the kingdom of mankind and He
appoints it to whomever He wills.
[22]"And you, his son, O Belshazzar,
have not humbled your heart (mind),
even though you knew all this.
[23]"And you have exalted yourself
against the Lord of heaven, and
the vessels of His house have been

5:11 ***a spirit of the holy gods.*** This is the same expression used by Nebuchadnezzar (4:8–9,18).
5:13 ***Daniel who is one of the sons of the exiles.*** Daniel was an old man by this time, possibly 80 years old or older.

9 Da 2:1 **11** Da 2:48; 4:8,9,18; Da 4:9 **12** Da 6:3; Da 1:7 **14** ver. 11,12 **15** ver. 7,8 **16** ver. 7 **18** Da 2:37,38; 4:17,22,25 **19** Jer 27:7; Da 3:4 **20** Da 4:30,37 **21** Da 4:32; Da 4:17,25 **22** 2Ch 33:23; 36:12 **23** ver. 3,4; Ps 115:5,6; Jer 10:23

brought before you, and you and your nobles, your wives and your concubines have been drinking wine from them; and you have praised the gods of silver and gold, of bronze, iron, wood and stone, which do not see or hear or understand. But the God who holds in His hand your breath of life and your ways you have not honored *and* glorified [but have dishonored and defied].

24 “Then the hand was sent from the presence [of the Most High God], and this inscription was written:

25 “This is the inscription that was written, ‘MENE, MENE, TEKEL, UPHARSIN [numbered, numbered, weighed, and divided].’

26 “This is the interpretation of the message: ‘MENE’—God has numbered the days of your kingdom and put an end to it;

27 ‘TEKEL’—you have been weighed on the scales [of righteousness] and found deficient;

28 ‘PERES’—your kingdom has been divided and given over to the Medes and Persians.”

29 Then Belshazzar gave the command, and Daniel was clothed with purple and a chain of gold was put around his neck, and a proclamation concerning him was issued [declaring] that he now had authority as the third *ruler* in the kingdom.

30 During that same night Belshazzar the [last] Chaldean king was slain [by troops of the invading army].

31 So Darius the Mede received the kingdom; he was about the age of sixty-two.

Daniel Serves Darius

6 IT SEEMED good to Darius [who became king after Belshazzar] to appoint over the kingdom 120 satraps who would be in charge throughout the kingdom,

2 and over them three chief commissioners (of whom Daniel was one), that these satraps might be accountable to them, so that the king would have no loss [from disloyalty or mismanagement].

3 Then this Daniel, because of the extraordinary spirit within him, began distinguishing himself among the commissioners and the satraps, and the king planned to appoint him over the entire realm.

4 Then the [other two] commissioners and the satraps began trying to find a reason to bring a complaint against Daniel concerning the [administration of the] kingdom; but they could find no reason for an accusation or *evidence of* corruption, because he was faithful [a man of high moral character and personal integrity], and no negligence or corruption [of any kind] was found in him.

5 Then these men said, “We will

5:25–28 ***MENE, MENE, TEKEL, UPHARSIN.*** MENE means “numbered.” The repetition is for emphasis. God had numbered the days of Belshazzar’s kingdom, and the time was up. TEKEL means “weighed.” God had weighed Belshazzar’s character, and he did not measure up. UPHARSIN (the plural of PERES) means “divided.” That very night Babylon would be divided and defeated by the Medes and the Persians.

5:30 ***During that same night.*** That very evening (October 12, 539 BC), Babylon fell to the Persian army commanded by Gubaru.

5:31 ***Darius the Mede.*** Darius the Mede is mentioned by name only in the Book of Daniel. He cannot be the famous Darius I Hystaspes because Darius I was not a Mede, and he lived too late (522–486 BC) to be a contemporary of Daniel. It is believed that “Darius the Mede” was Gubaru, a governor appointed by Cyrus. Ancient literary sources indicate that this official took over immediately in Babylon until Cyrus appointed his own son Cambyses as co-ruler around 538 BC. Why Gubaru might have been called Darius is uncertain, though ancient rulers often took other names for themselves.

6:3 ***the extraordinary spirit.*** This probably refers to Daniel’s surpassing ability to do his job well and perhaps also indicates a commendable attitude.

6:5 ***the law of his God.*** Daniel had such integrity that, even after a life spent in government circles, his enemies could find nothing against

27 Job 31:6; Ps 62:9; Jer 6:30 **28** Isa 21:2; ver. 31; Da 9:1; Da 6:28 **29** ver. 7 **30** Jer 51:31,39,57 **31** Da 9:1
CHAPTER 6 **3** Da 5:12 **4** Ecc 4:4

not find any basis for an accusation against this Daniel unless we find something against him in connection with the law of his God." [Acts 24:13–21; 1 Pet 4:12–16]

6 Then these commissioners and satraps agreed to approach the king and said to him, "King Darius, live forever!

7 "All the commissioners of the kingdom, the prefects and the satraps, the counselors and the governors have consulted *and* agreed together that the king should establish a *royal* statute and enforce an injunction that anyone who petitions (prays to) any god or man besides you, O king, during the next thirty days, shall be thrown into the den of lions.

8 "Now, O king, establish the injunction and sign the document so that it may not be changed, in accordance with the law of the Medes and Persians, which [insures that it] may not be altered *or* revoked."

9 So King Darius signed the document, that is, the injunction.

10 Now when Daniel knew that the document was signed, he went into his house (now in his roof chamber his windows were open toward Jerusalem); he continued to get down on his knees three times a day, praying and giving thanks before his God, as he had been doing previously. [Ps 5:7]

11 Then, by agreement, these men came [together] and found Daniel praying and making requests before his God.

12 Then they approached and spoke before the king regarding his injunction, "Have you not signed an injunction that anyone who petitions (prays to) any god or man except you, O king, within the *designated* thirty days, is to be thrown into the den of lions?" The king answered, "The statement is true, in accordance with the law of the Medes and Persians, which may not be altered *or* revoked."

13 Then they answered and said before the king, "Daniel, who is one of the exiles from Judah, does not pay any attention to you, O king, or to the injunction which you have signed, but keeps praying [to his God] three times a day."

14 Then, as soon as the king heard these words, he was deeply distressed [over what he had done] and set his mind on rescuing Daniel; and he struggled until the sun went down [trying to work out a way] to save him.

15 Then, by agreement, these same men came to the king and said, "Know, O king, that it is a law of the Medes and Persians that no injunction or statute which the king establishes may be altered *or* revoked."

Daniel in the Den of Lions

16 Then the king gave a command, and Daniel was brought and thrown into the den of lions. The king said to Daniel, "May your God, whom you constantly serve, rescue you Himself!" [Ps 34:7, 19; 37:39, 40; 50:15]

17 A stone was brought and laid over the mouth of the den; and the king sealed it with his own signet ring and with the signet rings of his nobles, so that nothing would be changed concerning Daniel.

18 Then the king returned to his palace and spent the night fasting; and no music or entertainment was brought before him, and he remained unable to sleep.

19 Then the king arose at dawn, at the break of day, and hurried to the den of lions.

20 When he had come near the den, he called out to Daniel with a troubled

---

him. His devotion to God was so well-known that these men were confident that Daniel would obey His law even if it would cost him his life.

6:13 ***one of the exiles from Judah.*** Daniel's accusers did not describe him as governor (v. 2), but as a captive from another land, in order to implicate him as a treasonous and dangerous person.

6:14 ***was deeply distressed.*** It is clear that Darius had not factored Daniel into the situation in the beginning. He never had the intention of harming him.

6 ver. 21; Neh 2:3; Da 2:4 **8** ver. 12,15; Est 1:19; 8:8 **10** 1Ki 8:44,48; Ps 5:7; Jnh 2:4; Ps 55:17; Ac 2:1,2,15; 3:1; 10:9 **12** Da 3:8; ver. 8 **13** Da 1:6; 5:13; Da 3:12 **14** Mk 6:26 **15** ver. 8 **17** La 3:53; Mt 27:66 **18** Da 2:1 **20** Da 3:15

voice. The king said to Daniel, "O Daniel, servant of the living God, has your God, whom you constantly serve, been able to rescue you from the lions?"
21Then Daniel spoke to the king,
"O king, live forever!
22"My God has sent His angel and
has shut the mouths of the lions so that they have not hurt me, because I was found innocent before Him; and also before you, O king, I have committed no crime." [2 Tim 4:17]
23Then the king was greatly pleased
and ordered that Daniel be taken out of the den. So Daniel was taken out of the den, and no injury whatever was found on him, because he believed in *and* relied on *and* trusted in his God.
24The king then gave a command,
and those men who had maliciously accused Daniel were brought and thrown into the den of lions, they, their children and their wives; and before they reached the bottom of the den, the lions overpowered them and crushed all their bones.
25Then Darius the king wrote to all
the peoples, nations, and *speakers of every* language who were living in all the land: "May peace abound to you!
26"I issue a decree that in all the
dominion of my kingdom men are to [reverently] fear and tremble before the God of Daniel,

For He is the living God, enduring
and steadfast forever,
And His kingdom is one which
will not be destroyed,
And His dominion will be forever.
27"He rescues and saves and
performs signs and wonders
In heaven and on earth—
He who has rescued Daniel from
the power of the lions."

28So this [man] Daniel prospered *and*
enjoyed success in the reign of Darius and in the reign of Cyrus the Persian.

Vision of the Four Beasts

7 IN THE first year of Belshazzar king of Babylon Daniel had a dream and visions appeared in his mind *as he lay* on his bed; then he wrote the dream down and related a summary of it.
2Daniel said, "I saw in my vision by
night, and behold, the four winds of heaven were stirring up the great sea (the nations).
3"And four great beasts, each differ-
ent from the other, were coming up out of the sea [in succession].
4"The first (the Babylonian Empire
under Nebuchadnezzar) was like a lion and had the wings of an eagle. I kept looking until its wings were plucked, and it was lifted up from the ground and made to stand on two feet like a man; a human mind was given to it. [Dan 2:37, 38]
5"And behold, another beast, a sec-
ond one (the Medo-Persian Empire), was like a bear, and it was raised up on one side (domain), and three ribs were in its mouth between its teeth; and it was told, 'Arise, devour much meat.'

6:23 *he believed in and relied on and trusted in his God.* Daniel's faithfulness got him into trouble; faith got him out of it (Heb 11:33)
6:24 *their children and their wives.* The entire families of the wicked conspirators were destroyed because the Persians, like the Hebrews and other peoples, considered guilt a collective responsibility (Nu 16:1 – 35; Jos 7).
6:28 *and in the reign of Cyrus.* Gubaru, or Darius, served Cyrus for about one year, after which Cyrus appointed his son Cambyses as regent over Babylon.
7:1 *the first year of Belshazzar.* Chapter 5 records Belshazzar's death, indicating that the Book of Daniel is not arranged chronologically.
7:3 *four great beasts.* These four beasts represent kings or kingdoms, like the four metals of the statue in chapter 2.
7:4 *like a lion and had the wings of an eagle.* There has been almost universal agreement from the early centuries until today that this beast represents Babylon. It is also agreed that the visions of chapters 2 and 7 speak of the same four kingdoms.
7:5 *like a bear.* The bear seems to represent Babylon's successor, the Medo-Persian Empire

21 Da 2:4 **22** Da 3:28; Heb 11:33 **23** Heb 11:33 **24** Dt 19:19; Est 9:10; See Dt 24:16; 2Ki 14:6 **25** Da 4:1 **26** Da 3:29; Ps 99:1; Da 4:34; Da 2:44; 4:3,34; Lk 1:33 **27** Da 4:3 **28** Da 1:21; Ezr 1:1,2 **CHAPTER 7** **1** Nu 12:6; Am 3:7; Da 2:28 **3** Rev 13:1 **4** Dt 28:49; 2Sa 1:23; Jer 48:40; Eze 17:3; Hab 1:8 **5** Da 2:39

6"After this I kept looking, and behold, another one (the Greek Empire of Alexander the Great), like a leopard, which had on its back four wings like those of a bird; the beast also had four heads (Alexander's generals, his successors), and power to rule was given to it. [Dan 2:39; 8:20–22]
7"After this I kept looking in the night visions, and behold, [I saw] a fourth beast (the Roman Empire), terrible and extremely strong; and it had huge iron teeth. It devoured and crushed and trampled down what was left with its feet. It was different from all the beasts that came before it, and it had ten horns (ten kings). [Dan 2:40–43; 7:23]
8"While I was considering the horns, behold, there came up among them another horn, a little one, and three of the first horns were pulled up by the roots before it; and behold, in this horn were eyes like the eyes of a man and a mouth boasting of great things.

The Ancient of Days Reigns

9"I kept looking
Until thrones were set up,
And the Ancient of Days (God) took His seat;
His garment was white as snow
And the hair of His head like pure wool.
His throne was flames of fire;
Its wheels were a burning fire.
[1 Kin 22:19; Ps 90:2; Ezek 1:26–28; Dan 7:13, 22; Matt 19:28; Rev 20:4]
10"A river of fire was flowing
And coming out from before Him;
A thousand thousands were attending Him,
And ten thousand times ten thousand were standing before Him;
The court was seated,
And the books were opened.
11"Then I kept looking because of the sound of the great *and* boastful words which the horn was speaking. I kept looking until the beast was slain, and its body destroyed and given to be burned with fire.
12"As for the rest of the beasts, their power was taken away; yet their lives were prolonged [for the length of their lives was fixed] for a predetermined time.

The Son of Man Presented

13"I kept looking in the night visions,
And behold, on the clouds of heaven
One like a Son of Man was coming,
And He came up to the Ancient of Days
And was presented before Him.
14"And to Him (the Messiah) was given dominion (supreme authority),

(2:38–39). The three ribs may represent the three kingdoms that Medo-Persia devoured — Babylon, Libya, and Egypt.

7:6 ***like a leopard.*** The leopard is believed to represent Greece. The Greeks, under the leadership of Alexander the Great, rapidly conquered the known world. ***four heads.*** After Alexander's death, his empire was divided into four different parts (8:8–22) — Macedonia, Egypt, Syria, and Thracia.

7:7 ***fourth beast.*** The last of the beasts may represent Rome (2:40).

7:9 ***Ancient of Days.*** "Ancient of Days" is a reference to God the Father as certified by the submission of the "one like a Son of Man" (vv. 13–14) and His role in judgment (v. 22).

7:10 ***And the books were opened.*** The books record the names and deeds of those who will be judged (Rev 20:12).

7:13 ***on the clouds of heaven.*** John uses the same expression to speak of Jesus coming in judgment (Rev 1:7). ***One like a Son of Man.*** The term "Son of Man" is an expression meaning "human," but clearly this "one like" the Son of Man was no ordinary human. Jewish and Christian expositors have both identified this individual as the Messiah. Jesus Himself used this name to emphasize His humanity (Mt 9:6; 10:23).

7:14 ***to Him (the Messiah) was given dominion.*** Jesus will reign over all things (1Co 15:27–28; Eph 1:20–23; Php 2:9–11; Rev 17:14; 19:10).

6 Da 8:8,22 **7** Da 2:40,41; Rev 13:1 **8** Da 8:9; Rev 9:7; Ps 12:3; Rev 13:5 **9** Rev 20:4; Ps 90:2; Ps 104:2; Rev 1:14; Eze 1:15 **10** Ps 50:3; Isa 30:33; 66:15; 1Ki 22:19; Ps 68:17; Rev 5:11; Rev 20:4 **11** Rev 19:20 **13** Eze 1:26; Mt 24:30; Rev 1:7 **14** Ps 2:6-8; Mt 28:18; Jn 3:35; 1Co 15:27; Eph 1:22; Da 3:4; Ps 145:13; Mic 4:7; Lk 1:33; Jn 12:34; Heb 12:28

Glory and a kingdom,
That all the peoples, nations, and
speakers of every language
Should serve *and* worship Him.
His dominion is an everlasting
dominion
Which will not pass away;
And His kingdom is one
Which will not be destroyed.
[Rev 5:1–10]

The Vision Interpreted

15 “As for me, Daniel, my spirit was
distressed *and* anxious within me, and
the visions [that appeared] in my mind
kept alarming (agitating) me.
16 “I approached one of those who
stood by and began asking him the
exact meaning of all this. So he told me
and explained to me the interpretation
of the things:
17 ‘These four great beasts are four
kings who will arise from the earth.
18 ‘But the saints (believers) of the
Most High [God] will receive the king-
dom and possess the kingdom forev-
er, for all ages to come.’ [Rom 8:17;
1 Pet 2:9; Rev 3:21]
19 “Then I wished to know the exact
meaning of the fourth beast, which
was different from all the others, ex-
tremely dreadful, with teeth of iron
and claws of bronze, which devoured,
crushed and trampled down what was
left with its feet,
20 and *the meaning* of the ten horns
(kings) that were on its head and the
other *horn* which came up later, and be-
fore which three of the horns fell, spe-
cifically, that horn which had eyes and
a mouth that boasted great *things* and
which looked larger than the others.
21 “As I kept looking, that horn was
making war with the saints (believers)
and overpowering them [Rev 13:7–9]
22 until the Ancient of Days came and

7:21 ***that horn was making war.*** The little horn's militaristic character is seen also in 11:38–39 and particularly in Revelation 13:1–10. There, in the guise of a beast, this blasphemous enemy of the saints prevails for 42 months. The connection between Daniel's "little horn" and John's "beast from the sea" is unmistakable.

18 Isa 60:12; 2Ti 2:11; Rev 2:26 **21** Rev 17:14 **22** Rev 1:6

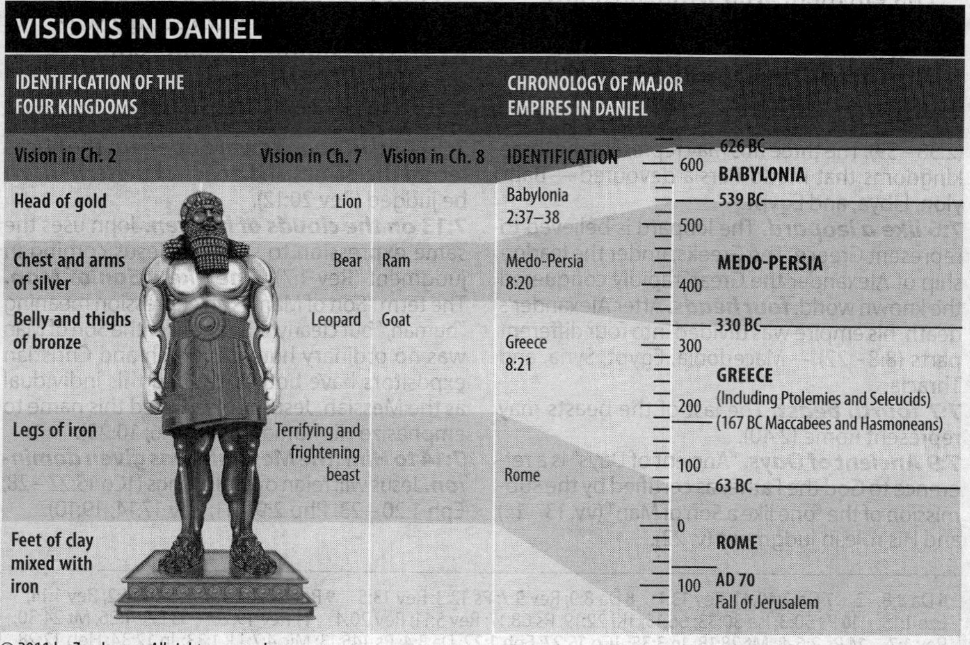

judgment was passed in favor of the saints of the Most High [God], and the time arrived when the saints (believers) took possession of the kingdom.

23 “Thus the angel said, ‘The fourth beast shall be a fourth kingdom on earth, which will be different from all other kingdoms and will devour the whole earth and tread it down, and crush it.

24 ‘As for the ten horns, out of this kingdom ten kings will arise; and another will arise after them, and he will be different from the former ones, and he will subdue three kings.

25 ‘He will speak words against the Most High [God] and wear down the saints of the Most High, and he will intend to change the times and the law; and they will be given into his hand for a time, [two] times, and half a time [three and one-half years]. [Rev 13:1–6]

26 ‘But the court [of the Most High] will sit *in judgment*, and his dominion will be taken away, [first to be] consumed [gradually] and [then] to be destroyed forever.

27 ‘Then the kingdom and the dominion and the greatness of all the kingdoms under the whole heaven will be given to the people of the saints (believers) of the Most High; His kingdom will be an everlasting kingdom, and all the dominions will serve and obey Him.’

28 “This is the end of the matter. As for me, Daniel, my [waking] thoughts were extremely troubling and alarming and my face grew pale; but I kept the matter [of the vision and the angel's explanation] to myself.”

Vision of the Ram and Goat

8 IN THE third year of the reign of King Belshazzar a [second] vision appeared to me, Daniel, [this was two years] after the one that first appeared to me.

2 I looked in the vision and it seemed that I was at the citadel of Susa, [the capital of Persia], which is in the province of Elam; and I looked in the vision and I saw myself by the Ulai Canal.

3 Then I raised my eyes and looked, and behold, there in front of the canal stood a [lone] ram (the Medo-Persian Empire) which had two horns. The two horns were high, but one (Persia) was higher than the other (Media), and the higher one came up last.

4 I saw the ram (Medo-Persia) charging westward and northward and southward; no beast could stand before him, nor was there anyone who could rescue [anything] from his power, but he did as he pleased and magnified *himself*. [Dan 8:20]

5 As I was observing [this], behold, a male goat (Greece) was coming from the west [rushing] across the face of the whole earth without touching the ground; and the goat had a conspicuous *and* remarkable horn (Alexander the Great) between his eyes. [Dan 8:21]

6 He came up to the ram that had the two horns, which I had seen standing

---

7:24 *the ten horns.* Some perceive the fourth beast as representing Rome, and the ten horns as the fragments of the Roman Empire. Others see the fourth beast as a revived Roman Empire and the ten horns as kings of a future realm.

7:25 *a time, [two] times, and half a time.* If the expression “time” is taken to mean a year, and “times” as two years, the three and a half years would exactly equal the 42 months mentioned in the Book of Revelation (Rev 13:1 – 10), half of the 70th “week” of years of 9:27. Some also believe that the expression does not indicate a specific number of years but instead a period of time that God in His mercy would shorten.

8:1 *In the third year.* After writing in Aramaic from 2:4 – 7:28, Daniel returns to writing in Hebrew.

8:3 *a [lone] ram (the Medo-Persian empire) which had two horns.* The ram represents Medo-Persia (v. 20). The two horns symbolize the peoples of Media and Persia.

8:5 *a male goat.* The goat represents Greece (v. 21). The remarkable horn symbolizes Alexander the Great (v. 21) who launched his attack against Persia in 334 BC. Within two years, he had essentially subdued the Persian Empire. His conquest was so rapid that it seemed as if he never touched the ground.

---

23 Da 2:40 **24** Rev 17:12 **25** Isa 37:23; Rev 17:6; Da 2:21; Rev 13:7; Rev 12:14 **26** ver. 10,22 **27** ver. 14,18; Lk 1:33; Jn 12:34; Rev 11:15; Isa 60:12 **28** Da 8:27; Lk 2:19 **CHAPTER 8** **1** Da 7:1 **2** Est 1:2 **4** Da 5:19

in front of the canal, and charged at him in [the fury of] his power *and* wrath.

7 [In my vision] I saw him come close to the ram (Medo-Persia), and he was filled with rage toward him; and the goat (Greece) struck the ram and shattered his two horns, and the ram had no strength to stand before him. So the goat threw him to the ground and trampled on him, and there was no one who could rescue the ram from his power.

8 Then the male goat magnified himself exceedingly, and when he was [young and] strong, the great horn (Alexander) was [suddenly] broken; and in its place there came up four prominent *horns* [among whom the kingdom was divided, one] toward [each of] the four winds of heaven.

The Little Horn

9 Out of one of them (Antiochus IV Epiphanes) came forth a rather small horn [but one of irreverent presumption and profane pride] which grew exceedingly powerful toward the south, toward the east, and toward the Beautiful *Land* (Israel). [Dan 8:23]

10 And [in my vision] this horn grew up to the host of heaven, and caused some of the host and some of the stars to fall to the earth, and it trampled on them.

11 Indeed, it magnified itself to be equal with the Commander of the host [of heaven]; and it took away from Him the daily sacrifice (burnt offering), and the place of His sanctuary was thrown down (profaned).

12 Because of the transgression [of God's people—their irreverence and ungodliness] the host will be given over *to the wicked horn,* along with the regular sacrifice; and righteousness *and* truth will be flung to the ground, and the horn will do as it pleases [by divine permission] and prosper.

13 Then I heard a holy one (angel) speaking, and another holy one said to the one who was speaking, "How much time will be required to complete the vision regarding the regular sacrifice, the transgression that brings horror, and the trampling underfoot of both the sanctuary and the host [of the people]?" [Luke 21:24]

14 He said to me, "For 2,300 evenings and mornings; then the sanctuary will be cleansed *and* properly restored."

Interpretation of the Vision

15 When I, Daniel, had seen the vision, I sought to understand it; then behold, standing before me was one who looked like a man.

16 And I heard the voice of a man between *the banks of* the Ulai, which called out and said, "Gabriel, give this man (Daniel) an understanding of the vision." [Dan 9:21; Luke 1:19, 26]

17 So he came near where I was standing, and when he came I was frightened and fell face downward; but he said to me, "Understand, son of man, that the [fulfillment of the] vision pertains to [events that will occur in] the time of the end."

18 Now as he (Gabriel) was speaking with me, I drifted into a deep sleep (unconsciousness) with my face to the

---

8:8 *the great horn (Alexander) was [suddenly] broken.* Alexander the Great died at the height of his career, before he was 33 years old. After his death, his empire was divided among his four generals (11:4).

8:9 *a rather small horn.* This horn is Antiochus Epiphanes, who ruled part of the Greek Empire from 175 to 164 BC.

8:11 *Commander of the host.* This is clearly God Himself. The "host" refers to God's people (12:3; Ge 15:5). Antiochus is remembered in infamy by the Jews because he desecrated the temple by setting up a statue of Zeus and sacrificing a pig on the holy altar.

8:14 *2,300 evenings and mornings.* This was the amount of time between Antiochus' pollution of the temple and the Maccabees' cleansing of it.

8:16 *Gabriel.* This is the first mention of the angel Gabriel. This angel is mentioned by name three other times (9:21; Lk 1:19,26).

---

8 ver. 22 **9** Da 11:21,25; Ps 48:2 **10** Da 11:28; Isa 14:13; Rev 12:4 **11** Da 11:36; Jos 5:14; Da 11:31; Ex 29:38 **12** Da 11:31; Ps 119:43; Isa 59:14; ver. 4 **13** Da 4:13; 1Pe 1:12 **15** 1Pe 1:10; Eze 1:26 **16** Da 12:6,7; Lk 1:19 **17** Eze 1:28; Rev 1:17 **18** Lk 9:32; Eze 2:2

ground; but he touched me and made
me stand [where I had stood before].
19He said, "Behold, I am going to let
you know what will happen during
the final time of the indignation *and*
wrath [of God upon the ungodly], for it
concerns the appointed time of the end.

The Ram's Identity

20"The ram which you saw with the
two horns represents the kings of Media and Persia.

The Goat

21"The shaggy (rough-coated) male
goat *represents* the kingdom of Greece,
and the great horn between his eyes is
the first king.
22"*Regarding* the shattered *horn* and
the four *others that* arose in its place,
four kingdoms will rise from *his* (Alexander's) nation, although not with
his power *and* heritage.

23"At the latter period of their reign,
When the transgressors have finished,
A king will arise
Insolent and skilled in intrigue *and* cunning.
24"His power will be mighty, but not by his own power;
And he will corrupt *and* destroy in an astonishing manner
And [he will] prosper and do exactly as he wills;
He shall corrupt *and* destroy mighty men and the holy people. [Dan 8:9–12; 2 Thess 2:3–10; Rev 13:4–10]
25"And through his shrewdness
He will cause deceit to succeed by his hand (influence);
He will magnify himself in his mind,
He will corrupt *and* destroy many who enjoy a false sense of security.
He will also stand up *and* oppose the Prince of princes,
But he will be broken, and that by no human hand [but by the hand of God]. [Rev 19:19, 20]
26"The vision of the evenings and the mornings
Which has been told [to you] is true.
But keep the vision a secret,
For it has to do with many days *in the now distant future*."

27And I, Daniel, was exhausted and
was sick for [several] days. Afterward
I got up and continued with the king's
business; but I was astounded at the
vision, and there was no one who could
explain it.

Daniel's Prayer for His People

9 IN THE first year of Darius the son
of Ahasuerus, of Median descent,
who was made king over the realm of
the Chaldeans—
2in the first year of his reign, I, Daniel, understood from the books the
number of years which, according to
the word of the LORD to Jeremiah the
prophet, must pass before the desolations [which had been] pronounced
on Jerusalem would end; and it was
seventy years. [Jer 25:11, 12; 29:10]
3So I directed my attention to the
Lord God to seek Him by prayer and
supplications, with fasting, sackcloth
and ashes.

8:24 *not by his own power.* Like the antichrist (2Th 2:9), Antiochus would be energized by Satan.
8:25 *broken, and that by no human hand.* According to the book of 2 Maccabees, Antiochus died of a painful disease.
9:2 *from the books.* The "books" were the Scriptures, specifically the Book of Jeremiah, which states that the captivity would last 70 years (Jer 25:11 – 12; 29:10 – 14). By this time, Daniel himself had been in captivity for about 67 years, and he knew that the punishment was nearly over.
9:3 – 4 Prayer and Fasting — There are many examples in Scripture of people who pray to learn the will of God. There are also some examples of people who do not pray and find themselves in trouble (Jos 9). Most Christians quickly learn that one of the most important ways we learn the will of God for our lives is through prayer. "If any of you lacks wisdom [to guide him through

19 Hab 2:3 **21** Da 11:3 **22** Da 11:4 **23** Dt 28:50 **24** Rev 17:13; Da 11:36; Da 7:25 **25** Da 11:21; Da 11:36; Da 11:36; Job 34:20; La 4:6 **26** Eze 12:27; Rev 22:10 **27** Da 7:28 **CHAPTER 9** **1** Da 1:21 **2** 2Ch 36:21; Jer 25:11 **3** Neh 1:4; Jer 29:12; Da 6:10

[4]I prayed to the LORD my God and confessed and said, "O Lord, the great and awesome God, who keeps His covenant and extends lovingkindness toward those who love Him and keep His commandments,
[5]we have sinned and committed wrong, and have behaved wickedly and have rebelled, turning away from Your commandments and ordinances.
[6]"Further, we have not listened to *and* heeded Your servants the prophets, who spoke in Your name to our kings, our princes and our fathers, and to all the people of the land.
[7]"Righteousness belongs to You, O Lord, but to us confusion *and* open shame, as it is this day—to the men of Judah, to the inhabitants of Jerusalem, and to all Israel, those who are nearby and those who are far away, in all the countries to which You have driven them, because of the [treacherous] acts of unfaithfulness which they have committed against You.
[8]"O LORD, to us belong confusion *and* open shame—to our kings, to our princes, and to our fathers—because we have sinned against You.
[9]"To the Lord our God *belong* mercy *and* lovingkindness and forgiveness, for we have rebelled against Him;
[10]and we have not obeyed the voice of the LORD our God by walking in His laws which He set before us through His servants the prophets.
[11]"Yes, all Israel has transgressed Your law, even turning aside, not obeying Your voice; so the curse has been poured out on us and the oath which is written in the Law of Moses the servant of God, because we have sinned against Him. [Lev 26:14–45; Deut 28:15–68]
[12]"And He has carried out completely His [threatening] words which He had spoken against us and against our rulers [the kings, princes, and judges] who ruled us, to bring on us a great tragedy; for under the whole heaven there has not been done anything [so dreadful] like that which [He commanded and] was done to Jerusalem.
[13]"Just as it is written in the Law of Moses, all this tragedy has come on us. Yet we have not wholeheartedly begged for forgiveness *and* sought the favor of the LORD our God by turning from our wickedness and paying attention to *and* placing value in Your truth. [Deut 4:29; 28:15ff]
[14]"Therefore the LORD has kept the tragedy ready and has brought it on us, for the LORD our God is [uncompromisingly] righteous *and* openly just in all His works which He does—He keeps His word; and we have not obeyed His voice.
[15]"And now, O Lord our God, who brought Your people out of the land of Egypt with a mighty hand and who made for Yourself a name, as it is today—we have sinned, we have been wicked.
[16]"O Lord, in accordance with all Your righteous *and* just acts, please let Your anger and Your wrath turn away from Your city Jerusalem, Your holy mountain. Because of our sins and the wickedness of our fathers, Jerusalem

---

a decision or circumstance], he is to ask of [our benevolent] God, who gives to everyone generously and without rebuke or blame, and it will be given to him" (Jas 1:5). See also Psalm 143:8–10 and James 4:2.

Other verses in the Bible link prayer with fasting. To fast is to abstain for a period of time from some important and necessary activity in our lives. The purpose of fasting is to be able to spend that time in prayer before God. Different kinds of fasting are possible. One may, for a time refrain from sleep (2Co 6:5; 11:27), marital sex (1Co 7:1–5), or food (Mt 4:1–2). There are also many examples of fasting in the Word: Moses in Deuteronomy 9:9, Elijah in 1 Kings 19:8, Daniel in Daniel 9:3, Ezra in Ezra 10:6, and Nehemiah in Nehemiah 1:4.

9:11 *the curse ... and the oath.* Covenant documents typically contained statements concerning the penalties for covenant violation (Lev 26:3–45; Dt 27–28). The most feared and devastating curse of all had come to pass when the people were deported from the land.

4 Ex 20:6; Dt 7:9 **5** 1Ki 8:47; Ps 106:6; Jer 14:7 **6** 2Ch 36:15 **7** Neh 9:33 **9** Ps 130:4,7 **11** Isa 1:4-6; Lev 26:14; Dt 27:15; La 2:17 **12** Zec 1:6; La 1:12; Eze 5:9; Am 3:2 **13** Dt 28:15; La 2:17; Isa 9:13; Jer 2:30; Hos 7:7 **14** Jer 31:28; Neh 9:33 **15** Ex 32:11; 1Ki 8:51; Neh 1:10; Ex 14:18; Neh 9:10; Jer 32:20 **16** 1Sa 12:7; Ps 31:1; Mic 6:4,5; Zec 8:3; Ex 20:5; La 2:16; Ps 79:4

and Your people *have become* an object of scorn *and* a contemptuous byword to all who are around us.

[17]"Now therefore, our God, listen to (heed) the prayer of Your servant (Daniel) and his supplications, and for Your own sake let Your face shine on Your desolate sanctuary.

[18]"O my God, incline Your ear and hear; open Your eyes and look at our desolations and the city which is called by Your name; for we are not presenting our supplications before You because of our own merits *and* righteousness, but because of Your great mercy *and* compassion.

[19]"O Lord, hear! O Lord, forgive! O Lord, listen and take action! Do not delay, for Your own sake, O my God, because Your city and Your people are called by Your name."

Gabriel Brings an Answer

[20]While I was still speaking and praying, and confessing my sin and the sin of my people Israel, and presenting my supplication before the LORD my God in behalf of the holy mountain of my God,

[21]while I was still speaking in prayer and extremely exhausted, the man Gabriel, whom I had seen in the earlier vision, came to me about the time of the evening sacrifice. [Dan 8:16]

[22]He instructed me and he talked with me and said, "O Daniel, I have now come to give you insight *and* wisdom and understanding.

[23]"At the beginning of your supplications, the command [to give you an answer] was issued, and I have come to tell you, for you are highly regarded *and* greatly beloved. Therefore consider the message and begin to understand the [meaning of the] vision.

Seventy Weeks and the Messiah

[24]"Seventy weeks [of years, or 490 years] have been decreed for your people and for your holy city (Jerusalem), to finish the transgression, to make an end of sins, to make atonement (reconciliation) for wickedness, to bring in everlasting righteousness (right-standing with God), to seal up vision and prophecy *and* prophet, and to anoint the Most Holy *Place*.

[25]"So you are to know and understand that from the issuance of the command to restore and rebuild Jerusalem until [the coming of] the Messiah (the Anointed One), the Prince, *there will be* seven weeks [of years] and sixty-two weeks [of years]; it will be built again, with [a city] plaza and moat, even in times of trouble.

[26]"Then after the sixty-two weeks [of years] the Anointed One will be cut off [and denied His Messianic kingdom] and have nothing [and no one to defend Him], and the people of the [other] prince who is to come will destroy the city and the sanctuary. Its end *will come* with a flood; even to the end there will be war; desolations are determined. [Is 53:7–9; Nah 1:8; Matt 24:6–14]

[27]"And he will enter into a binding *and* irrevocable covenant with the

---

9:21 *the time of the evening sacrifice.* The temple was in ruins, and regular daily sacrifices were impossible. Nevertheless, Daniel observed the ritual of worship by praying at the hour of the evening sacrifice. Daniel's prayer was his evening offering.

9:24 *Seventy weeks.* The word "weeks" can also be translated "sevens." Many scholars agree that the "sevens" are periods of seven years.

9:25 *the issuance of the command to restore and rebuild Jerusalem.* This may refer to the decree of Cyrus in Ezra 1, the decree of Darius in Ezra 6, the decree of Artaxerxes in Ezra 7, or the decree of Artaxerxes in Nehemiah 2.

9:26 *sixty-two weeks.* When the 7 weeks and 62 weeks (v. 25) are added together, they equal 483 years. If these years are added to the date of the decree of Artaxerxes in Nehemiah 2 (445 BC), with an adjustment to allow for a 360-day year, the end of the 69 weeks coincides with the date of the triumphal entry into Jerusalem just before the crucifixion. ***the [other] prince who is to come.*** This seems to be a reference to the antichrist.

17 Nu 6:25; La 5:18; Jn 16:24 **18** Isa 37:17; Ex 3:7; Jer 25:29 **21** Da 8:16 **23** Mt 24:15 **24** Isa 53:10; Rev 14:6; Ps 45:7 **25** Jn 1:41; Isa 55:4 **26** Isa 53:8; 1Pe 2:21; Mt 22:7; Lk 19:44 **27** Isa 42:6; Mt 26:28; Da 11:36

many for one week (seven years), but in the middle of the week he will stop the sacrifice and grain offering [for the remaining three and one-half years]; and on the wing of abominations *will come* one who makes desolate, even until the complete destruction, one that is decreed, is poured out on the one who causes the horror."

Daniel Is Terrified by a Vision

10 IN THE third year of Cyrus king of Persia a message was revealed to Daniel, who was named Belteshazzar; and the message was true and it referred to great conflict (warfare, misery). And he understood the message and had an understanding of the vision. [Dan 8:26; Rev 19:9]

2 In those days I, Daniel, had been mourning for three entire weeks.

3 I ate no tasty food, nor did any meat or wine enter my mouth; and I did not anoint (refresh, groom) myself at all for the full three weeks.

4 On the twenty-fourth day of the first month, as I was on the bank of the great river Hiddekel [which is the Tigris],

5 I raised my eyes and looked, and behold, there was a certain man dressed in linen, whose loins were girded with [a belt of] pure gold of Uphaz.

6 His body also was like beryl [with a golden luster], his face had the appearance of lightning, his eyes were like flaming torches, his arms and his feet like the gleam of burnished bronze, and the sound of his words was like the noise of a multitude [of people or the roaring of the sea]. [Rev 1:12–16; 19:6]

7 And I, Daniel, alone saw the vision [of this heavenly being], for the men who were with me did not see the vision; nevertheless, a great panic overwhelmed them, so they ran away to hide themselves.

8 So I was left alone and saw this great vision; yet no strength was left in me, for my normal appearance turned to a deathly pale, and I grew weak *and* faint [with fright].

9 Then I heard the sound of his words; and when I heard the sound of his words, I fell on my face in a deep sleep, with my face toward the ground.

Daniel Comforted

10 Then behold, a hand touched me and set me unsteadily on my hands and knees.

11 So he said to me, "O Daniel, you highly regarded *and* greatly beloved man, understand the words that I am about to say to you and stand upright, for I have now been sent to you." And while he was saying this word to me, I stood up trembling.

12 Then he said to me, "Do not be afraid, Daniel, for from the first day that you set your heart on understanding this and on humbling yourself before your God, your words were heard, and I have come in response to your words.

13 "But the prince of the kingdom of

9:27 ***in the middle of the week.*** That is, 3 – 1/2 years later. These 3 – 1/2 years of the rule of the antichrist seem to correspond with the "time, [two] times, and half a time" when the fourth beast rules (7:25) and with the 42-month rule of the beast from the sea (Rev 13:1 – 10). ***one who makes desolate.*** Antiochus committed an abomination by setting up an altar to the god Zeus in the holy place in the temple in Jerusalem (11:31). The antichrist will also commit an abomination of desolation against the living God. Jesus' reference to "the abomination of desolation ... spoken of by the prophet Daniel" (Mt 24:15) occurred long after the desolation caused by Antiochus and indicates that this verse is describing the abomination of the antichrist and not that of Antiochus.

10:2 ***three entire weeks.*** This period of time refers to Daniel's observance of the Passover and the Feast of Unleavened Bread, which took place during the first month of the year (Ex 12:1 – 20).

10:6 ***his face had the appearance of lightning.*** The description of this man is very much like Ezekiel's description of the glory of God (Eze 1:4 – 28) and John's description of the risen Christ (Rev 1:9 – 20).

10:13 ***the prince of the kingdom of Persia.*** This prince cannot be a human ruler because the conflict referred to here is in the spiritual, heavenly realm, as the allusion to the angel Michael

---

CHAPTER 10 **5** Rev 1:13 **6** Rev 1:15 **10** Da 9:21 **11** Da 9:23 **12** Rev 1:17; Da 9:3,4,22,23; Ac 10:4 **13** ver. 20; ver. 21; Da 12:1; Jude 9; Rev 12:7

Persia was standing in opposition to
me for twenty-one days. Then, behold,
Michael, one of the chief [of the celes-
tial] princes, came to help me, for I had
been left there with the kings of Persia.
14 “Now I have come to make you
understand what will happen to your
people in the latter days, for the vision
is in regard to the days yet to come.”
15 When he had spoken to me accord-
ing to these words, I turned my face to-
ward the ground and was speechless.
16 And behold, one who resembled
the sons of men touched my lips. Then
I opened my mouth and spoke and
said to him who was standing before
me, “O my lord, because of the vision
anguish has come upon me, and I have
retained no strength.
17 “For how can such a [weakened]
servant of my lord talk with such [a
being] as my lord? For now there re-
mains no strength in me, nor has any
breath been left in me.”
18 Then the one (Gabriel) whose
appearance was like that of a man
touched me again, and he strength-
ened me.
19 He said, “O man, highly regarded
and greatly beloved, do not be afraid.
Peace be to you; take courage and be
strong.” Now when he had spoken to
me, I was strengthened and said, “Let
my lord speak, for you have strength-
ened me.”
20 Then he said, “Do you understand
[fully] why I came to you? Now I shall
return to fight against the [hostile]
prince of Persia; and when I have gone,
behold, the prince of Greece is about
to come.
21 “But I (Gabriel) will tell you what is
inscribed in the writing of truth. There
is no one who stands firmly with me
and strengthens himself against these
[hostile spirit forces] except Michael,
your prince [the guardian of your na-
tion].

Conflicts to Come

11 “ALSO I, in the first year of Da-
rius the Mede, I (Gabriel) arose to
be an encouragement and a protection
for him.
2 “And now I will tell you the truth.
Behold, three more kings are going
to arise in Persia. Then a fourth will
become far richer than all of them.
When he becomes strong through his
riches he will stir up the whole *empire*
against the realm of Greece.
3 “Then a mighty [warlike, threaten-
ing] king will arise who will rule with
great authority and do as he pleases.
4 “But as soon as he (Alexander) has
risen, his kingdom will be broken [by
his death] and divided toward the four
winds of heaven [the north, south, east,
and west], but not to his descendants,

(also referred to as a prince) makes clear. This prince, therefore, must be understood as a satanic figure who was to supervise the affairs of Persia, inspiring its religious, social, and political structures to works of evil. The apostle Paul refers to “spiritual forces of wickedness in the heavenly (supernatural) places” (Eph 6:12). The prince of Persia apparently sought to detain the angel so that Daniel would be prevented from hearing more of God’s revelation (vv. 12 – 14). ***Michael.*** Michael seems to be one of the most powerful angels. He is mentioned three times in the Old Testament, all in the Book of Daniel (v. 21; 12:1), and twice in the New Testament (Jude 9; Rev 12:7).

10:20 ***against the [hostile] prince of Persia.*** Persia was under the ultimate dominion of an evil spirit from Satan (vv. 13 – 14), and so also was Greece. The succession of world powers follows the pattern of Daniel’s second vision (8:20 – 22).

11:1 ***the first year of Darius.*** This is the same year as that of the revelation of the 70 weeks, 539 BC.

11:2 ***three more kings.*** Darius (under Cyrus) was followed by Cambyses (530 – 522 BC), Gaumata (522 BC), Darius I (522 – 486 BC), and Xerxes (486 – 465 BC) — who was the richest king of all, due to the extent of the empire’s conquests and the severe taxation.

11:4 ***but not to his descendants.*** The “mighty king” of verse 3 fits with Alexander the Great, the first ruler of the Greek Empire. When Alexander died, his four generals carved up the Macedonian Empire. Antigonus ruled from southern Syria to central Asia; Cassander ruled over Macedonia;

---

14 Ge 49:1; Da 2:28; ver. 1; Da 8:26; Hab 2:3 **15** ver. 9; Da 8:18 **16** Da 8:15; ver. 10; Jer 1:9; ver. 8 **19** ver. 11; Jdg 6:23 **20** ver. 13 **21** ver. 13; Jude 9; Rev 12:7 **CHAPTER 11** **1** Da 9:1; Da 5:31 **3** Da 7:6; 8:5; ver. 16,36; Da 8:4 **4** Da 8:8; Da 8:22

nor according to the [Grecian] author-
ity with which he ruled, for his king-
dom will be torn out *and* uprooted and
given to others (his four generals) to
the exclusion of these.
5“Then the king of the South (Egypt)
will be strong, along with one of his
princes who will be stronger than he
and have dominance over him; his
domain will be a great dominion.
6“After some years the Syrian king
of the North and the Egyptian king
of the South will make an alliance;
the daughter (Berenice) of the king
of the South will come to the king of
the North to make an equitable *and*
peaceful agreement (marriage); but
she will not retain the power of her
position, nor will he retain his power.
She will be handed over with her atten-
dants and her father as well as he who
supported her in those times.
7“But out of a branch of her [familial]
roots will one (her brother, Ptolemy III
Euergetes I) arise in his place, and he
will come against the [Syrian] army
and enter the fortress of the king of
the North, and he will deal with them
and will prevail.
8“Also he will carry off to Egypt
their [Syrian] gods with their cast
images and their precious *and* costly
treasure of silver and of gold, and he
will refrain from waging war against
the king of the North for some years.
9“And the king of the North will
come into the realm of the king of the
South, but he will retreat to his own
country [badly defeated].
10“His sons will prepare for battle
and assemble a multitude of great forc-
es; which will keep on coming and
overflow [the land], and pass through,
so that they may again wage war as far
as his fortress.
11“The king of the South (Ptolemy
IV Philopator of Egypt) will be en-
raged and go out and fight with the
king of the North (Antiochus III the
Great); and the Syrian king will raise
a great multitude (army), but the mul-
titude shall be given into the hand of
the *Egyptian king*.
12“When the multitude (army) is cap-
tured *and* carried away, the heart of
the *Egyptian king* will be proud (arro-
gant), and he will cause tens of thou-
sands to fall, but he will not prevail.
13“For the king of the North will
again raise a multitude (army) greater
than the one before, and after several
years he will advance with a great
army and substantial equipment.
14“In those times many will rise up
against the king of the South (Egypt);
also the violent men among your own
people will arise in order to fulfill the
[earlier] visions, but they will fail.
15“Then the king of the North (Syria)
will come and build up siege ramps
and capture a well-fortified city. The
forces of the South will not stand *their*
ground, not even the finest troops,
for there will be no strength to stand
[against the Syrian king].
16“But he (Syria) who comes against
him (Egypt) will do exactly as he
pleases, and no one will be able to
stand against him; he (Antiochus III
the Great) will also stay for a time in
the Beautiful *and* Glorious Land [of
Israel], with destruction in his hand.

Ptolemy ruled in Egypt and southern Syria, including Palestine; Lysimachus ruled over Thrace. **11:5 *the king of the South.*** Alexander's general Ptolemy I Soter was the first king of the Southern Kingdom — that is, Egypt. **11:6 – 15 *After some years.*** The events described in these verses fit with the actual history of the divided Greek Empire. ***the daughter (Berenice) of the king.*** This refers to Berenice, the daughter of Ptolemy Philadelphus (285 – 246 BC) of Egypt. ***the king of the North.*** This is Antiochus II Theos (261 – 246 BC) of Syria. ***a branch of her [familial] roots.*** This is Berenice's brother, Ptolemy III Eurgetes (246 – 221 BC), who conquered Seleucus Callinicus (246 – 226 BC) of Syria (the king of the North). Seleucus did attempt a return attack on Egypt, but returned to Syria without accomplishing his goal. The kings of Egypt and Syria (the south and the north) continued to war against each other in the manner described in the prophecy. ***capture a well-fortified city.*** Antiochus of Syria defeated the fortified city of Sidon in 198 BC.

10 Isa 8:8; Da 9:26; ver. 7 **16** Da 8:4,7; Jos 1:5

17 "He will be determined to come with the power of his entire kingdom, and propose equitable conditions *and* terms of peace, which he will put into effect [by making an agreement with the king of the South]. He will also give him his daughter (Cleopatra I), *in an attempt* to overthrow the kingdom, but it will not succeed or be to his advantage.

18 "After this, he (Antiochus III the Great, King of Syria) will turn his attention to the islands *and* coastlands and capture many [of them]. But a commander (Lucius Scipio Asiaticus of Rome) will put an end to his aggression [toward Rome's territorial interests]; in fact, he will repay his insolence *and* turn his audacity back upon him.

19 "Then he will turn back toward the fortresses of his own land [of Syria], but he will stumble and fall and not be found.

20 "Then in his place one (his eldest son, Seleucus IV Philopator) will arise who will send an oppressor through the Jewel of his kingdom; yet within a few days he will be shattered, though not in anger nor in battle.

21 "And in his place [in Syria] will arise a despicable *and* despised person, to whom royal majesty *and* the honor of kingship have not been conferred, but he will come [without warning] in a time of tranquility and seize the kingdom by intrigue. [Dan 8:9–12, 23–25]

22 "The overwhelming forces [of the invading armies of Egypt] will be flooded away before him *and* smashed; and also the prince of the covenant [will be smashed].

23 "After an alliance is made with him he will work deceitfully, and he will go up and gain power with a small *force of* people.

24 "In a time of tranquility, [without warning] he will enter the most productive *and* richest parts of the kingdom [of Egypt], and he will accomplish that which his fathers never did, nor his fathers' fathers; he will distribute plunder, spoil and goods among them. He will devise plans against strongholds, but only for a time [decreed by God].

25 "He will stir up his strength and courage against [his former Egyptian ally] the king of the South (Ptolemy VI) with a great army; so the king of the South will prepare an extremely great and powerful army to wage war, but he will not stand, for schemes will be devised against him.

26 "Yes, those who eat his fine food will betray *and* destroy him (Ptolemy VI), and his army will be swept away, and many will fall down slain.

27 "And as for both of these kings, their hearts will be set on doing evil; they will speak lies over the same table, but it will not succeed, for the end is yet to come at the appointed time.

28 "Then he (Antiochus IV Epiphanes) will return to his land with great treasure (plunder); and his heart will be set against the holy covenant, and he will take action and return to his own land (Syria).

29 "At the time appointed [by God] he will return and come into the South, but this last time will not be successful as were the previous invasions [of Egypt].

11:17 *his daughter (Cleopatra I), in an attempt to overthrow the kingdom.* Antiochus III's daughter Cleopatra was given in marriage to Ptolemy V Epiphanes of Egypt in order to destroy or undermine Egypt, but Cleopatra sided with her husband over her father.

11:18 – 19 *the islands and coastland . . . his own land.* Antiochus III undertook a vigorous campaign into Asia Minor and the Aegean region. The Roman Lucius Cornelius Scipio defeated Antiochus. Having lost all that he had gained, Antiochus returned to his own land, where he was defeated and killed while trying to plunder a temple.

11:21 *a despicable and despised person.* Antiochus IV Epiphanes seized the throne through treachery and later defiled the temple in Jerusalem (v. 31; 9:27).

11:29 *he will return and come into the South.* After learning that Ptolemy VI and Ptolemy VII had formed a union against him, Antiochus returned to Egypt in 168 BC, but he was driven out by the Romans.

17 2Ch 20:3; Da 9:26 **19** Ps 37:36 **21** Da 7:8 **22** Da 8:10,11 **23** Da 8:25

30“For ships of Cyprus [in Roman
hands] will come against him; there-
fore he will be discouraged and turn
back [to Israel] and carry out his rage
against the holy covenant and take
action; so he will return and show
favoritism toward those [Jews] who
abandon (break) the holy covenant
[with God].
31“Armed forces of his will arise [in
Jerusalem] and defile *and* desecrate
the sanctuary, the [spiritual] strong-
hold, and will do away with the reg-
ular sacrifice [that is, the daily burnt
offering]; and they will set up [a pagan
altar in the sanctuary which is] the
abomination of desolation.
32“With smooth *words* [of flattery
and praise] he will turn to godlessness
those who [are willing to] disregard
the [Mosaic] covenant, but the people
who [are spiritually mature and] know
their God will display strength and
take action [to resist].
33“They who are wise *and* have spir-
itual insight among the people will
instruct many *and* help them under-
stand; yet for many days some [of them
and their followers] will fall by the
sword and by flame, by captivity and
by plunder.
34“Now when they fall they will re-
ceive a little help, and many will join
with them in hypocrisy.
35“Some of those who are [spiritually]
wise *and* have insight will fall [as mar-
tyrs] in order to refine, to purge and to
make those among God’s people pure,
until the end time; because it is yet to
come at the time appointed [by God].
36“Then the king (the Antichrist) will
do exactly as he pleases; he will exalt
himself and magnify himself above
every god and will speak astounding
and disgusting things against the God
of gods and he will prosper until the
indignation is finished, for that which
is determined [by God] will be done.
37“He will have no regard for the
gods of his fathers or for the desire of
women, nor will he have regard for any
other god, for he shall magnify himself
above them all.
38“Instead, he will honor a god of
fortresses, a god whom his fathers did
not know; he will honor him with gold
and silver, with precious stones and
with expensive things.

11:31 *abomination of desolation.* Antiochus defiled the sanctuary by sacrificing a pig on the altar. He put a stop to the daily sacrifices, and he set up an image of Zeus in the holy place. Jesus said that a similar thing would happen just prior to His return (Mt 24:15).

11:32 *the people who [are spiritually mature and] know their God.* The books of Maccabees record the story of Mattathias, the father of five sons, who refused to offer profane sacrifices and killed the king’s agents. He and his sons then fled to the mountains and began the famous Maccabean revolt.

11:32 Know God Through His Word—The highest knowledge to which men and women can attain is personal knowledge of God (Jer 9:24). One of the most valuable teachings of Scripture is that we can actually know God through His Word. To know God personally is to be saved and have eternal life (Jn 17:3). We gain this knowledge primarily through interaction with His Word in four ways: First, we listen to and receive God’s Word as the Holy Spirit interprets it and applies it to our hearts. Second, Scripture reveals God’s nature and character. We know God through understanding of the works He has done, which are explained in Scripture. Third, our knowledge of God moves from intellectual to personal when we accept the invitation He has given us and do what He commands. Fourth, our personal knowledge of God grows as we rejoice in the love He shows us in Scripture and express joy in response to what He has done for us and given us. The Word leads to knowledge of all that is true about God. This knowledge of God then produces fellowship with Him.

11:35 *it is yet to come at the time appointed.* Clearly, the trouble and wickedness of Antiochus’ reign was not the end. That is yet to come.

11:36 *Then the king.* Many ancient and modern interpreters have concluded that at this point a new person, the antichrist, is introduced. This king is distinguished from the king of the North (v. 40); therefore, he cannot be Antiochus Epiphanes. It appears that there is a gap of many years between verses 35 and 36, and this refers back to “the end time” which will come at the “time appointed” (v. 35).

11:38 *a god whom his fathers did not know.* This is probably a reference to self-worship (v. 37; 2Th 2:4).

30 Jer 2:10 **31** Da 8:11 **35** Da 12:10 **36** Da 7:8,25 **37** Isa 14:13

39"He will act against the strongest
fortresses with *the help of* a foreign
god; he will give great honor to those
who acknowledge him and he will
cause them to rule over the many, and
will parcel out land for a price.
40"At the end time the king of the
South will push *and* attack him (the
Antichrist), and the king of the North
will storm against him with chariots
and horsemen and with many ships;
and he will enter countries, overwhelm
them and pass through.
41"He shall also enter the Beautiful
and Glorious Land (Israel), and many
countries will fall, but these will be
rescued out of his hand: Edom, Moab,
and the foremost [core] of the people
of Ammon.
42"Then he will stretch out his hand
against other countries, but Egypt will
not be among the ones which escape.
43"He will have power over the trea-
sures of gold and silver and over all
the precious things of Egypt, and the
Libyans and the Ethiopians *will follow*
in his footsteps.
44"But rumors from the east and

11:40 *the end time.* This is the period just before the return of Christ (Mt 24:14).

40 Isa 21:1; Eze 38:4; Rev 9:16 **41** Isa 11:14 **43** Ex 11:8

PTOLEMIES AND SELEUCIDS

Soon after the death of Alexander the Great in 323 BC, his generals divided his empire into four parts, two of which—Egypt and Syria—were under the rule of the Ptolemies and Seleucids respectively. The Holy Land was controlled from Egypt by the Ptolemaic dynasty from 323 to 198, and was subsequently governed by the Seleucids of Syria from 198 to 142.

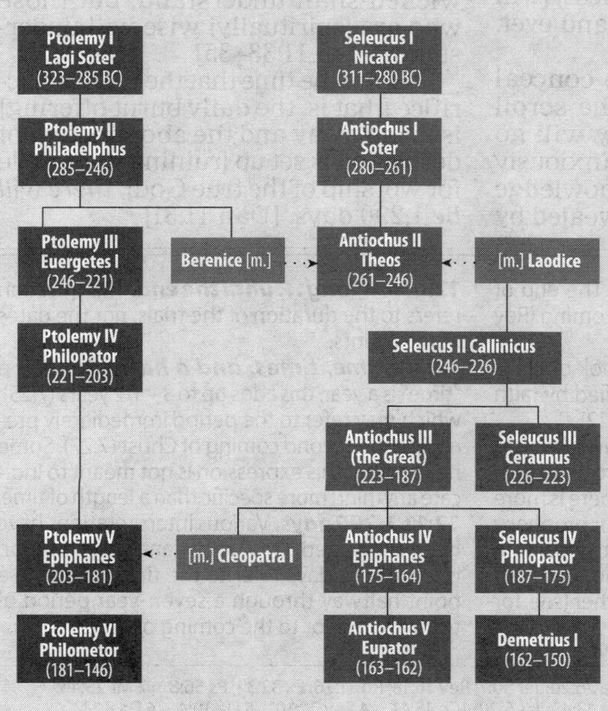

The Diadochi, as the successors of Alexander were called, struggled bitterly for power over his domain. At first Ptolemy I seized his own satrapy, Egypt and North Africa, which had splendid resources and natural defense capabilities. Seleucus gained Syria and Mesopotamia, and by 301 Lysimachus held Thrace and Asia Minor while Cassander ruled Macedon. The situation changed again by 277, when only three major Hellenistic kingdoms stabilized in Egypt, in Syria, and in Macedonia under the Antigonids (277–168). Each continued until the eventual triumph of Rome.

Daniel 11 treats the "king of the South" and the "king of the North," describing their conflicts, wars and alliances. Their hostility toward the people of God culminated in the "abomination that causes desolation" (11:31), identified historically with the reign of Antiochus IV Epiphanes (175–164). The Maccabean revolt followed, leading eventually to the founding of the Hasmonean dynasty.

Continued political rivalries in Judea brought the intervention of the Roman general Pompey in 63 BC. This event signaled the end of Jewish political independence, except for periods of brief autonomy during the ill-fated revolts of the first and second Christian centuries.

from the north will alarm *and* disturb
him, and he will set out with great fury
to destroy and to annihilate many.
45“He will pitch his palatial tents be-
tween the seas and the glorious Holy
Mountain (Zion); yet he will come to
his end with no one to help him [in his
final battle with God]. [2 Thess 2:4;
Rev 13:5–8]

The Time of the End

12 “NOW AT that [end] time Mi-
chael, the great [angelic] prince
who stands *guard* over the children
of your people, will arise. And there
will be a time of distress such as nev-
er occurred since there was a nation
until that time; but at that time your
people, everyone who is found written
in the Book [of Life], will be rescued.
2“Many of those who sleep in the
dust of the ground will awake (resur-
rect), these to everlasting life, but some
to disgrace and everlasting contempt
(abhorrence). [John 5:29]
3“Those who are [spiritually] wise
will shine brightly like the brightness
of the expanse of heaven, and those
who lead many to righteousness, [will
shine] like the stars forever and ever.
[Matt 13:43]
4“But as for you, Daniel, conceal
these words and seal up the scroll
until the end of time. Many will go
back and forth *and* search anxiously
[through the scroll], and knowledge
[of the purpose of God as revealed by
His prophets] will [greatly] increase.”
[Amos 8:12]
5Then I, Daniel, looked, and behold,
there stood two others, the one [angel]
on this bank of the river and the other
[angel] on that bank of the river.
6And one said to the man dressed in
linen, who was above the waters of the
river, “How long *will it be* until the end
of these wonders?” [Dan 10:5]
7And I heard the man dressed in
linen, who was above the waters of the
river, as he held up his right hand and
his left hand toward heaven, and swore
by Him who lives forever that it would
be for a time, times, and a half a time
(three and a half years); and as soon
as they finish shattering *and* crushing
the power of the holy people, all these
things will be finished.
8As for me, I heard, but I did not
understand; so I said, “My lord, what
will be the outcome of these things?”
9And the angel said, “Go *your way,*
Daniel, for the words are concealed
and sealed up until the end of time.
10“Many will be purged, purified
(made white) and refined, but the wick-
ed will behave wickedly. None of the
wicked shall understand, but those
who are [spiritually] wise will under-
stand. [Dan 11:33–35]
11“From the time that the regular sac-
rifice [that is, the daily burnt offering]
is taken away and the abomination of
desolation is set up [ruining the temple
for worship of the true God], *there will
be* 1,290 days. [Dan 11:31]

11:45 *with no one to help him.* The end of the king is sealed at Christ's second coming (Rev 19:11 – 21).

12:1 *written in the Book.* The book of life is God's record of those who are justified by faith (Ex 32:32; Ps 69:28; Lk 10:20; Rev 20:12).

12:2 *Many . . . who sleep . . . will awake.* This passage appears to refer to a general resurrection, while other passages suggest that there is more than one (Jn 5:25). It is not unusual for prophecy in the Old Testament to present events separated by a considerable span of time as if they occurred *in immediate relationship* to each other (see, for example, Isa 61:1 – 2).

12:6 *How long . . . until the end.* This question refers to the duration of the trials, not the dates of the events.

12:7 *a time, times, and a half a time.* If a "time" is a year, this adds up to 3 – 1/2 years (7:25), which may refer to the period immediately preceding the second coming of Christ (7:27). Some believe that this expression is not meant to indicate anything more specific than a length of time.

12:11 *1,290 days.* Various interpretations have been suggested. One significant interpretation is that these days refer to the time following a point halfway through a seven-year period of tribulation prior to the coming of Christ (9:27).

45 Ps 48:2; Rev 19:20 **CHAPTER 12** **1** Isa 26:20; Jer 30:7; Rev 16:18; Ro 11:26; Ex 32:32; Ps 56:8 **2** Mt 25:46; Jn 5:28; Ac 24:15; Isa 66:24; Ro 9:21 **3** Mt 13:43; Jas 5:20; 1Co 15:41 **4** Rev 22:10 **5** Da 10:4 **6** Da 8:13 **7** Dt 32:40; Da 4:34; Da 7:25; Lk 21:24; Da 8:24 **10** Zec 13:9; Hos 14:9; Jn 8:47

12“How blessed [happy, fortunate, spiritually prosperous] *and* beloved is he who waits expectantly [enduring without wavering for the period of tribulation] and comes to the 1,335 days!

13“But as for you (Daniel), go *your way* until the end [of your life]; for you will rest and rise *again* for your allotted inheritance at the end of the age.” [Heb 11:32–40]

12:12 *1,335 days.* The extra 45 days may be the amount of time that the last battles will take before the victory is completely established.
12:13 *you will rest and rise again for your allotted inheritance.* Daniel died before these things came to pass, but at the end he will be among those resurrected (v. 2).

13 Rev 14:13; Ps 1:5

THE BOOK OF

HOSEA

▸ **AUTHOR:** Few critics argue with the claim in 1:1 that Hosea is the author of this book. The author's place of birth is not given but his familiarity and obvious concern with the Northern Kingdom point to his living in Israel, rather than Judah. Hosea had a real compassion for his people. His personal suffering because of his wife, Gomer, gave him some understanding of God's grief over the people's sin, and this grief becomes the source of the unique tenderness and hope that characterizes Hosea's book.

▸ **TIMES:** c. 755 – 710 BC ▸ **KEY VERSE:** Hos 4:1

▸ **THEME:** Hosea was a contemporary of Isaiah, prophesying near the end of Israel's existence. It is clear from reading the text that Assyria was about to take over. In the second verse of Hosea, God tells Hosea to marry a prostitute named Gomer to provide a living illustration of God's faithfulness and Israel's unfaithfulness. By this, Hosea demonstrates that God loves us, as He did Israel, knowingly and in spite of all our propensities to reject His love for us.

Hosea's Wife and Children

1 THE WORD of the LORD that came
to Hosea the son of Beeri in the
days of Uzziah, Jotham, Ahaz and
Hezekiah, kings of Judah, and in the
days of Jeroboam the son of Joash
king of Israel.
[2]When the LORD first spoke through
Hosea, the LORD said to him, "Go, take
for yourself a wife of prostitution and
have children of [her] prostitution; for
the land commits great acts of prostitution by not following the LORD."
[3]So he went and took Gomer the
daughter of Diblaim, and she conceived and bore him a son.
[4]And the LORD said to him, "Name
him Jezreel; for yet in a little while I
will avenge the blood [that was shed
in the Valley] of Jezreel *and* inflict the
punishment for it on the house of Jehu,
and I will put an end to the kingdom
of the house of Israel. [2 Kin 10:1–11]
[5]"On that day I will break the bow
[of the military power] of Israel in the
Valley of Jezreel."
[6]Then Gomer conceived again and
gave birth to a daughter. And the LORD

1:2 – 3 *wife of prostitution.* Gomer may have been a common prostitute at the time Hosea married her, or perhaps she had participated in a ritual sexual act as part of a Baal cult. However, it is more likely that the descriptive phrase anticipates what Gomer would become following her marriage to Hosea. ***children of [her] prostitution.*** If Gomer was a prostitute when she married Hosea, this could refer to children that Gomer already had and that Hosea adopted at the time of marriage. A more likely possibility is that the title anticipates children born to a mother whose reputation and escapades would make their lineage suspect. Gomer's marital infidelity is a picture of Israel's idolatry and unfaithfulness to its covenant with God.

1:5 *break the bow.* This phrase means to destroy an opponent's military strength (1Sa 2:4; Ps 46:9; Jer 49:35).

1:6 *Lo-Ruhamah.* This means "not loved," foreshadowing the Lord's rejection of Israel.

CHAPTER 1 **1** 2Pe 1:21 **2** Hos 3:1; Dt 31:16; Ps 73:27; Jer 2:13; Eze 23:3 **4** 2Ki 10:11; 2Ki 15:10 **5** 2Ki 15:29 **6** 2Ki 17:6

said to Hosea, "Name her Lo-Ruhamah (not shown mercy), for I will no longer have mercy on the house of Israel, that I would ever forgive them.
7"But I will have mercy on the house of Judah and will rescue them by the LORD their God, and will not rescue them by bow, sword, war, horses, or horsemen." [Is 31:8; 37:33–35]
8Now when Gomer had weaned Lo-Ruhamah, she conceived and gave birth to a son.
9And the LORD said, "Name him Lo-Ammi (not my people), for you are not My people and I am not your God."

10Yet the number of the sons of Israel
Shall be like the sand of the sea,
Which cannot be measured or numbered;
And in the place
Where it is said to them,
"You are not My people,"
It will be said to them,
"*You are* the sons of the living God." [Gen 22:17; Rom 9:26]
11Then the sons of Judah and the sons of Israel shall be gathered together,
And they will appoint for themselves one leader,
And they will go up from the land,
For great *and* glorious will be the day of Jezreel. [Is 11:12, 13; Ezek 37:15–28]

Israel's Unfaithfulness Condemned

2 "[HOSEA,] SAY to your brothers, 'Ammi (you are my people),' and to your sisters, 'Ruhamah (you have been pitied and have obtained mercy).'

2"Contend with your mother (nation); contend,
For she is not my wife and I am not her husband;
And have her remove her [marks of] prostitution from her face
And her adultery from between her breasts [Is 50:1]
3Or I will strip her naked
And expose her as on the day she was born,
And make her like a wilderness
And make her like a parched land
And slay her with thirst.
4"Also, I will have no mercy on her children,
Because they are the children of prostitution.
5"For their mother has played the prostitute;
She who conceived them has acted shamefully,
For she said, 'I will pursue my lovers
Who give me my food and my water,
My wool and my flax, my oil and my [refreshing] drinks.'
6"Therefore, behold, I [the LORD God] will hedge up her way with thorns;
And I will build a wall against her [shutting off her way] so that she cannot find her paths.
7"She will [passionately] pursue her lovers, but she will not overtake them;
And she will seek them, but will not find them.
Then she will say, 'Let me go and return to my first husband,
For it was better for me then than now!'

1:9 *Lo-Ammi.* This means "not my people," threatening the termination of the Lord's covenant relationship with His people (Lev 26:12).
1:10 *Shall be like the sand of the sea.* The Lord would not reject His people forever. God would fulfill His promise to Abraham (Ge 22:17; 32:12).
2:2 *she is not my wife.* This may be a formal announcement of divorce or a realistic confession that the relationship between God and Israel had lost its vitality.
2:3 *And make her like a wilderness.* This simile pictures the loss of fertility, an appropriate punishment for a nation that had sought fertility by worshiping another god.
2:6–7 *She will [passionately] pursue her lovers.* This word draws attention to the strong passion the people of Israel felt for Baal. These verses anticipate the exile, when Israel would be separated from the idols of Baal.

7 2Ki 19:35; Zec 4:6 **10** Ge 32:12; 1Pe 2:10; Jn 1:12 **11** Isa 11:12 **CHAPTER 2** **2** Isa 50:1; Eze 16:25 **3** Jer 13:22; Eze 16:4; Am 8:11 **4** Jn 8:41 **5** ver. 8,12 **6** La 3:7,9 **7** Lk 15:18; Eze 16:8

8 "For she (Israel) has not noticed
nor understood *nor* realized
that it was I [the LORD God] who
gave her the grain and the new
wine and the oil,
And lavished on her silver and
gold,
Which they used for Baal *and*
made into his image.
9 "Therefore, I will return *and* take
back My grain at harvest
time
And My new wine in its
season.
I will also take away My wool and
My flax
Given to cover her nakedness.
10 "And now I will uncover her
lewdness *and* shame
In the sight of her lovers,
And no one will rescue her from
My hand.
11 "I will also put an end to all her
rejoicing,
Her feasts, her New Moons, her
Sabbaths,
And all her festivals.
12 "I will destroy her vines and her
fig trees
Of which she has said, 'These are
my wages
Which my lovers have given me.'
And I will make them a forest,
And the animals of the open
country will devour them.
13 "And I will punish her for the
[feast] days of the Baals,
When she used to offer sacrifices
and burn incense to them
And adorn herself with her
earrings *and* nose rings and her
jewelry,
And follow her lovers, so that she
forgot Me," says the LORD.

Restoration of Israel

14 "Therefore, behold, I will allure
Israel
And bring her into the
wilderness,
And I will speak tenderly to her [to
reconcile her to Me].
15 "Then I will give her her vineyards
from there,
And make the Valley of Achor a
door of hope *and* expectation
[anticipating the time when I
will restore My favor on her].
And she will sing there *and* respond
as in the days of her youth
As in the day when she came up
from the land of Egypt. [Ex 15:2;
Josh 7:24–26]
16 "It shall come about in that day,"
says the LORD,
"That you will call Me Ishi (my
husband)
And will no longer call Me Baali
(my Baal).
17 "For I will remove the names of the
Baals from her mouth,
So that they will no longer be
mentioned *or* remembered by
their names. [Ex 23:13]
18 "And in that day I will make a
covenant for Israel
With the animals of the open
country
And with the birds of the
heavens
And with the creeping things of
the ground.
And I will abolish the bow and the
sword and [banish] war from
the land
And will make them lie down in
safety.
19 "And I will betroth you (Israel) to
Me forever;

2:12 *animals of the open country.* The Lord would break down the nation's defenses and turn them into overgrown thickets inhabited by wild animals.

2:14 *I will allure Israel.* Having separated Israel from her lovers, the Lord would seek to win her back by making romantic overtures and wooing her with tender words of love.

2:15 *Valley of Achor.* This meant "valley of trouble." It was a reminder of the sin of Achan and God's discipline of the nation of Israel for his sin (Jos 7:24–26).

2:19–20 *betroth.* Betrothal was a binding commitment, the last step before the wedding and consummation of the marriage.

8 Isa 1:3 **10** Eze 16:37 **11** Am 8:10 **15** Jos 7:26; Jer 2:2; Eze 16:8; Ex 15:1 **17** Ex 23:13; Ps 16:4 **18** Job 5:23; Isa 2:4; Lev 26:5; Jer 23:6

Yes, I will betroth you to Me in
righteousness and in justice,
In lovingkindness *and* loyalty, and
in compassion.
20 "I will betroth you to Me in
stability *and* in faithfulness.
Then you will know (recognize,
appreciate) the LORD
[and respond with loving
faithfulness].

21 "It will come about in that day that
I will respond," says the LORD.
"I will respond to the heavens
[which ask for rain to pour on
the earth], and they will respond
to the earth [which begs for the
rain],
22 And the earth shall respond to the
grain and the new wine and the
oil [which beg it to bring them
forth],
And they will respond to Jezreel
[My Israel, who will now be
restored].
23 "I will sow her for Myself in the
land.
I will also have mercy on her who
had not obtained mercy;
And I will say to those who were
not My people,
'You are My people,'
And they will say, '*You are* my
God!' " [1 Pet 2:9, 10]

Hosea's Second Symbolic Marriage

3 THEN THE LORD said to me, "Go
again, love a woman (Gomer) who
is beloved by her husband and yet is
an adulteress, even as the LORD loves
the children of Israel, though they
turn to other gods and love the raisin
cakes [used in the feasts in pagan
worship]."
2 So I bought her for myself for fif-
teen pieces of silver and a homer and
a half of barley [the price of a common
slave].
3 And I said to her, "You shall stay
with me for many days. You shall not
play the prostitute nor shall you have a
man; so I will also be toward you [until
you have proved your faithfulness]."
4 For the sons of Israel will remain
for many days without king or prince,
without sacrifice or [idolatrous] pillar,
and without ephod or teraphim (house-
hold idols).
5 Afterward the sons of Israel will
return [in deep repentance] and seek
the LORD their God and [seek from
the line of] David their king [the King
of kings—the Messiah]; and they will
come trembling to the LORD and to His
goodness *and* blessing in the last days.
[Jer 30:9; Ezek 34:24]

3:1 – 2 *I bought her.* Gomer had become the property of another man. Hosea's purchase of Gomer symbolized God's great devotion, which moves Him to seek reconciliation even if it means subjecting Himself to humiliation (Php 2:8). One of the great truths presented in the Old Testament is God's undying love for Israel. From among all the ancient nations on Earth, He had chosen Israel.

3:1 The Extent of God's Love — People who think of the God of the Old Testament as a God of judgment and the God of the New Testament as a God of love should spend some time studying Hosea. In the book God instructs Hosea to marry a woman named Gomer who is consistently unfaithful. The Book of Hosea is a living parable about how far God will go to love Israel. While there is definitely judgment in Hosea, the consistent ongoing message is God will go to any extreme to demonstrate His love.

He is even willing to play the betrayed spouse in order to save us. He is willing to be an object of scorn and disrespect if that is what it takes to win us back to Him. God's own given law allows for the execution of both parties in an adulterous affair (Lev 20:10). God cares deeply about this sin. He cares more deeply about His people.

It is important to understand how much He takes the initiative. He does not wait passively for us to come to Him. He is faithful about the task of going after us. Even though there is every reason to reject and ignore us, God is right there working to win us in spite of the fact that we reject Him at every turn.

3:4 *pillar.* These were stone pillars used by the Canaanites in their worship of Baal and other gods (2Ki 3:2; 10:26 – 27; 17:10). ***ephod.*** This was a priestly garment.

---

20 Jer 31:33; Jn 17:3 **21** Zec 8:12 **23** Jer 31:27; Hos 1:6; Hos 1:10 **CHAPTER 3** **1** Hos 1:2; Jer 3:20 **3** Dt 21:13 **4** Hos 10:3; Ex 28:6; Jdg 17:5 **5** Hos 5:6; Jer 30:9; Eze 34:23,24; Isa 2:2; Jer 30:24; Eze 38:8

God's Controversy with Israel

4 HEAR THE word of the LORD,
you children of Israel,
For the LORD has a [legal] case
with the inhabitants of the land,
Because there is no faithfulness
[no steadfast love, no
dependability] or loyalty *or*
kindness
Or knowledge of God [from
personal experience with Him]
in the land.
2 There is [false] swearing *of*
oaths, deception (broken faith),
murder, stealing, and adultery;
They employ violence, so that
one [act of] bloodshed follows
closely on another.
3 Therefore the land [continually]
mourns,
And everyone who lives in it
languishes [in tragic suffering]
Together with the animals of the
open country and the birds of
the heavens;
Even the fish of the sea
disappear.
4 Yet let no one find fault, nor let
any rebuke [others];
For your people are like those who
contend with the priest.
5 So you will stumble in the
daytime,
And the [false] prophet will also
stumble with you in the night;
And I will destroy your mother
(Israel). [Ex 19:6]
6 My people are destroyed for lack
of knowledge [of My law, where
I reveal My will].
Because you [the priestly nation]
have rejected knowledge,
I will also reject you from being
My priest.
Since you have forgotten the law
of your God,
I will also forget your children.
7 The more they multiplied [in
numbers and increased in
power], the more they sinned
against Me;
I will change their glory into
shame.
8 They (the priests) feed on the sin
offering of My people
And set their heart on their
wickedness. [Lev 7:7, 8]
9 And it shall be: like people, like
priest [both are wicked and both
will be judged];
So I will punish them for their
ways
And repay them for their deeds.
10 They will eat, but not have enough;
They will play the prostitute, but
not increase [their descendants],
Because they have stopped giving
heed to the LORD.
11 Prostitution, wine, and new wine
take away the mind *and* the
[spiritual] understanding.
12 My people consult their [lifeless]
wooden idol, and their [diviner's]
wand gives them oracles.

4:1 ***a [legal] case.*** The Hebrew word refers to a formal complaint charging Israel with breaking the covenant. ***knowledge.*** This does not refer to intellectual awareness, but to recognition of God's authority as Israel's covenant Lord.
4:2 ***[false] swearing of oaths, deception (broken faith), murder, stealing, and adultery.*** Five of the Ten Commandments are mentioned here.
4:5 – 6 ***lack of knowledge.*** The priests had failed to teach God's law to the people (Mal 2:7). As a result, the priests would be the special object of God's judgment. He would terminate the priestly line.
4:7 – 8 ***They (the priests) feed on the sin offering of My people.*** The priests greedily accepted the meat from the people's hypocritical and empty sacrifices (6:6; 8:11 – 13).
4:10 ***play the prostitute.*** This refers to religious prostitution associated with Baal worship, not to immorality in general. The Israelites worshiped Baal in order to have good crops and many children, but they still would not have enough to eat, nor would they multiply in number.
4:12 ***their [diviner's] wand.*** This refers to wooden idols that Baal worshipers consulted for guidance.

CHAPTER 4 **1** Isa 1:18; Jer 4:22 **3** Am 5:16; Zep 1:3 **4** Dt 17:12 **5** Jer 15:8 **6** Isa 5:13 **7** 1Sa 2:30; Mal 2:9 **9** Isa 24:2; Jer 5:31 **10** Lev 26:26; Mic 6:14 **11** Isa 28:7 **12** Jer 2:27; Isa 44:20

For a spirit of prostitution has
led them astray [morally and
spiritually],
And they have played the
prostitute, *withdrawing*
themselves from their God.
13 They sacrifice on the tops of the
mountains
And burn incense on the hills,
Under oaks, poplars, and
terebinths,
Because the shade is pleasant
there.
Therefore your daughters play the
prostitute
And your brides commit adultery.
14 I will not punish your daughters
when they play the prostitute
Or your brides when they commit
adultery,
For the men themselves slip away
with prostitutes,
And they offer sacrifices with
temple prostitutes [who give
their bodies in honor of the idol].
So the people without
understanding [stumble and fall
and] come to ruin.

15 Though you, Israel, play the
prostitute [by worshiping idols],
Do not let Judah become guilty [of
the same thing];
And do not go to Gilgal [where
idols are worshiped],
Or go up to Beth-aven (House of
Wickedness),
Nor swear [oaths in idolatrous
worship, saying],
"As the LORD lives!"
16 For Israel is stubborn,
Like a stubborn heifer.
Can the LORD now pasture them
Like a lamb in a large field?
17 Ephraim is joined to idols,
So let him alone [to suffer the
consequences].
18 When their liquor is gone [and
their drinking parties are over],
They habitually go to play the
prostitute;
Ephraim's rulers continue to
dearly love shame [more than
her glory which is the LORD,
Israel's God].
19 The wind [of God's relentless
wrath] has wrapped up Israel in
its wings,
And [in captivity] they will be
ashamed because of their
sacrifices [to calves, to sun, to
moon, to stars, and to pagan
gods].

The People's Apostasy Rebuked

5 HEAR THIS *and* pay close
attention, O priests!
Give heed, O house of Israel!
Listen, O house of the king!
For the [pronounced] judgment
pertains to you *and* is meant for
you to hear,
Because you have been a snare at
Mizpah
And a net spread out over Tabor
(military strongholds on either
side of the Jordan River).
2 The revolters have gone deep into
depravity,
But I [the LORD God] will chastise
them all.
3 I know Ephraim, and Israel is not
hidden from Me;
For now, O Ephraim, you have
played the prostitute *and* have
worshiped idols;
Israel has defiled itself.
4 Their [immoral] practices will not
permit them
To return to their God,
For the spirit of prostitution is
within them

4:15 *Gilgal.* This was an important religious center in the north, known in Hosea's time for its hypocritical religious practices (9:15; 12:11; Am 4:4). ***Beth-aven.*** This means "house of iniquity," and is a sarcastic reference to the important religious center Bethel, which means "house of God" (Am 5:5).

4:17 – 19 *Ephraim.* This tribe was one of the largest tribes of Israel. It is used here to represent the entire Northern Kingdom.
5:4 *spirit of prostitution.* The people had an uncontrollable desire to worship other gods.

13 Isa 1:29; Eze 6:13; Am 7:17; Ro 1:28 **15** Hos 9:15; 1Ki 12:29; Am 8:14 **16** Jer 3:6 **17** Mt 15:14 **18** Mic 3:11 **19** Jer 51:1; Isa 1:29 **CHAPTER 5** **1** Hos 6:9 **2** Isa 29:15 **3** Am 3:2; Hos 4:17 **4** Hos 4:12

And they do not know the
LORD [they do not recognize,
appreciate, heed or cherish
Him].
5 But the pride *and* self-reliance of
Israel testifies against him.
Therefore Israel, and [especially]
Ephraim, stumble *and* fall in
their wickedness *and* guilt;
Judah also has stumbled with
them.
6 They will go with their flocks and
with their herds
To seek the LORD [diligently
searching for Him], but they will
not find Him;
He has withdrawn from them
[refusing to hear the prayers of
the unrepentant].
7 They have dealt treacherously
against the LORD,
For they have borne illegitimate
(pagan) children.
Now the New Moon will devour
them along with their land
[bringing judgment and
captivity].

8 Blow the horn in Gibeah,
The trumpet in Ramah [the lofty
hills on Benjamin's northern
border].
Sound the alarm at Beth-aven:
"Behind you *and* coming after you
[is the enemy], O Benjamin [be
on guard]!"
9 Ephraim will become a desolation
in the day of rebuke;
Among the tribes of Israel I
declare what is certain.
10 The princes of Judah are like those
who move a boundary *marker;*
I will pour out My wrath on them
like [an unrestrained flood of]
water. [Deut 19:14; Prov 22:28]
11 Ephraim is oppressed; he is
broken *and* crushed by [divine]
judgment,
Because he was determined
to follow *man's* command
(vanities, filth, secular precepts).
12 Therefore I am like a moth to
Ephraim
And like dry rot to the house of
Judah [in My judgment against
them].
13 When Ephraim saw his sickness,
And Judah his wound,
Then Ephraim went to Assyria
[instead of the LORD]
And sent to [Assyria's] great King
Jareb [for help].
But he cannot heal you
Nor will he cure you of your
wound [received in judgment].
14 For I *will be* like a lion to Ephraim
And like a young lion to the house
of Judah.
I, even I, will tear to pieces and go
on [tearing];
I will carry off [the prey] and there
will be no one to rescue *them.*
15 I will go away and return to My
place [on high]
Until they acknowledge their
offense *and* bear their guilt and
seek My face;
In their distress they will earnestly
seek Me, *saying,*

The Response to God's Rebuke

6 "COME AND let us return [in
repentance] to the LORD,

5:8–9 *Blow the horn.* This act signaled an emergency and mustered the fighting men to defend the land. The towns mentioned were north of Jerusalem, within or near the borders of Benjamin. The implication is that the enemy army had already swept through the north and was ready to invade Judah.
5:10 *move a boundary marker.* Stones were used to mark the boundaries of property. A thief could steal a part of someone's land by moving one. The law warned that altering a boundary in this way would bring a special judgment from God (Dt 19:14; 27:17; Pr 22:28).
5:12 *I am like a moth to Ephraim.* As a moth slowly destroys clothing, so the Lord would destroy Israel (Job 13:28; Isa 50:9; 51:8). ***dry rot.*** Elsewhere this word refers to bone or to decay (Pr 12:4; 14:30; Hab 3:16).
5:14–15 *like a young lion.* God would scatter His people as judgment for their treachery. But the purpose of the Lord's discipline was to drive the people to "earnestly" seek Him.

6 Pr 1:28 **7** Jer 3:20 **8** Joel 2:1; Isa 10:30; Jos 7:2 **10** Dt 19:14 **11** Dt 28:33; Mic 6:16 **12** Pr 12:4 **13** Jer 30:12; 2Ki 15:19 **14** La 3:10; Ps 50:22 **CHAPTER 6 1** Dt 32:39; Jer 30:17

For He has torn us, but He will
heal us;
He has wounded us, but He will
bandage us.
2 "After two days He will revive us;
On the third day He will raise us up
That we may live before Him.
[Is 26:19; Ezek 37:1–10]
3 "So let us know *and* become
personally acquainted with
Him; let us press on to know *and*
understand fully the [greatness
of the] LORD [to honor, heed, and
deeply cherish Him].
His appearing is prepared *and* is
as certain as the dawn,
And He will come to us [in
salvation] like the [heavy] rain,
Like the spring rain watering the
earth."

The Reply of the Lord

4 O Ephraim, what shall I do with
you?
O Judah, what shall I do with you?
For your [wavering] loyalty *and*
kindness are [transient] like the
morning cloud
And like the dew that goes away
early.
5 Therefore, I have hewn them in
pieces by [the words of] the
prophets;
I have slain them by the words of
My mouth;
My judgments [pronounced upon
them by the prophets] are
like the light that shines forth
[obvious to all].
6 For I desire *and* delight in
[steadfast] loyalty [faithfulness
in the covenant relationship],
rather than sacrifice,
And in the knowledge of God
more than burnt offerings.
[Matt 9:13; 12:7]
7 But they, like Adam, have
transgressed the covenant;
There they have dealt
treacherously against Me.
8 Gilead is a city of wrongdoers;
It is tracked with bloody
footprints.
9 And as bands of robbers [lie in]
wait for a man,
So a band of priests murder on the
road toward Shechem [covering
their crimes in that city of
refuge];
Certainly they have committed
crimes *and* outrages.
10 I have seen a horrible thing [sins
of every kind] in the house of
Israel!
Ephraim's prostitution (idolatry) is
there; Israel has defiled itself.
11 Also, O Judah, there is a harvest
[of divine judgment] appointed
for you,
When I restore the fortunes of My
people [who have been slaves to
the misery of sin].

Ephraim's Sin

7 WHEN I would heal Israel,
The sin (guilt) of Ephraim is
uncovered,
And the wickedness of Samaria,
Because they practice false
dealing;
The thief enters,
Bandits ravage *and* raid outside.
2 But they do not consider in their
hearts (minds)
That I remember [always] all their
wickedness.

6:3 ***like the [heavy] rain, Like the spring rain watering the earth.*** Two periods of rain are alluded to here. The heavy rains came in the autumn and softened the ground for plowing and sowing. The spring rains came in the spring and caused the plants to grow.
6:5 ***judgments [pronounced upon them by the prophets] are like the light that shines forth.*** This comparison suggests that God's judgment, like bright sunlight, was obvious to all; or that, like a bolt of lightning or a blinding flash of light, it came swiftly.
6:11 ***there is a harvest [of divine judgment] appointed for you.*** The comparison of God's judgment to a harvest indicates that the judgment was inevitable and implies that it would be thorough in its destruction.

2 1Co 15:4 **3** Isa 54:13; 2Sa 23:4; Ps 72:6; Job 29:23 **5** Jer 23:29 **6** Mt 9:13; Isa 1:11; Jn 17:3
CHAPTER 7 **1** Hos 5:1 **2** Jer 17:1

Now their deeds surround *and* entangle them;
They are before My face.
[3]They make the king glad with their wickedness,
And the princes with their lies.
[4]They are all adulterers;
Like the heat of an oven
When the baker ceases to stir *the fire*, [their passion smolders]
From the kneading of the dough until it is leavened.
[5]On the [special] day of our king, the princes became sick with the heat of wine;
The king stretched out his hand [in association] with scoffers (lawless people).
[6]As they approach their plotting,
Their mind burns [with intrigue] like an oven [while they lie in wait].
Their anger smolders all night;
In the morning it blazes like a flaming fire.
[7]They are all hot like an oven
And they consume their judges (rulers);
All their kings have fallen.
There is no one among them who calls to Me.

[8]Ephraim mixes himself with the [Gentile] nations [seeking favor with one country, then another];
Ephraim is a cake not turned [worthless; ready to be thrown away].
[9]Strangers have devoured his strength,
Yet he does not know it;
Gray hairs are sprinkled on him,
Yet he does not know.
[10]Though the pride of Israel testifies against him,
Yet they do not return [in repentance] to the LORD their God,
Nor seek *nor* search for *nor* desire Him [as essential] in spite of all this.
[11]Ephraim also is like a silly dove, without heart *or* good sense;
They call to Egypt [for help], they go to Assyria.
[12]When they go, I will spread My net over them;
I will bring them down like birds of the heavens [into Assyrian captivity].
I will chastise them in accordance with the proclamation (prophecy) to their congregation. [Lev 26:14–39; Deut 28:15–68]
[13]Woe (judgment is coming) to them, for they have wandered away from Me!
Devastation is theirs, because they have rebelled *and* trespassed against Me!
I would redeem them, but they speak lies against Me.
[14]They do not cry out to Me from their heart

7:4–7 *They are all hot like an oven.* The background for these verses is the political turmoil of the Northern Kingdom. During a 20-year period (752–732 BC), four Israelite kings were assassinated (2Ki 15). The dangerous, uncontrollable perpetuators of these crimes are described here. These conspirators were like a large baker's oven that has been heating up for several hours while the bread dough rises. By morning the fire in the oven can be destructive.

7:8 *Ephraim mixes himself with the [Gentile] nations.* Instead of depending on the Lord for political stability, Israel formed alliances with surrounding nations. The destructive outcome of this policy is compared to a cake that has been placed over a fire and left unturned.

7:9–10 *Gray hairs.* Israel did not recognize that its power was declining and its freedom was slipping away, like an aging man who is gradually overtaken by the signs of old age.

7:11–12 *Egypt . . . Assyria.* Israel was caught between these two superpowers. It tried to maintain its independence by playing one power against the other, but this vacillating policy didn't work. Israel was like a silly dove, flitting about from place to place.

7:13 *Woe (judgment is coming) to them.* When prophets spoke this way, they were saying a funeral dirge for those under the sentence of God's judgment.

7:14 *grain and new wine.* God sent a drought on Israel, but instead of the people turning to

---

3 Ro 1:32 **4** Jer 9:2 **7** Isa 64:7 **8** Ps 106:35 **9** Hos 8:7 **10** Hos 5:5; Isa 9:13 **11** Hos 11:11; Hos 5:13 **12** Lev 26:14; Dt 28:15; 2Ki 17:13 **13** Mic 6:4 **14** Job 35:9; Jer 3:10; Zec 7:5

When they wail on their beds [in
unbelieving despair];
For the sake of grain and new
wine they assemble themselves
[as if worshiping Baal];
They rebel against Me.
15 Although I trained and
strengthened their arms [for
victory over their enemies],
Yet they devise evil against Me.
16 They turn, but they do not turn
upward to the Most High.
They are like a poorly crafted bow
[that misses the mark];
Their princes shall fall by the sword
Because of the insolence of their
tongue.
This *will be* cause for their
mockery *and* disdain in the land
of Egypt.

Israel Reaps the Whirlwind

8 SET THE trumpet to your
lips [announcing impending
judgment]!
Like a [great] vulture *the enemy
comes* against the house of the
LORD,
Because they have broken My
covenant
And transgressed *and* rebelled
against My law.
2 Then they will cry out to Me,
"My God, we of Israel know You!"
3 Israel has rejected the good;
The enemy shall pursue him.
4 They set up kings, but not from Me
[therefore without My blessing];
They have appointed princes, but I
did not know it.
With their silver and their gold
they made idols for themselves,
That they might be cut off.
5 He has rejected your [pagan] calf,
O Samaria, *saying*,
"My wrath burns against them."
How long will they be incapable of
innocence?
6 For even this [loathsome calf] is
from Israel.
A craftsman made it, so it is not
God;
Surely the calf of Samaria will be
broken to pieces *and* go up in
flames.
7 For they sow the wind [in evil]
And they reap the whirlwind [in
disaster].
The standing grain has no growth;
It yields no grain.
If it were to yield, strangers would
swallow it up.
8 Israel is [as if] swallowed up [by
enemies];
They are now among the nations
Like a vessel [of cheap, coarse
pottery] that is useless.
9 For they have gone up to Assyria,
Like a wild donkey wandering
alone *and* taking her own way;
Ephraim has hired lovers (pagan
allies).
10 Yes, even though [with presents]
they hire *allies* among the
nations,

Him in repentance, the idolatrous Israelites demonstrated their devotion to Baal. According to Canaanite religious beliefs, prolonged drought was a signal that the storm god Baal had been temporarily defeated by the god of death and was imprisoned by the underworld. Baal's worshipers would mourn his death in hopes that their tears might facilitate his resurrection and the restoration of crops.

8:1 – 3 *Like a [great] vulture.* As a bird of prey would do, Assyria would invade Israel and take its people into captivity. ***we of Israel know You.*** Though Israel claimed to acknowledge the Lord's authority, it had violated His covenant and rejected the qualities the Lord regarded as good, such as justice, loyalty, and humility (Am 5:14 – 15; Mic 6:8).

8:4 *They set up kings.* This phrase alludes to the political turmoil surrounding the throne of the Northern Kingdom during the eighth century BC, when four kings were assassinated during a 20-year period (7:4 – 7).

8:6 *A craftsman made it.* Hosea reasoned that anything that is made with human hands cannot possibly qualify as a god.

8:9 – 10 *a wild donkey.* This comparison draws attention to Israel's free-spirited attitude and desire to live unrestrained by God's standards.

16 Ps 78:57; Ps 73:9; Hos 9:3,6 **CHAPTER 8** **1** Dt 28:49; Jer 4:13 **2** Ps 78:34; Titus 1:16 **4** 2Ki 15:13,17,25, Shallum, Menahem, Pekahiah **5** Jer 13:27 **7** Pr 22:8 **8** 2Ki 17:6; Jer 22:28 **9** Jer 2:24; Eze 16:33,34 **10** Eze 16:37; Isa 10:8; Eze 26:7; Da 2:37

Now I will gather them up;
And [in a little while] they will begin to grow weak *and* diminish
Because of the burden imposed by the king of princes [the king of Assyria].

11 For Ephraim has constructed many altars for sin;
They are altars intended for sinning [which multiply his guilt].
12 I wrote for him the ten thousand *precepts* of My law,
But they are regarded as a strange thing [which does not concern him].
13 As for My sacrificial offerings,
They sacrifice the meat [as a mere formality] and eat it,
But the LORD is not pleased with them *and* does not accept them.
Now He will remember *and* take into account their wickedness *and* guilt,
And punish them for their sins.
They will return [in captivity] to [another] Egypt [that is, Assyria]. [Deut 28:68]
14 For Israel has forgotten his Maker and built palaces [and pagan temples],
And Judah has built many fortified cities;
But I will send a fire upon their cities so that it may consume their palaces *and* fortresses. [Amos 1:4, 7, 10, 12, 14; 2:2, 5]

Ephraim Punished

9 DO NOT rejoice, O Israel, with exultation as do the [pagan] peoples,
For you have played the prostitute, *turning* away from your God.
You have loved *prostitutes'* earnings on every threshing floor [attributing the harvest to the Baals instead of to God].
2 The threshing floor and the wine press will no longer feed them,
And the new wine will fail them [because they failed to honor the God who provides].
3 They will not remain in the land of the LORD,
But Ephraim will return to [another] Egypt [in bondage]
And they will eat [ceremonially] unclean *food* in Assyria. [2 Kin 25:26; Ezek 4:13]
4 They will not pour out drink offerings of wine to the LORD;
Their sacrifices will not please Him.
Their bread will be like mourners' bread [eaten at funerals];
All who eat it will be [ceremonially] unclean,
For their bread will be for themselves;
It will not enter the house of the LORD [to be consecrated].
5 What will you do on the day of the appointed festival
And on the day of the feast of the LORD [when you are in exile]?
6 For behold, they will go away because of devastation *and* destruction;
Egypt will gather them up,
Memphis will bury them.
Weeds will take over their treasures of silver;
Thorns *will grow* in their tents.
7 The days of punishment have come;
The days of retribution are at hand;

8:14 *palaces . . . built many fortified cities.* True security comes from the Creator, but God's people trusted instead in their own efforts, symbolized by their important buildings.

9:1 – 2 *threshing floor.* Because of their association with the harvest, threshing floors were the site of agricultural festivals in which Israel offered up sacrifices to Baal. The Lord would take away the joy of the harvest by destroying the crops and leaving the threshing floors and wine vats empty.

9:3 *the land of the LORD.* Israel had forgotten that their land belonged to the Lord. He alone decided who would or would not live in it (Lev 25:23).

9:7 *The man [of God] who is inspired is [treated as if] demented.* The word translated "demented" or "mad" is used in 1 Samuel 21:15

---

12 Dt 4:6,8; Ps 119:18 **13** Zec 7:6; Jer 14:10 **14** Dt 32:18; Isa 29:23; Jer 17:27 **CHAPTER 9** **1** Jer 44:17
3 Lev 25:23; Jer 2:7; Hos 8:13; Eze 4:13 **4** Jer 6:20 **7** Mic 2:11

Let Israel know this!
The prophet is [considered] a fool;
The man [of God] who is inspired
is [treated as if] demented,
Because of the abundance of your
wickedness *and* guilt,
And *because* your deep
antagonism [toward God
and the prophets] is so great.
[Luke 21:22]
[8]Ephraim was a watchman with my
God, a [true] prophet [to warn
the nation];
But the snare of a bird catcher was
laid in all his paths.
And there is *only* deep hostility in
the house of his God (the land of
Israel).
[9]They have deeply corrupted
(perverted) themselves
As in the days of Gibeah.
The LORD will remember their
wickedness *and* guilt;
He will punish their sins. [Judg 20]
[10]I found Israel like grapes in the
wilderness [an unexpected and
refreshing delight];
I saw your fathers (ancestors) as
the first ripe fruit on the fig tree
in its first *season,*
But they came to Baal-peor and
consecrated themselves to
shamefulness [the worship of
Baal],
And [because of their spiritual and
physical adultery] they became
as detestable *and* loathsome as
the thing they loved.
[11]As for Ephraim, their glory will fly
away like a bird;
No birth, no pregnancy, and
[because of their impurity] no
conception.
[12]Even though they bring up their
children,
Yet I will bereave them until not
one is left.
Indeed, woe (judgment is coming)
to them when I look away *and*
withdraw [My blessing] from
them!
[13]Ephraim, as I have seen,
Is planted in a pleasant [and
prosperous] meadow like
Tyre;
But Ephraim will bring out his
children to the executioner [for
slaughter].
[14]Give them [the punishment they
deserve], O LORD! What will You
give?
Give them a miscarrying womb
and dry breasts.
[15]All their wickedness [says the
LORD] is focused in Gilgal;
Indeed, I came to hate them there!
Because of the wickedness of their
[idolatrous] practices
I will drive them out of My house
(the land of Israel)!
I will love them no longer;
All their princes are rebels.
[Hos 4:15; 12:11]
[16]Ephraim is stricken, their root is
dried up,
They will bear no fruit.
Even though they give birth,
I will slay the precious children of
their womb.
[17]My God will reject them *and* cast
them away
Because they did not listen to
Him;
And they will be wanderers
(fugitives) among the nations.

---

of David when he pretended to be a madman before the Philistine king.
9:8 *watchman.* He would look for approaching armies and then warn the people so that they could secure the city and prepare for battle (Eze 33:6). The prophets were like watchmen because they were sent by God to warn the people of judgment and urge them to repent (Eze 3:17).
9:9 *As in the days of Gibeah.* The reference here is to the rape and murder of a young woman by men of Gibeah, an event that started a civil war (Jdg 19). Those who witnessed this violent deed remarked that it was the worst crime committed in Israel's history until that time. However, the sins of Hosea's generation rivaled the infamous Gibeah.
9:14 *miscarrying womb.* Some women of Israel would be barren (v. 11); others would bear children, only to lose them to the invader's sword (vv. 12 – 13). Still others would conceive but miscarry.

9 Hos 10:9; Jdg 19:22 **10** Nu 25:3; Ps 106:28; Ps 81:12 **12** Dt 31:17 **13** Eze 26; 27; 28 **14** Lk 23:29 **15** Isa 1:23

Retribution for Israel's Sin

10 ISRAEL IS a luxuriant *and* prolific vine;
He produces fruit for himself.
The more his fruit,
The more altars he made [to Baal];
The richer his land,
The better he made the [idolatrous] pillars.
2 Their heart is divided (faithless);
Now they must bear their guilt *and* punishment.
The LORD will break down [the horns of] their altars;
He will destroy their *idolatrous* pillars.

3 Surely now they will say [in despair], "We have no [true] king,
For we do not revere the LORD;
And as for the king, what can he do for us [to rescue us]?"
4 They have spoken *empty (disingenuous)* words,
Swearing falsely to make covenants [they intend to break];
Therefore, judgment springs up like poisonous weeds in the furrows of the field.
5 The people of Samaria will fear *and* tremble
For the [idolatrous] calf of Beth-aven (House of Wickedness).
Indeed, its people will mourn over it
And its idolatrous priests will cry out *and* wail over it,
Over its glory, because the glory [of their calf god] has departed from it.
6 The golden calf itself will be carried to Assyria
As tribute to King Jareb;
Ephraim will be seized with shame
And Israel will be ashamed of his own counsel [to worship the calf and separate Israel from Judah].
7 As for Samaria, her king will be cut off *and* float away
Like a twig on the surface of the water.
8 Also the high places of Aven (Beth-aven), the sin of Israel, will be destroyed;
The thorn and the thistle will grow on their [pagan] altars,
And [in despair] they will say to the mountains,
"Cover us!" And to the hills, "Fall on us!" [Luke 23:30; Rev 6:16; 9:6]
9 O Israel, you have [willfully] sinned since the days of Gibeah;
There they (Israel) stand!
Will not the battle against the sons of wickedness overtake them at Gibeah? [Judg 20]
10 When it is my desire [to defend My righteousness], I will chastise them;
And [hostile] peoples will be gathered against them
When they are bound *and* punished for their double guilt [their revolt against the LORD and their worship of idols]. [Jer 2:13; Lam 3:31–33]

11 Ephraim is a trained heifer that loves to tread out the grain,
But I will come over her fair neck *with a heavy yoke* [for hard field work].
I will harness Ephraim;
Judah will plow and Jacob will harrow *and* rake for himself.

10:1 *Israel is a luxuriant and prolific vine.* This refers to God's blessings upon the nation, which contrast with the nation's ingratitude and idolatry.
10:4 *judgment springs up like poisonous weeds in the furrows of the field.* In much the same way judgment would replace God's blessings.
10:11 *loves to tread out.* Israel preferred to be unrestrained, like an unmuzzled heifer at the threshing floor that can simply lean down and eat grain. ***I will harness Ephraim.*** Israel's rebellious spirit necessitated harsh treatment, compared here to a farmer binding his calf to the yoke and forcing it to do hard labor. Threshing in this context refers to Israel's service to the Lord; plowing refers to the discipline that Israel had to acquire through judgment and exile.

CHAPTER 10 **1** Na 2:2; Hos 8:11 **2** 1Ki 18:21; Mt 6:24 **4** Am 5:7 **8** Dt 9:21; Isa 2:19; Lk 23:30 **10** Jer 16:16 **11** Mic 4:13

12 Sow with a view to righteousness
[that righteousness, like seed, may germinate];
Reap in accordance with mercy *and* lovingkindness.
Break up your uncultivated ground,
For it is time to seek *and* search diligently for the LORD [and to long for His blessing]
Until He comes to rain righteousness *and* His gift of salvation on you. [2 Cor 9:10]
13 You have plowed *and* planted wickedness, you have reaped the [willful] injustice [of oppressors],
You have eaten the fruit of lies.
Because you have trusted in your own way *and* your chariots, and in your many warriors,
14 Therefore an uproar will arise among your people,
And all your fortresses will be destroyed,
As Shalman destroyed Beth-arbel on the day of battle,
When mothers were dashed in pieces with their children. [2 Kin 17:3]
15 In this way it will be done to you at [idolatrous] Bethel because of your great wickedness;
At daybreak the king of Israel will be completely cut off.

God is the Loving Father of His People

11 WHEN ISRAEL was a child [a young nation], I loved him,
And I called My son out of Egypt. [Matt 2:15]
2 The more they [the prophets] called them [to repentance and obedience],
The more they went away from them;
They kept sacrificing to the Baals
And burning incense to the carved images.
3 Yet it is I who taught Ephraim to walk,
Taking them in My arms [nurturing the young nation];
But they did not know that I healed them.
4 I led them *gently* with cords of a man, with bonds of love [guiding them],
And I was to them as one who lifts up *and* eases the yoke [of the law] over their jaws;
And I bent down to them and fed them.
5 They will not return to the land of Egypt,
But Assyria will be their king [bringing them into captivity]
Because they refused to return *to Me*.
6 The sword will whirl against *and* fall on their cities,
And will demolish the bars of their gates *and* fortifications
And will consume them because of their counsels.
7 My people are bent on turning from Me;
Though the prophets call them to *the One* on high,
None at all exalts *Him*.

10:12 *Break up your uncultivated ground.* Plowing and planting are necessary preliminary steps for growing a crop, which eventually sprouts when the rain falls in season. In the same way, repentance would set the stage for restored blessing, which God would eventually rain down on His people.
11:3 *it is I who taught Ephraim to walk.* Like a father teaching his child to walk, the Lord patiently gave the people of Israel direction and cared for them tenderly when they experienced pain or injury.
11:4 *cords . . . bonds.* The Lord had placed restraints on Israel, but His regulations, rather than being overly strict or harsh, reflected His concern for the people's well-being. God did not drive them mercilessly but provided for their needs, like a farmer who periodically removes the yoke from an animal's neck so that it can eat.
11:6 *consume.* This is the same Hebrew word translated "fed them" in verse 4. The people of Israel had rejected the gentle Master who fed them and provided for their needs. As a result, they would be devoured by the swords of the invading Assyrians.

12 Jer 4:3 **13** Pr 22:8; Gal 6:7,8 **CHAPTER 11** **1** Mt 2:15; Ex 4:22 **3** Dt 1:31; Ex 15:26 **4** Lev 26:13; Ps 78:25 **7** Jer 3:6

8 How can I give you up,
O Ephraim?
How can I surrender you, O Israel?
How can I make you like Admah?
How can I treat you like Zeboiim?
My heart recoils within Me;
All My compassions are kindled
together [for My nation of
Israel]. [Deut 29:23]
9 I will not execute the fierceness of
My anger;
I will not return to Ephraim to
destroy him again.
For I am God and not man, the
Holy One in your midst [who
will not revoke My covenant],
And I will not come in wrath *or*
enter the city [in judgment].
10 They will walk after the LORD [in
obedience and worship],
Who will roar like a lion;
He will roar [summoning them]
And *His* sons will come trembling
from the west.
11 They will come trembling *and*
hurriedly like birds from
Egypt
And like doves from the land of
Assyria;
And I will settle them in their
houses [in the land of their
inheritance], declares the LORD.
12 Ephraim surrounds Me with lies
And the house of Israel with
deceit;
Judah is also unruly against God,
Even against the faithful Holy
One.

Ephraim Reminded

12 EPHRAIM FEEDS on the
[emptiness of the] wind
And [continually] pursues the
[parching] east wind [which
brings destruction];
Every day he multiplies lies and
violence.
Further, he makes a covenant with
Assyria
And (olive) oil is carried to Egypt
[to seek alliances]. [Is 30:6, 7]
2 The LORD also has a dispute
[a legal complaint and an
indictment] with Judah,
And He will punish Jacob in
accordance with his ways;
He will repay him in accordance
with his deeds.
3 In *their mother's* womb he took
his brother by the heel,
And in his maturity he contended
with God. [Gen 25:26; 27:36]
4 He wrestled with the angel and
prevailed;
He wept [in repentance] and
sought His favor.
He met Him at Bethel
And there God spoke with [him
and through him with] us—
[Gen 28:12–19; 32:28; 35:1–15]
5 Even the LORD, the God of hosts,
The name of Him [who spoke with
Jacob] is the LORD.
6 Therefore, return [in repentance]
to your God,
Observe *and* highly regard
kindness and justice,
And wait [expectantly] for your
God continually.
7 A merchant, in whose hand are
false *and* fraudulent balances;
He loves to oppress *and* exploit.
8 Ephraim said, "I have indeed
become rich [and powerful as a
nation];
I have found wealth for myself.
In all my labors they will not find
in me
Any wickedness that *would be*
sin." [Rev 3:17]

11:9 *For I am God and not man.* When human beings get angry, they are often incapable of tempering their anger with compassion, but God's emotions operate in perfect balance.
12:1 *oil is carried to Egypt.* Oil may have been used in a ritual ratifying a treaty or given as a sign of loyalty.

12:7 *in whose hand are false and fraudulent balances.* In violation of the Old Testament law (Lev 19:36), dishonest merchants sometimes rigged their scales so that they could give buyers less than what they thought they were purchasing (Pr 11:1; 16:11).

8 Jer 9:7; Ge 14:8 **9** Nu 23:19 **10** Joel 3:16 **11** Isa 60:8; Eze 28:25,26 **CHAPTER 12** **1** 2Ki 17:4; Isa 30:6 **2** Mic 6:2 **3** Ge 25:26; 32:28 **4** Ge 28:12 **5** Ex 3:15 **6** Mic 6:8 **7** Am 8:5 **8** Rev 3:17

9 But I *have been* the LORD your God
since [you became a nation in]
the land of Egypt;
I will make you live in tents again,
As in the days of the appointed *and*
solemn festival. [Lev 23:39–43]
10 I have also spoken to [you through]
the prophets,
And I gave [them] many visions [to
make My will known],
And through the prophets I gave
parables [to appeal to your sense
of right and wrong].
11 Is there wickedness (idolatry) in
Gilead?
Surely the people there are
worthless.
In Gilgal [they defy Me when] they
sacrifice bulls,
Yes, [after My judgment] their
[pagan] altars are like the stone
heaps
In the furrows of the fields.
12 Now Jacob (Israel) fled into the
open country of Aram (Paddan-aram), [Gen 28:2, 5]
And [there] Israel (Jacob) worked
and served for a wife,
And for a wife he kept *sheep*.
[Gen 29:18–20; 30:31; 31:38–41]
13 And by a prophet (Moses) the
LORD brought Israel up from
Egypt,
And by a prophet Israel was
preserved.
14 Ephraim has provoked most bitter
anger;
So his Lord will leave his bloodguilt
on him [invoking punishment]
And bring back to him his shame
and dishonor.

Ephraim's Idolatry

13 WHEN EPHRAIM spoke,
there was trembling *and* terror.
He exalted himself [above the
other tribes] in Israel;
But through [the worship of] Baal
he became guilty and died
[spiritually, and then came
ruin, sealing Israel's doom as a
nation].
2 And now they sin more and more,
And make for themselves molten
images,
Idols skillfully made from their
silver [as it pleased them],
All of them the work of the
craftsmen.
They say of these [very works of
their hands], "Let those who
sacrifice kiss *and* show respect
to the calves [as if they were
living gods]!"
3 Therefore they will be [swiftly
dissipated] like the morning
cloud
Or like dew which soon
disappears,
Like chaff which swirls with the
whirlwind from the threshing
floor,
And like smoke from the
chimney *or* through the
window [worthless and without
substance —they will vanish].
4 Yet I *have been* the LORD your God
Since [the time you became a
nation in] the land of Egypt;
And you were not to know any god
except Me,
For there is no savior besides Me.
5 I knew *and* regarded you *and*
cared for you in the wilderness,
In the land of drought.
6 When *they had* their pasture, they
became satisfied,
And being satisfied, their heart
became proud (self-centered);
Therefore they forgot Me.
7 So I will be like a lion to them;
Like a leopard I will watch *and* lie
in wait [ready to attack] by the
road [to Assyria].

12:9 *I will make you live in tents again.* During the Feast of the Tabernacles people lived in tents to commemorate the wilderness wandering (Lev 23:33–43).
13:2 *kiss and show respect to the calves.* This is a reference to the idolatrous practice of kissing images as a sign of homage (1Ki 19:18).
13:6–9 *So I will be like a lion to them.* God provided for Israel's needs and richly blessed the people, like a shepherd leading his flock to lush

9 Lev 23:42 **10** 2Ki 17:13 **12** Ge 28:5 **13** Ex 12:50 **14** Da 11:18 **CHAPTER 13** **3** Da 2:35 **4** Isa 43:11
5 Dt 2:7; 8:15 **6** Dt 8:12 **7** La 3:10; Jer 5:6

8 I will encounter them like a bear
robbed of her cubs,
And I will tear open their chests;
There I will also devour them like
a lioness,
As a wild beast would tear them.

9 It is your destruction, O Israel,
Because *you are* against Me, [and
have rebelled] against your help.
10 Where now is your king
That he may save you [when you
are attacked] in all your cities?
And your judges of whom you
asked,
"Give me a king and princes"?
11 I gave you a king in My anger,
And I took him away in My wrath
[as punishment].

12 The wickedness of Ephraim
[which is not yet completely
punished] is bound up [as in a
bag];
His sin is stored up [for judgment
and destruction].
13 The pains of childbirth come on
him;
But he is not a wise son,
For it is not the time to delay [his
chance at a new birth] as the
womb opens [but he ignores the
opportunity to change].
14 Shall I ransom them from the
power of Sheol (the place of the
dead)?
Shall I redeem them from death?
O death, where are your thorns?
O Sheol, where is your sting?
Compassion is hidden from My
eyes [because of their failure to
repent]. [1 Cor 15:55]

15 For though he flourishes among
the reeds (his fellow tribes),
An east wind (Assyria) will come,
The breath of the LORD rising from
the desert;
And Ephraim's spring will become
dry
And his fountain will be dried up.
Assyria will plunder his treasury
of every precious object.
16 Samaria will be found guilty [and
become desolate],
Because she rebelled against her
God;
They will fall by the sword,
Their infants will be dashed in
pieces,
And their pregnant women will be
ripped open.

Israel's Future Blessing

14 O ISRAEL, return [in
repentance] to the LORD your
God,
For you have stumbled *and* fallen
[visited by tragedy], because of
your sin.
2 Take the words [confessing your
guilt] with you and return to the
LORD.
Say to Him, "Take away all our
wickedness;
Accept what is good *and* receive us
graciously,
So that we may present the fruit of
our lips (gratitude). [Heb 13:15]
3 "Assyria will not save us;
We will not ride on horses [relying
on military might],
Nor will we say again to [the idols
who are] the work of our hands,

---

pasturelands. In return, Israel forgot the Lord. The Lord's relationship with Israel would change drastically from caring Shepherd to ravaging Predator. Ironically and tragically, Israel's rebellion had turned its Helper into a Destroyer.
13:12 ***bound up . . . stored up.*** God had kept a careful record of Israel's sins, to be revealed as evidence of guilt in the day of judgment.
13:13 ***The pains of childbirth.*** This metaphor illustrates Israel's spiritual insensitivity. When the crucial time of judgment arrived, Israel would respond unwisely, resulting in death. The nation's failure to repent is compared to a baby that is not positioned properly during labor and jeopardizes the life of both mother and child.
14:1 – 3 ***Take away all our wickedness.*** The final section of Hosea's prophecy begins with a call to repentance that includes a model prayer. The people of Israel were to pray for God's gracious forgiveness and renew their allegiance to Him by renouncing foreign alliances, their own military strength, and artificial gods.

8 2Sa 17:8 **10** Dt 32:38; 1Sa 8:5 **11** 1Sa 8:7 **12** Dt 32:34 **13** Isa 13:8 **14** 1Co 15:54; Jer 15:6 **15** Jer 4:11
16 2Ki 8:12 **CHAPTER 14** **1** Joel 2:13 **2** Heb 13:15 **3** Ps 33:17; Ps 10:14

'You are our gods.'
For in You [O LORD] the orphan
finds love *and* compassion *and*
mercy."

4 I will heal their apostasy *and*
faithlessness;
I will love them freely,
For My anger has turned away
from Israel.
5 I shall be like the dew to Israel;
He will blossom like the lily,
And he will take root like *the*
cedars of Lebanon.
6 His shoots will sprout,
And his beauty will be like the
olive tree
And his fragrance like *the cedars*
of Lebanon.
7 Those who live in his shadow
Will again raise grain,
And they will blossom like the
vine.
His renown *will be* like the wine of
Lebanon.

8 O Ephraim, what more have I to do
with idols?
It is I who have answered and will
care for you *and* watch over you.
I am like a luxuriant cypress tree;
With Me your fruit is found [which
is to nourish you].

9 Whoever is [spiritually] wise, let
him understand these things;
Whoever is [spiritually] discerning
and understanding, let him
know them.
For the ways of the LORD are
right,
And the righteous will walk in
them,
But transgressors will stumble *and*
fall in them. [Ps 107:43; Is 26:7;
Jer 9:12; Dan 12:10]

14:4 *I will heal their apostasy and faithlessness.* The grief-stricken Hosea does not tell us whether a reconciliation took place between him and his adulterous wife Gomer. But there is no question concerning the outcome between God and faithless Israel. Several beautiful figures of speech are employed by Hosea to describe the results and effects of God's love for Israel.

14:9 *For the ways of the LORD are right.* God's demands and principles are completely true. The wise person will choose to obey them, but the foolish person will ignore them and consequently stumble into judgment.

5 Pr 19:12 **6** Ps 52:8; Ge 27:27 **7** Ps 91:1 **9** Pr 10:29

THE BOOK OF JOEL

▸ **AUTHOR:** Although there are several other Joel's in the Bible, the prophet Joel is known only from this book. It has been suggested that he lived not far from Jerusalem and some think that Joel was possibly a priest as well as a prophet on account of references to the priesthood throughout the book (Joel 1:13 – 14; 2:17).

▸ **TIMES:** c. 835 BC ▸ **KEY VERSE:** Joel 2:11

▸ **THEME:** For the true agrarian society, crops are life itself. It is hard to imagine how devastating the natural disasters described in Joel are, and he uses these painful events as a megaphone to get the attention of the people. There is urgency in this call, because the day of the Lord is coming. This day will be a day of judgment or a day of blessing depending on where one stands with God.

1 THE WORD of the Lord that came to Joel, the son of Pethuel.

The Devastation of Locusts

2 Hear this, O elders,
Listen closely, all inhabitants of the land!
Has *such a thing as* this occurred in your days,
Or even in the days of your fathers?
3 Tell your children about it,
And let your children tell their children,
And their children the next generation.

4 What the gnawing locust has left, the swarming locust has eaten;
And what the swarming locust has left, the creeping locust has eaten;
And what the creeping locust has left, the stripping locust has eaten [in judgment of Judah].

5 Awake [from your intoxication], you drunkards, and weep;
Wail, all you drinkers of wine,
Because of the [fresh] sweet wine
That is cut off from your mouth.
6 For a [pagan and hostile] nation has invaded My land [like locusts],
Mighty and without number;
Its teeth are the teeth of a lion,
And it has the fangs of a lioness. [Rev 9:7, 8]
7 It has made My vine (My people) a waste *and* object of horror,
And splintered *and* broken My fig tree.
It has stripped them completely bare and thrown them away;
Their branches have become white. [Is 5:5, 6]

8 Wail like a virgin [bride] clothed with sackcloth
For the bridegroom of her youth [who has died].

1:2 *Has such a thing as this occurred in your days.* The calamity of recent days was unprecedented in the memory of the people.
1:4 *locust.* Many interpreters have viewed these locusts as foreign armies that attacked Judah in successive waves — Assyria, Babylon, Greece, and Rome. Yet literal locust plagues were one of the judgments promised if the people disobeyed God

CHAPTER 1 **2** Joel 2:2 **3** Ps 78:4 **4** Dt 28:38 **5** Isa 32:10 **6** Pr 30:23; Rev 9:8 **7** Isa 5:6 **8** Isa 22:12; Pr 2:17; Jer 3:4

9 The [daily] grain offering and the
drink offering are cut off
From the house of the LORD;
The priests mourn
Who minister to the LORD.
10 The field is ruined,
The ground mourns;
For the grain is ruined,
The new wine is dried up,
The fresh oil fails.
11 Be ashamed, O farmers;
Wail, O vinedressers,
For the wheat and for the barley,
Because the harvest of the field
has perished.
12 The vine dries up
And the fig tree fails;
The pomegranate, the palm also,
and the apple tree,
All the trees of the field dry up,
Indeed, joy dries up *and* withdraws
From the sons of men.

13 Clothe yourselves *with sackcloth*
And lament (cry out in grief),
O priests;
Wail, O ministers of the altar!
Come, spend the night in sackcloth
[and pray without ceasing],
O ministers of my God,
For the grain offering and the
drink offering
Are withheld from the house of
your God.

Starvation and Drought

14 Consecrate a fast,
Proclaim a solemn assembly,
Gather the elders
And all the inhabitants of the land
To the house of the LORD your God,
And cry out to the LORD [in
penitent pleadings].
15 Alas for the day!
For the [judgment] day of the LORD
is at hand,
And it will come [upon the nation]
as a destruction from the
Almighty. [Zeph 1:14–18]
16 Has not the food been cut off
before our eyes,
Joy and gladness from the house
of our God?
17 The seeds [of grain] shrivel under
the clods,
The storehouses are desolate *and*
empty,
The barns are in ruins
Because the grain is dried up.
18 How the animals groan!
The herds of cattle are bewildered
and wander aimlessly
Because they have no pasture;
Even the flocks of sheep suffer.
19 O LORD, I cry out to You,
For fire has devoured the pastures
of the wilderness,
And the flame has burned up all
the trees of the field.
20 Even the wild animals pant [in
longing] for You;
For the water brooks are dried up
And fire has consumed the
pastures of the wilderness.

The Terrible Visitation

2 BLOW THE trumpet in Zion
[warning of impending
judgment],

---

and broke their covenant with Him (Dt 28:38–42). Further, Joel's description of the damage done by the locusts compares with eyewitness reports. The impression given is one of overwhelming devastation.
1:9 *The [daily] grain offering and the drink offering.* This phrase refers to the wine offerings that accompanied the priests' morning and evening sacrifices (Ex 29:38–41). The devastation of the locust meant that no sacrifice could be offered.
1:10 *The ground mourns.* The land is personified as mourning because the three principle crops it produced — grain, grapes, and olives — had been destroyed (Dt 7:13; Ps 104:15).
1:15 *the [judgment] day of the LORD.* This phrase refers to a time of judgment and deliverance. Joel views the locust plague as a contemporary day of judgment that was serving as a token or forewarning of an even greater, future "day of the LORD."
1:17 *The seeds [of grain] shrivel.* This indicated further devastation in the land and an inability to replant the following year.

9 Joel 2:14 **10** Jer 12:11; Isa 24:7 **11** Jer 14:3,4 **12** ver. 10; Isa 24:11; Jer 48:33 **13** Jer 4:8 **14** 2Ch 20:3; Lev 23:36; 2Ch 20:13 **15** Jer 30:7; Isa 13:6,9 **16** See Dt 12:6,7 **18** Hos 4:3 **19** Ps 50:15; Jer 9:10 **20** Job 38:41; Ps 104:21; 1Ki 17:7 **CHAPTER 2** **1** Jer 4:5; Nu 10:5; Ob 15; Zep 1:14

Sound an alarm on My holy
mountain [Zion]!
Let all the inhabitants of the land
tremble *and* shudder in fear,
For the [judgment] day of the LORD
is coming;
It is close at hand, [Ezek 7:2–4;
Amos 5:16–20]
2 A day of darkness and gloom,
A day of clouds and of thick [dark]
mist,
Like the dawn spread over the
mountains;
There is a [pagan, hostile] people
numerous and mighty,
The like of which has never been
before
Nor will be again afterward
Even for years of many generations.
3 Before them a fire devours,
And behind them a flame burns;
Before them the land is like the
Garden of Eden,
But behind them a desolate
wilderness;
And nothing at all escapes them.
4 Their appearance is like the
appearance of horses,
And they run like war horses.
5 Like the noise of chariots
They leap on the tops of the
mountains,
Like the crackling of a flame of
fire devouring the stubble,
Like a mighty people set in battle
formation. [Rev 9:7, 9]
6 Before them the people are in
anguish;
All faces become pale [with terror].
7 They run like warriors;
They climb the wall like soldiers.
They each march [straight ahead]
in line,
And they do not deviate from their
paths.
8 They do not crowd each other;
Each one marches in his path.
When they burst through the
defenses (weapons),
They do not break ranks.
9 They rush over the city,
They run on the wall;
They climb up into the houses,
They enter at the windows like a
thief.
10 The earth quakes before them,
The heavens tremble,
The sun and the moon grow dark
And the stars lose their brightness.
[Rev 9:2–4; 16:14]
11 The LORD utters His voice before
His army,
For His camp is very great,
Because strong *and* powerful is he
who [obediently] carries out His
word.
For the day of the LORD is indeed
great and very terrible [causing
dread];
Who can endure it? [Is 26:20, 21;
34:1–4, 8; Rev 6:16, 17]
12 "Even now," says the LORD,
"Turn *and* come to Me with
all your heart [in genuine
repentance],
With fasting and weeping and
mourning [until every barrier
is removed and the broken
fellowship is restored];
13 Rip your heart to pieces [in sorrow
and contrition] and not your
garments."

2:1 *coming . . . close at hand.* The Bible presents the day of the Lord as an imminent reality. It is not something that we are gradually moving toward; rather, it is ever ready to burst in on us. At any moment, the day that is "nigh" may become present.
2:2 *darkness and gloom.* This phrase is used as a figure for misery, distress, and judgment (Isa 8:22; 60:2; Jer 13:16).
2:4 *Their appearance is like the appearance of horses.* Joel compared the speed and strength of the invaders to galloping horses.
2:11 *Who can endure it?* Nothing will be able to withstand the wrath of God (Mt 24:21 – 22).
2:13 *Rip your heart.* God is not satisfied with outward acts of repentance. Tearing one's garments was a customary way of expressing grief or remorse (Jos 7:6; 1Sa 4:12). However, like all outward acts, the tearing of a garment could be done without true sorrow or repentance. God required more than mere external words or actions; He wanted a change of heart and sorrow over sin.

2 Am 5:18; Joel 1:6; Ex 10:14 **3** Ge 2:8; Isa 51:3; Zec 7:14 **4** Rev 9:7 **5** Rev 9:9 **6** Jer 8:21; La 4:8; Na 2:10 **9** Jer 9:21; Jn 10:1 **10** Ps 18:7; Isa 13:10; Mt 24:29 **11** Jer 25:30; Jer 50:34; Rev 18:8; Jer 30:7; Am 5:18; Zep 1:15; Mal 3:2 **12** Jer 4:1; Hos 12:6 **13** Ps 34:18; Ge 37:34; 2Sa 1:11; Job 1:20; Ex 34:6

Now return [in repentance] to the
LORD your God,
For He is gracious and
compassionate,
Slow to anger, abounding in
lovingkindness [faithful to His
covenant with His people];
And He relents [His sentence of]
evil [when His people genuinely
repent].
14 Who knows whether He will relent
[and revoke your sentence],
And leave a blessing behind Him,
Even a grain offering and a drink
offering [from the bounty He
provides you]
For the LORD your God?
15 Blow a trumpet in Zion [warning
of impending judgment],
Dedicate a fast [as a day of
restraint and humility], call a
solemn assembly.
16 Gather the people, sanctify the
congregation,
Assemble the elders,
Gather the children and the
nursing infants.
Let the bridegroom come out of
his room
And the bride out of her bridal
chamber. [No one is excused
from the assembly.]
17 Let the priests, the ministers of the
LORD,
Weep between the porch and the
altar,
And let them say, "Have
compassion *and* spare Your
people, O LORD,
And do not make Your inheritance
(Israel) an object of ridicule,
Or a [humiliating] byword among
the [Gentile] nations.
Why should they say among the
peoples,
'Where is their God?' "

Deliverance Promised

18 Then the LORD will be jealous for
His land [ready to defend it since
it is rightfully and uniquely His]
And will have compassion on His
people [and will spare them].
19 The LORD will answer and say to
His people,
"Behold, I am going to send you
grain and new wine and oil,
And you will be satisfied *in full*
with them;
And I will never again make you
an object of ridicule among the
[Gentile] nations.
20 "But I will remove the northern
army far away from you,
And I will drive it into a parched
and desolate land,
With its forward guard into the
eastern sea (Dead Sea)
And with its rear guard into the
western sea (Mediterranean
Sea).
And its stench will arise and its
foul odor of decay will come up
[this is the fate of the northern
army in the final day of the
LORD],
For He has done great things."
[Is 34:1–4, 8; Amos 4:10]

2:14 *Who knows.* These words suggest that even at the last moment, the Lord would withhold His wrath and display His grace if the people would truly repent. As a result, agriculture would be restored and productivity would return. There would be food and drink for the people and for offerings to the Lord.

2:16 *bridegroom . . . And the bride.* According to Jewish tradition codified in the Mishnah, a couple could be excused from reciting daily prayers on their wedding day. But Joel excused no one from prayer at this time of spiritual emergency.

2:17 *Why should they say among the peoples.* This rhetorical question was designed to move God to intervene. Failure to come to Judah's aid might encourage the nations to make a mockery of Judah's God.

2:18 – 19 *jealous for His land.* The deep love of God for the land of Israel is coupled with His abiding love for the people. On every occasion in which God brought judgment on the land, there was the hope that one day His zeal for the land would lead to a renewal of blessing. Genuine repentance is the prerequisite for God's blessing. In response to repentance, God would bring restoration and blessing.

14 Jos 14:12; 2Ki 19:4; Hag 2:19; Joel 1:9,13 **15** Nu 10:3; Joel 1:14 **16** Ex 19:10; 1Co 7:5 **17** Eze 8:16; Mt 23:35; Ex 32:11,12; Ps 42:10 **18** Zec 1:14; Isa 60:10 **19** Joel 1:10; Mal 3:10 **20** Ex 10:19; Jer 1:14; Dt 11:24

21 Do not fear, O land; be glad and
rejoice,
For the LORD has done great
things! [Zech 12:8–10]
22 Do not be afraid, you animals of
the field,
For the pastures of the wilderness
have turned green;
The tree has produced its fruit,
And the fig tree and the vine have
yielded in full.
23 So rejoice, O children of Zion,
And delight in the LORD, your God;
For He has given you the early
[autumn] rain in vindication
And He has poured down the rain
for you,
The early [autumn] rain and the
late [spring] rain, as before.
24 And the threshing floors shall be
full of grain,
And the vats shall overflow with
new wine and oil.
25 "And I will compensate you for the
years
That the swarming locust has
eaten,
The creeping locust, the stripping
locust, and the gnawing locust—
My great army which I sent
among you.
26 "You will have plenty to eat and be
satisfied
And praise the name of the LORD
your God
Who has dealt wondrously with
you;
And My people shall never be put
to shame.
27 "And you shall know [without any
doubt] that I am in the midst of
Israel [to protect and bless you],
And that I am the LORD your God,
And there is no other;
My people will never be put to
shame.

The Promise of the Spirit

28 "It shall come about after this
That I shall pour out My Spirit on
all mankind;
And your sons and your daughters
will prophesy,
Your old men will dream dreams,
Your young men will see visions.
29 "Even on the male and female
servants
I will pour out My Spirit in those
days.

The Day of the LORD

30 "I will show signs *and* wonders
[displaying My power] in the
heavens and on the earth,
Blood and fire and columns of
smoke.
31 "The sun will be turned into
darkness
And the moon into blood
Before the great and terrible day
of the LORD comes. [Is 13:6,
9–11; 24:21–23; Ezek 32:7–10;
Matt 24:29, 30; Rev 6:12–17]
32 "And it shall come about that
whoever calls on the name of
the LORD
Will be saved [from the coming
judgment]

2:22 *For the pastures of the wilderness have turned green; The tree has produced its fruit.* The renewal of agriculture would be a sign that God had renewed prosperity and peace to His land.

2:28 – 32 *I shall pour out My Spirit on all mankind.* Peter quotes this passage on the Day of Pentecost (Ac 2:17 – 21) to explain the miracle of speaking in tongues. There are three main viewpoints regarding how Peter uses Joel's prophecy: (1) Some interpreters see a completer fulfillment of Joel's prophecy in the experience of the first believers on the Day of Pentecost. The outpouring of the Spirit ushered in the kingdom age. (2) Some interpreters believe that Peter was simply using Joel's prophecy as an illustration of what was happening. In effect, Peter was saying, "This is that same Holy Spirit which was spoken of by Joel." (3) Some others suggest that Joel's prophecy was partially fulfilled on the Day of Pentecost. The gift of the Holy Spirit was given, but the signs mentioned in verses 30 – 32 will be fulfilled later in connection with the return of Christ in great glory.

22 Joel 1:19 **23** Isa 41:16; Hab 3:18; Zec 10:7; Lev 26:4; Dt 11:14 **25** Joel 1:4 **26** Lev 26:5 **27** Lev 26:11; Isa 45:5 **28** Eze 39:29; Zec 12:10; Isa 54:13; Ac 21:9 **29** Gal 3:28 **30** Mt 24:29; Mk 13:24; Lk 21:11 **31** Isa 13:9,10; Mal 4:5 **32** Ro 10:13; Isa 46:13; Ro 11:26; Isa 11:11; Jer 31:7; Mic 4:7; Ro 9:27

For on Mount Zion and in
Jerusalem
There will be those who escape,
As the LORD has said,
Even among the remnant [of
survivors] whom the LORD calls.
[Acts 2:17–21; Rom 10:13]

The Nations Will Be Judged

3 "FOR BEHOLD, in those
[climactic] days and at that time,
When I restore the fortunes of
Judah and Jerusalem,
2 I will gather together all the
[Gentile] nations [that were
hostile to My people]
And bring them down into the
Valley of Jehoshaphat (the LORD
has judged).
And there I will deal with them
and enter into judgment with
them there
For [their treatment of] My people,
My inheritance, Israel,
Whom they have scattered among
the nations,
And [because] they have
encroached on My land *and*
divided it up.
3 "They have also cast lots for My
people,
And have traded a boy for a
prostitute
And have sold a girl for wine that
they may drink.
4 "Moreover, what are you to Me, O Tyre
and Sidon and all the [five small] re-
gions of Philistia? Will you pay Me
back for something [I have supposedly
done to you]? Even if you do pay Me
back, I will swiftly and speedily return
your deed [of retaliation] on your own
head. [Is 23; Ezek 26:1–18; Amos 1:6–
10; Zeph 2:4–7; Zech 9:2–7]
5 "Because you have taken My sil-
ver and My gold and have carried My
precious treasures to your temples *and*
palaces,
6 and have sold the children of Judah
and the children of Jerusalem to the
Greeks, so that you may send them far
away from their territory,
7 behold, I am going to stir them up
from the place where you have sold
them [and return them to their land],
and I shall return your action [of retal-
iation] on your own head.
8 "Also I will sell your sons and your
daughters into the hand of the children
of Judah, and they will sell them to the
Sabeans, to a distant nation," for the
LORD has spoken. [Is 14:2; 60:14]

9 Proclaim this among the [pagan]
nations:
Prepare a war! Stir up the mighty
men!
Let all the men of war come near,
let them come up!
10 Beat your plowshares into swords
And your pruning hooks into
spears;
Let the weak say, "I am strong!"
[Is 2:4; Mic 4:3]
11 Hurry and come, all you
surrounding nations,
And gather yourselves there;
Bring down, O LORD, Your mighty
ones (Your warriors).
12 Let the nations be stirred [to action]
And come up to the Valley of
Jehoshaphat,
For there I will sit to judge *and*
punish
All the surrounding nations.
13 Put in the sickle [of judgment], for
the harvest is ripe;
Come, tread [the grapes], for the
wine press is full;
The vats overflow, for the
wickedness [of the people]
is great. [Mark 4:29; Rev 14:15,
18–20]

3:2 *Valley of Jehoshaphat.* The name Jehoshaphat means "the Lord judges." The location of this valley is not known. Perhaps this was merely a symbolic name for the location of the great battle in the end times.

3:11 *nations . . . mighty ones.* Joel saw two different armies assembling for battle (Mk 8:38; Rev 19:14).

CHAPTER 3 **1** Jer 30:3; Eze 38:14 **2** Zec 14:2; Isa 66:16; Eze 38:22 **3** Ob 11; Na 3:10 **4** Am 1:6 **7** Isa 43:5,6; Jer 23:8 **8** Eze 23:42; Jer 6:20 **9** Eze 38:7 **10** Isa 2:4; Mic 4:3; Zec 12:8 **11** Ps 103:20; Isa 13:3 **12** Ps 96:13; Isa 2:4 **13** Mt 13:39; Rev 14:15; Jer 51:33; Isa 63:3; Rev 14:19

14 Multitudes, multitudes in the
valley of decision (judgment)!
For the day of the LORD is near
in the valley of decision
[when judgment is executed].
[Zech 14:1–9]
15 The sun and the moon grow dark
And the stars lose their brightness.
16 The LORD thunders *and* roars from
Zion
And utters His voice from
Jerusalem [in judgment of His
enemies],
And the heavens and the earth
tremble *and* shudder;
But the LORD is a refuge for His
people
And a stronghold [of protection]
to the children of Israel.
[Amos 9:11–15; Mic 4:1–3; 5:2;
Zeph 3:13–20; Zech 6:12, 13; 12:8,
9]
17 Then you will know *and*
understand fully that I am the
LORD your God,
Dwelling in Zion, My holy
mountain.
Then Jerusalem will be holy,
And strangers [who do not belong]
will no longer pass through it.

Judah Will Be Blessed

18 And in that day
The mountains will drip with
sweet wine
And the hills will flow with
milk;
And all the brooks *and* riverbeds
of Judah will flow with water,
And a fountain will go out from
the house of the LORD
To water the [desert] Valley
of Shittim. [Ezek 47:1–12;
Amos 9:13; Zech 14:8]
19 Egypt will become a waste,
And Edom will become a desolate
wilderness,
Because of their violence against
the children of Judah,
In whose land they have shed
innocent blood. [Ex 1:16;
Amos 1:11]
20 But Judah shall be inhabited
forever
And Jerusalem from generation to
generation.
21 And I shall avenge their
blood which I have not
avenged,
For the LORD dwells in Zion.

3:14 *the valley of decision.* This may be a symbolic name for the valley of Jehoshaphat (3:2), or it may refer to the option before the people to continue toward certain judgment or to turn to God in repentance (vv. 12 – 13).

3:18 *in that day.* These words indicate the prophetic future. Joel uses poetic imagery to describe the productivity of the land in the Messianic Age. The valley of Shittim was the location of the last encampment before the Israelites entered Canaan (Nu 25:1; Jos 3:1).

14 Joel 2:1 **16** Isa 51:5,6 **21** Isa 4:4

THE BOOK OF

AMOS

▸ **AUTHOR:** The only Old Testament appearance of the name Amos is in this book. Amos' objective appraisal of Israel's spiritual condition was not well received, not least because he was just a farmer from Judah. The author said of his background, "I am not a prophet [by profession], nor am I a prophet's son; I am a herdsman and a grower of sycamore figs" (7:14). He delivered his message in Bethel because it was the residence of the king of Israel and a center of idolatry.

▸ **TIMES:** c. 760 – 753 BC ▸ **KEY VERSES:** Am 3:1 – 2

▸ **THEME:** Amos was a contemporary of Isaiah and Hosea. The unusual aspect of his ministry is that he was a farmer and herdsman from Judah prophesying to the northern Israel. The issues he addresses are the usual prophetic concerns, but with a heavy emphasis on social justice. When injustice is rampant, expect God's judgment. No one is immune. In fact, the more God has given, the more God expects in response.

Judgment on Neighboring Nations

1 THE WORDS of Amos, who was
among the sheepherders of Tekoa,
which he saw [in a divine revelation]
concerning Israel in the days of Uzziah king of Judah, and in the days of
Jeroboam the son of Joash, king of Israel, two years before the earthquake.
[Zech 14:5]

2 And he said,
"The LORD thunders *and* roars
from Zion [in judgment]
And utters His voice from
Jerusalem;
Then the pastures of the shepherds
mourn,
And the summit of [Mount]
Carmel dries up [because of
God's judgment]." [Is 42:13;
Jer 25:30; Joel 3:16]

3 Thus says the LORD,
"For three transgressions
of Damascus and for four
(multiplied delinquencies)
I shall not reverse its punishment
or revoke My word concerning it,

1:1 – 2:16 *The words of Amos.* The Lord sent Amos, a Judean, to Bethel to prophesy of coming judgment on Israel. But in Bethel, Amos faced a hostile audience. Israel's first king, Jeroboam I, had made the town a center of pagan worship. Because the temple in Jerusalem was in Judah and not in the nation of Israel, Jeroboam had encouraged the Israelites to worship at Bethel instead of Jerusalem. Thus the Israelites who gathered at Bethel would regard Amos, a Judean, with suspicion. Yet Amos bravely condemned there the sins of Israel's neighbors. He also points to the iniquity of Israel and Judah. They both had rejected the God who had covenanted with them.

1:1 *Tekoa.* This town was about ten miles south of Jerusalem, in a region well-suited for raising sheep and goats.

1:3 *For three . . . and for four.* This stylistic device indicated the exhaustion of God's patience — the Syrians had continued to sin, again and again. This device is repeated as Amos speaks God's words against nation after sinful nation.

CHAPTER 1 **1** 2Sa 14:2; Am 7:10; Zec 14:5 **2** Joel 3:16; 1Sa 25:2; Isa 33:9 **3** Isa 8:4

Because they have threshed
Gilead [east of the Jordan
River] with sharp iron sledges
[having spikes that crushed and
shredded]. [2 Kin 10:32, 33]
4 "So I will send a fire [of war,
conquest, and destruction] upon
the house of Hazael,
And it shall devour the palaces
and strongholds of Ben-hadad
(Hazael's son).
5 "I also will break the bar [of the
gate] of Damascus,
And cut off *and* destroy the
inhabitant from the Valley of
Aven (Wickedness),
And the ruler who holds the
scepter, from Beth-eden
(Damascus);
And the people of Aram
[conquered by the Assyrians]
will go into exile to Kir,"
Says the LORD. [Ezek 30:17]

6 Thus says the LORD,
"For three transgressions of
Gaza [in Philistia] and for four
(multiplied delinquencies)
I will not reverse its punishment *or*
revoke My word concerning it,
Because [as slave traders] they
took captive the entire [Jewish]
population [of defenseless
Judean border villages, of which
none was spared]
And deported them to Edom [for
the slave trade]. [Joel 3:6]
7 "So I will send a fire [of war,
conquest, and destruction] on
the wall of Gaza
And it shall consume her
citadels.
8 "And I will cut off *and* destroy the
inhabitants from Ashdod,
And the ruler who holds the
scepter, from Ashkelon;
And I will unleash My power *and*
turn My hand [in judgment]
against Ekron,
And the rest of the Philistines [in
Gath and the towns dependent
on these four Philistine cities]
shall die,"
Says the Lord GOD. [Josh 13:3]

9 Thus says the LORD,
"For three transgressions of
Tyre and for four (multiplied
delinquencies)
I will not reverse its punishment *or*
revoke My word concerning it,
Because they [as middlemen]
deported an entire [Jewish]
population to Edom
And did not [seriously] remember
their covenant of brotherhood.
[1 Kin 5:1, 12; 9:12, 13]
10 "So I will send a fire [of war,
conquest, and destruction] on
the wall of Tyre,
And it shall consume her
citadels."

11 Thus says the LORD,
"For three transgressions of
Edom [the descendants of
Esau] and for four (multiplied
delinquencies)
I will not reverse its punishment *or*
revoke My word concerning it,
Because he pursued his brother
Jacob (Israel) with the sword,
Corrupting *and* stifling his
compassions *and* casting off all
mercy;
His destructive anger raged
continually,
And he maintained [and nurtured]
his wrath forever.

Gilead. This was the region on the east side of the Jordan from the Yarmuk River to the Dead Sea.

1:4 *I will send a fire . . . it shall devour the palaces.* Fire in an ancient city was a real threat. Cities were crowded with houses close together on very narrow streets; there was too little water to effectively fight them.

1:5 *the bar.* This was a large timber that barred the city gate from the inside. If it was broken, the city would lose its security and could be captured easily.

1:6 *Gaza.* This was one of the five principal cites of the Philistines.

1:11 *Edom.* This nation was located southeast of the Dead Sea. It controlled important caravan trade routes, and thus was deeply involved in commerce. Its citizens were descendants of Esau.

4 Jer 17:27 **5** Jer 51:30 **6** Jer 47:4,5 **7** Jer 47:1 **8** Zep 2:4; Ps 81:14; Eze 25:16 **9** Isa 23:1 **11** Isa 21:11; Jer 49:8

12 "So I will send a fire [of war,
conquest, and destruction] upon
Teman,
And it shall consume the citadels
of Bozrah [in Edom]."

13 Thus says the LORD,
"For three transgressions of the
children of Ammon and for four
(multiplied delinquencies)
I will not reverse its punishment *or*
revoke My word concerning it,
Because the Ammonites have
ripped open the pregnant
women of Gilead,
That they might enlarge their
border.
14 "So I will kindle a fire [of war,
conquest, and destruction] on
the wall of Rabbah [in Ammon]
And it shall devour its strongholds
Amid war cries *and* shouts of
alarm on the day of battle,
And a tempest on the day of the
whirlwind [when the enemy
captures the city].
15 "Their king shall go into exile,
He and his princes together," says
the LORD.

Judgment on Moab

2 THUS SAYS the LORD,
"For three transgressions of
Moab and for four (multiplied
delinquencies)
I will not reverse its punishment *or*
revoke My word concerning it,
Because he burned the bones
of the king of Edom [Esau's
descendant] into lime [and used
it to plaster a Moabite house].
2 "So I will send a fire [of war,
conquest, and destruction] upon
Moab
And it shall devour the
strongholds of Kerioth;
And Moab shall die amid tumult
and uproar,
With war cries *and* shouts of alarm
and the sound of the trumpet.
3 "I will also cut off *and* destroy the
ruler from its midst
And slay all the princes with him,"
says the LORD.

Judgment on Judah

4 Thus says the LORD,
"For three transgressions of
Judah and for four (multiplied
delinquencies)
I will not reverse its punishment *or*
revoke My word concerning it,
Because they have rejected the law
of the LORD [the sum of God's
instruction to His people]
And have not kept His
commandments;
But their lies [and their idols], after
which their fathers walked,
Caused them to go astray.
5 "So I will send a fire [of war,
conquest, and destruction by the
Babylonians] upon Judah
And it will devour the strongholds
of Jerusalem."

Judgment on Israel

6 Thus says the LORD,
"For three transgressions of
Israel and for four (multiplied
delinquencies)
I will not reverse its punishment *or*
revoke My word concerning it,
Because they sell the righteous
and innocent for silver
And the needy for the price of a
pair of sandals.

1:13 *Ammon.* The nation of Ammon was located east of Gilead on the edge of the desert. Its people were descended from one of the sons of Lot (Ge 19:36–38).

2:1 *burned the bones.* This act was believed to desecrate the remains of a deceased person, a heinous act in ancient times and a great dishonor to the person's memory.

2:6 *sell the righteous and innocent for silver.* In His law, God had instructed the Israelites to work off their debts through indentured service — administered humanely and for a strictly limited time (Lev 25:39–43; Dt 15:12). By Amos' day, those in power in Israel were taking advantage of the courts to sell debtors as slaves, termed "the righteous" here because they were the innocent victims of the corruption of the courts. ***for the price of a pair of sandals.*** This means for little or nothing.

12 Ob 9,10 **13** Jer 49:1; Eze 25:2 **14** Dt 3:11; Am 2:2 **15** Jer 49:3 **CHAPTER 2** **1** 2Ki 3:27 **2** Jer 48:41 **3** Nu 24:17; Jer 48:7 **4** Lev 26:14; Isa 28:15; Jer 16:19; Eze 20:13,16,18 **5** Jer 17:27; Hos 8:14 **6** Isa 29:21

ISRAEL AND JUDAH UNDER JEREBOAM II AND UZZIAH

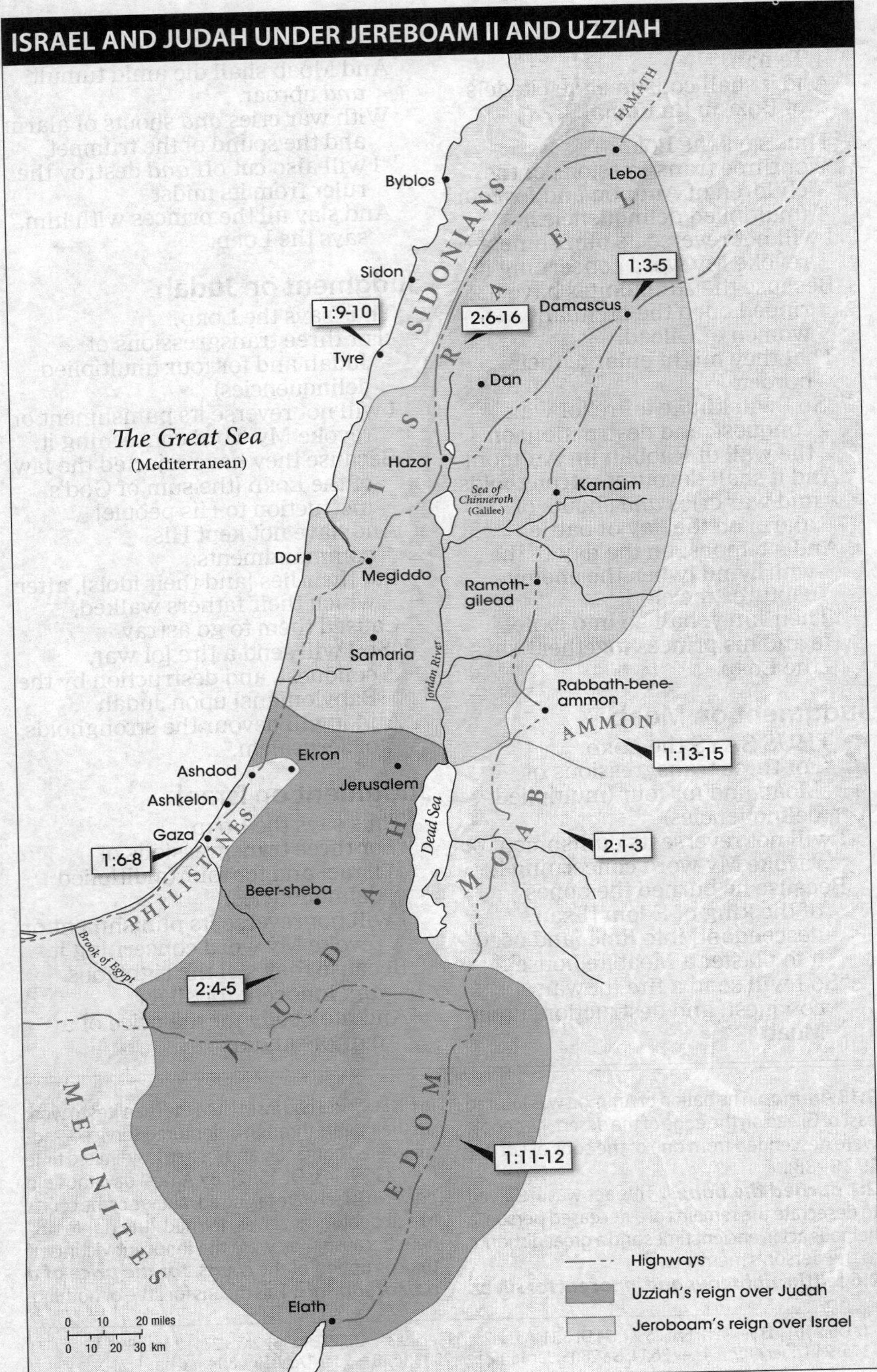

7 "These who pant after (long to see)
the dust of the earth on the head
of the helpless [as sign of their
grief and distress]
Also turn aside the way of the
humble;
And a man and his father will go
to the same girl
So that My holy name is profaned.
8 "They stretch out beside every
[pagan] altar on clothes taken
in pledge [to secure a loan,
disregarding God's command],
And in the house of their God
[in contempt of Him] they
frivolously drink the wine
[which has been] taken from
those who have been fined.
[Ex 22:26; Deut 24:12, 13]
9 "Yet it was I [not the false gods]
who destroyed the Amorite
before them,
Though his height was like the
height of the cedars,
And he was as strong as the oaks;
I even destroyed his fruit above
and his root below.
10 "Also it was I who brought you up
out of the land of Egypt,
And I led you forty years through
the wilderness
That you might possess the land of
the Amorite.
11 "Then I raised up some of your
sons to be prophets [who gave
you My revelation],
And some of your young men to be
Nazirites (dedicated ones).
Is this not true, O you children
of Israel?" says the LORD.
[Num 6:1–8]
12 "But you gave the Nazirites wine
to drink [despite their vows]
And commanded the prophets,
saying, 'You shall not prophesy!'
13 "Behold, I am weighted down
beneath you
As a cart that is weighted down
when it is full of sheaves.
14 "Flight will be lost to the swift [so
they will be unable to escape],
And the strong shall not
strengthen *nor* maintain his
power,
Nor shall the mighty man save his
own life.
15 "He who handles the bow will not
stand *his ground,*
The one who is swift of foot will
not escape,
Nor will he who rides the horse
save his life [from the invading
army].
16 "Even the bravest among the
warriors shall flee naked on that
day," says the LORD.

All the Families Are Guilty

3 HEAR THIS word that the LORD
has spoken against you, O children
of Israel, against the whole family
which I brought up from the land of
Egypt:

2 "I have known [chosen, cared for,
and loved] only you of all the
families of the earth;

2:7 *humble.* Those without power or influence should have been able to depend on the justice due them. Instead, justice was denied them. As a result, their lives were turned to poverty, oppression, and insecurity.
2:8 *clothes taken in pledge.* Clothing taken as security for a loan was supposed to be returned in the evening so that it could be used as bedding for the poor (Ex 22:26–27). The powerful in Israel were spreading the clothes out as beds for themselves beside the altars, in a show of empty, merciless piety.
2:9 *Yet it was I [not the false gods] who destroyed.* This emphatic statement underscores the fact that God had been Israel's champion, and the nation's success had not been its own doing. ***the Amorite.*** This refers to the previous inhabitants of the land of Canaan.
2:13 *I am weighted down beneath you.* This is a powerful metaphor of the burden of Israel's sin on the Lord. This is the same God Isaiah describes as measuring the waters of the earth in the hollow of His hand, measuring the heavens with the span of His hand, and weighing the mountains in His balance (Isa 40:12).
3:1 *the whole family which I brought up.* This phrase emphasizes the personal, intimate relationship that God had with Israel.
3:2 *I have known [chosen, cared for, and*

7 Am 5:12; Eze 22:11; Lev 20:3 **8** Ex 22:26; 1Co 8:10 **9** Nu 21:24; Dt 2:31; Isa 5:24; Mal 4:1 **10** Ex 12:51; Dt 2:7 **11** Nu 6:2; Jdg 13:5 **12** Isa 30:10; Jer 11:21; Mic 2:6 **13** Isa 1:14 **14** Jer 9:23; Ps 33:16 **CHAPTER 3** **2** Dt 7:6; Ps 147:19; Mt 11:22; Ro 2:9

Therefore I shall punish you for all
your wickedness."
3 Do two men walk together
unless they have made an
appointment?
4 Does a lion roar in the forest when
he has no prey?
Does a young lion growl from
his den if he has not captured
something?
5 Does a bird fall into a trap on the
ground when there is no bait in it?
Does a trap spring up from the
ground when it has caught
nothing at all? [Of course not!
So it is that Israel has earned
her impending judgment.]
6 If a trumpet is blown in a city
[warning of danger] will not the
people tremble?
If a disaster *or* misfortune occurs
in a city has not the LORD
caused it?
7 Surely the Lord GOD does nothing
Without revealing His secret plan
[of the judgment to come]
To His servants the prophets.
[Rev 10:7]
8 The lion has roared! Who will not
fear?
The Lord GOD has spoken [to
the prophets]! Who can but
prophesy? [Acts 4:20; 5:20, 29;
1 Cor 9:16]

9 Proclaim on the fortresses in Ash-
dod (Philistia) and on the citadels in
the land of Egypt, and say, "Assemble
yourselves on the mountains of Sa-
maria, and see the great confusion
within her and the oppressions *and*
abuse of authority in her midst.
10 "For they do not know how to do
right," says the LORD, "these who store
up violence and devastation [like trea-
sures] in their strongholds."
11 Therefore, thus says the Lord GOD,

"An adversary (Assyria), even one
surrounding the land,
Shall pull down your strength
from you
And your fortresses will be
looted."
12 Thus says the LORD,
"Just as the shepherd snatches
from the mouth of the lion a
couple of legs or a piece of the
[sheep's] ear [to prove to the
owner that he has not stolen the
animal],

loved] only you. God's relationship with Israel was not only intimate, it was exclusive. God had been faithful to Israel, yet Israel had not been faithful to God. For this reason, the nation would be judged.

3:2 Selection of Israel — The selection of Israel as a special nation to God was part of God's plan (Ro 11:2). Historically, the selection of Israel began with the Lord's promise to Abraham, "I will make you a great nation" (Ge 12:2). The name Israel actually comes from the new name which God gave to Abraham's grandson, Jacob, when they fought at the ford of Jabbok (Ge 32:28). This fact explains why his descendants are often called the children of Israel.

The motivation for the Lord's choice of Israel as His select nation did not lay in any special attraction the nation possessed. Its people were, in fact, the least in number among all the nations (Dt 7:6 – 8). Rather, the Lord chose them because of His love for them and because of His covenant with Abraham. This fact does not mean that God did not love other nations, because it was through Israel that He blessed all nations in Christ.

3:3 – 6 *Do two men walk together.* This series of rhetorical questions illustrates the seriousness, certainty, and righteousness of God's impending action against Israel. Each question is framed so as to require a resounding "no" as its answer.

3:11 *An adversary (Assyria), even one surrounding the land.* This verse pictures a formal sentencing of Israel in the presence of the witnesses whom God had called (v. 9). Sapping Israel's strength was exactly what Assyria did in the years following Amos' prophecies, finally putting an end to the nation in 722 BC.

3:12 *as the shepherd snatches from the mouth of the lion.* The hired shepherd was responsible to the owner for the safety of the sheep. He had to make good any loss, unless he could prove it was unavoidable. A lion taking a sheep was an unavoidable loss, but the shepherd had to prove that the lion had taken it. A couple of small bones or a piece of an ear was sufficient; the owner would recognize the lion's work. As complete as the destruction of a sheep by a lion would be the destruction of Israel that God would bring.

6 Isa 45:7 **7** Ge 6:13; Jn 15:15 **8** Ac 4:20 **10** Jer 4:22

So will the [remaining] children
of Israel living in Samaria be
snatched away
With the corner of a bed and [part
of] the damask covering of a
couch.
13 "Hear and testify against the
house of Jacob,"
Says the Lord GOD, the God of
hosts,
14 "On that day when I punish Israel's
transgressions,
I shall also punish the altars of
Bethel [with their golden calves];
And the horns of the altar shall be
cut off
And fall to the ground.
15 "And I shall tear down the winter
house with the summer house;
And the houses of ivory shall also
perish
And the great houses shall come to
an end,"
Says the LORD.

"Yet You Have Not Returned to Me"

4 HEAR THIS word, you [well-
fed, pampered] cows (women)
of Bashan who are on the
mountain of Samaria,
Who oppress the poor, who crush
the needy,
Who say to their husbands, "Bring
[the wine] now, and let us
drink!" [Ps 22:12; Ezek 39:18]
2 The Lord GOD has sworn [an oath]
by His holiness
That, "Behold, the days are
coming upon you
When they shall take you away
with meat hooks,
And the last of you with fish
hooks. [Ps 89:35]
3 "And you shall go out through the
breaches [made in the city wall],
Every woman straight before her
[unable to turn aside],
And you shall be cast to Harmon,"
Says the LORD.
4 "Come to Bethel [where the golden
calf is] and transgress;
In Gilgal [where idols are
worshiped] multiply
transgression;
Bring your sacrifices every
morning,
Your tithes every three days!
5 "Offer [by burning] a sacrifice of
thanksgiving of that which is
leavened,
And [boastfully] proclaim freewill
offerings, announce them.
For this you so love to do,
O children of Israel!"
Says the Lord GOD.
6 "I also gave you cleanness of teeth
[because of the famine] in all
your cities
And lack of bread in all your
places,
Yet you have not returned to Me
[in repentance]," says the LORD.
7 "Furthermore, I withheld the rain
from you

3:15 *the great houses shall come to an end.* The four houses mentioned here were all symbols of oppression. Many small inheritances had been stolen to form the large estates of the wealthy and powerful, where they built their opulent houses.
4:1 *cows (women) of Bashan.* This phrase refers to the well-fed women of Samaria. Bashan, the region east and northeast of the Sea of Galilee, was (and is) a prime grassland area renown for its cattle.
4:3 *breaches.* These were a symbol of the thoroughness of the destruction of the city and the homes that the people held so dear. In an undamaged city, the usual way in and out was the one main gate. But Samaria would be so ruined that the deportees would be driven straight through the breaches in the walls of their houses and their city.
4:6 – 11 *you have not returned to Me [in repentance], says the LORD.* This passage describes a series of five calamities that God had already sent upon the Israelites in an effort to drive them to repentance. A striking feature of this narrative is God's emphatic claim that the Israelites had brought these disasters on themselves. They had repeatedly failed to understand the implications of the disasters.

15 Jer 36:22; Jdg 3:20; 1Ki 22:39 **CHAPTER 4** **1** Ps 22:12; Eze 39:18 **2** Ps 89:35; Jer 16:16; Hab 1:15 **3** Eze 12:5 **4** Eze 20:39; Hos 4:15; Nu 28:3; Dt 14:28 **5** Lev 7:13; 22:18; Dt 12:6 **6** Isa 26:11; Jer 5:3; Hag 2:17

When *there were* still three
months until the harvest.
Then I would send rain on one
city,
And on another city I would not
send rain;
One piece of ground was
rained on,
While the part not rained on
would dry up.
8 "So [the people of] two or three
cities would stagger into one city
to drink water,
But would not be satisfied;
Yet you have not returned to Me
[in repentance]," says the LORD.
9 "I wounded you with blight [from
the hot, blasting east wind] and
with mildew;
And the caterpillar devoured
Your many gardens and
vineyards, your fig trees and
your olive trees;
Yet you have not returned to Me
[in repentance]," says the LORD.
10 "I sent a plague among you like
[those of] Egypt;
I killed your young men with
the sword and I captured your
horses,
I made the stench of your camp
rise up into your nostrils;
Yet you have not returned to Me
[in repentance]," says the LORD.
[2 Kin 8:12; 13:3, 7]
11 "I overthrew *and* destroyed
[some among] you, as [I, your]
God overthrew Sodom and
Gomorrah,
And you were [rescued] like a log
pulled out of the flame;
Yet you have not returned to Me
[in repentance]," says the LORD.
[Gen 19:24, 25; Is 13:19; Jer 49:18]
12 "Therefore this is what I shall do to
you, O Israel;
Because I will do this to you,
Prepare to meet your God [in
judgment], O Israel!"
13 For behold, He who forms the
mountains and creates the
wind
And declares to man what are His
thoughts,
He who makes the dawn into
darkness
And treads on the heights of the
earth—
The LORD God of hosts is His
name. [Ps 139:2; Dan 2:28]

"Seek Me that You May Live"

5 HEAR THIS word which I take up for you as a funeral song, O house of Israel:

2 She has fallen, she will not rise
again—
The virgin Israel.
She lies neglected on her land;
There is no one to raise her up.
3 For thus says the Lord GOD,
"The city which goes forth a
thousand *strong*
Will have a hundred left,
And the one which goes forth a
hundred *strong*
Will have ten left to the house of
Israel."

4 For thus says the LORD to the house
of Israel,

4:10 *like [those of] Egypt.* This fourth calamity suggests that God was reminding Israel of the ten plagues that preceded their exodus from Egypt; these included epidemic diseases and other disasters.
4:11 *you were [rescued] like a log pulled out of the flame.* This refers to a stick snatched from a fire with one end already ablaze. Here it was a vivid metaphor for God's last-minute rescue of most of Israel from the fate He brought upon some of its cities and territories.
4:12 *Prepare to meet your God [in judgment], O Israel.* Because Israel had not returned to God through these five calamities, it would have to meet God Himself. To be confronted — inescapably — by the God it had scorned and rejected would be a fate more terrible than Israel could imagine.
5:2 *The virgin Israel.* This term depicts the nation as a young maiden, cut off from her life before it had really begun. ***on her land.*** This is a reminder that the land had been God's gift to Israel. By their faithlessness, the people had turned God's gift into the place of their death and burial.

9 Dt 28:22; Hag 2:17; Joel 1:4 **10** Ex 9:3,6; Dt 28:27; Ps 78:50 **11** Ge 19:24; Isa 13:19 **12** Eze 13:5 **13** Ps 139:2; Da 2:28; Mic 1:3; Isa 47:4; Jer 10:16 **CHAPTER 5** **1** Jer 7:29 **4** Jer 29:13; Isa 55:3

"Seek Me [search diligently for Me
and regard Me as more essential
than food] so that you may live.
[2 Chr 15:2; Jer 29:13]
5 "But do not resort to Bethel [to
worship the golden calf]
Nor enter [idolatrous] Gilgal,
Nor cross over to Beersheba [and
its idols];
For Gilgal will certainly go into
captivity *and* exile,
And Bethel will come to nothing.
6 "Seek the LORD [search diligently
for Him and long for Him as
your most essential need] so that
you may live,
Or He will rush down like a
[devouring] fire, O house of
Joseph,
And there will be no one to quench
the flame for [idolatrous] Bethel,
7 "For those [shall be consumed]
who turn justice into wormwood
(bitterness)
And cast righteousness down to
the earth."

8 He who made the [cluster of
stars called] Pleiades and [the
constellation] Orion,
Who turns deep darkness into the
morning
And darkens the day into night,
Who calls for the waters of the sea
And pours them out on the surface
of the earth,
The LORD is His name.
9 It is He who causes [sudden]
destruction to flash forth on the
strong
So that destruction comes on the
fortress.

10 They hate the one who reprimands
[the unrighteous] in the [court
held at the city] gate [regarding
him as unreasonable and
rejecting his reprimand],
And they detest him who speaks
[the truth] with integrity *and*
honesty.
11 Therefore, because you impose
heavy rent on the poor
And demand a tribute (food-tax) of
grain from them,
Though you have built [luxurious]
houses of square stone,
You will not live in them;
You have planted beautiful
vineyards, but you will not
drink their wine.

5:6 *O house of Joseph.* This phrase refers to the whole nation.
5:8 *the [cluster of stars called] Pleiades.* This refers to a cluster of stars within the constellation Taurus, one of the twelve signs of the Zodiac. One of Israel's idolatries was astral worship. Far from being deities, Amos asserted, the constellations also were God's creations. ***Orion.*** This is a reference to a prominent constellation in the southern sky in the shape of a hunter.
5:10 *gate.* This was the location of the town court, where justice was to be upheld in all legal proceedings whether civil or criminal.
5:11 – 15 God's Justice — The Israelites in Amos' day had lost sight of God's commands to treat the poor compassionately. There is no record that Israel ever practiced the year of Jubilee (Lev 25:11) that is part of Old Testament law, for instance.

As many of the prophets did, Amos called on the Israelites to practice justice and see to it that the poor were not abused. He made it clear that the rich in his day were taking advantage of the poor. The justice system was ineffective because of rampant bribery. The prophets repeatedly made the point that the sacrifices were not enough. The sacrificial process needed to be connected with a response in behavior. God's justice demanded more than the sacrifices. It demanded obedience.

Amos teaches us to be observant about where this injustice is being practiced. He teaches us to look for movements, forces, or programs that can work against the accumulation of power and unjustly gained wealth.

One of the first things the Jerusalem church did when it formed was to put in place a system of some kind to care for the widows and orphans (Ac 6:1 – 4). Belief in God included an understanding of His desire for justice and the believer's need to act on it.
5:11 *And demand a tribute (food-tax) of grain from them.* To take grain taxes from the poor was to put them at risk of starvation if the harvest had not been bountiful. Yet the rich and powerful had sufficient resources to build

---

5 Am 4:4; Am 8:14; Hos 4:15 **7** Am 6:12 **8** Job 9:9; Ps 104:20; Job 38:34; Am 4:13 **10** Isa 29:21; 1Ki 22:8
11 Mic 6:15

12 For I know your transgressions are
many and your sins are great
(shocking, innumerable),
You who distress the righteous
and take bribes,
And turn away from the poor
in the [court of the city] gate
[depriving them of justice].
13 Therefore, he who is prudent *and*
has insight will keep silent at
such a [corrupt and evil] time,
for it is an evil time [when
people will not listen to truth
and will disregard those of good
character].

14 Seek (long for, require) good and
not evil, that you may live;
And so may the LORD God of hosts
be with you,
Just as you have said!
15 Hate evil and love good,
And establish justice in the [court
of the city] gate.
Perhaps the LORD God of hosts
Will be gracious to the remnant
of Joseph [that is, those who
remain after God's judgment].

16 Therefore, thus says the LORD God
of hosts, the Lord,

"There is wailing in all the public
plazas,
And in all the streets they say,
'Alas! Alas!'
And they call the farmers to
mourning [for those who have
died]
And professional mourners to
wailing.
17 "And in all vineyards *there is*
wailing,
For I will pass through your midst
[in judgment]," says the LORD.
[Ex 12:12]
18 Woe (judgment is coming) to you
who desire the day of the LORD
[expecting rescue from the
Gentiles]!
Why would you want the day of
the LORD?
It is darkness (judgment) and
not light [and rescue and
prosperity];
19 It is as if a man runs from a lion
[escaping one danger]
And a bear meets him [so he dies
anyway],
Or goes home, and leans with his
hand against the wall
And a snake bites him.
20 Will not the day of the LORD be
darkness, instead of light,
Even very dark with no brightness
in it?

21 "I hate, I despise *and* reject your
[sacred] feasts,
And I do not take delight in your
solemn assemblies.
22 "Even though you offer Me your
burnt offerings and your grain
offerings,
I will not accept them;
And I will not even look at the
peace offerings of your fattened
animals.
23 "Take the noise of your songs
away from Me [they are an
irritation]!

---

luxurious houses for themselves. God promised that the rich would not enjoy their luxury stolen from the lifeblood of the poor and powerless.

5:12 *your sins are great.* Israel's leaders did not sin incidentally or furtively; they sinned brazenly and habitually, as though God had never revealed Himself and His standards of justice and mercy.

5:18 *the day of the LORD.* The popular theology of Amos' time apparently looked forward to this day as the time of Israel's restoration to military, political, and economic greatness, perhaps to the greatness of the reigns of David and Solomon. Amos declared such hopes futile, even pitiable. What the people looked forward to as a day of light and triumph would rise upon them instead as a day of darkness and ruin.

5:19 *bear ... snake.* These images evoke the terror that follows when a person escapes a terrible danger and is exhausted and relieved, only to find a worse danger so close at hand that it is inescapable.

5:21–23 *feasts ... solemn assemblies.* By stating He would no longer accept Israel's sacrifices or listen to them, God was rejecting Israel's worship as hypocritical, dishonest, and meaningless.

12 Am 2:6; Isa 29:21 **13** Am 6:10 **14** Mic 3:11 **15** Ro 12:9; Joel 2:14 **16** Jer 9:17 **17** Ex 12:12 **18** Isa 5:19; Jer 17:15; Joel 2:2 **19** Jer 48:44 **21** Isa 1:11-16; Lev 26:31 **22** Isa 66:3; Mic 6:6,7

I shall not even listen to the
melody of your harps.
24 "But let justice run down like
waters
And righteousness like an
ever-flowing stream [flowing
abundantly].

25 "Did you bring Me sacrifices and
grain offerings during those forty
years in the wilderness, O house of
Israel? [Certainly not!]
26 "You carried along your king Sik-
kuth and Kayyun [your man-made
gods of Saturn], your images of your
star-god which you made for your-
selves [but you brought Me none of the
appointed sacrifices].
27 "Therefore, I will send you to go
into exile far beyond Damascus," says
the LORD, whose name is the God of
hosts. [Acts 7:42, 43]

"Those at Ease in Zion"

6 WOE (JUDGMENT IS COMING)
TO those who are at ease *and*
carefree in Zion (Judah)
And to those on the mountain of
Samaria who feel secure,
The distinguished men of the
foremost of nations,
To whom the house of Israel
comes. [Luke 6:24, 25]
2 Go over to Calneh [in Babylonia]
and look,
And from there go [north of
Damascus] to the great city of
Hamath;
Then go down to Gath of the
Philistines.
Are they better than these
kingdoms [of yours],
Or is their territory greater than
yours?
3 Do you put off the day of
punishment,
Yet cause the seat of violence to
come near?

4 Those who lie on [luxurious] beds
of ivory
And lounge around out on their
couches,
And eat lambs from the flock
And calves from the midst of the
stall,
5 Who improvise to the sound of the
harp—
Like David they have composed
songs for themselves—
[1 Chr 23:5]
6 Who drink wine from sacrificial
bowls
And anoint themselves with the
finest oils [reflecting their
unrestrained celebration];
Yet they are not grieved over
the ruin of Joseph (Israel).
[Gen 49:22, 23]
7 Therefore, they will now go
into exile with the first of the
captives,
And the cultic revelry *and*
banqueting of those who lounge
around [on their luxurious
couches] will pass away.

8 The Lord GOD has sworn [an oath]
by Himself—the LORD God of
hosts, says:
"I loathe *and* reject the [self-
centered] arrogance of Jacob
(Israel),
And I hate his palaces *and*
citadels;
Therefore, I shall hand over the
[idolatrous] city [of Samaria]
with all that it contains [to the
Assyrian invaders]."

6:3 *you put off the day of punishment.* This refers to those who insisted that Israel was too strong for destruction to fall upon the nation any time soon.
6:4 – 6 *lambs . . . calves*. This passage describes the extravagant living indulged in by the rich and paid for with the wealth stolen from the poor. Meat was a luxury for most families of the ancient Middle East, consumed only on special occasions. Meat on a daily basis was the privilege only of the rich and powerful. The upper classes of Israel were so engrossed in their own privileges and luxuries that they cared nothing for the affliction of their fellow Israelites, though it was their transgressions that had caused it.

24 Hos 6:6; Mic 6:8 **25** Dt 32:17; Jos 24:14; Isa 43:23 **26** 1Ki 11:33 **27** 2Ki 17:6; Am 4:13 **CHAPTER 6 1** Lk 6:24; Ex 19:5 **2** Jer 2:10; Isa 10:9; 2Ki 18:34; Na 3:8 **3** Eze 12:27; Am 5:18; Am 5:12; Ps 94:20 **5** Isa 5:12; 1Ch 23:5 **6** Ge 37:25 **8** Jer 51:14; Ps 47:4; Eze 24:21

[9]And it shall come to pass that if there remain ten men in one house, they shall die [by the pestilence that comes with war].
[10]Then one's uncle, or his undertaker, shall come to bring the [disease-infected] body out of the house, [to cremate it], and he will say to another in the farthest part of the house, "Is there anyone else with you?" And that one will say, "No one." Then he will respond, "Hush! Keep quiet! For the name of the LORD is not to be mentioned [even casually, for fear that we might invoke even more punishment]." [1 Sam 31:12]
[11]For behold, the LORD is going to command that the great house be smashed to pieces and the small house to fragments.

[12]Do horses run on rocks?
Do men plow rocks with oxen? [Of course not!]
Yet you have turned justice into poison
And the fruit of righteousness into wormwood (bitterness),
[13]You who [self-confidently] rejoice in Lo-debar (Nothing),
Who say, "Have we not by our own strength taken Karnaim (Strength) for ourselves?"
[14]"For behold, I am going to stir up a nation against you,
O house of Israel," says the LORD, the God of hosts,
"And they will afflict *and* torment you [to the entire limits of Israel] from the entrance of Hamath [in the north]
To the brook of the Arabah [in the south]."

Warning Through Visions

7 THUS THE Lord GOD showed me [a vision], and behold, He was forming a swarm of locusts when the spring crop began to sprout. And behold, the spring crop was after the king's mowing.
[2]And when the locusts had finished eating the plants of the land, then I said,

"O Lord GOD, please forgive!
How can Jacob stand,
For he is so small [that he cannot endure this]?"
[3]The LORD revoked this sentence.
"It shall not take place," said the LORD.

[4]Thus the Lord GOD showed me, and behold, the Lord GOD called for punishment with fire, and it devoured the great deep [underground sources of water] and began to consume the land.
[5]Then I said,

"O Lord GOD, please stop!
How can Jacob stand,
For he is so small [that he cannot endure this]?"
[6]The LORD revoked this sentence.
"This also shall not be," said the Lord GOD.

[7]Thus He showed me [a vision], and behold, the Lord was standing by a vertical wall with a plumb line in His hand [to determine if the wall was straight or if it needed to be destroyed]. [2 Kin 21:13; Is 34:11]

7:1 *the king's mowing.* These words imply that the king took the first harvest of hay as a tax. Thus a swarm of locusts devouring the late crop would leave the people with nothing for themselves, inflicting a crippling economic blow.
7:2 – 3 *How can Jacob stand.* If God carried out the threatened punishment, Jacob (the nation of Israel) might be destroyed. One function of the prophet was to serve as intercessor for the people before God. Amos prayed that the vision decreed in heaven might be halted before it was accomplished on earth. The basis of Amos' petition lay in the true assessment of Israel's position. They were not large and strong, as they thought; rather they were small and weak. In response to Amos' intercession, and out of His own love for Israel, God stayed His decree.
7:7 – 9 *a plumb line.* This apparatus is a string with a weight tied to one end, used to establish a vertical line so that a wall can be built straight. ***what do you see.*** Unlike the first two visions of natural disasters, the visions of the plumb line and the basket of summer fruit were not self-explanatory. God asked Amos what he saw,

10 Am 5:13; Am 8:3 **11** Isa 55:11; Am 3:15 **12** Hos 10:4 **14** Jer 5:15; 1Ki 8:65 **CHAPTER 7** **2** Isa 51:19 **3** Dt 32:36; Jnh 3:10; Jas 5:16 **5** ver. 2,3

[8]The LORD said to me, "Amos, what do you see?" And I said, "A plumb line." Then the Lord said,

"Behold, I am setting a plumb line
[as a standard]
Among My people Israel [showing
the defectiveness of the nation,
requiring judgment].
I shall not spare them any longer.
[The door of mercy is shut.]
[9]"And the [idolatrous] high places of
Isaac (Israel) will be devastated
and deserted,
And the sanctuaries of Israel will
be in ruins.
Then I shall rise up against
the house of Jeroboam with
the sword [and destroy the
monarchy]."

Amos Accused, Answers

[10]Then Amaziah, the priest of Bethel [site of the golden calf shrine], sent *word* to Jeroboam king of Israel, saying, "Amos has conspired against you in the midst of the house of Israel; the land is unable to endure all his words. [1 Kin 12:31, 32]
[11]"For in this way Amos has said, 'Jeroboam will die by the sword and Israel will certainly go from its land into exile.' "
[12]Then Amaziah said to Amos, "Go, you seer, run for your life [from Israel] to the land of Judah [your own country] and eat bread and live as a prophet there!
[13]"But do not prophesy any longer at Bethel, for it is the king's sanctuary and a royal residence." [Luke 10:10–12]
[14]Then Amos replied to Amaziah, "I am not a prophet [by profession], nor am I a prophet's son; I am a herdsman and a grower of sycamore figs.
[15]"But the LORD took me as I followed the flock and the LORD said to me, 'Go, prophesy to My people Israel.'
[16]"Now therefore, listen to the word of the LORD: You say, 'You shall not prophesy against Israel nor shall you speak against the house of Isaac.'
[17]"Therefore, thus says the LORD, 'Your wife shall become a prostitute in the city [when the Assyrians capture Samaria] and your sons and your daughters shall fall by the sword, and your land shall be divided by a measuring line; you yourself shall die in an unclean *and* defiled [pagan] land, and Israel shall certainly go from its land into exile.' "

Basket of Fruit and Israel's Captivity

8 THUS THE Lord GOD showed me [a vision], and behold, *there was* a basket of [overripe] summer fruit.
[2]And He said, "Amos, what do you see?" And I said, "A basket of summer fruit." Then the LORD said to me, "The

---

then explained the vision's meaning. Also unlike the first two visions, God did not give Amos opportunity to intercede, nor did He relent. These judgments would be executed. ***the house of Jeroboam.*** This is a metaphor for the nation.
7:10 – 11 ***Amaziah.*** Amaziah was the priest in charge of the temple at Bethel, who informed the king about the prophet who was making threats against the king's house. Amaziah was reacting to Amos' third vision which ended with God's promise to bring the sword against the house of Jeroboam. Amaziah regarded Amos' words as a political threat, and reported them not as a prophecy from God, but as Amos' call to revolt.
7:14 – 17 ***nor am I a prophet's son.*** Amos' answer to Amaziah came in two parts. First, he denied being a prophet by profession. He did not come from a family of prophets, nor had he been trained in prophecy. Amos made it clear that he had neither desired nor sought his prophetic task. ***You wife shall become a prostitute.*** The only way the spouse of an important official like Amaziah would be reduced to prostitution would be if all her family and all her resources were taken away and she were left to fend entirely for herself.
8:1 – 3 ***a basket of [overripe] summer fruit.*** The fruits that came at the end of the harvest in late summer included grapes, pomegranates, and figs. ***The end has come.*** Amos could not have discerned the meaning of this vision until God's pronouncement. Israel's wickedness was about to result in a harvest of judgment.

8 See 2Ki 21:13; Isa 28:17; La 2:8; Mic 7:18 **9** Fulfilled 2Ki 15:10 **10** 1Ki 12:32; 2Ki 14:23 **13** Am 2:12; 1Ki 12:32
14 1Ki 20:35; 2Ki 2:5; Zec 13:5 **16** Eze 21:2; Mic 2:6 **17** Jer 28:12; 29:21,32; Isa 13:16; La 5:11; Hos 4:13; Zec 14:2
CHAPTER 8 **2** Eze 7:2; Am 7:8

end has come for My people Israel.
I will spare them no longer [for the
nation is ripe for judgment].
3 “In that day, the songs of the palace
shall turn to wailing,” says the Lord
God. “There will be many dead bodies;
in [sacred] silence they will throw them
everywhere.”
4 Hear this, you who trample down
the needy, and do away with the poor
of the land,
5 saying,

“When will the New Moon
[festival] be over
So that we may sell grain,
And the Sabbath ended so that we
may open the wheat *market*,
Making the ephah [measure]
smaller and the shekel bigger
[that is, selling less for a higher
price]
And to cheat by falsifying the
scales,
6 So that we may buy the poor [as
slaves] for silver [since they are
unable to support themselves]
And the needy for a pair of
sandals,
And that we may sell the leftovers
of the wheat [as if it were a good
grade of grain]?”

7 The Lord has sworn [an oath] by
the pride of Jacob,
“Surely I shall never forget [nor
leave unpunished] any of their
[rebellious] acts.
8 “Because of this [coming
judgment] will the land not
quake
And everyone mourn who dwells
in it?
Indeed, all of it shall rise up like
the Nile,
And it will be tossed around [from
the impact of judgment]
And [afterward] subside again like
the Nile of Egypt.
9 “It shall come about in that day,”
says the Lord God,
“That I shall cause the sun to go
down at noon,
And I shall darken the earth in
broad daylight. [Ezek 32:7–10]
10 “And I shall turn your festivals *and*
feasts into mourning
And all your songs into dirges
(funeral poems to be sung);
And I shall cause sackcloth to be
put on everyone’s loins
And baldness on every head
[shaved for mourning].
And I shall make that time like *a
time of* mourning for an only
son [who has died],
And the end of it shall be like a
bitter day.

11 “Behold, the days are coming,”
says the Lord God,
“When I will send hunger over the
land,
Not hunger for bread or a thirst for
water,
But rather [a hunger] for hearing
the words of the Lord.
12 “People shall stagger from sea
to sea [to the very ends of the
earth]
And from the north even to the
east;
They will roam here and there
to seek the word of the Lord
[longing for it as essential for
life],

8:5 *Making the ephah [measure] smaller.* This was a way of cheating the customer of value received for price paid. ***shekel.*** This was a unit of money, so making it “bigger” was also a way of cheating.

8:12 – 13 *sea to sea.* This meant from the Dead Sea to the Mediterranean. ***the beautiful virgins And [even the vigorous] young men.*** This refers to those who are most vigorous to survive.

8:14 *Dan … Beersheba.* This was a phrase that indicated the limits of the Israelite territory. In Amos’ day, Beersheba was in the kingdom of Judah. Israel could swear oaths by the Lord, claiming they loyally worshiped Him from the extreme north to the extreme south of His land, but that would not relieve the famine of God’s word.

3 Am 5:23; Am 6:9,10 **4** Ps 14:4; Pr 30:14 **5** Neh 13:15; Mic 6:10 **6** Am 2:6 **7** Am 6:8; Hos 8:13 **8** Hos 4:3; Am 9:5 **9** Job 5:14; Isa 13:10; 59:9,10; Jer 15:9; Mic 3:6 **10** Isa 15:2,3; Jer 48:37; Eze 27:31; Jer 6:26; Zec 12:10 **11** 1Sa 3:1; Ps 74:9; Eze 7:26

But they will not find it.
[13]"In that day the beautiful virgins
And [even the vigorous] young men shall faint from thirst.
[14]"Those who swear [their oaths] by the sin (guilt) of Samaria *or* Ashimah (a pagan goddess),
Who say, 'By the life of your god [the golden calf], O Dan!'
And [swear], 'By the life of the way of [idolatrous] Beersheba,'
They shall fall and not rise again."

God's Judgment Unavoidable

9 I SAW [in a vision] the Lord standing at the altar, and He said,

"Destroy the capitals (tops) of the pillars so that the thresholds will shake,
And break them on the heads of all of the people!
Then I will kill the rest of them with the sword;
They will not have a fugitive who will get away,
Or a survivor who will escape.
[2]"Though they dig into Sheol [to hide in the deepest pit],
From there My hand will take them [for judgment];
And though they climb up to heaven [to hide in the realm of light],
From there will I bring them down [for judgment].
[3]"Though they hide on the summit of [Mount] Carmel,
I will track them down and take them from there;
And though they hide from My sight on the floor of the sea,
From there I shall command the serpent and it will bite them.
[4]"And though they go into captivity before their enemies,
From there I shall command the sword to kill them,
And I will set My eyes against them for evil (judgment, punishment) and not for good [that is, not for correction leading to restoration]."

[5]The Lord God of hosts [the Omnipotent Ruler],
It is He who touches the earth [in judgment] and it melts,
And all who dwell on it mourn [in despair and fear],
And all of it rises up like the Nile
And subsides like the Nile of Egypt;
[6]It is He who builds His upper chambers in the heavens
And has established His vaulted dome (the firmament of heaven) over the earth,
He who calls to the waters of the sea
And pours them out on the face of the earth—
The Lord is His name.

[7]"Are you [degenerate ones] not as the [despised] sons of Ethiopia to Me,
O sons of Israel?" says the Lord.
"Have I not brought up Israel from the land of Egypt,
And the Philistines from Caphtor and the Arameans (Syrians) from Kir?
[8]"Behold, the eyes of the Lord God are on the sinful [northern] kingdom [of Israel's ten tribes]
And I shall destroy it from the face of the earth;
But I shall not totally destroy the house of Jacob [that is, the entire nation of Israel],"
Says the Lord.

9:2 *Sheol ... heaven.* In this imagery, Israel's fugitives from God's judgment could escape neither up nor down; God would find them no matter where in the universe they fled.
9:3 *summit of [Mount] Carmel.* This peak represented the highest point on earth. Whether as high as that, or as low as the bottom of the sea, the earth would provide no escape.
9:8 *the sinful [northern] kingdom.* This is Israel. ***I shall not totally destroy.*** This was a glimmer of hope in a long passage of judgment and doom. God's judgment would be thorough, but a remnant would survive.

14 Hos 4:15; Dt 9:21; Am 5:5 **CHAPTER 9** **1** Ps 68:21; Hab 3:13; Am 2:14 **2** Ps 139:8; Jer 51:53 **4** Lev 26:33; 17:10 **5** Mic 1:4; Am 8:8 **6** Ps 104:3; Am 5:8; Am 4:13 **7** Jer 47:4; Dt 2:23; Jer 47:4; Am 1:5 **8** ver. 4; Jer 30:11; Ob 16,17

9 "For behold, I am commanding,
And I shall shake *and* sift the house of Israel among all nations [and cause it to tremble]
Like *grain* is shaken in a sieve [removing the chaff],
But not a kernel [of the faithful remnant] shall fall to the ground *and* be lost [from My sight]. [Lev 26:33; Deut 28:64; Hos 9:17]
10 "All the sinners among My people will die by the sword,
Those who say [defiantly], 'The disaster will not overtake or confront us.'

The Restoration of Israel

11 "In that day I shall raise up *and* restore the fallen tabernacle (booth) of David,
And wall up its breaches [in the city walls];
I will also raise up *and* restore its ruins
And rebuild it as it was in the days of old,
12 That they may possess the remnant of Edom (ancient enemies)
And all the nations that are called by My name,"
Says the LORD who does this. [Acts 15:15–17]
13 "Behold, the days are coming," says the LORD,
"When the plowman shall overtake the one who gathers the harvest,
And the one who treads the grapes [shall overtake] him who sows the seed [for the harvest continues until planting time];
When the mountains will drip sweet wine
And all the hills shall melt [that is, everything that was once barren will overflow with streams of blessing]. [Lev 26:5; Joel 3:18]
14 "Also I shall bring back the exiles of My people Israel,
And they will rebuild the deserted *and* ruined cities and inhabit them:
They will also plant vineyards and drink their wine,
And make gardens and eat their fruit.
15 "I will also plant them on their land,
And they shall never again be uprooted from their land
Which I have given them,"
Says the LORD your God.

9:9 *Like grain is shaken in a sieve.* Sifting grain was the final operation in cleaning it before gathering it into storage. In winnowing, all the chaff was blown away; only pebbles and small clumps of mud remained with the grain. The sieve was constructed with holes that were sized so other debris were retained in the sieve.

9:13 *the plowman shall overtake the one who gathers the harvest.* For this to happen it would mean such an abundant harvest that it would last all summer and would not be gathered until the plowing had started again. Grapes were harvested from mid-summer to early fall. The grain crop was sown after the plowing in late fall.

9:15 *plant them on their land.* God does not abandon His promises or His covenant, nor does He leave His people without hope. God's punishment is certain, but His restoration is just as certain. The word of hope for God's people of old is valid also for God's people of today.

10 Am 6:3 **11** Ac 15:16 **12** Ob 19; Nu 24:18 **13** Lev 26:5; Joel 3:18 **14** Jer 30:3; Isa 61:4 **15** Eze 34:28

THE BOOK OF

OBADIAH

▸ **AUTHOR:** Obadiah was an obscure prophet who probably lived in the Southern Kingdom of Judah. It is assumed, however, that he was not a priest since his father is not mentioned and nothing is given of his background. There are 13 Obadiah's in the Old Testament. Four of the better prospects for this Obadiah are: (1) the officer in Ahab's palace that hid God's prophets in a cave (1Ki 18:3); (2) one of the officials sent out by Jehoshaphat to teach the law in the cities of Judah (2Ch 17:7); (3) one of the overseers who took part in repairing the temple under Josiah (2Ch 34:12); or (4) a priest in the time of Nehemiah (Neh 10:5).

▸ **TIMES:** c. 840 BC ▸ **KEY VERSE:** Ob 10

▸ **THEME:** Obadiah is a prophecy against Edom, the nation that descended from Esau. Edom included the area south and east of the Dead Sea. Throughout most of Old Testament history, if Edom is mentioned, it is in the context of some kind of skirmish. This friction started when the king of Edom refused to let the Israelites cross his territory as they journeyed towards the promised land in Numbers 20:14 – 21. When Israel and Judah were taken into exile, Edom stood by and watched. The purpose of Obadiah seems clear. He is out to encourage the Israelites in the context of captivity. God will rescue his people.

Edom Will Be Humbled

1 THE VISION of Obadiah.

Thus says the Lord GOD concerning Edom—
We have heard a report from the LORD,
And an ambassador has been sent among the nations, *saying*,
"Arise, and let us rise up against Edom for battle [with the LORD as commander]!" [Ps 137:7; Is 34:1–15; 63:1–6; Jer 49:7–22; Ezek 25:12–14]
2 "Behold [Edom], I shall [humiliate you and] make you small among the nations;
You are greatly despised. [Ezek 35]
3 "The pride *and* arrogance of your heart have deceived you,
You who live in the clefts *and* lofty security of the rock (Sela),
Whose dwelling place is high,
Who say [boastfully] in your heart,
'Who will bring me down to earth?'
4 "Though you build [your nest] on high like the eagle,
Though you set your nest among the stars,
I will bring you down from there," says the LORD.

---

2 *I shall [humiliate you and] make you small.* God would bring about a reversal of Edom's inflated self-importance.
3 *Whose dwelling place is high.* Some of the mountain peaks of Edom reached over 6,000 feet. Jerusalem is about 2,300 feet above sea level. ***Who will bring me down to earth?*** Edom's presumed physical safety led the Edomites to become haughty; this would be their downfall.
4 *build [your nest] on high like the eagle.*

1 Isa 21:11; Eze 25:12; Joel 3:19; Mal 1:3; Jer 49:14 **3** Isa 14:13-15; Rev 18:7 **4** Job 20:6; Hab 2:9

5 "If thieves came to you,
If robbers by night—
How you will be ruined!—
Would they not steal only until
they had enough?
If grape gatherers came to you,
Would they not leave some grapes
for gleaning? [Jer 49:9]
6 "How Esau (Edom) shall be
ransacked [by men who come to
ravage with divine approval]!
How his hidden treasures shall be
searched out!
7 "All the men allied with you
Shall send you on your way to the
border;
The men who were at peace with
you
Shall deceive you and overpower
you;
Those who eat your bread [those
you trust]
Shall set a hostile ambush for you.
(There is no understanding of it.)
8 "Will I not on that day," says the
LORD,
"Destroy the wise men from Edom
[removing all wisdom]
And understanding from the
mountain of Esau?
9 "And your mighty men shall be
dismayed *and* demoralized,
O Teman,
So that everyone from the
mountain of Esau may be cut off
in the slaughter.

Edom Denounced

10 "Because of the violence you did
against your brother Jacob,
Shame shall cover you
[completely],
And you shall be cut off forever.
11 "On the day that [Jerusalem was
destroyed] you stood aloof [from
your brother Jacob]—
On the day that strangers took his
forces captive *and* carried off
his wealth,
And foreigners entered his gates
And cast lots for Jerusalem
[dividing the city for plunder]—
You too were like one of them
[collaborating with the enemy].
[Num 20:18–20; Amos 1:11, 12]
12 "Do not gaze *and* gloat [in
triumph] over your brother's
day,
The day when his misfortune
came.
Do not rejoice over the sons of
Judah
In the day of their destruction;
Do not speak arrogantly [jeering
and maliciously mocking]
In the day of their distress.
13 "Do not enter the gate of My
people
In the day of their disaster;
Yes, you, do not look [with delight]
on their misery
In the day of their ruin,
And do not loot treasures
In the day of their ruin.
14 "Do not stand at the crossroad
To cut down those [of Judah] who
escaped;
And do not hand over [to the
enemy] those [of Judah] who
survive
In the day of their distress.

Edom's physical location became a metaphor of the proud and haughty spirit that the nation had displayed at the time of Judah's distress. Trusting in its high places and mountainous strongholds, Edom reckoned that no one could bring it to account for its actions.

8 *Destroy the wise men from Edom.* The nation had a reputation for having many wise men among its citizens (Jer 49:7).

9 *O Teman.* This name comes from a son of Eliphaz, who was the firstborn son of Esau (Ge 36:9 – 11).

11 *On the day.* This refers to the time of Judah's distress. ***strangers . . . foreigners.*** These words are used to describe Judah's principal enemies, contrasted with the words of verse 10, "your brother." It was one thing for the Babylonians to attack Judah; for a nation like Edom to join the Babylonians against their own brothers was unthinkable.

13 *the day of their disaster.* This phrase is repeated three times in this verse. It refers to the day of God's judgment upon Judah, carried out by the hand of Nebuchadnezzar.

5 Jer 49:9; Dt 24:21 **7** Jer 38:22; Isa 19:11 **8** Job 5:12; Isa 29:14 **9** Ps 76:5; Jer 49:7 **10** Ge 27:41; Eze 35:9
11 Na 3:10 **12** Mic 4:11; Pr 17:5

The Day of the Lord and the Future

15 "For the [judgment] day of the
Lord draws near on all the
nations.
As you have done, it shall be done
to you [in retribution];
Your [evil] dealings will return
on your own head. [Ps 137:7–
9; Is 2:10–22; Zeph 3:8–20;
Zech 12:1–14; Rev 19:11–21]
16 "Because just as you [Edom]
drank on My holy mountain
[desecrating it in the revelry of
the destroyers],
So shall all the nations drink
continually [one by one, of My
wrath];
Yes, they shall drink and swallow
[the full measure of
punishment]
And become as though they had
never existed. [Rev 16:14–16]
17 "But on Mount Zion [in Jerusalem]
there shall be [deliverance for]
those who escape,
And it shall be holy [no pagan will
defile it];
And the house of Jacob shall
possess their [former]
possessions. [Ezek 36; Joel 2:32]
18 "Then the house of Jacob shall be
a fire
And the house of Joseph a flame
[in executing God's wrath];
But the house of Esau will be like
stubble.
They (Jacob) shall set them on
fire and consume them (the
Edomites),
So that there shall be no survivor
of the house of Esau,"
For the Lord has spoken.
[Ezek 25:12–14]
19 Then *those of* the Negev shall
possess the mountain of Esau,
And *those of* the Shephelah [shall
possess] the Philistine *plain;*
Also, [they shall] possess the fields
of Ephraim and the fields of
Samaria,
And Benjamin *will possess* Gilead
[across the Jordan River].
[Amos 9:12; Zeph 2:7]
20 And the exiles of this host of the
sons (descendants) of Israel
Who are *among* the Canaanites as
far as Zarephath,
And the exiles of Jerusalem who
are in Sepharad
Shall possess the cities of the
Negev.
21 The deliverers shall go up on
Mount Zion
To rule *and* judge the mountain of
Esau,
And the kingdom *and* the kingship
shall be the Lord's. [Zech 12:8,
9; Mal 1:2–5; Matt 24:27–30;
Luke 1:31–33; Acts 15:14–17]

---

15 *the [judgment] day of the Lord.* This is a technical term used by the prophets to indicate the day of God's judgment (Am 5:18–20). Here the term likely refers to the time when God would judge all the nations, including Edom, that had participated in Judah's destruction.

18 *house of Jacob ... house of Joseph.* Together these signify a unified Israel. God intends to rejoin the kingdoms of Israel and Judah as one people again.

20 *Zarephath.* This was a Phoenician city 14 miles north of Tyrus (1Ki 17:8–24). ***Sepharad.*** This was a city to which some Judeans were exiled. The restoration of Judah from exile, which these verses predict, was a sign to Judah and all nations that the God of Israel was not just a local God. He had not been defeated by the Babylonian god Marduk. The fact that He could allow His people to be carried into captivity in a foreign land and then bring them back to their own land was proof of His power and sovereignty over all the earth.

21 *deliverers.* The Judeans who had been taken into captivity would come back as deliverers, and they would reign over the people of Edom. ***the kingdom and the kingship shall be the Lord's.*** These were Obadiah's last words against all human arrogance, pride, and rebellion. Edom had thought itself indestructible; but the Lord humbled that nation and restored the fallen Judah. Many people are tempted to consider themselves beyond the reach of God. But God will bring them low, just as He will lift those who humble themselves before Him. And one great day, He will establish His just rule over all.

15 Eze 30:3; Hab 2:8 **16** Joel 3:17 **17** Am 9:8 **18** Zec 12:6 **19** Zep 2:7 **20** 1Ki 17:9; Jer 32:44 **21** Jas 5:20; Rev 11:15

THE BOOK OF

JONAH

▸ **AUTHOR:** Jonah was "the son of Amittai" and nothing more would be known about him were it not for a reference in 2 Kings 14:25 calling him a prophet in the reign of Jeroboam II of Israel. Jonah was a Galilean, contrary to the Pharisees claim that "no prophet arises out of Galilee." One Jewish tradition says that Jonah was the son of the widow of Zarephath whom Elijah raised from the dead (1Ki 17:8 – 24).

▸ **TIMES:** c. 760 BC ▸ **KEY VERSES:** Jnh 2:8 – 9

▸ **THEME:** The Book of Jonah directs us towards God's greatness and mercy. He will go to any lengths in order to assure that His message is heard. He makes it possible for people to repent and be redeemed no matter how decadent and far away from God they are. Jonah himself is a prime example of the power of storytelling, as he gives us an amazingly visual and memorable image of God's far reaching grace and His involvement in individual lives to accomplish His purposes.

Jonah's Disobedience

1 NOW THE word of the LORD came to Jonah the son of Amittai, saying,
[2]"Go to Nineveh, that great city, and proclaim [judgment] against it, for their wickedness has come up before Me." [Gen 10:11, 12]
[3]But Jonah ran away to Tarshish to escape from the presence of the LORD [and his duty as His prophet]. He went down to Joppa and found a ship going to Tarshish [the most remote of the Phoenician trading cities]. So he paid the fare and went down into the ship to go with them to Tarshish away from the presence of the LORD. [Gen 4:16; Job 1:12; 2:7]
[4]But the LORD hurled a great wind toward the sea, and there was a violent tempest on the sea so that the ship was about to break up. [Ps 107:23–27]
[5]Then the sailors were afraid, and each man cried out to his god; and to lighten the ship [and diminish the danger] they threw the ship's cargo into the sea. But Jonah had gone below into the hold of the ship and had lain down and was sound asleep.
[6]So the captain came up to him and said, "How can you stay asleep? Get

1:1 ***the word of the LORD.*** This phrase affirms the divine source of the message to Jonah (Jer 1:4; Hos 1:1; Joel 1:1; Mic 1:1). The name "Jonah" means "Dove."
1:2 ***Nineveh.*** Nineveh is located on the Tigris River, the capital of ancient Assyria (2Ki 19:36) for about a century. It was over 500 miles from Jonah's home near Nazareth.
1:3 ***a ship going to Tarshish.*** The location of this port city is uncertain, but it could be Tartessus on the southeast coast of Spain. The city represents the most distant place known to the Israelites. Joppa was about 50 miles southwest of Jonah's hometown in the opposite direction from Nineveh.
1:4 – 5 ***the LORD hurled a great wind.*** Throughout the Book of Jonah, the Lord shows Himself sovereign over every aspect of creation. In this case, the storm at sea was so ferocious that even the experienced mariners were afraid.

CHAPTER 1 **2** Ge 10:11; 18:20 **3** Jos 19:46; Ge 4:16 **4** Ps 107:25 **5** 1Sa 24:3 **6** Ps 107:28; Joel 2:14

up! Call on your god! Perhaps your
god will give a thought to us so that
we will not perish."
7 And they said to another, "Come, let
us cast lots, so we may learn who is to
blame for this disaster." So they cast
lots and the lot fell on Jonah.
8 Then they said to him, "Now tell us!
Who is to blame for this disaster? What
is your occupation? Where do you come
from? What is your country?"
9 So he said to them, "I am a Hebrew,
and I [reverently] fear *and* worship the
LORD, the God of heaven, who made
the sea and the dry land."
10 Then the men became extremely
frightened and said to him, "How could
you do this?" For the men knew that
he was running from the presence of
the LORD, because he had told them.
11 Then they said to him, "What
should we do to you, so that the sea
will become calm for us?"—for the sea
was becoming more and more violent.
12 Jonah said to them, "Pick me up
and throw me into the sea. Then the
sea will become calm for you, for I
know that it is because of me that this
great storm *has come* upon you."
13 Nevertheless, the men rowed hard
[breaking through the waves] to return
to land, but they could not, because the
sea became even more violent [surging
higher] against them.
14 Then they called on the LORD and
said, "Please, O LORD, do not let us
perish because of taking this man's
life, and do not make us accountable
for innocent blood; for You, O LORD,
have done as You pleased."
15 So they picked up Jonah and threw
him into the sea, and the sea stopped
its raging.
16 Then the men greatly feared the
LORD, and they offered a sacrifice to
the LORD and made vows.
17 Now the LORD had prepared (ap-
pointed, destined) a great fish to swal-
low Jonah. And Jonah was in the stom-
ach of the fish three days and three
nights. [Matt 12:40]

Jonah's Prayer

2 THEN JONAH prayed to the LORD
his God from the stomach of the
fish,
2 and said,

"I called out of my trouble *and*
distress to the LORD,
And He answered me;
Out of the belly of Sheol I cried for
help,
And You heard my voice. [Ps 120:1;
130:1; 142:1; Lam 3:55–58]
3 "For You cast me into the deep,
Into the [deep] heart of the seas,

1:9 *I am a Hebrew.* With these words, Jonah identified himself with the people of the Lord's covenant (Ge 14:13). ***I [reverently] fear and worship the LORD.*** Fear here indicates an ongoing activity of awe before the Lord, of piety in His presence, of obedience to His word, and of saving faith (Ge 22:12; Ex 20:20; Pr 1:7). Yet Jonah's actions contradicted his words.
1:10 *extremely frightened.* This is the same term for "fear" that Jonah used in his statement of piety (v. 9). But here the word means to be in terror; it refers to overwhelming dread (v. 16). God, the Creator of the universe, was after Jonah. And because God was after Jonah, He was after the sailors as well. They had every right to be afraid (Ge 12:18; Jdg 15:11).
1:14 *they called on the LORD.* Ironically, the pagan sailors prayed to the Lord on behalf of the Lord's rebellious prophet. Jonah needed God's grace as much as Nineveh did. ***as You pleased.*** The narrator skillfully uses the sailors' words to express one of the book's themes: the Lord is free to act as He wills.
1:17 *the LORD had prepared (appointed, destined) a great fish.* God sent the fish — not a whale, as is commonly thought — to rescue Jonah from drowning, not to punish him (ch. 2). Three days and three nights may refer to one full day and portions of two more (Ge 30:36; Ex 3:18; 1Sa 30:12). Jesus Christ said that His death and resurrection were foreshadowed by Jonah's experience (Mt 12:39–40; 16:4; Lk 11:29).
2:2 *I called . . . I cried.* These terms come from two different verbs. The first is a more general term meaning "to call aloud," with a wide range of usage in the Bible. The second is a term that means a "cry for help," particularly as a scream to God (Ps 5:2; 18:6; 22:24; 88:13; 119:146).

7 Jos 7:14; 1Sa 14:41 **8** Jos 7:19 **9** Ps 146:6; Ac 17:24 **12** Jn 11:50 **13** Pr 21:30 **14** Dt 21:8; Ps 115:3 **15** Ps 89:9; Lk 8:24 **16** Mk 4:41; Ac 5:11 **17** Mt 12:40; Lk 11:30 **CHAPTER 2** **2** Ps 120:1; La 3:55; Ps 65:2 **3** Ps 88:6; 42:7

And the currents surrounded *and* engulfed me;
All Your breakers and billowing waves passed over me. [Ps 42:7]
4 "Then I said, 'I have been cast out of Your sight.
Nevertheless I will look again toward Your holy temple.'
[Ps 31:22]
5 "The waters surrounded me, to the point of death.
The great deep engulfed me,
Seaweed was wrapped around my head. [Ps 69:1; Lam 3:54]
6 "I descended to the [very] roots of the mountains.
The earth with its bars closed behind me [bolting me in] forever,
Yet You have brought up my life from the pit (death), O LORD my God.
7 "When my soul was fainting within me,
I remembered the LORD,
And my prayer came to You,
Into Your holy temple.
8 "Those who regard *and* follow worthless idols
Turn away from their [living source of] mercy *and* lovingkindness.
9 "But [as for me], I will sacrifice to You
With the voice of thanksgiving;
I shall pay that which I have vowed.
Salvation is from the LORD!"

10 So the LORD commanded the fish,
and it vomited Jonah up onto the dry
land.

Nineveh Repents

3 NOW THE word of the LORD came
to Jonah the second time, saying,
2 "Go to Nineveh the great city and
declare to it the message which I am
going to tell you."
3 So Jonah went to Nineveh in accor-
dance with the word of the LORD. Now
Nineveh was an exceedingly great city,
a three days' walk [about sixty miles
in circumference].
4 Then on the first day's walk, Jonah
began to go through the city, and he
called out and said, "Forty days more
[remain] and [then] Nineveh will be
overthrown!"
5 The people of Nineveh believed *and*
trusted in God; and they proclaimed a
fast and put on sackcloth [in penitent
mourning], from the greatest even to
the least of them.
6 When word reached the king of
Nineveh [of Jonah's message from
God], he rose from his throne, took
off his robe, covered himself with
sackcloth and sat in the dust [in re-
pentance].

2:4 *I will look again toward Your holy temple.* The man who had run from God's presence was alone, yet he clung to the hope that God would not abandon him. The temple, the sanctuary in Jerusalem (Dt 12:5–7; Ps 48; 79:1; Heb 9:24), was the symbol of God's presence.
2:6 *the [very] roots of the mountains.* Jonah pictures himself so deep in the sea that it is as if he had found the deepest place possible. ***the pit.*** This term, along with hell (v. 2), is used to describe the realm of the dead (Job 33:24; Ps 30:9; 49:9).
2:9 *I will sacrifice to You . . . voice of thanksgiving.* This vow is common in the Psalms (Ps 13:6; 142:7). ***I shall pay that which I have vowed.*** Jonah declares that he will keep his promise, a pledge both to sacrifice and to acknowledge God's help (Job 22:27; Ps 50:14; 66:13; Ro 6:13; 1Pe 2:5).
2:10 *the LORD commanded the fish.* The focus in the story of Jonah is on the Lord's sovereign control over creation to bring about His purpose.
3:1–2 *the word of the LORD came to Jonah the second time.* Jonah's new commission was essentially the same as the one he had received in 1:1.
3:5 *The people of Nineveh believed and trusted in God.* The term used for God here is the general term for deity. In contrast, the sailors in chapter 1 proclaimed faith in the Lord, using the personal, covenant name for God (1:16). The fact that the writer does not use the personal name for God here may suggest that the Ninevites had a short-lived or imperfect understanding of God's message. History bears this out. We have no historical record of a lasting period of belief in Nineveh. Eventually the city was destroyed in 612 BC.

4 Ps 31:22; 1Ki 8:38 **5** Ps 69:1; La 3:54 **6** Ps 16:10 **7** Ps 18:6 **8** 2Ki 17:15; Jer 10:8 **9** Ps 50:14; Hos 14:2; Ps 3:8
CHAPTER 3 **4** Dt 18:22 **5** Mt 12:41; Lk 11:32 **6** Job 2:8

7He issued a proclamation and it
said, "In Nineveh, by the decree of the
king and his nobles: No man, animal,
herd, or flock is to taste anything. They
are not to eat or drink water.
8"But both man and animal must
be covered with sackcloth; and every
one is to call on God earnestly *and*
forcefully that each may turn from his
wicked way and from the violence that
is in his hands.
9"Who knows, God may turn [in
compassion] and relent and withdraw
His burning anger (judgment) so that
we will not perish." [Joel 2:13, 14]
10When God saw their deeds, that
they turned from their wicked way,
then God [had compassion and] re-
lented concerning the disaster which
He had declared that He would bring
upon them. And He did not do it.

Jonah's Displeasure Rebuked

4 BUT IT greatly displeased Jonah
and he became angry.
2He prayed to the LORD and said,
"O LORD, is this not what I said when
I was still in my country? That is why
I ran to Tarshish, because I knew that
You are a gracious and compassion-
ate God, slow to anger and great in
lovingkindness, and [when sinners
turn to You] You revoke the [sentence
of] disaster [against them]. [Ex 34:6]
3"Therefore now, O LORD, just take
my life from me, for it is better for me
to die than to live."
4Then the LORD said, "Do you have
a good reason to be angry?"
5Then Jonah went out of the city and
sat east of it. There he made himself
a shelter and sat under its shade so
that he could see what would happen
in the city.
6So the LORD God prepared a plant
and it grew up over Jonah, to be a shade
over his head to spare him from discom-
fort. And Jonah was extremely happy
about [the protection of] the plant.
7But God prepared a worm when
morning dawned the next day, and
it attacked the plant and it withered.
8When the sun came up God prepared
a scorching east wind, and the sun beat
down on Jonah's head so that he fainted
and he wished to die, and said, "It is
better for me to die than to live."
9Then God said to Jonah, "Do you
have a good reason to be angry about
[the loss of] the plant?" And he said, "I
have a [very] good reason to be angry,
angry enough to die!"
10Then the LORD said, "You had com-
passion on the plant for which you did
not work and which you did not cause
to grow, which came up overnight and
perished overnight.
11"Should I not have compassion on
Nineveh, the great city in which there
are more than 120,000 [innocent] per-
sons, who do not know *the difference*
between their right and left hand [and
are not yet accountable for sin], as well
as many [blameless] animals?"

3:10 *God [had compassion and] relented.* The Ninevites' repentance moved the Lord to extend grace and mercy to them.
4:1 *displeased.* Jonah's irritation belied the good news that the city would be spared God's judgment, but he was unable to appreciate the parallel. ***Jonah ... became angry.*** In contrast to God, Jonah had no compassion on the people of Nineveh.
4:5 *so that he could see what would happen in the city.* In his continuing stubbornness and lack of compassion, Jonah held out hope that God would judge Nineveh. This was God's chief complaint against him (Ps 58).
4:7 *God prepared a worm.* The Book of Jonah depicts the Lord as both sovereign and free to act in creation. God placed the worm in the plant to serve as His agent in Jonah's life.
4:9 *I have a [very] good reason to be angry.* Jonah's anger (v. 1) did not arise from a desire for justice, but from his own selfishness. He continued to justify his rebellious attitude. And again, God was merciful.
4:11 *have compassion.* The same word used to describe Jonah's feeling toward the plant in verse 10 is used for God's feeling toward the people of Nineveh. People are of more value than animals and animals of more value than plants, but the Lord has a concern that extends to all of His creation. The Lord's compassion comes from His character (v. 2; Joel 2:13 – 14).

7 2Ch 20:3; Joel 2:15 **8** Isa 58:6; Isa 59:6 **9** 2Sa 12:22; Joel 2:14 **10** Jer 18:8; Am 7:3,6 **CHAPTER 4** **2** Jnh 1:3; Ex 34:6; Ps 86:5; Joel 2:13 **3** 1Ki 19:4; ver. 8 **8** ver. 3 **11** Jnh 1:2; 3:2,3; Dt 1:39; Ps 36:6; 145:9

THE BOOK OF

MICAH

▸ **AUTHOR:** Micah was from Moresheth-gath (1:14) which was located about 25 miles southwest of Jerusalem, near Gath. Although Micah was not as politically aware as Isaiah or Daniel, he showed a profound concern for the suffering of the people and had a clear sense of his prophetic calling. A contemporary of Isaiah and Hosea, Micah may have been a farmer turned prophet like Amos.

▸ **TIMES:** c. 735 – 710 BC ▸ **KEY VERSE:** Mic 6:8

▸ **THEME:** Micah was from a town in southwestern Judah. His message was directed at both capital cities, Samaria and Jerusalem. He was probably around when the Assyrians destroyed Samaria in 722 BC, and may have even lived through the siege of Jerusalem by Assyria. Micah's message comes out of unique visions from God. In effect he saw things that others couldn't, such as the prophecy of Bethlehem as the birthplace of Christ.

Destruction in Israel and Judah

1 THE WORD of the LORD that came
to Micah of Moresheth in the days
of Jotham, Ahaz, and Hezekiah, kings
of Judah, which he saw [through divine revelation] concerning Samaria
and Jerusalem.

2 Hear, O peoples, all of you;
Listen closely, O earth and all that is in it,
And let the Lord GOD be witness [giving a testimony of the judgment] against you,
The Lord from His holy temple [in the heavens]. [1 Kin 22:28]
3 For behold, the LORD is coming down from His place
He shall come down and tread [in judgment] on the high places of the earth. [Zech 14:3, 4; Mal 4:2, 3; Matt 24:27–30; Rev 1:7; 19:11–16]
4 The mountains shall melt under Him
And the valleys shall be split
Like wax before the fire,
Like waters poured down a steep place.
5 All this is because of the rebellion *and* apostasy of Jacob
And for the sins of the house of Israel (the Northern Kingdom).
What is the rebellion *and* apostasy of Jacob?

1:1 *Micah.* The name means "Who is like the Lord?" The question presents a major biblical theme, the idea that God is incomparable (7:18; Dt 4:32 – 40; Ps 113:4 – 6). Micah's ministry centered on the Assyrian threat to Samaria, the capital of Israel, that was destroyed in 722 BC and Jerusalem, the capital of Judah.
1:3 *the LORD is coming.* This is the language of epiphany, the dramatic coming of God to earth, here in a solemn procession of judgment. In other texts the language of epiphany is used to describe God's dramatic acts of deliverance (Ps 18:7 – 19).
1:5 *Jacob.* The name is used to refer to the Northern Kingdom of Israel, whose transgression was centered in its capital Samaria. ***high places.*** Jerusalem, which was once "fair and beautiful in elevation" (Ps 48:2), was nothing more than another platform of pagan worship, like the "high places" of the Canaanites.

CHAPTER 1 **1** Jer 26:18 **2** Ps 11:4 **4** Am 9:5

Is it not [the abandonment of God
in order to worship the idols of]
Samaria?
What are the high places [of
idolatry] in Judah (the Southern
Kingdom)?
Are they not Jerusalem [the capital
and center of corruption]?
6 Therefore I [the LORD] shall make
Samaria a heap of ruins [and of
stones and arable land] in the
open country,
A place for planting vineyards;
And I will pour her stones down
into the ravine
And lay bare her foundations.
[2 Kin 19:25; Ezek 13:14]
7 All her idols shall be broken in
pieces,
All her earnings [from her
idolatry] shall be burned with
fire,
And all her images I shall make
desolate;
For from the earnings of a
prostitute she collected them,
And to the earnings of a prostitute
they shall return.

8 Because of this I [Micah] must
lament (mourn over with
expressions of grief) and wail,
I must go barefoot and naked
[without outer garments as if
robbed];
I must wail like the jackals
And lament [with a loud, mournful
cry] like the ostriches.
9 For Samaria's wound is incurable,
For it has come to Judah;
The enemy has reached the gate of
my people,
Even to Jerusalem.
10 Announce it not in Gath [in
Philistia],
Weep not at all [and in this way
betray your grief to Gentiles];
In Beth-le-aphrah (House of Dust)
roll in the dust [among your own
people].
11 Go on your way [into exile—
stripped of beauty, disarmed],
inhabitants of Shaphir
(Beautiful), in shameful
nakedness.
The inhabitant of Zaanan (Go Out)
does not go out [of the house];
The wailing of Beth-ezel (House of
Removal) will take away from
you its support.
12 For the inhabitant of Maroth
(Bitterness)
Writhes in pain [at its losses] and
waits anxiously for good,
Because a catastrophe has come
down from the LORD
To the gate of Jerusalem.
13 Harness the chariot to the team of
horses [to escape the invasion],
O inhabitant of Lachish—
She was the beginning of sin
To the Daughter of Zion
(Jerusalem)—
Because in you were found
The rebellious acts of Israel.
14 Therefore you will give parting
gifts
On behalf of Moresheth-gath
(Micah's home);
The houses of Achzib (Place of
Deceit) will become a deception
To the kings of Israel.

1:7 *from the earnings of a prostitute she collected them.* Idolatry is often described in the Hebrew Bible as spiritual adultery (Jer 3:1; Hos 4:15). Israel is pictured here as a wife who is unfaithful to her husband. This is not just a metaphor, however; the worship system of Canaan was sexual in nature.

1:8 *barefoot and naked.* Micah's words describe mourning rites in which outer garments were laid aside in deep humility. The mourning person thought no longer about himself but only about the calamity that had overcome his senses.

1:10 *in Gath.* The reference here is to the lament of David in his mourning over the death of Saul and Jonathan (2Sa 1:20). Just as it was unseemly then to have the bad news of God's people profaned in a foreign city, so it would be in the present circumstance.

1:12 *Maroth.* This name means "bitterness." The name Jerusalem suggests "peace." Thus, the inhabitants of the "town of bitterness" would be sickened with dread, and the inhabitants of the "town of peace" would experience God's judgments.

6 2Ki 19:25; Eze 13:14 **7** Hos 2:5 **8** Ps 102:6 **9** 2Ki 18:13 **10** 2Sa 1:20 **12** Am 3:6 **13** 2Ki 18:14 **14** 2Sa 8:2; 2Ki 18:14; Jos 15:44

15 Moreover, I will bring on you
The one who takes possession,
O inhabitant of Mareshah
(Prominent Place).
The glory (nobility) of Israel will
enter Adullam [seeking refuge].
[1 Sam 22:1]
16 Make yourself bald [in
mourning]—shave off your
hair
For the children of your delight;
Remain as bald as the eagle,
For your children will be taken
from you into exile.

Woe to Oppressors

2 WOE (JUDGMENT is coming) to
those who devise wickedness
And plot evil on their beds!
When morning comes, they
practice evil
Because it is in the power of their
hands.
2 They covet fields and seize them,
And houses, and take them away.
They oppress *and* rob a man and
his house,
A man and his inheritance. [Is 5:8;
Ex 20:17; Lev 25:23ff.]

3 Therefore, thus says the Lord,

"Behold, I am planning against
this family a disaster (exile)
[Like a noose] from which you
cannot remove your necks;
Nor will you be able to walk
haughtily *and* erect,
For it will be an evil time [of
subjugation to the invaders].
4 "On that day they shall take up
a [taunting, deriding] parable
against you
And wail with a doleful *and* bitter
song of mourning and say,
'We are completely destroyed!
God exchanges the inheritance of
my people;
How He removes it from me!
He divides our fields to the
rebellious [our captors].'
5 "Therefore, you will have no one
stretching a measuring line
[dividing the common land]
For you by lot in the assembly of
the Lord. [Rev 21:27]
6 'Do not speak out,' so they speak
out.
But if they do not speak out
concerning these things,
Reproaches will not be turned
back.
7 "Is it being said, O house of
Jacob:
'Is the Spirit of the Lord
impatient?
Or are these [prophesied
judgments] His doings?'
Do not My words do good
To the one walking uprightly?
8 "But lately My people have stood
up as an enemy [and have made
Me their antagonist].
You strip the ornaments off the
garment
Of those unsuspecting passers-by,
Like those returned from war.
9 "You evict the women (widows) of
My people,
Each one from her pleasant house;
From her [young, fatherless]
children you take away My
splendor *and* blessing forever
[by putting them among the
pagans, away from Me].

1:16 *shave off your hair.* This would have been the ultimate sign of mourning in a culture in which a man's hair was highly valued.
2:1 – 2 *devise wickedness . . . covet.* The ethical teaching of the prophets regularly included oracles of judgment against greed, theft, and oppression, actions of the powerful in attacking the weak. To covet is not just to have a passing thought; it is a determination to seize what is not one's own.
2:4 *He divides our fields.* God would take the property rights from those who had seized them illegally and give them to people who were even more reprobate than they were.
2:5 – 6 *no one stretching a measuring line*. Land-grabbers would no longer have a legitimate claim among God's people. God would dispossess them even as they had dispossessed others. ***Do not speak out***. These words may have been a strong warning to Micah not to be like the lying prophets who counseled that all was well in the land.

15 Jos 15:44; 2Ch 11:7 **16** Job 1:20; Isa 15:2; Jer 7:29; La 4:5 **CHAPTER 2** **4** 2Sa 1:17

10 "Arise and depart [because the captivity is inevitable],
For this [land] is not the place of rest
Because of the defilement that brings destruction,
A painful *and* terrible destruction.
11 "If a man walking in a false spirit [spouting deception]
Should lie and say,
'I will prophesy to you [O Israel] of wine and liquor (greed, sensual pleasure),'
He would be the acceptable spokesman of this people. [Jer 5:31]

12 "I shall most certainly assemble all of you, O Jacob;
I shall surely gather the remnant of Israel.
I shall bring them together like sheep in the fold [multiplying the nation];
Like a flock in the midst of its pasture.
The place will swarm with many people *and* hum loudly with noise.
13 "The breaker [the Messiah, who opens the way] shall go up before them [liberating them].
They will break out, pass through the gate and go out;
So their King goes on before them,
The LORD at their head." [Ex 23:20, 21; 33:14; Is 63:8, 9; Hos 3:5; Amos 9:11]

Rulers Denounced

3 AND I said,
"Hear now, heads of Jacob
And rulers of the house of Israel.
Is it not for you to know *and* administer justice?
2 "You who hate good and love evil,
Who tear the skin off my people
And their flesh from their bones;
3 You who eat the flesh of my people,
Strip off their skin from them,
Break their bones
And chop them in pieces as for the pot,
Like meat in a kettle."
4 Then they will cry to the LORD,
But He will not answer them;
Instead, He will even hide His face from them at that time [withholding His mercy]
Because they have practiced *and* tolerated *and* ignored evil acts. [Is 1:15]

5 Thus says the LORD concerning the
[false] prophets who lead my people
astray;

When they have *something good* to bite with their teeth,
They call out, "Peace,"
But against the one who gives them nothing to eat,
They declare a holy war.
6 Therefore *it will* be night (tragedy) for you—without vision,
And darkness (cataclysm) for you—without foresight.

2:12–13 *assemble ... gather ... bring them together*. The verbs are emphatic, demonstrating the certainty of God's determination to bring to pass His good pleasure on His people (Dt 30:1–6). ***They will break out*.** This phrase speaks of regathering Israel from wherever the people may have been scattered.

3:1 *Is it not for you to know and administer judgment?* The idea here is that one might not expect justice from pagan leaders in a faraway place. But the rulers of the people of God were expected to emphasize justice. Justice is one of the key concepts of the law (Dt 10:18; 32:4; 33:21). Perverting justice was strongly prohibited by God (Dt 16:19; 24:17), yet this was precisely what the leaders of Judah were doing. They had used their authority to destroy justice rather than to establish it among the people.

3:5–7 *concerning the [false] prophets*. This oracle was against false prophets who proclaimed peace, causing the people to be unprepared for trouble. These prophets would have neither true prophetic insight, nor help from the forbidden arts of divination. Finally, they would have nothing to say, for there would be no answer from God.

---

10 Dt 12:9; Lev 18:25; Jer 3:2 **12** Mic 4:6,7; Jer 31:10; Eze 36:37 **13** Hos 3:5; Isa 52:12 **CHAPTER 3** **1** Jer 5:4,5 **3** Ps 14:4; Eze 11:3 **4** Ps 18:41; Pr 1:28; Isa 1:15 **5** Isa 56:10,11; Eze 13:10; Mt 7:15; Eze 13:18 **6** Isa 8:20; Eze 13:23; Am 8:9

The sun shall go down on the [false] prophets,
And the day shall become dark *and* black over them.
7 The seers shall be ashamed
And the diviners discredited *and* embarrassed;
Indeed, they shall all cover their mouths [in shame]
Because there is no answer from God.
8 But in fact, I am filled with power,
With the Spirit of the LORD,
And with justice and might,
To declare to Jacob his transgression
And to Israel his sin.
9 Now hear this, you heads of the house of Jacob
And rulers of the house of Israel,
Who hate *and* reject justice
And twist everything that is straight,
10 Who build Zion with blood [and extortion and murder]
And Jerusalem with violent injustice.
11 Her leaders pronounce judgment for a bribe,
Her priests teach for a fee,
And her prophets foretell for money;
Yet they lean on the LORD, saying,
"Is not the LORD among us?
No tragedy *or* distress will come on us." [Is 1:10–15]
12 Therefore, on account of you
Zion shall be plowed like a field,
Jerusalem shall become a heap of ruins,
And the mountain of the house [of the LORD] *shall become* like a densely wooded hill. [Jer 26:17–19]

Peaceful Latter Days

4 BUT IT shall come about in the last days
That the mountain of the house of the LORD
Shall be established as the highest *and* chief of the mountains;
It shall be above the hills,
And peoples shall flow [like a river] to it.
2 And many nations shall come and say,
"Come, let us go up to the mountain of the LORD,
To the house of the God of Jacob,
That He may teach us about His ways
And that we may walk in His paths."
For the law shall go forward from Zion,
And the word of the LORD [the revelation about Him and His truth] from Jerusalem.
3 And He will judge between many peoples
And render decisions for strong and distant nations.
Then they shall hammer their swords into plowshares
And their spears into pruning hooks [so that the implements of war may become the tools of agriculture];
Nation shall not lift up sword against nation,

3:11 ***bribe . . . for a fee . . . money.*** The wicked leaders and prophets of Israel "worked" only when they could gain something from it. Needless to say, if justice had to be paid for, it would not be justice. ***Is not the LORD among us?*** Many people of Jerusalem believed that they would not be affected by God's judgment because God Himself dwelled in the holy temple in Jerusalem. They reasoned that, despite their evils, as long as God was in His temple they were safe — even from divine judgment. What people refused to believe was that God might leave His temple because of the sinfulness of the people (Eze 10).

4:1 ***in the last days.*** This is an indication of a prophecy of end times.

4:2 ***we may walk in His paths.*** Unlike the people of Micah's generation who were strangers to justice (3:1), the peoples of the coming kingdom will be obedient to God.

4:3 ***swords . . . spears.*** All weapons of destruction will be recycled into tools of production. There will finally be an end to conflict. War will not even be a subject for study any more.

7 Am 8:11 **8** Isa 58:1 **10** Jer 22:13; Eze 22:27; Zep 3:3 **11** Isa 1:23; Eze 22:12; Jer 6:13; Isa 48:2; Jer 7:4 **12** Jer 26:18; Ps 79:1; Mic 4:2 **CHAPTER 4** **1** Eze 17:22 **3** Isa 2:4; Joel 3:10; Ps 72:7

Nor shall they ever again train for
war. [Is 2:2–4; Joel 3:10]
4 Each of them shall sit [in security
and peace] under his vine
And under his fig tree,
With no one to make them afraid,
For the mouth of the [omnipotent]
LORD of hosts has spoken it.
[Zech 3:10]
5 For all the peoples [now] walk
Each in the name of his god [in a
transient relationship],
As for us, we shall walk [securely]
In the name of the LORD our [true]
God forever and ever.

6 "In that day," says the LORD,
"I shall assemble the lame,
And gather the outcasts [from
foreign captivity],
Even those whom I have caused
pain.
7 "I shall make the lame a [godly]
remnant
And the outcasts a strong nation;
And the LORD shall reign over
them in Mount Zion
From this time on and forever.
8 "As for you [Jerusalem], tower of
the flock [of Israel],
Hill *and* stronghold of the
Daughter of Zion (Jerusalem's
inhabitants),
To you the former dominion shall
come,
The kingdom of the Daughter of
Jerusalem [when the Messiah
reigns in Jerusalem, and
the times of the Gentiles are
fulfilled]. [Luke 21:24]

9 "Now, why do you cry out loudly?
Is there no king among you?
Has your counselor perished?
For agony has gripped you like a
woman in childbirth.
10 "Writhe in pain and labor to give
birth,
O Daughter of Zion,
Like a woman in childbirth;
For now you shall go out of the
city,
Live in the field,
And go to Babylon.
There you will be rescued;
There the LORD shall redeem you
From the hand of your enemies.
11 "Now many [conquering] nations
are assembled against you,
Who say, 'Let her be profaned
[through Gentile presence and
the temple's destruction],
And let our eyes gaze on *and* gloat
over Zion.'
12 "But they (Gentile nations) do not
know the thoughts of the LORD,
Nor do they understand His
purpose *and* plan;
For He has gathered them
(Gentiles) like sheaves to the
threshing floor [for destruction].
13 "Arise and thresh, O Daughter of
Zion!
For I will make your horn iron
And I will make your hoofs
bronze;
That you may beat many peoples
in pieces [trampling down your
enemies],
That you may devote to the
LORD their unjust gain (pagan
possessions)
And their wealth to the Lord of all
the earth. [Zech 12:1–8; 14:14]

Birth of the King in Bethlehem

5 "NOW GATHER yourself in
troops, O daughter of troops;
A state of siege has been placed
against us.

4:4 *vine . . . fig tree.* Both are symbols of peace and prosperity (Zec 3:10).
4:7 *remnant.* The majority of people in Israel did not live their lives in faith and dedication to the Lord. However, true faith never really died out in Israel, even in the worst of times.
4:9 – 10 *like a woman in childbirth.* The troubles of the present moment would lead finally to the birth of a deliverer. ***go to Babylon.*** This refers to the exile.
4:13 *Arise and thresh.* The nations would be gathered by the Lord like sheaves on the threshing floor (v. 12). This is a way of speaking of the final victory over all of Israel's foes.

4 1Ki 4:25; Zec 3:10 **5** Zec 10:12 **6** Eze 34:16; Ps 147:2; Eze 34:13 **7** Mic 2:12; Isa 9:6; Da 7:14; Lk 1:33; Rev 11:15 **9** Jer 8:19; Isa 13:8; Jer 30:6 **11** La 2:16; Ob 12 **12** Isa 55:8; Isa 21:10 **13** Jer 51:33; Da 2:44; Isa 18:7; Zec 4:14 **CHAPTER 5** **1** La 3:30

They shall strike the ruler of
Israel on the cheek with a rod
(scepter).
2 "But as for you, Bethlehem
Ephrathah,
Too little to be among the clans of
Judah;
From you One shall come forth for
Me [who is] to be Ruler in Israel,
His goings forth (appearances) are
from long ago,
From ancient days." [Gen 49:10;
Matt 2:5–12; John 7:42]
3 Therefore, He will give them up
until the time
When she who is in labor has
given birth to a child.
Then what is left of His kinsmen
Shall return to the children of
Israel.
4 And He shall stand and shepherd
and guide *His flock*
In the strength of the LORD,
In the majesty of the name of the
LORD His God;
And they shall dwell [secure in
undisturbed peace],
Because at that time He shall be
great [extending His authority]
[Even] to the ends of the earth.
[Ps 72:8; Is 40:11; Zech 9:10;
Luke 1:32, 33]
5 This One [the Messiah] shall be
our peace.

When the Assyrian invades our
land
And tramples on our citadels *and*
in our palaces,
Then shall we raise against him
Seven shepherds and eight princes
[an overpowering force] among
men. [Is 9:6; Eph 2:14]
6 They shall devastate the land of
Assyria with the sword and
The land of Nimrod within her
[own] gates.
And He (the Messiah) shall rescue
us from the Assyrian (all enemy
nations)
When he attacks our land
And when he tramples our
territory.
7 Then the remnant of Jacob
Shall be among many peoples
Like dew from the LORD,
Like showers on the grass [a
source of blessing]
Which [come suddenly and] do not
wait for man
Nor delay for the sons of men.
[Ps 72:6; 110:3]
8 The remnant of Jacob
Shall be among the nations,
In the midst of many peoples
Like a lion among the beasts of the
forest,
Like a young lion [suddenly
appearing] among the flocks of
sheep
Which, if he passes through,
Tramples down and tears into
pieces [the nations in judgment],
And there is no one to rescue.
9 Your hand will be lifted up against
your adversaries,
And all your enemies shall be cut
off *and* destroyed.

10 "And in that day," says the LORD,
"I will cut off your horses from
among you
And destroy your chariots [on
which you depend]. [Ps 20:7, 8;
Zech 9:10]

5:2 ***Bethlehem.*** This name means "House of Bread." ***Ephrathah.*** This locates the village in a known region in Judah (Ge 35:16). This prophecy figures significantly in the New Testament story of the visit of the wise men to the Christ child (Mt 2:1 – 12). ***goings forth.*** The birth of this Savior King would be unlike the birth of any other, because He was preexistent. He is "from everlasting."
5:3 ***she who is in labor.*** This probably refers to Zion (4:10). The metaphor refers to the deliverance in the end time of those who will be able to delight in the coming of God's kingdom (4:9 – 5:1).
5:7 ***dew ... showers.*** Jewish people are blessings from God on their neighbors.
5:10 ***I will cut off.*** It was God's intention to destroy the evils in Israel's society. Horses and chariots represent the pride of Israel's military power. Israel's tendency was to rely on its own military power rather than on the Lord.

2 Mt 2:6; Jn 7:42; 1Sa 23:23; Ex 18:25; Ge 49:10; Isa 9:6; Ps 90:2; Jn 1:1 **3** Mic 4:7,10 **4** Isa 40:11; Eze 34:23; Ps 72:8; Isa 52:13; Zec 9:10 **5** Ps 72:7; Isa 9:6 **6** Ge 10:8; Lk 1:71 **7** ver. 3; Dt 32:2; Ps 72:6 **10** Zec 9:10

11 "I will cut off the cities of your land
And tear down all your
fortifications.
12 "I will cut off witchcrafts *and*
sorceries from your hand,
And you shall have no more
fortune-tellers.
13 "I will also cut off your carved
images
And your *sacred* pillars from
among you,
So that you will no longer worship
and bow down
To the work of your hands.
14 "I will root out your Asherim
(symbols of the goddess
Asherah) from among you
And destroy your cities [which are
the centers of pagan worship].
[Deut 16:21]
15 "And in anger and wrath I shall
execute vengeance
On the nations which have not
obeyed [such vengeance as they
have not known before]."

God's Indictment of His People

6 HEAR NOW what the LORD is
saying,
"Arise, plead your case before the
mountains,
And let the hills [as witnesses]
hear your voice.
2 "Hear, O mountains, the
indictment of the LORD,
And you enduring foundations of
the earth,
For the LORD has a case (a legal
complaint) against His people,
And He will dispute (challenge)
Israel.
3 "O My people, what have I done to
you [since you have turned away
from Me]?
And how have I wearied you?
Answer Me.
4 "For I brought you up from the
land of Egypt
And ransomed you from the house
of slavery,
And I sent before you Moses
[to lead you], Aaron [the
high priest], and Miriam [the
prophetess].
5 "My people, remember now
What Balak king of Moab devised
[with his evil plan against Israel]
And what Balaam the son of Beor
answered him [turning the
curse into blessing for Israel],
[Remember what the LORD did for
you] from Shittim to Gilgal,
So that you may know the righteous
and saving acts [displaying the
power] of the LORD." [Num 23:7–
24; 24:3–24; Josh 3:1; 4:19]

What God Requires of Man

6 With what shall I come before the
LORD [to honor Him]
And bow myself before God on
high?
Shall I come before Him with
burnt offerings,
With yearling calves?
7 Will the LORD be delighted with
thousands of rams,
Or with ten thousand rivers of oil?
Shall I present my firstborn for my
acts of rebellion,
The fruit of my body for the sin of
my soul?
8 He has told you, O man, what is
good;
And what does the LORD require
of you
Except to be just, and to love [and
to diligently practice] kindness
(compassion),

6:1–2 *mountains . . . hills.* These were among the witnesses to the covenant that God made with His people (Dt 4:26; 32:1; Isa 1:2).
6:7 *Will the LORD be delighted.* The idea of bringing pleasure to God through sacrifice is found elsewhere in the Bible. God is pleased with those who do as He commands (Ge 4:1–8).

6:8 *what does the LORD require of you.* This verse speaks of the underlying attitudes that must accompany all true worship. The idea here is that God seeks certain characteristics of true worship from His people. ***be just . . . love [and to diligently practice] kindness . . . walk humbly.*** These three phrases summarize biblical

12 Isa 2:6 **13** Zec 13:2; Isa 2:8 **15** 2Th 1:8 **CHAPTER 6** **2** Ps 50:1,4; Hos 12:2; Isa 1:18 **3** Jer 2:5,31 **4** Dt 4:20 **5** Nu 22:5; Jos 24:9; Nu 25:1; Jdg 5:11 **7** Ps 50:9; Isa 1:11; Job 29:6; 2Ki 16:3; Eze 23:37 **8** Dt 10:12; 1Sa 15:22; Ge 18:19; Isa 1:17

And to walk humbly with
your God [setting aside any
overblown sense of importance
or self-righteousness]?
[Deut 10:12, 13]

9 The voice of the LORD shall call to
the city [of Jerusalem]—
And it is sound wisdom to heed
[solemnly] *and* fear Your name
[with awe-filled reverence];
"Hear, O tribe [the rod of
punishment]. Who has
appointed its time?
10 "Are there not still treasures
gained by wickedness
In the house of the wicked,
And a short (inaccurate) measure
[for grain] *that is* cursed?
[Deut 25:14–16]
11 "Can I [be guiltless and] justify
deceptive scales
And a bag of dishonest weights?
[1 Thess 4:6]
12 "For the rich men of the city are
full of violence [of every kind];
Her inhabitants speak lies
And their tongue is deceitful in
their mouth.
13 "So also I will make you sick,
striking you down,
Desolating *and* devastating you,
because of your sins.
14 "You shall eat, but you will not be
satisfied,
And your emptiness shall be
among you;
You will [try to] remove [your
goods and those you love] *for
safekeeping*
But you will fail to save *anything*,
And what you do save I shall give
to the sword.
15 "You shall sow but you shall not
reap;
You shall tread olives, but shall not
anoint yourself with oil,
And [you will extract juice from]
the grapes, but you shall not
drink the wine.
16 "For [you have kept] the statutes of
Omri [the idolatrous king],
And all the works of the [wicked]
house (dynasty) of Ahab;
And you walk in their counsels
and policies.
Therefore, I shall hand you over
for destruction *and* horror
And your [city's] inhabitants for
ridicule,
And you shall bear the rebuke *and*
scorn of My people."

The Prophet Acknowledges Injustice

7 WOE IS me (judgment is
coming)! For I am
Like one who gathers the summer
fruits, like one who gleans the
vintage grapes.
There is not a cluster of grapes to
eat,
No first-ripe fig which my appetite
craves.
2 The godly person [who is faithful
and loyal to God] has perished
from the earth,
And there is no upright *person*
[one with good character and
moral integrity] among men.
They all lie in wait to shed blood;
Each hunts the other with a net.
3 Concerning evil, both of their
hands pursue it and do it
diligently *and* thoroughly;

---

piety in true worship. The majority of the people of Israel had violated each of these standards repeatedly. ***with your God.*** It is the Lord who ultimately gives a person strength, courage, and ability to exercise the virtues of godly living. **7:1–2 *Woe is me.*** Micah was moved by the oracles of judgment that God delivered through him (1:8). ***There is not a cluster.*** For Micah, the harvest was over. There was nothing around him but undesirable fruit. ***The godly person . . . has perished.*** The norms of society had broken down; everyone was out to destroy someone else. **7:3–4 *both of their hands.*** The people were pursuing evil with gusto. The leaders of the state were leading the way in evil (3:11). ***The day of your watchmen.*** This refers to the time when people needed to be alert for the approach of an enemy army. In this context, judgment was imminent.

11 Hos 12:7 **12** Jer 9:3,5 **13** Lev 26:16; Ps 107:17 **14** Lev 26:26 **15** Am 5:11 **16** 1Ki 16:25; Hos 5:11; Isa 25:8
CHAPTER 7 **1** Isa 17:6; Isa 28:4 **2** Ps 12:1; Isa 57:1; Hab 1:15

The prince asks, also the judge, for
a bribe,
And a great man speaks the [evil]
desire of his soul.
So they twist the course of justice
between them.
4 The best of them is [injurious] like
a briar;
The most upright is [prickly] like a
thorn hedge.
The day of your watchmen [that
is, the time predicted by the
prophets]
And your punishment comes;
Now shall be their confusion.
5 Do not trust in a neighbor
[because of the moral corruption
in the land];
Do not have confidence in a friend.
Guard the doors of your mouth
From her who lies in your bosom.
[Luke 12:51–53]
6 For the son dishonors the father
and treats him contemptuously,
The daughter rises up [in hostility]
against her mother,
The daughter-in-law against her
mother-in-law—
A man's enemies are the
men (members) of his own
household. [Matt 10:21, 35, 36;
Mark 13:12, 13]

God Is the Source of Salvation and Light

7 But as for me, I will look
expectantly for the LORD *and*
with confidence in Him I will
keep watch;
I will wait [with confident
expectation] for the God of my
salvation.
My God will hear me.
8 Do not rejoice over me [amid my
tragedies], O my enemy!
Though I fall, I will rise;
Though I sit in the darkness [of
distress], the LORD is a light for
me.
9 I will bear the indignation *and*
wrath of the LORD
Because I have sinned against
Him,
Until He pleads my case and
executes judgment for me.
He will bring me out to the light,
And I will behold His [amazing]
righteousness *and* His
remarkable deliverance.
[Rom 10:1–4; 11:23–27]
10 Then my enemy [all the pagan
nations] shall see it,
And shame [for despising the LORD]
will cover her who said to me,
"Where is the LORD your God?"
My eyes will look on her [with
satisfaction at her judgment];
Now she (unbelievers) will be
trampled down
Like mud of the streets.
11 *It shall be* a day for building your
walls,
On that day the boundary [of
Israel] shall be [greatly]
extended. [Is 33:17; Amos 9:11]
12 It *shall be* a day when the Gentiles
will come to you
From Assyria and from the cities
of Egypt,
And from Egypt even to the river
Euphrates,
From sea to sea and from
mountain to mountain.
13 Yet the earth [beyond the land of
Israel] shall become desolate
because of those who dwell in it,
Because of the fruit of their deeds.
14 Shepherd *and* rule Your people
with Your scepter [of blessing],
The flock of Your inheritance *and*
Your possession
Which dwells alone [separate and
secure from attack] in the forest,
In the midst of a garden land.
Let them feed in Bashan and
Gilead
As in the days of old [the days of
Moses and Elijah].

7:7 *I will look expectantly for the LORD.* While there would need to be a watchman for the coming of an enemy army, Micah was going to look for the advent of the Lord.

7:8–9 *I have sinned.* This is the confession of the people in saving faith.

7:11–12 *On that day.* These words call attention to a future day, the time of the end.

4 Eze 2:6; Isa 55:13 **6** Mt 10:21 **8** Pr 24:17; Ps 37:24; Pr 24:16 **9** La 3:39 **10** Ps 35:26; 42:3 **12** Isa 11:16 **13** Jer 21:14 **14** Isa 37:24

15 "As in the days when you came out
from the land of Egypt,
I shall show you marvelous *and*
miraculous things."
16 The [pagan] nations shall see
[God's omnipotence in delivering
Israel] and be ashamed
Of all their might [which cannot
be compared to His].
They shall put their hand on their
mouth [in silent astonishment];
Their ears shall be deaf.
17 They shall lick the dust like a
serpent;
Like crawling things of the earth
They shall come trembling out of
their fortresses *and* hiding places.
They shall turn *and* come with
fear *and* dread to the LORD our
God
And they shall be afraid *and* stand
in awe before You [O LORD].
[Jer 33:9]

18 Who is a God like You, who
forgives wickedness
And passes over the rebellious
acts of the remnant of His
possession?
He does not retain His anger
forever,
Because He [constantly] delights
in mercy *and* lovingkindness.
19 He shall again have compassion
on us;
He will subdue *and* tread
underfoot our wickedness
[destroying sin's power].
Yes, You will cast all our sins
Into the depths of the sea.
[Ps 103:12]
20 You shall give truth to Jacob
And lovingkindness *and* mercy to
Abraham,
As You have sworn to our
forefathers
From the days of old. [Luke 1:54, 55]

7:16 – 17 *nations shall see [God's omnipotence in delivering Israel] and be ashamed.* The response of the wicked nations to the renewed mercies of God on His people would be terror. The nations would be humiliated because they had taunted Israel in the day of its trouble (vv. 8 – 10).

7:18 – 20 God's Mercy — There is a significant passage on mercy or love like this in every book in the Old Testament. God wants His people to succeed and be prosperous. He wants the best for them. He is always eager to restore them. He protects, directs, sustains, and covenants with them. His steadfast love is characterized by faithfulness in spite of constant wandering in unfaithfulness.

In the New Testament, it is also easy to find passages in every book where someone is being judged. Usually it's the religious people who have set themselves up in God's place or those who have turned away from God when they should know better who are condemned.

The Old Testament predicts, leads toward, and sets the scene for the ultimate judgment of the New Testament. The entire Bible consistently points to the kind of creatures we are because of the fall and sin. Only God has the ultimate solution in Christ. God subjects Himself to that ultimate judgment for us so that all of His love for us may be realized. It's a mystery that we can solve only in our hearts by accepting and believing its implications.

Every day our prayer needs to be, "Lord, My sins are ever with me. I deserve your judgment. Thank you for the great mercy I've received through Jesus' death for me. That He died in my place must always be the primary reality in my life."

7:18 *Who is a God like You.* These words speak of the incomparability of God. There is nothing in all of creation to compare with God (Isa 40:25).

7:20 *As You have sworn.* This last verse is reminiscent of God's promise to Abraham in Genesis 12, 15, and 22, and His promises to Jacob in Genesis 32. The Lord had sworn to fulfill His promises to the patriarchs. He would not — could not — leave His promise unfulfilled (Ps 89:33).

15 Ps 68:22 **16** Isa 26:11; Job 21:5 **17** Ps 72:9; Isa 49:23; Ps 18:45 **18** Ex 15:11; Ex 34:6; Jer 50:20; Mic 4:7; Ps 103:9; Isa 57:16 **20** Lk 1:72; Ps 105:9

THE BOOK OF

NAHUM

▸ **AUTHOR:** The only mention of Nahum in the Old Testament is found in 1:1 where he is called Nahum of Elkosh. Scholars have been unable to determine the exact location of Elkosh and numerous theories exist, but due to his interest in the triumph of Judah (1:15; 2:2), some believe Nahum to be a prophet of the Southern Kingdom.

▸ **TIMES:** c. 660 BC ▸ **KEY VERSES:** Na 1:7 – 8

▸ **THEME:** Nahum is unique in that it is a prophecy addressed completely to a nation other than Israel: Assyria and its capital Nineveh. While Nineveh may be powerful, her day of destruction is coming. Nineveh is not invincible. The message is that God's standards apply to all nations, not just Israel and Judah. They need to be prepared to live by those standards or face judgment.

God Is Awesome

1 THE ORACLE (a burdensome message—a pronouncement from God) concerning Nineveh [the capital city of Assyria]. The book of the vision of Nahum of Elkosh [which he saw in spirit and prophesied].

2 The LORD is a jealous and
avenging God [protecting and
demanding what is rightfully
and uniquely His];
The LORD avenges and He is full of
wrath.
The LORD takes vengeance on His
adversaries,
And He reserves wrath for His
enemies. [Ex 20:5]
3 The LORD is slow to anger and
great in power
And He will by no means leave *the
guilty* unpunished.
The LORD has His way in the
whirlwind and in the storm,
And the clouds are the dust
beneath His feet. [Ex 34:6, 7]
4 He rebukes the sea and dries
it up;
He dries up all the rivers
[illustrating His judgment].
Bashan [on the east] and [Mount]
Carmel [on the west] wither,
And [in the north] the blossoms of
Lebanon fade.
5 The mountains quake before Him
And the hills melt away;
Indeed the earth is shaken by His
presence—
Yes, the world and all that dwell
in it.
6 Who can stand before His
indignation [His great wrath]?
And who can stand up *and* endure
the fierceness of His anger?

1:2 *jealous and avenging God.* The repetition of words and the use of parallel terms are typical devices in Hebrew poetry for intensifying and sharpening the poet's message.
1:3 *whirlwind and in the storm ... clouds.* The peoples of the ancient Middle East worshiped nature gods, particularly deities associated with storms, clouds, and rainfall. In Canaan, this fixation on storms was centered in the worship of Baal and his consorts Anat and Asherah. The Scriptures testify that there are no gods but the Lord; it is He who rules and is above all creation.

CHAPTER 1 **1** Zep 2:13 **2** Ex 20:5; Dt 4:24; Jos 24:19 **3** Ex 34:6,7; Neh 9:17; Job 9:4; Ps 18:7 **4** Mt 8:26; Isa 33:9 **6** Mal 3:2

His wrath is poured out like fire
And the rocks are destroyed by
Him.
7 The LORD is good,
A strength *and* stronghold in the
day of trouble;
He knows [He recognizes, cares
for, and understands fully]
those who take refuge *and*
trust in Him. [Ps 1:6; Hos 13:5;
John 10:14, 27]
8 But with an overwhelming flood
[of judgment through invading
armies]
He will make a complete
destruction of its site
And will pursue His enemies into
darkness.

9 Whatever [plot] you [Assyrians]
devise against the LORD,
He will make a complete end of it;
Affliction [of God's people by the
hand of Assyria] will not occur
twice.
10 Like tangled thorn branches
[gathered for fuel],
And like those drowned in
drunkenness,
The people of Nineveh are
consumed [through fire]
Like stubble completely withered
and dry [in the day of the LORD's
wrath]. [Mal 4:1]
11 From you [O Nineveh],
One has gone forth who plotted
evil against the LORD,
A malevolent counselor [the king
of Assyria]. [2 Kin 19:20–23;
Is 10:5–7; 36:15–20]

12 This is what the LORD says,

"Though they are at full *strength*
and many in number,
Even so, they will be cut off and
pass away.
Though I have afflicted you *and*
caused you grief [O Jerusalem],
I will afflict you no longer.
[2 Kin 19:35–37; John 5:14]
13 "Now, I will break his yoke [of
taxation] off you,
And I will tear off your shackles."
[Is 14:25]

14 The LORD has given a command
concerning you [O king of
Nineveh]:
"Your name will no longer be
perpetuated.
I will cut off the carved idols and
cast images
From the temple of your gods;
I will prepare your grave,
For you are vile *and* unworthy."
[Is 37:38; Ezek 32:22, 23]

15 Behold, on the mountains the feet
of him who brings good news
[telling of Assyria's destruction],
Who announces peace *and*
prosperity!
Celebrate your feasts, O Judah;
Perform your vows.
For the wicked one [the king of
Assyria] will never again pass
through you;
He is completely cut off. [Is 52:7;
Rom 10:15]

The Overthrow of Nineveh

2 THE ONE who scatters has come
up against you [Nineveh].
Man the fortress *and* ramparts,
watch the road;
Strengthen your back [prepare
for battle], summon all your
strength.

1:8 *flood . . . complete destruction . . . darkness.* The judgment of the Lord will be inescapable. The word "flood" is both a poetic term for overwhelming devastation and a specific reference to the actual manner of Nineveh's fall. It is believed that the invaders of Nineveh entered the city through its flooded waterways (2:6).
1:11 *A malevolent counselor.* "Malevolent," or in some translations "wicked," is one of the harshest terms in biblical language, nearly a curse word. The term speaks of someone who is utterly worthless.
1:14 *you are vile and unworthy.* The only thing to be done with Nineveh was to dig a grave and bury it. The prophecy came true literally — the city was destroyed so completely that its very existence was questioned until its discovery by archaeologists in the nineteenth century (3:13 – 15).
2:1 *Man the fortress and ramparts.* These were sarcastic words to the people of Nineveh

7 Jer 33:11 **9** Ps 2:1; 1Sa 3:12 **10** 2Sa 23:6; Na 3:11; Mal 4:1

[2]For the LORD will restore the
splendor *and* majesty of Jacob
Like the splendor of [ancient and
united] Israel,
Even though destroyers have
destroyed them
And ruined their vine branches.
[Is 10:12]
[3]The shields of his soldiers [of
Media and Babylon] are colored
red;
The warriors are dressed in
scarlet.
The chariots blaze with fire of
[flashing] steel
When he is prepared *to march,*
And the cypress *spears* are
brandished [for battle].
[4]The chariots race madly in the
streets;
They rush wildly in the broad
plazas.
Their appearance is like torches;
They rush in various directions
like forked lightning.
[5]He remembers *and* summons his
nobles;
They stumble in their march
[terrified because of the attack].
They hurry to the city wall,
And the mantelet is prepared *and*
firmly set up.
[6]The gates of the rivers
[surrounding Nineveh] are
opened
And the palace [of sun-dried brick]
is dissolved [by the torrents].
[7]It is decreed:
Nineveh is stripped, and she is
carried away,
And her handmaids are moaning
like the sound of doves,
Beating on their breasts [in sorrow].

[8]Though Nineveh was like a pool of
water throughout her days,
Now her inhabitants are fleeing;
"Stop! Stop!" [a few cry,]
But no one turns back.
[9]Plunder the silver!
Plunder the gold!
For there is no end to the
treasure—
Wealth from every precious object.
[10]She is emptied! She is desolate and
waste!
Hearts melting [in fear] and knees
knocking!
Anguish is in the whole body,
And the faces of all grow pale!
[Is 13:7, 8]
[11]Where is the den of the lions
(Assyria)
And the feeding place of the young
lions,
Where the lion, lioness, and lion's
cub prowled
With nothing to fear?
[12]The lion [of Assyria] tore enough
for his cubs (Assyrian citizens),
Killed [enough prey] for his
lionesses,
And filled his lairs with prey
And his dens with torn flesh.

[13]"Behold, I am against you [Nin-
eveh]," declares the LORD of hosts, "and

---

and its leaders, as if they would be able to protect themselves against the wrath of the Lord.

2:3 *red . . . scarlet . . . blaze with fire.* These images speak of blood, violence, and warfare. Isaiah refers to the custom of the Assyrians of rolling their outer garments in blood before a battle (Isa 9:5) to strike terror in the hearts of their opponents. Here the tables would be turned. While others would have shields, chariots, and spears, the people of Nineveh would be bathed in blood—their own blood.

2:4 *The chariots race madly.* The Assyrians used chariots as formidable war machines. The proficiency of the chariot drivers underlies the imagery of this verse. But, as in the case of the shields and spears of verse 3, the chariots of Nineveh would not prevail, no matter how fast they drove.

2:6 *gates of the rivers.* The destruction of Nineveh is believed to have taken place when the besiegers entered the city through its flooded waterways. The attack came at flood time, when rivers undermined the walls and defenses of the city. Archaeologists have found evidence of flood debris that may be associated with the destruction of the city. Thus, the words of Nahum were fulfilled exactly.

2:11–12 *den of the lions.* Nineveh was the city of lions (v. 13). Yet, despite all the horrors that the lion of Nineveh had brought to other nations, it would no longer need to be feared by anyone. Although the Babylonians conquered the city, they were only God's instruments. Nineveh's greatest foe was God Himself.

I will burn your chariots in the smoke, and the sword will devour your young lions. I will cut off your prey from the land, and the voice of your messengers will no longer be heard."

Nineveh's Complete Ruin

3 WOE (JUDGMENT is coming) to the city of blood [guilty of murder and mayhem], completely full of lies and pillage;
Her prey never departs [alive].
[Ezek 24:6, 9, 10; Hab 2:12]
2 The noise of the [cracking of the] whip,
The noise of the rattling of the wheel,
Galloping horses
And rumbling *and* bounding chariots [in the assault of Nineveh]!
3 Horsemen charging,
Swords flashing, spears gleaming,
Many slain, a mass of corpses,
No end of corpses—
The horsemen stumble over the corpses!
4 All because of the many acts of prostitution of [Nineveh] the prostitute,
The charming *and* well-favored one, the mistress of sorceries,
Who betrays nations by her acts of prostitution (idolatry)
And families by her sorceries.
5 "Behold, I am against you," declares the LORD of hosts,
"And I will lift up your skirts over your face,
And I will let the nations look at your nakedness [O Nineveh]
And the kingdoms at your disgrace.
6 "I will throw filth on you
And make you vile *and* treat you with contempt,
And set you up as a spectacle.
7 "And it will come about that all who see you
Will shrink back *and* run from you and say,
'Nineveh is completely ruined!
Who will grieve for her?'
Where will I seek comforters for you?"
8 Are you better than Thebes,
Which was situated by the waters of the Nile,
With water surrounding her,
Whose defense was the sea (the Nile),
Whose wall *consisted* of the sea?
9 Ethiopia was her strength,
And Egypt too, without limits.
Put and Lubim were among her helpers.
10 Yet she became an exile;
She went into captivity.
Her young children were dashed to pieces
At the head of every street;
They cast lots for her honorable men,
And all her great men were bound with chains.
11 You too [Nineveh] will become drunk [with the cup of God's wrath];
You will be hidden.

3:4 *prostitution.* Any worship of gods other than the God of Scriptures is an act of spiritual prostitution. Nineveh was so adept at pagan practices that the city earned the descriptive title, "the mistress of witchcrafts."

3:6–7 *I will throw filth on you.* The Lord described the fate of Nineveh as comparable to a person on whom unspeakable filth was thrown. When Nineveh lay in ruins, no one would grieve for her. The nations would be glad that the city was gone.

3:8 *Thebes.* Thebes is derived from an Egyptian name meaning "city of the god Amon." The argument seems to suggest that, before its destruction, no one would have even dreamed of the fall of Thebes. But the destruction had happened — not long before the writing of the Book of Nahum. The city of Thebes was rebuilt only to be destroyed later during the Roman period (29 BC). Nineveh, however, would never be rebuilt.

3:11 *drunk . . . hidden . . . will search.* Nineveh would be like a helpless drunk hoping for strength but finding nowhere to turn for it.

CHAPTER 3 **4** Isa 47:9,12 **5** Na 2:13; Isa 47:2,3 **6** Heb 10:33 **7** Rev 18:10; Jer 15:5 **8** Am 6:2; Jer 46:25 **10** Ps 137:9; Isa 13:16; Hos 13:16; La 2:19; Joel 3:3; Ob 11 **11** Jer 25:17; Na 1:10

You too [Nineveh] will search
[in vain] for a refuge from the
enemy.
12 All your fortresses are [nothing
but] fig trees with ripe figs—
When shaken they fall into the
mouth of the eater.
13 Behold, your people are [as weak
and helpless as] women in your
midst!
The gates of your land are opened
wide to your enemies;
Fire consumes the bars across
your gates.
14 Draw water for a [long, continued]
siege!
Strengthen your fortresses!
Go down to the clay pits, trample
the mortar!
Prepare the brick kiln [to burn
bricks for the rampart]!
15 But there [in the very midst of
these preparations] the fire will
devour you;
The sword will cut you down;
It will devour you as the locust
does.
Multiply yourself like the creeping
locusts;
Multiply yourself like the
swarming locusts.
16 You have increased your traders
more than the [visible] stars of
heaven—
The creeping locust strips *and*
destroys and then flies away.
17 Your guardsmen are like the
swarming locusts.
Your marshals are like the hordes
of grasshoppers
Settling in the stone walls on a
cold day.
When the sun rises, they fly
away,
And no one knows the place where
they are.
18 Your shepherds are asleep, O king
of Assyria;
Your nobles are lying down [in
death].
Your people are scattered on the
mountains
And there is no one to gather
them.
19 There is no relief *and* healing for
your hurt;
Your wound is incurable.
All who hear the news about you
Clap their hands over [what has
happened to] you.
For on whom has your [unceasing]
evil not come continually?

3:16 – 17 *the sun rises.* The people of Nineveh would be like nocturnal insects that disappear at daylight.
3:19 *All who hear.* Every nation and people that had suffered under the abusive power of Nineveh would shout and clap upon hearing of the city's destruction. There would be no mourning for Nineveh.

12 Rev 6:13 **13** Jer 50:37; Ps 147:13; Jer 51:30 **14** Na 2:1 **15** Joel 1:4 **17** Rev 9:7 **18** Ex 15:16; Ps 76:6; Jer 50:18; Eze 31:3; 1Ki 22:17 **19** Mic 1:9; La 2:15; Zep 2:15

THE BOOK OF

HABAKKUK

▸ **AUTHOR:** In both the introduction to the book (1:1) and the closing psalm (3:1) the author identifies himself as Habakkuk the prophet. It is believed that he might have been a priest as he mentions in the closing psalm "For the choir director, on my stringed instruments" (3:19). Also, in the apocryphal book of Bel and the Dragon, Daniel is rescued a second time by the prophet Habakkuk.

▸ **TIMES:** c. 607 BC ▸ **KEY VERSE:** Hab 2:4

▸ **THEME:** This whole book of Habakkuk is really devoted to the question of "Lord, if you are all powerful, why is evil allowed to exist?" The events that seem to be precipitating this question are the victories of Babylon. God was using Babylon, a completely Godless nation, to punish Israel, God's own people. The answers God gives us to this question in Habakkuk solidly point us in one direction, but ultimately the answers are in faith in Him alone.

Chaldeans Used to Punish Judah

1 THE ORACLE (a burdensome message—a pronouncement from God) which Habakkuk the prophet saw.

2 O LORD, how long will I call for help
And You will not hear?
I cry out to You, "Violence!"
Yet You do not save.
3 Why do You make me see iniquity,
And cause me to look on wickedness?
For destruction and violence are before me;
Strife continues and contention arises.
4 Therefore, the law is ineffective *and* ignored
And justice is never upheld,
For the wicked surround the righteous;
Therefore, justice becomes perverted.

5 [The LORD replied,] "Look among the nations! See!
Be astonished! Wonder!
For I am doing something in your days—
You would not believe it if you were told. [Acts 13:40, 41]
6 "For behold, I am raising up the Chaldeans [who rule in Babylon],
That fierce and impetuous nation
Who march throughout the earth
To take possession of dwelling places that do not belong to them. [2 Kin 24:2]

1:2 *O LORD, how long.* This question is phrased as a formal complaint (Ps 13:1 – 2).
1:4 *the law is ineffective and ignored.* The revelation of God given at Mount Sinai had little impact on the hearts of people whose lives were focused on material success. These people had little interest in living by God's definition of what is fair and humane. ***wicked.*** God's chosen people committed and tolerated heinous acts through the corruption of the courts.
1:5 *Look among the nations.* The international scene during Habakkuk's lifetime was full of turmoil, with Assyria on the decline and Babylon on the rise.
1:6 *I am raising up.* God controls the nations for His own purposes (Da 2:21), sometimes indirectly and at other times directly.

CHAPTER 1 **2** La 3:8 **4** Jer 12:1 **5** Isa 29:14

7 "The Chaldeans are dreaded and
feared;
Their justice and authority
originate with themselves *and*
are defined only by their decree.
8 "Their horses are swifter than
leopards
And keener than [hungry] wolves
in the evening,
Their horsemen come galloping,
Their horsemen come from far
away;
They fly like an eagle swooping
down to devour.
9 "They all come for violence;
Their horde of faces moves
[eagerly] forward,
They gather prisoners like sand.
10 "They make fun of kings
And rulers are a laughing matter
to them.
They ridicule every stronghold
And heap up rubble [for earth
mounds] and capture it.
11 "Then they will sweep by like the
wind and pass on.
But they will be held guilty,
They [and all men] whose own
power *and* strength is their god."

12 Are You not from everlasting,
O LORD, my God, My Holy One?
We will not die.
O LORD, You have appointed the
Chaldeans [who rule in Babylon]
to execute [Your] judgment,
And You, O Rock, have established
them to correct *and* chastise.
[Deut 32:4]
13 Your eyes are too pure to approve
evil,
And You cannot look *favorably* on
wickedness.
Why then do You look favorably
On those who act treacherously?
Why are you silent when the
wicked (Chaldean oppressors)
destroy
Those more righteous than they?
14 Why do You make men like the
fish of the sea,
Like reptiles *and* creeping things
that have no ruler [and are
helpless against their enemies]?
15 *The Chaldeans* bring all of them
up with a hook,
And drag them away with a net,
And gather them together in their
fishing net;
So they rejoice and are glad.
16 Therefore, they offer sacrifices to
their net
And burn incense to their fishing
net;
Because through these things
their catch is large *and* they live
luxuriously,
And their food is plentiful.
17 Will they continue to empty their
net
And [mercilessly] go on destroying
nations without sparing?

God Answers the Prophet

2 I WILL stand at my guard post
And station myself on the tower;
And I will keep watch to see what
He will say to me,
And what answer I will give [as
His spokesman] when I am
reproved.
2 Then the LORD answered me and
said,
"Write the vision
And engrave it plainly on [clay]
tablets

1:7 *dreaded and feared.* Far from being humane, the Babylonians prided themselves on their arrogant use of raw power.
1:9 *They gather prisoners like sand.* The Babylonians resettled numerous conquered peoples with little regard for them as individuals.
1:12 *Are You not from everlasting.* Habakkuk's point seems to be that God's holiness should have prohibited Him from using a "dirty" instrument such as Babylon to accomplish His purposes in judging and reproving His own people.
1:16 *they offer sacrifices to their net.* This phrase speaks of the contemptuous pride of the Babylonians in their devices of destruction.
2:1 *I will stand ... on the tower.* Habakkuk stationed himself as a watchman to look at the nations, as God had commanded him. ***what He will say to me.*** Habakkuk's faith is seen in his anticipation of a response from God. ***when I am reproved.*** This phrase indicates the prophet's submission to God.

11 Da 5:4 **12** Isa 10:5-7 **16** Dt 8:17 **CHAPTER 2** **1** Isa 21:8,11 **2** Isa 8:1

So that the one who reads it will
run.
3 "For the vision is yet for the
appointed [future] time
It hurries toward the goal [of
fulfillment]; it will not fail.
Even though it delays, wait
[patiently] for it,
Because it will certainly come; it
will not delay. [Heb 10:37, 38]

4 "Look at the proud one,
His soul is not right within him,
But the righteous will live by
his faith [in the true God].
[Rom 1:17; Gal 3:11]
5 "Moreover, wine is treacherous
and betrays the arrogant man,
So that he does not stay at home.
His appetite is large like Sheol,
And he is like death, never
satisfied.
He gathers to himself all nations
And collects to himself all peoples
[as if he owned them].

6 "Will all these [victims of his
greed] not take up a taunting
song against him,
And in mocking derision against
him
Say, 'Woe (judgment is coming) to
him who increases that which is
not his—
How long [will he possess it]?
And [woe to him who] makes
himself wealthy with loans.'
7 "Will your creditors not rise up
suddenly,
And those who collect from you
awaken?
Then you will become plunder for
them.
8 "Because you [king of Babylon]
have looted many nations,
All peoples who are left will loot
you—
Because of human bloodshed and
for the violence done to the land,
To the city and all its inhabitants.

9 "Woe (judgment is coming) to him
who obtains wicked gain for his
house [and thinks by so doing]
To set his nest on high,
That he may be rescued from the
hand of evil.
10 "You have devised a shameful
thing for your house
By cutting off *and* putting an end
to many peoples;
So you are sinning against your
own life *and* forfeiting it.
11 "For the stone will cry out from the
wall [to accuse you—built in sin!]
And the rafter will answer it out of
the woodwork.

12 "Woe (judgment is coming) to
him who builds a city with
bloodshed
And establishes a town by
violence!
13 "Is it not indeed from the LORD of
hosts
That peoples labor [only] for the
fire [that will destroy their
work],

2:3 *the appointed [future] time.* This speaks of a determined time in God's eyes. ***Even though it delays, wait [patiently] for it.*** God knows His plan and the outworking of all things in accordance with His purposes. The godly are responsible to study and proclaim His revelation while awaiting its fulfillment. ***it will certainly come.*** The fulfillment of the vision would not take any longer than God had planned.
2:4 *the righteous will live by his faith.* True righteousness before God is linked to genuine faith in God. A proud person relies on self, power, position, and accomplishment; a righteous person relies on the Lord.
2:5 *all nations . . . all peoples.* These peoples of the earth should have been gathered together before the Lord in holy worship (Ps 117:1); instead, they became morsels for the rapacious appetite of Babylon.
2:6 *Woe (judgment is coming) to him.* A woe is an oracle of judgment consisting of two parts: a declaration of the wrong and a notice of impending judgment. The judgment usually applies the principle of the law of retribution.
2:7 *creditors.* This Hebrew term has the idea of "those who bite," suggesting sudden, hurtful attacks (Mic 3:5).
2:11 *the stone will cry out . . . the rafter will answer it out of the woodwork.* The whole structure of Israel's society called out for justice; every part reverberated with the need for righting wrongs.

---

3 Da 10:14; Heb 10:37 **4** Jn 3:36 **8** Isa 33:1 **9** Ob 4

And nations grow weary for
nothing [that is, things which
have no lasting value]?
14 "But [the time is coming when] the
earth shall be filled
With the knowledge of the glory of
the LORD,
As the waters cover the sea.
[Is 11:9]

15 "Woe (judgment is coming) to
you who make your neighbors
drink,
Who mix in your venom to make
them drunk
So that you may look at their
nakedness!
16 "You will be filled with disgrace
instead of honor.
Now drink and expose your own
nakedness!
The cup [of wrath] in the LORD's
right hand will come around to
you [O destroyer],
And utter disgrace will be on your
own glory. [Rev 16:19]
17 "For the violence done to Lebanon
will overwhelm you;
The destruction of the animals
will terrify you
On account of human bloodshed
and the violence done to the
land,
To the city and all its inhabitants.
18 "What profit is the carved image
when its maker has formed it?
It is only a cast image, and a
teacher of lies.
For its maker trusts in his own
creation [as his god]
When he makes speechless
idols.
19 "Woe (judgment is coming) to him
who says to the wooden image,
'Awake!'
And to the speechless stone,
'Arise!'
And that is your teacher?
Look, it is overlaid with gold and
silver,
And there is no breath at all
inside it.
20 "But the LORD is in His holy
temple.
Let all the earth hush *and* be
silent before Him." [Zeph 1:7;
Zech 2:13]

God's Salvation of His People

3 A PRAYER of Habakkuk the
prophet, set to wild *and* enthusi-
astic music.

2 O LORD, I have heard the report
about You and I fear.
O LORD, revive Your work in the
midst of the years,
In the midst of the years make it
known;
In wrath [earnestly] remember
compassion *and* love.

3 God [approaching from Sinai]
comes from Teman (Edom),
And the Holy One from Mount
Paran. *Selah (pause, and
calmly think of that).*
His splendor *and* majesty covers
the heavens
And the earth is full of His
praise.

2:14 *the glory of the LORD.* This speaks to the full manifestation of His person, significance, presence, and wonder. The true knowledge of God in the time of His kingdom on earth will be like the waters — all-embracing, inescapable, and fully enveloping.
2:16 *The cup [of wrath] in the LORD's right hand.* This represents the wrath of God (Isa 51:17,22; Rev 14:10; 16:19).
2:18 *teacher of lies.* Idolatry begins with deception, encourages deception, and calls for a commitment to deception (Isa 44:20).
2:20 *be silent before him.* The call to silence is not an invitation to worship, but a command to reflect on the terrible state of all who fall into the hands of the angry God (Zep 1:7).
3:2 *I have heard.* Habakkuk knew the stories of God's mighty acts as celebrated in song and in the feasts and festivals of Israel. These mighty acts included the exodus from Egypt, the miracles by the Red Sea, and the conquest of the land. ***revive ... make it known.*** Habakkuk prayed for God's renewed involvement in Israel. ***In the midst of the years.*** This was a way of calling for a quick response.

15 Hos 7:5

4 His brightness is like the sunlight;
He has [bright] rays *flashing* from His hand,
And there [in the sunlike splendor] is the hiding place of His power.
5 Before Him goes the pestilence [of judgment as in Egypt],
And [the burning] plague [of condemnation] follows at His feet [as in Sennacherib's army]. [Ex 7:2–4; 2 Kin 19:32–35]
6 He stood and measured the earth;
He looked and startled the nations,
Yes, the eternal mountains were shattered,
The ancient hills bowed low *and* collapsed.
His ways are eternal.
7 I [Habakkuk, in my vision] saw the tents of Cushan under distress;
The tent curtains of the land of Midian were trembling.

8 Did the LORD rage against the rivers,
Or was Your anger against the rivers,
Or was Your wrath against the [Red] Sea,
That You rode on Your horses,
On Your chariots of salvation?
9 Your bow was made bare;
The rods of chastisement were sworn. *Selah (pause, and calmly think of that).*
You split the earth with rivers [bringing waters to dry places]. [Ex 17:6; Num 20:11]
10 The mountains saw You and [they] trembled *and* writhed [as if in pain];
The downpour of waters swept by [as a deluge].
The deep uttered its voice *and* raged,
It lifted its hands high.
11 The sun and moon stood in their places [as before Joshua];
They went away at the light of Your [swift] arrows,
At the radiance *and* gleam of Your glittering spear. [Josh 10:12, 13]
12 In indignation You marched through the earth;
In anger You trampled *and* threshed the nations.
13 You went forth for the salvation of Your people,
For the salvation *and* rescue of Your anointed [people Israel].
You struck the head from the house of the wicked
To lay him open from the thigh to the neck. *Selah (pause, and calmly think of that).*
14 With the enemy's own spears, You pierced
The head of his hordes.
They stormed out to scatter us,
Rejoicing like those
Who secretly devour the oppressed [of Israel].
15 You have trampled on the sea with Your horses,
On the surge of many waters. [Ex 15:8]

16 I heard and my whole inner self trembled;
My lips quivered at the sound.
Decay *and* rottenness enter my bones,
And I tremble in my place.
Because I must wait quietly for the day of distress,
For the people to arise who will invade *and* attack us.
17 Though the fig tree does not blossom
And there is no fruit on the vines,
Though the yield of the olive fails
And the fields produce no food,
Though the flock is cut off from the fold

3:4 *the hiding place of His power.* God reveals evidence of His power, but its totality and greatness remain hidden.
3:8 *rivers . . . Sea.* The Lord had divided the Red Sea and the Jordan River for His people to cross (Ex 14:26 – 15:5; Jos 3:14 – 17). ***chariots of salvation.*** The appearance of the Lord was for the purpose of bringing deliverance to His people.
3:16 *I must wait quietly for the day of distress.* The prophet encouraged the godly not to be anxious in adversity.
3:17 God and Politics — Living in this physical, time bound reality we see only a small portion of what God created. It is the bigger part of creation

CHAPTER 3 **6** Na 1:5 **10** Ex 14:22 **15** Ps 77:19 **16** Ps 119:120

And there are no cattle in the stalls,
18 Yet I will [choose to] rejoice in the
LORD;
I will [choose to] shout in
exultation in the [victorious]
God of my salvation! [Rom 8:37]
19 The Lord GOD is my strength [my
source of courage, my invincible
army];
He has made my feet [steady and
sure] like hinds' feet
And makes me walk [forward
with spiritual confidence] on my
high places [of challenge and
responsibility].

For the choir director, on my stringed instruments.

---

we need to be aware of and try to understand. We ultimately live beyond what we see and feel now. Life, as currently defined, is only that proverbial shadow of what it shall be. Our struggle is to have the vision to see beyond.

The same can be said for the political realities Habakkuk complains about. A season of failing crops isn't that much different than living a few years under the rule of an incompetent or cruel despot. It is tough and life can be severely affected, but the ultimate realities of how the world functions and how God relates to it remain unchanged.

God is a just God and will bring about justice. A period of injustice does not imply God has lost sight of what is going on or that He is losing His grip on the events of the world. He has different immediate purposes or works in a completely different timeframe.

3:19 ***my strength.*** God will strengthen those who trust in Him (Ps 18:32,39). He will give those who live by faith the same confidence that a surefooted deer has in climbing mountains.

19 2Sa 22:34; Dt 32:13

THE BOOK OF

ZEPHANIAH

▸ **AUTHOR:** In the beginning of the book, Zephaniah traces his lineage back four generations to the godly King Hezekiah. This would make him the only prophet of royal descent. His use of the phrase "this place" in reference to Jerusalem indicates that he was probably an inhabitant of Judah's royal city.

▸ **TIMES:** c. 630 BC ▸ **KEY VERSES:** Zep 1:14 – 15

▸ **THEME:** A contemporary of Jeremiah, Zephaniah was written during the reign of Josiah, one of the good kings of Judah. The book follows a fairly familiar pattern for the prophets. Judgment is pronounced on Judah as well as several surrounding nations. After the judgment of the first two chapters, the third declares a restoration process that sounds strongly encouraging.

Day of Judgment on Judah

1 THE WORD of the LORD which came to Zephaniah the son of Cushi, the son of Gedaliah, the son of Amariah, the son of Hezekiah, in the days of Josiah the son of Amon, king of Judah:

2 "I will completely consume *and* sweep away all *things*
From the face of the earth [in judgment]," says the LORD.
3 "I will consume *and* sweep away man and beast;
I will consume *and* sweep away the birds of the air
And the fish of the sea,
And the stumbling blocks (idols) along with the wicked;
And I will cut off *and* destroy man from the face of the earth," declares the LORD.
4 "I will also stretch out My hand [in judgment] against Judah
And against all the inhabitants of Jerusalem.
And I will cut off *and* destroy the remnant of Baal from this place,
And the names *and* remembrance of the idolatrous priests along with the [false] priests,
5 And those who bow down *and* worship the host of heaven [the sun, the moon, and the stars] on their housetops
And those who bow down and swear [oaths] to [and pretend to worship] the LORD and [yet also] swear by [the pagan god called] Milcom [god of the Ammonites],
6 And those who have turned back from following the LORD,

1:1 ***Zephaniah*** means "Hidden in the Lord," a name that relates to the principal message the prophet presented (2:3). The names of the prophets were often significantly associated with the message that God gave them to present to the people.
1:2 – 3 ***I will completely consume and sweep away all things.*** The message of Zephaniah begins with a pronouncement of universal judgment (Ge 6 – 8). These words not only introduce the particular judgment that would be pronounced upon Judah (v. 4), but they also speak of the final judgment that will usher in the kingdom of God on earth (Rev 20:11 – 15).
1:4 – 6 ***I will cut off and destroy the remnant of Baal.*** Baal worship and its evils had led to the destruction of Israel and its capital Samaria

CHAPTER 1 **3** Hos 4:3 **4** Hos 10:5 **5** 2Ki 23:12; Jos 23:7 **6** Isa 1:4; Jer 2:13; Hos 7:7

And those who have not sought
the LORD [as their most
important need] or inquired of
Him."

7 [Hush!] Be silent before the Lord
GOD [there is no acceptable
excuse to offer]!
For the day [of the vengeance] of
the LORD is near,
For the LORD has prepared a
sacrifice (Judah),
He has set apart [for His use]
those who have accepted His
invitation [the Chaldeans who
rule Babylon]. [Hab 2:20]
8 "Then it will come about on the
day of the LORD's sacrifice
That I will punish the princes and
the king's sons
And all who are clothed in [lavish]
foreign apparel [reflecting their
paganism]. [Num 15:38, 39]
9 "On that day I will also punish all
those who leap over the *temple*
threshold,
Who fill their [pagan] lord's temple
with violence and deceit.
10 "On that day," declares the LORD,
"There will be the sound of crying
from the Fish (Damascus)
Gate [in the northern wall of
Jerusalem where invaders enter]
And wailing from the Second
Quarter [of the city],
And a loud crash from the hills.
11 "Wail [in anguish], you inhabitants
of the Mortar (Valley of Siloam),
For all the merchants of Canaan
will be silenced *and* destroyed;
All who weigh out silver will be
cut off.
12 "It will come about at that time
That I will search Jerusalem with
lamps
And I will punish the men
Who [like old wine] are stagnant
in spirit,
Who say in their hearts,
'The LORD will not do good, nor
will He do evil.'
13 "Furthermore, their wealth will
become plunder
And their houses a desolation.
Yes, they will build houses but not
live in them,
And plant vineyards but not drink
their wine." [Deut 28:30, 39;
Amos 5:11, 12]

14 The great [judgment] day of the
LORD is near,
Near and coming very quickly.
Listen! The [voice of the] day of the
LORD!
The warrior cries out bitterly
[unable to fight or to flee].
15 That day is a day of [the
outpouring of the] wrath [of
God],
A day of trouble and distress,
A day of destruction and
devastation,
A day of darkness and gloom,
A day of clouds and thick
darkness, [Jer 30:7; Joel 2:11;
Amos 5:18]
16 A day of trumpet and the battle
cry [of invaders]

---

in 722 BC. Likewise, Baal worship and its associations would lead to the destruction of Judah and its capital, Jerusalem, in 586 BC.
1:7 ***Be silent.*** This prophetic call for silence was for solemn preparation for the horror of divine wrath (Hab 2:20; Zec 2:13). ***sacrifice.*** The people of God were expected to prepare sacrifices for the Lord as acts of contrition and celebration. But rebels, scofflaws, idolaters, and apostates would themselves become God's sacrifice.
1:8–9 ***foreign apparel.*** This suggests two things: (1) acts of greed and extortion against the populace, amassing funds for exotic clothing; (2) participation in foreign religious rites associated with exotic clothing. ***leap over the temple threshold.*** This may refer to a pagan practice like the one mentioned in 1 Samuel 5:5. The priests of Dagon would not step on the doorway of the temple to Dagon because the hands and the head of Dagon had fallen there.
1:12–13 ***The LORD will not do good, nor will He do evil.*** The complacency of the wicked people led them to believe that God is similarly complacent. Foolishly these people believed that the Lord would be inactive, neither blessing nor cursing, neither benefiting nor punishing His people.

7 Hab 2:20; Zec 2:13; Isa 13:6; Isa 34:6; Jer 46:10 **8** Jer 39:6 **10** 2Ch 33:14 **11** Jas 5:1 **12** Jer 48:11; Ps 94:7 **13** Am 5:11; Mic 6:15 **14** Joel 2:1,11 **15** Isa 22:5; Jer 30:7 **16** Jer 4:19

Against the fortified cities
And against the high corner
towers (battlements).
17 I will bring distress on men
So that they will walk like the
blind [unable to find a way of
escape],
Because they have sinned against
the LORD;
Their blood will be poured out like
dust [and trampled underfoot],
And their flesh like dung.
18 Neither their silver nor their gold
Will be able to rescue them
On the day of the LORD's
indignation *and* wrath.
And the whole earth will be
consumed
In the fire of His jealous wrath,
For He shall make a full *and*
complete end,
Indeed a terrifying one,
Of all the inhabitants of the earth.
[Luke 21:35, 36; 2 Pet 3:10–13]

Judgments on Judah's Enemies

2 GATHER YOURSELVES
together [in repentance], yes,
gather [in submission],
O nation without shame,
2 Before the decree takes effect [and
the time for repentance is lost]—
The day passes like the chaff
[whirled by the wind]—
Before the burning *and* fierce
anger of the LORD comes upon
you,
Before the day of the wrath of the
LORD comes upon you.
3 Seek the LORD [search diligently
for Him and regard Him as the
foremost necessity of your life],
All you humble of the land
Who have practiced His
ordinances *and* have kept His
commandments;
Seek righteousness, seek humility
[regard them as vital].
Perhaps you will be hidden [and
pardoned and rescued]
In the day of the LORD's anger.

4 For [this is the fate of the
Philistines:] Gaza will be
abandoned
And Ashkelon a desolation;
[The people of] Ashdod will be
driven out at noon [in broad
daylight]
And Ekron will be uprooted *and*
destroyed.
5 Woe (judgment is coming) to the
inhabitants of the seacoast,
The nation of the Cherethites [in
Philistia]!
The word of the LORD is against
you,
O Canaan, land of the Philistines;
I will destroy you
So that no inhabitant will be left.
6 So the [depopulated] seacoast shall
be pastures,
With [deserted] meadows for
shepherds and folds for flocks.
7 The seacoast will belong
To the remnant of the house of
Judah;
They will pasture [their flocks] on it.
In the [deserted] houses of
Ashkelon [in Philistia] they [of
Judah] will lie down *and* rest in
the evening,
For the LORD their God will care
for them;
And restore their fortune
[permitting them to occupy the
land]. [Is 14:29–31; Amos 1:6–8]

1:17–18 *like the blind.* God's judgment would be so sudden and so overwhelming that the survivors would be in a state of shock, stumbling around in the dark.

2:1–3 *you will be hidden.* Zephaniah used a play on words with the meaning of his own name, "Hidden in the Lord." Even in the midst of the most calamitous of judgment scenes, the mercy and grace of the Lord is still available to a repentant people.

2:4–5 *Gaza . . . Ashkelon . . . Ashdod . . . Ekron.* The focus of the book moves from the description of divine judgment on Judah and Jerusalem to a description of divine judgment on the surrounding nations. The judgment begins with the nation to the west, Philistia, and its major cities.

---

17 Dt 28:29; Ps 79:3; Jer 9:22 **18** Eze 7:19; Zep 3:8; ver. 2,3 **CHAPTER 2** **1** Joel 2:16 **2** Job 21:18; Isa 17:13; 2Ki 23:26 **3** Am 5:6; Ps 76:9; Am 5:15 **4** Zec 9:5,6; Jer 6:4 **5** Eze 25:16; Jos 13:3 **6** Isa 17:2 **7** Mic 5:7,8; Lk 1:68; Jer 29:14

8 "I have heard the taunting of Moab
And the revilings of the sons of
Ammon,
With which they have taunted My
people
And become arrogant against
their territory [by violating
Israel's boundary and trying to
seize its land].
9 "Therefore, as I live," declares the
LORD of hosts,
The God of Israel,
"Moab will in fact become like
Sodom
And the sons of Ammon like
Gomorrah,
A land possessed by nettles and
salt pits,
And a perpetual desolation.
The remnant of My people will
plunder them
And what is left of My nation will
inherit them [as their own]."

10 This they shall have in return for
their pride, because they have taunt-
ed and become arrogant against the
people of the LORD of hosts.
11 The LORD will be terrifying *and*
awesome to them, for He will starve all
the gods of the earth; and all the coast-
lands of the nations will bow down *and*
worship Him, everyone from his own
place. [Joel 2:11; Zeph 1:4; 3:9]

12 "You also, O Ethiopians, will be
slain by My sword." [Is 18]
13 And the LORD will stretch out His
hand against the north
And destroy Assyria,
And He will make Nineveh a
desolation [a wasteland],
Parched as the desert. [Is 10:12;
Nah 1:1]

14 Flocks will lie down in her midst,
All the animals which range in
herds;
Both the pelican and the short-
eared owl
Will roost on the top of Nineveh's
pillars.
Birds will sing in the window,
Desolation will be on the
threshold;
For He has uncovered the cedar
paneling.
15 This is the joyous city
Which dwells carelessly [feeling so
secure],
Who says in her heart,
"I am, and there is no one besides
me."
What a desolation she has become,
A lair for [wild] animals!
Everyone who passes by her will
hiss [in scorn]
And wave his hand *in contempt*.
[Is 10:5–34; 47:8, 10]

Woe to Jerusalem and the Nations

3 WOE (JUDGMENT is coming)
to her who is rebellious and
defiled,
The tyrannical city [Jerusalem]!
2 She did not listen *and* heed the
voice [of God];
She accepted no correction.
She did not trust in the LORD [but
trusted her own power];
She did not draw near to her God
[but to the pagan gods of Baal or
Molech].
3 Her officials within her are
roaring lions;
Her judges are [as hungry as] the
wolves at evening,

2:11 ***The LORD will be terrifying and awe-some to them.*** There may be a double meaning in these words. For the righteous people of Judah and Jerusalem, there would be a response of awe and wonder before God, who had responded to the prayer of His servant. But for the wicked there would be quite another response, one of terror and dread. ***all the coastlands of the nations.*** Not only would there be a righteous remnant in Judah, there would also be people coming to God from the nations of the earth.
2:13–15 ***Birds will sing in the window.*** The presence of birds in the ruins of Nineveh attests to the severity of the destruction announced on these people. ***the joyous city.*** The rejoicing here is ironic, seen as an act of the city's complacency. Soon the judgment of God would descend suddenly, and the region would be useful only for herding animals.
3:3–4 ***officials ... judges ... prophets ... priests.*** God had designated these people to

8 Jer 48:27; Eze 25:3; Jer 49:1 **9** Isa 15; Am 1:13; Dt 29:33; ver. 7 **10** Isa 16:6; Jer 48:29 **11** Mal 1:11; Jn 4:21; Ge 10:5 **12** Isa 18:1; Jer 46:9; Ps 17:13 **13** Isa 10:12; Na 1:1 **14** ver. 6; Isa 13:21; Isa 34:11; Jer 22:14 **15** Isa 47:8; Rev 18:7; La 2:15; Na 3:19 **CHAPTER 3** **2** Jer 22:21; Jer 5:3 **3** Eze 22:27; Mic 3:9; Hab 1:8

They leave nothing for the
morning.
4 Her prophets are reckless and
treacherous men;
Her priests have profaned the
sanctuary;
They have done violence to the
law [by pretending their word
is God's word]. [Jer 23:11;
Ezek 22:26; Hos 9:7]
5 The LORD is righteous within her;
He will do no injustice.
Every morning He brings His
justice to light;
He does not fail.
But the unjust person knows no
shame.
6 "I [the LORD] have cut off *and*
destroyed nations [as a warning
to Judah];
Their corner towers (battlements)
are in ruins.
I have made their streets
desolate
So that no one passes by;
Their cities are destroyed
So that there is no man, there is no
inhabitant.
7 "I said, 'Most certainly you will
[reverently] fear Me;
Accept correction.'
So Jerusalem's dwelling will not
be cut off
In accordance with all that I
have appointed concerning her
[punishment],
But they were eager [even rising
early] to make all their deeds
corrupt. [Jer 7:13]
8 "Therefore [you of the godly
remnant of Judah, patiently]
wait for Me," declares the LORD,
"[Wait] for the day when I rise
up as a witness [against the
nations].
For it is My decision *and* My right
to gather the nations,
To assemble kingdoms,
To pour out on them My
indignation,
All [the heat of] My burning anger;
For [in that day] all the earth shall
be consumed
By the fire of My zeal.
9 "Then I will give to the peoples
[clear and pure speech from]
purified lips [which reflect their
purified hearts],
That all of them may call on the
name of the LORD,
To serve Him shoulder to shoulder
(united).

---

work for righteousness, but they were more wicked than the "regular" citizens of Jerusalem. These leaders were destroying and defrauding the weak, the needy, and the helpless.

3:8 *All [the heat of] My burning anger.* God's response to the wickedness of Jerusalem was to declare His judgment. He would use other nations to punish the city for its rebellion.

3:8 God's Purpose in Judgment—What we don't properly understand is that judgment should lead us to a restoration or improvement in a relationship. Judgment is never announced without grace being far behind. We live with the tension of knowing God's judgment hangs over us while at the same time knowing that forgiveness is readily available to us too. Such is the message of Zephaniah.

Judgment implies a necessary purification process. You can't get the impurities out without first identifying their presence. We want to think of ourselves as pure without going through any process of purification. We want grace without judgment, but it doesn't work that way. Judgment reflects the true state of our being, namely that we are sinful and in need of grace. Often the only way to understand our reality is to go through a judgment process.

Once the judgment is accepted and the proper response is made, we fully experience God's grace. He deals with our enemies (3:15). He quiets us with His love (3:17). He removes our burdens (3:18). God stands ready to gather us back to Himself (3:19). He restores our fortunes (3:20).

The commonly held thought that the writings of the Old Testament prophets are all gloom and doom is actually myth and misnomer. There's always hope and renewal in the prophetic message. There are always opportunities for repentance, forgiveness, and restoration. God's judgment is in fact good for us because the sin in our lives needs to be brought to light in order for us to be restored to full fellowship with God.

3:9–13 *purified lips.* One day human language will become a unifying element in the true worship of God. ***My worshipers.*** God's people would come from all nations to worship Him.

4 Hos 9:7; Eze 22:26 **5** Dt 32:4; Mic 3:11; Jer 3:3 **7** Jer 8:6; Ge 6:12 **8** Pr 20:22; Joel 3:2; Zep 1:18 **9** Isa 19:18

10 "From beyond the rivers of
Ethiopia
My worshipers, [the descendants
of] My dispersed ones,
Will bring My offerings.
11 "On that day you [Israel] will feel
no shame
Because of all your acts
By which you have rebelled *and*
sinned against Me;
Then I will remove from among
you
Your rejoicing ones who delight in
their pride;
And you will never again behave
arrogantly
On My holy mountain [Mount
Zion].

A Remnant of Israel

12 "But I will leave among you
A humble and lowly people,
And they will take refuge *and*
trust confidently in the name of
the LORD.
13 "The remnant of Israel will do no
wrong
Nor speak lies,
Nor will a deceitful tongue
Be found in their mouths;
For they will eat and lie down
With no one to make them tremble
and feel afraid."
14 Shout for joy, O Daughter of Zion!
Shout *in triumph,* O Israel!
Rejoice, be in high spirits *and*
glory with all your heart,
O Daughter of Jerusalem [in that
day]!
15 The LORD has taken away the
judgments against you;
He has cleared away your
enemies.
The King of Israel, even the LORD
[Himself], is in your midst;
You will no longer fear disaster.
16 In that day it will be said to
Jerusalem:
"Do not be afraid, O Zion;
Do not let your hands fall limp.
17 "The LORD your God is in your
midst,
A Warrior who saves.
He will rejoice over you with joy;
He will be quiet in His love
[making no mention of your past
sins],
He will rejoice over you with
shouts of joy.
18 "I will gather those [Israelites in
captivity] who grieve about the
appointed feasts—
They came from you, [O Zion];
On whom the reproach [of exile] is
a burden.
19 "Behold, at that time I am going to
deal
With all your oppressors;
I will save the lame
And gather the scattered,
And I will turn their shame into
praise and renown
In every land [where they have
suffered]. [Mic 4:6, 7]
20 "At that time I will bring you in,
Yes, at the time I gather you
together;
For I will make you a name and a
praise
Among all the peoples of the earth
When I restore your fortunes [and
freedom] before your eyes,"
Says the LORD.

3:20 *I will make you a name and a praise.* Ordinarily Scripture speaks of the praise that should be brought to God. Here we find the praise that God will bring to His people. ***Says the LORD.*** This is a solemn vow of God to do what He has promised. Zephaniah begins and ends with the strong assertion that the Lord is speaking. The implication is clear: "Listen and live!"

10 Ps 68:31; Ac 8:27 **11** Mt 3:9 **12** Isa 14:32 **13** Mic 4:7; Isa 60:21; Rev 14:5; Eze 34:28 **14** Isa 12:6 **15** Jn 1:49; Eze 48:35; Rev 7:15 **16** Isa 35:3,4; Heb 12:12 **17** ver. 15; Isa 62:5; Jer 32:41 **18** La 2:6 **19** Eze 34:16; Mic 4:6,7 **20** Isa 11:12; Eze 28:25

THE BOOK OF

HAGGAI

▸ **AUTHOR:** The authorship of the book is virtually uncontested as Haggai's name is mentioned nine times. Haggai is known only from this book and two other references to him in Ezra 5:1 and 6:14. Haggai returned from Babylon with the remnant and may well have been one of the few people who could remember the former temple before its destruction. Haggai was therefore very instrumental in the rebuilding of the temple.

▸ **TIMES:** c. 520 BC ▸ **KEY VERSES:** Hag 1:7 – 8

▸ **THEME:** Haggai is the first of the postexilic prophets, addressing the immediate problem of the rebuilding of the temple. The people had returned about 20 years earlier, but apathy and opposition were keeping the work from being completed. Haggai's concern is that neglect of the temple is a symptom of a bigger problem. God has dropped out of the Israelites' sight as a priority. The people are more concerned with building their materialistic lifestyles than they are with their relationship with God.

Haggai Begins Temple Building

1 IN THE second year of Darius the
king [of Persia], on the first day
of the sixth month (Aug 29, 520 B.C.),
the word of the LORD came by Haggai
the prophet to Zerubbabel the son of
Shealtiel, governor of Judah, and to
Joshua the son of Jehozadak, the high
priest, saying,
2"Thus says the LORD of hosts:
'These people say, "The time has not
come that the LORD's house (temple)
should be rebuilt." ' " [Ezra 1:1–6; 4:1–
6, 24; 5:1–3]
3Then the word of the LORD came by
Haggai the prophet, saying,
4"Is it time for you yourselves to live
in your [expensive] paneled houses
while this house [of the LORD] lies in
ruins?"
5Now therefore, thus says the LORD
of hosts, "Consider your ways *and*
thoughtfully reflect on your conduct!
6"You have planted much, but you
harvest little; you eat, but you do not
have *enough;* you drink, but you do
not have *enough* to be intoxicated;
you clothe yourselves, but no one is
warm *enough;* and he who earns wages earns them *just to put* them in a
bag with holes in it [because God has
withheld His blessing]."
7Thus says the LORD of hosts, "Consider your ways *and* thoughtfully reflect on your conduct!
8"Go up to the hill country, bring

1:2 *The time has not come.* The people had decided that rebuilding the Lord's dwelling among His people was not important.
1:4 *your [expensive] paneled houses.* Those who wanted to make their houses elaborate installed wood panels. The people of Haggai's time were making their homes elegant, rivaling royal residences and the holy temple itself. But they still did not feel that the "time was right" to begin working on the renewed temple. While this verse is not a blanket condemnation of elegant living among God's people, it certainly calls for a re-evaluation of priorities.
1:8 *that I may be pleased with it.* God's joy in

CHAPTER 1 **1** Ezr 4:24; 1Ch 3:17; Ezr 5:2; 1Ch 6:15 **3** Ezr 5:1 **4** 2Sa 7:2 **5** La 3:40 **6** Dt 28:38; Zec 8:10

lumber and rebuild My house (temple),
that I may be pleased with it and be
glorified," says the LORD [accepting it
as done for My glory].
9"You look for much [harvest], but
it comes to little; and even when you
bring that home, I blow it *away.* Why?"
says the LORD of hosts. "Because of My
house, which lies in ruins while each
of you runs to his own house [eager
to enjoy it].
10"Therefore, because of you [that is,
your sin and disobedience] the heavens
withhold the dew and the earth with-
holds its produce.
11"I called for a drought on the land
and the hill country, on the grain, on
the new wine, on the oil, on what the
ground produces, on men, on cattle,
and on all the labor of your hands."
12Then Zerubbabel the son of Sheal-
tiel and Joshua the son of Jehozadak,
the high priest, with all the remnant
of the people [who had returned from
exile], listened carefully *and* obeyed
the voice of the LORD their God and the
words of Haggai the prophet, since the
LORD their God had sent him. And the
people [reverently] feared the LORD.
13Then Haggai, the LORD's messen-
ger, spoke the LORD's message to the
people saying, " 'I am with you,' de-
clares the LORD."
14So the LORD stirred up the spirit of
Zerubbabel the son of Shealtiel, gover-
nor of Judah, and the spirit of Joshua
the son of Jehozadak, the high priest,
and the spirit of all the remnant of the
people; and they came and worked on
the house of the LORD of hosts, their
God,
15on the twenty-fourth day of the
sixth month (Sept 21, 520 B.C.) in the
second year of Darius the king.

The Builders Encouraged

2 ON THE twenty-first day of the
seventh month (Oct 17, 520 B.C., the
second year of Darius king of Per-
sia), the word of the LORD came by the
prophet Haggai, saying,
2"Speak now to Zerubbabel the son
of Shealtiel, governor of Judah, and
to Joshua the son of Jehozadak, the
high priest, and to the remnant of the
people, saying,
3'Who is left among you who saw
this house (temple) in its former glory?
And how do you see it now? Does it
not seem to you like nothing in com-
parison?
4'But now be courageous, Zerubba-
bel,' declares the LORD, 'be courageous
also, Joshua the son of Jehozadak, the
high priest, and be courageous, all you
people of the land,' declares the LORD,
'and work; for I am with you,' declares
the LORD of hosts.
5'As for the promise which I made
with you when you came out of Egypt,
My Spirit stands [firm and immovable]
and continues with you; do not fear!'
6"For thus says the LORD of hosts,
'Once more, in a little while, I am going
to shake the heavens and the earth,
the sea and the dry land. [Heb 12:26]
7'I will shake all the nations; and
they will come with the desirable

---

the temple is related to His pleasure in the people who would worship Him there. ***be glorified.*** Clearly God does not need to receive more glory (Ps 24:7 – 10); however, He gladly receives the adoration of His people.

1:13 *I am with you.* God's promise to Moses was, "Certainly I will be with you" (Ex 3:12). God's promise to the people of Judah was that the name of the Coming One would be Immanuel, meaning "God is with us" (Isa 7:14). Here God repeated the same message of comfort and encouragement.

2:3 *this house (temple) in its former glory.* The temple of Solomon was one of the wonders of the ancient world (1Ki 6). The older temple would have loomed large and magnificent, far outstripping the present structure. So even though the building was completed, there may have been the sense among some of the people that it was "as nothing."

2:6 *I am going to shake the heavens.* This is another way of speaking of the day of the Lord. The purpose of the day of the Lord is to prepare the earth for the glorious reign of Jesus Christ on earth (Mt 24:29; Rev 6:12 – 17).

---

9 Hag 2:16; Hag 2:17 **10** Lev 26:19; Dt 28:23; 1Ki 8:35 **11** 1Ki 17:1; 2Ki 8:1; Hag 2:17 **12** Ezr 5:2 **13** Mt 28:20; Ro 8:31 **14** 2Ch 36:22; Ezr 1:1; Hag 2:21; Ezr 5:2,8 **CHAPTER 2** **3** Ezr 3:12; Zec 4:10 **4** Zec 8:9 **5** Ex 29:45,46; Neh 9:20; Isa 63:11 **6** ver. 21; Heb 12:26; Joel 3:16 **7** Ge 49:10; Mal 3:1

and precious things of all nations,
and I will fill this house with glory
and splendor,’ says the LORD of hosts.
[Is 60:5; Matt 2:1–12]
8 ‘The silver is Mine and the gold is
Mine,’ declares the LORD of hosts.
9 ‘The latter glory of this house will
be greater than the former,’ says the
LORD of hosts, ‘and in this place I shall
give [the ultimate] peace *and* prosper-
ity,’ declares the LORD of hosts.”
10 On the twenty-fourth day of the
ninth month (Dec 18, 520 B.C.), in the
second year of Darius, the word of
the LORD came to Haggai the prophet,
saying,
11 “Thus says the LORD of hosts, ‘Ask
the priests for a ruling:
12 ‘If a man carries meat that is holy
[because it has been offered in sacrifice
to God] in the fold of his garment, and
he touches bread, or cooked food, or
wine, or oil, or any [kind of] food with
this fold, does what he touches become
holy [dedicated exclusively to God’s
service]?’ ” And the priests answered,
“No!” [Holiness is not transferrable.]
13 Then Haggai said, “If one who
is [ceremonially] unclean because of
[contact with] a corpse touches any
of these [articles of food], will it be
unclean?” And the priests answered,
“It will be unclean.” [Ceremonial un-
cleanness, like sin, is infectious.]
14 Then Haggai answered, “ ‘So is this
people. And so is this nation before
Me,’ declares the LORD, ‘and so is every
work of their hands; and what they
offer there [on the altar] is unclean
[because they who offer it are unclean].
15 ‘But now, do consider [what will
happen] from this day forward: before
one stone was placed on another in the
temple of the LORD,
16 from that time when one came to
a *grain* heap *expecting* twenty *mea-
sures*, there would be only ten; and
when one came to the wine vat to draw
out fifty measures, there would be only
twenty.
17 ‘I struck you and the work of your
hands with scorching wind, mildew,
and hail; yet you did not come back to
Me,’ declares the LORD.
18 ‘Do consider from this day for-
ward, from the twenty-fourth day of
the ninth month; from the day when
the temple of the LORD was founded,
consider:
19 Is the seed still in the barn? As to
the vine, the fig tree, the pomegranate,
and the olive tree—they have not pro-
duced. Yet from this day on I will bless
you [in the harvest of your crops].’ ”
20 And again the word of the LORD
came to Haggai on the twenty-fourth
day of the month (Dec 18, 520 B.C.),
saying,
21 “Speak to Zerubbabel governor of
Judah, saying, ‘I am going to shake
the heavens and the earth. [Hag 2:6;
Matt 1:12, 13]
22 ‘I will [in the distant future] over-
throw the thrones of kingdoms and
destroy the power of the kingdoms of
the [ungodly] nations; and I will over-
throw the chariots and those who ride
in them, and the horses and their riders
will go down, every one by the sword
of his brother [annihilating one anoth-
er]. [Dan 2:34, 35, 44, 45; Rev 19:11–21]
23 ‘On that day,’ declares the LORD of

2:9 *I shall give [the ultimate] peace.* Peace includes good health, well-being, and an abundant life. The term speaks of everything being as it ought to be.

2:12 *does what he touches become holy.* Since the role of the priest was to interpret God’s law, it was reasonable that questions on holiness should be addressed to them. Haggai asked whether holiness could be transferred by contact. The answer was no.

2:13 – 14 *It will be unclean.* The priests were asked if a religiously unclean person, someone who had touched a corpse, could contaminate someone else by touch. The answer was yes (Nu 19:11 – 13). The people had worked hard to rebuild the temple, only to be told that their worship would be unacceptable in the new temple. The existence of the temple itself guaranteed nothing. The hearts of the people had to be in harmony with the sacrifices being made.

---

9 Jn 1:14; Ps 85:8,9; Lk 2:14; Eph 2:14 **11** Lev 10:10,11; Dt 33:10; Mal 2:7 **13** Nu 19:11 **14** Titus 1:15 **15** Hag 1:5
16 Hag 1:6,9; Zec 8:10 **17** Dt 28:22; 1Ki 8:37; Am 4:9; Hag 1:9; Hag 1:11; Jer 5:3; Am 4:6,8-11 **18** Zec 8:9
19 Zec 8:12 **21** Hag 1:14; ver. 6,7 **22** Da 2:44; Mic 5:10; Zec 9:10

hosts, 'I will take you, Zerubbabel, the son of Shealtiel, My servant,' declares the LORD, 'and I will make you [through the Messiah, your descendant] like a signet ring, for I have chosen you [as the one with whom to renew My covenant to David's line],' " declares the LORD of hosts. [2 Sam 7:12, 16]

2:23 *a signet ring.* This was an item of great value in the ancient world. The owner used it much like we use our personal signature on checks or other important documents. God used this imagery to indicate that Zerubbabel was in His hand, that he was highly valued, and that he represented God's authority in his leadership of the people. Even though the people had been told they were still unclean in God's eyes (2:10 – 14), their leader Zerubbabel was encouraged to guide them through those spiritually trying times.

23 SS 8:6; Jer 22:24; Isa 42:1; 43:10

THE BOOK OF

ZECHARIAH

▸ **AUTHOR:** The universal testimony of the Jewish and Christian tradition affirms Zechariah as the author of the entire book. Like Jeremiah and Ezekiel, he was of priestly lineage and was a young man when he was called to prophesy. According to Jewish tradition, Zechariah was a member of the Great Synagogue that collected and preserved the canon of revealed Scripture. He was born in Babylon and brought to Palestine by his grandfather when the Jewish exiles returned under Zerubbabel and Joshua the high priest.

▸ **TIMES:** 520 – 470 BC ▸ **KEY VERSE:** Zec 9:9

▸ **THEME:** Zechariah's writings were designed to encourage the Israelites and inspire energy, identity, and vision during the rebuilding of the temple. Like Isaiah, Daniel, and Ezekiel, his prophecies are characterized by visions of God and the future. In this context, many would describe the book to be apocalyptic with similarities to Revelation. Probably, more than any of the other books, Zechariah makes concrete predictions about Christ, which are fulfilled in the New Testament. He also makes some startling predictions about Israel in the end times that have already seen fulfillment.

A Call to Repentance

1 IN THE eighth month of the second
year [of the reign] of Darius [the
king of Persia], the word of the LORD
came to Zechariah (the LORD remem-
bers) the son of Berechiah, the son of
Iddo, the prophet, saying, [Ezra 5:1]
2"The LORD was extremely angry
with your fathers.
3"Therefore say to the Jews, 'Thus
says the LORD of hosts (armies), "Re-
turn to Me," declares the LORD of hosts,
"and I shall return to you.
4"Do not be like your fathers, to
whom the former prophets proclaimed,
'Thus says the LORD of hosts, "Repent
[that is, change your way of thinking]
and return now from your evil way [of
life] and from your evil deeds." ' But
they did not listen or pay attention to
Me," declares the LORD. [2 Kin 17:13;
Is 45:22; Jer 18:11; Ezek 33:11]
5"Your fathers, where are they? And
the prophets, do they live forever?
6"But did not My words (warnings)
and My statutes, which I commanded
My servants the prophets, overtake
your fathers? Then they repented and
said, 'As the LORD of hosts planned to
do to us [in discipline and punishment],
in accordance with our ways and our
deeds, so has He dealt with us.' " ' "

1:1 *Zechariah.* The name means "Yahweh remembers," emphasizing God's faithfulness to His covenant promises and to His people.
1:3 *says the LORD of hosts.* The personal name translated "Lord" speaks of God's gracious nature as He relates to His people (Ex 3:14 – 16); the hosts are the angelic armies that await His every command. ***Return to Me.*** These words remind us of the depth of God's unconditional love.
1:5 – 6 *fathers . . . prophets.* The previous generation had been overtaken by God's judgment (Dt 28:15 – 68).

CHAPTER 1 **1** Ezr 4:24; Hag 1:1; Ezr 5:1; Mt 23:35 **3** Jer 25:5; 35:15; Mic 7:19; Mal 3:7; Lk 15:20; Jas 4:8 **4** 2Ch 36:15,16; Isa 31:6; Jer 3:12; 18:11; Eze 18:30; Hos 14:1 **6** Isa 55:1; La 1:18; 2:17

Patrol of the Earth

7 On the twenty-fourth day of the eleventh month (Feb 15, 519 B.C.), which is the month of Shebat, in the second year of [the reign of] Darius, the word of the LORD came to Zechariah the prophet, the son of Berechiah, the son of Iddo, as follows:

8 In the night I saw [a vision] and behold, a Man was riding on a red horse, and it stood among the myrtle trees that were in the ravine; and behind Him were horses: red, sorrel (reddish-brown), and white.

9 Then I said, "O my lord, what are these?" And the angel who was speaking with me said, "I will show you what these are."

10 And the Man who stood among the myrtle trees answered and said, "These are the ones whom the LORD has sent to go throughout the earth *and* patrol it."

11 And the men on the horses answered the Angel of the LORD who stood among the myrtle trees and said, "We have gone throughout the earth [patrolling it] and behold, all the earth sits at rest [in peace and free from war]."

12 Then the Angel of the LORD said, "O LORD of hosts, how long will You withhold mercy *and* compassion from Jerusalem and the cities of Judah, against which You have had indignation *and* anger these seventy years [of the Babylonian captivity]?"

13 And the LORD answered the angel who was speaking with me with gracious and comforting words.

14 So the angel who was speaking with me said to me, "Proclaim, 'Thus says the LORD of hosts, "I am jealous [with a burning, fiery passion] for Jerusalem and for Zion [demanding what is rightfully and uniquely mine] with a great jealousy.

15 "But I am very angry with the nations who are at ease *and* feel secure; for while I was only a little angry, they furthered the disaster [against the people of Israel]."

16 'Therefore, thus says the LORD, "I have returned to Jerusalem with mercy *and* compassion. My house shall be built in it," says the LORD of hosts, "and a measuring line shall be stretched out over Jerusalem." '

17 "Proclaim again, 'Thus says the LORD of hosts, "My cities shall again overflow with prosperity, and the LORD shall again comfort Zion and again choose Jerusalem." ' "

18 Then I looked up, and saw four horns (powers)!

19 So I asked the angel who was speaking with me, "What are these?" And he answered me, "These are the horns [the powerful Gentile nations] that have scattered Judah (the Southern Kingdom), Israel (the Northern Kingdom), and Jerusalem (capital city of Judah)."

1:7 – 6:15 *the word of the LORD.* This section contains a sequence of eight night visions concerning Israel's future, followed by the symbolic crowning of the high priest Joshua. Here Zechariah pursues the same end as Haggai, rebuilding the temple as the center of worship and world rule, and as a place of pilgrimage for the nations (8:20 – 23).

1:8 *myrtle.* This was an evergreen tree that was once very common in the vicinity of Jerusalem (Neh 8:15).

1:12 – 13 *Angel of the LORD.* This may be a conversation between the pre-incarnate Jesus and the first Person of the Trinity, God the Father (Ps 110:1 – 3). It is certainly an allusion to Jesus' role as Intercessor.

1:15 *I am very angry.* Here the anger of God was against the nations that He had used to punish His unrepentant people.

1:16 *a measuring line shall be stretched.* A measuring line was used to make measurements in preparation for new construction. The stretching of the line was a promise that the work would begin and that the completion of the task would follow.

1:18 *four horns.* Animal horns were often used by poets and prophets as symbols of powerful nations and their kings (Da 7:7 – 8,24). The horns that persecuted Israel and Judah included Assyria, Babylon, Medo-Persia, and later Greece.

---

8 Jos 5:13; Rev 6:4; Zec 6:2-7 **10** Heb 1:14 **11** Ps 103:20,21 **12** Jer 25:11,12; Da 9:2; Zec 7:5 **13** Jer 29:10 **14** Joel 2:18; Zec 8:2 **15** Isa 47:6 **16** Isa 12:1; 54:8; Zec 2:10; 8:3; Zec 2:1,2 **17** Isa 51:3; 14:1; Zec 2:12; 3:2 **19** Ezr 4:1,4,7; 5:3

[20]Then the LORD showed me four craftsmen.
[21]I asked, "What are these [horns and craftsmen] coming to do?" And he said, "These are the horns (powers) that have scattered Judah so that no man raised up his head [because of the suffering inflicted by the Gentile nations]. But these *craftsmen* have come to terrify them *and* make them panic, and throw down the horns of the nations who have lifted up their horns against the land of Judah in order to scatter it."

God's Favor to Zion

2 AND I looked up, and saw a man with a measuring line in his hand.
[2]So I said, "Where are you going?" And he said to me, "To measure Jerusalem, to see how wide it is and how long it is."
[3]And behold, the angel who was speaking with me was going out, and another angel was coming out to meet him,
[4]and he said to the second angel, "Run, speak to that young man, saying, 'Jerusalem will be inhabited [like villages] without walls [spreading out into the open country] because of the great number of people and livestock in it.
[5]'For I,' declares the LORD, 'will be a wall of fire around her [protecting her from enemies], and I will be the glory in her midst.' "
[6]"Hear this! Flee from [Babylon] the land of the north [which shall come under judgment]," declares the LORD, "for I have scattered you like the four winds of the heavens," declares the LORD.
[7]"Hear, Zion (Jerusalem)! Escape, you who are living with the daughter of Babylon!"
[8]For thus says the LORD of hosts, "After glory He has sent Me against the nations which plunder you—for he who touches you, touches the apple of His eye.
[9]"Behold, I will wave my hand over them and they shall become plunder for their own slaves. Then you shall know (recognize, understand fully) that the LORD of hosts has sent Me.
[10]"Sing for joy and rejoice, O Daughter of Zion; for behold, I am coming, and I will dwell in your midst," declares the LORD.
[11]"Many nations shall join themselves to the LORD in that day and shall be My people. And I will dwell in your midst, and you shall know (recognize, understand fully) that the LORD of hosts has sent Me to you. [Is 2:3; Mic 4:2]
[12]"The LORD will take possession of Judah as His portion in the holy land and will again choose Jerusalem.
[13]"Be still before the LORD, all mankind; for He is roused (raised up) from His holy habitation [in response to His persecuted people]." [Hab 2:20; Zeph 1:7]

Joshua, the High Priest

3 THEN THE guiding angel showed me Joshua the high priest [representing disobedient, sinful Israel] stand-

---

2:4–5 *inhabited [like villages] without walls.* Jerusalem will have no need for defensive fortifications because God's presence will guarantee its safety and security. These words refer ultimately to the future Jerusalem under the rule of its glorious king (Zep 3:15–19).

2:8–9 *the apple of His eye.* This refers to the pupil, an endearing expression suggesting how enormously important the Hebrew people are to God because of His covenant with them. Just as we protect our eyes from even the smallest particles of dust, so God protects and cares for His people.

2:12 *the holy land.* Surprisingly, this phrase occurs in the Old Testament only here. The land is "holy" because of the presence of God among His believing people.

3:1 *Satan.* The Hebrew is literally "the Satan," meaning "the Accuser." The picture is not unlike that of Job 1, where Satan stands before the Lord making accusations against people who follow God.

21 Ps 75:4,5 **CHAPTER 2** **1** Eze 40:3 **2** Rev 11:1 **4** Jer 31:27; Eze 36:10 **5** Isa 26:1; Isa 60:19 **6** Isa 48:20; Dt 28:64; Eze 17:21 **7** Rev 18:4 **8** Dt 32:10 **9** Isa 19:16; Zec 4:9 **10** Isa 12:6; Lev 26:12 **11** Isa 2:2,3; Zec 3:10; Ex 12:49; Eze 33:33 **12** Dt 32:9; Zec 1:17 **13** Hab 2:20; Ps 68:5; Isa 57:15 **CHAPTER 3** **1** Hag 1:1; Ps 109:6

ing before the Angel of the LORD, and Satan standing at Joshua's right hand to be his adversary *and* to accuse him.

2 And the LORD said to Satan, "The LORD rebuke you, Satan! Even the LORD, who [now and ever] has chosen Jerusalem, rebuke you! Is this not a log snatched *and* rescued from the fire?" [Jude 9]

3 Now Joshua was clothed with filthy (nauseatingly vile) garments and was standing before the Angel [of the LORD].

4 He spoke to those who stood before Him, saying, "Remove the filthy garments from him." And He said to Joshua, "See, I have caused your wickedness to be taken away from you, and I will clothe *and* beautify you with rich robes [of forgiveness]."

5 And I (Zechariah) said, "Let them put a clean turban on his head." So they put a clean turban on his head and clothed him with [rich] garments. And the Angel of the LORD stood by.

6 And the Angel of the LORD [solemnly and earnestly] admonished Joshua, saying,

7 "Thus says the LORD of hosts, 'If you will walk in My ways [that is, remain faithful] and perform My service, then you will also govern My house and have charge of My courts, and I will give you free access [to My presence] among these who are standing here.

The Branch

8 'Now listen, Joshua, the high priest, you and your colleagues who are sitting in front of you—indeed they are men who are a symbol [of what is to come]—for behold, I am going to bring in My servant the Branch [in Messianic glory]. [Is 4:2; Jer 23:5; 33:15; Zech 6:12]

9 'For behold, the stone which I have set before Joshua; on that one stone are seven eyes (symbolizing infinite intelligence, omniscience). Behold, I will engrave an inscription on it,' declares the LORD of hosts, 'and I will remove the wickedness *and* guilt of this land in a single day. [2 Chr 16:9; Jer 50:20; Zech 4:10]

10 'In that day,' declares the LORD of hosts, 'every one of you will invite his neighbor to sit under his vine and his fig tree [enjoying peace and prosperity in the kingdom].' " [Mic 4:1–4]

The Golden Lampstand and Olive Trees

4 AND THE angel who was speaking with me came back and awakened me, like a man who is awakened out of his sleep.

2 He said to me, "What do you see?" I said, "I see, and behold, a lampstand all of gold, with its bowl [for oil] on the top of it and its seven lamps on it with seven spouts belonging to each of the lamps which are on the top of it. [Matt 5:14, 16; Luke 12:35; Phil 2:15; Rev 1:20]

3 "And there are two olive trees by it, one on the right side of the bowl and the other on its left side [supplying it continuously with oil]." [Rev 11:4–13]

4 So I asked the angel who was speaking with me, "What are these, my lord?"

5 Then the angel who was speaking with me answered me, "Do you not know what these are?" And I said, "No, my lord."

3:3 *with filthy (nauseatingly vile) garments.* The high priest represented the people before God (Ex 28:29) and under no circumstances was he to become defiled or unclean (Ex 28:2; Lev 21:10–15). Joshua's garments were literally "befouled with excrement."

3:8 *the Branch.* Isaiah used this word and a similar one to describe the Messiah who will grow out of the root of the family of Jesse as a tender sprout shoots up from the ground (6:12; Isa 4:2; 11:1; 53:2). Joshua and his companions were "men wondered at" because the reinstitution of the priesthood made public God's continuing intention to fulfill His promises to His people.

4:2–3 *a lampstand all of gold.* This would remind people of the lampstand in the tabernacle and the temple.

2 Jude 9; Ro 8:33; Am 4:11; Ro 11:5 **3** Isa 64:6 **4** Isa 61:10; Lk 15:22 **5** Ex 29:6 **7** Lev 8:35; Eze 44:16; Dt 17:9; Zec 4:14 **8** Ps 71:7; Isa 8:18; Isa 42:1; Eze 34:23; Isa 11:1; Zec 6:12 **9** Ps 118:22; Isa 28:16; Rev 5:6; Jer 31:34; Mic 7:18 **10** Zec 2:11; Isa 36:16; Mic 4:4 **CHAPTER 4** **1** Zec 2:3; Da 8:18 **2** Rev 1:12; 4:5 **3** Rev 11:4

6 Then he said to me, "This [contin-
uous supply of oil] is the word of the
LORD to Zerubbabel [prince of Judah],
saying, 'Not by might, nor by power,
but by My Spirit [of whom the oil is a
symbol],' says the LORD of hosts.
7 'What are you, O great mountain
[of obstacles]? Before Zerubbabel [who
will rebuild the temple] *you will be-
come* a plain (insignificant)! And he
will bring out the capstone [of the new
temple] with loud shouts of "Grace,
grace to it!" ' " [Ezra 4:1–5, 24; Is 40:4]
8 Also the word of the LORD came to
me, saying,
9 "The hands of Zerubbabel have
laid the foundations of this house, and
his hands will finish it. Then you will
know (recognize, understand fully)
that the LORD of hosts has sent me [as
His messenger] to you.
10 "Who [with reason] despises the
day of small things (beginnings)? For
these seven [eyes] shall rejoice when
they see the plumb line in the hand
of Zerubbabel. They are the eyes of
the LORD which roam throughout the
earth." [Rev 5:6]
11 Then I said to him [who was speak-
ing with me], "What are these two olive
trees on the right side of the lampstand
and on its left?"
12 And a second time I said to him,
"What are these two olive branches
which are beside the two golden pipes
by which the golden oil is emptied?"
13 And he answered me, "Do you not
know what these are?" And I said, "No,
my lord."
14 Then he said, "These are the two
sons of fresh oil [Joshua the high
priest and Zerubbabel the prince of
Judah] who are standing by the Lord
of the whole earth [as His anointed
ones]." [Rev 11:4]

The Flying Scroll

5 AGAIN I looked up, and I saw a
scroll flying *in the air!*
2 And the angel said to me, "What
do you see?" And I answered, "I see a
flying scroll; its length is twenty cubits
(thirty feet) and its width is ten cubits
(fifteen feet)."
3 Then he said to me, "This is the
curse that is going out over the face
of the whole land; for everyone who
steals will be cut off according to the
writing on one side, and everyone who
swears [oaths falsely] shall be cut off
according to the writing on the other
side. [Is 24:6; Mal 3:8, 9]
4 "I will send the curse out," declares
the LORD of hosts, "and it will enter
the house of the thief and the house
of the one who swears falsely by My
name; and it will spend the night in
that house and consume it, both its
timber and its stones."
5 Then the angel who was speaking
with me came forward and said to
me, "Now look up and see what this
is going forth."
6 And I said, "What is it?" And he
said, "This is the ephah (grain basket)
going forth. This," he continued, "is
their appearance throughout the land
[Amos 8:5]
7 (and behold, a [round, flat] lead

4:6 *but by My Spirit.* The rebuilding of the temple, which had at last begun in earnest (Ezr 5:1 – 2; Hag 1:14), would be accomplished not by human strength or resources, but by the power of God's Spirit.

4:7 *O great mountain.* This was a figurative reference to the great obstacles the people faced in rebuilding the temple (Ezr 5:3 – 17). The setting of the "capstone" would mark the completion of the project. ***Grace, grace to it.*** This may be understood as a prayer for God's favor, or as a cry of admiration over the grace and beauty of the newly built temple.

4:11 – 14 *two olive trees . . . two sons of fresh oil.* These are identified as representatives of the religious and political offices in Israel, or of priest and king. Many identify the two branches with the high priest Joshua and the governor Zerubbabel.

5:4 *it will . . . consume it.* God's great love does not preclude the exercise of His judgment on those who violate His will. The judgment upon the disobedient would be certain and severe.

5:7 – 8 *This is Wickedness.* The woman sitting inside the ephah (basket) is a personification of sin.

---

6 Hos 1:7 **7** Jer 51:25; Mt 21:21; Ps 118:22; Ezr 3:11,13 **9** Ezr 3:10; Ezr 6:15; Zec 2:9,11; 6:15; Isa 48:16; Zec 2:8
10 Hag 2:3; 2Ch 16:9; Pr 15:3; Zec 3:9 **11** ver. 3 **14** Rev 11:4; Zec 3:7; See Jos 3:11,13; Zec 6:5
CHAPTER 5 **1** Eze 2:9 **3** Mal 4:6 **4** Lev 19:12; Zec 8:17; Mal 3:5; See Lev 14:45

cover was lifted up); and there sat a
woman inside the ephah."
8 Then he said, "This is Wickedness
(Godlessness)!" And he threw her back
down into the middle of the ephah and
threw the lead cover on its opening.
9 Then I looked up, and there were
two women coming out with the wind
in their wings; and they had wings like
the wings of a stork, and they lifted
up the ephah between the earth and
the heavens.
10 I said to the angel who was speak-
ing with me, "Where are they taking
the ephah?"
11 And he said to me, "To the land of
Shinar (Babylon) to build a temple for
her; and when it is prepared, she shall
be set there on her own pedestal."

The Four Chariots

6 NOW AGAIN I looked up, and four
chariots were coming out from be-
tween two mountains; and the moun-
tains were mountains of [firm, immov-
able] bronze (divine judgment).
2 The first chariot had red horses
(war, bloodshed), the second chari-
ot had black horses (famine, death),
[Rev 6:4–6]
3 the third chariot had white horses
(victory), and the fourth chariot had
strong dappled horses (death through
judgment). [Rev 6:2, 8]
4 Then I said to the angel who was
speaking with me, "What are these,
my lord?"
5 The angel answered me, "These are
the four spirits of the heavens, which
go out after presenting themselves be-
fore the Lord of all the earth, [Ps 104:4;
Matt 24:31]
6 with the chariot with the black
horses going toward the north country;
then the one with the white horses fol-
lows after them [because there are two
northern powers to overcome], and the
chariot with the dappled horses goes
toward the south country."
7 When the strong horses went out,
they were eager to patrol the earth.
And the LORD said, "Go, patrol the
earth." So they patrolled the earth
[watching and protecting it].
8 Then He called out to me and said
to me, "See, those who are going to the
north country have quieted My Spirit
[of wrath] in the north country."
9 The word of the LORD also came to
me, saying,
10 "Take *an offering* from the exiles,
from Heldai, from Tobijah, and from
Jedaiah [as representatives]; and you
go the same day and enter the house
of Josiah the son of Zephaniah, where
they have arrived from Babylon.

The Symbolic Crowns

11 "Take silver and gold [from them],
and make an *ornate* crown and set
it on the head of Joshua the son of
Jehozadak, the high priest.
12 "Then say to Joshua, 'Thus says the
LORD of hosts, "Behold (look, keep in
sight, watch), a Man (Messiah) whose
name is Branch, for He shall branch
out from His place (Israel, the Davidic
line); and He shall build the [ultimate]
temple of the LORD. [Is 4:2; Jer 23:5;
33:15; Zech 3:8]
13 "Yes, [you are to build a temple of
the LORD, but] it is He who shall build
the [ultimate] temple of the LORD, and

6:1 *chariots.* In ancient times two-wheeled and four-wheeled horse-drawn carts served as vehicles for transportation and for warfare. The war chariots usually had a crew of two or three men including a driver, an archer, and a defender who used a shield to protect the others.

6:5 *four spirits of the heavens.* These spirits were probably angels.

6:11 *make an ornate crown.* This crown was to be placed on the head of Joshua the high priest.

6:12 *He shall build the [ultimate] temple of the LORD.* Since the restoration temple (the second temple) was already being built and would be complete by Zerubbabel (4:9), the temple referred to here may be the future temple of the messianic kingdom (Isa 2:2 – 4; Eze 40 – 42; Mic 4:1 – 5; Hag 2:7 – 9). The Messiah Himself will build it. The temple of Zerubbabel was a prophetic symbol of the temple that is still to come.

6:13 *sit and rule . . . be a Priest.* In the Messiah

---

11 Jer 29:5,28; Ge 10:10 **CHAPTER 6** **2** Zec 1:8; Rev 6:5 **4** Zec 5:10 **5** Ps 104:4; Heb 1:7,14; 1Ki 22:19; Da 7:10; Zec 4:14; Lk 1:19 **6** Jer 1:14 **7** Ge 13:17; Zec 1:10 **8** Ecc 10:4 **11** Ex 29:6 **12** Lk 1:78; Jn 1:45; Zec 3:8; Mt 16:18; Eph 2:20; Heb 3:3 **13** Isa 22:24; Ps 110:4; Heb 3:1

He shall bear the honor *and* majesty [as the only begotten of the Father] and sit and rule on His throne. And He shall be a Priest on His throne, and the counsel of peace shall be between the two offices [Priest and King].” ’ [John 1:14; 17:5; Heb 2:9]

14“Now the crown shall become a reminder in the temple of the LORD to Helem, Tobijah, Jedaiah, and Hen the son of Zephaniah. [Matt 10:41]

15“And those who are far away will come and [help] build the temple of the LORD.” Then you shall know [without any doubt] that the LORD of hosts sent me (Zechariah) to you. And it will come about if you will diligently obey the [voice of the] LORD your God.

Hearts like Flint

7 IN THE fourth year of [the reign of] King Darius [of Persia], the word of the LORD came to Zechariah on the fourth day of the ninth month, *which is* Chislev (Dec 7, 518 B.C.).

2Now the people of Bethel had sent Sharezer and Regem-melech and their men to seek the favor of the LORD,

3speaking to the priests who belong to the house of the LORD of hosts and to the prophets, saying, “[Now that I am returned from exile] shall I weep in the fifth month [mourning the destruction of the temple], and fast as I have done these many years [in Babylon]?”

4Then the word of the LORD of hosts came to me (Zechariah), saying,

5“Speak to all the people of the land and to the priests, saying, ‘When you fasted and mourned in the fifth and seventh months these seventy years [that you were in exile], was it actually for Me that you fasted?

6‘When you eat and when you drink, do you not eat for yourselves and do you not drink for yourselves [to satisfy your own needs]?

7‘Should you not hear the words which the LORD proclaimed by the former prophets, when Jerusalem was inhabited and prosperous along with her cities around her, and the South (the Negev) and the foothills were inhabited?’ ”

8Then the word of the LORD came to Zechariah, saying,

9“Thus has the LORD of hosts said, ‘Dispense true justice and practice kindness and compassion, to each other;

10and do not oppress *or* exploit the widow or the fatherless, the stranger or the poor; and do not devise *or* even imagine evil in your hearts against one another.’

11“But they refused to listen *and* pay attention and turned a stubborn shoulder [stiffening themselves in resistance] and stopped up their ears.

12“They made their hearts [hard] like flint, so that they could not hear the law and the words which the LORD of hosts had sent by His Spirit through the former prophets. Therefore great wrath came from the LORD of hosts.

13“And just as He called and they

---

the two offices of king and priest will be united (Jn 1:49; Heb 3:1).

7:3 *the house of the LORD of hosts.* This refers to the temple in Jerusalem.

7:5 – 6 *was it actually for Me that you fasted.* The rhetorical question was designed to confront the people and priests with the selfish motives of their self-righteous fasting. Biblical fasting is meant to be time taken from the normal routines of preparing and eating food to express humility and dependence on God during a time of prayer. There was only one required fast in the law of Moses, the fast on the Day of Atonement (Lev 23:27).

7:9 – 10 *Dispense true justice.* Judicial decisions must be made without partiality or bias. ***practice kindness and compassion.*** Loving commitment and concern should guide our relationships with others. ***do not oppress.*** No advantage is to be taken of the helpless and less fortunate. ***do not devise or even imagine evil in your hearts against one another.*** Evil scheming against others is prohibited. Sacrifices and worship are of little interest to God if they are not accompanied by practical piety. Zechariah’s four admonitions highlight the practical social concerns that many of the prophets emphasized (Isa 1:11 – 17; Hos 6:6; Mic 6:6 – 8).

14 Ex 12:14; Mk 14:9 **15** Isa 57:19; Eph 2:13 **CHAPTER 7** **3** Dt 17:9; Mal 2:7; Zec 8:19 **5** Isa 58:5; Jer 41:1; Zec 1:12; Ro 14:6 **7** Jer 17:26 **9** Isa 58:6,7; Jer 7:23 **10** Ex 22:21; Isa 1:17; Jer 5:28; Ps 36:4; Mic 2:1 **11** Neh 9:29; Ac 7:57 **12** Eze 11:19; Neh 9:29; 2Ch 36:16; Da 9:11 **13** Pr 1:24; Isa 1:15; Mic 3:4

would not listen, so they called and
I would not listen," says the LORD of
hosts;
14 "but I scattered them with a storm
wind among all the nations whom they
have not known. Thus the land was
desolate after they had gone, so that
no one passed through or returned,
for they [by their sins] had made the
pleasant land desolate *and* deserted."

The Coming Peace and Prosperity of Zion

8 THEN THE word of the LORD of
hosts came [to me], saying,
2 "Thus says the LORD of hosts, 'I am
jealous for Zion with great jealousy [de-
manding what is rightfully and unique-
ly mine], and I am jealous for her with
great wrath [against her enemies].'
3 "Thus says the LORD, 'I shall return
to Zion and will dwell in the midst
of Jerusalem, and Jerusalem shall be
called the [faithful] City of Truth, and
the mountain of the LORD of hosts will
be called the Holy Mountain.'
4 "Thus says the LORD of hosts, 'Old
men and old women will again sit in
the streets (public places) of Jerusalem,
each man with his staff in his hand
because of his advanced age.
5 'And the streets of the city will be
filled with boys and girls playing in
its streets.'
6 "Thus says the LORD of hosts, 'If
it is difficult in the eyes of the rem-
nant of this people in those days [in
which this comes to pass], will it also
be difficult in My sight?' declares the
LORD of hosts. [Gen 18:14; Jer 32:17, 27;
Luke 18:27]
7 "Thus says the LORD of hosts, 'Be-
hold, I am going to save My people
from the east country and from the
west; [Is 43:5, 6]
8 and I will bring them home and
they will live in the midst of Jerusalem;
and they shall be My people, and I will
be their God in truth (faithfulness) and
in righteousness.'
9 "Thus says the LORD of hosts, 'Let
your hands be strong, you who in
these days hear these words from the
mouths of the prophets who, on the day
that the foundation of the house of the
LORD of hosts was laid, foretold that the
temple might be rebuilt.
10 'For before those days there were
no wages for man or animal; nor was
there any peace *or* success for him
who went out or came in because of
his enemies, for I set all men against
one another.
11 'But now [in this time since you
began to build] I will not treat the rem-
nant of this people as in the former
days,' declares the LORD of hosts.
12 'For there the seed will produce
peace *and* prosperity; the vine will
yield its fruit, and the ground will pro-
duce its increase, and the heavens will
give their dew. And I will cause the
remnant of this people to inherit *and*
possess all these things.
13 'And as you have been a curse
among the nations, O house of Judah
(Southern Kingdom) and house of
Israel (Northern Kingdom), so I will
save you, that you may be a blessing.
Fear not; let your hands be strong.'
[Jer 22:8, 9]
14 "For thus says the LORD of hosts,
'Just as I planned to do harm to you

8:1 – 3 *City of Truth.* This label will be valid only when the Messiah brings His righteous reign to that city. Then the land will be holy (2:12).
8:7 – 8 *east country . . . west.* These terms together represent all parts of the earth. ***My people . . . their God.*** This expression occurs in the descriptions of God's covenant relationship with His people (Ex 19:5; 29:45; Lev 26:12; Hos 2:23). With these words, Zechariah anticipates a renewal of God's covenant with His people (Jer 31:34).
8:10 *no wages . . . nor was there any peace.* Zechariah recounts the desperate situation in Judea before the work on the temple resumed in 520 BC (Hag 1:1,6,10 – 11; 2:16 – 17).
8:11 – 13 *let your hands be strong.* In view of God's gracious purposes and future plans for His people, they were called to be diligent in their present efforts to serve Him with sincere hearts (1Co 15:58).

14 Dt 28:64 **CHAPTER 8** **2** Na 1:2 **3** Isa 1:21; Isa 2:2,3; Jer 31:23 **4** 1Sa 2:31; Isa 65:20 **6** Ge 18:14; Lk 1:37 **7** Isa 11:11; Eze 37:21 **8** Jer 31:1,33; 4:2 **9** Hag 2:4; Ezr 5:1,2; Hag 2:18 **10** Hag 1:6,9 **12** Joel 2:22; Ps 67:6; Hag 1:10 **13** Jer 42:18; Ge 12:2; Ru 4:11 **14** Jer 31:28; 2Ch 36:16

when your fathers provoked Me to
wrath,' says the LORD of hosts, 'and I
did not relent,
15 so I have again planned in these
days to do good to Jerusalem and to
the house of Judah. Do not fear!
16 'These are the things which you
should do: speak the truth with one an-
other; judge with truth and pronounce
the judgment that brings peace in [the
courts at] your gates. [Eph 4:25]
17 'And let none of you devise *or* even
imagine evil in your heart against an-
other, and do not love lying *or* half-
truths; for all these things I hate,' de-
clares the LORD."
18 Then the word of the LORD of hosts
came to me (Zechariah), saying,
19 "Thus says the LORD of hosts,
'The fast of the fourth [month to
mourn the breaching of Jerusalem's
walls], the fast of the fifth [month to
mourn the temple's destruction], the
fast of the seventh [month to mourn
Gedaliah's assassination], and the fast
of the tenth [month to mourn the siege
of Jerusalem] will become times of joy
and gladness and cheerful feasts for
the house of Judah; so [to bring this
about] love truth and peace.' [Jer 39:2;
2 Kin 25:1, 2, 8, 25]
20 "Thus says the LORD of hosts, 'It
will come to pass that peoples and the
inhabitants of many cities will come
[to Jerusalem].
21 'The inhabitants of one [city] will
go to another, saying, "Let us go at
once to ask the favor of the LORD and to
seek the LORD of hosts. I will go also."
22 'So many peoples and powerful
nations will come to seek the LORD of
hosts in Jerusalem and to ask the LORD
for His favor.'
23 "Thus says the LORD of hosts, 'In
those days ten men [as representatives]
from all the nations will grasp the robe
of a Jew, saying, "Let us go with you,
for we have heard that God is with
you."'"

Prophecies against Neighboring Nations

9 THE ORACLE (a burdensome mes-
sage) of the word of the LORD is
against the land of Hadrach [in Syria],
with Damascus as its resting place (for
the eyes of men, especially of all the
tribes of Israel, are toward the LORD),
[Nah 1:1]

2 And Hamath also, which borders
  on it (Damascus),
Tyre and Sidon, though they are
  very wise.
3 For Tyre built herself an
  [impregnable] stronghold [on an
  island offshore],
And she has heaped up silver like
  dust
And gold like the mire of the
  streets.
4 Behold, the Lord will dispossess her
And throw her wealth into the sea;
And Tyre will be devoured by fire.
5 Ashkelon will see it and fear;
Gaza will writhe in pain,
And Ekron, for her hope *and*
  expectation, has been ruined.
The king will perish from Gaza,
And Ashkelon will not be
  inhabited.
6 And a mongrel race will live in
  Ashdod,
And I will put an end to the pride
  and arrogance of the
  Philistines.
7 I will take the blood from their
  mouths

8:16 – 17 *judge with truth and pronounce the judgment that brings peace.* Zechariah set forth the ethical obligations of a life of faith. He upheld these important values and condemned evil plans and false oaths.

8:20 – 23 *peoples . . . will come.* Here Zechariah announces a great turning of the nations to God. During the Messianic Era, a multitude of people from many cities will go to Jerusalem to "seek the LORD." These Gentiles will be included among the people of God by faith (Eph 2:13 – 19).

9:1 *oracle.* This word suggests that a weighty judgment must be declared.

9:7 *blood from their mouths . . . detestable things from between their teeth.* These

16 Eph 4:25 **17** Pr 3:29 **19** Jer 52:6,12; 2Ki 25:25; Jer 41:1,2; Jer 52:4; Est 8:17; ver. 16 **21** Isa 2:3; Mic 4:1,2 **22** Isa 60:3 **23** Isa 3:6; 1Co 14:25 **CHAPTER 9** **1** Jer 23:33; Am 1:3; 2Ch 20:12; Ps 145:15 **2** Jer 49:23; Isa 23; Eze 26; 1Ki 17:9; Eze 28:3 **4** Isa 23:1; Eze 26:17 **6** Am 1:8

And their detestable things from
between their teeth [those
repulsive, idolatrous sacrifices
eaten with the blood].
Then they too will be a remnant
for our God,
And be like a clan in Judah,
And Ekron will be like one of the
Jebusites.
8 Then I will camp around My house
[as a guard] because of an army,
Because of him who passes by and
returns;
And no oppressor will again
overrun them (Israel),
For now My eyes are upon them
[providentially protecting them].
9 Rejoice greatly, O Daughter of Zion!
Shout aloud, O Daughter of
Jerusalem!
Behold, your King (Messianic
King) is coming to you;
He is righteous and endowed with
salvation,
Humble *and* unassuming [in
submission to the will of the
Father] and riding on a donkey,
Upon a colt, the foal of a donkey.
10 I will cut off the [war] chariot from
Ephraim
And the [war] horse from Jerusalem,
And the bow of war will be cut off.
And He will speak [words of]
peace to the nations,
And His dominion shall be from
sea to sea [absolutely endless],
And from the River [Euphrates] to
the ends of the earth. [Ps 72:8]

Salvation of Judah and Ephraim

11 As for you also, because of the
blood of My covenant with you
[My chosen people, the covenant
that was sealed with blood]
I have freed your prisoners from
the waterless pit. [Gen 37:24;
Ex 24:4–8; Heb 9:16]
12 Return to the stronghold [of
security and prosperity],
O prisoners who have the hope;
Even today I am declaring that I
will restore double [your former
prosperity] to you [as firstborn
among nations]. [Ps 40:2; Is 40:2]
13 For I will bend Judah as My bow,
I will fit the bow with Ephraim [as
My arrow].
And I will stir up your sons,
O Zion, against your sons,
O Greece,
And will make you [Israel] like the
sword of a warrior.
14 Then the LORD will be seen
[hovering] over them [protecting
His people],
And His arrow will go forth like
lightning;
And the Lord GOD will blow the
trumpet
And will march in the windstorms
of the south.
15 The LORD of hosts shall defend *and*
protect them;
And they will devour [the
enemy] and trample down the
slingstones [that have missed
their mark],
And they will drink [of victory]
and be boisterous as with wine;
And they shall be filled like
sacrificial bowls [used to catch
the blood],
Drenched like the corners of the
[sacrificial] altar.
16 And the LORD their God shall save
them on that day
As the flock of His people;
For they are like the [precious]
jewels of a crown,

---

phrases refer to the cessation of unlawful and idolatrous practices (Lev 17:14; Isa 65:4; 66:17).

9:9 *Humble and unassuming . . . and riding on a donkey.* This prophecy was fulfilled on the day of the triumphal entry, when Jesus rode into Jerusalem on the colt of a donkey (Mt 21:2 – 7). The donkey was the mount of princes (Jdg 5:10; 10:4) and kings (2Sa 16:1 – 2).

9:14 *windstorms of the south.* This description, patterned after God's appearance at Sinai (Ex 19), reveals God's sovereignty and power to protect His own.

9:15 *they will drink.* The people will be filled with drink like sacrificial basins were filled with blood, and they will be filled with meat like the corners of a sacrificial altar (Ps 110:6).

8 Ps 34:7 **9** Zec 2:10; Jer 23:5; Lk 19:38 **10** Hos 1:7; Mic 5:10 **11** Isa 42:7 **12** Isa 49:9 **14** Ps 18:14; Isa 21:1 **16** Isa 62:3; Mal 3:17; Isa 11:12

Displayed *and* glittering in His land.
17 For how great is God's goodness and how great is His beauty!
And how great [He will make Israel's] goodliness and [Israel's] beauty!
Grain and new wine will make the young men and virgins flourish.

God Will Bless Judah and Ephraim

10 ASK *FOR* rain from the LORD at the time of the spring rain.
It is the LORD who makes the thunder clouds;
And He will give them showers of rain, grass in the field to everyone.
2 For the teraphim (household idols) speak wickedness (emptiness, worthlessness),
And the diviners see lying visions
And tell false dreams;
They comfort in vain.
Therefore the people wander like sheep,
They are afflicted *and* suffer because there is no shepherd.
3 "My anger is kindled against the shepherds [who are not true shepherds],
And I shall punish the male goats (leaders);
For the LORD of hosts has visited His flock, the house of Judah (the Southern Kingdom),
And will make them like His beautiful *and* majestic horse in the battle. [Ezek 34:1–10]
4 "From them (Judah) shall come the Cornerstone,
From them the tent peg,
From them the bow of battle,
From them every ruler, all of them together. [Jer 30:21]
5 "They will be like mighty men
Trampling down *their enemies* in the mire of the streets in the battle;
And they will fight because the LORD is with them,
And the [enemies'] riders on horses will be shamed.
6 "I will strengthen the house of Judah [making it superior],
And I will save the house of Joseph.
I will bring them back [and allow them to live securely],
Because I have had compassion on them.
They will be as though I had not rejected them,
For I am the LORD their God, and I will listen *and* answer them.
7 "Then Ephraim will be like a mighty warrior,
And their heart will rejoice as if from wine;
Yes, their children will see it and rejoice;
Their heart will rejoice *and* shout triumphantly in the LORD.
8 "I will whistle for them and gather them together,
For I have redeemed them;
And they will increase [again] as they have increased before [in Egypt]. [Ezek 36:10, 11]
9 "When I scatter them among the nations,
They will remember Me in far countries,

10:2 *no shepherd.* The metaphor of *shepherd* was often used in the ancient Middle East to represent a king or ruler (Eze 34:6 – 8,23 – 24). Here the emphasis was on the lack of spiritual leadership.
10:3 *the house of Judah.* God will strengthen Judah so that she can overthrow the oppressors.
10:4 – 5 *tent peg.* A peg firmly in place suggests permanence and endurance (Isa 22:23). ***bow of battle.*** This image pictures the strength necessary for military conquest (2Ki 13:17).
10:7 *as if from wine.* What was promised to Judah in verse 5 is here promised to Ephraim. Wine is used here as a symbol of abundant joy (Ps 104:15; Am 9:13; Jn 2:1 – 11).
10:9 *They will remember Me.* This phrase anticipates their turning to the Lord in repentance. ***will live.*** This implies more than mere survival.

17 Ps 31:19; Joel 3:18 **CHAPTER 10** **1** Jer 14:22; Dt 11:14; Joel 2:23 **2** Jer 10:8; Hab 2:18; Job 13:4; Eze 34:5 **3** Eze 34:17; Lk 1:68; SS 1:9 **4** Isa 28:16; Isa 22:23 **5** Ps 18:42 **6** Jer 3:18; Eze 37:21; Hos 1:7; Zec 13:9 **7** Ps 104:15 **8** Isa 5:26; Isa 49:19; Eze 36:37 **9** Hos 2:23; Dt 30:1

And with their children they will
live and come back [to Me and
the land I gave them].
10 "I will bring them (all Israel) back
home again from the land of
Egypt
And gather them from Assyria,
And I will bring them into the land
of Gilead and Lebanon [the land
on the east and on the west of
the Jordan]
Until no room can be found for
them.
11 "And they will pass through the
sea of distress *and* anxiety [with
the LORD leading His people, as
at the Red Sea]
And He will strike the waves in
the sea,
So that all the depths of the Nile
will dry up;
And the pride of Assyria will be
brought down
And the scepter [of the
taskmasters] of Egypt will pass
away.
12 "And I will strengthen Israel in the
LORD,
And they will walk [and glory] in
His name," declares the LORD.

The Doomed Flock

11 OPEN YOUR doors,
O Lebanon,
That fire may devour your cedars.
2 Wail, O cypress, for the cedar has
fallen,
Because the magnificent trees
have been destroyed;
Wail, O oaks of Bashan,
For the inaccessible forest [on the
steep mountainside] has come
down.
3 There is a sound of the shepherds'
wail,
For their splendor (grazing land) is
ruined;
There is a sound of the young
lions' roar,
For the pride of the Jordan is
ruined.

4 Thus says the LORD my God, "Pas-
ture the flock *doomed* for slaughter,
5 whose buyers slay them and go un-
punished, and those who sell them say,
'Blessed be the LORD, for I have become
rich!' And their own shepherds have no
pity on them *nor* protect them [from
the wolves].
6 "For I will no longer have pity on the
inhabitants of the land," declares the
LORD; "but behold, I will cause the men
to fall, each into the hand of another
and into the hands of his [foreign] king.
And the enemy will strike the land,
and I will not rescue the people from
their hand."
7 So I [Zechariah] pastured the
flock *doomed* for slaughter, truly [as
the name implies] the most miserable
of sheep. And I took two [shepherd's]
staffs, the one I called Favor (Grace)
and the other I called Union (Bonds);
so I pastured the flock.
8 Then I eliminated the three [incom-
petent, unfit] shepherds [the civil rul-
ers, the priests, and the prophets] in
one month, for I was impatient with
them, and they also were tired of me
and despised me. [Jer 2:8, 26; 18:18]

God promises spiritual life and blessing to the repentant.
10:12 *I will strengthen Israel.* The regathering will be accomplished by God's power as He gives strength to His people. ***they will walk [and glory] in His name.*** In the last days, Israel will return to the land as a believing nation (v. 8; 12:10 – 13:1; Ro 11:26).
11:7 *Favor ... Union.* These were the names of Zechariah's two staffs. The images suggest that he wanted the flock to enjoy God's favor and to experience national unity. According to Canaanite legend, the god Baal was given the two clubs named Driver and Chaser to battle the dark deities of the sea. It is appropriate that God's messenger Zechariah is given shepherd's staffs to guide the people, instead of clubs for fighting.
11:8 *three [incompetent, unfit] shepherds.* Some have suggested that the three shepherds represent classes of rulers in Israel: kings, priests, and prophets. Others suggest that they refer to the last three kings of Judah or to certain high priests of the Maccabean era.

10 Isa 11:11; Hos 11:11; Isa 49:20 **11** Isa 11:15; 14:25; Eze 30:13 **12** Mic 4:5 **CHAPTER 11** **1** Zec 10:10 **2** Isa 32:19 **5** Jer 2:3; 50:7; Dt 29:19; Hos 12:8 **7** Zep 3:12; Mt 11:5 **8** Hos 5:7

9So I said, "I will not pasture you.
What is to die, let it die, and what is to
be destroyed, let it be destroyed; and
let the survivors devour one another's
flesh."
10I took my staff, Favor, and broke it
in pieces, breaking the covenant which
I had made with all the peoples.
11So the covenant was broken on that
day, and thus the most wretched of the
flock who were watching me realized
that it was the word of the LORD.
12I said to them, "If it seems good to
you, give me my wages; but if not, do
not." So they weighed out thirty pieces
of silver as my wages.
13Then the LORD said to me, "Throw
it to the potter [as if to the dogs]—that
magnificent sum at which I am valued
by them!" So I took the thirty pieces
of silver and threw them to the potter
in the house of the LORD. [Matt 26:14,
15; 27:3–10]
14Then I broke my second staff,
Union, into pieces to break the broth-
erhood between Judah (the Southern
Kingdom) and Israel (the Northern
Kingdom).
15The LORD said to me, "Take again
for yourself the equipment [of a shep-
herd, but this time] of a foolish shep-
herd. [Ezek 34:2–6]
16"For behold, I am going to raise
up a [false] shepherd in the land who
will not care for the perishing, seek
the scattered, heal the broken, or feed
the healthy; but will eat the flesh of
the fat ones and tear off their hoofs [to
consume everything].
17"Woe (judgment is coming) to the
worthless *and* foolish shepherd
Who deserts the flock!
The sword will strike his arm
And his right eye!
His arm shall be totally withered
And his right eye completely
blinded." [Jer 23:1; John 10:12, 13]

Jerusalem to Be Attacked

12 THE ORACLE (a burdensome
message) of the word of the LORD
concerning Israel.
1Thus declares the LORD who stretch-
es out the heavens and lays the foun-
dation of the earth and forms the spirit
of man within him:
2"Behold, I am going to make Jeru-
salem a cup that causes reeling (stag-
gering) to all the surrounding peoples;
and when the siege is against Jerusa-
lem, it will also be against Judah.
3"And in that day I will make Jeru-
salem a heavy stone for all the peoples;
all who lift it will be severely injured.
And all the nations of the earth will
come *and* be gathered against it.
4"In that day," declares the LORD, "I
will strike every horse with panic and
his rider with madness; but I will open
My eyes *and* watch over the house of
Judah, and will strike every horse of
the [opposing] nations with blindness.
5"Then the clans of Judah will say
in their hearts, 'The inhabitants of Je-
rusalem are our strength in the LORD
of hosts, their God.'
6"In that day I will make the clans of

11:12 *thirty pieces of silver.* Zechariah, taking the role of the messianic shepherd, requested his wages for service rendered. This amount was the price of a slave. It was also the price paid to Judas for betraying Jesus (Mt 27:6–10).
11:15–16 *Take again for yourself the equipment [of a shepherd, but this time] of a foolish shepherd.* This phrase means to behave like one. ***eat the flesh of the fat ones and tear off their hoofs.*** These phrases express the savagery of a foolish shepherd.
11:17 *worthless and foolish shepherd.* He will be judged. His "arm," which should have been used to protect the sheep, will wither. His "right eye," which should have watched over the sheep, will be blinded.
12:1 *The oracle.* As in 9:1, the burden is a weighty judgment that the prophet must discharge. ***heavens . . . the earth . . . the spirit of man.*** Three phrases are used here in describing the greatness of God as Creator.
12:3 *heavy stone.* Jerusalem is compared to a heavy stone that brings injury to anyone who tries to remove it from its place.
12:6 *Judah.* Here, Judah is likened to (1) "a firepot in a woodpile" used to carry hot coals for

9 Jer 15:2 **11** Zep 3:12 **12** Mt 26:15; Ex 21:32 **13** Mt 27:9 **15** Eze 34:2 **17** Jer 23:1; Eze 34:2; Jn 10:12
CHAPTER 12 **1** Isa 42:5; 44:24; Nu 16:22; Ecc 12:7; Isa 57:16 **2** Isa 51:17 **3** ver. 4,6,8; Zec 13:1; Mt 21:44
4 Ps 76:6; Eze 38:4 **6** Ob 18

Judah like a firepot in a woodpile, and like a flaming torch among sheaves [of grain]. They will devour all the surrounding peoples on the right hand and on the left; and the people of Jerusalem will again live [securely] in their own place, in Jerusalem.

7"The LORD shall save the tents of Judah first, so that the glory of the house of David and the glory of the inhabitants of Jerusalem will not be magnified above Judah.

8"In that day the LORD will defend the people of Jerusalem, and the one who is impaired among them in that day [of persecution] will become [strong and noble] like David; and the house of David will be like God, like the Angel of the LORD [who is] before them.

9"And in that day I will seek to destroy all the nations that come against Jerusalem.

10"I will pour out on the house of David and on the people of Jerusalem, the Spirit of grace (unmerited favor) and supplication. And they will look at Me whom they have pierced; and they will mourn for Him as one mourns for an only son, and they will weep bitterly over Him as one who weeps bitterly over a firstborn. [John 19:37; Rev 1:7]

11"In that day there shall be a great mourning in Jerusalem, like the mourning of [the city of] Hadadrimmon in the Valley of Megiddo [over beloved King Josiah]. [2 Chr 35:22–25]

12"The land will mourn, every family by itself; the [royal] family of the house of David by itself and their wives by themselves; the family of the house of Nathan [David's son] by itself and their wives by themselves;

13the [priestly] family of the house of Levi by itself and their wives by themselves; the family of Shimei [grandson of Levi] by itself and their wives by themselves;

14all the families that remain, each by itself, and their wives by themselves [each with an overwhelming individual regret for having blindly rejected their Messiah].

False Prophets Ashamed

13 "IN THAT day a fountain shall be opened for the house of David and for the people of Jerusalem for [cleansing from] sin and impurity.

2"In that day," declares the LORD of hosts, "I will cut off the names of the idols from the land, and they will no longer be remembered. I will also remove the [false] prophets and the unclean spirit from the land.

3"And if anyone still [appears as a prophet and falsely] prophesies, then his father and his mother who gave birth to him will say to him, 'You shall not live, for you have spoken lies in the name of the LORD'; and his father and his mother who gave birth to him shall pierce him through when he prophesies.

4"And in that day the [false] prophets will each be ashamed of his vision when he prophesies, and they will not

---

the purpose of starting a fire, and (2) "a flaming torch" that could quickly ignite a field of cut grain.

12:10 ***Spirit of grace.*** These words refer to the gracious working of the Holy Spirit that leads to conviction and repentance (Jn 16:8–11). ***supplication.*** The Spirit will stimulate an attitude of repentance and prayer for God's mercy. There are many significant ministries of the Holy Spirit in the period of the Hebrew kingdom.

12:12–14 ***the house of David . . . the house of Levi . . . their wives by themselves.*** These words are quoted in the Talmud as an argument for separating men and women in worship. But the verse seems to indicate that each mourner will face his or her sorrow alone, without the comfort of companionship.

13:2 ***cut off the names of the idols.*** In ancient times, a person's name reflected his or her reputation. Zechariah anticipated the complete removal of the reputation and acknowledgement of false gods.

13:4 ***a hairy robe.*** This was the traditional clothing of a prophet. False prophets will deny that they are prophets, for fear of punishment, and will refuse to wear one (2Ki 1:8; Mt 3:4).

---

9 Hag 2:22 **10** Jer 31:9; 50:4; Eze 39:29; Joel 2:28; Jn 19:34; Rev 1:7; Jer 6:26; Am 8:10 **11** Ac 2:37; 2Ki 23:29 **12** Rev 1:7; Lk 3:31 **CHAPTER 13** **1** Heb 9:14 **2** Ex 23:13; 2Pe 2:1 **3** Dt 18:20 **4** Mic 3:6,7; 2Ki 1:8

wear a hairy robe [of true prophets] in
order to deceive,
5 but he will [deny his identity and]
say, 'I am no prophet. I work the
ground, because a man sold me as a
slave in my youth.'
6 "And one will say to him, 'What
are these wounds between your
arms?' Then he will answer, 'Those
wounds I received in the house of my
friends.'

7 "Awake, O sword, against My
    Shepherd,
And against the Man, My
    Associate,"
Declares the LORD of hosts.
"Strike the Shepherd so that the
    sheep [of the flock] may be
    scattered;
And I will turn My hand *and* stretch
    it out against the little ones [of the
    flock]. [Matt 26:31, 32]
8 "It will come about in all the
    land,"
Declares the LORD,
"Two parts in it will be cut off and
    perish,
But the third will be left alive.
    [Hos 2:23; Rom 11:5]
9 "And I will bring the third part
    through the fire,
Refine them as silver is refined,
And test them as gold is tested.
They will call on My name,
And I will listen *and* answer
    them;
I will say, 'They are My people,'
And they will say, 'The LORD is
    my God.' "

God Will Battle Jerusalem's Foes

14 BEHOLD, A day is coming for
the LORD when the spoil taken
from you (Jerusalem) will be divided
in your midst.
2 For I will gather all nations against
Jerusalem to battle, and the city will
be captured and the houses plundered
and the women ravished; and half of
the city will be exiled, but the rest of the
people will not be cut off from the city.
3 Then the LORD will go forth and
fight against those nations, as when
He fights on a day of battle.
4 In that day His feet shall stand on
the Mount of Olives, which lies before
Jerusalem on the east; and the Mount
of Olives will be split in half from the
east to the west by a very large valley,
and half of the mountain will move
toward the north and half of it toward
the south. [Is 64:1, 2]
5 You will flee by the valley of My
mountains, for the valley of the moun-
tains will reach to Azel; and you will
flee just as you fled from the earth-
quake in the days of Uzziah king of
Judah. Then the LORD my God will
come, and all the holy ones (believers,
angels) with Him. [Amos 1:1; Col 3:4;
1 Thess 4:14; Jude 14, 15]
6 In that day there will be no light; the
glorious ones (heavenly bodies) shall
be darkened.
7 But it will be a unique day which is
known to the LORD—not day and not
night, but at evening time there will
be light.

13:6 *wounds between your arms.* This is probably a reference to the profession of an ecstatic prophet who slashed himself on the back or breast. Self-inflicted wounds were thought to gain the attention and blessing of the gods (1Ki 18:28). Under questioning, the man declares that the wounds were received from friends so that he will not be found out as a false prophet and be put to death (v. 3).

13:7 *O sword.* The sword, an instrument of death, is likened to a warrior being roused for action. The Lord commands the sword to strike the Messiah. ***My Shepherd.*** This clearly indicates that the death of Jesus was not accident, but was divinely determined.

13:9 *Refine them.* The smelting pot uses intense heat to separate the dross from pure metal. ***test them.*** Once refined, precious metal must be analyzed to determine its value.

14:4 *Mount of Olives.* This is located east of Jerusalem and the Kidron valley: it is a north-south hill about 2,700 feet in elevation. The Messiah will return to the Mount of Olives, the very mountain from which He will have ascended after His time on earth. (Ac 1:10–11). On the day of Messiah's return, the mount will be split by a deep east-west valley.

5 Am 7:14 **7** Isa 40:11; Jn 10:30; Mt 26:31; Lk 12:32 **8** Ro 11:5 **9** Isa 48:10; 1Pe 1:6; Ps 50:15; Jer 30:22
CHAPTER 14 **1** Isa 13:9 **2** Joel 3:2 **4** Eze 11:23; Joel 3:12 **5** Am 1:1; Mt 24:30; Joel 3:11 **7** Mt 24:36; Isa 30:26

8 And in that day living waters will
flow out from Jerusalem, half of them
to the eastern sea (Dead Sea) and half
of them to the western sea (the Medi-
terranean); it will be in summer as well
as in winter.

God Will Be King over All

9 And the LORD shall be king over all
the earth; in that day the LORD shall
be *the only* one [worshiped], and His
name *the only* one.
10 All the land will be changed into
a plain from Geba to Rimmon, [the
Rimmon that is] south of Jerusalem;
but Jerusalem will rise and remain
[lifted up] on its site from Benjamin's
Gate to the place of the First Gate to
the Corner Gate, and from the Tower
of Hananel to the king's wine presses.
11 It will be inhabited, for there will
no longer be a curse, for Jerusalem will
dwell in security. [Rev 22:3]
12 Now this will be the plague with
which the LORD shall strike all the
peoples that have warred against Je-
rusalem: Their flesh will rot while they
stand on their feet, and their eyes will
rot in their sockets, and their tongue
will rot in their mouth.
13 In that day a great panic *and* dis-
may from the LORD will fall on them;
and they will seize one another's hand,
and the hand of the one will be raised
against the hand of the other.
14 Judah also will fight at Jerusalem;
and the wealth of all the surrounding
nations will be gathered together—
gold and silver and garments in great
abundance.
15 So like this plague [on men] there
will be the plague on the horses, mules,
camels, donkeys, and all the livestock
in those camps.
16 Then everyone who is left of all
the nations that went against Jeru-
salem will go up from year to year to
worship the King, the LORD of hosts,
and celebrate the Feast of Booths (Tab-
ernacles).
17 And it will be that whichever of
the families of the earth does not go
up to Jerusalem to worship the King,
the LORD of hosts, there will be no rain
on them.
18 If the family of Egypt does not go
up [to Jerusalem] and present them-
selves, then no *rain will fall* on them.
It will be the plague with which the
LORD will strike the nations who do not
go up to celebrate the Feast of Booths
(Tabernacles).
19 This will be the [consequent] pun-
ishment [for the sin] of Egypt, and the
[consequent] punishment [for the sin]
of all the nations that do not go up to
celebrate the Feast of Booths (Taber-
nacles).
20 In that day there will *be written*
on the little bells on the horses, "HOLY

14:8 *living waters.* This term describes running water from a spring or river, in contrast to the stale and stagnant water of a cistern (Jer 2:13). The water will flow from Jerusalem toward the eastern sea (the Dead Sea) and the western sea (the Mediterranean). In contrast with the seasonal streams that flow only during the rainy season, these streams will irrigate the land in both summer and winter.

14:11 *will be inhabited.* This is a contrast to the time of Nehemiah when the population of Jerusalem was sparse (Neh 7:4; 11:1). In the Lord's coming kingdom, the city will be inhabited and its citizens secure.

14:18–19 *Egypt.* In this passage, Egypt is used as an example of the nations that are unwilling to come to Jerusalem to worship King Messiah and celebrate the feast. It will be subject to divine judgment because it was a traditional enemy of Israel.

14:20–21 *HOLY TO THE LORD.* These words will be inscribed on the gold headband worn by the high priest (Ex 28:36). Holiness will so permeate Messiah's kingdom that even the lowly cooking pots will be holy. The name "Canaanite" here refers to the merchants who frequented Jerusalem and the temple courts with their wares (Neh 13:19–22; Mt 21:12; Jn 2:14). None will profiteer in the worship of God in the coming age. God's search for true worshipers will be realized in the company of devoted, holy people.

8 Eze 47:1 **9** Rev 11:15; Eph 4:5,6 **10** Zec 12:6; Neh 3:1 **11** Jer 31:40; Jer 23:6 **13** 1Sa 14:15,20; Jdg 7:22; 2Ch 20:23; Eze 38:21 **14** Eze 39:10,17 **15** ver. 12 **16** Isa 60:6; 66:23; Lev 23:34; Neh 8:14; Hos 12:9; Jn 7:2 **17** Isa 60:12 **18** Dt 11:10 **20** Isa 23:18

TO THE LORD." And the cooking pots in the LORD's house will be [holy to the LORD] like the bowls before the altar.
[21]Every cooking pot in [all the houses in] Jerusalem and in Judah will be holy to the LORD of hosts, and all who sacrifice will come and take them and boil [their sacrifices] in them. And in that day there will no longer be a Canaanite [that is, any godless or spiritually unclean person, whether Jew or Gentile] in the house of the LORD of hosts. [Eph 2:19–22]

21 Isa 35:8; Joel 3:17; Rev 21:27; 22:15; Eph 2:19-22

THE BOOK OF MALACHI

▸ **AUTHOR:** The only Old Testament mention of Malachi is in 1:1. Nothing else is known of Malachi, not even his father's name. But tradition holds that he too, like Zechariah, was a member of the Great Synagogue. He is generally accepted as the author of this book. It is likely that Malachi proclaimed his message when Nehemiah was absent from Judah between 432 BC and 425 BC, almost a century after Haggai and Zechariah began to prophesy. Thus, because of its place in history and the Old Testament, Malachi is a transitional book. Its primary themes are consistent with the rest of the Old Testament, but it also serves as a precursor to the New Testament.

▸ **TIMES:** c. 432 – 425 BC ▸ **KEY VERSE:** Mal 2:17

▸ **THEME:** In Malachi, the days of political upheaval are past, and the country is living in an uneventful waiting period. The people are waiting for Messiah to bring the glorious restoration of their nation to the renewed prominence of the Davidic and Solomonic period. There is a sense the people are losing touch with God during this rather uneventful time. The old problem with idol worship is gone, but other problems have taken its place. Malachi's role is to call them back to a genuine enduring faith in God. His dominant admonition is for a personal relationship with the living God, who seeks men to walk with Him (2:6).

God's Love for Jacob

1 THE ORACLE (burdensome message) of the word of the LORD to Israel through [My messenger] Malachi.
2 "I have loved you," says the LORD. But you say, "How *and* in what way have You loved us?" "Was not Esau Jacob's brother?" declares the LORD. "Yet I loved Jacob (Israel);
3 but [in comparison with My love for Jacob] I have hated Esau (Edom), and I have made his mountains a wasteland, and *have given* his inheritance to the jackals of the wilderness." [Rom 9:13, 16]
4 Though [impoverished] Edom says, "We have been beaten down, but we will return and build up the ruins." Thus says the LORD of hosts, "They may build, but I will tear down; and men will call them the Wicked Territory, the people against whom the LORD is indignant forever."
5 Your own eyes will see this and you will say, "The LORD is great *and* shall be magnified beyond the border

1:1 *to Israel.* In the postexilic period, the use of the word Israel for the people of Judah expresses the hope that the Lord was in the process of reasserting the fullness of His original promises to His people. The name "Malachi" means "My Messenger."
1:3 *I have hated Esau.* The contrast between the words *love* and *hate* here and in verse 2 seems too strong. But on many occasions in the Old Testament, the verb *hate* has the basic meaning "not to choose." God's love for Jacob was expressed in His electing grace in extending His covenant to Jacob and to his descendants (Ge 25:21 – 26; Isa 44:1 – 5). In His sovereign purpose, God set His love on the one and not the other. The term *hate* may carry the idea of indifference as well.

CHAPTER 1 **2** Dt 7:8; 10:15; Ro 9:13 **3** Jer 49:18; Eze 35:3; Ob 10 **5** Ps 35:27

of Israel!" [Is 34; 63:1–6; Jer 49:7–22;
Ezek 25:12–14; Obad 1]

Sin of the Priests

6" 'A son honors his father, and a
servant his master. Then if I am a Fa-
ther, where is My honor? And if I am
a Master, where is the [reverent] fear
and respect due Me?' says the LORD of
hosts to you, O priests, who despise My
name. But you say, 'How *and* in what
way have we despised Your name?'
7"You are presenting defiled food
upon My altar. But you say, 'How have
we defiled You?' By thinking that the
table of the LORD is contemptible *and*
may be despised.
8"When you [priests] present the
blind [animals] for sacrifice, is it not
evil? And when you present the lame
and the sick, is it not evil? Offer such
a thing [as a blind or lame or sick an-
imal] to your governor [as a gift or as
payment for your taxes]. Would he
be pleased with you? Or would he re-
ceive you graciously?" says the LORD
of hosts.
9"But now will you not entreat God's
favor, that He may be gracious to us?
With such an offering from your hand
[as an imperfect animal for sacrifice],
will He show favor to any of you?" says
the LORD of hosts.
10"Oh, that there were even one
among you [whose duty it is to minis-
ter to Me] who would shut the gates, so
that you would not kindle *fire on* My
altar uselessly [with an empty, worth-
less pretense]! I am not pleased with
you," says the LORD of hosts, "nor will
I accept an offering from your hand.
11"For from the rising of the sun,
even to its setting, My name shall be
great among the nations. In every
place incense is going to be offered
to My name, and a grain offering that
is pure; for My name shall be great
among the nations," says the LORD of
hosts.
12"But you [priests] profane it when
you say, 'The table of the Lord is de-
filed, and as for its fruit, its food is to
be despised.'
13"You also say, 'How tiresome this
is!' And you disdainfully sniff at it,"
says the LORD of hosts, "and you bring
what was taken by robbery, and the
lame or the sick [animals]; this you
bring as an offering! Should I receive
it with pleasure from your hand?" says
the LORD. [Lev 1:3; Deut 15:21]
14"But cursed is the swindler who
has a male in his flock and vows [to
offer] it, but sacrifices to the Lord a
blemished *or* diseased thing! For I am
a great King," says the LORD of hosts,
"and My name is to be [reverently and
greatly] feared among the nations."

Priests to Be Disciplined

2 "NOW, O priests, this command-
ment is for you.
2"If you do not listen, and if you do
not take it to heart to honor My name,"
says the LORD of hosts, "then I will
send the curse upon you and I will

1:6 ***A son honors his father.*** Here the Lord uses truisms: A father and a master can expect honor from those beneath them, but God was not receiving the honor due Him. ***if I am a Father.*** The image of God as Father is common in the New Testament, but less frequent in the Old Testament (Isa 63:16; 64:8).

1:8 ***the blind . . . lame and the sick.*** The demands of the holy worship of God had been made clear in the law. Only the very best should be presented as an offering to the Lord (Lev 1:3); no one was to come with an offering that was blemished or unclean (Lev 7:19–21).

1:11 ***great among the nations.*** God would one day receive praise from all the nations. Even the despised Gentiles would offer praise, while God's own people were profaning His holy name (Ps 87; 117).

1:14 ***I am a great King.*** The reputation of the Lord among His people was to have been the means whereby all the nations would be drawn to worship Him as well.

2:2 ***I will send the curse.*** At the passage of the people into the promised land, the Levites spread before the people the blessings of obedience and the curses on disobedience (Dt 27; 28). But

6 Ex 20:12; Lk 6:46; Mal 2:14 **7** Dt 15:21; Eze 41:22 **8** Lev 22:22; Job 42:8 **9** Hos 13:9 **10** 1Co 9:13; Isa 1:11 **11** Isa 59:19; Isa 60:3,5; 1Ti 2:8; Rev 8:3; Isa 66:19 **12** ver. 7 **13** Lev 22:20 **14** ver. 8; Ps 47:2; 1Ti 6:15
CHAPTER 2 **2** Dt 28:15

curse your blessings [on the people]. Indeed, I have cursed them already, because you are not taking it to heart.

3 “Behold, I am going to rebuke your seed, and I will spread the refuse on your faces, the refuse from the festival offerings; and you will be taken away with it [in disgrace].

4 “Then you will know [without any doubt] that I have sent this [new] commandment to you (priests), that My covenant may continue with Levi [the priestly tribe],” says the LORD of hosts.

5 “My covenant with Levi was [one of] life and peace, and I gave them to him as an object of reverence; so he [and the priests] feared Me and stood in reverent awe of My name.

6 “True instruction was in Levi’s mouth and injustice was not found on his lips. He walked with Me in peace and uprightness, and he turned many from wickedness.

7 “For the lips of the priest should guard *and* preserve knowledge [of My law], and the people should seek instruction from his mouth; for he is the messenger of the LORD of hosts.

8 “But as for you [priests], you have turned from the way and you have caused many to stumble by your instruction [in the law]. You have violated the covenant of Levi,” says the LORD of hosts.

9 “So I have also made you despised and abased before all the people, just as you are not keeping My ways but are showing partiality [to people] in [your administration of] the law.”

Sin in the Family

10 Do we not all have one Father? Has not one God created us? Why do we deal treacherously with one another, profaning the covenant of our fathers [with God]?

11 Judah has been treacherous (disloyal), and an repulsive act has been committed in Israel and in Jerusalem; for Judah has profaned the sanctuary of the LORD which He loves, and has married the daughter of a foreign god. [Ezra 9:2; Jer 2:3]

12 As for the man who does this, may the LORD cut off from the tents of Jacob to the last man those who do this [evil thing], awake and aware, even the one who brings an offering to the LORD of hosts.

13 This is another thing you do: you cover the altar of the LORD with tears, with [your own] weeping and sighing,

---

the priests were not obeying the law that they were supposed to uphold. They would therefore receive the curses.

2:3 *refuse.* This was the refuse in the sacrificed animal that should have been removed when the animal was prepared for sacrifice to the Lord.

2:6 *True instruction.* The priests of the Old Testament period had a twofold responsibility: they were to represent the people in holy worship before the living God, and they were to teach and apply God’s law to the people. ***in peace and uprightness.*** This refers to complete moral virtue in all things before the Lord.

2:7 *messenger.* In the Old Testaments, prophets were commonly called messengers. But apparently this is the only time in the Old Testament that priests are specifically called the messengers of the Lord (3:1).

2:10 God the Father of All — The Fatherhood of God applies in a general sense to everyone since all men and women are created by God in His image. God is the Father of the human race. Several Scriptures speak of God as “the Father of spirits” (Heb 12:9; Nu 16:22; Ecc 12:7). Paul even agrees with a heathen poet that all men are God’s offspring (Ac 17:28). James 3:9 says that men have been made in God’s image.

God is also the Father of all as sustainer of life. Every person is an object of His fatherly care (Mt 18:10) and a candidate for His Kingdom (Lk 18:16). Furthermore, God is not willing that any should perish (Mt 18:14; 1Ti 2:4). Even when men and women reject God, He still provides for them as He does believers with rain, fruitful seasons, food, and gladness (Mt 5:45; Ac 14:17).

2:11 *the sanctuary of the LORD which He loves.* The text presents the ideas of affection and revulsion which we usually think of in the verbs *to love* and *to hate*. Marriage is something God loves; divorce is something He hates (v. 16). The Lord’s people had polluted something in which God takes great pleasure.

2:13 *This is another thing you do.* The prophets at times spoke of the compounding sins of the

---

3 1Ki 14:10 **5** Nu 25:12; Eze 34:25; Dt 33:9 **6** Dt 33:10; Jer 23:22; Jas 5:20 **7** Dt 17:9; Gal 4:14 **8** Jer 18:15; Neh 13:29 **9** 1Sa 2:30 **10** 1Co 8:6; Job 31:15 **11** Ezr 9:1; Neh 13:23 **12** Neh 13:29

because the LORD no longer regards
your offering or accepts it with favor
from your hand.
14 But you say, "Why [does He reject
it]?" Because the LORD has been a wit-
ness between you and the wife of your
youth, against whom you have dealt
treacherously. Yet she is your marriage
companion and the wife of your cov-
enant [made by your vows].
15 But not one has done so who has
a remnant of the Spirit. And what did
that one do while seeking a godly off-
spring? Take heed then to your spir-
it, and let no one deal treacherously
against the wife of your youth.
16 "For I hate divorce," says the LORD,
the God of Israel, "and him who covers
his garment with wrong *and* violence,"
says the LORD of hosts. "Therefore keep
watch on your spirit, so that you do not
deal treacherously [with your wife]."
17 You have wearied the LORD with
your words. But you say, "In what way
have we wearied Him?" In that you say,
"Everyone who does evil is good in the
sight of the LORD, and He delights in
them," or [by asking], "Where is the
God of justice?"

The Purifier

3 "BEHOLD, I am going to send My
messenger, and he will prepare
and clear the way before Me. And the
Lord [the Messiah], whom you seek,
will suddenly come to His temple; the
Messenger of the covenant, in whom
you delight, behold, He is coming,"
says the LORD of hosts. [Matt 11:10;
Luke 1:13–17, 76]
2 "But who can endure the day of His
coming? And who can stand when He
appears? For He is like a refiner's fire
and like launderer's soap [which re-

---

people (Jer 2:13). Here, tears seem to be judged as hypocritical acts of insincere repentance (Isa 1:10–15).

2:14 *Why.* The feigned surprise of the people fooled no one, certainly not the Lord. ***witness.*** There are some whose witness may be challenged, but the Lord is not among them (3:5). ***wife of your youth.*** These men had not only married pagan wives, but they had divorced their first wives to make room for their new ones.

2:15–16 God and Marriage—While couples make the marriage covenant with each other, God is a party in the relationship too. He owns us and makes us one, all at the same time. Going back to Genesis 2:24, He designed men and women for each other; to be in relationship with each other, out of His wisdom for what was best for them. This design was the culminating action in the creation process. Out of it was to be the future of this race, this species that God created to rule with Him. Marriage is not just an institution for couples, but for society and God. In marriage we fulfill God's plan for the universe. God not only made the couple one, in a way He made Himself one with the couple too. It grieves Him when we can not or will not follow through with our part of this covenant.

The best way to carry on the faith is through children of functioning covenant marriages. This only confirms what all the statistics are increasingly telling us. When divorce rates started soaring in the 60's and 70's, many thought kids were resilient and handling the dissolution of their families well. Current studies, years later, indicate children of these divorces have significantly greater problems coping with life when compared with kids from intact families. While there is enormous complexity involved in a marriage relationship, nothing about it is more important in making it work than the commitment to maintain it.

2:15 *a remnant of the Spirit.* This somewhat difficult phrase most likely indicates the work of God's Holy Spirit in the life of the married couple. God has joined them, and by His Spirit He has worked on their behalf to strengthen them.

2:16 *treacherously.* To the Lord, attitudes of indifference to marriage vows and duties are the actions of a traitor.

2:17 *You have wearied the LORD.* God is wearied by people who do not submit to Him but who argue their points against His revelation. When justice comes, they will be sorry they asked (3:5).

3:1 *Messenger of the covenant.* This is a messianic title, referring to the One who will initiate the New Covenant (Jer 31:33–34; Mt 26:28; Heb 12:24). ***He is coming.*** As in Psalm 96:13, this dramatic wording indicates something that was just about to occur. However, it would be 400 years before these words would be fulfilled.

3:2 *like a refiner's fire and like launderer's soap.* These two images are vivid illustrations of the purifying process. The Savior King Himself will sift all people to prepare for His reign.

---

14 Pr 5:18; 2:17 **15** Mt 19:4; Ezr 9:2; 1Co 7:14 **16** Dt 24:1; Mt 5:32 **17** Isa 43:24 **CHAPTER 3** **1** Mt 11:10; Lk 1:76; Isa 40:3; Isa 63:9; Hag 2:7 **2** Mal 4:1; Rev 6:17; Isa 4:4; Mt 3:10

moves impurities and uncleanness].
[Rev 6:12–17]
3He will sit as a refiner and purifier
of silver, and He will purify the sons
of Levi [the priests], and refine them
like gold and silver, so that they may
present to the LORD [grain] offerings
in righteousness.
4“Then the offering of Judah and Jeru-
salem will be pleasing to the LORD as in
the days of old and as in ancient years.
5“Then I will come near you for
judgment; I will be a swift witness
against sorcerers, against adulterers,
against perjurers, and against those
who oppress the laborer in his wages
and widows and the fatherless, and
against those who turn away the alien
[from his right], and those who do not
fear Me [with awe-filled reverence],”
says the LORD of hosts. [Deut 24:17]
6“For I am the LORD, I do not change
[but remain faithful to My covenant
with you]; that is why you, O sons of
Jacob, have not come to an end.
7“Yet from the days of your fathers
you have turned away from My stat-
utes *and* ordinances and have not kept
them. Return to Me, and I will return to
you,” says the LORD of hosts. “But you
say, ‘How shall we return?’

You Have Robbed God

8“Will a man rob God? Yet you are
robbing Me! But you say, ‘In what way
have we robbed You?’ In tithes and
offerings [you have withheld].
9“You are cursed with a curse, for
you are robbing Me, this whole nation!
[Lev 26:14–17]
10“Bring all the tithes (the tenth) into
the storehouse, so that there may be
food in My house, and test Me now
in this,” says the LORD of hosts, “if I
will not open for you the windows of
heaven and pour out for you [so great]
a blessing until there is no more room
to receive it. [Mal 2:2]
11“Then I will rebuke the devour-
er (insects, plague) for your sake and
he will not destroy the fruits of the
ground, nor will your vine in the field
drop *its grapes* [before harvest],” says
the LORD of hosts.
12“All nations shall call you happy
and blessed, for you shall be a land of
delight,” says the LORD of hosts.
13“Your words have been harsh
against Me,” says the LORD. “But you say,
‘What have we spoken against You?’
14“You have said, ‘It is useless to
serve God. What profit is it if we keep
His ordinances, and walk around like
mourners before the LORD of hosts?
15‘So now we call the arrogant happy
and blessed. Evildoers are exalted *and*
prosper; and when they test God, they
escape [unpunished].’ ”

The Book of Remembrance

16Then those who feared the LORD
[with awe-filled reverence] spoke
to one another; and the LORD paid
attention and heard it, and a book of

3:3 *purify the sons of Levi.* Since the priests had come under such strong censure in this book (1:6 – 2:9), and since the prophet himself was likely a priest, these words would have had a special significance for him.

3:6 *For I am the LORD, I do not change.* We might expect these opening words to ensure the nation's doom. Instead, they give assurance of God's continuing mercy.

3:8 *tithes.* These were gifts to the Lord that the law required. There were three: two that were annual and one that came every three years. The tithe supported the priests and Levites, and also widows, orphans, and foreigners (Dt 14:28 – 29).

3:12 *All nations.* One of the ways in which other countries would be drawn to the worship of the Lord was by seeing how the people of Israel fared with the Lord as their God. ***a land of delight.*** The adjective indicates enjoyment, life that is genuinely pleasurable (1:10).

3:14 *What profit.* The people secretly entertained doubts about the value of following the Lord. In fact, they had not really “kept his ordinance.” The proper attitude is encouraged in Malachi 4:4.

3:16 *a book of remembrance.* God never forgets His promises. God teaches us to remember and value the good that people do (Php 4:8); He does the same as He commands us.

---

3 Isa 1:25; 1Pe 2:5 **4** Mal 1:11 **5** Zec 5:4; Jas 5:4 **6** Nu 23:19; Ro 11:29; Jas 1:17; La 3:22 **7** Ac 7:51; Zec 1:3; Mal 1:6 **8** Neh 13:10 **10** Pr 3:9; 1Ch 26:20; 2Ch 31:11; Neh 10:38; Ge 7:11; 2Ki 7:2; 2Ch 31:10 **11** Am 4:9 **12** Da 8:9 **13** Mal 2:17 **14** Job 21:14 **15** Ps 73:12; 95:9 **16** Ps 66:16; Heb 3:13; Ps 56:8; Isa 65:6; Rev 20:12

remembrance was written before Him
of those who fear the LORD [with an
attitude of reverence and respect] and
who esteem His name.
17 “They will be Mine,” says the LORD
of hosts, “on that day when I publicly
recognize them *and* openly declare
them to be My own possession [that is,
My very special treasure]. And I will
have compassion on them *and* spare
them as a man spares his own son who
serves him.”
18 Then you will again distinguish
between the righteous and the wicked,
between the one who serves God and
the one who does not serve Him.

Final Admonition

4 “FOR BEHOLD, the day is coming,
burning like a furnace, and all the
arrogant (proud, self-righteous, haugh-
ty), and every evildoer shall be stubble;
and the day that is coming shall set
them on fire,” says the LORD of hosts,
“so that it will leave them neither root
nor branch. [Is 5:21–25; Matt 3:12]
2 “But for you who fear My name
[with awe-filled reverence] the sun of
righteousness will rise with healing in
its wings. And you will go forward and
leap [joyfully] like calves [released]
from the stall.
3 “You will trample the wicked, for
they will be ashes under the soles of
your feet on the day that I do this,” says
the LORD of hosts.
4 “Remember [with thoughtful con-
cern] the Law of Moses My servant,
the statutes and the ordinances which
I commanded him on [Mount] Horeb
[to give] to all Israel.
5 “Behold, I am going to send you Eli-
jah the prophet before the coming of
the great and terrible day of the LORD.
[Matt 11:14; 17:10–13]
6 “He will turn the hearts of the fa-
thers to their children, and the hearts
of the children to their fathers [a recon-
ciliation produced by repentance], so
that I will not come and strike the land
with a curse [of complete destruction].”
[Luke 1:17]

3:17 *They will be Mine.* These words are exciting because we can sense in them the pride God has in His children.

3:18 *one who serves God.* Serving God means putting Him first, obeying His commands, and finding one's chief joy in life the advancement of the glory of His name.

4:2 *with healing in its wings.* The prophet compares the Savior to a bird whose comforting wings bring healing to the chicks that gather underneath (Ps 91:1 – 4).

4:5 *Elijah the prophet.* There are three ways in which this prophecy might be fulfilled: (1) John the Baptist, whom Malachi had already prophesied (3:1), was the first to fill the promise of the Elijah figure. John, like Elijah, was a minister of the Lord calling the people to repent and prepare for the coming of the Messiah (Mt 11:14). (2) Elijah appeared in person along with Moses at the transfiguration (Mt 17:1 – 8). (3) An Elijah-like figure will appear at the end times; he will call fire down from heaven just as Elijah did (1Ki 18:36; Rev 11:1 – 7).

4:6 *fathers to their children ... children to their fathers.* Malachi ends with a promise and a warning. As in every act of God announcing judgment, there is also an offer of His mercy (Jnh 4:2). ***a curse.*** The term is one of the harshest in Scripture. The Hebrew word suggests complete annihilation. This is the term translated "accursed" in the account of the destruction of Jericho (Jos 6:17).

17 Ex 19:5; Dt 7:6; Ps 135:4; Isa 62:3; Ps 103:13 **18** Ps 58:11 **CHAPTER 4** **1** Joel 2:31; 2Pe 3:7; Mal 3:18; Ob 18; Am 2:9 **2** Mal 3:16; Lk 1:78; Eph 5:14; Rev 2:28 **3** Mic 7:10 **4** Ex 20:3; Dt 4:10; Ps 147:19 **5** Mt 11:14; Lk 1:17; Joel 2:31 **6** Zec 14:12; 5:3

FROM MALACHI TO CHRIST

The Persian Period
450–330 BC

For about 200 years after Nehemiah's time the Persians controlled Judah, but the Jews were allowed to carry on their religious observances and were not interfered with. During this time Judah was ruled by high priests, who answered to the Persian authorities.

The Hellenistic Period
330–166 BC

In the late fourth century BC, Alexander the Great defeated the Persians repeatedly in battle and quickly conquered the eastern Mediterranean region, including Syria, Egypt, Persia and Babylonia. Alexander believed in the superiority of Greek culture and was convinced that it was the one force that could unify the world. Alexander permitted the Jews to observe their laws and even granted them exemption from tribute or tax during their sabbath years. When he built Alexandria in Egypt, he encouraged Jews to live there. The Greek conquest prepared the way for the translation of the Hebrew Old Testament into Greek (Septuagint version), beginning c. 250 BC.

The Hasmonean Period
166–63 BC

When this historical period began, the Jews were being greatly oppressed. The Ptolemies of Egypt had been tolerant of the Jews and their religious practices, but the Seleucid rulers of Syria were determined to force Hellenism on them. Copies of the Scriptures were ordered destroyed, and laws were enforced banning circumcision and other Jewish practices. The oppressed Jews revolted, led by Judas Maccabeus.

The Roman Period
Begins in 63 BC

In the year 63 BC, Pompey, the Roman general, captured Jerusalem, and the provinces in the Holy Land became subject to Rome. The Romans ruled at times through local vassal kings and at other times through Roman governors who were appointed by the emperors. Herod the Great was ruler of that whole region at the time of Jesus' birth.

410
400 BC
390
380
370
360
350
340
330
Rule of Alexander the Great
320
310
300
290
280
270
Rule of the Ptolemies of Egypt
260
250
240
230
220
210
200
190
Rule of the Seleucids of Syria
180
170
160
150
140
130
120
Hasmonean Dynasty
110
100
90
80
70
60
50
40
30
Herod the Great rules as king; subject to Rome
20
10
10
20
AD 30

Malachi c. 430 BC
334–323 Alexander the Great conquers the East
330–328 Alexander's years of power
320 Ptolemy (I) Soter conquers Jerusalem
311 Seleucus conquers Babylon; Seleucid dynasty begins
226 Antiochus (III) of Syria conquers the Holy Land
223–187 Antiochus becomes Seleucid ruler of Syria
198 Antiochus defeats Egypt and gains control of the Holy Land
175–164 Antiochus (IV) Epiphanes rules Syria; Judaism is prohibited
167 Mattathias and his sons rebel against Antiochus; Maccabean revolt begins
166–160 Judas Maccabeus's leadership
160–143 Jonathan is high priest
142–134 Simon becomes high priest; establishes Hasmonean dynasty (see map and essay, pp. 1572 – 1574)
134–104 John Hyrcanus enlarges the independent Jewish state
103 Aristobulus's rule
102–76 Alexander Janneus's rule
75–67 Rule of Salome Alexandra with Hyrcanus II as high priest
66–63 Battle between Aristobulus II and Hyrcanus II
63 Pompey invades the Holy Land; Roman rule begins
63–40 Hyrcanus II governs but is subject to Rome
40–37 Parthians conquer Jerusalem
37 Herod becomes ruler of the Holy Land
19 Herod's temple begun
4 Herod dies; Archelaus succeeds him

THE MACCABEAN-HASMONEAN PERIOD

SELEUCID KINGS		JEWISH LEADERS		PTOLEMAIC KINGS	
Seleucus I (Nicator)	321 – 281			Ptolemy I (Soter)	323 – 285
Antiochus I (Soter)	281 – 261				
Antiochus II (Theos)	261 – 246			Ptolemy II (Philadelphus)	285 – 246
Seleucus II (Callinicus)	246 – 225			Ptolemy III (Euergetes)	246 – 222
Seleucus III (Soter)	225 – 223			Ptolemy IV (Philopator)	221 – 205
Antiochus III (the Great)	223 – 187			Ptolemy V (Epiphanes)	204 – 180
Seleucus IV (Philopator)	187 – 175			Ptolemy VI (Philometor)	180 – 145
Antiochus IV (Epiphanes)	175 – 163	Mattathias Judas	166 166 – 160		
Antiochus V (Eupator)	163 – 162				
Demetrius I (Soter)	162 – 150	Jonathan	160 – 143		
Alexander Balas	150 – 145			Ptolemy VII (Neos Philopator)	145
Demetrius II (Nicator)	145 – 139	Simon	143 – 135	Ptolemy VII (Neos Philopator)	145
(Antiochus VI [Epiphanes Dionysus]) 145 – 142				Ptolemy VIII (Euergetes II or Physcon)	145 – 116
Antiochus VII (Sidetes)	139 – 129	John Hyrcanus I	135 – 104		
Demetrius II (Nicator)	129 – 125				
Antiochus VIII (Grypus)	125/4 – 113			Ptolemy IX (Soter II or Lathyrus)	116 – 110
Antiochus IX (Philopator Cyzicenus)	113 – 111				
Antiochus VIII (Grypus)	111 – 95	Aristobulus	104 – 103	Ptolemy X (Alexander)	110 – 109 108 – 88
Seleucus VI	95 – 54	Alexander Jannaeus	103 – 76		
Antiochus X (Eusebes)	94 – 83			Ptolemy IX (Soter II or Lathyrus)	88 – 80
Tigranes, King of Armenia	83 – 69	Salome Alexandra	76 – 67	Ptolemy XI (Alexander II)	80 (20 days)
				Ptolemy XII (Philopator Philadelphus Neos Dionysus or Auletes)	80 – 51
Antiochus XIII (Asiaticus)	69 – 65	Hyrcanus II Aristobulus	67 (3 months) 67 – 63	Cleopatra VII	51 – 30

THE NEW TESTAMENT

NEW TESTAMENT OVERVIEW

Matthew: A brief history of the life of Christ, pointing to Jesus as the promised Messiah.

Mark: The briefest and most fast-paced history of the life of Christ.

Luke: The history of the life of Christ, focusing on his important miracles and teachings.

John: The life of Christ, including many teachings and events not recorded by the other gospel authors.

Acts: The history of the apostles and the early Christian church.

Romans: Paul writes extensively on key realities of Christian belief and justification by faith alone.

1 Corinthians: Paul speaks to the errors of the church in Corinth.

2 Corinthians: Paul encourages the church in Corinth and defends his character.

Galatians: Paul's letter points out that believers are justified by faith, not by our own efforts.

Ephesians: Paul's positive letter focuses on God's amazing grace and urges the church to live in love.

Philippians: Paul writes on Christian contentment, unity and kindness.

Colossians: Paul warns his audience against following false teaching, focusing on Jesus' work of salvation.

1 Thessalonians: Paul encourages his listeners to continue to live in a way that pleases God.

2 Thessalonians: Paul encourages the church and talks about Jesus' second coming.

1 and 2 Timothy: Paul encourages and instructs his young student Timothy in his role as a pastor.

Titus: Paul encourages Titus in his role as a pastor.

Philemon: Paul asks a believing slave owner to treat a believing slave with kindness.

Hebrews: A discourse on how Jesus is the ultimate and permanent fulfillment of the Mosaic Law.

James: A letter from Jesus' brother on the necessity of combining faith with work.

1 and 2 Peter: The apostle warns and encourages his audience as they live their Christian lives.

1 John: John elegantly explains basic truths about the Christian life.

2 John: John warns a believing lady about false teachers.

3 John: John's letter to a believing man thanking him for his hospitality.

Jude: A letter warning Christians against those who try to deceive them.

Revelation: John's vision of the exalted Christ and the future of the church.

THE GOSPEL ACCORDING TO
MATTHEW

▸ **AUTHOR:** The early church uniformly attributed this Gospel to Matthew, and no tradition to the contrary ever emerged. This book was known early and accepted quickly. Matthew occupied the unpopular post of tax collector in Capernaum for the Roman government, and as a result he was no doubt disliked by his Jewish countrymen. He was chosen as one of the twelve apostles, and the last appearance of his name in the Bible is in Acts 1:13. Matthew's life from that point on is veiled in tradition.

▸ **TIMES:** c. 4 BC – AD 33 ▸ **KEY VERSES:** Mt 16:16 – 19

▸ **THEME:** Matthew is typically described as the story of Jesus written by a Jew for Jewish people. In this context it contains the most references to Jewish culture and the Old Testament of the Gospels. The author's main purpose seems to be proving to his Jewish readers that Jesus is their Messiah. Matthew is also the fullest systematic account of Christ's teachings. These 5 "blocks" of teaching are one of the key differences with the other Gospels: Chapters 5 – 7, The Sermon on the Mount; Chapter 10, The Mission Charge; Chapter 13, The Parables of the Kingdom; Chapter 18, The Church; Chapters 23 – 25, Judgment and the End of the World.

The Genealogy of Jesus the Messiah

1 THE RECORD of the genealogy of Jesus the Messiah, the son (descendant) of David, the son (descendant) of Abraham: [Ps 132:11; Is 11:1]
2 Abraham was the father of Isaac, Isaac the father of Jacob, and Jacob the father of Judah and his brothers [who became the twelve tribes of Israel].
3 Judah was the father of Perez and Zerah by Tamar, Perez was the father of Hezron, and Hezron the father of Ram.
4 Ram was the father of Aminadab, Aminadab the father of Nahshon, and Nahshon the father of Salmon.
5 Salmon was the father of Boaz by Rahab, Boaz was the father of Obed by Ruth, and Obed the father of Jesse.
6 Jesse was the father of David the king.

1:1 *genealogy.* Jesus' genealogy is crucial to His claim to be the Messiah, as it traces the lineage of Joseph, His recognized father, back to Abraham through David. It shows that from a legal standpoint, Jesus is qualified to rule from the throne of David.

1:3 *Tamar.* The mention of women in a Jewish genealogy is unusual. But in addition to Mary, four women are listed in this catalogue of names: Tamar, who was involved in a scandal with Judah (Ge 38); Rahab, the Canaanite harlot of Jericho (Jos 2:1 – 21); Ruth, who was not an Israelite, but a Moabite (Ru 1:4); and Bathsheba, the wife of Uriah, who committed adultery with David (2Sa 11:1 – 5). At the beginning of his Gospel, Matthew shows how God's grace forgives the darkest of sins and reaches beyond the nation of Israel to the world. He also points out that God can lift the lowest and place them in royal lineage.

CHAPTER 1 **1** Lk 3:23; Ps 132:11; Isa 11:1; Jer 23:5; Mt 22:42; Jn 7:42; Ac 2:30; Ro 1:3; Ge 12:3 **2** Ge 21:2; Ge 25:26; Ge 29:35 **3** Ge 38:27; Ru 4:18; 1Ch 2:5 **6** 1Sa 16:1; 17:12; 2Sa 12:24

David was the father of Solomon by Bathsheba who had been the wife of Uriah. [Ruth 4:18–22; 1 Chr 2:13–15]

7 Solomon was the father of Rehoboam, Rehoboam the father of Abijah, and Abijah the father of Asa.

8 Asa was the father of Jehoshaphat, Jehoshaphat the father of Joram, and Joram the father of Uzziah.

9 Uzziah was the father of Jotham, Jotham the father of Ahaz, and Ahaz the father of Hezekiah.

10 Hezekiah was the father of Manasseh, Manasseh the father of Amon, and Amon the father of Josiah.

11 Josiah became the father of Jeconiah [also called Coniah and Jehoiachin] and his brothers, at the time of the deportation (exile) to Babylon. [2 Kin 24:14; 1 Chr 3:15, 16]

12 After the deportation to Babylon: Jeconiah became the father of Shealtiel, and Shealtiel the father of Zerubbabel.

13 Zerubbabel was the father of Abihud, Abihud the father of Eliakim, and Eliakim the father of Azor.

14 Azor was the father of Zadok, Zadok the father of Achim, and Achim the father of Eliud.

15 Eliud was the father of Eleazar, Eleazar the father of Matthan, and Matthan the father of Jacob.

16 Jacob was the father of Joseph the husband of Mary, by whom Jesus was born, who is called the Messiah (Christ).

17 So all the generations from Abraham to David are fourteen; from David to the Babylonian deportation (exile), fourteen generations; and from the Babylonian deportation to the Messiah, fourteen generations.

Conception and Birth of Jesus

18 Now the birth of Jesus Christ was as follows: when His mother Mary had been betrothed to Joseph, before they came together she was found to be with child by [the power of] the Holy Spirit.

19 And Joseph her [promised] husband, being a just *and* righteous man and not wanting to expose her publicly to shame, planned to send her away *and* divorce her quietly.

20 But after he had considered this, an angel of the Lord appeared to him in a dream, saying, "Joseph, descendant of David, do not be afraid to take Mary as your wife, for the Child who has been conceived in her is of the Holy Spirit.

21 "She will give birth to a Son, and you shall name Him Jesus (The LORD is salvation), for He will save His people from their sins."

22 All this happened in order to fulfill what the Lord had spoken through the prophet [Isaiah]:

23 "BEHOLD, THE VIRGIN SHALL BE WITH CHILD AND GIVE BIRTH TO A SON, AND THEY SHALL CALL HIS NAME IMMANUEL"—which, when translated, means, "GOD WITH US." [Is 7:14]

24 Then Joseph awoke from his sleep and did as the angel of the Lord had commanded him, and he took *Mary* [to his home] as his wife,

25 but he kept her a virgin until she had given birth to a Son [her firstborn child]; and he named Him Jesus (The LORD is salvation).

1:16 *the husband of Mary.* Matthew was careful not to identify Jesus as the physical son of Joseph. The Greek pronoun translated "by whom" is feminine and refers to Mary. ***called the Messiah (Christ).*** The words "Messiah" (from the Hebrew) and "Christ" (from the Greek) both mean "Anointed One."

1:17 *Abraham . . . to the Messiah.* The genealogy is broken down into three groups of names with 14 generations in each list. A basic covenant is set forth in each period: the Abrahamic covenant, the Davidic covenant, and the New Covenant.

1:18 *betrothed.* In Jewish culture, this covenant was made about a year before the marriage. Engagement was understood to be as binding as a marriage covenant, therefore a legal divorce was required to withdraw from the agreement.

1:23 *BEHOLD . . . IMMANUEL.* The angel's message to Joseph indicated that Mary would fulfill the prophecy of Isaiah (Isa 7:14). "Jesus," the Greek form of "Joshua" means "salvation."

1:25 *kept her a virgin until.* The clear implication is that Mary was a virgin only until the birth of Jesus. The brothers and sisters of Jesus

7 1Ch 3:10 **10** 2Ki 20:21; 1Ch 3:13 **11** See 1Ch 3:15,16; 2Ki 24:14-16; 25:11; 2Ch 36:10; Jer 27:20; 52:11,15; Da 1:2 **12** 1Ch 3:17; Ezr 3:2; Neh 12:1; Hag 1:1 **18** Lk 1:27; Lk 1:35 **19** Dt 24:1 **20** Lk 1:35 **21** Lk 1:31; Ac 4:12; 5:31; 13:23,38 **23** Isa 7:14 **25** Ex:13:2; Lk 2:7,21

The Visit of the Magi

2 NOW WHEN Jesus was born in Bethlehem of Judea in the days of Herod the king (Herod the Great), magi (wise men) from the east came to Jerusalem, asking,

2 “Where is He who has been born King of the Jews? For we have seen His star in the east and have come to worship Him.” [Num 24:17; Jer 23:5; Zech 9:9]

3 When Herod the king heard this, he was disturbed, and all Jerusalem with him.

4 So he called together all the chief priests and scribes of the people and [anxiously] asked them where the Christ (the Messiah, the Anointed) was to be born.

5 They replied to him, “In Bethlehem of Judea, for this is what has been written by the prophet [Micah]:

6 ‘AND YOU, BETHLEHEM, IN THE LAND
OF JUDAH,
ARE NOT IN ANY WAY LEAST AMONG
THE LEADERS OF JUDAH;
FOR FROM YOU SHALL COME A
RULER
WHO WILL SHEPHERD MY PEOPLE
ISRAEL.’ ” [Mic 5:2]

7 Then Herod secretly sent for the magi and learned from them the [exact] time the star [had first] appeared.

8 Then he sent them to Bethlehem, saying, “Go and search carefully for the Child; and when you have found Him, report to me, so that I too may come and worship Him.”

9 After hearing the king, they went their way; and behold, the star, which they had seen in the east, went on before them [continually leading the way] until it came and stood over *the place* where the young Child was.

10 When they saw the star, they rejoiced exceedingly with great joy.

11 And after entering the house, they saw the Child with Mary His mother; and they fell down and worshiped Him. Then, after opening their treasure chests, they presented to Him gifts [fit for a king, gifts] of gold, frankincense, and myrrh.

12 And having been warned [by God] in a dream not to go back to Herod, the magi left for their own country by another way.

The Flight to Egypt

13 Now when they had gone, an angel of the Lord appeared to Joseph in a dream and said, “Get up! Take the Child and His mother and flee to Egypt, and remain there until I tell you; for Herod intends to search for the Child in order to destroy Him.”

14 So Joseph got up and took the Child and His mother while it was still night, and left for Egypt.

15 He remained there until the death of Herod. *This was* to fulfill what the Lord had spoken by the prophet [Hosea]: “OUT OF EGYPT I CALLED MY SON.” [Hos 11:1]

(13:55–56) were probably younger siblings born to Joseph and Mary after Jesus’ birth. Joseph could not have had children by a previous marriage, as some suppose, for then Jesus would not have been heir to the Davidic throne as the oldest son of Joseph.

2:1 *magi (wise men) from the east.* These “wise men” would have been of the same class as the “wise men” of Babylon over whom Daniel was made ruler (Da 2:48). ***to Jerusalem.*** Contrary to popular belief, the events of chapter two probably took place some months after Jesus’ birth. Herod murdered all the male children 2 years and under, going by the time the wise men said the star had appeared (and probably leaving a significant margin for error). In addition, it would have been strange for Mary and Joseph to offer the sacrifice of the poor (see Lev 12:8; Lk 2:24) if the wise men had just given them rich gifts.

2:7 *Then Herod.* This is Herod the Great, who reigned over Palestine for over thirty years. A crafty ruler and lavish builder, Herod had a reign marked by cruelty and bloodshed.

2:15 *to fulfill.* The prophecy quoted here, from Hosea 11:1, refers to the nation of Israel as God’s son coming out of Egypt in the exodus. Jesus is the genuine Son of God, and, as Israel’s Messiah, is the true Israel (Jn 15:1); therefore He gives fuller meaning to the prophecy of Hosea.

CHAPTER 2 **1** Lk 2:4,6; Ge 25:6; 1Ki 4:30 **2** Lk 2:11; Nu 24:17; Isa 60:3 **4** 2Ch 36:14; 2Ch 34:13; Mal 2:7 **6** Jn 7:42; Rev 2:27 **11** Ps 72:10; Isa 60:6 **12** Mt 1:20 **15** Hos 11:1

Herod Slaughters the Babies

16Then Herod, when he realized that
he had been tricked by the magi, was
extremely angry, and he sent [soldiers]
and put to death all the male children
in Bethlehem and in all that area who
were two years old and under, accord-
ing to the date which he had learned
from the magi.
17Then what had been spoken
through Jeremiah the prophet was
fulfilled:

18"A voice was heard in Ramah,
Weeping and great mourning,
Rachel weeping for her
children;
She refused to be comforted,
Because they were no more."
[Jer 31:15]

19But when Herod died, an angel
of the Lord appeared in a dream to
Joseph in Egypt, and said,
20"Get up! Take the Child and His
mother, and go to the land of Israel;
for those who sought the Child's life
are dead."
21Then Joseph got up, and took the
Child and His mother, and came into
the land of Israel.
22But when he heard that Archelaus
was ruling over Judea in place of his
father Herod [the Great], he was afraid
to go there. Then being warned *by*
God in a dream, he left for the region
of Galilee,
23and went and settled in a city called
Nazareth. *This was* to fulfill what was
spoken through the prophets: "He shall
be called a Nazarene."

2:18 *Rachel weeping for her children.* This prophecy comes from Jeremiah 31:15, in which Rachel, entombed near Bethlehem some 13 centuries before the Babylonian captivity, is seen weeping for her children as they are led away in 586 BC. In the slaughter of the male infants at the time of Christ's birth, Rachel is again seen weeping for the violent loss of her sons.

2:23 *Nazareth.* Those who lived in Nazareth were looked down upon (Jn 1:46). Perhaps God

17 Jer 31:15 **22** Mt 3:13; Lk 2:39 **23** Jn 1:45; Jdg 13:5; 1Sa 1:11

THE BIRTH OF JESUS AND THE FLIGHT INTO EGYPT

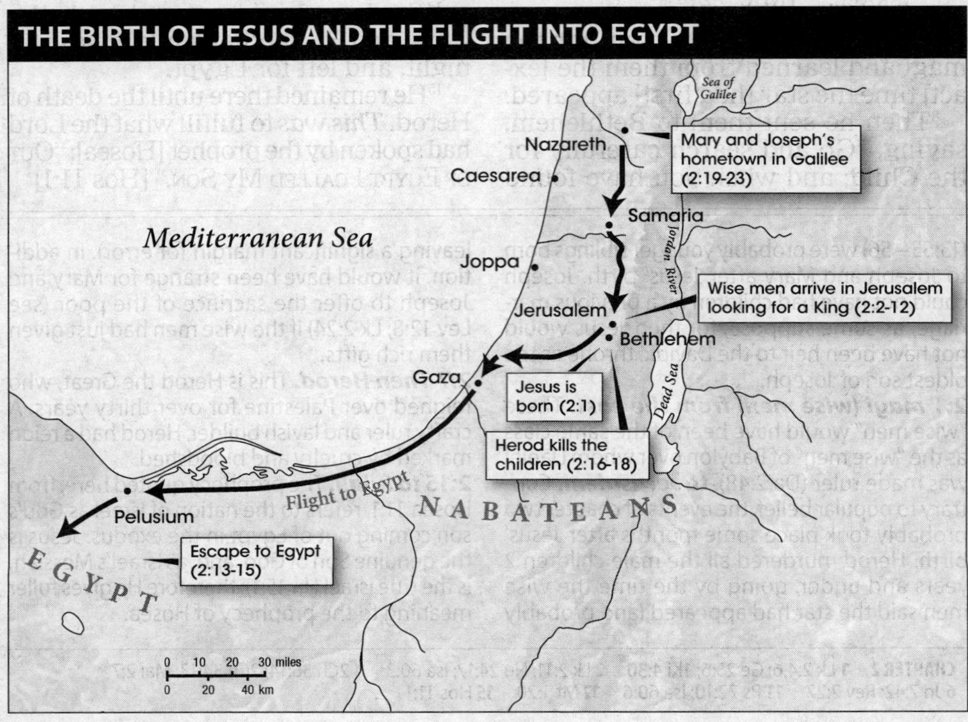

The Preaching of John the Baptist

3 IN THOSE days John the Baptist appeared, preaching in the Wilderness of Judea [along the western side of the Dead Sea] and saying,

2 "Repent [change your inner self—your old way of thinking, regret past sins, live your life in a way that proves repentance; seek God's purpose for your life], for the kingdom of heaven is at hand."

3 This is the one who was mentioned by the prophet Isaiah when he said,

"THE VOICE OF ONE SHOUTING IN THE WILDERNESS,
'PREPARE THE ROAD FOR THE LORD,
MAKE HIS HIGHWAYS STRAIGHT (level, direct)!' " [Is 40:3]

4 Now this same John had clothing made of camel's hair and a [wide] leather band around his waist; and his food was locusts and wild honey. [Lev 11:22; 2 Kin 1:8; Zech 13:4]

5 At that time Jerusalem was going out to him, and all Judea and all the district around the Jordan;

6 and they were being baptized by him in the Jordan River, as they confessed their sins.

7 But when he saw many of the Pharisees and Sadducees coming for baptism, he said to them, "You brood of vipers, who warned you to flee from the [divine] wrath *and* judgment to come?

8 "So produce fruit that is consistent with repentance [demonstrating new behavior that proves a change of heart, and a conscious decision to turn away from sin];

9 and do not presume to say to yourselves [as a defense], 'We have Abraham for our father [so our inheritance assures us of salvation]'; for I say to you that from these stones God is able to raise up children (descendants) for Abraham. [Luke 3:8]

10 "And already the axe [of God's judgment] is swinging toward the root of the trees; therefore every tree that does not bear good fruit is cut down and thrown into the fire.

11 "As for me, I baptize you with water because of [your] repentance [that is, because you are willing to change your inner self—your old way of thinking, regret your sin and live a changed life], but He (the Messiah) who is coming after me is mightier [more powerful, more noble] than I, whose sandals I am not worthy to remove [even as His slave]; He will baptize you [who truly repent] with the Holy Spirit and [you who remain unrepentant] with fire (judgment). [Luke 3:16]

---

chose this place for His Son to emphasize His humanness.

3:2 *Repent.* The Greek verb translated "repent" indicates a change of attitude. The basic idea is a recognition of sin and a reversal of thinking which changes one's life.

3:3 *PREPARE THE ROAD FOR THE LORD.* As roads were smoothed and straightened for the arrival of a king, so John was preparing a spiritual path for the Messiah. The quotation is from Isaiah 40:3.

3:7 *Pharisees and Sadducees.* The Pharisees and Sadducees were two prominent groups in Judaism at the time of Christ. The groups differed considerably in their beliefs. The Pharisees not only based their beliefs on the law of Moses, but also on a large body of oral tradition. They were devout and zealous, concerned with outward righteousness. The Sadducees were associated with a priestly caste, and in doctrine they held primarily to the first five books of Moses. They did not believe in the resurrection of the dead, and did not adhere to all the detailed laws of the Pharisees. Formerly enemies, the two groups seemed to unite against a common enemy: the long awaited Messiah.

3:11 *baptize.* Sometimes fire has connotations of judgment in Scripture, but here the fire of God's Spirit represents the transforming power of His grace and love. The baptism of all Jesus' disciples with water is an outward sign of the inward work of the Holy Spirit. It is the symbol of obedience to the command to believe in Christ's saving work of grace on the cross.

CHAPTER 3 **1** Mk 1:4,15; Lk 3:2,3; Jn 1:28; Jos 14:10 **2** Da 2:44; Mt 4:17; 10:7 **3** Isa 40:3; Mk 1:3; Lk 3:4; Jn 1:23; Lk 1:76 **4** Mk 1:6; 2Ki 1:8; Zec 13:4; Lev 11:22; 1Sa 14:25,26 **5** Mk 1:5; Lk 3:7 **6** Ac 19:4,18 **7** Mt 12:34; 23:33; Lk 3:7-9; Ro 5:9; 1Th 1:10 **9** Jn 8:33,39; Ac 13:26; Ro 4:1,11,16 **10** Mt 7:19; Lk 13:7,9; Jn 15:6 **11** Mk 1:8; Lk 3:16; Jn 1:15,26,33; Ac 1:5; 11:16; 19:4; Isa 4:4; 44:3; Mal 3:2; Ac 2:3,4; 1Co 12:13

[12]"His winnowing fork is in His hand, and He will thoroughly clear out His threshing floor; and He will gather His wheat (believers) into His barn (kingdom), but He will burn up the chaff (the unrepentant) with unquenchable fire."

The Baptism of Jesus

[13]Then Jesus came from Galilee to John at the Jordan [River], to be baptized by him. [Mark 1:9–11; Luke 3:21, 22; John 1:32]
[14]But John tried to prevent Him [vigorously protesting], saying, "It is I who need to be baptized by You, and do You come to me?"
[15]But Jesus replied to him, "Permit it just now; for this is the fitting way for us to fulfill all righteousness." Then John permitted [it and baptized] Him.
[16]After Jesus was baptized, He came up immediately out of the water; and behold, the heavens were opened, and he (John) saw the Spirit of God descending as a dove and lighting on Him (Jesus), [John 1:32]
[17]and behold, a voice from heaven said, "This is My beloved Son, in whom I am well-pleased *and* delight-ed!" [Ps 2:7; Is 42:1]

The Temptation of Jesus

4 THEN JESUS was led by the [Holy] Spirit into the wilderness to be tempted by the devil. [Luke 4:1–13]
[2]After He had gone without food for forty days and forty nights, He became hungry. [Ex 34:28; 1 Kin 19:8]
[3]And the tempter came and said to Him, "If You are the Son of God, command that these stones become bread."
[4]But Jesus replied, "It is written *and* forever remains written, 'MAN SHALL NOT LIVE BY BREAD ALONE, BUT BY EVERY WORD THAT COMES OUT OF THE MOUTH OF GOD.' " [Deut 8:3]
[5]Then the devil took Him into the holy city [Jerusalem] and placed Him on the pinnacle (highest point) of the temple. [Neh 11:1; Dan 9:24]
[6]And he said [mockingly] to Him, "If You are the Son of God, throw Yourself down; for it is written,

'HE WILL COMMAND HIS ANGELS
CONCERNING YOU [to serve, care for, protect and watch over You]';

and

'THEY WILL LIFT YOU UP ON *their* HANDS,
SO THAT YOU WILL NOT STRIKE
YOUR FOOT AGAINST A STONE.' "
[Ps 91:11, 12]

3:15 *to fulfill all righteousness.* This phrase does not suggest that Jesus came for baptism because He had sinned; the Lord Jesus was without sin (2Co 5:21; Heb 4:15). His baptism probably served several purposes. By being baptized, He confirmed the ministry of John and fulfilled the Father's will.

3:17 God, the Father of Christ — Most Christians eventually wonder how God may be called the Father of Christ and Christ, the Son of God. First, one must recognize that God is spirit (Jn 4:24), and Christ was the Son of God before He assumed a human body in Bethlehem (Jn 3:16; Gal 4:4). Passages which use terms implying physical origin must be taken in a figurative sense (Heb 1:5). Second, the title expresses a sonship relationship, unique from that of His disciples (Jn 20:17). He was begotten of God unlike anyone else (Jn 1:14; 3:16). The Nicean council in the fourth century used the phrase "very God of very God; begotten, not made, being of one substance with the Father" to describe this unique relationship. Third, the title describes equality with God. When Jesus claimed to be "one" with the Father, He was speaking of a unity of "substance" with the Father and thus equality in all the attributes of deity (Jn 10:30). The Jews understood this claim, because they took up stones to stone Him, protesting that "You . . . make Yourself out to be God" (Jn 10:33). Fourth, the title emphasizes Christ's role as the revealer of God. He alone possesses the knowledge of the Father (Jn 14:6–9; 1Jn 1:2), and He is the sole mediator of that knowledge (1Ti 2:5). Therefore, no one can know the Father except through the Son (Jn 14:6).

4:1–4 *It is written.* Satan did not lead Jesus into the place of temptation, the Holy Spirit did. Perhaps part of the reason for this was to show us how to deal with temptation. Jesus quoted the Word of God, showing the power of Scripture in battling with the evil one.

12 Mal 3:3; 4:1; Mt 13:30 **13** Mk 1:9; Lk 3:21; Mt 2:22 **16** Mk 1:10; Isa 11:2; 42:1; Lk 3:22; Jn 1:32 **17** Jn 12:28; Ps 2:7; Isa 42:1; Mt 17:5; Mk 1:11; Lk 9:35; Eph 1:6; Col 1:13; 2Pe 1:17 **CHAPTER 4** **1** Mk 1:12; Lk 4:1; See 1Ki 18:12; Eze 3:14; 8:3; 11:1,24; 40:2; 43:5; Ac 8:39 **4** Dt 8:3 **5** Neh 11:1; Isa 48:2; 52:1; Mt 27:53; Rev 11:2 **6** Ps 91:11,12

THE BAPTISM OF JESUS AND THE SOJOURN IN THE DESERT

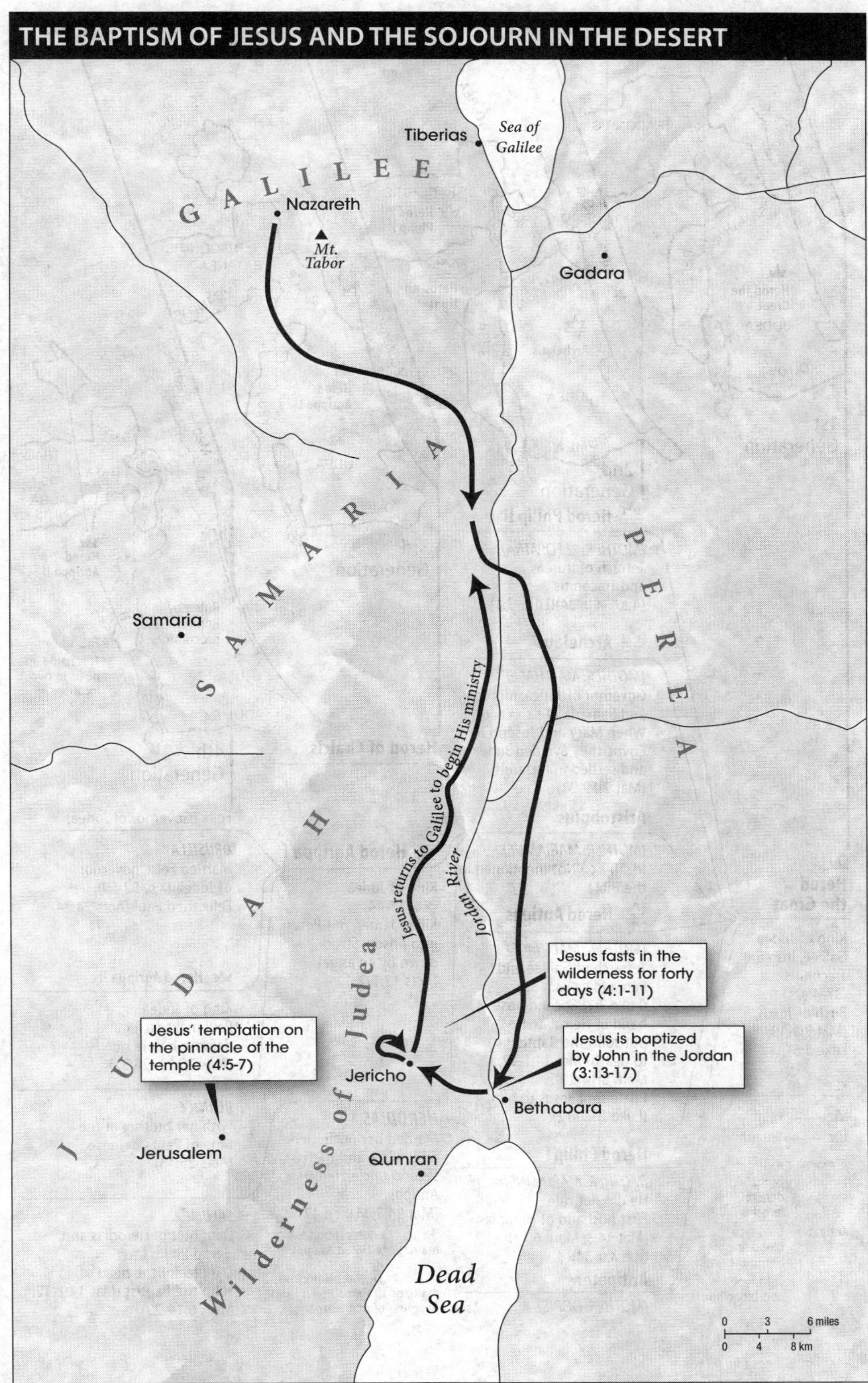

HOUSE OF HEROD

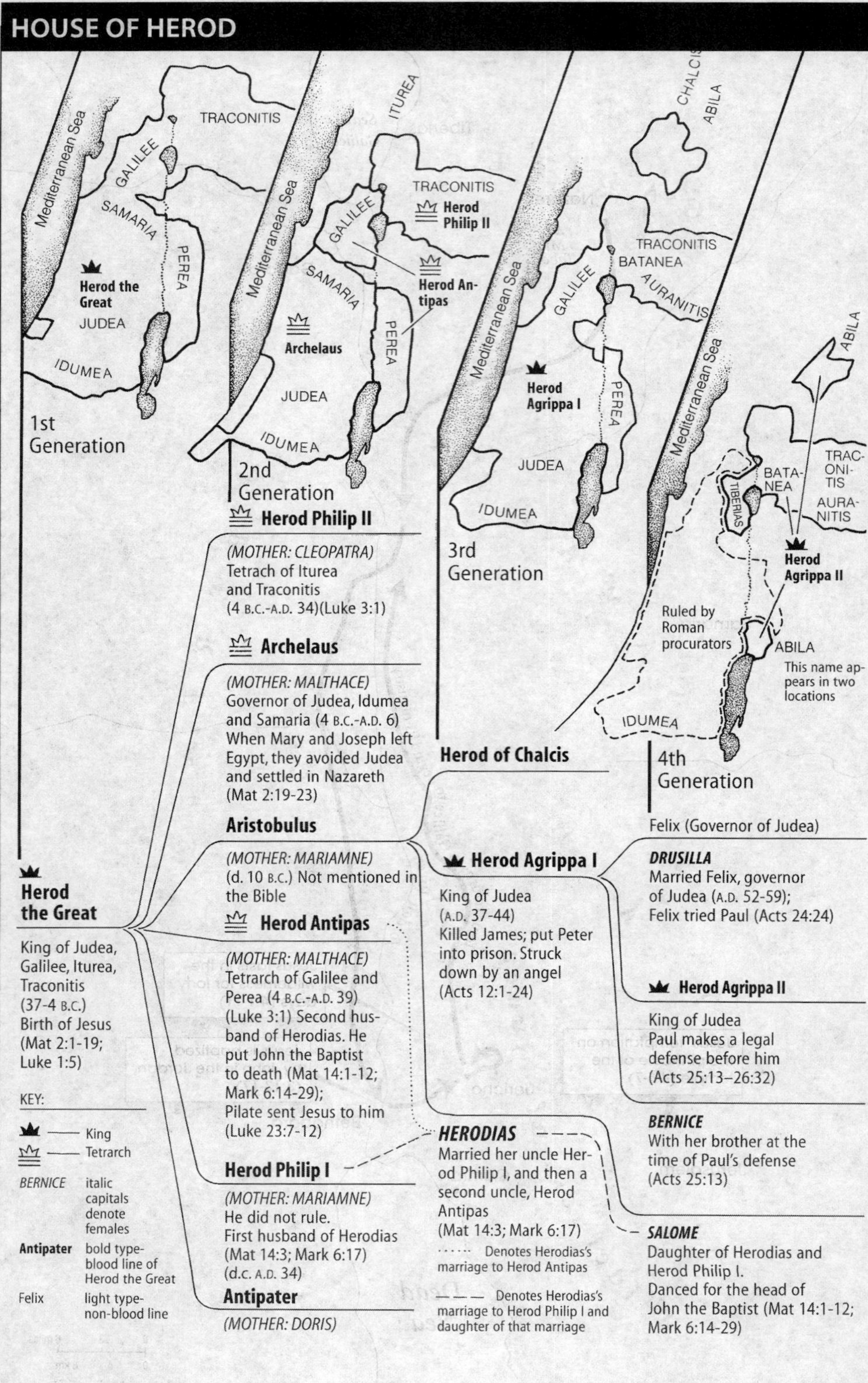

[7]Jesus said to him, "On the other hand,
it is written *and* forever remains writ-
ten, 'YOU SHALL NOT TEST THE LORD YOUR
GOD.' " [Deut 6:16]
[8]Again, the devil took Him up on a
very high mountain and showed Him
all the kingdoms of the world and the
glory [splendor, magnificence, and ex-
cellence] of them;
[9]and he said to Him, "All these things
I will give You, if You fall down and
worship me."
[10]Then Jesus said to him, "Go away,
Satan! For it is written *and* forever re-
mains written, 'YOU SHALL WORSHIP THE
LORD YOUR GOD, AND SERVE HIM ONLY.' "
[Deut 6:13]
[11]Then the devil left Him; and angels
came and ministered to Him [bringing
Him food and serving Him].

Jesus Begins His Ministry

[12]Now when Jesus heard that John
[the Baptist] had been arrested *and* put
in prison, He left for Galilee.
[13]And leaving Nazareth, He went
and settled in Capernaum, which is by
the sea, in the country of Zebulun and
Naphtali. [Mark 2:1]
[14]*This was* to fulfill what was spoken
by the prophet Isaiah:

[15]"THE LAND OF ZEBULUN AND THE LAND
OF NAPHTALI,
BY THE WAY OF THE SEA, BEYOND THE
JORDAN, GALILEE [in the district]
OF THE GENTILES—
[16]"THE PEOPLE WHO WERE SITTING
(living) IN [spiritual] DARKNESS
HAVE SEEN A GREAT LIGHT,
AND FOR THOSE WHO WERE SITTING
(living) IN THE LAND AND SHADOW
OF [spiritual and moral] DEATH,
UPON THEM A LIGHT HAS DAWNED."
[Is 9:1, 2]

[17]From that time Jesus began to
preach and say, "Repent [change your
inner self—your old way of thinking,
regret past sins, live your life in a way
that proves repentance; seek God's
purpose for your life], for the kingdom
of heaven is at hand."

The First Disciples

[18]As Jesus was walking by the Sea
of Galilee, He noticed two brothers,
Simon who was called Peter, and An-
drew his brother, casting a net into the
sea; for they were fishermen.
[19]And He said to them, "Follow Me
[as My disciples, accepting Me as your
Master and Teacher and walking the
same path of life that I walk], and I will
make you fishers of men."
[20]Immediately they left their nets
and followed Him [becoming His dis-
ciples, believing and trusting in Him
and following His example].
[21]And going on [further] from there
He noticed two other brothers, James
the *son* of Zebedee, and his brother
John, in the boat with their father Zeb-
edee, mending their nets; and He called
them [to follow Him as His disciples].
[22]Immediately they left the boat and
their father, and followed Him [becom-
ing His disciples, believing and trust-
ing in Him and following His example].

Ministry in Galilee

[23]And He went throughout all Gali-
lee, teaching in their synagogues and
preaching the good news (gospel) of
the kingdom, and healing every kind
of disease and every kind of sickness
among the people [demonstrating
and revealing that He was indeed the
promised Messiah].
[24]So the news about Him spread

4:10 *Satan.* Satan is not dispatched easily by anyone who merely says, "Go." The only way we can be victorious in temptation is through the blood and authority of Jesus Christ.

4:15 – 16 *GREAT LIGHT.* The passage quoted here (Isa 9:1 – 2) foretells the reign of the Messiah in the coming kingdom.

4:18 – 20 *I will make you fishers of men.* This allusion to Jeremiah 16:16 was used to call Peter and Andrew to a life of ministry.

4:23 *teaching ... preaching ... healing.* These words summarize Jesus' early ministry.

7 Dt 6:16 **10** Dt 6:13; 10:20; Jos 24:14; 1Sa 7:3 **11** Heb 1:14 **12** Mk 1:14; Lk 3:20; 4:14,31; Jn 4:43 **15** Isa 9:1,2 **16** Isa 42:7; Lk 2:32 **17** Mk 1:14; Mt 3:2; 10:7 **18** Mk 1:16-18; Lk 5:2; Jn 1:42 **19** Lk 5:10 **20** Mk 10:28; Lk 18:28 **21** Mk 1:19; Lk 5:10 **23** Mt 9:35; Mk 1:21,39; Lk 4:15,44; Mt 24:14; Mk 1:14; Mk 1:34

throughout all Syria; and they brought to Him all who were sick, those suffering with various diseases and pains, those under the power of demons, and epileptics, paralytics; and He healed them.

25 Large crowds followed Him from Galilee and the Decapolis and Jerusalem and Judea and the other side of the Jordan.

The Sermon on the Mount; The Beatitudes

5 WHEN JESUS saw the crowds, He went up on the mountain; and when He was seated, His disciples came to Him.

2 Then He *began* to teach them, saying,

3 "Blessed [spiritually prosperous, happy, to be admired] are the poor in spirit [those devoid of spiritual arrogance, those who regard themselves as insignificant], for theirs is the kingdom of heaven [both now and forever]. [Luke 6:20–23]

4 "Blessed [forgiven, refreshed by God's grace] are those who mourn [over their sins and repent], for they will be comforted [when the burden of sin is lifted]. [Is 61:2]

5 "Blessed [inwardly peaceful, spiritually secure, worthy of respect] are the gentle [the kind-hearted, the sweet-spirited, the self-controlled], for they will inherit the earth. [Ps 37:11]

6 "Blessed [joyful, nourished by God's goodness] are those who hunger and thirst for righteousness [those who actively seek right standing with God], for they will be [completely] satisfied. [Is 55:1, 2]

7 "Blessed [content, sheltered by God's promises] are the merciful, for they will receive mercy.

8 "Blessed [anticipating God's presence, spiritually mature] are the pure in heart [those with integrity, moral courage, and godly character], for they will see God. [Ps 24:3, 4]

9 "Blessed [spiritually calm with life-joy in God's favor] are the makers *and* maintainers of peace, for they will [express His character and] be called the sons of God. [Heb 12:14]

10 "Blessed [comforted by inner peace and God's love] are those who are persecuted for doing that which is morally right, for theirs is the kingdom of heaven [both now and forever].

11 "Blessed [morally courageous and spiritually alive with life-joy in God's goodness] are you when *people* insult you and persecute you, and falsely say all kinds of evil things against you because of [your association with] Me.

12 "Be glad and exceedingly joyful, for your reward in heaven is great [absolutely inexhaustible]; for in this same way they persecuted the prophets who were before you. [2 Chr 36:16]

Disciples and the World

13 "You are the salt of the earth; but if the salt has lost its taste (purpose), how can it be made salty? It is no longer good for anything, but to be thrown out and walked on by people [when the walkways are wet and slippery].

14 "You are the light of [Christ to] the world. A city set on a hill cannot be hidden;

15 nor does *anyone* light a lamp and

5:2 *He began to teach them.* The Sermon on the Mount wasn't given as the way of salvation for the lost, but as the way of life for the children of the kingdom. It was instruction for those who had responded to Jesus' invitation to repent.

5:3 – 12 The Beatitudes — In the Sermon on the Mount, Christ succinctly describes the basic character traits of those who will inherit the kingdom. The word *kingdom* usually implies someone who is on top, who rules and has authority over others. They are the privileged. In God's kingdom the people are not privileged because they are on top but because, by being on the bottom, they are in a better position to receive God's grace and favor. These characteristics are the reverse of what man generally values in the world. "Blessed" can also be translated as "Happy." The signs of being blessed aren't power or material wealth. The sign of being blessed is receiving the benefits of God's grace.

---

25 Mk 3:7 **CHAPTER 5** **1** Mk 3:13 **3** Lk 6:20; See Ps 51:17; Pr 16:19; 29:23; Isa 57:15; 66:2 **4** Isa 61:2,3; Lk 6:21; Jn 16:20; 2Co 1:7; Rev 21:4 **5** Ps 37:11; Ro 4:13 **6** Isa 55:1; 65:13 **7** Ps 41:1; Mk 11:25 **8** Ps 15:2; Heb 12:14; 1Co 13:12 **10** 2Co 4:17; 1Pe 3:14 **11** Lk 6:22; 1Pe 4:14 **12** Lk 6:23; Ac 5:41; 1Pe 4:13; Neh 9:26; Ac 7:52 **13** Mk 9:50; Lk 14:34 **14** Pr 4:18; Php 2:15 **15** Mk 4:21; Lk 8:16

put it under a basket, but on a lamp-
stand, and it gives light to all who are
in the house. [Mark 4:21; Luke 8:16;
11:33]
16 “Let your light shine before men
in such a way that they may see your
good deeds *and* moral excellence, and
[recognize and honor and] glorify your
Father who is in heaven.
17 “Do not think that I came to do
away with *or* undo the Law [of Moses]
or the [writings of the] Prophets; I did
not come to destroy but to fulfill.
18 “For I assure you *and* most solemn-
ly say to you, until heaven and earth
pass away, not the smallest letter or
stroke [of the pen] will pass from the
Law until all things [which it foreshad-
ows] are accomplished.
19 “So whoever breaks one of the
least [important] of these command-
ments, and teaches others to do the
same, will be called least [important]
in the kingdom of heaven; but whoever
practices and teaches them, he will be
called great in the kingdom of heaven.
20 “For I say to you that unless your
righteousness (uprightness, moral es-
sence) is more than that of the scribes
and Pharisees, you will never enter the
kingdom of heaven.

Personal Relationships

21 “You have heard that it was said to
the men of old, ‘YOU SHALL NOT MURDER,’
and ‘Whoever murders shall be guilty
before the court.’ [Ex 20:13; Deut 5:17;
16:18]
22 “But I say to you that everyone
who continues to be angry with his
brother *or* harbors malice against him
shall be guilty before the court; and
whoever speaks [contemptuously and
insultingly] to his brother, ‘Raca (You
empty-headed idiot)!’ shall be guilty
before the supreme court (Sanhedrin);
and whoever says, ‘You fool!’ shall be
in danger of the fiery hell.
23 “So if you are presenting your of-
fering at the altar, and *while* there you
remember that your brother has some-
thing [such as a grievance or legitimate
complaint] against you,
24 leave your offering there at the al-
tar and go. First make peace with your
brother, and then come and present
your offering.
25 “Come to terms quickly [at the ear-
liest opportunity] with your opponent
at law while you are with him on the
way [to court], so that your opponent
does not hand you over to the judge,
and the judge to the guard, and you are
thrown into prison. [Luke 12:58, 59]
26 “I assure you *and* most solemnly
say to you, you will not come out of
there until you have paid the last cent.
27 “You have heard that it was said,
‘YOU SHALL NOT COMMIT ADULTERY’;
[Ex 20:14; Deut 5:18]
28 but I say to you that everyone who
[so much as] looks at a woman with
lust for her has already committed
adultery with her in his heart.
29 “If your right eye makes you stum-
ble *and* leads you to sin, tear it out and
throw it away [that is, remove yourself
from the source of temptation]; for it is
better for you to lose one of the parts
of your body, than for your whole body
to be thrown into hell.
30 “If your right hand makes you
stumble *and* leads you to sin, cut it
off and throw it away [that is, remove
yourself from the source of tempta-
tion]; for it is better for you to lose one
of the parts of your body than for your
whole body to go into hell.

5:16 *Let your light shine.* The believer does not have inherent light, rather, we have reflective light. As Christ followers, we must make sure that we do not allow anything to come between us and our Source of light.

5:27 *ADULTERY.* Control of the heart and body begins with control of the eyes. Deeds of shame result from fantasies of shame. Jesus gives the sobering advice "if your right eye makes you stumble and leads you to sin, tear it out and throw it away." It should be clear here that Jesus is not advocating mutilating our bodies, but He is using a strong figure of speech to emphasize removing any temptation for evil, whatever the cost.

16 1Pe 2:12; Jn 15:8; 1Co 14:25 **17** Ro 10:4 **18** Lk 16:17 **19** Jas 2:10 **20** Ro 10:3 **21** Ex 20:13 **22** 1Jn 3:15; Jas 2:20 **23** Mt 8:4 **24** Job 42:8; 1Ti 2:8; 1Pe 3:7 **25** Pr 25:8; Lk 12:58; Ps 32:6; Isa 55:6 **27** Ex 20:14; Dt 5:18 **28** Job 31:1; Pr 6:25 **29** Mk 9:43; Col 3:5

AROUND THE SEA OF GALILEE

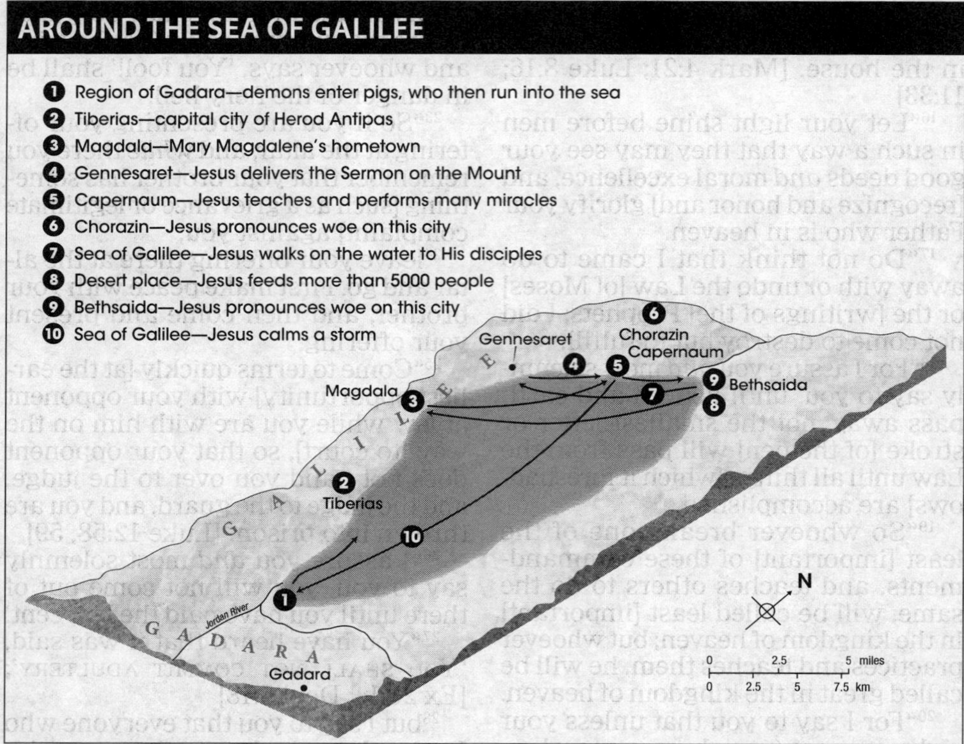

31"It has also been said, 'WHOEVER
DIVORCES HIS WIFE IS TO GIVE HER A CER-
TIFICATE OF DIVORCE';
32but I say to you that whoever di-
vorces his wife, except on grounds
of sexual immorality, causes her to
commit adultery; and whoever marries
a woman who has been divorced com-
mits adultery. [Deut 24:1–4; Luke 16:18]
33"Again, you have heard that it was
said to the men of old, 'YOU SHALL NOT
MAKE FALSE VOWS, BUT YOU SHALL FULFILL
YOUR VOWS TO THE LORD [as a religious
duty].'
34"But I say to you, do not make an
oath at all, either by heaven, for it is
the throne of God;
35or by the earth, for it is the footstool
of His feet; or by Jerusalem, for it is THE
CITY OF THE GREAT KING. [Ps 48:2; Is 66:1]
36"Nor shall you make an oath by
your head, for you are not able to make
a single hair white or black.
37"But let your statement be, 'Yes, yes'
or 'No, no' [a firm yes or no]; anything
more than that comes from the evil
one. [Lev 19:12; Num 30:2; Deut 23:21]
38"You have heard that it was said,
'AN EYE FOR AN EYE, AND A TOOTH FOR
A TOOTH [punishment that fits the of-
fense].' [Ex 21:24; Lev 24:20; Deut 19:21]
39"But I say to you, do not resist an
evil person [who insults you or vio-
lates your rights]; but whoever slaps

5:32 *sexual immorality.* This is a general term that includes premarital sex, extramarital infidelity, homosexuality, and bestiality.

5:38 *AN EYE FOR AN EYE.* This important Old Testament law (Ex 21:24–25; Lev 24:20; Dt 19:21), known as the *lex talionis* (law of retaliation), covered what type of punishment should be meted out to transgressors. It limited the retribution the offender would have to bear, preventing the "head for eye, jaw for tooth" vengeance typical of humans.

31 Dt 24:1; Jer 3:1; Mk 10:2 **32** Lk 16:18; Ro 7:3 **33** Mt 23:16; Ex 20:7; Lev 19:12; Dt 23:23 **34** Mt 23:16; Jas 5:12; Isa 66:1 **35** Ps 48:2 **37** Col 4:6; Jas 5:12 **38** Ex 21:24; Lev 24:20; Dt 19:21 **39** Pr 20:22; Lk 6:29; Ro 12:17; 1Co 6:7; 1Pe 3:9; Isa 50:6; La 3:30

you on the right cheek, turn the other toward him also [simply ignore insignificant insults or trivial losses and do not bother to retaliate—maintain your dignity, your self-respect, your poise]. [Luke 6:29, 30; Rom 12:17–21]

40“If anyone wants to sue you and take your shirt, let him have your coat also [for the Lord repays the offender].

41“And whoever forces you to go one mile, go with him two.

42“Give to him who asks of you, and do not turn away from him who wants to borrow from you. [Deut 15:8; Prov 24:29]

43“You have heard that it was said, ‘YOU SHALL LOVE YOUR NEIGHBOR (fellow man) and hate your enemy.’ [Lev 19:18; Ps 139:21, 22]

44“But I say to you, love [that is, unselfishly seek the best or higher good for] your enemies and pray for those who persecute you, [Prov 25:21, 22]

45so that you may [show yourselves to] be the children of your Father who is in heaven; for He makes His sun rise on those who are evil and on those who are good, and makes the rain fall on the righteous [those who are morally upright] and the unrighteous [the unrepentant, those who oppose Him].

46“For if you love [only] those who love you, what reward do you have? Do not even the tax collectors do that?

47“And if you greet only your brothers [wishing them God’s blessing and peace], what more [than others] are you doing? Do not even the Gentiles [who do not know the Lord] do that?

48“You, therefore, will be perfect [growing into spiritual maturity both in mind and character, actively integrating godly values into your daily life], as your heavenly Father is perfect. [Lev 19:2]

Giving to the Poor and Prayer

6 “BE [VERY] careful not to do your good deeds publicly, to be seen by men; otherwise you will have no reward [prepared and awaiting you] with your Father who is in heaven.

2“So whenever you give to the poor *and* do acts of kindness, do not blow a trumpet before you [to advertise it], as the hypocrites do [like actors acting out a role] in the synagogues and in the streets, so that they may be honored *and* recognized *and* praised by men. I assure you *and* most solemnly say to you, they [already] have their reward in full.

3“But when you give to the poor *and* do acts of kindness, do not let your left hand know what your right hand is doing [give in complete secrecy],

4so that your charitable acts will be done in secret; and your Father who sees [what is done] in secret will reward you.

5“Also, when you pray, do not be like the hypocrites; for they love to pray [publicly] standing in the synagogues and on the corners of the streets so that they may be seen by men. I assure you *and* most solemnly say to you, they [already] have their reward in full.

6“But when you pray, go into your most private room, close the door and pray to your Father who is in secret, and your Father who sees [what is done] in secret will reward you.

7“And when you pray, do not use meaningless repetition as the Gentiles do, for they think they will be heard because of their many words. [1 Kin 18:25–29]

8“So do not be like them [praying as they do]; for your Father knows what you need before you ask Him.

9“Pray, then, in this way:

5:41 ***forces.*** The Roman government could press anyone to carry a load as far as one mile.
5:45 ***children of your Father.*** In other words, “that you be like your heavenly Father who displays His love without discrimination.”
5:48 ***be perfect.*** God does not lower the standard to accommodate our sinfulness. He gives us the power to keep this righteousness standard.
6:2 ***they [already] have their reward.*** The only reward the hypocrites will ever receive is to be honored by man.
6:9 ***in this way.*** This does not mean to pray only

41 Mt 27:32 **42** Dt 15:8; Lk 6:30 **43** Lev 19:18; Dt 23:6; Ps 41:10 **44** Lk 6:27; Ro 12:14; Lk 23:34; Ac 7:60; 1Co 4:12; 1Pe 2:23 **45** Job 25:3 **46** Lk 6:32 **48** Ge 17:1; Lev 11:44; 19:2; Lk 6:36; Col 1:28; 4:12; Jas 1:4; 1Pe 1:15; Eph 5:1 **CHAPTER 6** **2** Ro 12:8 **4** Lk 14:14 **6** 2Ki 4:33 **7** Ecc 5:2; 1Ki 18:26 **9** Lk 11:2

'Our Father who is in heaven,
Hallowed be Your name.
[Luke 11:2–4]
10 'Your kingdom come,
Your will be done
On earth as it is in heaven.
11 'Give us this day our daily bread.
12 'And forgive us our debts, as
we have forgiven our debtors
[letting go of both the wrong
and the resentment].
13 'And do not lead us into
temptation, but deliver us from
evil. [For Yours is the kingdom
and the power and the glory
forever. Amen.]' [Luke 11:2–4]

14 "For if you forgive others their trespasses [their reckless and willful sins], your heavenly Father will also forgive you.

15 "But if you do not forgive others [nurturing your hurt and anger with the result that it interferes with your relationship with God], then your Father will not forgive your trespasses.

Fasting, The True Treasure, Wealth (Mammon)

16 "And whenever you are fasting, do not look gloomy like the hypocrites, for they put on a sad and dismal face [like actors, discoloring their faces with ashes or dirt] so that their fasting may be seen by men. I assure you *and* most solemnly say to you, they [already] have their reward in full. [Is 58:5]

17 "But when you fast, put oil on your head [as you normally would to groom your hair] and wash your face

18 so that your fasting will not be noticed by people, but by your Father who is in secret; and your Father who sees [what is done] in secret will reward you.

19 "Do not store up for yourselves [material] treasures on earth, where moth and rust destroy, and where thieves break in and steal.

20 "But store up for yourselves treasures in heaven, where neither moth nor rust destroys, and where thieves do not break in and steal;

21 for where your treasure is, there your heart [your wishes, your desires; that on which your life centers] will be also.

22 "The eye is the lamp of the body; so if your eye is clear [spiritually perceptive], your whole body will be full of light [benefiting from God's precepts].

23 "But if your eye is bad [spiritually blind], your whole body will be full of darkness [devoid of God's precepts]. So if the [very] light inside you [your inner self, your heart, your conscience] is darkness, how great *and* terrible is that darkness!

24 "No one can serve two masters; for either he will hate the one and love the other, or he will be devoted to the one and despise the other. You cannot serve God and mammon [money, possessions, fame, status, or whatever is valued more than the Lord].

The Cure for Anxiety

25 "Therefore I tell you, stop being worried *or* anxious (perpetually uneasy, distracted) about your life, as to what you will eat or what you will drink; nor about your body, as to what you will wear. Is life not more than food, and the body more than clothing? [Luke 12:22–31]

---

these words, but to remember the general topics of worship, request for both physical and spiritual needs, confession, and repentance of sins.

6:19 *Do not store up . . . on earth.* In other words, don't give priority to things that only last on earth, but instead put priority and energy into serving God.

6:24 Covetousness — God requires total allegiance and continuous subjection of our wills to Him. He asks for full commitment of our hearts and love for His service. We cannot serve God like that while under the influence of the god of money, urging us to make present, tangible, and worldly things the object of our thoughts and affections.

---

10 Mt 26:39; Ac 21:14; Ps 103:20 **11** See Job 23:12; Pr 30:8 **12** Mt 18:21 **13** Mt 26:41; 1Co 10:13; 2Pe 2:9; Rev 3:10; Jn 17:15; 1Ch 29:11 **14** Mk 11:25; Eph 4:32; Col 3:13 **15** Mt 18:35; Jas 2:13 **16** Isa 58:5 **17** Ru 3:3; Da 10:3 **19** Pr 23:4; 1Ti 6:17; Heb 13:5; Jas 5:1 **20** Mt 19:21; Lk 12:33; 18:22; 1Ti 6:19; 1Pe 1:4 **22** Lk 11:34 **24** Lk 16:13; Gal 1:10; 1Ti 6:17; Jas 4:4; 1Jn 2:15 **25** Ps 55:22; Lk 12:22; Php 4:6; 1Pe 5:7

26“Look at the birds of the air; they
neither sow [seed] nor reap [the harvest] nor gather [the crops] into barns,
and yet your heavenly Father keeps
feeding them. Are you not worth much
more than they?
27“And who of you by worrying can
add one hour to [the length of] his life?
[Ps 39:5–7]
28“And why are you worried about
clothes? See how the lilies *and* wildflowers of the field grow; they do not labor
nor do they spin [wool to make clothing],
29yet I say to you that not even Solomon
in all his glory *and* splendor dressed
himself like one of these. [1 Kin 10:4–7]
30“But if God so clothes the grass of
the field, which is alive *and* green today
and tomorrow is [cut and] thrown [as
fuel] into the furnace, *will He* not much
more *clothe* you? You of little faith!
31“Therefore do not worry *or* be anxious (perpetually uneasy, distracted),
saying, ‘What are we going to eat?’ or
‘What are we going to drink?’ or ‘What
are we going to wear?’
32“For the [pagan] Gentiles eagerly
seek all these things; [but do not worry,] for your heavenly Father knows
that you need them.
33“But first *and* most importantly
seek (aim at, strive after) His kingdom
and His righteousness [His way of doing and being right—the attitude and
character of God], and all these things
will be given to you also.
34“So do not worry about tomorrow;
for tomorrow will worry about itself.
Each day has enough trouble of its own.

Judging Others

7 “DO NOT judge *and* criticize *and*
condemn [others unfairly with an
attitude of self-righteous superiority
as though assuming the office of a
judge], so that you will not be judged
[unfairly].
2“For just as you [hypocritically]
judge others [when you are sinful and
unrepentant], so will you be judged;
and in accordance with your standard
of measure [used to pass out judgment],
judgment will be measured to you.
3“Why do you look at the [insignificant] speck that is in your brother’s eye,
but do not notice *and* acknowledge the
[egregious] log that is in your own eye?
4“Or how can you say to your brother,
‘Let me get the speck out of your eye,’
when there is a log in your own eye?
5“You hypocrite (play-actor, pretender), first get the log out of your own eye,
and then you will see clearly to take the
speck out of your brother’s eye.
6“Do not give that which is holy to
dogs, and do not throw your pearls
before pigs, for they will trample them
under their feet, and turn and tear you
to pieces.

Prayer and the Golden Rule

7“Ask *and* keep on asking and it
will be given to you; seek *and* keep on
seeking and you will find; knock *and*
keep on knocking and the door will be
opened to you. [Luke 11:9–13]
8“For everyone who keeps on asking
receives, and he who keeps on seeking
finds, and to him who keeps on knocking, it will be opened.
9“Or what man is there among you
who, if his son asks for bread, will
[instead] give him a stone?
10“Or if he asks for a fish, will [instead] give him a snake?
11“If you then, evil (sinful by nature)
as you are, know how to give good *and*
advantageous gifts to your children,
how much more will your Father who

6:27 *add one hour.* It seems that Jesus would bring a smile here; the mental picture either of growing taller, or of stretching time by worrying, helps us to see the futility of it.

7:1 – 2 *judge.* The point of this verse is that a Christian must not judge or criticize in a way that they themselves would not want to be judged or criticized. Every judgment that a person makes becomes a basis for his or her own judgment (Jas 3:1 – 2).

7:6 *dogs . . . pigs.* These insulting terms refer to people who are enemies of the gospel, as opposed to those who are merely unbelievers.

26 Job 38:41; Ps 147:9; Lk 12:24 **33** See 1Ki 3:13; Ps 37:25; Mk 10:30; Lk 12:31; 1Ti 4:8 **CHAPTER 7** **1** Lk 6:37; Ro 14:3; 1Co 4:3; Jas 4:11 **2** Mk 4:24; Lk 6:38 **3** Lk 6:41 **6** Pr 9:7,8; 23:9; Ac 13:45 **7** Mt 21:22; Mk 11:24; Lk 11:9; 18:1; Jn 14:13; 15:7; 16:23,24; Jas 1:5,6; 1Jn 3:22; 5:14,15 **8** Pr 8:17; Jer 29:12 **9** Lk 11:11 **11** Ge 6:5; 8:21

is in heaven [perfect as He is] give what is good *and* advantageous to those who keep on asking Him.

12 "So then, in everything treat others the same way you want them to treat you, for this is [the essence of] the Law and the [writings of the] Prophets.

The Narrow and Wide Gates

13 "Enter through the narrow gate. For wide is the gate and broad *and* easy to travel is the path that leads the way to destruction *and* eternal loss, and there are many who enter through it.

14 "But small is the gate and narrow *and* difficult to travel is the path that leads the way to [everlasting] life, and there are few who find it. [Deut 30:19; Jer 21:8]

A Tree and Its Fruit

15 "Beware of the false prophets, [teachers] who come to you dressed as sheep [appearing gentle and innocent], but inwardly are ravenous wolves. [Ezek 22:27]

16 "By their fruit you will recognize them [that is, by their contrived doctrine and self-focus]. Do people pick grapes from thorn bushes or figs from thistles? [Luke 6:43, 44]

17 "Even so, every healthy tree bears good fruit, but the unhealthy tree bears bad fruit.

18 "A good tree cannot bear bad fruit, nor can a bad tree bear good fruit.

19 "Every tree that does not bear good fruit is cut down and thrown into the fire.

20 "Therefore, by their fruit you will recognize them [as false prophets].

21 "Not everyone who says to Me, 'Lord, Lord,' will enter the kingdom of heaven, but only he who does the will of My Father who is in heaven.

22 "Many will say to Me on that day [when I judge them], 'Lord, Lord, have we not prophesied in Your name, and driven out demons in Your name, and done many miracles in Your name?'

23 "And then I will declare to them publicly, 'I never knew you; DEPART FROM ME [you are banished from My presence], YOU WHO ACT WICKEDLY [disregarding My commands].' [Ps 6:8]

The Two Foundations

24 "So everyone who hears these words of Mine and acts on them, will be like a wise man [a far-sighted, practical, and sensible man] who built his house on the rock. [Luke 6:47–49]

25 "And the rain fell, and the floods *and* torrents came, and the winds blew and slammed against that house; yet it did not fall, because it had been founded on the rock.

26 "And everyone who hears these words of Mine and does not do them, will be like a foolish (stupid) man who built his house on the sand.

27 "And the rain fell, and the floods *and* torrents came, and the winds blew and slammed against that house; and it fell—and great *and* complete was its fall."

28 When Jesus had finished [speaking] these words [on the mountain], the crowds were astonished *and* overwhelmed at His teaching;

29 for He was teaching them as one who had authority [to teach entirely of His own volition], and not as their scribes [who relied on others to confirm their authority].

Jesus Cleanses a Leper; The Centurion's Faith

8 WHEN JESUS came down from the mountain, large crowds followed Him.

2 And a leper came up to Him and

7:15 *Beware of the false prophets.* Deuteronomy 13:1 – 11 and 18:20 – 22 provide information on discerning and responding to false prophets. The way to tell a false teacher from teachers of the truth is by their fruits. Fruit does not only refer to deeds, but also to doctrine (16:12; 1Jn 4:1 – 3).

12 Lk 6:31; Lev 19:18; Mt 22:40; Ro 13:8; Gal 5:14; 1Ti 1:5 **13** Lk 13:24 **15** Dt 13:3; Jer 23:16; Mt 24:4,5; Mk 13:22; Ro 16:17; Eph 5:6; Col 2:8; 2Pe 2:1; 1Jn 4:1; Mic 3:5; 2Ti 3:5; Ac 20:29 **16** ver. 20; Lk 6:43 **17** Jer 11:19; Mt 12:33 **19** Mt 3:10; Lk 3:9; Jn 15:2 **21** Hos 8:2; Mt 25:11; Lk 6:46; 13:25; Ac 19:13; Ro 2:13; Jas 1:22 **22** Nu 24:4; Jn 11:51; 1Co 13:2 **23** Mt 25:12; Lk 13:25; 2Ti 2:19; Ps 5:5; 6:8; Mt 25:41 **24** Lk 6:47 **28** Mt 13:54; Mk 1:22; 6:2; Lk 4:32 **29** Jn 7:46 **CHAPTER 8** **2** Mk 1:40; Lk 5:12

bowed down before Him, saying, "Lord, if You are willing, You are able to make me clean (well)." [Mark 1:40–44; Luke 5:12–14]
[3]Jesus reached out His hand and touched him, saying, "I am willing; be cleansed." Immediately his leprosy was cleansed.
[4]And Jesus said to him, "See that you tell no one [about this]; but go, show yourself to the priest [for inspection] and present the offering that Moses commanded, as a testimony (evidence) to them [of your healing]." [Lev 14:2]
[5]As Jesus went into Capernaum, a centurion came up to Him, begging Him [for help], [Luke 7:1–10]
[6]and saying, "Lord, my servant is lying at home paralyzed, with intense *and* terrible, tormenting pain."
[7]Jesus said to him, "I will come and heal him."
[8]But the centurion replied to Him, "Lord, I am not worthy to have You come under my roof, but only say the word, and my servant will be healed.
[9]"For I also am a man subject to authority [of a higher rank], with soldiers subject to me; and I say to one, 'Go!' and he goes, and to another, 'Come!' and he comes, and to my slave, 'Do this!' and he does it."
[10]When Jesus heard this, He was amazed and said to those who were following Him, "I tell you truthfully, I have not found such great faith [as this] with anyone in Israel.
[11]"I say to you that many [Gentiles] will come from east and west, and will sit down [to feast at the table, and enjoy God's promises] with Abraham, Isaac, and Jacob in the kingdom of heaven [because they accepted Me as Savior],
[12]while the sons *and* heirs of the kingdom [the descendants of Abraham who will not recognize Me as Messiah] will be thrown out into the outer darkness; in that place [which is farthest removed from the kingdom] there will be weeping [in sorrow and pain] and grinding of teeth [in distress and anger]." [Ps 107:2, 3; Is 49:12; 59:19; Mal 1:11]
[13]Then Jesus said to the centurion, "Go; it will be done for you as you have believed." And the servant was restored to health at that very hour.

Peter's Mother-in-law and Many Others Healed

[14]When Jesus went into Peter's house [in Capernaum], He saw Peter's mother-in-law lying sick in bed with a fever. [Mark 1:29–34; Luke 4:38–41]
[15]He touched her hand and the fever left her; and she got up and served Him.
[16]When evening came, they brought to Him many who were under the power of demons; and He cast out the *evil* spirits with a word, and restored to health all who were sick [exhibiting His authority as Messiah],
[17]so that He fulfilled what was spoken by the prophet Isaiah: "HE HIMSELF TOOK OUR INFIRMITIES [upon Himself] AND CARRIED AWAY OUR DISEASES." [Is 53:4]

Discipleship Tested

[18]Now when Jesus saw a crowd around Him, He gave orders to cast off for the other side *of the Sea of Galilee.*
[19]Then [on His way to board the boat] a scribe [who was a respected and authoritative interpreter of the Law] came and said to Him, "Master, I will accompany You [as Your student] wherever You go." [Luke 9:57–60]

8:4 show yourself to the priest. This was no small undertaking. The sacrifice required was long and involved (Lev 14:4–32). In obeying the law of Moses, the leper also would be a powerful testimony to the religious authorities in Jerusalem that the Messiah had arrived.

8:10 I have not found . . . in Israel. Jesus makes it clear that just being a physical descendant of Abraham does not guarantee entrance into His kingdom. The true children of Abraham are those who share his faith in God (Gal 5:6–9).

8:17 TOOK OUR INFIRMITIES [upon Himself] AND CARRIED AWAY OUR DISEASES. This verse quotes Isaiah 53:4. Jesus healed because He had compassion on the people.

4 Mt 9:30; Mk 5:43; Lev 14:3,4,10; Lk 5:14 **5** Lk 7:1 **8** Lk 15:19,21; Ps 107:20 **11** Ge 12:3; Isa 2:2,3; 11:10; Mal 1:11; Lk 13:29; Ac 10:45; 11:18; 14:27; Ro 15:9; Eph 3:6 **12** Mt 21:43; Mt 13:42,50; 22:13; 24:51; 25:30; Lk 13:28; 2Pe 2:17; Jude 13 **14** Mk 1:29-31; Lk 4:38,39; 1Co 9:5 **16** Mk 1:32; Lk 4:40,41 **17** Isa 53:4; 1Pe 2:24 **19** Lk 9:57,58

[20]Jesus replied to him, "Foxes have holes and the birds of the air have nests, but the Son of Man has nowhere to lay His head." [Dan 7:13; Mark 8:31, 38; Luke 12:8; John 1:51; Acts 7:56]

[21]Another of the disciples said to Him, "Lord, let me first go and bury my father (collect my inheritance)." [Luke 9:59, 60]

[22]But Jesus said to him, "Follow Me [believing in Me as Master and Teacher], and allow the [spiritually] dead to bury their own dead."

[23]When He got into the boat, His disciples followed Him. [Mark 4:36–41; Luke 8:22–25]

[24]And suddenly a violent storm arose on the sea, so that the boat was being covered by the waves; but Jesus was sleeping.

[25]And the disciples went and woke Him, saying, "Lord, save us, we are going to die!"

[26]He said to them, "Why are you afraid, you men of little faith?" Then He got up and rebuked the winds and the sea, and there was [at once] a great *and* wonderful calm [a perfect peacefulness].

[27]The men wondered in amazement, saying, "What kind of man is this, that even the winds and the sea obey Him?"

Jesus Casts Out Demons

[28]When He arrived at the other side in the country of the Gadarenes, two demon-possessed men coming out of the tombs met Him. *They were* so extremely fierce *and* violent that no one could pass by that way. [Mark 5:1–17; Luke 8:26–37]

[29]And they screamed out, "What business do we have [in common] with each other, Son of God? Have You come to torment us before the appointed time [of judgment]?" [Judg 11:12; 2 Sam 16:10; Matt 25:41; Mark 5:7; Luke 4:34; Rev 20:10]

[30]Some distance from them a large herd of pigs was grazing.

[31]The demons *began* begging Him, "If You drive us out, send us into the herd of pigs."

[32]And He said to them, "Go!" So they came out [of the men] and went into the pigs, and the whole herd rushed down the steep bank into the sea and died in the water.

[33]The herdsmen ran away, and went to the city and reported everything, including what had happened to the men under the power of demons.

[34]And the whole city came out to meet Jesus; and as soon as they saw Him, they begged Him to leave their region.

A Paralytic Healed

9 AND JESUS, getting into a boat, crossed over *the Sea of Galilee* and came to [Capernaum] His own city.

[2]They brought to Him a man who was paralyzed, lying on a stretcher. Seeing their [active] faith [springing from confidence in Him], Jesus said to the paralytic, "Do not be afraid, son; your sins are forgiven [the penalty is paid, the guilt removed, and you are declared to be in right standing with God]." [Mark 2:3–12; Luke 5:18–26]

[3]And some of the scribes said to themselves, "This *man* blasphemes [by claiming the rights and prerogatives of God]!"

[4]But Jesus, knowing their thoughts, said, "Why do you think evil in your hearts?

[5]"For which is easier, to say, 'Your sins are forgiven *and* the penalty paid,' or to say, 'Get up and walk'? [Both are possible for God; both are impossible for man.]

8:28 – 29 *demon-possessed.* We learn several things about demons in this passage. They recognize the deity of Christ, they are limited in their knowledge, they know they will ultimately be judged by Christ (25:41; Jas 2:19; 2Pe 2:4; Jude 6; Rev 12:7 – 17), and they cannot act without the permission of higher authority.

9:2 *their [active] faith.* This refers to the faith of the paralytic as well as that of the men who were carrying him.

21 Lk 9:59,60; See 1Ki 19:20 **24** Mk 4:37; Lk 8:23 **26** Ps 65:7; 89:9; 107:29 **28** Mk 5:1; Lk 8:26 **34** See Dt 5:25; 1Ki 17:18; Lk 5:8; Ac 16:39 **CHAPTER 9 1** Mt 4:13 **2** Mk 2:3; Lk 5:18; Mt 8:10 **4** Ps 139:2; Mt 12:25; Mk 12:15; Lk 5:22; 6:8; 9:47; 11:17

6 “But so that you may know that the Son of Man has authority *and* the power on earth to forgive sins”—then He said to the paralytic, “Get up, pick up your stretcher and go home.”

7 And he got up and went home [healed and forgiven].

8 When the crowds saw this, they were awestruck, and glorified God *and* praised Him, who had given such authority *and* power to men.

Matthew Called

9 As Jesus went on from there, He saw a man named Matthew (Levi) sitting in the tax collector's booth; and He said to him, “Follow Me [as My disciple, accepting Me as your Master and Teacher and walking the same path of life that I walk].” And Matthew got up and followed Him. [Mark 2:14–22; Luke 5:27–39]

10 Then as Jesus was reclining *at the table* in *Matthew's* house, many tax collectors and sinners [including non-observant Jews] came and ate with Him and His disciples.

11 When the Pharisees saw this, they asked His disciples, “Why does your Master eat with tax collectors and sinners?”

12 But when Jesus heard *this*, He said, “Those who are healthy have no need for a physician, but [only] those who are sick.

13 “Go and learn what this [Scripture] means: ‘I DESIRE COMPASSION [for those in distress], AND NOT [animal] SACRIFICE,’ for I did not come to call [to repentance] the [self-proclaimed] righteous [who see no need to change], but sinners [those who recognize their sin and actively seek forgiveness].” [Hos 6:6; Mark 2:17; Luke 5:32]

The Question about Fasting

14 Then the disciples of John [the Baptist] came to Jesus, asking, “Why do we and the Pharisees often fast [as a religious exercise], but Your disciples do not fast?”

15 And Jesus replied to them, “Can the guests of the bridegroom mourn while the bridegroom is with them? The days will come when the bridegroom is taken away from them, and then they will fast.

16 “But no one puts a piece of unshrunk (new) cloth on an old garment; for the patch pulls away from the garment, and a worse tear results.

17 “Nor is new wine put into old wineskins [that have lost their elasticity]; otherwise the wineskins burst, and the [fermenting] wine spills and the wineskins are ruined. But new wine is put into fresh wineskins, so both are preserved.”

Miracles of Healing

18 While He was saying these things to them, a ruler (synagogue official) entered [the house] and kneeled down *and* worshiped Him, saying, “My daughter has just now died; but come and lay Your hand on her, and she will live.” [Mark 5:22–43; Luke 8:41–56]

19 Jesus got up and *began* to accompany the ruler, with His disciples.

20 Then a woman who had suffered from a hemorrhage for twelve years came up behind Him and touched the [tassel] fringe of His outer robe; [Matt 14:36]

21 for she had been saying to herself, “If I only touch His outer robe, I will be healed.”

22 But Jesus turning and seeing her said, “Take courage, daughter; your

---

9:10 *tax collectors.* Tax collectors were often despised not only because they were seen as traitors, working for the hated Roman government, but also because they generally collected more than necessary and pocketed the difference.

9:12–13 *Those who are healthy have no need.* Jesus refers ironically to the Pharisees as “the righteous.” They were not righteous, that was only how they perceived themselves because of their pious and scrupulous law keeping (Php 3:6). But God is more interested in a person's loyal love than the observance of external rituals.

9 Mk 2:14; Lk 5:27 **10** Mk 2:15; Lk 5:29 **11** Mt 11:19; Lk 5:30; 15:2; Gal 2:15 **13** Hos 6:6; Mic 6:6-8; Mt 12:7; 1Ti 1:15 **14** Mk 2:18; Lk 5:33; 18:12 **15** Jn 3:29; Ac 13:2,3; 14:23; 1Co 7:5 **18** Mk 5:22; Lk 8:41 **20** Mk 5:25; Lk 8:43 **22** Lk 7:50; 8:48; 17:19; 18:42

[personal trust and confident] faith [in Me] has made you well." And at once the woman was [completely] healed.

23 When Jesus came to the ruler's house, and saw the flute players [who were professional, hired mourners] and the [grieving] crowd making an uproar,

24 He said, "Go away; for the girl is not dead, but is sleeping." And they laughed *and* jeered at Him.

25 But when the crowd had been sent outside, Jesus went in and took her by the hand, and the girl got up.

26 And the news about this spread throughout all that district.

27 As Jesus went on from there, two blind men followed Him, screaming loudly, "Have mercy *and* compassion on us, Son of David (Messiah)!"

28 When He went into the house, the blind men came up to Him, and Jesus said to them, "Do you believe [with a deep, abiding trust] that I am able to do this?" They said to Him, "Yes, Lord."

29 Then He touched their eyes, saying, "According to your faith [your trust and confidence in My power and My ability to heal] it will be done to you."

30 And their eyes were opened. And Jesus sternly warned them: "See that no one knows this!"

31 But they went out and spread the news about Him throughout that whole district.

32 While they were going away, a mute, demon-possessed man was brought to Jesus.

33 And when the demon was driven out [by Jesus], the mute man spoke; and the crowds wondered in amazement, saying, "Never before has anything like this [miracle] been seen in Israel."

34 But the Pharisees were saying, "He casts out the demons by [the power of] the ruler of demons."

35 Jesus went throughout all the cities and villages [in Galilee], teaching in their synagogues and proclaiming the good news (gospel) of the kingdom, and healing every kind of disease and every kind of sickness [His words and His works reflecting His Messiahship].

36 When He saw the crowds, He was moved with compassion *and* pity for them, because they were dispirited and distressed, like sheep without a shepherd. [Zech 10:2]

37 Then He said to His disciples, "The harvest is [indeed] plentiful, but the workers are few.

38 "So pray to the Lord of the harvest to send out workers into His harvest."

The Twelve Disciples; Instructions for Service

10 JESUS SUMMONED His twelve disciples and gave them authority *and* power over unclean spirits, to cast them out, and to heal every kind of disease and every kind of sickness. [Mark 6:7; Luke 9:1]

2 Now these are the names of the twelve apostles (special messengers, personally chosen representatives): first, Simon, who is called Peter, and Andrew, his brother; James the son of Zebedee, and John his brother; [Mark 3:16–19; Luke 6:13–16]

3 Philip and Bartholomew (Nathanael); Thomas and Matthew (Levi) the tax collector; James the son of Alphaeus, and Thaddaeus (Judas, not Iscariot);

4 Simon the Cananaean (Zealot), and Judas Iscariot, the one who betrayed Him.

5 Jesus sent out these twelve, instructing them: "Do not go among the Gentiles, and do not go into a city of the Samaritans;

9:30 *See that no one knows this!* Jesus may have wanted to discourage the masses from coming to Him for physical healing alone, because His primary purpose was spiritual healing.

9:37 *harvest.* The harvest will mark the beginning of the Kingdom Age. For the lost it will mean doom, but for the saved it will mean blessing.

10:2 *the twelve.* The twelve are called disciples in verse 1; here they are called "apostles." The word "apostle" emphasizes delegated authority (1Th 2:6).

23 Mk 5:38; Lk 8:51; See 2Ch 35:25 **24** Ac 20:10 **27** Mt 15:22; Mk 10:47; Lk 18:38 **30** Mt 8:4; Lk 5:14 **31** Mk 7:36 **32** Mt 12:22; Lk 11:14 **34** Mt 12:24; Lk 11:15 **35** Mt 4:23 **36** Mk 6:34; Nu 27:17; 1Ki 22:17 **37** Lk 10:2; Jn 4:35 **38** 2Th 3:1 **CHAPTER 10** **1** Mk 3:13; Lk 6:13 **2** Jn 1:42 **4** Lk 6:15; Ac 1:13; Jn 13:26 **5** Mt 4:15; 2Ki 17:24; Jn 4:9

[6]but rather go to the lost sheep of the
house of Israel.
[7]"And as you go, preach, saying,
'The kingdom of heaven is at hand.'
[8]"Heal the sick, raise the dead,
cleanse the lepers, cast out demons.
Freely you have received, freely give.
[9]"Do not take gold, or silver, or [even]
copper money in your money belt,
[10]or a provision bag for your jour-
ney, or even two tunics, or sandals,
or a staff; for the worker deserves his
support.
[11]"Whatever city or village you enter,
ask who in it is worthy [who welcomes
you and your message], and stay at his
house until you leave [that city].
[12]"As you go into the house, give it
your greeting [that is, 'Peace be to this
house'].
[13]"If [the family living in] the house
is worthy [welcoming you and your
message], give it your [blessing of]
peace [that is, a blessing of well-being
and prosperity, the favor of God]. But
if it is not worthy, take back your *bless-
ing of* peace.
[14]"Whoever does not welcome you,
nor listen to your message, as you leave
that house or city, shake the dust [of it]
off your feet [in contempt, breaking all
ties]. [Mark 6:11; Acts 13:51]
[15]"I assure you *and* most solemnly
say to you, it will be more tolerable
on the day of judgment for the land of
Sodom and Gomorrah than for that
city [since it rejected the Messiah's
messenger].

A Hard Road before Them

[16]"Listen carefully: I am sending you
out like sheep among wolves; so be
wise as serpents, and innocent as doves
[have no self-serving agenda]. [Gen 3:1]
[17]"Beware of men [whose nature is to
act in opposition to God], for they will
hand you over to the courts and flog
you in their synagogues;
[18]and you will be brought before
governors and kings for My sake, as
witnesses to them and to the Gentiles.
[19]"But when they hand you over, do
not worry about how or what you are
to say; for what you are to say will
be given you within that [very] hour;
[Mark 13:11–13; Luke 21:12–19]
[20]for it is not you speaking, but the
Spirit of your Father speaking through
you.
[21]"Brother will betray brother to
death, and the father his child; and
children will rise up *and* rebel against
their parents and cause them to be put
death.
[22]"And you will be hated by everyone
because of [your association with] My
name, but it is the one who has patient-
ly persevered *and* endured to the end
who will be saved.
[23]"When they persecute you in one
city [because of your faith in Me], flee
to the next; for I assure you *and* most
solemnly say to you, you will not finish
going through all the cities of Israel
before the Son of Man comes.

The Meaning of Discipleship

[24]"A disciple is not above his teacher,
nor is a bond-servant above his master.
[25]"It is enough for the disciple to be
like his teacher, and the bond-servant
like his master. If they have called the
head of the house Beelzebul (Satan),
how much more [will they speak evil
of] the members of his household.
[2 Kin 1:2]
[26]"So do not be afraid of them, for
nothing is hidden that will not be

10:15 *more tolerable ... for the land of Sodom and Gomorrah.* This verse, together with 11:22–24, implies that there will be different degrees of judgment and torment for those who reject Christ.

10:18 *for My sake.* God would use Jewish rejection and persecution of the messengers to bring the gospel message to the Gentiles.

10:25 Persecution — Believers must know that what the world has called our Lord, it will call us. The world has hated Jesus without cause, and they will hate those who bear His name in the same way.

6 Mt 15:24; Ac 13:46; Isa 53:6; Jer 50:6; Eze 34:5; 1Pe 2:25 **7** Lk 9:2; Mt 3:2; Lk 10:9 **8** Ac 8:18 **9** 1Sa 9:7; Mk 6:8; Lk 9:3; 10:4; Mk 6:8 **10** Lk 10:7; 1Co 9:7; 1Ti 5:18 **11** Lk 10:8 **13** Lk 10:5; Ps 35:13 **14** Mk 6:11; Lk 9:5; 10:10,11; Neh 5:13; Ac 13:51 **15** Mt 11:22 **16** Lk 10:3; Ro 16:19; Eph 5:15; Php 2:15 **17** Mk 13:9; Lk 12:11; Ac 5:40 **18** Ac 12:1; 25:7,23; 2Ti 4:16 **19** Lk 21:14; Ex 4:12; Jer 1:7 **20** 2Sa 23:2; 2Ti 4:17 **21** Mic 7:6; Lk 21:16 **22** Lk 21:17; Da 12:12; Mk 13:13 **23** Mt 2:13; Ac 8:1; Mt 16:28 **24** Lk 6:40; Jn 15:20 **25** Mk 3:22; Jn 8:48 **26** Mk 4:22; Lk 8:17; 12:2,3

revealed [at the judgment], or kept secret that will not be made known [at the judgment]. [Mark 4:22; Luke 12:2–9]

27 “What I say to you in the dark (privately), tell in the light (publicly); and what you hear *whispered* in your ear, proclaim from the housetops [to many people].

28 “Do not be afraid of those who kill the body but cannot kill the soul; but rather be afraid of Him who can destroy both soul and body in hell.

29 “Are not two little sparrows sold for a copper coin? And yet not one of them falls to the ground apart from your Father's will.

30 “But even the very hairs of your head are all numbered [for the Father is sovereign and has complete knowledge].

31 “So do not fear; you are more valuable than many sparrows.

32 “Therefore, the one who confesses *and* acknowledges Me before men [as Lord and Savior, affirming a state of oneness with Me], that one I will also confess *and* acknowledge before My Father who is in heaven.

33 “But the one who denies *and* rejects Me before men, that one I will also deny *and* reject before My Father who is in heaven.

34 “Do not think that I have come to bring peace on the earth; I have not come to bring peace, but a sword [of division between belief and unbelief]. [Luke 12:51–53]

35 “For I have come to SET A MAN AGAINST HIS FATHER, AND A DAUGHTER AGAINST HER MOTHER, AND A DAUGHTER-IN-LAW AGAINST HER MOTHER-IN-LAW;

36 and A MAN'S ENEMIES WILL BE THE MEMBERS OF HIS [own] HOUSEHOLD [when one believes and another does not]. [Mic 7:6]

37 “He who loves father or mother more than Me is not worthy of Me; and he who loves son or daughter more than Me is not worthy of Me. [Luke 14:26]

38 “And he who does not take his cross [expressing a willingness to endure whatever may come] and follow Me [believing in Me, conforming to My example in living and, if need be, suffering or perhaps dying because of faith in Me] is not worthy of Me.

39 “Whoever finds his life [in this world] will [eventually] lose it [through death], and whoever loses his life [in this world] for My sake will find it [that is, life with Me for all eternity]. [Matt 16:25; Mark 8:35; Luke 9:24; 17:33; John 12:25]

The Reward of Service

40 “He who receives *and* welcomes you receives Me, and he who receives Me receives Him who sent Me. [Mark 9:37; Luke 10:16; John 13:20]

41 “He who receives *and* welcomes a prophet because he is a prophet will receive a prophet's reward; and he who receives a righteous (honorable) man because he is a righteous man will receive a righteous man's reward.

42 “And whoever gives to one of these little ones [these who are humble in rank or influence] even a cup of cold water to drink because he is my disciple, truly I say to you, he will not lose his reward.”

John's Questions

11 WHEN JESUS had finished giving instructions to His twelve disciples, He went on from there to teach and to preach in their [Galilean] cities.

2 Now when John [the Baptist] in prison heard about the activities of Christ, he sent *word* by his disciples [Luke 7:18–35]

10:32 *the one who confesses.* Every act of our lives will be evaluated at the judgment seat of Christ (2Co 5:10). To refuse to speak up for Christ because of intimidation or persecution will result in the believer's loss of reward and consequent loss of glory in the kingdom (Ro 8:17; 2Ti 2:12).

10:38 *does not take his cross.* “Taking up a cross” stands for commitment to the extent of being willing to die for something.

28 Isa 8:12,13; Lk 12:4; 1Pe 3:14 **30** 1Sa 14:45; Lk 21:18; Ac 27:34 **32** Lk 12:8; Ro 10:9; Rev 3:5 **33** Lk 9:26; 2Ti 2:12 **34** Lk 12:49 **35** Mic 7:6 **36** Ps 41:9; 55:13; Jn 13:18 **37** Lk 14:26 **38** Mk 8:34 **39** Lk 17:33; Jn 12:25 **40** Lk 9:48; Jn 12:44; Gal 4:14 **41** 1Ki 17:10; 2Ki 4:8 **42** Mt 25:40; Mk 9:41; Heb 6:10 **CHAPTER 11** **2** Lk 7:18; Mt 14:3

3 and asked Him, "Are You the Expected One (the Messiah), or should we look for someone else [who will be the promised One]?" [Gen 49:10; Num 24:17; Ps 40:7; 118:26; Is 59:20]

4 Jesus answered, "Go and report to John what you hear and see:

5 the BLIND RECEIVE [their] SIGHT and the lame walk, the lepers are cleansed [by healing] and the deaf hear, the dead are raised, and the POOR HAVE THE GOSPEL PREACHED TO THEM. [Is 35:5, 6; 61:1]

6 "And blessed [joyful, favored by God] is he who does not take offense at Me [accepting Me as the Messiah and trusting confidently in My message of salvation]." [Luke 7:23]

Jesus' Tribute to John

7 As these men were going away, Jesus began to speak to the crowds about John: "What did you go out in the wilderness to see? A reed shaken by the wind [which is commonplace]?

8 "What did you go out to see? A man dressed in soft *clothing* [entirely unsuited for the harsh desert]? Those who wear soft *clothing* are in the palaces of kings!

9 "But what did you [really] go out to see? A prophet? Yes, I tell you, and one [more eminent, more remarkable, and] far more than a prophet [who foretells the future].

10 "This is the one of whom it is written [by the prophet Malachi],

'BEHOLD, I SEND MY MESSENGER
AHEAD OF YOU,
WHO WILL PREPARE YOUR WAY BEFORE
YOU.' [Mal 3:1]

11 "I assure you *and* most solemnly say to you, among those born of women there has not risen *anyone* greater than John the Baptist; yet the one who is least in the kingdom of heaven is greater [in privilege] than he.

12 "From the days of John the Baptist until now the kingdom of heaven suffers violent assault, and violent men seize it by force [as a precious prize].

13 "For all the prophets and the Law prophesied up until John.

14 "And if you are willing to accept it, John himself is [the fulfillment of] Elijah [as the messenger] who was to come [before the kingdom]. [Mal 4:5]

15 "He who has ears to hear, let him hear *and* heed My words.

16 "But to what shall I compare this generation? It is like little children sitting in the market places, who call to the others,

17 and say 'We piped the flute for you [playing wedding], and you did not dance; we wailed sad dirges [playing funeral], and you did not mourn *and* cry aloud.'

18 "For John came neither eating nor drinking [with others], and they say, 'He has a demon!'

19 "The Son of Man came eating and drinking [with others], and they say, 'Look! A glutton and a drunkard, a friend of tax collectors and sinners [including non-observant Jews]!' Yet wisdom is justified *and* vindicated by her deeds [in the lives of those who respond to Me]."

The Unrepenting Cities

20 Then He began to denounce [the people in] the cities in which most of His miracles were done, because they did not repent [and change their hearts and lives].

21 "Woe (judgment is coming) to you, Chorazin! Woe to you, Bethsaida! For

---

11:3 *should we look.* John probably expected the Messiah to immediately judge Israel and establish His kingdom (3:2–12). Jesus' failure to do what John anticipated may have planted seeds of doubt in John's mind about whether Jesus was the Messiah. But doubt that inquires and does not weaken faith is not evil. John went to the right person for answers, and Jesus reassured him by pointing out the fulfillment of prophecy.

11:12 *violent men seize it by force.* This probably means that violent people forcibly oppose the kingdom with their hostility (23:13).

11:21 *Woe.* Jesus pronounced a direct judgment on Israel. They would be judged for seeing the Messiah and then rejecting Him.

3 Ge 49:10; Nu 24:17; Da 9:24; Jn 6:14 **5** Isa 29:18; 35:4-6; Jn 2:23; Ps 22:26; Isa 61:1; Lk 4:18; Jas 2:5 **6** Isa 8:14,15; Ro 9:32; 1Pe 2:8 **7** Lk 7:24; Eph 4:14 **9** Lk 1:76 **10** Mal 3:1; Mk 1:2; Lk 1:76 **12** Lk 16:16 **13** Mal 4:6 **14** Mal 4:5; Lk 1:17 **15** Mt 13:9; Lk 8:8; Rev 2:7,11,17,29; 3:6,13 **16** Lk 7:31 **19** Mt 9:10; Lk 7:35 **20** Lk 10:13 **21** Jnh 3:7

if the miracles done in you had been done in Tyre and Sidon [cities of the Gentiles], they would have repented long ago in sackcloth and ashes [their hearts would have been changed and they would have expressed sorrow for their sin and rebellion against God].

22 “Nevertheless I say to you, it will be more tolerable for [the pagan cities of] Tyre and Sidon on the day of judgment than for you.

23 “And you, Capernaum, are you to be exalted to heaven [for your apathy and unresponsiveness]? You will descend to Hades (the realm of the dead); for if the miracles done in you had been done in Sodom, it would have remained until this day.

24 “But I say to you, it will be more tolerable for the land of Sodom on the day of judgment, than for you.”

Come to Me

25 At that time Jesus said, “I praise You, Father, Lord of heaven and earth [I openly and joyfully acknowledge Your great wisdom], that You have hidden these things [these spiritual truths] from the wise and intelligent and revealed them to infants [to new believers, to those seeking God’s will and purpose].

26 “Yes, Father, for this way was well-pleasing in Your sight.

27 “All things have been handed over to Me by My Father; and no one fully knows *and* accurately understands the Son except the Father; and no one fully knows *and* accurately understands the Father except the Son, and anyone to whom the Son [deliberately] wills to reveal *Him*.

28 “Come to Me, all who are weary and heavily burdened [by religious rituals that provide no peace], and I will give you rest [refreshing your souls with salvation].

29 “Take My yoke upon you and learn from Me [following Me as My disciple], for I am gentle and humble in heart, and YOU WILL FIND REST (renewal, blessed quiet) FOR YOUR SOULS. [Jer 6:16]

30 “For My yoke is easy [to bear] and My burden is light.”

Sabbath Questions

12 AT THAT particular time Jesus went through the grainfields on the Sabbath, and His disciples were hungry and began to pick the heads of grain and eat them. [Deut 23:25; Mark 2:23–28; Luke 6:1–5]

2 But when the Pharisees saw this, they said to Him, “Look! Your disciples are doing what is unlawful on the Sabbath.” [Ex 20:10; 23:12; Deut 5:14]

3 He said to them, “Have you not read [in the Scriptures] what David did when he was hungry, he and those who accompanied him— [Lev 24:9; 1 Sam 21:1–6]

4 how he went into the house of God, and they ate the consecrated bread, which was not lawful for him to eat nor for those with him, but for the priests only?

5 “Or have you not read in the Law, that on the Sabbath the priests in the temple break [the sanctity of] the Sabbath and yet are innocent? [Num 28:9, 10]

6 “But I tell you that something greater than the temple is here.

7 “And if you had only known what this statement means, ‘I DESIRE COMPASSION [for those in distress], AND NOT [animal] SACRIFICE,’ you would not have condemned the innocent. [Hos 6:6; Matt 9:13]

Lord of the Sabbath

8 “For the Son of Man is Lord of the Sabbath.”

11:23 *Capernaum.* Capernaum, which is on the north shore of the Sea of Galilee was called “His own city” (9:1).

12:2 *is unlawful.* To desecrate the Sabbath was flagrant disobedience to the law of Moses (Nu 15:30 – 36). The Pharisees were trying to make Jesus into a lawbreaker and accuse Him of wrongdoing.

22 ver. 24; Mt 10:15 **23** See Isa 14:13; La 2:1 **24** Mt 10:15 **25** Lk 10:21; Ps 8:2; 1Co 1:19; 2:8; 2Co 3:14; Mt 16:17 **27** Mt 28:18; Lk 10:22; Jn 3:35; 13:3; 17:2; 1Co 15:27; Jn 1:18; 6:46; 10:15 **29** Jn 13:15; Php 2:5; 1Pe 2:21; 1Jn 2:6; Zec 9:9; Php 2:7,8; Jer 6:16 **30** 1Jn 5:3 **CHAPTER 12** **1** Dt 23:25; Mk 2:23; Lk 6:1 **3** 1Sa 21:6 **4** Ex 25:30; Lev 24:5; Ex 29:32; Lev 8:31; 24:9 **5** Nu 28:9; Jn 7:22 **6** 2Ch 6:18; Mal 3:1 **7** Hos 6:6; Mic 6:6-8; Mt 9:13

9 Leaving there, He went into their
synagogue. [Mark 3:1–6; Luke 6:6–11]
10 A man *was there* whose hand was
withered. And they asked Jesus, "Is it
lawful *and* permissible to heal on the
Sabbath?"—*they asked this* so that
they might accuse Him *and* bring
charges into court.
11 But He said to them, "What man is
there among you who, if he has only
one sheep and it falls into a pit on the
Sabbath, will not take hold of it and
lift it out?
12 "How much more valuable then
is a man than a sheep! So it is law-
ful *and* permissible to do good on the
Sabbath."
13 Then He said to the man, "Reach
out your hand!" The man reached out
and it was restored, as normal *and*
healthy as the other.
14 But the Pharisees went out and
conspired against Him, *discussing*
how they could destroy Him.
15 Being aware of this, Jesus left
there. Many followed Him, and He
healed all of them [who were sick],
16 and warned them not to tell [pub-
licly] who He was.
17 *This was* to fulfill what was spoken
by the prophet Isaiah:
18 "Behold, My Servant whom I have
chosen;
My Beloved in whom My soul is
well-pleased;
I will put My Spirit upon Him,
And He will proclaim justice to
the nations.
19 "He will not quarrel, nor cry out
loudly;
Nor will anyone hear His voice in
the streets.
20 "A battered reed He will not
break,
And a smoldering wick He will not
extinguish,
Until He leads justice to victory.
21 "And in His name the Gentiles (all
the nations of the world) will hope
[with confidence]." [Is 42:1–4]

The Pharisees Rebuked

22 Then a demon-possessed man
who was blind and mute was brought
to Jesus, and He healed him, so that
the mute man both spoke and saw.
[Mark 3:22–27; Luke 11:14, 15]
23 All the people wondered in amaze-
ment, and said, "Could this be the Son
of David (the Messiah)?"
24 But the Pharisees heard it and said,
"This man casts out demons only by
[the help of] Beelzebul (Satan) the
prince of the demons."
25 Knowing their thoughts Jesus said
to them, "Any kingdom that is divided
against itself is being laid waste; and
no city or house divided against itself
will [continue to] stand.
26 "If Satan casts out Satan [that is,
his demons], he has become divided
against himself *and* disunited; how
then will his kingdom stand?
27 "If I cast out the demons by [the
help of] Beelzebul (Satan), by whom
do your sons drive them out? For this
reason they will be your judges.
28 "But if it is by the Spirit of God
that I cast out the demons, then the
kingdom of God has come upon you
[before you expected it].
29 "Or how can anyone go into a
strong man's house and steal his prop-
erty unless he first overpowers *and*
ties up the strong man? Then he will
ransack *and* rob his house. [Is 49:24,
25; Mark 3:27]

The Unpardonable Sin

30 "He who is not with Me [once and
for all on My side] is against Me; and

12:14 *how they could destroy him.* Because of Jesus' view of the Sabbath, the Pharisees concluded that He was trying to overthrow the entire Mosaic system, and therefore had to be destroyed. Their antagonism toward Jesus was growing.

12:17–21 *spoken by the prophet Isaiah.* This quotation of Isaiah 42:1–4 shows that the Messiah's gentleness was just as had been prophesied, and also that the Gentiles would be included in His blessing.

9 Mk 3:1; Lk 6:6 **10** Lk 13:14; 14:3; Jn 9:16 **11** See Ex 23:4,5; Dt 22:4 **14** Mt 27:1; Mk 3:6; Lk 6:11; Jn 5:18; 10:39; 11:53 **15** See Mt 10:23; Mk 3:7; Mt 19:2 **16** Mt 9:30 **18** Isa 42:1; Mt 3:17; 17:5 **22** See Mt 9:32; Mk 3:11; Lk 11:14 **24** Mt 9:34; Mk 3:22; Lk 11:15 **25** Mt 9:4; Jn 2:25; Rev 2:23 **28** Da 2:44; 7:14; Lk 1:33; 11:20; 17:20,21 **29** Isa 49:24; Lk 11:21-23

he who does not [unequivocally] gather
with Me scatters. [Luke 9:50; 11:23]
31 “Therefore I say to you, every sin
and blasphemy [every evil, abusive, in-
jurious speaking, or indignity against
sacred things] will be forgiven people,
but blasphemy against the [Holy] Spir-
it will not be forgiven.
32 “Whoever speaks a word against
the Son of Man will be forgiven; but
whoever speaks against the Holy Spir-
it [by attributing the miracles done
by Me to Satan] will not be forgiven,
either in this age or in the *age* to come.
[Mark 3:29; Luke 12:10]

Words Reveal Character

33 “Either make the tree good and its
fruit good, or make the tree bad and
its fruit bad; for the tree is recognized
and judged by its fruit.
34 “You brood of vipers, how can you
speak good things when you are evil?
For the mouth speaks out of that which
fills the heart.
35 “The good man, from his [inner]
good treasure, brings out good things;
and the evil man, from his [inner] evil
treasure, brings out evil things.
36 “But I tell you, on the day of judg-
ment people will have to give an ac-
counting for every careless *or* useless
word they speak.
37 “For by your words [reflecting your
spiritual condition] you will be justi-
fied *and* acquitted of the guilt of sin;
and by your words [rejecting Me] you
will be condemned *and* sentenced.”

The Desire for Signs

38 Then some of the scribes and Phar-
isees said to Him, “Teacher, we want
to see a sign (attesting miracle) from
You [proving that You are what You
claim to be].”
39 But He replied and said to them,
“An evil and adulterous generation
[that is morally unfaithful to God]
craves *and* demands a [miraculous]
sign; but no sign will be given to it
except the sign of the prophet Jonah;
[Luke 11:29–32]
40 for just as JONAH WAS THREE DAYS
AND THREE NIGHTS IN THE BELLY OF THE
SEA MONSTER, so will the Son of Man
be three days and three nights in the
heart of the earth. [Jon 1:17]
41 “The men of Nineveh will stand up
[as witnesses] at the judgment against
this generation, and will condemn it
because they repented at the preaching
of Jonah; and now, something greater
than Jonah is here. [Jon 3:5]
42 “The Queen of the South (Sheba)
will stand up [as a witness] at the judg-
ment against this generation, and will
condemn it because she came from
the ends of the earth to listen to the
wisdom of Solomon; and now, some-
thing greater than Solomon is here.
[1 Kin 10:1; 2 Chr 9:1]
43 “Now when the unclean spirit has

12:31–32 *blasphemy.* The sin that shall not be forgiven is the stubborn refusal to heed the Holy Spirit's conviction and accept the salvation that Christ offers. Particularly in reference to the leaders of Israel, Jesus had offered them all the proof that could be expected, such as the ministry of John, the testimony of the Father, the prophecies of the Old Testament, His own testimony, and the substantiation of the Holy Spirit. Because the leaders rejected all proofs regarding Jesus as Messiah, nothing else would be given.

12:39 *the sign of the prophet Jonah.* The demand for signs was evidence of unbelief. The "sign of the prophet Jonah" is explained in verse 40 as the resurrection.

12:41–42 *The men of Nineveh ... The Queen of the South.* These terms represent Gentiles who come to faith because of the words of God's prophets and kings, lesser messengers than God's only Son.

12:43 *the unclean spirit.* This analogy seems to be describing the moral reformation that took place in Israel as a result of the ministries of John the Baptist and Jesus. The reformation, however, was not genuine, and therefore Israel's unbelief and hardness of heart was worse than before. In the same way, a person who decides to try religion without being born again, and then decides "it's not for me," is worse off than if they had never tried, because their hearts are hardened to God's voice.

---

31 Mk 3:28; Lk 12:10; Heb 6:4; 10:26,29; 1Jn 5:16; Ac 7:51 **32** Mt 11:19; 13:55; Jn 7:12,52; 1Ti 1:13 **33** Mt 7:17; Lk 6:43 **34** Mt 3:7; 23:33; Lk 6:45 **38** Mt 16:1; Mk 8:11; Lk 11:16; Jn 2:18; 1Co 1:22 **39** Isa 57:3; Mt 16:4; Mk 8:38; Jn 4:48 **40** Jnh 1:17 **41** Lk 11:32; See Jer 3:11; Eze 16:51; Ro 2:27; Jnh 3:5 **42** 1Ki 10:1; 2Ch 9:1; Lk 11:31 **43** Lk 11:24; Job 1:7; 1Pe 5:8

gone out of a man, it roams through
waterless (dry, arid) places in search
of rest, but it does not find it.
44“Then it says, ‘I will return to my
house from which I came.’ And when it
arrives, it finds *the place* unoccupied,
swept, and put in order.
45“Then it goes and brings with it
seven other spirits more wicked than
itself, and they go in and make their
home there. And the last condition
of that man becomes worse than the
first. So will it also be with this wicked
generation.”

Changed Relationships

46While He was still talking to the
crowds, it happened that His moth-
er and brothers stood outside, ask-
ing to speak to Him. [Mark 3:31–35;
Luke 8:19–21]
47Someone said to Him, “Look! Your
mother and Your brothers are standing
outside asking to speak to You.”
48But Jesus replied to the one who
told Him, “Who is My mother and who
are My brothers?”
49And stretching out His hand to-
ward His disciples [and all His oth-
er followers], He said, “Here are My
mother and My brothers!
50“For whoever does the will of My
Father who is in heaven [by believing
in Me, and following Me] is My brother
and sister and mother.”

Jesus Teaches in Parables

13 THAT SAME day Jesus went
out of the house and was sitting
beside the sea [of Galilee]. [Mark 4:1–
20; Luke 8:4–15]
2But such large crowds gathered
around Him that He got into a boat
and sat there [positioning Himself as a
teacher], while the whole crowd stood
on the shore.
3He told them many things in para-
bles, saying, “Listen carefully: a sower
went out to sow [seed in his field];
4and as he sowed, some *seed* fell
beside the road [between the fields],
and the birds came and ate it.
5“Other seed fell on rocky ground,
where they did not have much soil; and
at once they sprang up because they
had no depth of soil.
6“But when the sun rose, they were
scorched; and because they had no
root, they withered away.
7“Other seed fell among thorns, and
thorns came up and choked them out.
8“Other seed fell on good soil and
yielded grain, some a hundred times as
much [as was sown], some sixty [times
as much], and some thirty.
9“He who has ears [to hear], let him
hear *and* heed My words.”

An Explanation

10Then the disciples came to Him
and asked, “Why do You speak to the
crowds in parables?”
11Jesus replied to them, “To you it has
been granted to know the mysteries of
the kingdom of heaven, but to them it
has not been granted. [Mark 4:11]
12“For whoever has [spiritual wis-
dom because he is receptive to God’s
word], to him *more* will be given, and
he will be richly *and* abundantly sup-
plied; but whoever does not have [spir-
itual wisdom because he has devalued
God’s word], even what he has will
be taken away from him. [Matt 25:29;
Mark 4:25; Luke 8:18]
13“This is the reason I speak to the
crowds in parables: because while
[having the power of] seeing they do
not see, and while [having the power
of] hearing they do not hear, nor do
they understand *and* grasp [spiritual
things].
14“In them the prophecy of Isaiah is
being fulfilled, which says,

13:11 *To you it has been granted.* The purpose of this parable was to both reveal and conceal the truth. This hiding of the truth was a judgment for unbelief, as happened during Isaiah’s ministry (Isa 6:9 – 10).

13:14 – 15 Spiritual Death — Genesis 3 teaches

45 Heb 6:4; 10:26; 2Pe 2:20-22 **46** Mk 3:31; Lk 8:19-21; Mt 13:55; Mk 6:3; Jn 2:12; 7:3,5; Ac 1:14; 1Co 9:5; Gal 1:19
50 See Jn 15:14; Gal 5:6; 6:15; Col 3:11; Heb 2:11 **CHAPTER 13** **1** Mk 4:1 **2** Lk 8:4; Lk 5:3 **3** Lk 8:5 **8** Ge 26:12
9 Mt 11:15; Mk 4:9 **11** Mt 11:25; 16:17; Mk 4:11; 1Co 2:10; 1Jn 2:27 **12** Mt 25:29; Mk 4:25; Lk 8:18; 19:26
14 Isa 6:9; Eze 12:2; Mk 4:12; Lk 8:10; Jn 12:40; Ac 28:26,27; Ro 11:8; 2Co 3:14,15

‘YOU WILL HEAR *and* KEEP ON
HEARING, BUT NEVER UNDERSTAND;
AND YOU WILL LOOK *and* KEEP ON
LOOKING, BUT NEVER COMPREHEND;
15 FOR THIS NATION’S HEART HAS GROWN
HARD,
AND WITH THEIR EARS THEY HARDLY
HEAR,
AND THEY HAVE [tightly] CLOSED
THEIR EYES,
OTHERWISE THEY WOULD SEE WITH
THEIR EYES,
AND HEAR WITH THEIR EARS,
AND UNDERSTAND WITH THEIR HEART,
AND TURN [to Me]
AND I WOULD HEAL THEM
[spiritually].’ [Is 6:9]

16 “But blessed [spiritually aware, and favored by God] are your eyes, because they see; and your ears, because they hear. [Luke 10:23, 24]

17 “I assure you *and* most solemnly say to you, many prophets and righteous men [who were honorable and in right standing with God] longed to see what you see, and did not see it, and to hear what you hear, and did not hear it.

The Sower Explained

18 “Listen then to the [meaning of the] parable of the sower: [Mark 4:2–20; Luke 8:4–15]

19 “When anyone hears the word of the kingdom [regarding salvation] and does not understand *and* grasp it, the evil one comes and snatches away what was sown in his heart. This is the one on whom seed was sown beside the road.

20 “The one on whom seed was sown on rocky ground, this is the one who hears the word and at once welcomes it with joy;

21 yet he has no [substantial] root in himself, but is only temporary, and when pressure or persecution comes because of the word, immediately he stumbles *and* falls away [abandoning the One who is the source of salvation].

22 “And the one on whom seed was sown among thorns, this is the one who hears the word, but the worries *and* distractions of the world and the deceitfulness [the superficial pleasures and delight] of riches choke the word, and it yields no fruit.

23 “And the one on whom seed was sown on the good soil, this is the one who hears the word and understands *and* grasps it; he indeed bears fruit and yields, some a hundred times [as much as was sown], some sixty [times as much], and some thirty.” [Mark 4:2–20; Luke 8:4–15]

Weeds among Wheat

24 Jesus gave them another parable [to consider], saying, “The kingdom of heaven is like a man who sowed good seed in his field.

25 “But while his men were sleeping, his enemy came and sowed weeds [resembling wheat] among the wheat, and went away.

26 “So when the plants sprouted and formed grain, the weeds appeared also.

27 “The servants of the owner came to him and said, ‘Sir, did you not sow good seed in your field? Then how does it have weeds in it?’

28 “He replied to them, ‘An enemy has done this.’ The servants asked him, ‘Then do you want us to go and pull them out?’

29 “But he said, ‘No; because as you

---

us that, through sin, man died spiritually. Here, Christ quotes from Isaiah 6 to detail the meaning of spiritual death: Our ability to perceive spiritual reality is absent. Key spiritual senses don’t work as they were originally designed to work. We can’t see the implications of spiritual events. We can’t understand the meaning of spiritual words. It is as if our senses are dead. In order to have our spiritual senses restored, we need someone to heal us. Only Christ can provide the necessary healing to open our spiritual eyes and ears.

13:25 *his enemy came and sowed weeds.* These weeds closely resemble wheat, but do not produce good food. They are indistinguishable from the real wheat until the fruit appears. Just like the weeds among the wheat, genuine believers and counterfeits will be allowed to remain together.

15 Heb 5:11 **16** Mt 16:17; Lk 10:23,24; Jn 20:29 **17** Heb 11:13; 1Pe 1:10,11 **18** Mk 4:14; Lk 8:11 **19** Mt 4:23
20 Isa 58:2; Eze 33:31,32; Jn 5:35 **21** Mt 11:6; 2Ti 1:15 **22** Mt 19:23; Mk 10:23; Lk 18:24; 1Ti 6:9; 2Ti 4:10; Jer 4:3

pull out the weeds, you may uproot the wheat with them.

30 'Let them grow together until the harvest; and at harvest time I will tell the reapers, "First gather the weeds and tie them in bundles to be burned; but gather the wheat into my barn." ' "

The Mustard Seed

31 He gave them another parable [to consider], saying, "The kingdom of heaven is like a mustard seed, which a man took and sowed in his field; [Mark 4:30–32; Luke 13:18, 19]

32 and of all the seeds [planted in the region] it is the smallest, but when it has grown it is the largest of the garden herbs and becomes a tree, so that THE BIRDS OF THE AIR FIND SHELTER IN ITS BRANCHES." [Ezek 17:23]

The Leaven

33 He told them another parable, "The kingdom of heaven is like leaven, which a woman took and worked into three measures of flour until all of it was leavened." [Gen 18:6; Luke 13:21]

34 All these things Jesus said to the crowds in parables, and He said nothing to them without [using] a parable.

35 *This was* to fulfill what was spoken by the prophet:

"I WILL OPEN MY MOUTH IN PARABLES;
I WILL UTTER THINGS [unknown and unattainable] THAT HAVE BEEN HIDDEN [from mankind] SINCE THE FOUNDATION OF THE WORLD." [Ps 78:2]

The Weeds Explained

36 Then He left the crowds and went into the house. And His disciples came to Him saying, "Explain [clearly] to us the parable of the weeds in the field."

37 He answered, "The one who sows the good seed is the Son of Man,

38 and the field is the world; and [as for] the good seed, these are the sons of the kingdom; and the weeds are the sons of the evil *one;*

39 and the enemy who sowed them is the devil, and the harvest is the end of the age; and the reapers are angels.

40 "So just as the weeds are gathered up and burned in the fire, so will it be at the end of the age.

41 "The Son of Man will send out His angels, and they will gather out of His kingdom all things that offend [those things by which people are led into sin], and all who practice evil [leading others into sin],

42 and will throw them into the furnace of fire; in that place there will be weeping [over sorrow and pain] and grinding of teeth [over distress and anger].

43 "Then THE RIGHTEOUS [those who seek the will of God] WILL SHINE FORTH [radiating the new life] LIKE THE SUN in the kingdom of their Father. He who has ears [to hear], let him hear *and* heed My words. [Dan 12:3]

Hidden Treasure

44 "The kingdom of heaven is like a [very precious] treasure hidden in

---

13:31 *like a mustard seed.* The parable of the mustard seed shows that the number of people who will inherit the kingdom will be very small at first, but it will grow to be completely out of proportion to its initial size.

13:33 *like leaven.* Although leaven is sometimes used in Scripture to symbolize evil, here the kingdom of heaven is being compared to the dynamic character of yeast. When yeast is mixed with the dough, it expands from within, causing the dough to grow. Rather than being powered by outward armies or organizations, the kingdom of God will grow by the internal power of the Holy Spirit.

13:42 Hell — This verse describes the separation that comes between the righteous and the wicked at the end of the age. The place of their eternal dwelling is described as a "furnace of fire," perhaps because fire is one of man's most vivid concepts of suffering. Some think that there is no real, actual hell of fire, and that instead the wicked simply cease to exist, but this is difficult to support. The Scriptures consistently speak of hell as a real place of torment and anguish for all who do not receive the salvation that Jesus offers.

13:44 *like a [very precious] treasure.* The

30 Mt 3:12 **31** Isa 2:2,3; Mic 4:1; Mk 4:30; Lk 13:18 **33** Lk 13:20 **34** Mk 4:33 **35** Ps 78:2; Ro 16:25,26; 1Co 2:7; Eph 3:9; Col 1:26 **38** Mt 24:14; 28:19; Mk 16:15; Lk 24:47; Ro 10:18; Col 1:6; Ge 3:15; Jn 8:44; Ac 13:10; 1Jn 3:8 **39** Joel 3:13; Rev 14:15 **41** Mt 18:7; 2Pe 2:1,2 **42** Mt 3:12; Rev 19:20; 20:10; ver. 50; Mt 8:12 **43** Da 12:3; 1Co 15:42,43,58; ver. 9 **44** Php 3:7,8; Isa 55:1; Rev 3:18

a field, which a man found and hid again; then in his joy he goes and sells all he has and buys that field [securing the treasure for himself].

A Costly Pearl

45“Again, the kingdom of heaven is like a merchant in search of fine pearls,

46and upon finding a single pearl of great value, he went and sold all that he had and bought it.

A Dragnet

47“Again, the kingdom of heaven is like a dragnet which was lowered into the sea, and gathered *fish* of every kind,

48and when it was full, they dragged it up on the beach; and they sat down and sorted out the good *fish* into baskets, but the worthless ones they threw away.

49“So it will be at the end of the age; the angels will come and separate the wicked from the righteous

50and throw the wicked into the furnace of fire; in that place there will be weeping [over sorrow and pain] and grinding of teeth [over distress and anger].

51“Have you understood all these things [in the lessons of the parables]?” They said to Jesus, “Yes.”

52He said to them, “Therefore every scribe who has become a disciple of the kingdom of heaven is like the head of a household, who brings out of his treasure things that are new *and* fresh and things that are old *and* familiar.”

Jesus Revisits Nazareth

53When Jesus had finished these parables, He left there.

54And after coming to [Nazareth] His hometown, He *began* teaching them in their synagogue, and they were astonished, and said, “Where did this Man get this wisdom and these miraculous powers [what is the source of His authority]? [Mark 6:1–6; Luke 4:16, 23]

55“Is not this the carpenter’s son? Is not His mother called Mary? And are not His brothers, James and Joseph and Simon and Judas?

56“And His sisters, are they not [living here] among us? Where then did this Man get all this [wisdom and power]?”

57And they took offense at Him [refusing to believe in Him]. But Jesus said to them, “A prophet is not without honor except in his hometown and in his own household.”

58And He did not do many miracles there [in Nazareth] because of their unbelief.

John the Baptist Beheaded

14 AT THAT time Herod [Antipas], the tetrarch [who governed a portion of Palestine including Galilee and Perea], heard the reports about Jesus, [Luke 9:7–9]

2and said to his attendants, “This is John the Baptist; he has been raised from the dead, and that is why the miraculous powers are at work in him.”

3For Herod had John arrested and bound him and put him in prison [at the fortress of Machaerus, east of the Jordan, to keep him away] because of Herodias, the wife of his brother Philip, [Mark 6:17; Luke 3:19]

4for John had said to him, “It is not lawful (morally right) for you to have her [living with you as your wife].” [Lev 18:16; 20:21]

---

main point here is the immense value of the kingdom, which far outweighs any sacrifice or inconvenience one might encounter on earth.

13:47 *of every kind.* The responsibility of the disciples would be to catch as many “fish” of every kind as possible. The work of judging or sorting out the false catch, however, is a job that disciples are neither called nor equipped to do. That work is assigned to angels at Christ’s return.

14:3 *because of Herodias.* Herod had gone to Rome, where he met Herodias, the wife of his half brother Philip. After seducing Herodias, Herod divorced his own wife and married his sister-in-law. John had rebuked the king for his moral transgressions.

46 Pr 2:4; 3:14,15; 8:10,19 **47** Mt 22:10 **49** Mt 25:32 **52** SS 7:13 **54** Mt 2:23; Mk 6:1; Lk 4:16 **55** Isa 49:7; Mk 6:3; Lk 3:23; Jn 6:42; Mt 12:46; Mk 15:40 **57** Mt 11:6; Mk 6:3,4; Lk 4:24; Jn 4:44 **58** Mk 6:5,6 **CHAPTER 14** **1** Mk 6:14; Lk 9:7 **3** Mk 6:17; Lk 3:19,20 **4** Lev 18:16; 20:21

5 Although Herod wished to have him put to death, he feared the people, for they regarded John as a prophet.

6 But when Herod's birthday came, [his niece Salome], the daughter of Herodias danced [immodestly] before them and pleased *and* fascinated Herod,

7 so much that he promised with an oath to give her whatever she asked.

8 She, being coached by her mother [Herodias], said, "Give me here on a platter the head of John the Baptist."

9 The king was distressed, but because of his oaths, and because of his dinner guests, he ordered it to be given her.

10 He sent and had John beheaded in the prison.

11 His head was brought on a platter and given to the girl, and she brought it to her mother [Herodias].

12 And John's disciples came and took away the body and buried it. Then they went and told Jesus.

Five Thousand Fed

13 When Jesus heard *about John,* He left there privately in a boat and went to a secluded place. But when the crowds heard of this, they followed Him on foot from the cities. [Mark 6:32–44; Luke 9:10–17; John 6:1–13]

14 When He went ashore, He saw a large crowd, and felt [profound] compassion for them and healed their sick.

15 When evening came, the disciples came to Him and said, "This is an isolated place and the hour is already late; send the crowds away so that they may go into the villages and buy food for themselves."

16 But Jesus said to them, "They do not need to go away; you give them *something* to eat!"

17 They replied, "We have nothing here except five loaves and two fish."

18 He said, "Bring them here to Me."

19 Then He ordered the crowds to sit down on the grass, and He took the five loaves and the two fish and, looking up toward heaven, He blessed and broke the loaves and gave them to the disciples, and the disciples *gave them* to the people,

20 and they all ate and were satisfied. They picked up twelve full baskets of the leftover broken pieces.

21 There were about 5,000 men who ate, besides women and children.

Jesus Walks on the Water

22 Immediately He directed the disciples to get into the boat and go ahead of Him to the other side [of the Sea of Galilee], while He sent the crowds away. [Mark 6:45–52; John 6:15–21]

23 After He had dismissed the crowds, He went up on the mountain by Himself to pray. When it was evening, He was there alone.

24 But the boat [by this time] was already a long distance from land, tossed *and* battered by the waves; for the wind was against them.

25 And in the fourth watch of the night (3:00–6:00 a.m.) Jesus came to them, walking on the sea. [Mark 6:48; John 6:19]

26 When the disciples saw Him walking on the sea, they were terrified, and said, "It is a ghost!" And they cried out in fear.

27 But immediately He spoke to them, saying, "Take courage, it is I! Do not be afraid!" [Ex 3:14]

28 Peter replied to Him, "Lord, if it is [really] You, command me to come to You on the water."

29 He said, "Come!" So Peter got out of the boat, and walked on the water and came toward Jesus.

30 But when he saw [the effects of] the wind, he was frightened, and he began to sink, and he cried out, "Lord, save me!"

31 Immediately Jesus extended His hand and caught him, saying to him, "O you of little faith, why did you doubt?"

32 And when they got into the boat, the wind ceased.

33 Then those in the boat worshiped Him [with awe-inspired reverence], saying, "Truly You are the Son of God!"

34 When they had crossed over [the sea], they went ashore at Gennesaret.

5 Mt 21:26; Lk 20:6 **13** Mt 10:23; 12:15; Mk 6:32; Lk 9:10; Jn 6:1,2 **14** Mt 9:36; Mk 6:34 **15** Mk 6:35; Lk 9:12; Jn 6:5 **19** Mt 15:36 **23** Mk 6:46; Jn 6:16 **26** Job 9:8 **33** Ps 2:7; Mt 16:16; 26:63; Mk 1:1; Lk 4:41; Jn 1:49; 6:69; 11:27; Ac 8:37; Ro 1:4 **34** Mk 6:53

35And when the men of that place
recognized Him, they sent *word*
throughout all the surrounding district
and brought to Him all who were sick;
36and they begged Him to let them
merely touch the fringe of His robe;
and all who touched it were perfectly
restored. [Matt 9:20]

Tradition and Commandment

15 THEN SOME Pharisees and
scribes from Jerusalem came to
Jesus and said,
2"Why do Your disciples violate the
tradition (religious laws) handed down
by the [Jewish] elders? For Your disci-
ples do not [ceremonially] wash their
hands before they eat."
3He replied to them, "Why also do
you violate the commandment of God
for the sake of your tradition [handed
down by the elders]?
4"For God said [through Moses],
'HONOR YOUR FATHER AND MOTHER,' and,
'HE WHO SPEAKS EVIL OF *or* INSULTS *or*
TREATS IMPROPERLY FATHER OR MOTHER
IS TO BE PUT TO DEATH.' [Ex 20:12; 21:17;
Lev 20:9; Deut 5:16]
5"But you say, 'If anyone says to his
father or mother, "Whatever [money or
resource that] I have that would help
you is [already dedicated and] given
to God,"
6he is not to honor his father or his
mother [by helping them with their
need].' So by this you have invalidat-
ed the word of God [depriving it of
force and authority and making it of
no effect] for the sake of your tradition
[handed down by the elders].
7"You hypocrites (play-actors, pre-
tenders), rightly did Isaiah prophesy
of you when he said,

8'THIS PEOPLE HONORS ME WITH THEIR
LIPS,
BUT THEIR HEART IS FAR AWAY FROM
ME.
9'BUT IN VAIN DO THEY WORSHIP ME,
FOR THEY TEACH AS DOCTRINES THE
PRECEPTS OF MEN.' " [Is 29:13]

10After Jesus called the crowd to
Him, He said, "Listen and understand
this:
11It is not what goes into the mouth of
a man that defiles *and* dishonors him,
but what comes out of the mouth, this
defiles *and* dishonors him."
12Then the disciples came and said
to Jesus, "Do You know that the Phar-
isees were offended when they heard
you say this?"
13He answered, "Every plant which
My heavenly Father did not plant will
be torn up by the roots. [Is 60:21]
14"Leave them alone; they are blind
guides [leading blind followers]. If a
blind man leads a blind man, both will
fall into a pit."

The Heart of Man

15Peter asked Him, "Explain this
parable [about what defiles a person]
to us."
16And He said, "Are you still so dull
[and unable to put things together]?
17"Do you not understand that what-
ever goes into the mouth passes into
the stomach, and is eliminated?
18"But whatever [word] comes out

15:2 *the tradition (religious laws) handed down by the [Jewish] elders.* This was not the law of Moses, but oral tradition, based on interpretations of the law.
15:3 *tradition.* The scribes and Pharisees were placing their own views above the revelation of God, and yet claimed to be following Him.
15:7 *hypocrites.* The Pharisees had laid down many rigid and inflexible laws concerning diet, Sabbath day activities, ceremonial washings, and many other traditions. Not only did this reduce spiritual service to a harsh system of do's and don'ts, it also caused everyone, Pharisees included, to look for loopholes of escape from the burden of so many laws and rules. The ultimate outcome was religious hypocrisy. Christ came both to fulfill the law (5:17 – 18) and also to free us from its penalty (Gal 3:13).
15:18 *comes from the heart.* As we think in our hearts, or inner beings, so we are. The raw material

36 Mt 9:20; Mk 3:10; Lk 6:19; Ac 19:12 **CHAPTER 15** **1** Mk 7:1 **2** Mk 7:5 **4** Ex 20:12; Lev 19:3; Dt 5:16; Pr 23:22; Eph 6:2; Ex 21:17; Lev 20:9; Dt 27:16; Pr 20:20; 30:17 **5** Mk 7:11,12 **7** Mk 7:6 **8** Isa 29:13; Eze 33:31 **9** Isa 29:13; Col 2:18-22; Titus 1:14 **10** Mk 7:14 **11** Ac 10:15; Ro 14:14,17,20; 1Ti 4:4; Titus 1:15 **13** Jn 15:2; 1Co 3:12 **14** Isa 9:16; Mal 2:8; Mt 23:16; Lk 6:39 **15** Mk 7:17 **16** Mt 16:9; Mk 7:18 **17** 1Co 6:13 **18** Jas 3:6

of the mouth comes from the heart,
and this is what defiles *and* dishonors
the man.
[19]"For out of the heart come evil
thoughts *and* plans, murders, adulter-
ies, sexual immoralities, thefts, false
testimonies, slanders (verbal abuse,
irreverent speech, blaspheming).
[20]"These are the things which defile
and dishonor the man; but eating with
[ceremonially] unwashed hands does
not defile the man."

The Syrophoenician Woman

[21]After leaving there, Jesus with-
drew to the district of Tyre and Sidon.
[Mark 7:24–30]
[22]And a Canaanite woman from that
district came out and *began* to cry out
[urgently], saying, "Have mercy on
me, O Lord, Son of David (Messiah);
my daughter is cruelly possessed by
a demon."
[23]But He did not say a word in an-
swer to her. And His disciples came
and asked Him [repeatedly], "Send
her away, because she keeps shouting
out after us."
[24]He answered, "I was commissioned
by God *and* sent only to the lost sheep
of the house of Israel."
[25]But she came and *began* to kneel
down before Him, saying, "Lord, help
me!"
[26]And He replied, "It is not good (ap-
propriate, fair) to take the children's
bread and throw it to the pet dogs."
[27]She said, "Yes, Lord; but even the
pet dogs eat the crumbs that fall from
their [young] masters' table."
[28]Then Jesus answered her, "Wom-
an, your faith [your personal trust and
confidence in My power] is great; it will
be done for you as you wish." And her
daughter was healed from that moment.

Healing Crowds

[29]Jesus went on from there and
passed along by [the eastern shore
of] the Sea of Galilee. Then He went
up on the hillside and was sitting there.
[30]And great crowds came to Him,
bringing with them the lame, crippled,
blind, mute, and many others, and they
put them down at His feet; and He
healed them.
[31]So the crowd was amazed when
they saw the mute speaking, the crip-
pled restored, the lame walking, and
the blind seeing; and they praised *and*
glorified the God of Israel.

Four Thousand Fed

[32]Then Jesus called His disciples to
Him, and said, "I feel compassion for
the crowd, because they have been
with Me now three days and have
nothing [left] to eat; and I do not want
to send them away hungry, because
they might faint [from exhaustion] on
the way [home]." [Mark 8:1–21]
[33]The disciples said to Him, "Where
are we to get enough bread in this iso-
lated place to feed so large a crowd?"
[34]And Jesus asked them, "How many
loaves [of bread] do you have?" They
replied, "Seven, and a few small fish."
[35]He directed the crowd to sit down
on the ground,
[36]and He took the seven loaves
and the fish; and when He had given
thanks, He broke them and started
giving them to the disciples, and the
disciples [gave them] to the people.
[37]And they all ate and were satis-
fied, and they gathered up seven full
baskets of the broken pieces that were
left over.
[38][Among] those who ate were 4,000
men, not counting women and children.
[39]Then Jesus sent the crowds away,

---

of our actions is what we take into our minds and allow to settle in our hearts. David put it this way: "Your word I have treasured and stored in my heart, that I may not sin against You" (Ps 119:11). The other side is seen in Psalm 101:3 "I will set no worthless or wicked thing before my eyes." Paul says the believer must take "every thought and purpose captive to the obedience of Christ" (2Co 10:5).

15:22 *Have mercy on me, O Lord, Son of David.* The woman was a Gentile who would have had no natural claim on the Jewish Messiah.

15:31 *glorified the God of Israel.* The Gentiles believed and glorified Israel's God, while many in Israel remained blind to their Messiah.

19 Ge 6:5; 8:21; Pr 6:14; Jer 17:9; Mk 7:21 **21** Mk 7:24 **24** Mt 10:5,6 **26** Mt 7:6; Php 3:2 **29** Mk 7:31; Mt 4:18 **30** Isa 35:5,6; Mt 11:5; Lk 7:22 **32** Mk 8:1 **33** 2Ki 4:43 **36** Mt 14:19; 1Sa 9:13; Lk 22:19 **39** Mk 8:10

got into the boat and went to the dis-
trict of Magadan.

Pharisees Test Jesus

16 NOW THE Pharisees and Saddu-
cees came up, and testing Jesus
[to get something to use against Him],
they asked Him to show them a sign
from heaven [which would support His
divine authority].
2 But He replied to them, "When it is
evening, you say, '*It will be* fair weath-
er, for the sky is red.'
3 "And in the morning, '*It will be*
stormy today, for the sky is red and
has a threatening look.' You know
how to interpret the appearance of the
sky, but cannot interpret the signs of
the times?
4 "An evil and [morally] unfaithful
generation craves a [miraculous] sign;
but no sign will be given to it, except
the sign of [the prophet] Jonah." Then
He left them and went away. [Jon 3:4, 5]
5 When the disciples reached the oth-
er side *of the sea,* they realized that
they had forgotten to bring bread.
6 Jesus said to them, "Watch out and
be on your guard against the leaven of
the Pharisees and Sadducees."
7 They began to discuss this among
themselves, saying, "*He said that* be-
cause we did not bring bread."
8 But Jesus, aware of this, said, "You
men of little faith, why are you discuss-
ing among yourselves that you have
no bread?
9 "Do you still not understand or re-
member the five loaves for the five
thousand, and how many baskets you
picked up?
10 "Or the seven loaves for the four
thousand, and how many large baskets
you picked up?
11 "How is it that you fail to under-
stand that I was not talking to you
about bread? But beware of the leaven
of the Pharisees and Sadducees."
12 Then they understood that He did
not tell them to beware of the leaven
of bread, but of the [false] teaching of
the Pharisees and Sadducees.

Peter's Confession of Christ

13 Now when Jesus went into the re-
gion of Caesarea Philippi, He asked
His disciples, "Who do people say that
the Son of Man is?" [Mark 8:27–29;
Luke 9:18–20]
14 And they answered, "Some say
John the Baptist; others, Elijah; and
still others, Jeremiah, or [just] one of
the prophets."
15 He said to them, "But who do you
say that I am?"
16 Simon Peter replied, "You are the
Christ (the Messiah, the Anointed), the
Son of the living God."
17 Then Jesus answered him, "Blessed
[happy, spiritually secure, favored by
God] are you, Simon son of Jonah, be-
cause flesh and blood (mortal man) did
not reveal this to you, but My Father
who is in heaven.
18 "And I say to you that you are Peter,
and on this rock I will build My church;

16:11 – 12 *leaven*. In Scripture, leaven is often used as a symbol of evil. The doctrine of the Pharisees and Sadducees was hypocrisy and legalism, political opportunism, and spiritual hardness.

16:16 Church — Peter's confession "You are the Christ, the Son of the living God" is the foundation on which the church is built. Never mind how small the apostolic band may be, the church is indestructible, and with unsurpassed power overcomes Satan and cannot be overcome. The power comes from God, the Creator of the universe, Owner and Master of the church. All the church has is derived from and dependent on the Almighty Son of God.

16:18 The Origin of the Church — The church was a mystery (not clearly revealed) in the Old Testament. Christ prophesied in these words spoken to Peter, "on this rock I will build My church." There is a play here on the word *rock*, which also happens to be Peter's name. Jesus said, "you are Peter" (masculine, *petros*) and "on this rock" (feminine, *petra*) "I will build My church." The Holy Spirit came upon the church on the Day of Pentecost in response to Peter's sermon when "about 3,000 souls were added [to the body of believers]" (Ac 2:41). This group, along with the original disciples, became "the church."

CHAPTER 16 **1** Mt 12:38; Mk 8:11; Lk 11:16; 12:54-56; 1Co 1:22 **4** Mt 12:39 **5** Mk 8:14 **6** Lk 12:1 **9** Mt 14:17; Jn 6:9 **10** Mt 15:34 **13** Mk 8:27; Lk 9:18 **14** Mt 14:2; Lk 9:7-9 **16** Mt 14:33; Mk 8:29; Lk 9:20; Jn 6:69; 11:27; Ac 8:37; 9:20; Heb 1:2,5; 1Jn 4:15 **17** Eph 2:8; 1Co 2:10; Gal 1:16 **18** Jn 1:42; Eph 2:20; Rev 21:14; Job 38:17; Ps 9:13; 107:18; Isa 38:10

THE VISITS TO TYRE, SIDON AND CAESAREA PHILIPPI

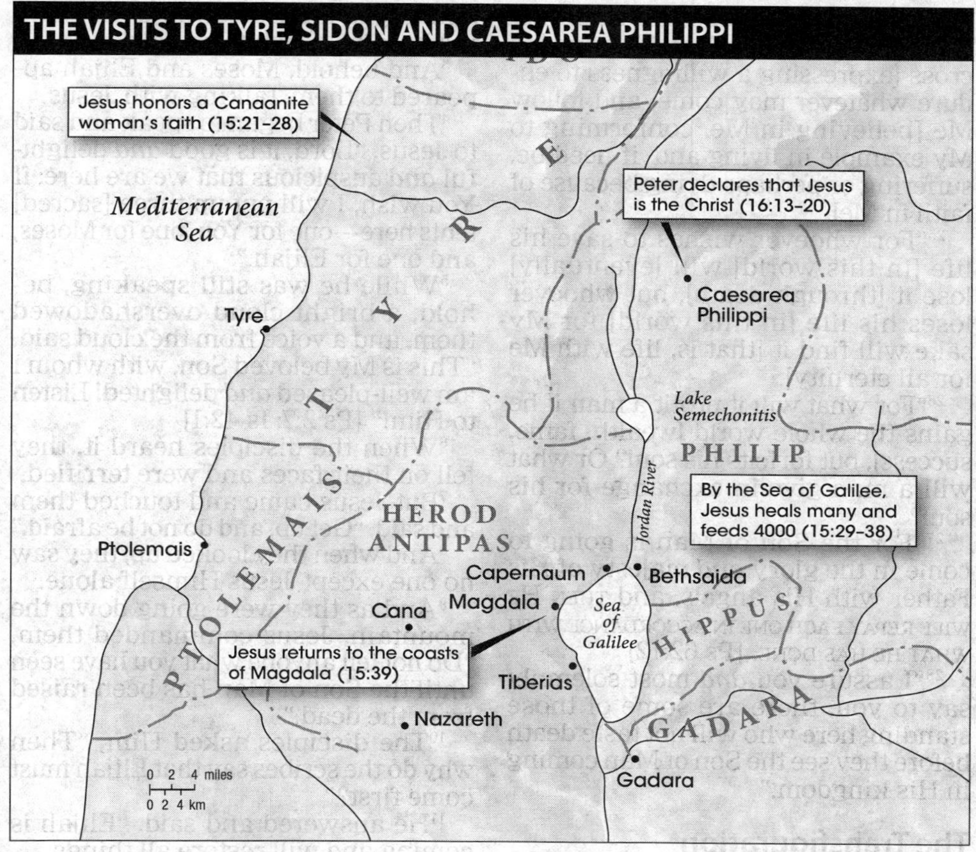

and the gates of Hades (death) will
not overpower it [by preventing the
resurrection of the Christ]. [Eph 1:22;
4:15; 5:23; Col 1:18]
19 "I will give you the keys (authority)
of the kingdom of heaven; and whatever you bind [forbid, declare to be
improper and unlawful] on earth will
have [already] been bound in heaven, and whatever you loose [permit,
declare lawful] on earth will have
[already] been loosed in heaven."
[Is 22:22; Matt 18:18]
20 Then He gave the disciples strict
orders to tell no one that He was the
Christ (the Messiah, the Anointed).

Jesus Foretells His Death

21 From that time on Jesus began to
show His disciples [clearly] that He
must go to Jerusalem, and endure
many things at the hands of the elders and the chief priests and scribes
(Sanhedrin, Jewish High Court), and
be killed, and be raised [from death to
life] on the third day. [Mark 8:31–9:1;
Luke 9:22–27]
22 Peter took Him aside [to speak to
Him privately] and began to reprimand
Him, saying, "May God forbid it! This
will never happen to You."
23 But Jesus turned and said to Peter, "Get behind Me, Satan! You are a
stumbling block to Me; for you are not
setting your mind on things of God,
but on things of man."

Discipleship Is Costly

24 Then Jesus said to His disciples,
"If anyone wishes to follow Me [as My

19 Mt 18:18; Jn 20:23 **20** Mt 17:9; Lk 9:21 **21** Mt 20:17; Mk 8:31; 9:31; 10:33; Lk 9:22; 18:31; 24:6,7
23 See 2Sa 19:22; Ro 8:7

disciple], he must deny himself [set
aside selfish interests], and take up his
cross [expressing a willingness to en-
dure whatever may come] and follow
Me [believing in Me, conforming to
My example in living and, if need be,
suffering or perhaps dying because of
faith in Me].
25“For whoever wishes to save his
life [in this world] will [eventually]
lose it [through death], but whoever
loses his life [in this world] for My
sake will find it [that is, life with Me
for all eternity].
26“For what will it profit a man if he
gains the whole world [wealth, fame,
success], but forfeits his soul? Or what
will a man give in exchange for his
soul?
27“For the Son of Man is going to
come in the glory *and* majesty of His
Father with His angels, and THEN HE
WILL REPAY EACH ONE IN ACCORDANCE WITH
WHAT HE HAS DONE. [Ps 62:12]
28“I assure you *and* most solemnly
say to you, there are some of those
standing here who will not taste death
before they see the Son of Man coming
in His kingdom.”

The Transfiguration

17 SIX DAYS later Jesus took with
Him Peter and James and John
the brother of James, and led them up
on a high mountain by themselves.
[Mark 9:2–8; Luke 9:28–36]
2And His appearance changed dra-
matically in their presence; and His
face shone [with heavenly glory, clear
and bright] like the sun, and His cloth-
ing became as white as light.
3And behold, Moses and Elijah ap-
peared to them, talking with Jesus.
4Then Peter began to speak and said
to Jesus, “Lord, it is good *and* delight-
ful *and* auspicious that we are here; if
You wish, I will put up three [sacred]
tents here—one for You, one for Moses,
and one for Elijah.”
5While he was still speaking, be-
hold, a bright cloud overshadowed
them, and a voice from the cloud said,
“This is My beloved Son, with whom I
am well-pleased *and* delighted! Listen
to Him!” [Ps 2:7; Is 42:1]
6When the disciples heard it, they
fell on their faces and were terrified.
7But Jesus came and touched them
and said, “Get up, and do not be afraid.”
8And when they looked up, they saw
no one except Jesus Himself alone.
9And as they were going down the
mountain, Jesus commanded them,
“Do not tell anyone what you have seen
until the Son of Man has been raised
from the dead.”
10The disciples asked Him, “Then
why do the scribes say that Elijah must
come first?”
11He answered and said, “Elijah is
coming and will restore all things;
12but I say to you that Elijah has
come already, and they did not rec-
ognize him, but did to him as they
wished. The Son of Man is also going
to suffer at their hands.”
13Then the disciples understood that
He had spoken to them about John the
Baptist. [Mal 4:5]

16:28 *not taste death.* In the transfiguration, Peter, James, and John saw a preview of the kingdom. Jesus was explaining that very soon those three disciples would see Him glorified as He will be in the kingdom.

17:3 *Moses and Elijah.* This amazing experience was not only to show the disciples that Jesus was God's Son, but also to show them that He supersedes the law and the prophets and that they were subordinate to Him. It also explained that what Jesus was doing was no mystery to the Old Testament. The Old Testament people had been long looking forward to the Messiah and His kingdom.

17:11 – 13 *Elijah.* Jesus indicates that the prophecies concerning Elijah had their fulfillment in John the Baptist, yet because the restoration is not complete, many conclude that the role of Elijah will be taken up by one of the two witnesses of Revelation 11:3 – 6.

24 Mk 8:34; Lk 9:23; 14:27; Ac 14:22; 1Th 3:3; 2Ti 3:12 **25** Lk 17:33; Jn 12:25 **26** Ps 49:7,8 **27** Mt 26:64; Mk 8:38; Lk 9:26; Da 7:10; Zec 14:5; Mt 25:31; Jude 14; Job 34:11; Ps 62:12; Pr 24:12; Jer 17:10; 32:19; Ro 2:6; 1Co 3:8; 2Co 5:10; 1Pe 1:17; Rev 2:23; 22:12 **28** Mk 9:1; Lk 9:27 **CHAPTER 17** **1** Mk 9:2; Lk 9:28 **5** 2Pe 1:17; Mt 3:17; Mk 1:11; Lk 3:22; Isa 42:1; Dt 18:15,19; Ac 3:22,23 **6** 2Pe 1:18 **7** Da 8:18; 9:21; 10:10,18 **9** Mt 16:20; Mk 8:30; 9:9 **10** Mal 4:5; Mt 11:14; Mk 9:11 **11** Mal 4:6; Lk 1:16,17; Ac 3:21 **12** Mt 11:14; Mk 9:12,13; Mt 14:3,10; Mt 16:21 **13** Mt 11:14

The Demoniac

14 When they approached the crowd,
a man came up to Jesus, kneeling be-
fore Him and saying, [Mark 9:14–27;
Luke 9:37–42]
15 "Lord, have mercy on my son, for
he is a lunatic (moonstruck) and suf-
fers terribly; for he often falls into the
fire and often into the water.
16 "And I brought him to Your disciples,
and they were not able to heal him."
17 And Jesus answered, "You unbe-
lieving and perverted generation, how
long shall I be with you? How long
shall I put up with you? Bring him
here to Me."
18 Jesus rebuked the demon, and
it came out of him, and the boy was
healed at once.
19 Then the disciples came to Jesus
privately and asked, "Why could we
not drive it out?"
20 He answered, "Because of your
little faith [your lack of trust and con-
fidence in the power of God]; for I
assure you *and* most solemnly say
to you, if you have [living] faith the
size of a mustard seed, you will say
to this mountain, 'Move from here to
there,' and [if it is God's will] it will
move; and nothing will be impossi-
ble for you. [Mark 11:23; Luke 17:6;
1 John 5:14]
21 "[But this kind of demon does not
go out except by prayer and fasting.]"
22 When they were gathering togeth-
er in Galilee, Jesus said to them, "The
Son of Man is going to be betrayed
and handed over to men [who are His
enemies];
23 and they will kill Him, and He
will be raised [from death to life] on
the third day." And they were deeply
grieved *and* distressed.

14 Mk 9:14; Lk 9:37 **20** Mt 21:21; Mk 11:23; Lk 17:6; 1Co 12:9; 13:2 **22** Mt 16:21; 20:17; Mk 8:31; 9:30,31; 10:33; Lk 9:22,44; 18:31; 24:6,7

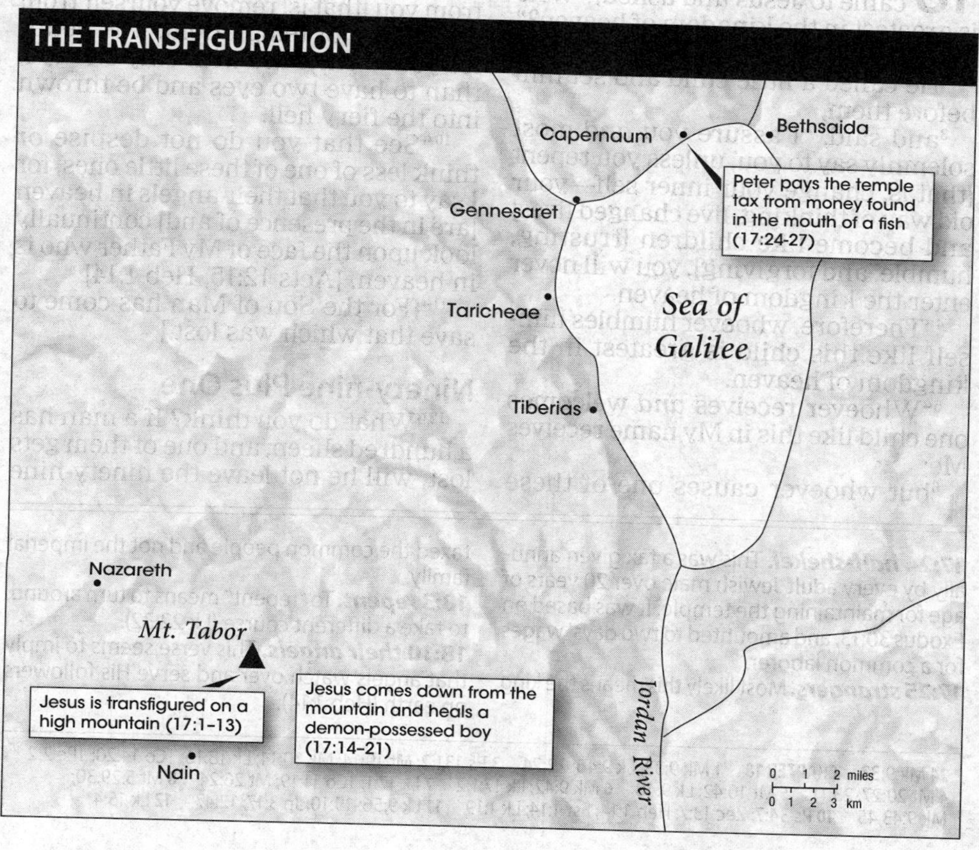

The Tribute Money

24 When they arrived in Capernaum, the collectors of the half-shekel [temple tax] went up to Peter and said, "Does not your teacher pay the half-shekel?" [Ex 30:13; 38:26]

25 Peter answered, "Yes." And when he came home, Jesus spoke to him first, saying, "What do you think, Simon? From whom do earthly rulers collect duties or taxes, from their sons or from strangers?"

26 When Peter said, "From strangers," Jesus said to him, "Then the sons are exempt [from taxation].

27 "However, so that we do not offend them, go to the sea and throw in a hook, and take the first fish that comes up; and when you open its mouth, you will find a shekel. Take it and give it to them [to pay the temple tax] for you and Me."

Rank in the Kingdom

18 AT THAT time the disciples came to Jesus and asked, "Who is greatest in the kingdom of heaven?" [Mark 9:33–37; Luke 9:46–48]

2 He called a little child and set him before them,

3 and said, "I assure you *and* most solemnly say to you, unless you repent [that is, change your inner self—your old way of thinking, live changed lives] and become like children [trusting, humble, and forgiving], you will never enter the kingdom of heaven.

4 "Therefore, whoever humbles himself like this child is greatest in the kingdom of heaven.

5 "Whoever receives *and* welcomes one child like this in My name receives Me;

6 but whoever causes one of these little ones who believe in Me to stumble *and* sin [by leading him away from My teaching], it would be better for him to have a heavy millstone [as large as one turned by a donkey] hung around his neck and to be drowned in the depth of the sea. [Mark 9:42; Luke 17:2]

Stumbling Blocks

7 "Woe (judgment is coming) to the world because of stumbling blocks *and* temptations to sin! It is inevitable that stumbling blocks come; but woe to the person on whose account *or* through whom the stumbling block comes! [Luke 17:1]

8 "If your hand or your foot causes you to stumble *and* sin, cut it off and throw it away from you [that is, remove yourself from the source of temptation]; it is better for you to enter life crippled or lame, than to have two hands or two feet and be thrown into everlasting fire.

9 "If your eye causes you to stumble *and* sin, pluck it out and throw it away from you [that is, remove yourself from the source of temptation]; it is better for you to enter life with only one eye, than to have two eyes and be thrown into the fiery hell.

10 "See that you do not despise *or* think less of one of these little ones, for I say to you that their angels in heaven [are in the presence of and] continually look upon the face of My Father who is in heaven. [Acts 12:15; Heb 1:14]

11 "[For the Son of Man has come to save that which was lost.]

Ninety-nine Plus One

12 "What do you think? If a man has a hundred sheep, and one of them gets lost, will he not leave the ninety-nine

---

17:24 *half-shekel.* This was a tax given annually by every adult Jewish male over 20 years of age for maintaining the temple. It was based on Exodus 30:13, and amounted to two days' wages for a common laborer.

17:25 *strangers.* Most likely this means the king taxed the common people and not the imperial family.

18:3 *repent.* To "repent" means to turn around, to take a different course (Lk 22:32).

18:10 *their angels.* This verse seems to imply that angels watch over and serve His followers on earth (Heb 1:14).

---

24 Mk 9:33 **CHAPTER 18** **1** Mk 9:33; Lk 9:46; 22:24 **3** Ps 131:2; Mt 19:14; Mk 10:14; Lk 18:16; 1Co 14:20; 1Pe 2:2 **4** Mt 20:27; 23:11 **5** Mt 10:42; Lk 9:48 **6** Mk 9:42; Lk 17:1,2 **7** Lk 17:1; 1Co 11:19; Mt 26:24 **8** Mt 5:29,30; Mk 9:43,45 **10** Ps 34:7; Zec 13:7; Heb 1:14; Est 1:14; Lk 1:19 **11** Lk 9:56; 19:10; Jn 3:17; 12:47 **12** Lk 15:4

on the mountain and go in search of
the one that is lost? [Luke 15:4–7]
13 “And if it turns out that he finds it,
I assure you *and* most solemnly say to
you, he rejoices over it more than over
the ninety-nine that did not get lost.
14 “So it is not the will of your Father
who is in heaven that one of these little
ones be lost.

Discipline and Prayer

15 “If your brother sins, go and show
him his fault in private; if he listens
and pays attention to you, you have
won back your brother.
16 “But if he does not listen, take along
with you one or two others, so that
EVERY WORD MAY BE CONFIRMED BY THE
TESTIMONY OF TWO OR THREE WITNESSES.
17 “If he pays no attention to them
[refusing to listen and obey], tell it to
the church; and if he refuses to listen
even to the church, let him be to you
as a Gentile (unbeliever) and a tax col-
lector. [Lev 19:17; Deut 19:15]
18 “I assure you *and* most solemnly
say to you, whatever you bind [forbid,
declare to be improper and unlaw-
ful] on earth shall have [already] been
bound in heaven, and whatever you
loose [permit, declare lawful] on earth
shall have [already] been loosed in
heaven. [Matt 16:19]
19 “Again I say to you, that if two be-
lievers on earth agree [that is, are of
one mind, in harmony] about anything
that they ask [within the will of God],
it will be done for them by My Father
in heaven. [1 John 5:14]
20 “For where two or three are gath-
ered in My name [meeting together
as My followers], I am there among
them.” [Ex 3:14]

Forgiveness

21 Then Peter came to Him and asked,
“Lord, how many times will my broth-
er sin against me and I forgive him *and*
let it go? Up to seven times?”
22 Jesus answered him, “I say to you,
not up to seven times, but seventy
times seven.
23 “Therefore the kingdom of heaven
is like a king who wished to settle ac-
counts with his slaves.
24 “When he began the accounting,
one who owed him 10,000 talents was
brought to him.
25 “But because he could not repay,
his master ordered him to be sold, with
his wife and his children and every-
thing that he possessed, and payment
to be made.
26 “So the slave fell on his knees and
begged him, saying, ‘Have patience
with me and I will repay you every-
thing.’
27 “And his master's heart was moved
with compassion and he released him
and forgave him [canceling] the debt.
28 “But that same slave went out and
found one of his fellow slaves who
owed him a hundred denarii; and he
seized him and *began* choking him,
saying, ‘Pay what you owe!’
29 “So his fellow slave fell on his
knees and begged him earnestly, ‘Have
patience with me and I will repay you.’

18:16 ***TWO OR THREE WITNESSES.*** The principle of witnesses is taken from Deuteronomy 19:15. Evidently, in this case they are to witness that the offended brother is acting in good faith and the right spirit in attempting to work towards reconciliation. They would also be witnesses to any agreement.

18:17 ***church.*** Unfortunately “discipline” has sometimes been reduced to a merely negative concept. To be sure, discipline includes the notion of punishment and correction, but church discipline in this context clearly has the restoration of the offender in view. Severe measures may sometimes need to be taken with an erring brother or sister, but restoration and reconciliation should always be the goal.

18:22 ***seventy times seven.*** Some translations say “seventy-seven times.” Whichever number is used, the point is the same: be ready to forgive over and over again, past counting. This verse does not only apply to forgiveness for seventy times seven different sins. Sometimes, we may have to consciously decide to forgive and let go of an old hurt again and again, “seventy times seven.”

15 Lev 19:17; Lk 17:3; Jas 5:20; 1Pe 3:1 **16** Dt 17:6; 19:15; Jn 8:17; 2Co 13:1; Heb 10:28 **17** Ro 16:17; 1Co 5:9; 2Th 3:6,14; 2Jn 10 **18** Mt 16:19; Jn 20:23; 1Co 5:4 **19** Mt 5:24; 1Jn 3:22; 5:14 **21** Lk 17:4 **22** Mt 6:14; Mk 11:25; Col 3:13 **25** 2Ki 4:1; Neh 5:8

30"But he was unwilling and he went
and had him thrown in prison until he
paid back the debt.
31"When his fellow slaves saw what
had happened, they were deeply
grieved and they went and reported
to their master [with clarity and in
detail] everything that had taken place.
32"Then his master called him and
said to him, 'You wicked *and* contempt-
ible slave, I forgave all that [great] debt
of yours because you begged me.
33'Should you not have had mercy
on your fellow slave [who owed you
little by comparison], as I had mercy
on you?'
34"And in wrath his master turned
him over to the torturers (jailers) until
he paid all that he owed.
35"My heavenly Father will also do
the same to [every one of] you, if each
of you does not forgive his brother
from your heart."

Concerning Divorce

19 NOW WHEN Jesus had finished
saying these things, He left Gali-
lee and went into the part of Judea that
is beyond the Jordan;
2and large crowds followed Him, and
He healed them there.
3And Pharisees came to Jesus, test-
ing Him and asking, "Is it lawful for
a man to divorce his wife for just any
reason?"
4He replied, "Have you never read
that He who created them from the
beginning MADE THEM MALE AND FEMALE,
5and said, 'FOR THIS REASON A MAN
SHALL LEAVE HIS FATHER AND MOTHER AND
SHALL BE JOINED INSEPARABLY TO HIS WIFE,
AND THE TWO SHALL BECOME ONE FLESH'?
[Gen 1:27; 2:24; Mark 10:7]
6"So they are no longer two, but one
flesh. Therefore, what God has joined
together, let no one separate."
7The Pharisees said to Him, "Why
then did Moses command us to GIVE
HER A CERTIFICATE OF DIVORCE AND SEND
HER AWAY?" [Deut 24:1–4]
8He said to them, "Because your
hearts were hard *and* stubborn Moses
permitted you to divorce your wives;
but from the beginning it has not been
this way.
9"I say to you, whoever divorces his
wife, except for sexual immorality,
and marries another woman commits
adultery."
10The disciples said to Jesus, "If the
relationship of a man with his wife is
like this, it is better not to marry."
11But He said to them, "Not all men
can accept this statement, but *only*
those to whom [the capacity to receive]
it has been given.
12"For there are eunuchs who have
been born that way from their mother's
womb [making them incapable of con-
summating a marriage]; and there are
eunuchs who have been made eunuchs
by men [for royal service]; and there
are eunuchs who have made them-
selves so for the sake of the kingdom of
heaven. He who is able to accept this,
let him accept it."

Jesus Blesses Little Children

13Then children were brought to
Jesus so that He might place His hands
on them [for a blessing] and pray; but
the disciples reprimanded them.

18:35 *forgive.* This verse is a serious warning (1Jn 4:20).

19:9 *divorces his wife.* When the Pharisees asked Jesus if divorce could ever be considered lawful, He did not fall into their trap. He took them back to Genesis and God's original intent in marriage, one man and one woman for life (vv. 4 – 5; Ge 1:27; 2:24). In spite of the "exception clause" one thing is surely clear: God hates divorce (Mal 2:15 – 16). Marriage is a divine arrangement that is intended to be permanent and inviolable. Straying from God's path always has tragic consequences.

19:12 *eunuchs.* The term eunuch refers to a castrated man, whether by surgery, accident, or birth. In the ancient world, eunuchs were put in charge of harems, because they had the physical strength and endurance of a man, but would not be a sexual threat to the women of the harem.

35 Pr 21:13; Mt 6:12; Mk 11:26; Jas 2:13 **CHAPTER 19** **1** Mk 10:1; Jn 10:40 **2** Mt 12:15 **4** Ge 1:27; 5:2; Mal 2:15 **5** Ge 2:24; Mk 10:5-9; Eph 5:31; 1Co 6:16; 7:2 **7** Dt 24:1; Mt 5:31 **9** Mt 5:32; Mk 10:11; Lk 16:18; 1Co 7:10 **10** Pr 21:19 **11** 1Co 7:2,7,9,17 **12** 1Co 7:32; 9:5,15 **13** Mk 10:13; Lk 18:15

JESUS' LAST JOURNEY TO JERUSALEM

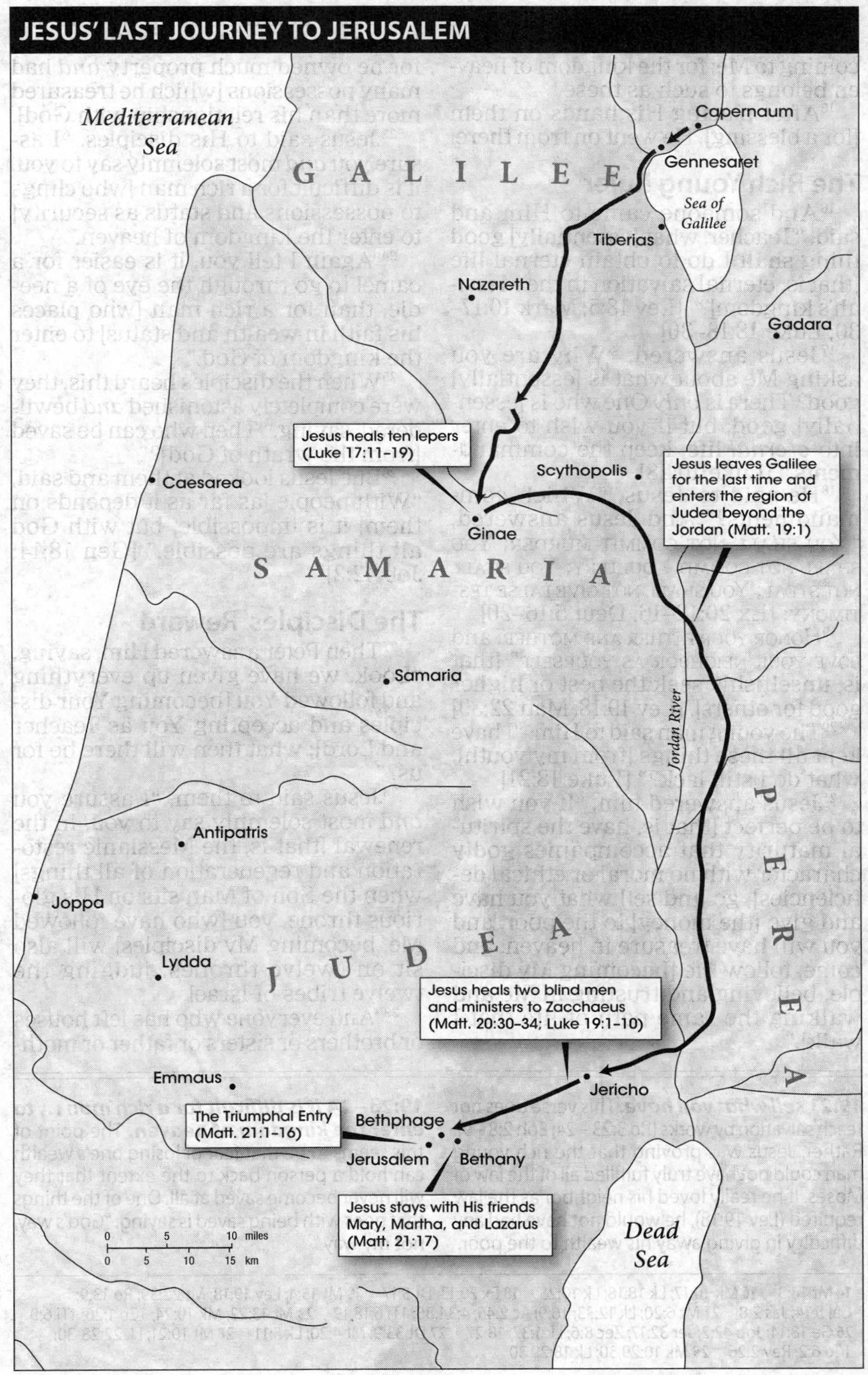

14 But He said, "Leave the children alone, and do not forbid them from coming to Me; for the kingdom of heaven belongs to such as these."

15 After placing His hands on them [for a blessing], He went on from there.

The Rich Young Ruler

16 And someone came to Him and said, "Teacher, what [essentially] good thing shall I do to obtain eternal life [that is, eternal salvation in the Messiah's kingdom]?" [Lev 18:5; Mark 10:17–30; Luke 18:18–30]

17 Jesus answered, "Why are you asking Me about what is [essentially] good? There is *only* One who is [essentially] good; but if you wish to enter into *eternal* life, keep the commandments." [Luke 10:28]

18 He said to Jesus, "Which commandments?" And Jesus answered, "You shall not commit murder; You shall not commit adultery; You shall not steal; You shall not give false testimony; [Ex 20:12–16; Deut 5:16–20]

19 Honor your father and mother; and love your neighbor as yourself" [that is, unselfishly seek the best or higher good for others]. [Lev 19:18; Matt 22:39]

20 The young man said to Him, "I have kept all these things [from my youth]; what do I still lack?" [Luke 18:21]

21 Jesus answered him, "If you wish to be perfect [that is, have the spiritual maturity that accompanies godly character with no moral or ethical deficiencies], go and sell what you have and give [the money] to the poor, and you will have treasure in heaven; and come, follow Me [becoming My disciple, believing and trusting in Me and walking the same path of life that I walk]."

22 But when the young man heard this, he left grieving *and* distressed, for he owned much property *and* had many possessions [which he treasured more than his relationship with God].

23 Jesus said to His disciples, "I assure you *and* most solemnly say to you, it is difficult for a rich man [who clings to possessions and status as security] to enter the kingdom of heaven.

24 "Again I tell you, it is easier for a camel to go through the eye of a needle, than for a rich man [who places his faith in wealth and status] to enter the kingdom of God."

25 When the disciples heard this, they were completely astonished *and* bewildered, saying, "Then who can be saved [from the wrath of God]?"

26 But Jesus looked at them and said, "With people [as far as it depends on them] it is impossible, but with God all things are possible." [Gen 18:14; Job 42:2]

The Disciples' Reward

27 Then Peter answered Him, saying, "Look, we have given up everything and followed You [becoming Your disciples and accepting You as Teacher and Lord]; what then will there be for us?"

28 Jesus said to them, "I assure you *and* most solemnly say to you, in the renewal [that is, the Messianic restoration and regeneration of all things] when the Son of Man sits on His glorious throne, you [who have followed Me, becoming My disciples] will also sit on twelve thrones, judging the twelve tribes of Israel.

29 "And everyone who has left houses or brothers or sisters or father or moth-

---

19:21 ***sell what you have.*** This verse does not teach salvation by works (Ro 3:23–24; Eph 2:8–9). Rather, Jesus was proving that the rich young man could not have truly fulfilled all of the law of Moses. If he really loved his neighbor as the law required (Lev 19:18), he would not have had any difficulty in giving away his wealth to the poor.

19:23–24 ***it is difficult for a rich man . . . to enter the kingdom of heaven.*** The point of this seems to be that fear of losing one's wealth can hold a person back to the extent that they will never become saved at all. One of the things that goes with being saved is saying, "God's way, not my way."

14 Mt 18:3 **16** Mk 10:17; Lk 18:18; Lk 10:25 **18** Ex 20:13; Dt 5:17 **19** Mt 15:4; Lev 19:18; Mt 22:39; Ro 13:9; Gal 5:14; Jas 2:8 **21** Mt 6:20; Lk 12:33; 16:9; Ac 2:45; 4:34,35; 1Ti 6:18,19 **23** Mt 13:22; Mk 10:24; 1Co 1:26; 1Ti 6:9 **26** Ge 18:14; Job 42:2; Jer 32:17; Zec 8:6; Lk 1:37; 18:27 **27** Dt 33:9; Mt 4:20; Lk 5:11 **28** Mt 10:21; Lk 22:28-30; 1Co 6:2; Rev 2:26 **29** Mk 10:29,30; Lk 18:29,30

er or children or farms for My name's sake will receive many times as much, and will inherit eternal life.

30"But many *who are* first [in this world] will be last [in the world to come]; and the last, first.

Laborers in the Vineyard

20 "FOR THE kingdom of heaven is like the owner of an estate who went out in the morning at dawn to hire workmen for his vineyard.

2"When he had agreed with the laborers for a denarius for the day, he sent them into his vineyard.

3"And he went out about the third hour (9:00 a.m.) and saw others standing idle in the market place;

4and he said to them, 'You also go into the vineyard, and I will pay you whatever is right (an appropriate wage).' And they went.

5"He went out about the sixth hour (noon) and the ninth hour (3:00 p.m.), and did the same thing.

6"And about the eleventh hour (5:00 p.m.) he went out and found others standing *around*, and he said to them, 'Why have you been standing here idle all day?'

7"They answered him, 'Because no one hired us.' He told them, 'You go into the vineyard also.'

8"When evening came, the owner of the vineyard said to his manager, 'Call the workers and pay them their wages, beginning with the last [to be hired] and ending with the first [to be hired].' [Lev 19:13; Deut 24:15]

9"Those who had been *hired* at the eleventh hour (5:00 p.m.) came and received a denarius each [a day's wage].

10"Now when the first [to be hired] came, they thought they would get more; but each of them also received a denarius.

11"When they received it, they protested *and* grumbled at the owner of the estate,

12saying, 'These men who came last worked [only] one hour, and yet you have made them equal [in wages] to us who have carried [most of] the burden and [worked in] the scorching heat of the day.'

13"But the owner of the estate replied to one of them, 'Friend, I am doing you no injustice. Did you not agree with me for a denarius?

14'Take what belongs to you and go, but I choose to give to this last man [hired] the same as I give to you.

15'Am I not lawfully permitted to do what I choose with what is mine? Or is your eye envious because I am generous?'

16"So those who are last [in this world] shall be first [in the world to come], and those who are first, last."

Death, Resurrection Foretold

17As Jesus was going up to Jerusalem, He took the twelve [disciples] aside, and along the way He said to them,

18"Listen carefully: we are going up to Jerusalem; and the Son of Man will be handed over to the chief priests and scribes (Sanhedrin, Jewish High Court), and they will [judicially] condemn Him *and* sentence Him to death,

19and will hand Him over to the Gentiles (Roman authorities) to be mocked and scourged and crucified, and He will be raised [to life] on the third day."

Preferred Treatment Asked

20Then [Salome] the mother of Zebedee's children [James and John] came up to Jesus with her sons and, kneeling down [in respect], asked a favor of Him. [Mark 10:35–45]

20:3 *third hour.* This was about 9:00 A.M.
20:5 *the sixth hour.* This was about noon, and the ninth hour was about 3:00 P.M.
20:6 *the eleventh hour.* This was about 5:00 P.M. There would be only an hour or so left in the working day.
20:16 *last [in this world] shall be first.* The workers who were collected without an agreement represent the Gentiles who are made equal with the Jewish people when salvation became available to all through Jesus Christ (Ro 11:15; Eph 2:13–15; 3:6).

30 Mt 20:16; 21:31,32; Mk 10:31; Lk 13:30 **CHAPTER 20** **15** Ro 9:21; Dt 15:9; Pr 23:6; Mt 6:23 **16** Mt 19:30; Mt 22:14 **17** Mk 10:32; Lk 18:31; Jn 12:12 **18** Mt 16:21 **19** Mt 27:2; Mk 15:1,16; Lk 23:1; Jn 18:28; Ac 3:13 **20** Mk 10:35; Mt 4:21

21 And He said to her, "What do you wish?" She answered Him, "Command that in Your kingdom these two sons of mine may sit [in positions of honor and authority] one on Your right and one on Your left."

22 But Jesus replied, "You do not realize what you are asking. Are you able to drink the cup [of suffering] that I am about to drink?" They answered, "We are able."

23 He said to them, "You will drink My cup [of suffering]; but to sit on My right and on My left this is not Mine to give, but it is for those for whom it has been prepared by My Father."

24 And when the [other] ten heard this, they were resentful *and* angry with the two brothers.

25 But Jesus called them to Himself and said, "You know that the rulers of the Gentiles have absolute power *and* lord it over them, and their great men exercise authority over them [tyrannizing them]. [Mark 10:42–45; Luke 22:25–27]

26 "It is not this way among you, but whoever wishes to become great among you shall be your servant,

27 and whoever wishes to be first among you shall be your [willing and humble] slave;

28 just as the Son of Man did not come to be served, but to serve, and to give His life as a ransom for many [paying the price to set them free from the penalty of sin]."

Sight for the Blind

29 As they were leaving Jericho, a large crowd followed Him. [Mark 10:46–52; Luke 18:35–43]

30 And two blind men were sitting by the road, and when they heard that Jesus was passing by, they cried out, "Lord, have mercy on us, Son of David (Messiah)!"

31 The crowd sternly told them to be quiet, but they cried out all the more, "Lord, Son of David (Messiah) have mercy on us!"

32 Jesus stopped and called them, and asked, "What do you want Me to do for you?"

33 They answered Him, "Lord, *we want* our eyes to be opened."

34 Moved with compassion, Jesus touched their eyes; and immediately they regained their sight and followed Him [as His disciples].

The Triumphal Entry

21 WHEN THEY approached Jerusalem and had reached Bethphage, at the Mount of Olives, Jesus sent two disciples [ahead], [Mark 11:1–10; Luke 19:29–38; John 12:12–15]

2 saying to them, "Go into the village opposite you, and at once you will find a donkey tied, and a colt with her; untie them and bring them to Me.

3 "If anyone says anything to you, you should say, 'The Lord needs them,' and without delay the owner will send them [with you]."

4 This happened so that what was spoken by the prophet would be fulfilled, saying:

5 "Tell the daughter of Zion (the
people of Jerusalem),
'Behold, your King is coming to
you,
Gentle and mounted on a donkey,
Even on a colt, the foal of a beast
of burden.' " [Is 62:11; Zech 9:9]

6 Then the disciples went and did as Jesus had instructed them,

7 and they brought the donkey and the colt, and placed their coats on them; and Jesus sat on the coats.

8 Most of the crowd spread their coats on the road [as before a king], while

---

20:26–27 *whoever wishes to become great.* The measure of greatness is not position, power, or prestige. It is service.

21:2 *a donkey tied.* This was prophesied in Zechariah 9:9.

21 Mt 19:28 **22** Mt 26:39,42; Mk 14:36; Lk 22:42; Jn 18:11; Lk 12:50 **23** Ac 12:2; Ro 8:17; 2Co 1:7; Rev 1:9; Mt 25:34 **24** Mk 10:41; Lk 22:24,25 **26** 1Pe 5:3; Mt 23:11; Mk 9:35; 10:43 **27** Mt 18:4 **28** Jn 13:4; Php 2:7; Lk 22:27; Jn 13:14; Isa 53:10,11; Da 9:24,26; Jn 11:51,52; 1Ti 2:6; Titus 2:14; 1Pe 1:19; Mt 26:28; Ro 5:15,19; Heb 9:28 **29** Mk 10:46; Lk 18:35 **30** Mt 9:27 **CHAPTER 21** **1** Mk 11:1; Lk 19:29; Zec 14:4 **5** Isa 62:11; Zec 9:9; Jn 12:15 **6** Mk 11:4 **7** 2Ki 9:13 **8** See Lev 23:40; Jn 12:13

others were cutting branches from the trees and spreading them on the road.
[9]The crowds that went ahead of Him, and those that followed Him, were shouting [in praise and adoration],

"Hosanna to the Son of David (Messiah);
BLESSED [praised, glorified] IS HE WHO COMES IN THE NAME OF THE LORD;
Hosanna in the highest [heaven]!" [Ps 118:26]

[10]When He entered Jerusalem, all the city was trembling [with excitement], saying, "Who is this?"
[11]And the crowds were saying, "This is the prophet Jesus, from Nazareth in Galilee."

Cleansing the Temple

[12]And Jesus entered the temple [grounds] and drove out [with force] all who were buying and selling [birds and animals for sacrifice] in the temple *area*, and He turned over the tables of the moneychangers [who made a profit exchanging foreign money for temple coinage] and the chairs of those who were selling doves [for sacrifice]. [Mark 11:15–18; Luke 19:45–47; John 2:14–16]
[13]Jesus said to them, "It is written [in Scripture], 'MY HOUSE SHALL BE CALLED A HOUSE OF PRAYER'; but you are making it a ROBBERS' DEN." [Is 56:7; Jer 7:11]
[14]And the blind and the lame came to Him in [the porticoes and courts of] the temple *area*, and He healed them.
[15]But when the chief priests and the scribes saw the wonderful *and* miraculous things that Jesus had done, and *heard* the boys who were shouting in [the porticoes and courts of] the temple [in praise and adoration], "Hosanna to the Son of David (the Messiah)," they became indignant
[16]and they said to Him, "Do You hear what these *children* are saying?" And Jesus replied to them, "Yes; have you never read [in the Scripture], 'OUT OF THE MOUTHS OF INFANTS AND NURSING BABIES YOU HAVE PREPARED *and* PROVIDED PRAISE FOR YOURSELF'?" [Ps 8:2]
[17]Then He left them and went out of the city to Bethany, and spent the night there.

The Barren Fig Tree

[18]Now early in the morning, as Jesus was coming back to the city, He was hungry. [Mark 11:12–14, 20–24]
[19]Seeing a lone fig tree at the roadside, He went to it and found nothing but leaves on it; and He said to it, "Never again will fruit come from you." And at once the fig tree withered.
[20]When the disciples saw it, they were astonished and asked, "How is it that the fig tree has withered away all at once?"
[21]Jesus replied to them, "I assure you *and* most solemnly say to you, if you have faith [personal trust and confidence in Me] and do not doubt *or* allow yourself to be drawn in two directions, you will not only do what was done to the fig tree, but even if you say to this mountain, 'Be taken up and thrown into the sea,' it will happen [if God wills it]. [1 John 5:14]
[22]"And whatever you ask for in prayer, believing, you will receive."

Authority Challenged

[23]When He entered the temple *area*, the chief priests and elders of the people came to Him as He was teaching

---

21:9 *Hosanna.* Hosanna literally means "save now." The people were using it as an exclamation of joyous praise, but also they expected the Messiah to save them from the oppression of the Romans.
21:19 *at once.* This does not necessarily mean instantly; it may have the idea of "very soon" as in Luke 19:11. (The account of this miracle in Mk 11:12–14,20–21 indicates some time passing.)
21:21 *faith.* Few if any besides our Savior will reach this kind of faith in its fullness. However, as each believer approaches such faith in prayer,

9 Ps 118:25,26; Mt 23:39 **10** Mk 11:15; Lk 19:45; Jn 2:13,15 **11** Mt 2:23; Lk 7:16; Jn 6:14; 7:40; 9:17 **12** Mk 11:11; Lk 19:45; Jn 2:15; Dt 14:25 **13** Isa 56:7; Jer 7:11; Mk 11:17; Lk 19:46 **16** Ps 8:2 **17** Mk 11:11; Jn 11:18 **18** Mk 11:12 **19** Mk 11:13 **20** Mk 11:20 **21** Mt 17:20; Jas 1:6; 1Co 13:2 **22** Mt 7:7; Mk 11:24; Lk 11:9; Jas 5:16; 1Jn 3:22; 5:14 **23** Mk 11:27; Lk 20:1; Ex 2:14; Ac 4:7; 7:27

and said, "By what [kind of] authority are You doing these things, and who gave You this authority [to exercise this power]?" [Mark 11:27–33; Luke 20:1–8]

24 Jesus replied to them, "I will also ask you a question, and if you tell Me the answer, then I will tell you by what authority I do these things.

25 "The baptism of John—from where did it come? From heaven [that is, ordained by God] or from men?" And they *began* debating among themselves [considering the implications of their answer], saying, "If we say, 'From heaven,' He will say to us, 'Then why did you not believe John?'

26 "But if we say, 'From men,' we are afraid of the [response of the] crowd; for they all regard John as a prophet."

27 So they answered Jesus, "We do not know." And He said to them, "Neither will I tell you by what [kind of] authority I do these things."

Parable of Two Sons

28 "What do you think? There was a man who had two sons, and he came to the first and said, 'Son, go and work in the vineyard today.'

29 "And he answered, 'I will not'; but afterward he regretted it *and* changed his mind and went.

30 "Then the man came to the second son and said the same thing; and he replied, 'I *will*, sir'; but he did not go.

31 "Which of the two did the will of the father?" The chief priests and elders replied, "The first one." Jesus said to them, "I assure you *and* most solemnly say to you that the tax collectors and the prostitutes will get into the kingdom of God before you.

32 "For John came to you [walking] in the way of righteousness and you did not believe him; but the tax collectors and the prostitutes did believe him; and you, seeing this, did not even change your mind afterward and believe him [accepting what he proclaimed to you].

Parable of the Landowner

33 "Listen to another parable. There was a landowner who PLANTED A VINEYARD AND PUT A WALL AROUND IT AND DUG A WINE PRESS IN IT, AND BUILT A TOWER, and rented it out to tenant farmers and went on a journey [to another country]. [Is 5:1–7; Mark 12:1–12; Luke 20:9–19]

34 "When the harvest time approached, he sent his servants to the tenants to get his [share of the] fruit.

35 "But the tenants took his servants and beat one, and killed another, and stoned a third.

36 "Again he sent other servants, more than the first time; and they treated them the same way.

37 "Finally he sent his own son to them, saying, 'They will respect my son *and* have regard for him.'

38 "But when the tenants saw the son, they said to themselves, 'This [man] is the heir; come on, let us kill him and seize his inheritance.'

39 "So they took the son and threw him out of the vineyard, and killed him.

40 "Now when the owner of the vineyard comes back, what will he do to those tenants?"

41 They said to Him, "He will put those despicable men to a miserable end, and rent out the vineyard to other tenants [of good character] who will pay him the proceeds at the *proper* seasons."

42 Jesus asked them, "Have you never read in the Scriptures:

'THE [very] STONE WHICH THE
BUILDERS REJECTED *and* THREW
AWAY,

---

his effort will be rewarded. Answers are always given, even to the feeblest prayers of faith.

21:33 ***PLANTED A VINEYARD.*** The owner of the vineyard was God; the vine-growers were the people of Israel. The slaves represent God's messengers, and the son is Jesus the Messiah.

21:42 ***CHIEF CORNERSTONE.*** The rejected stone was the Messiah, who became the chief

26 Mt 14:5; Mk 6:20; Lk 20:6 **31** Lk 7:29,50 **32** Mt 3:1; Lk 3:12,13 **33** Ps 80:9; SS 8:11; Isa 5:1; Jer 2:21; Mk 12:1; Lk 20:9; Mt 25:14 **34** SS 8:11,12 **35** 2Ch 24:21; 36:16; Neh 9:26; Mt 5:12; 23:34,37; Ac 7:52; 1Th 2:15; Heb 11:36,37 **38** Ps 2:8; Heb 1:2; Ps 2:2; Mt 26:3; 27:1; Jn 11:53; Ac 4:27 **39** Mt 26:50; Mk 14:46; Lk 22:54; Jn 18:12; Ac 2:23 **41** Lk 20:16; Lk 21:24; Heb 2:3; Ac 13:46; 15:7; 18:6; 28:28; Ro 9; 10; 11 **42** Ps 118:22; Isa 28:16; Mk 12:10; Lk 20:17; Ac 4:11; Eph 2:20; 1Pe 2:6,7

HAS BECOME THE CHIEF CORNERSTONE;
THIS IS THE LORD'S DOING,
AND IT IS MARVELOUS *and* WONDERFUL
IN OUR EYES'? [Ps 118:22, 23]
43 "Therefore I tell you, the kingdom
of God will be taken away from you
and given to [another] people who will
produce the fruit of it.
44 "And he who falls on this Stone will
be broken to pieces; but he on whom
it falls will be crushed." [Is 8:14, 15;
Dan 2:34, 35]
45 When the chief priests and the
Pharisees heard His parables, they
understood that He was talking about
them.
46 And although they were trying
to arrest Him, they feared the peo-
ple, because they regarded Jesus as
a prophet.

Parable of the Marriage Feast

22 JESUS SPOKE to them again in
parables, saying,
2 "The kingdom of heaven may be
compared to a king who gave a wed-
ding feast for his son.
3 "And he sent his servants to call
those who had [previously] been in-
vited to the wedding feast, but they
refused to come.
4 "Then he sent out some other ser-
vants, saying, 'Tell those who have
been invited, "Look, I have prepared
my dinner; my oxen and fattened
calves are butchered and everything
is ready; come to the wedding feast."'
5 "But they paid no attention [they
disregarded the invitation, treating it
with contempt] and went away, one to
his farm, another to his business.
6 "The rest [of the invited guests]
seized his servants and mistreated
them [insulting and humiliating them]
and killed them.
7 "The king was enraged [when he
heard this], and sent his soldiers and
destroyed those murderers and burned
their city.
8 "Then he said to his servants, 'The
wedding [feast] is ready, but those who
were invited were not worthy.
9 'So go to the main highways that
lead out of the city, and invite to the
wedding feast as many as you find.'
10 "Those servants went out into the
streets and gathered together all *the
people* they could find, both bad and
good; so the wedding hall was filled
with dinner guests [sitting at the ban-
quet table].
11 "But when the king came in to see
the dinner guests, he saw a man there
who was not dressed [appropriately]
in wedding clothes,
12 and he said, 'Friend, how did you
come in here without wearing the wed-
ding clothes [that were provided for
you]?' And the man was speechless
and without excuse.
13 "Then the king said to the atten-
dants, 'Tie him hand and foot, and
throw him into the darkness outside; in
that place there will be weeping [over
sorrow and pain] and grinding of teeth
[over distress and anger].'
14 "For many are called (invited, sum-
moned), but few are chosen."

Tribute to Caesar

15 Then the Pharisees went and con-
spired together plotting how to trap
Him by [distorting] what He said.
[Mark 12:13–17; Luke 20:20–26]

---

cornerstone, the one holding the whole building together (Ps 118:22–23).

22:11 *was not dressed [appropriately] in wedding clothes.* Like the others, this visitor had been invited to the wedding, but he failed to prepare himself for it. In Revelation, the garment of fine linen worn by the bride of the Lamb is said to be the righteous deeds of the saints (Rev 19:8). In this parable the garment may refer to the righteousness of Christ, graciously provided for us through His death. To refuse to put it on would mean a refusal of Christ's sacrifice.

22:14 *many are called (invited, summoned), but few are chosen.* All Israel has been invited, but only a few will accept and follow Jesus. Not all those invited will be among the chosen of God, for not all will believe.

---

43 Mt 8:12 **44** Isa 8:14,15; Zec 12:3; Lk 20:18; Ro 9:33; 1Pe 2:8; Isa 60:12; Da 2:44 **46** ver. 11; Lk 7:16; Jn 7:40
CHAPTER 22 **1** Lk 14:16; Rev 19:7,9 **4** Pr 9:2 **7** Da 9:26; Lk 19:27 **8** Mt 10:11; Ac 13:46 **10** Mt 13:38
11 2Co 5:3; Eph 4:24; Col 3:10,12; Rev 3:4; 16:15; 19:8 **13** Mt 8:12 **14** Mt 20:16 **15** Mk 12:13; Lk 20:20

16 They sent their disciples to Him,
along with the Herodians, saying,
"Teacher, we know that You are sin-
cere and that You teach the way of
God truthfully, without concerning
Yourself about [what] anyone [thinks
or says of Your teachings]; for You are
impartial *and* do not seek anyone's
favor [and You treat all people alike,
regardless of status].
17 "Tell us then, what do You think?
Is it permissible [according to Jewish
law and tradition] to pay a poll-tax to
Caesar, or not?"
18 But Jesus, aware of their malice,
asked, "Why are you testing Me, you
hypocrites?
19 "Show me the coin used for the
poll-tax." And they brought Him a de-
narius [a day's wage].
20 And Jesus said to them, "Whose
likeness and inscription is this?"
21 They said, "[The Emperor Tiberi-
us] Caesar's." Then He said to them,
"Then pay to Caesar the things that
are Caesar's; and to God the things
that are God's."
22 When they heard this, they were
caught off guard, and they left Him
and went away.

Jesus Answers the Sadducees

23 On that day some Sadducees, who
say that there is no resurrection [of the
dead], came to Him and asked Him a
question, [Mark 12:18–27; Luke 20:27–40]
24 saying, "Teacher, Moses said, 'IF A
MAN DIES, LEAVING NO CHILDREN, HIS BROTH-
ER AS NEXT OF KIN SHALL MARRY HIS WIDOW,
AND RAISE CHILDREN FOR HIS BROTHER.'
[Deut 25:5]
25 "Now there were seven brothers
among us; the first married and died,
and having no children left his wife to
his brother.
26 "The second also [died childless],
and the third, down to the seventh.
27 "Last of all, the woman died.
28 "So in the resurrection, whose wife
of the seven will she be? For they all
had *married* her."
29 But Jesus replied to them, "You are
all wrong because you know neither
the Scriptures [which teach the resur-
rection] nor the power of God [for He
is able to raise the dead].
30 "For in the resurrection neither do
men marry nor are *women* given in
marriage, but they are like angels in
heaven [who do not marry nor produce
children].
31 "But as to the resurrection of the
dead—have you not read [in the Scrip-
ture] what God said to you:
32 'I AM THE GOD OF ABRAHAM, AND THE
GOD OF ISAAC, AND THE GOD OF JACOB'?
He is not the God of the dead, but of
the living." [Ex 3:6]
33 When the crowds heard this, they
were astonished at His teaching.
34 Now when the Pharisees heard
that He had silenced (muzzled) the
Sadducees, they gathered together.
[Mark 12:28–31; Luke 10:25–28]
35 One of them, a lawyer [an expert in
Mosaic Law], asked Jesus *a question,*
to test Him:
36 "Teacher, which is the greatest com-
mandment in the Law?" [Mark 12:28]
37 And Jesus replied to him, " 'YOU
SHALL LOVE THE LORD YOUR GOD WITH ALL
YOUR HEART, AND WITH ALL YOUR SOUL, AND
WITH ALL YOUR MIND.' [Deut 6:5]
38 "This is the first and greatest com-
mandment.
39 "The second is like it, 'YOU SHALL
LOVE YOUR NEIGHBOR AS YOURSELF [that
is, unselfishly seek the best or higher
good for others].' [Lev 19:18; Matt 19:19]
40 "The whole Law and the [writings
of the] Prophets depend on these two
commandments."
41 Now while the Pharisees were
[still] gathered together, Jesus asked

22:21 *things that are Caesar's.* When one subjects one's self to the state and accepts its protection and benefits, one is obligated to support it and obey its laws until it becomes sinful to do so (Ro 13:1–7; 1Pe 2:13–17). But giving back to God what is His reaches far deeper than obedience to the state. Man has a duty to give himself to God, with all he is and all that he has.

21 Mt 17:25; Ro 13:7 **23** Mk 12:18; Lk 20:27; Ac 23:8 **24** Dt 25:5 **29** Jn 20:9 **30** 1Jn 3:2 **32** Ex 3:6,16; Mk 12:26; Lk 20:37; Ac 7:32; Heb 11:16 **33** Mt 7:28 **34** Mk 12:28 **35** Lk 10:25 **37** Dt 6:5; 10:12; 30:6; Lk 10:27 **39** Lev 19:18; Mt 19:19; Mk 12:31; Lk 10:27; Ro 13:9; Gal 5:14; Jas 2:8 **40** Mt 7:12; 1Ti 1:5 **41** Mk 12:35; Lk 20:41

them a question: [Mark 12:35–37; Luke 20:41–44]
[42]"What do you [Pharisees] think of the Christ (the Messiah, the Anointed)? Whose Son is He?" They said to Him, "*The son* of David."
[43]Jesus asked them, "How is it then that David by the inspiration of the Spirit, calls Him 'Lord,' saying,

[44]'THE LORD (the Father) SAID TO MY
LORD (the Son, the Messiah),
"SIT AT MY RIGHT HAND,
UNTIL I PUT YOUR ENEMIES UNDER
YOUR FEET" '? [Ps 110:1]

[45]"So then, if David calls Him (the Son, the Messiah) 'Lord,' how is He David's son?"
[46]No one was able to say a word to Him in answer, nor from that day on did anyone dare to question Him again.

Pharisaism Exposed

23 THEN JESUS spoke to the crowds and to His disciples,
[2]saying: "The scribes and Pharisees have seated themselves in Moses' chair [of authority as teachers of the Law];
[3]so practice and observe everything they tell you, but do not do as they do; for they preach [things], but do not practice *them.*
[4]"The scribes and Pharisees tie up heavy loads [that are hard to bear] and place them on men's shoulders, but they themselves will not lift a finger [to make them lighter].
[5]"They do all their deeds to be seen by men; for they make their phylacteries (tefillin) wide [to make them more conspicuous] and make their tassels long. [Ex 13:9; Num 15:38; Deut 6:8]
[6]"They love the place of distinction *and* honor at feasts and the best seats in the synagogues [those on the platform near the scrolls of the Law, facing the congregation],
[7]and to be greeted [with respect] in the market places *and* public forums, and to have people call them Rabbi.
[8]"But do not be called Rabbi (Teacher); for One is your Teacher, and you are all [equally] brothers.
[9]"Do not call *anyone* on earth [who guides you spiritually] your father; for One is your Father, He who is in heaven.
[10]"Do not *let yourselves* be called leaders *or* teachers; for One is your Leader (Teacher), the Christ.
[11]"But the greatest among you will be your servant.
[12]"Whoever exalts himself shall be humbled; and whoever humbles himself shall be raised to honor.

Eight Woes

[13]"But woe (judgment is coming) to you, [self-righteous] scribes and Pharisees, hypocrites, because you shut off the kingdom of heaven in front

---

22:42–45 *Christ . . . Whose Son is He?* The Old Testament foretold that the Messiah would come from David's royal line (2Sa 7:12–16; Ps 89:3–4,34–36; Isa 9:7; 16:5; 55:3–4).

22:44 *THE LORD (the Father) SAID TO MY LORD (the Son, the Messiah).* The Hebrew text of Psalm 110:1 uses two different Hebrew words for "Lord." The first, translated "LORD," is the name Yahweh, the proper name of Israel's God. The second "Lord" means "master." David, the great king of Israel, calls one of his offspring "Lord" or "master." The implication is that Jesus, the Son of David, is God. He is a human descendant of David, and also divine.

23:5 *phylacteries.* Phylacteries were small boxes containing specific Scripture passages, in fulfillment of Deuteronomy 6:8 (Ex 13:9,16; Pr 3:3; 6:21; 7:3). They were worn on the forehead or arm. In order to be seen as especially righteous, some Pharisees wore conspicuously large phylacteries.

23:7 *Rabbi.* The title "rabbi" means "teacher."

23:10 *Do not let yourselves be called leaders or teachers.* This verse is a warning against the human tendency to replace a personal relationship with God with following an earthly leader. No matter how dynamic or even how godly such a leader is, as soon as people start

---

44 Ps 110:1; Ac 2:34; 1Co 15:25; Heb 1:13; 10:12,13 **46** Lk 14:6; Mk 12:34; Lk 20:40 **CHAPTER 23** **2** Neh 8:4,8; Mal 2:7; Mk 12:38; Lk 20:45 **3** Ro 2:19 **4** Lk 11:46; Ac 15:10; Gal 6:13 **5** Mt 6:1,2,5,16; Nu 15:38; Dt 6:8; 22:12; Pr 3:3 **6** Mk 12:38,39; Lk 11:43; 20:46; 3Jn 9 **8** Jas 3:1; See 2Co 1:24; 1Pe 5:3 **9** Mal 1:6 **11** Mt 20:26,27 **12** Job 22:29; Pr 15:33; 29:23; Lk 14:11; 18:14; Jas 4:6; 1Pe 5:5 **13** Lk 11:52

JEWISH SECTS

PHARISEES	
Their roots can be traced to the Hasidim of the second century BC (see note on Mk 2:16).	(1) Along with the Torah, they accepted as equally inspired and authoritative all the commands set forth in the oral traditions preserved by the rabbis.
	(2) On free will and determination, they held to a mediating view that did not allow either human free will or the sovereignty of God to cancel out the other.
	(3) They accepted a rather developed hierarchy of angels and demons.
	(4) They believed in the immortality of the soul and in reward and retribution after death.
	(5) They believed in the resurrection of the dead.
	(6) The main emphasis of their teaching was ethical rather than theological.
SADDUCEES	
They probably had their beginning during the Hasmonean period (166–63 BC). Their demise occurred c. AD 70 with the fall of Jerusalem and the destruction of the temple.	(1) They considered only the books of Moses to be canonical Scripture, denying that the oral law was authoritative and binding.
	(2) They were very exacting in Levitical purity.
	(3) They attributed everything to free will.
	(4) They argued that there is neither resurrection of the dead nor a future life.
	(5) They rejected the idea of a spiritual world, including belief in angels and demons.
ESSENES	
They probably originated among the Hasidim, along with the Pharisees, from whom they later separated (1 Maccabees 2:42; 7:13). The Hasidim were a group of zealous Jews who took part with the Maccabeans in a revolt against the Syrians c. 165–155 BC. A group of Essenes probably moved to Qumran c. 150 BC, where they copied scrolls and deposited them in nearby caves (see essay, pp. 1574–1576).	(1) They strictly observed the purity laws of the Torah.
	(2) They practiced communal ownership of property.
	(3) They had a strong sense of mutual responsibility.
	(4) Daily worship was an important feature along with daily study of their sacred scriptures.
	(5) Solemn oaths of piety and obedience had to be taken.
	(6) Sacrifices were offered on holy days and during their sacred seasons, but not at the temple, which they considered to be corrupt.
	(7) Marriage was avoided by some but was not condemned in principle.
	(8) They attributed to fate everything that happened.
ZEALOTS	
They originated during the reign of Herod the Great c. 6 BC. A group of Zealots were among the last defenders against the Romans at Masada in AD 73.	(1) They opposed payment of taxes to a pagan emperor because they believed that allegiance was due to God alone.
	(2) They were fiercely loyal to Jewish tradition.
	(3) They endorsed the use of violence as long as it accomplished a good end.
	(4) They were opposed to the influence of Greek pagan culture in the Holy Land.

of people; for you do not enter yourselves, nor do you allow those who are [in the process of] entering to do so. [Luke 11:52]

14 "[Woe to you, scribes and Pharisees, hypocrites, because you swallow up widows' houses, and to cover it up you make long prayers; therefore you will receive the greater condemnation.]

15 "Woe to you, [self-righteous] scribes and Pharisees, hypocrites, because you travel over sea and land to make a single proselyte (convert to Judaism), and when he becomes a convert, you make him twice as much a son of hell as you are.

16 "Woe to you, blind guides, who say, 'Whoever swears [an oath] by the sanctuary of the temple, that is nothing (non-binding); but whoever swears [an oath] by the gold of the temple is obligated [as a debtor to fulfill his vow and keep his promise].'

17 "You fools and blind men! Which is more important, the gold or the sanctuary of the temple that sanctified the gold? [Ex 30:29]

18 "And [you scribes and Pharisees say], 'Whoever swears [an oath] by the altar, that is nothing (non-binding), but whoever swears [an oath] by the offering on it, he is obligated [as a debtor to fulfill his vow and keep his promise].'

19 "You [spiritually] blind men, which is more important, the offering, or the altar that sanctifies the offering?

20 "Therefore, whoever swears [an oath] by the altar, swears both by it and by everything [offered] on it.

21 "And whoever swears [an oath] by the sanctuary of the temple, swears by it and by Him who dwells within it. [1 Kin 8:13; Ps 26:8]

22 "And whoever swears [an oath] by heaven, swears both by the throne of God and by Him who sits upon it.

23 "Woe to you, [self-righteous] scribes and Pharisees, hypocrites! For you give a tenth (tithe) of your mint and dill and cumin [focusing on minor matters], and have neglected the weightier [more important moral and spiritual] provisions of the Law: justice and mercy and faithfulness; but these are the [primary] things you ought to have done without neglecting the others.

24 "You [spiritually] blind guides, who strain out a gnat [consuming yourselves with miniscule matters] and swallow a camel [ignoring and violating God's precepts]! [Lev 11:24; 27:30; Mic 6:8]

25 "Woe to you, [self-righteous] scribes and Pharisees, hypocrites! For you clean the outside of the cup and of the plate, but inside they are full of extortion *and* robbery and self-indulgence (unrestrained greed).

26 "You [spiritually] blind Pharisee, first clean the inside of the cup and of the plate [examine and change your inner self to conform to God's precepts], so that the outside [your public life and deeds] may be clean also.

27 "Woe to you, [self-righteous] scribes and Pharisees, hypocrites! For you are like whitewashed tombs which look beautiful on the outside, but inside are full of dead men's bones and everything unclean.

28 "So you, also, outwardly seem to be just *and* upright to men, but inwardly you are full of hypocrisy and lawlessness. [Ps 5:9]

29 "Woe to you, [self-righteous] scribes and Pharisees, hypocrites! For you build tombs for the prophets and decorate *and* adorn the monuments of the righteous,

---

looking to that person rather than to God, they have created an idol.

23:24 *swallow a camel.* The Pharisees would literally "strain out a gnat" in order not to violate Leviticus 11:41 – 43, but they swallowed "a camel" by neglecting mercy, justice, and faith.

23:25 – 26 *but inside.* The inside of the cup represents a person's character. Sometimes those who most loudly protest the sins of others are secretly guilty of those or worse sins themselves.

14 Mk 12:40; Lk 20:47; 2Ti 3:6; Titus 1:11 **16** ver. 24; Mt 15:14; Mt 5:33,34 **17** Ex 30:29 **19** Ex 29:37 **21** 1Ki 8:13; 2Ch 6:2; Ps 26:8; 132:14 **22** Ps 11:4; Mt 5:34; Ac 7:49 **23** Lk 11:42; 1Sa 15:22; Hos 6:6; Mic 6:8; Mt 9:13; 12:7 **25** Mk 7:4; Lk 11:39 **27** Lk 11:44; Ac 23:3 **29** Lk 11:47

30 and you say, 'If we had been *living*
in the days of our fathers, we would
not have joined them in *shedding* the
blood of the prophets.'
31 "So you testify against yourselves
that you are the descendants of those
who murdered the prophets.
32 "Fill up, then, the [allotted] mea-
sure *of the guilt* of your fathers' *sins*.
33 "You serpents, you spawn of vi-
pers, how can you escape the penalty
of hell?
34 "Therefore, take notice, I am send-
ing you prophets and wise men [in-
terpreters, teachers] and scribes [men
educated in the Mosaic Law and the
writings of the prophets]; some of
them you will kill and *even* crucify,
and some you will flog in your syn-
agogues, and pursue *and* persecute
from city to city,
35 so that on you will come *the guilt*
of all the blood of the righteous shed
on earth, from the blood of righteous
Abel to the blood of Zechariah [the
priest], the son of Berechiah, whom
you murdered between the temple
and the altar. [Gen 4:8; 2 Chr 24:21;
Luke 11:51]
36 "I assure you *and* most solemn-
ly say to you, [the judgment for] all
these things [these vile and murderous
deeds] will come on this generation.
[2 Chr 36:15, 16]

Lament over Jerusalem

37 "O Jerusalem, Jerusalem, who
murders the prophets and stones [to
death] those [messengers] who are sent
to her [by God]! How often I wanted to
gather your children together [around
Me], as a hen gathers her chicks under
her wings, and you were unwilling.
[Luke 13:34, 35]
38 "Listen carefully: your house is
being left to you desolate [completely
abandoned by God and destitute of
His protection]! [1 Kin 9:6, 7; Jer 22:5]
39 "For I say to you, you will not see
Me again [ministering to you publicly]
until you say, 'Blessed [to be celebrat-
ed with praise] is He who comes in the
name of the Lord!' " [Ps 118:26]

Signs of Christ's Return

24 JESUS LEFT the temple *area*
and was going on His way
when His disciples came up to Him to
call His attention to the [magnificent
and massive] buildings of the temple.
[Mark 13; Luke 21:5–36]
2 And He said to them, "Do you see
all these things? I assure you *and* most
solemnly say to you, not one stone here
will be left on another, which will not
be torn down."
3 While Jesus was seated on the
Mount of Olives, the disciples came to
Him privately, and said, "Tell us, when
will this [destruction of the temple]
take place, and what will be the sign
of Your coming, and of the end (com-
pletion, consummation) of the age?"
4 Jesus answered, "Be careful that no
one misleads you [deceiving you and
leading you into error].
5 "For many will come in My name
[misusing it, and appropriating the

23:35 *Abel.* Abel was the first person murdered in the Old Testament (Ge 4:8); Zechariah is the last. His death is recorded in 2 Chronicles 24:20–22, the last book of the Hebrew canon.

24:1 *temple.* The first temple, built by Solomon, was destroyed by the Babylonians in 586 BC. The second temple, built under the encouragement of Haggai and Zechariah, and the leadership of Zerubbabel and Joshua (Hag 1:1), was completed after considerable delay in 516 BC. This second temple was lavishly restored by Herod the Great, but not completed until AD 64. It stood completed for only six years, before it was reduced to rubble by the Romans. The devastation in AD 70 was so complete that the precise location is still unknown today.

24:4 *Be careful that no one misleads you.* Jesus' warning about being deceived was especially appropriate for the disciples. The destruction of Jerusalem did not necessarily mean the nearness of the end of the age. This principle was a point of confusion for them (Lk 19:11–27; Ac 1:6–7).

---

31 Ac 7:51,52; 1Th 2:15 **32** Ge 15:16; 1Th 2:16 **33** Mt 3:7; 12:34 **34** Mt 21:34,35; Lk 11:49; Ac 5:40; 7:58,59; 22:19; Mt 10:17; 2Co 11:24,25 **35** Rev 18:24; Ge 4:8; 1Jn 3:12; 2Ch 24:20,21 **37** Lk 13:34; 2Ch 24:21; Dt 32:11,12; Ps 17:8; 91:4 **39** Ps 118:26; Mt 21:9 **CHAPTER 24** **1** Mk 13:1; Lk 21:5 **2** 1Ki 9:7; Jer 26:18; Mic 3:12; Lk 19:44 **3** Mk 13:3; 1Th 5:1 **4** Eph 5:6; Col 2:8,18; 2Th 2:3; 1Jn 4:1 **5** ver. 24; Jer 14:14; 23:21,25; Jn 5:43; ver. 11

strength of the name which belongs
to Me], saying, ‘I am the Christ (the
Messiah, the Anointed),’ and they will
mislead many.
6“You will *continually* hear of wars
and rumors of wars. See that you are
not frightened, for *those things* must
take place, but that is not yet the end
[of the age].
7“For nation will rise against nation,
and kingdom against kingdom, and
there will be famines and earthquakes
in various places.
8“But all these things are *merely*
the beginning of birth pangs [of the
intolerable anguish and the time of
unprecedented trouble].
9“Then they will hand you over to
[endure] tribulation, and will put you
to death, and you will be hated by all
nations because of My name.
10“At that time many will be offend-
ed *and* repelled [by their association
with Me] *and* will fall away [from the
One whom they should trust] and will
betray one another [handing over be-
lievers to their persecutors] and will
hate one another.
11“Many false prophets will appear
and mislead many.
12“Because lawlessness is increased,
the love of most people will grow cold.
13“But the one who endures *and*
bears up [under suffering] to the end
will be saved.
14“This good news of the kingdom
[the gospel] will be preached through-
out the whole world as a testimony to
all the nations, and then the end [of the
age] will come.

Perilous Times

15“So when you see the ABOMINATION
OF DESOLATION [the appalling sacrilege
that astonishes and makes desolate],
spoken of by the prophet Daniel,
standing in the Holy Place (let the
reader understand), [Dan 9:27; 11:31;
12:11]
16then let those who are in Judea flee
to the mountains [for refuge].
17“Whoever is on the housetop must
not go down to get the things that are
in his house [because there will not be
enough time].
18“Whoever is in the field must not
turn back to get his coat.
19“And woe to those who are preg-
nant and to those who are nursing
babies in those days!

24:6 *must take place.* This indicates a divine or logical necessity. Such things will happen because of the people’s sin. False messiahs had existed before (Ac 5:36 – 38) and false preachers would come in the future (Ac 20:29; 2Co 11:13 – 15). Verses 4 – 6 may describe the first part of Daniel’s seventieth week (Da 9:25 – 27), but possibly they present a general picture of the present age.

24:7 *famines and earthquakes.* These disasters are more fully described in Revelation 6:1 – 8; 8:5 – 23; 9:13 – 21; 16:2 – 21).

24:10 Apostasy — Satan is a subtle adversary who works as an angel of light through false religious teachers (2Co 11:14 – 15), and many will be misled. Apostasy is also the result of persecution. Jesus speaks of “temporary” faith, and says that a falling away often occurs when “pressure or persecution comes because of the word” (13:21). Perseverance in faith and in the accompanying results of faith are positive evidence of a genuine Christian profession.

24:15 *ABOMINATION OF DESOLATION.* The abomination of desolation literally means “the abomination that makes desolate.” This prophecy comes from Daniel, specifically Daniel 9:27; 11:31; 12:11. Many believe that Daniel 11:31 refers to Antiochus IV, who desecrated the temple by sacrificing a pig on its altar and setting up an idol to Zeus in it. His actions were certainly a prelude to what the ultimate “man of sin” will do. In AD 70, Titus destroyed Jerusalem, burned the temple, and set up an idol to mock the Jews. Significantly, Paul speaks of the Antichrist at the end times also setting himself up as god (2Th 2:3 – 4; Rev 13:14 – 15).

24:16 *flee.* At the time of the war ending in the destruction of the temple in AD 70, many of the Christians did flee, hiding in the clefts of Petra. Some believe that the final fulfillment of this prophecy will occur in the future desecration of the temple (Da 9:27) and the subsequent setting up of an image of the “man of sin” in the most holy place.

7 2Ch 15:6; Isa 19:2; Hag 2:22; Zec 14:13 **9** Mt 10:17; Lk 21:12; Jn 16:2; Ac 4:2,3 **10** 2Ti 1:15; 4:10,16 **11** Ac 20:29; 2Pe 2:1; 1Ti 4:1 **13** Mt 10:22; Mk 13:13; Rev 2:10 **14** Mt 4:23; Ro 10:18; Col 1:6,23 **15** Mk 13:14; Lk 21:20; Da 9:27; 12:11; Da 9:23 **19** Lk 23:29

[20]"Pray that your flight [from persecution and suffering] will not be in winter, or on a Sabbath [when Jewish laws prohibit travel].
[21]"For at that time there will be a great tribulation (pressure, distress, oppression), such as has not occurred since the beginning of the world until now, nor ever will [again]. [Dan 12:1; Joel 2:2]
[22]"And if those days [of tribulation] had not been cut short, no human life would be saved; but for the sake of the elect (God's chosen ones) those days will be shortened.
[23]"Then if anyone says to you [during the great tribulation], 'Look! Here is the Christ,' or 'There *He is*,' do not believe *it*.
[24]"For false Christs and false prophets will appear and they will provide great signs and wonders, so as to deceive, if possible, even the elect (God's chosen ones).
[25]"Listen carefully, I have told you in advance.
[26]"So if they say to you, 'Look! He is in the wilderness,' do not go out there, or, 'Look! He is in the inner rooms [of a house],' do not believe it.
[27]"For just as the lightning comes from the east and flashes as far as the west, so will be the coming [in glory] of the Son of Man [everyone will see Him clearly].
[28]"Wherever the corpse is, there the vultures will flock together. [Job 39:30]

The Glorious Return

[29]"Immediately after the tribulation of those days THE SUN WILL BE DARKENED, AND THE MOON WILL NOT PROVIDE ITS LIGHT, AND THE STARS WILL FALL from the sky, and the powers of the heavens will be shaken. [Is 13:10; 34:4; Joel 2:10, 11; Zeph 1:15]
[30]"And at that time the sign of the Son of Man [coming in His glory] will appear in the sky, and then all the tribes of the earth [and especially Israel] will mourn [regretting their rebellion and rejection of the Messiah], and they will see the SON OF MAN COMING ON THE CLOUDS OF HEAVEN with power and great glory [in brilliance and splendor]. [Dan 7:13; Rev 1:7]
[31]"And He will send His angels with A LOUD TRUMPET and THEY WILL GATHER TOGETHER His elect (God's chosen ones) from the four winds, from one end of the heavens to the other. [Is 27:13; Zech 9:14]

Parable of the Fig Tree

[32]"Now learn this lesson from the fig tree: As soon as its young shoots become tender and it puts out its leaves, you know that summer is near; [Mark 13:28, 29; Luke 21:29–31]
[33]so you, too, when you see all these things [taking place], know for certain that He is near, right at the door.
[34]"I assure you *and* most solemnly say to you, this generation [the people living when these signs and events begin] will not pass away until all these things take place.
[35]"Heaven and earth [as now known] will pass away, but My words will not pass away.
[36]"But of that [exact] day and hour no one knows, not even the angels of

---

24:24 *signs and wonders.* Miracles by themselves do not prove that something is of God (7:21–23; 2Th 2:9; Rev 13:13–15). The teaching of those who perform signs and wonders must be tested against correct doctrine (Dt 13:1–5; 1Jn 4:1–3), and by the witness of God's Spirit (Jn 10:3–5,27).

24:29 *Immediately after.* This verse moves chronologically to the close of the tribulation, a period that will be marked by monumental cosmic disturbances (Isa 13:10; 34:4; Eze 32:7–8; Joel 2:30–31; 3:15; Hag 2:6; Zec 14:6; Rev 6:12–14).

24:34 *this generation.* "Generation" may mean "race," indicating that Israel as a people will not cease to exist before God fulfills His promises to them. Another possibility is that the word describes a particular era in which people will see the end times. That is, the events will occur so rapidly that all will happen within one generation. Perhaps both interpretations are true.

24:36 *that [exact] day and hour no one knows.* Mark 13:32 indicates that even Jesus

21 Da 9:26; Joel 2:2 **22** Isa 65:8,9; Zec 14:2 **23** Mk 13:21; Lk 17:23; 21:8 **24** Dt 13:1; 2Th 2:9; Rev 13:13; Jn 6:37; 10:28,29; Ro 8:28; 2Ti 2:19 **27** Lk 17:24 **28** Job 39:30; Lk 17:37 **29** Da 7:11; Eze 32:7; Joel 2:10; Am 8:9; Mk 13:24; Ac 2:20 **30** Da 7:13; Zec 12:12; Mk 13:26; Rev 1:7 **31** 1Co 15:52; 1Th 4:16 **32** Lk 21:29 **33** Jas 5:9 **34** Mt 16:28; Mk 13:30; Lk 21:32 **35** Ps 102:26; Isa 51:6; Jer 31:35; Mk 13:31; Lk 21:33 **36** Mk 13:32; Ac 1:7; 1Th 5:2; 2Pe 3:10; Zec 14:7

heaven, nor the Son [in His humanity],
but the Father alone.
37 “For the coming of the Son of Man
(the Messiah) will be just like the days
of Noah.
38 “For as in those days before the
flood they were eating and drinking,
marrying and giving in marriage, un-
til the [very] day when Noah entered
the ark,
39 and they did not know *or* under-
stand until the flood came and swept
them all away; so will the coming of
the Son of Man be [unexpected judg-
ment]. [Gen 6:5–8; 7:6–24]
40 “At that time two men will be in the
field; one will be taken [for judgment]
and one will be left.
41 “Two women *will be* grinding at the
mill; one will be taken [for judgment]
and one will be left.

Be Ready for His Coming

42 “So be alert [give strict attention,
be cautious and active in faith], for you
do not know which day [whether near
or far] your Lord is coming.
43 “But understand this: If the head of
the house had known what time of the
night the thief was coming, he would
have been on the alert and would not
have allowed his house to be broken
into. [Luke 12:39, 40]
44 “Therefore, you [who follow Me]
must also be ready; because the Son
of Man is coming at an hour when you
do not expect Him.
45 “Who then is the faithful and wise
servant whom his master has put in
charge of his household to give the oth-
ers [in the house] their food *and* supplies
at the proper time? [Luke 12:42–46]
46 “Blessed is that [faithful] servant
when his master returns and finds
him doing so.
47 “I assure you *and* most solemn-
ly say to you that he will put him in
charge of all his possessions.
48 “But if that servant is evil and says
in his heart, ‘My master is taking his
time [he will not return for a long
while],’
49 and begins to beat his fellow ser-
vants and to eat and drink with drunk-
ards;
50 the master of that servant will
come on a day when he does not ex-
pect him and at an hour of which he
is not aware,
51 and will cut him in two and put
him with the hypocrites; in that place
there will be weeping [over sorrow
and pain] and grinding of teeth [over
distress and anger].

Parable of Ten Virgins

25 “THEN THE kingdom of heav-
en will be like ten virgins, who
took their lamps and went to meet the
bridegroom.
2 “Five of them were foolish [thought-
less, silly, and careless], and five were
wise [far-sighted, practical, and sen-
sible].
3 “For when the foolish took their
lamps, they did not take any [extra]
oil with them,
4 but the wise took flasks of oil along
with their lamps.
5 “Now while the bridegroom was
delayed, they all began to nod off, and
they fell asleep.
6 “But at midnight there was a shout,
‘Look! The bridegroom [is coming]! Go
out to meet *him.*’
7 “Then all those virgins got up and
put their own lamps in order [trimmed
the wicks and added oil and lit them].
8 “But the foolish *virgins* said to the
wise, ‘Give us some of your oil, because
our lamps are going out.’
9 “But the wise replied, ‘No, other-
wise there will not be enough for us
and for you, *too;* go instead to the deal-
ers and buy *oil* for yourselves.’

Himself did not know the exact time of His return. When the Lord Jesus was on earth, He voluntarily limited His use of His divine attributes (Jn 17:4 – 5; Php 2:5 – 8). Therefore He became hungry, thirsty, and tired. In this instance, Jesus surrendered the use of His divine omniscience.

38 Ge 6:3-5; Lk 17:26; 1Pe 3:20 **40** Lk 17:34 **42** Mt 25:13; Lk 21:36 **43** Lk 12:39; 1Th 5:2; Rev 3:3 **44** 1Th 5:6 **45** Lk 12:42; Ac 20:28 **46** Rev 16:15 **47** Mt 25:21,23; Lk 22:29 **51** Mt 8:12; 25:30 **CHAPTER 25** **1** Eph 5:29,30; Rev 19:7; 21:2,9 **2** Mt 13:47; 22:10 **5** 1Th 5:6 **6** Mt 24:31; 1Th 4:16 **7** Lk 12:35

10 “But while they were going away to buy *oil,* the bridegroom came, and those who were ready went in with him to the wedding feast; and the door was shut *and* locked.

11 “Later the others also came, and said, ‘Lord, Lord, open [the door] for us.’

12 “But He replied, ‘I assure you *and* most solemnly say to you, I do not know you [we have no relationship].’

13 “Therefore, be on the alert [be prepared and ready], for you do not know the day nor the hour [when the Son of Man will come].

Parable of the Talents

14 “For it is just like a man who was *about* to take a journey, and he called his servants together and entrusted them with his possessions. [Luke 19:12–27]

15 “To one he gave five talents, to another, two, and to another, one, each according to his own ability; and then he went on his journey.

16 “The one who had received the five talents went at once and traded with them, and he [made a profit and] gained five more.

17 “Likewise the one who had two [made a profit and] gained two more.

18 “But the one who had received the one went and dug *a hole* in the ground and hid his master’s money.

19 “Now after a long time the master of those servants returned and settled accounts with them.

20 “And the one who had received the five talents came and brought him five more, saying, ‘Master, you entrusted to me five talents. See, I have [made a profit and] gained five more talents.’

21 “His master said to him, ‘Well done, good and faithful servant. You have been faithful *and* trustworthy over a little, I will put you in charge of many things; share in the joy of your master.’

22 “Also the one who had the two talents came forward, saying, ‘Master, you entrusted two talents to me. See, I have [made a profit and] gained two more talents.’

23 “His master said to him, ‘Well done, good and faithful servant. You have been faithful *and* trustworthy over a little, I will put you in charge of many things; share in the joy of your master.’

24 “The one who had received one talent also came forward, saying, ‘Master, I knew you to be a harsh *and* demanding man, reaping [the harvest] where you did not sow and gathering where you did not scatter *seed.*

25 ‘So I was afraid [to lose the talent], and I went and hid your talent in the ground. See, you have what is your own.’

26 “But his master answered him, ‘You wicked, lazy servant, you knew that I reap [the harvest] where I did not sow and gather where I did not scatter *seed.*

27 ‘Then you ought to have put my money with the bankers, and at my return I would have received my *money* back with interest.

28 ‘So take the talent away from him, and give it to the one who has the ten talents.’

29 “For to everyone who has [and values his blessings and gifts from God, and has used them wisely], more will be given, and [he will be richly supplied so that] he will have an abundance; but from the one who does not have [because he has ignored or disregarded his blessings and gifts from God], even what he does have will be taken away. [Matt 13:12; Luke 19:26]

25:10 *the bridegroom came.* Christ’s return is often compared to a wedding (22:1 – 14; Rev 19:7 – 8).

25:14 *entrusted them with his possessions.* The parable of the talents illustrates the faith required of God’s servants.

25:15 *talents.* A talent was a large sum of money, about six thousand denarii.

25:23 *I will put you in charge of many things.* The first two servants received the same reward, based on their faithfulness, not on the size of their responsibilities. The smallest task in

10 Lk 13:25 **11** Mt 7:21-23 **12** Ps 5:5; Hab 1:13; Jn 9:31 **13** Mt 24:42,44; Mk 13:33,35; Lk 21:36 **14** Lk 19:12; Mt 21:33 **15** Ro 12:6; 1Co 12:7,11,29; Eph 4:11 **21** ver. 34,46; Mt 24:47; Lk 12:44; 22:29,30; 2Ti 2:12; Heb 12:2; 1Pe 1:8 **23** ver. 21 **29** Mt 13:12; Mk 4:25; Lk 8:18; 19:26; Jn 15:2

THE LIFE OF CHRIST

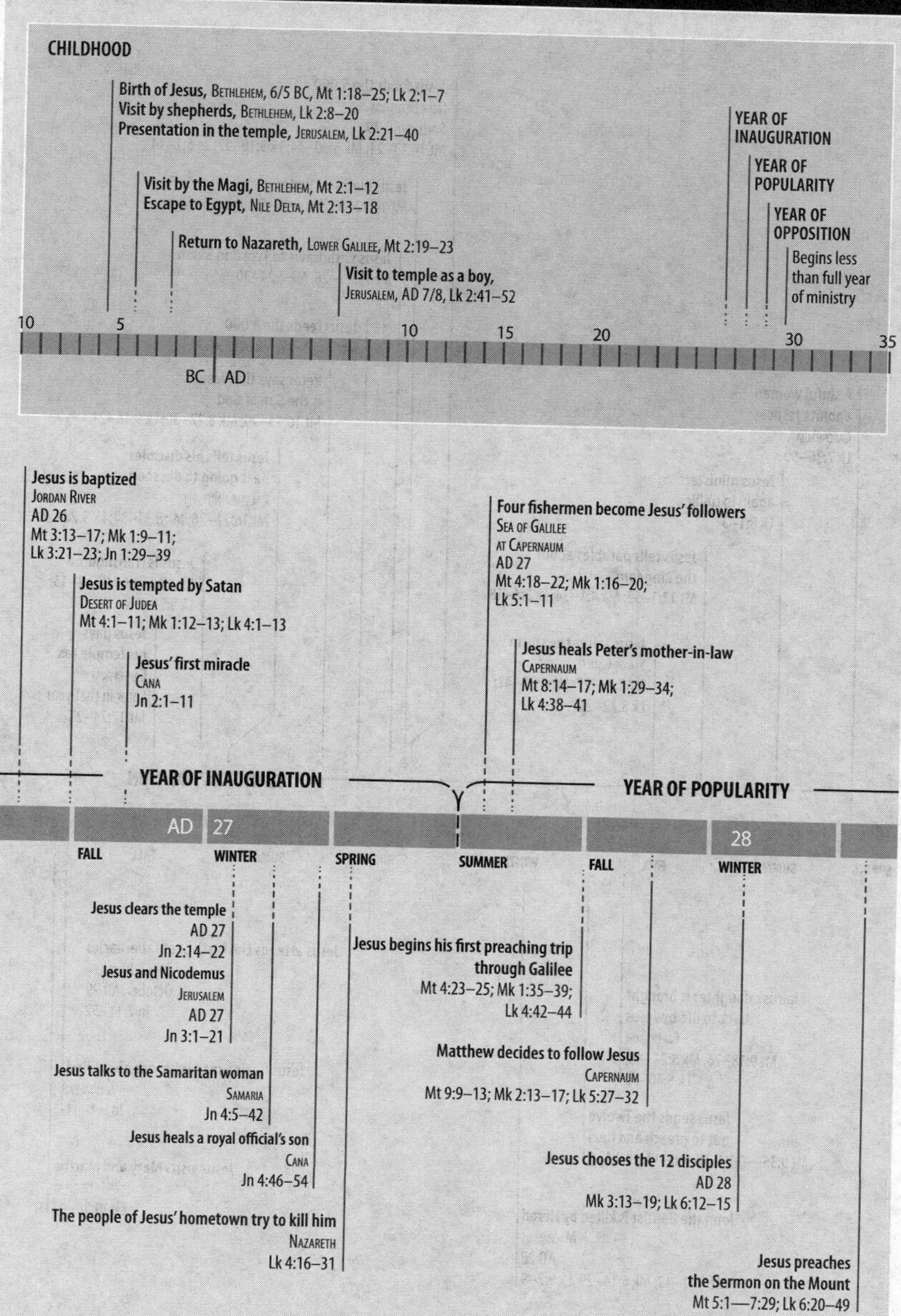

Dotted lines leading to the timeline are meant to define sequence of events only. All dates are approximate.

THE LIFE OF CHRIST CONT.

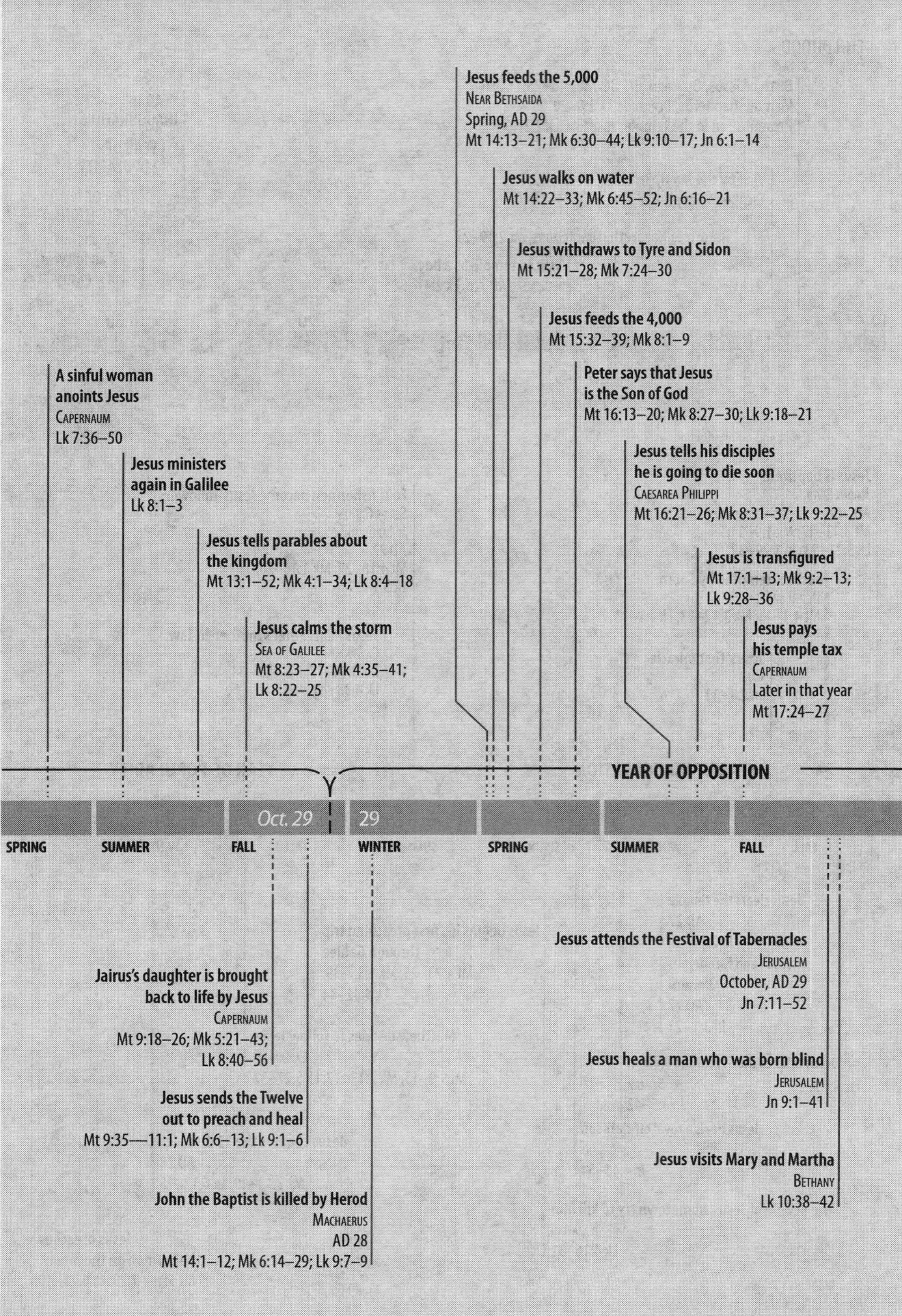

The most likely dates for Jesus' public ministry are AD 27–30; the next most likely option, however, is 30–33.

THE LIFE OF CHRIST CONT.

Jesus begins his last trip to Jerusalem
AD 30
Lk 17:11

Jesus blesses the little children
Across the Jordan
Mt 19:13–15; Mk 10:13–16; Lk 18:15–17

Jesus talks to the rich young man
Across the Jordan
Mt 19:16–30; Mk 10:17–31; Lk 18:18–30

Jesus again predicts his death and resurrection
Near the Jordan
Mt 20:17–19; Mk 10:32–34; Lk 18:31–34

Jesus heals blind Bartimaeus
Jericho
Mt 20:29–34; Mk 10:46–52; Lk 18:35–43

Jesus talks to Zacchaeus
Jericho
Lk 19:1–10

Jesus returns to Bethany to visit Mary and Martha
Bethany
Jn 11:55—12:1

THE LAST WEEK

The "Triumphal" Entry, Jerusalem, Sunday
Mt 21:1–11; Mk 11:1–10; Lk 19:29–44; Jn 12:12–19

Jesus curses the fig tree, Monday
Mt 21:18–19; Mk 11:12–14

Jesus clears the temple, Monday
Mt 21:12–13; Mk 11:15–18

The authority of Jesus questioned, Tuesday
Mt 21:23–27; Mk 11:27–33; Lk 20:1–8

Jesus teaches in the temple, Tuesday
Mt 21:28—23:39; Mk 12:1–44; Lk 20:9—21:4

Jesus anointed, Bethany, Tuesday
Mt 26:6–13; Mk 14:3–9; Jn 12:2–11

The plot against Jesus, Wednesday
Mt 26:14–16; Mk 14:10–11; Lk 22:3–6

The Last Supper, Thursday
Mt 26:17–29; Mk 14:12–25; Lk 22:7–20; Jn 13:1–38

Jesus comforts the disciples, Thursday
Jn 14:1—16:33

Gethsemane, Thursday
Mt 26:36–46; Mk 14:32–42; Lk 22:40–46

Jesus' arrest and trial, Thursday night and Friday
Mt 26:47—27:26; Mk 14:43—15:15; Lk 22:47—23:25; Jn 18:2—19:16

Jesus' crucifixion and death, Golgotha, Friday
Mt 27:27–56; Mk 15:16–41; Lk 23:26–49; Jn 19:17–30

The burial of Jesus, Joseph's Tomb, Friday
Mt 27:57–66; Mk 15:42–47; Lk 23:50–56; Jn 19:31–42

30 WINTER SPRING SUMMER FALL 31 WINTER SPRING SUMMER

AFTER THE RESURRECTION

The empty tomb, Jerusalem, Sunday
Mt 28:1–10; Mk 16:1–8; Lk 24:1–12; Jn 20:1–10

Mary Magdalene sees Jesus in the garden
Jerusalem, Sunday
Mt 16:9–11; Jn 20:11–18

Jesus appears to the two going to Emmaus
Sunday
Mk 16:12–13; Lk 24:13–35

Jesus appears to 10 disciples
Jerusalem, Sunday
Mk 16:14; Lk 24:36–43; Jn 20:19–25

Jesus appears to the 11 disciples
Jerusalem, One week later
Jn 20:26–31

Jesus talks with some of his disciples
Sea of Galilee, One week later
Jn 21:1–25

Jesus ascends to his Father in heaven
Mount of Olives, 40 days later
Mt 28:16–20; Mk 16:19–20; Lk 24:44–53

Jesus raises Lazarus from the dead
Bethany
Winter, AD 30
Jn 11:1–44

30 "And throw out the worthless ser-
vant into the outer darkness; in that
place [of grief and torment] there will
be weeping [over sorrow and pain]
and grinding of teeth [over distress
and anger].

The Judgment

31 "But when the Son of Man comes
in His glory *and* majesty and all the
angels with Him, then He will sit on
the throne of His glory. [Rev 20:4–6]
32 "All the nations will be gathered
before Him [for judgment]; and He will
separate them from one another, as a
shepherd separates his sheep from the
goats; [Ezek 34:17]
33 and He will put the sheep on His
right [the place of honor], and the goats
on His left [the place of rejection].
34 "Then the King will say to those on
His right, 'Come, you blessed of My Fa-
ther [you favored of God, appointed to
eternal salvation], inherit the kingdom
prepared for you from the foundation
of the world.
35 'For I was hungry, and you gave Me
something to eat; I was thirsty, and you
gave Me *something* to drink; I was a
stranger, and you invited Me in;
36 *I was* naked, and you clothed Me;
I was sick, and you visited Me [with
help and ministering care]; I was in
prison, and you came to Me [ignoring
personal danger].' [Is 58:7]
37 "Then the righteous will answer
Him, 'Lord, when did we see You hun-
gry, and feed You, or thirsty, and give
You something to drink?
38 'And when did we see You as a
stranger, and invite You in, or naked,
and clothe You?
39 'And when did we see You sick, or
in prison, and come to You?'
40 "The King will answer and say to
them, 'I assure you *and* most solemnly
say to you, to the extent that you did
it for one of these brothers of Mine,
even the least *of them*, you did it for
Me.' [Prov 19:17]
41 "Then He will say to those on His
left, 'Leave Me, you cursed ones, into the
eternal fire which has been prepared
for the devil and his angels (demons);
42 for I was hungry, and you gave Me
nothing to eat; I was thirsty, and you
gave Me nothing to drink;
43 I was a stranger, and you did not
invite Me in; naked, and you did not
clothe Me; sick, and in prison, and
you did not visit Me [with help and
ministering care].'
44 "Then they also [in their turn] will
answer, 'Lord, when did we see You
hungry, or thirsty, or as a stranger, or
naked, or sick, or in prison, and did
not minister to You?'
45 "Then He will reply to them, 'I as-
sure you *and* most solemnly say to you,
to the extent that you did not do it for one
of the least of these [my followers], you
did not do it for Me.' [Prov 14:31; 17:5]
46 "Then these [unbelieving people]
will go away into eternal (unending)
punishment, but those who are righ-
teous *and* in right standing with God
[will go, by His remarkable grace] into
eternal (unending) life." [Dan 12:2]

The Plot to Kill Jesus

26 WHEN JESUS had finished this
discourse, He said to His disciples,
2 "You know that the Passover is
coming in two days, and the Son of
Man is to be betrayed *and* handed
over for crucifixion." [Mark 14:1, 2;
Luke 22:1, 2]

God's work may receive a great reward if we are faithful in performing it (10:42).

25:32 – 40 Judgment — The final judgment will be according to the evidence, not according to what was professed but what was practiced. It will be not according to what was said, but what was done. These works cannot earn salvation, but they are works of love which reflect a life redeemed by the saving work of Christ through the Holy Spirit (Gal 5:6). Love for God is demonstrated by love for man (1Jn 4:20).

30 Mt 8:12; 24:51 **31** Zec 14:5; Mt 16:27; 19:28; Mk 8:38; Ac 1:11; 1Th 4:16; 2Th 1:7; Jude 14; Rev 1:7 **32** Ro 14:10; 2Co 5:10; Rev 20:12; Eze 20:38 **34** Ro 8:17; 1Pe 1:4,9; 3:9; Rev 21:7; Mt 20:23; Mk 10:40; 1Co 2:9; Heb 11:16 **35** Isa 58:7; Eze 18:7; Jas 1:27; Heb 13:2; 3Jn 5 **36** Jas 2:15,16; 2Ti 1:16 **40** Pr 14:31; 19:17; Mt 10:42; Mk 9:41; Heb 6:10 **41** Ps 6:8; Mt 7:23; Lk 13:27; Mt 13:40,42; 2Pe 2:4; Jude 6 **45** Pr 14:31; 17:5; Zec 2:8; Ac 9:5 **46** Dan 12:2; Jn 5:29; Ro 2:7 **CHAPTER 26** **2** Mk 14:1; Lk 22:1; Jn 13:1

3 Then the chief priests and the elders
of the people gathered in the courtyard
of the [elegant home of the Jewish] high
priest, whose name was Caiaphas,
4 and plotted together to arrest Jesus
by stealth and kill Him.
5 But they said, "It must not be during
the festival (Passover), otherwise there
might be a riot among the people."

The Anointing in Bethany

6 Now when Jesus was [back] in
Bethany, at the home of Simon the
leper, [Mark 14:3–9; John 12:1–8]
7 a woman came to Him with an ala-
baster vial of very expensive perfume
and she poured it on Jesus' head as He
reclined *at the table.*
8 But when the disciples saw it they
were indignant *and* angry, saying,
"Why all this waste [of money]?
9 "For this *perfume* might have been
sold at a high price and *the money*
given to the poor."
10 But Jesus, aware [of the malice] of
this [remark], said to them, "Why are
you bothering the woman? She has
done a good thing to Me.
11 "For you always have the poor with
you; but you will not always have Me.
[Deut 15:11; Mark 14:7]
12 "When she poured this perfume
on My body, she did it to prepare Me
for burial.
13 "I assure you *and* most solemnly
say to you, wherever this gospel [of
salvation] is preached in the whole
world, what this woman has done will
also be told in memory of her [for her
act of love and devotion]."

Judas' Bargain

14 Then one of the twelve [disciples],
who was called Judas Iscariot, went to
the chief priests
15 and said, "What are you willing to
give me if I hand Jesus over to you?"
And they weighed out thirty pieces of
silver. [Ex 21:32; Zech 11:12]
16 And from that moment Judas *be-
gan* looking for an opportune time
to betray Jesus. [Mark 14:10, 11;
Luke 22:3–6; John 6:71]
17 Now on the first day of Unleavened
Bread (Passover Week) the disciples
came to Jesus and asked, "Where
do You want us to prepare for You
to eat the Passover?" [Mark 14:12–16;
Luke 22:7–13]
18 He said, "Go into the city to a cer-
tain man, and say to him, 'The Teacher
says, "My time [to suffer and atone for
sin] is near; I *am to* keep the Passover
at your house with My disciples." ' "
19 [Accordingly] the disciples did as
Jesus had directed them, and they pre-
pared the Passover. [Deut 16:5–8]

The Last Passover

20 When evening came, Jesus was
reclining *at the table* with the twelve
disciples. [Mark 14:17–21]
21 And as they were eating, He said,
"I assure you *and* most solemnly say
to you that one of you will betray Me."
22 Being deeply grieved *and* extreme-
ly distressed, each one of them began
to say to Him, "Surely not I, Lord?"
23 Jesus answered, "He who has
dipped his hand in the bowl with Me
[as a pretense of friendship] will be-
tray Me.
24 "The Son of Man is to go [to the
cross], just as it is written [in Scripture]
of Him; but woe (judgment is coming)
to that man by whom the Son of Man is
betrayed! It would have been good for
that man if he had never been born."
[Ps 41:9]
25 And Judas, the betrayer, said,

26:14 ***one of the twelve.*** The enormity of Judas' sin is seen in these words: Jesus was betrayed by one of His own best friends.
26:15 ***thirty pieces of silver.*** Thirty pieces of silver was the price of a slave (Ex 21:32). Zechariah prophesied this sum (Zec 11:12 – 13).
26:21 ***one of you will betray Me.*** This statement indicates the Lord's omniscience. Repeatedly, Christ unveiled evidence of His deity to His disciples.

3 Ps 2:2; Jn 11:47; Ac 4:25 **6** Mk 14:3; Jn 11:1,2; 12:3; Mt 21:17 **8** Jn 12:4 **11** Dt 15:11; Jn 12:8; See Mt 18:20; 28:20; Jn 13:33; 14:19; 16:5,28; 17:11 **14** Mk 14:10; Lk 22:3; Jn 13:2,30; Mt 10:4 **15** Zec 11:12; Mt 27:3 **17** Ex 12:6,18; Mk 14:12; Lk 22:7 **20** Mk 14:17-21; Lk 22:14; Jn 13:21 **23** Ps 41:9; Lk 22:21; Jn 13:18 **24** Ps 22; Isa 53; Da 9:26; Mk 9:12; Lk 24:25,26,46; Ac 17:2,3; 26:22,23; 1Co 15:3; Jn 17:12

"Surely it is not I, Rabbi?" Jesus said to him, "You have said it yourself."

The Lord's Supper Instituted

26 Now as they were eating Jesus took bread, and after blessing it, He broke it and gave it to the disciples, and said, "Take, eat; this is My body." [Mark 14:22–25; Luke 22:17–20; 1 Cor 11:23–25]

27 And when He had taken a cup and given thanks, He gave it to them, saying, "Drink from it, all of you;

28 for this is My blood of the [new and better] covenant, which [ratifies the agreement and] is being poured out for many [as a substitutionary atonement] for the forgiveness of sins. [Ex 24:6–8]

29 "But I say to you, I will not drink of this fruit of the vine from now on until that day when I drink it new with you in My Father's kingdom."

30 After singing a hymn, they went out to the Mount of Olives.

31 Then Jesus said to them, "You will all fall away because of Me this night [disillusioned about Me, confused, and some even ashamed of Me], for it is written [in the Scriptures], 'I WILL STRIKE THE SHEPHERD, AND THE SHEEP OF THE FLOCK WILL BE SCATTERED.' [Zech 13:7]

32 "But after I am raised [to life], I will go ahead of you [leading the way] to Galilee."

33 Peter replied to Him, "Though they all fall away because of You [and doubt and disown You], I will never fall away!" [Mark 14:29–31; Luke 22:33, 34; John 13:37, 38]

34 Jesus said to him, "I assure you *and* most solemnly say to you, this night, before a rooster crows, you will [completely] deny Me three times."

35 Peter said to Jesus, "Even if I have to die with You, I will not deny You!" And all the disciples said the same thing.

The Garden of Gethsemane

36 Then Jesus came with them to a place called Gethsemane (olive-press), and He told His disciples, "Sit here while I go over there and pray." [Mark 14:32–42; Luke 22:40–46]

37 And taking with Him Peter and the two sons of Zebedee [James and John], He began to be grieved and greatly distressed.

38 Then He said to them, "My soul is deeply grieved, so that I am almost dying *of sorrow*. Stay here and stay awake *and* keep watch with Me."

39 And after going a little farther, He fell face down and prayed, saying, "My Father, if it is possible [that is, consistent with Your will], let this cup pass from Me; yet not as I will, but as You will."

40 And He came to the disciples and found them sleeping, and said to Peter, "So, you *men* could not stay awake *and* keep watch with Me for one hour?

41 "Keep *actively* watching and praying that you may not come into temptation; the spirit is willing, but the body is weak."

42 He went away a second time and prayed, saying, "My Father, if this cannot pass away unless I drink it, Your will be done."

26:26–28 *My body . . . My blood.* The Lord Jesus, at this last meal with His disciples before He went to the cross, instituted this ordinance for His church throughout this age. It is called "the Lord's Supper" (1Co 11:20). Using common everyday items, the bread and wine that could be found on any table, no matter how poor, He gave us a "remembrance" so that we would never forget that His broken body and shed blood bought salvation for us.

26:28 *My blood of the [new and better] covenant.* This refers to the new covenant promised in the Old Testament (Jer 31:31–34; 32:37–44; Eze 34:25–31; 37:26–28).

26:36 *Gethsemane.* The name "Gethsemane" means "oil press." This garden was east of Jerusalem on the Mount of Olives. In the place where olives were crushed and ground, the Anointed One was crushed.

26 Mk 14:22; Lk 22:19; 1Co 11:23; 1Co 10:16 **27** Mk 14:23 **28** See Ex 24:8; Lev 17:11; Jer 31:31; Mt 20:28; Ro 5:15; Heb 9:22 **29** Mk 14:25; Lk 22:18; Ac 10:41 **30** Mk 14:26 **31** Mk 14:27; Jn 16:32; Mt 11:6; Zec 13:7 **32** Mt 28:7,10; Mk 14:28; 16:7 **34** Mk 14:30; Lk 22:34; Jn 13:38 **36** Mk 14:32-35; Lk 22:39; Jn 18:1 **37** Mt 4:21 **38** Jn 12:27 **39** Mk 14:36; Lk 22:42; Heb 5:7; Jn 12:27; Mt 20:22; Jn 5:30; 6:38; Php 2:8 **41** Mk 13:33; 14:38; Lk 22:40,46; Eph 6:18

43 Again He came and found them sleeping, for their eyes were heavy.

44 So, leaving them again, He went away and prayed for the third time, saying the same words once more.

45 Then He returned to the disciples and said to them, "Are you still sleeping and resting? Listen, the hour [of My sacrifice] is at hand and the Son of Man is being betrayed into the hands of sinners [whose way and nature is to oppose God].

46 "Get up, let us go. Look, My betrayer is near!"

Jesus' Betrayal and Arrest

47 As Jesus was still speaking, Judas [Iscariot], one of the twelve [disciples], came up accompanied by a large crowd with swords and clubs, [who came as representatives] from the chief priests and elders of the people. [Mark 14:43–50; Luke 22:47–53; John 18:3–11]

48 Now the betrayer had given them a sign, saying, "Whomever I kiss, He is the one; seize Him."

49 Immediately Judas went to Jesus and said, "Greetings (rejoice), Rabbi!" And he kissed Him [in a deliberate act of betrayal].

50 Jesus said to Judas, "Friend, do what you came for." Then they came and seized Jesus and arrested Him.

51 And one of those who were with Jesus reached out and drew his sword, and struck [Malchus] the slave of the high priest and cut off his ear. [Mark 14:47; Luke 22:50; John 18:10]

52 Then Jesus said to him, "Put your sword back in its place; for all those who *habitually* draw the sword will die by the sword. [Gen 9:6]

53 "Do you think that I cannot appeal to My Father, and He will immediately provide Me with more than twelve legions of angels?

54 "How then will the Scriptures be fulfilled, that it must happen this way?"

55 At that moment Jesus said to the crowds, "Have you come out with swords and clubs to arrest Me as *you would* against a robber? Day after day I used to sit in the porches *and* courts of the temple teaching, and you did not arrest Me.

56 "But all this has taken place so that the Scriptures of the prophets would be fulfilled." Then all the disciples deserted Him and fled.

Jesus before Caiaphas

57 Those who had seized Jesus led Him away to Caiaphas, the high priest, where the scribes and the elders (Sanhedrin, Jewish High Court) had gathered [illegally] together. [Mark 14:53–65; Luke 22:66–71; John 18:12f, 19–24]

58 But Peter followed Him at a distance as far as the courtyard of the [elegant home of the Jewish] high priest, and went inside, and sat with the guards to see the outcome.

59 Now the chief priests and the whole Council (Sanhedrin, Jewish High Court) tried to get false witnesses to testify against Jesus, so that they might [have a reason to] put Him to death.

60 They found none, even though many false witnesses came forward. At last two came forward,

61 and testified, "This man said, 'I am able to tear down the temple of God and rebuild it in three days.' "

62 The high priest stood up and said to Jesus, "Have You no answer to give? What is it that these men are testifying against You?"

26:51 *one of those.* John 18:10 informs us that the impetuous swordsman was Peter. This action was performed with one of the two swords that the disciples had (Lk 22:38).

26:53 *twelve legions of angels.* A legion in the Roman army was about six thousand men. When one considers the power of one angel (Ex 32:23; 2Sa 24:15 – 17; 2Ki 19:35) the power of more than 72,000 angels is beyond comprehension. Jesus had all of heaven's power at His disposal, yet He refused to use it. His Father's will was for Him to go to the cross.

26:62 *Have You no answer to give?* In maintaining His silence, Jesus fulfilled the prophecy of Isaiah 53:7.

47 Mk 14:43; Lk 22:47; Jn 18:3; Ac 1:16 **49** 2Sa 20:9 **50** Ps 41:9; 55:13 **51** Jn 18:10 **52** Ge 9:6; Rev 13:10 **53** 2Ki 6:17; Da 7:10 **54** ver. 24; Isa 53:7; Lk 24:25,44,46 **56** La 4:20; See Jn 18:15 **57** Mk 14:53; Lk 22:54; Jn 18:12,13,24 **60** Ps 27:12; 35:11; Mk 14:55; Ac 6:13; Dt 19:15 **61** Mt 27:40; Jn 2:19 **62** Mk 14:60

63But Jesus kept silent. And the high
priest said to Him, "I call on You to
swear a binding oath by the living
God, that you tell us whether You are
the Christ, the Son of God."
64Jesus said to him, "You have [in
fact] said it; but more than that I tell
you [regardless of what you do with
Me now], in the future you will see [Me
revealed as] THE SON OF MAN SEATED AT
THE RIGHT HAND OF POWER, and COMING
ON THE CLOUDS OF HEAVEN." [Ps 110:1;
Dan 7:13]
65Then the high priest tore his robes
[in mock horror] and exclaimed, "He
has blasphemed [by making Himself
God's equal]! What further need have
we of witnesses *or* evidence? See,
you have now heard the blasphemy.
[Lev 24:16; Num 14:6]
66"What do you think?" They an-
swered, "He deserves to be put to
death."
67Then they spat in His face and
struck Him with their fists; and some
slapped Him, [Is 50:6]
68saying, "Prophesy to us, You Christ
(Messiah, Anointed); who was it that
struck You?"

Peter's Denials

69Now Peter was sitting outside in
the courtyard, and a servant-girl came
up to him and said, "You too were with
Jesus the Galilean." [Mark 14:66–72;
Luke 22:55–62; John 18:16–18, 25–27]
70But he denied it before them all,
saying, "I do not know what you are
talking about."
71And when he had gone out to the
gateway, another *servant-girl* saw him
and she said to the bystanders, "This
man was with Jesus the Nazarene."
72And again he denied it with an
oath, "I do not know the man."
73After a little while the bystanders
came up and said to Peter, "Surely you
are one of them too; for even your [Gal-
ilean] accent gives you away."
74Then he began to curse [that is, to
invoke God's judgment on himself]
and swear [an oath], "I do not know the
man!" And at that moment a rooster
crowed.
75And Peter remembered the [pro-
phetic] words of Jesus, when He had
said, "Before a rooster crows, you will
deny Me three times." And he went out-
side and wept bitterly [in repentance].

Judas' Remorse

27 WHEN IT was morning, all the
chief priests and the elders of the
people (Sanhedrin, Jewish High Court)
conferred together against Jesus, [plot-
ting how] to put Him to death [since
under Roman rule they had no power
to execute anyone];
2so they bound Him, and led Him
away and handed Him over to Pilate
the governor [of Judea, who had the au-
thority to condemn prisoners to death].

26:64 Second Coming — Throughout His ministry, Jesus had applied to Himself the Old Testament prophecies that were acknowledged as messianic by the Jewish teachers. Here, Jesus answers Caiaphas the high priest by combining two well-known messianic prophecies from Psalm 110:1 and Daniel 7:13. The first describes His enthronement and the other His second coming. The final word spoken by Christ to the Jews was about the certainty of His future return. About His first coming Jesus said, "For God did not send the Son into the world to judge and condemn the world" (Jn 3:17). But the time will come when all the world will see Him enthroned at the right hand of God and given all power and majesty as the judge of the ages.

26:74 *at that moment a rooster crowed.* Some have detected a contradiction between this passage and the account in Mark 14:72. Others believe that seeing a contradiction is a forced reading of the text. Matthew, Luke, and John make the simple statement that a rooster would crow (Lk 22:61; Jn 18:27), whereas Mark, which is believed to be based on Peter's memories, would include more exact details.

27:2 *Pilate.* Pontius Pilate was governor of Judea, Samaria, and Idumea from AD 26 to 36. Because the Jews did not have authority to execute Jesus, they brought Him to Pilate.

63 Isa 53:7; Mt 27:12; Lev 5:1; 1Sa 14:24,26 **64** Da 7:13; Mt 16:27; 24:30; 25:31; Lk 21:27; Jn 1:51; Ro 14:10; 1Th 4:16; Rev 1:7; Ps 110:1; Ac 7:55 **65** 2Ki 18:37 **66** Lev 24:16; Jn 19:7 **67** Isa 50:6; 53:3; Mt 27:30; Lk 22:63 **68** Mk 14:65; Lk 22:64 **69** Mk 14:66; Lk 22:55; Jn 18:16,17,25 **73** Lk 22:59 **74** Mk 14:71 **75** ver. 34; Lk 22:61; Jn 13:38 **CHAPTER 27** **1** Ps 2:2; Mk 15:1; Lk 22:66; 23:1; Jn 18:28 **2** Mt 20:19; Ac 3:13

3 When Judas, His betrayer, saw that Jesus was condemned, he was gripped with remorse and returned the thirty pieces of silver to the chief priests and the elders, [Ex 21:32]

4 saying, "I have sinned by betraying innocent blood." They replied, "What is that to us? See to that yourself!"

5 And throwing the pieces of silver into the temple sanctuary, he left; and went away and hanged himself.

6 The chief priests, picking up the pieces of silver, said, "It is not lawful to put these in the treasury [of the temple], because it is the price of blood."

7 So after consultation they used the money to buy the Potter's Field as a burial place for strangers.

8 Therefore that piece of ground has been called the Field of Blood to this day.

9 Then the words spoken by Jeremiah the prophet were fulfilled: "AND THEY TOOK THE THIRTY PIECES OF SILVER, THE PRICE OF HIM ON WHOM A PRICE HAD BEEN SET by the sons of Israel; [Jer 18:1, 2; 19:1–15; 32:6–9]

10 AND THEY GAVE THEM FOR THE POTTER'S FIELD, AS THE LORD DIRECTED ME." [Zech 11:13]

Jesus before Pilate

11 Now Jesus stood before [Pilate] the governor, and the governor asked Him, "Are you the King of the Jews?" [In affirmation] Jesus said to him, "*It is as* you say." [Mark 15:2–5; Luke 23:2, 3; John 18:29–37]

12 But when the charges were brought against Him by the chief priests and elders, He did not answer. [Is 53:7]

13 Then Pilate said to Him, "Do You not hear how many things they are testifying against You?"

14 But Jesus did not reply to him, not even to a single accusation, so that the governor was greatly astonished.

15 Now at the feast [of the Passover] the governor was in the habit of setting free any one prisoner whom the people chose. [Mark 15:6–15; Luke 23:18–25; John 18:39–19:16]

16 And at that time they were holding a notorious prisoner [guilty of insurrection and murder], called Barabbas.

17 So when they had assembled [for this purpose], Pilate said to them, "Whom do you want me to set free for you? Barabbas, or Jesus who is called Christ?"

18 For Pilate knew that it was because of jealousy that the chief priests and elders had handed Jesus over to him.

19 While he was seated on the judgment seat, his wife sent him *a message*, saying, "Have nothing to do with that righteous *and* innocent Man; for last night I suffered greatly in a dream because of Him."

20 But the chief priests and the elders persuaded the crowds to ask for Barabbas and to put Jesus to death.

21 The governor said to them, "Which of the two do you wish me to set free for you?" And they said, "Barabbas."

22 Pilate said to them, "Then what shall I do with Jesus who is called Christ?" They all replied, "Let Him be crucified!"

23 And he said, "Why, what has He done that is evil?" But they continued shouting all the louder, "Let Him be crucified!" [Mark 15:14; Luke 23:4, 14, 22; John 18:39; 19:4, 6]

24 So when Pilate saw that he was getting nowhere, but rather that a riot was breaking out, he took water and washed his hands [to ceremonially cleanse himself of guilt] in the presence of the crowd, saying, "I am innocent of this [righteous] Man's blood; see *to that* yourselves." [Deut 21:6–9; Ps 26:6]

25 And all the people answered, "Let [the responsibility for] His blood be on us and on our children!" [Josh 2:19]

27:25 *His blood be on us and on our children.* The sins of the fathers are visited on their children for those who hate God. But if anyone turns to Jesus and repents, He never fails to show His lovingkindness.

3 Mt 26:14 **5** 2Sa 17:23; Ac 1:18 **8** Ac 1:19 **9** Zec 11:12 **11** Mk 15:2; Lk 23:3; Jn 18:33; Jn 18:37; 1Ti 6:13 **12** Mt 26:63; Jn 19:9 **13** Mt 26:62; Jn 19:10 **15** Mk 15:6; Lk 23:17; Jn 18:39 **20** Mk 15:11; Lk 23:18; Jn 18:40; Ac 3:14 **24** Dt 21:6 **25** Dt 19:10; Jos 2:19; 2Sa 1:16; 1Ki 2:32; Ac 5:28

26 So he set Barabbas free for them; but after having Jesus severely whipped (scourged), he handed Him over to be crucified.

Jesus Is Mocked

27 Then the governor's soldiers took Jesus into the Praetorium, and they gathered the whole Roman cohort around Him. [Mark 15:16–20; John 19:1–3]

28 They stripped him and put a scarlet robe on Him [as a king's robe].

29 And after twisting together a crown of thorns, they put it on His head, and put a reed in His right hand [as a scepter]. Kneeling before Him, they ridiculed Him, saying, "Hail (rejoice), King of the Jews!"

30 They spat on Him, and took the reed and struck Him *repeatedly* on the head.

31 After they finished ridiculing Him, they stripped Him of the *scarlet* robe and put His own clothes on Him, and led Him away to crucify Him.

32 Now as they were coming out, they found a man of Cyrene named Simon, whom they forced into service to carry the cross of Jesus. [Mark 15:21; Luke 23:26]

The Crucifixion

33 And when they came to a place called Golgotha, which means Place of a Skull, [Mark 15:22–32; Luke 23:33–43; John 19:17–24]

34 they offered Him wine mixed with gall (myrrh, a bitter-tasting narcotic) to drink; but after tasting it, He refused to drink it.

35 And when they had crucified Him, they divided His clothes among them by casting lots. [Ps 22:18]

36 Then sitting down there, they *began* to keep watch over Him [to guard against any rescue attempt].

37 And above His head they put the accusation against Him which read, "THIS IS JESUS THE KING OF THE JEWS."

38 At the same time two robbers were crucified with Jesus, one on the right and one on the left.

39 Those who passed by were hurling abuse at Him *and* jeering at Him, wagging their heads [in scorn and ridicule], [Ps 22:7, 8; 109:25]

40 and they said [tauntingly], "You who would destroy the temple and rebuild it in three days, save Yourself [from death]! If You are the Son of God, come down from the cross."

41 In the same way the chief priests also, along with the scribes and elders, mocked Him, saying,

42 "He saved others [from death]; He cannot save Himself. He is the King of Israel; let Him now come down from the cross, and we will believe in Him *and* acknowledge Him.

43 "HE TRUSTS IN GOD; LET GOD RESCUE *Him* now, IF HE DELIGHTS IN HIM; for He said, 'I am the Son of God.' " [Ps 22:8]

27:27 *the Praetorium.* This was the official residence of the governor when he was in Jerusalem.
27:31 *crucify.* Crucifixion, a practice probably adopted from Persia, was considered by the Romans to be the cruelest form of execution. This punishment was reserved for the worst criminals. The offender usually died after two or three days of agonizing suffering, enduring not only incomprehensible pain, but also hunger, thirst, and exposure. The offenders' arms were nailed to a beam that was hoisted up and fixed to a post, to which their feet were nailed.
27:32 *Simon.* Simon probably was (or later became) a follower of Christ; it is unlikely that he would be referred to by name if he were a stranger to the Christian community (Mk 15:21).
27:34 *wine mixed with gall.* It is believed that this mixture was meant to dull the victim's pain. The prophetic words of Psalm 69:21 were fulfilled here.
27:35 *casting lots.* The soldiers fulfilled the prophetic words of Psalm 22:18.
27:38 *two robbers.* This is the fulfillment of Isaiah 53:12, he "was counted among the transgressors." Psalm 22:6 predicted the insults that would be directed at the Messiah.

26 Isa 53:5; Mk 15:15; Lk 23:16,24,25; Jn 19:1,16 **27** Mk 15:16; Jn 19:2 **28** Lk 23:11 **29** Ps 69:19; Isa 53:3 **30** Isa 50:6; Mt 26:67 **31** Isa 53:7 **32** Nu 15:35; 1Ki 21:13; Ac 7:58; Heb 13:12; Mk 15:21; Lk 23:26 **33** Mk 15:22; Lk 23:33; Jn 19:17 **34** See ver. 48; Ps 69:21 **35** Mk 15:24; Lk 23:34; Jn 19:24; Ps 22:18 **36** ver. 54 **37** Mk 15:26; Lk 23:38; Jn 19:19 **38** Isa 53:12; Mk 15:27; Lk 23:32,33; Jn 19:18 **39** Ps 22:7; 109:25; Mk 15:29; Lk 23:35 **40** Mt 26:61; Jn 2:19; Mt 26:63 **43** Ps 22:8

44 The robbers who had been crucified with Him also began to insult Him in the same way.

45 Now from the sixth hour (noon) there was darkness over all the land until the ninth hour (3:00 p.m.). [Mark 15:33–41; Luke 23:44–49]

46 About the ninth hour Jesus cried out with a loud [agonized] voice, "ELI, ELI, LAMA SABACHTHANI?" that is, "MY GOD, MY GOD, WHY HAVE YOU FORSAKEN ME?" [Ps 22:1]

47 When some of the bystanders there heard it, they *began* saying, "This man is calling for Elijah."

48 Immediately one of them ran, and took a sponge, soaked it with sour wine and put it on a reed, and gave Him a drink. [Ps 69:21; Mark 15:36f; Luke 23:36; John 19:29, 30]

49 But the rest said, "Let us see whether Elijah will come to save Him [from death]."

50 And Jesus cried out again with a loud [agonized] voice, and gave up His spirit [voluntarily, sovereignly dismissing and releasing His spirit from His body in submission to His Father's plan]. [John 10:18]

51 And [at once] the veil [of the Holy of Holies] of the temple was torn in two from top to bottom; the earth shook and the rocks were split apart. [Ex 26:31–35]

52 The tombs were opened, and many bodies of the saints (God's people) who had fallen asleep [in death] were raised [to life];

53 and coming out of the tombs after His resurrection, they entered the holy city (Jerusalem) and appeared to many people.

54 Now the centurion, and those who were with him keeping guard over Jesus, when they saw the earthquake and the things that were happening, they were terribly frightened *and* filled with awe, and said, "Truly this was the Son of God!"

55 There were also many women there looking on from a distance, who had accompanied Jesus from Galilee, ministering to Him.

56 Among them was Mary Magdalene, and Mary the mother of James and Joseph, and [Salome] the mother of Zebedee's sons [James and John].

Jesus Is Buried

57 When it was evening, there came a rich man from Arimathea, named Joseph, who was also a disciple of Jesus. [Mark 15:42–47; Luke 23:50–56; John 19:38–42]

58 He went to Pilate and asked for the body of Jesus [so that he might bury Him], and Pilate ordered that it be given *to him.*

27:45 *the sixth hour.* This would have been noon. The first hour began at sunrise (approximately 6:00 A.M.). ***darkness.*** The darkness could not have been due to a natural cause, such as an eclipse of the sun, since the Passover occurred during a full moon. This was a supernatural occurrence.

27:46 – 50 Atonement — Because God cannot tolerate sin, as Jesus took upon Himself the sin of the whole human race, God had to turn away. Jesus felt this separation, and many believe it was as much for the dread of this as for the physical pain that Jesus wept in the garden. Jesus' cry to God is a quote from Psalm 22:1, a messianic verse that the Jews should have understood.

27:50 *cried out again with a loud [agonized] voice.* The cry referred to here by Matthew was, "It is finished" (Jn 19:30). This was not a cry of exhaustion, but a cry of victory. The purpose for which Jesus came into the world had been accomplished. Redemption from sin had been purchased for all mankind.

27:51 *the veil [of the Holy of Holies] of the temple was torn in two from top to bottom.* The temple had two veils or curtains, one in front of the holy place and the other separating the holy place from the most holy place. These curtains were heavy and very strong and thick. It was the second of these that was torn, demonstrating that through the death of Jesus, there was now open access to God. Jesus' blood covered our sins from God's sight.

27:57 *a rich man from Arimathea.* Joseph's actions fulfilled the prophecy of Isaiah, "His grave was assigned with the wicked, but He was with a rich man in His death" (Isa 53:9).

---

44 Mk 15:32; Lk 23:39 **45** Am 8:9; Mk 15:33; Lk 23:44 **46** Heb 5:7; Ps 22:1 **48** Ps 69:21; Mk 15:36; Lk 23:36; Jn 19:29 **50** Mk 15:37; Lk 23:46 **51** Ex 26:31; 2Ch 3:14; Mk 15:38; Lk 23:45 **54** ver. 36; Mk 15:39; Lk 23:47 **55** Lk 8:2,3 **56** Mk 15:40 **57** Mk 15:42; Lk 23:50; Jn 19:38

[59]And Joseph took the body and wrapped it in a clean linen cloth (burial wrapping),
[60]and laid it in his own new tomb, which he had cut in the rock; and he rolled a large stone over the entrance of the tomb and went away.
[61]And Mary Magdalene was there, and the other Mary, sitting opposite the tomb.
[62]The next day, that is, *the day* after the [day of] preparation [for the Sabbath], the chief priests and the Pharisees assembled before Pilate,
[63]and said, "Sir, we have remembered that when He was still alive that deceiver said, 'After three days I will rise [from the dead].'
[64]"Therefore, give orders to have the tomb made secure *and* safeguarded until the third day, otherwise His disciples may come and steal Him *away* and tell the people, 'He has risen from the dead,' and the last deception [the reporting of His resurrection] will be worse than the first [the reporting that He is the Messiah]."
[65]Pilate said to them, "You have a guard [of soldiers]; go [with them], make the tomb as secure as you know how."
[66]So they went and made the tomb secure, and along with [stationing] a guard of soldiers [to be on watch] they set a seal on the stone.

Jesus Is Risen!

28 NOW AFTER the Sabbath, near dawn of the first *day* of the week, Mary Magdalene and the other Mary went to look at the tomb. [Mark 16:1–8; Luke 24:1–10, John 20:1–8]
[2]And a great earthquake had occurred, for an angel of the Lord descended from heaven and came and rolled away the stone [from the opening of the tomb], and sat on it.
[3]The angel's appearance was like lightning, and his clothes were as white as snow.
[4]The guards shook, paralyzed with fear [at the sight] of him and became like dead men [pale and immobile].
[5]But the angel said to the women, "Do not be afraid; for I know that you are looking for Jesus who has been crucified.
[6]"He is not here, for He has risen, just as He said [He would]. Come! See the place where He was lying.
[7]"Then go quickly and tell His disciples that He has risen from the dead; and behold, He is going ahead of you into Galilee [as He promised]. There you will see Him; behold, I have told you."
[8]So the women left the tomb quickly with fear and great joy, and ran to tell [the good news to] the disciples.
[9]And *as they went*, suddenly, Jesus met them, saying, "Rejoice!" And they went to Him and took hold of His feet [in homage] and worshiped Him [as the Messiah].
[10]Then Jesus said to them, "Do not be afraid; go and tell My brothers to leave for Galilee, and there they will see Me [just as I promised]."
[11]While they were on their way, some of the [Roman] guards went into the city and reported to the chief priests everything that had happened.
[12]And when the chief priests had gathered with the elders and had consulted together [to develop a plan of deception], they gave a sufficient sum of money [as a bribe] to the soldiers,
[13]and said, "You say this, 'His disciples came at night and stole Him while we were sleeping.'

28:2 *rolled away the stone.* The tomb was not opened to allow Christ to come out; it was opened to allow others to go in and see for themselves that it was empty.

28:6 *He has risen, just as He said.* Jesus predicted His resurrection to His disciples, even though they did not understand Him (12:40; 16:21; 17:9,23; 26:32).

28:7 *go quickly and tell.* This is always the divine order: to tell others the good news that Jesus is alive (v. 19).

---

60 Isa 53:9 **63** Mt 16:21; 17:23; 20:19; 26:61; Mk 8:31; 10:34; Lk 9:22; 18:33; 24:6,7; Jn 2:19 **66** Da 6:17
CHAPTER 28 **1** Mk 16:1; Lk 24:1; Jn 20:1; Mt 27:56 **2** See Mk 16:5; Lk 24:4; Jn 20:12 **3** Da 10:6 **6** Mt 12:40; 16:21; 17:23; 20:19 **7** Mt 26:32; Mk 16:7 **9** See Mk 16:9; Jn 20:14 **10** See Jn 20:17; Ro 8:29; Heb 2:11

14 "And if the governor (Pilate) hears about it, we will calm him down and keep you out of trouble."
15 So they took the money [they were paid for lying] and did as they were instructed; and this [fabricated] story was widely spread among the Jews, and is to the present day.

The Great Commission

16 Now the eleven disciples went to Galilee, to the mountain which Jesus had designated.
17 And when they saw Him, they worshiped *Him;* but some doubted [that it was really He].
18 Jesus came up and said to them, "All authority (all power of absolute rule) in heaven and on earth has been given to Me.
19 "Go therefore and make disciples of all the nations [help the people to learn of Me, believe in Me, and obey My words], baptizing them in the name of the Father and of the Son and of the Holy Spirit,
20 teaching them to observe everything that I have commanded you; and lo, I am with you always [remaining with you perpetually—regardless of circumstance, and on every occasion], even to the end of the age."

28:19 Why Share Our Faith — There are at least six compelling reasons for sharing our faith in Christ with those who have not experienced new life in Christ:

Because God has commanded us to do so (Ac 1:8).

Because it demonstrates our love for God. If we truly love Him we will keep His commandments (Jn 14:15).

Because all are lost without Christ (Ro 3:10,23).

Because this is God's chosen method: He could use angels, but He only uses redeemed sinners to tell lost sinners about Christ (Ro 10:14 – 17; 1Ti 1:15).

Because God desires to save all people (Ac 4:12; 1Ti 2:4; 2Pe 3:9).

Because faith grows best when each generation conscientiously strives to pass it on to the next.

28:20 *I am with you always.* Jesus is the true *Immanuel*, "God with us" (1:23; Heb 13:5 – 6; Rev 21:3).

16 ver. 7; Mt 26:32 **18** Da 7:13,14; Mt 11:27; 16:28; Lk 1:32; 10:22; Jn 3:35; 5:22; 13:3; 17:2; Ac 2:36; Ro 14:9; 1Co 15:27; Eph 1:10,21; Php 2:9,10; Heb 1:2; 2:8; 1Pe 3:22; Rev 17:14 **19** Mk 16:15; Isa 52:10; Lk 24:47; Ac 2:38,39; Ro 10:18; Col 1:23 **20** Ac 2:42

THE GOSPEL ACCORDING TO
MARK

▸ **AUTHOR:** According to Acts 12:12, Mark's mother Mary had a large house that was used as a meeting place for believers in Jerusalem. Barnabas was Mark's cousin (Col 4:10), but Peter may have been the person that led him to Christ (Peter called him "my son, Mark" in 1Pe 5:13). It was this close association with Peter that lent apostolic authority to Mark's Gospel, since Peter was evidently Mark's primary source of information. It has been suggested that Mark was referring to himself in his account of a "young man" in Gethsemane (14:51). Since all the disciples had abandoned Jesus (14:50), this little incident may have been a firsthand account.

▸ **TIMES:** c. AD 29 – 33 ▸ **KEY VERSES:** Mk 8:34 – 37

▸ **THEME:** Mark is the shortest and simplest of the Gospels. He doesn't seem to be telling the story in a way that appeals to a particular audience the way Matthew does. He also does not use the well-developed thematic structure that characterizes John. One of the most common phrases in the book is one that is translated "straightway" in the King James and "immediately" or "at once" in other translations. He uses this phrase frequently as he moves from one anecdote to another. Mark's quickly paced Gospel is often confrontational, as he tells the story of the gospel as clearly as possible. He wants the reader to respond, and almost seems to be saying "here is the truth, believe it, and let's get on with following Jesus."

The Preaching of John the Baptist

1 THE BEGINNING of the [facts regarding the] good news of Jesus Christ, the Son of God.
2 As it is written *and* forever remains in the [writings of the] prophet Isaiah:

"BEHOLD, I SEND MY MESSENGER
AHEAD OF YOU,
WHO WILL PREPARE YOUR WAY—
[Mal 3:1]
3 A VOICE OF ONE SHOUTING IN THE
WILDERNESS,
'PREPARE THE WAY OF THE LORD,
MAKE HIS PATHS STRAIGHT!' " [Is 40:3]

4 John the Baptist appeared in the wilderness preaching a baptism of repentance for the forgiveness of sins [that is, requiring a change of one's old way

---

1:1 *The beginning of the [facts regarding the] good news of Jesus Christ.* Writing three decades after the resurrection of Christ, Mark starts his narrative with a simple declaration of the good news about God's Son, the Lord Jesus Christ. The *gospel* refers to the basic story of the good news to be found in Christ's life, ministry, death, and resurrection.

1:2 – 3 *As it is written.* Other than by quoting Jesus, Mark makes only one reference to the Old Testament.

1:4 *John the Baptist appeared . . . preaching a baptism of repentance.* The mention of John without any introduction presupposes some knowledge of the Christian faith on the part of Mark's readers. ***the forgiveness of sins.*** This

CHAPTER 1 **1** Mt 14:33; Lk 1:35; Jn 1:34 **2** Mal 3:1; Mt 11:10; Lk 7:27 **3** Isa 40:3; Mt 3:3; Lk 3:4; Jn 1:15,23 **4** Mt 3:1; Lk 3:3; Jn 3:23

of thinking, turning away from sin and seeking God and His righteousness].
[5]And all the country of Judea and all the people of Jerusalem were *continually* going out to him; and they were being baptized by him in the Jordan River, as they confessed their sins.
[6]John wore clothing made of camel's hair and had a [wide] leather band around his waist, and he ate locusts and wild honey. [Lev 11:22; 2 Kin 1:8]
[7]And he was preaching, saying, "After me comes He who is mightier [more powerful, more noble] than I, and I am not worthy to stoop down and untie the straps of His sandals [even as His slave].
[8]"As for me, I baptized you [who came to me] with water [only]; but He will baptize you [who truly repent] with the Holy Spirit."

The Baptism of Jesus

[9]In those days Jesus came from Nazareth of Galilee and was baptized by John in the Jordan. [Matt 3:13–17; Luke 3:21, 22; John 1:32]
[10]Immediately coming up out of the water, he (John) saw the heavens torn open, and the Spirit like a dove descending on Him (Jesus);
[11]and a voice came out of heaven saying: "You are My beloved Son, in You I am well-pleased *and* delighted!" [Ps 2:7; Is 42:1]
[12]Immediately the [Holy] Spirit forced Him out into the wilderness.
[13]He was in the wilderness forty days being tempted [to do evil] by Satan; and He was with the wild animals, and the angels ministered *continually* to Him.

Jesus Preaches in Galilee

[14]Now after John [the Baptist] was arrested *and* taken into custody, Jesus went to Galilee, preaching the good news of [the kingdom of] God,
[15]and saying, "The [appointed period of] time is fulfilled, and the kingdom of God is at hand; repent [change your inner self—your old way of thinking, regret past sins, live your life in a way that proves repentance; seek God's purpose for your life] and believe [with a deep, abiding trust] in the good news [regarding salvation]."

---

phrase does not mean that one is baptized in order to receive forgiveness of sins. The Greek preposition translated *of* in English probably means "with a view to," signifying that baptism looks to the forgiveness that God gives through the gift of repentance.

1:5 *were being baptized by him.* John's baptizing was a recurring popular event that attracted large crowds. Mark vividly portrays the continuous stream of followers who flocked to John. As each person was baptized by John, he or she would admit to his or her individual sin and need for the Messiah.

1:7 *And he was preaching, saying.* The tense of these verbs indicates continuous action in past time. John's characteristic message was to promote expectancy and acceptance of the Lord Jesus Christ.

1:8 *I baptized you [who came to me] with water.* The water is a physical representation of the future life in the Spirit that people who followed the Messiah would have.

1:9 *Jesus . . . was baptized by John.* Because He had no sins to repent of, Jesus' baptism was unique. It showed His identity with John's work and with the sinner for whom He would die. It also foreshadowed His own death, burial, and resurrection for sinners.

1:11 *a voice came out of heaven.* Three times during Christ's earthly ministry a voice came from heaven. Here it was the Father's testimony to Christ's unique and divine Sonship. The other two confirming incidents were at the transfiguration (9:7) and on the day of Christ's triumphal entry into Jerusalem (Jn 12:28).

1:13 *angels ministered continually to Him.* Mark is the only Gospel that mentions these angels.

1:15 *kingdom of God.* The kingdom was the subject of much Old Testament prophecy, and the theme was familiar to Jesus' listeners. ***repent . . . and believe.*** These are both acts of faith. When a person accepts the only true and worthy object of faith, that person readily turns from inferior substitutes.

---

5 Mt 3:5 **6** Mt 3:4 **7** Mt 3:11; Jn 1:27; Ac 13:25 **8** Ac 1:5; 11:16; 19:4; Isa 44:3; Joel 2:28; Ac 2:4; 10:45; 11:15,16; 1Co 12:13 **9** Mt 3:13; Lk 3:21 **10** Mt 3:16; Jn 1:32 **11** Ps 2:7; Mt 3:17; Mk 9:7 **12** Mt 4:1; Lk 4:1 **13** Mt 4:11 **14** Mt 4:12; Mt 4:23 **15** Da 9:25; Gal 4:4; Eph 1:10; Mt 3:2; 4:17

[16]As Jesus was walking by the shore
of the Sea of Galilee, He saw Simon
[Peter] and Simon's brother, Andrew,
casting a net in the sea; for they were
fishermen.
[17]And Jesus said to them, "Follow
Me [as My disciples, accepting Me as
your Master and Teacher and walking
the same path of life that I walk], and I
will make you fishers of men."
[18]Immediately they left their nets
and followed Him [becoming His disciples, believing and trusting in Him
and following His example].
[19]Going on a little farther, He saw
James the son of Zebedee, and his
brother John, who were also in the
boat mending *and* cleaning the nets.
[20]Immediately Jesus called to them;
and they left their father Zebedee in
the boat with the hired workers, and
went away to follow Him [becoming
His disciples, believing and trusting
in Him and following His example].

1:19 *James . . . John.* The scenes of verses 16–20 are very colorful. Simon and Andrew are fishing when we encounter them. James and John are mending their nets. Such details indicate the testimony of an eyewitness, probably Peter.

16 Mt 4:18; Lk 5:4 **18** Mt 19:27; Lk 5:11 **19** Mt 4:21

FROM NAZARETH TO CANA AND CAPERNAUM

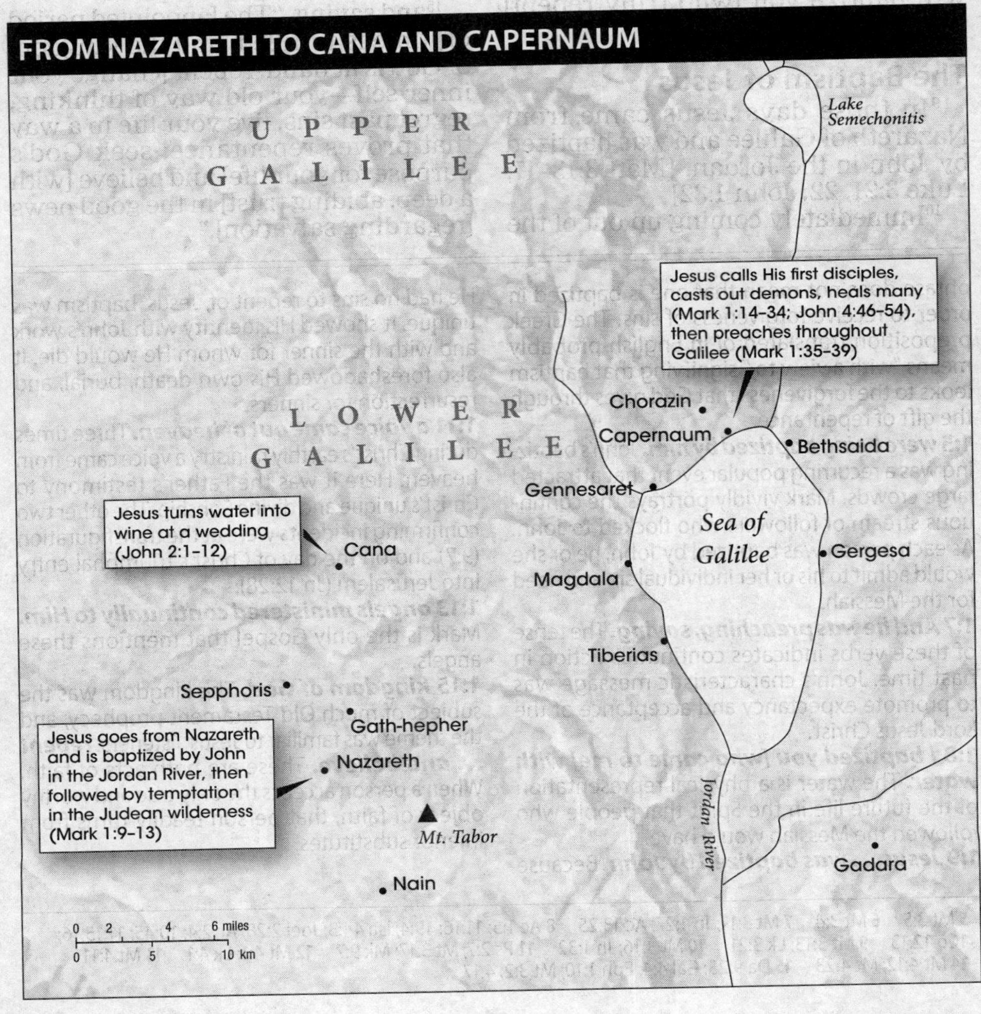

21 They went into Capernaum, and
immediately on the Sabbath Jesus
went into the synagogue and *began*
to teach. [Luke 4:31–37]
22 They were completely amazed at
His teaching; because He was teach-
ing them as one having [God-given]
authority, and not as the scribes.
23 Just then there was a man in their
synagogue with an unclean spirit; and
he cried out [terribly from the depths
of his throat],
24 saying, "What business do You
have with us, Jesus of Nazareth? Have
You come to destroy us? I know who
You are—the Holy One of God!"
25 Jesus rebuked him, saying, "Be
quiet (muzzled, silenced), and come
out of him!"
26 The unclean spirit threw the man
into convulsions, and screeching with
a loud voice, came out of him.
27 They were all so amazed that they
debated *and* questioned each other,
saying, "What is this? A new teaching
with authority! He commands even
the unclean spirits (demons), and they
obey Him."
28 Immediately the news about Him
spread everywhere throughout the dis-
trict surrounding Galilee.

Healing the Crowds

29 And immediately they left the syn-
agogue and went into the house of
Simon [Peter] and Andrew, accompa-
nied by James and John. [Matt 8:14–17;
Luke 4:38–41]
30 Now Simon's mother-in-law was
lying sick with a fever; and immedi-
ately they told Him about her.
31 Jesus went to her, and taking her
by the hand, raised her up; and the
fever left her, and she *began* to serve
them [as her guests].
32 Now when evening came, after the
sun had set [and the Sabbath Day had
ended, in a steady stream] they were
bringing to Him all who were sick and
those who were under the power of
demons,
33 until [it seemed as though] the
whole city had gathered together at
the door.
34 And Jesus healed many who were
suffering with various diseases; and
He drove out many demons, but would
not allow the demons to speak, be-
cause they knew Him [recognizing
Him as the Son of God].
35 Early in the morning, while it was
still dark, Jesus got up, left [the house],
and went out to a secluded place, and
was praying there.
36 Simon [Peter] and his companions
searched [everywhere, looking anx-
iously] for Him,
37 and they found Him and said,
"Everybody is looking for You!"
38 He replied, "Let us go on to the
neighboring towns, so I may preach
there also; that is why I came [from
the Father]."
39 So He went throughout Galilee,
preaching [the gospel] in their syna-
gogues and casting out demons.
40 And a leper came to Him, begging
Him and falling on his knees before
Him, saying, "If You are willing, You
are able to make me clean." [Matt 8:2–4;
Luke 5:12–14]
41 Moved with compassion [for his

1:21 *Capernaum.* This city is now in ruins, and sits beside the northern edge of the Sea of Galilee. It is mentioned 22 times in the Gospels. By contrast, only one recorded event during Christ's ministry occurred at Nazareth (Lk 4:16).

1:22 *They were completely amazed at His teaching.* Christ's teaching differed from that of scribes and Pharisees because He did not lean on the wisdom of other teachers and rabbis. His authority came from Himself.

1:28 *the news about Him spread everywhere throughout the district surrounding Galilee.* Mark notes the extent of recognition this great miracle brought Jesus. He also creates suspense by contrasting the people who received Christ with the Pharisees and rulers who worked to bring about His death.

1:35 *was praying there.* The verb tense indicates Jesus prayed continuously. Jesus' prayer life was successful because it was planned, private, and prolonged. He got up early enough, got far enough away, and stayed at it long enough.

21 Mt 4:13; Lk 4:31 **22** Mt 7:28 **24** Mt 8:29 **25** ver. 34 **26** Mk 9:20 **29** Mt 8:14; Lk 4:38 **32** Mt 8:16; Lk 4:40 **34** Mk 3:12; Lk 4:41; See Ac 16:17,18 **35** Lk 4:42 **38** Lk 4:43; Isa 61:1; Jn 16:28; 17:4 **39** Mt 4:23; Lk 4:44 **40** Mt 8:2; Lk 5:12

suffering], Jesus reached out with His hand and touched him, and said to him, "I am willing; be cleansed."

[42]The leprosy left him immediately and he was cleansed [completely healed and restored to health].

[43]And Jesus [deeply moved] admonished him sternly and sent him away immediately,

[44]saying to him, "See that you tell no one anything [about this]; but go, show yourself to the priest and offer for your purification what Moses commanded, as proof to them [that you are really healed]." [Lev 13:45; 14:2–32]

[45]But he went out and began to proclaim it freely and to spread the news [of his healing], to such an extent that Jesus could no longer openly enter a city [where He was known], but stayed out in the unpopulated places; yet people were still coming to Him from everywhere.

The Paralytic Healed

2 JESUS RETURNED to Capernaum, and a few days later the news went out that He was at home. [Matt 4:13]

[2]So many people gathered together that there was no longer room [for them], not even near the door; and Jesus was discussing with them the word [of God].

[3]Then they came, bringing to Him a paralyzed man, who was being carried by four men. [Matt 9:2–8; Luke 5:18–26]

[4]When they were unable to get to Him because of the crowd, they removed the roof above Jesus; and when they had dug out an opening, they let down the mat on which the paralyzed man was lying.

[5]When Jesus saw their [active] faith [springing from confidence in Him], He said to the paralyzed man, "Son, your sins are forgiven."

[6]But some of the scribes were sitting there debating in their hearts [the implication of what He had said],

[7]"Why does this man talk that way? He is blaspheming; who can forgive sins [remove guilt, nullify sin's penalty, and assign righteousness] except God alone?"

[8]Immediately Jesus, being fully aware [of their hostility] *and* knowing in His spirit that they were thinking this, said to them, "Why are you debating *and* arguing about these things in your hearts?

[9]"Which is easier, to say to the paralyzed man, 'Your sins are forgiven'; or to say, 'Get up, and pick up your mat and walk'?

[10]"But so that you may know that the Son of Man has the authority *and* power on earth to forgive sins"—He said to the paralyzed man,

[11]"I say to you, get up, pick up your mat and go home."

[12]And he got up and immediately picked up the mat and went out before them all, so that they all were astonished and they glorified *and* praised God, saying, "We have never seen anything like this!"

[13]Jesus went out again along the [Galilean] seashore; and all the people were coming to Him, and He was teaching them.

1:44 *tell no one anything.* Jesus' demand has several plausible explanations: (1) The report of Jesus' healing the man may have prejudiced the priest who needed to pronounce him clean; (2) Jesus did not want to be known primarily as a miracle worker, so He often commanded those who received His healing to remain quiet; and (3) the man's testimony would possibly have hastened the confrontation between Jesus and the religious leaders.

2:5 *saw their [active] faith.* Not only did the four men have faith, but the paralytic himself had it too. When Jesus announced to him, "your sins are forgiven," He was implicitly acknowledging the paralytic's trust that He was the Messiah.

2:6 – 7 *some of the scribes.* Mark notes the opposition of the scribes, who under their breath accused Jesus of blasphemy. In Christ's day the scribes were commonly called lawyers.

2:11 *get up, pick up your mat and go home.* By healing the paralytic, Jesus made His pronouncement of forgiveness far more credible.

2:13 *He was teaching them.* Jesus regularly taught the multitudes in retreat settings. This is

44 Lev 14:3,4,10 **45** Lk 5:15; Mk 2:13 **CHAPTER 2** **1** Mt 9:1 **7** Job 14:4; Isa 43:25 **9** Mt 9:5 **13** Mt 9:9

Levi (Matthew) Called

14 As He was passing by, He saw Levi
(Matthew) the son of Alphaeus sitting
in the tax collector's booth, and He said
to him, "Follow Me [as My disciple, ac-
cepting Me as your Master and Teacher
and walking the same path of life that
I walk]." And he got up and followed
Him [becoming His disciple, believing
and trusting in Him and following His
example]. [Matt 9:9–17; Luke 5:27–39]
15 And it happened that Jesus was
reclining *at the table* in Levi's house,
and many tax collectors and sinners
[including non-observant Jews] were
eating with Him and His disciples;
for there were many of them and they
were following Him.
16 When the scribes [belonging to the
sect] of the Pharisees saw that Jesus
was eating with the sinners [including
non-observant Jews] and tax collec-
tors, they asked His disciples, "Why
does He eat and drink with tax collec-
tors and sinners?"
17 When Jesus heard this, He said to
them, "Those who are healthy have no
need of a physician, but [only] those
who are sick; I did not come to call
the righteous, but sinners [who rec-
ognize their sin and humbly seek for-
giveness]."
18 Now John's disciples and the Phar-
isees were fasting [as a ritual]; and
they came and asked Jesus, "Why are
John's disciples and the disciples of the
Pharisees fasting, but Your disciples
are not doing so?"
19 Jesus answered, "The attendants
of the bridegroom cannot fast while
the bridegroom is [still] with them, can
they? As long as they have the bride-
groom with them, they cannot fast.
20 "But the days will come when the
bridegroom is [forcefully] taken away
from them, and they will fast at that
time.
21 "No one sews a patch of unshrunk
(new) cloth on an old garment; other-
wise the patch pulls away from it, the
new from the old, and the tear becomes
worse.
22 "No one puts new wine into old
wineskins; otherwise the [ferment-
ing] wine will [expand and] burst the
skins, and the wine is lost as well as
the wineskins. But new wine must be
put into new wineskins."

Question of the Sabbath

23 One Sabbath He was walking
along [with His disciples] through the
grainfields, and as they went along,
His disciples began picking the heads
of grain. [Deut 23:25; Matt 12:1–8;
Luke 6:1–5]
24 The Pharisees said to Him, "Look,
why are they doing what is unlawful
on the Sabbath?"
25 Jesus said to them, "Have you
never read [in the Scriptures] what
David did when he was in need and
was hungry, he and his companions;
[1 Sam 21:1–6]
26 how he went into the house of God
in the time of Abiathar the high priest,
and ate the sacred bread, which is not
lawful for anyone but the priests to eat,
and how he also gave it to the men who
were with him?" [1 Sam 21:1–6]

---

indicated by the continuous tense of the verbs used here. They kept on coming and Jesus kept on teaching.

2:18 *fasting.* Jesus was not against fasting, if properly observed. He gave guidelines for fasting in the Sermon on the Mount (Mt 6:16 – 18). Here, the Pharisees' fasting, perhaps twice each week (Lk 18:12), is contrasted with Jesus feasting probably at Levi's house.

2:21 – 22 *No one sews . . . No one puts.* Mark records only four of Jesus' parables — two of which he includes here. The comparison implies that the newness of His message, and of the new covenant to follow, cannot fit into the old molds of Judaism. The Old Testament was preparation for the New Testament (Gal 3:19 – 25).

2:24 *what is unlawful on the Sabbath.* The point to the Pharisees' accusation against Jesus and His disciples was that they had performed work on the Sabbath, but their charge was dubious. The act of plucking grain should not be confused with Sabbath work condemned by the law (Ex 31:15). This incident is further proof of rising opposition to Jesus' ministry.

14 Mt 9:9; Lk 5:27 **15** Mt 9:10 **17** Mt 9:12,13; 18:11; Lk 5:31,32; 19:10; 1Ti 1:15 **18** Mt 9:14; Lk 5:33 **23** Mt 12:1; Lk 6:1; Dt 23:25 **25** 1Sa 21:6 **26** Ex 29:32,33; Lev 24:9

27 Jesus said to them, "The Sabbath was made for man, not man for the Sabbath. [Ex 23:12; Deut 5:14]

28 "So the Son of Man is Lord even of the Sabbath [and He has authority over it]."

Jesus Heals on the Sabbath

3 AGAIN JESUS went into a synagogue; and a man was there whose hand was withered. [Matt 12:9–14; Luke 6:6–11]

2 The Pharisees were watching Jesus *closely to see* if He would heal him on the Sabbath, so that they might accuse Him [in the Jewish high court].

3 He said to the man whose hand was withered, "Get up and come forward!"

4 He asked them, "Is it lawful on the Sabbath to do good or to do evil, to save a life or to kill?" But they kept silent.

5 After looking around at them with anger, grieved at the hardness *and* arrogance of their hearts, He told the man, "Hold out your hand." And he held it out, and his hand was [completely] restored.

6 Then the Pharisees went out and immediately *began* conspiring with the Herodians [to plot] against Him, as to how they might [fabricate some legal grounds to] put Him to death.

7 Jesus withdrew to the sea with His disciples; and a large crowd from Galilee followed Him; and *also people* from Judea,

8 and from Jerusalem, and from Idumea, and [from the region] beyond the Jordan, and around Tyre and Sidon; a vast number of people came to Him because they were hearing about all [the things] that He was doing.

9 And He told His disciples to have a small boat stand ready for Him because of the many people, so that they would not crowd Him;

10 for He had healed many, and as a result all who had diseases pressed around Him to touch Him.

11 Whenever the unclean spirits saw Him, they fell down before Him and screamed out, "You are the Son of God!"

12 Jesus sternly warned them [again and again] not to tell who He was.

The Twelve Are Chosen

13 He went up on the hillside and called those whom He Himself wanted *and* chose; and they came to Him.

14 And He appointed twelve [disciples], so that they would be with Him [for instruction] and so that He could send them out to preach [the gospel as apostles—that is, as His special messengers, personally chosen representatives],

15 and to have authority *and* power to cast out demons.

16 He appointed the twelve: Simon (to whom He gave the name Peter), [Matt 10:2–4; Luke 6:13–16]

17 and James, the son of Zebedee, and John the brother of James (to them He gave the name Boanerges, that is, "Sons of Thunder");

3:5 *After looking around at them with anger.* It is possible, as Paul exhorts, to be angry and not sin (Eph 4:26). Jesus demonstrated this righteous anger. He was grieved with sin but did not sin Himself by retaliating or losing control of His emotions.

3:6 *Herodians.* The Pharisees were religious experts who should have led the people in righteousness. Instead they plotted Jesus' death with the Herodians, their bitter enemies. They were willing to set aside differences to destroy a common foe. The Herodians were Jews who supported Rome and the Herods in particular. Herod Antipas, a son of Herod the Great, ruled Galilee during the same time that Pilate served as Roman governor over Judea and Samaria.

3:11 – 12 *Jesus sternly warned them [again and again] not to tell who He was.* Jesus rebuked the demons who proclaimed "You are the Son of God." This was not because the demons incorrectly identified Jesus, but because their testimony was untrustworthy.

3:16 – 19 *(to whom He gave the name Peter).* Jesus gave Peter a new name because it was the Jewish custom to rename someone who had experienced a life-changing event. This renaming of the disciples has similarities to the renaming of Abram (Ge 17:3 – 5) and of Saul (Ac 9).

---

28 Mt 12:8 **CHAPTER 3** **1** Mt 12:9; Lk 6:6 **6** Mt 12:14; 22:16 **7** Lk 6:17 **11** Mk 1:23,24; Lk 4:41; Mt 14:33; Mk 1:1 **12** Mt 12:16; Mk 1:25,34 **13** Mt 10:1; Lk 6:12; 9:1 **16** Jn 1:42

18 and [He also appointed] Andrew, and Philip, and Bartholomew (Nathanael), and Matthew (Levi the tax collector), and Thomas, and James the son of Alphaeus, and Thaddaeus (Judas the son of James), and Simon the Zealot;

19 and Judas Iscariot, who betrayed Him.

20 Then He came to a house [in Capernaum], and a crowd formed again, so [many people] that Jesus and His disciples could not even eat a meal [together].

21 When His own family heard this they went to take custody of Him; for they were saying, "He is out of His mind."

22 The scribes who came down from Jerusalem were saying, "He is possessed by Beelzebul (Satan)," and "He is driving out the demons by the [power of the] ruler of the demons." [Matt 12:22–37; Luke 11:14–28]

23 So He called them to Himself and spoke to them in parables, "How can Satan drive out Satan?

24 "If a kingdom is divided [split into factions and rebelling] against itself, that kingdom cannot stand.

25 "And if a house is divided against itself, that house cannot stand.

26 "And if Satan has risen up against himself and is divided, he cannot stand, but is coming to an end.

27 "But no one can go into a strong man's house and steal his property unless he first overpowers *and* ties up the strong man, and then he will ransack *and* rob his house. [Is 49:24, 25; Matt 12:29]

28 "I assure you *and* most solemnly say to you, all sins will be forgiven the sons of men, and all the abusive *and* blasphemous things they say;

29 but whoever blasphemes against the Holy Spirit *and* His power [by attributing the miracles done by Me to Satan] never has forgiveness, but is guilty of an everlasting sin [a sin which is unforgivable in this present age as well as in the age to come]"— [Matt 12:32; Luke 12:10]

30 [Jesus said this] because the scribes and Pharisees were [attributing His miracles to Satan by] saying, "He has an unclean spirit."

31 Then His mother and His brothers arrived, and standing outside they sent *word* to Him and called for Him. [Matt 12:46–50; Luke 8:19–21]

32 A crowd was sitting around Him, and they said to Him, "Look! Your mother and Your brothers are outside asking for You."

33 And He replied, "Who are My mother and My brothers?"

34 Looking at those who were sitting in a circle around Him, He said, "Here are My mother and My brothers!

35 For whoever does the will of God [by believing in Me, and following Me], he is My brother and sister and mother."

Parable of the Sower and Soils

4 AGAIN JESUS began to teach beside the sea [of Galilee]. And a very large crowd gathered around Him, so

---

3:27 *strong man.* Whoever defeats Satan must be stronger than he. Jesus implies that He Himself has come to enter the house of the strong man, Satan, to seize his goods (1Jn 3:8).

3:28 – 30 *whoever blasphemes against the Holy Spirit.* This person places himself or herself outside the redeeming grace of God. It is apparently not a single act of defiant behavior, but a continued state of opposition entered into willingly. The tense of "they said" indicates a continued action, not a one time event. The words and works of Christ were spoken and performed by the power of the Holy Spirit. To attribute them to Satan is to call the work of heaven a work of hell. For such perverse belief there is no remedy. How someone can commit this sin today is a difficult question to answer, but those who persist in denigrating Christ by insulting His work or by attributing it to Satan may drive themselves past a point of no return (Mt 12:31 – 32).

3:31 *His mother and His brothers.* Opposition arose from Jesus' own immediate family. We are not told precisely what they wanted to say, but it likely involved a concern for Jesus' safety or reputation, since He was becoming widely known as a preaching prophet and a worker of miracles.

20 Mk 6:31 **21** Jn 7:5; 10:20 **22** Mt 9:34; 10:25; Lk 11:15; Jn 7:20; 8:48,52; 10:20 **23** Mt 12:25 **27** Isa 49:24; Mt 12:29 **28** Mt 12:31; Lk 12:10; 1Jn 5:16 **31** Mt 12:46; Lk 8:19 **CHAPTER 4** **1** Mt 13:1; Lk 8:4

He got into a boat [anchoring it a short
distance out] on the sea and sat down;
and the whole crowd was by the sea on
the shore. [Matt 13:1–15; Luke 8:4–15]
2 And He taught them many things
in parables, and in His teaching He
said to them,
3 "Listen! A sower went out to sow
seed;
4 and as he was sowing, some *seed*
fell by the road, and the birds came
and ate it up.
5 "Other *seed* fell on rocks where
there was not much soil; and imme-
diately a plant sprang up because the
soil had no depth.
6 "And when the sun came up, the
plant was scorched; and because it had
no root, it dried up *and* withered away.
7 "Other *seed* fell among thorns, and
the thorns came up and choked it, and
it yielded no grain.
8 "And other *seed* fell into good soil,
and as the plants grew and increased,
they yielded a crop and produced thir-
ty, sixty, and a hundred times [as much
as had been sown]."
9 And He said, "He who has ears to
hear, let him hear *and* heed My words."
10 As soon as He was alone, those
who were around Him, together with
the twelve [disciples], *began* asking
Him about [the interpretation of] the
parables.
11 He said to them, "The mystery of
the kingdom of God has been given to
you [who have teachable hearts], but
those who are outside [the unbelievers,
the spiritually blind] get everything in
parables,
12 so that THEY WILL CONTINUALLY LOOK
BUT NOT SEE, AND THEY WILL CONTINUALLY
HEAR BUT NOT UNDERSTAND, OTHERWISE
THEY MIGHT TURN [from their rejection of
the truth] AND BE FORGIVEN." [Is 6:9, 10;
Matt 13:11–15]

Explanation

13 Then He said to them, "Do you
not understand this parable? How will
you understand *and* grasp the mean-
ing of all the parables? [Matt 13:18–23;
Luke 8:11–15]
14 "The sower sows the word [of God,
the good news regarding the way of
salvation].
15 "These [in the first group] are the
ones along the road where the word
is sown; but when they hear, Satan
immediately comes and takes away the
word which has been sown in them.
16 "In a similar way these [in the
second group] are the ones on whom
seed was sown on rocky ground, who,
when they hear the word, immediately
receive it with joy [but accept it only
superficially];
17 and they have no real root in them-
selves, so they endure only for a little
while; then, when trouble or perse-
cution comes because of the word,
immediately they [are offended and
displeased at being associated with Me
and] stumble *and* fall away.
18 "And others are the ones on whom
seed was sown among the thorns;
these are the ones who have heard
the word,
19 but the worries *and* cares of the
world [the distractions of this age
with its worldly pleasures], and the
deceitfulness [and the false security
or glamour] of wealth [or fame], and
the passionate desires for all the oth-
er things creep in and choke out the
word, and it becomes unfruitful.

4:3 – 8 *A sower went out to sow seed.* The point of the parable is that the condition of the soil determines the potential for growth. The principle is true for Christians and non-Christians alike. Those who have become complacent and lackadaisical are not likely to receive the Word with benefit (Jas 1:2 – 25).

4:11 *The mystery of the kingdom of God has been given to you.* In Scripture, a mystery is a truth God has revealed or will reveal at the proper time (Ro 16:25 – 26). Jesus apparently used parables for several reasons. First, they are interesting and grab the listener's attention. Second, such stories are easily remembered. Third, they reveal truth to those who are ready spiritually to receive it. Fourth, they conceal truth from those who oppose Christ's message. Frequently Jesus' opponents failed to understand the lessons because of their own spiritual blindness (Mt 21:45 – 46).

2 Mk 12:38 **8** Jn 15:5; Col 1:6 **10** Mt 13:10; Lk 8:9 **11** 1Co 5:12; Col 4:5; 1Th 4:12; 1Ti 3:7 **12** Isa 6:9; Mt 13:14; Lk 8:10; Jn 12:40; Ac 28:26; Ro 11:8 **14** Mt 13:19 **19** 1Ti 6:9,17

20 “And those [in the last group] are the ones on whom seed was sown on the good soil; and they hear the word [of God, the good news regarding the way of salvation] and accept it and bear fruit—thirty, sixty, and a hundred times as much [as was sown].”

21 He said to them, “A lamp is not brought in to be put under a basket or under a bed, is it? Is it not [brought in] to be put on the lampstand? [Matt 5:15; Luke 8:16; 11:33]

22 “For nothing is hidden, except to be revealed; nor has anything been kept secret, but that it would come to light [that is, things are hidden only temporarily, until the appropriate time comes for them to be known]. [Matt 10:26–33; Luke 12:2–9]

23 “If anyone has ears to hear, let him hear *and* heed My words.”

24 Then He said to them, “Pay attention to what you hear. By your own standard of measurement [that is, to the extent that you study spiritual truth and apply godly wisdom] it will be measured to you [and you will be given even greater ability to respond]—and more will be given to you besides.

25 “For whoever has [a teachable heart], to him *more* [understanding] will be given; and whoever does not have [a yearning for truth], even what he has will be taken away from him.” [Matt 13:12; 25:29; Luke 8:18]

Parable of the Seed

26 Then He said, “The kingdom of God is like a man who throws seed on the ground;

27 and he goes to bed at night and gets up every day, and [in the meantime] the seed sprouts and grows; how [it does this], he does not know.

28 “The earth produces crops by itself; first the blade, then the head [of grain], then the mature grain in the head.

29 “But when the crop ripens, he immediately puts in the sickle [to reap], because [the time for] the harvest has come.”

Parable of the Mustard Seed

30 And He said, “How shall we picture the kingdom of God, or what parable shall we use to illustrate *and* explain it? [Matt 13:31, 32; Luke 13:18, 19]

31 “It is like a mustard seed, which, when it is sown on the ground, even though it is smaller than all the [other] seeds that are [sown] on the soil,

32 yet when it is sown, it grows up and becomes larger than all the garden herbs; and it puts out large branches, so that THE BIRDS OF THE SKY are able to MAKE NESTS *and* LIVE UNDER ITS SHADE.” [Ps 104:12; Ezek 17:23; 31:6]

33 With many such parables, Jesus spoke the word to them, as they were able to hear *and* understand it;

34 and He did not say *anything* to them without [using] a parable; He did, however, explain everything privately to His own disciples.

Jesus Stills the Sea

35 On that [same] day, when evening had come, He said to them, “Let us go over to the other side [of the Sea of Galilee].”

4:20 *hear the word . . . and accept it and bear fruit.* Only one soil produces fruit. Such a person recognizes God's call, determines to follow it, and experiences a profound transformation.

4:21 – 23 *A lamp.* These were small clay vessels that burned a wick set in olive oil. Like the lamp, Jesus' teachings reveal the motives of the human heart.

4:26 – 29 *The kingdom of God is like a man who throws seed on the ground.* Plants develop in a complex, intricate process that humans still do not fully understand even two thousand years after Jesus spoke these words. Yet plants grow and bear fruit and seeds just the same. God's kingdom likewise is growing, although we do not understand all that is happening. This parable, which appears only in Mark's Gospel, presents God's kingdom in brief, from first sowing to final reaping.

4:35 *go over to the other side.* The Sea of Galilee is about eight miles wide and twelve miles long. Its unique geography produces a

21 Mt 5:15; Lk 8:16; 11:33 **22** Mt 10:26 **23** ver. 9; Mt 11:15 **24** Mt 7:2; Lk 6:38 **25** Mt 13:12; 25:29; Lk 8:18; 19:26 **26** Mt 13:24 **29** Rev 14:15 **30** Mt 13:31; Lk 13:18; Ac 2:41; 4:4; 5:14; 19:20 **33** Mt 13:34; Jn 16:12 **35** Mt 8:18,23; Lk 8:22

36 So leaving the crowd, they took Him with them, just as He was, in the boat. And other boats were with Him. [Matt 8:23–27; Luke 8:22–25]

37 And a fierce windstorm began to blow, and waves were breaking over the boat, so that it was already being swamped.

38 But Jesus was in the stern, asleep [with His head] on the [sailor's leather] cushion. And they woke Him and said to Him, "Teacher, do You not care that we are about to die?"

39 And He got up and [sternly] rebuked the wind and said to the sea, "Hush, be still (muzzled)!" And the wind died down [as if it had grown weary] and there was [at once] a great calm [a perfect peacefulness].

40 Jesus said to them, "Why are you afraid? Do you still have no faith *and* confidence [in Me]?"

41 They were filled with great fear, and said to each other, "Who then is this, that even the wind and the sea obey Him?"

The Gerasene Demoniac

5 THEY CAME to the other side of the sea, to the region of the Gerasenes. [Matt 8:28–34; Luke 8:26–37]

2 When Jesus got out of the boat, immediately a man from the tombs with an unclean spirit met Him,

3 and the man lived in the tombs, and no one could bind him anymore, not even with chains.

4 For he had often been bound with shackles [for the feet] and with chains, and he tore apart the chains and broke the shackles into pieces, and no one was strong enough to subdue *and* tame him.

5 Night and day he was constantly screaming *and* shrieking among the tombs and on the mountains, and cutting himself with [sharp] stones.

6 Seeing Jesus from a distance, he ran up and bowed down before Him [in homage];

7 and screaming with a loud voice, he said, "What business do we have in common with each other, Jesus, Son of the Most High God? I implore you by God [swear to me], do not torment me!" [Matt 8:29; Luke 4:34]

8 For Jesus had been saying to him, "Come out of the man, you unclean spirit!"

9 He was asking him, "What is your name?" And he replied, "My name is Legion; for we are many."

10 And he *began* begging Him repeatedly not to send them out of the region.

11 Now there was a large herd of pigs grazing there on the mountain.

12 And *the demons* begged Him, saying, "Send us to the pigs so that we may go into them!"

13 Jesus gave them permission. And the unclean spirits came out [of the man] and entered the pigs. The herd, numbering about two thousand, rushed down the steep bank into the sea; and they were drowned [one after the other] in the sea.

14 The herdsmen [tending the pigs] ran away and reported it in the city and in the country. And *the people* came to see what had happened.

15 They came to Jesus and saw the man who had been demon-possessed sitting down, clothed and in his right mind, the man who had [previously] had the "legion" [of demons]; and they were frightened.

16 Those who had seen it described [in detail] to the people what had happened to the demon-possessed man, and [told them all] about the pigs.

---

greatly varying climate. It is 700 feet below sea level with mountains that rise 3,000–4,000 feet around it. It is not unusual for sudden windstorms to appear during the evening hours. The warm tropical air from the lake's surface rises and meets the colder air from the nearby hills. The resulting turbulences and winds can be treacherous.

4:41 *Who then is this.* Mark uses the disciples' question to evoke a similar response in the minds of his readers. Mark relates the works and words of the one he calls "Jesus Christ, the Son of God" (1:1).

5:1 *the region of the Gerasenes.* This area is on the eastern shore of the Sea of Galilee. The form of the name varies (Mt 8:28; Lk 8:26,37).

CHAPTER 5 **1** Mt 8:28; Lk 8:26 **12** Lev 11:7; Dt 14:8; Isa 65:4; Lk 15:15

17So the people began to beg with
Jesus to leave their region.
18As He was stepping into the boat,
the [Gentile] man who had been
demon-possessed was begging with
Him [asking] that he might go with
Him [as a disciple].
19Jesus did not let him [come], but
[instead] He said to him, "Go home to
your family and tell them all the great
things that the Lord has done for you,
and how He has had mercy on you."
20So he [obeyed and] went away and
began to publicly proclaim in Decapolis [the region of the ten Hellenistic
cities] all the great things that Jesus
had done for him; and all the people
were astonished.

Miracles and Healing

21When Jesus had again crossed
over in the boat to the other side [of the
sea], a large crowd gathered around
Him; and so He stayed by the seashore.
22One of the synagogue officials
named Jairus came up; and seeing
Him, fell at His feet [Matt 9:18–26;
Luke 8:41–56]
23and begged anxiously with Him,
saying, "My little daughter is at the
point of death; [please] come and lay
Your hands on her, so that she will be
healed and live."
24And Jesus went with him; and a
large crowd followed Him and pressed
in around Him [from all sides].
25A woman [in the crowd] had [suffered from] a hemorrhage for twelve
years,
26and had endured much [suffering] at
the hands of many physicians. She had
spent all that she had and was not helped
at all, but instead had become worse.
27She had heard [reports] about
Jesus, and she came up behind Him in
the crowd and touched His outer robe.
28For she thought, "If I just touch His
clothing, I will get well."
29Immediately her flow of blood was
dried up; and she felt in her body [and
knew without any doubt] that she was
healed of her suffering.
30Immediately Jesus, recognizing in
Himself that power had gone out from
Him, turned around in the crowd and
asked, "Who touched My clothes?"
31His disciples said to Him, "You
see the crowd pressing in around You
[from all sides], and You ask, 'Who
touched Me?' "
32Still He kept looking around to see
the woman who had done it.
33And the woman, though she was
afraid and trembling, aware of what
had happened to her, came and fell
down before Him and told Him the
whole truth.
34Then He said to her, "Daughter,

5:17 – 20 *the people began to beg with Jesus to leave their region.* Jesus was not well received in this region. His presence had cost financial loss to some, although it meant liberation to the demoniac. Jesus could have healed and saved in that region, but He was turned away by its fearful citizens. ***Decapolis.*** This literally means "ten cities." This largely Gentile, Greek-speaking area was an important strategic link in Rome's military defense.

5:22 *One of the synagogue officials.* Jairus was a lay leader charged with supervising services at the synagogue.

5:26 *had endured much [suffering] at the hands of many physicians.* Mark is not complimentary toward the physicians who had treated this woman.

5:29 – 30 *Immediately.* This word is used twice in this context. Both the woman and Jesus simultaneously knew what had happened. ***Who touched My clothes?*** Jesus turned when He was touched and confronted the woman before she disappeared. He wanted to correct any mistaken notion she may have had about her healing. It was not any magical quality of His clothing but His divine will that had made her well.

5:33 *told Him the whole truth.* Jesus' kind manner and tender words must have eased the fear this woman had of being revealed. Naturally, the time that Jesus took to care for the woman must have worried the already tense disciples.

5:34 *Daughter.* Jesus used this tender word to address this woman, and He noted that her faith made the difference, for it was correctly placed in Him. Faith itself does not heal — it is the proper object of that faith, Jesus, who heals.

17 Mt 8:34; Ac 16:39 **18** Lk 8:38 **21** Mt 9:1; Lk 8:40 **22** Mt 9:18; Lk 8:41 **25** Lev 15:25; Mt 9:20 **30** Lk 6:19; 8:46 **34** Mt 9:22; Mk 10:52; Ac 14:9

your faith [your personal trust and confidence in Me] has restored you to health; go in peace and be [permanently] healed from your suffering."

35 While He was still speaking, some people came from the synagogue official's house, saying [to Jairus], "Your daughter has died; why bother the Teacher any longer?"

36 Overhearing what was being said, Jesus said to the synagogue official, "Do not be afraid; only keep on believing [in Me and my power]."

37 And He allowed no one to go with Him [as witnesses], except Peter and James and John the brother of James.

38 They came to the house of the synagogue official; and He looked [with understanding] at the uproar *and* commotion, and people loudly weeping and wailing [in mourning].

39 When He had gone in, He said to them, "Why make a commotion and weep? The child has not died, but is sleeping."

40 They *began* laughing [scornfully] at Him [because they knew the child was dead]. But He made them all go outside, and took along the child's father and mother and His own [three] companions, and entered *the room* where the child was.

41 Taking the child's hand, He said [tenderly] to her, "Talitha kum!"—which translated [from Aramaic] means, "Little girl, I say to you, get up!"

42 The little girl immediately got up and *began* to walk, for she was twelve years old. And immediately they [who witnessed the child's resurrection] were overcome with great wonder *and* utter amazement.

43 He gave strict orders that no one should know about this, and He told them to give her *something* to eat.

Teaching at Nazareth

6 JESUS LEFT there and came to His hometown [Nazareth]; and His disciples followed Him. [Matt 13:54–58; Luke 4:16, 23]

2 When the Sabbath came, He began to teach in the synagogue; and many who listened to Him were astonished, saying, "Where did this man get these things [this knowledge and spiritual insight]? What is this wisdom [this confident understanding of the Scripture] that has been given to Him, and such miracles as these performed by His hands?

3 "Is this not the carpenter, the son of Mary, and the brother of James and Joses and Judas and Simon? Are His sisters not here with us?" And they were [deeply] offended by Him [and their disapproval blinded them to the fact that He was anointed by God as the Messiah].

4 Jesus said to them, "A prophet is not without honor (respect) except in his hometown and among his relatives and in his own household."

5 And He could not do a miracle there at all [because of their unbelief] except that He laid His hands on a few sick people and healed them.

6 He wondered at their unbelief.

And He was going around in the villages teaching.

The Twelve Sent Out

7 And He called the twelve [disciples] and began to send them out [as His special messengers] two by two, and gave them authority *and* power over the unclean spirits.

8 He told them to take nothing for the journey except a mere walking stick—no bread, no [traveler's] bag, no money in their belts—

5:43 *He gave strict orders.* The command to keep the miracle a secret was a temporary measure, for certainly the girl's appearance could not be hidden very long. Such orders would, however, allow Jesus to exit quietly. Jesus did not want to be known *primarily* as a miracle worker, lest people seek Him for the wrong reasons.

6:4 *A prophet is not without honor (respect) except in his hometown.* This maxim is still repeated and is still true today. Perhaps others were jealous of Jesus' popularity and huge following. Their envy even took the form of violence against Christ (Lk 4:29).

35 Lk 8:49 **39** Jn 11:11 **40** Ac 9:40 **43** Mt 8:4; 9:30; 12:16; 17:19; Mk 3:12; Lk 5:14 **CHAPTER 6** **1** Mt 13:54; Lk 4:16 **2** Jn 6:42 **3** See Mt 12:46; Gal 1:19; Mt 11:6 **4** Mt 13:57; Jn 4:44 **5** See Ge 19:22; 32:25; Mt 13:58; Mk 9:23 **6** Isa 59:16; Mt 9:35; Lk 13:22 **7** Mt 10:1; Mk 3:13,14; Lk 9:1

CANA AND NAZARETH REVISITED

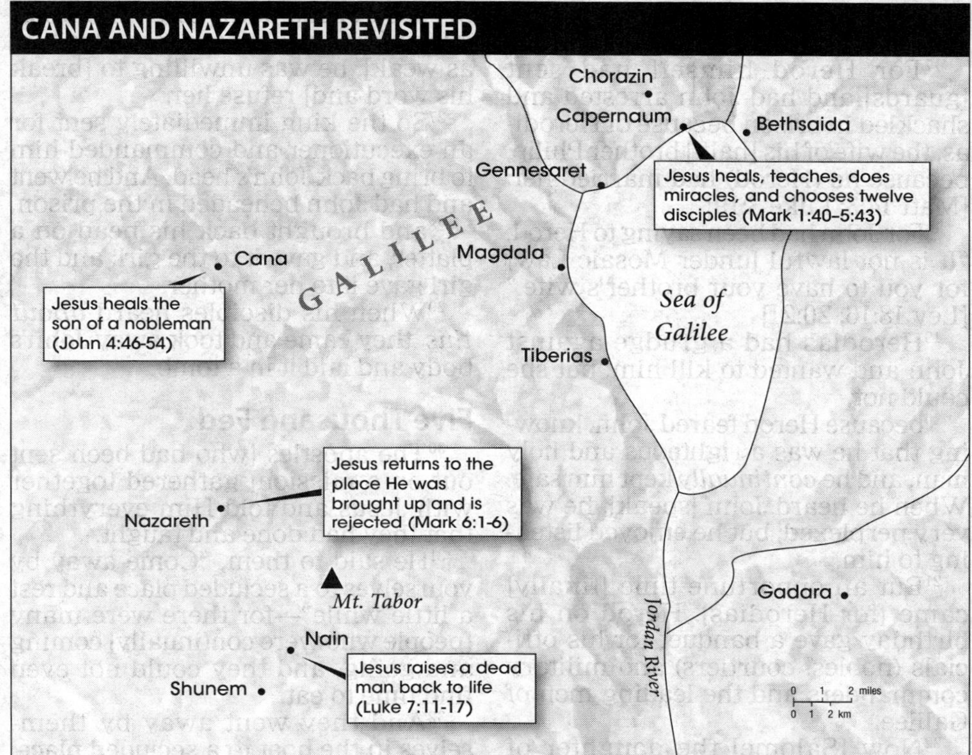

[9]but to wear sandals; and [He told
them] not to wear two tunics.
[10]And He told them, "Wherever you
go into a house, stay there until you
leave that town.
[11]"Any place that does not welcome
you or listen to you, when you leave
there, shake the dust off the soles
of your feet as a testimony against
them [breaking all ties with them
because they rejected My message]."
[Matt 10:14; Acts 13:51]
[12]So they went out and preached
that men should repent [that is, think
differently, recognize sin, turn away
from it, and live changed lives].
[13]And they were casting out many
demons and were anointing with oil
many who were sick, and healing
them.

John's Fate Recalled

[14]King Herod [Antipas] heard about
this, for Jesus' name *and* reputation
had become well known. People were
saying, "John the Baptist has been
raised from the dead, and that is why
these miraculous powers are at work
in Him."
[15]But others were saying, "He is Eli-
jah!" And others were saying, "It is a
prophet, like one of the prophets [of
old]."
[16]But when Herod heard [of it], he

6:14 *King Herod*. This is Herod Antipas, one of the sons of Herod the Great, the king who tried to kill the baby Jesus (Mt 2:1 – 18). After Herod the Great's death in 4 BC his kingdom was divided between Archaelaus, who received Judea and Samaria; Philip, who ruled Iturea and Trachonitis, north and east of Galilee; and Antipas, who controlled Galilee and Perea from 4 BC to AD 39. Jesus ministered largely in the territory ruled by Antipas.

9 Ac 12:8 **10** Mt 10:11; Lk 9:4; 10:7,8 **11** Mt 10:14; Lk 10:10; Ac 13:51; 18:6 **13** Jas 5:14 **14** Mt 14:1; Lk 9:7 **15** Mt 16:14; Mk 8:28 **16** Mt 14:2; Lk 3:19

kept saying, "John, whom I beheaded,
has risen [from the dead]!"
17 For Herod himself had sent
[guards] and had John arrested and
shackled in prison because of Herodi-
as, the wife of his [half-] brother Philip,
because he (Herod) had married her.
[Matt 14:3; Luke 3:19]
18 For John had been saying to Herod,
"It is not lawful [under Mosaic Law]
for you to have your brother's wife."
[Lev 18:16; 20:21]
19 Herodias had a grudge against
John and wanted to kill him, but she
could not,
20 because Herod feared John, know-
ing that he was a righteous and holy
man, and he *continually* kept him safe.
When he heard John [speak], he was
very perplexed; but he enjoyed listen-
ing to him.
21 But an opportune time [finally]
came [for Herodias]. Herod on his
birthday gave a banquet for his offi-
cials (nobles, courtiers) and military
commanders and the leading men of
Galilee.
22 Now [Salome] the daughter of
Herodias came in and danced [for the
men]. She pleased *and* beguiled Herod
and his dinner guests; and the king
said to the girl, "Ask me for whatever
you want and I will give it to you."
23 And he swore to her, "Whatever
you ask me, I will give it to you; up to
half of my kingdom." [Esth 5:3, 6]
24 She went out and said to her moth-
er, "What shall I ask for?" And Hero-
dias replied, "The head of John the
Baptist!"
25 And she rushed back to the king
and asked, saying, "I want you to give
me right now the head of John the
Baptist on a platter!"
26 The king was deeply grieved, but
because of his oaths and his dinner
guests [who might have regarded him
as weak], he was unwilling to [break
his word and] refuse her.
27 So the king immediately sent for
an executioner and commanded him
to bring back John's head. And he went
and had John beheaded in the prison,
28 and brought back his head on a
platter, and gave it to the girl; and the
girl gave it to her mother.
29 When his disciples heard *about
this,* they came and took away John's
body and laid it in a tomb.

Five Thousand Fed

30 The apostles [who had been sent
out on a mission] gathered together
with Jesus and told Him everything
that they had done and taught.
31 He said to them, "Come away by
yourselves to a secluded place and rest
a little while"—for there were many
[people who were continually] coming
and going, and they could not even
find time to eat.
32 And they went away by them-
selves in the boat to a secluded place.
[Matt 14:13–21; Luke 9:10–17; John 6:1–
13]
33 Many [people] saw them leaving,
and recognized *them* and ran there
together on foot from all the [surround-
ing] cities, and got there ahead of them.
34 When Jesus went ashore, He saw
a large crowd [waiting], and He was
moved with compassion for them be-
cause they were like sheep without a
shepherd [lacking guidance]; and He
began to teach them many things.
35 When the day was nearly gone,
His disciples came to Him and said,
"This is an isolated place, and it is al-
ready late;
36 send the crowds away so that they

6:18 *not lawful.* John's message to Herod was that his divorce was not lawful as grounds for remarriage. John's declaration could be based on Jesus' stern words about divorce (10:11 – 12) or on Leviticus 20:21, which prohibits a man from taking his brother's wife.

6:23 *up to half of my kingdom.* This is an expression meaning a large amount but with some limits.

6:34 *moved with compassion.* The Gospels record several times that when Jesus saw a need He responded compassionately (1:41). That compassion led to action, despite an obvious lack of food in this instance.

18 Lev 18:16; 20:21 **20** Mt 14:5; 21:26 **21** Mt 14:6; Ge 40:20 **23** Est 5:3,6; 7:2 **26** Mt 14:9 **30** Lk 9:10
31 Mt 14:13; Mk 3:20 **32** Mt 14:13 **34** Mt 9:36; 14:14; Lk 9:11 **35** Mt 14:15; Lk 9:12

may go into the surrounding countryside and villages and buy themselves something to eat."

37 But He replied, "You give them something to eat!" And they asked Him, "Shall we go and buy 200 denarii worth of bread and give it to them to eat?" [2 Kin 4:42–44]

38 He said to them, "How many loaves do you have? Go look!" And when they found out, they said, "Five [loaves], and two fish."

39 Then Jesus commanded them all to sit down by groups on the green grass.

40 They sat down in groups of hundreds and of fifties [so that the crowd resembled an orderly arrangement of colorful garden plots].

41 Taking the five loaves and two fish, He looked up to heaven and said a blessing [of praise and thanksgiving to the Father]. Then He broke the loaves and [repeatedly] gave them to the disciples to set before the people; and He divided up the two fish among them all.

42 They all ate and were satisfied.

43 And the disciples picked up twelve full baskets of the broken pieces [of the loaves], and of the fish.

44 Those who ate the loaves were five thousand men [not counting the women and children].

Jesus Walks on the Water

45 Jesus immediately insisted that His disciples get into the boat and go ahead [of Him] to the other side to Bethsaida, while He was dismissing the crowd. [Matt 14:22–32; John 6:15–21]

46 And after He said goodbye to them, He went to the mountain to pray.

47 Now when evening had come, the boat was in the middle of the sea, and Jesus was alone on the land.

48 Seeing the disciples straining at the oars, because the wind was against them, at about the fourth watch of the night (3:00–6:00 a.m.) He came to them, walking on the sea. And [acted as if] He intended to pass by them. [Matt 14:25; John 6:19]

49 But when they saw Him walking on the sea, they thought it was a ghost, and cried out [in horror];

50 for they all saw Him and were shaken *and* terrified. But He immediately spoke with them and said, "Take courage! It is I (I AM)! Stop being afraid." [Ex 3:14]

51 Then He got into the boat with them, and the wind ceased [as if exhausted by its own activity]; and they were completely overwhelmed,

52 because they had not understood [the miracle of] the loaves [how it revealed the power and deity of Jesus]; but [in fact] their heart was hardened [being oblivious and indifferent to His amazing works].

Healing at Gennesaret

53 When they had crossed over [the sea], they reached the land of Gennesaret and anchored at the shore.

54 They got out of the boat and immediately *people* recognized Him,

55 and ran throughout that surrounding countryside and began to carry around on their mats those who were sick, to any place where they heard He was.

56 And wherever He came into villages,

6:36 – 37 *send the crowds away.* The disciples sought to avoid responsibility for the hungry multitude.

6:39 – 40 *in groups of hundreds and of fifties.* Details such as sitting on the green grass, which is possible only in late winter and early spring, and the fact that the groups were counted are indications that an eyewitness, probably Peter, recounted this story to Mark.

6:43 *twelve full baskets of the broken pieces.* These were small baskets commonly carried by travelers. It is possible to conclude that the leftovers gave each disciple enough food for his own use.

6:51 *He got into the boat with them.* Three miracles are contained in this brief account (vv. 47 – 51); (1) In the darkness Jesus saw the disciples out in the storm miles away, (2) Jesus walked on the water, and (3) Jesus showed complete control over His creation when the wind ceased.

6:56 *wherever He came into villages, or*

---

37 Nu 11:13,22; 2Ki 4:43 **38** Mt 14:17; Lk 9:13; Jn 6:9; See Mt 15:34; Mk 8:5 **41** 1Sa 9:13; Mt 26:26 **45** Mt 14:22; Jn 6:17 **47** Mt 14:23; Jn 6:16,17 **48** See Lk 24:28 **52** Mk 8:17,18; Mk 3:5; 16:14 **53** Mt 14:34 **56** Mt 9:20; Mk 5:27,28; Ac 19:12

or cities, or the countryside, they were laying the sick in the market places and pleading with Him [to allow them] just to touch the fringe (tassel with a blue cord) of His robe; and all who touched it were healed.

Followers of Tradition

7 NOW THE Pharisees and some of the scribes came from Jerusalem and gathered around Him,

2 and they had seen that some of His disciples ate their bread with [ceremonially] impure hands, that is, unwashed [and defiled according to Jewish religious ritual].

3 (For the Pharisees and all of the Jews do not eat unless they carefully wash their hands, holding firmly to the traditions of the elders;

4 and *when they come* from the market place, they do not eat unless they cleanse themselves [completely according to ritual]; and there are many other things [oral, man-made laws and traditions handed down to them] which they follow diligently, such as the washing of cups and pitchers and copper utensils.)

5 So the Pharisees and scribes asked Jesus, "Why do Your disciples not live their lives according to the tradition of the elders, but [instead] eat their bread with [ceremonially] unwashed hands?"

6 He replied, "Rightly did Isaiah prophesy about you hypocrites (play-actors, pretenders), as it is written [in Scripture],

'THESE PEOPLE HONOR ME WITH THEIR LIPS,
BUT THEIR HEART IS FAR FROM ME.
7 'THEY WORSHIP ME IN VAIN [their worship is meaningless and worthless, a pretense],
TEACHING THE PRECEPTS OF MEN AS DOCTRINES [giving their traditions equal weight with the Scriptures].' [Is 29:13]

8 "You disregard *and* neglect the commandment of God, and cling [faithfully] to the tradition of men."

9 He was also saying to them, "You are experts at setting aside *and* nullifying the commandment of God in order to keep your [man-made] tradition *and* regulations.

10 "For Moses said, 'HONOR YOUR FATHER AND YOUR MOTHER [with respect and gratitude]'; and, 'HE WHO SPEAKS EVIL OF HIS FATHER OR MOTHER MUST BE PUT TO DEATH'; [Ex 20:12; 21:17; Lev 20:9; Deut 5:16]

11 but you [Pharisees and scribes] say, 'If a man tells his father or mother, "Whatever I have that would help you is Corban, (that is to say, *already* a gift to God)," '

12 then you no longer let him do anything for his father or mother [since helping them would violate his vow of Corban];

13 so you nullify the [authority of the] word of God [acting as if it did not apply] because of your tradition which you have handed down [through the elders]. And you do many things such as that."

cities, or the countryside. Mark summarizes Jesus' healing ministry, noting how widespread it was.

7:3 – 4 *For the Pharisees.* These two verses explain the tradition of handwashing and various kinds of ceremonial uncleanness. Mark's intended readers in Rome likely needed more background on the Jewish faith to understand this controversy.

7:5 *the tradition of the elders.* This phrase refers to a series of rules meant to bolster the ceremonial law of the Jews. Its authority was not supported by Scripture. The question indirectly challenged Jesus, for as the disciples' teacher He was judged responsible for their actions.

7:6 – 7 *hypocrites.* The term originally referred to actors who wore masks on stage as they played different characters. Thus the Pharisees were not genuinely religious; they were merely playing a part for all to see.

7:11 – 13 *but you [Pharisees and scribes] say.* This shows the absolute contrast between God's will and man's empty tradition. ***Corban.*** This was evidently a pious-sounding evasion of the requirement of honoring one's parents by supporting them financially.

CHAPTER 7 **1** Mt 15:1 **5** Mt 15:2 **6** Isa 29:13 **10** Ex 20:12; Dt 5:16; Mt 15:4; Ex 21:17; Lev 20:9; Pr 20:20 **11** Mt 15:5; 23:18

The Heart of Man

14 After He called the people to Him again, He *began* saying to them, "Listen [carefully] to Me, all of you, [hear] and understand [what I am saying]:

15 there is nothing outside a man [such as food] which by going into him can defile him [morally or spiritually]; but the things which come out of [the heart of] a man are what defile *and* dishonor him.

16 ["If anyone has ears to hear, let him hear."]

17 When Jesus had left the crowd and gone into the house, His disciples asked Him about the parable.

18 And He said to them, "Are you, too, so foolish *and* lacking in understanding? Do you not understand that whatever goes into the man from outside cannot defile *and* dishonor him,

19 since it does not enter his heart, but [only] his stomach, and [from there it] is eliminated?" (*By this, He* declared all foods ceremonially clean.)

20 And He said, "Whatever comes from [the heart of] a man, that is what defiles *and* dishonors him.

21 "For from within, [that is] out the heart of men, come base *and* malevolent thoughts *and* schemes, acts of sexual immorality, thefts, murders, adulteries,

22 acts of greed *and* covetousness, wickedness, deceit, unrestrained conduct, envy *and* jealousy, slander *and* profanity, arrogance *and* self-righteousness and foolishness (poor judgment).

23 "All these evil things [schemes and desires] come from within and defile *and* dishonor the man."

The Syrophoenician Woman

24 Jesus got up and left there and went to the region of Tyre [and Sidon, the coastal area of Phoenicia]. He entered a house and did not want anyone to know *about it;* but it was impossible for Him to be hidden [from the public]. [Matt 15:21–28]

25 Instead, after hearing about Him, a woman whose little daughter had an unclean spirit immediately came and fell at His feet.

26 Now the woman was a Gentile (Greek), a Syrophoenician by nationality. And she kept pleading with Him to drive the demon out of her daughter.

27 He was saying to her, "First let the children [of Israel] be fed, for it is not right to take the children's bread and throw it to the pet dogs (non-Jews)."

28 But she replied, "Yes, Lord, but even the pet dogs under the table eat the children's crumbs."

29 And He said to her, "Because of this answer [reflecting your humility and faith], go [knowing that your request is granted]; the demon has left your daughter [permanently]."

30 And returning to her home, she found the child lying on the couch [relaxed and resting], the demon having gone.

31 Soon after this Jesus left the region of Tyre, and passed through Sidon to the Sea of Galilee, through the region of Decapolis [the ten Hellenistic cities].

32 They brought to Him a man who was deaf and had difficulty speaking, and they begged Jesus to place His hand on him.

33 Jesus, taking him aside by himself, away from the crowd, put His fingers into the man's ears, and after spitting,

---

7:24 *the region of Tyre.* This city is the farthest Jesus traveled from Israel during his public ministry.

7:27 *to the pet dogs.* Jesus is not attempting to insult the woman by using this metaphor. In fact, He is testing her faith. Matthew records Jesus' reaction to her reply, "Woman, your faith ... is great" (Mt 15:28).

7:28 *But she replied.* The woman understood Jesus' test and persistently replied that even during the meal the dogs consume the children's crumbs that fall from the table.

7:32–35 *a man who was deaf.* The healing of this deaf man (who also had a speech impediment) is one of the two miracles recorded by Mark only. (The other is the healing of the blind man in 8:22–26.)

14 Mt 15:10 **16** Mt 11:15 **17** Mt 15:15 **21** Ge 6:5; 8:21; Mt 15:19 **24** Mt 15:21 **31** Mt 15:29 **32** Mt 9:32; Lk 11:14 **33** Mk 8:23; Jn 9:6

He touched the man's tongue [with the saliva];

[34]and looking up to heaven, He sighed deeply and said to the man, "Ephphatha," which [in Aramaic] means, "Be opened *and* released!"

[35]And his ears were opened, his tongue was released, and he *began* speaking plainly.

[36]Jesus commanded them not to tell anyone; but the more He ordered them, the more widely they continued to proclaim it.

[37]They were thoroughly astounded *and* completely overwhelmed, saying, "He has done everything well! He even makes the deaf hear and the mute speak!"

Four Thousand Fed

8 IN THOSE days, when there was again a large crowd [gathered before Him] and they had nothing to eat, Jesus called His disciples and told them, [Matt 15:32–39]

[2]"I feel compassion for the crowd; they have been with Me now for three days and have nothing [left] to eat.

[3]"If I send them away to their homes hungry, they will faint [from exhaustion] on the road; because some of them have come a long way."

[4]His disciples replied to Him, "Where will anyone be able to find enough bread here in this isolated place to feed these people?"

[5]He asked them, "How many loaves [of bread] do you have?" They said, "Seven."

[6]He directed the people to sit down on the ground; and taking the seven loaves, He gave thanks and broke them, and [repeatedly] gave them to His disciples to set before them, and they served the crowd.

[7]They also had a few small fish; and when Jesus had blessed them [and given thanks], He ordered these [fish] to be set before them as well.

[8]And the people ate and were satisfied; and they picked up seven large baskets full of the broken pieces that were left over.

[9]About four thousand [men] were there [besides women and children]; and He sent them away.

[10]Then immediately He got into the boat with His disciples and went to the district of Dalmanutha.

[11]The Pharisees came out and began to argue [contentiously and debate] with Him, demanding from Him a sign from heaven, to test Him [because of their unbelief].

[12]He groaned *and* sighed deeply in His spirit and said, "Why does this generation demand a sign? I assure you *and* most solemnly say to you, no sign will be given to this generation!"

[13]Leaving them, He again boarded the boat and left for the other side.

[14]Now the disciples had forgotten to bring bread, and they had only one loaf with them in the boat.

[15]Jesus repeatedly ordered them, saying, "Watch out! Beware of the leaven of the Pharisees and the leaven of Herod."

[16]They *began* discussing this with one another, saying, "It is because we have no bread [that He said this]."

[17]Jesus, aware of this [discussion],

8:8 *seven large baskets.* There was one basket for each original loaf. These baskets were much larger than the 12 small personal baskets mentioned in 6:43. It was the kind of larger basket that was used to lower Paul over the wall of Damascus (Ac 9:25).

8:10 *Dalmanutha.* This was probably on the western side of the Sea of Galilee, about three miles north of modern Tiberias and about five miles southwest of Capernaum. This is the only time it is mentioned in the New Testament.

8:11 *The Pharisees came out and began to argue [contentiously and debate] with Him.* The Pharisees' testing of Jesus was crafty and devious. Obviously these men did not heed the many signs and wonders that Jesus had already performed. John 20:30–31 indicates that the signs were meant to produce faith. It is doubtful that the Pharisees would have changed their minds even if they had seen another miracle.

8:17–21 *Do you still not see or understand?* The disciples continued to show a lack of spiritual

34 Mk 6:41; Jn 11:41; 17:1; Jn 11:33,38 **35** Isa 35:5,6 **36** Mk 5:43 **CHAPTER 8** **1** Mt 15:32 **5** Mt 15:34; See Mk 6:38 **7** Mt 14:19; Mk 6:41 **10** Mt 15:39 **11** Mt 12:38; 16:1; Jn 6:30 **14** Mt 16:5 **15** Mt 16:6; Lk 12:1 **17** Mk 6:52

said to them, "Why are you discussing [the fact] that you have no bread? Do you still not see or understand? Are your hearts hardened? [Is 6:9, 10]

18 "THOUGH YOU HAVE EYES, DO YOU NOT SEE? AND THOUGH YOU HAVE EARS, DO YOU NOT HEAR *and* LISTEN [to what I have said]? And do you not remember, [Jer 5:21]

19 when I broke the five loaves for the five thousand, how many baskets full of broken pieces you picked up?" They answered, "Twelve."

20 "And [when I broke] the seven [loaves] for the four thousand, how many large baskets full of broken pieces did you pick up?" And they answered, "Seven."

21 And He was saying to them, "Do you still not understand?"

22 Then they came to Bethsaida; and some people brought a blind man to Jesus and begged Him to touch him.

23 Taking the blind man by the hand, He led him out of the village; and after spitting on his eyes and laying His hands on him, He asked him, "Do you see anything?"

24 And he looked up and said, "I see people, but [they look] like trees, walking around."

25 Then again Jesus laid His hands on his eyes; and the man stared intently and [his sight] was [completely] restored, and he *began* to see everything clearly.

26 And He sent him to his home, saying, "Do not even enter the village."

Peter's Confession of Christ

27 Then Jesus and His disciples went out to the villages of Caesarea Philippi; and on the way He asked His disciples, "Who do people say that I am?" [Matt 16:13–16; Luke 9:18–20]

28 They answered Him, "John the Baptist; and others say Elijah; but others, one of the prophets."

29 And He asked them, "But who do you say that I am?" Peter replied to Him, "You [in contrast to the others] are the Christ (the Messiah, the Anointed)."

30 Then Jesus strictly warned them not to tell anyone about Him.

31 And He began to teach them that the Son of Man must [of necessity] suffer many things and be rejected [as the Messiah] by the elders and the chief priests and the scribes, and must be put to death, and after three days rise [from death to life]. [Matt 16:21–28; Luke 9:22–27]

32 He was stating the matter plainly [not holding anything back]. Then Peter took Him aside and began to reprimand Him.

33 But turning around [with His back to Peter] and seeing His disciples, He rebuked Peter, saying, "Get behind Me, Satan; for your mind is not set on God's will *or* His values and purposes, but on what pleases man."

34 Jesus called the crowd together with His disciples, and said to them,

---

discernment despite the miracles they had witnessed. Jesus' rebuke was intended to make them recall what God had done for them.

8:27 ***Caesarea Philippi.*** This city is about 25 miles north of Bethsaida and the Sea of Galilee. It stands on the southern edge of Mount Hermon. One of the sources of the Jordan River springs forth from under a large rocky cliff that rises a hundred or more feet above the village. The name Philippi distinguishes this town from Caesarea by the sea.

8:29 ***But who do you say that I am?*** Jesus emphatically asks His disciples for their understanding. ***you.*** Prominent in Jesus' question is the word "you." ***You . . . are the Christ.*** Peter answers for the group. Jesus wants His disciples to grasp firmly His true identity before He reveals to them the necessity of His coming death and resurrection. In Mark's Gospel, only the disciples come to understand who Jesus is.

8:30 ***not to tell anyone about Him.*** Jesus' warning may seem strange. Its explanation lies in the fact that the Jews expected the Messiah to be a political liberator. Jesus' first coming was meant to accomplish another kind of liberation—release from sin. Hence Jesus was careful not to use the name Messiah publicly, for it was misunderstood by the Jewish people, their leaders, and the Roman authorities.

---

19 Mt 14:20; Mk 6:43; Lk 9:17; Jn 6:13 **20** ver. 8; Mt 15:37 **21** ver. 17; Mk 6:52 **23** Mk 7:33 **26** Mt 8:4; Mk 5:43 **27** Mt 16:13; Lk 9:18 **28** Mt 14:2 **29** Mt 16:16; Jn 6:69; 11:27 **30** Mt 16:20 **31** Mt 16:21; 17:22; Lk 9:22 **34** Mt 10:38; 16:24; Lk 9:23; 14:27

“If anyone wishes to follow Me [as My
disciple], he must deny himself [set
aside selfish interests], and take up
his cross [expressing a willingness to
endure whatever may come] and follow
Me [believing in Me, conforming to
My example in living and, if need be,
suffering or perhaps dying because of
faith in Me].
35 “For whoever wishes to save his
life [in this world] will [eventually]
lose it [through death], but whoever
loses his life [in this world] for My sake
and the gospel’s will save it [from the
consequences of sin and separation
from God]. [Matt 10:39; Luke 17:33;
John 12:25]
36 “For what does it benefit a man
to gain the whole world [with all its
pleasures], and forfeit his soul?
37 “For what will a man give in ex-
change for his soul *and* eternal life [in
God’s kingdom]?
38 “For whoever is ashamed [here
and now] of Me and My words in this
adulterous and sinful generation, the
Son of Man will also be ashamed of
him when He comes in the glory of His
Father with the holy angels.”

The Transfiguration

9 AND JESUS said to them, “I assure
you *and* most solemnly say to you,
there are some of those who are stand-
ing here who will not taste (experience)
death before they see the kingdom of
God after it has come with power.”
2 Six days later, Jesus took with Him
Peter and James and John, and led them
up on a high mountain by themselves.
And He was transfigured (changed in
form) before them [and began to shine
brightly with divine and regal glory];
[Matt 17:1–8; Luke 9:28–36]
3 and His clothes became radiant *and*
dazzling, intensely white, as no laun-
derer on earth can whiten them.
4 Elijah appeared to them along with
Moses, and they were having a conver-
sation with Jesus.
5 Peter responded and said to Jesus,
“Rabbi (Master), it is good for us to be
here; let us make three [sacred] tents—
one for You, and one for Moses, and
one for Elijah.”
6 For he did not [really] know what
to say because they were terrified [and
stunned by the miraculous sight].
7 Then a cloud formed, overshadow-
ing them, and a voice came out of the
cloud, “This is My beloved Son. Listen
to Him *and* obey Him!”
8 Suddenly they looked around and
no longer saw anyone with them, ex-
cept Jesus alone.
9 As they were coming down from
the mountain, Jesus expressly ordered
them not to tell anyone what they had
seen, until the Son of Man had risen
from the dead.
10 So they [carefully and faithfully]
kept the matter to themselves, discuss-
ing *and* questioning [with one another]
what it meant to rise from the dead.
11 They asked Him, saying, “Why do
the scribes say that Elijah must come
first [before the Messiah comes]?”
[Mal 4:5, 6]
12 He answered them, “Elijah does
come first and restores *and* reestab-
lishes all things. And yet how is it
written of the Son of Man that He will
suffer many things [grief and physi-
cal distress] and be treated with con-
tempt [utterly despised and rejected]?
[Is 53:3]
13 “But I say to you that Elijah has
in fact come [already], and they did to

8:38 *when He comes in the glory.* This is the first glimpse of the fulfillment of all history (1Co 15:24 – 28). Those who will reign with Christ invest their lives in that which will last (v. 35). Those who are willing to confess Him today will be rewarded before the Father in heaven (Mt 5:10 – 12; 2Ti 2:11 – 13; Rev 2:26 – 28).

9:4 *Elijah.* Elijah is mentioned in Malachi 4:5 – 6 in connection with the future coming of Christ. This is why people asked John the Baptist if he was Elijah (Jn 1:21). Moses was the lawgiver and liberator, while Elijah was the first of the great prophets. Their presence confirmed the reality that Jesus is the Messiah of Peter’s confession.

35 Jn 12:25 **38** Mt 10:33; Lk 9:26; 12:9; See Ro 1:16; 2Ti 1:8; 2:12 **CHAPTER 9** **1** Mt 16:28; Lk 9:27; Mt 24:30 **2** Mt 17:1; Lk 9:28 **3** Da 7:9 **9** Mt 17:9 **11** Mal 4:5; Mt 17:10 **12** Ps 22:6; Isa 53:2; Da 9:26; Lk 23:11; Php 2:7 **13** Mt 11:14; 17:12; Lk 1:17

him whatever they wished, just as it is written [in Scripture] of him."

All Things Possible

14 When they came [back] to the [other nine] disciples, they saw a large crowd around them, and scribes questioning *and* arguing with them. [Matt 17:14–18; Luke 9:37–42]

15 Immediately, when the entire crowd saw Jesus, they were startled and *began* running up to greet Him.

16 He asked them, "What are you discussing with them?"

17 One of the crowd replied to Him, "Teacher, I brought You my son, possessed with a spirit which makes him unable to speak;

18 and whenever it seizes him [intending to do harm], it throws him down, and he foams [at the mouth], and grinds his teeth and becomes stiff. I told Your disciples to drive it out, and they could not do it."

19 He replied, "O unbelieving (faithless) generation, how long shall I be with you? How long shall I put up with you? Bring him to Me!"

20 They brought the boy to Him. When the [demonic] spirit saw Him, immediately it threw the boy into a convulsion, and falling to the ground he *began* rolling around and foaming *at the mouth*.

21 Jesus asked his father, "How long has this been happening to him?" And he answered, "Since childhood.

22 "The demon has often thrown him both into fire and into water, intending to kill him. But if You can do anything, take pity on us and help us!"

23 Jesus said to him, "[You say to Me,] 'If You can?' All things are possible for the one who believes *and* trusts [in Me]!"

24 Immediately the father of the boy cried out [with a desperate, piercing cry], saying, "I do believe; help [me overcome] my unbelief."

25 When Jesus saw that a crowd was rapidly gathering [around them], He rebuked the unclean spirit, saying to it, "You deaf and mute spirit, I command you, come out of him and never enter him again!"

26 After screaming out and throwing him into a terrible convulsion, it came out. The boy looked so much like a corpse [so still and pale] that many [of the spectators] said, "He is dead!"

27 But Jesus took him by the hand and raised him; and he stood up.

28 When He had gone indoors, His disciples *began* asking Him privately, "Why were we unable to drive it out?"

29 He replied to them, "This kind [of unclean spirit] cannot come out by anything but prayer [to the Father]."

Death and Resurrection Foretold

30 They went on from there and *began* to go through Galilee. Jesus did not want anyone to know it,

31 because He was teaching His disciples [and preparing them for the future]. He told them, "The Son of Man is to be betrayed *and* handed over to men [who are His enemies], and they will kill Him; and when He has been killed, He will rise [from the dead] three days later."

32 But they did not understand this statement, and they were afraid to ask Him [what He meant].

33 They arrived at Capernaum; and when He was in the house, He asked them, "What were you discussing *and* arguing about on the road?" [Matt 18:1–5; Luke 9:46–48]

34 But they kept quiet, because on the road they had discussed *and* debated with one another which one [of them] was the greatest.

35 Sitting down [to teach], He called the twelve [disciples] and said to them, "If anyone wants to be first, he must

9:24 *I do believe; help [me overcome] my unbelief.* These words express the dilemma that even those who believe can be nagged by doubt and hopelessness. This man took the correct course by appealing to Jesus for help.

14 Mt 17:14; Lk 9:37 **17** Mt 17:14; Lk 9:38 **20** Mk 1:26; Lk 9:42 **23** Mt 17:20; Mk 11:23; Lk 17:6; Jn 11:40 **28** Mt 17:19 **31** Mt 17:22; Lk 9:44 **33** Mt 18:1; Lk 9:46; 22:24 **35** Mt 20:26,27; Mk 10:43

be last of all [in importance] and a servant of all."

36 Taking a child, He set him before them; and taking him in His arms, He said to them,

37 "Whoever receives *and* welcomes one child such as this in My name receives Me; and whoever receives Me receives not [only] Me, but Him who sent Me." [Matt 10:40; Luke 10:16; John 13:20]

Dire Warnings

38 John said to Him, "Teacher, we saw someone casting out demons in Your name, and we tried to stop him because he was not accompanying us [as Your disciple]." [Luke 9:49, 50]

39 But Jesus said, "Do not stop him; for there is no one who will perform a miracle in My name, and be able soon afterward to speak evil of Me.

40 "For he who is not against us is for us. [Num 11:27–29]

41 "For whoever gives you a cup of water to drink because of your name as followers of Christ, I assure you *and* most solemnly say to you, he will not lose his reward.

42 "But whoever causes one of these little ones who believe *and* trust in Me to stumble [that is, to sin or lose faith], it would be better for him if a heavy millstone [one requiring a donkey's strength to turn it] were hung around his neck and he were thrown into the sea. [Matt 18:6; Luke 17:2]

43 "If your hand causes you to stumble *and* sin, cut it off [that is, remove yourself from the source of temptation]! It is better for you to enter life crippled, than to have two hands and go into hell, into the unquenchable fire,

44 [where THEIR WORM DOES NOT DIE, AND THE FIRE IS NOT PUT OUT.] [Is 66:24]

45 "If your foot causes you to stumble *and* sin, cut it off [that is, remove yourself from the source of temptation]! It would be better for you to enter life lame than to have two feet and be thrown into hell,

46 [where THEIR WORM DOES NOT DIE, AND THE FIRE IS NOT PUT OUT.] [Is 66:24]

47 "If your eye causes you to stumble *and* sin, throw it out [that is, remove yourself from the source of temptation]! It would be better for you to enter the kingdom of God with one eye, than to have two eyes and be thrown into hell,

48 where THEIR WORM [that feeds on the dead] DOES NOT DIE, AND THE FIRE IS NOT PUT OUT. [Is 66:24]

49 "For everyone will be salted with fire.

50 "Salt is good *and* useful; but if salt has lost its saltiness (purpose), how will you make it salty? Have salt within yourselves *continually*, and be at peace with one another."

Jesus' Teaching about Divorce

10 GETTING UP, He left there (Capernaum) and went to the region of Judea and beyond the Jordan; and crowds gathered around Him again *and* accompanied Him, and as was His custom, He once more *began* to teach them.

2 Pharisees came to Jesus to test Him [intending to trick Him into saying something wrong], and asked Him, "Is it lawful [according to Scripture] for a man to divorce his wife *and* send her away?"

3 He replied to them, "What did Moses command you?"

4 They said, "Moses allowed *a man* TO WRITE A CERTIFICATE OF DIVORCE AND TO SEND HER AWAY." [Deut 24:1–4]

9:40 ***For he who is not against us is for us.*** Jesus is not endorsing all who claim to follow Him. Rather, this statement was meant to remind the disciples that God's work was not necessarily restricted to their small group.

9:49 ***For everyone will be salted with fire.*** This phrase may refer to the trials and judgments that all will face — believers with trials that purify faith, unbelievers with the eternal fire of God's judgment.

10:4 ***A CERTIFICATE OF DIVORCE.*** This was a document signed before witnesses. Its intent was to limit frivolous divorces. In Jesus' day, the

36 Mt 18:2; Mk 10:16 **37** Mt 10:40; Lk 9:48 **38** Nu 11:28; Lk 9:49 **39** 1Co 12:3 **40** See Mt 12:30 **41** Mt 10:42 **42** Mt 18:6; Lk 17:1 **43** Dt 13:6; Mt 5:29; 18:8 **44** Isa 66:24 **49** Lev 2:13; Eze 43:24 **50** Mt 5:13; Lk 14:34; Eph 4:29; Col 4:6; Ro 12:18; 14:19; 2Co 13:11; Heb 12:14 **CHAPTER 10** **1** Mt 19:1; Jn 10:40; 11:7 **2** Mt 19:3 **4** Dt 24:1; Mt 5:31; 19:7

[5]But Jesus said to them, "Because of your hardness of hearts [your callousness and insensitivity toward your wives and the provision of God] he wrote you this precept.
[6]"But from the beginning of creation *God* MADE THEM MALE AND FEMALE. [Gen 1:27; 5:2]
[7]"FOR THIS REASON A MAN SHALL LEAVE HIS FATHER AND HIS MOTHER [to establish a home with his wife], [Matt 19:5]
[8]AND THE TWO SHALL BECOME ONE FLESH; so that they are no longer two, but [are united as] one flesh. [Gen 2:24]
[9]"Therefore, what God has united *and* joined together, man must not separate [by divorce]."
[10]In the house the disciples *began* questioning Him again about this.
[11]And He said to them, "Whoever divorces his wife and marries another woman commits adultery against her;
[12]and if a woman divorces her husband and marries another man, she commits adultery."

Jesus Blesses Little Children

[13]People were bringing children to Him so that He would touch *and* bless them, but the disciples reprimanded them *and* discouraged them [from coming].
[14]But when Jesus saw this, He was indignant and He said to them, "Allow the children to come to Me; do not forbid them; for the kingdom of God belongs to such as these.
[15]"I assure you *and* most solemnly say to you, whoever does not receive *and* welcome the kingdom of God like a child will not enter it at all."
[16]And He took the children [one by one] in His arms and blessed them [with kind, encouraging words], placing His hands on them.

The Rich Young Ruler

[17]As He was leaving on His journey, a man ran up and knelt before Him and asked Him, "Good Teacher [You who are essentially good and morally perfect], what shall I do to inherit eternal life [that is, eternal salvation in the Messiah's kingdom]?" [Matt 19:16–29; Luke 18:18–30]
[18]Jesus said to him, "Why do you call Me good? No one is [essentially] good [by nature] except God alone.
[19]"You know the commandments: 'DO NOT MURDER, DO NOT COMMIT ADULTERY, DO NOT STEAL, DO NOT TESTIFY FALSELY, Do not defraud, HONOR YOUR FATHER AND MOTHER.' " [Ex 20:12–16; Deut 5:16–20]
[20]And he replied to Him, "Teacher, I have [carefully] kept all these [commandments] since my youth."
[21]Looking at him, Jesus felt a love (high regard, compassion) for him, and He said to him, "You lack one thing: go and sell all your property and give [the money] to the poor, and you will have [abundant] treasure in heaven; and come, follow Me [becoming My disciple, believing and trusting in Me and walking the same path of life that I walk]."
[22]But the man was saddened at Jesus' words, and he left grieving, because he owned much property *and* had many possessions [which he treasured more than his relationship with God].
[23]Jesus looked around and said to His disciples, "How difficult it will be

---

interpretation of this custom varied widely. The disciples of Hillel allowed divorce for almost any reason, but the followers of Shammai permitted divorce only for sexual impurity.

10:11 ***Whoever divorces his wife.*** Mark includes no exception to Christ's prohibition of divorce, nor is any exception listed in Luke 16:18, Romans 7:1 – 2, or 1 Corinthians 7:10 – 11. Compare Matthew 5:32 where the exception is made.

10:18 ***No one is [essentially] good [by nature] except God alone.*** This reply is a claim to deity, which Jesus asks the young ruler to recognize.

10:19 ***Do not.*** Jesus recounts the Seventh, Sixth, Eighth, Ninth, and Fifth Commandments. ***Do not defraud.*** Jesus inserts this phrase just before the Fifth Commandment. All of these commands concern the fair and ethical treatment of other people (Ex 20:12 – 17).

6 Ge 1:27; 5:2 **7** Ge 2:24; 1Co 6:16; Eph 5:31 **11** Mt 5:32; 19:9; Lk 16:18; Ro 7:3; 1Co 7:10,11 **13** Mt 19:13; Lk 18:15 **14** 1Co 14:20; 1Pe 2:2 **15** Mt 18:3 **17** Mt 19:16; Lk 18:18 **19** Ex 20; Ro 13:9 **21** Mt 6:19,20; 19:21; Lk 12:33; 16:9 **23** Mt 19:23; Lk 18:24

for those who are wealthy [and cling
to possessions and status as security]
to enter the kingdom of God!"
24The disciples were amazed *and*
bewildered by His words. But Jesus
said to them again, "Children, how
difficult it is [for those who place their
hope and confidence in riches] to enter
the kingdom of God!
25"It is easier for a camel to go
through the eye of a needle than for
a rich man [who places his faith in
wealth or status] to enter the kingdom
of God."
26They were completely *and* utterly
astonished, and said to Him, "Then
who can be saved [from the wrath of
God]?"
27Looking at them, Jesus said, "With
people [as far as it depends on them] it
is impossible, but not with God; for all
things are possible with God."
28Peter started saying to Him, "Look,
we have given up everything and fol-
lowed You [becoming Your disciples
and accepting You as Teacher and
Lord]."
29Jesus said, "I assure you *and* most
solemnly say to you, there is no one
who has given up a house or brothers
or sisters or mother or father or chil-
dren or farms, for My sake and for the
gospel's sake,
30who will not receive a hundred
times as much now in the present
age—houses and brothers and sisters
and mothers and children and farms—
along with persecutions; and in the age
to come, eternal life.
31"But many *who are* first will be
last, and the last, first."

Jesus' Sufferings Foretold

32Now they were on the road going
up to Jerusalem, and Jesus was walk-
ing on ahead of them; and they were
perplexed [at what Jesus had said],
and those who were following were
alarmed *and* afraid. And again He
took the twelve [disciples] aside and
began telling them what was going to
happen to Him,
33*saying*, "Listen very carefully: we
are going up to Jerusalem, and the Son
of Man will be betrayed *and* handed
over to the chief priests and the scribes;
and they will condemn Him to death
and hand Him over to the Gentiles
(Romans).
34"They will mock *and* ridicule Him
and spit on Him, and whip (scourge)
Him and kill *Him*, and three days later
He will rise [from the dead]."
35James and John, the two sons of
Zebedee, came to Him, saying, "Teach-
er, we want You to do for us whatever
we ask of You." [Matt 20:20, 21]
36And He replied to them, "What do
you want Me to do for you?"
37They said to Him, "Grant that we
may sit [with You], one on Your right
and one on *Your* left, in Your glory
[Your majesty and splendor in Your
kingdom]."
38But Jesus said to them, "You do
not know what you are asking. Are
you able to drink the cup that I drink,
or to be baptized with the baptism [of

10:25–27 *It is easier.* This comparison of a camel going through a needle is a literal one. In human terms, it is not just difficult, but totally impossible, for a rich man to be saved. But it is also impossible for anyone at all to be saved apart from God's grace and power. God provides the means of salvation, enlightens the sinner's understanding, and regenerates the believing soul.

10:30 *in the present age.* This is the time between Christ's first and second comings. Mark alone mentions that persecutions will follow as well — a point his Roman readers may have already known.

10:37 *one on Your right and one on Your left.* To be seated at a king's right hand was to take the position of the most prominence; the person seated at the left hand ranked just below that (Lk 22:24–30). Jesus had to remind the disciples again about the price of greatness in God's kingdom.

10:38 *drink the cup that I drink, or to be baptized with the baptism.* These phrases are references to the suffering and death that awaited Jesus (14:36). Jesus wanted His disciples to understand the mocking, scourging, beating, and torture He would have to endure.

24 Job 31:24; Ps 52:7; 62:10; 1Ti 6:17 **27** Jer 32:17; Mt 19:26; Lk 1:37 **28** Mt 19:27; Lk 18:28 **30** 2Ch 25:9; Lk 18:30 **31** Mt 19:30; 20:16; Lk 13:30 **32** Mt 20:17; Lk 18:31; Mk 8:31; 9:31; Lk 9:22; 18:31 **35** Mt 20:20

suffering and death] with which I am
baptized?"
39 And they replied to Him, "We are
able." Jesus told them, "The cup that I
drink you will drink, and you will be
baptized with the baptism with which
I am baptized.
40 "But to sit on My right or left, this
is not Mine to give; but it is for those
for whom it has been prepared [by My
Father]."
41 Hearing this, the [other] ten be-
came indignant with James and John.
42 Calling them to Himself, Jesus said
to them, "You know that those who are
recognized as rulers of the Gentiles
lord it over them; and their powerful
men exercise authority over them [tyr-
annizing them].
43 "But this is not how it is among
you; instead, whoever wishes to be-
come great among you must be your
servant,
44 and whoever wishes to be first *and*
most important among you must be
slave of all.
45 "For even the Son of Man did not
come to be served, but to serve, and
to give His life as a ransom for many."

Bartimaeus Receives His Sight

46 Then they came to Jericho. And as
He was leaving Jericho with His disci-
ples and a large crowd, a blind beggar,
Bartimaeus, the son of Timaeus, was
sitting beside the road [as was his cus-
tom]. [Matt 20:29–34; Luke 18:35–43]
47 When Bartimaeus heard that it
was Jesus of Nazareth, he began to
shout and say, "Jesus, Son of David
(Messiah), have mercy on me!"
48 Many sternly rebuked him, telling
him to keep still *and* be quiet; but he
kept on shouting out all the more, "Son
of David (Messiah), have mercy on me!"
49 Jesus stopped and said, "Call him."
So they called the blind man, telling
him, "Take courage, get up! He is call-
ing for you."
50 Throwing his cloak aside, he
jumped up and came to Jesus.
51 And Jesus said, "What do you want
Me to do for you?" The blind man said
to Him, "Rabboni (my Master), let me
regain my sight."
52 Jesus said to him, "Go; your faith
[and confident trust in My power] has
made you well." Immediately he re-
gained his sight and *began* following
Jesus on the road. [Is 42:6, 7]

The Triumphal Entry

11 WHEN THEY were nearing Je-
rusalem, at Bethphage and Beth-
any near the Mount of Olives, Jesus
sent two of His disciples, [Matt 21:1–9;
Luke 19:29–38; John 12:12–15]
2 saying to them, "Go into the village
in front of you, and immediately as you
enter it, you will find a [donkey's] colt
tied, which has never been ridden by
anyone; untie it and bring it here.
3 "If anyone asks you, 'Why are you
doing this?' say, 'The Lord needs it';
and immediately he will send it here."
4 So they went away [to the village]
and found a colt tied outside at a gate
in the street, and they untied it.

10:45 The Ministry of Christ — He is Savior. Sinful men to be saved (1Ti 1:15); Christ's qualifications to be Savior (Jn 10:18 – 38); His humiliating death (Jn 19:18); bodily resurrection to guarantee our salvation (1Co 15:13 – 22); and results of salvation (Jn 5:24). It is no wonder that, in light of these realities, Paul speaks of Christ as "our great God and Savior" (Titus 2:13).

He is High Priest. The high priest brought the people before God on the Day of Atonement (Lev 16:32 – 33). Jesus is eminently qualified to be our High Priest: appointed by God (Heb 5:5), eternal (Heb 7:24 – 25), sinless (Heb 7:26), His offering was final (Heb 9:28), and His mediation is effective (Ro 8:34; Heb 7:25; 1Jn 2:1). As the only qualified High Priest for men and women, Jesus Christ thus constitutes the only way to God (1Ti 2:5).

He is King. King implies sovereign authority and rule over all. This right belongs only to Jesus Christ who is called "Lord of lords and King of kings" (Rev 17:14; 19:16). He is destined to rule as king and every knee must ultimately bow and acknowledge His authority (Php 2:10). Those who acknowledge Christ as King and Lord in this life will reign with Him; those who do not will be judged by Him (Rev 20:11 – 15).

---

41 Mt 20:24 **42** Lk 22:25 **43** Mt 20:26,28; Mk 9:35; Lk 9:48 **45** Jn 13:14; Php 2:7; Mt 20:28; 1Ti 2:6; Titus 2:14
46 Mt 20:29; Lk 18:35 **52** Mt 9:22; Mk 5:34 **CHAPTER 11** **1** Mt 21:1; Lk 19:29; Jn 12:14

5 Some of the people who were standing there said to them, "What are you doing, untying the colt?"

6 They replied to them just as Jesus had directed, and they allowed them to go.

7 They brought the colt to Jesus and put their coats on it, and He sat on it.

8 And many [of the people] spread their coats on the road [as an act of tribute and homage before a new king], and others [scattered a layer of] leafy branches which they had cut from the fields [honoring Him as Messiah]. [2 Kin 9:13]

9 Those who went in front and those who were following [Him] were shouting [in joy and praise],

"Hosanna (Save, I pray)!
Blessed (praised, glorified) is He
who comes in the name of the
Lord! [Ps 118:26]
10 "Blessed is the coming kingdom of
our father David!
Hosanna in the highest [heaven]!"

11 Jesus entered Jerusalem and went to the temple [enclosure]; and after looking around at everything, He left for Bethany with the twelve [disciples], because it was already late [in the day].

12 On the next day, when they had left Bethany, He was hungry. [Matt 21:18–22]

13 Seeing at a distance a fig tree in leaf, He went to see if He would find anything on it. But He found nothing but leaves, for it was not the season for figs.

14 He said to it, "No one will ever eat fruit from you again!" And His disciples were listening [to what He said].

Jesus Drives Moneychangers from the Temple

15 Then they came to Jerusalem. And He entered the temple [grounds] and began driving out [with force] the people who were selling and buying [animals for sacrifice] in the temple area, and overturned the tables of the moneychangers [who made a profit exchanging foreign money for temple coinage] and the seats of those who were selling doves; [Matt 21:12–16; Luke 19:45–47; John 2:13–16]

16 and He would not permit anyone to carry merchandise *or* household wares through the temple [grounds, using the temple area irreverently as a shortcut].

17 He *began* to teach and say to them, "Is it not written, 'My house shall be called a house of prayer for all the nations'? But you have made it a robbers' den." [Is 56:7; Jer 7:11]

18 The chief priests and the scribes heard this and *began* searching for a way to destroy Him; for they were afraid of Him, since the entire crowd was struck with astonishment at His teaching.

19 When evening came, Jesus and His disciples would leave the city.

20 In the morning, as they were passing by, the disciples saw that the fig tree had withered away from the roots up.

21 And remembering, Peter said to Him, "Rabbi (Master), look! The fig tree which You cursed has withered!"

22 Jesus replied, "Have faith in God [constantly].

23 "I assure you *and* most solemnly say to you, whoever says to this

---

11:8 – 11 *Bethany.* Jesus retired there each night, perhaps staying in a friend's home. But in view of the fact that Jesus appears to have had no breakfast the next day (v. 12), He and the twelve may have camped outside this night.

11:13 *it was not the season for figs.* Passover always comes in March or April, and fig season is not until May or June. However, fig trees generally produce a number of buds in March, leaves in April, and ripe fruit later on. Jesus was looking for the edible buds, the lack of which indicated that the tree would be fruitless that year.

11:17 *ROBBERS' DEN.* Jesus was referring to the practice of cheating people, both Israelites and those of other nations, either through a crooked exchange of money or by selling inferior products.

11:21 *The fig tree which You cursed has withered!* The passage emphasizes the power of true faith. Some have suggested that the fig tree represented Israel, which bore no fruit and would soon face the judgment of God.

8 Mt 21:8 **9** Ps 118:26 **10** Ps 148:1 **11** Mt 21:12 **12** Mt 21:18 **13** Mt 21:19 **15** Mt 21:12; Lk 19:45; Jn 2:14 **17** Isa 56:7; Jer 7:11 **18** Mt 21:45,46; Lk 19:47; Mt 7:28; Mk 1,22; Lk 4:32 **20** Mt 21:19 **23** Mt 17:20; 21:21; Lk 17:6

mountain, 'Be lifted up and thrown into the sea!' and does not doubt in his heart [in God's unlimited power], but believes that what he says is going to take place, it will be done for him [in accordance with God's will]. [Matt 17:20; Luke 17:6; 1 John 5:14]

24 "For this reason I am telling you, whatever things you ask for in prayer [in accordance with God's will], believe [with confident trust] that you have received them, and they will be *given* to you.

25 "Whenever you stand praying, if you have anything against anyone, forgive him [drop the issue, let it go], so that your Father who is in heaven will also forgive you your transgressions *and* wrongdoings [against Him and others].

26 ["But if you do not forgive, neither will your Father in heaven forgive your transgressions."]

Jesus' Authority Questioned

27 They came again to Jerusalem. And as Jesus was walking in the [courts and porches of the] temple, the chief priests, the scribes, and the elders came to Him, [Matt 21:23–27; Luke 20:1–8]

28 and *began* saying to Him, "By what authority are You doing these things, or who gave You this authority to do these things?"

29 Jesus said to them, "I will ask you one question, and you answer Me, and then I will tell you by what authority I do these things.

30 "Was the baptism of John [the Baptist] from heaven [that is, ordained by God] or from men? Answer Me."

31 They *began* discussing it with each other, saying, "If we say, 'From heaven,' He will say, 'Then why did you not believe him?'

32 "But shall we say, 'From men?' "—they were afraid [to answer because] of the crowd, for everyone considered John to have been a real prophet.

33 So they replied to Jesus, "We do not know." And Jesus said to them, "Neither will I tell you by what authority I do these things."

Parable of the Vineyard Owner

12 JESUS BEGAN to speak to them [the chief priests, scribes and elders who were questioning Him] in parables: "A man PLANTED A VINEYARD AND PUT A WALL AROUND IT, AND DUG A PIT FOR THE WINE PRESS AND BUILT A TOWER; and he rented it out to tenant farmers and left the country. [Is 5:1, 2; Matt 21:33–46; Luke 20:9–19]

2 "When the *harvest* season came he sent a servant to the tenants, in order to collect from them some of the fruit of the vineyard.

3 "They took him and beat him and sent him away empty-handed.

4 "Again he sent them another servant, and they [threw stones and] wounded him in the head, and treated him disgracefully.

5 "And he sent another, and that one they killed; then many others—some they beat and some they killed.

6 "He still had one man left *to send*, a beloved son; he sent him last of all to them, saying, 'They will respect my son.'

7 "But those tenants said to each other, 'This *man* is the heir! Come on, let us kill him [and destroy the evidence], and his inheritance will be ours!'

11:29–30 *answer Me.* The intent of Jesus' question was to expose once again the insincerity of His detractors. ***baptism of John.*** This refers to the authority of John's baptism. ***from heaven.*** Was it ordained by God and worthy of obedience? ***from men.*** Or was it of human contrivance and void of any spiritual authority and reality?

12:1 *Jesus began to speak to them . . . in parables.* Parables usually get across a significant truth, but the details are not meant to correspond exactly with particular spiritual realities. In this parable, the owner of the vineyard represents God, but God Himself was never so mistaken as to assume they would respect His Son. God is omniscient, whereas the vineyard owner in the parable is not. This story illustrates the immense patience God had with Israel.

24 Mt 7:7; Lk 11:9; Jn 14:13; 15:7; 16:24; Jas 1:5,6 **25** Mt 6:14; Col 3:13 **26** Mt 18:35 **27** Mt 21:23; Lk 20:1 **32** Mt 3:5; 14:5; Mk 6:20 **CHAPTER 12 1** Mt 21:33; Lk 20:9

8“So they took him and killed him,
and threw his body outside the vine-
yard.
9“What will the owner of the vine-
yard do? He will come and destroy the
tenants, and will give the vineyard to
others.
10“Have you not even read this Scrip-
ture:

‘THE STONE WHICH THE BUILDERS
REGARDED AS UNWORTHY *and*
REJECTED,
THIS [very stone] HAS BECOME THE
CHIEF CORNERSTONE
11THIS CAME ABOUT FROM THE LORD,
AND IT IS MARVELOUS *and* WONDERFUL
IN OUR EYES’?” [Ps 118:22, 23]

12And they were looking for a way
to seize Him, but they were afraid of
the crowd; for they knew that He spoke
this parable in reference to [and as a
charge against] them. And so they left
Him and went away.

Jesus Answers the Pharisees, Sadducees and Scribes

13Then they sent some of the Phar-
isees and Herodians to Jesus in order
to trap Him into *making* a statement
[that they could use against Him].
[Matt 22:15–22; Luke 20:20–26]
14They came and said to Him,
“Teacher, we know that You are truth-
ful and have no personal bias toward
anyone; for You are not influenced by
outward appearances *or* social status,
but in truth You teach the way of God.
Is it lawful [according to Jewish law
and tradition] to pay the poll-tax to
[Tiberius] Caesar, or not?
15“Should we pay [the tax] or should
we not pay?” But knowing their hy-
pocrisy, He asked them, “Why are you
testing Me? Bring Me a coin (denarius)
to look at.”
16So they brought one. Then He
asked them, “Whose image and in-
scription is this?” They said to Him,
“Caesar’s.”
17Jesus said to them, “Pay to Caesar
the things that are Caesar’s, and to
God the things that are God’s.” And
they were greatly amazed at Him.
18Some Sadducees (who say that
there is no resurrection) came to Him,
and *began* questioning Him, saying,
[Matt 22:23–33; Luke 20:27–38]
19“Teacher, Moses wrote for us [a
law] that IF A MAN’S BROTHER DIES and
leaves a wife BUT LEAVES NO CHILD, HIS
BROTHER IS TO MARRY THE WIDOW AND RAISE
UP CHILDREN FOR HIS BROTHER. [Deut 25:5]
20“There were seven brothers; the
first [one] took a wife, and died leaving
no children.
21“The second brother married her,
and died leaving no children; and the
third likewise;
22and so all seven [married her and
died, and] left no children. Last of all
the woman died also.
23“In the resurrection, whose wife
will she be? For all seven [brothers]
were married to her.”
24Jesus said to them, “Is this not why
you are wrong, because you know nei-
ther the Scriptures [that teach the res-
urrection] nor the power of God [who
is able to raise the dead]?
25“For when they rise from the dead,
they do not marry nor are they giv-

12:12 *they were looking for a way to seize Him.* Only as the final points of the parable were made did these evil men realize that Jesus was speaking of them.
12:14 *You are truthful and have no personal bias toward anyone.* This comment was intended as a compliment. The teachers recognized that Jesus was partial to no one. The question, however, was a lose-lose proposition: a *yes* answer would alienate Jews who opposed Rome, while a *no* answer could be taken as treason against the state.
12:18 *Sadducees* were an elite group of religious leaders who denied the existence of angels, the immortality of the soul, and the resurrection. They rejected the oral traditions and accepted only the validity of the Pentateuch, the first five books of the Old Testament.
12:19 – 22 *Moses wrote for us.* The custom of marrying the widow of one’s brother was supported by Deuteronomy 25:5 – 6, but it was not absolutely binding (Dt 25:7 – 10).

10 Ps 118:22 **12** Mt 21:45,46; Mk 11:18; Jn 7:25,30,44 **13** Mt 22:15; Lk 20:20 **18** Mt 22:23; Lk 20:27; Ac 23:8 **19** Dt 25:5 **25** 1Co 15:42,49,52

en in marriage, but are like angels in heaven.

26 "But concerning the raising of the dead, have you not read in the book of Moses, in the *passage* about the *burning* bush, how God spoke to him, saying, 'I AM THE GOD OF ABRAHAM, AND THE GOD OF ISAAC, AND THE GOD OF JACOB'? [Ex 3:2–6]

27 "He is not the God of the dead, but of the living; you are greatly mistaken *and* you are deceiving yourselves!"

28 Then one of the scribes [an expert in Mosaic Law] came up and listened to them arguing [with one another], and noticing that Jesus answered them well, asked Him, "Which commandment is first *and* most important of all?" [Matt 22:34–40; Luke 10:25–28]

29 Jesus answered, "The first *and* most important *one* is: 'HEAR, O ISRAEL, THE LORD OUR GOD IS ONE LORD;

30 AND YOU SHALL LOVE THE LORD YOUR GOD WITH ALL YOUR HEART, AND WITH ALL YOUR SOUL (life), AND WITH ALL YOUR MIND (thought, understanding), AND WITH ALL YOUR STRENGTH.' [Deut 6:4, 5]

31 "This is the second: 'YOU SHALL [unselfishly] LOVE YOUR NEIGHBOR AS YOURSELF.' There is no other commandment greater than these." [Lev 19:18]

32 The scribe said to Him, "Admirably answered, Teacher; You truthfully stated that HE IS ONE, AND THERE IS NO OTHER BUT HIM;

33 AND TO LOVE HIM WITH ALL THE HEART AND WITH ALL THE UNDERSTANDING AND WITH ALL THE STRENGTH, AND TO [unselfishly] LOVE ONE'S NEIGHBOR AS ONESELF, is much more than all burnt offerings and sacrifices." [1 Sam 15:22; Hos 6:6; Mic 6:6–8; Heb 10:8]

34 When Jesus saw that he answered thoughtfully *and* intelligently, He said to him, "You are not far from the kingdom of God." And after that, no one would dare to ask Him any more questions.

35 Jesus *began* to say, as He taught in [a portico or court of] the temple, "How can the scribes say that the Christ is the son of David? [Matt 22:41–46; Luke 20:41–44]

36 "David himself said [when inspired] by the Holy Spirit,

'THE LORD (the Father) SAID TO MY
LORD (the Son, the Messiah),
"SIT AT MY RIGHT HAND,
UNTIL I PUT YOUR ENEMIES UNDER
YOUR FEET." ' [Ps 110:1]

37 "David himself calls Him (the Son, the Messiah) 'Lord'; so how can it be that He is David's Son?" The large crowd enjoyed hearing Jesus *and* listened to Him with delight.

38 In [the course of] His teaching He was saying, "Beware of the scribes, who like to walk around in long robes [displaying their prominence], and *like*

12:26–27 *I AM THE GOD OF ABRAHAM . . . ISAAC . . . JACOB.* Jesus quotes from the law — the Book of Exodus — to make His point. God said I am the God of the three patriarchs mentioned, not "I was their God, but now they are dead." He still is their God because they are still alive. Their souls not only live after death, but their bodies will be raised anew as well.

12:28 *Which commandment is first.* In Judaism, these words (quoted from Dt 6:4–5) are known as the *Shema*. It is described by Jews as the most important words a Jew can know. Jesus quotes these words at the beginning of answering the question, "What commandment is the foremost of all?" We should be driven to the cross. There, we understand His love for us and are constantly motivated to seek to love Him better because of what He has done. We can only be thankful at the comprehensiveness of His love. Even though we sin every day of our lives, He forgives. We just need to keep coming to Him for that forgiveness.

12:29 *HEAR, O ISRAEL.* This phrase from Deuteronomy 6:4 is commonly called the Shema (from a Hebrew word meaning "to hear") and is repeated by Jews the world over, as expressing the essence of their faith in God.

12:35 *in [a portico or court of] the temple.* This does not refer to the sanctuary itself, where only the priests were allowed to minister. The temple environs included a number of porticos and courts. One was designated especially for women, another for men. Gentiles could view the temple from an outer area.

26 Ex 3:6 **28** Mt 22:35 **29** Dt 6:4; Lk 10:27 **31** Lev 19:18; Mt 22:39; Ro 13:9; Gal 5:14; Jas 2:8 **32** Dt 4:39; Isa 45:6,14; 46:9 **33** 1Sa 15:22; Hos 6:6; Mic 6:6-8 **34** Mt 22:46 **35** Mt 22:41; Lk 20:41 **36** 2Sa 23:2; Ps 110:1 **38** Mk 4:2; Mt 23:1; Lk 20:46; Lk 11:43

to receive respectful greetings in the market places,

39 and [they love] the chief seats in the synagogues and the places of distinction *and* honor at banquets,

40 [these scribes] who devour (confiscate) widows' houses, and offer long prayers for appearance's sake [to impress others]. These men will receive greater condemnation."

The Widow's Mite

41 And He sat down opposite the [temple] treasury, and *began* watching how the people were putting money into the treasury. And many rich people were putting in large sums. [Luke 21:1–4]

42 A poor widow came and put in two small copper coins, which amount to a mite.

43 Calling His disciples to Him, He said to them, "I assure you *and* most solemnly say to you, this poor widow put in [proportionally] more than all the contributors to the treasury.

44 "For they all contributed from their surplus, but she, from her poverty, put in all she had, all she had to live on."

Things to Come

13 AS HE was coming out of the temple [grounds], one of His disciples said to Him, "Teacher, look what wonderful stones and what wonderful buildings!" [Matt 24; Luke 21:5–36]

2 Jesus replied to him, "You see these great buildings? Not one stone will be left on another which will not be torn down!"

3 As He was sitting on the Mount of Olives opposite the temple, Peter and James and John and Andrew asked Him privately,

4 "Tell us, when will these things happen, and what will be the sign when all these things are about to be fulfilled?"

5 Jesus began to say to them, "Be careful *and* see to it that no one misleads you.

6 "Many will come in My name [misusing My name or claiming to be the Messiah], saying, 'I am *He!*' and will deceive *and* mislead many.

7 "When you hear of wars and rumors of wars, do not be alarmed (frightened, troubled); *these things* must take place, but the end is not yet.

8 "For nation will rise up against nation, and kingdom against kingdom; there will be earthquakes in various places; there will be famines. These things are the beginning of the birth pangs [the intolerable anguish and suffering].

9 "But be on your guard; they will turn you over to courts, and you will be beaten in synagogues, and you will stand [as accused] before governors and kings for My sake, as a testimony to them.

10 "The gospel [that is, the good news regarding the way of salvation] must first be preached to all the [Gentile] nations. [Col 1:6, 23]

11 "When they take you and turn you over [to the court], do not worry beforehand about what to say, but say whatever is given to you [by God] in

---

12:43–44 *this poor widow put in [proportionally] more than all the contributors to the treasury.* Jesus' comparison of the percentages contributed by the rich and the poor reminds us that God measures not how much we give, but how much we retain. Those with greater income have an obligation to return a larger percentage of it to God's work.

13:1–2 *what wonderful stones and what wonderful buildings!* The disciples' excitement over the temple's tremendous construction was a natural reaction to splendid and majestic architecture; each stone weighed several tons. Josephus described its magnificence. There was nothing like it in all the world. Begun by Herod the Great in 20 BC, the temple was later completed by Herod's descendants some time before AD 66. Its beautiful white marble stones with gold ornamentation reached 100 feet high. Surrounding it were colonnaded walkways, courtyards, and stairways that filled 20 acres of the most prominent landscape in all Jerusalem.

13:11–12 *the Holy Spirit.* The promise given that the Holy Spirit will guide one's speech in the hour of trial applies first to the twelve and only secondarily to others who will experience

40 Mt 23:14 **41** Lk 21:1; 2Ki 12:9 **43** 2Co 8:12 **44** Dt 24:6; 1Jn 3:17 **CHAPTER 13** **1** Mt 24:1; Lk 21:5 **2** Lk 19:44 **4** Mt 24:3; Lk 21:7 **5** Jer 29:8; Eph 5:6; 1Th 2:3 **8** Mt 24:8 **9** Mt 10:17,18; 24:9; Rev 2:10 **10** Mt 24:14 **11** Mt 10:19; Lk 12:11; 21:14; Ac 2:4; 4:8,31

that hour; for it is not you who speak,
but it is the Holy Spirit [who will speak
through you].
12 “Brother will betray brother to [be
put to] death, and a father [will hand
over] his child; and children will rise
up *and* take a stand against parents
and have them put to death.
13 “You will be hated by everyone
because of [your association with]
My name, but the one who [patiently
perseveres empowered by the Holy
Spirit and] endures to the end, he will
be saved.
14 “But when you see the ABOMINATION
OF DESOLATION standing [in the temple
sanctuary] where it ought not to be (let
the reader understand) then those who
are in Judea must flee to the mountains. [Dan 9:27; 11:31; 12:11]
15 “Whoever is on the housetop must
not go down [to enter the house], or
go inside to take anything out of his
house;
16 whoever is in the field must not
turn back to get his coat.
17 “And woe to those women who are
pregnant and to those who are nursing
babies in those days!
18 “Pray that it will not occur in winter,
19 for at that time there will be such
tribulation as has not occurred, from
the beginning of the creation which
God made, until now—and never will
[be again].
20 “And if the Lord had not shortened the days, no human life would
have been saved; but for the sake of the
elect, whom He chose [for Himself], He
shortened the days. [Dan 12:1]
21 “Then if anyone says to you, ‘Look,
here is the Christ (the Messiah, the
Anointed)!’ or, ‘Look, *He is* there!’ do
not believe it;
22 for false Christs and false prophets will arise, and they will provide
signs and wonders in order to deceive,
if [such a thing were] possible, even
the elect [those God has chosen for
Himself].
23 “But be on your guard; I have told
you everything in advance.

The Return of Christ

24 “But in those days, after [the suffering and distress of] that tribulation,
THE SUN WILL BE DARKENED, AND THE MOON
WILL NOT GIVE ITS LIGHT, [Is 13:10]
25 AND THE STARS WILL BE FALLING from
the sky, and the powers that are in the
heavens will be shaken. [Is 34:4]
26 “Then they will see THE SON OF MAN
COMING IN CLOUDS with great power and
glory [in royal majesty and splendor].
[Dan 7:13, 14]
27 “And then He will send out the angels, and will gather together His elect
[those He has chosen for Himself] from
the four winds, from the farthest end of
the earth to the farthest end of heaven.
28 “Now learn this lesson from the fig
tree: as soon as its branch becomes tender and it puts out its leaves, you recognize that summer is near. [Matt 24:32,
33; Luke 21:29–31]
29 “Even so, you too, when you see
these things happening, know [for certain] that He is near, *right* at the door.
30 “I assure you *and* most solemnly

persecution. But this promise does not assure escape from persecution or even freedom from being put to death.

13:13 *the one who ... endures to the end, he will be saved.* This is not referring to regeneration or justification but to physical deliverance from affliction (vv. 19 – 20). The ones who physically endure will be delivered into Christ's messianic kingdom.

13:14 *standing [in the temple sanctuary] where it ought not.* This phrase refers to the presence of an idol standing in the temple. Daniel's prediction primarily referred to Antiochus Ephiphanes' placement of sacrifices to Zeus on the temple's altar. Some believe that the destruction of the Herodian temple in AD 70 fulfilled Jesus' prediction. Others still await its fulfillment in the blasphemous actions of the antichrist in the last days (2Th 2:3 – 4).

13:28 – 29 *when you see these things happening.* Jesus likened the signs of His second coming to the sprouts of growth and leaves on a

12 Mic 7:6; Mt 10:21; 24:10; Lk 21:16 **13** Mt 24:9; Lk 21:17; Da 12:12; Mt 10:22; 24:13; Rev 2:10 **14** Mt 24:15; Da 9:27; Lk 21:21 **17** Lk 21:23 **19** Da 9:26; 12:1; Joel 2:2; Mt 24:21 **21** Mt 24:23; Lk 17:23; 21:8 **23** 2Pe 3:17 **24** Da 7:10; Zep 1:15; Mt 24:29 **26** Da 7:13,14; Mt 16:27; 24:30; Mk 14:62; Ac 1:11; 1Th 4:16; 2Th 1:7,10; Rev 1:7 **28** Mt 24:32; Lk 21:29

say to you, this generation [the people living when these signs and events begin] will not pass away until all these things take place.

31 “Heaven and earth [as now known] will pass away, but My words will not pass away.

32 “But of that [exact] day or hour no one knows, not even the angels in heaven, nor the Son [in His humanity], but the Father *alone*.

33 “Be on guard and stay constantly alert [and pray]; for you do not know when the *appointed* time will come.

34 “It is like a man away on a journey, *who* when he left home put his servants in charge, each with his *particular* task, and also ordered the doorkeeper to be *continually* alert.

35 “Therefore, be *continually* on the alert—for you do not know when the master of the house is coming, whether in the evening, or at midnight, or when the rooster crows, or in the morning—

36 [stay alert,] in case he should come suddenly *and* unexpectedly and find you asleep *and* unprepared.

37 “What I say to you I say to everyone, ‘Be on the alert [stay awake and be continually cautious]!’ ”

Death Plot and the Anointing in Bethany

14 IT WAS now two days before the Passover and [the festival of] Unleavened Bread, and the chief priests and the scribes were searching for a deceitful way to arrest Jesus and kill *Him;* [Matt 26:2–5; Luke 22:1, 2]

2 but they were saying, “Not during the festival, for the people might riot.”

3 While He was in Bethany [as a guest] at the home of Simon the leper, and reclining *at the table*, a woman came with an alabaster vial of very costly *and* precious perfume of pure nard; and she broke the vial and poured the perfume over His head.

4 But there were some who were indignantly *remarking* to one another, “Why has this perfume been wasted?

5 “For this perfume might have been sold for more than three hundred denarii [a laborer’s wages for almost a year], and *the money* given to the poor.” And they scolded her.

6 But Jesus said, “Let her alone; why are you bothering her *and* causing trouble? She has done a good *and* beautiful thing to Me.

7 “For you always have the poor with you, and whenever you wish you can do something good to them; but you will not always have Me. [Deut 15:11]

8 “She has done what she could; she has anointed My body beforehand for the burial.

9 “I assure you *and* most solemnly say to you, wherever the good news [regarding salvation] is proclaimed

---

fig tree. Both point to the glories to come — the full flowering of the earth and return of Christ.

13:32 ***But of that [exact] day or hour no one knows.*** As one who was fully God and at the same time fully man, Jesus possessed all the attributes of deity, including omnipotence and omniscience. He knew what was in people’s hearts (2:8), and He could still the waves (4:39). When Jesus became a man, however, He voluntarily placed certain knowledge in the hands of the Father. Of course today, glorified in heaven, Jesus now knows the day and hour of His return.

13:34 – 36 ***It is like a man away on a journey.*** Jesus’ parable of the absent master of the house is unique to Mark. The point of the parable is that the master could return at any time so all servants must be vigilant and watchful (Lk 19:11 – 27).

14:3 ***alabaster.*** Alabaster is a translucent stone still used to make ornamented jewelry boxes and other items of value. ***perfume of pure nard.*** This was a precious perfume imported from India, made from plants that grow in the high elevations of the Himalayas. This perfume is mentioned in the Song of Solomon (1:12; 4:13 – 14).

14:7 ***For you always have the poor with you.*** Jesus’ statement does not show callousness towards the poor (Dt 15:7 – 11). His compassion for those overwhelmed by sickness and poverty appears frequently in the Gospels, and He encouraged others to meet their needs (10:21). But He also wanted people to give freely and of their own volition. No one can coerce a gift from another; no one should criticize another’s

---

31 Isa 40:8 **33** Mt 24:42; 25:13; Lk 12:40; 21:34; Ro 13:11; 1Th 5:6 **34** Mt 24:45; 25:14 **35** Mt 24:42,44
CHAPTER 14 **1** Mt 26:2; Lk 22:1; Jn 11:55; 13:1 **3** Mt 26:6; Jn 12:1,3; See Lk 7:37

throughout the world, what she has
done will be told in memory of her."
10 Then Judas Iscariot, who was one
of the twelve [disciples], went to the
chief priests to betray Jesus to them.
[Matt 26:14–16; Luke 22:3–6; John 6:71]
11 When they heard this they were
delighted, and promised to give him
money. And he *began* looking for an
opportune time to betray Jesus.

The Last Passover

12 On the first day [of the festival] of
Unleavened Bread, when [as was cus-
tomary] they sacrificed the Passover
lamb, His disciples asked Him, "Where
do You want us to go and prepare for
You to eat the Passover?" [Matt 26:17–
19; Luke 22:7–13]
13 And He sent two of His disciples,
saying to them, "Go into the city, and a
man carrying a jar of water will meet
you; follow him;
14 and say to the owner of the *house*
he enters, 'The Teacher asks, "Where
is My guest room in which I may eat
the Passover with My disciples?"'
15 "He will show you a large upstairs
room, furnished and ready [with car-
pets and dining couches]; prepare [the
supper] for us there."
16 The disciples left and went to the
city and found everything just as He
had told them, and they prepared the
Passover.
17 When it was evening, He came with
the twelve [disciples]. [Matt 26:20–25]
18 While they were reclining *at the*
table, Jesus said, "I assure you *and*
most solemnly say to you that one of
you will betray Me—one who is eating
with Me." [Ps 41:9]
19 They began to be grieved *and* deep-
ly distressed and to say to Him one by
one, "Surely not I?"
20 And He replied, "It is one of the
twelve [disciples], one who is dipping
bread in the bowl with Me.
21 "For the Son of Man goes [to the
cross] just as it is written [in Scripture]
of Him; but woe to that man by whom
the Son of Man is betrayed! *It would*
have been good for that man if he had
not been born."

The Lord's Supper

22 While they were eating, Jesus took
bread and blessed it [giving thanks
and praise], and He broke it, and gave
it to them and said, "Take it. This is My
body." [Matt 26:26–29; Luke 22:17–20;
1 Cor 11:23–25]
23 And when He had taken a cup [of
wine] and given thanks, He gave it
to them, and they all drank from it.
[Ex 24:8]
24 And He said to them, "This is
My blood of the [new] covenant, [My
blood] which is being poured out for
many [for the forgiveness of sins].
25 "I assure you *and* most solemnly
say to you, I will not drink again of the
fruit of the vine until that day when I
drink it new in the kingdom of God."
26 After they had sung a hymn, they
went out to the Mount of Olives.

---

gift; and no one can read the heart of a giver. A giver's motive is known only to God.

14:14 – 15 *a large upstairs room.* There is reason to suspect that the master of the house may have been Mark's father. Mark himself may have been the young man of verses 51 and 52. Acts 12:12 indicates that this house was later used as a gathering place for many believers who prayed together. Tradition has it that this was also the "upper room" of Acts 1:13 where over 100 believers met on Pentecost.

14:19 *Surely not I?* In Greek this is actually a negative question that implies a negative answer. The phrase means "It is not I, is it?" Matthew and John both identify the culprit as Judas, even though Mark does not (Mt 26:25; Jn 13:26).

14:24 *This is My blood.* This means that the contents of this cup represented Jesus' blood that would be shed for our sins. The sprinkling of blood was required to institute the Mosaic covenant in Exodus 29:12 (Heb 9:18 – 22). In the same way, Jesus' blood shed on the cross initiated the new covenant. His blood was shed for many. He died on the cross in the place of many sinners from every nation. He paid the price for all of their sins. All those who believe in Him will receive eternal life.

14:26 *After they had sung a hymn.* What they sang was no doubt from the Psalms. Frequently

10 Mt 26:14; Lk 22:3,4 **12** Mt 26:17; Lk 22:7 **17** Mt 26:20 **21** Mt 26:24; Lk 22:22 **22** Mt 26:26; Lk 22:19; 1Co 11:23 **26** Mt 26:30

[27]Jesus said to them, "You will all fall
away [and be ashamed and be afraid
to be associated with Me as disciples],
because it is written, 'I WILL STRIKE THE
SHEPHERD, AND THE SHEEP WILL BE SCAT-
TERED.' [Zech 13:7]
[28]"But after I have been raised [from
the dead], I will go ahead of you to
Galilee."
[29]But Peter said to Him, "Even if they
all fall away [and desert You, ashamed
and afraid of being associated with
You], yet I will not [do so]!"
[30]Jesus said to him, "I assure you *and*
most solemnly say to you, this very
night, before a rooster crows twice,
you will deny [that you even know] Me
three times." [Matt 26:34; John 13:38]
[31]But Peter kept saying insistently,
"If I have to die with You, I will not
deny You!" And they all were saying
the same thing as well.

Jesus in Gethsemane

[32]Then they went to a place called
Gethsemane; and Jesus said to His
disciples, "Sit down here until I have
prayed." [Matt 26:36–46; Luke 22:40–46]
[33]He took Peter and James and John
with Him, and He began to be deeply
distressed and troubled [extremely
anguished at the prospect of what was
to come].
[34]And He said to them, "My soul is
deeply grieved *and* overwhelmed with
sorrow, to the point of death; remain
here and keep watch."
[35]After going a little farther, He fell
to the ground [distressed by the weight
of His spiritual burden] and *began* to
pray that if it were possible [in the Fa-
ther's will], the hour [of suffering and
death for the sins of mankind] might
pass from Him.
[36]He was saying, "Abba, Father! All
things are possible for You; take this
cup [of judgment] away from Me; but
not what I will, but what You will."
[37]And He came back and found them
sleeping, and He said to Peter, "Simon,
are you asleep? Were you unable to
keep watch for one hour?
[38]"Keep [actively] watching and
praying so that you do not come into
temptation; the spirit is willing, but the
body is weak."
[39]He went away again and prayed,
saying the same words.
[40]And again He came back and
found them sleeping, because their
eyes were very heavy; and they did not
know how to answer Him.
[41]He came back a third time and said

Psalms 113 – 118 were used in connection with the Passover.

14:30 *before a rooster crows twice.* Only Mark mentions Christ's prediction of Peter's denial. The incident would have remained vivid in Peter's mind when he related the story to Mark.

14:34 *My soul is deeply grieved and overwhelmed with sorrow.* The crushing realization of having to bear the sin of the world and to lose, even temporarily, the fellowship of God the Father was nearly more than Jesus' soul could bear.

14:35 *the hour . . . might pass from Him.* This is a reference to the time Jesus would bear the punishment for the sin of the world in His own body, becoming, as it were, sin for all.

14:38 Temptation by the Flesh — *Flesh* in the Bible often means something other than the substance of the human body. It is used constantly to refer to the carnal, sinful principle within man that is opposed to God (Ro 8:7). The actions produced by the flesh are given in detail in Galatians 5:19 – 21. Among these are all types of sexual immorality, impurity, hatred, anger, envy, and drunkenness. A person whose life is characterized by these sins cannot be a true Christian and is under the wrath of God (Gal 5:21; Eph 2:3). Though the flesh is not eradicated for the Christian, he does have the power to deny it (Ro 7:15 – 25). He possesses a new nature empowered by the Holy Spirit. The solution to the urges of the flesh lies in acknowledging that the power of sin was nullified by Jesus' death (Ro 6:11) and in living under the control of the Spirit's power (Gal 5:16). The latter is a moment-by-moment dependence in faith on the Spirit's power. The believer must choose by an act of his will to benefit from the Spirit's enablement.

14:39 – 41 *He went away again.* The three apostles were exhorted to watch and pray several times, and no doubt truly desired to uphold their Lord in His deepest hour of need. Yet physical fatigue overcame spiritual alertness.

---

27 Mt 26:31; Zec 13:7 **28** Mk 16:7 **29** Mt 26:33,34; Lk 22:33,34; Jn 13:37,38 **32** Mt 26:36; Lk 22:39; Jn 18:1 **34** Jn 12:27 **36** Ro 8:15; Gal 4:6; Heb 5:7; Jn 5:30; 6:38 **38** Ro 7:23; Gal 5:17 **41** Jn 13:1

to them, "Are you still sleeping and resting? Enough [of that]! The hour has come. Look, the Son of Man is being betrayed into the hands of sinners.

42 "Get up, let us go. Look, my betrayer is near!"

Betrayal and Arrest

43 And at once, while He was still speaking, Judas [Iscariot], one of the twelve [disciples], came up, and with him a crowd of men with swords and clubs, *who came* from the chief priests, the scribes, and the elders [of the Sanhedrin]. [Matt 26:47–56; Luke 22:47–53; John 18:3–11]

44 Now the betrayer had given them a signal, saying, "Whomever I kiss, He is the one; seize Him and lead Him away safely [under guard]."

45 When Judas came, immediately he went up to Jesus and said, "Rabbi (Master)!" and he kissed Him [forcefully].

46 They laid hands on Him and seized Him.

47 But one of the bystanders [Simon Peter] drew his sword and struck [Malchus] the slave of the high priest and cut off his ear. [Matt 26:51; Luke 22:50; John 18:10]

48 Jesus said to them, "Have you come out with swords and clubs to arrest Me, as *you would* against a robber?

49 "Day after day I was with you, teaching in the [courts and porches of the] temple, and you did not seize Me; but *this has happened* so that the Scriptures would be fulfilled."

50 Then all of His disciples abandoned Him and fled.

51 A young man was following Him, wearing [only] a linen sheet over *his* naked *body;* and some men seized him.

52 But pulling free of the linen sheet, he escaped [from them] naked.

Jesus before His Accusers

53 They led Jesus away to the high priest, and all the chief priests and the elders and the scribes (Sanhedrin, Jewish High Court) gathered together. [Matt 26:57–68; Luke 22:66–71; John 18:12f, 19–24]

54 Peter had followed Him at a distance, right into the courtyard of the high priest; and he was sitting with the officers [guards and servants] and warming himself at the fire.

55 Now the chief priests and the entire Council (Sanhedrin, Jewish High Court) were trying to obtain testimony against Jesus [which they could use] to have Him [condemned and] executed, but they were not finding any.

56 For many [people] were giving false testimony against Him, but their testimonies were not consistent.

57 Some stood up and *began* to give false testimony against Him, saying,

58 "We heard Him say, 'I will destroy this temple (sanctuary) that was made with hands, and in three days I will build another made without hands.' " [John 2:19–21]

59 Not even in this respect was their testimony consistent.

60 The high priest stood up and came forward and asked Jesus, "Have You no answer to give [in response] to what these men are testifying against You?"

61 But Jesus kept silent and gave no answer at all. Again the high priest was questioning Him, and saying to Him,

---

14:43 *and with him a crowd of men.* Judas came with a detachment of troops (Jn 18:3). It was one-tenth of a Roman legion or roughly 600 men. **14:50–52 *young man.*** Only Mark tells of this incident and many believe that this young man was Mark himself. How else would he have known this story, and why else should he have included it? If it was Mark, and if the Last Supper was at his home that evening, he could easily have risen from bed, pulled on a linen sheet, and followed the disciples.

14:61 *Jesus kept silent.* Jesus remained silent before Pilate and Herod Antipas. Finally they could find nothing substantial with which to charge Him. ***the Christ (the Messiah, the Anointed), the Son of the Blessed One.*** The trial was over, and Jesus stood falsely condemned for blasphemy, which in this context means laying

42 Mt 26:46; Jn 18:1,2 **43** Mt 26:47; Lk 22:47; Jn 18:3 **48** Mt 26:55; Lk 22:52 **49** Ps 22:6; Isa 53:7; Lk 22:37; 24:44 **50** ver. 27; Ps 88:8 **53** Mt 26:57; Lk 22:54; Jn 18:13 **55** Mt 26:59 **58** Mk 15:29; Jn 2:19 **60** Mt 26:62 **61** Isa 53:7; Mt 26:63

"Are You the Christ (the Messiah, the
Anointed), the Son of the Blessed One?"
62 Jesus said, "I am; and you will [all]
see THE SON OF MAN SEATED [with au-
thority] AT THE RIGHT HAND OF POWER (the
Father), and COMING WITH THE CLOUDS OF
HEAVEN." [Ps 110:1; Dan 7:13]
63 Then tearing his robe [to express
his indignation], the high priest said,
"What further need do we have of wit-
nesses? [Num 14:6]
64 "You have heard the blasphemy
[that is, His claim to be the Son of God].
What is your decision?" And they all
condemned Him to be [guilty and] de-
serving of death. [Lev 24:16]
65 And some began to spit on Him,
and to blindfold Him, and to beat Him
with their fists, and to say to Him,
"Prophesy [by telling us who hit you]!"
Then the officers took custody of Him
and struck him in the face.

Peter's Denials

66 While Peter was down below in the
courtyard, one of the servant-girls of
the high priest came, [Matt 26:69–75;
Luke 22:55–62; John 18:16–18, 25–27]
67 and when she saw Peter warming
himself, she looked intently at him
and said, "You were with Jesus the
Nazarene, too."
68 But he denied it, saying, "I neither
know nor understand what you are
talking about." Then he went out [of
the courtyard] to the porch, [and a
rooster crowed.]
69 The servant-girl saw him, and be-
gan once more to tell the bystanders,
"This [man] is *one* of them."
70 But again he denied it. After a little
while, the bystanders again said to
Peter, "You are in fact *one* of them, for
[it is clear from your accent, that] you
are a Galilean, too."
71 But he began to invoke a curse [on
himself] and to swear [an oath], "I do
not know this man you are talking
about!"
72 Immediately a rooster crowed the
second time. And Peter remembered
what Jesus said to him: "Before a roost-
er crows twice, you will deny Me three
times." And thinking of this, he began
weeping [in anguish].

Jesus before Pilate

15 EARLY IN the morning the
chief priests, with the elders and
scribes and the whole Council (Sanhe-
drin, Jewish High Court), immediately
consulted together; and they bound
Jesus, they took Him away [violently]
and handed Him over to Pilate. [Is 53:8]
2 Pilate questioned Him, "Are You the
King of the Jews?" And He replied to
him, "It is as you say." [Matt 27:11–14;
Luke 23:2, 3; John 18:29–37]
3 The chief priests *began* accusing
Him of many things.
4 Then Pilate again asked Him,
"Have You no answer [to give]? See
how many charges they are bringing
against You!"
5 But Jesus gave no further answer;
so Pilate was perplexed. [Is 53:7]
6 Now at the [Passover] feast Pilate
used to set free for them any one prison-
er whom they requested. [Matt 27:15–
26; Luke 23:18–25; John 18:39–19:16]

---

claim to deity. Naturally, this is the boast of a liar or a lunatic — unless He is the Almighty God in human flesh, as Jesus was (Php 2:5 – 8; 1Jn 1:1 – 3).

14:71 – 72 *a rooster crowed.* We are not told that Peter thought at all about Jesus' words. If he did, maybe he tried to conceal his identity more carefully, but to no avail. Each of the other Gospel writers tells us that the cock crowed immediately upon Peter's final denial (Mt 26:74; Lk 22:60; Jn 18:27). This time he thought about it, and he wept.

15:1 – 3 *consulted together.* Rather than murdering Jesus privately, the Jewish politicians decided to seek Pilate's approval so they could execute the "blasphemer legally." Their charges included many things but apparently centered on treason. Jesus claimed to be a king, thus defying Caesar (Lk 23:2). This crime was punishable in the Roman Empire by death. Pilate must have concluded that the charges against Jesus were groundless, for Mark tells us he desired to release Him.

62 Mt 24:30; 26:64; Lk 22:69 **66** Mt 26:58,69; Lk 22:55; Jn 18:16 **69** Mt 26:71; Lk 22:58; Jn 18:25 **70** Mt 26:73; Lk 22:59; Jn 18:26; Ac 2:7 **72** Mt 26:75 **CHAPTER 15** **1** Ps 2:2; Mt 27:1; Lk 22:66; 23:1; Jn 18:28; Ac 3:13; 4:26 **2** Mt 27:11 **4** Mt 27:13 **5** Isa 53:7; Jn 19:9 **6** Mt 27:15; Lk 23:17; Jn 18:39

[7]The man called Barabbas was
imprisoned with the insurrectionists
(revolutionaries) who had committed
murder in the civil rebellion.
[8]The crowd came up and began ask-
ing Pilate to do as he usually did for
them.
[9]Pilate answered them, saying, "Do
you want me to set free for you the
King of the Jews?"
[10]For he was aware that the chief
priests had turned Jesus over to him
because of envy *and* resentment.
[11]But the chief priests stirred up the
crowd to get him to release Barabbas
for them instead.
[12]Again Pilate answered, "Then
what shall I do with Him whom you
call the King of the Jews?"
[13]They screamed back, "Crucify
Him!"
[14]But Pilate asked them, "Why, what
has He done that is evil?" But they
screamed all the more, "Crucify Him!"
[15]So Pilate, wishing to satisfy the
crowd, set Barabbas free for them;
and after having Jesus scourged, he
handed Him over [to his soldiers] to
be crucified. [Is 53:5]

Jesus Is Mocked

[16]The soldiers led Him away into
the palace (that is, the Praetorium),
and they called together the entire
[Roman] battalion [of 600 soldiers].
[Matt 27:27–31]
[17]They dressed Him up in [a ranking
Roman officer's robe of] purple, and
after twisting [together] a crown of
thorns, they placed it on Him;
[18]and they began saluting *and* mock-
ing Him: "Hail, King of the Jews!"
[19]They kept beating Him on the head
with a reed and spitting on Him, and
kneeling and bowing in [mock] hom-
age to Him. [Is 50:6]
[20]After they had mocked Him, they
took off the purple robe and put His
own clothes on Him. And they led Him
out [of the city] to crucify Him.
[21]They forced into service a passer-
by coming in from the countryside,
Simon of Cyrene (the father of Alex-
ander and Rufus), to carry His cross.
[Matt 27:32; Luke 23:26]

The Crucifixion

[22]Then they brought Him to the place
[called] Golgotha, which is translat-
ed, Place of a Skull. [Matt 27:33–44;
Luke 23:33–43; John 19:17–24]
[23]They tried to give Him wine mixed
with myrrh [to dull the pain], but He
would not take it.
[24]And they crucified Him, and divid-
ed up His clothes among themselves,
casting lots for them to see who should
take what. [Ps 22:18]
[25]It was the third hour (9:00 a.m.)
when they crucified Him. [Ps 22:14–16]
[26]The inscription of the accusation
against Him had been written [above
Him]: "THE KING OF THE JEWS."
[27]They crucified two robbers with
Him, one on His right and one on His
left.
[28][And the Scripture was fulfilled
which says, "He was counted with the
transgressors."] [Is 53:12]
[29]Those who were passing by were
insulting Him with abusive *and* inso-
lent language, wagging their heads
[as a sign of contempt], and saying,
"Ha! You who would destroy the tem-
ple and rebuild it in [only] three days,
[John 2:19]

15:15 *after having Jesus scourged.* This word, used only twice in the New Testament (Mt 27:26 and here), describes a punishment more severe than flogging or beating. The prisoner was beaten with a whip fashioned of numerous strips of leather attached to a handle. To the leather strips were tied sharp pieces of bone and metal, which could rip and tear one's skin to shreds.

15:22 *Golgotha* is an Aramaic word. The hill may have resembled the bony features of a skull or was called this because it was a place of death. The name Calvary comes from the Latin word for skull.
15:25 *the third hour.* This was 9 A.M., using a common Jewish system of marking the day. Jesus suffered on the cross until at least 3 P.M., the ninth hour of verse 34.

11 Mt 27:20; Ac 3:14 **15** Mt 27:26; Jn 19:1,16 **16** Mt 27:27 **21** Mt 27:32; Lk 23:26 **22** Mt 27:33; Lk 23:33; Jn 19:17 **23** Mt 27:34 **24** Ps 22:18; Lk 23:34; Jn 19:23 **25** See Mt 27:45; Lk 23:44; Jn 19:14 **26** Mt 27:37; Jn 19:19 **27** Mt 27:38 **28** Isa 53:12; Lk 22:37 **29** Ps 22:7; Mk 14:58; Jn 2:19

30save Yourself by coming down
from the cross!"
31In the same way the chief priests
also, along with the scribes, were ridi-
culing *and* mocking *Him* among them-
selves and saying, "He saved others
[from death]; He cannot save Himself!
[Ps 22:7, 8]
32"Let the Christ (the Messiah, the
Anointed), the King of Israel, now
come down from the cross, so that
we may see and believe *and* trust [in
Him]!" Those who were crucified with
Him were also insulting Him.
33When the sixth hour (noon) came,
darkness covered the whole land until
the ninth hour (3:00 p.m.). [Matt 27:45–
56; Luke 23:44–49]
34And at the ninth hour Jesus cried
out with a loud voice, "Eloi, Eloi, lama
sabachthani?"—which is translated,
"My God, My God, why have You for-
saken Me?" [Ps 22:1]
35Some of the bystanders heard
Him and said, "Look! He is calling
for Elijah!"
36Someone ran and filled a sponge
with sour wine, put it on a reed and
gave Him a drink, saying, "Let us
see whether Elijah is coming to take
Him down." [Ps 69:21; Matt 27:48, 50;
Luke 23:36; John 19:29, 30]
37But Jesus uttered a loud cry, and
breathed out His last [voluntarily, sov-
ereignly dismissing and releasing His
spirit from His body in submission to
His Father's plan].
38And the veil [of the Holy of Holies]
of the temple was torn in two from top
to bottom.
39When the centurion, who was
standing opposite Him, saw the way
He breathed His last [being fully in
control], he said, "Truly this man was
the Son of God!"
40Now some women also were
watching from a distance, among
whom were Mary Magdalene, and
Mary the mother of James the Less
and of Joses, and Salome. [John 19:25]
41When Jesus was in Galilee, they
used to accompany him and minis-
ter to Him; and *there were* also many
other women who came up with Him
to Jerusalem.

Jesus Is Buried

42When evening had already
come, because it was the preparation
day, that is, the day before the Sab-
bath, [Deut 21:22, 23; Matt 27:57–61;
Luke 23:50–56; John 19:38–42]
43Joseph of Arimathea came, a
prominent *and* respected member of
the Council (Sanhedrin, Jewish High
Court), who was himself waiting for
the kingdom of God—and he coura-
geously dared to go in before Pilate,
and asked for the body of Jesus.
44Pilate wondered if He was dead

15:32 ***Let the Christ.*** Jesus was mockingly called the Christ or Messiah by the chief priests and scribes. Their offer to believe in Christ if He would descend from the cross was not believable.

15:37 ***Jesus uttered a loud cry.*** Frequently, crucifixion produced a coma or unconsciousness prior to death, but Jesus was in control of all His faculties until the moment when He voluntarily gave up His life (Jn 10:17–18).

15:38 ***the veil [of the Holy of Holies] of the temple.*** The significance of this event is that access to God is now open to all. No longer through priests and the blood of bulls and goats do we approach God, but through the torn veil, which also symbolizes Jesus' broken and torn body (Heb 10:20).

15:40–41 ***some women also were watching.*** These women were true disciples of Christ. They had ministered to Jesus' needs and would be the first witnesses of His resurrection. Mark does not name Jesus' mother here but includes other prominent women. Three Marys were present along with many other women and Salome. She was the mother of the disciples James and John (Mt 27:56).

15:43 ***Joseph of Arimathea.*** He is identified as a prominent member of the Sanhedrin. To ask Pilate for the body of Jesus was not just a gesture of kindness. It was an act of bravery, which placed Joseph in opposition to the Sanhedrin and identified him as a follower of Jesus.

32 Mt 27:44; Lk 23:39 **33** Mt 27:45; Lk 23:44 **34** Ps 22:1; Mt 27:46 **36** Mt 27:48; Jn 19:29; Ps 69:21 **37** Mt 27:50; Lk 23:46; Jn 19:30 **38** Mt 27:51; Lk 23:45 **39** Mt 27:54; Lk 23:47 **40** Mt 27:55; Lk 23:49; Ps 38:11 **41** Lk 8:2,3 **42** Mt 27:57; Lk 23:50; Jn 19:38 **43** Lk 2:25,38

by this time [only six hours after being crucified], and he summoned the centurion and asked him whether He was already dead.

45 And when he learned from the centurion [that Jesus was in fact dead], he gave the body to Joseph [by granting him permission to remove it].

46 So Joseph purchased a [fine] linen cloth [for wrapping the body], and after taking Jesus down [from the cross], he wrapped Him in the linen cloth and placed Him in a tomb which had been cut out of rock. Then he rolled a [large, wheel-shaped] stone against the entrance of the tomb. [Is 53:9]

47 Mary Magdalene and Mary the *mother* of Joses were [carefully] watching to see where He was laid.

The Resurrection

16 WHEN THE Sabbath was over, Mary Magdalene, Mary the *mother* of James, and Salome purchased [sweet-smelling] spices, so that they might go and anoint Him. [Matt 28:1–8; Luke 24:1–10; John 20:1–8]

2 Very early on the first day of the week, they came to the tomb when the sun had risen.

3 And they were saying to one another, "Who will roll back the stone for us from the entrance of the tomb?"

4 Looking up, they saw that the stone had been rolled away, though it was extremely large.

5 Entering the tomb, they saw a young man sitting on the right, wearing a [long, stately] white robe; and they were amazed *and* bewildered.

6 And he said to them, "Do not be amazed; you are looking for Jesus the Nazarene, who was crucified. He has risen; He is not here. See, [here is] the place where they laid Him. [Ps 16:10]

7 "But go, tell His disciples and Peter, 'He is going ahead of you to Galilee; you will see Him there, just as He told you.' " [Mark 14:28]

8 They went out and fled from the tomb, for they were seized with trembling and astonishment; and they said nothing [about it] to anyone, because they were afraid.

9 [Now Jesus, having risen [from death] early on the first day of the week, appeared first to Mary Magdalene, from whom He had cast out seven demons.

10 She went and reported it to those who had been with Him, while they were mourning and weeping.

11 When they heard that He was alive and had been seen by her, they did not believe it.

12 After that, He appeared in a different form to two of them as they were walking along the way to the country. [Luke 24:13–35]

13 They returned [to Jerusalem] and told the others, but they did not believe them either.

The Disciples Commissioned

14 Later, Jesus appeared to the eleven [disciples] themselves as they were reclining *at the table;* and He called

---

16:5 – 6 *a young man sitting on the right, wearing a [long, stately] white robe.* Mark does not identify the young man with the robe as an angel, but he is there to explain the mystery that confronts the women. ***He has risen.*** In the passive voice, this indicates that an act of God accomplished the raising up of Jesus.

16:9 – 20 *Now Jesus, having risen.* The authenticity of these last twelve verses has been disputed. Those who doubt Mark's authorship of this passage point to two fourth-century manuscripts that omit these verses. Others believe that they should be included because even these two manuscripts leave space for all or some of these verses, indicating that their copyists knew of their existence. The difficulty is in knowing whether the space is for this longer version of Mark's ending or for one of the alternate endings found in the manuscripts. Important early church fathers endorsed this passage, and it does not seem likely that Mark would end his story on a note of fear (v. 8).

16:14 *to the eleven.* After Judas' demise (Mt 27:3 – 5; Ac 1:16 – 18), the disciples were known

46 Mt 27:59,60; Lk 23:53; Jn 19:40 **CHAPTER 16** **1** Mt 28:1; Lk 24:1; Jn 20:1; Lk 23:56 **2** Lk 24:1; Jn 20:1 **5** Lk 24:3; Jn 20:11 **6** Mt 28:5 **7** Mt 26:32; Mk 14:28 **8** Mt 28:8; Lk 24:9 **9** Lk 8:2 **10** Lk 24:10; Jn 20:18 **11** Lk 24:11 **12** Lk 24:13 **14** Lk 24:36; Jn 20:19; 1Co 15:5

them to account for their unbelief and
hardness of heart, because they had
not believed those who had seen Him
after He had risen [from death].
15 And He said to them, "Go into all
the world and preach the gospel to all
creation.
16 "He who has believed [in Me] and
has been baptized will be saved [from
the penalty of God's wrath and judg-
ment]; but he who has not believed will
be condemned.
17 "These signs will accompany those
who have believed: in My name they
will cast out demons, they will speak
in new tongues;
18 they will pick up serpents, and if
they drink anything deadly, it will not
hurt them; they will lay hands on the
sick, and they will get well."
19 So then, when the Lord Jesus had
spoken to them, He was taken up into
heaven and sat down at the right hand
of God. [Ps 110:1]
20 And they went out and preached
everywhere, while the Lord was work-
ing with them and confirming the
word by the signs that followed.]

---

for a while as the eleven. Jesus upbraided these disciples for not believing the accounts of eyewitnesses, but He pronounced a blessing on "they who did not see [Me] and yet believed" (Jn 20:29).

16:19 *He was taken up into heaven.* This was the final sign that Jesus was the Son of God.

15 Mt 28:19; Jn 15:16; Col 1:23 **16** Jn 3:18; Ac 2:38; 16:30-32; Ro 10:9; 1Pe 3:21; Jn 12:48 **17** Lk 10:17; Ac 5:16; Ac 2:4; 1Co 12:10 **18** Lk 10:19; Ac 28:5; 5:15; Jas 5:14 **19** Ac 1:2,3; Lk 24:51; Ps 110:1; Ac 7:55 **20** Ac 5:12; 1Co 2:4,5; Heb 2:4

THE GOSPEL ACCORDING TO

LUKE

▸ **AUTHOR:** It is evident from the prologues to Luke and Acts (1:1 – 4; Ac 1:1 – 5) that both books were addressed to a man called Theophilus as a two-volume work. Acts begins with a summary of Luke and continues the story from where the Gospel of Luke concludes. Luke may have been a Hellenistic Jew, but it is more likely that he was a Gentile (this would make him the only Gentile contributor to the New Testament). It has been suggested that Luke may have been a Greek physician to a Roman family who at some point was set free and given Roman citizenship. Luke was not an eyewitness of the events in his Gospel, but he relied on the testimony of apostolic eyewitness and reliable written sources.

▸ **TIMES:** c. 4 BC – AD 33 ▸ **KEY VERSE:** Lk 19:10

▸ **THEME:** The beginning of Luke makes reference to the fact that there was a great deal of oral tradition concerning Jesus circulating during the first century. The rapid growth of the church (over 3,000 on the Day of Pentecost alone) meant that there would have been potential for significant variety in stories about Jesus. Luke's stated agenda is reliability. Where Matthew goes to great lengths to tie Jesus' story to the history of the Jews, Luke is more interested in where the story fits in the history of the human race. Throughout the book, Christ reaches out to people from a variety of social strata, nationalities, and cultures. Luke sees Jesus as the Savior of the whole world.

Introduction

1 SINCE [AS is well known] many have undertaken to compile an orderly account of the things which have been fulfilled among us [by God],
2exactly as they were handed down to us by those [with personal experience] who from the beginning [of Christ's ministry] were eyewitnesses and ministers of the word [that is, of the teaching concerning salvation through faith in Christ],
3it seemed fitting for me as well, [and so I have decided] after having carefully searched out *and* investigated all the events accurately, from the *very* beginning, to write an orderly account for you, most excellent Theophilus; [Acts 1:1]
4so that you may know the exact truth about the things you have been

---

1:1 ***many have undertaken to compile.*** Luke makes it clear that he was not the first to write a narrative of the ministry of Jesus.
1:2 ***eyewitnesses.*** These verses suggest that Luke was not an eyewitness to the events of Jesus' ministry, but that he had access to statements of those who were.
1:3 ***an orderly account.*** Luke gave his narrative a basic structure. Not every part is in chronological sequence, but the broad sequence is Christ's ministry in Galilee, His travel to Jerusalem, and His struggles in Jerusalem. The order of events shows how Jesus gradually revealed Himself and how opposition to Him grew.
1:4 ***the exact truth.*** Theophilus was likely a young Gentile believer. He not only needed to know the truth and accuracy of what the church taught, but he also needed to be reassured. He might well

CHAPTER 1 **2** Heb 2:3; 1Pe 5:1; 2Pe 1:16; Mk 1:1; Jn 15:27 **3** Ac 15:19; 1Co 7:40; Ac 11:4; Ac 1:1 **4** Jn 20:31

taught [that is, the history and doctrine
of the faith].

Birth of John the Baptist Foretold

5 In the days of Herod [the Great],
king of Judea, there was a certain priest
whose name was Zacharias, of the divi-
sion of Abijah. His wife was a descen-
dant of Aaron [the first high priest of
Israel], and her name was Elizabeth.
6 They both were righteous (ap-
proved) in the sight of God, walking
blamelessly in all the commandments
and requirements of the Lord.
7 But they were childless, because
Elizabeth was barren, and they were
both far advanced in years.
8 Now it happened while Zachari-
as was serving as priest before God
in the *appointed* order of his priestly
division,
9 as was the custom of the priest-
hood, he was chosen by lot to enter
[the sanctuary of] the temple of the
Lord and burn incense [on the altar of
incense]. [Ex 30:7]
10 And all the congregation was pray-
ing outside [in the court of the temple]
at the hour of the incense offering.
11 And an angel of the Lord appeared
to him, standing to the right of the altar
of incense.
12 When Zacharias saw *the angel,* he
was troubled and overcome with fear.
13 But the angel said to him, "Do not
be afraid, Zacharias, because your pe-
tition [in prayer] was heard, and your
wife Elizabeth will bear you a son, and
you will name him John.
14 "You will have great joy and delight,
and many will rejoice over his birth,
15 for he will be great *and* distin-
guished in the sight of the Lord; and
will never drink wine or liquor, and he
will be filled with *and* empowered to
act by the Holy Spirit while still in his
mother's womb. [Num 6:3]
16 "He will turn many of the sons
of Israel back [from sin] to [love and
serve] the Lord their God.
17 "It is he who will go *as a forerunner*
before Him in the spirit and power of
Elijah, TO TURN THE HEARTS OF THE FATHERS
BACK TO THE CHILDREN, and the disobedient
to the attitude of the righteous [which is
to seek and submit to the will of God]—
in order to make ready a people [perfect-
ly] prepared [spiritually and morally] for
the Lord." [Is 40:3; Mal 4:5, 6]
18 And Zacharias said to the angel,
"How will I be certain of this? For I am
an old man and my wife is advanced
in age."
19 The angel replied and said to him,
"I am Gabriel; I stand *and* minister
in the [very] presence of God, and I
have been sent [by Him] to speak to
you and to bring you this good news.
[Dan 8:16; 9:21]

---

have been wondering what he as a Gentile was doing in a movement which was originally Jewish.

1:5 *Herod.* He was appointed by the Roman emperor and reigned over Judea, Samaria, Galilee, Perea, and Syria from 37 to 4 BC.

1:7 *Elizabeth was barren.* Being childless was a grave disappointment in ancient Israel (1Sa 1). The Scriptures record a number of times when God blessed a barren woman by giving her a son (Ge 18:11; 21:2).

1:8 – 9 *the custom of the priesthood.* Zacharias served for one week twice a year at the temple, one of perhaps 18,000 priests who served in a year.

1:13 *Do not be afraid.* Angels often calmed the fears of those to whom they appeared (v. 30; 2:10; Ge 15:1; Da 10:12; Mt 1:20; Ac 18:9; Rev 1:17).

1:14 *joy and delight.* Joy is a major theme throughout the writings of Luke (vv. 44,47,58; 2:10; 10:20; 13:17; 15:5 – 7; Ac 5:41).

1:15 *will never drink wine or liquor.* As with Samuel and Samson, a vow was imposed on the child that indicated his special consecration to the Lord. ***filled with and empowered to act by the Holy Spirit.*** Being filled with the Spirit means being directed by Him and obedient to Him (Eph 5:18).

1:17 *in the spirit and power of Elijah.* John was the forerunner of the Messiah. This description recalls Matthew 3:1 – 6. John's ministry paralleled Elijah, for both prophets called Israel to repentance (1Ki 17:18).

1:19 *Gabriel.* Two angels are named in the Bible

5 Mt 2:1; 1Ch 24:10; Neh 12:4 **6** Ge 7:1; 1Ki 9:4; 2Ki 20:3 **8** 1Ch 24:19; 2Ch 8:14 **9** Ex 30:7,8; 1Ch 23:13; 2Ch 29:11 **10** Lev 16:17 **11** Ex 30:1 **12** Jdg 6:22; 13:22; Da 10:8; Lk 2:9; Ac 10:4; Rev 1:17 **13** ver. 60,63 **14** ver. 58 **15** Nu 6:3; Jdg 13:4; Lk 7:33; Jer 1:5; Gal 1:15 **16** Mal 4:5,6 **17** Mal 4:5; Mt 11:14; Mk 9:12 **18** Ge 17:17 **19** Da 8:16; 9:21-23; Mt 18:10; Heb 1:14

[20]"Listen carefully, you will be *continually* silent and unable to speak until the day when these things take place, because you did not believe what I told you; but my words will be fulfilled at their proper time."
[21]The people [outside in the court] were waiting for Zacharias, and were wondering about his *long* delay in the temple.
[22]But when he did come out, he was unable to speak to them. They realized that he had seen a vision in the temple; and he kept making signs to them, and remained mute.
[23]When his time of priestly service was finished, he returned to his home.
[24]Now after this his wife Elizabeth became pregnant, and for five months she secluded herself completely, saying,
[25]"This is how the Lord has dealt with me in the days when He looked with favor on *me*, to take away my disgrace among men." [Gen 30:23; Is 4:1]

Jesus' Birth Foretold

[26]Now in the sixth month [of Elizabeth's pregnancy] the angel Gabriel was sent from God to a city in Galilee called Nazareth,
[27]to a virgin betrothed to a man whose name was Joseph, a descendant of the house of David; and the virgin's name was Mary.
[28]And coming to her, the angel said, "Greetings, favored one! The Lord is with you."
[29]But she was greatly perplexed at what he said, and kept carefully considering what kind of greeting this was.
[30]The angel said to her, "Do not be afraid, Mary, for you have found favor with God.
[31]"Listen carefully: you will conceive in your womb and give birth to a son, and you shall name Him Jesus.
[32]"He will be great *and* eminent and will be called the Son of the Most High; and the Lord God will give Him the throne of His father David;
[33]and He will reign over the house of Jacob (Israel) forever, and of His kingdom there shall be no end." [Is 9:6, 7; Dan 2:44]
[34]Mary said to the angel, "How will this be, since I am a virgin *and* have no intimacy with any man?"
[35]Then the angel replied to her, "The Holy Spirit will come upon you, and the power of the Most High will overshadow you [like a cloud]; for that reason the holy (pure, sinless) Child shall be called the Son of God. [Ex 40:34; Is 7:14]
[36]"And listen, even your relative Elizabeth has also conceived a son in her old age; and she who was called barren is now in her sixth month.
[37]"For with God nothing [is or ever] shall be impossible."
[38]Then Mary said, "Behold, *I am* the servant of the Lord; may it be done to me according to your word." And the angel left her.

---

who function as messengers. Michael is the other one (Da 8:16; 9:21; 10:13,21; Jude 9; Rev 12:7).

1:25 ***my disgrace.*** In ancient Israel barrenness was seen as a cause for shame. The "opening of the womb" indicated God's grace (Ge 21:6; 30:23; 1Sa 1: 2). In this verse, Elizabeth praises the Lord for mercifully blessing her even as He moved His plan for all of human history forward.

1:32 ***Most High.*** This phrase is another way of referring to the majesty of God. ***David.*** Jesus fulfilled God's promise to David concerning an unending dynasty.

1:34 ***How will this be.*** Mary did not ask for a sign, so this remark does not reflect unbelief. She accepts her role without question in verse 38, and thus is a model of faith, even though she does not fully understand everything. The work of God in Mary introduces something unknown before or after; the birth into the human race of One who is both God and man.

1:35 ***The Holy Spirit will come upon you.*** This is a direct declaration of Jesus' divine conception. The child's conception means He is uniquely set apart.

1:38 ***servant.*** This term suggests humility before the Lord and a readiness for faithful and obedient

20 Eze 3:26; 24:27 **23** 2Ki 11:5; 1Ch 9:25 **25** Ge 30:23; Isa 4:1; 54:1,4 **27** Mt 1:18; Lk 2:4,5 **28** Da 9:23; 10:19; Jdg 6:12 **29** ver. 12 **31** Isa 7:14; Mt 1:21; Lk 2:21 **32** Mk 5:7; 2Sa 7:11; Ps 132:11; Isa 9:6,7; 16:5; Jer 23:5; Rev 3:7 **33** Da 2:44; 7:14,27; Ob 21; Mic 4:7; Jn 12:34; Heb 1:8 **35** Mt 1:20; Mt 14:33; 26:63,64; Mk 1:1; Jn 1:34; 20:31; Ac 8:37; Ro 1:4 **37** Ge 18:14; Jer 32:17; Zec 8:6; Mt 19:26; Mk 10:27; Lk 18:27; Ro 4:21

Mary Visits Elizabeth

39 Now at this time Mary arose and
hurried to the hill country, to a city of
Judah (Judea),
40 and she entered the house of Zach-
arias and greeted Elizabeth.
41 When Elizabeth heard Mary's
greeting, her baby leaped in her womb;
and Elizabeth was filled with the Holy
Spirit *and* empowered by Him.
42 And she exclaimed loudly, "Blessed
[worthy to be praised] are you among
women, and blessed is the fruit of your
womb!
43 "And how has it *happened* to me,
that the mother of my Lord would
come to me?
44 "For behold, when the sound of
your greeting reached my ears, the
baby in my womb leaped for joy.
45 "And blessed [spiritually fortu-
nate and favored by God] is she who
believed *and* confidently trusted that
there would be a fulfillment of the
things that were spoken to her [by the
angel sent] from the Lord."

The Magnificat

46 And Mary said,
"My soul magnifies *and* exalts the
Lord,
47 And my spirit has rejoiced in God
my Savior.
48 "For He has looked [with loving
care] on the humble state of His
maidservant;
For behold, from now on all
generations will count me blessed
and happy *and* favored by God!
49 "For He who is mighty has done
great things for me;
And holy is His name [to be
worshiped in His purity,
majesty, and glory].
50 "AND HIS MERCY IS UPON GENERATION
AFTER GENERATION
TOWARD THOSE WHO [stand in great
awe of God and] FEAR HIM.
FROM GENERATION TO GENERATION.
[Ps 103:17]
51 "He has done mighty deeds with
His [powerful] arm;
He has scattered *those who were*
proud in the thoughts of their
heart.
52 "He has brought down rulers from
their thrones,
And exalted those who were
humble.
53 "HE HAS FILLED THE HUNGRY WITH
GOOD THINGS;
And sent the rich away empty-
handed.
54 "He has helped His servant Israel,
In remembrance of His mercy,
55 Just as He promised to our fathers,
To Abraham and to his
descendants forever." [Gen 17:7;
18:18; 22:17; 1 Sam 2:1–10;
Mic 7:20]

56 And Mary stayed with Elizabeth
for about three months, and then re-
turned to her home.

John Is Born

57 Now the time had come for Eliza-
beth to give birth, and she gave birth
to a son.
58 Her neighbors and relatives heard
that the Lord had shown His great
mercy toward her, and they were re-
joicing with her.

---

service, which should characterize every believer. Paul uses the masculine form of this word to describe himself (Ro 1:1).

1:46 *My soul magnifies and exalts the Lord.* The following hymn gets its name, the "Magnificat," from the Latin word for *magnifies*. Mary's hymn is a recital of what God had done for her and for others in the past.

1:48 *all generations will count me blessed.* Mary went from being a poor unknown Hebrew girl to the most honored woman in the history of the world.

1:50 *MERCY.* This term expresses the Old Testament concept of God's loyal, gracious, faithful love (Ps 103).

1:51 – 53 *He has scattered those who were proud.* These verses portray a "reversal" in the end times, when those who have abused power will be judged and those who have suffered persecution will be exalted.

39 Jos 21:9 **42** Jdg 5:24 **46** 1Sa 2:1; Ps 34:2,3; Hab 3:18 **48** 1Sa 1:11; Ps 138:6; Lk 11:27 **49** Ps 71:19; 126:2,3; Ps 111:9 **50** Ge 17:7; Ex 20:6; Ps 103:17 **51** Ps 98:1; 118:15; Isa 40:10; Ps 33:10; 1Pe 5:5 **52** 1Sa 2:6; Job 5:11; Ps 113:6 **53** 1Sa 2:5; Ps 34:10 **54** Ps 98:3; Jer 31:3 **55** Ge 17:19; Ps 132:11; Gal 3:16

59 It happened that on the eighth day they came to circumcise the child [as required by the Law], and they intended to name him Zacharias, after his father; [Gen 17:12; Lev 12:3]

60 but his mother answered, "No indeed; instead he will be called John."

61 And they said to her, "None of your relatives is called by that name."

62 Then they made signs to his father, as to what he wanted him called.

63 And he asked for a *writing* tablet and wrote as follows, "His name is John." And they were all astonished.

64 At once Zacharias' mouth was opened and his tongue *freed,* and he *began* speaking, praising *and* blessing *and* thanking God.

65 Then fear came on all their neighbors; and all these things were discussed throughout the hill country of Judea.

66 All who heard these things kept them in mind, saying, "What then will this little boy *turn out to* be?" For the hand of the Lord was certainly with him [to bring about his birth].

Zacharias' Prophecy

67 Now Zacharias his father was filled with the Holy Spirit *and* empowered by Him, and he prophesied, saying,

68 "Blessed (praised, glorified) be the
Lord, the God of Israel,
Because He has visited us and
brought redemption to His
people,
69 And He has raised up a horn of
salvation [a mighty and valiant
Savior] for us
In the house of David His
servant—
70 Just as He promised by the mouth
of His holy prophets from the
most ancient times—
71 Salvation FROM OUR ENEMIES,
And FROM THE HAND OF ALL WHO HATE
US; [Ps 106:10]
72 To show mercy [as He promised] to
our fathers,
And to remember His holy
covenant [the promised blessing],
73 The oath which He swore to
Abraham our father,
74 To grant us that we, being rescued
from the hand of our enemies,
Might serve Him without fear,
75 In holiness [being set apart] and
righteousness [being upright]
before Him all our days.
76 "And you, child, will be called a
prophet of the Most High;
For you will go on BEFORE THE LORD
(the Messiah) TO PREPARE HIS
WAYS; [Is 40:3; Mal 4:5]
77 To give His people the knowledge
of salvation
By the forgiveness of their sins,
78 Because of the tender mercy of our
God,
With which the Sunrise (the
Messiah) from on high will
dawn *and* visit us, [Mal 4:2]
79 TO SHINE UPON THOSE WHO SIT IN
DARKNESS AND IN THE SHADOW OF
DEATH,
To guide our feet [in a straight
line] into the way of peace *and*
serenity." [Is 9:2]

80 The child continued to grow and to become strong in spirit, and he

---

1:67 *Zacharias his father was filled with the Holy Spirit . . . and he prophesied.* The presence of the Holy Spirit enabled Zacharias to announce God's promise. Zacharias's hymn is called the "Benedictus" from its first word in the Latin Vulgate translation. There are three types of prophecy in the Bible: foretelling future events, forthtelling the Word of God, and praising God. Zacharias's prophecy includes all three.

1:69 *horn of salvation.* The horn of an ox is a symbol of power (Dt 33:17; 1Sa 2:10; 2Sa 22:3; Ps 75:4 – 5,10; 132:17; Eze 29:21).

1:77 *knowledge of salvation.* John's task was to prepare the people by informing them of their need to repent (3:1 – 14) and of the One who was coming (3:15 – 18).

1:78 *the Sunrise (the Messiah) from on high will dawn and visit us.* This phrase is a reference to the coming of the Messiah (Nu 24:17; Mal 4:2).

59 Ge 17:12; Lev 12:3 **60** ver. 13 **66** Lk 2:19; Ge 39:2; Ps 80:17; Ac 11:21 **67** Joel 2:28 **68** 1Ki 1:48; Ps 41:13; Ex 3:16; Ps 111:9; Lk 7:16 **69** Ps 132:17 **70** Jer 23:5; Da 9:24 **72** Lev 26:42; Eze 16:60 **73** Ge 12:3; Heb 6:13 **74** Ro 6:18; Heb 9:14 **75** Jer 32:39; Eph 4:24; 2Th 2:13 **76** Isa 40:3; Mal 3:1; Mt 11:10 **77** Mk 1:4 **79** Isa 9:2; Mt 4:16 **80** Lk 2:40; Mt 3:1

lived in the deserts until the day of
his public appearance to Israel [as
John the Baptist, the forerunner of
the Messiah].

Jesus' Birth in Bethlehem

2 NOW IN those days a decree went
out from [the emperor] Caesar Au-
gustus, that all the inhabited world (the
Roman Empire) should be registered
[in a census].
2 This was the first census taken
while Quirinius was governor of Syria.
3 And everyone went to register for
the census, each to his own city.
4 So Joseph also went up from Gali-
lee, from the city of Nazareth, to Judea,
to the city of David which is called
Bethlehem, because he was of the
house and family of David,
5 in order to register with Mary, who
was betrothed to him, and was with
child. [Matt 1:18–25]
6 While they were there [in Bethle-
hem], the time came for her to give
birth,
7 and she gave birth to her Son, her
firstborn; and she wrapped Him in
[swaddling] cloths and laid Him in a
manger, because there was no [private]
room for them in the inn.
8 In the same region there were shep-
herds staying out in the fields, keeping
watch over their flock by night.
9 And an angel of the Lord suddenly
stood before them, and the glory of the
Lord flashed *and* shone around them,
and they were terribly frightened.
10 But the angel said to them, "Do not
be afraid; for behold, I bring you good
news of great joy which will be for all
the people.
11 "For this day in the city of David
there has been born for you a Savior,
who is Christ the Lord (the Messiah).
[Mic 5:2]
12 "And this will be a sign for you [by
which you will recognize Him]: you
will find a Baby wrapped in [swad-
dling] cloths and lying in a manger."
[1 Sam 2:34; 2 Kin 19:29; Is 7:14]
13 Then suddenly there appeared
with the angel a multitude of the heav-
enly host (angelic army) praising God
and saying,

14 "Glory to God in the highest
[heaven],
And on earth peace among men
with whom He is well-pleased."

15 When the angels had gone away
from them into heaven, the shepherds
began saying one to another, "Let us
go straight to Bethlehem, and see this
[wonderful] thing that has happened
which the Lord has made known to
us."
16 So they went in a hurry and found
their way to Mary and Joseph, and the
Baby as He lay in the manger.
17 And when they had seen this, they
made known what had been told them
about this Child,
18 and all who heard it were astound-
ed *and* wondered at what the shep-
herds told them.
19 But Mary treasured all these
things, giving careful thought to them
and pondering them in her heart.
20 The shepherds returned, glorifying

2:1 – 2 *Augustus.* This was the Roman emperor from 31 BC to AD 14. ***Quirinius.*** Quirinius was the governor or administrator of a major census organized to facilitate the collection of taxes.
2:3 – 4 *to register.* The registration, following Jewish custom took place at a person's ancestral home (2Sa 24). The journey from Nazareth to Bethlehem was about 90 miles, at least a three-day trip.
2:9 *glory.* This word refers to evidence of God's majestic presence, later associated with Jesus (Ac 7:55). In this scene, the glory is the appearance of light in the midst of darkness.
2:11 *Savior, who is Christ the Lord.* These three titles together summarize the saving work of Jesus and His sovereign position. What God was called in 1:47, Jesus is called here. The word Christ means "Anointed," referring to Jesus' royal, messianic position. The word Lord was the title of a ruler.
2:14 *peace among men.* Peace is not for everyone, but for those who please God.

CHAPTER 2 **2** Ac 5:37 **4** 1Sa 16:1; Jn 7:42; Mt 1:16 **5** Mt 1:18 **7** Mt 1:25 **9** Lk 1:12 **10** Ge 12:3; Mt 28:19; Mk 1:15; Col 1:23 **11** Isa 9:6; Mt 1:21; Mt 1:16; 16:16; Ac 2:36; Php 2:11 **13** Ge 28:12; Ps 103:20; 148:2; Da 7:10; Heb 1:14; Rev 5:11 **14** Lk 19:38; Eph 1:6; Isa 57:19; Ro 5:1; Eph 2:17; Col 1:20; Jn 3:16; Eph 2:4,7; 2Th 2:16; 1Jn 4:9 **19** Ge 37:11; Lk 1:66

and praising God for all that they had
heard and seen, just as it had been
told them.

Jesus Presented at the Temple

[21]At the end of eight days, when He
was to be circumcised, He was named
Jesus, the name given [to Him] by the
angel [Gabriel] before He was conceived in the womb.
[22]And when the time for their purification came [that is, the mother's
purification and the baby's dedication]
according to the Law of Moses, they
brought Him up to Jerusalem to present Him to the Lord [set apart as the
Firstborn] [Lev 12:1–4]
[23](as it is written in the Law of the
Lord, "EVERY *firstborn* MALE THAT OPENS
THE WOMB SHALL BE CALLED HOLY [set
apart and dedicated] TO THE LORD)"
[Ex 13:1, 2, 12; Num 8:17]
[24]and [they came also] to offer a sacrifice according to what is said in the
Law of the Lord [to be appropriate
for a family of modest means], "A PAIR
OF TURTLEDOVES OR TWO YOUNG PIGEONS."
[Lev 12:6–8]
[25]Now there was a man in Jerusalem
whose name was Simeon; and this
man was righteous and devout [carefully observing the divine Law], and
looking for the Consolation of Israel;
and the Holy Spirit was upon him.
[26]It had been revealed to him by the
Holy Spirit that he would not die before he had seen the Lord's Christ (the
Messiah, the Anointed).
[27]Prompted by the Spirit, he came
into the temple [enclosure]; and when
the parents brought in the child Jesus,
to do for Him the custom required by
the Law,
[28]Simeon took Him into his arms,
and blessed *and* praised *and* thanked
God, and said,

[29]"Now, Lord, You are releasing
Your bond-servant to leave [this
world] in peace,
According to Your word;
[30]For my eyes have seen Your
Salvation, [Is 52:10]
[31]Which You have prepared in the
presence of all peoples,
[32]A LIGHT FOR REVELATION TO THE
GENTILES [to disclose what was
previously unknown],
And [to bring] the praise *and*
honor *and* glory of Your people
Israel." [Is 42:6; 49:6]

[33]And His [legal] father and His
mother were amazed at what was said
about Him.
[34]Simeon blessed them and said to
Mary His mother, "Listen carefully:
this *Child* is appointed *and* destined
for the fall and rise of many in Israel,
and for a sign that is to be opposed—
[Is 8:14, 15]
[35]and a sword [of deep sorrow] will
pierce through your own soul—so that
the thoughts of many hearts may be
revealed."
[36]There was a prophetess, Anna, the
daughter of Phanuel, of the tribe of
Asher. She was very old, and had lived
with her husband for seven years after
her marriage, [Josh 19:24]
[37]and then as a widow to the age
of eighty-four. She did not leave the
[area of the] temple, but was serving

2:21 *At the end of eight days.* According to the law, a Jewish boy was to be circumcised on his eighth day (Ge 17:12; Lev 12:3).

2:25 *Consolation of Israel.* Simeon was waiting for the comforter of Israel, a hope that parallels the hope of national deliverance expressed in the two hymns of chapter one. This deliverance would involve the work of the Messiah, as verse 26 suggests.

2:32 *A LIGHT FOR REVELATION TO THE GENTILES.* This is the first explicit statement in Luke that includes both Jew and Gentile. Salvation is portrayed as light (1:79). It would be a revelation to Gentiles because they would be able to participate in God's blessing with a fullness that had not been revealed in the Old Testament (Eph 2:11 – 3:7).

2:36 *There was a prophetess, Anna.* Anna's work as a prophetess in the temple court suggests that she addressed all who would listen to her, as did Miriam (Ex 15:20), Deborah (Jdg 4:4), and Huldah (2Ki 22:14).

21 Ge 17:12; Lev 12:3; Lk 1:59; Mt 1:21,25; Lk 1:31 **22** Lev 12:2 **23** Ex 13:2; 22:29; Nu 3:13 **24** Lev 12:2 **25** ver. 38; Isa 40:1; Mk 15:43 **26** Ps 89:48; Heb 11:5 **27** Mt 4:1 **29** Ge 46:30; Php 1:23 **30** Isa 52:10 **32** Isa 9:2; 42:6; 49:6; 60:1-3; Mt 4:16; Ac 13:47; 28:28 **34** Isa 8:14; Hos 14:9; Mt 21:44; Ro 9:32; 1Co 1:23; 2Co 2:16; 1Pe 2:7,8; Ac 28:22 **35** Ps 42:10; Jn 19:25 **37** Ac 26:7; 1Ti 5:5

and worshiping night and day with
fastings and prayers.
[38]She, too, came up at that very mo-
ment and *began* praising *and* giving
thanks to God, and continued to speak
of Him to all who were looking for
the redemption *and* deliverance of
Jerusalem.

Return to Nazareth

[39]And when they had done every-
thing [in connection with Jesus' birth]
according to the Law of the Lord, they
went back to Galilee, to their own city,
Nazareth.
[40]And the Child continued to grow
and become strong [in spirit], filled
with wisdom; and the grace (favor,
spiritual blessing) of God was upon
Him. [Judg 13:24]

Visit to Jerusalem

[41]Now His parents went to Jerusa-
lem every year for the Passover Feast.
[Deut 16:1–8; Ex 23:15]
[42]And when He was twelve years old,
they went up *to Jerusalem*, according
to the custom of the Feast;
[43]and as they were returning [to
Nazareth], after spending the required
number of days [at the Feast], the boy
Jesus remained behind in Jerusalem.
Now His parents did not know this,
[44]but supposed Him to be in the car-
avan, and traveled a day's journey; and
[then] they *began* searching [anxious-
ly] for Him among their relatives and
acquaintances.
[45]When they did not find Him, they
went back to Jerusalem looking for
Him [everywhere].

2:41 ***to Jerusalem every year.*** The annual pilgrimage to Jerusalem was customary for many who lived outside the city. The laws commanded three pilgrimages for the men each year: Passover, Pentecost, and the Feast of Tabernacles (Ex 23:14–17; Dt 16:16).

38 ver. 25; Mk 15:43; Lk 24:21 **40** ver. 52; Lk 1:80 **41** Ex 23:15,17; 34:23; Dt 16:1,16

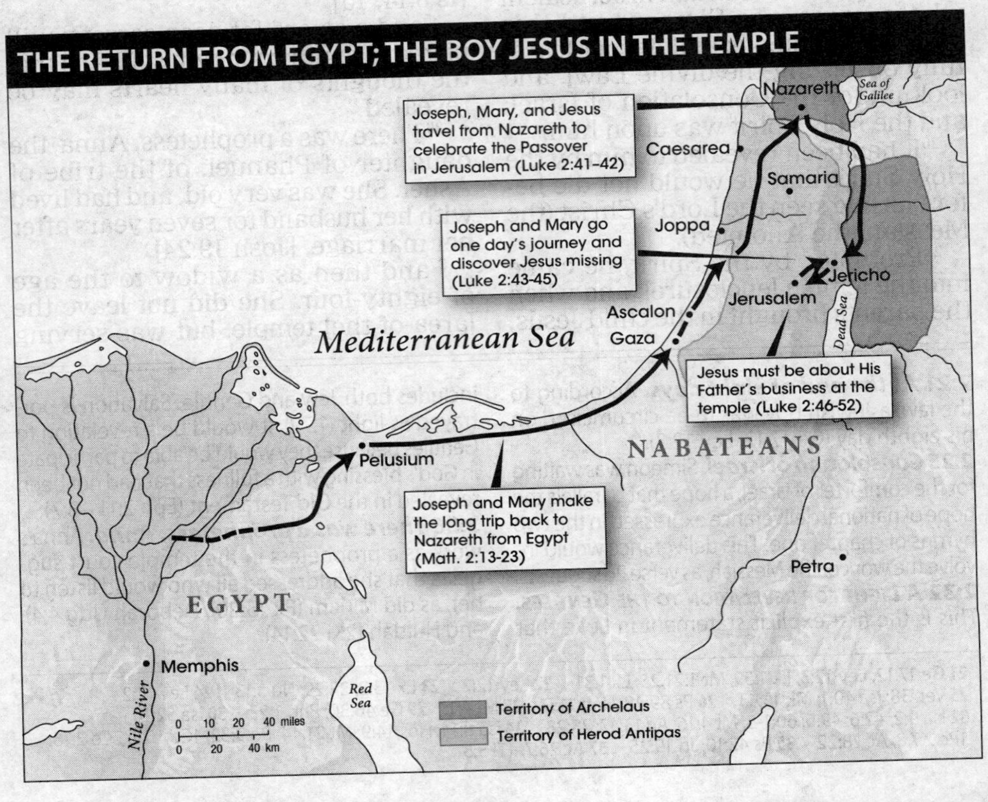

46 Three days later they found Him in
the [court of the] temple, sitting among
the teachers, both listening to them
and asking them questions.
47 All who heard Him were amazed
by His intelligence *and* His under-
standing and His answers.
48 When they saw Him, they were
overwhelmed; and His mother said
to Him, "Son, why have You treated
us like this? Listen, Your father and
I have been [greatly distressed and]
anxiously looking for You."
49 And He answered, "Why did you
have to look for Me? Did you not know
that I had to be in My Father's *house*?"
50 But they did not understand what
He had said to them.
51 He went down to Nazareth with
them, and was continually submissive
and obedient to them; and His mother
treasured all these things in her heart.
52 And Jesus kept increasing in wis-
dom and in stature, and in favor with
God and men. [1 Sam 2:26]

John the Baptist Preaches

3 NOW IN the fifteenth year of [Em-
peror] Tiberius Caesar's reign—
when Pontius Pilate was governor
of Judea, and Herod [Antipas] was
tetrarch of Galilee, and his brother
Philip was tetrarch of the region of
Ituraea and Trachonitis, and Lysanias
was tetrarch of Abilene—
2 in the high priesthood of Annas and
Caiaphas [his son-in-law], the word of
God came to John, the son of Zacha-
rias, in the wilderness.
3 And he went into all the coun-
try around the Jordan, preaching a
baptism of repentance for the forgive-
ness of sin;
4 as it is written *and* forever remains
written in the book of the words of
Isaiah the prophet,

"THE VOICE OF ONE SHOUTING IN THE
WILDERNESS,
'PREPARE THE WAY OF THE LORD,
MAKE HIS PATHS STRAIGHT.
5 'EVERY RAVINE SHALL BE FILLED UP,
AND EVERY MOUNTAIN AND HILL SHALL
BE LEVELED;
AND THE CROOKED [places] SHALL BE
MADE STRAIGHT,
AND THE ROUGH ROADS SMOOTH;
6 AND ALL MANKIND SHALL SEE THE
SALVATION OF GOD.' " [Is 40:3–5]

7 So he *began* saying to the crowds
who were coming out to be baptized by
him, "You brood of vipers, who warned
you to flee from the wrath [of God that
is] to come?
8 "Therefore produce fruit that is wor-
thy of [and consistent with your] repen-
tance [that is, live changed lives, turn
from sin and seek God and His righ-
teousness]. And do not *even* begin to say
to yourselves [as a defense], 'We have
Abraham for our father [and so our heri-
tage assures us of salvation]'; for I say to
you that from these stones God is able
to raise up children (descendants) for

2:49 *I had to be in My Father's house.* This is the first indication in Luke's Gospel that Jesus knew He had a unique mission and a unique relationship to the Father.

3:1 – 2 *Tiberius Caesar . . . Pontius Pilate . . . Herod . . . Annas . . . Caiaphas.* The various rulers that Luke lists show the complexity of the historical and political situation in Israel during Jesus' day. A first century Israelite had to deal with the edicts of the Roman emperor, the regulations of the governor over Israel, and the judgments of the religious leaders of Israel.

3:4 – 6 *PREPARE THE WAY OF THE LORD.* This citation from Isaiah 40:3 – 5 declares the coming of God's deliverance. Luke cites the text more fully than Matthew or Mark. He carries the passage through to its mention of salvation being seen by all flesh (v. 6), thus highlighting that the gospel is for all people. The preparation for the arrival of a king typically meant that a road was prepared for his journey. This is what Isaiah compares to the arrival of God's salvation.

3:8 *Therefore produce fruit.* John the Baptist warned that the fruits of repentance are necessary, not the claim of an ancestral connection to Abraham. External genealogical connections would not change one's attitude to God.

47 Mt 7:28; Mk 1:22; Lk 4:22,32; Jn 7:15,46 **49** Jn 2:16 **50** Lk 9:45; 18:34 **51** ver. 19; Da 7:28 **52** ver. 40; 1Sa 2:26 **CHAPTER 3** **2** Jn 11:49,51; 18:13; Ac 4:6 **3** Mt 3:1; Mk 1:4; Lk 1:77 **4** Isa 40:3; Mt 3:3; Mk 1:3; Jn 1:23 **6** Ps 98:2; Isa 52:10; Lk 2:10 **7** Mt 3:7

Abraham [for God can replace the un-
repentant, regardless of their heritage,
with those who are obedient]. [Matt 3:9]
9 “Even now the axe [of God’s judg-
ment] is swinging toward the root of
the trees; so every tree that does not
produce good fruit is being cut down
and thrown into the fire.”
10 The crowds asked him, “Then what
are we to do?”
11 And John replied, “The man who
has two tunics is to share with him
who has none; and he who has food is
to do the same.”
12 Even *some* tax collectors came to
be baptized, and they asked, “Teacher,
what are we to do?”
13 And he told them, “Collect no more
than the *fixed amount* you have been
ordered to [collect].”
14 *Some* soldiers asked him, “And
what about us, what are we to do?”
And he replied to them, “Do not ex-
tort money from anyone or harass *or*
blackmail *anyone*, and be satisfied
with your wages.”
15 Now the people were in a state of
expectation, and all were wondering in
their hearts about John, as to whether
he was the Christ (the Messiah, the
Anointed).
16 John answered them all by saying,
“As for me, I baptize you [only] with
water; but One who is mightier [more
powerful, more noble] than I is coming,
and I am not fit to untie the strap of
His sandals [even as His slave]. He will
baptize you [who truly repent] with
the Holy Spirit and [you who remain
unrepentant] with fire. [Matt 3:11]
17 “His winnowing fork is in His hand
to thoroughly clear His threshing floor,
and to gather the wheat (believers) into
His barn (kingdom); but He will burn
up the chaff (the unrepentant) with
unquenchable fire.”
18 So with many other appeals *and*
various admonitions John preached
the good news (gospel) to the people.
19 But when Herod [Antipas] the
tetrarch was *repeatedly* reprimanded
[and convicted by John’s disapproval]
for having Herodias, his brother’s wife
[as his own], and for all the wicked
things that Herod had done, [Matt 14:3;
Mark 6:17]
20 he also added this to them all: he
locked up John in prison.

Jesus’ Baptism

21 Now when all the people were bap-
tized, Jesus was also baptized, and
while He was praying, the [visible]
heaven was opened, [Matt 3:13–17;
Mark 1:9–11; John 1:32]
22 and the Holy Spirit descended on
Him in bodily form like a dove, and a
voice came from heaven, “You are My
Son, My Beloved, in You I am well-
pleased *and* delighted!” [Ps 2:7; Is 42:1]

3:11 *two tunics.* One was an undergarment, and the other was an outer garment. A person did not need two when another person had none.
3:12 *tax collectors.* These men were Jewish agents employed by those who had purchased the right to collect taxes for the Roman state. Tax collectors often added interest to cover their own expenses and to pad their income. They were disliked both for their business practices and for their support of the occupying state.
3:16–17 *the Holy Spirit and [you who remain unrepentant] with fire.* These two facets of Christ’s work relate to His first and second comings. As a result of Christ’s work at His first coming, believers are placed into one family (1Co 12:13) and commended to the care of the Holy Spirit. When Christ comes a second time, He will come with the fire of judgment. ***winnowing fork.*** This tool was a wooden forklike shovel that lifted the grain in the air so that the wind could separate it from the chaff.
3:19–20 *all the wicked things that Herod had done.* Herod had divorced his wife to marry his own niece Herodias, who already had been the wife of his brother Philip. Not only was the divorce a problem, so was marrying such a close relative (Lev 18:16; 20:21).
3:22 *You are My Son, My Beloved, in You I am well-pleased and delighted.* This statement combines two ideas. The idea of God’s Son comes from Psalm 2:7, a psalm about God’s chosen King. The idea of pleasure comes from the image of the Servant in Isaiah 42:1. The fact that Jesus is both King and Servant is fundamental to Jesus’ identity.

9 Mt 7:19 **10** Ac 2:37 **11** Lk 11:41; 2Co 8:14; Jas 2:15,16; 1Jn 3:17; 4:20 **12** Mt 21:32; Lk 7:29 **13** Lk 19:8
14 Ex 23:1; Lev 19:11 **16** Mt 3:11 **17** Mic 4:12; Mt 13:30 **19** Mt 14:3; Mk 6:17 **21** Mt 3:13; Jn 1:32

CAPERNAUM SYNAGOGUE

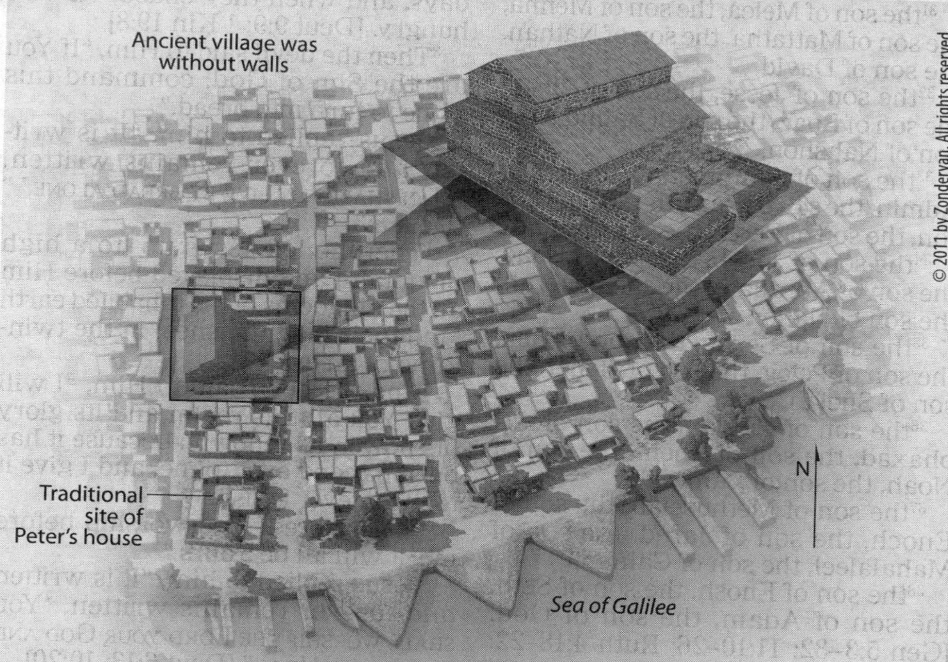

Capernaum was more than a seaside fishing village in the days of Jesus. It was the place that Jesus chose to be the center of his ministry to the entire region of Galilee, and it possessed ideal characteristics as a point of dissemination for the gospel.

There were good reasons for this. The town itself was named Kephar Nahum, "village of [perhaps the prophet] Nahum," and was the centerpiece of a densely populated region having a bicultural flavor. On the one hand, there were numerous synagogues in Galilee (in addition to the one in Capernaum), where the ferment of Jewish religious life was profound. On the other hand, there was Hellenism, a pervasive culture already centuries old and potent in its paganism—a lifestyle that influenced manners, dress, architecture and political institutions as well.

Archaeological work at Capernaum has revealed a section of the pavement of a first-century synagogue below the still-existing ruins of the fourth-century one on the site. A private house later made into a church and a place of pilgrimage has yielded some evidence that may link it to the site of Simon Peter's house (Lk 4:38).

Genealogy of Jesus

23 When He began His ministry,
Jesus Himself was about thirty years
of age, being, as was supposed, the son
of Joseph, the son [by marriage] of Eli,
24 the son of Matthat, the son of Levi,
the son of Melchi, the son of Jannai,
the son of Joseph,
25 the son of Mattathias, the son of
Amos, the son of Nahum, the son of
Hesli, the son of Naggai,
26 the son of Maath, the son of Mattathias, the son of Semein, the son of
Josech, the son of Joda,
27 the son of Joanan, the son of Rhesa, the son of Zerubbabel, the son of
Shealtiel, the son of Neri,
28 the son of Melchi, the son of Addi,
the son of Cosam, the son of Elmadam,
the son of Er,
29 the son of Joshua, the son of
Eliezer, the son of Jorim, the son of
Matthat, the son of Levi,
30 the son of Simeon, the son of

23 See Nu 4:3,35,39,43,47; Mt 13:55; Jn 6:42

Judah, the son of Joseph, the son of
Jonam, the son of Eliakim,
31 the son of Melea, the son of Menna,
the son of Mattatha, the son of Nathan,
the son of David,
32 the son of Jesse, the son of Obed,
the son of Boaz, the son of Salmon, the
son of Nahshon,
33 the son of Amminadab, the son of
Admin, the son of Ram, the son of Hez-
ron, the son of Perez, the son of Judah,
34 the son of Jacob, the son of Isaac,
the son of Abraham, the son of Terah,
the son of Nahor,
35 the son of Serug, the son of Reu,
the son of Peleg, the son of Heber, the
son of Shelah,
36 the son of Cainan, the son of Ar-
phaxad, the son of Shem, the son of
Noah, the son of Lamech,
37 the son of Methuselah, the son of
Enoch, the son of Jared, the son of
Mahalaleel, the son of Cainan,
38 the son of Enosh, the son of Seth,
the son of Adam, the son of God.
[Gen 5:3–32; 11:10–26; Ruth 4:18–22;
1 Chr 1:1–4, 24–28; 2:1–15]

The Devil Tempts Jesus

4 NOW JESUS, full of [and in per-
fect communication with] the Holy
Spirit, returned from the Jordan and
was led by the Spirit in the wilderness
[Matt 4:1–11]
2 for forty days, being tempted by the
devil. And He ate nothing during those
days, and when they ended, He was
hungry. [Deut 9:9; 1 Kin 19:8]
3 Then the devil said to Him, "If You
are the Son of God, command this
stone to turn into bread."
4 Jesus replied to him, "It is writ-
ten *and* forever remains written,
'MAN SHALL NOT LIVE BY BREAD ALONE.' "
[Deut 8:3]
5 Then he led Jesus up [to a high
mountain] and displayed before Him
all the kingdoms of the inhabited earth
[and their magnificence] in the twin-
kling of an eye.
6 And the devil said to Him, "I will
give You all this realm and its glory
[its power, its renown]; because it has
been handed over to me, and I give it
to whomever I wish.
7 "Therefore if You worship before
me, it will all be Yours."
8 Jesus replied to him, "It is written
and forever remains written, 'YOU
SHALL WORSHIP THE LORD YOUR GOD AND
SERVE ONLY HIM.' " [Deut 6:13; 10:20]
9 Then he led Jesus to Jerusalem and
had Him stand on the pinnacle (highest
point) of the temple, and said [mock-
ingly] to Him, "If You are the Son of
God, throw Yourself down from here;
10 for it is written *and* forever remains
written,

4:1–13 Temptation of Christ—Hebrews 2:18 makes the point that, because Christ was tempted, He is able to help those who are being tempted. We can see two examples of this quite plainly. The temptations are about security and power. In becoming man, Jesus gave up both (Php 2:5–11). Jesus didn't cling to any of what was by nature and identity rightfully His. In doing so, He had to trust fully in the Father for His life and very being. He can truly identify with our temptations. His experience wasn't just like ours are. No one ever gave up more power. No one of greater stature has ever been in such an insecure position. He can be there for us because He has been there before us.
4:3 *If You are the Son of God.* This is a conditional statement. In other words, Satan was saying: "Let's assume for the sake of argument that You are the Son of God." In fact, Satan was challenging Jesus' identity and authority.
4:4 *It is written.* Jesus responded to Satan's temptation by quoting Deuteronomy 8:3. Jesus refused to operate independently of God. The Spirit had led Him into the wilderness to prepare Him for His ministry, so eating at Satan's instruction would have shown a lack of dependence on the Father.
4:5 *all the kingdoms of the inhabited earth.* This temptation was an attempt to offer Jesus power by the wrong means. Satan's method involved a detour around the cross, an inducement to "take the easy way" to power.
4:10–11 *HE WILL COMMAND HIS ANGELS CONCERNING YOU TO GUARD and PROTECT YOU.* Satan cited Psalm 91:11–12, reminding Jesus of God's promise of protection. However, the mere use of

31 Zec 12:12; 2Sa 5:14; 1Ch 3:5 **32** Ru 4:18; 1Ch 2:10 **34** Ge 11:24,26 **36** See Ge 11:12; 5:6; 11:10 **38** Ge 5:12
CHAPTER 4 **1** Mt 4:1; Mk 1:12; ver. 14; Lk 2:27 **2** Ex 34:28; 1Ki 19:8 **4** Dt 8:3 **6** Jn 12:31; 14:30; Rev 13:2,7
8 Dt 6:13; 10:20 **9** Mt 4:5 **10** Ps 91:11

'HE WILL COMMAND HIS ANGELS
CONCERNING YOU TO GUARD *and*
PROTECT YOU,'
11 and,
'THEY WILL LIFT YOU UP ON *their*
HANDS,
SO THAT YOU DO NOT STRIKE YOUR FOOT
AGAINST A STONE.' " [Ps 91:11, 12]

12 Jesus replied to him, "It is said [in
Scripture], 'YOU SHALL NOT TEMPT THE
LORD YOUR GOD [to prove Himself to
you].' " [Deut 6:16; Matt 4:7]
13 When the devil had finished every
temptation, he [temporarily] left Him
until a more opportune time.

Jesus' Public Ministry

14 Then Jesus went back to Galilee in
the power of the Spirit, and the news
about Him spread through the entire
region.
15 And He *began* teaching in their
synagogues and was praised *and* glo-
rified *and* honored by all.
16 So He came to Nazareth, where
He had been brought up; and as was
His custom, He entered the synagogue
on the Sabbath, and stood up to read.
17 The scroll of the prophet Isaiah
was handed to Him. He unrolled the
scroll and found the place where it was
written, [Is 61:1, 2]

18 "THE SPIRIT OF THE LORD IS UPON ME
(the Messiah),
BECAUSE HE HAS ANOINTED ME TO
PREACH THE GOOD NEWS TO THE POOR.
HE HAS SENT ME TO ANNOUNCE
RELEASE (pardon, forgiveness) TO
THE CAPTIVES,
AND RECOVERY OF SIGHT TO THE BLIND,
TO SET FREE THOSE WHO ARE OPPRESSED
(downtrodden, bruised, crushed
by tragedy),
19 TO PROCLAIM THE FAVORABLE YEAR
OF THE LORD [the day when
salvation and the favor of God
abound greatly]." [Is 61:1, 2]

20 Then He rolled up the scroll [having
stopped in the middle of the verse],
gave it back to the attendant and sat
down [to teach]; and the eyes of all
those in the synagogue were [atten-
tively] fixed on Him.
21 He began speaking to them: "To-
day this Scripture has been fulfilled
in your hearing *and* in your presence."
22 And [as He continued on] they all
were speaking well of Him, and were
in awe *and* were wondering about the
words of grace which were coming
from His lips; and they were saying,
"Is this not Joseph's son?"
23 So He said to them, "You will no
doubt quote this proverb to Me, 'Phy-
sician, heal Yourself! Whatever [mir-
acles] that we heard were done [by
You] in Capernaum, do here in Your
hometown as well.' "
24 Then He said, "I assure you *and*

---

biblical words does not always reveal God's will, particularly if they are placed in the wrong context.
4:12 ***YOU SHALL NOT TEMPT THE LORD YOUR GOD.*** In response to Satan's third temptation, Jesus cited Deuteronomy 6:16. God is to be trusted, not tested. The Deuteronomy passage refers to Israel's attempt to test God at Meribah (Ex 17:1 – 7). Jesus would not repeat the nation's error of unfaithfulness to God.
4:16 – 17 ***stood up to read.*** Most synagogue services had a reading from the Law and one from the Prophets, with an exposition that tied the texts together. Jesus expounded Isaiah 61.
4:18 – 19 ***HE HAS SENT ME.*** By citing Isaiah 61, Jesus was claiming to be a royal figure and to have a prophetic mission (v. 24). ***RELEASE (pardon, forgiveness) TO THE CAPTIVES.*** In the Old Testament, captivity refers to Israel's exile (1:68 – 74); here captivity refers to sin (1:77; 7:47; 24:47; Ac 2:38; 5:31; 10:43; 13:38; 26:18). ***THOSE WHO ARE OPPRESSED.*** This was originally the call of Israel, but the nation had failed in its assignment (Isa 58:6). ***THE FAVORABLE YEAR OF THE LORD.*** This phrase is an allusion to the year of Jubilee when every fiftieth year all debt was forgiven and slaves were given their freedom (Lev 25:10).
4:20 ***He rolled up the scroll.*** Jesus closed the book in the middle of the sentence. He did not continue because the next phrase — "the day of vengeance of our God" — was not being fulfilled then.

---

12 Dt 6:16 **13** Jn 14:30; Heb 4:15 **14** Mt 4:12; Jn 4:43; ver. 1; Ac 10:37 **16** Mt 2:23; 13:54; Mk 6:1; Ac 13:14; 17:2 **18** Isa 61:1 **22** Ps 45:2; Mt 13:54; Mk 6:2; Lk 2:47; Jn 6:42 **23** Mt 4:13; 11:23; Mt 13:54; Mk 6:1 **24** Mt 13:57; Mk 6:4; Jn 4:44

most solemnly say to you, no prophet
is welcome in his hometown.
25 “But in truth I say to you, there
were many widows in Israel in the
days of Elijah, when the sky was
closed up for three years and six
months, when a great famine came
over all the land;
26 and yet Elijah was not sent [by the
Lord] to a single one of them, but only
to Zarephath *in the land* of Sidon, to a
woman who was a widow. [1 Kin 17:1,
8–16; 18:1]
27 “And there were many lepers in
Israel in the time of Elisha the proph-
et; and not one of them was cleansed
[by being healed] except Naaman the
Syrian.” [2 Kin 5:1–14]
28 As they heard these things [about
God’s grace to these two Gentiles], *the
people* in the synagogue were filled
with a great rage;
29 and they got up and drove Him out
of the city, and led Him to the crest of
the hill on which their city had been
built, in order to hurl Him down the
cliff.
30 But passing [miraculously] through
the crowd, He went on His way.
31 Then He came down [from the hills
of Nazareth] to Capernaum, a city of
Galilee [on the shore of the sea], and
He was teaching them on the Sabbath;
[Mark 1:21–28]
32 and they were surprised [almost
overwhelmed] at His teaching, because
His message was [given] with authori-
ty *and* power *and* great ability.
33 There was a man in the synagogue
who was possessed by the spirit of an
unclean demon; and he cried out with
a loud *and* terrible voice,
34 “Let us alone! What business do
we have [in common] with each other,
Jesus of Nazareth? Have You come to
destroy us? I know who You are—the
Holy One of God!”
35 But Jesus rebuked him, saying, “Be
silent (muzzled, gagged) and come out
of him!” And when the demon had
thrown the man down among them,
he came out of him without injuring
him in any way.
36 They were all astonished *and* in
awe, and *began* saying to one anoth-
er, “What is this message? For with
authority and power He commands
the unclean spirits and they come out!”
37 And the news about Him spread
into every place in the surrounding
district (Galilee).

Many Are Healed

38 Then Jesus got up and left the syn-
agogue and went to Simon’s (Peter’s)
house. Now Simon’s mother-in-law
was suffering from a high fever, and
they asked Him to help her. [Matt 8:14–
17; Mark 1:29–34]
39 Standing over her, He rebuked the
fever, and it left her; and immediately
she got up and *began* serving them [as
her guests].
40 While the sun was setting [mark-
ing the end of the Sabbath day], all
those who had any *who were* sick
with various diseases brought them
to Jesus; and laying His hands on each
one of them, He was healing them [ex-
hibiting His authority as Messiah].
[Matt 8:16, 17; Mark 1:32–34]
41 Demons also were coming out of
many people, shouting, “You are the
Son of God!” But He rebuked them
and would not allow them to speak,
because they knew that He was the
Christ (the Messiah, the Anointed).
42 When daybreak came, Jesus left
[Simon Peter’s house] and went to a
secluded place; and the crowds were

4:34 *What business do we have [in common] with each other.* The demon knew that Jesus possessed divine authority, and he wanted nothing to do with Him.
4:35–36 *rebuked.* This term in Aramaic was a technical term for calling evil into submission. Jesus’ authority over evil forces is clear.
4:41 *You are the Son of God.* This confession, unique to the Gospel of Luke, shows the close connection Luke makes between Jesus’ sonship and messiahship.

25 1Ki 17:9; 18:1; Jas 5:17 **27** 2Ki 5:14 **30** Jn 8:59; 10:39 **31** Mt 4:13; Mk 1:21 **32** Mt 7:28,29 **33** Mk 1:23 **34** ver. 41; Ps 16:10; Da 9:24; Lk 1:35 **38** Mt 8:14; Mk 1:29 **40** Mt 8:16; Mk 1:32 **41** Mk 1:34; 3:11; ver. 34,35; Mk 1:25,34 **42** Mk 1:35

searching for Him, and [they] came
to Him and tried to keep Him from
leaving them.
[43]But He said, "I must preach [the
good news of] the kingdom of God to
the other cities also, because I was sent
for this purpose."
[44]So He continued preaching in the
synagogues of Judea [the country of
the Jews, including Galilee].

The First Disciples

5 NOW IT happened that while
Jesus was standing by the Lake of
Gennesaret (Sea of Galilee), with the
people crowding all around Him and
listening to the word of God;
[2]that He saw two boats lying at the
edge of the lake, but the fishermen had
gotten out of them and were washing
their nets.
[3]He got into one of the boats, which
was Simon's, and asked him to put out
a little distance from the shore. And
He sat down and *began* teaching the
crowds from the boat.
[4]When He had finished speaking,
He said to Simon [Peter], "Put out into
the deep water and lower your nets for
a catch [of fish]."
[5]Simon replied, "Master, we worked
hard all night [to the point of exhaus-
tion] and caught nothing [in our nets],
but at Your word I will [do as you say
and] lower the nets [again]."
[6]When they had done this, they
caught a great number of fish, and their
nets were [at the point of] breaking;
[7]so they signaled to their partners in
the other boat to come and help them.
And they came and filled both of the
boats [with fish], so that they began
to sink.
[8]But when Simon Peter saw this, he
fell down at Jesus' knees, saying, "Go
away from me, for I am a sinful man,
O Lord!"
[9]For he and all his companions were
completely astounded at the catch of
fish which they had taken;
[10]and so were James and John, sons
of Zebedee, who were partners with
Simon [Peter]. Jesus said to Simon,
"Have no fear; from now on you will
be catching men!"
[11]After they had brought their boats
to land, they left everything and fol-
lowed Him [becoming His disciples,
believing and trusting in Him and fol-
lowing His example].

The Leper and the Paralytic

[12]While Jesus was in one of the cit-
ies, there came a man covered with [an
advanced case of] leprosy; and when
he saw Jesus, he fell on his face and
begged Him, saying, "Lord, if You are
willing, You can make me clean *and*
well." [Matt 8:2–4; Mark 1:40–44]
[13]And Jesus reached out His hand
and touched him, saying, "I am willing;
be cleansed." And immediately the
leprosy left him.
[14]Jesus ordered him to tell no one
[that he might happen to meet], "But
go and show yourself to the priest,

4:43 *kingdom of God.* In Luke, the kingdom is referred to thirty times and six times in Acts. Jesus announced the rule of God through His person, in dealing with sin (24:47), in distributing the Spirit as He mediates blessing from God's side (24:49), and in reigning with His followers according to the Old Testament promise (Ps 2:7–12; Ac 3:18–22).

5:1 *Gennesaret.* This is another name for the Sea of Galilee and the Sea of Tiberias.

5:5 *at Your word I will [do as you say and] lower the nets.* This is Peter's statement of faith. The fisherman noted that he and his companions had just failed to make a catch at the best time for fishing, the evening. The circumstances were not good for a catch at the time of Jesus' command, but Peter chose to obey His word and let down his nets anyway.

5:12 *leprosy.* This term was used broadly in the ancient world. It included psoriasis, lupus, and ringworm. Lepers were isolated from the rest of society (Lev 13:45–46), but could be restored to the community when they recovered (Lev 14).

5:14 *show yourself to the priest.* Jesus commanded that the regulation of Leviticus 14 be followed in silencing the healed leper. Jesus sought to avoid drawing excessive attention to His healing ministry.

44 Mk 1:39 **CHAPTER 5** **1** Mt 4:18; Mk 1:16 **4** Jn 21:6 **8** 2Sa 6:9; 1Ki 17:8 **10** Mt 4:19; Mk 1:17 **11** Mt 4:20; 19:27; Mk 1:18; Lk 18:28 **12** Mt 8:2; Mk 1:40 **14** Mt 8:4; Lev 14:4,10,21,22

and make an offering for your purification, just as Moses commanded, as a testimony (witness) to them [that this is a work of Messiah]." [Lev 13:49; 14:2–32]

15 But the news about Him was spreading farther, and large crowds kept gathering to hear Him and to be healed of their illnesses.

16 But Jesus Himself would often slip away to the wilderness and pray [in seclusion].

17 One day as He was teaching, there were Pharisees and teachers of the Law sitting there who had come from every village of Galilee and Judea and from Jerusalem. And the power of the Lord was *present* with Him to heal.

18 *Some* men came carrying on a stretcher a man who was paralyzed, and they tried to bring him in and lay him down in front of Jesus. [Matt 9:2–8; Mark 2:3–12]

19 But finding no way to bring him in because of the crowd, they went up on the roof [and removed some tiles to make an opening] and lowered him through the tiles with his stretcher, into the middle *of the crowd,* in front of Jesus.

20 When Jesus saw their [active] faith [springing from confidence in Him], He said, "Man, your sins are forgiven."

21 The scribes and the Pharisees began to consider *and* question [the implications of what He had said], saying, "Who is this man who speaks blasphemies [by claiming the rights and prerogatives of God]? Who can forgive sins [that is, remove guilt, nullify sin's penalty, and assign righteousness] except God alone?"

22 But Jesus, knowing their [hostile] thoughts, answered them, "Why are you questioning [these things] in your hearts?

23 "Which is easier, to say, 'Your sins are forgiven you,' or to say, 'Get up and walk'?

24 "But, in order that you may know that the Son of Man (the Messiah) has authority *and* power on earth to forgive sins"—He said to the paralyzed man, "I say to you, get up, pick up your stretcher and go home."

25 He immediately stood up before them, picked up his stretcher, and went home glorifying *and* praising God.

26 They were all astonished, and they *began* glorifying God; and they were filled with [reverential] fear and kept saying, "We have seen wonderful *and* incredible things today!"

Call of Levi (Matthew)

27 After this Jesus went out and noticed a tax collector named Levi (Matthew) sitting at the tax booth; and He said to him, "Follow Me [as My disciple, accepting Me as your Master and Teacher and walking the same path of life that I walk]." [Matt 9:9–17; Mark 2:14–22]

28 And he left everything behind and got up and *began* to follow Jesus [as His disciple].

29 Levi (Matthew) gave a great banquet for Him at his house; and there was a large crowd of tax collectors

---

5:21 ***blasphemies.*** The charge of the scribes and the Pharisees was that Jesus' claim dishonored God. This was a serious charge; the conviction of blasphemy would eventually lead to Jesus' death (22:70–71).

5:23 ***Which is easier.*** Jesus posed a riddle to His audience. From an external point of view, it would seem easier to declare sins forgiven than to actually heal a person. In reality, however, one has to possess more authority to forgive sin. Jesus linked the healing to what it represented, the forgiveness of sin. Jesus forgave the man's sins and healed him at the same time.

5:24 ***Son of Man.*** This is an Aramaic idiom that refers to a human being, meaning "someone" or "I." Jesus used this idiom as a title, taken from Daniel 7:13. In the Book of Daniel, the phrase "Son of man" describes a figure who shares authority with the Ancient of Days.

5:29 ***with them.*** In ancient Israel the table was a place where spiritual points were taught and where fellowship occurred.

15 Mt 4:25; Mk 3:7; Jn 6:2 **16** Mt 14:23; Mk 6:46 **18** Mt 9:2; Mk 2:3 **21** Mt 9:3; Mk 2:6,7; Ps 32:5; Isa 43:25
27 Mt 9:9; Mk 2:13,14 **29** Mt 9:10; Mk 2:15; Lk 15:1

and others who were reclining *at the table* with them.

30 The Pharisees and their scribes [seeing those with whom He was associating] *began* murmuring in discontent to His disciples, asking, "Why are you eating and drinking with the tax collectors and sinners [including non-observant Jews]?"

31 And Jesus replied to them, "It is not those who are healthy who need a physician, but [only] those who are sick.

32 "I did not come to call the [self-proclaimed] righteous [who see no need to repent], but sinners to repentance [to change their old way of thinking, to turn from sin and to seek God and His righteousness]."

33 Then they said to Him, "The disciples of John [the Baptist] often practice fasting and offer prayers [of special petition], and so do the *disciples* of the Pharisees; but Yours eat and drink."

34 Jesus said to them, "Can you make the wedding guests of the bridegroom fast while he is with them?

35 "But days [for mourning] will come when the bridegroom is [forcefully] taken away from them. They will fast in those days."

36 He also told them a parable: "No one tears a piece of cloth from a new garment and puts it on an old one; otherwise he will both tear the new, and the piece from the new will not match the old.

37 "And no one puts new wine into old wineskins; otherwise the new [fermenting] wine will [expand and] burst the skins and it will be spilled out, and the skins will be ruined.

38 "But new wine must be put into fresh wineskins.

39 "And no one, after drinking old *wine*, wishes for new; for he says, 'The old is fine.' "

Jesus Is Lord of the Sabbath

6 ONE SABBATH while Jesus was passing through fields of standing grain, it happened that His disciples were picking the heads of grain, rubbing them in their hands, and eating them. [Deut 23:25; Matt 12:1–8; Mark 2:23–28]

2 But some of the Pharisees said, "Why are you doing what is unlawful on the Sabbath?" [Ex 20:10; 23:12; Deut 5:14]

3 Jesus replied to them, "Have you not even read [in the Scriptures] what David did when he was hungry, he and those who were with him— [1 Sam 21:1–6]

4 how he went into the house of God, and took and ate the consecrated bread, which is not lawful [for anyone] to eat except the priests alone, and [how he also] gave it to the men who were with him?" [Lev 24:9]

5:33 *fasting.* The Pharisees fasted twice a week, on Mondays and Thursdays (18:12), as well as on the Day of Atonement (Lev 16:29). They also fasted as an act of penitence (Isa 58:1 – 9) and to recall four times a year the destruction of Jerusalem (Zec 7:3,5; 8:19). The goal of fasting was to dedicate oneself to prayer and to focus on God. John led an ascetic life, which his followers also imitated (7:24 – 28; Mt 11:1 – 19).

5:35 *days [for mourning] will come.* The image of the removal of the bridegroom is the first hint in Jesus' ministry of His fast approaching death.

5:37 *puts new wine into old wineskins.* This would not work because as the new wine fermented, it would stretch the old skin and break it, ruining the wineskin and wasting the wine.

6:1 *picking . . . rubbing . . . eating.* According to Jewish tradition, the disciples were reaping, threshing, and preparing food, and so were violating the commandment not to work on the Sabbath. It is clear that at this point the Pharisees were watching Jesus carefully (v. 7).

6:3 – 4 *consecrated bread.* This was bread that was taken from the twelve loaves placed on a table in the holy place and changed once a week (Ex 25:30; 39:36; Lev 24:5 – 9). Jesus pointed out that if David and his men could violate the law to satisfy their hunger, His disciples could do the same.

---

32 Mt 9:13; 1Ti 1:15 **33** Mt 9:14; Mk 2:18 **36** Mt 9:16,17; Mk 2:21,22 **CHAPTER 6** **1** Mt 12:1; Mk 2:23 **2** Ex 20:10
3 1Sa 21:6 **4** Lev 24:9

5 Jesus was saying to them, "The Son of Man (the Messiah) is Lord [even] of the Sabbath."

6 On another Sabbath He went into the synagogue and taught, and a man was present whose right hand was withered. [Matt 12:9–14; Mark 3:1–6]

7 The scribes and the Pharisees were watching Him closely [with malicious intent], to see if He would [actually] heal [someone] on the Sabbath, so that they might find *a reason* to accuse Him.

8 But He was aware of their thoughts, and He said to the man with the withered hand, "Get up and come forward." So he got up and stood *there*.

9 Then Jesus said to them, "I ask you directly: Is it lawful to do good on the Sabbath or to do evil, to save a life or to destroy it?"

10 After looking around at them all, He said to the man, "Stretch out your hand!" And he did, and his hand was [fully] restored.

11 But the scribes and Pharisees were filled with senseless rage [and lacked spiritual insight], and discussed with one another what they might do to Jesus.

Choosing the Twelve

12 Now at this time Jesus went off to the mountain to pray, and He spent the whole night in prayer to God.

13 When day came, He called His disciples and selected twelve of them, whom He also named apostles (special messengers, personally chosen representatives): [Matt 10:2–4; Mark 3:16–19]

14 Simon, whom He also named Peter, and his brother Andrew; and [the brothers] James and John; and Philip, and Bartholomew [also called Nathanael];

15 and Matthew (Levi, the tax collector) and Thomas; and James *the son* of Alphaeus, and Simon who was called the Zealot;

16 Judas [also called Thaddaeus] *the son* of James, and Judas Iscariot, who became a traitor [to the Lord].

17 Then Jesus came down with them and stood on a level place; and *there was* a large crowd of His disciples, and a vast multitude of people from all over Judea and Jerusalem and the coastal region of Tyre and Sidon,

18 who had come to listen to Him and to be healed of their diseases. Even those who were troubled by unclean spirits (demons) were being healed.

19 All the people were trying to touch Him, because [healing] power was coming from Him and healing them all.

The Beatitudes

20 And looking toward His disciples, He began speaking: "Blessed [spiritually prosperous, happy, to be admired] are you *who are* poor [in spirit, those devoid of spiritual arrogance, those who regard themselves as insignificant], for the kingdom of God is yours [both now and forever]. [Matt 5:3–12]

21 "Blessed [joyful, nourished by God's goodness] are you who hunger now [for righteousness, actively seeking right standing with God], for you will be [completely] satisfied. Blessed [forgiven, refreshed by God's grace]

6:5 *Lord [even] of the Sabbath.* Regardless of the laws and customs that the Pharisees cited, Jesus has authority over the Sabbath. Jesus' claim of divine authority here is similar to His claim of authority to forgive sins in 5:21,24.

6:11 *senseless rage.* The term here means irrational or mindless anger. The parallels in Matthew 12:14 and Mark 3:6 make it clear that the Pharisees started to plot against Jesus in earnest after this confrontation.

6:17 *level place.* This probably refers to a plateau on a mountain. The setting and the contents of the sermon that follows suggest that Luke is providing a shorter version of the Sermon on the Mount, omitting those portions that have to do with the law.

6:20 *Blessed . . . are you.* Blessed means "happy," referring to the special joy and favor that comes upon those who experience God's grace.

6 Mt 12:9; Mk 3:1; See Lk 13:14; 14:3; Jn 9:16 **13** Mt 10:1 **14** Jn 1:42 **16** Jude 1 **17** Mt 4:25; Mk 3:7
19 Mt 14:36; Mk 5:30; Lk 8:46 **20** Mt 5:3; 11:5; Jas 2:5 **21** Isa 55:1; 65:13; Mt 5:6; Isa 61:3; Mt 5:4

are you who weep now [over your sins and repent], for you will laugh [when the burden of sin is lifted].

22 “Blessed [morally courageous and spiritually alive with life-joy in God’s goodness] are you when people hate you, and exclude you [from their fellowship], and insult you, and scorn your name as evil because of [your association with] the Son of Man.

23 “Rejoice on that day and leap for joy, for your reward in heaven is great [absolutely inexhaustible]; for their fathers used to treat the prophets in the same way.

24 “But woe (judgment is coming) to you who are rich [and place your faith in possessions while remaining spiritually impoverished], for you are [already] receiving your comfort in full [and there is nothing left to be awarded to you].

25 “Woe to you who are well-fed (gorged, satiated) now, for you will be hungry. Woe *to you* who laugh now [enjoying a life of self-indulgence], for you will mourn and weep [and deeply long for God].

26 “Woe *to you* when all the people speak well of you *and* praise you, for their fathers used to treat the false prophets in the same way.

27 “But I say to you who hear [Me and pay attention to My words]: Love [that is, unselfishly seek the best or higher good for] your enemies, [make it a practice to] do good to those who hate you,

28 bless *and* show kindness to those who curse you, pray for those who mistreat you.

29 “Whoever strikes you on the cheek, offer him the other one also [simply ignore insignificant insults or losses and do not bother to retaliate—maintain your dignity]. Whoever takes away your coat, do not withhold your shirt from him either. [Matt 5:39–42]

30 “Give to everyone who asks of you. Whoever takes away what is yours, do not demand it back.

31 “Treat others the same way you want them to treat you.

32 “If you [only] love those who love you, what credit is that to you? For even sinners love those who love them.

33 “If you do good to those who do good to you, what credit is that to you? For even sinners do the same.

34 “If you lend [money] to those from whom you expect to receive [it back], what credit is that to you? Even sinners lend to sinners expecting to receive back the same *amount*.

35 “But love [that is, unselfishly seek the best or higher good for] your enemies, and do good, and lend, expecting nothing in return; for your reward will be great (rich, abundant), and you will be sons of the Most High; because He Himself is kind *and* gracious

---

6:22 *because of [your association with] the Son of Man.* Identification with Jesus usually leads to rejection and hardship, but the disciple who has left all to follow Jesus understands what placing Jesus first means. He or she also recognizes that God is aware of all suffering.

6:24 *woe.* A woe is a cry of pain that results from misfortune. Just as God presented blessings for obedience and curses for disobedience in *Deuteronomy* 28, Jesus presented blessings and woes to His disciples who were anticipating the kingdom. The same blessings and woes apply to believers today when their works are evaluated (1Co 3:12–15; 2Co 5:10; 1Jn 2:28; Rev 22:12).

6:27–28 *Love . . . your enemies.* The threat of religious persecution was very real when Jesus presented His command for extraordinary love. The reference to a cursing enemy suggests a context of religious persecution.

6:30 *do not demand it back.* The commands of verses 29 and 30 are expressed in such absolute terms that they force the listener to reflect on them by contrasting them with the normal responses people would have to such injustices.

6:35 *He Himself is kind and gracious and good to the ungrateful and the wicked.* The practice of loving one’s enemies is modeled by God Himself.

22 Mt 5:11; 1Pe 2:19; 3:14; 4:14; Jn 16:2 **23** Mt 5:12; Ac 5:41; Col 1:24; Jas 1:2; Ac 7:51 **24** Am 6:1; Jas 5:1; Lk 12:21; Mt 6:2,5,16; Lk 16:25 **25** Isa 65:13; Pr 14:13 **26** Jn 15:19; 1Jn 4:5 **27** ver. 35; Ex 23:4; Pr 25:21; Mt 5:44; Ro 12:20 **28** Lk 23:34; Ac 7:60 **29** Mt 5:39; 1Co 6:7 **30** Dt 15:7,8,10; Pr 21:26; Mt 5:42 **31** Mt 7:12 **32** Mt 5:46 **34** Mt 5:42 **35** ver. 27,30; Ps 37:26; Mt 5:45

and good to the ungrateful and the
wicked.
36"Be merciful (responsive, compas-
sionate, tender) just as your [heavenly]
Father is merciful.
37"Do not judge [others self-
righteously], and you will not be
judged; do not condemn [others when
you are guilty and unrepentant], and
you will not be condemned [for your
hypocrisy]; pardon [others when they
truly repent and change], and you will
be pardoned [when you truly repent
and change]. [Matt 7:1–5]
38"Give, and it will be given to you.
They will pour into your lap a good
measure—pressed down, shaken to-
gether, and running over [with no
space left for more]. For with the stan-
dard of measurement you use [when
you do good to others], it will be mea-
sured to you in return."
39He also told them a parable: "Can a
blind man guide [another] blind man?
Will they not both fall into a hole in
the ground?
40"A student is not superior to his
teacher; but everyone, after he has
been completely trained, will be like
his teacher.
41"Why do you look at the speck that
is in your brother's eye, but do not no-
tice *or* consider the log that is in your
own eye?
42"How can you say to your broth-
er, 'Brother, allow me to take out the
speck that is in your eye,' when you
yourself do not see the log that is in
your own eye? You hypocrite (play
actor, pretender), first take the log out
of your own eye, and then you will see
clearly to take out the speck that is in
your brother's eye.
43"For there is no good tree which
produces bad fruit, nor, on the other
hand, a bad tree which produces good
fruit. [Matt 7:16, 18]
44"For each tree is known *and* iden-
tified by its own fruit. For figs are not
picked from thorn bushes, nor is a clus-
ter of grapes picked from a briar bush.
45"The [intrinsically] good man pro-
duces what is good *and* honorable *and*
moral out of the good treasure [stored]
in his heart; and the [intrinsically] evil
man produces what is wicked *and* de-
praved out of the evil [in his heart]; for
his mouth speaks from the overflow
of his heart.

A Secure Foundation

46"Why do you call Me, 'Lord, Lord,'
and do not practice what I tell you?
47"Everyone who comes to Me and
listens to My words and obeys them,
I will show you whom he is like:
[Matt 7:24–27]
48he is like a [far-sighted, practical,
and sensible] man building a house,
who dug deep and laid a foundation on
the rock; and when a flood occurred,
the torrent burst against that house
and yet could not shake it, because it
had been securely built *and* founded
on the rock.
49"But the one who has [merely]
heard and has not practiced [what I
say], is like a [foolish] man who built a
house on the ground without *any* foun-
dation, and the torrent burst against it;
and it immediately collapsed, and the
ruin of that house was great."

Jesus Heals a Centurion's Slave

7 AFTER HE had finished all that
He had to say in the hearing of
the people, He went to Capernaum.
[Matt 8:5–13]

6:38 *good measure.* This illustration comes from the marketplace where grain was poured out, shaken down, and then filled to overflowing so the buyer received the full amount purchased. Such is the full measure that will be returned to one who has been generous.
6:46 *Lord, Lord.* Jesus pointed out that those who called Him by this title of respect acknowledged submission to Him. However when these same people ignored His teaching, they were guilty of hypocrisy.
7:1 *Capernaum.* This city was on the northwest shore of the Sea of Galilee. It was an important town in northern Galilee with an economy

36 Mt 5:48 **37** Mt 7:1 **38** Pr 19:17; Ps 79:12; Mt 7:2; Mk 4:24; Jas 2:13 **39** Mt 15:14 **40** Mt 10:24; Jn 13:16; 15:20 **41** Mt 7:3 **43** Mt 7:16,17 **44** Mt 12:33 **45** Mt 12:35; Mt 12:34 **46** Mal 1:6; Mt 7:21; 25:11; Lk 13:25 **47** Mt 7:24 **CHAPTER 7** **1** Mt 8:5

2 Now a [Roman] centurion's slave,
who was highly regarded by him, was
sick and on the verge of death.
3 When the centurion heard about
Jesus, he sent some Jewish elders to
Him, asking Him to come and save the
life of his slave.
4 When they reached Jesus, they
pleaded with Him earnestly [to come],
saying, "He is worthy for You to do
this for him,
5 because he loves our nation and
he built us our synagogue [at his own
expense]."
6 And Jesus went with them. But
when He was near the house, the cen-
turion sent friends to Him, saying,
"Lord, do not trouble Yourself further,
for I am not worthy for You to come
under my roof.
7 "Therefore I did not even consider
myself worthy to come to You. But
just speak a word, and my slave will
be healed.
8 "For I also am a man subject to au-
thority, with soldiers under me; and I
say to this one, 'Go,' and he goes, and
to another, 'Come,' and he comes, and
to my slave, 'Do this,' and he does it."
9 Now when Jesus heard this, He was
amazed at him, and turned and said
to the crowd that was following Him,
"I say to you, not even in Israel have I
found such great faith [as this man's]."
10 When the messengers who had
been sent returned to the house, they
found the slave in good health.
11 Soon afterward Jesus went to a
city called Nain [near Nazareth], and
His disciples and a large crowd accom-
panied Him.
12 Now as He approached the city
gate, a dead man was being carried
out—the only son of his mother, and
she was a widow. And a large crowd
from the city was with her [in the fu-
neral procession].
13 When the Lord saw her, He felt
[great] compassion for her, and said
to her, "Do not weep."
14 And He came up and touched the
bier [on which the body rested], and
the pallbearers stood still. And He
said, "Young man, I say to you, arise
[from death]!"
15 The man who was dead sat up and
began to speak. And *Jesus* gave him
back to his mother.
16 Fear *and* profound awe gripped
them all, and they *began* glorifying
and honoring *and* praising God, say-
ing, "A great prophet has arisen among
us!" and, "God has visited His people
[to help and care for and provide for
them]!"
17 This news about Him spread
through all of Judea and in all the sur-
rounding countryside. [1 Kin 17:17–24;
2 Kin 4:32–37]

A Delegation from John

18 John's disciples brought word to
him [in prison] of all these things.
[Matt 11:2–19]
19 John called two of his disciples and
sent them to the Lord, saying, "Are
You the Expected One (the Messiah),
or should we look for someone else?"
20 So the men came to Jesus and said,
"John the Baptist sent us to You to ask,
'Are You the Expected One (the Mes-
siah), or should we look for someone
else?' "
21 At that very hour Jesus healed
many *people* of sicknesses and infir-
mities and evil spirits; and He gave
[the gracious gift of] sight to many
who were blind.
22 So He replied to them, "Go and tell
John about everything you have seen

---

centered on fishing and agriculture. Heavily Jewish, it was the center for Jesus' Galilean ministry (4:31–44).

7:5 *built us our synagogue.* The Roman government regarded synagogues as valuable because their moral emphasis helped maintain order.

7:9 *not even in Israel.* The Centurion's example of faith came from outside the nation of Israel. This is one of only two cases where Jesus "wondered" (Mk 6:6).

7:12 *a dead man was being carried out.* This was a funeral procession. The cemetery was located outside the city gates. Funerals were

14 Lk 8:54; Jn 11:43; Ac 9:40; Ro 4:17 **16** Lk 1:65; Lk 24:19; Jn 4:19; 6:14; 9:17; Lk 1:68 **18** Mt 11:2 **22** Mt 11:4; Isa 35:5; Lk 4:18

and heard: the BLIND RECEIVE SIGHT, the
lame walk, the lepers are cleansed, the
deaf hear, the dead are raised up, and
the POOR HAVE THE GOOD NEWS (gospel)
PREACHED TO THEM. [Is 29:18, 19; 35:5,
6; 61:1]
23 "Blessed [joyful, spiritually fa-
vored] is he who does not take offense
at Me."
24 When John's messengers left,
Jesus began speaking to the crowds
about John: "What did you go out to
the wilderness to see? A reed shaken
by the wind?
25 "But what did you go out to see? A
man dressed in soft clothing [entirely
unsuited for the harsh wilderness]?
Those who wear splendid clothing and
live in luxury are in royal palaces!
26 "But what did you [really] go out to
see? A prophet? Yes, I say to you, and
one far more [eminent and remark-
able] than a prophet [who foretells the
future].
27 "This is the one of whom it is writ-
ten [by the prophet Malachi],

'BEHOLD, I SEND MY MESSENGER
AHEAD OF YOU,
WHO WILL PREPARE YOUR WAY BEFORE
YOU.' [Mal 3:1]

28 "I tell you, among those born of wom-
en there is no one greater than John;
yet he who is least in the kingdom of
God is greater [in privilege] than he."
29 All the people and the tax collectors
who heard Jesus, acknowledged [the
validity of] God's justice, having been
baptized with the baptism of John.
30 But the Pharisees and the lawyers
[who were experts in the Mosaic Law]
annulled *and* set aside God's purpose
for themselves, not having been bap-
tized by John.
31 "To what then shall I compare the
people of this generation [who set aside
God's plan], and what are they like?
32 "They are like children sitting in
the market place and calling to one
another, and saying, 'We played the
flute for you [pretending to be at a wed-
ding], and you did not dance; we sang
a dirge [pretending to be at a funeral],
and you did not weep [so nothing we
did appealed to you].'
33 "For John the Baptist has come nei-
ther eating bread nor drinking wine,
and you say, 'He has a demon!'
34 "The Son of Man has come eating
and drinking, and you say, 'Look, a
man who is a glutton and a [heavy]
wine-drinker, a friend of tax collectors
and sinners [including non-observant
Jews].'
35 "Yet wisdom is vindicated *and*
shown to be right by all her children
[by the lifestyle, moral character, and
good deeds of her followers]."

The Anointing in Galilee

36 One of the Pharisees asked Jesus
to eat with him, and He went into the
Pharisee's house [in the region of Gal-
ilee] and reclined *at the table.*

---

normally held the day of death because keeping a body overnight rendered a house unclean.

7:24–26 *Jesus began speaking to the crowds about John.* The questions that Jesus asked were designed to emphasize that John the Baptist played a special role in God's plan. The crowds did not go out to the wilderness to see scenery or a man dressed in special clothes, but to see a prophet.

7:28 *he who is least in the kingdom of God.* Jesus emphasizes the contrast between the old and new eras. John was the greatest prophet ever born. But the lowest person in the new era of God's kingdom is higher that the greatest prophet of the old era.

7:31–34 *To what then shall I compare.* Jesus made a comparison between children playing a game in the marketplace and the present generation of Israel, referring especially to the Jewish religious leaders. The leaders were like the children in that they complained no matter what tune was played. John the Baptist refused to eat bread or drink wine, and the religious leaders dismissed him as demon-possessed. In contrast, Jesus, the Son of Man, was accused of living loosely and associating with sinners. No matter what the style of God's messenger was, the religious leaders complained and rejected him.

7:36 *One of the Pharisees asked Jesus to eat with him.* This event is not the same as the

24 Mt 11:7 **27** Mal 3:1 **29** Mt 3:5; Lk 3:12 **30** Ac 20:27 **31** Mt 11:16 **33** Mt 3:4; Mk 1:6; Lk 1:15 **35** Mt 11:19 **36** Mt 26:6; Mk 14:3; Jn 11:2

[37]Now there was a woman in the city who was [known as] a sinner; and when she found out that He was reclining *at the table* in the Pharisee's house, she brought an alabaster vial of perfume;
[38]and standing behind Him at His feet, weeping, she began wetting His feet with her tears, and wiped them with the hair of her head, and [respectfully] kissed His feet [as an act signifying both affection and submission] and anointed them with the perfume.
[39]Now when [Simon] the Pharisee who had invited Him saw this, he said to himself, "If this Man were a prophet He would know who and what sort of woman this is who is touching Him, that she is a [notorious] sinner [an outcast, devoted to sin]."

Parable of Two Debtors

[40]Jesus, answering, said to the Pharisee, "Simon, I have something to say to you." And he replied, "Teacher, say it."
[41]"A certain moneylender had two debtors: one owed him five hundred denarii, and the other fifty.
[42]"When they had no means of repaying [the debts], he freely forgave them both. So which of them will love him more?"
[43]Simon answered, "The one, I take it, for whom he forgave more." Jesus said to him, "You have decided correctly."
[44]Then turning toward the woman, He said to Simon, "Do you see this woman? I came into your house [but you failed to extend to Me the usual courtesies shown to a guest]; you gave Me no water for My feet, but she has wet My feet with her tears and wiped them with her hair [demonstrating her love].
[45]"You gave Me no [welcoming] kiss, but from the moment I came in, she has not ceased to kiss My feet.
[46]"You did not [even] anoint My head with [ordinary] oil, but she has anointed My feet with [costly and rare] perfume.
[47]"Therefore I say to you, her sins, which are many, are forgiven, for she loved much; but he who is forgiven little, loves little."
[48]Then He said to her, "Your sins are forgiven."
[49]Those who were reclining *at the table* with Him began saying among themselves, "Who is this who even forgives sins?"
[50]Jesus said to the woman, "Your faith [in Me] has saved you; go in peace [free from the distress experienced because of sin]."

Ministering Women

8 SOON AFTERWARD, Jesus *began* going around from one city and village to another, preaching and proclaiming *the good news of* the kingdom of God. The twelve [disciples] were with Him,
[2]and *also* some women who had been healed of evil spirits and diseases: Mary, called Magdalene [from the city of Magdala in Galilee], from whom seven demons had come out,
[3]and Joanna, the wife of Chuza, Herod's household steward, and Susanna, and many others who were contributing to their support out of their private means [as was the custom for a rabbi's disciples].

---

one in Matthew 26:6–13; Mark 14:3–9; and John 12:1–8. The event described in those passages occurred in the house of a leper, a place where no Pharisee would ever have gone.

7:37 *alabaster vial.* This was made of soft stone to preserve the quality of the precious and expensive perfume. There is humility and devotion in the woman's act of service, as well as a great deal of courage, as she performed the deed in front of a crowd that knew her as a sinner.

7:44–46 *Do you see this woman?* Jesus contrasted the actions of the woman with the actions of the Pharisee Simon, implying that the woman knew more about forgiveness than Simon (v. 47).

8:1–3 *Mary, called Magdalene.* Because she is introduced here, it is unlikely that she was the sinful woman of 7:36–50. ***Joanna.*** This is an example of how some women of means used their wealth to benefit the work of God.

39 Lk 15:2 **46** Ps 23:5 **47** 1Ti 1:14 **48** Mt 9:2; Mk 2:5 **49** Mt 9:3; Mk 2:7 **50** Mt 9:22; Mk 5:34; 10:52; Lk 8:48; 18:42 **CHAPTER 8** **2** Mt 27:55,56; Mk 16:9

Parable of the Sower

4 When a large crowd was gathering
together, and people from city after
city were coming to Him, He spoke [to
them] using a parable: [Matt 13:2–9;
Mark 4:1–9]
5 "The sower went out to sow his
seed; and as he sowed, some fell beside
the road and it was trampled under-
foot, and the birds of the sky ate it up.
6 "And some *seed* fell on [shallow soil
covering] the rocks, and as soon as it
sprouted, it withered away, because it
had no moisture.
7 "Other *seed* fell among the thorns,
and the thorns grew up with it and
choked it out.
8 "And some fell into good soil, and
grew up and produced a crop a hun-
dred times as great." As He said these
things, He called out, "He who has
ears to hear, let him hear *and* heed
My words."
9 Now His disciples *began* asking
Him what this parable meant.
10 And He said, "To you [who have
been chosen] it has been granted to
know *and* recognize the mysteries of
the kingdom of God, but to the rest it
is in parables, so that *though* SEEING
THEY MAY NOT SEE, AND HEARING THEY MAY
NOT UNDERSTAND. [Is 6:9, 10; Jer 5:21;
Ezek 12:2]
11 "Now [the meaning of] the parable
is this: The seed is the word of God
[concerning eternal salvation].
12 "Those beside the road are the peo-
ple who have heard; then the devil
comes and takes the message [of God]
away from their hearts, so that they
will not believe [in Me as the Messiah]
and be saved.
13 "Those on the rocky *soil are* the
people who, when they hear, receive
and welcome the word with joy; but
these have no *firmly grounded* root.
They believe for a while, and in time
of trial *and* temptation they fall away
[from Me and abandon their faith].
14 "The *seed* which fell among the
thorns, these are the ones who have
heard, but as they go on their way they
are suffocated with the anxieties and
riches and pleasures of this life, and
they bring no fruit to maturity.
15 "But as for that *seed* in the good
soil, these are the ones who have heard
the word with a good and noble heart,
and hold on to it tightly, and bear fruit
with patience.

Parable of the Lamp

16 "Now no one lights a lamp and then
covers it with a container [to hide it],
or puts it under a bed; instead, he puts
it on a lampstand, so that those who
come in may see the light. [Matt 5:15;
Mark 4:21; Luke 11:33]
17 "For there is nothing hidden that
will not become evident, nor *anything*
secret that will not be known and come
out into the open.
18 "So be careful how you listen; for
whoever has [a teachable heart], to him
more [understanding] will be given;
and whoever does not have [a long-
ing for truth], even what he thinks
he has will be taken away from him."
[Matt 13:12; 25:29; Mark 4:25]
19 Then Jesus' mother and His brothers

8:10 *kingdom . . . parables.* Jesus' parables both concealed and revealed truths. The disciples were privileged to learn the truths of parables. For other listeners, the parables served as judgments that concealed truth, as the reference to Isaiah 6:9 indicates. On occasion, a parable was understood by an outsider but was not accepted, thus still functioning as a message of judgment (20:9 – 19).

8:13 *believe for a while . . . fall away.* Brief and superficial encounters with the Word of God will not stand times of testing. A person needs to meditate on the truths in Scripture and establish them as principles for living in order to withstand the trials and temptations that will inevitably come.

8:14 *anxieties and riches and pleasures of this life.* According to this parable, these three are the great obstacles to spiritual fruitfulness. The concerns of life can squelch spiritual growth. This type of "soil" is viewed as tragically unsuccessful (2Ti 2:4; 4:10).

8:19 – 20 *Then Jesus' mother and His brothers came up toward Him.* Jesus' family was concerned about the direction of His ministry

---

4 Mt 13:2; Mk 4:1 **9** Mt 13:10; Mk 4:10 **10** Isa 6:9; Mk 4:12 **11** Mt 13:18; Mk 4:14 **16** Mt 5:15; Mk 4:21; Lk 11:33 **17** Mt 10:26; Lk 12:2 **18** Mt 13:12; 25:29; Lk 19:26 **19** Mt 12:46; Mk 3:31

came up toward Him, but they could
not reach Him because of the crowd.
[Matt 12:46–50; Mark 3:31–35]
20 And He was told, "Your mother and
Your brothers are standing outside,
asking to see You."
21 But He answered, "My mother and
My brothers are these who listen to the
word of God and do it!"

Jesus Calms the Sea

22 Now on one of *those* days Jesus
and His disciples got into a boat, and
He said to them, "Let us cross over to
the other side of the lake (Sea of Gal-
ilee)." So they set out. [Matt 8:23–27;
Mark 4:36–41]
23 But as they were sailing, He fell
asleep. And a fierce gale of wind swept
down [as if through a wind tunnel]
on the lake, and they *began* to be
swamped, and were in great danger.
24 They came to Jesus and woke Him,
saying, "Master, Master, we are about
to die!" He got up and rebuked the
wind and the raging, violent waves,
and they ceased, and it became calm
[a perfect peacefulness].
25 And He said to them, "Where is
your faith [your confidence in Me]?"
They were afraid and astonished, say-
ing to one another, "Who then is this,
that He commands even the winds and
the sea, and they obey Him?"

The Demoniac Cured

26 Then they sailed to the country of
the Gerasenes, which is east of Galilee.
[Matt 8:28–34; Mark 5:1–17]
27 Now when Jesus stepped out on
land, He was met by a man from the
city [of Gerasa] who was possessed
with demons. For a long time he had
worn no clothes, and was not living in
a house, but among the tombs.
28 Seeing Jesus, he cried out [with a
terrible voice from the depths of his
throat] and fell down before Him [in
dread and terror], and shouted loudly,
"What business do we have [in com-
mon] with each other, Jesus, Son of
the Most High God? I beg You, do not
torment me [before the appointed time
of judgment]!"
29 Now He was [already] command-
ing the unclean spirit to come out of
the man. For it had seized him [vio-
lently] many times; and he was kept
under guard and bound with chains
and shackles, but he would break the
bonds and be driven by the demon into
the desert.
30 Then Jesus asked him, "What is
your name?" And he answered, "Le-
gion"; because many demons had en-
tered him.
31 They *continually* begged Him not
to command them to go into the abyss.
[Rev 9:1]
32 Now a large herd of pigs was
feeding there on the mountain. *The
demons* begged Jesus to allow them
to enter the pigs, and He gave them
permission.
33 Then the demons came out of the
man and entered the pigs; and the herd
rushed down the steep bank into the
lake and was drowned.

(Mk 3:31 – 35). Though some have suggested that the brothers here were sons of Joseph by a previous marriage or cousins of Jesus, most likely they were the sons of Joseph and Mary. Joseph's absence here may mean that he had died by this time.

8:23 *a fierce gale of wind.* The calming of the wind is the first of four miracles in verses 22 – 56 that demonstrate Jesus' authority over a variety of phenomena — nature, demons, disease, and death. This miracle took place on the Sea of Galilee. Cool air rushing down the ravines and hills of the area collides with warm air from the Sea of Galilee, causing sudden and strong storms.

8:25 *Where is your faith.* Jesus' question was a rebuke of His disciples. Because God was aware of their situation, they could trust in His protection, for He was powerful enough to control the winds and waves.

8:28 *Son of the Most High God.* The demon's confession recalls the angel's announcement to Mary in 1:31 – 32 and the demonic confessions of 4:34,41.

8:30 *Legion.* This name reflects the fact that the man was possessed by multiple demons. A legion was a Roman military unit of about 6,000 soldiers.

8:31 *the abyss.* This is an allusion to the underworld and the destruction of judgment (Ro 10:7).

22 Mt 8:23; Mk 4:35 **26** Mt 8:28; Mk 5:1 **31** Rev 20:3 **32** Job 1:12; 12:16; Rev 20:7

[34]When the herdsmen saw what had
happened, they ran away and told it in
the city and out in the country.
[35]*And people* came out to see what
had happened. They came to Jesus,
and found the man from whom the
demons had gone out, sitting at Jesus'
feet, clothed and in his right mind
(mentally healthy); and they were
frightened.
[36]Those who had seen it told them
how the man who had been demon-
possessed had been healed.
[37]Then all the people of the country of
the Gerasenes and the surrounding dis-
trict asked Him to leave them, because
they were overwhelmed with fear. So
Jesus got into the boat and returned
[to the west side of the Sea of Galilee].
[38]But the man from whom the de-
mons had gone out kept begging Him,
pleading to go with Him; but Jesus sent
him away, saying,
[39]"Return home and tell [about] all
the great things God has done for you."
So the man went away, proclaiming
throughout the whole city what great
things Jesus had done for him.

Miracles of Healing

[40]Now as Jesus was returning [to
Galilee], the people welcomed Him,
for they had all been expecting Him.
[41]Now a man named Jairus, a syna-
gogue official, came [to Him]; and he
fell at Jesus' feet and *began* begging
Him to come to his house; [Matt 9:18–26; Mark 5:22–43]
[42]for he had an only daughter, about
twelve years old, and she was dying.
But as Jesus went, the people were
crowding against Him [almost crush-
ing Him].
[43]And a woman who had [suffered
from] a hemorrhage for twelve years
[and had spent all her money on phy-
sicians], and could not be healed by
anyone,
[44]came up behind Him and touched
the fringe of His outer robe, and imme-
diately her bleeding stopped.
[45]Jesus said, "Who touched Me?"
While they all were denying it, Peter
[and those who were with him] said,
"Master, the people are crowding and
pushing against You!"
[46]But Jesus said, "Someone did touch
Me, because I was aware that power
[to heal] had gone out of Me."
[47]When the woman saw that she
had not escaped notice, she came up
trembling and fell down before Him.
She declared in the presence of all
the people the reason why she had
touched Him, and how she had been
immediately healed.
[48]He said to her, "Daughter, your
faith [your personal trust and confi-
dence in Me] has made you well. Go in
peace (untroubled, undisturbed well-
being)."
[49]While He was still speaking, some-
one from the synagogue official's
house came and said [to Jairus], "Your
daughter is dead; do not inconvenience
the Teacher any further."
[50]But Jesus, hearing this, answered
him, "Do not be afraid *any longer;* only
believe *and* trust [in Me and have faith
in My ability to do this], and she will
be made well."
[51]When He came to the house, He
allowed no one to enter with Him, ex-
cept Peter and John and James, and
the girl's father and mother.
[52]Now they were all weeping loudly
and mourning for her; but He said,
"Do not weep, for she is not dead, but
is sleeping."
[53]Then they *began* laughing scorn-
fully at Him *and* ridiculing Him, know-
ing [without any doubt] that she was
dead.
[54]But Jesus took hold of her hand
and spoke, saying, "Child, arise!"
[55]And her spirit returned, and she

8:44 *her bleeding stopped.* This condition not only would have been embarrassing, it would have made the woman unclean (Lev 15:25–31). It took great courage for her to seek out Jesus. Note that her action was not criticized, but commended (v. 48).

8:52 *sleeping.* "Sleeping" was a common metaphor for death. Here it indicates that the girl's death was not permanent.

37 Mt 8:34; Ac 16:39 **38** Mk 5:18 **41** Mt 9:18; Mk 5:22 **43** Mt 9:20 **46** Mk 5:30; Lk 6:19 **49** Mk 5:35 **52** Jn 11:11,13 **54** Lk 7:14; Jn 11:43

got up immediately; and He ordered
that she be given *something* to eat.
56Her parents were greatly aston-
ished [by the miracle]; but He instruct-
ed them to tell no one what had hap-
pened.

Ministry of the Twelve

9 NOW JESUS called together the
twelve [disciples] and gave them
[the right to exercise] power and au-
thority over all the demons and to heal
diseases.
2Then He sent them out [on a brief
journey] to preach the kingdom of God
and to perform healing. [Matt 10:5]
3And He said to them, "Take nothing
for *your* journey [that might encumber
you]—neither a walking stick, nor bag,
nor bread, nor money; and do not *even*
have two tunics apiece.
4"Whatever house you enter, stay
there until you leave that city [to go
to another].
5"And as for all those who do not
welcome you, when you leave that city,
shake the dust off your feet [break-
ing all ties with them] as a testimony
against them [that they rejected My
message]."
6So they *began* going from village
to village, preaching the gospel and
healing *the sick* everywhere.
7Now Herod [Antipas] the tetrarch
[who governed a portion of Palestine
including Galilee and Perea] heard
about all that was being done [by
Jesus], and he was thoroughly per-
plexed, because it was said by some
that John [the Baptist whom he had
ordered beheaded] had been raised
from the dead, [Matt 14:1, 2]
8and by others that Elijah had ap-
peared, and by others that one of the
[other] prophets of old had been res-
urrected.
9Herod said, "I personally had John
beheaded. Who is this man about
whom I hear such things?" And he
kept trying to see Jesus.
10When the apostles returned, they
told Him all that they had done. He
took them with Him and He private-
ly withdrew [across the Jordan] to a
city called Bethsaida. [Matt 14:13–21;
Mark 6:32–44; John 6:5–13]
11But when the crowds learned of it,
they followed Him; and He welcomed
them and He *began* talking to them
about the kingdom of God, and healing
those who needed to be healed.

Five Thousand Fed

12Now the day was ending, and the
twelve [disciples] came and said to
Him, "Send the crowd away, so that
they may go into the surrounding vil-
lages and countryside and find lodg-
ing, and get provisions; because here
we are in an isolated place."
13But He said to them, "You give
them *something* to eat." They said,
"We have no more than five loaves
and two fish—unless perhaps we go
and buy food for all these people."
[2 Kin 4:42–44]
14(For there were about 5,000 men.)
And He said to His disciples, "Have
them sit down *to eat* in groups of about
fifty each."
15They did so, and had them all sit
down.
16Then He took the five loaves and
the two fish, and He looked up to heav-
en [and gave thanks] and blessed them,
and broke *them* and kept giving *them*
to the disciples to set before the crowd.
17They all ate and were [completely]

9:2 *to preach . . . to perform healing.* The entire nation of Israel needed to see the evidence of the kingdom of God and make a decision concerning the King. Jesus commissioned His disciples to spread the word about God's kingdom through preaching and healing.

9:11 *talking . . . healing.* Jesus had the same two-pronged ministry that the twelve disciples had: preaching and healing (v. 2). The topic of Jesus' preaching was always the kingdom of God.

9:13 – 17 *about 5,000 men.* This is the only miracle of Jesus' ministry that appears in all four Gospels. The feeding of the 5,000 demonstrated Jesus' ability to provide.

56 Mt 8:4; 9:30; Mk 5:43 **CHAPTER 9** **1** Mt 10:1; Mk 3:13; 6:7 **2** Mt 10:7,8; Mk 6:12; Lk 10:1,9 **3** Mt 10:9; Mk 6:8; Lk 10:4; 22:35 **4** Mt 10:11; Mk 6:10 **5** Mt 10:14; Ac 13:51 **6** Mk 6:12 **7** Mk 14:1; 6:14 **9** Lk 23:8 **10** Mk 6:30; Mt 14:13 **12** Mt 14:15; Mk 6:35; Jn 6:1,5

satisfied; and the broken pieces which
they had left over were [abundant and
were] picked up—twelve baskets full.
18Now it happened that as Jesus
was praying privately, the disciples
were with Him, and He asked them,
"Who do the crowds say that I am?"
[Matt 16:13–16; Mark 8:27–29]
19They answered, "John the Baptist,
and some say, Elijah; but others, that
one of the ancient prophets has come
back to life."
20And He said to them, "But who do
you say that I am?" Peter replied, "The
Christ (the Messiah, the Anointed) of
God!"
21But He strictly warned and admon-
ished them not to tell this to anyone,
22saying, "The Son of Man must suf-
fer many things and be rejected [as the
Messiah] by the elders and chief priests
and scribes (Sanhedrin, Jewish High
Court), and be put to death, and on the
third day be raised up [from death to
life]." [Matt 16:21–28; Mark 8:31–9:1]
23And He was saying to them all, "If
anyone wishes to follow Me [as My dis-
ciple], he must deny himself [set aside
selfish interests], and take up his cross
daily [expressing a willingness to en-
dure whatever may come] and follow
Me [believing in Me, conforming to
My example in living and, if need be,
suffering or perhaps dying because of
faith in Me].
24"For whoever wishes to save his
life [in this world] will [eventually] lose
it [through death], but whoever loses
his life [in this world] for My sake, he
is the one who will save it [from the
consequences of sin and separation
from God].
25"For what does it profit a man if he
gains the whole world [wealth, fame,
success], and loses or forfeits himself?
26"For whoever is ashamed [here and
now] of Me and My words, the Son of
Man will be ashamed of him when He
comes in His glory and *the glory* of
the [heavenly] Father and of the holy
angels.
27"But I tell you truthfully, there are
some among those standing here who
will not taste death before they see the
kingdom of God."

The Transfiguration

28Now about eight days after these
teachings, He took along Peter and
John and James and went up on
the mountain to pray. [Matt 17:1–8;
Mark 9:2–8]
29As He was praying, the appear-
ance of His face became different [ac-
tually transformed], and His clothing
became white *and* flashing with the
brilliance of lightning.
30And behold, two men were talking
with Him; and they were Moses and
Elijah,
31who appeared in glory, and were
speaking of His departure [from

9:20 *The Christ (the Messiah, the Anointed) of God.* The emphasis here is on the messianic role of Jesus. He is the Promised One who was ushering in a new era. However, Jesus would soon reveal to the disciples that His messiahship would have elements of suffering that the disciples did not expect (vv. 22 – 23).

9:22 *must suffer . . . be rejected . . . be put to death . . . be raised up.* This is the first of several predictions in Luke of Jesus' suffering and vindication (v. 44; 12:50; 13:31 – 33; 17:25; 18:31 – 33). The disciples struggled to understand what Jesus was saying (v. 45; 18:34). They could not comprehend how Jesus' predictions fit into God's plan. Only after Jesus' resurrection and His explanation of the Scriptures to them did they begin to understand (24:25 – 27,44 – 49).

9:23 *take up his cross daily.* Although Jesus offered salvation as a free gift (Jn 1:12; 3:16 – 18), He also warned that following Him would entail suffering and hardship (Mt 5:10 – 12; Ro 8:17; 2Th 1:5).

9:24 – 25 *For what does it profit a man if he gains the whole world.* It makes no sense to attempt to save our lives on earth only to lose everything when our lives quickly and inevitably pass away. The wise course is to invest our earthly resources — our time, talents, and wealth — in what is eternal.

9:31 *speaking of His departure.* This important allusion to the central Old Testament event

18 Mt 16:13; Mk 8:27 **19** ver. 7,8; Mt 14:2 **20** Mt 16:16; Jn 6:69 **21** Mt 16:20 **22** Mt 16:21; 17:22 **23** Mt 10:38; 16:24; Mk 8:34; Lk 14:27 **25** Mt 16:26; Mk 8:36 **26** Mt 10:33; Mk 8:38; 2Ti 2:12 **27** Mt 16:28; Mk 9:1 **28** Mt 17:1; Mk 9:2

earthly life], which He was about to bring to fulfillment at Jerusalem.

32 Now Peter and those who were with him had been overcome with sleep; but when they were fully awake, they saw His glory *and* splendor *and* majesty, and the two men who were standing with Him.

33 And as these [men, Moses and Elijah] were leaving Him, Peter said to Jesus, "Master, it is delightful *and* good for us to be here; we should make three [sacred] tents; one for You, one for Moses, and one for Elijah"—not realizing what he was saying.

34 But even as he was saying this, a cloud formed and *began* to overshadow them; and they were [greatly] afraid as they entered the cloud.

35 Then a voice came out of the cloud, saying, "This is My beloved Son, My Chosen One; listen *and* obey *and* yield to Him!"

36 When the voice had ceased, Jesus was found *there* alone. And they kept silent, and told no one at that time any of the things which they had seen [concerning the divine manifestation]. [2 Pet 1:16–19]

37 On the next day, when they came down from the mountain, a large crowd met Him. [Matt 17:14–18; Mark 9:14–27]

38 And a man from the crowd shouted for help, "Teacher, I beg You to look at my son, because he is my only child;

39 and a spirit seizes him, and suddenly he cries out, and it throws him into a convulsion so that he foams *at the mouth;* and only with [great] difficulty does it leave him, mauling *and* bruising him *as it leaves.*

40 "I begged Your disciples to cast it out, but they could not."

41 Jesus answered, "You unbelieving and perverted generation! How long shall I be with you and put up with you? Bring your son here [to Me]."

42 Even while the boy was coming, the demon slammed him down and threw him into a [violent] convulsion. But Jesus rebuked the unclean spirit, and healed the boy and gave him back to his father.

43 They were all amazed [practically overwhelmed] at the [evidence of the] greatness of God *and* His majesty *and* His wondrous work. [Mark 9:30–32]

But while they were still awed by everything Jesus was doing, He said to His disciples,

44 "Let these words sink into your ears: the Son of Man is going to be betrayed *and* handed over to men [who are His enemies]."

45 However, they did not understand this statement. Its meaning was kept hidden from them so that they would not grasp it; and they were afraid to ask Him about it.

The Test of Greatness

46 An argument started among them as to which of them might be the greatest [surpassing the others in esteem and authority]. [Matt 18:1–5; Mark 9:33–37]

47 But Jesus, knowing what they were thinking in their heart, took a child and had him stand beside Him,

48 and He told them, "Whoever welcomes this child in My name welcomes Me; and whoever welcomes

---

of salvation is unique to Luke's account of the transfiguration. The comparison is made between Jesus' death and the journey to salvation that the nation of Israel experienced under Moses.

9:34 ***cloud.*** This is an allusion to the presence of God (Ex 40:35).

9:41 ***unbelieving and perverted generation.*** This rebuke suggests that the disciples lacked the faith to cast out the spirit described in verses 38 – 40. There is also a hint of a competitive spirit among the disciples (v. 46).

9:45 ***they were afraid to ask.*** The indication here is that the disciples still had much to learn. Their fear shows that they understood something about what Jesus said, but they did not understand how and why Jesus could say such things about Himself, since He was the Messiah. The suffering of the Messiah was something the disciples did not yet understand. They would continue to be confused in their understanding of how such suffering fit into God's plan until Jesus' death and resurrection (24:25 – 26,43 – 49).

32 Da 8:18; 10:9 **35** Mt 3:17; Ac 3:22 **36** Mt 17:9 **37** Mt 17:14; Mk 9:14,17 **44** Mt 17:22 **45** Mk 9:32; Lk 2:50; 18:34 **46** Mt 18:1; Mk 9:34 **48** Mt 10:40; 18:5; Mk 9:37; Jn 12:44; 13:20; Mt 23:11,12

Me [also] welcomes Him who sent Me;
for the one who is least among all of
you [that is, the one who is genuinely
humble—the one with a realistic self-
view]—he is the one who is [truly]
great."
49 John replied, "Master, we saw
someone driving out demons in Your
name; and we tried to stop him be-
cause he does not follow along with
us." [Mark 9:38–40]
50 But Jesus told him, "Do not stop
him; for he who is not against you is
for you." [Matt 12:30]
51 Now when the time was approach-
ing for Him to be taken up [to heaven],
He was determined to go to Jerusalem
[to fulfill His purpose].
52 He sent messengers on ahead of
Him, and they went into a Samaritan
village to make arrangements for Him;
53 but the people would not welcome
Him, because He was traveling toward
Jerusalem.
54 When His disciples James and
John saw this, they said, "Lord, do
You want us to command fire to come
down from heaven and destroy them?"
[2 Kin 1:9–16]
55 But He turned and rebuked them
[and He said, "You do not know what
kind of spirit you are;
56 for the Son of Man did not come to
destroy men's lives, but to save them."]
And they journeyed on to another
village.

Exacting Discipleship

57 As they were going along the road,
someone said to Him, "I will follow You
wherever You go." [Matt 8:19–22]
58 And Jesus told him, "Foxes have
holes and the birds of the air have
nests, but the Son of Man has no place
to lay His head."
59 He said to another, "Follow Me [ac-
cepting Me as Master and Teacher]."
But he said, "Lord, allow me first to
go and bury my father." [Matt 8:21, 22]
60 But He said to him, "Allow the
[spiritually] dead to bury their own
dead; but as for you, go and spread
the news about the kingdom of God."
61 Another also said, "I will follow
You, Lord [as Your disciple]; but first
let me say goodbye to those at my
home."
62 But Jesus said to him, "No one who
puts his hand to the plow and looks
back [to the things left behind] is fit
for the kingdom of God."

The Seventy Sent Out

10 NOW AFTER this the Lord ap-
pointed seventy others, and sent
them out ahead of Him, two by two,
into every city and place where He
was about to go.
2 He was saying to them, "The har-
vest is abundant [for there are many
who need to hear the good news about
salvation], but the workers [those

9:51 *He was determined to go to Jerusalem.* This is the first indication that Jesus' attention was turning toward His final suffering in Jerusalem (v. 53; 13:22; 17:11; 18:31; 19:11,28,41). Luke's Gospel uniquely emphasizes this journey to Jerusalem.

9:52 *Samaritan.* These people were the descendants of Jews who had married Gentiles after the fall of the Northern Kingdom, Israel. The Samaritans eventually developed their own religious rites which they practiced on Mount Gerizim instead of at the temple in Jerusalem. Though there was deep hostility between Jews and Samaritans, Jesus ministered to both groups.

9:54 *command fire to come down.* James and John wanted Jesus to bring judgment upon the Samaritan villages that refused to respond to His message, just as Elijah had done in 2 Kings 1:9 – 16. Their demand for judgment was antithetical to Jesus' loving response (v. 56).

9:59 *allow me first to go and bury my father.* This aspiring disciple placed family responsibilities ahead of following Jesus. The concerns of home were this man's stumbling block.

9:62 *fit for the kingdom.* This remark of Jesus demonstrates the seriousness of commitment to Him.

10:2 *The harvest is abundant.* The picture of a great harvest suggests that a positive response awaited the laborers, even in the face of much rejection.

49 Mk 9:38; See Nu 11:28 **50** See Mt 12:30; Lk 11:23 **51** Mk 16:19; Ac 1:2 **53** Jn 4:4,9 **54** 2Ki 1:10,12 **56** Jn 3:17; 12:47 **57** Mt 8:19 **59** Mt 8:21 **61** See 1Ki 19:20 **CHAPTER 10** **1** Mt 10:1; Mk 6:7 **2** Mt 9:37; Jn 4:35; 2Th 3:1

available to proclaim the message of salvation] are few. Therefore, [prayerfully] ask the Lord of the harvest to send out workers into His harvest.

3 “Go your way; listen carefully: I am sending you out like lambs among wolves.

4 “Do not carry a money belt, a provision bag, or [extra] sandals; and do not greet anyone along the way [who would delay you].

5 “Whatever house you enter, first say, ‘Peace [that is, a blessing of well-being and prosperity, the favor of God] to this house.’

6 “And if anyone of peace is there [someone who is sweet-spirited and hospitable], your [blessing of] peace will rest on him; but if not, it will return to you.

7 “Stay in that house, eating and drinking what they provide, for the laborer is worthy of his wages. Do not move from house to house. [Deut 24:15]

8 “Whenever you go into a city and they welcome you, eat what is set before you;

9 and heal those in it who are sick [authenticating your message], and say to them, ‘The kingdom of God has come near to you.’

10 “But whatever city you enter and they do not welcome you, go out into its streets and say,

11 ‘Even the dust of your city which clings to our feet we wipe off *in protest* against you [breaking all ties]; yet understand this, that the kingdom of God has come near [and you rejected it].’

12 “I tell you, it will be more bearable in that day [of judgment] for Sodom than for that city. [Gen 19:24–28]

13 “Woe (judgment is coming) to you, Chorazin! Woe to you, Bethsaida! For if the miracles performed in you had been performed in Tyre and Sidon, they would have repented *and* changed their minds long ago, sitting in sackcloth and ashes [to show deep regret for sin].

14 “However, it will be more tolerable for Tyre and Sidon in the judgment than for you.

15 “And you, Capernaum, will not be exalted to heaven, will you? You will descend to Hades (the realm of the dead).

16 “The one who listens to you listens to Me; and the one who rejects you rejects Me; and the one who rejects Me rejects Him [My heavenly Father] who sent Me.”

The Joyous Results

17 The seventy returned with joy, saying, “Lord, even the demons are subject to us in Your name.”

18 He said to them, “I watched Satan fall from heaven like [a flash of] lightning.

19 “Listen carefully: I have given you authority [that you now possess] to tread on serpents and scorpions, and [the ability to exercise authority] over all the power of the enemy (Satan); and nothing will [in any way] harm you.

20 “Nevertheless do not rejoice at this, that the spirits are subject to you, but

---

10:3 *lambs among wolves.* This image from Isaiah 40:11 was a popular one in Judaism.

10:13 *if the miracles performed in you had been performed.* Jesus’ remark was meant to wake the people up to what their rejection of Him signified.

10:16 *The one who listens to you listens to Me.* Hearing the messenger is the same as hearing the One who sent him. Authority resides not in the messenger, but in the person the messenger represents, the source of the message.

10:18 *I watched Satan.* This verse provides a commentary on what the disciples’ healing ministry meant. The reversal of the effects of sin and death, which Satan introduced through his deception in Genesis 3 is portrayed graphically as Satan falling from heaven. Jesus’ ministry and what grows out of it represents the defeat of Satan, sin, and death.

10:19 – 20 *I have given you authority.* This passage records the transmission of Jesus’ power to His immediate circle of disciples. It should be

---

3 Mt 10:16 **4** Mt 10:9; Mk 6:8; Lk 9:3; 2Ki 4:29 **5** Mt 10:12 **7** Mt 10:11; 1Co 10:27; Mt 10:10; 1Co 9:4; 1Ti 5:18 **9** Lk 9:2; ver. 11; Mt 3:2; 4:17; 10:7 **11** Mt 10:14; Lk 9:5; Ac 13:51; 18:6 **12** Mt 10:15; Mk 6:11 **13** Mt 11:21; Eze 3:6 **15** Mt 11:23; See Ge 11:4; Dt 1:28; Isa 14:13; Jer 51:53; See Eze 26:20; 32:18 **16** Mt 10:40; Mk 9:37; Jn 13:20; 1Th 4:8; Jn 5:23 **17** ver. 1 **18** Jn 12:31; 16:11; Rev 9:1; 12:8,9 **19** Mk 16:18; Ac 28:5 **20** Ex 32:32; Ps 69:28; Isa 4:3; Da 12:1; Php 4:3; Heb 12:23; Rev 13:8; 20:12

rejoice that your names are recorded in heaven." [Ex 32:32; Ps 69:28; Dan 12:1; Rev 3:5]

21 In that very hour He was overjoyed *and* rejoiced greatly in the Holy Spirit, and He said, "I praise You, O Father, Lord of heaven and earth, that You have hidden these things [relating to salvation] from the wise and intelligent, and have revealed them to infants [the childlike and untaught]. Yes, Father, for this way was [Your gracious will and choice, and was] well-pleasing in Your sight.

22 "All things have been transferred *and* turned over to Me by My Father and no one knows who the Son is except the Father, or who the Father is except the Son, and anyone to whom the Son wishes to reveal Him."

23 Then turning to His disciples, Jesus said privately, "Blessed [joyful, spiritually enlightened, and favored by God] are the eyes which see what you see, [Matt 13:16, 17]

24 for I say to you that many prophets and kings longed to see what you see, and they did not see it; and to hear what you hear, and did not hear it."

25 And a certain lawyer [an expert in Mosaic Law] stood up to test Him, saying, "Teacher, what must I do to inherit eternal life?" [Matt 22:34–40; Mark 12:28–31]

26 Jesus said to him, "What is written in the Law? How do you read it?"

27 And he replied, "YOU SHALL LOVE THE LORD YOUR GOD WITH ALL YOUR HEART, AND WITH ALL YOUR SOUL, AND WITH ALL YOUR STRENGTH, AND WITH ALL YOUR MIND; AND YOUR NEIGHBOR AS YOURSELF." [Lev 19:18; Deut 6:5]

28 Jesus said to him, "You have answered correctly; DO THIS *habitually* AND YOU WILL LIVE." [Lev 18:5; Ezek 20:11; Matt 19:17]

29 But he, wishing to justify *and* vindicate himself, asked Jesus, "And who is my neighbor?"

Parable of the Good Samaritan

30 Jesus replied, "A man was going down from Jerusalem to Jericho, and he encountered robbers, who stripped him of his clothes [and belongings], beat him, and went their way [unconcerned], leaving him half dead.

31 "Now by coincidence a priest was going down that road, and when he saw him, he passed by on the other side.

32 "Likewise a Levite also came down to the place and saw him, and passed by on the other side [of the road].

---

noted that similar power was not given beyond that circle of disciples.

10:22 *All things have been transferred and turned over to Me.* This is Jesus' declaration of total authority as the Son of God (Jn 10:18; 17:2). Jesus declares His unique relationship with God the Father. The Lord reveals Himself only through Jesus. To know God, one must know His Son, Jesus.

10:25 – 26 *what must I do to inherit eternal life?* The question posed by the lawyer is really a challenge, since the verse speaks of the testing of Jesus. This is a similar, though probably distinct, event from Matthew 22:34 – 40 and Mark 12:28 – 34. To inherit something is to receive it. In other words, the man was asking, "What must I do to share in the reward at the resurrection of the righteous at the end?"

10:27 *YOU SHALL LOVE THE LORD . . . AND YOUR NEIGHBOR.* The lawyer responded to Jesus' question by quoting Deuteronomy 6:5, a text that was recited twice a day by every faithful Jew. This text summarized the central ethical standard of the law.

10:28 *DO THIS habitually AND YOU WILL LIVE.* Jesus was not saying that righteousness is the result of works. Rather He was saying that love for and obedience to God will be a natural result of placing one's faith in the Lord.

10:29 *who is my neighbor?* This question was an attempt to limit the demands of the law by suggesting that some people are neighbors while others are not. The lawyer was looking for minimal obedience while Jesus was looking for absolute obedience.

10:30 *Jerusalem to Jericho.* This was a 17 mile journey on a road known to harbor many robbers.

10:31 – 33 *priest . . . Levite . . . Samaritan.* Part of the beauty of the story of the Good Samaritan is the reversal of stereotypes. The priest and Levite traditionally would have been the "good guys." The Samaritan would have been a "bad guy," a person who compromised in religious matters. However, the Samaritan knew how to

21 Mt 11:25 **22** Mt 28:18; Jn 3:35; 5:27; 17:2; Jn 1:18; 6:44,46 **23** Mt 13:16 **24** 1Pe 1:10 **25** Mt 19:16; 22:35 **27** Dt 6:5; Lev 19:18 **28** Lev 18:5; Neh 9:29; Eze 20:11,13,21; Ro 10:5 **29** Lk 16:15 **31** Ps 38:11

33“But a Samaritan (foreigner),
who was traveling, came upon him;
and when he saw him, he was deeply
moved with compassion [for him],
34and went to him and bandaged
up his wounds, pouring oil and wine
on *them* [to sooth and disinfect the
injuries]; and he put him on his own
pack-animal, and brought him to an
inn and took care of him.
35“On the next day he took out two
denarii (two days’ wages) and gave
them to the innkeeper, and said, ‘Take
care of him; and whatever more you
spend, I will repay you when I return.’
36“Which of these three do you think
proved himself a neighbor to the man
who encountered the robbers?”
37He answered, “The one who
showed compassion *and* mercy to
him.” Then Jesus said to him, “Go and
constantly do the same.”

Martha and Mary

38Now while they were on their way,
Jesus entered a village [called Betha-
ny], and a woman named Martha wel-
comed Him into her home. [John 11:1]
39She had a sister named Mary, who
seated herself at the Lord’s feet and was
continually listening to His teaching.
40But Martha was very busy *and* dis-
tracted with all of her serving respon-
sibilities; and she approached Him and
said, “Lord, is it of no concern to You
that my sister has left me to do the
serving alone? Tell her to help me *and*
do her part.”
41But the Lord replied to her, “Mar-
tha, Martha, you are worried and
bothered *and* anxious about so many
things;
42but *only* one thing is necessary, for
Mary has chosen the good part [that
which is to her advantage], which will
not be taken away from her.”

Instruction about Prayer

11 IT HAPPENED that while Jesus
was praying in a certain place,
after He finished, one of His disciples
said to Him, “Lord, teach us to pray
just as John also taught his disciples.”
2He said to them,

“When you pray, say:
‘Father, hallowed be Your name.
Your kingdom come.
3‘Give us each day our daily bread.
4‘And forgive us our sins,
For we ourselves also forgive
everyone who is indebted to
us [who has offended or
wronged us].
And lead us not into temptation
[but rescue us from evil].’ ”

Parable of Persistence

5Then He said to them, “Suppose one
of you has a friend, and goes to him at
midnight and says, ‘Friend, lend me
three loaves [of bread];
6for a friend of mine who is on a
journey has just come to *visit* me, and
I have nothing to serve him’;
7and from inside he answers, ‘Do not

---

treat his neighbor. The neighbor here was not someone the Samaritan knew or even someone of the same race, just someone in need.

10:36 *Which . . . proved himself a neighbor.* The central issue is not determining who one’s neighbor is, but being a good neighbor to all.

11:1 *Lord, teach us to pray.* The Lord’s Prayer illustrates the variety of requests that one can and should make to God, as well as displaying the humble attitude that should accompany prayer. The use of the plural pronoun *us* throughout the prayer shows that it is not just the prayer of one person for his or her own personal needs, but a community prayer.

11:2 *Your kingdom come.* The reference here is to God’s program and promise. This is more affirmation than request, highlighting the petitioner’s submission to God’s will and the desire to see God’s work come to pass.

11:4 *For we ourselves also forgive.* The petitioner recognizes that if mercy is to be sought from God, then mercy must be shown to others. We need to adopt the same standard that we expect others to follow. ***lead us not into temptation.*** This remark is often misunderstood as suggesting that perhaps God can lead us into sin. The point is that if one is to avoid sin, one must follow where God leads. In short, the petitioner asks God for the spiritual protection necessary to avoid falling into sin.

33 Jn 4:9 **38** Jn 11:1; 12:2,3 **39** 1Co 7:32; Lk 8:35; Ac 22:3 **42** Ps 27:4 **CHAPTER 11** **2** Mt 6:9

bother me; the door has already been
shut and my children and I are in bed;
I cannot get up and give you *anything*.'
8 "I tell you, even though he will not
get up and give him *anything just* because he is his friend, yet because of
his persistence *and* boldness he will
get up and give him whatever he needs.
9 "So I say to you, ask *and* keep on
asking, and it will be given to you;
seek *and* keep on seeking, and you
will find; knock *and* keep on knocking,
and the door will be opened to you.
[Matt 7:7–11]
10 "For everyone who keeps on asking [persistently], receives; and he who
keeps on seeking [persistently], finds;
and to him who keeps on knocking
[persistently], the door will be opened.
11 "What father among you, if his son
asks for a fish, will give him a snake
instead of a fish?
12 "Or if he asks for an egg, will give
him a scorpion?
13 "If you, then, being evil [that is,
sinful by nature], know how to give
good gifts to your children, how much
more will your heavenly Father give
the Holy Spirit to those who ask *and*
continue to ask Him!"

Pharisees' Blasphemy

14 And [at another time] Jesus was
casting out a demon, and it was [controlling a man so as to make him]
mute; when the demon had gone out,
the mute man spoke. And the crowds
were awed. [Matt 12:22–24]
15 But some of them said, "He drives
out demons by [the power of] Beelzebul (Satan), the ruler of the demons."
16 Others, trying to test Him, were
demanding of Him a sign from heaven.
17 But He, *well* aware of their
thoughts *and* purpose, said to them,
"Every kingdom divided against itself
is doomed to destruction; and a house
divided against itself falls.
18 "If Satan also is divided against
himself, how will his kingdom stand
and continue to survive? For you are
saying that I drive out demons by [the
power of] Beelzebul.
19 "Now if I drive out the demons by
Beelzebul, by whom do your sons [the
Jewish exorcists] drive them out? For
this reason they will be your judges.
20 "But if I drive out the demons by
the finger of God, then the kingdom of
God has already come upon you.
21 "When the strong man, fully
armed, guards his own house, his belongings are undisturbed *and* secure.
22 "But when someone stronger than
he attacks and overpowers him, he
robs him of all his armor on which
he had relied and divides his [goods
as] spoil.
23 "He who is not with Me [believing
in Me as Lord and Savior] is against
Me [there is no impartial position];
and he who does not gather with Me
[assisting in My ministry], scatters.
24 "When the unclean spirit comes
out of a person, it roams through waterless places in search [of a place] of

---

11:17 – 18 *you are saying that I drive out demons by [the power of] Beelzebul.* The attribution of Jesus' miracles to Satan was not only blasphemous, it was illogical. If Satan had cast out the demon (v. 14), he would have been destroying the result of his own work.
11:20 *the finger of God.* This phrase is an allusion to God's power, like that demonstrated in the exodus (Ex 8:19; Dt 9:10; Ps 8:3). ***the kingdom of God has already come upon you.*** Jesus' miracles represented the arrival of God's power and promise — in short, His rule. That rule comes in and through Jesus. The miracles of Jesus demonstrated God's victory over the forces of evil. The kingdom program, depicted as drawing near, will be consummated at the return of Jesus when this rule is manifested over every creature.
11:22 *But when someone stronger than he.* Jesus portrays Himself as someone stronger than Satan who overruns Satan's house and gives the spoils of victory to those who are His (Eph 4:8 – 9).
11:23 *He who is not with Me.* Jesus' ministry forces everyone to make a choice. Neutrality is not an option. Either Jesus comes from God or He does not. Not to align with Jesus is to be against Him.

8 Lk 18:1 **9** Mt 7:7; 21:22; Mk 11:24; Jn 15:7; Jas 1:6; 1Jn 3:22 **11** Mt 7:9 **14** Mt 9:32; 12:22 **15** Mt 9:34; 12:24 **16** Mt 12:38; 16:1 **17** Mt 12:25; Mk 3:24; Jn 2:25 **20** Ex 8:19 **21** Mt 12:29; Mk 3:27 **22** Isa 53:12; Col 2:15 **23** Mt 12:30 **24** Mt 12:43

rest; and not finding any, it says, 'I will go back to my house (person) from which I came.'
[25]"And when it comes, it finds the place swept and put in order.
[26]"Then it goes and brings seven other spirits more evil than itself, and they go in [the person] and live there; and the last state of that person becomes worse than the first."
[27]Now while Jesus was saying these things, one of the women in the crowd raised her voice and said to Him, "Blessed (happy, favored by God) is the womb that gave birth to You and the breasts at which You nursed!"
[28]But He said, "On the contrary, blessed (happy, favored by God) are those who hear the word of God and continually observe it."

The Sign of Jonah

[29]Now as the crowds were increasing [in number], He began to say, "This [present] generation is a wicked generation; it seeks a sign (attesting miracle), but no sign will be given to it except the sign of Jonah [the prophet]. [Matt 12:39–42]
[30]"For just as Jonah became a sign to the people of Nineveh, so will the Son of Man also be [a sign] to this generation. [Jon 3:4–10]
[31]"The Queen of the South (the kingdom of Sheba) will rise up in the judgment with the men of this generation and condemn them, because she came from the ends of the earth to listen to the wisdom of Solomon, and look, something greater than Solomon is here. [1 Kin 10:1–13; 2 Chr 9:1–12]
[32]"The men of Nineveh will stand up [as witnesses] at the judgment with this generation and condemn it, because they repented at the preaching of Jonah, and look, something greater than Jonah is here. [Jon 3:5]
[33]"No one lights a lamp and then puts it in a cellar nor under a basket [hiding the light], but [instead it is put] on the lampstand, so that those who come in may see the light. [Matt 5:15; Mark 4:21; Luke 8:16]
[34]"The eye is the lamp of your body. When your eye is clear [spiritually perceptive, focused on God], your whole body also is full of light [benefiting from God's precepts]. But when it is bad [spiritually blind], your body also is full of darkness [devoid of God's word].
[35]"Be careful, therefore, that the light that is in you is not darkness.
[36]"So if your whole body is illuminated, with no dark part, it will be entirely bright [with light], as when the lamp gives you light with its bright rays."

Woes upon the Pharisees

[37]Now after Jesus had spoken, a Pharisee asked Him to have lunch with him. He went in [the Pharisee's home] and reclined *at the table* [without ceremonially washing His hands].
[38]The Pharisee noticed this and was surprised that Jesus did not first ceremonially wash before the meal.
[39]But the Lord said to him, "Now you Pharisees clean the outside of the cup and plate [as required by tradition]; but inside you are full of greed and wickedness.
[40]"You foolish ones [acting without reflection or intelligence]! Did not He

---

11:26 ***the last state.*** Jesus' point is that experiencing God's blessing and then ignoring it leaves one callous towards the work of God and exposed to the control of demonic forces.

11:29 ***the sign of Jonah.*** This refers to his prophetic call to repentance rather than to the resurrection foreshadowed by Jonah's return from the belly of the great fish.

11:36 ***your whole body is illuminated.*** A person can become like light, a living picture of what God's Word teaches, by concentrating on the light of the truth.

11:39 ***clean the outside of the cup.*** These condemnations by Jesus are similar to those in Matthew 23. The Pharisees washed the outside of cups, making sure that the cups had not become unclean through contact with a dead insect (Lev 11:31–38). Jesus pointed out that the Pharisees concerned themselves with outward appearances and ritual cleanness, while

---

26 Jn 5:14; Heb 6:4; 10:26; 2Pe 2:20 **27** Lk 1:28,48 **28** Mt 7:21; Lk 8:21; Jas 1:25 **29** Mt 12:38,39 **30** Jnh 1:17; 2:10 **31** 1Ki 10:1 **32** Jnh 3:5 **33** Mt 5:15; Mk 4:21; Lk 8:16 **34** Mt 6:22 **38** Mk 7:3 **39** Mt 23:25; Titus 1:15

who made the outside make the inside
also?
41 “But give that which is within as
charity [that is, acts of mercy and com-
passion, not as a public display, but as
an expression of your faithfulness to
God], and then indeed all things are
clean for you.
42 “But woe (judgment is coming)
to you Pharisees, because you [self-
righteously] tithe the mint and rue and
every [little] garden herb [tending to
all the minutiae], and yet disregard *and*
neglect justice and the love of God; but
these are the things you should have
done, without neglecting the others.
[Lev 27:30; Mic 6:8]
43 “Woe to you Pharisees, because
you love the best seats in the syna-
gogues and to be respectfully greeted
in the market places.
44 “Woe to you! For you are like graves
which are unmarked, and people walk
over them without being aware of it
[and are ceremonially unclean].”
45 One of the lawyers [an expert
in the Mosaic Law] answered Him,
“Teacher, by saying this, You insult
us too!”
46 But He said, “Woe to you lawyers
as well, because you weigh men down
with burdens [man-made rules, un-
reasonable requirements] which are
hard to bear, and you yourselves will
not even touch the burdens with one
of your fingers [to lighten the load].
47 “Woe to you! For you repair *or*
build tombs for the prophets, and it
was your fathers who killed them.
48 “So you are witnesses and approve
the deeds of your fathers, because they
[actually] killed them, and you repair
or build their tombs.
49 “For this reason also the wisdom
of God said [in the Scriptures], ‘I will
send them prophets and apostles, some
of whom they will put to death and
some they will persecute,
50 so that charges may be brought
against this generation [holding them
responsible] for the blood of all the
prophets shed since the foundation of
the world,
51 from the blood of Abel to the blood
of Zechariah [the priest], who was
murdered between the altar and the
house *of God.* Yes, I tell you, charges
will be brought against this genera-
tion.’ [Gen 4:8; 2 Chr 24:20, 21; Zech 1:1;
Matt 23:35]
52 “Woe to you lawyers, because you
have taken away the key to knowl-
edge (scriptural truth). You yourselves
did not enter, and you held back those
who were entering [by your flawed
interpretation of God’s word and your
man-made tradition].” [Matt 23:13]
53 When He left there, the scribes and
the Pharisees began to be very hostile
[toward Him] and to interrogate Him
on many subjects,
54 plotting against Him to catch *Him*
in something He might say.

---

what was inside, what really counts, was full of selfishness and evil.

11:42 *tithe mint and rue.* Some Pharisees took the strictest interpretation and counted almost anything, including spices. However, they neglected two basic things that the prophets also had warned about: love and justice (Mic 6:8; Zec 7:8 – 10).

11:46 *burdens.* This term refers to a ship’s cargo. The idea is that a heavy strain was being imposed on the people and yet, in the end, this burden did not bring them close to God. Here Jesus rebuked the tradition that had grown up around the law of Moses.

11:47 – 48 *you repair or build tombs for the prophets.* Jesus made a biting, ironic comparison between the current generation of Israel and the generations of the past. Jesus was saying that the current generation finished the job of slaying the prophets that the previous generation had started. The building and care of tombs was supposed to be an act of honoring the prophets, but Jesus pointed out that something else was really going on.

11:52 *Woe to you lawyers.* Jesus charged the lawyers with doing the opposite of what they claimed their calling to be. Rather than bringing people nearer to God, they had removed the possibility of their entering into that knowledge, and had prevented others from understanding it as well.

---

41 Isa 58:7; Da 4:27; Lk 12:33 **42** Mt 23:23 **43** Mt 23:6; Mk 12:38,39 **44** Mt 23:27; Ps 5:9 **46** Mt 23:4
47 Mt 23:29 **49** Mt 23:34 **51** Ge 4:8; 2Ch 24:20,21 **52** Mt 23:13 **54** Mk 12:13

God Knows and Cares

12 IN THE meantime, after so many thousands of the people had gathered that they were stepping on one another, Jesus began speaking first *of all* to His disciples, “Be *continually* on your guard against the leaven of the Pharisees [that is, their pervasive, corrupting influence and teaching], which is hypocrisy [producing self-righteousness].

2 “But there is nothing [so carefully] concealed that it will not be revealed, nor so hidden that it will not be made known. [Matt 10:26–33; Mark 4:22]

3 “For that reason, whatever you have said in the dark will be heard in the light, and what you have whispered behind closed doors will be proclaimed on the housetops.

4 “I say to you, My friends, do not be afraid of those who kill the body and after that have nothing more that they can do.

5 “But I will point out to you whom you should fear: fear the One who, after He has killed, has authority *and* power to hurl [you] into hell; yes, I say to you, [stand in great awe of God and] fear Him!

6 “Are not five sparrows sold for two copper coins? Yet not one of them has [ever] been forgotten in the presence of God.

7 “Indeed the very hairs of your head are all numbered. Do not be afraid; you are far more valuable than many sparrows.

8 “I say to you, whoever declares openly *and* confesses Me before men [speaking freely of Me as his Lord], the Son of Man also will declare openly *and* confess him [as one of His own] before the angels of God.

9 “But he who denies Me before men will be denied in the presence of the angels of God.

10 “And everyone who speaks a word against the Son of Man, it will be forgiven him; but he who blasphemes against the Holy Spirit [that is, whoever intentionally discredits the Holy Spirit by attributing the authenticating miracles done by Me to Satan], it will not be forgiven him [for him there is no forgiveness]. [Matt 12:31; Mark 3:28–30]

11 “When they bring you before the synagogues and the magistrates and the authorities, do not be worried about how you are to defend yourselves or what you are to say;

12 for the Holy Spirit will teach you in that very hour what you ought to say.”

Covetousness Denounced

13 Someone from the crowd said to Him, “Teacher, tell my brother to divide the *family* inheritance with me.”

14 But He said to him, “Man, who appointed Me a judge or an arbitrator over [the two of] you?”

15 Then He said to them, “Watch out and guard yourselves against every form of greed; for not even when one has an overflowing abundance does his life consist of *nor* is it derived from his possessions.”

12:1–2 *leaven.* This represents the presence of corruption. Unleavened bread is what the Jews ate at Passover (Ex 12:14–20). The corruption in view here is hypocrisy. Practicing hypocrisy is senseless because eventually all deeds—both good and evil—will be exposed.

12:4 *do not be afraid of those who kill the body.* This verse anticipates the presence of severe religious persecution in response to Jesus' remarks in Luke 11:39–54.

12:5 *fear Him.* Even in the context of physical persecution, the only One believers should fear is God, who sees how we live and judges us. Jesus was not guaranteeing physical preservation in this life, but was opening the prospect of deliverance in the next life.

12:6 *two copper coins.* These coins, the smallest in circulation, were worth about one-sixteenth of a basic day's wages.

12:14 *who appointed Me a judge.* Jesus refuses to enter into a dispute over money, which is clearly dividing a family. Such disputes over money destroy relationships, so Jesus tells a parable that explains the danger of focusing on wealth.

CHAPTER 12 **1** Mat 16:6; Mk 8:15; Mt 16:12 **2** Mt 10:26; Mk 4:22; Lk 8:17 **4** Isa 51:7,8,12,13; Jer 1:8; Mt 10:28; Jn 15:14,15 **8** Mt 10:32; Mk 8:38; 2Ti 2:12; 1Jn 2:23 **10** Mt 12:31,32; Mk 3:28; 1Jn 5:16 **11** Mt 10:19; Mk 13:11 **14** Jn 18:36 **15** 1Ti 6:7

Parable of the Wealthy Fool

16 Then He told them a parable, saying, "There was a rich man whose land was very fertile *and* productive.

17 "And he began thinking to himself, 'What shall I do, since I have no place [large enough in which] to store my crops?'

18 Then he said, 'This is what I will do: I will tear down my storehouses and build larger ones, and I will store all my grain and my goods there.

19 'And I will say to my soul, "Soul, you have many good things stored up, [enough] for many years; rest *and* relax, eat, drink and be merry (celebrate continually)." '

20 "But God said to him, 'You fool! This *very* night your soul is required of you; and *now* who will own all the things you have prepared?' [Job 27:8; Jer 17:11]

21 "So it is for the one who continues to store up *and* hoard possessions for himself, and is not rich [in his relationship] toward God."

22 Jesus said to His disciples, "For this reason I tell you, do not worry about your life, as to what you will eat; or about your body, as to what you will wear. [Matt 6:25–33]

23 "For life is more than food, and the body more than clothes.

24 "Consider the ravens, for they neither sow [seed] nor reap [the crop]; they have no storehouse or barn, and yet God feeds them. How much more valuable are you than the birds!

25 "And which of you by worrying can add one hour to his life's span?

26 "So if you are not even able to do a very little thing [such as that], why are you worried about the rest?

27 "Consider the lilies *and* wildflowers, how they grow [in the open field]. They neither labor nor spin [wool to make clothing]; yet I tell you, not even Solomon in all his glory *and* splendor dressed himself like one of these. [1 Kin 10:4–7]

28 "But if this is how God clothes the grass which is in the field today and tomorrow is thrown into the furnace, how much more *will He clothe* you? You of little faith!

29 "So as for you, do not seek what you will eat and what you will drink; nor have an anxious *and* unsettled mind.

30 For all the [pagan] nations of the world greedily seek these things; and your [heavenly] Father [already] knows that you need them.

31 "But [strive for and actively] seek His kingdom, and these things will be given to you as well.

32 "Do not be afraid *and* anxious, little flock, for it is your Father's good pleasure to give you the kingdom.

33 "Sell your possessions (show compassion) and give [donations] to the poor. Provide money belts for yourselves that do not wear out, an unfailing *and* inexhaustible treasure in the heavens, where no thief comes near and no moth destroys.

34 "For where your treasure is, there your heart will be also.

Be in Readiness

35 "Be dressed and ready for active service, and keep your lamps continuously burning.

12:18–19 *This is what I will do.* Including verse 17, the word "I" appears six times, showing the selfish focus this man has as a result of his fortune. His plan is to store his abundant resources for himself, as though the assets were his alone and should be hoarded. This focus on the self is what Jesus is condemning.

12:27–29 *God clothes the grass.* This illustration indicates that God cares enough to provide beauty for the parts of His creation that have a short life. Why should we worry if God takes such care of even the smallest blade of grass? The Lord knows our problems and will provide us with what we need.

12:33 *Sell your possessions.* In contrast to the world's hoarding of possessions, the disciple must be generous with what God gives. By serving God and others, you can invest in your eternal future. You cannot take possessions with you in the next life, but you can store up an eternal treasure by giving to others (Php 4:17).

12:34 *where your treasure is.* What people

---

19 Ecc 11:9; 1Co 15:32; Jas 5:5 **20** Job 20:22; 27:8; Ps 52:7; Jas 4:14; Ps 39:6; Jer 17:11 **21** ver. 33; Mt 6:20; 1Ti 6:18,19; Jas 2:5 **22** Mt 6:25 **24** Job 38:41; Ps 147:9 **31** Mt 6:33 **32** Mt 11:25,26 **33** Mt 19:21; Ac 2:45; 4:34; Mt 6:20; Lk 16:9; 1Ti 6:19 **35** Eph 6:14; 1Pe 1:13; Mt 25:1

[36]"Be like men who are waiting for their master when he returns from the wedding feast, so that when he comes and knocks they may immediately open *the door* for him.

[37]"Blessed (happy, prosperous, to be admired) are those servants whom the master finds awake *and* watching when he arrives. I assure you *and* most solemnly say to you, he will prepare himself *to serve,* and will have them recline *at the table,* and will come and wait on them.

[38]"Whether he comes in the second watch (before midnight), or even in the third (after midnight), and finds them so [prepared and ready], blessed are those *servants.*

[39]"But be sure of this, that if the head of the house had known at what time the thief was coming, he [would have been awake and alert, and] would not have allowed his house to be broken into. [Matt 24:43, 44]

[40]"You too, be *continually* ready; because the Son of Man is coming at an hour that you do not expect."

[41]Peter said, "Lord, are You addressing this parable to us [disciples], or to everyone else as well?"

Parable of the Faithful Steward

[42]The Lord said, "Who then is the faithful and wise steward [of the estate], whom his master will put in charge over his household, to give *his servants* their portion of food at the proper time? [Matt 24:45–51]

[43]"Blessed (happy, prosperous, to be admired) is that servant whom his master finds so doing when he arrives.

[44]"I assure you *and* most solemnly say to you, he will put him in charge of all his possessions.

[45]"But if that servant says in his heart, 'My master is taking his time in coming,' and begins to beat the servants, both men and women, and to eat and drink and get drunk,

[46]the master of that servant will come on a day when he does not expect him and at an hour he does not know, and will cut him in pieces, and assign him a place with the unbelievers.

[47]"And that servant who knew his master's will, and yet did not get ready or act in accord with his will, will be beaten with many lashes [of the whip],

[48]but the one who did not know it and did things worthy of a beating, will receive only a few [lashes]. From everyone to whom much has been given, much will be required; and to whom they entrusted much, of him they will ask all the more. [Num 15:29, 30; Deut 25:2, 3]

Christ Divides Men

[49]"I have come to cast fire (judgment) on the earth; and how I wish that it were already kindled!

[50]"I have a baptism [of great suffering]

---

consider valuable is where their energy will be spent. Knowing God and investing in His purposes should be the treasure we seek.

12:38 *Whether he comes in the second watch (before midnight), or even in the third (after midnight).* This verse speaks of a return at an unusually late hour. The exact time referred to depends on which system of time was used. In the Roman system the second and third watch would be 9 P.M. to 3 A.M. By the Jewish method it would be 10 P.M. to 6 A.M.

12:41 *to us [disciples], or to everyone else.* Peter asked if Jesus' teaching was for the disciples only or for all people. Jesus did not answer the question directly. Instead He described a variety of categories of servants. Servants are those who belong to the Master and have their stewardship evaluated (19:11 – 27). Several responses, from faithfulness to blatant disobedience, are described in verses 42 – 48. The issue is who lives life in a way that looks for, and takes seriously, the return of Jesus (1Jn 2:28).

12:45 *begins to beat the servants, both men and women.* This servant is depicted as consciously doing the opposite of caring for others, and of treating the Master's return as irrelevant.

12:46 *will cut him in pieces.* The image of being slain indicates the severity of this judgment, especially in contrast to the whippings of verses 47 and 48.

12:49 *I have come to cast fire (judgment) on the earth.* Fire is an image associated with

37 Mt 24:46 **39** Mt 24:43; 1Th 5:2; 2Pe 3:10; Rev 3:3; 16:15 **40** Mt 24:44; 25:13; Mk 13:33; Lk 21:34,36; 1Th 5:6; 2Pe 3:12 **42** Mt 24:45; 25:21; 1Co 42 **44** Mt 24:47 **45** Mt 24:48 **47** Nu 15:30; Dt 25:2; Jn 9:41; 15:22; Ac 17:30; Jas 4:17 **48** Lev 5:17; 1Ti 1:13 **49** ver. 51 **50** Mt 20:22; Mk 10:38

with which to be baptized, and how [greatly] I am distressed until it is accomplished!

[51]"Do you suppose that I came to grant peace on earth? No, I tell you, but rather division [between believers and unbelievers]; [Matt 10:34–36]

[52]for from now on five in one household will be divided [over Me], three against two and two against three.

[53]"They will be divided, father against son and son against father, mother against daughter and daughter against mother, mother-in-law against daughter-in-law and daughter-in-law against mother-in-law." [Mic 7:6]

[54]He also said to the crowds, "When you see a cloud rising in the west, you immediately say, 'It is going to rain,' and that is how it turns out.

[55]"And when [you see that] a south wind is blowing, you say, 'It will be a hot day,' and it happens.

[56]"You hypocrites (play-actors, pretenders)! You know how to analyze *and* intelligently interpret the appearance of the earth and sky [to forecast the weather], but why do you not intelligently interpret this present time?

[57]"And why do you not even on your own initiative judge what is right?

[58]"For while you are going with your opponent [at law] to appear before a magistrate, on the way make an effort to settle, so that he does not drag you before the judge, and the judge does not [rule against you and] turn you over to the officer, and the officer does not throw you into prison. [Matt 5:25, 26]

[59]"I say to you, you [absolutely] will not get out of there until you have paid the very last cent."

Call to Repent

13 JUST AT that time some people came who told Jesus about the Galileans whose blood Pilate [the governor] had mixed with their sacrifices.

[2]Jesus replied to them, "Do you think that these Galileans were worse sinners than all *other* Galileans because they have suffered in this way?

[3]"I tell you, no; but unless you repent [change your old way of thinking, turn from your sinful ways and live changed lives], you will all likewise perish.

[4]"Or do you assume that those eighteen on whom the tower in Siloam fell and killed were worse sinners than all the others who live in Jerusalem?

[5]"I tell you, no; but unless you repent [change your old way of thinking, turn from your sinful ways and live changed lives], you will all likewise perish."

Parable of the Fig Tree

[6]Then He *began* telling them this parable: "A certain man had a fig tree that had been planted in his vineyard; and he came looking for fruit on it, but did not find any;

[7]so he said to the vineyard-keeper, 'For three years I have come looking for fruit on this fig tree and have found

---

God's judgment (Jer 5:14; 23:29). Jesus' coming brings judgment on those who refuse to accept Him and divides the believers from the faithless.

12:54 – 55 *a cloud rising in the west.* In Palestine, a western breeze meant moisture coming from the Mediterranean Sea. A south wind meant hot air coming from the desert.

12:56 *You hypocrites.* Jesus rebuked His audience for being able to discern the weather but not what God was doing through Him.

13:1 *Pilate.* Pilate was known for his insensitivity to the Jewish people early in his rule. The event probably occurred during the Feast of the Passover or Tabernacles, when Galileans most likely would have been at the temple.

13:5 *unless you repent.* The manner in which a person dies is not a measure of righteousness; what is important is not to die outside of God's grace and care. The way to avoid such a fate is to repent, to come to God through the care of the Physician Jesus (5:32).

13:6 *a fig tree.* This tree often represents God's blessing, or a people who have a special relationship with God (Mic 7:1 – 2). The man in this parable represents God; the fig tree represents Israel.

13:7 *For three years.* A fig tree was often given some time to bear good fruit since its root structure was complex and took time to develop. Three years would have been enough for the tree to yield some fruit.

---

51 ver. 49; Mt 10:34; Mic 7:6; Jn 7:43; 9:16; 10:19 **52** Mt 10:35 **54** Mt 16:2 **58** Pr 25:8; Mt 5:25; See Ps 32:6; Isa 55:6 **CHAPTER 13** **6** Isa 5:2; Mt 21:19

none. Cut it down! Why does it even
use up the ground [depleting the soil
and blocking the sunlight]?'
8"But he replied to him, 'Let it alone,
sir, [just] one more year until I dig
around it and put in fertilizer;
9and if it bears fruit after this, fine;
but if not, cut it down.' "

Healing on the Sabbath

10Now Jesus was teaching in one of
the synagogues on the Sabbath.
11And there was a woman who for
eighteen years had had an illness
caused by a spirit (demon). She was
bent double, and could not straighten
up at all.
12When Jesus saw her, He called her
over and said to her, "Woman, you are
released from your illness."
13Then He laid His hands on her;
and immediately she stood erect again
and she *began* glorifying *and* praising
God.
14But the leader of the synagogue,
indignant because Jesus had healed
on the Sabbath, *began* saying to the
crowd in response, "There are six days
in which work ought to be done; so
come on those days and be healed, and
not on the Sabbath day." [Ex 20:9, 10]
15But the Lord replied to him, "You
hypocrites (play-actors, pretenders)!
Does not each one of you on the Sab-
bath untie his ox or his donkey from
the stall and lead it away to water it?
16"And this woman, a daughter (de-
scendant) of Abraham whom Satan
has bound for eighteen long years,
should she not have been released
from this bond on the Sabbath day?"
17As He was saying this, all His op-
ponents were being humiliated; and
the entire crowd was rejoicing over
all the glorious things that were being
done by Him.

Parables of Mustard Seed and Leaven

18So this led Him to say, "What is
the kingdom of God like? And to what
shall I compare it? [Matt 13:31, 32;
Mark 4:30–32]
19"It is like a mustard seed, which
a man took and planted in his own
garden; and it grew and became a
tree, and THE BIRDS OF THE SKY FOUND
SHELTER *and* NESTED IN ITS BRANCHES."
[Ezek 17:23; Dan 4:12]
20And again He said, "To what shall
I compare the kingdom of God?
21"It is like leaven, which a woman
took and hid in three peck measures
of flour until it was all leavened."
[Matt 13:33]

Teaching in the Villages

22Jesus journeyed on through cities
and villages, teaching and making His
way toward Jerusalem.
23And someone asked Him, "Lord,
will only a few be saved [from the pen-
alties of the last judgment]?" And He
said to them,
24"Strive to enter through the nar-
row door [force aside unbelief and the
attractions of sin]; for many, I tell you,
will try to enter [by their own works]
and will not be able.
25"Once the head of the house gets up
and closes the door, and you begin to
stand outside and knock on the door
[again and again], saying, 'Lord, open
to us!' then He will answer you, 'I do
not know where you are from [for you
are not of My household].'
26"Then you will begin to say, 'We
ate and drank in Your presence, and
You taught in our streets';
27but He will say to you, 'I do not
know where you are from; DEPART FROM
ME, ALL YOU EVILDOERS!' [Ps 6:8]

13:15 *hypocrites.* When the ruler of the synagogue became indignant regarding Jesus' healing on the Sabbath (vv. 10–14), Jesus pointed out that basic compassion was shown to animals on the Sabbath, so how much more compassion should be shown to a suffering woman (v. 16)?

13:18–19 *mustard.* A tree of the mustard family would grow to about twelve feet. The image of birds nesting in the trees is found frequently in the Old Testament (Ps 104:12; Eze 17:22–24; Da 4:10–12).

13:26 *We ate and drank . . . You taught.* The appeal here is by people who experience

13 Mk 16:18; Ac 9:17 **14** Ex 20:9; Mt 12:10; Mk 3:2; Lk 6:7; 14:3 **15** Lk 14:5 **16** Lk 19:9 **18** Mt 13:31; Mk 4:30 **22** Mt 9:35; Mk 6:6 **24** Mt 7:13; See Jn 7:34; 8:21; 13:33; Ro 9:31 **25** Ps 32:6; Isa 55:6; Mt 25:10; Lk 6:46; Mt 7:23; 25:12 **27** ver. 25; Mt 7:23; 25:41; Ps 6:8; Mt 25:41

28"In that place there will be weeping
[in sorrow and pain] and grinding of
teeth [in distress and anger] when you
see Abraham and Isaac and Jacob and
all the prophets in the kingdom of God,
but yourselves being thrown out *and*
driven away.
29"And *people* will come from east
and west, and from north and south,
and they will sit down [and feast at the
table] in the kingdom of God.
30"And behold, *some* are last who
will be first, and *some* are first who
will be last."
31At that very hour some Pharisees
came up and said to Him, "Leave and
go away from here, because Herod
[Antipas] wants to kill You."
32And He said to them, "Go and
tell that fox [that sly, cowardly man],
'Listen carefully: I cast out demons
and perform healings today and to-
morrow, and on the third *day* I reach
My goal.'
33"Nevertheless I must travel on to-
day and tomorrow and the *day* after
that—for it cannot be that a prophet
would die outside of Jerusalem.
34"O Jerusalem, Jerusalem, who
kills the prophets and stones [to death]
those [messengers] who are sent to her
[by God]! How often I have wanted to
gather your children together [around
Me], just as a hen *gathers* her young
under her wings, but you were not
willing! [Matt 23:37–39]
35"Listen carefully: your house is left
to you desolate [abandoned by God and
destitute of His protection]; and I say to
you, you will not see Me until *the time*
comes when you say, 'BLESSED [to be
celebrated with praise] IS HE WHO COMES
IN THE NAME OF THE LORD!' " [Ps 118:26;
Jer 22:5]

Jesus Heals on the Sabbath

14 IT HAPPENED one Sabbath,
when He went for a meal at the
house of one of the ruling Pharisees,
that they were watching Him close-
ly *and* carefully [hoping to entrap
Him].
2And there in front of Him was a man
who had dropsy (extreme swelling).
3And Jesus asked the lawyers and
the Pharisees, "Is it lawful to heal on
the Sabbath, or not?"
4But they kept silent. Then He took
hold of the man and healed him, and
sent him on his way.
5Then He said to them, "Which one
of you, having a son or an ox that falls
into a well, will not immediately pull
him out on the Sabbath day?"
6And they were unable to reply to
this.

Jesus' presence. The passage primarily involves those Jews who witnessed Jesus' ministry. They were trying to gain entry into God's presence based simply on the fact that they had observed Jesus. Jesus refused them. Pointing out that it was not enough for them to have been close to Him. In order to have a relationship with God, one must embrace Jesus and come to know Him.

13:29 *east . . . west . . . north . . . south.* People would come from all corners of the earth for entrance into God's kingdom. This passage alludes to the inclusion of Gentiles.

13:30 *some are last who will be first.* There will be many surprises in God's kingdom. Those who are despised on earth — some Gentiles, for example — will be greatly honored in the kingdom. Conversely, those who are considered influential and powerful on earth — the Jewish religious leaders of Jesus' day, for example — will be excluded from the kingdom.

13:32 *Go and tell that fox.* Herod is portrayed as more curious than hostile. The reference here is to Herod's cunning. Jesus' reply seems to take the Pharisees' warning at face value.

13:34 *O Jerusalem, Jerusalem.* The double address indicates Jesus' deep sorrow (2Sa 18:33; Jer 22:29). The city had executed many of God's messengers. Stephen makes a similar point about the nation of Israel in Acts 7:51 – 53.

13:35 *BLESSED [to be celebrated with praise] IS HE.* This is a citation of Psalm 118:26. The people of Israel would not see the Messiah again until they were ready to receive Him and recognize that He was sent from God. Psalm 118 reflects the greeting of a priest to a group entering the temple. Jesus used the language of this psalm to illustrate God's greeting to Him.

28 Mt 8:12; 13:42; 24:51; Mt 8:11 **30** Mt 19:30; 20:16; Mk 10:31 **32** Heb 2:10 **34** Mt 23:37 **35** Lev 26:31,32; Ps 69:25; Isa 1:7; Da 9:27; Mic 3:12; Ps 118:26; Mt 21:9; Mk 11:10; Lk 19:38; Jn 12:13 **CHAPTER 14** **3** Mt 12:10 **5** Ex 23:5; Dt 22:4; Lk 13:15

Parable of the Guests

7 Now Jesus *began* telling a parable to the invited guests when He noticed how they had been selecting the places of honor *at the table*, saying to them,

8 "When you are invited by someone to a wedding feast, do not sit down [to eat] at the place of honor, since a more distinguished person than you may have been invited by the host, [Prov 25:6, 7]

9 and he who invited both of you will come and say to you, 'Give this man your place,' and then, in disgrace you proceed to take the last place.

10 "But when you are invited, go and sit down [to eat] at the last place, so that when your host comes, he will say to you, 'Friend, move up higher'; and then you will be honored in the presence of all who are at the table with you.

11 "For everyone who exalts himself will be humbled [before others], and he who *habitually* humbles himself (keeps a realistic self-view) will be exalted."

12 Jesus also went on to say to the one who had invited Him, "When you give a luncheon or a dinner, do not invite your friends or your brothers or your relatives or wealthy neighbors, otherwise they may also invite you in return and that will be your repayment.

13 "But when you give a banquet *or* a reception, invite the poor, the disabled, the lame, and the blind,

14 and you will be blessed because they cannot repay you; for you will be repaid at the resurrection of the righteous (the just, the upright)."

15 When one of those who were reclining *at the table* with Him heard this, he said to Him, "Blessed (happy, prosperous, to be admired) is he who will eat bread in the kingdom of God!"

Parable of the Dinner

16 But Jesus said to him, "A man was giving a big dinner, and he invited many *guests;*

17 and at the dinner hour he sent his servant to tell those who had been invited, 'Come, because everything is ready now.'

18 "But they all alike began to make excuses. The first one said to him, 'I have purchased a piece of land and I have to go out and see it; please consider me excused.'

19 "Another one said, 'I have purchased five yoke of oxen, and I am going to try them out; please consider me excused.'

20 "And another said, 'I have [recently] married a wife, and for that reason I am unable to come.' [Deut 24:5]

21 "So the servant came back and reported this to his master. Then [his master,] the head of the household, became angry [at the rejections of his invitation] and said to his servant, 'Go out quickly into the streets and the lanes of the city and bring in here the poor and the disabled and the blind and the lame.'

22 "And the servant [after returning] said, 'Sir, what you commanded has been done, and still there is room.'

23 "Then the master told the servant, 'Go out into the highways and along

---

14:7 *they had been selecting the places of honor.* In ancient times the best seats at a meal were those next to the host.

14:17 *those who had been invited.* In the ancient world, invitations to a feast were sent out well in advance of the meal. Then on the day of the feast, servants would announce the start of the meal. This parable is similar to the one in Matthew 22:1 – 4, but was probably spoken on a different occasion.

14:20 *I have [recently] married a wife.* While the Old Testament exempted a man from military duty because of marriage (Dt 20:7; 24:5), marriage was not an excuse for avoiding social duties. The general point here is that the man regarded his own affairs as more important than the feast.

14:21 *poor and the disabled and the blind and the lame.* This list matches that of verse 13. The disabled were excluded from full participation in Jewish worship (Lev 21:17 – 23). The master's second invitation extended the scope of the offer to those who were rejected by society.

14:23 *Go out into the highways.* The master's second invitation extended beyond the city

10 Pr 25:6,7 **11** Job 22:29; Ps 18:27; Pr 29:23; Mt 23:12; Lk 18:14; Jas 4:6; 1Pe 5:5 **13** Neh 8:10,12 **15** Rev 19:9 **16** Mt 22:2 **17** Pr 9:2,5

the hedges, and compel them to come
in, so that my house may be filled [with
guests].
24 ‘For I tell you, not one of those who
were invited [and declined] will taste
my dinner.’ ”

Discipleship Tested

25 Now large crowds were going
along with Jesus; and He turned and
said to them,
26 “If anyone comes to Me, and does
not hate his own father and mother
and wife and children and brothers
and sisters, yes, and even his own life
[in the sense of indifference to or rela-
tive disregard for them in comparison
with his attitude toward God]—he can-
not be My disciple.
27 “Whoever does not carry his own
cross [expressing a willingness to en-
dure whatever may come] and follow
after Me [believing in Me, conforming
to My example in living and, if need
be, suffering or perhaps dying because
of faith in Me] cannot be My disciple.
28 “For which one of you, when he
wants to build a watchtower [for his
guards], does not first sit down and cal-
culate the cost, to see if he has enough
to finish it?
29 “Otherwise, when he has laid a
foundation and is unable to finish [the
building], all who see it will begin to
ridicule him,
30 saying, ‘This man began to build
and was not able to finish!’
31 “Or what king, when he sets out to
meet another king in battle, will not
first sit down and consider whether
he is strong enough with ten thousand
men to encounter the one who is com-
ing against him with twenty thousand?
32 “Or else [if he feels he is not pow-
erful enough], while the other [king]
is still a far distance away, he sends
an envoy and asks for terms of peace.
33 “So then, none of you can be My
disciple who does not [carefully con-
sider the cost and then for My sake]
give up all his own possessions.
34 “Therefore, salt is good; but if salt
has become tasteless, with what will
it be seasoned?
35 “It is fit neither for the soil nor for
the manure pile; it is thrown away. He
who has ears to hear, let him hear *and*
heed My words.”

The Lost Sheep

15 NOW ALL the tax collectors
and sinners [including non-
observant Jews] were coming near
Jesus to listen to Him.
2 Both the Pharisees and the scribes
began muttering *and* complaining,
saying, “This man accepts *and* wel-
comes sinners and eats with them.”
3 So He told them this parable:
4 “What man among you, if he has a
hundred sheep and loses one of them,
does not leave the ninety-nine in the
wilderness and go after the one which
is lost, [searching] until he finds it?
[Matt 18:12–14]
5 “And when he has found it, he lays
it on his shoulders, rejoicing.
6 “And when he gets home, he calls
together his friends and his neighbors,
saying to them, ‘Rejoice with me, be-
cause I have found my lost sheep!’
7 “I tell you, in the same way there

---

limits, encouraging even more people to come to the feast. This may picture the inclusion of Gentiles in God’s salvation (Isa 49:6). The instruction to *compel* them to come in does not mean to force people in, but to urge them.

14:34 *salt is good.* In the ancient world, salt was often used as a catalyst for burning fuel such as cattle dung. The salt of the time was impure and could lose its strength over time, becoming useless. Jesus’ point is that the same is true of a “saltless” disciple.

15:1 *tax collectors and sinners.* The three parables of chapter 15 explain why Jesus associated with the despised groups while the Pharisees and scribes did not. The parables in this chapter are found only in Luke.

15:4 *a hundred sheep.* This was a medium-sized flock. The average herd ran from 20 to 200 head, while a flock of 300 or more was considered large.

15:7 *people who have no need of repentance.* This phrase is a rhetorical way of describing the scribes and Pharisees. A similar

24 Mt 21:43; 22:8; Ac 13:46 **26** Dt 13:6; 33:9; Mt 10:37; Ro 9:13; Rev 12:11 **27** Mt 16:24; Mk 8:34; Lk 9:23; 2Ti 3:12
28 Pr 24:27 **34** Mt 5:13; Mk 9:50 **CHAPTER 15** **1** Mt 9:10 **2** Ac 11:3; Gal 2:12 **4** Mt 18:12 **6** 1Pe 2:10,25 **7** Lk 5:32

will be more joy in heaven over one
sinner who repents than over ninety-
nine righteous people who have no
need of repentance.

The Lost Coin

8 “Or what woman, if she has ten
silver coins [each one equal to a day’s
wages] and loses one coin, does not
light a lamp and sweep the house and
search carefully until she finds it?
9 “And when she has found it, she
calls together her [women] friends and
neighbors, saying, ‘Rejoice with me,
because I found the lost coin!’
10 “In the same way, I tell you, there
is joy in the presence of the angels of
God over one sinner who repents [that
is, changes his inner self—his old way
of thinking, regrets past sins, lives his
life in a way that proves repentance;
and seeks God’s purpose for his life].”

The Prodigal Son

11 Then He said, “A certain man had
two sons.
12 “The younger of them [inappropri-
ately] said to his father, ‘Father, give me
the share of the property that falls to
me.’ So he divided the estate between
them. [Deut 21:15–17]
13 “A few days later, the younger son
gathered together everything [that he
had] and traveled to a distant country,
and there he wasted his fortune in
reckless *and* immoral living.
14 “Now when he had spent every-
thing, a severe famine occurred in that
country, and he began to do without
and be in need.
15 “So he went and forced himself on
one of the citizens of that country, who
sent him into his fields to feed pigs.
16 “He would have gladly eaten the
[carob] pods that the pigs were eating
[but they could not satisfy his hunger],
and no one was giving *anything* to
him. [Jer 30:14]
17 “But when he [finally] came to
his senses, he said, ‘How many of my
father’s hired men have more than
enough food, while I am dying here
of hunger!
18 ‘I will get up and go to my father,
and I will say to him, “Father, I have
sinned against heaven and in your
sight.
19 “I am no longer worthy to be called
your son; [just] treat me like one of
your hired men.” ’
20 “So he got up and came to his fa-
ther. But while he was still a long way
off, his father saw him and was moved
with compassion *for him,* and ran and
embraced him and kissed him.
21 “And the son said to him, ‘Father,

---

description is found in 5:31, where it is said that some do not need a physician. The scribes and Pharisees believed that they did not need to repent because they were not lost.

15:8 *ten silver coins.* A drachma was a silver coin equal to a day’s wage for a basic laborer. The woman needed a lamp because she lived in a windowless house. Her broom for sweeping would have been made of palm twigs.

15:15 *to feed pigs.* Feeding pigs was an insulting job for a Jewish person, since pigs were unclean according to the law of Moses.

15:20 *his father saw him and was moved with compassion.* Many scholars feel that the emphasis on the son in this parable causes people to miss the more important point, namely, the importance of the father’s welcoming role. Still others think it could even be called the Parable of the Elder Brother. Interestingly, both brothers underestimate their father’s love and grace. The younger brother is slow to realize the extent and permanence of his father’s love. The elder brother has trouble understanding that the restored relationship with the younger son is vital to the life of the father. What makes the dramatic conversion possible is the younger son’s knowledge that he will be accepted when he returns. While there are consequences to his behavior (his money is gone), he is welcomed to be a part of the family again. In many ways the welcome is even more than he could have hoped for. What is amazing about grace is that it is always more than we expect or deserve.

15:21 *no longer worthy to be called your son.* Despite his awareness of being accepted by his father, the son continued his confession of his sin. He then asked to become one of his father’s servants. Similarly, a sinner realizes that he or she brings nothing to and deserves nothing from God, but must rely completely on God’s mercy.

---

12 Mk 12:44 **20** Ac 2:39; Eph 2:13,17 **21** Ps 51:4

I have sinned against heaven and in your sight; I am no longer worthy to be called your son.'
[22]"But the father said to his servants, 'Quickly bring out the best robe [for the guest of honor] and put it on him; and give him a ring for his hand, and sandals for his feet. [Gen 41:42; Zech 3:4]
[23]'And bring the fattened calf and slaughter it, and let us [invite everyone and] feast and celebrate;
[24]for this son of mine was [as good as] dead and is alive again; he was lost and has been found.' So they began to celebrate.
[25]"Now his older son was in the field; and when he returned and approached the house, he heard music and dancing.
[26]"So he summoned one of the servants and *began* asking what this [celebration] meant.
[27]"And he said to him, 'Your brother has come, and your father has killed the fattened calf because he has received him back safe and sound.'
[28]"But the elder brother became angry *and* deeply resentful and was not willing to go in; and his father came out and *began* pleading with him.
[29]"But he said to his father, 'Look! These many years I have served you, and I have never neglected *or* disobeyed your command. Yet you have never given me [so much as] a young goat, so that I might celebrate with my friends;
[30]but when this [other] son of yours arrived, who has devoured your estate with immoral women, you slaughtered that fattened calf for him!'
[31]"The father said to him, 'Son, you are always with me, and all that is mine is yours.
[32]'But it was fitting to celebrate and rejoice, for this brother of yours was [as good as] dead and *has begun* to live. He was lost and has been found.'"

The Unjust Steward (Manager)

16 NOW JESUS was also saying to the disciples, "There was a certain rich man who had a manager [of his estate], and accusations [against this man] were brought to him, that this man was squandering his [master's] possessions.
[2]"So he called him and said to him, 'What is this I hear about you? Give an accounting of your management [of my affairs], for you can no longer be [my] manager.'
[3]"The manager [of the estate] said to himself, 'What will I do, since my master is taking the management away from me? I am not strong enough to dig [for a living], and I am ashamed to beg.
[4]'I know what I will do, so that when I am removed from the management, people [who are my master's debtors] will welcome me into their homes.'
[5]"So he summoned his master's debtors one by one, and he said to the first, 'How much do you owe my master?'
[6]"He said, 'A hundred measures of [olive] oil.' And he said to him, 'Take your bill, and sit down quickly and write fifty.'
[7]"Then he said to another, 'And how much do you owe?' He said, 'A hundred measures of wheat.' He said to him, 'Take your bill, and write eighty.'
[8]"And his master commended the unjust manager [not for his misdeeds,

15:24 *dead . . . alive again . . . lost . . . found.* The total transformation of the prodigal son is summarized in these two contrasts. Such a transformation is a reason to celebrate. It is also the reason Jesus chose to associate with the lost.
15:28 *the elder brother became angry.* The elder brother's unhappiness over a fatted calf (v. 27) being killed to celebrate the return of his undisciplined brother illustrates the response of the Pharisees and scribes at the prospect of sinners becoming acceptable to God.

16:1 *a manager.* This was a servant who supervised and administered an estate. The charge brought against this manager is incompetence.
16:8 *And his master commended the unjust manager.* The master recognized the foresight in the steward's generosity. It is debatable whether the steward was dishonest and robbed the master by such reductions or was shrewd in using his authority to discount the goods (vv. 6–7). The fact that the master commended the steward may suggest that the master was not robbed

24 ver. 32 **32** ver. 24 **CHAPTER 16** **2** Ecc 11:9,10; Ro 14:12; 2Co 5:10; 1Pe 4:5 **8** Jn 12:36; Eph 5:8; 1Th 5:5

PARABLES OF JESUS

PARABLE	MATTHEW	MARK	LUKE
Lamp under a bowl	5:14–15	4:21–22	8:16; 11:33
Wise and foolish builders	7:24–27		6:47–49
New cloth on an old coat	9:16	2:21	5:36
New wine in old wineskins	9:17	2:22	5:37–38
Sower and the soils	13:3–8, 18–23	4:3–8,14–20	8:5–8,11–15
Weeds	13:24–30,36–43		
Mustard seed	13:31–32	4:30–32	13:18–19
Yeast	13:33		13:20–21
Hidden treasure	13:44		
Valuable pearl	13:45–46		
Net	13:47–50		
Owner of a house	13:52		
Lost sheep	18:12–14		15:4–7
Unmerciful servant	18:23–34		
Workers in the vineyard	20:1–16		
Two sons	21:28–32		
Tenants	21:33–44	12:1–11	20:9–18
Wedding banquet	22:2–14		
Fig tree	24:32–35	13:28–29	21:29–31
Faithful and wise servant	24:45–51		12:42–48
Ten virgins	25:1–13		
Bags of gold (minas)	25:14–30		19:12–27
Sheep and goats	25:31–46		
Growing seed		4:26–29	
Watchful servants		13:35–37	12:35–40
Moneylender			7:41–43
Good Samaritan			10:30–37
Friend in need			11:5–8
Rich fool			12:16–21
Unfruitful fig tree			13:6–9
Lowest seat at the feast			14:7–14
Great banquet			14:16–24
Cost of discipleship			14:28–33
Lost coin			15:8–10
Lost (prodigal) son			15:11–32
Shrewd manager			16:1–8
Rich man and Lazarus			16:19–31
Master and his servant			17:7–10
Persistent widow			18:2–8
Pharisee and tax collector			18:10–14

but] because he had acted shrewdly
[by preparing for his future unem-
ployment]; for the sons of this age [the
non-believers] are shrewder in relation
to their own kind [that is, to the ways
of the secular world] than are the sons
of light [the believers].
9“And I tell you [learn from this],
make friends for yourselves [for eter-
nity] by means of the wealth of un-
righteousness [that is, use material
resources as a way to further the work
of God], so that when it runs out, they
will welcome you into the eternal
dwellings.
10“He who is faithful in a very little
thing is also faithful in much; and he
who is dishonest in a very little thing
is also dishonest in much.
11“Therefore if you have not been
faithful in the *use of* earthly wealth,
who will entrust the true *riches* to you?
12“And if you have not been faith-
ful in *the use of* that [earthly wealth]
which belongs to another [whether
God or man, and of which you are a
trustee], who will give you that which
is your own?
13“No servant can serve two masters;
for either he will hate the one and love
the other, or he will stand devotedly
by the one and despise the other. You
cannot serve *both* God and mammon
[that is, your earthly possessions or
anything else you trust in and rely on
instead of God].”
14Now the Pharisees, who were lov-
ers of money, were listening to all these
things and were sneering *and* ridicul-
ing Him.
15So He said to them, “You are the
ones who declare yourselves just *and*
upright in the sight of men, but God
knows your hearts [your thoughts,
your desires, your secrets]; for that
which is highly esteemed among
men is detestable in the sight of God.
[1 Sam 16:7; Prov 21:2]
16“The Law and the [writings of the]
Prophets were proclaimed until John;
since then the gospel of the kingdom
of God has been *and* continues to be
preached, and everyone tries forcefully
to go into it.
17“Yet it is easier for heaven and
earth to pass away than for a single
stroke of a letter of the Law to fail *and*
become void.
18“Whoever divorces his wife and
marries another commits adultery, and
he who marries one who is divorced
from her husband commits adultery.
[Matt 5:31, 32]

The Rich Man and Lazarus

19“Now there was a certain rich man
who was habitually dressed in expen-
sive purple and fine linen, and cele-
brated *and* lived joyously in splendor
every day.
20“And a poor man named Lazarus,
was laid at his gate, covered with sores.
21“He [eagerly] longed to eat the
crumbs which fell from the rich man's
table. Besides, even the dogs were com-
ing and licking his sores.
22“Now it happened that the poor
man died and his spirit was carried
away by the angels to Abraham's
bosom (paradise); and the rich man
also died and was buried.
23“In Hades (the realm of the dead),

---

and that the steward's reduction was the result of either an adherence to the law or a lowering of the steward's own commission.

16:9 *wealth of unrighteousness.* This is money and should be used generously to build works that last. Money is called unrighteous because it often manifests unrighteousness and selfishness in people (1Ti 6:6–10,17–19; Jas 1:9–11; 5:1–6).

16:19 *dressed in expensive purple.* Purple clothes were extremely expensive because they were made with a special dye extracted from a kind of snail.

16:20–21 *licking his sores.* To have his sores licked by dogs threatened Lazarus with infection as well as ritual uncleanness, since dogs fed on garbage, including dead animals.

16:22 *Abraham's bosom.* This was the blessed place of the dead. Angelic escorts for the dead were also known in Judaism. This verse indicates that the dead know their fate immediately.

9 Da 4:27; Mt 6:19; 19:21; Lk 11:41; 1Ti 6:17-19 **10** Mt 25:21; Lk 19:17 **13** Mt 6:24 **14** Mt 23:14 **15** Lk 10:29; Ps 7:9; 1Sa 16:7 **16** Mt 4:17; 11:12,13; Lk 7:29 **17** Ps 102:26,27; Isa 40:8; 51:6; Mt 5:18; 1Pe 1:25 **18** Mt 5:32; 19:9; Mk 10:11; 1Co 7:10,11

being in torment, he looked up and saw Abraham far away and Lazarus in his bosom (paradise).

[24]"And he cried out, 'Father Abraham, have mercy on me, and send Lazarus so that he may dip the tip of his finger in water and cool my tongue, because I am in severe agony in this flame.'

[25]"But Abraham said, 'Son, remember that in your lifetime you received your good things [all the comforts and delights], and Lazarus likewise bad things [all the discomforts and distresses]; but now he is comforted here [in paradise], while you are in severe agony.

[26]'And besides all this, between us and you [people] a great chasm has been fixed, so that those who want to come over from here to you will not be able, and none may cross over from there to us.'

[27]"So the rich man said, 'Then, father [Abraham], I beg you to send Lazarus to my father's house—

[28]for I have five brothers—in order that he may *solemnly* warn them *and* witness to them, so that they too will not come to this place of torment.'

[29]"But Abraham said, 'They have [the Scriptures given by] Moses and the [writings of the] Prophets; let them listen to them.'

[30]"He replied, 'No, father Abraham, but if someone from the dead goes to them, they will repent [they will change their old way of thinking and seek God and His righteousness].'

[31]"And he said to him, 'If they do not listen to [the messages of] Moses and the Prophets, they will not be persuaded even if someone rises from the dead.' "

Instructions

17 JESUS SAID to His disciples, "Stumbling blocks [temptations and traps set to lure one to sin] are sure to come, but woe (judgment is coming) to him through whom they come! [Matt 18:7]

[2]"It would be better for him if a millstone [as large as one turned by a donkey] were hung around his neck and he were hurled into the sea, than for him to cause one of these little ones to stumble [in sin and lose faith]. [Matt 18:6; Mark 9:42]

[3]"Pay attention *and* always be on guard [looking out for one another]! If your brother sins *and* disregards God's precepts, solemnly warn him; and if he repents *and* changes, forgive him.

[4]"Even if he sins against you seven times a day, and returns to you seven times and says, 'I repent,' you must forgive him [that is, give up resentment and consider the offense recalled and annulled]."

[5]The apostles said to the Lord, "Increase our faith [our ability to confidently trust in God and in His power]."

[6]And the Lord said, "If you have [confident, abiding] faith in God [even as small] as a mustard seed, you could say to this mulberry tree [which has very strong roots], 'Be pulled up by the roots and be planted in the sea'; and [if the request was in agreement with the will of God] it would have obeyed you. [Matt 17:20; Mark 11:23; 1 John 5:14]

16:24 *I am in severe agony in this flame.* The rich man desired relief from his suffering. The image of thirst for the experience of judgment is common (Isa 5:13; 65:13; Hos 2:3).
16:29 *They have [the Scriptures given by] Moses and the [writings of the] Prophets.* Abraham made it clear that the rich man's brothers should have known what to do, since they had the message of God in the ancient writings. The point here is that generosity with money and care for the poor were taught in the Old Testament (Dt 14:28–29; Isa 3:14–15; Mic 6:10–11).
17:1–2 *woe (judgment is coming) to him.* Jesus warned that judgment awaits those who cause others to stumble. The severe form of the warning suggests that false teaching, or leading someone into apostasy, is in view here. ***a millstone.*** This was a heavy stone used in a grinding mill.

24 Zec 14:12; Isa 66:24; Mk 9:44 **25** Job 21:13; Lk 6:24 **29** Isa 8:20; 34:16; Jn 5:39,45; Ac 15:21; 17:11 **31** Jn 12:10,11 **CHAPTER 17** **1** Mt 18:6,7; Mk 9:42; 1Co 11:19 **3** Mt 18:15,21; Lev 19:17; Pr 17:10; Jas 5:19 **6** Mt 17:20; 21:21; Mk 9:23; 11:23

7 “Which of you who has a servant
plowing or tending sheep will say to
him when he comes in from the field,
‘Come at once and sit down to eat?’
8 “Will he not instead say to him,
‘Prepare something for me to eat,
and *appropriately* clothe yourself [for
service] and serve me while I eat and
drink; then afterward you may eat
and drink?’
9 “He does not thank the servant just
because he did what he was ordered to
do, does he?
10 “So you too, when you have done
everything that was assigned *and*
commanded you, say, ‘We are unwor-
thy servants [undeserving of praise or
a reward, for we have not gone beyond
our obligation]; we have *merely* done
what we ought to do.’ ”

Ten Lepers Cleansed

11 While Jesus was on the way to
Jerusalem, He was passing [along the
border] between Samaria and Galilee.
12 As He entered a village, He was met
by ten lepers who stood at a distance;
13 and they raised their voices and
called out, “Jesus, Master, have mercy
on us!”
14 When He saw them, He said to
them, “Go and show yourselves to the
priests.” And as they went, they were
[miraculously] healed *and* made clean.
[Lev 14:2–32]
15 One of them, when he saw that he
was healed, turned back, glorifying
and praising *and* honoring God with
a loud voice;
16 and he lay face downward at Jesus’
feet, thanking Him [over and over]. He
was a Samaritan.
17 Then Jesus asked, “Were not ten [of
you] cleansed? Where are the [other]
nine?
18 “Was there no one found to return
and to give thanks *and* praise to God,
except this foreigner?”
19 Jesus said to him, “Get up and go
[on your way]. Your faith [your per-
sonal trust in Me and your confidence
in God’s power] has restored you to
health.”
20 Now having been asked by the
Pharisees when the kingdom of God
would come, He replied, “The kingdom
of God is not coming with signs to be
observed *or* with a visible display;
21 nor will people say, ‘Look! Here it
is!’ or, ‘There it is!’ For the kingdom
of God is among you [because of My
presence].”

Second Coming Foretold

22 Then He said to the disciples, “The
time will come when you will long to
see [even] one of the days of the Son of
Man, and you will not see it.
23 “They will say to you, ‘Look [the
Messiah is] there!’ *or* ‘Look [He is]
here!’ Do not go away [to see Him],
and do not run after *them.*
24 “For just like the lightning, when
it flashes out of one part of the sky,
gives light to the other part of the sky,
so [visible] will the Son of Man be in
His day.
25 “But first He must suffer many

17:20 *kingdom of God.* In ancient Israel there was an expectation that the kingdom of God would come with cosmic signs (Joel 2:28–32). Jesus’ concept of the kingdom of God, however, was broader than the time of the final consummation.

17:21 *among you.* This verse indicates that there was an aspect of kingdom promise involved in Jesus’ first coming. The kingdom of God is among earthly kingdoms today; but one day the kingdom of God will swallow up all rival kingdoms (Rev 11:15). In verses 22–37, Jesus makes it clear that the kingdom has two phases — one now and one to come. In the beginning of His kingdom on earth, God first prepares a King to rule; then He gathers a people for Him to rule over; then He gives the Ruler a realm in which to reign. The kingdom of God is not the same as the church, though the church is a part of the kingdom. The kingdom now is the presence of God alongside earthly kingdoms. One day, however, Jesus will rule over all, and He will share that rule with His people (Rev 2:26–27; 5:9–10; 20:4–6).

---

8 Lk 12:37 **10** Job 22:3; 35:7; Ps 16:2; Mt 25:30; Ro 3:12; 11:35; 1Co 9:16,17; Php 11 **11** Lk 9:51,52; Jn 4:4 **12** Lev 13:46 **14** Lev 13:2; 14:2; Mt 8:4; Lk 5:14 **19** Mt 9:22; Mk 5:34; 10:52; Lk 7:50; 8:48; 18:42 **21** ver. 23; Ro 14:17 **22** See Mt 9:15; Jn 17:12 **23** Mt 24:23; Mk 13:21; Lk 21:8 **24** Mt 27:27 **25** Mk 8:31; 9:31; 10:33; Lk 9:22

things and be repudiated *and* rejected *and* considered unfit [to be the Messiah] by this [unbelieving] generation.

26 “And just as it was in the days of Noah, so it will be in the time of [the second coming of] the Son of Man:

27 the people were eating, they were drinking, they were marrying, they were being given in marriage, [they were indifferent to God] until the day that Noah went into the ark, and the flood came and destroyed them all. [Gen 6:5–8; 7:6–24]

28 “It was the same as it was in the days of Lot. People were eating, they were drinking, they were buying, they were selling, they were planting, they were building [carrying on business as usual, without regard for their sins];

29 but on the [very] day that Lot left Sodom it rained fire and brimstone (burning sulfur) from heaven and destroyed them all.

30 “It will be just the same on the day that the Son of Man is revealed. [Gen 18:20–33; 19:24, 25]

31 “On that day, whoever is on the housetop, with his belongings in the house, must not come down [and go inside] to take them out; and likewise whoever is in the field must not turn back.

32 “Remember [what happened to] Lot’s wife [when she looked back]! [Gen 19:26]

33 “Whoever seeks to save his life will [eventually] lose it [through death], and whoever loses *his life* [in this world] will keep it [from the consequences of sin and separation from God]. [Matt 10:39; 16:25; Mark 8:35; Luke 9:24; John 12:25]

34 “I tell you, on that night [when Messiah comes again] there will be two [sleeping] in one bed; the one (the non-believer) will be taken [away in judgment] and the other (the believer) will be left.

35 “There will be two women grinding [at the mill] together; the one (the non-believer) will be taken [away in judgment] and the other (the believer) will be left.

36 [“Two men will be in the field; one will be taken and the other will be left.”]

37 And they asked Him, “Where, Lord?” He answered, “Where the corpse is, there the vultures will be gathered.”

Parables on Prayer

18 NOW JESUS was telling the disciples a parable to make the point that at all times they ought to pray and not give up *and* lose heart,

2 saying, “In a certain city there was a judge who did not fear God and had no respect for man.

3 “There was a [desperate] widow in that city and she kept coming to him and saying, ‘Give me justice *and* legal protection from my adversary.’

4 “For a time he would not; but later he said to himself, ‘Even though I do not fear God nor respect man,

5 yet because this widow *continues* to bother me, I will give her justice

---

17:26 *in the days of Noah.* At that time people paid little attention to God and faced judgment as a result (Ge 6:5 – 13). The same will be the case at Jesus’ return.

17:32 *Lot’s wife.* This woman represents those who are attached to earthly things, those whose hearts are still in this world. Like Lot’s wife, such people will perish (Ge 19:26).

17:34 – 37 *one (the non-believer) will be taken.* This phrase suggests judgment such as when the soldiers took Jesus to crucify Him. Verse 37 makes it clear that those who are taken are taken to final judgment. The vultures will be gathered. When judgment comes, it will be final and terrible, with the stench of death and the presence of vultures everywhere. No one will need to look for the place of judgment; the presence of the birds will reveal where the carcasses are.

18:2 *a judge.* The Romans allowed the Jews to manage most of their own affairs. This judge did not fear God, and was therefore probably a secular judge, not a religious one. The dishonest judge represents corrupted power.

18:5 *this widow continues to bother me.* The persistence of the widow is the lesson of the

26 Ge 7; Mt 24:37 **28** Ge 19 **29** Ge 19:16,24 **30** 2Th 1:7 **31** Mt 24:17; Mk 13:15 **32** Ge 19:26 **33** Mt 10:39; 16:25; Mk 8:35; Lk 9:24; Jn 12:25 **34** Mt 24:40,41; 1Th 4:17 **37** Job 39:30; Mt 24:28 **CHAPTER 18** **1** Lk 11:5; 21:36; Ro 12:12; Eph 6:18; Col 4:2; 1Th 5:17 **5** Lk 11:8

and legal protection; otherwise by
continually coming she [will be an
intolerable annoyance and she] will
wear me out.' "
6 Then the Lord said, "Listen to what
the unjust judge says!
7 "And will not [our just] God defend
and avenge His elect [His chosen ones]
who cry out to Him day and night?
Will He delay [in providing justice] on
their behalf?
8 "I tell you that He will defend *and*
avenge them quickly. However, when
the Son of Man comes, will He find
[this kind of persistent] faith on the
earth?"

The Pharisee and the Tax Collector

9 He also told this parable to some
people who trusted in themselves *and*
were confident that they were righ-
teous [posing outwardly as upright
and in right standing with God], and
who viewed others with contempt:
10 "Two men went up into the temple
[enclosure] to pray, one a Pharisee and
the other a tax collector.
11 "The Pharisee stood [ostentatious-
ly] and began praying to himself [in
a self-righteous way, saying]: 'God, I
thank You that I am not like the rest
of men—swindlers, unjust (dishon-
est), adulterers—or even like this tax
collector.
12 'I fast twice a week; I pay tithes of
all that I get.'
13 "But the tax collector, standing at
a distance, would not even raise his
eyes toward heaven, but was striking
his chest [in humility and repentance],
saying, 'God, be merciful *and* gracious
to me, the [especially wicked] sinner
[that I am]!'
14 "I tell you, this man went to his home
justified [forgiven of the guilt of sin and
placed in right standing with God] rath-
er than the other man; for everyone who
exalts himself will be humbled, but he
who humbles himself [forsaking self-
righteous pride] will be exalted."
15 Now they were also bringing their
babies to Him, so that He would touch
and bless them, and when the disciples
noticed it, they *began* reprimanding
them.
16 But Jesus called them to Himself,
saying [to the apostles], "Allow the
children to come to Me, and do not
forbid them, for the kingdom of God
belongs to such as these.
17 "I assure you *and* most solemnly
say to you, whoever does not receive the
kingdom of God [with faith and humil-
ity] like a child will not enter it at all."

The Rich Young Ruler

18 A certain ruler asked Him, "Good
Teacher [You who are essentially and
morally good], what shall I do to in-
herit eternal life [that is, eternal sal-
vation in the Messiah's kingdom]?"
[Matt 19:16–29; Mark 10:17–30]
19 Jesus said to him, "Why do you
call Me good? No one is [essentially
and morally] good except God alone.

---

parable. God is a counterexample to the judge. God does not begrudge answering prayer. Jesus' point is that, if an insensitive judge will respond to the continual requests of a widow, God will certainly respond to the continual prayers of believers.

18:11 – 12 *God, I thank You.* The tone of the prayer reveals the Pharisee's problem. He uses the pronoun "I" five times in two verses. The Pharisee's attitude seems to be that God should be grateful to him for his commitment. The man obviously looked down on other people and was proud of his fasting and tithing.

18:13 *God, be merciful and gracious to me, the [especially wicked] sinner.* This is an example of the humble spirit of repentance that Jesus commends. The tax collector knew that he could not say or bring anything to enhance his standing with God. He knew that only God's mercy and grace, and not his own works, could deliver him.

18:16 *But Jesus called them.* Jesus used the thoughtlessness of his disciples to make two points: (1) all people, even little children, are important to God; and (2) the kingdom of God consists of those who respond to Him with the trust that a little child gives to a parent.

7 Rev 6:10 **8** Heb 10:37; 2Pe 3:8,9 **9** Lk 10:29; 16:15 **11** Ps 135:2; Isa 1:15; 58:2; Rev 3:17 **14** Job 22:29; Mt 23:12; Lk 14:11; Jas 4:6; 1Pe 5:5 **15** Mt 19:13; Mk 10:13 **16** 1Co 14:20; 1Pe 2:2 **17** Mk 10:15 **18** Mt 19:16; Mk 10:17

20“You know the commandments: ‘DO NOT COMMIT ADULTERY, DO NOT MURDER, DO NOT STEAL, DO NOT TESTIFY FALSELY, HONOR YOUR FATHER AND YOUR MOTHER.’ ” [Ex 20:12–16; Deut 5:16–20]

21He replied, “I have kept all these things from my youth.”

22When Jesus heard this, He said to him, “You still lack one thing; sell everything that you have and distribute the money to the poor, and you will have [abundant] treasure in heaven; and come, follow Me [becoming My disciple, believing and trusting in Me and walking the same path of life that I walk].”

23But when he heard these things, he became very sad, for he was extremely rich.

24Jesus looked at him and said, “How difficult it is for those who are wealthy to enter the kingdom of God!

25“For it is easier for a camel to go through the eye of a needle than for a rich man [who places his faith in wealth or status] to enter the kingdom of God.”

26And those who heard it said, “Then who can be saved?”

27But He said, “The things that are impossible with people are possible with God.” [Gen 18:14; Jer 32:17]

28Peter said, “Look, we have left all [things—homes, families, businesses] and followed You.”

29And He said to them, “I assure you *and* most solemnly say to you, there is no one who has left house or wife or brothers or parents or children for the sake of the kingdom of God,

30who will not receive many times as much in this present age and in the age to come, eternal life.”

31Then taking the twelve [disciples] aside, He said to them, “Listen carefully: we are going up to Jerusalem, and all things that have been written through the prophets about the Son of Man will be fulfilled *and* completed. [Is 53:1–12]

32“He will be betrayed *and* handed over to the Gentiles (Roman authorities), and will be mocked *and* ridiculed and insulted *and* abused and spit on, [Is 50:6]

33and after they have scourged Him, they will kill Him; and on the third day He will rise [from the dead].” [Ps 16:10]

34But the disciples understood none of these things [about the approaching death and resurrection of Jesus]. This statement was hidden from them, and they did not grasp the [meaning of the] things that were said [by Jesus].

Bartimaeus Receives Sight

35As He was approaching Jericho [on His way to Jerusalem], it happened that a blind man was sitting beside the road begging. [Matt 20:29–34; Mark 10:46–52]

36Now when he heard a crowd going by, he *began* to ask what this was [about].

37They told him, “Jesus of Nazareth is passing by.”

18:22 *sell everything that you have and distribute the money to the poor.* This was a radical test of the ruler's concern for others (12:33 – 34). Jesus was determining whether the ruler's treasure (Mt 6:19 – 21) lay with God or money (16:13). Jesus was not establishing a new requirement for being saved. He was examining the ruler's orientation to God by directly confronting him with the very thing that was hindering him — namely, his wealth.

18:24 – 25 *For it is easier for a camel to go through the eye of a needle.* Jesus used this figure of speech to emphasize the difficulty of turning from wealth to find salvation. Because many Jewish people believed that wealth was evidence of God's blessing, Jesus' statements would have been shocking to His audience.

18:34 *the disciples understood none of these things.* The disciples may have understood something of what Jesus said, but they could not understand why God's Chosen One would have to face such suffering. For those who were expecting the Promised One to be an exalted figure who would deliver God's people, it would be very difficult to reconcile such an expectation with such terrible suffering.

20 Ex 20:12,16; Dt 5:16-20; Ro 13:9; Eph 6:2; Col 3:20 **22** Mt 6:19,20; 19:21; 1Ti 6:19 **24** Pr 11:28; Mt 19:23; Mk 10:23 **27** Jer 32:17; Zec 8:6; Mt 19:26; Lk 1:37 **28** Mt 19:27 **29** Dt 33:9 **30** Job 42:10 **31** Mt 16:21; 17:22; 20:17; Mk 10:32; Ps 22; Isa 53 **32** Mt 27:2; Lk 23:1; Jn 18:28; Ac 3:13 **34** Mk 9:32; Lk 2:50; 9:45; Jn 10:6; 12:16 **35** Mt 20:29; Mk 10:46

38So he shouted out, saying, "Jesus,
Son of David (Messiah), have mercy
on me!"
39Those who were leading the way
were sternly telling him to keep quiet;
but he screamed all the more, "Son of
David, have mercy on me!"
40Then Jesus stopped and ordered
that the blind man be led to Him; and
when he came near, Jesus asked him,
41"What do you want Me to do for
you?" He said, "Lord, let me regain
my sight!"
42Jesus said to him, "Regain your
sight; your [personal trust and confi-
dent] faith [in Me] has made you well."
43Immediately he regained his sight
and *began* following Jesus, glorify-
ing *and* praising *and* honoring God.
And all the people, when they saw it,
praised God.

Zacchеus Converted

19 JESUS ENTERED Jericho and
was passing through.
2And there was a man called Zac-
cheus; he was a chief tax collector [a
superintendent to whom others report-
ed], and he was rich.
3Zaccheus was trying to see who
Jesus was, but he could not see be-
cause of the crowd, for he was short
in stature.
4So he ran on ahead [of the crowd]
and climbed up in a sycamore tree in
order to see Him, for He was about to
pass through that way.
5When Jesus reached the place, He
looked up and said to him, "Zaccheus,
hurry and come down, for today I must
stay at your house."
6So Zaccheus hurried and came
down, and welcomed Jesus with joy.
7When the people saw it, they all
began muttering [in discontent], "He
has gone to be the guest of a man who
is a [notorious] sinner."
8Zaccheus stopped and said to the
Lord, "See, Lord, I am [now] giving
half of my possessions to the poor,
and if I have cheated anyone out of
anything, I will give back four times
as much." [Ex 22:1; Lev 6:5; Num 5:6, 7]
9Jesus said to him, "Today salvation
has come to this household, because
he, too, is a [spiritual] son of Abraham;
10for the Son of Man has come to
seek and to save that which was lost."

Parable of Money Usage

11While they were listening to these
things, Jesus went on to tell a parable,
because He was near Jerusalem, and
they assumed that the kingdom of God
was going to appear immediately [as
soon as He reached the city].
12So He said, "A nobleman went to a
distant country to obtain for himself a
kingdom, and [then] to return.
13"So he called ten of his servants,
and gave them ten minas [one apiece,
each equal to about a hundred days'
wages] and said to them, 'Do business
[with this] until I return.'
14"But his citizens [the residents of
his new kingdom] hated him and sent

18:38 ***Son of David.*** Note the irony in this verse. The blind man recognized who Jesus was more clearly than many people who were blessed with physical sight. The blind man's cry for mercy demonstrated his belief that Jesus had the power to heal him.
19:2 ***Zaccheus.*** This was the chief tax collector which meant he most likely bid for the right to collect taxes and then hired another tax collector to actually gather the money.
19:7 ***they all began muttering.*** The crowd was not happy with Jesus' choice of who to honor with His fellowship. In the crowd's opinion, Zaccheus was a sinner. Tax collectors often took for themselves a high percentage of what they demanded. They were hated and despised in ancient Israel.
19:11 ***they assumed that.*** Evidently the disciples believed that Jesus' arrival in Jerusalem would signal the arrival of the kingdom of God. Jesus' parable in verses 12 – 27 was designed to dispel this misconception. Note that the disciples raised the same question in Acts 1:6.
19:13 ***ten minas.*** Each servant received about four months' wages for the average worker. The master, symbolizing Jesus Himself, wants to see fruit, or dividends from his investment. Did his servants put the money they received to good use?

42 Lk 17:19 **43** Lk 5:26; Ac 4:21; 11:18 **CHAPTER 19** **7** Mt 9:11; Lk 5:30 **8** Lk 3:14; Ex 22:1; 1Sa 12:3; 2Sa 12:6 **9** Ro 4:11,12,16; Gal 3:7; Lk 13:16 **10** Mt 18:11; See Mt 10:6; 15:24 **11** Ac 1:6 **12** Mt 25:14; Mk 13:34 **14** Jn 1:11

a delegation after him, saying, 'We do not want this man to be a king over us.'
15"When he returned, after receiving the kingdom, he ordered that these servants, to whom he had given the money, be called to him, that he might find out what business they had done.
16"The first one came before him and said, 'Lord, your mina has made ten more minas.'
17"And he said to him, 'Well done, good servant! Because you proved yourself faithful *and* trustworthy in a very little thing, you shall [now] have authority over ten cities [in my kingdom].'
18"The second one came and said, 'Lord, your mina has made five minas.'
19"And he said to him also, 'And you shall take charge over five cities.'
20"Then another came and said, 'Lord, here is your mina, which I have kept laid up in a handkerchief [for safekeeping].
21'I was [always] afraid of you, because you are a stern man; you pick up what you did not lay down and you reap what you did not sow.'
22"He said to the servant, 'I will judge *and* condemn you by your own words, you worthless servant! Did you [really] know that I was a stern man, picking up what I did not lay down and reaping what I did not sow?
23'Then why did you not [at the very least] put my money in a bank? Then on my return, I would have collected it with interest.'
24"Then he said to the bystanders, 'Take the mina away from him and give it to the one who has the ten minas.'
25"And they said to him, 'Lord, he has ten minas *already!*'
26"[Jesus explained,] 'I tell you that to everyone who has [because he valued his gifts from God and has used them wisely], *more* will be given; but from the one who does not have [because he disregarded his gifts from God], even what he has will be taken away.'
27"[The king ended by saying,] 'But as for these enemies of mine who did not want me to be king over them, bring them here and kill them in my presence.' "

The Triumphal Entry

28After saying these things, Jesus went on ahead [of them], going up to Jerusalem.
29When He approached Bethphage and Bethany, at the mount that is called Olivet, He sent two of the disciples, [Matt 21:1–9; Mark 11:1–10; John 12:12–15]
30saying, "Go into the village ahead of you; there, as you enter, you will find a [donkey's] colt tied, on which no one has ever sat. Untie it and bring it here.
31"If anybody asks you, 'Why are you untying the colt?' you will say, 'The Lord needs it.' "
32So those who were sent left and found the colt just as He had told them.
33As they were untying the colt, its owners asked them, "Why are you untying the colt?"
34They said, "The Lord needs it."
35They brought it to Jesus, and they threw their robes over the colt and put Jesus on it. [Zech 9:9]
36As He rode along, people were spreading their coats on the road [as an act of homage before a king]. [2 Kin 9:13]
37As soon as He was approaching

19:20–23 *I was [always] afraid of you.* The unfaithful servant's excuse for failure reflects a negative view of the nobleman. If the servant had really feared the master, he would have done something with the money. Even putting the money in the bank would have yielded interest.
19:31–34 *The Lord needs it.* Such borrowing of an animal was not as strange as it may appear. There was an ancient custom by which a political or religious leader could commandeer property for short-term use. Jesus was entering Jerusalem to celebrate the Passover and the Feast of Unleavened Bread, festivals that commemorated the great act of God's deliverance of the nation. Such feasts were often celebrated at this time with the hope that God's decisive deliverance would come.

17 Mt 25:21; Lk 16:10 **21** Mt 25:24 **22** 2Sa 1:16; Job 15:6; Mt 12:37; Mt 25:26 **26** Mt 13:12; 25:29; Mk 4:25; Lk 8:18 **28** Mk 10:32 **29** Mt 21:1; Mk 11:1 **35** 2Ki 9:13; Mt 21:7; Mk 11:7; Jn 12:14

[Jerusalem], near the descent of the Mount of Olives, the entire multitude of the disciples [all those who were or claimed to be His followers] began praising God [adoring Him enthusiastically and] joyfully with loud voices for all the miracles *and* works of power that they had seen,
38 shouting,

"BLESSED (celebrated, praised) IS
THE KING WHO COMES IN THE NAME
OF THE LORD!
Peace in heaven and glory
(majesty, splendor) in the
highest [heaven]!" [Ps 118:26]

39 Some of the Pharisees from the crowd said to Him, "Teacher, rebuke Your disciples [for shouting these Messianic praises]."
40 Jesus replied, "I tell you, if these [people] keep silent, the stones will cry out [in praise]!" [Hab 2:11]
41 As He approached *Jerusalem*, He saw the city and wept over it [and the spiritual ignorance of its people],
42 saying, "If [only] you had known on this day [of salvation], even you, the things which make for peace [and on which peace depends]! But now they have been hidden from your eyes.
43 "For a time [of siege] is coming when your enemies will put up a barricade [with pointed stakes] against you, and surround you [with armies] and hem you in on every side, [Is 29:3; Jer 6:6; Ezek 4:2]
44 and they will level you to the ground, you [Jerusalem] and your children within you. They will not leave in you one stone on another, all because you did not [come progressively to] recognize [from observation and personal experience] the time of your visitation [when God was gracious toward you and offered you salvation]."

Traders Driven from the Temple

45 Jesus went into the temple [enclosure] and began driving out those who were selling, [Matt 21:12, 13; Mark 11:15–17; John 2:13–16]
46 saying to them, "It is written, 'MY HOUSE SHALL BE A HOUSE OF PRAYER'; but you have made it a ROBBERS' DEN." [Is 56:7; Jer 7:11]
47 He was teaching day after day in the temple [porches and courts]; but the chief priests and scribes and the leading men among the people were seeking [a way] to put Him to death,
48 and they could not find anything that they could do, for all the people [stayed close to Him and] were hanging on to every word He said.

Jesus' Authority Questioned

20 ON ONE of the days, as Jesus was instructing the people in the temple [area] and preaching the good news (gospel), the chief priests and the scribes along with the elders confronted *Him*, [Matt 21:23–27; Mark 11:27–33]
2 and said to Him, "Tell us by what *kind of* authority You are doing these things? Or who is the one who gave You this authority?"

19:41 ***wept over it.*** Jesus knew that so many of the people of Israel had rejected Him that the nation would suffer judgment, in the form of the terrible destruction that came on Jerusalem in AD 70.
19:43 ***put up a barricade [with pointed stakes] against you, and surround you.*** This is a prediction of Rome's successful siege of Jerusalem under Titus. The details reflect a divine judgment for covenant unfaithfulness, similar to the Babylonian destruction of Jerusalem in 586 BC (Isa 29:1 – 4; Jer 6:6 – 21; Eze 4:1 – 3).
19:45 ***Jesus went into the temple.*** Jesus cleansed the temple in anger after seeing that the place of prayer had become an excuse for corrupt commerce. Merchants were selling sacrificial animals in the outer court of the temple (the court of the Gentiles) at exorbitant prices. Money changers were making an excessive profit exchanging currencies for the temple shekel. John records a temple cleansing in John 2:13 – 22, but it is not clear whether that event is the same as this one in Luke. Since John places the event early in Jesus' ministry, Jesus might have cleansed the temple twice.

38 Ps 118:26; Lk 13:35; Lk 2:14; Eph 2:14 **40** Hab 2:11 **41** Jn 11:35 **43** Isa 29:3,4; Jer 6:3,6; Lk 21:20
44 1Ki 9:7,8; Mic 3:12; Mt 24:2; Mk 13:2; Lk 21:6; Da 9:24; Lk 1:68,78; 1Pe 2:12 **45** Mt 21:12; Mk 11:11,15; Jn 2:14,15
46 Isa 56:7; Jer 7:11 **47** Mk 11:18; Jn 7:19; 8:37 **CHAPTER 20** **1** Mt 21:23 **2** Ac 4:7; 7:27

3 Jesus replied, "I will also ask you a
question. You tell Me:
4 "The baptism of John [the Baptist]—
was it from heaven [that is, ordained
by God] or from men?"
5 They discussed *and* debated it
among themselves, saying, "If we say,
'From heaven,' He will say, 'Why did
you not believe him?'
6 "But if we say, 'From men,' all the
people will stone us to death, for they
are *firmly* convinced that John was a
prophet."
7 So they replied that they did not
know from where *it came*.
8 Then Jesus said to them, "Nor am I
telling you by what [kind of] authority
I do these things."

Parable of the Vineyard Owner

9 Then He began to tell the people
this parable: "A man planted a vine-
yard and leased it to tenant farmers,
and went on a journey for a long
time [to another country]. [Is 5:1–7;
Matt 21:33–46; Mark 12:1–12]
10 "At *harvest* time he sent a servant
[as his representative] to the tenants,
so that they would give him *his share*
of the fruit of the vineyard; but the
tenants beat the servant and sent him
away empty-handed.
11 "So he again sent another servant;
they also beat him and dishonored *and*
treated him disgracefully and sent him
away empty-handed.
12 "And he sent yet a third; and this
one too they wounded and threw out
[of the vineyard].
13 "Then the owner of the vineyard
said, 'What shall I do? I will send my
beloved son; perhaps they will have
respect for him.'
14 "But when the tenants saw him,
they discussed it among themselves,
saying, 'This [man] is the heir; let us
kill him so that the inheritance will
be ours.'
15 "So they threw the son out of the
vineyard and killed him. What, then,
will the owner of the vineyard do to
them?
16 "He will come and put these ten-
ants to death and will give the vine-
yard to others." When the chief priests,
the scribes, and the elders heard this,
they said, "May it never be!"
17 But Jesus looked at them and said,
"What then is [the meaning of] this
that is written:

'The [very] Stone which the
builders rejected,
This became the chief
Cornerstone'? [Ps 118:22, 23]

18 "Everyone who falls on that stone will
be broken *and* shattered in pieces; and
on whomever it falls, it will crush him."
[Is 8:14, 15; Dan 2:34, 35]

20:4 *The baptism of John [the Baptist]—was it from heaven [that is, ordained by God] or from men?* Here as throughout the Gospel of Luke, the ministries of John the Baptist and Jesus are linked. Jesus' question presented the Pharisees with a dilemma. If they recognized John's ministry as coming from heaven, they would be recognizing the same divine origin of Jesus' similar "independent" Spirit directed ministry. But if the Pharisees denied that John was sent by God they risked angering the majority of the people, who believed that John's ministry was divinely directed (vv. 5–6).

20:9 *A man planted a vineyard.* The imagery of the vineyard recalls the subject of Jesus' parable in 13:6–9. This parable is also found in Matthew 21:33–44 and Mark 12:1–12, with some slight variations of detail in each account.

20:14 *This [man] is the heir; let us kill him.* The vinedressers hoped that with the son gone, the inheritance would fall to those who worked the property, a transfer that was possible in the ancient world. It should be noted that the details of this parable do not represent the thinking of those who crucified Jesus. The leaders of Israel thought they were stopping someone who was dangerous to Judaism, not that they were going to inherit Jesus' kingdom.

20:17 *The [very] Stone which the builders rejected.* This passage, taken from Psalm 118:22, pictures the exaltation of the Righteous One, Jesus, after His rejection. Opposition will not stop God from making the One who is rejected the center of His work of salvation.

20:18 *Everyone who falls on that stone.* Jesus is the stone. Anyone who goes against the stone will be destroyed. Jesus' statement is similar to a late Jewish proverb: "If the stone falls on the

---

6 Mt 14:5; 21:26; Lk 7:29 **9** Mt 21:33; Mk 12:1 **17** Ps 118:22; Mt 21:42 **18** Da 2:34,35; Mt 21:44

Tribute to Caesar

[19]The scribes and the chief priests tried to [find a way to] arrest Him at that very hour, but they were afraid of the people; because they understood that He spoke this parable against them.
[20]So they watched [for a chance to trap] Him. They sent spies who pretended to be upright *and* sincere, in order that they might catch Him in some statement [that they could distort and use against Him], so that they could turn Him over to the control and authority of [Pilate] the governor. [Matt 22:15–22; Mark 12:13–17]
[21]They asked Him, "Teacher, we know that You speak and teach correctly, and that You show no partiality to anyone, but teach the way of God truthfully.
[22]"Is it lawful [according to Jewish law and tradition] for us to pay taxes (tribute money) to Caesar or not?"
[23]But He saw through their trickery and said to them,
[24]"Show Me a [Roman] denarius. Whose image and inscription does the coin have?" They answered, "[the Emperor Tiberius] Caesar's."
[25]He said to them, "Then pay to Caesar the things that are Caesar's, and to God the things that are God's."
[26]They were not able to seize on anything He said in the presence of the people; and being unnerved at His reply, they were silent.

Is There a Resurrection?

[27]Now some of the Sadducees (who say that there is no resurrection) came to Him [Matt 22:23–33; Mark 12:18–27]
[28]and they questioned Him, saying, "Teacher, Moses wrote for us [a law that] IF A MAN'S BROTHER DIES, leaving a wife AND NO CHILDREN, HIS BROTHER SHOULD MARRY THE WIFE AND RAISE CHILDREN FOR HIS BROTHER. [Deut 25:5, 6]
[29]"Now there were seven brothers; and the first took a wife and died childless.
[30]"And the second,
[31]and the third married her, and in the same way all seven died, leaving no children.
[32]"Finally the woman also died.
[33]"So in the [life after] resurrection, whose wife does she become? For all seven had married her."
[34]Jesus said to them, "The sons of this [world and present] age marry and [the women] are given in marriage;
[35]but those who are considered worthy to gain that [other world and that future] age and the resurrection from the dead, neither marry nor are given in marriage;
[36]and they cannot die again, because they are [immortal] like the angels (equal to, angel-like). And they are children of God, being participants in the resurrection.
[37]"But [as for the fact] that the dead are raised [from death], even Moses

---

pot, alas for the pot; If the pot falls on the stone, alas for the pot." The imagery for the stone is also found in 1 Peter 2:4–8.

20:22 *Is it lawful . . . for us to pay taxes (tribute money) to Caesar.* This question concerned the poll tax to Rome, which was different from the taxes collected by the tax collectors. The poll tax was a citizenship tax paid directly to Rome, as an indication that Israel was subject to that Gentile nation. The Pharisees' query was a trick question. If Jesus answered yes, the people would be angry because He respected a foreign power. If He answered no, He could be charged with sedition.

20:24 *Whose image and inscription does the coin have?* Jesus' reply was clever. He had the Pharisees pull out a coin, indicating that they already recognized Roman sovereignty by using Roman coins themselves. A penny was a silver coin that had a picture of the emperor Tiberius on it.

20:27 *Sadducees.* The Sadducees, the Pharisees, and the Essenes were three major divisions in first-century Judaism. The Sadducees rejected the oral traditions that the Pharisees too stringently obeyed. Instead they based their teaching only on the first five books of the Old Testament. They also denied that there could be a resurrection.

20:36 *they are [immortal] like the angels.* The everlasting life of a resurrected person makes that person something like an angel. Paul explains further that in the resurrection we will be given resurrection bodies similar to Christ's

20 Mt 22:15 **21** Mt 22:16; Mk 12:14 **27** Mt 22:23; Mk 12:18; Ac 23:6,8 **36** 1Co 15:42,49,52; 1Jn 3:2; Ro 8:23 **37** Ex 3:6

showed, in the *passage about the burning* bush, when he calls the Lord THE GOD OF ABRAHAM, THE GOD OF ISAAC, AND THE GOD OF JACOB. [Ex 3:6]
38"Now He is not the God of the dead, but of the living [so these forefathers will be among the resurrected]; for all live [in a definite relationship] to Him."
39Some of the scribes replied, "Teacher, you have spoken well [so that there is no room for blame]."
40And they did not dare to question Him further about anything [because of the wisdom He displayed in His answers].
41Then He said to them, "How *is it that* people say that the Christ (the Messiah, the Anointed) is David's son? [Matt 22:41–46; Mark 12:35–37]
42"For David himself says in the book of Psalms,

'THE LORD (the Father) SAID TO MY
LORD (the Son, the Messiah),
"SIT AT MY RIGHT HAND,
43 UNTIL I MAKE YOUR ENEMIES A
FOOTSTOOL FOR YOUR FEET." '
[Ps 110:1]

44"So David calls Him (the Son) 'Lord,' and how *then* is He David's son?"
45And with all the people listening, He said to His disciples,
46"Beware of the scribes, who like to walk around in long robes [displaying their prominence], and love respectful greetings in the [crowded] market places, and chief seats in the synagogues and places of honor at banquets.
47"These [men] who confiscate *and* devour widows' houses, and for a pretense [to appear devout] offer long prayers. These [men] will receive the greater [sentence of] condemnation."

The Widow's Gift

21 LOOKING UP, He saw the rich people putting their gifts into the treasury. [Mark 12:41–44]
2And He saw a poor widow putting in two small copper coins.
3He said, "Truly I say to you, this poor widow has put in [proportionally] more than all *of them;*
4for they all put in gifts from their abundance; but she out of her poverty put in all she had to live on."
5As some were talking about the temple, that it was decorated with beautiful stones and consecrated offerings [of magnificent gifts of gold which were displayed on the walls and hung in the porticoes], He said, [Matt 24; Mark 13]
6"As for all these things which you see, the time will come when there will not be one stone left on another that will not be torn down."
7They asked Him, "Teacher, when will these things happen? And what will be the sign when these things are about to happen?"
8He said, "Be careful *and* see to it that you are not misled; for many will

---

(1Co 15:25 – 58). This will be a new experience that will not necessarily parallel experiences on this earth, such as marriage.

20:41 – 42 *How is it that people say.* Here Jesus takes His turn at raising a theological issue. The dilemma He poses is how the Messiah could be called the Son of David, when David himself gave Him the title *Lord, my Lord*. This is a citation from Psalm 110:1. The Messiah was David's descendant and yet David gave Him the respect due to a superior, the reverse of what normally occurred in ancient times. Jesus was not denying the title *Son of David* to the Messiah, He was simply noting that the title *Lord*, meaning "Master," is more central. Even David one day will bow at the Messiah's feet and confess that He is Lord (Php 2:10).

21:2 *two small copper coins.* These were the smallest currency available.

21:5 *consecrated offerings.* These were gift offerings for the decoration of the temple and included gold and silver-plated gates, grapevine clusters, and Babylonian linen tapestries which hung from the temple veil. Even Tacitus, the Roman historian, called it an "immensely opulent temple."

21:6 *there will not be one stone left on another.* Jesus noted that the beautiful place of worship was temporary and would be destroyed. He was referring to the fall of Jerusalem in AD 70, which itself was a picture of the destruction of the last days.

21:8 *Be careful and see to it that you are not misled.* The first century and early second

38 Ro 6:10,11 **41** Mt 22:42; Mk 12:35 **42** Ps 110:1; Ac 2:34 **45** Mt 23:1; Mk 12:38 **46** Mt 23:5; Lk 11:43 **47** Mt 23:14
CHAPTER 21 **1** Mk 12:41 **3** 2Co 8:12 **5** Mt 24:1; Mk 13:1 **6** Lk 19:44 **8** Mt 24:4; Mk 13:5; Eph 5:6; 2Th 2:3

come in My name [appropriating for themselves the name Messiah which belongs to Me alone], saying, ‘I am *He,*’ and, ‘The time is near!’ Do not follow them.

9 “When you hear of wars and disturbances [civil unrest, revolts, uprisings], do not panic; for these things must take place first, but the end will not *come* immediately.”

Things to Come

10 Then Jesus told them, “Nation will rise against nation and kingdom against kingdom. [2 Chr 15:6; Is 19:2]

11 “There will be violent earthquakes, and in various places famines and [deadly and devastating] pestilences (plagues, epidemics); and there will be terrible sights and great signs from heaven.

12 “But before all these things, they will lay their hands on you and will persecute you, turning you over to the synagogues and prisons, and bringing you before kings and governors for My name’s sake. [Matt 10:19–22; Mark 13:11–13]

13 “This will be a time *and* an opportunity for you to testify [about Me].

14 “So make up your minds not to prepare beforehand to defend yourselves;

15 for I will give you [skillful] words and wisdom which none of your opponents will be able to resist or refute.

16 “But you will be betrayed *and* handed over even by parents and brothers and relatives and friends, and they will put *some* of you to death,

17 and you will be *continually* hated by everyone because of [your association with] My name.

18 “But not a hair of your head will perish. [1 Sam 14:45]

19 “By your [patient] endurance [empowered by the Holy Spirit] you will gain your souls.

20 “But when you see Jerusalem surrounded by [hostile] armies, then understand [with confident assurance] that her complete destruction is near.

21 “At that time, those who are in Judea must flee to the mountains, and those who are inside the city (Jerusalem) must get out, and those who are [out] in the country must not enter the city;

22 for these are days of vengeance [of rendering full justice or satisfaction], so that all things which are written will be fulfilled.

23 “Woe to those women who are pregnant and to those who are nursing babies in those days! For great trouble *and* anguish will be on the land, and wrath *and* retribution on this people [Israel].

24 “And they will fall by the edge of the sword, and will be led captive

---

century were times of great messianic fervor in Judaism, as the Israelites sought freedom from Roman rule. Many people claimed to be the Messiah. Jesus warned his disciples not to be fooled by such claims.

21:12 *synagogues and prisons . . . kings and governors.* These references indicate that all nations would share responsibility for the massacre of the disciples.

21:15 *I will give you [skillful] words and wisdom.* Jesus promises the disciples that the Holy Spirit will assist them in giving testimony (12:11 – 12). The initial fulfillment of this promise is found in Acts 4:8 – 14; 7:54; and 26:24 – 30.

21:16 *you will be betrayed.* The persecution of the disciples would be painful and severe. Identifying with Jesus often means risking the rejection and denunciation of family, and in some cases martyrdom.

21:20 *complete destruction.* This passage compared the desecration of the temple to what occurred in 167 BC, when Antiochus Epiphanes erected an altar to Zeus in the temple. A similar desecration of the temple site occurred during the destruction of Jerusalem in AD 70.

21:22 *days of vengeance.* Jerusalem had become an object of divine judgment because of its unfaithfulness. Jesus warned of this consequence throughout His ministry (13:9,34 – 35; 19:41 – 44). The premise for such judgment goes back to the curses of the Mosaic covenant and the Old Testament prophets’ warnings of coming judgment (Dt 28:49 – 57; 32:35; Jer 6:1 – 8; 26:1 – 9; Hos 9:7).

10 Mt 24:7 **12** Mk 13:9; Rev 2:10; Ac 4:3; 5:18; 12:4; 16:24; Ac 25:23; 1Pe 2:13 **13** Php 1:28; 2Th 1:5 **14** Mt 10:19; Mk 13:11; Lk 12:11 **15** Ac 6:10 **16** Mic 7:6; Mk 13:12; Ac 7:59; 12:2 **17** Mt 10:22 **18** Mt 10:30 **20** Mt 24:15; Mk 13:14 **22** Da 9:26,27; Zec 11:1 **23** Mt 24:19 **24** Da 9:27; 12:7; Ro 11:25

into all nations; and Jerusalem will be
trampled underfoot by the Gentiles un-
til the times of the Gentiles are fulfilled
(completed). [Is 63:18; Dan 8:13]

The Return of Christ

25 "There will be signs (attesting
miracles) in the sun and moon and
stars; and on the earth [there will be]
distress *and* anguish among nations,
in perplexity at the roaring *and* toss-
ing of the sea and the waves, [Is 13:10;
Joel 2:10; Zeph 1:15]
26 people fainting from fear and ex-
pectation of the [dreadful] things com-
ing on the world; for the [very] powers
of the heavens will be shaken.
27 "Then they will see THE SON OF
MAN COMING IN A CLOUD with [transcen-
dent, overwhelming] power [subdu-
ing the nations] and with great glory.
[Dan 7:13, 14]
28 "Now when these things begin to
occur, stand tall and lift up your heads
[in joy], because [suffering ends as]
your redemption is drawing near."

Parable of the Fig Tree

29 Then He told them a parable:
"Look at the fig tree and all the trees;
[Matt 24:32, 33; Mark 13:28, 29]
30 as soon as they put out leaves, you
see it and know for yourselves that
summer is near.
31 "So you too, when you see these
things happening, know [without any
doubt] that the kingdom of God is near.
32 "I assure you *and* most solemnly
say to you, this generation [those living
at that definite period of time preced-
ing the second coming] will not pass
away until everything takes place.
33 "Heaven and earth will pass away,
but My words will not pass away.
34 "But be on guard, so that your
hearts are not weighed down *and* de-
pressed with the giddiness of debauch-
ery and the nausea of self-indulgence
and the worldly worries of life, and
then that day [when the Messiah re-
turns] will not come on you suddenly
like a trap;
35 for it will come upon all those who
live on the face of all the earth.
36 "But keep alert at all times [be at-
tentive and ready], praying that you
may have the strength *and* ability [to
be found worthy and] to escape all
these things that are going to take
place, and to stand in the presence of
the Son of Man [at His coming]."
37 Now in the daytime Jesus was
teaching in [the porches and courts
of] the temple, but at night He would go
out and spend the night on the mount
that is called Olivet.
38 And early in the morning all the
people would come to Him in the tem-
ple to listen to Him.

Preparing the Passover

22 NOW THE Festival of Unleav-
ened Bread, which is called the
Passover, was approaching. [Lev 23:4, 5;
Ezek 45:21; Matt 26:2–5; Mark 14:1, 2]

21:27 *SON OF MAN COMING IN A CLOUD.* The reference here is to the authoritative return of Jesus. The allusion to the cloud and the figure comes from Daniel 7:13 – 14, with its picture of One who receives authority from the Ancient of Days. Jesus viewed this text in terms of an apocalyptic deliverance. The image of the cloud is important, since God is identified as riding the clouds in the Old Testament (Ex 34:5; Ps 104:3). The Son of Man has divine authority to judge the world.
21:29 – 30 *as soon as they put out leaves.* The tender buds that appear every spring on trees show that summer is approaching; the appearance of the signs Jesus describes will warn of the coming of the end times.
21:33 *will not pass away.* The disciples had the assurance that Jesus' promises concerning the end times were more certain than creation itself. God made an unconditional and unilateral covenant, and He will keep it (Ge 12:1 – 3; 15:18 – 21; Ps 89).
21:34 *be on guard.* Though the events of the end times may not come to pass for a long time, believers should continue to look for their arrival. The day of Jesus' return should not take us by surprise. We should live as if it is imminent.
22:1 *the Festival of Unleavened Bread.* This feast took place immediately following Passover

---

25 Mt 24:29; Mk 13:24; 2Pe 3:10,12 **26** Mt 24:29 **27** Mt 24:30; Rev 1:7; 14:14 **28** Ro 8:19,23 **29** Mt 24:32; Mk 13:28 **33** Mt 24:35 **34** Ro 13:13; 1Th 5:6; 1Pe 4:7 **35** 1Th 5:2; 2Pe 3:10; Rev 3:3; 16:15 **36** Mt 24:42; 25:13; Mk 13:33; Lk 18:1; Ps 1:5; Eph 6:13 **37** Jn 8:1,2; Lk 22:39 **CHAPTER 22** **1** Mt 26:2; Mk 14:1

[2]The chief priests and the scribes were looking for a way to put Him to death; for they were afraid of the people [who listened devotedly to His teaching, and who respected His spiritual wisdom].

[3]Then Satan entered Judas, the one called Iscariot, who was one of the twelve [disciples].

[4]And he went away and discussed with the chief priests and officers how he might betray Him *and* hand Him over to them.

[5]They were delighted and agreed with him to give him money.

[6]So he consented, and *began* looking for a good opportunity to betray Jesus to them [at a time when He was] separated from the crowd [because the people might riot or stop them from seizing Him].

[7]Then came the *preparation* day of Unleavened Bread on which the Passover *lamb* had to be sacrificed. [Ex 12:18–20; Deut 16:5–8; Matt 26:17–19; Mark 14:12–16]

[8]So Jesus sent Peter and John, saying, "Go and prepare the Passover meal for us, so that we may eat it."

[9]They asked Him, "Where do You want us to prepare it?"

[10]He replied, "When you have entered the city, a man carrying an *earthen* jar of water will meet you; follow him into the house that he enters.

[11]"And say to the owner of the house, 'The Teacher asks, "Where is the guest room in which I may eat the Passover with My disciples?"'

[12]"Then he will show you a large upstairs room, furnished [with carpets and dining couches]; prepare the meal there."

[13]They left and found it just as He had told them; and they prepared the Passover.

The Lord's Supper

[14]When the hour [for the meal] had come, Jesus reclined *at the table*, and the apostles with Him.

[15]He said to them, "I have earnestly wanted to eat this Passover with you before I suffer;

[16]for I say to you, I will not eat it again until it is fulfilled in the kingdom of God."

[17]And when He had taken a cup and given thanks, He said, "Take this and share it among yourselves; [Matt 26:26–29; Mark 14:22–25; 1 Cor 11:23–25]

[18]for I say to you, I will not drink of the fruit of the vine from now on until the kingdom of God comes."

[19]And when He had taken bread and given thanks, He broke it and gave it to them, saying, "This is My body which is given for you; do this in remembrance of Me."

[20]And in the same way *He took* the cup after they had eaten, saying, "This cup, which is poured out for you, is the new covenant [ratified] in My blood.

[21]"But listen, the hand of the one betraying Me is with Mine on the table. [Ps 41:9]

(Ex 12:1 – 20; Dt 16:1 – 8). The two feasts were often considered as one. Passover commemorated the night of the tenth plague in Egypt. The Feast of Unleavened Bread celebrated the exodus.

22:4 *officers.* These were Levites who were members of the temple guard. They were the ones who could make the arrest.

22:11 – 12 *guest room.* Such rooms were often made available to the thousands of pilgrims who came to Jerusalem for the celebration of Passover and the Feast of Unleavened Bread. Such a room would contain couches for guests at the feasts to recline for the meal. Access to the room was probably gained by stairs on the outside of the house.

22:19 *My body . . . do this in remembrance.* Jesus instituted a new meal which is not only a memorial of His death, but also a fellowship meal of unity. It is a proclamation and a symbol of the believer's anticipation of Jesus' return, when all God's promises will be fulfilled (1Co 10:16 – 17; 11:23 – 26).

22:20 *This cup . . . is the new covenant.* The wine of the Lord's Supper depicts the giving of life, a sacrifice of blood, which inaugurated the new covenant for those who respond to Jesus' offer of salvation (Heb 8:8,13; 9:11 – 28).

2 Ps 2:2; Jn 11:47; Ac 4:27 **3** Mt 26:14; Mk 14:10; Jn 13:2,27 **5** Zec 11:12 **7** Mt 26:17; Mk 14:12 **14** Mt 26:20; Mk 14:17 **16** Lk 14:15; Ac 10:41; Rev 19:9 **18** Mt 26:29; Mk 14:25 **19** Mt 26:26; Mk 14:22; 1Co 11:24 **20** 1Co 10:16 **21** Ps 41:9; Mt 26:21,23; Mk 14:18; Jn 13:21,26

22 “For indeed, the Son of Man is
going as it has been determined; but
woe (judgment is coming) to that man
by whom He is betrayed *and* handed
over!”
23 And they began to discuss among
themselves which one of them it might
be who was going to do this.

Who Is Greatest?

24 Now a dispute also arose among
them as to which of them was regarded
to be the greatest.
25 Jesus said to them, “The kings of
the Gentiles have absolute power *and*
lord it over them; and those in authority over them are called ‘Benefactors.’
[Matt 20:25–28; Mark 10:42–45]
26 “But it is not to be this way with
you; on the contrary, the one who is
the greatest among you must become
like the youngest [and least privileged],
and the [one who is the] leader, like
the servant.
27 “For who is the greater, the one
who reclines *at the table* or the one
who serves? Is it not the one who reclines *at the table*? But I am among
you as the one who serves.
28 “You are those who have remained
and have stood by Me in My trials;
29 and just as My Father has granted
Me a kingdom, I grant you [the privilege]
30 that you may eat and drink at My
table in My kingdom, and you will sit
on thrones judging the twelve tribes
of Israel.
31 “Simon, Simon (Peter), listen! Satan has demanded *permission* to sift
[all of] you like grain; [Job 1:6–12;
Amos 9:9]
32 but I have prayed [especially] for
you [Peter], that your faith [and confidence in Me] may not fail; and you,
once you have turned back again [to
Me], strengthen *and* support your
brothers [in the faith].”
33 And Peter said to Him, “Lord, I am
ready to go with You both to prison and
to death!” [Matt 26:33–35; Mark 14:29–31; John 13:37, 38]
34 Jesus said, “I say to you, Peter,
before the rooster crows today, you
will [utterly] deny three times that you
know Me.”
35 And He said to them, “When I sent
you out without a money belt and [provision] bag and [extra] sandals, did
you lack anything?” They answered,
“Nothing.”
36 Then He said to them, “But now,
he who has a money belt is to take it
along, and also his [provision] bag, and
he who has no sword is to sell his coat
and buy one.
37 “For I tell you that this [Scripture]
which is written must be completed
and fulfilled in Me: ‘AND HE WAS COUNTED WITH THE CRIMINALS’; for that which
refers to Me has its fulfillment [and is
settled].” [Is 53:12]
38 They said, “Lord, look, here are
two swords.” And He said to them, “It
is enough.”

The Garden of Gethsemane

39 And He came out and went, as was
His habit, to the Mount of Olives; and
the disciples followed Him.
40 When He arrived at the place
[called Gethsemane], He said to them,
“Pray *continually* that you may not
fall into temptation.” [Matt 26:36–46;
Mark 14:32–42]

22:30 eat and drink . . . sit on thrones judging. This is a promise of future blessing and authority. The disciples were promised a seat at the *banquet of victory and the right* to help Jesus rule over Israel on His return (Mt 19:28; 2Ti 2:12).

22:32 I have prayed [especially] for you . . . you have turned back again [to Me]. The Greek word for *you* here is singular, referring specifically to Peter. In effect, Jesus restored Peter even before his fall (vv. 54 – 62), and He instructed the disciple to shepherd the saints by strengthening them.

22:37 this [Scripture] which is written. Jesus cited Isaiah 53:12, which describes a righteous one who suffers as a criminal. Jesus noted that His death would fulfill Isaiah's prediction.

---

22 Mt 26:24; Ac 2:23; 4:28 **23** Mt 26:22; Jn 13:22,25 **24** Mk 9:34; Lk 9:46 **25** Mt 20:25; Mk 10:42 **26** Mt 20:26; 1Pe 5:3; Lk 9:48 **27** Lk 12:37; Mt 20:28; Jn 13:13,14; Php 2:7 **28** Heb 4:15 **29** Mt 24:47; Lk 12:32 **30** Mt 8:11; Lk 14:15; Rev 19:9; Ps 49:14; Mt 19:28; 1Co 6:2; Rev 3:21 **31** 1Pe 5:8; Am 9:9 **32** Jn 17:9,11,15 **34** Mt 26:34; Mk 14:30; Jn 13:38 **35** Mt 10:9; Lk 9:3; 10:4 **37** Isa 53:12; Mk 15:28 **39** Mt 26:36; Mk 14:32; Jn 18:1; Lk 21:37 **40** ver. 46; Mt 6:13; 26:41; Mk 14:38

41And He withdrew from them about
a stone's throw, and knelt down and
prayed,
42saying, "Father, if You are willing,
remove this cup [of divine wrath] from
Me; yet not My will, but [always] Yours
be done."
43Now an angel appeared to Him
from heaven, strengthening Him.
44And being in agony [deeply dis-
tressed and anguished; almost to the
point of death], He prayed more intent-
ly; and His sweat became like drops
of blood, falling down on the ground.
[Heb 5:7]
45When He rose from prayer, He
came to the disciples and found them
sleeping from sorrow,
46and He said to them, "Why are you
sleeping? Get up and pray that you
may not fall into temptation."

Judas Betrays Jesus

47While He was still speaking, a
crowd *came*, and the man called Judas,
one of the twelve [disciples], was lead-
ing the way for them. He approached
Jesus to kiss Him. [Matt 26:47–56;
Mark 14:43–50; John 18:3–11]
48And Jesus said to him, "Judas, are
you betraying the Son of Man with a
kiss?"
49When those who were around Him
saw what was about to happen, they
said, "Lord, should we strike with the
sword?"
50And one of them struck the slave of
the high priest and cut off his right ear.
[Matt 26:51; Mark 14:47; John 18:10]
51But Jesus replied, "Stop! No more
of this." And He touched the ear and
healed him.
52Then Jesus said to the chief priests
and officers of the temple and elders
[of the Sanhedrin] who had come out
against Him, "Have you come out with
swords and clubs as you would against
a robber?
53"Day after day when I was with you
in the temple, you did not lay hands on
Me; but this hour and the power *and*
authority of darkness are yours."

Peter's Denials

54Then they seized Him, and led
Him *away* and brought Him to the
[elegant] house of the [Jewish] high
priest. And Peter was following at a
[safe] distance.
55After they had kindled a fire in
the middle of the courtyard and had
sat down together, Peter sat among
them. [Matt 26:69–75; Mark 14:66–72;
John 18:16–18, 25–27]
56And a servant-girl, seeing him as
he sat in the firelight and looking in-
tently at him, said, "This man was with
Him too."
57But Peter denied it, saying, "Wom-
an, I do not know Him!"
58A little later someone else saw him
and said, "You are one of them too."
But Peter said, "Man, I am not!"
59After about an hour had passed,
another man *began* to insist, "This
man was with Him, for he is a Gali-
lean too."
60But Peter said, "Man, I do not know
what you are talking about." Immedi-
ately, while he was still speaking, a
rooster crowed.
61The Lord turned and looked at Pe-
ter. And Peter remembered the word of
the Lord, how He had told him, "Before
a rooster crows today, you will deny
Me three times."

22:42 *this cup.* This is a figure of speech for wrath (Ps 11:6; 75:7–8; Jer 25:15–16; Eze 23:31–34).
22:43 *strengthening Him.* God's answer to Jesus' prayer did not allow His Son to avoid suffering. However, God did provide angelic help for Jesus to face what was coming. Sometimes God answers prayer by eliminating trials; sometimes He answers by strengthening us in the midst of them.
22:52 *as you would against a robber.* The Greek term for *robber* was used of both highway bandits and revolutionaries. Jesus rebuked His captors for treating Him as though He were a dangerous lawbreaker.
22:59 *for he is a Galilean.* According to Mark

41 Mt 26:39; Mk 14:35 **42** Jn 5:30; 6:38 **43** Mt 4:11 **44** Jn 12:27; Heb 5:7 **46** ver. 40 **47** Mt 26:47; Mk 14:43; Jn 18:3 **50** Mt 26:51; Mk 14:47 **52** Mt 26:55; Mk 14:48 **53** Jn 12:27 **54** Mt 26:57; Mt 26:58; Jn 18:15 **55** Mt 26:69; Mk 14:66; Jn 18:17,18 **58** Mt 26:71; Mk 14:69; Jn 18:25 **59** Mt 26:73; Mk 14:70; Jn 18:26 **61** Mt 26:75; Mk 14:72; Mt 26:34,75; Jn 13:38

[62]And he went out and wept bitterly
[deeply grieved and distressed].
[63]Now the men who were holding
Jesus in custody were mocking *and*
ridiculing Him [and treating Him with
contempt] and beating Him.
[64]They blindfolded Him and asked,
"Prophesy, who is it that struck You?"
[65]And they were saying many other
[evil and slanderous] things against
Him, blaspheming [speaking sacrile-
giously and abusively about] Him.

Jesus before the Sanhedrin

[66]When day came, the Council of the
elders of the people (Sanhedrin, Jew-
ish High Court) assembled, both chief
priests and scribes; and they led Jesus
away to the council *chamber*, saying,
[67]"If You are the Christ (the Messiah,
the Anointed), tell us." But He said to
them, "If I tell you, you will not believe
[what I say],
[68]and if I ask a question, you will
not answer.
[69]"But from now on, THE SON OF MAN
WILL BE SEATED AT THE RIGHT HAND of the
power OF GOD." [Ps 110:1]
[70]And they all said, "Are You the Son
of God, then?" He replied, "*It is just as*
you say."
[71]Then they asked, "What further
need of testimony do we have? For we
ourselves have heard it from His own
mouth."

Jesus before Pilate

23 THEN THE whole assembly got
up and brought Him before Pi-
late.
[2]They began to accuse Jesus, as-
serting, "We found this Man mislead-
ing *and* perverting our nation and
forbidding us to pay taxes to Cae-
sar, and claiming that He Himself is
Christ (the Messiah, the Anointed),
a King." [Matt 27:11–14; Mark 15:2–5;
John 18:29–37]
[3]So Pilate asked Him, "Are You the
King of the Jews?" And He answered
him, "*It is just as* you say."
[4]Then Pilate said to the chief priests
and the crowds, "I find no guilt in this
Man."
[5]But they were insistent and said,
"He stirs up the people [to rebel], teach-
ing throughout Judea, starting from
Galilee even as far as here [in Jeru-
salem]."
[6]When Pilate heard it, he asked
whether the man was a Galilean.
[7]And when he learned that He be-
longed to the jurisdiction of Herod
[Antipas, the tetrarch of Galilee], he

14:70, Peter's accent gave him away as being from the same region as Jesus.

22:66 *the elders of the people . . . assembled.* The description here is of a major morning trial that involved all the Jewish religious leaders, the entire council or Sanhedrin. This trial violated various Jewish legal rules given in later sources: meeting on the morning of a feast; meeting at Caiaphas's home; trying a defendant without defense; and reaching the verdict in one day instead of the two days that were required for capital cases.

22:69 *AT THE RIGHT HAND of the power OF GOD.* Jesus' reply here alludes to the regal enthronement image of Psalm 110:1. This reply is what convicted Him. Apparently what offended Jesus' audience was His claim to sit in God's presence and to exercise divine authority. In effect, His answer to their question about being the Christ was more than they expected. It was not blasphemous to claim to be Messiah. What was blasphemous was the claim to be the Judge of Jewish people, with God's authority.

23:2 *began to accuse.* Three charges were lodged against Jesus: (1) perverting the nation, (2) forbidding payment of taxes to Rome, and (3) claiming to be the Christ. The first charge, which was a general complaint, involved disturbing the peace. The other two charges could have been construed as challenges to Rome. The second charge was a blatant lie (20:20–26). The third charge was true, but not in the threatening sense that the prosecutors suggested. A three-part Roman procedure was followed at the trial; charges, examination, and verdict.

23:5 *they were insistent.* By mentioning the charge that Jesus stirred up the people, the leaders suggested that Pilate risked being found derelict in his duty if he let Jesus go.

23:7 *jurisdiction of Herod.* Herod was responsible for Galilee, so Pilate "passed the buck" for the ruling and showed political courtesy at the same time.

---

63 Mt 26:67,68; Mk 14:65 **66** Mt 27:1; Ac 4:26; See Ac 22:5 **67** Mt 26:63; Mk 14:61 **69** Mat 26:64; Mk 14:62; Heb 1:3; 8:1 **70** Mt 26:64; Mk 14:62 **71** Mt 26:65; Mk 14:63 **CHAPTER 23** **1** Mt 27:2; Mk 15:1; Jn 18:28 **2** Ac 17:7; See Mt 17:27; 22:21; Mk 12:17; Jn 19:12 **3** Mt 27:11; 1Ti 6:13 **4** 1Pe 2:22 **7** Lk 3:1

sent Him to Herod, who was also in Jerusalem at that time.

Jesus before Herod

8 When Herod saw Jesus, he was exceedingly pleased. He had wanted to see Him for a long time because of what he had heard about Him, and was hoping to see some [miraculous] sign [even something spectacular] done by Him.

9 And he questioned Him at some length, but Jesus made no reply. [Is 53:7]

10 The chief priests and the scribes were standing there, *continually* accusing Him heatedly.

11 And Herod with his soldiers, after treating Him with contempt and mocking *and* ridiculing Him, dressed Him in a gorgeous robe and sent Him back to Pilate. [Is 53:8]

12 Now that very day Herod and Pilate became friends with each other—before this they had been enemies.

Pilate Seeks Jesus' Release

13 Pilate summoned the chief priests and the rulers and the people,

14 and said to them, "You brought this man before me as one who corrupts *and* incites the people to rebellion. After examining Him before you, I have found no guilt in this Man regarding the charges which you make against Him.

15 "No, nor has Herod, for he sent Him back to us; and indeed, He has done nothing to deserve death.

16 "Therefore I will punish Him [to teach Him a lesson] and release Him."

17 [Now he was obligated to release to them one prisoner at the Feast.]

18 But they [loudly] shouted out all together, saying, "Away with this Man, and release Barabbas to us!" [Matt 27:15–26; Mark 15:6–15; John 18:39–19:16]

19 (He was one who had been thrown into prison for an insurrection that happened in the city, and for murder.)

20 Pilate addressed them again, wanting to release Jesus,

21 but they kept shouting out, "Crucify, crucify Him!"

22 A third time he said to them, "Why, what wrong has He done? I have found no guilt [no crime, no offense] in Him *demanding* death; therefore I will punish Him [to teach Him a lesson] and release Him."

23 But they were insistent *and* unrelenting, demanding with loud voices that Jesus be crucified. And their voices *began* to prevail *and* accomplish their purpose.

24 Pilate pronounced sentence that their demand be granted.

25 And he released the man they were asking for who had been thrown into prison for insurrection and murder, but he handed over Jesus to their will.

Simon Bears the Cross

26 When they led Him away, they seized a man, Simon of Cyrene, who was coming in [to the city] from the country, and placed on him the cross to carry behind Jesus. [Matt 27:32; Mark 15:21]

27 Following Him was a large crowd of the people, including women who were mourning and wailing for Him.

28 But Jesus, turning toward them,
said, "Daughters of Jerusalem, do not
weep for Me, but weep for yourselves
and for your children. 29 "For behold,
the days are coming when they will
say, 'Blessed are the barren, and the

23:16 *punish Him . . . and release Him.* Pilate hoped that a public whipping might satisfy the crowd and tame Jesus, avoiding the need to resort to the death penalty.

23:18–19 *Away with this Man.* The entire crowd is portrayed as wanting Jesus to die. Luke makes it clear that Jesus' death was not only instigated by Jewish officials but approved by the Jewish people.

23:26 *Simon of Cyrene* was recruited to carry Jesus' cross. He was from a leading city of Libya.

23:28 *do not weep for Me.* Though He was dying, Jesus pointed out that their weeping should be for Jerusalem and its inhabitants, since judgment

---

8 Lk 9:9; Mt 14:1; Mk 6:14 **11** Isa 53:3 **12** Ac 4:27 **13** Mt 27:23; Mk 15:14; Jn 18:38; 19:4 **14** ver. 1,2,4 **16** Mt 27:26; Jn 19:1 **17** Mt 27:15; Mk 15:6; Jn 18:39 **18** Ac 3:14 **24** Mt 27:26; Mk 15:15; Jn 19:16 **26** Mt 27:32; Mk 15:21; See Jn 19:17 **29** Mt 24:19; Lk 21:23

wombs that have not given birth, and
the breasts that have never nursed.'
30“Then they will begin TO SAY TO
THE MOUNTAINS, 'FALL ON US!' AND TO THE
HILLS, 'COVER US!' [Is 2:19, 20; Hos 10:8;
Rev 6:16]
31“For if they do these things when
the tree is green, what will happen
when it is dry?”
32Two others also, who were crim-
inals, were being led away to be exe-
cuted with Him. [Is 53:12]

The Crucifixion

33When they came to the place called
The Skull, there they crucified Him
and the criminals, one on the right
and one on the left. [Matt 27:33–44;
Mark 15:22–32; John 19:17–24]
34And Jesus was saying, “Father,
forgive them; for they do not know
what they are doing.” And they cast
lots, dividing His clothes among them-
selves. [Ps 22:18]
35Now the people stood by, watch-
ing; but even the rulers ridiculed *and*
sneered at Him, saying, “He saved oth-
ers [from death]; let Him save Himself
if He is the Christ (the Messiah, the
Anointed) of God, His Chosen One.”
36The soldiers also mocked Him,
coming up to Him and [cruelly] of-
fering Him sour wine, [Ps 69:21;
Matt 27:48; Mark 15:36f; John 19:29, 30]
37and sarcastically saying, “If you
are [really] the King of the Jews, save
Yourself [from death]!”
38Now there was also an inscription
above Him: “THIS IS THE KING OF
THE JEWS.”
39One of the criminals who had been
hanged [on a cross beside Him] kept
hurling abuse at Him, saying, “Are You
not the Christ? Save Yourself and us
[from death]!”
40But the other one rebuked him,
saying, “Do you not even fear God,
since you are under the same sentence
of condemnation?
41“We *are suffering* justly, because
we are getting what we deserve for
what we have done; but this Man has
done nothing wrong.”
42And he was saying, “Jesus, [please]
remember me when You come into
Your kingdom!”
43Jesus said to him, “I assure you
and most solemnly say to you, today
you will be with Me in Paradise.”
[2 Cor 12:4; Rev 2:7]
44It was now about the sixth hour
(noon), and darkness came over the
whole land until the ninth hour (3:00
p.m.), [Matt 27:45–56; Mark 15:33–41;
John 19:14]
45because the sun was obscured; and
the veil [of the Holy of Holies] of the
temple was torn in two [from top to
bottom]. [Ex 26:31–35]
46And Jesus, crying out with a loud
voice, said, “Father, INTO YOUR HANDS I
COMMIT MY SPIRIT!” Having said this, He
breathed His last. [Ps 31:5]
47Now when the centurion saw what
had taken place, he *began* praising *and*

---

was going to fall on the city (19:41 – 44). Jerusalem here represents the entire nation of Israel.

23:31 *what will happen when it is dry.* The idea here seems to be “If this is what is done to a live tree, what will happen to the dead one?” In other words, “If Jesus, the living tree, has not been spared, how much more will dead wood not be spared.” This is Jesus' final lament over the nation of Israel.

23:33 *the place called The Skull.* The name of the place in Aramaic is Golgotha, which means “skull.” Calvary is the Latin name for Golgotha. Possibly the name referred to a geographical feature of the locale, something that resembled a skull.

23:36 *sour wine.* The drink referred to here was probably wine vinegar, which was inexpensive and quenched thirst better than water. It was a drink of the poor.

23:44 *sixth hour ... ninth hour.* The first hour was sunrise, so the time was 12 P.M. to 3 P.M. During these three hours, signs of creation revealed that the hour was not one of light but of darkness (22:53).

23:47 *Certainly this Man was innocent.* If Jesus was righteous and innocent, then He is who He claimed to be. Thus a second figure

---

30 Isa 2:19; Hos 10:8; Rev 6:16; 9:6 **31** Pr 11:31; Jer 25:29; Eze 20:47; 21:3,4; 1Pe 4:17 **32** Isa 53:12; Mt 27:38 **33** Mt 27:33; Mk 15:22; Jn 19:17,18 **34** Mt 5:44; Ac 7:60; 1Co 4:12; Ac 3:17; Mt 27:35; Mk 15:24; Jn 19:23 **35** Ps 22:17; Zec 12:10; Mt 27:39; Mk 15:29 **38** Mt 27:37; Mk 15:26; Jn 19:19 **39** Mt 27:44; Mk 15:32 **44** Mt 27:45; Mk 15:33 **45** Mt 27:51; Mk 15:38 **46** Ps 31:5; 1Pe 2:23; Mt 27:50; Mk 15:37; Jn 19:30 **47** Mt 27:54; Mk 15:39

honoring God, saying, "Certainly this
Man was innocent."
48 All the crowds who had gathered
for this spectacle, when they saw what
had happened, *began* to return [to their
homes], beating their breasts [as a sign
of mourning or repentance].
49 And all His acquaintances and the
women who had accompanied Him
from Galilee were standing at a dis-
tance, watching these things.

Jesus Is Buried

50 A man named Joseph, who was
a member of the Council (Sanhedrin,
Jewish High Court), a good and honor-
able man [Matt 27:57–61; Mark 15:42–
47; John 19:38–42]
51 (he had not consented to the Coun-
cil's plan and action) *a man* from Ari-
mathea, a city of the Jews, who was
waiting for *and* expecting the kingdom
of God;
52 this man went to Pilate and asked
for the body of Jesus.
53 And [after receiving permission]
he took it down and wrapped it in a
linen [burial] cloth and laid Him in a
tomb cut into the rock, where no one
had yet been laid.
54 It was the day of preparation [for
the Sabbath], and the Sabbath was
dawning.
55 Now the women who had come
with Him from Galilee followed [close-
ly], and saw the tomb and how His
body was laid.
56 Then they went back and pre-
pared spices and ointments *and* sweet-
smelling herbs.
And on the Sabbath they rested in
accordance with the commandment
[forbidding work]. [Ex 12:16; 20:10]

The Resurrection

24 BUT ON the first day of the
week, at early dawn, the women
went to the tomb bringing the spices
which they had prepared [to finish
anointing the body]. [Matt 28:1–8;
Mark 16:1–8; John 20:1–8]
2 And they found the [large, circular]
stone rolled back from the tomb,
3 but when they went inside, they did
not find the body of the Lord Jesus.
4 While they were perplexed *and*
wondering about this, suddenly, two
men in dazzling clothing stood near
them;
5 and as the women were terrified
and were bowing their faces to the
ground, the men said to them, "Why
are you looking for the living One
among the dead?
6 "He is not here, but has risen. Re-
member how He told you, while He
was still in Galilee,
7 saying that the Son of Man must
be handed over to sinful men, and be
crucified, and on the third day rise
[from death to life]." [Ps 16:10]
8 And they remembered His words,
9 and after returning from the tomb,
they reported all these things to the
eleven [apostles] and to all the rest.
10 Now they were Mary Magda-
lene and Joanna [the wife of Chuza,
Herod's steward] and Mary the *mother*
of James; also the other women with
them were telling these things to the
apostles.

---

besides the thief on the cross had insight into Jesus' death.

23:52 *the body of Jesus.* There is no doubt that Jesus died. Efforts to explain the resurrection as something like a return from a coma are more impossible than the idea of the resurrection itself.

23:54 *the day of preparation.* Jesus was buried late on Friday, on the day called Preparation when everything was made ready for the Sabbath, the day when no labor could take place.

24:2 *they found the [large, circular] stone rolled back.* Matthew 28:2 mentions that an earthquake moved the stone, which would have fit in a channel in front of the entrance to the tomb. Moving the stone would have been possible, though difficult, for a group of people. The earthquake settles the question of how the stone was moved.

24:11 *they would not believe them.* Skepticism reigned among the disciples. It is clear that

49 Ps 38:11; Mt 27:55; Mk 15:40; See Jn 19:25 **50** Mt 27:57; Mk 15:42; Jn 19:38 **51** Mk 15:43; Lk 2:25,38 **53** Mt 27:59; Mk 15:46 **54** Mt 27:62 **55** Lk 8:2; Mk 15:47 **56** Mk 16:1; Ex 20:10 **CHAPTER 24** **1** Mt 28:1; Mk 16:1; Jn 20:1; Lk 23:56 **2** Mt 28:2; Mk 16:4 **3** ver. 23; Mk 16:5 **4** Jn 20:12; Ac 1:10 **6** Mt 16:21; 17:23; Mk 8:31; 9:31; Lk 9:22 **8** Jn 2:22 **9** Mt 28:8; Mk 16:10 **10** Lk 8:3

RESURRECTION APPEARANCES

APPEARANCE	PLACE	TIME	MATTHEW	MARK	LUKE	JOHN	ACTS	1 CO
The empty tomb	Jerusalem	Resurrection Sunday	28:1–10	16:1–8	24:1–12	20:1–9		
To Mary Magdalene in the garden	Jerusalem	Resurrection Sunday		16:9–11		20:11–18		
To other women	Jerusalem	Resurrection Sunday	28:9–10					
To two people going to Emmaus	Road to Emmaus	Resurrection Sunday		16:12–13	24:13–32			
To Peter	Jerusalem	Resurrection Sunday			24:34			15:5
To the ten disciples in the upper room	Jerusalem	Resurrection Sunday			24:36–43	20:19–25		
To the 11 disciples in the upper room	Jerusalem	Following Sunday		16:14		20:26–31		15:5
To seven disciples fishing	Sea of Galilee	Some time later				21:1–23		
To the 11 disciples on a mountain	Galilee	Some time later	28:16–20	16:15–18				
To more than 500	Unknown	Some time later						15:6
To James	Unknown	Some time later						15:7
To his disciples at his ascension	Mount of Olives	40 days after Jesus' resurrection			24:44–49		1:3–8	
To Paul	Damascus	Several years later					9:1–19 22:3–16 26:9–18	9:1

11 But their report seemed to them like idle talk *and* nonsense, and they would not believe them.

12 But Peter got up and ran to the tomb. Stooping [at the small entrance] and looking in, he saw only the linen wrappings; and he went away, wondering about what had happened. [John 20:3–6]

The Road to Emmaus

13 And then, that very day two of them were going to a village called Emmaus, which was about seven miles from Jerusalem. [Mark 16:12]

14 And they were talking with each other about all these things which had taken place.

---

they did not expect a resurrection. The disciples thought the women's story was nonsense.

24:12 *Peter got up and ran.* Having already experienced a fulfilled prediction of the Lord (22:54 – 62), Peter hurried to the tomb to check out the women's story. It is hard to say whether Peter believed in the resurrection when he left the tomb. At that point he was probably more amazed than anything else.

11 ver. 25 **12** Jn 20:3 **13** Mk 16:12

15 While they were talking and discussing it, Jesus Himself came up and *began* walking with them.

16 But their eyes were [miraculously] prevented from recognizing Him.

17 Then Jesus asked them, "What are you discussing with one another as you walk along?" And they stood still, looking brokenhearted.

18 One *of them*, named Cleopas, answered Him, "Are you the only stranger visiting Jerusalem who is unaware of the things which have happened here in these [recent] days?"

19 He asked, "What things?" And they replied, "The things about Jesus of Nazareth, who was a prophet powerful in deed and word in the sight of God and all the people,

20 and how the chief priests and our rulers handed Him over to be sentenced to death, and crucified Him.

21 "But we were hoping that it was He who was going to redeem Israel *and* set our nation free. Indeed, besides all this, it is the third day since these things happened.

22 "And also some of the women among us shocked us. They were at the tomb early in the morning,

23 and they did not find His body. Then they came back, saying that they had even seen a vision of angels who said that He was alive!

24 "Some of those who were with us went to the tomb and found it just exactly as the women had said, but they did not see Him."

25 Then Jesus said to them, "O foolish men, and slow of heart to trust *and* believe in everything that the prophets have spoken!

26 "Was it not necessary for the Christ to suffer these things and [only then to] enter His glory?"

27 Then beginning with Moses and [throughout] all the [writings of the] prophets, He explained *and* interpreted for them the things referring to Himself [found] in all the Scriptures.

28 Then they approached the village where they were going, and He acted as if He were going farther.

29 But they urged Him [not to go on], saying, "Stay with us, because it is almost evening, and the day has just about ended." So He went inside to stay with them.

30 And it happened that as He reclined *at the table* with them, He took the bread and blessed it, and breaking it, He *began* giving it to them.

31 Then their eyes were [suddenly] opened [by God] and they [clearly] recognized Him; and He vanished from their sight.

32 They said to one another, "Were not our hearts burning within us while He was talking with us on the road and opening the Scriptures to us?"

33 They got up that very hour and went back to Jerusalem, and found the eleven [apostles] gathered together and those who were with them,

34 saying, "The Lord has really risen and has appeared to Simon [Peter]!"

35 They *began* describing in detail what had happened on the road, and how Jesus was recognized by them when He broke the bread.

24:19 – 21 *Jesus of Nazareth, who was a prophet.* These disciples on the road to Emmaus regarded Jesus as the Revealer of God's way and the Doer of His work.

24:23 *He was alive!* The women reported that there was no body found in Jesus' tomb, and that angels had announced to them that Jesus lives. The fact that the men were still sad indicates that they did not believe the report.

24:25 *slow of heart to trust and believe.* Jesus, who at this time was still not known to the travelers, rebuked His companions and reminded them of the things that the prophets taught.

24:27 *Then beginning with Moses.* Going from the books of Moses to the Prophets, Jesus provided an overview of God's plan in the Scriptures. This plan is present throughout the entire Old Testament (Ac 3:22 – 26; 10:43).

15 Mt 18:20 **16** Jn 20:14; 21:4 **18** Jn 19:25 **19** Mt 21:11; Lk 7:16; Jn 3:2; 4:19; 6:14; Ac 2:22; Ac 7:22 **20** Lk 23:1; Ac 13:27 **21** Lk 1:68; 2:38; Ac 1:6 **22** ver. 9,10; Mt 28:8; Mk 16:10; Jn 20:18 **24** ver. 12 **26** Ac 17:3; 1Pe 1:11 **27** ver. 45; Ge 3:15; 22:18; 26:4; 49:10; Nu 21:9; Dt 18:15; Ps 16:9,10; 22; 132:11; Isa 7:14; 9:6; 40:10,11; 50:6; Jer 23:5; 33:14,15; Eze 34:23; 37:25; Da 9:24; Mic 7:20; Mal 3:1; 4:2; See Jn 1:45 **28** Ge 32:26; 42:7; Mk 6:48 **29** Ge 19:3; Ac 16:15 **30** Mt 14:19 **34** 1Co 15:5

Other Appearances

36 While they were talking about this,
Jesus Himself [suddenly] stood among
them and said to them, "Peace be to
you."
37 But they were startled and terrified
and thought that they were seeing a
spirit.
38 And He said, "Why are you trou-
bled, and why are doubts rising in your
hearts?
39 "Look at [the marks in] My hands
and My feet, [and see] that it is I Myself.
Touch Me and see; a spirit does not
have flesh and bones, as you see that
I have." [John 20:20–27]
40 After saying this, He showed them
His hands and His feet.
41 While they still did not believe it
because of their joy and amazement,
He asked them, "Do you have anything
here to eat?"
42 They gave Him a piece of broiled
fish,
43 and He took it and ate it in front of
them. [Acts 10:40, 41]
44 Then He said to them, "This is
what I told you while I was still with
you, everything which has been writ-
ten about Me in the Law of Moses and
the [writings of the] Prophets and the
Psalms must be fulfilled."
45 Then He opened their minds to
[help them] understand the Scriptures,
46 and said, "And so it is written, that
the Christ (the Messiah, the Anointed)
would suffer and rise from the dead on
the third day, [Hos 6:2]
47 and that repentance [necessary] for
forgiveness of sins would be preached
in His name to all the nations, begin-
ning from Jerusalem.
48 "You are witnesses of these things.
49 "Listen carefully: I am sending
the Promise of My Father [the Holy
Spirit] upon you; but you are to re-
main in the city [of Jerusalem] until
you are clothed (fully equipped) with
power from on high." [John 14:26;
Acts 1:4]

The Ascension

50 Then He led them out as far as
Bethany, and lifted up His hands and
blessed them. [Matt 21:17; Acts 1:9–12]
51 While He was blessing them, He
left them and was taken up into heaven.
52 And they worshiped Him and re-
turned to Jerusalem with great joy
[fully understanding that He lives and
that He is the Son of God];
53 and they were continually in the
temple blessing *and* praising God.

24:39 *flesh and bones.* Jesus pointed out that a raised body is not a disembodied spirit. The presence of his body indicates that Jesus had been raised and that He was not a hallucination. He was raised in the same physical body in which He had been put to death. The difference was that His resurrected body is not corruptible and not subject to death.

24:46 *Christ (the Messiah, the Anointed) would suffer and rise from the dead.* Two parts of God's plan had been fulfilled. Jesus had been crucified and raised from the dead. Old Testament texts that predict these events are Psalm 22 and Psalm 118:22.

24:49 *the Promise of My Father.* This is a reference to the baptism of the Holy Spirit at Pentecost (Ac 2:4). It was promised in Jeremiah 31:31 – 33, and in Joel 2:28. Peter called this coming of the Spirit "the beginning" (Ac 11:15) because the real fulfillment of God's promise of salvation would start in those people united by the Spirit to establish the church.

36 Mk 16:14; Jn 20:19; 1Co 15:5 **37** Mk 6:49 **39** Jn 20:20 **41** Ge 45:26; Jn 21:5 **43** Ac 10:41 **44** ver. 6; Mt 16:21; 17:22; 20:18; Mk 8:31; Lk 9:22; 18:31 **45** Ac 16:14 **46** Ps 22; Ac 17:3 **47** Da 9:24; Ac 13:38; Ps 22:27; Jer 31:34; Mic 4:2 **48** Ac 1:8 **49** Isa 44:3; Joel 2:28 **50** Ac 1:12 **51** Mk 16:19 **52** Mt 28:9 **53** Ac 2:46

THE GOSPEL ACCORDING TO

JOHN

▸ **AUTHOR:** Jesus nicknamed John and his brother, James, "Sons of Thunder" (Mk 3:17). John was evidently among the Galileans who followed John the Baptist until they were called to follow Jesus at the outset of His public ministry. These Galileans were later called to become full-time disciples of the Lord (Lk 5:1 – 11), and John was among the twelve men who were selected to be apostles (Lk 6:12 – 16). The author of this Gospel is identified only as the disciple "whom Jesus loved" (Jn 13:23; 19:26; 21:7), but attention to detail concerning geography and Jewish culture in the Gospel lend credibility to the author's claim to be an eyewitness. The strong testimony of the early church relates this eyewitness to the apostle John.

▸ **TIMES:** c. AD 29 – 33 ▸ **KEY VERSES:** Jn 20:30 – 31

▸ **THEME:** John is a great book for new or young Christians because it intentionally helps the reader understand the significance of Jesus. What becomes increasingly clear as you read the Gospel of John is that Jesus does not fit the image of someone who is simply a nice moral teacher. Only a lunatic would make the claims He makes for Himself unless He was who He said He was. John leaves no room for indecision. Like the many people Jesus encounters in the book, as you read, you must either reject Him or accept Him, and say in the end like Thomas: "My Lord and my God" (20:28). This Gospel is an incredibly powerful presentation of Jesus.

The Deity of Jesus Christ

1 IN THE beginning [before all time]
was the Word (Christ), and the
Word was with God, and the Word
was God Himself. [Gen 1:1; Is 9:6]
2He was [continually existing] in
the beginning [co-eternally] with God.
3All things were made *and* came into
existence through Him; and without
Him not even one thing was made that
has come into being.
4In Him was life [and the power to
bestow life], and the life was the Light
of men.
5The Light shines on in the darkness, and the darkness did not under-

1:1 ***In the beginning.*** Genesis 1:1 starts with the moment of creation and moves forward to the creation of humanity. John 1:1 starts with creation and contemplates eternity past. ***the Word was with God.*** This suggests a face-to-face relationship. In the ancient world, it was important that persons of equal station be on the same level when seated across from one another.
1:3 ***All things were made and came into existence through Him.*** God the Father created the world (Ge 1:1) through God the Son (Col 1:16; Heb 1:2). All creation was made through Him. Thus, He is the Creator God.
1:4 ***Light of men.*** This image conveys the concept of revelation. As the light, Jesus Christ reveals both sin and God to humans (Ps 36:9). Later in this Gospel, Christ declares Himself to be both the life (11:25) and the light (8:12). Death and darkness flee when the life and light enter.
1:5 ***Light shines on in the darkness.*** Although

CHAPTER 1 **1** Pr 8:22; 1Jn 1:1; Pr 8:30; Jn 17:5; 1Jn 5:7 **2** Ge 1:1 **3** Ps 33:6; Eph 3:9; Col 1:16 **4** 1Jn 5:11; Jn 8:12 **5** Jn 3:19

stand it *or* overpower it *or* appropriate
it *or* absorb it [and is unreceptive to it].
[Gen 1:3]

The Witness of John the Baptist

[6]There came a man commissioned
and sent from God, whose name was
John. [Mal 3:1]
[7]This man came as a witness, to tes-
tify about the Light, so that all might
believe [in Christ, the Light] through
him.
[8]John was not the Light, but came
to testify about the Light.
[9]There it was—the true Light [the
genuine, perfect, steadfast Light]
which, coming into the world, enlight-
ens everyone. [Is 49:6]
[10]He (Christ) was in the world, and
though the world was made through
Him, the world did not recognize Him.
[11]He came to that which was His
own [that which belonged to Him—His
world, His creation, His possession],
and those who were His own [people—
the Jewish nation] did not receive *and*
welcome Him.
[12]But to as many as did receive *and*
welcome Him, He gave the right [the
authority, the privilege] to become
children of God, *that is,* to those who
believe in (adhere to, trust in, and rely
on) His name— [Is 56:5]
[13]who were born, not of blood [nat-
ural conception], nor of the will of the
flesh [physical impulse], nor of the
will of man [that of a natural father],
but of God [that is, a divine and super-
natural birth—they are born of God—
spiritually transformed, renewed,
sanctified].

The Word Made Flesh

[14]And the Word (Christ) became
flesh, and lived among us; and we [ac-
tually] saw His glory, glory as belongs
to the [One and] only begotten *Son*
of the Father, [the Son who is truly
unique, the only One of His kind, who
is] full of grace and truth (absolutely
free of deception). [Is 40:5]
[15]John testified [repeatedly] about
Him and has cried out [testifying
officially for the record, with valid-
ity and relevance], "This was He of
whom I said, 'He who comes after
me has a higher rank than I *and* has
priority over me, for He existed be-
fore me.' "
[16]For out of His fullness [the super-
abundance of His grace and truth] we
have all received grace upon grace

Satan and his forces resist the light, they cannot thwart its power. In short, Jesus is life and light; those who accept Him are "sons of light" (12:35–36). As the creation of light was the beginning of the original creation, so, when believers receive the light, they become part of the new creation (2Co 4:3–6).

1:7 *as a witness.* This phrase means "to testify" or "to declare." John uses the word translated *witness* 33 times as a verb and 14 times as a noun in his Gospel. The term is particularly important to his purpose, which is to record adequate witnesses to Jesus as the Messiah so that individuals might believe Him (20:30–31). ***believe.*** This word means "to trust." John uses this verb almost 100 times in his Gospel to express what must take place for a person to receive the gift of eternal life.

1:11 *receive.* This means "to receive with favor" and implies "welcome." Instead of a welcome mat, Jesus had a door slammed in His face. The themes of rejection and reception (v. 12) introduced in the prologue (1:1–18) appear repeatedly throughout the Gospel of John.

1:12 *He gave the right.* This phrase refers to the legitimate entitlement to the position of children of God. By believing, undeserving sinners can become full members of God's family.

1:14 *the Word (Christ) became flesh.* The Son of God who was from eternity became human, with limitations in time and space (Php 2:5–8). This is the doctrine of the incarnation: God became human. Nothing of the essential nature of deity was lost in this event; we might rephrase *became* as "took to Himself." John uses the word *flesh* to refer to the physical nature of humans, not to our sinful disposition. ***lived among us.*** The Greek word for *tent* or *lived* was also used in the Greek Old Testament for the tabernacle, where the presence of God dwelt. ***only One.*** This means unique, one of a kind.

1:16 *grace upon grace.* The background of this doubled term, as well as the use of the term in

6 Mal 3:1; Mt 3:1; Lk 3:2 **7** Ac 19:4 **9** Isa 49:6 **10** Heb 1:2 **11** Lk 19:14 **12** Gal 3:26 **13** 1Pe 1:23 **14** Mt 1:16; Lk 1:31; Gal 4:4; Heb 2:11; Isa 40:5; Col 1:19 **15** Jn 3:32; Mt 3:11; Mk 1:7; Lk 3:16; Col 1:17 **16** Col 1:19

[spiritual blessing upon spiritual bless-
ing, favor upon favor, and gift heaped
upon gift].
17For the Law was given through
Moses, but grace [the unearned, unde-
served favor of God] and truth came
through Jesus Christ. [Ex 20:1]
18No one has seen God [His es-
sence, His divine nature] at any time;
the [One and] only begotten God [that
is, the unique Son] who is in the inti-
mate presence of the Father, He has
explained Him [and interpreted and
revealed the awesome wonder of the
Father]. [Prov 8:30]

The Testimony of John

19This is the testimony of John [the
Baptist] when the Jews sent priests and
Levites to him from Jerusalem to ask
him, "Who are you?"
20And he confessed [truthfully] and
did not deny [that he was only a man],
but acknowledged, "I am not the Christ
(the Messiah, the Anointed)!"
21They asked him, "What then?
Are you Elijah?" And he said, "I am
not." "Are you the [promised] Prophet?"
And he answered, "No." [Deut 18:15,
18; Mal 4:5]
22Then they said to him, "Who are
you? *Tell us,* so that we may give an
answer to those who sent us. What do
you say about yourself?"
23He said, "I am THE VOICE OF ONE
SHOUTING IN THE WILDERNESS, 'MAKE
STRAIGHT THE WAY OF THE LORD,' as the
prophet Isaiah said." [Is 40:3]
24Now they had been sent from the
Pharisees.
25They asked him, "Why then are
you baptizing, if you are not the Christ,
nor Elijah, nor the Prophet?"
26John answered them, "I baptize
[only] in water, but among you there
stands One whom you do not recog-
nize *and* of whom you know nothing.
[Mal 3:1]
27"It is He [the preeminent One] who
comes after me, the strap of whose
sandal I am not worthy to untie [even
as His slave]."
28These things occurred in Bethany
across the Jordan [at the Jordan River
crossing], where John was baptizing.
29The next day he saw Jesus coming
to him and said, "Look! The Lamb of
God who takes away the sin of the
world! [Ex 12:3; Is 53:7]
30"This is He on behalf of whom I
said, 'After me comes a Man who has
a higher rank than I *and* has priority
over me, for He existed before me.'
31"I did not recognize Him [as the

---

verse 17, is found in Exodus 32 – 34. Moses and the people had received grace, but they were in tremendous need of more grace (Ex 33:13).

1:18 *No one has seen God.* God is Spirit (4:24) and is invisible (Col 1:15; 1Ti 1:17) unless God chooses to reveal Himself. Humans cannot look at God and live (Ex 33:20). However, the Son is in intimate relationship with the Father, face-to-face with God (1:1; 6:46; 1Jn 1:2). God became visible to human eyes in the man Jesus. It is through seeing the Son that we see God.

1:19 – 20 *the Jews.* This refers to the Jewish leaders or the council (the Sanhedrin), who would be responsible for examining anyone thought to be a prophet, to see if the person was true or false.

1:23 *MAKE STRAIGHT.* When a king traveled, roads were built so that the royal chariot would not have to travel over rough terrain or be stuck in the mud. Isaiah was saying that before God appeared to manifest His glory, a voice would be heard, inviting Israel to make straight the way by which God Himself would come.

1:24 *the Pharisees.* The Pharisees were an influential sect that numbered about 6,000. As strict interpreters of the law in Israel, they were extremely zealous for ritual and tradition.

1:27 *strap of whose sandal I am not worthy to untie.* Undoing the shoe strap was the job of a slave. The Jewish Talmud says, "Everything that a servant will do for his master, a scholar shall perform for his teacher, except the menial task of loosing his sandal thong." Thus, John was saying that "Jesus Christ is the living Lord and I am the voice, His servant and slave. Actually, I'm not even worthy to be His slave."

1:29 *The Lamb of God.* Jesus Christ is the Lamb that God would give as a sacrifice not only for Israel, but for the whole world (Isa 52:13 – 53:12).

---

17 Ex 20:1; Ro 5:21; Jn 8:32 **18** Ex 33:20; Mt 11:27; 1Ti 6:16; 1Jn 4:9 **19** Jn 5:33 **20** Lk 3:15; Ac 13:25 **21** Mal 4:5; Dt 18:15 **23** Mt 3:3; Isa 40:3 **26** Mt 3:11; Mal 3:1 **27** Ac 19:4 **28** Jdg 7:24; Jn 10:40 **29** Ex 12:3; Isa 53:7; Ac 8:32; 1Pe 1:19; Rev 5:6; Isa 53:11; 1Co 15:3; Gal 1:4; Heb 1:3; 2:17; 9:28; 1Pe 2:24; 3:18; 1Jn 2:2; 3:5; Rev 1:5 **30** ver. 15,27 **31** Mal 3:1; Mt 3:6; Lk 1:17,76,77; 3:3,4

Messiah]; but I came baptizing in water
so that He would be [publicly] revealed
to Israel."
32 John gave [further] evidence [tes-
tifying officially for the record, with
validity and relevance], saying, "I
have seen the Spirit descending as a
dove out of heaven, and He remained
upon Him. [Matt 3:13–17; Mark 1:9–11;
Luke 3:22, 23]
33 "I did not recognize Him [as the
Messiah], but He who sent me to bap-
tize in water said to me, 'He upon
whom you see the Spirit descend and
remain, this One is He who baptizes
with the Holy Spirit.'
34 "I myself have [actually] seen [that
happen], and my testimony is that this
is the Son of God!"

Jesus' Public Ministry, First Converts

35 Again the next day John was
standing with two of his disciples,
36 and he looked at Jesus as He
walked along, and said, "Look! The
Lamb of God!"
37 The two disciples heard him say
this, and they followed Jesus.
38 And Jesus turned and saw them
following Him, and asked them, "What
do you want?" They answered Him,
"Rabbi (which translated means Teach-
er), where are You staying?"
39 He said to them, "Come, and you
will see." So they went [with Him] and
saw where He was staying; and they
stayed with Him that day, for it was
about the tenth hour.
40 One of the two who heard what
John said and [as a result] followed
Jesus was Andrew, Simon Peter's
brother.
41 He first looked for *and* found his
own brother Simon and told him, "We
have found the Messiah" (which trans-
lated means the Christ).
42 Andrew brought Simon to Jesus.
Jesus looked at him and said, "You
are Simon the son of John. You shall
be called Cephas (which is translated
Peter)."
43 The next day Jesus decided to go
into Galilee, and He found Philip and
said to him, "Follow Me [as My disci-
ple, accepting Me as your Master and
Teacher, and walking the same path
of life that I walk]."
44 Now Philip was from Bethsaida,
the city of Andrew and Peter.
45 Philip found Nathanael and told
him, "We have found the One Mo-
ses in the Law and also the Prophets
wrote about—Jesus from Nazareth,
the son of Joseph [according to public
record]."
46 Nathanael answered him, "Can
anything good come out of Nazareth?"
Philip replied, "Come and see."
47 Jesus saw Nathanael coming to-
ward Him, and said of him, "Here is an
Israelite indeed [a true descendant of
Jacob], in whom there is no guile *nor*
deceit *nor* duplicity!"
48 Nathanael said to Jesus, "How do
You know [these things about] me?"
Jesus answered, "Before Philip called
you, when you were still under the fig
tree, I saw you."

1:33 *this One is He who baptizes with the Holy Spirit.* Seven times, the New Testament mentions this ministry of Jesus. Five are prophetic (Mt 3:11; Mk 1:8; Lk 3:16; Ac 1:5); one is historical (Ac 11:16–18); one is doctrinal (1Co 12:13).

1:42 *Cephas.* This is the Aramaic word for "rock" (Mt 16:18).

1:45 *Nathanael.* This name is not mentioned in the Synoptic Gospels. But in every list of the apostles in Matthew, Mark, and Luke, the name Bartholomew is listed with Philip, as Nathanael is linked with Philip here. It is likely that Nathanael and Bartholomew were the same person.

1:46 *Nazareth.* Nathanael knew that the Old Testament prophets had predicted that the Messiah would be born in Bethlehem. Furthermore, Nazareth was an obscure village. Nathanael simply could not fathom that such a significant person as the Messiah could come from such an insignificant place as Nazareth.

1:48–49 *under the fig tree.* In the Old Testament, this expression often suggests being safe and at leisure (1Ki 4:25; Mic 4:4; Zec 3:10).

---

32 Mt 3:16; Mk 1:10; Jn 5:32 **33** Mt 3:11; Ac 2:4; 10:44 **36** ver. 29 **42** Mt 16:18 **44** Jn 12:21 **45** Jn 21:2; Ge 3:15; 49:10; Dt 18:18; See Lk 24:27; Isa 4:2; 7:14; 9:6; Mic 5:2; Zec 6:12; See more on Lk 24:27; Mt 2:23; Lk 2:4 **46** Jn 7:41,42 **47** Ps 32:2; 73:1; Jn 8:39; Ro 2:28; 9:6

49 Nathanael answered, "Rabbi (Teacher), You are the Son of God; You are the King of Israel."

50 Jesus replied, "Because I said to you that I saw you under the fig tree, do you believe [in Me]? You will see greater things than this."

51 Then He said to him, "I assure you *and* most solemnly say to you, you will see heaven opened and the angels of God ascending and descending on the Son of Man [the bridge between heaven and earth]." [Gen 28:12; Dan 7:13]

Miracle at Cana

2 ON THE third day there was a wedding at Cana of Galilee, and the mother of Jesus was there;

2 and both Jesus and His disciples were invited to the wedding.

3 When the wine was all gone, the mother of Jesus said to Him, "They have no *more* wine."

4 Jesus said to her, "[Dear] woman, what is that to you and to Me? My time [to act and to be revealed] has not yet come." [Eccl 3:1]

5 His mother said to the servants, "Whatever He says to you, do it."

6 Now there were six stone waterpots set there for the Jewish custom of purification (ceremonial washing), containing twenty or thirty gallons each.

7 Jesus said to the servants, "Fill the waterpots with water." So they filled them up to the brim.

8 Then He said to them, "Draw *some* out now and take it to the headwaiter [of the banquet]." So they took it *to him*.

9 And when the headwaiter tasted the water which had turned into wine, not knowing where it came from (though the servants who had drawn the water knew) he called the bridegroom,

10 and said to him, "Everyone else serves his best wine first, and when *people* have drunk freely, *then he serves* that which is not so good; but you have kept back the good wine until now."

11 This, the first of His signs (attesting miracles), Jesus did in Cana of Galilee, and revealed His glory [displaying His deity and His great power openly], and His disciples believed [confidently] in Him [as the Messiah—they adhered to, trusted in, and relied on Him]. [Deut 5:24; Ps 72:19]

12 After this He went down to Capernaum, He and His mother and brothers and His disciples; and they stayed there a few days.

First Passover—Cleansing the Temple

13 Now the Passover of the Jews was approaching, so Jesus went up to Jerusalem.

2:1 – 2 ***Cana.*** This city was about four and a half miles northwest of Nazareth. ***the mother of Jesus was there; and both Jesus and His disciples were invited.*** This suggests that Jesus and His disciples were invited because of Mary. Her forwardness in asking Jesus to help when the wine ran out (v. 3) may indicate that she was in some way related to the family holding the wedding.

2:3 ***They have no more wine.*** Hospitality in the East was a sacred duty. A wedding feast often lasted for a week. To run out of wine at such an important event would have been humiliating for the bride and groom. The family of Jesus was not wealthy, and it is likely their relatives and acquaintances were not either. This may have been a "low-budget" wedding feast.

2:6 ***six stone waterpots.*** Each waterpot held 20 – 30 gallons, for a total of 120 – 180 gallons of the finest wine (v. 10). ***Jewish custom of purification.*** Jewish tradition required several kinds of ceremonial washings. Strict Jews washed their hands before a meal, between courses, and after the meal. This "purifying" extended not only to washing hands, but also to washing cups and vessels (Mk 7:3 – 4).

2:11 ***This, the first of His signs.*** In the Gospel of John, the miracles of Jesus are called signs, indicating that they pointed to His messiahship. This sign signified Christ's glory — that is, His deity. When Jesus transformed water into wine, He demonstrated His power.

2:13 ***the Passover of the Jews.*** Every male Jew was required to go to Jerusalem three times

---

49 Mt 14:33; 21:5; Jn 18:37 **51** Ge 28:12; Mt 4:11; Lk 2:9,13; 22:43; Ac 1:10 **CHAPTER 2** **1** See Jos 19:28 **4** Jn 19:26; 2Sa 16:10; Jn 7:6 **6** Mk 7:3 **9** Jn 4:46 **11** Jn 1:14 **12** Mt 12:46 **13** Ex 12:14; Dt 16:1; Jn 5:1

MIRACLES OF JESUS

HEALING MIRACLES	MATTHEW	MARK	LUKE	JOHN
Man with leprosy	8:2–4	1:40–42	5:12–13	
Roman centurion's servant	8:5–13		7:1–10	
Peter's mother-in-law	8:14–15	1:30–31	4:38–39	
Two men from Gadara	8:28–34	5:1–15	8:27–35	
Paralyzed man	9:2–7	2:3–12	5:18–25	
Woman with bleeding	9:20–22	5:25–29	8:43–48	
Two blind men	9:27–31			
Mute, demon-possessed man	9:32–33			
Man with a shriveled hand	12:10–13	3:1–5	6:6–10	
Blind, mute, demon-possessed man	12:22		11:14	
Canaanite woman's daughter	15:21–28	7:24–30		
Demon-possessed boy	17:14–18	9:17–29	9:38–43	
Two blind men (including Bartimaeus)	20:29–34	10:46–52	18:35–43	
Deaf mute		7:31–37		
Demon-possessed man in synagogue		1:23–26	4:33–35	
Blind man at Bethsaida		8:22–26		
Crippled woman			13:11–13	
Man with abnormal swelling			14:1–4	
Ten men with leprosy			17:11–19	
The high priest's servant			22:50–51	
Official's son at Capernaum				4:46–54
Sick man at pool of Bethesda				5:1–9
Man born blind				9:1–7
MIRACLES SHOWING POWER OVER NATURE				
Calming the storm	8:23–27	4:37–41	8:22–25	
Walking on water	14:25	6:48–51		6:19–21
Feeding the 5,000	14:15–21	6:35–44	9:12–17	6:6–13
Feeding the 4,000	15:32–38	8:1–9		
Coin in fish's mouth	17:24–27			
Fig tree withered	21:18–22	11:12–14,20–25		
Large catch of fish			5:4–11	
Water turned into wine				2:1–11
Another large catch of fish				21:1–11
MIRACLES OF RAISING THE DEAD				
Jairus's daughter	9:18–19,23–25	5:22–24,38–42	8:41–42,49–56	
Widow's son at Nain			7:11–15	
Lazarus				11:1–44

14 And in the temple [enclosure] He
found the people who were selling
oxen and sheep and doves, and the
money changers sitting *at their tables.*
[Matt 21:12ff; Mark 11:15, 17]
15 He made a whip of cords, and
drove them all out of the temple, with
the sheep and the oxen; and He scat-
tered the coins of the money changers
and overturned their tables;
16 then to those who sold the doves
He said, "Take these things away! Stop
making My Father's house a place of
commerce!" [Ps 93:5]
17 His disciples remembered that it is
written [in the Scriptures], "ZEAL (love,
concern) FOR YOUR HOUSE [and its honor]
WILL CONSUME ME." [Ps 69:9]
18 Then the Jews retorted, "What sign
(attesting miracle) can You show us
as [proof of] your authority for doing
these things?"
19 Jesus answered them, "Destroy
this temple, and in three days I will
raise it up."
20 Then the Jews replied, "It took
forty-six years to build this temple,
and You will raise it up in three days?"
21 But He was speaking of the temple
which was His body.
22 So when He had risen from the dead,
His disciples remembered what He had
said. And they believed *and* trusted in
and relied on the Scripture and the
words that Jesus had spoken. [Ps 16:10]
23 Now when He was in Jerusalem at
the Passover feast, many believed in
His name [identifying themselves with
Him] after seeing His signs (attesting
miracles) which He was doing.
24 But Jesus, for His part, did not en-
trust Himself to them, because He knew
all *people* [and understood the superfi-
ciality and fickleness of human nature],
25 and He did not need anyone to
testify concerning man [and human
nature], for He Himself knew what
was in man [in their hearts—in the
very core of their being]. [1 Sam 16:7]

The New Birth

3 NOW THERE was a certain man
among the Pharisees named Nico-
demus, a ruler (member of the Sanhe-
drin) among the Jews,
2 who came to Jesus at night and said

---

a year — for the Feast of Passover, the Feast of Pentecost, and the Feast of Tabernacles (Ex 23:14 – 19; Lev 23). ***Jerusalem.*** The Synoptic Gospels concentrate on Jesus' Galilean ministry. John focuses on Jesus' ministry in Jerusalem.

2:14 *And in the temple [enclosure] He found the people who were selling oxen and sheep and doves.* The Synoptic Gospels place the cleansing of the temple at the conclusion of Jesus' ministry (Mt 21:12 – 13), whereas John puts it at the beginning. Apparently, Jesus cleansed the temple two different times. The law of Moses required that any animal offered in sacrifice be unblemished and that every Jewish male over 19 years of age pay a temple tax (Lev 1:3; Dt 17:1). As a result, tax collectors and inspectors of sacrificial animals were present at the temple. However, these officials would not accept secular coins because they had an image of the Roman emperor. To put such coins into the temple treasury was thought to be an offense. Accordingly, merchants and moneychangers set up shop and charged high prices for changing currency and for sacrificial animals.

2:19 *Destroy this temple.* Jesus was not talking about the physical building; He was referring to His body, as John emphasizes in verse 21. Jesus was speaking of His death. ***I will raise it up.*** Note that Jesus did not say, "I will build it again." He was referring to His resurrection, three days after His death.

2:20 *forty-six years.* Herod the Great began restoring the temple in 20 BC. The work was not finished at the time of this conversation. In fact, it was not completed until around AD 64 under Herod Agrippa.

2:23 *many believed in His name.* This was saving faith. John's purpose in recording Jesus' miracles was for people to believe and have eternal life (20:30 – 31).

2:24 *But Jesus, for His part, did not entrust Himself.* This word is the same Greek word translated *believe* in verse 23. There is a play on words here. These individuals trusted Jesus, but Jesus did not entrust Himself to them.

3:2 *at night.* The fact that Nicodemus came to Jesus at night may reveal the timidity of his faith (12:42); however, his faith was developing (7:50 – 51; 19:39).

---

14 Mt 21:12; Mk 11:15; Lk 19:45 **16** Lk 2:49 **17** Ps 69:9 **18** Mt 12:38; Jn 6:30 **19** Mt 26:61; 27:40; Mk 14:58; 15:29 **21** Col 2:9; Heb 8:2; 1Co 3:16; 6:19; 2Co 6:16 **22** Lk 24:8 **25** 1Sa 16:7; 1Ch 28:9; Mt 9:4; Mk 2:8; Jn 6:64; 16:30; Ac 1:24; Rev 2:23 **CHAPTER 3** **2** Jn 7:50; 19:39; 9:16,33; Ac 2:22; Ac 10:38

JESUS' VISITS TO JERUSALEM

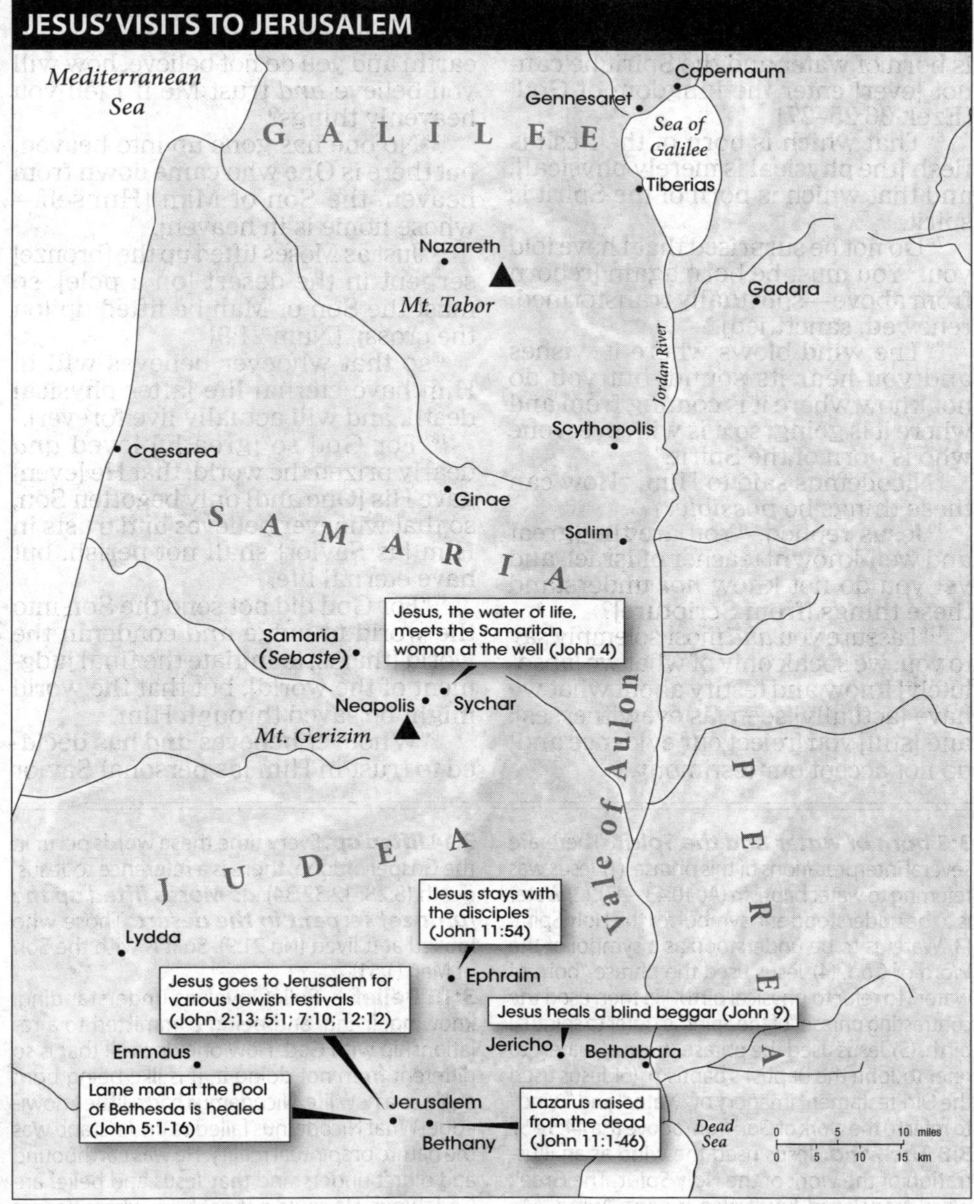

to Him, "Rabbi (Teacher), we know
[without any doubt] that You have
come from God as a teacher; for no
one can do these signs [these wonders,
these attesting miracles] that You do
unless God is with him."
³Jesus answered him, "I assure you
and most solemnly say to you, unless
a person is born again [reborn from
above—spiritually transformed, re-
newed, sanctified], he cannot [ever] see
and experience the kingdom of God."
⁴Nicodemus said to Him, "How can a
man be born when he is old? He cannot
enter his mother's womb a second time
and be born, can he?"

3 Jn 1:13; Gal 6:15; Titus 3:5; Jas 1:18; 1Pe 1:23; 1Jn 3:9

[5]Jesus answered, "I assure you *and*
most solemnly say to you, unless one
is born of water and the Spirit he can-
not [ever] enter the kingdom of God.
[Ezek 36:25–27]
[6]"That which is born of the flesh is
flesh [the physical is merely physical],
and that which is born of the Spirit is
spirit.
[7]"Do not be surprised that I have told
you, 'You must be born again [reborn
from above—spiritually transformed,
renewed, sanctified].'
[8]"The wind blows where it wishes
and you hear its sound, but you do
not know where it is coming from and
where it is going; so it is with everyone
who is born of the Spirit."
[9]Nicodemus said to Him, "How can
these things be *possible?*"
[10]Jesus replied, "You are the [great
and well-known] teacher of Israel, and
yet you do not know *nor* understand
these things [from Scripture]?
[11]"I assure you *and* most solemnly say
to you, we speak only of what we [abso-
lutely] know and testify about what we
have [actually] seen [as eyewitnesses];
and [still] you [reject our evidence and]
do not accept our testimony.
[12]"If I told you earthly things [that
is, things that happen right here on
earth] and you do not believe, how will
you believe *and* trust Me if I tell you
heavenly things?
[13]"No one has gone up into heaven,
but there is One who came down from
heaven, the Son of Man [Himself—
whose home is in heaven].
[14]"Just as Moses lifted up the [bronze]
serpent in the desert [on a pole], so
must the Son of Man be lifted up [on
the cross], [Num 21:9]
[15]so that whoever believes will in
Him have eternal life [after physical
death, and will actually live forever].
[16]"For God so [greatly] loved *and*
dearly prized the world, that He [even]
gave His [One and] only begotten Son,
so that whoever believes *and* trusts in
Him [as Savior] shall not perish, but
have eternal life.
[17]"For God did not send the Son into
the world to judge *and* condemn the
world [that is, to initiate the final judg-
ment of the world], but that the world
might be saved through Him.
[18]"Whoever believes *and* has decid-
ed to trust in Him [as personal Savior

3:5 *born of water and the Spirit.* There are several interpretations of this phrase. (1) Jesus was referring to water baptism (Ac 10:43–47). (2) Water is to be understood as a symbol for the Holy Spirit. (3) Water is to be understood as a symbol of the Word of God. (4) Jesus used the phrase "born of water" to refer to physical birth. He then used the contrasting phrase "of the Spirit" to refer to spiritual birth. (5) Jesus used the phrase "born of water" to refer to John the Baptist's baptism. (6) Jesus used the Old Testament imagery of "water" and "wind" to refer to the work of God from above (Isa 44:3–5).

3:8 *The wind.* Jesus used the wind as an illustration of the work of the Holy Spirit. The Greek word translated *Spirit* also means "wind." As the wind seemingly blows where it wills, so the Holy Spirit sovereignly works. Likewise, no one knows the origin or destination of the wind, but everyone knows it is there. The same is true of the Holy Spirit.

3:12 *heavenly things.* This refers to events like Christ's ascension (6:61–62) and the coming of the Holy Spirit (16:7).

3:14 *lifted up.* Every time these words occur in the Gospel of John, there is a reference to Jesus' death (8:28; 12:32,34). ***as Moses lifted up the [bronze] serpent in the desert.*** Those who looked at it lived (Nu 21:9). So it is with the Son of Man (1:51).

3:16 Belief — Belief involves understanding, knowing, living, and being committed to a relationship with God. How one does all that is so different from not doing it, it is like being born again to a new life. Nicodemus had a little knowledge. What Nicodemus failed to understand was the nature of spiritual reality. He was earthbound and didn't understand that Jesus and belief are God things. He could not get from where he was to where Jesus was on the road of his understanding. He needed to accept a new road, namely the one Jesus was walking, toward Him. Jesus draws us to that light, His light. We have to respond to it as Nicodemus did over time (Jn 7:50; 19:39). Belief involves internalizing these truths with our whole hearts and minds, being born again, letting all of ourselves be exposed to, and by, that light.

5 Mk 16:16; Ac 2:38 **8** Ecc 11:5; 1Co 2:11 **9** Jn 6:52,60 **11** Mt 11:27; Jn 1:18; 7:16; 8:28; ver. 32 **13** Pr 30:4; Jn 6:33,38; Ac 2:34; 1Co 15:47; Eph 4:9 **14** Nu 21:9; Jn 8:28; 12:32 **15** ver. 36; Jn 6:47 **16** Ro 5:8; 1Jn 4:9 **17** Lk 9:56; Jn 5:45; 8:15; 12:47; 1Jn 4:14 **18** Jn 5:24; 6:40,47; 20:31

and Lord] is not judged [for this one, there is no judgment, no rejection, no condemnation]; but the one who does not believe [and has decided to reject Him as personal Savior and Lord] is judged already [that one has been convicted and sentenced], because he has not believed *and* trusted in the name of the [One and] only begotten Son of God [the One who is truly unique, the only One of His kind, the One who alone can save him].

19 “This is the judgment [that is, the cause for indictment, the test by which people are judged, the basis for the sentence]: the Light has come into the world, and people loved the darkness rather than the Light, for their deeds were evil. [Is 5:20]

20 “For every wrongdoer hates the Light, and does not come to the Light [but shrinks from it] for fear that his [sinful, worthless] activities will be exposed *and* condemned.

21 “But whoever practices truth [and does what is right—morally, ethically, spiritually] comes to the Light, so that his works may be plainly shown to be what they are—accomplished in God [divinely prompted, done with God’s help, in dependence on Him].”

John’s Last Testimony

22 After these things Jesus and His disciples went into the land of Judea, and there He spent time with them and baptized. [John 4:1, 2]

23 Now John was also baptizing at Aenon near Salim, because there was an abundance of water there; and *people* were coming and were being baptized—

24 for John had not yet been thrown into prison.

25 Therefore there arose a controversy between John’s disciples and a Jew in regard to purification (ceremonial washing).

26 So they came to John and said to him, “Rabbi (Teacher), the Man who was with you on the other side of the Jordan [at the Jordan River crossing]—and to whom you have testified—look, He is baptizing too, and everyone is going to Him!”

27 John replied, “A man can receive nothing [he can claim nothing at all] unless it has been granted to him from heaven [for there is no other source than the sovereign will of God].

28 “You yourselves are my witnesses that I stated, ‘I am not the Christ (the Messiah, the Anointed),’ but, ‘I have [only] been sent ahead of Him [as His appointed forerunner and messenger to announce and proclaim His coming].’ [Mal 3:1]

29 “He who has the bride is the bridegroom; but the friend of the bridegroom, who stands by and listens to him, rejoices greatly because of the bridegroom’s voice. So this pleasure *and* joy of mine is now complete. [Song 5:1]

30 “He must increase [in prominence], but I must decrease. [Is 9:7]

3:20 *For every wrongdoer hates the Light.* People offer many excuses for not accepting Christ. Some cite the presence of hypocrites in the church. Others claim inability to believe some of the truths about Christ or the gospel. These are merely attempts to conceal a heart in rebellion against God. The ultimate reason people do not come to Christ is that they do not want to.

3:26 *they came to John.* John the Baptist’s disciples were loyal to him. They were deeply concerned that one of his “disciples,” Jesus, was competing with and surpassing him. In their astonishment, they exaggerated the predicament, saying, “all men come to him.” They were concerned that John was losing his audience to another preacher.

3:27 *John replied.* John the Baptist clarified the relationship between himself and Jesus. First, he talked about himself (vv. 27 – 29); then he talked about Jesus (vv. 30 – 36). John explained that he could not accept the position of supremacy that his disciples wanted to thrust upon him because he had not received it from heaven.

3:29 *friend of the bridegroom.* John compared himself to this person who was generally appointed to arrange the preliminaries of the wedding, to manage the wedding, and to preside at the wedding feast.

19 Jn 1:4,9-11; 8:12 **20** Job 24:13; Eph 5:13 **22** Jn 4:2 **23** 1Sa 9:4; Mt 3:5,6 **24** Mt 14:3 **26** Jn 1:7,15,27,34 **27** 1Co 4:7; Heb 5:4; Jas 1:17 **28** Jn 1:20,27; Mal 3:1; Mk 1:2; Lk 1:17 **29** Mt 22:2; 2Co 11:2; Eph 5:25,27; Rev 21:9; SS 5:1

[31]"He who comes from [heaven] above is above all *others;* he who is of the earth is from the earth and speaks [about things] of the earth [his viewpoint and experience are earthly]. He who comes from heaven is above all.
[32]"What He has [actually] seen and heard, of that He testifies; and yet no one accepts His testimony [as true].
[33]"Whoever receives His testimony has set his seal [of approval] to this: God is true [and he knows that God cannot lie].
[34]"For He whom God has sent speaks the words of God [proclaiming the Father's own message]; for God gives the [gift of the] Spirit without measure [generously and boundlessly]! [Deut 18:18]
[35]"The Father loves the Son and has given *and* entrusted all things into His hand. [Dan 7:14]
[36]"He who believes *and* trusts in the Son *and* accepts Him [as Savior] has eternal life [that is, already possesses it]; but he who does not believe the Son *and* chooses to reject Him, [disobeying Him and denying Him as Savior] will not see [eternal] life, but [instead] the wrath of God hangs over him *continually.*" [Heb 3:18]

Jesus Goes to Galilee

4 SO WHEN the Lord learned that the Pharisees had been told that Jesus was making and baptizing more disciples than John
[2](although Jesus Himself was not baptizing, but His disciples were),
[3]He left Judea and returned again to Galilee.
[4]Now He had to go through Samaria.
[5]So He arrived at a Samaritan town called Sychar, near the tract of land that Jacob gave to his son Joseph;
[6]and Jacob's well was there. So Jesus, tired as He was from His journey, sat down by the well. It was then about the sixth hour (noon).

The Samaritan Woman

[7]Then a woman from Samaria came to draw water. Jesus said to her, "Give Me a drink"—
[8]For His disciples had gone off into the city to buy food—
[9]The Samaritan woman asked Him, "How is it that You, being a Jew, ask me, a Samaritan woman, for a drink?"

3:31 *He who comes from [heaven] above.* This is a reference to Christ. ***he who is of the earth.*** This refers to John the Baptist. John emphasized his earthly origin and its limitations. John proclaimed divine truth on earth; Jesus, on the other hand, is from heaven and above all.
3:33 *has set his seal.* In a society where many could not read, seals were used to convey a clear message, even to the illiterate. A seal indicated ownership to all and expressed a person's personal guarantee. To receive Jesus' testimony is to certify that God is true regarding what He has sealed.
3:34 *God gives [the gift of] the Spirit without measure.* Unlike human teachers, Jesus was not given the Spirit in a limited way (Isa 11:1 – 2). All three Persons of the Trinity are referred to in this verse; God the Father sent Christ the Son, and gave Him the Holy Spirit without measure.
4:1 *So when.* This refers the reader back to 3:22 – 36. Christ's success in winning disciples had created jealousy among John's followers and provoked questions among the Pharisees. Since Jesus did not want to be drawn into a controversy over baptism at this stage of His ministry, He left Judea for Galilee (v. 3).
4:4 *He had to go through Samaria.* The shortest route from Judea in the south to Galilee in the north went through Samaria. The journey took three days if He wanted to travel the direct route. The Jews often avoided Samaria by going around it along the Jordan River. The hatred between the Jews and Samaritans went back to the days of the exile. Samaria was the region between Judea and Galilee. When the Northern Kingdom was exiled to Assyria, King Sargon repopulated the area with captives from other lands. The intermarriage of these foreigners and the Jews who had been left complicated the ancestry of the Samaritans. The Jews hated the Samaritans and considered them to be no longer "pure" Jews.

31 ver. 13; Jn 8:23; Mt 28:18; Jn 1:15,27; Ro 9:5; 1Co 15:47; Jn 6:33; 1Co 15:47; Eph 1:21; Php 2:9 **32** ver. 11; Jn 8:26; 15:15 **33** Ro 3:4; 1Jn 5:10 **34** Jn 7:16; Jn 1:16 **35** Mt 11:27; 28:18; Lk 10:22; Jn 5:20,22; 13:3; 17:2; Heb 2:8 **36** ver. 15,16; Jn 1:12; 6:47; Ro 1:17; 1Jn 5:10 **CHAPTER 4 1** Jn 3:22,26 **5** Ge 33:19; 48:22; Jos 24:32 **9** 2Ki 17:24; Lk 9:52,53; Ac 10:28

(For Jews have nothing to do with Sa-
maritans.)
10 Jesus answered her, “If you knew
[about] God’s gift [of eternal life], and
who it is who says, ‘Give Me a drink,’
you would have asked Him [instead],
and He would have given you living
water (eternal life).”
11 She said to Him, “Sir, You have
nothing to draw with [no bucket and
rope] and the well is deep. Where then
do You get that living water?
12 “Are You greater than our father
Jacob, who gave us the well, and who
used to drink from it himself, and his
sons and his cattle also?”
13 Jesus answered her, “Everyone
who drinks this water will be thirsty
again.
14 “But whoever drinks the water that
I give him will never be thirsty again.
But the water that I give him will be-
come in him a spring of water [satis-
fying his thirst for God] welling up
[continually flowing, bubbling within
him] to eternal life.”
15 The woman said to Him, “Sir, give
me this water, so that I will not get
thirsty nor [have to continually] come
all the way here to draw.”
16 At this, Jesus said, “Go, call your
husband and come back.”
17 The woman answered, “I do not
have a husband.” Jesus said to her,
“You have correctly said, ‘I do not have
a husband’;
18 for you have had five husbands,
and the man you are now living with
is not your husband. You have said this
truthfully.”
19 The woman said to Him, “Sir, I see
that You are a prophet.
20 “Our fathers worshiped on this
mountain, but you *Jews* say that the
place where one ought to worship is
in Jerusalem [at the temple].”
21 Jesus replied, “Woman, believe Me,
a time is coming [when God’s kingdom
comes] when you will worship the Fa-
ther neither on this mountain nor in
Jerusalem.
22 “You [Samaritans] do not know
what you worship; we [Jews] do know
what we worship, for salvation is from
the Jews.
23 “But a time is coming and is al-
ready here when the true worshipers
will worship the Father in spirit [from
the heart, the inner self] and in truth;
for the Father seeks such people to be
His worshipers.
24 “God is spirit [the Source of life, yet
invisible to mankind], and those who
worship Him must worship in spirit
and truth.”
25 The woman said to Him, “I know
that Messiah is coming (He who is
called Christ—the Anointed); when
that One comes, He will tell us every-
thing [we need to know].”
26 Jesus said to her, “I who speak to
you, am *He* (the Messiah).”
27 Just then His disciples came, and
they were surprised to find Him talking
with a woman. However, no one said,
“What are You asking about?” or,
“Why are You talking to her?”
28 Then the woman left her water jar,
and went into the city and began tell-
ing the people,
29 “Come, see a man who told me
all the things that I have done! Can
this be the Christ (the Messiah, the
Anointed)?”

4:16 *Go, call your husband.* Jesus mentioned the woman’s husband in order to expose her sin (v. 18).

4:20 *you Jews say . . . in Jerusalem.* The Jews insisted that the exclusive place of worship was Jerusalem. But the Samaritans had set up a rival worship site on Mount Gerizim, which, according to their tradition, was where Abraham went to sacrifice Isaac and where later on he met Melchizedek.

4:24 *God is spirit . . . worship in spirit and truth.* God is not limited by time and space. When people are born of the Spirit, they can commune with God anywhere. *Spirit* is the opposite of what is material and earthly, for example, Mount Gerizim. Christ makes worship a matter of the heart. *Truth* is what is in harmony with the nature and will of God. The issue is not where a person worships, but how and whom.

4:29 *all the things that I have done.* In her

---

10 Isa 12:3; 44:3; Jer 2:13; Zec 13:1; 14:8 **14** Jn 6:35,58; 7:38 **15** Jn 6:34; 17:2,3; Ro 6:23; 1Jn 5:20 **19** Lk 7:16; 24:19; Jn 6:14 **20** Jdg 9:7; Dt 12:5,11; 1Ki 9:3; 2Ch 7:12 **21** Mal 1:11; 1Ti 2:8 **22** 2Ki 17:29; Isa 2:3; Lk 24:47; Ro 9:4,5 **23** Php 3:3; Jn 1:17 **24** 2Co 3:17 **25** ver. 29,39 **26** Mt 26:63,64; Mk 14:61,62 **29** ver. 25

[30]So the people left the city and were
coming to Him.
[31]Meanwhile, the disciples were
urging Jesus [to have a meal], saying,
"Rabbi (Teacher), eat."
[32]But He told them, "I have food to
eat that you do not know about."
[33]So the disciples said to one another,
"Has anyone brought Him *something*
to eat?"
[34]Jesus said to them, "My food is to
do the will of Him who sent Me and to
completely finish His work.
[35]"Do you not say, 'It is still four
months until the harvest comes?' Look,
I say to you, raise your eyes and look
at the fields *and* see, they are white
for harvest.
[36]"Already the reaper is receiving
his wages and he is gathering fruit
for eternal life; so that he who plants
and he who reaps may rejoice together.
[37]"For in this *case* the saying is true,
'One [person] sows and another reaps.'
[38]"I sent you to reap [a crop] for
which you have not worked. Others
have worked and you have been priv-
ileged to reap the results of their work."

The Samaritans

[39]Now many Samaritans from that
city believed in Him *and* trusted Him
[as Savior] because of what the woman
said when she testified, "He told me all
the things that I have done."
[40]So when the Samaritans came to
Jesus, they asked Him to remain with
them; and He stayed there two days.
[41]Many more believed in Him [with
a deep, abiding trust] because of His
word [His personal message to them];
[42]and they told the woman, "We no
longer believe *just* because of what you
said; for [now] we have heard *Him* for
ourselves and know [with confident
assurance] that this One is truly the
Savior of [all] the world."
[43]After the two days He went on
from there into Galilee.
[44]For Jesus Himself declared that
a prophet has no honor in his own
country.
[45]So when He arrived in Galilee, the
Galileans welcomed Him, since they
had seen all the things that He did in
Jerusalem at the feast; for they too
came to the feast.

Healing a Nobleman's Son

[46]So Jesus came again to Cana of
Galilee, where He had turned the wa-
ter into wine. And there was a certain
royal official whose son was sick in
Capernaum.
[47]Having heard that Jesus had come
back from Judea to Galilee, he went
to *meet* Him and began asking Him
to come down and heal his son; for he
was at the point of death.
[48]Then Jesus said to him, "Unless
you [people] see [miraculous] signs and
wonders, you [simply] will not believe."
[49]The royal official pleaded with
Him, "Sir, do come down [at once] be-
fore my child dies!"
[50]Jesus said to him, "Go; your son
lives!" The man believed what Jesus
said to him and started home.
[51]As he was already going down
[the road], his servants met him and
reported that his son was living [and
was healthy].
[52]So he asked them at what time he
began to get better. They said, "Yester-

---

excitement, the woman exaggerated. She did not report what Jesus actually told her, but what He could have told her. Note the woman's spiritual journey. She first viewed Christ as a Jew (v. 9), then as a prophet (v. 19), and finally as the Messiah.

4:36 *receiving his wages.* The reaper of a spiritual harvest receives wages — that is, fruit which brings joy. In this case, Jesus sowed by giving the message to the woman. The disciples were going to reap the harvest that He had sown.

4:42 *Savior of [all] the world.* This title is used only here and in 1 John 4:14. The Jews of Jesus' day taught that to approach God, one first had to be a Jew. By including this incident in the Gospel, John demonstrates that Jesus is for all people of the world.

4:46 *a certain royal official.* This was probably someone who was in the service of the king. Herod Antipas was technically the "tetrarch" of Galilee, but he was referred to as a king.

34 Job 23:12; Jn 6:38; 17:4; 19:30 **35** Mt 9:37; Lk 10:2 **36** Da 12:3 **39** ver. 29 **42** Jn 17:8; 1Jn 4:14
44 Mt 13:57 **45** Jn 2:23; 3:2; Dt 16:16 **46** Jn 2:1,11 **48** 1Co 1:22

day during the seventh hour the fever
left him."
[53]Then the father realized that it was
at that *very* hour when Jesus had said
to him, "Your son lives"; and he and his
entire household believed *and* confi-
dently trusted [in Him as Savior].
[54]This is the second sign (attesting
miracle) that Jesus performed [in
Cana] after He had come from Judea
to Galilee [revealing that He is the
Messiah].

The Healing at Bethesda

5 LATER ON there was a Jewish
feast (festival), and Jesus went up
to Jerusalem.
[2]Now in Jerusalem, near the Sheep
Gate, there is a pool, which is called in
Hebrew (Jewish Aramaic) Bethesda,
having five porticoes (alcoves, colon-
nades).
[3]In these *porticoes* lay a great num-
ber of people who were sick, blind,
lame, withered, [waiting for the stir-
ring of the water;
[4]for an angel of the Lord went down
into the pool at appointed seasons and
stirred up the water; the first one to
go in after the water was stirred was
healed of his disease.]
[5]There was a certain man there who
had been ill for thirty-eight years.
[6]When Jesus noticed him lying there
[helpless], knowing that he had been *in
that condition* a long time, He said to
him, "Do you want to get well?"
[7]The invalid answered, "Sir, I have
no one to put me in the pool when the
water is stirred up, and while I am
coming [to get into it myself], someone
else steps down ahead of me."
[8]Jesus said to him, "Get up; pick up
your pallet and walk."
[9]Immediately the man was healed
and recovered his strength, and picked
up his pallet and walked.
Now that day was the Sabbath.
[10]So the Jews kept saying to the man
who had been healed, "It is the Sab-
bath, and you are not permitted to pick
up your pallet [because it is unlawful]."
[11]He answered them, "The Man
who healed me *and* gave me back my
strength was the One who said to me,
'Pick up your pallet and walk.' "
[12]They asked him, "Who is the Man
who told you, 'Pick up *your pallet* and
walk'?"
[13]Now the man who had been healed
did not know who it was, for Jesus had
slipped away [unnoticed] since there
was a crowd in that place.
[14]Afterward, Jesus found him in the
temple and said to him, "See, you are
well! Stop sinning or something worse
may happen to you."
[15]The man went away and told the
Jews that it was Jesus who had made
him well.
[16]For this reason the Jews began to
persecute Jesus *continually* because
He was doing these things on the Sab-
bath.
[17]But Jesus answered them, "My Fa-
ther has been working until now [He
has never ceased working], and I too
am working."

5:2 *the Sheep Gate.* This gate was in the wall of Jerusalem near the temple, through which sheep were brought for sacrifice.
5:9 *picked up his pallet and walked.* Carrying a bed on the Sabbath was considered a violation of the law of Moses (v. 10).
5:10 *you are not permitted.* The law of Moses taught that the Sabbath must be different from other days. On it, neither people nor animals could work. The prophet Jeremiah had prohibited carrying burdens or working on the Sabbath (Jer 17:21–22). Over the years, the Jewish leaders had amassed thousands of rules and regulations concerning the Sabbath. By Jesus' day, they had 39 different classifications of work. According to them, carrying furniture and even providing medical treatment on the Sabbath were forbidden. Jesus did not break the law. He violated the *traditions* of the Pharisees which had grown up around the law.
5:16 *the Jews began to persecute Jesus.* This is the first recorded declaration of open hostility toward Jesus in the Gospel of John.
5:17 *My Father.* Jesus is the unique Son of God. Here He claims not only a unique relationship with God the Father, but also equality with God

CHAPTER 5 **1** Lev 23:2; Dt 16:1; Jn 2:13 **2** Neh 3:1; 12:39 **8** Mt 9:6; Mk 2:11; Lk 5:24 **9** Jn 9:14 **10** Ex 20:10; Neh 13:19; Jer 17:21; Mt 12:2; Mk 2:24; Lk 6:2 **14** Mt 12:45; Jn 8:11 **17** Jn 9:4; 14:10

Jesus' Equality with God

[18]This made the Jews more determined than ever to kill Him, for not only was He breaking the Sabbath [from their viewpoint], but He was also calling God His own Father, making Himself equal with God.

[19]So Jesus answered them by saying, "I assure you *and* most solemnly say to you, the Son can do nothing of Himself [of His own accord], unless it is something He sees the Father doing; for whatever things the Father does, the Son [in His turn] also does in the same way.

[20]"For the Father *dearly* loves the Son and shows Him everything that He Himself is doing; and *the Father* will show Him greater works than these, so that you will be filled with wonder.

[21]"Just as the Father raises the dead and gives them life [and allows them to live on], even so the Son also gives life to whom He wishes.

[22]"For the Father judges no one, but has given all judgment [that is, the prerogative of judging] to the Son [placing it entirely into His hands],

[23]so that all will give honor (reverence, homage) to the Son just as they give honor to the Father. [In fact] the one who does not honor the Son does not honor the Father who has sent Him.

[24]"I assure you *and* most solemnly say to you, the person who hears My word [the one who heeds My message], and believes *and* trusts in Him who sent Me, has (possesses now) eternal life [that is, eternal life actually begins—the believer is transformed], and does not come into judgment *and* condemnation, but has passed [over] from death into life.

Two Resurrections

[25]"I assure you *and* most solemnly say to you, a time is coming and is [here] now, when the dead will hear the voice of the Son of God, and those who hear it will live.

[26]"For just as the Father has life in Himself [and is self-existent], even so He has given to the Son to have life in Himself [and be self-existent].

[27]"And He has given Him authority to execute judgment, because He is a Son of Man [sinless humanity, qualifying Him to sit in judgment over mankind]. [Dan 7:13, 14]

[28]"Do not be surprised at this; for a time is coming when all those who are in the tombs will hear His voice,

[29]and they will come out—those who did good things [will come out] to a resurrection of [new] life, but those who did evil things [will come out] to

---

in nature. Since God continually does good works without allowing Himself to stop on the Sabbath, the Son does likewise, since He is equal with God. Certainly the Jewish leaders understood the implications of Jesus' claims (v. 18).

5:19 *the Son can do nothing of Himself.* Action by the Son apart from the Father is impossible because of the unity of the Father and the Son (v. 17). ***whatever things the Father does, the Son [in His turn] also does.*** Here is a claim of deity and unity with the Father.

5:22 *all judgment . . . to the Son.* The Jews recognized that God alone had the right to judge humanity. In claiming that the Father committed all judgment to Him, Jesus again claimed equality with God.

5:24 Never-Ending Life—One of the primary features of the new life that we have in Christ is that it is an eternal or everlasting life. This truth completely changes how we look at our present lives and at the future. It needs to be seen as something we possess even now (Jn 10:28). We have entered into a new, personal relationship with God that gives us a spiritual vitality and fullness of life that we lacked before (Jn 17:3). It will be completely fulfilled in the future when we are bodily redeemed (Ro 8:23). The greatness of this spiritual reality constitutes a wonderful incentive to vigorously proclaim the gospel to those who are still dead in *trespasses and sins* (Eph 2:1).

5:26 *For.* This indicates that this verse explains the previous verse. Christ can give life because He Himself possesses life. He not only has a part in giving it, He is the source of it. This is another testimony to Jesus' deity because only God has life in Himself.

5:29 *resurrection of [new] life . . . resurrection of judgment.* Two separate resurrections are presented here in the fashion of the Old

18 Jn 7:19; Jn 10:30; Php 2:6 **19** ver. 30; Jn 8:28; 9:4 **20** Mt 3:17; Jn 3:35 **21** Lk 7:14; 8:54; Jn 11:25 **22** Mt 11:27; 28:18; Jn 3:35; 17:2; Ac 17:31; 1Pe 4:5 **23** 1Jn 2:23 **24** Jn 3:16,18; 6:40,47; 8:51; 1Jn 3:14 **25** Eph 2:1,5; 5:14; Col 2:13 **27** Ac 10:42; 17:31; Da 7:13 **29** Isa 26:19; 1Co 15:52; Da 12:2; Mt 25:32,33,46

a resurrection of judgment [that is, to
be sentenced]. [Dan 12:2; Rev 20:11–15]
30“I can do nothing on my own ini-
tiative *or* authority. Just as I hear, I
judge; and My judgment is just (fair,
righteous, unbiased), because I do not
seek My own will, but only the will of
Him who sent Me.
31“If I *alone* testify about Myself, My
testimony is not valid.
32“There is another [My Father] who
testifies about Me, and I know [without
any doubt] that His testimony on My
behalf is true *and* valid.

Testimony of John

33“You have sent [an inquiry] to John
[the Baptist] and he has testified [as an
eyewitness] to the truth.
34“But the testimony I receive is not
from man [a merely human witness];
but I say these things so that you may
be saved [that is, have eternal life].
35“John was the lamp that kept on
burning and shining [to show you the
way], and you were willing for a while
to rejoice in his light. [John 1:23–25]

Testimony of Works

36“But the testimony which I have is
far greater than *the testimony of* John;
for the works that the Father has given
Me to finish—the very same works
[that is, the miracles and proofs of My
deity] that I am [now] doing—testify
about Me, [by providing evidence] that
the Father has sent Me.

Testimony of the Father

37“And the Father who sent Me has
Himself testified about Me. You have
never heard His voice nor seen His
form [His majesty and greatness—
what He is like].
38“You do not have His word (Scrip-
ture) abiding in you [actually living
in your hearts and minds], because
you do not believe in Him whom He
has sent.

Testimony of the Scripture

39“You search *and* keep on searching
and examining the Scriptures because
you think that in them you have eternal
life; and yet it is those [very Scriptures]
that testify about Me;
40and still you are unwilling to come
to Me so that you may have life.
41“I do not receive glory *and* approv-
al from men;
42but I know you *and* recognize that
you do not have the love of God in
yourselves.
43“I have come in My Father’s name
and with His power, and you do not
receive Me [because your minds are
closed]; but if another comes in his
own name *and* with no authority or
power except his own, you will re-
ceive him *and* give your approval to
an imposter.
44“How can you believe [in Me],
when you [seek and] receive glory
and approval from one another, and
yet you do not seek the glory *and* ap-
proval which comes from the *one and*
only God?
45“Do not think that I [am the One
who] will accuse you before the Father.
There [already] is one who accuses
you: Moses, [the very one] in whom
you have placed your hope [for sal-
vation].

Testament prophets, who often grouped together events of the future without distinction of the time (Isa 61:2). Jesus was teaching the universality of resurrection, not the timing of it.

5:31–32 My testimony is not valid. If Christ were the only one bearing witness of what He was claiming, His witness would not be accepted. According to Jewish legal practice, a person’s testimony about himself was not accepted in court. So, in this case, Jesus offered another witness—John the Baptist (v. 33).

5:42 the love of God. This love is not love from God but love for God. Love from God is evidenced in Christ (3:16; Ro 5:8). Since God loves us, we should love Him (Dt 6:5; 1Jn 4:19).

5:45 in whom you have placed your hope. Christ will not have to accuse the people on judgment day because the one in whom they place

---

30 ver. 19; Mt 26:39; Jn 4:34; 6:38 **31** Jn 8:14; Rev 3:14 **32** Mt 3:17; 17:5; Jn 8:18; 1Jn 5:6 **33** Jn 1:15,19,27,32 **35** 2Pe 1:19; Mt 13:20; Mk 6:20 **36** 1Jn 5:9; Jn 3:2; 10:25; 15:24 **37** Mt 3:17; 17:5; Jn 6:27; 8:18; Dt 4:12; Jn 1:18; 1Ti 1:17; 1Jn 4:12 **39** ver. 46; Isa 8:20; 34:16; Lk 16:29; Ac 17:11; Dt 18:15,18; Lk 24:27 **40** Jn 1:11; 3:19 **41** ver. 34; 1Th 2:6 **44** Jn 12:43; Ro 2:29 **45** Ro 2:12

46"For if you believed *and* relied on
[the Scriptures written by] Moses, you
would believe Me, for he wrote about
Me [personally]. [Gen 3:15; 22:18; 49:10;
Num 24:17; Deut 18:15]
47"But if you do not believe his writ-
ings, how will you believe My words?"

Five Thousand Fed

6 AFTER THIS, Jesus went to the oth-
er side of the Sea of Galilee (or Sea
of Tiberias). [Matt 14:13–21; Mark 6:32–
44; Luke 9:10–17; John 6:23; 21:1]
2A large crowd was following Him
because they had seen the signs (at-
testing miracles) which He *continually*
performed on those who were sick.
3And Jesus went up on the moun-
tainside and sat down there with His
disciples.
4Now the Passover, the feast of the
Jews, was approaching. [Ex 12:1–36]
5Jesus looked up and saw that a
large crowd was coming toward Him,
and He said to Philip, "Where will we
buy bread for these *people* to eat?"
6But He said this to test Philip, be-
cause He knew what He was about
to do.
7Philip answered, "Two hundred de-
narii (200 days' wages) worth of bread
is not enough for each one to receive
even a little."
8One of His disciples, Andrew, Si-
mon Peter's brother, said to Him,
9"There is a little boy here who has
five barley loaves and two fish; but
what are these for so many people?"
10Jesus said, "Have the people sit
down [to eat]." Now [the ground] there
was [covered with] an abundance of
grass, so the men sat down, about
5,000 in number.
11Then Jesus took the loaves, and
when He had given thanks, He distrib-
uted them to those who were seated;
the same also with the fish, as much
as they wanted.
12When they had eaten enough, He
said to His disciples, "Gather up the left-
over pieces so that nothing will be lost."
13So they gathered them up, and they
filled twelve large baskets with pieces
from the five barley loaves which were
left over by those who had eaten.
14When the people saw the sign
(attesting miracle) that He had done,
they *began* saying, "This is without a
doubt the promised Prophet who is to
come into the world!" [Deut 18:15, 18;
John 1:21; Acts 3:22]

Jesus Walks on the Water

15Then Jesus, knowing that they
were going to come and take Him by
force to make Him king, withdrew
again to the mountainside by Himself.
16When evening came, His disciples
went down to the sea,
17and they got into a boat and started

their trust, Moses, will. The people will be condemned by the very law they professed to keep.
5:46 *for he wrote about Me.* Moses wrote about Christ in the promises to the patriarchs, in the history of the deliverance from Egypt, in the symbolic institutions of the law, and in the prediction of a Prophet like himself (Lk 24:25 – 26). If the people had believed Moses, they would have received Jesus gladly. Over 300 Old Testament prophecies were specifically fulfilled in the first coming of Christ.
6:1 *Sea of Galilee (or Sea of Tiberias).* John's use of the name Tiberias is an indication that his Gospel was written for those outside of Palestine. The Jewish people called this body of water the Lake of Genessaret. The Romans called it Tiberias, after the city built on its western shore by Herod Antipas and named for the Emperor Tiberius.
6:7 *Two hundred denarii.* One denarius was a day's wage for a laborer or field hand (Mt 20:2). Two hundred denarii would have been almost two-thirds of a year's wages.
6:9 *barley loaves.* These were an inexpensive food of the common people and the poor.
6:10 – 11 *about 5,000 in number . . . He distributed them to those who were seated.* This is the only miracle of Jesus that is recounted in all four Gospels.
6:15 *to make Him king.* Moses had not only miraculously provided food for the Israelites, he had also led them out of bondage in Egypt. Perhaps these men felt that Jesus could lead them

46 Ge 3:15; 12:3; 18:18; 22:18; 49:10; Dt 18:15,18; Jn 1:45; Ac 26:22 **CHAPTER 6** **1** Mt 14:15; Mk 6:35; Lk 9:10,12 **4** Lev 23:5,7; Dt 16:1; Jn 2:13; 5:1 **5** Mt 14:14; Mk 6:35; Lk 9:12 **7** See Nu 11:21,22 **9** 2Ki 4:43 **14** Ge 49:10; Dt 18:15,18; Mt 11:3; Jn 1:21; 4:19,25; 7:40 **16** Mt 14:23; Mk 6:47

to cross the sea to Capernaum. It was already dark, and Jesus had still not come [back] to them.

18 The sea was getting rough *and* rising high because a strong wind was blowing.

19 Then, when they had rowed three or four miles [and were near the center of the sea], they saw Jesus walking on the sea and approaching the boat; and they were [terribly] frightened.

20 But Jesus said to them, "It is I (I AM); do not be afraid." [Matt 14:27; John 8:58]

21 Then they were willing to take Him on board the boat, and immediately the boat reached the [shore of the] land to which they were going.

22 The next day the crowd that stood on the other side of the sea realized that there had been only one small boat there, and that Jesus had not boarded the boat with His disciples, but that His disciples had gone away alone.

23 [Now some] other small boats from Tiberias had come in near the place where they ate the bread after the Lord had given thanks.

24 So when the crowd saw that neither Jesus nor His disciples were there, they boarded the small boats themselves and came to Capernaum looking for Jesus.

25 And when they found Him on the other side of the sea, they asked Him, "Rabbi, when did You get here?"

Words to the People

26 Jesus answered, "I assure you *and* most solemnly say to you, you have been searching for Me, not because you saw the signs (attesting miracles), but because you ate the loaves and were filled.

27 "Do not work for food that perishes, but for food that endures [and leads] to eternal life, which the Son of Man will give you; for God the Father has authorized Him *and* put His seal on Him."

28 Then they asked Him, "What are we to do, so that we may *habitually* be doing the works of God?"

29 Jesus answered, "This is the work of God: that you believe [adhere to, trust in, rely on, and have faith] in the One whom He has sent."

30 So they said to Him, "What sign (attesting miracle) will You do that we may see it and believe You? What [supernatural] work will You do [as proof]?

31 "Our fathers ate the manna in the wilderness; as it is written [in Scripture], 'HE GAVE THEM BREAD OUT OF HEAVEN TO EAT.' " [Ex 16:15; Neh 9:15; Ps 78:24]

32 Then Jesus said to them, "I assure you *and* most solemnly say to you, it is not Moses who has given you the bread out of heaven, but it is My Father who gives you the true bread out of heaven.

33 "For the Bread of God is He who comes down out of heaven, and gives life to the world."

34 Then they said to Him, "Lord, always give us this bread."

35 Jesus replied to them, "I am the Bread of Life. The one who comes to Me will never be hungry, and the one who believes in Me [as Savior] will

---

out of bondage to the Romans. Christ was at the zenith of His popularity, and the temptation to take the kingdom without the cross must have been great (Mt 4:8 – 10).

6:19 – 21 *they saw Jesus walking on the sea.* This miracle, the fifth sign recorded by John, pointed to Jesus' deity. Only God could walk on water, calm the sea, and supernaturally transport the disciples to their destination.

6:27 *Do not work for food.* The impression that one must work for eternal life is quickly corrected when Jesus adds "which the Son of Man will give you." The Son provides *life* as a gift (4:10).

6:31 *HE GAVE THEM BREAD OUT OF HEAVEN.* There was a tradition that said the Messiah would cause manna to fall from heaven as Moses did (Ex 16:4,15). The people probably also saw this "miracle worker" as the perpetual provider of physical needs rather than spiritual ones.

6:32 *My Father.* The crowd misrepresented the truth, so Jesus corrected them. The manna had not come from Moses; it had been provided by God. Moreover, God still gives *true bread* — that is, eternal life (v. 33).

27 Jn 4:14; Mt 3:17; 17:5; Mk 1:11; 9:7; Lk 3:22; 9:35; Jn 5:37; Ac 2:22; 2Pe 1:17 **29** 1Jn 3:23 **30** Mt 12:38; 16:1; Mk 8:11; 1Co 1:22 **31** Ex 16:15; Nu 11:7; Neh 9:15; 1Co 10:3; Ps 78:24 **34** See Jn 4:15 **35** ver. 48,58; Jn 4:14; 7:37

never be thirsty [for that one will be sustained spiritually].

36 “But as I told you, you have seen Me and still you do not believe.

37 “All that My Father gives Me will come to Me; and the one who comes to Me I will most certainly not cast out [I will never, never reject anyone who follows Me].

38 “For I have come down from heaven, not to do My own will, but to do the will of Him who sent Me.

39 “This is the will of Him who sent Me, that of all that He has given Me I lose nothing, but that I [give new life and] raise it up at the last day.

40 “For this is My Father’s will *and* purpose, that everyone who sees the Son and believes in Him [as Savior] will have eternal life, and I will raise him up [from the dead] on the last day.”

Words to the Jews

41 Now the Jews murmured *and* found fault with Him because He said, “I am the Bread that came down out of heaven.”

42 They kept saying, “Is this not Jesus, the son of Joseph, whose father and mother we know? How does He now [have the arrogance to] say, ‘I have come down out of heaven’?”

43 So Jesus answered, “Stop murmuring among yourselves.

44 “No one can come to Me unless the Father who sent Me draws him [giving him the desire to come to Me]; and I will raise him up [from the dead] on the last day.

45 “It is written in the prophets, ‘AND THEY WILL ALL BE TAUGHT OF GOD.’ Everyone who has listened to and learned from the Father, comes to Me. [Is 54:13]

46 “Not that anyone has seen the Father, except He [who was with the Father and] who is from God; He [alone] has seen the Father.

47 “I assure you *and* most solemnly say to you, he who believes [in Me as Savior—whoever adheres to, trusts in, relies on, and has faith in Me—already] has eternal life [that is, now possesses it].

48 “I am the Bread of Life [the Living Bread which gives and sustains life].

49 “Your fathers ate the manna in the wilderness, and they died.

50 “This is the Bread that comes down out of heaven, so that one may eat of it and not die.

51 “I am the Living Bread that came down out of heaven. If anyone eats of this Bread [believes in Me, accepts Me as Savior], he will live forever. And the Bread that I will give for the life of the world is My flesh (body).”

52 Then the Jews *began* to argue with one another, saying, “How can this man give us His flesh to eat?”

53 And Jesus said to them, “I assure you *and* most solemnly say to you, unless you eat the flesh of the Son of Man and drink His blood [unless you believe in Me as Savior and believe in the saving power of My blood which will be shed for you], you do not have life in yourselves.

54 “The one who eats My flesh and drinks My blood [believes in Me, accepts Me as Savior] has eternal life [that is, now possesses it], and I will raise him up [from the dead] on the last day.

6:39–40 *My Father’s will.* This is twofold: (1) that all who come to the Son will be received and not lost; (2) that all who see and believe on the Son will have eternal life.

6:42 *the son of Joseph.* The religious leaders’ proof that Jesus was not from heaven was that they knew His parents. To them, there was nothing supernatural about Jesus’ origin.

6:48–49 *I am the Bread of Life.* Those who believe in Him have life (v. 47). The manna in the wilderness did not ultimately sustain life. Those who ate it eventually died because it could not provide eternal life.

6:53–58 *eats My flesh and drinks My blood.* Jesus had made it abundantly clear in this context that eternal life is gained by believing (vv. 29,35,40,47). These verses teach that the benefits of Jesus’ death must be appropriated, by faith, by each individual.

36 ver. 26,64 **37** ver. 45; Mt 24:24; Jn 10:28,29; 2Ti 2:19; 1Jn 2:19 **38** Mt 26:39; Jn 5:30; 4:34 **39** Jn 10:28; 17:12; 18:9 **40** ver. 27,47,54; Jn 3:15,16; 4:14 **42** Mt 13:55; Mk 6:3; Lk 4:22 **44** ver. 65; SS 1:4 **45** Isa 54:13; Jer 31:34; Mic 4:2; Heb 8:10; ver. 37 **46** Jn 1:18; Mt 11:27; Lk 10:22; Jn 7:29 **47** Jn 3:16,18 **48** ver. 33,35 **49** ver. 31 **50** ver. 51,58 **51** Jn 3:13; Heb 10:5 **52** Jn 7:43; 9:16; 10:19 **53** Mt 26:16 **54** ver. 27,40; Jn 4:14

55“For My flesh is true [spiritual]
food, and My blood is true [spiritual]
drink.
56“He who eats My flesh and drinks
My blood [believes in Me, accepts Me
as Savior] remains in Me, and I [in the
same way remain] in him.
57“Just as the living Father sent Me,
and I live because of the Father, even
so the one who feeds on Me [believes
in Me, accepts Me as Savior] will also
live because of Me.
58“This is the Bread which came
down out of heaven. It is not like [the
manna that] our fathers ate and they
[eventually] died; the one who eats this
Bread [believes in Me, accepts Me as
Savior] will live forever.”

Words to the Disciples

59He said these things in a syna-
gogue while He was teaching in Caper-
naum.
60When many of His disciples heard
this, they said, “This is a difficult *and*
harsh *and* offensive statement. Who
can [be expected to] listen to it?”
61But Jesus, aware that His disci-
ples were complaining about it, asked
them, “Does this cause you to stumble
and take offense?
62“*What* then [will you think] if you
see the Son of Man ascending to [the
realm] where He was before?
63“It is the Spirit who gives life; the
flesh conveys no benefit [it is of no
account]. The words I have spoken
to you are spirit and life [providing
eternal life].
64“But [still] there are some of you
who do not believe *and* have faith.”
For Jesus knew from the beginning
who did not believe, and who would
betray Him.
65And He was saying, “This is the
reason why I have told you that no
one can come to Me unless it has been
granted him [that is, unless he is en-
abled to do so] by the Father.”

Peter's Confession of Faith

66As a result of this many of His dis-
ciples abandoned Him, and no longer
walked with Him.
67So Jesus said to the twelve [disci-
ples], “You do not want to leave too,
do you?”
68Simon Peter answered, “Lord, to
whom shall we go? You [alone] have
the words of eternal life [you are our
only hope].
69“We have believed *and* confidently
trusted, and [even more] we have come
to know [by personal observation and
experience] that You are the Holy One
of God [the Christ, the Son of the living
God].”
70Jesus answered them, “Did I not
choose you, the twelve [disciples]? And
yet one of you is a devil (ally of Satan).”
71Now He was speaking of Judas,
the son of Simon Iscariot; for he, one
of the twelve [disciples], was about to
betray Him.

Jesus Teaches at the Feast

7 AFTER THIS, Jesus walked [from
place to place] in Galilee, for He
would not walk in Judea because the
Jews were seeking to kill Him.
2Now the Jewish Feast of Taberna-
cles (Booths) was approaching.
3So His brothers said to Him, “Leave
here and go to Judea, so that Your

6:60 *This is a difficult and harsh and offensive statement.* It was hard for the Jewish learners to accept the idea of eating flesh and drinking blood. Jews were forbidden to even taste blood.
6:63 *It is the Spirit who gives life.* Jesus was trying to get the religious leaders to see beyond the physical aspects of His teaching to the real issue — namely, that if they believed on Him they would have eternal life.

7:2 *Feast of Tabernacles.* This was one of the three great Jewish religious festivals (Passover and Pentecost were the other two). It was called the Feast of Tabernacles (Booths) because for seven days the people lived in makeshift shelters or lean-tos made of branches and leaves. The feast commemorated the days when the Israelites wandered in the wilderness and lived in tents (Lev 23:40 – 43).
7:3 – 4 *His brothers.* Jesus' brothers argued, “If

56 1Jn 3:24; 4:15,16 **58** ver. 49-51 **60** ver. 66; Mt 11:6 **62** Mk 16:19; Jn 3:13; Ac 1:9; Eph 4:8 **63** 2Co 3:6 **64** ver. 36; Jn 2:24,25; 13:11 **65** ver. 44,45 **66** ver. 60 **68** Ac 5:20 **69** Mt 16:16; Mk 8:29; Lk 9:20; Jn 1:49; 11:27 **70** Lk 6:13; Jn 13:27 **CHAPTER 7** **1** Jn 5:16,18 **2** Lev 23:34 **3** Mt 12:46; Mk 3:31; Ac 1:14

disciples [there] may also see the
works that You do.
4“No one does anything in secret
when he wants to be *known* publicly.
If You [must] do these things, show
Yourself openly to the world *and* make
Yourself known!”
5For not even His brothers believed
in Him.
6So Jesus said to them, “My time
has not yet come; but any time is right
for you.
7“The world cannot hate you [since
you are part of it], but it does hate Me
because I denounce it *and* testify that
its deeds are evil.
8“Go up to the feast yourselves. I am
not going up to this feast because My
time has not yet fully come.”
9Having said these things to them,
He stayed behind in Galilee.
10But [afterward], when His brothers
had gone up to the feast, He went up
too, not publicly [with a caravan], but
quietly [because He did not want to
be noticed].
11So the Jews kept looking for Him
at the feast and asking, “Where is He?”
12There was a lot of whispered dis-
cussion *and* murmuring among the
crowds about Him. Some were saying,
“He is a good man”; others said, “No,
on the contrary, He misleads the peo-
ple [giving them false ideas].”
13Yet no one was speaking out open-
ly *and* freely about Him for fear of [the
leaders of] the Jews.
14When the feast was already half
over, Jesus went up into the temple
[court] and *began to* teach.
15Then the Jews were perplexed.
They said, “How did this man become
learned [so versed in the Scriptures and
theology] without formal training?”
16Jesus answered them by saying,
“My teaching is not My own, but His
who sent Me.
17“If anyone is willing to do His will,
he will know whether the teaching is
of God or whether I speak on My own
accord *and* by My own authority.
18“He who speaks on his own accord
seeks glory *and* honor for himself. But
He who seeks the glory *and* the honor
of the One who sent Him, He is true,
and there is no unrighteousness *or*
deception in Him.
19“Did not Moses give you the Law?
And yet not one of you keeps the Law.
Why do you want to kill Me [for not
keeping it]?”
20The crowd answered, “You have
a demon [You are out of Your mind]!
Who wants to kill You?”
21Jesus replied, “I did one work, and
you are all astounded. [John 5:1–9]
22“For this reason Moses has given
you [God’s law regarding] circumci-
sion (not that it originated with Moses,
but with the patriarchs) and you cir-
cumcise a man [even] on the Sabbath.
23“If, to avoid breaking the Law of
Moses, a man undergoes circumcision
on the Sabbath, why are you angry
with Me for making a man’s whole
body well on the Sabbath?
24“Do not judge by appearance [su-
perficially and arrogantly], but judge
fairly *and* righteously.”
25Then some of the people of Jeru-
salem said, “Is this not the Man they
want to kill?
26“Look, He is speaking publicly, and
they say nothing to Him! Is it possible

You are really working miracles and thus claiming to be the Messiah, do not hide in obscure Galilee. If you are doing miracles at all, then do them in Jerusalem at the Feast to convince the whole nation.” These words were sarcastic, as verse 5 explains.

7:14 *When the feast was already half over.* This would have been the fourth day of the seven-day feast. During the first half of the festival, Jesus remained in seclusion (v. 10). During the second half, He began to teach publicly. This is the first mention in the Gospel of John of Jesus teaching in the temple.

7:15 *without formal training.* Jesus never attended a rabbinical school. Similar bewilderment was later expressed regarding Jesus’ disciples (Ac 4:13).

5 Mk 3:21 **6** Jn 2:4; 8:20 **7** Jn 15:19; 3:19 **8** Jn 8:20 **11** Jn 11:56 **12** Jn 9:16; 10:19; ver. 40; Mt 21:46; Lk 7:16; Jn 6:14 **13** Jn 9:22; 12:42; 19:38 **15** Mt 13:54; Mk 6:2; Lk 4:22; Ac 2:7 **16** Jn 3:11; 8:28; 12:49; 14:10,24 **17** Jn 8:43 **18** Jn 5:41; 8:50 **19** Ex 24:3; Dt 33:4; Jn 1:17; Ac 7:38; Mt 12:14; Mk 3:6; Jn 5:16,18; 10:31,39; 11:53 **20** Jn 8:48,52; 10:20 **22** Lev 12:3; Ge 17:10 **23** Jn 5:8,9,16 **24** Dt 1:16; Pr 24:23; Jn 8:15; Jas 2:1 **26** ver. 48

that the rulers really know that this is
the Christ?
27“But we know where this Man is
from; whenever the Christ comes, no
one will know where He is from.”
28Then Jesus called out as He taught
in the temple, “You know Me and
know where I am from; and I have
not come on my own initiative [as self-
appointed], but He who sent Me is true,
and Him you do not know.
29“I know Him Myself because I am
from Him [I came from His very pres-
ence] and it was He [personally] who
sent Me.”
30So they were eager to arrest Him;
but no one laid a hand on Him, because
His time had not yet come.
31But many from the crowd believed
in Him. And they kept saying, “When
the Christ comes, will He do more
signs *and* exhibit more proofs than
this Man?”
32The Pharisees heard the crowd
muttering these things [under their
breath] about Him, and the chief
priests and Pharisees sent guards to
arrest Him.
33Therefore Jesus said, “For a little
while longer I am [still] with you, and
then I go to Him who sent Me.
34“You will look for Me, and will not
[be able to] find Me; and where I am,
you cannot come.”
35Then the Jews said among them-
selves, “Where does this Man intend
to go that we will not find Him? Does
He intend to go to the Dispersion [of
Jews scattered and living] among the
Greeks, and teach the Greeks?
36“What does this statement of His
mean, ‘You will look for Me, and will
not [be able to] find Me; and where I
am, you cannot come’?”
37Now on the last and most impor-
tant day of the feast, Jesus stood and
called out [in a loud voice], “If any-
one is thirsty, let him come to Me and
drink!
38“He who believes in Me [who ad-
heres to, trusts in, and relies on Me], as
the Scripture has said, ‘From his inner-
most being will flow *continually* rivers
of living water.’ ” [Is 58:11; John 4:14]
39But He was speaking of the [Holy]
Spirit, whom those who believed in
Him [as Savior] were to receive *after-
ward*. The Spirit had not yet been giv-
en, because Jesus was not yet glorified
(raised to honor).

Division of People over Jesus

40Listening to these words, some of
the people said, “This is certainly the
Prophet!” [Deut 18:15, 18; John 1:21;
6:14; Acts 3:22]
41Others said, “This is the Christ (the
Messiah, the Anointed)!” But others
said, “Surely the Christ is not going to
come out of Galilee, is He?

7:28–29 *You know Me and know where I am from.* Jesus reminded the leaders that they knew His origin. Their problem was that they did not know God, who sent Jesus. He explained to them that He knew God, was from God, and was sent by God.

7:32 *to arrest Him.* The Jewish leaders decided earlier that they wanted to kill Christ (5:16), but this is the first real attempt on His life.

7:37–39 *the last and most important day of the feast.* On each day of the feast, the people came with palm branches and marched around the great altar. A priest took a golden pitcher filled with water from the pool of Siloam, carried it to the temple, and poured it on the altar as an offering to God. This dramatic ceremony was a memorial of the water that flowed from the rock when the Israelites traveled through the wilderness. On the last day of the feast, the people marched seven times around the altar in memory of the seven circuits around the walls of Jericho.

7:38 *as the Scripture has said.* The reference is not to a single passage, but to the general emphasis of such passages as Deuteronomy 18:15, Isaiah 58:11, and Zechariah 14:8. In contrast to the small amount of water poured out each day during the feast, there will be a river of water coming out of those who believe in Christ. Not only will they be satisfied themselves, but they will also become a river so that others may drink and be satisfied (v. 39).

7:40–42 *Christ comes from the descendants of David.* These people knew that the Messiah was to come from Bethlehem (Mic 5:2). However, they did not know that Jesus had been born there.

27 Mt 13:55; Mk 6:3; Lk 4:22 **28** Jn 8:14; 5:43; 8:42; Jn 5:32; 8:26; Ro 3:4; Jn 1:18; 8:55 **29** Mt 11:27; Jn 10:15
30 Mk 11:18; Lk 19:47; 20:19; Jn 8:37; ver. 44 **31** Mt 12:23; Jn 3:2; 8:30 **33** Jn 13:33; 16:16 **34** Hos 5:6; Jn 8:21; 13:33
35 Isa 11:12; Jas 1:1; 1Pe 1:1 **37** Lev 23:36; Isa 55:1; Jn 6:35; Rev 22:17 **38** Dt 18:15; Pr 18:4; Isa 12:3; 44:3; Jn 4:14
39 Isa 44:3; Joel 2:28; Jn 16:7; Ac 2:17,33,38; Jn 12:16; 16:7 **40** Dt 18:15; Jn 1:21; 6:14 **41** Jn 4:42; 6:69; ver. 52; Jn 1:46

42 “Does the Scripture not say that
the Christ comes from the descendants
of David, and from Bethlehem, the
village where David lived?” [Ps 89:3,
4; Mic 5:2]
43 So the crowd was divided because
of Him.
44 Some of them wanted to arrest
Him, but no one laid hands on Him.
45 Then the guards went [back] to
the chief priests and Pharisees, who
asked them, “Why did you not bring
Him [here with you]?”
46 The guards replied, “Never [at any
time] has a man talked the way this
Man talks!”
47 Then the Pharisees said to them,
“Have you also been deluded *and*
swept off your feet?
48 “Has any of the rulers or Pharisees
believed in Him?
49 “But this [ignorant, contemptible]
crowd that does not know the Law is
accursed *and* doomed!”
50 Nicodemus (the one who came to
Jesus before and was one of them)
asked,
51 “Does our Law convict someone
without first giving him a hearing and
finding out what he is [accused of]
doing?”
52 They responded, “Are you also
from Galilee? Search [and read the
Scriptures], and see [for yourself] that
no prophet comes from Galilee!”
53 [And everyone went to his own
house.

The Adulterous Woman

8 BUT JESUS went to the Mount of
Olives.
2 Early in the morning He came back
into the temple [court], and all the peo-
ple were coming to Him. He sat down
and *began* teaching them.
3 Now the scribes and Pharisees
brought a woman who had been caught
in adultery. They made her stand in the
center *of the court*,
4 and they said to Him, “Teacher, this
woman has been caught in the very
act of adultery.
5 “Now in the Law Moses commanded
us to stone such women [to death]. So
what do You say [to do with her—what
is Your sentence]?” [Deut 22:22–24]
6 They said this to test Him, hoping
that they would have grounds for ac-
cusing Him. But Jesus stooped down
and began writing on the ground with
His finger.
7 However, when they persisted in
questioning Him, He straightened up
and said, “He who is without [any]
sin among you, let him be the first to
throw a stone at her.” [Deut 17:7]
8 Then He stooped down again and
started writing on the ground.
9 They listened [to His reply], and
they *began* to go out one by one, start-
ing with the oldest ones, until He was
left alone, with the woman [standing
there before Him] in the center *of the
court*.
10 Straightening up, Jesus said to her,
“Woman, where are they? Did no one
condemn you?”
11 She answered, “No one, Lord!”
And Jesus said, “I do not condemn you
either. Go. From now on sin no more.”]

Jesus Is the Light of the World

12 Once more Jesus addressed the
crowd. He said, “I am the Light of the

They thought He was from Galilee. They knew the Scripture, but they did not take the time to know the Messiah (5:39).
8:2 *He sat down.* Teachers in ancient Israel sat when they taught. Jesus assumed the position of an authoritative teacher.
8:4 – 5 *in the Law Moses commanded us to stone such women.* Stoning was specified in certain cases of adultery (Dt 22:23 – 24), though not all. (It is not clear why the authorities intended to punish the woman but not the man.) In the Greek text, the pronoun *you* is emphatic. The religious leaders were trying to trap Jesus into saying something that was contrary to the law.
8:6 *to test Him.* If Jesus had said not to stone her, He would have contradicted Jewish law. If He had said to stone her, He would have run counter to Roman law, which did not permit Jews to carry

42 Ps 132:11; Jer 23:5; Mic 5:2; Mt 2:5; Lk 2:4; 1Sa 16:1,4 **43** ver. 12; Jn 9:16; 10:19 **44** ver. 30 **48** Jn 12:42; Ac 6:7; 1Co 1:20,26; 2:8 **50** Jn 3:2 **51** Dt 1:17; 17:8; 19:15 **52** ver. 41; Isa 9:1,2; Mt 4:15; Jn 1:46 **CHAPTER 8** **5** Lev 20:10; Dt 22:22 **7** Dt 17:7; Ro 2:1 **9** Ro 2:22 **11** Lk 9:56; 12:14; Jn 3:17; Jn 5:14 **12** Jn 1:4,5,9; 3:19; 9:5; 12:35,36,46

world. He who follows Me will not
walk in the darkness, but will have
the Light of life."
13 Then the Pharisees told Him, "You
are testifying on Your own behalf;
Your testimony is not valid."
14 Jesus replied, "Even if I do testify
on My own behalf, My testimony is
valid, because I know where I came
from and where I am going; but you do
not know where I come from or where
I am going.
15 "You judge according to human
standards [just by what you see]. I do
not judge anyone.
16 "But even if I do judge, My judg-
ment is true *and* My decision is right;
for I am not alone [in making it], but I
and the Father who sent Me [make the
same judgment].
17 "Even in your own law it is writ-
ten that the testimony of two per-
sons is true [valid and admissible].
[Deut 19:15]
18 "I am One [of the Two] who testifies
about Myself, and My Father who sent
Me testifies about Me."
19 Then the Pharisees said to Him,
"Where is this Father of Yours?" Jesus
answered, "You know neither Me nor
My Father; if you knew Me, you would
know My Father also."
20 Jesus said these things in the trea-
sury, as He taught in the temple [court-
yard]; and no one seized Him, because
His time had not yet come.
21 Then He said again to them, "I
am going away, and you will look for
Me, and you will die [unforgiven and
condemned] in your sin. Where I am
going, you cannot come."
22 So the Jews were asking [among
themselves], "Will He kill Himself? Is
that why He says, 'Where I am going,
you cannot come'?"
23 He said to them, "You are from
below, I am from above; you are of this
world, I am not of this world.
24 "That is why I told you that you will
die [unforgiven and condemned] in
your sins; for if you do not believe that
I am *the One* [I claim to be], you will
die in your sins." [Ex 3:14; Matt 24:5;
Mark 13:6; Luke 21:8]
25 So they said to Him, "Who are You
[anyway]?" Jesus replied, "What have
I been saying to you from the begin-
ning?
26 "I have many things to say and
judge concerning you, but He who sent
Me is true; and I say to the world [only]
the things that I have heard from Him."
27 They did not realize [or have the
spiritual insight to understand] that He
was speaking to them about the Father.
28 So Jesus said, "When you lift up
the Son of Man [on the cross], you will
know then [without any doubt] that I
am *He,* and that I do nothing on My
own authority, but I say these things
just as My Father taught Me.
29 "And He who sent Me is [always]
with Me; He has not left Me alone, be-
cause I always do what pleases Him."

out their own executions (18:31). What Jesus wrote on the ground is a matter of conjecture.

8:13 *Your testimony is not valid.* This phrase does not mean "false"; it means "not sufficient." The Pharisees challenged Jesus on legal grounds because no man on trial in a Jewish court was allowed to testify on his own behalf. Their point was that, if Jesus were the only one testifying as to who He claimed to be, it would not be enough to prove His case.

8:14 *My testimony is valid.* In 5:31 Jesus argued on the basis of legality and offered other witnesses. Sometimes, however, an individual is the only one who knows the facts about himself. Thus, self-disclosure is the only way to truth (7:29; 13:3).

8:15 *according to human standards.* The religious leaders formed conclusions based on human standards and an imperfect, external, and superficial examination. Jesus did not judge according to human standards or outward appearances.

8:24 *I am.* This was God's designation of Himself (Ex 3:14). Jesus was claiming to be God. This assertion was not understood by the religious leaders at this time. Later, Jesus' claim to be the "I Am" (v. 58) prompted the Jewish leaders to seek His life (v. 59).

13 Jn 5:31 **14** Jn 7:28; 9:29 **15** Jn 7:24; 3:17; 12:47; 18:36 **16** Jn 16:32 **17** Dt 17:6; 19:15; Mt 18:16; 2Co 13:1; Heb 10:28 **18** Jn 5:37 **19** Jn 16:3; Jn 14:7 **20** Mk 12:41; Jn 7:30; Jn 7:8 **21** Jn 7:34; 13:33; ver. 24 **23** Jn 3:31; Jn 15:19; 17:16; 1Jn 4:5 **24** ver. 21; Mk 16:16 **26** Jn 7:28; 3:32; 15:15 **28** Jn 3:14; 12:32; Ro 1:4; Jn 5:19,30; Jn 3:11 **29** Jn 14:10; ver. 16; Jn 4:34; 5:30; 6:38

30 As He said these things, many believed in Him.

The Truth Will Make You Free

31 So Jesus was saying to the Jews who had believed Him, "If you abide in My word [continually obeying My teachings and living in accordance with them, then] you are truly My disciples.

32 "And you will know the truth [regarding salvation], and the truth will set you free [from the penalty of sin]."

33 They answered Him, "We are Abraham's descendants and have never been enslaved to anyone. What do You mean by saying, 'You will be set free'?"

34 Jesus answered, "I assure you *and* most solemnly say to you, everyone who practices sin *habitually* is a slave of sin.

35 "Now the slave does not remain in a household forever; the son [of the master] does remain forever.

36 "So if the Son makes you free, then you are unquestionably free.

37 "I know that you are Abraham's descendants; yet you plan to kill Me, because My word has no place [to grow] in you [and it makes no change in your heart].

38 "I tell the things that I have seen at My Father's side [in His very presence]; so you also do the things that you heard from your father."

39 They answered, "Abraham is our father." Jesus said to them, "If you are [truly] Abraham's children, then do the works of Abraham *and* follow his example.

40 "But as it is, you want to kill Me, a Man who has told you the truth, which I heard from God. This is not the way Abraham acted.

41 "You are doing the works of your [own] father." They said to Him, "We are not illegitimate children; we have one [spiritual] Father: God."

42 Jesus said to them, "If God were your Father [but He is not], you would love *and* recognize Me, for I came from God [out of His very presence] and have arrived *here*. For I have not even come on My own initiative [as self-appointed], but He [is the One who] sent Me.

43 "Why do you misunderstand what I am saying? It is because [your spiritual ears are deaf and] you are unable to hear [the truth of] My word.

44 "You are of *your* father the devil, and it is your will to practice the desires [which are characteristic] of your father. He was a murderer from

---

8:31 God's Word Confirms — The Bible establishes the truth in our own hearts in several ways. **It confirms our salvation.** In Jesus' own words in the Gospel of John: "I assure you and most solemnly say to you, the person who hears My word [the one who heeds My message], and believes and trusts in Him who sent Me, has (possesses now) eternal life [that is, eternal life actually begins — the believer is transformed], and does not come into judgment and condemnation, but has passed [over] from death into life." (Jn 5:24). Compare John 3:16; 6:27,35,37,40; 10:27 – 29; Romans 8:1.
It confirms the hand of God in all of life's bitter disappointments. Romans 8:28 provides reassurance and comfort in these crucial situations: "And we know [with great confidence] that God [who is deeply concerned about us] causes all things to work together [as a plan] for good for those who love God, to those who are called according to *His* plan and purpose."
It confirms our forgiveness when we sin. Repeatedly, the Bible assures us that all confessed sin is instantly and eternally forgiven (Ps 32:5; 103:12; Isa 38:17).

8:33 *have never been enslaved to anyone.* The Pharisees' objection is startling. In their past, the Israelites had been in bondage to the Egyptians, the Assyrians, and the Babylonians. At the time they spoke, Israel was under the power of Rome.

8:39 *Abraham is our father.* The Pharisees believed that being a descendant of Abraham guaranteed them a place in heaven.

8:41 *We are not illegitimate children.* From ancient times, this has been interpreted as a sneer, as if to say, "We are not illegitimate children, but You are." Apparently gossip had

---

30 Jn 7:31; 10:42; 11:45 **32** Ro 6:14,18,22; Jas 1:25; 2:12 **33** Lev 25:42; Mt 3:9 **34** Rom 6:16; 2Pe 2:19 **35** Gal 4:30 **36** Ro 8:2; Gal 5:1 **37** Jn 7:19 **38** Jn 3:32; 5:19,30; 14:10,24 **39** Mt 3:9; Ro 2:28; 9:7; Gal 3:7,29 **40** ver. 37; ver. 26 **41** Isa 63:16; 64:8; Mal 1:6 **42** 1Jn 5:1; Jn 16:27; 17:8,25; Jn 5:43; 7:28,29 **43** Jn 7:17 **44** Mt 13:38; 1Jn 3:8; Jude 6

the beginning, and does not stand in the truth because there is no truth in him. When he lies, he speaks what is natural to him, for he is a liar and the father of lies *and* half-truths.

45"But because I speak the truth, you
do not believe Me [and continue in your unbelief].

46"Which one of you [has proof and]
convicts Me of sin? If I speak truth, why do you not believe Me?

47"Whoever is of God *and* belongs to
Him hears [the truth of] God's words; for this reason you do not hear them: because you are not of God *and* you are not in fellowship with Him."

48The Jews answered Him, "Are we
not right when we say You are a Samaritan and [that You] have a demon [and are under its power]?"

49Jesus answered, "I do not have a
demon. On the contrary, I honor My Father, and you dishonor Me.

50"However, I am not seeking glory
for Myself. There is One who seeks [glory for Me] and judges [those who dishonor Me].

51"I assure you *and* most solemnly
say to you, if anyone keeps My word [by living in accordance with My message] he will indeed never, ever see *and* experience death."

52The Jews said to Him, "Now we
know that You have a demon [and are under its power]. Abraham died, and also the prophets; yet You say, 'If anyone keeps My word, he will never, ever taste of death.'

53"Are You greater than our father
Abraham, who died? The prophets died too! Whom do You make Yourself out to be?"

54Jesus answered, "If I glorify My-
self, My glory is [worth] nothing. It is My Father who glorifies Me, of whom you say, 'He is our God.'

55Yet you do not know Him, but I
know Him fully. If I said I did not know Him, I would be a liar like you. But I do know Him and keep His word.

56"Your father Abraham [greatly]
rejoiced to see My day (My incarnation). He saw it and was delighted." [Heb 11:13]

57Then the Jews said to Him, "You
are not even fifty years old, and You [claim to] have seen Abraham?"

58Jesus replied, "I assure you *and*
most solemnly say to you, before Abraham was born, I Am." [Ex 3:14]

59So they picked up stones to throw
at Him, but Jesus concealed Himself and left the temple.

Healing the Man Born Blind

9 WHILE HE was passing by, He
noticed a man [who had been] blind from birth.

2His disciples asked Him, "Rabbi
(Teacher), who sinned, this man or his parents, that he would be born blind?"

3Jesus answered, "Neither this man
nor his parents sinned, but it was so that the works of God might be displayed *and* illustrated in him.

4"We must work the works of Him

---

followed Jesus for many years, alleging that He had been conceived out of wedlock.

8:53 *Are You greater than our father Abraham.* Abraham and the prophets kept God's word and died. Jesus was claiming not that He would prevent physical death, but that He could give eternal life. To the Jewish leaders, this was proof that Jesus was demon-possessed.

8:58 – 59 *I Am.* Jesus was not just claiming to have lived before Abraham; He was claiming eternal existence. He was claiming to be God Himself (Ex 3:14). This time the Jewish leaders understood that Jesus was claiming to be God, so they took up stones to stone Him for blasphemy (Lev 24:16).

9:1 *a man [who had been] blind from birth.* Most likely he was a beggar. Beggars waited by the gates of the temple for gifts from worshipers. Therefore, it is likely that this scene took place near the temple.

9:2 *who sinned.* It was commonly supposed that sickness was a result of sin. It would follow that sin committed by a baby still in the womb or sin committed by parents could result in a baby being born with a disease. Jesus rejected both suggestions (v. 3).

47 Jn 10:26; 1Jn 4:6 **48** ver. 52; Jn 7:20; 10:20 **50** Jn 5:41; 7:18 **51** Jn 5:24; 11:26 **52** Zec 1:5; Heb 11:13 **54** Jn 5:41; 16:14; 17:1; Ac 3:13 **55** Jn 7:28,29 **56** Lk 10:24; Heb 11:13 **58** Ex 3:14; Isa 43:13; Jn 17:5,24; Col 1:17; Rev 1:8 **59** Jn 10:31,39; 11:8; Lk 4:30 **CHAPTER 9** **2** ver. 34 **3** Jn 11:4 **4** Jn 4:34; 5:19,36; 11:9; 12:35; 17:4

who sent Me while it is day; night is
coming when no one can work.
5“As long as I am in the world, I am
the Light of the world [giving guidance
through My word and works].”
6When He had said this, He spat on
the ground and made mud with His
saliva, and He spread the mud [like an
ointment] on the man’s eyes.
7And He said to him, “Go, wash in
the pool of Siloam” (which is trans-
lated, Sent). So he went away and
washed, and came back seeing.
8So the neighbors, and those who
used to know him as a beggar, said,
“Is not this the man who used to sit
and beg?”
9Some said, “It is he.” Still others
said, “No, but he looks like him.” But
he kept saying, “I am the man.”
10So they said to him, “How were
your eyes opened?”
11He replied, “The Man called Jesus
made mud and smeared it on my eyes
and told me, ‘Go to Siloam and wash.’
So I went and washed, and I received
my sight!”
12They asked him, “Where is He?”
He said, “I do not know.”

Controversy over the Man

13Then they brought the man who
was formerly blind to the Pharisees.
14Now it was on a Sabbath day that
Jesus made the mud and opened the
man’s eyes.
15So the Pharisees asked him again
how he received his sight. And he said
to them, “He smeared mud on my eyes,
and I washed, and now I see.”
16Then some of the Pharisees said,
“This Man [Jesus] is not from God, be-
cause He does not keep the Sabbath.”
But others said, “How can a man who
is a sinner (a non-observant Jew) do
such signs *and* miracles?” So there was
a difference of opinion among them.
17Accordingly they said to the blind
man again, “What do you say about
Him, since He opened your eyes?”
And he said, “[It must be that] He is
a prophet!”
18However, the Jews did not believe
that he had been blind and had re-
ceived his sight until they called the
man’s parents.
19They asked them, “Is this your son,
who you say was born blind? Then
how does he now see?”
20His parents answered, “We know
that this is our son, and that he was
born blind;
21but as to how he now sees, we do
not know; or who has opened his eyes,
we do not know. Ask him [and stop
asking us]; he is of age, he will speak
for himself *and* give his own account
of it.”
22His parents said this because they
were afraid of [the leaders of] the Jews;
for the Jews had already agreed that
if anyone acknowledged Jesus to be
the Christ, he would be put out of the
synagogue (excommunicated).
23Because of this his parents said,
“He is of age; ask him.”
24So a second time they called the
man who had been [born] blind, and
said to him, “Give God glory *and* praise
[for your sight]! We know this Man
[Jesus] is a sinner [separated from
God].”
25Then he answered, “I do not know
whether He is a sinner [separated from
God]; but one thing I do know, that
though I was blind, now I see.”

9:7 pool of Siloam. Hezekiah had a tunnel cut through solid rock to transport water from Gihon into the city of Jerusalem, to the pool of Siloam (2Ki 20:20; 2Ch 32:30). John emphasizes that the name Siloam means “sent,” because Jesus had just announced that He had been sent by God (v. 4).

9:22 put out of the synagogue. To take this action was a form of excommunication. The Jews had three types of excommunication: one lasting 30 days, during which the person could not come within six feet of anybody else; one for an indefinite time, during which the person was excluded from all fellowship and worship; and one that meant absolute expulsion forever. These judgments were very serious because no one could conduct business with a person who was excommunicated.

5 Jn 1:5,9; 3:19; 8:12; 12:35,46 **6** Mk 7:33; 8:23 **7** Neh 3:15; See 2Ki 5:14 **11** ver. 6,7 **16** ver. 33; Jn 3:2; Jn 7:12,43; 10:19 **17** Jn 4:19; 6:14 **22** Jn 7:13; 12:42; 19:38; Ac 5:13; ver. 34; Jn 16:2 **24** Jos 7:19; 1Sa 6:5; ver. 16

26 So they said to him, "What did He [actually] do to you? How did He open your eyes?"

27 He answered, "I already told you and you did not listen. Why do you want to hear it again *and* again? Do you want to become His disciples, too?"

28 And [at that remark] they stormed at him and jeered, "You are His disciple, but we are disciples of Moses!

29 "We know [for certain] that God has spoken to Moses, but as for this Man, we do not know where He is from."

30 The man replied, "Well, this is astonishing! You do not know where He comes from, and yet He opened my eyes!

31 "We know [according to your tradition] that God does not hear sinners; but if anyone fears God and does His will, He hears him.

32 "Since the beginning of time it has never been heard that anyone opened the eyes of a person born blind.

33 "If this Man were not from God, He would not be able to do anything [like this because God would not hear His prayer]."

34 They answered him, "You were born entirely in sins [from head to foot], and you [presume to] teach us?" Then they threw him out [of the synagogue].

Jesus Affirms His Deity

35 Jesus heard that they had put him out [of the synagogue], and finding him, He asked, "Do you believe in the Son of Man?"

36 He answered, "Who is He, Sir? Tell me so that I may believe in Him."

37 Jesus said to him, "You have both seen Him, and [in fact] He is the one who is talking with you."

38 And he said, "Lord, I believe [in You and Your word]!" And he worshiped Him [with reverence and awe].

39 Then Jesus said, "I came into this world for judgment [to separate those who believe in Me from those who reject Me—to declare judgment on those who choose to be separated from God], so that the sightless would see, and those who see would become blind."

40 Some Pharisees who were with Him heard these things and said to Him, "Are we also blind?"

41 Jesus said to them, "If you were blind [to spiritual things], you would have no sin [and would not be blamed for your unbelief]; but since you claim to have [spiritual] sight, [you have no excuse so] your sin *and* guilt remain. [Prov 26:12]

Parable of the Good Shepherd

10 "I ASSURE you *and* most solemnly say to you, he who does not enter by the door into the sheepfold, but climbs up from some other place [on the stone wall], that one is a thief and a robber.

2 "But he who enters by the door is the shepherd of the sheep [the protector and provider].

3 "The doorkeeper opens [the gate] for this man, and the sheep hear his voice *and* pay attention to it. And [knowing that they listen] he calls his own sheep by name and leads them out [to pasture].

4 "When he has brought all his own *sheep* outside, he walks on ahead of

---

9:30–33 *it has never been heard.* There is no healing of a blind man recorded anywhere in the Old Testament.
9:38 *Lord, I believe.* Note the progression throughout this chapter of the healed man's understanding of the person of Christ. First, he called Jesus "The Man" (v. 11); then, "a prophet" (v. 17); and finally, he realized that Jesus is the Son of God (vv. 35–38).

10:1 *sheepfold.* A sheepfold was a walled enclosure or high fence made with stakes and having one door or gate; often the enclosure was a cave. ***some other place.*** The Pharisees had secured their power by illegitimate means.
10:3 *The doorkeeper.* The doorkeeper was the undershepherd. ***calls his own sheep by name.*** The naming of sheep was an ancient practice (Ps 147:4; Isa 40:26).

29 Jn 8:14 **30** Jn 3:10 **31** Job 27:9; 35:12; Ps 18:41; 34:15; 66:18; Pr 1:28; 15:29; 28:9; Isa 1:15; Jer 11:11; 14:12; Eze 8:18; Mic 3:4; Zec 7:13 **33** ver. 16 **34** ver. 2 **35** Mt 14:33; 16:16; Mk 1:1; Jn 10:36; 1Jn 5:13 **37** Jn 4:26 **39** Jn 5:22,27; 3:17; 12:47; Mt 13:13 **40** Ro 2:19 **41** Jn 15:22,24

JESUS' SEVEN "I AM" STATEMENTS

Jesus' "I am" statements would have particular significance to the first-century Jewish listener. God had revealed Himself to Moses with a resounding "I AM" (Ex. 3:14). Now Jesus was using the same words to describe Himself (4:26; 6:20; 13:19).

TITLE	REFERENCE	CONTEXT	SIGNIFICANCE
"I am the bread of life."	6:35, 41, 48, 51	After Jesus had fed the five thousand and the people wanted more free food.	As bread sustains physical life, so Christ offers and sustains spiritual life. The nourishment and satisfaction He offers are permanent.
"I am the light of the world."	8:12	During the Feast of Tabernacles. At this feast a huge candelabra was lit in the women's court of the temple. It reminded the Israelites of the pillar of fire which guided their ancestors during the wilderness wanderings.	To a world stumbling about in the darkness of sin, Christ offers Himself as a constant guide. Light is also symbolic of holiness.
"I am the door of the sheep."	10:7, 9	During a discourse with Israel's religious leaders in which Jesus in essence declared them to be unfit shepherds of the nation.	Shepherds guided their flocks into stone enclosures each night to protect them. These structures had no doors. The shepherd would sit or lie in the opening to prevent predators from attacking. Thus Jesus was describing His care and constant devotion to those who are His.
"I am the good shepherd."	10:11, 14	Same as above.	Unlike hirelings who might run away and leave the flock unprotected, Jesus is committed to caring for and keeping watch over His people.
"I am the resurrection and the life."	11:25	After Lazarus had died.	Jesus is the Lord of all life and possesses the power to raise the dead. Death is not the final word, for all who are in Christ will live forever.
"I am the way, the truth, and the life."	14:6	When the disciples were confused about Jesus' statements about heaven.	Jesus is the one and only way to the Father. He is the source of all truth and the source for all knowledge about God. He offers to spiritually dead people the very life of God.
"I am the true vine."	15:1, 5	In the Upper Room discourse on the night of His arrest.	The Old Testament contains many references to Israel as God's vine (Ps. 80:8; Is. 5:1–7; Ezek. 15; Hos. 10:1). But because of the nation's unfruitfulness, Jesus came to fulfill God's plan. By attaching ourselves to Christ, we enable His life to flow in and through us. Then we cannot help but bear fruit that will honor the Father. In this metaphor, He is the Gardener.

them, and the sheep follow him be-
cause they know his voice *and* recog-
nize his call.
5“They will never follow a stranger,
but will run away from him, because
they do not know the voice of strang-
ers.”
6Jesus used this figure of speech
with them, but they did not understand
what He was talking about.
7So Jesus said again, “I assure you
and most solemnly say to you, I am
the Door for the sheep [leading to life].
8“All who came before Me [as false
messiahs and self-appointed leaders]
are thieves and robbers, but the [true]
sheep did not hear them.
9“I am the Door; anyone who enters
through Me will be saved [and will live
forever], and will go in and out [freely],
and find pasture (spiritual security).
10“The thief comes only in order to
steal and kill and destroy. I came that
they may have *and* enjoy life, and have
it in abundance [to the full, till it over-
flows].
11“I am the Good Shepherd. The
Good Shepherd lays down His [own]
life for the sheep. [Ps 23; Is 40:11]
12“But the hired man [who merely
serves for wages], who is neither the
shepherd nor the owner of the sheep,
when he sees the wolf coming, deserts
the flock and runs away; and the wolf
snatches the sheep and scatters *them*.
13“The *man runs* because he is a
hired hand [who serves only for wages]
and is not concerned about the [safety
of the] sheep.
14“I am the Good Shepherd, and I
know [without any doubt those who
are] My own and My own know Me
[and have a deep, personal relationship
with Me]—
15even as the Father knows Me and I
know the Father—and I lay down My
[very own] life [sacrificing it] for *the
benefit of* the sheep.
16“I have other sheep [beside these]
that are not of this fold. I must bring
those also, and they will listen to My
voice *and* pay attention to My call, and

10:7 *I am the Door.* In verses 1 – 5, Jesus is the shepherd; here, He is the door. Some shepherds lay down across the entry of the sheepfold at night to sleep. Wild beasts would be discouraged from entering, and sheep would not exit. Thus, the shepherd was also the door.

10:10 *have it in abundance.* The thieves take life; the shepherd gives it. Abundant life includes salvation, nourishment, healing (v. 9), and much more. *Life* here refers to eternal life, God's life. It speaks not only of endlessness, but of quality of life. With Christ, life on earth can reach much higher quality, and then in heaven it will be complete and perfect.

10:11 The Ministry of Jesus — Jesus' most important teachings are: the kingdom of God (Mt 5 – 7; 24 – 25); His divine authority over men (Mt 7:28 – 29; Mk 2:10); His own role as God and Messiah demonstrated by miracles and signs; the significance of His death and resurrection (Mt 16:21; Lk 24:26); the relationship which His disciples and subsequent believers are to share with Him (Jn 13 – 16); and the urgency of His commission to believers to make disciples (Mt 28:19 – 20). The most significant events of His earthly life, His death, and resurrection, are central to the entire Christian faith (1Co 15:14).

The death of Christ was a humiliating physical death (Jn 19:18,33) that constituted a spiritual separation from God (Mt 27:46). Within this moment there occurred the inexplicable mystery of the Father punishing the Son for the sins of the world (1Pe 3:18; 2Co 5:21). The greatest crime of human history was in the plan of God (Ac 2:23) and became the basis of salvation for sinners (Isa 53:5). The resurrection of Christ demonstrated that His death, by which believing sinners are justified, was valid (1Co 15:12 – 20). The historical evidence for the resurrection is plentiful: the many separate accounts of post-resurrection appearances, the empty tomb, and the transformed disciples. It is the power of the resurrection that empowers Christians today to live the Christian life (Eph 1:19 – 20; Php 3:10).

10:16 *I have other sheep.* These were not Jews in heathen lands, but Gentiles. The Jewish people had asked if Jesus would go and teach the Gentiles (7:35). Jesus now declared that He had sheep among the despised heathen. ***one flock.*** This anticipates the salvation of the Gentiles and the formation of the church, in which converted Jews and Gentiles would form one spiritual body (Gal 3:28; Eph 2:16).

CHAPTER 10 **9** Jn 14:6; Eph 2:18 **11** Isa 40:11; Eze 34:12,23; 37:24; Heb 13:20; 1Pe 2:25; 5:4 **12** Zec 11:16,17 **14** 2Ti 2:19 **15** Mt 11:27; Jn 15:13 **16** Isa 56:8; Eze 37:22; Eph 2:14; 1Pe 2:25

they will become one flock with one
Shepherd. [Ezek 34:23; Eph 2:13–18]
17 "For this reason the Father loves
Me, because I lay down My [own] life
so that I may take it back.
18 "No one takes it away from Me, but
I lay it down voluntarily. I am autho-
rized *and* have power to lay it down
and to give it up, and I am authorized
and have power to take it back. This
command I have received from My
Father."
19 A division [of opinion] occurred
again among the Jews because of these
words [of His].
20 Many of them said, "He has a de-
mon and He is mad [insane—He raves
and rambles]. Why listen to Him?"
21 Others were saying, "These are not
the words *and* thoughts of one pos-
sessed by a demon. Can a demon open
the eyes of the blind?"

Jesus Asserts His Deity

22 At that time the Feast of Dedication
took place at Jerusalem.
23 It was winter, and Jesus was walk-
ing in the temple [area] in Solomon's
portico.
24 So the Jews surrounded Him and
began saying to Him, "How long are
You going to keep us in suspense? If
You are [really] the Christ (the Mes-
siah, the Anointed), tell us so plainly
and openly."
25 Jesus answered them, "I have told
you so, yet you do not believe. The
works that I do in My Father's name
testify concerning Me [they are My
credentials and the evidence declaring
who I am].
26 "But you do not believe Me [so you
do not trust and follow Me] because
you are not My sheep.
27 "The sheep that are My own hear
My voice *and* listen to Me; I know
them, and they follow Me.
28 "And I give them eternal life, and
they will never, ever [by any means]
perish; and no one will ever snatch
them out of My hand.
29 "My Father, who has given *them*
to Me, is greater *and* mightier than all;
and no one is able to snatch *them* out
of the Father's hand.
30 "I and the Father are One [in es-
sence and nature]."
31 Again the Jews picked up stones
to stone Him.
32 Jesus answered them, "I showed
you many good works [and many acts
of mercy] from the Father; for which of
them are you stoning Me?"
33 The Jews answered Him, "We
are not going to stone You for a good
work, but for blasphemy, because You,
a *mere* man, make Yourself out to be
God."
34 Jesus answered them, "Is it not
written in your Law, 'I SAID, YOU ARE
GODS [human judges representing God,
not divine beings]'? [Ps 82:6]

10:19–21 ***Many of them said . . . Others were saying.*** After Jesus' analogy of the good shepherd, the editorial comment by John is fitting. In the analogy, Jesus was the good shepherd whose sheep hear His voice, implying that there are sheep who do not hear His voice. John's comment indicates that some believe and others do not. This is the same division that occurred in 9:16.

10:22 ***the Feast of Dedication.*** This festival was celebrated for eight days. In 167 BC Antiochus Epiphanes desecrated the temple in Jerusalem, as prophesied in Daniel 11:31. The Maccabeans restored and purified the temple. In commemoration of the restoration, the Feast of Dedication was instituted. Today it is also known as the Feast of Lights or Hanukkah.

10:27–29 ***hear . . . follow.*** The following of the sheep is a metaphor for faith. Other metaphors for faith in this Gospel include drinking water (4:14), eating bread (6:50–51), eating flesh, and drinking blood (6:54).

10:30 ***I and the Father are One.*** The Jewish opponents understood that Jesus was claiming to be God (vv. 31,33).

10:34 ***YOU ARE GODS.*** In the Old Testament, judges were called gods. They exercised godlike judicial sovereignty. Psalm 82:6, the verse quoted here, refers to judges who violate the law. Jesus' argument was that, if the divine name had been applied by God to mere men, there could be neither blasphemy nor folly in its application to the incarnate Son of God Himself.

17 Isa 53:7,8,12; Heb 2:9 **18** Jn 2:19; Jn 6:38; 15:10; Ac 2:24,32 **19** Jn 7:43; 9:16 **20** Jn 7:20; 8:48,52 **21** Ex 4:11; Ps 94:9; 146:8; Jn 9:6,7,32,33 **23** Ac 3:11; 5:12 **25** ver. 38; Jn 3:2; 5:36 **26** Jn 8:47 **27** ver. 4,14 **29** Jn 14:28; Jn 17:2,6 **30** Jn 17:11,22 **31** Jn 8:59 **33** Jn 5:18 **34** Ps 82:6

35“If He called them gods, men to
whom the word of God came (and the
Scripture cannot be undone *or* an-
nulled *or* broken),
36[if that is true] then do you say of
Him whom the Father sanctified *and*
set apart *for Himself* and sent into the
world, ‘You are blaspheming,’ because
I said, ‘I am the Son of God’?
37“If I do not do the works of My Fa-
ther [that is, the miracles that only God
could perform], then do not believe Me.
38“But if I am doing them, even if you
do not believe Me *or* have faith in Me,
[at least] believe the works [that I do—
admit that they are the works of God],
so that you may know and keep on
knowing [clearly—without any doubt]
that the Father is in Me, and I am in the
Father [that is, I am One with Him].”
39So they tried again to seize Him,
but He eluded their grasp.
40He went back again across the Jor-
dan to the place where John was first
baptizing, and He was staying there.
41Many came to Him, and they were
saying, “John did not perform a single
sign (attesting miracle), but everything
John said about this Man was true *and*
accurate.”
42And many there believed *and* con-
fidently trusted in Him [accepting Him
as Savior, and following His teaching].

The Death and Resurrection of Lazarus

11 NOW A certain man named
Lazarus was sick. He was from
Bethany, the village where Mary and
her sister Martha lived.
2It was the Mary who anointed the
Lord with perfume and wiped His feet
with her hair, whose brother Lazarus
was sick. [John 12:3]
3So the sisters sent *word* to Him, say-
ing, “Lord, he [our brother and Your
friend] whom You love is sick.”
4When Jesus heard this, He said,
“This sickness will not end in death;
but [on the contrary it is] for the glory
and honor of God, so that the Son of
God may be glorified by it.”
5Now Jesus loved *and* was con-
cerned about Martha and her sister
and Lazarus [and considered them
dear friends].
6So [even] when He heard that
Lazarus was sick, He stayed in the
same place two more days.
7Then He said to His disciples, “Let
us go back to Judea.”
8The disciples said to Him, “Rabbi
(Teacher), the Jews were only recently
going to stone You, and You are [think-
ing of] going back there again?”
9Jesus answered, “Are there not
twelve hours [of light] in the day? Any-
one who walks in the daytime does not
stumble, because he sees [by] the light
of this world.
10“But if anyone walks in the night,
he stumbles, because there is no light
in him.”
11He said this, and after that said,
“Our friend Lazarus has fallen asleep;
but I am going *there* to wake him.”
12The disciples answered, “Lord, if
he has fallen asleep, he will recover.”
13However, Jesus had spoken of his
death, but they thought that He was
referring to natural sleep.
14So then Jesus told them plainly,
“Lazarus is dead.
15“And for your sake I am glad that I
was not there, so that you may believe.
But let us go to him.”
16Then Thomas, who was called
Didymus (the twin), said to his fellow

11:1 *Bethany.* This was a small village on the southeast slope of the Mount of Olives. It was located about two miles from Jerusalem.
11:4 *not end in death.* This phrase means not having death as its final result.
11:6–8 *He stayed in the same place two more days.* God's purpose was to glorify His Son (v. 4) and to cause the disciples to grow (v. 15). Had Jesus immediately rushed to Lazarus' bedside and healed him, Lazarus would not have died and Jesus would not have been able to manifest His glory by raising Lazarus.
11:16 *Let us go too, that we may die with Him.* While the Lord saw their development in

35 Ro 13:1 **36** Jn 6:27; Jn 3:17; 5:36,37; 8:42; ver. 30; Jn 5:17,18; Lk 1:35; Jn 9:35,37 **37** Jn 15:24 **38** Jn 5:36; 14:10,11; Jn 14:10,11; 17:21 **39** Jn 7:30,44; 8:59 **40** Jn 1:28 **41** Jn 3:30 **42** Jn 8:30; 11:45 **CHAPTER 11** **1** Lk 10:38,39 **2** Mt 26:7; Mk 14:3; Jn 12:3 **4** ver. 40; Jn 9:3 **6** Jn 10:40 **8** Jn 10:31 **9** Jn 9:4 **10** Jn 12:35 **11** Dt 31:16; Da 12:2; Mt 9:24; Ac 7:60; 1Co 15:18,51

disciples, "Let us go too, that we may
die with Him."
17So when Jesus arrived, He found
that Lazarus had already been in the
tomb four days.
18Bethany was near Jerusalem,
about two miles away;
19and many of the Jews had come to
see Martha and Mary, to comfort them
concerning [the loss of] their brother.
20So when Martha heard that Jesus
was coming, she went to meet Him, while
Mary remained sitting in the house.
21Then Martha said to Jesus, "Lord, if
You had been here, my brother would
not have died.
22"Even now I know that whatever
You ask of God, God will give to You."
23Jesus told her, "Your brother will
rise [from the dead]."
24Martha replied, "I know that he
will rise [from the dead] in the resur-
rection on the last day."
25Jesus said to her, "I am the Resur-
rection and the Life. Whoever believes
in (adheres to, trusts in, relies on) Me
[as Savior] will live even if he dies;
26and everyone who lives and be-
lieves in Me [as Savior] will never die.
Do you believe this?"
27She said to Him, "Yes, Lord; I have
believed *and* continue to believe that
You are the Christ (the Messiah, the
Anointed), the Son of God, He who
was [destined and promised] to come
into the world [and it is for You that the
world has waited]."
28After she had said this, she left
and called her sister Mary, privately
whispering [to her], "The Teacher is
here and is asking for you."
29And when she heard this, she got
up quickly and went to Him.
30Now Jesus had not yet entered the
village, but was still at the place where
Martha had met Him.
31So when the Jews who were with
her in the house comforting her, saw
how quickly Mary got up and left, they
followed her, assuming that she was
going to the tomb to weep there.
32When Mary came [to the place]
where Jesus was and saw Him, she
fell at His feet, saying to Him, "Lord, if
You had been here, my brother would
not have died."
33When Jesus saw her sobbing, and
the Jews who had come with her also
sobbing, He was deeply moved in spirit
[to the point of anger at the sorrow
caused by death] and was troubled,
34and said, "Where have you laid
him?" They said, "Lord, come and see."
35Jesus wept.
36So the Jews were saying, "See how
He loved him [as a close friend]!"
37But some of them said, "Could not
this Man, who opened the blind man's
eyes, have kept this man from dying?"
38So Jesus, again deeply moved with-
in [to the point of anger], approached the
tomb. It was a cave, and a boulder was
lying against it [to cover the entrance].
39Jesus said, "Take away the stone."
Martha, the sister of the dead man,
said to Him, "Lord, by this time there
will be an offensive odor, for he has
been *dead* four days! [It is hopeless!]"
40Jesus said to her, "Did I not say to
you that if you believe [in Me], you will
see the glory of God [the expression of
His excellence]?"
41So they took away the stone. And
Jesus raised His eyes [toward heaven]
and said, "Father, I thank You that You
have heard Me.
42"I knew that You always hear Me
and listen to Me; but I have said this
because of the people standing around,
so that they may believe that You have
sent Me [and that You have made Me
Your representative]."
43When He had said this, He shouted
with a loud voice, "Lazarus, come out!"

---

faith, Thomas saw their deaths. Yet, in his loyalty, he followed anyway.

11:33 *troubled.* This word means to be stirred up, disturbed. Jesus was moved by the mourning of Mary and indignant at the hypocritical lamentations of His enemies.

11:37 *Could not this Man.* Some people misinterpreted Jesus' tears as powerlessness. They complained that He had healed others, but now was impotent.

11:43 *Lazarus.* Augustine once said that, if Jesus had not designated Lazarus by name, all the

22 Jn 9:31 **24** Lk 14:14; Jn 5:29 **25** Jn 5:21; 6:39,40,44; 3:36; 1Jn 5:10 **27** Mt 16:16; Jn 4:42; 6:14,69 **31** ver. 19 **32** ver. 21 **35** Lk 19:41 **37** Jn 9:6 **40** ver. 4,23 **42** Jn 12:30

44 Out came the man who had been dead, his hands and feet *tightly* wrapped in burial cloths (linen strips), and with a [burial] cloth wrapped around his face. Jesus said to them, "Unwrap him and release him."

45 So then, many of the Jews who had come to [be with] Mary and who were eyewitnesses to what Jesus had done, believed in Him.

46 But some of them went back to the Pharisees and told them what Jesus had done.

Conspiracy to Kill Jesus

47 So the chief priests and Pharisees convened a council [of the leaders in Israel], and said, "What are we doing? For this man performs many signs (attesting miracles).

48 "If we let Him go on like this, everyone will believe in Him, and the Romans will come and take away both our [holy] place (the temple) and our nation."

49 But one of them, Caiaphas, who was the high priest that year [the year of Christ's crucifixion], said to them, "You know nothing at all!

50 "Nor do you understand that it is expedient *and* politically advantageous for you that one man die for the people, and that the whole nation not perish."

51 Now he did not say this [simply] on his own initiative; but being the high priest that year, he [was unknowingly used by God and] prophesied that Jesus was going to die for the nation, [Is 53:8]

52 and not only for the nation, but also for the purpose of gathering together into one body the children of God who have been scattered abroad. [Is 49:6]

53 So from that day on they planned together to kill Him.

54 For that reason Jesus no longer walked openly among the Jews, but left there *and* went to the district that borders on the uninhabited wilderness, to a town called Ephraim; and He stayed there with the disciples.

55 Now the Passover of the Jews was approaching, and many from the country went up to Jerusalem before Passover to purify themselves [ceremonially, so that they would be able to participate in the feast].

56 So they were looking for Jesus as they stood in the temple [area], and saying among themselves, "What do you think? Will He not come to the feast at all?"

57 Now the chief priests and Pharisees had given orders that if anyone knew where He was, he was to report it so that they might arrest Him.

Mary Anoints Jesus

12 SIX DAYS before the Passover, Jesus went to Bethany, where Lazarus was, whom He had raised from the dead. [Matt 26:6–13; Mark 14:3–9]

2 So they gave a supper for Him there. Martha was serving, and Lazarus was one of those reclining *at the table* with Him.

---

graves would have been emptied at His command (5:28). Raising Lazarus from the dead is the seventh sign of Jesus' messiahship, the greatest miracle of all, giving life back to the dead.

11:49 – 52 *it is expedient.* In the opinion of Caiaphas, Jesus should die rather than plunge the nation into destruction. John adds that by virtue of his office Caiaphas pronounced a message of God unconsciously. Caiaphas was a prophet in spite of himself. John also saw in Caiaphas' words a prophecy that Jesus should die not only for Israel but for the Gentiles as well.

11:53 *they planned together to kill Him.* Humanly speaking, the resurrection of Lazarus was a major factor that led to the plot by the Jewish religious leaders to kill Christ. At this point the council decided informally, if not formally, to put Jesus to death. It is ironic that these men believed they could put to death permanently One who could raise the dead.

12:1 *Six days before the Passover.* If the crucifixion took place on a Friday, this dinner occurred during the evening of the previous Saturday. Verse 12 seems to support this conclusion because the Jerusalem entry took place on Sunday.

44 Jn 20:7 **45** Jn 2:23; 10:42; 12:11,18 **47** Ps 2:2; Mt 26:3; Mk 14:1; Lk 22:2; Jn 12:19; Ac 4:16 **49** Lk 3:2; Jn 18:14; Ac 4:6 **50** Jn 18:14 **52** Isa 49:6; 1Jn 2:2; Jn 10:16; Eph 2:14-17 **54** Jn 4:1,3; 7:1; See 2Ch 13:19 **55** Jn 2:13; 5:1; 6:4 **56** Jn 7:11 **CHAPTER 12** **1** Jn 11:1,43 **2** Mt 26:6; Mk 14:3

3 Then Mary took a pound of very expensive perfume of pure nard, and she poured it on Jesus' feet and wiped His feet with her hair; and the house was filled with the fragrance of the perfume.

4 But Judas Iscariot, one of His disciples, the one who was going to betray Him, said,

5 "Why was this perfume not sold for three hundred denarii and [the money] given to the poor?"

6 Now he said this, not because he cared about the poor [for he had never cared about them], but because he was a thief; and since he had the money box [serving as treasurer for the twelve disciples], he used to pilfer what was put into it.

7 So Jesus said, "Let her alone, so that she may keep [the rest of] it for the day of My burial.

8 "You always have the poor with you, but you do not always have Me."

9 A large crowd of Jews learned that He was there [at Bethany]; and they came, not only because of Jesus, but also to see Lazarus, whom He had raised from the dead.

10 So the chief priests planned to kill Lazarus also,

11 because on account of him many of the Jews were going away [from the teaching and traditions of the Jewish leaders] and believing in Jesus [following Him as Savior and Messiah].

The Triumphal Entry

12 The next day, when the large crowd who had come to the *Passover* feast heard that Jesus was coming to Jerusalem, [Matt 21:4–9; Mark 11:7–10; Luke 19:35–38]

13 they took branches of palm trees [in homage to Him as King] and went out to meet Him, and they *began* shouting *and* kept shouting "Hosanna! BLESSED (celebrated, praised) IS HE WHO COMES IN THE NAME OF THE LORD, even the King of Israel!" [Ps 118:26]

14 And Jesus, finding a young donkey, sat on it; just as it is written [in Scripture],

15 "DO NOT FEAR, DAUGHTER OF ZION; BEHOLD, YOUR KING IS COMING, SEATED ON A DONKEY'S COLT." [Zech 9:9]

16 His disciples did not understand [the meaning of] these things at first; but when Jesus was glorified *and* exalted, they remembered that these things had been written about Him and had been done to Him.

17 So the people, who were with Him when He called Lazarus out of the tomb and raised him from the dead, continued to tell others *about Him*.

18 For this reason the crowd went to meet Him, because they heard that He had performed this [miraculous] sign.

19 Then the Pharisees [argued and] said to one another, "You see that your efforts are futile. Look! The whole world has gone [running] after Him!"

Greeks Seek Jesus

20 Now there were some Greeks (Gentiles) among those who were going up to worship at the feast;

21 these came to Philip, who was from

12:3 *expensive perfume.* Judas Iscariot said that this perfume cost 300 denarii. One denarius was a laborer's wage for one day. Thus, the perfume cost approximately a year's wages. ***poured it on Jesus' feet.*** Mary also anointed Jesus' head. The custom of that time was to anoint the heads of guests. Anointing Jesus' head was an act of honor; anointing His feet was a display of devotion.

12:10 – 11 *the chief priests planned to kill Lazarus also.* The chief priests were mostly Sadducees. They had an additional reason to kill Lazarus. He was a living refutation of their doctrine that there was no resurrection (11:57; Ac 23:8). Yet this was not a meeting of the Jewish council, nor was it a formal sentence of death. The ultimate motivation for wanting to kill Lazarus was that, because of him, many were believing in Jesus.

12:13 – 15 *the King of Israel.* Until this point, Jesus had discouraged expressions of support from the people (6:15; 7:1 – 8). Here, He allowed public enthusiasm. He entered Jerusalem on the back of a young donkey. This act fulfilled prophecy (Zec 9:9) and as such was a symbolic proclamation that Jesus is the Messiah.

12:20 *to worship at the feast.* This verse indicates that these Greeks were Jewish proselytes.

3 Lk 10:38,39; Jn 11:2 **6** Jn 13:29 **8** Mt 26:11; Mk 14:7 **9** Jn 11:43,44 **10** Lk 16:31 **11** ver. 18; Jn 11:45 **12** Mt 21:8; Mk 11:8; Lk 19:35,36 **13** Ps 118:25,26 **14** Mt 21:7 **15** Zec 9:9 **16** Lk 18:34; Jn 7:39; Jn 14:26 **18** ver. 11 **19** Jn 11:47,48 **20** Ac 17:4; 1Ki 8:41,42; Ac 8:27 **21** Jn 1:44

JESUS' TRIAL, JUDGMENT AND CRUCIFIXION

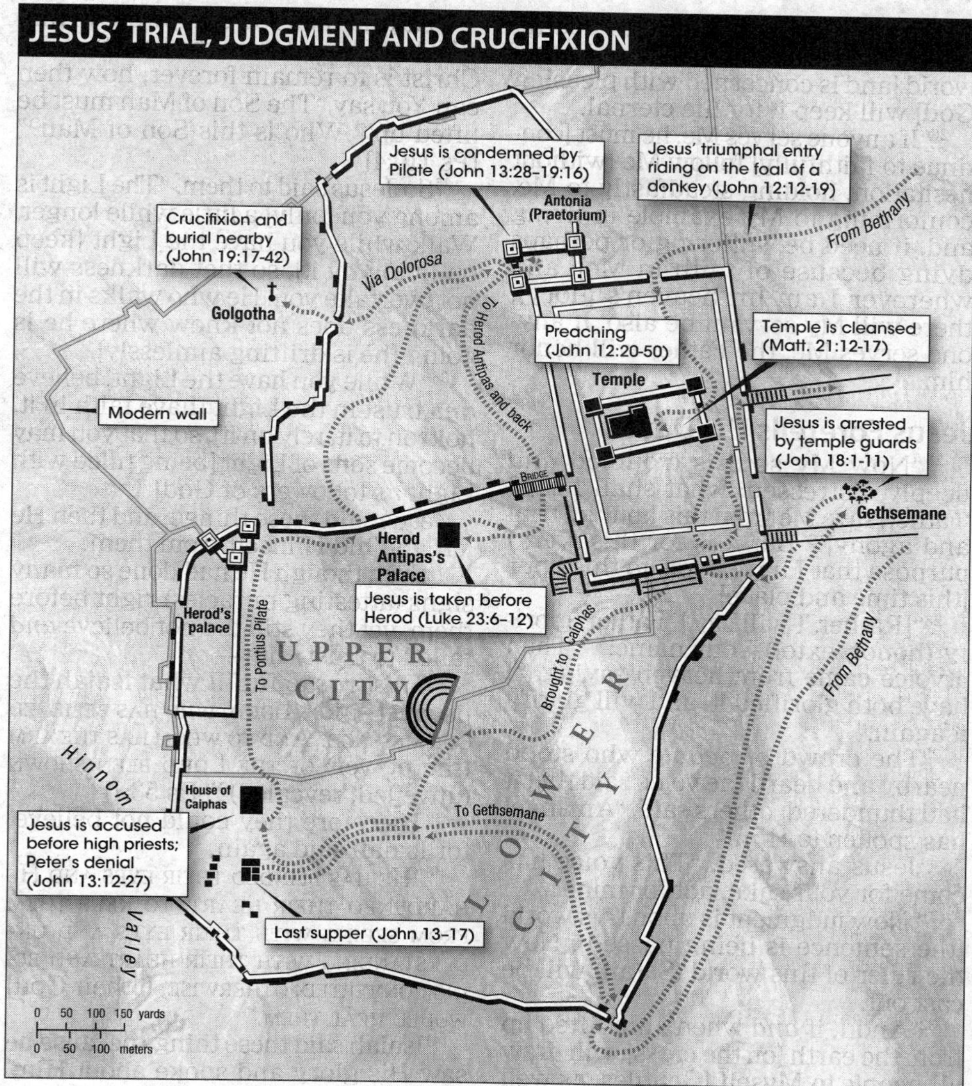

Bethsaida in Galilee, with a request,
saying, "Sir, we wish to see Jesus."
22Philip came and told Andrew; then
Andrew and Philip went and told Jesus.
23And Jesus answered them, "The
hour has come for the Son of Man to
be glorified *and* exalted.
24"I assure you *and* most solemnly
say to you, unless a grain of wheat
falls into the earth and dies, it remains
alone [just one grain, never more]. But
if it dies, it produces much grain *and*
yields a harvest.
25"The one who loves his life

By recording this incident, perhaps John was hinting that the salvation rejected by many of the Jews was already passing to the Gentiles. ***12:24 unless a grain of wheat . . . dies.*** When a seed dies, it produces fruit. Life comes by death. This principle is not only true in nature, but it is also true spiritually. Jesus was speaking first and foremost of Himself. He is the grain of wheat.

23 Jn 13:32; 17:1 **24** 1Co 15:36 **25** Mt 10:39; 16:25; Mk 8:35; Lk 9:24; 17:33

[eventually] loses it [through death], but the one who hates his life in this world [and is concerned with pleasing God] will keep it for life eternal.

26 “If anyone serves Me, he must [continue to faithfully] follow Me [without hesitation, holding steadfastly to Me, conforming to My example in living and, if need be, suffering or perhaps dying because of faith in Me]; and wherever I am [in heaven’s glory], there will My servant be also. If anyone serves Me, the Father will honor him.

Jesus Foretells His Death

27 “Now My soul is troubled *and* deeply distressed; what shall I say? ‘Father, save Me from this hour [of trial and agony]’? But it is for this [very] purpose that I have come to this hour [this time and place].

28 “[Rather, I will say,] ‘Father, glorify (honor, extol) Your name!’ ” Then a voice came from heaven saying, “I have both glorified it, and will glorify it again.”

29 The crowd *of people* who stood nearby and heard the voice said that it had thundered; others said, “An angel has spoken to Him!”

30 Jesus answered, “This voice has come for your sake, not for mine.

31 “Now judgment is upon this world [the sentence is being passed]. Now the ruler of this world (Satan) will be cast out.

32 “And I, if *and* when I am lifted up from the earth [on the cross], will draw all *people* to Myself [Gentiles, as well as Jews].”

33 He said this to indicate the kind of death by which He was to die.

34 At this the crowd answered Him, “We have heard from the Law that the Christ is to remain forever; how then can You say, ‘The Son of Man must be lifted up’? Who is this Son of Man?” [Ps 110:4]

35 So Jesus said to them, “The Light is among you [only] a little while longer. Walk while you have the Light [keep on living by it], so that darkness will not overtake you. He who walks in the darkness does not know where he is going [he is drifting aimlessly].

36 “While you have the Light, believe *and* trust in the Light [have faith in it, hold on to it, rely on it], so that you may become sons of Light [being filled with Light as followers of God].”

Jesus said these things, and then He left and hid Himself from them.

37 Even though He had done so many signs (attesting miracles) right before them, yet they still did not believe *and* failed to trust Him—

38 *This was* to fulfill what Isaiah the prophet said: “LORD, WHO HAS BELIEVED OUR MESSAGE? AND TO WHOM HAS THE ARM (the power) OF THE LORD BEEN SHOWN (unveiled, revealed)?” [Is 53:1]

39 Therefore they could not believe, for Isaiah said again,

40 “HE HAS BLINDED THEIR EYES AND HE HARDENED THEIR HEART, TO KEEP THEM FROM SEEING WITH THEIR EYES AND UNDERSTANDING WITH THEIR HEART AND BEING CONVERTED; OTHERWISE, I [their God] WOULD HEAL THEM.”

41 Isaiah said these things because he saw His glory and spoke about Him. [Is 6:9, 10]

42 Nevertheless, even many of the leading men believed in Him [as Sav-

---

His death would produce much fruit and would result in many living for God.

12:27 *Now My soul is troubled.* Jesus’ agony over His impending death was not confined to Gethsemane, where He prayed for the cup to pass from Him (Mt 26:39). He felt the agony and expressed it almost a week before Gethsemane.

12:35 – 36 *while you have the Light.* Instead of answering the people’s questions (v. 34), Jesus gave them a warning. Jesus is the light. He wanted the people to believe and abide in Him (v. 46).

12:42 – 43 *Nevertheless.* This word marks a stark contrast between these believers and the

---

26 Jn 14:3; 17:24; 1Th 4:17 **27** Mt 26:38,39; Lk 12:50; Jn 13:21; Lk 22:53; Jn 18:37 **28** Mt 3:17 **30** Jn 11:42 **31** Mt 12:29; Lk 10:18; Jn 14:30; 16:11; Ac 26:18; 2Co 4:4; Eph 2:2; 6:12 **32** Jn 3:14; 8:28; Ro 5:18; Heb 2:9 **33** Jn 18:32 **34** Ps 89:36,37; 110:4; Isa 9:7; 53:8; Eze 37:25; Da 2:44; 7:14,27; Mic 4:7 **35** Jn 1:9; 8:12; 9:5; Jer 13:16; Eph 5:8; Jn 11:10; 1Jn 2:11 **36** Lk 16:8; Eph 5:8; 1Th 5:5; 1Jn 2:9-11; Jn 8:59; 11:54 **38** Isa 53:1; Ro 10:16 **40** Isa 6:9,10; Mt 13:14 **41** Isa 6:1 **42** Jn 7:13; 9:22

ior and Messiah], but because of the Pharisees they would not confess it, for fear that [if they acknowledged Him openly] they would be put out of the synagogue (excommunicated);

43 for they loved the approval of men more than the approval of God.

44 But Jesus loudly declared, "The one who believes *and* trusts in Me does not believe [only] in Me but [also believes] in Him who sent Me.

45 "And whoever sees Me sees the One who sent Me.

46 "I have come as Light into the world, so that everyone who believes *and* trusts in Me [as Savior—all those who anchor their hope in Me and rely on the truth of My message] will not continue to live in darkness.

47 "If anyone hears My words and does not keep them, I do not judge him; for I did not come to judge *and* condemn the world [that is, to initiate the final judgment of the world], but to save the world.

48 "Whoever rejects Me and refuses to accept My teachings, has one who judges him; the *very* word that I spoke will judge *and* condemn him on the last day.

49 "For I have never spoken on My own initiative *or* authority, but the Father Himself who sent Me has given Me a commandment *regarding* what to say and what to speak. [Deut 18:18, 19]

50 "I know that His commandment is eternal life. So the things I speak, I speak [in accordance with His exact instruction,] just as the Father has told Me."

The Lord's Supper

13 NOW BEFORE the Passover Feast, Jesus knew that His hour had come [and it was time] for Him to leave this world *and* return to the Father. Having [greatly] loved His own who were in the world, He loved them [and continuously loves them with His perfect love] to the end (eternally).

2 It was during supper, when the devil had already put [the thought of] betraying Jesus into the heart of Judas Iscariot, Simon's son,

3 that Jesus, knowing that the Father had put everything into His hands, and that He had come from God and was [now] returning to God,

4 got up from supper, took off His [outer] robe, and taking a [servant's] towel, He tied it around His waist.

Jesus Washes the Disciples' Feet

5 Then He poured water into the basin and began washing the disciples' feet and wiping them with the towel which was tied around His waist.

6 When He came to Simon Peter, he said to Him, "Lord, are You going to wash my feet?"

7 Jesus replied to him, "You do not realize now what I am doing, but you will [fully] understand it later."

8 Peter said to Him, "You will never wash my feet!" Jesus answered, "Unless I wash you, you have no part with Me [we can have nothing to do with each other]."

9 Simon Peter said to Him, "Lord, [in that case, wash] not only my feet, but also my hands and my head!"

10 Jesus said to him, "Anyone who has bathed needs only to wash his feet, and is completely clean. And you [My disciples] are clean, but not all *of you*."

---

unbelief spoken of in verses 37 – 41. These men were genuine believers. Their problem was that they feared the opinions of their fellow leaders. Such believers will be ashamed at Christ's return (1Jn 2:28).

12:47 *I do not judge him.* Christ will judge, but at His first coming He did not come to judge but to save (3:17).

13:1 *to the end.* This phrase means either "to the last" or "utterly and completely." What follows in verses 1 – 11 demonstrates Jesus' complete love. Jesus loved His disciples, even though He knew that one would betray Him, another would deny Him, and all would desert Him for a time.

13:8 *no part with Me.* The washing was a symbol of spiritual cleansing (vv. 10 – 11). If Peter did not participate in the cleansing, he would not enjoy fellowship with Christ (1Jn 1:9).

---

43 Jn 5:44 **44** Mk 9:37; 1Pe 1:21 **45** Jn 14:9 **46** ver. 35,36; Jn 3:19; 9:5,39 **47** Jn 5:45; 8:15,26; Jn 3:17 **48** Lk 10:16; Dt 18:19; Mk 16:16 **49** Jn 8:38; 14:10; Dt 18:18 **CHAPTER 13** **1** Mt 26:2; Jn 12:23; 17:1,11 **2** Lk 22:3 **3** Mt 11:27; 28:18; Jn 3:35; 17:2; Ac 2:36; 1Co 15:27; Heb 2:8 **4** Lk 22:27; Php 2:7,8 **6** Mt 3:14 **7** ver. 12 **8** Jn 3:5; 1Co 6:11; Eph 5:26; Titus 3:5; Heb 10:22 **10** Jn 15:3

11 For He knew who was going to
betray Him; for that reason He said,
"Not all of you are clean."
12 So when He had washed their feet
and put on His [outer] robe and re-
clined *at the table* again, He said to
them, "Do you understand what I have
done for you?
13 "You call Me Teacher and Lord,
and you are right in doing so, for *that
is who* I am.
14 "So if I, the Lord and the Teacher,
washed your feet, you ought to wash
one another's feet as well.
15 "For I gave you [this as] an exam-
ple, so that you should do [in turn] as
I did to you.
16 "I assure you *and* most solemnly
say to you, a slave is not greater than
his master, nor is one who is sent great-
er than the one who sent him.
17 "If you know these things, you are
blessed [happy and favored by God] if
you put them into practice [and faith-
fully do them].
18 "I am not speaking of all of you. I
know whom I have chosen; but [this
has happened] in order that the Scrip-
ture may be fulfilled: 'HE WHO EATS MY
BREAD HAS RAISED UP HIS HEEL AGAINST ME
[as My enemy].' [Ps 41:9]
19 "From now on I am telling you
[what will happen] before it occurs, so
that when it does take place you may
believe that I am *He* [who I say I am—
the Christ, the Anointed, the Messiah].
20 "I assure you *and* most solemnly say
to you, the one who receives *and* wel-
comes whomever I send receives Me;
and the one who receives Me receives
Him who sent Me [in that same way]."

Jesus Predicts His Betrayal

21 After Jesus had said these things,
He was troubled in spirit, and testi-
fied and said, "I assure you *and* most
solemnly say to you, one of you will
betray Me *and* hand Me over."
22 The disciples *began* looking at one
another, puzzled *and* disturbed as to
whom He could mean.
23 One of His disciples, whom Jesus
loved (esteemed), was leaning against
Jesus' chest.
24 So Simon Peter motioned to him
(John) and [quietly] asked [him to ask
Jesus] of whom He was speaking.
25 Then leaning back against Jesus'
chest, he (John) asked Him [privately],
"Lord, who is it?"
26 Jesus answered, "It is the one to
whom I am going to give this piece [of
bread] after I have dipped it." So when
He had dipped the piece of bread [into
the dish], He gave it to Judas, *son* of
Simon Iscariot.
27 After [Judas had taken] the piece of
bread, Satan entered him. Then Jesus
said to him, "What you are going to do,
do quickly [without delay]."
28 But no one reclining *at the table*
knew why He said *this* to him.
29 Some thought that, since Judas
[as the treasurer of the group] had the
money box, Jesus was telling him,
"Buy what we need for the feast," or
that he was to give something to the
poor.
30 After taking the piece of bread,
he went out immediately; and it was
night.
31 So when Judas had left, Jesus said,

13:13 *Teacher and Lord.* These were the ordinary titles of respect given to a rabbi.
13:18 *HAS RAISED UP HIS HEEL.* Jesus quoted Psalm 41:9 to explain the action of Judas. Lifting up one's heel was a gesture of insult or a preparation to kick. The blow had not yet been given. This was the attitude of Judas at that moment. He was eating with the disciples, but he was ready to strike.
13:23 *whom Jesus loved.* The disciple is never named in Scripture, but the tradition of the early church designates him as John, the author of this Gospel. ***leaning against Jesus' chest.*** At this time people did not generally sit at a table to eat. They reclined on the left side of a low platform, resting on the left elbow and eating with the right hand, their feet extended outward. Reclining in such a way, a man's head was near the chest of the person on his left.

11 Jn 6:64 **13** Mt 23:8; Lk 6:46; 1Co 8:6; 12:3; Php 2:11 **14** Lk 22:27; Ro 12:10; Gal 6:1,2; 1Pe 5:5 **15** Mt 11:29; Php 2:5; 1Pe 2:21; 1Jn 2:6 **16** Mt 10:24; Lk 6:40; Jn 15:20 **17** Jas 1:25 **18** ver. 21; Ps 41:9; Mt 26:23 **19** Jn 14:29; 16:4 **20** Mt 10:40; 25:40; Lk 10:16 **21** Mt 26:21; Mk 14:18; Lk 22:21; Jn 12:27; Ac 1:17; 1Jn 2:19 **23** Jn 19:26; 20:2; 21:7,20 **27** Lk 22:3; Jn 6:70 **29** Jn 12:6 **31** Jn 12:23; Jn 14:13; 1Pe 4:11

"Now is [the time for] the Son of Man [to
be] glorified, and God is glorified in Him;
32 [if God is glorified in Him,] God
will also glorify Him (the Son) in Him-
self, and will glorify Him at once.
33 "Little children, I am with you
[only] a little longer. You will look for
Me and, as I told the Jews, so I tell you
now, 'Where I am going, you are not
able to come.' [John 8:21]
34 "I am giving you a new command-
ment, that you love one another. Just
as I have loved you, so you too are to
love one another.
35 "By this everyone will know that
you are My disciples, if you have love
and unselfish concern for one another."
36 Simon Peter said to Him, "Lord,
where are You going?" Jesus an-
swered, "Where I am going, you can-
not follow Me now; but you will be able
to follow later."
37 Peter said to Him, "Lord, why
cannot I follow You now? I will lay
down my life for You!" [Matt 26:33–35;
Mark 14:29–31; Luke 22:33, 34]
38 Jesus answered, "Will you [really]
lay down your life for Me? I assure you
and most solemnly say to you, before a
rooster crows you will deny *and* com-
pletely disown Me three times.

Jesus Comforts His Disciples

14 "DO NOT let your heart be trou-
bled (afraid, cowardly). Believe
[confidently] in God *and* trust in Him,
[have faith, hold on to it, rely on it, keep
going and] believe also in Me.
2 "In My Father's house are many
dwelling places. If it were not so, I
would have told you, because I am
going there to prepare a place for you.
3 "And if I go and prepare a place for
you, I will come back again and I will
take you to Myself, so that where I am
you may be also.
4 "And [to the place] where I am go-
ing, you know the way."
5 Thomas said to Him, "Lord, we do
not know where You are going; so how
can we know the way?"
6 Jesus said to him, "I am the [only]
Way [to God] and the [real] Truth and
the [real] Life; no one comes to the
Father but through Me.

Jesus' Oneness with the Father

7 "If you had [really] known Me, you
would also have known My Father.
From now on you know Him, and have
seen Him."
8 Philip said to Him, "Lord, show us
the Father and then we will be satis-
fied."
9 Jesus said to him, "Have I been with
you for so long a time, and you do not
know Me yet, Philip, *nor* recognize
clearly who I am? Anyone who has
seen Me has seen the Father. How can
you say, 'Show us the Father?'

13:33 ***Little children*** is an expression of tender affection used nowhere else in the Gospels. John did not forget the expression; he used it repeatedly in 1 John.

13:35 ***By this.*** Unbelievers recognize Jesus' disciples not by their doctrinal distinctives, nor by dramatic miracles, nor even by their love for the lost. They recognize His disciples by their deeds of love for one another.

13:36 ***Lord, where are you going?*** This question Jesus had already addressed twice before, indicating that Peter completely missed the point of what Jesus said in verses 34 and 35.

13:37 ***I will lay down my life for You!*** Peter was ready to die for Jesus. Unfortunately, he was not ready, at this point, to live for Him. Later Peter would die for Christ (21:18 – 19). Church tradition states that Peter was crucified upside down, at his request, for he felt himself unworthy to be crucified like his Lord.

14:3 ***I will come back again and I will take you.*** Peter may have failed Jesus (13:38), but Christ will not fail to return for Peter and for everyone else who has believed in Him (1Th 4:16 – 17).

14:6 ***the [only] Way [to God]and the [real] Truth and the [real] Life.*** Through His death and resurrection, Jesus is the way to the Father. He is also the truth and the life. As truth, He is the revelation of God. As life, He is the source of our very beings.

32 Jn 12:23 **33** Jn 8:21 **34** Lev 19:18; Jn 15:12,17; Eph 5:2; 1Th 4:9; Jas 2:8; 1Pe 1:22; 1Jn 2:7; 3:11,23 **35** 1Jn 2:5; 4:20 **36** Jn 21:18; 2Pe 1:14 **37** Mt 26:33; Mk 14:29; Lk 22:33 **CHAPTER 14** **1** ver. 27 **2** Jn 13:33 **3** Ac 1:11; Jn 12:26; 17:24; 1Th 4:17 **6** Heb 9:8; Jn 8:32; Jn 11:25; Jn 10:9 **7** Jn 8:19 **9** Jn 12:45; Col 1:15; Heb 1:3

10 “Do you not believe that I am in the Father, and the Father is in Me? The words I say to you I do not say on My own initiative *or* authority, but the Father, abiding *continually* in Me, does His works [His attesting miracles and acts of power].

11 “Believe Me that I am in the Father and the Father is in Me; otherwise believe [Me] because of the [very] works themselves [which you have witnessed].

12 “I assure you *and* most solemnly say to you, anyone who believes in Me [as Savior] will also do the things that I do; and he will do even greater things than these [in extent and outreach], because I am going to the Father.

13 “And I will do whatever you ask in My name [as My representative], this I will do, so that the Father may be glorified *and* celebrated in the Son. [Ex 3:14]

14 “If you ask Me anything in My name [as My representative], I will do it.

15 “If you [really] love Me, you will keep *and* obey My commandments.

Role of the Spirit

16 “And I will ask the Father, and He will give you another Helper (Comforter, Advocate, Intercessor—Counselor, Strengthener, Standby), to be with you forever—

17 the Spirit of Truth, whom the world cannot receive [and take to its heart] because it does not see Him or know Him, *but* you know Him because He (the Holy Spirit) remains with you *continually* and will be in you.

18 “I will not leave you as orphans [comfortless, bereaved, and helpless]; I will come [back] to you.

19 “After a little while the world will no longer see Me, but you will see Me; because I live, you will live also.

20 “On that day [when that time comes] you will know for yourselves that I am in My Father, and you *are* in Me, and I *am* in you.

21 “The person who has My commandments and keeps them is the one who [really] loves Me; and whoever [really] loves Me will be loved by My Father, and I will love him and reveal Myself to him [I will make Myself real to him].”

22 Judas (not Iscariot) asked Him, “Lord, what has happened that You are going to reveal Yourself to us and not to the world?”

23 Jesus answered, “If anyone [really] loves Me, he will keep My word (teaching); and My Father will love him, and We will come to him and make Our dwelling place with him.

24 “One who does not [really] love Me does not keep My words. And the word (teaching) which you hear is not Mine, but is the Father’s who sent Me.

14:12 *greater things.* Jesus had accomplished the greatest things possible, including raising the dead. How could He say that believers would do greater things? The answer is seen in the extent of what the apostles did. Jesus’ work on earth was confined to Palestine; the apostles would preach everywhere and see the conversion of thousands. Peter’s message at Pentecost brought more followers to Jesus than did Jesus’ entire earthly ministry. The disciples were able to do this work because Christ would go to the Father and send the Holy Spirit to empower them.

14:17 *the Spirit of Truth.* This is another name for the Holy Spirit because He is truth and guides us into all truth (1Co 2:13; 2Pe 1:21).

14:18 *as orphans [comfortless, bereaved, and helpless].* He would not abandon them. He would come to them. There are three suggested interpretations as to when that statement would be fulfilled: (1) after the resurrection, (2) at Pentecost, in the person of the Holy Spirit, and (3) at the second coming.

14:23 *If anyone [really] loves Me, he will keep My word.* In response to Judas’ question (v. 22), Jesus explained that His manifestation to the disciples would be in response to their love and obedience. ***make Our dwelling place with him.*** If a believer loves and obeys the Lord, he or she will experience fellowship with God.

14:24 *One who does not [really] love Me does not keep My words.* If a person does not love Jesus, he or she will not obey Him.

---

10 Jn 10:38; 17:21,23; 5:19; 8:28 **11** Jn 10:38 **12** Mt 21:21; Mk 16:17; Lk 10:17 **13** Mt 7:7; 21:22; Mk 11:24; Lk 11:9; Jn 15:7,16; 16:23,24; Jas 1:5; 1Jn 3:22; 5:14 **15** ver. 21,23; Jn 15:10; 1Jn 5:3 **16** Jn 15:26; 16:7; Ro 8:15 **17** Jn 15:26; 16:13; 1Jn 4:6; 1Co 2:14; 1Jn 2:27 **18** Mt 28:20; ver. 3,28 **19** Jn 16:16; 1Co 15:20 **20** Jn 10:38 **21** 1Jn 2:5; 5:3 **22** Lk 6:16 **23** 1Jn 2:24; Rev 3:20 **24** Jn 5:19

25 "I have told you these things while
I am still with you.
26 "But the Helper (Comforter, Ad-
vocate, Intercessor—Counselor,
Strengthener, Standby), the Holy Spir-
it, whom the Father will send in My
name [in My place, to represent Me
and act on My behalf], He will teach
you all things. And He will help you
remember everything that I have told
you. [Matt 5:7, 13, 24, 25; Luke 24:49;
John 14:16; Acts 1:4]
27 "Peace I leave with you; My [per-
fect] peace I give to you; not as the
world gives do I give to you. Do not
let your heart be troubled, nor let it
be afraid. [Let My perfect peace calm
you in every circumstance and give
you courage and strength for every
challenge.]
28 "You heard Me tell you, 'I am going
away, and I am coming *back* to you.' If
you [really] loved Me, you would have
rejoiced, because I am going [back]
to the Father, for the Father is greater
than I.
29 "I have told you now before it hap-
pens, so that when it does take place,
you may believe *and* have faith [in Me].
30 "I will not speak with you much
longer, for the ruler of the world (Sa-
tan) is coming. And he has no claim on
Me [no power over Me nor anything
that he can use against Me];
31 but so that the world may know
[without any doubt] that I love the Fa-
ther, I do exactly as the Father has com-
manded Me [and act in full agreement
with Him]. Get up, let us go from here.

Jesus Is the Vine—Followers Are Branches

15 "I AM the true Vine, and My
Father is the vinedresser.
2 "Every branch in Me that does not
bear fruit, He takes away; and every
branch that continues to bear fruit, He
[repeatedly] prunes, so that it will bear
more fruit [even richer and finer fruit].
3 "You are already clean because of
the word which I have given you [the
teachings which I have discussed with
you].
4 "Remain in Me, and I [will remain]
in you. Just as no branch can bear fruit
by itself without remaining in the vine,
neither can you [bear fruit, producing
evidence of your faith] unless you re-
main in Me.
5 "I am the Vine; you are the branch-
es. The one who remains in Me and I in
him bears much fruit, for [otherwise]
apart from Me [that is, cut off from vi-
tal union with Me] you can do nothing.
6 "If anyone does not remain in Me,
he is thrown out like a [broken off]
branch, and withers *and* dies; and they
gather such branches and throw them
into the fire, and they are burned.
7 "If you remain in Me and My words
remain in you [that is, if we are vitally
united and My message lives in your
heart], ask whatever you wish and it
will be done for you.
8 "My Father is glorified *and* honored
by this, when you bear much fruit,
and prove yourselves to be My [true]
disciples.

Disobedience is a serious matter, for Jesus' words are the words of God.
14:30 *has no claim on Me.* These words indicate Jesus' sinlessness. Jesus' yielding to what was about to happen did not mean that Satan had any power over Him. Jesus would soon voluntarily yield to the death of the cross, in loving obedience to the Father (v. 31).
15:2 *Every branch in Me.* The emphasis of *in Me* in this passage is on deep, abiding fellowship. Jesus' purpose was to move His disciples from servants to friends (vv. 13 – 15). This would involve a process of discipline in regard to His commandments. ***prunes.*** This word carries the sense of purging. Once the fruit is on the vine, the vinedresser cleanses the fruit of bugs and diseases. The spiritual counterpart is cleansing which is done through the Word (v. 3).
15:6 *If anyone does not remain in Me.* Not abiding in Christ has serious consequences: (1) the person *is thrown out like a branch*, indicating the loss of fellowship; (2) the person *withers and dies*, indicating a loss of vitality; (3) the person is *burned*, indicating a loss of reward.
15:8 *by this.* Notice the striking parallel between this verse and 13:35. ***fruit.*** The love of 13:35 is

---

26 Lk 24:49; Jn 15:26; Jn 2:22; 12:16; 1Jn 2:20 **27** Php 4:7; Col 3:15 **28** ver. 3,18; Jn 16:16; 20:17; Jn 5:18; 10:30; Php 2:6 **29** Jn 13:19; 16:4 **30** Jn 12:31; 16:11 **31** Jn 10:18; Php 2:8; Heb 5:8 **CHAPTER 15** **2** Mt 15:13 **3** Jn 13:10; Eph 5:26; 1Pe 1:22 **4** Col 1:23; 1Jn 2:6 **5** Hos 14:8; Php 1:11; 4:13 **6** Mt 3:10; 7:19 **7** Jn 16:23 **8** Mt 5:16; Php 1:11; Jn 8:31

[9]"I have loved you just as the Father has loved Me; remain in My love [and do not doubt My love for you].

[10]"If you keep My commandments *and* obey My teaching, you will remain in My love, just as I have kept My Father's commandments and remain in His love.

[11]"I have told you these things so that My joy *and* delight may be in you, and that your joy may be made full *and* complete *and* overflowing.

Disciples' Relation to Each Other

[12]"This is My commandment, that you love *and* unselfishly seek the best for one another, just as I have loved you.

[13]"No one has greater love [nor stronger commitment] than to lay down his own life for his friends.

[14]"You are my friends if you keep on doing what I command you.

[15]"I do not call you servants any longer, for the servant does not know what his master is doing; but I have called you [My] friends, because I have revealed to you everything that I have heard from My Father.

[16]"You have not chosen Me, but I have chosen you and I have appointed *and* placed *and* purposefully planted you, so that you would go and bear fruit *and* keep on bearing, and that your fruit will remain *and* be lasting, so that whatever you ask of the Father in My name [as My representative] He may give to you.

[17]"This [is what] I command you: that you love *and* unselfishly seek the best for one another.

Disciples' Relation to the World

[18]"If the world hates you [and it does], know that it has hated Me before *it hated* you.

[19]"If you belonged to the world, the world would love [you as] its own *and* would treat you with affection. But you are not of the world [you no longer belong to it], but I have chosen you out of the world. And because of this the world hates you.

[20]"Remember [and continue to remember] that I told you, 'A servant is not greater than his master.' If they persecuted Me, they will also persecute you. If they kept My word, they will keep yours also.

[21]"But they will do all these [hurtful] things to you for My name's sake [because you bear My name and are identified with Me], for they do not know the One who sent Me.

[22]"If I had not come and spoken to them, they would not have [the guilt of their] sin; but now they have no excuse for their sin.

[23]"The one who hates Me also hates My Father.

[24]"If I had not done among them the works (attesting miracles) which no one else [ever] did, they would not have

---

pictured here. The text has come full circle in showing how strategic it is for disciples to love each other, as Christ's method of evangelizing the lost. Where there is good fruit, there are also seeds for propagation.

15:11 ***that your joy may be made full.*** This phrase is an expression peculiar to John (3:29; 16:24; 17:13; 1Jn 1:4; 2Jn 12). It describes a believer's experience of Christ's love: complete joy.

15:14 ***if you keep on doing.*** Jesus is our model for love (v. 13). Intimacy with Him is the motive for loving as He loves. If believers obey His command to love, they enjoy the intimacy of His friendship. Not that friendship, unlike sonship, is a once-for-all gift, but develops as the result of obeying Jesus' command to love.

15:15 ***I do not call you servants.*** Until this point, Jesus had called His disciples servants (12:26; 13:13 – 16). A servant does what he is told and sees what his master does, but does not necessarily know the meaning or purpose of it. ***friends.*** A friend knows what is happening because friends develop deep fellowship by communicating with one another.

15:22 – 23 ***not have [the guilt of their] sin . . . no excuse for their sin.*** The world's hatred of Jesus was a sin against God, for He revealed the Father Himself to them.

10 Jn 14:15 **11** Jn 16:24; 17:13; 1Jn 1:4 **12** Jn 13:34; 1Th 4:9; 1Pe 4:8; 1Jn 3:11 **13** Jn 10:11; Ro 5:7,8; Eph 5:2; 1Jn 3:16 **14** Mt 12:50; Jn 14:15 **15** Ge 18:17; Jn 17:26 **16** Jn 6:70; 13:18; 1Jn 4:10; Mt 28:19; Mk 16:15; Col 1:6; ver. 7 **18** 1Jn 3:13 **19** 1Jn 4:5; Jn 17:14 **20** Mt 10:24; Lk 6:40; Eze 3:7 **21** Mt 10:22; 24:9 **22** Jn 9:41; Ro 1:20; Jas 4:17 **23** 1Jn 2:23 **24** Jn 3:2

[the guilt of their] sin; but now [the fact is that] they have both seen [these works] and have hated Me [and continue to hate Me] and My Father as well.

25 "But [this is so] that the word which has been written in their Law would be fulfilled, 'THEY HATED ME WITHOUT A CAUSE.' [Ps 35:19; 69:4]

26 "But when the Helper (Comforter, Advocate, Intercessor—Counselor, Strengthener, Standby) comes, whom I will send to you from the Father, *that is* the Spirit of Truth who comes from the Father, He will testify *and* bear witness about Me.

27 "But you will testify also *and* be My witnesses, because you have been with Me from the beginning.

Jesus' Warning

16 "I HAVE told you these things so that you will not stumble *or* be caught off guard *and* fall away.

2 "They will put you out of the synagogues *and* make you outcasts. And a time is coming when whoever kills you will think that he is offering service to God.

3 "And they will do these things because they have not known the Father or Me.

4 "I have told you these things [now], so that when their time comes, you will remember that I told you about them. I did not say these things to you at the beginning, because I was with you.

The Holy Spirit Promised

5 "But now I am going to Him who sent Me; and none of you asks Me, 'Where are You going?'

6 "But because I have said these things to you, sorrow has filled your hearts [and taken complete possession of them].

7 "But I tell you the truth, it is to your advantage that I go away; for if I do not go away, the Helper (Comforter, Advocate, Intercessor—Counselor, Strengthener, Standby) will not come to you; but if I go, I will send Him (the Holy Spirit) to you [to be in close fellowship with you].

8 "And He, when He comes, will convict the world about [the guilt of] sin [and the need for a Savior], and about righteousness, and about judgment:

9 about sin [and the true nature of it], because they do not believe in Me [and My message];

10 about righteousness [personal integrity and godly character], because I am going to My Father and you will no longer see Me;

11 about judgment [the certainty of it], because the ruler of this world (Satan) has been judged *and* condemned.

12 "I have many more things to say

15:26–27 *He will testify.* As the disciples spoke, the Holy Spirit would bring inner conviction to unbelievers concerning Christ. This in turn would make the disciples witnesses for Jesus.

16:2 *They will put you out of the synagogues.* The persecution that the disciples would face included excommunication and even execution. Excommunication had economic as well as religious implications because much of the life of an ancient Jew revolved around the synagogue.

16:7 *it is to your advantage.* The disciples must have thought, "How can it be to our advantage to be alone? The Romans hate us because they see us as disturbers of the peace. The Jewish leaders hate us because they see us as blasphemers." Jesus explained the benefits of His departure. When Jesus left, the believers would have (1) the provision of the Holy Spirit (vv. 7–15); (2) the potential of full joy (vv. 16–24); (3) the possibility of fuller knowledge (vv. 25–28); (4) the privilege of peace (vv. 29–33).

16:8 *convict.* The Holy Spirit would demonstrate the truth of Christ beyond the fear of contradiction. The Holy Spirit convicts unbelievers through believers who witness about Christ (15:26–27). Believers are the mouthpiece for God's voice.

16:11 *about judgment.* Satan, the ruler of the world, rules in the hearts of unregenerate people and blinds their minds (1Co 2:6–8). Satan was judged at the cross, and the Holy Spirit would convince people of the judgment to come. Satan has been judged, so all who side with him will be judged with him.

16:12 *you.* Here, this refers to the apostles. Technically, what the Lord says about the ministry of the Holy Spirit in verses 12–15 applies primarily

---

25 Ps 35:19; 69:4 **26** Lk 24:49; Jn 14:17; Ac 2:33; 1Jn 5:6 **27** Lk 24:48; Ac 1:21; 2:32; 3:15; 4:20,33; 5:32; 10:39; 13:31; 1Pe 5:1; 2Pe 1:16; Lk 1:2; 1Jn 1:1 **CHAPTER 16** **1** Mt 11:6; 24:10; 26:31 **2** Jn 9:22; Ac 8:1; 9:1; 26:9,10 **3** Jn 15:21; Ro 10:2; 1Co 2:8; 1Ti 1:13 **4** Jn 13:19; 14:29 **5** Jn 7:33; 14:28 **7** Jn 7:39; 14:16,26; 15:26; Ac 2:33; Eph 4:8 **9** Ac 2:22 **10** Ac 2:32; Jn 5:32 **11** Ac 26:18; Lk 10:18; Eph 2:2; Col 2:15; Heb 2:14 **12** Mk 4:33; 1Co 3:2; Heb 5:12

to you, but you cannot bear [to hear] them now.

[13]"But when He, the Spirit of Truth, comes, He will guide you into all the truth [full and complete truth]. For He will not speak on His own initiative, but He will speak whatever He hears [from the Father—the message regarding the Son], and He will disclose to you what is to come [in the future].

[14]"He will glorify *and* honor Me, because He (the Holy Spirit) will take from what is Mine and will disclose it to you.

[15]"All things that the Father has are Mine. Because of this I said that He [the Spirit] will take from what is Mine and will reveal it to you.

Jesus' Death and Resurrection Foretold

[16]"A little while, and you will no longer see Me; and again a little while, and you will see Me."

[17]Some of His disciples said to one another, "What does He mean when He tells us, 'A little while, and you will not see Me; and again a little while, and you will see Me'; and, 'because I am going to My Father'?"

[18]So they were saying, "What does He mean when He says, 'A little while'? We do not know what He is talking about."

[19]Jesus knew that they wanted to ask Him, so He said to them, "Are you wondering among yourselves about what I meant when I said, 'A little while, and you will not see Me, and again a little while, and you will see Me'?

[20]"I assure you *and* most solemnly say to you, that you will weep and grieve [in great mourning], but the world will rejoice. You will be sorrowful, but your sorrow will be turned into joy.

[21]"A woman, when she is in labor, has pain because her time [to give birth] has come; but when she has given birth to the child, she no longer remembers the anguish because of her joy that a child has come into the world.

[22]"So for now you are in grief; but I will see you again, and [then] your hearts will rejoice, and no one will take away from you your [great] joy.

Prayer Promises

[23]"In that day you will not [need to] ask Me about anything. I assure you *and* most solemnly say to you, whatever you ask the Father in My name [as My representative], He will give you.

[24]"Until now you have not asked [the Father] for anything in My name; but now ask *and* keep on asking and you will receive, so that your joy may be full *and* complete.

[25]"I have told you these things in figurative language (veiled language, proverbs); the hour is now coming when I will no longer speak to you in figures of speech, but I will tell you plainly about the Father.

---

to the apostles. That ministry was threefold: (1) He would guide them into all truth (v. 13); (2) He would tell them of the future (v. 13); (3) He would help them glorify Christ (vv. 14–15). Jesus' words were fulfilled in the apostles' preaching and writings.

16:13 *Spirit of Truth.* The phrase means that the Holy Spirit is the source of truth (14:17; 15:26). ***guide.*** The Holy Spirit would not compel or carry the disciples into truth. He would lead; their job was to follow.

16:14 *glorify and honor Me.* The Holy Spirit glorifies Christ by declaring Him or making Him known. It is the work of the Holy Spirit to throw light on Jesus Christ, who is the image of the invisible God. Christ is to be on center stage; that is the desire of both the Father and the Spirit. The apostles received truth from the Holy Spirit, truth about things to come, and truth about Christ. Then, under the guidance of the Holy Spirit, they wrote those truths in documents known today as the New Testament.

16:18 *A little while.* The biggest question weighing on the disciples' minds was the time factor. They simply did not understand the strange intervals marked by their separation from Jesus.

16:21 *A woman, when she is in labor.* Jesus used the example of a pregnant woman whose sorrow is transformed into joy in the birth of a child.

13 Jn 14:17; Jn 14:26; 1Jn 2:20 **15** Mt 11:27; Jn 3:35 **16** Jn 13:3 **21** Isa 26:17 **22** Lk 24:41; Jn 14:1,27; 20:20; Ac 2:46; 13:52; 1Pe 1:8 **23** Mt 7:7; Jn 14:13; 15:16 **24** Jn 15:11

26 “In that day you will ask in My
name, and I am not saying to you that
I will ask the Father on your behalf
[because it will be unnecessary];
27 for the Father Himself [tenderly]
loves you, because you have loved Me
and have believed that I came from
the Father.
28 “I came from the Father and have
come into the world; again, I am leav-
ing the world and going to the Father.”
29 His disciples said, “Ah, now You
are speaking plainly to us and not in
figures of speech!
30 “Now we know that You know all
things, and have no need for anyone
to question You; because of this we
believe [without any doubt] that you
came from God.”
31 Jesus answered them, “Do you now
[at last] believe?
32 “Take careful notice: an hour is
coming, and has arrived, when you
will all be scattered, each to his own
home, leaving Me alone; and yet I
am not alone, because the Father is
with Me.
33 “I have told you these things, so
that in Me you may have [perfect]
peace. In the world you have tribula-
tion *and* distress *and* suffering, but be
courageous [be confident, be undaunt-
ed, be filled with joy]; I have overcome
the world.” [My conquest is accom-
plished, My victory abiding.]

The High Priestly Prayer

17 WHEN JESUS had spoken these
things, He raised His eyes to
heaven [in prayer] and said, “Father,
the hour has come. Glorify Your Son,
so that Your Son may glorify You.
2 “Just as You have given Him power
and authority over all mankind, [now
glorify Him] so that He may give eter-
nal life to all whom You have given Him
[to be His—permanently and forever].
3 “Now this is eternal life: that they
may know You, the only true [supreme
and sovereign] God, and [in the same
manner know] Jesus [as the] Christ
whom You have sent.
4 “I have glorified You [down here] on
the earth by completing the work that
You gave Me to do.
5 “Now, Father, glorify Me togeth-
er with Yourself, with the glory *and*
majesty that I had with You before the
world existed.
6 “I have manifested Your name [and
revealed Your very self, Your real self]
to the people whom You have given Me
out of the world; they were Yours and
You gave them to Me, and they have
kept *and* obeyed Your word.
7 “Now [at last] they know [with con-
fident assurance] that all You have
given Me is from You [it is really and
truly Yours].
8 “For the words which You gave Me
I have given them; and they received

16:26 *I will ask the Father on your behalf.* Because Jesus provides forgiveness of sins through His death and now intercedes for all believers at the right hand of the Father (Heb 7:25), we have direct access to the Father. We do not need the intercession of a priest, because Jesus acts as our High Priest before God.

16:31 *Do you now [at last] believe?* We continue in the Christian life the same way we begin, by believing in Jesus. The more we learn of Christ, the more we have to believe. The more we place our trust in Jesus, the more we receive. The more we receive, the more we can accomplish for His glory.

16:33 *tribulation.* This is literally “pressure” and figuratively means “affliction” or “distress.”

17:1 – 2 *the hour has come.* Throughout the Gospel of John, Jesus referred to the cross as His “hour” (2:4; 7:30; 8:20; 12:23; 13:1). The time for Him to die had arrived. ***Glorify Your Son.*** Jesus was asking that His mission to the world would be made known through the cross. The reasons for this request are twofold: (1) that *Your Son may glorify You.* In the cross, Jesus reveals the Father to the world, that is, His love and justice, and (2) that, through Jesus’ death on the cross, God would provide forgiveness of sins and *give eternal life* to all those who believe in His Son.

17:3 *that they may know You.* Eternal life consists of a growing knowledge of the only true God as opposed to false gods.

27 Jn 14:21; Jn 3:13 **28** Jn 13:3 **30** Jn 21:17; Jn 17:8 **32** Mt 26:31; Mk 14:27; Jn 20:10; Jn 8:29 **33** Isa 9:6; Ro 5:1; Eph 2:14; 2Ti 3:12; Ro 8:37; 1Jn 4:4 **CHAPTER 17** **1** Jn 12:23 **2** Da 7:14; Mt 11:27; Jn 3:35; Php 2:10; Heb 2:8; ver. 6,9,24; Jn 6:37 **3** Isa 53:11; Jer 9:24; 1Co 8:4; 1Th 1:9; Jn 3:34 **4** Jn 13:31; Jn 4:34; Jn 14:31 **5** Php 2:6; Col 1:15; Heb 1:3 **6** Ps 22:22; Jn 6:37 **8** Jn 8:28; Jn 16:27

and accepted them and truly understood [with confident assurance] that I came from You [from Your presence], and they believed [without any doubt] that You sent Me.
9"I pray for them; I do not pray for the world, but for those You have given Me, because they belong to You;
10and all things that are Mine are Yours, and [all things that are] Yours are Mine; and I am glorified in them.
11"I am no longer in the world; yet they are still in the world, and I am coming to You. Holy Father, keep them in Your name, *the name* which You have given Me, so that they may be one just as We are.
12"While I was with them, I was keeping them in Your name which You have given Me; and I guarded them *and* protected them, and not one of them was lost except the son of destruction, so that the Scripture would be fulfilled. [Ps 41:9; John 6:70]

The Disciples in the World

13"But now I am coming to You; and I say these things [while I am still] in the world so that they may experience My joy made full *and* complete *and* perfect within them [filling their hearts with My delight].
14"I have given to them Your word [the message You gave Me]; and the world has hated them because they are not of the world *and* do not belong to the world, just as I am not of the world *and* do not belong to it.
15"I do not ask You to take them out of the world, but that You keep them *and* protect them from the evil one.
16"They are not of the world, just as I am not of the world.
17"Sanctify them in the truth [set them apart for Your purposes, make them holy]; Your word is truth.
18"Just as You commissioned *and* sent Me into the world, I also have commissioned *and* sent them (believers) into the world.
19"For their sake I sanctify Myself [to do Your will], so that they also may be sanctified [set apart, dedicated, made holy] in [Your] truth.
20"I do not pray for these alone [it is not for their sake only that I make this request], but also for [all] those who [will ever] believe *and* trust in Me through their message,
21that they all may be one; just as You, Father, are in Me and I in You, that they also may be one in Us, so that the world may believe [without any doubt] that You sent Me.

Their Future Glory

22"I have given to them the glory *and* honor which You have given Me, that they may be one, just as We are one;

17:11 *keep them in Your name.* This verse reveals Jesus' sensitivity to the plight of His disciples brought on by His departure. He was going to the Father, but they would be left behind. Jesus asked the Father to keep them true to the revelation of God that Jesus had given to them while He was with them. The disciples would have a new union with the Father and Son through the future indwelling of the Holy Spirit.

17:14 – 16 *of the world.* This verse has profound implications for discipleship. Our desire should not be to isolate ourselves from the world, but to use Christ's Word and the Holy Spirit's power to serve Him while our life lasts. Yet, at the same time, we should not become like the world, succumbing to the evil influences of the world.

17:17 *Sanctify them.* This means "to set apart." There are two ways to understand this statement: (1) as separate for holiness, or (2) as set apart for service. According to the first view, Jesus was praying not only that the disciples should be kept from evil, but that they should advance in holiness.

17:21 *that they all may be one.* The present tense of the verb "to be" indicates that Jesus was praying for the unity that takes place through the sanctification of believers. This is what Jesus was commanding in 13:34 – 35.

17:22 *the glory.* This is the revelation of Jesus Christ through His disciples and is the means to unity. Such unity begins with belief and correct thinking about Jesus and God the Father, that is, with doctrine. But correct belief must bear fruit — a life that demonstrates God's love and produces unity between all believers.

---

9 1Jn 5:19 **10** Jn 16:15 **11** Jn 13:1; 1Pe 1:5; Jude 1; Jn 10:30 **12** Heb 2:13; 1Jn 2:19; Jn 6:70; Ps 109:8; Ac 1:20
14 1Jn 3:13; Jn 8:23 **15** Mt 6:13; Gal 1:4; 1Jn 5:18 **17** Ac 15:9; Eph 5:26; 1Pe 1:22; Ps 119:142,151 **18** Jn 20:21
19 1Co 1:2; 1Th 4:7; Heb 10:10 **21** Jn 10:16; Ro 12:5; Gal 3:28; Jn 10:38 **22** Jn 14:20; 1Jn 1:3

[23]I in them and You in Me, that they may be perfected *and* completed into one, so that the world may know [without any doubt] that You sent Me, and [that You] have loved them, just as You have loved Me.

[24]"Father, I desire that they also, whom You have given to Me [as Your gift to Me], may be with Me where I am, so that they may see My glory which You have given Me, because You loved Me before the foundation of the world.

[25]"O just *and* righteous Father, although the world has not known You *and* has never acknowledged You [and the revelation of Your mercy], yet I have *always* known You; and these [believers] know [without any doubt] that You sent Me;

[26]and I have made Your name known to them, and will *continue to* make it known, so that the love with which You have loved Me may be in them [overwhelming their heart], and I [may be] in them."

Judas Betrays Jesus

18 HAVING SAID these things, Jesus left with His disciples and went across the ravine of the Kidron. There was a garden there, which He and His disciples entered.

[2]Now Judas, who was betraying Him, knew the place, because Jesus had often met there with His disciples.

[3]So Judas, having obtained the *Roman* cohort and some officers from the high priests and the Pharisees, came there with lanterns and torches and weapons. [Matt 26:47–56; Mark 14:43–50; Luke 22:47–53]

[4]Then Jesus, knowing all that was about to happen to Him, went to them and asked, "Whom do you want?"

[5]They answered Him, "Jesus the Nazarene." Jesus said, "I am *He*." And Judas, who was betraying Him, was also standing with them.

[6]When Jesus said, "I am *He*," they drew back and fell to the ground.

[7]Again He asked them, "Whom do you want?" And they said, "Jesus the Nazarene."

[8]Jesus answered, "I told you that I am *He*; so if you want Me, let these men go on their way."

[9]*This was* to fulfill *and* verify the words He had spoken, "Of those whom You have given Me, I have not lost even one." [John 6:39; 17:12]

[10]Then Simon Peter, who had a sword, drew it and struck the high priest's servant, cutting off his right ear. The servant's name was Malchus.

[11]So Jesus said to Peter, "Put the sword [back] in its sheath! Shall I not drink the cup which My Father has given Me?"

Jesus before Annas and Caiaphas

[12]So the cohort and their commander and the officers of the Jews arrested Jesus and bound Him,

[13]and led Him to Annas first; for he was the father-in-law of Caiaphas, who was high priest that year.

[14]It was Caiaphas who had advised the Jews that it was expedient for one man to die on behalf of the people. [John 11:49, 50]

17:23 *I in them and You in Me.* The mutual indwelling of the Father in the Son and the Son in the church is also the means to unity, the ultimate expression of God's love (13:35; Ro 8:17).

18:1 *ravine of the Kidron.* A brook was located in a ravine that was between Jerusalem and the Mount of Olives.

18:3 *officers.* These were members of the temple police under the command of the Jewish council, the Sanhedrin.

18:13 *Annas.* Annas was high priest from AD 7 to 14. He was deposed by the Romans. Then Caiaphas, Annas' son-in-law, was appointed to the position and served from AD 18 to 37. However, according to Jewish law the high priest was a lifetime position, so the Jews still considered Annas to be high priest. Therefore, they took Jesus to Annas first.

---

23 Col 3:14 **24** Jn 12:26; 1Th 4:17; ver. 5 **25** Jn 15:21; 16:3; Jn 7:29; 8:55; 10:15; ver. 8; Jn 16:27 **26** ver. 6; Jn 15:15; Jn 15:9 **CHAPTER 18** **1** Mt 26:36; Mk 14:32; Lk 22:39; 2Sa 15:23 **2** Lk 21:37; 22:39 **3** Mt 26:47; Mk 14:43; Lk 22:47; Ac 1:16 **9** Jn 17:12 **10** Mt 26:51; Mk 14:47; Lk 22:49,50 **11** Mt 20:22; 26:39,42 **13** See Mt 26:57; Lk 3:2 **14** Jn 11:50

15 Simon Peter and another disciple were following Jesus. Now that disciple was known to the high priest, so he went with Jesus into the courtyard of the [residence of the] high priest;

16 but Peter was standing outside at the door. So the other disciple (John), who was known to the high priest, went out and spoke to the doorkeeper, and brought Peter inside. [Matt 26:69–75; Mark 14:66–72; Luke 22:55–62]

17 Then the servant girl who kept the door said to Peter, "You are not one of this Man's disciples, are you?" He said, "I am not."

18 Now the servants and the officers had made a fire of coals, because it was cold, and they were standing and warming themselves. And Peter was with them, standing and warming himself.

19 Then the high priest questioned Jesus about His disciples and about His teaching. [Matt 26:59–68; Mark 14:55–65; Luke 22:63–71]

20 Jesus answered him, "I have spoken openly to the world. I always taught in a synagogue and in the temple [area], where all the Jews *habitually* congregate; and I said nothing in secret.

21 "Why question Me? Question those who have heard what I said to them. They know what I said."

22 But when He said this, one of the officers who was standing nearby struck Jesus [in the face], saying, "Is that how You answer the high priest?"

23 Jesus replied, "If I have said *anything* wrong, make a formal statement about the wrong; but if [I spoke] properly, why did you strike Me?"

24 So Annas sent Him bound to Caiaphas the high priest.

Peter's Denial of Jesus

25 Now Simon Peter was [still] standing and warming himself. So they said to him, "You are not one of His disciples, are you?" He denied it and said, "I am not." [Matt 26:71–75; Mark 14:69–72; Luke 22:58–62]

26 One of the high priest's servants, a relative of the one whose ear Peter cut off, said, "Did I not see you with Him in the garden?"

27 So Peter denied it again, and immediately a rooster crowed.

Jesus before Pilate

28 Then the Jews led Jesus from Caiaphas to the Praetorium (governor's palace). Now it was early and the Jews did not enter the Praetorium so that they would not be [ceremonially] unclean, but might [be able to] eat [and participate in the Feast of Unleavened Bread which began after] the Passover [supper].

29 So Pilate came out to them and asked, "What accusation do you bring against this Man?" [Matt 27:11–14; Mark 15:2–5; Luke 23:2, 3]

30 They answered, "If He were not a criminal, we would not have handed Him over to you [for judgment]."

31 Then Pilate said to them, "Take Him yourselves and judge Him accord-

---

18:15 *another disciple.* Although this other disciple is never identified, the consensus is that he was John, the author of this Gospel.

18:21 *Question those who have heard.* According to the law, the witnesses for the defense had to be called first. Jesus should not have been questioned until witnesses had testified.

18:27 *Peter denied it again.* For the third time, Peter denied the Lord, as Jesus had said he would (13:38). In the upper room, Peter had boasted that he would remain true to the Lord to the end (13:37; Mt 26:33,35). In the garden he surrendered to the desires of his body by sleeping three times when the Lord had commanded the disciples to stay up in prayer (Mk 14:34–42). Now he submitted to the pressure of the world and denied the Lord three times.

18:28 *Praetorium.* This was probably the Roman governor's official residence, probably the Fortress Antonia near the temple.

18:29–30 *What accusation.* Pilate was not ignorant of the accusation. He was merely requesting that it be formally stated.

18:31 *We are not permitted to put anyone*

15 Mt 26:58; Mk 14:54; Lk 22:54 **16** Mt 26:69; Mk 14:66; Lk 22:54 **20** Mt 26:55; Lk 4:15; Jn 7:14,26,28; 8:2 **22** Jer 20:2; Ac 23:2 **24** Mt 26:57 **25** Mt 26:69,71; Mk 14:69; Lk 22:58 **27** Mt 26:74; Mk 14:72; Lk 22:60; Jn 13:38 **28** Mt 27:2; Mk 15:1; Lk 23:1; Ac 3:13; Ac 10:28; 11:3

ing to your own law." The Jews said, "We are not permitted to put anyone to death."

32 *This was* to fulfill the word which Jesus had spoken to indicate by what manner of death He was going to die. [John 12:32–34]

33 So Pilate went into the Praetorium again, and called Jesus and asked Him, "Are You the King of the Jews?"

34 Jesus replied, "Are you saying this on your own initiative, or did others tell you about Me?"

35 Pilate answered, "I am not a Jew, am I? Your own people and their chief priests have handed You over to me. What have You done [that is worthy of death]?"

36 Jesus replied, "My kingdom is not of this world [nor does it have its origin in this world]. If My kingdom were of this world, My servants would be fighting [hard] to keep Me from being handed over to the Jews; but as it is, My kingdom is not of this world."

37 So Pilate said to Him, "Then You are a King?" Jesus answered, "You say [correctly] that I am a King. This is why I was born, and for this I have come into the world, to testify to the truth. Everyone who is of the truth [who is a friend of the truth and belongs to the truth] hears *and* listens carefully to My voice." [Dan 7:13, 14; Luke 1:32, 33]

38 Pilate said to Him [scornfully], "What is truth?"

And when he had said this, he went out to the Jews again and told them, "I find no guilt in Him [no crime, no cause for an accusation].

39 "But you have a custom that I release someone for you at the Passover. So shall I release for you the King of the Jews?" [Matt 27:15–26; Mark 15:6–15; Luke 23:18–25]

40 Then they all shouted back again, "Not this Man, but Barabbas!" Now Barabbas was a robber.

The Crown of Thorns

19 SO THEN Pilate took Jesus and had Him scourged (flogged, whipped).

2 And the soldiers twisted together a crown of thorns and put it on His head, and put a purple robe around Him; [Matt 27:27–30; Mark 15:16–19]

3 and they kept coming up to Him, saying [mockingly], "Hail, King of the Jews [Good health! Peace! Long life to you, King of the Jews]!" And they slapped Him *in the face.* [Is 53:3, 5, 7]

4 Then Pilate came out again and said to them, "Look, I am bringing Him out to you so that you may know that I find no guilt in Him [no crime, no cause for an accusation]."

5 So Jesus came out, wearing the crown of thorns and the purple robe, and *Pilate* said to them, "Look! The Man!"

---

to death. The Romans did not allow the Jews to impose capital punishment. These Jewish leaders had no interest in a just trial; they simply wanted permission from Rome to have Jesus executed. **18:34** ***Are you saying this on your own initiative.*** In reply to Pilate, Jesus gave no violent protest of innocence, nor was He sullenly defiant. Jesus politely but directly asked whether Pilate was asking on his own initiative or whether the charge was secondhand. If Pilate's question originated with him, he was using *king* in the Roman sense of political ruler. If not, then *king* was being used in the Jewish sense of the messianic king. **18:38** ***What is truth?*** This question has been interpreted as (1) a cynical denial of the possibility of knowing truth; (2) a contemptuous jest at anything so impractical as abstract truth; and (3) a desire to know what no one had been able to tell him. ***no guilt.*** This is a legal term meaning that there were no grounds for a criminal charge. **18:39** ***you have a custom.*** It appears that some in the crowd suggested that a prisoner should be released in honor of the Passover (Mk 15:8,11). Pilate jumped at the possible compromise. By promising to release Jesus on account of the custom rather than by proclaiming Him innocent, Pilate would avoid insulting the Jewish leaders, who had already pronounced Him guilty. **19:4** ***I am bringing Him out to you.*** Perhaps Pilate was appealing to the people's compassion so that he could release Jesus.

32 Mt 20:19; Jn 12:32,33 **33** Mt 27:11 **36** 1Ti 6:13; Da 2:44; 7:14; Lk 12:14; Jn 6:15; 8:15 **37** Jn 8:47; 1Jn 3:19; 4:6 **38** Mt 27:24; Lk 23:4; Jn 19:4,6 **39** Mt 27:15; Mk 15:6; Lk 23:17 **40** Ac 3:14; Lk 23:19 **CHAPTER 19** **1** Mt 20:19; 27:26; Mk 15:15; Lk 18:33 **4** ver. 6; Jn 18:38

6 When the chief priests and officers saw Him, they shouted, "Crucify [Him]! Crucify [Him]!" Pilate said to them, "Take Him yourselves and crucify Him, for I find no guilt in Him [no crime, no cause for an accusation]." [Luke 23:4, 14, 22; John 18:38; 19:4]

7 The Jews answered him, "We have a law [regarding blasphemy], and according to that law He should die, because He made Himself out to be the Son of God." [Lev 24:16]

8 So when Pilate heard this said, he was [even] more alarmed *and* afraid.

9 He went into the Praetorium again and said to Jesus, "Where are You from?" But Jesus did not answer him. [Is 53:7]

10 So Pilate said to Him, "You do not speak to me? Do You not know that I have authority to release You, and I have authority to crucify You?"

11 Jesus answered, "You would have no authority over Me at all if it had not been given to you from above. For this reason the sin *and* guilt of the one who handed Me over to you is greater [than your own]."

12 As a result of this, Pilate kept making efforts to release Him, but the Jews kept screaming, "If you release this Man, you are no friend of Caesar! Anyone who makes himself out [to be] a king opposes Caesar [and rebels against the emperor]!"

13 When Pilate heard this, he brought Jesus out, and sat down on the judgment seat at a place called The Pavement, but in Hebrew, Gabbatha.

14 Now it was the day of Preparation for the Passover [week], and it was about the sixth hour. He said to the Jews, "Look, your King!"

15 But they shouted, "Away with *Him*, away with *Him*, crucify Him!" Pilate said to them, "Shall I crucify your King?" The chief priests answered, "We have no king but Caesar!"

The Crucifixion

16 Then he handed Him over to them to be crucified.

17 So they took Jesus, and He went out, bearing His own cross, to the place called the Place of the Skull, which is called in Hebrew, Golgotha. [Matt 27:33–44; Mark 15:22–32; Luke 23:33–43]

18 There they crucified Him, and with Him two others, one on either side, and Jesus between them. [Is 53:12]

19 Pilate also wrote an inscription [on a placard] and put it on the cross. And it was written: "JESUS THE NAZARENE, THE KING OF THE JEWS." [Matt 27:33–44; Mark 15:22–32; Luke 23:33–43]

20 And many of the Jews read this inscription, for the place where Jesus was crucified was near the city; and it was written in Hebrew, in Latin, and in Greek.

21 Then the chief priests of the Jews said to Pilate, "Do not write, 'The King

---

19:7 *We have a law.* The Jewish leaders were telling Pilate, "If you are appealing to us, we say that, according to our law, He must die." As governor, Pilate was bound by Roman custom to respect Jewish law. ***He made Himself out to be the Son of God.*** The Jewish leaders were accusing Jesus of violating the laws against blasphemy (Lev 24:16).

19:9 *Jesus did not answer him.* Three times Pilate had publicly pronounced Jesus innocent (18:38; 19:4,6).

19:12 *you are no friend of Caesar.* The Jews shifted their focus from the religious charge (v. 7) to the political charge (18:33), which they backed up with an appeal to Caesar's own political interest. This new plea forced Pilate to choose between yielding to an indefinite sense of right or escaping the danger of an accusation from Rome.

19:19 *wrote an inscription.* It was a Roman custom to write the name of the condemned person and his crime on a plaque to be placed above his head at execution.

19:20 *written in Hebrew, in Latin, and in Greek.* Multilingual inscriptions were common. The title was written in the local, common, and official languages of the day. Everyone could read the message in his or her own language.

---

6 Ac 3:13 **7** Lev 24:16; Mt 26:65; Jn 5:18; 10:33 **9** Isa 53:7; Mt 27:12,14 **11** Lk 22:53; Jn 7:30 **12** Lk 23:2; Ac 17:7 **14** Mt 27:62 **15** Ge 49:10 **16** Mt 27:26,31; Mk 15:15; Lk 23:24 **17** Mt 27:31,33; Mk 15:21,22; Lk 23:26,33; Nu 15:36; Heb 13:12 **19** Mt 27:37; Mk 15:26; Lk 23:38

of the Jews'; but, 'He said, "I am King of the Jews."' "
[22]Pilate replied, "What I have written I have written [and it remains written]."
[23]Then the soldiers, when they had crucified Jesus, took His outer clothes and made four parts, a part for each soldier, and also the tunic. But the tunic was seamless, woven [in one piece] from the top throughout. [Matt 27:35; Mark 15:24; Luke 23:34]
[24]So they said to one another, "Let us not tear it, but cast lots for it, *to decide* whose it will be." *This was* to fulfill the Scripture, "THEY DIVIDED MY OUTER CLOTHING AMONG THEM, AND FOR MY CLOTHING THEY CAST LOTS." [Ps 22:18]
[25]So the soldiers did these things.

But standing by the cross of Jesus were His mother, His mother's sister [Salome], Mary the *wife* of Clopas, and Mary Magdalene. [Mark 15:40]
[26]So Jesus, seeing His mother, and the disciple whom He loved (esteemed) standing near, said to His mother, "[Dear] woman, look, [here is] your son!"
[27]Then He said to the disciple (John), "Look! [here is] your mother [protect and provide for her]!" From that hour the disciple took her into his own *home.*
[28]After this, Jesus, knowing that all was now finished, said in fulfillment of the Scripture, "I am thirsty." [Ps 69:21]
[29]A jar full of sour wine was placed there; so they put a sponge soaked in the sour wine on [a branch of] hyssop and held it to His mouth. [Matt 27:48, 50; Mark 15:36f; Luke 23:36]
[30]When Jesus had received the sour wine, He said, "It is finished!" And He bowed His head and [voluntarily] gave up His spirit.

Care of the Body of Jesus

[31]Since it was the day of Preparation [for the Sabbath], in order to prevent the bodies from hanging on the cross on the Sabbath (for that Sabbath was a high holy day) the Jews asked Pilate to have their legs broken [to hasten death] and the bodies taken away.
[32]So the soldiers came and broke the legs of the first man, and of the other who had been crucified with Him.
[33]But when they came to Jesus and saw that He was already dead, they did not break His legs.
[34]But one of the soldiers pierced His side with a spear, and immediately blood and water came [flowing] out.
[35]And he (John, the eyewitness) who has seen it has testified, and his testimony is true; and he knows that he is telling the truth, so that you also [who read this] may believe.
[36]For these things took place to fulfill the Scripture, "NOT A BONE OF HIS

19:23 *the soldiers.* According to Roman law, the garments of a condemned criminal belonged to the executioners. Jesus had two items of clothing. The cloak was a large, loose garment. The tunic was a close-fitting garment that went from the neck to the knees.

19:24 *cast lots.* The outer garment could be conveniently divided, but the inner garment could not. Thus, the soldiers divided the outer one and cast lots for the inner one. Unknowingly, the soldiers fulfilled David's prophecy in Psalm 22:18.

19:30 *It is finished!* Having fulfilled every command of the Father and every prophecy of Scripture, Jesus voluntarily died. This was not a cry of exhaustion, but of completion. Jesus had done what He had agreed to do.

19:31 *the day of Preparation.* This day was Friday, the day before the Sabbath Day. Bodies should not remain on the cross. It is ironic that in the midst of a deliberate judicial murder the Jews were scrupulous about keeping the ceremonial law. According to Jewish law (Dt 21:23), it was necessary to remove the bodies of executed criminals before sunset. To avoid breaking the law, the Jews requested that the legs of the condemned be broken so that the men would die quickly and could be removed from their crosses. With his legs broken, a victim could no longer lift his body in order to breathe and would soon suffocate.

19:34 *one of the soldiers pierced His side with a spear.* After the soldier did this, blood and water came out, indicating that Jesus was already dead. Only blood would have flowed from a living body.

19:35 *he (John, the eyewitness) who has seen it.* John's words can be trusted because

---

23 Mt 27:35; Mk 15:24; Lk 23:34 **24** Ps 22:18 **25** Mt 27:55; Mk 15:40; Lk 23:49; Lk 24:18 **26** Jn 13:23; 20:2; 21:7,20,24; Jn 2:4 **27** Jn 1:11; 16:32 **28** Ps 69:21 **29** Mt 27:48 **30** Jn 17:4 **31** ver. 42; Mk 15:42; Dt 21:23 **34** 1Jn 5:6,8 **36** Ex 12:46; Nu 9:12; Ps 34:20

SHALL BE BROKEN." [Ex 12:46; Num 9:12; Ps 34:20]

37 And again another Scripture says, "THEY SHALL LOOK AT HIM WHOM THEY HAVE PIERCED." [Zech 12:10]

38 And after this, Joseph of Arimathea—a disciple of Jesus, but secretly for fear of the Jews—asked Pilate to let him take away the body of Jesus; and Pilate gave him permission. So he came and took away His body. [Matt 27:57–61; Mark 15:42–47; Luke 23:50–56]

39 Nicodemus, who had first come to Him at night, also came bringing a mixture of myrrh and aloes, [weighing] about a hundred [Roman] pounds.

40 So they took Jesus' body and bound it in linen wrappings with the fragrant spices, as is the burial custom of the Jews.

41 Now there was a garden at the place where He was crucified, and in the garden a new tomb [cut out of solid rock] in which no one had yet been laid.

42 Therefore, because of the Jewish day of Preparation, and since the tomb was nearby, they laid Jesus there.

The Empty Tomb

20 NOW ON the first day of the week Mary Magdalene came to the tomb early, while it was still dark, and saw the stone [already] removed from the [groove across the entrance of the] tomb. [Matt 28:1–8; Mark 16:1–8; Luke 24:1–10]

2 So she ran and went to Simon Peter and to the other disciple (John), whom Jesus loved (esteemed), and said to them, "They have taken away the Lord out of the tomb, and we do not know where they have laid Him!"

3 So Peter and the other disciple left, and they were going to the tomb. [Luke 24:12]

4 And the two were running together, but the other disciple outran Peter and arrived at the tomb first.

5 Stooping down and looking in, he saw the linen wrappings [neatly] lying *there;* but he did not go in.

6 Then Simon Peter came up, following him, and went into the tomb and saw the linen wrappings [neatly] lying *there;*

7 and the [burial] face-cloth which had been on Jesus' head, not lying with the [other] linen wrappings, but rolled up in a place by itself.

8 So the other disciple, who had reached the tomb first, went in too; and he saw [the wrappings and the face-cloth] and believed [without any doubt that Jesus had risen from the dead].

9 For as yet they did not understand the Scripture, that He must rise from the dead. [Ps 16:10]

10 Then the disciples went back again to their own homes.

11 But Mary [who had returned] was standing outside the tomb sobbing; and so, as she wept, she stooped down and looked into the tomb;

12 and she saw two angels in white sitting *there,* one at the head and one at the feet, where the body of Jesus had lain.

13 And they said to her, "Woman, why

---

he is giving an eyewitness account, so that his readers will believe that Jesus is the Savior.

20:2 *They have taken away the Lord.* Mary Magdalene jumped to the wrong conclusion.

20:5 *the linen wrappings [neatly] lying.* No one who came to steal the body would have taken the time to unwrap it and leave the clothes behind.

20:6 *saw the linen.* The Greek term implies an intense stare, in contrast to the more casual look described in verse 5. Peter went into the tomb to get a good look. He carefully examined the place where Jesus' body had been.

20:9 *they did not understand the Scripture.* The disciples believed because of what they saw in the tomb (v. 8), not because of what they knew from Old Testament passages describing the Savior's resurrection (Lk 24:25–27). Jesus had prophesied His death and resurrection in the disciples' presence, but the disciples had not understood what He was talking about.

---

37 Ps 22:16,17; Zec 12:10; Rev 1:7 **38** Mt 27:57; Mk 15:42; Lk 23:50; Jn 9:22; 12:42 **39** Jn 3:1,2; 7:50 **40** Ac 5:6 **42** Isa 53:9; ver. 31 **CHAPTER 20** **1** Mt 28:1; Mk 16:1; Lk 24:1 **2** Jn 13:23; 19:26; 21:7,20,24 **3** Lk 24:12 **5** Jn 19:40 **7** Jn 11:44 **9** Ps 16:10; Ac 2:25-31; 13:34,35 **11** Mk 16:5

THE RESURRECTION AND ASCENSION

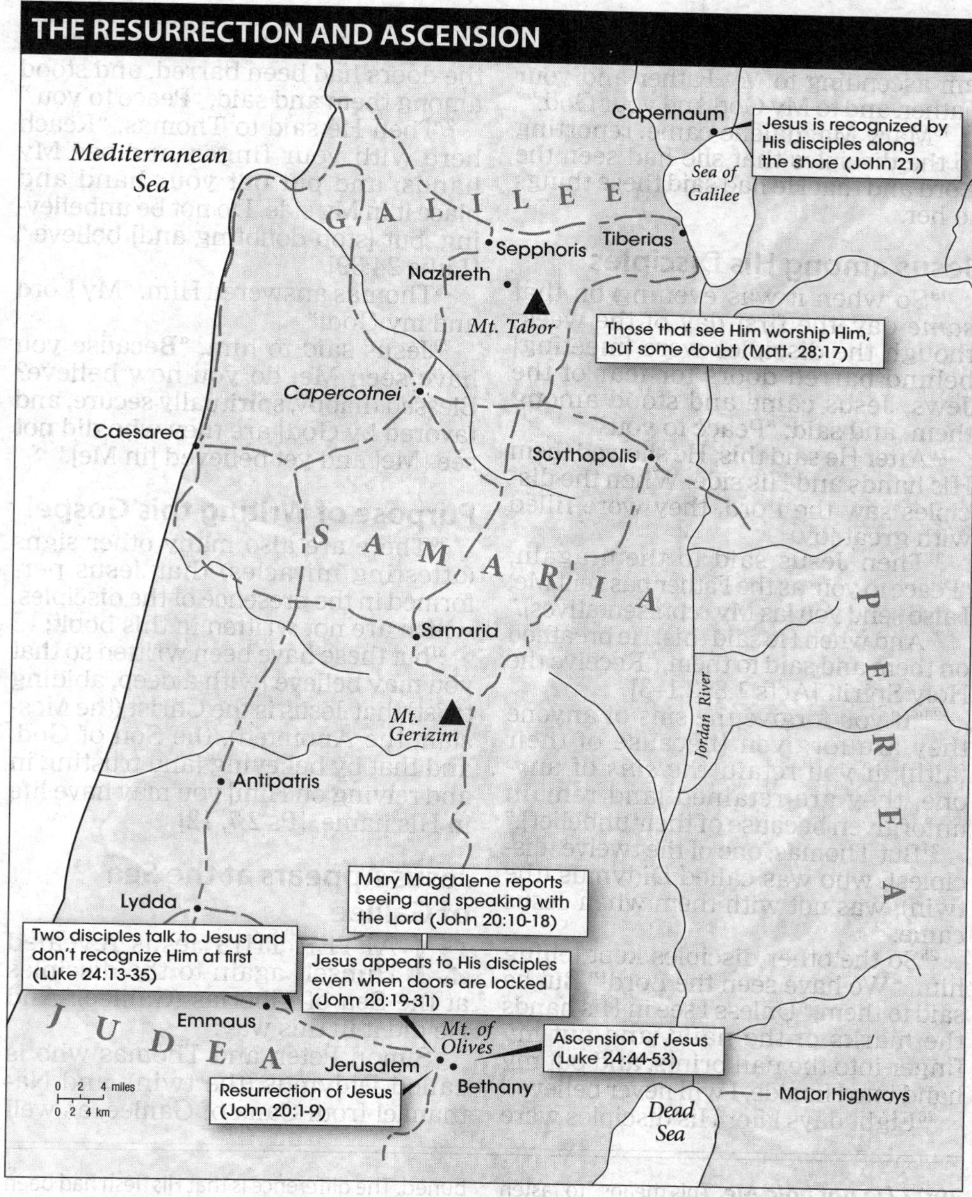

are you crying?" She told them, "Because they have taken away my Lord, and I do not know where they have laid Him."

14After saying this, she turned around and saw Jesus standing *there*, but she did not know that it was Jesus.

15Jesus said to her, "Woman, why are you crying? For whom are you looking?" Supposing that He was the gardener, she replied, "Sir, if you are the one who has carried Him away *from here*, tell me where you have put Him, and I will take Him away."

16Jesus said to her, "Mary!" She turned and said to Him in Hebrew, "Rabboni!" (which means, Teacher).

17Jesus said to her, "Do not hold Me,

14 Mt 28:9; Mk 16:9; Lk 24:16,31; Jn 21:4

for I have not yet ascended to the Father;
but go to My brothers and tell them, 'I
am ascending to My Father and your
Father, and to My God and your God.' "
18 Mary Magdalene came, reporting
to the disciples that she had seen the
Lord and that He had said these things
to her.

Jesus among His Disciples

19 So when it was evening on that
same day, the first day of the week,
though the disciples were [meeting]
behind barred doors for fear of the
Jews, Jesus came and stood among
them, and said, "Peace to you."
20 After He said this, He showed them
His hands and His side. When the dis-
ciples saw the Lord, they were filled
with great joy.
21 Then Jesus said to them again,
"Peace to you; as the Father has sent Me,
I also send you [as My representatives]."
22 And when He said this, He breathed
on them and said to them, "Receive the
Holy Spirit. [Acts 1:8; 2:1–3]
23 "If you forgive the sins of anyone
they are forgiven [because of their
faith]; if you retain *the sins* of any-
one, they are retained [and remain
unforgiven because of their unbelief]."
24 But Thomas, one of the twelve [dis-
ciples], who was called Didymus (the
twin), was not with them when Jesus
came.
25 So the other disciples kept telling
him, "We have seen the Lord!" But he
said to them, "Unless I see in His hands
the marks of the nails, and put my
finger into the nail prints, and put my
hand into His side, I will never believe."
26 Eight days later His disciples were
again inside *the house,* and Thomas
was with them. Jesus came, though
the doors had been barred, and stood
among them and said, "Peace to you."
27 Then He said to Thomas, "Reach
here with your finger, and see My
hands; and put out your hand and
place it in My side. Do not be unbeliev-
ing, but [stop doubting and] believe."
[Luke 24:39]
28 Thomas answered Him, "My Lord
and my God!"
29 Jesus said to him, "Because you
have seen Me, do you now believe?
Blessed [happy, spiritually secure, and
favored by God] are they who did not
see [Me] and yet believed [in Me]."

Purpose of Writing this Gospel

30 There are also many other signs
(attesting miracles) that Jesus per-
formed in the presence of the disciples,
which are not written in this book;
31 but these have been written so that
you may believe [with a deep, abiding
trust] that Jesus is the Christ (the Mes-
siah, the Anointed), the Son of God;
and that by believing [and trusting in
and relying on Him] you may have life
in His name. [Ps 2:7, 12]

Jesus Appears at the Sea of Galilee

21 AFTER THIS Jesus revealed
Himself again to the disciples
at the Sea of Tiberias (Galilee). And
He did it in this way:
2 Simon Peter, and Thomas who is
called Didymus (the twin), and Na-
thanael from Cana of Galilee, as well

20:17 *Do not hold Me.* This means "to fasten oneself to." Evidently Mary had grabbed Christ and was holding on to Him as if she would never turn Him loose.
20:19 *Jesus came and stood among them.* Christ's appearance was miraculous because the doors were shut. Jesus, as God, could perform a variety of miracles without requiring a change in His humanity. Here Christ's body was a physical body, the same body in which He died and was buried. The difference is that His flesh had been changed to take on immortality and incorruptibility (1Co 15:53).
20:31 *that you may believe.* John states the purpose of his book, which was to convince his readers that Jesus is the Christ, the Messiah who fulfilled God's promises to Israel. Jesus is the Son of God, God in the flesh. By believing these things, a person obtains eternal life (1:12).

17 Ps 22:22; Mt 28:10; Ro 8:29; Heb 2:11; Jn 16:28; Eph 1:17 **18** Mt 28:10; Lk 24:10 **19** Mk 16:14; Lk 24:36; 1Co 15:5 **20** Jn 16:22 **21** Mt 28:18; Jn 17:18,19; 2Ti 2:2; Heb 3:1 **23** Mt 16:10; 18:18 **24** Jn 11:16 **27** 1Jn 1:1 **29** 2Co 5:7; 1Pe 1:8 **30** Jn 21:25 **31** Lk 1:4; Jn 3:15,16; 5:24; 1Pe 1:8,9 **CHAPTER 21** **2** Jn 1:45; Mt 4:21

as [John and James] the sons of Zebedee, and two others of His disciples were together.

3 Simon Peter said to them, "I am going fishing." They said, "And we are coming with you." So they went out and got into the boat; and that night they caught nothing.

4 As morning was breaking, Jesus [came and] stood on the beach; however, the disciples did not know that it was Jesus.

5 So Jesus said to them, "Children, do you have any fish [to eat along with your bread]?" They answered, "No."

6 And He said to them, "Cast the net on the right-hand side of the boat (starboard) and you will find some." So they cast [the net], and then they were not able to haul it in because of the great catch of fish.

7 Then that disciple (John) whom Jesus loved (esteemed) said to Peter, "It is the Lord!" So when Simon Peter heard that it was the Lord, he put on his outer tunic (for he was stripped *for work*) and threw himself into the sea [and swam ashore].

8 But the other disciples came in the small boat, for they were not far from shore, only about a hundred yards away, dragging the net full of fish.

9 So when they got out on the beach, they saw a charcoal fire set up and fish on it *cooking*, and bread.

10 Jesus said to them, "Bring some of the fish which you have just caught."

11 So Simon Peter went aboard and hauled the net to land, full of large fish, a hundred and fifty-three [of them]; and although there were so many, the net was not torn.

Jesus Provides

12 Jesus said to them, "Come *and* have breakfast." None of the disciples dared to ask Him, "Who are You?" They knew [without any doubt] that it was the Lord.

13 Jesus came and took the bread and gave it to them, and likewise the fish.

14 This was now the third time that Jesus appeared to the disciples, after He had risen from the dead.

The Love Motivation

15 So when they had finished breakfast, Jesus said to Simon Peter, "Simon, *son* of John, do you love Me more than these [others do—with total commitment and devotion]?" He said to Him, "Yes, Lord; You know that I love You [with a deep, personal affection, as for a close friend]." Jesus said to him, "Feed My lambs."

16 Again He said to him a second time, "Simon, *son* of John, do you love Me [with total commitment and devotion]?" He said to Him, "Yes, Lord; You know that I love You [with a deep, personal affection, as for a close friend]." Jesus said to him, "Shepherd My sheep."

17 He said to him the third time, "Simon, *son* of John, do you love Me [with a deep, personal affection for Me, as for a close friend]?" Peter was grieved that He asked him the third time, "Do you [really] love Me [with a deep, personal affection, as for a close friend]?" And he said to Him, "Lord, You know everything; You know that I love You [with a deep, personal affection, as for a close friend]." Jesus said to him, "Feed My sheep.

Our Times Are in His Hand

18 "I assure you *and* most solemnly say to you, when you were younger you dressed yourself and walked wherever you wished; but when you grow old, you will stretch out your hands *and*

21:4 *the disciples did not know.* Perhaps the apostles did not recognize Jesus because they were preoccupied with their work, as Mary Magdalene had been with her sorrow (20:14). In addition, there was not much light at this time of day.
21:7 *Peter . . . threw himself into the sea.* John was the first to recognize the Lord; Peter was the first to act.
21:17 *You know that I love You.* Peter denied the Lord at least three times. Here, he affirmed his love for the third time.

4 Jn 20:14 **5** Lk 24:41 **6** Lk 5:4,6,7 **7** Jn 13:23; 20:2 **12** Ac 10:41 **14** See Jn 20:19,26 **16** Ac 20:28; Heb 13:20; 1Pe 2:25; 5:2,4 **17** Jn 2:24,25; 16:30 **18** Jn 13:36; Ac 12:3,4

MAJOR ARCHAEOLOGICAL FINDS RELATING TO THE NEW TESTAMENT

SITE OR ARTIFACT	LOCATION —ISRAEL	RELATING SCRIPTURE
Caiaphas' ossuary	Jerusalem	Mt 26:3
Herod's temple	Jerusalem	Lk 1:9
Herod's winter palace	Jericho	Mt 2:4
The Herodium (site of Herod's tomb)	Near Bethlehem	Mt 2:19
Masada	Near western shore of Dead Sea	Cf. Lk 21:20
Early synagogue	Capernaum	Mt 4:13; Mk 1:21
Pool of Siloam	Jerusalem	Jn 9:7
Pool of Bethesda	Jerusalem	Jn 5:2
Pilate inscription	Caesarea	Lk 3:1
Inscription: Gentile entrance to temple sanctuary	Jerusalem	Ac 21:27–29
Skeletal remains of crucified man	Jerusalem	Mk 15:24
Peter's house	Capernaum	Mt 4:13; Lk 4:38
Jacob's well	Nablus	Jn 4:5–6
SITE OR ARTIFACT	**LOCATION —ASIA MINOR**	**RELATING SCRIPTURE**
Derbe inscription	Kerti Hüyük	Ac 14:20
Sergius Paulus inscription	Kythraia, Cyprus	Ac 13:6–7
Zeus altar (Satan's throne?)	Pergamum	Rev 2:13
Fourth-century BC walls	Assos	Ac 20:13–14
Artemis temple and altar	Ephesus	Ac 19:27–28
Ephesian theater	Ephesus	Ac 19:29
Silversmith shops	Ephesus	Ac 19:24
Artemis statues	Ephesus	Ac 19:35
SITE OR ARTIFACT	**LOCATION —GREECE**	**RELATING SCRIPTURE**
Erastus inscription	Corinth	Ro 16:23
Synagogue inscription	Corinth	Ac 18:4
Meat market inscription	Corinth	1Co 10:25
Cult dining rooms (in Asclepius and Demeter temples)	Corinth	1Co 8:10; 10:14
Court (bema)	Corinth	Ac 18:12
Marketplace (bema)	Philippi	Ac 16:19
Starting gate for races	Isthmia	1Co 9:24,26
Gallio inscription	Delphi	Ac 18:12
Egnatian Way	Neapolis (Kavalla), Philippi, Amphipolis, Apollonia, Thessalonica	Cf. Ac 16:11–12; 17:1
Politarch inscription	Thessalonica	Ac 17:6
SITE OR ARTIFACT	**LOCATION —ITALY**	**RELATING SCRIPTURE**
Tomb of Augustus	Rome	Lk 2:1
Mamertine Prison	Rome	2Ti 1:16–17; 2:9; 4:6–8
Appian Way	Puteoli to Rome	Ac 28:13–16
Golden House of Nero	Rome	Cf. Ac 25:10; 1Pe 2:13
Arch of Titus	Rome	Cf. Lk 19:43–44; 21:6,20

arms, and someone else will dress you,
and carry you where you do not wish
to go."
19 Now He said this to indicate the
kind of death by which Peter would
glorify God. And after saying this,
He said to him, "Follow Me [walk the
same path of life that I have walked]!"
20 Peter turned and saw the disciple
whom Jesus loved following them;
the one who also had leaned back on
His chest at the supper and had said,
"Lord, who is it that is going to betray
You?"
21 So when Peter saw him, he asked
Jesus, "Lord, and what about this man
[what is in his future]?"
22 Jesus said to him, "If I want him to
stay alive until I come [again], what *is*
that to you? You follow Me!"
23 So this word went out among the
brothers that this disciple (John) was
not going to die; yet Jesus did not say
to him that he was not going to die,
but *only*, "If I want him to stay alive
until I come [again], what *is that* to
you?"
24 This is the *same* disciple who is
testifying to these things and has re-
corded them; and we know [without
any doubt] that his testimony is true.
25 And there are also many other
things which Jesus did, which if they
were recorded one by one, I suppose
that even the world itself could not con-
tain the books that would be written.

21:20–21 *the disciple whom Jesus loved.* This is commonly considered to be John, the author of this Gospel.

21:24 *This is the same disciple.* This is basically John's signature to his Gospel.

21:25 *there are also many other things which Jesus did.* The Gospel of John is truthful (v. 24), but it is not exhaustive.

19 2Pe 1:14 **20** Jn 13:23,25; 20:2 **22** Mt 16:27,28; 25:31; 1Co 4:5; 11:26; Rev 2:25; 3:11; 22:7,20 **24** Jn 19:35; 3Jn 12 **25** Jn 20:30; Am 7:10

THE

ACTS

OF THE APOSTLES

▸ **AUTHOR:** There are many "we" sections in Acts that imply the author was present for these events (16:10 – 17; 20:5 – 21:18; 27:1 – 28:16). These sections of Acts are the historical record of an eyewitness. For the remainder of this book, Luke no doubt followed the same careful investigative procedures that he used in writing his Gospel (Lk 1:1 – 4). As a close traveling companion of Paul, Luke had access to the principal eyewitness for chapters 13 – 18. It is also likely that he had opportunities to interview such key witnesses in Jerusalem as Peter and John for the information in chapters 13 – 28. Twentieth-century archeological discoveries have strikingly confirmed the trustworthiness and precision of Luke as an historian.

▸ **TIMES:** c. AD 33 – 62 ▸ **KEY VERSES:** Ac 2:42 – 47

▸ **THEME:** Acts is the record of how the events surrounding Jesus' life and death and resurrection resulted in this worldwide movement called the church. The book is certainly not a comprehensive history. Acts is more like a photo album of snapshots. It is the record of an eyewitness who wrote about what he saw and what seemed to be the critical events in the beginnings of the church and its movement out of Jerusalem to the rest of the world. One could say that the Book of Acts is an elaboration on Acts 1:8: "But you will receive power and ability when the Holy Spirit comes upon you; and you will be My witnesses [to tell people about Me] both in Jerusalem and in all Judea, and Samaria, and even to the ends of the earth."

Introduction

1 THE FIRST account I made, Theophilus, was [a continuous report] about all the things that Jesus began to do and to teach [Luke 1:1–4]
[2]until the day when He ascended *to heaven*, after He had by the Holy Spirit given instruction to the apostles (special messengers) whom He had chosen.
[3]To these [men] He also showed Himself alive after His suffering [in Gethsemane and on the cross], by [a series of] many infallible proofs *and* unquestionable demonstrations, appearing to them over *a period of* forty days and talking to them about the things concerning the kingdom of God.
[4]While being together *and* eating with them, He commanded them not to leave Jerusalem, but to wait for what the Father had promised, "Of which," *He said*, "you have heard Me speak. [John 14:16, 26; 15:26]
[5]"For John baptized with water, but you will be baptized *and* empowered *and* united with the Holy Spirit, not long from now."

1:3 *many infallible proofs*. This is the only time the Greek word *tekmerion* occurs, emphasizing the certainty of the resurrection.

1:5 Baptism — The promised Holy Spirit (Isa 32:15; Joel 2:28 – 32) is a gift to believers after the glorification of Jesus (Jn 7:39). John baptized

CHAPTER 1 **1** Lk 1:3 **2** Mk 16:19; 1Ti 3:16; Mt 28:19; Jn 20:21 **3** Mk 16:14 **4** Lk 24:43,49; Jn 14:16 **5** Mt 3:11; Joel 3:18

6 So when they had come together,
they asked Him *repeatedly,* "Lord,
are You at this time reestablishing
the kingdom *and* restoring it to Israel?"
7 He said to them, "It is not for you to
know the times or epochs which the
Father has fixed by His own authority.
8 "But you will receive power *and*
ability when the Holy Spirit comes
upon you; and you will be My witness-
es [to tell people about Me] both in Je-
rusalem and in all Judea, and Samaria,
and even to the ends of the earth."

The Ascension

9 And after He said these things, He
was caught up as they looked on, and
a cloud took Him up out of their sight.
10 While they were looking intent-
ly into the sky as He was going, two
men in white clothing suddenly stood
beside them,
11 who said, "Men of Galilee, why do
you stand looking into the sky? This
[same] Jesus, who has been taken up
from you into heaven, will return in
just the same way as you have watched
Him go into heaven."

The Upper Room

12 Then the disciples returned to Je-
rusalem from the mount called Olivet
(Olive Grove), which is near Jerusalem,
[only] a Sabbath day's journey (less
than one mile) away.
13 When they had entered *the city,*
they went upstairs to the upper room
where they were staying [indefinitely];
that is, Peter, and John and [his broth-
er] James, and Andrew, Philip and
Thomas, Bartholomew (Nathanael)
and Matthew, James *the son* of Al-
phaeus, and Simon the Zealot, and
Judas (Thaddaeus) the son of James.
14 All these with one mind *and* one
purpose were continually devoting
themselves to prayer, [waiting togeth-
er] along with the women, and Mary
the mother of Jesus, and with His
brothers.
15 Now on one of these days Peter
stood up among the brothers and sis-
ters (a gathering of about a hundred
and twenty believers was there) and
he said,
16 "Brothers and sisters, it was nec-
essary that the Scripture be fulfilled,
which the Holy Spirit foretold by the
lips of David [king of Israel] about
Judas [Iscariot], who acted as guide
to those who arrested Jesus.
17 "For he (Judas) was counted among
us and received his share [by divine
allotment] in this ministry."
18 (Now Judas Iscariot acquired a
piece of land [indirectly] with the
[money paid him as a] reward for his
treachery, and falling headlong, his
body burst open in the middle and all
his intestines poured out.

---

for forgiveness of sins, but the outpouring of the Spirit resulted from Christ's victory and exaltation to God's right hand (2:33). Believers are sealed until redemption (Eph 1:13), made one body, and caused to drink of one Spirit (1Co 12:13). The baptism of the Spirit is the immersion in the Spirit and uniting of believers into one body.

1:8 Living by Faith — God designed the Christian life to be one lived in the power of the Holy Spirit. Believers must appropriate, daily, by faith, the power of the Holy Spirit to live as Christians (Ro 8:4–5). This means that the believer trusts the Spirit to empower him in specific instances such as resisting temptation, being faithful, and sharing one's faith. There is no secret formula that makes the Spirit's power operational in our lives. Scripture tells us that the Spirit dwells and operates in us (1Co 6:9). We have to learn by experience through interaction with God to understand how that dynamic works. First the disciples received the Holy Spirit. Then he gave them power and finally the disciples were told they would be Christ's witness to the very ends of the earth. Effective witness requires that we first learn to rely on the Spirit to help us.

1:14 with one mind and one purpose. The disciples were like-minded; the people put aside personal positions and took on a common goal. True unity is an act of grace.

6 Mt 24:3; Isa 1:26 **7** 1Th 5:1 **8** Ac 2:1,4; Lk 24:49; Lk 24:48 **9** Lk 24:51; ver. 2 **10** Mt 28:3; Mk 16:5; Lk 24:4; Jn 20:12; Ac 10:3,30 **11** Ac 2:7; 13:31; Da 7:13; Mt 24:30; Mk 13:26; Lk 21:27; Jn 14:3; 1Th 1:10; 4:16; 2Th 1:10; Rev 1:7 **12** Lk 24:52 **13** Ac 9:37,39; 20:8; Mt 10:2-4; Lk 6:15; Jude 1 **14** Ac 2:1,46; Lk 23:49,55; Mt 13:55 **15** Rev 3:4 **16** Ps 41:9; Jn 13:18; Lk 22:47; Jn 18:3 **17** Mt 10:4; Lk 6:16; ver. 25; Ac 12:25; 20:24; 21:19 **18** Mt 27:5,7,8; Mt 26:15; 2Pe 2:15

19All the people in Jerusalem learned
about this, so in their own dialect—
Aramaic—they called the piece of land
Hakeldama, that is, Field of Blood.)
20"For in the book of Psalms it is
written,

'LET HIS PLACE OF RESIDENCE BECOME
DESOLATE,
AND LET THERE BE NO ONE TO LIVE IN IT';
and [again],
'LET ANOTHER TAKE HIS POSITION AS
OVERSEER.' [Ps 69:25; 109:8]

21"So of the men who have accompa-
nied us during all the time that the
Lord Jesus spent with us,
22beginning with the baptism by
John [at the outset of Jesus' ministry]
until the day when He was taken up
from us—one of these men *must* be-
come a witness with us [to testify] of
His resurrection."
23And they put forward two men,
Joseph, the one called Barsabbas (who
was surnamed Justus), and Matthias.
24They prayed and said, "You, Lord,
who know all hearts [their thoughts,
motives, desires], show us which one
of these two You have chosen
25to occupy this ministry and apos-
tleship which Judas left to go to his
own place [of evil]."
26And they cast lots for them, and the
lot fell to Matthias; and he was added
to the eleven apostles.

The Day of Pentecost

2 WHEN THE day of Pentecost had
come, they were all together in one
place,
2and suddenly a sound came from
heaven like a rushing violent wind,
and it filled the whole house where
they were sitting.
3There appeared to them tongues
resembling fire, which were being dis-
tributed [among them], and they rested
on each one of them [as each person
received the Holy Spirit].
4And they were all filled [that is, dif-
fused throughout their being] with the
Holy Spirit and began to speak in other
tongues (different languages), as the
Spirit was giving them the ability to
speak out [clearly and appropriately].
5Now there were Jews living in Je-
rusalem, devout *and* God-fearing men
from every nation under heaven.
6And when this sound was heard, a
crowd gathered, and they were bewil-
dered because each one was hearing
those in the upper room speaking in
his own language *or* dialect.
7They were completely astonished,
saying, "Look! Are not all of these who
are speaking Galileans?
8"Then how is it that each of us hears
in our own language *or* native dialect?
9"[Among us there are] Parthians,
Medes and Elamites, and people of
Mesopotamia, Judea and Cappadocia,
Pontus and Asia [Minor],
10Phrygia and Pamphylia, Egypt and
the districts of Libya around Cyrene,
and the visitors from Rome, both Jews
and proselytes (Gentile converts to
Judaism),
11Cretans and Arabs—we all hear
them speaking in our [native] tongues
about the mighty works of God!"
12And they were beside themselves
with amazement and were greatly per-
plexed, saying one to another, "What
could this mean?"
13But others were laughing *and* jok-
ing *and* ridiculing them, saying, "They
are full of sweet wine *and* are drunk!"

Peter's Sermon

14But Peter, standing with the eleven,
raised his voice and addressed them:
"Men of Judea and all you who live in
Jerusalem, let this be explained to you;
listen closely *and* pay attention to what
I have to say.
15"These people are not drunk, as
you assume, since it is [only] the third
hour of the day (9:00 a.m.);

2:4 *tongues.* This means "diverse languages" and was essential to the rapid worldwide spread of the gospel. Those gathered for Pentecost came from around the known world and had various "mother tongues."

20 Ps 69:25; Ps 109:8 **22** ver. 9; ver. 8; Jn 15:27; Ac 4:33 **23** Ac 15:22 **24** 1Sa 16:7; 1Ch 28:9; 29:17; Jer 11:20; 17:10; Ac 15:8; Rev 2:23 **25** ver. 17 **CHAPTER 2** **1** Lev 23:15; Dt 16:9; Ac 20:16; Ac 1:14 **2** Ac 4:31 **4** Ac 1:5; Mk 16:17; Ac 10:46; 19:6; 1Co 12:10,28,30; 13:1; 14:2 **7** Ac 1:11 **15** 1Th 5:7

[16]but this is [the beginning of] what
was spoken of through the prophet
Joel:

[17]'And it shall be in the last days,'
says God,
'That I will pour out My Spirit
upon all mankind;
And your sons and your daughters
shall prophesy,
And your young men shall see
[divinely prompted] visions,
And your old men shall dream
[divinely prompted] dreams;
[18]Even on My bond-servants, both
men and women,
I will in those days pour out My
Spirit
And they shall prophesy.
[19]'And I will bring about wonders in
the sky above
And signs (attesting miracles) on
the earth below,
Blood and fire and smoking vapor.
[20]'The sun shall be turned into
darkness
And the moon into blood,
Before the great and glorious day
of the Lord comes.
[21]'And it shall be that everyone
who calls upon the name of
the Lord [invoking, adoring,
and worshiping the Lord
Jesus] shall be saved (rescued
spiritually).' [Joel 2:28–32]

[22]"Men of Israel, listen to these
words: Jesus of Nazareth, a Man ac-
credited *and* pointed out *and* attest-
ed to you by God with [the power to
perform] miracles and wonders and
signs which God worked through Him
in your [very] midst, just as you your-
selves know—
[23]this *Man,* when handed over [to
the Roman authorities] according to
the predetermined decision and fore-
knowledge of God, you nailed to a
cross and put to death by the hands of
lawless *and* godless men.
[24]"But God raised Him up, releasing
Him *and* bringing an end to the agony
of death, since it was impossible for
Him to be held in death's power.
[25]"For David says of Him,

'I saw the Lord constantly before
me;
For He is at my right hand, so that
I will not be shaken [from my
state of security].
[26]'Therefore my heart rejoiced and
my tongue exulted exceedingly;
Moreover my flesh also will live
in hope [that is, will encamp in
anticipation of the resurrection];
[27]'For You will not forsake me *and*
abandon my soul to Hades (the
realm of the dead),
Nor let Your Holy One undergo
decay [after death].
[28]'You have made known to me the
ways of life;
You will fill me [infusing my soul]
with joy with Your presence.'
[Ps 16:8–11]

[29]"Brothers, I may confidently *and*
freely say to you regarding the pa-
triarch David that he both died and
was buried, and his tomb is with us
to this day.
[30]"And so, being a prophet and
knowing fully that God had sworn to
him with an oath that He would seat
one of his descendants on his throne,
[2 Sam 7:12–16; Ps 132:11]
[31]he foresaw and spoke [prophetical-
ly] of the resurrection of the Christ (the
Messiah, the Anointed), that He was
not abandoned [in death] to Hades (the
realm of the dead), nor did His body
undergo decay. [Ps 16:10]
[32]"God raised this Jesus [bodily from
the dead], and of that [fact] we are all
witnesses.

2:17 *VISIONS . . . DREAMS.* The Holy Spirit was poured out on the church at the beginning of this final age of Scripture.

17 Isa 44:3; Eze 11:19; Joel 2:28; Zec 12:10; Jn 7:38; Ac 10:45; Ac 21:9 **18** Ac 21:4,9; 1Co 12:10; 14:1 **19** Joel 2:30 **20** Mt 24:29; Mk 13:24; Lk 21:25 **21** Ro 10:13 **22** Jn 3:2; 14:10,11; Ac 10:38; Heb 2:4 **23** Mt 26:24; Lk 22:22; Ac 3:18; Ac 5:30 **24** Ro 8:11; 1Co 6:14; 2Co 4:14; Eph 1:20; Col 2:12; 1Th 1:10; Heb 13:20 **25** Ps 16:8 **29** Ac 13:36 **30** 2Sa 7:12; Ps 132:11; Lk 1:32; Ro 1:3; 2Ti 2:8 **31** Ps 16:10 **32** ver. 24; Ac 1:8

33 “Therefore having been exalted
to the right hand of God, and having
received from the Father the promise
of the Holy Spirit, He has poured out
this [blessing] which you both see and
hear.
34 “For David did not ascend into the
heavens, yet he himself says,

‘The Lord [the Father] said to my
Lord [the Son],
“Sit at My right hand,
35 Until I make Your enemies a
footstool for Your feet.” ’
[Ps 110:1]

36 “Therefore let all the house of Israel
recognize beyond all doubt that God
has made Him both Lord and Christ
(Messiah, Anointed)—this Jesus whom
you crucified.”

The Ingathering

37 Now when they heard this, they
were cut to the heart [with remorse
and anxiety], and they said to Peter
and the rest of the apostles, “Brothers,
what are we to do?”
38 And Peter said to them, “Repent
[change your old way of thinking,
turn from your sinful ways, accept
and follow Jesus as the Messiah] and
be baptized, each of you, in the name of
Jesus Christ because of the forgiveness
of your sins; and you will receive the
gift of the Holy Spirit.
39 “For the promise [of the Holy
Spirit] is for you and your children
and for all who are far away [includ-
ing the Gentiles], as many as the Lord
our God calls to Himself.” [Is 57:19;
Joel 2:32]
40 And Peter solemnly testified and
continued to admonish *and* urge them
with many more words, saying, “Be
saved from this crooked *and* unjust
generation!”
41 So then, those who accepted his
message were baptized; and on that
day about 3,000 souls were added [to
the body of believers].
42 They were continually *and* faith-
fully devoting themselves to the in-
struction of the apostles, and to fel-
lowship, to eating meals together and
to prayers.
43 A sense of awe was felt by every-
one, and many wonders and signs (at-
testing miracles) were taking place
through the apostles.
44 And all those who had believed
[in Jesus as Savior] were together and
had all things in common [consider-
ing their possessions to belong to the
group as a whole].
45 And they *began* selling their prop-
erty and possessions and were sharing
the proceeds with all [the other believ-
ers], as anyone had need.
46 Day after day they met in the tem-
ple [area] continuing with one mind,
and breaking bread in various private

2:37 Conviction of the Holy Spirit — Peter's preaching was extremely effective, for it came "in [its inherent] power and in the Holy Spirit and with great conviction" (1Th 1:5). The result was they were "cut to the heart." Their response was, "Brothers, what are we to do?" The reality was that conviction by the Holy Spirit brought about a real search for an answer. Such a consciousness of sin is an indispensable prerequisite to conversion.

2:38 *Repent.* Peter called the Jews to turn their backs on their former lives and change. Faith involves an action of belief by those who accept Jesus.

2:42–47 Being in the Church — Converts were apparently immediately incorporated into the body of believers that became the church. Being involved in the Jerusalem church clearly must have changed the lives of these new believers dramatically. This was manifested in several ways: (1) they devoted themselves to new teaching; (2) they thought differently about all their possessions; (3) they became people of prayer; (4) they ate together and worshiped together with unified hearts. They weren't just saved from sin. They were saved to Christ and to this new body called the church, which of course is also His. We are called to be a part of one another's lives. We are to learn, share, pray, and worship together. As a body of believers, God expects us to have great concern for our fellow believers and to help one another mature.

---

33 Php 2:9; Heb 10:12; Jn 14:26; 16:7,13; Ac 10:45; Eph 4:8 **34** Ps 110:1; Mt 22:44; 1Co 15:25; Eph 1:20; Heb 1:13 **37** Zec 12:10; Lk 3:10; Ac 9:6 **38** Lk 24:47; Ac 3:19 **39** Joel 2:28; Ac 3:25; Ac 11:15,18; Eph 2:13 **42** Ac 1:14; Ro 12:12; Eph 6:18; Col 4:2; Heb 10:25 **43** Mk 16:17; Ac 5:12 **44** Ac 4:32,34 **45** Isa 58:7 **46** Ac 1:14; Lk 24:53; Ac 20:7

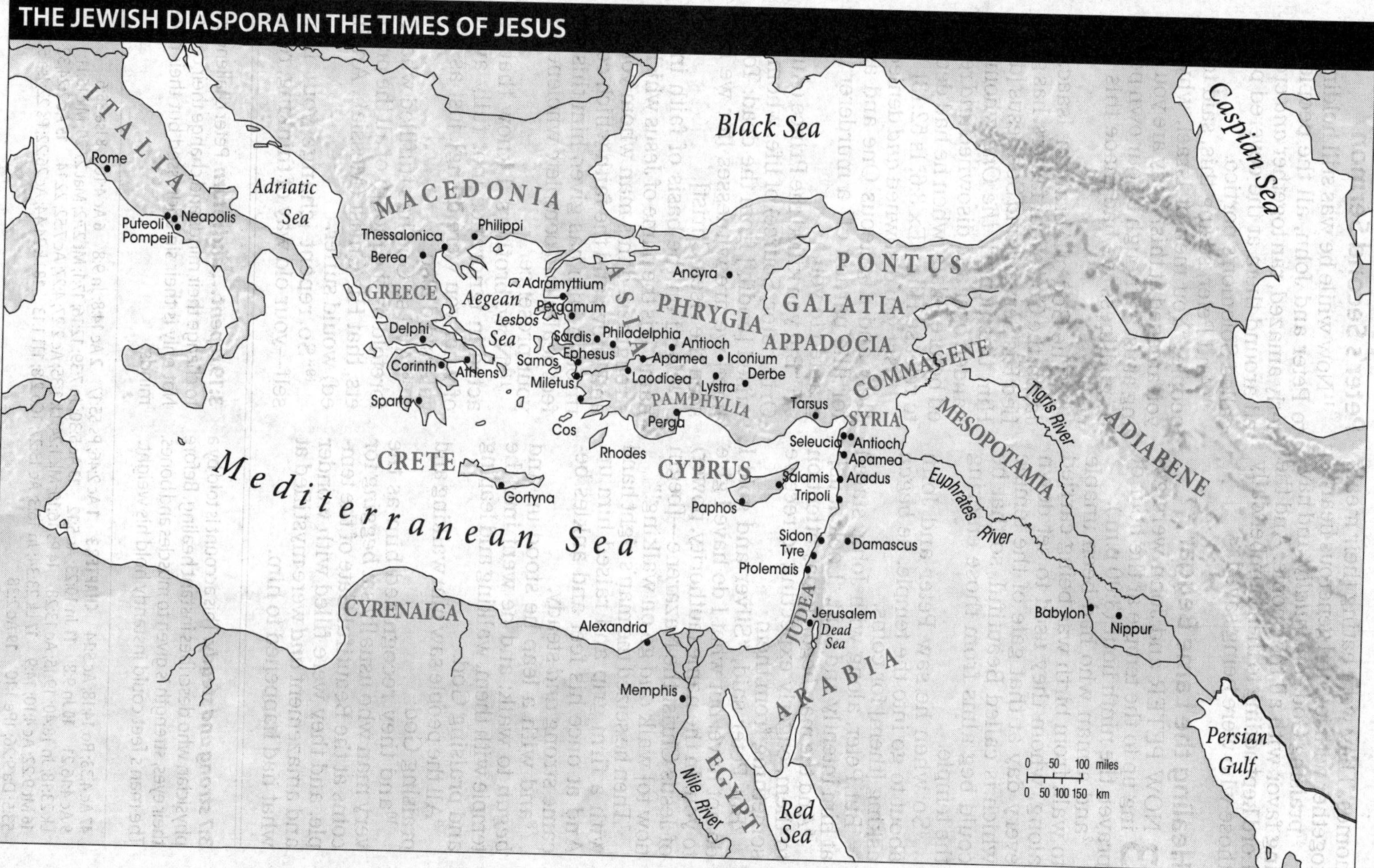
THE JEWISH DIASPORA IN THE TIMES OF JESUS
ITALIA
Rome
Puteoli
Pompeii
Neapolis
Adriatic Sea
MACEDONIA
Philippi
Thessalonica
Berea
GREECE
Delphi
Corinth
Athens
Sparta
Aegean Sea
Lesbos
Adramyttium
Pergamum
Sardis
Philadelphia
Ephesus
Samos
Miletus
Cos
Rhodes
ASIA
PHRYGIA
Antioch
Apamea
Laodicea
Iconium
Lystra
Derbe
PAMPHYLIA
Perga
Ancyra
Black Sea
PONTUS
GALATIA
APPADOCIA
COMMAGENE
Tarsus
SYRIA
Seleucia
Antioch
Apamea
Aradus
Tripoli
CYPRUS
Salamis
Paphos
CRETE
Gortyna
Mediterranean Sea
CYRENAICA
Alexandria
Memphis
EGYPT
Nile River
Red Sea
Sidon
Tyre
Ptolemais
Damascus
JUDEA
Jerusalem
Dead Sea
ARABIA
MESOPOTAMIA
Tigris River
Euphrates River
ADIABENE
Babylon
Nippur
Caspian Sea
Persian Gulf
0 50 100 miles
0 50 100 150 km

homes. They were eating their meals together with joy and generous hearts,

47 praising God *continually*, and having favor with all the people. And the Lord kept adding to their number daily those who were being saved.

Healing the Lame Beggar

3 NOW PETER and John were going up to the temple at the hour of prayer, the ninth hour (3:00 p.m.),

2 and a man who had been unable to walk from birth was being carried along, whom they used to set down every day at that gate of the temple which is called Beautiful, so that he could beg alms from those entering the temple.

3 So when he saw Peter and John about to go into the temple, he *began* asking [them] for coins.

4 But Peter, along with John, stared at him intently and said, "Look at us!"

5 And the man *began* to pay attention to them, eagerly expecting to receive something from them.

6 But Peter said, "Silver and gold I do not have; but what I do have I give to you: In the name (authority, power) of Jesus Christ the Nazarene—[begin now to] walk *and* go on walking!"

7 Then he seized the man's right hand with a firm grip and raised him up. And at once his feet and ankles became strong *and* steady,

8 and with a leap he stood up and *began* to walk; and he went into the temple with them, walking and leaping and praising God.

9 All the people saw him walking and praising God;

10 and they recognized him as the very man who usually sat *begging* for coins at the Beautiful Gate of the temple, and they were filled with wonder and amazement *and* were mystified at what had happened to him.

Peter's Second Sermon

11 Now while he was still holding on to Peter and John, all the people, utterly amazed, ran together *and* crowded around them at the covered porch called Solomon's portico.

12 And Peter, seeing this, said to the people, "You men of Israel, why are you amazed at this? Why are you staring at us, as though by our own power or godliness we had made this man walk?

13 "The God of Abraham, Isaac, and Jacob, the God of our fathers, has glorified His Servant *and* Son Jesus [doing Him this honor], *the One* whom you handed over and disowned *and* rejected before Pilate, when he had decided to release Him. [Ex 3:6; Is 52:13]

14 "But you disowned *and* denied the Holy and Righteous One and asked for [the pardon of] a murderer to be granted to you.

15 "But you killed the Prince (Author, Originator, Source) of life, whom God raised [bodily] from the dead. To this [fact] we are witnesses [for we have seen the risen Christ].

16 "And on the basis of faith in His name, it is the name of Jesus which has strengthened this man whom you see and know; and the faith which *comes* through Him has given him this perfect health *and* complete wholeness in your presence.

17 "Now, brothers, I know that you acted in ignorance [not fully aware of what you were doing], just as your rulers did also.

18 "And so God has fulfilled what He foretold by the mouth of all the prophets, that His Christ (Messiah, Anointed) would suffer.

19 "So repent [change your inner self—your old way of thinking, regret

---

3:7 *strong and steady.* This account is told by a physician who describes instant healing. Before their eyes, strength is given to muscles and bones. The man's feet could instantly hold his weight.

3:19 *repent . . . and return.* Peter challenges all to change their minds and change their courses. Not only is their sin addressed but their closed minds.

47 Ac 4:33; Ro 14:18; Ac 5:14 **CHAPTER 3** **1** Ac 2:46; Ps 55:17 **2** Ac 14:8; Jn 9:8 **6** Ac 4:10 **8** Isa 35:6 **9** Ac 4:16,21 **10** Jn 9:8 **11** Jn 10:23; Ac 5:12 **13** Ac 5:30; Jn 7:39; 12:16; 17:1; Mt 27:2; Mat 27:20; Mk 15:11; Lk 23:18; Jn 18:40; 19:15; Ac 13:28 **14** Ps 16:10; Mk 1:24; Lk 1:35; Ac 2:27; 4:27; Ac 7:52; 22:14 **15** Ac 2:24,32 **16** Mt 9:22; Ac 4:10; 14:9 **17** Lk 23:34; Jn 16:3; Ac 13:27; 1Co 2:8; 1Ti 1:13 **18** Lk 24:44; Ac 26:22; Ps 22; Isa 50:6; 53:5; Da 9:26; 1Pe 1:10 **19** Ac 2:38

past sins] and return [to God—seek
His purpose for your life], so that your
sins may be wiped away [blotted out,
completely erased], so that times of re-
freshing may come from the presence
of the Lord [restoring you like a cool
wind on a hot day];
20 and that He may send [to you]
Jesus, the Christ, who has been ap-
pointed for you,
21 whom heaven must keep until the
time for the [complete] restoration of
all things about which God promised
through the mouth of His holy proph-
ets from ancient time.
22 "Moses said, 'THE LORD GOD WILL
RAISE UP FOR YOU A PROPHET LIKE ME FROM
YOUR COUNTRYMEN; YOU SHALL LISTEN TO
HIM *and* OBEY everything He tells you.
23 'And it will be that every person
that does not listen to *and* heed that
Prophet will be utterly destroyed from
among the people.' [Deut 18:15–19]
24 "Indeed, all the prophets who have
spoken, from Samuel and those who
came after him, also announced these
days.
25 "You are the sons (descendants)
of the prophets and [heirs] of the cov-
enant which God made with your fa-
thers, saying to Abraham, 'AND IN YOUR
SEED (descendant) ALL THE FAMILIES OF
THE EARTH SHALL BE BLESSED.' [Gen 22:18;
Gal 3:16]
26 "*It was* for you first *of all that* God
raised up His Servant *and* Son [Jesus],
and sent Him to bless you by turning
every one *of you* from your wicked
ways." [Acts 2:24; 3:22]

Peter and John Arrested

4 AND WHILE Peter and John were
talking to the people, the priests
and the captain [who was in charge
of the temple area and] of the temple
guard and the Sadducees came up to
them,
2 being extremely disturbed *and* thor-
oughly annoyed because they were
teaching the people and proclaiming
in [the case of] Jesus the resurrection
of the dead.
3 So they arrested them and put them
in jail until the next day, because it
was evening.
4 But many of those who heard the
message [of salvation] believed [in
Jesus and accepted Him as the Christ].
And the number of the men came to be
about 5,000.
5 On the next day, their magistrates
and elders and scribes (Sanhedrin,
Jewish High Court) were gathered to-
gether in Jerusalem;
6 and Annas the high priest *was
there*, and Caiaphas and John and
Alexander, and all others who were
of high-priestly descent.
7 When they had put the men in front
of them, they repeatedly asked, "By
what sort of power, or in what name
[that is, by what kind of authority], did
you do this [healing]?"
8 Then Peter, filled with [the power
of] the Holy Spirit, said to them, "Rul-
ers and elders of the people [members
of the Sanhedrin, the Jewish High
Court],

3:22 Messiah — Peter draws on the witness of the prophets who foretold the suffering of Christ. He quotes Moses, who spoke of a prophet like himself from among the Jews (Dt 18:15 – 17). The crucified, risen, and ascended Jesus has fulfilled this role perfectly as God's anointed Servant sent to atone for humans. Jesus carried God's authority; the words of Jesus must be heeded since they give life to the dying sinner. A person greater than Moses has come to fulfill the prophets. Peter is proclaiming that Jesus is the deliberate fulfillment of God's promise for redemption.

4:1 *Sadducees.* The Sadducees were skeptics who rejected all of the Old Testament except the books of Moses, and who denied the resurrection from the dead. Peter's teaching about the resurrection challenged their beliefs and teaching.

4:5 magistrates and elders and scribes. The Sanhedrin, which consisted of 70 men plus the high priest, was the highest Jewish court. The group consisted of the wealthiest, most educated, and most powerful Jewish men in Israel.

4:8 The Filling of the Holy Spirit — This is the second description in the Book of Acts of someone being filled with the Holy Spirit (see 2:4; 4:31; 9:17; 13:9). The initial filling accompanies

---

21 Ac 1:11; Mt 17:11; Lk 1:70 **22** Dt 18:15,18,19; Ac 7:37 **25** Ac 2:39; Ro 9:4,8; 15:8; Gal 3:26; Ge 12:3; 18:18; 22:18; 26:4; 28:14; Gal 3:8 **26** Mt 10:5; 15:24; Lk 24:47; Ac 13:32,33,46; ver. 22; Mt 1:21 **CHAPTER 4** **6** Lk 3:2; Jn 11:49; 18:13 **7** Ex 2:14; Mt 21:23; Ac 7:27 **8** Lk 12:11,12

9 if we are being put on trial today [to interrogate us] for a good deed done to [benefit] a disabled man, as to how this man has been restored to health,

10 let it be known *and* clearly understood by all of you, and by all the people of Israel, that in the name of Jesus Christ the Nazarene, whom you [demanded be] crucified [by the Romans and], whom God raised from the dead—in this name [that is, by the authority and power of Jesus] this man stands here before you in good health.

11 "This Jesus is the STONE WHICH WAS DESPISED *and* REJECTED by you, THE BUILDERS, *but* WHICH BECAME THE CHIEF CORNERSTONE. [Ps 118:22]

12 "And there is salvation in no one else; for there is no other name under heaven that has been given among people by which we must be saved [for God has provided the world no alternative for salvation]."

Threat and Release

13 Now when the men of the Sanhedrin (Jewish High Court) saw the confidence *and* boldness of Peter and John, and grasped the fact that they were uneducated and untrained [ordinary] men, they were astounded, and *began* to recognize that they had been with Jesus.

14 And seeing the man who had been healed standing *there* with them, they had nothing to say in reply.

15 But after ordering them to step out of the Council [chamber], they *began* to confer among themselves,

16 saying, "What are we to do with these men? For the fact that an extraordinary miracle has taken place through them is public knowledge *and* clearly evident to all the residents of Jerusalem, and we cannot deny it.

17 "But to keep it from spreading further among the people *and* the nation, let us [sternly] warn them not to speak again to anyone in this name."

18 So they sent for them, and commanded them not to speak [as His representatives] or teach at all in the name of Jesus [using Him as their authority].

19 But Peter and John replied to them, "Whether it is right in the sight of God to listen to you *and* obey you rather than God, you must judge [for yourselves];

20 for we, on our part, cannot stop telling [people] about what we have seen and heard."

21 When the rulers and Council members had threatened them further, they let them go, finding no way to punish them because [of their fear] of the people, for they were all praising *and* glorifying *and* honoring God for what had happened;

22 for the man to whom this sign (attesting miracle) of healing had happened was more than forty years old.

23 After Peter and John were released, they returned to their own [people] and reported everything that the chief priests and elders had said to them.

24 And when they heard it, they raised their voices together to God and said, "O Sovereign Lord [having complete power and authority], it is You who MADE THE HEAVEN AND THE EARTH AND THE SEA, AND EVERYTHING THAT IS IN THEM, [Ex 20:11; Ps 146:6]

25 who by the Holy Spirit, *through* the mouth of our father David, Your servant, said,

---

the baptism in the Spirit. This filling brought boldness for God's work. Jesus had promised His disciples that they would stand before kings and rulers and that the Spirit of God within them would implant in their minds exactly what to say to these leaders (Mt 10:16–20).

4:19 listen to you and obey you rather than God. There is no authority apart from God. When human authority rejects God's authority, it becomes twisted and loses its right to demand compliance (5:29). God's people are responsible to obey the government because it has been set in place by God, but when government directs against God's will, the Author of authority has the higher claim on our allegiance. We must resist any command that is against God's will (Ex 1; Da 3; Heb 11:23).

10 Ac 3:6,16; Ac 2:24 **11** Ps 118:22; Isa 28:16; Mt 21:42 **12** Mt 1:21; Ac 10:43; 1Ti 2:5,6 **13** Mt 11:25; 1Co 1:27 **14** Ac 3:11 **16** Jn 11:47; Ac 3:9,10 **18** Ac 5:40 **19** Ac 5:29 **20** Ac 1:8; 2:32; Ac 22:15; 1Jn 1:1,3 **21** Mt 21:26; Lk 20:6,19; 22:2; Ac 5:26; Ac 3:7,8 **23** Ac 12:12 **24** 2Ki 19:15 **25** Ps 2:1

'WHY DID THE NATIONS (Gentiles)
BECOME ARROGANT *and* RAGE,
AND THE PEOPLES DEVISE FUTILE
THINGS [against the Lord]?
26'THE KINGS OF THE EARTH TOOK THEIR
STAND [to attack],
AND THE RULERS WERE ASSEMBLED
TOGETHER
AGAINST THE LORD AND AGAINST
HIS ANOINTED (the Christ, the
Messiah).' [Ps 2:1, 2]

27"For in this city there were gathered
together against Your holy Servant
Jesus, whom You anointed, both Herod
and Pontius Pilate, along with the Gen-
tiles and the peoples of Israel,
28to do whatever Your hand and Your
purpose predestined [before the cre-
ation of the world] to occur [and so
without knowing it, they served Your
own purpose].
29"And now, Lord, observe their
threats [take them into account] and
grant that Your bond-servants may
declare Your message [of salvation]
with great confidence,
30while You extend Your hand to
heal, and signs and wonders (attesting
miracles) take place through the name
[and the authority and power] of Your
holy Servant *and* Son Jesus."
31And when they had prayed, the
place where they were meeting together
was shaken [a sign of God's presence];
and they were all filled with the Holy
Spirit and *began* to speak the word of
God with boldness *and* courage.

Sharing among Believers

32Now the company of believers was
of one heart and soul, and not one [of
them] claimed that anything belonging
to him was [exclusively] his own, but
everything was common property *and*
for the use of all.
33And with great ability *and* power
the apostles were *continuously* testi-
fying to the resurrection of the Lord
Jesus, and great grace [God's remark-
able lovingkindness and favor and
goodwill] rested richly upon them all.
34There was not a needy person
among them, because those who were
owners of land or houses were selling
them, and bringing the proceeds of
the sales
35and placing *the money* down at the
apostles' feet. Then it was distributed
to each as anyone had need.
36Now Joseph, a Levite and native
of Cyprus, who was surnamed Bar-
nabas by the apostles (which trans-
lated means Son of Encouragement),
37sold a field belonging to him and
brought the money and set it at the
apostles' feet.

Fate of Ananias and Sapphira

5 NOW A man named Ananias, with
his wife Sapphira, sold a piece of
property,
2and with his wife's full knowledge
[and complicity] he kept back some of
the proceeds, bringing only a portion
of it, and set it at the apostles' feet.
3But Peter said, "Ananias, why has
Satan filled your heart to lie to the
Holy Spirit and [secretly] keep back
for yourself some of the proceeds [from
the sale] of the land?
4"As long as it remained [unsold],
did it not remain your own [to do with
as you pleased]? And after it was sold,
was the money not under your control?
Why is it that you have conceived this

5:3 Filled with Satan — Satan is the father of lies (Jn 8:44). When Ananias and Sapphira deliberately lied, they took upon themselves the moral character of the one who is behind all lies, the devil himself. A person who is listening to Satan begins to act like Satan; his or her thoughts and actions are "filled with Satan" rather than reflecting the filling and direction of the Holy Spirit. Satan or a demon cannot possess someone who is filled with the Holy Spirit, but by listening to Satan rather than the Holy Spirit a believer can behave like one who belongs to Satan rather than one who belongs to God.

5:4 Holy Spirit — This passage confirms the deity of the Holy Spirit. The Holy Spirit is the third

27 Mt 26:3; Lk 22:2; 23:1,8; Lk 1:35; Lk 4:18; Jn 10:36 **28** Ac 2:23; 3:18 **29** ver. 13,31; 9:27; 13:46; 14:3; 19:8; 26:26; Eph 6:19 **30** Ac 2:43; 5:12; Ac 3:6,16; ver. 27 **31** Ac 2:2,4; 16:26; ver. 29 **32** Ac 5:12; Ro 15:5,6; 2Co 13:11; Php 1:27; 2:2; 1Pe 3:8; Ac 2:44 **33** Ac 1:8,22; Ac 2:45 **34** Ac 2:45 **35** ver. 37; Ac 5:2; 2:45; 6:1 **37** ver. 34,35; Ac 5:1,2 **CHAPTER 5** **3** Nu 30:2; Dt 23:21; Ecc 5:4; Lk 22:3

act [of hypocrisy and deceit] in your
heart? You have not [simply] lied to
people, but to God."
5And hearing these words, Ananias
fell down suddenly and died; and great
fear *and* awe gripped those who heard
of it.
6And the young men [in the con-
gregation] got up and wrapped up the
body, and carried it out and buried it.
7Now after an interval of about three
hours his wife came in, not knowing
what had happened.
8Peter asked her, "Tell me whether
you sold your land for so much?" And
she said, "Yes, for so much."
9Then Peter said to her, "How could
you two have agreed together to put
the Spirit of the Lord to the test? Look!
The feet of those who have buried your
husband are at the door, and they will
carry you out also."
10And at once she fell down at his
feet and died; and the young men came
in and found her dead, and they car-
ried her out and buried her beside her
husband.
11And great fear *and* awe gripped
the whole church, and all who heard
about these things.
12At the hands of the apostles many
signs and wonders (attesting miracles)
were *continually* taking place among
the people. And by common consent
they all met together [at the temple] in
[the covered porch called] Solomon's
portico.
13But none of the rest [of the people,
the non-believers] dared to associate
with them; however, the people were
holding them in high esteem *and* were
speaking highly of them.
14More *and* more believers in the
Lord, crowds of men and women, were
constantly being added to *their number*,
15to such an extent that they even
carried their sick out into the streets
and put them on cots and sleeping
pads, so that when Peter came by at
least his shadow might fall on one of
them [with healing power].
16And the people from the towns in
the vicinity of Jerusalem were coming
together, bringing the sick and those
who were tormented by unclean spir-
its, and they were all being healed.

Imprisonment and Release

17But the high priest stood up, along
with all his associates (that is, the sect
of the Sadducees), and they were filled
with jealousy *and* resentment.
18They arrested the apostles and put
them in a public jail.
19But during the night an angel of
the Lord opened the prison doors, and
leading them out, he said,
20"Go, stand and *continue* to tell the
people in the temple [courtyards] the
whole message of this Life [the eter-
nal life revealed by Christ and found
through faith in Him]."
21When they heard this, they went
into the temple [courtyards] about day-
break and *began* teaching.
Now when the high priest and his
associates arrived, they called together
the Council (Sanhedrin, Jewish High
Court), even all the council of elders of
the sons of Israel, and sent word to the
prison for the apostles to be brought
[before them].
22But when the officers arrived, they
did not find them in the prison; and
they came back and reported,
23"We found the prison securely
locked and the guards standing at the
doors, but when we opened [the doors],
we found no one inside."
24Now when the captain of the tem-

Person of the triune Godhead. To lie to Him (v. 3) is to lie to God.

5:12 *signs and wonders.* These are miraculous occurrences that point to a warning, instruction, or encouragement from God. The signs and wonders which were done among the people at this time gave credibility to the apostles as messengers from God.

5:19 Angels — The word "angel" simply means "messenger." The phrase "angel of the Lord" is commonly used in the Old Testament to refer to spiritual messengers of God.

5 ver. 10,11 **6** Jn 19:40 **9** ver. 3; Mt 4:7 **10** ver. 5 **11** ver. 5; Ac 2:43; 19:17 **12** Ac 2:43; 14:3; 19:11; Ro 15:19; 2Co 12:12; Heb 2:4; Ac 3:11; 4:32 **13** Jn 9:22; 12:42; 19:38; Ac 2:47; 4:21 **15** Mt 9:21; 14:36; Ac 19:12 **16** Mk 16:17,18; Jn 14:12 **17** Ac 4:1,2,6 **18** Lk 21:12 **19** Ac 12:7; 16:26 **20** Jn 6:68; 17:3; 1Jn 5:11 **21** Ac 4:5,6 **24** Lk 22:4; Ac 4:1

ple *guard* and the chief priests heard these things, they were greatly perplexed, wondering what would come of this.

25 But someone came and told them, "The men whom you put in prison are standing [right here] in the temple [area], teaching the people!"

26 Then the captain went with the officers and brought them back, without hurting them (because they were afraid of the people, worried that they might be stoned).

27 So they brought them and presented them before the Council (Sanhedrin, Jewish High Court). The high priest questioned them,

28 saying, "We gave you strict orders not to continue teaching in this name, and yet you have filled Jerusalem with your teaching and you intend to bring this Man's blood on us [by accusing us as His murderers]."

29 Then Peter and the apostles replied, "We must obey God rather than men [we have no other choice].

30 "The God of our fathers raised up Jesus, whom you had put to death by hanging Him on a cross [and you are responsible]. [Deut 21:22, 23]

31 "God exalted Him to His right hand as Prince and Savior *and* Deliverer, in order to grant repentance to Israel, and [to grant] forgiveness of sins.

32 "And we are witnesses of these things; and so is the Holy Spirit, whom God has bestowed on those who obey Him."

Gamaliel's Counsel

33 Now when they heard this, they were infuriated and they intended to kill the apostles.

34 But a Pharisee named Gamaliel, a teacher of the Law [of Moses], highly esteemed by all the people, stood up in the Council (Sanhedrin, Jewish High Court) and ordered that the men be taken outside for a little while.

35 Then he said to the Council, "Men of Israel, be careful in regard to what you propose to do to these men.

36 "For some time ago Theudas rose up, claiming to be somebody [of importance], and a group of about four hundred men allied themselves with him. But he was killed, and all who followed him were scattered and came to nothing.

37 "After this man, Judas the Galilean rose up, [and led an uprising] during the time of the census, and drew people after him; he was also killed, and all his followers were scattered.

38 "So in the present case, I say to you, stay away from these men and let them alone, for if this plan or action is of men [merely human in origin], it will fail *and* be destroyed;

39 but if it is of God [and it appears that it is], you will not be able to stop them; or else you may even be found fighting against God!"

40 The Council (Sanhedrin, Jewish High Court) took his advice; and after summoning the apostles, they flogged them and ordered them not to speak in the name of Jesus, and released them.

41 So they left the Council, rejoicing that they had been considered worthy [dignified by indignity] to suffer shame for [the sake of] His name.

42 And every single day, in the temple [area] and in homes, they did not stop teaching and telling the good news of Jesus as the Christ (the Messiah, the Anointed).

Choosing of the Seven

6 NOW ABOUT this time, when the number of disciples was increasing, a complaint was made by the Hellenists (Greek-speaking Jews) against the [native] Hebrews, because their

5:32 *witnesses of these things.* The witness of the believer is vitally related to the Holy Spirit. Jesus had said that the Holy Spirit would be a witness and that the apostles would be witnesses.

26 Mt 21:26 **28** Ac 4:18; Ac 2:23,36; 3:15; 7:52; Mt 23:35; 27:25 **29** Ac 4:19 **30** Ac 3:13,15; 22:14; Ac 10:39; 13:29; Gal 3:13; 1Pe 2:24 **31** Ac 2:33,36; Php 2:9; Heb 2:10; 12:2; Ac 3:15; Mt 1:21; Lk 24:47; Ac 3:26; 13:38; Eph 1:7; Col 1:14 **32** Jn 15:26,27; Ac 2:4; 10:44 **33** Ac 2:37; 7:54 **34** Ac 22:3 **38** Pr 21:30; Isa 8:10; Mt 15:13 **39** Lk 21:15; 1Co 1:25; Ac 7:51; 9:5; 23:9 **40** Ac 4:18; Mt 10:17; 23:34; Mk 13:9 **41** Mt 5:12; Ro 5:3; 2Co 12:10; Php 1:29; Heb 10:34; Jas 1:2; 1Pe 4:13,16 **42** Ac 2:46; Ac 4:20,29 **CHAPTER 6** **1** Ac 2:41; 4:4; 5:14; ver. 7; Ac 9:29; 11:20; Ac 4:35

widows were being overlooked in the daily serving *of food*.

2 So the Twelve called the disciples together and said, "It is not appropriate for us to neglect [teaching] the word of God in order to serve tables *and* manage the distribution of food.

3 "Therefore, brothers, choose from among you seven men with good reputations [men of godly character and moral integrity], full of the Spirit and of wisdom, whom we may put in charge of this task.

4 "But we will [continue to] devote ourselves [steadfastly] to prayer and to the ministry of the word."

5 The suggestion pleased the whole congregation; and they selected Stephen, a man full of faith [in Christ Jesus], and [filled with and led by] the Holy Spirit, and Philip, Prochorus, Nicanor, Timon, Parmenas, and Nicolas (Nikolaos), a proselyte (Gentile convert) from Antioch.

6 They brought these men before the apostles; and after praying, they laid their hands on them [to dedicate and commission them for this service].

7 And the message of God kept on growing *and* spreading, and the number of disciples continued to increase greatly in Jerusalem; and a large number of the priests were becoming obedient to the faith [accepting Jesus as Messiah and acknowledging Him as the Source of eternal salvation].

8 Now Stephen, full of grace (divine blessing, favor) and power, was doing great wonders and signs (attesting miracles) among the people.

9 However, some men from what was called the Synagogue of the Freedmen (freed Jewish slaves), both Cyrenians and Alexandrians, and some from Cilicia and [the province of] Asia, rose up and questioned *and* argued with Stephen.

10 But they were not able to successfully withstand *and* cope with the wisdom *and* the intelligence [and the power and inspiration] of the Spirit by whom he was speaking.

11 Then [to attack him another way] they secretly instructed men to say, "We have heard this man [Stephen] speak blasphemous (slanderous, sacrilegious, abusive) words against Moses and *against* God."

12 And they provoked *and* incited the people, as well as the elders and the scribes, and they came up to Stephen and seized him and brought him before the Council (Sanhedrin, Jewish High Court).

13 They presented false witnesses who said, "This man never stops speaking against this holy place and the Law [of Moses];

14 for we have heard him say that this Jesus the Nazarene will tear down this place and will change the traditions *and* customs which Moses handed down to us."

15 Then all those who were sitting in the Council, stared [intently] at him, and they saw that Stephen's face was like the face of an angel.

The apostles were conscious that they were indwelt by the Holy Spirit of God, and that their witness depended upon this filling. There is a tremendous lesson here for every believer. No one can be a witness for Christ and a herald of the gospel by individual initiative. Empowerment must come from the Holy Spirit.

6:3 *full of the Spirit and of wisdom.* The men's lives were consistent with their confession of faith. They knew the will of God and understood how to carry it out in their lives (Eph 5:15 – 18). They could be trusted with responsibility and authority.

6:6 *laid their hands on them.* This was not done in order for the men to receive the Holy Spirit, because the seven men were already "full of the Spirit" (vv. 3,5). Instead the apostles were conferring on these men the responsibility of carrying out the ministry. The laying on of hands was a meaningful tradition that dated back to the days of Moses (Nu 27:23); it identified people with the ministries to be performed.

6:8 *full of grace (divine blessing, favor) and power.* Stephen had the gifts, the boldness, and the brilliance to be a powerful witness; yet even his witness would be rejected by the religious leaders. Hearts are opened only by God, not by our gifts, boldness, or brilliance.

2 Ex 18:17 **3** Dt 1:13; Ac 1:21; 16:2; 1Ti 3:7 **4** Ac 2:42 **5** Ac 11:24; Ac 8:5,26; 21:8; Rev 2:6,15 **6** Ac 1:24; 8:17; 9:17; 13:3; 1Ti 4:14; 5:22; 2Ti 1:6 **7** Ac 12:24; 19:20; Col 1:6; Jn 12:42 **10** Lk 21:15; Ac 5:39; See Ex 4:12; Isa 54:17 **11** 1Ki 21:10,13; Mt 26:59,60 **14** Ac 25:8; Da 9:26

Stephen's Defense

7 NOW THE high priest asked [Ste-
phen], "Are these charges true?"
2 And he answered, "Brothers and
fathers, listen to me! The God of glory
[the Shekinah, the radiance of God] ap-
peared to our father Abraham when he
was in Mesopotamia, before he lived in
Haran, [Gen 11:31; 15:7; Ps 29:3]
3 and He said to him, 'LEAVE YOUR
COUNTRY AND YOUR RELATIVES, AND COME
TO THE LAND THAT I WILL SHOW YOU.'
[Gen 12:1]
4 "Then he left the land of the Chal-
deans and settled in Haran. And from
there, after his father died, *God* sent
him to this country in which you now
live. [Gen 11:31; 12:5; 15:7]
5 "But He did not give him inheritable
property, not even enough ground to
take a step on, yet He promised that HE
WOULD GIVE IT TO HIM AS A POSSESSION, AND
TO HIS DESCENDANTS AFTER HIM. [Gen 12:7;
17:8; Deut 2:5]
6 "And this is, in effect, what God
spoke [to him]: That his DESCENDANTS
WOULD BE ALIENS (strangers) IN A FOREIGN
LAND, AND THAT THEY WOULD BE ENSLAVED
AND MISTREATED FOR FOUR HUNDRED YEARS.
7 " 'AND I WILL JUDGE ANY NATION TO
WHOM THEY WILL BE IN BONDAGE,' said
God, 'AND AFTER THAT THEY WILL COME
OUT AND SERVE ME [in worship] IN THIS
PLACE.' [Gen 15:13, 14; Ex 3:12]
8 "And God gave Abraham a cov-
enant [a formal agreement to be strict-
ly observed] of [which] circumcision
[was the sign]; and so [under these cir-
cumstances] Abraham became the fa-
ther of Isaac, and circumcised him on
the eighth day; and Isaac [became the
father] of Jacob, and Jacob [became
the father] of the twelve patriarchs.
[Gen 17:10–14; 21:2–4; 25:26; 29:31–35;
30:1–24; 35:16–26]
9 "The [ten elder] patriarchs, *over-
whelmed* with jealousy, sold [their
younger brother] Joseph into [slav-
ery in] Egypt; but God was with him,
[Gen 37:11, 28; 45:4]
10 and He rescued him from all his
suffering, and gave him favor and
wisdom in the sight of Pharaoh, king
of Egypt, and he made Joseph gov-
ernor over Egypt and over his entire
household. [Gen 39:2, 3, 21; 41:40–46;
Ps 105:21]
11 "Now a famine came over all Egypt
and Canaan, bringing great distress
and our fathers could not find food
[for their households and livestock].
[Gen 41:54, 55; 42:5]
12 "But when Jacob heard that there
was grain in Egypt, he sent our fathers
there the first time. [Gen 42:2]
13 "And on the second *visit* Joseph
identified himself to his brothers, and
Joseph's family *and* background were
revealed to Pharaoh. [Gen 45:1–4]
14 "Then Joseph sent and invited Ja-
cob his father and all his relatives to
come to him, seventy-five persons in
all. [Gen 45:9, 10]
15 "And Jacob (Israel) went down into
Egypt, and there he died, as did our
fathers; [Gen 49:33]
16 and [from Egypt] their bodies were
taken back to Shechem and placed in
the tomb which Abraham had pur-
chased for a sum of money from the
sons of Hamor in Shechem. [Gen 50:13;
Josh 24:32]
17 "But as the time [for the fulfillment]
of the promise which God had made to

7:8 *circumcision.* This covenant and its outward symbol were given to Abraham that he might never forget God's promise to bless him. Abraham was saved by faith in God (Ge 15:6); the symbol of circumcision was an outward sign of the inward reality of his faith. God's blessing was not based on the physical fact of circumcision but on genuine faith.

7:16 *Shechem.* At the time of Stephen's defense, Shechem was the center of Samaritan life. Mount Gerazim, the Samaritan worship center, was located nearby. Stephen's point was not to speak against the temple in Jerusalem, but to point out that God had been speaking and moving in the lives of His people not only in Jerusalem or the temple. The most important address God

CHAPTER 7 **2** Ac 22:1 **3** Ge 12:1 **4** Ge 11:31; 12:4,5 **5** Ge 12:7; 13:15; 15:3,18; 17:8; 26:3 **6** Ge 15:13,16; Ex 12:40; Gal 3:17 **7** Ex 3:12 **8** Ge 17:9-11; 21:2-4; Ge 25:26; Ge 29:31; 30:5; 35:18,23 **9** Ge 37:4,11,28; Ps 105:17; Ge 39:2,21,23 **10** Ge 41:37; 42:6 **11** Ge 41:54 **12** Ge 42:1 **13** Ge 45:4,16 **14** Ge 45:9,27; Ge 46:27; Dt 10:22 **15** Ge 46:5; 49:33; Ex 1:6 **16** Ex 13:19; Jos 24:32; Ge 23:16; 33:19 **17** ver. 6; Ge 15:13; Ex 1:7-9; Ps 105:24,25

Abraham was approaching, the [He-
brew] people increased and multiplied
in Egypt, [Deut 10:22]
18 until [the time when] THERE AROSE
ANOTHER KING OVER EGYPT WHO DID NOT
KNOW JOSEPH [nor his history and the
merit of his service to Egypt]. [Ex 1:7, 8]
19 "He shrewdly exploited our race
and mistreated our fathers, forcing
them to expose their [male] babies so
that they would die. [Ex 1:7–11, 15–22]
20 "It was at this [critical] time that
Moses was born; and he was lovely in
the sight of God, and for three months
he was nourished in his father's house.
[Ex 2:2]
21 "Then when he was set outside [to
die], Pharaoh's daughter rescued him
and claimed him for herself, and cared
for him as her own son. [Ex 2:5, 6, 10]
22 "So Moses was educated in all the
wisdom *and* culture of the Egyptians,
and he was a man of power in words
and deeds.
23 "But when he reached the age of
forty, it came into his heart to visit his
brothers, the sons of Israel.
24 "And when he saw one [of them]
being treated unfairly, he defended
the oppressed man and avenged him
by striking *and* killing the Egyptian.
25 "He expected his countrymen to
understand that God was granting
them freedom through him [assuming
that they would accept him], but they
did not understand.
26 "Then on the next day he sudden-
ly appeared to two of them as they
were fighting, and he tried to reconcile
them, saying, 'Men, you are brothers;
why do you wrong one another?'
27 "But the man who was injuring his
neighbor pushed Moses away, saying,
'WHO APPOINTED YOU RULER AND JUDGE
OVER US?
28 'DO YOU INTEND TO KILL ME AS YOU
KILLED THE EGYPTIAN YESTERDAY?'
29 "At this remark MOSES FLED AND
BECAME AN EXILE IN THE LAND OF MIDIAN,
where he fathered two sons. [Ex 2:11–
15, 22; 18:3, 4]
30 "After forty years had passed, AN
ANGEL APPEARED TO HIM IN THE WILDER-
NESS OF MOUNT SINAI, IN THE FLAME OF A
BURNING THORN BUSH.
31 "When Moses saw it, he was aston-
ished at the sight; but as he went near
to look more closely, the voice of the
Lord came [to him, saying]:
32 'I AM THE GOD OF YOUR FATHERS, THE
GOD OF ABRAHAM AND OF ISAAC AND OF
JACOB.' Moses trembled with fear and
did not dare to look.
33 "THEN THE LORD SAID TO HIM, 'RE-
MOVE THE SANDALS FROM YOUR FEET, FOR
THE PLACE WHERE YOU ARE STANDING IS
HOLY GROUND [worthy of reverence and
respect].
34 'I HAVE MOST CERTAINLY SEEN THE OP-
PRESSION OF MY PEOPLE IN EGYPT AND HAVE
HEARD THEIR GROANING, AND I HAVE COME
DOWN TO RESCUE THEM. NOW COME, AND I
WILL SEND YOU TO EGYPT [as My messen-
ger].' [Ex 3:1–10]
35 "This Moses whom they rejected,
saying, 'WHO MADE YOU A RULER AND A
JUDGE?' is the very one whom God sent
to be both a ruler and a deliverer, with
the [protecting and helping] hand of
the Angel who appeared to him in the
thorn bush. [Ex 2:14]
36 "This man led them out [of Egypt]
after performing wonders and signs in
the land of Egypt and at the Red Sea
and in the wilderness for forty years.
[Ex 7:3; 14:21; Num 14:33]

---

made to His people was at Mount Sinai, which is nowhere near Jerusalem.

7:19 Persecution — Pharaoh enslaved and mistreated the Hebrews, and at the same time he feared their strength. It was his fear that led him to seek their destruction, persecuting them and destroying their children. It is easy to recognize the enormity and evil of the Egyptian persecution of the Jews as a race and a nation, but the ancient Egyptians are not the only ones guilty of such sin. Some of those claiming the name of Christ in recent times have been guilty of mistreating or even enslaving those of different ethnic background. Feelings of racial superiority have no place in the heart of a Christian.

19 Ex 1:22 **20** Ex 2:2; Heb 11:23 **21** Ex 2:3-10 **22** Lk 24:19 **23** Ex 2:11,12 **27** See Lk 12:14; Ac 4:7 **29** Ex 2:15,22; 4:20; 18:3,4 **30** Ex 3:2 **32** Mt 22:32; Heb 11:16 **33** Ex 3:5; Jos 5:15 **34** Ex 3:7 **35** Ex 14:19; Nu 20:16 **36** Ex 12:41; 33:1; Ex 7; 8; 9; 10; Ps 105:27; Ex 14:21; Ex 16:1

37 "This is the Moses who said to the children of Israel, 'GOD WILL RAISE UP FOR YOU A PROPHET LIKE ME FROM YOUR COUNTRYMEN.' [Deut 18:15, 18]

38 "This is the one who was in the congregation in the wilderness together with the Angel who spoke to him on Mount Sinai, and *who was* with our fathers; and he received living oracles [divine words that still live] to be handed down to you. [Ex 19]

39 "Our fathers were unwilling to be subject to him [and refused to listen to him]. They rejected him, and in their hearts turned back to Egypt. [Num 14:3, 4]

40 "THEY SAID TO AARON, 'MAKE FOR US GODS WHO WILL GO BEFORE US; FOR THIS MOSES WHO LED US OUT OF THE LAND OF EGYPT, WE DO NOT KNOW WHAT HAS HAPPENED TO HIM.' [Ex 32:1, 23]

41 "In those days they made a calf and brought a sacrifice to the idol, and rejoiced *and* celebrated over the works of their hands. [Ex 32:4, 6]

42 "But God turned away [from them] and handed them over to serve the host of heaven. As it is written *and* forever remains written in the book of the prophets, 'IT WAS NOT [really] TO ME THAT YOU OFFERED VICTIMS AND SACRIFICES FOR FORTY YEARS IN THE WILDERNESS, WAS IT, O HOUSE OF ISRAEL? [Jer 19:13]

43 'YOU ALSO TOOK ALONG THE TABERNACLE (portable temple) OF MOLOCH AND THE STAR OF THE GOD ROMPHA, THE IMAGES WHICH YOU MADE TO WORSHIP; AND I WILL REMOVE YOU BEYOND BABYLON [carrying you away into exile].' [Amos 5:25–27]

44 "Our fathers had the tabernacle of testimony in the wilderness, just as God directed Moses to make it according to the pattern which he had seen. [Ex 25:9–40]

45 "Our fathers also brought it in [with them into the land] with Joshua when they dispossessed the nations whom God drove out before our fathers, [and so it remained here] until the time of David, [Deut 32:49; Josh 3:14–17]

46 who found favor (grace, spiritual blessing) in the sight of God and asked that he might [be allowed to] find a dwelling place for the God of Jacob. [2 Sam 7:8–16; Ps 132:1–5]

47 "But it was Solomon who built a house for Him. [1 Kin 6]

48 "However, the Most High [the One infinitely exalted above humanity] does not dwell in *houses* made by human hands; as the prophet [Isaiah] says, [1 Kin 8:27]

49 'HEAVEN IS MY THRONE,
AND THE EARTH IS THE FOOTSTOOL FOR MY FEET;
WHAT KIND OF HOUSE WILL YOU BUILD FOR ME?' says the Lord,
'OR WHAT PLACE IS THERE FOR MY REST?
50 'WAS IT NOT MY HAND THAT MADE ALL THESE THINGS?' [Is 66:1, 2]

51 "You stiff-necked *and* stubborn people, uncircumcised in heart and

---

7:38 The Meaning of the Church — In modern English the word *church* is used five ways: (1) a building designated as a place of worship; (2) all who profess faith in Christ; (3) a denomination; (4) a single organized local church; and (5) the body of Christ, that is, the universal church. While all of these may be legitimate uses for modern English, the word *church* is used in the New Testament in only the last two senses — a local congregation or the body of Christ, the universal church. At its root, the word *church* means a "called-out group." It is used for the nation of Israel (Ac 7:38), which was a group of people who were called out of the rest of the world to have a special national relationship to God. It is used for a local church (1Th 1:1; Rev 2:1) and for the universal church, the body of Christ (Col 1:18). The universal church comprises all believers from the Day of Pentecost until God completes His plan for the world. The local church is a local, visible, temporal manifestation of the universal church.

7:44 *tabernacle*. The ancient tabernacle had been the focus of the Israelites' national worship. Even after the miraculous deliverance from Egypt there was a tendency among the people to forget God. The tabernacle was a constant testimony of God's presence no matter where the people went. Paul tells us that we are the tabernacle, the temple

37 Dt 18:15; Mt 17:5 **38** Ex 19:3; Isa 63:9; Gal 3:19; Heb 2:2; Ex 21:1; Dt 5:27; Jn 1:17; Ro 3:2 **40** Ex 32:1 **41** Dt 9:16; Ps 106:19 **42** Ps 81:12; 2Th 2:11; Dt 4:19; 2Ki 21:3; Am 5:25 **44** Ex 25:40; Heb 8:5 **45** Jos 3:14; Neh 9:24; Ps 44:2 **46** 2Sa 7:1; Ps 89:19; 1Ch 22:7 **47** 1Ki 8:20 **48** 1Ki 8:27; 2Ch 2:6 **49** Isa 66:1,2; Mt 5:34 **51** Ex 32:9; Lev 26:41; Dt 10:16; Jer 4:4

ears, you are always actively resisting
the Holy Spirit. You are doing just as
your fathers did. [Ex 33:3, 5; Num 27:14;
Is 63:10; Jer 6:10; 9:26]
52"Which one of the prophets did
your fathers not persecute? They killed
those who proclaimed beforehand the
coming of the Righteous One, whose
betrayers and murderers you have now
become;
53you who received the law as ordained *and* delivered to you by angels,
and yet you did not obey it!"

Stephen Put to Death

54Now when they heard this [accusation and understood its implication],
they were cut to the heart, and they
began grinding their teeth [in rage]
at him.
55But he, being full of the Holy Spirit
and led by Him, gazed into heaven and
saw the glory [the great splendor and
majesty] of God, and Jesus standing
at the right hand of God;
56and he said, "Look! I see the heavens opened up [in welcome] and the
Son of Man standing at the right hand
of God!"
57But they shouted with loud voices,
and covered their ears and together
rushed at him [considering him guilty
of blasphemy].
58Then they drove him out of the
city and *began* stoning him; and the
witnesses placed their outer robes at
the feet of a young man named Saul.
[Acts 22:20]
59They continued stoning Stephen as
he called on *the Lord* and said, "Lord
Jesus, receive *and* accept *and* welcome
my spirit!"
60Then falling on his knees [in worship], he cried out loudly, "Lord, do
not hold this sin against them [do not
charge them]!" When he had said this,
he fell asleep [in death].

Saul Persecutes the Church

8 SAUL WHOLEHEARTEDLY approved of Stephen's death.
And on that day a great *and* relentless persecution broke out against the
church in Jerusalem; and the believers
were all scattered throughout the regions of Judea and Samaria, except
for the apostles.
2Some devout men buried Stephen,
and mourned greatly over him [expressing a personal sense of loss].
3But Saul *began* ravaging the church
[and assaulting believers]; entering
house after house and dragging off
men and women, putting them in prison.

Philip in Samaria

4Now those [believers] who had been
scattered went from place to place
preaching the word [the good news of
salvation through Christ].
5Philip [the evangelist] went down
to the city of Samaria and *began*
proclaiming Christ (the Messiah, the
Anointed) to them. [Acts 6:5]
6The crowds gathered and were paying close attention to everything Philip
said, as they heard [the message] and

---

of God (1Co 3:16). We can never move beyond God's reach, for we carry His presence with us.

7:58 *drove him out of the city.* Because Jewish law did not allow an execution within the walls of the holy city, the religious leaders took Stephen outside the city. Jerusalem is situated in a stony area and this made Stephen's hasty (and illegal) execution easy. His executioners had plenty of rocks at hand, they only had to bend over and pick them up (see Jn 10:31).

7:59–60 Death — Scripture affirms, and experience confirms, the universality of death. It comes to kings and commoners, saints and sinners alike. Christians die, as well as unbelievers. No one likes to think of dying violently, but Stephen's death shows that even this end can be met with courage and peace. In both life and death Stephen sought to imitate his Lord, and he departed without resentment, praying for the pardon of his foes.

8:5 *Samaria.* In the first century, the Jews and Samaritans hated one another. The Jews considered the Samaritans half-breeds and religious deviants. Following the fall of the Northern Kingdom of Israel in 722 BC, Samaria had been

---

52 2Ch 36:16; Mt 21:35; 1Th 2:15; Ac 3:14 **53** Ex 20:1; Gal 3:19 **54** Ac 5:33 **55** Ac 6:5 **56** Mt 3:16; Da 7:13 **58** Lk 4:29; Heb 13:12; Lev 24:16; Dt 13:9 **59** Ac 9:14; Ps 31:5; Lk 23:46 **60** Ac 9:40; Mt 5:44; Lk 6:28 **CHAPTER 8** **1** Ac 7:58; Ac 11:19 **2** Ge 23:2; 50:10; 2Sa 3:31 **3** Ac 7:58; 1Co 15:9; Gal 1:13; Php 3:6; 1Ti 1:13 **4** Mt 10:23 **5** Ac 6:5

saw the [miraculous] signs which he was doing [validating his message].
[7]For unclean spirits (demons), shouting loudly, were coming out of many who were possessed; and many who had been paralyzed and lame were healed.
[8]So there was great rejoicing in that city.
[9]Now there was a man named Simon, who previously practiced magic in the city and amazed the people of Samaria, claiming to be someone great.
[10]They all paid [a great deal of] attention to him, from the least to the greatest, saying, "This man is what is called the Great Power of God!"
[11]They were paying attention to him because for a long time he had mystified *and* dazzled them with his magic.
[12]But when they believed Philip as he preached the good news about the kingdom of God and the name of Jesus Christ, they were being baptized, both men and women.
[13]Even Simon believed [Philip's message of salvation]; and after being baptized, he continued on with Philip, and as he watched the *attesting* signs and great miracles taking place, he was constantly amazed.
[14]When the apostles in Jerusalem heard that [the people of] Samaria had accepted the word of God, they sent Peter and John to them.
[15]They came down and prayed for them that they might receive the Holy Spirit;
[16]for He had not yet fallen on any of them; they had simply been baptized in the name of the Lord Jesus [as His possession].
[17]Then Peter and John laid their hands on them [one by one], and they received the Holy Spirit.
[18]Now when Simon saw that the Spirit was given through the laying on of the apostles' hands, he offered them money,
[19]saying, "Give me this authority *and* power too, so that anyone on whom I lay my hands may receive the Holy Spirit."
[20]But Peter said to him, "May your money be destroyed along with you, because you thought you could buy the [free] gift of God with money!
[21]"You have no part or share in this matter, because your heart (motive, purpose) is not right before God. [Ps 78:37]
[22]"So repent of this wickedness of yours, and pray to the Lord that, if possible, this thought of your heart may be forgiven you.
[23]"For I see that you are provoked by bitterness and bound by sin." [Deut 29:18; Is 58:6]
[24]But Simon answered, "Pray to the Lord for me both of you, so that nothing of what you have said will come upon me."

An Ethiopian Receives Christ

[25]So, when Peter and John had given their testimony and preached the word of the Lord, they started back to Jerusalem, preaching the good news [about salvation] in many Samaritan villages [along the way].
[26]But an angel of the Lord said to

---

resettled by colonists brought to the land by the Assyrians. These colonists intermarried with the remaining Jews, and the Samaritans of the New Testament era were descendants of these mixed marriages. Because of their mixed heritage and their rejection of the temple in Jerusalem and most of the Old Testament Scriptures (the Samaritans only accepted the five books of Moses), the Jews considered them to be unclean. The amazing work of the Holy Spirit in forming one fellowship out of Jewish and Samaritan believers indicates that there is no room for racial or ethnic division in His church (Gal 3:26–28).

8:14–15 *that they might receive the Holy Spirit*. This episode clearly showed the Samaritans that salvation did come through the Jews, and that the Scriptures they had previously rejected were actually God's message. It also showed the Jewish believers that God had accepted the Samaritan believers fully into His family. The dependence of the Samaritans upon the Jews to receive the gift of the Holy Spirit

7 Mk 16:17 **9** Ac 13:6; Ac 5:36 **12** Ac 1:3 **15** Ac 2:38 **16** Ac 19:2; Mt 28:19; Ac 2:38; Ac 10:48; 19:5 **17** Ac 6:6; 19:6; Heb 6:2 **20** Mt 10:8; See 2Ki 5:16; Ac 2:38; 10:45; 11:17 **22** Da 4:27; 2Ti 2:25 **23** Heb 12:15 **24** Ge 20:7,17; Ex 8:8; Nu 21:7; 1Ki 13:6; Job 42:8; Jas 5:16

Philip, "Get up and go south to the road that runs from Jerusalem down to Gaza." (This is a desert road).
27So he got up and went; and there was an Ethiopian eunuch [a man of great authority], a court official of Candace, queen of the Ethiopians, who was in charge of all her treasure. He had come to Jerusalem to worship,
28and he was returning, and sitting in his chariot he was reading [the scroll of] the prophet Isaiah.
29Then the [Holy] Spirit said to Philip, "Go up and join this chariot."
30Philip ran up and heard the man reading the prophet Isaiah, and asked, "Do you understand what you are reading?"
31And he said, "Well, how could I [understand] unless someone guides me [correctly]?" And he invited Philip to come up and sit with him.
32Now this was the passage of Scripture which he was reading:

"LIKE A SHEEP HE WAS LED TO THE SLAUGHTER;
AND AS A LAMB BEFORE ITS SHEARER IS SILENT,
SO HE DOES NOT OPEN HIS MOUTH.
33"IN HUMILIATION HIS JUDGMENT WAS TAKEN AWAY [justice was denied Him].
WHO WILL DESCRIBE HIS GENERATION?
FOR HIS LIFE IS TAKEN FROM THE EARTH." [Is 53:7, 8]

34The eunuch replied to Philip, "Please *tell me*, about whom does the prophet say this? About himself or about someone else?"
35Then Philip spoke and beginning with this Scripture he preached Jesus to him [explaining that He is the promised Messiah and the source of salvation].
36As they continued along the road, they came to some water; and the eunuch exclaimed, "Look! Water! What forbids me from being baptized?"
37[Philip said to him, "If you believe with all your heart, you may." And he replied, "I do believe that Jesus Christ is the Son of God."]
38And he ordered that the chariot be stopped; and both Philip and the eunuch went down into the water, and Philip baptized him.
39When they came up out of the water, the Spirit of the Lord [suddenly] took Philip [and carried him] away [to a different place]; and the eunuch no longer saw him, but he went on his way rejoicing.
40But Philip found himself at Azotus, and as he passed through he preached the good news [of salvation] to all the cities, until he came to Caesarea [Maritima].

The Conversion of Saul

9 NOW SAUL, still breathing threats and murder against the disciples of the Lord [and relentless in his search for believers], went to the high priest,
2and he asked for letters [of authority] from him to the synagogues at

---

was the healing sign that the two sides were to become one.

8:27 *had come to Jerusalem to worship.* Many Gentiles in the first century had grown weary of the multiple gods and loose morals of their own cultures. In their search for something more, some of them came to Judaism. One who accepted Judaism, obeying all the law of Moses (including circumcision and baptism), was called a *proselyte*. Gentiles who did not become proselytes but did attend the Jewish synagogues to listen to the Scriptures were called *God-fearers*. We cannot be sure which category the Ethiopian eunuch fell into.

8:35 *preached Jesus to him.* First-century Jews did not speak much about a suffering Messiah. The Jewish people, facing the yoke of Roman rule, believed that the Messiah would come as the Lion of Judah, a delivering king, not a weak lamb. They believed and taught that the suffering One spoken of by Isaiah was the suffering nation of Israel. Philip's explanation of the passage gave a very different view, showing Jesus as the Messiah who came to suffer and die in order to redeem sinners.

9:2 *synagogues.* The early Jewish believers in Jesus were still attending the synagogues, gathering places where Jews came together to hear the Scriptures read and expounded upon. Part of Saul's mission was apparently to let the

27 Zep 3:10; Jn 12:20 **32** Isa 53:7,8 **35** Lk 24:27; Ac 18:28 **36** Ac 10:47 **37** Mt 28:19; Mk 16:16; Mt 16:16; Jn 6:69; 9:35,38; 11:27; Ac 9:20; 1Jn 4:15; 5:5,13 **39** 1Ki 18:12; 2Ki 2:16; Eze 3:12,14 **CHAPTER 9** **1** Ac 8:3; Gal 1:13; 1Ti 1:13

Damascus, so that if he found any men
or women there belonging to the Way
[believers, followers of Jesus the Mes-
siah], men and women alike, he could
arrest them *and* bring them bound
[with chains] to Jerusalem.
3 As he traveled he approached Da-
mascus, and suddenly a light from
heaven flashed around him [displaying
the glory and majesty of Christ];
4 and he fell to the ground and heard
a voice [from heaven] saying to him,
"Saul, Saul, why are you persecuting
and oppressing Me?"
5 And Saul said, "Who are You,
Lord?" And He *answered*, "I am Jesus
whom you are persecuting,
6 now get up and go into the city, and
you will be told what you must do."
7 The men who were traveling with
him [were terrified and] stood speech-
less, hearing the voice but seeing no one.
8 Saul got up from the ground, but
though his eyes were open, he could
see nothing; so they led him by the
hand and brought him into Damascus.
9 And he was unable to see for three
days, and he neither ate nor drank.
10 Now in Damascus there was a dis-
ciple named Ananias; and the Lord
said to him in a vision, "Ananias." And
he answered, "Here I am, Lord."
11 And the Lord said to him, "Get up
and go to the street called Straight,
and ask at the house of Judas for a
man from Tarsus named Saul; for he
is praying [there],
12 and in a vision he has seen a man
named Ananias come in and place his
hands on him, so that he may regain
his sight."
13 But Ananias answered, "Lord, I
have heard from many people about
this man, especially how much suffer-
ing *and* evil he has brought on Your
saints (God's people) at Jerusalem;
14 and here [in Damascus] he has
authority from the high priests to put
in chains all who call on Your name
[confessing You as Savior]."
15 But the Lord said to him, "Go, for
this man is a [deliberately] chosen in-
strument of Mine, to bear My name
before the Gentiles and kings and the
sons of Israel;
16 for I will make clear to him how
much he must suffer *and* endure for
My name's sake."
17 So Ananias left and entered the
house, and he laid his hands on Saul
and said, "Brother Saul, the Lord
Jesus, who appeared to you on the
road as you came [to Damascus], has
sent me so that you may regain your
sight and be filled with the Holy Spirit
[in order to proclaim Christ to both
Jews and Gentiles]."
18 Immediately something like scales
fell from Saul's eyes, and he regained his
sight. Then he got up and was baptized;
19 and he took some food and was
strengthened.

Saul Begins to Preach Christ

For several days [afterward] Saul
remained with the disciples who were
at Damascus.
20 And immediately he *began* pro-
claiming Jesus in the synagogues, say-
ing, "This Man is the Son of God [the
promised Messiah]!"
21 All those who heard him continued
to be amazed and said, "Is this not the

Damascus synagogues know beyond any doubt that the followers of "The Way" did not have the approval of the Sanhedrin.

9:4–5 Messiah — Apparently unimpressed by the witness of the dying Stephen (7:59), Saul needed a more serious, personal jolt to awaken his spiritual awareness. The light that blinded Saul prepared him to receive the True Light that came into the world to dispel the darkness of sin. This personal encounter with the risen Christ changed Saul from a fire-breathing persecutor into a dynamic preacher who was not ashamed to publicly claim the crucified Man from Galilee as his Lord and Savior.

9:17 *Jesus, who appeared to you.* Saul was not dreaming on the road to Damascus but instead had seen the resurrected Lord.

---

3 Ac 22:6; 26:12; 1Co 15:8 **4** Mt 25:40 **6** Lk 3:10; ch 2:37; 16:30 **7** Da 10:7; See Ac 22:9; 26:13 **10** Ac 22:12 **11** Ac 21:39; 22:3 **13** ver. 1 **14** ver. 21; Ac 7:59; 1Co 1:2; 2Ti 2:22 **15** Ac 13:2; 22:21; Ro 1:1; 1Co 15:10; Gal 1:15; Eph 3:7,8; 1Ti 2:7; 2Ti 1:11; Ro 1:5; 11:13; Gal 2:7,8; Ac 25:22,23; 26:1 **16** Ac 20:23; 21:11; 2Co 11:23 **17** Ac 22:12,13; Ac 8:17; Ac 2:4; 4:31; 8:17; 13:52 **19** Ac 26:20 **21** ver. 1; Ac 8:3; Gal 1:13,23

THE LIFE OF PAUL

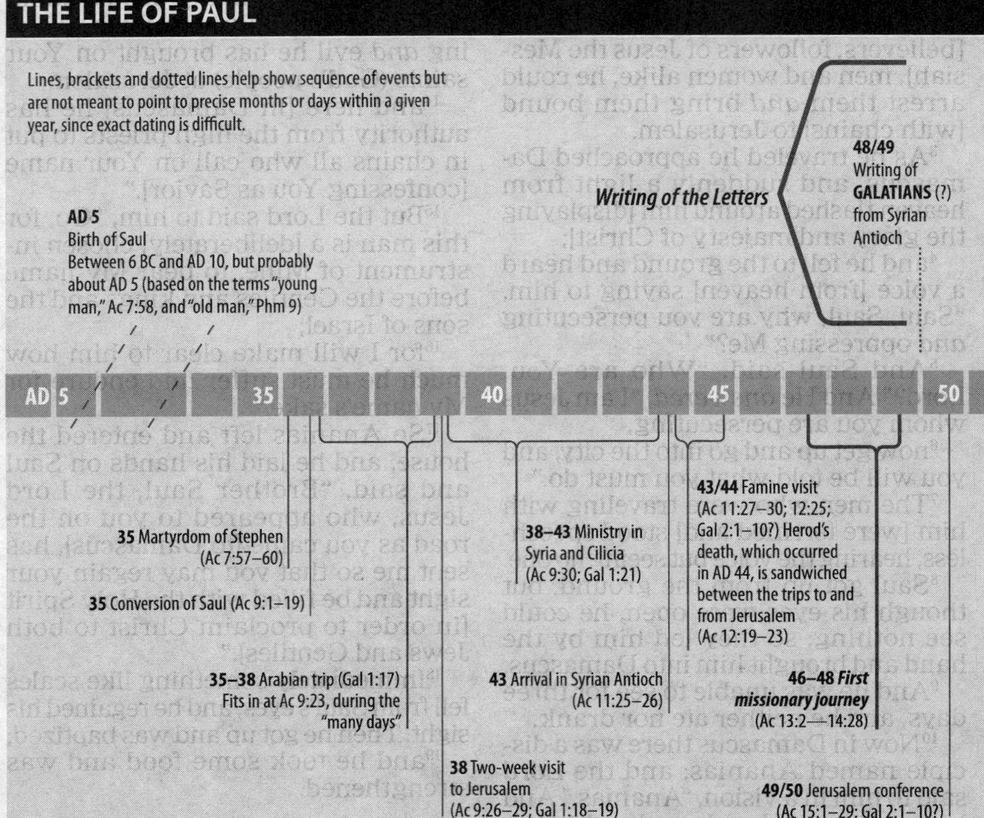

man who in Jerusalem attacked those
who called on this name [of Jesus],
and had come here [to Damascus] for
the express purpose of bringing them
bound [with chains] before the chief
priests?"
22But Saul increased in strength
more and more, and continued to perplex the Jews who lived in Damascus
by examining [theological evidence]
and proving [with Scripture] that this
Jesus is the Christ (the Messiah, the
Anointed).
23After considerable time had passed
[about three years or so], the Jews plotted together to kill him,
24but their plot became known to Saul.
They were also watching the city's gates
day and night so they could kill him;
25but his disciples took him at night
and let him down through *an opening*
in the wall, lowering him in a large
basket.
26When he arrived in Jerusalem, he
tried to join the disciples; but they were
all afraid of him, not believing that he
really was a disciple.
27However, Barnabas took him and
brought him to the apostles, and described to them how Saul had seen
the Lord on the road [to Damascus],
and how He had spoken to him, and
how at Damascus Saul had preached
openly *and* spoken confidently in the
name of Jesus.
28So he was with them, moving
around freely [as one among them] in
Jerusalem, speaking out boldly in the
name of the Lord.
29He was talking and arguing with

22 Ac 18:28 **23** Ac 23:12; 2Co 11:26 **24** 2Co 11:32 **25** Jos 2:15; 1Sa 19:12 **26** Ac 22:17; Gal 1:17,18 **27** Ac 4:36; 13:2; ver. 20,22 **28** Gal 1:18 **29** Ac 6:1; 11:20; ver. 23; 2Co 11:26

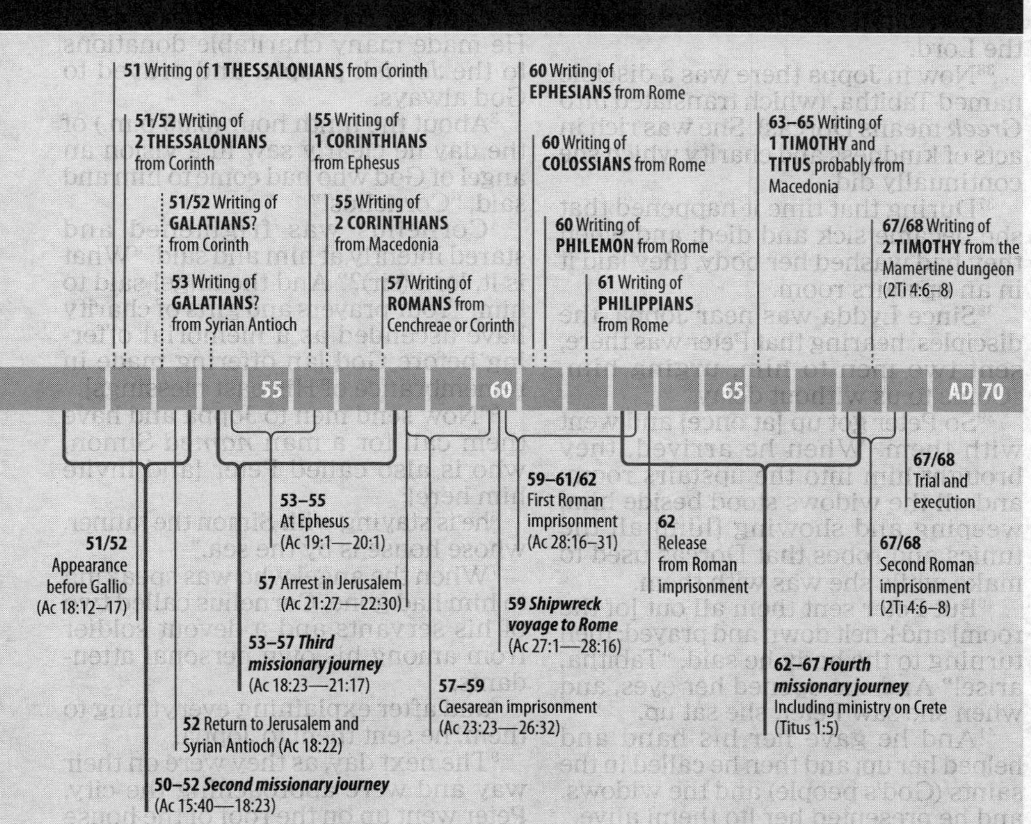

the Hellenists (Greek-speaking Jews); but they were attempting to kill him.
30When the brothers found out [about the plot], they brought him down to Caesarea [Maritima] and sent him off to Tarsus [his home town].
31So the church throughout Judea and Galilee and Samaria enjoyed peace [without persecution], being built up [in wisdom, virtue, and faith]; and walking in the fear of the Lord and in the comfort *and* encouragement of the Holy Spirit, it continued to grow [in numbers].

Peter's Ministry

32Now as Peter was traveling throughout *the land,* he went down to [visit] the saints (God's people) who lived at Lydda.
33There he found a man named Aeneas, who had been bedridden for eight years and was paralyzed.
34Peter said to him, "Aeneas, Jesus Christ heals you. Get up and make your bed." Immediately Aeneas got up.
35Then all who lived at Lydda and

9:30 *Tarsus.* Saul's hometown was about three hundred miles north of Jerusalem and about ten miles inland from the Mediterranean Sea. Tarsus was a well known university city, surpassed in educational opportunities only by Athens and Alexandria.

9:31 *peace.* This rest was not due solely to Saul's conversion. Tiberius, the emperor of Rome, died around this time. He was replaced by Caligula, who wanted to erect a statue of himself in the temple at Jerusalem. The attention of the Jewish religious leaders was directed towards this new threat, and the emerging church was given a short season of respite.

31 See Ac 8:1 **32** Ac 8:14 **34** Ac 3:6,16; 4:10 **35** 1Ch 5:16; Ac 11:21

the plain of Sharon saw [what had happened to] him, and they turned to the Lord.
36 Now in Joppa there was a disciple named Tabitha, (which translated *into Greek* means Dorcas). She was rich in acts of kindness and charity which she continually did.
37 During that time it happened that she became sick and died; and when they had washed her body, they laid it in an upstairs room.
38 Since Lydda was near Joppa, the disciples, hearing that Peter was there, sent two men to him, urging him, "Come to us without delay."
39 So Peter got up [at once] and went with them. When he arrived, they brought him into the upstairs room; and all the widows stood beside him, weeping and showing [him] all the tunics and robes that Dorcas used to make while she was with them.
40 But Peter sent them all out [of the room] and knelt down and prayed; then turning to the body he said, "Tabitha, arise!" And she opened her eyes, and when she saw Peter, she sat up.
41 And he gave her his hand and helped her up; and then he called in the saints (God's people) and the widows, and he presented her [to them] alive.
42 This became known all over Joppa, and many came to believe in the Lord [that is, to adhere to and trust in and rely on Jesus as Christ and Savior].
43 And so it was that Peter stayed in Joppa for many days with Simon, a tanner.

Cornelius' Vision

10 NOW AT Caesarea [Maritima] *there was* a man named Cornelius, a centurion of what was known as the Italian Regiment,
2 a devout man and one who, along with all his household, feared God. He made many charitable donations to the *Jewish* people, and prayed to God always.
3 About the ninth hour (3:00 p.m.) of the day he clearly saw in a vision an angel of God who had come to him and said, "Cornelius!"
4 Cornelius was frightened and stared intently at him and said, "What is it, lord (sir)?" And the angel said to him, "Your prayers and gifts of charity have ascended as a memorial offering before God [an offering made in remembrance of His past blessings].
5 "Now send men to Joppa and have them call for a man *named* Simon, who is also called Peter [and invite him here];
6 he is staying with Simon the tanner, whose house is by the sea."
7 When the angel who was speaking to him had gone, Cornelius called two of his servants and a devout soldier from among his own personal attendants;
8 and after explaining everything to them, he sent them to Joppa.
9 The next day, as they were on their way and were approaching the city, Peter went up on the roof of the house about the sixth hour (noon) to pray,
10 but he became hungry and wanted something to eat. While the meal was being prepared he fell into a trance;
11 and he saw the sky opened up, and an object like a great sheet descending, lowered by its four corners to the earth,
12 and it contained all *kinds of* four-footed animals and crawling creatures of the earth and birds of the air.
13 A voice came to him, "Get up, Peter, kill and eat!"
14 But Peter said, "Not at all, Lord,

10:1 – 11:18 The following two chapters mark an important turning point in the Book of Acts. Those who were scattered by persecution from Jerusalem had been preaching the gospel only to Jews (11:19). At this point, they began to overcome their prejudices and carry the message of Christ to the Gentiles.

10:6 Simon the tanner. God cut away Peter's prejudices by having him stay for many days with one whose trade Peter likely considered repulsive. Since a tanner (one who makes leather) is constantly working with animals dead from various causes, he would spend much of his life "ceremonially unclean."

36 1Ti 2:10; Titus 3:8 **37** Ac 1:13 **40** Mt 9:25; Ac 7:60; Mk 5:41,42; Jn 11:43 **42** Jn 11:45 **43** Ac 10:6
CHAPTER 10 **2** ver. 22; Ac 8:2; 22:12; ver. 35 **3** ver. 30; Ac 11:13 **6** Ac 9:43; Ac 11:14 **9** Ac 11:5 **11** Ac 7:56; Rev 19:11 **14** Lev 11:4; 20:25; Dt 14:3,7; Eze 4:14

for I have never eaten anything that is common (unholy) and [ceremonially] unclean."

[15]And the voice came to him a second time, "What God has cleansed *and* pronounced clean, no longer consider common (unholy)."

[16]This happened three times, and then immediately the object was taken up into heaven.

[17]Now Peter was still perplexed *and* completely at a loss as to what his vision could mean when the men who had been sent by Cornelius, having asked directions to Simon's house, arrived at the gate.

[18]And they called out to ask whether Simon, who was also called Peter, was staying there.

[19]While Peter was thoughtfully considering the vision, the Spirit said to him, "Now listen, three men are looking for you.

[20]"Get up, go downstairs and go with them without hesitating *or* doubting, because I have sent them Myself."

[21]Peter went down to the men and said, "I am the one you are looking for. For what reason have you come?"

[22]They said, "Cornelius, a centurion, an upright and God-fearing man well spoken of by all the Jewish people, was *divinely* instructed by a holy angel to send for you *to come* to his house and hear what you have to say."

[23]So Peter invited them in and gave them lodging [for the night].

Peter at Caesarea

The next day Peter got up and left with them, and some of the brothers from Joppa went with him.

[24]On the following day he [and the others] entered Caesarea. Cornelius was waiting for them, and had called together his relatives and close friends.

[25]When Peter arrived, Cornelius met him, and fell down at his feet and worshiped *him*.

[26]But Peter raised him up, saying, "Stand up; I too am only a man."

[27]As Peter talked with him, he entered [the house] and found a large group of people assembled.

[28]He said to them, "You know that it is unlawful for a Jewish man to associate with *or* befriend a Gentile, or to visit him; and yet God has shown me that I am not to call anyone common or [ceremonially] unclean.

[29]"Therefore when I was sent for, I came without raising an objection. So I ask for what reason have you sent for me?"

[30]Cornelius said, "Four days ago to this hour, I was praying in my house during the ninth hour (3:00–4:00 p.m.); and a man [dressed] in bright, dazzling clothing suddenly stood before me,

[31]and he said, 'Cornelius, your prayer has been heard, and your acts of charity have been remembered before God [so that He is about to help you].

[32]'Therefore send *word* to Joppa and invite Simon, who is also called Peter, to come to you. He is staying at the house of Simon the tanner by the sea.'

[33]"So I sent for you at once, and you have been kind enough to come. Now then, we are all here present before God to listen to everything that you have been instructed by the Lord [to say]."

Gentiles Hear Good News

[34]Opening his mouth, Peter said: "Most certainly I understand now that God is not one to show partiality [to people as though Gentiles were excluded from God's blessing],

[35]but in every nation the person who fears God and does what is right [by seeking Him] is acceptable *and* welcomed by Him.

10:15 *What God has cleansed and pronounced clean, no longer consider common.* Food may have been his first consideration, but Peter would soon understand the greater message. The vision was a sign from heaven that Jews were no longer to call Gentiles unclean.

---

15 ver. 28; Mt 15:11; Ro 14:14,17,20; 1Co 10:25; 1Ti 4:4; Titus 1:15 **19** Ac 11:12 **20** Ac 15:7 **22** Ac 22:12 **23** Ac 11:12 **26** Ac 14:14 **28** Jn 4:9; 18:28; Ac 11:3; Gal 2:12; Ac 15:8,9; Eph 3:6 **30** Ac 1:10; Mt 28:3; Mk 16:5; Lk 24:4 **31** Da 10:12; Heb 6:10 **34** Dt 10:17; 2Ch 19:7; Job 34:19; Ro 2:11; Gal 2:6; Eph 6:9; Col 3:25; 1Pe 1:17 **35** Ac 15:9; Ro 2:13; 3:22; 10:12,13; 1Co 12:13; Gal 3:28; Eph 2:13

36“You know the message which He sent to the sons of Israel, announcing the good news of peace through Jesus Christ, who is Lord of all—

37you know the things that have taken place throughout Judea, starting in Galilee after the baptism preached by John—

38how God anointed Jesus of Nazareth with the Holy Spirit and with great power; and He went around doing good and healing all who were oppressed by the devil, because God was with Him. [Is 61:1–3; Luke 4:18–21]

39“We are [personally] eyewitnesses of everything that He did both in the land of the Jews and in Jerusalem [in particular]. They also put Him to death by hanging Him on a cross;

40God raised Him [to life] on the third day and caused Him to be plainly seen,

41not to all the people, but to witnesses who were chosen *and* designated beforehand by God, *that is*, to us who ate and drank together with Him after He rose from the dead. [Luke 24:42, 43; John 21:12–15]

42“He commanded us to preach to the people [both Jew and Gentile], and to solemnly testify that He is the One who has been appointed *and* ordained by God as Judge of the living and the dead.

43“All the prophets testify about Him, that through His name everyone who believes in Him [whoever trusts in and relies on Him, accepting Him as Savior and Messiah] receives forgiveness of sins.”

44While Peter was still speaking these words, the Holy Spirit fell on all those who were listening to the message [confirming God’s acceptance of Gentiles].

45All the circumcised believers who came with Peter were amazed, because the gift of the Holy Spirit had been poured out even on the Gentiles.

46For they heard them talking in [unknown] tongues (languages) and exalting *and* magnifying *and* praising God. Then Peter said,

47“Can anyone refuse water for these people to be baptized, since they have received the Holy Spirit just as we did?”

48And he ordered that they be baptized in the name of Jesus Christ. Then they asked him to stay there for a few days.

Peter Reports at Jerusalem

11 NOW THE apostles and the believers who were throughout Judea heard [with astonishment] that the Gentiles also had received *and* accepted the word of God [the message concerning salvation through Christ].

2So when Peter went up to Jerusalem, those of the circumcision [certain Jewish believers who followed the Law] took issue with him [for violating Jewish customs],

3saying, “You went to uncircumcised men and [even] ate with them!”

4But Peter began [at the beginning] and explained [the events] to them step by step, saying,

5“I was in the city of Joppa praying; and in a trance I saw a vision of an object coming down from heaven, like a huge sheet being lowered by the four corners; and [it descended until] it came right down to me,

6and looking closely at it, I saw *all kinds of* the four-footed animals of the earth and the wild beasts and the crawling creatures and the birds of the air [both clean and unclean according to the Law],

7and I also heard a voice saying to me, ‘Get up, Peter; kill and eat.’

8“But I said, ‘Not at all, Lord; for

10:44 ***the Holy Spirit fell on all those who were listening to the message.*** Following the plan laid out by Jesus before His ascension (1:8), the good news had reached the Jews, the Samaritans, and now the Gentiles. All were united by the same faith in the same Lord with the same gift of the Holy Spirit.

11:2 ***those of the circumcision.*** This term refers to Jewish believers in Jesus who taught that Gentiles had to become Jews (be circumcised

36 Isa 57:19; Eph 2:14; Col 1:20; Mt 28:18; Ro 10:12; 1Co 15:27; Eph 1:20; 1Pe 3:22; Rev 17:14 **37** Lk 4:14 **38** Lk 4:18; Heb 1:9; Jn 3:2 **39** Ac 2:32; Ac 5:30 **40** Ac 2:24 **41** Jn 14:17,22; Ac 13:31; Lk 24:30; Jn 21:13 **42** Mt 28:19; Ac 1:8; Jn 5:22; Ac 17:31; Ro 14:9; 2Co 5:10; 2Ti 4:1; 1Pe 4:5 **43** Isa 53:11; Jer 31:34; Da 9:24; Mic 7:18; Zec 13:1; Mal 4:2; Ac 26:18; Ro 10:11; Gal 3:22 **44** Ac 4:31 **45** ver. 23; Ac 11:18; Gal 3:14 **47** Ac 11:17 **48** 1Co 1:17; Ac 2:38; 8:16 **CHAPTER 11** **2** Ac 10:45 **3** Ac 10:28; Gal 2:12 **4** Lk 1:3 **5** Ac 10:9

nothing common (unholy) or [ceremonially] unclean has ever entered my mouth.'

[9]"But the voice from heaven answered a second time, 'What God has cleansed *and* pronounced clean, no longer consider common (unholy).'

[10]"This happened three times, and everything was drawn up again into heaven.

[11]"And right then the three men who had been sent to me from Caesarea arrived at the house where we were *staying*.

[12]"The Spirit told me to go with them without the slightest hesitation. So these six brothers also went with me and we went to the man's house.

[13]"And Cornelius told us how he had seen the angel standing in his house, saying, 'Send *word* to Joppa and have Simon, who is also called Peter, brought here;

[14]he will bring a message to you by which you will be saved [and granted eternal life], you and all your household.'

[15]"When I began to speak, the Holy Spirit fell on them just as *He did* on us at the beginning [at Pentecost]. [Acts 2:1–4]

[16]"Then I remembered the word of the Lord, how He used to say, 'John baptized with water, but you will be baptized with the Holy Spirit.'

[17]"So, if God gave Gentiles the same gift [equally] as He gave us after we accepted *and* believed *and* trusted in the Lord Jesus Christ [as Savior], who was I to interfere *or* stand in God's way?"

[18]When they heard this, they quieted down and glorified *and* praised God, saying, "Then God has also granted to the Gentiles repentance *that leads* to *eternal* life [that is, real life after earthly death]."

The Church at Antioch

[19]So then [since they were unaware of these developments] those who were scattered because of the persecution that occurred in connection with [the stoning of] Stephen traveled as far as Phoenicia and Cyprus and Antioch, without telling the message [of salvation through Christ] to anyone except Jews.

[20]But there were some of them, men of Cyprus and Cyrene, who came to Antioch and *began* speaking to the Greeks as well, proclaiming [to them] the good news about the Lord Jesus.

[21]And the hand (the power and presence) of the Lord was with them, and a great number who believed turned to the Lord [for salvation, accepting and drawing near to Jesus as Messiah and Savior].

[22]The news of this reached the ears of the church in Jerusalem, and they sent Barnabas to Antioch.

[23]When he arrived and saw the grace of God [that was bestowed on them], he rejoiced and *began* to encourage them all with an unwavering heart to stay true *and* devoted to the Lord.

[24]For Barnabas was a good man [privately and publicly—his godly character benefited both himself and others] and *he was* full of the Holy Spirit and full of faith [in Jesus the Messiah, through whom believers have everlasting life]. And a great number of people were brought to the Lord.

[25]And Barnabas left for Tarsus to search for Saul;

[26]and when he found him, he brought him back to Antioch. For an entire year they met [with others] in the church and instructed large numbers; and it was in Antioch that the disciples were

---

and keep the law of Moses) in order to become Christians.

11:16 *baptized with the Holy Spirit*. This is found seven times in the New Testament (1:5; Mt 3:11; Mk 1:8; Lk 3:16; Jn 1:33; 1Co 12:13) and refers to an act by Christ for believers.

11:22–23 *Antioch*. Seleucus I founded the city of Antioch, naming it after his father. The city was cosmopolitan, attracting people of various cultures and ethnic backgrounds—including people from Persia, India, and even China. The gospel proclaimed in Antioch would have tremendous potential for reaching other areas of the world.

11:26 *called Christians*. Originally, the believers had called themselves "followers of The Way." Although the term "Christian" was apparently

12 Jn 16:13; Ac 10:19; 15:7; Ac 10:23 **13** Ac 10:30 **15** Ac 2:4 **16** Mt 3:11; Jn 1:26,33; Ac 1:5; 19:4; Isa 44:3; Joel 2:28; 3:18 **17** Ac 15:8,9; Ac 10:47 **18** Ro 10:12,13; 15:9,16 **19** Ac 8:1 **20** Ac 6:1; 9:29 **21** Lk 1:66; Ac 2:47; Ac 9:35 **22** Ac 9:27 **23** Ac 13:43; 14:22 **24** Ac 6:5; ver. 21; Ac 5:14 **25** Ac 9:30

first called Christians. [Acts 26:28;
1 Pet 4:16]
27 Now at this time some prophets
came down from Jerusalem to Antioch.
28 One of them named Agabus stood
up and prophesied through the [Holy]
Spirit that a severe famine would come
on the entire world. And this did hap-
pen during the reign of Claudius.
29 So the disciples decided to send
a contribution, each according to his
individual ability, to the believers who
lived in Judea.
30 And this they did, sending the con-
tribution to the elders by Barnabas
and Saul.

Peter's Arrest and Escape

12 NOW AT that time Herod [Agrip-
pa I] the king [of the Jews] arrest-
ed some who belonged to the church,
intending to harm them.
2 And he had James the brother of
John put to death with a sword;
3 and when he saw that it pleased the
Jews, he proceeded to have Peter arrest-
ed as well. This was during the days of
Unleavened Bread [the Passover week].
4 When he had seized Peter, he put
him in prison, turning him over to four
squads of soldiers of four each to guard
him [in rotation throughout the night],
planning after the Passover to bring him
out before the people [for execution].
5 So Peter was kept in prison, but
fervent *and* persistent prayer for him
was being made to God by the church.
6 The very night before Herod was to
bring him forward, Peter was sleeping
between two soldiers, bound with two
chains, and sentries were in front of
the door guarding the prison.
7 Suddenly, an angel of the Lord ap-
peared [beside him] and a light shone
in the cell. The angel struck Peter's
side and awakened him, saying, "Get
up quickly!" And the chains fell off
his hands.
8 The angel said to him, "Prepare
yourself and strap on your sandals [to
get ready for whatever may happen]."
And he did so. Then the angel told him,
"Put on your robe and follow me."
9 And Peter went out following *the
angel.* He did not realize that what was
being done by the angel was real, but
thought he was seeing a vision.
10 When they had passed the first
guard and the second, they came to
the iron gate that leads into the city. Of
its own accord it swung open for them;
and they went out and went along one
street, and at once the angel left him.
11 When Peter came to his senses, he
said, "Now I know for certain that the
Lord has sent His angel and has res-
cued me from the hand of Herod and
from all that the Jewish people were
expecting [to do to me]."
12 When he realized what had hap-
pened, he went to the house of Mary
the mother of John, who was also
called Mark, where many [believers]
were gathered together and were pray-

---

given to them by nonbelievers, they adopted it for themselves. Its essential meaning, "Christ-follower" is appropriate for those who have given their lives into the keeping of Jesus, the Messiah.

11:29 – 30 Benevolence — Christians must exercise responsibility and charity (love) towards all men, and especially to other believers (Gal 6:10). The Christians at Antioch are an example of well implemented Christian giving. All gave in accordance with their means (2Co 8:3). The gifts were placed in the charge of trustworthy Christians (2Co 8:20 – 21), who could ensure a responsible delivery and administration of the gifts.

12:1 – 3 *Herod [Agrippa I] the king.* This is Herod Agrippa I, the nephew of Herod Antipas who murdered John the Baptist, and the grandson of Herod the Great who had the children of Bethlehem put to death in his search for Jesus. Herod was not a Jew but an Edomite. The Jews resented the fact that a son of Edom was given the position of king of the Jews.

12:11 rescued me from the hand of Herod. Why was Peter's life spared while James' life was taken? The answer is the sovereign will of God. If we believe that God is good and wise, we can trust that what He allowed to happen was part of His wise plan for the good of all His people.

---

27 Ac 2:17; 13:1; 15:32; 21:9; 1Co 12:28; Eph 4:11 **28** Ac 21:10 **29** Ro 15:26; 1Co 16:1; 2Co 9:1 **30** Ac 12:25
CHAPTER 12 **2** Mt 4:21; 20:23 **3** Ex 12:14,15; 23:15 **4** Jn 21:18 **7** Ac 5:19 **9** Ps 126:1; Ac 10:3,17; 11:5
10 Ac 16:26 **11** Ps 34:7; Da 3:28; 6:22; Heb 1:14; Job 5:19; Ps 33:18,19; 34:22; 41:2; 97:10; 2Co 1:10; 2Pe 2:9
12 Ac 4:23; Ac 15:37; ver. 5

ing *continually* [and had been praying all night].

13 When he knocked at the door of the gateway, a servant-girl named Rhoda came to answer.

14 Recognizing Peter's voice, in her joy she failed to open the gate, but ran in and announced that Peter was standing in front of the gateway.

15 They said to her, "You are out of your mind!" But she kept insisting that it was so. They kept saying, "It is his angel!" [Matt 18:10; Heb 1:14]

16 But [meanwhile] Peter continued knocking; and when they opened *the door* and saw him, they were completely amazed.

17 But motioning to them with his hand to be quiet *and* listen, he described how the Lord had led him out of the prison. And he said, "Report these things to James and the brothers and sisters." Then he left and went to another place.

18 Now when day came, there was no small disturbance among the soldiers over what had become of Peter.

19 When Herod had searched for him and could not find him, he interrogated the guards and commanded that they be led away *to execution*. Then he went down from Judea to Caesarea [Maritima] and spent some time there.

Death of Herod

20 Now Herod [Agrippa I] was extremely angry with the people of Tyre and Sidon; and their delegates came to him in a united group, and after persuading Blastus, the king's chamberlain [to support their cause], they asked for peace, because their country was fed by [imports of grain and other goods from] the king's country.

21 On an appointed day Herod dressed himself in his royal robes, sat on his throne (tribunal, rostrum) and *began* delivering a speech to the people.

22 The assembled people kept shouting, "It is the voice of a god and not of a man!"

23 And at once an angel of the Lord struck him down because he did not give God the glory [and instead permitted himself to be worshiped], and he was eaten by worms and died [five days later].

24 But the word of the Lord [the good news about salvation through Christ] continued to grow and spread [increasing in effectiveness].

25 Barnabas and Saul came back from Jerusalem when they had completed their mission, bringing with them John, who was also called Mark. [Acts 11:28–30]

First Missionary Journey

13 NOW IN the church at Antioch there were prophets [who spoke a new message of God to the people] and teachers: Barnabas, Simeon who was called Niger, Lucius of Cyrene, Manaen who had been brought up with Herod [Antipas] the tetrarch, and Saul.

2 While they were serving the Lord and fasting, the Holy Spirit said, "Set apart for Me Barnabas and Saul (Paul) for the work to which I have called them."

3 Then after fasting and praying, they laid their hands on them [in approval and dedication] and sent them away [on their first journey].

12:22 *the voice of a god.* The Jewish historian Josephus also provides an account of this display, informing us that in an attempted appeasement of the king the people confessed that he was "more than mortal."

13:2–4 Holy Spirit — God reveals His will to those who are sensitive to His leading. The believers in Antioch heard from the Lord as they were praying and fasting. Most often, God does not speak to us out of the blue. He speaks to us when we are listening. The Holy Spirit gave distinct direction to the listening, sensitive believers of the first century, and He leads believers in the same way today.

13:3 *laid their hands on them.* The laying on of hands was the church's way of identifying with and affirming the mission to which God had called a particular person.

15 Ge 48:16; Mt 18:10 **17** Ac 13:16; 19:33; 21:40 **20** 1Ki 5:9,11; Eze 27:17 **23** 1Sa 25:38; 2Sa 24:17; Ps 115:1
24 Isa 55:11; Ac 6:7; 19:20; Col 1:6 **25** Ac 13:5,13; 15:37; ver. 12 **CHAPTER 13 1** Ac 14:26; Ac 11:22; Ro 16:21
2 Nu 8:14; Ac 9:15; 22:21; Ro 1:1; Gal 1:15; 2:9; Mt 9:38; Ac 14:26; Ro 10:15; Eph 3:7,8; 1Ti 2:7; 2Ti 1:11; Heb 5:4
3 Ac 6:6

4 So then, being sent out by the Holy
Spirit, they went down to Seleucia, and
from there they sailed to Cyprus.
5 When Barnabas and Saul arrived
at Salamis, they *began* to preach the
word of God [proclaiming the message
of eternal salvation through faith in
Christ] in the synagogues of the Jews;
and they also had John [Mark] as their
assistant.
6 When they had traveled through
the entire island [of Cyprus] as far as
Paphos, they found a sorcerer, a Jewish
false prophet named Bar-Jesus,
7 who was [closely associated] with
the proconsul [of the province], Sergi-
us Paulus, an intelligent *and* sensible
man. He called for Barnabas and Saul
and wanted to hear the word of God
[concerning eternal salvation through
faith in Christ].
8 But Elymas the sorcerer (for that is
how his name is translated) opposed
them, trying to turn the proconsul
away from *accepting* the faith.
9 But Saul, who was also *known as*
Paul, filled with the Holy Spirit *and*
led by Him, looked steadily at Elymas,
10 and said, "You [Elymas] who are
full of every [kind of] deceit, and ev-
ery [kind of] fraud, you son of the
devil, enemy of everything that is
right *and* good, will you never stop
perverting the straight paths of the
Lord? [Hos 14:9]
11 "Now, watch! The hand of the Lord
is on you, and you will be blind, [so
blind that you will be] unable to see the
sun for a time." Immediately a mist and
darkness fell upon him, and he groped
around, seeking people to lead him by
the hand.
12 The proconsul believed [the mes-
sage of salvation] when he saw what
had happened, being astonished at the
teaching concerning the Lord.
13 Now Paul and his companions
sailed from Paphos and came to Per-
ga in Pamphylia; but John [Mark] left
them and went back to Jerusalem.
14 Now they went on from Perga and
arrived at Antioch in Pisidia, and on
the Sabbath day they went into the
synagogue and sat down.
15 After the reading of the Law and
the [writings of the] Prophets, the of-
ficials of the synagogue sent *word* to
them, saying, "Brothers (kinsmen), if
you have any word of encouragement
for the people, say it."
16 So Paul stood up, and motioning
with his hand, he said,
"Men of Israel, and you who fear
God, listen!
17 "The God of this people Israel
chose our fathers and made the people
great *and* numerous during their stay
[as foreigners] in the land of Egypt,
and then with an uplifted arm He led
them out of there. [Ex 6:1, 6]
18 "For a period of about forty years
He put up with their behavior in the
wilderness. [Deut 1:31]
19 "When He had destroyed seven
nations in the land of Canaan, He
gave their land [to our ancestors] as
an inheritance—this took about four
hundred and fifty years. [Deut 7:1;
Josh 14:1, 2]
20 "After this, He gave *them* judges
until the prophet Samuel.
21 "Then they asked for a king, and
God gave them Saul the son of Kish,
a man of the tribe of Benjamin, for
forty years.
22 "And when He had removed him,
He raised up David to be their king: of
him He testified and said, 'I HAVE FOUND
DAVID the son of Jesse, A MAN AFTER MY
OWN HEART [conforming to My will and
purposes], who will do all My will.'
[1 Sam 13:14; Ps 89:20; Is 44:28]
23 "From this man's descendants
God has brought to Israel a Savior,
[in the person of] Jesus, according to
His promise.

13:6–12 *Sergius Paulus.* Luke presents this man as the first Gentile ruler to believe the gospel. There is no evidence that Sergius Paulus was a God-fearer or had ever shown any interest in Judaism prior to this time. This pagan government official was amazed at the power of God and believed the truth.

4 Ac 4:36 **5** ver. 46; Ac 12:25; 15:37 **6** Ac 8:9 **8** Ex 7:11; 2Ti 3:8 **9** Ac 4:8 **10** Mt 13:38; 1Jn 3:8 **11** 1Sa 5:6 **13** Ac 15:38 **14** Ac 16:13 **15** Lk 4:16; Heb 13:22 **16** Ac 10:35 **17** Dt 7:6,7; Ac 7:17 **18** Ex 16:35 **19** Jos 14:1 **20** Jdg 2:16; 1Sa 3:20 **21** 1Sa 8:5 **22** 1Sa 15:23; 1Sa 16:13; Ps 89:20; 1Sa 13:14 **23** Isa 11:1; Ps 132:11; Mt 1:21

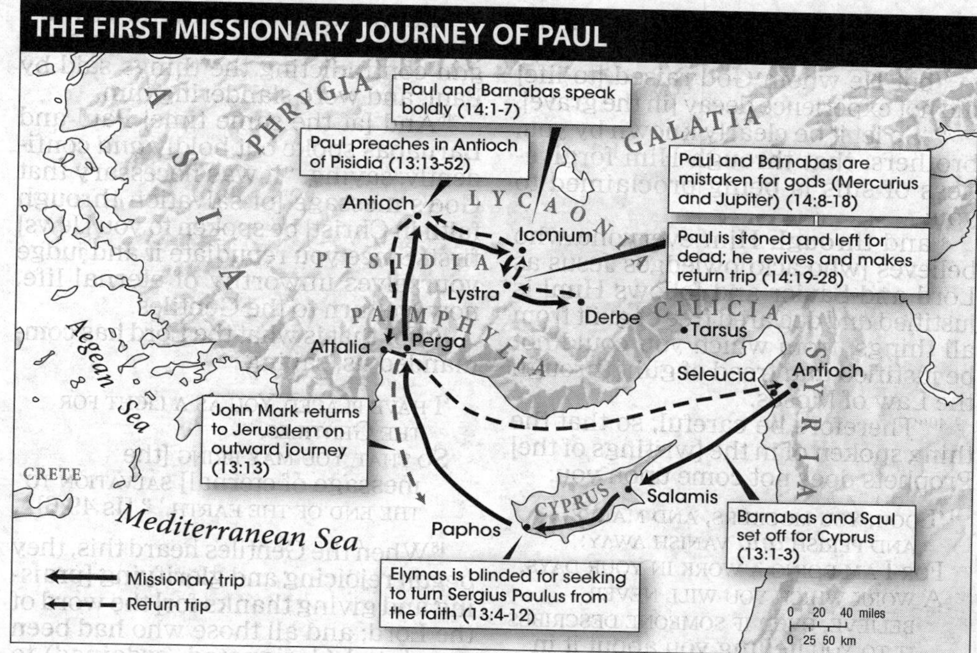

24"Before His coming John [the Baptist] had preached a baptism of repentance to all the people of Israel.
25"And as John was finishing his course [of ministry], he kept saying, 'What *or* who do you think that I am? I am not He [the Christ]; but be aware, One is coming after me whose sandals I am not worthy to untie [even as His slave]!'
26"Brothers, sons of Abraham's family, and those among you who fear God, to us has been sent the message of this salvation [obtained through faith in Jesus Christ]. [Ps 107:20]
27"For those who live in Jerusalem, and their rulers, who failed to recognize *or* understand both Jesus and the voices of the prophets which are read every Sabbath, have fulfilled these [very prophecies] by condemning Him.
28"And though they found no cause *or* charge deserving death, they asked Pilate to have Him executed.
29"And when they had finished carrying out everything that was written [in Scripture] about Him, they took Him down from the cross and laid Him in a tomb.
30"But God raised Him from the dead;
31and for many days (forty) He appeared to those who came up with Him from Galilee to Jerusalem, the very ones who are now His witnesses to the people.
32"And we are bringing you the good news of the promise made to our fathers (ancestors),
33that God has *completely* fulfilled this *promise* to our children by raising up Jesus, as it is also written in the second Psalm, 'YOU ARE MY SON; TODAY I HAVE BEGOTTEN (fathered) YOU.' [Ps 2:7]
34"And [as for the fact] that He raised Him from the dead, never again to return to decay [in the grave], He has spoken in this way: 'I WILL GIVE YOU THE HOLY AND SURE *blessings* OF DAVID [those blessings and mercies that were promised to him].' [Is 55:3]
35"For this reason He also says in another *Psalm*, 'YOU WILL NOT ALLOW YOUR HOLY ONE TO SEE DECAY.' [Ps 16:10]
36"For David, after he had served the purpose of God in his own generation, fell asleep and was buried among his

24 Mt 3:1; Lk 3:3 **25** Mk 1:7 **26** Mt 10:6 **27** Lk 23:34 **28** Mt 27:22 **29** Lk 18:31; Mt 27:59 **30** Mt 28:6 **31** Mt 28:16 **32** Ge 3:15 **33** Heb 1:5 **34** Isa 55:3 **35** Ps 16:10 **36** Ac 2:29

fathers and experienced decay [in the grave];

37 but He whom God raised [to life] did not experience decay [in the grave].

38 "So let it be clearly known by you, brothers, that through Him forgiveness of sins is being proclaimed to you;

39 and through Him everyone who believes [who acknowledges Jesus as Lord and Savior and follows Him] is justified *and* declared free of guilt from all things, from which you could not be justified *and* freed of guilt through the Law of Moses.

40 "Therefore be careful, so that the thing spoken of in the [writings of the] Prophets does not come upon you:

41 'Look, you mockers, and marvel,
and perish *and* vanish away;
For I am doing a work in your days,
A work which you will never
believe, even if someone describes
it to you [telling you about it in
detail].' " [Hab 1:5]

42 As Paul and Barnabas were leaving [the synagogue], the people kept begging that these things might be spoken to them on the next Sabbath.

43 When the congregation of the synagogue had been dismissed, many of the Jews and the devout converts to Judaism followed Paul and Barnabas, who, talking to them were urging them to continue in the grace of God.

Paul Turns to the Gentiles

44 On the next Sabbath almost the entire city gathered together to hear the word of the Lord [about salvation through faith in Christ].

45 But when the Jews saw the crowds, they were filled with jealousy and *began* contradicting the things said by Paul, and were slandering him.

46 And [at the same time] Paul and Barnabas spoke out boldly *and* confidently, saying, "It was necessary that God's message [of salvation through faith in Christ] be spoken to you [Jews] first. Since you repudiate it and judge yourselves unworthy of eternal life, now we turn to the Gentiles.

47 "For that is what the Lord has commanded us, saying,

'I have placed You as a light for
the Gentiles,
So that You may bring [the
message of eternal] salvation to
the end of the earth.' " [Is 49:6]

48 When the Gentiles heard this, they *began* rejoicing and glorifying [praising and giving thanks for] the word of the Lord; and all those who had been appointed (designated, ordained) to eternal life [by God] believed [in Jesus as the Christ and their Savior].

49 And so the word of the Lord [regarding salvation] was being spread through the entire region.

50 But the Jews incited the devout, prominent women and the leading men of the city, and instigated persecution against Paul and Barnabas, and drove them forcibly out of their district.

51 But they shook its dust from their feet *in protest* against them and went to Iconium. [Matt 10:14; Mark 6:11]

52 And the disciples were continually filled [throughout their hearts and souls] with joy and with the Holy Spirit.

13:39 everyone who believes . . . is justified and declared free of guilt from all things. "Justified" is a technical legal term declaring that a person is acquitted and absolved. Because of Jesus' death on the cross, our sin debt has been paid. Everyone who accepts this payment is justified before God, considered righteous through the blood of Christ.

13:45 the Jews. When Luke refers to "the Jews," he is not speaking of all Jewish people, but rather of the Jewish religious establishment, which opposed the gospel.

13:52 Joy — The pursuit of happiness doesn't always lead to the possession of joy. Joy does not come from circumstances but from the presence of God. It is a fruit of the spirit, poured into a believer's life by the grace of God. The believers in this passage were not filled with joy because their lives were comfortable, or because they were wealthy or powerful, but

38 Jer 31:34 **39** Isa 53:11 **40** Hab 1:5 **43** Ac 11:23; 14:22; Titus 2:11; Heb 12:15; 1Pe 5:12 **45** Ac 18:6; 1Pe 4:4; Jude 10 **46** ver. 26; Mt 10:6; Ac 3:26; Ro 1:16; Ex 32:10; Dt 32:21; Isa 55:5; Mt 21:43; Ro 10:19; Ac 18:6; 28:28 **47** Isa 42:6; 49:6; Lk 2:32 **48** Ac 2:47 **50** 2Ti 3:11 **51** Mt 10:14; Mk 6:11; Lk 9:5; Ac 18:6 **52** Mt 5:12; Jn 16:22; Ac 2:46

Acceptance and Opposition

14 NOW IN Iconium Paul and Barnabas went into the Jewish synagogue together and spoke in such a way [with such power and boldness] that a large number of Jews as well as Greeks believed [and confidently accepted Jesus as Savior];

2 but the unbelieving Jews [who rejected Jesus as Messiah] stirred up and embittered the minds of the Gentiles against the believers.

3 So Paul and Barnabas stayed for a long time, speaking boldly *and* confidently for the Lord, who continued to testify to the word of His grace, granting that signs and wonders (attesting miracles) be done by them.

4 But the people of the city were divided; some were *siding* with the Jews, and some with the apostles.

5 When there was an attempt by both the Gentiles and the Jews, together with their rulers, to shamefully mistreat and to stone them,

6 they, aware of the situation, escaped to Lystra and Derbe, [taking refuge in the] cities of Lycaonia, and the neighboring region;

7 and there they continued to preach the good news.

8 Now at Lystra a man sat who was unable to use his feet, for he was crippled from birth and had never walked.

9 This man was listening to Paul as he spoke, and Paul looked intently at him and saw that he had faith to be healed,

10 and said with a loud voice, "Stand up on your feet." And he jumped up and *began* to walk.

11 And the crowds, when they saw what Paul had done, raised their voices, shouting in the Lycaonian language, "The gods have come down to us in human form!"

12 They began calling Barnabas, Zeus [chief of the Greek gods], and Paul, Hermes [messenger of the Greek gods], since he took the lead in speaking.

13 The priest of Zeus, whose *temple* was at the entrance of the city, brought bulls and garlands to the city gates, and wanted to offer sacrifices with the crowds.

14 But when the apostles Barnabas and Paul heard about it, they tore their robes and rushed out into the crowd, shouting,

15 "Men, why are you doing these things? We too are only men of the same nature as you, bringing the good news to you, so that you turn from these useless *and* meaningless things to the living God, WHO MADE THE HEAVEN AND THE EARTH AND THE SEA AND EVERYTHING THAT IS IN THEM. [Ex 20:11; Ps 146:6]

16 "In generations past He permitted all the nations to go their own ways;

17 yet He did not leave Himself without some witness [as evidence of Himself], in that He kept constantly doing good things *and* showing you kindness, and giving you rains from heaven and productive seasons, filling your hearts with food and happiness."

18 Even saying these words, with difficulty they prevented the people from offering sacrifices to them.

19 But Jews arrived from Antioch and Iconium, and having won over the crowds, they stoned Paul and dragged him out of the city, thinking he was dead. [2 Cor 11:25; 2 Tim 3:11]

20 But the disciples formed a circle around him, and he got up and went back into the city; and the next day he went on with Barnabas to Derbe.

---

because they saw God working and had His Holy Spirit in their lives.

14:11 ***The gods have come down.*** The Roman poet Ovid told of an ancient legend in which Zeus and Hermes came to the Phrygian hill country disguised as mortals seeking lodging. After being turned away from a thousand homes, they found refuge in the humble cottage of an elderly couple. In appreciation for the couple's hospitality, the gods transformed the cottage into a splendid temple and then destroyed all the houses of the inhospitable people. The people probably remembered this ancient legend, and wanted to make sure they did not make the same mistake their ancestors did.

CHAPTER 14 **3** Mk 16:20; Heb 2:4 **4** Ac 13:2,3 **5** 2Ti 3:11 **6** Mt 10:23 **8** Ac 3:2 **10** Isa 35:6 **11** Ac 8:10; 28:6 **13** Da 2:46 **14** Mt 26:65 **15** Ac 10:26; Jas 5:17; Rev 19:10; 1Sa 12:21; 1Ki 16:13; Jer 14:22; Am 2:4; 1Co 8:4; 1Th 1:9; Ge 1:1; Ps 33:6; 146:6; Rev 14:7 **16** Ps 81:12; Ac 17:30; 1Pe 4:3 **17** Ac 17:27; Ro 1:20; Lev 26:4; Dt 11:14; 28:12; Job 5:10; Ps 65:10; 68:9; 147:8; Jer 14:22; Mt 5:45 **19** Ac 13:45; 2Co 11:25; 2Ti 3:11

21 They preached the good news to that city and made many disciples, then they returned to Lystra and to Iconium and to Antioch,

22 strengthening *and* establishing the hearts of the disciples; encouraging them to remain firm in the faith, saying, "It is through many tribulations *and* hardships that we must enter the kingdom of God."

23 When they had appointed elders for them in every church, having prayed with fasting, they entrusted them to the Lord in whom they believed [and joyfully accepted as the Messiah].

24 Then they passed through Pisidia and came to Pamphylia.

25 When they had spoken the word [of salvation through faith in Christ] in Perga, they went down to Attalia.

26 From there they sailed back to Antioch, where they had been entrusted to the grace of God for the work which they had now completed.

27 Arriving *there,* they gathered the church together and *began* to report [in great detail] everything that God had done with them and how He had opened to the Gentiles a door of faith [in Jesus as the Messiah and Savior].

28 And they stayed there a long time with the disciples.

The Council at Jerusalem

15 SOME MEN came down from Judea and *began* teaching the brothers, "Unless you are circumcised in accordance with the custom of Moses, you cannot be saved." [Gen 17:9–14]

2 Paul and Barnabas disagreed greatly and debated with them, so it was determined that Paul and Barnabas and some of the others from their group would go up to Jerusalem to the apostles and the elders [and confer with them] concerning this issue.

3 So, after being supplied *and* sent on their way by the church, they went through both Phoenicia and Samaria telling in detail the conversion of the Gentiles, and they brought great joy to all the believers.

4 When they arrived in Jerusalem, they were received warmly by the church and the apostles and the elders, and they reported to them all the things that God had accomplished through them.

5 But some from the sect of the Pharisees who had believed [in Jesus as the Messiah] stood up and said, "It is necessary to circumcise the Gentile converts and to direct them to observe the Law of Moses."

6 The apostles and the elders came together to consider this matter.

7 After a long debate, Peter got up and said to them, "Brothers, you know that in the early days God made a choice among you, that by my mouth the Gentiles would hear the message of the gospel and believe.

8 "And God, who knows *and* understands the heart, testified to them, giving them the Holy Spirit, just as He also did to us;

9 and He made no distinction between us and them, cleansing their hearts by faith [in Jesus].

10 "Now then, why are you testing God by placing a yoke on the neck of the disciples which neither our fathers nor we have been able to endure?

11 "But we believe that we are saved through the [precious, undeserved] grace of the Lord Jesus [which makes

---

14:23 ***appointed elders.*** The process outlined in 6:1–7 for selecting the seven men to serve the Jerusalem believers may provide a clue to the process used for selecting elders here. Both the assembly and the apostles were involved in the selection process.

15:11 ***we are saved through the [precious, undeserved] grace of the Lord Jesus.*** These are the last words of Peter in the Book of Acts. He leaves us with the eternal truth that we are saved through faith by grace alone. The emphasis in the narrative now moves from Peter to Paul, and his outreach to the Gentiles.

21 Mt 28:19 **22** Ac 11:23; 13:43; Mt 10:38; 16:24; Lk 22:28; Ro 8:17; 2Ti 2:12; 3:12 **23** Titus 1:5 **26** Ac 13:1,3; Ac 15:40 **27** Ac 15:4,12; 21:19; 1Co 16:9; 2Co 2:12; Col 4:3; Rev 3:8 **CHAPTER 15** **1** Gal 2:12; ver. 5; Jn 7:22; Gal 5:2; Php 3:2; Col 2:8,11,16; Ge 17:10; Lev 12:3 **2** Gal 2:1 **3** Ro 15:24; 1Co 16:6,11; Ac 14:27 **4** ver. 12; Ac 14:27 **5** ver. 1 **7** Ac 10:20; 11:12 **8** 1Ch 28:9; Ac 1:24; Ac 10:44 **9** Ro 10:12; Ac 10:15,28; 1Co 1:2; 1Pe 1:22 **10** Mt 23:4; Gal 5:1 **11** Ro 3:24; Eph 2:8; Titus 2:11; 3:4,5

us free of the guilt of sin and grants us eternal life], in just the same way as they are."

12 All the people remained silent, and they listened [attentively] to Barnabas and Paul as they described all the signs and wonders (attesting miracles) that God had done through them among the Gentiles.

James' Judgment

13 When they had finished speaking, James replied, "Brothers, listen to me.
14 "Simeon (Simon Peter) has described how God first concerned Himself about taking from among the Gentiles a people for His name [to honor Him and be identified with Him].
15 "The words of the Prophets agree with this, just as it is written [in Scripture],

16 'After these things I will return,
And I will rebuild the tent of
David which has fallen;
I will rebuild its ruins,
And I will restore it,
17 So that the rest of mankind may
seek the Lord,
And all the Gentiles upon whom
My name has been invoked,'
18 Says the Lord,
Who has been making these things
known from long ago. [Is 45:21;
Jer 12:15; Amos 9:11, 12]

19 "Therefore it is my judgment that we do not trouble *and* make it difficult for those who are turning to God among the Gentiles [by putting obstacles in their way],
20 but that we write to them that they are to abstain from anything that has been contaminated by [being offered to] idols and from sexual impurity and from [eating the meat of] what has been strangled and from [the consumption of] blood.
21 "For from ancient generations [the writing of] Moses has been preached in every city, since he is read *aloud* in the synagogues every Sabbath."
22 Then the apostles and the elders, together with the whole church, decided to select some of their men to go to Antioch with Paul and Barnabas—Judas, who was called Barsabbas, and Silas [also called Silvanus, both], leading men among the brothers.
23 With them they sent the following letter: "The apostles and the brothers who are the elders, to the brothers and sisters who are from the Gentiles in Antioch, Syria, and Cilicia, Greetings.

24 "Since we have heard that some of our men have troubled you with *their* teachings, causing distress *and* confusion—men to whom we gave no *such* orders *or* instructions—

15:13 *James.* James was the leader of the church in Jerusalem until he was stoned to death at the insistence of the high priest in AD 62. It is believed that this James is the Lord's brother, the son of Mary and Joseph, who did not believe until the Lord appeared to him privately after the Resurrection (1Co 15:7).

15:19 – 20 *abstain from anything that has been contaminated by [being offered to] idols.* The Jerusalem council understood that it was not necessary for Gentiles to keep the whole of the law in order to be believers in Jesus, but also recognized that they did not have the background of moral teaching the Jewish believers had. They needed both reassurance as to their acceptance as true Christians and teaching for a godly life. In looking at the present application of these requirements, it is important to remember that Acts is a transitional book, documenting the beginning of the Christian movement. Sexual purity and food regulations are both addressed more thoroughly elsewhere in the New Testament (1Co 6 – 8).

15:20 Fornication — Illicit sexual relationships were not a matter of shame or sin among the Gentiles as they were among the Jews. In fact, many pagan religious practices included prostitution and sexual orgies. This made the need for teaching on sexual purity doubly urgent for the new Gentile believers. They would be constantly presented with temptation, not only for sexual sin but for returning to their old ways of worship. They needed to hear God's strict prohibition of such behavior.

12 Ac 14:27 **13** Ac 12:17 **14** ver. 7 **16** Am 9:11 **19** See ver. 23; 1Th 1:9 **20** Ge 35:2; Ex 20:3,23; Eze 20:30; 1Co 8:1; 10:20,28; Rev 2:14; 1Co 6:9; Gal 5:19; Eph 5:3; Col 3:5; 1Th 4:3; 1Pe 4:3; Ge 9:4; Lev 3:17; Dt 12:16 **21** Ac 13:15,27 **22** Ac 1:23 **24** ver. 1; Gal 2:4; 5:12; Titus 1:10,11

25 it has been decided by us, having
met together, to select men
and send them to you with
our beloved Barnabas and
Paul,
26 men who have risked their lives
for the name of our Lord Jesus
Christ.
27 "So we have sent Judas and Silas,
who will report by word of
mouth the same things [that we
decided in our meeting].
28 "For it seemed good to the Holy
Spirit and to us not to place on
you any greater burden than
these essentials:
29 that you abstain from things
sacrificed to idols, and from
[consuming] blood, and from
[eating the meat of] things
that have been strangled,
and from sexual impurity.
If you keep yourselves from
these things, you will do well.
Farewell."

30 So when they were sent off, they
went down to Antioch; and after as-
sembling the congregation, they de-
livered the letter.
31 And when they had read it, the peo-
ple rejoiced greatly at the encourage-
ment *and* comfort [it brought them].
32 Judas and Silas, who were them-
selves prophets (divinely inspired
spokesmen), encouraged and strength-
ened the believers with many words.
33 After spending some time there,
they were sent back by the brothers
with [the greeting of] peace to those
who had sent them.
34 [However, Silas decided to stay
there.]
35 But Paul and Barnabas remained
in Antioch, and with many others also
continued teaching and proclaiming
the good news, the word of the Lord
[concerning eternal salvation through
faith in Christ].

Paul's Second Missionary Journey

36 After some time Paul said to Bar-
nabas, "Let us go back and visit the
brothers and sisters (believers) in ev-
ery city where we preached the mes-
sage of the Lord, and see how they
are doing."
37 Now Barnabas wanted to take [his
cousin] John, who was called Mark,
along with them.
38 But Paul kept insisting that they
should not take along with them the
one who had quit *and* deserted them in
Pamphylia and had not gone on with
them to the work.
39 And it became such a sharp dis-
agreement that they separated from
one another, and Barnabas took [John]
Mark with him and sailed away to
Cyprus.
40 But Paul chose Silas [who was
again in Antioch] and set out [on his
second journey], commended by the
brothers to the grace *and* favor of the
Lord.
41 And he traveled through Syria and
Cilicia, strengthening the churches.

The Macedonian Vision

16 NOW PAUL traveled to Derbe
and also to Lystra. A disciple
named Timothy was there, the son of
a Jewish woman who was a believer
[in Christ], however, his father was a
Greek.
2 Timothy was well spoken of by the
brothers and sisters who were in Lys-
tra and Iconium.

15:39 *that they separated from one another.* Even though Paul and Barnabas had a heated disagreement, it is important to note that they did not bring their disagreement into the church fellowship, forcing others to take sides and causing more dissension. Instead, they simply parted ways, each continuing to faithfully serve the Lord. Later, the disagreement was apparently resolved, for Paul wrote to Timothy when he was imprisoned, asking for Mark to be sent to him, "for he is very helpful to me for the ministry" (2Ti 4:11).

26 Ac 13:50 **29** ver. 20; Ac 21:25; Rev 2:14,20; Lev 17:14 **32** Ac 14:22; 18:23 **33** 1Co 16:11; Heb 11:31 **35** Ac 13:1 **36** Ac 13:4,13,14,51; 14:1,6,24,25 **37** Ac 12:12,25; 13:5; Col 4:10; 2Ti 4:11; Php 24 **38** Ac 13:13 **40** Ac 14:26 **41** Ac 16:5 **CHAPTER 16** **1** Ac 14:6; Ac 19:22; Ro 16:21; 1Co 4:17; Php 2:19; 1Th 3:2; 1Ti 1:2; 2Ti 1:2; 2Ti 1:5 **2** Ac 6:3

THE SECOND MISSIONARY JOURNEY OF PAUL

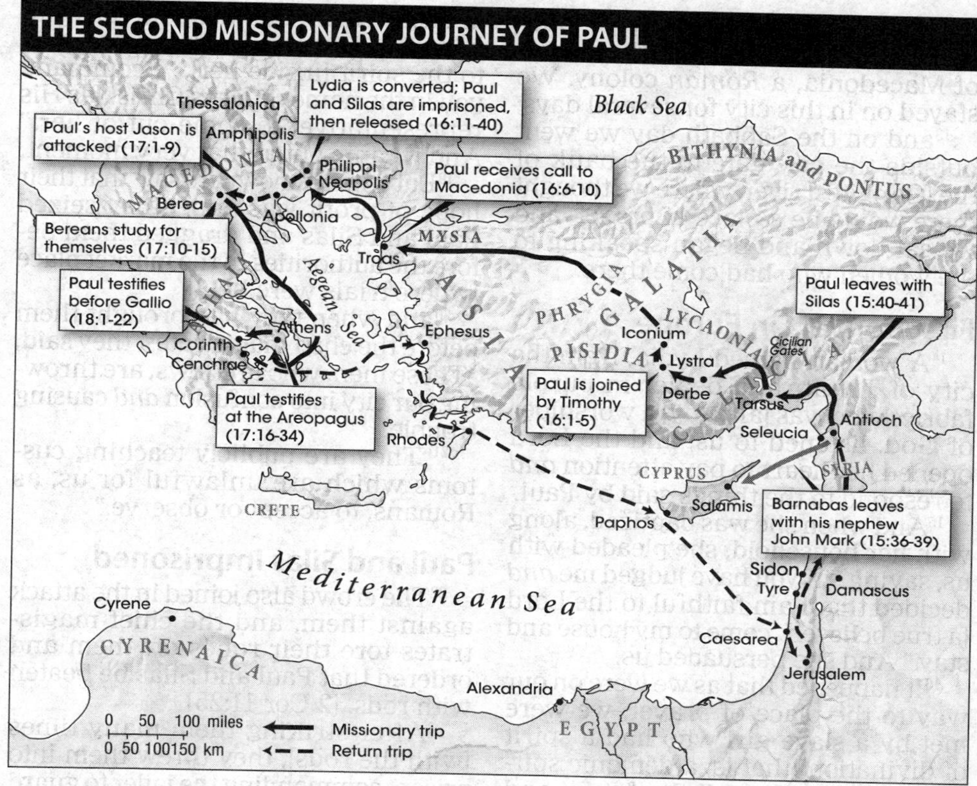

[3]Paul wanted Timothy to go with
him [as a missionary]; and he took
him and circumcised him because of
the Jews who were in those places,
since they all knew that his father was
a Greek.
[4]As they traveled from town to town,
they delivered the decrees decided on
by the apostles and elders who were in
Jerusalem, for the churches to observe.
[5]So the churches were strengthened
in the faith, and they *continually* in-
creased in number day after day.
[6]Now they passed through the ter-
ritory of Phrygia and Galatia, after
being forbidden by the Holy Spirit to
speak the word in [the west coast prov-
ince of] Asia [Minor];
[7]and after they came to Mysia, they
tried to go into Bithynia, but the Spirit
of Jesus did not permit them;
[8]so passing by Mysia, they went
down to Troas.
[9]Then a vision appeared to Paul in
the night: a man from [the Roman
province of] Macedonia was standing
and pleading with him, saying, "Come
over to Macedonia and help us!"
[10]And when he had seen the vision,
we (including Luke) tried to go on into
Macedonia at once, concluding that
God had called us to preach the gospel
to them.
[11]So setting sail from Troas, we ran
a direct course to Samothrace, and the
next day [went on] to Neapolis;

16:3 *circumcised him.* According to Jewish law, Timothy should have been circumcised and raised a Jew, even with a Gentile father. For whatever reason, this had not happened, and the fact that he was an uncircumcised Jew would limit his effectiveness with Jewish Christians. The issue was not law but effectiveness.

3 1Co 9:20; Gal 2:3; See Gal 5:2 **4** Ac 15:28,29 **5** Ac 15:41 **8** 2Co 2:12; 2Ti 4:13 **9** Ac 10:30 **10** 2Co 2:13

12 and from there [we came] to Philip-
pi, which is a leading city of the district
of Macedonia, a *Roman* colony. We
stayed on in this city for several days;
13 and on the Sabbath day we went
outside the city gate to the bank of
the [Gangites] river, where we thought
there would be a place of prayer, and
we sat down and began speaking to
the women who had come there.

First Convert in Europe

14 A woman named Lydia, from the
city of Thyatira, a dealer in purple
fabrics who was [already] a worshiper
of God, listened to us; and the Lord
opened her heart to pay attention *and*
to respond to the things said by Paul.
15 And when she was baptized, along
with her household, she pleaded with
us, saying, "If you have judged me *and*
decided that I am faithful to the Lord
[a true believer], come to my house and
stay." And she persuaded us.
16 It happened that as we were on our
way to the place of prayer, we were
met by a slave-girl who had a spirit
of divination [that is, a demonic spir-
it claiming to foretell the future and
discover hidden knowledge], and she
brought her owners a good profit by
fortune-telling.
17 She followed after Paul and us and
kept screaming *and* shouting, "These
men are servants of the Most High
God! They are proclaiming to you the
way of salvation!"
18 She continued doing this for sever-
al days. Then Paul, being greatly an-
noyed *and* worn out, turned and said
to the spirit [inside her], "I command
you in the name of Jesus Christ [as His
representative] to come out of her!"
And it came out at that very moment.
19 But when her owners saw that their
hope of profit was gone, they seized
Paul and Silas and dragged them be-
fore the authorities in the market place
[where trials were held],
20 and when they had brought them
before the chief magistrates, they said,
"These men, who are Jews, are throw-
ing our city into confusion *and* causing
trouble.
21 "They are publicly teaching cus-
toms which are unlawful for us, as
Romans, to accept or observe."

Paul and Silas Imprisoned

22 The crowd also joined in the attack
against them, and the chief magis-
trates tore their robes off them and
ordered that Paul and Silas be beaten
with rods. [2 Cor 11:25]
23 After striking them many times
[with the rods], they threw them into
prison, commanding the jailer to guard
them securely.
24 He, having received such a [strict]
command, threw them into the inner
prison (dungeon) and fastened their feet
in the stocks [in an agonizing position].
25 But about midnight when Paul and
Silas were praying and singing hymns
of praise to God, and the prisoners
were listening to them;

16:12 *Philippi.* Named after the father of Alexander the Great, Philippi was a Roman colony loyal to the empire. The city itself was organized by the state of Rome and functioned as a military outpost. Because of its proximity to the sea as well as to one of the major roads to Europe, Philippi was a commercial center in Macedonia. Its influence throughout the region made it a good place to begin preaching the gospel of Jesus Christ.

16:13 *where we thought there would be a place of prayer.* According to Jewish custom, a congregation consisted of ten households. If ten male household heads could be found in a city, a synagogue was formed. If not, a place of prayer was established. Philippi did not have a synagogue, but Paul was still able to find the God-fearers of the city.

16:25 Praise — Paul and Silas were praying and singing hymns of praise to God at midnight in spite of the fact that they had been arrested, stripped naked, and beaten, confined to an inner cell and clamped into an uncomfortable position. They could praise God because their joy was not based on circumstances but on a relationship. Jesus Christ and His love and grace are the same, no matter where you are or what is happening to you.

12 Php 1:1 **14** Lk 24:45 **15** Ge 19:3; 33:11; Jdg 19:21; Lk 24:29; Heb 13:2 **16** 1Sa 28:7; Ac 19:24
18 See Mk 1:25,34; Mk 16:17 **19** Ac 19:25,26; Mt 10:18 **20** 1Ki 18:17; Ac 17:6 **22** 2Co 6:5; 11:23,25; 1Th 2:2

26 suddenly there was a great earth-
quake, so [powerful] that the very
foundations of the prison were shaken
and at once all the doors were opened
and everyone's chains were unfas-
tened.
27 When the jailer, shaken out of
sleep, saw the prison doors open, he
drew his sword and was about to kill
himself, thinking that the prisoners
had escaped.
28 But Paul shouted, saying, "Do not
hurt yourself, we are all here!"
29 Then the jailer called for torches
and rushed in, and trembling with fear
he fell down before Paul and Silas,
30 and after he brought them out [of
the inner prison], he said, "Sirs, what
must I do to be saved?"

The Jailer Converted

31 And they answered, "Believe in the
Lord Jesus [as your personal Savior
and entrust yourself to Him] and you
will be saved, you and your household
[if they also believe]."
32 And they spoke the word of the
Lord [concerning eternal salvation
through faith in Christ] to him and to
all who were in his house.
33 And he took them that *very* hour
of the night and washed their *bloody*
wounds, and immediately he was bap-
tized, he and all his *household*.
34 Then he brought them into his
house and set food before them, and re-
joiced greatly, since he had believed in
God with his entire family [accepting
with joy what had been made known
to them about the Christ].
35 Now when day came, the chief
magistrates sent their officers, saying,
"Release those men."
36 And the jailer repeated the words
to Paul, *saying*, "The chief magistrates
have sent *word* to release you; so come
out now and go in peace."
37 But Paul said to them, "They have
beaten us in public without a trial, men
who are Romans, and have thrown us
into prison; and now they are sending
us out secretly? No! Let them come
here themselves and bring us out!"
38 The officers reported this message
to the chief magistrates, and when they
heard that the prisoners were Romans,
they were frightened;
39 so they came [to the prison] and
appealed to them [with apologies], and
when they brought them out, they kept
begging them to leave the city.
40 So they left the prison and went to
Lydia's *house;* and when they had seen
the brothers and sisters, they encour-
aged *and* comforted them, and left.

Paul at Thessalonica

17 NOW AFTER Paul and Silas had
traveled through Amphipolis
and Apollonia, they came to Thessa-
lonica, where there was a synagogue
of the Jews.

16:31 It Begins with Faith — Paul and Silas's answer to the Philippian jailer's question is the essence of salvation; *Believe in the Lord Jesus and you will be saved*. This verse raises two questions: What does it mean to believe, and what does it mean to be saved? Belief includes but is more than just an intellectual assent. Belief includes the idea of total trust, dependence, and submission of oneself to Christ as Lord (King, Master). To be saved is to be delivered. We are delivered from the very presence of sin and evil (Satan and hell) and will be delivered into the very presence of God (Christ and heaven). We receive this new life by faith — believing that we are sinful, that Jesus died for our sins, that His death was in our place, and that His payment for sin is fully acceptable in God's sight. Faith can be summarized in the acrostic:

Forsaking
All
I
Take
Him

16:33 – 34 Family — This man assumed spiritual leadership of his family by being the first to repent, to humble himself before God and ask for forgiveness and a change of life. By his example, the rest of his family was won. In the same way, every believing father has the responsibility to set the example of spiritual commitment, and to teach his family all he knows of following Christ.

16:37 *Romans.* Paul was not simply seeking

---

26 Ac 4:31; 5:19; 12:7,10 **30** Lk 3:10; Ac 2:37; 9:6 **31** Jn 3:16,36; 6:47; 1Jn 5:10 **34** Lk 5:29; 19:6 **37** Ac 22:25 **39** Mt 8:34 **40** ver. 14

2And Paul entered the synagogue, as
was his custom, and for three Sabbaths
he engaged in discussion *and* friendly
debate with them from the Scriptures,
3explaining and pointing out [scriptural evidence] that it was necessary
for the Christ to suffer and rise from
the dead, and *saying*, "This Jesus,
whom I am proclaiming to you, is the
Christ (the Messiah, the Anointed)."
4And some of them were persuaded
to believe and joined Paul and Silas,
along with a large number of the God-fearing Greeks and many of the leading women.
5But the [unbelieving] Jews became
jealous, and taking along some thugs
from [the lowlifes in] the market place,
they formed a mob and set the city in
an uproar; and then attacking Jason's
house tried to bring Paul and Silas out
to the people.
6But when they failed to find them,
they dragged Jason and some brothers
before the city authorities, shouting,
"These men who have turned the world
upside down have come here too;
7and Jason has welcomed them [into
his house and protected them]! And
they all are saying things contrary to
the decrees of Caesar, [actually] claiming that there is another king, Jesus."
8They stirred up the crowd and the
city authorities who heard these things.
9And when they had taken security
(bail) from Jason and the others, they
let them go.

Paul at Berea

10The brothers immediately sent
Paul and Silas away by night to Berea;
and when they arrived, they entered
the Jewish synagogue.
11Now these people were more noble *and* open-minded than those in
Thessalonica, so they received the
message [of salvation through faith
in the Christ] with great eagerness,
examining the Scriptures daily to see
if these things were so.
12As a result many of them became
believers, together with a number of
prominent Greek women and men.
13But when the Jews of Thessalonica
learned that the word of God [concerning eternal salvation through faith in
Christ] had also been preached by Paul
at Berea, they came there too, agitating
and disturbing the crowds.
14So at that time the brothers immediately sent Paul away to go as far
as the sea; but Silas and Timothy remained there [at Berea].
15Those who escorted Paul brought
him to Athens; and [after] receiving
instructions [from Paul] for Silas and
Timothy to join him as soon as possible, they left.

Paul at Athens

16Now while Paul was waiting for
them at Athens, his spirit was greatly
angered when he saw that the city was
full of idols.
17So he had discussions in the synagogue with the Jews and the God-fearing *Gentiles*, and in the market
place day after day with any who happened to be there.
18And some of the Epicurean and
Stoic philosophers began to engage in
conversation with him. And some said,
"What could this idle babbler [with his
eclectic, scrap-heap learning] have in
mind to say?" Others said, "He seems
to be a proclaimer of strange deities"—

---

self-justification, he was protecting the infant church in Philippi. By forcing a public statement of their innocence, he minimized the possibility that the new believers would be regarded as "friends of criminals and troublemakers."

17:7 *things contrary to the decrees of Caesar.* In AD 49 the Roman emperor Caligula expelled all Jews from Rome due to riots ignited by a group of zealous Jews. Paul's accusers were trying to paint him as a revolutionary who was bringing sedition to Thessalonica.

17:18 *this idle babbler.* This word is literally "seed picker." The philosophers were saying that Paul was like a gutter sparrow, picking up bits and scraps of knowledge without fully digesting or thinking about what he taught.

CHAPTER 17 **2** Lk 4:16; Ac 9:20; 13:5,14; 14:1; 16:13; 19:8 **3** Lk 24:26,46; Ac 18:28; Gal 3:1 **4** Ac 28:24; Ac 15:22,27,32,40 **5** Ro 16:21 **6** Ac 16:20 **7** Lk 23:2; Jn 19:12; 1Pe 2:13 **10** ver. 14; Ac 9:25 **11** Isa 34:16; Lk 16:29; Jn 5:39 **14** Mt 10:23 **15** Ac 18:5 **16** 2Pe 2:8

because he was preaching the good
news about Jesus and the resurrection.
19 They took him and brought him to
the Areopagus (Hill of Ares, the Greek
god of war), saying, "May we know
what this [strange] new teaching is
which you are proclaiming?
20 "For you are bringing some startling *and* strange things to our ears;
so we want to know what they mean."
21 (Now all the Athenians and the
foreigners visiting there used to spend
their [leisure] time in nothing other
than telling or hearing something new.)

Sermon on Mars Hill

22 So Paul, standing in the center of
the Areopagus, said: "Men of Athens,
I observe [with every turn I make
throughout the city] that you are very
religious *and* devout in all respects.
23 "Now as I was going along and
carefully looking at your objects of
worship, I came to an altar with this inscription: 'TO AN UNKNOWN GOD.'
Therefore what you already worship as
unknown, this I proclaim to you.
24 "The God who created the world
and everything in it, since He is Lord
of heaven and earth, does not dwell in
temples made with hands;
25 nor is He served by human hands,
as though He needed anything, because it is He who gives to all [people]
life and breath and all things. [Is 42:5]
26 "And He made from one *man* every
nation of mankind to live on the face
of the earth, having determined their
appointed times and the boundaries of
their lands *and* territories.
27 "This was so that they would seek
God, if perhaps they might grasp for
Him and find Him, though He is not
far from each one of us.
28 "For in Him we live and move and
exist [that is, in Him we actually have
our being], as even some of your own
poets have said, 'For we also are His
children.'
29 "So then, being God's children,
we should not think that the Divine
Nature (deity) is like gold or silver or
stone, an image formed by the art and
imagination *or* skill of man.
30 "Therefore God overlooked *and*
disregarded the *former* ages of ignorance; *but* now He commands all
people everywhere to repent [that is,
to change their old way of thinking,
to regret their past sins, and to seek
God's purpose for their lives],
31 because He has set a day when
He will judge the *inhabited* world in
righteousness by a Man whom He has
appointed *and* destined for that task,
and He has provided credible proof
to everyone by raising Him from the
dead." [Ps 9:8; 96:13; 98:9]
32 Now when they heard [the term]
resurrection from the dead, some
mocked *and* sneered; but others said,
"We will hear from you again about
this matter."
33 So Paul left them.

17:19 *Areopagus.* Just southwest of the Acropolis in Athens was a hill called the Hill of Ares (Mars, in Latin), the god of war. This was where court was held concerning questions of religion and morals. In Athens, the gospel message was examined by the supposed experts of philosophy and religion.

17:23 An Unknown God — In the sixth century BC it was said that a poet from Crete named Epimenides turned aside a horrible plague from the people of Athens by appealing to a god of whom the people had never heard. An altar was built to honor this god, and its inscription caught Paul's attention. Knowing that the Athenians had no background in the Old Testament Scriptures as did the Jews in the synagogues, Paul began his discourse with what they were already familiar with: their own legends and observation.

17:31 Resurrection — Christ has been raised from the dead not only for the purpose of returning to heaven and resuming His fellowship with the Father, a fellowship interrupted only by the alienation and abandonment at the cross. He has gone from His tomb to the right hand of His Father to intercede for us. One day, however, the mantle of Judge will be placed on Him, and we will stand before our Judge, not our High Priest. The world has yet to see the last of Jesus Christ.

17:32 *some mocked.* Though they embraced the idea of the soul living on, the Greeks were

24 Ac 14:15; Mt 11:25; Ac 7:48 **25** Ps 50:8; Ge 2:7; Nu 16:22; Job 12:10; 27:3; 33:4; Isa 42:5; 57:16; Zec 12:1 **26** Dt 32:8 **27** Ro 1:20; Ac 14:17 **28** Col 1:17; Heb 1:3; Titus 1:12 **29** Isa 40:18 **30** Ac 14:16; Ro 3:25; Lk 24:47; Titus 2:11,12; 1Pe 1:14; 4:3 **31** Ac 10:42; Ro 2:16; 14:10; Ac 2:24

34 But some men joined him and be-
lieved; among them were Dionysius,
[a judge] of the *Council of* Areopagus,
and a woman named Damaris, and
others with them.

Paul at Corinth

18 AFTER THIS Paul left Athens
and went to Corinth.
2 There he met a Jew named Aquila,
a native of Pontus, who had recently
come from Italy with his wife, Pris-
cilla, because [the Roman Emperor]
Claudius had issued an edict that all
the Jews were to leave Rome. Paul
went to see them,
3 and because he was of the same
trade, he stayed with them; and they
worked *together* for they were tent-
makers.
4 And he reasoned *and* debated in
the synagogue every Sabbath, trying
to persuade Jews and Greeks;
5 but when Silas and Timothy came
down from Macedonia (northern
Greece), Paul *began* devoting himself
completely to [preaching] the word,
and solemnly testifying to the Jews
that Jesus is the Christ (the Messiah,
the Anointed).
6 But since the Jews kept resisting
and opposing him, and blaspheming
[God], he shook out his robe and said
to them, "Your blood (damnation) be
on your own heads! I am innocent of it.
From now on I will go to the Gentiles."
[Acts 13:46]
7 Then he moved on from there and
went to the house of a man named Titius
Justus, who worshiped God and whose
house was next door to the synagogue.
8 Crispus, the leader of the syna-
gogue, believed in the Lord together
with his entire household [joyfully
acknowledging Him as Messiah and
Savior]; and many of the Corinthians
who heard [Paul's message] were be-
lieving and being baptized.
9 One night the Lord said to Paul in a
vision, "Do not be afraid anymore, but
go on speaking and do not be silent;
10 for I am with you, and no one will
attack you in order to hurt you, be-
cause I have many people in this city."
[Is 43:5; Jer 1:8]
11 So he settled *there* for a year and
six months, teaching them the word
of God [concerning eternal salvation
through faith in Christ].
12 But when Gallio was proconsul of
Achaia (southern Greece), the Jews
made a united attack on Paul and
brought him before the judgment seat,
13 declaring, "This man is persuading
people to worship God in violation of
the law [of Moses]."
14 But when Paul was about to reply,
Gallio said to the Jews, "If it were a
matter of some misdemeanor or seri-
ous crime, O Jews, I would have reason
to put up with you;
15 but since it is merely a question [of
doctrine within your religion] about
words and names and your own law,

---

repulsed by the idea of a bodily resurrection because they considered the body to be evil. This idea, known as *dualism* was derived from the teachings of Socrates and Plato. It held that everything physical is evil and everything spiritual is good. Therefore, the body and what is done with it is not important because it will be discarded at the end of life.

18:1 *Corinth.* Corinth was the political capital of Achaia. It was also a center for the worship of Aphrodite, the goddess of fertility, and it housed the major temple of Apollo. Because of the sensuous nature of the religious cult of Aphrodite, Corinth had a reputation for being a city of immorality. Beginning in the fifth century BC, the Greeks used a word meaning "to act like a Corinthian" as a symbol for sexual immorality.

18:3 *tent-makers.* All young rabbinical students had to learn a trade. The province of Cilicia, from which Paul came, was noted for its cloth made from goats' hair. It is likely that Paul's skill involved making such cloth.

18:7 *Titius Justus.* Most Romans had three names. This man's name was Titius Justus. Based on Paul's letter to the Corinthians, it is likely that Justus was the man called Gaius mentioned in 1 Corinthians 1:14.

CHAPTER 18 **2** Ro 16:3; 1Co 16:19; 2Ti 4:19 **3** Ac 20:34; 1Co 4:12; 1Th 2:9; 2Th 3:8 **4** Ac 17:2 **5** Ac 17:14,15; ver. 28; Job 32:18; Ac 17:3 **6** Ac 13:45; Neh 5:13; Mt 10:14; Ac 13:51; Lev 20:9,11,12; 2Sa 1:16; Eze 18:13; 33:4; Eze 3:18,19; 33:9; Ac 20:26; Ac 13:46; 28:28 **8** 1Co 1:14 **9** Ac 23:11 **10** Jer 1:18,19 **14** Ac 23:29; 25:11,19

THE THIRD MISSIONARY JOURNEY OF PAUL

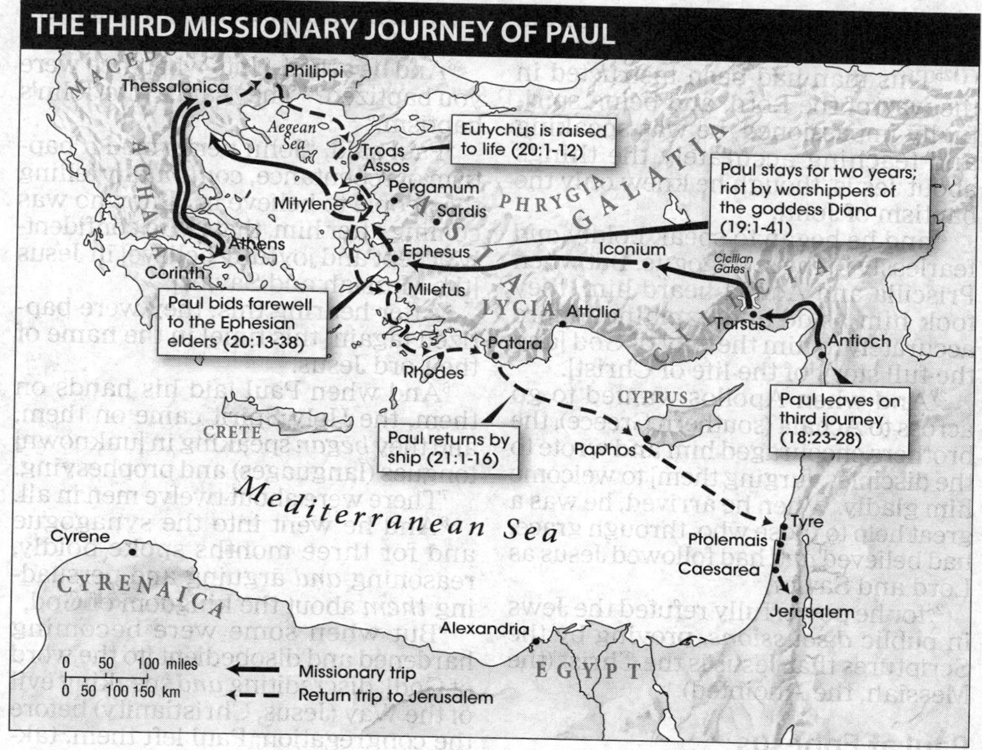

see to it yourselves; I am unwilling to
judge these matters."
16 And he drove them away from the
judgment seat.
17 Then the Greeks all seized Sos-
thenes, the leader of the synagogue,
and *began* beating him right in front
of the judgment seat; but Gallio paid
no attention to any of this. [1 Cor 1:1]
18 Paul stayed for a while longer, and
then told the brothers and sisters good-
bye and sailed for Syria; and he was
accompanied by Priscilla and Aquila.
At Cenchrea [the southeastern port of
Corinth] he had his hair cut, because
he was keeping a [Nazirite] vow [of
abstention].
19 Then they arrived in Ephesus, and
he left the others there; but he entered
the synagogue and reasoned *and* de-
bated with the Jews.
20 When they asked him to stay for a
longer time, he refused;
21 but after telling them goodbye and
saying, "I will return again if God is
willing," he set sail from Ephesus.
22 When he had landed at Caesarea,
he went up and greeted the church [at
Jerusalem], and then went down to
Antioch.

Paul's Third Missionary Journey

23 After spending some time *there*, he
left and traveled through the territory
of Galatia and Phrygia, strengthening
and encouraging all the disciples.
24 Now a Jew named Apollos, a native
of Alexandria, came to Ephesus. He

18:18 *had his hair cut.* Paul had his hair cut as part of a Nazirite vow he had made (see Nu 6:5). Such a vow had to be fulfilled in Jerusalem where the hair would be presented to God.

18:24 *Apollos, a native of Alexandria.* This Jew with a Greek name was from the second largest city in the Roman Empire. Alexandria was a seaport on the northern coast of Egypt. Founded

17 1Co 1:1 **18** Nu 6:18; Ac 21:24; Ro 16:1 **21** Ac 19:21; 20:16; 1Co 4:19; Heb 6:3; Jas 4:15 **23** Gal 1:2; 4:14; Ac 14:22; 15:32,41 **24** 1Co 1:12; 3:5,6; 4:6; Titus 3:13

was an eloquent *and* cultured man, and
well versed in the [Hebrew] Scriptures.
25 This man had been instructed in
the way of the Lord, and being spiri-
tually impassioned, he was speaking
and teaching accurately the things
about Jesus, though he knew only the
baptism of John;
26 and he began to speak boldly *and*
fearlessly in the synagogue. But when
Priscilla and Aquila heard him, they
took him aside and explained more
accurately to him the way of God [and
the full story of the life of Christ].
27 And when Apollos wanted to go
across to Achaia (southern Greece), the
brothers encouraged him and wrote to
the disciples, [urging them] to welcome
him gladly. When he arrived, he was a
great help to those who, through grace,
had believed *and* had followed Jesus as
Lord and Savior,
28 for he powerfully refuted the Jews
in public *discussions*, proving by the
Scriptures that Jesus is the Christ (the
Messiah, the Anointed).

Paul at Ephesus

19 IT HAPPENED that while Apol-
los was in Corinth, Paul went
through the upper [inland] districts
and came down to Ephesus, and found
some disciples.
2 He asked them, "Did you receive
the Holy Spirit when you believed [in
Jesus as the Christ]?" And they said,
"No, we have not even heard that there
is a Holy Spirit."
3 And he asked, "Into what then were
you baptized?" They said, "Into John's
baptism."
4 Paul said, "John performed a bap-
tism of repentance, *continually* telling
the people to believe in Him who was
coming after him, that is, [to confident-
ly accept and joyfully believe] in Jesus
[the Messiah and Savior]."
5 After hearing this, they were bap-
tized [again, this time] in the name of
the Lord Jesus.
6 And when Paul laid his hands on
them, the Holy Spirit came on them,
and they *began* speaking in [unknown]
tongues (languages) and prophesying.
7 There were about twelve men in all.
8 And he went into the synagogue
and for three months spoke boldly,
reasoning *and* arguing and persuad-
ing *them* about the kingdom of God.
9 But when some were becoming
hardened and disobedient [to the word
of God], discrediting *and* speaking evil
of the Way (Jesus, Christianity) before
the congregation, Paul left them, tak-
ing the disciples with him, and went
on holding daily discussions in the
lecture hall of Tyrannus [instead of in
the synagogue].
10 This continued for two years, so
that all the inhabitants of [the west
coast province of] Asia [Minor], Jews
as well as Greeks, heard the word of

---

by Alexander the Great, the city was very cosmopolitan. Egyptians, Romans, and Greeks all lived there; over one quarter of the population was Jewish. The Greek translation of the Hebrew Scriptures had been produced in that city about 150 years before the birth of Jesus The city was famous for its great library and was considered the cultural and educational center of the world.

19:3 *John's baptism.* Baptism was a ritual used by the Jews as a picture of cleansing and purification. Gentiles who converted to Judaism would go through the rite of purification as their first act of worship. They would dip themselves in water as a sign of being cleansed from their old way of life. Before entering into the temple to worship, Jews would dip themselves in ritual bathing pools to show their desire for purification. John's baptism was a symbol of repentance from sin and a looking ahead to the coming of the Messiah.

19:6 *laid his hands on them.* The Holy Ghost was received without the laying on of hands in 10:44–48. By laying on his hands here, Paul was demonstrating his apostolic authority. He was also affirming the unity of the new church in Ephesus with the church in Jerusalem. Both were empowered by the Holy Spirit to speak in foreign tongues.

19:10 *all the inhabitants of [the west coast province of] Asia ... heard.* From Ephesus, other churches were born in Asia Minor—in Colosse, Smyrna, Pergamos, Thyatira, Sardis, Philadelphia, and Laodicea. Paul and his students

25 Ro 12:11; Ac 19:3 **27** 1Co 3:6 **28** ver. 5; Ac 9:22; 17:3 **CHAPTER 19** **1** 1Co 1:12; 3:5,6 **2** Ac 8:16; See 1Sa 3:7 **3** Ac 18:25 **4** Mt 3:11; Jn 1:15,27,30; Ac 1:5; 11:16; 13:24,25 **5** Ac 8:16 **6** Ac 6:6; 8:17; 2:4; 10:46 **8** Ac 17:2; 18:4; Ac 1:3; 28:23 **9** 2Ti 1:15; 2Pe 2:2; Jude 10; ver. 23; See Ac 9:2; 22:4; 24:14 **10** See Ac 20:31

the Lord [concerning eternal salvation through faith in Christ].

Miracles at Ephesus

11God was doing extraordinary *and* unusual miracles by the hands of Paul,
12so that even handkerchiefs *or* face-towels or aprons that had touched his skin were brought to the sick, and their diseases left them and the evil spirits came out [of them].
13Then some of the traveling Jewish exorcists also attempted to call the name of the Lord Jesus over those who had evil spirits, saying, "I implore you *and* solemnly command you by the Jesus whom Paul preaches!"
14Seven sons of one [named] Sceva, a Jewish chief priest, were doing this.
15But the evil spirit retorted, "I know *and* recognize *and* acknowledge Jesus, and I know about Paul, but as for you, who are you?"
16Then the man, in whom was the evil spirit, leaped on them and subdued all of them and overpowered them, so that they ran out of that house [in terror, stripped] naked and wounded.
17This became known to all who lived in Ephesus, both Jews and Greeks. And fear fell upon them all, and the name of the Lord Jesus was magnified *and* exalted.
18Many of those who had become believers were coming, confessing and disclosing their [former sinful] practices.
19And many of those who had practiced magical arts collected their books and [throwing book after book on the pile] began burning them in front of everyone. They calculated their value and found it to be 50,000 pieces of silver.
20So the word of the Lord [concerning eternal salvation through faith in Christ] was growing greatly and prevailing.
21Now after these events, Paul determined in the Spirit that he would travel through Macedonia and Achaia (most of the Greek mainland), and go to Jerusalem, saying, "After I have been there, I must also see Rome [and preach the good news of salvation]."
22And after sending two of his assistants, Timothy and Erastus, to Macedonia [ahead of him], he stayed on in [the west coast province of] Asia [Minor] for a while.
23About that time there occurred no small disturbance concerning the Way (Jesus, Christianity).
24Now a man named Demetrius, a silversmith, who made silver shrines of [the goddess] Artemis (Diana), was bringing no small profit to the craftsmen.
25These [craftsmen] he called together, along with the workmen of similar *trades,* and said, "Men, you are well aware that we make a good living from this business.
26"You see and hear that not only at Ephesus, but almost all over [the province of] Asia, this Paul has persuaded [people to believe his teaching] and has misled a large number of people, claiming that gods made by [human] hands are not *really* gods *at all.*
27"Not only is there danger that this trade of ours will be discredited, but also that the [magnificent] temple of the great goddess Artemis will be discredited, and that she whom all Asia and the world worship will even be dethroned *and* lose her glorious magnificence."
28When they heard this, they were filled with rage, and they *began* shouting, "Great is Artemis of the Ephesians!"
29Then the city was filled with

clearly did more than study. They must have actively evangelized as well.

19:13 *the name of the Lord Jesus.* The use of magical names in incantations was common in the ancient world. These practitioners had latched onto the name of Jesus to use as an incantation, but they discovered that it was not enough to know the name of Jesus; they needed to know Jesus personally.

19:29 *the amphitheater.* This amphitheater seated 25,000 people.

11 Mk 16:20; Ac 14:3 **12** See 2Ki 4:29; Ac 5:15 **13** Mt 12:27; See Mk 9:38; Lk 9:49 **17** Lk 1:65; 7:16; Ac 2:43; 5:5,11 **18** Mt 3:6 **20** Ac 6:7; 12:24 **21** Ro 15:25; Gal 2:1; Ac 20:22; Ac 18:21; 23:11; Ro 15:24-28 **22** Ro 16:23; 2Ti 4:20 **23** 2Co 1:8; See Ac 9:2 **24** Ac 16:16,19 **26** Ps 115:4; Isa 44:10-20; Jer 10:3 **29** Ro 16:23; 1Co 1:14; Ac 20:4; 27:2; Col 4:10; Php 24

confusion; and people rushed togeth-
er [as a group] into the amphitheater,
dragging along with them Gaius and
Aristarchus, Macedonians who were
Paul's traveling companions.
30 Paul wanted to go into the [pagan]
assembly, but the disciples would not
let him.
31 Even some of the Asiarchs (offi-
cials) who were his friends sent *word*
to him and repeatedly warned him not
to venture into the amphitheater.
32 Now some shouted one thing and
some another, for the gathering was in
confusion and most of the people did
not know why they had come together.
33 Some of the crowd advised Alexan-
der [to speak], since the Jews had pushed
him forward; and Alexander motioned
with his hand [for attention] and intend-
ed to make a defense to the people.
34 But when they realized that he was
a Jew, a single outcry went up from
the crowd as they shouted for about
two hours, "Great is Artemis of the
Ephesians!"
35 After the town clerk had quieted
the crowd, he said, "Men of Ephesus,
what person is there who does not
know that the city of the Ephesians
is the guardian of the temple of the
great Artemis and of that [sacred stone
image of her] which fell from the sky?
36 "So, since these things cannot be
denied, you ought to be quiet *and* stay
calm and not do anything rash.
37 "For you have brought these men
here who are neither temple robbers
nor blasphemers of our goddess.
38 "So then, if Demetrius and the
craftsmen who are with him have a
complaint against anyone, the courts
are in session and proconsuls are
available; let them bring charges
against one another there.
39 "But if you want anything beyond
this, it will be settled in the lawful as-
sembly.
40 "For we are running the risk of
being accused of rioting in regard to
today's events, and since there is no
reason for it, we will be unable to give
an account *and* justify this disorderly
gathering."
41 And when he had said these things,
he dismissed the assembly.

Paul in Macedonia and Greece

20 AFTER THE uproar had end-
ed, Paul sent for the disciples,
and when he had encouraged them he
told them goodbye, and set off to go to
Macedonia.
2 After he had gone through those
districts and had encouraged the be-
lievers, he came to Greece.
3 And he stayed three months, and
when a plot was formed against him
by the Jews as he was about to set sail
for Syria, he decided to return through
Macedonia (northern Greece).
4 He was accompanied by Sopater
of Berea, *the son* of Pyrrhus, and by
Aristarchus and Secundus of the Thes-
salonians, and by Gaius of Derbe, and
Timothy, and Tychicus and Trophimus
of Asia.
5 These men went on ahead and
were waiting for us (including Luke)
at Troas.
6 We sailed from Philippi after the
days of Unleavened Bread (Passover
week), and within five days we reached
them at Troas, where we stayed for
seven days.
7 Now on the first day of the week
(Sunday), when we were gathered

19:40 *we are running the risk.* The riot at Ephesus could have brought the discipline of Rome down upon the city. The *Pax Romana*, the peace that the Roman Empire brought to the Mediterranean world, was very important to Rome. The Romans would not tolerate any kind of uprising or rebellion. Ephesus risked losing its freedom and being ruled directly by the Roman army.

20:2 *encouraged.* This word has a full range of meanings, from rebuking in a certain way to comforting. Encouragement includes instruction, appeal, affirmation, exhortation, warning, and correction.

20:7 The Lord's Supper — Although the phrase "to break bread" could mean an ordinary meal, it more likely refers to the observance of

33 1Ti 1:20; 2Ti 4:14; Ac 12:17 **CHAPTER 20** **1** 1Co 16:5; 1Ti 1:3 **3** Ac 9:23; 23:12; 25:3; 2Co 11:26 **4** Ac 19:29; 27:2; Col 4:10; Ac 19:29; Ac 16:1; Eph 6:21; Col 4:7; 2Ti 4:12; Titus 3:12; Ac 21:29; 2Ti 4:20 **6** Ex 12:14,15; 23:15; Ac 16:8; 2Co 2:12; 2Ti 4:13 **7** 1Co 16:2; Rev 1:10; Ac 2:42,46; 1Co 10:16; 11:20

together to break bread (share communion), Paul *began* talking with them, intending to leave the next day; and he kept on with his message until midnight.
[8]Now there were many lamps in the upper room where we were assembled,
[9]and there was a young man named Eutychus ("Lucky") sitting on the window sill. He was sinking into a deep sleep, and as Paul kept on talking longer and longer, he was completely overcome by sleep and fell down from the third story; and he was picked up dead.
[10]But Paul went down and threw himself on him and embraced him, and said [to those standing around him], "Do not be troubled, because he is alive."
[11]When Paul had gone back upstairs and had broken the bread and eaten, he talked [informally and confidentially] with them for a long time—until daybreak [in fact]—and then he left.
[12]They took the boy [Eutychus] home alive, and were greatly comforted *and* encouraged.

Troas to Miletus

[13]But we went on ahead to the ship and set sail for Assos, intending to take Paul on board there; for that was what he had arranged, intending himself to go [a shorter route] by land.
[14]So when he met us at Assos, we took him on board and sailed on to Mitylene.
[15]Sailing from there, we arrived the next day [at a point] opposite Chios; the following day we crossed over to Samos, and the next day we arrived at Miletus [about 30 miles south of Ephesus].
[16]Paul had decided to sail on past Ephesus so that he would not end up spending time [unnecessarily] in [the province of] Asia (modern Turkey); for he was in a hurry to be in Jerusalem, if possible, on the day of Pentecost.

Farewell to Ephesus

[17]However, from Miletus he sent *word* to Ephesus and summoned the elders of the church [to meet him there].
[18]And when they arrived he said to them:
"You know well how I [lived when I] was with you, from the first day that I set foot in Asia [until now],
[19]serving the Lord with all humility and with tears and trials which came on me because of the plots of the Jews [against me];
[20][you know] how I did not shrink back in fear from telling you anything that was for your benefit, or from teaching you in public meetings, and from house to house,
[21]solemnly [and wholeheartedly] testifying to both Jews and Greeks, urging them to turn in repentance to God and [to have] faith in our Lord Jesus Christ [for salvation].
[22]"And now, compelled by the Spirit *and* obligated by my convictions, I am going to Jerusalem, not knowing what will happen to me there,
[23]except that the Holy Spirit solemnly [and emphatically] affirms to me in city after city that imprisonment and suffering await me.
[24]"But I do not consider my life as

---

the Lord's Supper in obedience to Christ's command. The "breaking of bread" appears to be the primary purpose for the gathering, with Paul's sermon rising naturally in a group of people who had gathered to remember Christ.

20:13–16 *to go [a shorter route] by land.* The distance between Troas and Assos was about thirty miles by sea, but Paul chose to go over land on foot.

20:17 *elders.* The words "elder" (literally, one who is older) and "overseer" (v. 28) appear to be used in the New Testament as interchangeable terms for the leaders of a particular fellowship.

20:22 *compelled by the Spirit.* Some say that Paul was out of the will of God in going to Jerusalem after the warnings of bonds and afflictions. But there is no evidence that Paul was rebelling against God. On the contrary, Jesus Himself confirmed that the trip was part of His good and perfect will (23:11).

8 Ac 1:13 **10** 1Ki 17:21; 2Ki 4:34; Mt 9:24 **16** Ac 18:21; 19:21; 21:4,12; Ac 24:17; Ac 2:1; 1Co 16:8 **18** Ac 18:19; 19:1,10 **19** ver. 3 **20** ver. 27 **21** Ac 18:5; Mk 1:15; Lk 24:27; Ac 2:38 **22** Ac 19:21 **23** Ac 21:4,11; 1Th 3:3 **24** Ac 21:13; Ro 8:35; 2Co 4:16; 2Ti 4:7; Ac 1:17; 2Co 4:1; Gal 1:1; Titus 1:3

something of value *or* dear to me, so
that I may [with joy] finish my course
and the ministry which I received from
the Lord Jesus, to testify faithfully
of the good news of God's [precious,
undeserved] grace [which makes us
free of the guilt of sin and grants us
eternal life].

25 "And now, listen carefully: I know
that none of you, among whom I went
about preaching the kingdom, will see
me again.

26 "For that reason I testify to you on
this [our parting] day that I am inno-
cent of the blood of all people.

27 "For I did not shrink from declar-
ing to you the whole purpose *and* plan
of God.

28 "Take care *and* be on guard for
yourselves and for the whole flock over
which the Holy Spirit has appointed
you as overseers, to shepherd (tend,
feed, guide) the church of God which
He bought with His own blood.

29 "I know that after I am gone, [false
teachers like] ferocious wolves will
come in among you, not sparing the
flock;

30 even from among your own selves
men will arise, speaking perverse *and*
distorted things, to draw away the dis-
ciples after themselves [as their fol-
lowers].

31 "Therefore be *continually* alert, re-
membering that for three years, night
or day, I did not stop admonishing *and*
advising each one [of you] with tears.

32 "And now I commend you to God
[placing you in His protective, lov-
ing care] and [I commend you] to the
word of His grace [the counsel and
promises of His unmerited favor]. His
grace is able to build you up and to give
you the [rightful] inheritance among
all those who are sanctified [that is,
among those who are set apart for
God's purpose—all believers].

33 "I had no desire for anyone's silver
or gold or [expensive] clothes.

34 "You know personally that these
hands ministered to my own needs
[working in manual labor] and to
[those of] the people who were with me.

35 "In everything I showed you [by
example] that by working hard in this
way you must help the weak and re-
member the words of the Lord Jesus,
that He Himself said, 'It is more blessed
[and brings greater joy] to give than to
receive.' "

36 When he had said these things, he
knelt down and prayed with them all.

37 And they *began* to weep openly
and threw their arms around Paul's
neck, and repeatedly kissed him,

38 grieving *and* distressed especially
over the word which he had spoken,
that they would not see him again.
And they accompanied him to the ship.

Paul Sails from Miletus

21 WHEN WE had torn ourselves
away from them and set sail, we
ran a straight course and came to Cos,
and on the next day to Rhodes, and
from there to Patara;

2 and after finding a ship crossing
over to Phoenicia, we went on board
and set sail.

3 After we came in sight of Cyprus,

20:28 Church — The elders or overseers of God's flock must be men who are appointed not just by other men, but by the Holy Spirit of God. The leadership of the church is a solemn responsibility, and it should only be accepted by those who are convinced that they have been both called and equipped by the Holy Spirit to do this work. An elder has the responsibility to follow the example of our Chief Shepherd, Jesus Christ, as a servant leader.

20:35 It is more blessed [and brings greater joy] to give. This saying of Jesus is not found in the Gospels, but it has been recorded here through Paul's knowledge of it.

21:2 a ship crossing over to Phoenicia. In the summer months, the wind of the Aegean Sea blows from the north, beginning very early in the morning. In the late afternoon the wind dies away. Sunset brings a dead calm, and later a gentle southerly breeze blows. If a ship was

---

25 ver. 38; Ro 15:23 **26** Ac 18:6; 2Co 7:2 **27** ver. 20; Lk 7:30; Jn 15:15; Eph 1:11 **28** 1Ti 4:16; 1Pe 5:2; 1Co 12:28; Eph 1:7,14; Col 1:14; Heb 9:12; 1Pe 1:19; Rev 5:9; See Heb 9:14 **29** Mt 7:15; 2Pe 2:1 **30** 1Ti 1:20; 1Jn 2:19 **31** Ac 19:10 **32** Heb 13:9; Ac 9:31; Ac 26:18; Eph 1:18; Col 1:12; 3:24; Heb 9:15; 1Pe 1:4 **33** 1Sa 12:3; 1Co 9:12; 2Co 7:2; 11:9; 12:17 **34** Ac 18:3; 1Co 4:12; 1Th 2:9; 2Th 3:8 **35** Ro 15:1; 1Co 9:12; 2Co 11:9,12; 12:13; Eph 4:28; 1Th 4:11; 5:14; 2Th 3:8 **36** Ac 7:60; 21:5 **37** Ge 45:14; 46:29 **38** ver. 25

leaving it on our left (port side), we sailed on to Syria and put in at Tyre; for there the ship was to unload her cargo.
4After looking up the disciples [in Tyre], we stayed there [with them] seven days; and they kept telling Paul through the [Holy] Spirit not to set foot in Jerusalem.
5When our days there came to an end, we left and proceeded on our journey, while all of the disciples, with their wives and children, escorted us on our way until *we were* outside the city. After kneeling down on the beach and praying, we told one another goodbye.
6Then we boarded the ship, and they returned to their homes.
7When we had completed the voyage from Tyre, we landed [twenty miles to the south] at Ptolemais, and after greeting the believers, we stayed with them for one day.
8On the next day we left and came to Caesarea, and we went to the house of Philip the evangelist, who was one of the seven [deacons], and stayed with him. [Acts 6:3–6]
9He had four virgin daughters who had the gift of prophecy.
10As we were staying there for some time, a prophet named Agabus came down from Judea.
11And coming to [see] us, he took Paul's [wide] band (belt, sash) and bound his own feet and hands, and said, "This is what the Holy Spirit says: 'In this same way the Jews in Jerusalem will bind the man who owns this band, and they will hand him over to the Gentiles (pagans).' "
12Now when we had heard this, both we and the local residents *began* pleading with Paul trying to persuade him not to go up to Jerusalem.
13Then Paul replied, "What are you doing, weeping and breaking my heart [like this]? For I am ready not only to be bound *and* imprisoned, but even to die at Jerusalem for the name of the Lord Jesus."
14And since he would not be dissuaded, we stopped pleading *and* fell silent, saying, "The Lord's will be done!"

Paul at Jerusalem

15After this we got ready and started on our way up to Jerusalem.
16Some of the disciples from Caesarea also came with us, taking us to [the house of] Mnason, a man from Cyprus, a disciple of long standing with whom we were to lodge.
17When we arrived in Jerusalem, the brothers and sisters welcomed us gladly.
18On the next day Paul went with us to [see] James, and all the elders *of the church* were present.
19After greeting them, Paul *began* to give a detailed account of the things that God had done among the Gentiles through his ministry.
20And when they heard it, they *began* glorifying *and* praising God; and they said to him, "You see, brother, how

---

heading down the coast, it would typically anchor at evening and wait for the winds of the morning.
21:4 *through the [Holy] Spirit*. Because of this warning, many have thought that Paul's insistence in going to Jerusalem was disobedience to God's will. However, it is more likely that this was simply a warning to let him know what to expect in the future. Paul was obviously very sensitive to the Holy Spirit (16:6), and felt that he had received specific instructions to go to Jerusalem (20:22). Later Jesus Himself encouraged Paul concerning his decision to go (23:11).
21:10–14 *bound his own feet and hands*. The Holy Spirit did not forbid Paul to go to Jerusalem, but warned him of what it would cost him.
21:17 Fellowship — Fellowship means more than chatting over coffee and cookies, or sharing a potluck supper. Christian fellowship essentially means sharing one another's lives, participating in both the joy and sorrow of our brothers and sisters in Christ. Christian community extends beyond geography, class, color, and gender. As parts of one glorious whole, the body of Christ, believers rejoice in one another's joy, and reach out a helping hand for another's need.

CHAPTER 21 **4** ver. 12; Ac 20:23 **5** Ac 20:36 **6** Jn 1:11 **8** Eph 4:11; 2Ti 4:5; Ac 6:5; 8:26,40 **9** Joel 2:28; Ac 2:17 **10** Ac 11:28 **11** ver. 33; Ac 20:23 **13** Ac 20:24 **14** Mt 6:10; 26:42; Lk 11:2; 22:42 **17** Ac 15:4 **18** Ac 15:13; Gal 1:19; 2:9 **19** Ac 15:4,12; Ro 15:18,19; Ac 1:17; 20:24 **20** Ac 22:3; Ro 10:2; Gal 1:14

PAUL'S VOYAGE TO ROME

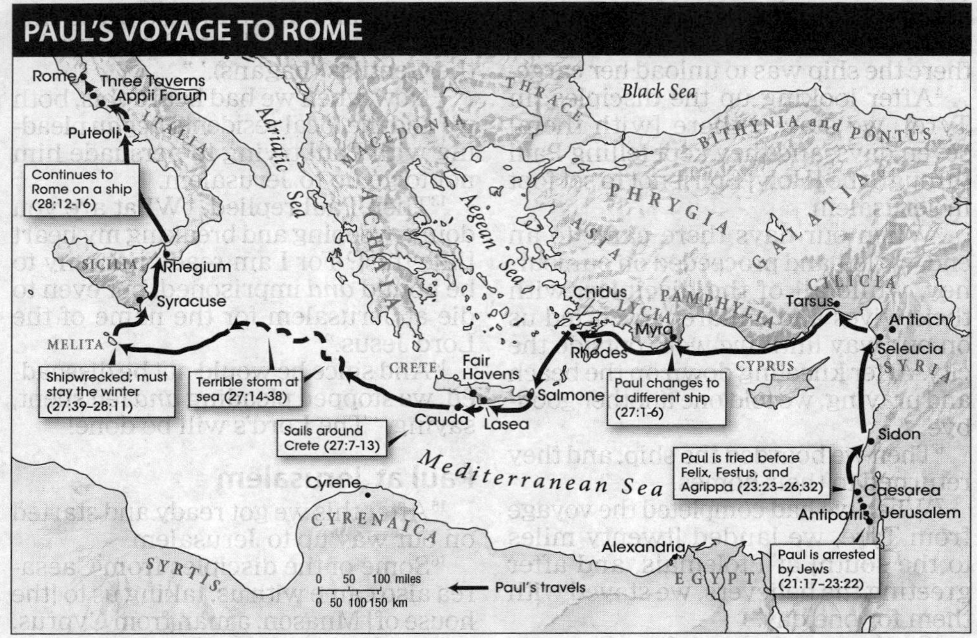

many thousands of believers there are
among the Jews, and they are all enthu-
siastic supporters of the Law [of Moses].
21 "Now they have been told about
you, that you are teaching all the Jews
who are *living* among the Gentiles to
turn away from [the Law of] Moses,
advising them not to circumcise their
children or to live according to the
[Mosaic] customs.
22 "What then should be done? They
will certainly hear that you have arrived.
23 "Therefore do just what we tell you.
We have four men who have taken a
vow;
24 take these men and purify your-
self along with them, and pay their
expenses [for the temple offerings] so
that they may shave their heads. Then
everyone will know that there is noth-
ing to the things they have been told
about you, but that you yourself also
follow and keep the Law.
25 "But with regard to the Gentiles
who have believed [in Christ], we have
sent them a letter with our decision
that they should abstain from meat
sacrificed to idols and from [consum-
ing] blood and from [the meat of] what
has been strangled and from sexual
immorality."
26 Then Paul took the [four] men, and
the next day he purified himself along
with them [by submitting to the ritual].
He went into the temple to give notice
of [the time] when the days of puri-
fication [ending each vow] would be
fulfilled and the usual offering could
be presented on behalf of each one.

Paul Seized in the Temple

27 When the seven days [required
to complete the ritual] were almost
over, [some] Jews from [the province
of] Asia [Minor], caught sight of him
in the temple, and *began* to stir up the
crowd, and they seized him,
28 shouting, "Men of Israel, help us!
This is the man who teaches all men

21:25 *they should abstain from.* The spiritual unity of the body of believers is realized in its diversity, not in its conformity. From our diverse backgrounds and cultures we honor the same Lord.

21:28 *defiled this holy place.* The temple in

24 Nu 6:2,13,18; Ac 18:18 **25** Ac 15:20,29 **26** Ac 24:18; Nu 6:13 **27** Ac 24:18; Ac 26:21 **28** Ac 24:5,6

everywhere against our people and
the Law and this place. And besides,
he has brought Greeks into the temple
and has defiled this holy place."
29 For they had previously seen
Trophimus the Ephesian in the city
with Paul, and they assumed that he
had brought the man into the temple
[beyond the court of the Gentiles].
30 Then the whole city was provoked
and confused, and the people rushed
together. They seized Paul and dragged
him out of the temple, and immediately
the gates were closed.
31 Now while they were trying to kill
him, word came to the commander of
the [Roman] garrison that all Jerusa-
lem was in a state of upheaval.
32 So he immediately took soldiers
and centurions and ran down among
them. When the people saw the com-
mander and the soldiers, they stopped
beating Paul.
33 Then the commander came up and
arrested Paul, and ordered that he be
bound with two chains. Then he asked
who he was and what he had done.
34 But some in the crowd were shout-
ing one thing and others something
else; and since he could not determine
the facts because of the uproar, he or-
dered that Paul be taken to the bar-
racks [in the tower of Antonia].
35 When Paul got to the steps, he was
carried by the soldiers because of the
violence of the mob;
36 for the majority of the people kept
following them, shouting, "Away with
him! [Kill him!]"
37 Just as Paul was about to be taken
into the barracks, he asked the com-
mander, "May I say something to you?"
And the man replied, "Do you know
Greek?
38 "Then you are not [as I assumed]
the Egyptian who some time ago
stirred up a rebellion and led those
4,000 men of the Assassins out into
the wilderness?"
39 Paul said, "I am a Jew from Tarsus
in Cilicia (Mersin Province, Turkey),
a citizen of no insignificant city; and
I beg you, allow me to speak to the
people."
40 When the commander had given
him permission, Paul, standing on the
steps, gestured with his hand to the
people; and when there was a great
hush, he spoke to them in the Hebrew
dialect (Jewish Aramaic), saying,

Paul's Defense before the Jews

22 "BRETHREN AND fathers
(kinsmen), hear my defense
which I now offer to you."
2 When they heard that he was ad-
dressing them in the Hebrew dialect,
they became even more quiet. And he
continued,
3 "I am a Jew, born in Tarsus of Cili-
cia, but brought up in this city, educat-
ed at the feet of Gamaliel according to
the strictness of the law of our fathers,
being ardent *and* passionate for God
just as all of you are today.
4 "I persecuted *and* pursued the fol-
lowers of this Way to the death, bind-
ing them with chains and putting [fol-
lowers of Jesus] both men and women
into prisons,
5 as the high priest and all the Coun-
cil of the elders (Sanhedrin, Jewish
High Court) can testify; because from
them I received letters to the brothers,

New Testament times was surrounded by three courts. The innermost court was the court of Israel, where Jewish men could offer sacrifices. The second court was the court of Women where Jewish families could gather for prayer and worship. The outer court was the court of Gentiles, open to all who would worship God. The penalty for any Gentile who went beyond this court was death.

21:38 ***you are not [as I assumed] the Egyptian.*** An assassin claiming to be a prophet had come to Jerusalem in AD 54, and led four thousand Jews up to the Mount of Olives, promising that at his word the walls of Jerusalem would fall and the Roman Empire would be destroyed. The uprising was crushed, leaving four hundred Jews dead and another two hundred as prisoners. The Egyptian escaped into the desert with some of his followers.

29 Ac 20:4 **30** Ac 26:21 **32** Ac 23:27; 24:7 **33** ver. 11; Ac 20:23 **36** Lk 23:18; Jn 19:15; Ac 22:22 **38** See Ac 5:36 **39** Ac 9:11; 22:3 **40** Ac 12:17 **CHAPTER 22 1** Ac 7:2 **3** Ac 21:39; 2Co 11:22; Php 3:5; Dt 33:3; Ac 5:34; Ac 26:5; Ac 21:20; Gal 1:14; Ro 10:2 **4** Ac 8:3; 26:9-11; Php 3:6; 1Ti 1:13 **5** Lk 22:66; Ac 4:5; Ac 9:2; 26:10,12

and I was on my way to Damascus in
order to bring those [believers] who
were there to Jerusalem in chains to
be punished.
6“But as I was on my way, approach-
ing Damascus about noontime, a great
blaze of light suddenly flashed from
heaven *and* shone around me.
7“And I fell to the ground and heard
a voice saying to me, ‘Saul, Saul, why
are you persecuting Me?’
8“And I replied, ‘Who are You, Lord?’
And He said to me, ‘I am Jesus the
Nazarene, whom you are persecuting.’
9“Now those who were with me saw
the light, but did not understand the
voice of the One who was speaking
to me.
10“And I asked, ‘What shall I do,
Lord?’ And the Lord answered me,
‘Get up and go into Damascus. There
you will be told all that is appointed
and destined for you to do.’
11“But since I could not see because
of the [glorious intensity and dazzling]
brightness of that light, I was led by the
hand by those who were with me and
came into Damascus.
12“And one Ananias, a devout man
according to the standard of the Law,
and well spoken of by all the Jews who
lived there,
13came to [see] me, and standing
near, he said to me, ‘Brother Saul,
receive your sight!’ And at that very
moment I [recovered my sight and]
looked up at him.
14“And he said, ‘The God of our fa-
thers has appointed you to know His
will, [and to progressively understand
His plan with clarity and power] and
to see the Righteous One [Jesus Christ,
the Messiah] and to hear a message
from His [own] mouth.
15‘For you will be His witness to all
men *testifying* of what you have seen
and heard.
16‘Now, why do you delay? Get up
and be baptized, and wash away your
sins by calling on His name [for sal-
vation].’
17“Then it happened when I had re-
turned to Jerusalem and was praying
in the temple [enclosure], that I fell into
a trance (vision);
18and I saw Him saying to me, ‘Hur-
ry and get out of Jerusalem quickly,
because they will not accept your tes-
timony about Me.’
19“And I said, ‘Lord, they themselves
know [without any doubt] that in one
synagogue after another I used to im-
prison and beat those who believed in
You [and Your message of salvation].
20‘And when the blood of Your wit-
ness Stephen was being shed, I also
was standing nearby approving *and*
consenting [to his death], and guarding
the coats of those who were killing
him.’
21“And the Lord said to me, ‘Go, I will
send you far away to the Gentiles.’ ”
22They listened to Paul until [he
made] this [last] statement, but now
they raised their voices and shouted,
“Away with such a man from the earth!
He is not fit to live!”
23And as they were shouting and
throwing off their coats [getting ready
to stone Paul] and tossing dust into the
air [expressing their anger],
24the commander ordered him to be
brought into the barracks, stating that
he was to be interrogated with a whip
in order to learn why the people were
shouting against him that way.
25But when they had stretched him
out with the *leather* straps [in prepa-
ration for the whip], Paul said to the
centurion who was standing by, “Is

22:16 ***calling on His name.*** Calling on the name of the Lord is what brings salvation, not the physical act of baptism (Ro 10:9 – 13). Baptism is the public declaration of one’s repentance and new life.
22:24 ***with a whip.*** The scourge was a leather whip, studded with pieces of metal or bone, fastened to a wooden handle. The victim was stretched out on the floor or bound to a pillar to be beaten. Scourging was a cruel torture, designed to maim or kill the victim.

6 Ac 9:3; 26:12,13 **9** Da 10:7; Ac 9:7 **12** Ac 9:17; 10:22; 1Ti 3:7 **14** Ac 3:13; 5:30; 9:15; 26:16; 1Co 9:1; 15:8; Ac 3:14; 7:52; 1Co 11:23; Gal 1:12 **15** Ac 23:11; Ac 4:20; 26:16 **16** Ac 2:38; Heb 10:22; Ac 9:14; Ro 10:13 **17** Ac 9:26; 2Co 12:2 **18** ver. 14; Mt 10:14 **19** ver. 4; Ac 8:3; Mt 10:17 **20** Ac 7:58; Lk 11:48; Ac 8:1; Ro 1:32 **21** Ac 9:15; 13:2,46,47; 18:6; 26:17; Ro 1:5; 11:13; 15:16; Gal 1:15,16; 2:7,8; Eph 3:7,8; 1Ti 2:7; 2Ti 1:11 **22** Ac 21:36; Ac 25:24 **25** Ac 16:37

it legal for you to whip a man who is a Roman *citizen* and uncondemned [without a trial]?"

26 When the centurion heard *this*, he went to the commander and said to him, "What are you about to do? This man is a Roman!"

27 So the commander came and asked Paul, "Tell me, are you a Roman?" And he said, "Yes."

28 The commander replied, "I purchased this citizenship [of mine] for a large sum of money [so how did you acquire yours?]." Paul said, "But I was actually born a *citizen*."

29 So those who were about to interrogate him *by torture* immediately let him go; and the commander was also afraid when he realized that Paul was a Roman and he had put him in chains.

30 But on the next day, wanting to know the real reason why Paul was being accused by the Jews, he released him and ordered the chief priests and the whole Council (Sanhedrin, Jewish High Court) to assemble; and brought Paul down and presented him before them.

Paul before the Council

23 THEN PAUL, looking intently at the Council (Sanhedrin, Jewish High Court), said, "Kinsmen, I have lived my life before God with a perfectly good conscience until this very day."

2 [At this] the high priest Ananias ordered those who stood beside him to strike Paul on the mouth.

3 Then Paul said to him, "God is going to strike you, you whitewashed wall! Do you actually sit to judge me according to the Law, and yet in violation of the Law order me to be struck?"

4 But those who stood near Paul said, "Are you insulting the high priest of God?"

5 Paul said, "I was not aware, brothers, that he was high priest; for it is written, 'YOU SHALL NOT SPEAK EVIL OF A RULER OF YOUR PEOPLE.' " [Ex 22:28]

6 But recognizing that one group were Sadducees and the other Pharisees, Paul *began* affirming loudly in the Council *chamber*, "Kinsmen, I am a Pharisee, a son of Pharisees; I am on trial for the hope and resurrection of the dead!"

7 When he said this, an angry dispute erupted between the Pharisees and the Sadducees, and the [whole crowded] assembly was divided [into two factions].

8 For the Sadducees say that there is no [such thing as a] resurrection, nor an angel, nor a spirit, but the Pharisees [speak out freely and] acknowledge [their belief in] them all.

9 Then a great uproar occurred, and some of the scribes of the Pharisees' party stood up and *began* to argue heatedly [in Paul's favor], saying, "We find nothing wrong with this man; suppose a spirit or an angel has [really] spoken to him?"

10 And as the dissension became even greater, the commander, fearing that Paul would be torn to pieces by them, ordered the troops to go down and forcibly take him from them, and bring him to the barracks.

22:28 born a citizen. Roman citizenship was originally limited to free Romans, but later it was offered to many others in the empire, either as a reward for outstanding service, or in exchange for a high price. Because Paul's father was a Roman citizen (how he became a citizen is unknown), Paul was born a citizen. Ultimately, God used Paul's Roman citizenship to spread the gospel to Rome.

23:1 Conscience—The human conscience is given as a tool, enabling us to tell right from wrong, and to evaluate our own actions. The problem is that the conscience of fallen humans is not a reliable guide. Because humans are not "basically good," an untrained conscience will not necessarily lead toward right. The conscience must be trained by good teaching. It can be rendered useless if it is seared or defiled; it can be deadened by constantly ignoring it. In order to provide useful guidance, the conscience must be recharged by the Holy Spirit. It must be kept clear by confession of sins, and refusing to accept violations.

CHAPTER 23 **1** Ac 24:16; 1Co 4:4; 2Co 1:12; 4:2; 2Ti 1:3; Heb 13:18 **2** 1Ki 22:24; Jer 20:2; Jn 18:22 **3** Lev 19:35; Dt 25:1,2; Jn 7:51 **5** Ac 24:17; Ex 22:28; Ecc 10:20; 2Pe 2:10; Jude 8 **6** Ac 26:5; Php 3:5; Ac 24:15,21; 26:6; 28:20 **8** Mt 22:23; Mk 12:18; Lk 20:27 **9** Ac 25:25; 26:31; 22:7,17,18; Ac 5:39

11 On the following night the Lord
stood near Paul and said, “Be brave;
for as you have solemnly *and* faithfully
witnessed about Me at Jerusalem, so
you must also testify at Rome.”

A Conspiracy to Kill Paul

12 Now when day came, the Jews
formed a conspiracy and bound them-
selves under an oath (curse), saying
that they would not eat or drink until
they had killed Paul.
13 There were more than forty [men]
who formed this plot [and swore this
oath].
14 They went to the chief priests and
elders and said, “We have bound our-
selves under a solemn oath not to taste
anything [neither food nor drink] until
we have killed Paul.
15 “So now you, along with the Coun-
cil (Sanhedrin, Jewish High Court),
notify the commander to bring Paul
down to you, as if you were going to
investigate his case more thoroughly.
But we are ready to kill him before he
comes near [the place].”
16 But the son of Paul’s sister heard of
their [planned] ambush, and he went
to the barracks and told Paul.
17 Then Paul, calling in one of the
centurions, said, “Take this young man
to the commander, for he has some-
thing to tell him.”
18 So he took him and led him to the
commander and said, “Paul the prison-
er called for me and asked me to bring
this young man to you, because he has
something to tell you.”
19 The commander took him by the
hand and stepping aside, *began* to ask
him privately, “What is it that you have
to tell me?”
20 And he said, “The Jews have
agreed to ask you to bring Paul down
to the Council (Sanhedrin, Jewish High
Court) tomorrow, as if they were going
to interrogate him more thoroughly.
21 “But do not listen to them, for more
than forty of them are lying in wait for
him, and they have bound themselves
with an oath not to eat or drink until
they have killed him. Even now they are
ready, just waiting for your promise.”
22 So the commander let the young
man leave, instructing him, “Do not
tell anyone that you have given me this
information.”

Paul Moved to Caesarea Maritima

23 Then summoning two of the cen-
turions, he said, “Have two hundred
soldiers ready by the third hour of the
night (9:00 p.m.) to go as far as Caes-
area, with seventy horsemen and two
hundred spearmen;
24 also provide mounts for Paul to
ride, and bring him safely to Felix the
governor.”
25 And [after instructing the centu-
rions] he wrote a letter to this effect:
26 “Claudius Lysias, to the most excel-
lent governor Felix, greetings.
27 “This man was seized [as a pris-
oner] by the Jews and was about to
be killed by them, when I came upon
him with the troops and rescued him,
having learned that he was a Roman
citizen.

28 “And wanting to know the
exact charge which they were
making against him, I brought
him down to their Council
(Sanhedrin, Jewish High Court);
29 and I discovered that he was
accused in regard to questions
and issues in their Law, but
[he was] under no accusation
that would call for the
penalty of death or [even] for
imprisonment.

30 “When I was told that there would
be a plot against the man, I sent him
to you immediately, also directing his
accusers to bring their charges against
him before you.”

23:11 ***also testify at Rome.*** Because of the earlier warnings of his friends (21:4,10 – 14), Paul may have begun to doubt his decision. The Lord gave Paul special encouragement at this time, that he was indeed doing just what God wanted him to do.

11 Ac 18:9; 27:23,24 **12** ver. 21,30; Ac 25:3 **20** ver. 12; Ac 20:3 **27** Ac 21:33; 24:7 **28** Ac 22:30 **29** Ac 18:15; 25:19; Ac 26:31 **30** ver. 20; Ac 24:8; 25:6

31 So the soldiers, in compliance with
their orders, took Paul and brought
him to Antipatris during the night.
32 And the next day, leaving the
horsemen to go on with him, they re-
turned to the barracks.
33 When these [horsemen] reached
Caesarea, they delivered the letter to
the governor, and also presented Paul
to him.
34 After reading the letter, he asked
which province Paul was from, and
when he learned that he was from Cili-
cia [an imperial province],
35 he said, "I will hear your case when
your accusers have arrived," giving
orders that Paul be kept under guard
in Herod's Praetorium (the governor's
official residence).

Paul before Felix

24 FIVE DAYS later, the high priest
Ananias came down [from Je-
rusalem to Caesarea] with some el-
ders and an attorney *named* Tertullus
[acting as spokesman and counsel].
They presented to the governor their
[formal] charges against Paul.
2 After Paul had been summoned,
Tertullus began the complaint [against
him], saying *to the governor:*
"Since through you we have attained
great peace, and since by your fore-
sight reforms are being carried out
for this nation,
3 in every way and in every place,
most excellent Felix, we acknowledge
this with all gratitude.
4 "But so that I do not weary you fur-
ther, I beg you to grant us, by your
kindness, a brief hearing.
5 "For we have found this man to be
a public menace and one who insti-
gates dissension among all the Jews
throughout the world, and a ringleader
of the [heretical] sect of the Nazarenes.
6 "He even tried to desecrate the tem-
ple, but we took him into custody [and
we intended to judge him by our Law,
7 but Lysias the commander came,
and with great force took him out of
our hands,
8 and ordered his accusers to come
before you.] By interrogating him
yourself concerning all these mat-
ters you will be able to determine [the
truth about] these things with which
we charge him."
9 The Jews also joined in the attack,
declaring *and* insisting that these
things were so.
10 When the governor nodded for him
to speak, Paul answered,
"Knowing that for many years you
have been a judge over this nation, I
make my defense cheerfully *and* with
good courage.
11 As you can easily verify, it has
been no more than twelve days since
I went up to Jerusalem to worship.
12 "Neither in the temple, nor in the
synagogues, nor *elsewhere* in the city
did they find me carrying on a dis-
cussion *or* disputing with anybody or
causing a crowd to gather.
13 "Nor can they present evidence
to you to prove what they now bring
against me.
14 "But I confess this to you, that ac-
cording to the Way, which they call a
[divisive and heretical] sect, I do wor-
ship *and* serve the God of our fathers,
[confidently] believing everything that
is in accordance with the Law [of Mo-
ses] and that is written in the Prophets;
15 having [the same] hope in God
which these men cherish themselves,
that there shall certainly be a resurrec-

23:33 *the governor.* Antonius Felix governed Judea from AD 52 to 60. Felix had been a slave, but had gained the status of freedman under the emperor Claudius. Because Felix's brother was a friend of the emperor, Felix's political career blossomed, even though he was not popular among his peers. The writer Tacitus described him as "exercising the powers of a king with the character of a slave."

24:14 *the Way.* Paul openly admitted that he was a follower of "the Way" (those who followed Jesus), but he contended that he still believed the Law and the Prophets. That is, he was a follower of Judaism, a religion which enjoyed the protection of Rome.

34 Ac 21:39 **35** Ac 24:1,10; 25:16; Mt 27:27 **CHAPTER 24** **1** Ac 21:27; Ac 23:2,30,35; 25:2 **5** Lk 23:2; Ac 6:13; 16:20; 17:6; 21:28; 1Pe 2:12,15 **6** Ac 21:28; Jn 18:31 **7** Ac 21:33 **8** Ac 23:30 **11** ver. 17; Ac 21:26 **12** Ac 25:8; 28:17 **14** See Am 8:14; Ac 9:2; 2Ti 1:3; Ac 26:22; 28:23 **15** Ac 23:6; 26:6,7; 28:20; Da 12:2; Jn 5:28,29

tion of [the dead], both of the righteous and of the wicked.
16"In view of this, I also do my best *and* strive always to have a clear conscience before God and before men.
17"Now after several years I came [to Jerusalem] to bring to my people charitable contributions and offerings.
18"They found me in the temple presenting these *offerings*, after I had undergone [the rites of] purification, without any crowd or uproar. But *there were* some Jews from [the west coast province of] Asia [Minor],
19who ought to have been here before you to present their charges, if they have anything against me.
20"Or else let these men tell what crime they found [me guilty of] when I stood before the Council (Sanhedrin, Jewish High Court),
21other than for this one statement which I had shouted out as I stood among them, 'For the resurrection of the dead I am on trial before you today.' "
22But Felix, having a rather accurate understanding about the Way, put them off, saying, "When Lysias the commander comes down, I will decide your case."
23Then he ordered the centurion to keep Paul in custody, but to let him have some freedom, and [he told the centurion] not to stop any of his friends from providing for his needs.
24Several days later Felix came with his wife Drusilla, who was a Jewess. He sent for Paul and listened to him talk about faith in Christ Jesus.
25But as he was discussing righteousness, self-control [honorable behavior, personal integrity], and the judgment to come, Felix became frightened and said, "Go away for now, and when I find [a convenient] time I will send for you."
26At the same time he was also hoping to get money from Paul [as a bribe]; so he continued to send for him quite often and talked with him.
27But after two years had passed, Felix was succeeded [in office] by Porcius Festus; and wishing to do the Jews a favor, Felix left Paul imprisoned.

Paul before Festus

25 NOW FESTUS arrived in the province, and three days later he went up to Jerusalem from Caesarea [Maritima].
2And [there in Jerusalem] the chief priests and the leading men of the Jews brought charges against Paul [before Festus], and they repeatedly pleaded with him,
3asking as a concession against Paul, that he would have him brought to Jerusalem; (*meanwhile* planning an ambush to kill him on the way).
4Festus answered that Paul was being held in custody in Caesarea [Maritima] and that he himself was about to leave shortly.
5"So," he said, "let those who are in a position of authority among you go there with me, and if there is anything criminal about the man, let them bring charges against him."
6Now after Festus had spent no more

24:16 Conscience—There is a connection between Paul's belief in future judgment and his desire to maintain a clear conscience before God and man. The intensity of Paul's desire may be seen from the verb translated "to do my best," which occurs only here in the New Testament. Paul's desire to have a good conscience toward God and man reflects the summary of duties of the law of love toward God and neighbor. The conscience needs to be enlightened and purified by Scripture in regard to our responsibilities toward God and man.

24:22 having a rather accurate understanding about the Way. Felix's wife Drusilla was Jewish, and part of the Herodian family. Felix had governed Judea and Samaria for six years. He had ample opportunity to understand both Judaism and "the Way" as he must have observed the workings of the early church in Jerusalem.

24:27 after two years. Around AD 60, a riot broke out in Caesarea. Felix crushed it with such force that he was removed from office.

16 Ac 23:1 **17** Ac 11:29,30; 20:16; Ro 15:25; 2Co 8:4; Gal 2:10 **18** Ac 21:26,27; 26:21 **19** Ac 23:30; 25:16 **21** Ac 23:6; 28:20 **22** ver. 7 **23** Ac 27:3; 28:16 **26** Ex 23:8 **27** Ex 23:2; Ac 12:3; 25:9,14 **CHAPTER 25** **2** ver. 15; Ac 24:1 **3** Ac 23:12,15 **5** ver. 18; Ac 18:14

than eight or ten days among them, he went down to Caesarea, and on the next day he took his seat on the tribunal (the judicial bench), and ordered Paul to be brought [before him].

7 After Paul arrived, the Jews who had come down from Jerusalem stood around him, bringing many serious charges against him which they were not able to prove,

8 while Paul declared in his own defense, "I have done no wrong *and* committed no offense either against the Law of the Jews or against the temple or against Caesar."

9 But Festus, wishing to do the Jews a favor, answered Paul, "Are you willing to go up to Jerusalem and stand trial there in my presence [before the Jewish Sanhedrin] on these *charges?*"

10 Paul said, "I am standing before Caesar's tribunal, where I ought to be tried. I have done nothing wrong to the Jews, as you also very well know.

11 "Therefore, if I am guilty and have committed anything worthy of death, I do not try to escape death; but if there is nothing to the accusations which these men are bringing against me, no one can hand me over to them. I appeal to Caesar (Emperor Nero)."

12 Then Festus, after conferring with [the men who formed] his council, answered, "You have appealed to Caesar; to Caesar you shall go."

13 Now several days later, Agrippa [II] the king and Bernice [his sister] arrived at Caesarea and paid their respects to Festus [the new governor].

14 While they were spending many days there, Festus laid Paul's case before the king, saying, "There is a man here who was left as a prisoner by Felix.

15 "When I was at Jerusalem, the chief priests and the elders of the Jews [told me about him and] brought charges against him, petitioning for a sentence of condemnation against him.

16 "I told them that it was not the custom of the Romans to hand over any man [for punishment] before the accused meets his accusers face to face and has the opportunity to defend himself against the charges.

17 "So after they arrived together here, I did not delay, but on the next day took my place on the tribunal and ordered that the man be brought before me.

18 "When his accusers stood up, they brought no charges against him of crimes that I was expecting [neither civil nor criminal actions],

19 instead they had some points of disagreement with him about their own religion and about one Jesus, a man who had died, but whom Paul kept asserting *and* insisting [over and over] to be alive.

20 "And I, being at a loss as to how to investigate these things, asked whether he was willing to go to Jerusalem and be tried there regarding these matters.

21 "But when Paul appealed to be held in custody for a decision by the Emperor [Nero], I ordered him to be kept in custody until I *could* send him to Caesar."

22 Then Agrippa said to Festus, "I would like to hear the man myself." "Tomorrow," Festus replied, "you will hear him."

Paul before Agrippa

23 So the next day Agrippa and [his sister] Bernice came with great pageantry, and they went into the auditorium accompanied by the military commanders and the prominent men of the city. At the command of Festus, Paul was brought in.

24 Then Festus said, "King Agrippa and all you gentlemen present with us, you see this man [Paul] about whom all the Jewish people appealed to me, both

---

25:11 *appeal to Caesar.* If a Roman citizen thought he was not getting justice in a provincial court, he could appeal to the emperor himself. If the appeal was declared valid, all other proceedings in the lower courts ceased and the prisoner was sent to Rome for the disposition of his case.

7 Mk 15:3; Lk 23:2,10; Ac 24:5,13 **8** Ac 6:13; 24:12; 28:17 **9** Ac 24:27; ver. 20 **11** ver. 25; Ac 18:14; 23:29; 26:31; Ac 26:32; 28:19 **14** Ac 24:27 **15** ver. 2,3 **16** ver. 4,5 **17** ver. 6 **19** Ac 18:15; 23:29 **22** See Ac 9:15 **24** ver. 2,3,7; Ac 22:22

at Jerusalem and here, loudly insisting that he ought not to live any longer.

25 "But I found that he had done nothing worthy of death; however, since he appealed to the Emperor [Nero], I decided to send him [to Rome].

26 "But I have nothing specific about him to write to my lord. So I have brought him before *all of* you, and especially before you, King Agrippa, so that after the investigation has taken place, I will have something to put in writing.

27 "For it seems absurd *and* unreasonable to me to send a prisoner [to Rome] without indicating the charges against him."

Paul's Defense before Agrippa

26 THEN AGRIPPA said to Paul, "You are [now] permitted to speak on your own behalf." At that, Paul stretched out his hand [as an orator] and made his defense [as follows]:

2 "I consider myself fortunate, King Agrippa, since it is before you that I am to make my defense today regarding all the charges brought against me by the Jews,

3 especially because you are an expert [fully knowledgeable, experienced and unusually conversant] in all the Jewish customs and controversial issues; therefore, I beg you to listen to me patiently.

4 "So then, all the Jews know my manner of life from my youth up, which from the beginning was spent among my own nation [the Jewish people], and in Jerusalem.

5 "They have known me for a long time, if they are willing to testify to it, that according to the strictest sect of our religion, I have lived as a Pharisee.

6 "And now I am standing trial for the hope of the promise made by God to our fathers. [Acts 13:32, 33]

7 "Which hope [of the Messiah and the resurrection] our twelve tribes [confidently] expect to realize as they serve *and* worship *God* in earnest night and day. And for this hope, O King, I am being accused by Jews!

8 "Why is it thought incredible by [any of] you that God raises the dead?

9 "So then, I [once] thought to myself that it was my duty to do many things in opposition to the name of Jesus of Nazareth.

10 "And this is just what I did in Jerusalem; I not only locked up many of the saints (God's people) in prison after receiving authority from the chief priests, but also when they were being condemned to death, I cast my vote against them.

11 "And I often punished them [making them suffer] in all the synagogues and tried to force them to blaspheme; and in my extreme rage at them, I kept hunting them even to foreign cities [harassing and persecuting them].

12 "While so engaged, as I was traveling to Damascus with the authority and commission *and* full power of the chief priests,

13 at midday, O King, I saw on the way a light from heaven surpassing the brightness of the sun, shining all around me and those who were traveling with me.

14 "And when we all had fallen to the ground, I heard a voice in the Hebrew dialect (Jewish Aramaic) saying to me, 'Saul, Saul, why are you persecuting Me? It is hard for you to kick [repeatedly] against the goads [offering pointless resistance].'

15 "And I said, 'Who are You, Lord?' And the Lord said, 'I am Jesus whom you are persecuting.

16 'Get up and stand on your feet. I have appeared to you for this purpose,

---

26:5 *I have lived as a Pharisee.* Paul was not some stranger or foreigner trying to start a new religion. He was a Jew, and a member of the religious body which took God's law most seriously.

26:6–7 Hope — Paul faced a real paradox in his trial before Agrippa. He had been a faithful Pharisee, looking forward to the fulfillment of their common hope, the coming of the Messiah, and

25 Ac 23:9,29; 26:31; ver. 11,12 **CHAPTER 26** **5** Ac 22:3; 23:6; 24:15,21; Php 3:5 **6** Ac 23:6; Ge 3:15; 22:18; 26:4; 49:10; Dt 18:15; 2Sa 7:12; Ps 132:11; Isa 4:2; 7:14; 9:6; 40:10; Jer 23:5; 33:14-16; Eze 34:23; 37:24; Da 9:24; Ac 13:32; Ro 15:8; Titus 2:13 **7** Jas 1:1; Lk 2:37; 1Th 3:10; 1Ti 5:5; Php 3:11 **9** Jn 16:2; 1Ti 1:13 **10** Ac 8:3; Gal 1:13; Ac 9:14,21; 22:5 **11** Ac 22:19 **12** Ac 9:3; 22:6 **16** Ac 22:15

to appoint you [to serve] as a minister
and as a witness [to testify, with authority,] not only to the things which
you have seen, but also to the things
in which I will appear to you,
17[choosing you for Myself and] rescuing you from the *Jewish* people and
from the Gentiles, to whom I am sending you, [Ezek 2:1, 3]
18to open their [spiritual] eyes so that
they may turn from darkness to light
and from the power of Satan to God,
that they may receive forgiveness *and*
release from their sins and an inheritance among those who have been
sanctified (set apart, made holy) by
faith in Me.' [Is 42:7, 16]
19"So, King Agrippa, I was not disobedient to the heavenly vision,
20but I openly proclaimed first to
those at Damascus, then at Jerusalem
and throughout the region of Judea,
and *even* to the Gentiles, that they
should repent [change their inner self—
their old way of thinking] and turn
to God, doing deeds *and* living lives
which are consistent with repentance.
21"Because of this *some* Jews seized
me in the temple and tried to kill me.
22"But I have had help from God to
this day, and I stand [before people]
testifying to small and great alike, stating nothing except what the Prophets
and Moses said would come to pass—
23that the Christ (the Messiah, the
Anointed) was to suffer, and that He
by being the first to rise from the dead
[with an incorruptible body] would
proclaim light (salvation) both to the
Jewish people and to the Gentiles."
24While Paul was making this defense, Festus said loudly, "Paul, you are
out of your mind! Your great education
is turning you toward madness."
25But Paul replied, "I am not out of
my mind, most excellent *and* noble
Festus, but [with a sound mind] I am
uttering rational words of truth *and*
reason.
26"For [your majesty] the king understands these things, and [therefore] I am also speaking to him with
confidence *and* boldness, since I am
convinced that none of these things
escape his notice; for this has not been
done in a corner [hidden from view,
in secret].
27"King Agrippa, do you believe the
[writings of the] Prophets [their messages and words]? I know that you do."
28Then Agrippa said to Paul, "In a
short time [and with so little effort]
you [almost] persuade me to become
a Christian."
29And Paul replied, "Whether in a
short time or long, I wish to God that
not only you, but also all who hear
me today, might become such as I am,
except for these chains."
30Then the king stood up, and [with
him] the governor and Bernice, and
those who were sitting with them;
31and after they had gone out, they
began saying to one another, "This
man is not doing anything worthy of
death or [even] of imprisonment."
32And Agrippa said to Festus, "This
man could have been set free if he
had not appealed to Caesar (Emperor
Nero)."

---

eventually the resurrection of the dead. Now that the Messiah had come, and Paul began proclaiming the truth of His atonement and resurrection, he was being persecuted by the very ones who had once shared his hope.

26:20 *that they should repent*. Repentance indicates a complete change in thinking, an "about face" of the mind and heart. Genuine repentance is evidenced by changed behavior.

26:22–23 Christ — Paul makes it clear that Jesus stood firmly in the tradition of the Hebrew Law and Prophets, and specifically identifies Him as the promised Messiah. The suffering and death of the Messiah were ordained by God and proclaimed by His prophets. The resurrection of Jesus provided evidence of the control God was exercising over the process of redemption. This triumphant event removed the purely local and national character of Christ's work, and gave His message of salvation worldwide dimensions, as had been prophesied (Isa 60:3; Mal 1:11).

17 Ac 22:21 **18** Isa 35:5; 42:7; Lk 1:79; Jn 8:12; 2Co 4:4; Eph 1:18; 1Th 5:5; 2Co 6:14; Eph 4:18; 5:8; Col 1:13; 1Pe 2:9; Lk 1:77; Eph 1:11; Col 1:12; Ac 20:32 **20** Ac 9:20,22; 11:26; chs. 13,14; 16-21; Mt 3:8 **21** Ac 21:30 **22** Lk 24:27; Ac 24:14; 28:23; Ro 3:21; Jn 5:46 **23** Lk 24:26; 1Co 15:20; Col 1:18; Rev 1:5; Lk 2:32 **24** 2Ki 9:11; Jn 10:20; 1Co 1:23; 2:13,14; 4:10 **29** 1Co 7:7 **31** Ac 23:9,29; 25:25 **32** Ac 25:11

Paul Is Sent to Rome

27 NOW WHEN it was determined that we (including Luke) would sail for Italy, they turned Paul and some other prisoners over to a centurion of the Augustan Regiment named Julius.

2 And going aboard a ship from Adramyttian which was about to sail for the ports along the [west] coast [province] of Asia [Minor], we put out to sea; and Aristarchus, a Macedonian from Thessalonica, accompanied us.

3 The next day we landed at Sidon; and Julius, treating Paul with [thoughtful] consideration, allowed him to go to his friends *there* and be cared for *and* refreshed.

4 From there we put out to sea and sailed to the leeward (sheltered) side of Cyprus [for protection from weather] because the winds were against us.

5 When we had sailed across the sea along the coasts of Cilicia and Pamphylia, we landed at Myra in Lycia [on the south coast of Asia Minor].

6 There the centurion [Julius] found an Alexandrian ship [a grain ship of the Roman fleet] sailing for Italy, and he put us aboard it.

7 For a number of days we sailed slowly and arrived with difficulty off Cnidus; then, because the wind did not allow us to go farther, we sailed under the leeward (sheltered) side of Crete, off Salmone;

8 and hugging the shore with difficulty, we came to a place called Fair Havens, near the city of Lasea [on the south side of Crete].

9 Now much time had been lost, and navigation was dangerous, because even [the time for] the fast (Day of Atonement) was already over, so Paul *began* to strongly warn them,

10 saying, "Men, I sense [after careful thought and observation] that this voyage will certainly be a disaster and with great loss, not only of the cargo and the ship, but also of our lives."

11 However, the centurion [Julius, ranking officer on board] was persuaded by the pilot and the owner of the ship rather than by what Paul said.

12 Because the harbor was not well situated for wintering, the majority [of the sailors] decided to put to sea from there, hoping somehow to reach Phoenix, a harbor of Crete facing southwest and northwest, and spend the winter *there.*

13 So when the south wind blew softly, thinking that they had obtained their goal, they weighed anchor and sailed along Crete, hugging the coast.

Shipwreck

14 But soon afterward a violent wind, called Euraquilo [a northeaster, a tempestuous windstorm like a typhoon], came rushing down from the island;

15 and when the ship was caught in it and could not head against the wind [to gain stability], we gave up and [letting her drift] were driven along.

16 We ran under the shelter of a small island [twenty-five miles south of Crete] called Clauda, and with great difficulty we were able to get the *ship's* skiff on the deck *and* secure it.

17 After hoisting the skiff [on board], they used support lines [for frapping] to undergird *and* brace the ship's hull; and fearing that they might run aground on *the shallows of* Syrtis [off the north coast of Africa], they let down the sea anchor *and* lowered the sails and were driven along [backwards with the bow into the wind].

18 On the next day, as we were being violently tossed about by the storm [and taking on water], they began to jettison the cargo;

19 and on the third day they threw the ship's tackle (spare lines, blocks, miscellaneous equipment) overboard

---

27:4 *the winds were against us.* This happened just before the winter storms increased, and sailing became difficult. Paul was being sent to Rome by ship at the worst time of year for sailing.

27:14 *Euraquilo.* This was a name given to the northeasterly storms which blow up on the Mediterranean Sea at this time of year.

CHAPTER 27 **1** Ac 25:12,25 **2** Ac 19:29 **3** Ac 24:23; 28:16 **9** The fast was on the tenth day of the seventh month; Lev 23:27,29 **19** Jnh 1:5

with their own hands [to further re-
duce the weight].
20 Since neither sun nor stars ap-
peared for many days, and no small
storm kept raging about us, from then
on all hope of our being saved was
[growing worse and worse and] grad-
ually abandoned.
21 After they had gone a long time
without food [because of seasickness
and stress], Paul stood up before them
and said, "Men, you should have fol-
lowed my advice and should not have
set sail from Crete, and brought on this
damage and loss.
22 "But *even* now I urge you to keep
up your courage *and* be in good spirits,
because there will be no loss of life
among you, but *only loss* of the ship.
23 "For this very night an angel of
the God to whom I belong and whom
I serve stood before me,
24 and said, 'Stop being afraid, Paul.
You must stand before Caesar; and
behold, God has given you [the lives
of] all those who are sailing with you.'
25 "So keep up your courage, men,
for I believe God *and* have complete
confidence in Him that it will turn out
exactly as I have been told;
26 but we must run [the ship] aground
on some island."
27 The fourteenth night had come
and we were drifting *and* being driven
about in the Adriatic Sea, when about
midnight the sailors *began* to suspect
that they were approaching some land.
28 So they took soundings [using a
weighted line] and found [the depth
to be] twenty fathoms (120 feet); and
a little farther on they sounded again
and found [the depth to be] fifteen fath-
oms (90 feet).
29 Then fearing that we might run
aground somewhere on the rocks, they
dropped four anchors from the stern
[*to slow the ship*] and kept wishing for
daybreak to come.
30 But as the sailors were trying to
escape [secretly] from the ship and
had let down the skiff into the sea,
pretending that they were going to lay
out anchors from the bow,
31 Paul said to the centurion and the
soldiers, "Unless these men remain on
the ship, you cannot be saved."
32 Then the soldiers cut away the
ropes that held the skiff and let it fall
and drift away.
33 While they waited for the day to
dawn, Paul encouraged them all [and
told them] to have some food, saying,
"This is the fourteenth day that you
have been constantly on watch and go-
ing without food, having eaten nothing.
34 "So I urge you to eat some food,
for this is for your survival; for not a
hair from the head of any of you will
perish."
35 Having said this, he took bread and
gave thanks to God in front of them
all, and he broke it and began to eat.
36 Then all of them were encouraged
and their spirits improved, and they
also ate some food.
37 All told there were two hundred
and seventy-six of us aboard the ship.
38 After they had eaten enough, they
began to lighten the ship by throwing
the wheat [from Egypt] overboard into
the sea.
39 When day came, they did not rec-
ognize the land, but they noticed a bay
with a beach, and they decided to run
the ship ashore there if they could.
40 So they cut the cables *and* severed
the anchors and left them in the sea
while at the same time unlashing the
ropes of the rudders; and after hoisting
the foresail to the wind, they headed
steadily for the beach.
41 But striking a reef with waves
breaking in on either side, they ran
the ship aground. The prow (forward
point) stuck fast and remained immov-
able, while the stern *began* to break up
under the [violent] force *of the waves.*
42 The soldiers' plan was to kill the
prisoners, so that none of them would
dive overboard *and* swim [to land] and
escape;
43 but the centurion, wanting to save
Paul, kept them from [carrying out]
their plan. He commanded those who
could swim to jump overboard first
and get to the shore;

23 Ac 23:11; Da 6:16; Ro 1:9; 2Ti 1:3 **25** Lk 1:45; Ro 4:20,21; 2Ti 1:12 **26** Ac 28:1 **34** 1Ki 1:52; Mt 10:30; Lk 12:7; 21:18 **35** 1Sa 9:13; Mt 15:36; Mk 8:6; Jn 6:11; 1Ti 4:3,4 **37** Ac 2:41; 7:14; Ro 13:1; 1Pe 3:20 **41** 2Co 11:25

44 and [he commanded] the rest *to follow,* some on [floating] planks, and others on various things from the ship. And so it was that all of them were brought safely to land.

Safe at Malta

28 AFTER WE were safe [on land], we found out that the island was called Malta.

2 And the natives showed us extraordinary kindness *and* hospitality; for they kindled a fire and welcomed us all, since it had begun to rain and was cold.

3 But when Paul had gathered a bundle of sticks and laid them on the fire, a viper crawled out because of the heat and fastened itself on his hand.

4 When the natives saw the creature hanging from his hand, they *began* saying to one another, "Undoubtedly this man is a murderer, and though he has been saved from the sea, Justice [the avenging goddess] has not permitted him to live."

5 Then Paul [simply] shook the creature off into the fire and suffered no ill effects.

6 But they stood watching *and* expecting him to swell up or suddenly drop dead. But after they had waited a long time and had seen nothing unusual happen to him, they changed their minds and *began* saying that he was a god.

7 In the vicinity of that place there were estates belonging to the leading man of the island, named Publius, who welcomed and entertained us hospitably for three days.

8 And it happened that the father of Publius was sick [in bed] with recurring attacks of fever and dysentery; and Paul went to him, and after he had prayed, he laid his hands on him and healed him.

9 After this occurred, the rest of the people on the island who had diseases were coming to him and being healed.

10 They also gave us many honors [gifts and courtesies expressing respect]; and when we were setting sail, they supplied us with all the things we needed.

Paul Arrives at Rome

11 At the end of three months we set sail on a ship which had wintered at the island, an Alexandrian ship with the Twin Brothers [Castor and Pollux] as its figurehead.

12 We landed at Syracuse [on Sicily] and stayed there three days.

13 From there we sailed around and arrived at Rhegium [on Italy's southern tip]; and a day later a south wind came up, and on the second day we arrived at Puteoli.

14 There we found some believers and were invited to stay with them for seven days. And so we came to Rome.

15 And the brothers and sisters, having heard news about us, came from as far away as the Forum of Appius and Three Inns to meet us. When Paul saw them, he thanked God and was encouraged.

16 When we entered Rome, Paul was allowed to stay by himself [in rented quarters] with the soldier who was guarding him.

17 Three days later he called together the leaders of the Jews; and when they had gathered, he said to them, "Kinsmen, though I have done nothing against our people or against the customs of our fathers, yet I was turned over as a prisoner from Jerusalem into the hands of the Romans.

18 "After they had interrogated me, they were ready to release me because I was not guilty of any offense deserving death.

28:8 *sick [in bed] with recurring attacks of fever.* This fever was possibly Malta fever, which was common in Malta, Gibraltar, and other Mediterranean islands. The microorganism has since been traced to the milk of the Maltese goats. The fever usually lasted four months, but sometimes could last as long as two or three years.

28:17 *leaders of the Jews.* By this time, the decree of the emperor Claudius (18:2) had been allowed to lapse, and Jews had returned to Rome.

44 ver. 22 **CHAPTER 28** **1** Ac 27:26 **2** Ro 1:14; 1Co 14:11; Col 3:11 **5** Mk 16:18; Lk 10:19 **6** Ac 14:11
8 Jas 5:14,15; Mk 6:5; 7:32; 16:18; Lk 4:40; Ac 19:11,12; 1Co 12:9,28 **10** Mt 15:6; 1Ti 5:17 **16** Ac 24:25; 27:3
17 Ac 24:12,13; Ac 21:33 **18** Ac 22:24; 24:10; 25:8

19 "But when the Jews objected [to my
release], I was forced to appeal to Cae-
sar (Emperor Nero), not because I had
any charge to make against my nation.
20 "For this reason I have asked to
see you and talk with you, since it is
for the sake of the hope of Israel (the
Messiah, the resurrection) that I am
bound with this chain."
21 They said to him, "We have not
received [any] letters about you from
Judea, nor have any of the [Jewish]
brothers come here and reported or
said anything bad about you.
22 "But we would like to hear from
you what your views are [that is, ex-
actly what you believe]; for in regard
to this sect (Christianity), we are ful-
ly aware that it is denounced every-
where."
23 When they had set a day for Paul,
they came to his lodging in large
numbers. And he carefully explained
[Christianity] to them from morning
until evening, solemnly testifying
about the kingdom of God and trying
to persuade them concerning Jesus,
both from the Law of Moses and from
the [writings of the] Prophets.
24 Some were persuaded by what he
said, but others would not believe.
25 They disagreed among themselves
and they *began* to leave after Paul had
made one *last* statement: "The Holy
Spirit rightly spoke through Isaiah the
prophet to your fathers, saying,

26 'Go to this people and say,

"You will keep on hearing, but will
not understand,
You will keep on seeing, but will
not perceive;
27 "For the heart (the understanding,
the soul) of this people has
become dull (calloused),
And with their ears they scarcely
hear,
And they have shut their eyes [to
the truth];
Otherwise they might see with
their eyes,
And hear with their ears,
And understand with their heart
and return [to Me],
And I would heal them." '
[Is 6:9, 10]

28 "Therefore let it be known to you
that [this message of] the salvation of
God has been sent to the Gentiles; they
indeed will listen!" [Ps 67:2]
29 [And when he had said these
things, the Jews left, arguing among
themselves.]
30 And Paul lived there for two full
years [at his own expense] in his own
rented lodging and welcomed all who
came to him,
31 preaching *and* proclaiming the
kingdom of God and teaching about
the Lord Jesus Christ with all open-
ness *and* boldness, unhindered *and*
unrestrained.

28:20 Hope — The hope of Israel and the hope which Paul had found in Christ were not two different things. Wherever he went, he proclaimed Christ to the Jews as the fulfillment of their hope. That hope included not only the resurrection; it also included the Messiah and His kingdom. Paul is careful to emphasize that the hope which he now proclaims does not undermine the hope of Israel but rather is its divine fulfillment. His devotion to the hope of the fathers was the cause that brought about his imprisonment and put him in chains. His demeanor before these Jewish leaders in Rome must have been impressive. As he stood before these men whose influence could result in life or death for him, there was no quaking or fear. He had that hope which made him secure, whatever happened.

28:30 *two full years.* Paul wrote four of the New Testament letters (Ephesians, Philippians, Colossians, and Philemon) during this period.

28:31 *preaching . . . teaching.* Apparently Paul's case had not been decided when Luke finished this book. It is thought that Paul was in fact released (there was really no case against him), and actually went to Spain as he desired (Ro 15:24). Titus 1:5 implies that Paul ministered on the island of Crete (something not mentioned in Acts), and many believe that Paul resumed his missionary travel for a few more years before his final arrest, condemnation, and execution, sometime around AD 67.

19 Ac 25:11 **20** Ac 26:6,7,29; Eph 3:1; 4:1; 6:20; 2Ti 1:16; Php 10,13 **22** Lk 2:34; Ac 24:5,14; 1Pe 2:12; 4:14 **23** Lk 24:27; Ac 17:3; 19:8; See Ac 26:6,22 **24** Ac 14:4; 19:9 **26** Isa 6:9; Jer 5:21; Eze 12:2; Mt 13:14; Mk 4:12; Lk 8:10; Jn 12:40; Ro 11:8 **28** Mt 21:41; Ac 13:46; 18:6; 26:17,18; Ro 11:11 **31** Ac 4:31; Eph 6:19

THE LETTER OF PAUL TO THE

ROMANS

▸ **AUTHOR:** All critical schools agree on the Pauline authorship of this foundational book. The vocabulary, style, logic, and theological development are consistent with Paul's other epistles. He wrote Romans in AD 57, near the end of his third missionary journey, evidently during his three-month stay in Greece (Ac 20:3 – 6), more specifically, in Corinth. The church in Rome was well-known (1:8), and it had been established for several years by the time of this letter. The believers were probably numerous, and evidently they met in several places (Ro 16:1 – 16). The historian Tacitus even referred to the Christians who were persecuted there under Nero in AD 64 as an "immense multitude," as the gospel filled the gap left by the practically defunct polytheism of Roman religion.

▸ **TIMES:** c. AD 57 ▸ **KEY VERSES:** Ro 1:16 – 17

▸ **THEME:** Most scholars feel that Paul probably wrote this letter from Corinth, shortly before going to Jerusalem with the relief funds for the believers there. At this point in his life and ministry, his theology has been fully developed through years of study and interaction with people as he preached the gospel. Romans systematically explains what Christ did, why He did it, and what has happened as a result. It speaks to what we are as humans and how God has interacted with us through Christ. It lays out God's plan for the world, clarifying what has happened and is still happening in biblical history. In this way, Paul forces us to deal with all the false versions of reality inspired by our fallen human nature as opposed to God's gracious, sustaining plan.

The Gospel Exalted

1 PAUL, A bond-servant of Christ
Jesus, called as an apostle (special
messenger, personally chosen represen-
tative), set apart for [preaching] the gos-
pel of God [the good news of salvation],
2 which He promised beforehand
through His prophets in the sacred
Scriptures—
3 [the good news] regarding His Son,
who, as to the flesh [His human na-
ture], was born a descendant of David
[to fulfill the covenant promises],
4 and [as to His divine nature] ac-
cording to the Spirit of holiness was
openly designated to be the Son of
God with power [in a triumphant and
miraculous way] by *His* resurrection
from the dead: Jesus Christ our Lord.
5 It is through Him that we have re-
ceived grace and [our] apostleship to
promote obedience to the faith *and*
make disciples for His name's sake
among all the Gentiles,
6 and you also are among those who
are called of Jesus Christ to belong
to Him;

1:1 *bond-servant.* A bond-servant is a slave. Paul is talking about a slavery taken voluntarily out of love (see Ex 21:1 – 6), unlike the forced slavery known to so many in the Roman Empire.

1:4 *designated.* Jesus did not become the Son of God by the resurrection. Instead, the resurrection proved that Jesus was the Son of God.

CHAPTER 1 **1** 1Ti 1:11; Ac 9:15 **2** Ac 26:6; Gal 3:8 **3** Gal 4:4 **4** Ac 13:33; Heb 9:14 **5** Eph 3:8; Ac 6:7; 9:15

[7][I am writing] to all who are beloved of God in Rome, called to be saints (God's people) *and* set apart for a sanctified life, [that is, set apart for God and His purpose]: Grace to you and peace [inner calm and spiritual well-being] from God our Father and from the Lord Jesus Christ.
[8]First, I thank my God through Jesus Christ for all of you, because your faith [your trust and confidence in His power, wisdom, and goodness] is being proclaimed in all the world.
[9]For God, whom I serve with my spirit by *preaching* the gospel of His Son, is my witness as to how continuously I mention you
[10]in my prayers; always pleading that somehow, by God's will, I may now at last come to you.
[11]For I long to see you so that I may share with you some spiritual gift, to strengthen *and* establish you;
[12]that is, that we may be mutually encouraged *and* comforted by each other's faith, both yours and mine.
[13]I do not want you to be unaware, brothers and sisters, that many times I have planned to come to you, (and have been prevented so far) so that I may have some fruit [of my labors] among you, even as *I have* among the rest of the Gentiles.
[14]I have a duty to perform *and* a debt to pay both to Greeks and to barbarians [the cultured and the uncultured], both to the wise and to the foolish.
[15]So, for my part, I am ready *and* eager to preach the gospel also to you who are in Rome.
[16]I am not ashamed of the gospel, for it is the power of God for salvation [from His wrath and punishment] to everyone who believes [in Christ as Savior], to the Jew first and also to the Greek.
[17]For in the gospel the righteousness of God is revealed, *both springing* from faith *and leading* to faith [disclosed in a way that awakens more faith]. As it is written *and* forever remains written, "THE JUST *and* UPRIGHT SHALL LIVE BY FAITH." [Hab 2:4]

Unbelief and Its Consequences

[18]For [God does not overlook sin and] the wrath of God is revealed from heaven against all ungodliness and unrighteousness of men who in their wickedness suppress *and* stifle the truth,
[19]because that which is known about God is evident within them [in their inner consciousness], for God made it evident to them.
[20]For ever since the creation of the world His invisible attributes, His eternal power and divine nature, have been clearly seen, being understood through His workmanship [all His creation, the

---

1:14 *barbarians.* Paul is referring to the non-Greek Gentile populations, such as the northern European peoples, the Britons, the Gauls, and the Celts.

1:17 *from faith and leading to faith.* Faith is at the beginning of the salvation process, and it is the goal as well. Paul had faith that God, through the Holy Spirit, could and would build true righteousness in him. For the believer this means prayerful self-examination, prayer to do better, and careful response to those inner nudges that say, "don't say that ... have pity ... encourage him," etc.

1:18 – 19 There Are No Excuses — Someone once said there were two points they understood about God: (1) "There is a God"; and (2) "I am not Him." Theologians use the term "general revelation" to describe the concept Paul is teaching here in Romans 1. God has revealed Himself through His creation so that everyone can understand that He exists and that He has created the world and man with a purpose. God created man with an inner sense that there is something bigger out there, something that transcends mankind. That something is God and He requires recognition. The created world points us to God, but we suppress that truth, preferring to put ourselves in the place of God, in effect saying, "There is no God but me." Paul further says that, because the revelation is so clear, we have no excuse for missing it, no legitimate reason for our blindness. People who do not see it are guilty of not acknowledging the most basic reality there is.

7 1Co 1:2; 1Co 1:3 **8** 1Co 1:4; Ro 16:19 **9** Ro 9:1; Ac 27:23; 1Th 3:10 **11** Ro 15:29 **12** Titus 1:4 **13** 1Th 2:18; Php 4:17 **16** Ps 40:9,10; Mk 8:38; 1Co 1:18; Lk 2:30; Ac 13:26 **17** Ro 3:21; Hab 2:4; Jn 3:36; Gal 3:11 **18** Ac 17:30; Eph 5:6 **19** Ac 14:17; Jn 1:9 **20** Ps 19:1; Ac 14:17

wonderful things that He has made],
so that they [who fail to believe and
trust in Him] are without excuse *and*
without defense. [Ps 19:1–4; Eph 2:10]
21 For even though they knew God [as
the Creator], they did not honor Him
as God or give thanks [for His won-
drous creation]. On the contrary, they
became worthless in their thinking
[godless, with pointless reasonings,
and silly speculations], and their fool-
ish heart was darkened.
22 Claiming to be wise, they became
fools,
23 and exchanged the glory *and* maj-
esty *and* excellence of the immortal
God for an image [worthless idols] in
the shape of mortal man and birds and
four-footed animals and reptiles.
24 Therefore God gave them over in
the lusts of their own hearts to [sexual]
impurity, so that their bodies would be
dishonored among them [abandoning
them to the degrading power of sin],
25 because [by choice] they ex-
changed the truth of God for a lie, and
worshiped and served the creature
rather than the Creator, who is blessed
forever! Amen. [Jer 2:11]
26 For this reason God gave them over
to degrading *and* vile passions; for
their women exchanged the natural
function for that which is unnatural [a
function contrary to nature],
27 and in the same way also the men
turned away from the natural function
of the woman and were consumed with
their desire toward one another, men
with men committing shameful acts
and in return receiving in their own
bodies the inevitable *and* appropriate
penalty for their wrongdoing.
28 And since they did not see fit to
acknowledge God *or* consider Him
worth knowing [as their Creator], God
gave them over to a depraved mind,
to do things which are improper *and*
repulsive,
29 until they were filled (permeated,
saturated) with every kind of unrigh-
teousness, wickedness, greed, evil; full
of envy, murder, strife, deceit, malice
and mean-spiritedness. They are gos-
sips [spreading rumors],
30 slanderers, haters of God, insolent,
arrogant, boastful, inventors [of new
forms] of evil, disobedient *and* disre-
spectful to parents,
31 without understanding, untrust-
worthy, unloving, unmerciful [without
pity].
32 Although they know God's righ-
teous decree *and* His judgment, that
those who do such things deserve
death, yet they not only do them, but
they even [enthusiastically] approve
and tolerate others who practice them.

The Impartiality of God

2 THEREFORE YOU have no ex-
cuse *or* justification, everyone
of you who [hypocritically] judges

1:25 *lie.* This refers to the kind of wrong thinking that led to idol worship. This "lie" refuses to honor both God's law and His authority. When people stop knowing that God created the universe, that it is His, they adopt all kinds of wrong thinking about sin, society, morality, and especially, the role of God Himself.

1:27 *committing shameful acts.* Homosexuality is sin (Lev 18:22), and the actions that are part of this lifestyle are called "shameful" by God. In this passage Paul explains that homosexual sin is the result of men having rejected God and exchanged what is natural for the unnatural. The problems from this way of living are themselves the "recompense" for this choice.

1:29 – 32 *were filled (permeated, saturated) with every kind of unrighteousness.* These verses contain one of the most complete lists of sin in all of Scripture. This passage addresses not only the fact that God judges rightly that these sins are deserving of death, but it also addresses the idea that approving of these sins is something God judges.

2:1 – 4 *judges.* Paul points out in this passage that anyone who judges others condemns himself, for in this list of sins is something that everyone has been guilty of in one way or another. Paul asks if the judgers realize that it is God in His goodness who leads one to repentance, and that only God can judge rightly. Only He can judge the actions of the heart and person without condemning Himself, for only He is without sin.

---

21 2Ki 17:15; Jer 2:5; Eph 4:17 **22** Jer 10:14 **23** Dt 4:16; Ps 106:20; Isa 40:18 **24** Ps 81:12; Ac 7:42; Eph 4:18; 1Co 6:18; 1Th 4:4; Lev 18:22 **25** 1Th 1:9; 1Jn 5:20; Isa 44:20; Jer 10:14 **26** Lev 18:22; Eph 5:12 **28** Eph 5:4 **32** Ro 2:2; Ro 6:21; Ps 50:18; Hos 7:3 **CHAPTER 2** **1** Ro 1:20; 2Sa 12:5; Mt 7:1,2; Jn 8:9

and condemns others; for in passing
judgment on another person, you
condemn yourself, because you who
judge [from a position of arrogance
or self-righteousness] are *habitually*
practicing the very same things [which
you denounce].
2 And we know that the judgment
of God falls justly *and* in accordance
with truth on those who practice such
things.
3 But do you think this, O man, when
you judge *and* condemn those who
practice such things, and yet do the
same yourself, that you will escape
God's judgment *and* elude His verdict?
4 Or do you have no regard for the
wealth of His kindness and tolerance
and patience [in withholding His
wrath]? Are you [actually] unaware *or*
ignorant [of the fact] that God's kind-
ness leads you to repentance [that is,
to change your inner self, your old
way of thinking—seek His purpose
for your life]?
5 But because of your callous stub-
bornness and unrepentant heart you
are [deliberately] storing up wrath for
yourself on the day of wrath when
God's righteous judgment will be
revealed.
6 He WILL PAY BACK TO EACH PERSON
ACCORDING TO HIS DEEDS [justly, as his
deeds deserve]: [Ps 62:12; Prov 24:12]
7 to those who by persistence in doing
good seek [unseen but certain heaven-
ly] glory, honor, and immortality, [He
will give the gift of] eternal life.
8 But for those who are selfishly am-
bitious *and* self-seeking and disobe-
dient to the truth but responsive to
wickedness, [there will be] wrath and
indignation.
9 *There will be* tribulation and an-
guish [torturing confinement] for ev-
ery human soul who does [or permits]
evil, to the Jew first and also to the
Greek,
10 but glory and honor and *inner*
peace [will be given] to everyone who
habitually does good, to the Jew first
and also to the Greek.
11 For God shows no partiality [no
arbitrary favoritism; with Him one
person is not more important than
another]. [Deut 10:17; 2 Chr 19:7]
12 For all who have sinned without
the Law will also perish without [re-
gard to] the Law, and all who have
sinned under the Law will be judged
and condemned by the Law.
13 For it is not those who merely hear
the Law [as it is read aloud] who are
just *or* righteous before God, but it is
those who [actually] obey the Law who
will be justified [pronounced free of
the guilt of sin and declared acceptable
to Him].
14 When Gentiles, who do not have
the Law [since it was given only to
Jews], do instinctively the things the
Law requires [guided only by their con-
science], they are a law to themselves,
though they do not have the Law.
15 They show that the essential re-
quirements of the Law are written

2:4 *repentance.* Literally, this means "to change one's mind." In this context it means to reject one's sinful habits and turn to God.

2:7 – 8 *doing good . . . eternal life.* According to these verses it might seem that "eternal life" can be gained by "doing good." But Romans clearly teaches justification by faith (3:22). The subject of this verse is judgment, not justification. Jesus said that "on the day of judgment people will have to give an accounting for every careless or useless word they speak" (Mt 12:36). Even Christians will see both the good and the evil that they have done. They are justified (considered righteous and therefore not punished for their sins because they have accepted Christ's death on their behalf) but they still have to see what they have done according to God's righteous judgment. Good works are "a good foundation for the future" (1Ti 6:17 – 19).

2:12 *without the Law.* Gentiles, who did not receive the Mosaic law, were sometimes described by this term.

2:14 *do instinctively the things the Law requires.* Gentiles who still do such things as honor their parents, respond in kindness, or live honestly, show that they do have the idea of a basic moral law and the concepts of right and wrong.

4 Eph 1:7; Ro 3:25; Ex 34:6; Isa 30:18; 2Pe 3:9 **5** Dt 32:34; Jas 5:3 **6** Job 34:11; Ps 62:12; Pr 24:12; Jer 17:10; 2Co 5:10 **8** Job 24:13; 2Th 1:8 **9** Am 3:2; Lk 12:47; 1Pe 4:17 **10** 1Pe 1:7 **11** Dt 10:17; Job 34:19; Ac 10:34; Eph 6:9 **13** Jas 1:22; 1Jn 3:7

in their hearts; and their conscience
[their sense of right and wrong, their
moral choices] bearing witness and
their thoughts alternately accusing or
perhaps defending them
16 on that day when, as my gospel
proclaims, God will judge the secrets
[all the hidden thoughts and concealed
sins] of men through Christ Jesus.
[Eccl 12:14]

The Jew Is Condemned by the Law

17 But if you bear the name "Jew" and
rely on the Law [for your salvation]
and boast in [your special relationship
to] God,
18 and [if you claim to] know His
will and approve the things that are
essential *or* have a sense of what is
excellent, based on your instruction
from the Law,
19 and [if you] are confident that you
are a [qualified] guide to the blind
[those untaught in theology], a light
to those who are in darkness,
20 and [that you are] a corrector of
the foolish, a teacher of the [spiritually]
childish, having in the Law the embodi-
ment of knowledge and of the truth—
21 well then, you who teach others,
do you not teach yourself? You who
preach against stealing, do you steal
[in ways that are discrete, but just as
sinful]?
22 You who say that one must not
commit adultery, do you commit adul-
tery? You who detest idols, do you rob
[pagan] temples [of valuable idols and
offerings]? [Deut 7:25; Acts 19:37]
23 You who boast in the Law, do you
[repeatedly] dishonor God by breaking
the Law?
24 For, "THE NAME OF GOD IS BLASPHEMED
AMONG THE GENTILES BECAUSE OF YOU," just
as it is written [in Scripture]. [Is 52:5;
Ezek 36:20]
25 Circumcision [the sign of the cov-
enant of Abraham] is indeed of value
if you practice the Law; but if you *ha-
bitually* break the Law, your circum-
cision has become uncircumcision [it
is meaningless in God's sight].
26 So if the uncircumcised man keeps
the requirements of the Law, will not
his uncircumcision be regarded [by
God] as circumcision?
27 Then he who is physically uncir-
cumcised but keeps [the spirit of] the
Law will judge you who, even though
you have the written code and circum-
cision, break the Law.
28 For he is not a [real] Jew who is
only one outwardly, nor is [true] cir-
cumcision something external and
physical.
29 But he is a Jew who is one inwardly;
and [true] circumcision is *circumcision*
of the heart, by the Spirit, not by [the
fulfillment of] the letter [of the Law]. His
praise is not from men, but from God.

All the World Guilty

3 THEN WHAT is the advantage of
the Jew? Or what is the benefit of
circumcision?
2 Great in every respect. To begin
with, the Jews were entrusted with
the oracles of God [His very words].
[Ps 147:19]

2:16 *secrets.* According to the gospel that Paul preached, God will judge not only people's actions, but their motives, or "secrets."

2:17–25 Self-Righteousness — Paul speaks of the lamentable disparity between the truth that the Jews knew, and their practice of the truth. Boasting about having God's law, while breaking the law in their lives, brings upon them the strongest condemnation, and establishes the truth that the law can only condemn.

2:29 *by the Spirit, not by [the fulfillment of] the letter.* The internal circumcision of the heart is the work of the Holy Spirit. God condemns external observance if it is not the product of a righteous heart (Isa 1:10–18).

3:2 *oracles of God.* The entire Old Testament, the laws and the covenants that have been given by God Himself to the nation of Israel are the "oracles," or the things that God has "spoken."

16 Ecc 12:14; Mt 25:31; Rev 20:12; Jn 5:22; Ac 10:42; 1Ti 1:11 **17** Mt 3:9; Jn 8:33; Mic 3:11; Isa 48:2 **18** Dt 4:8; Php 1:10 **19** Mt 15:14; Jn 9:34 **20** 2Ti 3:5 **21** Ps 50:16; Mt 23:3 **22** Mal 3:8 **23** ver. 17 **24** 2Sa 12:14; Isa 52:5; Eze 36:20 **25** Gal 5:3 **26** Ac 10:34 **27** Mt 12:41 **28** Mt 3:9; Jn 8:39; Gal 6:15 **29** 1Pe 3:4; Php 3:3; Ro 7:6; 1Co 4:5; 2Co 10:18; 1Th 2:4 **CHAPTER 3** **2** Dt 4:7; Ps 147:19

3 What then? If some did not believe
or were unfaithful [to God], their lack
of belief will not nullify *and* make in-
valid the faithfulness of God *and* His
word, will it?
4 Certainly not! Let God be found
true [as He will be], though every per-
son *be found* a liar, just as it is written
[in Scripture],

"THAT YOU MAY BE JUSTIFIED IN YOUR
WORDS,
AND PREVAIL WHEN YOU ARE JUDGED
[by sinful men]." [Ps 51:4]

5 But if our unrighteousness demon-
strates the righteousness of God, what
shall we say? God is not wrong to in-
flict His wrath [on us], is He? (I am
speaking in purely human terms.)
6 Certainly not! For *otherwise*, how
will God judge the world?
7 But [as you might say] if through
my lie God's truth was magnified *and*
abounded to His glory, why am I still
being judged as a sinner?
8 And why not say, (as some slander-
ously report and claim that we teach)
"Let us do evil so that good may come
of it"? Their condemnation [by God]
is just.
9 Well then, are we [Jews] better
off than they? Not at all; for we have
already charged that both Jews and
Greeks (Gentiles) are under the control
of sin *and* subject to its power.
10 As it is written *and* forever remains
written,

"THERE IS NONE RIGHTEOUS [none that
meets God's standard], NOT EVEN
ONE. [Ps 14:3]
11 "THERE IS NONE WHO UNDERSTANDS,
THERE IS NONE WHO SEEKS FOR GOD.
[Ps 14:2]
12 "ALL HAVE TURNED ASIDE, TOGETHER
THEY HAVE BECOME USELESS;
THERE IS NONE WHO DOES GOOD, NO,
NOT ONE." [Ps 53:1–3]
13 "THEIR THROAT IS AN OPEN GRAVE;
THEY [habitually] DECEIVE WITH
THEIR TONGUES."
"THE VENOM OF ASPS IS BENEATH THEIR
LIPS." [Ps 5:9; 140:3]
14 "THEIR MOUTH IS FULL OF CURSING AND
BITTERNESS." [Ps 10:7]
15 "THEIR FEET ARE SWIFT TO SHED BLOOD,
16 DESTRUCTION AND MISERY ARE IN THEIR
PATHS,
17 AND THEY HAVE NOT KNOWN THE PATH
OF PEACE." [Is 59:7, 8]
18 "THERE IS NO FEAR OF GOD [and His
awesome power] BEFORE THEIR
EYES." [Ps 36:1]

19 Now we know that whatever the
Law [of Moses] says, it speaks to those
who are under the Law, so that [the ex-
cuses of] every mouth may be silenced
[from protesting] and that all the world
may be held accountable to God [and
subject to His judgment].
20 For no person will be justified
[freed of guilt and declared righteous]
in His sight by [trying to do] the works
of the Law. For through the Law we
become conscious of sin [and the rec-
ognition of sin directs us toward repen-
tance, but provides no remedy for sin].

Justification by Faith

21 But now the righteousness of
God has been clearly revealed [inde-
pendently and completely] apart from
the Law, though it is [actually] con-
firmed by the Law and the [words and
writings of the] Prophets.
22 This righteousness of God comes
through faith in Jesus Christ for all

3:16 ***DESTRUCTION AND MISERY.*** In verses 10 – 18, Paul quotes without formal introduction a number of different verses from the Old Testament. In these passages it is shown that man not only does not seek God, but apart from Him they lack true goodness and will treat each other with violence, cursing, being quick to kill, and finding only "destruction and misery."

3:18 ***FEAR OF GOD.*** This is an Old Testament expression for respect and reverence for God.

3:20 ***justified.*** A legal term used of the defendant in a trial, "justified" means "declared righteous." No one will be declared righteous by doing what God requires in the law.

3 Heb 4:2; Nu 23:19; 2Ti 2:13 **4** Job 40:8; Jn 3:33; Ps 62:9; Ps 51:4 **5** Gal 3:15 **6** Ge 18:25 **8** Ro 5:20 **9** Gal 3:22 **10** Ps 14:1-3 **13** Ps 5:9; Jer 5:16; Ps 140:3 **14** Ps 10:7 **15** Pr 1:16; Isa 59:7,8 **18** Ps 36:1 **19** Jn 10:34; Job 5:16; Ps 107:42; Ro 2:2 **20** Ps 143:2; Ac 13:39; Gal 2:16; Ro 7:7 **21** Ac 15:11; Ro 1:17; Jn 5:46; 1Pe 1:10 **22** Ro 4; Ro 10:12; Gal 3:28; Col 3:11

those [Jew or Gentile] who believe [and
trust in Him and acknowledge Him
as God's Son]. There is no distinction,
[1 Cor 12:13; Gal 3:28]
23 since all have sinned and *continu-
ally* fall short of the glory of God,
24 and are being justified [declared
free of the guilt of sin, made acceptable
to God, and granted eternal life] as
a gift by His [precious, undeserved]
grace, through the redemption [the
payment for our sin] which is [provid-
ed] in Christ Jesus,
25 whom God displayed publicly [be-
fore the eyes of the world] as a [life-
giving] sacrifice of atonement *and* rec-
onciliation (propitiation) by His blood
[to be received] through faith. *This
was* to demonstrate His righteousness
[which demands punishment for sin],
because in His forbearance [His delib-
erate restraint] He passed over the sins
previously committed [before Jesus'
crucifixion].
26 *It was* to demonstrate His righ-
teousness at the present time, so that
He would be just and the One who jus-
tifies those who have faith in Jesus [and
rely confidently on Him as Savior].
27 Then what becomes of [our] boast-
ing? It is excluded [entirely ruled out,
banished]. On what principle? On [the
principle of good] works? No, but on
the principle of faith.
28 For we maintain that an individual
is justified by faith distinctly apart
from works of the Law [the observance
of which has nothing to do with justi-
fication, that is, being declared free of
the guilt of sin and made acceptable
to God].
29 Or is God *the God* of Jews only? Is
He not also *the God* of Gentiles [who
were not given the Law]? Yes, of Gen-
tiles also,
30 since indeed it is one [and the same]
God who will justify the circumcised
by faith [which began with Abraham]
and the uncircumcised through [their
newly acquired] faith.
31 Do we then nullify the Law by this
faith [making the Law of no effect, over-
throwing it]? Certainly not! On the con-
trary, we confirm *and* establish *and* up-

3:23 Universal Sin — We generally avoid the word *sin*. We want to call it something other than what it is because we don't like the implications of the word. We don't like being told we're rebels, that we're flawed and bent in our very natures, and that there is nothing we can do about it on our own (Ge 3:6 – 7). We have this innate sense that we can overcome the problem with a little more effort or maturity. Even that innate sense is an illustration of the problem. The bold hard facts always point us back to Paul's conclusions; "we're sinners," period.

3:24 *redemption.* Those who believe are "justified," that is, declared righteous, freely, by God's grace or favor. Christ Jesus died to provide "redemption," (or to "buy back," in the same way we "redeem" a promissory note). He died to pay the price required to ransom sinners. He transfers His righteousness to those who believe in Him, and on the basis of Christ's righteousness alone, believers can approach God's throne with praise.

3:25 *reconciliation (propitiation).* By His death, Christ satisfied the justice of God. The word "reconciliation" or "propitiation" refers to appeasement. No man can ever appease God, for His wrath over sin and His judgment of sin is totally just. But God in His mercy provided that appeasement through Jesus Christ, who died on the cross to pay for the sins of the world and to open the way for sinners to come before our Holy God.

3:27 *principle of faith.* The "principle of faith" is a kind of play on words. Paul has been talking about the fact that the law (translated "principle" here) does not give people a right relationship with God. The only "law" about having this relationship is that it must be by "faith," not by deeds, whether people are Jewish or Gentile. We can never earn our salvation.

3:31 *nullify the Law.* In this passage the question of making the law void, or as nothing, and "establishing the law" means that if salvation is received by faith, it would seem like the law was of no value. But actually the fact that Christ came, which was promised through the whole Old Testament, and that He kept the law perfectly, establishes the law as being valid. Only after salvation can people keep the law at all, as Jesus explained in Matthew 22:40, for the law is summed up in loving God and loving our neighbor.

---

23 Ro 11:32; Gal 3:22 **24** Ro 4:16; Eph 2:8; Titus 3:5,7; Mt 20:28; Eph 1:7; Col 1:14; 1Ti 2:6; Heb 9:12; 1Pe 1:18 **25** Lev 16:15; 1Jn 2:2; 4:10; Col 1:20; Ac 17:30; Heb 9:15 **27** Ro 2:17,23; 1Co 1:29; Eph 2:9 **28** ver. 20-22; Gal 2:16 **30** Ro 10:12; Gal 3:8,20

hold the Law [since it convicts us all of sin, pointing to the need for salvation].

Justification by Faith Evidenced in Old Testament

4 WHAT THEN shall we say that Abraham, our forefather humanly speaking, has found? [Has he obtained a favored standing?]

2 For if Abraham was justified [that is, acquitted from the guilt of his sins] by works [those things he did that were good], he has something to boast about, but not before God.

3 For what does the Scripture say? "ABRAHAM BELIEVED IN (trusted, relied on) GOD, AND IT WAS CREDITED TO HIS ACCOUNT AS RIGHTEOUSNESS (right living, right standing with God)." [Gen 15:6]

4 Now to a laborer, his wages are not credited as a favor *or* a gift, but as an obligation [something owed to him].

5 But to the one who does not work [that is, the one who does not try to earn his salvation by doing good], but believes *and* completely trusts in Him who justifies the ungodly, his faith is credited to him as righteousness (right standing with God).

6 And in this same way David speaks of the blessing on the one to whom God credits righteousness apart from works:

7 "BLESSED *and* HAPPY *and* FAVORED
ARE THOSE WHOSE LAWLESS ACTS
HAVE BEEN FORGIVEN,
AND WHOSE SINS HAVE BEEN COVERED
UP *and* COMPLETELY BURIED.
8 "BLESSED *and* HAPPY *and* FAVORED IS
THE MAN WHOSE SIN THE LORD WILL
NOT TAKE INTO ACCOUNT *nor* CHARGE
AGAINST HIM." [Ps 32:1, 2]

9 Is this blessing only for the circumcised, or also for the uncircumcised? For we say, "FAITH WAS CREDITED TO ABRAHAM AS RIGHTEOUSNESS."

10 How then was it credited [to him]? Was it after he had been circumcised, or before? Not after, but while [he was] uncircumcised.

11 He received the sign of circumcision, a seal *or* confirmation of the righteousness which he had by faith while [he was still] uncircumcised—this was so that he would be the [spiritual] father of all who believe without being circumcised—so that righteousness would be credited to them,

12 and [that he would be] the [spiritual] father of those circumcised who are not only circumcised, but who also walk in the steps of the faith of our father Abraham which he had before he was circumcised.

13 For the promise to Abraham or to his descendants that he would be heir of the world was not through [observing the requirements of] the Law, but through the righteousness of faith. [Gen 17:4–6; 22:16–18]

14 If those who are [followers] of the Law are [the true] heirs [of Abraham], then faith [leading to salvation] is of no effect *and* void, and the promise [of God] is nullified.

15 For the Law results in [God's] wrath [against sin], but where there is no law, there is no violation [of it either].

16 Therefore, [inheriting] the promise depends entirely on faith [that is, confident trust in the unseen God], in order that *it may be given* as an act of grace [His unmerited favor and mercy], so that the promise will be [legally] guaranteed to all the descendants [of Abraham]—not only for those [Jewish believers] who keep the Law, but also for those [Gentile believers] who share the faith of Abraham, who is the [spiritual] father of us all—

17 (as it is written [in Scripture], "I HAVE MADE YOU A FATHER OF MANY

4:1 *humanly speaking.* The term "humanly speaking" means "by his own labor."

4:16 *Abraham, who is the [spiritual] father of us all.* God's promises to Abraham were not based on any performance or ritual, but on Abraham's belief, so Abraham is the "father" of all who believe.

4:17 *gives life to the dead.* The description of God as one who "gives life to the dead" refers not

---

CHAPTER 4 **1** Isa 51:2; Mt 3:9; Jn 8:33; 2Co 11:22 **2** Ro 3:20,27 **3** Ge 15:6; Gal 3:6; Jas 2:23 **4** Ro 11:6 **5** Jos 24:2 **7** Ps 32:1,2 **11** Ge 17:10; ver. 12,16; Lk 19:9; Gal 3:7 **13** Ge 17:4; Gal 3:29 **14** Gal 3:18 **15** Ro 3:20; 7:8,10,11; 1Co 15:56; 2Co 3:7,9; Gal 3:10; 1Jn 3:4 **16** Ro 3:24; Gal 3:22; Isa 51:2; Ro 9:8 **17** Ge 17:5; Ro 8:11; Eph 2:1,5; Ro 9:26; 1Co 1:28; 1Pe 2:10

NATIONS") in the sight of Him in whom
he believed, that is, God who gives life
to the dead and calls into being that
which does not exist. [Gen 17:5]
18 In hope against hope Abraham
believed that he would become a fa-
ther of many nations, as he had been
promised [by God]: "So [numberless]
SHALL YOUR DESCENDANTS BE." [Gen 15:5]
19 Without becoming weak in faith
he considered his own body, now as
good as dead [for producing children]
since he was about a hundred years
old, and [he considered] the deadness
of Sarah's womb. [Gen 17:17; 18:11]
20 But he did not doubt *or* waver in
unbelief concerning the promise of
God, but he grew strong *and* empow-
ered by faith, giving glory to God,
21 being fully convinced that God had
the power to do what He had promised.
22 Therefore his faith WAS CREDITED TO
HIM AS RIGHTEOUSNESS (right standing
with God). [Gen 15:6]
23 Now not for his sake alone was
it written that it was credited to him,
24 but for our sake also—to whom
righteousness will be credited, as those
who believe in Him who raised Jesus
our Lord from the dead—
25 who was betrayed *and* crucified
because of our sins, and was raised
[from the dead] because of our justifi-
cation [our acquittal—absolving us of
all sin before God].

Results of Justification

5 THEREFORE, SINCE we have
been justified [that is, acquitted of
sin, declared blameless before God]
by faith, [let us grasp the fact that] we
have peace with God [and the joy of
reconciliation with Him] through our
Lord Jesus Christ (the Messiah, the
Anointed).
2 Through Him we also have access
by faith into this [remarkable state of]
grace in which we [firmly and safely
and securely] stand. Let us rejoice in
our hope *and* the confident assurance
of [experiencing and enjoying] the
glory of [our great] God [the manifes-
tation of His excellence and power].
3 And not only *this*, but [with joy] let
us exult in our sufferings *and* rejoice in
our hardships, knowing that hardship
(distress, pressure, trouble) produces
patient endurance;
4 and endurance, proven character
(spiritual maturity); and proven char-
acter, hope *and* confident assurance
[of eternal salvation].
5 Such hope [in God's promises] nev-
er disappoints *us*, because God's love
has been abundantly poured out with-
in our hearts through the Holy Spirit
who was given to us.
6 While we were still helpless [power-
less to provide for our salvation], at the
right time Christ died [as a substitute]
for the ungodly.
7 Now it is an extraordinary thing
for one to willingly give his life even
for an upright man, though perhaps
for a good man [one who is noble and
selfless and worthy] someone might
even dare to die.
8 But God clearly shows *and* proves
His own love for us, by the fact that
while we were still sinners, Christ died
for us.
9 Therefore, since we have now been
justified [declared free of the guilt of
sin] by His blood, [how much more

---

only to God making Abraham and Sarah's dead reproductive systems alive, but also to the fact that God could and did resurrect Jesus. That is the kind of God He is; belief in the resurrection is central to Christianity, and also to our belief in our own eternal life through Christ.

5:1 Justification — God's gracious justification of the believer does not take place by stages or degrees. It is an instantaneous judicial "not guilty" declaration, based on the perfect obedience and the once-for-all sacrifice of Christ. The believer now has peace with God through Jesus Christ, full pardon of his sins, and the title to eternal life. The crowning gift is an abiding joy and peace in the Lord, which remains in spite of outside circumstances.

18 Ge 15:5 **19** Ge 17:17; 18:11; Heb 11:11 **21** Ps 115:3; Lk 1:37; Heb 11:19 **23** Ro 15:4; 1Co 10:6 **24** Ac 2:24 **25** Isa 53:5,6; Ro 3:25; Gal 1:4; Heb 9:28; 1Co 15:17; 1Pe 1:21 **CHAPTER 5** **1** Isa 32:17; Jn 16:33; Eph 2:14 **2** Jn 10:9; Eph 2:18; 1Co 15:1; Heb 3:6 **3** Mt 5:11; Ac 5:41; 2Co 12:10; Php 2:17; Jas 1:2; Jas 1:3 **4** Jas 1:12 **5** Php 1:20; 2Co 1:22; Eph 1:13 **6** Ro 4:25 **8** Jn 15:13 **9** Eph 2:13; 1Jn 1:7; 1Th 1:10

certain is it that] we will be saved from the wrath *of God* through Him.

[10]For if while we were enemies we were reconciled to God through the death of His Son, *it is* much more *certain,* having been reconciled, that we will be saved [from the consequences of sin] by His life [that is, we will be saved because Christ lives today].

[11]Not only that, but we also rejoice in God [rejoicing in His love and perfection] through our Lord Jesus Christ, through whom we have now received *and* enjoy our reconciliation [with God]. [Jer 9:24]

[12]Therefore, just as sin came into the world through one man, and death through sin, so death spread to all people [no one being able to stop it or escape its power], because they all sinned.

[13]Sin was [committed] in the world before the Law [was given], but sin is not charged [against anyone] when there is no law [against it].

[14]Yet death ruled [over mankind] from Adam to Moses [the Lawgiver], even over those who had not sinned as Adam did. Adam is a type of Him (Christ) who was to come [but in reverse—Adam brought destruction, Christ brought salvation]. [Gen 5:5; 7:22; Deut 34:5]

[15]But the free gift [of God] is not like the trespass [because the gift of grace overwhelms the fall of man]. For if many died by one man's trespass [Adam's sin], much more [abundantly] did God's grace and the gift [that comes] by the grace of the one Man, Jesus Christ, overflow to [benefit] the many.

[16]Nor is the gift [of grace] like *that which came* through the one who sinned. For on the one hand the judgment [following the sin] *resulted* from one trespass and brought condemnation, but on the other hand the free gift *resulted* from many trespasses and brought justification [the release from sin's penalty for those who believe].

[17]For if by the trespass of the one (Adam), death reigned through the one (Adam), much more *surely* will those who receive the abundance of grace and the free gift of righteousness reign in [eternal] life through the One, Jesus Christ.

[18]So then as through one trespass [Adam's sin] there resulted condemnation for all men, even so through one act of righteousness there resulted justification of life to all men.

[19]For just as through one man's disobedience [his failure to hear, his carelessness] the many were made sinners, so through the obedience of the one Man the many will be made righteous *and* acceptable to God *and* brought into right standing with Him.

[20]But the Law came to increase *and* expand [the awareness of] the trespass [by defining and unmasking sin]. But where sin increased, [God's remarkable, gracious gift of] grace [His unmerited favor] has surpassed it *and* increased all the more,

[21]so that, as sin reigned in death, so also grace would reign through righteousness which brings eternal life through Jesus Christ our Lord.

5:12 *one man.* The "one man" is Adam.

5:13 *charged.* This refers to charging something to one's account, as by an entry made into a ledger. In other words, sin was present in the world from Adam to Moses, but God did not keep an account of *sins before the giving* of the law because there was no law to obey or disobey. Those after Adam and before Moses did not sin like Adam because there were no prohibitions similar to the law of Moses. But they did sin, and the way we know this is that "death reigned." They all died.

5:19 *the many will be made righteous.* Through the sanctifying work of the Holy Spirit, the believer who has been declared righteous by God is continually becoming more righteous in thought and action.

5:20 *where sin increased . . . grace . . . increased all the more.* Once the law had been revealed, the sin which was already there became much more obvious because it had been explicitly illustrated how wrong it was. But grace was even bigger than the sin. Sin can never exceed the grace provided by God, and it loses its threat when compared to the infinite grace of God.

10 Ro 8:32; 2Co 5:18; Eph 2:16; Jn 14:19 **11** Gal 4:9 **12** Ge 3:6; 1Co 15:21; Ge 2:17 **13** 1Jn 3:4 **14** 1Co 15:21
15 Isa 53:11 **18** Jn 12:32; Heb 2:9 **20** Jn 15:22; Gal 3:19; Lk 7:47

Believers Are Dead to Sin, Alive to God

6 WHAT SHALL we say [to all this]?
Should we continue in sin *and* prac-
tice sin as a habit so that [God's gift
of] grace may increase *and* overflow?
2 Certainly not! How can we, the very
ones who died to sin, *continue to* live
in it any longer?
3 Or are you ignorant of the fact that
all of us who have been baptized into
Christ Jesus were baptized into His
death?
4 We have therefore been buried with
Him through baptism into death, so
that just as Christ was raised from the
dead through the glory *and* power of
the Father, we too might walk *habit-
ually* in newness of life [abandoning
our old ways].
5 For if we have become one with
Him [permanently united] in the like-
ness of His death, we will also certain-
ly be [one with Him and share fully] *in
the likeness* of His resurrection.
6 We know that our old self [our hu-
man nature without the Holy Spirit]
was nailed to the cross with *Him,* in
order that our body of sin might be
done away with, so that we would no
longer be slaves to sin.
7 For the person who has died [with
Christ] has been freed from [the power
of] sin.
8 Now if we have died with Christ, we
believe that we will also live [together]
with Him,
9 because we know [the self-evident
truth] that Christ, having been raised
from the dead, will never die again;
death no longer has power over Him.
10 For the death that He died, He died
to sin [ending its power and paying the
sinner's debt] once and for all; and the
life that He lives, He lives to [glorify]
God [in unbroken fellowship with Him].
11 Even so, consider yourselves to be
dead to sin [and your relationship to it
broken], but alive to God [in unbroken
fellowship with Him] in Christ Jesus.
12 Therefore do not let sin reign in
your mortal body so that you obey its
lusts *and* passions.
13 Do not go on offering members of
your body to sin as instruments of wick-
edness. But offer yourselves to God [in
a decisive act] as those alive [raised]
from the dead [to a new life], and
your members [all of your abilities—
sanctified, set apart] as instruments of
righteousness [yielded] to God.
14 For sin will no longer be a mas-
ter over you, since you are not under
Law [as slaves], but under [unmerited]
grace [as recipients of God's favor and
mercy].
15 What then [are we to conclude]?
Shall we sin because we are not under
Law, but under [God's] grace? Certain-
ly not!
16 Do you not know that when you
continually offer yourselves to some-
one to do his will, you are the slaves of
the one whom you obey, either [slaves]
of sin, which leads to death, or of obe-
dience, which leads to righteousness
(right standing with God)?
17 But thank God that though you
were slaves of sin, you became obedi-
ent with all your heart to the standard
of teaching in which you were instruct-
ed *and* to which you were committed.
18 And having been set free from sin,
you have become the slaves of righ-
teousness [of conformity to God's will
and purpose].
19 I am speaking in [familiar] human
terms because of your natural lim-
itations [your spiritual immaturity].
For just as you presented your bodily
members as slaves to impurity and to
[moral] lawlessness, leading to fur-
ther lawlessness, so now offer your
members [your abilities, your talents]
as slaves to righteousness, leading to
sanctification [that is, being set apart
for God's purpose].

6:6 *nailed to the cross with Him*. Simply put, a believer is not the same person he or she was before conversion. A believer is a new creation in Christ (2Co 5:17).

CHAPTER 6 **1** Ro 3:8 **2** Gal 2:19; Col 3:3 **3** Gal 3:27; 1Co 15:29 **4** Col 2:12; Ro 8:11; 1Co 6:14; Jn 2:11; Gal 6:15 **5** Php 3:10 **6** Gal 2:20; Col 2:11 **7** 1Pe 4:1 **8** 2Ti 2:11 **9** Rev 1:18 **10** Heb 9:27; Lk 20:38 **11** ver. 2; Gal 2:19 **12** Ps 19:13 **13** Ro 7:5; Col 3:5; Jas 4:1; Ro 12:1; 1Pe 2:24; 4:2 **14** Ro 7:4,6; 8:2; Gal 5:18 **15** 1Co 9:21 **16** Mt 6:24; Jn 8:34; 2Pe 2:19 **17** 2Ti 1:13 **18** Jn 8:32; 1Co 7:22; Gal 5:1; 1Pe 2:16

[20]When you were slaves of sin, you were free in regard to righteousness [you had no desire to conform to God's will].
[21]So what benefit did you get at that time from the things of which you are now ashamed? [None!] For the outcome of those things is death!
[22]But now since you have been set free from sin and have become [willing] slaves to God, you have your benefit, resulting in sanctification [being made holy and set apart for God's purpose], and the outcome [of this] is eternal life.
[23]For the wages of sin is death, but the free gift of God [that is, His remarkable, overwhelming gift of grace to believers] is eternal life in Christ Jesus our Lord.

Believers United to Christ

7 OR DO you not know, brothers and sisters (for I am speaking to those who know the Law), that the Law has jurisdiction [to rule] over a person as long as he lives?
[2]For the married woman [as an example] is bound *and* remains bound by law to her husband while he lives; but if her husband dies, she is released *and* exempt from the law concerning her husband.
[3]Accordingly, she will be designated as an adulteress if she unites herself to another man while her husband is alive. But if her husband dies, she is free from the law [regarding marriage], so that she is not an adulteress if she marries another man.
[4]Therefore, my fellow believers, you too died to the Law through the [crucified] body of Christ, so that you may belong to another, to Him who was raised from the dead, in order that we may bear fruit for God.
[5]When we were *living* in the flesh [trapped by sin], the sinful passions, which were awakened by [that which] the Law [identifies as sin], were at work in our body to bear fruit for death [since the willingness to sin led to death and separation from God].
[6]But now we have been released from the Law *and* its penalty, having died [through Christ] to that by which we were held captive, so that we serve [God] in the newness of the Spirit and not in the oldness of the letter [of the Law].
[7]What shall we say then? Is the Law sin? Certainly not! On the contrary, if it had not been for the Law, I would not have recognized sin. For I would not have known [for example] about coveting [what belongs to another, and would have had no sense of guilt] if the Law had not [repeatedly] said, "YOU SHALL NOT COVET." [Ex 20:17; Deut 5:21]
[8]But sin, finding an opportunity

6:23 New Life: A Free Gift — This passage gets at the central point of the Christian gospel. When we are separated from God, sin directs our lives and there is a wage, a consequence, for that sin: death and permanent separation from God. In stark contrast, we do not earn a wage from God. His gifts are free and abundant — the gift of eternal life. There is nothing that one can do to earn this incredible gift. Eternal life is just that — eternal — it never ceases. All fear of death and its effects can end. Instead of being separated from God for all eternity, Christians will have union with Him. Jesus Christ accomplished all of this on the cross once and for all.

7:3 Adultery — In this passage Paul uses the marriage relationship as an illustration of the believer's relationship to the law and Christ. A wife cannot leave her husband and marry another without committing adultery, but if her husband is dead, she is free to marry another. In the same way, believers must count the law (reconciliation with God by works) dead, in order to "marry" Christ and have a new life. Believers cannot live by the law and by Grace, any more than a woman can have two husbands.

7:6 newness of the Spirit . . . oldness of the letter. Believers have a new life in the Holy Spirit, not in trying to gain life by obeying ancient or old laws.

7:8 without the Law sin is dead. Sin can exist without the law, but without a standard of right and wrong, there can be no judgment of what is sin and what is not.

---

20 Jn 8:34 **21** Ro 7:5; Ro 1:32 **22** Jn 8:32 **23** Ge 2:17; Ro 5:12; Jas 1:15; Ro 2:7; 1Pe 1:4 **CHAPTER 7**
2 1Co 7:39 **3** Mt 5:32 **4** Gal 2:19; 5:18; Col 2:14; Gal 5:22 **5** Ro 6:13; Ro 6:21; Gal 5:19; Jas 1:15 **6** Ro 2:29; 2Co 3:6 **7** Ro 3:20; Ex 20:17; Dt 5:21; Ac 20:33 **8** Ro 4:15; 1Co 15:56

through the commandment [to express
itself] produced in me every kind of
coveting *and* selfish desire. For with-
out the Law sin is dead [the recognition
of sin is inactive].
9 I was once alive without [knowl-
edge of] the Law; but when the com-
mandment came [and I understood its
meaning], sin became alive and I died
[since the Law sentenced me to death].
[Ps 73:22]
10 And the *very* commandment which
was intended to bring life, actually
proved to bring death for me. [Lev 18:5]
11 For sin, seizing its opportunity
through the commandment, beguiled
and completely deceived me, and using
it as a weapon killed me [separating
me from God].
12 So then, the Law is holy, and the
commandment is holy and righteous
and good.
13 Did that which is good [the Law],
then become death to me? Certainly not!
But sin, in order that it might be revealed
as sin, was producing death in me by
[using] this good thing [as a weapon],
so that through the commandment sin
would become exceedingly sinful.

The Conflict of Two Natures

14 We know that the Law is spiritual,
but I am *a creature* of the flesh [world-
ly, self-reliant—carnal and unspiritu-
al], sold into slavery to sin [and serving
under its control].
15 For I do not understand my own ac-
tions [I am baffled and bewildered by
them]. I do not practice what I want *to
do*, but I am doing the very thing I hate
[and yielding to my human nature, my
worldliness—my sinful capacity].
16 Now if I *habitually* do what I do
not want to do, [that means] I agree
with the Law, *confessing* that it is good
(morally excellent).
17 So now [if that is the case, then] it
is no longer I who do it [the disobedi-
ent thing which I despise], but the sin
[nature] which lives in me.
18 For I know that nothing good lives
in me, that is, in my flesh [my human
nature, my worldliness—my sinful
capacity]. For the willingness [to do
good] is present in me, but the doing
of good is not.
19 For the good that I want to do, I do
not do, but I practice the very evil that
I do not want.
20 But if I am doing the very thing I do
not want to do, I am no longer the one
doing it [that is, it is not me that acts],
but the sin [nature] which lives in me.
21 So I find *it to be* the law [of my
inner self], that evil is present in me,
the one who wants to do good.
22 For I joyfully delight in the law of
God in my inner self [with my new
nature], [Ps 1:2]
23 but I see a different law *and* rule
of action in the members of my body
[in its appetites and desires], waging
war against the law of my mind *and*
subduing me and making me a pris-
oner of the law of sin which is within
my members.
24 Wretched *and* miserable man that
I am! Who will [rescue me and] set
me free from this body of death [this
corrupt, mortal existence]?
25 Thanks be to God [for my deliver-
ance] through Jesus Christ our Lord!
So then, on the one hand I myself with
my mind serve the law of God, but on
the other, with my flesh [my human
nature, my worldliness, my sinful ca-
pacity—I serve] the law of sin.

Escape from Bondage

8 THEREFORE THERE is now no
condemnation [no guilty verdict,
no punishment] for those who are in

7:9 when the commandment came [and I understood its meaning], sin became alive. Oddly enough, the very rules against certain behaviors arouse the desire to perform those evil acts.
7:13 become death to me. The problem is not the law; the problem is sin. Through the law, sin is shown for what it is, and realization that we are "dead" in sin. We cannot really "be good," even when we know what that is.
8:1 Condemnation — God's justification ("not guilty"), once pronounced, is final. Christ's death blots out the sins of His people, and when His

---

10 Lev 18:5; Eze 20:11,13,21; 2Co 3:7 **12** Ps 19:8; 119:38; 1Ti 1:8 **14** 2Ki 17:17 **15** Gal 5:17 **18** Ge 6:5; 8:21
22 Ps 1:2; 2Co 4:16; Eph 3:16; Col 3:9,10 **23** Gal 5:17; Ro 6:13,19 **25** 1Co 15:57 **CHAPTER 8** **1** Gal 5:16

Christ Jesus [who believe in Him as personal Lord and Savior]. [John 3:18]

2 For the law of the Spirit of life [which is] in Christ Jesus [the law of our new being] has set you free from the law of sin and of death.

3 For what the Law could not do [that is, overcome sin and remove its penalty, its power] being weakened by the flesh [man's nature without the Holy Spirit], God did: He sent His own Son in the likeness of sinful man as an offering for sin. And He condemned sin in the flesh [subdued it and overcame it in the person of His own Son], [Lev 7:37]

4 so that the [righteous and just] requirement of the Law might be fulfilled in us who do not live our lives in the ways of the flesh [guided by worldliness and our sinful nature], but [live our lives] in the ways of the Spirit [guided by His power].

5 For those who are *living* according to the flesh set their minds on the things of the flesh [which gratify the body], but those who are *living* according to the Spirit, [set their minds on] the things of the Spirit [His will and purpose].

6 Now the mind of the flesh is death [both now and forever—because it pursues sin]; but the mind of the Spirit is life and peace [the spiritual well-being that comes from walking with God—both now and forever];

7 the mind of the flesh [with its sinful pursuits] is actively hostile to God. It does not submit itself to God's law, since it cannot,

8 and those who are in the flesh [living a life that caters to sinful appetites and impulses] cannot please God.

9 However, you are not [living] in the flesh [controlled by the sinful nature] but in the Spirit, if in fact the Spirit of God lives in you [directing and guiding you]. But if anyone does not have the Spirit of Christ, he does not belong to Him [and is not a child of God]. [Rom 8:14]

10 If Christ lives in you, though your [natural] body is dead because of sin, your spirit is alive because of righteousness [which He provides].

11 And if the Spirit of Him who raised Jesus from the dead lives in you, He who raised Christ Jesus from the dead will also give life to your mortal bodies through His Spirit, who lives in you.

12 So then, brothers and sisters, we have an obligation, but not to our flesh [our human nature, our worldliness, our sinful capacity], to live according to the [impulses of the] flesh [our nature without the Holy Spirit]—

13 for if you are living according to the [impulses of the] flesh, you are going to die. But if [you are living] by the [power of the Holy] Spirit you are *habitually* putting to death the *sinful* deeds of the body, you will [really] live *forever*.

14 For all who are *allowing themselves to* be led by the Spirit of God are sons of God.

15 For you have not received a spirit of slavery leading again to fear [of God's judgment], but you have received the

---

work is applied to the believer, there is no room for condemnation, for God's justice has removed all grounds for it forever. This does not mean that the believer does not still deal with overcoming sin on a regular basis, but through the work of the Holy Spirit, he can be free from the tyranny of sin, and for the love of Christ, live in a way that pleases his Savior.

8:3 *the Law could not do.* The law can point out sin, but it cannot do anything about sin itself.

8:4 *the [righteous and just] requirement of the Law might be fulfilled in us.* The believer gains the righteous standard of the law — love — not by means of the law, but by being in Christ and walking "after the Spirit."

8:15 God the Father — God is the Father of all who believe in Christ in a special sense not shared by unbelievers. God is called their Father, first of all, because they have a new standing before Him. While unbelievers are the offspring of God because He created them (Ac 17:28 – 29), they do not have the standing of sons or daughters. Their standing is rather as condemned sinners before God the Judge (Jn 3:18; Rev 20:11).

2 Ro 6:18,22; 1Co 15:45; Ro 7:24,25 **3** Ac 13:39; Heb 7:18; 2Co 5:21; Gal 3:13 **4** ver. 1 **5** Jn 3:6; Gal 5:22 **6** Gal 6:8 **7** Jas 4:4; 1Co 2:14 **9** Jn 3:34; Gal 4:6 **11** Ac 2:24; 1Co 6:14; 2Co 4:14 **12** Ro 6:7,14 **13** Gal 6:8; Eph 4:22 **14** Gal 5:18 **15** 1Co 2:12; Heb 2:15; 2Ti 1:7; 1Jn 4:18; Isa 56:5; Mk 14:36

Spirit of adoption as sons [the Spirit
producing sonship] by which we [joy-
fully] cry, "Abba! Father!"
16 The Spirit Himself testifies *and*
confirms together with our spirit [as-
suring us] that we [believers] are chil-
dren of God.
17 And if [we are His] children, [then
we are His] heirs also: heirs of God
and fellow heirs with Christ [sharing
His spiritual blessing and inheritance],
if indeed we share in His suffering so
that we may also share in His glory.
[John 17:24; Gal 3:29; 4:7; Eph 1:3, 11;
3:6; Heb 6:12]
18 For I consider [from the standpoint
of faith] that the sufferings of the pres-
ent life are not worthy to be compared
with the glory that is about to be re-
vealed to us *and* in us!
19 For [even the whole] creation [all
nature] waits eagerly for the children
of God to be revealed.
20 For the creation was subjected to
frustration *and* futility, not willingly
[because of some intentional fault on
its part], but by the will of Him who
subjected it, in hope [Eccl 1:2]
21 that the creation itself will also be
freed from its bondage to decay [and
gain entrance] into the glorious free-
dom of the children of God.
22 For we know that the whole cre-
ation has been moaning together as
in the pains of childbirth until now.
[Jer 12:4, 11]
23 And not only this, but we too, who
have the first fruits of the Spirit [a joy-
ful indication of the blessings to come],
even we groan inwardly, as we wait
eagerly for [the sign of] our adoption as
sons—the redemption *and* transforma-
tion of our body [at the resurrection].
[2 Cor 5:2, 4; Eph 4:30]
24 For in this hope we were saved [by
faith]. But hope [the object of] which
is seen is not hope. For who hopes for
what he already sees?
25 But if we hope for what we do not
see, we wait eagerly for it with patience
and composure.

Our Victory in Christ

26 In the same way the Spirit [comes
to us and] helps us in our weakness.
We do not know what prayer to offer
or how to offer it as we should, but the
Spirit Himself [knows our need and
at the right time] intercedes on our
behalf with sighs *and* groanings too
deep for words.
27 And He who searches the hearts
knows what the mind of the Spirit is,
because the Spirit intercedes [before
God] on behalf of God's people in ac-
cordance with God's will. [Ps 139:1, 2]
28 And we know [with great confi-
dence] that God [who is deeply con-
cerned about us] causes all things to
work together [as a plan] for good for
those who love God, to those who are
called according to His plan *and* pur-
pose.
29 For those whom He foreknew [and
loved and chose beforehand], He also
predestined to be conformed to the
image of His Son [and ultimately share
in His complete sanctification], so that
He would be the firstborn [the most
beloved and honored] among many
believers.
30 And those whom He predestined,
He also called; and those whom He
called, He also justified [declared free

When a person believes in Christ as Savior, his estate is changed from condemnation to sonship. This new standing grants to all believers the legal right and spiritual privileges of divine sonship: "heirs of God and fellow heirs with Christ" (Ro 8:17). He gives them new life (Jn 3:3). This relationship then is a family one involving many of the same realities that exist between an earthly father and child: birth of the child (Jn 3:3); partaking of the father's nature (2Pe 1:4); the father's care for the child (Mt 6:32 – 33; 7:9 – 11): and the father's discipline of the child (Heb 12:6 – 8). Furthermore, this new Father-child relationship carries with it new brothers and sisters (Heb 13:1). The one who believes in Christ as Savior enters into the Father-child relationship with God solely on the grounds of Christ's sonship (Ro 8:17; Heb 2:17).

---

16 Eph 1:13 **17** Ac 26:18; Php 1:29 **18** 2Co 4:17; 1Pe 1:6 **19** 2Pe 3:13 **20** Ge 3:19 **22** Jer 12:11 **23** 2Co 5:5; Eph 1:14; 2Co 5:2; Lk 20:36; Lk 21:28; Eph 4:30 **24** 2Co 5:7; Heb 11:1 **26** Mt 20:22; Jas 4:3; Eph 6:18 **27** 1Ch 28:9; Ac 1:24; 1Jn 5:14 **28** 2Ti 1:9 **29** 2Ti 2:19; Eph 1:5; 2Co 3:18; 1Jn 3:2; Col 1:15; Heb 1:6 **30** 1Pe 2:9; 1Co 6:11; Jn 17:22; Eph 2:6

of the guilt of sin]; and those whom
He justified, He also glorified [raising
them to a heavenly dignity].
31 What then shall we say to all these
things? If God is for us, who can be
[successful] against us? [Ps 118:6]
32 He who did not spare [even] His
own Son, but gave Him up for us all,
how will He not also, along with Him,
graciously give us all things?
33 Who will bring any charge against
God's elect (His chosen ones)? It is God
who justifies us [declaring us blame-
less and putting us in a right relation-
ship with Himself].
34 Who is the one who condemns us?
Christ Jesus is the One who died [to
pay our penalty], and more *than that*,
who was raised [from the dead], and
who is at the right hand of God inter-
ceding [with the Father] for us.
35 Who shall ever separate us from
the love of Christ? Will tribulation, or
distress, or persecution, or famine, or
nakedness, or danger, or sword?
36 Just as it is written *and* forever
remains written,

"For Your sake we are put to death
all day long;
We are regarded as sheep for the
slaughter." [Ps 44:22]

37 Yet in all these things we are more
than conquerors *and* gain an over-
whelming victory through Him who
loved us [so much that He died for us].
38 For I am convinced [and continue
to be convinced—beyond any doubt]
that neither death, nor life, nor angels,
nor principalities, nor things present
and threatening, nor things to come,
nor powers,
39 nor height, nor depth, nor any oth-
er created thing, will be able to sep-
arate us from the [unlimited] love of
God, which is in Christ Jesus our Lord.

Concern for Israel

9 I AM telling the truth in Christ, I
am not lying, my conscience testi-
fies with me [enlightened and prompt-
ed] by the Holy Spirit,
2 that I have great sorrow and un-
ceasing anguish in my heart.
3 For [if it were possible] I would wish
that I myself were accursed, [separat-
ed, banished] from Christ for the sake
[of the salvation] of my brothers, my
natural kinsmen, [Ex 32:32]
4 who are Israelites, to whom belongs
the adoption as sons, the glory (She-
kinah), the [special] covenants [with
Abraham, Moses, and David], the giv-
ing of the Law, the [system of temple]
worship, and the [original] promises.
[Ex 4:22; Hos 11:1]
5 To them belong the patriarchs, and
from them, according to His natural
descent, *came* the Christ (the Messiah,
the Anointed), He who is exalted *and*
supreme over all, God blessed forever.
Amen.

8:38 – 39 The Ultimate Security — The first chapters of Romans contain the most complete and systematic presentation of the gospel in the Scriptures. This passage is the bottom-line statement. Nothing can separate us from the love of God that is in Christ. Sadly, too often we hear those words and aren't able to apply them to how we live on a day-to-day basis. Satan is known as a deceiver. He will always try to persuade us that God's love is less than what it is. No matter what the circumstances, no matter how much we mess up, no matter how many powerful forces there are that would try to damage our relationship with Him, God will be there for us with His love.

8:39 *will be able to separate us.* Christ created all things, "in heaven and on earth, [things] visible and invisible," and He was "before all things, and in Him all things hold together" (Col 1:16 – 17). If God, who was from the beginning, is for us, no created thing can separate us from His love. Our security in Him is absolute.

9:1 Conscience — This word is used by Paul for the witness within a person which scrutinizes, examines, and renders a verdict on behavior. Paul is saying in the passage that his conscience verifies the truthfulness of his statement that he has great grief over the Jew's rejection of the gospel. The Holy Spirit is the revealer of truth to the soul, and only as the mind and heart are taught

31 Nu 14:9; Ps 118:6 **32** Ro 5:6,10; Ro 4:25 **33** Isa 50:8,9; Rev 12:10 **34** Job 34:29; Mk 16:19; Col 3:1; Heb 1:3; Heb 7:25; 9:24; 1Jn 2:1 **36** Ps 44:22; 2Co 4:11 **37** 1Co 15:57; 1Jn 4:4 **38** Eph 1:21 **CHAPTER 9** **1** 2Co 1:23; Gal 1:20; 1Ti 2:7 **2** Ro 10:1 **3** Ex 32:32 **4** Ex 4:22; Dt 14:1; 1Sa 4:21; 1Ki 8:11; Ac 3:25; Ps 147:19; Heb 9:1; Ac 13:32; Eph 2:12 **5** Dt 10:15; Lk 3:23; Jer 23:6; Heb 1:8

6 However, it is not as though God's word has failed [coming to nothing]. For not all who are descended from Israel (Jacob) are [the true] Israel;

7 and they are not all the children of Abraham because they are his descendants [by blood], but [the promise was]: "YOUR DESCENDANTS WILL BE NAMED THROUGH ISAAC" [though Abraham had other sons]. [Gen 21:9–12]

8 That is, it is not the children of the body [Abraham's natural descendants] who are God's children, but it is the children of the promise who are counted as [Abraham's true] descendants.

9 For this is what the promise said: "ABOUT THIS TIME [next year] I WILL COME, AND SARAH SHALL HAVE A SON." [Gen 18:10]

10 And not only that, but this too: Rebekah conceived *twin sons* by one man [under the same circumstances], by our father Isaac;

11 and though *the twins* were not yet born and had not done anything *either* good or bad, so that God's purpose [His choice, His election] would stand, not because of works [done by either child], but because of [the plan of] Him who calls them,

12 it was said to her, "THE OLDER (Esau) WILL SERVE THE YOUNGER (Jacob)." [Gen 25:21–23]

13 As it is written *and* forever remains written, "JACOB I LOVED (chose, protected, blessed), BUT ESAU I HATED (held in disregard compared to Jacob)." [Mal 1:2, 3]

14 What shall we say then? Is there injustice with God? Certainly not!

15 For He says to Moses, "I WILL HAVE MERCY ON WHOMEVER I HAVE MERCY, AND I WILL HAVE COMPASSION ON WHOMEVER I HAVE COMPASSION." [Ex 33:19]

16 So then God's choice is not dependent on human will, nor on human effort [the totality of human striving], but on God who shows mercy [to whomever He chooses—it is His sovereign gift].

17 For the Scripture says to Pharaoh, "I RAISED YOU UP FOR THIS VERY PURPOSE, TO DISPLAY MY POWER IN [dealing with] YOU, AND SO THAT MY NAME WOULD BE PROCLAIMED IN ALL THE EARTH." [Ex 9:16]

18 So then, He has mercy on whom He wills (chooses), and He hardens [the heart of] whom He wills.

19 You will say to me then, "Why does He still blame me [for sinning]? For who [including myself] has [ever] resisted His will *and* purpose?"

20 On the contrary, who are you, O man, who answers [arrogantly] back to God *and* dares to defy Him? Will the thing which is formed say to him who formed it, "Why have you made me like this?" [Is 29:16; 45:9]

21 Does the potter not have the right over the clay, to make from the same lump [of clay] one object for honorable

---

by Scripture and governed by the Holy Spirit is the voice of conscience a reliable guide in life.

9:6 *not all who are descended from Israel.* What about the Jewish people? They had the law, the covenants, and the promises. God has not changed His mind about His chosen people. He always intended for them to understand His whole message, up to and including the Messiah (Christ), as Paul has just explained. But God has, throughout history, always worked with those who believed, not just according to bloodline.

9:15 *I WILL HAVE MERCY.* God does not "owe" any of us salvation. He has mercy on us in spite of the way we act, not because of the way we act.

9:20 *answers [angrily] back to God.* Herein lies the divine tension. The Lord says that He does not wish for any to perish, but for all to come to repentance (2Pe 3:9). But He also says that no one comes to Jesus unless the Father draws him (Jn 6:44). He has mercy on whom He desires, and He hardens whom He desires (v. 18). Paul insists on God's right to do as He pleases. Even though God both draws and hardens, He also says that who He is and His worthiness to be worshiped are made plain in creation, so man is without excuse (Ro 1:18–21). The question is not, "Why are some saved and some condemned?" Everyone deserves condemnation and it is only by God's grace that anyone is saved. We can be sure that whatever God does, it will be righteous, and there is a bigger picture than we can understand from our finite point of view. The only real question is, "How can I be saved?"

6 Nu 23:19; Jn 8:39; Gal 6:16 **7** Gal 4:23; Ge 21:12 **8** Gal 4:28 **9** Ge 18:10 **10** Ge 25:21 **11** Ro 4:17 **12** Ge 25:23 **13** Mal 1:2,3; Mt 10:37 **14** Dt 32:4; Job 8:3 **15** Ex 33:19 **17** Gal 3:8; Ex 9:16 **19** 2Ch 20:6; Da 4:35 **20** Isa 29:16 **21** Pr 16:4; 2Ti 2:20

use [something beautiful or distinctive]
and another for common use [something ordinary or menial]?
22What if God, although willing to
show His [terrible] wrath and to make
His power known, has tolerated with
great patience the objects of His wrath
[which are] prepared for destruction?
[Prov 16:4]
23And what if He has done so to
make known the riches of His glory
to the objects of His mercy, which He
has prepared beforehand for glory,
24*including* us, whom He also called,
not only from among the Jews, but also
from among the Gentiles?
25Just as He says in [the writings of
the prophet] Hosea:

"I WILL CALL THOSE WHO WERE NOT MY
PEOPLE, 'MY PEOPLE,'
AND [I will call] HER WHO WAS NOT
BELOVED, 'BELOVED.' " [Hos 2:23]
26"AND IT SHALL BE THAT IN THE PLACE
WHERE IT WAS SAID TO THEM, 'YOU
ARE NOT MY PEOPLE,'
THERE THEY SHALL BE CALLED SONS OF
THE LIVING GOD." [Hos 1:10]

27And Isaiah calls out concerning
Israel: "THOUGH THE NUMBER OF THE SONS
OF ISRAEL BE LIKE THE SAND OF THE SEA,
IT IS ONLY THE REMNANT [a small believing minority] THAT WILL BE SAVED [from
God's judgment];
28FOR THE LORD WILL EXECUTE HIS WORD
UPON THE EARTH [He will conclude His
dealings with mankind] COMPLETELY
AND WITHOUT DELAY." [Is 10:22, 23]
29It is as Isaiah foretold,

"IF THE LORD OF HOSTS HAD NOT LEFT
US SEED [future generations from
which a believing remnant of
Israelites came],
WE WOULD HAVE BECOME LIKE SODOM,
AND WOULD HAVE RESEMBLED
GOMORRAH [totally rejected and
destroyed]!" [Is 1:9]

30What shall we say then? That Gentiles, who did not pursue righteousness
[who did not seek salvation and a right
relationship with God, nevertheless] obtained righteousness, that is, the righteousness which is produced by faith;
31whereas Israel, [though always]
pursuing the law of righteousness,
did not succeed in fulfilling the law.
[Is 51:1]
32And why not? Because it was not
by faith [that they pursued it], but as
though it were by works [relying on
the merit of their works instead of their
faith]. They stumbled over the stumbling Stone [Jesus Christ]. [Is 8:14; 28:16]
33As it is written *and* forever remains
written,

"BEHOLD I AM LAYING IN ZION A STONE
OF STUMBLING AND A ROCK OF
OFFENSE;
AND HE WHO BELIEVES IN HIM
[whoever adheres to, trusts
in, and relies on Him] WILL
NOT BE DISAPPOINTED [in his
expectations]." [Is 28:16]

The Word of Faith Brings Salvation

10 BROTHERS AND sisters, my
heart's desire and my prayer to
God for Israel is for their salvation.
2For I testify about them that they
have a certain enthusiasm for God,
but not in accordance with [correct
and vital] knowledge [about Him and
His purposes].
3For not knowing about God's
righteousness [which is based on faith],

9:32 *stumbled.* Being committed to righteousness by works, Israel "stumbled" over the righteousness of faith offered in Christ, just as God had already seen they would and declared through the prophet Isaiah (v. 33).

10:3 Self-Righteousness — There are two things which hinder people from submitting themselves to God's plan of salvation. The first is ignorance of God's own righteous character, and the second is human pride. No one is ever a candidate for Christ's righteousness unless he sees himself as utterly devoid of all possibility of attaining it on his own merits.

22 1Th 5:9; 1Pe 2:8 **23** Col 1:27; Ro 8:28-30 **24** Ro 3:29 **25** Hos 2:23 **26** Hos 1:10 **27** Isa 10:22; Ro 11:5 **28** Isa 28:22 **29** Isa 1:9; La 3:22; Isa 13:19; Jer 50:40 **30** Ro 4:11; Ro 1:17 **31** Ro 10:2; Gal 5:4 **32** Lk 2:34; 1Co 1:23 **33** Ps 118:22; Isa 8:14; 28:16; Mt 21:42; 1Pe 2:6-8; Ro 10:11 **CHAPTER 10** **2** Ac 21:20; 22:3; Ro 9:31; Gal 1:14 **3** Ro 1:17; Php 3:9

and seeking to establish their own [righteousness based on works], they did not submit to God's righteousness.

4 For Christ is the end of the law [it leads to Him and its purpose is fulfilled in Him], for [granting] righteousness to everyone who believes [in Him as Savior].

5 For Moses writes that the man who practices the righteousness which is based on law [with all its intricate demands] shall live by it. [Lev 18:5]

6 But the righteousness based on faith [which produces a right relationship with Him] says the following: "DO NOT SAY IN YOUR HEART, 'WHO WILL ASCEND INTO HEAVEN?' that is, to bring Christ down;

7 or, 'WHO WILL DESCEND INTO THE ABYSS?' that is, to bring Christ up from the dead [as if we had to be saved by our own efforts, doing the impossible]." [Deut 30:12, 13]

8 But what does it say? "THE WORD IS NEAR YOU, IN YOUR MOUTH AND IN YOUR HEART"—that is, the word [the message, the basis] of faith which we preach—[Deut 30:14]

9 because if you acknowledge *and* confess with your mouth that Jesus is Lord [recognizing His power, authority, and majesty as God], and believe in your heart that God raised Him from the dead, you will be saved.

10 For with the heart a person believes [in Christ as Savior] resulting in his justification [that is, being made righteous—being freed of the guilt of sin and made acceptable to God]; and with the mouth he acknowledges *and* confesses [his faith openly], resulting in *and* confirming [his] salvation.

11 For the Scripture says, "WHOEVER BELIEVES IN HIM [whoever adheres to, trusts in, and relies on Him] WILL NOT BE DISAPPOINTED [in his expectations]." [Is 28:16]

12 For there is no distinction between Jew and Gentile; for the same *Lord* is Lord over all [of us], and [He is] abounding in riches (blessings) for all who call on Him [in faith and prayer].

13 For "WHOEVER CALLS ON THE NAME OF THE LORD [in prayer] WILL BE SAVED." [Joel 2:32]

14 But how will people call on Him in whom they have not believed? And how will they believe in Him of whom they have not heard? And how will they hear without a preacher (messenger)?

15 And how will they preach unless they are commissioned *and* sent [for that purpose]? Just as it is written *and* forever remains written, "HOW BEAUTIFUL ARE THE FEET OF THOSE WHO BRING GOOD NEWS OF GOOD THINGS!" [Is 52:7]

16 But they did not all pay attention to the good news [of salvation]; for Isaiah says, "LORD, WHO HAS BELIEVED OUR REPORT?" [Is 53:1]

17 So faith *comes* from hearing [what is told], and what is heard *comes* by the [preaching of the] message concerning Christ.

18 But I say, did they not hear? Indeed they have;

"THEIR VOICE [that of creation
bearing God's message] HAS
GONE OUT TO ALL THE EARTH,
AND THEIR WORDS TO THE [farthest]
ENDS OF THE WORLD." [Ps 19:4, 7–11]

19 But I say, did Israel fail to understand [that the gospel was to go also to the Gentiles]? First Moses says,

"I WILL MAKE YOU JEALOUS OF THOSE
WHO ARE NOT A NATION (Gentiles);
WITH A NATION THAT LACKS
UNDERSTANDING I WILL MAKE YOU
ANGRY." [Deut 32:21]

10:4 *For Christ is the end of the law.* Christ fulfilled all the requirements of the law, and He is also the opening to the only way of righteousness we can ever have.

10:8 *THE WORD IS NEAR YOU.* Righteousness by faith is not far off and inaccessible, but it is as near as a person's mouth and heart.

10:11 *WHOEVER.* Paul emphasizes the universal offer of salvation.

4 Mt 5:17; Gal 3:24 **5** Lev 18:5; Neh 9:29; Eze 20:11; Gal 3:12 **6** Dt 30:12 **8** Dt 30:14 **9** Mt 10:32; Lk 12:8; Ac 8:37 **11** Isa 28:16; 49:23; Jer 17:7 **12** Ac 15:9; Ro 3:22; Ac 10:36; 1Ti 2:5; Eph 1:7; 2:4,7 **13** Joel 2:32; Ac 2:21; Ac 9:14 **14** Titus 1:3 **15** Isa 52:7; Na 1:15 **16** Isa 53:1; Jn 12:38 **18** Ps 19:4; Mt 24:14; Mk 16:15; Col 1:6,23; 1Ki 18:10; Mt 4:8 **19** Ro 11:11; Titus 3:3

[20]Then Isaiah is very bold and says,
"I HAVE BEEN FOUND BY THOSE WHO DID NOT SEEK ME;
I HAVE SHOWN MYSELF TO THOSE WHO DID NOT [consciously] ASK FOR ME." [Is 65:1]

[21]But of Israel he says, "ALL DAY LONG I HAVE STRETCHED OUT MY HANDS [in compassion] TO A DISOBEDIENT AND OBSTINATE PEOPLE." [Is 65:2]

Israel Is Not Cast Away

11 I SAY then, has God rejected *and* disowned His people? Certainly not! For I too am an Israelite, a descendant of Abraham, of the tribe of Benjamin. [1 Sam 12:22; Jer 31:37; 33:24–26; Phil 3:5]
[2]God has not rejected His [chosen] people whom He foreknew. Or do you not know what the Scripture says of Elijah, how he pleads with God against Israel? [Ps 94:14; 1 Kin 19]
[3]"Lord, THEY HAVE KILLED YOUR PROPHETS, THEY HAVE TORN DOWN YOUR ALTARS, AND I ALONE AM LEFT [of the prophets], AND THEY ARE SEEKING MY LIFE."
[4]But what is God's response to him? "I HAVE KEPT for Myself SEVEN THOUSAND MEN WHO HAVE NOT BOWED THE KNEE TO BAAL." [1 Kin 19:18]
[5]So too then, at the present time there has come to be a remnant [a small believing minority] according to *God's* gracious choice.
[6]But if it is by grace [God's unmerited favor], it is no longer on the basis of works, otherwise grace is no longer grace [it would not be a gift but a reward for works].
[7]What then? Israel failed to obtain what it was seeking [that is, God's favor by obedience to the Law], but the elect [those chosen few] obtained it, while the rest of them became hardened *and* callously indifferent;
[8]just as it is written [in Scripture],
"GOD GAVE THEM A SPIRIT OF STUPOR,
EYES THAT DO NOT SEE AND EARS THAT DO NOT HEAR,
[a spiritual apathy that has continued] TO THIS VERY DAY."
[Deut 29:4; Is 29:10]

[9]And David says,
"LET THEIR TABLE (abundance) BECOME A SNARE AND A TRAP,
A STUMBLING BLOCK AND A RETRIBUTION TO THEM. [Ps 69:22]
[10]"LET THEIR EYES BE DARKENED SO THAT THEY DO NOT SEE,
AND MAKE THEIR BACKS BEND [under their burden] FOREVER." [Ps 69:23]

[11]So I say, have they stumbled so as to fall [to spiritual ruin]? Certainly not! But by their transgression [their rejection of the Messiah] salvation *has come* to the Gentiles, to make Israel jealous [when they realize what they have forfeited].
[12]Now if Israel's transgression means riches for the world [at large] and their failure means riches for the Gentiles, how much more will their fulfillment *and* reinstatement be!
[13]But *now* I am speaking to you who are Gentiles. Inasmuch then as I am an apostle to the Gentiles, I magnify my ministry,
[14]in the hope of somehow making my fellow countrymen jealous [by stirring them up so that they will seek the truth] and *perhaps* save some of them.
[15]For if their [present] rejection [of salvation] is for the reconciliation of the world [to God], what will their acceptance [of salvation] be but [nothing less than] life from the dead?

11:1 *has God rejected and disowned His people?* Paul points out that he himself is an Israelite, and was chosen by God to be a believer and an apostle. As he develops this thought, Paul reminds us that there has always been a remnant of Israelites whom God has kept true to Himself.

11:8 – 10 *EARS THAT DO NOT HEAR.* Paul quotes Isaiah and David to show that Israel's spiritual indifference was a continual pattern.

20 Isa 65:1 **21** Isa 65:2 **CHAPTER 11** **1** 1Sa 12:22; Jer 31:37; 2Co 11:22; Php 3:5 **2** Ro 8:29 **3** 1Ki 19:10 **4** 1Ki 19:18 **5** Ro 9:27 **6** Ro 4:4,5; Dt 9:4,5; Gal 5:4 **7** Ro 9:31 **8** Isa 29:10; Dt 29:4; Isa 6:9; Jer 5:21; Eze 12:2; Mt 13:14; Jn 12:40; Ac 28:26 **9** Ps 69:22 **10** Ps 69:23 **11** Ac 13:46; 18:6; Ro 10:19 **13** Ac 9:15; Gal 1:16; Eph 3:8; 1Ti 2:7 **14** 1Co 9:22; 1Ti 4:16; Jas 5:20

16 If the first portion [of dough offered as the first fruits] is holy, so is the *whole* batch; and if the root (Abraham, the patriarchs) is holy, so are the branches (the Israelites). [Num 15:19–21]

17 But if some of the branches were broken off, and you [Gentiles], being like a wild olive shoot, were grafted in among them to share with them the rich root of the olive tree,

18 do not boast over the [broken] branches *and* exalt yourself at their expense. If you do boast *and* feel superior, *remember that* it is not you who supports the root, but the root that *supports* you.

19 You will say then, "Branches were broken off so that I might be grafted in."

20 That is true. They were broken off because of their unbelief, but you stand by your faith [as believers understanding the truth of Christ's deity]. Do not be conceited, but [rather stand in great awe of God and] fear [Him];

21 for if God did not spare the natural branches [because of unbelief], He will not spare you either.

22 Then appreciate the gracious kindness and the severity of God: to those who fell [into spiritual ruin], severity, but to you, God's *gracious* kindness—if you continue in His kindness [by faith and obedience to Him]; otherwise you too will be cut off.

23 And even they [the unbelieving Jews], if they do not continue in their unbelief, will be grafted in; for God has the power to graft them in again.

24 For if you were cut off from what is by nature a wild olive tree, and against nature were grafted into a cultivated olive tree, how much easier will it be to graft these who are the natural *branches* back into [the original parent stock of] their own olive tree?

25 I do not want you, believers, to be unaware of this mystery [God's previously hidden plan]—so that you will not be wise in your own opinion—that a partial hardening has [temporarily] happened to Israel [to last] until the full number of the Gentiles has come in;

26 and so [at that time] all Israel [that is, all Jews who have a personal faith in Jesus as Messiah] will be saved; just as it is written [in Scripture],

"The Deliverer (Messiah) will
come from Zion,
He will remove ungodliness from
Jacob." [Is 59:20, 21]

27 "This is My covenant with them,
When I take away their sins."
[Is 27:9; Jer 31:33]

28 From the standpoint of the gospel, the Jews [at present] are enemies [of God] for your sake [which is for your benefit], but from the standpoint of God's choice [of the Jews as His people], they are still loved by Him for the sake of the fathers.

29 For the gifts and the calling of God are irrevocable [for He does not withdraw what He has given, nor does He change His mind about those to whom He gives His grace or to whom He sends His call].

30 Just as you once were disobedient *and* failed to listen to God, but have now obtained mercy because of their disobedience,

31 so they too have now become disobedient so that they too may one day receive mercy because of the mercy shown to you.

32 For God has imprisoned all in disobedience so that He may show mercy to all [Jew and Gentile alike].

33 Oh, the depth of the riches and wisdom and knowledge of God! How unsearchable are His judgments *and*

11:25 *mystery.* The mystery is that Israel has been temporarily and partially hardened, but God has not rejected them.

11:26 *all Israel.* "All Israel" does not mean that every individual in the nation will turn to the Lord. It means that the nation as a whole will be saved, just as the nation as a whole (but not every individual in it) is now rejecting the Lord.

16 Lev 23:10; Jas 1:18 **17** Jer 11:16; Ac 2:39; Eph 2:12 **18** 1Co 10:12 **20** Ro 12:16; Pr 28:14; Isa 66:2 **22** 1Co 15:2; Heb 3:6; Jn 15:2 **23** 2Co 3:16 **25** Ro 12:16; 2Co 3:14; Lk 21:24; Rev 7:9 **26** Ps 14:7; Isa 59:20 **27** Isa 27:9; Jer 31:31; Heb 8:8 **28** Dt 7:8 **29** Nu 23:19 **30** Eph 2:2; Col 3:7 **32** Ro 3:9 **33** Ps 36:6; Job 11:7; Ps 92:5

decisions and how unfathomable *and*
untraceable are His ways!
34For who has known the mind of the
Lord, or who has been His counselor?
[Is 40:13, 14]
35Or who has first given to Him that
it would be paid back to him?
36For from Him [all things originate]
and through Him [all things live and
exist] and to Him are all things [di-
rected]. To Him be glory *and* honor
forever! Amen.

Dedicated Service

12 THEREFORE I urge you, broth-
ers and sisters, by the mercies of
God, to present your bodies [dedicating
all of yourselves, set apart] as a living
sacrifice, holy and well-pleasing to
God, *which is* your rational (logical,
intelligent) act of worship.
2And do not be conformed to this
world [any longer with its superficial
values and customs], but be trans-
formed *and* progressively changed [as
you mature spiritually] by the renew-
ing of your mind [focusing on godly
values and ethical attitudes], so that
you may prove [for yourselves] what
the will of God is, that which is good
and acceptable and perfect [in His plan
and purpose for you].
3For by the grace [of God] given to
me I say to everyone of you not to think
more highly of himself [and of his im-
portance and ability] than he ought to
think; but to think so as to have sound
judgment, as God has apportioned to
each a degree of faith [and a purpose
designed for service].
4For just as in one [physical] body
we have many parts, and these parts
do not all have the same function *or*
special use,
5so we, who are many, are [neverthe-
less just] one body in Christ, and indi-
vidually [we are] parts one of another
[mutually dependent on each other].
6Since we have gifts that differ ac-
cording to the grace given to us, *each
of us is to use them accordingly:* if
[someone has the gift of] prophecy, [let
him speak a new message from God to
His people] in proportion to the faith
possessed;
7if service, in the act of serving; or
he who teaches, in the act of teaching;
8or he who encourages, in the act of

12:1 *living sacrifice.* In the Old Testament sacrificial system, the "job" of the sacrificial lamb was ended with its death. An individual or household selected an animal according to the dictated forms, and it was sacrificed to cover sins. Since Christ became the final atonement for sin, we no longer need the old system. But Paul is calling believers to consider their whole life as a sacrifice dedicated to God and His purposes, a "living" sacrifice, both holy and single-minded.

12:2 Walking in the Spirit—Confession of sin in itself is not enough to enable the believer to automatically walk in the Spirit. He or she must learn to yield their whole self to God (Ro 6:13; Jas 4:7). This involves both the body (Ro 12:1; 1Co 6:20) and the mind (Ro 12:2), since what is conceived in the mind is carried out by the body. One's whole being must be presented by a decisive act of the will to God for His service. Yielding leads not only to dedication but also can result in separation: "do not be conformed to this world" (Ro 12:2). Finally, yielding includes transformation of the mind. This work is said to be accomplished through a lifetime of "renewing" the mind. Man's mind has been darkened by sin (Ro 8:7; Col 1:21) and must be brought to the place where it thinks as God thinks (Eph 4:23). This renewing is said to come especially through prayer in everything (Php 4:6 – 7) and through constant meditation on the Word of God (Ps 119:1). This transformation is a lifelong process that will not be completed until we are with Christ (Php 1:6; 1Jn 3:2).

12:4 – 5 Fellowship—A believer must not view himself exclusively as an individual, but must also see himself as part of the whole, as a member of "one body." Fellowship in the New Testament sense is not merely companionship, but a partnership, a responsibility to one another that is financial, practical, and spiritual.

12:6 *prophecy.* In its narrower sense, "prophecy" means the revealing of God's will in a particular situation (Ac 13:1 – 3).

34 Job 15:8; Isa 40:13; Jer 23:18; Job 36:22 **35** Job 35:7 **36** Col 1:16; Heb 13:21; Rev 1:6 **CHAPTER 12**
1 2Co 10:1; 1Pe 2:5; Ro 6; Heb 10:20 **2** 1Jn 2:15; Eph 4:23; Col 3:10; 1Th 4:3 **3** Gal 2:9; Pr 25:27; Eph 4:7
4 1Co 12:12; Eph 4:16 **5** 1Co 10:17; Eph 1:23 **6** 1Co 12:4; ver. 3; Ac 11:27 **7** Eph 4:11 **8** Ac 15:32; Mt 6:1-3;
Ac 20:28; 2Co 9:7

encouragement; he who gives, with generosity; he who leads, with diligence; he who shows mercy [in caring for others], with cheerfulness.

[9]Love is to be sincere *and* active [the real thing—without guile and hypocrisy]. Hate what is evil [detest all ungodliness, do not tolerate wickedness]; hold on tightly to what is good.

[10]Be devoted to one another with [authentic] brotherly affection [as members of one family], give preference to one another in honor;

[11]never lagging behind in diligence; aglow in the Spirit, *enthusiastically* serving the Lord;

[12]*constantly* rejoicing in hope [because of our confidence in Christ], steadfast *and* patient in distress, devoted to prayer [continually seeking wisdom, guidance, and strength],

[13]contributing to the needs of God's people, pursuing [the practice of] hospitality.

[14]Bless those who persecute you [who cause you harm or hardship]; bless and do not curse [them]. [Matt 5:44; Luke 6:28]

[15]Rejoice with those who rejoice [sharing others' joy], and weep with those who weep [sharing others' grief].

[16]Live in harmony with one another; do not be haughty [conceited, self-important, exclusive], but associate with humble people [those with a realistic self-view]. Do not overestimate yourself. [Prov 3:7]

[17]Never repay anyone evil for evil. Take thought for what is right *and* gracious *and* proper in the sight of everyone. [Prov 20:22]

[18]If possible, as far as it depends on you, live at peace with everyone.

[19]Beloved, never avenge yourselves, but leave the way open for God's wrath [and His judicial righteousness]; for it is written [in Scripture], "VENGEANCE IS MINE, I WILL REPAY," says the Lord. [Deut 32:35]

[20]"BUT IF YOUR ENEMY IS HUNGRY, FEED HIM; IF HE IS THIRSTY, GIVE HIM A DRINK; FOR BY DOING THIS YOU WILL HEAP BURNING COALS ON HIS HEAD." [Prov 25:21, 22]

[21]Do not be overcome *and* conquered by evil, but overcome evil with good.

Be Subject to Government

13 LET EVERY person be subject to the governing authorities. For there is no authority except from God [granted by His permission and sanction], and those which exist have been put in place by God. [Prov 8:15]

[2]Therefore whoever resists [governmental] authority resists the ordinance of God. And those who have resisted it will bring judgment (civil penalty) on themselves.

[3]For [civil] authorities are not a source of fear for [people of] good behavior, but for [those who do] evil. Do you want to be unafraid of authority? Do what is good and you will receive approval *and* commendation.

[4]For he is God's servant to you for good. But if you do wrong, [you should] be afraid; for he does not carry the [executioner's] sword for nothing. He is God's servant, an avenger who brings punishment on the wrongdoer.

[5]Therefore one must be subject [to civil authorities], not only to escape the punishment [that comes with wrongdoing], but also as a matter of principle [knowing what is right before God].

[6]For this same reason you pay taxes, for *civil authorities* are God's servants, devoting themselves to governance.

[7]Pay to all what is due: tax to whom tax *is due*, customs to whom customs, respect to whom respect, honor to whom honor.

12:9 *Love.* There are three words used for love in the New Testament: "self-sacrificial love," "brotherly love," and "kindly affection," the last of which is used in this verse. The greatest proof of the truth of the gospel message and of the reality of Jesus' love is the love believers show to each other.

12:20 *BURNING COALS.* Freed from vengeance, believers can give themselves to mercy, even toward their enemies. Such unexpected acts

---

9 1Ti 1:5; Ps 34:14 **10** Heb 13:1; Php 2:3 **12** Lk 10:20; Lk 21:19; Lk 18:1 **13** 1Co 16:1; 1Ti 3:2 **14** Mt 5:44 **15** 1Co 12:26 **16** Php 2:2; Jer 45:5; Pr 3:7 **17** Mt 5:39; 2Co 8:21 **18** Heb 12:14 **19** Lev 19:18; Dt 32:35 **20** Mt 5:44 **CHAPTER 13** **1** 1Pe 2:13; Da 2:21 **2** Titus 3:1 **3** 1Pe 2:14 **5** Ecc 8:2; 1Pe 2:19 **7** Mt 22:21; Lk 20:25

8 Owe nothing to anyone except to love *and* seek the best for one another; for he who [unselfishly] loves his neighbor has fulfilled the [essence of the] law [relating to one's fellowman]. [Matt 22:36–40]

9 The commandments, "YOU SHALL NOT COMMIT ADULTERY, YOU SHALL NOT MURDER, YOU SHALL NOT STEAL, YOU SHALL NOT COVET," and any other commandment are summed up in this statement: "YOU SHALL LOVE YOUR NEIGHBOR AS YOURSELF." [Ex 20:13–17; Lev 19:18]

10 Love does no wrong to a neighbor [it never hurts anyone]. Therefore [unselfish] love is the fulfillment of the Law.

11 Do this, knowing that this is a critical time. It is already the hour for you to awaken from your sleep [of spiritual complacency]; for our salvation is nearer to us now than when we first believed [in Christ].

12 The night [this present evil age] is almost gone and the day [of Christ's return] is almost here. So let us fling away the works of darkness and put on the [full] armor of light.

13 Let us conduct ourselves properly *and* honorably as in the [light of] day, not in carousing and drunkenness, not in sexual promiscuity and irresponsibility, not in quarreling and jealousy.

14 But clothe yourselves with the Lord Jesus Christ, and make no provision for [nor even think about gratifying] the flesh in regard to its improper desires.

Principles of Conscience

14 AS FOR the one whose faith is weak, accept him [into your fellowship], but not for [the purpose of] quarreling over his opinions.

2 One man's faith permits him to eat everything, while the weak *believer* eats *only* vegetables [to avoid eating ritually unclean meat or something previously considered unclean].

3 The one who eats [everything] is not to look down on the one who does not eat, and the one who does not eat must not criticize *or* pass judgment on the one who eats [everything], for God has accepted him.

4 Who are you to judge the servant of another? Before his own master he stands [approved] or falls [out of favor]. And he [who serves the Master—the Lord] will stand, for the Lord is able to make him stand.

5 One person regards one day as better [or more important] than another, while another regards every day [the same as any other]. Let everyone be fully convinced (assured, satisfied) in his own mind.

6 He who observes the day, observes it for the Lord. He who eats, eats for the Lord, since he gives thanks to God; while he who abstains, abstains for the Lord and gives thanks to God.

---

of mercy might even bring them to shame and repentance.

13:9 ***AS YOURSELF.*** This is not a command to love ourselves. It is a recognition that we do love ourselves, and a command to love others just as genuinely and sincerely.

13:10 ***love.*** "Love" excludes murder, adultery, stealing, and lying. Therefore when we love, we automatically fulfill the prohibitions of the law.

14:1 ***faith is weak.*** Those whose faith is weak are not unbelievers, but they have not yet understood (or are not able to understand) some of the deeper thinking about the not so clearly defined situations that a Christian faces.

14:5 ***one day as better [or more important] than another.*** This verse probably relates to the holy days of the Old Testament ceremonial law. The exhortation does not mean it is wrong to have strong convictions, but that all people must have their own convictions. Concerning "disputable matters," things that are not clearly defined as sin, we as Christians are supposed to think deeply about these things, and decide what we think best pleases the Lord. We are not supposed to live by default, doing what most others are doing, or being swayed by the strongest voice. We may find that we need to change our original conclusions, but we must do so thoughtfully, not impulsively. We must not condemn others who come to a different conclusion.

8 Gal 5:14; 1Ti 1:5 **9** Ex 20:13; Mt 19:18; Lev 19:18; Mk 12:31; Jas 2:8 **10** Mt 22:40 **11** 1Co 15:34; Eph 5:14 **12** Eph 5:11; 6:13 **13** Php 4:8; Pr 23:20; 1Co 6:9; Jas 3:14 **14** Gal 3:27; Eph 4:24; Gal 5:16 **CHAPTER 14** **1** 1Co 8:9 **2** 1Co 10:25; Titus 1:15 **3** Col 2:16 **4** Jas 4:12 **5** Gal 4:10 **6** Gal 4:10; 1Co 10:31; 1Ti 4:3

7 None of us lives for himself [for his own benefit, but for the Lord], and none of us dies for himself [but for the Lord].

8 If we live, we live for the Lord, and if we die, we die for the Lord. So then, whether we live or die, we are the Lord's.

9 For Christ died and lived again for this reason, that He might be Lord of both the dead and the living.

10 But you, why do you criticize your brother? Or you again, why do you look down on your [believing] brother *or* regard him with contempt? For we will all stand before the judgment seat of God [who alone is judge].

11 For it is written [in Scripture],

"As I live, says the Lord, every
knee shall bow to Me,
And every tongue shall give praise
to God." [Is 45:23]

12 So then, each of us will give an account of himself to God.

13 Then let us not criticize one another anymore, but rather determine this—not to put an obstacle or a stumbling block *or* a source of temptation in another believer's way.

14 I know and am convinced [as one] in the Lord Jesus that nothing is unclean [ritually defiled, and unholy] in itself; but [nonetheless] it is unclean to anyone who thinks it is unclean.

15 If your brother is being hurt *or* offended because of food [that you insist on eating], you are no longer walking in love [toward him]. Do not let what you eat destroy *and* spiritually harm one for whom Christ died.

16 Therefore do not let what is a good thing for you [because of your freedom to choose] be spoken of as evil [by someone else];

17 for the kingdom of God is not *a matter of* eating and drinking [what one likes], but of righteousness and peace and joy in the Holy Spirit.

18 For the one who serves Christ in this way [recognizing that food choice is secondary] is acceptable to God and is approved by men.

19 So then, let us pursue [with enthusiasm] the things which make for peace and the building up of one another [things which lead to spiritual growth].

20 Do not, for the sake of food, tear down the work of God. All things indeed are [ceremonially] clean, but they are wrong for the person who eats and offends [another's conscience in the process].

21 It is good [to do the right thing and] not eat meat or drink wine, or do any-

---

14:12 *account of himself to God.* We must give an account to God for these conclusions we have reached about how to live, and in light of that, we want to be sure that our conclusions do not cause someone else to stumble.

14:14 *unclean.* "Unclean" means common, and refers to the things prohibited by the Jewish ceremonial law. If anyone considers some activity to be wrong, then for him it is wrong to engage in that activity.

14:15 Selfishness — This chapter concerns weak and strong Christians and their attitudes toward each other in practical matters within the church. If a stronger brother fails to consider the scruples of the weaker brother, the stronger brother violates the obligations of love. He is selfishly putting his own desires above the real needs of one who is weak in faith.

14:16 *good thing for you ... be spoken of as evil.* Even if you have decided that eating certain foods is in accord with your understanding of what is pleasing to God, if it causes another believer to be grieved by the choice you have made, you should be eager to change. Your freedom should not look like license or gluttony. The kingdom of God is a lot more important than the things we eat and drink.

14:21 *offends.* A believer does not have to abandon his own convictions, but love should cause him to carefully observe how what he does affects others. It is a sin (v. 23) to do something that you are really convinced is wrong, even if others think it is all right. In light of this, if a believer is influencing another to violate his conscience, even if the believer is not violating his own conscience, he has caused the other brother to "stumble," and that should not happen.

7 1Co 6:19; Gal 2:20; 1Th 5:10; 1Pe 4:2 **9** 2Co 5:15; Ac 10:36 **10** Mt 25:31; 2Co 5:10 **11** Isa 45:23 **12** Mt 12:36; Gal 6:5; 1Pe 4:5 **13** 1Co 8:9 **14** 1Co 10:25; 1Co 8:7 **15** 1Co 8:11 **16** Ro 12:17 **17** 1Co 8:8 **18** 2Co 8:21 **19** Ro 12:18; 1Co 14:12; 1Th 5:11 **20** ver. 15; Mt 15:11; 1Co 8:9 **21** 1Co 8:13

thing that offends your brother *and* weakens him spiritually.

22 The faith which you have [that gives you freedom of choice], have as your own conviction before God [just keep it between yourself and God, seeking His will]. Happy is he who has no reason to condemn himself for what he approves.

23 But he who is uncertain [about eating a particular thing] is condemned if he eats, because he is not *acting* from faith. Whatever is not from faith is sin [whatever is done with doubt is sinful].

Self-denial on Behalf of Others

15 NOW WE who are strong [in our convictions and faith] ought to [patiently] put up with the weaknesses of those who are not strong, and not just please ourselves.

2 Let each one of us [make it a practice to] please his neighbor for his good, to build him up spiritually.

3 For even Christ did not please Himself; but as it is written [in Scripture], "THE REPROACHES OF THOSE WHO REPROACHED YOU (the Father) FELL ON ME (the Son)." [Ps 69:9]

4 For whatever was written in earlier times was written for our instruction, so that through endurance and the encouragement of the Scriptures we might have hope *and* overflow with confidence in His promises.

5 Now may the God who gives endurance and who supplies encouragement grant that you be of the same mind with one another according to Christ Jesus,

6 so that with one accord you may with one voice glorify *and* praise *and* honor the God and Father of our Lord Jesus Christ.

7 Therefore, [continue to] accept *and* welcome one another, just as Christ has accepted *and* welcomed us to the glory of [our great] God.

8 For I tell you that Christ has become a servant *and* a minister to the circumcision (Jews) on behalf of God's truth, to confirm *and* verify the promises made to the fathers,

9 and for the Gentiles to glorify God for His mercy [to them, since God had no covenant with them]. As it is written *and* forever remains written,

"THEREFORE I PRAISE YOU AMONG THE GENTILES,
AND SING PRAISES TO YOUR NAME."
[Ps 18:49]

10 Again it says,

"REJOICE *and* CELEBRATE, O GENTILES,
ALONG WITH HIS PEOPLE."
[Deut 32:43]

11 And again,

"PRAISE THE LORD ALL YOU GENTILES,
AND LET ALL THE PEOPLES PRAISE
HIM!" [Ps 117:1]

12 Again Isaiah says,

"THERE SHALL BE A ROOT OF JESSE,
HE WHO ARISES TO RULE [as King]
OVER THE GENTILES,
IN HIM SHALL THE GENTILES HOPE."
[Is 11:1, 10; Rev 5:5; 22:16]

13 May the God of hope fill you with all joy and peace in believing [through the experience of your faith] that by the power of the Holy Spirit you will abound in hope *and* overflow with confidence in His promises.

15:3 *Christ.* Jesus Christ is the ultimate model for the strong believer. He "did not regard equality with God a thing to be grasped . . . but emptied Himself" (Php 2:5 – 7) so that He could clearly represent God and His cause.

15:9 *As it is written.* Paul quotes from all three divisions of the Old Testament (the Law, the Prophets, and the Psalms) and from three great Jewish leaders (Moses, David, and Isaiah) to demonstrate that God's purpose was always to bless the Gentiles through Israel.

15:12 *ROOT OF JESSE.* This is a title for the Messiah (Christ). Jesse was the father of David, and the Messiah was to be the Son of David. The Messiah is both the Origin and the Offspring of David.

---

22 1Jn 3:21 **23** Titus 1:15 **CHAPTER 15** **1** Gal 6:1; Ro 14:1 **2** 1Co 10:33; Ro 14:19 **3** Mt 26:39; Ps 69:9 **4** 1Co 10:11 **5** 1Co 1:10 **6** Ac 4:24 **7** Ro 14:1,3; Ro 5:2 **8** Mt 15:24; Jn 1:11; Ac 3:25; 2Co 1:20 **9** Jn 10:16; Ps 18:49 **10** Dt 32:43 **11** Ps 117:1 **12** Isa 11:1; Rev 5:5 **13** Ro 12:12

14 Personally I am convinced about you, my brothers and sisters, that you yourselves are full of goodness, amply filled with all [spiritual] knowledge, and competent to admonish *and* counsel *and* instruct one another.

15 Still, on some points I have written to you very boldly *and* without reservation to remind you [about them] again, because of the grace that was given to me from God,

16 to be a minister of Christ Jesus to the Gentiles. I minister as a priest the gospel of God, in order that my offering of the Gentiles may become acceptable [to Him], sanctified [made holy and set apart for His purpose] by the Holy Spirit.

17 In Christ Jesus, then, I have found [legitimate] reason for boasting in things related [to my service] to God.

18 For I will not [even] presume to speak of anything except what Christ has done through me [as an instrument in His hands], resulting in the obedience of the Gentiles [to the gospel], by word and deed,

19 with the power of signs and wonders, [and all of it] in the power of the Spirit. So [starting] from Jerusalem and as far *away* as Illyricum, I have fully preached the gospel [faithfully preaching the good news] of Christ [where it had not before been preached].

20 Accordingly I set a goal to preach the gospel, not where Christ's name was already known, so that I would not build on another man's foundation;

21 but [instead I would act on this goal] as it is written [in Scripture],

> "They who had no news of Him
> shall see,
> And they who have not heard
> [of Him] shall understand."
> [Is 52:15]

22 This [goal—my commitment to this principle] is the reason why I have often been prevented from coming to you [in Rome].

23 But now, with no further place for work in these regions, and since I have longed for many years to come to you—

24 whenever I go [on my trip] to Spain—I hope to see you as I pass through [Rome], and to be helped on my journey there by you, after I have first enjoyed your company for a little while.

25 But for now, I am going to Jerusalem to serve the saints (Jewish believers).

26 For [Gentile believers in] Macedonia and Achaia have been pleased to make a contribution for the poor among the saints (Jewish believers) in Jerusalem.

27 They were pleased to do it, and they are indebted to them. For if the Gentiles have come to share in their spiritual things, then they are indebted to serve them also in [tangible] material things.

28 Therefore, when I have finished this [mission] and have safely given to them what has been raised, I will go on by way of you to Spain.

29 I know that when I do come to you, I will come in the abundant blessing of Christ.

30 I urge you, believers, by our Lord Jesus Christ and by the love of the Spirit, to join together with me in your prayers to God in my behalf,

---

15:25–26 Kindness — One of the New Testament commands is that Christians display kindness toward other believers (12:10). The Macedonian believers had just gathered a love offering for the needy saints in Jerusalem. Such kindness is a response to God's wonderful kindness to us. In fact, wanting to reach out to others is an evidence of our new birth, and as we bless others in this way, we will find ourselves receiving similar blessings of kindness (Lk 6:38).

15:28 *Spain.* No one knows for sure if Paul ever got to Spain, but he had it on his travel itinerary.

15:29 *when I do come to you.* Paul did get to Rome, but not in the time frame or way he had thought. God had a special plan for Paul. The Lord would give him the opportunity to testify

14 2Pe 1:12; 1Jn 2:21; 1Co 8:1 **15** Ro 1:5; 12:3; Gal 1:15; Eph 3:7,8 **16** Ro 11:13; Gal 2:7-9; 1Ti 2:7; 2Ti 1:11; Isa 66:20; Php 2:17 **17** Heb 5:1 **18** Ac 21:19; Gal 2:8; Ro 1:5; 16:26 **19** Ac 19:11; 2Co 12:12 **20** 2Co 10:13,15,16 **21** Isa 52:15 **22** Ro 1:13; 1Th 2:17 **23** Ac 19:21; Ro 1:11 **24** Ac 15:3 **25** Ac 19:21; 24:17 **26** 1Co 16:1; 2Co 8:1 **27** Ro 11:17; 1Co 9:11; Gal 6:6 **28** Php 4:17 **29** Ro 1:11 **30** Php 2:1; 2Co 1:11; Col 4:12

31 [and pray] that I may be rescued from the unbelievers in Judea, and that my service for Jerusalem may be acceptable to the saints (Jewish believers) *there;*

32 so that by God's will I may come to you with joy and find rest in your company.

33 May the God of peace be with you all! Amen.

Greetings and Love Expressed

16 NOW I introduce *and* commend to you our sister Phoebe, a deaconess (servant) of the church at Cenchrea,

2 that you may receive her in the Lord [with love and hospitality], as God's people ought to receive one another. And that you may help her in whatever matter she may require assistance from you, for she has been a helper of many, including myself.

3 Greet Prisca and Aquila, my fellow workers in Christ Jesus,

4 who risked their own necks [endangering their very lives] for my life. To them not only do I give thanks, but also all the churches of the Gentiles.

5 Also *greet* the church that meets in their house. Greet my beloved Epaenetus, who is the first convert to Christ from [the west coast province of] Asia [Minor].

6 Greet Mary, who has worked so hard for you.

7 Greet Andronicus and Junias, my kinsmen and [once] my fellow prisoners, who are held in high esteem in *the estimation of* the apostles, and who were [believers] in Christ before me.

8 Greet Ampliatus, my beloved in the Lord.

9 Greet Urbanus, our fellow worker in Christ, and my beloved Stachys.

10 Greet Apelles, the one tested *and* approved in Christ. Greet those who belong to the *household* of Aristobulus.

11 Greet my kinsman Herodion. Greet those of the *household* of Narcissus, who are in the Lord.

12 Greet those workers in the Lord, Tryphaena and Tryphosa. Greet my beloved Persis, who has worked hard in the Lord.

13 Greet Rufus, an eminent *and* choice man in the Lord, also his mother [who has been] a mother to me as well.

14 Greet Asyncritus, Phlegon, Hermes, Patrobas, Hermas, and the brothers who are with them.

15 Greet Philologus and Julia, Nereus and his sister, and Olympas, and all God's people who are with them.

16 Greet one another with a holy kiss. All the churches of Christ greet you.

17 I urge you, brothers and sisters, to keep your eyes on those who cause dissensions and create obstacles *or* introduce temptations [for others] to commit sin, [acting in ways] contrary to the doctrine which you have learned. Turn away from them.

18 For such people do not serve our Lord Christ, but their own appetites and base desires. By smooth and flattering speech they deceive the hearts of the unsuspecting [the innocent and the naive].

19 For *the report of* your obedience has reached everyone, so that I rejoice over you, but I want you to be wise in what is good and innocent in what is evil.

20 The God of peace will soon crush Satan under your feet.

---

of his faith in the emperor's court, but he would do so as a prisoner (Ac 28).

16:3 – 4 *Prisca and Aquila.* This married couple is never mentioned separately, perhaps because they ministered so effectively together. Like Paul, they were tentmakers, and worked with him in Corinth and Ephesus. (Ac 18:1 – 3,18,26).

16:8 – 10 *Ampliatus . . . Urbanus . . . Stachys . . . Apelles.* These were common slave names. ***Aristobulus.*** This was a familiar Greek name, and this man may have been the owner of the previously mentioned men, if they were indeed slaves.

31 2Th 3:2; 2Co 8:4 **32** Ro 1:10; Ac 18:21; 1Co 4:19; Jas 4:15; 1Co 16:18; 2Co 7:13; 2Ti 1:16; Php 7,20 **33** Ro 16:20; 1Co 14:33; 2Co 13:11; Php 4:9; 1Th 5:23; 2Th 3:16; Heb 13:20 **CHAPTER 16** **1** Ac 18:18 **2** Php 2:29; 3Jn 5,6 **3** Ac 18:2,18,26 **5** 1Co 16:19; Col 4:15; Php 2; 1Co 16:15 **7** Gal 1:22 **13** 2Jn 1 **16** 1Co 16:20; 2Co 13:12 **17** Ac 15:1; 1Co 5:9; 2Ti 3:5 **18** Php 3:19; 1Ti 6:5; Col 2:4; 2Ti 3:6 **19** Ro 1:8; Mt 10:16 **20** Ro 15:33; Ge 3:15; 1Co 16:23

The [wonderful] grace of our Lord
Jesus be with you.
21 Timothy, my fellow worker, sends
his greetings to you, as do Lucius, Ja-
son and Sosipater, my kinsmen.
22 I, Tertius, the writer (scribe) of this
letter, greet you in the Lord.
23 Gaius, who is host to me and to the
whole church here, greets you. Eras-
tus, the city treasurer, and our brother
Quartus, greet you.
24 [The grace of our Lord Jesus Christ
be with you all. Amen.]
25 Now to Him who is able to estab-
lish *and* strengthen you [in the faith]
according to my gospel and the preach-
ing of Jesus Christ, according to the
revelation of the mystery [of the plan of
salvation] which has been kept secret
for long ages past,
26 but now has been disclosed and
through the prophetic Scriptures has
been made known to all the nations,
according to the commandment of the
eternal God, *leading them* to obedi-
ence to the faith,
27 to the only wise God, through Jesus
Christ, be the glory forevermore! Amen.

16:23 *Gaius.* "Gaius" of Corinth (1Co 1:14) not only gave Paul lodging, but offered his house as a meeting place for the church.

16:25 *mystery.* Paul speaks of his message as a "mystery" (see 11:25) because God's complete plan of salvation was at first hidden but now was being revealed. Part of the mystery is that the church will consist of both Jews and Gentiles united in one body of Christ (Eph 3:1 – 13).

21 Ac 16:1; Heb 13:23; Ac 13:1; Ac 17:5; Ac 20:4 **23** 1Co 1:14; Ac 19:22 **24** 1Th 5:28 **25** Eph 3:20; Ro 2:16; Eph 1:9; Col 1:26 **26** Eph 1:9; Ac 6:7

THE FIRST LETTER OF PAUL TO THE

CORINTHIANS

▸ **AUTHOR:** Pauline authorship of 1 Corinthians is almost universally accepted. Instances of this widely held belief can be found as early as AD 95, when Clement of Rome wrote to the Corinthian church and cited this epistle in regard to the continuing problem of factions among themselves. Paul taught the Word of God in Corinth for eighteen months in AD 51 and 52, leaving Apollos to preach and teach in his absence. When Paul was in Ephesus during his third missionary journey, he became disturbed by reports of discord in the church of Corinth. First Corinthians is a record of Paul's initial response to these problems.

▸ **TIMES:** c. AD 56 ▸ **KEY VERSE:** 1Co 1:10

▸ **THEME:** The basic theme of this epistle is the application of Christian principles to carnality in the individual as well as in the church. Paul is responding to a letter he received from the Corinthians concerning five behavioral problems that are causing dissension in one way or another: 1) Divisions in the church; 2) A case of incest; 3) Court cases between members; 4) The abuse of Christian "freedom"; 5) The chaos occurring in connection with celebration of the Lord's Supper.

Paul's ethical responses to the various behaviors of the Corinthian church are based on a theological understanding of what it means to be a part of the people of God in a complex multi-cultural, pagan environment.

Appeal to Unity

1 PAUL, CALLED as an apostle (spe-
cial messenger, personally chosen
representative) of Jesus Christ by the
will of God, and our brother Sosthenes,
2 To the church of God in Corinth, to
those sanctified (set apart, made holy)
in Christ Jesus, who are selected *and*
called as saints (God's people), togeth-
er with all those who in every place
call on *and* honor the name of our Lord
Jesus Christ, their *Lord* and ours:
3 Grace to you and peace [inner calm
and spiritual well-being] from God
our Father and the Lord Jesus Christ.
4 I thank my God always for you be-
cause of the grace of God which was
given you in Christ Jesus,
5 so that in everything you were
[exceedingly] enriched in Him, in all
speech [empowered by the spiritual
gifts] and in all knowledge [with in-
sight into the faith].
6 In this way our testimony about
Christ was confirmed *and* established
in you,

1:1 ***by the will of God.*** The Corinthian church greatly valued human wisdom. This misplaced emphasis had caused some in the church to challenge Paul's authority. They forgot that Jesus Christ Himself had called him to his ministry as an apostle of Christ.

1:2 ***sanctified (set apart, made holy) in Christ Jesus.*** Holiness comes from our position in Christ, not from our own goodness. Jesus' death in payment for our sins makes a believer holy forever in God's eyes (Heb 10:14). But in everyday living, sanctification involves small daily changes.

CHAPTER 1 **1** Ro 1:1; 2Co 1:1 **2** Ac 15:9; Ro 1:7; 1Co 8:6; Ro 3:22 **3** Ro 1:7; 2Co 1:2 **4** Ro 1:8 **5** 1Co 12:8 **6** 2Ti 1:8; Rev 1:2

7 so that you are not lacking in any
spiritual gift [which comes from the
Holy Spirit], as you eagerly wait [with
confident trust] for the revelation of our
Lord Jesus Christ [when He returns].
8 And He will also confirm you to
the end [keeping you strong and free
of any accusation, so that you will be]
blameless *and* beyond reproach in the
day [of the return] of our Lord Jesus
Christ.
9 God is faithful [He is reliable, trust-
worthy and ever true to His promise—
He can be depended on], and through
Him you were called into fellowship
with His Son, Jesus Christ our Lord.
10 But I urge you, believers, by the
name of our Lord Jesus Christ, that
all of you be in full agreement in what
you say, and that there be no divisions
or factions among you, but that you be
perfectly united in your way of think-
ing and in your judgment [about mat-
ters of the faith].
11 For I have been informed about
you, my brothers and sisters, by those
of Chloe's *household*, that there are
quarrels *and* factions among you.
12 Now I mean this, that each one of
you says, "I am [a disciple] of Paul," or
"I am [a disciple] of Apollos," or "I am
[a disciple] of Cephas (Peter)," or "I am
[a disciple] of Christ."
13 Has Christ been divided [into dif-
ferent parts]? Was Paul crucified for
you? Or were you baptized into the
name of Paul? [Certainly not!]
14 I thank God that I did not baptize
any of you except Crispus and Gaius,
[Acts 18:8; Rom 16:23]
15 so that no one would say that you
were baptized into my name.
16 Now I also baptized the household
of Stephanas; beyond that, I do not
know if I baptized anyone else.
17 For Christ did not send me [as an
apostle] to baptize, but [commissioned
and empowered me] to preach the good
news [of salvation]—not with clever
and eloquent speech [as an orator], so
that the cross of Christ would not be
made ineffective [deprived of its saving
power].

The Wisdom of God

18 For the message of the cross is
foolishness [absurd and illogical] to
those who are perishing *and* spiritu-
ally dead [because they reject it], but
to us who are being saved [by God's
grace] it is [the manifestation of] the
power of God.
19 For it is written *and* forever re-
mains written,

"I WILL DESTROY THE WISDOM OF THE
WISE [the philosophy of the
philosophers],
AND THE CLEVERNESS OF THE CLEVER
[who do not know Me] I WILL
NULLIFY." [Is 29:14]

20 Where is the wise man (philosopher)?
Where is the scribe (scholar)? Where
is the debater (logician, orator) of this
age? Has God not exposed the foolish-
ness of this world's wisdom?

1:7 *not lacking in any spiritual gift.* The Corinthians were richly blessed with spiritual gifts because God was giving them everything they needed to do His will (12:14–27).

1:10 *united in your way of thinking.* Christian unity is not uniformity of appearance, but unity of direction, and the bond of mutual love and esteem (Eph 4:14–16).

1:14 *Crispus and Gaius.* Crispus was the ruler of the synagogue in Corinth when Paul began to preach there (Ac 18:8). He was instrumental in the conversion of many other Christians. Gaius may be the same person who hosted Paul and the entire church (Ro 16:23).

1:16 *Stephanas.* Stephanas was one of Paul's first converts in Achaia, the region of which Corinth was the capital. Paul praised him and his household for their devotion to the ministry and for their assistance (16:15). Stephanus was one of the couriers who took correspondence to and from Corinth.

1:17 *not send me [as an apostle] to baptize, but [commissioned and empowered me] to preach the good news.* Paul's primary ministry was not baptism, but preaching the truth. Baptism naturally follows conversion, but is secondary in importance.

1:20 *Where is the wise man.* All human efforts to find favor with God fall woefully short (Ro

---

7 Php 3:20; Titus 2:13; 2Pe 3:12 **8** 1Th 3:13; Col 1:22 **9** Isa 49:7; 1Th 5:24; Jn 15:4 **10** 2Co 13:11; 1Pe 3:8 **12** 1Co 3:4; Ac 18:24; Jn 1:42 **13** 2Co 11:4 **14** Ac 18:8; Ro 16:23 **16** 1Co 16:15 **17** 1Co 2:4 **18** 2Co 2:15; Ac 17:18; 1Co 15:2; Ro 1:16 **19** Isa 29:14 **20** Isa 33:18; Job 12:17; Isa 44:25; Ro 1:22

21 For since the world through all its
[earthly] wisdom failed to recognize
God, God in His wisdom was well-
pleased through the foolishness of
the message preached [regarding sal-
vation] to save those who believe [in
Christ and welcome Him as Savior].
22 For Jews demand signs (attesting
miracles), and Greeks pursue [worldly]
wisdom *and* philosophy,
23 but we preach Christ crucified, [a
message which is] to Jews a stumbling
block [that provokes their opposition],
and to Gentiles foolishness [just utter
nonsense],
24 but to those who are the called,
both Jews and Greeks (Gentiles),
Christ is the power of God and the
wisdom of God. [Rom 8:28]
25 [This is] because the foolishness
of God [is not foolishness at all and]
is wiser than men [far beyond human
comprehension], and the weakness of
God is stronger than men [far beyond
the limits of human effort].
26 Just look at your own calling, be-
lievers; not many [of you were con-
sidered] wise according to human
standards, not many powerful *or* in-
fluential, not many of high *and* noble
birth.
27 But God has selected [for His pur-
pose] the foolish things of the world to
shame the wise [revealing their igno-
rance], and God has selected [for His
purpose] the weak things of the world
to shame the things which are strong
[revealing their frailty].
28 God has selected [for His purpose]
the insignificant (base) things of the
world, and the things that are despised
and treated with contempt, [even] the
things that are nothing, so that He
might reduce to nothing the things
that are,
29 so that no one may [be able to]
boast in the presence of God.
30 But it is from Him that you are in
Christ Jesus, who became to us wis-
dom from God [revealing His plan of
salvation], and righteousness [making
us acceptable to God], and sanctifica-
tion [making us holy and setting us
apart for God], and redemption [pro-
viding our ransom from the penalty
for sin],
31 so then, as it is written [in Scrip-
ture], "HE WHO BOASTS *and* GLORIES,
LET HIM BOAST *and* GLORY IN THE LORD."
[Jer 9:24]

Paul's Reliance upon the Spirit

2 AND WHEN I came to you, broth-
ers and sisters, proclaiming to you
the testimony of God [concerning sal-
vation through Christ], I did not come
with superiority of speech or of wis-
dom [no lofty words of eloquence or of
philosophy as a Greek orator might do];
2 for I made the decision to know
nothing [that is, to forego philosophical
or theological discussions regarding
inconsequential things and opinions
while] among you except Jesus Christ,
and Him crucified [and the meaning of
His redemptive, substitutionary death
and His resurrection].
3 I came to you in [a state of] weak-
ness and fear and great trembling.
4 And my message and my preaching
were not in persuasive words of wis-
dom [using clever rhetoric], but [they
were delivered] in demonstration of the
[Holy] Spirit [operating through me]
and of [His] power [stirring the minds
of the listeners and persuading them],
5 so that your faith would not rest on
the wisdom *and* rhetoric of men, but on
the power of God.

3:9–28). Only through faith in Christ can we be saved from our sins.

1:27 *the foolish things of the world.* God's plan of salvation does not conform to the world's priorities. Yet in reality, eternal salvation is more valuable than anything else.

1:28 *the insignificant (base) things . . . that are despised.* Corinth had a large slave population, and many of these slaves became followers of Christ. Slaves were despised by the free-born and the well to do.

21 Mt 11:25; Lk 10:21; Ro 1:20 **22** Mt 12:38; Mk 8:11; Jn 4:48 **23** Isa 8:14; Lk 2:34; Jn 6:60; Gal 5:11; 1Co 2:14 **24** Ro 1:4; Col 2:3 **26** Jn 7:48 **27** Mt 11:25 **28** Ro 4:17; 1Co 2:6 **29** Ro 3:27; Eph 2:9 **30** ver. 24; Jer 23:5; Ro 4:25; 2Co 5:21; Jn 17:19; Eph 1:7 **31** Jer 9:23 **CHAPTER 2** **1** 1Co 1:17; 1Co 1:6 **2** Gal 6:14; Php 3:8 **3** Ac 18:1; 2Co 4:7 **4** 2Pe 1:16; Ro 15:19 **5** 2Co 4:7

6 Yet we do speak wisdom among those *spiritually* mature [believers who have teachable hearts and a greater understanding]; but [it is a higher] wisdom not [the wisdom] of this *present* age nor of the rulers *and* leaders of this age, who are passing away;

7 but we speak God's wisdom in a mystery, the *wisdom* once hidden [from man, but now revealed to us by God, that wisdom] which God predestined before the ages to our glory [to lift us into the glory of His presence].

8 None of the rulers of this age recognized *and* understood this *wisdom;* for if they had, they would not have crucified the Lord of glory;

9 but just as it is written [in Scripture],

"THINGS WHICH THE EYE HAS NOT SEEN
AND THE EAR HAS NOT HEARD,
AND WHICH HAVE NOT ENTERED THE
HEART OF MAN,
ALL THAT GOD HAS PREPARED FOR THOSE
WHO LOVE HIM [who hold Him
in affectionate reverence, who
obey Him, and who gratefully
recognize the benefits that He
has bestowed]." [Is 64:4; 65:17]

10 For God has unveiled them *and* revealed *them* to us through the [Holy] Spirit; for the Spirit searches all things [diligently], even [sounding and measuring] the [profound] depths of God [the divine counsels and things far beyond human understanding].

11 For what person knows the thoughts and motives of a man except the man's spirit within him? So also no one knows the *thoughts* of God except the Spirit of God.

12 Now we have received, not the spirit of the world, but the [Holy] Spirit who is from God, so that we may know *and* understand the [wonderful] things freely given to us by God.

13 We also speak of these things, not in words taught *or* supplied by human wisdom, but in those taught by the Spirit, combining *and* interpreting spiritual *thoughts* with spiritual *words* [for those being guided by the Holy Spirit].

14 But the natural [unbelieving] man does not accept the things [the teachings and revelations] of the Spirit of God, for they are foolishness [absurd and illogical] to him; and he is incapable of understanding them, because they are spiritually discerned *and* appreciated, [and he is unqualified to judge spiritual matters].

15 But the spiritual man [the spiritually mature Christian] judges all things [questions, examines and applies what the Holy Spirit reveals], yet is himself judged by no one [the unbeliever cannot judge and understand the believer's spiritual nature].

16 For WHO HAS KNOWN THE MIND *and* PURPOSES OF THE LORD, SO AS TO INSTRUCT HIM? But we have the mind of Christ [to be guided by His thoughts and purposes]. [Is 40:13]

2:7 *mystery.* God's plan was kept hidden, known only to Him, until He chose to reveal it (Eph 3:1–11). This is in contrast to the teachings of the Gnostics, a group of false religious teachers who would infiltrate the early church (1Jn 2:18–27). They claimed that there existed a body of secret knowledge that was only available to those initiated into an inner circle of spiritual teachers.

2:13 *interpreting spiritual thoughts with spiritual words.* These words are difficult to translate and interpret. The two references to "spiritual" may mean interpreting spiritual truths to spiritual persons, or else combining spiritual truths with spiritual words (2Ti 3:16; 2Pe 1:20–21).

3:2 *I fed you with milk.* Paul did not expect the Corinthians to be mature when they first accepted Christ. Yet they should have grown in their faith — that is, become sanctified. The behavior of Christians should begin to line up with their righteous position in Christ.

3:3 *You are still worldly.* An immature Christian naturally lacks many Christian traits, but no one should expect this condition to last. Paul was surprised that the Corinthians had not yet grown into spiritual maturity or become able to distinguish between good and evil (Heb 5:14).

3:13 *the day.* This is the time when Christ will judge the merits of His servants' work (2Co 5:10), not whether they receive forgiveness of sin. Likewise, the fire does not refer to the eternal fire of damnation (Rev 20:10) but to the evaluation of believers' works (Rev 22:12).

6 1Co 14:20; Heb 5:14; 2Co 1:12; 1Co 1:28 **7** Eph 3:5; Col 1:26 **8** Mt 11:25; Lk 23:34 **9** Isa 64:4 **10** Mt 13:11
11 Pr 20:27; Jer 17:9; Ro 11:33 **12** Ro 8:15 **14** Mt 16:23; 1Co 1:18,23; Jude 19 **15** 1Jn 4:1

Foundations for Living

3 HOWEVER, BROTHERS and sis-
ters, I could not talk to you as to
spiritual people, but [only] as to worldly
people [dominated by human nature],
mere infants [in the new life] in Christ!
2 I fed you with milk, not solid food;
for you were not yet able *to receive it.*
Even now you are still not ready.
3 You are still worldly [controlled by
ordinary impulses, the sinful capacity].
For as long as there is jealousy and strife
and discord among you, are you not
unspiritual, and are you not walking
like ordinary men [unchanged by faith]?
4 For when one *of you* says, "I am [a
disciple] of Paul," and another, "I am
[a disciple] of Apollos," are you not
[proving yourselves unchanged, just]
ordinary people?
5 What then is Apollos? And what is
Paul? Just servants through whom you
believed [in Christ], even as the Lord
appointed to each his task.
6 I planted, Apollos watered, but God
[all the while] was causing the growth.
7 So neither is the one who plants
nor the one who waters anything, but
[only] God who causes the growth.
8 He who plants and he who waters
are one [in importance and esteem,
working toward the same purpose];
but each will receive his own reward
according to his own labor.
9 For we are God's fellow workers
[His servants working together]; you
are God's cultivated field [His garden,
His vineyard], God's building. [Is 61:3]
10 According to the [remarkable]
grace of God which was given to me [to
prepare me for my task], like a skillful
master builder I laid a foundation, and
now another is building on it. But each
one must be careful how he builds on it,
11 for no one can lay a foundation
other than the one which is [already]
laid, which is Jesus Christ.
12 But if anyone builds on the founda-
tion with gold, silver, precious stones,
wood, hay, straw,
13 each one's work will be clearly
shown [for what it is]; for the day [of
judgment] will disclose it, because it is
to be revealed with fire, and the fire will
test the quality *and* character *and* worth
of each person's work. [2 Cor 5:10]
14 If any person's work which he has
built [on this foundation, that is, any
outcome of his effort] remains [and
survives this test], he will receive a
reward.
15 But if any person's work is burned
up [by the test], he will suffer the loss
[of his reward]; yet he himself will be
saved, but only as [one who has barely
escaped] through fire. [Job 23:10]
16 Do you not know *and* understand
that you [the church] are the temple of
God, and that the Spirit of God dwells
[permanently] in you [collectively and
individually]?
17 If anyone destroys the temple of
God [corrupting it with false doctrine],
God will destroy the destroyer; for the
temple of God is holy (sacred), and that
is what you are.
18 Let no one deceive himself. If any-
one among you thinks that he is wise
in this age, let him become a fool [dis-
carding his worldly pretensions and
acknowledging his lack of wisdom], so
that he may become [truly] wise. [Is 5:21]
19 For the wisdom of this world is
foolishness (absurdity, stupidity) be-
fore God; for it is written [in Scrip-
ture], "[He is] THE ONE WHO CATCHES THE
WISE *and* CLEVER IN THEIR CRAFTINESS;"
[Job 5:13]
20 and again, "THE LORD KNOWS THE
THOUGHTS of the [humanly] wise, THAT
THEY ARE USELESS." [Ps 94:11]
21 So let no one boast in men [about
their wisdom, or of having this or

3:21 *all things are yours.* The Stoic literature of the time, which the Corinthians would have known, often spoke of the wise man as possessing everything. Everything God has done in the church, and in the entire universe, benefits all believers. There is no place for foolish boasting or competition among Christians.

16 Job 15:8; Jn 15:15 **CHAPTER 3** **1** 1Co 2:15; 1Co 2:14; Heb 5:13 **2** Heb 5:12; 1Pe 2:2; Jn 16:12 **3** Gal 5:20; Jas 3:16 **5** 2Co 3:3; Ro 12:3; 1Pe 4:11 **6** Ac 18:4; 2Co 10:14; Ac 18:24; 19:1; 2Co 3:5 **7** 2Co 12:11; Gal 6:3 **8** Ps 62:12; Ro 2:6; Gal 6:4,5 **9** Ac 15:4; 2Co 6:1; Eph 2:20; Col 2:7; Heb 3:3,4 **10** Ro 1:5; 12:3; 1Co 4:15 **11** Isa 28:16; Mt 16:18; 2Co 11:4; Eph 2:20 **13** 1Pe 1:7; Lk 2:35 **16** 2Co 6:16 **18** Pr 3:7 **19** Job 5:13 **20** Ps 94:11 **21** 2Co 4:5

that one as a leader]. For all things
are yours,
22 whether Paul or Apollos or Cephas
(Peter) or the world or life or death or
things present or things to come; all
things are yours,
23 and you belong to Christ; and
Christ belongs to God.

Servants of Christ

4 SO THEN, let us [who minister] be
regarded as servants of Christ and
stewards (trustees, administrators) of
the mysteries of God [that He chooses
to reveal].
2 In this case, moreover, it is required
[as essential and demanded] of stew-
ards that one be found faithful *and*
trustworthy.
3 But [as for me personally] it matters
very little to me that I may be judged by
you or *any* human court [on this point];
in fact, I do not even judge myself.
4 I am aware of nothing against my-
self *and* I feel blameless, but I am not
by this acquitted [before God]. It is the
Lord who judges me.
5 So do not go on passing judgment
before the appointed time, *but wait*
until the Lord comes, for He will both
bring to light the [secret] things that
are hidden in darkness and disclose
the motives of the hearts. Then each
one's praise will come from God.
6 Now I have applied these things
[that is, the analogies about factions]
to myself and Apollos for your benefit,
believers, so that you may learn from
us not to go beyond what is written [in
Scripture], so that none of you will be-
come arrogant *and* boast in favor of one
[minister or teacher] against the other.
7 For who regards you as superior *or*
what sets you apart as special? What
do you have that you did not receive
[from another]? And if in fact you re-
ceived it [from God or someone else],
why do you boast as if you had not re-
ceived it [but had gained it by yourself]?
8 [You behave as if] you are already
filled [with spiritual wisdom and in
need of nothing more]. Already you
have become rich [in spiritual gifts]!
You [in your conceit] have ascended
your thrones *and* become kings with-
out us; and how I wish [that it were
true and] that you did reign as kings,
so that we might reign with you.
9 For, I think, God has exhibited us
apostles at the end of the line, like men
sentenced to death [and paraded as
prisoners in a procession], because we
have become a spectacle to the world
[a show in the world's amphitheater],
both to angels and to men.
10 We are [regarded as] fools for
Christ, but you are so wise in Christ;
we are weak, but you are strong; you
are highly esteemed, but we are dis-
honored.
11 To this present hour we are both
hungry and thirsty; we are *continually*
poorly dressed, and we are roughly
treated, and wander homeless.
12 We work [for our living], working
hard with our own hands. When we
are reviled *and* verbally abused, we
bless. When we are persecuted, we
take it patiently *and* endure.
13 When we are slandered, we *try to
be* conciliatory *and* answer softly. We
have become like the scum of the world,
the dregs of all things, even until now.
14 I do not write these things to shame
you, but to warn *and* advise you as my
beloved children.

4:5 *do not go on passing judgment.* While believers can benefit from the constructive evaluations of other believers, their ultimate Judge is the Lord Himself. We cannot know the whole picture, and we must be careful not to make premature evaluations of others.

4:6 *become arrogant and boast.* Greeks considered humility to be a fault, a characteristic of slaves. To the Christian, however, it exemplifies the attitude of Christ (Php 2:5 – 8).

4:10 *fools for Christ.* True strength is found in understanding our weakness and Christ's sufficiency (2Co 12:7 – 10; Php 4:11 – 13).

23 Ro 14:8; 2Co 10:7; Gal 3:29 **CHAPTER 4** **1** Mt 24:45; Col 1:25; Lk 12:42; Titus 1:7 **5** Mt 7:1; Ro 2:1; Rev 20:12; Ro 2:29; 2Co 5:10 **6** 1Co 1:12; Ro 12:3; 1Co 3:21 **7** Jn 3:27 **8** Rev 3:17 **9** Ps 44:22; Heb 10:33 **10** 1Co 2:3; Ac 17:18; 2Co 13:9 **11** Php 4:12; Ro 8:35; Ac 23:2 **12** Ac 18:3; 20:34; 1Th 2:9; 2Th 3:8; 1Ti 4:10; Mt 5:44; Lk 6:28; 23:34; Ac 7:60; Ro 12:14 **13** La 3:45 **14** 1Th 2:11

15 For even if you were to have ten
thousand teachers [to guide you] in
Christ, yet you would not have many
fathers [who led you to Christ and as-
sumed responsibility for you], for I
became your father in Christ Jesus
through the good news [of salvation].
16 So I urge you, be imitators of me
[just as a child imitates his father].
17 For this reason I have sent Timothy
to you, who is my beloved and faithful
child in the Lord, and he will remind you
of my way of life in Christ [my conduct
and my precepts for godly living], just
as I teach everywhere in every church.
18 Now some of you have become ar-
rogant *and* pretentious, as though I
were not coming to see you.
19 But I will come to you soon, if the
Lord is willing, and I will find out not
just the talk of these arrogant people,
but [evaluate] their [spiritual] pow-
er [whether they live up to their own
claims].
20 For the kingdom of God is not
based on talk but on power.
21 Which do you prefer? Shall I come
to you with a rod [of discipline and
correction], or with love and a gentle
spirit?

Immorality Rebuked

5 IT IS actually reported [every-
where] that there is sexual immo-
rality among you, a kind of immorality
that is condemned even among the
[unbelieving] Gentiles: that someone
has [an intimate relationship with] his
father's wife. [Deut 22:30; 27:20]
2 And you are proud *and* arrogant!
You should have mourned in shame
so that the man who has done this
[disgraceful] thing would be removed
from your fellowship!
3 For I, though absent [from you] in
body but present in spirit, have already
passed judgment on him who has com-
mitted this [act], as if I were present.
4 In the name of our Lord Jesus, when
you are assembled, and I am with you in
spirit, with the power of our Lord Jesus,
5 you are to hand over this man to
Satan for the destruction of his body,
so that his spirit may be saved in the
day of the Lord Jesus.
6 Your boasting [over the supposed
spirituality of your church] is not good
[indeed, it is vulgar and inappropriate].
Do you not know that [just] a little leav-
en ferments the whole batch [of dough,
just as a little sin corrupts a person or
an entire church]?
7 Clean out the old leaven so that you
may be a new batch, just as you are,
still unleavened. For Christ our Pass-
over Lamb has been sacrificed.
8 Therefore, let us celebrate the feast,
not with old leaven, nor with leaven of
vice *and* malice and wickedness, but
with the unleavened bread of sincerity
and [untainted] truth. [Ex 12:19; 13:7;
Deut 16:3]
9 I wrote you in my [previous] letter
not to associate with [sexually] immor-
al people—

5:1 *sexual immorality.* The sexual immorality of incest was forbidden by Old Testament law (Lev 18:8; Dt 22:30) and by Roman law. The phrase "his father's wife" probably indicates that the woman was the offender's stepmother. Paul does not specify any discipline for the woman, which may indicate that she was not a believer.

5:2 *proud and arrogant! You should have mourned in shame.* The Corinthian Christians had a twisted view of grace that caused them to be proud of their tolerance of the sexual offender. They believed that, because God's grace is limitless, living in sin was no problem.

5:6 *a little leaven.* The backdrop for this passage is the Passover (Ex 12). In commemoration of their ancestors' hurried departure from Egypt, Jewish families would carefully remove all leaven (yeast) from their homes in preparation for the celebration of the Passover. In the New Testament, leaven is often used as a symbol of sin. Yeast spreads through a batch of dough, and unchallenged sin can soon contaminate the whole church. The sexual offender was guilty of sin, but the whole congregation was also guilty of ignoring the man's disobedience.

5:9 *my [previous] letter.* It is believed that this refers to an earlier letter which has been lost.

15 Ac 18:11; Gal 4:19; Jas 1:18 **16** 1Co 11:1; 1Th 1:6 **17** Ac 19:22; Php 2:19; 1Ti 1:2; 2Ti 1:2; 1Co 11:2; 1Co 7:17; 1Co 14:33 **18** 1Co 5:2 **19** Ac 19:21; 2Co 1:15; Ac 18:21; Heb 6:3; Jas 4:15 **20** 1Th 1:5 **21** 2Co 10:2
CHAPTER 5 **1** Eph 5:3; Lev 18:8; 2Co 7:12 **2** 1Co 4:18; 2Co 7:7 **3** Col 2:5 **4** Mt 16:19; Jn 20:23; 2Co 2:10 **5** Ps 109:6; 1Ti 1:20; Ac 26:18 **6** 1Co 3:21; Gal 5:9; 2Ti 2:17 **7** Isa 53:7; 1Pe 1:19; Jn 19:14 **8** Ex 12:15; Dt 16:3; Mt 16:6; Mk 8:15; Lk 12:1 **9** 2Co 6:14; Eph 5:11

[10]not meaning the immoral people of this world, or the greedy ones and swindlers, or idolaters, for then you would have to get out of the world *and* human society altogether!

[11]But actually, I have written to you not to associate with any so-called [Christian] brother if he is sexually immoral or greedy, or is an idolater [devoted to anything that takes the place of God], or is a reviler [who insults or slanders or otherwise verbally abuses others], or is a drunkard or a swindler—you must not so much as eat with such a person. [2 Thess 3:6]

[12]For what business is it of mine to judge outsiders (non-believers)? Do you not judge those who are within *the church* [to protect the church as the situation requires]?

[13]God *alone* sits in judgment on those who are outside [the faith]. REMOVE THE WICKED ONE FROM AMONG YOU [expel him from your church]. [Deut 17:7]

Lawsuits Discouraged

6 DOES ANY one of you, when he has a complaint (civil dispute) with another [believer], dare to go to law before unrighteous men (non-believers) instead of [placing the issue] before the saints (God's people)?

[2]Do you not know that the saints (God's people) will [one day] judge the world? If the world is to be judged by you, are you not competent to try trivial (insignificant, petty) cases?

[3]Do you not know that we [believers] will judge angels? How much more then [as to] matters of this life?

[4]So if you have lawsuits dealing with matters of this life, are you appointing those as judges [to hear disputes] who are of no account in the church?

[5]I say this to your shame. Can it be that there is not one wise man among you who [is governed by integrity and] will be able *and* competent to decide [private disputes] between his fellow believers,

[6]but *instead,* brother goes to law against brother, and that before [judges who are] unbelievers?

[7]Why, the very fact that you have lawsuits with one another is already a defeat. Why not rather be wronged? Why not rather be defrauded?

[8]On the contrary, it is you who wrong and defraud, and you do this even to your brothers and sisters.

[9]Do you not know that the unrighteous will not inherit *or* have any share in the kingdom of God? Do not be deceived; neither the sexually immoral, nor idolaters, nor adulterers, nor effeminate [by perversion], nor those who participate in homosexuality,

[10]nor thieves, nor the greedy, nor drunkards, nor revilers [whose words are used as weapons to abuse, insult, humiliate, intimidate, or slander], nor swindlers will inherit *or* have any share in the kingdom of God.

[11]And such were some of you [before

5:10 *of this world.* Christians are called to influence the world, not to run away from it (Mt 5:13 – 16). They are agents of God to carry the light of Jesus Christ into a dark world (Php 2:14 – 16; 1Pe 2:11 – 12).

6:9 *kingdom of God.* This term seems to refer to a future time when God will rule the earth in righteousness (Mt 6:10; Lk 11:2).

6:11 Changed Life — The greatest proof of the new birth is a changed life. The child of God now suddenly loves the following:

He loves Jesus. Before conversion the sinner might hold Christ in high esteem, but after conversion he loves the Savior (1Jn 5:1 – 2).

He loves the Bible. We should love God's Word as the psalmist did in Psalm 119. There he expresses his great love for God's Word 17 times.

He loves other Christians. "We know that we have passed out of death into Life, because we love the brothers and sisters" (1Jn 3:14).

He loves his enemies. (Mt 5:43 – 45).

He loves the souls of all people. Like Paul, he too can cry out for the conversion of loved ones. "Brothers and sisters, my heart's desire and my prayer to God for Israel is for their salvation" (Ro 10:1).

He loves the pure life. John says, if one loves the world, the love of the Father is not in him (1Jn 2:15 – 17).

He loves to talk to God. "Speak to one another

---

10 1Co 10:27; 1Co 1:20; Jn 17:15; 1Jn 5:19 **11** Mt 18:17; Ro 16:17; 2Jn 10; Gal 2:12 **12** Mk 4:11; Col 4:5; 1Th 4:12; 1Co 6:1-4 **13** Dt 13:5 **CHAPTER 6** **2** Ps 49:14; Da 7:22; Mt 19:28; Lk 22:30 **3** 2Pe 2:4 **4** 1Co 5:12 **7** Pr 20:22; Mt 5:39; Lk 6:29 **8** 1Th 4:6 **9** Gal 5:21; Eph 5:5; 1Ti 1:9 **11** 1Co 12:2; Heb 10:22

you believed]. But you were washed
[by the atoning sacrifice of Christ],
you were sanctified [set apart for God,
and made holy], you were justified [de-
clared free of guilt] in the name of the
Lord Jesus Christ and in the [Holy]
Spirit of our God [the source of the be-
liever's new life and changed behavior].

The Body Is the Lord's

12 Everything is permissible for
me, but not all things are beneficial.
Everything is permissible for me, but
I will not be enslaved by anything [and
brought under its power, allowing it to
control me].
13 Food is for the stomach and the
stomach for food, but God will do away
with both of them. The body is not in-
tended for sexual immorality, but for
the Lord, and the Lord is for the body
[to save, sanctify, and raise it again
because of the sacrifice of the cross].
14 And God has not only raised the
Lord [to life], but will also raise us up
by His power.
15 Do you not know that your bodies
are members of Christ? Am I there-
fore to take the members of Christ
and make them part of a prostitute?
Certainly not!
16 Do you not know that the one who
joins himself to a prostitute is one body
with her? For He says, "THE TWO SHALL
BE ONE FLESH." [Gen 2:24]
17 But the one who is united *and*
joined to the Lord is one spirit *with*
Him.
18 Run away from sexual immorality
[in any form, whether thought or behav-
ior, whether visual or written]. Every
other sin that a man commits is outside
the body, but the one who is sexually
immoral sins against his own body.
19 Do you not know that your body
is a temple of the Holy Spirit who is
within you, whom you have [received
as a gift] from God, and that you are
not your own [property]?
20 You were bought with a price [you
were actually purchased with the pre-
cious blood of Jesus and made His
own]. So then, honor *and* glorify God
with your body.

---

in psalms and hymns and spiritual songs, [offering praise by] singing and making melody with your heart to the Lord" (Eph 5:19).

6:13 *Food is for the stomach and the stomach for food.* The stomach's purpose is to digest food, but it is not the purpose of the body to commit immorality. Furthermore, by design God put restrictions on both eating and sexual activity. Eating to the point of gluttony and having sex outside of marriage both violate God's intent and are sinful.

6:15 *your bodies are members of Christ.* Becoming a Christ follower is not just a "spiritual experience." Our bodies belong to Jesus as well as our souls, and nothing that we do with our bodies is apart from our relationship with Jesus Christ.

6:16 *one body.* God designed sex as part of the intense "one flesh" bond between husband and wife, so sex is not a one-dimensional physical act. It involves soul, spirit, and emotions as well. Broken sexual relationships tear away at a person's very being in a way that nothing else does.

6:19 The Work of the Holy Spirit — The Holy Spirit is sometimes referred to as the *Paraclete*. The first part of that word, "para," is a preposition that means "coming alongside." As the Spirit comes alongside of us, it ministers in the following ways:

The Holy Spirit indwells Christians. The Bible teaches that believers are indwelt and are the "temple of the Holy Spirit" (1Co 6:19). The purpose of this indwelling ministry is to empower the newly created nature (2Co 5:17; Eph 3:16).

The Holy Spirit fills believers. We are admonished to "be filled with the [Holy] Spirit" (Eph 5:18). We are then to be subject to the control of the Spirit in contrast to being controlled by the lures of the world.

The Holy Spirit sanctifies the believer (Ro 15:16; 2Th 2:13).

The Holy Spirit produces fruit in the life of the believer. This fruit is described by Paul: "But the fruit of the Spirit ... is love ... joy, [inner] peace, patience ... kindness, goodness, faithfulness, gentleness, self-control" (Gal 5:22 – 23).

The Holy Spirit gives gifts to Christians (Ro 12:6 – 8; 1Co 12:1 – 11; Eph 4:7 – 12). These are abilities given to every Christian (1Co 7:7; 1Pe 4:10). The purpose of these gifts is to glorify God (Rev 4:11) and to edify the body of Christ (Eph 4:12 – 13).

The Holy Spirit teaches believers. He will

---

12 1Co 10:23 **13** Mt 15:17; Ro 14:17; Col 2:22; 1Th 4:3; Eph 5:23 **14** Ro 6:5,8; 2Co 4:14; Eph 1:19 **15** Ro 12:5; Eph 4:12; 5:30 **16** Ge 2:24; Mt 19:5; Eph 5:31 **17** Jn 17:21; Eph 4:4 **18** Ro 6:12; Heb 13:4; Ro 1:24; 1Th 4:4 **19** 2Co 6:16; Ro 14:7 **20** Ac 20:28; Gal 3:13; Heb 9:12; 1Pe 1:18; 2Pe 2:1; Rev 5:9

Teaching on Marriage

7 NOW AS to the matters of which you wrote: It is good (beneficial, advantageous) for a man not to touch a woman [outside marriage].

[2]But because of [the temptation to participate in] sexual immorality, let each man have his own wife, and let each woman have her own husband.

[3]The husband must fulfill his [marital] duty to his wife [with good will and kindness], and likewise the wife to her husband.

[4]The wife does not have [exclusive] authority over her own body, but the husband *shares with her;* and likewise the husband does not have [exclusive] authority over his body, but the wife *shares with him.*

[5]Do not deprive each other [of marital rights], except perhaps by mutual consent for a time, so that you may devote yourselves [unhindered] to prayer, but come together again so that Satan will not tempt you [to sin] because of your lack of self-control.

[6]But I am saying this as a concession, not as a command.

[7]I wish that all the people were as I am; but each person has his own gift from God, one of this kind and one of that.

[8]But I say to the unmarried and to the widows, [that as a practical matter] it is good if they remain [single and entirely devoted to the Lord] as I am.

[9]But if they do not have [sufficient] self-control, they should marry; for it is better to marry than to burn *with passion.*

[10]But to the married [believers] I give instructions—not I, but the Lord—that the wife is not to separate from her husband,

[11](but even if she does leave him, let her remain single or else be reconciled to her husband) and that the husband should not leave his wife.

[12]To the rest I declare—I, not the Lord [since Jesus did not discuss this]—that if any [believing] brother has a wife who does not believe [in Christ], and she consents to live with him, he must not leave her.

[13]And if any [believing] woman has an unbelieving husband, and he consents to live with her, she must not leave him.

[14]For the unbelieving husband is sanctified [that is, he receives the blessings granted] through his [Christian] wife, and the unbelieving wife is sanctified through her believing husband. Otherwise your children would be [ceremonially] unclean, but as it is they are holy.

[15]But if the unbelieving partner leaves, let him leave. In such cases the [remaining] brother or sister is not [spiritually or morally] bound. But God has called us to peace.

[16]For how do you know, wife, whether you will save your husband [by leading him to Christ]? Or how do you know, husband, whether you will save your wife [by leading her to Christ]?

[17]Only, let each one live the life which the Lord has assigned him, and to which God has called him [for each person is unique and is accountable for

---

instruct us in all spiritual things as we read the Word of God (Jn 14:26) and abide in the Son of God (1Jn 2:24–27).

6:20 *bought with a price.* With His death, Jesus Christ paid the cost to redeem us from our slavery to sin (Eph 1:7; 1Pe 1:18–19).

7:6 *concession, not as a command.* The Corinthians seemed to be caught by two extreme false positions: the false concept that physical activity does not affect the spirit, and the opposite incorrect idea that any kind of physical relationship is evil. Sexual relationships in marriage are good and God given, yet Paul also outlines the value of celibacy.

7:11 *remain single.* This statement is consistent with Jesus' teaching (Mk 10:9–12).

7:16 *how do you know.* First Peter 3:1–6 reminds us that consistent obedience to God can make a skeptical spouse into a believing one, but there are no guarantees.

7:17 *live the life which the Lord has assigned him.* Social status is unimportant to God. He is interested in faithfulness.

CHAPTER 7 **1** ver. 8,26 **3** Ex 21:10; 1Pe 3:7 **5** Joel 2:16; Zec 7:3; See Ex 19:15; 1Sa 21:4; 1Th 3:5 **6** 2Co 8:8; 11:17 **7** Ac 26:29; 1Co 9:5; 1Co 12:11 **8** ver. 1,26 **9** 1Ti 5:14 **10** Mal 2:14; Mt 5:32; 19:6,9; Mk 10:11; Lk 16:18 **14** Mal 2:15 **15** Ro 12:18; 14:19; 1Co 14:33 **16** 1Pe 3:1 **17** 1Co 4:17

his choices and conduct, let him walk
in this way]. This is the rule I make in
all the churches.
18Was anyone at the time of his call-
ing [from God already] circumcised?
He is not to become uncircumcised.
Has anyone been called while uncir-
cumcised? He is not to be circumcised.
[Gal 5:1–3]
19Circumcision is nothing, and un-
circumcision is nothing, but *what mat-
ters is* keeping the commandments
of God.
20Each one should remain in the con-
dition in which he was [when he was]
called.
21Were you a slave when you were
called? Do not worry about that [since
your status as a believer is equal to
that of a freeborn believer]; but if you
are able to gain your freedom, do that.
22For he who was a slave when he
was called in the Lord is a freedman
of the Lord, likewise he who was free
when he was called is a slave of Christ.
23You were bought with a price [a
precious price paid by Christ]; do not
become slaves to men [but to Christ].
24Brothers, let each one remain with
God in that *condition* in which he was
[when he was] called.
25Now concerning the virgins [of
marriageable age] I have no command
of the Lord, but I give my opinion as one
who by the Lord's mercy is trustworthy.
26I think then that because of the im-
pending distress [that is, the pressure
of the current trouble], it is good for a
man to remain as he is.
27Are you bound to a wife? Do not
seek to be released. Are you unmar-
ried? Do not seek a wife.
28But if you do marry, you have not
sinned [in doing so]; and if a virgin
marries, she has not sinned [in doing
so]. Yet those [who marry] will have
troubles (special challenges) in this
life, and I am trying to spare you that.
29But I say this, believers: the time
has been shortened, so that from now
on even those who have wives should
be as though they did not;
30and those who weep, as though
they did not weep; and those who re-
joice, as though they did not rejoice;
and those who buy, as though they did
not possess [anything];
31and those who use the world [tak-
ing advantage of its opportunities], as
though they did not make full use of
it. For the outward form of this world
[its present social and material nature]
is passing away.
32But I want you to be free from con-
cern. The unmarried man is concerned
about the things of the Lord, how he
may please the Lord;
33but the married man is concerned
about worldly things, how he may
please his wife,
34and *his interests* are divided. The
unmarried woman or the virgin is con-
cerned about the matters of the Lord,
how to be holy *and* set apart both in
body and in spirit; but a married wom-
an is concerned about worldly things,
how she may please her husband.
35Now I say this for your own benefit;
not to restrict you, but to promote what
is appropriate and secure undistracted
devotion to the Lord.
36But if any man thinks that he is not
acting properly *and* honorably toward
his virgin *daughter*, [by not permitting
her to marry], if she is past her youth,
and it must be so, let him do as he
wishes, he does not sin; let her marry.
37But the man who stands firmly
committed in his heart, having no
compulsion [to yield to his daughter's

7:27 bound to a wife . . . released. Considering the clear prohibition against divorce and remarriage (v. 10 – 11), this verse is most likely referring to couples who are betrothed but not yet married.
7:36 – 38 his virgin daughter. One interpretation of this verse is that this refers to a virgin daughter, although the word "daughter" is not actually in the Greek text. A second interpretation suggests that the *any man* of verse 36 refers to a fiancé who is maintaining, although with difficulty, a celibate state with a virgin he is (or has been) engaged to.

18 Ac 15:1; Gal 5:2 **19** Gal 5:6; Jn 15:14; 1Jn 2:3; 3:24 **22** Jn 8:36; Ro 6:18; Php 16; 1Co 9:21; Gal 5:13; Eph 6:6; 1Pe 2:16 **23** 1Pe 1:18; See Lev 25:42 **25** 2Co 8:8; 1Ti 1:16; 1Ti 1:12 **26** ver. 1,8 **29** Ro 13:11; 1Pe 4:7; 2Pe 3:8,9 **31** 1Co 9:18; Ps 39:6; Jas 1:10; 4:14; 1Pe 1:24; 4:7; 1Jn 2:17 **32** 1Ti 5:5 **34** Lk 10:40

request], and has authority over his own will, and has decided in his own heart to keep his own virgin [daughter from being married], he will do well.

38 So then both the father who gives his virgin *daughter* in marriage does well, and he who does not give her in marriage will do better.

39 A wife is bound [to her husband by law] as long as he lives. But if her husband dies, she is free to marry whomever she wishes, only [provided that he too is] in the Lord.

40 But in my opinion a widow is happier if she stays as she is. And I think that I also have the Spirit of God [in this matter].

Take Care with Your Liberty

8 NOW ABOUT food sacrificed to idols, we know that we all have knowledge [concerning this]. Knowledge [alone] makes [people self-righteously] arrogant, but love [that unselfishly seeks the best for others] builds up *and* encourages others to grow [in wisdom].

2 If anyone imagines that he knows *and* understands anything [of divine matters, without love], he has not yet known as he ought to know.

3 But if anyone loves God [with awe-filled reverence, obedience and gratitude], he is known by Him [as His very own and is greatly loved].

4 In this matter, then, of eating food offered to idols, we know that an idol is nothing in the world [it has no real existence], and that there is no God but one. [Deut 6:4]

5 For even if there are so-called gods, whether in heaven or on earth, as indeed there are many gods and many lords,

6 yet for us there is but one God, the Father, who is the source of all things, and we *exist* for Him; and one Lord, Jesus Christ, by whom are all things [that have been created], and we [believers exist and have life and have been redeemed] through Him. [Mal 2:10]

7 However, not all [believers] have this knowledge. But some, being accustomed [throughout their lives] to [thinking of] the idol until now [as real and living], still eat food as if it were sacrificed to an idol; and because their conscience is weak, it is defiled (guilty, ashamed).

8 Now food will not commend us to God *nor* bring us close to Him; we are no worse off if we do not eat, nor are we better if we do eat.

9 Only be careful that this liberty of yours [this power to choose] does not somehow become a stumbling block [that is, a temptation to sin] to the weak [in conscience].

10 For if someone sees you, a person having knowledge, eating in an idol's temple, then if he is weak, will he not be encouraged to eat things sacrificed to idols [and violate his own convictions]?

11 For through your knowledge (spiritual maturity) this weak man is ruined [that is, he suffers in his spiritual life], the brother for whom Christ died.

12 And when you sin against the brothers and sisters in this way and

---

7:40 *I think that I also have the Spirit of God.* The Holy Spirit enabled Paul to speak with apostolic authority and also with spiritual wisdom. **8:4 *there is no God but one.*** The Corinthian believers who claimed to have knowledge readily admitted that an idol is nothing (Isa 37:19; Jer 16:20; Gal 4:8) and that there is only one God (Dt 6:4). Therefore, since an idol is nothing, and since the whole world belongs to God, food which has been offered to idols is not contaminated (10:19,25 – 26). **8:7 *accustomed [throughout their lives] to [thinking of] the idol.*** Even though it is true that an idol is not a real god, a new believer leaving a life of idol worship is still accustomed to thinking of the idol as real. Because of this strong association, eating meat sacrificed to an idol might still feel like paying honor to the idol, and thus seem vile and contaminating. A person who still feels the pull of the old worship is right to flee from all remembrances of it (10:20 – 23). **8:12 *wound their weak conscience.*** The believer is given responsibility for a weaker brother's

---

38 Heb 13:4 **39** Ro 7:2; 2Co 6:14 **40** ver. 25; 1Th 4:8 **CHAPTER 8** **1** Ac 15:20; 1Co 10:19; Ro 14:14; Ro 14:3 **2** 1Co 13:8,9; Gal 6:3; 1Ti 6:4 **3** Ex 33:12; Na 1:7; Mt 7:23; Gal 4:9 **4** Isa 41:24; Dt 4:39; 6:4; Isa 44:8; Mk 12:29; Eph 4:6; 1Ti 2:5 **5** Jn 10:34 **6** Mal 2:10; Eph 4:6; Ac 17:28; Ro 11:36; Jn 13:13; Ac 2:36; Eph 4:5; Php 2:11; Jn 1:3; Col 1:16; Heb 1:2 **7** 1Co 10:28; Ro 14:14 **8** Ro 14:17 **9** Gal 5:13; Ro 14:13 **10** 1Co 10:28 **11** Ro 14:15 **12** Mt 25:40

wound their weak conscience [by confusing them], you sin against Christ.

13 Therefore, if [my eating a certain] food causes my brother to stumble (sin), I will not eat [such] meat ever again, so that I will not cause my brother to stumble.

Paul's Use of Liberty

9 AM I not free [unrestrained and exempt from any obligation]? Am I not an apostle? Have I not seen Jesus our [risen] Lord [in person]? Are you not [the result and proof of] my work in the Lord?

2 If I am not [considered] an apostle to others, at least I am one to you; for you are the seal *and* the certificate *and* the living evidence of my apostleship in the Lord [confirming and authenticating it].

3 This is my defense to those who would put me on trial *and* interrogate me [concerning my authority as an apostle]:

4 Have we not the right to our food and drink [at the expense of the churches]?

5 Have we not the right to take along with us a believing wife, as do the rest of the apostles and the Lord's brothers and Cephas (Peter)?

6 Or is it only Barnabas and I who have no right to stop doing manual labor [in order to support our ministry]?

7 [Consider this:] Who at any time serves as a soldier at his own expense? Who plants a vineyard and does not eat its fruit? Or who tends a flock and does not use the milk of the flock?

8 Do I say these things only from a man's perspective? Does the Law not endorse the same principles?

9 For it is written in the Law of Moses, "YOU SHALL NOT MUZZLE AN OX WHILE IT IS TREADING OUT THE GRAIN [to keep it from eating the grain]." Is it [only] for oxen that God cares? [Deut 25:4]

10 Or does He speak entirely for our sake? Yes, it was written for our sake: The plowman ought to plow in hope, and the thresher to thresh in hope of sharing the harvest.

11 If we have sown [the good seed of] spiritual things in you, is it too much if we reap material things from you?

12 If others share in this rightful claim over you, do not we even more? However, we did not exercise this right, but we put up with everything so that we will not hinder [the spread of] the good news of Christ.

13 Do you not know that those who officiate in the sacred services of the temple eat from the temple [offerings of meat and bread] and those who regularly attend the altar have their share from the [offerings brought to the] altar? [Deut 18:1]

14 So also [on the same principle] the Lord directed those who preach the gospel to get their living from the gospel.

15 But I have used none of these privileges, nor am I writing this [to suggest] that any such provision be made for me now. For it would be better for me to die than to have anyone deprive me of my boast [in this matter of financial support].

16 For if I [merely] preach the gospel, I have nothing to boast about, for I am compelled [that is, absolutely obligated to do it]. Woe to me if I do not preach the good news [of salvation]!

17 For if I do this work of my own free will, then I have a reward; but if it is not of my will [but by God's choosing],

---

conscience. It is sin to cause another to fall or to be wounded in the conscience. God is warning believers to stay away from questionable things.

9:1 *an apostle.* Paul could claim the title of apostle because he had seen the resurrected Lord (Ac 1:21 – 22), and the church in Corinth was his work in the Lord, a seal of his apostleship.

9:14 *get their living from the gospel.* God commands that ministers of the gospel be supported. Even as the priests in Israel were

---

13 Ro 14:21; 2Co 11:29 **CHAPTER 9** **1** Ac 9:15; 13:2; 26:17; 2Co 12:12; Gal 2:7,8; 1Ti 2:7; 2Ti 1:11; Ac 9:3,17; 18:9; 22:14,18; 1Co 15:8; 1Co 3:6 **2** 2Co 12:12 **4** 1Th 2:6 **5** Mt 13:55; Gal 1:19; Mt 8:14 **6** 2Th 3:8 **7** 2Co 10:4; 1Ti 1:18; Dt 20:6; Jn 21:15; 1Pe 5:2 **9** Dt 25:4; 1Ti 5:18 **10** 2Ti 2:6 **11** Ro 15:27; Gal 6:6 **12** Ac 20:33; 1Th 2:6; 2Co 11:12 **13** Lev 6:16 **14** Mt 10:10; Lk 10:7; Gal 6:6 **15** Ac 18:3; 2Co 11:10 **16** Ro 1:14 **17** 1Co 3:8,14; Gal 2:7; Col 1:25

I have been entrusted with a [sacred] stewardship.

18 What then is my reward? [Just this:] that, when I preach the gospel, I may offer the gospel without charge [to everyone], so as not to take advantage of my rights [as a preacher and apostle] in [preaching] the gospel.

19 For though I am free from all men, I have made myself a slave to everyone, so that I may win more [for Christ].

20 To the Jews I became as a Jew, so that I might win Jews [for Christ]; to men under the Law, [I became] as one under the Law, though not being under the Law myself, so that I might win those who are under the Law.

21 To those who are without (outside) the Law, [I became] as one without the Law, though [I am] not without the law of God, but under the law of Christ, so that I might win those who are without law.

22 To the weak I became [as the] weak, to win the weak. I have become all things to all men, so that I may by all means [in any and every way] save some [by leading them to faith in Jesus Christ].

23 And I do all this for the sake of the gospel, so that I may share in its blessings along with you.

24 Do you not know that in a race all the runners run [their very best to win], but only one receives the prize? Run [your race] in such a way that you may seize the prize *and* make it yours!

25 Now every athlete who [goes into training and] competes in the games is disciplined *and* exercises self-control in all things. They do it to win a crown that withers, but we [do it to receive] an imperishable [crown that cannot wither].

26 Therefore I do not run without a definite goal; I do not flail around like one beating the air [just shadow boxing].

27 But [like a boxer] I strictly discipline my body and make it my slave, so that, after I have preached [the gospel] to others, I myself will not somehow be disqualified [as unfit for service].

Avoid Israel's Mistakes

10 FOR I do not want you to be unaware, believers, that our fathers were all under the cloud [in which God's presence went before them] and they all passed [miraculously and safely] through the [Red] Sea; [Ex 13:21; 14:22, 29]

2 And all [of them] were baptized into Moses [into his safekeeping as their leader] in the cloud and in the sea;

3 and all [of them] ate the same spiritual food; [Ex 16:4, 35]

4 and all [of them] drank the same spiritual drink, for they were drinking from a spiritual rock which followed them; and the rock was Christ. [Ex 17:6; Num 20:11]

5 Nevertheless, God was not well-pleased with most of them, for they were scattered along the ground in the wilderness [because their lack of self-control led to disobedience which led to death]. [Num 14:29, 30]

6 Now these things [the warnings and admonitions] took place as exam-

---

supported for their work, New Testament ministers were to be provided for as well (1Ti 5:17 – 18).

9:20 *To the Jews I became as a Jew.* In order to relate to the Jews in Jerusalem, Paul made a Nazirite vow in the temple (Ac 21:23 – 24).

9:21 *under the law of Christ.* Paul was not lawless; he was differentiating between the law of the Old Covenant and the broader law of Christ which includes great freedom and flexibility for the believer whose heart is obedient to Christ's will (11:1; Ro 13:8; Gal 6:2).

9:27 *will not somehow be disqualified.* A careful distinction should be made between the *prize* and the *gift*. The free gift of justification cannot be the result of good works (Ro 4:1 – 8). The prize or crown, however, is the reward for endurance and suffering for the cause of Christ (Php 1:29; 2Ti 2:12).

10:1 *under the cloud.* When the ancient Israelites were wandering in the wilderness, the pillar of cloud was the visible manifestation of God's presence with them.

10:6 *crave evil things.* The first failure of the Israelites was that they were not satisfied with

18 1Co 10:33; 1Co 7:31 **19** ver. 1; Gal 5:13; Mt 18:15; 1Pe 3:1 **20** Ac 16:3; 18:18 **21** Gal 3:2; Ro 2:12; 1Co 7:22 **22** Ro 15:1; 2Co 11:29; 1Co 10:33; Ro 11:14 **24** Gal 2:2; 2Ti 4:7 **25** Jas 1:12; Rev 2:10 **26** 2Ti 2:5 **27** Ro 8:13; Col 3:5; Ro 6:18; Jer 6:30; 2Co 13:5 **CHAPTER 10** **1** Ex 13:21; 14:22; Ps 78:13 **3** Ex 16:15; Ps 78:24 **4** Ex 17:6; Ps 78:15 **5** Nu 14:29; Ps 106:26 **6** Nu 11:4

ples for us, so that we would not crave evil things as they did. [Num 11:4, 34]
7 Do not be worshipers of handmade gods, as some of them were; just as it is written [in Scripture], "THE PEOPLE SAT DOWN TO EAT AND DRINK [after sacrificing to the golden calf at Horeb], AND STOOD UP TO PLAY [indulging in immoral activities]." [Ex 32:6]
8 We must not indulge in [nor tolerate] sexual immorality, as some of them did, and twenty-three thousand [suddenly] fell [dead] in a single day! [Num 25:1–18]
9 We must not tempt the Lord [that is, test His patience, question His purpose or exploit His goodness], as some of them did—and they were killed by serpents. [Num 21:5, 6]
10 And do not murmur [in unwarranted discontent], as some of them did—and were destroyed by the destroyer. [Num 16:41, 49]
11 Now these things happened to them as an example *and* warning [to us]; they were written for our instruction [to admonish and equip us], upon whom the ends of the ages have come.
12 Therefore let the one who thinks he stands firm [immune to temptation, being overconfident and self-righteous], take care that he does not fall [into sin and condemnation].
13 No temptation [regardless of its source] has overtaken *or* enticed you that is not common to human experience [nor is any temptation unusual or beyond human resistance]; but God is faithful [to His word—He is compassionate and trustworthy], and He will not let you be tempted beyond your ability [to resist], but along with the temptation He [has in the past and is now and] will [always] provide the way out as well, so that you will be able to endure it [without yielding, and will overcome temptation with joy].
14 Therefore, my beloved, run [keep far, far away] from [any sort of] idolatry [and that includes loving anything more than God, or participating in anything that leads to sin and enslaves the soul].
15 I am speaking as to wise *and* sensible people; judge [carefully and thoughtfully consider] for yourselves what I say.
16 Is the cup of blessing which we bless [at the Lord's Supper] not a sharing in the blood of Christ? [Indeed it is.] Is the bread which we break not a sharing in the body of Christ? [Indeed it is.]
17 Since there is one bread, we [believers] who are many are [united into] one body; for we all partake of the one bread [which represents the body of Christ].
18 Consider the people of Israel; are those who eat the sacrifices not partners of the altar [united in their worship of the same God]? [Indeed they are.] [Lev 7:6]
19 What do I mean then? That a thing offered to idols is anything [special or changed simply because it is offered], or that an idol is anything?

God's provision (Nu 11:4 – 34). It is not that the food they craved was evil in itself, but their lack of trust in God was sin.

10:7 *worshipers of handmade gods.* The Israelites had seen God's mighty hand work on their behalf, yet they still fell into idolatry and sexual immorality. Knowledge alone does not protect against sin — obedience is a heart issue.

10:12 *take care that he does not fall.* The Corinthians may have had the attitude that, since they were justified by God, nothing could happen to them. The discipline of God, however, is not to be taken lightly. No one can sin without consequences (Gal 6:7 – 8).

10:14 *run [keep far, far away] from [any sort of] idolatry.* This was not a simple thing to do in ancient Greek culture, where the worship of multiple gods was deeply ingrained. There were idols on street corners and in houses. Various civic societies paid homage to their favorite gods. Cities adopted certain gods as their special protectors. The pagan temples were frequented often, especially in Corinth with its temple prostitution. Most of the food in the marketplace had been offered in worship to different gods.

7 ver. 14; Ex 32:6 **8** Rev 2:14; Ps 106:29 **9** Ex 17:2,7; Nu 21:6 **10** Ex 16:2; Nu 14:37; Ex 12:23 **11** Ro 15:4; Php 4:5; Heb 10:25 **12** Ro 11:20 **13** 1Co 1:9; Ps 125:3; 2Pe 2:9 **14** 2Co 6:17 **15** 1Co 8:1 **16** Mt 26:26; Ac 2:42 **17** 1Co 12:27 **18** Ro 4:12; Ro 4:1; 2Co 11:18; Lev 3:3 **19** 1Co 8:4

20 On the contrary, the things which the Gentiles (pagans) sacrifice, they sacrifice to demons [in effect], and not to God; and I do not want you to become partners with demons [by eating at feasts in pagan temples]. [Deut 32:17]

21 You cannot drink [both] the Lord's cup and the cup of demons. You cannot share in both the Lord's table and the table of demons [thereby becoming partners with them].

22 Do we [really] provoke the Lord to jealousy [when we eat food sacrificed to handmade "gods" at pagan feasts]? Are we [spiritually] stronger than He? [Certainly not! He knows that the idols are nothing. But we deeply offend Him.] [Deut 32:21; Eccl 6:10; Is 45:9]

23 All things are lawful [that is, morally legitimate, permissible], but not all things are beneficial *or* advantageous. All things are lawful, but not all things are constructive [to character] *and* edifying [to spiritual life].

24 Let no one seek [only] his own good, but [also] that of the other person.

25 [Regarding meat offered to idols:] Eat anything that is sold in the meat market without asking any questions for the sake of your conscience,

26 FOR THE [whole] EARTH IS THE LORD'S, AND EVERYTHING THAT IS IN IT. [Ps 24:1; 50:12]

27 If one of the unbelievers invites you [to a meal at his home] and you want to go, eat whatever is served to you without asking questions [about its source] for the sake of your conscience.

28 But if anyone says to you, "This meat has been offered in sacrifice to an idol," do not eat it, out of consideration for the one who told you, and for conscience's sake—

29 and by conscience I mean for the sake of the other *man's,* not yours. For why is my freedom [of choice] judged by another's conscience [another's ethics—another's sense of right and wrong]?

30 If I take my share [of food] with thankfulness, why am I accused because of something for which I give thanks?

31 So then, whether you eat or drink or whatever you do, do all to the glory of [our great] God.

32 Do not offend Jews or Greeks or even the church of God [but live to honor Him];

33 just as I please everyone in all things [as much as possible adapting myself to the interests of others], not seeking my own benefit but that of the many, so that they [will be open to the message of salvation and] may be saved.

Christian Order

11 IMITATE ME, just as I *imitate* Christ.

2 I praise *and* appreciate you because you remember me in everything and you firmly hold to the traditions [the substance of my instructions], just as I have passed them on to you.

10:20 *sacrifice to demons.* While the idols themselves are worthless, powerless, and certainly not gods, behind the statues and images is the very real evil and power of Satan and his demons. Anytime that worship is being directed at something that is not God, we can be sure that Satan is behind it.

10:22 *provoke the Lord to jealousy.* To participate in idolatrous activity is to deny that God is the only one worthy of worship.

10:23 *All things are lawful.* Though we have freedom, we also have a responsibility to help others in their Christian growth. Our first duty is to others, not to ourselves.

10:25 *Eat anything that is sold.* Paul himself did not ask whether meat was sacrificed in the temple, because pagan worship could not contaminate what God had made clean (Ps 24:1; Ac 10:15).

10:28 *for conscience's sake.* Believers do not need to fearfully ask whether the meat they are eating has been sacrificed to idols — it doesn't make any difference to the food itself. However, a Christian may give the impression to others, by eating sacrificed food, that he himself is also still involved in idol worship.

---

20 Lev 17:7; Dt 32:17; Ps 106:37 **21** 2Co 6:15; Dt 32:38 **22** Dt 32:21; Eze 22:14 **23** 1Co 6:12 **24** Ro 15:1,2; 1Co 13:5 **25** 1Ti 4:4 **26** Ex 19:5; Ps 24:1 **27** Lk 10:7 **28** 1Co 8:10,12; Dt 10:14; Ps 24:1 **29** Ro 14:16 **30** Ro 14:6; 1Ti 4:3,4 **31** Col 3:17; 1Pe 4:11 **32** Ro 14:13; 1Co 8:13; Ac 20:28; 1Ti 3:5 **33** Ro 15:2; ver. 24 **CHAPTER 11** **1** Eph 5:1; Php 3:17 **2** 1Co 4:17; 1Co 7:17

3 But I want you to understand that
Christ is the head (authority over) of
every man, and man is the head of
woman, and God is the head of Christ.
4 Every man who prays or prophesies
with *something* on his head dishonors
his head [and the One who is his head].
5 And every woman who prays or
prophesies when she has her head un-
covered disgraces her head; for she is
one and the same as the woman whose
head is shaved [in disgrace].
6 If a woman does not cover her head,
she should have her hair cut off; and if
it is disgraceful for a woman to have
her hair cut off or her head shaved, she
should cover her head.
7 A man ought not have his head cov-
ered [during worship], since he is the
image and [reflected] glory of God; but
the woman is [the expression of] man's
glory. [Gen 1:26]
8 For man does not originate from
woman, but woman from man;
[Gen 2:21–23]
9 for indeed man was not created for
the sake of woman, but woman for the
sake of man. [Gen 2:18]
10 Therefore the woman ought to
have a *sign of* authority on her head,
for the sake of the angels [so as not to
offend them].
11 Nevertheless, woman is not inde-
pendent of man, nor is man indepen-
dent of woman.
12 For as the woman originates from
the man, so also man is born through
the woman; and all things [whether
male or female] originate from God
[as their Creator].
13 Judge for yourselves; is it proper
for a woman to offer prayer to God
[publicly] with her head uncovered?
14 Does not common sense itself
teach you that if a man has long hair,
it is a dishonor to him,
15 but if a woman has long hair, it is
her ornament *and* glory? For her long
hair is given to her as a covering.
16 Now if anyone is inclined to be con-
tentious [about this], we have no other
practice [in worship than this], nor do
the churches of God [in general].
17 But in giving this next instruction,
I do not praise you, because when you
meet together it is not for the better but
for the worse.
18 For, in the first place, when you

11:3 *the head.* The term "head" primarily means "authority" when used in the context of human relationships, but it can also mean "source" or "origin." The relationship between men and women does not involve inferiority; in the parallel clause Christ is not inferior to God the Father. Just as Christ and God are equally divine, men and women are equal in God's image. But Jesus and God the Father have different roles in God's plan of salvation, and so also men and women are given different roles in life and in the church.
11:4 *prays or prophesies.* This may refer to intercessory prayer similar to that of Old Testament prophets (Ge 20:7; 1Sa 12:23; Jer 27:18), or Anna (Lk 2:36 – 38), or to the combination of tongues and prayer (14:13 – 16; Ac 2:4; 10:46). The term "prophesy" means to speak forth the words of God (14:3).
11:5 *every woman who prays or prophesies.* It is difficult from this passage alone to tell exactly what a woman's role is to be in the Christian assembly, but it appears that women did minister to other believers through prayer and prophecy (see also 1Ti 2:11 – 14). ***shaved.*** For a woman to have her head shaved was a sign of public disgrace.
11:9 *woman for the sake of man.* This does not mean that women are inferior to men; it refers only to the purposes of God for men and women in the creative order, and the woman's God-given role of "helper" (Ge 2:20).
11:10 *authority.* Some think that this might be a symbol of the woman's authority to prophesy in the new church age; others believe that it might refer to a symbol of the man's authority over the woman and her willingness to submit to God's order. ***for the sake of the angels.*** Evidently God's angels are present at the meetings of the church and actually learn of God's work of grace through the lives and worship of God's people (Eph 3:10).
11:11 *woman is not independent of man, nor is man independent of woman.* Men and women need each other, and as creatures of God, both depend on Him. Neither man nor woman can have any claim to special status other than what God has purposed for them as their Creator.

3 Eph 5:23; Ge 3:16; 1Ti 2:11; Jn 14:28; Php 2:7-9 **4** 1Co 12:10 **5** Ac 21:9; Dt 21:12 **6** Nu 5:18 **7** Ge 1:26 **8** Ge 2:21 **9** Ge 2:18 **10** Ge 24:65; Ecc 5:6 **11** Gal 3:28 **16** 1Ti 6:4; 1Co 7:17 **18** 1Co 1:10,11

meet together in church, I hear that
there are divisions among you; and in
part I believe it,
19 for [doubtless] there have to be factions among you, so that those who are of approved character may be clearly recognized among you.
20 So when you meet together, it is not to eat the Lord's Supper,
21 for when you eat, each one hurries to get his own supper first [not waiting for others or the poor]. So one goes hungry while another gets drunk.
22 What! Do you not have houses in which to eat and drink? Or do you show contempt for the church of God and humiliate those [impoverished believers] who have nothing? What will I say to you? Shall I praise you for this? In this I will not praise you!

The Lord's Supper

23 For I received from the Lord Himself that [instruction] which I passed on to you, that the Lord Jesus on the night in which He was betrayed took bread;
24 and when He had given thanks, He broke it and said, "This is (represents) My body, which is [offered as a sacrifice] for you. Do this in [affectionate] remembrance of Me."
25 In the same way, after supper *He took* the cup, saying, "This cup is the new covenant [ratified and established] in My blood; do this, as often as you drink it, in [affectionate] remembrance of Me."
26 For every time you eat this bread and drink this cup, you are [symbolically] proclaiming [the fact of] the Lord's death until He comes [again].
27 So then whoever eats the bread or drinks the cup of the Lord in a way that is unworthy [of Him] will be guilty of [profaning and sinning against] the body and blood of the Lord.
28 But a person must [prayerfully] examine himself [and his relationship to Christ], and only when he has done so should he eat of the bread and drink of the cup.
29 For anyone who eats and drinks [without solemn reverence and heartfelt gratitude for the sacrifice of Christ], eats and drinks a judgment on himself if he does not recognize the body [of Christ].
30 That [careless and unworthy participation] is the reason why many among you are weak and sick, and a number sleep [in death].
31 But if we evaluated *and* judged ourselves honestly [recognizing our shortcomings and correcting our behavior], we would not be judged.
32 But when we [fall short and] are judged by the Lord, we are disciplined [by undergoing His correction] so that we will not be condemned [to eternal punishment] along with the world.
33 So then, my brothers and sisters, when you come together to eat [the Lord's Supper], wait for one another [and see to it that no one is left out].
34 If anyone is too hungry [to wait], let him eat at home, so that you will not come together for judgment [on your-

---

11:19 *those who are of approved character.* Paul is here being sarcastic, suggesting that some individuals within the church felt that they alone were truly approved of by the Lord, and trying to separate themselves from other believers whom they felt to be unapproved or less-approved by God than themselves. He condemns this attitude in these verses.
11:20 *the Lord's Supper.* The Lord's Supper was the centerpiece of early Christian worship. Gathered around one table, fellow believers met with the Lord and with each other in unity. Christ had expressed this type of humility and unity when He instituted the Supper (Mt 26:26 – 30; Mk 14:22 – 26; Lk 22:14 – 23).
11:26 *you are [symbolically] proclaiming [the fact of] the Lord's death until He comes.* The Lord's Supper looks back to Christ's death and forward to His second coming (Mt 26:29; Mk 14:25; Lk 22:18).
11:30 *sleep.* The death of Christians is often referred to as "sleep" (15:18; 1Th 4:15 – 16). In this passage, it refers to untimely death, a punishment suffered by some Christians who failed to examine themselves at the Lord's Supper (v. 28).

19 Mt 18:7; Lk 17:1; 1Ti 4:1; Lk 2:35; 1Jn 2:19 **21** 2Pe 2:13; Jude 12 **22** 1Co 10:32; Jas 2:6 **23** 1Co 15:3; Mt 26:26; Lk 22:19 **26** Jn 14:3; Ac 1:11 **27** Jn 6:51 **28** 2Co 13:5 **31** Ps 32:5; 1Jn 1:9 **32** Ps 94:12 **34** Titus 1:5; 1Co 4:19

selves]. About the remaining matters [of which I was informed], I will take care of them when I come.

The Use of Spiritual Gifts

12 NOW ABOUT the spiritual *gifts* [the special endowments given by the Holy Spirit], brothers and sisters, I do not want you to be uninformed.

2 You know that when you were pagans, *you were* led off after speechless idols; however you were led off [whether by impulse or habit].

3 Therefore I want you to know that no one speaking by the [power and influence of the] Spirit of God can say, "Jesus be cursed," and no one can say, "Jesus is [my] Lord," except by [the power and influence of] the Holy Spirit.

4 Now there are [distinctive] varieties of *spiritual* gifts [special abilities given by the grace and extraordinary power of the Holy Spirit operating in believers], but it is the same Spirit [who grants them and empowers believers].

5 And there are [distinctive] varieties of ministries *and* service, but it is the same Lord [who is served].

6 And there are [distinctive] ways of working [to accomplish things], but it is the same God who produces all things in all *believers* [inspiring, energizing, and empowering them].

7 But to each one is given the manifestation of the Spirit [the spiritual illumination and the enabling of the Holy Spirit] for the common good.

8 To one is given through the [Holy] Spirit [the power to speak] the message of wisdom, and to another [the power to express] the word of knowledge *and* understanding according to the same Spirit;

9 to another [wonder-working] faith [is given] by the same [Holy] Spirit, and to another the [extraordinary] gifts of healings by the one Spirit;

10 and to another the working of miracles, and to another prophecy [foretelling the future, speaking a new message from God to the people], and to another discernment of spirits [the ability to distinguish sound, godly doctrine from the deceptive doctrine of man-made religions and cults], to another *various* kinds of [unknown] tongues, and to another interpretation of tongues.

11 All these things [the gifts, the achievements, the abilities, the empowering] are brought about by one and the same [Holy] Spirit, distributing to each one individually just as He chooses.

12 For just as the body is one and yet has many parts, and all the parts, though many, form [only] one body, so it is with Christ.

13 For by one [Holy] Spirit we were all baptized into one body, [spiritually transformed—united together] whether Jews or Greeks (Gentiles), slaves or free, and we were all made to drink of one [Holy] Spirit [since the same Holy Spirit fills each life]. [Rom 3:22; Gal 3:28]

14 For the [human] body does not

12:1 – 10 Using Spiritual Gifts — Spiritual gifts are discussed in detail in four passages of the New Testament: Romans 12:3 – 8; 1 Corinthians 12:1 – 10; Ephesians 4:11 – 12; and 1 Peter 4:10 – 11. These lists are not exhaustive but are to be regarded as representative of spiritual gifts. They are given by the Spirit of God to accomplish God's purpose in the world and for the edification of the church, the body of Christ. Every believer has been given spiritual gifts (Ro 12:5 – 6; 1Co 12:7; 1Pe 4:10). The gifts belong to God and are given for the believer to use for the glory of God (1Pe 4:11).

12:3 *cursed . . . Lord.* A person speaking by the Holy Spirit will never curse Jesus; by the same token, no one can genuinely proclaim the lordship of Jesus without the enabling of the Spirit.

12:4 *gifts.* These gifts are spiritual capacities that God gives to individual Christians, through which He may strengthen His people.

12:13 *by one [Holy] Spirit.* "By" here may also be translated "in," speaking of location. Christ places each new member of the body in the Holy Spirit for His care and safekeeping (2Co 1:22).

CHAPTER 12 **1** 1Co 14:1,37 **2** Eph 2:11; 1Th 1:9; 1Pe 4:3; Ps 115:5 **3** Mk 9:39; 1Jn 4:2; Mt 16:17; Jn 15:26 **4** Ro 12:4; 1Pe 4:10; Eph 4:4 **5** Ro 12:6; Eph 4:11 **6** Eph 1:23 **7** Ro 12:6; Eph 4:7 **8** 1Co 2:6,7; 2Co 8:7 **9** Mt 17:19; 2Co 4:13; Mk 16:18; Jas 5:14 **10** Mk 16:17; Gal 3:5; Ro 12:6; 1Jn 4:1; Ac 2:4 **11** Ro 12:6; 2Co 10:13; Jn 3:8 **12** Ro 12:4,5; Eph 4:4; Gal 3:16 **13** Ro 6:5; Gal 3:28; Col 3:11; Jn 6:63

consist of one part, but of many [limbs
and organs].
[15]If the foot says, "Because I am not
a hand, I am not *a part* of the body,"
is it not on the contrary still *a part* of
the body?
[16]If the ear says, "Because I am not
an eye, I am not *a part* of the body,"
is it not on the contrary still *a part* of
the body?
[17]If the whole body were an eye,
where would the hearing be? If the
whole [body] were an ear, where would
the sense of smell be?
[18]But now [as things really are], God
has placed *and* arranged the parts in
the body, each one of them, just as He
willed *and* saw fit [with the best bal-
ance of function].
[19]If they all were a single *organ*,
where would [the rest of] the body be?
[20]But now [as things really are] there
are many parts [different limbs and
organs], but a single body.
[21]The eye cannot say to the hand,
"I have no need of you," nor again the
head to the feet, "I have no need of you."
[22]But quite the contrary, the parts of
the body that seem to be weaker are
[absolutely] necessary;
[23]and as for those *parts* of the body
which we consider less honorable,
these we treat with greater honor; and
our less presentable parts are treated
with greater modesty,
[24]while our more presentable parts
do not require it. But God has com-
bined the [whole] body, giving greater
honor to that part which lacks it,
[25]so that there would be no division
or discord in the body [that is, lack of
adaptation of the parts to each other],
but that the parts may have the same
concern for one another.
[26]And if one member suffers, all the
parts share the suffering; if one mem-
ber is honored, all rejoice with it.
[27]Now you [collectively] are Christ's
body, and individually [you are] mem-
bers of it [each with his own special
purpose and function].
[28]So God has appointed *and* placed
in the church [for His own use]: first
apostles [chosen by Christ], second
prophets [those who foretell the future,
those who speak a new message from
God to the people], third teachers, then
those who work miracles, then those
with the gifts of healings, the helpers,
the administrators, and speakers in
various kinds of [unknown] tongues.
[29]Are all apostles? Are all prophets?
Are all teachers? Are all workers of
miracles?
[30]Do all have gifts of healing? Do all
speak with tongues? Do all interpret?
[31]But earnestly desire *and* strive for
the greater gifts [if acquiring them is
going to be your goal].
And yet I will show you a still more
excellent way [one of the choicest grac-
es and the highest of them all: unself-
ish love].

The Excellence of Love

13 IF I speak with the tongues of
men and of angels, but have not
love [for others growing out of God's

12:18 *God has placed and arranged the parts in the body.* We should neither boast in what we do nor think too little of ourselves. Each one of us is important to God and has a mission to accomplish here on earth.
12:28 *apostles.* The term "apostle" or "sent one" refers generally to missionaries (15:7; Ro 16:7; 2Co 11:5, 12:11; Gal 1:17 – 19). Other times the term is limited to the small group who witnessed the resurrected Christ and were given a special mission by Him as His representatives (9:1; 15:5,8).
12:31 *earnestly desire and strive for the greater gifts.* This phrase has generally been interpreted as Paul's exhortation to the Corinthians to seek after the more spiritually profitable gifts, yet it is possible that Paul is stating that the Corinthians were improperly desiring the gifts that would bring attention to themselves. In other words, he would be telling them that, although they desire this sort of gift, he wants to show them a more excellent way.
13:1 – 13 Love — The word *love* is also translated *charity.* The more one reads 1 Corinthians 13, the more one has to face the fact that we don't naturally have that kind of love in us. The only way to get it is to get it from God. Love comes

18 ver. 28; Ro 12:3 **27** Ro 12:5; Eph 1:23; 4:12; 5:23,30; Col 1:24; Eph 5:30 **28** Eph 4:11; 2:20; 3:5; Ac 13:1; Ro 12:6; ver. 10; ver. 9; Nu 11:17; Ro 12:8; 1Ti 5:17; Heb 13:17,24 **31** 1Co 14:1,39

love for me], then I have become only a noisy gong or a clanging cymbal [just an annoying distraction].
[2]And if I have *the gift of* prophecy [and speak a new message from God to the people], and understand all mysteries, and [possess] all knowledge; and if I have all [sufficient] faith so that I can remove mountains, but do not have love [reaching out to others], I am nothing.
[3]If I give all my possessions to feed *the poor,* and if I surrender my body to be burned, but do not have love, it does me no good at all.
[4]Love endures with patience *and* serenity, love is kind *and* thoughtful, and is not jealous *or* envious; love does not brag and is not proud *or* arrogant.
[5]It is not rude; it is not self-seeking, it is not provoked [nor overly sensitive and easily angered]; it does not take into account a wrong *endured.*
[6]It does not rejoice at injustice, but rejoices with the truth [when right and truth prevail].
[7]Love bears all things [regardless of what comes], believes all things [looking for the best in each one], hopes all things [remaining steadfast during difficult times], endures all things [without weakening].
[8]Love never fails [it never fades nor ends]. But as for prophecies, they will pass away; as for tongues, they will cease; as for the gift of special knowledge, it will pass away.
[9]For we know in part, and we prophesy in part [for our knowledge is fragmentary and incomplete].
[10]But when that which is complete *and* perfect comes, that which is incomplete *and* partial will pass away.
[11]When I was a child, I talked like a child, I thought like a child, I reasoned like a child; when I became a man, I did away with childish things.
[12]For now [in this time of imperfection] we see in a mirror dimly [a blurred reflection, a riddle, an enigma], but then [when the time of perfection comes we will see reality] face to face. Now I know in part [just in fragments], but then I will know fully, just as I have been fully known [by God].
[13]And now there remain: faith [abiding trust in God and His promises], hope [confident expectation of eternal salvation], love [unselfish love for others growing out of God's love for me], these three [the choicest graces]; but the greatest of these is love.

Prophecy a Superior Gift

14 PURSUE [THIS] love [with eagerness, make it your goal], yet earnestly desire *and* cultivate the spiritual *gifts* [to be used by believers for the benefit of the church], but especially that you may prophesy [to foretell the future, to speak a new message from God to the people].
[2]For one who speaks in an *unknown* tongue does not speak to people but to God; for no one understands him *or* catches his meaning, but by the Spirit he speaks mysteries [secret truths, hidden things].
[3]But [on the other hand] the one

---

from God (1Jn 4:7). We're not very good at this kind of loving, and the only way we can be is through the empowering work of the Holy Spirit. It is tough because it means dependency on God for that which we cannot do by ourselves. It is tough because the objects of our love often act in unlovable ways or they reject our love when we give it. It is tough because we have to keep coming back with more love, even when it is rejected.

13:8 ***Love never fails.*** This uncompromising and bold affirmation introduces the contrast with the spiritual gifts which will not last. Paul wants the Corinthians to know that all the gifts would one day no longer be needed, but charity, or love.

13:10 ***when that which is complete and perfect comes.*** The Greek word for "perfect" means "end" or "completion." Most likely, this is a reference to the second coming of Christ and the completion of all things, but some have interpreted this as referring to the completion of the New Testament canon.

14:3 ***prophesies.*** In this sense, prophecy incorporates all speaking gifts that edify the church (Ro 12:6; 1Pe 4:11).

CHAPTER 13 **2** 1Co 12:8-10,28; 14:1; See Mt 7:22; Mt 17:20; Mk 11:23; Lk 17:6 **3** Mt 6:1,2 **4** Pr 10:12; 1Pe 4:8 **5** 1Co 10:24; Php 2:4 **6** Ps 10:3; Ro 1:32; 2Jn 4 **7** Ro 15:1; Gal 6:2; 2Ti 2:24 **9** 1Co 8:2 **12** 2Co 3:18; 5:7; Php 3:12; Mt 18:10; 1Jn 3:2 **CHAPTER 14** **1** 1Co 12:31; Nu 11:25,29 **2** Ac 2:4; 10:46

who prophesies speaks to people for
edification [to promote their spiritual
growth] and [speaks words of] encour-
agement [to uphold and advise them
concerning the matters of God] and
[speaks words of] consolation [to com-
passionately comfort them].
[4]One who speaks in a tongue edifies
himself; but one who prophesies edifies
the church [promotes growth in spiritu-
al wisdom, devotion, holiness, and joy].
[5]Now I wish that all of you spoke in
unknown tongues, but *even* more [I
wish] that you would prophesy. The
one who prophesies is greater [and
more useful] than the one who speaks
in tongues, unless he translates *or*
explains [what he says], so that the
church may be edified [instructed, im-
proved, strengthened].
[6]Now, believers, if I come to you
speaking in *unknown* tongues, how
will I benefit you unless I also speak
to you [clearly] either by revelation [re-
vealing God's mystery], or by knowl-
edge [teaching about God], or by proph-
ecy [foretelling the future, speaking a
new message from God to the people],
or by instruction [teaching precepts
that develop spiritual maturity]?
[7]Yet *even* lifeless things, whether
flute or harp, when producing a sound,
if they do not produce distinct [musi-
cal] tones, how will anyone [listening]
know what is piped or played?
[8]And if the [war] bugle produces
an indistinct sound, who will prepare
himself for battle?
[9]So it is with you, if you speak words
[in an unknown tongue] that are not
intelligible *and* clear, how will anyone
understand what you are saying? You
will be talking into the air [wasting
your breath]!
[10]There are, I suppose, a great many
kinds of languages in the world [un-
known to us], and none is lacking in
meaning.
[11]But if I do not know the meaning
of the language, I will [appear to] be a
foreigner to the one who is speaking
[since he knows exactly what he is
saying], and the one who is speaking
will [appear to] be a foreigner to me.
[12]So it is with you, since you are so
very eager to have spiritual gifts *and*
manifestations of the Spirit, strive to
excel in ways that will build up the
church [spiritually].
[13]Therefore let one who speaks in
a tongue pray that he may [be gifted
to] translate *or* explain [what he says].
[14]For if I pray in a tongue, my spirit
prays, but my mind is unproductive
[because it does not understand what
my spirit is praying].
[15]Then what am I to do? I will pray
with the spirit [by the Holy Spirit that
is within me] and I will pray with the
mind [using words I understand]; I
will sing with the spirit [by the Holy
Spirit that is within me] and I will sing
with the mind [using words I under-
stand].
[16]Otherwise if you bless [and give
thanks to God] in the spirit only, how
will any outsider *or* someone who is
not gifted [in spiritual matters] say
the "Amen" [of agreement] to your
thanksgiving, since he does not know
what you are saying? [1 Chr 16:36;
Ps 106:48]
[17]You are giving thanks well enough
[in a way that God is glorified], but
the other person [who does not under-
stand you] is not edified [and spiritu-
ally strengthened since he cannot join
in your thanksgiving].
[18]I thank God that I speak in [un-
known] tongues more than all of you;
[19]nevertheless, in public worship I
would rather say five *understandable*
words in order to instruct others, than
ten thousand words in a tongue [which
others cannot understand].

Instruction for the Church

[20]Brothers and sisters, do not be
children [immature, childlike] in your

14:11 *I do not know the meaning.* Paul underlines the original purpose of all spiritual gifts: they must serve the church (vv. 13 – 14; 12:7). Tongues must convey meaning or else they fail to help those who listen.

14:16 *Amen.* The word "amen" means "truly" or "so

6 ver. 26 **15** Eph 5:19; Col 3:16; Ps 47:7 **16** 1Co 11:24 **20** Ps 131:2; Mt 11:25; 18:3; 19:14; Ro 16:19; 1Co 3:1; Eph 4:14; Heb 5:12,13; Mt 18:3; 1Pe 2:2

thinking; be infants in [matters of] evil [completely innocent and inexperienced], but in your minds be mature [adults].
21It is written in the Law, "BY MEN OF STRANGE TONGUES AND BY THE LIPS OF FOREIGNERS I WILL SPEAK TO THIS PEOPLE, AND NOT EVEN THEN WILL THEY LISTEN TO ME," says the Lord. [Is 28:11, 12]
22Therefore, [unknown] tongues are [meant] for a [supernatural] sign, not to believers but to unbelievers [who might be receptive]; while prophecy [foretelling the future, speaking a new message from God to the people] is not for unbelievers but for believers.
23So then, if the whole church gathers together and all of you speak in [unknown] tongues, and outsiders *or* those who are not gifted [in spiritual matters] or unbelievers come in, will they not say that you are out of your mind?
24But if all prophesy [foretelling the future, speaking a new message from God to the people], and an unbeliever or outsider comes in, he is convicted [of his sins] by all, and he is called to account by all [because he can understand what is being said];
25the secrets of his heart are laid bare. And so, falling on his face, he will worship God, declaring that God is really among you.
26What then is *the right course,* believers? When you meet together, each one has a psalm, a teaching, a revelation (disclosure of special knowledge), a tongue, *or* an interpretation. Let everything be constructive *and* edifying *and* done for the good of all the church.
27If anyone speaks in a tongue, *it should be limited* to two or at the most three, and *each one speaking* in turn, and one must interpret [what is said].
28But if there is no one to interpret, the one [who wishes to speak in a tongue] must keep silent in church; let him speak to himself and to God.
29Let two or three prophets speak [as inspired by the Holy Spirit], while the rest pay attention *and* weigh carefully what is said.
30But if an inspired revelation is made to another who is seated, then the first one must be silent.
31For [in this way] you can all prophesy one by one, so that everyone may be instructed and everyone may be encouraged;
32for the spirits of prophets are subject to the prophets [the prophecy is under the speaker's control, and he can stop speaking];
33for God [who is the source of their prophesying] is not *a God* of confusion *and* disorder but of peace *and* order.
As [is the practice] in all the churches of the saints (God's people),
34the women should be silent in the churches, for they are not authorized to speak, but are to take a subordinate place, as the Law says.
35If there is anything they want to learn [that is, if they have questions about anything being said or taught], they are to ask their own husbands at

---

be it" (Jn 3:5). Saying "amen" indicated agreement with what was being said (Dt 27:14–26; Rev 5:14).
14:29 ***two or three.*** The meetings of the church should be characterized by orderliness and moderation. ***weigh.*** No one, not even a person exercising a spiritual gift, is exempt from accountability to the church (6:5; 11:29–31).
14:32 ***subject to the prophets.*** Paul anticipated that some might excuse disorder by claiming that they could not prevent themselves from prophesying when God brought a revelation to them. He explained that the Holy Spirit does not overpower the person through whom He speaks.
14:34 ***women should be silent.*** This command is the subject of much debate, for it seems to contradict the fact that Paul spoke of women prophesying in 1 Corinthians 11:5. It has been suggested that Paul was addressing a particular problem in the Corinthian church, a group of women who were disruptive, but the prohibition is repeated at a different time to a different group of people (1Ti 2:11–12). This verse has also been interpreted as a prohibition on women interpreting prophecy, judging the prophets, or speaking in tongues. Others believe that women do prophesy and minister, but only to other women, or

21 Jn 10:34; Isa 28:11,12 **23** Ac 2:13 **25** Isa 45:14; Zec 8:23 **26** ver. 6; 1Co 12:8-10; 1Co 12:7; 2Co 12:19; Eph 4:12 **29** 1Co 12:10 **30** 1Th 5:19,20 **32** 1Jn 4:1 **33** 1Co 11:16 **34** 1Ti 2:11,12; Ge 3:16

home; for it is improper for a woman
to talk in church.
36 Did the word of the Lord originate
from you [Corinthians], or has it come
to you only [so that you know best
what God requires]?
37 If anyone thinks *and* claims that he
is a prophet [a true spokesman for God]
or spiritually astute [filled with and
energized by the Holy Spirit], let him
recognize that the things which I write
to you are the Lord's commandment.
38 If anyone does not recognize this
[that it is a command of the Lord], he
is not recognized [by God].
39 Therefore, believers, desire ear-
nestly to prophesy [to foretell the fu-
ture, to speak a new message from
God to the people], and do not forbid
speaking in *unknown* tongues.
40 But all things must be done ap-
propriately and in an orderly manner.

The Fact of Christ's Resurrection

15 NOW BROTHERS and sisters,
let me remind you [once again]
of the good news [of salvation] which I
preached to you, which you welcomed
and accepted and on which you stand
[by faith].
2 By this *faith* you are saved [reborn
from above—spiritually transformed,
renewed, and set apart for His pur-
pose], if you hold firmly to the word
which I preached to you, unless you
believed in vain [just superficially and
without complete commitment].
3 For I passed on to you as of first
importance what I also received, that
Christ died for our sins according to
[that which] the Scriptures [foretold],
[Is 53:5–12]
4 and that He was buried, and that He
was [bodily] raised on the third day ac-
cording to [that which] the Scriptures
[foretold], [Ps 16:9, 10]
5 and that He appeared to Cephas
(Peter), then to the Twelve.
6 After that He appeared to more
than five hundred brothers and sisters
at one time, the majority of whom are
still alive, but some have fallen asleep
[in death].
7 Then He was seen by James, then
by all the apostles,
8 and last of all, as to one untimely
(prematurely, traumatically) born, He
appeared to me also. [Acts 9:1–9]
9 For I am the least [worthy] of the
apostles, and not fit to be called an
apostle, because I [at one time] fiercely
oppressed *and* violently persecuted the
church of God.
10 But by the [remarkable] grace of

---

in a setting other than public church meetings, such as Priscilla and Aquila instructing Apollos (Ac 18:24 – 28).

14:40 *appropriately and in an orderly manner.* This verse is the key to all church practice. In worship and teaching, as in all of life, believers should demonstrate self-control and consideration.

15:3 – 4 Gospel Message — Paul makes it clear here that evangelism should be centered on the gospel of Christ. The central point of the good news is Christ's death and resurrection. The four key points about that gospel are:

God's Word says all are sinners, condemned to hell (Isa 53:6; Ro 3:10 – 11,23; 5:8,12; Rev 20:15).

There is nothing a sinner can do on his own to save himself (Isa 64:6; Eph 2:9).

Christ was born, crucified, and resurrected to save lost people from their sin (Jn 3:16; 1Ti 1:15).

To be saved, a sinner must believe God's Word and invite Christ into his or her heart by faith (Jn 5:24; Ac 16:31).

15:3 *according to [that which] the Scriptures [foretold].* Christ lived and died in accordance with the prophecies about Him in the Old Testament (Ps 16:10; Isa 53:8 – 10).

15:8 *untimely (prematurely, traumatically) born.* This is probably Paul's comment on the unique way that he became an apostle. Unlike the other apostles, who had the benefit of an initial training period with Christ, Paul became an apostle abruptly, with no opportunity for earthly contact with Christ or His teaching.

15:9 *fiercely oppressed and violently persecuted the church.* The story of Paul's persecuting and conversion is told in Acts 9, 22; Ephesians 3:8; 1 Timothy 1:15 – 16.

37 2Co 10:7; 1Jn 4:6 **39** 1Co 12:31; 1Th 5:20 **40** ver. 33 **CHAPTER 15** **1** Gal 1:11; Ro 5:2 **2** Ro 1:16; 1Co 1:21; Gal 3:4 **3** 1Co 11:2,23; Gal 1:12; Ps 22:15; Isa 53:5,6; Da 9:26; Zec 13:7; Lk 24:26,46; Ac 3:18; 26:23; 1Pe 1:11; 2:24 **4** Ps 16:10; Isa 53:10; Hos 6:2; Lk 24:26; Ac 2:25; 1Pe 1:11 **5** Lk 24:34; Mt 28:17; Mk 16:14; Lk 24:36; Jn 20:19 **7** Lk 24:50; Ac 1:3,4 **8** Ac 9:4; 22:14,18 **9** Eph 3:8; Ac 8:3; Php 3:6 **10** Eph 3:7,8; 2Co 11:23; 12:11; Mt 10:20; Ro 15:18; 2Co 3:5; Gal 2:8; Eph 3:7; Php 2:13

God I am what I am, and His grace
toward me was not without effect. In
fact, I worked harder than all of the
apostles, though it was not I, but the
grace of God [His unmerited favor and
blessing which was] with me.
11 So whether it was I or they, this is
what we preach, and this is what you
believed *and* trusted in *and* relied on
with confidence.
12 Now if Christ is preached as raised
from the dead, how is it that some
among you say that there is no resur-
rection of the dead?
13 But if there is no resurrection of the
dead, then not even Christ has been
raised;
14 and if Christ has not been raised,
then our preaching is vain [useless,
amounting to nothing], and your faith
is also vain [imaginary, unfounded,
devoid of value and benefit—not based
on truth].
15 We are even discovered to be false
witnesses [misrepresenting] God, be-
cause we testified concerning Him that
He raised Christ, whom He did not
raise, if in fact the dead are not raised.
16 For if the dead are not raised, then
Christ has not been raised, either;
17 and if Christ has not been raised,
your faith is worthless *and* powerless
[mere delusion]; you are still in your
sins [and under the control and pen-
alty of sin].
18 Then those also who have fallen
asleep in Christ are lost.
19 If we who are [abiding] in Christ
have hoped only in this life [and this
is all there is], then we are of all people
most miserable *and* to be pitied.

The Order of Resurrection

20 But now [as things really are]
Christ has *in fact* been raised from
the dead, [and He became] the first
fruits [that is, the first to be resurrected
with an incorruptible, immortal body,
foreshadowing the resurrection] of
those who have fallen asleep [in death].
[Col 1:18]
21 For since [it was] by a man that
death *came* [into the world], it is also
by a Man that the resurrection of the
dead *has come.*
22 For just as in Adam all die, so also
in Christ all will be made alive.
23 But each in his own order: Christ
the first fruits, then those who are
Christ's [own will be resurrected with

15:12 *no resurrection.* These opponents of Paul may have been denying the reality of Christ's resurrection. They may also have been teaching that resurrection is only spiritual and not physical; or they may have been teaching that the resurrection had already happened (2Ti 2:18). Whatever the case, they contradicted the essential teaching that Christ had been physically raised from the dead and that all believers in Him will someday also be resurrected.

15:15 *false witnesses.* In verses 5 – 8 Paul listed several people, including himself, who had witnessed the resurrected Christ. To deny the resurrection was to call these people liars.

15:17 Resurrection — There are many biblical scholars these days who say that the resurrection was an invented story out of some kind of "faith" process. They relegate the critical event that defines Christianity to the imaginations of some well-meaning but deluded Palestinian peasants. Paul goes to great pains to put the resurrection in the realm of fact, not opinion or imagination. He talks about the eyewitness testimony of hundreds (v. 6). He references his own story of personal confrontation with Christ (v. 8). In the end he says that if the resurrection isn't a fact, then he is absolutely lost (v. 19). This sounds like a man who staked his entire life on an indisputable fact.

15:19 *miserable.* If Christ did not rise, then He is just another dead prophet with no power over sin or death, and the Christian's hope of eternal life is a lie.

15:20 *first fruits.* The "first fruit" is the first installment of a crop, which anticipates and guarantees the ultimate offering of the whole crop (16:15; Ro 8:23). Because Christ rose from the dead, those who are asleep in Christ (1Th 4:15 – 16) have a guarantee of their own resurrection.

15:21 *by a man that death came.* The first man, Adam, transgressed God's law and brought sin and death into the world (Ge 2:17; 3:19; Ro 5:12 – 21); the second man, Jesus Christ, was the perfect sacrifice to take away sin and to bring life and resurrection to those who believe in Him (Ro 5:15 – 21).

15:23 *each in his own order.* The believers who

13 1Th 4:14 **15** Ac 2:24; 4:10,33 **17** Ro 4:25 **19** 2Ti 3:12 **20** 1Pe 1:3; Ac 26:23; Rev 1:5 **21** Ro 5:12; Jn 11:25; Ro 6:23 **23** 1Th 4:15

incorruptible, immortal bodies] at His coming.

24 After that comes the end (completion), when He hands over the kingdom to God the Father, after He has made inoperative *and* abolished every ruler and every authority and power.

25 For Christ must reign [as King] until He has put all His enemies under His feet. [Ps 110:1]

26 The last enemy to be abolished *and* put to an end is death.

27 For HE (the Father) HAS PUT ALL THINGS IN SUBJECTION UNDER HIS (Christ's) FEET. But when He says, "All things have been put in subjection [under Christ]," it is clear that He (the Father) who put all things in subjection to Him (Christ) is excepted [since the Father is not in subjection to His own Son]. [Ps 8:6]

28 However, when all things are subjected to Him (Christ), then the Son Himself will also be subjected to the One (the Father) who put all things under Him, so that God may be all in all [manifesting His glory without any opposition, the supreme indwelling and controlling factor of life].

29 Otherwise, what will those do who are being baptized for the dead? If the dead are not raised at all, why are people even baptized for them?

30 [For that matter] why are we [running such risks and putting ourselves] in danger [nearly] every hour [if there is no resurrection]?

31 I assure you, believers, by the pride which I have in you in [your union with] Christ Jesus our Lord, I die daily [I face death and die to self].

32 What good has it done me if, [merely] from a human point of view, I fought with wild animals at Ephesus? If the dead are not raised [at all], LET US EAT AND DRINK [enjoying ourselves now], FOR TOMORROW WE DIE. [Is 22:13; 2 Cor 1:8, 9]

33 Do not be deceived: "Bad company corrupts good morals."

34 Be sober-minded [be sensible, wake up from your spiritual stupor] as you ought, and stop sinning; for some [of you] have no knowledge of God [you are disgracefully ignorant of Him, and ignore His truths]. I say this to your shame.

35 But someone will say, "How are the dead raised? And with what kind of body will they come?"

36 You fool! Every time you plant *seed* you sow something that does not come to life [germinating, springing up and growing] unless it *first* dies.

37 The seed you sow is not the body (the plant) which it is going to become, but it is a bare seed, perhaps of wheat or some other grain.

38 But God gives it a body just as He planned, and to each kind of seed a body of its own [is given]. [Gen 1:11]

39 All flesh is not the same. There is one kind for humans, another for animals, another for birds, and another for fish.

40 There are also heavenly bodies [sun, moon and stars] and earthly bodies [humans, animals, and plants], but the glory *and* beauty of the heavenly is

---

have died will be the first to rise at Christ's coming and be reunited with their physical bodies. Following this is the removal of all living Christians from the earth (1Th 4:13 – 18).

15:29 *baptized for the dead.* It may be that some of the Corinthians had for some reason been baptized on behalf of others who had died without baptism. Paul does not address whether this practice was right or wrong (although his use of "they" rather than "we" indicates that he did not participate), but makes the point that their own actions are inconsistent with their beliefs. There would be no point in doing anything for the dead if there is no resurrection.

15:30 *in danger.* If this life is all there is, it would make more sense to take the position of the Epicureans, seeking pleasure and avoiding pain.

15:32 *wild animals at Ephesus.* This may be a figurative reference to Paul's enemies at Ephesus (Ac 19).

15:36 *unless it first dies.* Difficulty understanding the nature of the resurrection should not cause a person to doubt its reality any more than not understanding how a seed becomes a plant should cause disbelief in the coming harvest.

24 Da 7:14 **25** Ps 110:1; Ac 2:34; Eph 1:22 **26** 2Ti 1:10; Rev 20:14 **27** Ps 8:6 **28** Php 3:21; 1Co 3:23; 11:3 **30** 2Co 11:26; Gal 5:11 **31** 1Th 2:19; Ro 8:36; 2Co 4:10 **32** 2Co 1:8; Ecc 2:24; Isa 22:13; Lk 12:19 **33** 1Co 5:6 **34** Ro 13:11; Eph 5:14; 1Th 4:5; 1Co 6:5 **35** Eze 37:3 **36** Jn 12:24

one kind, and the *glory* of the earthly
is another.
41 There is a glory *and* beauty of the
sun, another glory of the moon, and yet
another [distinctive] glory of the stars;
and one star differs from another in
glory *and* brilliance.
42 So it is with the resurrection of the
dead. The [human] body that is sown
is perishable *and* mortal, it is raised
imperishable *and* immortal. [Dan 12:3]
43 It is sown in dishonor, it is raised
in glory; it is sown in weakness, it is
raised in strength;
44 it is sown a natural body [mortal,
suited to earth], it is raised a spiritual
body [immortal, suited to heaven]. As
surely as there is a physical body, there
is also a spiritual *body*.
45 So it is written [in Scripture], "The
first MAN, Adam, BECAME A LIVING SOUL
(an individual);" the last Adam (Christ)
became a life-giving spirit [restoring
the dead to life]. [Gen 2:7]
46 However, the spiritual [the immor-
tal life] is not first, but the physical [the
mortal life]; then the spiritual.
47 The first man [Adam] is from the
earth, earthy [made of dust]; the sec-
ond Man [Christ, the Lord] is from
heaven. [Gen 2:7]
48 As is the earthly man [the man of
dust], so are those who are of earth;
and as is the heavenly [Man], so are
those who are of heaven.
49 Just as we have borne the image of
the earthly [the man of dust], we will
also bear the image of the heavenly
[the Man of heaven].

The Mystery of Resurrection

50 Now I say this, believers, that flesh
and blood cannot inherit *nor* be part
of the kingdom of God; nor does the
perishable (mortal) inherit the imper-
ishable (immortal).
51 Listen very carefully, I tell you a
mystery [a secret truth decreed by God
and previously hidden, but now re-
vealed]; we will not all sleep [in death],
but we will all be [completely] changed
[wondrously transformed],
52 in a moment, in the twinkling of an
eye, at [the sound of] the last trumpet
call. For a trumpet will sound, and
the dead [who believed in Christ] will
be raised imperishable, and we will
be [completely] changed [wondrously
transformed].
53 For this perishable [part of us] must
put on the imperishable [nature], and
this mortal [part of us that is capable of
dying] must put on immortality [which
is freedom from death].
54 And when this perishable puts
on the imperishable, and this mortal
puts on immortality, then the Scripture
will be fulfilled that says, "DEATH IS
SWALLOWED UP in victory (vanquished
forever). [Is 25:8]
55 "O DEATH, WHERE IS YOUR VICTORY?
O DEATH, WHERE IS YOUR STING?" [Hos 13:14]
56 The sting of death is sin, and the
power of sin [by which it brings death]
is the law;
57 but thanks be to God, who gives
us the victory [as conquerors] through
our Lord Jesus Christ.
58 Therefore, my beloved brothers and
sisters, be steadfast, immovable, always
excelling in the work of the Lord [al-
ways doing your best and doing more
than is needed], being *continually*
aware that your labor [even to the point
of exhaustion] in the Lord is not futile
nor wasted [it is never without purpose].

15:44 *natural body . . . spiritual body.* The contrast is not between a material body and an immaterial body, but between a body subject to death and a body that is immortal.

15:54 *DEATH IS SWALLOWED UP in victory.* Satan's apparent victories in the garden of Eden (Ge 3:13) and at the cross (Mk 15:22 – 24) were reversed by Jesus' death and resurrection (Col 2:13 – 15).

15:58 *your labor [even to the point of exhaustion] in the Lord is not futile nor wasted.* We are looking forward to eternal life because of the hope of the resurrection; everything we do on this earth matters for eternity.

42 Da 12:3; Mt 13:43 **43** Php 3:21 **45** Ge 2:7; Ro 5:14; Jn 5:21; Php 3:21; Col 3:4 **47** Jn 3:31; Ge 3:19; Jn 3:13 **48** Php 3:20 **49** Ge 5:3; Ro 8:29; 2Co 3:18; Php 3:21; 1Jn 3:2 **50** Mt 16:17; Jn 3:3,5 **51** 1Th 4:15; Php 3:21 **52** Zec 9:14; Mt 24:31; Jn 5:25 **53** 2Co 5:4 **54** Isa 25:8; Rev 20:14 **55** Hos 13:14 **56** Ro 4:15 **57** Ro 7:25; 1Jn 5:4 **58** 2Pe 3:14; 1Co 3:8

Instructions and Greetings

16 NOW CONCERNING the money
collected for [the relief of] the
saints [in Jerusalem], you are to do
the same as I directed the churches of
Galatia *to do.*
2 On the first day of every week each
one of you is to put something aside, in
proportion to his prosperity, and save
it so that no collections [will need to]
be made when I come.
3 When I arrive, I will send whomev-
er you approve with letters [of autho-
rization] to take your gift [of charity
and love] to Jerusalem;
4 and if it is fitting for me to go too,
they will accompany me.
5 I will visit you after I go through
Macedonia, for I am only passing
through Macedonia;
6 but it may be that I will stay with
you [for a while], or even spend the
winter, so that you may send me on my
way to wherever I may go *afterward.*
7 For I do not wish to see you right
now *just* in passing, but I hope to re-
main with you for some time [later on],
if the Lord permits.
8 But I will stay in Ephesus until Pen-
tecost,
9 because a wide door for effective
service has opened to me [in Ephesus, a
very promising opportunity], and there
are many adversaries. [Acts 19:23–41]
10 If Timothy comes, see to it that
[you put him at ease, so that] he has
nothing to fear in regard to you, for he
is [devotedly] doing the Lord's work,
just as I am.
11 So allow no one to treat him with
disdain [as if he were inconsequential].
But send him off [cordially, and speed
him on his way] in peace, so that he
may come to me, for I am expecting
him [to come along] with the *other*
brothers.
12 As for our brother Apollos, I have
strongly encouraged him to visit you
with the other brothers. It was not at
all his desire to come now, but he will
come when he has the opportunity.
13 Be on guard; stand firm in your
faith [in God, respecting His precepts
and keeping your doctrine sound]. Act
like [mature] men *and* be courageous;
be strong. [Ps 31:24]
14 Let everything you do be done in
love [motivated and inspired by God's
love for us].
15 Brothers and sisters, you know that
those of the household of Stephanas
were the first converts in Achaia, and
that they have devoted themselves for
ministry to God's people—now I urge
you
16 to be subject to such leaders [treat-
ing them with courtesy and respect],
and to everyone who helps in the work
and labors [for the benefit of your-
selves and the church].
17 I rejoice because Stephanas and
Fortunatus and Achaicus have ar-
rived, for they have made up for your
absence.
18 They have refreshed my spirit as
well as yours. So fully acknowledge
such men *and* deeply appreciate them.
19 The churches of Asia send you

16:2 *the first day of every week.* It appears that the custom of believers meeting on the first day of the week began early in Christian history. ***put something aside.*** The Old Testament tithe was not adopted by the New Testament church, though certainly Christ practiced it. New Testament believers were encouraged to give liberally, but never a specified amount or percentage (Ro 12:8). Considering the New Testament teachings on generosity and self-sacrifice, believers should probably expect to give much more than ten percent.

16:13 *Act like [mature] men.* This phrase emphasizes bravery as well as maturity. Paul's command to do everything with love serves as a balance to these strong exhortations.

16:17 *Stephanas and Fortunatus and Achaicus.* These were probably the ones who confirmed the bad report brought by Chloe's household in 1 Corinthians 1:11.

16:19 *Aquila and Prisca.* Aquila and Prisca were tentmakers who had met Paul in Corinth. They followed him to Ephesus and made their

---

CHAPTER 16 **1** Ac 11:29; Gal 2:10 **2** Ac 20:7 **3** 2Co 8:19 **4** 2Co 8:19 **5** Ac 19:21; 2Co 1:16 **6** Ac 15:3; Ro 15:24 **7** Ac 18:21; Jas 4:15 **9** Ac 14:27; 2Co 2:12; Col 4:3; Ac 19:9 **10** Ac 19:22; Php 2:20; 1Th 3:2 **11** 1Ti 4:12; Ac 15:33 **12** 1Co 1:12 **13** Mt 24:42; 1Th 5:6; 1Pe 5:8; Php 1:27; 1Th 3:8; 2Th 2:15; Eph 6:10; Col 1:11 **14** 1Pe 4:8 **15** 1Co 1:16; Ro 16:5; 2Co 8:4; Heb 6:10 **16** Heb 13:17; 6:10 **17** 2Co 11:9; Php 2:30 **18** Col 4:8; Php 2:29 **19** Ro 16:5

their greetings. Aquila and Prisca, together with the church [that meets] in their house, send you their warm greetings in the Lord.

[20] All the believers greet you. Greet one another with a holy kiss.

[21] This greeting is in my own hand—Paul.

[22] If anyone does not love the Lord [does not obey and respect and believe in Jesus Christ and His message], he is to be accursed. Maranatha (O our Lord, come)!

[23] The grace of our Lord Jesus [His unmerited favor, His spiritual blessing, His profound mercy] be with you.

[24] My love be with all of you in Christ Jesus. Amen.

---

house available for the meetings of the church (Ro 16:3 – 5). They would have been known to many in the Corinthian church.

16:20 *holy kiss.* In the ancient world (as in many cultures still today), a kiss was a common form of friendly or affectionate greeting.

16:22 *be accursed.* Paul does not condemn unbelievers, but rather unbelievers condemn themselves by ignoring the claims of the Creator on their lives.

20 Ro 16:16 **21** Col 4:18 **22** Eph 6:24; Gal 1:8,9; Jude 14,15 **23** Ro 16:20

THE SECOND LETTER OF PAUL TO THE

CORINTHIANS

▸ **AUTHOR:** External and internal evidence amply support the Pauline authorship of this letter. There is an interval of about a year between these two letters to the Corinthians. Since Paul's first letter, the Corinthian church had been swayed by false teachers who stirred the people against Paul. They claimed he was fickle, arrogant, unimpressive in appearance and speech, and unqualified to be an apostle of Jesus Christ. During this time Paul has paid them what must have been an unpleasant visit and then wrote them another letter, which we do not have (2:1 – 4). Paul wrote 2 Corinthians in AD 56 in Macedonia and sent the letter to the church with Titus and another brother (8:16).

▸ **TIMES:** c. AD 56 ▸ **KEY VERSES:** 2Co 4:5 – 6

▸ **THEME:** As Paul writes this letter, he is looking forward to yet another visit, and it appears that the Corinthians have listened to him and things are getting on the right track. There are still some problems though. The key issue seems to be Paul's leadership. He spends a good deal of the letter establishing his authority and the need to exercise it, which makes the letter intensely personal. In it we can see the depth of his relationship with the Corinthians, and we get an understanding of the hardships Paul went through for these people on his missionary journeys. Most importantly we see a faith that is so focused that Paul is ready to endure anything to see it spread.

Introduction

1 PAUL, AN apostle (special messenger, personally chosen representative) of Christ Jesus (the Messiah) by the will of God, and Timothy *our* brother,

To the church of God which is at Corinth, and to all the saints (God's people) throughout Achaia (southern Greece):

2 Grace to you and peace [inner calm and spiritual well-being] from God our Father and the Lord Jesus Christ.

3 Blessed [gratefully praised and adored] be the God and Father of our Lord Jesus Christ, the Father of mercies and the God of all comfort,

4 who comforts *and* encourages us in every trouble so that we will be able to comfort *and* encourage those who are in any kind of trouble, with the comfort with which we ourselves are comforted by God.

5 For just as Christ's sufferings are ours in abundance [as they overflow to His followers], so also our comfort [our reassurance, our encouragement, our consolation] is abundant through

---

1:4 *who comforts and encourages us in every trouble.* God comforts us for our own encouragement and also to make us comforters of others. The comfort that God gives to us becomes a gift that we can give to others (7:6; Ac 9:10 – 19).

1:5 *Christ's sufferings.* Jesus warned His disciples that they would experience the same kind of suffering that He did for the sake of the gospel (Jn 15:20).

CHAPTER 1 **1** 1Co 1:1; Eph 1:1; Col 1:1; 1Ti 1:1; 2Ti 1:1; Php 1:1; Col 1:2 **2** Ro 1:7; 1Co 1:3; Gal 1:3; Php 1:2; Col 1:2; 1Th 1:1; 2Th 1:2 **3** Eph 1:3; 1Pe 1:3 **5** Ac 9:4; 2Co 4:10

Christ [it is truly more than enough to endure what we must].

[6]But if we are troubled *and* distressed, it is for your comfort and salvation; or if we are comforted *and* encouraged, it is for your comfort, which works [in you] when you patiently endure the same sufferings which we experience.

[7]And our hope for you [our confident expectation of good for you] is firmly grounded [assured and unshaken], since we know that just as you share *as partners* in our sufferings, so also you share *as partners* in our comfort.

[8]For we do not want you to be uninformed, brothers and sisters, about our trouble in [the west coast province of] Asia [Minor], how we were utterly weighed down, beyond our strength, so that we despaired even of life [itself].

[9]Indeed, we felt within ourselves that we had received the sentence of death [and were convinced that we would die, but this happened] so that we would not trust in ourselves, but in God who raises the dead.

[10]He rescued us from so great a *threat of* death, and will *continue to* rescue us. On Him we have set our hope. And He will again rescue us [from danger and draw us near],

[11]while you join in helping us by your prayers. Then thanks will be given by many persons on our behalf for the gracious gift [of deliverance] granted to us through *the prayers of* many [believers].

Paul's Integrity

[12]This is our [reason for] proud confidence: our conscience testifies that we have conducted ourselves in the world [in general], and especially toward you, with pure motives and godly sincerity, not in human wisdom, but in the grace of God [that is, His gracious lovingkindness that leads people to Christ and spiritual maturity].

[13]For we write you nothing other than what you read and understand [there is no double meaning in what we say]. And I hope you will [accurately] understand [divine things] until the end;

[14]just as you have [already] partially understood us, [and one day will recognize] that you can be proud of us just as we are of you, in the day of our Lord Jesus.

[15]It was with this confidence that I planned at first to visit you, so that you might receive twice a token of grace;

[16]that is, [I wanted] to visit you on my way to Macedonia, and [then] to come back to you [on my return] from Macedonia, and have you send me on my way to Judea.

[17]So then, was I indecisive *or* capricious when I was [originally] planning this? Or the things I plan, do I plan in a self-serving way like a worldly man, ready to say, "Yes, yes" and "No, no" [at the same time]?

[18]But [as surely as] God is faithful *and* means what He says, our message to you is not "Yes" and "No" [at the same time].

[19]For the Son of God, Jesus Christ, who was preached among you by us, by me, Silvanus, and Timothy, was not "Yes" and "No," but has proved to be "Yes" in Him [true and faithful, the divine "Yes" affirming God's promises].

[20]For as many as are the promises of God, in Christ they are [all answered] "Yes." So through Him we say our "Amen" to the glory of God.

[21]Now it is God who establishes *and* confirms us [in joint fellowship] with

---

1:8 *Asia.* This is the Roman province in western Asia Minor, present day Turkey. The trouble that Paul speaks of is likely the riots in Ephesus (Ac 19:23–41).

1:12 *godly sincerity.* The Corinthians certainly were well acquainted with Paul's character, since he had spent 18 months with them (Ac 18:11).

1:19 *not "Yes" and "No."* Paul's preaching was not inconsistent or contradictory. Instead, his preaching reflected the truthfulness and faithfulness of God, because his teaching was based on the Scriptures and the teachings of Christ.

1:21 *anointed us.* God confirmed Paul and his fellow workers by anointing them, the special

6 2Co 4:15 **7** Ro 8:17; 2Ti 2:12 **8** Ac 19:23; 1Co 15:32; 16:9 **9** Jer 17:5,7 **10** 2Pe 2:9 **11** Ro 15:30; Php 1:19; Php 22; 2Co 4:15 **12** 2Co 2:17; 1Co 2:4 **14** 2Co 5:12; Php 2:16; 1Th 2:19 **15** 1Co 4:19; Ro 1:11 **16** 1Co 16:5,6 **17** 2Co 10:2 **19** Mk 1:1; Lk 1:35; Ac 9:20; Heb 13:8 **20** Ro 15:8 **21** 1Jn 2:20

you in Christ, and who has anointed us [empowering us with the gifts of the Spirit];
22it is He who has also put His seal on us [that is, He has appropriated us and certified us as His] and has given us the [Holy] Spirit in our hearts as a pledge [like a security deposit to guarantee the fulfillment of His promise of eternal life].
23But I call on God as my soul's witness, that it was to spare you [pain and discouragement] that I did not come again to Corinth—
24not that we rule [like dictators] over your faith, but *rather* we work with you for [the increase of] your joy; for in your faith you stand firm [in your strong conviction that Jesus of Nazareth—the Messiah—is the Son of God, through whom we obtain eternal salvation].

Reaffirm Your Love

2 BUT I made up my mind not to grieve you with another painful visit.
2For if I cause you grief [by a well-deserved rebuke], who then provides me enjoyment but the very one whom I have made sad?
3And I wrote this same thing to you, so that when I came, I would not be filled with sorrow by those who ought to make me glad, for I trusted in you *and* felt confident that my joy would be shared by all of you.
4For I wrote to you out of great distress and with an anguished heart, and with many tears, not to cause you sorrow but to make you realize the [overflowing] love which I have especially for you.
5But if someone has caused [all this] sorrow, he has caused it not to me, but in some degree—not to put it too severely—[he has distressed and grieved] all of you.
6For such a one this punishment by the majority is sufficient,
7so instead [of further rebuke, now] you should rather [graciously] forgive and comfort *and* encourage him, to keep him from being overwhelmed by excessive sorrow.
8Therefore I urge you to reinstate him in your affections *and* reaffirm your love for him.
9For this was my purpose in writing, to see if you would stand the test, whether you are obedient *and* committed to following my instruction in all things.
10If you forgive anyone anything, I too forgive [that one]; and what I have forgiven, if I have forgiven anything, has been for your sake in the presence of [and with the approval of] Christ,
11to keep Satan from taking advantage of us; for we are not ignorant of his schemes.
12Now when I arrived at Troas to *preach* the good news of Christ, even though a door [of opportunity] opened for me in the Lord,
13my spirit could not rest because I did not find my brother Titus *there;* so saying goodbye to them, I left for Macedonia.
14But thanks be to God, who always

---

mark of service to God which was given to kings and priests in the Old Testament. This anointing probably refers to special empowerment by the Holy Spirit, similar to the anointing that John described in 1 John 2:20,27.

1:22 *put His seal on us.* Sealing indicates ownership and security. The *sealing* and the *giving* of the Holy Spirit are also linked. The Holy Spirit is a guarantee, the down payment that there is more spiritual blessing to come and that the believer will receive eternal life.

2:5 *caused [all this] sorrow.* This is probably a reference to the incestuous man of 1 Corinthians 5.

2:7 *forgive and comfort and encourage him.* The purpose of church discipline is repentance and restoration. Forgiveness should always follow the correction, just as Christ instructed (Mt 18:15–35).

2:12 *Troas.* Troas was a city on the Aegean coast, where Paul had received his call to preach the gospel in Macedonia (Ac 16:8).

22 Eph 4:30; 2Ti 2:19; Rev 2:17; 2Co 5:5; Eph 1:14 **23** Ro 1:9; 2Co 11:31; Gal 1:20; Php 1:8; 1Co 4:21; 2Co 2:3; 12:20; 13:2,10 **24** 1Co 3:5; 1Pe 5:3; Ro 11:20; 1Co 15:1 **CHAPTER 2** **1** 2Co 1:23 **3** 2Co 12:21; 2Co 8:22; Gal 5:10 **4** 2Co 7:8,9 **5** 1Co 5:1; Gal 4:12 **6** 1Co 5:4,5; 1Ti 5:20 **7** Gal 6:1 **9** 2Co 10:6 **12** Ac 16:8; 1Co 16:9 **13** 2Co 7:5,6 **14** SS 1:3

leads us in triumph in Christ, and
through us spreads *and* makes evident
everywhere the sweet fragrance of the
knowledge of Him.
15 For we are the *sweet* fragrance of
Christ [which ascends] to God, [dis-
cernible both] among those who are
being saved and among those who are
perishing;
16 to the *latter* one an aroma from
death to death [a fatal, offensive odor],
but to the other an aroma from life to
life [a vital fragrance, living and fresh].
And who is adequate *and* sufficiently
qualified for these things?
17 For we are not like many, [acting
like merchants] peddling God's word
[shortchanging and adulterating God's
message]; but from pure [uncompro-
mised] motives, as [commissioned and
sent] from God, we speak [His mes-
sage] in Christ in the sight of God.

Ministers of a New Covenant

3 ARE WE starting to commend our-
selves again? Or do we need, like
some [false teachers], letters of recom-
mendation to you or from you? [No!]
2 You are our letter [of recommenda-
tion], written in our hearts, recognized
and read by everyone.
3 You show that you are a letter from
Christ, delivered by us, written not
with ink but with the Spirit of the liv-
ing God, not on tablets of stone but
on tablets of human hearts. [Ex 24:12;
31:18; 32:15, 16; Jer 31:33]
4 Such is the confidence *and* stead-
fast reliance *and* absolute trust that
we have through Christ toward God.
5 Not that we are sufficiently quali-
fied in ourselves to claim anything as
coming from us, but our sufficiency
and qualifications come from God.
6 He has qualified us [making us suf-
ficient] as ministers of a new covenant
[of salvation through Christ], not of
the letter [of a written code] but of the
Spirit; for the letter [of the Law] kills [by
revealing sin and demanding obedi-
ence], but the Spirit gives life. [Jer 31:31]
7 Now if the ministry of death, en-
graved in letters on stones [the cov-
enant of the Law which led to death
because of sin], came with such glory
and splendor that the Israelites were
not able to look steadily at the face
of Moses because of its glory, [a bril-
liance] that was fading, [Ex 34:29–35]
8 how will the ministry of the Spirit
[the new covenant which allows us to
be Spirit-filled] fail to be even more
glorious *and* splendid?
9 For if the ministry that brings con-
demnation [the old covenant, the Law]
has glory, how much more does glory
overflow in the ministry that brings
righteousness [the new covenant which
declares believers free of guilt and sets
them apart for God's special purpose]!
10 Indeed, what had glory [the Law],
in this case no longer has glory be-
cause of the glory that surpasses it
[the gospel].
11 For if that [Law] which fades away
came with glory, *how* much more *must*

2:16 *death to death.* The gospel message gives life to those who choose to accept it, but it represents death and judgment to those who reject it.

3:2 *You are our letter.* Paul sometimes did use letters of recommendation (8:22; Ro 16:1; 1Co 16:10; Col 4:10), but he did not need one for the Corinthians. They already knew him personally and had personally benefited from his ministry. Paul's love for the Corinthians was known to all who were acquainted with him. One of the qualifications for ministry is love for people, both God's people and the lost.

3:6 *not of the letter.* The "letter" is the old covenant of law. The "letter" kills because no one can be perfect enough to keep the whole law all the time, and the penalty for breaking it is death.

3:7 *ministry of death.* Though the law itself is holy (Ro 7:12), the ministry of the law is the ministry of death because the law defines and convicts of sin but offers no salvation.

3:9 *ministry that brings righteousness.* God declares righteous those who believe in His Son, and then the Holy Spirit empowers the believer to live righteously. This first work of God is called justification, and the second is called sanctification.

---

15 1Co 1:18; 2Co 4:3 **16** Lk 2:34; Jn 9:39; 1Pe 2:7; 1Co 15:10 **17** 2Pe 2:3; 2Co 1:12 **CHAPTER 3** **1** 2Co 5:12; Ac 18:27 **2** 1Co 9:2 **3** 1Co 3:5; Ex 24:12; Ps 40:8; Eze 11:19; Heb 8:10 **5** Jn 15:5; 1Co 15:10 **6** 1Co 3:5; Eph 3:7; Col 1:25; Jer 31:31; Mt 26:28; Heb 8:6,8; Ro 2:27; Ro 3:20; Gal 3:10; Jn 6:63; Ro 8:2 **7** Ro 7:10; Ex 34:1; Dt 10:1; Ex 34:29 **8** Gal 3:5 **9** Ro 1:17

that [gospel] which remains *and* is permanent abide in glory *and* splendor!

12 Since we have such a [glorious] hope *and* confident expectation, we speak with great courage,

13 and we are not like Moses, *who* used to put a veil over his face so that the Israelites would not gaze at the end of the glory which was fading away.

14 But [in fact] their minds were hardened [for they had lost the ability to understand]; for until this very day at the reading of the old covenant the same veil remains unlifted, because it is removed [only] in Christ.

15 But to this day whenever Moses is read, a veil [of blindness] lies over their heart;

16 but whenever a person turns [in repentance and faith] to the Lord, the veil is taken away.

17 Now the Lord is the Spirit, and where the Spirit of the Lord is, *there* is liberty [emancipation from bondage, true freedom]. [Is 61:1, 2]

18 And we all, with unveiled face, *continually* seeing as in a mirror the glory of the Lord, are *progressively* being transformed into His image from [one degree of] glory to [even more] glory, which comes from the Lord, [who is] the Spirit.

Paul's Apostolic Ministry

4 THEREFORE, SINCE we have this ministry, just as we received mercy [from God, granting us salvation, opportunities, and blessings], we do not get discouraged *nor* lose our motivation.

2 But we have renounced the disgraceful things hidden because of shame; not walking in trickery or adulterating the word of God, but by stating the truth [openly and plainly], we commend ourselves to everyone's conscience in the sight of God.

3 But even if our gospel is [in some sense] hidden [behind a veil], it is hidden [only] to those who are perishing;

4 among them the god of this world [Satan] has blinded the minds of the unbelieving to prevent them from seeing the illuminating light of the gospel of the glory of Christ, who is the image of God.

5 For we do not preach ourselves, but Jesus Christ as Lord, and ourselves [merely] as your bond-servants for Jesus' sake.

6 For God, who said, "Let light shine out of darkness," is the One who has shone in our hearts to give us the Light of the knowledge of the glory *and* majesty of God [clearly revealed] in the face of Christ. [Gen 1:3]

7 But we have this *precious* treasure [the good news about salvation] in [unworthy] earthen vessels [of human frailty], so that the grandeur *and* surpassing greatness of the power will be [shown to be] from God [His sufficiency] and not from ourselves.

8 We are pressured in every way [hedged in], but not crushed; perplexed

---

3:11 *that [gospel] which remains.* The new covenant supersedes the old covenant established at Mount Sinai between God and the nation of Israel.

3:18 *from [one degree of] glory to [even more] glory.* As believers behold the glory of God in the Word of God, the Spirit of God changes their hearts and actions to make them more and more like Jesus Christ.

4:2 *adulterating the word of God.* Apparently Paul had been accused of being crafty (12:16) and of being deceitful in the way that he preached. In fact, his ministry was based on the truthfulness of the word of God.

4:4 *blinded the minds of the unbelieving.* Because of Satan's deception, sometimes what the world thinks is obviously true is painfully wrong (Pr 14:12). ***image of God.*** Jesus Christ is God's Son, and He perfectly reveals God the Father to us. Human beings have been created in the image of God, but through sin they have fallen from a perfect relationship with God. Jesus Christ is restoring believers to what they were originally created to be (3:18; Ge 1:26).

4:8 *but not crushed.* As believers we will face trials, but we must remember that God controls trials and uses them to strengthen His people. God's glory is manifested through broken vessels,

---

12 2Co 7:4; Eph 6:19 **13** Ex 34:33; Ro 10:4; Gal 3:23 **14** Isa 6:10; Ac 28:26 **16** Ex 34:34; Ro 11:23; Isa 25:7 **17** 1Co 15:45 **18** 1Co 13:12; 2Co 4:4,6; Ro 8:29 **CHAPTER 4** **1** 2Co 3:6; 1Co 7:25 **2** 2Co 2:17; 2Co 6:4,7; 2Co 5:11 **3** 1Co 1:18 **4** Eph 6:12; Jn 12:40; 2Co 3:8,9; Jn 1:18; Heb 1:3 **5** 1Co 1:13; 10:33; 1Co 9:19 **6** Ge 1:3; 2Pe 1:19; 1Pe 2:9 **7** 2Co 5:1; 1Co 2:5 **8** 2Co 7:5

[unsure of finding a way out], but not driven to despair;

9 hunted down *and* persecuted, but not deserted [to stand alone]; struck down, but never destroyed;

10 always carrying around in the body the dying of Jesus, so that the [resurrection] life of Jesus also may be shown in our body.

11 For we who live are constantly [experiencing the threat of] being handed over to death for Jesus' sake, so that the [resurrection] life of Jesus also may be evidenced in our mortal body [which is subject to death].

12 So *physical* death is [actively] at work in us, but [spiritual] life [is actively at work] in you.

13 Yet we have the same spirit of faith as he had, who wrote *in Scripture*, "I BELIEVED, THEREFORE I SPOKE." We also believe, therefore we also speak, [Ps 116:10]

14 knowing that He who raised the Lord Jesus will also raise us with Jesus and will present us [along] with you in His presence.

15 For all [these] things are for your sake, so that as [God's remarkable, undeserved] grace reaches to more and more people it may increase thanksgiving, to the glory of [our great] God.

16 Therefore we do not become discouraged [spiritless, disappointed, or afraid]. Though our outer self is [progressively] wasting away, yet our inner *self* is being [progressively] renewed day by day.

17 For our momentary, light distress [this passing trouble] is producing for us an eternal weight of glory [a fullness] beyond all measure [surpassing all comparisons, a transcendent splendor and an endless blessedness]!

18 So we look not at the things which are seen, but at the things which are unseen; for the things which are visible are temporal [just brief and fleeting], but the things which are invisible are everlasting *and* imperishable.

The Temporal and Eternal

5 FOR WE know that if the earthly tent [our physical body] which is our house is torn down [through death], we have a building from God, a house not made with hands, eternal in the heavens.

2 For indeed in this *house* we groan, longing to be clothed with our [immortal, eternal] celestial dwelling,

3 so that by putting it on we will not be found naked.

4 For while we are in this tent, we groan, being burdened [often weighed down, oppressed], not that we want to be unclothed [separated by death from the body], but to be clothed, so that what is mortal [the body] will be swallowed up by life [after the resurrection].

5 Now He who has made us *and* prepared us for this very purpose is God, who gave us the [Holy] Spirit as a pledge [a guarantee, a down payment on the fulfillment of His promise].

6 So then, being always filled with good courage *and* confident hope, and knowing that while we are at home

---

through people who endure troubles by relying on His power.

4:9 *struck down.* This literally happened (Ac 14:19). In Lystra a crowd stoned Paul, leaving him for dead. But the Lord spared his life so that he could continue to preach the gospel and testify to God's deliverance.

4:12 *life [is actively at work] in you.* Had Paul not been willing to risk death to bring the gospel to Corinth, the Corinthians would not have received eternal life.

4:17 *producing for us.* Afflictions produce glory, but the glory is far greater than the affliction (Mk 10:30).

5:2 *we groan.* Along with the rest of creation, our spirits cry out for what we were meant to be (Ro 8:22–23).

5:5 *a pledge.* The Holy Spirit's work in believers' lives can be compared to a down payment, or a pledge (1:22). The presence of the Holy Spirit assures believers that God has purchased them. They are no longer slaves to sin, but are now His children.

---

9 Ps 37:24 **10** Php 3:10; Ro 8:17 **11** Ro 8:36 **12** 2Co 13:9 **13** 2Pe 1:1; Ps 116:10 **14** Ro 8:11; 1Co 6:14 **15** Col 1:24; 2Ti 2:10; 2Co 1:11 **16** Ro 7:22; Col 3:10 **17** Mt 5:12; Ro 8:18; 1Pe 1:6 **18** Ro 8:24; Heb 11:1
CHAPTER 5 **1** Job 4:19 **2** Ro 8:23 **3** Rev 3:18 **4** 1Co 15:53 **5** Isa 29:23; Eph 2:10; Ro 8:23; Eph 1:14

in the body we are absent from the
Lord—
7for we walk by faith, not by sight
[living our lives in a manner consis-
tent with our confident belief in God's
promises]—
8we are [as I was saying] of good
courage *and* confident hope, and pre-
fer rather to be absent from the body
and to be at home with the Lord.
9Therefore, whether we are at home
[on earth] or away from home [and
with Him], it is our [constant] ambition
to be pleasing to Him.
10For we [believers will be called to
account and] must all appear before
the judgment seat of Christ, so that
each one may be repaid for what has
been done in the body, whether good or
bad [that is, each will be held respon-
sible for his actions, purposes, goals,
motives—the use or misuse of his time,
opportunities and abilities].
11Therefore, since we know the fear
of the Lord [and understand the im-
portance of obedience and worship],
we persuade people [to be reconciled
to Him]. But we are plainly known to
God [He knows everything about us];
and I hope that we are plainly known
also in your consciences [your God-
given discernment].
12We are not commending ourselves
to you again, but are giving you an
occasion to be [rightfully] proud of
us, so that you will have *an answer*
for those who take pride in [outward]
appearances [the virtues they pretend
to have] rather than what is [actually]
in heart.
13If we are out of our mind [just un-
stable fanatics as some critics say], it
is for God; if we are in our right mind,
it is for your benefit.
14For the love of Christ controls *and*
compels us, because we have conclud-
ed this, that One died for all, therefore
all died;
15and He died for all, so that all those
who live would no longer live for them-
selves, but for Him who died and was
raised for their sake.
16So from now on we regard no one
from a human point of view [accord-
ing to worldly standards and values].
Though we have known Christ from a
human point of view, now we no longer
know Him *in this way*.
17Therefore if anyone is in Christ
[that is, grafted in, joined to Him by
faith in Him as Savior], *he is* a new
creature [reborn and renewed by the
Holy Spirit]; the old things [the previ-
ous moral and spiritual condition] have

5:8 *be at home with the Lord.* This is one of the passages indicating where believers will go after death; they will be with Jesus in heaven (Lk 23:43; Php 1:23).

5:9 *our [constant] ambition.* Pleasing the Lord should always be our first concern in this life, since it is the only thing which will carry over into the next life.

5:10 *what has been done in the body.* The believer will either be approved or ashamed (5:3; Lk 19:11–26; 1Co 3:14–15; 9:27; 1Jn 2:28; 2Jn 7–8).

5:11 *fear of the Lord.* This is the fear of standing before the Lord and having one's life exposed and evaluated. The reality of giving an account to the Lord motivated Paul to persuade people, in this context meaning to convince the Corinthians of his sincerity and integrity.

5:14 *love of Christ.* This phrase can mean either Christ's love for us or our love for Christ.

5:15 *for Him.* Believers are united with Jesus both in His death and in His resurrection, and therefore they participate in the new creation. That is, they receive the benefits of being restored by Christ to what God had originally created them to be (Ge 1:26; 1Co 15:45–49).

5:17 Our New Nature—The term "new nature" refers to the spiritual transformation that occurs within people when they believe in Christ as Savior. New does not mean renewed, renovated, reformed, or rehabilitated. It means completely and distinctly new, with a new family, a new set of values, new motivations, and a whole new life. The old man is still present in the new life and expresses himself in sinful deeds such as lying (Eph 4:22; Col 3:9). The new man, to be visible, must be *put on*, as one would put on a new suit of clothes (Col 3:10). In other words, the new nature must be cultivated or nurtured by spiritual decisiveness to grow in Christ. We must not revert to putting

---

7 Ro 8:24; Heb 11:1 **8** Php 1:23 **10** Ro 14:10; Gal 6:7; Eph 6:8; Rev 22:12 **11** Heb 10:31; Jude 23; 2Co 4:2 **12** 2Co 3:1; 2Co 1:14 **13** 2Co 11:1,16 **14** Ro 5:15 **15** Ro 6:11; 1Co 6:19; Gal 2:20 **16** Mt 12:50; Col 3:11; Jn 6:63 **17** Ro 8:9; Gal 5:6; Isa 65:17; Eph 2:15; Rev 21:5

passed away. Behold, new things have come [because spiritual awakening brings a new life].

18 But all *these* things are from God, who reconciled us to Himself through Christ [making us acceptable to Him] and gave us the ministry of reconciliation [so that by our example we might bring others to Him],

19 that is, that God was in Christ reconciling the world to Himself, not counting people's sins against them [but canceling them]. And He has committed to us the message of reconciliation [that is, restoration to favor with God].

20 So we are ambassadors for Christ, as though God were making His appeal through us; we [as Christ's representatives] plead with you on behalf of Christ to be reconciled to God.

21 He made Christ who knew no sin to [judicially] be sin on our behalf, so that in Him we would become the righteousness of God [that is, we would be made acceptable to Him and placed in a right relationship with Him by His gracious lovingkindness].

Their Ministry Commended

6 WORKING TOGETHER *with Him,* we strongly urge you not to receive God's grace in vain [by turning away from sound doctrine and His merciful kindness].

2 For He says,

"AT THE ACCEPTABLE TIME (the time of grace) I LISTENED TO YOU,
AND I HELPED YOU ON THE DAY OF SALVATION."

Behold, now is "THE ACCEPTABLE TIME," behold, now is "THE DAY OF SALVATION"—[Is 49:8]

3 we put no obstruction in anyone's path, so that the ministry will not be discredited,

4 but we commend ourselves in every way as servants of God: in great endurance, in sufferings, in hardships, in distresses,

5 in beatings, in imprisonments, in riots, in labors, in sleepless nights, in hunger,

6 in purity *and* sincerity, in knowledge *and* spiritual insight, in patience, in kindness, in the Holy Spirit, in genuine love,

7 in [speaking] the word of truth, in the power of God; by the weapons of righteousness for the right hand [like holding the sword to attack] and for the left [like holding the shield to defend],

8 amid glory and dishonor; by evil report and good report; *branded* as deceivers and yet [vindicated as] truthful;

9 as unknown [to the world], yet well-known [by God and His people]; as

---

on the old suit of the former life; rather, we must continue to grow in this new life (Eph 5:8).

5:18 *ministry of reconciliation.* Reconciliation is the change of relation from enmity to peace. We who have been reconciled to God through Christ have the privilege of telling others that they can be reconciled to Him as well.

5:19 *reconciling the world to Himself.* God could change His relationship toward us because our sins have been imputed (charged) to Christ instead of to us. If we believe in Jesus, God counts Jesus' righteousness as our righteousness (v. 21).

5:20 *ambassadors.* Ambassadors are representatives of the sovereign who sends them, the "stand in" for their own ruler in a foreign country. Christians have been called by their King to serve as ambassadors in a world that is in rebellion against Him, with the responsibility to bring a message of peace and of reconciliation.

6:1 *in vain.* Believers who live for themselves may have received the grace of God, but they will miss out on a heavenly reward for their service to Him. Paul encourages those who have been saved to work out or develop their salvation (Php 2:12). The Corinthians were failing at this very point. They were saved and stuck, so to speak.

6:4 *in great endurance.* Believers must not expect that it will be easy or comfortable to be a disciple, but it will be more deeply fulfilling than anything else could be.

18 Ro 5:10; Eph 2:16; Col 1:20 **19** Ro 3:24 **20** Job 33:23; Mal 2:7; Eph 6:20; 2Co 6:1 **21** Isa 53:6,9; Gal 3:13; 1Pe 2:22; 1Jn 3:5; Ro 1:17; 10:3 **CHAPTER 6** **1** 1Co 3:9; 2Co 5:20; Heb 12:15 **2** Isa 49:8 **3** Ro 14:13; 1Co 9:12; 10:32 **4** 1Co 4:1 **5** 2Co 11:23 **7** 2Co 7:14; 1Co 2:4; 2Co 10:4; Eph 6:11; 2Ti 4:7 **9** 2Co 4:2; 5:11; 1Co 4:9; 2Co 1:9; 4:10,11; Ps 118:18

dying, yet we live; as punished, yet not killed;

10 as sorrowful, yet always rejoicing; as poor, yet bestowing riches on many; as having nothing, yet possessing all things.

11 We are speaking freely to you, Corinthians [we are keeping nothing back], and our heart is opened wide. [Is 60:5; Ezek 33:22]

12 There is no limit to our affection for you, but you are limited in your own affection [for us].

13 Now in the same way as a fair exchange [for our love toward you]—I am speaking as [I would] to children—open wide [your hearts] *to us* also.

14 Do not be unequally bound together with unbelievers [do not make mismatched alliances with them, inconsistent with your faith]. For what partnership can righteousness have with lawlessness? Or what fellowship can light have with darkness?

15 What harmony can there be between Christ and Belial (Satan)? Or what does a believer have in common with an unbeliever?

16 What agreement is there between the temple of God and idols? For we are the temple of the living God; just as God said:

"I WILL DWELL AMONG THEM AND WALK
AMONG THEM;
AND I WILL BE THEIR GOD, AND THEY
SHALL BE MY PEOPLE. [Ex 25:8;
29:45; Lev 26:12; Jer 31:1;
Ezek 37:27]

17 "SO COME OUT FROM AMONG
UNBELIEVERS AND BE SEPARATE,"
says the Lord,
"AND DO NOT TOUCH WHAT IS UNCLEAN;
And I will graciously receive you
and welcome you [with favor],
[Is 52:11]
18 And I will be a Father to you,
And you will be My sons and
daughters,"
Says the Lord Almighty. [Is 43:6;
Hos 1:10]

Paul Reveals His Heart

7 THEREFORE, SINCE we have these [great and wonderful] promises, beloved, let us cleanse ourselves from everything that contaminates body and spirit, completing holiness [living a consecrated life—a life set apart for God's purpose] in the fear of God.

2 Make room for us *in your hearts;* we have wronged no one, we have corrupted no one, we have cheated no one.

3 I do not say *this* to condemn *you,* for I have said before that you are [nested] in our hearts [and you will remain there] to die together and to live together [with us].

4 Great is my confidence in you; great is my pride *and* boasting on your behalf. I am filled [to the brim] with comfort; I am overflowing with joy in spite of all our trouble.

5 For even when we arrived in Macedonia our bodies had no rest, but we were oppressed at every turn—

6:14 *unequally bound together with unbelievers.* This verse has most often been applied to the subject of marriage, warning believers not to bind themselves for life to one who does not love the Lord.
6:15 *Belial.* This term for Satan occurs only here in the New Testament. It refers to one who is vile and wicked and who causes destruction.
6:16 *we are the temple.* This reference to Leviticus 26:11 – 12 and Ezekiel 37:27 reminds believers of their relationship with God. Since the Holy Spirit is living in them, they are God's new dwelling place (1Co 6:19).
6:17 *BE SEPARATE.* Paul was not encouraging isolation from unbelievers (1Co 9:5 – 13) but discouraging compromise with their sinful values and practices. He was urging them (and us) to maintain integrity in the world just as Christ did (Jn 15:14 – 16; Php 2:14 – 16).
7:1 *completing holiness.* This means dedicating ourselves to Christ and living righteously (Heb 6:1).
7:3 *you are [nested] in our hearts.* Paul was not throwing his weight around or trying to be controlling. He loved the Corinthians and wanted the very best for them.

11 2Co 7:3 **12** 2Co 12:15 **13** 1Co 4:14 **14** Dt 7:2,3; 1Co 5:9; 1Sa 5:2,3; 1Ki 18:21; 1Co 10:21; Eph 5:7,11 **16** 1Co 3:16; 6:19; Eph 2:21; Heb 3:6; Ex 29:45; Lev 26:12; Jer 31:33; 32:38; Eze 11:20; Zec 13:9 **17** Isa 52:11; Rev 18:4 **18** Jer 31:1,9; Rev 21:7 **CHAPTER 7** **1** 1Jn 3:3 **2** Ac 20:33 **3** 2Co 6:11,12 **4** 2Co 3:12; 1Co 1:4; Php 2:17; Col 1:24 **5** 2Co 2:13; 2Co 4:8; Dt 32:35

conflicts *and* disputes without, fears
and dread within.
6 But God, who comforts *and* encour-
ages the depressed *and* the disquieted,
comforted us by the arrival of Titus.
7 And not only by his arrival, but also
by [his account of] the encouragement
which he received in regard to you. He
told us about your longing [for us], your
mourning [over sin], *and* how eagerly
you took my part and supported me,
so that I rejoiced even more.
8 For even though I did grieve you
with my letter, I do not regret it [now];
though I did regret it —for I see that
the letter hurt you, though only for a
little while—
9 yet I am glad now, not because you
were hurt *and* made sorry, but because
your sorrow led to repentance [and you
turned back to God]; for you felt a grief
such as God meant you to feel, so that
you might not suffer loss in anything
on our account.
10 For [godly] sorrow that is in ac-
cord with *the will of* God produces
a repentance without regret, *leading*
to salvation; but worldly sorrow [the
hopeless sorrow of those who do not
believe] produces death.
11 For [you can look back and] see
what an earnestness *and* authentic
concern this godly sorrow has pro-
duced in you: what vindication of
yourselves [against charges that you
tolerate sin], what indignation [at sin],
what fear [of offending God], what
longing [for righteousness and justice],
what passion [to do what is right], what
readiness to punish [those who sin
and those who tolerate sin]! At every
point you have proved yourselves to be
innocent in the matter.
12 So even though I wrote to you [as
I did], it was not for the sake of the
offender nor for the sake of the one
offended, but in order to make evident
to you before God how earnestly you
do care for us [and your willingness to
accept our authority].
13 It is for this reason that we are
comforted *and* encouraged.
And in addition to our comfort, we
were especially delighted at the joy
of Titus, because you have refreshed
his spirit.
14 For if I have boasted to him at all
concerning you, I was not disappoint-
ed. But just as everything we ever said
to you was true, so our boasting [about
you] to Titus has proved true also.
15 His affection is greater than ever
as he remembers the obedience [to his
guidance] that all of you exhibited,
and how you received him with the
greatest respect.
16 I rejoice that in everything I have
[perfect] confidence in you.

Great Generosity

8 NOW, BROTHERS and sisters, we
want to tell you about the grace of
God which has been evident in the
churches of Macedonia [awakening in
them a longing to contribute];
2 for during an ordeal of severe dis-
tress, their abundant joy and their deep
poverty [together] overflowed in the
wealth of their lavish generosity.
3 For I testify that according to their
ability, and beyond their ability, *they
gave* voluntarily,
4 begging us insistently for the priv-
ilege of participating in the service
for [the support of] the saints [in
Jerusalem].
5 Not only [did they give materially]
as we had hoped, but first they gave
themselves to the Lord and to us [as His
representatives] by the will of God [dis-
regarding their personal interests and
giving as much as they possibly could].

7:10 *produces a repentance.* A person can be sorry that he or she was caught in sin, or sorry to have to bear the consequences, without repenting of sin. True sorrow leads to a change of heart and a turning to God. Repentance means changing direction, and results in spiritual deliverance.

8:1 *Macedonia.* Macedonia corresponds to the northern part of present day Greece. Paul had established churches in the Macedonian cities of Philippi, Thessalonica, and Berea.

6 2Co 1:4; See 2Co 2:13 **8** 2Co 2:4 **10** 2Sa 12:13; Mt 26:75; Pr 17:22 **12** 2Co 2:4 **13** Ro 15:32 **15** 2Co 2:9; Php 2:12 **16** 2Th 3:4; Php 8,21 **CHAPTER 8** **2** Mk 12:44 **4** Ac 11:29; 24:17; Ro 15:25,26; 1Co 16:1,3,4; 2Co 9:1

6 So we urged Titus that, as he began it, he should also complete this gracious work among you as well.

7 But just as you excel in everything, [and lead the way] in faith, in speech, in knowledge, in genuine concern, and in your love for us, see that you excel in this gracious work [of giving] also.

8 I am not saying *this* as a command [to dictate to you], but to prove, by [pointing out] the enthusiasm of others, the sincerity of your love as well.

9 For you are recognizing [more clearly] the grace of our Lord Jesus Christ [His astonishing kindness, His generosity, His gracious favor], that though He was rich, yet for your sake He became poor, so that by His poverty you might become rich (abundantly blessed).

10 I give you *my* opinion in this matter: this is to your advantage, who were the first to begin a year ago not only to take action [to help the believers in Jerusalem], but also [the first] to desire *to do it.*

11 So now finish this, so that your eagerness in desiring it may be equaled by your completion of it, according to your ability.

12 For if the eagerness [to give] is there, it is acceptable according to what one has, not according to what he does not have.

13 For it is not [intended] that others be relieved [of their responsibility] and that you be burdened [unfairly], but that there be equality [in sharing the burden]—

14 at this present time your surplus [over necessities] *is going* to *supply* their need, so that [at some other time] their surplus may be *given* to *supply* your need, that there may be equality;

15 as it is written [in Scripture], "HE WHO *gathered* MUCH DID NOT HAVE TOO MUCH, AND HE WHO *gathered* LITTLE DID NOT LACK." [Ex 16:18]

16 But thanks be to God who puts the same genuine concern for you in the heart of Titus.

17 For Titus not only accepted our appeal, but was so very interested in you that he has gone to *visit* you of his own accord.

18 And we have sent along with him the brother who is praised in the gospel [ministry] throughout all the churches;

19 and not only *this,* but he has also been appointed by the churches to travel with us in regard to this gracious offering which we are administering for the glory of the Lord Himself, and *to show* our eagerness [as believers to help one another].

20 We are taking precaution so that no one will [find anything with which to] discredit us in our administration of this generous gift.

21 For we have regard for what is honorable [and above suspicion], not only in the sight of the Lord, but also in the sight of men.

22 We have sent with them our brother, whom we have often tested and found to be diligent in many things, but who is now even more diligent [than ever] because of his great confidence in you.

23 As for Titus, *he is* my partner and fellow worker in your service; and as for the [other two] brothers, *they are* [special] messengers of the churches, a glory *and* credit to Christ.

24 Therefore, show these men, in the sight of the churches, the proof of your love and our reason for being proud of you.

God Gives Most

9 NOW IT is unnecessary for me to write to you about the offering [that is to be made] for the saints [in Jerusalem];

8:8 *prove . . . the sincerity of your love.* Generosity is the natural result of sincere love.

8:9 *you might become rich.* Jesus offers forgiveness, justification, regeneration, eternal life, and glorification. He purchased us from slavery to sin, giving us the position of children of God with free access to His presence.

8:10 *to your advantage.* Giving in this life is an investment for eternity (Mt 6:19 – 21).

---

6 ver. 17; 2Co 12:18 **7** 1Co 1:5; 12:13; 2Co 9:8 **8** 1Co 7:6 **9** Mt 8:20; Lk 9:58; Php 2:6,7 **10** 1Co 7:25; Pr 19:17; Mt 10:42; 1Ti 6:18, 19; Heb 13:16; 2Co 9:2 **12** Mk 12:43,44; Lk 21:3 **15** Ex 16:18 **17** ver. 6 **18** 2Co 12:18 **19** 1Co 16:3,4; 2Co 4:15 **21** Ro 12:17; Php 4:8; 1Pe 2:12 **23** Php 2:25 **24** 2Co 7:14; 9:2
CHAPTER 9 **1** Ac 11:29; Ro 15:26; 1Co 16:1; 2Co 8:4; Gal 2:10

[2]for I know your eagerness [to promote this cause], and I have [proudly] boasted to the people of Macedonia about it, telling them that Achaia has been prepared since last year [for this contribution], and your enthusiasm has inspired the majority of them [to respond].
[3]Still, I am sending the brothers [on to you], so that our pride in you may not be an empty boast in this case, and so that you may be prepared, just as I told them you would be;
[4]otherwise, if any Macedonians come with me and find you unprepared, we—to say nothing of yourselves—will be humiliated for being so confident.
[5]That is why I thought it necessary to urge these brothers to go to you [before I come] and make arrangements in advance for this generous, previously promised gift of yours, so that it would be ready, not as something extorted [or wrung out of you], but as a [voluntary and] generous gift.
[6]Now [remember] this: he who sows sparingly will also reap sparingly, and he who sows generously [that blessings may come to others] will also reap generously [and be blessed].
[7]Let each one give [thoughtfully and with purpose] just as he has decided in his heart, not grudgingly or under compulsion, for God loves a cheerful giver [and delights in the one whose heart is in his gift]. [Prov 22:9]
[8]And God is able to make all grace [every favor and earthly blessing] come in abundance to you, so that you may always [under all circumstances, regardless of the need] have complete sufficiency in everything [being completely self-sufficient in Him], and have an abundance for every good work *and* act of charity.
[9]As it is written *and* forever remains written,

"He [the benevolent and generous person] SCATTERED ABROAD, HE GAVE TO THE POOR,
HIS RIGHTEOUSNESS ENDURES FOREVER!" [Ps 112:9]

[10]Now He who provides seed for the sower and bread for food will provide and multiply your seed for sowing [that is, your resources] and increase the harvest of your righteousness [which shows itself in active goodness, kindness, and love]. [Is 55:10; Hos 10:12]
[11]You will be enriched in every way so that you may be generous, and this [generosity, administered] through us is producing thanksgiving to God [from those who benefit].
[12]For the ministry of this service (offering) is not only supplying the needs of the saints (God's people), but is also overflowing through many expressions of thanksgiving to God.
[13]Because of this act of ministry, they will glorify God for your obedience to the gospel of Christ which you confess, as well as for your generous

---

9:4 *any Macedonians.* Paul was in Macedonia when he wrote this letter (2:13; 7:5). When he made his visit to Corinth he would no doubt bring traveling companions from Macedonia.

9:6–8 Giving—There is no better indicator of growth in the new life than in the area of giving. This passage and others deal with several aspects of giving:

Giving should be done generously, even extravagantly (2Co 9:6).
Giving should be done cheerfully (2Co 9:7).
Giving should be regular (1Co 16:2).
Giving should be systematic (1Co 16:2).
Giving should be proportionate (2Co 8:3).

God is not primarily concerned about the amount of the gift, but with the motive that lies behind it. The person who fails to honor God with his money actually robs God (Mal 3:8), not because it impoverishes God but because it denies the God-ordained means for the support of His work and His ministers. For the child of God who honors God with his money, God promises abundant blessing (Mal 3:10; Lk 6:38) and the provision of his every need (Php 4:19).

9:6 *also reap sparingly.* The law of the harvest is referred to repeatedly in Scripture (Pr 11:24–25; 19:17; Lk 6:38; Gal 6:7). If you do not plant, you will have no harvest.

9:8 *God is able.* God sees to it that the generous giver will not suffer want. Instead, God generously provides for those who give so that they can continue to do so.

2 2Co 8:19; 2Co 8:24; 2Co 8:10 **3** 2Co 8:6,17 **6** Pr 11:24 **7** Dt 15:7; Ex 35:5; Pr 11:25; Ro 12:8; 2Co 8:12 **8** Pr 11:24; Php 4:19 **9** Ps 112:9 **10** Isa 55:10; Hos 10:12; Mt 6:1 **11** 2Co 1:11 **12** 2Co 8:14 **13** Mt 5:16; Heb 13:16

participation [in this gift] for them and for all [the other believers in need],

14 and they also long for you while they pray on your behalf, because of the surpassing measure of God's grace [His undeserved favor, mercy, and blessing which is revealed] in you.

15 Now thanks be to God for His indescribable gift [which is precious beyond words]!

Paul Describes Himself

10 NOW I, Paul, urge you by the gentleness and graciousness of Christ—I who am meek [so they say] when with you face to face, but bold [outspoken and fearless] toward you when absent!

2 I ask that when I do come I will not be driven to the boldness that I intend to show toward those few who regard us as if we walked according to the flesh [like men without the Spirit].

3 For though we walk in the flesh [as mortal men], we are not carrying on our [spiritual] warfare according to the flesh *and* using the weapons of man.

4 The weapons of our warfare are not physical [weapons of flesh and blood]. Our weapons are divinely powerful for the destruction of fortresses.

5 *We are* destroying sophisticated arguments and every exalted *and* proud thing that sets itself up against the [true] knowledge of God, and *we are* taking every thought *and* purpose captive to the obedience of Christ,

6 being ready to punish every act of disobedience, when your own obedience [as a church] is complete.

7 You are looking [only] at the outward appearance of things. If anyone is confident that he is Christ's, he should reflect *and* consider this, that just as he is Christ's, so too are we.

8 For even though I boast rather freely about the authority the Lord gave us for building you up and not for destroying you, I will not be ashamed [of the truth],

9 nor do I want to seem to be trying to frighten you with my letters;

10 for they say, "His letters are weighty and forceful *and* impressive, but his personal presence is unimpressive and his speech contemptible [of no account]."

11 Let such people realize that what we say by word in letters when we are absent, is the same as what *we are* in action when present.

12 We do not have the audacity to put ourselves in the same class or compare ourselves with some who [supply testimonials to] commend themselves. When they measure themselves by themselves and compare themselves with themselves, they lack wisdom *and* behave like fools.

13 We, on the other hand, will not boast beyond our proper limit, but [will keep] within the limits of our commission (territory, authority) which God has granted to us as a measure, which reaches *and* includes even you.

14 We are not overstepping the limits of our province, as if we did not [legitimately] reach to you, for we were the [very] first to come even as far as you with the good news of Christ.

15 We do not go beyond our proper limit, boasting in the work of other men, but we have the hope that as your faith [in Christ and His divine power] continues to grow, our field among you may be greatly expanded [but still within the limits of our commission],

16 so that *we may* preach the gospel even in the lands beyond you, but not

---

9:15 *indescribable gift.* Our gifts can never compare with God's sacrifice for us.

10:4 *our warfare.* The world is hostile to Christ and His followers because the world is following Satan. The life of a believer is not one of ease but a constant spiritual battle.

10:8 *building you up.* Paul's exhortation was aimed at correcting abuses, not the tearing down of the church.

10:16 *lands beyond you.* Paul states in Romans that his ambition was to preach the gospel in Spain (Ro 15:24).

14 2Co 8:1 **15** Jas 1:17 **CHAPTER 10** **1** Ro 12:1; 2Co 12:5 **2** 1Co 4:21; 2Co 13:2,10 **4** Eph 6:13; 1Th 5:8; 1Ti 1:18; 2Ti 2:3; Ac 7:22; 1Co 2:5; Jer 1:10 **5** 1Co 1:19 **6** 2Co 13:2,10; 2Co 7:15 **7** Jn 7:24; 1Co 14:37; 1Jn 4:6; 1Co 3:23; 2Co 11:23 **8** 2Co 13:10; 2Co 7:14 **10** 1Co 2:3,4; Gal 4:13; 1Co 1:17 **12** 2Co 5:12 **13** ver. 15 **14** 1Co 3:5 **15** Ro 15:20

to boast in work already accomplished in another one's field of activity.
[17]However, "LET HIM WHO BOASTS BOAST IN THE LORD." [Jer 9:24]
[18]For it is not he who commends *and* praises himself who is approved [by God], but it is the one whom the Lord commends *and* praises.

Paul Defends His Apostleship

11 I WISH you would bear with me [while I indulge] in a little foolishness; but indeed you are bearing with me [as you read this].
[2]I am jealous for you with a godly jealousy because I have promised you to one husband, to present you as a pure virgin to Christ. [Hos 2:19, 20]
[3]But I am afraid that, even as the serpent beguiled Eve by his cunning, your minds may be corrupted *and* led away from the simplicity of [your sincere and] pure devotion to Christ. [Gen 3:4]
[4]For [you seem willing to allow it] if one comes and preaches another Jesus whom we have not preached, or if you receive a different spirit from the one you received, or a different gospel from the one you accepted. You tolerate all this beautifully [welcoming the deception].
[5]Yet I consider myself in no way inferior to the [so-called] super-apostles.
[6]But even if I am unskilled in speaking, yet I am not [untrained] in knowledge [I know what I am talking about]; but we have made this evident to you in every way, in all things.
[7]Or did I [perhaps] sin by humbling myself so that you might be exalted *and* honored, because I preached God's gospel to you free of charge?
[8]I robbed other churches by accepting [more than their share of] financial support for my ministry to you.
[9]And when I was with you and ran short [financially], I did not burden any of you; for what I needed was fully supplied by the brothers (Silas and Timothy) who came from Macedonia (the church at Philippi). So I kept myself from being a burden to you in any way, and will continue to do so. [Phil 4:15, 16]
[10]As the truth of Christ is in me, my boast [of independence] will not be silenced in the regions of Achaia (southern Greece).
[11]Why? Because I do not love you [or wish you well, or have regard for your welfare]? God knows [that I do]!
[12]But what I am doing I will keep doing, [for I am determined to keep this independence] in order to cut off the claim of those who want an opportunity to be regarded just as we are in the things they brag about.
[13]For such men are counterfeit apostles, deceitful workers, masquerading as apostles of Christ.
[14]And no wonder, since Satan himself masquerades as an angel of light.
[15]So it is no great surprise if his servants also masquerade as servants of righteousness, but their end will correspond with their deeds.
[16]I repeat then, let no one think that I am foolish; but even if you do, at least accept me as foolish, so that I too may boast a little.

11:2 *jealous.* Usually jealousy has a negative connotation to us—we confuse jealousy with envy or spite. The word has the same root as "zealous," and it can mean a sincere and energetic protection of the rights or purity of a person or place.
11:3 *simplicity.* In this sense, simplicity indicates sincerity or lack of double motives or cunning.
11:6 *unskilled in speaking.* Paul may have lacked gifts as a professional speaker, but he did not lack knowledge since he had received direct revelation from the Lord (Gal 1:11–12).
11:7 *free of charge.* Professional philosophers and teachers in Greek society charged for teaching.
11:14 *masquerades as an angel of light.* Don't make the mistake of believing that evil always appears grotesque, ugly, or repulsive. Satan's main tool is deception and he is quite capable of making evil appear beautiful.

17 Isa 65:16; Jer 9:24; 1Co 1:31 **18** Pr 27:2; Ro 2:29; 1Co 4:5 **CHAPTER 11** **1** ver. 16; 2Co 5:13 **2** Gal 4:17; Hos 2:19; 1Co 4:15; Col 1:28; Lev 21:13 **3** Ge 3:4; Jn 8:44; Eph 6:24; Col 2:4,8; 1Ti 1:3 **4** Gal 1:7,8 **5** 1Co 15:10 **6** 1Co 1:17; Eph 3:4; 2Co 12:12 **9** Ac 20:33; 1Th 2:9; Php 4:10; 2Co 12:14 **10** Ro 9:1; 1Co 9:15 **11** 2Co 6:11 **12** 1Co 9:12 **13** Ac 15:24; Ro 16:18; Gal 1:7; Php 1:15; 2Pe 2:1; Rev 2:2; Php 3:2; Titus 1:10 **14** Gal 1:8 **15** Php 3:19

[17]What I say in this confident boast-
ing, I say not as the Lord would [with
His authority], but foolishly.
[18]Since many boast [of worldly
things and brag] about human accom-
plishments, I will boast too.
[19]For you, being so wise, gladly tol-
erate *and* accept the foolish [like me]!
[20]For you tolerate it if anyone makes
you his slave; or devours you *and* your
possessions; or takes advantage of you;
or acts presumptuously; or hits you in
the face.
[21]To my shame, I must say, we have
been too weak [in comparison to those
pseudo-apostles who take advantage
of you].
But in whatever anyone else dares
to boast—I am speaking foolishly—I
also dare to boast.
[22]Are they Hebrews? So am I. Are
they Israelites? So am I. Are they de-
scendants of Abraham? So am I.
[23]Are they [self-proclaimed] servants
of Christ?—I am speaking as if I were
out of my mind—I am more so [for I
exceed them]; with far more labors,
with far more imprisonments, beaten
times without number, and often in
danger of death.
[24]Five times I received from the Jews
thirty-nine *lashes.* [Deut 25:3]
[25]Three times I was beaten with
rods, once I was stoned. Three times I
was shipwrecked, a night and a day I
have spent *adrift* on the sea;
[26]many times on journeys, [exposed
to] danger from rivers, danger from
bandits, danger from my own country-
men, danger from the Gentiles, danger
in the city, danger in the wilderness,
danger on the sea, danger among
those posing as believers;
[27]in labor and hardship, often unable
to sleep, in hunger and thirst, often
[driven to] fasting [for lack of food], in
cold and exposure [without adequate
clothing].
[28]Besides those external things,
there is the daily [inescapable] pres-
sure of my concern for all the churches.
[29]Who is weak, and I do not feel [his]
weakness? Who is made to sin, and I
am not on fire [with sorrow and con-
cern]?
[30]If I must boast, I will boast of the
things that reveal my weakness [the
things by which I am made weak in
the eyes of my opponents].
[31]The God and Father of the Lord
Jesus, He who is blessed *and* to be
praised forevermore, knows that I am
not lying.
[32]In Damascus the governor (eth-
narch) under King Aretas guarded the
city of Damascus in order to arrest me,
[33]and I was [actually] let down in a
basket through a window in the wall,
and slipped through his fingers.

Paul's Vision

12 IT IS necessary to boast, though
nothing is gained by it; but I will
go on to visions and revelations of the
Lord.
[2]I know a man in Christ who four-
teen years ago—whether in the body
I do not know, or out of the body I do

11:17 ***I say not as the Lord would.*** This kind of boasting was not characteristic of the Lord. Jesus Christ was an example of humility (Php 2:5 – 11).
11:18 ***about human accomplishments.*** The false apostles measured themselves by their own standards rather than by God's.
11:21 ***we have been too weak.*** Paul's critics had accused him of being weak (10:10). He sarcastically said that he was too weak to rule the Corinthians harshly as the false apostles had done.
11:23 ***as if I were out of my mind.*** Paul acknowledged the silliness of such bragging. He knew that only God had made his preaching and service effective. Paul's credentials were superior to those of the false teachers on every point of experience and background, but even so his ministry had authority only because he received it from God.
12:1 ***visions and revelations.*** This boasting may have been to counter similar claims by the false teachers.
12:2 ***fourteen years.*** Paul wrote 2 Corinthians in AD 56; 14 years earlier would have been AD 42,

17 1Co 7:6 **19** 1Co 4:10 **20** Gal 2:4 **21** 2Co 10:10; Php 3:4 **22** Ac 22:3; Ro 11:1; Php 3:5 **23** 1Co 15:10; Ac 9:16; 1Co 15:30 **24** Dt 25:3 **25** Ac 16:22; 14:19; 27:41 **26** Ac 9:23; Ac 14:5 **27** Ac 20:31; 1Co 4:11 **28** Ac 20:18; Ro 1:14 **29** 1Co 8:13 **30** 2Co 12:5 **31** Ro 1:9; Gal 1:20; 1Th 2:5; Ro 9:5 **32** Ac 9:24
CHAPTER 12 **2** Ro 16:7; Gal 1:22; Ac 22:17

not know, [only] God knows—such a
man was caught up to the third heaven.
[Luke 23:43]
3 And I know that such a man—
whether in the body or out of the body
I do not know, [only] God knows—
4 was caught up into Paradise and
heard inexpressible words which man
is not permitted to speak [words too
sacred to tell].
5 On behalf of such a man [and his
experiences] I will boast; but in my
own behalf I will not boast, except in
regard to my weaknesses.
6 If I wish to boast, I will not be fool-
ish, because I will be speaking the
truth. But I abstain [from it], so that
no one will credit me with more than
[is justified by what] he sees in me or
hears from me.

A Thorn in the Flesh

7 Because of the surpassing great-
ness *and* extraordinary nature of the
revelations [which I received from
God], for this reason, to keep me from
thinking of myself as important, a
thorn in the flesh was given to me, a
messenger of Satan, to torment *and*
harass me—to keep me from exalting
myself! [Job 2:6]
8 Concerning this I pleaded with the
Lord three times that it might leave me;
9 but He has said to me, "My grace
is sufficient for you [My loving-
kindness and My mercy are more
than enough—always available—
regardless of the situation]; for [My]
power is being perfected [and is com-
pleted and shows itself most effec-
tively] in [your] weakness." There-
fore, I will all the more gladly boast
in my weaknesses, so that the power
of Christ [may completely enfold me
and] may dwell in me.
10 So I am well pleased with weak-
nesses, with insults, with distresses,
with persecutions, and with difficul-
ties, for the sake of Christ; for when I
am weak [in human strength], then I
am strong [truly able, truly powerful,
truly drawing from God's strength].
11 Now I have become foolish; you
have forced me [by questioning my
apostleship]. Actually I should have
been commended by you [instead of
being treated disdainfully], for I was
not inferior to those super-apostles,
even if I am nobody.
12 The signs that indicate a genuine
apostle were performed among you
fully *and* most patiently—signs and
wonders and miracles.
13 For in what respect were you
treated as inferior to the rest of the
churches, except [for the fact] that I
did not burden you [with my financial
support]? Forgive me [for doing you]
this injustice!
14 Now for the third time I am ready
to visit you. I will not burden you [fi-
nancially], because I do not want what
is yours [not your money or your pos-
sessions], but you. For children are not
responsible to save up for their parents,
but parents for their children.
15 But I will very gladly spend [my
own resources] and be utterly spent
for your souls. If I love you greatly, am
I to be loved less [by you]?

---

probably when he was in Antioch (Ac 11:26). ***third heaven.*** It was common to speak of three "heavens:" The first is the atmosphere where the birds fly; the second is the place of the sun, moon, and stars; the third is where God dwells. **12:7** ***thorn in the flesh.*** Most commentators interpret Paul's thorn as a physical ailment, and many suggest that it was eye trouble on the basis of Galatians 4:15. It is also possible that "flesh" is a reference to the fallen human nature, in which case the thorn could be a temptation, or it could refer to persecution or opposition. ***messenger of Satan.*** God permitted Satan to afflict Paul as He did Job (Job 1 – 2).
12:11 ***forced me.*** Only the fact that the Corinthians had listened to the silly slander against Paul had made him waste time on boasting.
12:12 ***signs that indicate a genuine apostle.*** God has often used miracles as supernatural evidences of His authority in a new work (Ac 14:3).
12:14 ***the third time.*** It is not clear whether Paul had already made two previous visits to Corinth,

4 Lk 23:43 **5** 2Co 11:30 **6** 2Co 11:16 **7** See Eze 28:24; Gal 4:13; Job 2:7; Lk 13:16 **8** Dt 3:23; Mt 26:44 **9** 2Co 11:30; 1Pe 4:14 **10** Ro 5:3; 2Co 7:4; 2Co 13:4 **11** 2Co 11:1,16; 2Co 11:5; Gal 2:6-8; 1Co 3:7; Eph 3:8 **12** Ro 15:18; 1Co 9:2; 2Co 4:2 **13** 1Co 1:7; 1Co 9:12; 2Co 11:9; 2Co 11:7 **14** 2Co 13:1; Ac 20:33; 1Co 10:33; 1Co 4:14 **15** Jn 10:11; 2Co 1:6; Col 1:24; 2Ti 2:10; 2Co 6:12,13

16 But be that as it may, I did not burden you [with my support]. But [some say that] I was sly and took you by trickery.

17 Did I take advantage of you *or* make any money off you through any of the messengers I sent you? [Certainly not!]

18 I urged Titus to go, and I sent the brother with him. Titus did not take advantage of you, did he? [No!] Did we not conduct ourselves in the same spirit and walk in the same steps? [Of course!]

19 All this time you have been thinking that we are [merely] defending ourselves to you. It is in the sight of God that we have been speaking [as one] in Christ; and everything, dearly beloved, is to strengthen you [spiritually].

20 For I am afraid that perhaps when I come I may find you not to be as I wish, and that you may find me not as you wish—that perhaps *there may be* strife, jealousy, angry tempers, disputes, slander, gossip, arrogance and disorder;

21 I am afraid that when I come again my God may humiliate me before you, and I may mourn over many of those who have sinned in the past and not repented of the impurity, sexual immorality and decadence which they formerly practiced.

Examine Yourselves

13 THIS IS the third time that I am visiting you. EVERY FACT SHALL BE SUSTAINED *and* CONFIRMED BY THE TESTIMONY OF TWO OR THREE WITNESSES. [Deut 19:15]

2 I have already warned those who have sinned in the past and all the rest *as well,* and I warn them now even though I am absent [from you] as I did when I was with you the second time, that if I come back I will not spare *anyone,*

3 since you seek [forensic] proof that Christ is speaking in *and* through me. He is not weak *or* ineffective in dealing with you, but powerful within you.

4 For even though He was crucified in weakness [yielding Himself], yet He lives [resurrected] by the power of God [His Father]. For we too are weak in Him [as He was humanly weak], yet we are alive *and* well [in fellowship] with Him because of the power of God *directed* toward you.

5 Test *and* evaluate yourselves *to see* whether you are in the faith *and* living your lives as [committed] believers. Examine yourselves [not me]! Or do you not recognize this about yourselves [by an ongoing experience] that Jesus Christ is in you—unless indeed you fail the test *and* are rejected as counterfeit?

6 But I hope you will acknowledge that we do not fail the test *nor* are we to be rejected.

7 But I pray to God that you may do nothing wrong. Not so that we [and our teaching] may appear to be approved, but that you may continue doing what is right, even though we [by comparison] may seem to have failed.

8 For we can do nothing against the truth, but only for the truth [and the gospel—the good news of salvation].

9 We are glad when we are weak [since God's power comes freely through us], but you [by comparison] are strong. We also pray for this, that

---

or whether this refers to the third attempt to visit. We know that he had tried to come and had been prevented at least once (1:15–16,23; 2:1–4).

13:4 *in weakness.* Christ appeared to be weak when He was crucified, but He was raised by the power of God; similarly, Paul was weak, but by the power of God he would live with Christ in strength toward them.

13:5 *Examine yourselves.* Paul did not doubt that they were true believers (1:1,24; 7:1; 8:1; 12:14). He wanted them to ask themselves whether they were walking according to the gospel that they professed. He wanted them to apply the same standard to themselves that they were applying to him.

13:9 *complete.* The Greek word for "complete" was used to describe the setting of bones and the reconciliation of alienated friends.

16 2Co 11:9 **17** 2Co 7:2 **18** 2Co 8:6,18 **19** 2Co 5:12; Ro 9:1; 2Co 11:31; 1Co 10:33 **20** 1Co 4:21; 2Co 13:2,10 **21** 2Co 2:1,4; 2Co 13:2; 1Co 5:1 **CHAPTER 13** **1** 2Co 12:14; Nu 35:30; Dt 17:6; Mt 18:16; Jn 8:17; Heb 10:28 **2** 2Co 10:2; 2Co 12:21; 2Co 1:23 **3** Mt 10:20; 1Co 5:4; 1Co 9:2 **4** Php 2:7,8; 1Pe 3:18; Ro 6:4; 2Co 10:3,4 **5** Ro 8:10; Gal 4:19; 1Co 9:27 **7** 2Co 6:9 **9** 1Co 4:10; 2Co 11:30; 1Th 3:10

you be made complete [fully restored,
growing and maturing in godly char-
acter and spirit—pleasing your heav-
enly Father by the life you live].
10 For this reason I am writing these
things while absent from you, so that
when I come, I will not need to deal
severely [with you], in my use of the
authority which the Lord has given me
[to be used] for building you up and not
for tearing you down.
11 Finally, believers, rejoice! Be made
complete [be what you should be], be
comforted, be like-minded, live in
peace [enjoy the spiritual well-being
experienced by believers who walk
closely with God]; and the God of
love and peace [the source of loving-
kindness] will be with you.
12 Greet one another with a holy kiss.
13 All God's people greet you.
14 The grace of the Lord Jesus Christ
and the love of God, and the fellowship
of the Holy Spirit be with you all.

13:14 *the fellowship of the Holy Spirit.* At the end of his letter, Paul identifies the solution to many of the Corinthians' problems. The Holy Spirit, who dwelled in each of them, could empower them to live righteously. Furthermore, the Spirit could reconcile them to each other. They could love and encourage each other instead of fighting each other (12:20). They needed God's grace, not selfishness; God's love, not anger; and communion, not conflict.

10 1Co 4:21; 2Co 12:20,21 **11** Ro 12:16,18; Ro 15:33 **12** Ro 16:16; 1Co 16:20; 1Th 5:26; 1Pe 5:14 **14** Ro 16:24; Php 2:1

THE LETTER OF PAUL TO THE
GALATIANS

▸ **AUTHOR:** The Pauline authorship and the unity of this epistle are virtually unchallenged. The first verse clearly identifies the author as, "Paul, an apostle" as does 5:2, "Notice, it is I, Paul, who tells you." In fact, Paul actually wrote, or at least finished, Galatians by his own hand (6:11) instead of dictating it to a secretary, as was his usual practice. There is some controversy as to whether Paul was writing to the North Galatians or the South Galatians. If the former theory is correct, this epistle was written sometime during Paul's third missionary journey in AD 53 – 56. If the latter theory is correct, this epistle was written before the Jerusalem Council (Ac 15) in AD 49, right after the first missionary journey. Regardless of the timing of its writing, Galatians affords us a clear glimpse into the ministry and theology of Paul as a Jewish Christian.

▸ **TIMES:** c. AD 49 – 53 ▸ **KEY VERSES:** Gal 2:20 – 21

▸ **THEME:** The big question for the church in its first generation was "Did a person have to become a Jew before they could be a Christian?" There were many Jews who thought this was the case. Three things happened to move the church away from this perspective: Peter's vision as recorded in Acts 10; the decision of the Jerusalem Council in Acts 15 that Gentiles didn't need to adopt all the Jewish customs; and Paul's received revelation that he was to deliver to the Gentiles. Even with all this evidence, there were still some Jews who followed Paul around and attempted to teach Jewish regulations to his newly planted churches. Paul was furious at these events and used this letter to set the record straight. Christ brought freedom and died for people of all cultures, an idea that was a new paradigm for many of the Jews who were stuck in a "God loves us most" mode. Paul goes to great lengths to review with the Galatians what he had taught them and where this teaching had come from.

Introduction

1 PAUL, AN apostle (not commissioned *and* sent from men nor through the agency of man, but through Jesus Christ—the Messiah— and God the Father, who raised Him from the dead),
[2]and all the brothers who are with me,
To the churches of Galatia:
[3]Grace to you and peace [inner calm

1:1 ***an apostle.*** Paul calls himself this title to assert his divinely given authority to speak to the problem confronting the Galatian churches. ***through Jesus Christ — the Messiah — and God the Father.*** Paul makes reference to his unique call to be an apostle (vv. 15 – 16) which came to him at the same time as his salvation on the road to Damascus (Ac 26:12 – 18).
1:2 ***To the churches of Galatia.*** Galatians is a circular letter, intended for several churches.
1:3 ***Grace to you and peace.*** These words are a variation from the standard greeting of ancient

CHAPTER 1 **1** Ac 9:6; Titus 1:3; Ac 2:24 **2** Php 2:22; 1Co 16:1 **3** 1Th 1:1

and spiritual well-being] from God our Father and the Lord Jesus Christ,
[4]who gave Himself [as a sacrifice to atone] for our sins [to save and sanctify us] so that He might rescue us from this present evil age, in accordance with the will *and* purpose *and* plan of our God and Father—
[5]to Him be [ascribed all] the glory through the ages of the ages. Amen.

Perversion of the Gospel

[6]I am astonished *and* extremely irritated that you are so quickly shifting your allegiance *and* deserting Him who called you by the grace of Christ, for a different [even contrary] gospel;
[7]which is really not another [gospel]; but there are [obviously] some [people masquerading as teachers] who are disturbing *and* confusing you [with a misleading, counterfeit teaching] and want to distort the gospel of Christ [twisting it into something which it absolutely is not].
[8]But even if we, or an angel from heaven, should preach to you a gospel contrary to that which we [originally] preached to you, let him be condemned to destruction!
[9]As we have said before, so I now say again, if anyone is preaching to you a gospel different from that which you received [from us], let him be condemned to destruction!
[10]Am I now trying to win the favor *and* approval of men, or of God? Or am I seeking to please someone? If I were still trying to be popular with men, I would not be a bond-servant of Christ.

Paul Defends His Ministry

[11]For I want you to know, believers, that the gospel which was preached by me is not man's gospel [it is not a human invention, patterned after any human concept].
[12]For indeed I did not receive it from man, nor was I taught it, but *I received it* through a [direct] revelation of Jesus Christ.
[13]You have heard of my career *and* former manner of life in Judaism, how I used to hunt down *and* persecute the church of God extensively and [with fanatical zeal] tried [my best] to destroy it.
[14]And [you have heard how] I surpassed many of my contemporaries among my countrymen in [my advanced study of the laws of] Judaism, as I was extremely loyal to the traditions of my ancestors.
[15]But when God, who had chosen me *and* set me apart before I was born,

---

letters in Paul's time. Paul adds the Greek word for the traditional Hebrew greeting, "peace."
1:4 *rescue us from this present evil age.* This passage is similar to Colossians 1:13, which states, "For He has rescued us and has drawn us to Himself from the dominion of darkness, and has transferred us to the kingdom of His beloved Son." Both passages develop this truth based on Christ's redemptive work (Col 1:14), implying that the word "rescue" refers to sanctification in the face of temptations of this present age.
1:6–7 *astonished.* Use of this word reveals Paul's ongoing shock at the Galatians' defection from the gospel of God's undeserved grace. The Galatians had unwittingly fallen for a different message.
1:8–9 *if anyone.* Paul's concern for the purity of the gospel message is revealed by his assertion that he would condemn to destruction anyone who taught a false gospel.
1:10 *seeking to please someone.* This was neither Paul's motivation nor the source of his authority (v. 1). Paul continually sought the approval of God. He did not base his decisions on the opinions of other people. Instead he single-mindedly aimed at pleasing God (Php 3:14).
1:13–14 *manner of life in Judaism.* This refers to the Jewish way of life, which was based partly on the Old Testament and partly on additional traditions (Mt 15:2).
1:15–17 *chosen me and set me apart ... called me through His grace.* Paul related that God had chosen him to be an apostle (v. 1) before his birth, not unlike Jeremiah's call to be a prophet (Jer 1:5). Paul, like the Judaizers in Galatia, had previously tried to earn his salvation by works (v. 14). He needed no human validation because of the way he had received his message.

---

4 Mt 20:28; Ro 4:25; Titus 2:14; Heb 2:5; 1Jn 5:19 **6** Gal 5:8 **7** 2Co 11:4; Ac 15:1; 2Co 2:17 **8** 1Co 16:22
9 Dt 4:2; Pr 30:6; Rev 22:18 **10** 1Th 2:4; 1Sa 24:7; Mt 28:14; 1Th 2:4; Jas 4:4 **11** 1Co 15:1 **12** 1Co 15:1; Eph 3:3
13 Ac 9:1; 1Ti 1:13; Ac 8:3 **14** Ac 26:9; Php 3:6; Jer 9:14; Mt 15:2; Mk 7:5 **15** Isa 49:1,5

and called me through His grace, was
pleased [Is 49:1; Jer 1:5]
16 to reveal His Son in me so that I
might preach Him among the Gentiles
[as the good news—the way of salva-
tion], I did not immediately consult
with anyone [for guidance regarding
God's call and His revelation to me].
17 Nor did I [even] go up to Jerusalem
to those who were apostles before me;
but I went to Arabia *and* stayed awhile,
and afterward returned once more to
Damascus.
18 Then three years later I did go up
to Jerusalem to get acquainted with
Cephas (Peter), and I stayed with him
fifteen days.
19 But I did not see any other apostle
except James, the [half] brother of the
Lord.
20 (Now in what I am writing to you, I
assure you as if I were standing before
God that I am not lying.)
21 Then I went into the regions of Syr-
ia and Cilicia.
22 And I was still unknown by sight
to the churches which were in Christ in
Judea (Jerusalem and the surrounding
region);
23 they only kept hearing, "He who
used to persecute us is now preaching
the [good news of the] faith which he
once was trying to destroy."
24 And they were glorifying God [as
the Author and Source of what had
taken place and all that had been ac-
complished] in me.

The Council at Jerusalem

2 THEN AFTER a period of fourteen
years I again went up to Jerusalem,
[this time] with Barnabas, taking Titus
along also.
2 I went up [to Jerusalem] because of
a [divine] revelation, and I put before
them the gospel which I preach among
the Gentiles. But *I did so* in private
before those of reputation, for fear that
I might be running or had run [the
course of my ministry] in vain.
3 But [all went well, for] not even Ti-
tus, who was with me, was compelled
[as some had anticipated] to be cir-
cumcised, despite the fact that he was
a Greek.
4 My concern was because of the
false brothers [those people masquer-
ading as Christians] who had been
secretly smuggled in [to the commu-
nity of believers]. They had slipped in
to spy on the freedom which we have
in Christ Jesus, in order to bring us
back into bondage [under the Law of
Moses].
5 But we did not yield to them even
for a moment, so that the truth of the
gospel would continue to remain with
you [in its purity].
6 But from those who were of high
reputation (whatever they were—in

1:19 *James, the [half] brother of the Lord.* This reference indicates that the "apostles" were not always restricted to "the twelve."
2:1 *fourteen years.* This timeframe may refer to twelve full years plus fractions of the first and last years (1:18). The span could date from Paul's previous visit to Jerusalem, but more likely from his conversion.
2:3 *Titus.* One of Paul's companions was a kind of "test-case" Gentile. ***circumcised.*** This term introduces a central topic of the Jewish false teachers, one which Paul addresses repeatedly in Galatians (5:2 – 3,6). Unlike Timothy, whom Paul had circumcised because Timothy's mother was Jewish, Titus was not circumcised. Circumcising him would have been a sign to all other Gentiles that following Jewish law was required for a person to become a Christian. As Paul explains in this letter, circumcising Titus would be a rejection of the good news that salvation is God's gift to those who believe in His Son.
2:4 *false brothers.* This phrase apparently indicates that, although these people passed themselves off convincingly as Christians, there was reason to view their profession as a sham. These pseudo-Christians did not announce their purpose, which was to curtail Christian liberty (5:1,13).
2:6 *those who were of high reputation.* While Paul recognized the leadership roles of James, Peter, and John, he pointed out that they were in no way superior to him in their understanding of the gospel.

---

16 2Co 4:6; Ac 9:15; Eph 3:8; Mt 16:17; Eph 6:12 **18** Ac 9:26 **19** 1Co 9:5; Mt 13:55 **20** Ro 9:1 **21** Ac 9:30 **22** 1Th 2:14; Ro 16:7 **CHAPTER 2** **1** Ac 15:2 **2** Ac 15:12; Php 2:16; 1Th 3:5 **4** Ac 15:1; 2Co 11:26; Gal 3:25; Gal 4:3,9 **5** ver. 14 **6** Gal 6:3; Ac 10:34; Ro 2:11; 2Co 12:11

terms of individual importance—
makes no difference to me; God shows
no partiality—He is not impressed with
the positions that people hold nor does
He recognize distinctions such as fame
or power)—well, those who were of
reputation contributed nothing to me
[that is, they had nothing to add to
my gospel message nor did they im-
pose any new requirements on me].
[Deut 10:17]
7 But on the contrary, they saw that
I had been entrusted with the gospel
to the uncircumcised (Gentiles), just as
Peter *had been* [entrusted to proclaim
the gospel] to the circumcised (Jews);
8 (for He who worked effectively for
Peter *and* empowered him in his minis-
try to the Jews also worked effectively
for me *and* empowered me in my min-
istry to the Gentiles).
9 And recognizing the grace [that God
had] bestowed on me, James and Cephas
(Peter) and John, who were reputed to
be pillars [of the Jerusalem church],
gave to me and Barnabas the right hand
of fellowship, so that we could go to the
Gentiles [with their blessing] and they
to the circumcised (Jews).
10 *They asked* only [one thing], that
we remember the poor, the very thing
I was also eager to do.

Peter (Cephas) Opposed by Paul

11 Now when Cephas (Peter) came
to Antioch, I opposed him face to face
[about his conduct there], because he
stood condemned [by his own actions].
12 Before certain men came from
James, he used to eat [his meals] with
the Gentiles; but when the men [from
Jerusalem] arrived, he *began* to with-
draw and separate himself [from the
Gentile believers], because he was
afraid of those from the circumcision.
13 The rest of the Jews joined him in
this hypocrisy [ignoring their knowl-
edge that Jewish and Gentile Chris-
tians were united, under the new cov-
enant, into one faith], with the result
that even Barnabas was carried away
by their hypocrisy.
14 But when I saw that they were not
being straightforward about the truth
of the gospel, I told Cephas (Peter) in
front of everyone, "If you, being a Jew,
live [as you have been living] like a
Gentile and not like a Jew, how is it
that you are [now virtually] forcing the
Gentiles to live like Jews [if they want
to eat with you]?"
15 [I went on to say] "We are Jews by
birth and not sinners from among the
Gentiles;
16 yet we know that a man is not jus-
tified [and placed in right standing
with God] by works of the Law, but
[only] through faith in [God's beloved
Son,] Christ Jesus. And even we [as
Jews] have believed in Christ Jesus,
so that we may be justified by faith in
Christ and not by works of the Law. By
observing the Law no one will ever be

2:7 – 10 *uncircumcised . . . circumcised.* There were not two different gospels. Rather, the primary scope of Paul's apostolic ministry was to the Gentiles (Ro 11:13), while Peter's apostleship was, first and foremost, targeted toward the Jews. ***remember the poor.*** Almost certainly, this is a reference to the poor among the church in Judea (Ac 11:29 – 30).
2:11 – 12 *Antioch.* This city was the largest of the Roman province of Syria. It became a center for missionary outreach to other Gentile cities in Asia Minor and Macedonia (Ac 13:1 – 3).
2:14 *they were not being straightforward about the truth of the gospel.* Peter's hypocritical example implied that Gentiles had to behave like Jews in order to receive God's grace. It had already been decided (vv. 1 – 5) that it was not proper to compel Gentiles to live as Jews, because salvation was through faith alone.
2:15 – 17 *We are Jews by birth.* Paul is not denying that those who are Jews by birth are sinners, as are all Gentiles (Ro 3:23). Rather he is implying that Jews enjoy spiritual privileges (Ro 9:4 – 5) that should make them more knowledgeable about how to be justified before God (3:6; Ge 15:6). The Jews should have been aware that no person can be declared righteous or justified by obedience to the law of Moses (3:10 – 21).

7 Ac 13:46; Ro 11:13; 2Ti 1:11; 1Th 2:4 **8** Ac 9:15; 1Co 15:10; Gal 3:5 **9** Mt 16:18; Rev 21:14; Ro 1:5; 1Co 15:10; Eph 3:8 **10** Ac 11:30; Ro 15:25 **11** Ac 15:35 **12** Ac 10:28 **14** ver. 5; 1Ti 5:20; Ac 10:28 **15** Ac 15:10; Mt 9:11; Eph 2:3 **16** Ac 13:38; Ro 1:17; Gal 3:24; Ps 143:2; Ro 3:20

justified [declared free of the guilt of
sin and its penalty]. [Ps 143:2]
17 "But if, while we seek to be justified
in Christ [by faith], we ourselves are
found to be sinners, does that make
Christ an advocate *or* promoter of our
sin? Certainly not!
18 "For if I [or anyone else should]
rebuild [through word or by practice]
what I once tore down [the belief that
observing the Law is essential for sal-
vation], I prove myself to be a trans-
gressor.
19 "For through the Law I died to
the Law *and* its demands on me [be-
cause salvation is provided through
the death and resurrection of Christ],
so that I might [from now on] live to
God.
20 "I have been crucified with Christ
[that is, in Him I have shared His cru-
cifixion]; it is no longer I who live, but
Christ lives in me. The *life* I now live
in the body I live by faith [by adhering
to, relying on, and completely trusting]
in the Son of God, who loved me and
gave Himself up for me.
21 "I do not ignore *or* nullify the [gra-
cious gift of the] grace of God [His
amazing, unmerited favor], for if righ-
teousness *comes* through [observing]
the Law, then Christ died needlessly.
[His suffering and death would have
had no purpose whatsoever.]"

Faith Brings Righteousness

3 O YOU foolish *and* thoughtless *and*
superficial Galatians, who has be-
witched you [that you would act like
this], to whom—right before your
very eyes—Jesus Christ was publicly
portrayed as crucified [in the gospel
message]?
2 This is all I want to ask of you: did
you receive the [Holy] Spirit as the
result of obeying [the requirements of]
the Law, or was it the result of hearing
[the message of salvation and] with
faith [believing it]?
3 Are you so foolish *and* senseless?
Having begun [your new life by faith]
with the Spirit, are you now being per-
fected *and* reaching spiritual maturity
by the flesh [that is, by your own works
and efforts to keep the Law]?
4 Have you suffered so many
things *and* experienced so much all
for nothing—if indeed it was all for
nothing?
5 So then, does He who supplies you
with His [marvelous Holy] Spirit and
works miracles among you, do it as a
result of the works of the Law [which
you perform], or because you [believe
confidently in the message which you]
heard with faith?
6 Just as Abraham BELIEVED GOD, AND
IT WAS CREDITED TO HIM AS RIGHTEOUS-
NESS, [as conformity to God's will

2:17–19 ***make Christ an advocate or promoter of our sin.*** Paul strongly rejects the erroneous conclusion that being justified by faith in Christ actually made Jews sinners. Those who attempt to be justified through "the works of the law" are "under a curse" (3:10). If anyone attempts to reassert the "works of the law" as having any part in the justification before God, the law itself convicts that person. The law itself is not sinful; its purpose is to convince individuals of their personal, spiritual deadness in sin outside of faith in Christ (Ro 7:7–13).

3:1 ***O you foolish and thoughtless and superficial Galatians.*** This phrase does not indicate lack of intelligence, but lack of wisdom. Paul wonders whether something like an evil spell had prevented the Galatians from recalling the gospel of the crucified Christ.

3:3 ***Having begun [your new life by faith] with the Spirit . . . now being perfected and reaching spiritual maturity by the flesh.*** The Galatians were mistakenly trying to achieve perfection through their own efforts, especially through circumcision.

3:6 ***Abraham BELIEVED GOD.*** There are several reasons for Paul's reference to Abraham's faith as an example: (1) Abraham was the father of the Jewish nation (Ge 12:1–3); (2) Abraham is the clearest example of justification in the Old Testament; (3) the Judaizers almost certainly were pointing back to Abraham, probably in connection with circumcision (2:3; 5:2–3). The example of Abraham's faith is also developed in Romans 4 and Hebrews 11.

---

17 1Jn 3:8 **19** Ro 8:2; 6:14; Ro 6:11; 2Co 5:15; Heb 9:14 **20** Ro 6:6; 2Co 5:15; 1Pe 4:2; Eph 5:2; Titus 2:14 **21** Heb 7:11; Ro 11:6 **CHAPTER 3** **1** Gal 5:7; Gal 2:14 **2** Ac 2:38; Eph 1:13; Heb 6:4; Ro 10:16 **3** Gal 4:9; Heb 7:16 **4** Heb 10:35; 2Jn 8 **6** Ge 15:6; Ro 4:3,9; Jas 2:23

and purpose—so it is with you also].
[Gen 15:6]
[7]So understand that it is the people
who live by faith [with confidence in
the power and goodness of God] who
are [the true] sons of Abraham.
[8]The Scripture, foreseeing that God
would justify the Gentiles by faith,
proclaimed the good news [of the Sav-
ior] to Abraham in advance [with this
promise], *saying*, "IN YOU SHALL ALL THE
NATIONS BE BLESSED." [Gen 12:3]
[9]So then those who are people of
faith [whether Jew or Gentile] are
blessed *and* favored by God [and de-
clared free of the guilt of sin and its
penalty, and placed in right standing
with Him] along with Abraham, the
believer.
[10]For all who depend on the Law
[seeking justification and salvation
by obedience to the Law and the ob-
servance of rituals] are under a curse;
for it is written, "CURSED (condemned
to destruction) IS EVERYONE WHO DOES
NOT ABIDE BY ALL THINGS WRITTEN IN THE
BOOK OF THE LAW, SO AS TO PRACTICE THEM."
[Deut 27:26]
[11]Now it is clear that no one is justi-
fied [that is, declared free of the guilt of
sin and its penalty, and placed in right
standing] before God by the Law, for
"THE RIGHTEOUS (the just, the upright)
SHALL LIVE BY FAITH." [Hab 2:4]
[12]But the Law does not rest on *or*
require faith [it has nothing to do with
faith], but [instead, the Law] *says*, "HE
WHO PRACTICES THEM [the things pre-
scribed by the Law] SHALL LIVE BY THEM
[instead of faith]." [Lev 18:5]
[13]Christ purchased our freedom *and*
redeemed us from the curse of the Law
and its condemnation by becoming a
curse for us—for it is written, "CURSED
IS EVERYONE WHO HANGS [crucified] ON A
TREE (cross)"— [Deut 21:23]
[14]in order that in Christ Jesus the
blessing of Abraham might also come
to the Gentiles, so that we would all
receive [the realization of] the promise
of the [Holy] Spirit through faith.

Intent of the Law

[15]Brothers and sisters, I speak in
terms of human relations: even though
a last will and testament is just a hu-
man covenant, yet when it has been
signed *and* made legally binding, no
one sets it aside or adds to it [modify-
ing it in some way].
[16]Now the promises [in the cov-
enants] were decreed to Abraham and
to his seed. God does not say, "And to
seeds (descendants, heirs)," as if [refer-
ring] to many [persons], but as to one,
"And to your Seed," who is [none other
than] Christ. [Gen 13:15; 17:8]
[17]This is what I mean: the Law, which
came into existence four hundred and
thirty years later [after the covenant
concerning the coming Messiah], does
not *and* cannot invalidate the covenant
previously established by God, so as to
abolish the promise. [Ex 12:40]
[18]For if the inheritance [of what was
promised] is based on [observing] the

3:7 *the people who live by faith.* These are the spiritual sons of Abraham, even if they are not Jews. They are part of God's people.

3:8–9 *Scripture.* Here, Scripture is personified as a preacher who foretells that Abraham and his example of faith (Ge 15:6) would become a life-changing blessing to all nations (Ge 12:3; Mt 28:19) as the gospel spread. All who have faith, as Abraham did, join in his "blessed" status.

3:10 *CURSED (condemned to destruction) IS EVERYONE.* The quotation from Deuteronomy 27:26 says that those who do not keep the whole law are cursed, proving that all are cursed who follow the law, because all fall short of the law's standards (Ro 1:17; 3:10,18,23).

3:13 *the curse of the Law.* Paul knew that many of his readers would perceive that they were actually under the curse of the law. For them, as for us, it is incredibly comforting to know that Christ became that curse for us on the cross (Dt 21:23).

3:16 *to Abraham and to his seed.* Jesus Christ is the fulfillment of the covenant (v. 15) God made with Abraham. Although in one sense all Jews are the physical seed of Abraham, Christ is the final focus of God's promises, the ultimate seed.

---

7 Jn 8:39 **8** Ro 9:17; Ge 12:3; Ac 3:25 **10** Dt 27:26; Jer 11:3 **11** Gal 2:16; Hab 2:4; Ro 1:17; Heb 10:38
12 Ro 4:4,5; Lev 18:5; Ro 10:5 **13** Ro 8:3; 2Co 5:21; Dt 21:23 **14** Ro 4:9; Isa 32:15; Eze 11:19; Ac 2:33 **15** Heb 9:17
16 Ge 12:3; 1Co 12:12 **17** Ex 12:40; Ro 4:13 **18** Ro 8:17; Ro 4:14

Law [as these false teachers claim], it is no longer based on a promise; however, God granted it to Abraham [as a gift] by virtue of His promise.

[19]Why, then, the Law [what was its purpose]? It was added [after the promise to Abraham, to reveal to people their guilt] because of transgressions [that is, to make people conscious of the sinfulness of sin], and [the Law] was ordained through angels *and* delivered to Israel by the hand of a mediator [Moses, the mediator between God and Israel, to be in effect] until the Seed would come to whom the promise had been made.

[20]Now the mediator *or* go-between [in a transaction] is not [needed] for just one *party;* whereas God is *only* one [and was the only One giving the promise to Abraham, but the Law was a contract between two, God and Israel; its validity depended on both].

[21]Is the Law then contrary to the promises of God? Certainly not! For if a *system of* law had been given which could impart life, then righteousness (right standing with God) would actually have been based on law.

[22]But the Scripture has imprisoned everyone [everything—the entire world] under sin, so that [the inheritance, the blessing of salvation] which was promised through faith in Jesus Christ might be given to those who believe [in Him and acknowledge Him as God's precious Son].

[23]Now before faith came, we were kept in custody under the Law, [perpetually] imprisoned [in preparation] for the faith that was destined to be revealed,

[24]with the result that the Law has become our tutor *and* our disciplinarian *to guide us* to Christ, so that we may be justified [that is, declared free of the guilt of sin and its penalty, and placed in right standing with God] by faith.

[25]But now that faith has come, we are no longer under [the control and authority of] a tutor *and* disciplinarian.

[26]For you [who are born-again have been reborn from above—spiritually transformed, renewed, sanctified and] are all children of God [set apart for His purpose with full rights and privileges] through faith in Christ Jesus.

[27]For all of you who were baptized into Christ [into a spiritual union with the Christ, the Anointed] have clothed yourselves with Christ [that is, you have taken on His characteristics and values].

[28]There is [now no distinction in regard to salvation] neither Jew nor Greek, there is neither slave nor free, there is neither male nor female; for you [who believe] are all one in Christ Jesus [no one can claim a spiritual superiority]. [Rom 3:22; 1 Cor 12:13]

3:19–20 *Why, then, the Law [what was its purpose]?* The purpose of the law of Moses was not to justify humankind in God's eyes (2:16). Rather, the law was added after God's promise to Abraham to clarify the issue of sin until Christ, the seed, came.

3:21–22 *Is the Law then contrary to the promises of God?* The relationship of the law and the promises is one of need and fulfillment. The law was not designed by God to give eternal life and righteousness. Rather, the law showed humanity's need for the promise of life through faith in Jesus Christ (v. 9; 2:16).

3:23–25 *kept in custody under the Law . . . tutor and disciplinarian.* Paul gives two different illustrations concerning the function of the law until Christ came (4:4–5). The law acted as a jailor to hold humankind in custody until faith in Christ was revealed. But the law also served as a teacher. A teacher in ancient Greek culture would accompany the children in his care, instructing and disciplining them when necessary. The law was like a teacher because it both corrected and instructed the Israelites in God's ways until Christ was revealed and such a schoolmaster was no longer needed (4:1–2).

3:28 *There is . . . neither Jew nor Greek.* The context of this verse is justification by faith in Christ Jesus. Racial, social, and gender distinctions that so easily divide in no way hinder a person from coming to Christ in order to receive His mercy. All people equally can become God's heirs and recipients of His eternal promises (4:5–7).

---

19 Jn 15:22; Ro 4:15; Ac 7:53; Ex 20:19; Jn 1:17 **20** Ro 3:29 **22** Ro 11:32; 4:11 **24** Ro 10:4; Ac 13:39 **26** Jn 1:12; Ro 8:14 **27** Ro 6:3; Ro 13:14 **28** Ro 10:12; Jn 10:16; Eph 2:14

29And if you belong to Christ [if you
are in Him], then you are Abraham's
descendants, and [spiritual] heirs according to [God's] promise.

Sonship in Christ

4 NOW WHAT I mean [when I talk
about children and their guardians] is this: as long as the heir is a
child, he does not differ at all from
a slave even though he is the [future
owner and] master of all [the estate];
2but he is under [the authority of]
guardians and household administrators *or* managers until the date set
by his father [when he is of legal age].
3So also we [whether Jews or Gentiles], when we were children (spiritually immature), were kept like slaves
under the elementary [man-made religious or philosophical] teachings of
the world.
4But when [in God's plan] the proper time had fully come, God sent His
Son, born of a woman, born under the
[regulations of the] Law,
5so that He might redeem *and* liberate those who were under the Law, that
we [who believe] might be adopted as
sons [as God's children with all rights
as fully grown members of a family].
[Rom 11:17–24]
6And because you [really] are [His]
sons, God has sent the Spirit of His
Son into our hearts, crying out, "Abba!
Father!"
7Therefore you are no longer a slave
(bond-servant), but a son; and if a son,
then also an heir through [the gracious
act of] God [through Christ].
8But at that time, when you did not
know [the true] God *and* were unacquainted with Him, you [Gentiles] were
slaves to those [pagan] things which by
[their very] nature were not *and* could
not be gods *at all*.
9Now, however, since you have
come to know [the true] God [through
personal experience], or rather to be
known by God, how is it that you are
turning back again to the weak and
worthless elemental principles [of religions and philosophies], to which you
want to be enslaved all over again?
10[For example,] you observe [particular] days and months and seasons
and years.
11I fear for you, that perhaps I have
labored [to the point of exhaustion]
over you in vain.
12Believers, I beg of you, become as
I am [free from the bondage of Jewish
ritualism and ordinances], for I *have
become* as you are [a Gentile]. You did
me no wrong [when I first came to you;
do not do it now].
13On the contrary, you know that it
was because of a physical illness that

4:1 – 2 *until the date set by his father.* In ancient society a child had to wait until the proper time before he could inherit what was his. Paul uses this idea to explain why God delayed Jesus Christ's coming, leaving people with His law as a guide (3:23 – 25).

4:4 – 5 *born under the [regulations of the] Law.* This means Christ was subject to the Jewish law (Mt 5:17 – 19), further establishing His identification with all people who are subject to the law. ***redeem.*** This verb was used in the context of buying from a slave market. It describes Christ's supreme and final payment for the sins of humanity. His death on the cross frees those who believe in Him from the curse of the law and slavery to sin. This decisive payment and resulting freedom clear the way for Christians to become God's sons.

4:6 *God has sent the Spirit.* Just as "God sent His Son" when "the proper time had fully come" in world history (v. 4), so God has also sent the Spirit at just the right time for every person who believes in Christ.

4:9 *how is it that you are turning back again.* The Galatians had come to know God through faith in Jesus Christ (Jn 17:2 – 3). He had adopted them as His own sons, but they were turning back to the law that had once enslaved them.

4:12 *I beg of you.* To get beyond the present dilemma, Paul appeals to the Galatians to follow his example (1Co 11:1). He had abandoned the ceremonial rules and regulations connected with Judaism so that he could freely preach the gospel of Christ to Jew and Gentile alike in the cities of Galatia. They too should not hinder the gospel of Christ with laws and regulations.

29 Ge 21:10; Heb 11:18; Ro 8:17 **CHAPTER 4** **3** Col 2:8; Heb 9:10 **4** Ge 49:10; Mk 1:15; Jn 1:14; Heb 2:14; Ge 3:15; Isa 7:14; Mt 1:23; Mt 5:17; Lk 2:27 **5** Mt 20:28; Heb 9:12; Jn 1:12; Eph 1:5 **6** Ro 5:5 **7** Ro 8:16 **8** Eph 2:12; 1Th 4:5; Ro 1:25; 1Co 12:2; 1Th 1:9 **9** 1Co 8:3; Col 2:20; Heb 7:18 **10** Ro 14:5 **11** 1Th 3:5 **12** 2Co 2:5 **13** 1Co 2:3

I [remained and] preached the gospel to you the first time;

14 and even though my physical condition was a trial to you, you did not regard it with contempt, or scorn *and* reject me; but you received me as an angel of God, even as Christ Jesus *Himself.*

15 What then has become of that sense of blessing *and* the joy that you once had [from your salvation and your relationship with Christ]? For I testify of you that, if possible, you would have torn out your own eyes and given them to me [to replace mine].

16 So have I become your enemy by telling you the truth?

17 These men [the Judaizers] eagerly seek you [to entrap you with honeyed words and attention, to win you over to their philosophy], not honorably [for their purpose is not honorable or worthy of consideration]. They want to isolate you [from us who oppose them] so that you will seek them.

18 Now it is always pleasant to be eagerly sought after [provided that it is] for a good purpose, and not just when I am with you [seeking you myself—but beware of the others doing it].

19 My little children, for whom I am again in [the pains of] labor until Christ is [completely and permanently] formed within you—

20 how I wish that I were with you now and could change my tone, because I am perplexed in regard to you.

Bond and Free

21 Tell me, you who are bent on being under the Law, do you not listen to [what] the Law [really says]?

22 For it is written that Abraham had two sons, one by the slave woman [Hagar] and one by the free woman [Sarah]. [Gen 16:15; 21:2, 9]

23 But the child of the slave woman was born according to the flesh *and* had an ordinary birth, while the son of the free woman was born in fulfillment of the promise.

24 Now these facts are about to be used [by me] as an allegory [that is, I will illustrate by using them]: for these *women* can represent two covenants: one [covenant originated] from Mount Sinai [where the Law was given] that bears children [destined] for slavery; she is Hagar.

25 Now Hagar is (represents) Mount Sinai in Arabia and she corresponds to the present Jerusalem, for she is in slavery with her children.

26 But the Jerusalem above [that is, the way of faith, represented by Sarah] is free; she is our mother.

27 For it is written [in the Scriptures],

"REJOICE, O BARREN WOMAN WHO HAS NOT GIVEN BIRTH;
BREAK FORTH INTO A [joyful] SHOUT, YOU WHO ARE NOT IN LABOR;
FOR THE DESOLATE WOMAN HAS MANY MORE CHILDREN
THAN SHE WHO HAS A HUSBAND."
[Is 54:1]

4:17 – 18 *They want to isolate you.* Paul was strongly implying that the false teachers in Galatia were making the same mistake he had made prior to his conversion. Their zeal for the law was blinding them to the freedom and truth to be found in Jesus Christ.

4:19 *My little children.* Paul calls the Galatians children because of their lack of spiritual growth and depth. The apostle also portrays himself as the Galatians' "spiritual mother." He was feeling the labor pains of their birth all over again because they had fallen into serious error.

4:21 – 22 *slave woman . . . free woman.* To clinch his argument about the bondage of the law and freedom found in Christ, Paul uses as examples the two sons of Abraham, Ishmael and Isaac. Ishmael was born of a slave woman, Hagar, and Isaac was born of Sarah, a free woman (Ge 16:15; 21:2). Paul counters the Jewish false teachers' zeal for the law with an argument based on the Law, the Pentateuch. He uses allegory to prove his point because it was a rhetorical technique the false teachers used. In other words, Paul was demonstrating that he could argue from the law just as well as they could, but to prove that the law of Moses pointed to the Messiah, Jesus Christ.

4:26 *Jerusalem above.* This phrase represents the Jewish hope of heaven finally coming to earth (Rev 21 – 22). Paul was strongly implying that the question at hand was not allegiance to Jerusalem,

14 Mal 2:7; Lk 10:16 **17** Ro 10:2 **19** 1Co 4:15 **22** Ge 16:15; Ge 21:2 **23** Ro 9:7,8; Heb 11:11 **24** Dt 33:2 **26** Isa 2:2 **27** Isa 54:1

[28]And we, [believing] brothers and sisters, like Isaac, are children [not merely of physical descent, like Ishmael, but are children born] of promise [born miraculously].
[29]But as at that time the child [of ordinary birth] born according to the flesh persecuted the son *who was born* according to [the promise and working of] the Spirit, so it is now also. [Gen 21:9]
[30]But what does the Scripture say?

> "Cast out the bondwoman [Hagar]
> and her son [Ishmael],
> For never shall the son of the
> bondwoman be heir *and* share the
> inheritance with the son of the
> free woman." [Gen 21:10]

[31]So then, believers, we [who are born again—reborn from above—spiritually transformed, renewed, and set apart for His purpose] are not children of a slave woman [the natural], but of the free woman [the supernatural].

Walk by the Spirit

5 IT WAS for this freedom that Christ set us free [completely liberating us]; therefore keep standing firm and do not be subject again to a yoke of slavery [which you once removed].
[2]Notice, it is I, Paul, who tells you that if you receive circumcision [as a supposed requirement of salvation], Christ will be of no benefit to you [for you will lack the faith in Christ that is necessary for salvation].
[3]Once more I solemnly affirm to every man who receives circumcision [as a supposed requirement of salvation], that he is under obligation *and* required to keep the whole Law.
[4]You have been severed from Christ, if you seek to be justified [that is, declared free of the guilt of sin and its penalty, and placed in right standing with God] through the Law; you have fallen from grace [for you have lost your grasp on God's unmerited favor and blessing].
[5]For we [not relying on the Law but] through the [strength and power of the Holy] Spirit, by faith, are waiting [confidently] for the hope of righteousness [the completion of our salvation].
[6]For [if we are] in Christ Jesus neither circumcision nor uncircumcision means anything, but only faith activated *and* expressed *and* working through love.
[7]You were running [the race] well; who has interfered *and* prevented you from obeying the truth?
[8]This [deceptive] persuasion is not from Him who called you [to freedom in Christ].
[9]A little leaven [a slight inclination to error, or a few false teachers] leavens

---

but allegiance to which Jerusalem — the new or the old? Would the Galatians follow the short-sighted present Jerusalem and its legalism or the liberty of the heavenly Jerusalem?
4:28 – 30 *And we, [believing] brothers and sisters, like Isaac, are children . . . of promise.* This portion of Paul's allegory is based on Genesis 21:9 – 10. Isaac was continually persecuted by his older half brother Ishmael. Eventually, Ishmael and his mother Hagar were expelled because Ishmael had no standing in God's eyes as an heir of Abraham. In creating a parallel between the story from Genesis and the Galatians' situation, Paul points out that (1) the persecution by the Jewish legalists of his day was not unexpected, and (2) it would not go on indefinitely because the legalists would soon be cast out.
4:31 – 5:1 *So then.* This phrase represents the conclusion of the previous section, while "therefore" signals that Paul is going to apply this spiritual truth to the lives of the Galatian believers.
5:2 – 3 *if you receive circumcision.* The legalistic Jewish teachers in Galatia were urging believers to be circumcised (6:12 – 13). Paul points out that circumcision would change the entire orientation of salvation away from God's grace to one's own actions. One who is circumcised in an attempt to gain God's acceptance is obligated to keep the whole law, which history has abundantly demonstrated no one can do (Ro 3:10 – 18).
5:5 *hope of righteousness.* We can be assured that we will be declared righteous before the Lord on that last day because we have a foretaste of that righteousness from the Spirit who lives within us (2Co 5:5).
5:9 – 10 *leaven.* This symbolizes the intruders, with their false doctrine and its sinister influence. They were taking the gospel of free forgiveness

28 Ac 3:25 **29** Ge 21:9; Gal 5:11 **30** Gal 3:8,22; Ge 21:10; Jn 8:35 **31** Jn 8:36 **CHAPTER 5** **1** Ro 6:18; Ac 15:10 **2** Ac 15:1 **3** Gal 3:10 **4** Ro 9:31; Heb 12:15 **5** Ro 8:24 **6** Col 3:11; 1Th 1:3 **7** 1Co 9:24; Gal 3:1 **8** Gal 1:6 **9** 1Co 5:6

THE FRUIT OF THE SPIRIT

The aspects of the fruit of the Spirit advocated by Paul in Galatians 5:22–23 occur not only here but also elsewhere in the Scriptures. Most of the attributes are those by which God himself lives.

ASPECT	GK NUMBER*	DEFINITION	ATTRIBUTE OF GOD	ATTRIBUTE FOR CHRISTIANS
love	26	sacrificial, unmerited deeds to help a needy person	Ex 34:6; Jn 3:16; Ro 5:8; 1Jn 4:8,16	Jn 13:34–35; Ro 12:9,10; 1Pe 1:22; 1Jn 4:7,11–12,21
joy	5915	an inner happiness not dependent on outward circumstances	Ps 104:31; Isa 62:5; Lk 15:7,10	Dt 12:7,12,18; Ps 64:10; Isa 25:9; Php 4:4; 1Pe 1:8
peace	1645	harmony in all relationships	Isa 9:6–7; Eze 34:25; Jn 14:27; Heb 13:20	Isa 26:3; Ro 5:1; 12:18; 14:17; Eph 2:14–17
patience	3429	putting up with others, even when one is severely tried	Ro 9:22; 1Ti 1:16; 1Pe 3:20; 2Pe 3:9,15	Eph 4:2; Col 1:11; Heb 6:12; Jas 5:7–8,10
kindness	5983	doing thoughtful deeds for others	Ro 2:4; 11:22; Eph 2:7; Titus 3:4	1Co 13:4; Eph 4:32; Col 3:12
goodness	20	showing generosity to others	Ne 9:25,35; Ps 31:19; Mk 10:18	Ro 15:14; Eph 5:9; 2Th 1:11
faithfulness	4411	trustworthiness and reliability	Ps 33:4; 1Co 1:9; 10:13; Heb 10:23; 1Jn 1:9	Lk 16:10–12; 2Th 1:4; 2Ti 4:7; Titus 2:10
gentleness	4559	meekness and humility	Zec 9:9; Mt 11:29	Isa 66:2; Mt 5:5; Eph 4:2; Col 3:12
self-control	1602	victory over sinful desires		Pr 16:32; Titus 1:8; 2:12; 1Pe 5:8–9; 2Pe 1:6

*The numbers refer to the Greek dictionary entry numbers in Goodrick & Kohlenberger, *The NIV Exhaustive Concordance*.

the whole batch [it perverts the concept of faith and misleads the church].
10 I have confidence in you in the Lord that you will adopt no other view [contrary to mine on the matter]; but the one who is disturbing you, whoever he is, will have to bear the penalty.
11 But as for me, brothers, if I am still preaching circumcision [as I had done before I met Christ; and as some accuse me of doing now, as necessary for salvation], why am I still being persecuted [by Jews]? In that case the stumbling block of the cross [to unbelieving Jews] has been abolished.
12 I wish that those who are troubling you [by teaching that circumcision is necessary for salvation] would even [go all the way and] castrate themselves!
13 For you, my brothers, were called to freedom; only do not let your freedom *become* an opportunity for the

away from the Galatians. The one who causes such harm will experience God's judgment (2Co 5:10).
5:11 *the stumbling block of the cross.* The cross is a stumbling block to people because it proclaims God's unmerited grace and leaves no place for people's good works.
5:13 *freedom.* Christian liberty is the freedom to serve one another in love (vv. 5–6). As we grow in our knowledge of the Word of God, understand and apply its meaning, we should increasingly be involved in serving God and our fellow believers. The Spirit of God has given us spiritual gifts, but those gifts are worthless unless they are used in the service of God and His church. Paul often

10 2Co 2:3; Gal 1:7; 2Co 10:6 **11** Gal 6:12; 1Co 15:30; 1:23 **12** Jos 7:25; Ac 15:1,2 **13** 1Co 8:9; 1Pe 2:16; 1Co 9:19

sinful nature (worldliness, selfishness),
but through love serve *and* seek the
best for one another.
14 For the whole Law [concerning hu-
man relationships] is fulfilled in one
precept, "YOU SHALL LOVE YOUR NEIGHBOR
AS YOURSELF [that is, you shall have an
unselfish concern for others and do
things for their benefit]." [Lev 19:18]
15 But if you bite and devour one an-
other [in bickering and strife], watch out
that you [along with your entire fellow-
ship] are not consumed by one another.
16 But I say, walk *habitually* in the
[Holy] Spirit [seek Him and be respon-
sive to His guidance], and then you
will certainly not carry out the desire
of the sinful nature [which responds
impulsively without regard for God
and His precepts].
17 For the sinful nature has its desire
which is opposed to the Spirit, and the
[desire of the] Spirit opposes the sinful
nature; for these [two, the sinful nature
and the Spirit] are in direct opposition
to each other [continually in conflict], so
that you [as believers] do not [always] do
whatever [good things] you want to do.
18 But if you are guided *and* led by the
Spirit, you are not subject to the Law.
19 Now the practices of the sinful
nature are *clearly* evident: they are
sexual immorality, impurity, sensual-
ity (total irresponsibility, lack of self-
control),
20 idolatry, sorcery, hostility, strife,
jealousy, fits of anger, disputes, dissen-
sions, factions [that promote heresies],
21 envy, drunkenness, riotous behav-
ior, and *other* things like these. I warn
you beforehand, just as I did previous-
ly, that those who practice such things
will not inherit the kingdom of God.
22 But the fruit of the Spirit [the result
of His presence within us] is love [un-
selfish concern for others], joy, [inner]

---

uses the figure of the human body to sho w the importance of each part serving the others (Ro 12:4–5; 1Co 12:12–31). While some parts of the body have more prominent places of service than others, all are equally important. To maintain strength, health, and vitality, every part of the body must function and serve all the other parts of the body. This is also true of the spiritual or new life. We will grow in the new life, become strong, and maintain good spiritual health as we use the talents and abilities that God has given us to meet the needs of the other parts of the body.

5:14 *the whole Law.* The Christian does not live under the law of Moses, but instead under "the law of Christ" (6:2). Living in Christ empowers us to love others, which is the fulfillment of the law (Mt 22:36–40).

5:16 *walk habitually in the [Holy] Spirit.* The only consistent way to overcome the sinful desires of our human nature (the flesh) is to live step-by-step in the power of the Holy Spirit as He works through our spirit.

5:17 *the sinful nature has its desire which is opposed to the Spirit.* The potential of the sinful nature energized by Satan in the life of the Christian should not be underestimated. Given free rein, the sinful nature will direct our choices, making us do what we know we should not do. This inner conflict between the sinful nature and the Spirit is very real. Although the precise meaning of sinful nature is unclear, Paul's intent is plain. The desires of our sinful nature are at odds with what the Holy Spirit desires for us: to be free from sin.

5:19–21 The Human Condition — The last part of Galatians 5 contrasts *practices of the sinful nature with fruit of the Spirit.* The practices of the sinful nature here are represented by those kinds of activities that are characteristic of our old natures. Without God, our lives are dominated by these more obvious sins and less obvious sinful attitudes. It is our sinful nature to be this way. Those who operate with these sins as a regular part of their lives, with no sense of guilt, demonstrate their need for salvation. It is the role of the Spirit to change these sinful behaviors. Paul points out that, if changes are not occurring, then there is a need for the Spirit that comes with the gift of salvation.

5:22–24 The New Nature — While the deeds of the sinful nature portray a disintegrating life, the fruit of the Spirit describes a life where things are working harmoniously. It points to qualities of personality and to behaviors that make us function as better people. It points to what God wants to see in us and should see in us as we mature in the faith.

5:22 *fruit of the Spirit.* This analogy is reminiscent of Jesus' teaching on the vine, branches, and fruitful harvest.

---

14 Mt 7:12; Jas 2:8; Mt 22:39 **16** Ro 6:12; 1Pe 2:11 **17** Ro 7:23; Ro 7:15 **18** Ro 6:14 **19** Eph 5:3 **21** 1Co 6:9
22 Jn 15:2; Eph 5:9; Col 3:12; Ro 15:14; 1Co 13:7

peace, patience [not the ability to wait, but how we act while waiting], kindness, goodness, faithfulness,
[23]gentleness, self-control. Against such things there is no law.
[24]And those who belong to Christ Jesus have crucified the sinful nature together with its passions and appetites.
[25]If we [claim to] live by the [Holy] Spirit, we must also walk by the Spirit [with personal integrity, godly character, and moral courage—our conduct empowered by the Holy Spirit].
[26]We must not become conceited, challenging *or* provoking one another, envying one another.

Bear One Another's Burdens

6 BROTHERS, IF anyone is caught in any sin, you who are spiritual [that is, you who are responsive to the guidance of the Spirit] are to restore such a person in a spirit of gentleness [not with a sense of superiority or self-righteousness], keeping a watchful eye on yourself, so that you are not tempted as well.
[2]Carry one another's burdens and in this way you will fulfill the requirements of the law of Christ [that is, the law of Christian love]. [John 13:34]
[3]For if anyone thinks he is something [special] when [in fact] he is nothing [special except in his own eyes], he deceives himself.
[4]But each one must carefully scrutinize his own work [examining his actions, attitudes, and behavior], and then he can have the personal satisfaction and inner joy of doing something commendable without comparing himself to another.
[5]For every person will have to bear [with patience] his own burden [of faults and shortcomings for which he alone is responsible].
[6]The one who is taught the word [of God] is to share all good things with his teacher [contributing to his spiritual and material support].
[7]Do not be deceived, God is not mocked [He will not allow Himself to be ridiculed, nor treated with contempt nor allow His precepts to be scornfully set aside]; for whatever a man sows, this *and* this only is what he will reap.
[8]For the one who sows to his flesh [his sinful capacity, his worldliness, his disgraceful impulses] will reap from the flesh ruin *and* destruction, but the one who sows to the Spirit will from the Spirit reap eternal life.
[9]Let us not grow weary *or* become discouraged in doing good, for at the proper time we will reap, if we do not give in.
[10]So then, while we [as individual believers] have the opportunity, let us do good to all people [not only being helpful, but also doing that which

---

5:24 ***have crucified the sinful nature.*** Those who have mastered these sinful desires are those who have kept their focus on God (Jer 9:23 – 24; Da 11:32; Jn 17:3; Heb 12:1 – 3).
6:1 ***restore such a person in a spirit of gentleness.*** A believer devastated by sin needs to be approached gently by fellow believers.
6:2 ***the law of Christ.*** This phrase is probably referring to the summation of the law: "Love you neighbor" (5:14; Mt 22:39; Jn 13:34 – 35). Bearing the burdens of one another is precisely what Christ expects of all believers. The Greek word for *burdens* refers to something beyond the normal capacity to carry.
6:7 – 8 ***the one who sows to his flesh.*** The principle of sowing and reaping was known to everyone in a largely agricultural society. It would be foolish for Christians to think that they could escape the harvest of destruction and judgment if they persist in sin. ***ruin and destruction.*** This is a term used for a field in which the produce is too rotten to harvest (Heb 6:8). ***the one who sows to the Spirit will from the Spirit reap eternal life.*** This does not mean that everlasting life is earned by works. Rather, Paul is saying that everlasting life is the glorious end of those who follow the guidance of the Spirit (Ro 6:22). Jesus said that He came so that we might have life and have it more abundantly (Jn 10:10). In this life, through the indwelling of the Spirit, Christians are developing a capacity to experience Christ to the fullest in the life to come.
6:9 ***doing good.*** The apostle has argued at length that such works cannot justify (2:16) or

---

23 1Ti 1:9 **24** Ro 6:6; 1Pe 2:11 **25** Ro 8:4,5 **26** Php 2:3 **CHAPTER 6** **1** Ro 14:1; 1Co 2:15; 1Co 4:21; 1Co 7:5 **2** Ro 15:1; 1Th 5:14; Jas 2:8 **3** Ro 12:3; 1Co 8:2; 2Co 3:5 **4** 1Co 11:28; Lk 18:11 **5** Ro 2:6; 1Co 3:8 **6** 1Co 9:11 **7** 1Co 6:9; Job 13:9; Ro 2:6; 2Co 9:6 **8** Job 4:8 **9** 1Co 15:58; Mt 24:13; Rev 2:10 **10** Jn 9:4; Titus 3:8; Eph 2:19

promotes their spiritual well-being], and especially [be a blessing] to those of the household of faith (born-again believers).

11 See with what large letters I am writing to you with my own hand.

12 Those who want to make a good impression in public [before the Jews] try to compel you to be circumcised, just so they will escape being persecuted for [faithfulness to] the cross of Christ.

13 For even the circumcised [Jews] themselves do not [really] keep the Law, but they want to have you circumcised so that they may boast in your flesh [that is, in the fact that they convinced you to be circumcised].

14 But far be it from me to boast [in anything or anyone], except in the cross of our Lord Jesus Christ, through whom the world has been crucified to me, and I to the world.

15 For neither is circumcision anything [of any importance], nor uncircumcision, but [only] a new creation [which is the result of a new birth—a spiritual transformation—a new nature in Christ Jesus].

16 Peace and mercy be upon all who walk by this rule [who discipline themselves and conduct their lives by this principle], and upon the [true] Israel of God (Jewish believers). [Ps 125:5]

17 From now on let no one trouble me [by making it necessary for me to justify my authority as an apostle, and the absolute truth of the gospel], for I bear on my body the branding-marks of Jesus [the wounds, scars, and other outward evidence of persecutions—these testify to His ownership of me].

18 The grace of our Lord Jesus Christ be with your spirit, my brothers and sisters. Amen.

---

sanctify (3:3) anyone. However, good works are, in fact, an important fruit of the life of faith (5:5) that God has planned for each believer (Eph 2:8 – 10).

6:12 ***make a good impression.*** The Judaizers were trying to appear spiritual by becoming circumcised and demanding that others become circumcised (5:2 – 12). By teaching that all Christians should become circumcised, the Judaizers were trying to make Christianity into a sect of Judaism. This would have two advantages. First, they could counter the persecution that they suffered from the zealous Jews. Second, they could include themselves with an officially sanctioned religion of the Roman Empire, Judaism.

6:13 ***even the circumcised [Jews] themselves do not [really] keep the Law.*** The Judaizers knew that they were unable to keep the entire law even though they were required to do so. They still attempted to persuade the Galatians to be circumcised so that they could boast about having them as their followers.

6:16 ***the [true] Israel of God.*** This probably refers to the remnant of believing Jews (Ro 11:1 – 2,7). They are Abraham's spiritual descendants (3:6 – 9) because they believe in God and rely on His grace.

6:17 ***I bear on my body.*** Paul's scars branded him as a slave for Christ (Ro 1:1). Such marks far outweighed the "mark" of circumcision so valued by the false teachers in Galatia (vv. 12 – 15).

12 Gal 2:3,14; Php 3:18; Gal 5:11 **14** Php 3:3,7; Ro 6:6 **15** 1Co 7:19; 2Co 5:17 **16** Ps 125:5; Php 3:16; Ro 2:29 **17** 2Co 1:5 **18** 2Ti 4:22

THE LETTER OF PAUL TO THE

EPHESIANS

▸ **AUTHOR:** All internal and external evidence strongly supports the Pauline authorship of Ephesians. In recent years, however, critics have turned to internal grounds to challenge this unanimous ancient tradition. It has been argued that the vocabulary and style are different from other Pauline epistles, but this overlooks Paul's flexibility under different circumstances (as in Romans and 2 Corinthians). The theology of Ephesians in some ways reflects a later development, but this must be attributed to Paul's own growth and meditation on the church as the body of Christ. Ephesians was written during his first Roman imprisonment in AD 60–62, perhaps around the same time as Philippians, Colossians, and Philemon.

▸ **TIMES:** c. AD 60–61 ▸ **KEY VERSES:** Eph 4:1–3

▸ **THEME:** Ephesians is like a grand landscape whose subject is the whole world. Paul paints a richly textured picture of God's plan to bless the world through Christ. God is bringing light to darkness, healing to brokenness and reconciliation to the separated. Central to this teaching is the role of the church in the world and the gifts God has given it. God will bring about these things through the church. Once we understand and believe all that God has done and is doing, it is our responsibility to obey and live in light of His actions. Paul gives us much more than the theory in Ephesians. He makes critical connections between big picture theology and the practical implications for living the day-to-day Christian life.

The Blessings of Redemption

1 PAUL, AN apostle (special messenger, personally chosen representative) of Christ Jesus (the Messiah, the Anointed), by the will of God [that is, by His purpose and choice],
To the saints (God's people) who are at Ephesus and are faithful *and* loyal *and* steadfast in Christ Jesus:
2 Grace to you and peace [inner calm and spiritual well-being] from God our Father and the Lord Jesus Christ.
3 Blessed *and* worthy of praise be the God and Father of our Lord Jesus Christ, who has blessed us with every spiritual blessing in the heavenly realms in Christ,
4 just as [in His love] He chose us in Christ [actually selected us for Himself as His own] before the foundation of

---

1:1–2 *saints.* In the New Testament all believers are set apart by God in Christ. ***Grace be to you and peace.*** The salutations in the New Testament epistles follow the form of the typical first-century letter. The writer is mentioned first and the recipient next, followed by a blessing or best wishes for good health. The difference here lies in the content of the blessing: pagan letters mentioned non-existent gods and goddesses such as Diana or Apollo; the apostles call upon the one true God and His Son Jesus Christ to bless their readers.
1:3 *every spiritual blessing.* God does not guarantee health, wealth, and prosperity to the New Testament believer. The blessings of Christianity are largely spiritual.
1:4–5 *love.* In this instance the Greek *agape* is

CHAPTER 1 **1** 2Co 1:1; Ro 1:7; 2Co 1:1; 1Co 4:17 **2** Gal 1:3 **3** 2Co 1:3 **4** Ro 8:28; 1Pe 1:2; Lk 1:75

the world, so that we would be holy
[that is, consecrated, set apart for Him,
purpose-driven] and blameless in His
sight. In love
5He predestined *and* lovingly
planned for us to be adopted to Himself
as [His own] children through Jesus
Christ, in accordance with the kind
intention *and* good pleasure of His
will—
6to the praise of His glorious grace
and favor, which He so freely bestowed
on us in the Beloved [His Son, Jesus
Christ].
7In Him we have redemption [that is,
our deliverance and salvation] through
His blood, [which paid the penalty for
our sin and resulted in] the forgiveness
and complete pardon of our sin, in ac-
cordance with the riches of His grace
8which He lavished on us. In all wis-
dom and understanding [with practical
insight]
9He made known to us the mystery
of His will according to His good plea-
sure, which He purposed in Christ,
10with regard to the fulfillment of
the times [that is, the end of history,
the climax of the ages]—to bring all
things together in Christ, [both] things
in the heavens and things on the earth.
11In Him also we have received
an inheritance [a destiny—we were
claimed by God as His own], having
been predestined (chosen, appoint-
ed beforehand) according to the pur-
pose of Him who works everything
in agreement with the counsel *and*
design of His will,
12so that we who were the first to
hope in Christ [who first put our con-
fidence in Him as our Lord and Savior]
would exist to the praise of His glory.
13In Him, you also, when you heard
the word of truth, the good news of
your salvation, and [as a result] be-
lieved in Him, were stamped with the
seal of the promised Holy Spirit [the
One promised by Christ] as owned
and protected [by God]. [John 7:39;
Acts 2:33]
14The Spirit is the guarantee [the first
installment, the pledge, a foretaste] of
our inheritance until the redemption of
God's own [purchased] possession [His
believers], to the praise of His glory.
15For this reason, because I have
heard of your faith in the Lord Jesus
and your love for all God's people,
16I do not cease to give thanks for
you, remembering you in my prayers;
17[I always pray] that the God of our
Lord Jesus Christ, the Father of glory,
may grant you a spirit of wisdom and
of revelation [that gives you a deep and
personal and intimate insight] into the
true knowledge of Him [for we know
the Father through the Son].

---

used. That love is a love that is by choice or one's will, not just a sentimental feeling. ***He predestinated and lovingly planned for us.*** Predestination is not a cold-hearted determinism or set fate, but rather a loving choice on God's part.

1:6 *the Beloved.* This title is messianic, referring to God's Son, Jesus.

1:7 *redemption.* The word means "buy back" or "ransom." In ancient times, one could buy back a person who was sold into slavery. In the same way, Christ through His death bought us from our slavery to sin. ***His blood.*** The blood of Christ is the means by which our redemption comes. The Old Testament and the New both clearly teach that there is no forgiveness without the shedding of blood.

1:9 *the mystery.* This is not a puzzle to solve, or knowledge only for the few and the initiated, as in the mystery religions of Paul's day. In Paul's use, the word *mystery* refers to an aspect of God's will that was once hidden or obscure, but now was being revealed by God (Ro 11:25).

1:14 *the guarantee [the first installment, the pledge, a foretaste] of our inheritance.* The Greek word for *earnest* can also be used to indicate an engagement ring. As Christ is the bridegroom and the church is the bride, so the Holy Spirit is the down payment, the earnest money in the long-awaited marriage of the two (Rev 19:7). ***[purchased] possession.*** The Old Testament described the nation of Israel as God's special treasure, one He had purchased by His mighty acts of deliverance during the exodus (Ex 19:5). Here Paul describes Christians as a purchased possession, bought with the blood of Christ.

---

5 Ro 8:29; Jn 1:12; 1Co 1:21 **6** Ro 3:24; Mt 3:17 **7** Heb 9:12; Ro 3:24 **9** Ro 16:25; 2Ti 1:9 **10** Gal 4:4; 1Co 3:22; Col 1:20 **11** Ro 8:17; ver. 5; Isa 46:10 **12** 2Th 2:13; Jas 1:18 **13** Jn 1:17; 2Co 1:22 **14** 2Co 5:5; Ro 8:23; Ac 20:28; 1Pe 2:9 **15** Col 1:4 **16** Ro 1:9 **17** Jn 20:17; Col 1:9

18 And [I pray] that the eyes of your heart [the very center and core of your being] may be enlightened [flooded with light by the Holy Spirit], so that you will know *and* cherish the hope [the divine guarantee, the confident expectation] to which He has called you, the riches of His glorious inheritance in the saints (God's people),

19 and [so that you will begin to know] what the immeasurable *and* unlimited *and* surpassing greatness of His [active, spiritual] power is in us who believe. These are in accordance with the working of His mighty strength

20 which He produced in Christ when He raised Him from the dead and seated Him at His own right hand in the heavenly *places,*

21 far above all rule and authority and power and dominion [whether angelic or human], and [far above] every name that is named [above every title that can be conferred], not only in this age *and* world but also in the one to come.

22 And He put all things [in every realm] in subjection under Christ's feet, and appointed Him as [supreme and authoritative] head over all things in the church, [Ps 8:6; Col 1:18]

23 which is His body, the fullness of Him who fills *and* completes all things in all [believers].

Made Alive in Christ

2 AND YOU [He made alive when you] were [spiritually] dead *and* separated from Him because of your transgressions and sins,

2 in which you once walked. You were following the ways of this world [influenced by this present age], in accordance with the prince of the power of the air (Satan), the spirit who is now at work in the disobedient [the unbelieving, who fight against the purposes of God].

3 Among these [unbelievers] we all once lived in the passions of our flesh [our behavior governed by the sinful self], indulging the desires of human nature [without the Holy Spirit] and [the impulses] of the [sinful] mind. We were, by nature, children [under the sentence] of [God's] wrath, just like the rest [of mankind].

4 But God, being [so very] rich in mercy, because of His great *and* wonderful love with which He loved us,

5 even when we were [spiritually] dead *and* separated from Him because of our sins, He made us [spiritually] alive together with Christ (for by His grace—His undeserved favor and mercy—you have been saved from God's judgment). [Rom 6:1–10]

6 And He raised us up together with Him [when we believed], and seated us with Him in the heavenly *places,* [because we are] in Christ Jesus,

7 [and He did this] so that in the ages to come He might [clearly] show the immeasurable *and* unsurpassed riches of His grace in [His] kindness toward us in Christ Jesus [by providing for our redemption].

8 For it is by grace [God's remarkable compassion and favor drawing you

---

1:18 – 19 *the eyes of your heart.* This phrase refers to spiritual understanding. To describe this, Paul uses words that picture eyes that have been brightened with divine illumination.
1:21 *not only in this age and world but also in the one to come.* The Jews of Christ's time understood the end times to be divided into two time periods, the age in which they were living and the coming age. The Messiah, called "the Coming One," would rule in the age which is to come.
2:2 *in which you once walked.* Walking is a biblical expression that pictures a believer's steady normal progress with God (Ps 1:1). Believers are saved so that they can have a lifestyle characterized by good works (v. 10). ***prince of the power of the air.*** This is a reference to Satan.
2:4 – 7 *we were [spiritually] dead and separated from Him because of our sins.* Because of Adam's sin, the entire human race is spiritually dead. Only God can grant new life and save us from this predicament. Out of His mercy, God gave His Son for us while we were yet His enemies. He loved us long before we loved Him (1Jn 4:9 – 10).
2:8 – 10 *you have been saved ... through faith.* The grace of God is the source of salvation; faith is the channel, not the cause. God alone

---

18 Ac 26:18; Eph 2:12 **19** Col 2:12 **20** Ac 2:24; Ps 110:1 **21** Php 2:9,10; Ro 8:38 **22** Mt 28:18; Heb 2:7 **23** Ro 12:5; Col 2:9; 1Co 12:6 **CHAPTER 2** **1** Col 2:13; Eph 4:18 **2** Col 1:21; Eph 6:12; Col 3:6 **3** 1Pe 4:3; Gal 5:16; Ps 51:5 **4** Ro 10:12 **5** Ro 5:6,8; Ro 6:4,5 **6** Eph 1:20 **7** Titus 3:4 **8** 2Ti 1:9; Ro 4:16; Mt 16:17

to Christ] that you have been saved
[actually delivered from judgment and
given eternal life] through faith. And
this [salvation] is not of yourselves
[not through your own effort], but it is
the [undeserved, gracious] gift of God;
9not as a result of [your] works [nor
your attempts to keep the Law], so that
no one will [be able to] boast *or* take
credit in any way [for his salvation].
10For we are His workmanship
[His own master work, a work of
art], created in Christ Jesus [reborn
from above—spiritually transformed,
renewed, ready to be used] for good
works, which God prepared [for us]
beforehand [taking paths which He
set], so that we would walk in them
[living the good life which He pre-
arranged and made ready for us].
[Rom 1:20]
11Therefore, remember that at one
time you Gentiles by birth, who are
called "Uncircumcision" by those who
called themselves "Circumcision," [it-
self a mere mark] *which is* made in the
flesh by human hands—
12*remember* that at that time you
were separated from Christ [exclud-
ed from any relationship with Him],
alienated from the commonwealth of
Israel, and strangers to the covenants
of promise [with no share in the sacred
Messianic promise and without knowl-
edge of God's agreements], having no
hope [in His promise] and [living] in
the world without God.
13But now [at this very moment] in
Christ Jesus you who once were [so
very] far away [from God] have been
brought near by the blood of Christ.
14For He Himself is our peace *and*
our bond of unity. He who made both
groups—[Jews and Gentiles]—*into* one
body and broke down the barrier, the
dividing wall [of spiritual antagonism
between us],
15by abolishing in His [own cruci-
fied] flesh the hostility *caused by* the
Law with its commandments *con-
tained* in ordinances [which He satis-
fied]; so that in Himself He might make
the two into one new man, thereby
establishing peace.
16And [that He] might reconcile them
both [Jew and Gentile, united] in one
body to God through the cross, thereby
putting to death the hostility.
17AND HE CAME AND PREACHED THE
GOOD NEWS OF PEACE TO YOU [Gentiles]
WHO WERE FAR AWAY, AND PEACE TO THOSE
[Jews] WHO WERE NEAR. [Is 57:19]
18For it is through Him that we both
have a [direct] way of approach in one
Spirit to the Father.
19So then you are no longer strang-
ers and aliens [outsiders without rights
of citizenship], but you are fellow cit-
izens with the saints (God's people),
and are [members] of God's household,
20having been built on the founda-
tion of the apostles and prophets, with
Christ Jesus Himself as the [chief] Cor-
nerstone,
21in whom the whole structure is
joined together, and it continues [to
increase] growing into a holy temple
in the Lord [a sanctuary dedicated,

saves. Salvation never originates in the efforts of people; it always arises out of the lovingkindness of God. ***the [undeserved, gracious] gift of God.*** We cannot do anything to earn our salvation.

2:14 ***the barrier, the dividing wall.*** This was vividly portrayed by an actual partition in the temple area, with a sign warning that any Gentile going beyond the Court of the Gentiles would receive swift and sudden death.

2:15 ***one new man.*** In the early days of Christianity, the church was largely made up of Jews. But, under the direction of God's Spirit, the believers witnessed to Gentiles (Ac 10), who then soon outnumbered the Jewish members. As the two groups learned to work together, they became something completely new.

2:20 ***the apostles and prophets.*** The early church was established on the teaching and preaching of the apostles. They were the foundation of the church.

2:21 ***joined together.*** This idea pictures the process in Roman construction whereby laborers would turn huge rocks around until they fit each other perfectly.

10 Isa 19:25 **11** Col 2:11 **12** Col 1:21; Eze 13:9; Ro 9:4,8; 1Th 4:13; Gal 4:8 **13** Gal 3:28; Ac 2:39 **14** Mic 5:5; Jn 10:16 **15** Col 2:14; Col 1:22; Gal 6:15 **16** Col 1:20-22; Ro 6:6 **17** Isa 57:19; Ps 148:14 **18** Jn 10:9; 1Co 12:13 **19** Php 3:20; Gal 6:10 **20** 1Pe 2:4; Mt 16:18; 1Co 12:28; Ps 118:22 **21** 1Co 3:17

set apart, and sacred to the presence
of the Lord].
22 In Him [and in fellowship with one
another] you also are being built to-
gether into a dwelling place of God in
the Spirit.

Paul's Stewardship

3 FOR THIS reason [because I preach
that you and believing Jews are
joint heirs] I, Paul, am the prisoner
of Christ Jesus on behalf of you Gen-
tiles—
2 assuming that you have heard of
the stewardship of God's grace that
was entrusted to me [to share with you]
for your benefit;
3 and that by [divine] revelation the
mystery was made known to me, as I
have already written in brief. [Eph 1:9]
4 By referring to this, when you read
it you can understand my insight into
the mystery of Christ,
5 which in other generations was not
disclosed to mankind, as it has now
been revealed to His holy apostles and
prophets by the [Holy] Spirit;
6 [it is this:] that the Gentiles are now
joint heirs [with the Jews] and mem-
bers of the same body, and joint par-
takers [sharing] in the [same divine]
promise in Christ Jesus through [their
faith in] the good news [of salvation].
7 Of this [gospel] I was made a min-
ister by the gift of God's grace given
me through the working of His power.
8 To me, [though I am] the very least
of all the saints (God's people), this
grace [which is undeserved] was gra-
ciously given, to proclaim to the Gen-
tiles the good news of the incompre-
hensible riches of Christ [that spiritual
wealth which no one can fully under-
stand],
9 and to make plain [to everyone]
the plan of the mystery [regarding the
uniting of believing Jews and Gentiles
into one body] which [until now] was
kept hidden through the ages in [the
mind of] God who created all things.
10 So now through the church the
multifaceted wisdom of God [in all its
countless aspects] might now be made
known [revealing the mystery] to the
[angelic] rulers and authorities in the
heavenly *places*.
11 *This is* in accordance with [the
terms of] the eternal purpose which He
carried out in Christ Jesus our Lord,
12 in whom we have boldness and
confident access through faith in Him
[that is, our faith gives us sufficient
courage to freely and openly approach
God through Christ].
13 So I ask you not to lose heart at my
sufferings on your behalf, for they are
your glory *and* honor.
14 For this reason [grasping the great-
ness of this plan by which Jews and
Gentiles are joined together in Christ]
I bow my knees [in reverence] before
the Father [of our Lord Jesus Christ],
15 from whom every family in heaven
and on earth derives its name [God—
the first and ultimate Father].
16 May He grant you out of the rich-
es of His glory, to be strengthened
and spiritually energized with power
through His Spirit in your inner self,
[indwelling your innermost being and
personality],
17 so that Christ may dwell in your
hearts through your faith. And may
you, having been [deeply] rooted and
[securely] grounded in love,
18 be fully capable of comprehending
with all the saints (God's people) the
width and length and height and depth

3:5–6 *the Gentiles are now joint heirs.* In Old Testament times people had only partial knowledge of God and His works. While Genesis pointed to the fact that God's grace would come to the Gentiles (Ge 12:3), no one understood that they would also be fully equal with the Jews.
3:10 *multifaceted wisdom.* God's ways are not only "mysterious," but also varied. Angels are also learning about God's wisdom as they watch His grace working in us (1Co 11:10).
3:17 *Christ may dwell in your hearts.* Christ actually resides or makes His home in the believer's heart.

22 1Pe 2:5 **CHAPTER 3** **1** Ac 21:33; Col 1:24 **2** Ro 1:5; Ac 9:15 **3** Ac 22:17; Ro 16:25 **5** Ro 16:25 **6** Gal 3:28 **7** Ro 15:16; 1:5; Ro 15:18 **8** 1Co 15:9; Col 1:27 **9** Ro 16:25; Ps 33:6 **10** 1Pe 1:12; Col 1:16; 1Ti 3:16 **12** Heb 4:16 **13** Php 1:14; 2Co 1:6 **15** Eph 1:10 **16** Php 4:19; Col 1:11; Ro 7:22 **17** Jn 14:23; Col 1:23 **18** Eph 1:18; Ro 10:3

of His love [fully experiencing that amazing, endless love];
[19]and [that you may come] to know [practically, through personal experience] the love of Christ which far surpasses [mere] knowledge [without experience], that you may be filled up [throughout your being] to all the fullness of God [so that you may have the richest experience of God's presence in your lives, completely filled and flooded with God Himself].
[20]Now to Him who is able to [carry out His purpose and] do superabundantly more than all that we dare ask or think [infinitely beyond our greatest prayers, hopes, or dreams], according to His power that is at work within us,
[21]to Him be the glory in the church and in Christ Jesus throughout all generations forever and ever. Amen.

Unity of the Spirit

4 SO I, the prisoner for the Lord, appeal to you to live a life worthy of the calling to which you have been called [that is, to live a life that exhibits godly character, moral courage, personal integrity, and mature behavior—a life that expresses gratitude to God for your salvation],
[2]with all humility [forsaking self-righteousness], and gentleness [maintaining self-control], with patience, bearing with one another in [unselfish] love.
[3]Make every effort to keep the oneness of the Spirit in the bond of peace

---

3:21 The Purpose of the Church — The ultimate purpose of the church is to bring honor and glory to Jesus Christ. It does this as it fulfills its three purposes related to God's plan for the world. **Worship** — As the church worships, it continually declares to believers and the world God's view of reality. God is the world's Creator and Sustainer. Through Jesus Christ, God has redeemed the world and provided a way of salvation for people who rebel against Him. **Evangelism** — The Great Commission in Matthew 28 clearly points to evangelism as a primary purpose for the church. "Teaching" implies that there is more to evangelism than simply declaring the good news. Evangelism should lead to discipleship, which involves the work of helping the new believer reach full maturity in Christ. This happens much as a parent raises children, nurturing them in every way possible so that they can grow. Christ makes baptism an important element in this process. In baptism, one indicates that he has been identified with Christ in His death, burial, and resurrection and that he wishes to be identified with the church. **Edification** — Ephesians 4:12 points to the fact that the saints need to be built up (that is equipped) to fully do the work of the church, namely the ministry of Christ to the world. This involves making believers aware of everything they have in Christ and how the Spirit's gifts enable them to serve the body of Christ effectively.
4:1 *live a life worthy of the calling to which you have been called.* The second half of Ephesians, like that of a number of Paul's epistles, emphasizes the behavior that should result from the doctrines or beliefs taught in the first half.
4:2 *humility [forsaking self-righteousness], and gentleness [maintaining self-control], with patience.* These are the attitudes that Jesus demonstrated when He was on earth (Php 2:5–8). These attitudes do not come naturally, but must be cultivated by the determination to place others above ourselves. Only the Spirit can empower us to treat people this way consistently.
4:3 Person of the Holy Spirit — Many people make the serious error of thinking of the Holy Spirit as only some kind of vague principle or an influence. On the contrary, the Holy Spirit is as much a person (individual existence of a conscious being) as the Father and the Son. **The personality of the Holy Spirit.** The Bible speaks of the mind (Ro 8:27) and will (1Co 2:11) of the Spirit. He is often described as speaking directly to men in the Book of Acts. During Paul's second missionary journey, the apostle was forbidden by the Spirit to visit a certain mission field (Ac 16:6–7) and then was instructed to proceed toward another field of service (Ac 16:10). It was God's Spirit who spoke directly to Christian leaders in the Antioch church, commanding them to send Paul and Barnabas on their first missionary journey (Ac 13:2). **The deity of the Holy Spirit.** He is not only a distinct being, but He is also God. As is God the Father, He too is everywhere at once (Ps 139:7). As the Son is eternal, the Holy Spirit has also existed forever (Heb 9:14). He is often referred to as God in the Bible (Ac 5:3–4). Finally, the Holy Spirit is equal with the Father and Son. This is

---

19 Eph 1:23 **20** Ro 16:25; 1Co 2:9; Col 1:29 **21** Ro 11:36 **CHAPTER 4** **1** Php 1,9; Php 1:27 **2** Ac 20:19 **3** Col 3:14

[each individual working together to make the whole successful].

4 *There is* one body [of believers] and one Spirit—just as you were called to one hope when called [to salvation]—

5 one Lord, one faith, one baptism,

6 one God and Father of us all who is [sovereign] over all and [working] through all and [living] in all.

7 Yet grace [God's undeserved favor] was given to each one of us [not indiscriminately, but in different ways] in proportion to the measure of Christ's [rich and abundant] gift.

8 Therefore it says,

"When He ascended on high,
He led captivity captive,
And He bestowed gifts on men."
[Ps 68:18]

9 (Now this *expression*, "He ascended," what does it mean except that He also had *previously* descended [from the heights of heaven] into the lower parts of the earth?

10 He who descended is the *very* same as He who also has ascended high above all the heavens, that He [His presence] might fill all things [that is, the whole universe]).

11 And [His gifts to the church were varied and] He Himself appointed some as apostles [special messengers, representatives], some as prophets [who speak a new message from God to the people], some as evangelists [who spread the good news of salvation], and some as pastors and teachers [to shepherd and guide and instruct],

12 [and He did this] to fully equip *and* perfect the saints (God's people) for works of service, to build up the body of Christ [the church];

13 until we all reach oneness in the faith and in the knowledge of the Son of God, [growing spiritually] to become a mature believer, reaching to the measure of the fullness of Christ [manifesting His spiritual completeness and exercising our spiritual gifts in unity].

14 So that we are no longer children [spiritually immature], tossed back and forth [like ships on a stormy sea] and carried about by every wind of [shifting] doctrine, by the cunning *and* trickery of [unscrupulous] men, by the deceitful scheming of people ready to do anything [for personal profit].

15 But speaking the truth in love [in all things—both our speech and our lives expressing His truth], let us grow

---

seen during the baptism of Christ (Mt 3:16–17) and is mentioned by Jesus Himself just prior to His ascension from the Mount of Olives (Mt 28:19–20).

4:7 *grace [God's undeserved favor] was given ... in proportion to the measure of Christ's [rich and abundant] gift.* Like Peter (1Pe 4:10), Paul taught that all Christians have a spiritual gift or gifts. The gifts are given sovereignly by the ascended Christ in order to build up the church (1Co 12:11). Thus the body of Christ is to function like a machine in which every part is essential for getting a job done. But, unlike a machine, the body of Christ should maintain itself and build every one of its members up so that they can do good works (1Co 12:7).

4:8 *When He ascended on high.* Paul quotes Psalm 68:18 to picture the ascended Messiah triumphant over Satan and his hosts, distributing spiritual gifts to His people.

4:11 *apostles ... prophets ... evangelists ... pastors and teachers.* Apostles, meaning "envoys" or "ambassadors," in its strict sense refers to those who saw Christ in resurrected form and were specially chosen by Christ to tell others about Him from their eyewitness accounts. Prophets delivered direct revelations from God. They foretold God's actions in the future and they proclaimed what God had already said in the Scriptures. Evangelists play a major role in bringing people into the body of Christ. Pastors function as shepherds. They feed, nurture, care for, and protect the members of the body. The Greek ties in teacher with pastor.

4:12–13 *fully equip and perfect the saints for works of service ... to build up the body of Christ.* Three stages of growth are presented here. Leaders are responsible to perfect, or equip. The well-equipped saints do the work of the ministry, and the result is that the body is built up. The final goal is maturity, truth, and love.

---

4 Ro 12:5 **5** 1Co 1:13; Jude 3; Heb 6:6 **6** Mal 2:10; Ro 11:36 **7** 1Co 12:11 **8** Ps 68:18; Jdg 5:12 **9** Jn 3:13 **10** Ac 1:9; Ac 2:33 **11** 1Co 12:28; Ac 21:8; Ac 20:28; Ro 12:7 **12** 1Co 12:7; 1Co 14:26; Col 1:24 **13** Col 2:2; 1Co 14:20 **14** Isa 28:9; Heb 13:9; Mt 11:7; Ro 16:18 **15** 2Co 4:2; Eph 1:22; Col 1:18

up in all *things* into Him [following His example] who is the Head—Christ.

16 From Him the whole body [the church, in all its various parts], joined and knitted *firmly* together by what every joint supplies, when each part is working properly, causes the body to grow *and* mature, building itself up in [unselfish] love.

The Christian's Walk

17 So this I say, and solemnly affirm together with the Lord [as in His presence], that you must no longer live as the [unbelieving] Gentiles live, in the futility of their minds [and in the foolishness and emptiness of their souls],

18 for their [moral] understanding is darkened *and* their reasoning is clouded; [they are] alienated *and* self-banished from the life of God [with no share in it; this is] because of the [willful] ignorance *and* spiritual blindness that is [deep-seated] within them, because of the hardness *and* insensitivity of their heart.

19 And they, [the ungodly in their spiritual apathy], having become callous *and* unfeeling, have given themselves over [as prey] to unbridled sensuality, eagerly craving the practice of every kind of impurity [that their desires may demand].

20 But you did not learn Christ in this way!

21 If in fact you have [really] heard Him and have been taught by Him, just as truth is in Jesus [revealed in His life and personified in Him],

22 that, regarding your previous way of life, you put off your old self [completely discard your former nature], which is being corrupted through deceitful desires,

23 and be *continually* renewed in the spirit of your mind [having a fresh, untarnished mental and spiritual attitude],

24 and put on the new self [the regenerated and renewed nature], created in God's image, [godlike] in the righteousness and holiness of the truth [living in a way that expresses to God your gratitude for your salvation].

25 Therefore, rejecting all falsehood [whether lying, defrauding, telling half-truths, spreading rumors, any such as these], SPEAK TRUTH EACH ONE WITH HIS NEIGHBOR, for we are all parts of one another [and we are all parts of the body of Christ]. [Zech 8:16]

26 BE ANGRY [at sin—at immorality, at injustice, at ungodly behavior], YET DO NOT SIN; do not let your anger [cause you shame, nor allow it to] last until the sun goes down. [Ps 4:4]

27 And do not give the devil an opportunity [to lead you into sin by holding a grudge, or nurturing anger, or harboring resentment, or cultivating bitterness].

28 The thief [who has become a believer] must no longer steal, but instead he must work hard [making an honest living], producing that which is good with his own hands, so that he will have *something* to share with those in need.

29 Do not let unwholesome [foul, profane, worthless, vulgar] words ever come out of your mouth, but only such *speech* as is good for building up others, according to the need *and* the occasion, so that it will be a blessing to those who hear [you speak].

30 And do not grieve the Holy Spirit of God [but seek to please Him], by whom you were sealed *and* marked [branded as God's own] for the day of redemption [the final deliverance from the consequences of sin]. [Eph 1:13, 14; Phil 3:20, 21]

4:16 *every joint . . . each part.* There are no insignificant parts in the body (1Co 12:14 – 27). Anything that builds up believers and the church can be said to be edifying.

4:22 – 24 *you put off your old self.* Paul compares the Christian life to stripping off the dirty clothes of a sinful past and putting on the snowy white robes of Christ's righteousness.

4:30 *the Holy Spirit of God.* We should never push away, ignore, or reject the Holy Spirit. If we would remember that the One who lives in us is God's own Spirit, we would be much more

16 Col 2:19 **17** Col 3:7; Ro 1:21 **18** Ac 26:18; 1Th 4:5; Ro 1:21 **19** 1Ti 4:2; 1Pe 4:3 **22** Col 2:11; 3:7 **23** Col 3:10 **24** Ro 6:4 **25** Zec 8:16; Ro 12:5 **26** Ps 37:8 **27** 1Pe 5:9 **28** Ac 20:35; Lk 3:11 **29** Col 3:8; 1Th 5:11; Col 3:16 **30** Isa 7:13; Lk 21:28

31 Let all bitterness and wrath and
anger and clamor [perpetual animosi-
ty, resentment, strife, fault-finding] and
slander be put away from you, along
with every kind of malice [all spiteful-
ness, verbal abuse, malevolence].
32 Be kind *and* helpful to one another,
tender-hearted [compassionate, under-
standing], forgiving one another [read-
ily and freely], just as God in Christ
also forgave you.

Be Imitators of God

5 THEREFORE BECOME imitators
of God [copy Him and follow His
example], as well-beloved children
[imitate their father];
2 and walk *continually* in love [that
is, value one another—practice em-
pathy and compassion, unselfishly
seeking the best for others], just as
Christ also loved you and gave Himself
up for us, an offering and sacrifice to
God [slain for you, so that it became]
a sweet fragrance. [Ezek 20:41]
3 But sexual immorality and all [mor-
al] impurity [indecent, offensive be-
havior] or greed must not even be hint-
ed at among you, as is proper among
saints [for as believers our way of life,
whether in public or in private, reflects
the validity of our faith].
4 Let there be no filthiness and sil-
ly talk, or coarse [obscene or vulgar]
joking, *because* such things are not
appropriate [for believers]; but instead
speak of your thankfulness [to God].
5 For be sure of this: no immoral, im-
pure, or greedy person—for that one
is [in effect] an idolater—has any in-
heritance in the kingdom of Christ and
God [for such a person places a higher
value on something other than God].
6 Let no one deceive you with empty
arguments [that encourage you to sin],
for because of these things the wrath
of God comes upon the sons of dis-
obedience [those who habitually sin].
[Lev 18:24, 25]
7 So do not participate *or* even asso-
ciate with them [in the rebelliousness
of sin].
8 For once you were darkness, but
now you are Light in the Lord; walk
as children of Light [live as those who
are native-born to the Light]
9 (for the fruit [the effect, the result]
of the Light consists in all goodness
and righteousness and truth),
10 trying to learn [by experience]
what is pleasing to the Lord [and let-
ting your lifestyles be examples of
what is most acceptable to Him—your
behavior expressing gratitude to God
for your salvation].
11 Do not participate in the worthless
and unproductive deeds of darkness,
but instead expose them [by exempli-
fying personal integrity, moral cour-
age, and godly character];
12 for it is disgraceful even to mention
the things that such people practice
in secret.
13 But all things become visible when
they are exposed by the light [of God's
precepts], for it is light that makes
everything visible.
14 For this reason He says,

"Awake, sleeper,
And arise from the dead,
And Christ will shine [as dawn]
upon you *and* give you light."
[Is 26:19; 51:17; 52:1; 60:1, 2]

15 Therefore see that you walk care-
fully [living life with honor, purpose,
and courage; shunning those who
tolerate and enable evil], not as the
unwise, but as wise [sensible, intelli-
gent, discerning people],
16 making the very most of your time
[on earth, recognizing and taking ad-

---

selective about what we think, read, watch, say, and do.

5:1 *Therefore become imitators of God.* Believers are to follow the example of God's actions. He loved us when we were still His enemies.

5:12 *in secret.* This verse effectively bans Christians from indulging in the modern preoccupation with examining the lurid details of evils such as the occult and other perverted practices.

5:16 *making the very most of your time.* This

31 Col 3:8,19; Jas 4:11; Titus 3:3 **32** 2Co 2:10; Mk 11:25 **CHAPTER 5** **1** Lk 6:36 **2** 1Th 4:9; Gal 1:4; 2Co 2:15 **3** Ro 6:13; 1Co 5:1 **4** Mt 12:35; Ro 1:28 **5** 1Co 6:9; Col 3:5; Rev 22:15 **6** Jer 29:8; Ro 1:18 **8** Isa 9:2; 2Co 3:18; Lk 16:8 **9** Gal 5:22 **10** Ro 12:2 **11** Ro 6:21; 1Ti 5:20 **12** Ro 1:24 **13** Jn 3:20 **14** Isa 60:1; Jn 5:25 **15** Col 4:5 **16** Col 4:5; Ecc 11:2

vantage of each opportunity and using it with wisdom and diligence], because the days are [filled with] evil.

17 Therefore do not be foolish *and* thoughtless, but understand *and* firmly grasp what the will of the Lord is.

18 Do not get drunk with wine, for that is wickedness (corruption, stupidity), but be filled with the [Holy] Spirit *and* constantly guided by Him. [Prov 23:20]

19 Speak to one another in psalms and hymns and spiritual songs, [offering praise by] singing and making melody with your heart to the Lord;

20 always giving thanks to God the Father for all things, in the name of our Lord Jesus Christ;

21 being subject to one another out of reverence for Christ.

Marriage Like Christ and the Church

22 Wives, be *subject* to your own husbands, as [a service] to the Lord.

23 For the husband is head of the wife, as Christ is head of the church, Himself *being* the Savior of the body.

24 But as the church is subject to Christ, so also wives should be subject to their husbands in everything [respecting both their position as protector and their responsibility to God as head of the house].

25 Husbands, love your wives [seek the highest good for her and surround her with a caring, unselfish love], just as Christ also loved the church and gave Himself up for her,

26 so that He might sanctify the

---

means taking advantage of opportunities for service. Paul exhorts us to use as much time as is possible for advancing Christ's purposes in this world.

5:18 ***drunk with wine.*** Just as a person who is drunk is under the control of alcohol, so a Spirit-filled believer is controlled by the Spirit. ***filled.*** Filling is a step beyond the sealing of the Holy Spirit (1:13). Sealing is an action God took at the point of our new birth. The tense of the Greek word translated *filled* indicates that filling is a moment-by-moment repeatable action. To be filled with the Spirit is to be controlled by the Spirit and is therefore crucial to successfully living the Christian life. The imperative says that the believer is to be filled with the presence of the Spirit so that he comes to know God in all His fullness, living in relationship with Him. Out of this relationship, the believer is able to manifest Christlike character. The certainty of being filled with the Spirit may be confirmed by the believer's faith and life. The believer must, of course, believe God's Word that meeting the conditions will result in the filling. The Spirit-filled person will exhibit the Christlike character described in Galatians 5:22 – 23 as the fruit of the Spirit. Included in that list are all the vibrant, attractive qualities desired by all Christians. Any Christian may be transformed by the filling of the Spirit and possess these qualities.

5:19 ***singing and making melody.*** Most believe that these words refer to three larger categories: (1) the 150 psalms in the Psalter, (2) hymns or compositions addressed directly to God, and (3) spiritual songs, hymns about the Christian experience.

5:21 – 22 ***being subject.*** Verse 21 completes the thought of the previous verses (vv. 18 – 20), which address how being filled with the Spirit manifests itself in the believer's life. It also introduces the next section (5:22 – 6:4), about how members of a Christian family should relate to each other. The Greek word for *being subject* does not refer to being under the absolute control of another but to voluntarily place oneself under the authority of another.

5:22 – 24 ***Wives, be subject.*** Just as Christ is not inferior to the Father, but is the second Person in the Trinity, so wives are equal to their own husbands. Yet, in a marriage relationship, a husband and wife have different roles. A wife's voluntary submission arises out of her own submission to Christ.

5:25 ***Husbands, love.*** Paul does not emphasize the husband's authority; instead, he calls on husbands to love self-sacrificially. Husbands are to emulate Christ's love, the kind of love that is willing to lay down one's life for another. ***Christ also loved the church.*** The relationship between Christ and the church was initiated by Christ, who loved the church and gave Himself for it. The details of that relationship are described with seven images:

"The Shepherd and the sheep" emphasizes both the warm leadership and protection of Christ and the helplessness and dependency of believers (Jn 10:1 – 18).

"The vine and the branches" points out the

---

17 Col 4:5; Ro 12:2; 1Th 4:3 **18** Pr 20:1 **19** Ac 16:25 **20** Ps 34:1; 1Pe 2:5 **21** Php 2:3 **22** Ge 3:16; Eph 6:5 **23** 1Co 11:3; Col 1:18; Eph 1:23 **24** Titus 2:9 **25** Col 3:19; Ac 20:28 **26** Jn 3:5

church, having cleansed her by the washing of water with the word [of God],

[27]so that [in turn] He might present the church to Himself in glorious splendor, without spot or wrinkle or any such thing; but that she would be holy [set apart for God] and blameless.

[28]Even so husbands should *and* are morally obligated to love their own wives as [being in a sense] their own bodies. He who loves his own wife loves himself.

[29]For no one ever hated his own body, but [instead] he nourishes *and* protects and cherishes it, just as Christ does the church,

[30]because we are members (parts) of His body.

[31]FOR THIS REASON A MAN SHALL LEAVE HIS FATHER AND HIS MOTHER AND SHALL BE JOINED [and be faithfully devoted] TO HIS WIFE, AND THE TWO SHALL BECOME ONE FLESH. [Gen 2:24]

[32]This mystery [of two becoming one] is great; but I am speaking with reference to [the relationship of] Christ and the church.

[33]However, each man among you [without exception] is to love his wife as his very own self [with behavior worthy of respect and esteem, always seeking the best for her with an attitude of lovingkindness], and the wife [must see to it] that she respects *and* delights in her husband [that she notices him and prefers him and treats him with loving concern, treasuring him, honoring him, and holding him dear]. [1 Pet 3:2]

Family Relationships

6 CHILDREN, OBEY your parents in the Lord [that is, accept their guidance and discipline as His representatives], for this is right [for obedience teaches wisdom and self-discipline].

[2]HONOR [esteem, value as precious] YOUR FATHER AND YOUR MOTHER [and be respectful to them]—this is the first commandment with a promise—

[3]SO THAT IT MAY BE WELL WITH YOU, AND THAT YOU MAY HAVE A LONG LIFE ON THE EARTH. [Ex 20:12]

[4]Fathers, do not provoke your children to anger [do not exasperate them to the point of resentment with de-

---

necessity for Christians to depend on Christ's sustaining strength for growth (Jn 15:1 – 8).

"Christ as high priest" and "the church as a kingdom of priests" stress the joyful worship, fellowship, and service which the church can render to God through Christ (Heb 5:1 – 10; 7:1; 8:6; 1Pe 2:5 – 9).

"The cornerstone and building stones" (Mt 21:42) accents the foundational value of Christ to everything the church is and does, as well as Christ's value to the unity of believers. Love is to be the mortar which solidly holds the living stones together (1Co 3:9; 13:1 – 13; Eph 2:19 – 22; 1Pe 2:5).

"The head and many-membered body," the church is a vibrant organism, not merely an organization; it draws its vitality and direction from Christ, the Head, and each believer has a unique and necessary place in its growth (1Co 12:12 – 13,27; Eph 4:4).

"The last Adam and new creation" presents Christ as the initiator of a new creation of believers as Adam was of the old creation (1Co 15:22,45; 2Co 5:17).

"The bridegroom and bride" beautifully emphasizes the intimate fellowship and co-ownership existing between Christ and the church (Eph 5:25 – 33; Rev 19:7 – 8; 21:9).

5:31 ***THE TWO SHALL BECOME ONE FLESH.*** Paul quotes Genesis 2:24, which teaches that the special union between husband and wife supersedes the original family ties.

5:32 ***This mystery . . . is great.*** A sacred secret revealed is that Christian marriage parallels the union that exists spiritually between Christ and His bride, the church.

6:1 – 4 ***Children, obey . . . Fathers, do not provoke.*** This paragraph has the beautiful balance we expect to find in God's Word: children are to obey their parents, and parents are to treat their children in such a way that the children will want to obey.

6:4 Parenting — The father is the parent responsible for setting the pattern for the child's obedience in the family. The father's responsibility is set forth in two ways: First, what the father is *not to do* — "do not provoke your children to anger." He is not to overdiscipline them or rule

---

27 Col 1:22; SS 4:7 **30** Ge 2:23 **31** Mt 19:5; 1Co 6:16 **33** Col 3:19; 1Pe 3:6 **CHAPTER 6** **1** Col 3:20 **2** Ex 20:12 **4** Col 3:21; Ge 18:19

mands that are trivial or unreasonable or humiliating or abusive; nor by showing favoritism or indifference to any of them], but bring them up [tenderly, with lovingkindness] in the discipline and instruction of the Lord.

5 Slaves, be obedient to those who are your earthly masters, with respect for authority, and with a sincere heart [seeking to please them], as [service] to Christ—

6 not in the way of eye-service [working only when someone is watching you and only] to please men, but as slaves of Christ, doing the will of God from your heart;

7 rendering service with goodwill, as to the Lord, and not [only] to men,

8 knowing that whatever good thing each one does, he will receive this back from the Lord, whether [he is] slave or free.

9 You masters, do the same [showing goodwill] toward them, and give up threatening *and* abusive words, knowing that [He who is] both their true Master and yours is in heaven, and that there is no partiality with Him [regardless of one's earthly status].

The Armor of God

10 In conclusion, be strong in the Lord [draw your strength from Him and be empowered through your union with Him] and in the power of His [boundless] might.

11 Put on the full armor of God [for His precepts are like the splendid armor of a heavily-armed soldier], so that you may be able to [successfully] stand up against all the schemes *and* the strategies *and* the deceits of the devil.

12 For our struggle is not against flesh and blood [contending only with physical opponents], but against the rulers, against the powers, against the world forces of this [present] darkness, against the spiritual *forces* of wickedness in the heavenly (supernatural) *places*.

13 Therefore, put on the complete armor of God, so that you will be able to [successfully] resist *and* stand your ground in the evil day [of danger], and having done everything [that the crisis demands], to stand firm [in your place, fully prepared, immovable, victorious].

14 So stand firm *and* hold your ground, HAVING TIGHTENED THE WIDE BAND

---

the household in such a way that the child can only react in a rage. Second, what the father is *to do* — "but bring them up ... in the discipline and instruction of the Lord." "Bring them up" involves three ideas:

It is a continuous job. As long as the child is a dependent, the father is to be responsible for providing for the child so that he becomes what God wants him to be.

It is a loving job. To "bring up" means literally to nourish tenderly; children should be objects of tender, loving care.

It is a job that involves nurture and admonition. The child needs to be nurtured physically and spiritually. He also needs corrective discipline that will be effective in bringing about obedience to the Word of God (Pr 13:24; 19:18; 29:15 – 17).

6:5 *Slaves, be obedient.* The word "slaves" can also be translated "bondservants." They made up a large percentage of the population of the Roman Empire. These people were considered mere property and could be abused and even killed by their masters with no resulting investigation by the state. In the church, wealthy slave owners and their slaves broke bread together at the Lord's Table as equals.

6:6 *not in the way of eye-service.* Servants and employees should serve faithfully even when no one is looking. After all, God sees all that we do.

6:11 *the full armor of God.* This equipment is the believer's protection against evil and the devil. Paul presented the extended metaphor of the battle dress roughly according to the order in which the various pieces were put on.

6:12 *For our struggle is not.* The real battle is not with human cultists, false religionists, atheists, agnostics, and pseudo-Christians, but with the demonic beings working through them.

6:14 *TRUTH.* This is a reference to integrity, a life of practical truthfulness and honesty. ***BREASTPLATE.*** In Roman times this went completely around the body and was made of hard leather or metal. ***RIGHTEOUSNESS.*** This is not the righteousness of Christ, which all believers possess, but the practical, righteous character and deeds of the believer.

---

5 1Ti 6:1; 2Co 7:15; Php 2:12; 1Ch 29:17; Col 3:22 **6** Col 3:22 **8** Ro 2:6; Col 3:24; Gal 3:28 **9** Col 4:1; Ro 2:11
11 2Co 6:7 **12** Ro 8:38; Lk 22:53 **13** 2Co 10:4; Eph 5:16 **14** Isa 11:5; 1Pe 1:13; Isa 59:17

OF TRUTH (personal integrity, moral
courage) AROUND YOUR WAIST and HAVING
PUT ON THE BREASTPLATE OF RIGHTEOUSNESS
(an upright heart), [Is 11:5]
15 and having strapped on YOUR FEET
THE GOSPEL OF PEACE IN PREPARATION [to
face the enemy with firm-footed sta-
bility and the readiness produced by
the good news]. [Is 52:7]
16 Above all, lift up the [protective]
shield of faith with which you can ex-
tinguish all the flaming arrows of the
evil *one*.
17 And take THE HELMET OF SALVATION,
and the sword of the Spirit, which is
the Word of God. [Is 59:17]
18 With all prayer and petition pray
[with specific requests] at all times [on
every occasion and in every season]
in the Spirit, and with this in view,
stay alert with all perseverance and
petition [interceding in prayer] for all
God's people.
19 And *pray* for me, that words may
be given to me when I open my mouth,
to proclaim boldly the mystery of the
good news [of salvation],
20 for which I am an ambassador in
chains. And *pray* that in *proclaiming* it
I may speak boldly *and* courageously,
as I should.
21 Now, so that you may know how I
am and what I am doing, Tychicus, the
beloved brother and faithful minister
in the Lord, will tell you everything.
22 I have sent him to you for this very
purpose, so that you may know how
we are, and that he may comfort *and*
encourage *and* strengthen your hearts.
23 Peace be to the brothers and sis-
ters, and love joined with faith, from
God the Father and the Lord Jesus
Christ.
24 Grace be with all who love our
Lord Jesus Christ with undying *and*
incorruptible *love*.

6:15 *THE GOSPEL OF PEACE IN PREPARATION.* This may mean either that the gospel is the firm foundation on which Christians are to stand or that the Christian soldier should be ready to go out to defend and spread the gospel.

6:16 *shield of faith.* The Christian's shield offers protection against all forms of evil. Flaming arrows could not penetrate the fireproof shield of the ancient Roman soldier, nor can the assaults of Satan penetrate to the believer who places his or her faith in God.

6:17 *the sword of the Spirit.* This is the only offensive weapon in the believer's armor. This weapon is not necessarily the Bible as a whole, but the specific word that needs to be spoken in a specific situation.

6:21 – 24 *that you may know how I am and what I am doing.* The last verses of Ephesians reveal Paul's appreciation of the ministry of others, especially the ministry of Tychicus (Col 4:7). The fact that this letter does not conclude with personal greetings, as Paul's other letters do, may indicate that this was a circular letter, one intended for a number of churches around Ephesus.

15 Isa 52:7 **16** 1Jn 5:4 **17** 1Th 5:8; Heb 4:12 **18** Lk 18:1; Mt 26:41; Php 1:4 **19** Ac 4:29; 2Co 3:12 **20** 2Co 5:20; Php 1:20 **21** Ac 20:4 **22** Col 4:8 **23** 1Pe 5:14

THE LETTER OF PAUL TO THE
PHILIPPIANS

▸ **AUTHOR:** The external and internal evidence for the Pauline authorship of Philippians is very strong, and there is scarcely any doubt that anyone but Paul wrote it. Paul's "Macedonian Call" in Troas during his second missionary journey led to his ministry in Philippi with the conversion of Lydia and others. Internal evidence suggests that the epistle was written from Rome (1:3; 4:22), although some commentators argue for Caesarea or Ephesus. It seems that during the writing of this letter Paul's life was at stake, and he was evidently awaiting the verdict of the Imperial Court (2:20–26).

▸ **TIMES:** c. AD 62 ▸ **KEY VERSES:** Php 4:4–7

▸ **THEME:** Even though Paul probably wrote this letter while imprisoned in Rome, the letter is often called the Epistle of Joy. It gives us valuable insight into key areas of the Christian life by helping understand how we should identify with Christ in a variety of circumstances. We gain some insight into what Christian relationships should look like and what the content of our prayers for each other should be. Philippians also provides great insight in setting spiritual direction and determining practical priorities. Christians desiring to mature in the Lord will return to study it often.

Thanksgiving

1 PAUL AND Timothy, bond-servants of Christ Jesus (the Messiah, the Anointed),

To all the saints (God's people) in Christ Jesus who are at Philippi, including the overseers and deacons:

[2]Grace to you and peace [inner calm and spiritual well-being] from God our Father and the Lord Jesus Christ.

[3]I thank my God in every remembrance of you,

[4]always offering every prayer of mine with joy [and with specific requests] for all of you,

[5][thanking God] for your participation *and* partnership [both your comforting fellowship and gracious contributions] in [advancing] the good news [regarding salvation] from the first day [you heard it] until now.

1:1–11 ***To all the saints.*** This term means "holy ones" (those who are separated to God) and refers to all the believers in Philippi. ***overseers.*** This refers to those who watch over the spiritual welfare of the local church. ***deacons.*** This is a reference to those who serve the congregation in special service capacities. They were charged with handling the physical and material concerns of the church (Ac 6:1–7). In the first few verses, Paul reveals his great love for the Philippians. He thinks of them often (vv. 3–6), he is concerned about them (vv. 7–8), and he regularly prays for them (vv. 9–11).

1:3 ***I thank.*** The tense of the Greek verb indicates that Paul was continually thankful to God for the Philippian Christians. ***in every remembrance of you.*** Every time God brought them to his mind, Paul gave thanks.

1:4 ***joy.*** This is the first of five uses of the Greek word for *joy* in the letter (v. 25; 2:2,29; 4:1). Paul also uses the Greek word for *rejoice* eight times in this letter (v. 18; 2:17–18,28; 3:1; 4:4).

1:5 ***partnership.*** This term is a commercial term for a joint-partnership in a business venture in which all parties actively participate to ensure

CHAPTER 1 1 1Co 1:2 2 1Pe 1:2 3 1Co 1:4 5 Ro 12:13

6 I am convinced *and* confident of
this very thing, that He who has begun
a good work in you will [continue to]
perfect *and* complete it until the day of
Christ Jesus [the time of His return].
[Rom 14:10]
7 It is right for me to feel this way
about you, because [you have me in
your heart as] I have you in my heart,
since both in my imprisonment and in
the defense and confirmation of the
good news [regarding salvation], all
of you share in [His matchless] grace
with me.
8 For God is my witness, how I long
for all of you with the affection of
Christ Jesus [whose great love fills me].
9 And this I pray, that your love may
abound more and more [displaying it-
self in greater depth] in real knowledge
and in practical insight,
10 so that you may learn to recognize
and treasure what is excellent [iden-
tifying the best, and distinguishing
moral differences], and that you may
be pure and blameless until the day of
Christ [actually living lives that lead
others away from sin];
11 filled with the fruit of righteous-
ness which comes through Jesus
Christ, to the glory and praise of God
[so that His glory may be both revealed
and recognized].

The Gospel Is Preached

12 Now I want you to know, believers,
that what has happened to me [this
imprisonment that was meant to stop
me] has actually served to advance [the
spread of] the good news [regarding
salvation].
13 My imprisonment in [the cause of]
Christ has become common knowl-
edge throughout the whole praetorian
(imperial) guard and to everyone else.
14 Because of my chains [seeing that
I am doing well and that God is ac-
complishing great things], most of the
brothers have renewed confidence in
the Lord, and have far more courage
to speak the word of God [concerning
salvation] without fear [of the conse-
quences, seeing that God can work His
good in all circumstances].
15 Some, it is true, are [actually]
preaching Christ out of envy and

---

the success of the business. In the Christian community, the word expresses intimacy with Christ (1Co 1:9).

1:6 *until.* This word can also be translated "as far as." It expresses progress toward a goal and indicates that a time is coming when God will completely finish His work among the Philippian Christians.

1:7 *right.* This word conveys a sense of moral uprightness and is often translated throughout the New Testament as "righteous." In this context, the word indicates that Paul's thoughts regarding the Philippians were in perfect accord with God's will. ***confirmation.*** Used only here and in Hebrews 6:16 in the New Testament, this word is a legal and commercial term meaning "a validating guarantee."

1:8 *the affection of Christ Jesus.* The word translated "affection" literally means the internal organs, regarded by the first century reader as the center of the deepest feelings. Whereas the heart is the seat of reflection, Paul now speaks of his deep feelings for the believers. His feelings for the Philippians were like those of Jesus Christ, who loved them and died for them.

1:9 *love.* The kind of love that Paul sought for the believers is the highest form of Christian love, based on a lasting, unconditional commitment, not on an unstable emotion. ***knowledge.*** The first of two terms on which a directed love is built, knowledge suggests an intimate understanding based on a relationship with a person. Here the focus of this knowledge is God. ***insight.*** Found only here in the New Testament, the Greek word means moral or ethical understanding based on both the intellect and the senses.

1:12 *advance.* This word could suggest a pioneer beating or cutting a path through a densely forested area. Paul's imprisonment was a strategic advance in the kingdom of God because it was clearing the way for the gospel to penetrate the ranks of the Roman military.

1:13 *praetorian (imperial) guard.* This is a force consisting of several thousand highly trained, elite soldiers of the Roman Empire who were headquartered at Rome. For the one to two years that Paul had been under house arrest in Rome, different soldiers had taken turns guarding him. Although Paul could not go to the world to preach, in this way God brought the world to Paul. In an ironic twist, they were the captives and Paul was free to preach.

6 Jn 6:29 **8** Ro 1:9; Gal 1:20 **10** Ro 12:2; Ac 24:16; 1Co 1:8 **11** Eph 2:10; Col 1:6; Jn 15:8 **13** Php 4:22 **15** Php 2:3

rivalry [toward me—for no better reason than a competitive spirit or misguided ambition], but others out of goodwill *and* a loyal spirit [toward me].

16The latter [preach Christ] out of love, because they know that I have been put here [by God on purpose] for the defense of the gospel;

17but the former preach Christ [insincerely] out of selfish ambition [just self-promotion], thinking that they are causing me distress in my imprisonment.

18What then [does it matter]? So long as in every way, whether in pretense [for self-promotion] or in all honesty [to spread the truth], Christ is being preached; and in this I rejoice.

Yes, and I will rejoice [later as well],
19for I know [with confidence] that this will turn out for my deliverance *and* spiritual well-being, through your prayers and the [superabundant] supply of the Spirit of Jesus Christ [which upholds me].

20It is my own eager expectation and hope, that [looking toward the future] I will not disgrace myself *nor* be ashamed in anything, but that with courage *and* the utmost freedom of speech, even now as always, Christ will be magnified *and* exalted in my body, whether by life or by death.

To Live Is Christ

21For to me, to live is Christ [He is my source of joy, my reason to live] and to die is gain [for I will be with Him in eternity].

22If, however, it is to be life here *and* I am to go on living, this *will mean* useful *and* productive service for me; so I do not know which to choose [if I am given that choice].

23But I am hard-pressed between the two. I have the desire to leave [this world] and be with Christ, for that is far, far better;

24yet to remain in my body is more necessary *and* essential for your sake.

25Since I am convinced of this, I know that I will remain and continue with all of you for your progress and joy in the faith,

26so that your rejoicing for me may overflow in Christ Jesus through my coming to you again.

27Only [be sure to] lead your lives in a manner [that will be] worthy of the gospel of Christ, so that whether I do come and see you or remain absent, I will hear about you that you are standing firm in one spirit [and one purpose], with one mind striving side by side [as if in combat] for the faith of the gospel.

28And in no way be alarmed *or* intimidated [in anything] by your opponents,

---

1:18 *in pretense [for self-promotion] or in all honesty.* Whether the preaching was done for false motives or pure, whether for appearance's sake or for the sake of what was right, Paul was pleased that the gospel was being spread.

1:20 *be magnified.* Paul was committed to ensuring that Christ would be made even more conspicuous in his own life than ever. He was not relying on himself to magnify Christ but looked to the Holy Spirit (v. 19) to magnify Christ in him (Jn 16:14).

1:21 *Christ . . . gain.* Paul would experience gain in his own death because He would be with Christ (v. 23). In fact, Paul may have been expressing his confidence that his imprisonment had furthered the gospel; God would also use his death to further His kingdom.

1:22 *I do not know which to choose.* Paul was in a dilemma because he clearly saw the advantages of both life and death, for the Christian life meant an opportunity to minister to people like the Philippians (v. 24), while death meant being with Christ his Savior.

1:25 *your progress.* Paul was not satisfied that the Philippian Christians should simply be saved, but that they should advance to maturity in Christ.

1:27 *lead your lives.* The word used could refer to discharging the obligations of a citizen. Because Philippi held the privileged status of a Roman colony, its citizens understood the responsibilities associated with citizenship. Paul here commanded them to shift their perspective from the earthly realm to the heavenly one. They should live in this world as citizens of another world, the heavenly kingdom. Their conduct should reveal their heavenly citizenship.

1:28 *alarmed or intimidated.* This phrase is used for the terror of a panicked horse. The

19 2Co 1:11 **20** Ro 8:19; 5:5; Eph 6:19 **23** 2Co 5:8; 2Ti 4:6 **25** Php 2:24 **26** 2Co 1:14 **27** Eph 4:1; 1Th 2:12; 1Co 1:10; Ac 2:36 **28** 2Th 1:5; Ro 8:17

for such [constancy and fearlessness on your part] is a [clear] sign [a proof and a seal] for them of [their impending] destruction, but [a clear sign] for you of deliverance *and* salvation, and that *too,* from God.
29For you have been granted [the privilege] for Christ's sake, not only to believe *and* confidently trust in Him, but also to suffer for His sake,
30[and so you are] experiencing the same [kind of] conflict which you saw me endure, and which you hear to be mine now.

Be Like Christ

2 THEREFORE IF there is any encouragement *and* comfort in Christ [as there certainly is in abundance], if there is any consolation of love, if there is any fellowship [that we share] in the Spirit, if [there is] any [great depth of] affection and compassion,
2make my joy complete by being of the same mind, having the same love [toward one another], knit together in spirit, intent on one purpose [and living a life that reflects your faith and spreads the gospel—the good news regarding salvation through faith in Christ].
3Do nothing from selfishness or empty conceit [through factional motives, or strife], but with [an attitude of] humility [being neither arrogant nor self-righteous], regard others as more important than yourselves.
4Do not *merely* look out for your own personal interests, but also for the interests of others.
5Have this same attitude in yourselves which was in Christ Jesus [look to Him as your example in selfless humility],
6who, although He existed in the form *and* unchanging essence of God [as One with Him, possessing the fullness of all the divine attributes—the entire nature of deity], did not regard equality with God a thing to be grasped *or* asserted [as if He did not already possess it, or was afraid of losing it];
7but emptied Himself [without renouncing or diminishing His deity, but only temporarily giving up the outward

---

Philippians are not to be terror-stricken in the face of their enemies.
1:29 *to suffer for His sake.* Suffering matures us as Christians in the present (Jas 1:2–4) and enables us to be glorified with Christ in the future (Ro 8:17).
2:1 *If . . . if . . . if.* The conditional clauses in this verse indicate certainties, not "maybes." Each *if* here expresses the idea of "since," and each following clause may be considered to be true.
2:2 *being of the same mind.* In this verse the apostle sets forth a fourfold appeal that expresses one major idea — namely, the unity of the church. Paul is strongly emphasizing the unity that should exist between believers and how they must single-mindedly strive together to advance the gospel of Jesus Christ.
2:3 *regard others as more important than yourselves.* This verb indicates a thorough analysis of the facts in order to reach a correct conclusion about the matter. In other words, each Philippian Christian was to properly assess himself or herself. Such an assessment would lead to valuing others.
2:5 *Have this same attitude.* All godly action begins with the "renewing of the mind." Right thinking produces right actions. Our actions are the fruit of our deepest thoughts. ***in yourselves.*** Thinking and being like Christ are requirements not only for an individual but also for the corporate body of believers. Together, we need to think and act like one being, like the Person of Jesus Christ.
2:6 *did not regard equality with God a thing to be grasped or asserted.* Because Christ was God, He did not look on sharing God's nature as "a thing to be grasped," as though He did not already possess it, or "asserted," as though He might lose it.
2:7 *emptied Himself.* Christ did this by taking on the form of a servant. In doing this, He did not empty Himself of any part of His essence as God. Instead, He gave up His privileges as God and took upon Himself existence as a man. While remaining completely God, He became completely human. ***form.*** Jesus added to His divine essence (v. 6) a servant's essence, that is, the essential characteristics of a human being

29 Ro 5:3; Eph 2:8 **30** Col 2:1; Ac 16:19; 1Th 2:2 **CHAPTER 2 1** 2Co 13:14; Col 3:12 **2** Jn 3:29; Ro 12:16; 1Co 1:10 **3** Gal 5:26; Jas 3:14; Ro 12:10; 1Pe 5:5 **4** 1Co 13:5 **5** Mt 11:29; 1Pe 2:21 **6** 2Co 4:4; Col 1:15 **7** Ps 22:6; Isa 53:3; Da 9:26; Mk 9:12; Isa 42:1; Eze 34:23; Zec 3:8; Mt 20:28; Lk 22:27; Jn 1:14; Ro 1:3; Gal 4:4

expression of divine equality and His rightful dignity] by assuming the form of a bond-servant, and being made in the likeness of men [He became completely human but was without sin, being fully God and fully man].
[8]After He was found in [terms of His] outward appearance as a man [for a divinely-appointed time], He humbled Himself [still further] by becoming obedient [to the Father] to the point of death, even death on a cross.
[9]For this reason also [because He obeyed and so completely humbled Himself], God has highly exalted Him and bestowed on Him the name which is above every name,
[10]so that at the name of Jesus EVERY KNEE SHALL BOW [in submission], of those who are in heaven and on earth and under the earth, [Is 45:23]
[11]and that every tongue will confess *and* openly acknowledge that Jesus Christ is Lord (sovereign God), to the glory of God the Father.
[12]So then, my dear ones, just as you have always obeyed [my instructions with enthusiasm], not only in my presence, but now much more in my absence, continue to work out your salvation [that is, cultivate it, bring it to full effect, actively pursue spiritual maturity] with awe-inspired fear and trembling [using serious caution and critical self-evaluation to avoid anything that might offend God or discredit the name of Christ].
[13]For it is [not your strength, but it is] God who is effectively at work in you, both to will and to work [that is, strengthening, energizing, and creating in you the longing and the ability to fulfill your purpose] for His good pleasure.
[14]Do everything without murmuring or questioning [the providence of God],
[15]so that you may prove yourselves to be blameless *and* guileless, innocent *and* uncontaminated, children of God without blemish in the midst of a [morally] crooked and [spiritually] perverted generation, among whom you are seen as bright lights [beacons shining out clearly] in the world [of darkness],
[16]holding out *and* offering to everyone the word of life, so that in the day of Christ I will have reason to rejoice greatly because I did not run [my race] in vain nor labor without result.
[17]But even if I am being poured out as a drink offering on the sacrifice and service of your faith [for preaching the

---

seeking to fulfill the will of another. Paul does not say that Christ exchanged the form of God for the form of a servant, involving a loss of deity or the attributes of deity. Rather, in the incarnation, Christ continued in the very nature of God but added to Himself the nature of a servant.

2:8 *He humbled Himself.* Jesus willingly took the role of a servant; no one forced Him to do it. ***obedient.*** Although He never sinned and did not deserve to die, He chose to die so that the sins of the world could be charged to His account. Subsequently, He could credit His righteousness to the account of all who believe in Him (2Co 5:21; Gal 1:4). ***even death on a cross.*** Paul describes the depths of Christ's humiliation by reminding his readers that Christ died by the cruelest form of capital punishment, crucifixion. The Jews viewed death on a cross as a curse from God (Dt 21:23; Gal 3:13).

2:11 *confess.* The term Paul uses is a strong, intensive verb, which means "agree with" or "say the same thing." Essentially Paul is saying that everyone will unanimously affirm what God the Father has already stated (Isa 45:23): that Jesus Christ is Lord.

2:12 *work out.* The Greek term speaks of the present deliverance of the Philippians. The word translated *work out* is used by a first century author to speak of digging silver out of silver mines. Thus, salvation can be compared to a huge gift that needs to be unwrapped for one's thorough enjoyment. Note that Paul is encouraging the Philippians to develop and *work out* their salvation, but not to work *for* their salvation.

2:15 *crooked and [spiritually] perverted generation.* Paul describes the world as being the opposite of Christian. On the one hand, the world is turned away from the truth, while on the other hand, it exerts a corrupting influence that is opposed to the truth.

2:17 *poured out.* Paul was probably saying that he was presently being offered as a living

---

8 Mt 26:39; Heb 5:8 **9** Ac 2:33; Heb 2:9; 1:4 **10** Isa 45:23; Mt 28:18 **11** Jn 13:13; Ac 2:36 **12** Php 1:5; Eph 6:5 **13** 2Co 3:5 **14** 1Pe 4:9; Ro 14:1 **15** Mt 5:45; Eph 5:1; 1Pe 2:12; Dt 32:5; Eph 5:8 **16** 2Co 1:14; 1Th 2:19; Gal 2:2 **17** 2Ti 4:6; Ro 15:16; 2Co 7:4; Col 1:24

message of salvation], still I rejoice and
share my joy with you all. [Num 28:7;
2 Tim 4:6]
[18]You too, rejoice in the same way
and share your joy with me.

Timothy and Epaphroditus

[19]But I hope in the Lord Jesus to send
Timothy to you soon, so that I may
also be encouraged by learning news
about you.
[20]For I have no one else [like him
who is] so kindred a spirit who will be
genuinely concerned for your [spiritu-
al] welfare.
[21]For the others [who deserted me
after my arrest] all seek [to advance]
their own interests, not those of Jesus
Christ.
[22]But you know of Timothy's tested
worth *and* his proven character, that he
has served with me to advance the gos-
pel like a son *serving* with his father.
[23]Therefore, I hope [that it is His will]
to send him immediately, just as soon
as I see how my case turns out;
[24]and I trust [confidently] in the Lord
that soon I also will be coming *to you.*
[25]However, I thought it necessary to
send *back* to you Epaphroditus, [who
has been] my brother and companion
and fellow soldier, who was also *sent
as* your messenger to take care of my
needs.
[26]For he has been longing for all of
you and was distressed because you
had heard that he was sick.
[27]He certainly was sick and close to
death. But God had mercy on him, and
not only on him but also on me, so that
I would not have sorrow upon sorrow.
[28]So I have sent him all the more ea-
gerly so that when you see him again
you may rejoice and I may be less con-
cerned *about you.*
[29]Welcome him *home* in the Lord
with great joy, and appreciate *and* hon-
or men like him;
[30]because he came close to death for
the work of Christ, risking his life to
complete what was lacking in your ser-
vice to me [which distance prevented
you from rendering personally].

The Goal of Life

3 FINALLY, MY fellow believers,
continue to rejoice *and* delight in
the LORD. To write the same things
again is no trouble for me, and it is a
safeguard for you.
[2]Look out for the dogs [the Juda-
izers, the legalists], look out for the
troublemakers, look out for the false
circumcision [those who claim circum-
cision is necessary for salvation];
[3]for we [who are born-again have
been reborn from above—spiritually

---

sacrifice on behalf of the faith of the Philippians. ***sacrifice.*** This means primarily the act of offering something to God.

2:19 *Timothy.* He had accompanied Paul on his second missionary journey, during which time they had established the church at Philippi. Timothy was apparently well loved by the Philippians, and he in turn exhibited a great concern for them.

2:22 *like a son serving with his father.* In New Testament times a son who served his father did so to learn the family trade. Serving in this way meant learning all about the business and being willing to obey the teacher in order to become as skillful as possible in the work.

2:25 *Epaphroditus.* He was a Philippian Christian sent by the church in Philippi to take a gift to Paul and to assist Paul in his ministry.

2:27 *sick and close to death.* Paul was making certain that the Philippians understood the effort that Epaphroditus had made for the cause of Christ. His condition had been far worse than perhaps they had imagined. Paul viewed Epaphroditus' healing as God's direct intervention.

3:2 *Look out for the dogs.* In New Testament times, dogs were hated scavengers. The term came to be used for all who had morally impure minds. ***the false circumcision.*** Paul here points sarcastically and specifically to those who desire to reinstate Jewish religious practices as necessary for salvation. He suggests that these people do not even understand the truth about the Old Testament practice of circumcision.

3:3 *the true circumcision.* Paul defines this as a matter of the heart and not of the flesh. He reveals three aspects: (1) worshiping God in the Spirit; (2) rejoicing in Christ; and (3) placing no

---

19 Ro 16:21 **20** Ps 55:13 **21** 1Co 10:24; 13:5; 2Ti 4:10 **22** 1Co 4:17; 1Ti 1:2 **24** Php 1:25 **25** Php 4:18; Php 2; 2Co 8:23; 2Co 11:9 **26** Php 1:8 **29** 1Co 16:18; 1Th 5:12; 1Ti 5:17 **30** 1Co 16:17 **CHAPTER 3** **1** 2Co 13:11; 1Th 5:16 **2** Gal 5:15; Ro 2:28 **3** Dt 30:6; Jer 4:4; Ro 7:6; Gal 6:14

transformed, renewed, set apart for
His purpose and] are the *true* circum-
cision, who worship in the Spirit of
God and glory *and* take pride *and* exult
in Christ Jesus and place no confi-
dence [in what we have or who we are]
in the flesh—
4 though I myself might have [some
grounds for] confidence in the flesh [if
I were pursuing salvation by works]. If
anyone else thinks that he has reason
to be confident in the flesh [that is, in
his own efforts to achieve salvation], I
have far more:
5 circumcised when I was eight days
old, of the nation of Israel, of the tribe
of Benjamin, a Hebrew of Hebrews [an
exemplary Hebrew]; as to the [obser-
vance of the] Law, a Pharisee;
6 as to my zeal [for Jewish tradition],
a persecutor of the church; and as to
righteousness [supposed right living]
which [my fellow Jews believe] is in the
Law, I proved myself blameless.
7 But whatever *former* things were
gains to me [as I thought then], these
things [once regarded as advance-
ments in merit] I have come to consider
as loss [absolutely worthless] for the
sake of Christ [and the purpose which
He has given my life].
8 But more than that, I count every-
thing as loss compared to the priceless
privilege *and* supreme advantage of
knowing Christ Jesus my Lord [and
of growing more deeply and thor-
oughly acquainted with Him—a joy
unequaled]. For His sake I have lost
everything, and I consider it all gar-
bage, so that I may gain Christ,
9 and may be found in Him [believ-
ing and relying on Him], not having
any righteousness of my own derived
from [my obedience to] the Law *and* its
rituals, but [possessing] that [genuine
righteousness] which comes through
faith in Christ, the righteousness
which comes from God on the basis
of faith.
10 *And this, so* that I may know Him
[experientially, becoming more thor-
oughly acquainted with Him, under-
standing the remarkable wonders of
His Person more completely] and [in
that same way experience] the power
of His resurrection [which overflows
and is active in believers], and [that I
may share] the fellowship of His suffer-
ings, by being *continually* conformed
[inwardly into His likeness even] to His
death [dying as He did];
11 so that I may attain to the resurrec-
tion [that will raise me] from the dead.
12 Not that I have already obtained it
[this goal of being Christlike] or have
already been made perfect, but I ac-
tively press on so that I may take hold
of that [perfection] for which Christ

---

confidence in any human honor or accomplishment as a means to reach God.

3:5 *eight days old.* Paul's parents obeyed God's law and had Paul circumcised on the appropriate day after his birth (Lev 12:2 – 3). ***tribe of Benjamin.*** This tribe was highly regarded because it had produced the first king of Israel and had remained loyal to David. ***Hebrew of Hebrews.*** This description of Paul may indicate that (1) both his parents were Jews, (2) he was a model Jew, or (3) he was educated completely as a Jew. ***Pharisee.*** They rigorously followed and defended the letter of the Jewish law.

3:7 *loss.* This word indicates that which is damaged or of no further use (v. 8). Those things that Paul thought to be important became unimportant after confronting the resurrected Messiah.

3:8 *garbage.* This word means anything that is detestable or worthless. All things of this world are garbage compared to Christ. Even our righteousness is like filthy rags (Isa 64:6).

3:10 *power of His resurrection.* Paul does not say the power "in" His resurrection, which would specify the power of the one-time event of His resurrection. Rather, Paul seeks the ongoing power that is the day-to-day experience of being in Christ. ***fellowship of His sufferings.*** Paul sees the value of participating in the persecutions or struggles that naturally accompany one who is in partnership with Christ and His sufferings. ***being continually conformed [inwardly into His likeness even] to His death.*** Paul desires to imitate Christ — even in His death. In other words, Paul wants to be completely obedient to God the Father, just as Jesus was obedient to His Father's will (Lk 22:42).

3:12 *perfect.* The Greek term means mature or complete, finished. It does not specifically mean

---

4 2Co 11:18 **5** Ro 11:1; 2Co 11:22; Ac 23:6 **6** Ac 22:3; Ro 10:5; Lk 1:6 **7** Mt 13:44 **8** Isa 53:11 **9** Ro 10:3; Ro 1:17 **10** Ro 6:3-5; 8:17 **11** Ac 26:7 **12** 1Ti 6:12; Heb 12:23

Jesus took hold of me *and* made me His
own. [1 Cor 9:24; 1 Tim 6:12]
[13]Brothers and sisters, I do not consider that I have made it my own yet;
but one thing *I do:* forgetting what *lies*
behind and reaching forward to what
lies ahead,
[14]I press on toward the goal to win
the [heavenly] prize of the upward call
of God in Christ Jesus.
[15]All of us who are mature [pursuing
spiritual perfection] should have this
attitude. And if in any respect you have
a different attitude, that too God will
make clear to you.
[16]Only let us stay true to what we
have already attained.
[17]Brothers and sisters, together follow my example and observe those
who live by the pattern we gave you.
[18]For there are many, of whom I have
often told you, and now tell you even
with tears, who live as enemies of the
cross of Christ [rejecting and opposing
His way of salvation],
[19]whose fate is destruction, whose
god is *their* belly [their worldly appetite, their sensuality, their vanity], and
whose glory is in their shame—who
focus their mind on earthly *and* temporal things.
[20]But [we are different, because] our
citizenship is in heaven. And from
there we eagerly await [the coming
of] the Savior, the Lord Jesus Christ;
[21]who, by exerting that power which
enables Him even to subject everything to Himself, will [not only] transform [but completely refashion] our
earthly bodies so that they will be like
His glorious *resurrected* body.

Think of Excellence

4 THEREFORE, MY fellow believers,
whom I love and long for, my delight and crown [my wreath of victory],
in this way stand firm in the Lord, my
beloved.
[2]I urge Euodia and I urge Syntyche
to agree *and* to work in harmony in
the Lord.
[3]Indeed, I ask you too, my true companion, to help these women [to keep
on cooperating], for they have shared
my struggle in the [cause of the] gospel,
together with Clement and the rest of
my fellow workers, whose names are
in the Book of Life. [Dan 12:1; Mal 3:16,
17; Rev 3:5; 21:27]
[4]Rejoice in the Lord always [delight,
take pleasure in Him]; again I will say,
rejoice! [Ps 37:4]

---

a moral or sinless perfection. Paul is not speaking of moral perfection or righteousness but of reaching the state of completion as a Christian. ***take hold.*** This phrase adds the idea of overtaking by surprise to the sense of seizing some object. Paul urgently wants to "take hold of" God as God had taken hold of him.

3:13 *forgetting.* Paul was indicating that it is an ongoing process. He might even be implying that he wanted to forget everything so that he would not rest on his past successes in Christ, but continue to labor for the Lord.

3:16 *let us stay true.* Paul commands the Philippians to conduct themselves as soldiers who "march in line" together, organized each in his proper position.

3:17 *example.* The word indicates an exact representation of the original. The example of Paul's life is so evident that one can readily see it and use it as a pattern for living.

3:19 *glory is in their shame.* The things in which they take pride actually are the things that will bring "disgrace" or "humiliation" to them, things of which they should have been ashamed.

3:20 *citizenship is in heaven.* Here Paul presents a direct contrast to the earthly focus of enemies of the cross in v. 19. The eager desire of Christians is not earthly things, but a heavenly Person, the Savior.

3:21 *like His glorious resurrected body.* Our bodies now are weak and susceptible to sin, disease, and death. But God will change our bodies to resemble Christ's glorious resurrection body.

4:2 *Euodia . . . Syntyche.* What is written here is all that is known about the two women and their dispute. Paul does not take sides in the argument, but instead encourages them to be reconciled.

4:4 *Rejoice in the Lord.* The joy of Christians is not based on agreeable circumstances; instead, it is based on their relationship to God. Christians will

---

13 Lk 9:62; Heb 6:1 **14** 2Ti 4:7; Heb 3:1 **15** 1Co 2:6; Gal 5:10 **16** Ro 12:16; 15:6; Gal 6:16 **17** 1Co 11:1; 1Th 1:6; 1Pe 5:3 **18** Gal 1:7; 2:21 **19** 2Co 11:15; 1Ti 6:5; Titus 1:11; Hos 4:7; Gal 6:13; Ro 8:5 **20** Eph 2:6; Col 3:1,3; Ac 1:11; 1Co 1:7; 1Th 1:10 **21** 1Co 15:43; Col 3:4; Eph 1:19; 1Co 15:26 **CHAPTER 4** **1** Php 1:8; 2Co 1:14; Php 2:16; Php 1:27 **2** Php 3:16 **3** Ro 16:3; Ex 32:32; Ps 69:28; Da 12:1 **4** Ro 12:12; 1Th 5:16; 1Pe 4:13

5 Let your gentle *spirit* [your gra-
ciousness, unselfishness, mercy, tol-
erance, and patience] be known to all
people. The Lord is near.
6 Do not be anxious *or* worried about
anything, but in everything [every cir-
cumstance and situation] by prayer
and petition with thanksgiving, con-
tinue to make your [specific] requests
known to God.
7 And the peace of God [that peace
which reassures the heart, that peace]
which transcends all understanding,
[that peace which] stands guard over
your hearts and your minds in Christ
Jesus [is yours]. [John 14:27]
8 Finally, believers, whatever is true,
whatever is honorable *and* worthy of
respect, whatever is right *and* con-
firmed by God's word, whatever is pure
and wholesome, whatever is lovely *and*
brings peace, whatever is admirable
and of good repute; if there is any ex-
cellence, if there is anything worthy
of praise, think *continually* on these
things [center your mind on them, and
implant them in your heart].
9 The things which you have learned
and received and heard and seen in
me, practice these things [in daily life],
and the God [who is the source] of
peace *and* well-being will be with you.

God's Provisions

10 I rejoiced greatly in the Lord, that
now at last you have renewed your
concern for me; indeed, you were con-
cerned about me *before*, but you had
no opportunity to show it.
11 Not that I speak from [any per-
sonal] need, for I have learned to be
content [and self-sufficient through
Christ, satisfied to the point where I am
not disturbed or uneasy] regardless of
my circumstances.
12 I know how to get along and live
humbly [in difficult times], and I also
know how to enjoy abundance *and*
live in prosperity. In any and every cir-
cumstance I have learned the secret [of
facing life], whether well-fed or going
hungry, whether having an abundance
or being in need.
13 I can do all things [which He has
called me to do] through Him who
strengthens *and* empowers me [to ful-
fill His purpose—I am self-sufficient
in Christ's sufficiency; I am ready
for anything and equal to anything
through Him who infuses me with
inner strength and confident peace.]
14 Nevertheless, it was right of you
to share [with me] in my difficulties.
15 And you Philippians know that in
the early days of preaching the gos-
pel, after I left Macedonia, no church
shared with me in the matter of giving
and receiving except you alone;
16 for even in Thessalonica you sent
a gift more than once for my needs.
17 Not that I seek the gift itself, but I
do seek the profit which increases to

---

face trouble in this world, but they should rejoice in the trials they face because they know God is using those situations to improve their character.

4:6 *Do not be anxious or worried about anything.* Paul prohibits the Philippians from worrying about their own problems. Instead, they are to commit their problems to God in prayer, trusting that He will provide deliverance.

4:7 *stands guard.* Paul's choice of a military term "keep" or "guard" implies that the mind is in a battle zone and needs to be "protected by a military guard" since the purpose of such a guard in a wartime situation is either to prevent a hostile invasion or to keep the inhabitants of a besieged city from escaping.

4:9 *learned.* This verb conveys not only the concept of "increasing in intellectual knowledge," but also the idea of "learning by habitual practice." In some areas of their Christian development, the Philippians had been excellent disciples of Paul, practicing what he had taught.

4:11 *content.* The word literally means "self-sufficient." In Stoic philosophy this Greek word described a person who dispassionately accepted whatever circumstances brought. For the Greeks, this contentment came from personal sufficiency. But for Paul, true sufficiency is found in the strength of Christ.

4:17 *account.* Paul uses business terminology. The Philippians' gift was producing spiritual profit, just as money deposited in a bank account accrues interest. But Paul was not as concerned

5 Heb 10:25; 1Pe 4:7 **6** Ps 55:22; Pr 16:3; Mt 6:25 **7** Jn 14:27; Ro 5:1; Col 3:15 **8** 1Th 5:22 **9** Php 3:17; Ro 15:33
10 2Co 11:9 **11** 1Ti 6:6 **12** 1Co 4:11 **13** Jn 15:5 **14** Php 1:7 **15** 2Co 11:8 **17** Titus 3:14

your [heavenly] account [the blessing
which is accumulating for you].
[18]But I have received everything in
full and more; I am amply supplied,
having received from Epaphroditus
the gifts you sent me. They are the
fragrant aroma of an offering, an ac-
ceptable sacrifice which God welcomes
and in which He delights.
[19]And my God will liberally supply
(fill until full) your every need accord-
ing to His riches in glory in Christ Jesus.
[20]To our God and Father be the glory
forever and ever. Amen.
[21]Remember me to every saint in
Christ Jesus. The brothers who are
with me greet you.
[22]All God's people wish to be remem-
bered to you, especially those of Cae-
sar's household.
[23]The grace of the Lord Jesus Christ
be with your spirit.

---

with their gift as with the development in the Philippians of the spiritual ability to give.

4:20 ***Amen.*** The Jewish practice of closing prayers with the word *amen* carried over to the Christian church as well. When found at the end of a sentence, as it is here, the word can be translated "so be it" or "may it be fulfilled." At the beginning of a sentence, it means "surely," "truly," or "most assuredly."

18 Php 2:25; Heb 13:16; 2Co 9:12 **19** Ps 23:1; Eph 1:7 **20** Ro 16:27 **21** Gal 1:2 **22** Php 1:13 **23** Ro 16:24

THE LETTER OF PAUL TO THE

COLOSSIANS

▸ **AUTHOR:** The external testimony to the Pauline authorship of Colossians is ancient and consistent, and the internal evidence is also very good. It not only claims to be written by Paul (1:1,23; 4:18), but the personal details and close parallels with Ephesians and Philemon make the case even stronger. It is evident from 1:4 – 8 and 2:1 that Paul had never visited the church at Colosse, which was founded by Epaphras. On his third missionary journey, Paul devoted almost three years to an Asian ministry centered in Ephesus (Ac 19:10; 20:31), and Epaphras probably came to Christ during this time. He then carried the gospel to cities like Colosse in the Lycus valley. Epaphras visited Paul in prison (4:12) and his report concerning the church in Colosse prompted this epistle.

▸ **TIMES:** c. AD 60 – 61 ▸ **KEY VERSES:** Col 2:9 – 10

▸ **THEME:** The problem of the Colossian church was similar to what we experience in many churches today. This is often called syncretism, the tendency to regard other philosophies and religions as equally valid as Christianity. The people in Colosse wanted to believe Christian truth, but they also wanted to hang on to their old beliefs as well by blending them with the gospel. Paul's purpose in this letter is to settle once and for all the issue of Christ's centrality and supremacy. He writes to restore Jesus, the Messiah, to the center of these believers' lives. Here we can see Paul's unwavering confidence in the incomparability of Christ, as it has completely shaped his views on all of life. He writes to introduce the Colossians to this same vision.

Thankfulness for Spiritual Attainments

1 PAUL, AN apostle (special messenger, personally chosen representative) of Christ Jesus (the Messiah, the Anointed) by the will of God, and Timothy our brother,

[2]To the saints and faithful believers in Christ [who are] at Colossae: Grace to you and peace [inner calm and spiritual well-being] from God our Father.

[3]We give thanks to God, the Father of our Lord Jesus Christ, as we pray always for you,

[4]for we have heard of your faith in Christ Jesus [how you lean on Him with absolute confidence in His power, wisdom, and goodness], and of the

---

1:1 ***an apostle.*** Paul calls himself an apostle, a word whose root means "to send." The Greek word was first used for a cargo ship or fleet, but later denoted a commander of a fleet. The New Testament employs the word to signify an approved spokesman sent as a personal representative.
1:2 ***saints.*** The Greek term means "holy people." The essence of "holiness" is being set apart to God. All believers are saints, not because they are perfect, but because they belong to God. ***in Christ.*** This is a favorite expression of the apostle Paul, used some 80 times in his letters.
1:4 – 8 ***faith . . . love . . . hope.*** Paul often uses these three terms together (Ro 5:2 – 5; 1Co 13:13; 1Th 1:3; 5:8). Faith is in Christ. Love flows from

CHAPTER 1 **1** Eph 1:1 **2** 1Co 4:17; Gal 1:3 **3** 1Co 1:4; Eph 1:16; Php 1:3 **4** Eph 1:15; Heb 6:10

[unselfish] love which you have for all
the saints (God's people);
5because of the [confident] hope [of
experiencing that] which is reserved
and waiting for you in heaven. You
previously heard of this *hope* in the
message of truth, the gospel [regarding
salvation]
6which has come to you. Indeed, just
as in the whole world *the gospel* is con-
stantly bearing fruit and spreading [by
God's power], just as *it has been doing*
among you ever since the day you first
heard *of it* and understood the grace
of God in truth [becoming thoroughly
and deeply acquainted with it].
7You learned it from [our represen-
tative] Epaphras, our beloved fellow
bond-servant, who is a faithful minis-
ter of Christ on our behalf
8and he also has told us of your love
[well-grounded and nurtured] in the
[Holy] Spirit.
9For this reason, since the day we
heard about it, we have not stopped
praying for you, asking [specifically]
that you may be filled with the knowl-
edge of His will in all spiritual wisdom
[with insight into His purposes], and
in understanding [of spiritual things],
10so that you will walk in a manner
worthy of the Lord [displaying admi-
rable character, moral courage, and
personal integrity], to [fully] please
Him in all things, bearing fruit in ev-
ery good work and steadily growing
in the knowledge of God [with deeper
faith, clearer insight and fervent love
for His precepts];
11[we pray that you may be] strength-
ened *and* invigorated with all power,
according to His glorious might, to
attain every kind of endurance and
patience with joy;
12giving thanks to the Father, who
has qualified us to share in the inher-
itance of the saints (God's people) in
the Light.

The Incomparable Christ

13For He has rescued us *and* has
drawn us to Himself from the domin-
ion of darkness, and has transferred
us to the kingdom of His beloved Son,
14in whom we have redemption [be-
cause of His sacrifice, resulting in]
the forgiveness of our sins [and the
cancellation of sins' penalty].
15He is the exact living image [the
essential manifestation] of the unseen

---

faith and proves the genuineness of one's faith (Jas 2:14–26). Hope refers to the result of faith, the treasure laid up in heaven.

1:9 *all spiritual wisdom ... and in understanding.* *Wisdom* is the practical outworking of knowledge (Jas 3:17), and that knowledge cannot be separated from the spiritual understanding that comes through the discernment given by the Holy Spirit.

1:10 *walk in a manner worthy of the Lord.* Paul wanted the Colossians to live in a manner that adequately reflected what God had done for them and was doing in them. Being "worthy of God" is a phrase that occurs in ancient pagan inscriptions throughout Asia. It pictures someone's life being weighed on scales to determine its worth.

1:12 *qualified us.* Believers can never be qualified on their own; instead, God must make them sufficient through Jesus Christ. The tense of the verb points to "qualifying" as an act in the past rather than a process.

1:13 *rescued ... transferred.* God has liberated believers from the dominion of darkness. The apostle uses the common symbolism of light and darkness for good and evil, for God's kingdom and Satan's kingdom, that is found throughout the New Testament. The kingdom from which believers have been rescued is the kingdom of darkness.

1:14 *redemption.* The Greek word points naturally to the payment of a price or ransom for the release of a slave. They are freed from bondage to sin by forgiveness through the blood of Jesus (Eph 1:7).

1:15 *firstborn ... of all creation.* Verses 15–20 are thought to be an early Christian hymn celebrating the supremacy of Christ. *Firstborn* could denote a priority in time or in rank. The word does not describe Christ as the first being created in time because the hymn proclaims that all things were "created by Him" and that "He is before all things." Being firstborn referred more to rank and privilege than to order of birth.

5 1Pe 1:4 **6** Mt 24:14; Eph 3:2; Titus 2:11 **7** Php 23; 2Co 11:23; 1Ti 4:6 **8** Ro 15:30 **9** Eph 1:15; 1Co 1:5; Ro 12:2; Eph 1:8 **10** Php 1:27; 1Th 4:1; Heb 13:21 **11** Eph 3:16; 4:2; Ac 5:41 **12** Eph 5:20; Eph 1:11 **13** Eph 6:12; 2Pe 1:11 **14** Eph 1:7 **15** 2Co 4:4; Rev 3:14

God [the visible representation of the invisible], the firstborn [the preeminent one, the sovereign, and the originator] of all creation.
[16]For by Him all things were created in heaven and on earth, [things] visible and invisible, whether thrones or dominions or rulers or authorities; all things were created *and* exist through Him [that is, by His activity] and for Him.
[17]And He Himself existed *and* is before all things, and in Him all things hold together. [His is the controlling, cohesive force of the universe.] [Prov 8:22–31]
[18]He is also the head [the life-source and leader] of the body, the church; and He is the beginning, the firstborn from the dead, so that He Himself will occupy the first place [He will stand supreme and be preeminent] in everything. [1 Cor 15:20]
[19]For it pleased the *Father* for all the fullness [of deity—the sum total of His essence, all His perfection, powers, and attributes] to dwell [permanently] in Him (the Son),
[20]and through [the intervention of] the Son to reconcile all things to Himself, making peace [with believers] through the blood of His cross; through Him, [I say,] whether things on earth or things in heaven.
[21]And although you were at one time estranged *and* alienated and hostile-minded [toward Him], *participating* in evil things,
[22]yet Christ has now reconciled you [to God] in His physical body through death, in order to present you before the Father holy and blameless and beyond reproach—
[23][and He will do this] if you continue in the faith, well-grounded and steadfast, and not shifting away from the [confident] hope [that is a result] of the gospel that you have heard, which

---

1:16 *all things were created and exist through Him [that is, by His activity] and for Him.* Not only did Jesus create all things, everything was created for His purposes (Heb 1:2, where Christ is said to be the "heir and lawful owner of all things").

1:18 *head [the life-source and leader] of the body.* No one should underestimate the significance of the church, for it is in fact Christ's body. The sovereign Creator of the universe, as Head of the church, provides leadership and oversight over it.

1:19 *fullness.* The opponents of Paul, and later the Greek Gnostics, seem to have used this word as a technical term for the sphere between heaven and earth where a hierarchy of angels lived. The Gnostics viewed Christ as one of many spirits existing in this hierarchy between God and all people. However, Paul used the term *fullness* to refer to the complete embodiment of God.

1:20–22 Jesus Pays the Price — Salvation is a free gift, but it is not a cheap one. It costs us nothing, but it cost God dearly — it cost Jesus His life. In physically dying on the cross, Jesus sacrificed Himself and satisfied the debt that we had incurred through sin, so that it is possible for God and man to be reconciled. As Jesus hung on the cross, He cried, *My God, My God, why have You forsaken me?* (Mt 27:46). Jesus was separated from God the Father so that we do not have to be. This is the heart of the atonement (becoming *at one* with God). The marvel of it all is that He did this while we were His enemies: *But God clearly shows and proves His own love for us, by the fact that while we were still sinners, Christ died for us* (Ro 5:8).

1:20–21 *reconcile all things.* This phrase shows the significance of Christ's work on the cross. It does not mean that all people will be saved, since many passages clearly say that unbelievers will suffer eternal separation from God (Mt 25:46).

1:22 *holy and blameless and beyond reproach.* We who were once enemies of God and alienated by our own wicked works will one day be presented as above reproach on account of Christ's death for us.

1:23 *if you continue in the faith.* The perseverance of the Colossians was proof of the reconciling work of Christ on their behalf. ***all creation under heaven.*** Paul uses this exaggeration to illustrate the rapid spread of the gospel. Compare Acts 17:6 where the apostles are said to have turned the world upside down, even though their ministry, up to that point, had been limited to a small portion of the eastern Mediterranean region.

---

16 Heb 1:2; Eph 1:21; Heb 2:10 **17** Jn 17:5 **18** 1Co 11:3; Rev 1:5 **19** Jn 1:16 **20** Eph 2:14; 2Co 5:18; Eph 1:10
21 Eph 2:1; Titus 1:15 **22** Eph 2:15; Eph 5:27 **23** Eph 3:17; Jn 15:6; Ro 10:18; Ac 1:17

was proclaimed in all creation under heaven, and of which [gospel] I, Paul, was made a minister.

24 Now I rejoice in my sufferings on your behalf. And with my own body I supplement whatever is lacking [on our part] of Christ's afflictions, on behalf of His body, which is the church.

25 In *this church* I was made a minister according to the stewardship which God entrusted to me for your sake, so that I might make the word of God fully known [among you]—

26 *that is,* the mystery which was hidden [from angels and mankind] for ages and generations, but has now been revealed to His saints (God's people).

27 God [in His eternal plan] chose to make known to them how great for the Gentiles are the riches of the glory of this mystery, which is Christ in *and* among you, the hope *and* guarantee of [realizing the] glory.

28 We proclaim Him, warning and instructing everyone in all wisdom [that is, with comprehensive insight into the word and purposes of God], so that we may present every person complete in Christ [mature, fully trained, and perfect in Him—the Anointed].

29 For this I labor [often to the point of exhaustion], striving with His power *and* energy, which so greatly works within me.

You Are Built Up in Christ

2 FOR I want you to know how great a struggle I have for you and for those [believers] at Laodicea, and for all who [like yourselves] have never seen me face to face.

2 [For my hope is] that their hearts may be encouraged as they are knit together in [unselfish] love, so that they may have all the riches that come from the full assurance of understanding [the joy of salvation], resulting in a true [and more intimate] knowledge of the mystery of God, *that is,* Christ,

3 in whom are hidden all the treasures of wisdom and knowledge [regarding the word and purposes of God].

4 I say this so that no one will deceive you with persuasive [but thoroughly deceptive] arguments.

5 For even though I am absent [from you] in body, nevertheless I am with you in spirit, delighted to see your good discipline [as you stand shoulder to shoulder and form a solid front] and to see the stability of your faith in Christ [your steadfast reliance on Him and your unwavering confidence in His power, wisdom, and goodness].

6 Therefore as you have received Christ Jesus the Lord, walk in [union with] Him [reflecting His character in the things you do and say—living lives that lead others away from sin],

7 having been deeply rooted [in Him] and *now* being *continually* built up in Him and [becoming increasingly more] established in your faith, just as you were taught, and overflowing in it with gratitude.

8 See to it that no one takes you captive through philosophy and empty deception [pseudo-intellectual babble], according to the tradition [and

---

1:24 *my sufferings on your behalf.* Paul is making the point that a Christian will endure the sufferings that Christ would be enduring if He were still in the world (2Co 1:5; 4:11).

1:26 – 27 *mystery.* In Greek pagan religions, a mystery was a secret teaching reserved for a few spiritual teachers who had been initiated into an inner circle. Paul uses the word to refer to knowledge that had been "hidden for ages and generations" but was now being revealed by God. The mystery is that Christ now lives within Gentile believers.

2:1 *Laodicea.* It was a sister city of Colosse about 11 miles away. The two churches were to share their letters from Paul.

2:2 – 3 *knowledge of the mystery of God.* Paul reminds the Colossians that true knowledge will be acknowledged by bringing people together in Christian love in the church. The Gnostics thought only certain "knowledgeable" people could join their elite group; Paul teaches that every believer has access to complete wisdom found in Christ.

2:8 *philosophy.* This verse has been used at times to teach that Christians should not study or

---

24 2Co 7:4; Eph 3:1,13; 2Co 1:5; Eph 1:23 **25** Gal 2:7 **26** 1Co 2:7; 2Ti 1:10 **27** 2Co 2:14; Ro 9:23; 1Ti 1:1 **28** Ac 20:20; Eph 5:27 **29** 1Co 15:10; Col 2:1; Eph 1:19 **CHAPTER 2** **1** Php 1:30 **2** 2Co 1:6; Col 3:14; Php 3:8 **3** 1Co 1:24 **4** Ro 16:18 **5** 1Th 2:17; 1Co 14:40; 1Pe 5:9 **6** 1Th 4:1 **7** Eph 2:21 **8** Gal 1:14; 4:3,9

musings] of *mere* men, following the
elementary principles of this world,
rather than following [the truth—the
teachings of] Christ.
9 For in Him all the fullness of Deity
(the Godhead) dwells in bodily form
[completely expressing the divine es-
sence of God].
10 And in Him you have been made
complete [achieving spiritual stature
through Christ], and He is the head
over all rule and authority [of every
angelic and earthly power].
11 In Him you were also circumcised
with a circumcision not made with
hands, but by the [spiritual] circum-
cision of Christ in the stripping off of
the body of the flesh [the sinful carnal
nature],
12 having been buried with Him in
baptism and raised with Him [to a new
life] through [your] faith in the work-
ing of God, [as displayed] when He
raised Christ from the dead.
13 When you were dead in your sins
and in the uncircumcision of your
flesh (worldliness, manner of life), God
made you alive together with Christ,
having [freely] forgiven us all our sins,
14 having canceled out the certificate
of debt consisting of legal demands
[which were in force] against us and
which were hostile to us. And this cer-
tificate He has set aside *and* completely
removed by nailing it to the cross.
15 When He had disarmed the rulers
and authorities [those supernatural
forces of evil operating against us], He
made a public example of them [exhib-
iting them as captives in His triumphal
procession], having triumphed over
them through the cross.
16 Therefore let no one judge you in
regard to food and drink or in regard
to [the observance of] a festival or a
new moon or a Sabbath day.
17 Such things are only a shadow of
what is to come *and* they have only
symbolic value; but the substance [the
reality of what is foreshadowed] be-
longs to Christ.
18 Let no one defraud you of your
prize [your freedom in Christ and your
salvation] by insisting on mock humili-
ty and the worship of angels, going into
detail about *visions* [he claims] he has
seen [to justify his authority], puffed
up [in conceit] by his unspiritual mind,
19 and not holding fast to the head [of
the body, Jesus Christ], from whom the
entire body, supplied and knit togeth-
er by its joints and ligaments, grows
with the growth [that can come only]
from God.

---

read philosophy. This is not Paul's meaning. Paul himself was adept at philosophy, evidenced by his interaction with the Stoic and Epicurean philosophers in Athens (Ac 17:1 – 34). Paul was warning the believers not to be taken in by any philosophy that does not conform to a proper knowledge of Christ. The false teachers at Colosse had combined worldly philosophies with the gospel.

2:9 *all the fullness of Deity (the Godhead) dwells in bodily form.* In this verse Paul clearly proclaims the incarnation, the fact that God became a man bodily. This contradicts the Gnostic idea of the inherent evil of physical bodies and the claim that Jesus is merely a spirit.

2:10 *you have been made complete.* Paul emphasizes the sufficiency of Christ in order to refute the Gnostics and the Judaizers who respectively believed that special knowledge or works were necessary to make a Christian complete.

2:12 – 13 *buried with Him in baptism.* Baptism is the symbol of the believer's association with Christ's death on the cross. Water baptism itself does not bring forgiveness of sins, but Paul uses the rite to help explain the work of the Spirit. The early church would never have understood the idea of an unbaptized Christian.

2:15 *rulers and authorities.* These words allude to Satan and the fallen angels. Paul is describing Christ's victory on the cross over the powers that opposed Him and that were against God's faithful people. To describe this victory, Paul uses the spectacle of the military triumph, when prisoners of war were stripped and paraded before the populace behind the conquering general.

2:16 – 19 *mock humility.* People who do not champion salvation in Christ alone often appear to be humble. But their search for a new spiritual experience or advocacy of some work as necessary for salvation is actually human pride. They do not want to submit to God's plan of salvation.

9 Jn 1:14 **10** 1Pe 3:22; Col 1:16 **11** Dt 10:16; Ro 6:6 **12** Eph 1:19; Ac 2:24 **14** Eph 2:15 **15** Isa 53:12; Eph 6:12 **16** Ro 14:2,3; Ro 14:5 **17** Heb 8:5 **19** Eph 4:15

[20]If you have died with Christ to the elementary principles of the world, why, as if you were still living in the world, do you submit to rules *and* regulations, such as,
[21]"Do not handle [this], do not taste [that], do not [even] touch!"?
[22](these things all perish with use)— in accordance with the commandments and teachings of men. [Is 29:13]
[23]These practices indeed have the appearance [that popularly passes as that] of wisdom in self-made religion and mock humility and severe treatment of the body (asceticism), but are of no value against sinful indulgence [because they do not honor God].

Put On the New Self

3 THEREFORE IF you have been raised with Christ [to a new life, sharing in His resurrection from the dead], keep seeking the things that are above, where Christ is, seated at the right hand of God. [Ps 110:1]
[2]Set your mind *and* keep focused *habitually* on the things above [the heavenly things], not on things that are on the earth [which have only temporal value].
[3]For you died [to this world], and your [new, real] life is hidden with Christ in God.
[4]When Christ, who is our life, appears, then you also will appear with Him in glory.
[5]So put to death *and* deprive of power the evil longings of your earthly body [with its sensual, self-centered instincts] immorality, impurity, *sinful* passion, evil desire, and greed, which is [a kind of] idolatry [because it replaces your devotion to God].
[6]Because of these [sinful] things the [divine] wrath of God is coming on the sons of disobedience [those who fail to listen and who routinely and obstinately disregard God's precepts],
[7]and in these [sinful things] you also once walked, when you were *habitually* living in them [without the knowledge of Christ].
[8]But now rid yourselves [completely] of all these things: anger, rage, malice, slander, and obscene (abusive, filthy, vulgar) language from your mouth.
[9]Do not lie to one another, for you have stripped off the old self with its *evil* practices,
[10]and have put on the new [spiritual] self who is being *continually* renewed in true knowledge in the image of Him who created the new self— [Gen 1:26]
[11]*a renewal* in which there is no [distinction between] Greek and Jew, circumcised and uncircumcised, [nor between nations whether] barbarian or Scythian, [nor in status whether] slave or free, but Christ is all, and in all [so believers are equal in Christ, without distinction].
[12]So, as God's own chosen people, who are holy [set apart, sanctified for

2:20–23 *submit to rules and regulations.* Since believers have been released from ritualistic observances, why should they let others bind them down again (Ro 6:3–14)? No human work can be added to the merit of Christ's death. His work on the cross is the only acceptable work in God's eyes.

3:1–4 *Set your mind . . . on the things above.* The false teachers were instructing the Colossians to concentrate on temporal observances; in contrast, Paul instructs them to concentrate on the eternal realities of heaven. The Greek verb for *set* emphasizes an ongoing decision. Christians must continually discipline themselves to focus on eternal realities instead of the temporal realities of this earth.

3:9–10 *old self . . . new [spiritual] self.* These two terms do not refer to the Christian's fleshly and spiritual natures. Instead, Paul describes our former unredeemed life as the old self and our life as God's child as the new self. The new self has the image of the new creation in Christ, just as the old self bears the image of our fallen nature. The old self is under an old master, Satan, while the new self has a new master, the Spirit of God living within.

3:11 *barbarian.* In the Roman Empire a person who did not speak Greek was despised. ***Scythian.*** An uncultured person who came from the area around the Black Sea.

20 Ro 6:3,5; Gal 4:3,9 **21** 1Ti 4:3 **22** Titus 1:14 **23** 1Ti 4:8 **CHAPTER 3** **1** Eph 1:20 **3** Ro 6:2; 2Co 5:7 **4** 1Jn 3:2; Jn 14:6; 1Co 15:43 **5** Ro 8:13; Ro 6:13; Eph 5:3; Eph 5:5 **6** Rev 22:15; Eph 2:2 **7** 1Co 6:11 **8** Eph 4:22; Eph 4:29 **9** Eph 4:25; Eph 4:22 **10** Ro 12:2; Eph 4:23; Eph 2:10 **11** Gal 3:28; Eph 1:23 **12** 1Pe 1:2; Gal 5:22

His purpose] and well-beloved [by God Himself], put on a heart of compassion, kindness, humility, gentleness, and patience [which has the power to endure whatever injustice or unpleasantness comes, with good temper];
13bearing graciously with one another, and willingly forgiving each other if one has a cause for complaint against another; just as the Lord has forgiven you, so should you forgive.
14Beyond all these things put on *and* wrap yourselves in [unselfish] love, which is the perfect bond of unity [for everything is bound together in agreement when each one seeks the best for others].
15Let the peace of Christ [the inner calm of one who walks daily with Him] be the controlling factor in your hearts [deciding and settling questions that arise]. To this *peace* indeed you were called as members in one body [of believers]. And be thankful [to God always].
16Let the [spoken] word of Christ have its home within you [dwelling in your heart and mind—permeating every aspect of your being] as you teach [spiritual things] and admonish *and* train one another with all wisdom, singing psalms and hymns and spiritual songs with thankfulness in your hearts to God.
17Whatever you do [no matter what it is] in word or deed, do everything in the name of the Lord Jesus [and in dependence on Him], giving thanks to God the Father through Him.

Family Relations

18Wives, be subject to your husbands [out of respect for their position as protector, and their accountability to God], as is proper *and* fitting in the Lord.
19Husbands, love your wives [with an affectionate, sympathetic, selfless love that always seeks the best for them] and do not be embittered *or* resentful toward them [because of the responsibilities of marriage].
20Children, obey your parents [as God's representatives] in all things, for this [attitude of respect and obedience] is well-pleasing to the Lord [and will bring you God's promised blessings].
21Fathers, do not provoke *or* irritate *or* exasperate your children [with demands that are trivial or unreasonable or humiliating or abusive; nor by favoritism or indifference; treat them tenderly with lovingkindness], so they will not lose heart *and* become discouraged *or* unmotivated [with their spirits broken].
22Servants, in everything obey those who are your masters on earth, not only with external service, as those who merely please people, but with sincerity of heart because of your fear of the Lord.
23Whatever you do [whatever your task may be], work from the soul [that is, put in your very best effort], as [something done] for the Lord and not for men,
24knowing [with all certainty] that it is from the Lord [not from men] that you will receive the inheritance which is your [greatest] reward. It is the Lord Christ whom you [actually] serve.
25For he who does wrong will be punished for his wrongdoing, and [with God] there is no partiality [no special treatment based on a person's position in life].

Fellow Workers

4 MASTERS, [ON your part] deal with your slaves justly and fairly, knowing that you also have a Master in heaven. [Lev 25:43, 53]
2Be persistent *and* devoted to prayer,

3:18–23 *be subject.* See notes on Ephesians 5:19–31.
3:22–25 *the inheritance which is your [greatest] reward.* The strong motivation to serve someone well is found in the future reward that Christ gives to those who are faithful in this service. We normally think we receive eternal rewards for spiritual practices like reading the Bible, prayer, or evangelism. Here, Paul asserts that all work done to the honor of Christ will bring an eternal reward (1:22–23; 2:18).

13 Mk 11:25 **14** 1Pe 4:8; 1Co 13; Eph 4:3 **15** Php 4:7; 1Co 7:15; Eph 4:4 **16** Eph 5:19 **17** 1Co 10:31 **18** 1Pe 3:1; Eph 5:3 **19** Eph 5:25; 4:31 **20** Eph 6:1; Eph 5:24 **21** Eph 6:4 **22** Eph 6:5; 1Ti 6:1; Titus 2:9; 1Pe 2:18; ver. 20; Php 16 **23** Eph 6:6,7 **24** Eph 6:8; 1Co 7:22 **25** Ro 2:11; Eph 6:9; 1Pe 1:17; Dt 10:17 **CHAPTER 4** **1** Eph 6:9 **2** Lk 18:1; Ro 12:12; Col 2:7

being alert *and* focused in your prayer
life with *an attitude of* thanksgiving.
3 At the same time pray for us, too,
that God will open a door [of oppor-
tunity] to us for the word, to proclaim
the mystery of Christ, for which I have
been imprisoned;
4 that I may make it clear [and speak
boldly and unfold the mystery] in the
way I should.
5 Conduct yourself with wisdom in
your interactions with outsiders (non-
believers), make the most of each op-
portunity [treating it as something
precious].
6 Let your speech at all times be gra-
cious *and* pleasant, seasoned with salt,
so that you will know how to answer
each one [who questions you].
7 As to all my affairs, Tychicus, who
is a much-loved brother and faithful
assistant and fellow bond-servant in
the Lord, will give you all the informa-
tion. [Eph 6:21]
8 I have sent him to you for this very
purpose, that you may know how we
are doing and that he may encourage
your hearts;
9 and with him is Onesimus, our faith-
ful and beloved brother, who is one of
you. They will let you know everything
about the situation here [in Rome].
10 Aristarchus, my fellow prisoner,
wishes to be remembered to you; as
does Mark, the cousin of Barnabas
(about whom you received instructions;
if he comes to you, welcome him);
11 and from Jesus, who is called Jus-
tus. These are the only fellow workers
for the kingdom of God who are from
the circumcision (Jewish Christians),
and they have proved to be an encour-
agement *and* a comfort to me.
12 Epaphras, who is one of you and
a bond-servant of Christ Jesus, sends
you greetings. [He is] always striving
for you in his prayers, praying with
genuine concern, [pleading] that you
may [as people of character and cour-
age] stand firm, [spiritually mature]
and fully assured in all the will of God.
13 For I testify for him that he has
worked strenuously for you and for
the believers in Laodicea and those in
Hierapolis.
14 Luke, the beloved physician, and
Demas greet you.
15 Give my greetings to the brothers
and sisters at Laodicea, and to Nym-
pha and the church that meets in her
house.
16 When this letter has been read
among you, see that it is read in the
church of the Laodiceans; and also
that you in turn read my letter [that is
coming to you] from Laodicea.
17 And say to Archippus, "See to it
that you fulfill [carefully the duties of]
the ministry which you have received
in the Lord."
18 I, Paul, write this greeting with
my own hand. Remember my chains.
May grace (God's unmerited favor and
blessing) be with you.

4:5 *Conduct yourself with wisdom in your interactions with outsiders.* Early Christians were often viewed with suspicion, distrust, and disdain. They were considered atheists because they would not worship the gods of Rome and Greece. Many labeled them as unpatriotic because they would not burn incense before the image of the emperor. Some even accused the early Christians of participating in orgies because of their talk of "love feasts" (Jude 12). Others harbored suspicions that Christians were really cannibals who ate and drank the blood and body of the Lord. With such misrepresentations of Christian belief and practice running rampant, it was very important for misunderstandings to be dispelled by the virtuous and impeccable lives of Christian believers.

4:9 *Onesimus.* This slave of Philemon probably accompanied Tychicus to Colosse. Paul's letter to Philemon would have been carried along with the letter to the Colossians. It dealt with a personal situation between Onesimus and his master.

4:10–15 *Mark.* This is the author of the Gospel of Mark.

4:18 *I, Paul, write this greeting with my own hand.* The apostle dictated his letters to a secretary, but it was his custom to give a greeting in his own handwriting at the end (2Th 2:1; 3:17). This served to personalize and authenticate the letter.

3 Eph 6:19; 1Co 16:9; 2Co 2:12; Eph 6:19; Eph 6:20; Php 1:7 **5** Eph 5:15; Eph 5:16 **6** Ecc 10:12; Mk 9:50; 1Pe 3:15 **8** Eph 6:22 **9** Php 10 **10** Ac 19:29; Ac 15:37; 2Ti 4:11 **12** Php 23; Ro 15:30; Mt 5:48; 1Co 2:6 **14** 2Ti 4:11; 2Ti 4:10 **15** Ro 16:5; 1Co 16:19 **16** 1Th 5:27 **17** Php 2; 1Ti 4:6 **18** 1Co 16:21; 2Th 3:17; Heb 13:3; Heb 13:25

THE FIRST LETTER OF PAUL TO THE

THESSALONIANS

▸ **AUTHOR:** First Thessalonians went unchallenged as a Pauline Epistle until the nineteenth century, when radical critics claimed that its lack of doctrinal content made its authenticity suspect. But this is a weak objection on two counts: (1) the proportion of doctrinal teaching in Paul's epistles varies widely, and (2) 4:13 – 5:11 is a foundational passage for New Testament eschatology (future events). Paul had quickly grounded the Thessalonians in Christian doctrine, and the only problematic issue when this epistle was written concerned the matter of Christ's return. Paul planted the Thessalonian church on his second missionary journey, and wrote this epistle as a response to a good report regarding the church from Timothy in AD 51.

▸ **TIMES:** c. AD 51 ▸ **KEY VERSES:** 1Th 3:12 – 13

▸ **THEME:** In that Paul's time in Thessalonica was cut short, Paul used these letters to clarify some of his teaching. After a review of the basics, the primary issues covered in 1 Thessalonians are what happens when people die and the timing of the second coming of Christ. In that there were so many people around at that time that had seen Jesus, the promise of His return was met with anxious expectation. We tend to be blasé about it because we have watched so many predictions concerning the end times come and go, but this book will help us to sharpen and renew our expectations.

Thanksgiving for These Believers

1 PAUL, SILVANUS (Silas), and Timothy,
To the church of the Thessalonians in God the Father and the Lord Jesus Christ: Grace to you and peace [inner calm and spiritual well-being from God].
[2]We give thanks to God always for all of you, *continually* mentioning you in our prayers;
[3]recalling unceasingly before our God and Father your work energized by faith, and your service motivated

1:1 ***Silvanus.*** Silvanus is the Roman form of the name Silas. After Paul had separated from Barnabas (Ac 15:36 – 40), Silas became Paul's traveling companion on the second missionary journey, and he may have served as Paul's secretary. He was a leader of the Jerusalem church (Ac 15:22 – 23), and he accompanied Paul and Barnabas to Antioch to deliver the decree of the Jerusalem council (Ac 15:22 – 23). He and Paul suffered a beating at Philippi (Ac 16:22 – 24), and he had helped found the church at Thessalonica (Ac 17:1 – 4). ***Timothy.*** Timothy was also with Paul on the second missionary journey. Paul considered him like a son and loved him dearly (Ac 16:3; 1Ti 1:2). This letter is a response to Timothy's report from the church in Thessalonica. ***To the church.*** The Greek word *ekklesia* was a familiar term meaning any gathering or assembly. In its New Testament usage this word calls to mind the relationship of believers in Thessalonica as a body.
1:3 ***unwavering hope.*** The believers at Thessalonica fixed their hope solidly on the return of Jesus Christ (v. 10). Notice that each of the virtues has Christ as its object. Jesus is constantly the

CHAPTER 1 **1** 1Pe 5:12; Eph 1:2 **2** Ro 1:8 **3** 1Th 2:13; Jn 6:29; Ro 16:6

by love and unwavering hope in [the
return of] our Lord Jesus Christ.
[1 Thess 1:10]
4Brothers and sisters beloved by
God, we know that He has chosen you;
5for our good news [regarding salva-
tion] came to you not only in word, but
also in [its inherent] power and in the
Holy Spirit and with great conviction
[on our part]. You know what kind of
men we proved to be among you for
your benefit.
6You became imitators of us and
[through us] of the Lord, after you
welcomed our message in [a time of]
great trouble with the joy supplied by
the Holy Spirit;
7so that you became an example to
all the believers in Macedonia and in
Achaia.
8For the word of the Lord has re-
sounded from you *and* has echoed [like
thunder], not only in Macedonia and
Achaia, but in every place [the news of]
your [great] faith in God has spread,
so that we never need to say anything
about it.
9For they themselves report about
us, *telling* what kind of reception we
had among you, and how you turned
to God from idols to serve the living
and true God,
10and to [look forward and confi-
dently] wait for [the coming of] His
Son from heaven, whom He raised
from the dead—Jesus, who [personal-
ly] rescues us from the coming wrath
[and draws us to Himself, granting us
all the privileges and rewards of a new
life with Him].

Paul's Ministry

2 FOR YOU know, brothers and sis-
ters, that our coming to you has
not been ineffective (fruitless, in vain),
2but after we had already suf-
fered and been outrageously treated
in Philippi, as you know, yet in [the
strength of] our God we summoned
the courage to proclaim boldly to you

---

focus. This is a good standard for evaluating any Christian service.

1:5 *our good news.* Paul had preached the gospel to them clearly when he was with them. For three weeks he had "engaged in discussion and friendly debate with them from the Scriptures, explaining and pointing out [scriptural evidence] that it was necessary for the Christ to suffer and rise from the dead" (Ac 17:2–3). This message was far different from the messianic expectations that Paul knew from his own training as a Pharisee. The Jews of that day were not looking for a suffering savior but a conquering champion.

1:5 Sharing Our Faith — In order to share our faith successfully, we must keep the following rules in mind:

First, we must be clean vessels. God reminds Isaiah the prophet of this: "purify yourselves, you who carry the articles of the Lord" (Isa 52:11). David prays for forgiveness and cleansing, and a willing spirit. He states, "Then I will teach transgressors Your ways, and sinners shall be converted and return to You" (Ps 51:13).

We must be able to clearly give out the simple facts of the gospel without getting bogged down with profound theological concepts. Philip the evangelist demonstrated how to do this when he dealt with the Ethiopian eunuch in the desert. "Then Philip spoke and beginning with this Scripture he preached Jesus to him" (Ac 8:35).

We must avoid arguments and stick to the basic issues of man's sin and Christ's sacrifice.

We must use the Word of God. Paul's tremendous success as an evangelist can be linked directly to his constant use of God's Word (Ac 17:2; 18:28; 2Ti 2:15; 3:14–17).

We must depend upon the Spirit of God (Jn 3:15; Ac 6:10; 1Co 2:4).

1:6 *imitators of us.* As we focus on Jesus we will reflect His image to others (2Co 3:18).

1:8 *the word of the Lord has resounded from you.* Since Thessalonica was a port city on the much-traveled Egnatian Way, those who saw the virtuous life and persistent faith of the Thessalonican Christians would spread the word throughout the entire region.

1:10 *rescues us from the coming wrath.* Because Christ endured God's wrath at Calvary, all who are in Christ will escape that wrath. They have nothing to fear.

2:2 *in Philippi.* Paul and Silas were beaten and put in the stocks in Philippi (Ac 16:22–24).

4 Col 3:12 **5** Mk 16:20; 2Co 6:6; Heb 2:3 **6** 1Co 4:16; Php 3:17; Ac 5:41; Heb 10:34 **8** Ro 10:18; 1:8; 2Th 1:4 **9** 1Th 2:1; 1Co 12:2; Gal 4:8 **10** Ro 2:7; 2Pe 3:12; Ac 1:11; Ac 2:24; Ro 5:9 **CHAPTER 2** **1** 1Th 1:5,9 **2** Ac 16:22; 1Th 1:5; Php 1:30

the good news of God [regarding salvation] amid great opposition.
3For our appeal does not *come* from delusion or impure motives, nor [is it motivated] by deceit [our message is complete, accurate, and based on the truth—it does not change].
4But just as we have been approved by God to be entrusted with the gospel [that tells the good news of salvation through faith in Christ], so we speak, not as [if we were trying] to please people [to gain power and popularity], but *to please* God who examines our hearts [expecting our best].
5For as you well know, we never came with words of flattery nor with a pretext for greed—God is our witness—
6nor did we seek glory *and* honor from people, neither from you nor from anyone else, though as apostles of Christ we had the power to assert our authority.
7But we behaved gently when we were among you, like a devoted *mother* tenderly caring for her own children.
8Having such a deep affection for you, we were delighted to share with you not only God's good news but also our own lives, because you had become so very dear to us.
9For you remember, believers, our labor and hardship. We worked night and day [practicing our trade] in order not to be a [financial] burden to any of you while we proclaimed the gospel of God to you.
10You are witnesses, and so is God, how unworldly and just and blameless was our behavior toward you who believe [in our Lord Jesus Christ].
11For you know how we were exhorting and encouraging and imploring each one of you just as a father does [in dealing with] his own children, [guiding you]
12to live lives [of honor, moral courage, and personal integrity] worthy of the God who [saves you and] calls you into His own kingdom and glory.
13And we also thank God continually for this, that when you received the word of God [concerning salvation] which you heard from us, you welcomed it not as the word of [mere] men, but as it truly is, the word of God, which is effectually at work in you who believe [exercising its inherent, supernatural power in those of faith].
14For you, brothers and sisters, became imitators of the churches of God in Christ Jesus that are in Judea, because you too suffered the same [kind of] persecution from your own countrymen, as they did from the Jews,
15who killed both the Lord Jesus and the prophets, and harassed *and* drove us out; and [they] continue to be highly displeasing to God and [to show themselves] hostile to all people,
16forbidding us from speaking to the Gentiles (non-Jews) so that they may be saved. So, as always, they fill up [to the brim] the measure of their sins [allotted to them by God]. But [God's] wrath has come upon them at last [completely and forever]. [Gen 15:16]
17But since we were taken away from

2:5 *words of flattery.* Far from flattering, Paul preached boldly that everyone was a sinner who needed to be saved by the grace of God.
2:9 *labor.* This word indicates strenuous work that produces weariness. Paul made tents to provide for his financial needs (Ac 18:3), showing that his ministry was motivated by an unselfish desire to promote the well-being of others rather than to advance his own needs.
2:13 *effectually at work.* Gentile Christians in Thessalonica could contrast the pure Word of God, with its transforming effect, with the immoral pagan religions, which only perverted people even more. Likewise, Jewish believers could contrast the love and grace of God in the gospel to the legalism and pride often produced by the Jewish religion.
2:16 *fill up [to the brim] the measure of their sins.* The implication is that God will allow a nation, group, or individual to go only so far in sin before He brings judgment upon them (Ge 15:16).

3 2Co 7:2 **4** 1Co 7:25; Titus 1:3; Gal 1:10; Pr 17:3 **5** 2Co 2:17; Ro 1:9 **6** 1Ti 5:17; 1Co 9:4; 2Co 11:9; 1Co 9:1 **7** 1Co 2:3 **8** Ro 1:11; 15:29; 2Co 12:15 **9** Ac 20:34; 2Th 3:8; 2Co 12:13 **10** 1Th 1:5; 2Co 7:2 **12** Col 1:10; 1Co 1:9; 2Th 2:14 **13** 1Th 1:3; Gal 4:14 **14** Gal 1:22; Ac 17:5 **15** Ac 2:23; Mt 5:12; Est 3:8 **16** Lk 11:52; Ac 13:50; Ge 15:16; Mt 23:32; Mt 24:6 **17** 1Co 5:3; Col 2:5; 1Th 3:10

you, believers, for a little while—in
person, but not in heart—we endeav-
ored, with great longing to see you
face to face.
18For we wanted to come to you—I,
Paul, again and again [wanted to
come], but Satan hindered us.
19For who is [the object of] our hope
or joy or our victor's wreath of trium-
phant celebration [when we stand] in
the presence of our Lord Jesus at His
coming? Is it not you?
20For you are [indeed] our glory and
our joy!

Encouragement of Timothy's Visit

3 THEREFORE, WHEN we could
no longer endure our separation
[from you], we thought it best to be left
behind, alone at Athens,
2and so we sent Timothy, our brother
and God's servant in [spreading] the
good news of Christ, to strengthen and
encourage you [exhorting, comforting,
and establishing you] in regard to your
faith,
3so that no one would be unsettled
by these difficulties [to which I have
referred]. For you know that we have
been destined for this [as something
unavoidable in our position].
4For even when we were with you,
we warned you plainly in advance that
we were going to experience persecu-
tion; and so, as you know, it has come
to pass.
5For this reason, when I could no lon-
ger endure the suspense, I sent *some-
one* to find out about your faith [how
you were holding up under pressure],
for fear that somehow the tempter had
tempted you and our work [among you]
would prove to be ineffective.
6But now that Timothy has come
back to us from [his visit with] you,
and has brought us good news of your
[steadfast] faith and [the warmth of
your] love, and [reported] that you al-
ways think kindly of us *and* treasure
your memories of us, longing to see us
just as we long to see you,
7for this reason, brothers and sisters,
during all our distress and suffering
we have been comforted *and* greatly
encouraged about you because of your
faith [your unwavering trust in God—
placing yourselves completely in His
loving hands];
8because now we *really* live [in spite
of everything], if you stand firm in
the Lord.
9For what [adequate] thanks can we
offer to God for you in return for all the
joy *and* delight we have before our God
on your account?
10We continue to pray night and day
most earnestly that we may see you
face to face, and may complete what-
ever may be imperfect *and* lacking in
your faith.
11Now may our God and Father
Himself, and Jesus our Lord guide our
steps to you [by removing the obstacles
that stand in our way].
12And may the Lord cause you to in-
crease and excel *and* overflow in love
for one another, and for all people, just
as we also do for you;

2:18 *Satan hindered us.* Satan has a vested interest in hindering the spread of the gospel, and we may be sure that when we are engaged in the Lord's work, we will experience spiritual attacks and opposition of various kinds.

3:1 *Athens.* When forced to leave Thessalonica, Paul and Silas went to Berea, the next city west of Thessalonica. The Thessalonian Jews who had opposed Paul learned that he was at Berea, and went there also to stir up opposition. Paul's friends then escorted him south to Athens (Ac 17:13–15).

3:3 *unsettled by these difficulties.* The Bible teaches that those who live godly lives should expect persecution (2Ti 3:12). In fact, Christ warned His disciples that they would experience the same type of rejection He had experienced (Jn 15:18–21). But such suffering should not make us depressed. Instead we should rejoice that we are allied with His name (Mt 5:10–12).

3:12 *increase and excel and overflow in love for one another.* Christ had told His disciples that His followers would be identified by their love for one another (Jn 13:35).

18 Ro 1:13 **19** 2Co 1:14; Pr 16:31; 1Co 15:23 **CHAPTER 3** **1** ver. 5; Ac 17:15 **2** Ro 16:21; 1Co 16:10 **3** Eph 3:13; Ac 9:16; 1Co 4:9; 2Ti 3:12 **4** Ac 20:24 **5** ver. 1; 1Co 7:5; 2Co 11:3; Gal 2:2 **6** Ac 18:1; Php 1:8 **7** 2Co 1:4 **8** Php 4:1 **9** 1Th 1:2 **10** Ac 26:7; Ro 15:32; 1Th 2:17; Col 4:12 **11** Mk 1:3 **12** 1Th 4:10

13 so that He may strengthen *and* establish your hearts without blame in holiness in the sight of our God and Father at the coming of our Lord Jesus with all His saints (God's people).

Sanctification and Love

4 FINALLY, BELIEVERS, we ask and admonish you in the Lord Jesus, that you follow the *instruction* that you received from us about how you ought to walk and please God (just as you are actually doing) and that you excel even more and more [pursuing a life of purpose and living in a way that expresses gratitude to God for your salvation].

2 For you know what commandments *and* precepts we gave you by the *authority of* the Lord Jesus.

3 For this is the will of God, that you be sanctified [separated and set apart from sin]: that you abstain *and* back away from sexual immorality;

4 that each of you know how to control his own body in holiness and honor [being available for God's purpose and separated from things profane],

5 not [to be used] in lustful passion, like the Gentiles who do not know God *and* are ignorant of His will;

6 and that [in this matter of sexual misconduct] no man *shall* transgress and defraud his brother because the Lord is the avenger in all these things, just as we have told you before and solemnly warned you.

7 For God has not called us to impurity, but to holiness [to be dedicated, and set apart by behavior that pleases Him, whether in public or in private].

8 So whoever rejects *and* disregards this is not [merely] rejecting man but the God who gives His Holy Spirit to you [to dwell in you and empower you to overcome temptation].

9 Now concerning brotherly love, you have no need for *anyone* to write you, for you have been [personally] taught by God to love one another [that is, to have an unselfish concern for others and to do things for their benefit]. [Lev 19:18; John 13:34]

10 For indeed you already do practice it toward all the believers throughout Macedonia [by actively displaying your love and concern for them]. But we urge you, brothers and sisters, that you excel [in this matter] more and more,

11 and to make it your ambition to live quietly *and* peacefully, and to mind your own affairs and work with your hands, just as we directed you,

12 so that you will behave properly toward outsiders [exhibiting good

---

3:13 ***all His saints.*** The word saints means "holy ones" or "those set apart." It can be used to apply to believers, or to holy angels. Angels will participate in the second coming (4:16; Jude 14; Rev 19:14).

4:1 ***how you ought to walk.*** The Christian life not only begins with faith, but it continues as a daily walk of faith. Christians are not to live like unsaved Gentiles (Eph 4:17), instead they are to walk worthy of their calling from God (Eph 4:1). John exhorts Christians to walk in the light, that is, in the revealed will of God (1Jn 1:7).

4:3 ***abstain and back away from sexual immorality.*** A major problem for the early church was maintaining sexual purity (1Co 5:1,9 – 11). Pagan religions often included sexual orgies as part of their rites of worship, and temple prostitutes were dedicated to various gods. In contrast, Christianity taught that the body is God's temple (1Co 6:18 – 20). The body should be honored as created by God and should be sanctified in keeping with its holy purpose.

4:10 ***excel [in this matter] more and more.*** These believers already had a good record of loving one another, but Paul desired that love to increase. This was the commandment of Jesus (Jn 13:34 – 35; 15:12,17) and is an important basis of evangelism. In a world that is filled with self-serving individuals, the genuine love of Christians should attract others to the faith.

4:11 ***make it your ambition to live quietly and peacefully.*** This does not refer to a lack of activity but rather to an inner quietness and peace befitting the Christian faith (2Th 3:12; 1Ti 2:11). ***work with your hands.*** Usually people who are busy running other people's affairs do not run their own affairs well. A Christian's house should be in order as a testimony to others.

---

13 1Co 1:8; Php 1:10; Zec 14:5 **CHAPTER 4** **1** Php 1:27; 1Th 2:12; Col 1:10 **3** Ro 12:2; Eph 5:27; Col 3:5 **4** Ro 6:19 **5** Col 3:5; Eph 4:17; 1Co 15:34 **6** 2Th 1:8 **7** Lev 11:44 **8** Lk 10:16; 1Co 2:10 **9** 1Th 5:1; Jer 31:34; Mt 22:39 **10** 1Th 1:7; 1Th 3:12 **11** 2Th 3:11; Ac 20:35; Eph 4:28 **12** Ro 13:13

character, personal integrity, and moral courage worthy of the respect of the outside world], and be dependent on no one *and* in need of nothing [be self-supporting].

Those Who Died in Christ

13Now we do not want you to be un-
informed, believers, about those who are asleep [in death], so that you will not grieve [for them] as the others do who have no hope [beyond this present life].
14For if we believe that Jesus died
and rose again [as in fact He did], even so God [in this same way—by raising them from the dead] will bring with Him those [believers] who have fallen asleep in Jesus.
15For we say this to you by the Lord's
[own] word, that we who are still alive and remain until the coming of the Lord, will in no way precede [into His presence] those [believers] who have fallen asleep [in death].
16For the Lord Himself will come
down from heaven with a shout of command, with the voice of the archangel and with the [blast of the] trumpet of God, and the dead in Christ will rise first.
17Then we who are alive and remain
[on the earth] will *simultaneously* be caught up (raptured) together with them [the resurrected ones] in the clouds to meet the Lord in the air, and so we will always be with the Lord! [John 14:3; 1 Cor 15:52; 2 Cor 5:8; Phil 1:23; Col 3:4]
18Therefore comfort *and* encourage
one another with these words [concerning our reunion with believers who have died].

The Day of the Lord

5 NOW AS to the times and dates, brothers and sisters, you have no need for anything to be written to you.
2For you yourselves know perfectly
well that the day of the [return of the] Lord is coming just as a thief [comes unexpectedly and suddenly] in the night.
3While they are saying, "Peace and
safety [all is well and secure!]" then [in a moment unforeseen] destruction will come upon them suddenly like labor pains on a woman with child, and they will absolutely not escape [for there will be no way to escape the judgment of the Lord].
4But you, believers, [all you who be-
lieve in Christ as Savior and acknowledge Him as God's Son] are not in

---

4:14 *those [believers] who have fallen asleep.* Some believe this phrase indicates that departed Christians are unconscious until the second coming. But the Bible indicates that to be absent from our present body is to be present with the Lord Jesus (5:10; 2Co 5; 8; Php 1:23). When a Christian dies, it is the body that sleeps. The soul goes to heaven.
4:16 *come down from heaven with a shout.* Accompanying the descent of Christ from heaven will be the voice of an archangel, perhaps Michael, who is portrayed as the leader of the army of God (Da 10:13,21; Jude 9; Rev 12:7–9). The only other angel named in Scripture is Gabriel, who is given a prominent role as a messenger of God (Da 8:16; 9:21; Lk 1:19,26). ***the dead in Christ will rise.*** Clearly this will be a physical resurrection in which bodily existence will be restored, as confirmed in 1 Corinthians 15:51–53. The resurrected bodies of Christians will be like the body of Christ (1Jn 3:2), incorruptible and immortal, and yet they will be bodies of flesh and bone (Lk 24:39–40; Jn 20:20,25,27).
4:17 *caught up.* The English word *rapture* comes from the Latin for "caught up."
5:2 *the day of the [return of the] Lord.* This expression was familiar to those who knew the Hebrew Scriptures. The day of the Lord in the Old Testament was characterized by two phases: God's judgment against sinful people and God's eternal reign over His people. God's judgment will be a time of darkness and an expression of His wrath (Joel 2:1–2; Am 5:18–20; Zep 1:14–15). His reign will also be a time blessing (Isa 2:1–3; 11:1–9; 30:23–26; Zec 14:1,7–11,20–21; Mt 19:28; Ac 3:19–21).
5:4 *not in spiritual darkness.* Though the day of the Lord will overtake the unsaved world unexpectedly, it will not overtake Christians, because they will be looking forward to and expecting it. The fact that Christ could come at any moment

---

13 Lev 19:28; 2Sa 12:20; Eph 2:12 **14** 1Co 15:13,23 **15** 1Ki 13:17; 1Co 15:51 **16** Mt 24:30; Ac 1:11; 1Co 15:52; 1Co 15:23 **17** 1Co 15:51; Ac 1:9; Jn 17:24 **18** 1Th 5:11 **CHAPTER 5** **1** Mt 24:3; 1Th 4:9 **2** 2Pe 3:10 **3** Isa 13:6-9; Hos 13:13 **4** Ro 13:12

spiritual darkness [nor held by its power], that the day [of judgment] would overtake you [by surprise] like a thief;

5 for you are all sons of light and sons of day. We do not belong to the night nor to darkness.

6 So then let us not sleep [in spiritual indifference] as the rest [of the world does], but let us keep wide awake [alert and cautious] and let us be sober [self-controlled, calm, and wise].

7 For those who sleep, sleep at night, and those who are drunk get drunk at night.

8 But since we [believers] belong to the day, let us be sober, having put on the breastplate of faith and love, and as a helmet, the hope *and* confident assurance of salvation.

9 For God has not destined us to [incur His] wrath [that is, He did not select us to condemn us], but to obtain salvation through our Lord Jesus Christ,

10 who died [willingly] for us, so that whether we are awake (alive) or asleep (dead) [at Christ's appearing], we will live together with Him [sharing eternal life].

11 Therefore encourage *and* comfort one another and build up one another, just as you are doing.

Christian Conduct

12 Now we ask you, brothers and sisters, to appreciate those who diligently work among you [recognize, acknowledge, and respect your leaders], who are in charge over you in the Lord and who give you instruction,

13 and [we ask that you appreciate them and] hold them in the highest esteem in love because of their work [on your behalf]. Live in peace with one another.

14 We [earnestly] urge you, believers, admonish those who are out of line [the undisciplined, the unruly, the disorderly], encourage the timid [who lack spiritual courage], help the [spiritually] weak, be very patient with everyone [always controlling your temper]. [Is 35:4]

15 See that no one repays another with evil for evil, but always seek that which is good for one another and for all people.

16 Rejoice always *and* delight in your faith;

17 be unceasing *and* persistent in prayer;

18 in every situation [no matter what the circumstances] be thankful *and* continually give thanks *to God;* for this is the will of God for you in Christ Jesus.

19 Do not quench [subdue, or be unresponsive to the working and guidance of] the [Holy] Spirit.

20 Do not scorn *or* reject gifts of prophecy *or* prophecies [spoken revelations—words of instruction or exhortation or warning].

21 But test all things carefully [so

---

should motivate unbelievers to accept His forgiveness, and believers to live daily for Him.

5:8 *sober.* A sober life is not only free from drunkenness, but awake to spiritual realities.

5:9 *not destined us to [incur His] wrath.* There will be wrath at the day of the Lord, but it will be God's wrath on the unbelieving world that has spurned and mocked Christ (Rev 6:12 – 17).

5:12 *Now we ask you.* Significantly, Paul combines prophecy with practical teachings for the Christian life. God never intended prophecy to just be a field for academic debate, but to be a truth that would provide believers hope and direction in their lives.

5:16 *Rejoice always.* Regardless of difficult circumstances, a Christian always has grounds for rejoicing. The Lord is a sovereign Ruler and will accomplish His purpose. Christian joy is not based on circumstances, but on a growing awareness of God and the certain future of eternal life with Christ (Rev 21:1 – 7).

5:17 *be unceasing and persistent in prayer.* To pray without ceasing seems impossible, but a person can develop an attitude and habit of constant prayer. No matter what else is going on, we should be aware of God's presence with us, and turn to Him with every thought and action.

5 Eph 5:8 **6** Mt 25:5; 1Pe 5:8 **7** Lk 21:34; Ac 2:15 **8** Eph 6:14 **9** Ro 9:22; 2Th 2:13 **10** 2Co 5:15 **11** 1Th 4:18 **12** 1Co 16:18 **13** Mk 9:50 **14** 2Th 3:11; Heb 12:12; Ro 14:1; Gal 5:22 **15** Lev 19:18; Gal 6:10 **16** 2Co 6:10 **17** Eph 6:18 **19** Eph 4:30 **20** 1Co 14:1 **21** 1Jn 4:1; Php 4:8

you can recognize what is good]. Hold
firmly to that which is good.
22 Abstain from every form of evil
[withdraw and keep away from it].
23 Now may the God of peace Him-
self sanctify you through and through
[that is, separate you from profane
and vulgar things, make you pure and
whole and undamaged—consecrated
to Him—set apart for His purpose];
and may your spirit and soul and body
be kept complete and [be found] blame-
less at the coming of our Lord Jesus
Christ.
24 Faithful *and* absolutely trust-
worthy is He who is calling you [to
Himself for your salvation], and He
will do it [He will fulfill His call by
making you holy, guarding you, watch-
ing over you, and protecting you as
His own].
25 Brothers and sisters, pray for us.
26 Greet all the believers with a holy
kiss [as brothers and sisters in God's
family].
27 I solemnly charge you by the Lord
to have this letter read before all the
congregation.
28 The grace of our Lord Jesus Christ
be with you.

5:23 *spirit and soul and body.* Every part of the Christian life should bear evidence that we are set apart as holy to God.

5:26 *a holy kiss.* A kiss was a customary greeting among friends (as it still is in some cultures), something like our modern handshake.

22 1Th 4:12 **23** Php 4:9; 1Th 3:13; 1Co 1:8 **24** 1Co 1:9 **25** Col 4:3 **26** Ro 16:16 **27** Col 4:16 **28** Ro 16:20

THE SECOND LETTER OF PAUL TO THE
THESSALONIANS

▸ **AUTHOR:** The external attestation to the authenticity of 2 Thessalonians as a Pauline Epistle is even stronger than that for 1 Thessalonians. Internally the vocabulary, style, and doctrinal content support the claims in 1:1 and 3:17 that it was written by Paul. This letter was probably written a few months after 1 Thessalonians, while Paul was still in Corinth with Silas and Timothy (1:1; Ac 18:5).

▸ **TIMES:** c. AD 51 ▸ **KEY VERSES:** 2Th 2:2 – 3

▸ **THEME:** This letter to the Thessalonians appears to have been written fairly soon after the first one. He provides some further clarification on some of the same issues he addressed in the first letter. There appears to still be some confusion about the events of the end times, which he clarifies. He also wisely encourages the believers in the basics he has taught them in his role as a caring pastor.

Thanksgiving for Faith and Perseverance

1 PAUL, SILVANUS (Silas), and Tim-
othy,
To the church of the Thessalonians
in God our Father and the Lord Jesus
Christ:
2 Grace to you and peace [inner calm
and spiritual well-being] from God the
Father and the Lord Jesus Christ.
3 We ought always *and* indeed are
morally obligated [as those in debt] to
give thanks to God for you, brothers and
sisters, as is fitting, because your faith
is growing ever greater, and the [un-
selfish] love of each one of you toward
one another is continually increasing.
4 Therefore, we speak of you with
pride among the churches of God for
your steadfastness [your unflinching
endurance, and patience] and your
firm faith in the midst of all the per-
secution and [crushing] distress which
you endure.
5 *This is* a positive proof of the righ-
teous judgment of God [a sign of His
fair verdict], so that you will be consid-
ered worthy of His kingdom, for which
indeed you are suffering.
6 For after all it is *only* just for God
to repay with distress those who dis-
tress you,
7 and to *give* relief to you who are so
distressed and to us as well when the

1:1 ***Silvanus (Silas), and Timothy.*** Silvanus (Latin for Silas) had been Paul's traveling companion ever since the start of the second missionary journey. He had participated in the founding of the church at Thessalonica (Ac 17:1 – 4). Timothy also accompanied Paul on his second missionary journey. His report from the Thessalonian church had been the occasion for writing 1 Thessalonians (1Th 3:6 – 8). ***To the church.*** The Greek word *ekklesia* means "gathering" or "assembly."

1:5 ***considered worthy of His kingdom.*** If believers handle their persecutions properly, they will be counted worthy of great reward in the coming kingdom of God (Mt 5:12; 1Pe 2:19 – 20). Christians are called to endure suffering in this world, for they will receive a far greater reward in the next (2Ti 2:12).

1:7 – 8 ***when the Lord Jesus is revealed.***

CHAPTER 1 **1** 2Co 1:19; 1Th 1:1 **2** 1Co 1:3 **3** 1Th 1:2; 2Th 2:13 **4** 2Co 7:14; 1Th 2:19; 1Th 1:3; 1Th 2:14 **5** Php 1:28; 1Th 2:14 **6** Rev 6:10 **7** Rev 14:13; 1Th 4:16; Jude 14

Lord Jesus is revealed from heaven with
His mighty angels in a flame of fire,
8 dealing out [full and complete] ven-
geance to those who do not [seek to]
know God and to those who ignore
and refuse to obey the gospel of our
Lord Jesus [by choosing not to respond
to Him].
9 These people will pay the penalty
and endure the punishment of ever-
lasting destruction, banished from
the presence of the Lord and from the
glory of His power,
10 when He comes to be glorified in
His saints on that day [that is, glorified
through the changed lives of those
who have accepted Him as Savior and
have been set apart for His purpose],
and to be marveled at among all who
have believed, because our testimony
to you was believed *and* trusted [and
confirmed in your lives].
11 With this in view, we constantly
pray for you, that our God will count
you worthy of your calling [to faith]
and with [His] power fulfill every de-
sire for goodness, and complete [your]
every work of faith,
12 so that the name of our Lord Jesus
will be glorified in you [by what you
do], and you in Him, according to the
[precious] grace of our God and the
Lord Jesus Christ.

Man of Lawlessness

2 NOW IN regard to the coming of
our Lord Jesus Christ and our gath-
ering together to *meet* Him, we ask
you, brothers and sisters, [Mark 13:27;
1 Thess 2:19; 4:15–17]
2 not to be quickly unsettled or
alarmed either by a [so-called prophet-
ic revelation of a] spirit or a message
or a letter [alleged to be] from us, to
the effect that the day of the Lord has
[already] come.
3 Let no one in any way deceive *or*
entrap you, for *that day will not come*
unless the apostasy comes first [that
is, the great rebellion, the abandon-
ment of the faith by professed Chris-
tians], and the man of lawlessness is
revealed, the son of destruction [the
Antichrist, the one who is destined
to be destroyed], [Dan 7:25; 8:25;
1 Tim 4:1]

Presently the Lord Jesus is enthroned in glory at the right hand of the Father (Jn 17:5). Stephen saw this glory before he was martyred (Ac 7:55–56), but one day, and it may be soon, "every eye will see Him" (Rev 1:7). ***in a flame of fire.*** Some believe that this is the fulfillment of John the Baptist's prophecy of the One who would "baptize with fire" (Mt 3:11–12; Lk 3:16–17).

1:8 *do not [seek to] know . . . refuse to obey.* Those who do not know are the unbelieving Gentiles, those who do not obey are the unbelieving Jews who knew about God and rejected His Son (Ro 10:1,16).

1:12 *glorified in you.* Christ will be glorified not only among, but also in the saints, for believers reflect His glory.

2:1 *to the coming of our Lord.* After writing 1 Thessalonians, Paul had received word that the believers in Thessalonica were being misled by false teachers who were confusing the believers with erroneous ideas about the second coming. ***gathering together to meet Him.*** This will be the first time that the whole church, including every believer, will be gathered before the Lord to worship Him. The phrase seems to refer to the event described in 1 Thessalonians 4:17, where Paul speaks of meeting the Lord in the air.

2:2 *the day of the Lord has [already] come.* The false teaching was that the day of the Lord (1Th 5:2–4) had already come, bringing with it the tribulations they were experiencing. Thus, some Thessalonian believers thought that they had missed the second coming.

2:3 *apostasy.* The Greek word translated "apostasy" is the word commonly used to describe a military rebellion. In the Scriptures, the word is used of rebellion against God. Some have therefore interpreted this verse to refer to a general defection from the truth, perhaps even by those professing to be the church. This apostasy would prepare the way for the antichrist. ***the man of lawlessness.*** Paul does not use the title "antichrist" for this man, but his description parallels John's description of the antichrist (1Jn 2:18; Rev 13). The man of lawlessness will lead the world into rebellion against God (v. 10), perform wonders through Satan's power (v. 9), and finally will present himself as a god to be worshiped (v. 4).

8 Heb 12:29; 2Pe 3:7; Rev 21:8; Ps 79:6; Ro 2:8 **9** Php 3:19; 2Pe 3:7; Dt 33:2; Isa 2:19 **10** Ps 89:7; 68:35 **11** ver. 5; 1Th 1:3 **12** 1Pe 1:7 **CHAPTER 2** **1** 1Th 4:16; Mt 24:31; Mk 13:27 **2** Mt 24:4; Eph 5:6 **3** Mt 24:4; Eph 5:6; 1Ti 4:1; Da 7:25; Rev 13:11; Jn 17:12

4 who opposes and exalts himself [so proudly and so insolently] above every so-called god or object of worship, so that he [actually enters and] takes his seat in the temple of God, publicly proclaiming that he himself is God. [Ezek 28:2; Dan 11:36, 37]

5 Do you not remember that when I was still with you, I was telling you these things?

6 And you know what restrains him now [from being revealed]; it is so that he will be revealed at his own [appointed] time.

7 For the mystery of lawlessness [rebellion against divine authority and the coming reign of lawlessness] is already at work; [but it is restrained] only until he who now restrains it is taken out of the way.

8 Then the lawless one [the Antichrist] will be revealed and the Lord Jesus will slay him with the breath of His mouth and bring him to an end by the appearance of His coming. [Is 11:4]

9 The coming of the [Antichrist, the lawless] one is through the activity of Satan, [attended] with great power [all kinds of counterfeit miracles] and [deceptive] signs and false wonders [all of them lies],

10 and by unlimited seduction to evil *and* with all the deception of wickedness for those who are perishing, because they did not welcome the love of the truth [of the gospel] so as to be saved [they were spiritually blind, and rejected the truth that would have saved them].

11 Because of this God will send upon them a misleading influence, [an activity of error and deception] so they will believe the lie,

12 in order that all may be judged *and* condemned who did not believe the truth [about their sin, and the need for salvation through Christ], but *instead* took pleasure in unrighteousness.

13 But we should *and* are [morally] obligated [as debtors] always to give thanks to God for you, believers beloved by the Lord, because God has chosen you from the beginning for salvation through the sanctifying work of the Spirit [that sets you apart for God's purpose] and by your faith in the truth [of God's word that leads you to spiritual maturity].

14 It was to this end that He called you through our gospel [the good news of Jesus' death, burial, and resurrection], so that you may obtain *and* share in the glory of our Lord Jesus Christ.

15 So then, brothers and sisters, stand firm and hold [tightly] to the traditions which you were taught, whether by word *of mouth* or by letter from us.

16 Now may our Lord Jesus Christ Himself and God our Father, who has loved us and given us everlasting comfort *and* encouragement and the good [well-founded] hope [of salvation] by *His* grace,

17 comfort *and* encourage and

2:4 *takes his seat in the temple of God.* This is the ultimate fulfillment of the "abomination of desolation" spoken of by Daniel (Da 7:23; 9:26; 11:31,36 – 37; 12:11) and Jesus (Mt 24:15; Mk 13:14).
2:7 *is already at work.* The evil and deception that the man of sin embodies already exist in this world (1Jn 2:18). Anyone who opposes Christ and His church and seeks to deceive others into worshiping false gods is against Christ (antichrist). ***taken out of the way.*** Many believe that this verse refers to the rapture of the church (1Th 4:16 – 17), and the cessation of the Holy Spirit working through believers to restrain the power of sin in this world. There are a variety of other interpretations for the identity of the restrainer, including the Roman state, or the principle of law and government embodied in the state.
2:8 *the Lord Jesus will slay him . . . and bring him to an end.* Although the man of lawlessness will be revealed as extremely powerful (Rev 13:7), he will be destroyed by Christ and cast into the lake of fire when the Lord comes (Rev 19:19 – 20).
2:14 *obtain and share in the glory.* The Thessalonians have already been saved (v. 13), and called, but they must respond to God's work in them. Through the power of the Holy Spirit (v. 13), believers on this earth prepare for a future with Christ by living in a holy manner (1:10; 1Th 4:1 – 2).
2:17 *comfort and encourage and strengthen your hearts.* It is interesting to note that Paul

---

4 Isa 14:13; Rev 13:6; 1Co 8:5 **7** 1Jn 2:18 **8** Da 7:10; Isa 11:4; Heb 10:27 **9** Jn 8:41; Rev 18:23; Dt 13:1; Rev 19:20 **10** 2Co 2:15 **11** Ro 1:24; 1Ti 4:1 **12** Ro 1:32 **13** 2Th 1:3; 1Th 1:4; Eph 1:4; 1Pe 1:2 **14** 1Pe 5:10 **15** 1Co 16:13; 11:2 **16** 2Th 1:1,2; Rev 1:5; 1Pe 1:3 **17** 1Co 1:8

strengthen your hearts [keeping them steadfast and on course] in every good work and word.

Exhortation

3 FINALLY, BROTHERS and sisters,
pray *continually* for us that the
word of the Lord will spread rapidly
and be honored [triumphantly cele-
brated and glorified], just as it was
with you;
2and [pray] that we will be rescued
from perverse and evil men; for not
everyone has the faith.
3But the Lord is faithful, and He will
strengthen you [setting you on a firm
foundation] and will protect *and* guard
you from the evil *one*.
4We have confidence in the Lord
concerning you, that you are doing and
will *continue* to do the things [which]
we command.
5May the Lord direct your hearts
into the love of God and into the stead-
fastness *and* patience of Christ.
6Now we command you, believers, in
the name of our Lord Jesus Christ *and*
by His authority, that you withdraw
and keep away from every brother or
sister who leads an undisciplined life
and does not live in accordance with
the tradition *and* teaching that you
have received from us.
7For you yourselves know how you
ought to follow our example, because
we did not act in an undisciplined *or*
inappropriate manner when we were
with you [we were never idle or lazy,
nor did we avoid our duties],
8nor did we eat anyone's bread with-
out paying for it, but with labor and
hardship we worked night and day [to
pay our own way] so that we would not
be a *financial* burden on any of you [for
our support];
9not because we do not have a right
to such support, but [we provided our
own financial support] to offer our-
selves as a model for you, so that you
would follow our example.
10For even while we were with you,
we used to give you this order: if any-
one is not willing to work, then he is
not to eat, either.
11Indeed, we hear that some among
you are leading an undisciplined *and*
inappropriate life, doing no work at all,
but acting like busybodies [meddling
in other people's business].
12Now such people we command
and exhort in the Lord Jesus Christ to
settle down *and* work quietly and earn
their own food *and* other necessities
[supporting themselves instead of de-
pending on the hospitality of others].
13And as for [the rest of] you, believ-

---

uses the singular form of these verbs, with the plural subject of "Lord Jesus Christ Himself and God our Father," supporting the trinity and equality of God (1Th 3:11).

3:2 *perverse and evil men.* These may have been the unbelieving Jews in Corinth who were persecuting Paul at the time he wrote this letter (Ac 18:12 – 13). Justice in this world may never come for Christians, but they can certainly pray for deliverance from the wicked.

3:5 *direct your hearts.* The heart, the seat of a person's will and emotions, is the place where spiritual renewal begins. There God plants love and patience, traits that will produce a harvest of good works.

3:6 *command.* This is not just a friendly suggestion, but a binding order with the authority of Jesus Christ. ***withdraw.*** Among other things, this would include not allowing the person to participate in love feasts and the Lord's Supper (1Co 5:9 – 12; Mt 18:15 – 17).

3:9 *not because we do not have a right.* It is right for the church to financially support those who do the Lord's work (Lk 10:7; 1Co 9:6 – 14; Gal 6:6; 1Ti 5:17 – 18).

3:11 *doing no work at all.* Some Thessalonians, apparently using the impending return of the Lord as an excuse, had refused to work and were expecting others in the church to feed them. In his previous letter, Paul had already exhorted them to work (1Th 4:11 – 12). Since they had not heeded, the time had come to take further steps. While believers must always act with gentleness and love toward one another, it is wrong to enable another person to continue in sin.

3:12 *work quietly.* The cure for gossips and busybodies is hard work. There is much truth in the saying "Satan finds work for idle hands."

CHAPTER 3 **1** Eph 6:19 **2** Ro 15:31; Ac 28:24; Ro 10:16 **3** 1Co 1:9; Jn 17:15; 2Pe 2:9 **4** 2Co 7:16 **5** 1Ch 29:18 **6** Ro 16:17; 1Co 5:11; 1Th 4:11; 2Th 2:15 **7** 1Co 4:16; 1Th 2:10 **8** Ac 18:3; 2Co 11:9 **9** 1Co 9:6; ver. 7 **10** 1Th 4:11 **11** ver. 6; 1Ti 5:13 **12** 1Th 4:11; Eph 4:28 **13** Gal 6:9

ers, do not grow tired *or* lose heart in doing good [but continue doing what is right without weakening].

14 Now if anyone [in the church] does not obey what we say in this letter, take special note of that person and do not associate with him, so that he will be ashamed *and* repent.

15 Do not regard him as an enemy, but keep admonishing him as a [believing] brother.

16 Now may the Lord of peace Himself grant you His peace at all times *and* in every way [that peace and spiritual well-being that comes to those who walk with Him, regardless of life's circumstances]. The Lord be with you all. [John 14:27]

17 I, Paul, write you this final greeting with my own hand. This is the distinguishing mark in every letter [of mine, that shows it is genuine]. It is the way I write [my handwriting and signature].

18 The grace of our Lord Jesus Christ be with all of you.

3:15 *as a [believing] brother.* The disobedient one is not an enemy, but one who needs compassionate correction.

3:18 *our Lord Jesus Christ.* Not only is Jesus our ultimate hope, it is He who lovingly strengthens us to endure trials.

14 Mt 18:17 **15** Lev 19:17; Titus 3:10 **16** Ro 15:33 **17** 1Co 16:21 **18** Ro 16:24

THE FIRST LETTER OF PAUL TO

TIMOTHY

▸ **AUTHOR:** The external evidence solidly supports the position that Paul wrote the letters to Timothy and Titus. Only Romans and 1 Corinthians have better attestation among the Pauline Epistles. Pauline authorship of the Pastoral Epistles requires Paul's release from his Roman imprisonment (Ac 28), the continuation of his missionary endeavors, and his imprisonment for a second time in Rome. Unfortunately, the order of events can only be reconstructed from hints, because there is no concurrent history paralleling Acts to chronicle the last years of the apostle. It is most probable that Paul wrote 1 Timothy from Macedonia in AD 62 or 63 while Timothy was serving as his representative in Ephesus.

▸ **TIMES:** c. AD 62–63 ▸ **KEY VERSES:** 1Ti 3:15–16

▸ **THEME:** The letters to Timothy and Titus are generally called the "Pastoral" Epistles. They are pastoral in tone and in the subject matter they address. While covering much of the apostolic instruction on the life and doctrine of the church, they also provide some guidelines on how Christians in the church should relate to society. One of the overriding concerns of the books is that truth be valued and guarded. Too often today, truth is subjective and culturally conditioned to the point where people don't even have problems believing mutually contradictory ideas. Paul speaks of the value of truth in his own apostolic role, and he stands against false teachers who would distort the truth for their own ends.

Misleadings in Doctrine and Living

1 PAUL, AN apostle (special messenger, personally chosen representative) of Christ Jesus by the commandment of God our Savior, and of Christ Jesus (the Messiah, the Anointed) our Hope [the fulfillment of our salvation],
2 to Timothy, my true son in the faith: Grace, mercy, and peace [inner calm and spiritual well-being] from God the Father and Christ Jesus our Lord.
3 As I urged you when I was on my way to Macedonia, stay on at Ephesus so that you may instruct certain individuals not to teach any different doctrines,
4 nor to pay attention to legends (fables, myths) and endless genealogies, which give rise to useless speculation *and* meaningless arguments rather than

1:1 ***apostle (special messenger, personally chosen representative) of Christ Jesus.*** The Greek word for "apostle" means "sent one." Paul was an ambassador sent by Christ (Ac 9).
1:2 ***Timothy.*** Timothy was a young believer from Lystra who traveled with Paul during his second and third missionary journeys.
1:3 ***that you may instruct.*** Paul's request that Timothy stay in Ephesus to minister to the believers there demonstrates Paul's confidence in the young man.
1:4 ***legends (fables, myths) and endless genealogies.*** The errors that Paul left Timothy to correct in Ephesus appear to have been primarily

CHAPTER 1 **1** Ac 9:15; Titus 1:3; Col 1:27 **2** Ac 16:1; Titus 1:4; Gal 1:3 **3** Ac 20:1; Gal 1:6,7 **4** Titus 1:14; 1Ti 6:4

advancing God's program *of instruction*
which is grounded in faith [and requires
surrendering the entire self to God in
absolute trust and confidence].
5But the goal of our instruction is love
[which springs] from a pure heart and
a good conscience and a sincere faith.
6Some individuals have wandered
away from these things into empty
arguments *and* useless discussions,
7wanting to be teachers of the Law
[of Moses], even though they do not
understand the terms they use or the
subjects about which they make [such]
confident declarations.
8Now we know [without any doubt]
that the Law is good, if one uses it
lawfully *and* appropriately,
9understanding the fact that law is
not enacted for the righteous person
[the one in right standing with God],
but for lawless and rebellious people,
for the ungodly and sinful, for the irreverent and profane, for those who kill
their fathers or mothers, for murderers,
10for sexually immoral persons, for
homosexuals, for kidnappers *and* slave
traders, for liars, for perjurers—and
for whatever else is contrary to sound
doctrine,
11according to the glorious gospel
of the blessed God, with which I have
been entrusted.
12I thank Christ Jesus our Lord, who
has granted me [the needed] strength
and made me able for this, because
He considered me faithful *and* trustworthy, putting me into service [for
this ministry],
13even though I was formerly a blasphemer [of our Lord] and a persecutor
[of His church] and a shameful *and*
outrageous *and* violent aggressor [toward believers]. Yet I was shown mercy because I acted out of ignorance in
unbelief.
14The grace of our Lord [His amazing, unmerited favor and blessing]
flowed out in superabundance [for me,
together] with the faith and love which
are [realized] in Christ Jesus.
15This is a faithful *and* trustworthy
statement, deserving full acceptance
and approval, that Christ Jesus came
into the world to save sinners, among
whom I am foremost.
16Yet for this reason I found mercy,
so that in me as the foremost [of sinners], Jesus Christ might demonstrate
His perfect patience as an example *or*
pattern for those who would believe in
Him for eternal life.

Jewish in nature. The Jews tended to place a lot of importance on the genealogies and also on allegorical interpretations of the law.

1:6 *empty arguments and useless discussions.* Gossip, speculation, and criticism should not come from the lips of believers.

1:8 *Law.* The proper function of the law is to make sinners aware of their sinfulness (Ro 3:20).

1:10 *perjurers.* The term "perjure" is more significant than simply "lie," as it deals with false promises. To swear an oath and then not carry through is a serious thing indeed.

1:13 *Yet I was shown mercy.* Paul found mercy and forgiveness even after his intense persecution of the church. God surely offers salvation to all people (2:4).

1:14 *grace.* Grace is God's undeserved, unearned, freely given favor.

1:15–16 Believing Jesus — Jesus came to earth to save sinners. Paul knew this firsthand. When he became a Christian, Paul realized the extent of his sin in terms of both his past sins and his current tendencies. But he also knew exactly where he stood in Christ as a believer. The mercy of God can only be acquired through belief. Paul reminds Timothy here of God's perfect patience and mercy and urges others to come to faith and receive the benefit of new and everlasting life, as he has. Eternal life can only begin with belief. It is an active choice of the individual. We must believe that Jesus is the saving Christ or reject Him. Paul says, *I found mercy, so that in me as the foremost [of sinners], Jesus Christ might demonstrate His perfect patience as an example or pattern for those who would believe in Him for eternal life.* If you have never believed in Jesus, take this opportunity to tell God how you feel. Believe in Jesus as Savior and begin on the path of a new life.

1:16 *believe in Him.* As stated over 185 times in the New Testament, the sole condition for salvation is belief, having faith or trust in Jesus

---

5 Ro 13:8; Gal 5:14; 2Ti 2:22 **6** 1Ti 6:4,20 **7** 1Ti 6:4 **8** Ro 7:12 **9** Gal 3:19 **10** 2Ti 4:3; Titus 1:9 **11** 1Co 9:17; Gal 2:7; Col 1:25 **12** 2Co 12:9; 1Co 7:25; 2Co 3:5 **13** Ac 8:3; Jn 4:21 **14** Ro 5:20; 2Ti 1:13; Lk 7:47 **15** 2Ti 2:11; Mt 9:13 **16** 2Co 4:1; Ac 13:39

17 Now to the King of the ages [eternal],
immortal, invisible, the only God, be
honor and glory forever and ever. Amen.
18 This command I entrust to you,
Timothy, my son, in accordance with
the prophecies previously made con-
cerning you, so that [inspired and aid-
ed] by them you may fight the good
fight [in contending with false teachers],
19 keeping your faith [leaning com-
pletely on God with absolute trust and
confidence in His guidance] and having
a good conscience; for some [people]
have rejected [their moral compass] and
have made a shipwreck of their faith.
20 Among these are Hymenaeus and
Alexander, whom I have handed over
to Satan, so that they will be disci-
plined *and* taught not to blaspheme.

A Call to Prayer

2 FIRST OF all, then, I urge that pe-
titions (specific requests), prayers,
intercessions (prayers for others) and
thanksgivings be offered on behalf of
all people,
2 for kings and all who are in [po-
sitions of] high authority, so that we
may live a peaceful and quiet life in
all godliness and dignity.
3 This [kind of praying] is good and
acceptable *and* pleasing in the sight of
God our Savior,
4 who wishes all people to be saved
and to come to the knowledge *and*
recognition of the [divine] truth.
5 For there is [only] one God, and
[only] one Mediator between God and
mankind, the Man Christ Jesus,
6 who gave Himself as a ransom [a
substitutionary sacrifice to atone] for
all, the testimony given at the right *and*
proper time.
7 And for this matter I was appointed
a preacher and an apostle—I am tell-
ing the truth, I am not lying [when I
say this]—a teacher of the Gentiles in
faith and truth.
8 Therefore I want the men in every
place to pray, lifting up holy hands,
without anger and disputing *or* quar-
reling *or* doubt [in their mind].

Christ. The gospel (or "good news") is that Jesus Christ, God's Son, gave up His heavenly kingdom for a time to become a human. As a man, He died for our sins, was buried, and rose on the third day. All who place their trust in Jesus will be saved from the coming judgment and from the present power of sin. To add any other condition to faith for salvation is to make it dependent on our own works (Ro 11:6; Gal 2:16).

1:20 *handed over to Satan.* Paul did not have some sort of authority over these men to have them "handed over" in the sense that they would now belong to Satan. Rather, Paul had stopped trying to exhort them, or show them the way they should go. They would not listen, so Paul had to say, "so be it, go your own way."

2:4 *who wishes all people to be saved.* God desires that all men would be saved, although this does not mean that He will force this to happen. Only those who believe in Christ will receive salvation (Ro 1:16 – 17; 3:21 – 26; 5:17). Christ died for the sins of the entire world, but only those who believe will receive the benefits of His sacrifice. ***and to come to the knowledge and recognition of the [divine] truth.*** God not only wants our salvation (justification), He also wants us to grow in truth (sanctification) so that we will not be led astray by false teachers.

2:5 *one God.* This is the central truth of the Hebrew Scriptures. The only living God desires that all should be saved. He is the only one to whom our prayers should be addressed. ***Mediator.*** This is a concept that came from the ceremonial worship in the Old Testament. In the tabernacle and later in the temple, the priests mediated between God and Israel by offering sacrifices to atone for the sins of the people. In their position of mediator, the priests were the only ones eligible to enter into the holy place, the place where God had made His presence known. When Jesus came, He came as the Mediator between man and God. Through Him we can be eligible to enter into God's holy presence.

2:6 *a ransom.* The Greek word translated "ransom" is found only here in the New Testament. It specifically refers to a ransom paid for a slave.

2:7 *in faith and truth.* Paul was called not only to preach the gospel to the Gentiles, but also to guide their growth in truth.

2:8 *men.* The Greek word translated "men" in this verse refers specifically to males as distinguished from females. Some believe that this verse means specifically public worship, while others believe

---

17 Ps 10:16; Ro 1:23; Heb 11:27; Ro 16:27; 1Ch 29:11 **18** 2Ti 2:2; 1Ti 4:14; 2Ti 2:3 **20** 2Ti 2:17; 4:14; 1Co 5:5; Ac 13:45
CHAPTER 2 **2** Ezr 6:10; Ro 13:1 **3** Ro 12:2; 2Ti 1:9 **4** Eze 18:23; Titus 2:11; Jn 17:3; 2Ti 2:25 **5** Gal 3:20; Heb 9:15
6 Mk 10:45; 1Co 1:6; 2Ti 1:8; Ro 5:6; Eph 1:9 **7** Eph 3:7,8; Ro 9:1; Gal 1:16 **8** Lk 23:34; Ps 134:2

Women Instructed

[9]Likewise, *I want* women to adorn
themselves modestly *and* appropri-
ately and discreetly in proper cloth-
ing, not with [elaborately] braided
hair and gold or pearls or expensive
clothes,
[10]but instead *adorned* by good deeds
[helping others], as is proper for wom-
en who profess to worship God.
[11]A woman must quietly receive in-
struction with all submissiveness.
[12]I do not allow a woman to teach
or exercise authority over a man, but
to remain quiet [in the congregation].
[13]For Adam was formed first [by God
from the earth], then Eve; [Gen 2:7,
21, 22]
[14]and it was not Adam who was de-
ceived, but the woman who was led
astray and fell into sin. [Gen 3:1–6]
[15]But *women* will be preserved
(saved) through [the pain and dan-
gers of] the bearing of children if they
continue in faith and love and holiness
with self-control *and* discretion.

Overseers and Deacons

3 THIS IS a faithful *and* trustworthy
saying: if any man [eagerly] seeks
the office of overseer (bishop, superin-
tendent), he desires an excellent task.

---

it refers to life in general. ***lifting up holy hands.*** This is a Hebrew way of praying (1Ki 8:22; Ps 141:2). "Holy" means morally and spiritually clean.

2:9 *appropriately and discreetly.* This word is also translated "with propriety," which means reverence and respect, shrinking away from what is inappropriate. ***in proper clothing.*** Modesty means more than just covering up enough. It means not flaunting one's wealth, or one's jewels, or one's name brands, as well as not flaunting one's body.

2:10 *good deeds.* A Christian woman's beauty should be found in her godly character and her love for the Lord as demonstrated in all types of good deeds.

2:11 *quietly . . . with all submissiveness.* These verses are not easy to understand, and there are many differences of opinion as to their meaning. The Scripture here does actually say just what it looks like: that women must be silent and submissive. It is universally accepted that this is referring to times of public worship, although the Bible makes it clear that a woman must submit to her husband (Eph 5:22; Col 3:18), but the concept of submission also applies to all believers. Philippians 4:5 says, "Let your gentle spirit be known to all people. The Lord is near." Being submissive means not being unruly or argumentative. There are times when it is proper for a woman to teach, pray, or prophesy (1Co 11), but apparently this is not supposed to happen in public worship.

2:12 *to teach or exercise authority.* It seems best to understand this passage as saying that women may exercise their spiritual gifts in a variety of ministries in the local assembly, as long as those gifts are exercised under the appropriate leadership of men. We have problems understanding the roles of men and women in the church. Often we want to ignore the subject altogether and say that men and women are entirely equal, the alternative being that men become despotic and tyrannical, while women become spiritually weak with no teaching and no opportunity to use their God-given gifts. Men and women are equal in God's eyes in terms of their value as people and eligibility for spiritual growth and relationship with God, but He created this difference in roles. Many tend to feel that this role difference is because of the fall, but God did create men and women to be different. The mess and confusion we have with our God-given positions is the result of the fall.

2:14 *it was not Adam who was deceived.* This seems to point to the fact that Adam sinned with his eyes open; he knew what he was doing. Eve sinned because she was deceived. Paul's arguments from creation and the fall seem to indicate that the prohibitions in verses 9 – 12 are permanent, not cultural.

2:15 *will be preserved (saved) through [the pain and dangers of] the bearing of children.* This is a very difficult verse to understand and no one agrees about what it means. We know that it does not mean "saved" in terms of receiving eternal life, because the Bible elsewhere makes it very clear we are saved by faith alone (Ro 1:16 – 17; 3:23 – 26; 5:17; Jn 3:15 – 18). Some think that it has to do with daily sanctification and the woman's special task of bearing children. Others say it is referring to being delivered from the desire to dominate by recognizing one's appropriate place in God's creation order. Still others believe that it refers specifically to the birth of Jesus Christ, the seed born of woman prophesied in Genesis 3:15.

3:1 *overseer.* This means a person who oversees a congregation. The words "overseer" and "elder" are used interchangeably for the same office (Titus 1:5 – 7).

---

9 1Pe 3:3 **10** 1Pe 3:4 **12** 1Co 14:34 **13** Ge 1:27; 1Co 11:8 **14** Ge 3:6; 2Co 11:3

[2]Now an overseer must be blameless
and beyond reproach, the husband
of one wife, self-controlled, sensible,
respectable, hospitable, able to teach,
[3]not addicted to wine, not a bully *nor*
quick-tempered *and* hot-headed, but
gentle *and* considerate, free from the
love of money [not greedy for wealth
and its inherent power—financially
ethical].
[4]*He must* manage his own house-
hold well, keeping his children under
control with all dignity [keeping them
respectful and well-behaved]
[5](for if a man does not know how to
manage his own household, how will
he take care of the church of God?).
[6]and *He must* not be a new convert,
so that he will not [behave stupidly and]
become conceited [by appointment to
this high office] and fall into the [same]
condemnation incurred by the devil [for
his arrogance and pride]. [Is 14:12–14]
[7]And he must have a good reputation
and be well thought of by those outside
the church, so that he will not be dis-
credited and fall into the devil's trap.
[8]Deacons likewise *must be* men wor-
thy of respect [honorable, financially
ethical, of good character], not double-
tongued [speakers of half-truths], not
addicted to wine, not greedy for dis-
honest gain,
[9]but upholding *and* fully understand-
ing the mystery [that is, the true doc-
trine] of the [Christian] faith with a
clear conscience [resulting from behav-
ior consistent with spiritual maturity].
[10]These men must first be tested;
then if they are found to be blameless
and beyond reproach [in their Chris-
tian lives], let them serve as deacons.
[11]Women must likewise be worthy of
respect, not malicious gossips, but self-
controlled, [thoroughly] trustworthy
in all things.
[12]Deacons must be husbands of *only*
one wife, and good managers of *their*
children and their own households.
[13]For those who have served well as
deacons gain a high standing [having
a good reputation among the congre-
gation], and great confidence in the
faith which is [founded on and cen-
tered] in Christ Jesus.
[14]I hope to come to you before long,
but I am writing these instructions
to you
[15]in case I am delayed, so that you
will know how people ought to conduct

3:2 *blameless.* The idea is not that an overseer is sinless, but that he displays mature, consistent Christian conduct that gives no reason for anyone to accuse him of anything. ***husband of one wife.*** This phrase is also subject to much disagreement. Many feel that it means "a one-woman kind of man," indicating a lifestyle of fidelity. Others feel that it is more specific, and prohibits a divorced and remarried man from the elder position. Certainly it is an exclusion of any one who is sexually immoral or a polygamist.

3:3 *a bully.* This word is also translated "violent." An overseer is not to be a quarrelsome man.

3:7 *good reputation.* An overseer must have a good reputation in the community. A non-Christian should not be able to reproach or insult an elder because of his behavior. The elder's good testimony avoids the traps of Satan.

3:8 *Deacons.* Deacons fill a second leadership position in the local assembly. The Greek word for deacon means "servant." ***not double-tongued.*** This speaks specifically of the dangers of gossip, especially changing sides or changing a story to fit the audience.

3:9 *mystery [that is, the true doctrine] of the [Christian] faith.* The mystery of the faith is the coming of God in the flesh (v. 16). The Son of God becoming a human in order to serve humanity (Mk 10:43–45) is the embodiment of service.

3:11 *Women must likewise be.* Some believe here that Paul is speaking of another office in the local body, that of "deaconess," godly women who serve under the leadership of the elders. Others, however, believe that this verse refers to the wives of the deacons, and not to an office. It could be assumed that both are true, and that the deacon and his wife are supposed to work together as a team, serving the church. The original language leaves the verse open to interpretation, since the Greek uses one word to mean both woman and wife.

3:15 *pillar and foundation of the truth.* Misconduct and disorder in the local church weaken the support of God's truth in the world. We as believers have a tremendous responsibility to

---

CHAPTER 3 **2** Titus 1:6; 2Ti 2:24 **3** 2Ti 2:24; 1Pe 5:2 **4** Titus 1:6 **7** Ac 22:12; 1Co 5:12; 2Ti 2:26 **8** Ac 6:3; Eze 44:21 **9** 1Ti 1:19 **11** Titus 2:3 **13** Mt 25:21 **15** Eph 2:21; 2Ti 2:20

themselves in the household of God, which is the church of the living God, the pillar and foundation of the truth.

16 And great, we confess, is the mystery [the hidden truth] of godliness:

He (Jesus Christ) who was
revealed in human flesh,
Was justified *and* vindicated in the
Spirit,
Seen by angels,
Preached among the nations,
Believed on in the world,
Taken up in glory.

Apostasy

4 BUT THE [Holy] Spirit explicitly *and* unmistakably declares that in later times some will turn away from the faith, paying attention instead to deceitful *and* seductive spirits and doctrines of demons,

2 [misled] by the hypocrisy of liars whose consciences are seared as with a branding iron [leaving them incapable of ethical functioning],

3 who forbid marriage and *advocate* abstaining from [certain kinds of] foods which God has created to be gratefully shared by those who believe and have [a clear] knowledge of the truth.

4 For everything God has created is good, and nothing is to be rejected if it is received with gratitude;

5 for it is sanctified [set apart, dedicated to God] by means of the word of God and prayer.

A Good Minister's Discipline

6 If you point out these instructions to the brothers and sisters, you will be a good servant of Christ Jesus, *constantly* nourished [through study] on the words of the faith and of the good [Christian] doctrine which you have closely followed.

7 But have nothing to do with irreverent folklore *and* silly myths. On the other hand, discipline yourself for the purpose of godliness [keeping yourself spiritually fit].

8 For physical training is of some value, but godliness (spiritual training) is of value in everything *and* in every way, since it holds promise for the present life and for the life to come.

9 This is a faithful *and* trustworthy saying worthy of full acceptance *and* approval.

10 It is for this that we labor and strive [often called to account], because we have fixed our [confident] hope on the living God, who is the Savior of all

---

keep the name of our Lord without spot or criticism from the nonbelieving world.

3:16 *revealed in human flesh.* This refers to Christ's incarnation, the fact that Jesus became man (Jn 1:14). ***justified and vindicated in the Spirit.*** This is the work of the Holy Spirit in Jesus' ministry and resurrection (Mt 3:15 – 17; Jn 16:7 – 10; Ro 1:4). ***Seen by angels.*** This refers to the angelic witness of Christ's ministry and resurrection. ***Preached among the nations.*** This refers to the preaching of Christ to the Gentiles (Col 1:23). ***Believed on in the world.*** This is the response of individuals to God's plan of salvation (Col 1:18 – 25). ***Taken up in glory.*** Christ ascended to heaven and is seated at God's right hand there (Ac 1:9; Heb 1:3 – 4).

4:1 *the [Holy] Spirit explicitly and unmistakably declares.* When Paul speaks of the Holy Spirit's words here, he may be referring to various prophecies inspired by the Holy Spirit concerning defection from God's truth (Da 7:25; 8:23; Mt 24:4 – 12), or also he may have been referring to a revelation the Spirit had given him.

4:5 *sanctified.* Sanctified means "set apart," or "made holy." Paul is saying that God has sanctified all the good things He created, from marriage to the food we eat. Nothing is less in accord with God than to begin forbidding the good things He made for us.

4:7 *irreverent folklore and silly myths.* Paul is merely using these terms to describe the superstitions and thoughtless beliefs that were prevalent.

4:8 *of some value.* This contrasts the short-term value of physical exercise with the long-term benefits of godliness for all things.

4:10 *Savior of all people.* This describes God as the One who gives life, breath, and existence to all.

---

16 Jn 1:14; 1Jn 1:2; Mt 3:16; Ro 1:4; Mt 28:2; Mk 16:5; Ac 10:34; Ro 10:18; Col 1:6,23; Lk 24:51 **CHAPTER 4**
1 Jn 16:13; 2Th 2:3; 2Ti 3:1; 1Pe 1:20; 2Ti 3:13; Rev 16:14; Da 11:35; Rev 9:20 **2** Mt 7:15; Eph 4:19 **3** 1Co 7:28; Ro 14:3; Ge 1:29; Ro 14:6 **4** Ro 14:14 **6** 2Ti 3:14 **7** 2Ti 2:16; Titus 1:14; Heb 5:14 **8** 1Co 8:8; 1Ti 6:6; Ps 37:4 **10** 1Co 4:11; Ps 36:6

people, especially of those who believe [in Him, recognize Him as the Son of God, and accept Him as Savior and Lord].

[11]Keep commanding and teaching these things.

[12]Let no one look down on [you because of] your youth, but be an example *and* set a pattern for the believers in speech, in conduct, in love, in faith, and in [moral] purity.

[13]Until I come, devote yourself to public reading [of Scripture], to preaching and to teaching [the sound doctrine of God's word].

[14]Do not neglect the spiritual gift within you, [that special endowment] which was intentionally bestowed on you [by the Holy Spirit] through prophetic utterance when the elders laid their hands on you [at your ordination].

[15]Practice *and* work hard on these things; be absorbed in them [completely occupied in your ministry], so that your progress will be evident to all.

[16]Pay close attention to yourself [concentrate on your personal development] and to your teaching; persevere in these things [hold to them], for as you do this you will ensure salvation both for yourself and for those who hear you.

Honor Widows

5 DO NOT sharply reprimand an older man, but appeal to him as [you would to] a father, to younger men as brothers,

[2]to older women as mothers, to younger women as sisters, in all purity [being careful to maintain appropriate relationships].

[3]Honor *and* help those widows who are truly widowed [alone, and without support].

[4]But if a widow has children or grandchildren [who are adults], see to it that these first learn to show great respect to their own family [as their religious duty and natural obligation], and to compensate their parents *or* grandparents [for their upbringing]; for this is acceptable *and* pleasing in the sight of God.

[5]Now a woman who is really a widow and has been left [entirely] alone [without adequate income] trusts in God and continues in supplications and prayers night and day.

[6]Whereas she who lives for pleasure *and* self-indulgence is *spiritually* dead even while she *still* lives.

[7]Keep instructing [the people to do] these things as well, so that they may be blameless *and* beyond reproach.

[8]If anyone fails to provide for his own, and especially for those of his own family, he has denied the faith [by disregarding its precepts] and is worse than an unbeliever [who fulfills his obligation in these matters].

[9]A widow is to be put on the list [to receive regular assistance] only if she is over sixty years of age, [having been] the wife of one man,

---

4:12 *be an example.* Timothy, in spite of youth, was to set an example in five areas: "in speech"; "in conduct," or behavior; "in love," which is the love of God; "in faith," meaning trust in God; "in purity," both in thought and action. These are qualities every believer should strive after, practice, and desire.
4:16 *ensure salvation . . . for yourself.* This is not a reference to justification by works, but to sanctification, which is the Christian's daily walk of faith (Mk 8:34–38; Jn 12:25–26). Timothy's example and hard work in teaching would serve to help others with their walk also.
5:2 *all purity.* Believing men must respect the purity of a young woman as the purity of a sister.
5:3 *truly widowed.* This refers to a woman who when widowed is left with no family at all, as opposed to those widows who still have living children or other relations.
5:4 *show great respect to their own family.* Honoring our parents includes caring for them physically and financially as they grow older.
5:8 *fails to provide for his own.* A believer is to provide for his family and this seems to include any of his relatives that need help. Failure to do this denies the faith he has said to believe in and smirches the name of Christianity.
5:9 *put on the list.* Many believe the list referred to here was a list of widows whom the church was to assist. Some have maintained that this was an official order of widows. These women were to pray for the church and practice works of charity (vv. 5,10).

12 Titus 2:7 **14** 2Ti 1:6; 1Ti 1:18; Ac 6:6 **16** Ac 20:28; Eze 33:9 **CHAPTER 5** **1** Lev 19:32 **4** Ge 45:10; Mt 15:4; Eph 6:1,2 **5** 1Co 7:32; Lk 2:37; Ac 26:7 **6** Jas 5:5 **8** Isa 58:7; Gal 6:10; 2Ti 3:5; Titus 1:16; Mt 18:17

[10]and has a reputation for good deeds;
[she is eligible] if she has brought up
children, if she has shown hospitality
to strangers, if she has washed the feet
of the saints (God's people), if she has
assisted the distressed, and has devoted herself to doing good in every way.
[11]But refuse [to enroll the] younger
widows, for when they feel their natural desires in disregard of Christ, they
wish to marry *again*,
[12]and so they incur condemnation
for having set aside their previous
pledge.
[13]Now at the same time, they also
learn to be idle as they go from house
to house; and not only idle, but also
gossips and busybodies [meddlers
in things that do not concern them],
talking about things they should not
mention.
[14]So I want younger *widows* to get
married, have children, manage their
households, and not give opponents
of the faith any occasion for slander.
[15]Some [widows] have already
turned away [from the faith] to follow
Satan.
[16]If any believing woman has [dependent] widows [in her household],
she must assist them [according to
her ability]; and the church must not
be burdened [with them], so that it
may assist those who are truly widows [those who are all alone and are
dependent].

Concerning Elders

[17]The elders who perform their leadership duties well are to be considered
worthy of double honor (financial support), especially those who work hard
at preaching and teaching [the word
of God concerning eternal salvation
through Christ].
[18]For the Scripture says, "YOU SHALL
NOT MUZZLE THE OX WHILE IT IS TREADING
OUT THE GRAIN [to keep it from eating],"
and, "The worker is worthy of his wages [he deserves fair compensation]."
[Deut 25:4; Luke 10:7]
[19]Do not accept an accusation
against an elder unless it is based on
[the testimony of at least] two or three
witnesses. [Deut 19:15]
[20]As for those [elders] who continue
in sin, reprimand them in the presence
of all [the congregation], so that the
rest will be warned.
[21]I solemnly charge you in the presence of God and of Christ Jesus and of
His chosen angels that you guard *and*
keep these rules without bias, doing
nothing out of favoritism.
[22]Do not hurry to lay hands on anyone [ordaining and approving someone for ministry or an office in the
church, or in reinstating expelled offenders], and thereby share in the sins
of others; keep yourself free from sin.
[23]No longer continue drinking [only]
water, but use a little wine for the sake

5:13 – 14 *idle ... gossips and busybodies.* An old saying tells us "Idle hands are the devil's workshop." Do not allow yourself to become so idle that you begin to gossip. As odd as it may sound, it will happen. Employ yourself with the tasks God has set before you. Look around. There are lots of things we as believers should be doing.

5:18 *Scripture says.* Paul quotes two passages: Deuteronomy 25:4 and Luke 10:7. The quotation from Luke is especially interesting as it shows that Paul considered the Gospels to be Scripture as well as the Old Testament.

5:19 *Do not accept an accusation against an elder.* Charges against elders are to be factual, not based on a single opinion or rumor.

5:20 *those [elders] who continue in sin.* This seems to refer to elders who fail in their leadership, whether in the church, in their social relationships, or in their home life. Public rebuke is to serve as a warning to other believers. Sin is a serious matter, especially for those who are in leadership, setting an example for others (1Pe 4:14).

5:22 *Do not hurry.* This verse is believed to be warning against too quickly restoring a leader who has fallen. Correction in love and restoration to fellowship should occur as soon as possible, but restoration to leadership should not be made without time and biblical evaluation. Not only does this apply to former leaders, it is a caution not to share responsibility for someone else's sins by restoring or appointing someone who is not qualified.

10 Ac 16:15; Heb 13:2; 1Pe 4:9; Ge 19:2 **13** 2Th 3:11 **14** 1Co 7:9; Titus 2:8 **16** ver. 3,5 **17** Php 2:29; Ac 28:10 **18** Dt 25:4; 1Co 9:9; Lev 19:13; Dt 24:14; Mt 10:10 **19** Dt 19:15 **20** Titus 1:13; Dt 13:11 **21** 1Ti 6:13; 2Ti 2:14 **22** Ac 6:6; 2Ti 1:6; 2Jn 11 **23** Ps 104:15

of your stomach and your frequent illnesses.

[24]The sins of some people are conspicuous, leading the way for them into judgment [so that they are clearly not qualified for ministry]; but the sins of others appear later [for they are hidden and follow behind them].

[25]Likewise, good deeds are quite evident, and those which are otherwise cannot be hidden [indefinitely].

Instructions to Those Who Minister

6 ALL WHO are under the yoke as bond-servants (slaves) are to regard their own masters as worthy of honor *and* respect so that the name of God and the teaching [about Him] will not be spoken against.

[2]Those who have believing masters are not to be disrespectful toward them because they are brothers [in Christ], but they should serve them even better, because those who benefit from their kindly service are believers and beloved. Teach and urge these [duties and principles].

[3]If anyone teaches a different doctrine and does not agree with the sound words of our Lord Jesus Christ, and with the doctrine *and* teaching which is in agreement with godliness (personal integrity, upright behavior),

[4]he is conceited and woefully ignorant [understanding nothing]. He has a morbid interest in controversial questions and disputes about words, which produces envy, quarrels, verbal abuse, evil suspicions,

[5]and perpetual friction between men who are corrupted in mind and deprived of the truth, who think that godliness is a source of profit [a lucrative, money-making business—withdraw from them].

[6]But godliness *actually* is a source of great gain when accompanied by contentment [that contentment which comes from a sense of inner confidence based on the sufficiency of God].

[7]For we have brought nothing into the world, so [it is clear that] we cannot take anything out of it, either.

[8]But if we have food and clothing, with these we will be content.

[9]But those who [are not financially ethical and] crave to get rich [with a compulsive, greedy longing for wealth] fall into temptation and a trap and into many foolish and harmful desires that plunge people into ruin and destruction [leading to personal misery].

[10]For the love of money [that is, the greedy desire for it and the willingness to gain it unethically] is a root of all sorts of evil, and some by longing for it have wandered away from the faith and pierced themselves [through and through] with many sorrows.

[11]But as for you, O man of God, flee from these things; aim at *and* pursue righteousness [true goodness, moral

---

5:25 *evident . . . cannot be hidden.* Unnoticed good works always come to light, if not in this life, at the judgment seat, but even sins hidden from men cannot be concealed from God.

6:1 *bond-servants.* This serves as an example of how believers should act in the workplace. We are Christians, who are to represent our faith, and Christ Himself. If we do this badly, we minimize not only our faith, but the power and testimony of Christ.

6:2 *these [duties and principles].* This probably refers to the contents of the entire letter to Timothy.

6:9 *those who [are not financially ethical and] crave to get rich.* Inside of every man there is a "God-shaped void." Many unbelievers try to fill this inner longing with wealth and possessions. Greed drives people to temptation and foolish and harmful desires. This is not an ailment of unbelievers only. Many believers also try to gain material things rather than the imperishable things of righteousness, godliness, faith, love, perseverance, and gentleness (v. 11). These are the things we should pursue with all of our being.

6:10 *love of money.* Money in and of itself is not a problem, but the love of money is. Christians can be so blinded by greed that they no longer see the need for holy living. A life focused on material things brings only pain.

24 Gal 5:19 **CHAPTER 6** **1** Eph 6:5; Col 3:22; Titus 2:9; 1Pe 2:18; Isa 52:5; Ro 2:24; Titus 2:5,8 **2** Col 4:1 **3** 2Ti 1:13; Titus 1:1,9 **4** 1Co 8:2 **5** 1Co 11:16; 2Pe 2:3; Ro 16:17 **6** Ps 37:16; Heb 13:5 **7** Job 1:21 **8** Ge 28:20; Heb 13:5 **9** Pr 15:27; 1Ti 1:19 **10** Dt 16:19 **11** 2Ti 2:22; Dt 33:1

conformity to the character of God], godliness [the fear of God], faith, love, steadfastness, and gentleness. [2 Tim 3:17]

12 Fight the good fight of the faith [in the conflict with evil]; take hold of the eternal life to which you were called, and [for which] you made the good confession [of faith] in the presence of many witnesses.

13 I *solemnly* charge you in the presence of God, who gives life to all things, and [in the presence] of Christ Jesus, who made the good confession [in His testimony] before Pontius Pilate,

14 to keep all His precepts without stain or reproach until the appearing of our Lord Jesus Christ,

15 which He will bring about in His own time—He who is the blessed and only Sovereign [the absolute Ruler], the King of those who reign as kings and Lord of those who rule as lords,

16 He alone possesses immortality [absolute exemption from death] and lives in unapproachable light, whom no man has ever seen or can see. To Him be honor and eternal power *and* dominion! Amen.

17 As for the rich in this present world, instruct them not to be conceited *and* arrogant, nor to set their hope on the uncertainty of riches, but on God, who richly *and* ceaselessly provides us with everything for our enjoyment.

18 *Instruct them* to do good, to be rich in good works, to be generous, willing to share [with others].

19 In this way storing up for themselves the *enduring* riches of a good foundation for the future, so that they may take hold of that which is truly life.

20 O Timothy, guard *and* keep safe the deposit [of godly truth] entrusted to you, turn away from worldly and godless chatter [with its profane, empty words], and the contradictions of what is falsely called "knowledge"—

21 which some have professed and by doing so have erred (missed the mark) *and* strayed from the faith.

Grace be with you.

6:12 *take hold of the eternal life.* Use the hope of everlasting life with the Savior as your lifeline, your comfort, and your guide.

6:14 *the appearing of our Lord Jesus Christ.* The imminent return of Christ should be a motive for godly living (1Jn 2:28).

6:16 *immortality.* This may also be translated "without death." Jesus is God, and can therefore never die.

6:20 *what is falsely called "knowledge."* Gnosticism (from the Greek word for knowledge) is a heresy that teaches that salvation comes through secret knowledge of spiritual mysteries.

6:21 *Grace be with you.* The Greek word for "you" here is plural, including the whole church. God's grace to us as sinners is indeed amazing.

12 1Ti 1:18; Php 3:12; Heb 13:23 **13** 1Ti 5:21; 1Sa 2:6; Jn 18:37 **14** Php 1:6 **15** 1Ti 1:11,17 **16** Jn 6:46; Eph 3:21 **17** Lk 12:21; Pr 23:5; 1Th 1:9; Ac 14:17 **18** Jas 2:5; Ro 12:13; Gal 6:6 **19** Mt 6:20 **20** 2Ti 1:14; Titus 1:14

THE SECOND LETTER OF PAUL TO

TIMOTHY

▸ **AUTHOR:** Fearing for their own lives, the Asian believers failed to support Paul after his second Roman imprisonment and his first defense before the Imperial Court (1:15; 4:16). Now he was in a cold Roman cell (4:13) without hope of acquittal in spite of the success of his initial defense. Under these conditions, Paul wrote this epistle in the fall of AD 67, hoping that Timothy would be able to visit him before the approaching winter (4:21).

▸ **TIMES:** c. AD 66 – 67 ▸ **KEY VERSES:** 2Ti 3:14 – 17

▸ **THEME:** This is likely the last of Paul's writings that we have. He writes this letter from a prison cell where he is being kept like a common criminal. He knows that his work on earth is nearing its conclusion, and these are then his last words of counsel to his trusted companion in ministry. One can sense his weariness, but also his strongly held conviction about what is necessary for the continued growth of the church. One can also clearly see the hope that sustains him as he looks forward to going home to Christ.

Timothy Charged to Guard His Trust

1 PAUL, AN apostle (special messenger, personally chosen representative) of Christ Jesus (the Messiah, the Anointed) by the will of God, according to the promise of life that is in Christ Jesus,
[2]to Timothy, my beloved son: Grace, mercy, and peace [inner calm and spiritual well-being] from God the Father and Christ Jesus our Lord.
[3]I thank God, whom I worship *and* serve with a clear conscience the way my forefathers did, as I constantly remember you in my prayers night and day,
[4]and as I recall your tears, I long to see you so that I may be filled with joy.
[5]I remember your sincere *and* unqualified faith [the surrendering of your entire self to God in Christ with confident trust in His power, wisdom and goodness, a faith] which first lived in [the heart of] your grandmother Lois and your mother Eunice, and I am confident that it is in you as well.
[6]That is why I remind you to fan into flame the gracious gift of God, [that inner fire—the special endowment] which is in you through the laying on of my hands [with those of the elders at your ordination].
[7]For God did not give us a spirit of

1:1 ***the promise of life.*** This message of life stands in ironic contrast to the fact that Paul was writing from a Roman prison, facing his execution.
1:3 ***my forefathers.*** Paul's forefathers were the patriarchs of the faith: Abraham, Isaac, and Jacob. Paul had great love for Israel (Ro 9:1 – 5). The reason that he connects himself to Israel's forefathers may be to demonstrate that he is not advocating a new religion but one of which the godly of the past are also a part.
1:5 ***Lois . . . Eunice.*** The prayers, witness, and faith of his godly mother and grandmother were central factors in the spiritual development of Timothy (1Ti 2:15).

CHAPTER 1 **1** 2Co 1:1; Eph 3:6; Heb 9:15 **2** 1Ti 1:2 **3** Ro 1:8; Eph 1:16; Ac 22:3; Ro 1:9; 1Th 1:2 **4** 2Ti 4:9,21 **5** 1Ti 1:5; Ac 16:1 **6** 1Ti 4:14 **7** Ro 8:15; Ac 1:8

timidity *or* cowardice *or* fear, but [He has given us a spirit] of power and of love and of sound judgment *and* personal discipline [abilities that result in a calm, well-balanced mind and self-control].

8 So do not be ashamed to testify about our Lord or about me His prisoner, but with me take your share of suffering for the gospel [continue to preach regardless of the circumstances], in accordance with the power of God [for His power is invincible],

9 for He delivered us *and* saved us and called us with a holy calling [a calling that leads to a consecrated life—a life set apart—a life of purpose], not because of our works [or because of any personal merit—we could do nothing to earn this], but because of His own purpose and grace [His amazing, undeserved favor] which was granted to us in Christ Jesus before the world began [eternal ages ago],

10 but now [that extraordinary purpose and grace] has been fully disclosed *and* realized by us through the appearing of our Savior Christ Jesus who [through His incarnation and earthly ministry] abolished death [making it null and void] and brought life and immortality to light through the gospel,

11 for which I was appointed a preacher and an apostle and a teacher [of this good news regarding salvation].

12 This is why I suffer as I do. Still, I am not ashamed; for I know Him [and I am personally acquainted with Him] whom I have believed [with absolute trust and confidence in Him and in the truth of His deity], and I am persuaded [beyond any doubt] that He is able to guard that which I have entrusted to Him until that day [when I stand before Him]. [1 Cor 1:8, 3:13; Phil 1:6]

13 Keep *and* follow the pattern of sound teaching (doctrine) which you have heard from me, in the faith and love which are in Christ Jesus.

14 Guard [with greatest care] *and* keep unchanged, the treasure [that precious truth] which has been entrusted to you [that is, the good news about salvation through personal faith in Christ Jesus], through [the help of] the Holy Spirit who dwells in us.

15 You are aware of the fact that all who are in [the province of] Asia turned away *and* deserted me, Phygelus and Hermogenes among them.

16 The Lord grant mercy to the family of Onesiphorus, because he often refreshed me *and* showed me kindness [comforting and reviving me like fresh air] and he was not ashamed of my chains [for Christ's sake];

17 but [instead] when he reached Rome, he eagerly searched for me and found me—

18 the Lord grant to him that he may find mercy from the Lord on that [great] day. You know very well how many things he did for me *and* what a help he was at Ephesus [you know better than I can tell you].

1:8 *do not be ashamed to testify.* To testify is to be a witness for the Lord; the Greek term is the source of the English word *martyr*. Church tradition says that most of the apostles died as martyrs.
1:9 *not because of our works.* It is impossible for people to earn their way into heaven. Salvation is by grace, the unearned and undeserved favor of God.
1:10 *abolished death.* Knowing that leaving our earthly bodies simply means that we will live forever with the Lord effectively robs death of its dread. The same gospel that offers us the forgiveness of sins and draws us to holy living also announces life and immortality. Believing the gospel, we begin to live in the power of an endless life (1Jn 5:11 – 13,20).
1:12 *which I have entrusted.* It is certain that God will keep our "deposit" safe. Paul was preparing for imminent death, but in spite of this he was hopeful. He had spent his time, resources, and even his life on proclaiming the gospel, and this investment in Christ's kingdom would bring him an abundant reward in eternity (Lk 19:15; 1Co 3:10 – 15; Rev 11:15,18).
1:14 *the treasure.* This is the truth of the kingdom of God (Mt 13:44 – 45; 1Ti 6:20).

8 Ro 1:16; 1Ti 2:6; Eph 3:1; Col 1:24 **9** 1Ti 1:1; Heb 3:1; Ro 3:20; Ro 8:28; Ro 16:25 **10** Eph 1:9; 1Co 15:54
11 Ac 9:15; 1Ti 2:7 **12** Eph 3:1; 1Pe 4:19; 1Ti 6:20 **13** Titus 1:9; Heb 10:23; Ro 2:20; 1Ti 6:3; 1Ti 1:14 **14** Ro 8:11
15 Ac 19:10 **16** Mt 5:7; Php 7; Ac 28:20 **18** 2Th 1:10; Heb 6:10

Be Strong

2 SO YOU, my son, be strong [con-
stantly strengthened] *and* empow-
ered in the grace that is [to be found
only] in Christ Jesus.
2 The things [the doctrine, the pre-
cepts, the admonitions, the sum of my
ministry] which you have heard me
teach in the presence of many wit-
nesses, entrust [as a treasure] to reli-
able *and* faithful men who will also be
capable *and* qualified to teach others.
3 Take with me your share of hard-
ship [passing through the difficulties
which you are called to endure], like a
good soldier of Christ Jesus.
4 No soldier in active service gets
entangled in the [ordinary business]
affairs of civilian life; [he avoids them]
so that he may please the one who
enlisted him to serve.
5 And if anyone competes as an ath-
lete [in competitive games], he is not
crowned [with the wreath of victory]
unless he competes according to the
rules.
6 The hard-working farmer [who la-
bors to produce crops] ought to be the
first to receive his share of the crops.
7 Think over the things I am saying
[grasp their application], for the Lord
will grant you insight *and* understand-
ing in everything.
8 Remember Jesus Christ [the ever-
living Lord who has] risen from the
dead, [as the prophesied King] de-
scended from David [king of Israel],
according to my gospel [the good news
that I preach], [Ps 16:10]
9 for that [gospel] I am suffering even
to [the point of] wearing chains like a
criminal; but the word of God is not
chained *or* imprisoned!
10 For this reason I [am ready to] pa-
tiently endure all things for the sake of
those who are the elect (God's chosen
ones), so that they too may obtain the
salvation which is in Christ Jesus and
with it the reward of eternal glory.
11 This is a faithful *and* trustworthy
saying:

If we died with Him, we will also
live with Him;
12 If we endure, we will also reign
with Him;
If we deny Him, He will also deny
us;
13 If we are faithless, He remains
faithful [true to His word and
His righteous character], for He
cannot deny Himself.

An Unashamed Workman

14 Remind *the people* of these facts,
and solemnly charge *them* in the pres-
ence of God to avoid petty controversy
over words, which does no good, and
[upsets and undermines and] ruins [the
faith of] those who listen.
15 Study *and* do your best to present
yourself to God approved, a workman
[tested by trial] who has no reason to
be ashamed, accurately handling *and*
skillfully teaching the word of truth.
16 But avoid all irreverent babble and
godless chatter [with its profane, emp-
ty words], for it will lead to further
ungodliness,

2:1 *strong . . . in the grace that is [to be found only] in Christ Jesus.* The emphasis is on the strength of Christ, not on Timothy's own power. If we trust in ourselves, we are doomed to fail.
2:2 *entrust [as a treasure] to reliable and faithful men.* Since the time of Christ, there has been an endless chain of Christian discipleship (Mt 28:18 – 20).
2:8 *descended from David.* Jesus is the fulfillment of all the promises that God gave to David (2Sa 7:11 – 16).
2:11 *If we died . . . we will also live.* Believers are united with Christ in His death and resurrection (Ro 6:3 – 11).
2:12 *If we endure.* Persevering in our faith, even in the face of hardship or persecution, will result in a reward when Christ returns (Lk 19:11 – 27; Ro 8:17; Rev 3:21).
2:13 *faithless.* This word describes an immature believer who lives for self and not for the Savior (1Co 3:1 – 3,15). ***He remains faithful.*** For Christ to abandon us would be contrary to His faithful nature (Jn 10:27 – 30; Heb 10:23; 13:5).
2:15 *Study.* The position of teaching God's word

CHAPTER 2 **1** 1Ti 1:2; Eph 6:10 **3** 1Ti 1:18 **4** 1Co 9:25 **5** 1Co 9:25 **8** Ro 1:3,4; 1Co 15:1; Ro 2:16 **9** Ac 9:16; Eph 3:1; Ac 28:31; Eph 6:19 **10** Eph 3:13; 2Co 1:6 **11** Ro 6:5,8 **12** Ro 8:17; 1Pe 4:13; Mt 10:33; Mk 8:38 **13** Ro 3:3; Nu 23:19 **14** 1Ti 5:21 **16** 1Ti 4:7

[17]and their teaching will spread like gangrene. So it is with Hymenaeus and Philetus,
[18]who have deviated from the truth. They claim that the resurrection has already taken place, and they undermine the faith of some.
[19]Nevertheless, the firm foundation of God [which He has laid] stands [sure and unshaken despite attacks], bearing this seal: "The Lord knows those who are His," and, "Let everyone who names the name of the Lord stand apart from wickedness *and* withdraw from wrongdoing." [Num 16:5; Is 26:13]
[20]Now in a large house there are not only vessels *and* objects of gold and silver, but also vessels *and* objects of wood and of earthenware, and some are for honorable (noble, good) use and some for dishonorable (ignoble, common).
[21]Therefore, if anyone cleanses himself from these *things* [which are dishonorable—disobedient, sinful], he will be a vessel for honor, sanctified [set apart for a special purpose and], useful to the Master, prepared for every good work.
[22]Run away from youthful lusts—pursue righteousness, faith, love, and peace with those [believers] who call on the Lord out of a pure heart.
[23]But have nothing to do with foolish and ignorant speculations [useless disputes over unedifying, stupid controversies], since you know that they produce strife *and* give birth to quarrels.
[24]The servant of the Lord must not participate in quarrels, but must be kind to everyone [even-tempered, preserving peace, and he must be], skilled in teaching, patient *and* tolerant when wronged.
[25]He must correct those who are in opposition with courtesy *and* gentleness in the hope that God may grant that they will repent and be led to the knowledge of the truth [accurately understanding and welcoming it],
[26]and that they may come to their senses and *escape* from the trap of the devil, having been held captive by him to do his will.

"Difficult Times Will Come"

3 BUT UNDERSTAND this, that in the last days dangerous times [of great stress and trouble] will come [difficult days that will be hard to bear].
[2]For people will be lovers of self [narcissistic, self-focused], lovers of money [impelled by greed], boastful, arrogant, revilers, disobedient to parents, ungrateful, unholy *and* profane,
[3][and they will be] unloving [devoid of natural human affection, calloused and inhumane], irreconcilable, malicious gossips, devoid of self-control [intemperate, immoral], brutal, haters of good,
[4]traitors, reckless, conceited, lovers of [sensual] pleasure rather than lovers of God,
[5]holding to a form of [outward] godliness (religion), although they have denied its power [for their conduct nullifies their claim of faith]. Avoid such people *and* keep far away from them.

---

is a position of great responsibility, not to be taken lightly (Jas 3:1).
2:18 *already taken place.* This was probably an early form of Gnosticism, a body of teaching which emphasized the "spiritual," and considered the physical world and the human body unreal and unimportant.
2:21 *Master.* This is a strong term for God's authority over the lives of believers, regardless of their level of spiritual maturity.
2:22 *Run away . . . pursue.* When we run toward righteousness, we are running away from sin. The two are completely opposite, and a person cannot follow both at once.
2:25 *correct . . . with courtesy and gentleness.* The aim of correction is repentance or a change of thinking, not self-justification or the pleasure of argument.
2:26 *come to their senses and escape.* False teaching has an intoxicating effect that dulls the mind to God's truth.
3:5 *a form of [outward] godliness.* This is an outward appearance of reverence for God. Denying its power describes religious activity

---

18 1Co 15:12 **19** Mt 24:24; Na 1:7; Jn 10:14 **20** Ro 9:21 **21** Isa 52:11; 2Ti 3:17 **22** Ac 9:14; 1Co 1:2; 1Ti 1:5 **23** 1Ti 1:4 **24** Titus 3:2; 1:9 **25** Gal 6:1; 1Ti 6:11; Ac 8:22; 1Ti 2:4 **26** 1Ti 3:7 **CHAPTER 3** **1** 1Ti 4:1 **2** Php 2:21; 2Pe 2:3; Jude 16; 1Ti 6:4; 1Ti 1:20; Ro 1:30 **3** Ro 1:31; Ro 1:31; 2Pe 3:3 **4** 2Pe 2:10; Php 3:19 **5** 1Ti 5:8; 1Ti 6:5

6 For among them are those who worm their way into homes and captivate *morally* weak *and* spiritually-dwarfed women weighed down by [the burden of their] sins, easily swayed by various impulses,

7 always learning *and* listening to anybody who will teach them, but never able to come to the knowledge of the truth.

8 Just as Jannes and Jambres [the court magicians of Egypt] opposed Moses, so these *men* also oppose the truth, men of depraved mind, unqualified *and* worthless [as teachers] in regard to the faith. [Ex 7:11]

9 But they will not get very far, for their meaningless nonsense *and* ignorance will become obvious to everyone, as was that of Jannes and Jambres.

10 Now you have diligently followed [my example, that is] my teaching, conduct, purpose, faith, patience, love, steadfastness,

11 persecutions, and sufferings—such as happened to me at Antioch, at Iconium, and at Lystra; what persecutions I endured, but the Lord rescued me from them all! [2 Cor 12:10]

12 Indeed, all who delight in pursuing righteousness *and* are determined to live godly lives in Christ Jesus will be hunted *and* persecuted [because of their faith].

13 But evil men and impostors will go on from bad to worse, deceiving and being deceived.

14 But as for you, continue in the things that you have learned and of which you are convinced [holding tightly to the truths], knowing from whom you learned *them*,

15 and how from childhood you have known the sacred writings (Hebrew Scriptures) which are able to give you the wisdom that leads to salvation through faith which is in Christ Jesus [surrendering your entire self to Him and having absolute confidence in His wisdom, power and goodness].

16 All Scripture is God-breathed [given by divine inspiration] and is profitable for instruction, for conviction [of sin], for correction [of error and restoration to obedience], for training in righteousness [learning to live in conformity to God's will, both publicly and privately—behaving honorably with personal integrity and moral courage];

17 so that the man of God may be complete *and* proficient, outfitted *and* thoroughly equipped for every good work.

"Preach the Word"

4 I SOLEMNLY charge you in the presence of God and of Christ Jesus, who is to judge the living and the dead, and by His appearing and His kingdom:

2 preach the word [as an official messenger]; be ready when the time is right and *even* when it is not [keep your sense of urgency, whether the oppor-

---

that is not connected to a living relationship with Jesus Christ. This kind of religion provokes God's anger (Isa 1:10 – 18; Mt 23:25 – 28).

3:8 *Jannes and Jambres.* They are not named in the Old Testament, but according to Jewish tradition, Jannes and Jambres were two of the Egyptian magicians who opposed Moses (Ex 7:11).

3:12 *will be hunted and persecuted.* God does not promise deliverance *from* persecution, but deliverance *through* it. Persecution is one of the means that God uses to bring about our growth and sanctification (2:12; Mt 5:10 – 12; Rev 2:10).

3:16 *God-breathed.* Scripture was freely produced by human writers, but the original Author is God Himself. God "breathed out" the Scriptures so that they are not only human words, but simultaneously and ultimately the very utterances of God. Thus, Scripture is true in all that it affirms and is completely authoritative (1Pe 1:20 – 21). The Bible not only "contains God's words," it *is* God's Word. Therefore the Scriptures are fully consistent and inerrant, authoritative and trustworthy.

3:17 *every good work.* Paul emphasizes the essential link between knowing God's Word and applying it to one's daily life. Right doctrine should produce right practice.

4:2 *inexhaustible patience.* Patience and doctrine are two necessary components of an effective ministry. True spiritual growth occurs

---

6 Mt 23:14; Titus 1:11 **7** 1Ti 2:4 **8** Ex 7:11; 1Ti 6:5; Ro 1:28 **9** Ex 7:12 **10** 1Ti 4:6 **11** Ac 13:45; 14:2; Ac 14:19; Ps 34:19 **12** Ps 34:19 **13** 2Th 2:11 **14** 2Ti 1:13 **15** Jn 5:39 **16** 2Pe 1:20; Ro 15:4 **17** 1Ti 6:11; 2Ti 2:21 **CHAPTER 4** **1** 1Ti 5:21; Ac 10:42 **2** 1Ti 5:20; Titus 1:13; 1Ti 4:13

tunity seems favorable or unfavorable,
whether convenient or inconvenient,
whether welcome or unwelcome]; cor-
rect [those who err in doctrine or be-
havior], warn [those who sin], exhort
and encourage [those who are grow-
ing toward spiritual maturity], with
inexhaustible patience and [faithful]
teaching.
3 For the time will come when people
will not tolerate sound doctrine *and*
accurate instruction [that challenges
them with God's truth]; but *wanting*
to have their ears tickled [with some-
thing pleasing], they will accumulate
for themselves [many] teachers [one
after another, chosen] to satisfy their
own desires *and* to support the errors
they hold,
4 and will turn their ears away from
the truth and will wander off into
myths *and* man-made fictions [and
will accept the unacceptable].
5 But as for you, be clear-headed in
every situation [stay calm and cool
and steady], endure every hardship
[without flinching], do the work of an
evangelist, fulfill [the duties of] your
ministry.
6 For I am already being poured out
as a drink offering, and the time of my
departure [from this world] is at hand
and I will soon go free. [Num 15:1–12;
28:7; Phil 2:17]
7 I have fought the good *and* wor-
thy *and* noble fight, I have finished
the race, I have kept the faith [firmly
guarding the gospel against error].
8 In the future there is reserved for me
the [victor's] crown of righteousness
[for being right with God and doing
right], which the Lord, the righteous
Judge, will award to me on that [great]
day—and not to me only, but also to all
those who have loved *and* longed for
and welcomed His appearing.

Personal Concerns

9 Make every effort to come to me
soon;
10 for Demas, having loved [the plea-
sures of] this present world, has de-
serted me and gone to Thessalonica;
Crescens *has gone* to Galatia, Titus to
Dalmatia.
11 Only Luke is with me. Get Mark
and bring him with you, for he is very
helpful to me for the ministry.
12 But Tychicus I have sent to Ephe-
sus.
13 When you come bring the coat that
I left at Troas with Carpus, and the
books, especially the parchments.
14 Alexander the coppersmith did me
great harm; [but that is no concern
of mine, for] the Lord will repay him
according to his actions.
15 Be on guard against him yourself,
because he vigorously opposed our
message.
16 At my first trial no one supported
me [as an advocate] *or* stood with me,
but they all deserted me. May it not be
counted against them [by God].
17 But the Lord stood by me and

---

over a period of time, through consistent teaching and application of God's Word.

4:6 *drink offering.* This is an offering performed by pouring wine out on the ground or altar (Nu 28:11 – 31). Paul's life was already being poured out in service to Christ.

4:7 *fought the good and worthy and noble fight.* Paul did not make these comments until the end of his race, when he was about to die. He did not presume or rely on his past service. Instead, he persevered, struggled, and served God until the end (1Co 9:24 – 27).

4:8 *loved and longed for and welcomed His appearing.* These are the believers who have lived faithfully in the hope of His return (Titus 2:11 – 15; 1Jn 2:28).

4:11 *Mark.* Mark's desertion of Paul in Pamphylia on his first missionary journey had led to the separation of Paul and Barnabas at the beginning of Paul's second missionary journey (Ac 15:36 – 40). Later Paul and Mark were reconciled, and Mark served Paul in the ministry (Col 4:10). It is believed that Mark later wrote the Gospel of Mark.

4:12 *Tychicus.* Tychicus was Paul's faithful coworker (Ac 20:4; Eph 6:21; Col 4:7).

4:14 *Alexander.* This may be the person named in 1 Timothy 1:20 or Acts 19:33, who caused harm to Paul's ministry in Ephesus.

3 2Ti 3:1; 1Ti 1:10; 2Ti 3:6 **4** 1Ti 1:4 **5** 2Ti 1:8; Ac 21:8 **6** Php 2:17; Php 1:23; 2Pe 1:14 **7** Php 3:14; Heb 12:1 **8** Jas 1:12; 2Ti 1:12 **10** Col 4:14; 1Jn 2:15 **11** 2Ti 1:15; Col 4:14; Ac 12:25 **12** Ac 20:4; Eph 6:21 **14** Ac 19:33; 2Sa 3:39; Ps 28:4 **16** Ac 7:60 **17** Ac 23:11; 9:15; Ps 22:21

strengthened *and* empowered me, so
that through me the [gospel] message
might be fully proclaimed, and that all
the Gentiles might hear it; and I was
rescued from the mouth of the lion.
[18]The Lord will rescue me from every evil assault, and He will bring me
safely into His heavenly kingdom; to
Him be the glory forever and ever.
Amen.
[19]Give my greetings to Prisca and
Aquila, and to the household of Onesiphorus.
[20]Erastus stayed on at Corinth, but I
left Trophimus sick at Miletus.
[21]Try your best to come [to me] before winter. Eubulus wishes to be remembered to you, as do Pudens and
Linus and Claudia and all the brothers
and sisters.
[22]The Lord be with your spirit. Grace
be with you.

4:19 *Prisca and Aquila.* Prisca is a form of the name Priscilla. Paul had met Priscilla and Aquila in Corinth on his second missionary journey (Ac 18:1 – 3), and they had assisted in God's work in Ephesus (Ac 18:18 – 19).

4:20 *Trophimus.* Trophimus, a member of the church of Ephesus (Ac 21:29), had traveled with Paul to Jerusalem (Ac 20:4).

18 Ps 121:7; Ro 11:36; Gal 1:5; Heb 13:21 **19** Ac 18:2; Ro 16:3 **20** Ac 19:22; Ro 16:23; Ac 20:4 **21** ver. 9 **22** Gal 6:18; Php 25

THE LETTER OF PAUL TO

TITUS

▸ **AUTHOR:** Titus was one of Paul's Gentile converts. He probably worked with Paul during his time at Ephesus on his third missionary journey. Later he also worked in Corinth and this letter indicates that Paul is commissioning him to work on the island of Crete. Paul wrote this letter about AD 63, perhaps from Corinth, taking advantage of the journey of Zenas and Apollos (3:13), whose destination would take them by way of Crete.

▸ **TIMES:** c. AD 63 ▸ **KEY VERSE:** Titus 3:8

▸ **THEME:** Paul's instructions to Titus are similar to those he gives to Timothy. He gives him instructions about the leadership and organization of the church and guidance in dealing with the opposition of those who would contradict his teaching. His tone is that of a seasoned leader passing on the essential instructions to a valued disciple.

Salutation

1 PAUL, A bond-servant of God
and an apostle (special messen-
ger, personally chosen representative)
of Jesus Christ, for the faith of God's
chosen ones and [to lead and encour-
age them to recognize and pursue] the
knowledge of the truth which leads to
godliness,
2 based on the hope *and* divine guar-
antee of eternal life, [the life] which
God, who is ever truthful *and* without
deceit, promised before the ages of
time began,
3 and at the appointed time has made
known His word *and* revealed it as His
message, through preaching, which
was entrusted to me according to the
command of God our Savior—
4 To Titus, my true child in a com-
mon faith: Grace and peace [inner
calm and spiritual well-being] from
God the Father and Christ Jesus our
Savior.

1:2 We Can Trust God — Often Christians will doubt our position with God simply because we do not *feel* saved. We don't understand that the basis for our standing is the promise of God and not emotional feelings. One helpful way to see these promises is in relation to the Trinity:

The promise and work of the Father. He has promised to graciously accept in Christ all repenting sinners (Eph 1:6 and Col 3:3). This means a Christian has the right to be in heaven someday, for he is in Christ. God guarantees us that He will work out all things for our ultimate good (Ro 8:28).

The promise and work of the Son. He has promised us eternal life (Jn 5:24) and abundant life (Jn 10:10). This promise covers not only our final destiny in heaven, but also our present Christian service here on earth. He is, in fact, right now praying for us and ministering to us at His Father's right hand (Heb 8:1; 9:24).

The promise and work of the Holy Spirit. The Holy Spirit is said to indwell the believer (Jn 14:16). In addition, He places all believing sinners into the body of Christ, thus assuring us of union with God's family (1Co 12:13).

1:3 *preaching*. Paul places the emphasis on the message, not on the messenger. Christ is the center of our faith, not any one preacher (1Co 9:16; 2Co 4:5).

CHAPTER 1 **1** 2Ti 2:25; 1Ti 3:16 **2** 2Ti 1:1; 2:13; Ro 16:25 **3** 2Ti 1:10; 1Th 2:4 **4** 2Co 2:13; Eph 1:2

Qualifications of Elders

5 For this reason I left you *behind* in Crete, so that you would set right what remains *unfinished*, and appoint elders in every city as I directed you,

6 *namely*, a man of unquestionable integrity, the husband of one wife, having children who believe, not accused of being immoral or rebellious.

7 For the overseer, as God's steward, must be blameless, not self-willed, not quick-tempered, not addicted to wine, not violent, not greedy for dishonest gain [but financially ethical].

8 And *he must be* hospitable [to believers, as well as strangers], a lover of what is good, sensible (upright), fair, devout, self-disciplined [above reproach—whether in public or in private].

9 He must hold firmly to the trustworthy word [of God] as it was taught to him, so that he will be able both to give accurate instruction in sound [reliable, error-free] doctrine and to refute those who contradict [it by explaining their error].

10 For there are many rebellious men who are empty talkers [just windbags] and deceivers; especially those of the circumcision [those Jews who insist that Gentile believers must be circumcised and keep the Law in order to be saved].

11 They must be silenced, because they are upsetting whole families by teaching things they should not teach for the purpose of dishonest *financial* gain.

12 One of them [Epimenides, a Cretan], a prophet of their own, said, "Cretans are always liars, evil beasts, lazy gluttons."

13 This description is true. So rebuke them sharply so that they will be sound in the faith *and* free from doctrinal error,

14 not paying attention to Jewish myths and the commandments *and* rules of men who turn their backs on the truth.

15 To the pure, all things are pure; but to the corrupt and unbelieving, nothing is pure; both their mind and their conscience are corrupted.

16 They profess to know God [to rec-

1:5 *appoint elders.* The Greek words for "elder" and "overseer" seem to have been used interchangeably by Paul (v. 7). "Elder" perhaps speaks more of the office and its authority, while "overseer" may speak more of the person's function and the ministry of oversight (Ac 20:17).
1:6 *husband of one wife.* The exact application of this phrase is debated; some believe that it merely forbids polygamy, while others believe that it also prohibits a man who is divorced and remarried. It is clearly emphasizing the importance of marital faithfulness (Mt 19:5). ***children who believe.*** The man must have a good relationship with his wife, and he should also have children who demonstrate faithfulness to God. If a man has children who reject the ways of God, or who are out of control, this reflects on the father's ability to lead others outside his home.
1:9 *refute.* The word *refute* here means to rebuke in such a way as to produce repentance and confession of sin (Jn 16:8). A rebuke can have the positive results of producing change in a person's life.
1:10 *those of the circumcision.* Apparently there were Jewish Christians in the churches of Crete who were limiting the Christian freedom of Gentile Christians by requiring an adherence to Jewish laws (Gal 3).
1:12 *Cretans are always liars.* Paul is quoting the Cretan poet Epimenides, who wrote these words around 600 BC. The Cretans were so much regarded as liars in the Mediterranean world that the expression "to Cretanize" meant "to lie."
1:14 *Jewish myths.* These were probably legends about Old Testament figures, like some that survive to this day in non-biblical writings.
1:15 *To the pure . . . to the corrupt and unbelieving.* Paul highlights the mistaken asceticism of the Cretan false teachers. They had identified certain foods and practices as defiled when in reality it was their minds that were defiled and unbelieving. On the other hand, to the pure, all things are pure. The Cretan believers had placed their trust in Christ, focusing their minds on Him, and therefore they would be empowered by God's Spirit to lead pure lives. Jesus taught the same principle in Matthew 15:11. Physical objects or external practices do not defile a person, but a mind focused on evil thoroughly corrupts.

---

5 1Co 11:34 **6** 1Ti 3:2; 1Ti 3:4 **7** Mt 24:45; Lev 10:9 **8** 1Ti 3:2 **9** 1Ti 1:10 **10** 1Ti 1:6; Ac 15:1 **11** 2Ti 3:6; 1Ti 6:5 **12** Ac 17:28 **13** 2Co 13:10; Titus 2:2 **14** 1Ti 1:4; Isa 29:13 **15** 1Co 6:12 **16** 2Ti 3:5; Ro 1:28

ognize and be acquainted with Him],
but by *their* actions they deny *and*
disown Him. They are detestable and
disobedient and worthless for good
work of any kind.

Duties of the Older and Younger

2 BUT AS for you, teach the things
which are in agreement with sound
doctrine [which produces men and
women of good character whose life-
style identifies them as true Christians].
2 Older men are to be temperate,
dignified, sensible, sound in faith, in
love, in steadfastness [Christlike in
character].
3 Older women similarly are to be
reverent in their behavior, not mali-
cious gossips nor addicted to much
wine, teaching what is right *and* good,
4 so that they may encourage the
young women to tenderly love their
husbands and their children,
5 to be sensible, pure, makers of a
home [where God is honored], good-
natured, being subject to their own
husbands, so that the word of God will
not be dishonored.
6 In a similar way urge the young
men to be sensible *and* self-controlled
and to behave wisely [taking life se-
riously].
7 And in all things show yourself to
be an example of good works, with pu-
rity in doctrine [having the strictest re-
gard for integrity and truth], dignified,
8 sound *and* beyond reproach in in-
struction, so that the opponent [of the
faith] will be shamed, having nothing
bad to say about us.
9 Urge bond-servants to be subject to
their own masters in everything, to be
pleasing and not talk back,
10 not stealing [things, regardless of
value], but proving themselves trust-
worthy, so that in every respect they
will adorn *and* do credit to the teaching
of God our Savior.
11 For the [remarkable, undeserved]
grace of God that brings salvation has
appeared to all men.
12 It teaches us to reject ungodliness
and worldly (immoral) desires, and to
live sensible, upright, and godly lives
[lives with a purpose that reflect spir-
itual maturity] in this present age,
13 awaiting *and* confidently expect-
ing the [fulfillment of our] blessed hope
and the glorious appearing of our great
God and Savior, Christ Jesus,
14 who [willingly] gave Himself [to
be crucified] on our behalf to redeem
us *and* purchase our freedom from all
wickedness, and to purify for Himself
a chosen *and* very special people to be

2:1 *sound doctrine.* "Sound" means "healthy." Right thinking is the raw material for right actions (Ps 119:11; Pr 23:7; Ro 12:2; Jas 1:13 – 15). Our actions will naturally reveal the direction of our thoughts.
2:2 *Older men.* Maturity is not determined simply by age or even by how much a person knows; it is determined by how skilled a person is in applying the truth to life and in distinguishing good from evil (Heb 5:13 – 14).
2:4 *love their husbands and their children.* This is not just romantic or emotional love, but the commitment of a woman to the welfare of her husband and children.
2:5 *being subject to their own husbands.* Women are not under the authority of men in general, but rather the authority of their own husbands (Eph 5:21). ***will not be dishonored.*** The older women are to teach the younger women so that their actions will glorify God, build His kingdom, and strengthen the family. Failure to follow Paul's instructions will result in the word of God being maligned in the pagan community.
2:6 *young men.* Young men are to pursue the character qualities that older men should possess already.
2:7 *example of good works.* More people will learn from our daily actions than from what we say.
2:11 *appeared.* Christ came the first time in grace to save men from their sins; the second time He will come in glory to reign (v. 13).
2:13 *awaiting and confidently expecting the [fulfillment of our] blessed hope.* Paul reminded Timothy that there is a special crown awaiting all "who have loved ... His appearing" (2Ti 4:8). ***our great God and Savior, Christ Jesus.*** This is one of the strongest statements of the deity of Christ in the New Testament.
2:14 *redeem.* "Redeem" means "to purchase." With His death on the cross, Christ paid the

CHAPTER 2 **1** 1Ti 1:10 **5** 1Co 14:34; Ro 2:24 **7** 1Ti 4:12; Eph 6:24 **8** 1Ti 6:3; Neh 5:9 **9** Eph 6:5; Eph 5:24 **10** Mt 5:16 **11** Ro 5:15; Lk 3:6 **12** Lk 1:75; 1Pe 4:2 **13** 1Co 1:7; Ac 24:15; Col 3:4 **14** Gal 1:4; Heb 9:14; Ex 15:16; Eph 2:10

His own possession, *who are* enthusiastic for doing what is good. [Deut 14:2; Ps 130:8; Ezek 37:23]

15 Tell *them* these things. Encourage and rebuke with full authority. Let no one disregard *or* despise you [conduct yourself and your teaching so as to command respect].

Godly Living

3 REMIND PEOPLE to be subject to rulers and authorities, to be obedient, to be ready *and* willing to do good,

2 to slander *or* abuse no one, to be kind *and* conciliatory and gentle, showing unqualified consideration *and* courtesy toward everyone.

3 For we too once were foolish, disobedient, deceived, enslaved to various *sinful* desires and pleasures, spending *and* wasting our life in malice and envy, hateful, hating one another.

4 But when the goodness *and* kindness of God our Savior and *His* love for mankind appeared [in human form as the Man, Jesus Christ],

5 He saved us, not because of any works of righteousness that we have done, but because of His own compassion *and* mercy, by the cleansing of the new birth (spiritual transformation, regeneration) and renewing by the Holy Spirit,

6 whom He poured out richly upon us through Jesus Christ our Savior,

7 so that we would be justified [made free of the guilt of sin] by His [compassionate, undeserved] grace, and that we would be [acknowledged as acceptable to Him and] made heirs of eternal life [actually experiencing it] according to our hope (His guarantee).

8 This is a faithful *and* trustworthy saying; and concerning these things I want you to speak with great confidence, so that those who have believed God [that is, those who have trusted in, relied on, and accepted Christ Jesus as Savior,] will be careful to participate in doing good *and* honorable things. These things are excellent [in themselves] and profitable for the people.

9 But avoid foolish *and* ill-informed *and* stupid controversies and genealogies and dissensions and quarrels about the Law, for they are unprofitable and useless.

10 After a first and second warning

---

price to release us from the bondage of sin (Ro 6:6–7,17,20; Eph 1:7). God's purpose in redeeming us is not only to save us from hell; He also wants to free us from sin so that we can produce good works that glorify Him (Eph 2:8–10).

3:1 *Remind people.* The Cretans notoriously lacked the virtue of good citizenship (1:12). Disobedience permeated the Cretan's lifestyle, both in the church (v. 10) and in government. Believers who got along with civil authorities and who lived peacefully with their neighbors would reflect positively on their faith and would glorify God.

3:5 *not because of any works of righteousness.* Paul has been exhorting Titus to emphasize good works in his ministry with the Cretans, and he wants to make it clear that such good works have no value in saving a person. It is solely on the basis of God's mercy that we are delivered from the penalty of our sin. ***cleansing of the new birth.*** This phrase refers to the work of the Holy Spirit, in whom we are "born again" (Jn 3:3,6), given a new nature and cleansed from old sin. ***renewing by the Holy Spirit.*** There are three works performed by the Holy Spirit in preparing nonbelievers to become Christians. **(1) The Holy Spirit restrains.** Satan would enjoy nothing more than to destroy people before they make their decision to accept Christ as Savior. But the Holy Spirit prevents this from occurring (Isa 59:19). **(2) The Holy Spirit convicts.** Mankind's sin and righteousness are exposed by the Holy Spirit (Jn 16:8). Two examples of such conviction are Felix, a Roman governor who "trembled" under conviction (Ac 24:25), and King Agrippa, who was almost persuaded in Acts 26:28. **(3) The Holy Spirit regenerates.** When a repenting sinner accepts Christ as Savior, he is given a new nature by the Holy Spirit (2Co 5:17). Jesus carefully explained this ministry of the Holy Spirit to Nicodemus (Jn 3:3–7).

3:7 *we would be [acknowledged as acceptable to Him and] made heirs.* God justifies believers so that they might become co-heirs with Jesus Christ in His coming reign (Ro 8:17; 2Ti 2:12).

3:10 *reject a divisive man.* A sinner must always be given ample opportunity to repent, but

15 2Ti 4:2 **CHAPTER 3** **1** 1Pe 2:13; Col 1:10; Heb 13:21 **2** Eph 4:31; 2Ti 2:24; Php 4:5; Eph 4:2; Col 3:12 **3** 1Co 6:11; 1Pe 4:3 **4** Titus 2:11; 1Ti 2:3 **5** Ro 3:20; 2Ti 1:9; Jn 3:3; 1Pe 3:21 **6** Eze 36:25; Joel 2:28 **7** Ro 3:24; 8:23; Titus 1:2 **8** 1Ti 1:15; Titus 2:14 **9** 1Ti 1:4; 2Ti 2:14 **10** 2Co 13:2; Mt 18:17

reject a divisive man [who promotes heresy and causes dissension—ban him from your fellowship and have nothing more to do with him],
11well aware that such a person is twisted and is sinning; he is convicted *and* self-condemned [and is gratified by causing confusion among believers].

Personal Concerns

12When I send Artemas or [perhaps] Tychicus to you, make every effort to come to me at Nicopolis, for I have decided to spend the winter there.
13Do your best to help Zenas the lawyer and Apollos on their way; see that they are supplied *and* lack nothing.
14Our people must learn to do good deeds to meet necessary demands [whatever the occasion may require], so that they will not be unproductive.
15All who are with me greet you. Greet those who love us in the faith.
Grace be with all of you.

---

if he insists on continuing in sin, the church is required to let him go (Mt 18:15 – 17; 2Th 3:14 – 15).

3:12 *Tychicus.* Tychicus, one of Paul's assistants, is also mentioned in Acts 20:4; Ephesians 6:21; Colossians 4:7; 2 Timothy 4:12.

3:13 *Apollos.* Apollos was a fellow worker of Paul's (1Co 16:12), an Alexandrian who had been taught by Priscilla and Aquila and who had eloquently preached the gospel at Ephesus and Corinth (Ac 18:24 – 19:1).

3:14 *not be unproductive.* Justification is a free gift from God, but we will be rewarded according to what we do on this earth (Rev 22:12). It would be a tragedy to stand ashamed at Christ's return (1Jn 2:28).

11 Ac 13:46 **12** Ac 20:4 **13** Ac 18:24 **14** ver. 8; Ro 15:28; Php 1:11

THE LETTER OF PAUL TO

PHILEMON

▸ **AUTHOR:** Though some critics deny its authenticity, the general consensus of scholarship recognizes Philemon as Paul's work. There could have been no doctrinal motive for its forgery, and it is supported externally by consistent tradition and internally by no less than three references to Paul (Phile 1,9,19).

▸ **TIMES:** c. AD 60 – 61 ▸ **KEY VERSES:** Philemon 16 – 17

▸ **THEME:** Paul wrote this letter to a slave owner in the church at Colosse. Apparently, Onesimus, the slave of Philemon, had stolen from him and had run away, an act punishable by death under Roman law. Onesimus had since met Paul and become a Christian. Paul's letter is a personal appeal in an effort to help them reconcile and renew their relationship.

Salutation

1 PAUL, A prisoner [for the sake] of
Christ Jesus (the Messiah, the Anoint-
ed), and our brother Timothy,
To Philemon our dearly beloved
friend and fellow worker,
2 and to [your wife] Apphia our sister,
and to Archippus our fellow soldier [in
ministry], and to the church that meets
in your house:
3 Grace to you and peace [inner calm
and spiritual well-being] from God our
Father and the Lord Jesus Christ.

Philemon's Love and Faith

4 I thank my God always, making
mention of you in my prayers,
5 because I hear of your love and of
your faith which you have toward the
Lord Jesus and toward all the saints
(God's people).
6 I pray that the sharing of your faith
may become effective *and* powerful
because of your *accurate* knowledge
of every good thing which is ours in
Christ.
7 For I have had great joy and comfort
and encouragement from your love,
because the hearts of the saints (God's
people) have been refreshed through
you, my brother.
8 Therefore [on the basis of these
facts], though I have enough confi-
dence in Christ to order you to do what
is appropriate,
9 yet for love's sake I prefer to appeal
to you—since I am such a person as
Paul, an old man, and now also a pris-
oner [for the sake] of Christ Jesus—

---

1 – 2 *To Philemon . . . and to the church.* Paul addresses the letter to Philemon and the Colossian church, but this intensely personal epistle uses the singular "I" and "you," demonstrating that the letter is Paul's personal plea to Philemon. It was written at the same time as the letter to the Colossians, and doubtless carried by the same messenger.

2 *Apphia . . . Archippus.* Apphia may have been the wife of Philemon; Archippus may have been Philemon's son, or perhaps an elder in the Colossian church (Col 4:17).

6 *faith may become effective.* Working faith is a sharing faith; it is the acknowledgment of what Christ has done in the believer's life (Eph 3:17 – 19).

9 *Paul, an old man.* The apostle is either speaking of his old age, or of the office of an elder.

1 ver. 9; Eph 3:1; 4:1; 2Ti 1:8; Php 2:25 **2** Col 4:17; Php 2:25; Ro 16:5; 1Co 16:19 **3** Eph 1:2 **4** Eph 1:16; 1Th 1:2; 2Th 1:3 **5** Eph 1:15; Col 1:4 **6** Php 1:9 **7** ver. 20; 2Co 7:13; 2Ti 1:16 **8** 1Th 2:6 **9** ver. 1

A Plea for Onesimus to be Freed

[10]I appeal to you for my [own spiritual] child Onesimus, whom I have fathered [in the faith] while a captive in these chains.
[11]Once he was useless to you, but now he is indeed useful to you as well as to me.
[12]I have sent him back to you in person, that is, *like sending* my very heart.
[13]I would have chosen to keep him with me, so that he might minister to me on your behalf during my imprisonment for the gospel;
[14]but I did not want to do anything without first getting your consent, so that your goodness would not be, in effect, by compulsion but of your own free will.
[15]Perhaps it was for this reason that he was separated from you for a while, so that you would have him back forever,
[16]no longer as a slave, but [as someone] more than a slave, as a brother [in Christ], especially dear to me, but how much more to you, both in the flesh [as a servant] and in the Lord [as a fellow believer]. [Col 4:9]
[17]So if you consider me a partner, welcome *and* accept him as you would me.
[18]But if he has wronged you in any way or owes you anything, charge that to my account;
[19]I, Paul, write this with my own hand, I will repay it *in full* (not to mention to you that you owe to me even your own self as well).
[20]Yes, brother, let me have some benefit *and* joy from you in the Lord; refresh my heart in Christ.
[21]I write to you [perfectly] confident of your obedient compliance, since I know that you will do even more than I ask.
[22]At the same time also prepare a guest room for me [in expectation of a visit], for I hope that through your prayers I will be [granted the gracious privilege of] coming to you [at Colossae].
[23]Greetings to you from Epaphras, my fellow prisoner here in [the cause of] Christ Jesus,
[24]and from Mark, Aristarchus, Demas, and Luke, my fellow workers.
[25]The grace of the Lord Jesus Christ be with your spirit.

---

11 *useless . . . useful.* Paul uses an interesting play on words here. Having mentioned Onesimus, whose name means "useful," the apostle describes him as someone who was formerly useless, but who has become useful through the work of Christ in his life.
14 *by compulsion . . . free will.* Service for Christ is never forced. Paul has given Philemon several good reasons to forgive Onesimus, but here he returns to the foundation of his argument: Philemon's actions must proceed from his own love (v. 9).
18 *wronged you.* Onesimus had probably stolen something from Philemon when he left. ***charge that to my account.*** This accounting imagery reminds us of the theological truth that our sins were charged over to Christ even though He had not earned them. Forgiveness is costly (Isa 53:6).
19 *my own hand.* Paul wrote this personal letter himself, and therefore it could be considered a legal document obligating him to pay the damages that Onesimus had caused.
22 *prepare a guest room for me.* It is believed that Paul wrote this letter during his imprisonment in Rome (Ac 28), and that he was released shortly afterwards. He was probably not at liberty for very long, but it is possible that he was able to visit Colosse before his second imprisonment and execution.
23 – 24 *Epaphras . . . Mark, Aristarchus, Demas, and Luke.* These five co-workers are also mentioned in Colossians 4:10 – 14.

10 Col 4:9; 1Co 4:15; Gal 4:19 **13** 1Co 16:17; Php 2:30 **14** 2Co 9:7 **15** Ge 45:5,8 **16** Mt 23:8; 1Ti 6:2; Col 3:22 **17** 2Co 8:23 **20** ver. 7 **21** 2Co 7:16 **22** Php 1:25; 2:24; 2Co 1:11 **23** Col 1:7; 4:12 **24** Ac 12:12,25; Ac 19:29; 27:2; Col 4:10; Col 4:14; 2Ti 4:11 **25** 2Ti 4:22

THE LETTER TO THE

HEBREWS

▸ **AUTHOR:** The origin of Hebrews is unknown. Uncertainty plagues not only its authorship, but also its date and its readership. Hebrews 13:18 – 24 tells us that this book was not anonymous to the original readers; they evidently knew the author. For some reason, however, early church tradition is divided over the identity of the author. Part of the church attributed it to Paul, others preferred Barnabas, Luke, or Clement, and some chose anonymity. Some aspects of the language style and theology of Hebrews are very similar to Paul's Epistles. However, significant stylistic differences have led the majority of biblical scholars to reject Pauline authorship of this book.

▸ **TIMES:** c. AD 64 – 68 ▸ **KEY VERSES:** Heb 4:14 – 16

▸ **THEME:** Hebrews was written for a group of Jewish Christians who were thinking about returning to their original faith. The author goes to great lengths to convince them to stay with their new faith. Point by point he goes through a whole series of arguments showing how Judaism was a foreshadowing of Christ. Everything promising about Old Testament Judaism is fulfilled in Christ. The new way is the superior way, as Christ and the faith that He established supersedes what has gone before. Understanding Jewish faith and practice, and the role of Moses and Aaron in biblical history, is a prerequisite to understanding Hebrews.

God's Final Word in His Son

1 GOD, HAVING spoken to the fathers long ago in [the voices and writings of] the prophets in many separate revelations [each of which set forth a portion of the truth], and in many ways,
2has in these last days spoken [with finality] to us in [the person of One who is by His character and nature] His Son [namely Jesus], whom He appointed heir *and* lawful owner of all things, through whom also He created the universe [that is, the universe as a space-time-matter continuum].
3The Son is the radiance *and* only expression of the glory of [our awesome] God [reflecting God's Shekinah

1:2 *in . . . His Son.* This could be rephrased as "in such a person as a Son." The emphasis rests on the character of the revelation. It is a revelation of the Son, a revelation not so much in what He has said as in who He is and what He has done. **1:3 *radiance . . . of the glory.*** The author of Hebrews is emphasizing that this is not a reflected brightness like the light of the moon. Instead, this is an inherent brightness like a ray from the sun. Jesus' glorious brightness comes from being essentially divine. ***perfect imprint.*** In Greek literature the word was used for stamping a coin from the die. ***upholding.*** This means to "bear" or "carry," referring to movement and progress toward a final end. The Son not only created the universe by His powerful word, but also maintains and directs its course. He is the Governor of the universe. ***sat down.*** This suggests the formal act of assuming the office of High Priest and implies a contrast to the Levitical priest, who never finished his work and sat down (10:11 – 13).

CHAPTER 1 **1** Nu 12:6 **2** Eph 1:10; Jn 1:17; Ps 2:8; Jn 1:3 **3** Jn 1:14; Jn 1:4; Rev 4:11; Heb 7:27; Ps 110:1

glory, the Light-being, the brilliant light of the divine], and the exact representation *and* perfect imprint of His [Father's] essence, and upholding *and* maintaining *and* propelling all things [the entire physical and spiritual universe] by His powerful word [carrying the universe along to its predetermined goal]. When He [Himself and no other] had [by offering Himself on the cross as a sacrifice for sin] accomplished purification from sins *and* established our freedom from guilt, He sat down [revealing His completed work] at the right hand of the Majesty on high [revealing His Divine authority],

4 having become as much superior to angels, since He has inherited a more excellent *and* glorious name than they [that is, Son—the name above all names].

5 For to which of the angels did the Father ever say,

"You are My Son,
Today I have begotten (fathered)
You [established You as a Son, with kingly dignity]"?

And again [did He ever say to the angels],

"I shall be a Father to Him
And He shall be a Son to Me"?
[2 Sam 7:14; Ps 2:7]

6 And when He again brings the firstborn [highest-ranking Son] into the world, He says,

"And all the angels of God are to worship Him." [Ps 97:7]

7 And concerning the angels He says,

"Who makes His angels winds,
And His ministering servants flames of fire [to do His bidding]." [Ps 104:4]

8 But about the Son [the Father says to Him],

"Your throne, O God, is forever and ever,
And the scepter of [absolute] righteousness is the scepter of His kingdom.
9 "You have loved righteousness [integrity, virtue, uprightness in purpose] and have hated lawlessness [injustice, sin].
Therefore God, Your God, Has anointed You
With the oil of gladness above Your companions." [Ps 45:6, 7]

10 And,

"You, Lord, laid the foundation of the earth in the beginning,
And the heavens are the works of Your hands;
11 They will perish, but You remain [forever and ever];
And they will all wear out like a garment,
12 And like a robe You will roll them up;
Like a garment they will be changed.
But You are the same [forever],
And Your years will never end."
[Ps 102:25–27]

13 But to which of the angels has the Father ever said,

1:5 *Today I have begotten (fathered) You.* This probably refers to the day Christ sat down at the Father's right hand after He accomplished His work as the Messiah.
1:6 *And when He again brings the firstborn.* This is a reference to the second coming. "Firstborn" refers to rank, meaning one who ranks above all others (Ps 89:27).
1:7 *Ministering servants.* The Son is superior to angels because He is the Sovereign who is worshiped, while the angels are *ministering servants* of God. The author of Hebrews quotes Psalm 104 because that psalm places angels in a long list of created objects which God sovereignly controls.
1:9 *Companions.* This term comes from a word that means "close associates" or "partners." The concept of believers being partners with Christ is key in Hebrews (3:1,14; 6:4; 12:8). The term refers to those who will be participants with Christ in His reign.
1:10 – 12 *You, Lord.* The context of Psalm 102 here indicates that the Lord is the One who would appear in the future to Israel and the nations (Ps 102:12 – 16).

4 Php 2:9,10 **5** Ps 2:7; Ac 13:33; 2Sa 7:14 **6** Ro 8:29; Dt 32:43 **7** Ps 104:4 **8** Ps 45:6,7 **9** Isa 61:1 **10** Ps 102:25 **11** Isa 34:4 **13** Ps 110:1; Lk 20:42

"Sit at My right hand [together
with me in royal dignity],
Until I make your enemies
A footstool for your feet [in
triumphant conquest]"?
[Ps 110:1]

14 Are not all the angels ministering spirits sent out [by God] to serve (accompany, protect) those who will inherit salvation? [Of course they are!]

Give Heed

2 FOR THIS reason [that is, because of God's final revelation in His Son Jesus and because of Jesus' superiority to the angels] we must pay much closer attention than ever to the things that we have heard, so that we do not [in any way] drift away from truth.
2 For if the message given through angels [the Law given to Moses] was authentic *and* unalterable, and every violation and disobedient act received an appropriate penalty,
3 how will we escape [the penalty] if we ignore such a great salvation [the gospel, the new covenant]? For it was spoken at first by the Lord, and it was confirmed to us *and* proved authentic by those who *personally* heard [Him speak],
4 [and besides this evidence] God also testifying with them [confirming the message of salvation], both by signs and wonders and by various miracles [carried out by Jesus and the apostles] and by [granting to believers the] gifts of the Holy Spirit according to His own will.

Earth Subject to Man

5 It was not to angels that God subjected the [inhabited] world of the future [when Christ reigns], about which we are speaking.
6 But one has [solemnly] testified somewhere [in Scripture], saying,

"What is man, that You are
mindful of him,
Or the son of man, that You
graciously care for him?
7 "You have made him for a little
while lower [in status] than the
angels;
You have crowned him with glory
and honor,
And set him over the works of
Your hands;
8 You have put all things in
subjection under his feet
[confirming his supremacy]."

Now in putting all things in subjection to man, He left nothing outside his control. But at present we do not yet see all things subjected to him. [Ps 8:4–6]

Jesus Briefly Humbled

9 But we do see Jesus, who was made lower than the angels for a little while

---

1:14 *those who will inherit salvation.* Salvation here is not justification because it is in the future, not in the past. The reference is to believers who inherit the kingdom or rule in God's kingdom as a reward for their service to the Son (9:28; Col 3:24).
2:1 *drift away.* The author's audience was marked by immaturity and spiritual sluggishness (5:11–12). The author warned them not to be carried away by the popular opinions that surrounded them. Instead, they were to hold fast to Christ's words because they were the words of God.
2:3 *how will we escape.* If the people who heard the message delivered through angels were justly punished when they disobeyed the law, how can believers expect to escape punishment when they neglect the even greater message delivered through the greater Messenger, the Son?
2:4 *signs and wonders.* This phrase refers to the miracles performed by the Holy Spirit through the Lord and His apostles in fulfillment of the ancient promises regarding the coming of the Messiah (Ac 2:22,43; 4:30; 5:12; 6:8; 14:3; 15:12; 1Co 12:12).
2:6–8 *And set him over the works of Your hands.* Since the Son's humanity might appear to be an obstacle to the claim of His superiority, the author of Hebrews cites Psalm 8, a lyrical reflection on Genesis 1, to prove that God has placed humanity over all created things, which includes the angelic world.

14 Ps 103:20; Mt 18:10; Ro 8:17 **CHAPTER 2** **2** Dt 33:2; Ac 7:53; Nu 15:30 **3** Heb 10:28; Mt 4:17; Lk 1:2 **4** Mk 16:20; Ac 2:22; 1Co 12:4,7,11; Eph 1:5,9 **5** 2Pe 3:13 **6** Job 7:17 **8** Mt 28:18; Eph 1:22; 1Co 15:25 **9** Php 2:7-9; Ac 2:33; Jn 3:16; 2Co 5:15; 1Jn 2:2; Rev 5:9

[by taking on the limitations of humanity], crowned with glory and honor because of His suffering of death, so that by the grace of God [extended to sinners] He might experience death for [the sins of] everyone.

[10]For it was fitting for God [that is, an act worthy of His divine nature] that He, for whose sake are all things, and through whom are all things, in bringing many sons to glory, should make the author *and* founder of their salvation perfect through suffering [bringing to maturity the human experience necessary for Him to be perfectly equipped for His office as High Priest].

[11]Both Jesus who sanctifies and those who are sanctified [that is, spiritually transformed, made holy, and set apart for God's purpose] are all from one *Father;* for this reason He is not ashamed to call them brothers and sisters,

[12]saying,

"I WILL DECLARE YOUR (the Father's)
NAME TO MY BRETHREN (believers),
IN THE MIDST OF THE CONGREGATION I
WILL SING YOUR PRAISE." [Ps 22:22]

[13]And again [He says],

"MY TRUST *and* CONFIDENT HOPE WILL
BE PLACED IN HIM."

And again,

"HERE I AM, I AND THE CHILDREN WHOM
GOD HAS GIVEN ME." [Is 8:17, 18]

[14]Therefore, since [these His] children share in flesh and blood [the physical nature of mankind], He Himself in a similar manner also shared in the same [physical nature, but without sin], so that through [experiencing] death He might make powerless (ineffective, impotent) him who had the power of death—that is, the devil—

[15]and [that He] might free all those who through [the haunting] fear of death were held in slavery throughout their lives.

[16]For, as we all know, He (Christ) does not take hold of [the fallen] angels [to give them a helping hand], but He does take hold of [the fallen] descendants of Abraham [extending to them His hand of deliverance]. [Is 41:8, 9]

[17]Therefore, *it was essential that* He had to be made like His brothers (mankind) in every respect, so that He might [by experience] become a merciful and faithful High Priest in things related to God, to make atonement (propitiation) for the people's sins [thereby wiping away the sin, satisfying divine justice, and providing a

---

2:10 *founder of their salvation.* The Greek word here means "leader" or "originator." The word describes a pioneer or pathfinder. Jesus' endurance of sufferings on this earth makes Him our leader. He not only endured them but also triumphed over sin, death, and Satan through them.

2:12 *TO MY BRETHREN.* Psalm 22 is quoted here. In it, the Messiah refers to "My brethren," identifying Himself with all those who place their faith in God.

2:14 – 16 *He might make powerless ... free all.* Having established the unity between the Son and believer, the author concludes that there are two purposes of this close identification. The Son became human so that He could destroy the devil and release those who were in bondage to sin.

2:16 *descendants of Abraham.* The author may have used the expression because the recipients of this letter were primarily Jewish believers. The author is pointing out that Christ came to the aid of Abraham's sons, not the angelic hosts.

2:17 *in things related to God.* Jesus participated in our nature and in our sufferings on earth so that He could be a sympathetic Mediator between God and humanity. He understands our weaknesses and intercedes for us in the presence of God the Father. ***make atonement.*** This term refers to the satisfaction of the claims of a holy and righteous God against sinners who have broken His law. Christ appeased God's righteous wrath by dying on the cross in our place (Ro 3:21 – 26). Although completely sinless, Christ voluntarily submitted to the penalty of sin, His agonizing death on the cross. This voluntary sacrifice of Himself for our welfare satisfied the justice and holiness of God. The benefits of His sacrifice are applied to all who place their faith in Him.

10 Lk 24:46; Ro 11:36; Ac 5:31; Lk 13:32 **11** Heb 10:10; Ac 17:26; Mt 28:10; Jn 20:17 **12** Ps 22:22 **13** Ps 18:2; Isa 12:2; Isa 8:18; Jn 10:29 **14** Jn 1:14; Php 2:7; 1Co 15:54; Col 2:15 **15** Lk 1:74; 2Ti 1:7 **17** Php 2:7; Heb 4:15

way of reconciliation between God
and mankind].
[18]Because He Himself [in His hu-
manity] has suffered in being tempted,
He is able to help *and* provide immedi-
ate assistance to those who are being
tempted *and* exposed to suffering.

Jesus Our High Priest

3 THEREFORE, HOLY brothers and
sisters, who share in the heavenly
calling, [thoughtfully and attentively]
consider the Apostle and High Priest
whom we confessed [as ours when
we accepted Him as Savior], namely,
Jesus;
[2]He was faithful to Him who ap-
pointed Him [Apostle and High Priest],
as Moses also was *faithful* in all God's
house. [Num 12:7]
[3]Yet Jesus has been considered wor-
thy of much greater glory *and* honor
than Moses, just as the builder of a
house has more honor than the house.
[4]For every house is built by someone,
but the builder of all things is God.
[5]Now Moses was faithful in [the ad-
ministration of] all God's house, [but
only] as a *ministering* servant, [his
ministry serving] as a testimony of
the things which were to be spoken
afterward [the revelation to come in
Christ]; [Num 12:7]
[6]but Christ is faithful as a Son over
His [Father's] house. And we are His
house if we hold fast our confidence
and sense of triumph in our hope [in
Christ].
[7]Therefore, just as the Holy Spirit
says,

"TODAY IF YOU HEAR HIS VOICE,
[8]DO NOT HARDEN YOUR HEARTS
AS [your fathers did] IN THE
REBELLION [of Israel at Meribah],
ON THE DAY OF TESTING IN THE
WILDERNESS,
[9]WHERE YOUR FATHERS TRIED ME BY
TESTING [My forbearance and
tolerance],
AND SAW MY WORKS FOR FORTY YEARS
[And found I stood their test].
[10]"THEREFORE I WAS ANGERED WITH THIS
GENERATION,
AND I SAID, 'THEY ALWAYS GO ASTRAY
IN THEIR HEART,
AND THEY DID NOT KNOW MY WAYS
[nor become progressively better
and more intimately acquainted
with them]';

2:18 *He Himself [in His humanity] has suffered in being tempted.* Christ's suffering included temptation. He experienced the lure of sin, but He never surrendered Himself to it. He knows what it is like to be tempted, so He knows how to assist those who are being tempted.
3:2 *in all God's house.* This phrase is taken from Numbers 12:7. "House" refers to the tabernacle, the center of Israelite worship. Moses had faithfully obeyed God's instructions concerning the tabernacle. In the same way, Jesus had been obedient to the mission the Father had given Him. Through obedience, God established a new house of God, the church.
3:3–4 *worthy of much greater glory and honor than Moses.* The implication is that the covenant established through Jesus' death is more glorious than the covenant established at Mount Sinai.
3:5 *as a ministering servant.* The author of Hebrews continues the comparison between Moses and Jesus. While Moses was faithful as a servant, Christ's faithfulness was greater because it was performed by a Son. ***things which were to be spoken afterward.*** Moses' work pointed forward to Christ (9:10; 10:3). The regulations of the law of Moses pointed out both the sin of humanity and the need for a perfect sacrifice to reconcile people to their holy Creator.
3:7–11 *DO NOT HARDEN YOUR HEARTS.* The author of Hebrews quotes Psalm 95:7–11 to warn the Jewish Christians about hardening their hearts to God and the salvation He offers. Moses' generation had refused to trust in God to provide for their needs in the wilderness (Ex 17:1–7), and the readers of this letter were also in danger. ***MY REST.*** This is a key concept in Hebrews. In the Old Testament, the conquest of the promised land and the cessation of fighting in the land was viewed as a form of rest (Dt 3:20; 12:9; 25:19; Jos 11:23; 21:44; 22:4). In the New Testament, "rest" speaks of the believer's eternal home and the joy that he or she will experience in Jesus' presence (4:1).

18 Heb 4:15,16 **CHAPTER 3** **1** Ro 1:7; 1Co 1:2; Php 3:14; 2Pe 1:10; Ro 15:8 **2** Nu 12:7 **3** Zec 6:12; Mt 16:18 **4** Eph 2:10; Heb 1:2 **5** ver. 2; Ex 14:31; Dt 3:24; Dt 18:19 **6** Heb 1:2; 1Co 3:16; Mt 10:22; Ro 5:2; Col 1:23 **7** Ac 1:16; Ps 95:7

[11]So I SWORE [an oath] IN MY WRATH,
'THEY SHALL NOT ENTER MY REST [the promised land].' " [Ps 95:7–11]

The Peril of Unbelief

[12]Take care, brothers and sisters, that there not be in any one of you a wicked, unbelieving heart [which refuses to trust and rely on the Lord, a heart] that turns away from the living God.
[13]But continually encourage one another every day, as long as it is called "Today" [and there is an opportunity], so that none of you will be hardened [into settled rebellion] by the deceitfulness of sin [its cleverness, delusive glamour, and sophistication].
[14]For we [believers] have become partakers of Christ [sharing in all that the Messiah has for us], if only we hold firm our newborn confidence [which originally led us to Him] until the end,
[15]while it is said,

"TODAY [while there is still opportunity] IF YOU HEAR HIS VOICE,
DO NOT HARDEN YOUR HEART, AS WHEN THEY PROVOKED ME [in the rebellion in the desert at Meribah]." [Ps 95:7, 8]

[16]For who were they who heard and yet provoked *Him* [with rebellious acts]? Was it not all those who came out of Egypt led by Moses?
[17]And with whom was He angry for forty years? Was it not with those who sinned, whose dead bodies were scattered in the desert?
[18]And to whom did He swear [an oath] that they would not enter His rest, but to those who disobeyed [those who would not listen to His word]?
[19]So we see that they were not able to enter [into His rest—the promised land] because of unbelief *and* an unwillingness to trust in God. [Num 14:1–35]

The Believer's Rest

4 THEREFORE, WHILE the promise of entering His rest still remains *and* is freely offered today, let us fear, in case any one of you may seem to come short of reaching it *or* think he has come too late.
[2]For indeed we have had the good news [of salvation] preached to us, just as the Israelites also [when the good news of the promised land came to them]; but the message they heard did not benefit them, because it was not united with faith [in God] by those who heard.
[3]For we who believe [that is, we who personally trust and confidently rely on God] enter that rest [so we have His inner peace now because we are confident in our salvation, and assured of His power], just as He has said,

"AS I SWORE [an oath] IN MY WRATH,
THEY SHALL NOT ENTER MY REST,"

[this He said] although His works were completed from the foundation of the world [waiting for all who would believe]. [Ps 95:11]
[4]For somewhere [in Scripture] He

3:12 – 13 *unbelieving heart.* In essence, unbelief is a stubborn refusal to trust in the truthfulness of His word. It is a grave sin because it leads us away from God.
3:14 *partakers of Christ.* This is the same word translated *companions* in 1:9. Believers will be partners with Christ in His future kingdom (Rev 2:26 – 27).
3:15 – 19 *And with whom was He angry.* The Jewish Christians to whom this letter was addressed were in danger of following in their ancestors' footsteps. They were tempted to doubt the words of Jesus. With the rhetorical questions in these verses, the author of Hebrews was encouraging them to place their faith firmly in Christ.
4:2 *good news [of salvation] preached.* This is the translation of a single Greek word meaning "the good news was announced."
4:4 *GOD RESTED.* The theme of rest has its beginning in God's own rest after creation. The fact that Genesis makes no mention of the evening of the seventh day of creation provides a basis for some Jewish commentators to conclude that the rest of God lasts throughout all history.

14 ver. 6 **15** ver. 7 **16** Nu 14:2 **17** Nu 14:22; Ps 106:26 **18** Nu 14:30 **CHAPTER 4** **1** Heb 12:15 **3** Heb 3:14; Ps 95:11 **4** Ex 20:11

has said this about the seventh day:
"AND GOD RESTED ON THE SEVENTH DAY
FROM ALL HIS WORKS"; [Gen 2:2]
[5]and again in this, "THEY SHALL NOT
ENTER MY REST." [Ps 95:11]
[6]Therefore, since the promise re-
mains for some to enter His rest, and
those who formerly had the good news
preached to them failed to [grasp it and
did not] enter because of [their unbelief
evidenced by] disobedience,
[7]He again sets a definite day, [a new]
"Today," [providing another oppor-
tunity to enter that rest by] saying
through David after so long a time,
just as has been said before [in the
words already quoted],

> "TODAY IF YOU HEAR HIS VOICE,
> DO NOT HARDEN YOUR HEARTS."
> [Ps 95:7, 8]

[8][This mention of a rest was not a ref-
erence to their entering into Canaan.]
For if Joshua had given them rest, God
would not speak about another day [of
opportunity] after that.
[9]So there remains a [full and com-
plete] Sabbath rest for the people of God.
[10]For the one who has once entered
His rest has also rested from [the wea-
riness and pain of] his [human] labors,
just as God rested from [those labors
uniquely] His own. [Gen 2:2]
[11]Let us therefore make every effort
to enter that rest [of God, to know and
experience it for ourselves], so that no
one will fall by *following* the same ex-
ample of disobedience [as those who
died in the wilderness].
[12]For the word of God is living and
active *and* full of power [making it
operative, energizing, and effective].
It is sharper than any two-edged
sword, penetrating as far as the di-
vision of the soul and spirit [the com-
pleteness of a person], and of both
joints and marrow [the deepest parts
of our nature], exposing *and* judging
the very thoughts and intentions of
the heart.
[13]And not a creature exists that
is concealed from His sight, but all
things are open *and* exposed, and re-
vealed to the eyes of Him with whom
we have to give account.
[14]Inasmuch then as we [believers]
have a great High Priest who has [al-
ready ascended and] passed through
the heavens, Jesus the Son of God, let
us hold fast our confession [of faith
and cling tenaciously to our absolute
trust in Him as Savior].
[15]For we do not have a High Priest
who is unable to sympathize *and*
understand our weaknesses *and*
temptations, but One who has been
tempted [knowing exactly how it feels
to be human] in every respect as *we
are, yet* without [committing any] sin.
[16]Therefore let us [with privilege]
approach the throne of grace [that is,
the throne of God's gracious favor]
with confidence *and* without fear, so
that we may receive mercy [for our
failures] and find [His amazing] grace
to help in time of need [an appropri-
ate blessing, coming just at the right
moment].

4:9 *rest.* The word used here is different from the word used in verses 1,3,5,10–11; 3:11,18. Jews commonly taught that the Sabbath foreshadowed the world to come, and they spoke of "a day of which shall be all Sabbath."
4:11 *make every effort to enter that rest.* The rest is not automatic. Determined diligence is required. The danger is that believers today, like the Israelites of the past, will not stand, but will fall in disobedience.
4:13 *open and exposed.* This phrase suggests complete exposure and defenselessness before God.
4:15 *sympathize.* This word means "to suffer with" and expresses the feeling of one who has entered into suffering.
4:16 *approach.* This command strongly contrasts with God's command at Mt Sinai: "go not up into the mount, or touch the border of it" (Ex 19:12). Because of Christ's priestly work, believers can approach God's presence. ***with confidence.*** This word carries with it the idea of "fearlessness" or "courageousness." Believers should boldly approach God in prayer because He is our gracious High Priest who sits at God's right hand interceding for us.

6 Heb 3:19 **7** Ps 95:7 **12** Ps 147:15; Jer 23:29; Isa 49:2; Eph 6:17; Rev 1:16; 1Co 14:25 **13** Ps 90:8; Job 26:6
14 Heb 7:26; Heb 10:23 **15** Isa 53:3; Lk 22:28; 2Co 5:21; 1Pe 2:22 **16** Eph 2:18

The Perfect High Priest

5 FOR EVERY high priest chosen from among men is appointed [to act] on behalf of men in things relating to God, so that he may offer both gifts and sacrifices for sins.

2 He is able to deal gently with the *spiritually* ignorant and misguided, since he is also subject to *human* weakness;

3 and because of this [human weakness] he is required to offer *sacrifices* for sins, for himself as well as for the people.

4 And besides, one does not appropriate for himself the honor [of being high priest], but he who is called by God, just as Aaron was.

5 So too Christ did not glorify Himself so as to be made a high priest, but He [was exalted and appointed by the One] who said to Him,

"You are My Son,
Today I have begotten (fathered)
You [declared Your authority
and rule over the nations]";
[Ps 2:7]

6 just as He also says in another place,

"You are a priest [appointed]
forever
According to the order of
Melchizedek." [Ps 110:4]

7 In the days of His earthly life, Jesus offered up both [specific] petitions and [urgent] supplications [for that which He needed] with fervent crying and tears to the One who was [always] able to save Him from death, and He was heard because of His reverent submission toward God [His sinlessness and His unfailing determination to do the Father's will].

8 Although He was a Son [who had never been disobedient to the Father], He learned [active, special] obedience through what He suffered.

9 And having been made perfect [uniquely equipped and prepared as Savior and retaining His integrity amid opposition], He became the source of eternal salvation [an eternal inheritance] to all those who obey Him, [Is 45:17]

10 being designated by God as High Priest according to the order of Melchizedek. [Ps 110:4]

11 Concerning this we have much to say, and it is hard to explain, since you have become dull *and* sluggish in [your spiritual] hearing *and* disinclined to listen.

12 For though by this time you ought to be teachers [because of the time you have had to learn these truths], you actually need someone to teach you again the elementary principles of God's word [from the beginning], and you have come to be *continually* in need of milk, not solid food.

13 For everyone who lives on milk is [doctrinally inexperienced and] unskilled in the word of righteousness, since he is a *spiritual* infant.

5:1–4 *high priest.* He represents the people and thus must identify with their human nature. But he also represents God to the people and thus must be called by God to his office.

5:2 *ignorant and misguided.* This phrase describes those who unintentionally sin (Nu 15:30–36).

5:8 *He learned [active, special] obedience.* Jesus experienced all of what a person goes through on this earth. He knows how difficult it is to obey God completely, just as He understands the attraction of temptation (2:18).

5:9 *having been made perfect.* This phrase does not suggest that Jesus had not been perfect before. It means that He successfully carried out God's plan for Him. He endured suffering and temptation so that He could truly function as our High Priest, understanding our weaknesses and interceding before God for us.

5:12 *elementary principles.* The phrase refers to the letters of the alphabet in writing or to addition and subtraction tables in arithmetic. They are principles out of which everything else develops.

5:13 *unskilled in the word of righteousness.* The readers of this letter did not necessarily lack information concerning righteousness; they lacked experience in practicing the information they had.

CHAPTER 5 **1** Heb 8:3 **3** Lev 4:3 **4** 2Ch 26:18; Jn 3:27; Ex 28:1 **5** Jn 8:54; Ps 2:7 **6** Ps 110:4 **7** Mt 26:39; Mk 14:36; Jn 17:1; Ps 22:1; Mt 27:46; Mt 26:53; Mk 14:36; Mt 26:37; Mk 14:33; Lk 22:43; Jn 12:27 **8** Heb 3:6; Php 2:8 **11** Jn 16:12; 2Pe 3:16; Mt 13:15 **12** 1Co 3:1 **13** 1Co 13:11; Eph 4:14; 1Pe 2:2

THE "GREATER THANS" IN HEBREWS

One of the author's main points in Hebrews is that Jesus is greater than all those things associated with the Jewish religion and way of life. Sometimes he actually uses the words "greater than"; sometimes he does not. But in all cases the theme is clear.

THEME	PASSAGE IN HEBREWS
Jesus is greater than the prophets.	1:1–3
Jesus is greater than the angels.	1:4–14; 2:5
Jesus is greater than Moses.	3:1–6
Jesus is greater than Joshua.	4:6–11
Jesus is greater than the Aaronic high priests.	5:1–10; 7:26—8:2
Jesus is greater than the Levitical priests.	6:20—7:25
Jesus as the high priest in the order of Melchizedek is greater than Abraham.	7:1–10
Jesus' ministry is greater than the tabernacle ministry.	8:3–6; 9:1–28
Jesus' new covenant is greater than the old covenant.	8:7–13
Jesus' sacrifice is greater than the OT sacrifices.	10:1–14
Experiencing Jesus is greater than the experience on Mount Sinai.	12:18–24

Adapted from *The Expositor's Bible Commentary* - Abridged Edition: The New Testament, by Kenneth L. Barker; John R. Kohlenberger III.

14But solid food is for the [spiritually]
mature, whose senses are trained by
practice to distinguish between what
is morally good and *what is* evil.

The Peril of Falling Away

6 THEREFORE LET us get past the
elementary stage in the teachings
about the Christ, advancing on to
maturity *and* perfection *and* spiritu-
al completeness, [doing this] without
laying again a foundation of repen-
tance from dead works and of faith
toward God,
2of teaching about washings (ritual
purifications), the laying on of hands,
the resurrection of the dead, and eter-
nal judgment. [These are all important
matters in which you should have been
proficient long ago.]
3And we will do this [that is, proceed
to maturity], if God permits.
4For [it is impossible to restore to
repentance] those who have once been

6:1 *repentance from dead works.* This phrase refers to a change of mind about the demands of the law of Moses (9:14). Even though the law was good (1Ti 1:8), it was weak because of the weakness of our sinful nature (Ro 8:3). What is needed for salvation is not lifeless works that cannot save, but faith directed toward God.
6:2 *laying on of hands.* This action was used to impart the Holy Spirit (Ac 8:17–18; 19:6). It was also used for ordination of the ministry (Ac 6:6; 13:3). This practice is also found in the Old Testament in commissioning someone to a public office (Nu 27:18,23; Dt 34:9) or in the context of presenting a sacrificial offering to the Lord (Lev 1:4; 3:2; 4:4; 8:14; 16:21). ***eternal judgment.*** This refers to the belief that everyone will be judged by the great Judge.
6:4–6 *and then have fallen away.* This difficult passage has been interpreted in various ways. Some insist that the author is speaking of nominal Christians who heard the truth and appeared to believe in Christ but were not sincere in their faith. Others view these verses as a hypothetical argument. In other words, the author is using this hypothetical case to warn the spiritually immature. These two positions are supported by passages that speak of God's consistency in His work, that nothing can separate us from His love

14 Isa 7:15; 1Co 2:14 **CHAPTER 6** **1** Php 3:12-14; Heb 5:12; Heb 9:14 **2** Ac 19:4,5; 8:14; 19:6; Ac 17:31; Ac 24:25; Ro 2:16 **3** Ac 18:21 **4** Mt 12:31; Heb 10:26; 2Pe 2:20; 1Jn 5:16; Heb 10:32; Jn 4:10; 6:32; Eph 2:8; Gal 3:2,5; Heb 2:4

enlightened [spiritually] and who have tasted *and* consciously experienced the heavenly gift and have shared in the Holy Spirit,

5 and have tasted *and* consciously experienced the good word of God and the powers of the age (world) to come,

6 and then have fallen away—it is impossible to bring them back again to repentance, since they again nail the Son of God on the cross [for as far as they are concerned, they are treating the death of Christ as if they were not saved by it], and are holding Him up again to public disgrace.

7 For soil that drinks the rain which often falls on it and produces crops useful to those for whose benefit it is cultivated, receives a blessing from God;

8 but if it persistently produces thorns and thistles, it is worthless and close to being cursed, and it ends up being burned. [Gen 3:17, 18]

Better Things for You

9 But, beloved, even though we speak to you in this way, we are convinced of better things concerning you, and of things that accompany salvation.

10 For God is not unjust so as to forget your work and the love which you have shown for His name in ministering to [the needs of] the saints (God's people), as you do.

11 And we desire for each one of you to show the same diligence [all the way through] so as to realize *and* enjoy the full assurance of hope until the end,

12 so that you will not be [spiritually] sluggish, but [will instead be] imitators of those who through faith [lean on God with absolute trust and confidence in Him and in His power] and by patient endurance [even when suffering] are [now] inheriting the promises.

13 For when God made the promise to Abraham, He swore [an oath] by Himself, since He had no one greater by whom to swear,

14 saying, "I WILL SURELY BLESS YOU AND I WILL SURELY MULTIPLY YOU." [Gen 22:16, 17]

15 And so, having patiently waited, he realized the promise [in the miraculous birth of Isaac, as a pledge of what was to come from God].

16 Indeed men swear [an oath] by one greater *than themselves,* and with them [in all disputes] the oath *serves* as confirmation [of what has been said] and is an end of the dispute.

17 In the same way God, in His desire to show to the heirs of the promise the unchangeable nature of His purpose, intervened *and* guaranteed it with an oath,

18 so that by two unchangeable things [His promise and His oath] in which it is impossible for God to lie, we who have fled [to Him] for refuge would have strong encouragement *and* indwelling strength to hold tightly to the hope set before us.

19 This hope [this confident assurance] we have as an anchor of the soul [it cannot slip and it cannot break down under whatever pressure bears upon it]—a safe and steadfast hope that enters within the veil [of

---

(Jn 6:39–40; 10:27–29; Ro 8:28–30). But another group of commentators insists that the author is speaking of genuine Christians who renounce Christ. They point out that those who "tasted and consciously experienced the heavenly gift" fall away. Passages such as 2 Corinthians 11:1–4; 2 Timothy 2:17–18; 1 John 2:21–25 are in support of this position. Whatever way one interprets this passage, it is clear that the author of Hebrews has given us a clear warning not to renounce Christ or spurn His offer of salvation.

6:6 *bring them back.* In other words, it is impossible for continuous effort on the part of anyone in the Christian community to restore an apostate back to fellowship with God. Continuing Christian immaturity is dangerous.

6:13–15 *Abraham.* Here is an example of faith and patience in God's promise (v. 12). He waited 25 years from the time the promise was first made until Isaac, the promised son, was born (Ge 12:3–4; 15:4; 18:10; 21:5).

6:18 *two unchangeable things.* These things are God's Word and God's oath. Since God does not lie and since He is all-powerful, He will fulfill all His promises.

5 Heb 2:5 **6** Heb 10:29 **7** Ps 65:10 **8** Isa 5:6 **10** Pr 14:31; Mt 10:42; 25:40; Jn 13:20; Ro 3:4; 2Th 1:6,7; 1Th 1:3; Ro 15:25; 2Co 8:4; 2Ti 1:18 **11** Heb 3:6,14; Col 2:2 **12** Heb 10:36 **13** Ge 22:16,17; Ps 105:9; Lk 1:73 **16** Ex 22:11 **17** Heb 11:9; Ro 11:29 **18** Heb 12:1 **19** Lev 16:15; Heb 9:7

the heavenly temple, that most Holy Place in which the very presence of God dwells], [Lev 16:2]
[20]where Jesus has entered [in advance] as a forerunner for us, having become a High Priest forever according to the order of Melchizedek. [Ps 110:4]

Melchizedek's Priesthood Like Christ's

7 FOR THIS Melchizedek, king of Salem, priest of the Most High God, met Abraham as he returned from the slaughter of the kings and blessed him,
[2]and Abraham gave him a tenth of all [the spoil]. He is, first of all, by the translation *of his name,* king of righteousness, and then he is also king of Salem, which means king of peace.
[3]Without [any record of] father or mother, nor ancestral line, without [any record of] beginning of days (birth) nor ending of life (death), but having been made like the Son of God, he remains a priest without interruption *and* without successor.
[4]Now pause *and* consider how great this man was to whom Abraham, the patriarch, gave a tenth of the spoils.
[5]It is true that those descendants of Levi who are charged with the priestly office are commanded in the Law to collect tithes from the people—which means, from their kinsmen—though these have descended from Abraham.
[6]But this person [Melchizedek] who is not from their Levitical ancestry received tithes from Abraham and blessed him who possessed the promises [of God].
[7]Yet it is beyond all dispute that the lesser person is *always* blessed by the greater one.
[8]Furthermore, here [in the Levitical priesthood] tithes are received by men who are subject to death; but in that case [concerning Melchizedek], *they are received* by one of whom it is testified that he lives on [perpetually].
[9]A person might even say that Levi [the father of the priestly tribe] himself, who received tithes, paid tithes through Abraham [the father of all Israel and of all who believe],
[10]for Levi was still in the loins (unborn) of his forefather [Abraham] when Melchizedek met him (Abraham).
[11]Now if perfection [a perfect fellowship between God and the worshiper] had been attained through the Levitical priesthood (for under it the people were given the Law) what further need was there for another *and* different

---

6:20 *forerunner.* This word was used in the second century AD for the smaller boats sent into the harbor by larger ships unable to enter due to the buffeting of the weather. These smaller boats carried the anchor through the breakers inside the harbor and dropped it there, securing the larger ship. *Forerunner* also presupposes that others will follow. Thus, Jesus is like a runner boat that has taken our anchor into port and secured it there.

7:1 *Melchizedek.* The name means "king of righteousness." ***Salem*** means "peace." The ideal king rules in righteousness, which assures peace (Isa 32:17).

7:3 *Without [any record of] father or mother, nor ancestral line.* Genesis, a book with many genealogies, has none for Melchizedek. The author is not saying that Melchizedek was born without a father and mother, only that there is no record of his birth in the genealogies of Genesis. This description of Melchizedek prefigures the eternal priesthood of Jesus. Like Melchizedek, Jesus is both a Priest and a King belonging to a righteous priesthood that is independent of Aaron's.

7:4 *patriarch.* In the Greek text this word is emphatic. The greatness of Abraham, the one who possessed the promises of God (v. 6), underscores the even greater rank of Melchizedek, the priest of righteousness.

7:8 – 10 *tithes are received by men who are subject to death.* Melchizedek was not only superior to Abraham, but he was also superior to the Levitical priesthood in two ways: first, the Levitical priests were mortal. In contrast, Melchizedek seems to be immortal. At least, the Old Testament does not record his death. Second, in a sense, Levi paid tithes to Melchizedek through Abraham's gift. Because he was descended from Abraham, he is counted as having paid tithes to Melchizedek.

---

20 Heb 4:14; 8:1; 9:24; 3:1; 5:6,10; 7:17 **CHAPTER 7** **1** Ge 14:18 **4** Ge 14:20 **5** Nu 18:21,26 **6** Ge 14:19; Ro 4:13 **8** Heb 5:6; 6:20 **11** ver. 18,19; Gal 2:21; Heb 8:7

kind of priest to arise, one in the man-
ner of Melchizedek, rather than one
appointed to the order of Aaron?
12 For when there is a change in
the priesthood, there is of necessity
a change of the law [concerning the
priesthood] as well.
13 For the One of whom these things
are said belonged [not to the priestly
line of Levi but] to another tribe, from
which no one has officiated *or* served
at the altar.
14 For it is evident that our Lord de-
scended from [the tribe of] Judah,
and Moses mentioned nothing about
priests in connection with that tribe.
15 And this becomes even more ev-
ident if another priest arises in the
likeness of Melchizedek, [Ps 110:4]
16 who has become *a priest,* not on
the basis of a physical *and* legal re-
quirement in the Law [concerning his
ancestry as a descendant of Levi], but
on the basis of the power of an inde-
structible *and* endless life.
17 For it is attested [by God] of Him,

"You (Christ) are a Priest forever
According to the order of
Melchizedek." [Ps 110:4]

18 For, on the one hand, a former com-
mandment is cancelled because of its
weakness and uselessness [because of
its inability to justify the sinner before
God]
19 (for the Law never made anything
perfect); while on the other hand a bet-
ter hope is introduced through which
we now *continually* draw near to God.
20 And indeed it was not without the
taking of an oath [that Christ was
made priest]
21 (for those *Levites* who formerly
became priests [received their office]
without [its being confirmed by the
taking of] an oath, but this One [was
designated] with an oath through the
One who said to Him,

"The Lord has sworn
And will not change His mind *or*
regret it,
'You (Christ) are a Priest
forever' "). [Ps 110:4]

22 And so [because of the oath's greater
strength and force] Jesus has become
the certain guarantee of a better cov-
enant [a more excellent and more ad-
vantageous agreement; one that will
never be replaced or annulled].
23 The [former successive line of]
priests, on the one hand, existed in
greater numbers because they were
each prevented by death from continu-
ing [perpetually in office];
24 but, on the other hand, Jesus holds
His priesthood permanently *and* with-
out change, because He lives on forever.
25 Therefore He is able also to save for-
ever (completely, perfectly, for eternity)
those who come to God through Him,
since He always lives to intercede *and*
intervene on their behalf [with God].
26 It was fitting for us to have such a
High Priest [perfectly adapted to our
needs], holy, blameless, unstained [by
sin], separated from sinners and exalt-
ed higher than the heavens;

7:12 *change.* This word means removal (12:27). If the Melchizedek priesthood removed the Levitical priesthood, then the Mosaic law is also removed. In short, the believer is not under the law but instead relies on the righteousness of Christ (Ro 6:14; Gal 3:24–25).
7:15–18 *but on the basis of the power of an indestructible and endless life.* This point is proved by Psalm 110:4, quoted in verse 17. Jesus is a different kind of priest, another indication that the law has been changed. There has been a *disannulling,* a putting away, of the law.
7:25 *He is able also to save.* Christ is able to save because He is fully God and fully human (2:18; 4:15). Since this verse speaks to Jesus' present intercession for us, the word "save" in this verse speaks of our sanctification, the continuing process by which we are freed from the power of sin. This continuing process of salvation will eventually be completed in our glorification, when we are saved from the presence of sin.
7:26–28 *no day by day need, like those high priests.* The high priest offered an annual sacrifice on the Day of Atonement for the atonement of the people's sins (9:7; 10:1), but the priests also offered sacrifices every day before

14 Isa 11:1; Mt 1:3; Lk 3:33; Ro 1:3; Rev 5:5 **17** Ps 110:4; Heb 6:20 **18** Ro 8:3; Gal 4:9 **19** Ac 13:39; Ro 3:20,21,28; Heb 6:18; Ro 5:2; Eph 2:18; Heb 4:16 **21** Ps 110:4 **22** Heb 8:6 **25** Ro 8:34; 1Ti 2:5; 1Jn 2:1 **26** Heb 4:15; Eph 1:20; 4:10

27 who has no day by day need, like those high priests, to offer sacrifices, first of all for his own [personal] sins and then for those of the people, because He [met all the requirements and] did this once for all when He offered up Himself [as a willing sacrifice].

28 For the Law appoints men as high priests who are weak [frail, sinful, dying men], but the word of the oath [of God], which came after [the institution of] the Law, *permanently appoints* [as priest] a Son who has been made perfect forever. [Ps 110:4]

A Better Ministry

8 NOW THE main point of what we have to say *is this:* we have such a High Priest, [the Christ] who is seated [in the place of honor] at the right hand of the throne of the Majesty (God) in heaven, [Ps 110:1]

2 a Minister (Officiating Priest) in the holy places and in the true tabernacle, which is erected not by man, but by the Lord.

3 For every high priest is appointed to offer both gifts and sacrifices; so it is essential for this One also to have something to offer.

4 Now if He were [still living] on earth, He would not be a priest at all, for there are priests who offer the gifts [to God] in accordance with the Law.

5 They serve as a pattern and foreshadowing of [what has its true existence and reality in] the heavenly things (sanctuary). For when Moses was about to erect the tabernacle, he was warned *by God*, saying, "SEE THAT YOU MAKE it all [exactly] ACCORDING TO THE PATTERN WHICH WAS SHOWN TO YOU ON THE MOUNTAIN." [Ex 25:40]

6 But as it is, Christ has acquired a [priestly] ministry which is more excellent [than the old Levitical priestly ministry], for He is the Mediator (Arbiter) of a better covenant [uniting God and man], which has been enacted *and* rests on better promises.

A New Covenant

7 For if that first *covenant* had been faultless, there would have been no occasion for a second one *or* an attempt to institute another one [the new covenant].

8 However, God finds fault with them [showing its inadequacy] when He says,

"BEHOLD, THE DAYS WILL COME, SAYS THE LORD,
WHEN I WILL MAKE *and* RATIFY A NEW COVENANT
WITH THE HOUSE OF ISRAEL AND WITH THE HOUSE OF JUDAH;
9 NOT LIKE THE COVENANT THAT I MADE WITH THEIR FATHERS
ON THE DAY WHEN I TOOK THEM BY THE HAND
TO LEAD THEM OUT OF THE LAND OF EGYPT;
FOR THEY DID NOT ABIDE IN MY COVENANT,
AND SO I WITHDREW MY FAVOR *and* DISREGARDED THEM, SAYS THE LORD.
10 "FOR THIS IS THE COVENANT THAT I WILL MAKE WITH THE HOUSE OF ISRAEL

---

the Lord (Ex 29:36). In contrast Jesus offered Himself once, a perfect, sinless sacrifice for the sins of all. Since Jesus is perfect, He did not have to offer sacrifices for His own sins.

8:2 *holy places.* This term refers to the heavenly reality represented by the most holy place (9:2,8,24; 10:19; 13:11). The reality is the presence of God. Our High Priest serves there and desires to bring us there (10:19).

8:8 *A NEW COVENANT.* This covenant is the "better covenant" of verse 6. This covenant was made with Israel and Judah, yet the church enjoys the spiritual blessings of this covenant now. The Abrahamic covenant was made with Abraham and his physical descendants (Ge 17:7). Yet the Abrahamic covenant also contained spiritual promise (Ge 12:3) in which the church participates (Ro 11:11 – 27; Gal 3:13 – 14). The new covenant in fact is a fulfillment of the spiritual redemption promise in the Abrahamic and Davidic covenants (Mt 26:26 – 29; Lk 22:20).

8:10 – 12 *AFTER THOSE DAYS, SAYS THE LORD.* There are four provisions of the new covenant: (1) God's law will be written on believers' minds

---

27 Lev 9:7; Lev 16:15; Ro 6:10 **28** Heb 5:1,2; Heb 2:10; 5:9 **CHAPTER 8** **1** Eph 1:20; Col 3:1; Heb 10:12 **2** Heb 9:8,11,12 **3** Heb 5:1; Eph 5:2; Heb 9:14 **5** Col 2:17; Heb 9:23; Ex 25:40; Nu 8:4; Ac 7:44 **6** 2Co 3:6,8; Heb 7:22 **7** Heb 7:11,18 **8** Jer 31:31 **10** Heb 10:16; Zec 8:8

After those days, says the Lord:
I will imprint My laws upon
their minds [even upon their
innermost thoughts and
understanding],
And engrave them upon their
hearts [effecting their
regeneration].
And I will be their God,
And they shall be My people.
11 "And it will not be [necessary]
for each one to teach his fellow
citizen,
Or each one his brother, saying,
'Know [by experience, have
knowledge of] the Lord,'
For all will know [Me by
experience and have knowledge
of] Me,
From the least to the greatest
of them.
12 "For I will be merciful *and*
gracious toward their
wickedness,
And I will remember their sins no
more." [Jer 31:31–34]

13 When God speaks of "A new *covenant*," He makes the first one obsolete. And whatever is becoming obsolete (out of use, annulled) and growing old is ready to disappear.

The Old and the New

9 NOW EVEN the first *covenant* had regulations for divine worship and for the earthly sanctuary. [Ex 25:10–40]
2 A tabernacle (sacred tent) was put up, the outer one *or* first section, in which were the lampstand and the table with [its loaves of] the sacred showbread; this is called the Holy Place. [Lev 24:5, 6]
3 Behind the second veil there was another tabernacle [the inner one or second section] known as the Holy of Holies, [Ex 26:31–33]
4 having the golden altar of incense and the ark of the covenant covered entirely with gold. This contained a golden jar which held the manna, and the rod of Aaron that sprouted, and the [two stone] tablets of the covenant [inscribed with the Ten Commandments]; [Ex 16:32–34; 30:1–6; Num 17:8–10]
5 and above the ark were the [golden] cherubim of glory overshadowing the mercy seat; but we cannot now go into detail about these things.
6 Now when these things have been prepared in this way, the priests continually enter the outer [or first section of the] tabernacle [that is, the Holy Place] performing [their ritual acts of] the divine worship,
7 but into the second [inner tabernacle, the Holy of Holies], only the high priest *enters* [and then only] once a year, and never without [bringing a sacrifice of] blood, which he offers [as a substitutionary atonement] for himself and for the sins of the people committed in ignorance. [Lev 16:15]
8 By this the Holy Spirit signifies that

---

and hearts. (2) Believers will have a relationship with God fulfilling the promise of Leviticus 26:12 (2Co 6:16). (3) All will know God. No longer will Pharisees and scribes have to teach the intricacies of the law to the people. (4) God will forgive the sins of believers and remember them no more. The continual sacrifice of animals for the atonement of sin will cease.

8:13 *becoming obsolete (out of use, annulled) and growing old.* At the time the author of Hebrews wrote these words, the ceremonies of the Mosaic covenant were still being conducted in the temple in Jerusalem. In AD 70 the Roman general Titus destroyed the temple, fulfilling these words.

9:2–5 *A tabernacle (sacred tent) was put up.* These verses simply describe the furniture of the tabernacle. The tabernacle courtyard contained an altar for animal sacrifice and a laver for ceremonial washings. The tabernacle was divided into two rooms by a veil. The first part was the sanctuary or holy place, housing the lampstand, the table for the showbread, and the altar of incense. The second room was the most holy place, containing the ark of the covenant, in which were stored the symbols of the Mosaic covenant.

9:7–8 *once a year.* In the provisions of the Mosaic covenant, access to God was limited. The fact that the high priest had such little access himself

11 Isa 54:13; Jn 6:45; 1Jn 2:27 **12** Ro 11:27 **13** 2Co 5:17 **CHAPTER 9** **1** Ex 25:8 **2** Ex 26:1; Ex 26:35; Ex 25:31; Ex 25:23 **3** Ex 26:31 **4** Ex 25:10; Ex 16:33; Nu 17:10; Ex 25:16; Dt 10:2 **5** Lev 16:2 **6** Nu 28:3 **7** Ex 30:10; Heb 7:27 **8** Heb 10:19; Jn 14:6

the way into the Holy Place [the true Holy of Holies and the presence of God] has not yet been disclosed as long as the first *or* outer tabernacle is still standing [that is, as long as the Levitical system of worship remains a recognized institution],
[9]for this [first or outer tabernacle] is a symbol [that is, an archetype or paradigm] for the present time. Accordingly both gifts and sacrifices are offered which are incapable of perfecting the conscience *and* renewing the [inner self of the] worshiper.
[10]For they [the gifts, sacrifices, and ceremonies] deal only with [clean and unclean] food and drink and various ritual washings, [mere] external regulations for the body imposed [to help the worshipers] until the time of reformation [that is, the time of the new order when Christ will establish the reality of what these things foreshadow—a better covenant].
[11]But when Christ appeared as a High Priest of the good things to come [that is, true spiritual worship], *He entered* through the greater and more perfect tabernacle, not made with hands, that is to say, not a part of this [material] creation.
[12]He went once for all into the Holy Place [the Holy of Holies of heaven, into the presence of God], and not through the blood of goats and calves, but through His own blood, having obtained *and* secured eternal redemption [that is, the salvation of all who personally believe in Him as Savior].
[13]For if the sprinkling of [ceremonially] defiled persons with the blood of goats and bulls and the ashes of a [burnt] heifer is sufficient for the cleansing of the body, [Lev 16:6, 16; Num 19:9, 17, 18]
[14]how much more will the blood of Christ, who through the eternal [Holy] Spirit *willingly* offered Himself unblemished [that is, without moral or spiritual imperfection as a sacrifice] to God, cleanse your conscience from dead works *and* lifeless observances to serve the ever living God?
[15]For this reason He is the Mediator *and* Negotiator of a new covenant [that is, an entirely new agreement uniting God and man], so that those who have been called [by God] may receive [the fulfillment of] the promised eternal inheritance, since a death has taken place [as the payment] which redeems them from the sins *committed* under the *obsolete* first covenant.
[16]For where there is a will *and* testament involved, the death of the one who made it must be established,
[17]for a will *and* testament takes effect [only] at death, since it is never in force as long as the one who made it is alive.
[18]So even the first *covenant* was not put in force without [the shedding of] blood.
[19]For when every commandment in the Law had been read by Moses to

---

indicates the striking failure of the Mosaic covenant to bring believers into the presence of God.

9:9 are incapable of perfecting the conscience and renewing the [inner self of the] worshiper. The Mosaic covenant covered sins of ignorance (v. 7), but not premeditated sins or the sinful nature of all people (Ps 51). In other words, the old system was lacking. It did not completely reconcile the people to God.

9:12 through His own blood. Christ obtained eternal redemption. His sacrifice never has to be repeated because it is perfect.

9:13 ashes of a [burnt] heifer. These were mixed with water and were used to cleanse a person who had become ceremonially defiled by touching a corpse (Nu 19:11 – 13). The author of Hebrews points out that these ceremonies could purify only a person's exterior, not a person's heart.

9:14 the eternal [Holy] Spirit. All three persons of the Trinity are involved in cleansing. The defilement is internal, not external (v. 13). Christ's death has the power to purify a person's mind and soul.

9:15 redeems. Christ paid the price to free us from our own sin. His death substitutes for our death, the penalty of our sins. Like the Israelites, believers receive an inheritance, but our inheritance is eternal (v. 14).

9 Gal 3:21 **10** Col 2:16; Nu 19:7; Eph 2:15 **11** Heb 3:1; Heb 10:1; Heb 8:2 **12** Heb 10:4; Eph 1:7; Col 1:14; Zec 3:9; Da 9:24 **13** Lev 16:14; Nu 19:2 **14** 1Jn 1:7; Ro 1:4; Heb 10:22; Heb 6:1; Lk 1:74 **15** 1Ti 2:5; Heb 7:22; Ro 3:25; Heb 3:1 **17** Gal 3:15 **18** Ex 24:6 **19** Ex 24:5,6; Lev 14:4

all the people, he took the blood of the calves and goats [which had been sacrificed], together with water and scarlet wool and with a bunch of hyssop, and he sprinkled both the scroll itself and all the people,

20 saying, "THIS IS THE BLOOD OF THE COVENANT [that seals and ratifies the agreement] WHICH GOD ORDAINED *and* COMMANDED [me to deliver to] YOU." [Ex 24:6–8]

21 And in the same way he sprinkled both the tabernacle and all the containers *and* sacred utensils of worship with the blood.

22 In fact under the Law almost everything is cleansed with blood, and without the shedding of blood there is no forgiveness [neither release from sin and its guilt, nor cancellation of the merited punishment].

23 Therefore it was necessary for the [earthly] copies of the heavenly things to be cleansed with these, but the heavenly things themselves required far better sacrifices than these.

24 For Christ did not enter into a holy place made with hands, a mere copy of the true one, but [He entered] into heaven itself, now to appear in the very presence of God on our behalf;

25 nor did He [enter into the heavenly sanctuary to] offer Himself again and again, as the high priest enters the Holy Place every year with blood that is not his own.

26 Otherwise, He would have needed to suffer over and over since the foundation of the world; but now once for all at the consummation of the ages He has appeared *and* been publicly manifested to put away sin by the sacrifice of Himself.

27 And just as it is appointed *and* destined for all men to die once and after this [comes certain] judgment,

28 so Christ, having been offered once *and* once for all to bear [as a burden] the sins of many, will appear a second time [when he returns to earth], not to deal with sin, but to bring salvation to those who are eagerly *and* confidently waiting for Him.

One Sacrifice of Christ Is Sufficient

10 FOR SINCE the Law has only a shadow [just a pale representation] of the good things to come—not the very image of those things—it can never, by offering the same sacrifices continually year after year, make perfect those who approach [its altars].

2 For if it were otherwise, would not these sacrifices have stopped being offered? For the worshipers, having once [for all time] been cleansed, would no longer have a consciousness of sin.

3 But [as it is] these [continual] *sacrifices* bring a fresh reminder of sins [to be atoned for] year after year,

4 for it is impossible for the blood of bulls and goats to take away sins.

5 Therefore, when Christ enters into the world, He says,

"SACRIFICE AND OFFERING YOU HAVE NOT DESIRED,
BUT [instead] YOU HAVE PREPARED A BODY FOR ME [to offer];

9:24 *Christ did not enter into a holy place made with hands.* Christ's sacrifice was better than sacrifices made under the Mosaic covenant because Christ did not enter a man-made sanctuary, which was a copy; instead, He entered the true sanctuary, which is in heaven — the very presence of God.

9:26 *but now once.* Christ's sacrifice was better than the sacrifices made under the Mosaic covenant because He did not offer an annual sacrifice of animals but offered Himself once for all time.

10:1 – 4 *not the very image of those things.* The sacrifices of the Mosaic covenant prefigured Christ's ultimate sacrifice of Himself. Therefore, these imperfect sacrifices of mere animals could not completely purify the person who offered them. If they had been able to, these sacrifices would have ceased. Instead of thoroughly atoning for the sins of the people, the annual sacrifice on the Day of Atonement was a visible reminder of the people's sins.

10:5 – 7 *TO DO YOUR WILL.* The Old Testament prophets had warned the Israelites that sacrifices alone would not please God. He desired

20 Ex 24:8; Mt 26:28 **21** Ex 29:12; Lev 8:15 **22** Lev 17:11 **23** Heb 8:5 **24** Heb 6:20; Heb 8:2; Ro 8:34; 1Jn 2:1 **25** ver. 7 **26** Heb 7:27; 1Co 10:11 **27** Ge 3:19; Ecc 3:20; 2Co 5:10 **28** Ro 6:10; 1Pe 3:18; 2:24; 1Jn 3:5; Mt 26:28; Ro 5:15; Titus 2:13 **CHAPTER 10** **1** Col 2:17; Heb 9:9,11; ver. 14 **3** Heb 9:7 **4** Mic 6:6,7 **5** Ps 40:6

[6] IN BURNT OFFERINGS AND *sacrifices*
FOR SIN YOU HAVE TAKEN NO
DELIGHT.
[7] "THEN I SAID, 'BEHOLD, I HAVE COME
TO DO YOUR WILL, O GOD—
[TO FULFILL] WHAT IS WRITTEN OF
ME IN THE SCROLL OF THE BOOK.' "
[Ps 40:6–8]

[8] After saying [in the citation] above,
"YOU HAVE NEITHER DESIRED, NOR HAVE
YOU TAKEN DELIGHT IN SACRIFICES AND OF-
FERINGS AND WHOLE BURNT OFFERINGS AND
sacrifices FOR SIN" (which are offered
according to the Law)
[9] then He said, "BEHOLD, I HAVE COME TO
DO YOUR WILL." [And so] He does away
with the first [covenant as a means
of atoning for sin based on animal
sacrifices] so that He may inaugurate
and establish the second [covenant by
means of obedience]. [Ps 40:6–8]
[10] And in accordance with this will
[of God] we [who believe in the mes-
sage of salvation] have been sanctified
[that is, set apart as holy for God and
His purposes] through the offering of
the body of Jesus Christ (the Messiah,
the Anointed) once for all.
[11] Every priest stands [at his altar of
service] ministering daily, offering the
same sacrifices over and over, which
are never able to strip away sins [that
envelop and cover us];
[12] whereas Christ, having offered the
one sacrifice [the all-sufficient sacri-
fice of Himself] for sins for all time,
SAT DOWN [signifying the completion of
atonement for sin] AT THE RIGHT HAND OF
GOD [the position of honor],
[13] waiting from that time onward UN-
TIL HIS ENEMIES ARE MADE A FOOTSTOOL FOR
HIS FEET. [Ps 110:1]
[14] For by the one offering He has per-
fected forever *and* completely cleansed
those who are being sanctified [bring-
ing each believer to spiritual comple-
tion and maturity].
[15] And the Holy Spirit also adds His
testimony to us [in confirmation of
this]; for after having said,

[16] "THIS IS THE COVENANT THAT I WILL
MAKE WITH THEM
AFTER THOSE DAYS, SAYS THE LORD:
I WILL IMPRINT MY LAWS UPON THEIR
HEART,
AND ON THEIR MIND I WILL INSCRIBE
THEM [producing an inward
change],"

He then says,

[17] "AND THEIR SINS AND THEIR LAWLESS
ACTS
I WILL REMEMBER NO MORE [no longer
holding their sins against
them]." [Jer 31:33, 34]

[18] Now where there is [absolute] for-
giveness *and* complete cancellation
of the penalty of these things, there is
no longer any offering [to be made to
atone] for sin.

A New and Living Way

[19] Therefore, believers, since we
have confidence *and* full freedom to
enter the Holy Place [the place where
God dwells] by [means of] the blood
of Jesus,
[20] by this new and living way which
He initiated *and* opened for us through

---

obedience as well (Ps 51:16–17; Isa 1:13–17; Mk 12:33). This messianic psalm indicates that Jesus' obedience to God the Father was one of the reasons His sacrifice was better than the Old Testament sacrifices.

10:8–9 *He does away with the first ... so that He may inaugurate and establish the second.* The author is explaining Psalm 40. The verb translated "does away with" means "abolishes." The imperfect sacrifices were abolished so that the perfect Sacrifice could impart true life.

10:11–12 *SAT DOWN.* Sitting indicates that His work of atonement is finished. His final words on the cross, "It is finished," declare this spiritual reality (Jn 19:30).

10:16–18 *I WILL REMEMBER NO MORE.* This phrase does not mean to forget, but not to hold sin against us any longer.

10:19 *Therefore.* The author has spent five chapters explaining the superiority of Christ's priesthood to the Levitical priesthood and the superiority of the new covenant to the Mosaic covenant. Unlike the Israelites, who approached God at Mount Sinai with fear and trembling (Ex

10 Jn 17:19; Heb 9:12 **11** Nu 28:3; ver. 4 **12** Col 3:1 **13** Ps 110:1; Ac 2:35 **14** ver. 1 **16** Heb 8:10,12 **19** Eph 2:18; Heb 9:8,12 **20** Jn 10:9; Heb 9:3

the veil [as in the Holy of Holies], that is, through His flesh,
[21]and since we have a great *and* wonderful Priest [Who rules] over the house of God,
[22]let us approach [God] with a true *and* sincere heart in unqualified assurance of faith, having had our hearts sprinkled *clean* from an evil conscience and our bodies washed with pure water.
[23]Let us seize *and* hold tightly the confession of our hope without wavering, for He who promised is reliable *and* trustworthy *and* faithful [to His word];
[24]and let us consider [thoughtfully] how we may encourage one another to love and to do good deeds,
[25]not forsaking our meeting together [as believers for worship and instruction], as is the habit of some, but encouraging *one another;* and all the more [faithfully] as you see the day [of Christ's return] approaching.

Christ or Judgment

[26]For if we go on willfully *and* deliberately sinning after receiving the knowledge of the truth, there no longer remains a sacrifice [to atone] for our sins [that is, no further offering to anticipate],
[27]but a kind of awful *and* terrifying expectation of [divine] judgment and THE FURY OF A FIRE *and* BURNING WRATH WHICH WILL CONSUME THE ADVERSARIES [those who put themselves in opposition to God]. [Is 26:11]
[28]Anyone who has ignored *and* set aside the Law of Moses is put to death without mercy on *the testimony of* two or three witnesses. [Deut 17:2–6]
[29]How much greater punishment do you think he will deserve who has rejected *and* trampled under foot the Son of God, and has considered unclean *and* common the blood of the covenant that sanctified him, and has insulted the Spirit of grace [who imparts the unmerited favor and blessing of God]? [Ex 24:8]
[30]For we know Him who said, "VENGEANCE IS MINE [retribution and the deliverance of justice rest with Me], I WILL REPAY [the wrongdoer]." And again, "THE LORD WILL JUDGE HIS PEOPLE." [Deut 32:35, 36]
[31]It is a fearful *and* terrifying thing to fall into the hands of the living God [incurring His judgment and wrath].
[32]But remember the earlier days,

20:18 – 21), believers can approach God with boldness (3:6; 4:16; 10:35) because we possess Christ's righteousness and not our own.

10:20 *His flesh.* The Old Testament high priest passed through a veil to get to the most holy place. Now, believers enter God's presence through Christ's flesh, meaning His sacrificial death.

10:22 *our hearts sprinkled . . . our bodies washed.* Our consciences can be cleansed through the blood of Christ (9:14). Just as the high priest washed before entering the most holy place (Lev 16:3 – 4), so believers are cleansed before they come before the Holy One.

10:24 – 25 *encourage one another to love and to do good deeds.* The Greek word translated "encourage" carries the sense of "convulsion." In this context the word speaks forcefully of the tremendous impact believers can have on each other. That is why the author exhorts the Hebrews to gather together. Evidently, some believers had stopped attending the worship services of the church, perhaps because they feared persecution.

10:26 *willfully and deliberately sinning.* The reference here is not to an occasional act of sin (which can be confessed and forgiven) but to a conscious rejection of God. The Old Testament speaks in Numbers 15:30 – 31 of committing willful sin. A person who sinned presumptuously was to be cut off from the people. To sin deliberately after receiving the knowledge of the truth is apostasy. If a Christian rejects God's provision for his or her salvation, there is no other remedy for sins, since forgiveness for sins can only be found in Christ's perfect sacrifice.

10:29 *Spirit of grace.* This is a reference to the Holy Spirit, the agent of God's gracious gift of salvation. A believer who commits these offenses will be judged with a punishment worse than physical death.

---

21 Heb 4:14; 1Ti 3:15 **22** Heb 4:16; Eph 3:12; Heb 9:14; Eze 36:25 **23** Heb 4:14; 1Co 1:9; 2Th 3:3 **25** Ac 2:42; Ro 13:11; Php 4:5; 2Pe 3:9 **26** Nu 15:30; 2Pe 2:20 **27** Zep 1:18; 2Th 1:8 **28** Heb 2:2; Mt 18:16 **29** Heb 2:3; 1Co 11:29; Mt 12:31; Eph 4:30 **30** Dt 32:35,36 **31** Lk 12:5 **32** Gal 3:4; Heb 6:4; Php 1:29; Col 2:1

when, after being [spiritually] enlightened, you [patiently] endured a great conflict of sufferings,

33 sometimes by being made a spectacle, publicly exposed to insults and distress, and sometimes by becoming companions with those who were so treated.

34 For you showed sympathy *and* deep concern for those who were imprisoned, and you joyfully accepted the [unjust] seizure of your belongings *and* the confiscation of your property, conscious of the fact that you have a better possession and a lasting one [prepared for you in heaven].

35 Do not, therefore, fling away your [fearless] confidence, for it has a glorious *and* great reward.

36 For you have need of patient endurance [to bear up under difficult circumstances without compromising], so that when you have carried out the will of God, you may receive *and* enjoy to the full what is promised.

37 For yet in a very little while,
He who is coming will come, and
will not delay.
38 But My righteous one [the one
justified by faith] shall live
by faith [respecting man's
relationship to God and trusting
Him];
And if he draws back [shrinking in
fear], My soul has no delight in
him. [Hab 2:3, 4]

39 But our way is not that of those who shrink back to destruction, but [we are] of those who believe [relying on God through faith in Jesus Christ, the Messiah] *and* by this confident faith preserve the soul.

The Triumphs of Faith

11 NOW FAITH is the assurance (title deed, confirmation) of things hoped for (divinely guaranteed), and the evidence of things not seen [the conviction of their reality—faith comprehends as fact what cannot be experienced by the physical senses].

2 For by this [kind of] faith the men of old gained [divine] approval.

3 By faith [that is, with an inherent trust and enduring confidence in the power, wisdom and goodness of God] we understand that the worlds (universe, ages) were framed *and* created [formed, put in order, and equipped for their intended purpose] by the word of God, so that what is seen was not made out of things which are visible.

4 By faith Abel offered to God a more acceptable sacrifice than Cain, through which it was testified of him that he was righteous (upright, in right standing with God), and God testified by accepting his gifts. And though he died, yet through [this act of] faith he still speaks. [Gen 4:3–10]

5 By faith [that pleased God] Enoch was caught up *and* taken to heaven so that he would not have a glimpse of death; and he was not found because God had taken him; for even before he was taken [to heaven], he received the testimony [still on record] that he had walked with God *and* pleased Him. [Gen 5:21–24]

6 But without faith it is impossible to [walk with God and] please Him, for

---

10:35 *Do not, therefore, fling away your [fearless] confidence.* For the recipients of Hebrews to return to the safety of Judaism would mean a loss of eternal reward at the judgment seat of Christ.

11:1 *Now faith is.* This verse is not a definition of faith, but a description of what faith does. ***assurance.*** This means "essence" or "reality." Faith treats things hoped for as reality. ***evidence.*** This means "proof." Faith itself proves that what is unseen is real, such as the believer's rewards at the return of Christ (2Co 4:18).

11:4 *a more acceptable sacrifice than Cain.* Evidently, Cain offered his sacrifice without faith (Ge 4). ***still speaks.*** Abel still speaks to us because his righteous deeds have been recorded in Scripture.

11:6 *comes.* This word is used repeatedly in Hebrews to refer to the privilege of drawing near to God (4:16; 7:25; 10:1,22). Here, the author of

33 1Co 4:9; Php 1:7 **34** 2Ti 1:16; Mt 5:12; Mt 6:20 **35** Mt 5:12 **36** Lk 21:19; Col 3:24 **37** Lk 18:8; Hab 2:3,4 **38** Ro 1:17; Gal 3:11 **39** 2Pe 2:20; Ac 16:31; 1Th 5:9; 2Th 2:14 **CHAPTER 11** **1** Ro 8:24; 2Co 4:18 **2** ver. 39 **3** Ge 1:1; Ps 33:6; Jn 1:3; 2Pe 3:5 **4** Ge 4:4; 1Jn 3:12 **5** Ge 5:22

whoever comes [near] to God must [necessarily] believe that God exists and that He rewards those who [earnestly and diligently] seek Him.

7 By faith [with confidence in God and His word] Noah, being warned *by God* about events not yet seen, in reverence prepared an ark for the salvation of his family. By this [act of obedience] he condemned the world and became an heir of the righteousness which comes by faith. [Gen 6:13–22]

8 By faith Abraham, when he was called [by God], obeyed by going to a place which he was to receive as an inheritance; and he went, not knowing where he was going.

9 By faith he lived as a foreigner in the promised land, as in a strange *land,* living in tents [as nomads] with Isaac and Jacob, who were fellow heirs of the same promise. [Gen 12:1–8]

10 For he was [waiting expectantly and confidently] looking forward to the city which has foundations, [an eternal, heavenly city] whose architect and builder is God.

11 By faith even Sarah herself received the ability to conceive [a child], even [when she was long] past the normal age for it, because she considered Him who had given her the promise to be reliable *and* true [to His word]. [Gen 17:19; 18:11–14; 21:2]

12 So from one man, though he was [physically] as good as dead, were born *as many descendants* AS THE STARS OF HEAVEN IN NUMBER, AND INNUMERABLE AS THE SAND ON THE SEASHORE. [Gen 15:5, 6; 22:17; 32:12]

13 All these died in faith [guided and sustained by it], without receiving the [tangible fulfillment of God's] promises, only having seen (anticipated) them and having welcomed them from a distance, and having acknowledged that they were strangers and exiles on the earth. [Gen 23:4; Ps 39:12]

14 Now those who say such things make it clear that they are looking for a country of their own.

15 And if they had been thinking of that *country* from which they departed [as their true home], they would have had [a continuing] opportunity to return.

16 But the truth is that they were longing for a better country, that is, a heavenly one. For that reason God is not ashamed [of them or] to be called their God [even to be surnamed their God—the God of Abraham, Isaac, and Jacob]; for He has prepared a city for them. [Ex 3:6, 15; 4:5]

17 By faith Abraham, when he was tested [that is, as the testing of his faith was still in progress], offered up Isaac, and he who had received the promises [of God] was ready to sacrifice his only son [of promise]; [Gen 22:1–10]

18 to whom it was said, "THROUGH ISAAC YOUR DESCENDANTS SHALL BE CALLED." [Gen 21:12]

19 For he considered [it reasonable to believe] that God was able to raise *Isaac* even from among the dead. [Indeed, in the sense that he was prepared to sacrifice Isaac in obedience to God] Abraham did receive him back [from the dead] figuratively speaking.

Hebrews explains that faith is mandatory for those who approach Him. ***rewards.*** God rewards not only those who seek Him, but also those who do good works in the Holy Spirit's power (Rev 22:12).

11:8 *not knowing where he was going.* Abraham placed his trust in God. Faith means obediently stepping into the unknown (v. 1). Abraham did this, and God considered him righteous because of it (Ge 15:6; Ro 4:1 – 12).

11:15 *opportunity to return.* The patriarchs and Sarah did not return to Ur, even though they could have if they had wanted to. The recipients of Hebrews were to follow the patriarchs' example and refuse to return to the religion of their ancestors, a religious system that no longer provided atonement for sin (8:7 – 13).

11:17 – 19 *Abraham ... tested.* Abraham believed that God could raise Isaac from the dead (Ge 22:5), if necessary. The incident is figurative of what God has done for us. Isaac was as good as dead, but God provided a ram to sacrifice in his place (Ge 22:9 – 14).

7 Ge 6:13; 1Pe 3:20; Ro 3:22; Php 3:9 **8** Ge 12:1; Ac 7:2-4 **9** Ge 12:8; Heb 6:17 **10** Heb 12:22; Rev 21:10 **11** Ge 17:19; 18:11,14; Lk 1:36; Ro 4:21 **12** Ro 4:19; Ro 4:18 **13** ver. 39; Jn 8:56; Ge 23:4; 1Ch 29:15; Ps 39:12; 1Pe 1:17 **14** Heb 13:14 **16** Ex 3:6,15; Mt 22:32; Ac 7:32; Heb 13:14 **17** Ge 22:1; Jas 2:21 **18** Ge 21:12; Ro 9:7 **19** Ro 4:17

20 By faith Isaac blessed Jacob and Esau [believing what God revealed to him], even regarding things to come. [Gen 27:27–29, 39, 40]

21 By faith Jacob, as he was dying, blessed each of the sons of Joseph, and bowed in worship, *leaning* on the top of his staff. [Gen 48]

22 By faith Joseph, when he was dying, referred to [the promise of God for] the exodus of the sons of Israel [from Egypt], and gave instructions concerning [the burial of] his bones [in the land of the promise]. [Gen 50:24, 25; Ex 13:19]

23 By faith Moses, after his birth, was hidden for three months by his parents, because they saw he was a beautiful *and* divinely favored child; and they were not afraid of the king's (Pharaoh's) decree. [Ex 1:22; 2:2; Acts 7:20]

24 By faith Moses, when he had grown up, refused to be called the son of Pharaoh's daughter, [Ex 2:10, 15]

25 because he preferred to endure the hardship of the people of God rather than to enjoy the passing pleasures of sin.

26 He considered the reproach of the Christ [that is, the rebuke he would suffer for his faithful obedience to God] to be greater wealth than all the treasures of Egypt; for he looked ahead to the reward [promised by God].

27 By faith he left Egypt, being unafraid of the wrath of the king; for he endured [steadfastly], as seeing Him who is unseen. [Ex 2:15]

28 By faith he kept the Passover and the sprinkling of the blood [on the doorposts], so that the destroyer of the firstborn would not touch them (the firstborn of Israel). [Ex 12:21–30]

29 By faith the people [of Israel] crossed the Red Sea as though *they were passing* through dry land; but when the Egyptians attempted it they were drowned. [Ex 14:21–31]

30 By faith the walls of Jericho fell down after they had been encircled for seven days [by Joshua and the sons of Israel]. [Josh 6:12–21]

31 By faith Rahab the prostitute was not destroyed along with those who were disobedient, because she had welcomed the spies [sent by the sons of Israel] in peace. [Josh 2:1–21; 6:22–25]

32 And what more shall I say? For time will fail me if I tell of Gideon, Barak, Samson, Jephthah, of David and Samuel and the prophets, [Judg 4; 5; 6–8; 11; 12; 13–16; 1 Sam 1–30; 2 Sam 1–24; 1 Kin 1; 2; Acts 3:24]

33 who by faith [that is, with an enduring trust in God and His promises] subdued kingdoms, administered justice, obtained promised blessings, closed the mouths of lions, [Dan 6]

34 extinguished the power of [raging] fire, escaped the edge of the sword, out of weakness were made strong, became mighty *and* unbeatable in battle, putting enemy forces to flight. [Dan 3]

35 Women received back their dead by resurrection; and others were tortured [to death], refusing to accept release [offered on the condition of denying their faith], so that they would be resurrected to a better life; [1 Kin 17:17–24; 2 Kin 4:25–37]

36 and others experienced the trial of

11:26 *the reproach of the Christ.* This phrase refers to the earthly disgrace Christ received. Like Christ, Moses chose to suffer the indignities associated with God's people, instead of embracing the worldly pleasures of Pharaoh's court.

11:28 *sprinkling of the blood.* God told Moses to sprinkle blood on the doorposts. Moses believed God's word and heeded His warning, and, as a result, the firstborn of every Israelite family was saved (Ex 12:1 – 13).

11:35 *Women received back their dead.* This is probably a reference to the raising of the son of the widow of Zarephath (1Ki 17:17 – 24) and of the Shunammite woman (2Ki 4:32 – 37). But the author of Hebrews also points out that not all who had faith won victories, at least not in the same hour. ***tortured.*** This is usually understood to be an allusion to the heroic martyrs of Maccabean times, who were well-known.

20 Ge 27:27 **21** Ge 48:5; 47:31 **22** Ge 50:24 **23** Ex 2:2; 1:16 **24** Ex 2:10 **25** Ps 84:10 **26** Heb 13:13; Heb 10:35 **27** Ex 10:28; ver. 13 **28** Ex 12:21 **29** Ex 14:22 **30** Jos 6:20 **31** Jos 6:23; Jos 2:1 **32** Jdg 6:11; Jdg 13:24; Jdg 12:7; 1Sa 16:1; 1Sa 1:20 **33** 2Sa 7:11; Jdg 14:5; 1Sa 17:34 **34** Da 3:25; 1Sa 20:1; 2Ki 20:7; Jdg 15:8 **35** 1Ki 17:22; Ac 22:25 **36** Ge 39:20; Jer 20:2

mocking and scourging [amid torture], and even chains and imprisonment.

37 They were stoned [to death], they were sawn in two, they were lured with tempting offers [to renounce their faith], they were put to death by the sword; they went about wrapped in the skins of sheep and goats, utterly destitute, oppressed, cruelly treated

38 (people of whom the world was not worthy), wandering in deserts and mountains and [living in] caves and holes in the ground.

39 And all of these, though they gained [divine] approval through their faith, did not receive [the fulfillment of] what was promised,

40 because God had us in mind *and* had something better for us, so that they [these men and women of authentic faith] would not be made perfect [that is, completed in Him] apart from us.

Jesus, the Example

12 THEREFORE, SINCE we are surrounded by so great a cloud of witnesses [who by faith have testified to the truth of God's absolute faithfulness], stripping off every unnecessary weight and the sin which so easily *and* cleverly entangles us, let us run with endurance *and* active persistence the race that is set before us,

2 [looking away from all that will distract us and] focusing our eyes on Jesus, who is the Author and Perfecter of faith [the first incentive for our belief and the One who brings our faith to maturity], who for the joy [of accomplishing the goal] set before Him endured the cross, disregarding the shame, and sat down at the right hand of the throne of God [revealing His deity, His authority, and the completion of His work]. [Ps 110:1]

3 Just consider *and* meditate on Him who endured from sinners such bitter hostility against Himself [consider it all in comparison with your trials], so that you will not grow weary and lose heart.

A Father's Discipline

4 You have not yet struggled to the point of shedding blood in your striving against sin;

5 and you have forgotten the divine word of encouragement which is addressed to you as sons,

"MY SON, DO NOT MAKE LIGHT OF THE
DISCIPLINE OF THE LORD,
AND DO NOT LOSE HEART *and* GIVE UP
WHEN YOU ARE CORRECTED BY HIM;
6 FOR THE LORD DISCIPLINES *and*
CORRECTS THOSE WHOM HE LOVES,
AND HE PUNISHES EVERY SON WHOM
HE RECEIVES *and* WELCOMES [TO
HIS HEART]." [Prov 3:11, 12]

7 You must submit to [correction for the purpose of] discipline; God is dealing with you as with sons; for what son is there whom his father does not discipline?

8 Now if you are exempt from correction *and* without discipline, in which all [of God's children] share, then you

---

11:40 *made perfect.* This phrase means "made complete." This completion, the realization of all of God's promises in Christ's coming kingdom, awaits all believers.

12:1 *cloud of witnesses.* This refers to the people of faith mentioned in chapter 11. They are not actually spectators watching us; they are witnesses testifying to the truth of the faith (11:2,4–6).

12:2 *Perfecter.* Christ has done everything necessary for us to endure in our faith. He is our example and model. ***the joy [of accomplishing the goal] set before Him.*** His attention was not on the agonies of the cross, but on the crown, not on the suffering, but on the reward.

12:3 *consider.* This thought involves the idea of comparison, as an accountant would compare the various columns of a balance sheet. Believers should compare their sufferings to the torture Christ endured on their behalf (v. 4).

12:8 *then you are illegitimate children and not sons.* In Roman society an illegitimate son was one who had no inheritance rights.

37 1Ki 21:13; Ac 7:58; 2Ki 1:8; Mt 3:4; Zec 13:4 **38** 1Ki 18:4 **39** ver. 2,13 **40** Heb 5:9 **CHAPTER 12** **1** Col 3:8; 1Co 9:24; Ro 12:12 **2** Lk 24:26; Php 2:8; Ps 110:1; 1Pe 3:22 **3** Mt 10:24; Jn 15:20; Gal 6:9 **4** 1Co 10:13 **5** Job 5:17 **6** Ps 94:12; Jas 1:12 **7** Dt 8:5 **8** 1Pe 5:9

are illegitimate children and not sons [at all].

9 Moreover, we have had earthly fathers who disciplined us, and we submitted *and* respected them [for training us]; shall we not much more willingly submit to the Father of spirits, and live [by learning from His discipline]?

10 For our earthly fathers disciplined us for only a short time as seemed best to them; but He *disciplines us* for our good, so that we may share His holiness.

11 For the time being no discipline brings joy, but seems sad *and* painful; yet to those who have been trained by it, afterwards it yields the peaceful fruit of righteousness [right standing with God and a lifestyle and attitude that seeks conformity to God's will and purpose].

12 So then, strengthen hands that are weak and knees that tremble. [Is 35:3]

13 Cut through *and* make smooth, straight paths for your feet [that are safe and go in the right direction], so that *the leg* which is lame may not be put out of joint, but rather may be healed.

14 *Continually* pursue peace with everyone, and the sanctification without which no one will [ever] see the Lord.

15 See to it that no one falls short of God's grace; that no root of resentment springs up and causes trouble, and by it many be defiled;

16 and [see to it] that no one is immoral or godless like Esau, who sold his own birthright for a *single* meal. [Gen 25:29–34]

17 For you know that later on, when he wanted [to regain title to] his inheritance of the blessing, he was rejected, for he found no opportunity for repentance [there was no way to repair what he had done, no chance to recall the choice he had made], even though he sought for it with [bitter] tears. [Gen 27:30–40]

Contrast of Sinai and Zion

18 For you have not come [as did the Israelites in the wilderness] to *a mountain* that can be touched and to a blazing fire, and to gloom and darkness and a raging windstorm,

19 and to the blast of a trumpet and a sound of words [such that] those who heard it begged that nothing more be said to them. [Ex 19:12–22; 20:18–21; Deut 4:11, 12; 5:22–27]

20 For they could not bear the command, "IF EVEN A WILD ANIMAL TOUCHES THE MOUNTAIN, IT WILL BE STONED [to death]." [Ex 19:12, 13]

21 In fact, so terrifying was the sight, that Moses said, "I AM FILLED WITH FEAR and trembling." [Deut 9:19]

22 But you have come to Mount Zion and to the city of the living God, the heavenly Jerusalem, and to myriads of angels [in festive gathering],

23 and to the general assembly and assembly of the firstborn who are registered [as citizens] in heaven, and to God, who is Judge of all, and to

---

12:11 *the peaceful fruit of righteousness.* This phrase suggests that the result of God's discipline is peace and righteousness.

12:18 – 24 *For you have not come [as did the Israelites in the wilderness] to a mountain.* In these verses, the author of Hebrews contrasts the Mosaic covenant with the new covenant by contrasting two mountains: Mount Sinai and Mount Zion. At Mount Sinai, the Israelites received the law from God with fear and trembling, for God displayed at that time His awesome power (Ex 19:10 – 20:26). In contrast, Christian believers have come to a heavenly Jerusalem on Mount Zion through Jesus' blood. This mountain is a celebration of the Holy One, attended by angels, believers, and righteous people. The author makes the contrast between the two covenants vivid and then once again exhorts his readers not to reject Christ's offer of salvation (vv. 25 – 29).

12:23 *righteous (the redeemed in heaven) who have been made perfect.* This phrase refers to all believers who have died. They are righteous because they have been justified and perfect because they are now "complete" in heaven.

9 Job 12:10 **10** Lev 11:44 **11** Jas 3:18 **12** Job 4:3,4 **13** Pr 4:26; Gal 6:1 **14** Ps 34:14; 2Ti 2:22; Mt 5:8; 2Co 7:1 **15** Gal 5:4; Heb 3:12 **16** Eph 5:3; Ge 25:33 **17** Ge 27:34 **18** Dt 4:11 **19** Ex 20:19; Dt 5:5 **20** Ex 19:13 **21** Ex 19:16 **22** Gal 4:26; Rev 3:12; Php 3:20; Dt 33:2; Ps 68:17 **23** Jas 1:18; Lk 10:20; Ps 94:2; Php 3:12

the spirits of the righteous (the redeemed in heaven) who have been made perfect [bringing them to their final glory],

24 and to Jesus, the Mediator of a new covenant [uniting God and man], and to the sprinkled blood, which speaks [of mercy], a better *and* nobler *and* more gracious message than *the blood* of Abel [which cried out for vengeance]. [Gen 4:10]

The Unshaken Kingdom

25 See to it that you do not refuse [to listen to] Him who is speaking [to you now]. For if those [sons of Israel] did not escape when they refused [to listen to] him who warned them on earth [revealing God's will], how much less will we *escape* if we turn our backs on Him who warns from heaven? [Heb 2:1–4]

26 His voice shook the earth [at Mount Sinai] then, but now He has given a promise, saying, "YET ONCE MORE I WILL SHAKE NOT ONLY THE EARTH, BUT ALSO THE [starry] HEAVEN." [Hag 2:6]

27 Now this [expression], "Yet once more," indicates the removal *and* final transformation of all those things which can be shaken—that is, of that which has been created—so that those things which cannot be shaken may remain. [Ps 102:26]

28 Therefore, since we receive a kingdom which cannot be shaken, let us show gratitude, and offer to God pleasing service *and* acceptable worship with reverence and awe;

29 for our God is [indeed] a consuming fire. [Deut 4:24]

The Changeless Christ

13 LET LOVE of your fellow believers continue.

2 Do not neglect to extend hospitality to strangers [especially among the family of believers—being friendly, cordial, and gracious, sharing the comforts of your home and doing your part generously], for by this some have entertained angels without knowing it. [Gen 18:1–8; 19:1–3; Judg 6:11–24; 13:6–20]

3 Remember those who are in prison, as if you were their fellow prisoner, and those who are mistreated, since you also are in the body [and subject to physical suffering].

4 Marriage *is to be held* in honor among all [that is, regarded as something of great value], and the *marriage* bed undefiled [by immorality or by any sexual sin]; for God will judge the sexually immoral and adulterous.

5 Let your character [your moral essence, your inner nature] be free from the love of money [shun greed—be financially ethical], being content with what you have; for He has said, "I WILL NEVER [under any circumstances] DESERT YOU [nor give you up nor leave you without support, nor will I in any degree leave you helpless], NOR WILL I FORSAKE *or* LET YOU DOWN *or* RELAX MY HOLD ON YOU [assuredly not]!" [Josh 1:5]

6 So we take comfort *and* are encouraged *and* confidently say,

---

12:25 *Him who warns from heaven.* This is a reference to Christ, who spoke on earth and is now in heaven.

12:29 *our God is [indeed] a consuming fire.* The author concludes his lengthy warning to those who are tempted to abandon the faith (2:1 – 12:29) with a vivid description of God's judgment (Dt 4:24). The Lord will judge His people (10:27,30).

13:2 *entertained angels.* This is a reference to men in the Old Testament who encounter heavenly beings. These men included Abraham (Ge 18), Lot (Ge 19), and Gideon (Jdg 6). The idea is that, when you practice hospitality, you may be helping a messenger of God without realizing it.

13:5 *I WILL NEVER [under any circumstances] DESERT YOU . . . NOR WILL I FORSAKE . . . YOU.* This quotation is one of the emphatic statements in the New Testament. In Greek it contains two double negatives, similar to saying in English, "I will never, ever, ever forsake you." Jesus uses the same technique to express the certainty of eternal life for believers (Jn 10:28).

24 Heb 9:15; Ex 24:8; Ge 4:10 **25** Heb 2:2,3 **26** Ex 19:18; Hag 2:6 **27** 2Pe 3:10 **29** Ex 24:17; Dt 4:24
CHAPTER 13 **1** Ro 12:10; 1Pe 1:22 **2** Mt 25:35; 1Ti 3:2; Ge 18:3 **3** Mt 25:26 **4** 1Co 6:9 **5** Php 4:11; Ge 28:15
6 Ps 27:1

"THE LORD IS MY HELPER [in time of
need], I WILL NOT BE AFRAID.
WHAT WILL MAN DO TO ME?" [Ps 27:1;
118:6]

7Remember your leaders [for it was they] who brought you the word of God; and consider the result of their conduct [the outcome of their godly lives], and imitate their faith [their conviction that God exists and is the Creator and Ruler of all things, the Provider of eternal salvation through Christ, and imitate their reliance on God with absolute trust and confidence in His power, wisdom, and goodness].
8Jesus Christ is [eternally changeless, always] the same yesterday and today and forever.
9Do not be carried away by diverse and strange teachings; for it is good for the heart to be established *and* strengthened by grace and not by foods [rules of diet and ritualistic meals], which bring no benefit *or* spiritual growth to those who observe them.
10We have an altar from which those who serve the tabernacle (sacred tent) have no right to eat.
11For the bodies of those animals whose blood is brought into the sanctuary by the high priest *as an offering* for sin, are burned outside the camp. [Lev 16:27]
12Therefore Jesus also suffered *and* died outside the [city] gate so that He might sanctify *and* set apart for God as holy the people [who believe] through [the shedding of] His own blood.
13So, let us go out to Him outside the camp, bearing His contempt [the disgrace and shame that He had to suffer]. [Lev 16:27]
14For here we have no lasting city, but we are seeking *the city* which is to come.

God-pleasing Sacrifices

15Through Him, therefore, let us at all times offer up to God a sacrifice of praise, which is the fruit of lips that thankfully acknowledge *and* confess *and* glorify His name. [Lev 7:12; Is 57:19; Hos 14:2]
16Do not neglect to do good, to contribute [to the needy of the church as an expression of fellowship], for such sacrifices are always pleasing to God.
17Obey your [spiritual] leaders and submit to them [recognizing their authority over you], for they are keeping watch over your souls *and* continually

---

13:9 *strange teachings.* This implies ideas foreign to the gospel message. Many of the ideas which the author was confronting were Jewish in origin — pertaining to ritual observances, sacrificial feasts, and various laws identifying what was clean and unclean.

13:11 *burned outside the camp.* The believer has a sacrifice, Jesus Christ. He atoned for the sins of humanity with His death on the cross. But, unlike the high priests from the Old Testament, believers receive their sustenance from Christ in a symbolic way, by believing in Him (Jn 6:41 – 58).

13:15 – 16 *sacrifice of praise.* Although the Old Testament sacrifices are now obsolete (8:13), believers are to offer spiritual sacrifices which include their praise, their possessions, and even their lives (Ro 12:1 – 2).

13:15 Worship — Since worship encompasses thought, feeling, and deed, there are many expressions of it. Worship especially includes praise and thanksgiving which may be expressed privately or publicly, whether by grateful declarations (Heb 13:15) or by joyful singing (Ps 100:2; Eph 5:19; Col 3:16). Portions of early Christian hymns of worship have been preserved in the New Testament (Php 2:5 – 11; 1Ti 3:16; 2Ti 2:11 – 13). One very important expression of worship for the church is remembering the death of Christ through the Lord's Supper (1Co 11:26). The Lord's Supper was instituted by Christ Himself (Mt 26:26 – 28) and judged by Paul to be taken very seriously (1Co 11:28 – 32). Since worship means giving something to God, the cheerful giving of money to God's work is certainly an act of worship (2Co 9:7). The exercise of one of the spiritual gifts in ministry to the body of Christ constitutes worship as service (1Co 12) as does faithfully occupying a church office (Eph 4:11; 1Ti 3:1 – 13; Titus 1:5 – 9). In fact, presenting ourselves (mind and body) to God to serve in any context is described as an act of worship in Romans 12:1. In this manner our whole lives become acts of worship.

---

7 ver. 17; Heb 6:12 **8** Jn 8:58 **9** Eph 4:14; Col 2:4,8; Ro 14:17; 1Ti 4:3 **10** 1Co 9:13 **11** Ex 29:14 **12** Ac 7:58 **13** 1Pe 4:14 **14** Mic 2:10; Php 3:20 **15** Eph 5:20; Lev 7:12; Hos 14:2 **16** Ro 12:13; 2Co 9:12; Php 4:18 **17** Php 2:29; 1Ti 5:17; Eze 3:17

guarding your spiritual welfare as
those who will give an account [of
their stewardship of you]. Let them
do this with joy and not with grief
and groans, for this would be of no
benefit to you.
[18]Keep praying for us, for we are
convinced that we have a good con-
science, seeking to conduct ourselves
honorably [that is, with moral courage
and personal integrity] in all things.
[19]And I urge all of you to pray ear-
nestly, so that I may be restored to
you soon.

Benediction

[20]Now may the God of peace [the
source of serenity and spiritual well-
being] who brought up from the dead
our Lord Jesus, the great Shepherd
of the sheep, through the blood *that
sealed and ratified* the eternal cov-
enant, [Is 55:3; 63:11; Ezek 37:26;
Zech 9:11]
[21]equip you with every good thing
to carry out His will *and* strengthen
you [making you complete and perfect
as you ought to be], accomplishing in
us that which is pleasing in His sight,
through Jesus Christ, to whom be the
glory forever and ever. Amen.
[22]I call on you, brothers and sisters,
listen [patiently] to this message of
exhortation *and* encouragement, for I
have written to you briefly.
[23]Notice that our brother Timothy
has been released [from prison]. If he
comes soon, I will see you [along with
him].
[24]Give our greetings to all of your
[spiritual] leaders and to all of the saints
(God's people). Those [Christians] from
Italy send you their greetings.
[25]Grace be with you all.

13:20 ***great Shepherd of the sheep.*** Having laid down His life for them (Jn 10:15) and now continuing to make intercession for them (7:25), this is another description of Jesus' ministry.
13:22 ***message of exhortation.*** This phrase refers to the whole Epistle to the Hebrews. It is an exhortation not to depart from the living God (3:12), but to go on to maturity (6:1) and endure in the faith to the end (3:6,14).
13:24 ***Those [Christians] from Italy.*** This phrase may refer to people living in Italy, or else to people from there who were now living elsewhere. Because of its ambiguity, this phrase does not reveal the location of the author or of the recipients.

18 Eph 6:19; Ac 23:1 **20** Ro 15:33; Ro 4:24; Gal 1:1; 1Pe 2:25; Zec 9:11 **21** 1Pe 5:10; Php 2:13; Gal 1:5 **22** 1Pe 5:12 **23** 1Th 3:2; 1Ti 6:12 **24** ver. 7,17 **25** Titus 3:15

THE LETTER OF

JAMES

▸ **AUTHOR:** Four men are named James in the New Testament, one of which is the Lord's brother (Mt 13:55; Mk 6:3; Gal 1:19). Tradition points to this prominent figure as the author of the epistle, and this best fits the evidence of Scripture. The brevity and limited doctrinal emphasis of James kept it from wide circulation, and by the time it became known in the church as a whole, there was uncertainty about the identity of the James in 1:1. Growing recognition that it was written by the Lord's brother led to its acceptance as a canonical book.

▸ **TIMES:** c. AD 46 – 49 ▸ **KEY VERSES:** James 1:19 – 22

▸ **THEME:** James is for the practical person. While most of Paul's Epistles have a theological and practical section, there isn't much theoretical or systematic theology in this book. The subject matters covered in James are the issues we face daily if not hourly. How do we respond to trials and temptation? What are we doing with our money? Do we keep our tongues under control? Are we acting on our faith? What are we doing with our prayer lives? The main point of all these questions James raises is that saving faith needs to result in changed behavior.

Testing Your Faith

1 JAMES, A bond-servant of God
and of the Lord Jesus Christ,
To the twelve [Hebrew] tribes [scat-
tered abroad among the Gentiles] in
the dispersion: Greetings (rejoice)!
2 Consider it nothing but joy, my
brothers and sisters, whenever you
fall into various trials.
3 Be assured that the testing of your
faith [through experience] produces
endurance [leading to spiritual matu-
rity, and inner peace].
4 And let endurance have its perfect
result *and* do a thorough work, so that
you may be perfect and completely
developed [in your faith], lacking in
nothing.
5 If any of you lacks wisdom [to guide
him through a decision or circum-

1:1 *To the twelve [Hebrew] tribes.* This salutation probably means the letter is for Jewish Christians living outside of Palestine. The letter was not intended for one specific church but was to be passed around among various local assemblies.
1:2 *trials.* These are outward circumstances — conflicts, sufferings, and troubles — encountered by all believers. Trials are not pleasant and may be extremely grievous, but believers are to consider them as opportunities for rejoicing. Troubles and difficulties are a tool which refines and purifies our faith, producing patience and endurance.
1:3 *testing of your faith.* The word that is translated into this phrase occurs only here and in 1 Peter 1:7. The term was used for coins that were genuine and not debased. The aim of trying is not to destroy or afflict, but to purge and refine. "Patience" here transcends the idea of bearing affliction; it includes the idea of standing fast under pressure, with a staying power that turns adversities into opportunities.
1:5 *wisdom.* The starting point for wisdom is a genuine reverence for the Almighty (Ps 111:10; Pr 9:10) and a steadfast confidence that God

CHAPTER 1 **1** Ac 12:17; Titus 1:1; Ac 26:7; Dt 32:26; Jn 7:35; Ac 2:5; 1Pe 1:1 **2** Ac 5:41; 1Pe 1:6 **3** Ro 5:3
5 1Ki 3:9; Pr 2:3; Mt 7:7; Lk 11:9; Jn 14:13; Jer 29:12; 1Jn 5:14

stance], he is to ask of [our benevolent]
God, who gives to everyone generously
and without rebuke *or* blame, and it
will be given to him.
6 But he must ask [for wisdom] in
faith, without doubting [God's willing-
ness to help], for the one who doubts is
like a billowing surge of the sea that is
blown about and tossed by the wind.
7 For such a person ought not to think
or expect that he will receive anything
[at all] from the Lord,
8 *being* a double-minded man, un-
stable *and* restless in all his ways [in
everything he thinks, feels, or decides].
9 Let the brother in humble circum-
stances glory in his high position [as a
born-again believer, called to the true
riches and to be an heir of God];
10 and the rich man *is to glory* in be-
ing humbled [by trials revealing hu-
man frailty, knowing true riches are
found in the grace of God], for like the
flower of the grass he will pass away.
11 For the sun rises with a scorching
wind and withers the grass; its flower
falls off and its beauty fades away; so
too will the rich man, in the midst of
his pursuits, fade away. [Is 40:6, 7]
12 Blessed [happy, spiritually pros-
perous, favored by God] is the man
who is steadfast under trial *and* perse-
veres when tempted; for when he has
passed the test *and* been approved, he
will receive the [victor's] crown of life
which *the Lord* has promised to those
who love Him.
13 Let no one say when he is tempted,
"I am being tempted by God" [for temp-
tation does not originate from God, but
from our own flaws]; for God cannot
be tempted by [what is] evil, and He
Himself tempts no one.
14 But each one is tempted when he
is dragged away, enticed *and* baited
[to commit sin] by his own [worldly]
desire (lust, passion).
15 Then when the illicit desire has
conceived, it gives birth to sin; and
when sin has run its course, it gives
birth to death.
16 Do not be misled, my beloved
brothers and sisters.
17 Every good thing given and every
perfect gift is from above; it comes
down from the Father of lights [the
Creator and Sustainer of the heavens],
in whom there is no variation [no ris-
ing or setting] or shadow cast by His
turning [for He is perfect and never
changes].
18 It was of His own will that He gave
us birth [as His children] by the word
of truth, so that we would be a kind of
first fruits of His creatures [a prime
example of what He created to be set
apart to Himself—sanctified, made
holy for His divine purposes].
19 Understand this, my beloved broth-
ers and sisters. Let everyone be quick
to hear [be a careful, thoughtful listen-
er], slow to speak [a speaker of care-
fully chosen words and], slow to anger
[patient, reflective, forgiving];
20 for the [resentful, deep-seated]
anger of man does not produce the
righteousness of God [that standard of
behavior which He requires from us].

---

controls all circumstances, guiding them to His good purposes (Ro 8:28).

1:8 *double-minded.* This person is literally one with "two souls." If one part of a person is set on God and the other is set on this world (Mt 6:24), there will be constant conflict within.

1:12 *will receive the [victor's] crown of life.* The Bible describes the believer's reward (2Co 5:10; Rev 22:12) under various vivid images, such as precious metals (1Co 3:8 – 14), garments (Rev 3:5,18; 19:7 – 8), and crowns (1Co 9:25; Rev 2:10; 3:11).

1:13 *He Himself tempts no one.* Enticement to sin does not come from God. God will never deliberately lead a person to commit sin because that would not only go against His nature, but it would also be opposed to His purpose of molding His creation into His holy image. Yet, God does sometimes place His people in adverse circumstances for the purpose of building godly character (Ge 22:1,12).

1:19 *quick to hear . . . slow to speak . . . slow to anger.* These three exhortations reveal the outline of this letter (1:21 – 2:26 for "swift to hear"; 3:1 – 18 for "slow to speak"; 4:1 – 5:18 for "slow to wrath").

---

6 Mk 11:24; 1Ti 2:8 **8** Jas 4:8 **10** Job 14:2; Ps 37:2; 1Co 7:31 **12** Job 5:17; Pr 3:11; 1Co 9:25; 2Ti 4:8; Mt 10:22 **15** Job 15:35; Ps 7:14; Ro 6:21 **17** Jn 3:27; Nu 23:19 **18** Jn 1:13; 1Co 4:15; Eph 1:12; Rev 14:4 **19** Ecc 5:1; Pr 10:19; Ecc 5:2; Pr 14:17

21 So get rid of all uncleanness and all that remains of wickedness, and with a humble spirit receive the word [of God] which is implanted [actually rooted in your heart], which is able to save your souls.

22 But prove yourselves doers of the word [actively and continually obeying God's precepts], and not merely listeners [who hear the word but fail to internalize its meaning], deluding yourselves [by unsound reasoning contrary to the truth].

23 For if anyone only listens to the word without obeying it, he is like a man who looks very carefully at his natural face in a mirror;

24 for *once* he has looked at himself and gone away, he immediately forgets what he looked like.

25 But he who looks carefully into the perfect law, the *law* of liberty, and faithfully abides by it, not having become a [careless] listener who forgets but an active doer [who obeys], he will be blessed *and* favored by God in what he does [in his life of obedience].

26 If anyone thinks himself to be religious [scrupulously observant of the rituals of his faith], and does not control his tongue but deludes his *own* heart, this person's religion is worthless (futile, barren).

27 Pure and unblemished religion [as it is expressed in outward acts] in the sight of our God and Father is this: to visit *and* look after the fatherless and the widows in their distress, and to keep oneself uncontaminated by the [secular] world.

The Sin of Partiality

2 MY FELLOW believers, do not practice your faith in our glorious Lord Jesus Christ with *an attitude* of partiality [toward people—show no favoritism, no prejudice, no snobbery].

2 For if a man comes into your meeting place wearing a gold ring and fine clothes, and a poor man in dirty clothes also comes in,

3 and you pay special attention to the one who wears the fine clothes, and say to him, "You sit here in this good seat," and you tell the poor man, "You stand over there, or sit down [on the floor] by my footstool,"

4 have you not discriminated among yourselves, and become judges with wrong motives?

5 Listen, my beloved brothers and sisters: has not God chosen the poor of this world to be rich in faith and [as believers to be] heirs of the kingdom which He promised to those who love Him?

6 But you [in contrast] have dishonored the poor man. Is it not the rich who oppress *and* exploit you, and personally drag you into the courts of law?

7 Do they not blaspheme the precious name [of Christ] by which you are called?

8 If, however, you are [really] fulfilling the royal law according to the Scripture, "YOU SHALL LOVE YOUR NEIGHBOR AS YOURSELF [that is, if you have an

---

1:21 *with a humble spirit receive the word [of God] which is implanted.* The believer should have a teachable spirit — without resisting, disputing, or questioning. Receiving God's Word this way will save the believer's soul.

1:22 *prove yourselves doers of the word . . . and not merely listeners.* Believers who hear the Word of God (v. 19) must receive it with a teachable spirit (v. 21), applying it to their daily lives. To hear and not obey is to be deceived.

1:25 *the perfect law, the law of liberty.* Loving God and loving one's neighbor sum up the law (Ro 13:8 – 10). But it is Christ's love (Eph 3:17 – 19) which frees us from our sins to truly love others (Jn 8:36 – 38; Gal 5:13).

1:27 *fatherless and the widows.* These people were among the most unprotected and needy classes in ancient societies (Eze 22:7). Pure religion does not merely give material goods for the relief of the distressed; it also oversees their care (Ac 6:1 – 7).

2:5 *heirs of the kingdom.* This inheritance means more than entering the kingdom; it also involves ruling with Christ (1Co 6:9; Gal 5:21; 2Ti 2:12).

21 Col 3:8; 1Pe 2:1; Ac 13:26; Ro 1:16; Eph 1:13; Titus 2:11 **22** Mt 7:21; Ro 2:13; 1Jn 3:7 **23** Lk 6:47 **25** 2Co 3:18; Jas 2:12; Jn 13:17 **26** Ps 34:13; 1Pe 3:10 **27** Isa 1:16; Mt 25:36; Ro 12:2; 1Jn 5:18 **CHAPTER 2** **1** 1Co 2:8; Lev 19:15; Dt 1:17; Mt 22:16; Jude 16 **5** Jn 7:48; Lk 12:21; Ex 20:6; Pr 8:17 **6** 1Co 11:22; Ac 13:50 **8** Lev 19:18; Mt 22:39

unselfish concern for others and do
things for their benefit]" you are doing
well. [Lev 19:18]
9 But if you show partiality [preju-
dice, favoritism], you are committing
sin and are convicted by the Law as
offenders.
10 For whoever keeps the whole Law
but stumbles in one *point*, he has be-
come guilty of [breaking] all of it.
11 For He who said, "Do not commit
adultery," also said, "Do not murder."
Now if you do not commit adultery, but
you murder, you have become guilty
of transgressing the [entire] Law.
[Ex 20:13, 14; Deut 5:17, 18]
12 Speak and act [consistently] as
people who are going to be judged
by the law of liberty [that moral law
that frees obedient Christians from
the bondage of sin].
13 For judgment *will be* merciless to
one who has shown no mercy; but [to
the one who has shown mercy] mercy
triumphs [victoriously] over judgment.

Faith and Works

14 What is the benefit, my fellow be-
lievers, if someone claims to have faith
but has no [good] works [as evidence]?
Can that [kind of] faith save him? [No,
a mere claim of faith is not sufficient—
genuine faith produces good works.]
15 If a brother or sister is without [ad-
equate] clothing and lacks [enough]
food for each day,
16 and one of you says to them, "Go in
peace [with my blessing], [keep] warm
and feed yourselves," but he does not
give them the necessities for the body,
what good does that do?
17 So too, faith, if it does not have
works [to back it up], is by itself dead
[inoperative and ineffective].
18 But someone may say, "You [claim
to] have faith and I have [good] works;
show me your [alleged] faith without
the works [if you can], and I will show
you my faith by my works [that is, by
what I do]."
19 You believe that God is one; you
do well [to believe that]. The demons
also believe [that], and shudder *and*
bristle [in awe-filled terror—they have
seen His wrath]! [Deut 6:4; 11:13–21;
Mark 12:29]
20 But are you willing to recognize,
you foolish [spiritually shallow] per-
son, that faith without [good] works
is useless?
21 Was our father Abraham not
[shown to be] justified by works [of
obedience which expressed his faith]
when he offered Isaac his son on the al-
tar [as a sacrifice to God]? [Gen 22:1–14]
22 You see that [his] faith was working
together with his works, and as a result
of the works, his faith was completed

2:9 *if you show partiality [prejudice, favoritism], you are committing sin.* James alludes to Leviticus 19:15, which prohibits favoritism to either the poor or the rich.
2:10 *he has become guilty of [breaking] all.* God does not allow selective obedience. We cannot choose to obey the parts of the law that are to our own liking and disregard the rest. Some of the Pharisees were guilty of this. They carefully observed some of the requirements of the law, such as keeping the Sabbath, and ignored others, such as honoring their parents (Mt 15:1–7). Sin is a violation of the perfect righteousness of God, who is the Lawgiver. James is saying that the whole divine law has to be accepted as an expression of God's will for His people. The violation of even one Commandment separates an individual from God and His purposes.
2:14 *What is the benefit.* James is implying in this verse that faith in Christ will demonstrate itself in love for others (Jn 13:34–35).
2:19 *The demons also believe [that], and shudder.* While they believe, the demons do not love Him (Mt 8:29). Their kind of belief does not lead to love, submission, and obedience; instead, it leads to hatred, rebellion, and disobedience.
2:21 *justified.* James is using the word justified to mean "proved." We prove to others our genuine faith in Christ through our works. But the justification that comes through faith is before God, and we do not "prove" ourselves to Him; instead, God declares us righteous through our association with Christ, the One who died for our sins (Ro 3:28).
2:22 *faith . . . works.* These two should be together; there is a close relationship between the two. Faith produces works; and works make faith perfect, meaning "mature" or "complete."

9 ver. 1 **10** Dt 27:26; Mt 5:19; Gal 3:10 **11** Ex 20:13 **12** Jas 1:25 **13** Job 22:6; 1Jn 4:17 **14** Mt 7:26; Mt 15:11 **15** Lk 3:11 **16** 1Jn 3:18 **18** Jas 3:13 **21** Ge 22:9 **22** Heb 11:17

[reaching its maturity when he ex-
pressed his faith through obedience].
23 And the Scripture was fulfilled
which says, "ABRAHAM BELIEVED GOD, AND
THIS [faith] WAS CREDITED TO HIM [by God]
AS RIGHTEOUSNESS *and* AS CONFORMITY TO
HIS WILL," and he was called the friend
of God. [Gen 15:6; 2 Chr 20:7; Is 41:8]
24 You see that a man (believer) is
justified by works and not by faith
alone [that is, by acts of obedience a
born-again believer reveals his faith].
25 In the same way, was Rahab the
prostitute not justified by works too,
when she received the [Hebrew] spies
as guests *and* protected them, and sent
them away [to escape] by a different
route? [Josh 2:1–21]
26 For just as the [human] body with-
out the spirit is dead, so faith without
works [of obedience] is also dead.

The Tongue Is a Fire

3 NOT MANY [of you] should be-
come teachers [serving in an offi-
cial teaching capacity], my brothers
and sisters, for you know that we [who
are teachers] will be judged by a higher
standard [because we have assumed
greater accountability and more con-
demnation if we teach incorrectly].
2 For we all stumble *and* sin in many
ways. If anyone does not stumble in
what he says [never saying the wrong
thing], he is a perfect man [fully de-
veloped in character, without serious
flaws], able to bridle his whole body
and rein in his entire nature [taming
his human faults and weaknesses].
3 Now if we put bits into the hors-
es' mouths to make them obey us, we
guide their whole body as well.
4 And look at the ships. Even though
they are so large and are driven by
strong winds, they are still directed
by a very small rudder wherever the
impulse of the helmsman determines.
5 In the same sense, the tongue is a
small part of the body, and yet it boasts
of great things.
See [by comparison] how great a
forest is set on fire by a small spark!
6 And the tongue is [in a sense] a fire,
the *very* world of injustice *and* unrigh-
teousness; the tongue is set among our
members as that which contaminates
the entire body, and sets on fire the
course of our life [the cycle of man's
existence], and is itself set on fire by
hell (Gehenna).
7 For every species of beasts and
birds, of reptiles and sea creatures,
is tamed and has been tamed by the
human race.
8 But no one can tame the *human*
tongue; it is a restless evil [undisci-
plined, unstable], full of deadly poison.
9 With it we bless our Lord and Fa-
ther, and with it we curse men, who
have been made in the likeness of God.
10 Out of the same mouth come *both*
blessing and cursing. These things, my
brothers, should not be this way [for we
have a moral obligation to speak in a
manner that reflects our fear of God
and profound respect for His precepts].
11 Does a spring send out from the
same opening *both* fresh and bitter
water?
12 Can a fig tree, my brothers, pro-
duce olives, or a grapevine produce
figs? Nor can salt water produce fresh.

Wisdom from Above

13 Who among you is wise and intel-
ligent? Let him by his good conduct
show his [good] deeds with the gen-
tleness *and* humility of *true* wisdom.
14 But if you have bitter jealousy and
selfish ambition in your hearts, do not

3:1 *we [who are teachers] will be judged by a higher standard.* James does not give the warning of condemnation to others without applying it to himself.
3:7 – 8 *no one can tame the human tongue.* The instincts of animals can be subdued through conditioning and punishment, but the sinful nature that inspires evil words is beyond our control. Only the work of the Holy Spirit within us can bring this destructive force under control.
3:9 *we bless our Lord and Father.* James is pointing out the inconsistency of blessing God while cursing people who are created in His image.

23 Ge 15:6; Ro 4:3; Gal 3:6; 2Ch 20:7; Isa 41:8 **25** Heb 11:31 **CHAPTER 3** **1** Mt 23:8; Lk 6:37 **2** 1Ki 8:46; 2Ch 6:36; Pr 20:9; Ps 34:13; 1Pe 3:10; Mt 12:37 **3** Ps 32:9 **5** Pr 12:18; Ps 12:3 **6** Pr 16:27; Mt 15:11 **8** Ps 140:3 **9** Ge 1:26 **13** Gal 6:4; Jas 2:18; Jas 1:21 **14** Ro 13:13; Ro 2:17

be arrogant, and [as a result] be in defiance of the truth.

15 This [superficial] wisdom is not that which comes down from above, but is earthly (secular), natural (unspiritual), *even* demonic.

16 For where jealousy and selfish ambition exist, there is disorder [unrest, rebellion] and every evil thing *and* morally degrading practice.

17 But the wisdom from above is first pure [morally and spiritually undefiled], then peace-loving [courteous, considerate], gentle, reasonable [and willing to listen], full of compassion and good fruits. It is unwavering, without [self-righteous] hypocrisy [and self-serving guile].

18 And the seed whose fruit is righteousness (spiritual maturity) is sown in peace by those who make peace [by actively encouraging goodwill between individuals].

Things to Avoid

4 WHAT LEADS to [the unending] quarrels and conflicts among you? Do they not come from your [hedonistic] desires that wage war in your [bodily] members [fighting for control over you]?

2 You are jealous *and* covet [what others have] and your lust goes unfulfilled; so you murder. You are envious and cannot obtain [the object of your envy]; so you fight and battle. You do not have because you do not ask [it of God]. [1 John 3:15]

3 You ask [God for something] and do not receive it, because you ask with wrong motives [out of selfishness or with an unrighteous agenda], so that [when you get what you want] you may spend it on your [hedonistic] desires.

4 You adulteresses [disloyal sinners—flirting with the world and breaking your vow to God]! Do you not know that being the world's friend [that is, loving the things of the world] is being God's enemy? So whoever chooses to be a friend of the world makes himself an enemy of God.

5 Or do you think that the Scripture says to no purpose that the [human] spirit which He has made to dwell in us lusts with envy? [Gen 6:5]

6 But He gives us more and more grace [through the power of the Holy Spirit to defy sin and live an obedient life that reflects both our faith and our gratitude for our salvation]. Therefore, it says, "GOD IS OPPOSED TO THE PROUD *and* HAUGHTY, BUT [continually] GIVES [the gift of] GRACE TO THE HUMBLE [who turn away from self-righteousness]." [Prov 3:34]

7 So submit to [the authority of] God. Resist the devil [stand firm against him] and he will flee from you.

3:16 *there is disorder.* On the other hand, God brings harmony and wisdom (1Co 14:33). Anyone who is involved in envy and strife is confused. This confusion corrupts human relationships. It is likely that the Jewish Christians to whom James was writing were going through turmoil because of sinful acts like the ones mentioned here. James wanted his readers to set aside their petty attitudes and seek reconciliation.

4:1 *conflicts among you.* The source of problems is the conflict between desires for pleasure and the desire for God's will, an attitude that the Holy Spirit has placed within us.

4:3 *you ask with wrong motives.* Some might have protested James's admonition (vv. 1 – 2) by claiming that they had not received an answer to their prayers (Mt 7:7). James responds by suggesting that they were praying for the wrong things. Instead of praying for their sinful desires, they should have been praying for God's good will for them.

4:4 *whoever chooses.* This verse does not speak of God's attitude toward the believer, but of the believer's attitude toward God. The difference between the world and God is so vast that, as we move toward the world, we alienate ourselves from God. In the world, sin is considered acceptable and pleasurable. Ultimately the world has lost its awareness of sin, and thus sin has become habitual.

4:6 *GOD IS OPPOSED TO THE PROUD.* James quotes from Proverbs 3:34 to prove his point. Those who submit to divine wisdom will receive the necessary grace from God to put into practice the kind of life James describes (3:13 – 18). On the other hand, those who elevate themselves will face a formidable foe (v. 4). God Himself will fight against their plans, because they are not on His side.

---

15 Php 3:19 **16** 1Co 3:3; Gal 5:20 **17** 1Co 2:6; Ro 12:9; 1Pe 1:22 **18** Pr 11:18 **CHAPTER 4** **1** Ro 7:23; Gal 5:17 **3** Job 27:9; Ps 18:41; 66:18 **4** Ps 73:27; 1Jn 2:15; Jn 15:19; Gal 1:10 **5** Ge 6:5; Nu 11:29 **6** Job 22:29; Ps 138:6; Pr 3:34; Mt 23:12 **7** Eph 4:27; 1Pe 5:9

8Come close to God [with a contrite heart] and He will come close to you. Wash your hands, you sinners; and purify your [unfaithful] hearts, you double-minded [people].

9Be miserable and grieve and weep [over your sin]. Let your [foolish] laughter be turned to mourning and your [reckless] joy to gloom.

10Humble yourselves [with an attitude of repentance and insignificance] in the presence of the Lord, and He will exalt you [He will lift you up, He will give you purpose].

11Believers, do not speak against *or* slander one another. He who speaks [self-righteously] against a brother or judges his brother [hypocritically], speaks against the Law and judges the Law. If you judge the Law, you are not a doer of the Law but a judge of it.

12There is *only* one Lawgiver and Judge, the One who is able to save and to destroy [the one God who has the absolute power of life and death]; but who are you to [hypocritically or self-righteously] pass judgment on your neighbor?

13Come now [and pay attention to this], you who say, "Today or tomorrow we will go to such and such a city, and spend a year there and carry on our business and make a profit."

14Yet you do not know [the least thing] about what may happen in your life tomorrow. [What is secure in your life?] You are *merely* a vapor [like a puff of smoke or a wisp of steam from a cooking pot] that is visible for a little while and then vanishes [into thin air].

15Instead you ought to say, "If the Lord wills, we will live and we will do this or that."

16But as it is, you boast [vainly] in your pretension *and* arrogance. All such boasting is evil.

17So any person who knows what is right to do but does not do it, to him it is sin.

Misuse of Riches

5 COME [QUICKLY] now, you rich [who lack true faith and hoard and misuse your resources], weep and howl over the miseries [the woes, the judgments] that are coming upon you.

2Your wealth has rotted *and* is ruined and your [fine] clothes have become moth-eaten.

3Your gold and silver are corroded, and their corrosion will be a witness against you and will consume your flesh like fire. You have stored up your treasure in the last days [when it will do you no good].

4Look! The wages that you have [fraudulently] withheld from the laborers who have mowed your fields are crying out [against you for vengeance]; and the cries of the harvesters have come to the ears of the Lord of Sabaoth. [1 Sam 1:3]

5On the earth you have lived luxuriously *and* abandoned yourselves to soft living and led a life of wanton pleasure [self-indulgence, self-gratification]; you have fattened your hearts in a day of slaughter.

6You have condemned and have put to death the righteous *man;* he offers you no resistance.

Exhortation

7So wait patiently, brothers and sisters, until the coming of the Lord.

4:9 *Be miserable and grieve and weep.* When a believer who has fallen into sin responds to God's call for repentance, he or she should place laughter and joy aside to reflect on the sin with genuine sorrow (2Co 7:9 – 10). In this verse, laughter seems to refer to the loud revelry of pleasure-loving people. They immerse themselves in a celebration of their sins in an effort to forget God's judgment. A Christian should never laugh at sin. However, Christian sorrow leads to repentance; repentance leads to forgiveness; and forgiveness leads to true joy over one's reconciliation with God (Ps 32:1; 126:2; Pr 15:13).

4:13 *we will go ... and make a profit.* The problem here is not the plan or the concept of planning; it is leaving God out of the plan (v. 15).

5:2 – 3 *your [fine] clothes.* In the ancient world, food, costly clothing, and precious metals were

---

8 2Ch 15:2; Isa 1:16; 1Pe 1:22; 1Jn 3:3; Jas 1:8 **9** Mt 5:4 **10** Job 22:29 **11** 1Pe 2:1; Mt 7:1 **12** Mt 10:28; Ro 14:4 **13** Pr 27:1 **14** Job 7:7 **15** Ac 18:21 **16** 1Co 5:6 **17** Lk 12:47; Jn 9:41 **CHAPTER 5** **1** Pr 11:28; Lk 6:24 **2** Job 13:28; Mt 6:20 **3** Ro 2:5 **4** Lev 19:13; Dt 24:15 **5** Job 21:13; Am 6:1 **6** Jas 2:6 **7** Dt 11:14; Hos 6:3

The farmer waits [expectantly] for the
precious harvest from the land, being
patient about it, until it receives the
early and late rains.
8 You too, be patient; strengthen
your hearts [keep them energized and
firmly committed to God], because the
coming of the Lord is near.
9 Do not complain against one an-
other, believers, so that you will not
be judged [for it]. Look! The Judge is
standing right at the door.
10 As an example, brothers and sis-
ters, of suffering and patience, take
the prophets who spoke in the name
of the Lord [as His messengers and
representatives].
11 You know we call those blessed
[happy, spiritually prosperous, favored
by God] who were steadfast *and* en-
dured [difficult circumstances]. You
have heard of the *patient* endurance
of Job and you have seen the Lord's
outcome [how He richly blessed Job].
The Lord is full of compassion and is
merciful. [Job 1:21, 22; 42:10; Ps 111:4]
12 But above all, my fellow believers,
do not swear, either by heaven or by
earth or with any other oath; but let
your yes be [a truthful] yes, and your
no be [a truthful] no, so that you may
not fall under judgment. [Matt 5:34–37]
13 Is anyone among you suffering?
He must pray. Is anyone joyful? He is
to sing praises [to God].
14 Is anyone among you sick? He
must call for the elders (spiritual lead-
ers) of the church and they are to pray
over him, anointing him with oil in the
name of the Lord;
15 and the prayer of faith will restore
the one who is sick, and the Lord will
raise him up; and if he has committed
sins, he will be forgiven.
16 Therefore, confess your sins to
one another [your false steps, your
offenses], and pray for one another,
that you may be healed *and* restored.
The heartfelt *and* persistent prayer of
a righteous man (believer) can accom-
plish much [when put into action and
made effective by God—it is dynamic
and can have tremendous power].
17 Elijah was a man with a nature like
ours [with the same physical, mental,
and spiritual limitations and short-
comings], and he prayed intensely for
it not to rain, and it did not rain on the
earth for three years and six months.
[1 Kin 17:1]
18 Then he prayed again, and the sky
gave rain and the land produced its
crops [as usual]. [1 Kin 18:42–45]
19 My brothers and sisters, if anyone
among you strays from the truth *and*
falls into error and [another] one turns
him back [to God],
20 let the [latter] one know that the
one who has turned a sinner from the
error of his way will save that one's
soul from death and cover a multitude
of sins [that is, obtain the pardon of the
many sins committed by the one who
has been restored].

---

conspicuous signs of wealth. James pronounces judgment and destruction on all three.

5:12 – 13 ***do not swear.*** James is not forbidding a believer from taking an oath in court or invoking God as witness to some significant statement (1Th 2:5). Instead, he is prohibiting the ancient practice of appealing to a variety of different objects to confirm the veracity of one's statement. This practice was extremely close to idolatry, for it implied that such objects contained spirits. The warning in these verses can serve as a reminder to us to watch what we say. We should not use God's name in a reckless manner, and we should be careful to speak the truth.

5:14 ***anointing him with oil.*** This may refer to medicinal treatment (Lk 10:34). Yet, in this passage, it most likely refers to the healing power of the Holy Spirit, for verse 15 speaks of prayer saving the person. In either case, there is no indication that calling the elders excludes the use of a physician or medicine.

5:15 ***the prayer of faith.*** Whether a believer is healed through medicine or through miraculous means, all healing is ultimately from the Lord. That is why prayers should be consistently offered for the sick.

5:16 ***The heartfelt and persistent prayer.*** This can mean that (1) prayer is effective when it is used, or (2) heartfelt prayer accomplishes great results.

8 Php 4:5; 1Pe 4:7 **9** Jas 4:11; Mt 24:33 **10** Mt 5:12 **11** Ps 94:12; Job 2:10; Job 42:10; Nu 14:18 **12** Mt 5:34 **13** Eph 5:19 **14** Mk 6:13 **15** Isa 33:24 **16** Nu 11:2; Jn 9:31 **17** Ac 14:15; 1Ki 17:1; Lk 4:25 **18** 1Ki 18:42,45 **19** Mt 18:15 **20** Ro 11:14; Pr 10:12; 1Pe 4:8

THE FIRST LETTER OF
PETER

▸ **AUTHOR:** The early church universally acknowledged the authenticity and authority of 1 Peter. It is likely that Peter used Silvanus as his scribe (5:12). This epistle was addressed to Christians throughout Asia Minor, indicating the spread of the gospel in regions not evangelized when Acts was written. It was written from Babylon (5:13), but scholars are divided as to whether this refers literally to Babylon in Mesopotamia or symbolically to Rome. It is probably the latter as tradition consistently indicates that Peter spent the last few years of his life in Rome.

▸ **TIMES:** c. AD 63 – 64 ▸ **KEY VERSES:** 1Pe 4:12 – 13

▸ **THEME:** First Peter was probably written to the Roman provinces of Turkey at the beginning of Nero's persecutions of Christians. Its primary message is one of comfort, hope, and encouragement. He asks the readers to hold fast to the faith in the midst of the coming persecution. In these letters we get a picture of a mature Peter who has incorporated Christ's crucifixion and death and resurrection into his thinking about suffering. He fully understands, and even looks forward to, the glory that is to come after the sufferings of this life.

A Living Hope, and a Sure Salvation

1 PETER, AN apostle (special messenger, personally chosen representative) of Jesus Christ,
To those [elect—both Jewish and Gentile believers] who live as exiles, scattered throughout Pontus, Galatia, Cappadocia, Asia [Minor], and Bithynia, who are chosen [Heb 13:14]
[2]according to the foreknowledge of God the Father by the sanctifying work of the Spirit to be obedient to Jesus Christ and to be sprinkled with His blood: May grace and peace [that special sense of spiritual well-being] be yours in increasing abundance [as you walk closely with God]. [John 14:27]
[3]Blessed [gratefully praised and adored] be the God and Father of our Lord Jesus Christ, who according to His abundant *and* boundless mercy

---

1:1 ***exiles.*** This term conveys the idea of being dispersed, much like the Jewish exiles of the Old Testament who were not living in their homeland but in Babylon.
1:2 ***sanctifying work of the Spirit.*** Sanctification is the ongoing process whereby the Holy Spirit works in believers, making their lives holy, separated from their old ways and to God in order to be more like him. ***sprinkled with His blood.*** This concept, the second reason why God chooses us, draws our attention to three situations in the Old Testament when the Israelites were sprinkled with the blood of animals: (1) Moses' sprinkling of blood on the Israelites at Mount Sinai to symbolize their initiation into the covenant (Ex 24:5 – 8); (2) the sprinkling of Aaron and his sons to be the priests of Israel (Ex 29:19 – 21); and (3) the sprinkling of the blood performed by the priest over healed lepers to symbolize their cleansing (Lev 14:1 – 9). Any of these three cases could be the one that Peter has in mind here.
1:3 ***according to His abundant and boundless mercy.*** Our salvation is grounded in God's mercy, His act of compassion toward us despite

CHAPTER 1 **1** Jn 7:35; Ac 2:5,9; Jas 1:1 **2** Eph 1:4; Ro 8:29; 2Th 2:13; Heb 12:24; Ro 1:7 **3** Eph 1:3; Titus 3:5; Jn 3:3,5; Jas 1:18; 1Co 15:20

has caused us to be born again [that is, to be reborn from above—spiritually transformed, renewed, and set apart for His purpose] to an ever-living hope *and* confident assurance through the resurrection of Jesus Christ from the dead, [Matt 28:1–9; Mark 16:6; Luke 24:6; John 20:1–18]

[4]
[born anew] into an inheritance which is imperishable [beyond the reach of change] and undefiled and unfading, reserved in heaven for you,

[5]
who are being protected *and* shielded by the power of God through *your* faith for salvation that is ready to be revealed [for you] in the last time.

[6]
In this you rejoice greatly, even though now for a little while, if necessary, you have been distressed by various trials,

[7]
so that the genuineness of your faith, which is much more precious than gold which is perishable, even though tested *and* purified by fire, may be found to result in [your] praise and glory and honor at the revelation of Jesus Christ.

[8]
Though you have not seen Him, you love Him; and though you do not even see Him now, you believe *and* trust in Him and you greatly rejoice *and* delight with inexpressible and glorious joy,

[9]
receiving as the result [the outcome, the consummation] of your faith, the salvation of your souls.

[10]
Regarding this salvation, the prophets who prophesied about the grace [of God] that *was intended for* you, searched carefully and inquired [about this future way of salvation],

[11]
seeking to find out what person or what time the Spirit of Christ within them was indicating as He foretold the sufferings of Christ and the glories [destined] to follow.

[12]
It was revealed to them that their services [their prophecies regarding grace] were not [meant] for themselves *and* their time, but for you, in these things [the death, resurrection, and glorification of Jesus Christ] which have now been told to you by those who preached the gospel to you by the [power of the] Holy Spirit [who was] sent from heaven. Into these things even the angels long to look.

[13]
So prepare your minds for action, be completely sober [in spirit—steadfast, self-disciplined, spiritually and morally alert], fix your hope completely on the grace [of God] that

---

our condition of sinfulness. ***has caused us to be born again.*** God has given believers a new, spiritual life that enables us to live in an entirely different dimension than the one our physical birth allowed.

1:4 *inheritance.* The Greek word here suggests both a present and a future reality. God has already determined what we will one day experience in its totality. ***reserved.*** God has set aside in heaven a wonderful inheritance that is waiting for us even now.

1:7 *that the genuineness of your faith.* As the purity of gold is brought forth by intense heat, so the reality and purity of our faith are revealed as a result of the fiery trials we face. Ultimately the testing of our faith not only demonstrates our final salvation but also develops our capacity to bring glory to the Lord Jesus Christ when He comes into His kingdom and we reign with Him (Ro 8:17; 2Ti 2:12; Rev 5:9 – 12).

1:10 *the prophets.* Peter indicates that the Old Testament prophets knew of the gracious salvation we would one day receive and, as a result, studied it carefully and intensively.

1:12 *by the [power of the] Holy Spirit.* Although humans may preach God's message of salvation, ultimately the Holy Spirit is the One who proclaims these great truths. Even the angels are amazed at what a wonderful salvation God has enacted on our behalf (Eph 3:10).

1:13 *prepare your minds for action.* Just as people in biblical times would gather up their long robes and tie them around their waists so that they could move quickly and freely, we need to do whatever it takes to focus our thoughts on those things that allow us to serve God successfully, all the while eliminating any thoughts that would trip us up (Heb 12:1). ***be completely sober.*** Peter's concern here is primarily using mentally or spiritually sound judgment. ***fix your hope completely.*** We need to exhibit confidence that God will accomplish all that He promised He would do (v. 3; Ro 8:24 – 25).

4 Col 1:5 **5** Jn 10:28 **6** Mt 5:12; 2Co 4:17 **7** Jas 1:3; Job 23:10; Pr 17:3; Ro 2:7 **8** 1Jn 4:20; Jn 20:29 **9** Ro 6:22 **10** Ge 49:10 **11** 2Pe 1:21 **12** Da 9:24; Heb 11:13; Ac 2:4; Da 8:13 **13** Eph 6:14; Lk 21:34; Ro 13:13; 1Co 1:7

is coming to you when Jesus Christ is
revealed.
14 [Live] as obedient children [of
God]; do not be conformed to the evil
desires *which governed you* in your
ignorance [before you knew the re-
quirements and transforming power
of the good news regarding salvation].
15 But like the Holy One who called
you, be holy yourselves in all *your*
conduct [be set apart from the world
by your godly character and moral
courage];
16 because it is written, "You shall
be holy (set apart), for I am holy."
[Lev 11:44, 45; 19:2]
17 If you address as Father, the One
who impartially judges according to
each one's work, conduct yourselves
in [reverent] fear [of Him] *and* with
profound respect for Him throughout
the time of your stay *on earth*.
18 For you know that you were not re-
deemed from your useless [spiritually
unproductive] way of life inherited [by
tradition] from your forefathers with
perishable things like silver and gold,
19 but [you were actually purchased]
with precious blood, like that of a
[sacrificial] lamb unblemished and
spotless, *the priceless blood* of Christ.
[Lev 22:20]
20 For He was foreordained (fore-
known) before the foundation of the
world, but has appeared [publicly] in
these last times for your sake
21 and through Him you believe [con-
fidently] in God [the heavenly Father],
who raised Him from the dead and
gave Him glory, so that your faith and
hope are [centered and rest] in God.
22 Since by your obedience to the
truth you have purified yourselves for
a sincere love of the believers, [see that
you] love one another from the heart
[always unselfishly seeking the best
for one another],
23 for you have been born again [that
is, reborn from above—spiritually
transformed, renewed, and set apart
for His purpose] not of seed which
is perishable but [from that which is]
imperishable *and* immortal, *that is*,
through the living and everlasting
word of God.
24 For,

"All flesh is like grass,
And all its glory like the flower
of grass.
The grass withers
And the flower falls off,
25 But the word of the Lord endures
forever."

And this is the word [the good news
of salvation] which was preached to
you. [Is 40:6–8]

As Newborn Babes

2 SO PUT aside every trace of mal-
ice and all deceit and hypocrisy
and envy and all slander *and* hateful
speech;
2 like newborn babies [you should]
long for the pure milk of the word, so
that by it you may be nurtured *and*

1:17 *in [reverent] fear.* For Christians, this phrase should be understood as something between terror and reverential awe. We need to remember that God is both our merciful Savior (vv. 3,18 – 21) and our holy Judge (vv. 15 – 17).

1:19 *a [sacrificial] lamb.* Peter describes Christ as the ultimate sacrificial Lamb, who is offered in our place to pay the price for our sins. The analogy here may be a reference either to the Passover lamb (Ex 12:3 – 6) or to the many lambs without blemish that were offered as part of the Old Testament sacrificial system (Lev 23:12; Nu 6:14; 28:3).

1:20 *foreordained.* God has known (v. 2) the One who would bring salvation, even as He has known those to whom that salvation is offered and secured (Ro 11:2). ***but has appeared.*** This phrase contrasts with the first half of the verse. What was known only to God before the creation of the world is now made known to us.

1:22 *purified yourselves.* We accomplish the purification of our souls by obedience to God's truth.

2:2 *that by it you may be nurtured and grow.* The purpose of studying God's truth is not only to learn more, but to become mature in the faith.

14 Ro 12:2; Ac 17:30 **15** 2Co 7:1 **16** Lev 11:44 **17** Dt 10:17; Heb 12:28; Heb 11:13 **18** 1Co 6:20; Eze 20:18 **19** Ac 20:28; Ex 12:5 **20** Ro 3:25; Gal 4:4 **21** Ac 2:24,33 **22** Ac 15:9; Heb 13:1 **23** Jn 1:13; Jas 1:18 **24** Isa 40:6 **25** Isa 40:8; Jn 1:1 **CHAPTER 2** **1** Heb 12:1 **2** Mt 18:3; 1Co 3:2

grow in respect to salvation [its ultimate fulfillment],
[3]if in fact you have [already] tasted the goodness *and* gracious kindness of the Lord. [Ps 34:8]

As Living Stones

[4]Come to Him [the risen Lord] as to a living Stone which men rejected *and* threw away, but which is choice and precious in the sight of God. [Ps 118:22; Is 28:16]
[5]You [believers], like living stones, are being built up into a spiritual house for a holy *and* dedicated priesthood, to offer spiritual sacrifices [that are] acceptable *and* pleasing to God through Jesus Christ.
[6]For this is contained in Scripture:

"BEHOLD, I AM LAYING IN ZION
A CHOSEN STONE, A PRECIOUS
(honored) CORNERSTONE,
AND HE WHO BELIEVES IN HIM
[whoever adheres to, trusts
in, and relies on Him] WILL
NEVER BE DISAPPOINTED [in his
expectations]." [Is 28:16]

[7]This precious value, then, is for you who believe [in Him as God's only Son—the Source of salvation]; but for those who disbelieve,

"THE [very] STONE WHICH THE
BUILDERS REJECTED
HAS BECOME THE CHIEF
CORNERSTONE," [Ps 118:22]

[8]and,

"A STONE OF STUMBLING AND A ROCK OF
OFFENSE";

for they stumble because they disobey the word [of God], and to this they [who reject Him as Savior] were also appointed. [Is 8:14]
[9]But you are A CHOSEN RACE, A royal PRIESTHOOD, A CONSECRATED NATION, A [special] PEOPLE FOR *God's* OWN POSSESSION, so that you may proclaim the excellencies [the wonderful deeds and virtues and perfections] of Him who called you out of darkness into His marvelous light. [Ex 19:5, 6]
[10]Once you were NOT A PEOPLE [at all], but now you are GOD'S PEOPLE; once you had NOT RECEIVED MERCY, but now you have RECEIVED MERCY. [Hos 2:23]
[11]Beloved, I urge you as aliens and strangers [in this world] to abstain from the sensual urges [those dishonorable desires] that wage war against the soul.
[12]Keep your behavior excellent among the [unsaved] Gentiles [conduct

---

2:4 *living Stone.* This phrase anticipates the Old Testament quotations in verses 6–8. Jesus, as a living stone, is superior to the Old Testament temple.
2:5 *stones.* Christians are part of God's great spiritual building project. Referenced here are stones that are shaped and ready for use in construction, as opposed to natural rock. ***a holy and dedicated priesthood.*** Unlike the Old Testament priesthood, in which only those who were born into a certain tribe could be priests, all who are reborn into God's family, that is, all believers, are priests who have the privilege and responsibility of offering spiritual sacrifices to God (Ro 12:1–2; Heb 13:15–16).
2:6 *A PRECIOUS (honored) CORNERSTONE.* Jesus is the foundation stone from which the placement of all other living stones in the spiritual house (v. 5) is determined (Isa 28:16). In ancient buildings, the cornerstone was first situated on the foundation and then all of the other stones were aligned to it. Thus as part of the house of God, we need to keep our focus on our Cornerstone (Heb 12:2).
2:9 *A CHOSEN RACE.* God has not left to chance who will be part of a unique body of people, a group who will serve Him. ***A ROYAL PRIESTHOOD.*** Believers are transformed not only internally (v. 5), which describes us as being made into a "holy priesthood" but also externally. We are a priesthood that functions in a ruling capacity, as kings. ***A CONSECRATED NATION.*** Believers are a unified group of people who are set apart for God's use. ***A [special] PEOPLE.*** God protects those whom He has adopted into His family.
2:11 *aliens and strangers.* With these words, Peter reminds believers (1:1) that this earth is not our home. We are foreigners here, traveling to our eternal home, heaven.
2:12 *day of visitation.* This term probably refers to the final day of judgment when all people,

3 Heb 6:5 **4** Ps 118:22; Ac 4:11 **5** Eph 2:21; Heb 3:6; Isa 61:6; Hos 14:2; Mal 1:11; Php 4:18 **6** Isa 28:16
7 Ps 118:22 **8** Isa 8:14; 1Co 1:23; Ro 9:22 **9** Dt 10:15; Rev 5:10; Isa 62:12; Dt 4:20; Ac 26:18 **10** Hos 1:9
11 Ps 39:12; Gal 5:16; Jas 4:1 **12** Php 2:15; Mt 5:16

yourself honorably, with graciousness and integrity], so that for whatever reason they may slander you as evildoers, yet by observing your good deeds they may [instead come to] glorify God in the day of visitation [when He looks upon them with mercy].

Honor Authority

13 Submit yourselves to [the authority of] every human institution for the sake of the Lord [to honor His name], whether it is to a king as one in a position of power,

14 or to governors as sent by him to bring punishment to those who do wrong, and to praise *and* encourage those who do right.

15 For it is the will of God that by doing right you may silence (muzzle, gag) the [culpable] ignorance *and* irresponsible criticisms of foolish people.

16 *Live* as free people, but do not use your freedom as a cover *or* pretext for evil, but [use it and live] as bond-servants of God.

17 Show respect for all people [treat them honorably], love the brotherhood [of believers], fear God, honor the king.

18 Servants, be submissive to your masters with all [proper] respect, not only to those who are good and kind, but also to those who are unreasonable.

19 For this *finds* favor, if a person endures the sorrow of suffering unjustly because of an awareness of [the will of] God.

20 After all, what kind of credit is there if, when you do wrong and are punished for it, you endure it patiently? But if when you do what is right and patiently bear [undeserved] suffering, this *finds* favor with God.

Christ Is Our Example

21 For [as a believer] you have been called for this purpose, since Christ suffered for you, leaving you an example, so that you may follow in His footsteps.

22 HE COMMITTED NO SIN, NOR WAS DECEIT EVER FOUND IN HIS MOUTH. [Is 53:9]

23 While being reviled *and* insulted, He did not revile *or* insult in return; while suffering, He made no threats [of vengeance], but kept entrusting *Himself* to Him who judges fairly.

24 He personally carried our sins in His body on the cross [willingly offering Himself on it, as on an altar of sacrifice], so that we might die to sin [becoming immune from the penalty

---

believers and unbelievers alike, will fall on their knees and acknowledge who Jesus Christ is and what He has done through His people.

2:13 *to [the authority of] every human institution.* This phrase suggests that the submission of Christians in not to be exercised solely in relation to civil authorities (v. 14), but to all kinds of rules that Christians encounter (2:18; 3:1).

2:13 Our Responsibility to Human Government — As children of God, our responsibility to human government is threefold:

We are to recognize and accept that the powers that be are ordained by God (Ro 13:1). This truth even applies to governments that are anti-Christian. If a given law is clearly anti-scriptural, the believer is required to obey God rather than man (Da 3; 6; Ac 4:18 – 20).

We are to pay our taxes to human government (Mt 17:24; 22:21; Ro 13:7).

We are to pray for the leaders in human government (1Ti 2:1 – 3).

2:16 *as a cover or pretext for evil.* This may be understood either as an excuse made up before the fact, or after the fact.

2:18 *be submissive . . . with all [proper] respect.* Workers are to take their responsibilities seriously, even when serving the worst of bosses.

2:20 *what kind of credit.* There is no advantage to believers for successfully enduring a deserved punishment for wrongdoing, yet there is great value when we honor God with our actions when we are unfairly condemned by others (3:17). ***patiently bear.*** Patience and perseverance in the face of suffering please God.

2:24 *He personally carried our sins.* The Greek wording emphasizes Jesus' personal involvement in the act of paying the price for our sins. ***that we might die to sin . . . and live for righteousness.*** The purpose of Christ's bearing our sins is that we might live to please Him.

13 Ro 13:1 **14** Ro 13:3,4 **15** Titus 2:8 **16** Gal 5:1; 1Co 7:22 **17** Ro 12:10; Heb 13:1; Ro 13:7 **18** Eph 6:5
19 Mt 5:10 **21** Mt 16:24; 1Jn 2:6 **22** Isa 53:9 **23** Isa 53:7; Lk 23:46 **24** Heb 9:28; Ro 7:6; Isa 53:5

and power of sin] and live for righteousness; for by His wounds you [who believe] have been healed.

25 For you were continually wandering like [so many] sheep, but now you have come back to the Shepherd and Guardian of your souls. [Is 53:5, 6]

Godly Living

3 IN THE same way, you wives, be submissive to your own husbands [subordinate, not as inferior, but out of respect for the responsibilities entrusted to husbands and their accountability to God, and so partnering with them] so that even if some do not obey the word [of God], they may be won over [to Christ] without discussion by the *godly* lives of their wives, [Eph 5:22]

2 when they see your modest and respectful behavior [together with your devotion and appreciation—love your husband, encourage him, and enjoy him as a blessing from God].

3 Your adornment must not be *merely* external—with interweaving *and* elaborate knotting of the hair, and wearing gold jewelry, or [being superficially preoccupied with] dressing in *expensive* clothes;

4 but let it be [the inner beauty of] the hidden person of the heart, with the imperishable quality *and* unfading charm of a gentle and peaceful spirit, [one that is calm and self-controlled, not overanxious, but serene and spiritually mature] which is very precious in the sight of God.

5 For in this way in former times the holy women, who hoped in God, used to adorn themselves, being submissive to their own husbands *and* adapting themselves to them;

6 just as Sarah obeyed Abraham [following him and having regard for him as head of their house], calling him lord. And you have become her daughters if you do what is right without being frightened by any fear [that is, being respectful toward your husband but not giving in to intimidation, nor allowing yourself to be led into sin, nor to be harmed].

7 In the same way, you husbands, live with *your wives* in an understanding way [with great gentleness and tact, and with an intelligent regard for the marriage relationship], as with someone physically weaker, since she is a woman. Show her honor *and* respect as a fellow heir of the grace of life, so that your prayers will not be hindered *or* ineffective.

8 Finally, all of you be like-minded [united in spirit], sympathetic, brotherly, kindhearted [courteous and compassionate toward each other as members of one household], and humble in spirit;

9 and never return evil for evil or insult for insult [avoid scolding, berating,

---

2:25 *Guardian.* No one else is qualified to be the one Shepherd and Guardian of our souls — only Christ is. For this reason the New Testament regularly describes the church and its congregations as having more than one leader (Titus 1:5).

3:1 *may be won over [to Christ] without discussion.* A godly wife does not preach to her non-Christian husband with words but with the Christ-like beauty of her daily life. The goal is to see that husband become a Christian.

3:3 *Your adornment must not be merely external.* Christians are to spend more time developing their inner character than attempting to make themselves look beautiful on the outside (1Sa 16). Peter is not condemning women who wear jewelry. He is emphasizing the importance of a woman's character.

3:4 *gentle and peaceful spirit.* Peter encourages Christian wives to exhibit attitudes that do not demand personal rights, attitudes that are not harsh and grating but are soothing and tranquil.

3:6 *calling him lord.* Sarah was not worshiping Abraham; she was showing him respect.

3:7 *husbands, live with your wives in an understanding way.* A Christian husband should be intimately aware of his wife's needs, her strengths and weaknesses, and her goals and desires. He should know as much about her as possible in order to respond in the best way to her.

3:9 *evil for evil.* Peter encourages Christians to act like the Lord Jesus. He endured suffering and ridicule in silence, entrusting His just cause to the ultimate Judge.

---

25 Isa 53:6; Eze 34:23; Heb 13:20 **CHAPTER 3** **1** 1Co 14:34; 1Co 7:16; Mt 18:15 **2** 1Pe 2:12 **3** 1Ti 2:9 **4** Ro 2:29 **6** Ge 18:12 **7** 1Co 7:3; 12:23; Job 42:8; Mt 18:19 **8** Ro 12:16; Ro 12:10; Heb 13:1; Eph 4:32 **9** Pr 17:13; Mt 25:34

and any kind of abuse], but on the
contrary, give a blessing [pray for one
another's well-being, contentment, and
protection]; for you have been called
for this very purpose, that you might
inherit a blessing [from God that brings
well-being, happiness, and protection].
10 For,

"THE ONE WHO WANTS TO ENJOY
LIFE AND SEE GOOD DAYS [good—
whether apparent or not],
MUST KEEP HIS TONGUE FREE FROM EVIL
AND HIS LIPS FROM SPEAKING GUILE
(treachery, deceit).
11 "HE MUST TURN AWAY FROM
WICKEDNESS AND DO WHAT IS RIGHT.
HE MUST SEARCH FOR PEACE [with
God, with self, with others] AND
PURSUE IT EAGERLY [actively—not
merely desiring it].
12 "FOR THE EYES OF THE LORD ARE
[looking favorably] UPON THE
RIGHTEOUS (the upright),
AND HIS EARS ARE ATTENTIVE TO THEIR
PRAYER (eager to answer),
BUT THE FACE OF THE LORD IS AGAINST
THOSE WHO PRACTICE EVIL."
[Ps 34:12–16]

13 Now who is there to hurt you if you
become enthusiastic for what is good?
14 But even if you should suffer for
the sake of righteousness [though it
is not certain that you will], you are
still blessed [happy, to be admired and
favored by God]. DO NOT BE AFRAID OF
THEIR INTIMIDATING THREATS, NOR BE TROU-
BLED *or* DISTURBED [by their opposition].
15 But in your hearts set Christ apart
[as holy—acknowledging Him, giving
Him first place in your lives] as Lord.
Always be ready to give a [logical]
defense to anyone who asks you to
account for the hope *and* confident as-
surance [elicited by faith] that is within
you, yet [do it] with gentleness and
respect. [Is 8:12, 13]
16 And see to it that your conscience
is entirely clear, so that every time you
are slandered *or* falsely accused, those
who attack *or* disparage your good
behavior in Christ will be shamed [by
their own words].
17 For it is better that you suffer [un-
justly] for doing what is right, if that
should be God's will, than [to suffer
justly] for doing wrong.
18 For indeed Christ died for sins once
for all, the Just *and* Righteous for the
unjust *and* unrighteous [the Innocent
for the guilty] so that He might bring
us to God, having been put to death in
the flesh, but made alive in the Spirit;
19 in which He also went and preached
to the spirits *now* in prison,
20 who once were disobedient, when
the *great* patience of God was wait-
ing in the days of Noah, during the
building of the ark, in which a few,
that is, eight persons [Noah's family],

3:12 *EYES ... EARS.* Peter uses this imagery to remind his readers that God knows everything about believers, especially their suffering, and that He listens and responds to their cries for help (Heb 4:12–16).

3:15 *in your hearts set Christ apart ... as Lord.* Believers should acknowledge the eternal holiness of Christ by revering Him as the Lord of the universe who is in control of all things. ***to give a [logical] defense.*** Peter assumes that the Christian faith will be falsely accused. He therefore encourages Christians to have rational answers to respond to those false accusations.

3:17 *For it is better.* Peter is not encouraging believers to seek out situations in which they will experience suffering. Instead, he is saying that believers should make certain that when they suffer, it is the result of having been faithful to God rather than because they have done evil (2:19).

3:19–20 *spirits now in prison.* The Greek term translated *spirits* can refer to human spirits, angels, or demons. There are three main interpretations: (1) Some interpret these verses as describing Jesus as going to the place where fallen angels are incarcerated and declaring His final victory over evil in His work on the cross; (2) Others hold that *spirits* refers to human spirits. Thus Christ preached to human beings who had died in Noah's day and were in the realm of the dead (hell or hades); and (3) Another major interpretation understands this passage as describing Christ preaching through Noah to the unbelievers of his day.

10 Ps 34:12; Jas 1:26; Rev 14:5 **11** Ps 37:27; 3Jn 11; Ro 12:18; Heb 12:14 **12** Jn 9:31; Jas 5:16 **13** Pr 16:7 **14** Jas 1:12; 1Pe 2:19; Isa 8:12,13 **15** Ps 119:46; Col 4:6; 2Ti 2:25 **16** Heb 13:18; Titus 2:8 **18** Ro 5:6; 2Co 13:4; Col 1:21; Ro 1:4 **19** 1Pe 1:12; Isa 42:7 **20** Ge 6:3,5; Heb 11:7; Ge 7:7

were brought safely through the water. [Gen 6–8]

21Corresponding to that [rescue through the flood], baptism [which is an expression of a believer's new life in Christ] now saves you, not by removing dirt from the body, but by an appeal to God for a good (clear) conscience, [demonstrating what you believe to be yours] through the resurrection of Jesus Christ,

22who has gone into heaven and is at the right hand of God [that is, the place of honor and authority], with [all] angels and authorities and powers made subservient to Him.

Keep Fervent in Your Love

4 THEREFORE, SINCE Christ suffered in the flesh [and died for us], arm yourselves [like warriors] with the same purpose [being willing to suffer for doing what is right and pleasing God], because whoever has suffered in the flesh [being like-minded with Christ] is done with [intentional] sin [having stopped pleasing the world],

2so that he can no longer spend the rest of his natural life living for human appetites *and* desires, but [lives] for the will *and* purpose of God.

3For the time already past is [more than] enough for doing what the [unsaved] Gentiles like to do—living [unrestrained as you have done] in a course of [shameless] sensuality, lusts, drunkenness, carousing, drinking parties, and wanton idolatries.

4In [connection with] all this, they [the unbelievers] are resentful *and* surprised that you do not [think like them, value their values and] run [hand in hand] with *them* into the same excesses of dissipation *and* immoral freedom, and they criticize *and* abuse *and* ridicule you *and* make fun of your values.

5But they will [have to] give an account to Him who is ready to judge *and* pass sentence on the living and the dead.

6For this is why the good news [of salvation] was preached [in their lifetimes] even to those who are dead, that though they were judged in the flesh as men are, they may live in the spirit according to [the will and purpose of] God.

7The end *and* culmination of all things is near. Therefore, be sound-minded and self-controlled for the purpose of prayer [staying balanced and focused on the things of God so that your communication will be clear, reasonable, specific and pleasing to Him.]

8Above all, have fervent *and* unfailing love for one another, because love covers a multitude of sins [it overlooks unkindness and unselfishly seeks the best for others]. [Prov 10:12]

4:1 *is done with [intentional] sin.* Those who serve God faithfully in the midst of suffering take on a different attitude toward sin than what they previously held. Sin no longer holds the same grip on them.

4:3 *wanton idolatries.* The idea here is that some forms of idolatry may have been detestable even to the civil authorities. Of course, all types of idolatry are hateful to God.

4:5 *they will [have to] give an account.* Although unbelievers think they are free to do as they please, they are greatly mistaken. There are consequences to what they do. One day they will stand defenseless before God and give an account of all of their wickedness (Rev 20:11 – 15).

4:6 *to those who are dead.* There are four main interpretations of Peter's meaning here: (1) Some see a connection between the gospel preached in this verse and the proclamation of Christ in 3:19 – 20. Accordingly, they understand this verse to be about Christ offering salvation to those who lived in pre-Christian times; (2) Another group of commentators also connects this preaching to 3:19 – 20, but holds that this verse is speaking of Christ preaching the gospel only to the righteous people of Old Testament times; (3) Peter was speaking of the gospel which was preached to believers who are now dead; and (4) Peter is referring to the spiritually dead. The gospel was being preached to them so that they could come alive spiritually.

4:8 *love covers a multitude of sins.* Peter is not suggesting that one Christian's love atones for another Christian's sins. Rather, by introducing this proverb from the Old Testament (Pr 10:12), he is reminding us that love does not stir up sins. We

21 Eph 5:26; Titus 3:5; Ro 10:10; 1Pe 1:3 **22** Ps 110:1; Ro 8:34; Ro 8:38; 1Co 15:24 **CHAPTER 4** **1** 1Pe 3:18; Gal 5:24 **2** Ro 14:7; Gal 2:20; Jn 1:13 **3** Eze 44:6; Eph 2:2; 1Th 4:5; Titus 3:3 **4** Ac 13:45 **5** Ac 10:42; Ro 14:10; 2Ti 4:1 **6** 1Pe 3:19 **7** Ro 13:12; Mt 26:41; Lk 21:34 **8** Col 3:14; Heb 13:1; Pr 10:12; 1Co 13:7

9 Be hospitable to one another without complaint.

10 Just as each one of you has received a *special* gift [a spiritual talent, an ability graciously given by God], employ it in serving one another as [is appropriate for] good stewards of God's multi-faceted grace [faithfully using the diverse, varied gifts and abilities granted to Christians by God's unmerited favor].

11 Whoever speaks [to the congregation], *is to do so* as one who speaks the oracles (utterances, the very words) of God. Whoever serves [the congregation] *is to do so* as one who serves by the strength which God [abundantly] supplies, so that in all things God may be glorified [honored and magnified] through Jesus Christ, to whom belongs the glory and dominion forever and ever. Amen.

Share the Sufferings of Christ

12 Beloved, do not be surprised at the fiery ordeal which is taking place to test you [that is, to test the quality of your faith], as though something strange *or* unusual were happening to you.

13 But insofar as you are sharing Christ's sufferings, keep on rejoicing, so that when His glory [filled with His radiance and splendor] is revealed, you may rejoice with great joy.

14 If you are insulted *and* reviled for [bearing] the name of Christ, you are blessed [happy, with life-joy and comfort in God's salvation regardless of your circumstances], because the Spirit of glory and of God is resting on you [and indwelling you—He whom they curse, you glorify]. [Is 11:2]

15 Make sure that none of you suffers as a murderer, or a thief, or any sort of criminal [in response to persecution], or as a troublesome meddler interfering in the affairs of others;

16 but if *anyone suffers* [ill-treatment] as a Christian [because of his belief], he is not to be ashamed, but is to glorify God [because he is considered worthy to suffer] in this name.

17 For it is the time [destined] for judgment to begin with the household of God; and if *it begins* with us, what will the outcome be for those who do not respect *or* believe *or* obey the gospel of God?

18 AND IF IT IS DIFFICULT FOR THE RIGHTEOUS TO BE SAVED, WHAT WILL BECOME OF THE GODLESS AND THE SINNER? [Prov 11:31]

19 Therefore, those who are ill-treated *and* suffer in accordance with the will of God must [continue to] do right and commit their souls [for safe-keeping] to the faithful Creator.

Serve God Willingly

5 THEREFORE, I strongly urge the elders among you [pastors, spiritual leaders of the church], as a fellow elder and as an eyewitness [called to testify] of the sufferings of Christ, as well as one who shares in the glory that is to be revealed:

---

can demonstrate our love for our fellow believers by truly forgiving them and not talking openly about their past sins.

4:9 ***Be hospitable.*** In New Testament times, hospitality typically meant housing and feeding travelers for two to three days with no expectation of payment in return.

4:10 ***Just as each one of you has received a special gift.*** Every believer is gifted to serve. ***stewards.*** These are managers or trustees who will be held accountable for using their gift in the best interest of the One who gave it to them.

4:12 ***do not be surprised.*** Apparently Peter's readers were astonished that they had to suffer as Christians, especially to the extent that they were suffering. ***fiery ordeal.*** The Greek word translated here was also used to speak of the intense fire that burned away impurities in metals.

4:17 ***it is the time [destined] for judgment to begin.*** Judgment does not always imply condemnation in Scripture. When used in relation to Christians, it consistently refers to the evaluation of a believer's works for the purpose of reward (1Co 3:10 – 15).

5:1 ***one who shares.*** This phrase speaks of sharing in Christ's reign in the coming kingdom (Ro 8:17; Rev 2:26 – 28; 5:9 – 10). Peter considers himself to be already participating partly in the glory that one day he will experience fully.

---

9 Heb 13:2; 2Co 9:7 **10** Ro 12:6; Mt 24:45; Titus 1:7; 1Co 12:4; Eph 4:11 **11** Jer 23:22; 1Co 3:10; Eph 5:20; 1Ti 6:16 **12** 1Co 3:13 **13** Ac 5:41; Ro 8:17 **14** 2Co 12:10; Jas 1:12 **15** 1Pe 2:20; 1Th 4:11 **16** Ac 5:41 **17** Isa 10:12; Lk 23:31; Lk 10:12 **18** Lk 23:31 **19** 2Ti 1:12 **CHAPTER 5** **1** Php 9; Lk 24:48; Ac 1:8; Rev 1:9

2 shepherd *and* guide *and* protect the flock of God among you, exercising oversight not under compulsion, but voluntarily, according to *the will of* God; and not [motivated] for shameful gain, but with wholehearted enthusiasm;

3 not lording it over those assigned to your care [do not be arrogant or overbearing], but be examples [of Christian living] to the flock [set a pattern of integrity for your congregation].

4 And when the Chief Shepherd (Christ) appears, you will receive the [conqueror's] unfading crown of glory.

5 Likewise, you younger men [of lesser rank and experience], be subject to your elders [seek their counsel]; and all of you, clothe yourselves with humility toward one another [tie on the servant's apron], for GOD IS OPPOSED TO THE PROUD [the disdainful, the presumptuous, and He defeats them], BUT HE GIVES GRACE TO THE HUMBLE. [Prov 3:34]

6 Therefore humble yourselves under the mighty hand of God [set aside self-righteous pride], so that He may exalt you [to a place of honor in His service] at the appropriate time, [John 3:30]

7 casting all your cares [all your anxieties, all your worries, and all your concerns, once and for all] on Him, for He cares about you [with deepest affection, and watches over you very carefully]. [Ps 55:22]

8 Be sober [well balanced and self-disciplined], be alert *and* cautious at all times. That enemy of yours, the devil, prowls around like a roaring lion [fiercely hungry], seeking someone to devour.

9 But resist him, be firm in *your* faith [against his attack—rooted, established, immovable], knowing that the same experiences of suffering are being experienced by your brothers and sisters throughout the world. [You do not suffer alone.]

10 After you have suffered for a little while, the God of all grace [who imparts His blessing and favor], who called you to His *own* eternal glory in Christ, will Himself complete, confirm, strengthen, and establish you [making you what you ought to be].

11 To Him be dominion (power, authority, sovereignty) forever and ever. Amen.

12 By Silvanus, our faithful brother (as I consider him), I have written to you briefly, to counsel and testify that this is the true grace [the undeserved favor] of God. Stand firm in it!

13 She [the church] who is in Babylon, chosen together with you, sends you greetings, and *so does* my son [in the faith], Mark.

14 Greet one another with a kiss of love.

To all of you who are in Christ, may there be peace.

5:2 *shepherd and guide and protect the flock of God.* An ancient Israelite shepherd would go before his sheep to lead them; he would not drive the sheep in front of him. Church leaders should lead the people of God in the same way; feeding, protecting, and guiding them (Jn 21:15 – 17). Christian leaders should also remember that they have been given responsibility for tending a flock that belongs to God, not to themselves. ***not [motivated] for shameful gain.*** Christian leaders need to make certain that their work is not motivated by money, but by a passion for the good of those believers put in their charge (1Ti 3:3,8; Titus 1:11).

5:3 *not lording it over.* Echoing a command that Peter heard directly from Jesus during His earthly ministry, Peter reminds all Christian leaders that they need to perform the role of servants, not masters, to those whom God has assigned to their care (Mt 20:25 – 28; Mk 10:42 – 45).

5:8 *That enemy of yours.* Satan is our avowed enemy. He never ceases from being hostile toward us; he is constantly accusing us before God (Job 1:9 – 2:7; Zec 3:1; Lk 22:31; Rev 12:10). ***like a roaring lion.*** Satan is both cunning and cruel. He attacks when least expected and desires to destroy completely those whom he attacks.

5:10 *establish you.* As a consequence of our facing the attacks of our enemy, God will build in us a firm foundation that makes us steadfast and immovable.

5:11 *dominion(power, authority, sovereignty) forever and ever.* God is in control of all things both in this world and throughout eternity.

2 Ac 20:28; 1Co 9:17; 1Ti 3:3 **3** Eze 34:4; Ps 33:12; Php 3:17 **4** Heb 13:20; 2Ti 4:8 **5** Ro 12:10; Jas 4:6; Isa 57:15 **6** Jas 4:10 **7** Ps 37:5; Heb 13:5 **8** Lk 21:34; Job 1:7 **9** Eph 6:11; Ac 14:22 **10** 1Co 1:9; 2Co 4:17; Heb 13:21; 2Th 2:17 **11** Rev 1:6 **12** 2Co 1:19; Heb 13:22; Ac 20:24 **13** Ac 12:12 **14** Ro 16:16; Eph 6:23

THE SECOND LETTER OF

PETER

▸ **AUTHOR:** No other book in the New Testament poses as many problems of authenticity as does 2 Peter. But in spite of the external and internal problems, the traditional position of Petrine authorship overcomes more difficulties than any other option. This epistle was written just before the apostle's death (1:14), probably from Rome.

▸ **TIMES:** c. AD 64–66 ▸ **KEY VERSES:** 2Pe 1:20–21

▸ **THEME:** While 1 Peter deals with suffering and persecution caused by people outside the church, 2 Peter deals more with the need for the true spiritual knowledge and maturity in the face of false teachers who would distort the faith from inside the church. He gives his readers insight into the thinking of the false teachers and encourages opposition to them. He also urges watchfulness for Christ's return through all the events at the end of the age.

Growth in Christian Virtue

1 SIMON PETER, a bond-servant and apostle (special messenger, personally chosen representative) of Jesus Christ,

To those who have received *and* possess [by God's will] a precious faith of the same kind as ours, by the righteousness of our God and Savior, Jesus Christ:

2Grace and peace [that special sense of spiritual well-being] be multiplied to you in the [true, intimate] knowledge of God and of Jesus our Lord.

3For His divine power has bestowed on us [absolutely] everything necessary for [a dynamic spiritual] life and godliness, through true *and* personal knowledge of Him who called us by His own glory and excellence.

4For by these He has bestowed on us His precious and magnificent promises [of inexpressible value], so that by them you may escape from the immoral freedom that is in the world because

---

1:1 *apostle.* With this term Peter identifies himself as an authorized spokesman for the truth that Christ proclaimed. In verses 1–4 Peter describes the resources his readers have that will make growth in grace and knowledge possible. His apostleship is the first of these resources. ***a precious faith.*** Anyone who has faith in Jesus has the same access to God as any other believer. This access is the second great resource that Peter's readers possess.

1:2 *the [true, intimate] knowledge of God.* The Greek word translated *knowledge* is a key word in this letter. It describes a special kind of knowledge, a kind that is complete. Since our knowledge of Jesus grows as we mature in the faith, we will experience His grace and peace on many different occasions in our Christian walk.

1:3 *divine power.* This power is identified as the "power of His resurrection" (Php 3:10; 4:13). This power is the third resource for godly living that Peter lists in this letter. ***glory and excellence.*** These words suggest the qualities of Jesus that attract believers to Him. The glory that John saw in Jesus (Jn 1:14) was His authority and power.

1:4 *precious and magnificent promises.* This phrase refers to the numerous offers of divine provision found in Scripture. These promises offer us the glory and virtue of Christ as the basis for our growing participation in the divine nature. We have Christ within us, as He promised (Jn 14:23),

---

CHAPTER 1 **1** Eph 4:5 **2** Da 4:1 **3** 1Th 2:12 **4** 2Co 7:1; 2Co 3:18; Heb 12:10

of disreputable desire, and become sharers of the divine nature.
[5]For this very reason, applying your diligence [to the divine promises, make every effort] in [exercising] your faith to, develop moral excellence, and in moral excellence, knowledge (insight, understanding),
[6]and in *your* knowledge, self-control, and in *your* self-control, steadfastness, and in *your* steadfastness, godliness,
[7]and in *your* godliness, brotherly affection, and in *your* brotherly affection, [develop Christian] love [that is, learn to unselfishly seek the best for others and to do things for their benefit].
[8]For as these *qualities* are yours and are increasing [in you as you grow toward spiritual maturity], they will keep you from being useless and unproductive in regard to the true knowledge *and* greater understanding of our Lord Jesus Christ.
[9]For whoever lacks these *qualities* is blind—shortsighted [closing his spiritual eyes to the truth], having become oblivious to the fact that he was cleansed from his old sins.
[10]Therefore, believers, be all the more diligent to make certain about His calling and choosing you [be sure that your behavior reflects and confirms your relationship with God]; for by doing these things [actively developing these virtues], you will never stumble [in your spiritual growth and will live a life that leads others away from sin];
[11]for in this way entry into the eternal kingdom of our Lord and Savior Jesus Christ will be abundantly provided to you.
[12]Therefore, I will always be ready to remind you of these things, even though you *already* know them and are established in the truth which is held firmly in your grasp.
[13]I think it right, as long as I am in this *earthly* tent, to inspire you by reminding you,
[14]knowing that the laying aside of this *earthly* tent of mine is imminent, as our Lord Jesus Christ has made clear to me.
[15]Moreover, I will diligently endeavor [to see to it] that even after my departure you will be able, at all times, to call these things to mind.

Eyewitnesses

[16]For we did not follow cleverly devised stories *or* myths when we made known to you the power and coming of our Lord Jesus Christ, but we were eyewitnesses of His majesty [His grandeur, His authority, His sovereignty].

---

to enable us to become increasingly Christ-like (2Co 3:18).

1:5 *moral excellence.* This term is the same word used in verse 3 in reference to Christ's character. We cannot produce virtue ourselves; but we can choose to obey the promptings of the Holy Spirit who lives in us.

1:6 *steadfastness.* A person who exercises self-control will not easily succumb to discouragement or the temptation to quit. Viewing all circumstances as coming from the hand of a loving Father who is in control of all things is the secret of perseverance.

1:9 *blind.* This kind of person is one who looks only at earthly and material values — what is close at hand — and does not see the eternal spiritual realities. Concerned only with this present life, such a person becomes blind to the things of God, forgetting the wonderful sense of cleansing that comes from turning oneself over to Christ.

1:11 *entry . . . abundantly.* Peter distinguishes between a just-barely-made-it entrance into the eternal kingdom and a richly abundant one. The Scripture indicates that fruitful and faithful living here will be rewarded by greater privileges and rewards in glory (Rev 22:12).

1:15 *I will diligently endeavor . . . after my departure.* Several early church fathers took these words to be Peter's promise to leave behind a testimony of the truth for his readers, which they considered to be the Gospel of Mark.

1:16 *cleverly devised stories or myths.* Peter countered the false teacher's faith claims with an eyewitness account. Peter himself had actually seen the power and the coming of the Lord Jesus Christ. These are the twin themes of this letter; the power of Jesus available for holy living and the coming of Jesus as the glorious hope of each believer.

---

5 2Pe 3:18; 1Pe 3:7 **7** Gal 6:10; 1Th 3:12 **8** Jn 15:2; Titus 3:14 **9** 1Jn 2:9; Eph 5:26; Heb 9:14 **10** 1Jn 3:19 **12** Php 3:1; 1Jn 2:21; 1Pe 5:12 **13** 2Co 5:1 **14** 2Ti 4:6; Jn 21:18,19 **16** 1Co 1:17; Mk 9:2; 1Jn 1:1

17 For when He was invested with honor and [the radiance of the Shekinah] glory from God the Father, such a voice as this came to Him from the [splendid] Majestic Glory [in the bright cloud that overshadowed Him, saying], "This is My Son, My Beloved Son in whom I am well-pleased *and* delighted"— [Matt 17:5]

18 and we [actually] heard this voice made from heaven when we were together with Him on the holy mountain. [Matt 17:6]

19 So we have the prophetic word made more certain. You do well to pay [close] attention to it as to a lamp shining in a dark place, until the day dawns *and* light breaks through the gloom and the morning star arises in your hearts. [Num 24:17]

20 But understand this first of all, that no prophecy of Scripture is *a matter* of *or* comes from one's own [personal or special] interpretation,

21 for no prophecy was ever made by an act of human will, but men moved by the Holy Spirit spoke from God.

The Rise of False Prophets

2 BUT [in those days] false prophets arose among the people, just as there will be false teachers among you, who will subtly introduce destructive heresies, even denying the Master who bought them, bringing swift destruction on themselves.

2 Many will follow their shameful ways, and because of them the way of truth will be maligned.

3 And in *their* greed they will exploit you with false arguments *and* twisted doctrine. Their sentence [of condemnation which God has decreed] from a time long ago is not idle [but is still in force], and their destruction *and* deepening misery is not asleep [but is on its way].

4 For if God did not [even] spare angels that sinned, but threw them into hell and sent them to pits of gloom to be kept [there] for judgment;

5 and if He did not spare the ancient world, but protected Noah, a preacher of righteousness, with seven others, when He brought [the judgment of] a

---

1:19 *we have the prophetic word made more certain.* As strong as an eyewitness account (vv. 16–18) may be, there is an even stronger confirmation that Jesus is who He said He was. The written Scriptures are even more trustworthy than the personal experience of the apostle Peter.

1:20 *one's own [personal or special] interpretation.* Although some have taken this phrase to mean that no individual Christian has the right to interpret prophecy for himself or herself, the context and the Greek word for *interpretation* indicates another meaning for the verse. The Greek word for *interpretation* can also mean "origin." In the context of verse 21, it is clear that Peter is speaking of Scripture's "origin" from God Himself and not the credentials of the one who interprets it. There is no private source for the Bible; the prophets did not supply their own solutions or explanations to the mysteries of life. Rather, God spoke through them; He alone is responsible for what is written in Scripture.

2:1 *destructive heresies.* Peter is addressing here the ethical implication of false teaching. The Greek word translated *destructive* means "shameful" or "deliberately immoral." The false teachers gloried in the privileges of Christianity but treated its moral demands with indifference.

2:3 *sentence . . . destruction and deepening misery.* Peter turns from the description of the false teachers to a description of their fate. Verses 4–8 provide examples of judgment of false teachers of the past.

2:4 *angels that sinned.* There are two main interpretations of this passage, depending on one's understanding of Genesis 6:1–6. Some think that Peter is referring to "sons of God" in Genesis 6:2. According to this interpretation, the "sons of God" were angels who rebelled against God and their role in creation. They began to engage in forbidden practices with the daughters of men. Their conduct was met with immediate judgment. A second group of commentators balk at the suggestion of sexual relations between angels and women. They consider this verse to simply be a reference to those angels who fell with Satan.

2:5 *not spare the ancient world.* Peter's second example of God's judgment is the flood (3:6).

17 Mt 3:17; Lk 9:35 **18** Mt 17:6 **19** Ps 119:105; Jn 5:35; Rev 22:16 **20** Ro 12:6 **21** 2Ti 3:16; 1Pe 1:11; 2Sa 23:2; Ac 1:16 **CHAPTER 2** **1** Dt 13:1; Mt 24:11; 1Jn 4:1; Jude 4; 1Co 6:20; Heb 10:29; Rev 5:9; Php 3:19 **3** Ro 16:18; Titus 1:11; 2Co 2:17; Dt 32:35; Jude 4,15 **4** Job 4:18; Jude 6; Jn 8:44; Lk 8:31; Rev 20:2 **5** Ge 7:1; Heb 11:7; 1Pe 3:20; 1Pe 3:19; 2Pe 3:6

flood upon the world of the ungodly; [Gen 6–8; 1 Pet 3:20]
[6]and if He condemned the cities of Sodom and Gomorrah to destruction by reducing them to ashes, having made them an example to those who would live ungodly *lives* thereafter; [Gen 19:24]
[7]and if He rescued righteous Lot, who was tormented by the immoral conduct of unprincipled *and* ungodly men [Gen 19:16, 29]
[8](for that just man, while living among them, felt his righteous soul tormented day after day by what he saw and heard of their lawless acts),
[9]then [in light of the fact that all this is true, be sure that] the Lord knows how to rescue the godly from trial, and how to keep the unrighteous under punishment until the day of judgment,
[10]and especially those who indulge in the corrupt passions of the sin nature, and despise authority.
Presumptuous *and* reckless, self-willed *and* arrogant [creatures, despising the majesty of the Lord], they do not tremble when they revile angelic majesties,
[11]whereas *even* angels who are superior in might and power do not bring a reviling (defaming) accusation against them before the Lord. [Jude 8]
[12]But these [false teachers], like unreasoning animals, [mere] creatures of instinct, born to be captured and destroyed, reviling things they do not understand, will also perish in their own corruption [in their destroying they will be destroyed],
[13]suffering wrong [destined for punishment] as the wages of doing wrong. They count it a delight to revel in the daytime [living luxuriously]. They are stains and blemishes [on mankind], reveling in their deceptions even as they feast with you.
[14]They have eyes full of adultery, constantly looking for sin, enticing *and* luring away unstable souls. Having hearts trained in greed, [they are] children of a curse.
[15]Abandoning the straight road [that is, the right way to live], they have gone astray; they have followed the way of [the false teacher] Balaam the son of Beor, who loved the reward of wickedness; [Num 22:5, 7]
[16]but he was rebuked for his own transgression: a mute donkey spoke

preacher of righteousness. This is a reference to Noah because his righteous life put to shame the immoral lives of his neighbors. Noah's building of the ark would certainly have given him the opportunity to explain the coming judgment and to invite people to repent and believe in God. But the entreaties fell on deaf ears, just as the truth of Christ's atonement fell on the deaf ears of the false teachers of Peter's day. Such indifference and unbelief brought the ungodly of Noah's world to certain destruction.

2:6 *Sodom and Gomorrah.* These cities are Peter's third example of God's judgment. Genesis 19 makes it clear that sexual perversion was the primary cause of their destruction.

2:9 – 10 *Presumptuous and reckless, self-willed and arrogant.* These words describe the character and methods of false teachers. Their actions are characterized by boldness; they recklessly defy both God and man. Behind their presumption is a commitment to their own desires.

2:12 *like unreasoning animals, [mere] creatures of instinct.* False teachers are compared to animals in their behavior because they act in ignorance of the realities of death and judgment. Like animals they also react only to present circumstances, without giving thought to the consequences of their actions.

2:13 *revel in the daytime.* Even pagan societies thought it strange and unnatural to hold drunken riots in the daylight. However, the false teachers had no qualms about practicing their erroneous concept of Christian liberty in clear daylight.

2:14 *eyes full of adultery.* They could not cease from sin because their fantasizing had become habitual. As a consequence, they convinced unstable souls in the church that adultery was acceptable Christian behavior and lured them into sexual immorality.

2:15 – 16 *followed the way of [the false teacher] Balaam.* The account of Balaam in Numbers 22 – 24 is used here, as well as in Jude 11 and Revelation 2:14, to depict the danger of forsaking the right way and going astray.

6 Ge 19:24; Dt 29:23; Nu 26:10 **7** Ge 19:16 **8** Ps 119:139; Eze 9:4 **9** Ps 34:17; 1Co 10:13 **10** Jude 4,7,8 **11** Jude 9 **12** Jude 10 **13** Php 3:19; Ro 13:13; Jude 12; 1Co 11:20 **14** Jude 11 **15** Nu 22:5; Jude 11

with a man's voice and restrained the prophet's madness. [Num 22:21–31]

17These [false teachers] are springs without water and mists driven by a tempest, for whom is reserved the gloom of black darkness.

18For uttering arrogant *words* of vanity [pompous words disguised to sound scholarly or profound, but meaning nothing and containing no spiritual truth], they beguile *and* lure *using* lustful desires, by sensuality, those who barely escape from the ones who live in error.

19They promise them liberty, when they themselves are the slaves of depravity—for by whatever anyone is defeated *and* overcome, to that [person, thing, philosophy, or concept] he is *continually* enslaved.

20For if, after they have escaped the pollutions of the world by [personal] knowledge of our Lord and Savior Jesus Christ, they are again entangled in them and are overcome, their last condition has become worse for them than the first.

21For it would have been better for them not to have [personally] known the way of righteousness, than to have known it and then to have turned back from the holy commandment [verbally] handed on to them.

22The thing spoken of in the true proverb has happened to them, "THE DOG RETURNS TO HIS OWN VOMIT," and, "A sow is washed only to wallow [again] in the mire." [Prov 26:11]

Purpose of This Letter

3 BELOVED, I am now writing you this second letter. In this [as in the first one], I am stirring up your untainted mind to remind you,

2that you should remember the words spoken in the past [about the future] by the holy prophets and the commandment of the Lord and Savior *given* by your apostles [His personally chosen representatives].

The Coming Day of the Lord

3First of all, know [without any doubt] that mockers will come in the last days with their mocking, following after their own human desires

4and saying, "Where is the promise of His coming [what has become of it]? For ever since the fathers fell asleep [in death], all things have continued [exactly] as they did from the beginning of creation."

5For they willingly forget [the fact] that the heavens existed long ago by the word of God, and the earth was formed out of water and by water,

6through which the world at that time was destroyed by being flooded with water. [Gen 1:6–8; 7:11]

7But by His word the present heav-

2:17 *springs . . . mists.* Peter accuses the heretical teachers of awakening false expectations, like wells that contain no water or storm clouds that darken but produce no rain.

2:20 *they have escaped.* The subject of this phrase is the heretical teachers who are called "slaves of depravity" in verse 19. This verse seems to indicate that the teachers had formerly turned from the pollution of the world through a full and experiential knowledge of Christ. Now, however, they have fallen again into immorality, even becoming teachers of sinful lifestyles. ***their last condition has become worse for them than the first.*** This phrase is almost certainly taken from Jesus' words in Matthew 12:45 and probably reflects Peter's memory of that occasion.

2:22 *spoken of in the true proverb.* Jews considered dogs and pigs among the lowest of animals, so Peter chooses these animals to describe people who have known the truth but have turned away from it.

3:2 *words spoken in the past.* The only way Peter's readers could recognize the errors of the heretical teachers was to compare their teaching with the teaching of the holy prophets and apostles. As Peter had already reminded his readers in 1:21, "men moved by the Holy Spirit" spoke words that were therefore utterly reliable.

3:4 *fathers fell asleep.* This refers to the Old Testament patriarchs. ***all things have continued.*** The basis for denying the supernatural reappearance of Jesus is that nothing of that nature has occurred in the past.

---

17 Jude 12,13 **18** Jude 16; Ac 2:40 **19** Gal 5:13; Jn 8:34; Ro 6:16 **20** Mt 12:45; Lk 11:26; Heb 6:4; ver. 18; 2Pe 1:2 **21** Lk 12:47 **22** Pr 26:11 **CHAPTER 3** **1** 2Pe 1:13 **2** Jude 17 **3** 2Pe 2:10 **4** Isa 5:19; Jer 17:15; Eze 12:22; Mt 24:48; Lk 12:45 **5** Ge 1:6,9; Ps 33:6; Heb 11:3; Ps 24:2; Col 1:17 **6** Ge 7:11 **7** ver. 10; Mt 25:41; 2Th 1:8

ens and earth are being reserved for
fire, being kept for the day of judgment
and destruction of the ungodly people.
8 Nevertheless, do not let this one
fact escape your notice, beloved, that
with the Lord one day is like a thou-
sand years, and a thousand years is
like one day. [Ps 90:4]
9 The Lord does not delay [as though
He were unable to act] *and* is not slow
about His promise, as some count slow-
ness, but is [extraordinarily] patient
toward you, not wishing for any to
perish but for all to come to repentance.

A New Heaven and Earth

10 But the day of the Lord will come
like a thief, and then the heavens will
vanish with a [mighty and thunderous]
roar, and the [material] elements will
be destroyed with intense heat, and
the earth and the works that are on it
will be burned up.
11 Since all these things are to be de-
stroyed in this way, what kind of peo-
ple ought you to be [in the meantime]
in holy behavior [that is, in a pattern
of daily life that sets you apart as a
believer] and in godliness [displaying
profound reverence toward our awe-
some God],
12 [while you earnestly] look for and
await the coming of the day of God.
For on this day the heavens will be
destroyed by burning, and the [mate-
rial] elements will melt with intense
heat! [Is 34:4]
13 But in accordance with His prom-
ise we expectantly await new heavens
and a new earth, in which righteous-
ness dwells. [Is 65:17; 66:22]
14 So, beloved, since you are looking
forward to these things, be diligent
and make every effort to be found
by Him [at His return] spotless and
blameless, in peace [that is, inwardly
calm with a sense of spiritual well-
being and confidence, having lived a
life of obedience to Him].
15 And consider the patience of our
Lord [His delay in judging and aveng-
ing wrongs] as salvation [that is, allow-
ing time for more to be saved]; just as
our beloved brother Paul also wrote to
you according to the wisdom given to
him [by God],
16 speaking about these things as he
does in all of his letters. In which there
are some things that are difficult to
understand, which the untaught and
unstable [who have fallen into error]
twist *and* misinterpret, just as *they do*
the rest of the Scriptures, to their own
destruction.
17 Therefore, [let me warn you] be-
loved, knowing these things before-
hand, be on your guard so that you are
not carried away by the error of un-
principled men [who distort doctrine]
and fall from your own steadfastness
[of mind, knowledge, truth, and faith],
18 but grow [spiritually mature] in the
grace and knowledge of our Lord and
Savior Jesus Christ. To Him be glory
(honor, majesty, splendor), both now
and to the day of eternity. Amen.

3:8 *a thousand years.* God will surely accomplish His purposes and promises, even though it may appear that He is slow in doing so. His timing is always perfect.

3:10 *day of the Lord.* This phrase describes the end-time events, the second coming (Da 9:24–27; 1Th 5:2; 2Th 2:1–12). Peter's description requires the unlimited power of God in dissolving the very elements of the universe, from which He will create a new heaven and a new earth (v. 13; Rev 21:22).

3:11 *what kind of people.* The primary purpose of prophetic teaching is not to satisfy our curiosity but to motivate us to change our lives. Rather than work for things that will ultimately be destroyed, we should work for things that are eternal.

3:16 *the untaught and unstable . . . twist and misinterpret.* *Untaught* refers to one whose mind is untrained and undisciplined in habits of thought. *Unstable* refers to one whose conduct is not properly established.

8 Ps 90:4 **9** Hab 2:3; Heb 10:37; Isa 30:18; 1Pe 3:20; Eze 33:11; Ro 2:4; 1Ti 2:4 **10** Mt 24:43; Lk 12:39; 1Th 5:2; Ps 102:26; Isa 51:6; Mt 24:35; Ro 8:12 **11** 1Pe 1:15 **12** 1Co 1:7; Titus 2:13; Ps 50:3; Isa 34:4; Mic 1:4 **13** Isa 65:17; 66:22; Rev 21:1 **14** 1Co 1:8; 15:58; Php 1:10; 1Th 3:13 **15** Ro 2:4; 1Pe 3:20 **16** Ro 8:19; 1Co 15:24; 1Th 4:15 **17** Mk 13:23; Eph 4:14 **18** Eph 4:15; 1Pe 2:2; 2Ti 4:18; Rev 1:6

THE FIRST LETTER OF
JOHN

▸ **AUTHOR:** First John was universally accepted without dispute as authoritative by the early church. The internal evidence supports this tradition because the "we" (apostles), "you" (readers), and "they" (false teachers) phraseology places the writer in the sphere of apostolic eyewitness (1:1 – 3; 4:14). John's name was well-known to the readers, and it was unnecessary for him to mention it. The style and vocabulary of 1 John are so similar to those of the Fourth Gospel that most scholars acknowledge these books to be by the same hand. First John was probably written in Ephesus after the Gospel of John, but the date cannot be fixed with certainty.

▸ **TIMES:** c. AD 89 – 95 ▸ **KEY VERSES:** 1Jn 1:3 – 4

▸ **THEME:** Shortly after the church began, people like the Gnostics continually tried to recast the gospel in their own terms. Gnosticism made a distinction between the material or carnal, which was evil to them, and the spiritual, which was pure. John writes as one who knew Jesus personally, physically, and spiritually. He wants the reader to take the Christ he knew at face value. John wants his readers to believe the truth of his experience of Jesus and not the philosophical speculation of the Gnostics. In these letters we see the same themes as John's Gospel, light and darkness, truth and falsehood, life and death, love and hate. John weaves these themes together with a straightforward skill and fatherly care.

Introduction, The Incarnate Word

1 [I AM writing about] what existed from the beginning, what we have heard, what we have seen with our eyes, what we have looked at and touched with our hands, concerning the Word of Life [the One who existed even before the beginning of the world, Christ]—
2 and the Life [an aspect of His being] was manifested, and we have seen [it as eyewitnesses] and testify and declare to you [the Life], the eternal Life who was [already existing] with the Father and was [actually] made visible to us [His followers]—
3 what we have seen and heard we also proclaim to you, so that you too may have fellowship [as partners] with

---

1:1 – 4 *the Word of Life.* These verses emphasize the personal experience of the apostles with the incarnate Word. The memory of Jesus Christ burned in the mind of John as he reflected on the three and one-half years that he and the other disciples were with the Lord. Now he wanted to be sure that the churches under his care enjoyed fellowship with the resurrected Lord and other disciples.
1:2 *the Life [an aspect of His being] was manifested.* The life was not hidden or obscured so that few, if any, could find it. Rather, this life was made known openly and had its origin in God the Father. God had provided truth about Himself in nature and through the prophets of old, but the revelation in His Son (Heb 1:1 – 2) is God's finest and clearest presentation of Himself.
1:3 *have fellowship.* The idea of this word carries both the thought of a positive relationship

CHAPTER 1 **1** Jn 1:1,14; 2Pe 1:16; Lk 24:39; Jn 20:27 **2** Jn 1:4; 14:6; Ro 16:26; 1Ti 3:16; Jn 21:24; 1Jn 5:20; Jn 1:1 **3** Jn 17:21; 1Co 1:9

us. And indeed our fellowship [which is a distinguishing mark of born-again believers] is with the Father, and with His Son Jesus Christ.

4We are writing these things to you so that our joy [in seeing you included] may be made complete [by having you share in the joy of salvation].

God Is Light

5This is the message [of God's promised revelation] which we have heard from Him and now announce to you, that God is Light [He is holy, His message is truthful, He is perfect in righteousness], and in Him there is no darkness at all [no sin, no wickedness, no imperfection].

6If we say that we have fellowship with Him and yet walk in the darkness [of sin], we lie and do not practice the truth;

7but if we [really] walk in the Light [that is, live each and every day in conformity with the precepts of God], as He Himself is in the Light, we have [true, unbroken] fellowship with one another [He with us, and we with Him], and the blood of Jesus His Son cleanses us from all sin [by erasing the stain of sin, keeping us cleansed from sin in all its forms and manifestations].

8If we say we have no sin [refusing to admit that we are sinners], we delude ourselves and the truth is not in us. [His word does not live in our hearts.]

9If we [freely] admit that we have sinned *and* confess our sins, He is faithful and just [true to His own nature and promises], and will forgive our sins and cleanse us *continually* from all unrighteousness [our wrongdoing, everything not in conformity with His will and purpose].

10If we say that we have not sinned [refusing to admit acts of sin], we make Him [out to be] a liar [by contradicting Him] and His word is not in us.

Christ Is Our Advocate

2 MY LITTLE children (believers, dear ones), I am writing you these things so that you will not sin *and* violate God's law. And if anyone sins, we have an Advocate [who will intercede for us] with the Father: Jesus Christ the righteous [the upright, the just One, who conforms to the Father's will in every way—purpose, thought, and action].

2And He [that same Jesus] is the propitiation for our sins [the atoning sacrifice that holds back the wrath of God that would otherwise be directed

---

that people share and participation in a common interest or goal.

1:5 *God is Light.* This is God's nature, in His essential being, just as He is Spirit (Jn 4:24) and love (4:8). Light refers to God's moral character. ***no darkness at all.*** God is holy, untouched by any evil or sin. Because God is light, those who desire fellowship with Him must also be pure.

1:6 *fellowship with Him and yet walk in the darkness.* To walk in darkness means to live contrary to the moral character of God, to live a sinful life. To claim fellowship with God without living a moral life or practicing the truth is to live a lie, since God cannot compromise His holiness to accommodate sin.

1:8–9 *If we ... confess.* To confess is to agree with God, to admit that we are sinners in need of His mercy. If a believer confesses his or her specific sins to God, He will cleanse all unrighteousness from that person. Forgiveness and cleansing are guaranteed because God is faithful to His promises. Those promises are legitimated because God is just. God can maintain His perfect character and yet forgive us because of the perfect and righteous sacrifice of Jesus, His own Son (2:2).

1:10 *His word is not in us.* A person who denies committing sinful acts does not have the Word of God changing his or her life.

2:1 *My little children ... that you will not sin.* John's statements about sin (1:8 – 10) were designed to make believers aware of sin's ever-present danger and to put them on guard against it. According to Greek grammar, the *if* before *anyone sins* carries the added sense of "and it is assumed that we all do." This statement is not an encouragement to sin but a warning to all Christians to be on guard against sinful tendencies.

2:2 *propitiation.* This act brings about the merciful removal of guilt through divine forgiveness. In the Greek Old Testament, the Greek term for

---

4 Jn 16:24 **5** 1Jn 3:11; Jn 1:9 **6** 2Co 6:14 **7** 1Co 6:11; Eph 1:7; Heb 9:14; 1Pe 1:19; Rev 1:5 **8** Job 9:2; Ecc 7:20; Jas 3:2; 1Jn 2:4 **9** Ps 32:5; Ps 51:2 **CHAPTER 2** **1** Heb 7:25 **2** Ro 3:25; 2Co 5:18; Jn 1:29

at us because of our sinful nature—
our worldliness, our lifestyle]; and
not for ours alone, but also for [the
sins of all believers throughout] the
whole world.
3And this is how we know [daily, by
experience] that we have come to know
Him [to understand Him and be more
deeply acquainted with Him]: if we
habitually keep [focused on His pre-
cepts and obey] His commandments
(teachings).
4Whoever says, "I have come to
know Him," but does not *habitual-
ly* keep [focused on His precepts and
obey] His commandments (teachings),
is a liar, and the truth [of the divine
word] is not in him.
5But whoever *habitually* keeps His
word *and* obeys His precepts [and
treasures His message in its entire-
ty], in him the love of God has truly
been perfected [it is completed and has
reached maturity]. By this we know
[for certain] that we are in Him:
6whoever says he lives in Christ [that
is, whoever says he has accepted Him
as God and Savior] ought [as a moral
obligation] to walk *and* conduct him-
self just as He walked *and* conducted
Himself.
7Beloved, I am not writing a new
commandment to you, but an old com-
mandment which you have had from
the beginning; the old commandment
is the message which you have heard
[before from us]. [John 13:34, 35]
8On the other hand, I am writing
a new commandment to you, which
is true *and* realized in Christ and in
you, because the darkness [of moral
blindness] is clearing away and the
true Light [the revelation of God in
Christ] is already shining.
9The one who says he is in the
Light [in consistent fellowship with
Christ] and yet *habitually* hates (works
against) his brother [in Christ] is in the
darkness until now.
10The one who loves *and* unselfishly
seeks the best for his [believing] broth-
er lives in the Light, and in him there
is no occasion for stumbling *or* offense
[he does not hurt the cause of Christ
or lead others to sin].
11But the one who *habitually* hates
(works against) his brother [in Christ]
is in [spiritual] darkness and is walk-
ing in the darkness, and does not know
where he is going because the dark-
ness has blinded his eyes.
12I am writing to you, little chil-
dren (believers, dear ones), because
your sins have been forgiven for His

---

propitiation was used for the sacrificial mercy seat on which the high priest placed the blood of the Israelites' sacrifices (Ex 25:17–22). This practice indicates that God's righteous wrath had to be appeased somehow. God sent His Son and satisfied His own wrath with Jesus' sacrifice on the cross. Our sins made it necessary for Jesus to suffer the agonies of the crucifixion; but God demonstrated His love and justice by providing His own Son.

2:3 ***we have come to know Him.*** The New Testament speaks of knowing God in two senses. One who has trusted Christ knows Him (Jn 17:3), that is to say, has met Him. One who has previously met the Lord can also come to know Him intimately (Php 3:10). In this verse John is talking about knowing the Lord intimately.

2:6 ***lives in Christ.*** Living in Christ means pursuing habitual obedience. It has the idea of settling down in Christ or resting in Him. It is evidenced by a life modeled after Christ. ***ought [as a moral obligation] to walk and conduct himself.*** The admonition to live by the teaching of Jesus reveals that this conformity comes from us. The Christian, as a child of God, ought to obey God because of a sincere desire to do so. It should be a joy to follow in the footsteps of the One who died for us.

2:8 ***new commandment.*** This refers to love (v. 10). It may be that John is simply repeating the statement of Christ in John 13:34. The command to love reached its truest and fullest expression in the life of Christ. He demonstrated what true love is by coming into our world and giving His life for us.

2:11 ***the one who habitually hates (works against) his brother.*** Hating one's brother opposes the teaching of Christ to love one another. The idea that one could hate a brother and yet claim fellowship with God shows the utter darkness that has blinded the Christian to the truth.

---

4 1Jn 1:6; 1Jn 1:8 **5** Jn 14:21,23; 1Jn 4:12; 1Jn 4:13 **6** Jn 15:4; Mt 11:29; 1Pe 2:21 **7** 2Jn 5; 2Jn 5 **8** Jn 13:34; Ro 13:12; Jn 1:9 **9** 1Co 13:2; 2Pe 1:9 **10** 1Jn 3:14; 2Pe 1:10 **12** Lk 24:47

name's sake [you have been pardoned and released from spiritual debt through His name because you have confessed His name, believing in Him as Savior].

13 I am writing to you, fathers [those believers who are spiritually mature], because you know Him who has existed from the beginning. I am writing to you, young men [those believers who are growing in spiritual maturity], because you have been victorious *and* have overcome the evil one. I have written to you, children [those who are new believers, those spiritually immature], because you have come to know the Father.

14 I have written to you, fathers, because you know Him who has existed from the beginning. I have written to you, young men, because you are strong *and* vigorous, and the word of God remains [always] in you, and you have been victorious over the evil one [by accepting Jesus as Savior].

Do Not Love the World

15 Do not love the world [of sin that opposes God and His precepts], nor the things that are in the world. If anyone loves the world, the love of the Father is not in him.

16 For all that is in the world—the lust *and* sensual craving of the flesh and the lust *and* longing of the eyes and the boastful pride of life [pretentious confidence in one's resources or in the stability of earthly things]—these do not come from the Father, but are from the world.

17 The world is passing away, and with it its lusts [the shameful pursuits and ungodly longings]; but the one who does the will of God *and* carries out His purposes lives forever.

18 Children, it is the last hour [the end of this age]; and just as you heard that the antichrist is coming [the one who will oppose Christ and attempt to replace Him], even now many antichrists (false teachers) have appeared, which confirms our belief that it is the last hour.

19 They went out from us [seeming at first to be Christians], but they were not *really* of us [because they were not truly born again and spiritually transformed]; for if they had been of us, they would have remained with us; but *they went out* [teaching false doctrine], so that it would be clearly shown that none of them are of us.

20 But you have an anointing from the Holy One [you have been set apart,

---

2:15 *Do not love the world.* These words may be rephrased as "stop loving the world." John's readers were acting in a way that was inconsistent with the relationship with Christ. "World" here is the morally evil system opposed to all that God is and holds dear. In this sense, the "world" is the satanic system opposing Christ's kingdom on this earth (v. 16; 3:1; 4:4; 5:19; Jn 12:31; Eph 6:11 – 12; Jas 4:4).

2:16 *lust and sensual craving of the flesh and the lust and longing of the eyes and the boastful pride of life.* The world is characterized by these three lusts, which have been interpreted as corresponding to the three different ways Eve was tempted in the garden (Ge 3:6), or the three different temptations Jesus experienced (Lk 4:1 – 12). However, the correspondences are not close enough to make it certain that John was alluding to either of these. Instead, John was probably making a short list of the different ways believers could be lured away from a loving God. *Lust of the flesh* refers to desires of sinful sensual pleasure. *The lust of the eyes* refers to covetousness or materialism. *The pride of life* refers to being proud about one's position in this world.

2:17 *passing away.* John highlights the brevity of life. To be consumed with this life is to be unprepared for the next.

2:18 *antichrists.* This word is a combination of two Greek words: *anti*, meaning "instead of" or "against"; and *christos*, meaning "anointed one." *Antichrists* most likely means those who seek to take the place of Christ.

2:20 *anointing.* This is a reference to either the Holy Spirit or to Scripture. This anointing is the protection that believers have against the false teachers. The true Anointed One, Jesus, also has representatives who are anointed. One of the main heresies the first century church faced was Gnosticism, whose followers claimed to have secret knowledge of the truth that led to salvation. Here John was opposing this teaching by asserting that all believers knew the truth.

---

13 1Jn 1:1 **14** Eph 6:10 **15** Ro 12:2; Mt 6:24 **16** Ecc 5:11 **17** 1Co 7:31; 1Pe 1:24 **18** Jn 21:5; Heb 1:2; 2Th 2:3; Mt 24:5; 2Jn 7; 1Ti 4:1; 2Ti 3:1 **19** Dt 13:13; Mt 24:24; Jn 6:37; 1Co 11:19 **20** 2Co 1:21; Heb 1:9; Ac 3:14; Jn 16:13

specially gifted and prepared by the Holy Spirit], and all of you know [the truth because He teaches us, illuminates our minds, and guards us from error].

21 I have not written to you because you do not know the truth, but because you do know it, and because no lie [nothing false, no deception] is of the truth.

22 Who is the liar but the one who denies that Jesus is the Christ (the Messiah, the Anointed)? This is the antichrist [the enemy and antagonist of Christ], the one who denies *and* consistently refuses to acknowledge the Father and the Son.

23 Whoever denies *and* repudiates the Son does not have the Father; the one who confesses *and* acknowledges the Son has the Father also.

24 As for you, let that remain in you [keeping in your hearts that message of salvation] which you heard from the beginning. If what you heard from the beginning remains in you, you too will remain in the Son and in the Father [forever].

The Promise Is Eternal Life

25 This is the promise which He Himself promised us—eternal life.

26 These things I have written to you with reference to those who are trying to deceive you [seducing you and leading you away from the truth and sound doctrine].

27 As for you, the anointing [the special gift, the preparation] which you received from Him remains [permanently] in you, and you have no need for anyone to teach you. But just as His anointing teaches you [giving you insight through the presence of the Holy Spirit] about all things, and is true and is not a lie, and just as His anointing has taught you, you must remain in Him [being rooted in Him, knit to Him].

28 Now, little children (believers, dear ones), remain in Him [with unwavering faith], so that when He appears [at His return], we may have [perfect] confidence and not be ashamed and shrink away from Him at His coming.

29 If you know that He is *absolutely* righteous, you know [for certain] that everyone who practices righteousness [doing what is right and conforming to God's will] has been born of Him.

Children of God Love One Another

3 SEE WHAT an incredible quality of love the Father has shown to us, that we would [be permitted to] be named *and* called *and* counted the children of God! And so we are! For this reason the world does not know us, because it did not know Him.

2 Beloved, we are [even here and] now children of God, and it is not yet made clear what we will be [after His coming]. We know that when He comes *and* is revealed, we will [as His children] be like Him, because we will see Him just as He is [in all His glory].

2:22 – 23 *that Jesus is the Christ.* In John's epistles, denying that Jesus came in the flesh is to deny His status as the Anointed One. A person cannot worship God while denying Jesus' full deity and full humanity.
2:28 *ashamed and shrink away from Him at His coming.* The shame is the result of not having had a lifestyle of obedience when Christ returns.
3:1 *what an incredible quality of love.* John stands in amazement of God's love. But the greater amazement and appreciation is for the fact that God's love is expressed to human beings and that Christians are included in His family.

3:2 We Have a New Family — One of the primary benefits of becoming a Christian is that we also become part of Christ's family. The Bible refers to this change as being *born again* (Jn 3:3). When an individual places his faith in Christ as Savior, he is born again into a new, spiritual, familial relationship with God (Gal 3:26). He gains God as Father (Eph 4:6) and other Christians as brothers and sisters (Heb 3:1). God also adopts us when we become His children (Eph 1:5). This image implies a dramatic transformation of status from slave to son (Gal 4:1 – 5). One is no longer in bondage to the master but becomes a free son possessing all

22 2Jn 7 **23** Jn 15:23; 2Jn 9; 1Jn 4:15 **24** 2Jn 6; Jn 14:23 **25** Jn 17:3 **26** 2Jn 7 **27** ver. 20,21; Jn 14:26 **28** 1Jn 3:2; 1Jn 4:17 **29** Ac 22:14; 1Jn 3:7,10 **CHAPTER 3** **1** Jn 1:12; 16:3 **2** Isa 56:5; Ro 8:15,18; 2Co 4:17; Ro 8:29; 2Pe 1:4; Ps 16:11; Mt 5:8

3And everyone who has this hope
[confidently placed] in Him purifies
himself, just as He is pure (holy, un-
defiled, guiltless).
4Everyone who practices sin also
practices lawlessness; and sin is
lawlessness [ignoring God's law by
action or neglect or by tolerating
wrongdoing—being unrestrained by
His commands and His will].
5You know that He appeared [in vis-
ible form as a man] in order to take
away sins; and in Him there is [abso-
lutely] no sin [for He has neither the
sin nature nor has He committed sin
or acts worthy of blame].
6No one who abides in Him [who re-
mains united in fellowship with Him—
deliberately, knowingly, and habitual-
ly] practices sin. No one who *habitually*
sins has seen Him or known Him.
7Little children (believers, dear
ones), do not let anyone lead you
astray. The one who practices righ-
teousness [the one who strives to live a
consistently honorable life—in private
as well as in public—and to conform
to God's precepts] is righteous, just as
He is righteous.
8The one who practices sin [separat-
ing himself from God, and offending
Him by acts of disobedience, indiffer-
ence, or rebellion] is of the devil [and
takes his inner character and moral
values from him, not God]; for the dev-
il has sinned *and* violated God's law
from the beginning. The Son of God
appeared for this purpose, to destroy
the works of the devil.
9No one who is born of God [de-
liberately, knowingly, and habitual-
ly] practices sin, because God's seed
[His principle of life, the essence of
His righteous character] remains [per-
manently] in him [who is born again—
who is reborn from above—spiritually
transformed, renewed, and set apart
for His purpose]; and he [who is born
again] cannot *habitually* [live a life
characterized by] sin, because he is
born of God *and* longs to please Him.
10By this the children of God and the
children of the devil are clearly iden-
tified: anyone who does not practice
righteousness [who does not seek God's
will in thought, action, and purpose]
is not of God, nor is the one who does
not [unselfishly] love his [believing]
brother.
11For this is the message which you
[believers] have heard from the begin-
ning [of your relationship with Christ],
that we should [unselfishly] love *and*
seek the best for one another;
12and not be like Cain, who was of
the evil one and murdered his brother
[Abel]. And why did he murder him?
Because Cain's deeds were evil, and
his brother's were righteous.
13Do not be surprised, believers, if
the world hates you.
14We know that we have passed out

---

the rights and privileges of sonship. One of these benefits is the right to call God *Abba*, an affectionate term meaning "Father" (Ro 8:15). A marvelous relationship is possible when one becomes a part of the family of God. As in any family, there are also responsibilities. The Christian must exhibit the family character and grow into spiritual maturity.

3:3 *everyone who has this hope.* Knowing that Christ is morally pure helps a person pursue purity even more.

3:4 *sin.* This verse is not referring to occasional sin but a consistent lifestyle of sin. ***lawlessness.*** This is active rebellion against the law.

3:5–6 *No one who abides in Him ... practices sin.* Habitually sinful conduct indicates an absence of fellowship with Christ. Thus, if we claim to be a Christian but sin is our way of life, our status as children of God can legitimately be questioned.

3:8 *destroy the works of the devil.* A person who sins is of the devil in the sense that he is participating in the devil's activity (2:19). Thus John is indicating that it is possible for believers to do that which is of the devil (Mk 8:31–33; Jas 3:6).

3:10 *children of the devil.* Believers who sin are not expressing their nature as children of God; instead, they are following the devil's pattern.

3:14 *have passed out of death into Life.* The tense of the verb "have passed" indicates that something experienced in the past has continuing and abiding results in the present. Thus John is saying that Christians, who have experienced Christ's salvation in the past, should

---

3 1Jn 4:17 **4** Ro 4:15 **5** 1Jn 1:2; Isa 53:5,6; 2Co 5:21; Heb 4:15; 1Pe 2:22 **6** 1Jn 2:4 **7** 1Jn 2:26; Ro 2:13
8 Mt 13:38; Jn 8:44; Lk 10:18; Jn 16:11 **9** 1Jn 5:18; 1Pe 1:23 **10** 1Jn 2:29; 1Jn 4:8 **11** 1Jn 1:5; Jn 13:34; 2Jn 5
12 Ge 4:4,8; Heb 11:4 **13** Jn 17:14 **14** 1Jn 2:10; 1Jn 2:9,11

of death into Life, because we love the brothers and sisters. He who does not love remains in [spiritual] death.

[15]Everyone who hates (works against) his brother [in Christ] is [at heart] a murderer [by God's standards]; and you know that no murderer has eternal life abiding in him. [Matt 5:21–23]

[16]By this we know [and have come to understand the depth and essence of His precious] love: that He [willingly] laid down His life for us [because He loved us]. And we ought to lay down our lives for the believers.

[17]But whoever has the world's goods (adequate resources), and sees his brother in need, but has no compassion for him, how does the love of God live in him?

[18]Little children (believers, dear ones), let us not love [merely in theory] with word or with tongue [giving lip service to compassion], but in action and in truth [in practice and in sincerity, because practical acts of love are more than words].

[19]By this we will know [without any doubt] that we are of the truth, and will assure our heart *and* quiet our conscience before Him

[20]whenever our heart convicts us [in guilt]; for God is greater than our heart and He knows all things [nothing is hidden from Him because we are in His hands].

[21]Beloved, if our heart does not convict us [of guilt], we have confidence [complete assurance and boldness] before God;

[22]and we receive from Him whatever we ask because we [carefully and consistently] keep His commandments and do the things that are pleasing in His sight [habitually seeking to follow His plan for us].

[23]This is His commandment, that we believe [with personal faith and confident trust] in the name of His Son Jesus Christ, and [that we unselfishly] love *and* seek the best for one another, just as He commanded us.

[24]The one who *habitually* keeps His commandments [obeying His word and following His precepts, abides and] remains in Him, and He in him. By this we know *and* have the proof that He [really] abides in us, by the Spirit whom He has given us [as a gift].

Testing the Spirits

4 BELOVED, DO not believe every spirit [speaking through a self-proclaimed prophet]; instead test the spirits to see whether they are from God, because many false prophets *and* teachers have gone out into the world.

---

demonstrate their salvation by loving their fellow believers in the present.

3:18 ***not love [merely in theory] with word or with tongue.*** This phrase means to speak loving words but to stop short of doing anything to prove that love. The opposite of living in word is loving *in deed and in truth*.

3:20 ***our heart convicts us.*** This will happen when we recognize that we do not measure up to the standard of love and feel insecure in approaching God. Our conscience may not acknowledge the loving deeds we have done in the power of the Holy Spirit, but God does, and He is superior to our heart. Unlike our conscience, God takes everything into account, including Christ's atoning work for us. God is more compassionate and understanding toward us than we sometimes are toward ourselves.

3:24 We Have a Witness — Some of the benefits of being a believer are best described as being spiritual or even mystical. The whole idea of abiding in Christ while He abides in us is one of those concepts. Abide is best understood as "remain with." God doesn't come and go in our lives. He carries on a permanent relationship with us because He is always there for us and in us. We sense His presence primarily through the work of the Holy Spirit, whose role it is to stand beside us and comfort us. It happens in our hearts and minds and is largely invisible. Yet, it is also what most accurately describes the most important aspect of our day-to-day life as Christians. As we abide in Christ, He nourishes us spiritually the same way a vine gives nourishment to its branches (Jn 15:16).

4:1 ***false prophets.*** These persons obey evil spirits. A true prophet is one who receives direct

---

15 Mt 5:21; Gal 5:21 **16** Jn 3:16 **17** Dt 15:7; Lk 3:11; 1Jn 4:20 **18** Eze 33:31; Ro 12:9; Eph 4:15 **19** Jn 18:37 **20** 1Co 4:4 **21** Job 22:26; Heb 10:22 **22** Ps 34:15; Pr 15:29; Jer 29:12; Mt 7:8; Jn 8:29 **23** Jn 6:29; Mt 22:39; Jn 13:34; Eph 5:2; 1Jn 2:8,10 **24** Jn 14:23; 17:21; Ro 8:9 **CHAPTER 4** **1** Jer 29:8; Mt 24:4; 1Co 14:29; 1Th 5:21; Rev 2:2; Mt 24:5; Ac 20:30; 1Ti 4:1; 2Pe 2:1

2 By this you know *and* recognize
the Spirit of God: every spirit that ac-
knowledges *and* confesses [the fact]
that Jesus Christ has [actually] come in
the flesh [as a man] is from God [God
is its source];
3 and every spirit that does not con-
fess Jesus [acknowledging that He has
come in the flesh, but would deny any
of the Son's true nature] is not of God;
this is the *spirit* of the antichrist, which
you have heard is coming, and is now
already in the world.
4 Little children (believers, dear ones),
you are of God *and* you belong to Him
and have [already] overcome them [the
agents of the antichrist]; because He
who is in you is greater than he (Satan)
who is in the world [of sinful mankind].
5 They [who teach twisted doctrine]
are of the world *and* belong to it; there-
fore they speak from the [viewpoint of
the] world [with its immoral freedom
and baseless theories—demanding
compliance with their opinions and
ridiculing the values of the upright],
and the [gullible one of the] world lis-
tens closely *and* pays attention to them.
6 We [who teach God's word] are from
God [energized by the Holy Spirit], and
whoever knows God [through personal
experience] listens to us [and has a
deeper understanding of Him]. Whoev-
er is not of God does not listen to us. By
this we know [without any doubt] the
spirit of truth [motivated by God] and
the spirit of error [motivated by Satan].

God Is Love

7 Beloved, let us [unselfishly] love *and*
seek the best for one another, for love
is from God; and everyone who loves
[others] is born of God and knows God
[through personal experience].
8 The one who does not love has not
become acquainted with God [does not
and never did know Him], for God is
love. [He is the originator of love, and it
is an enduring attribute of His nature.]
9 By this the love of God was dis-
played in us, in that God has sent His
[One and] only begotten Son [the One
who is truly unique, the only One of
His kind] into the world so that we
might live through Him.
10 In this is love, not that we loved
God, but that He loved us and sent His
Son to be the propitiation [that is, the
atoning sacrifice, and the satisfying
offering] for our sins [fulfilling God's
requirement for justice against sin and
placating His wrath].
11 Beloved, if God so loved us [in this
incredible way], we also ought to love
one another.
12 No one has seen God at any time.
But if we love one another [with un-
selfish concern], God abides in us, and
His love [the love that is His essence
abides in us and] is completed *and*
perfected in us.
13 By this we know [with confident
assurance] that we abide in Him and
He in us, because He has given to us
His [Holy] Spirit.

---

revelation from God. A false prophet claims to have received direct revelation from God but in fact promotes erroneous ideas.

4:2 ***Jesus Christ has [actually] come in the flesh.*** This test seems to be aimed at Docetists. They taught that Christ did not have a physical body. The test may also be aimed at the followers of Cerinthus who claimed that Jesus and "the Christ" were two separate beings, one physical and the other spiritual. In this letter, John is careful to use the name and the title of Jesus Christ together to clearly express the complete union of the two titles in one person.

4:4 ***he (Satan) who is in the world.*** This phrase refers to the devil.

4:8 ***has not become acquainted with God.*** The knowledge of God here refers to an intimate, experiential knowledge (v. 6; 2:3) of God, rather than just information about God. John never says that those who do not love are not born of God (v. 7). Yet it is impossible to know God intimately without loving others, for God is love. Anyone in whom God dwells reflects His character. To claim to know God while failing to love others is to make a false claim (1:6).

4:13 ***that we abide in Him and He in us.*** Mutual abiding refers to the fellowship we have with God as a result of our salvation. The evidence that God abides in us and we in Him is the experience of the Holy Spirit dwelling in us. In the remainder

---

2 1Co 12:3 **3** 2Jn 7; 2Th 2:7 **4** 1Jn 5:4; Jn 12:31; Eph 2:2 **5** Jn 3:31; 15:19 **6** Jn 8:47; Isa 8:20 **7** 1Jn 3:10,11 **8** 1Jn 2:4; ver. 16 **9** Jn 3:16; 1Jn 5:11 **10** Jn 15:16; Ro 5:8; Titus 3:4; 1Jn 2:2 **11** Mt 18:33; 1Jn 3:16 **12** Jn 1:18; 1Ti 6:16; 1Jn 2:5 **13** Jn 14:20

14 We [who were with Him in person] have seen and testify [as eyewitnesses] that the Father has sent the Son to be the Savior of the world.

15 Whoever confesses *and* acknowledges that Jesus is the Son of God, God abides in him, and he in God.

16 We have come to know [by personal observation and experience], and have believed [with deep, consistent faith] the love which God has for us. God is love, and the one who abides in love abides in God, and God abides *continually* in him.

17 In this [union and fellowship with Him], love is completed *and* perfected with us, so that we may have confidence in the day of judgment [with assurance and boldness to face Him]; because as He is, so are we in this world.

18 There is no fear in love [dread does not exist]. But perfect (complete, full-grown) love drives out fear, because fear involves [the expectation of divine] punishment, so the one who is afraid [of God's judgment] is not perfected in love [has not grown into a sufficient understanding of God's love].

19 We love, because He first loved us.

20 If anyone says, "I love God," and hates (works against) his [Christian] brother he is a liar; for the one who does not love his brother whom he has seen, cannot love God whom he has not seen.

21 And this commandment we have from Him, that the one who loves God should also [unselfishly] love his brother *and* seek the best for him.

Overcoming the World

5 EVERYONE WHO believes [with a deep, abiding trust in the fact] that Jesus is the Christ (the Messiah, the Anointed) is born of God [that is, reborn from above—spiritually transformed, renewed, and set apart for His purpose], and everyone who loves the Father also loves the *child* born of Him.

2 By this we know [without any doubt] that we love the children of God: [expressing that love] when we love God and obey His commandments.

3 For the [true] love of God is this: that we *habitually* keep His commandments *and* remain focused on His precepts. And His commandments *and* His precepts are not difficult [to obey].

4 For everyone born of God is victorious *and* overcomes the world; and this is the victory that has conquered *and* overcome the world—our [continuing, persistent] faith [in Jesus the Son of God].

5 Who is the one who is victorious *and* overcomes the world? It is the one who believes *and* recognizes the fact that Jesus is the Son of God.

6 This is He who came through water and blood [His baptism and death], Jesus Christ—not by the water only, but by the water and the blood. It is the [Holy] Spirit who testifies, because the Spirit is the truth. [He is the essence and origin of truth itself.]

7 For there are three witnesses:

8 the Spirit and the water and the blood; and these three are in agreement [their testimony is perfectly consistent].

9 If we accept [as we do] the testimony of men [that is, if we are willing to take the sworn statements of fallible humans as evidence], the testimony of God is greater [far more authoritative]; for this is the testimony of God, that He has testified regarding His Son.

10 The one who believes in the Son of God [who adheres to, trusts in, and relies confidently on Him as Savior] has the testimony within himself [be-

---

of this passage, John explains how a believer can know that the Spirit is working in his or her life.

4:15 *Whoever confesses.* To be a Christian, a person must believe that Jesus is the Son of God.

5:1 *born of God.* This condition happens when one believes or trusts in Jesus Christ. Only correct, sincere belief produces spiritual birth. This birth is reflected in love for others who also have been born into the family of God (2:3 – 11).

5:6 *through water and blood.* This phrase has been interpreted at least four ways: (1) as Jesus' baptism and death; (2) as His incarnation; (3) as the water and blood that flowed from His side on the cross; and (4) as the baptism of the believer and the Lord's

14 Jn 1:14; 3:17 **15** Ro 10:9 **16** ver. 8; 1Jn 3:24 **17** Jas 2:13; 1Jn 3:3 **18** ver. 12 **20** 1Jn 2:4; ver. 12 **21** Mt 22:37; Jn 13:34 **CHAPTER 5** **1** Jn 1:12; 1Jn 2:22,23; Jn 1:13; Jn 15:23 **3** Jn 14:15; 2Jn 6; Mic 6:8 **4** Jn 16:33 **5** 1Co 15:57 **6** Jn 19:34; 14:17; 1Ti 3:16 **7** Jn 1:1; Rev 19:13; Jn 10:30 **9** Jn 8:17; Mt 3:16 **10** Ro 8:16; Jn 3:33

cause he can speak authoritatively about Christ from his own personal experience]. The one who does not believe God [in this way] has made Him [out to be] a liar, because he has not believed in the evidence that God has given regarding His Son.

[11]And the testimony is this: God has given us eternal life [we already possess it], and this life is in His Son [resulting in our spiritual completeness, and eternal companionship with Him].

[12]He who has the Son [by accepting Him as Lord and Savior] has the life [that is eternal]; he who does not have the Son of God [by personal faith] does not have the life.

This Is Written That You May Know

[13]These things I have written to you who believe in the name of the Son of God [which represents all that Jesus Christ is and does], so that you will know [with settled and absolute knowledge] that you [already] have eternal life.

[14]This is the [remarkable degree of] confidence which we [as believers are entitled to] have before Him: that if we ask anything according to His will, [that is, consistent with His plan and purpose] He hears us.

[15]And if we know [for a fact, as indeed we do] that He hears *and* listens to us in whatever we ask, we [also] know [with settled and absolute knowledge] that we have [granted to us] the requests which we have asked from Him.

[16]If anyone sees his brother committing a sin that does not *lead* to death, he will pray *and* ask [on the believer's behalf] and *God* will for him give life to those whose sin is not *leading* to death. There is a sin *that leads* to death; I do not say that one should pray for this [kind of sin].

[17]All wrongdoing is sin, and there is sin that does not *lead* to death [one can repent of it and be forgiven].

[18]We know [with confidence] that anyone born of God does not *habitually* sin; but He (Jesus) who was born of God [carefully] keeps *and* protects him, and the evil one does not touch him.

[19]We know [for a fact] that we are of God, and the whole world [around us] lies in the power of the evil one [opposing God and His precepts].

[20]And we [have seen and] know [by personal experience] that the Son of God has [actually] come [to this world], and has given us understanding *and* insight so that we may [progressively and personally] know Him who is true; and we are in Him who is true—in His Son Jesus Christ. This is the true God and eternal life.

[21]Little children (believers, dear ones), guard yourselves from idols—[false teachings, moral compromises, and anything that would take God's place in your heart].

Supper. Most scholars favor the first interpretation. John is correcting the false teacher, Cerinthus, who claimed that the Spirit came on Jesus at His baptism but left Him before His death (4:2 – 3).

5:11 ***the testimony is this.*** God's witness or testimony is that He has given us eternal life in his Son. Eternal life is not a wage to be earned, but a gift to be received from God (Ro 6:23).

5:14 – 15 ***according to His will.*** The key to knowing that God hears is to pray this way.

5:16 – 17 ***There is a sin that leads to death.*** This phrase may refer to blaspheming the Holy Spirit, rejecting Christ as Savior, rejecting the humanity or deity of Jesus, a specific sin such as murder (3:12,15), or a life of habitual sin. Whatever it is, the sin seems to be a flagrant violation of the sanctity of the Christian community (Ac 5:1 – 11; 1Co 5:5; 11:30). In other words, John is encouraging us to help fellow believers who are straying; we can be the tools God uses to restore an erring brother or sister to the true fellowship.

5:18 – 20 ***We know.*** This phrase introduces three concluding absolute truths. The general idea of this concluding section is that a proper relationship with God results in confidence of our position in Christ with a hostile world.

5:21 ***idols.*** This term may refer to literal idols, foods sacrificed to idols, false ideas in contrast to God's truth, or doctrines of false teachers. John has just reminded his readers of the true God (v. 20). It is appropriate that he closes by exhorting them to stay away from false gods.

11 1Jn 2:25; 1Jn 4:9 **12** Jn 3:36 **13** Jn 20:31; 1Jn 1:1,2 **14** 1Jn 3:22 **16** Job 42:8; Jas 5:14; Mt 12:31; Mk 3:29; Heb 6:4,6; Jer 7:16; Jn 17:9 **17** 1Jn 3:4 **18** 1Pe 1:23; Jas 1:27 **19** Gal 1:4 **20** Lk 24:45; Jn 17:3; Isa 9:6; Ac 20:28; Titus 2:13; ver. 11,12 **21** 1Co 10:14

THE SECOND LETTER OF
JOHN

▸ **AUTHOR:** Second John was not widely circulated at the beginning because of its brevity and subject matter. Its strong resemblance to the tone and style of 1 John and the Fourth Gospel support the early tradition that John was the author of this epistle sometime after AD 90.

▸ **TIMES:** c. AD 89 – 95 ▸ **KEY VERSES:** 2Jn 9 – 10

▸ **THEME:** The addressee of 2 John is a woman in a local church that apparently had a strong friendship with John. The apostle writes to warn her about showing hospitality to false teachers. He cautions her against unwittingly aiding these teachers who were sowing seeds of heresy and hurting the church.

Walk According to His Commandments

1 THE ELDER [of the church ad-
dresses this letter] to the elect (chosen)
lady and her children, whom I love in
truth—and not only I, but also all who
know *and* understand the truth—
2 because of the truth which lives in
our hearts and will be with us forever:
3 Grace, mercy, and peace (inner
calm, a sense of spiritual well-being)
will be with us, from God the Father
and from Jesus Christ, the Father's
Son, in truth and love.
4 I was greatly delighted to find *some*
of your children walking in truth, just as
we have been commanded by the Father.
5 Now I ask you, lady, not as if *I were*
writing to you a new commandment,
but [simply reminding you of] the one
which we have had from the begin-
ning, that we love *and* unselfishly seek
the best for one another.
6 And this is love: that we walk in
accordance with His commandments
and are guided continually by His pre-
cepts. This is the commandment, just
as you have heard from the beginning,
that you should [always] walk in love.
7 For many deceivers [heretics, pos-
ing as Christians] have gone out into
the world, those who do not acknowl-
edge *and* confess the coming of Jesus
Christ in the flesh (bodily form). This
[person, the kind who does this] is the

---

1 *The elder.* This is probably the apostle John. The title can refer either to an old man, an older person deserving respect, or a church leader. ***the elect (chosen) lady*** may be a specific person, or the phrase may be a figurative description of the local church.
4 *walking in truth.* This phrase means having an authentic relationship with God. Our walk with the Lord, if genuine, must be based upon His word.
6 *His commandments.* God's love is the basis of His desire for our obedience, and it is the reason He has revealed His will in His word. We prove our obedience to Christ by demonstrating love toward one another. Love is an unlimited resource readily available to us, and it is tremendously effective in furthering the work of Christ.
7 *coming of Jesus Christ in the flesh.* These words refer to the Incarnation, the fact that Jesus is the God-man. The humanity of Jesus provides a test by which false teachers can be identified. The Gnostic heresy, against which John wrote in 1 and 2 John, included a denial of the physical body of Christ. People who deny the physical reality of Jesus are not Christians, but antichrists.

1 3Jn 1; Col 1:5 **3** 1Ti 1:2 **4** 3Jn 3 **5** 1Jn 3:11; Jn 13:34 **6** 1Jn 2:5,24 **7** 1Jn 4:1; 1Jn 4:2; 1Jn 2:22

deceiver and the antichrist [that is, the
antagonist of Christ].
8Watch yourselves, so that you do
not lose what we have accomplished
together, but that you may receive
a full *and* perfect reward [when He
grants rewards to faithful believers].
9Anyone who runs on ahead and does
not remain in the doctrine of Christ
[that is, one who is not content with
what He taught], does not have God; but
the one who *continues* to remain in the
teaching [of Christ does have God], he
has both the Father and the Son.
10If anyone comes to you and does
not bring this teaching [but diminishes
or adds to the doctrine of Christ], do
not receive *or* welcome him into your
house, and do not give him a greeting
or any encouragement;
11for the one who gives him a greet-
ing [who encourages him or wishes
him success, unwittingly] participates
in his evil deeds.
12I have many things to write to you,
but I prefer not to do so with paper
(papyrus) and black (ink); but I hope
to come to you and speak with you
face to face, so that your joy may be
complete. [Num 12:8]
13The children of your elect (chosen)
sister greet you.

---

8 *Watch yourselves.* Being seduced by false teachers is one way that Christians can lose their reward at the judgment. With this in mind, John writes that the reason to guard against deceivers is our own desire not to lose our reward at the judgment seat of Christ.

9 *runs on ahead.* This phrase has the strong sense of running too far ahead. Departure from Christ into doctrinal error indicates that a person does not have God.

10 *this teaching.* Jesus is completely human and completely divine. A Christian should not only refuse to receive false teachers in the sense of supporting them while they visit the community, a Christian should also avoid appearing to endorse their teachings. The proper response to deceivers is to reject them as unbelievers. This shows how seriously we should take the Scriptures and how careful we should be in evaluating the teachings of everyone.

8 Mk 13:9; Gal 3:4 **9** 1Jn 2:23 **10** Ro 16:17 **12** 3Jn 13; Jn 17:13 **13** 1Pe 5:13

THE THIRD LETTER OF

JOHN

▸ **AUTHOR:** Much like 2 John, this letter had a very limited circulation in the early church, but was accepted as authoritative on account of its apostolic authorship. Its style and vocabulary strongly resemble that of John's Gospel and other epistles.

▸ **TIMES:** c. AD 89 – 95 ▸ **KEY VERSE:** 3Jn 11

▸ **THEME:** Third John has two main purposes. The first is to commend Gaius for being hospitable to itinerant missionaries. The second is to advise Gaius about Diotrephes, a man in the church who refuses to help the same kind of missionaries and who even gossips about them.

You Walk in the Truth

1THE ELDER [of the church ad-
dresses this letter] to the beloved *and*
esteemed Gaius, whom I love in truth.
2Beloved, I pray that in every way
you may succeed *and* prosper and be
in good health [physically], just as [I
know] your soul prospers [spiritually].
3For I was greatly pleased when
[some of the] brothers came [from time
to time] and testified to your [faithful-
ness to the] truth [of the gospel mes-
sage], *that is,* how you are walking
in truth.
4I have no greater joy than this, to
hear that my [spiritual] children are
living [their lives] in the truth.
5Beloved, you are acting faithful-
ly in what you are providing for the
brothers, and especially *when they
are* strangers;
6and they have testified before the
church of your love *and* friendship.
You will do well to [assist them and]
send them on their way in a manner
worthy of God.
7For these [traveling missionaries]
went out for the sake of the Name [of
Christ], accepting nothing [in the way
of assistance] from the Gentiles.
8So we ought to support such people
[welcoming them as guests and provid-
ing for them], so that we may be fellow
workers for the truth [that is, for the
gospel message of salvation].
9I wrote something to the church;
but Diotrephes, who loves to put him-
self first, does not accept what we say
and refuses to recognize my authority.
10For this reason, if I come, I will call
attention to what he is doing, unjustly
accusing us with wicked words *and*
unjustified charges. And not satisfied

---

2 may succeed and prosper and be in good health. John's greeting may imply that Gaius was physically weak though spiritually strong. More probably John is simply following the pattern of greetings common to Greek letters.

4 my [spiritual] children. This is a description Paul uses of those he has led to saving faith in Christ (1Co 4:14 – 17) and may indicate that Gaius was one of John's converts. It may also be a term John uses to describe those under his pastoral care as reflected in 1 John 2:1,12,18; 3:7,18; 4:4; 5:21.

5 – 12 you are acting faithfully. In these verses, John affirms Gaius' responsibility to assist Demetrius despite the opposition of Diotrephes and his expulsion of those who receive traveling missionaries.

7 Gentiles. In this case the term refers to unbelievers, not to Gentile Christians. The majority

1 2Jn 1 **3** 2Jn 4 **4** 1Co 4:15; Php 10 **7** 1Co 9:12,15

with this, he refuses to receive the [missionary] brothers himself, and also forbids those who want to [welcome them] and puts *them* out of the church.
11 Beloved, do not imitate what is evil,
but [imitate] what is good. The one who practices good [exhibiting godly character, moral courage and personal integrity] is of God; the one who practices [or permits or tolerates] evil has not seen God [he has no personal experience with Him and does not know Him at all]. [1 John 3:6]
12 Demetrius has received a *good*
testimony *and* commendation from everyone—and from the truth [the standard of God's word] itself; and we add our testimony *and* speak well of him, and you know that our testimony is true.
13 I had many things [to say when
I began] to write to you, but I prefer not to put it down with pen (reed) and black (ink);
14 but I hope to see you soon, and we
will speak face to face. [Num 12:8]
15 Peace be to you. The friends [here]
greet you. Greet the friends [personally] by name.

---

of Christians in the churches of Asia Minor were Gentile converts rather than Jewish.

11 *has not seen God.* Our sin is a result of a faulty vision of God. Therefore, the Scriptures encourage us to look at Christ (2Co 3:18; 4:16 – 18; Heb 12:2 – 3), for the day when we see Him perfectly will be the day that we will be like Him (1Jn 3:2 – 3).

12 *from the truth [the standard of God's word] itself.* Demetrius' life measured up to the teaching of Scripture and Christ's commands. His conduct matched his theology.

11 Ps 37:27; Isa 1:16,17; 1Pe 3:11; 1Jn 2:29; 3:6,9 **12** 1Ti 3:7; Jn 21:24 **13** 2Jn 12

THE LETTER OF
JUDE

▸ **AUTHOR:** In spite of its limited subject matter and size, Jude was accepted as authentic and quoted by early church fathers. It is unlikely that the author is the apostle Jude (Lk 6:16), but rather Jude the brother of Jesus and James (called Judas in Mt 13:55 and Mk 6:3). Because of the silence of the New Testament and tradition concerning Jude's later years, we cannot know where or when this epistle was written.

▸ **TIMES:** c. AD 66–80 ▸ **KEY VERSE:** Jude 3

▸ **THEME:** Jude's letter is hard hitting, short, and right to the point. False teachers are on the loose in the church and Jude wants to make sure his readers understand the destructive implications of their teaching. He urges Christians to resist these false teachers and to defend the faith and the body of truth received from the apostles that they have come to know and believe. He finishes by reminding them of the hope they have in knowing Christ is coming again.

The Warnings of History to the Ungodly

1JUDE, A bond-servant of Jesus
Christ, and brother of James, [writes
this letter],
To those who are the called (God's
chosen ones, the elect), dearly loved by
God the Father, and kept [secure and
set apart] for Jesus Christ:
2May mercy and peace and love be
multiplied to you [filling your heart
with the spiritual well-being and se-
renity experienced by those who walk
closely with God].
3Beloved, while I was making every
effort to write you about our common
salvation, I was compelled to write to
you [urgently] appealing that you fight
strenuously for [the defense of] the
faith which was once for all handed
down to the saints [the faith that is the
sum of Christian belief that was given
verbally to believers].
4For certain people have crept in un-
noticed [just as if they were sneaking
in by a side door]. They are ungodly
persons whose condemnation was
predicted long ago, for they distort
the grace of our God into decadence
and immoral freedom [viewing it as
an opportunity to do whatever they
want], and deny *and* disown our only
Master and Lord, Jesus Christ.
5Now I want to remind you, although

2 *peace.* This is the state of a person who rests in God completely for salvation and protection.
3 *common salvation.* Jude intended to write a more general doctrinal letter, but the present crisis demanded this short, pointed attack on doctrinal error.
4 *distort the grace of our God into decadence and immoral freedom.* The teaching of grace can be dangerous when perverted by false teachers or carnal people who believe that because they have been saved by grace they may live as they please (Ro 6:1–2).
5 *destroyed those who did not believe.* The Israelites of the exodus had a magnificent beginning in Egypt but a disastrous ending in the wilderness. That we have begun with the Lord

1 Ac 1:13; Jn 17:11; 1Pe 1:5; Ro 1:7 **2** 1Pe 1:2; 2Pe 1:2 **3** Titus 1:4; Php 1:27; 2Ti 1:13 **4** Gal 2:4; 2Pe 2:1; Ro 9:22; 2Pe 2:10; Titus 2:11; Titus 1:16 **5** 1Co 10:9; Nu 14:29; Ps 106:26

you are fully informed once for all,
that the Lord, after saving a people
out of the land of Egypt, subsequently
destroyed those who did not believe
[who refused to trust and obey and
rely on Him]. [Num 14:27–37]
6And angels who did not keep their
own designated place of power, but
abandoned their proper dwelling
place, [these] He has kept in eternal
chains under [the thick gloom of ut-
ter] darkness for the judgment of the
great day,
7just as Sodom and Gomorrah and
the adjacent cities, since they in the
same way as these *angels* indulged in
gross immoral freedom *and* unnatural
vice and sensual perversity. They are
exhibited [in plain sight] as an exam-
ple in undergoing the punishment of
everlasting fire. [Gen 19:1–29]
8Nevertheless in the same way, these
dreamers [who are dreaming that God
will not punish them] also defile the
body, and reject [legitimate] authority,
and revile *and* mock angelic majesties.
9But even the archangel Michael,
when he was disputing with the devil
(Satan), and arguing about the body
of Moses, did not dare bring an abu-
sive condemnation against him, but
[simply] said, "The Lord rebuke you!"
[Deut 34:5, 6; Zech 3:2]
10But these men sneer at anything
which they do not understand; and
whatever they do know by [mere] in-
stinct, like unreasoning *and* irratio-
nal beasts—by these things they are
destroyed.
11Woe to them! For they have gone
the [defiant] way of Cain, and for profit
they have run headlong into the error
of Balaam, and perished in the rebel-
lion of [mutinous] Korah. [Gen 4:3–8;
Num 16:22–24; 2 Pet 2:15]
12These men are hidden reefs [el-
ements of great danger to others] in
your love feasts when they feast to-
gether with you without fear, looking
after [only] themselves; [they are like]
clouds without water, swept along by
the winds; autumn trees without fruit,
doubly dead, uprooted *and* lifeless;
13wild waves of the sea, flinging up
their own shame like foam; wander-
ing stars, for whom the gloom of deep
darkness has been reserved forever.
14It was about these people that
Enoch, in the seventh *generation*
from Adam, prophesied, when he said,
"Look, the Lord came with myriads of
His holy ones

---

does not mean that we will have the glorious conclusion we might have envisioned at the beginning or our salvation journey. The false believers who had infiltrated God's people would be judged, just like the false believers who rejected God in the wilderness (Nu 25:1–9).

6 *angels.* These are not holy angels of God. Instead these angels could be those who had previously fallen with Satan. Some think that these angels are "the sons of God" of Genesis 6:2, who took on human form and married women before the flood.

8 *reject [legitimate] authority.* The false teachers even despised those who were placed in positions of authority in local congregations. They not only preferred error to truth but also demeaned and rejected those who taught the truth.

9 *arguing about the body of Moses.* Jude's description here is probably taken from an apocryphal book called *The Assumption of Moses*, written in the first century AD. There is no record in the Bible itself of the archangel's encounter with Satan, or a detailed account of Moses' body.

11 *For they have gone the [defiant] way of Cain.* The heretics are compared to three Old Testament failures. Cain did not place his faith in the Lord. The "way of Cain" is the way of pride and self-righteousness (Ge 4:3–8; Heb 11:4; 1Jn 3:12). ***Balaam.*** He was the epitome of the sin of greed (Nu 31:16). ***Korah.*** This was the Levite Korah (Nu 16:1–3; 31–35) who resented the prominent positions of Moses and Aaron as God's representatives. The Lord brought judgment on him and his followers for rebelling against those He had place in authority.

13 *wild waves . . . flinging . . . wandering stars.* These godless people put on a great show but lacked any substance. They boasted of liberty but placed the people of God in bondage to sin (2Pe 2:19). After they had done their evil deeds and made their profits, they, like wandering stars, moved on to other places to exploit God's people again.

---

6 Jn 8:44; 2Pe 2:4; Rev 20:10 **7** Ge 19:24; 2Pe 2:6 **8** 2Pe 2:10; Ex 22:28 **9** Da 10:13; 2Pe 2:11; Zec 3:2 **10** 2Pe 2:12 **11** 1Jn 3:12; 2Pe 2:15; Nu 16:1 **12** 2Pe 2:13; 1Co 11:21; Pr 25:14; 2Pe 2:17; Eph 4:14; Mt 15:13 **13** Isa 57:20; Php 3:19; 2Pe 2:17 **14** Ge 5:18; Dt 33:2

15 to execute judgment upon all, and to convict all the ungodly of all the ungodly deeds they have done in an ungodly way, and of all the harsh *and* cruel things ungodly sinners have spoken against Him."
16 These *people* are [habitual] murmurers, griping *and* complaining, following after their own desires [controlled by passion]; they speak arrogantly, [pretending admiration and] flattering people to *gain an* advantage.

Keep Yourselves in the Love of God

17 But as for you, beloved, remember the [prophetic] words spoken by the apostles of our Lord Jesus Christ.
18 They used to say to you, "In the last days there will be scoffers, following after their own ungodly passions." [2 Pet 3:3, 4]
19 These are the ones who are [agitators] causing divisions—worldly-minded [secular, unspiritual, carnal, merely sensual—unsaved], devoid of the Spirit.
20 But you, beloved, build yourselves up on [the foundation of] your most holy faith [continually progress, rise like an edifice higher and higher], pray in the Holy Spirit,
21 and keep yourselves in the love of God, waiting anxiously *and* looking forward to the mercy of our Lord Jesus Christ [which will bring you] to eternal life.
22 And have mercy on some, who are doubting;
23 save others, snatching them out of the fire; and on some have mercy but with fear, loathing even the clothing spotted *and* polluted by their shameless immoral freedom. [Amos 4:11; Zech 3:2–4]
24 Now to Him who is able to keep you from stumbling *or* falling into sin, and to present you unblemished [blameless and faultless] in the presence of His glory with triumphant joy *and* unspeakable delight,
25 to the only God our Savior, through Jesus Christ our Lord, be glory, majesty, dominion, and power, before all time and now and forever. Amen.

---

15 *ungodly.* This word is repeated four times, making the verse one of the most striking in the letter. In view of the wicked nature of evil persons, how could the church allow them to stay in their midst?
18 *there will be scoffers.* One of the main tactics that the false teachers used to gain credibility was to tear down godly leaders.
22–23 *have mercy on some.* We have certain obligations to other believers. First, we need to show compassion to those in any kind of spiritual or physical need. Second, we need to use discernment in helping our brothers and sisters in the church. Some will require tender care and patience to help them grow in Christ. With others we may need to use drastic action to rescue them from the temptations of sin. ***loathing even the clothing spotted and polluted by their shameless immoral freedom.*** This is a metaphor for staying wary of sin — as Paul says, "keeping a watchful eye on yourself, so that you are not tempted as well" (Gal 6:1).
24 *unblemished.* This is a Greek word used of sacrificial animals that had no blemish and thus were fit to be offered to God. Only God can save us, cleanse us from our sins, and present us to Himself as faultless, for God is the Author and Finisher of our faith (Heb 12:2).

15 1Sa 2:3; Ps 31:18 **16** 2Pe 2:18; Pr 28:21 **17** 2Pe 3:2 **18** 1Ti 4:1; 2Pe 2:1 **19** Pr 18:1; Jas 3:15 **20** Col 2:7; Ro 8:26 **21** Titus 2:13; 2Pe 3:12 **23** Ro 11:14; Am 4:11; Zec 3:2; Zec 3:4,5 **24** Eph 3:20; Col 1:22 **25** Ro 16:27

THE REVELATION TO JOHN

▸ **AUTHOR:** The style, symmetry, and plan of Revelation show that it was written by one author, four times named "John" (Rev 1:1,4,9; 22:8). Because of its contents and its address to seven churches, Revelation quickly circulated and became widely known and accepted in the early church. From the beginning, Revelation was considered an authentic work of the apostle John, the same John who wrote the Gospel and Epistles. Revelation was written at a time when Roman hostility to Christianity was erupting into overt persecution. It is likely that John wrote this book in AD 95 or 96 when the severe persecution of Christians began under the emperor Domitian.

▸ **TIMES:** c. AD 95 – 96 ▸ **KEY VERSES:** Rev 19:11 – 15

▸ **THEME:** John wrote this book late in his life while in exile on the island of Patmos off the coast of Asia. It is safe to say that no book of the Bible has generated more theories of interpretation over the last two millennia. In this context, probably one of the best approaches to interpreting and understanding Revelation is to concentrate on the major themes, such as worship. When the reader does that, one finds great comfort and assurance in the book. Many scholars think the purpose of the book is to provide comfort in the midst of persecution and difficult times, as the form of the book is in the tradition of Jewish apocalyptic literature that is designed to communicate hope through symbolic imagery.

The Revelation of Jesus Christ

1 *THIS IS* the revelation of Jesus Christ [His unveiling of the divine mysteries], which God [the Father] gave to Him to show to His bond-servants (believers) the things which must soon take place [in their entirety]; and He sent and communicated it by His angel (divine messenger) to His bond-servant John,
2who testified *and* gave supporting evidence to the word of God and to the testimony of Jesus Christ, *even* to everything that he saw [in his visions].
3Blessed (happy, prosperous, to be admired) is he who reads and those who hear the words of the prophecy, and who keep the things which are written in it [heeding them and taking them to heart]; for the time [of fulfillment] is near.

1:1 ***revelation.*** The word "revelation," which means "unveiling," or "disclosure," indicates that this book is a type of literature known as *apocalyptic literature*, or literature which reveals hidden things. ***of Jesus Christ.*** This revelation is both from Jesus Christ and about Him. ***John.*** John is the human writer, and Jesus is the divine Author. **1:3** ***Blessed.*** The word "blessed" means "spiritually happy." Even though some of the words of this book speak of terrifying and solemn times, it is a blessing to know how thoroughly the Lord holds all time and all times in His hands. Those who take time to read and try to understand this book will find themselves blessed by the hope of heaven and by the nearness of our Lord and Savior.

CHAPTER 1 **1** Jn 3:32; Rev 22:16 **2** 1Co 1:6; 1Jn 1:1 **3** Lk 11:28; Jas 5:8

Message to the Seven Churches

4John, to the seven churches that
are in [the province of] Asia: Grace
[be granted] to you and peace [inner
calm and spiritual well-being], from
Him Who is [existing forever] and
Who was [continually existing in the
past] and Who is to come, and from
the seven Spirits that are before His
throne, [Is 11:2]
5and from Jesus Christ, the faithful
and trustworthy Witness, the First-
born of the dead, and the Ruler of the
kings of the earth. To Him who [al-
ways] loves us and who [has once for
all] freed us [or washed us] from our
sins by His own blood (His sacrificial
death)— [Ps 89:27]
6and formed us into a kingdom [as
His subjects], priests to His God and
Father—to Him be the glory *and* the
power *and* the majesty and the domin-
ion forever and ever. Amen. [Ex 19:6;
Is 61:6]
7BEHOLD, HE IS COMING WITH THE
CLOUDS, and every eye will see Him,
even those who pierced Him; and all
the tribes (nations) of the earth will
mourn over Him [realizing their sin
and guilt, and anticipating the coming
wrath]. So it is to be. Amen. [Dan 7:13;
Zech 12:10]
8"I am the Alpha and the Omega
[the Beginning and the End]," says the
Lord God, "Who is [existing forever]
and Who was [continually existing
in the past] and Who is to come, the
Almighty [the Omnipotent, the Ruler
of all]." [Is 9:6]

The Patmos Vision

9I, John, your brother and compan-
ion in the tribulation and kingdom and
patient endurance *which are* in Jesus,
was on the island called Patmos, [ex-
iled there] because of [my preaching
of] the word of God [regarding eternal
salvation] and the testimony of Jesus
Christ.
10I was in the Spirit [in special com-
munication with the Holy Spirit and
empowered to receive and record the
revelation from Jesus Christ] on the
Lord's Day, and I heard behind me a
loud voice like the *sound* of a trumpet,
11saying, "Write on a scroll what you
see [in this revelation], and send it to
the seven churches—to Ephesus and
to Smyrna and to Pergamum and to
Thyatira and to Sardis and to Phila-
delphia and to Laodicea."
12Then I turned to see the voice that
was speaking with me. And after turn-
ing I saw seven golden lampstands;
13and in the midst of the lampstands

1:4 *the seven churches.* The seven churches are in the Roman province of Asia, which today is southwestern Turkey. The churches fit within a square 50 miles on each side, and their names are given in order going clockwise from the southwest.

1:5 *Firstborn of the dead.* This phrase refers to the resurrection of Christ, the first to come back from the dead. This is the basis of the hope of resurrection held by Christians (1Co 15:20 – 24).

1:7 *COMING WITH THE CLOUDS . . . EVERY EYE.* "Coming with the clouds" recalls Daniel's vision of the Son of Man (Da 7:13; Mt 24:30) and the ascension of Christ (Ac 1:11). "Every eye" indicates that Christ will be universally visible at His second coming.

1:8 *Alpha and the Omega.* The Lord's description of Himself as the first and last letters of the Greek alphabet means that He is the beginning and the end of all creation.

1:9 *tribulation.* The apostle Paul said there would be many tribulations (Ac 14:22), and John identifies both the suffering of others and his own exile on Patmos as part of the "troubles." The great tribulation is the time when the wrath of God is poured out on the earth (Mk 13:14 – 23); that time is explained in greater detail in this book.

1:12 *seven golden lampstands.* The seven lampstands represent the seven churches.

1:13 *someone like the Son of Man.* The term "Son of Man" echoes Daniel 7:13. Comparisons of these two passages, along with Jesus' common use of the name "Son of Man" for Himself, indicate that Christ is the subject of verses 12 – 18.

4 Ex 3:14; Jn 1:1; Zec 3:9 **5** Jn 8:14; 1Ti 6:13; Col 1:18; Rev 17:14; Jn 13:34; Gal 2:20; Heb 9:14; 1Jn 1:7 **6** 1Pe 2:5; 1Ti 6:16 **7** Da 7:13; Zec 12:10 **8** Isa 41:4; Rev 4:8 **9** Php 1:7; Ro 8:17; 2Ti 2:12; Rev 6:9 **10** Ac 10:10; 2Co 12:2; Jn 20:26; Rev 4:1 **11** ver. 8; ver. 17 **12** Ex 25:37; Zec 4:2 **13** Rev 2:1; Eze 1:26; Da 7:13; 10:16; Da 10:5; Rev 15:6

I saw someone like the Son of Man, dressed in a robe reaching to His feet, and with a golden sash wrapped around His chest. [Dan 7:13; 10:5]

14 His head and His hair were white like white wool, [glistening white] like snow; and His [all-seeing] eyes were [flashing] like a flame of fire [piercing into my being]. [Dan 7:9]

15 His feet were like burnished [white-hot] bronze, refined in a furnace, and His voice was [powerful] like the sound of many waters. [Dan 10:6]

16 In His right hand He held seven stars, and from His mouth came a sharp two-edged sword [of judgment]; and His face [reflecting His majesty and the Shekinah glory] was like the sun shining in [all] its power [at midday]. [Ex 34:29]

17 When I saw Him, I fell at His feet as though dead. And He placed His right hand on me and said, "Do not be afraid; I am the First and the Last [absolute Deity, the Son of God], [Is 44:6]

18 and the Ever-living One [living in and beyond all time and space]. I died, but see, I am alive forevermore, and I have the keys of [absolute control and victory over] death and of Hades (the realm of the dead).

19 "So write the things which you have seen [in the vision], and the things which are [now happening], and the things which will take place after these things.

20 "As for the mystery of the seven stars which you saw in My right hand, and the seven golden lampstands: the seven stars are the angels (divine messengers) of the seven churches, and the seven lampstands are the seven churches.

Message to Ephesus

2 "TO THE angel (divine messenger) of the church in Ephesus write:

"These are the words of the One who holds [firmly] the seven stars [which are the angels or messengers of the seven churches] in His right hand, the One who walks among the seven golden lampstands (the seven churches):

2 'I know your deeds and your toil, and your patient endurance, and that you cannot tolerate those who are evil, and have tested *and* critically appraised those who call themselves apostles (special messengers, personally chosen representatives, of Christ), and [in fact] are not, and have found them to be liars *and* impostors;

3 and [I know that] you [who believe] are enduring patiently and are bearing up for My name's sake, and that you have not grown weary [of being faithful to the truth].

4 'But I have *this* [charge] against you, that you have left your first love [you have lost the depth of love that you first had for Me].

1:14 *white.* The white appearance is parallel to the description of the "Ancient of Days" in Daniel 7:9, and of Christ on the mount of transfiguration (Mt 17:2). The similarity of descriptions demonstrates the purity and eternality of both God the Father and God the Son. Overcoming believers will also be "dressed in white clothing" (3:5; 19:8) in Christ's presence, symbolizing purity.

1:16 *sharp two-edged sword.* The sword coming out of Christ's mouth is symbolic of the judging power of the Word of God (Isa 49:2; Heb 4:12).

1:18 *keys of [absolute control and victory over] death and of Hades.* Christ has authority over those who have died physically and over their present resting place, which will be emptied and destroyed at the time of the great white throne judgment (20:11 – 15). "Hades" is the place where the dead rest. The Hebrew word *Sheol,* (the place where the dead go) and the Greek words *Hades,* or *Gehenna* (a place of eternal punishment), are both translated *hell* in some contexts. The parable that Jesus told (Lk 16:20 – 25) describes the rich man in torment in hell, and the beggar "far away" with Abraham. There was a great chasm between them.

1:20 *angels.* Angels are created spirit beings who minister to believers (Heb 1:14).

2:1 *Ephesus.* Ephesus was the most important city in Asia Minor when Revelation was written. It was the center of the worship of Artemis (or Diana; Ac 19:28), the goddess of fertility. It was a strategic commercial center and a great seaport.

---

14 Da 7:9; 10:6 **15** Eze 1:7; Da 10:6; Eze 43:2; Da 10:6; Rev 14:2 **16** Rev 2:1; Isa 49:2; Eph 6:17; Heb 4:12; Ac 26:13 **17** Eze 1:28; Da 8:18; 10:10; Isa 41:4; 44:6; 48:12; Rev 22:13 **18** Ro 6:9; Rev 4:9; Ps 68:20; Rev 20:1 **19** Rev 2:1; Rev 4:1 **20** Mal 2:7; Rev 2:1; Zec 4:2; Mt 5:15; Php 2:15 **CHAPTER 2** **1** Rev 1:13,16 **2** Ps 1:6; Rev 3:1,8; 1Jn 4:1; 2Co 11:13; 2Pe 2:1 **3** Gal 6:9; Heb 12:3,5

5 'So remember *the heights* from which you have fallen, and repent [change your inner self—your old way of thinking, your sinful behavior—seek God's will] and do the works you did at first [when you first knew Me]; otherwise, I will visit you and remove your lampstand (the church, its impact) from its place—unless you repent.
6 'Yet you have this [to your credit], that you hate the works *and* corrupt teachings of the Nicolaitans [that mislead and delude the people], which I also hate.
7 'He who has an ear, let him hear *and* heed what the Spirit says to the churches. To him who overcomes [the world through believing that Jesus is the Son of God], I will grant [the privilege] to eat [the fruit] from the tree of life, which is in the Paradise of God.' [Gen 2:9; 3:24; 1 John 5:5]

Message to Smyrna

8 "And to the angel (divine messenger) of the church in Smyrna write:

"These are the words of the First and the Last [absolute Deity, the Son of God] who died and came to life [again]: [Is 44:6]
9 'I know your suffering and your poverty (but you are rich), and how you are blasphemed *and* slandered by those who say they are Jews and are not, but are a synagogue of Satan [they are Jews only by blood, and do not believe and truly honor the God whom they claim to worship].
10 'Fear nothing that you are about to suffer. Be aware that the devil is about to throw some of you into prison, that you may be tested [in your faith], and for ten days you will have tribulation. Be faithful to the point of death [if you must die for your faith], and I will give you the crown [consisting] of life. [Rev 3:10, 11]
11 'He who has an ear, let him hear *and* heed what the Spirit says to the churches. He who overcomes [the world through believing that Jesus is the Son of God] will not be hurt by the second death (the lake of fire).' [1 John 5:5; Rev 20:14]

Message to Pergamum

12 "And to the angel (divine messenger) of the church in Pergamum write:

"These are the words of Him who has *and* wields the sharp two-edged sword [in judgment]:
13 'I know where you dwell, [a place] where Satan sits enthroned. Yet you are holding fast to My name, and you did not deny My faith even in the days of Antipas, My witness, My faithful

---

2:5 *remember.* A generation earlier the same church was commended for love (Eph 1:15; 6:24).
2:6 *Nicolaitans.* The Nicolaitans were a heretical group that troubled the churches at Ephesus and Pergamos (v. 15). Apparently their teaching and practice were immoral, perhaps even idolatrous (v. 14).
2:7 *Paradise.* Jesus told the believing thief on the cross that he would be with Jesus in paradise (Lk 23:42). Paul uses the term interchangeably with "the third heaven" (2Co 12:2,4).
2:8 *Smyrna.* Smyrna was an important seaport 35 miles north of Ephesus. The presence of a Roman imperial cult and a large Jewish population made life difficult for believers in Smyrna. However, the churches of Smyrna and Philadelphia are the only two of the seven not rebuked by Christ in some way.
2:10 *crown [consisting] of life.* The Greek crown or garland of green leaves was given to winners in athletic events. James 1:12 also promises the crown of life to believers who persevere under trial.
2:11 *second death.* The second death refers to the experience of eternal death in the lake of fire (20:14–15). No believer will suffer the second death.
2:12 *Pergamum.* Pergamum was the ancient capital of the province of Asia. It was said to be the place where parchment was first used. Pergamum means "citadel" in Greek. It was located 50 miles north of Smyrna and was situated on a high hill dominating the valley below. ***two-edged sword.*** The two-edged sword is the powerful word of the Lord (1:16; Heb 4:12).
2:13 *Satan sits enthroned.* "Where Satan sits enthroned" implies that Satan's authority and power were honored either openly or in effect. ***Antipas.*** Antipas (not Herod Antipas) had already

5 Mt 21:41 **7** Mt 11:15; 13:9,43; Rev 3:6,13; Rev 22:2,14; Ge 2:9 **8** Rev 1:8,17 **9** Lk 12:21; 1Ti 6:18; Jas 2:5; Ro 2:17; Rev 3:9 **10** Mt 10:22; Mt 24:13; Jas 1:12; Rev 3:11 **11** Rev 13:9; Rev 20:1; 21:8 **12** Rev 1:16

one, who was killed (martyred) among
you, where Satan dwells.
14‘But I have a few things against you,
because you have there some [among
you] who are holding to the [corrupt]
teaching of Balaam, who taught Ba-
lak to put a stumbling block before
the sons of Israel, [enticing them] to
eat things that had been sacrificed to
idols and to commit [acts of sexual]
immorality. [Num 25:1, 2; 31:16]
15‘You also have some who in the
same way are holding to the teaching
of the Nicolaitans.
16‘Therefore repent [change your
inner self—your old way of thinking,
your sinful behavior—seek God’s will];
or else I am coming to you quickly,
and I will make war *and* fight against
them with the sword of My mouth [in
judgment].
17‘He who has an ear, let him hear
and heed what the Spirit says to the
churches. To him who overcomes [the
world through believing that Jesus
is the Son of God], to him I will give
[the privilege of eating] *some* of the
hidden manna, and I will give him a
white stone with a new name engraved
on the stone which no one knows ex-
cept the one who receives it.’ [Ps 78:24;
Is 62:2; 1 John 5:5]

Message to Thyatira

18“And to the angel (divine messen-
ger) of the church in Thyatira write:
“These are the words of the Son of
God, who has eyes [that flash] like a
flame of fire [in righteous judgment],
and whose feet are like burnished
[white-hot] bronze: [Dan 10:6]
19‘I know your deeds, your love and
faith and service and patient endur-
ance, and that your last deeds are more
numerous *and* greater than the first.
20‘But I have this [charge] against
you, that you tolerate the woman Jez-
ebel, who calls herself a prophetess
[claiming to be inspired], and she teach-
es and misleads My bond-servants
so that they commit [acts of sexual]
immorality and eat food sacrificed to
idols. [1 Kin 16:31; 2 Kin 9:22, 30]
21‘I gave her time to repent [to change
her inner self and her sinful way of
thinking], but she has no desire to repent
of her immorality *and* refuses to do so.
22‘Listen carefully, I will throw her
on a bed *of sickness*, and those who
commit adultery with her [I will bring]
into great anguish, unless they repent
of her deeds.
23‘And I will kill her children (fol-
lowers) with pestilence [thoroughly
annihilating them], and all the church-
es will know [without any doubt] that
I am He who searches the minds and
hearts [the innermost thoughts, pur-
poses]; and I will give to each one of
you [a reward or punishment] accord-
ing to your deeds. [Ps 62:12; Jer 17:10]
24‘But to the rest of you in Thyatira,
who do not hold this teaching, who
have not explored *and* known the
depths of Satan, as they call them—I
place no other burden on you,

---

suffered martyrdom, thus receiving the promised “crown of life.”

2:14 *teaching of Balaam.* The background for this teaching is in the Old Testament (Nu 22:1 – 25:31). Balak hired Balaam to turn the hearts of Israel away from the Lord. Apparently seduction similar to that which Balaam instigated was taking place at the church at Pergamum, especially in relation to idols and sexual immorality (Ac 15:20).

2:18 *Thyatira.* Thyatira was a city with a large military detachment about 30 miles southeast of Pergamum. Recognized for its wool and dye industries, the city was also noted for its trade guilds. ***eyes [that flash] like a flame . . . feet are like burnished [white-hot] bronze.*** This is essentially the same wording as Daniel 10:6.

2:24 *depths of Satan.* The deep things may be secrets known by those initiated into the things of the devil. When the apostle Paul addressed the subject of walking in the Light (the revelation of Christ), he not only said not to participate in the unfruitful deeds of darkness, but he went on to say that it is disgraceful even to speak of those things done in secret (Eph 5:11 – 12).

14 Nu 24:14; 25:1; 31:16; 2Pe 2:15; Jude 11; Ac 15:29; 1Co 8:9; 10:19,20; 1Co 6:13 **16** Isa 11:4; 2Th 2:8; Rev 1:16 **17** Rev 3:12; 19:12 **18** Rev 1:14,15 **19** ver. 2 **20** 1Ki 16:31; 21:25; 2Ki 9:7; Ex 34:15; Ac 15:20 **21** Rev 9:20 **23** 1Sa 16:7; Jer 11:20; Jn 2:24; Ac 1:24; Ro 8:27; Ps 62:12; 2Co 5:10 **24** Ac 15:28

25 except to hold tightly to what you have until I come.

26 'And he who overcomes [the world through believing that Jesus is the Son of God] and he who keeps My deeds [doing things that please Me] until the [very] end, TO HIM I WILL GIVE AUTHORITY *and* POWER OVER THE NATIONS; [1 John 5:5]

27 AND HE SHALL SHEPHERD *and* RULE THEM WITH A ROD OF IRON, AS THE EARTHEN POTS ARE BROKEN IN PIECES, as I also have received *authority* [and power to rule them] from My Father; [Ps 2:8, 9]

28 and I will give him the Morning Star.

29 'He who has an ear, let him hear *and* heed what the Spirit says to the churches.'

Message to Sardis

3 "TO THE angel (divine messenger) of the church in Sardis write:

"These are the words of Him who has the seven Spirits of God and the seven stars: 'I know your deeds; you have a name (reputation) that you are alive, but [in reality] you are dead.

2 'Wake up, and strengthen *and* reaffirm what remains [of your faithful commitment to Me], which is about to die; for I have not found [any of] your deeds completed in the sight of My God *or* meeting His requirements.

3 'So remember *and* take to heart the lessons you have received and heard. Keep *and* obey them, and repent [change your sinful way of thinking, and demonstrate your repentance with new behavior that proves a conscious decision to turn away from sin]. So then, if you do not wake up, I will come like a thief, and you will not know at what hour I will come to you.

4 'But you [still] have a few people in Sardis who have not soiled their clothes [that is, contaminated their character and personal integrity with sin]; and they will walk with Me [dressed] in white, because they are worthy (righteous).

5 'He who overcomes [the world through believing that Jesus is the Son of God] will accordingly be dressed in white clothing; and I will never blot out his name from the Book of Life, and I will confess *and* openly acknowledge his name before My Father and before His angels [saying that he is one of Mine]. [Ps 69:28; Dan 12:1; Matt 10:32; 1 John 5:5]

6 'He who has an ear, let him hear *and* heed what the Spirit says to the churches.'

Message to Philadelphia

7 "And to the angel (divine messenger) of the church in Philadelphia write:

"These are the words of the Holy One, the True One, He who has the key [to the house] of David, He who

---

2:28 ***the Morning Star.*** The Morning Star is Christ Himself in 22:16. For the believer, Christ's presence is the light in the dark and difficult times. The morning star (the planet Venus, which can be seen in the sky just before sunrise) is the harbinger of day; it is easy to see how the return of Christ could be paralleled with the morning star. When Satan is referred to as the morning star, that is thought to be a description of what Satan was like before he rebelled (Isa 14:12).
3:1 ***Sardis.*** Sardis, located 30 miles southeast of Thyatira, had been the capital of Lydia. The worship of the Roman Caesar and Artemis, goddess of fertility, were active here.
3:3 ***like a thief.*** Christ's warning that He will come as unexpectedly as a thief echoes His repeated emphasis in Matthew 24:36–25:13 (see also 16:15).
3:5 ***Book of Life.*** The Book of Life is the list of the redeemed (20:11–15; Ex 32:32–33).
3:7 ***Philadelphia.*** Philadelphia, which means "brotherly love" in Greek, was a small city located about 40 miles southeast of Sardis. Its location, vineyards, and wine production made it wealthy and commercially important. ***key [to the house] of David.*** This key represents the authority of the One who opens and shuts the door in the Davidic kingdom (Isa 22:22), a prerogative that is Christ's as the rightful "son of David" (Mt 1:1).

---

25 Rev 3:11 **26** Jn 6:29; 1Jn 3:23; Mt 19:28; Lk 22:29; 1Co 6:3 **27** Ps 2:8,9; Da 7:22 **28** 2Pe 1:19 **29** ver. 7
CHAPTER 3 **1** Rev 1:4,16; Rev 2:2; Eph 2:1,5 **3** 1Ti 6:20; 2Ti 1:13; ver. 19; Mt 24:42; Mk 13:33; Lk 12:39; 1Th 5:2,6; 2Pe 3:10 **4** Ac 1:15; Jude 23; Rev 4:4; 6:11 **5** Rev 19:8; Ex 32:32; Php 4:3; Lk 12:8 **6** Rev 2:7 **7** Ac 3:14; 1Jn 5:20; Isa 22:22; Lk 1:32; Mt 16:19; Job 12:14

opens and no one will [be able to] shut, and He who shuts and no one opens: [Is 22:22]

8 ‘I know your deeds. See, I have set before you an open door which no one is able to shut, for you have a little power, and have kept My word, and have not renounced *or* denied My name. [1 Cor 16:9; Col 4:3, 4]

9 ‘Take note, I will make *those* of the synagogue of Satan, who say that they are Jews and are not, but lie—I will make them come and bow down at your feet and *make them* know [without any doubt] that I have loved you. [Is 45:14; 49:23; 60:14]

10 ‘Because you have kept the word of My endurance [My command to persevere], I will keep you [safe] from the hour of trial, that *hour* which is about to come on the whole [inhabited] world, to test those who live on the earth. [Mark 13:9; 2 Thess 2:1–12]

11 ‘I am coming quickly. Hold tight what you have, so that no one will take your crown [by leading you to renounce the faith].

12 ‘He who overcomes [the world through believing that Jesus is the Son of God], I will make him a pillar in the temple of My God; he will most certainly never be put out of it, and I will write on him the name of My God, and the name of the city of My God, the new Jerusalem, which descends out of heaven from My God, and My [own] new name. [Is 62:2; Ezek 48:35; 1 John 5:5]

13 ‘He who has an ear, let him hear *and* heed what the Spirit says to the churches.’

Message to Laodicea

14 “To the angel (divine messenger) of the church in Laodicea write:

“These are the words of the Amen, the trusted *and* faithful and true Witness, the Beginning *and* Origin of God’s creation:

15 ‘I know your deeds, that you are neither cold (invigorating, refreshing) nor hot (healing, therapeutic); I wish that you were cold or hot.

16 ‘So because you are lukewarm (spiritually useless), and neither hot nor cold, I will vomit you out of My mouth [rejecting you with disgust].

17 ‘Because you say, “I am rich, and have prospered *and* grown wealthy, and have need of nothing,” and you do not know that you are wretched and miserable and poor and blind and naked [without hope and in great need], [Hos 12:8]

18 I counsel you to buy from Me gold that has been heated red hot *and* refined by fire so that you may become *truly* rich; and white clothes [representing righteousness] to clothe yourself so that the shame of your nakedness will not be seen; and *healing* salve to put on your eyes so that you may see.

19 ‘Those whom I [dearly and tenderly] love, I rebuke and discipline [showing them their faults and instructing them]; so be enthusiastic and repent [change your inner self—your old way of thinking, your sinful behavior—seek God’s will]. [Prov 3:11, 12; Heb 5:8; 12:5–7]

20 ‘Behold, I stand at the door [of the church] and *continually* knock. If anyone hears My voice and opens the door, I will come in and eat with him (restore him), and he with Me.

3:8 *an open door which no one is able to shut.* The door, in this context, seems to be entrance into heaven and “the new Jerusalem” (v. 12; chs. 21 – 22).

3:10 *keep you [safe] from the hour of trial.* Christ’s promise to keep the believers from the hour of trial is often considered a promise that He will remove them before the period of unparalleled tribulation (1Th 4:16 – 18). Others believe that this means that believers will not be removed, but will be protected during the trial. The “hour of trial” is another way of referring to the unparalleled judgment of the “great tribulation” (7:14) predicted in Daniel 12:1 and Matthew 24:21.

3:14 *Laodicea.* Laodicea was 45 miles southeast of Philadelphia and 90 miles east of Ephesus. It was a wealthy city with thriving banks, a textile industry, and a medical school. The city was also known for its sparse water supply. All of these characteristics are played upon in Christ’s message to the church.

8 ver. 1; 1Co 16:9 **9** Rev 2:9; Isa 49:23 **10** 2Pe 2:9; Lk 2:1; Isa 24:17 **11** Php 4:5; Rev 2:25; Rev 2:10 **12** 1Ki 7:21; Gal 2:9; Rev 14:1; Heb 12:22; Rev 22:4 **13** Rev 2:7 **14** Isa 65:16; Rev 19:11; Col 1:15 **15** ver. 1 **17** Hos 12:8; 1Co 4:8 **18** Isa 55:1; Mt 13:44; 2Co 5:3; Rev 7:13 **19** Job 5:17; Pr 3:11; Heb 12:5,6 **20** SS 5:2; Lk 12:37; Jn 14:23

21 'He who overcomes [the world through believing that Jesus is the Son of God], I will grant to him [the privilege] to sit beside Me on My throne, as I also overcame and sat down beside My Father on His throne. [1 John 5:5]

22 'He who has an ear, let him hear *and* heed what the Spirit says to the churches.' "

Scene in Heaven

4 AFTER THIS I looked, and behold, a door standing open in heaven! And the first voice which I had heard, like *the sound* of a [war] trumpet speaking with me, said, "Come up here, and I will show you what must take place after these things."

2 At once I was in [special communication with] the Spirit; and behold, a throne stood in heaven, with One seated on the throne. [Ezek 1:26]

3 And He who sat there appeared like [the crystalline sparkle of] a jasper stone and [the fiery redness of] a sardius stone, and encircling the throne *there was* a rainbow that looked like [the color of an] emerald. [Ezek 1:28; Rev 21:11, 19]

4 Twenty-four [other] thrones surrounded the throne; and seated on these thrones were twenty-four elders dressed in white clothing, with crowns of gold on their heads.

The Throne and Worship of the Creator

5 From the throne came flashes of lightning and [rumbling] sounds and peals of thunder. Seven lamps of fire were burning in front of the throne, which are the seven Spirits of God; [Ex 19:16–20a]

6 and in front of the throne *there was something* like a sea *or* large expanse of glass, like [the clearest] crystal. In the center and around the throne were four living creatures who were full of eyes in front and behind [seeing everything and knowing everything that is around them]. [Ps 99:1; Is 6:2, 3; Ezek 1:5, 18]

7 The first living creature was like a lion, the second creature like a calf (ox), the third creature had the face of a man, and the fourth creature was like a flying eagle. [Ezek 1:10]

8 And the four living creatures, each one of them having six wings, are full of eyes all over and within [underneath their wings]; and day and night they never stop saying,

"HOLY, HOLY, HOLY [is the] LORD GOD,
THE ALMIGHTY [the Omnipotent,
the Ruler of all], WHO WAS AND
WHO IS AND WHO IS TO COME [the
unchanging, eternal God]."
[Is 6:1–3; Rev 1:4]

9 Whenever the living creatures give glory and honor and thanksgiving to Him who sits on the throne, to Him who lives forever and ever, [Ps 47:8]

10 the twenty-four elders fall down before Him who sits on the throne, and they worship Him who lives forever and ever; and they throw down their crowns before the throne, saying,

11 "Worthy are You, our Lord and
God, to receive the glory and the
honor and the power; for You
created all things, and because
of Your will they exist, and were
created *and* brought into being."
[Ps 19:1]

4:4 *dressed in white ... crowns.* The white robes point to those who are confirmed in righteousness. The crowns are for those who possess ruling authority, and possibly also indicate that the elders have already been judged and rewarded.

4:6 *four living creatures.* These creatures are remarkably similar to the cherubim (angels) that Ezekiel saw close to God's throne (Eze 1:4 – 10).

4:7 *lion ... calf ... man ... eagle.* This description recalls the four cherubim in Ezekiel 1:4 – 10.

4:10 *throw down their crowns before the throne.* This act symbolizes the willing surrender of their authority in light of the worthiness of God as Creator. Because no one but God can create, He alone should be worshiped and recognized as sovereign.

21 Mt 19:28; Lk 22:30; 2Ti 2:12 **22** Rev 2:7 **CHAPTER 4** **1** Rev 1:10; Rev 11:12; Rev 1:19 **2** Rev 1:10; Isa 6:1; Eze 1:26; Da 7:9 **3** Eze 1:28 **4** Rev 11:16; Rev 3:4,5 **5** Rev 8:5; Ex 37:23; 2Ch 4:20; Eze 1:13; Zec 4:2; Rev 1:4 **6** Ex 38:8; Rev 15:2; Eze 1:5 **7** Nu 2:2; Eze 1:10 **8** Isa 6:2,3; Rev 1:8; Rev 1:4 **9** Rev 1:18 **10** Rev 5:8,14 **11** Rev 5:12; Ge 1:1; Ac 17:24; Eph 3:9

The Scroll with Seven Seals

5 I SAW in the right hand of Him who was seated on the throne a scroll written on the inside and on the back, closed *and* sealed with seven seals. [Is 29:11; Ezek 2:9, 10; Dan 12:4]

2 And I saw a strong angel announcing with a loud voice, "Who is worthy [having the authority and virtue] to open the scroll and to break its seals?"

3 And no one in heaven or on earth or under the earth [in Hades, the realm of the dead] was able to open the scroll or look into it.

4 And I *began* to weep greatly because no one was found worthy to open the scroll or look into it.

5 Then one of the [twenty-four] elders said to me, "Stop weeping! Look closely, the Lion of the tribe of Judah, the Root of David, has overcome *and* conquered! He can open the scroll and [break] its seven seals." [Gen 49:9, 10; Is 11:1, 10; Rev 22:16]

6 And there between the throne (with the four living creatures) and among the elders I saw a Lamb (Christ) standing, [bearing scars and wounds] as though it had been slain, with seven horns (complete power) and with seven eyes (complete knowledge), which are the seven Spirits of God who have been sent [on duty] into all the earth. [Is 53:7; Zech 3:8, 9; 4:10]

7 And He came and took the scroll from the right hand of Him who sat on the throne.

8 And when He had taken the scroll, the four living creatures and the twenty-four elders fell down before the Lamb (Christ), each one holding a harp and golden bowls full of fragrant incense, which are the prayers of the saints (God's people).

9 And they sang a new song [of glorious redemption], saying,

"Worthy *and* deserving are You
to take the scroll and to break
its seals; for You were slain
(sacrificed), and with Your blood
You purchased *people* for God
from every tribe and language
and people and nation. [Ps 33:3]

10 "You have made them to be a
kingdom [of royal subjects] and
priests to our God; and they will
reign on the earth." [Ex 19:6;
Is 61:6; Rev 20:6]

Angels Exalt the Lamb

11 Then I looked, and I heard the voice of many angels around the throne and [the voice] of the living creatures and the elders; and they numbered myriads of myriads, and thousands of thousands (innumerable), [Dan 7:10]

12 saying in a loud voice,

"Worthy *and* deserving is the
Lamb that was sacrificed to
receive power and riches and
wisdom and might and honor
and glory and blessing."

13 And I heard every created thing that is in heaven or on earth or under the earth [in Hades, the realm of the dead] or on the sea, and everything that is in them, saying [together],

"To Him who sits on the throne,
and to the Lamb (Christ), be
blessing and honor and glory
and dominion forever and ever."
[Dan 7:13, 14]

5:1 ***a scroll.*** The scroll apparently contains the judgments and redemption seen in later chapters. It may also be the book that was sealed in Daniel 12:4. There appears to be an allusion to the scroll the Lord handed Ezekiel (Ezek 2:9 – 10). ***sealed with seven seals.*** A scroll cannot be unrolled until the seals have all been opened.

5:5 ***Lion of the tribe of Judah, the Root of David.*** Both of these titles are messianic titles (Ge 49:8 – 10, Isa 11:1,10).

5:7 ***took the scroll.*** The Lamb taking the scroll from the Father demonstrates that judgment and authority over the earth is committed to the Son (Da 7:13 – 14). The scroll may be the same one that was sealed in Daniel 12:9.

CHAPTER 5 **1** Eze 2:9; Isa 29:11; Da 12:4 **5** Ge 49:9; Heb 7:14; Isa 11:1,10; Rev 22:16; Rev 6:1 **6** Isa 53:7; Jn 1:29; 1Pe 1:19; Zec 3:9; Rev 4:5 **7** Rev 4:2 **8** Rev 4:8,10; Rev 14:2; Ps 141:2 **9** Ps 40:3; Rev 4:11; Ac 20:28; Ro 3:24; 1Co 6:20; Eph 1:7; Col 1:14; Heb 9:12; 1Pe 1:18; 2Pe 2:1; 1Jn 1:7; Da 4:1 **10** Ex 19:6; 1Pe 2:5 **11** Ps 68:17; Da 7:10; Heb 12:22 **12** Rev 4:11 **13** Php 2:10; 1Ch 29:11; Ro 9:5; 16:27; 1Ti 6:16; 1Pe 4:11; 5:11; Rev 6:16

14 And the four living creatures kept saying, "Amen." And the elders fell down and worshiped [Him who lives forever and ever].

The First Seal—The Conqueror

6 THEN I saw as the Lamb (Christ) broke one of the seven seals [of the scroll initiating the judgments], and I heard one of the four living creatures call out as with a voice of thunder, "Come."

2 I looked, and behold, a white horse [of victory] whose rider carried a bow; and a crown [of victory] was given to him, and he rode forth conquering and to conquer. [Ps 45:4, 5; Zech 1:8; 6:1–8]

The Second Seal—War

3 When He (the Lamb) broke the second seal, I heard the second living creature call out, "Come."

4 And another, a fiery red horse [of bloodshed], came out; and its rider was empowered to take peace from the earth, so that men would slaughter one another; and a great sword [of war and violent death] was given to him. [Zech 1:8; 6:1–8]

The Third Seal—Famine

5 When He (the Lamb) broke open the third seal, I heard the third living creature call out, "Come." I looked, and behold, a black horse [of famine]; and the rider had in his hand a pair of scales (a balance). [Zech 6:1–8]

6 And I heard *something* like a voice in the midst of the four living creatures saying, "A quart of wheat for a denarius (a day's wages), and three quarts of barley for a denarius; and do not damage the oil and the wine." [2 Kin 6:25]

The Fourth Seal—Death

7 When He (the Lamb) broke open the fourth seal, I heard the voice of the fourth living creature call out, "Come."

8 So I looked, and behold, an ashen (pale greenish gray) horse [like a corpse, representing death and pestilence]; and its rider's name was Death; and Hades (the realm of the dead) was following with him. They were given authority *and* power over a fourth part of the earth, to kill with the sword and with famine and with plague (pestilence, disease) and by the wild beasts of the earth. [Ezek 14:21; Hos 13:14]

The Fifth Seal—Martyrs

9 When He (the Lamb) broke open the fifth seal, I saw underneath the altar the souls of those who had been slaughtered because of the word of God, and because of the testimony which they had maintained [out of loyalty to Christ].

10 They cried in a loud voice, saying, "O Lord, holy and true, how long now before You will sit in judgment and avenge our blood on those [unregenerate ones] who dwell on the earth?" [Gen 4:10; Ps 79:10; 94:3; Zech 1:12]

11 Then they were each given a white robe; and they were told to rest *and* wait quietly for a little while longer, until *the number of* their fellow servants and their brothers and sisters who were to be killed even as they had been, would be completed.

6:2 *white horse . . . conquering.* Because the first rider is on a white horse and is conquering, some take it to be Christ (19:11). If so, His full conquest is considerably delayed (19:11 – 20:6). Another view is that this is a spirit of conquest and delusion (Mt 23:3 – 6). The bow suggests that the rider is a warrior. The crown suggests that he is a ruler.

6:8 *ashen.* The color of the "ashen" horse is the color of a corpse. It is fitting that this pale horse is ridden by a figure named "Death." This fourth judgment is the inevitable consequence of the first three. ***sword . . . famine . . . plague.*** These plagues are the same means that God used to bring the nation of Israel to repentance (1Ki 8:33 – 39; 1Ch 21:12), and in Revelation a godly nucleus does arise as a result of these judgments (7:3 – 8).

6:9 *underneath the altar.* Sacrificial blood was poured beside the base of the altar in the temple (Ex 29:12).

14 Rev 19:4; Rev 4:9,10 **CHAPTER 6** **1** Rev 5:5-7; Rev 4:7 **2** Zec 6:3; Rev 19:11; Ps 45:4,5 LXX; Zec 6:11; Rev 14:14 **3** Rev 4:7 **4** Zec 6:2 **5** Rev 4:7; Zec 6:2 **6** Rev 9:4 **7** Rev 4:7 **8** Zec 6:3; Eze 14:21; Lev 26:22 **9** Rev 8:3; 14:18; Rev 20:4; Rev 1:9; 2Ti 1:8; Rev 19:10 **10** See Zec 1:12; Rev 3:7; Rev 11:18 **11** Rev 3:4,5; Heb 11:40

The Sixth Seal—Terror

[12]I looked when He (the Lamb) broke
open the sixth seal, and there was a
great earthquake; and the sun became
black as sackcloth [made] of hair, and
the whole moon became like blood;
[Joel 2:10, 31]
[13]and the stars of the sky fell to the
earth, like a fig tree shedding its late
[summer] figs when shaken by a strong
wind. [Is 34:4]
[14]The sky was split [separated from
the land] and rolled up like a scroll, and
every mountain and island were dis-
lodged *and* moved out of their places.
[15]Then the kings of the earth and the
great men and the military command-
ers and the wealthy and the strong and
everyone, [whether] slave or free, hid
themselves in the caves and among the
rocks of the mountains;
[16]and they called to the mountains
and the rocks, "Fall on us and hide us
from the face of Him who sits on the
throne, and from the [righteous] wrath
and indignation of the Lamb; [Is 2:19–
21; Hos 10:8]
[17]for the great day of their wrath
and vengeance *and* retribution has
come, and who is able to [face God
and] stand [before the wrath of the
Lamb]?" [Joel 2:11; Mal 3:2; Jude 14;
Rev 19:11–16]

An Interlude

7 AFTER THIS I saw four angels
stationed at the four corners of the
earth, holding back the four winds of
the earth so that no wind would blow
on the earth or on the sea or on any
tree. [Zech 6:5]
[2]Then I saw another angel coming
up from the rising of the sun, holding
the seal of the living God; and with
a loud voice he called out to the four
angels to whom it was granted [to have
authority and power] to harm the earth
and the sea,
[3]saying, "Do not harm the earth
nor the sea nor the trees until we seal
(mark) the bond-servants of our God
on their foreheads." [Ezek 9:4]

The 144,000

[4]And I heard how many were sealed,
a hundred and forty-four thousand;
[twelve thousand] sealed from every
tribe of the sons of Israel:

[5]Twelve thousand were sealed
from the tribe of Judah, twelve
thousand from the tribe of
Reuben, twelve thousand from
the tribe of Gad,
[6]twelve thousand from the tribe of
Asher, twelve thousand from the
tribe of Naphtali, twelve thousand
from the tribe of Manasseh,
[7]twelve thousand from the tribe
of Simeon, twelve thousand
from the tribe of Levi, twelve
thousand from the tribe of
Issachar,
[8]twelve thousand from the tribe of
Zebulun, twelve thousand from
the tribe of Joseph, and twelve
thousand from the tribe of
Benjamin were sealed (marked,
redeemed, protected).

6:12 – 13 *sun . . . moon . . . stars.* The effects of the great earthquake on the sun, moon, and stars are worded similarly to Matthew 24:29, placing these events in proximity to the coming of the Son of Man (Mt 24:30).
6:14 *split . . . rolled up.* When the sky is rolled back, the people on earth can see "Him who sits on the throne" (v. 16). They will suddenly see that God is not far away or non-existent and they will have to be accountable to Him.
6:17 *who is able to [face God and] stand.* This rhetorical question is answered in the surrounding context. The unbelievers, no matter how strong, cannot stand. Those who are protected by the Lord are enabled to stand, whether on earth (7:1 – 8) or in God's presence in heaven (7:9 – 17).
7:3 *seal.* The seal was a mark of ownership or authority. In ancient times a seal was fixed to a document by pressing a carved stamp or signet into a lump of clay or wax at the point where the document was opened and closed.
7:4 *a hundred and forty-four thousand.* Those sealed are all the children of Israel, fulfilling the promise that when the "full number of the Gentiles has come" all Israel will be saved (Ro 11:25 – 27).
7:5 – 8 *Judah.* Judah is placed first in this list of

12 Rev 16:18; Joel 2:10; 3:15; Mt 24:29; Ac 2:20 **13** Rev 8:10; 9:1 **14** Ps 102:26; Isa 34:4; Heb 1:12; Jer 3:23; 4:24; Rev 16:20 **15** Isa 2:19 **16** Hos 10:8; Lk 23:30 **17** Isa 13:6; Zep 1:14; Rev 16:14; Ps 76:7 **CHAPTER 7** **1** Da 7:2; Rev 9:4 **3** Rev 6:6; Rev 22:4 **4** Rev 9:16; Rev 14:1

A Multitude from the Tribulation

9 After these things I looked, and this is what I saw: a vast multitude which no one could count, [gathered] from every nation and from all the tribes and peoples and languages [of the earth], standing before the throne and before the Lamb (Christ), dressed in white robes, with palm branches in their hands;

10 and in a loud voice they cried out, saying,

"Salvation [belongs] to our God who is seated on the throne, and to the Lamb [our salvation is the Trinity's to give, and to God the Trinity we owe our deliverance]."

11 And all the angels were standing around the throne and *around* the [twenty-four] elders and the four living creatures; and they fell to their faces before the throne and worshiped God,

12 saying,

"Amen! Blessing and glory *and* majesty and wisdom and thanksgiving and honor and power and might belong to our God forever and ever. Amen."

13 Then one of the elders responded, saying to me, "These who are dressed in the long white robes—who are they, and from where did they come?"

14 I said to him, "My lord, you know [the answer]." And he said to me, "These are the people who come out of the great tribulation (persecution), and they have washed their robes and made them white in the blood of the Lamb [because of His atoning sacrifice]. [Gen 49:11; Dan 12:1]

15 "For this reason, they are [standing] before the throne of God; and they serve Him [in worship] day and night in His temple; and He who sits on the throne will spread His tabernacle over them *and* shelter *and* protect them [with His presence]. [Rev 21:3]

16 "They will hunger no longer, nor thirst anymore; nor will the sun beat down on them, nor any [scorching] heat; [Is 49:10; Ps 121:6]

17 for the Lamb who is in the center of the throne will be their Shepherd, and He will guide them to springs of the waters of life; and God will wipe every tear from their eyes [giving them eternal comfort]." [Ps 23:2; Is 25:8; Ezek 34:23; Rev 21:4]

The Seventh Seal—the Trumpets

8 WHEN HE (the Lamb) broke open the seventh seal, there was silence in heaven for about half an hour [in awe of God's impending judgment]. [Zeph 1:7]

2 Then I saw the seven angels who stand before God, and seven trumpets were given to them.

3 Another angel came and stood at the altar. He had a golden censer, and much incense was given to him, so that he might add it to the prayers of all the saints (God's people) on the golden altar in front of the throne. [Ps 141:2]

4 And the smoke *and* fragrant aroma

---

the Israelite tribes because Christ, the Messiah, is the "Lion of the tribe of Judah" (5:5; Ge 49:8–10). ***Reuben.*** Reuben is next as Jacob's firstborn (Ge 49:3–4). Dan and Ephraim are omitted, perhaps because of their gross idolatry during the period of the judges, demonstrated by the incident in the territory of Dan (Jdg 18). ***Joseph.*** Joseph and his son Manasseh are both included, bringing the number of tribes to twelve.

7:14 *great tribulation.* This vast multitude has come out of the great tribulation, referring to "the hour of trial, that hour which is about to come on the whole [inhabited] world" (3:10). In view of the great loss of life during this time period, martyrdom is most likely the means of their escape. Tribulation was already being experienced by the church in John's day (2:10; Ac 14:22). However, the great tribulation, predicted in Daniel 12:1, will be of an intensity "such as has not occurred since the beginning of the world until now, nor ever will be" (Mt 24:21).

8:1 *seventh seal.* When the seventh seal is broken, the book can finally be opened.

---

9 Ro 11:25; Rev 5:9; ver. 14; Rev 3:5,18; 4:4; 6:11 **10** Ps 3:8; Isa 43:11; Jer 3:23; Hos 13:4; Rev 19:1; Rev 5:13 **11** Rev 4:6 **12** Rev 5:13,14 **13** ver. 9 **14** Rev 6:9; 17:6; Isa 1:18; See Zec 3:3-5 **15** Isa 4:5,6; Rev 21:3 **16** Isa 49:10; Ps 121:6; Rev 21:4 **17** Ps 23:1; 36:8; Jn 10:11,14; Isa 25:8; Rev 21:4 **CHAPTER 8** **1** Rev 6:1 **2** Mt 18:10; Lk 1:19; 2Ch 29:25-28 **3** Rev 5:8; Ex 30:1; Rev 6:9 **4** Ps 141:2; Lk 1:10

of the incense, with the prayers of the
saints (God's people), ascended before
God from the angel's hand.
5 So the angel took the censer and
filled it with fire from the altar, and
hurled it to the earth; and there were
peals of thunder *and* loud rumblings
and sounds and flashes of lightning and
an earthquake. [Lev 16:12; Ezek 10:2]
6 Then the seven angels who had the
seven trumpets prepared themselves to
sound them [initiating the judgments].
7 The first [angel] sounded [his
trumpet], and there was [a storm of]
hail and fire, mixed with blood, and
it was hurled to the earth; and a third
of the earth was burned up, and a
third of the trees were burned up, and
all the green grass was burned up.
[Ex 9:13–35]
8 The second angel sounded [his
trumpet], and *something* like a great
mountain blazing with fire was hurled
into the sea; and a third of the sea was
turned to blood; [Jer 51:25]
9 and a third of the living creatures
that were in the sea died, and a third
of the ships were destroyed.
10 The third angel sounded [his trum-
pet], and a great star fell from heaven,
burning like a torch [flashing across
the sky], and it fell on a third of the riv-
ers and on the springs of [fresh] waters.
11 The name of the star is Worm-
wood; and a third of the waters be-
came wormwood, and many people
died from the waters, because they had
become bitter (toxic).
12 Then the fourth angel sounded [his
trumpet], and a third of the sun and a
third of the moon and a third of the
stars were struck, so that a third of
them would be darkened and a third
of the daylight would not shine, and
the night in the same way [would not
shine]. [Ex 10:21–23]
13 Then I looked, and I heard a soli-
tary eagle flying in midheaven [for all
to see], saying with a loud voice, "Woe,
woe, woe [great wrath is coming] to
those who dwell on the earth, because
of the remaining blasts of the trumpets
which the three angels are about to
sound [announcing ever greater judg-
ments]!"

The Fifth Trumpet—the Bottomless Pit

9 THEN THE fifth angel sounded
[his trumpet], and I saw a star
(angelic being) that had fallen from
heaven to the earth; and the key of the
bottomless pit (abyss) was given to him
(the star-angel). [Rev 20:1]
2 He opened the bottomless pit, and
smoke like the smoke of a great fur-
nace flowed out of the pit; and the sun
and the atmosphere were darkened
by the smoke from the pit. [Gen 19:28;
Ex 19:18; Joel 2:10]
3 Then out of the smoke came locusts

8:7 *hail . . . fire . . . blood.* This blend of destruction and horror sounds like a combination of the first and seventh plagues of God upon Egypt (Ex 7:19 – 20; 9:22 – 25).

8:11 *Wormwood.* Wormwood is a plant found in the Middle East, known for its bitter taste. Here and elsewhere (La 3:19) the term is figurative for bitterness. Normally wormwood is not poisonous, but the plague of the third trumpet involves effects far more potent than the taste of this bitter plant: many men die from the water.

8:13 *Woe, woe, woe.* The "woes" refer to the impact of the three remaining trumpet judgments on the unbelieving inhabitants of the earth. The first woe is the fifth trumpet (9:12); the second woe is the sixth trumpet (11:14). The third woe "is coming quickly" and may be the same as the seventh trumpet (11:15 – 19), although that is not stated. If not, the final woe may be focused on Babylon, the great harlot, because of the climactic use of "woe" in 18:10,16, and 19.

9:1 *star (angelic being) that had fallen from heaven.* The star may be a demon (v. 11), Satan himself (12:9), or an angel serving God (20:1). ***bottomless pit.*** The pit is the interim jail for some demons (Lk 8:31). It is also the place of origin of the beast (11:7; 17:8). Furthermore, it will be the place where Satan will be imprisoned during Christ's reign (20:2 – 3).

9:3 *locusts.* Locusts, or grasshoppers, were greatly feared in agricultural societies because they devoured crops. In Exodus 10:12 – 15, a

---

5 Rev 16:18; 2Sa 22:8; 1Ki 19:11; Ac 4:31 **7** Eze 38:22; Rev 16:2; Isa 2:13; Rev 9:4 **8** Jer 51:25; Am 7:4; Rev 16:3; Eze 14:19 **9** Rev 16:3 **10** Isa 14:12; Rev 9:1; Rev 16:4 **11** Ru 1:20; Ex 15:23 **12** Isa 13:10; Am 8:9 **13** Rev 14:6; 19:17; Rev 9:12; 11:14 **CHAPTER 9** **1** Lk 10:18; Rev 8:10; ver. 2,11; Lk 8:31; Rev 17:8; 20:1 **3** Ex 10:4; Jdg 7:12; ver. 10

upon the earth, and power [to hurt]
was given to them, like the power
which the earth's scorpions have.
[Ex 10:12–15]
4They were told not to hurt the grass
of the earth, nor any green thing, nor
any tree, but [to hurt] only the peo-
ple who do not have the seal (mark of
ownership, protection) of God on their
foreheads. [Ezek 9:4]
5They were not permitted to kill any-
one, but to torment *and* cause them
extreme pain for five months; and their
torment was like the torment from a
scorpion when it stings a man.
6And in those days people will seek
death and will not find it; and they
will long to die [to escape the pain],
but [will discover that] death evades
them. [Job 3:21]
7The locusts resembled horses pre-
pared *and* equipped for battle; and on
their heads appeared to be [something
like] golden crowns, and their faces
resembled human faces. [Joel 2:4]
8They had hair like the hair of wom-
en, and their teeth were like *the teeth*
of lions. [Joel 1:6]
9They had breastplates (scales) like
breastplates made of iron; and the
[whirring] noise of their wings was
like the [thunderous] noise of countless
horse-drawn chariots charging [at full
speed] into battle. [Joel 2:5]
10They have tails like scorpions,
and stingers; and in their tails is their
power to hurt people for five months.
[Joel 2:6]
11They have as king over them, the
angel of the abyss (the bottomless pit);
in Hebrew his name is Abaddon (de-
struction), and in Greek he is called
Apollyon (destroyer-king).
12The first woe has passed; behold,
two woes are still coming after these
things.

The Sixth Trumpet—Army from the East

13Then the sixth angel sounded [his
trumpet], and I heard a solitary voice
from the four horns of the golden altar
which stands before God,
14saying to the sixth angel who had
the trumpet, "Release the four angels
who are bound at the great river Eu-
phrates."
15So the four angels, who had been
prepared for the [appointed] hour and
day and month and year, were released
to kill a third of mankind.
16The number of the troops of cav-
alry was twice ten thousand times
ten thousand (two hundred million); I
heard the number of them.
17And this is how I saw the horses
and their riders in my vision: *the rid-*
ers had breastplates [the color] of fire
and of hyacinth (sapphire blue) and
of brimstone (yellow); and the heads
of the horses looked like the heads of
lions; and from out of their mouths
came fire and smoke and brimstone
(burning sulfur).
18A third of mankind was killed by
these three plagues—by the fire and
the smoke and the brimstone that
came from the mouths of the horses.

---

plague of locusts wiped out what was left of Egypt's crops. Joel 1:2 tells of an invasion of locusts that the Lord used to judge unrepentant Judah, which was a foreshadowing of the day of the Lord. ***scorpions.*** Scorpions sting with their tails, causing great pain and even death (v. 10).
9:11 ***angel of the abyss.*** The angel of the abyss is demonic and controls the demonic locusts (3:10). If this angel serves God, this is another instance where the activity of Satan or his demons is under the Lord's sovereign control (2Co 12:7,9).
9:14 ***great river Euphrates.*** This river is the eastern boundary of the land promised to Abraham for his descendants (Ge 15:18), as well as the geographic area from which powerful enemies like Assyria and Babylon came to invade Israel (Isa 8:5 – 8). It may represent the seat of Satan's former victory (in the garden of Eden).
9:18 ***A third of mankind.*** A third of mankind could number in the billions. Coupled with the former destruction of one-fourth of humanity (6:8), over one-half of the world's population will have been killed.

4 Rev 6:6; 7:3; Rev 8:7; See Ex 12:23; Eze 9:4; Rev 7:3 **5** ver. 10; Rev 11:7 **6** Job 3:21; Isa 2:19; Jer 8:3; Rev 6:16 **7** Joel 2:4; Na 3:17; Da 7:8 **8** Joel 1:6 **9** Joel 2:5-7 **10** ver. 5 **11** Eph 2:2; ver. 1 **12** Rev 8:13 **14** Rev 16:12 **16** Ps 68:17; Da 7:10; Eze 38:4; Rev 7:4 **17** 1Ch 12:8; Isa 5:28,29

19 For the power of the horses [to do
harm] is in their mouths and in their
tails; for their tails are like serpents
and have heads, and it is with them
that they do harm.
20 The rest of mankind, who were not
killed by these plagues, did not repent
even then of the works of their hands,
so as to cease worshiping *and* paying
homage to the demons and the idols of
gold and of silver and of bronze and
of stone and of wood, which can nei-
ther see nor hear nor walk; [Ps 115:4–7;
135:15–17; Is 17:8]
21 and they did not repent of their
murders nor of their sorceries (drugs,
intoxications) nor of their [sexual] im-
morality nor of their thefts.

The Angel and the Little Book

10 THEN I saw another mighty
angel coming down from heav-
en, clothed in a cloud, with a rainbow
(halo) over his head; and his face was
like the sun, and his feet (legs) were
like columns of fire; [Ex 13:21, 22;
Ezek 1:26–28; Dan 7:13; Matt 17:2]
2 and he had a little book (scroll) open
in his hand. He set his right foot on
the sea and his left foot on the land;
[Ezek 2:9; Hos 11:10]
3 and he shouted with a loud voice,
like the roaring of a lion [compelling
attention and inspiring awe]; and when
he had shouted out, the seven peals of
thunder spoke with their own voic-
es [uttering their message in distinct
words]. [Ps 29]
4 And when the seven peals of thun-
der had spoken, I was about to write;
but I heard a voice from heaven saying,
"Seal up the things which the seven
peals of thunder have spoken and do
not write them down." [2 Cor 12:4]
5 Then the angel whom I had seen
standing on the sea and the land raised
his right hand [to swear an oath] to
heaven, [Deut 32:40; Dan 12:6, 7]
6 and swore [an oath] by [the name
of] Him who lives forever and ever, WHO
CREATED HEAVEN AND THE THINGS IN IT, AND
THE EARTH AND THE THINGS IN IT, AND THE
SEA AND THE THINGS IN IT, that there will
be delay no longer, [Neh 9:6]
7 but when it is time for the trumpet
call of the seventh angel, when he is
about to sound, then the mystery of
God [that is, His hidden purpose and
plan] is finished, as He announced
the gospel to His servants the proph-
ets. [Dan 12:6; Rom 11:25; 1 Cor 15:55;
2 Thess 2:7]
8 Then the voice which I heard from
heaven, *I heard* again speaking to me,
and saying, "Go, take the book (scroll)
which is open in the hand of the angel
who is standing on the sea and on the
land."
9 So I went up to the angel and told
him to give me the little book. And he
said to me, "Take it and eat it; it will
make your stomach bitter, but in your
mouth it will be as sweet as honey."
[Ezek 2:8, 9; 3:1–3]
10 So I took the little book from the
angel's hand and ate it, and in my
mouth it was as sweet as honey; but
once I had swallowed it, my stomach
was bitter. [Ps 119:103; Jer 15; 16]
11 Then they said to me, "You must

10:1 *mighty angel.* This mighty angel could be the "strong angel" of 5:2 or the angel "possessing great authority" of 18:1. It is unlikely that this is Michael, who is referred to by name elsewhere (12:7; Da 12:1) or Christ, since He is never called an angel in the New Testament. Furthermore, unlike Christ, this angel comes to earth before the time of tribulation is over.

10:2 *little book.* The little book is not the same as the book that was unsealed in 6:1 – 8:1. It is more like the scroll eaten by Ezekiel (Eze 2:9 – 3:3), although this scroll caused John's stomach to become bitter (vv. 9 – 10), not just his spirit (Eze 3:14).

10:10 *sweet . . . bitter.* The Word of God is always sweet, but the soberness of the judgments and what this will mean to the "peoples and nations and languages and kings," to whom John must prophesy, is enough to turn John's stomach. It is a terrible thing to contemplate the fate of those who refuse to repent (9:21).

---

19 Isa 9:15 **20** Dt 31:29; Lev 17:7; Dt 32:17; Ps 106:37; 1Co 10:20; Ps 115:4; 135:15; Da 5:23 **21** Rev 22:15
CHAPTER 10 **1** Eze 1:28; Mt 17:2; Rev 1:16; Rev 1:15 **2** Mt 28:18 **3** Rev 8:5 **4** Da 8:26; 12:4,9 **5** Ex 6:8; Da 12:7
6 Neh 9:6; Rev 4:11; 14:7; Da 12:7; Rev 16:17 **7** Rev 11:15 **8** ver. 4 **9** Jer 15:16; Eze 2:8 **10** Eze 3:3; 2:10

prophesy again concerning many peo-
ples and nations and languages and
kings.” [Jer 1:10]

The Two Witnesses

11 THEN THERE was given to me
a measuring rod like a staff; and
someone said, “Rise and measure the
temple of God and the altar [of in-
cense], and [count] those who worship
in it. [Ezek 40–42]
2“But leave out the court [of the Gen-
tiles] which is outside the temple and
do not measure it, because it has been
given to the Gentiles (the nations);
and they will trample the holy city
for forty-two months (three and one-
half years). [Dan 8:9–14; Zech 12:3;
Luke 21:24]
3“And I will grant *authority* to My
two witnesses, and they will prophe-
sy for twelve hundred and sixty days
(forty-two months; three and one-
half years), dressed in sackcloth.”
[Deut 18:18; Mal 4:5; Mark 9:4]
4These [witnesses] are the two olive
trees and the two lampstands which
stand before the Lord of the earth.
[Zech 4:3, 11–14]
5And if anyone wants to harm them,
fire comes out of their mouth and de-
vours their enemies; so if anyone wants
to harm them, he must be killed in this
way. [2 Kin 1:10–12; Jer 5:14]
6These [two witnesses] have the
power [from God] to shut up the sky,
so that no rain will fall during the days
of their prophesying [regarding judg-
ment and salvation]; and they have
power over the waters (seas, rivers)
to turn them into blood, and to strike
the earth with every [kind of] plague,
as often as they wish. [Ex 7:14–19;
1 Kin 17:1]
7When they have finished their tes-
timony *and* given their evidence, the
beast that comes up out of the abyss
(bottomless pit) will wage war with
them, and overcome them and kill
them. [Dan 7:3, 7, 21]
8And their dead bodies *will lie ex-
posed* in the open street of the great
city (Jerusalem), which in a spiritual
sense is called [by the symbolic and al-
legorical names of] Sodom and Egypt,
where also their Lord was crucified.
[Is 1:9]
9Those from the peoples and tribes

11:1 *measuring rod like a staff.* John's measuring rod is much like that used by Ezekiel (Eze 40:3 – 5) in his vision of measuring the temple.
11:3 *two witnesses.* The two unnamed witnesses are strikingly similar to Elijah (vv. 5 – 6; 1Ki 17; Mal 4:5) and Moses (v. 6; Ex 7 – 11), who appeared together with Christ on the Mount of Transfiguration (Lk 9:29 – 32). ***twelve hundred and sixty days.*** Forty-two months (v. 2) is the same length of time as twelve hundred and sixty days (12:6). Almost certainly "a time and times and half a time" (12:14) is also a period of three and a half years made up of 42 thirty-day months. These expressions draw from the prophecies in Daniel (Da 12:6 – 7,11 – 12). ***sackcloth.*** Sackcloth is a sign of mourning.
11:4 *two olive trees ... two lampstands.* The witnesses are described as olive trees and lampstands, linking them to the vision in Zechariah 4 of "the two sons of fresh oil ... who are standing by the Lord of the whole earth" (Zec 4:14). The passage in Zechariah refers to Zerubbabel and Joshua the priest. But the overarching principle for these and all other witnesses for the Lord is that their testimony to the truth is "Not by might, nor by power, but by My Spirit" (Zec 4:6).
11:6 *no rain ... waters ... into blood ... plague.* The power to prevent rain identifies the witnesses with Elijah (Jas 5:17), and turning the water into blood and striking the earth with plagues is reminiscent of Moses in Egypt (Ex 7:11 – 21).
11:7 *abyss.* The beast, who emerges as the satanically empowered world ruler (13; 17), comes from the abyss, as did the demonic locust plague of the fifth trumpet (9:1 – 10).
11:8 *great city.* The great city in Revelation is often Babylon (14:8), which possibly represents Rome (1Pe 5:13). But the further description "where also their Lord was crucified" seems to refer to Jerusalem. ***Sodom and Egypt.*** Sodom is the prototype for the moral degeneration of this great city (Ge 19) and Egypt was the prototype for its rampant idolatry.

CHAPTER 11 **1** Eze 40:3; Rev 21:15; Nu 23:18 **2** Eze 40:17; Ps 79:1; Lk 21:24; Da 8:10; Rev 13:5 **3** Rev 20:4; Rev 19:10; Rev 12:6 **4** Ps 52:8; Jer 11:16; Zec 4:3 **5** 2Ki 1:10; Jer 1:10; Eze 43:3; Hos 6:5; Nu 16:29 **6** 1Ki 17:1; Jas 5:16 **7** Lk 13:32; Rev 13:1,11; Rev 9:2; Da 7:21; Zec 14:2 **8** Rev 14:8; Heb 13:12 **9** Rev 17:15; Ps 79:2,3

and languages and nations look at
their dead bodies for three and a half
days, and will not allow their dead
bodies to be laid in a tomb.
10And those [non-believers] who live
on the earth will gloat over them and
rejoice; and they will send gifts [in celebration] to one another, because these
two prophets tormented *and* troubled
those who live on the earth.
11But after three and a half days,
the breath of life from God came into
them, and they stood on their feet; and
great fear *and* panic fell on those who
were watching them. [Ezek 37:5, 10]
12And the two witnesses heard a
loud voice from heaven saying to them,
"Come up here." Then they ascended
into heaven in the cloud, and their enemies watched them. [2 Kin 2:11]
13And in that [very] hour there was
a great earthquake, and a tenth of the
city fell *and* was destroyed; seven thousand people were killed in the earthquake, and the rest [who survived]
were overcome with terror, and they
glorified the God of heaven [as they
recognized His awesome power].
14The second woe is past; behold, the
third woe is coming quickly.

The Seventh Trumpet—Christ's Reign Foreseen

15Then the seventh angel sounded
[his trumpet]; and there were loud voices in heaven, saying,
"The kingdom (dominion, rule) of
the world has become *the kingdom*
of our Lord and of His Christ; and He
will reign forever and ever." [Ps 22:28;
Dan 2:31–45; 7:13, 14, 27; Zech 14:9]
16And the twenty-four elders, who sit
on their thrones before God, fell face
downward and worshiped God,
17saying,
"To You we give thanks, O Lord
God Almighty [the Omnipotent, the
Ruler of all], Who are and Who were,
because You have taken Your great
power *and* the sovereignty [which is
rightly Yours] and have [now] begun
to reign.
18"And the nations (Gentiles) became
enraged, and Your wrath *and* indignation came, and the time came for
the dead to be judged, and [the time
came] to reward Your bond-servants
the prophets and the saints (God's people) and those who fear Your name,
the small and the great, and [the time
came] to destroy the destroyers of the
earth." [Ps 2:1; 2 Thess 1:3–12]
19And the temple of God which is in
heaven was opened; and the ark of His
covenant appeared in His temple, and
there were flashes of lightning, loud
rumblings and peals of thunder and
an earthquake and a great hailstorm.
[1 Kin 8:1–12]

The Woman, Israel

12 AND A great sign [warning of an
ominous and frightening future
event] appeared in heaven: a woman
clothed with the sun, with the moon
beneath her feet, and on her head a
crown of twelve stars.
2She was with child (the Messiah)

11:14 *second woe.* The second woe includes the sixth trumpet (9:12 – 21) and a second interlude (10:1 – 11:13). ***third woe.*** The third woe is apparently the seventh trumpet (vv. 15 – 19), since it "is coming quickly" and 8:13 relates the woes to the last three blasts of the trumpet. The final woe may extend further since the word "woe" recurs in 12:12.

11:17 – 18 *To You we give thanks.* The 24 elders (4:10 – 11; 5:8 – 10) praise God's power and wrath, and the corresponding distribution of reward and judgment. This stanza of heavenly thanksgiving seems to reflect on the fulfillment of the great messianic prophecy in Psalm 2.

11:19 *ark of His covenant.* The ark of the covenant made by Moses disappeared at the time of the Babylonian captivity (2Ch 36:18 – 19). The ark represented God's presence, leadership, and protection of Israel (Nu 10:33 – 36; Jos 3:3,15 – 17).

12:1 *woman clothed with the sun.* The woman is the nation Israel. To Israel belongs the covenant and the promises. If Satan can make even one of those promises fail, he will have "won." This is

---

10 Rev 12:12; Est 9:19; Rev 16:10 **11** ver. 9; Eze 37:5 **12** Isa 14:13; Isa 60:8; Ac 1:9; 2Ki 2:1 **13** Rev 6:12; Rev 16:19; Jos 7:19 **14** Rev 8:13 **15** Rev 10:7; Isa 27:13; Rev 12:10; Da 2:44 **16** Rev 4:4 **17** Rev 16:5; Rev 19:6 **18** ver. 2,9; Da 7:9; Rev 19:5; Rev 13:10 **19** Rev 15:5,8; Rev 8:5; Rev 16:21 **CHAPTER 12** **2** Isa 66:7; Gal 4:19

and she cried out, being in labor and in pain to give birth. [Rom 9:4, 5]

The Red Dragon, Satan

[3]Then another sign [of warning] was seen in heaven: behold, a great fiery red dragon (Satan) with seven heads and ten horns, and on his heads were seven royal crowns (diadems). [Dan 7:7]

[4]And his tail swept [across the sky] *and* dragged away a third of the stars of heaven and flung them to the earth. And the dragon stood in front of the woman who was about to give birth, so that when she gave birth he might devour her child. [Dan 8:10; Rev 12:9]

The Male Child, Christ

[5]And she gave birth to a Son, a male *Child,* who is destined to rule (shepherd) all the nations with a rod of iron; and her Child was caught up to God and to His throne. [Ps 2:8, 9; 110:1, 2]

[6]Then the woman fled into the wilderness where she had a place prepared by God, so that she would be nourished there for a thousand two hundred and sixty days (forty-two months; three and one-half years).

The Angel, Michael

[7]And war broke out in heaven, Michael [the archangel] and his angels waging war with the dragon. The dragon and his angels fought,

[8]but they were not strong enough *and* did not prevail, and there was no longer a place found for them in heaven. [2 Pet 2:4; Jude 6]

[9]And the great dragon was thrown down, the age-old serpent who is called the devil and Satan, he who *continually* deceives *and* seduces the entire inhabited world; he was thrown down to the earth, and his angels were thrown down with him. [Gen 3:1, 14, 15; Zech 3:1; John 13:2; 2 Cor 11:3; Rev 20:8]

[10]Then I heard a loud voice in heaven, saying,

"Now the salvation, and the power, and the kingdom (dominion, reign) of our God, and the authority of His Christ have come; for the accuser of our [believing] brothers and sisters has been thrown down [at last], he

---

why the dragon stands over the woman in such a predatory manner (v. 4).

12:3 ***great fiery red dragon.*** The sign of the dragon is interpreted in verse 9 as Satan, who first appeared in Scripture as the serpent in the garden of Eden (Ge 3). The imagery is in keeping with Old Testament and extra-biblical usage (Isa 27:1). ***seven heads and ten horns . . . seven royal crowns.*** The dragon with the seven heads and ten horns refers to Satan and the empire over which he rules during the course of time. The seven heads, ten horns, and seven diadems refer to Satan's brilliance, power, and glory as "god of this world" (2Co 4:4). This description is almost identical to that of the beast from the sea in 13:1.

12:4 ***a third of the stars.*** This image may refer to the rebellion of a third of the angelic host following Satan. ***devour her child.*** The attempt of the dragon to devour the newborn Christ Child reveals that the strategy of Herod to kill the baby Jesus (Mt 2:3 – 16) was satanically inspired.

12:5 ***male Child, who is destined to rule.*** The male child who will rule with a rod of iron is the messianic figure of Psalm 2:8 – 9; however, there is no earthly rule over all nations at this point. From the perspective of this heavenly scene, the Child-ruler is soon caught up to the throne of God, apparently referring to the ascension of Christ (Ac 1:9).

12:6 ***a thousand two hundred and sixty days.*** The detailed way in which this same length of time is expressed ("a time and times and half a time," v. 14), suggests half of a literal seven-year tribulation period (Da 9:27).

12:7 – 8 ***Michael.*** Michael is an archangel (Jude 9). According to Daniel 12:1, he is a special guardian angel for the nation of Israel. Apparently he commands an army of angels. Michael and the heavenly forces are victorious, making heaven off-limits to Satan and his demons. (In Job 1 and 1Ki 22:22 it is clear that at one time Satan did have access to heaven).

12:9 ***to the earth.*** The devil's expulsion from heaven "to the earth" means that this world becomes his base of operations, and that his anger is vented toward the remaining inhabitants of the earth (v. 12). It is likely that the end times will be the greatest period of spiritual warfare (Eph 6:10 – 18) in history.

---

3 Rev 17:3,9,10; Rev 13:1 **4** Rev 9:10,19; Rev 17:18; Da 8:10; ver. 2; Ex 1:16 **5** Ps 2:9; Rev 19:15 **6** ver. 4; Rev 11:3 **7** Da 10:13; Rev 20:2 **9** Lk 10:18; Jn 12:31; Ge 3:1,4; Rev 20:2; Rev 20:3; Rev 9:1 **10** Rev 11:15; Job 1:9; Zec 3:1

who accuses them *and* keeps bringing charges [of sinful behavior] against them before our God day and night. [Job 1:6–11]

[11]"And they overcame *and* conquered him because of the blood of the Lamb and because of the word of their testimony, for they did not love their life *and* renounce their faith even when faced with death. [Zech 3:1–10; Rom 8:33, 34]

[12]"Therefore rejoice, O heavens and you who dwell in them [in the presence of God]. Woe to the earth and the sea, because the devil has come down to you in great wrath, knowing that he has *only* a short time [remaining]!" [Is 44:23; 49:13]

[13]And when the dragon saw that he was thrown down to the earth, he persecuted the woman who had given birth to the male *Child*.

[14]But the two wings of the great eagle were given to the woman, so that she could fly into the wilderness to her place, where she was nourished for a time and times and half a time (three and one-half years), away from the presence of the serpent (Satan). [Ex 19:4; Deut 32:10, 11; Is 40:31; Dan 7:25; 12:7]

[15]And the serpent hurled water like a river out of his mouth after the woman, so that he might cause her to be swept away with the flood.

[16]But the earth helped the woman, and the earth opened its mouth and swallowed up the river which the dragon had hurled out of his mouth. [Ex 15:12]

[17]So the dragon was enraged with the woman, and he went off to wage war on the rest of her children (seed), those who keep *and* obey the commandments of God and have the testimony of Jesus [holding firmly to it and bearing witness to Him].

The Beast from the Sea

13 AND THE dragon (Satan) stood on the sandy shore of the sea. [Dan 7:7]

Then I saw a [vicious] beast coming up out of the sea with ten horns and seven heads, and on his horns were ten royal crowns (diadems), and on his heads were blasphemous names.

[2]And the beast that I saw resembled a leopard, but his feet were like those of a bear, and his mouth was like that of a lion. And the dragon gave him his power and his throne and great authority.

[3]*I saw* one of his heads which

12:11 ***blood of the Lamb . . . word of their testimony . . . did not love their life.*** The heavenly defeat of Satan (vv. 7 – 9) is followed by reference to his earthly setbacks, including the crucifixion of Christ, the verbal witness of believers, and the martyrdom of some of the believers. The fact that these witnesses were willing to die for their testimony showed that they knew that Christ had defeated death.

12:14 ***a time.*** A "time" probably equals one year, so the period of protection here is three and a half years, which corresponds to the length of the two witnesses' testimony in 11:3. It is also equivalent to the period of the beast's authority ("forty-two months" in 13:5), which includes his ability to "wage war against the saints (God's people) and to overcome them" (13:7; Da 7:25; Ps 122:7).

12:17 ***rest of her children.*** The rest of the children are believers in Christ.

13:1 ***blasphemous names.*** The blasphemous names may be the common claim of ancient Roman emperors to be divine, or blasphemy against the name of the true God (vv. 5 – 6) as Daniel predicted of the willful king during the tribulation period (Da 11:36).

13:1 – 2 ***beast.*** The parallel to the four beasts (especially the fourth) in Daniel 7, and the explanation of the beast given in 17:8 – 11 make it seem that the beast symbolizes both a revived Roman Empire, which exercises universal authority, and a specific ruler, whom John calls the "antichrist" (1Jn 2:18).

13:3 ***fatal wound.*** The apparently fatal wound that was healed is a satanic attempt to mimic the wounds of Christ from His crucifixion, which Christ still carries after the resurrection. This is part of the fulfillment of the prophecy of the "great power . . . and [deceptive] signs and false wonders . . . and with all the deception of wickedness" that accompany the "lawless one" (2Th 2:8 – 12).

---

11 Ro 16:20; Lk 14:26 **12** Ps 96:11; Isa 49:13; Rev 18:20; Rev 8:13; Rev 10:6 **13** ver. 5 **14** Ex 19:4; ver. 6; Rev 17:3; Da 7:25 **15** Isa 59:19 **17** Ge 3:15; Rev 11:7; Rev 14:12; 1Co 2:1; 1Jn 5:10 **CHAPTER 13** **1** Da 7:2,7; Rev 12:3 **2** Da 7:6; Da 7:5; Da 7:4; Rev 12:9; Rev 12:4 **3** ver. 12,14; Rev 17:8

seemed to have a fatal wound, but his fatal wound was healed; and the entire earth *followed* after the beast in amazement.

4 They fell down *and* worshiped the dragon because he gave his authority to the beast; they also worshiped the beast, saying, "Who is like (as great as) the beast, and who is able to wage war against him?"

5 And the beast was given a mouth (the power of speech), uttering great things *and* arrogant and blasphemous words, and he was given freedom *and* authority to act *and* to do as he pleased for forty-two months (three and a half years). [Dan 7:8]

6 And he opened his mouth to speak blasphemies (abusive speech, slander) against God, to blaspheme His name and His tabernacle, and those who live in heaven.

7 He was also permitted to wage war against the saints (God's people) and to overcome them, and authority *and* power over every tribe and people and language and nation. [Dan 7:21, 25]

8 All the inhabitants of the earth will fall down *and* worship him, *everyone* whose name has not been written since the foundation of the world in the Book of Life of the Lamb who has been slain [as a willing sacrifice].

9 If anyone has an ear, let him hear.

10 If anyone *is destined* for captivity, he will go into captivity; if anyone kills with a sword, he must be killed with a sword. Here is [the call for] the patient endurance and the faithfulness of the saints [which is seen in the response of God's people to difficult times]. [Jer 15:2]

The Beast from the Earth

11 Then I saw another beast rising up out of the earth; he had two horns like a lamb and he spoke like a dragon. [Matt 7:15, 16]

12 He exercises all the authority of the first beast in his presence [when the two are together]. And he makes the earth and those who inhabit it worship the first beast, whose deadly wound was healed.

13 He performs great signs (awe-inspiring acts), even making fire fall from the sky to the earth, right before peoples' eyes.

14 And he deceives those [unconverted ones] who inhabit the earth [into believing him] because of the signs which he is given [by Satan] to perform in the presence of the [first] beast, telling those who inhabit the earth to make an image to the beast who was wounded [fatally] by the sword and has come back to life. [Deut 13:1–5; Mark 13:22; 2 Thess 2:9, 10]

15 And he is given power to give breath to the image of the beast, so that the image of the beast will even [appear to] speak, and cause those who

---

13:4 *worshiped the dragon . . . also . . . the beast.* Any false worship or idolatry is ultimately demonic and satanic (1Co 10:20 – 22).

13:5 *forty-two months.* Forty-two months is the duration of the beast's worldwide supremacy, in keeping with the prophecy of Daniel 7:25.

13:9 *If anyone has an ear, let him hear.* This phrase is used frequently in the Bible. It seems to imply that what has just been said has a wider context, or a significant present application. The statement is not just for future reference. Therefore, widespread spiritual delusion and blasphemy, as well as persecution and martyrdom, should not surprise believers at any point in history.

13:11 *another beast.* This beast's actions described in verses 12 – 17 make it virtually certain that he is the false prophet spoken of in 16:13; 19:20; 20:10. The two beasts may symbolize the intermingling of religious power and of secular, political power during the Roman period and during the last days. ***lamb.*** This is the only place in Revelation where "lamb" does not refer to Christ. The lamb with two horns is an emblem of Jewish worship and religious authority.

13:12 – 15 *great signs.* Calling fire from heaven and giving speech to the image of the first beast are persuasive signs of power. These signs are similar to those performed by the two witnesses (11:5 – 6). The performance of great signs and the power of Satan is part of the mass deception prophesied by Paul in 2 Thessalonians 2:8 – 12.

4 Rev 18:18 **5** Da 7:8; Rev 11:2 **6** Jn 1:14; Col 2:9 **7** Da 7:21; Rev 11:7,18 **8** Ex 32:32; Da 12:1; Php 4:3; Rev 3:5; Rev 17:8 **9** Rev 2:7 **10** Isa 33:1; Ge 9:6; Mt 26:52; Rev 14:12 **11** Rev 11:7 **12** ver. 3 **13** Dt 13:1; Mt 24:24; 2Th 2:9; Rev 16:14; 1Ki 18:38; 2Ki 1:10 **14** Rev 12:9; 2Th 2:9; 2Ki 20:7 **15** Rev 16:2

do not bow down *and* worship the im-
age of the beast to be put to death.
[Dan 3:5]
16 Also he compels all, the small and
the great, and the rich and the poor,
and the free men and the slaves, to be
given a mark on their right hand or on
their forehead [signifying allegiance
to the beast],
17 and that no one will be able to buy
or sell, except the one who has the
mark, *either* the name of the beast or
the number of his name.
18 Here is wisdom. Let the person
who has enough insight calculate
the number of the beast, for it is the
[imperfect] number of a man; and his
number is six hundred and sixty-six.

The Lamb and the 144,000 on Mount Zion

14 THEN I looked, and this is what
I saw: the Lamb stood [firm-
ly established] on Mount Zion, and
with Him a hundred and forty-four
thousand who had His name and
His Father's name inscribed on their
foreheads [signifying God's own pos-
session]. [Joel 2:32]
2 And I heard a voice from heaven,
like the sound of great waters and like
the rumbling of mighty thunder; and
the voice that I heard [seemed like mu-
sic and] was like *the sound* of harpists
playing on their harps.
3 And they sang a new song before
the throne [of God] and before the four
living creatures and the elders; and
no one could learn the song except
the hundred and forty-four thousand
who had been purchased (ransomed,
redeemed) from the earth. [Rev 7:4–8]
4 These are the ones who have not
been defiled [by relations] with wom-
en, for they are celibate. These are the
ones who follow the Lamb wherever
He goes. These have been purchased
and redeemed from among men [of Is-
rael] as the first fruits [sanctified and
set apart for special service] for God
and the Lamb. [Mark 8:34]
5 No lie was found in their mouth, for
they are blameless (spotless, untainted,
beyond reproach).

The Angel with the Gospel

6 Then I saw another angel flying in
midheaven, with an eternal gospel to
preach to the inhabitants of the earth,
to every nation and tribe and language
and people; [Rom 1:1–4; 1 Cor 15:3–5;
Gal 1:6,7]
7 and he said with a loud voice, "Fear
God [with awe and reverence], and
give Him glory [and honor and praise
in worship], because the hour of His
judgment has come; [with all your
heart] worship Him who created the
heaven and the earth, the sea and the
springs of water."

13:16 *to be given a mark.* The mark is some sort of identifiable proof of ownership and loyalty, an evil counterfeit of the seal on the foreheads of the servants of God (7:3; 14:1).
13:18 *Let the person who has enough insight calculate . . . six hundred and sixty-six.* No one knows exactly what this means. It is the number of the beast, and the number of a man, so the beast is merely a man, not a god. We can be sure that this man's "number" will someday be understood in relation to the number 666, and that when the people who are living at the time of the fulfillment of the prophecies in this book need to understand this clearly, the Lord will make it plain. In the meantime, the warning is enough for all that will hear.
14:5 *they are blameless.* This statement is not a reference to sinless perfection, but it is stating that they are considered pure before God. They have been sealed by God because of their belief in Christ (v. 1; 7:4).
14:6–7 *angel . . . eternal gospel.* The angel who preaches the gospel to "every nation and tribe and language and people" helps to fulfill God's promise that the gospel "will be preached throughout the whole world as a testimony to all the nations" (Mt 24:14) before Christ returns. The word "gospel," which literally means "good news," is used in Revelation only once. Even at this late stage in God's judgment He continues to offer everlasting life to the world (Jn 3:16). The gospel message at this point beseeches unbelievers to fear God and give glory to Him, and to escape the hour of His judgment.

16 Rev 14:9 **17** Rev 14:11; Rev 15:2 **18** Rev 17:9; Rev 15:2; Rev 21:17 **CHAPTER 14** **1** Rev 5:6; Rev 7:4; Rev 13:16 **2** Rev 1:15; Rev 5:8 **3** Rev 5:9; ver. 1 **4** 2Co 11:2; Rev 3:4; Rev 5:9; Jas 1:18 **5** Ps 32:2; Zep 3:13; Eph 5:27; Jude 24 **6** Rev 8:13; Eph 3:9; Titus 1:2; Rev 13:7 **7** Rev 11:18; Neh 9:6; Ps 33:6; 124:8; 146:5,6; Ac 14:15; 17:24

Doom for Proud Babylon

8 Then another angel, a second one,
followed, saying, "Fallen, fallen is Bab-
ylon the great, she who has made all
nations drink the wine of the passion
of her immorality [corrupting them
with idolatry]." [Is 21:9; Dan 4:30, 31;
Rev 17:2]

Doom for Worshipers of the Beast

9 Then another angel, a third one, fol-
lowed them, saying with a loud voice,
"Whoever worships the beast and his
image and receives the mark [of the
beast] on his forehead or on his hand,
10 he too will [have to] drink of the
wine of the wrath of God, mixed undi-
luted into the cup of His anger; and he
will be tormented with fire and brim-
stone (flaming sulfur) in the presence
of the holy angels and in the pres-
ence of the Lamb (Christ). [Gen 19:24;
Jer 25:15, 16; Luke 12:9]
11 "And the smoke of their torment
ascends forever and ever; and they
have no rest day and night—those
who worship the beast and his image,
and whoever receives the mark of his
name." [Is 34:10; Mark 9:48]
12 Here is [encouragement for] the
steadfast endurance of the saints
(God's people), those who *habitually*
keep God's commandments and their
faith in Jesus.

13 Then I heard [the distinct words
of] a voice from heaven, saying,
"Write, 'Blessed (happy, prosperous,
to be admired) are the dead who
die in the Lord from now on!'" "Yes,
[blessed indeed]," says the Spirit, "so
that they may rest *and* have relief
from their labors, for their deeds do
follow them."

The Reapers

14 Again I looked, and this is what I
saw: a white cloud, and sitting on the
cloud was One like the Son of Man,
with a crown of gold on His head and a
sharp sickle [of swift judgment] in His
hand. [Dan 7:13, 14; Matt 13:30, 40–42]
15 And another angel came out of the
temple, calling with a loud voice to
Him who was sitting upon the cloud,
"Put in Your sickle and reap [at once],
for the hour to reap [in judgment] has
arrived, because the earth's harvest is
fully ripened." [Joel 3:13]
16 So He who was sitting on the cloud
cast His sickle over the earth, and the
earth was reaped (judged).
17 Then another angel came out of
the temple (sanctuary) in heaven, and
he also had a sharp sickle.
18 And another angel came from
the altar, the one who has power over
fire; and he called with a loud voice to
him who had the sharp sickle, saying,
"Put in your sharp sickle and reap the
clusters of grapes from the vine of the
earth, because her grapes are ripe [for
judgment]." [Luke 9:54]
19 So the angel swung his sickle to the
earth and harvested the grapevine of
the earth, and threw the grapes into
the great wine press of the wrath *and*
indignation of God [as judgment of the
rebellious world]. [Is 63:3]
20 And *the grapes in* the wine press
were trampled *and* crushed outside the
city, and blood poured from the wine
press, *reaching* up to the horses' bri-
dles, for a distance of sixteen hundred
stadia. [Joel 3:13; Heb 13:12]

14:8 *Babylon.* Babylon is first mentioned in Revelation here, and it becomes the focus of God's judgment in the following sections (chs. 16–18).
14:13 *Blessed.* "Blessed" signals the second of seven beatitudes in Revelation (1:3; 16:15; 19:9; 20:6; 22:7,14). Six of the seven are clustered in the latter third of the book, perhaps as promises to encourage exemplary Christian response in the extremely difficult circumstances of the end times.
14:16 *cast His sickle.* The power of the Son of Man (Jesus Christ) is shown in that, with one swing of His sickle, the harvest of the earth is reaped. This pictures the events of chapters 16–19 as parts of one rapid succession of judgment, which is experienced by the inhabitants of the entire world.

8 Isa 21:9; Rev 18:2; Jer 51:7; Rev 16:19; 17:2,5; 18:3,10 **9** Rev 13:14 **10** Ps 75:8; Isa 51:17; Jer 25:15; Rev 18:6; Rev 16:19; Rev 20:10; Rev 19:20 **11** Isa 34:10 **12** Rev 13:10; Rev 12:17 **13** Ecc 4:1,2; 1Co 15:18; 1Th 4:16; 2Th 1:7; Heb 4:9,10 **14** Eze 1:26; Da 7:13; Rev 6:2 **15** Rev 16:17; Joel 3:13; Mt 13:39; Jer 51:33; Rev 13:12 **18** Rev 16:8; Joel 3:13 **19** Rev 19:15 **20** Isa 63:3; La 1:15; Heb 13:12; Rev 19:14

A Scene of Heaven

15 THEN I saw another sign in heaven, great and wonderful [a warning of terrifying and horrible events]: seven angels who had seven plagues (afflictions, calamities), *which are* the last, because with them the wrath of God is finished [that is, it is completely expressed and reaches its zenith]. [Lev 26:21]

2 Then I saw something like a sea *or* large expanse of glass mixed with fire, and those who were victorious over the beast and over his image and over the number corresponding to his name were standing on the sea *or* large expanse of glass, holding harps of God [worshiping Him]. [Rev 4:6; 7:9–17]

3 And they sang the song of Moses, the bond-servant of God, and the song of the Lamb, saying,

"Great and wonderful *and* awe-inspiring are Your works [in judgment],

O Lord God, the Almighty [the
Omnipotent, the Ruler of all];
Righteous and true are Your
ways,
O King of the nations! [Ex 15:1–8;
Ps 145:17]

4 "Who will not fear [reverently]
and glorify Your name, O Lord
[giving You honor and praise in
worship]?
For You alone are holy;
For ALL THE NATIONS SHALL COME AND
WORSHIP BEFORE YOU,
FOR YOUR RIGHTEOUS ACTS [Your just
decrees and judgments] HAVE
BEEN REVEALED *and* DISPLAYED."
[Ps 86:9; Jer 10:7; Phil 2:9–11]

5 After these things I looked, and the temple (sanctuary) of the tabernacle of the testimony in heaven was opened,

6 and the seven angels who had the seven plagues (afflictions, calamities) came out of the temple, arrayed in linen, pure *and* gleaming, and wrapped around their chests were golden sashes.

7 Then one of the four living creatures gave to the seven angels seven golden bowls full of the wrath *and* indignation of God, who lives forever and ever. [Rev 4:6]

8 And the temple was filled with smoke from the glory *and* radiance *and* splendor of God and from His power; and no one was able to enter the temple until the seven plagues of the seven angels were finished. [Ex 33:9, 10; 1 Kin 8:10, 11; Is 6:4; Ezek 44:4]

Six Bowls of Wrath

16 THEN I heard a loud voice from the temple, saying to the seven angels, "Go and pour out on the earth the seven bowls of the wrath *and* indignation of God." [Ps 69:24; Is 66:6]

2 So the first *angel* went and poured out his bowl on the earth; and loathsome and malignant sores came on the people who had the mark of the beast and who worshiped his image. [Ex 9:10, 11; Deut 28:35]

3 The second *angel* poured out his bowl into the sea, and it turned into blood like that of a corpse [foul and disgusting]; and every living thing in the sea died.

4 Then the third *angel* poured out his bowl into the rivers and the springs of water; and they turned into blood. [Ex 7:17–21]

15:1 *another sign.* The previous sign was about the woman clothed with the sun (12:1). This sign is "great and wonderful" because it deals with the seven last plagues sent by the Lord. The plagues, "the seven bowls of the wrath and indignation of God" (16:1), are much stronger and more widespread than the trumpet judgments in 8:2 – 11:19. The wrath of God is complete with the seven last plagues (15:1 – 19:5). They are immediately followed by the second coming and the marriage supper of the Lamb (19:6 – 21).

15:3 *song of Moses.* The song of Moses is a reference to Exodus 15:1 – 18 in which Israel celebrated its deliverance from Pharaoh's army (Ex 14). This song was sung by Jews in their Sabbath gatherings, as well as by early Christians at Easter. ***song of the Lamb.*** The song of the Lamb celebrates the finished work of God, when all

CHAPTER 15 **1** Rev 12:1,3; Rev 21:9; Rev 14:10 **2** Rev 4:6; Mt 3:11; Rev 13:15; Rev 5:8 **3** Ex 15:1; Dt 32:4; Ps 111:2; Ps 145:17; Hos 14:9 **4** Ex 15:14; Jer 10:7; Isa 66:23 **5** Nu 1:50 **6** ver. 1; Ex 28:6; Eze 44:17 **7** Rev 4:6; 1Th 1:9 **8** Ex 40:34; 2Ch 5:14; 2Th 1:9 **CHAPTER 16** **1** Rev 15:1; 14:10 **2** Rev 8:7; Ex 9:9-11; Rev 13:16; Rev 13:14 **3** Rev 8:8; Ex 7:17; Rev 8:9 **4** Rev 8:10; Ex 7:20

5And I heard the angel of the waters saying, "Righteous *and* just are You, Who are and Who were, O Holy One, because You judged these things;

6for they have poured out the blood of the saints (God's people) and the prophets, and You [in turn] have given them blood to drink. They deserve Your judgment." [Ps 79:3]

7And I heard [another from] the altar saying, "Yes, O Lord God, the Almighty [the Omnipotent, the Ruler of all], Your judgments are true and fair *and* righteous." [Ps 119:137]

8Then the fourth *angel* poured out his bowl on the sun, and it was given power to scorch humanity with [raging] fire.

9People were [severely] burned by the great heat; and they reviled the name of God who has power over these plagues, but they did not repent [of their sin] and glorify Him.

10Then the fifth *angel* poured out his bowl on the throne of the beast, and his kingdom was plunged into darkness; and people gnawed their tongues because of the pain [of their excruciating anguish and severe torment], [Ex 10:21]

11and they blasphemed the God of heaven because of their anguish and their sores (abscesses, boils); and they did not repent of what they had done *nor* hate their wickedness.

12Then the sixth *angel* poured out his bowl on the great river, the Euphrates; and its water was dried up, so that the way would be prepared for [the coming of] the kings from the east. [Is 11:15, 16]

Armageddon

13And I saw three loathsome spirits like frogs, *leaping* from the mouth of the dragon (Satan) and from the mouth of the beast (Antichrist, dictator) and from the mouth of the false prophet; [Ex 8:3; 1 Kin 22:21–23]

14for they are [actually] the spirits of demons, performing [miraculous] signs. And they go out to the kings of the entire inhabited earth, to gather them together for the war of the great day of God, the Almighty.

15("Behold, I am coming like a thief.

---

of His righteous acts have been revealed, from creation to atonement to judgment.

16:6 *saints.* Saints are those who are set apart because of their relationship with Jesus Christ. ***prophets.*** The prophets are God's spokesmen. Probably this passage is referring both to the saints and prophets (11:3 – 18) who have been killed and persecuted during the tribulation as well as those from past history. Jesus referred to the pattern of killing prophets (Mt 23:35) when He spoke to the Pharisees of the coming judgment.

16:8 *fourth . . . bowl.* The fourth bowl and the fourth trumpet both affect the sun, but in the bowl judgment the sun's heat is intensified instead of diminished.

16:9 – 10 *did not repent.* They cannot argue against the existence or power of God, but even so they will not repent and give glory to God. The good news of Christ is still in effect even just before His return (19:11 – 21), though it is apparently rejected by all unbelievers who are still alive.

16:12 *sixth . . . bowl.* The sixth bowl involves the Euphrates River, as does the sixth trumpet (9:14). Both judgments deal with demonically inspired military forces. The army of two hundred million (9:16) will kill a third of all humankind (9:18); the army of verses 12 – 14 will do battle against God (19:19 – 21).

16:13 – 14 *loathsome spirits . . . go out to the kings.* The kings of the earth recoil in fear before the judgment of the Lamb (6:15 – 16), yet because of the deceptive words of the demons, they are willing to wage war against God. The difference seems to be their confidence in the power of the beast, since they reason, "who is able to wage war against him?" (13:4). ***great day of God.*** The battle of that great day takes place at Armageddon (Mount of Megiddo) (v. 16; 19:17 – 21).

16:15 *Blessed.* This is the third of seven beatitudes in Revelation (see note after 14:13). Jesus warned believers to be vigilant because of the unexpected timing of His return (Mt 24:43 – 44). The warning to watch is a reminder of the parable of the ten virgins (Mt 25:1 – 13) who were told

5 Rev 15:3; Rev 1:4,8 **6** Mt 23:34; Rev 13:15; Rev 11:18; Isa 49:26 **7** Rev 15:3; Rev 13:10 **8** Rev 8:12; Rev 9:17,18 **9** ver. 11,21; Da 5:22; Rev 11:13 **10** Rev 13:2; Rev 9:2; Rev 11:10 **11** ver. 9,21; ver. 2; ver. 9 **12** Rev 9:14; Jer 50:38; Isa 41:2,25 **13** 1Jn 4:1; Rev 12:3,9; Rev 19:20 **14** 1Ti 4:1; Jas 3:15; 2Th 2:9; Lk 2:1; Rev 17:14 **15** Mt 24:43; 2Co 5:3

Blessed is he who stays awake and
who keeps his clothes [that is, stays
spiritually ready for the Lord's re-
turn], so that he will not be naked—
spiritually unprepared—and men will
not see his shame.") [Matt 24:42–44;
1 Thess 5:2–4]
16 And they (demons) gathered the
kings and armies of the world together
at the place which in Hebrew is called
Har-Magedon (Armageddon).

Seventh Bowl of Wrath

17 Then the seventh *angel* poured
out his bowl into the air, and a loud
voice came out of the temple from the
throne [of God], saying, "It is done.
[It is all over, it is all accomplished, it
has come.]"
18 And there were flashes of light-
ning and loud rumblings and peals
of thunder; and there was a massive
earthquake—nothing like it has ever
occurred since mankind originated on
the earth, so severe and far-reaching
was that earthquake. [Ex 19:16–18;
Dan 12:1]
19 The great city was split into three
parts, and the cities of the nations fell.
And God kept in mind Babylon the
great, to give her the cup of the wine
of His fierce *and* furious wrath.
20 Then every island fled away, and
no mountains could be found.
21 And giant hailstones, as heavy as a
talent, fell from the sky on the people;
and people reviled *and* spoke abusively
of God for the plague of the hail, be-
cause the plague was so very great.
[Ex 9:22–25]

The Doom of Babylon

17 THEN ONE of the seven angels
who had the seven bowls came
and spoke with me, saying, "Come
here, I will show you the judgment
and doom of the great prostitute who
is seated on many waters [influencing
nations], [Jer 51:13]
2 *she* with whom the kings of the
earth have committed *acts of* immo-
rality, and the inhabitants of the earth
have become intoxicated with the wine
of her immorality." [Jer 25:15, 16]
3 And the angel carried me away in
the Spirit into a wilderness; and I saw
a woman sitting on a scarlet beast that
was entirely covered with blasphe-
mous names, having seven heads and
ten horns. [Acts 10:10, 11]
4 The woman was dressed in purple
and scarlet, and adorned with gold,
precious stones and pearls, [and she
was] holding in her hand a gold cup
full of the abominations and the filth
of her [sexual] immorality. [Jer 51:7]
5 And on her forehead a name was
written, a mystery: "BABYLON THE
GREAT, THE MOTHER OF PROS-
TITUTES (false religions, heresies)
AND OF THE ABOMINATIONS OF
THE EARTH."
6 I saw that the woman was drunk
with the blood of the saints (God's

---

to "Therefore, be on the alert [be prepared and ready], for you do not know the day nor the hour."

16:17 *It is done.* The seventh bowl is the climax of all of Revelation's judgments. This is God's final act of judgment before Christ comes.

16:19 *Babylon.* Babylon may refer to the rebuilt ancient city, or it may be a symbolic name for Rome (17:9). It may also be a way of referring to any proud human society that attempts to exist apart from God. Babylon's classic manifestations of rebellion against God are the Tower of Babel (Ge 11:1–9) and the Babylonian Empire under Nebuchadnezzar (Da 4:30).

17:1 *judgment and doom of the great prostitute.* Babylon is called "the prostitute" in verses 1,5,16, and 19:2. Her habitual immorality was introduced in 14:8, as was her imminent and well-deserved judgment. Both the kings of the earth and the inhabitants of the earth are seduced into committing spiritual adultery with Babylon. The indication is that she made them drunk with power, material possessions, false worship, and pride. The wine of Babylon's immorality (14:8) is judged forcefully and finally by God in the "wine of His fierce and furious wrath" (16:19).

16 Rev 19:19 **17** Rev 21:6 **18** Rev 4:5; 11:13; Da 12:1 **19** Rev 14:8; 17:18; 18:5; Isa 51:17; Rev 14:10 **20** Rev 6:14 **21** Rev 11:19; ver. 9,11; Ex 9:23 **CHAPTER 17** **1** Rev 21:9; Rev 16:19; Na 3:4; Rev 19:2; Jer 51:13 **2** Rev 18:3; Jer 51:7; Rev 18:3 **3** Rev 12:6,14; Rev 12:3; Rev 13:1; ver. 9; ver. 12 **4** Rev 18:12; Da 11:38; Jer 51:7; Rev 18:6; Rev 14:8 **5** 2Th 2:7 **6** Rev 18:24; Rev 13:15; Rev 6:9,10

people), and with the blood of the wit-
nesses of Jesus [who were martyred].
When I saw her, I wondered in amaze-
ment.
7 But the angel said to me, "Why do
you wonder? I will explain to you the
mystery of the woman and of the beast
that carries her, which has the seven
heads and ten horns.
8 "The beast that you saw was [once],
but [now] is not, and he is about to
come up out of the abyss (the bottom-
less pit, the dwelling place of demons)
and go to destruction (perdition). And
the inhabitants of the earth, whose
names have not been written in the
Book of Life from the foundation of
the world, will be astonished when
they see the beast, because he was
and is not and is yet to come [to earth].
[Dan 7:3]
9 "Here is the mind which has wis-
dom [and this is what it knows about
the vision]. The seven heads are seven
hills on which the woman sits;
10 and they are seven kings: five of
whom have fallen, one exists *and* is
reigning; the other [the seventh] has
not yet come, and when he does come,
he must remain a little while.
11 "And the beast that [once] was but
is not, is himself also an eighth *king*
and is one of the seven, and he goes to
destruction (perdition).
12 "The ten horns that you saw are
ten kings who have not yet received a
kingdom, but [together] they receive
authority as kings for a single hour
[for a common purpose] along with
the beast. [Dan 7:20–24]
13 "These [kings] have one purpose
[one mind, one common goal], and
they give their power and authority
to the beast.

Victory for the Lamb

14 "They will wage war against the
Lamb (Christ), and the Lamb will tri-
umph *and* conquer them, because He
is Lord of lords and King of kings, and
those who are with Him *and* on His
side are the called and chosen (elect)
and faithful." [Dan 2:47; 1 Tim 6:15;
Rev 19:16]
15 Then the angel said to me, "The
waters which you saw, where the pros-
titute is seated, are peoples and multi-
tudes and nations and languages.
16 "And the ten horns which you
saw, and the beast, these will hate the

17:9 *seven hills.* Most interpreters understand this as a reference to the seven hills along the Tiber River, a well-known designation of the city of Rome.
17:10 *five of whom have fallen.* The five that have fallen would be past kingdoms, perhaps Egypt, Assyria, Babylon, Medo-Persia, and Greece. ***one exists and is reigning.*** The Roman Empire was the current power at the time of this writing. ***has not yet come.*** People speculate that the future kingdom may be a revived Roman Empire.
17:11 *the beast . . . is one of the seven.* The beast is related to the seventh king, but also has a separate identity. It seems that the eighth world empire may be some form of a revived Roman Empire over which the antichrist establishes the imperial authority of a dictator. He will overcome three horns, or nations (Da 7:20), and will claim universal authority.
17:12 *a single hour.* The time frame for these events may coincide with 16:14, in which the preparations for the battle at Armageddon are described.
17:14 *wage war against the Lamb.* The Lamb (Christ) will easily overcome the ten kings at His second coming (19:19 – 21). The beast and his forces are allowed by God to "wage war against the saints (God's people) and to overcome them" (13:7). Many of those whom the beast defeated and even killed are now numbered in the conquering army of the Lamb. The Lord's army is composed of the called, chosen, and faithful, probably the heavenly soldiers of 19:14.
17:16 – 17 *ten horns . . . will hate the prostitute.* Since this description is similar to God's judgment on Babylon in 18:8, it seems that the Lord uses the forces of the beast as His instrument of judgment on the kingdom of the antichrist (ch. 18) before they themselves are destroyed (19:19 – 21). With the advent of the beast as a supreme ruler given to self-deification (Da 11:36; Mt 24:15; 2Th 2), Satan has originated an entirely new order. This order is so radically different from the great prostitute (vv. 1 – 6) that the beast, or perhaps the political aspect of Babylon, turns upon and destroys the religious aspect of Babylon.

8 Rev 11:7; Rev 13:3,10; Rev 13:8 **9** Rev 13:1,18 **11** ver. 8 **12** Da 7:20; Zec 1:18 **14** Rev 16:14; Dt 10:17; 1Ti 6:15; Rev 19:16; Jer 50:44; Rev 14:4 **15** Isa 8:7; Rev 13:7 **16** Jer 50:41; Rev 16:12; Eze 16:37; Rev 18:16; Rev 18:8

prostitute and will make her desolate
and naked [stripped of her power and
influence], and will eat her flesh and
completely consume her with fire.
17 “For God has put it in their hearts
to carry out His purpose by agreeing
together to surrender their kingdom to
the beast, until the [prophetic] words
of God will be fulfilled.
18 “The woman whom you saw is the
great city, which reigns over *and* dominates *and* controls the kings *and* the
political leaders of the earth.”

Babylon Is Fallen

18 AFTER THESE things I saw another angel coming down from
heaven, possessing great authority,
and the earth was illuminated with his
splendor *and* radiance. [Ex 34:29–35;
1 Tim 6:16]
2 And he shouted with a mighty
voice, saying, “Fallen, fallen [certainly
to be destroyed] is Babylon the great!
She has become a dwelling place for
demons, a dungeon haunted by every
unclean spirit, and a prison for every
unclean and loathsome bird.
3 “For all the nations have drunk
from the wine of the passion of her
[sexual] immorality, and the kings *and*
political leaders of the earth have committed immorality with her, and the
merchants of the earth have become
rich by the wealth *and* economic power
of her sensuous luxury.” [Jer 25:15, 27]
4 And I heard another voice from
heaven, saying, “Come out of her, my
people, so that you will not be a partner in her sins and receive her plagues;
[Is 48:20; Jer 50:8]
5 for her sins (crimes, transgressions)
have piled up as high as heaven, and
God has remembered her wickedness
and crimes [for judgment]. [Jer 51:9]
6 “Repay to her even as she has repaid *others,* and pay back [to her] double [her torment] in accordance with
what she has done; in the cup [of sin
and suffering] which she mixed, mix
a double portion [of perfect justice] for
her. [Ps 137:8]
7 “To the degree that she glorified
herself and reveled *and* gloated in her
sensuality [living deliciously and luxuriously], to that same degree impose on
her torment *and* anguish, and mourning
and grief; for in her heart she boasts, ‘I
SIT AS A QUEEN [on a throne] AND I AM NOT
A WIDOW, and will never, ever see mourning *or* experience grief.’ [Is 47:8, 9]
8 “For this reason in a single day her
plagues (afflictions, calamities) will
come, pestilence and mourning and
famine, and she will be burned up
with fire *and* completely consumed;
for strong *and* powerful is the Lord
God who judges her.

Laments for Babylon

9 “And the kings *and* political leaders
of the earth, who committed immorality and lived luxuriously with her, will
weep and beat their chests [in mourning] over her when they see the smoke
of her burning, [Ezek 26:16, 17]
10 standing a long way off, in fear of
her torment, saying, ‘Woe, woe, the
great city, the strong city, Babylon! In
a single hour your judgment has come.’
11 “And merchants of the earth will
weep and grieve over her, because no
one buys their cargo (goods, merchandise) anymore— [Ezek 27:36]

17:18 *the great city.* The woman in John’s vision is the great city Babylon (16:19), yet she is also the ancient “mother of prostitutes” (v. 5). The satanic influence of this city over the world’s leaders has continued from Babel through Babylon to Rome (vv. 9–10), its classic manifestation in the first century AD.
18:4 *Come out.* The command echoes Isaiah 52:11 and especially Jeremiah 51:45, prophecies proclaimed at a time when the Babylonian Empire was ripe for judgment.
18:9–19 *weep and beat their chests [in mourning] over her.* This section is framed like an ancient lament and is especially similar in content to Ezekiel’s lament over the destruction of Tyre (Eze 27).

17 2Th 2:11; Rev 10:7 **18** Rev 16:19; Rev 12:4 **CHAPTER 18** **1** Rev 17:1; Eze 43:2 **2** Isa 13:19; Jer 51:8; Isa 13:21; Jer 50:39; Isa 14:23; Mk 5:2 **3** Rev 14:8; Isa 47:15 **4** Isa 48:20; Jer 50:8; 2Co 6:17 **5** Ge 18:20; Jer 51:9; Jnh 1:2; Rev 16:19 **6** Ps 137:8; Jer 50:15; Rev 14:10; Rev 16:19 **7** Eze 28:2; Isa 47:7,8; Zep 2:15 **8** ver. 10; Isa 47:9; Rev 17:16; Jer 50:34; Rev 11:17 **9** Eze 26:16; Jer 50:46; Rev 19:3 **10** Isa 21:9; Rev 14:8; ver. 17,19 **11** Eze 27:27

12 cargoes of gold and silver and pre-
cious stones and pearls and fine linen
and purple and silk and scarlet; all
kinds of citron (scented) wood and
every article of ivory and every ar-
ticle of very costly *and* lavish wood
and bronze and iron and marble;
[Ezek 27:12, 13, 22]
13 and cinnamon and spices and in-
cense and perfume and frankincense
and wine and olive oil and fine flour
and wheat; of cattle and sheep, and
cargoes of horses and chariots *and* car-
riages; and of slaves and human lives.
14 "The ripe fruits *and* delicacies
of your soul's desire have gone from
you, and all things that were luxurious
and extravagant are lost to you, never
again to be found.
15 "The merchants who handled these
articles, who grew wealthy from [their
business with] her, will stand a long
way off in fear of her torment, weeping
and mourning aloud,
16 saying, 'Woe, woe, for the great
city that was robed in fine linen, in
purple and scarlet, gilded *and* adorned
with gold, with precious stones, and
with pearls; [Ezek 27:31, 36]
17 because in one hour all the vast
wealth has been laid waste.' And ev-
ery ship captain *or* navigator, and ev-
ery passenger and sailor, and all who
make their living by the sea, stood a
long way off, [Is 23:14; Ezek 27:26–30]
18 and exclaimed as they watched the
smoke of her burning, saying, 'What
could be compared to the great city?'
19 "And they threw dust on their
heads and were crying out, weeping
and mourning, saying, 'Woe, woe, for
the great city, where all who had ships
at sea grew rich from her great wealth,
because in one hour she has been laid
waste!' [Ezek 27:30–34]
20 "Rejoice over her, O heaven, and
you saints (God's people) and apostles
and prophets [who were martyred],
because God has executed vengeance
for you [through righteous judgment]
upon her." [Is 44:23; Jer 51:48, 49]

The Divine Sentence upon Babylon

21 Then a single powerful angel
picked up a boulder like a great mill-
stone and flung it into the sea, saying,
"With such violence will Babylon the
great city be hurled down [by the sud-
den, spectacular judgment of God], and
will never again be found. [Jer 51:63,
64; Ezek 26:21]
22 "And the sound of harpists and
musicians and flutists and trumpet-
ers will never again be heard in you,
and no skilled artisan of any craft
will ever again be found in you, and
the sound of the millstone [grinding
grain] will never again be heard in you
[for commerce will no longer flourish,
and normal life will cease]. [Is 24:8;
Ezek 26:13]
23 "And never again will the light of a
lamp shine in you, and never again will
the voice of the bridegroom and bride
be heard in you; for your merchants
were the great *and* prominent men
of the earth, because all the nations
were deceived *and* misled by your sor-
cery [your magic spells and poisonous
charm].
24 "And in Babylon was found the
blood of prophets and of saints (God's
people) and of all those who have been
slaughtered on the earth." [Gen 4:10;
Jer 51:49]

18:20 *Rejoice . . . heaven, and you saints (God's people) and apostles and prophets.* This call to rejoice is a compressed introduction to the longer praise hymn in 19:1 – 5. Judgment for killing God's prophets is mentioned in 16:6, but this is the only place in Revelation other than 21:14 where Christ's apostles are mentioned. If specific apostles are in mind here, Peter and Paul's deaths at the hands of the state in Rome probably apply. If Babylon is the symbol of all the enemies of God and His people, and not just the Babylonian or Roman manifestations, even the killing of James in Acts 12:1 – 2 is being avenged here.

12 Rev 17:4 **13** Eze 27:13 **15** ver. 3,11 **16** Rev 17:4 **17** ver. 10; Isa 23:14; Eze 27:29 **18** Eze 27:30; Rev 13:4 **19** Jos 7:6; 1Sa 4:12; Job 2:12; Eze 27:30; ver. 8 **20** Isa 44:23; 49:13; Jer 51:48; Lk 11:49; Rev 19:2 **21** Jer 51:64; Rev 12:8; 16:20 **22** Jer 7:34; 16:9; 25:10; Eze 26:13 **23** Jer 25:10; 7:34; 16:9; 25:10; 33:11; Isa 23:8; 2Ki 9:22; Rev 17:2,5 **24** Rev 17:6; Jer 51:49

The Fourfold Hallelujah

19 AFTER THESE things I heard something like the great *and* mighty shout of a vast multitude in heaven, exclaiming,

"Hallelujah! Salvation and glory (splendor, majesty) and power (dominion, might) belong to our God;

2 BECAUSE HIS JUDGMENTS ARE TRUE AND RIGHTEOUS. He has judged [convicted and pronounced sentence on] the great prostitute (idolatress) who was corrupting *and* ruining *and* poisoning the earth with her adultery (idolatry), and HE HAS IMPOSED THE PENALTY FOR THE BLOOD OF HIS BOND-SERVANTS ON HER." [Deut 32:43; Ps 19:9]

3 And a second time they said, "Hallelujah! HER SMOKE SHALL ASCEND FOREVER AND EVER." [Is 34:10]

4 Then the twenty-four elders and the four living creatures also fell down and worshiped God who sits on the throne, saying, "Amen. Hallelujah (praise the Lord)!" [Ps 106:48]

5 Then from the throne there came a voice, saying,

"Praise our God, all you bond-servants of His, you who fear Him, the small (common) and the great (distinguished)." [Ps 115:13]

Marriage of the Lamb

6 Then I heard *something* like the shout of a vast multitude, and like the boom of many pounding waves, and like the roar of mighty peals of thunder, saying,

"Hallelujah! For the Lord our God, the Almighty, [the Omnipotent, the Ruler of all] reigns.

7 "Let us rejoice and shout for joy! Let us give Him glory *and* honor, for the marriage of the Lamb has come [at last] and His bride (the redeemed) has prepared herself." [Ps 118:24]

8 She has been permitted to dress in fine linen, dazzling white and clean—for the fine linen signifies the righteous acts of the saints [the ethical conduct, personal integrity, moral courage, and godly character of believers].

9 Then the angel said to me, "Write, 'Blessed are those who are invited to the marriage supper of the Lamb.' " And he said to me [further], "These are the true *and* exact words of God." [Is 25:6–8; Matt 26:29; Luke 13:29]

10 Then I fell down at his feet to worship him, but he [stopped me and] said to me, "You must not do that; I am a fellow servant with you and your brothers and sisters who have *and* hold the testimony of Jesus. Worship God [alone]. For the testimony of Jesus is the spirit of prophecy [His life and teaching are the heart of prophecy]." [Acts 10:25, 26; 2 Pet 1:21]

The Coming of Christ the Conqueror

11 And I saw heaven opened, and behold, a white horse, and He who was riding it is called Faithful and True (trustworthy, loyal, incorruptible, steady), and in righteousness He judges and wages war [on the rebellious nations]. [2 Thess 1:7–10]

12 His eyes are a flame of fire, and on His head are many royal crowns; and He has a name inscribed [on Him] which no one knows *or* understands except Himself.

13 He is dressed in a robe dipped in blood, and His name is called The Word of God. [John 1:1, 14]

14 And the armies of heaven, dressed in fine linen, [dazzling] white and clean, followed Him on white horses.

15 From His mouth comes a sharp sword (His word) with which He may

---

19:9 ***Blessed.*** This is the fourth of the seven beatitudes in Revelation (see note for 14:13). ***marriage supper.*** The marriage supper of John's day would begin on the evening of the wedding, but the celebration might continue for days. The marriage supper here is a time of joyous feasting to be enjoyed by the saints.

19:15 ***sharp sword.*** The sharp sword that comes

CHAPTER 19 **1** Rev 11:15; Rev 4:11; 7:10,12 **2** Rev 15:3; Dt 32:43 **3** Isa 34:10; Rev 14:11 **4** Rev 4:4,6; 1Ch 16:36; Neh 5:13; 8:6; Rev 5:14 **5** Ps 134:1; Rev 11:18; 20:12 **6** Eze 1:24; Rev 14:2; Rev 11:15 **7** Mt 22:2; 25:10; 2Co 11:2; Eph 5:32; Rev 21:2,9 **8** Ps 45:13; Eze 16:10; Rev 3:18; Ps 132:9 **9** Mt 22:2; Lk 14:15; Rev 22:6 **10** Rev 22:8; Ac 10:26; Rev 22:9; 1Jn 5:10; Rev 12:17 **11** Rev 15:5; Rev 6:2; Rev 3:14; Isa 11:4 **12** Rev 1:14; Rev 6:2; Rev 2:17 **13** Isa 63:2,3; Jn 1:1; 1Jn 5:7 **14** Rev 14:20; Mt 28:3; Rev 4:4 **15** Isa 11:4; 2Th 2:8; Rev 1:16; Ps 2:9; Rev 2:27; Isa 63:3; Rev 14:19

strike down the nations, and He will
rule them with a rod of iron; and He
will tread the wine press of the fierce
wrath of God, the Almighty [in judg-
ment of the rebellious world]. [Ps 2:9;
Is 11:4; Rev 1:16]
16 And on His robe and on His thigh
He has a name inscribed, "KING OF
KINGS, AND LORD OF LORDS."
[Deut 10:17]

Doom of the Beast and False Prophet

17 Then I saw a single angel stand-
ing in the sun, and with a loud voice
he shouted to all the birds that fly in
midheaven, saying, "Come, gather to-
gether for the great supper of God,
[Ezek 39:4, 17–20]
18 so that you may feast on the flesh
of kings, the flesh of commanders, the
flesh of powerful *and* mighty men, the
flesh of horses and of those who sit on
them, and the flesh of all humanity, both
free men and slaves, both small and
great [in a complete conquest of evil]."
19 Then I saw the beast and the kings
and political leaders of the earth with
their armies gathered to make war
against Him who is mounted on the
[white] horse and against His army.
20 And the beast (Antichrist) was
seized *and* overpowered, and with
him the false prophet who, in his pres-
ence, had performed [amazing] signs
by which he deceived those who had
received the mark of the beast and
those who worshiped his image; these
two were hurled alive into the lake of
fire which blazes with brimstone.
21 And the rest were killed with the
sword which came from the mouth
of Him who sat on the horse, and all
the birds fed ravenously *and* gorged
themselves with their flesh.

Satan Bound

20 AND THEN I saw an angel de-
scending from heaven, holding
the key of the abyss (the bottomless
pit) and a great chain was in his hand.
2 And he overpowered *and* laid
hold of the dragon, that old serpent
[of primeval times], who is the devil
and Satan, and bound him [securely]
for a thousand years (a millennium);
[Rev 12:7–9, 12, 15]
3 and the angel hurled him into the
abyss, and closed it and sealed it above
him [preventing his escape or rescue],
so that he would no longer deceive *and*
seduce the nations, until the thousand
years were at an end. After these things
he must be liberated for a short time.

The Millennial Reign

4 And then I saw thrones, and sitting
on them were those to whom judgment
[that is, the authority to act as judges]
was given. And *I saw* the souls of those

---

out of Christ's mouth is the two-edged sword spoken of in 1:16. ***rod of iron.*** Christ will rule with a rod of iron in fulfillment of the messianic prophesies in Psalm 2:8 – 9 and Isaiah 11:4.

19:20 – 21 *beast . . . false prophet . . . hurled alive into the lake of fire.* The lake of fire is the eternal destiny of all unbelievers (20:10,14 – 15). They are apparently the first to suffer the torment of the lake. The rest of the beast's allies are killed by the word from the mouth of the victorious Christ. Apparently all those who now suffer death go to Hades (Mt 16:18), to which Jesus has the keys (1:8), until death and Hades are emptied and cast into the lake of fire (20:13 – 15).

20:1 *angel.* The angel here may be the same one who had the key to the bottomless pit in 9:1 – 2.

20:2 – 3 *abyss . . . closed it . . . until the thousand years.* The abyss is presently the place of imprisonment of some demons (Lk 8:31) and will be the place from which the beast ascends (17:8). Thus, it is fitting that the devil will be held there for a thousand years. The dragon of 12:3,9, known as Satan, was in control of the serpent in the garden of Eden (Ge 3). God has a plan for Satan. He will be shut up in the abyss for a thousand years and then will be briefly released to deceive the nations one final time (vv. 7 – 9) before being cast into the lake of fire (v. 10). ***must be liberated.*** This phrase indicates that Satan will not escape from the pit but instead will be allowed to go forth from the pit to fulfill God's plan.

20:4 *thrones . . . reigned.* This may be a partial

---

16 ver. 12; Da 2:47; 1Ti 6:15; Rev 17:14 **17** ver. 21; Eze 39:17 **18** Eze 39:18 **19** Rev 16:16 **20** Rev 16:13; Rev 13:12; Da 7:11; Rev 20:10; Rev 14:10 **21** ver. 15; ver. 17,18; Rev 17:16 **CHAPTER 20** **1** Rev 1:18 **2** 2Pe 2:4; Jude 6; Rev 12:9 **3** Da 6:17; Rev 12:9 **4** Da 7:9; Mt 19:28; Lk 22:30; 1Co 6:2,3; Rev 6:9; Rev 13:12; Rev 13:15; Ro 8:17; 2Ti 2:12; Rev 5:10

who had been beheaded because of their testimony of Jesus and because of the word of God, and those who had refused to worship the beast or his image, and had not accepted his mark on their forehead and on their hand; and they came to life and reigned with Christ for a thousand years. [Dan 7:9, 22, 27]

[5]The rest of the dead [the nonbelievers] did not come to life again until the thousand years were completed. This is the first resurrection.

[6]Blessed (happy, prosperous, to be admired) and holy is the person who takes part in the first resurrection; over these the second death [which is eternal separation from God, the lake of fire] has no power *or* authority, but they will be priests of God and of Christ and they will reign with Him a thousand years. [Ex 19:6; 1 Pet 2:5, 9; Rev 1:6; 5:10]

The Final Rebellion

[7]And when the thousand years are completed, Satan will be released from his prison (the abyss), [8]and will come out to deceive *and* mislead the nations which are in the four corners of the earth—[including] Gog and Magog—to gather them together for the war; their number is like the sand of the seashore. [Ezek 38:2; 39:1, 6]

[9]And they swarmed up over the broad plain of the earth and surrounded the camp of the saints (God's people) and the beloved city [Jerusalem]; but fire came down from heaven and consumed them. [2 Kin 1:10–12; Ezek 38:2, 22]

[10]And the devil who had deceived them was hurled into the lake of fire and burning brimstone (sulfur), where the beast (Antichrist) and false prophet are also; and they will be tormented day and night, forever and ever.

The Final Judgment

[11]And I saw a great white throne and Him who was seated upon it, from whose presence earth and heaven fled away, and no place was found for them [for this heaven and earth

---

fulfillment of Daniel 7:18,27. The aspect of judgment in ruling is referred to in 1 Corinthians 6:2 – 4. At the onset of the kingdom, authority is officially transferred from angels to men (Heb 2:5,8). Christ, as the second Adam, fulfills God's original purpose for the earth. A new world order is established with the overcoming saints of the church age ruling together with Christ in His kingdom (Ro 8:17). Incredible as it may seem, with a perfect Ruler who is totally just, totally kind, and totally wise, there will still be men who will rebel (vv. 7 – 9).
20:5 *did not come to life again.* The resurrection of the dead will not encompass all people at the same time (Da 12:2; Jn 5:29). This passage indicates that there will be a first resurrection of dead believers before the thousand years of Christ's reign (1Co 15:23,52) and a final resurrection after the millennium is finished, before the great white throne judgment (vv. 11 – 13). It is generally considered that this is the time of resurrection of the Old Testament saints as well as those martyred in the great tribulation.
20:6 *Blessed.* This is the fifth of the seven beatitudes in Revelation (see note for 14:13). All look forward to life with Christ beyond the first resurrection (v. 5). Resurrection is assured for all believers. But the blessedness mentioned here belongs more precisely to those martyrs who will have a part as rulers with Christ in the first resurrection. ***second death.*** The second death is the everlasting death of torment in the lake of fire for unbelievers who face the great white throne judgment (vv. 11 – 15). John has previously stated that the one who overcomes will not be hurt by the second death (2:11).
20:8 *Gog and Magog.* Gog and Magog was a common rabbinical title for the nations in rebellion against the Lord, and the names recall the prophesied invasion of Israel in Ezekiel 38:18. Some hold that the battle of verses 8 – 9 is the one spoken of in Ezekiel, but there are major differences as well as similarities in the two passages.
20:9 *beloved city.* The beloved city may symbolically refer to the home of God's people. However, the new Jerusalem is commonly called "the city of My God" (3:12) and "the holy city" (21:2). The city here may be the renewed earthly Jerusalem, ready to give way to the everlasting sinless glory of the new Jerusalem (21:1 – 22:5).
20:11 *great white throne.* The great white throne is a picture of God's holy rule and

---

6 Rev 2:11; Isa 61:6; 1Pe 2:9; Rev 1:6; ver. 4 **7** ver. 2 **8** ver. 3,10; Eze 38:2; 39:1; Rev 16:14 **9** Isa 8:8; Eze 38:9
10 ver. 8; Rev 19:20; Rev 14:10 **11** 2Pe 3:7; Rev 21:1; Da 2:35

are passing away]. [Is 51:6; Matt 24:35;
2 Pet 3:10–12]
12 And I saw the dead, the great and
the small, standing before the throne,
and books were opened. Then another
book was opened, which is *the Book*
of Life; and the dead were judged
according to what they had done as
written in the books [that is, every-
thing done while on earth]. [Jer 17:10;
Rom 2:6]
13 And the sea gave up the dead who
were in it, and death and Hades (the
realm of the dead) surrendered the
dead who were in them; and they were
judged *and* sentenced, every one ac-
cording to their deeds.
14 Then death and Hades [the realm
of the dead] were thrown into the lake
of fire. This is the second death, the
lake of fire [the eternal separation
from God]. [Matt 25:41; 1 Cor 15:26]
15 And if anyone's name was not
found written in the Book of Life, he
was hurled into the lake of fire.

The New Heaven and Earth

21 THEN I saw a new heaven and
a new earth; for the first heaven
and the first earth had passed away
(vanished), and there is no longer any
sea. [Is 65:17; 66:22]
2 And I saw the holy city, new Jerusa-
lem, coming down out of heaven from
God, arrayed like a bride adorned for
her husband; [John 14:2, 3; Gal 4:26;
Heb 11:10]
3 and then I heard a loud voice from
the throne, saying, "See! The taberna-
cle of God is among men, and He will
live among them, and they will be His
people, and God Himself will be with
them [as their God,] [Lev 26:11, 12;
Ezek 37:27; John 1:14; 1 Cor 3:16, 17]
4 and He will wipe away every tear

---

judgment. The One occupying the throne may be God the Father (1Co 15:24–28) or both the Father and the Lamb (Christ), as in the new Jerusalem (22:1–3). ***earth and heaven fled away.*** There is no place for this sin-polluted creation in the new heaven and new earth (21:1–22:5). The earth and all of its works will be burned up (2Pe 3:10–13).

20:12 ***the dead.*** The dead, called "the rest of the dead" (v. 5), are raised and made to stand before God's throne of judgment. ***books.*** The books are thought to refer to the record of all works done in this life. Since all have sinned and fall short of God's standard (Ro 3:23), the opening of these books will certainly lead to eternal sentences in the lake of fire. ***Book of Life.*** The Book of Life is God's register of those who have believed in Jesus (17:8). Although no one can be judged acceptable based on works (Eph 2:8–9), many will be saved by God's grace received by faith in Jesus Christ.

20:14 ***death and Hades.*** Death and Hades refers not only to dying, but to existence beyond the grave (1:18; 6:8). If one considers "death" as a place, it would be the place where the body lies, and Hades, or hell, would be the place for the soul. The picture here is of all human bodies being given up to God's judgment. While unbelieving humanity is judged according to its works, death and hell, the Lord's final enemy (1Co 15:26), is also destroyed by being cast into the lake of fire. ***second death.*** The second death is spiritual and eternal, the just punishment of the wicked. The first death is physical dying. Both are included in the overall meaning of the death that came upon the human race because of Adam and Eve's sin (Ge 2:16–17; 3:1–19; Ro 5:12).

20:15 ***not found written in the Book of Life.*** Only those who have accepted Jesus Christ as their Savior will be found in the book. The rejection of the eternal gospel results in eternal condemnation (14:6–7).

21:1 ***new.*** "New" here suggest freshness, not just a second beginning. This is the fulfillment of the prophecies of Isaiah 65:17; 66:22 and 2 Peter 3:13. Significantly, this eternal renewal has already begun in the life of the believer because, using the same term, Paul says, "if anyone is in Christ, he is a new creature" (2Co 5:17). ***passed away (vanished), and there is no longer any sea.*** The present heaven and earth, including the sea, were burned up in the great white throne judgment (20:11–13). There will be a continuation of some features of the present creation in the new heaven and new earth, yet the drastic difference in the new eternal state is obvious from the fact that there will be no more sea, which was a major part of the original creation (Ge 1:6–10).

21:2 ***bride.*** Christ's bride (v. 9) is the new Jerusalem, the redeemed inhabitants of the holy city (vv. 3–7; 24–27).

12 Rev 19:5; Da 7:10; Ps 69:28; Da 12:1; Php 4:3; Rev 3:5; Jer 17:10; 32:19; Mt 16:27; Ro 2:6; Rev 2:23 **13** Rev 6:8; ver. 12 **14** 1Co 15:26; Rev 21:8 **15** Rev 19:20 **CHAPTER 21** **1** Isa 65:17; 2Pe 3:13; Rev 20:11 **2** Isa 52:1; Gal 4:26; Heb 11:10; 12:22; Rev 3:12; Isa 54:5; 2Co 11:2 **3** Lev 26:11; Eze 43:7; 2Co 6:16 **4** Isa 25:8; 1Co 15:26; Rev 20:14; Isa 35:10; 61:3; 65:19

from their eyes; and there will no longer be death; there will no longer be sorrow *and* anguish, or crying, or pain; for the former order of things has passed away." [Is 25:8; 35:10]

5 And He who sits on the throne said, "Behold, I am making all things new." Also He said, "Write, for these words are faithful and true [they are accurate, incorruptible, and trustworthy]." [Is 43:19]

6 And He said to me, "It is done. I am the Alpha and the Omega, the Beginning and the End. To the one who thirsts I will give [water] from the fountain of the water of life without cost. [Is 55:1]

7 "He who overcomes [the world by adhering faithfully to Christ Jesus as Lord and Savior] will inherit these things, and I will be his God and he will be My son. [2 Sam 7:14; 1 John 5:5]

8 "But as for the cowards and unbelieving and abominable [who are devoid of character and personal integrity and practice or tolerate immorality], and murderers, and sorcerers [with intoxicating drugs], and idolaters *and* occultists [who practice and teach false religions], and all the liars [who knowingly deceive and twist truth], their part will be in the lake that blazes with fire and brimstone, which is the second death."

The New Jerusalem

9 Then one of the seven angels who had the seven bowls filled with the seven final plagues came and spoke with me, saying, "Come here, I will show you the bride, the wife of the Lamb."

10 And he carried me away in the Spirit to a vast and lofty mountain, and showed me the holy (sanctified) city of Jerusalem coming down out of heaven from God, [Ezek 40:2]

11 having God's glory [filled with His radiant light]. The brilliance of it resembled a rare *and* very precious jewel, like jasper, shining *and* clear as crystal.

12 It had a massive and high wall, with twelve [large] gates, and at the gates [were stationed] twelve angels; and on the gates the names of the twelve tribes of the sons of Israel were written. [Ex 28:21; Ezek 48:30–34]

13 On the east side [there were] three gates, on the north three gates, on the south three gates, and on the west three gates.

14 And the wall of the city had twelve foundation stones, and on them the twelve names of the twelve apostles of the Lamb (Christ).

15 The one who was speaking with me had a gold measuring rod to measure the city, and its gates and its wall.

16 The city is laid out as a square, its length being the same as its width; and he measured the city with his rod—twelve thousand stadia (about 1,400 miles); its length and width and height are equal.

17 He measured its wall also—a hundred forty-four cubits (about 200 feet), *according to* man's measurements, which are [also] angelic [measurements].

18 The wall was built of jasper; and

21:6 ***It is done.*** For the third time, it is done. The first statement of "finishing" was on the cross (Jn 19:30), the second was at the end of God's wrath (16:17), and the third is when there is no more death, a new heaven and a new earth. ***water of life.*** The water of life may be recalling Jesus' references to living water in John 4:14 and 7:38, in connection with eternal life and life in the Holy Spirit. This water is further described in 22:1. A similar offer of God's grace to him who spiritually thirsts is repeated in 22:17.

21:12 ***twelve [large] gates . . . twelve tribes.*** The description of the high wall and the twelve gates echoes Ezekiel 48:30–35. It is a glorious picture of the place that Israel holds in the new Jerusalem when the New Covenant with Israel is at last fulfilled.

21:14 ***twelve foundation stones . . . apostles.*** This picture calls to mind Paul's imagery of the apostles as the foundation of the house of God in Ephesians 2:20.

5 Rev 4:2,9; 20:11; Isa 43:19; 2Co 5:17; Rev 19:9 **6** Rev 16:17; Rev 1:8; Isa 12:3; Jn 4:10; 7:37 **7** Zec 8:8; Heb 8:10 **8** 1Co 6:9; Gal 5:19; Eph 5:5; 1Ti 1:9; Heb 12:14; Rev 20:14 **9** Rev 15:1; Rev 19:7 **10** Rev 1:10; Eze 48 **11** Rev 22:5 **12** Eze 48:31-34 **13** Eze 48:31-34 **14** Mt 16:18; Gal 2:9; Eph 2:20 **15** Eze 40:3; Zec 2:1

the city was pure gold, transparent like clear crystal. [1 Kin 6:30]

19 The foundation stones of the wall of the city were adorned with every kind of precious stone. The first foundation stone was jasper; the second, sapphire; the third, chalcedony; the fourth, emerald; [Ex 28:17–20; Is 54:11, 12]

20 the fifth, sardonyx; the sixth, sardius; the seventh, chrysolite (yellow topaz); the eighth, beryl; the ninth, topaz; the tenth, chrysoprase; the eleventh, jacinth; the twelfth, amethyst.

21 And the twelve gates were twelve pearls; each separate gate was of one single pearl. And the street (broad way) of the city was pure gold, like transparent crystal.

22 I saw no temple in it, for the Lord God Almighty [the Omnipotent, the Ruler of all] and the Lamb are its temple.

23 And the city has no need of the sun nor of the moon to give light to it, for the glory (splendor, radiance) of God has illumined it, and the Lamb is its lamp *and* light. [Is 24:23; 60:19, 20]

24 The nations [the redeemed people from the earth] will walk by its light, and the kings of the earth will bring into it their glory. [Is 60:1–5]

25 By day (for there will be no night there) its gates will never be closed [in fear of evil]; [Is 60:11]

26 and they will bring the glory (splendor, majesty) and the honor of the nations into it;

27 and nothing that defiles *or* profanes *or* is unwashed will ever enter it, nor anyone who practices abominations [detestable, morally repugnant things] and lying, but only those [will be admitted] whose names have been written in the Lamb's Book of Life. [Dan 12:1]

The Perfect Life

22 THEN THE angel showed me a river of the water of life, clear as crystal, flowing from the throne of God and of the Lamb (Christ), [Ezek 47:1–12]

2 in the middle of its street. On either side of the river was the tree of life, bearing twelve *kinds of* fruit, yielding its fruit every month; and the leaves of the tree were for the healing of the nations. [Gen 2:9; 3:22]

3 There will no longer exist anything that is cursed [because sin and illness and death are gone]; and the throne of God and of the Lamb will be in it, and His bond-servants will serve *and* worship Him [with great awe and joy and loving devotion]; [Zech 14:21]

4 they will [be privileged to] see His face, and His name will be on their foreheads. [Ps 17:15; Matt 5:48; 1 John 3:2]

5 And there will no longer be night; they have no need for lamplight or sunlight, because the Lord God will illumine them; and they will reign [as kings] forever and ever. [Zech 14:7; Rev 1:6]

21:19 – 20 ***every kind of precious stone.*** The exact color of some of the stones is uncertain, but it is probable that jasper is colorless, sapphire is blue, chalcedony is green or greenish-blue, emerald is bright green, sardonyx has layers of red and white, sardius is blood red, chrysolite is yellow, beryl is blue or blue-green, topaz is golden, and amethyst is purple or violet.

22:2 ***tree of life.*** The tree of life in the original creation was in the middle of the garden of Eden (Ge 2:9), from which all of humanity was excluded after sin entered the world (Ge 3:22 – 24). Ezekiel's apocalyptic vision included trees bearing fruit every month with medicinal leaves (Eze 47:12). Since only one tree of life is mentioned here, even though it is on both sides of the river, it is probably meant as a parallel to Genesis 2, implying that a new, better, and everlasting Eden has come.

22:3 ***no longer exist anything that is cursed.*** The affliction of sin, especially on the human race and creation (Ge 3:14 – 19), will be erased. As God had fellowship with Adam and Eve before their fall into sin (Ge 3:8), so the Lord will again be with His servants eternally. In turn, His servants will worship and serve Him (Ro 12:1).

22:4 ***see His face.*** The believer's hope today

19 Isa 54:11 **21** Rev 22:2 **22** Jn 4:23 **23** Isa 24:23; 60:19,20 **24** Isa 60:3; 66:12 **25** Isa 60:11; Isa 60:20; Zec 14:7; Rev 22:5 **26** ver. 24 **27** Isa 35:8; 52:1; 60:21; Joel 3:17; Rev 22:14; Php 4:3 **CHAPTER 22** **1** Eze 47:1; Zec 14:8 **2** Eze 47:12; Rev 21:21; Ge 2:9; Rev 2:7; Rev 21:24 **3** Zec 14:11; Eze 48:35 **4** Mt 5:8; 1Co 13:12; 1Jn 3:2; Rev 14:1 **5** Rev 21:23; Ps 36:9; Da 7:27; Ro 5:17; 2Ti 2:12

You Are Invited to be Blessed

6 Then he said to me, "These words are faithful and true." And the Lord, the God of the spirits of the prophets, has sent His angel [as a representative] to show His bond-servants the things that must soon take place.

7 "And behold, I am coming quickly. Blessed (happy, prosperous, to be admired) is the one who heeds *and* takes to heart *and* remembers the words of the prophecy [that is, the predictions, consolations, and warnings] contained in this book (scroll)."

8 I, John, am the one who heard and saw these things. And when I heard and saw them, I fell down to worship before the feet of the angel who showed me these things.

9 But he said to me, "Do not do that. I am a fellow servant with you and your brothers the prophets and with those who heed *and* remember [the truths contained in] the words of this book. Worship God."

10 And he said to me, "Do not seal up the words of the prophecy of this book, for the time [of their fulfillment] is near.

11 "Let the one who does wrong, still do wrong; and the one who is filthy (vile, impure), still be filthy; and the one who is righteous (just, upright), still be righteous; and the one who is holy, still be holy." [Dan 12:10]

12 "Behold, I (Jesus) am coming quickly, and My reward is with Me, to give to each one according to the merit of his deeds (earthly works, faithfulness). [Is 40:10; Jer 17:10; Matt 16:27; 2 Cor 5:10]

13 "I am the Alpha and the Omega, the First and the Last, the Beginning and the End [the Eternal One]." [Is 44:6; 48:12; John 10:30]

14 Blessed (happy, prosperous, to be admired) are those who wash their robes [in the blood of Christ by believing and trusting in Him—the righteous who do His commandments], so that they may have the right to the tree of life, and may enter by the gates into the city. [Gen 2:9; 3:22, 24]

15 Outside are the dogs [the godless, the impure, those of low moral character] and the sorcerers [with their intoxicating drugs, and magic arts], and the immoral persons [the perverted, the molesters, and the adulterers], and the murderers, and the idolaters, and everyone who loves and practices lying (deception, cheating).

---

is to see the Lord face to face (1Co 13:12), something neither Moses nor any other human was previously allowed to do (Ex 33:20).

22:7 *Blessed.* "Blessed" begins the sixth of seven beatitudes in Revelation (see note after 14:13). And indeed, those who pay attention to this book will be blessed. The Lord has shown the things that must come to pass, the things that His servants must pay attention to, the ultimate fate of unbelievers, and a beautiful glimpse of eternity, which leaves all believers with an eagerness for the return of the Lord.

22:11 *wrong . . . filthy . . . righteous . . . holy.* This verse, on the surface, seems to be a statement that believers and unbelievers will live out their lives true to their nature until the final judgment (20:12 – 15). However, because this book is to be read before the events it foretells take place, it is almost certainly an implied, indirect evangelistic appeal based on the continuing offer of the gospel (v. 17; 14:6 – 7).

22:12 – 13 *My reward is with Me.* The rewarding of each believer according to his or her works is taught in 2 Corinthians 5:10. Christ's rewards are meant to provide a powerful incentive for an obedient life. Little wonder that the apostle Paul rigorously disciplined himself so that he would not be disqualified from the prize (1Co 9:24 – 27; Php 3:10 – 14). The judgment seat of Christ can be a time of great regret (1Co 3:5 – 10), or it can be an occasion of supreme joy (2Co 5:9 – 11). After Christ comes again, He will give rewards to His own. This can be counted on because Christ is in control of all history and all eternity.

22:14 *Blessed.* This is the last of the seven beatitudes in Revelation (see note after 14:13). This beatitude is speaking of those justified by faith who express that faith in obedience (Eph 2:8 – 10).

22:15 *dogs.* According to the context of Deuteronomy 23:18, a "dog" is a male prostitute.

---

6 Rev 19:9; Rev 1:1 **7** Rev 3:11; Rev 1:3 **8** Rev 19:10 **9** Rev 19:10 **10** Da 8:26; Rev 1:3 **11** Eze 3:27; Da 12:10; 2Ti 3:13 **12** ver. 7; Isa 40:10; Rev 20:12 **13** Isa 41:4 **14** Da 12:12; 1Jn 3:24; Rev 2:7; Rev 21:27 **15** 1Co 6:9; Gal 5:19; Col 3:6; Php 3:2

The Final Invitation

16“I, Jesus, have sent My angel to tes-
tify to you *and* to give you assurance of
these things for the churches. I am the
Root (the Source, the Life) and the Off-
spring of David, the radiant *and* bright
Morning Star.” [Num 24:17; Is 11:1, 10]
17The [Holy] Spirit and the bride (the
church, believers) say, “Come.” And let
the one who hears say, “Come.” And let
the one who is thirsty come; let the one
who wishes take *and* drink the water
of life without cost. [Is 55:1]
18I testify *and* warn everyone who
hears the words of the prophecy of
this book [its predictions, consolations,
and admonitions]: if anyone adds [any-
thing] to them, God will add to him the
plagues (afflictions, calamities) which
are written in this book; [Deut 4:2]
19and if anyone takes away from *or*
distorts the words of the book of this
prophecy, God will take away [from
that one] his share from the tree of
life and from the holy city (new Jeru-
salem), which are written in this book.
20He who testifies *and* affirms these
things says, “Yes, I am coming quick-
ly.” Amen. Come, Lord Jesus.
21The grace of the Lord Jesus (the
Christ, the Messiah) be with all [the
saints—all believers, those set apart
for God]. Amen.

22:16 *Root (the Source, the Life) and the Offspring of David.* Jesus is both the Source and Son of David, echoing the words of Isaiah 11:1,10. Jesus is both greater than David and the rightful heir to the throne of David.

22:17 *Come.* This book, so full of the pictures of the fulfillment of God’s righteous judgment, still closes with the sweet and compelling invitation to come to Christ. This is one of the reasons it is “blessed” to read this book.

22:18 – 19 *adds [anything] to . . . takes away.* The Book of Revelation was intended to be heard and obeyed (v. 7; 1:3), not tampered with. The person who either adds to or takes away from its contents will receive from God the strictest punishment, a punishment with eternal consequences.

22:20 *I am coming quickly.* The fact that Jesus is coming quickly within the scope of God’s overall plan for this creation is a repeated theme in Revelation (3:11; 22:7 – 12). John adds the hope of all believers to the declaration of Christ with his prayer, “Come, Lord Jesus.”

22:21 *grace.* The grace of our Lord Jesus Christ begins and concludes the Book of Revelation (1:4), implying that the message of grace and the free gift of eternal life in Christ (Eph 2:8 – 9), not merely the message of judgment upon unbelievers, can be found in this book.

16 Rev 1:1; Rev 5:5; Nu 24:17; Zec 6:12; 2Pe 1:19 **17** Rev 21:2,9; Isa 55:1; Jn 7:37 **18** Dt 4:2; Pr 30:6 **19** Ex 32:33; Ps 69:28; Rev 21:2 **20** ver. 12; Jn 21:25; 2Ti 4:8 **21** Ro 16:20

Theological Notes Index by Location

Theological Notes Index by Title

Topical Index

–Fought against Edomites ... 1Ch 18:12–13
–Killed Abner ... 2Sa 2:18–27
–Fought against Ammonites ... 2Sa 10:9–10
–Wanted to kill Shimei ... 2Sa 16:5–12
–Fought against Absalom ... 2Sa 18:2,5,12
–Fought against Sheba ... 2Sa 20:1–6,10
–Fought against Philistines ... 2Sa 21:15–17

ABNER

–Cousin of Saul ... 1Sa 14:50
–Commander of Saul's army ... 1Sa 17:55–57
–Chided by David for carelessness ... 1Sa 26:5–16
–Made Ish-Bosheth king after Saul ... 2Sa 2:8–10
–Defeated by David's men ... 2Sa 2:12–17
–Defected to David ... 2Sa 3:8–21
–Killed by Joab and Abishai ... 2Sa 3:22–39

ABORTION

A. Law regarding accidental loss of a child ... Ex 21:22

B. What is said about a fetus
–It is called a child ... Mt 1:20
–It has conscious awareness ... Lk 1:36,41,44
–Sinful nature is present at conception ... Ps 51:5

C. How God relates to a fetus
–God cares for a conceived child ... Isa 46:3
–God forms a child ... Ps 139:13–15
Isa 44:2,24
–God plans a child's life ... Ps 139:16
Isa 49:1
Jer 1:5
Gal 1:15

ABRAHAM

A. Family data
–Line of Shem ... 1Ch 1:24–27
–Son of Terah ... Ge 11:26–27
–Original name: Abram ... Ge 11:27
–Husband of Sarai ... Ge 11:29
–Father of Ishmael with Hagar ... Ge 16:1–4,15–16
–Father of Isaac with Sarah ... Ge 21:1–3
–Father of many children with Keturah ... Ge 25:1–4
–Died at 175 years old ... Ge 25:7–8

B. Covenant with the Lord
1. Called while in Ur ... Ge 12:1–3
Ac 7:2–4

2. Received promises
–Land and descendants ... Gen13:14–17
Ge 15:18–21
Ge 22:15–18
–A son by Sarah ... Ge 17:16
Ge 18:9–15

3. Given circumcision as a sign ... Ge 17:1–14, 23–27
Ro 4:9–12

4. Declared righteous through faith ... Ge 15:6
Ro 4:3,20–24
Gal 3:6–9

5. Covenant sealed by sacrifice ... Ge 15:8–21

6. Name changed to Abraham ... Ge 17:5
Neh 9:7

7. Covenant remembered ... Lk 1:68–75
Heb 6:13–15

C. Travels and significant events
–Left Ur ... Ge 11:31
–Went to Canaan ... Ge 12:1–6
Ac 7:2–4
–Deceived Pharaoh about Sarai ... Ge 12:10–20
–Divided land with Lot, settled in Hebron ... Ge 13:1–18
–Rescued Lot from four kings ... Ge 14:1–16
–Blessed by Melchizedek ... Ge 14:17–20
Heb 7:1–7
–Declared righteous through faith ... Ge 15:6
–Fathered Ishmael with Hagar ... Ge 16:1–16
–Entertained three visitors ... Ge 18:1–15
–Interceded for the city of Sodom ... Ge 18:16–33
–Deceived Abimelech about Sarah ... Ge 20:1–10
–Fathered Isaac with Sarah ... Ge 21:1–3
–Sent Hagar and Ishmael away ... Ge 21:8–21
Gal 4:22–30
–Made a covenant with Abimelech ... Ge 21:22–32
–Tested by command to sacrifice Isaac ... Ge 22:1–18
Heb 11:17–19
–Bought field for Sarah's burial ... Ge 23:1–20
–Secured wife for Isaac ... Ge 24:1–67
–Fathered children with Keturah ... Ge 25:1–6
–Died ... Ge 25:7–11

D. Titles ascribed to him
–Mighty prince ... Ge 23:5–6
–Servant of God ... Ge 26:24
–Friend of God ... Isa 41:8
Jas 2:23
–Prophet ... Ge 20:7
–Father of Israel ... Ex 3:15
Mt 3:9
–Father of all believers ... Ro 4:11–12,16
Gal 3:7

E. Significance in New Testament
–Jesus is a son of Abraham ... Mt 1:1
–His true seed is Christ ... Gal 3:15–16,29
–Jesus preceded him ... Jn 8:57–58
–Rejoiced to see Jesus' day ... Jn 8:56
–Showed greatness of Christ by giving a tithe to Melchizedek ... Heb 7:4–10
–Lived by faith ... Heb 11:8–12, 17–19
–Believed in the power of the resurrection ... Ro 4:17–21
–Became the father of believers ... Ro 4:11–12
Gal 3:7
–His faith preceded the law ... Ro 4:9–11,13–16
Gal 3:17–19
–Cast out the sons of the law ... Gal 4:21–31
–Demonstrated faith by works ... Jas 2:20–24

ABSALOM

–Son of David by Maacah ... 2Sa 3:3
1Ch 3:2
–Killed Amnon for rape of Tamar ... 2Sa 13:23–33
–Fled to Geshur ... 2Sa 13:36–38
–Allowed by David to return ... 2Sa 14:1–24
–Reconciled with David ... 2Sa 14:28–33
–Rebelled against David ... 2Sa 15:1–12
–David fled from him ... 2Sa 15:13–37
–Accepted the advice of Hushai ... 2Sa 16:15–17:23
–Fought against David's men ... 2Sa 18:1–8
–Killed by Joab ... 2Sa 18:9–18
–Mourned by David ... 2Sa 18:19–19:8

ACCESS TO GOD

A. The command to approach God
–In the Old Testament ... Isa 55:6
Am 5:4,6
–In the New Testament ... Mt 7:7
Lk 11:9
Jas 4:8

B. How can we approach God?
1. From God's standpoint
–The Father draws us to himself ... Jn 6:44
–Jesus is the way to the Father ... Jn 14:6
Ro 5:2
Eph 3:12
1Pe 3:18

–The Spirit enables us to come near .... Eph 2:18
2. From our standpoint
–We must believe .... Ro 5:2; Heb 11:6
–We must live clean, obedient lives .... Ps 24:3–5; Mt 5:8
–We must pray to the Father .... Mt 6:6
–We must call upon God's name . . . Ps 145:18

C. Promises to those who approach God
–We will find God.................. Dt 4:29; 2Ch 15:2
–God will listen to us 2Ki 13:4
–God will forgive us................ 2Ch 7:14
–God will make a covenant with us . . . Isa 55:3
–God will bless us.................. Ps 65:4
–We can have confidence before God .... Eph 3:12; Heb 4:16; 1Jn 5:14

See also PRAYER

ACHAN

–Son of Carmi, of tribe of Judah........ Jos 7:1
–Stole things from Jericho............ Jos 7:1
–His sin caused defeat at Ai............ Jos 7:3–12
–His sin revealed .... Jos 7:13–23
–Stoned to death...................... Jos 7:24–26
–A lesson for Israel.................... Jos 22:18–20

ACHISH

–King of Gath before whom David feigned insanity 1Sa 21:10–15
–Gave David town of Ziklag 1Sa 27:1–7
–Trusted David 1Sa 27:10–12
–Philistines asked him to expel David 1Sa 29:1–11
–Still king in time of Solomon.......... 1Ki 2:39–40

ADAM

A. The first Adam
1. The creation of Adam
–Made in God's image............ Ge 1:26–27
–Made from dust of the earth...... Ge 2:7
–Became a living being........... Ge 2:7; 1Co 15:45
–Woman was created from him . . . Ge 2:21–23
2. The work of Adam
–Was placed in Eden .... Ge 2:8
–Took care of Eden............... Ge 2:15
–Named the animals .... Ge 2:19–20
–Work cursed after the fall ....Ge 3:17–19
–Was banished from Eden .... Ge 3:23–24
3. Marriage of Adam and Eve
–Was established by God .... Ge 2:23–24
–Eve tempted her husband ....Ge 3:6; 1Ti 2:14
–Adam blamed Eve .... Ge 3:12
–Adam and Eve had children...... Ge 4:1–2; Ge 4:25–5:4
4. Temptation and fall of Adam
–God warned Adam not to sin..... Ge 2:16–17
–Adam disobeyed God .... Ge 3:1–6
–God pronounced punishment .... Ge 3:16–19
–Adam died .... Ge 5:5
–Sin and death passed on to all humans .... Ro 5:12,15–17,19
–God condemns us for Adam's sin. . . Ro 5:16,18

B. The second Adam (Christ)............ 1Co 15:45
1. Prophecy concerning him in Eden .... Ge 3:15
2. Christ as the second Adam
–Descended from the first Adam . . . Lk 3:23–38
–Obedient to God's will.......... Ro 5:19
–Victorious over the devil......... Mt 4:1–11; 1Jn 3:8
3. Results for believers
–They receive righteousness and life........................ Ro 5:15–18; 1Co 15:22
–They will receive new bodies like his .... 1Co 15:46–49; Php 3:20–21

ADONIJAH

–Son of David by Haggith 2Sa 3:4; 1Ch 3:2
–Attempted to be king after David...... 1Ki 1:5–27
–David made Solomon king instead..... 1Ki 1:28–53
–Wanted Abishag as wife.............. 1Ki 2:13–22
–Killed at Solomon's command......... 1Ki 2:23–25

ADOPTION

–*Becoming someone's child by a legal act*

A. In human relationships
–Abram wants to adopt .... Ge 15:2–4
–Pharaoh's daughter adopts Moses . . . Ex 2:10
–Mordecai adopts Esther .... Est 2:7
–A wife adopts a maid's son .... Ge 16:1–3; Ge 30:1–5; Ge 30:9–12

B. In the God-man relationship
1. It is rooted in God's eternal love . . . Eph 1:4–5; Ro 8:29; 1Jn 3:1
2. Israel is God's adopted child....... Ex 4:22–23; Dt 14:2; Jer 31:9; Hos 11:1; Ro 9:4
3. Christians are God's adopted children
–We become children by God's grace .... Eph 1:5–6
–We become children through faith in Christ................ Jn 1:12–13; Gal 3:26
–We can call God Father.......... Mt 6:9; Ro 8:15; Gal 4:6–7
–We become siblings of Christ...... Mk 3:34–35; Heb 2:11–12
–We are united as one body in Christ......................... Eph 2:11–13,19; Eph 3:6
–Our adoption is completed only at the resurrection ....Ro 8:19,23; 1Jn 3:2
4. Results of being God's children
–We receive the rights of inheritance...................... Ro 8:17; Gal 4:7
–We must walk in light .... Jn 12:35–36; Eph 5:8–10; 1Th 5:4–5
–We must live as obedient children....................... 1Pe 1:14–16
–We must live in peace .... Mt 5:9; Eph 2:17–19
–We must live in love.............. Mt 5:44–45; Lk 6:35
–We must separate ourselves from evil .... 2Co 6:17–18; Php 2:15
–We are subject to God's discipline..................... Heb 12:5–11
–We can expect suffering........... Ro 8:18,22

ADULLAM
- –A city in southwest Judah . . . . Jos 15:21,33,35
- –Judah married a woman from there . . . Ge 38:1–2
- –David hid his followers in a cave near it 1Sa 22:1–2
- –David's men risked getting water from Bethlehem 2Sa 23:13–17; 1Ch 11:15–19
- –Fortified by Rehoboam 2Ch 11:5–10
- –Judgment prophesied against it . . . . Mic 1:15
- –Established again after the exile . . . . . . Neh 11:30

ADULTERY
–Sexual unfaithfulness to one's spouse

A. Related theme
- ADULTERY is a theme of Hosea . . . . . Hos 4:13

B. Old Testament perspective
1. Laws against adultery
   - –In the Ten Commandments . . . . Ex 20:14; Dt 5:18
   - –Various laws on adultery . . . . Lev 20:10; Nu 5:12–31; Dt 22:22–24
2. Examples of adultery
   - –Judah and Tamar . . . . Ge 38:15–18
   - –David and Bathsheba 2Sa 11:2–5
   - –Others in Judah. . . . . Jer 5:7–9; Jer 29:23
3. Characteristics of adultery
   - –Is a sin against one's spouse and God. . . . . Ge 39:7–9; 2Sa 12:13; Ps 51:4
   - –Is personally dangerous . . . . Pr 2:16–19; Pr 6:25–29,32
   - –Defiles a whole nation. . . . . Jer 3:1; Jer 23:10–15; Eze 33:26

C. New Testament perspective
1. The sin of adultery
   - –Starts in a sinful heart. . . . . Mt 15:19
   - –Considered a sinful action . . . . .Ro 7:2–3; Jas 2:11; 2Pe 2:14
   - –Sinful even in thought. . . . . Mt 5:27–28
   - –Remarriage as adultery . . . . Mt 5:31–32; Mt 19:8–9
2. Results of adultery
   - –Leads to God's judgment. . . . . Heb 13:4
   - –Leads to exclusion from the kingdom . . . . Gal 5:19–21; 1Co 6:9; Rev 22:15
3. Pardon promised for adulterers. . . . Jn 8:3–11; 1Co 6:11

D. Spiritual adultery
- –References in the Old Testament. . . . Jer 3:6–10,20; Eze 16:32–35; Hos 1:2
- –References in the New Testament. . . Mt 12:39; Jas 4:4
- –God judges spiritual adultery. . . . . . . Jer 5:11–17; Eze 16:37–42; Mk 8:38
- –God desires faithfulness to Christ . . . 2Co 11:2

See also MARRIAGE

AFFLICTION
See PAIN

AGABUS
- –A prophet in the early church . . . . Ac 11:27–28
- –Predicted a severe famine for the world . . . . Ac 11:28
- –Predicted Paul's arrest in Jerusalem . . . Ac 21:10–11

AGAG
- –King of Amalekites; spared by Saul. . . . 1Sa 15:7–9,20
- –Killed by Samuel 1Sa 15:32–33

AGRIPPA
- –King who visited Festus . . . . Ac 25:13–22
- –Paul spoke before him. . . . . Ac 25:23–26:23
- –Paul invited him to believe. . . . . Ac 26:25–27
- –Rejected the gospel . . . . Ac 26:28
- –Declared Paul innocent. . . . . Ac 26:31–32

AHAB
A. Personal data
- –Son of Omri; king of Israel 1Ki 16:28–29
- –Husband of Jezebel 1Ki 16:31

B. Significant events
- –Promoted Baal worship. 1Ki 16:31–33
- –Opposed by Elijah 1Ki 17:1
- –Contest on Mount Carmel. 1Ki 18:16–39
- –Defeated Ben-Hadad 1Ki 20:1–34
- –Coveted Naboth's vineyard 1Ki 21:1–16
- –Fought against king of Aram 1Ki 22:29–30
- –Accidentally killed in battle. 1Ki 22:34–38

C. Prophesied against
- –By an unnamed prophet 1Ki 20:35–43
- –By Elijah. 1Ki 21:17–29
- –By Micaiah. 1Ki 22:9–28

D. Subsequent history
- –Elisha told Jehu to destroy Ahab's family 2Ki 9:6–10
- –House of Ahab destroyed 2Ki 10:1–17
- –Name became a symbol of wickedness . . . . 2Ch 21:6,13; 2Ch 22:3–4; Mic 6:16

AHAZ
- –Son of Jotham; king of Judah 2Ki 16:1; 2Ch 28:1
- –Worshiped idols 2Ki 16:1–4,10–18; 2Ch 28:1–4, 22–25
- –Fought against Aram and Israel. . . . . . . 2Ki 16:5–6; Isa 7:1
- –Defeated by Aram and Israel. 2Ch 28:5–15
- –Fought against Edom and Philistia 2Ch 28:16–19
- –Sought help from Assyria 2Ki 16:7–9
- –Refused a sign from the Lord . . . . Isa 7:2–17
- –His death 2Ki 16:19–20

AHAZIAH
A. Son of Ahab; king of Israel 1Ki 22:51
- –Worshiped idols 1Ki 22:52–53
- –Made an alliance with Jehoshaphat 2Ch 20:36–37
- –Died while seeking advice from Baal. 2Ki 1:1–17

B. Son of Jehoram; king of Judah. 2Ki 8:25–26; 2Ch 22:1–2
- –Worshiped idols 2Ki 8:27; 2Ch 22:3–4
- –Allied with Joram, king of Israel. . . . 2Ki 8:28–29
- –Killed by Jehu while visiting Joram 2Ki 9:14–29; 2Ch 22:1–9
- –Only surviving son was Joash. 2Ki 11:1–3

AHIMELECH
A. Priest at Nob during Saul's time 1Sa 21:1
- –Gave David consecrated bread 1Sa 21:2–6

–Gave David Goliath's sword 1Sa 21:8–9
–Betrayed to Saul by Doeg 1Sa 22:9–16
–Killed by Doeg with other priests ... 1Sa 22:17–19
–Son Abiathar escaped to join David .. 1Sa 22:20–23
B. Grandson of Ahimelech 2Sa 8:17
–Co-priest with Zadok during David's reign 1Ch 18:16; 1Ch 24:6,31
C. One of David's warriors 1Sa 26:6

AHITHOPHEL

–A counselor of David 2Sa 15:12
–Joined Absalom against David 2Sa 15:31–37
–Advised Absalom 2Sa 16:15–23
–Absalom rejected his counsel 2Sa 17:1–14
–Committed suicide 2Sa 17:23

AI

–A city in Palestine, east of Bethel ...... Jos 7:2
–Abram built an altar near there .... Ge 12:8
–Joshua's troops were initially defeated there .... Jos 7:3–5
–After Achan's death, Ai was destroyed .... Jos 8:1–29
–Later rebuilt, with Israelites settling there .... Ezr 2:2,28

ALCOHOL

A. Terms used in the Bible
–Beer and wine .... 1Sa 1:15; Pr 31:4,6
–Fermented drink .... Nu 6:3; Jdg 13:4,7
–Mixed wine .... Pr 9:2; Pr 23:30
–Old wine and new wine .... Am 9:13; Lk 5:37–39
B. Various uses for alcohol
–In family meals .... Ge 27:25
–In public feasting .... Est 1:7–8,10; Da 5:1–4
–At weddings .... Jn 2:3
–As an offering to God .... Ex 29:38,40; Lev 23:12–13
–As a tithe .... Dt 12:17; Neh 13:5
–In barter exchange 2Ch 2:10
–As a commodity for commerce .... Eze 27:18
–As medicine .... Lk 10:34; 1Ti 5:23
–As a drug for pain .... Pr 31:6; Mk 15:23
–As a means to become drunk .... Ge 9:20–21
C. Positive aspects of alcohol
–A blessing from God .... Joel 2:19
–Can help one celebrate .... Jn 2:1–11
–Can give enjoyment .... Ps 104:15; Zec 9:17
–Can aid in happiness .... Ecc 10:19
–Can help to refresh someone 2Sa 16:2
–Can help one's health 1Ti 5:23
D. Dangers of using alcohol
–Loosens morals .... Ge 9:21–22
–Inflames an individual .... Isa 5:11–12
–Destroys health 1Sa 25:36–37
–Impairs judgment .... Pr 31:4–5; Isa 28:7
–Raises tempers .... Pr 20:1
–Leads to poverty .... Pr 23:21
–Leads to sorrow .... Pr 23:29–30
–Creates disunity in the church 1Co 11:18–21
E. Drunkenness forbidden .... Isa 5:11–12,22; Ro 13:13; 1Co 5:11; 1Co 6:9–10; Eph 5:18
F. Symbolic uses of alcohol
–Symbolizes the blood of Christ .... Mt 26:27–29
–Symbolizes the gospel of salvation .... Isa 55:1
–Symbolizes the judgment of God ... Ps 75:8; Jer 25:15–16; Rev 14:10
–Symbolizes the sins of the antichrist .... Rev 17:2; Rev 18:3

ALIEN

–A citizen of one country residing in another

A. Aliens within the nation of Israel
1. Who were they?
–Those leaving Egypt with Israelites .... Ex 12:38
–Unconquered nations in Canaan .... Jos 9:26–27; 1Ki 9:20–21
–Captives taken in war .... Dt 21:10–11
–Slaves purchased .... Lev 25:44–46
–Foreigners hired in Israel 1Ki 9:27
–Foreigners attracted to Israel 2Ch 6:32–33
2. How were they to be treated?
–God had a special love for them ... Dt 10:18; Ps 146:9
–They were not to be oppressed ... Ex 22:21; Ex 23:9; Lev 19:33–34
–They enjoyed equal protection ... Lev 24:22; Lev 25:35; Dt 1:16–17; Dt 24:17–21
–They shared equal responsibility ... Ex 20:8–10; Nu 15:14–16
–Israel condemned for oppressing them .... Ps 94:6; Eze 22:7,29
B. God's people as aliens
1. In the Old Testament
–Abraham in Canaan .... Ge 17:8; Ge 23:4
–Jacob in Canaan .... Ge 28:4
–Moses in Midian .... Ex 18:3
–Israelites in Egypt .... Ge 15:13; Ex 23:9
–Israelites in Canaan .... Lev 25:23; 1Ch 29:15; Ps 39:12; Ps 119:19
–Israelites in Babylon .... La 5:2
–Their true homeland was elsewhere .... Heb 11:13–15
2. In the New Testament
–We are called aliens 1Pe 1:17; 1Pe 2:11
–We are not part of this world .... Jn 17:14,16
–Our true home is heaven .... Php 3:20–21; Col 3:1,3; Heb 11:16
–We must not love the world .... Ro 12:2; 1Jn 2:15–17
–We may not alienate people in the church .... Eph 2:19–22; Heb 13:1–2

ALTAR

A. Altars used in heathen religions
1. Such altars built .... Ex 32:5; 1Ki 16:32–33; 1Ki 18:26; Ac 17:23

2. Such altars destroyed
   - –At God's command. Ex 34:13; Dt 7:5
   - –By Moses. Ex 32:20
   - –By Gideon. Jdg 6:25–28
   - –By all the Israelites. 2Ki 11:18; 2Ch 31:1
   - –By various kings. 2Ki 18:4; 2Ki 23:12; 2Ch 14:3,5
   - –By the Lord himself. Hos 10:2

B. Altars used in the worship of the Lord

1. Such altars built or rebuilt by:
   - –Noah. Ge 8:20
   - –Abram. Ge 12:7–8; Ge 13:18
   - –Isaac. Ge 26:25
   - –Jacob. Ge 35:6–7
   - –Moses. Ex 17:15
   - –Joshua. Jos 8:30
   - –Gideon. Jdg 6:24
   - –Samuel. 1Sa 7:17
   - –Saul. 1Sa 14:35
   - –David. 2Sa 24:25
   - –Solomon. 2Ch 8:12
   - –Asa. 2Ch 15:8
   - –Elijah. 1Ki 18:30–32
   - –Hezekiah's men. 2Ch 29:18
   - –Manasseh. 2Ch 33:16
   - –Jeshua and Zerubbabel. Ezr 3:2–3
2. Altars located in
   - –The tabernacle. Ex 37:25–38:7
   - –Solomon's temple. 2Ch 4:1,19
   - –The second temple. Ezr 7:17
   - –Ezekiel's temple. Eze 43:13–27
   - –Herod's temple. Lk 1:11
3. Purpose of altars to the Lord
   - –To sacrifice to the Lord. Ge 8:20; Ge 12:7–8
   - –To make atonement for God's people. Lev 16:18–20
   - –To burn incense to the Lord. Ex 30:1–10
   - –To function as memorials. Ex 17:15; Jos 22:26–27
4. Altars in the Christian religion
   - –Christ's cross is our altar. Heb 13:10–12
   - –No need for sacrifice after Christ came. Heb 9:6–15, 23–28; Heb 10:1–18
   - –The heavenly altar of incense. Rev 6:9; Rev 8:3–5

AMALEKITES

A. Their identity
- –The descendants of Amalek, grandson of Esau. Ge 36:15–16
- –Lived in the Negev (south Canaan). Nu 13:29

B. Their wars
- –Defeated by Kedorlaomer and his allies. Ge 14:5–7
- –Defeated by Israelites in the desert. Ex 17:8–13
- –Defeated the disobedient Israelites. Nu 14:41–45
- –Allied with Eglon against Israelites. Jdg 3:12–13
- –Allied with Midianites against Israelites. Jdg 6:3,33
- –Defeated by Gideon. Jdg 7:12,22–24
- –Defeated by King Saul. 1Sa 14:47–48; 1Sa 15:1–9
- –King Agag killed by Samuel. 1Sa 15:32–33
- –Defeated by David. 1Sa 27:8–9; 1Sa 30:1–19
- –An Amalekite soldier killed King Saul. 2Sa 1:4–15

C. Important data concerning them
- –They had no fear of God. Dt 25:17–18
- –Moses prophesied their complete destruction. Ex 17:14; Dt 25:17–19
- –Balaam predicted their destruction. Nu 24:20
- –Destruction completed by the Simeonites. 1Ch 4:42–43

AMASA

- –Nephew of David. 1Ch 2:17
- –Commander of Absalom's forces. 2Sa 17:25
- –Came back to David. 2Sa 19:13
- –Killed by Joab. 2Sa 20:4–13

AMAZIAH

A. Son of Joash; king of Judah. 2Ki 14:1–2
- –Killed his father's assassins. 2Ki 14:5–6
- –Raised a large army. 2Ch 25:5–6
- –Defeated Edom. 2Ki 14:7; 2Ch 25:7–13
- –Worshiped Edom's gods. 2Ch 25:14
- –Rebuked by a prophet. 2Ch 25:15–16
- –Defeated by Israel. 2Ki 14:8–14; 2Ch 25:17–24
- –Killed by conspirators. 2Ch 25:27

B. Idolatrous priest who opposed Amos. Am 7:10–17

AMBITION

–A goal one sets in life

A. Related theme
PRIORITIES is a theme of Haggai. Hag 1:4

B. Examples of proper ambitions
- –Witnessing to unbelievers. Ro 15:20
- –Being fully devoted to the Lord. 1Co 7:32,34
- –Desiring the greater gifts, especially love. 1Co 12:31–13:7
- –Pleasing God in everything. 2Co 5:9
- –Striving for perfection, unity and peace. 2Co 13:11
- –Forging ahead in service to Christ. Php 3:12–14
- –Leading a quiet, diligent life. 1Th 4:11
- –Pursuing righteousness and godliness. 1Ti 6:11; 2Ti 2:22

C. Examples of improper ambitions
- –Competing with others in the kingdom. Mk 10:35–45; Php 1:15,17
- –Serving one's own selfish wants. Php 2:3; Jas 2:14–16
- –Seeking riches. 1Ki 3:7–12; Lk 12:13–21; 1Ti 6:9–10
- –Attempting to glorify oneself. Ge 11:3–4; Da 4:28–30
- –Attempting to displace God. Eze 28:2; 2Th 2:3–4

See also PRIDE

AMMONITES

A. Their identity
- –Descendants of Ben-Ammi, son of Lot. Ge 19:38
- –Related to the Moabites. Ge 19:36–38
- –Given land east of the Jordan. Dt 2:19; Dt 3:16
- –Served the god Molech. 1Ki 11:7,33

B. Significant Ammonites
- –Nahash: besieged Jabesh. 1Sa 11:1–2
- –Hanun: opposed David. 2Sa 10:1–4

–Zelek: one of David's mighty men . . . 1Ch 11:39
–Naamah: the mother of Rehoboam . . . 1Ki 14:21,31
–Zabad: conspired against Joash . . . 2Ch 24:26
–Tobiah: opposed Nehemiah . . . Neh 2:10,19; Neh 4:3,7–8

C. Their wars
–Allied with Eglon against Israelites . . . Jdg 3:12–13
–Allied with Philistines against Israelites . . . Jdg 10:7–9,17–18
–Defeated by Jephthah . . . Jdg 11:4–33
–Defeated by Saul . . . 1Sa 11:1–11; 1Sa 14:47
–Defeated by David's army . . . 2Sa 10:1–14; 2Sa 12:26–31; 1Ch 19:1–15; 1Ch 20:1
–Allied with Moabites against Jehoshaphat . . . 2Ch 20:1
–They and Moabites destroyed each other . . . 2Ch 20:22–24
–Defeated by Uzziah . . . 2Ch 26:8
–Defeated by Jotham . . . 2Ch 27:5
–Allied against Jehoiakim . . . 2Ki 24:1–2
–Plotted against rebuilding of Jerusalem . . . Neh 2:19; Neh 4:1–3,7–8

D. Important data concerning them
1. During the time of Moses and Joshua
–Not attacked by the Israelites . . . Dt 2:19,37
–Refused to give food to Israelites . . . Dt 23:4
–Not allowed to join the Israelites . . . Dt 23:4; Neh 13:1–8
–Half of their land given to Gad . . . Jos 13:25
2. During the time of the kings
–Israelites worshiped their gods . . . Jdg 10:6; 1Ki 11:5,7
–David used them to kill Uriah . . . 2Sa 12:9
–Solomon intermarried with them . . . 1Ki 11:1; 1Ki 14:21
3. Numerous Jews intermarried with them . . . Ezr 9:1; Neh 13:23–27
4. Prophecies concerning their destruction . . . Isa 11:12–14; Jer 49:1–5; Eze 21:28–32; Eze 25:1–7; Am 1:13–15; Zep 2:8–11

AMNON

–Firstborn of David . . . 2Sa 3:2
–Raped Tamar . . . 2Sa 13:1–19
–Killed by Absalom . . . 2Sa 13:20–29
–David mourned for him . . . 2Sa 13:37

AMON

A. Son of Manasseh; king of Judah . . . 2Ki 21:18–19
–Promoted idolatry . . . 2Ki 21:20–22
–Assassinated . . . 2Ki 21:23–24

B. Ruler of city of Samaria under Ahab . . . 1Ki 22:26; 2Ch 18:25

AMORITES

A. Their identity
–Descendants of Canaan, grandson of Noah . . . Ge 10:6,15–16
–One of the Canaanite nations . . . Ex 33:2
–Lived in hill country, east of the Jordan . . . Nu 13:29; Jos 2:10
–Boundaries given . . . Jos 12:2–5

B. Significant Amorites
–Mamre, Eshcol, Aner: friends of Abram . . . Ge 14:13
–Sihon and Og: fought against Israelites . . . Nu 21:21,33; Dt 4:46–47

C. Their wars
–Defeated by Kedorlaomer and his allies . . . Ge 14:5–7
–Sihon and Og defeated by the Israelites . . . Nu 21:21–31
–They defeated disobedient Israelites . . . Dt 1:42–45
–Five Amorite kings defeated by Joshua . . . Jos 10:5–26

D. Important data concerning them
1. Exceptionally sinful . . . Ge 15:16; 2Ki 21:11
2. God promised their land to the Israelites . . . Ex 3:8,17; Ex 34:11
3. Political relationship with Israelites
–Land given to tribe of Reuben . . . Jos 13:15,21
–Israelites told to destroy them . . . Dt 7:1–6; Dt 20:16–18
–Israelites did not destroy them . . . Jos 13:2,4; Jdg 1:34–36
–Amorites and Israelites at peace . . . 1Sa 7:14
–Became slaves of Israelites . . . 1Ki 9:20–21; 2Ch 8:7–8
4. Religious relationship with Israelites
–Israelites must not worship their gods . . . Jos 24:14–15
–Israelites worshiped their gods . . . Jdg 6:10
5. Intermarried with the Israelites . . . Jdg 3:5–6; Ezr 9:1–2

AMOS

A. Prophet from Tekoa . . . Am 1:1
–Originally a farmer and shepherd . . . Am 7:14
–Confronted the prophet Amaziah . . . Am 7:10–17

B. Ancestor of Jesus . . . Lk 3:25

ANANIAS

A. Husband of Sapphira . . . Ac 5:1
–Kept back part of their money . . . Ac 5:2
–Died for lying to God . . . Ac 5:3–10

B. Disciple in Damascus who baptized Saul/Paul . . . Ac 9:10–17
–Commissioned Paul . . . Ac 22:12–16

C. High priest at Paul's arrest . . . Ac 23:2; Ac 24:1

ANCESTRY

–Those from whom one has descended

A. Related theme
GENEALOGY is a theme of 1 Chronicles . . . 1Ch 9:1

B. Physical ancestry of the Israelites
–Genealogies were important . . . Ge 5:1–32; Ge 46:8–26; 1Ch 1:1–9:44; Ezr 2:3–61; Mt 1:1–17; Lk 3:23–38
–Priests had to prove ancestry . . . Ezr 2:62; Neh 7:64
–Israelites proud of Abraham as father . . . Isa 41:8; Isa 51:2; Lk 3:8; Jn 8:31–33

C. Ancestry of Jesus
–A descendant of Adam .... Lk 3:38
–A descendant of Abraham .... Mt 1:1
Ro 9:5
–A descendant of David .... Mt 1:1
Ro 1:3

D. Spiritual ancestry of God's people
1. Physical ancestry insufficient to be saved .... Ro 9:6–7
2. Requirements for becoming true children of Abraham
–We must be chosen by God .... Ro 9:10–13
–We must believe in Jesus .... Ro 4:11,16
Gal 3:7,26–29
–We must do God's will .... Jn 8:39–40
3. True children of Abraham
–Are heirs of God .... Ro 8:17
Gal 3:29
–Include both Jews and Gentiles .... Ro 4:16–17
Eph 3:6

ANDREW

–Brother of Simon Peter .... Mt 4:18
–Fisherman .... Mk 1:16–18
–Disciple of John the Baptist .... Jn 1:35–40
–Introduced Peter to Jesus .... Jn 1:41–42
–Became a disciple of Jesus .... Mt 4:18
–Introduced little boy to Jesus .... Jn 6:8
–Introduced Greeks to Jesus .... Jn 12:21–22
–Asked Jesus about destruction of temple .... Mk 13:3
–One of the apostles .... Ac 1:13

ANGEL

–Spiritual beings created by God

A. Their origin and nature
–They are spirits .... Heb 1:14
–They were created by God .... Ps 148:2,5
Col 1:16
–They were created early in creation .... Job 38:6–7
–They were created good .... Ge 1:31
–They are not to be worshiped .... Col 2:18
Rev 19:10
–They do not marry or die .... Lk 20:35–36
–Some angels rebelled against God 2Pe 2:4

B. Names and ranks of good angels
–Michael .... Da 12:1
Jude 9
Rev 12:7
–Gabriel .... Da 9:21
Lk 1:19,26
–Archangels 1Th 4:16
–Seraphs .... Isa 6:2
–Cherubim .... Eze 10:1–3
–Rulers and authorities .... Eph 3:10
Col 1:16
–Thrones and powers .... Col 1:16
–There are numerous angels .... Rev 5:11

C. Duties of good angels
1. General duties
–They revealed the law .... Ac 7:38
Gal 3:19
Heb 2:2
–They bring messages from God .... Zec 1:14–17
Ac 10:3–6
–They praise and worship God .... Heb 1:6
Rev 5:11–12
–They provide for God's people 1Ki 19:5–8
Mt 4:11
Heb 1:14
–They protect God's people .... Ps 91:11
Da 6:22
Ac 12:7–10
–Some serve as guardian angels .... Mt 18:10
Ac 12:15
–They give guidance to God's people .... Ac 8:26
Ac 27:23–24
–They interpret God's will .... Da 7:16
Zec 1:9,13–14
–They carry out God's will .... Nu 22:22
Ps 103:20–21
Mt 28:2
–They punish God's enemies 2Ki 19:35
Ac 12:23
Rev 14:17–16:21
2. Duties connected with Christ
–Gabriel announced conception to Mary .... Lk 1:26–38
–An angel announced conception to Joseph .... Mt 1:20–21
–An angel announced his birth .... Lk 2:9–12
–Angels sang at his birth .... Lk 2:13–14
–An angel warned Joseph to flee to Egypt .... Mt 2:13
–An angel told Joseph to return .... Mt 2:19–20
–Angels strengthened Christ .... Mt 4:11
Lk 22:43
–Angels were available to help him .... Mt 26:53
–An angel rolled away the stone .... Mt 28:2
–Angels announced his resurrection .... Mt 28:5–7
Lk 24:23
Jn 20:11–13
–Angels were present at his ascension .... Ac 1:11
–Angels will return with Christ .... Mt 25:31
2Th 1:7

D. Evil angels
1. Satan is their leader .... Job 1:6
Zec 3:1
Mt 4:10
2. Duties
–They oppose good angels .... Rev 12:7–9
–They work through false teachers 2Th 2:9–10
1Ti 4:1–2
–They try to separate believers from God .... Ro 8:38–39
–They oppose Christ and his church .... Rev 12:3–6, 13–17
–They do evil to humans .... Job 2:6–8
Mt 13:38–39
Lk 13:11,16
–They tempt humans to sin .... Mt 4:3
1Pe 5:8
–They accuse us before God .... Zec 3:1

ANGEL OF THE LORD

A. To whom did he appear?
–To Hagar .... Ge 16:7
Ge 21:17
–To Abraham .... Ge 22:11,15
–To Jacob .... Ge 31:11–13
–To Moses .... Ex 3:2
–To the Israelites in the exodus .... Ex 14:19
–To Balaam .... Nu 22:22–36
–To Joshua .... Jdg 2:1,4
–To Gideon .... Jdg 6:11
–To Samson's parents .... Jdg 13:21–22
–To David 1Ch 21:16
–To Elijah 2Ki 1:3–6
–To Daniel .... Da 6:22

B. What tasks did he perform?
–Delivered messages from the Lord .... Ge 22:15–18

–Protected God's people 2Ki 19:34–35
–Redeemed God's people .... Isa 63:9
–Punished God's people 2Sa 24:16–17
–Destroyed God's enemies .... Ex 23:23

C. How can we identify him as God (Jesus)?
–He uses "I" when he brings a message.......... Ge 16:10; Ge 22:16–17; Ge 31:13; Ex 3:6; Jdg 6:14
–He describes himself as holy .... Ex 3:2,5
–He carries out God's judgment 2Sa 24:16; 2Ki 19:35
–God's name is in him .... Ex 23:20–23
–He takes on a human appearance... Jos 5:13–15; Jdg 13:6,10,21

ANGER

A. Human anger
1. Expressed by such people as:
–Cain......................... Ge 4:5–6
–Jacob .... Ge 30:2
–Moses .... Ex 11:8
–Saul 1Sa 20:30
–David........................ 2Sa 6:8
–Naaman 2Ki 5:11
–Nehemiah.................... Neh 5:6
–Jonah........................ Jnh 4:1,9
2. Control of our anger
–We must refrain from anger ..... Ps 37:8; Eph 4:31
–We must be slow to anger .... Jas 1:19–20
–We must keep our temper in check .... Pr 16:32
–In our anger we must not sin ..... Ps 4:4; Eph 4:26–27
3. Anger puts us in danger of hell .... Mt 5:21–22
4. We must let God avenge sin .... Ps 94:1; Ro 12:19; 2Th 1:6–8

B. The anger of Jesus
–At injustice........................ Mk 3:5; Mk 10:14
–At the misuse of God's house........ Jn 2:12–17
–In the final judgment .... Rev 6:16–17

C. The anger of God
1. God's anger is righteous .... Ro 3:5–6; Rev 16:5–6
2. Reasons for his anger
–The worship of idols............. 1Ki 14:9,15,22; 2Ch 34:25
–Sin .... Dt 9:7; 2Ki 22:13; Ro 1:18
–Unbelief .... Ps 78:21–22; Jn 3:36
–Unjust treatment of others........ Isa 10:1–4; Am 2:6–7
–Refusal to repent.................. Isa 9:13,17; Ro 2:5
3. Expressions of his anger
–In temporal judgments .... Nu 11:1,33; Isa 10:5; La 1:12
–In the day of the Lord .... Ps 110:5; Zep 1:15,18; Ro 2:5,8; Rev 11:18
4. God's control of his anger
–God is slow to anger............. Ex 34:6; Ps 103:8
–God's mercy overshadows his anger .... Ps 30:5; Isa 54:8; Hos 11:8–11
–God will turn away his anger .... Ps 78:38; Isa 48:9; Da 9:16
–Believers are spared from God's anger .... Ro 5:9; 1Th 1:10; 1Th 5:9

ANIMALS

A. Animals mentioned in the Bible
–Antelope .... Dt 14:5
–Ape............................. 1Ki 10:22
–Baboon 1Ki 10:22
–Bear 1Sa 17:34–37
–Behemoth .... Job 40:15–24
–Camel .... Lev 11:4
–Cattle (bull, cow, calf) .... 1Sa 6:7; Ps 68:30
–Coney........................... Lev 11:5
–Deer .... Ps 42:1
–Dog............................. Mt 15:26–27
–Donkey .... Mt 21:2,5
–Fish............................. Jn 21:3–11
–Fox .... Mt 8:20
–Gazelle .... Dt 14:5
–Goat .... Ge 30:35
–Horse .... Ge 47:17
–Hyena .... Isa 13:22
–Ibex .... Dt 14:5
–Jackal .... Isa 13:21
–Leopard......................... Isa 11:6
–Leviathan .... Job 41:1
–Lion .... Ge 49:9
–Mule............................ 2Sa 18:9
–Ox.............................. Ex 22:1,4
–Pig .... Mk 5:11–16
–Rabbit .... Lev 11:6
–Rat .... Isa 66:17
–Rodent.......................... Isa 2:20
–Sheep (ram, ewe, lamb)............ Ge 32:14; 2Sa 12:1–4
–Weasel.......................... Lev 11:29
–Wolf .... Isa 11:6

B. Animals used as symbols
1. Behemoth: symbolizes power ...... Job 40:15–24
2. Deer
–Symbolizes the thirsty soul ...... Ps 42:1
–Symbolizes the joy of the redeemed.................... Isa 35:6; Hab 3:19
3. Dog
–Symbolizes God's judgment....... 1Ki 21:19,23–24; Rev 22:15
–Symbolizes a fool................ Pr 26:11
–Symbolizes an enemy .... Ps 22:16,20
4. Donkey: symbolizes gentleness.... Zec 9:9
5. Fish
See FISH
6. Fox
–Symbolizes that which threatens us .... SS 2:15
–Symbolizes slyness .... Lk 13:32
7. Horse
See HORSE
8. Lamb
See LAMB
9. Lion
See LION

10. Ox: symbolizes faithfulness .... Isa 1:3
11. Wolf: symbolizes a false prophet ... Mt 7:15; Acts 20:29

See also BIRDS
INSECTS
REPTILES

ANNA

–A prophetess from the tribe of Asher... Lk 2:36
–Elderly widow .... Lk 2:36–37
–Witnessed to others about baby Jesus... Lk 2:28

ANNAS

–High priest when John the Baptist ministered .... Lk 3:2
–Father-in-law of Caiaphas, the high priest .... Jn 18:13
–Jesus on trial before him .... Jn 18:13,19–23
–Sent Jesus to Caiaphas .... Jn 18:24
–Peter and John on trial before him..... Ac 4:5–7

ANOINTING

–Pouring oil on God's servants

A. Purposes of anointing with oil
1. For beautifying oneself .... Ru 3:3; Ps 104:15
2. For healing .... Lk 10:34; Jas 5:14
3. For dedicating officials to God..... Ex 29:7; 1Sa 10:1; 1Ki 19:16
4. For dedicating things to God
–Jacob's stone pillow .... Ge 28:18
–The tabernacle and its utensils ... Ex 40:9–11

B. Which officials received an anointing?
1. In the Old Testament
a. Prophets .... 1Ki 19:16; Ps 105:15
b. Priests .... Ex 29:1,7; Lev 8:12
c. Kings
–Specific examples 1Sa 10:1; 1Sa 16:1,13; 1Ki 19:16
–Kings called "the Lord's anointed" 1Sa 12:3; 1Sa 26:9; 2Ch 6:42
2. In the New Testament
a. Jesus, anointed by the Holy Spirit
–Prophesied .... Ps 2:2; Isa 61:1; Da 9:25–26
–Performed at his baptism...... Mt 3:16; Jn 1:32–33
b. Christians, anointed by the Holy Spirit.............. 2Co 1:21; I John 2:20,27

ANTICHRIST

A. Anyone who opposes Christ
–Called an antichrist 1Jn 2:18,22; 1Jn 4:3; 2Jn 7
–Called a false Christ.............. Mt 24:24; Mk 13:22

B. The antichrist
1. Given the title "the antichrist" 1Jn 2:18
2. Symbols of the antichrist
–Daniel's little horn .... Da 7:8,24–26
–The king who exalts himself ..... Da 11:36–45
–The abomination that causes desolation .... Mk 13:14
–The man of lawlessness 2Th 2:3–4,8–10
–The beast .... Rev 11:7; Rev 13:1,11
3. Characteristics of the antichrist
–He is controlled by Satan .... 2Th 2:9; Rev 13:2
–He opposes God .... Da 7:25; Da 11:36; 2Th 2:4; Rev 13:6
–He teaches false views of Christ... 1Jn 2:22; 1Jn 4:3; 2Jn 7
–He lies and deceives humanity ... 1Jn 2:22; 2Jn 7
–He performs counterfeit miracles.................. 2Th 2:9; Rev 13:3; Rev 19:20
–He persecutes Christians .... Rev 13:7
–He gains political control of the world................ Da 7:25; Da 11:40–45; Rev 13:7
–He gains economic control of the world................ Rev 13:16–17
–He gains religious control of the world................ 2Th 2:4; Rev 13:11–14
4. The end of the antichrist
–He is now being restrained........ 2Th 2:6–7
–He will be destroyed at Christ's return.................. 2Th 2:8
–He will be thrown into the lake of fire .... Rev 19:20; Rev 20:10

ANTIOCH

A. The capital of Syria
1. Important Christian events at Antioch
–First Gentile church located there......................... Ac 11:19–21
–Barnabas sent there............. Ac 11:22–24
–Paul brought there by Barnabas.................... Ac 11:25–26
–Disciples first called Christians there......................... Ac 11:26
–Agabus prophesied there .... Ac 11:27
–Peter and Paul had conflict there...Gal 2:11–14
–Sent delegates to council in Jerusalem .... Ac 15:1–3
–Church heard report of the council...................... Ac 15:22–31
2. Antioch as a missionary church
–Church sent out Paul and Barnabas.................... Ac 13:1–3
–Paul and Barnabas reported to them.................... Ac 14:26–27
–Paul's second journey began from there.................. Ac 15:35–40
–Paul returned there after second journey................ Acts18:22
–Paul's third journey began from there.................. Ac 18:23

B. An important town in Pisidia
–Paul preached the gospel there ..... Ac 13:14–48
–Word spread from there throughout region .... Ac 13:49
–Antioch Jews ran Paul out of town........................ Ac 13:50–51
–Paul made brief return visit .... Ac 14:21–23
–Paul recalled persecution that occurred there 2Ti 3:11

ANXIETY
–The experience of worry and concern

A. The experience of anxiety
 1. Appropriate concern
 –For other family members .... 1Sa 10:2; Lk 2:48
 –At the thought of having sinned... Ps 139:23–24
 –For not being able to understand a vision .... Da 7:15
 –For the welfare of other Christians .... 2Co 11:28–29; Php 2:20,26,28
 2. Inappropriate anxiety
 –For life's basic necessities........ Ecc 2:22–23; Eze 4:16–17; Mt 6:25–34; Lk 12:22–31
 –For trivial, unnecessary things... Lk 10:41
 –For the cares of this life.......... Mk 4:18–19
 3. Anxiety weighs us down.......... Pr 12:25

B. The cure for anxiety
 –We must not be anxious .... Ecc 11:10; Mt 6:31; 1Co 7:32
 –God promises to remove anxiety... Ps 94:19
 –God promises to take care of us .... Mt 6:34; 1Pe 5:7
 –We must rely on Jesus .... Lk 21:14–15
 –We must pray...................... Php 4:6

See also PROVIDENCE

APOLLOS
–Jewish Christian from Alexandria..... Ac 18:24–25
–Instructed by Aquila and Priscilla..... Ac 18:26
–Ministered at Corinth .... Ac 18:27–28; Ac 19:1; 1Co 3:4–9
–Urged to revisit Corinth 1Co 16:12
–Messenger for Paul to Titus .... Titus 3:13

APOSTASY
–Falling away from the truth
 See FALLING AWAY

APOSTLE
–Someone sent out on an official commission

A. Related themes
 PETER AND PAUL is a theme of Acts .... Ac 19:11
 DEFENSE is a theme of Galatians ... Gal 1:10
 SELF-DEFENSE is a theme of 2 Corinthians.................... 2Co 12:19

B. Jesus was an apostle, sent out by God .... Heb 3:1

C. Apostles sent out by Jesus
 1. The twelve disciples as apostles
 –Commissioned before his resurrection .... Mt 10:5–10
 –Commissioned after his resurrection .... Mt 28:19; Ac 1:8
 2. Paul as an apostle
 –His call from the risen Christ .... Ac 9:5–6; Ac 22:8–10,18; Ac 26:15–18
 –His defense of his apostleship .... 1Co 9:1–2; 2Co 10:1–11:33; 2Co 12:11–13; Gal 1:1–2:10
 –His calling as apostle to the Gentiles.................... Ro 11:13; Ro 15:16; Gal 2:8–9
 3. Others called apostles
 –Barnabas, with Paul............. Ac 14:4
 –James, the Lord's brother......... Gal 1:19
 –Andronicus and Junias............ Ro 16:7
 –Silas and Timothy, with Paul..... 1Th 2:6

D. The duties of Christ's apostles
 –Apostleship is one of God's gifts.... 1Co 12:28; Eph 4:11
 –Forming the foundation of the church.......................... Eph 2:20; Rev 21:14
 –Witnessing about Christ............ Ac 1:8
 –Teaching true doctrine .... Ac 2:42
 –Ministering the word of God .... Ac 6:2,4
 –Making important decisions for the church .... Ac 15:1–2; Gal 2:1–3,7–10

E. The signs of apostleship
 –Having seen the risen Christ........ Ac 1:21–22; 1Co 9:1
 –Performing signs, wonders and miracles 2Co 12:12
 –Being persecuted for the Lord....... Ac 5:40–41; 2Co 11:22–33

AQUILA
–Husband of Priscilla; tentmakers...... Ac 18:1–3
–Invited Paul to live with them .... Ac 18:3
–Traveled with Paul to Ephesus .... Ac 18:18–19
–Instructed Apollos .... Ac 18:26
–Paul considered him a fellow worker.............................. Ro 16:3
–Church met in their house .... Ro 16:4

ARAM, ARAMEANS
See DAMASCUS

ARK OF THE TESTIMONY
A. Its construction
 –Made of acacia wood, overlaid with gold .... Ex 25:10–11; Ex 37:1–2
 –Had gold rings for poles .... Ex 25:12–15; Ex 37:3–5
 –Its lid was the atonement cover..... Ex 25:17–21; Ex 37:6–9

B. Its contents
 –A pot of manna .... Ex 16:32–34
 –Aaron's staff that had budded ...... Nu 17:10–11
 –The Ten Commandments .... Dt 10:1–2; 1Ki 8:9
 –All three mentioned together....... Heb 9:4

C. Its symbolism
 –Symbolized God's presence among his people................ Ex 30:6
 –Symbolized the power of God .... Nu 10:35–36; Ps 132:8
 –Sprinkled blood symbolized forgiveness of sin.............. Lev 16:15–16

D. Its history
 1. During the time of Moses and Joshua
 –Placed in the Most Holy Place of tabernacle................. Ex 26:34
 –Went before the Israelites on journey .... Nu 10:33
 –Instrumental in crossing the Jordan................... Jos 3:1–3,14–17
 –Instrumental in the capture of Jericho.................... Jos 6:4–11
 –Joshua prayed before the ark after Ai............................ Jos 7:6
 –Present at covenant renewal at Mount Ebal................ Jos 8:30–33

ARMAGEDDON

ARTAXERXES

ASA

ASAHEL

ASAPH

ASCENSION
–The return of Jesus to heaven

ASHER

ASIA

–Area east of the Aegean Sea (present-day Turkey)

ASSURANCE

–Being certain of our salvation

ASSYRIANS

2. Country of Assyria was beautiful........ Eze 31:3–9
3. Character of the Assyrians
   - –A godless nation........ Isa 10:6
   - –A powerful nation........ 2Ki 19:11,17; Isa 28:2
   - –A proud nation........ 2Ki 19:23–24; Isa 10:12; Eze 31:3,10
   - –A cruel nation........ Na 3:1–4
4. God used Assyrians to punish Israelites........ 2Ki 17:7–17; Isa 7:17–25; Isa 10:5–6
5. Prophecies concerning them
   - –Assyrians to be destroyed........ Isa 10:5,12–19; Isa 30:31–33; Na 2:1–13; Zep 2:13–15
   - –Israelites to be called back from Assyria........ Isa 11:11–16; Isa 27:12–13; Hos 11:11; Mic 7:11–12; Zec 10:8–12
   - –Assyrians to worship the Lord someday........ Isa 19:23–25

ATHALIAH

- –Daughter of Ahab........ 2Ki 8:26
- –Wife of Jehoram and mother of Ahaziah........ 2Ki 8:18,26; 2Ch 22:2
- –Made herself queen by killing Ahaziah's sons........ 2Ki 11:1–2; 2Ch 22:10–12
- –Ruled for six years........ 2Ki 11:3
- –Killed when Joash was made king........ 2Ki 11:4–16; 2Ch 23:1–15

ATHLETICS

A. References to athletic activities in the Bible
- –Wrestling........ Ge 32:24–25
- –Slinging........ Jdg 20:16
- –Archery........ 1Sa 20:18–22,35–40
- –Running........ 2Sa 18:19–26
- –Boxing........ 1Co 9:26
- –Competing in the games........ 1Co 9:25

B. Athletics used in symbolic ways
1. Archery: Job felt like God's target........ Job 16:12–13
2. Ball-throwing: symbol of God's judgment........ Isa 22:17–18
3. Running races
   - –Running in the path of God's commands........ Ps 119:32
   - –Running the Christian race........ Heb 12:1–2
   - –Not running in vain........ Gal 2:2; Php 2:16
4. Wrestling: symbol of struggling with Satan........ Eph 6:12
5. The games
   - –The necessity of strict training........ 1Co 9:24–27
   - –Competing according to the rules........ 2Ti 2:5
6. The crown or prize awaiting believers........ 1Co 9:25; Php 3:13–14; 2Ti 2:5; 2Ti 4:8; 1Pe 5:4

ATONEMENT

–Procedure of reconciling sinners to God

A. Elements involved in atonement
- –Sin of humanity........ Isa 6:7; Isa 27:9; Da 9:24; Jn 1:29
- –Blood must be shed........ Lev 16:14,18; Heb 9:19–22
- –Substitutionary sacrifice is offered........ Lev 4:13–20; Lev 5:5–10; Isa 53:4–7; 1Jn 2:2
- –Guilt is transferred to the substitute........ Lev 1:3–4; Lev 16:21–22; 2Co 5:21
- –Forgiveness is granted........ Lev 4:26,31,35; Ro 3:23–25

B. Old Testament Day of Atonement
- –Description of the Day of Atonement........ Lev 16:2–34; Lev 23:26–32; Nu 29:7–11
- –Involved only the high priest........ Heb 9:7
- –Performed in the Most Holy Place........ Lev 16:2, 16–20; Heb 9:8,25
- –Done once a year........ Ex 30:10; Lev 16:34; Heb 9:7
- –Year of Jubilee began on Day of Atonement........ Lev 25:9

C. Atonement accomplished by Christ
1. Symbolized in Old Testament sacrifices
   - –The Passover lamb........ Ex 12:1–7,12–13; 1Co 5:7
   - –A lamb that takes away sin........ Isa 53:7; Jn 1:29,36; 1Pe 1:18–19; Rev 5:6
   - –The Day of Atonement........ Heb 9:7–14,23–28
2. Fulfilled in the New Testament
   - –Sacrifice of Christ atones for sin........ Ro 3:25; 1Co 5:7; Heb 9:28; 1Jn 2:2; 1Jn 4:10
   - –Christ presented his blood to God........ Heb 9:12,14
3. The results of Christ's atoning blood
   - –Our sins are forgiven........ Eph 1:7
   - –We are purified from sin........ 1Jn 1:7
   - –We are freed from sin........ Rev 1:5
   - –We are redeemed........ Ro 3:24–25; 1Pe 1:18
   - –We are saved........ Ro 5:9
   - –We are reconciled with God........ Ro 5:10; Col 1:20
   - –We have peace with God........ Col 1:20
   - –We are made holy........ Heb 13:12
   - –We are reconciled to other Christians........ Eph 2:14–17
   - –The power of the devil is destroyed........ Col 2:15; Heb 2:14

AUTHORITY

–The ability to exercise power over others

A. Related themes
1. AUTHORITY is a theme of:
   - –Matthew........ Mt 7:29
   - –John........ Jn 10:18

2. LEADERSHIP is a theme of:
- –Ezra . . . . Ezr 7:10
- –Nehemiah. Neh 13:25
- –1 Timothy 1Ti 4:16

B. Human authority

1. Given as a gift from God and Christ
- –To humans for ruling creation. . . . Ge 1:28; Ps 8:6–8
- –To kings for ruling people . . . . Ps 72:1; Ro 13:1–5
- –To prophets for speaking . . . . Dt 18:18
- –To disciples for casting out demons . . . . Mk 6:7,13
- –To apostles for forgiving sins. . . . . Jn 20:22–23
- –To apostles for founding the church . . . . Mt 16:19; Mt 18:18
- –To church leaders for building the church. . . . . 2Co 10:8; 2Co 13:10; Eph 4:11–13; Titus 2:15
- –To saints for judging the world . . . 1Co 6:2–3

2. Exercised by humans
- –Often done by exerting power. . . . Mt 20:25; Mk 10:42; Lk 22:25
- –Christian authority defined by service . . . . Mt 20:26–28; Mk 10:43–45; Lk 22:26–27

See SERVANT

3. Misused by humans
- –In ascribing power to ourselves, not God . . . . Dt 8:10–18
- –In depending on ourselves, not God . . . . Ps 147:10–11
- –In oppressing the poor . . . . Ps 10:2–11
- –In exalting power rather than wisdom . . . . Ecc 9:12–18

C. Divine authority

1. Authority of God
- –Power and authority ascribed to him. . . . . 2Ch 20:6; Ps 66:3,5–7; Jude 25
- –His authority may not be questioned. Ro 9:20–21
- –Even Satan under his control. . . . . Job 1:6–12; Job 2:1–7

2. Authority of Jesus

a. While on earth
- –To cast out evil spirits. . . . . Mk 1:34
- –To preach the word . . . . Mt 7:28–29
- –To forgive sins . . . . Mk 2:5–12
- –To give eternal life. . . . . Jn 17:2
- –To control nature . . . . Mk 4:39–41
- –To raise the dead . . . . Jn 10:17–18; Jn 11:23–27, 38–44
- –To judge . . . . Jn 5:27–30

b. Now in heaven
- –All authority given to him . . . . . Mt 28:18; Php 2:9–11
- –Has authority at God's right hand. . . . . Eph 1:20–23; Col 2:9–10
- –Controls history . . . . Rev 5:1–5
- –Is ruler of the kings of the earth. . . . . Rev 1:5
- –Is King of kings and Lord of lords. Rev 17:14; Rev 19:16

AWE

–*Reverence for the Lord*

See FEAR

BAASHA

- –Killed Nadab to become king of Israel . . . 1Ki 15:27–28
- –Killed rest of Jeroboam's family 1Ki 15:29–30
- –Fought against Asa of Judah 1Ki 15:16–22,32
- –Evil reign for twenty-four years 1Ki 15:33–34
- –Jehu prophesied against him. 1Ki 16:1–4
- –Family killed by Zimri 1Ki 16:9–13

BABYLON

A. Identity and early history of the city
- –Descendants of Ham . . . . Ge 10:6,8–10
- –City is built by Nimrod . . . . Ge 10:8–10
- –Rebellion against God at the Tower of Babel. . . . . Ge 11:1–9

B. The nation of Babylon

1. Significant Babylonians
- –Merodach-Baladan: paid visit to Hezekiah. 2Ki 20:12–13
- –Nebuchadnezzar. 2Ki 24:1

  See NEBUCHADNEZZAR
- –Nebuzaradan: commander of army 2Ki 24:8
- –Evil-Merodach: released Jehoiachin. 2Ki 25:27
- –Belshazzar: saw handwriting on the wall . . . . Da 5:1

2. Chronological history
- –Under the control of Assyria 2Ki 17:24
- –Envoys visited Hezekiah. 2Ki 20:12–18
- –Invaded Judah during Jehoiakim's reign 2Ki 24:1–2
- –Exiles deported with Jehoiachin. . . 2Ki 24:10–16
- –Nebuchadnezzar's dream. . . . . Da 2:1–49
- –Nebuchadnezzar's image and fiery furnace. . . . . Da 3:1–30
- –King Zedekiah's revolt 2Ch 36:13
- –Nebuchadnezzar marched on Jerusalem . . . . Jer 52:4–5
- –Jerusalem totally destroyed. . . . . . 2Ki 25:4,8–10; Jer 52:12–14
- –A second group deported 2Ki 25:11; 2Ch 36:20
- –Nebuchadnezzar's madness and restoration . . . . Da 4:1–37
- –A third group deported . . . . Jer 52:24–27
- –King Belshazzar's banquet . . . . . . Da 5:1–4
- –Medes took over Babylon . . . . Da 5:30–31

3. Jews in Babylon
- –Three waves of exiles . . . . Jer 52:28–30
- –Daniel and friends in royal service . . . . Da 1:1–21
- –Ezekiel saw visions . . . . Eze 1:1–28
- –Jews encouraged to settle there . . . Jer 29:1–7
- –Seventy years of exile . . . . Jer 25:11; 2Ch 36:21
- –Jews experienced grief . . . . Ps 137:1–6
- –Jews allowed to return under Persians. . . . . 2Ch 36:22–23; Ezr 1:1–4

4. Characteristics of the Babylonians

a. A powerful nation
- –A naval power . . . . Isa 43:14
- –A military power . . . . Jer 5:15–17; Jer 51:34
- –A worldwide kingdom . . . . Da 2:37–38; Da 4:22
- –A glorious nation . . . . Da 4:28–30,36
- –A wealthy people . . . . Jer 51:13

b. A wicked nation
- –They trusted in wickedness ... Isa 47:10
- –They were idolatrous ... Jer 50:38
- –They engaged in sacrilegious feasting ... Da 5:1–3
- –They were cruel ... Isa 14:4,16–17; Hab 1:6–7
- –They showed arrogance against God ... Isa 14:13–14

5. Prophecies concerning Babylon
- –They will conquer the world ... Jer 21:3–10; Jer 27:1–11; Eze 21:18–23; Eze 29:19
- –they will be destroyed ... Isa 13:1–14:23; Isa 14:3–22; Isa 21:1–10; Isa 47:1–15; Jer 50:1–51:58

C. New Testament references to Babylon

1. As a symbol of the Roman empire ... 1Pe 5:13

2. As a symbol of the power of the antichrist
- –Inspires people to sin ... Rev 14:8; Rev 18:2–5
- –Persecutes the church ... Rev 17:5–6; Rev 18:24
- –Makes war with the Lamb ... Rev 17:9–18
- –Will be destroyed completely ... Rev 18:2–10, 16–24

BALAAM

A. Personal data
- –Son of Beor ... Nu 22:5
- –Lived in Mesopotamia ... Dt 23:4
- –Considered a prophet ... 2Pe 2:16
- –Killed by Israelites ... Nu 31:8; Jos 13:22

B. His history
- –Asked by Balak to curse Israelites ... Nu 22:4–8
- –Commanded by God not to go ... Nu 22:9–13
- –Asked by Balak a second time ... Nu 22:15–17
- –Permitted to go ... Nu 22:18–20
- –Met by an angel on the way ... Nu 22:21–35
- –Uttered blessings instead of curses . Nu 23:1–24:10
- –Prophesied about Christ ... Nu 24:15–19
- –Advised Balak to intermarry with Israelites ... Nu 31:15–16
- –Returned home ... Nu 24:25

C. New Testament references
- –Considered an example of greed ... 2Pe 2:14–15; Jude 11
- –Considered a teacher of immorality ... Rev 2:14

BALAK

- –Moabite king, frightened by Israelites ... Nu 22:1–4
- –Hired Balaam to curse Israelites ... Nu 22:4–20; Jos 24:9
- –Encouraged Moabites to marry Israelites ... Rev 2:14

BANNER

–A flag or insignia

A. How banners were used
- –To designate different families ... Nu 2:2
- –To rally troops ... SS 6:4
- –To send messages ... Isa 13:2; Isa 18:3

B. The banner used as a symbol
- –The Lord as our Banner ... Ex 17:15
- –Jesus Christ as a banner for all nations ... Isa 11:10
- –The banner of love ... SS 2:4
- –God rallies us to his banner ... Ps 60:4
- –God rallies all nations to his banner ... Isa 11:12; Isa 49:22–23
- –We lift up victory banners ... Ps 20:5
- –We raise a banner for the nations ... Isa 62:10–11
- –God rallies armies to use in judgment ... Isa 5:26–29; Isa 13:2

BAPTISM

–The sacrament of initiation

A. Baptism of John the Baptist
- –Where John baptized ... Jn 1:28; Jn 3:23
- –He baptized many people ... Mt 3:5–6
- –He baptized Jesus ... Mt 3:13–15
- –His baptism symbolized repentance ... Mt 3:11
- –His baptism meant to reveal Jesus ... Jn 1:31
- –His baptism looked ahead to Spirit baptism ... Lk 3:16

B. Baptism by Jesus' disciples ... Jn 3:22; Jn 4:1–2

C. Christian baptism

1. It was commanded by Jesus ... Mt 28:19–20; Mk 16:16

2. It was done in the name
- –Of the Father, the Son, the Holy Spirit ... Mt 28:19
- –Of Jesus Christ ... Ac 2:38; Ac 10:48
- –Of the Lord Jesus ... Ac 19:5

3. It was typified in the Old Testament
- –In the story of the flood ... 1Pe 3:19–21
- –In the rite of circumcision ... Col 2:11–12
- –In the crossing of the Red Sea ... 1Co 10:2

4. Occurrences of Christian baptism
- –Three thousand on Pentecost ... Ac 2:41
- –New believers in Samaria ... Ac 8:12
- –Ethiopian eunuch ... Ac 8:36–38
- –Saul at his conversion ... Ac 9:18
- –Cornelius and his friends ... Ac 10:48
- –Lydia and her household ... Ac 16:15
- –Philippian jailer and his household ... Ac 16:33
- –New believers in Corinth ... Ac 18:8
- –Gaius, Crispus, household of Stephanas ... 1Co 1:14–16
- –New believers at Ephesus ... Ac 19:1–7

5. Symbolism of Christian baptism
- –Forgiveness of sins ... Ac 2:38
- –Washing away of sin ... Ac 22:16
- –Spiritual rebirth ... Titus 3:5
- –Salvation ... 1Pe 3:21
- –Dying with Christ ... Ro 6:3–4; Col 2:12
- –Spiritual circumcision ... Col 2:11–12
- –Inclusion in the body of Christ ... 1Co 12:13
- –Unity in the body of Christ ... Eph 4:3–6
- –Being clothed with Christ ... Gal 3:27

6. Characteristics of Christian baptism
- –Only one baptism ... Eph 4:5
- –Done with water ... Ac 8:36–38; Ac 10:47
- –Faith is essential ... Mk 16:16; Ac 8:12; Ac 16:31–34
- –Repentance is essential ... Ac 2:38

–Linked with receiving the Holy Spirit ... Ac 2:38; Ac 10:44–48; Ac 19:2–6
–Separated from receiving the Spirit ... Ac 8:14–17
–Administered to households ... Ac 16:15,33; 1Co 1:16

BAPTISM OF THE HOLY SPIRIT

A. Jesus was baptized with the Holy Spirit ... Mt 3:16; Jn 1:32–33

B. Jesus baptized with the Holy Spirit
–Prophesied by John ... Mt 3:11; Lk 3:16
–Prophesied by Jesus ... Ac 1:5
–Fulfilled at Pentecost ... Ac 2:1–4

C. Relationship to water baptism
–Water baptism linked with Spirit baptism ... Ac 2:38–39; Ac 9:17–18; Ac 10:44–48; Ac 19:1–6
–Water baptism separated from Spirit baptism ... Ac 8:12,14–17
–Born of water and the Spirit ... Jn 3:5
–Baptized by one Spirit into one body ... 1Co 12:13
–Washing of rebirth and renewal by Spirit ... Titus 3:5

BARABBAS

–Prisoner at the time of Jesus ... Mt 27:16
–Committed murder and insurrection ... Mk 15:7; Jn 18:40
–Received freedom in place of Jesus ... Mt 27:17–26; Ac 3:13–14

BARAK

–Warrior who fought with Deborah against Sisera ... Jdg 4:6–16
–Sang song with Deborah ... Jdg 5:1–31
–Considered an example of faith ... Heb 11:32

BARNABAS

A. Personal data
–Originally named Joseph ... Ac 4:36
–Full of the Holy Spirit and faith ... Ac 11:24
–Sold property, brought proceeds to the church ... Ac 4:37
–Considered a prophet and teacher ... Ac 13:1
–Considered an apostle ... Ac 14:14

B. Relationship with Paul
–Brought Paul to the apostles ... Ac 9:27
–Brought Paul to Antioch ... Ac 11:25–26
–Brought gift with Paul to Jerusalem ... Ac 11:28–29
–Accompanied Paul on missionary journey ... Ac 13–14
–Went to Jerusalem for conference ... Ac 15:1–2,12; Gal 2:1–9
–Conflict with Paul over John Mark ... Ac 15:36–40
–Conflict with Paul over eating with Gentiles ... Gal 2:11–13
–Fellow worker with Paul ... 1Co 9:6; Col 4:10

BARTHOLOMEW

–Disciple of Jesus ... Mk 3:18
–One of the apostles ... Mt 10:3; Ac 1:13
–Probably also known as Nathanael ... Jn 1:45–49

BARUCH

–Son of Neriah ... Jer 32:12
–Jeremiah's secretary and friend ... Jer 32:12–16; Jer 36:4–32
–Forced to go to Egypt ... Jer 43:1–7
–Received comforting message from Jeremiah ... Jer 45:1–5

BARZILLAI

–Gileadite who aided David ... 2Sa 17:27–29
–Unable to go with David because of age ... 2Sa 19:31–39

BATHSHEBA

–Wife of Uriah ... 2Sa 11:3
–Committed adultery with David ... 2Sa 11:4
–Sent message she was pregnant ... 2Sa 11:5
–Became wife of David after Uriah was killed ... 2Sa 11:27
–First child died ... 2Sa 12:13–23
–Mother of Solomon ... 2Sa 12:24
–Influenced David to make Solomon king ... 1Ki 1:11–31
–Pleaded with Solomon for Adonijah ... 1Ki 2:13–25

BEERSHEBA

A. History of Beersheba
–Southernmost city in the land of Israel ... Jdg 20:1
–Hagar fled there from Sarah ... Ge 21:14–19
–Abraham made a treaty with Abimelech there ... Ge 21:22–31
–Abraham lived there a while ... Ge 22:19
–Isaac made a treaty with Abimelech there ... Ge 26:23–33
–Jacob stopped there on the way to Egypt ... Ge 46:1–5
–Allotted to tribe of Judah ... Jos 15:21,28
–Later allotted to tribe of Simeon ... Jos 19:1–2
–Samuel's sons served as judges there ... 1Sa 8:1–3
–Elijah escaped there from Jezebel ... 1Ki 19:3
–Became a center of idolatry ... 2Ki 23:8; Am 8:14
–Resettled after the exile ... Neh 11:27,30

B. Appearances of God there
–To Hagar, to give her water ... Ge 21:17–19
–To Isaac, to bless him ... Ge 26:23–25
–To Jacob, to reassure him ... Ge 46:1–4
–To Elijah, to strengthen him ... 1Ki 19:3–7

BELSHAZZAR

–King of Babylon ... Da 7:1
–Gave a huge feast ... Da 5:1–4
–Saw handwriting on the wall ... Da 5:5–29
–Killed by the Medes ... Da 5:30–31

BENEVOLENCE

See THE RICH AND THE POOR
STEWARDSHIP

BEN-HADAD

A. King of Damascus ... 1Ki 15:18
–Made treaty with Asa ... 1Ki 15:18–19
–Fought against Israelite cities ... 1Ki 15:20–21

B. Another king of Damascus ... 1Ki 20:1
–Fought against Ahab ... 1Ki 20:2–12
–Defeated by Ahab ... 1Ki 20:13–21
–Fought Israel again the next year ... 1Ki 20:26–28
–Again defeated by Ahab ... 1Ki 20:29–30
–Made peace with Israelites ... 1Ki 20:31–34
–Later besieged Samaria ... 2Ki 6:24
–Siege miraculously lifted ... 2Ki 7:5–7
–Killed by Hazael ... 2Ki 8:7–15

C. Another king of Damascus — 2Ki 13:24
- –Son of Hazael — 2Ki 13:24
- –Defeated by Jehoash three times — 2Ki 13:25
- –Amos prophesied against him — Am 1:3–5

BENJAMIN

A. Twelfth son of Jacob, second of Rachel — Ge 35:16–24
- –Name means "son of my right hand" — Ge 35:16–18
- –Favored by Jacob — Ge 42:4
- –Accompanied brothers to Egypt — Ge 43:1–15
- –Royal cup found in his sack — Ge 44:1–13
- –Judah interceded for him — Ge 44:18–34
- –Moved to Egypt with his family — Ge 46:8,19
- –Father of ten sons — Ge 46:21
- –Blessed by Jacob — Ge 49:27

B. Tribe descended from Benjamin
- –Blessed by Moses — Dt 33:12
- –Numbered — Nu 1:36–37; Nu 26:38–41
- –Allotted land — Jos 18:11–28
- –Failed to possess land fully — Jdg 1:21
- –Nearly obliterated — Jdg 20–21
- –King Saul from this tribe — 1Sa 10:20–24
- –Sided with Ish-Bosheth after Saul's death — 2Sa 2:8–11
- –Turned to David — 1Ch 12:23,29
- –The apostle Paul was from this tribe — Ro 11:1; Php 3:5
- –One of the tribes of the 144,000 — Rev 7:8

BETHANY

- –A town on the Mount of Olives — Lk 19:29
- –Less than two miles from Jerusalem — Jn 11:18
- –The hometown of Mary, Martha and Lazarus — Jn 11:1
- –Jesus stayed there after triumphal entry — Mk 11:11
- –Jesus anointed by Mary there — Mt 26:6–13; Mk 14:3–9; Jn 12:1–8
- –Jesus ascended into heaven from there — Lk 24:50–51

BETHEL

A. Identity of Bethel
- –Originally called Luz — Ge 28:19
- –Close to Ai — Jos 12:9
- –On the border between Ephraim and Benjamin — Jos 16:1–2; Jos 18:11–13
- –Originally given to Benjamin — Jos 18:21–22
- –Later belonged to Ephraim — Jdg 4:5; 1Ch 7:20,28
- –Southernmost city of northern kingdom — 1Ki 12:26–29

B. History of Bethel
- –Abram built an altar near there — Ge 12:8; Ge 13:3
- –Jacob had a dream there — Ge 28:10–17
- –Jacob returned there with his family — Ge 35:1–7
- –Ephraim attacked the city and took it — Jdg 1:22–26
- –Samuel served as judge there — 1Sa 7:15–16
- –Prophet spoke against Jeroboam there — 1Ki 13:1–6
- –Abijah captured it from Jeroboam — 2Ch 13:19–20
- –Youths mocked Elisha and were killed — 2Ki 2:23–24
- –Amos prophesied against Israel there — Am 7:10–13
- –Josiah destroyed Jeroboam's altars — 2Ki 23:15
- –Resettled after exile — Neh 11:31

C. Religious importance of Bethel
- –God appeared to Jacob there — Ge 28:10–19; Ge 35:9–15
- –God was "the God of Bethel" — Ge 31:13
- –People inquired of the Lord there — Jdg 20:18; Jdg 21:2–3
- –The ark was kept there for a while — Jdg 20:26–27
- –Jeroboam set up golden calf there — 1Ki 12:28–32
- –A company of prophets lived there — 2Ki 2:2–3,23
- –Became known for its idolatry — Am 4:4
- –Prophesied against because of idolatry — Hos 10:15; Am 3:14; Am 5:5–6

BETHLEHEM

A. Identity of Bethlehem
- –Originally called Ephrath — Ge 35:19
- –A city given to Judah — Ru 1:1
- –Known as "the town of David" — Lk 2:4,11

B. Important events at Bethlehem
- –Rachel buried there — Ge 35:19–20
- –Ibzan judged there — Jdg 12:8–10
- –Home of Elimelech and Naomi — Ru 1:1,19–22
- –Ruth married Boaz there — Ru 4:11–13
- –David anointed king there — 1Sa 16:4–13
- –Philistines controlled it for a while — 2Sa 23:14–17
- –Rehoboam fortified it — 2Ch 11:5–6

C. Jesus and Bethlehem
- –Micah prophesied Messiah to be born there — Mic 5:2; Mt 2:3–6; Jn 7:42
- –Jesus was born in Bethlehem — Mt 2:1; Lk 2:1–7
- –Herod killed babies there — Mt 2:16–18

BETHSAIDA

- –A town in Galilee — Jn 12:21
- –Three of the disciples came from there — Jn 1:44
- –Feeding of five thousand occurred there — Lk 9:10–17
- –Jesus healed a blind man there — Mk 8:22–26
- –Jesus denounced it for unbelief — Mt 11:20–22; Lk 10:13–14

BEZALEL

- –Craftsman filled with God's Spirit — Ex 31:1–3; Ex 35:30–31
- –Supervised building of the tabernacle — Ex 31:4–11; Ex 36:1–5

BILDAD

- –One of Job's friends who tried to comfort him — Job 2:11–13
- –His first speech — Job 8:1–22
- –His second speech — Job 18:1–21
- –His third speech — Job 25:1–6
- –Offered sacrifices to God after Job's restoration — Job 42:7–9

BILHAH

- –Servant of Rachel — Ge 29:29
- –Mother of Dan and Naphtali — Ge 30:1–7; Ge 35:25
- –Reuben slept with her — Ge 35:22

BIRDS

A. Birds mentioned in the Bible
- –Bat — Lev 11:19

–Birds of prey............ Ge 15:11
–Carrion birds............ Eze 39:4
–Chicken............ Mt 23:37
–Cormorant............ Lev 11:17
–Dove............ SS 2:12,14
–Eagle............ Jer 49:16
–Falcon............ Dt 14:13
–Gull............ Lev 11:16
–Hawk............ Lev 11:16
–Heron............ Lev 11:19
–Hoopoe............ Lev 11:19
–Kite (various types)............ Lev 11:14
–Mourning dove............ Isa 38:14
–Osprey............ Lev 11:18
–Ostrich............ Job 39:13–18
–Owl (various types)............ Isa 34:11
–Partridge............ 1Sa 26:20
–Pigeon............ Lev 5:7,11
–Quail............ Nu 11:31–32
–Raven............ Ge 8:7
–Rooster............ Mt 26:74
–Sparrow............ Ps 84:3
–Stork............ Lev 11:19
–Swallow............ Pr 26:2
–Swift............ Jer 8:7
–Thrush............ Jer 8:7
–Vulture (various types)............ Lev 11:13

B. Birds used as symbols
1. The dove
–Symbolizes mourning............ Isa 38:14
Isa 59:11
–Symbolizes renewal............ Ge 8:10–12
–Symbolizes the Holy Spirit............ Mt 3:16
–Symbolizes innocence............ Mt 10:16
2. The eagle
–Symbolizes deliverance............ Ex 19:4
Rev 12:14
–Symbolizes power............ Jer 4:13
Eze 17:3,7
–Symbolizes youthfulness............ Ps 103:5
Isa 40:31
3. The sparrow
–Symbolizes God's protecting care............ Ps 84:3
Mt 10:29–31

BLASPHEMY

–Bringing reproach against God

A. How can one blaspheme God?
–By speaking against God............ Lev 24:11,16
Mt 26:64–65
Ac 6:11
–By speaking against God's word............ Ac 6:11
–By engaging in idolatry............ Neh 9:18,26
Eze 20:27–28
–By persecuting the church............ 1Ti 1:13
–By oppressing the poor............ Jas 2:2–7
–By bearing a sacrilegious name............ Rev 13:1

B. Regulations concerning blasphemy
–Prohibited by the law of God............ Ex 20:7
Ex 22:28
–Punishable by death............ Lev 24:13–16,23
Mt 26:65–66

C. Jesus is charged with blasphemy
–For claiming to forgive sins............ Mt 9:2–3
Mk 2:7
–For claiming to be Son of Man............ Mt 26:64–65
–For claiming to be God............ Jn 10:33

D. Blasphemy against Holy Spirit
–Linked with calling Jesus an agent of Satan............ Mt 12:24–27
Mk 3:22–26
–Considered an unforgivable sin............ Mt 12:31–32
Mk 3:29
Lk 12:10

BLESSING

A. Human blessings
1. Blessing sacred things
–Sacrifices............ 1Sa 9:13
–The cup in the Lord's Supper............ 1Co 10:16
2. Blessing other human beings
–A father blesses his sons............ Ge 27:1–40
Ge 48:15–16
–A family blesses a daughter leaving............ Ge 24:60
–Moses blesses the Israelites............ Dt 33
–Leaders bless the people............ Ex 39:43
Jos 22:6–7
2Sa 6:18
1Ki 8:14
2Ch 31:8
–Priests bless the people............ Nu 6:24–26
1Sa 2:20
2Ch 30:27
–A prophet blesses the people............ Nu 23:11,25–26
–The people bless the king............ 1Ki 8:66
–A blessing used as a greeting............ Ru 2:4
1Sa 15:13
–Children bless their mother............ Pr 31:28
–The command to bless one's enemies............ Lk 6:28
Ro 12:14

B. Divine blessings
1. What/whom does God bless?
–Nature............ Ge 1:22
–The Sabbath............ Ex 20:11
–The work of his people............ Dt 28:8,12
–Humanity in general............ Ge 1:28
–His covenant people............ Ge 9:1
Ge 24:1
Dt 2:7
–God-fearing individuals............ Ps 1:1–3
Pr 3:13
Pr 16:20
–Those who live by godly principles............ Ps 41:1
Prov14:21
Mt 5:3–11
–The home of the righteous............ Pr 3:33
–Nations other than Israel............ Ge 39:5
Isa 19:25
Jer 4:2
2. What are God's blessings?
a. Material blessings given to us
–General statements............ Dt 7:13–14
Dt 28:2–14
–Peace and prosperity............ Eze 34:26
–Health, happiness and long life............ Ps 21:3–5
–Children and a happy home............ Ps 128:1–6
–Abundant crops and food............ Ps 67:6–7
Mal 3:10–12
Ac 14:17
–Showers of blessing............ Eze 34:26–30
b. Spiritual blessings given to us
–General statements............ Jn 1:16–17
1Co 9:23
Eph 1:3
–God's favor and grace............ Ps 5:12
–Forgiveness of sins............ Ps 32:1–2
Ro 4:7–8
–Salvation............ Ro 10:12–13
–Being part of God's people............ Ro 15:27
–Eternal joy............ Ps 21:6

–Spiritual strength and peace .. Ps 29:11
–Having God as a shepherd ... Ps 28:9

c. The blessing of Abraham
–First mentioned to Abram ..... Ge 12:2–3
–Repeated to Abraham......... Ge 22:17–18
–Repeated to Isaac.............. Ge 26:3–5
–Repeated to Jacob .... Ge 28:13–15
–Repeated regarding David's line............... Ps 72:17
–Fulfilled in Christ for the Jews................... Ac 3:24–26
–Fulfilled in Christ for the Gentiles .... Gal 3:8–9,14

3. Who are blessed by the Lord?
–Those who avoid sin............ Ps 1:1
–Those who take refuge in the Lord...................... Ps 2:12
–Those whose sins are forgiven ... Ps 32:1
–Those who trust in the Lord...... Ps 40:4
–Those who show concern for the weak .... Ps 41:1
–Those chosen by the Lord........ Ps 65:4
–Those who dwell in God's house... Ps 84:4
–Those disciplined by the Lord .... Ps 94:12
–Those who fear the Lord......... Ps 112:1
–Those who walk according to God's law.................... Ps 119:1–2
–Those who find wisdom in the Lord.................... Pr 3:13
–Those who wait for the Lord ..... Isa 30:18
–Those who follow the way of Jesus .... Mt 5:3–12; Lk 6:20–22
–Those who confess Jesus as God's Son................ Mt 16:16–17
–Those who hear and obey God's word .... Lk 11:28
–Those who persevere in their faith .... Jas 1:12
–Those who die in the Lord .... Rev 14:13
–Those invited to Christ's marriage feast .... Rev 19:9

BLOOD

A. Blood referred to literally
–In a human being 2Sa 20:12
–In an animal..................... Ge 9:4

B. Blood used as a symbol

1. Blood symbolizes life
–Abel's blood meant his life .... Ge 4:10
–Eating blood means eating life ... Dt 12:23
–"Shedding blood" means taking a life.................. Ge 9:5; Hab 2:8,17; Mt 27:24
–"Being innocent of blood" means not being responsible for physical death .... Mt 27:24
–"Being innocent of blood" means not being responsible for spiritual death .... Eze 3:17–19; Ac 18:6

2. Blood used in Old Testament sacrifices
–Examples .... Lev 1:5,11; Lev 3:2,8,13; Lev 16:14–16
–Shed blood symbolized forgiveness .... Lev 17:11; Heb 9:22

3. The blood shed by Christ

a. What happened to it
–It flowed from the cross .... Jn 19:34
–It was presented to God in heaven .... Heb 9:12,24–28

b. What it accomplishes
–Our forgiveness .... Eph 1:7; Heb 9:22; Rev 1:5
–Our redemption .... Ac 20:28; Heb 9:12; 1Pe 1:18–19
–Our atonement .... Ro 3:25
–Our justification.............. Ro 5:9
–Our reconciliation .... Eph 2:13–16
–Our cleansing................ Heb 9:14; 1Jn 1:7; Rev 7:14
–Our holiness .... Heb 10:29; Heb 13:12
–Our new life .... Jn 6:53–56
–Establishment of the new covenant .... Lk 22:20; 1Co 11:25
–Power over Satan............. Rev 12:11

BOASTING

See PRIDE

BOAZ

–Bethlehemite....................... Ru 2:1
–Acted kindly to Ruth .... Ru 2:8–16
–Married Ruth....................... Ru 4:1–13
–Became ancestor of David .... Ru 4:18–22; 1Ch 2:12–15
–Became ancestor of Jesus............. Mt 1:5–16; Lk 3:23–32

BODY

A. The human body

1. Refers to the physical body
–Originally fashioned by God ..... Ge 2:7,22
–Now formed in the womb .... Ps 139:13,15–16; Isa 44:2
–Refers to one's outward appearance.................... Ge 25:25; SS 5:10–16
–We clothe the body............. Mt 6:25
–Refers to the sexual side of humans 1Co 7:4
–The body must be controlled ..... 1Th 4:4; Jas 3:2
–The body can be healthy......... Pr 3:8
–The body can become ill......... Ps 38:3,7
–The body can suffer............. 1Pe 4:1
–The body remains behind at death 1Sa 31:10; 1Ki 13:24–25

2. Refers to the whole human person
–It experiences life and peace Prov14:30
–It experiences freedom .... Mk 5:29
–We can discipline it 1Co 9:27
–We can love or hate it........... Eph 5:29
–It can be washed by God.......... Heb 10:22
–It can yearn for God............. Ps 63:1
–It can please God .... Ro 12:1
–It can reveal the living Jesus ..... 2Co 4:10; Php 1:20

3. Effects of sin on the human body/person
–It becomes an instrument of sin ... Ro 6:12–13,19; Ro 7:5
–It becomes subject to death ...... Ge 3:19; Ps 90:3–5; Ro 8:10

4. Effects of salvation on the human body/person
–It receives new life .... Ro 8:11
–It becomes a member of Christ ... 1Co 6:15
–It becomes a temple of the Spirit .. 1Co 6:19
–It seeks to do God's will.......... Ro 6:13,19

–It must honor God. . . . . Ro 12:1
1Co 5:20
Php 1:20

5. The future of the Christian's body
–Our bodies will be resurrected . . . Jn 5:28–29
Jn 11:23–24
1Co 15:42–44
–Our bodies will be redeemed. . . . . Ro 8:23
–We will receive new bodies, like Jesus. 1Co 15:52–54
Php 3:21

B. The body of Christ

1. His physical body
–Jesus came in a human body. 1Ti 3:16
1Jn 4:2–3
–Jesus was conceived by the Holy Spirit . . . . Lk 1:35
–Jesus suffered in his body 1Pe 4:1
–Jesus sacrificed himself in his body. . . . . Heb 10:10
–Jesus died in his body . . . . Ro 7:4
1Pe 3:18
–Jesus' body was buried . . . . Mt 27:58–60
Jn 19:38–40
–Jesus' body was raised to life. . . . . Ac 2:31–32
–Jesus received a glorified body . . . Php 3:21

2. Spiritual significance of his body
a. His body symbolized by bread in the Lord's Supper . . . . Mt 26:26
1Co 10:16
1Co 11:24
b. The church as the body of Christ
–Identified as such. . . . . Col 1:24
–Christ as the head of his body . . . . Eph 1:22–23
Col 1:18
–Christ as Savior of his body . . . Eph 5:23
–Emphasis on one body . . . . Ro 12:4–5
1Co 10:16–17
–Emphasis on unity in the body. 1Co 12:25–26
Eph 2:14–16
Eph 4:3–4,12–13
–Each member in the body important 1Co 12:14–24

BOLDNESS

See COURAGE

BOOK

A. In the Old Testament

1. Books of the law and prophecy
–The book(s) of God. . . . . Ex 32:32–33
Ps 139:16
Da 7:10
–The Book of the Covenant . . . . Ex 24:7
–The Book of the Law . . . . Dt 28:61
Neh 8:1,3,8,18
–The Book of Moses. . . . . Ezr 6:18
–The book of Jeremiah's prophecies. . . . . Jer 25:13
Jer 30:2–3
–The book of the vision of Nahum . . . . Na 1:1
–The Book of Truth . . . . Da 10:21

2. Books of history and poetry
–The Book of the Wars of the Lord . . . . Nu 21:14
–The Book of Jashar . . . . Jos 10:12–13
–The book of the annals of King David. 1Ch 27:24
–The book of the annals of Solomon 1Ki 11:41
–The book of the annals of the kings. 1Ki 14:19,29
–The book of Jeremiah's Laments. . . 2Ch 35:25
–The book of the annals of Persian kings. . . . . Est 2:23

3. No end to the making of books . . . . Ecc 12:12

B. In the New Testament

1. References to parts of the Old Testament
–The book of Moses. . . . . Mk 12:26
–The Book of the Law . . . . Gal 3:10
–The book of the prophets . . . . Ac 7:42
–The book of Isaiah . . . . Lk 3:4
Ac 8:28
–The Book of Psalms. . . . . Lk 20:42
Ac 1:20

2. References to parts of the New Testament
–The Gospel of Luke . . . . Ac 1:1
–The Gospel of John . . . . Jn 20:30
–The Revelation of John . . . . Rev 22:7,18–19

3. God's special books
–The scroll of history. . . . . Rev 5:1–5
–The book of life. . . . . Php 4:3
Rev 3:5
Rev 21:27
–The books opened on the judgment day. . . . . Rev 20:12

BORN AGAIN

–Spiritual rebirth by the power of Jesus

A. Why is spiritual rebirth necessary?
–Because we are dead in sin. . . . . Eph 2:1,4–5
Col 2:13
–Because we need the Spirit. . . . . Jn 3:3–6

B. How does spiritual rebirth take place?
–By a decision of God. . . . . Jn 1:13
–By a decision of Jesus, the Son of God . . . . Jn 5:21
–By an act of God through Christ . . . . Col 2:13
–By the Holy Spirit . . . . Jn 3:6
Titus 3:5
–Through the word of God . . . . Jas 1:18
1Pe 1:23
–Through believing in Jesus 1Jn 5:1

C. What does spiritual rebirth result in?
–Salvation and new life. . . . . Titus 3:5
–Entrance into God's kingdom . . . . . . Jn 3:3
–Being a new creation 2Co 5:17
Eph 4:24
–Victory over a sinful life . . . . Ro 6:4–7
1Jn 3:9
1Jn 5:4,18
–Ability to do what is right 1Jn 2:29
–Ability to love one another 1Jn 4:7
–Safety from the evil one 1Jn 5:18

BREAD

A. Physical bread

1. Bread as a food
–Bread is eaten . . . . Ge 14:18
1Ki 17:6
Mt 14:16–17
–Bread stands for life's necessities. . . . . Dt 8:3
Ps 37:25
Pr 30:8
Mt 6:11

2. God's use of bread
–God tested Israel by giving only manna. . . . . Dt 8:3
–God tested Israel by a lack of bread . . . . Nu 21:5
–God punished Israel by cutting off bread . . . . Lev 26:26
La 1:11

B. Bread in Old Testament worship
- 1. Used in fellowship offerings....... Lev 7:11–13
- 2. Used in Aaron's ordination........ Lev 8:2,26,31–32
- 3. The Bread of the Presence
  - –Placed in tabernacle.................. Ex 25:30
  - –Placed in the temple.............. 2Ch 4:19
  - –Twelve loaves for twelve tribes ... Lev 24:5–8
  - –David was given this bread .... 1Sa 21:3–6; Mt 12:3–4
- 4. First bread from each harvest offered to God.................. Nu 15:19–21
- 5. The Feast of Unleavened Bread
  - –A reminder of bread used in the exodus.................. Ex 12:8–20
  - –Regulations given.................. Lev 23:6; Dt 16:3–4
  - –Celebrated in Israel's history.......... Jos 5:11; 2Ch 30:21–27; 2Ch 35:17–19; Ezr 6:22
  - –Celebrated at the time of Jesus ... Mt 26:17
  - –Celebrated in the early church ... Ac 20:6

C. Bread related to Jesus
- 1. Physical bread
  - –Feeding of the five thousand ..... Mt 14:13–21; Mk 6:35–44; Lk 9:12–17; Jn 6:5–13
  - –Feeding of the four thousand..... Mt 15:29–38; Mk 8:1–9
  - –A parable on bread.............. Lk 11:5–8
  - –Jesus served bread in the upper room .... Mt 26:26
- 2. Bread used symbolically
  - –Jesus as bread of life .... Jn 6:35,41,48,51
  - –"This [bread] is my body"........ Mk 14:22; Lk 22:19; 1Co 11:23–24
  - –Participating in the body of Christ.................. 1Co 10:16
  - –Being one body in Christ 1Co 10:17

BROTHERS AND SISTERS

A. Natural use of brother and sister
- 1. People with the same parents....... Ge 4:2,8; Ge 34:13–15
- 2. People with the same father .... Ge 20:12; Ge 37:2,4,8
- 3. Any relative
  - –Members of the same tribe....... 2Sa 19:11–12
  - –Members of the Israelite nation... Dt 1:16; Dt 18:15; Isa 66:20; Hos 2:1; Ro 9:3–4
  - –People with the same ancestors (Esau/Jacob)................ Nu 20:14; Dt 2:8

B. Brothers and sisters of Jesus
- 1. Names
  - –James .... Mt 13:55; Gal 1:19
  - –Joseph .... Mt 13:55
  - –Simon .... Mt 13:55
  - –Judas .... Mt 13:55; Jude 1
- 2. Relationship to Jesus
  - –Wanted to see Jesus .... Mt 12:46–47
  - –Gave advice to Jesus .... Jn 7:3
  - –Did not believe in Jesus......... Jn 7:5
  - –Later became disciples of Jesus ... Ac 1:14
  - –Went on missionary excursions ... 1Co 9:5
  - –James became a leader of the church................ Ac 15:13–21; Gal 2:9

C. Spiritual use of brother and sister
- –Christ is our brother............... Ro 8:29; Heb 2:11
- –We are brothers and sisters of Christ .... Mt 12:50
- –Christians are brothers and sisters of one another .... Mt 23:8; 1Co 6:6; Phm 16
- –Specific references to sisters .... Ro 16:1; Phm 2; Jas 2:15; 2Jn 13

D. Living as Christian brothers and sisters
- –Be concerned about a brother or sister in need.................. Jas 2:15; 1Jn 3:17
- –Forgive each other .... Mt 5:23–24; Mt 18:15,21–22
- –Love each other.................. Ro 12:10; 1Th 4:9–10; Heb 13:1; 1Pe 1:22; 1Pe 2:17; 1Jn 4:20–21
- –Overlook social differences .... Phm 15–16; Gal 3:28
- –Discipline an errant brother or sister...................... 1Co 5:11; 2Th 3:6,14–15
- –Do not judge each other........... Ro 14:10,13; 1Co 6:5–7; Jas 4:11
- –Do not destroy each other.......... 1Co 8:9–13

BUILDING

A. Building in a physical sense
- 1. Things built to honor the Lord
  - –Altars .... Ge 12:8; Ge 35:1
  - –The tabernacle .... Ex 35:8–38:20
  - –The temple 1Ki 6:1–38
- 2. Things built against God's will
  - –The tower of Babel .... Ge 11:4
  - –Altars to pagan gods .... Ex 32:5; 1Ki 12:26–31

B. Building in a spiritual sense
- 1. Christians as builders
  - –Of their own lives on Christ and his words............... Mt 7:24–27; 1Co 3:12–15; Col 2:7
  - –Of themselves in the faith....... Jude 20
  - –Of the church into a unified body .... Eph 2:21; Eph 4:16
  - –Of other Christians in love....... Ro 15:2; 1Co 8:1; 1Th 5:11
- 2. The Lord as a builder
  - –Of Jerusalem .... Ps 147:2
  - –Of the house of David 2Sa 7:27; 1Ki 11:38
  - –Of the nation of Judah.......... Jer 31:4
  - –Of our homes.................. Ps 127:1
  - –Of the church................... Mt 16:18
  - –Of a place in heaven for his people .... Jn 14:1–2; 2Co 5:1

–Of the new Jerusalem ... Heb 11:10
–Christ is the cornerstone ... Ps 118:22–23; 1Pe 2:6

CAESAREA

–A seacoast city ... Ac 9:30; Ac 18:22
–Roman capital of Palestine ... Ac 12:19–20; Ac 23:23–24
–Philip's home and headquarters for preaching ... Ac 8:40; Ac 21:8
–Cornelius stationed there ... Ac 10:1
–Peter preached to Cornelius there ... Ac 10:23–48
–Paul imprisoned for two years there ... Ac 24:1,27
–Paul on trial before Felix there ... Ac 24:1–21
–Paul appealed to Caesar there ... Ac 25:6–12
–Paul spoke to Agrippa there ... Ac 25:13–26:32

CAIAPHAS

–A high priest at the time of John the Baptist ... Lk 3:2
–Son-in-law of Annas, the high priest ... Jn 18:13
–Spoke prophetically about Jesus ... Jn 11:49–53
–Jesus on trial before him ... Mt 26:57–67; Jn 18:24
–Peter and John on trial before him ... Ac 4:5–7

CAIN

A. History in the Old Testament
 –Firstborn son of Adam ... Ge 4:1
 –The first farmer ... Ge 4:2
 –Offered an unsatisfactory offering ... Ge 4:3,5
 –Murdered his brother Abel ... Ge 4:8; 1Jn 3:12
 –Became a wanderer ... Ge 4:10–16
 –His marriage and family ... Ge 4:17–18
B. Significance in the New Testament
 –Considered a symbol of evil ... Jude 11
 –Did not offer a sacrifice in faith ... Heb 11:4
 –Serves as warning not to hate others ... 1Jn 3:11–13

CALEB

–Son of Jephunneh; of tribe of Judah ... Nu 13:6
–One of the chosen spies of Canaan ... Nu 13:1–2,6
–Gave a positive report ... Nu 13:30
–Pled with Israelites to have faith ... Nu 14:6–9
–Allowed to enter Canaan ... Nu 14:30–32
–Given city of Hebron ... Jos 14:6–15; Jdg 1:20
–Gave daughter to be wife of Othniel ... Jdg 1:12–15

CALENDAR

See MONTH

CALL, CALLING

–God's summoning us to himself

A. Basic meanings of "call"
 –To summon to a conference ... Ge 3:9; Ac 4:18
 –To pray to the Lord ... Ge 4:26; Ro 10:13
 –To name something/someone ... Ge 2:19; Lk 1:60
 –To make someone one's own ... Isa 43:1; 1Pe 2:9
 –To appoint someone to service ... Ex 3:4–5; Mk 1:19–20
B. The call to become God's children
 1. What is its nature?
  –It is heavenward ... Php 3:14; Heb 3:1
  –It is irrevocable ... Ro 11:29
  –It is linked to our election ... Ro 8:30; 2Th 2:13–14
  –More are called than chosen ... Mt 22:14
 2. What must we do?
  –We must repent ... Lk 5:32; Ac 2:38–39; Ac 17:30
  –We must call on God's name ... Ac 9:21; Ro 10:12
  –We must confirm God's call by our lives ... 2Pe 1:5–10
 3. What are its results?
  –We are justified and glorified ... Ro 8:28–30
  –We have fellowship with Jesus ... 1Co 1:9
  –We enter God's kingdom ... 1Th 2:12; 2Pe 1:9–10
  –We enter God's light ... 1Pe 2:9
  –We enter Christ's glory ... 2Th 2:14
  –We have Christian hope ... Eph 4:4
  –We receive our inheritance ... Heb 9:15
  –We will conquer along with the Lamb ... Rev 17:14
C. The call to live a holy life
 1. Basic call ... Eph 4:1; 1Th 1:4; 2Ti 1:9
 2. What that call involves
  –Patient suffering ... 1Pe 2:20–21
  –Working for peace ... 1Co 7:15; Col 3:15
  –Serving one another ... Gal 5:13
  –Working as an apostle ... Ro 1:1
  –Working as missionaries ... Ac 13:2
D. The means used by God to call us
 –The Holy Spirit ... 1Th 1:5
 –Grace ... Gal 1:15
 –The message of the gospel ... 2Th 2:14; Ro 10:14

CANAAN, CANAANITES

A. Related themes
 SETTLEMENT is a theme of Joshua ... Jos 19:51
 HOMECOMING is a theme of Ezra ... Ezr 2:1
B. Identity
 –Canaanites were descendants of Ham ... Ge 10:6,15–17
 –Various Canaanite nations ... Ge 15:19–21; Ex 3:8; Nu 13:29; Dt 7:1
 –Borders of Canaan given ... Ge 10:18–19
C. Relationship to God's people
 1. Land promised to Abraham and descendants ... Ge 15:18–21; Ge 17:8; Ex 6:4; Ps 105:11
 2. Brief history of God's people in Canaan
  –Abraham wandered there ... Ge 17:8
  –Isaac lived there ... Ge 26:1–6
  –Jacob left Canaan for Egypt ... Ge 46:5–6
  –Under Joshua, Israelites conquered Canaan ... Jos 12:1–24
  –Land divided out to the twelve tribes ... Jos 14:1–5
  –Northern tribes removed from Canaan ... 2Ki 17:18,22–23
  –People of Judah exiled into Babylon ... 2Ki 24:14
  –Jews returned to Canaan ... Ezr 1:1–5

3. The destruction of the Canaanites
   - –God promised to destroy them ... Ex 23:23,27–31; Ex 34:11
   - –God ordered Israelites to destroy them ... Nu 33:51–53; Dt 20:16–17
   - –Israelites to make no alliance with them ... Ex 23:32; Dt 7:2–4
   - –Canaan was never fully taken ... Jos 13:1–5; Jdg 1:27–36
   - –Some still existed at the time of Jesus ... Mt 15:22

D. Significance of Canaan
- –Promised inheritance for Israelites ... Nu 26:52–56

  See INHERITANCE
- –A symbol of God's final land of rest ... Heb 4:1–11

CAPERNAUM

A. Jesus' ministry at Capernaum
- –Headquarters of Jesus' Galilean ministry ... Mt 4:13–17; Jn 2:12
- –Jesus taught there ... Mk 1:21–22; Lk 4:31–32
- –Jesus spoke about the bread of life there ... Jn 6:24–59

B. Miracles of Jesus at Capernaum
- –Demon cast out ... Mk 1:21–27; Lk 4:31–37
- –Healing of Peter's mother-in-law ... Mk 1:29–31; Lk 4:38–39
- –Healing of official's son ... Jn 4:46–54
- –Healing of paralytic man ... Mk 2:1–12
- –Healing of centurion's servant ... Mt 8:5–13; Lk 7:1–10
- –Healing of many people ... Mk 1:32–34; Lk 4:40–41
- –Paying temple tax from a fish ... Mt 17:24–27

C. Jesus denounced Capernaum for unbelief ... Mt 11:23–24; Lk 10:15

CASTING LOTS

A. Occasions for casting lots

1. Decisions of God's people through casting lots
   - –Choosing a goat on Day of Atonement ... Lev 16:8
   - –Dividing Canaan for the tribes of Israel ... Jos 18:6–10
   - –Determining a guilty party ... 1Sa 14:40–44
   - –Assigning duties to priests and Levites ... 1Ch 24:5,31; 1Ch 26:13–16; Lk 1:5–9
   - –Deciding who would live in Jerusalem ... Neh 11:1
   - –Choosing a replacement for Judas ... Ac 1:26
2. Decisions by heathens through casting lots
   - –Haman's choice of a day for killing Jews ... Est 3:7
   - –Detection of Jonah by sailors ... Jnh 1:7
   - –Owners of conquered Israelites ... Joel 3:3; Ob 11; Na 3:10
   - –Recipient of Jesus' garment ... Mt 27:35

B. God controls the casting of lots ... Pr 16:33

C. Urim and Thummim likely a form of casting lots ... Ex 28:30; Lev 8:8; Nu 27:21; Dt 33:8; 1Sa 28:6

CEPHAS

See PETER

CHARIOT

A. Uses for the chariot

1. For royalty to ride in ... Ge 41:43; 1Ki 18:44
2. For important officials to ride in ... 2Ki 5:21; Ac 8:28–30
3. For use in war
   - –The Egyptians ... Ex 14:7
   - –The Canaanites ... Jos 11:4,6,9
   - –The Philistines ... 1Sa 13:5
   - –The Arameans ... 1Ki 22:31–33
   - –The Assyrians ... 2Ki 19:23
   - –The Israelites ... 1Ch 18:4
   - –The Cushites ... 2Ch 14:9
   - –The Babylonians ... Eze 23:15,23–24
4. For use in pagan worship ... 2Ki 23:11

B. The chariot referred to symbolically
- –Elijah's ascension in a fiery chariot ... 2Ki 2:11–12
- –The clouds are God's chariot ... Ps 104:3
- –God's heavenly host are charioteers ... 2Ki 6:15–17; Ps 68:17
- –God executes judgment by his chariots ... Isa 66:15–16

CHASTISEMENT

See DISCIPLINE

CHILDREN

A. Proper opinion of children
- –A gift from God ... Ge 4:1; Ge 33:5
- –A heritage from the Lord ... Ps 127:3–5
- –A blessing from God ... Lk 1:42
- –A crown to the aged ... Pr 17:6

B. Familiar stories involving children
- –Abraham's willingness to sacrifice Isaac ... Ge 22:1–19
- –The baby Moses ... Ex 2:1–10
- –Jephthah's daughter ... Jdg 11:29–40
- –The call of Samuel ... 1Sa 3:1–18
- –David anointed king ... 1Sa 16:1–13
- –David killed a lion and a bear ... 1Sa 17:34–37
- –Elijah raised a dead boy ... 1Ki 17:17–24
- –Elisha raised a dead boy ... 2Ki 4:8–37
- –Joash became king at 7 years old ... 2Ki 11:4–12,21; 2Ch 23:1–11; 2Ch 24:1
- –Josiah became king at 8 years old ... 2Ki 22:1–2; 2Ch 34:1–2
- –Jesus raised a girl from the dead ... Mt 9:22–25; Mk 5:35–43; Lk 8:49–56
- –Jesus raised a boy from the dead ... Lk 7:11–15
- –Jesus used a boy's lunch to feed a crowd ... Jn 6:1–13
- –Jesus called children to come to him ... Mt 19:13–15; Mk 10:13–16; Lk 18:15–17

C. God's relationship to children

1. Blesses barren women with children ... Ps 113:9
   - –Sarah ... Ge 21:1–3

CHOOSING

CHRIST

CHRISTIAN

CHURCH

–God's called-out people

C. Titles ascribed to the church
- –God's building . . . 1Co 3:9
- –God's field . . . 1Co 3:9
- –The temple of the Holy Spirit . . . 1Co 6:19
- –The church of God . . . 2Co 1:1
- –A pure virgin . . . 2Co 11:2
- –The Jerusalem that is above . . . Gal 4:26
- –The Israel of God . . . Gal 6:16
- –The body of Christ . . . Eph 1:22–23
- –A holy temple . . . Eph 2:21
- –The bride of Christ . . . Eph 5:25–28
- –A chosen people . . . 1Pe 2:9
- –A royal priesthood . . . 1Pe 2:9
- –A holy nation . . . 1Pe 2:9
- –A people belonging to God . . . 1Pe 2:9
- –The flock of God . . . 1Pe 5:2
- –The wife of the Lamb . . . Rev 21:9–10

D. Characteristics of the New Testament church

1. Saved by Christ's blood . . . Ac 20:28; Eph 5:25–27
2. Usually met in homes . . . Ro 16:5; Col 4:15; Phm 2
3. Held worship services . . . Ac 20:7–11; 1Co 14:26–28; Heb 10:25
4. Shared in the sacraments
   - –Baptism . . . Ac 18:8; 1Co 12:13
   - –Lord's Supper (breaking bread) . . . Ac 2:42; Ac 20:7; 1Co 11:23–33
5. Experienced unity
   - –Into one body . . . Ro 12:5; Eph 4:13
   - –As one flock with one shepherd . . . Jn 10:16
6. Enjoyed fellowship . . . Ac 2:42; 1Jn 1:3–7
7. Helped each other . . . Ac 4:32–37; 2Co 8:1–5
8. Evangelized others . . . Ro 1:8; 1Th 1:8–10
9. Grew . . . Ac 4:4; Ac 5:14; Ac 16:5
10. Was organized . . . Ac 14:23; Php 1:1; 1Ti 3:1–13; Titus 1:5–9
11. Had problems . . . 1Co 1:11–12; 1Co 11:17–22; Gal 3:1–5
12. Had to exercise discipline . . . Mt 18:15–17; 1Co 5:1–5; 2Th 3:11–15; Titus 3:10–11
13. Experienced persecution . . . Ac 8:1–3; Ac 17:5–9; 1Th 2:14–15

See also BROTHERS AND SISTERS
DEACON
ELDER
FELLOWSHIP
GROWTH
MISSION
SACRAMENT
UNITY
WORSHIP

CIRCUMCISION

–The cutting off of the foreskin of males

A. Occurrences of circumcision
- –Abraham and his household . . . Ge 17:23–27
- –Isaac . . . Ge 21:4; Ac 7:8
- –All males in the city of Shechem . . . Ge 34:24
- –Moses' son . . . Ex 4:24–25
- –The Israelites at Gilgal . . . Jos 5:2–3
- –John the Baptist . . . Lk 1:59
- –Jesus . . . Lk 2:21
- –The apostle Paul . . . Php 3:5
- –Timothy . . . Ac 16:3

B. Circumcision in the Old Testament
- –Done at eight days . . . Ge 17:12
- –A sign of the covenant . . . Ge 17:9–14
- –A sign of Abraham's faith . . . Ro 4:11
- –Must be accompanied by heart circumcision . . . Dt 10:16; Dt 30:6; Jer 4:4

C. Circumcision in the New Testament

1. Controversy in early church
   - –A pro-circumcision faction in the church . . . Ac 11:2–3; Gal 2:12; Gal 6:12–13; Titus 1:10
   - –Discussed by leaders in Jerusalem . . . Ac 15:1–22; Gal 2:4
   - –Decision: circumcision unnecessary . . . Ac 15:6–29; Gal 2:1–3,15–16
2. Discussion in Paul's letters
   - –Physical circumcision means nothing . . . 1Co 7:19; Gal 5:6; Col 3:11
   - –Circumcision not needed for salvation . . . Ro 4:9–12; Gal 2:2–3; 1Co 7:18
   - –True circumcision involves obedience . . . Ro 2:25
   - –True circumcision is of the heart . . . Ro 2:28–29
   - –True worshipers are true circumcision . . . Php 3:3
   - –Christians are circumcised in baptism . . . Col 2:11–12

CITY

A. Major cities mentioned in the Bible
- –Antioch . . . Ac 11:19–20
- –Athens . . . Ac 17:15
- –Babel/Babylon . . . Ge 11:9; Da 4:30
- –Caesarea . . . Ac 23:23
- –Corinth . . . Ac 18:1
- –Damascus . . . 2Sa 8:6
- –Ephesus . . . Ac 19:1
- –Jericho . . . Jos 6:1
- –Jerusalem . . . 2Sa 5:6–7
- –Nineveh . . . Jnh 1:2
- –Philippi . . . Ac 16:12
- –Rome . . . Ac 28:14
- –Samaria . . . 1Ki 16:24
- –Sodom and Gomorrah . . . Ge 18:20

B. Types of Israelite cities
- –The capital city . . . 2Sa 5:6–9; 1Ki 16:24
- –Cities for defense . . . 2Ch 11:5–12
- –Chariot cities . . . 2Ch 1:14
- –Cities for storage . . . 2Ch 8:4,6
- –Cities for the Levites . . . Nu 35:1–5,7
- –Cities of refuge . . . Nu 35:6–15; Dt 19:1–3; Jos 20:1–9

C. Critical importance of cities
1. Defense of cities
–Usually fortified with walls ...... Nu 13:28
Dt 3:5
Jos 6:5
2Ch 11:5–13
–Besieged by armies 1Ki 20:1
2Ki 16:5
–Kingdom fell when the city was entered 2Ki 17:5–6
2Ki 25:1–7
2. Cities as centers for missions
a. Jonah sent to Nineveh .... Jnh 1:2
b. Disciples evangelized cities ..... Mt 10:23
c. Paul preached in cities
–Antioch .... Ac 11:25–26
–Paphos on Cyprus .... Ac 13:6–12
–Antioch of Pisidia .... Ac 13:14–49
–Philippi .... Ac 16:12–40
–Thessalonica 1Th 1:7–10
–Corinth .... Ac 18:1–17
–Ephesus .... Ac 19:1–41

D. The city used as a symbol
–Of total rebellion against God ...... Rev 18:1–24
See BABYLON
–Of the church and of heaven .... Heb 12:22–23
Rev 21:1–4
See JERUSALEM

CLEANNESS

A. The Old Testament regarding clean/unclean
1. How did one become unclean?
–By eating unclean foods .... Lev 11:1–23
–Through childbirth .... Lev 12:1–8
–Through skin diseases .... Lev 13:1–14:57
–Through discharges from the body .... Lev 15:1–33
–By touching a dead body .... Nu 5:2
–By worshiping false gods .... Jer 13:25–27
Hos 8:5
–Through a life of sin .... Isa 64:5–7
2. How could one become clean?
–By washing self and clothes ...... Ex 19:10–14
Ex 30:18–21
Lev 22:6
–By certain sacrifices and ceremonies .... Lev 12:6–8
Lev 14:1–11
–By turning to the Lord .... Ps 51:2,7
Isa 4:4
Isa 6:5–7

B. Inward cleansing from sin
1. The need for such cleansing .... Mt 23:25–28
2. God's promise for such cleansing ... Jer 3k 36:25,33
3. The process of such cleansing
–The believer must ask for it ...... Ps 51:2,7
1Jn 1:9
–It takes place in the heart .... Ps 24:3–4
Mk 7:18–23
–It occurs through Christ's blood ... Heb 9:14
Heb 10:19–22
1Jn 1:7
–It occurs through the word of God .... Eph 5:25–27
4. The results of such cleansing
–It leads to a life of holiness 2Co 7:1
–It leads to a life of purity 1Jn 3:3
–It leads to a life of love 1Pe 1:22

CLOTHING

A. Purposes and uses of clothing
1. Clothing for natural uses
–To cover nakedness .... Ge 3:7,21
–To keep warm .... Pr 31:21
–To trade in business .... Pr 31:24
Ac 16:14
2. Clothing for religious purposes
–To use in special service to God .. Ex 28:1–5
–To symbolize a message from God 1Ki 11:29–32
–To appoint a prophet as successor 1Ki 19:19
2Ki 2:13–14
3. Clothing used for display
–Special favor to a child .... Ge 37:3–4
–Honor to a citizen .... Est 6:11
–One's wealth .... Mt 11:8
–One's power .... Ac 12:21
–One's position as ruler .... Ge 41:42
–One's self-righteousness .... Mt 23:5
–Mourning .... Ge 37:34
2Sa 3:31
Job 1:20
–Sorrow for sin .... Ezr 9:3
–Shock .... Mk 14:63
Ac 14:14

B. Significant garments in the Bible
–Garments sewn by God for Adam and Eve .... Ge 3:21
–The robe of Joseph from his father ... Ge 37:3–4
–The garments stolen by Achan ..... Jos 7:20–21
–The purple robe put on Jesus .... Mk 15:17
–The seamless garment of Jesus at the cross .... Mt 27:35
Mk 15:24
Jn 19:23–24

C. Clothing used as a symbol
–Taking off a garment means putting off sin .... Eph 4:22
Col 3:9
–Putting on a garment means putting on Jesus .... Ro 13:14
Gal 3:27
–Receiving a new garment symbolizes forgiveness .... Zec 3:3–5
Mt 22:11–13
Rev 3:5
–Being clothed with white robes in heaven .... Rev 7:9,13–14

COMFORT

–*Consolation and strength in a time of need*

A. Related theme
COMFORT is a theme of Nahum ..... Na 2:2

B. People who need comfort
–Those grieving Gen37:33–35
Job 2:11
Isa 61:2
Mt 5:4
–Those in a new country .... Ru 2:13
–Those facing troubles .... Ps 71:21
Isa 51:19
–Those downcast 2Co 7:6
–Those being punished for sin .... Isa 40:1
La 1:9,17
2Co 2:6–7

C. Sources of comfort
1. Human comfort given by
–Spouses .... Ge 24:67
2Sa 12:24
–Children .... Ge 37:33–35
–Friends .... Job 2:11–13
Jn 11:19
–Prophets .... Isa 40:1–2
1Co 14:3

–Preachers .... Isa 61:1–2
2Co 1:4–6
1Th 2:11–12
–Any Christian 2Co 2:6–7
Col 4:11

2. Divine comfort given through
–God .... Isa 51:3,12
Isa 57:18
Isa 66:13
Zec 1:17
–The God of all comfort .... Jer 8:18
2Co 1:3
–God's rod and staff .... Ps 23:4
–God's promises .... Ps 119:50,76
–Jesus Christ .... Jn 14:27
Jn 16:33
–Christ's love .... Php 2:1
–The Holy Spirit as Counselor .... Jn 14:16,26
Jn 15:5–7

COMPASSION

–Deep feeling of concern for suffering and needy people

A. Related themes

1. CONCERN is a theme of:
–Nehemiah .... Neh 2:2
–1 Thessalonians 1Th 2:17

2. SOCIAL CONCERN is a theme of:
–Deuteronomy .... Dt 26:12
–Luke .... Lk 7:22

B. Human compassion commanded
–In the Old Testament .... Mic 6:8
Zec 7:9
–In the New Testament .... Gal 6:2
Eph 4:32
Col 3:12
1Pe 3:8

C. The compassion of Christ
–To people without leaders .... Mt 9:36
Mk 6:34
–To sick people .... Mt 14:14
Mt 20:34
Mk 1:41
–To hungry people .... Mt 15:32
Mk 8:2
–To a grieving widow .... Lk 7:13
–To all of us in our weaknesses .... Heb 4:15

D. The compassion of God

1. A chief characteristic of God
–God is the God of compassion 2Co 1:3
–He is compassionate .... Ex 34:6
Ps 103:8
Jnh 4:2
–He is full of compassion .... Ps 116:5
Jas 5:11
–His compassions never fail .... La 3:22

2. His expressions of compassion
–To Adam and Eve when they sinned .... Ge 3:15
–To the Israelites in Egypt .... Ex 3:7
–To the Israelites in the desert .... Neh 9:17–21
–To the Israelites groaning under enemies .... Jdg 2:18
–To the Israelites in exile .... Isa 54:7–8
Jer 42:11–12
–To all of us as sinners .... Ps 51:1
Ps 103:8–12
Mic 7:19
–To aliens and the oppressed .... Ex 22:27
Dt 10:18–19

See also MERCY

CONFESSION

A. Related theme
CONFESSION is a theme of Psalms ... Ps 51:2

B. Confession of sin before God

1. Examples of people confessing sin
–Aaron .... Nu 12:11
–David 2Sa 12:13
Ps 32:5
Ps 38:18
Ps 51:1–5
–Nehemiah .... Neh 1:6–7
–Isaiah .... Isa 6:5
–Peter .... Lk 5:8
–A tax collector .... Lk 18:13

2. Those who may confess sin
–Individual sinners .... Lev 5:5
Mt 6:12
–Priests on behalf of the people ... Lev 16:21
Ezr 9:5–10:1
–Prophets on behalf of the people ... Isa 6:5
Isa 59:12–15
Jer 14:7,20–21
Da 9:7–11

3. The results of confessing sin
–We receive God's mercy .... Pr 28:13
–We receive God's forgiveness .... Ps 32:5
1Jn 1:9
–We are justified .... Lk 18:13–14
–We receive healing .... Jas 5:16
–We become purified 1Jn 1:9

C. Confession of faith in Jesus Christ

1. Such confession is necessary to be saved .... Mt 10:32–33
Ro 10:9–10

2. Earliest confessions of faith
–"Jesus is Lord" .... Jn 20:28
Ro 10:9
1Co 12:3
Php 2:11
–"Jesus is the Christ" .... Mt 16:16
Jn 20:31
Ac 17:2–3
1Jn 2:22
–"Jesus is the Son of God" .... Mt 16:16
Mt 27:54
Jn 20:31
1Jn 4:15

3. Other elements added to confessions
–Certain teachings about Christ 1Jn 4:2–3
2Jn 7
–Trustworthy sayings 1Ti 1:15
1Ti 4:9–10
2Ti 2:11
Titus 3:8

4. Brief creeds in the New Testament ... 1Co 15:3–5
1Ti 3:16
2Ti 2:11–13
Titus 3:4–7

CONFIDENCE

See ASSURANCE

CONSCIENCE

–An inner voice defining right and wrong

A. Everyone has a conscience .... Ro 2:14–15

B. Our conscience and sin
–It helps us do what is right .... Ro 2:15
2Co 1:12
–It accuses us of sin 2Sa 24:10
Ac 2:37
1Co 8:7
–It can be distorted .... Pr 30:20
Eph 4:19
1Ti 4:2
–A good conscience can be rejected ... 1Ti 1:19

C. Our conscience and Christ
- –It becomes cleansed through Christ .... Heb 9:14; Heb 10:19,22
- –It inspires us to love others 1Ti 1:5
- –It inspires us to obey God's law 1Jn 3:21–22
- –We must hold a clear conscience .... Ac 24:16; 1Ti 3:9; Heb 13:18

D. Our conscience and other Christians
- –A weak Christian has a weak conscience 1Co 8:7,10; 1Co 10:27–29
- –A weak Christian's faith can be destroyed .... Ro 14:14–15; 1Co 8:11
- –We must protect a weak Christian ... Ro 14:13,15, 19–21; 1Co 8:9–13; 1Co 10:27–32
- –We must not judge another's conscience .... Ro 14:1–13; 1Co 10:29

CONTENTMENT
See COVETING

CONVERSION
See REPENTANCE

CORINTH

A. Events of the church in Corinth
- –Paul preached there for one and a half years .... Ac 18:1–11
- –Paul's trial before Gallio .... Ac 18:12–17
- –Apollos sent there .... Ac 18:27–19:1
- –First (lost) letter of Paul to them 1Co 5:9–10
- –Paul's second letter to them 1Co 1:1–2
- –Timothy sent there 1Co 4:17; 1Co 16:10–11
- –Paul's third (lost) letter to them 2Co 2:3–4; 2Co 7:8–12
- –Titus sent there 2Co 7:5–7
- –Paul's fourth letter to them 2Co 1:1
- –Titus sent there again 2Co 8:16–24
- –Paul's visit there for three months .. Ac 20:2–3
- –Paul's collection among them ...... Ro 15:25–27; 1Co 16:1–4; 2Co 8:6–15; 2Co 9:1–15

B. Character of the church in Corinth
- –Most held to the teachings of Paul .. 1Co 11:2; 1Co 15:1–2
- –Disunified 1Co 1:11–12
- –Spiritually immature 1Co 3:1–2; 1Co 14:20
- –Proud; tolerated sinners 1Co 5:1–2
- –Lack of concern for weak Christians 1Co 8:9–13
- –Lack of love for each other 1Co 11:17–22
- –Trouble over speaking in tongues ... 1Co 14:1–20
- –Some denied the resurrection 1Co 15:12
- –Some challenged Paul's leadership 2Co 10:1–11; 2Co 11:13–21

CORNELIUS
- –Roman centurion who feared God ..... Ac 10:1–2
- –Received vision from God .... Ac 10:3–8
- –Peter preached to him .... Ac 10:23–43
- –Received Holy Spirit .... Ac 10:44–46
- –Became a baptized Christian .... Ac 10:47–48

COUNSELOR
–One who gives advice and direction for life

A. Human counselors

1. A class of people called counselors . . Isa 3:3
2. Wise counsel
   - –Good counsel is necessary .... Pr 15:22; Pr 22:20–21
   - –Wisdom counsels us .... Pr 8:12–16
   - –God's law counsels us .... Ps 119:24
   - –David had wise counselors 1Ch 27:32–33
   - –Jeremiah was a good counselor ... Jer 38:14–27
3. Foolish counsel
   - –Wicked counselors must be rejected .... Job 21:16; Ps 1:1
   - –Rehoboam followed foolish counselors 1Ki 12:1–15
   - –The Babylonians had poor counselors .... Isa 47:13

B. God as counselor
- –The Lord as counselor .... Ps 16:7; Ps 73:24; Isa 28:29
- –Christ, the Wonderful Counselor ... Isa 9:6
- –The Holy Spirit as Counselor .... Isa 11:2; Jn 14:16,26; Jn 15:26; Jn 16:7

COURAGE
–The ability to face danger in spite of fear

A. Remarkable stories of courage
- –Moses and Aaron confronting Pharaoh .... Ex 5:1–4; Ex 10:24–29
- –Ehud killing Eglon .... Jdg 3:15–30
- –Gideon against the Midianites ...... Jdg 7:1–24
- –Jonathan against the Philistines 1Sa 14:1–14
- –David against Goliath 1Sa 17:26–50
- –Elijah on Mount Carmel 1Sa 18:1–40
- –Esther approaching King Ahasuerus (Xerxes) .... Est 5:1–8
- –Daniel's three friends and the fiery furnace .... Da 3:1–30
- –Daniel and the lions' den .... Da 6:1–23
- –The apostles facing the Sanhedrin . . . Ac 4:1–22; Ac 5:17–41
- –Saul (Paul) preaching in Damascus .... Ac 9:20–25
- –Paul heading to Jerusalem .... Ac 21:10–14

B. The command to be courageous
- –To the Israelites from Moses .... Dt 31:6
- –To the Israelites from Joshua .... Jos 10:25
- –To Joshua from Moses .... Dt 31:7,23
- –To Joshua from the Lord .... Jos 1:6–9,18
- –To Solomon from David 1Ch 22:13; 1Ch 28:20
- –To judges from King Jehoshaphat ... 2Ch 19:11
- –To the Israelites from Hezekiah 2Ch 32:7
- –To Peter from Jesus .... Mt 14:27
- –To the disciples from Jesus .... Mk 6:50
- –To Paul from the Lord .... Ac 23:11
- –To all of us .... 1Co 16:13; Heb 3:6

C. Aspects of courage

1. When do we need courage?
   - –As we face dangers and difficulties .... Jos 1:6–9; 1Co 16:13
   - –As we face the future .... Ro 8:37–39; 2Co 5:1–7
2. Who is our source of courage?
   - –God .... Ge 26:24; Jos 1:9; Ps 18:29–50; Ps 46:1–2
   - –Christ .... Php 4:13; Col 1:11; Rev 1:17–18
   - –The Holy Spirit .... Ac 4:8–13

COVENANT

–An agreement established between two parties

A. Related themes

1. COVENANT is a theme of:
   - –Genesis .... Ge 17:4
   - –Exodus .... Ex 24:3
   - –2 Samuel 2Sa 23:5
2. RENEWAL is a theme of:
   - –Deuteronomy .... Dt 29:12
   - –Joshua .... Jos 24:25
   - –Malachi .... Mal 3:7

B. Covenants between humans

1. Examples of human covenants
   - –Between Isaac and Abimelech .... Ge 26:26–31
   - –Between Jacob and Laban .... Ge 31:43–54
   - –Between Joshua and the Gibeonites .... Jos 9:3–15
   - –Between David and Jonathan 1Sa 18:3
   - –Between David and Abner 2Sa 3:12–16
   - –Between Jehoiada and the guards 2Ki 11:4–12
   - –Between Joash and the people ... 2Ki 11:17
   - –Between Zedekiah and the people .... Jer 34:8–10
2. Elements in a covenant
   - –Promises 1Sa 20:14–17
   - –Stipulations 2Sa 3:13
   - –Oaths .... Ge 31:53
   - –Responsibilities 2Ki 12:8
   - –Witnesses .... Ge 31:45–48; 1Sa 20:42
   - –Implied threats .... Ge 31:53

C. Covenants between God and humans

1. Examples of such covenants
   - –With Adam before the fall .... Ge 2:15–17
   - –With Adam after the fall .... Ge 3:14–19
   - –With Noah .... Ge 9:1–19
   - –With Abram .... Ge 12:1–3
   - –With Israel at Sinai .... Ex 19:5–8
   - –With Israel before entering Palestine .... Dt 29–30
   - –With Israel in the promised land ... Jos 24:1–27
   - –With David 2Sa 7:14–17
   - –With the returned exiles .... Neh 9:38–10:39
   - –Future covenant of peace .... Eze 34:25–31
   - –The new covenant .... Jer 31:33–34
2. The covenants with Adam
   - a. First covenant (before the fall)
     - –Requirement was obedience .... Ge 2:16–17
     - –Promise was life .... Ge 3:22
     - –Penalty was death .... Ge 2:17
     - –Adam and Eve disobeyed ...... Ge 3:1–6
     - –God pronounced punishment .... Ge 3:14–19
     - –Christ perfectly obeyed God's will .... Jn 6:38; Ro 5:18–19; 2Co 5:21; Heb 4:15
     - –Christ's death reversed Adam's .... Ro 5:15–19
   - b. Second covenant (after the fall)
     - –Conflict between Satan and humans .... Ge 3:15
     - –God promised Satan's defeat .... Ge 3:15
     - –Fulfilled in Satan's defeat by Christ .... Ro 16:20; Heb 2:14; 1Jn 3:8
3. The covenant with Abraham
   - a. Where is it mentioned?
     - –First mentioned to Abram ...... Ge 12:2–3
     - –Repeated to Abraham .... Ge 22:17–18
     - –Repeated to Isaac .... Ge 26:3–5
     - –Repeated to Jacob .... Ge 28:13–15
     - –Repeated to Moses .... Ex 6:2–4
     - –Celebrated by the psalmists ... Ps 105:7–11
     - –Acknowledged by the returned exiles .... Neh 9:7–8
   - b. What are its elements?
     - –Several promises .... Ge 12:2–3
     - –No conditions attached .... Ge 12:2–3
     - –Faith came later .... Ge 15:6
     - –Law of circumcision followed faith .... Ge 17:3–14
   - c. How was it fulfilled in Christ?
     - –John the Baptist began fulfillment .... Lk 1:72–75
     - –Peter preached its fulfillment .... Ac 3:25
     - –Its center is faith in Christ ..... Gal 3:6–9
     - –The law follows faith .... Ro 4:9–13
4. The covenant of the law made at Mount Sinai
   - a. Where is it mentioned?
     - –First made at Mount Sinai ..... Ex 19:3–6
     - –Confirmed by the Israelites .... Ex 24:1–8
     - –Renewed at the border of Canaan .... Dt 29
     - –Renewed at Mount Ebal .... Jos 8:30–35
     - –Renewed at Shechem .... Jos 24:1–27
     - –Rejected by the ten tribes 2Ki 17:7–20
     - –Renewed under Josiah 2Ch 34:29–33
     - –Broken by the nation of Judah .... Jer 31:32
     - –Renewed by the returned exiles .... Neh 9:38–10:39
   - b. What are its elements?
     - –Centered on the law of God .... Ex 34:27–28; Dt 4:13–14
     - –Required obedience .... Ex 24:7; Ex 34:10–11; Dt 29:9
     - –Linked with blessings and curses .... Dt 28; Jos 8:34–35
     - –Did not annul covenant with Abraham .... Gal 3:15–17
     - –Pointed out human sin .... Ro 3:20,23; Gal 3:19
     - –Increased sin .... Ro 5:20
     - –Prepared for the coming of Christ .... Gal 3:23–25
   - c. How was it fulfilled in Christ?
     - –He fulfilled the law .... Mt 5:17
     - –He perfectly obeyed the law ... Ro 5:18–19; 2Co 5:21; Heb 4:15
     - –He died the death of a curse ... Gal 3:10–13
     - –His death removed the curse from us .... Gal 3:13–14
5. The covenant with David
   - a. Where is it mentioned?
     - –First promised to David 2Sa 7:4–17
     - –Celebrated by David 2Sa 23:5
     - –Mentioned to Solomon 1Ki 2:2–4
     - –Celebrated by Solomon 1Ki 8:22–26
     - –Mentioned to Jeroboam 1Ki 11:34–36
     - –Reaffirmed during Jehoram's reign 2Ki 8:19
     - –Celebrated by psalmists .... Ps 89:3; Ps 132:10–12
     - –Reaffirmed by Isaiah .... Isa 9:6–7
     - –Reaffirmed by Ezekiel .... Eze 37:24–25
   - b. What are its elements?
     - –Several promises 2Sa 7:9–16
     - –No conditions attached 2Sa 7:15–16

c. How was it fulfilled in Christ?
- –Mentioned by Gabriel to Mary .... Lk 1:32–33
- –Preached by Paul............ Ac 13:22–23,34
- –Hinted at in book of Hebrews .... Heb 1:8
- –Jesus is the Son of David........ Mt 1:1; Ro 1:3
- –Jesus is a king who rules...... Jn 18:33–37; 1Co 15:24–25; Rev 19:16

6. The new covenant

a. Where is it promised?
- –Through Jeremiah........... Jer 31:33–34; Jer 32:38–40
- –Through Ezekiel .... Eze 16:60–62; Eze 34:25–31
- –Through Hosea .... Hos 2:18–20

b. What are its elements?
- –Several promises........... Jer 31:33–34
- –No conditions attached.......... Jer 31:33–34

c. How was it fulfilled in Christ?
- –Asserted by Christ in the upper room .... Lk 22:20; 1Co 11:25
- –Mentioned by Paul............ 2Co 3:6
- –Explained in book of Hebrews .... Heb 8:6–13; Heb 9:15–28; Heb 10:11–18; Heb 12:22–24

7. God's relationship to his covenants
- –He establishes his covenant...... Ge 6:18; Ge 17:7; Ex 6:4; Eze 16:60–62
- –He is faithful to his covenant..... Dt 7:9; 1Ki 8:23; Neh 9:32; Da 9:4
- –He remembers his covenant...... Ex 2:24; Ps 105:8; Ps 111:5; Eze 16:60; Lk 1:72

COVETING

–The sinful desire for what belongs to someone else; greed

A. The command against coveting
- –In the Old Testament .... Ex 20:17; Dt 5:21; Dt 7:25
- –In the New Testament .... Ro 7:7–11; Eph 5:3; Col 3:5

B. Coveting often leads to other sins 1Ti 6:10; 1Jn 2:15–16
- –To deceit (Jacob) .... Ge 27:18–26
- –To adultery (David) 2Sa 11:1–5
- –To disobedience to God (Achan) .... Jos 7:20–21
- –To hypocritical worship (Saul) 1Sa 15:9–23
- –To murder (Ahab) 1Ki 21:1–14
- –To theft (Gehazi) 2Ki 5:20–24
- –To family disharmony Prov15:27
- –To lying (Ananias and Sapphira) ... Ac 5:1–10

C. Contentment as the answer to coveting
- –The command to be content........ Lk 3:14; 1Ti 6:8; Heb 13:5
- –The experience of Paul .... Php 4:11–12

CREATION

A. Related theme

BEGINNINGS is a theme of Genesis .... Ge 1:1

B. The work of creation
- –Accounts of creation .... Ge 1:1–2:3; Ge 2:4–24; Job 38:4–38; Ps 104:1–26
- –Done out of nothing............ Heb 11:3
- –Done in six days .... Ge 1:3–31; Ex 20:11; Ex 31:17

C. Creation as the work of God
- –God as the creator............ Ge 1:1; Isa 44:24; Ac 4:24
- –Accomplished through Christ ...... Jn 1:3,10; Col 1:16; Heb 1:2
- –The Holy Spirit involved in creation .... Job 33:4; Ps 104:30

D. Creation reveals God
- –His glory............ Ps 19:1
- –His power............ Isa 40:26,28
- –His divine nature .... Ro 1:20
- –His wisdom............ Ps 104:24
- –His love .... Ps 33:5–6

E. Creation after Adam and Eve sinned
- –Was cursed by God............ Ge 3:14,17–19
- –Was subjected to frustration ...... Ro 8:20
- –Praises God .... Ps 145:10; Ps 148:1–5; Isa 55:12
- –Eagerly awaits redemption......... Ro 8:19
- –Will someday be liberated .... Ro 8:21
- –Will someday be recreated......... Isa 65:17; 2Pe 3:10–13; Rev 21:1

F. Humans commanded to rule creation .... Ge 1:26,28; Ps 8:6–8; Ps 115:16

CREED

See CONFESSION

CROSS

A. Jesus and the cross

1. What it involved
- –The means to bring about Jesus' death .... Jn 19:17–18; Ac 5:30
- –Was the death of a curse........ Gal 3:13
- –Planned by God .... Lk 24:26–27; Ac 2:23
- –Carried out by humans.......... Ac 2:23; Ac 5:30
- –Showed Jesus' obedience........ Php 2:8

2. What it accomplished
- –Redeemed us from the curse of God .... Gal 3:10,13
- –Took away our sins .... Col 2:13–14; 1Pe 2:24
- –Reconciled us with God .... Eph 2:16; Col 1:20
- –Gave us eternal life............ Jn 3:14–15
- –Brought about victory over Christ's enemies .... Col 2:15

B. The message of the cross
- –Was preached by the apostles ...... Ac 2:23; Ac 8:32–35; Ac 13:28–29; 1Co 1:23; 1Co 2:1–2
- –Was a stumbling block to Jews 1Co 1:23
- –Was foolishness to Gentiles 1Co 1:18,23

C. Believers and the cross
- –They are crucified with Christ ..... Gal 2:20
- –Their sinful nature is put to death ... Ro 6:6; Gal 5:24; 1Pe 2:24
- –They are crucified to the world ..... Gal 6:14
- –They must carry their cross .... Mt 10:38

CROWN

A. Examples of those who wore a crown
- –Priests .... Lev 8:9; Zec 6:9–11
- –Kings .... 2Sa 12:30; SS 3:11
- –Queens .... Est 1:11; Est 2:17
- –Christ with a crown of thorns .... Mt 27:29; Jn 19:2,5
- –Christ with a royal crown .... Rev 14:14; Rev 19:12

B. Crowns used as a symbol

1. In the present life
- –God crowns humans with glory and honor .... Ps 8:5
- –God crowns us with salvation .... Ps 149:4
- –God crowns us with love .... Ps 103:4
- –God crowns us with blessings ..... Pr 10:6
- –A good wife is her husband's crown .... Pr 12:4
- –Gray hair is a crown of splendor ... Pr 16:31
- –Grandchildren are a crown to the aged .... Pr 17:6
- –Christians are a crown to Paul .... 1Th 2:19; Php 4:1

2. In the life hereafter
- –God will be a glorious crown for us .... Isa 28:5
- –Christians will be a crown for God .... Isa 62:3
- –Everlasting joy will crown us .... Isa 35:10
- –We receive an everlasting crown 1Co 9:25
- –We receive a crown of righteousness 2Ti 4:8
- –We receive a crown of life .... Jas 1:12; Rev 2:10
- –We receive a crown of glory 1Pe 5:4

CURSE, CURSING

A. The curse as a result of sin

1. Warnings of the curse
- –Principle stated .... Dt 11:26–28; Pr 3:33; Jer 11:3
- –Extended list of curses .... Dt 27:15–26; Dt 28:15–68

2. Expressions of the curse

a. In the Old Testament
- –On the serpent .... Ge 3:14
- –On Cain .... Ge 4:9–12
- –On Canaan .... Ge 9:25
- –On Simeon and Levi .... Ge 49:7–9
- –On any who disobey the law .... Dt 27:26
- –On those who dishonor God .... Mal 2:2
- –On the land .... Ge 3:17; Isa 24:6; Jer 23:10; Jer 44:22; Mal 4:6

b. In the New Testament
- –On those not kind to the needy .... Mt 25:41–46
- –On those who refuse the gospel .... Gal 1:8–9
- –On those who do not love the Lord 1Co 16:22
- –On those who fall away from Christ .... Heb 6:4–8
- –On all sinners .... Gal 3:10

3. Removal of the curse by Christ's cross .... Gal 3:13

B. Human cursing

1. Cursing God
- –Humans may not curse God ...... Ex 20:7; Dt 5:11; 1Co 12:3
- –Penalty for cursing God was death .... Lev 24:10–16; 1Ki 21:13; Job 2:9

See also BLASPHEMY

2. Cursing other humans

a. Examples
- –Balak's desire to curse Israel .... Nu 23:11,25
- –Joshua cursed rebuilders of Jericho .... Jos 6:26
- –Citizens of Shechem cursed Abimelech .... Jdg 9:26–27
- –Goliath cursed David 1Sa 17:43
- –Shimei cursed David 2Sa 16:5–7
- –Curses on greedy people ...... Pr 11:26
- –Non-Christians curse Christians 1Co 4:12

b. The command not to curse other humans .... Ex 21:17; Pr 20:20; Pr 30:10–11; Jas 3:10–12

c. We must bless instead of curse ... Lk 6:28; Ro 12:14

CYRUS

- –Persian king .... 2Ch 36:22; Da 6:28
- –Allowed Israel to return from exile 2Ch 36:23
- –Commanded rebuilding of the temple ... Ezr 1:1–4
- –His decree recalled .... Ezr 6:1–5
- –Called shepherd of the Lord .... Isa 44:28
- –Called anointed of the Lord .... Isa 45:1–13

DAMASCUS

A. Identity and location
- –Capital city of the Arameans or Syrians .... 1Ki 15:18; Isa 7:8
- –Arameans were descendants of Shem .... Ge 10:22–23

B. Significant Arameans
- –Eliezer: servant of Abram .... Ge 15:2
- –Three kings called Ben-Hadad *See* BEN-HADAD
- –Naaman: the leprous commander ... 2Ki 5:1 *See* NAAMAN
- –Hazael: king after Ben-Hadad ...... 2Ki 8:15 *See* HAZAEL
- –Rezin: allied with Israel against Ahaz .... Isa 7:1–9

C. Significant events of Damascus/Syria

1. Old Testament
- –Abram passed through it .... Ge 14:15
- –David conquered it 2Sa 8:5–6; 1Ch 18:5–6
- –Twenty thousand Aramean soldiers defeated by Joab 2Sa 10:6–19

–Asa made a treaty with its king . . . 1Ki 15:18–20; 2Ch 16:2
–Elisha prophesied there . . . 2Ki 8:7–13
–Jeroboam II conquered it . . . 2Ki 14:28
–Joash defeated by the Arameans . . . 2Ch 24:23–25
–Israel allied with it against Judah . . . 2Ki 16:5; Isa 7:1–2
–Ahaz defeated by the Arameans . . . 2Ch 28:5
–Assyria captured it. . . 2Ki 16:9; Isa 8:3–7

2. New Testament
–News of Jesus went to Syria. . . Mt 4:24
–Saul went there to persecute Christians . . . Ac 9:1–2
–Saul converted near there. . . Ac 9:3–9
–Saul/Paul preached there . . . Ac 9:19–22; Gal 1:17–18
–Paul escaped from there in a basket . . . Ac 9:23–25; 2Co 11:32–33
–Paul traveled through Syria. . . Ac 15:41; Gal 1:21

D. Prophecies against Damascus . . . Isa 17:1–14; Jer 49:23–27; Am 1:3–5; Zec 9:1

DAN

A. Son of Jacob by Bilhah. . . Ge 35:25
–Name means "vindicated" . . . Ge 30:4–6
–Went to Egypt with family . . . Ge 46:8,23
–Father of one son. . . Ge 46:23
–Blessed by Jacob. . . Ge 49:16–17

B. Tribe descended from Dan . . . Nu 26:42
–Blessed by Moses . . . Dt 33:22
–Numbered. . . Nu 1:38–39; Nu 26:43
–Allotted land . . . Jos 19:40–48; Eze 48:1
–Failed to possess the land fully . . . Jdg 1:34–35
–Failed to support Deborah . . . Jdg 5:17
–Samson was a Danite. . . Jdg 13:2,24–25
–Stole Micah's priest . . . Jdg 18:1–26

C. A city in Israel . . . Ge 14:14
–At one time called Leshem . . . Jos 19:47
–Also called Laish . . . Jdg 18:27–31
–Northernmost city in land of Israel . . . Jdg 20:1
–Jeroboam set up golden calf there . . . 1Ki 12:25–30
–Conquered by Ben-Hadad. . . 1Ki 15:20

DANCING

A. There is a time to dance . . . Ecc 3:4

B. Occasions for dancing

1. Appropriate
–To praise and worship God . . . Ex 15:20–21; Ps 68:24–25; Ps 149:3; Ps 150:4
–To express human elation. . . 1Sa 18:6–7; 2Sa 6:16; Jer 31:4

2. Inappropriate
–In pagan worship . . . Ex 32:5–6,19; 1Ki 18:26–29; 1Co 10:7
–Herodias before Herod . . . Mt 14:6

3. Dancing ceases at a time of sorrow . . . La 5:15; Mt 11:17

C. God's blessing turns sorrow into dancing . . . Ps 30:11

DANIEL

A. Hebrew exile to Babylon . . . Da 1:6
–Educated in Babylonia. . . Da 1:3–5
–Name changed to Belteshazzar. . . Da 1:7
–Refused non-Jewish food . . . Da 1:8–21
–Interpreted dreams of Nebuchadnezzar . . . Da 2:24–47; Da 4:4–27
–Interpreted handwriting on the wall. . . Da 5:1–28
–Survived the lions' den . . . Da 6:1–23
–Recorded visions. . . Da 7:1–12:13
–Jesus referred to his prophecy. . . Mt 24:15

B. Son of David and Abigail. . . 1Ch 3:1

DARIUS

A. King of the Medes; conquered Babylon . . . Da 5:31
–Son of Ahasuerus (Xerxes). . . Da 9:1

B. A later king of Persia . . . Ezr 4:5; Hag 1:1,15
–Asked to order rebuilding of temple to stop . . . Ezr 5:3–17
–Allowed rebuilding of temple. . . Ezr 6:1–12

DARKNESS

A. Physical darkness
–Created by God . . . Isa 45:7
–Originally covered the earth . . . Ge 1:2
–Separated from light . . . Ge 1:4
–Called night . . . Ge 1:5
–Comes when the sun sets . . . Ge 15:17
–God can see things in the dark . . . Ps 139:11–12; Da 2:22

B. Darkness as a symbol

1. For the mysteriousness of God. . . Ex 20:21; Ps 18:9; Ps 97:2

2. For afflictions. . . Job 18:6,18; Isa 59:9; La 3:1–2

3. For ignorance about God. . . Job 37:19; Isa 60:2; 1Jn 2:8

4. For sin and evil
–Sinful deeds are deeds of darkness . . . Ro 13:12; Eph 5:11
–The way of the wicked is darkness . . . Pr 2:13; Pr 4:19; 1Th 5:4–5
–Living in sin is walking in darkness . . . Jn 3:19; 1Jn 1:6; 1Jn 2:9,11

5. For judgment from God . . . Joel 2:2; Am 5:18,20; Rev 16:10

6. For the realm of Satan . . . Lk 22:53; Eph 6:12; Col 1:13

7. For hell as a place of punishment . . . Mt 8:12; 2Pe 2:17; Jude 13

C. Antidotes to darkness as evil

1. God
–His first act was to dispel darkness . . . Ge 1:2–3
–He surrounds himself with light. . . Ps 104:1–2; 1Ti 6:16
–He is the God of light . . . 1Jn 1:5

2. Jesus
–Jesus came to dispel darkness.... Jn 1:4–9
Jn 3:19–21
Jn 12:46
–Jesus is the light of the world.... Jn 8:12
Jn 9:5

3. Heaven
–God's light permeates heaven .... Isa 60:19–20
Rev 21:23
–Heaven has no night .... Zec 14:7
Rev 22:5

See also LIGHT

DAVID

A. Related theme
DAVID is a theme of 1 Chronicles.... 1Ch 28:4

B. Personal data

1. Ancestry
–Son of Jesse .... Ru 4:17–22
1Ch 2:13–15
–Youngest in the family 1Sa 16:10–13

2. Wives
–Michal, daughter of Saul......... 1Sa 18:2–27
–Abigail, widow of Nabal.......... 1Sa 25:39–44
–Bathsheba, widow of Uriah 2Sa 11
–Many wives and concubines 2Sa 5:13–15

3. Descendants
–Solomon 2Sa 12:24
–Amnon 2Sa 13:1
–Absalom 2Sa 13:1
–Adonijah........................ 1Ki 1:5–6
–Many sons 2Sa 3:2–5
1Ch 3:1–9
–Jesus was the Son of David ...... Mt 1:1–17
Lk 3:31

4. Occupations
–A shepherd...................... 1Sa 16:11
1Sa 17:20,34–37
–A musician...................... 1Sa 16:14–23
2Sa 23:1
–A psalmist 1Ch 16:7
Ps 3–34, etc
Lk 20:42
–A prophet 2Sa 23:1–2
Ac 2:25–31
–A king.......................... 2Sa 5:3–4

C. David's life during Saul's reign

1. His anointing as future king....... 1Sa 16:1–13

2. His work in Saul's service
–Played music for Saul 1Sa 16:14–23
1Sa 18:10
–Killed Goliath 1Sa 17:4–51
–Became a mighty warrior......... 1Sa 18:2–7

3. Saul's reaction to David
–Was jealous of him.............. 1Sa 18:6–9,12,29
–Tried to kill him 1Sa 18:10–11
1Sa 19:1–18

4. David's flights
–To Nob.......................... 1Sa 21:1
–To Gath......................... 1Sa 21:10
–To the cave of Adullam 1Sa 22:1
–To Keilah 1Sa 23:7
–To desert strongholds 1Sa 23:14–24
–To the land of the Philistines 1Sa 27:1–3
–David spared Saul's life.......... 1Sa 24:1–21
1Sa 26:1–25

5. His military victories
–Killed two hundred Philistines ... 1Sa 18:24–27
–Saved town of Keilah............ 1Sa 23:1–6
–Defeated Amalekites............. 1Sa 30:1–31
–Not allowed to fight on side
of Philistines 1Sa 29:1–11

6. His covenant with Jonathan........ 1Sa 18:1–4
1Sa 20:16–17
1Sa 23:15–18

7. His lament over Saul and Jonathan 2Sa 1:17–27

D. David's life as king

1. His fight to become king
–Became king of Judah............ 2Sa 2:1–11
–Fought with Saul's supporters.... 2Sa 2:8–4:12
–Became king of all Israel 2Sa 5:1–4
1Ch 11:1–3

2. His military accomplishments
–Conquered Jerusalem............ 2Sa 5:6–10
1Ch 11:4–9
–Conquered Philistines........... 2Sa 5:17–25
2Sa 21:15–22
1Ch 14:8–17
–Conquered Ammonites.......... 2Sa 10:1–19
1Ch 19:1–19
–Conquered many others 2Sa 8:1–14
1Ch 18:1–13
–Avenged the Gibeonites 2Sa 21:1–14
–Organized army and
government................ 1Ch 27:1–34
–Had many mighty men 2Sa 23:8–39
1Ch 11–12
–Numbered his army; angered
the Lord..................... 2Sa 24:1–17
1Ch 21:1–19

3. His involvement in Israel's worship
–Brought ark to Jerusalem......... 2Sa 6:1–19
–Planned the temple.............. 1Ch 22:1–19
1Ch 28:8–29:9
–Organized Israel's worship 1Ch 15:16–16:43
–Organized priests and Levites.... 1Ch 23:26

4. God's covenant with him.......... 2Sa 7:1–17
See COVENANT

5. David's sin and its consequences
–His sin with Bathsheba.......... 2Sa 11:1–5
–Attempt at cover-up 2Sa 11:6–27
–Sin exposed by Nathan........... 2Sa 12:1–14
–Death of his son 2Sa 12:15–23
–Absalom's revolt................ 2Sa 14:1–18:8
–Death of Absalom............... 2Sa 18:9–18
–David mourned Absalom's death . 2Sa 18:33–19:4
–Return to Jerusalem............. 2Sa 19:9–43
–Sheba's revolt 2Sa 20:1–22

6. His last days
–Abishag took care of him 1Ki 1:1–4
–Appointed Solomon king 1Ki 1:28–2:9
–Gave charge to Solomon......... 1Ki 2:1–9
–His last words 2Sa 23:1–7
–His death 1Ki 2:10–12

E. His spiritual life

1. Positive qualities
–Depended on the Lord............ 1Sa 17:45–47
Ps 27:1–6
–Trusted in the Lord............. Ps 25:1–5
–Praised God.................... 1Ch 16:7–10
Ps 9:1–2
–Was concerned about God's
house 1Ch 17:1–2
1Ch 22:5
–Respected those in authority..... 1Sa 24:5
1Sa 26:9–11
–Was faithful to his promises 2Sa 9:1–13
–Repented of his sin............. 2Sa 12:13
Ps 32:3–5

2. Negative qualities
–Took pride in his military power... 2Sa 24:1–10
–Committed adultery with
Bathsheba................... 2Sa 11:1–5
–Committed a murder indirectly ... 2Sa 11:14–17

F. New Testament significance
- –Jesus is David's Son .... Mt 1:1; 2Ti 2:8
- –Jesus is the Root of David .... Rev 5:5; Rev 22:16
- –Jesus sat on David's throne .... Lk 1:30–33
- –David confessed Jesus to be Lord ... Mt 22:42–43
- –David was not a legalist .... Lk 6:1–5
- –David prophesied the resurrection .. Ac 2:25–31
- –David believed righteousness came through faith .... Ro 4:6–8
- –David was a hero of faith .... Heb 11:32–33
- –God spoke through David .... Heb 4:7

DAY

A. Meanings of the word "day"

1. The period of light after the night
   - –Light called "day" by God .... Ge 1:5
   - –"Day and night" .... Ge 8:22; Est 4:16; Jn 9:4–5
   - –Divided into twelve hours .... Mt 20:1–12; Jn 11:9
2. The time period of twenty-four hours .... Ge 1:5,13,19; Ge 8:4–5,13–14; Ex 2:11,13
3. A synonym for "time"
   - –The day of creation .... Dt 4:32
   - –The day of the exodus 1Ki 8:16
   - –The day of the giving of the law ... Nu 15:23
   - –A day of disaster .... Dt 32:35
   - –To the present day .... Jos 4:9
   - –The day of one's death .... Jdg 13:7
   - –The day Jerusalem was built ...... Jer 32:31
   - –The day the temple was built ..... Hag 2:18
   - –The day of salvation 2Co 6:2

B. The day of the Lord

1. In the Old Testament, it can refer to:
   - –The time of God's judgment ...... Joel 1:15; Am 5:18; Am 8:11–14; Zep 1:14–17
   - –The time of Israel's restoration ... Isa 10:20; Isa 11:10–11; Zec 9:16
   - –The first coming of Christ .... Mal 3:1–3
   - –The outpouring of the Spirit ..... Joel 2:28–31
   - –The kingdom of Christ .... Isa 4:2–6; Mic 4:1–7
   - –The end of the world .... Isa 24:21–23; Isa 27:12–13; Zec 14:1–3
2. In the New Testament, it can refer to:
   - –The day of the final battle ...... Rev 16:14
   - –The day of Christ's return .... Mk 13:24–27; 1Co 1:7–8; 2Co 1:14
   - –The day of judgment 1Co 3:12–15; 1Th 5:2–3; 2Pe 3:12
   - –The day of God's wrath .... Ro 2:5–6
   - –The day of blessing for Christians 1Co 1:8; 2Ti 4:8

DEACON

A. Often translated "servant"
- –Used of Jesus .... Ro 15:8
- –Used of Paul 1Co 3:5
- –Used of Timothy 1Ti 4:6
- –Used of any follower of Christ ..... Jn 12:26

B. An office in the New Testament church .... Php 1:1
- –Assistants to apostles .... Ac 6:1–4
- –Qualifications given .... Ac 6:3; 1Ti 3:8–13
- –Possibly women were deaconesses ... Ro 16:1; 1Ti 3:11

DEATH

A. Physical death

1. Phrases used
   - –Dying .... Ge 5:5,8,11,24
   - –Returning to the dust .... Ge 3:19; Ecc 12:7
   - –Lying down in the dust .... Job 7:21
   - –Going to one's fathers .... Ge 15:15
   - –Resting with one's fathers .... Dt 31:16; 2Sa 7:12
   - –Being gathered to one's people ... Ge 25:8; Ge 49:29
   - –Breathing one's last .... Ge 35:29; Lk 23:46
   - –Going down to the grave .... Ge 37:35; 1Ki 2:6,9
   - –Falling asleep .... Jn 11:11; Ac 7:60
   - –Being asleep .... Ps 76:5; Da 12:2
   - –Being away from the body 2Co 5:8
   - –Departing .... Php 1:23; 2Ti 4:6; 2Pe 1:15
2. All human beings die .... Ecc 8:8; Heb 9:27
   - –First examples .... Ge 4:8; Ge 5:5–20,25–31
   - –Two exceptions: Enoch and Elijah .... Ge 5:21–24; 2Ki 2:11–12
3. Death came as a result of sin
   - –A result of Adam's sin .... Ge 2:17; Ro 5:12; 1Co 15:21–22
   - –The wages of sin for everyone .... Ro 6:23
4. Death was conquered by Christ
   - –He was raised from the dead ...... Ro 6:9
   - –He holds the keys of death .... Rev 1:18
   - –He releases us from fear of death .... Heb 2:15
   - –He will destroy death completely 1Co 15:26,53–57
5. What is death for believers?
   - –Falling asleep in Christ 1Co 15:18; 1Th 4:14
   - –Gain .... Php 1:21
   - –Precious to God .... Ps 116:15; Rev 14:13
   - –The entrance into peace .... Isa 57:1–2
   - –The entrance into glory .... Ps 73:24
   - –Clothes us with our heavenly dwelling 2Co 5:4
   - –Prepares us to receive a crown ... 2Ti 4:8
6. What is death for the wicked?
   - –Without salvation .... Eze 3:19; Jn 8:21
   - –Without hope .... Job 8:13; Pr 11:7
   - –A judgment from God .... Nu 16:29–30; Lk 12:20
   - –The pathway to hell .... Lk 16:22–23; Ac 1:25
   - –Not pleasurable to God .... Eze 18:23,32

–Something for them to fear . . . . . . Job 27:19–21
Pr 10:24

B. Spiritual death

1. Its origin

–Came as a result of sin . . . . Ge 2:17
Ro 5:12
Ro 6:23

–Is part of the sinful human nature. . . . . Ro 8:6

2. Who are spiritually dead?

–Everyone who does not have Christ. . . . . Eph 2:1,5
Col 2:13
1Jn 5:12

–Those seeking personal pleasure. . . . . Eph 4:17–19
1Ti 5:6

–Those not serving God by good works. . . . . Heb 6:1
Heb 9:14
Rev 3:1–2

3. How can one overcome spiritual death?

–Through faith in Christ. . . . . Eph 2:4–5
Eph 5:14
1Jn 5:12

–By repenting and turning to God . . . . Lk 15:17–24
Rev 3:1–3

C. Eternal death

1. Phrases used to describe eternal death

–Eternal punishment . . . . Mt 25:46
–Hell . . . . Mt 5:29–30
–The eternal fire . . . . Mt 25:41
–The lake of burning sulfur . . . . Rev 19:20
–The lake of fire . . . . Rev 20:15
–Shut out from God's presence 2Th 1:9
–The darkness outside. . . . . Mt 25:30
–The blackest darkness. . . . . Jude 13
–The second death . . . . Rev 20:6
–The coming wrath 1Th 1:10

2. What is its origin?

–Came as a result of sin . . . . Ge 2:17
Ro 5:12
Ro 6:23
Jas 1:15

–Symbolized by removal from Eden. . . . . Ge 3:22–24

3. Who are subject to eternal death?

–The devil and his angels 2Pe 2:4
Rev 20:10

–The antichrist 2Th 2:8
Rev 19:20

–Those who worship the beast . . . . Rev 14:9–11
–Those who choose the broad road . . . . Mt 7:13
–Those who live a wicked life . . . . . Ro 1:28–31
–Those who do not love the needy . . . . Mt 25:41–46
–Those who do not believe in Jesus . . . . Jn 3:36
–False teachers in the church. 2Pe 2:1–17
–Godless, greedy people in the church. . . . . Jude 4,8–13

4. Jesus conquered eternal death. 1Co 15:20,54–57
2Ti 1:10

5. Who will escape eternal death?

–Those who believe in Jesus . . . . . . Jn 3:16,18,36
Jn 11:25–26

–Those who are raised with Christ. . . . . Ro 6:5–11
–Those who keep the word of God . . . . Jn 8:51
–Those who choose the narrow road . . . . Mt 7:14
–Those who are kind to the needy. . . . . Mt 25:34–40
–Those who do not worship the beast . . . . Rev 20:4–6

DEBORAH

A. Rebekah's nurse. Ge 35:8

B. A prophetess. . . . . Jdg 4:4

–Judged Israel . . . . Jdg 4:5
–Fought Sisera's army with Barak . . . Jdg 4:6–10,14–16
–Deborah's song of triumph . . . . Jdg 5:1–31

DEBT

–What is owed to another person

A. Financial debts

1. Regulated by Old Testament laws

–No interest to be charged . . . . Ex 22:25
Lev 25:36–37
Dt 15:8
Dt 23:19–20

–Security to be returned . . . . Ex 22:26–27
Dt 24:10–13

–The seventh year for canceling debts. . . . . Dt 15:1–6
–The Year of Jubilee for canceling debts. . . . . Lev 25:8–54

2. Examples of oppressed debtors

–Numerous people in David's time. 1Sa 22:2
–A widow in Elisha's day 2Ki 4:1–7
–The poor in Amos's day . . . . Am 2:6–8
–Many Israelites in Nehemiah's day . . . . Neh 5:1–13

3. Warnings against cosigning for a debt . . . . Pr 6:1–5
Pr 11:15
Pr 17:18
Pr 22:26–27

4. Debts in the New Testament world

–Borrowing was common. . . . . Lk 6:34
–Jesus used imagery of debt in parables . . . . Mt 18:23–35
Lk 7:41–42
Lk 11:5–8
Lk 16:1–9

–Jesus used imagery of interest in parables . . . . Mt 25:14–30
Lk 19:12–27

–We must lend without expecting return. . . . . Lk 6:35
–We must pay what is owed . . . . Ro 13:7

B. Debts used as a symbol

1. Debt symbolizes sin . . . . Mt 6:12–15
Mt 18:23–35
Lk 7:41–48

2. Debt symbolizes our Christian obligations

–Paul's debt to preach the gospel . . . Ro 1:14
1Co 9:16

–Our debt to love others . . . . Ro 13:8
–The Gentile debt to Jews. . . . . Ro 15:25–27

DEMETRIUS

–Silversmith in Ephesus . . . . Ac 19:24
–Incited a riot over evangelism there. . . . Ac 19:25–29
–Told to work through legal channels . . . Ac 19:38–40

DEMONS

–Evil spirits that can afflict humans

A. The characteristics of demons

1. Their identity

–They are related to false gods Dt 32:17; Ps 106:37; 1Co 10:20; Rev 9:20
–They are also called evil spirits Mk 5:12–13; 1Ti 4:1
2. Their behavior
–Insane raving Mk 1:23–24; Mk 5:2–5
–Self-destructive behavior Mk 5:5; Mk 9:22
–Convulsions Mk 9:18,20
–Could cause physical ailments Mt 12:22
–Could speak Mk 1:34; Mk 5:12
–Could perform miracles Rev 16:13–14
B. The relationship of demons to Jesus
1. They recognized Jesus Mt 8:28–29; Mk 1:23–24; Ac 19:13–16
2. They were driven out in the name of Jesus
–By Jesus himself Mk 1:23–24, 32–34; Mk 5:1–13; Mk 9:14–27
–By the followers of Jesus Mk 16:17; Lk 10:17; Ac 5:16; Ac 16:16–18
3. Jesus' power over demons demonstrates
–That he was not influenced by Beelzebub Mt 12:25–29; Mk 3:23–27; Lk 11:17–22
–That the kingdom of God worked in Jesus Mt 12:28; Lk 11:20

DEPRAVITY
See SIN

DEPRESSION
–The feeling of despair over life's problems
A. Examples of depressed people
–Moses Nu 11:10–15
–Elijah 1Ki 19:1–4
–Job Job 3:1–26
–The psalmist Ps 42:1–11
–The Teacher Ecc 2:20
–Jonah Jnh 4:3
B. Perspectives for depressed people
–Being reminded of God's presence 1Ki 19:11–13
–Experiencing the Holy Spirit Isa 61:1–3; Jn 16:6–7
–Placing hope and trust in God Ps 31:24; Ps 42:5,11; Heb 6:18–19
–Casting anxiety on God 1Pe 5:7
–Receiving the support of believers 1Sa 20:41–42; Job 2:11–13; Job 42:10–11; 1Th 5:11

DESPAIR
See DEPRESSION

DEVIL
See SATAN

DEVOTION
See MEDITATION

DINAH
–Daughter of Jacob Ge 30:21; Ge 46:15
–Raped by Shechem Ge 34:1–4
–Avenged by Simeon and Levi Ge 34:25–29

DISCIPLESHIP
–Following the lifestyle outlined by Jesus
A. Related theme
DISCIPLESHIP is a theme of Matthew Mt 10:25
B. Who are called disciples?
–Twelve chosen followers of Jesus Mk 3:16–19
–Believers in Jesus Ac 6:7; Ac 9:1; Ac 11:26
C. What is expected of disciples?
–Commitment to Jesus Mt 8:19–22; Mk 1:17–18; Lk 14:26–27
–Humble service Mk 10:43–44
–Following teachings of the Sermon on the Mount Mt 5:1–7:27
–Doing the will of God Mt 12:49–50
–Loving one another Jn 13:34–35; Jn 15:9–17
–Sharing with one another Ac 4:32–37; Ac 11:28–29
–Making disciples of all nations Mt 28:19
D. What happens to Jesus' disciples?
–They receive eternal life Mk 10:29–30
–Jesus teaches them Lk 11:2–4
–Jesus acknowledges them before his Father Mt 10:32
–They are called Christians Ac 11:26
–They may have to suffer Jn 15:20; 2Ti 3:12
–They may experience rejection Mt 10:22,34–35; Jn 15:18,21; Jn 17:14
–They need strengthening Ac 14:21–22; Ac 18:23

DISCIPLINE
–Measures taken to ensure conformity to the accepted standard
A. Related theme
DISCIPLINE is a theme of 1 Corinthians 1Co 5:5
B. Methods of discipline
1. Human discipline
–By instruction and warning Pr 1:2–4,8–10; 2Ti 4:2; Titus 2:15
–By the rod Pr 13:24; Pr 22:15
2. God's discipline of us
–By instruction and warning Jer 7:27–28; Jer 17:23
–By adversity and affliction Lev 26:23–26; Job 33:19; Ps 39:10–11; Jer 2:30
C. Motives of discipline
–Love 2Sa 7:14–15; Pr 3:12; Heb 12:6; Rev 3:19
–Desire for another's growth and improvement Job 5:17; Pr 25:12; Pr 29:15; Heb 12:10
D. Types of discipline
1. Self-discipline Ro 6:12–14; Ro 8:13; 1Co 9:26–27

2. Discipline in the home .... Pr 13:24
Pr 15:5
Pr 19:18

3. Mutual discipline
–Between friends .... Pr 17:10
Pr 27:5–6
Pr 28:23
–Among believers............ Lk 17:3
1Th 5:11,14–15
2Th 3:15

4. Church discipline
a. Done through preaching the word............ 2Ti 3:16–17
2Ti 4:2
Titus 2:15

b. Done through direct measures
–Rebuke sinners publicly....... 1Ti 5:20
Titus 1:13
–Have nothing to do with sinners............ Ro 16:17
1Co 5:9–11
2Th 3:6,14
Titus 3:10
–Remove sinners from the church............ 1Co 5:1–5,13
1Ti 1:20

DIVORCE

–The breaking of the marital bond

A. Physical divorce

1. Divorce in the Old Testament
–Not part of God's original plan.... Ge 2:24
Mt 19:8
–Allowed and regulated .... Dt 22:13–19, 28–29
Dt 24:1–4
–Evidence of human stubbornness .... Mt 19:8
–Priests not to marry divorcees.... Lev 21:7,14
–Hated by God............ Mal 2:16
–Defiled the land............ Jer 3:1–2
–Required for those with idolatrous wives............ Ezr 10:2–17

2. Divorce in the New Testament
–Marriage considered binding..... Mt 19:3–6
Ro 7:2–3
–Permitted by Jesus for unfaithfulness .... Mt 5:31–33
Mt 19:9
–Permitted by Paul in mixed marriages 1Co 7:12–15
–Divorce was a pardonable sin .... Jn 4:17–18,39–42

B. Spiritual divorce

1. A result of sin and idolatry .... Isa 50:1
Jer 3:2

2. Northern kingdom: divorced by God .... Jer 3:8

3. Southern kingdom of Judah
–Equally as adulterous as Israel ... Jer 3:8–11
–Temporary separation through the exile............ Isa 50:1
Isa 54:7
–Taken back by God as spouse .... Isa 54:6–8
Isa 62:4–5

See also ADULTERY
MARRIAGE

DOCTRINE

–True teachings concerning faith and life

A. Related themes

1. DIRECTION is a theme of Proverbs Pr 3:5
2. DEFENSE is a theme of Colossians Col 2:8
3. DISCERNMENT is a theme of 2 John............ 2Jn 10
4. FALSE DOCTRINE is a theme of 1 Timothy 1Ti 1:3
5. FALSE TEACHERS is a theme of:
–2 Peter 2Pe 2:1
–Jude .... Jude 4

B. The importance of knowing doctrine
–Stressed in the Old Testament...... Ps 78:1–8
Pr 7:1–5
Pr 13:14
–Stressed in the New Testament..... 1Co 11:2
2Th 2:15
2Ti 1:13
Titus 1:9
Titus 2:1

See also CONFESSION
EDUCATION

C. Concern over false doctrine

1. The identity of false teachers
–The teachers of the law .... Mt 23:2–4,16–22
Mk 12:38–40
Lk 20:46–47
1Ti 1:6–7
–Teachers of unsound doctrine.... 1Ti 4:1–3
2Ti 4:3–4
Titus 1:9–11
–Teachers who distort the truth ... Ac 20:29–30
2Ti 2:17–18
–Teachers who introduce heresies... 2Pe 2:1
2Jn 7
–Teachers who cause divisions....... Ro 16:17
1Ti 6:3–5
–Teachers who promote immorality 2Ti 3:6–8
Rev 2:14,20

2. Commands concerning false teachers
–Watch out for them............ Mk 12:38
Lk 20:46
Ac 20:31
2Jn 8
–Command them to stop teaching... 1Ti 1:3–4
Titus 1:10–11,13–14
–Withdraw from them............ Ro 16:17
2Ti 2:16–18
2Jn 10–11

DOEG

–An Edomite; Saul's head shepherd..... 1Sa 21:7
–Reported to Saul about priests of Nob... 1Sa 22:9–10
–Killed the priests of Nob for Saul 1Sa 22:18–19
–David wrote a psalm about the incident .... Ps 52:1–9

DOG

See ANIMALS

DORCAS

–Disciple in Joppa who died............ Ac 9:36–37
–Raised to life by God via Peter .... Ac 9:38–41

DOUBT

–A questioning of one's faith

A. Examples of believers who doubted
–Abram............ Ge 12:10–20
Ge 15:2–3
Ge 16:1–4
Ge 20:1–13
–Moses............ Ex 33:15–19
–Gideon............ Jdg 6:36–37,39
–John the Baptist .... Mt 11:2–3
–Peter............ Mt 14:28–31
–Martha .... Jn 11:39
–Some disciples............ Mt 28:17
–Thomas............ Jn 20:24–25

B. Ending doubt
- 1. How doubts were ended
  - –Abram, by believing God's word... Ge 15:6
  - –Moses, by seeing God's glory .... Ex 33:21–23
  - –Gideon, by throwing out the fleece.......... Jdg 6:36–40
  - –John, by seeing Christ's miracles.......... Mt 11:4–6
  - –Peter, by reaching out to Christ... Mt 14:30–31
  - –Thomas, by seeing the risen Christ.......... Jn 20:26–29
- 2. God wants us to overcome doubt... Mk 11:22–24; Jas 1:6; Jude 22

DOVE
See BIRDS

DREAMS AND VISIONS
A. Dreams and visions in general
- –Closely related.......... Da 7:1–2
- –Used by God for revelation.......... Nu 12:6
- –Authenticity must be tested .... Dt 13:1–5
- –God alone can interpret dreams .... Ge 40:8; Ge 41:16; Da 2:27–28

B. Examples of dreams and visions used for revelation
- 1. Dreams
  - –Jacob.......... Ge 28:12–16
  - –Joseph.......... Ge 37:5–9
  - –Pharaoh, interpreted by Joseph.......... Ge 41:1–36
  - –Solomon.......... 1Ki 3:5
  - –Nebuchadnezzar, interpreted by Daniel.......... Da 2:24–47; Da 4:4–27
  - –Joseph, husband of Mary........ Mt 1:20–21
- 2. Visions
  - –Abram.......... Ge 15:1
  - –Jacob.......... Ge 46:2
  - –Samuel.......... 1Sa 3:10–15
  - –Various prophets .... Isa 1:1; Da 7:1; Ob 1; Mic 1:1; Na 1:1
  - –Cornelius .... Ac 10:3–6
  - –Peter.......... Ac 10:9–17
  - –Paul.......... Ac 18:9

C. Warnings against those who feign dreams.......... Jer 23:25–28; Eze 13:3–9; Zec 10:2; Jude 8

DROUGHT
See HUNGER AND THIRST

DRUGS
See ALCOHOL

DRUNKENNESS
See ALCOHOL

DUST
A. Humans are creatures of dust
- –Created from the dust of the ground .... Ge 2:7; Ecc 3:20; 1Co 15:47
- –Pictures human frailty .... Ps 103:14
- –Will return to the dust.......... Ge 3:19; Ps 104:29; Ecc 12:7

B. Dust used as a symbol
- –Dust symbolizes a large number.... Ge 13:16; Nu 23:10
- –Rain turned into dust as God's judgment .... Dt 28:24
- –Dust on the head expresses grief ... Job 2:12; Isa 47:1
- –Sitting in dust expresses repentance.......... Jnh 3:6
- –Lying in dust expresses humiliation .... Ps 44:25; Ps 113:7
- –Lying down in dust means death ... Job 7:21; Ps 7:5
- –Enemies licking the dust means defeat .... Ps 72:9; Mic 7:17
- –Shaking dust off the feet means rejection.......... Mt 10:14; Ac 13:51
- –Throwing dust in the air expresses shock.......... Ac 22:23

EAGLE
See BIRDS

EAR
A. The human ear
- 1. Uses for the human ear
  - –To hear 2Sa 7:22
  - –To acquire wisdom and knowledge .... Pr 2:2; Pr 18:15
  - –To wear earrings .... Ge 35:4
  - –To designate, by piercing, a permanent servant .... Ex 21:6
- 2. Types of human ears
  - –The ear eager to listen to Jesus ... Mt 11:15
  - –The ear eager to listen to the Spirit.......... Rev 2:7,11,17,29
  - –The understanding ear .... Job 13:1
  - –The deaf ear.......... Isa 43:8
  - –The closed ear.......... Jer 6:10
  - –The uncircumcised ear .... Ac 7:51
  - –The ear itching to hear falsehood.......... 2Ti 4:3

B. The ears of God
- –His ears are attentive to our prayers.......... Ps 34:15; 1Pe 3:12
- –His ears hear the cries of the oppressed.......... Jas 5:4
- –His ear is not dull .... Isa 59:1
- –His ears hear insolence.......... 2Ki 19:28
- –He closes his ears to sinners.......... Eze 8:18
- –We can ask God to give ear to us.... Ps 5:1; Ps 17:1,6; Ps 130:2

EARTH
A. God and the earth
- 1. His actions regarding it
  - –He created it.......... Ge 1:1
  - –He laid its foundations.......... Heb 1:10
  - –He suspended it in space.......... Job 26:7
  - –He called forth plants from it.......... Ge 1:11
  - –He called forth animals from it .... Ge 1:24
  - –He made people from it.......... Ge 2:7
  - –He filled it with his creatures..... Ps 104:24
  - –He holds it firmly .... Ps 75:3
  - –He governs it .... Job 34:12–15
  - –He will judge it .... Ps 96:13
  - *See also* CREATION PROVIDENCE

2. His relationship to it
–He owns it ... Ps 24:1
1Co 10:26
–He is King over all of it ... Ps 47:2,7,9
–He loves it ... Ps 33:5
–His glory fills it ... Isa 6:3
–His knowledge will fill it ... Isa 11:9
Hab 2:14
–It is his footstool ... Isa 66:1
Mt 5:35

B. Humans and the earth
–Made from the earth ... Ge 2:7
1Co 15:47
–It is given to humans ... Ps 115:16
–Humans must fill and rule it ... Ge 1:28
Ge 9:7
Ps 8:6–8
–Believers shall inherit it ... Mt 5:5
Ro 4:13

C. The earth and sin
–Ground cursed after Adam's sin ... Ge 3:17–19
–Earth groans as a result of sin ... Ro 8:22
–Earth became the domain for Satan ... Rev 12:9
–Earth waits for redemption ... Ro 8:20–21
–God will someday make a new earth ... Isa 65:17
2Pe 3:13
Rev 21:1

EARTHQUAKE

–At the Lord's appearance to Elijah ... 1Ki 19:11–12
–At the Lord's judgment of Jerusalem ... Isa 29:5–6
–During the reign of Uzziah ... Am 1:1
Zec 14:5
–After the death of Christ ... Mt 27:54
–At the resurrection of Christ ... Mt 28:2
–During Paul's imprisonment in Philippi ... Ac 16:26
–As a sign of Christ's coming ... Mt 24:4–8
Mk 13:3–8
Lk 21:7–11
–In the great tribulation ... Rev 6:12
Rev 11:13
–In God's final judgment ... Rev 16:17–18

EDOMITES

A. Their identity
–The descendants of Esau (Edom) ... Ge 25:30
Ge 36:8–9
–Lived in hill country, southeast of Israel ... Ge 36:9
–Country also called Mount Seir ... Ge 32:3
–Territory bordered on Judah ... Jos 15:21

B. Significant Edomites
–Numerous kings listed ... Ge 36:31–39
1Ch 1:43–50
–Doeg: head shepherd of King Saul ... 1Sa 21:7
1Sa 22:9,18–19
–Hadad: fought against Solomon ... 1Ki 11:14–22

C. Their wars
–Defeated by King Saul ... 1Sa 14:47
–Defeated by David ... 2Sa 8:11–14
1Ch 18:11–13
–Defeated Moab with Israel and Judah ... 2Ki 3:1–27
–Allied with Moab against Jehoshaphat ... 2Ch 20:1,10
–Their warriors killed by Moabites and Ammonites ... 2Ch 20:22–24
–Defeated Jehoram of Judah ... 2Ki 8:20–22
2Ch 21:8–10
–Defeated by King Amaziah ... 2Ki 14:7
2Ch 25:10–12
–Defeated King Ahaz of Judah ... 2Ch 28:17

D. Important data concerning them
–Refused passage to Israelites in desert ... Nu 20:14–21
–Israelites passed around their country ... Nu 21:4
Jdg 11:17–18
–Solomon intermarried with them ... 1Ki 11:1
–Prophecies concerning their destruction ... Isa 34:4–15
Jer 49:7–22
Eze 25:12–14
Eze 35:1–15
Am 1:11–12
Ob 1–21

EDUCATION

A. People as educators
1. Primary educators: parents
–A never-ending task ... Dt 4:9
Dt 6:4–7
Pr 1:8
Pr 6:20
–Done by fathers ... Ge 18:19
Ps 44:1
Eph 6:4
–Done by mothers ... Pr 6:20
2Ti 1:5
2Ti 3:15
2. Officials authorized by a government ... Ezr 7:6,10
2Ch 17:7–9
Neh 8:7–8
Ac 7:22
3. Authorized religious officials ... Mk 12:28
Jn 3:10
Ac 22:3
4. The apostles ... Mt 28:20
Ac 2:42
Ac 4:2
5. People gifted by the Spirit ... 1Co 12:28–29
Eph 4:11
6. Any mature Christian ... Heb 5:11–14

B. The content of education
–The law of God ... Dt 6:6–7
Dt 33:10
–The praiseworthy deeds of God ... Ps 78:4–6
–The holy Scriptures ... 2Ti 3:14–17
–General knowledge and wisdom ... Da 1:17
Col 2:3

C. The foundation of education
–The fear of God ... Ps 111:10
Pr 1:7
Pr 9:10
–Knowing the Lord Jesus Christ ... 1Co 1:30
Col 2:3

D. Purpose of education
–To impart information ... Ps 78:4–6
–To inspire trust and obedience ... Ps 78:7–8
Pr 22:19
–To inspire wisdom ... Pr 4:5–8
–To attain skill in holy living ... Ge 18:19
Pr 1:2–4
2Ti 3:17
–To prepare for adulthood ... Pr 22:6

EGLON

A. City in Canaan ... Jos 10:3
–Its king joined others against the city of Gibeon ... Jos 10:3–8
–Defeated by Joshua ... Jos 10:9–14

B. King of Moab ... Jdg 3:12–14
–Killed by Ehud ... Jdg 3:16–23

EGYPT

A. Names and geography

1. Other terms for Egypt
   - –The land of Ham ... Ps 105:23
   - –The land of slavery ... Ex 20:2
   - –The South ... Da 11:5
   - –Rahab ... Isa 51:9–10

2. Areas of Egypt
   - –Upper and Lower Egypt ... Isa 11:11
   - –The Nile River ... Eze 29:3
   - –The land of Goshen ... Ge 47:6
   - –Rameses, a district in Goshen ... Ge 47:11
   - –Pithom and Rameses: built by Israelites ... Ex 1:11
   - –Memphis, the capital city ... Hos 9:6
   - –Thebes ... Eze 30:14
   - –Tahpanhes, the city to which Jews fled ... Jer 43:8; Jer 44:1

B. Important Egyptians
   - –Their kings were called Pharaohs *See* PHARAOH
   - –Hagar: servant of Sarai ... Ge 16:1
   - –Potiphar: owner of Joseph ... Ge 39:1
   - –Shishak: ransacked the temple ... 1Ki 14:25–26

C. Interaction with God's people

1. During the time of the patriarchs
   - –Abram went to Egypt during famine ... Ge 12:10–20
   - –Joseph sold there by merchants ... Ge 37:28
   - –Joseph became governor of Egypt ... Ge 41:33–45
   - –Joseph's brothers bought grain there ... Ge 42:1–26; Ge 43:1–44:3
   - –Jacob and his sons moved there ... Ge 46:1–47:12

2. At the time of the exodus *See* EXODUS

3. During the time of the kings
   - –Solomon intermarried with them ... 1Ki 3:1
   - –Solomon ruled territory to its border ... 1Ki 4:21
   - –Solomon traded with them ... 1Ki 10:28–29; 2Ch 1:16–17
   - –Enemies of Solomon fled there ... 1Ki 11:14–18; 1Ki 11:40
   - –Gained victory over Rehoboam ... 1Ki 14:25–26; 2Ch 12:1–12
   - –Hoshea allied with them against Syria ... 2Ki 17:4
   - –Josiah killed in a battle against them ... 2Ki 23:29–30; 2Ch 35:20–24
   - –Jehoahaz deposed by king of Egypt ... 2Ki 23:33–35; 2Ch 36:2–4
   - –Jews fled there after death of Gedaliah ... 2Ki 25:25–26
   - –Jeremiah forced to go there ... Jer 43:4–7

4. In the New Testament
   - –Jesus and his parents fled there ... Mt 2:13–15
   - –Egyptian Jews in Jerusalem on Pentecost ... Ac 2:10

D. Prophecies concerning Egypt
   - –God's people to be enslaved there ... Ge 15:13
   - –God's people to be freed ... Ge 15:14; Ex 3:7–10
   - –Judgment against Egypt ... Isa 19:1–17; Jer 46:2–26; Eze 29:3–30:26
   - –Judgment on those who seek help from Egypt ... Isa 30:1–3; Isa 31:1–4; Jer 2:18–19, 36–37; Jer 42:7–22; Hos 7:11–16
   - –God will call his people back from Egypt ... Isa 11:10–11; Isa 27:12–13
   - –God will call his Son from Egypt ... Hos 11:1; Mt 2:15
   - –Egyptians will someday worship the Lord ... Isa 19:18–25; Isa 45:14; Mic 7:11–13

EHUD

- –Left-handed judge of Israel ... Jdg 3:15
- –Killed Eglon ... Jdg 3:16–23
- –Led Israelites against Moabites ... Jdg 3:26–30

ELAH

- –Son of Baasha ... 1Ki 16:6
- –Became king of Israel ... 1Ki 16:6,8
- –Murdered by Zimri ... 1Ki 16:9–10

ELDER

A. Elders in the Old Testament
   - –Assisted in government ... Nu 11:16–17
   - –Advised kings ... 1Ki 12:6–7
   - –Judged the people ... Dt 22:13–19
   - –Witnessed legal matters ... Ru 4:2–11
   - –Performed religious rituals ... Ex 12:21
   - –Represented the tribes ... 1Ki 8:1–3
   - –Helped educate the people ... Ex 19:7

B. Elders in the New Testament

1. In Jewish society
   - –Leaders of the people ... Mt 27:12; Ac 24:1
   - –Established religious tradition ... Mt 15:2

2. In the church
   - –Synonymous with "overseer" ... Titus 1:6–7
   - –Appointed by the apostles ... Ac 14:23; Titus 1:5
   - –Qualifications given ... 1Ti 3:1–7; Titus 1:5–9
   - –Directed the affairs of church ... 1Ti 5:17
   - –Preached and taught the truth ... 1Ti 3:2; 1Ti 5:17
   - –Guarded against false teaching ... Ac 20:29–31; Titus 1:9
   - –Served as pastors ... Ac 20:28; Jas 5:14; 1Pe 5:1–3
   - –Church members should submit to them ... 1Th 5:12; Heb 13:7,17

3. Twenty-four elders in heaven
   - –They are seated on thrones ... Rev 4:4; Rev 11:16
   - –They worship God ... Rev 4:10; Rev 5:8–14; Rev 7:11–12; Rev 19:4

ELEAZAR

- –Son of Aaron ... Ex 6:23–25
- –Became high priest after Aaron ... Nu 20:26–28; Dt 10:6
- –Took census with Moses ... Nu 26:1–4
- –Aided Joshua in dividing up Canaan ... Jos 14:1
- –His death ... Jos 24:33

ELECTION

–Being chosen by God

A. Related theme
CHOOSING is a theme
of Deuteronomy ... Dt 7:6

B. Examples of people chosen by God

1. In the Old Testament
–Abraham ... Ge 18:19
–Jacob ... Ge 25:23
–Moses ... Ps 106:23
–Aaron ... Nu 17:1–8
–Saul ... 1Sa 10:24
–David ... 1Sa 16:1,12
2Sa 6:21
–People of Israel ... Isa 41:8–9
–Servant of the Lord ... Isa 42:1

2. In the New Testament
–Jesus, God's Son ... Lk 9:35
–The disciples ... Jn 15:16
–Paul ... Ac 9:15
Gal 1:15
–The church ... 1Pe 2:9
–Individual Christians ... Eph 1:4
1Pe 1:2

C. The basis of election
–God's love ... Dt 10:14–15
Eph 1:4
2Ti 1:9
–God's grace ... Ro 11:5–6
–God's faithfulness to his
promises ... Dt 7:7–8
–God's decision to fulfill his
purposes ... Ro 9:11
–God's foreknowledge ... Ro 8:29
1Pe 1:2
–Not based on human works ... Ro 9:11–12

D. The purposes of election

1. For God
–To show his grace ... Ro 11:5–6
Eph 1:7
–To redeem his children ... Eph 1:5,7
2Th 2:13

2. For the elect
–To come to faith ... Ac 13:48
2Th 2:13
–To assure us of salvation ... Isa 41:9–10
Ro 8:33–34
2Pe 1:10
–To praise God ... Eph 1:11–12
–To become like Christ ... Ro 8:29
–To do good works ... Eph 2:10
Col 3:12
–To bear fruit ... Jn 15:16
–To witness to others ... Isa 42:1,6–7
Ac 9:15

ELI

–High priest ... 1Sa 1:9
–Blessed Hannah ... 1Sa 1:12–18
–Raised Samuel ... 1Sa 2:11–21
–Grieved over his sons'
wickedness ... 1Sa 2:22–25
–Did not restrain his sons ... 1Sa 3:13
–Prophet spoke against him ... 1Sa 2:27–36
–His death ... 1Sa 4:12–22

ELIHU

–Younger friend of Job ... Job 32:4
–Angry with Job and his friends ... Job 32:2–3
–Gave a lengthy speech ... Job 32:6–37:24

ELIJAH

A. His life as a prophet of God
–Predicted drought in Israel ... 1Ki 17:1
Jas 5:17
–Fed by ravens ... 1Ki 17:2–6
–Stayed with a widow in Zarephath ... 1Ki 17:7–16
–Raised the widow's dead son ... 1Ki 17:17–24
–Challenged Baal's prophets to
a contest ... 1Ki 18:19–26
–Prayed for fire from heaven ... 1Ki 18:30–39
–Killed the prophets of Baal ... 1Ki 18:40
–Prayed for rain ... 1Ki 18:41–45
–Fled from Jezebel ... 1Ki 19:1–3
–Prayed that he might die ... 1Ki 19:4–5
–Strengthened by the Lord ... 1Ki 19:6–18
–Anointed Elisha as successor ... 1Ki 19:19–21
–Confronted Ahab after death
of Naboth ... 1Ki 21:17–29
–Prophesied death of Azariah ... 2Ki 1:3–17
–Taken to heaven without dying ... 2Ki 2:11–12

B. Later references
–Malachi prophesied his return ... Mal 4:5–6
–John the Baptist likened to him ... Mt 17:9–13
Mk 9:9–13
–Jesus compared to him ... Mt 16:14
–Jesus compared his rejection
to Elijah's ... Lk 4:24–26
–Appeared to Jesus in the
transfiguration ... Mt 17:1–8
Mk 9:1–8
–Paul recalled a remnant in
Elijah's day ... Ro 11:2–5
–His prayers are an example for us ... Jas 5:17–18

ELIMELECH

–Husband of Naomi ... Ru 1:2
–Fled to Moab during famine ... Ru 1:1
–Died in Moab ... Ru 1:3

ELIPHAZ

A. Firstborn son of Esau ... Ge 36:4,10

B. One of Job's friends who tried to
comfort him ... Job 2:11
–His first speech ... Job 4:1–5:27
–His second speech ... Job 15:1–35
–His third speech ... Job 22:1–30
–Offered sacrifices to God after
Job's restoration ... Job 42:7–9

ELISHA

A. His association with Elijah
–Anointed by Elijah as successor ... 1Ki 19:16–21
–Accompanied Elijah on his
last day ... 2Ki 2:1–8
–Inherited Elijah's cloak ... 2Ki 2:9–13
–Divided the Jordan with Elijah's
cloak ... 2Ki 2:14

B. His ministry
–Purified bad water ... 2Ki 2:19–22
–Pronounced a curse on mocking
young men ... 2Ki 2:23–25
–Aided Israelites in the defeat
of Moab ... 2Ki 3:11–20
–Increased widow's oil ... 2Ki 4:1–7
–Raised Shunammite's son ... 2Ki 4:8–37
–Purified food by a miracle ... 2Ki 4:38–41
–Fed a hundred men by a miracle ... 2Ki 4:42–44
–Healed Naaman's leprosy ... 2Ki 5:1–19
–Caused axhead to float ... 2Ki 6:1–7
–Captured Arameans ... 2Ki 6:8–23
–Advised king of Israel ... 2Ki 6:24–8:6
–Prophesied end to siege
of Arameans ... 2Ki 7:1–2
–Prophesied Ben-Hadad's death ... 2Ki 8:7–15
–Anointed Jehu as king of Israel ... 2Ki 9:1–3
–Prophesied victory for Jehoash ... 2Ki 13:14–17
–His death ... 2Ki 13:20

–Quarreled with Gideon .... Jdg 8:1–3
–Quarreled with Jephthah .... Jdg 12:1–6
–Many joined kingdom of Judah during Asa's reform 2Ch 15:8–9

C. A synonym for the northern kingdom .... Isa 7:17
Hos 5:5

ESAU

A. His birth
–Firstborn of Isaac .... Ge 25:25
–Twin with Jacob .... Ge 25:26
–Also called Edom .... Ge 25:30

B. Significant events
–Became a hunter .... Ge 25:27
–Sold his birthright .... Ge 25:29–34
–His blessing stolen by Jacob .... Ge 27:1–40
–Wanted to kill Jacob .... Ge 27:41
–Married pagan women .... Ge 26:34
Ge 28:6–9
–Reconciled to Jacob .... Ge 33:1–17
–With Jacob, buried Isaac .... Ge 35:29

C. His descendants .... Ge 36:1–43
See EDOMITES

D. Later significance of Esau
–Descendants to be obliterated .... Ob 1–21
Jer 49:7–22
–Jacob chosen over him .... Mal 1:2–3
–Demonstrates God's purpose of election .... Ro 9:11–13
–His rejection for not repenting .... Heb 12:16–17

ESTHER

–Daughter of Abihail .... Est 2:15
–Cousin of Mordecai .... Est 2:7
–Chosen queen by Ahasuerus (Xerxes) .... Est 2:8–18
–Objected to appearing before Ahasuerus (Xerxes) .... Est 4:10–11
–Asked for a fast .... Est 4:15–16
–Risked her life by approaching Ahasuerus (Xerxes) .... Est 5:1–2
–Foiled Haman's plan to kill Jews .... Est 7:1–8
–Caused Haman's execution .... Est 7:9–10
–Her plan preserved the Jews .... Est 8:1–9:17
–Decreed celebration of Purim .... Est 9:18–32

ETERNAL

–Without end in time

A. Eternity related to humans
1. The human body does not live forever .... Ecc 12:7
See DEATH
2. Eternal life for believers
–Jesus came to give eternal life .... Jn 11:25–26
2Ti 1:10
1Jn 5:11–12
–We receive eternal life through faith .... Jn 3:16,36
1Jn 5:13
–We receive eternal salvation through Christ .... Heb 5:9
Heb 9:12
–We have an eternal house in heaven 2Co 5:1
–We are called into God's eternal glory 1Pe 5:10
–We enter an eternal *kingdom* 2Pe 1:11
–We receive an eternal inheritance .... Heb 9:15
3. Eternal punishment for the wicked .... Mt 25:46
2Th 1:9
Rev 21:8

B. Eternity related to God
1. His being and person
–God is the eternal God .... Dt 33:27
–God is the eternal Rock .... Isa 26:4
–God is from everlasting to everlasting .... Ps 90:2
–God lives forever .... Isa 57:15
–God's name endures forever .... Ps 135:13
–God is not bound by time .... Ps 90:4
2Pe 3:8
Rev 1:8
2. His attributes
–He does not change .... Ps 102:27
Mal 3:6
Heb 13:8
–His love endures forever 2Ch 7:3,6
Ps 136:1–26
–His righteousness endures forever .... Ps 111:3
2Co 9:9
–His faithfulness endures forever .... Ps 100:5
Ps 117:2
–His purpose for humanity is eternal .... Eph 3:11
–His power is eternal .... Ro 1:20
3. His kingdom
–God is the eternal King 1Ti 1:17
–His kingdom is eternal .... Ps 145:13
Da 4:3,34
–Christ reigns forever and ever .... Rev 11:15
4. His everlasting covenant
–With Abraham, Isaac, Jacob .... Ge 17:7–8
1Ch 16:17
–With David 2Sa 7:13–16
2Sa 23:5
–With us in the new covenant .... Isa 55:3
Jer 32:40
Eze 37:26
5. God's word is eternal .... Ps 119:89
Isa 40:8
1Pe 1:24–25

EUPHRATES

–One of the rivers of Eden .... Ge 2:14
–Abraham came from beyond it .... Jos 24:2–3
–Israel's borders to expand there .... Ge 15:18
Dt 11:22–25
–Hittites controlled it .... Jos 1:4
–David expanded kingdom to it 2Sa 8:3
1Ch 18:3
–Solomon's kingdom bordered on it 1Ki 4:21
Ps 72:8
–Assyrians controlled it 2Ki 23:29
Isa 8:7–8
–Babylon controlled it 2Ki 24:1
Jer 46:2
–Christ's kingdom to reach to it .... Zec 9:9–10
–Army of the final battle to come from there .... Rev 9:14
Rev 16:12

EVANGELISM

See MISSION

EVE

A. Eve in the Old Testament
1. Her history
–Made in God's image .... Ge 1:27
Ge 5:1–2
–Made from Adam's rib .... Ge 2:22
–Became Adam's wife .... Ge 2:23–24
–Entered conversation with serpent .... Ge 3:1–5

–Ate forbidden fruit with Adam . . . Ge 3:6
–Tried to hide from God . . . . Ge 3:8
–Blamed serpent for her sin . . . . Ge 3:13
–Received curse from God . . . . Ge 3:16
–Banished with Adam from Eden . . . Ge 3:23
–Mother of Cain, Abel and Seth . . . Ge 4:1–2,25

2. Her significance as mother of all humans. . . . . Ge 3:20

B. Eve in the New Testament
–Significance of Eve being created after Adam. 1Co 11:8; 1Ti 2:13
–Significance of Eve deceived by serpent 2Co 11:3

EXAMPLE

A. Old Testament people as examples
1. As warnings. 1Co 10:6–11; 2Ti 3:8
2. As models for Christian behavior
–Job in his perseverance. . . . . Jas 5:10–11
–Elijah in his prayers. . . . . Jas 5:16–18
–Numerous saints in their faith. . . . Heb 11:4–40

B. Christ as an example
–His humility. . . . . Php 2:5–8
–His love . . . . Jn 15:12–13; Eph 5:2
–His service . . . . Jn 13:14–15
–His gentleness . . . . Mt 11:29
–His consideration of others. . . . . Ro 15:2–3
–His grace of giving 2Co 8:7–9
–His forgiveness . . . . Col 3:13
–His purity 1Jn 3:3
–His unjust suffering 1Pe 2:20–23
–His obedience to the Father . . . . Jn 15:10
–His general walk of life 1Jn 2:6

C. Paul as an example
–Thessalonians followed his example 1Th 1:6
–Churches encouraged to imitate him . . . . 1Co 4:16; 1Co 11:1; Php 3:17; 2Th 3:7,9

D. Christians as examples
–The Thessalonians were examples. . . 1Th 1:7
–Church leaders must be examples . . . 1Ti 4:12; Titus 2:7; 1Pe 5:3
–We must all be examples. . . . . Mt 5:16; Php 2:14–15; 1Pe 2:12

EXHORTATION

See ENCOURAGEMENT

EXILE

–The captivity of the people of Judah by the Babylonians

A. Judah carried away into Babylon
1. The story of the exile told 2Ki 24:11–16; 2Ki 25:11
2. Three waves of exiles. . . . . Jer 52:28–30
–Daniel in the first . . . . Da 1:1–6
–Ezekiel in the second. . . . . Eze 1:1–3
–Remainder of the people in the third. 2Ch 36:20
3. Reasons for the exile
–Because of the sins of Manasseh. . 2Ki 21:10–15; Jer 15:1–4
–Because of Judah's idolatry . . . . . . Dt 28:45–52; Isa 40:2; Jer 5:7–17; Eze 6:1–8
–Because Judah failed to heed prophets. 2Ch 36:15–20
4. Lessons the Jews learned in the exile
–That God was everywhere . . . . Eze 11:16
–That God was Redeemer. . . . . Isa 59:12–20
–That God still loved them . . . . Jer 30:10–11, 18–22; Eze 34:20–31
–That the Law was important . . . . . Ezr 7:10; Neh 8:1–9

B. The return from exile
–Occurred after seventy years. . . . . . . Jer 25:11
–God remembered his promises . . . . . Jer 29:10
–God remembered his covenant . . . . . Eze 16:60
–Cyrus decreed the Jews could return . . . . 2Ch 36:23; Ezr 1:2–4
–The Jews returned in two groups . . . Ezr 1:5–6; Ezr 7:1–9

EXODUS

–The escape of the Israelites from Egypt

A. Related themes
FREEDOM is a theme of Exodus. . . . . Ex 6:6
JOURNEY is a theme of Numbers . . . Nu 9:18

B. Jacob and his sons in Egypt
–Moved to Egypt. . . . . Ge 46:1–27
–Became slaves of the Egyptians . . . . Ex 1:8–14

C. God's deliverance of his people from Egypt
1. God's choosing of a deliverer
–Moses preserved at birth . . . . Ex 2:1–10
–Moses called as deliverer . . . . Ex 3:7–22
–Aaron appointed to assist Moses . Ex 4:13–17, 27–31
2. The process of deliverance
–Signs given to Moses . . . . Ex 4:1–9
–The first appearance before Pharaoh. . . . . Ex 5:1–5
–The second appearance before Pharaoh. . . . . Ex 7:10–13
–The first nine plagues . . . . Ex 7:14–10:29
–The preparation for the tenth plague . . . . Ex 11:1–12:28
–The slaying of the firstborn in Egypt. . . . . Ex 12:29–30
–The escape from Egypt. . . . . Ex 12:31–39
–The pursuit of the Israelites . . . . . . Ex 14:5–9
–The crossing of the Red Sea. . . . . . . Ex 14:10–22,29
–The drowning of the Egyptians . . . Ex 14:23–28
3. God's motive in the exodus
–Faithfulness to his promises . . . . . Ge 15:13–16; Dt 7:8–9
–His love for his people. . . . . Dt 7:8–9; Hos 11:1

D. Israelite remembrance of the exodus
–Sung after crossing the Red Sea . . . . Ex 15:1–21
–Celebrated annually in the Passover . . Ex 13:3–16
–Recalled in the Ten Commandments. . Ex 20:2; Dt 5:6
–Celebrated by psalmists . . . . Ps 66:5–6; Ps 78:12–14; Ps 105:26–39; Ps 106:8–12
–Taught by prophets. . . . . Isa 43:16–21; Isa 63:11–14; Hos 12:9,13; Na 1:4

E. The exodus in the New Testament
–As an affirmation of God's power. . . Ac 13:17; Ro 9:17
–As a picture of salvation in Christ . . 1Co 10:1–4
–As an example of God's care . . . . Jn 6:31–33
–As an example of human faith. . . . . . Heb 11:29
–As a warning against disobedience . . . Heb 3:7–4:2; Jude 5

EYE

A. The human eye

1. The physical eyes
   - –Leah's weak eyes .... Ge 29:17
   - –Lovers' eyes .... SS 1:15; SS 7:4
   - –Cruelty in eyes being gouged out ... Jdg 16:21; 2Ki 25:7
2. Figurative use of eyes
   - –Enlightened eyes symbolize knowledge .... Ps 19:8; Eph 1:18
   - –Opened eyes symbolize knowledge .... Ge 3:5,7
   - –Bright eyes symbolize well-being 1Sa 14:27
   - –Dim eyes symbolize grief .... Job 17:7
   - –Winking eyes express mockery .. Ps 35:19
   - –Winking eyes plot perversity ..... Pr 16:30
   - –Dissatisfied eyes express greed .. Pr 27:20
   - –Closed eyes express spiritual blindness .... Isa 6:10; Mt 13:15
   - –Lustful eyes 1Jn 2:16
   - –Eyes full of adultery 2Pe 2:14
   - –Haughty eyes .... Ps 18:27
   - –A jealous eye 1Sa 18:9

B. The eye of God
- –Symbolizes God's all-knowing nature .... Ps 139:16; Pr 15:3
- –Symbolizes God's holiness .... Hab 1:13
- –Symbolizes God watching over us .. Ezr 5:5; Ps 33:18
- –Symbolizes Christ's control of history .... Rev 5:6

EZEKIEL

A. Family background and history
- –A priest .... Eze 1:3
- –Carried into exile .... Eze 1:1
- –Called to be prophet .... Eze 2:1–3:11
- –Married; wife died .... Eze 24:18

B. His symbolic actions as a prophet
- –City of Jerusalem on a clay tablet ... Eze 4:1–3
- –Lying immobile for more than a year .... Eze 4:4–8
- –Strange diet during the "siege" of Jerusalem .... Eze 4:9–17
- –A strange haircut .... Eze 5:1–4
- –Packing his belongings for exile ... Eze 12:1–16
- –Shuddering while eating his food ... Eze 12:17–20
- –Groaning in public .... Eze 20:6–7
- –Not mourning when his wife died ... Eze 24:15–24
- –A prophecy using sticks .... Eze 37:15–28

C. His parables as a prophet
- –The parable of the useless vine ..... Eze 15:1–8
- –The parable of the wife turned prostitute .... Eze 16:1–63
- –The parable of two eagles and a vine .... Eze 17:1–24
- –The parable of the lion .... Eze 19:1–9
- –The parable of the two adulterous sisters .... Eze 23:1–49

EZRA

- –A priest .... Ezr 7:1–5
- –A teacher of the Law .... Ezr 7:6–10
- –Led exiles back to Jerusalem .... Ezr 8:15–36
- –Concerned about intermarriage .... Ezr 9:1–4
- –Prayed about intermarriage problem .. Ezr 9:5–15
- –Corrected intermarriage problem .... Ezr 10:1–17
- –Read Law at the Feast of Tabernacles .. Neh 8:1–8
- –Participated in dedication of wall of Jerusalem .... Neh 12:31–36

FACE

A. The human face

1. Significance of the human face
   - –Seeing a face means meeting a person .... Ge 43:3,5; 2Sa 14:28,32
   - –Talking face to face 2Jn 12; 3Jn 14
   - –A radiant face means closeness to God .... Ex 34:29–30
   - –One can slap a face in anger 1Ki 22:24
   - –One can spit in a face in disgust .. Mt 26:67
2. Emotions expressed by the face
   - –The cheerful face .... Pr 15:13
   - –The face bowed down in respect .. Ge 48:12; 1Sa 25:23
   - –The downcast face .... Ge 4:5–6; Lk 24:17
   - –The sad face .... Neh 2:3–4
   - –The face hidden in fear .... Ex 3:6
   - –The terrified face .... Da 5:6,9
   - –The face bowed down in grief .... Jos 7:10
   - –The face turned away in grief 2Ki 20:2
   - –The face turned away in shame ... Ezr 9:6
   - –The face covered with shame .... Ps 69:7

B. The face of God
- –God's face synonymous with himself .... Hos 5:15
- –God's glory seen in the face of Christ 2Co 4:6
- –Seeing God face to face .... Ge 32:30; 1Co 13:12
- –Seeking God's face in prayer .... Ps 24:6; Ps 27:8
- –God's face shining on us in blessing .... Nu 6:24–26; Ps 4:6
- –God's face hidden from our sins .... Ps 51:9
- –God's face hidden in judgment ..... Dt 31:17–18; Ps 13:1–2
- –God's face set against evildoers .... Lev 20:3,5; Ps 34:16; Eze 15:7; 1Pe 3:12

FAITH

–Belief in a person or a teaching

A. Related themes
1. BELIEVE is a theme of John ...... Jn 20:31
2. FAITH is a theme of:
   - –Galatians .... Gal 3:22
   - –James .... Jas 5:15
3. INDIVIDUALISM is a theme of Ezekiel .... Eze 18:4

B. What are the basic elements of faith?
1. Trust in God and commitment to Christ .... Ge 15:6; Pr 3:5; Ro 3:22; Heb 11:1
2. True knowledge of God and Christ
   - –Truths of the faith are important ... 1Ti 3:9; 1Ti 4:1
   - –They must be based on God's word 2Ti 3:16
   - –They are worth fighting for ...... Jude 3

C. What must we believe?
1. We must believe in:
   - –God .... Ex 14:31; Jn 14:1

–Christ . . . . Jn 2:11
Ac 16:31
–The name of the Son of God 1Jn 3:23
–The prophets . . . . Ex 14:31
2Ch 20:20

2. We must believe
a. What God has said
–The commandments of God . . . Ps 119:66
–The writings of the Old Testament . . . . Lk 24:25
Jn 5:46–47
Ac 26:27
–The gospel . . . . Mk 1:15
1Co 15:1–2
–The holy Scriptures 2Ti 3:14–15
–The promises of God . . . . Ro 4:20–21
–Things God has said to us . . . . . Ge 15:6
b. What God teaches about Jesus
–That Jesus is the Christ . . . . Jn 20:31
1Jn 5:1
–That Jesus is God's Son 1Jn 5:5
–That Jesus was raised from the dead . . . . Ro 10:9
–Summary creed 1Co 15:3–11

See also CONFESSION
DOCTRINE

D. Where does faith come from?
–From God, as a gift . . . . Eph 2:8
Php 1:29
–From the Father and the Son . . . . . Eph 6:23
–From the power of God in us . . . 1Co 2:5
–From the Holy Spirit 1Co 12:9
–From hearing the gospel . . . . Jn 17:20
Ac 15:7
Ro 10:14,17
–From reading the Scriptures . . . . Jn 20:31
1Jn 5:13

E. What happens when we believe?
–We receive forgiveness of sin . . . . Ac 10:43
–We are justified . . . . Ro 3:28
Gal 2:16
–We are saved . . . . Ac 16:30–31
Ro 10:9
–We receive eternal life . . . . Jn 3:14–16
–We become free from condemnation . . . . Jn 3:17
–We become free from spiritual death . . . . Jn 11:25–26
–We become God's children . . . . Jn 1:12
Gal 3:26
–We become children of light . . . . Jn 12:36
–We gain access to God . . . . Eph 3:12
–We enter God's rest . . . . Heb 4:3
–Our hearts are purified . . . . Ac 15:9
–We are sanctified . . . . Ac 26:18
–The word of God goes to work in us 1Th 2:13
–We receive peace with God . . . . Ro 5:1
–We experience joy . . . . Ac 16:34
–We gain security in God's power 1Pe 1:5

F. What must we do as believers?
–Live by faith 2Co 5:7
Gal 2:20
–Walk by faith . . . . Ro 4:12
–Face everything by faith . . . . Heb 11:33–39
–Remain true to the faith . . . . Ac 14:22
–Continue in the faith . . . . Col 1:23
–Stand firm in the faith 1Co 16:13
1Pe 5:9
–Fight for the faith 1Ti 6:12
Jude 3
–Increase our faith . . . . Lk 17:5
–Grow in faith 2Th 1:3
Jude 20
–Please God by our faith . . . . Heb 11:6
–Combine faith with hope and love . . . 1Co 13:2,13
Gal 5:6
1Th 1:3
–Do everything by faith . . . . Ro 14:22–23
–Pray in faith . . . . Jas 1:5–6
–Tell others about our faith 2Co 4:13–14
–Demonstrate faith by good works . . . Jas 2:14–26
–Overcome sin by our faith 1Jn 5:4–5
–Fight the devil by our faith . . . . Eph 6:16

G. Striking examples of faith
–Abraham . . . . Ro 4:1–3,9–21
–Numerous Old Testament people . . . Heb 11:4–40
–Daniel's three friends . . . . Da 3:16–18
–Daniel . . . . Da 6:1–11
–A centurion . . . . Mt 8:5–10
–A sick woman . . . . Mt 9:20–22
–A Canaanite woman . . . . Mt 15:22–28
–Blind Bartimaeus . . . . Mk 10:46–52
–A sinful woman . . . . Lk 7:36–50
–Martha . . . . Jn 11:21–27
–Thomas . . . . Jn 20:24–29
–Philippian jailer . . . . Ac 16:29–34
–Lois, Eunice and Timothy 2Ti 1:5
–Paul 2Ti 1:12

FAITHFULNESS

–Remaining steadfast to one's commitments

A. Related themes
FAITHFULNESS is a theme of:
–Judges . . . . Jdg 2:18
–2 Kings 2Ki 8:19
–Lamentations . . . . La 3:23

B. Human faithfulness
1. Faithfulness is an aspect of the fruit of the Spirit . . . . Gal 5:22
2. Examples of those who were faithful
–Abraham . . . . Neh 9:8
–Moses . . . . Nu 12:7
–Hezekiah 2Ch 31:20
–The Zadokite priests . . . . Eze 48:11
–Timothy 1Co 4:17
–Epaphras . . . . Col 1:7
–Onesimus . . . . Col 4:9
–Silas 1Pe 5:12
3. We must be faithful
–In obeying God's commands . . . . . . Dt 11:13
–In our walk before God 1Ki 2:4
–In serving God 2Ch 19:9
–In our prayer life . . . . Ro 12:12
–In the use of our gifts 1Pe 4:10
–In persevering until death . . . . Rev 2:10
4. God's promises to those who are faithful
–He is faithful to them . . . . Ps 18:25
–His eyes are on them . . . . Ps 101:6
–He preserves them . . . . Ps 31:23
–He guards their lives . . . . Ps 97:10
–He protects them . . . . Pr 2:8
–He blesses them . . . . Dt 11:13–15
–He rewards them . . . . Mt 25:21–23
–He does not forsake them . . . . Ps 37:28
–He guarantees them life . . . . Eze 18:9

C. God's faithfulness
1. God is faithful in himself
–He is the faithful God . . . . Dt 7:9
Heb 10:23
–He abounds in faithfulness . . . . Ps 86:15
–His faithfulness is great . . . . La 3:23
–He will remain faithful 2Ti 2:13
2. God is faithful in his actions
–He is faithful in all he does . . . . Ps 33:4
Ps 111:7–8
–He is faithful to his covenant . . . . . Ps 78:24–28

–He keeps all his promises........ Ge 21:1–2; 1Ki 8:20; Ac 13:23,32–33
–Christ fulfills all God's promises.................... 2Co 1:18,20

3. God is faithful in his relationship to us
–In his love for us................ Ps 89:24; Ps 143:1
–In helping us.................. 1Co 10:13
–In protecting us.................. Ps 91:4; 2Th 3:3
–In forgiving us.................. 1Jn 1:9

4. God's word is faithful............ 2Sa 7:28; Ps 19:7; Rev 21:5

FALLING AWAY

–Falling away from the faith, backsliding, apostasy

A. Falling away in the Old Testament

1. Examples
–At Mount Sinai.................. Ex 32:1–35
–During the time of the judges.... Jdg 2:10–12
–In Israel........................ 1Ki 16:30–33
–In Judah........................ 2Ch 24:17–19
–A regular pattern................ Ps 106:6–47

2. Causes
–Mixed marriages................ Nu 25:1–3; Neh 13:26–27
–Poor examples of kings.......... 1Ki 16:29–33; 2Ki 21:1–11

3. Judgment for those who fall away.......................... Dt 13:13–18; 2Ki 21:12–15

B. Falling away in the New Testament

1. Examples
–At the time of Jesus............ Jn 6:66
–In the early church.............. 1Ti 1:19–20; 2Ti 2:17–18; 2Pe 2:20–21
–Future severe apostasy.......... Mt 24:12; 2Th 2:3; 2Ti 3:1,5

2. Causes
–Influence of deceiving spirits..... 1Ti 4:1
–False teachers.................. Ac 20:29–30; Rev 2:14–15
–Human desires.................. 2Ti 4:3–4
–Love of world.................. 2Ti 4:10
–Hardened hearts................ Ac 7:51–52; Ac 28:26–27
–Persecution.................... Mt 24:9–10
–A time of testing................ Lk 8:13

3. Judgment for those who fell away
–Judgment from God............ Heb 10:26–31; Jude 11–15
–Removal from God's kingdom.... Rev 2:5
–Impossible to renew to repentance.................... Heb 6:4–8

4. The antidote to falling away
–Heed the warning not to fall away.................... Heb 3:12; 2Pe 3:17
–Depend on God................ Ro 8:35–39; 1Co 10:13; Jude 24
–Remain steadfast in faith........ Heb 6:11–12; Jude 20–21
–Continue reading God's word.... 2Ti 3:14–17
–Keep growing in Christian character........................ 2Pe 1:5–10
–Associate with other believers... Heb 3:13; Heb 10:24

FAMILY

A. Related theme
FAMILY is a theme of Ruth.......... Ru 2:20

B. The establishment of the family
–Marriage begun in the Garden of Eden...................... Ge 2:18–24
–The first children, given by God.... Ge 4:1–2
–The family built by God............ Ps 127:1–6
–The family blessed by God......... Ps 128:1–6
–The central unit in God's covenant... Ge 17:7; Jos 24:15

C. Responsibilities in the family

1. The father as head
–Head of the family.............. Ex 6:14
–Head of the wife................ Eph 5:23–24
–Must love his wife.............. Eph 5:25–33; 1Pe 3:7
–Must supervise religious observances................ Ge 35:1–7; Ex 12:3; 1Sa 1:21
–Must supervise education of children.................... Ps 44:1; Ps 78:3; Eph 6:4
–Must care for the children's needs........................ 2Co 12:14; Col 3:21

2. The role of the mother
–Submissive to her husband........ Eph 5:24; 1Pe 3:1–6
–Training children................ Pr 1:8; Pr 6:20
–Takes an important role in home...................... 1Sa 1:9–28; Pr 31:10–31; 2Ti 1:5

3. The place of children
–A blessing from the Lord........ Ps 127:3–5
–Must honor parents.............. Ex 20:12; Lev 19:3
–Must obey parents.............. Dt 21:18–21; Eph 6:1–3; Col 3:20

D. Things that disturb or destroy the family
–Jealousy and hatred.............. Ge 4:3–8
–Lack of respect toward parents.... Ge 9:21–22
–Parents picking favorites.......... Ge 25:27–28
–Rivalry and selfishness............ Ge 27:1–41
–Polygamy........................ Ge 30:1–2; 1Sa 1:1–6
–Lack of discipline................ 1Sa 2:22–25
–Lust and incest.................. 2Sa 13:1–21
–Personal ambition................ Jdg 9:1–5; 2Sa 15:1–17
–Mixed marriages................ Neh 13:23–27
–Materialism.................... 1Ti 6:6–10
–False teaching.................. Titus 1:10–11

E. New Testament teachings on the family
–Salvation took place in households........................ Ac 16:15,31–34; Ac 18:8; 1Co 1:16; 1Co 16:15
–Children of believers are holy...... 1Co 7:14
–A well-ordered family was important...................... 1Ti 3:4–5,12; Titus 1:6
–Care for members in the family circle........................ 1Ti 5:4,8,16

F. The family used figuratively
–As a picture of the nation of Israel... Ps 115:9–12

–As a picture of the church.......... Gal 6:10
Eph 2:19
Heb 2:11
1Pe 4:17

See also CHILDREN
FATHER
MARRIAGE
MOTHER

FAMINE

See HUNGER AND THIRST

FASTING

–Voluntarily depriving oneself of food

A. In the Old Testament

1. Occasions for fasting
–To prepare to receive God's law ... Ex 34:28
Dt 9:9,18
–To prepare for the Day of Atonement .... Lev 16:29,31
–To show sorrow at time of death ... 1Sa 31:13
2Sa 1:12
–To show sorrow for sin 1Ki 21:27
Neh 9:1
Jnh 3:6–9
–To show humility .... Ps 35:13
–To pray in time of national need ... 2Ch 20:3
Ezr 8:21
Est 4:16
Joel 2:15–17
–To accompany deep personal prayer 2Sa 12:16,21
Neh 1:4
Da 9:3–4

2. Prophets criticized fasting as outward show .... Isa 58:3–7
Jer 14:12
Zec 7:4–10

B. In the New Testament

1. Occasions for fasting
–A regular pattern for many Jews .. Mt 9:14
Lk 2:37
Ac 23:12–14
–Paul after his conversion .... Ac 9:9
–To prepare for mission work ..... Ac 13:2–3
Ac 14:23
–Not done by Jesus' disciples...... Mt 9:14

2. Jesus criticized fasting as outward show .... Mt 6:16–18
Lk 18:9–14

FATHER

A. Various meanings of father
–Creator .... Jas 1:17
–Source or originator.............. Ge 4:20–21
–Caretaker .... Job 29:16
–Counselor .... Ge 45:8
–A respected prophet 2Ki 6:21
–A respected priest................ Jdg 17:10
–One's male parent .... Ge 4:18
–One's grandfather................ Ge 28:13
–One's great-grandfather 1Ki 15:11
–One's ancestors in general .... Jos 24:6
2Ki 21:22

B. The father in the family

1. Duties of a father
–Supervise religious observances... Ge 35:1–7
Ex 12:3
1Sa 1:21
–Responsible for education of children.................... Ge 18:19
Dt 4:9–10
Eph 6:5
–Responsible for discipline of children.................. Dt 8:4
Pr 3:11–12
–Care for his children's needs 2Co 12:14
Col 3:21
–Give blessing to his children ..... Ge 27:27–29, 39–40
Ge 49:1–28

2. Responsibility of children
–Respect their fathers .... Ex 20:12
Lev 19:3
–Obey their fathers............... Ex 20:12
Eph 6:1
Col 3:20

C. Spiritual use of father
–Abraham as the father of believers... Ro 4:11,16–17
Gal 3:7
–Paul as the father of his churches ... 1Co 4:15
1Th 2:11–12
–God as Father of Jesus Christ ...... Jn 17:1,5
Eph 1:3
–God as Father of everyone .... Mal 2:10
Ac 17:28–29
–God as Father of his chosen people... Isa 63:16
Jer 31:9
–God as Father of believers in Jesus. . Mt 6:9
Jn 1:12–13
Gal 1:1,4
–Christians can call God "Abba" (Father)........................... Ro 8:15
Gal 4:6
–The devil as father of the ungodly ... Jn 8:44
1Jn 3:10–12

FEAR

–One's apprehension in a frightening situation; reverence

A. Fear as being afraid

1. Why did people experience fear?
–Fear of seeing God .... Ex 3:6
–Fear of a vision of angels .... Mt 28:4
Lk 2:8–9
–Fear of the unknown .... Lk 9:34,45
–Fear of punishment for sin .... Ge 3:8–10
Ge 18:15
Ac 24:25
–Fear of danger.................. Ac 27:17,29
–Fear of being killed .... Ge 26:7
1Ki 19:3
–Fear of losing one's life .... Jnh 1:5
Mt 14:30
–Fear of losing one's loved ones ... Ge 31:31
Ge 42:4
–Fear of bringing unpleasant news....................... 1Sa 3:15
2Sa 12:18
–Fear of an enemy 1Sa 28:5
Jn 20:19
–Fear of a person in authority ..... Neh 2:2
–Fear of what another person might do 1Sa 18:12,15
–Fear of what others might say..... Gal 2:12
–Fear of the future .... Ge 21:17

2. The command not to be afraid
–Given by God................... Ge 21:17
Ge 26:24
Ac 18:9
–Given by Moses................. Ex 14:13
Ex 20:20
–Given by Joshua .... Jos 10:25
–Given by Samuel................ 1Sa 12:20
–Given by Elijah 1Ki 17:13
–Given by David 1Ch 22:13
–Given by the prophet Jahaziel.... 2Ch 20:15,17

–Given by Hezekiah 2Ch 32:7
–Given by Isaiah .... Isa 44:2,8
–Given by Jeremiah .... Jer 42:11
–Given by Jesus .... Mt 14:27; Mk 5:36; Lk 12:4,7,32; Jn 6:20
–Given by an angel .... Lk 1:13,30; Lk 2:10; Ac 27:23–24

3. How to conquer fear
–By trusting in God .... Ps 56:4,11
–By believing in Jesus .... Mk 5:36
–By knowing God is with us .... Ge 26:24; Dt 31:6,8; Ps 23:4; Isa 43:5
–By knowing Jesus is with us .... Jn 6:20; Ac 18:9–10
–By knowing God is our Savior .... Ps 27:1,3
–By knowing God is our refuge .... Ps 46:1–2; Ps 91:1–6; Heb 13:6
–By knowing God will fight for us .... Dt 3:22; Dt 20:3–4; 2Ch 20:15–17
–By obeying the Lord 1Sa 12:20–21; 1Ch 22:12–13

4. Courage as the answer to fear
See COURAGE

B. Fear as reverence for the Lord

1. The command to fear the Lord .... Dt 6:13; Jos 24:14; 2Ch 19:7; Ps 33:8; Pr 3:7; Ecc 12:13

2. Examples of those who feared the Lord
–Noah .... Heb 11:7
–Abraham .... Ge 22:12
–Joseph .... Ge 42:18
–Job .... Job 1:1
–David .... Ps 5:7
–Hezekiah .... Jer 26:19
–Nehemiah .... Neh 5:15
–The early church .... Ac 9:31

3. Reasons for fearing the Lord
–His awesome power .... Ex 20:18–20
–His glory .... Lk 2:9
–His holiness .... Rev 15:4
–His majesty .... Ps 96:4–6
–His greatness 1Sa 12:24
–His forgiveness .... Ps 130:4
–His faithfulness .... Ps 119:38

4. Benefits of fearing God
–A way to praise God .... Ps 22:23
–A way to serve God .... Ps 2:11
–A way to obey God .... Ecc 12:13
–A way to fight evil .... Pr 8:13; Pr 16:6
–A way to become wise .... Ps 111:10; Pr 1:7
–A way to lengthen life .... Pr 10:27
–God loves those who fear him .... Ps 103:11,13,17
–God saves those who fear him .... Ps 85:9
–God protects those who fear him .... Ps 60:4; Pr 14:26–27
–God blesses those who fear him .... Ps 115:12–13
–God provides for those who fear him .... Ps 34:9; Ps 111:5

FEASTS

A. Religious feasts

1. Commanded in the Old Testament
–Passover .... Ex 12:1–14; Lev 23:5; Nu 9:1–14; Dt 16:1–7
–Unleavened Bread .... Ex 12:15–20; Ex 13:3–10; Lev 23:6–8; Nu 28:17–25; Dt 16:3–4,8
–Firstfruits .... Lev 23:9–14
–Weeks (Harvest, Pentecost) .... Ex 23:16; Lev 23:15–21; Nu 28:26–31; Dt 16:9–12
–Trumpets .... Lev 23:23–25; Nu 29:1–6
–Day of Atonement .... Lev 16:1–34; Nu 29:7–11
–Tabernacles (Ingathering, Booths) .... Ex 23:16; Lev 23:33–43; Nu 29:12–34; Dt 16:13–15
–Sacred Assembly .... Lev 23:36; Nu 29:35–38
–Purim .... Est 9:27–28

2. Celebrations in the Old Testament
–Passover .... Jos 5:10; 2Ki 23:21–23; 2Ch 30:1–20; 2Ch 35:1–17; Ezr 6:19–21
–Unleavened Bread .... Jos 5:11; 2Ch 30:21–27; 2Ch 35:17–19; Ezr 6:22
–Day of Atonement .... Neh 9:1–38
–Tabernacles (Booths) .... Ezr 3:4; Neh 8:13–18
–Purim .... Est 9:18–32

3. Celebrations in the New Testament
–Passover .... Mt 26:1–2,17–29; Mk 14:12–25; Lk 22:7–38; Jn 2:13–25; Jn 11:55–56; Jn 13:1–30
–Unleavened Bread .... Mt 26:17; Mk 14:1,12; Lk 22:1,7
–Weeks (Pentecost) .... Ac 2:1–41
–Tabernacles (Booths) .... Jn 7:2–36
–Sacred Assembly .... Jn 7:37–44
–Dedication (Hanukkah) .... Jn 10:22–39
–The Lord's Supper .... Mt 26:26–29; Mk 14:22–25; Lk 22:17–20; 1Co 11:17–26

4. Criticism when feasts became empty rituals
–In the Old Testament .... Isa 1:14; Isa 5:12; Hos 2:11; Am 5:21–23
–In the New Testament .... 2Pe 2:13; Jude 12

B. Non-religious occasions for feasting
–At weanings .... Ge 21:8
–At the signing of a treaty .... Ge 26:30
–At marriages .... Ge 29:21–22; Jdg 14:10
–At a coronation 1Ki 1:41

c. To purify his people .... Isa 48:10
Mal 3:3

3. Negative uses of fire
–To express his wrath .... Dt 32:22
Ps 89:46
–To judge sinners on earth .... Ge 19:24–25
Lev 10:2
Nu 11:1–2
2Ki 1:10,12
–To punish eternally in hell .... Mt 5:22
2Th 1:7–8
Jas 3:6
Rev 18:17–18

FIRSTFRUITS

A. Firstfruits in the Old Testament
1. Firstfruits to be dedicated to God
–Firstborn son .... Ex 13:1–2
–Firstborn of livestock .... Ex 13:1–2
–Firstfruits of the crops .... Ex 23:16
Lev 23:9
–Firstfruits of grain, wine, oil, wool .... Dt 18:4
2Ch 31:5
–Firstfruits of fruit trees .... Lev 19:23–24
–Firstfruits of everything grown .... Dt 26:2
Pr 3:9
2. Rules and regulations
a. General
–In the laws of Moses .... Lev 2:11–16
Lev 23:9–14
Dt 26:1–15
–After the exile .... Neh 10:35
Neh 12:44
–In the new temple .... Eze 44:30
b. Must be brought to the Lord's house .... Ex 23:19
Ex 34:26
c. Must precede eating of harvested crops .... Lev 23:14

B. Firstfruits as symbol in the New Testament
–Christ as the firstfruits of those raised 1Co 15:20,23
–The Holy Spirit as our first blessing .... Ro 8:23
–The Holy Spirit as a guaranteed deposit 2Co 1:22
2Co 5:5
Eph 1:14
–Early Christians as firstfruits of others .... Jas 1:18

FISH

A. Fish in the Old Testament
–A food for humans .... Nu 11:5
Neh 13:16
–Humans given dominion over fish ... Ge 1:26,28
Ps 8:6–8
–The great fish that swallowed Jonah .... Jnh 1:17
Mt 12:40

B. Fish in the New Testament
1. Several disciples were fishermen .... Mt 4:18–21
Jn 21:1–3
2. Miracles with fish
–Miraculous catch of fish .... Lk 5:4–7
Jn 21:4–11
–Feeding the multitude with two fish .... Mk 6:37–44
Jn 6:1–11
–Tax money in the mouth of a fish ... Mt 17:24–27
3. Parable concerning fish and net ... Mt 13:47–48

FOLLY

A. Characteristics of the fool
–Begins with a denial of God .... Ps 14:1
–Does not trust in God 2Ch 16:7–9
–Trusts in self .... Pr 28:26
–Has no desire to get wisdom .... Pr 1:7,22
Pr 17:16
–Spurns discipline .... Pr 15:5
–Finds pleasure in evil .... Pr 10:23
Titus 3:3
–Is rebellious .... Ps 107:17
–Engages in senseless merriment ..... Ecc 7:4–6
–Loves to quarrel .... Pr 20:3
–Does not control anger .... Pr 29:9,11
–Comes to ruin .... Pr 10:8,10,14

See also WISDOM

B. Special aspects of foolishness in the New Testament
–The foolishness of preaching 1Co 1:21–24
–The foolishness of God is wiser than human wisdom 1Co 1:25
–Being fools for Christ's sake 1Co 3:18
1Co 4:10
–Paul's speech of the fool 2Co 11:16–12:13

FOOL

See FOLLY

FOOT

A. The human foot
1. Symbolic uses of the human foot
–Washing feet in ceremonial cleansing .... Ex 30:17–21
–Washing feet as a sign of courtesy .... Ge 18:4
–Washing feet as a sign of repentance .... Lk 7:37–48
–Washing feet as a sign of servanthood .... Jn 13:3–15
–Cutting off feet as a punishment ... 2Sa 4:12
2. Metaphors concerning the foot
a. Dominion: everything under our feet .... Ps 8:6
b. Security: feet on solid rock ...... Ps 40:2
c. Gratitude: falling down at one's feet .... Lk 17:16
d. Victory
–Trampling underfoot .... Mic 7:10
–Placing feet on the neck .... Jos 10:24
–Enemies as one's footstool ..... Ps 110:1
Ac 2:35
e. Submission: falling down at one's feet 1Sa 25:24
2Sa 22:40
Rev 19:10
f. Rejection: shaking dust off one's feet .... Mt 10:14
Ac 13:51
g. Sin
–Straying feet .... Ps 44:18
–Stumbling feet .... Ps 116:8
h. Miscellaneous
–Beautiful feet of gospel preachers .... Isa 52:7
Ro 10:15
–God's word as a lamp to our feet .... Ps 119:105

B. The feet of God
–Bowing down at his feet in submission .... Dt 33:3
–The earth as God's footstool .... Isa 66:1
Mt 5:35
–The ark as God's footstool 1Ch 28:2

FORGET

A. Human forgetting
1. What we ought to forget
–Our troubles ... Ge 41:51
Isa 65:16
–The trials of the past ... Isa 43:18
Php 3:13
–Our sin and the shame it brings ... Isa 54:4
Eze 39:26
2. What we ought not to forget
–The Lord ... Dt 6:12
Isa 17:10
Jer 2:32
–God's mighty acts ... Dt 4:9
Ps 78:7,11
–God's covenant with us ... Dt 4:23,31
2Ki 17:38
–God's law ... Ps 119:61,83,109
–God's patience with us ... 2Pe 3:9–10
–God's benefits to us ... Ps 103:2
–The teachings of our parents ... Pr 3:6
Pr 4:5

B. Divine forgetting
1. What God forgets
–The sins of those who repent ... Isa 43:25
Jer 31:34
Heb 8:12
–Those who persistently refuse to believe ... Jer 23:39–40
2. What God does not forget
–His people ... Isa 44:21
Isa 49:21
–Our good deeds and love ... Heb 6:10
–Even the smallest of his creatures ... Lk 12:6
–The sins of those who refuse to repent ... Am 8:7
3. Praying that God will not forget
–Us ... Ps 13:1
–The helpless ... Ps 10:12
–Those who are afflicted ... Ps 74:19

See also REMEMBER

FORGIVENESS

–Pardon for human sins and shortcomings

A. Related theme
FORGIVENESS is a theme of Philemon ... Phm 17

B. Human forgiveness of others
1. Examples
–Esau of his brother Jacob ... Ge 33:4
–Joseph of his brothers ... Ge 50:15–21
–The father of his wayward son ... Lk 15:17–24
–Jesus of his enemies ... Lk 23:34
–Stephen of his enemies ... Ac 7:60
–Paul of those deserting him ... 2Ti 4:16
2. Required of Christians ... Mt 18:35
Lk 11:4
Eph 4:32
Col 3:13

C. God's forgiveness of us
1. Why does God forgive?
–Because of his compassion ... Ex 34:6–7
Mic 7:19
–Because of his love ... Ps 51:1
–Because of his grace ... Ps 103:8
–Because of his mercy ... Isa 55:7
2. How does God forgive?
–Always by shedding of blood ... Heb 9:22
–Foreshadowed by Old Testament sacrifice ... Lev 4:1–5:13
–Fulfilled by the blood of Christ ... Col 1:14
Col 2:13–14
Heb 9:14,28
–Jesus can forgive sins ... Mk 2:1–11
3. What happens to our sins?
–They go out of sight ... Isa 38:17
–They go out of reach ... Ps 103:12
Mic 7:19
–They go out of mind ... Isa 43:25
Jer 31:34
–They go out of existence ... Ps 51:1–2,7,9
Isa 44:22
Ac 3:19
4. How do we receive forgiveness?
–We must confess our sins ... Ps 32:5
1Jn 1:9
–We must repent of our sins ... Ac 2:38
Ac 3:19
–We must believe in Christ ... Lk 24:47
Ac 10:43
Ac 13:38

FORNICATION

See SEXUAL STANDARDS

FREEDOM

–Being liberated from bondage

A. Related themes
FREEDOM is a theme of:
–Exodus ... Ex 6:6
–Galatians ... Gal 5:13

B. Freedom from human slavery
1. In the Old Testament
–God delivered his enslaved people ... Ex 1:11
Ex 6:6–7
Ex 20:2
–God forbade slavery among Hebrews ... Ex 21:2
Dt 15:12–15
Jer 34:8–17
–Prophets spoke against slavery ... 2Ki 4:1–7
Neh 5:4–8
2. In the New Testament
–Apostles accepted slavery ... Eph 6:5–8
Col 3:22–25
1Pe 2:18–19
–Slaves were to be treated as brothers and sisters ... Phm 15–16

See also SLAVERY

C. Spiritual freedom
1. Who sets us free?
–God ... Ro 6:17–18
–Christ ... Jn 8:34–36
Gal 2:4
Gal 5:1
–The Holy Spirit ... Ro 8:15
2Co 3:17
2. From what are we set free?
–From sin ... Jn 8:36
Ro 6:7
–From sin and death ... Ro 8:2
–From fear of death ... Heb 2:15
–From fear ... Ro 8:15
–From the law ... Ro 7:6
Gal 3:23–25
Jas 1:25
–From the curse of the law ... Gal 3:13–14
–From bondage to decay ... Ro 8:21
–From the basic principles of the world ... Gal 4:3–4
Col 2:20–22

–To witness to Christ 1Co 12:1–3
–To build up the church 1Co 12:7
1Co 14:3,5,12,26
1Pe 4:10
–To demonstrate God's grace in us ... Ro 12:6
–To praise God 1Co 14:24–25
1Pe 4:11

C. Gifts are subordinate to love
–The greatest way is the way of love ... 1Co 12:31–13:3
–Gifts will disappear 1Co 13:8–10
–Love will always remain 1Co 13:13

D. Warning against gifts that deceive
–False prophets can do wonders and signs .... Mt 24:24
–The antichrist will do counterfeit signs 2Th 2:9
Rev 13:13–14
–We must test the spirits 1Jn 4:1

GLORY

–The grandeur and majesty of God

A. Related theme
GLORY OF CHRIST is a theme of Colossians
Col 1:27

B. God and his glory
1. Glory belongs to God 1Ch 29:11
Ps 29:1,3
Ps 96:7
Ro 11:36

2. God dwells in awesome majesty ... Job 37:22
Ps 93:1
Ps 145:5

3. God's name is glorious .... Dt 28:58
1Ch 29:13
Ps 8:1
Ps 79:9

4. God reveals his glory
–In Jesus Christ .... Isa 40:5
Jn 1:14
–In the Tent of Meeting .... Ex 40:34–35
–In the temple 2Ch 5:14
Eze 10:4
Eze 43:5
–In his works .... Ps 19:1
Ps 111:3
–Through Moses .... Ex 34:29–35
–On Mount Sinai .... Ex 24:15–17
–To Isaiah .... Isa 6:3
–To his people through his redemption .... Isa 44:23
Isa 46:13
–To Ezekiel .... Eze 1:28
–To the shepherds of Bethlehem ... Lk 2:9
–To Stephen .... Ac 7:55
–To the whole world .... Ps 97:6
Isa 66:18
Hab 2:14

C. Jesus and his glory
1. He is the Lord of glory 1Co 2:8
Jas 2:1

2. He has God's glory
–Had it from the beginning .... Jn 17:5
–Surpassed glory of the Old Testament 2Co 3:7–11
–Now exalted in glory 1Ti 3:16
Rev 5:12–13
–Will return in glory .... Mt 24:30
Mt 25:31

3. He revealed God's glory
–In human flesh .... Jn 1:14
Heb 1:3
–In his actions .... Jn 2:11
Jn 11:40–44
–In his transfiguration .... Lk 9:29–30
2Pe 1:16–19
–In his death .... Jn 12:23–24
–In the resurrection .... Lk 24:26
Php 3:21

D. The Spirit and his glory
–Called the Spirit of glory 1Pe 4:14
–His ministry is glorious 2Co 3:8

E. Believers and the glory of God
1. The present
–We fall short of his glory .... Ro 3:23
–Christ came to bring us to glory ... Lk 2:29–32
Col 1:27
–We receive God's glory through Christ .... Jn 17:22
2Co 4:6
–We receive the Spirit of glory 1Pe 4:14
–We must reflect his glory 1Co 10:31
2Co 3:18
–We must pray that his glory will endure .... Ps 104:31

2. The future
–We will be brought into his glory .... Heb 2:10
Jude 24
–We will share in Christ's glory .... Ro 8:17–18
1Pe 5:10
–Our new bodies will bear his glory 1Co 15:42–43
Php 3:21
–We will receive a crown of glory ... 1Pe 5:4

GOD

A. Related themes
1. GOD is a theme of:
–Genesis .... Ge 28:13
–Proverbs .... Pr 16:4
–Isaiah .... Isa 54:5

2. UNIVERSAL GOD is a theme of:
–Ruth .... Ru 1:16
–Ezekiel .... Eze 1:1
–Jonah .... Jnh 1:2

B. The being of God
See HOLY SPIRIT
JESUS CHRIST
TRINITY

C. Names of God
–God .... Ge 1:1
–Lord .... Ge 4:1,4
–Lord God .... Ge 2:4
–God Most High .... Ge 14:18–20
–The Sovereign Lord .... Ge 15:2
–God Almighty .... Ge 17:1
–The Eternal God .... Ge 21:33
–The God of Bethel .... Ge 31:13
–God of Abraham, Isaac, Jacob ...... Ex 3:6
–I AM WHO I AM .... Ex 3:14
–The God of the Hebrews .... Ex 3:18
–Jealous .... Ex 34:14
–The God of Israel 1Sa 1:17
–God, the Rock 2Sa 22:47
–The Lord, the God of heaven .... Ezr 1:2
–The Mighty One, God, the Lord ..... Ps 50:1
–God the King .... Ps 145:1
–The Holy One of Israel .... Isa 1:4
–The Mighty One of Israel .... Isa 1:24

D. Characteristics of God
1. Divine characteristics
–Holy .... Lev 11:44
–Eternal .... Ps 90:2
–Infinite 1Ki 8:27
–Immortal 1Ti 1:17
–Invisible .... Jn 1:18
–All-knowing .... Ps 147:5

–Everywhere present . . . Ps 139:7–21
–All-powerful . . . Isa 40:6–7
–Unchanging . . . Mal 3:6
–Incomparable . . . Isa 40:18,25
–Righteous . . . Ps 145:17
–Perfect . . . Mt 5:48
–Awesome and majestic . . . Ex 15:11
–Gracious . . . Ex 34:6
–Spirit . . . Jn 4:24

2. Human characteristics ascribed to him

a. Physical characteristics
–Face of God . . . Nu 6:25–26
See FACE
–Ears of God . . . Neh 1:6
See EAR
–Eyes of God . . . 2Ch 16:9
See EYE
–Nostrils of God . . . Ex 15:8
–Mouth of God . . . Dt 8:3
See MOUTH
–Voice of God . . . Ex 15:26
See VOICE
–Hands of God . . . Ezr 7:9
See HAND
–Fingers of God . . . Ps 8:3
–Arms of God . . . Dt 33:27
–Shoulders of God . . . Dt 33:12
–Back of God . . . Ex 33:21–22
–Feet of God . . . Ps 18:9
See FOOT

b. Physical actions
–God sits . . . Ps 102:12
–God stands . . . Ge 28:13
–God walks . . . Ge 3:8
–God comes down . . . Ge 11:5
–God goes up . . . Ge 17:22
–God marches . . . Zec 9:14
–God rides . . . Ps 68:33
–God soars . . . 2Sa 22:11
–God shoots arrows . . . 2Sa 22:15
–God reaches down . . . 2Sa 22:17
–God rests . . . Ge 2:2
–God sleeps . . . Ps 44:23

c. Emotional characteristics
–God loves . . . Ex 34:6
1Jn 4:8–10
–God is compassionate . . . Ex 3:7
–God is patient . . . 2Pe 3:9
–God laughs . . . Ps 2:4
–God becomes angry . . . Dt 9:7
–God grieves . . . Ge 6:6
–God is jealous . . . Ex 34:14
–God fears . . . Dt 32:26–27
–God hates . . . Ps 5:5

E. Our response to God
–We should trust in him . . . Jn 14:1
See TRUST
–We should hope in him . . . Ps 131:3
See HOPE
–We should believe him . . . Ge 15:6
See FAITH
–We should fear him . . . Dt 6:13
See FEAR
–We should praise him . . . Ps 150:1–6
See PRAISE
–We should worship him . . . Ps 96:9
See WORSHIP
–We should stand in awe of him . . . Hab 3:2
–We should honor him . . . Pr 3:9
–We should glorify him . . . Ps 34:3
–We should thirst for him . . . Ps 42:2

GOLD

A. Uses for gold

1. In Israelite worship
–The tabernacle structure . . . Ex 26:29,32
–The tabernacle furniture . . . Ex 25:10–40
Ex 30:3–5
–Priestly garments . . . Ex 28:11–36
–The temple structure . . . 2Ch 3:4–6
–The temple furniture . . . 2Ch 4:7–8,20–22

2. In pagan worship
–The golden calf in the desert . . . Ex 32:1–4
–The golden calves of Jeroboam . . . 1Ki 12:26–30
–Other idols . . . Isa 2:20
Hos 8:4

3. For personal wealth . . . 2Ch 9:13
Ecc 2:8
Mt 10:9

4. For gifts . . . 2Ch 9:9
Ezr 2:69
Mt 2:11

5. For jewelry . . . Ge 24:22
Ex 32:2
Jdg 8:24,26

6. For royal display . . . 2Ch 9:15–16
Est 1:6–7

B. Value of gold for God's people

1. Positive: a blessing from God . . . Ge 13:2
Isa 60:6,17

2. Negative
–Spiritual values worth more than gold . . . Ps 19:10
Pr 3:13–14
1Pe 1:7
–Gold valueless in redemption . . . 1Pe 1:18

C. Gold as a symbol
–For saints surviving God's testing . . . Job 23:10
–For trustworthy spiritual values . . . 1Co 3:12–13
Rev 3:18
–For the new heaven . . . Rev 21:18,21

GOLIATH

–A Philistine giant . . . 1Sa 17:4–7
–Taunted the Israelite army . . . 1Sa 17:8–11
–David offered to fight him . . . 1Sa 17:32–37
–David killed him . . . 1Sa 17:48–51
–David obtained his sword . . . 1Sa 21:9

GOMORRAH

See SODOM AND GOMORRAH

GOSPEL

–*The good news of salvation for humanity*

A. Terms used to describe the gospel
–The gospel of God . . . Ro 1:1
–The glorious gospel of God . . . 1Ti 1:11
–The gospel of God's grace . . . Ac 20:24
–The gospel of God's Son . . . Ro 1:9
–The gospel of our Lord Jesus . . . 2Th 1:8
–The gospel of Christ . . . Ro 15:19
–The gospel of the glory of Christ . . . 2Co 4:4
–The gospel about Jesus Christ . . . Mk 1:1
–The gospel of the kingdom . . . Mt 24:14
–The gospel of salvation . . . Eph 1:13
–The gospel of peace . . . Eph 6:15
–The eternal gospel . . . Rev 14:6

B. The gospel in the Old Testament
–First revealed to Adam and Eve . . . Ge 3:15
–Revealed to Abraham . . . Ge 12:2–3
Ge 18:18
Ge 22:18
Gal 3:8
–Revealed to Israel through prophets . . . Isa 40:9
Isa 52:7–10
Isa 61:6
Ro 1:1–2

C. The gospel in the New Testament

1. The proclaimers of the gospel
–The angel at Christ's birth . . . Lk 2:10

–John the Baptist ... Lk 3:18
–Jesus Christ ... Mk 1:14–15
Lk 4:43
–The twelve disciples ... Lk 9:6
–The twelve apostles ... Ac 5:42
–Peter and John ... Ac 8:25
Ac 15:7
–Philip ... Ac 8:12,40
–Paul ... Ac 14:7
Ro 15:19
–Unnamed missionaries ... 1Pe 1:12
–Our responsibility ... Mt 24:14
Mt 28:19

2. The content of the gospel
–The basic story about Jesus ... Mk 1:1
1Co 15:1–8,11
–Jesus is the Christ ... Ac 5:42
–Humans should repent ... Mk 1:15
–Salvation is by faith in Jesus ... Ro 1:16–17
–God gives us his grace ... Ac 20:24
–Both Jew and Gentile can be saved ... Eph 3:6–7
–Jesus will return as judge ... Ro 2:16
–How believers should live ... Php 1:27

3. The characteristics of the gospel
–It reveals the glory of Christ ... 2Co 4:4
–It is eternal ... 1Pe 1:25
Rev 14:6
–It demonstrates God's power ... Ro 1:16
–It calls us ... 2Th 2:14
–It saves us ... 1Co 15:2
–It gives us peace ... Eph 6:15
–It gives us hope ... Col 1:23
–It gives us life ... 2Ti 1:10
–It grows and bears fruit ... Col 1:6
–It tolerates no rival ... Gal 1:6–9

4. The response to the gospel
–We should believe it ... Heb 4:2
–We should obey it ... 2Co 9:13
2Th 1:8
Heb 4:6
–We should not be ashamed of it ... Ro 1:16
–We should live in line with its truth ... Gal 2:14
Php 1:27
–We should serve it ... 2Co 8:18
–We should continue in it ... Col 1:23
–We should promote it ... 1Co 9:16
–We should defend it ... Php 1:7,16
Jude 3
–We should preach it ... Mk 16:15
Ac 8:4
Ro 15:19–20
1Co 9:16
–We may have to suffer for it ... 2Ti 1:8
2Ti 2:8–9

GOVERNMENT

–The rule of humans by other humans

A. Phases of civil government among the Israelites/Jews

1. Rule by the fathers (patriarchs)
–Abram ... Ge 14:13–16
–Isaac ... Ge 26:26–32
–Jacob ... Ge 34:5,30–31
Ge 46:5–27

2. Rule by God's chosen leader
–Moses ... Ex 3:7–12
Ex 18:13–26
–Moses and Aaron ... Nu 17:1–13
–Joshua ... Dt 31:1–8
Jos 1:1–11

3. Rule by God's chosen judges
See JUDGE, JUDGMENT

4. Rule through God's chosen kings
–Israel asked for a king ... 1Sa 8:4–22
–Israel's first king, Saul ... 1Sa 10:20–26
–David anointed as king ... 1Sa 16:1–13
–David's line to be the royal line ... 2Sa 7:8–16
See KING

5. Rule by foreign kings
–The Babylonians ... 2Ch 36:15–21
Da 1:1–6
–The Persians ... Ezr 1:1–4
Isa 44:28–45:6
–The Herods of Idumea ... Mt 2:1–8,16–22
–The Romans ... Mt 27:11–14
Jn 18:28–40

B. Principles of government

1. God and human government
–God is the real ruler ... Dt 33:5
Jdg 8:23
1Ch 29:23
Ps 29:10–11
Isa 33:22
–God rules through anointed servants ... Ps 45:6–7
Isa 45:1

2. Humans in the government
–They derive authority from God ... Da 4:17
Jn 19:11
Ro 13:1,4
–God's people may serve pagan governments ... Neh 2:1–9
Neh 5:14–18
Est 8:1–2
Da 1:17–21

C. Our responsibility to government
–We must respect it ... 1Sa 14:6–7
1Sa 26:7–11
1Pe 2:17
–We must submit to it ... Ro 13:1,5
Titus 3:1
1Pe 2:13–14
–We must support it with taxes ... Mt 22:15–21
Ro 13:6–7
–We must pray for it ... 1Ti 2:1–2
–Occasionally we may have to disobey it ... Ac 5:29

GRACE

–God's free and undeserved favor

A. Related themes
GRACE is a theme of:
–Genesis ... Ge 25:33
–Judges ... Jdg 6:13
–Job ... Job 42:10
–Jonah ... Jnh 3:10
–Romans ... Ro 11:6

B. Grace comes as a gift
–From God ... Eph 2:8
1Pe 5:10
–From the Father ... Ps 84:11
Jas 1:17
–From Christ, the Son ... Jn 1:17
1Co 1:4
–From the Holy Spirit ... Zec 12:10
Heb 10:29

C. How can we receive grace?
–We must accept Christ ... Jn 1:14,16
2Co 8:9
Eph 1:6–7
–We must be humble ... Pr 3:34
Jas 4:6
–We cannot earn it by good works ... Ro 11:6
2Ti 1:9

–We cannot earn it by keeping the law . . . . Ro 6:14
Gal 2:16

D. Examples of those who received grace
–Abraham. . . . . Gal 3:18
–Paul . . . . Eph 3:2
1Ti 1:12–16
–All believers. . . . . Eph 1:7–8

E. What happens to believers through grace?
–They are chosen . . . . Ro 11:5
–They are called . . . . Gal 1:15
–They believe. . . . . Ac 18:27
–They are justified . . . . Ro 3:24
Titus 3:7
–They receive righteousness . . . . Ro 5:17
–They are saved . . . . Ac 15:11
Titus 2:11
–They are redeemed. . . . . Ro 3:24
–They are forgiven . . . . Eph 1:7
–They receive many good things . . . . Ro 8:32
Jas 1:17
–They receive spiritual gifts. . . . . Ro 12:6
Eph 4:7–12
–They receive encouragement. 2Th 2:16
–They receive help in time of need . . . Heb 4:16
–They are able to bear up under suffering. 2Co 12:9
–They have hope 2Th 2:16
–They are glorified in Christ 2Th 1:12

F. Relationship of believers to grace
–They are under grace. . . . . Ro 6:14
–They stand in grace . . . . Ro 5:2
–They are what they are by grace. . . . 1Co 15:10
–They abound in grace 2Co 9:8
1Ti 1:14
–They share in God's grace . . . . Php 1:7
–They may approach God's throne of grace. . . . . Heb 4:16
–They are strengthened by grace . . . . Heb 13:9
–They must grow in grace 2Pe 3:18
–They must not receive grace in vain 2Co 6:1
–They can fall away from grace . . . . . Gal 5:4
Heb 6:4–6

G. The wicked experience grace. . . . . Isa 26:10
Mt 5:45
Ac 14:17

GRAVE (SHEOL)

–Sheol is a Hebrew word of uncertain meaning

A. Where everyone goes at death. . . . . . . Isa 14:9–11
–The righteous. . . . . Ge 37:35
Ps 88:3–5
–The wicked. . . . . Nu 16:30
Eze 32:21,27

B. Characteristics
–A place of darkness and corruption . . . . Job 17:13–16
–A place of inactivity . . . . Ps 6:5
Ps 31:17
Ecc 9:10
Isa 38:18
–The opposite of the heavens. . . . . Ps 139:8
Am 9:2
–The opposite of life . . . . Pr 15:24
–It is never satisfied . . . . Pr 27:20
Isa 5:14
Hab 2:5

C. Resurrection takes place from there. . . . Ps 16:10–11
Ps 49:14–15

GREAT TRIBULATION

–A time of intense distress at the end of the world

A. General tribulation
See PAIN

B. The Great Tribulation
–Only use of the specific term . . . . Rev 7:14
–A time of great distress . . . . Isa 24:1–20
Da 12:1
Mt 24:15–28
–The time is limited . . . . Da 9:24–27
–Dominated by the antichrist. . . . . Rev 13:11–17
–Ends with the destruction of Babylon . . . . Rev 14:8
Rev 18:1–24
–Shortened for the sake of the elect . . . Mt 24:22

GREECE, GREEK

–A Roman province, south of Macedonia

A. Paul's ministry in Greece
1. Greece is also called Achaia. . . . . . . Ac 18:12,27
Ro 15:26
1Co 16:15
2. Ministry in Athens
–Paul preached to Jews and Greeks there. . . . . Ac 17:16–17
–Altar to unknown god located there . . . . Ac 17:22–23
–Paul's sermon to the Areopagus . . . Ac 17:22–31
3. Ministry in Corinth
See CORINTH

B. The Greeks
–Greeks wanted to speak with Jesus . . . . Jn 12:20–21
–God-fearing Greeks joined with Jews. . . . . Ac 17:4,17
–Grecian Jews in the early church. . . . . Ac 6:1
Ac 9:29
–Paul preached to Jews and Greeks . . . Ac 18:4
Ac 20:21
–"Greek" sometimes meant any non-Jew 1Co 1:22–24
Gal 2:3
Col 3:11
–In the church, neither Jew nor Greek . . . . Gal 3:28
Col 3:11

GREED

See THE RICH AND THE POOR

GRIEF

A. Related theme
LAMENT is a theme of Lamentations. . . . . La 1:16

B. Human grief
1. Occasions for human grief
–Death of a loved one. . . . . Ge 37:34–35
2Sa 18:33
–A loved one likely to die soon 2Sa 12:15–17
Mt 17:23
–A loved one departing . . . . Jn 16:19–20
–Experiencing pain and suffering . . . . Ps 10:12–13
Ps 31:9–13
1Pe 1:6
–Seeing the pain of others . . . . Job 30:25
Jer 48:36
–Feeling sorrow for sin . . . . Neh 8:8–11
Jas 4:8–9
–Being punished for sin. . . . . La 1:4–5
2Co 2:5–7
–Seeing the sin of others. 1Sa 16:1
–Not being able to bear children. . . . 1Sa 1:10–11,15–16
–Children marrying outside the faith . . . . Ge 26:34–35

–Children choosing the way of folly .... Pr 10:1; Pr 17:21
–One's relatives not receiving Christ .... Ro 9:2–3; 2Co 12:21

2. The answer to human grief
–Receiving comfort from friends ... Job 2:11–13; Jn 11:19; Ro 12:15
–Receiving comfort from the Lord .... Ps 23:4; Isa 61:2; Mt 5:4
–Seeing the risen Christ .... Jn 20:20; 1Th 4:13–14
–Experiencing salvation 2Co 7:9–10; 1Pe 1:5–6
–Knowing that God does not reject us .... La 3:31–33
–Knowing that God turns grief into joy .... Isa 61:3; Jer 31:13; Jn 16:20
–Knowing that God will wipe away all tears .... Isa 25:8; Rev 21:4

C. Divine grief
1. The grief of the Triune God
–Grief of the Father .... Ge 6:6–7; 1Sa 15:10–11
–Grief of the Son .... Lk 19:41–44; Jn 11:33–35
–Grief of the Holy Spirit .... Isa 63:10; Eph 4:30

2. Occasions for divine grief
–Grief because of human sin .... Ge 3:6–7; 1Sa 15:10–11; Eze 6:9–10
–Grief because of punishment for sin .... 2Sa 24:16; Jer 42:10; Lk 19:41–44

GROWTH

A. Related themes
GROWTH is a theme of Esther .... Est 4:8
MATURITY is a theme of Hebrews .. Heb 6:1
SEARCHING is a theme of Ecclesiastes .... Ecc 2:3

B. Natural growth
–Of plants .... Ps 90:5–6
–Of human beings .... Lk 1:80; Lk 2:40
–Of political power 2Sa 3:1

C. Numerical growth of the church
1. Parables of growth
–Parable of the sower .... Mt 13:3–9,18–23
–Parable of the weeds .... Mt 13:24–30, 36–43
–Parable of the mustard seed .... Mt 13:31–32
–Parable of the yeast .... Mt 13:33

2. Growth of the New Testament church .... Ac 4:4; Ac 5:14; Ac 6:7; Ac 9:31; Ac 16:5

D. Spiritual growth of Christians
1. What shows lack of growth?
–Inadequate knowledge of God's truth .... Ac 18:24–28; Ac 19:1–6
–Lack of doctrinal soundness .... Eph 4:14
–Jealousy and quarreling 1Co 3:1–3
–Living a life of evil 1Co 14:20
–Inability to understand deeper truths .... Heb 5:12–14

2. How does growth take place?
–By study of God's word 1Pe 2:1–3
–By increasing our knowledge of God .... Col 1:10
–By deepening our faith .... Eph 4:13
–By showing love .... Eph 4:15–16
–By developing Christian character 2Pe 1:5–8

3. God wants us to grow and bear fruit .... Ps 1:1–3; Ps 92:12–15; Jn 15:2,4–5,16

GUILT

–The condition of one who breaks the law

A. Guilt in the Old Testament
1. Standing guilty before God
–Because of deliberate sin .... Lev 6:1–4
–Because of unintentional sin .... Lev 5:2–4,14–17
–Guilty even before birth .... Ps 51:5
–Dressed in dirty clothes .... Isa 64:6; Zec 3:3–4
–God knows our guilt .... Ps 69:5
–God does not leave guilt unpunished .... Ex 34:7; Na 1:3

2. Feeling guilty because of sin .... 2Sa 24:10; Ezr 9:5–7,15; Ps 38:4

3. Resolving guilt before God
–The call to acknowledge guilt .... Jer 3:13; Hos 5:15
–The guilt offering .... Lev 5:14–6:7; Lev 7:1–6
–Confession and forgiveness .... Ps 32:5; Isa 6:5–7

B. Guilt in the New Testament
1. The reality of guilt
–Christ's coming convicts us of guilt .... Jn 15:22,24
–The Spirit convicts us of guilt .... Jn 16:7–8
–One sin makes us guilty of breaking the whole law .... Jas 2:10
–All stand guilty before God .... Ro 3:19,23
–All are guilty because of Adam's sin .... Ro 5:12–14

2. The resolution of guilt
–We must confess our sins 1Jn 1:9
–We must draw near to God in faith .... Heb 10:22
–We become free of guilt through Christ .... Ro 5:15–18

See also CONFESSION
FORGIVENESS
SIN

HAGAR

–Egyptian servant of Sarai .... Ge 16:1
–Given to Abram to conceive a child .... Ge 16:3
–Driven away by Sarai while pregnant ... Ge 16:5–16
–Gave birth to Ishmael .... Ge 25:12
–Driven away after birth of Isaac .... Ge 21:9–21
–Story interpreted by Paul .... Gal 4:21–31

HAGGAI

–A post-exilic prophet .... Ezr 5:1
–Encouraged rebuilding of temple .... Ezr 6:14

Hag 1:12–13
–Warned God's people of dangers of selfishness...................... Hag 1:3–11

HAM

–Son of Noah........................ Ge 5:32
1Ch 1:4
–Laughed at Noah's nakedness......... Ge 9:20–27
–Father of Canaan..................... Ge 9:18
1Ch 1:8–16

HAMAN

–Agagite noble honored by Ahasuerus (Xerxes)........................ Est 3:1–2
–Angry when Mordecai would not bow down.............................. Est 3:2–5
–Plotted to execute Jews................ Est 3:6–15
–Built gallows to hang Mordecai .... Est 5:9–14
–Forced to honor Mordecai .... Est 6:1–13
–Plot exposed by Esther .... Est 7:1–8
–Hanged on his own gallows........... Est 7:9–10

HAND

A. The human hand

1. What the human hand does
   –Works............................ Ps 90:17
   –Holds............................ Rev 7:9
   –Writes........................... Gal 6:11
   –Touches.......................... 1Jn 1:1
   –Claps............................ Ps 47:1
   –Fights........................... Ps 18:34
   –Blesses.......................... Lev 9:22
   –Lifts up in prayer 1Ti 2:8
   –Lifts up in praise................. Ps 134:2
   –Takes oath before God .... Ge 14:22
2. Significance of the right hand
   –Place of honor .... Ps 45:9
   –Position of power 1Ki 2:19
   –Used to confirm an agreement ... Gal 2:9
3. Laying on of hands
   a. In the Old Testament
   –Ordained Levites.............. Nu 8:10
   –Ordained leaders.............. Nu 27:18,22–23
   –Transferred guilt .... Lev 16:20–21
   b. In the New Testament
   –Conferred healing............ Mk 6:5
   Lk 4:40
   Ac 28:8
   –Transferred the Holy Spirit.... Ac 8:17
   Ac 9:17
   Ac 19:6
   –Ordained missionaries......... Ac 13:3
   –Ordained church officers........ Ac 6:6
   1Ti 4:14
   2Ti 1:6

B. The hand of God

1. What it does
   –It saves us........................ Ex 6:1
   Dt 5:15
   –It guides us....................... Ezr 7:9
   –It provides for us.................. Ps 104:28
   –It protects us .... Ps 139:10
   –It receives our spirits.............. Ps 31:5
   –It pleads with us .... Isa 65:2
   –It chastises us .... Ps 32:4
   –It punishes unbelievers .... Ex 7:5
2. Significance of the right hand of God
   –His hand of power .... Ps 17:7
   Ps 73:23
   Ps 118:15–16
   –Sitting at his right hand as ruler.. Ps 110:1
   Ac 2:33
   Eph 1:20
   Heb 1:3

HANNAH

–Wife of Elkanah 1Sa 1:1–2
–Prayed to have a child................ 1Sa 1:9–18
–Gave birth to Samuel.................. 1Sa 1:19–20
–Dedicated Samuel to the Lord's work .. 1Sa 1:24–28
–Prayed at Samuel's dedication 1Sa 2:1–10
–Blessed by Eli 1Sa 2:18–20
–Gave birth to other children........... 1Sa 2:21

HARAN

A. The father of Lot .... Ge 11:27
–Died in Ur......................... Ge 11:28

B. A city in Mesopotamia
–Terah, Abram and Lot emigrated there .... Ge 11:31
Ac 7:4
–Abram set out from there for Canaan............................ Ge 12:4
–Abraham sent there to find a wife for Isaac .... Ge 24:1–4
–Jacob fled there.................... Ge 28:10
–Home of Laban, Leah and Rachel... Ge 29:4–6
–Jacob lived there twenty years ..... Ge 31:41
–Belonged to Assyrian empire........ 2Ki 19:12

HARVEST

A. The importance of harvests

1. Events were calculated by harvest times.......................... Ge 30:14
   Jdg 15:1
   Ru 1:22
2. Israelite feasts centered around harvest
   –Feast of the Firstfruits.......... Lev 23:9–14
   –Feast of Weeks .... Lev 23:15–21
   –Feast of Tabernacles .... Lev 23:33–43
3. Provision made for the poor at harvesttime...................... Lev 19:9–10
   Dt 24:19–22
   Ru 2:1–9

B. God's use of harvests
–Abundant harvest demonstrated his love .... Dt 8:7–9
Ps 23:1
Ps 144:12–15
–God chastised by means of crop failure and famine............... Isa 17:10–11
Joel 1:8–12
Hag 1:5–6

C. Harvesting used as a metaphor

1. To picture mission work
   –Pray for workers in God's harvest........................ Mt 9:37–38
   –The fields ripe for harvest .... Jn 4:35–36
2. To picture God's judgment .... Isa 17:1–5
   Jer 51:33
3. To picture the end of the world
   –Gathering the saints .... Mt 13:24–30, 36–43
   –Judging God's enemies .... Rev 14:14–19
   Joel 3:12–13
4. The law of the harvest
   –Reaping what we sow 2Co 9:6
   Gal 6:7
   –Sowing evil and reaping trouble... Job 4:8
   Pr 22:8
   Hos 10:13
   –Sowing good and reaping blessing........................ Hos 10:12
   Gal 6:8–9

HAZAEL

–A servant of King Ben-Hadad of Aram...2Ki 8:7–8

–Anointed by Elijah as king over Aram . . . 1Ki 19:15
–Asked Elisha about Ben-Hadad 2Ki 8:8–9
–Murdered Ben-Hadad 2Ki 8:14–15
–Became king of Aram 2Ki 8:15
–Fought against Israel and Judah 2Ki 8:28
2Ch 22:5–6
–Conquered part of Israel 2Ki 10:32–33
2Ki 13:22
–Gained power over Joash 2Ki 12:17–18
–Succeeded by son Ben-Hadad 2Ki 13:24
–Judgment prophesied against him . . . . . Am 1:3–5

HEAD

A. The human head

1. Literal use
–Hand put on the head in blessing . . . Ge 48:14–18
–People were anointed on the head . . . . Ex 29:7
1Sa 10:1
–Anointing head with oil meant blessings . . . . Ps 23:5
–Crowns were put on the head 1Ch 20:2
Est 2:17
–No razor on the head of a Nazirite . . . . Nu 6:5–6
Jdg 13:5
–Cutting off the head, a sign of victory 1Sa 17:51
1Sa 31:9
–Woman's covered head showed submission 1Co 11:5,10
–A bowed head showed reverence . . . Ge 24:26
Ge 43:28
Ex 4:31
–A bowed head showed grief . . . . . . Ps 35:14
–Dust on one's head showed sorrow 1Sa 4:12
–Pulling hair from the head showed sorrow . . . . Ezr 9:3
–Shaving hair from the head showed grief . . . . Job 1:20
Isa 15:2
–Ashes on one's head showed shame 2Sa 13:19
–Shaking the head showed disdain . . . . Job 16:4
Ps 22:7
Mt 27:39

2. Figurative use
–Blessings crown the head . . . . Pr 10:6
–Joy crowns the head . . . . Isa 35:10
Isa 51:11
–Blood on one's head meant guilt . . . 2Sa 1:15–16
Eze 33:4
–Lifting up one's head meant pride . . . . Ps 83:2
–From head to foot meant the whole body . . . . Dt 28:35
Isa 1:6
–The Lord gives grace by lifting a head . . . . Ps 3:3
Ps 27:5–6
–Heaping coals of fire on the head . . . . Pr 25:22
Ro 12:20
–Jesus had nowhere to lay his head . . . . Mt 8:20

B. Head as a symbolic word

1. Political leadership
–Heads as leaders of the clans of Israel . . . . Nu 1:16
Jos 14:1
–Heads as leaders of the tribes . . . . Nu 30:1
–Heads as leaders of families 2Ch 1:2
Ezr 2:68
–A head as the king of a country . . . Isa 7:8–9

2. Husband as the head of his wife . . . 1Co 11:3,8–10
Eph 5:23

3. Christ as the head
–Head of all creation . . . . Eph 1:10
–Head of every man 1Co 11:3
–Head of the church . . . . Eph 5:23
Col 1:18
Col 2:19

HEALING

A. Roles in healing

1. God is the ultimate healer . . . . Dt 32:39
Ps 103:3
Jer 30:17

2. Human elements that play a role
–Faith . . . . Mt 13:58
Mk 5:34
Lk 18:42
–Prayer . . . . Jas 5:14–16
–Intercession . . . . Nu 12:10–15
1Ki 13:6
–A cheerful heart . . . . Pr 17:22
–Positive words . . . . Pr 16:24

B. Physical healing of the body

1. Medical care used 2Ki 20:7
Lk 10:34–35
1Ti 5:23

2. Miracles performed
–Directly by God . . . . Ge 20:17
–By prophets 1Ki 17:17–24
2Ki 5:1–14
–By Jesus . . . . Mt 4:24
–By followers of Jesus . . . . Ac 5:15–16
Ac 28:8
–By agents of Satan 2Th 2:9
Rev 13:3

3. Spiritual gifts of miracles and healing 1Co 12:9–10,28

See also MIRACLE

C. Spiritual healing
–Received by the land 2Ch 7:13–14
–Received by people 2Ch 30:18–20
Hos 14:4
1Pe 2:24
–Performed by Jesus with physical healing . . . . Mk 2:5–11

HEART

–The center of the human being

A. Basic concept of the heart

1. The wellspring of all life . . . . Pr 4:23
Lk 6:45

2. Combined with other basic human elements
–The heart and soul . . . . Dt 6:5
1Sa 14:7
Mt 22:37
–The heart and body . . . . Ps 16:9
–The heart and mind . . . . Ps 26:2
Mt 22:37
Rev 2:23
–The heart and spirit . . . . Ps 51:10,17
Eze 18:31
–The heart and flesh . . . . Ps 73:26
Ps 84:2
–The heart and thoughts . . . . Ps 139:23
–The heart and understanding . . . . Pr 3:5

B. What the heart controls

1. Human emotions
–The glad heart . . . . Ex 4:14
Ac 2:26

–The singing heart ... Eph 5:19
–The heart that loves ... Dt 6:5
SS 3:1–3
–The heart that takes delight ... Ecc 2:10
Jer 15:16
–The excited heart ... Lk 24:32
–The courageous heart ... 1Sa 10:26
Ps 27:14
–The heart that is encouraged ... Col 2:2
2Th 2:17
–The thankful heart ... Col 3:16
–The repentant heart ... Ps 51:17
–The humble heart ... Mt 11:29
–The compassionate heart ... Lk 7:13
–The anxious heart ... Pr 12:25
–The discouraged heart ... Jos 2:11
–The troubled heart ... Jn 12:27
–The grieving heart ... 1Sa 2:33
La 2:18
–The tormented heart ... La 2:11
–The broken heart ... Eze 21:6
–The heavy heart ... Pr 25:20
–The anguished heart ... Isa 65:14
Jer 4:19
Ro 9:2
–The fearful heart ... Dt 28:67
Jos 5:1
–The angry heart ... Ps 39:3
Pr 19:3

2. The human will
–To do according to one's heart ... 1Sa 2:35
1Ch 28:2
–To decide in the heart ... 2Ch 6:7
–To devote the heart ... 1Ch 22:19
–To direct the heart ... 2Th 3:5
–To turn the heart ... 1Ki 8:58
Ps 119:36
–To incline the heart ... Dt 5:29
–To win over the heart ... 2Sa 19:14
–To yield the heart ... Jos 24:23
–To agree with one heart ... Jer 32:39
Ac 4:32
–To be moved in the heart ... Ex 35:21
–The purposes of the heart ... Jer 23:20
–The motives of the heart ... 1Co 4:5
–The desires of the heart ... Ps 21:2
Ro 10:1
–The willing heart ... 2Ch 29:31
–The unrepentant heart ... Ro 2:5
–The hardened heart ... Ex 4:21
Pr 28:14

3. The human intelligence
–To acknowledge in the heart ... Dt 4:39
–To know in the heart ... Dt 8:5
–To take something to heart ... Ex 7:23
Ecc 7:2
–To fix words in the heart ... Dt 11:18
–To lay up words in the heart ... Job 22:22
Pr 4:21
–To search the heart ... Ps 4:4
–To say in the heart ... Ro 10:6
–To muse in the heart ... Ps 77:6
–To ponder in the heart ... Lk 2:19
–To think in the heart ... Mk 2:8
–To understand in the heart ... Pr 2:2
–To meditate in the heart ... Ps 19:14
–To pray in the heart ... Ge 24:45
1Sa 1:13
–To believe in the heart ... Ro 10:9
–To be wise in the heart ... Pr 2:10
Pr 10:8
–To doubt in the heart ... Mk 11:23
–To harbor deceit in the heart ... Pr 26:24
Jer 17:9
–To devise evil in the heart ... Ps 140:2
–The thoughts of the heart ... Ge 6:5
Lk 2:35

C. Key elements in the human heart
1. Characteristics of the unregenerate heart
–Proud ... Pr 18:12
–Foolish ... Pr 12:23
–Deceitful ... Jer 17:9
–Rebellious ... Jer 5:23
–Perverse ... Pr 11:20
–Evil ... Ge 6:5
–Wicked ... Pr 6:18
–Callous ... Ps 119:70
–Malicious ... Ps 28:3
–Hardened ... Eph 4:18
–Darkened ... Ro 1:21
–Deluded ... Isa 44:20
–Unrepentant ... Ro 2:5
–Unbelieving ... Heb 3:12
–Gone astray ... Ps 95:10
–Devoted to idols ... Eze 11:21
–Filled with schemes to do wrong ... Ecc 8:11
–Filled with madness ... Ecc 9:3
–Far from God ... Isa 29:13
Mk 7:6

2. What the regenerate heart does
–Cries out for the living God ... Ps 84:2
–Seeks God ... Ps 119:2,10
–Responds to God ... 2Ki 22:19
–Trusts in the Lord ... Pr 3:5
–Loves the Lord ... Dt 6:5
Mt 22:37
–Praises the Lord ... Ps 9:1
–Sings to the Lord ... Ps 30:12
–Rejoices in the Lord ... 1Sa 2:1
–Rejoices in salvation ... Ps 13:5
–Is grateful to God ... Col 3:16
–Obeys God's law ... Ps 119:34,69,112
Eph 6:6
–Hides God's word within ... Ps 119:11
–Is on fire for God's word ... Jer 20:9
–Meditates on God and his word ... Ps 19:14
–Is upright ... Ps 7:10
–Speaks the truth ... Ps 15:2
–Is steadfast and secure ... Ps 57:7
Ps 112:7–8
–Is pure ... Ps 24:4
Mt 5:8
–Is wise ... Pr 10:8
–Is sincere ... Ac 2:46
Heb 10:22
–Is unafraid and courageous ... Ps 27:3,14
–Is contrite ... Ps 51:17
–Is circumcised ... Dt 10:16
Ro 2:29
–Walks blamelessly ... Ps 101:2
–Loves others ... 1Pe 1:22

D. God's relationship to the human heart
–He knows it ... 1Sa 16:7
–He searches it ... Ps 7:9
Jer 17:10
–He tests it ... 1Ch 29:17
1Th 2:4
–He influences it ... Ezr 7:27
–He directs it ... Pr 21:1
–He opens it ... Ac 16:14
–He touches it ... 1Sa 10:26
–He makes light shine in it ... 2Co 4:6
–He cleanses it ... Heb 10:22
–He writes his law on it ... Jer 31:33
–He strengthens it ... 1Th 3:13
–He keeps it loyal ... 1Ch 29:18
–He gives a new heart ... Ps 51:10
Eze 11:19

HEAVEN

A. What is heaven?

1. Part of God's creation .... Ge 1:1
 –A component of the universe..... Ex 20:4; Php 2:10
 –Where God placed sun, moon and stars .... Ge 1:14–18; Dt 4:19
 –Where precipitation comes from... Ge 8:2; Job 38:29; Isa 55:10
2. The place where God dwells
 –His dwelling place .... 1Ki 8:30; Mt 6:9
 –His sanctuary .... Ps 102:19
 –Where his throne is .... Ps 2:4; Isa 63:15
 –Where Christ ascended.......... Lk 24:51; Heb 9:24

B. What does God do from heaven?

1. Actions in Bible history
 –God talked to his people .... Ge 22:11,15
 –God made the Israelites hear him .... Dt 4:36
 –God heard his people when they prayed.................... Neh 9:27–28
 –God sent bread .... Ex 16:4,13–15; Neh 9:15
 –God sent fire of judgment......... 2Ki 1:12
 –God sent fire for sacrifice......... 1Ch 21:26
 –God revealed mysteries.......... Da 2:18–19; Ac 10:10–16
2. Continuing actions
 –God reigns .... Ps 99:1–2
 –God observes human actions....... Ps 14:2; Ps 102:19
 –God blesses his people .... Dt 26:15
 –God hears our prayers........... 2Ch 6:21,23, 25,27
 –God saves us .... Ps 57:3
 –God sends his Holy Spirit......... 1Pe 1:12
 –God reveals his wrath .... Ro 1:18
 –Christ prepares a place for us .... Jn 14:2–3
 –Christ will return from heaven 1Th 4:16

C. Our relationship to heaven

1. How can we enter heaven?
 –We must be chosen and called.... 2Pe 1:10–11
 –We must be born again .... Jn 3:5
 –We must trust in God and in Jesus.......................... Jn 14:1–2
 –We must have our names recorded there .... Lk 10:20
 –We must be righteous .... Mt 5:19–20
 –We must live holy lives .... Rev 22:14–15
 –We must do the will of God ...... Mt 7:21
 –We must be humble .... Mt 18:3–4
 –We must be poor in spirit .... Mt 5:3
 –We must overcome............... Rev 2:7; Rev 21:7
 –We must receive new bodies 1Co 15:50–54
2. What should our attitude be toward heaven?
 –We should lay up treasures there........................ Mt 6:20
 –We should sacrifice everything *for it* .... Mt 13:44–46
 –We should long for it 2Co 5:2
 –We should eagerly look for it...... 2Pe 3:13
 –We should hope for it............ Col 1:5
 –In spirit we are already there..... Eph 2:6; Php 3:20; Col 3:1

D. Aspects of the present heaven

1. Positive
 –God dwells there................ 1Ki 8:30
 –Christ dwells there at God's right hand .... Ac 7:55–56; Eph 1:20
 –Christ intercedes for us there..... Heb 9:24
 –There is joy there .... Lk 15:7,10
 –There is comfort there........... Lk 16:22–25
 –Satan has been cast out of there... Rev 12:7–9
2. Negative
 –God reveals his wrath from there........................ 1Sa 2:10; Ro 1:18
 –Powers of evil intrude there....... Job 1:6–7; Eph 6:12
 –Wars occur there .... Rev 12:7
 –Saints cry out from there .... Rev 6:9–11
 –Saints do not yet have new bodies...................... 1Co 15:48–54
 –It must be destroyed and renewed..................... 2Pe 3:7,10,12–13; Rev 21:1

E. What the new heaven will be like

1. It will be free from:
 –Death.......................... Lk 20:35–36; Rev 21:4
 –Pain, sorrow and crying.......... Isa 65:19–23; Rev 21:4
 –Night .... Rev 22:5
 –Hunger and thirst............... Rev 7:16
 –The curse of God .... Rev 22:3
 –Wicked people.................. Rev 22:15
2. For believers, it will be:
 –Eternal 2Co 5:1
 –A place of eternal light .... Rev 22:5
 –The home of righteousness 2Pe 3:13
 –The place of harmony and unity.. Isa 65:25
 –The place of eternal praise to God .... Rev 7:15
 –The place of exquisite beauty .... Rev 21:10–21
 –The place of purity.............. Rev 21:27
 –The place of the tree of life....... Rev 22:1–2

HEBRON

–A city, originally called Kiriath Arba ... Jos 14:15
–Also called Mamre................. Ge 23:19
–Abram built an altar and lived there ... Ge 13:18
–Abraham and Sarah's burial plot located there .... Ge 23:1–19
–Allied with other cities against Gibeonites .... Jos 10:1–5
–Defeated by Joshua .... Jos 10:6–26; Jos 11:21
–Given to Caleb...................... Jos 14:13–15; Jdg 1:9–10,20
–Later given to Kohathites 1Ch 6:54–56
–David ruled from there for seven years 2Sa 2:1–4; 1Ki 2:11
–Soldiers joined David there 1Ch 12:23–40
–David anointed king of all Israel there 2Sa 5:1–3; 1Ch 11:1–3
–Absalom crowned king there 2Sa 15:7–10

HEIR

See INHERITANCE

HELL

A. A place of punishment
 –For fallen angels 2Pe 2:4

–For the devil and his angels Mt 25:41
–For the beast and the false prophet Rev 19:20
–For those who worship the beast Rev 14:9–11
–For wicked humans Rev 21:8
–For those who reject the gospel Mt 10:11–15

B. Hints of hell in the Old Testament
–The wicked perish in death Ps 49:10–15
–There will be judgment for the wicked Job 24:21–24
–There will be eternal punishment Isa 66:24; Da 12:2

C. Description of hell in the New Testament
–A place of separation from God 2Th 1:9
–The second death Rev 21:8
–The place of condemnation Mt 23:33
–The place of torment Lk 16:23
–The place of weeping and the grinding of teeth Mt 8:12; Mt 25:30
–The place where body and soul is destroyed Mt 10:28
–Eternal punishment Mt 25:46
–Everlasting destruction 2Th 1:9
–Everlasting chains Jude 6
–Eternal fire Mt 18:8; Jude 7
–The lake of fire Rev 20:15
–The blackest darkness Jude 13

HERESY
See DOCTRINE

HEROD
A. Herod the Great
–King of Judea at time of Jesus' birth Mt 2:1; Lk 1:5
–Magi contacted him Mt 2:1–8
–Ordered babies in Bethlehem killed Mt 2:16

B. Herod Antipas
–Tetrarch of Galilee Mt 14:1; Lk 3:1
–Beheaded John the Baptist Mt 14:3–12
–Worried about Jesus Lk 9:7–9
–Jesus called him a fox Lk 13:31–32
–Participated in trial of Jesus Lk 23:6–15

C. Herod Agrippa
–Persecuted the early church Ac 12:1
–Killed James Ac 12:2
–Arrested Peter Ac 12:3–19
–Died a miserable death from God Ac 12:19–23

HERODIAS
–Wife of Herod Antipas Mt 14:3–4; Mk 6:17
–Told daughter to ask for John's severed head Mt 14:6–11; Mk 6:21–27

HEZEKIAH
–King of Judah 2Ch 29:1
–Purified the temple 2Ch 29:3–19
–Restored proper sacrifices 2Ch 29:20–36
–Celebrated the Passover for two weeks 2Ch 30:1–27
–Cleansed land of idols 2Ch 31:1
–Organized priests and Levites 2Ch 31:2–19
–Collected Solomon's proverbs Pr 25:1
–Sought the Lord for help against Assyria 2Ch 32:1–20; Isa 36:1–37:20
–Witnessed the destruction of Sennacherib 2Ch 32:21–23; Isa 37:36–37
–Had fatal illness 2Ki 20:1
–Illness healed by God through prayer 2Ki 20:2–11; Isa 38:2–8
–Sang a song after his recovery Isa 38:9–20
–Judged for sin of pride 2Ki 20:12–21; Isa 39:1–8

HILKIAH
–High priest during time of Josiah 2Ki 22:4
–Reported his finding of the Book of the Law 2Ki 22:8; 2Ch 34:14–15
–Questioned Huldah about the Law 2Ki 22:14; 2Ch 34:22
–Ordered by Josiah to cleanse the temple 2Ki 23:4; 2Ch 34:9–11
–Became administrator of the temple 2Ch 35:8

HIRAM
–King of Tyre 2Sa 5:11
–Helped David build his palace 2Sa 5:11–12; 1Ch 14:1
–Helped Solomon build the temple 1Ki 5:1–12; 2Ch 2:3–18
–Scorned towns that Solomon gave him 1Ki 9:10–13
–Helped build Solomon's navy 1Ki 9:26–28; 2Ch 8:17–18
–Engaged in extensive trade 1Ki 10:11–12

HITTITES
A. Their identity
–Descendants of Canaan, grandson of Noah Ge 10:6,15
–One of the seven Canaanite nations Ex 33:2

B. Significant Hittites
–Ephron: sold Abraham a burial plot Ge 23:10–20
–Judith and Basemath: wives of Esau Ge 26:34
–Ahimelech: a soldier with David 1Sa 26:6
–Uriah: husband of Bathsheba 2Sa 11:3–24; 1Ki 15:5

C. Their wars
–Allied with others against Joshua Jos 11:1–5
–Defeated by Joshua Jos 12:7–8

D. Important data concerning them
–Controlled much land in Moses' time Nu 13:27–29; Jos 1:4
–God promised their land to his people Ex 3:8,17; Ex 34:11
–Israelites told to destroy them completely Dt 7:1–6; Dt 20:17
–Israelites did not destroy them completely Jdg 3:5
–Solomon traded with them 1Ki 10:29
–Many became Solomon's slaves 1Ki 9:20–21; 2Ch 8:7–8
–Intermarried with the Israelites Jdg 3:5–6; 1Ki 11:1; Ezr 9:1–2

HOLINESS
–*Being set apart from sin; purity*

A. Related theme
HOLINESS is a theme of Leviticus Lev 19:12

B. The holiness of God
1. In the Old Testament
–He is holy Ps 99:3,5,9

–He is called the Holy One of Israel ... Ps 22:3
Isa 30:11–12,15
–His Spirit is holy ... Isa 63:10
–His name is holy ... Ps 111:9
–His throne is holy ... Ps 47:8
–He is majestic in holiness ... Ex 15:11
–His holiness has splendor ... 1Ch 16:29
–He is surrounded by holiness ... Isa 6:3
–He is unique in his holiness ... 1Sa 2:2
–He swears by his holiness ... Am 4:2
–He will show himself holy ... Isa 5:16
–His words are holy ... Jer 23:9
–His arm is holy ... Isa 52:10

2. In the New Testament
–The Father is holy ... Mt 6:9
Jn 17:11
–The Son is holy ... Lk 1:35
Ac 4:27,30
–The Spirit is holy ... Ac 2:4
Ro 1:4

C. The holiness of God's people

1. Israel in the Old Testament
–They were holy to the Lord ... Jer 2:3
–They were a holy people ... Ex 19:6
Dt 7:6
–They formed a holy race ... Ezr 9:2
–They were expected to be holy ... Lev 11:44–45
Lev 19:12
–The priests were holy ... Lev 21:5–6

2. Christians in the New Testament
–They are a holy people ... Col 3:12
1Pe 2:9
–They are a holy temple ... Eph 2:21
–They are saints (holy ones) ... 2Co 1:1
Eph 1:1
–They are sanctified (made holy) ... 1Co 6:11
–They are chosen to be holy ... Eph 1:4
–They are called to a holy life ... 1Th 4:7
–They must live holy lives ... Heb 12:14
1Pe 1:15–16
–They are to serve God in holiness ... Lk 1:74–75
–They must purify themselves in holiness ... 2Co 7:1
–They will be presented to God as holy ... Col 1:22

D. The holiness of special things

1. Referred to in the Old Testament
–The ground where one meets God ... Ex 3:4–5
–The Holy Place and the Most Holy Place ... Ex 26:33
–The altar in the tabernacle ... Ex 29:37
–The garments of the priests ... Ex 28:2–4
–The turban of the priest ... Ex 39:30–31
–The furnishings used by the priests ... Nu 4:15
–The guilt offering ... Lev 7:1
–Anything given to the Lord ... Lev 27:9,14,21,28
–The camp of the Israelites ... Dt 23:14
–The temple ... Hab 2:20
–The Sabbath ... Ex 16:23
–The Year of Jubilee ... Lev 25:12
–Mount Zion in Jerusalem ... Ps 2:6
Isa 27:13
–The city of Jerusalem ... Neh 11:1

2. Referred to in the New Testament
–The angels ... Ac 10:22
1Th 3:13
–The city of Jerusalem ... Mt 4:5
–The Scriptures ... Ro 1:2
2Ti 3:15
–The law of God ... Ro 7:12
–A Christian's faith ... Jude 20
–A Christian's hands in prayer ... 1Ti 2:8
–The kiss of greeting among Christians ... 1Co 16:20
1Th 5:26

See also SANCTIFICATION

HOLY SPIRIT

A. Related theme
HOLY SPIRIT is a theme of Acts ... Ac 13:2

B. The Spirit's divine nature

1. Called God ... Lk 1:32,35
Ac 5:3–4

2. United with the Father and Son ... Mt 28:19
2Co 13:14

3. Has characteristics of God
–Eternal ... Heb 9:14
–Everywhere present ... Ps 139:7–10
–All-knowing ... 1Co 2:10–11
–Has great power ... Ac 1:8
Ro 15:19
–Raised Christ from the dead ... 1Pe 3:18
–Performs miracles ... Mt 12:28
Ro 15:19
–Involved in creation ... Ge 1:2
–Gives spiritual life to us ... Jn 3:3–8

C. The Spirit as a person
–He teaches ... Jn 14:26
–He hears and speaks ... Jn 16:13
–He testifies about Christ ... Jn 15:26
–He encourages ... Ac 9:31
–He counsels ... Jn 14:16
–He convicts people of sin ... Jn 16:8
–He prays for us ... Ro 8:27
–He sends people out ... Ac 13:4
–He experiences grief ... Eph 4:30
–He can be resisted ... Ac 7:51
–He can be tested ... Ac 5:9

D. The Spirit's work

1. In the Old Testament
–Involved in creation ... Ge 1:2
–Gave life to God's creatures ... Ps 104:30
–Guided God's people ... Isa 63:11–13
–Instructed God's people ... Neh 9:20
–Led God's people in the right way ... Ps 143:10
–Inspired God's people to do right ... Ps 51:10–22
–Admonished God's people ... Neh 9:30
–Reacted to human evil ... Ge 6:3
–Gave artistic ability to individuals ... Ex 31:2–3
–Gave his power to Israel's leaders ... Jdg 6:34
1Sa 16:13
Zec 4:6
–Lived among God's people ... Hag 2:5
–Inspired the prophets ... Nu 11:29
Mic 3:8
Zec 7:12
2Pe 1:21
–Spoke through the psalmists ... 2Sa 23:2
Ac 1:16,20
Heb 3:7–11
–Old Testament prophecies on the Spirit ... Isa 11:1–3
Isa 32:15
Isa 42:1
Isa 44:3
Isa 61:1–3
Eze 39:29
Joel 2:28–32

2. In the life of Jesus Christ
- –Jesus was conceived by the Spirit ... Lk 1:34–35
- –He received the Spirit at his baptism ... Lk 3:21–22
- –He was filled with the Spirit ... Lk 4:1
- –He ministered in the power of the Spirit ... Mt 12:15–21; Lk 4:18–21
- –He cast out demons by the Spirit ... Mt 12:28
- –He offered himself to God through the Spirit ... Heb 9:14
- –He was raised by the Spirit ... Ro 8:11; 1Ti 3:16; 1Pe 3:18
- –He promised to send the Spirit ... Jn 15:26
- –He sent the Spirit on Pentecost ... Ac 2:33
- –The Spirit is the Spirit of Jesus ... Ac 16:7; Ro 8:98; Gal 4:6

3. In the church
- –The Spirit came at Pentecost ... Ac 2:1–4
- –He dwells in the church ... 1Co 3:16–17; Eph 2:22
- –He appoints officers for the church ... Ac 20:28
- –He directs decisions of the church ... Ac 15:28
- –He chooses missionaries ... Ac 13:2
- –He sends out missionaries ... Ac 13:4
- –He directs the mission enterprise ... Ac 8:29,39; Ac 16:6–7

4. In individuals
- –The Spirit dwells in us ... Jn 14:16–17; Ro 8:11; 1Co 6:19
- –He convicts us of sin ... Jn 16:7–11
- –He gives us new life ... Jn 3:5–6; Titus 3:5
- –He makes us realize God's love ... Ro 5:5
- –He gives us power to witness ... Ac 1:8; Ac 6:9–10
- –He teaches us what to say ... Lk 12:12
- –He reveals God's secrets to us ... 1Co 2:10–16
- –He brings Christ's presence to us ... Jn 14:16–18
- –He keeps us in touch with God ... Ro 8:26; Jude 20
- –He teaches us about Christ ... Jn 14:26; Jn 15:26
- –He enables us to find the truth ... 1Jn 4:1–6
- –He encourages us ... Ac 9:31
- –He controls us ... Ro 8:9
- –He gives us joy and peace ... Ro 14:17
- –He draws us into fellowship ... 2Co 13:14; Php 2:1
- –He enables us to live the Christian life ... Ro 8:5–9
- –He works his fruit in us ... Gal 5:16–25
- –He sanctifies us ... Ro 15:16; 2Th 2:13
- –He gives us gifts ... 1Co 12:4–11
  See GIFTS OF THE SPIRIT
- –He gives us his sword to fight Satan ... Eph 6:17
- –He prays for us in times of crisis ... Ro 8:26
- –He will raise us from the dead ... Ro 8:11

E. The Spirit in our life

1. How to receive the Spirit
- –We must repent of our sins ... Ac 2:37–38
- –We must believe in Jesus ... Ac 11:15–17; Ro 8:9; Gal 3:2–3,14; Eph 1:13
- –We must be baptized in Jesus' name ... Ac 2:38; Ac 19:1–6
- –We must pray to receive him ... Lk 11:13; Ac 8:15

2. Being filled with the Holy Spirit

a. His filling is a gift for all believers
- –Old Testament promise ... Joel 2:28–29
- –New Testament fulfillment ... Ac 2:17–18
- –New Testament promise to us ... Ac 2:38; Ro 8:9

b. Persons filled with the Holy Spirit
- –Bezalel ... Ex 31:2–5
- –Samson ... Jdg 14:19
- –Saul ... 1Sa 10:10
- –John the Baptist ... Lk 1:15
- –Elizabeth ... Lk 1:47
- –Zechariah ... Lk 1:67
- –The disciples on Pentecost ... Ac 2:4
- –Peter before the Jewish council ... Ac 4:8
- –The early Christians at prayer ... Ac 4:31
- –Paul in his preaching ... Ac 13:9
- –New Christians ... Ac 13:52

c. Persons full of the Holy Spirit
- –Jesus ... Lk 4:1
- –The first deacons ... Ac 6:3
- –Stephen ... Ac 6:5
- –Barnabas ... Ac 11:24

d. The command to be filled with the Spirit
- –To Paul at his conversion ... Ac 9:17
- –To all Christians ... Eph 5:18

3. Being sealed with the Spirit ... 2Co 1:21–22; 2Co 5:5; Eph 1:13–14

4. Baptized with the Spirit

HOME
See FAMILY

HOMOSEXUALITY
See SEXUAL STANDARDS

HONESTY
See INTEGRITY

HOPE
–*Certainty in the present and firm expectation for the future*

A. Related themes

1. HOPE is a theme of:
- –Isaiah ... Isa 9:7
- –Jeremiah ... Jer 23:5
- –Amos ... Am 9:11
- –Micah ... Mic 4:1
- –Zephaniah ... Zep 3:15
- –Haggai ... Hag 2:7
- –1 Thessalonians ... 1Th 1:10
- –2 Thessalonians ... 2Th 2:3
- –1 Peter ... 1Pe 1:3
- –Revelation ... Rev 21:3

2. RESTORATION is a theme of:
- –Ezekiel ... Eze 36:24
- –Joel ... Joel 2:32

B. The nature of hope

1. Basic concept of hope
- –It is linked with faith ... 1Co 13:13; Heb 11:1
- –It is linked with trust ... Ps 33:20–21; Ro 15:13
- –It is linked with expectation ... Ro 4:18–19; Titus 1:2

2. In whom/what do we hope?
 –In God . . . . Ps 42:5,11; Ps 130:7; 1Ti 6:17
 –In Jesus Christ . . . . Ro 15:12; 1Co 15:19; Eph 1:12; Php 2:19
 –In the name of God . . . . Ps 52:9
 –In the word of God . . . . Ps 119:74; Ps 130:5
 –In the promises of God . . . . Ac 26:6
 –In the resurrection of the dead . . . Ac 23:6
3. For what do we hope?
 –God's righteousness . . . . Gal 5:5
 –Salvation . . . . Ro 8:24–25; 1Th 5:8
 –God's saving arm . . . . Isa 51:5
 –Liberation from bondage to decay . . . . Ro 8:20–21
 –The resurrection . . . . Ac 2:26; Ac 26:7
 –The glory of God . . . . Ro 5:2; 2Co 3:11–12
 –Our glorious inheritance . . . . Eph 1:18
 –The appearance of Jesus Christ . . . Titus 2:13; 1Jn 3:2–3
 –A crown of righteousness 2Ti 4:8
 –A crown of glory 1Pe 5:4
 –A crown of life . . . . Rev 2:10
 –Eternal life . . . . Titus 1:2; Titus 3:7

C. Jesus Christ and our hope
1. He is called our hope
 –He is our hope 1Ti 1:1
 –He is the hope of Israel . . . . Ac 28:20
 –He is the hope of glory . . . . Col 1:27
2. He fulfilled the hope of the Old Testament
 –Jesus confirms the promises of God . . . . Ac 26:6–7; Ro 15:8
 –All promises of God fulfilled in him 2Co 1:20

D. Hope in the Christian life
1. The choice we face
 –Hope in humans or in God . . . . Ps 33:16–19
 –Hope in riches or in God 1Ti 6:17
 –Without God, there is no hope . . . . Eph 2:12; 1Th 4:13
2. Attaining hope
 –We are called to only one hope . . . Eph 1:18; Eph 4:4
 –We must set our hope fully on Jesus 1Pe 1:13
 –We must believe the resurrection . . . 1Pe 1:3
 –We must abound in hope . . . . Ro 15:13; 1Co 13:13
 –We must never lose our hope . . . . . Ps 25:5
3. The benefits of hope
 –Causes us to praise God . . . . Ps 71:14
 –Causes us to rejoice . . . . Ro 5:2; Ro 12:12
 –Renews our strength . . . . Isa 40:31
 –Inspires us to a life of purity 1Jn 3:3
 –*Inspires us to persevere* 1Th 1:3
 –Cures the downcast soul . . . . Ps 42:5,11; La 3:20–21
 –Will never disappoint us . . . . Isa 49:23; Ro 5:5
 –Our hope is like a stabilizing anchor . . . . Heb 6:18–19
4. We should defend our hope 1Pe 3:15

HOPHNI

–Son of Eli, brother of Phinehas 1Sa 1:3
–A wicked priest 1Sa 2:12–17
–Scorned his father's rebuke 1Sa 2:22–25
–His death prophesied as a sign 1Sa 2:30–34
–Brought the ark into battle 1Sa 4:4
–Killed in the battle 1Sa 4:11,17

HOREB

See SINAI

HORSE

A. Literal uses of horses
1. Military
 –Description of the war-horse . . . . . Job 39:19–25
 –Pharaoh's horses . . . . Ex 14:9,23
 –Canaanite horses . . . . Jos 11:4
 –Solomon's horses 2Ch 1:14–16
 –Syrian horses 2Ki 6:14–15
2. Non-military uses
 –Horses used to reinforce royal power 2Sa 15:1; 1Ki 1:5
 –Horse riding to honor a person . . . Est 6:6–11
 –Horses as livestock . . . . Ge 47:17
 –Horses used in farm labor . . . . Isa 28:28
 –Horses used for transportation . . . Isa 66:20
 –Horses used to bring messages . . . Est 8:10
3. Relying on horses
 –They cannot bring victory . . . . Ps 33:16–17
 –Trust in God instead of horses . . . . Ps 20:7; Isa 31:1

B. Figurative use of horses
 –Horses of fire carried Elijah to heaven 2Ki 2:11
 –God's people becoming like the proud horse . . . . Zec 10:3
 –God's angels using horses and chariots 2Ki 6:17
 –God's power symbolized in his horses . . . . Hab 3:8,15
 –The returning Lord riding a white horse . . . . Rev 19:11–13

HOSEA

–A prophet, son of Beeri . . . . Hos 1:1
–His wife pictured unfaithful Israel . . . . . Hos 1:2–11
–Became reconciled with his wife . . . . . . Hos 3:1–3

HOSHEA

A. Original name of Joshua . . . . Nu 13:16
B. Last king of Israel 2Ki 17:1
 –Murdered Pekah to get throne 2Ki 15:30
 –Captured and deported by Assyria . . . 2Ki 17:2–6

HOSPITALITY

See KINDNESS

HULDAH

–A prophetess 2Ki 22:14
–Visited by Hilkiah during Josiah's reign 2Ki 22:12–20; 2Ch 34:19–28

HUMILITY

–*Lowliness; freedom from pride*

A. Related theme
 HUMILITY is a theme of 1 Corinthians 1Co 1:29
B. What humility involves
 –A childlike attitude . . . . Mt 18:1–4

–Repentance .... Isa 66:2
Lk 18:13–14
–Submission before God 2Ch 34:27
Da 5:22–23
–Seeking God's face in prayer 2Ch 7:14
–Fasting .... Ezr 8:21
Ps 35:13
–Following God's laws .... Jer 44:10
Zep 2:3
–Working for justice and mercy .... Mic 6:6–8
–Opposite of pride .... Pr 3:34
Da 4:37
1Pe 5:5

C. Humility in our lives
1. The command to be humble
–We must humble ourselves .... Eph 4:2
1Pe 5:6
–We must walk humbly with God .... Mic 6:8
–We must clothe ourselves with humility .... Col 3:12
1Pe 5:5
–We must consider others better than ourselves .... Php 2:3
–We must avoid false humility .... Col 2:18,23
2. The benefits of humility
–God saves the humble .... Ps 18:27
1Co 1:26–29
–God gives the humble grace .... Pr 3:34
Jas 4:6
–God raises the lowly .... Job 5:11
Mt 23:12
Lk 1:52
–God revives the lowly .... Isa 57:15
–God honors the humble .... Pr 15:33
Pr 18:12
–God rewards the humble .... Pr 22:4
–God blesses the humble 2Ch 7:14
–God holds the humble in esteem .... Isa 66:2
–God guides and teaches the humble .... Ps 25:9
–With humility comes wisdom .... Pr 11:2

D. Examples of humility
1. The supreme example: Jesus Christ
–In his coming to earth 2Co 8:9
–In his lowliness .... Mt 11:29
–In his life of service .... Lk 22:27
–In his submission to God's will .... Jn 6:38
–In his sufferings .... Isa 53:1–9
–In his washing of the disciples' feet .... Jn 13:4–5
–In his triumphal entry .... Mt 21:5,7
–In his death on the cross .... Php 2:5–8
2. Other examples
–The Israelites in the desert .... Dt 8:3
–Ahab 1Ki 21:29
–Josiah 2Ki 22:19
–Rehoboam and his people 2Ch 12:5–12
–Job .... Job 42:2–6
–Isaiah .... Isa 6:1–6
–John the Baptist .... Jn 3:27–30
–Peter .... Lk 5:8–9
–Paul .... Ac 20:19

HUNGER AND THIRST

A. Examples of famines and droughts
–Worldwide famine in Joseph's day .... Ge 41:53
–Famine in Bethlehem .... Ru 1:1
–Famine in David's time 2Sa 21:1
–Drought and famine in Elijah's day 1Ki 17:1
–Famine in Elisha's day 2Ki 6:25
2Ki 8:1
–Famine in Jerusalem 2Ki 25:3
–Famine in Nehemiah's day .... Neh 5:3
–Famine predicted by Agabus .... Ac 11:27–28

B. How times of hunger and thirst were used:
1. By God
–To fulfill his plan for his people .... Ge 15:13–14
Ge 41:56–42:3
Ge 46:3–4
–To humble and teach the Israelites .... Ex 16:2–3
Dt 8:2–3
–To get people to look to God for help .... Jdg 6:3–6
Ps 107:4–9
–To punish stubborn disobedience .... Dt 28:47–48
Isa 65:11–13
–To bring judgment on sinners .... Isa 9:18–21
Am 4:6,9
2. By Jesus
–To demonstrate his compassion .... Mk 6:34–44
Mk 8:1–9
–To show he was bread from heaven .... Jn 6:33,48–51
3. By the church
–To show kindness to the needy .... Ac 11:28–30
2Co 8:13–15
–To show church unity .... Ro 15:25–27

C. Spiritual hunger and thirst
1. The reality of such hunger and thirst
–Physical bread cannot satisfy .... Dt 8:3
Mt 4:4
–Prediction of a famine of God's word .... Am 8:11–12
2. Satisfying such hunger and thirst
–God promises to satisfy .... Isa 55:1–3
Mt 5:6
–Jesus is the bread of life .... Jn 6:35,48–58
1Co 10:16
–Jesus is the water of life .... Jn 4:13–14
Jn 7:37–38

HUR

–A chief magistrate of the Israelites .... Ex 24:14
–With Aaron, supported Moses' hand .... Ex 17:10–12

HUSHAI

–Friend of David 2Sa 15:37
–Conspired with David to outwit Absalom 2Sa 15:32–37
–Foiled Absalom's revolt by giving poor advice 2Sa 16:15–17:16

HYPOCRISY

–Open display of religion without genuine commitment

A. Related theme
HYPOCRISY is a theme of James .... Jas 3:9

B. Description of hypocrisy
–Displaying religion with no love for God .... Isa 29:13
Mt 6:2–6,16–18
Mt 23:5–7
–Claiming love for God, mistreating others .... Mk 12:38–40
1Jn 3:17
1Jn 4:20
–Not practicing what one preaches .... Mt 23:3
Ro 2:17–24
–Sticking only to the letter of the law .... Mt 23:16–23
Lk 13:15–16
–Criticizing another for one's own sins .... Mt 7:3–5
Mk 7:6–13

ICHABOD

IDOLATRY

–The worship of false gods

IMAGE OF GOD

INCARNATION

See JESUS CHRIST

INCENSE

–Incense on the Day of Atonement .... Lev 16:12–13; 1Ch 6:49

b. Regulations concerning incense . Ex 30:9,34–38; Lev 10:1–2; Nu 16:35–38

c. Continued in the New Testament.................. Lk 1:8–9

d. Incense detestable if insincere... Isa 1:13; Jer 6:20

B. Incense as symbolic of prayer .... Ps 141:2; Lk 1:10; Rev 5:8; Rev 8:3–4

INHERITANCE

A. Inheritance in the Old Testament

1. Family inheritance

–Firstborn son received birthright...Ge 25:29–34; Dt 21:15–17

–Firstborn son received double share .... Dt 21:17

–If no sons, daughters inherit ..... Nu 27:1–8

–If no children, next of kin inherit .. Nu 27:9

–Land had to stay within the tribe... Nu 36:7; 1Ki 21:3

–Each allotted land was an inheritance .... Nu 26:53,56

2. Israel's inheritance

–Canaan: the land of God's inheritance .... Dt 4:21; 1Ki 8:36; Ps 78:55

–Promised to Abram .... Ge 12:7; Ge 15:18–21

–Land divided as inheritance to Israelites .... Jos 11:23

–To remain an heir required obedience .... Dt 4:25–27; 2Ki 21:12–15

–Inheritance lost in the exile ...... Ps 79:1–8

–Inheritance regained in the return........................ Neh 11:20; Isa 65:8–9; Eze 36:12

3. Spiritualizing the inheritance

–The Lord as the people's inheritance .... Ps 73:26; Ps 142:5

–The people as the Lord's inheritance .... Dt 4:20; Isa 47:6

–God's inheritance to include Gentiles .... Ps 2:8; Jer 10:16

B. Inheritance in the New Testament

1. Jesus is the heir .... Heb 1:2

2. We become heirs

–When we become sons of God.... Gal 4:7

–When we believe in Jesus........ Ro 4:13; Heb 6:12

–When we receive God's grace .... Gal 3:18

–We become co-heirs with Christ.. Ro 8:17

3. What we are to inherit

–The earth .... Mt 5:5

–The kingdom of light........... Col 1:12

–The kingdom of heaven.......... Mt 25:34

–The kingdom of God 1Co 6:9

–Eternal life .... Mt 19:29; Titus 3:7

–Everything....................... Rev 21:7

4. The nature of our inheritance

–It is given by God and his word... Ac 20:32

–It is received as a reward .... Col 3:24

–It is kept in heaven for us 1Pe 1:4

–It is imperishable 1Co 15:50–53; 1Pe 1:4

–It is eternal....................... Heb 9:15

–It is guaranteed by the Spirit..... Eph 1:13–14

–It can be lost through disobedience................. Mt 25:41–46; Heb 4:6,11

INSECTS

A. Insects and other small creatures mentioned in Bible

–Ant.............................. Pr 6:6

–Bee.............................. Jdg 14:8

–Cricket.......................... Lev 11:22

–Flea............................. 1Sa 24:14

–Fly .... Ex 8:21–24

–Gadfly .... Jer 46:20

–Gnat............................. Ex 8:16–18

–Grasshopper..................... Ps 78:46

–Hornet .... Jos 24:12

–Katydid......................... Lev 11:22

–Leech........................... Pr 30:15

–Locust .... Joel 1:4

–Maggot .... Ex 16:20,24

–Moth............................ Job 27:18

–Scorpion .... Dt 8:15

–Spider .... Job 8:14

–Worm........................... Jnh 4:7

B. God's use of insects

–Some suitable for food, some not ... Lev 11:21–24

–Sometimes used as a judgment ..... Ex 8:16–32; Joel 1:2–12

–Ants used to teach us lessons...... Pr 6:6–8

–Moths used as a symbol of destruction .... Mt 6:19–20

–Honey used as a symbol of God's blessing .... Dt 11:9

INSPIRATION OF SCRIPTURE

–The Bible as God's written word

A. Scripture is inspired by God

1. Basic statement.................. 2Ti 3:16; 2Pe 1:21

2. Affirmations in the Old Testament

–God put words in prophets' mouths.......................... Dt 18:18; Isa 51:16; Jer 1:9

–The Spirit spoke through David... 2Sa 23:2

–"This is what the Lord says" ..... Isa 43:1; Jer 6:16

–"The word of the Lord came to..."... 1Ki 17:2; Eze 1:3

3. Affirmations in the New Testament

–David spoke by the Holy Spirit ... Mk 12:36; Ac 4:25

–God speaks in the Old Testament... Heb 4:3,7; Heb 8:8

–The Spirit speaks in the Old Testament .... Ac 28:25; Heb 3:7

–In the Old Testament, "It is written" .... Mt 4:4,6,10; 1Co 1:19,31

–The Scriptures cannot be broken.......................... Jn 10:35

–The Scriptures must be fulfilled .... Mt 5:18; Mt 24:35; Lk 24:44

B. Characteristics of the inspired word of God

–Trustworthy...................... 2Sa 7:28; Ps 111:7–8; Jn 17:17

–Eternally fixed........ Ps 119:89
Isa 40:8
–Unbreakable .... Mt 5:18
Jn 10:35
–A sure guide for life .... Ps 119:105
2Ti 3:16–17
–Effective in its purposes .... Jer 23:29
Heb 4:12

C. How Bible writers received their material
–In various ways........ Heb 1:1
–By direct speech from God........ Ex 34:27–28
Nu 12:8
Jer 30:1–2
–By angels .... Zec 1:12–17
Ac 7:53
–By visions........ Ge 15:1
Mic 1:1
–By dreams .... Da 7:1
See DREAMS AND VISIONS
–By an inner impulse from God........ Jer 20:9
2Pe 1:21
–By eyewitness accounts........ Lk 1:2
1Jn 1:1–4
–By careful research .... Lk 1:3–4

INTEGRITY

–Honesty in life and adherence to moral principle

A. Examples of those showing integrity
–Job .... Job 2:3
–David........ 1Ch 28:17
Ps 78:72
–Financial officials of the temple 2Ki 12:9–15
–Hananiah .... Neh 7:2
–Jesus .... Mt 22:16

B. Expectation of living in integrity and honesty
–Linked with observing all God's commands 1Ki 9:4
–Preferred above wealth........ Pr 28:6
–Expected of the upright........ Pr 11:3
–Expected of Christian leaders........ Titus 2:7
–Required in business dealings........ Lev 19:36
Dt 25:15
Pr 16:11

C. Blessings of living in integrity and honesty
–We please God........ 1Ch 29:17
–We gain a good reputation .... Pr 16:13
–We receive God's protection........ Pr 2:7
–We gain security for ourselves .... Ps 25:21
Pr 10:9
–We gain security for future generations 1Ki 9:4–5

See also TRUTH

INTERCESSION

–The prayer of one person for another

A. Related theme
INTERCESSION is a theme of Numbers........ Nu 14:19

B. Human intercession
1. Examples of intercession by officials
–By leaders........ Ex 32:11–14
Nu 14:13–19
Jos 7:6–9
–By priests .... Lev 5:10
Lev 16:21
Ezr 9:5–15
–By prophets 1Sa 7:5–6
1Ki 13:6
Da 9:3–19
Jas 5:17–18
–By kings 2Sa 24:17
1Ki 8:33–51
–By apostles........ Ac 8:15
Eph 3:14–19
Php 1:9–11
Col 1:9–12
–By elders........ Jas 5:14

2. Examples of intercession by individuals
a. In the Old Testament
–Abraham for Lot .... Ge 18:23–32
–David for his sick child........ 2Sa 12:16
–David for Solomon 1Ch 29:19
–Job for his children........ Job 1:5
–A psalmist for the people........ Ps 20:1–5
Ps 25:22
–A psalmist for all nations........ Ps 67:3–5
b. In the New Testament
–Stephen for his persecutors........ Ac 7:60
–Peter for Dorcas........ Ac 9:40
–Paul for a sick man .... Ac 28:8
–Paul for Timothy........ 2Ti 1:3
–Paul for Philemon .... Phm 4
–Christians for their persecutors........ Mt 5:44
–The church for Peter........ Ac 12:5,12
–The church for missionaries........ Mt 9:38
Ac 13:3
Heb 13:18
–The church for Paul........ Ro 15:31–32
Eph 6:19–20
–The church for each other .... Jas 5:16
–The church for all people........ 1Ti 2:1–2

3. The purposes of human intercession
–For averting judgment........ Ge 18:23–32
Nu 14:13–19
–For escape from danger .... Ac 12:5,12
Ro 15:31
–For God's blessings .... Nu 6:24–26
1Ki 18:41–45
–For the Holy Spirit's power........ Ac 8:15–17
Eph 3:14–17
–For healing........ 1Ki 17:20–21
Ac 28:8
Jas 5:14–16
–For forgiveness .... Ezr 9:5–15
Ac 7:60
–For the ability to rule well........ 1Ch 29:19
1Ti 2:2
–For Christian growth........ Php 1:9–11
Col 1:10–11
–For effective pastors........ 2Ti 1:3–7
–For effective mission work........ Mt 9:38
Eph 6:19–20
–For the salvation of others .... Ro 10:1–4
–For others to praise God .... Ps 67:3–5

C. Divine intercession
1. The intercession of Christ
–For his followers........ Lk 22:32
Jn 14:16
Jn 17:6–26
–For his enemies........ Lk 23:34
–Continual intercession for us........ Ro 8:34
Heb 7:24
Heb 9:24
1Jn 2:1
2. The Spirit as intercessor .... Ro 8:26–27

INTEREST

See DEBT

ISAAC

A. History of Isaac
–Promised son of Abraham and Sarah .... Ge 17:19
1Ch 1:28

–Had dream at Bethel — Ge 28:10–22
–God renewed Abraham's covenant with him — Ge 28:13–15

2. At Haran
–Arrived in Haran — Ge 29:1–8
–Met and stayed at Uncle Laban's — Ge 29:9–14
–Served Laban for Leah and Rachel — Ge 29:16–30
–Became father of many children — Ge 29:31–30:24
–Worked for wages to be paid in goats — Ge 30:25–43
–Decided to return to Canaan — Ge 31:1–21
–Pursued by Laban — Ge 31:22–55

3. Upon return to Canaan
–Devised scheme to make peace with Esau — Ge 32:1–21
–Wrestled with God — Ge 32:22–26
–Name changed to Israel — Ge 32:27–30
–Reconciled with Esau — Ge 33:1–17
–Settled in Shechem — Ge 33:18–20
–Returned to Bethel — Ge 35:1–15
–Grieved over disappearance of Joseph — Ge 37:31–35
–Sent sons to Egypt during famine — Ge 42:1–5; Ge 43:1–15

4. In Egypt
–Moved to Egypt — Ge 46:1–7
–Met Pharaoh — Ge 47:7–11
–Blessed Ephraim and Manasseh — Ge 48:1–20
–Blessed each of his sons — Ge 49:1–28; Heb 11:21
–His death — Ge 49:29–33
–Buried back in Canaan — Ge 50:1–14

C. Significance in the New Testament
–Samaritans considered Jacob their father — Jn 4:7–12
–Demonstrates God's purpose in election — Ro 9:11–13
–Is an example of faith — Heb 11:21

D. Name became a synonym for all Israelites — Nu 23:7; Ps 14:7; Isa 43:1,22,28; Ro 11:26

JAEL

–Woman who killed Sisera — Jdg 4:17–22
–Praised by Deborah — Jdg 5:24–27

JAIR

–Judge from Gilead — Jdg 10:3–5

JAIRUS

–Synagogue ruler whose daughter Jesus raised — Mk 5:22–43; Lk 8:41–56

JAMES

A. A disciple of Jesus
–Son of Zebedee and brother of John — Mt 4:21–22; Mk 3:17
–Originally a fisherman — Mt 4:21
–Wanted hostile Samaritans killed — Lk 9:52–55
–Observed the transfiguration — Mt 17:1–13; Mk 9:1–13
–Sought top place in Jesus' kingdom — Mk 10:35–45
–Accompanied Jesus to Gethsemane — Mt 26:36–46
–One of the apostles — Ac 1:13
–Killed by Herod — Ac 12:2

B. Another disciple of Jesus
–Son of Alphaeus — Mt 10:3; Mk 3:18
–One of the apostles — Ac 1:13

C. Son of Joseph and Mary — Mt 13:55
–A brother of the Lord Jesus — Gal 1:19
–Brother of Jude — Jude 1
–Did not believe in Jesus — Jn 7:3–5
–Met the risen Lord — 1Co 15:7
–Stayed with believers before Pentecost — Ac 1:13
–Became leader of the Jerusalem church — Ac 12:17; Gal 2:9,12
–Proposed solution at the council in Jerusalem — Ac 15:12–21
–Visited by Paul — Ac 21:18; Gal 1:19
–Wrote the letter of James — Jas 1:1

JAPHETH

–Son of Noah — Ge 5:32; 1Ch 1:4–5
–With Shem, covered his father with a garment — Ge 9:23
–Blessed by Noah — Ge 9:27
–Sons listed — Ge 10:2–5

JEALOUSY

–An emotion expressing possessiveness; related to zeal

A. Jealousy as a positive emotion

1. In humans
–Jealous for the things of the Lord — Nu 25:11–13; 1Ki 19:10,14
–Jealous for faithfulness in marriage — Pr 6:34; SS 8:6
–Jealous for the purity of the church — 2Co 11:2

2. In God
–He is jealous for his people — Joel 2:18; Zec 1:14; Zec 8:2
–He jealously tolerates no rivals — Ex 20:5; Jos 24:19; 1Co 10:21–22
–Sin arouses him to jealousy — Ps 78:58; Na 1:2
–His name is Jealous — Ex 34:14

B. Jealousy as a negative emotion

1. Sins that it leads to
–To envy — Ge 37:11; Ps 106:16–18
–To discontent — Ge 30:1
–To quarreling — 1Co 3:3–4
–To verbal abuse — Ac 13:45
–To intense anger — Pr 27:4
–To persecution — Ac 5:17–18

2. The command to get rid of jealousy — Ro 13:13; 2Co 12:20; Gal 5:20

JECONIAH

See JEHOIACHIN

JEHOAHAZ

A. Son of Jehu; king of Israel — 2Ki 13:1–9

B. Son of Josiah; king of Judah — 2Ki 23:31–34; 2Ch 36:1–4

JEHOASH

A. A king of Judah
See JOASH

B. Son of Jehoahaz; king of Israel 2Ki 13:10–11
- –Defeated Arameans three times 2Ki 13:14–25
- –Defeated Amaziah, king of Judah 2Ki 14:1–16; 2Ch 25:17–24

JEHOIACHIN

- –Son of Jehoiakim; king of Judah 2Ki 24:8–9; 2Ch 36:8–9
- –Brought to Babylon by Nebuchadnezzar 2Ki 24:10–15; 2Ch 36:10; Jer 24:1
- –Freed from prison in Babylon 2Ki 25:27–30; Jer 52:31–34

JEHOIADA

- –A priest during Athaliah's reign 2Ki 11:1–4
- –Son-in-law of King Jehoram 2Ch 22:11
- –Helped hide Joash for six years in temple 2Ch 22:11–12
- –Arranged for crowning of Joash as king 2Ki 11:5–16; 2Ch 23:1–15
- –Decided to rid the land of idols 2Ki 11:17–20; 2Ch 23:16–17
- –Managed the temple 2Ch 23:18–21
- –Advised Joash 2Ki 12:2; 2Ch 24:2
- –With Joash, repaired the temple 2Ki 12:4–16; 2Ch 24:3–14
- –His death 2Ch 24:15–16

JEHOIAKIM

- –Son of Josiah; king of Judah 2Ki 23:34
- –Had conflict with Nebuchadnezzar 2Ki 24:1–6; 2Ch 36:5–8
- –Killed the prophet Uriah Jer 26:20–23
- –Burned scroll of Jeremiah's prophecies Jer 36:16–26

JEHORAM

A. Son of Jehoshaphat; king of Judah 2Ki 8:16–19; 2Ch 21:4–7
- –Warred against Edom 2Ki 8:20–22
- –Prophesied against by Elijah 2Ch 21:12–15
- –Warred against the Philistines 2Ch 21:16–17
- –Killed by the Lord 2Ch 21:18–19

B. A king of Israel

JEHOSHAPHAT

- –Son of Asa; king of Judah 1Ki 22:41–44; 2Ch 17:1
- –Strengthened his kingdom 2Ch 17:2–19
- –Joined with Ahab of Israel against Aram 1Ki 22:1–33; 2Ch 18:1–32
- –Appointed judges 2Ch 19:4–11
- –Joined with Joram of Israel against Moab 2Ki 3:5–27
- –Miraculously delivered from Moab and Ammon 2Ch 20:1–26
- –Prayed intensely to the Lord 2Ch 20:5–12
- –Punished for alliance with Israel 2Ch 20:35–37

JEHU

A. Prophet who spoke against Baasha 1Ki 16:1–4,12

B. King of Israel 2Ki 9:6
- –Elijah told to anoint him king 1Ki 19:16
- –Anointed by servant of Elisha 2Ki 9:1–13
- –Appointed to obliterate house of Ahab 2Ki 9:6–10
- –Killed Joram and Ahaziah 2Ki 9:14–29; 2Ch 22:7–9
- –Killed Jezebel 2Ki 9:30–37
- –Killed relatives of Ahab 2Ki 10:1–17
- –Killed ministers of Baal 2Ki 10:18–29
- –His death 2Ki 10:30–36

JEPHTHAH

- –Judge from Gilead Jdg 11:1–3
- –Delivered Israel from Ammon Jdg 11:4–33
- –Made a rash vow affecting his daughter Jdg 11:30–40
- –Punished the Ephraimites Jdg 12:1–6
- –His death Jdg 12:7

JEREMIAH

- –Prophet to kingdom of Judah Jer 1:1–3
- –Called by the Lord Jer 1:4–19
- –Composed laments at Josiah's death 2Ch 35:25
- –His life threatened for continuing to prophesy Jer 11:18–23; Jer 26:1–16
- –Put in stocks Jer 20:1–3
- –Opposed by Hananiah Jer 28:1–17
- –Wrote scroll that was burned by king Jer 36:1–26
- –Rewrote the scroll Jer 36:27–32
- –Imprisoned; Zedekiah sought his advice Jer 37:1–21
- –Charged with treason and thrown into cistern Jer 38:1–13
- –Zedekiah sought his advice again Jer 38:14–27
- –Purchased field just before Jerusalem destroyed Jer 32:1–15
- –Taken with some of the people to Egypt Jer 43:1–7

JERICHO

A. Identity
- –Located in a valley Dt 34:3
- –Near the Jordan River Nu 33:50
- –Called "City of the Palms" Dt 34:3

B. History of the city

1. In the Old Testament
   - –Rahab lived there Jos 2:1
   - –Israelites spied it out Jos 2:1–21
   - –Israelites camped opposite it Jos 3:16
   - –Israelites marched around it Jos 6:1–15
   - –Its walls collapsed Jos 6:20
   - –All except Rahab destroyed Jos 6:21–25
   - –Joshua pronounced curse on rebuilding it Jos 6:26
   - –Curse fulfilled when Hiel rebuilt it 1Ki 16:34
   - –A company of prophets stationed there 2Ki 2:5
   - –It was reinhabited 2Ch 28:15; Neh 3:2
2. In the New Testament
   - –Good Samaritan headed toward it Lk 10:30–35
   - –Jesus healed Bartimaeus there Mk 10:46–52; Lk 18:35–43
   - –Jesus healed two blind men there Mt 20:29–34
   - –Zacchaeus lived there Lk 19:1–10

JEROBOAM

A. First king of the northern kingdom
- –An official of king Solomon 1Ki 11:26–28
- –Ahijah prophesied he would be king 1Ki 11:29–39
- –Fled to Egypt 1Ki 11:40
- –Led rebellion against Rehoboam 1Ki 12:18–19
- –Became king of the northern kingdom 1Ki 12:20
- –Instituted idolatry 1Ki 12:25–33
- –Judged for idolatry 1Ki 13:1–6; 1Ki 14:1–18
- –His death 1Ki 14:19–20

B. Son of Jehoash; king of Israel 2Ki 14:23–29
 –Denounced by Amos ...... Am 7:10–11

JERUB-BAAL

See GIDEON

JERUSALEM

A. Related theme
 JERUSALEM is a theme of 2 Samuel 2Sa 6:12

B. Important names for this city
 –Salem ...... Ge 14:18; Ps 76:2
 –The Jebusite city ...... Jos 18:28
 –Jebus 1Ch 11:4
 –Jerusalem 2Sa 5:6
 –Zion ...... 2Sa 5:7; Ps 48:12
 –The City of David 2Sa 6:12,16; 1Ki 2:10
 –The city of the Great King ...... Ps 48:2
 –The city of God ...... Ps 46:4; Ps 87:3
 –The city of the Lord ...... Isa 60:14
 –The City of Righteousness ...... Isa 1:26
 –The City of Truth ...... Zec 8:3
 –The holy city ...... Neh 11:1,18; Isa 48:2
 –the Lord is there ...... Eze 48:35
 –Moriah ...... Ge 22:1–2; 2Ch 3:1
 –Ariel ...... Isa 29:1

C. Significant historical events of Jerusalem
 –Abraham's "sacrifice" of Isaac ...... Ge 22:1–18
 –King of Jerusalem conquered by Joshua ...... Jos 10:1–14
 –City given to the tribe of Benjamin ... Jos 18:28
 –Conquered by David; became his capital 2Sa 5:6–10
 –Temple built there 2Ch 3:1
 –Became capital of the southern kingdom 1Ki 14:21
 –Destroyed by Nebuchadnezzar 2Ch 36:19
 –The center of Jewish life after exile ...... Ezr 1:5; Mt 2:1,3
 –Jesus entered it as king ...... Mt 21:9–10
 –Jesus was crucified there ...... Lk 9:31; Lk 24:18
 –Holy Spirit poured out there ...... Ac 2:1–5
 –Gospel spread out from there ...... Lk 24:47; Ac 1:8
 –First council of the church held there ...... Ac 15:1–2; Gal 2:1–5
 –Jesus predicted its destruction ...... Lk 19:42–44; Lk 21:20–24

D. Spiritual significance of Jerusalem
 –The city chosen by God 1Ki 11:13
 –The place where God put his Name ...... Dt 12:11; 1Ki 14:21
 –The city that Jews prayed toward ... 1Ki 8:44; Da 6:10
 –The place from which God's word comes ...... Isa 2:3
 –The place from which God rules ... Ps 48:1–3,12–14; Ps 99:1–2
 –The place from which the Messiah rules ...... Isa 9:6–7
 –The site of history's final battle ...... Zec 14:1–5; Rev 20:7–10
 –A symbol of the church ...... Gal 4:26; Heb 12:22
 –Heaven as the new Jerusalem ...... Rev 3:12; Rev 21:2,10–27

JESSE

–Grandson of Boaz and Ruth; father of David ...... Ru 4:17–22
–Visited by Samuel 1Sa 16:1–13
–Had eight sons 1Sa 16:8–11; 1Sa 17:12
–Sent David to enter Saul's service 1Sa 16:18–20
–Sent David to visit his brothers at battle 1Sa 17:17–19

JESUS CHRIST

A. Related themes
 1. SON OF GOD is a theme of Mark ... Mk 14:61
 2. JESUS = GOD/MAN is a theme of:
  –John ...... Jn 1:1
  –Hebrews ...... Heb 4:15
 3. ACTION is a theme of Mark ...... Mk 1:41

B. His divine nature
 1. Preexistence with God
  –Asserted in the Old Testament ... Isa 9:6–7; Mic 5:2
  –Asserted in the New Testament ... Jn 1:1; Php 2:6; Col 1:15–17; Rev 1:4,8
 2. Divine names ascribed to him
  –God ...... Jn 1:1; Heb 1:8; 1Jn 5:20
  –God the One and Only ...... Jn 1:18
  –God over all ...... Ro 9:5
  –God with us ...... Isa 7:14; Mt 1:23
  –Our God and Savior ...... Titus 2:13; 2Pe 1:1
  –Lord ...... Ac 2:36; Ro 10:9; Php 2:11; Col 2:6
  –Lord of all ...... Ac 10:36
  –Lord and God ...... Jn 20:28
  –Lord and Savior 2Pe 1:11; 2Pe 2:20; 2Pe 3:18
  –Lord of glory 1Co 2:8
  –Lord of lords ...... Rev 17:14; Rev 19:16
  –Alpha and Omega ...... Rev 1:8; Rev 21:5–6
  –The Living One ...... Rev 1:18
  –The Holy One of God ...... Mk 1:24
  –The Holy and Righteous One ...... Ac 3:14
  –The "I am" ...... Jn 8:58
 3. His relationship with the Father
  –Equal with the Father ...... Jn 5:18; Jn 10:33; Php 2:6
  –One with the Father ...... Jn 10:33; Jn 17:22
 4. Divine qualities ascribed to him
  –Has the fullness of God ...... Col 2:9
  –Was involved in creation ...... Jn 1:3; Col 1:16; Heb 1:2
  –Has the glory of God ...... Jn 1:14; Heb 1:3
  –Preserves creation ...... Col 1:17; Heb 1:3
  –Is present everywhere ...... Mt 28:20

–Is all-powerful .... Mt 28:18; Php 3:21
–Knows everything .... Jn 2:24–25; Jn 6:61,64
–Is unchanging .... Heb 1:12; Heb 13:8
–Has the power to forgive sins .... Mk 2:5–11; Lk 7:48
–Receives worship from people .... Mt 2:11; Rev 5:11–14
–Receives worship from angels .... Heb 1:6
–We must believe in him as we do in God .... Jn 14:1; Ac 16:31–34

C. His human nature

1. Had a human genealogy .... Mt 1:1–17; Lk 3:23–28

2. His birth and childhood
–Conceived in Mary's womb .... Mt 1:20; Lk 1:26–37
–His human birth .... Mt 1:25; Lk 2:1–7
–Circumcised on the eighth day .... Lk 2:21
–Visited the temple as a boy .... Lk 2:41–51
–Grew as anyone else does .... Lk 2:52

3. His suffering, death and burial
–Bloody sweat in the garden .... Lk 22:44
–Death on the cross .... Mt 27:50; Jn 19:33; Php 2:7–8
–Blood and water flowed from his wound .... Jn 19:34–35
–Body taken down from the cross .... Lk 23:53
–Body prepared and laid in a tomb .... Jn 19:39–41
–Burial clothes used .... Jn 20:6–7

4. His resurrection and ascension
–His resurrection on Easter Sunday .... Mt 28:1–15; Lk 24:1–8
–His appearances for forty days .... Lk 24:9–49; Jn 20:1–29; Ac 1:1–5
–His body still a human body .... Lk 24:40–43; Jn 20:24–29
–His ascension into heaven .... Lk 24:50–51; Ac 1:9–11

5. He had human characteristics
–Could be touched .... Mk 5:27–32; Jn 20:27; 1Jn 1:1
–Became hungry .... Mt 4:2; Mt 21:18
–Became thirsty .... Jn 19:28
–Became tired .... Jn 4:6
–Needed sleep .... Mt 8:20; Mk 4:38
–Showed compassion .... Mt 9:36; Mk 8:2
–Showed anger and indignation .... Mk 10:14; Jn 2:13–16
–Wept .... Lk 19:41; Jn 11:35

6. His human nature specifically mentioned
–He became flesh .... Jn 1:14
–He shared our humanity .... Heb 2:14
–He is like us in all things except sin .... Heb 2:17; Heb 4:15
–We must acknowledge that Jesus came in the flesh 1Jn 4:2; 2Jn 7

D. His most important names
–Jesus, our Savior .... Mt 1:21
–Immanuel .... Mt 1:23
–Christ, the Messiah .... Mt 16:16; Ac 17:3
–The Son of God .... Mk 1:1; Jn 20:31
–The Holy One of God .... Mk 1:24
–The capstone .... Mk 12:10
–The Word of God .... Jn 1:1; Rev 19:13
–The Lamb of God .... Jn 1:36
–The bridegroom of the church .... Jn 3:29
–The Prophet .... Jn 6:14
–The bread of life .... Jn 6:48
–The light of the world .... Jn 8:12
–The good shepherd .... Jn 10:11; Heb 13:20; 1Pe 5:4
–The resurrection and the life .... Jn 11:25
–The King of Israel .... Jn 12:13
–The way, the truth, the life .... Jn 14:6
–King of the Jews .... Jn 19:19–21
–The author of life .... Ac 3:15
–Prince and Savior .... Ac 5:31
–Son of Man .... Ac 7:56
–Judge of the living and the dead .... Ac 10:42
–Lord .... Ro 10:9; Php 2:11
–The Lord of glory 1Co 2:8
–Our Passover lamb 1Co 5:8
–The second Adam 1Co 15:45–47
–Husband of the church 2Co 11:2
–Head of the church .... Col 1:18
–The mediator 1Ti 2:5
–The righteous Judge 2Ti 4:8
–Great high priest .... Heb 4:14
–Alpha and Omega .... Rev 1:8
–The lion of the tribe of Judah .... Rev 5:5
–Lord of lords .... Rev 17:14
–The Root and Offspring of David .... Rev 22:16
–The bright Morning Star .... Rev 22:16

E. His work on earth and in heaven

1. His work on earth
–Did his Father's will .... Mt 26:39; Jn 4:34; Jn 6:38
–Fulfilled the Old Testament .... Mt 5:17
–Came to seek and save the lost .... Lk 19:10
–Came to give us eternal life .... Jn 10:10,28
–Gave his life as a ransom for many .... Mk 10:45
–Made an atoning sacrifice .... Ro 3:25; 1Jn 2:2
–Died for our sins .... 1Co 15:3; Gal 1:4; 1Pe 3:18
–Reconciled us to God .... 2Co 5:18–19; Eph 2:14–17
–Rose again for our justification .... Ro 4:25
–Destroyed the works of Satan .... Heb 2:14; 1Jn 3:8

2. His work as God's Anointed One
–Called the Anointed One .... Ps 2:2; Ac 4:26
–His anointing as Prophet .... Jn 6:14; Ac 3:21–23; Heb 1:1
–His anointing as Priest .... Heb 6:20; Heb 9:11–14, 23–28
–His anointing as King .... Jn 12:13; Rev 19:13–16

3. His work as the exalted Lord in heaven
   - –Sent out the Spirit............... Jn 15:26; Ac 2:32–33
   - –Rules the world at God's right hand........................ 1Co 15:25; Heb 1:3–4
   - –Rules the church at God's right hand........................ Eph 1:20–22; Col 1:18
   - –Makes intercession for us........ Ro 8:34; Heb 7:25
   - –Will overcome all his enemies.... 1Co 15:26–28; Rev 17:14; Rev 19:11–21
   - –Will come again to take us to himself 1Th 5:16–17
   - –Will come again to judge humanity.................... Ac 10:42; 2Co 5:10; 2Ti 4:1

See also TRINITY

JETHRO

- –Father-in-law of Moses; priest of Midian .... Ex 3:1
- –Also called Reuel .... Nu 10:29
- –Owned flocks of sheep .... Ex 2:16–20
- –Permitted Moses to return to Egypt from Midian....................... Ex 4:18
- –Brought wife and sons to Moses in desert .... Ex 18:1–7
- –Acknowledged power of the Lord ..... Ex 18:9–12
- –Advised Moses to appoint judges for Israel......................... Ex 18:13–27

JEW

A. Their identity
   - –Name given to God's people in Babylon .... Est 3:4–6; Est 8:9; Jer 32:12; Jer 44:1
   - –Jews returned to Jerusalem .... Ezr 5:1,5; Neh 4:1–2
   - –Jews lived all over the world .... Zec 8:23; Ac 24:5

B. The Jews in the New Testament

1. Their history
   - –Many opposed Jesus .... Jn 5:15–16; Jn 9:22
   - –They asked for Jesus' death....... Jn 19:4–12; 1Th 2:14–16
   - –First Christians were Jews....... Ac 2:5–14
   - –Jews continued to become believers .... Ac 14:1; Ac ts17:4,12
   - –The Jews persecuted the apostles... Ac 9:23; Ac 13:50; Ac 17:5–9,13

2. Paul and the Jews
   - –Paul was proud to be a Jew .... Php 3:4–5
   - –His message was to the Jew first............................ Ac 13:46; Ro 1:16
   - –Jews were as sinful as Gentiles.... Ro 2:9–10
   - –Christ is Savior of Jew and Gentile......................... Ro 10:12–13; 1Co 1:24
   - –True Jews marked by inner regeneration................... Ro 2:28–29
   - –Paul's sorrow over Jews rejecting Jesus.............. Ro 9:1–5
   - –Salvation of Gentiles would arouse Jews .... Ro 11:13–15

JEZEBEL

- –Sidonian wife of Ahab................. 1Ki 16:31
- –Promoted Baal worship 1Ki 16:32–33
- –Killed prophets of the Lord 1Ki 18:4,13
- –Opposed Elijah 1Ki 19:1–2
- –Had Naboth killed 1Ki 21:1–15
- –Death prophesied 1Ki 21:23
- –Killed by Jehu 2Ki 9:30–37
- –Became a symbol of wickedness ...... Rev 2:20

JOAB

- –Nephew of David 1Ch 2:16
- –Commander of David's army.......... 2Sa 8:16
- –Defeated Ish-Bosheth and his army.... 2Sa 2:10–32
- –Killed Abner 2Sa 3:22–27
- –Captured the city of Jerusalem........ 1Ch 11:6
- –Defeated Ammon 2Sa 10:7–19; 1Ch 19:8–19
- –Put Uriah in front line of battle....... 2Sa 11:16–24
- –Defeated Rabbah 1Ch 20:1–3
- –Devised plan to reconcile David and Absalom 2Sa 14:1–24
- –Killed Absalom........................ 2Sa 18:9–15
- –Rebuked David's grief over Absalom's death..................... 2Sa 19:1–8
- –Put down Sheba's revolt 2Sa 20:1–22
- –Tried to convince David not to number his men 2Sa 24:1–4
- –Numbered David's men................ 2Sa 24:9
- –Supported Adonijah over Solomon 1Ki 1:7
- –Killed under Solomon's orders 1Ki 2:28–34

JOASH

- –Son of Ahaziah; king of Judah 2Ki 11:2
- –Sheltered from Athaliah............... 2Ki 11:2–3; 2Ch 22:11–12
- –Proclaimed king by Jehoiada at seven years of age 2Ki 11:4–12,21; 2Ch 23:1–11
- –Repaired the temple................... 2Ki 12:1–16; 2Ch 24:1–14
- –Gave temple objects to king of Aram... 2Ki 12:17–18
- –Later led the people into idolatry 2Ch 24:17–19
- –Assassinated 2Ki 12:20; 2Ch 24:23–25

JOB

- –A God-fearing man from Uz .... Job 1:1
- –Very wealthy.......................... Job 1:1–3
- –His righteousness tested by disaster ... Job 1:6–22
- –His righteousness tested by affliction .. Job 2:7–8
- –His three friends tried to comfort him...Job 2:11–13
- –Cursed the day of his birth............ Job 3:1–26
- –Gave rebuttals to Eliphaz............. Job 6:1–7:21; Job 16:1–17:16; Job 23:1–24:25
- –Gave rebuttals to Bildad .... Job 9:1–10:22; Job 19:1–29; Job 26:1–31:40
- –Gave rebuttals to Zophar .... Job 12:1–13:28; Job 21:1–34
- –Repented.............................. Job 42:1–6
- –Prayed for his friends .... Job 42:10
- –Was made prosperous again .... Job 42:10–17
- –Considered an example of righteousness .... Eze 14:14,20
- –Considered an example of perseverance.................. Jas 5:11

JOCHEBED

- –Mother of Moses and Aaron .... Ex 6:20; Nu 26:59
- –Hid Moses from the Egyptians .... Ex 2:1–2
- –Hid Moses among the reeds........... Ex 2:3–4
- –Was asked to take care of Moses ...... Ex 2:7–10
- –Considered an example of faith .... Heb 11:23

JOHN

A. John the Baptist
- –His birth announced to his father Zechariah ..... Lk 1:11–20
- –Mother Elizabeth conceived ..... Lk 1:23–25
- –His birth ..... Lk 1:57–66
- –Ministered in the Desert of Judea ..... Mt 3:1–12; Mk 1:2–8
- –Preached a baptism of repentance ..... Lk 3:7–14; Ac 13:24; Ac 19:3–4
- –Witnessed concerning Jesus ..... Mt 3:11–12; Mk 1:7–8; Jn 1:29–36
- –Said Jesus must become greater ..... Jn 3:25–30
- –Baptized Jesus ..... Mt 3:13–17; Lk 3:21–22
- –Expressed doubts about Jesus ..... Mt 11:2–6; Lk 7:18–23
- –Arrested by Herod ..... Mt 4:12; Mk 1:14
- –Beheaded by Herod ..... Mt 14:1–12; Mk 6:14–29
- –Fulfilled prophecy about Elijah ..... Mt 11:7–19; Mk 9:11–13

B. A disciple of Jesus

1. Events during Jesus' lifetime
- –Son of Zebedee and brother of James ..... Mt 4:21–22; Mk 3:17
- –Originally a fisherman ..... Mt 4:21
- –Uneducated ..... Ac 4:13
- –Wanted hostile Samaritans killed ..... Lk 9:52–55
- –Observed the transfiguration ..... Mt 17:1–13; Mk 9:2–13
- –Sought top place in Jesus' kingdom ..... Mk 10:35–45
- –With Peter, prepared for the Passover ..... Lk 22:8
- –Accompanied Jesus to Gethsemane ..... Mt 26:36–45
- –Was called the disciple whom Jesus loved ..... Jn 13:23; Jn 19:26; Jn 20:2; Jn 21:7,20
- –Jesus committed his mother to him ..... Jn 19:26–27
- –Ran to the tomb on Easter Sunday ..... Jn 20:2–8
- –Breakfast with Jesus after resurrection ..... Jn 21:1–14

2. Events after Jesus' ascension
- –One of the apostles ..... Ac 1:13
- –Healed a lame man with Peter ..... Ac 3:1–8
- –Arrested with Peter ..... Ac 4:1–3
- –Questioned before the Sanhedrin ..... Ac ts4:7–21
- –Sent to new Christians in Samaria Ac 8:14–17
- –Involved in the council at Jerusalem ..... Gal 2:9
- –Wrote letters as "the elder" 2Jn 1; 3Jn 1
- –Exiled to Patmos ..... Rev 1:9
- –The prophet who wrote Revelation ..... Rev 1:1–33; Rev 22:8

C. Cousin of Barnabas

JONAH

- –Prophet in the days of Jeroboam II 2Ki 14:25
- –Called to preach to city of Nineveh ..... Jnh 1:1–2
- –Fled to Tarshish ..... Jnh 1:3
- –His flight caused a storm ..... Jnh 1:4–12
- –Thrown overboard ..... Jnh 1:13–16
- –Swallowed by fish ..... Jnh 1:17
- –Prayed while inside the fish ..... Jnh 2:1–9
- –Called a second time to preach to Nineveh ..... Jnh 3:1–4
- –Reproved by the Lord ..... Jnh 4:1–11
- –His life considered a sign of resurrection ..... Mt 12:39–41; Lk 11:29–32

JONATHAN

- –Oldest son of King Saul 1Sa 14:49
- –Attacked Philistines 1Sa 13:3–4; 1Sa 14:1–14
- –Ate honey in disobedience to Saul 1Sa 14:24–45
- –Became David's best friend 1Sa 18:1
- –Made covenant with David 1Sa 18:3–4; 1Sa 20:16–17; 1Sa 23:16–18
- –Informed David of Saul's plans 1Sa 19:1–3
- –Interceded for David 1Sa 19:4–6
- –Warned David to flee 1Sa 20:18–42
- –Killed in battle 1Sa 31:2

JORAM

A. Son of Ahab; king of Israel 2Ki 1:17; 2Ki 3:1–3
- –Fought with Jehoshaphat against Moab 2Ki 3:4–27
- –Wounded in battle against Hazael 2Ki 8:25–29; 2Ch 22:5–6
- –Killed by Jehu 2Ki 9:14–26; 2Ch 22:7–8

B. King of Judah

JORDAN

–The river flowing from the Sea of Galilee to the Dead Sea

A. In the time of the patriarchs
- –Well-watered plain where Lot settled ..... Ge 13:10–11
- –Jacob crossed it, going to Haran ..... Ge 32:10
- –Jacob's sons mourned Jacob's death there ..... Ge 50:10–11

B. In the time of Moses and Joshua
- –Israelites camped along it ..... Nu 22:1
- –A census taken there ..... Nu 26:1–4
- –Some Israelites given land east of the Jordan ..... Nu 32:1–33; Nu 34:10–15
- –Israelites crossed the Jordan ..... Jos 3:1–17; Ps 114:3,5
- –Twelve stones from the Jordan formed a memorial ..... Jos 4:1–9
- –Canaanites afraid because of the crossing ..... Jos 5:1

C. In the time of the judges and kings
- –Controlling the Jordan important in war ..... Jdg 3:28; Jdg 7:24–25; Jdg 12:5–6
- –David fled from Absalom across the Jordan 2Sa 17:21–22
- –Elijah miraculously crossed the Jordan 2Ki 2:7–8
- –Elisha miraculously crossed the Jordan 2Ki 2:13–14
- –Naaman cured by washing in the Jordan 2Ki 5:9–14
- –Axhead floated in the Jordan 2Ki 6:1–7

D. In the New Testament
- –John the Baptist baptized there ..... Mt 3:6; Mk 1:5; Lk 3:3

–Jesus was baptized in the Jordan ... Mt 3:13–17; Mk 1:9–11; Lk 3:21–22

–Jesus ministered across the Jordan ... Mt 19:1; Mk 10:1; Jn 10:40–42

JOSEPH

A. Son of Jacob by Rachel

1. His life in Canaan
   - –His birth ... Ge 30:24
   - –Name means "may he add" ... Ge 30:24
   - –Favored by Jacob, hated by brothers ... Ge 37:3–4
   - –His dreams ... Ge 37:5–11
   - –Sold by brothers to Midianites ... Ge 37:12–36
2. His life in Egypt
   - –Served under Potiphar ... Ge 39:1–19
   - –Put into prison ... Ge 39:20–23
   - –Interpreted dreams of Pharaoh's servants ... Ge 40:1–19
   - –Interpreted dreams of Pharaoh ... Ge 41:14–40
   - –Was appointed ruler in Egypt ... Ge 41:41–57
   - –Father of two sons ... Ge 41:50–52
   - –Treated brothers harshly during famine ... Ge 42:6–24
   - –Ordered return of money to his brothers ... Ge 42:25–28
   - –Had meal with all his brothers ... Ge 43:26–34
   - –Ordered silver cup put in Benjamin's sack ... Ge 44:1–13
   - –Revealed himself to his brothers ... Ge 45:1–15
   - –Invited his family to live in Egypt ... Ge 45:16–28
   - –Brought Jacob and sons to Egypt ... Ge 46:1–47:12
   - –Joseph's administration ... Ge 47:13–26
   - –Had Jacob bless Ephraim and Manasseh ... Ge 48:1–22
   - –Blessed by Jacob ... Ge 49:22–26
   - –His death ... Ge 50:22–26; Heb 11:22
   - –Bones taken back to Canaan ... Jos 24:32
3. Tribe divided into Ephraim and Manasseh ... Dt 33:13–17
   - *See* EPHRAIM, MANASSEH
   - –One of the tribes of the 144,000 ... Rev 7:8

B. Husband of Mary, mother of Jesus ... Mt 1:16; Lk 1:27
- –Considered not marrying Mary ... Mt 1:18–19
- –Visited by angel ... Mt 1:20–24
- –Went to Bethlehem during census ... Lk 2:1–5
- –Gave name "Jesus" to Mary's son ... Mt 1:25
- –Circumcised Jesus; presented him in the temple ... Lk 2:21–24
- –Took Mary and Jesus to Egypt ... Mt 2:13–15
- –Returned and settled in Nazareth ... Mt 2:19–23
- –Went to Jerusalem for Passover ... Lk 2:41–51

C. A rich man from Arimathea ... Mt 27:57
- –A member of the Jewish Council ... Mk 15:43
- –Had not consented to Jesus' crucifixion ... Lk 23:51
- –A secret disciple of Jesus ... Jn 19:38
- –With Nicodemus, prepared Jesus' body ... Jn 19:39–40
- –Buried Jesus in Joseph's own tomb ... Mt 27:58–60; Mk 15:43–46; Jn 19:41–42

D. A companion of Paul

JOSHUA

A. Son of Nun; name changed from Hoshea ... Nu 13:8,16; 1Ch 7:27

1. Ministry under Moses
   - –Fought Amalekites ... Ex 17:9–14
   - –Accompanied Moses on Mount Sinai ... Ex 24:13; Ex 32:17
   - –Spied out Canaan ... Nu 13:8,16–25
   - –Encouraged Israelites to enter Canaan ... Nu 14:6–9
   - –Allowed to enter land ... Nu 14:30
   - –Appointed as Moses' successor ... Nu 27:12–23; Dt 31:1–8
2. Leader of Israelites into Canaan
   - –Encouraged by the Lord as leader ... Jos 1:1–9
   - –Charged Israel to conquer Canaan ... Jos 1:10–16
   - –Led Israelites through the Jordan ... Jos 3:1–17
   - –Had stone memorial built at the Jordan ... Jos 4:1–9
   - –Circumcised Israelites ... Jos 5:1–9
   - –Visited by commander of the Lord ... Jos 5:13–15
   - –Conquered Jericho ... Jos 6:1–25
   - –Defeated at Ai ... Jos 7:1–5
   - –Conquered Ai ... Jos 8:1–28
   - –Deceived by Gibeonites ... Jos 9:1–27
   - –Conquered five kings at Gibeon ... Jos 10:1–28
   - –Conquered southern Canaan ... Jos 10:29–43
   - –Conquered northern Canaan ... Jos 11:1–12:24
   - –Renewed covenant ... Jos 8:30–35; Jos 24:1–27
   - –Divided land among tribes ... Jos 14:1–5
   - –His farewell ... Jos 23:1–16
   - –His death ... Jos 24:28–31

B. High priest during time of Zerubbabel ... Hag 1:1,12,14
- –Also called Jeshua ... Ezr 3:2
- –Rebuilt the altar of the Lord ... Ezr 3:2–6
- –Helped rebuild the temple ... Ezr 5:2
- –Zechariah's vision of Joshua's trial in heaven ... Zec 3:1–9
- –A crown for him ... Zec 6:9–15

JOSIAH

- –Son of Amon; king of Judah ... 2Ki 21:24; 2Ch 33:25
- –Began reign when eight years old ... 2Ki 22:1; 2Ch 34:1
- –Purged the land of idolatry ... 2Ki 23:4–20,24–25; 2Ch 34:3–7
- –A prophecy concerning his reign ... 1Ki 13:2
- –Repaired the temple ... 2Ki 22:3–7; 2Ch 34:8–13
- –Book of Law discovered ... 2Ki 22:8–20; 2Ch 34:14–28
- –Renewed the covenant ... 2Ki 23:1–3; 2Ch 34:29–32
- –Celebrated the Passover ... 2Ki 23:21–23; 2Ch 35:1–19
- –Killed by Pharaoh Neco ... 2Ki 23:29–30; 2Ch 35:20–27

JOTHAM

A. Youngest son of Gideon ... Jdg 9:5
- –Spoke to Shechemites against Abimelech ... Jdg 9:7–20
- –Fled to Beer ... Jdg 9:21

B. Son of Uzziah; king of Judah ... 2Ki 15:32–38
- –Reigned while Uzziah had leprosy ... 2Ch 26:21
- –Repaired temple and walls of Jerusalem ... 2Ch 27:1–4
- –Defeated Ammonites ... 2Ch 27:5–6
- –His death ... 2Ch 27:8–9

JOY

A. Related themes
JOY is a theme of:
- –Luke ... Lk 24:52
- –Philippians ... Php 4:4

B. The nature of true joy
1. It centers in God
   - –In the Father ... Ps 32:11; Ro 5:11
   - –In the Son ... Jn 15:11; Php 4:4
   - –In the Holy Spirit ... Ro 14:17; Ro 15:13; Gal 5:22
2. It can be experienced even while suffering ... Mt 5:11–12; Ac 5:41; Ro 5:3; Col 1:24; Jas 1:2–3; 1Pe 4:13
3. One aspect of the fruit of the Spirit ... Gal 5:22
4. Our joy should never end ... Php 4:4; 1Th 5:16

C. Reasons for joy
1. Expressed in the Old Testament
   a. Personal joy
   - –For salvation ... Isa 12:3; Isa 52:8–9
   - –For forgiveness ... Ps 51:7–8
   - –For personal wellbeing ... Dt 12:17–18; 1Ch 12:40
   - –For God's protection ... Ps 5:11–12; Ps 31:7–8
   - –For life in the presence of God ... Ps 16:11; Ps 21:6
   - –For a happy home ... Pr 5:18; Pr 23:24–25

   b. National joy
   - –At religious feasts ... 2Ch 30:23–25; Neh 8:12,17; Est 8:16–17
   - –At coronations ... 1Sa 11:15; 1Ki 1:39–40
   - –At the dedication of the temple ... 1Ki 8:65–66; Ezr 3:10–13
   - –For all that the Lord does ... Ps 98:1–9; Ps 100:1–2
   - –For victory over enemies ... 1Sa 18:6–7; 2Ch 20:27–28
   - –For the return from exile ... Ps 126:1–3; Jer 31:10–13
2. In the New Testament
   - –For the birth of Jesus ... Mt 2:10; Lk 2:10,20
   - –For the resurrection of Jesus ... Mt 28:8; Lk 24:41,52
   - –For salvation ... Ac 13:48; 1Pe 1:8–9
   - –For our names in the book of life ... Lk 10:20
   - –For miraculous healing ... Ac 8:7–8
   - –For privilege of preaching about Christ ... Php 1:18
   - –For one sinner who repents ... Lk 15:7,10
   - –For the wedding of the Lamb ... Rev 19:7

JUDAH

A. Son of Jacob by Leah ... Ge 35:23; 1Ch 2:1
- –Name means "praise" ... Ge 29:35
- –Spoke against killing brother Joseph ... Ge 37:25–27
- –Married a woman from Adullam ... Ge 38:1–5
- –Engaged in illicit sex with Tamar ... Ge 38:12–24
- –Fathered Perez and Zerah by Tamar ... Ge 38:27–30
- –Promised to be security for Benjamin ... Ge 43:8–10
- –Interceded for Benjamin before Joseph ... Ge 44:18–34
- –Went to Egypt with family ... Ge 46:8,12
- –Father of five sons ... Ge 46:12
- –Blessed by Jacob ... Ge 49:8–12

B. Tribe of Judah
- –Blessed by Moses ... Dt 33:7
- –Numbered ... Nu 1:27; Nu 26:22
- –Allotted land ... Jos 15; Eze 48:7
- –Failed to fully possess the land ... Jos 15:63; Jdg 1:1–20
- –David was from this tribe ... 1Ch 28:2–4; Mt 1:2–6
- –David ruled this tribe first ... 2Sa 2:1–4
- –Became the name for the southern kingdom ... 1Ki 12:21–22; 1Ki 14:21–22
- –Taken captive to Babylon ... 2Ki 24:1–16
- –Returned from exile ... Ezr 1:1–5
- –One of the tribes of the 144,000 ... Rev 7:5

JUDAS

A. Disciple of Jesus, called Iscariot ... Mt 10:4; Mk 3:19
- –Criticized Mary for wastefulness ... Jn 12:4–5
- –Treasurer of disciples; pilfered money ... Jn 12:6
- –Satan entered into him ... Lk 22:3; Jn 13:27
- –Agreed with Jews to betray Jesus ... Mt 26:14–16; Mk 14:10–11
- –Identified as betrayer in upper room ... Mt 26:25; Jn 13:21–30
- –Betrayed Jesus with a kiss ... Mt 26:47–49; Mk 14:43–45; Lk 22:47–48
- –Returned money to the Jews ... Mt 27:3–5
- –Committed suicide ... Mt 27:5
- –Died a horrible death ... Ac 1:18–19
- –Better not to have been born ... Mk 14:21
- –Called a devil ... Jn 6:70–71
- –Jesus said he was doomed to destruction ... Jn 17:12
- –Replaced by Matthias ... Ac 1:15–26

B. Another disciple of Jesus; son of James ... Lk 6:16; Jn 14:22
- –Probably also called Thaddaeus ... Mt 10:3; Mk 3:18
- –One of the apostles ... Ac 1:13

C. Brother of Jesus and James ... Mt 13:55; Mk 6:3
- –Also called Judge ... Jude 1

D. A Christian prophet ... Ac 15:22–32
- –Also called Barsabbas ... Ac 15:22

JUDE

See JUDAS

JUDEA

A. A district governed by the Romans
- –Located west of the Jordan River ... Mt 19:1

- –Ruled by King Herod at birth of Jesus.......... Mt 2:1–3; Lk 1:5
- –Ruled by Herod's son Archelaus.... Mt 2:22
- –Governed by Pilate.......... Lk 3:1
- –Ruled by Herod Agrippa.......... Ac 12:1–3,19

B. Important towns in Judea
- –Jerusalem.......... Mt 2:1; Ac 26:20
- –Bethlehem.......... Mt 2:1; Lk 2:4
- –Arimathea.......... Lk 23:51

C. John the Baptist preached in Desert of Judea.......... Mt 3:1

D. Jesus and Judea
- –Born in Bethlehem of Judea.......... Mt 2:1–6
- –Preached in synagogues of Judea... Lk 4:44
- –Ministered in Judean countryside .. Jn 3:22
- –News about Jesus spread throughout Judea.......... Lk 7:17; Lk 23:5
- –Many from Judea followed Jesus ... Mt 4:25; Mk 3:8; Lk 6:17
- –Jesus crucified in Judea.......... 1Th 2:14–15

E. The apostles and Judea
- –Gospel was to spread throughout Judea.......... Ac 1:8
- –Residents of Judea present at Pentecost.......... Ac 2:5–9
- –Christians scattered throughout Judea.......... Ac 8:1
- –Famine aid for Christians in Judea.......... Ac 11:29; Ro 15:25–26
- –Christians there suffered persecution.......... 1Th 2:14–16

JUDGE, JUDGMENT

A. Related themes

1. JUDGMENT is a theme of:
   - –Exodus.......... Ex 34:7
   - –2 Kings.......... 2Ki 17:22
   - –Isaiah.......... Isa 65:6
   - –Jeremiah.......... Jer 6:19
   - –Ezekiel.......... Eze 24:21
   - –Hosea.......... Hos 6:5
   - –Amos.......... Am 6:8
   - –Obadiah.......... Ob 18
   - –Micah.......... Mic 1:6
   - –Nahum.......... Na 3:7
   - –Zephaniah.......... Zep 1:4
   - –Revelation.......... Rev 16:5
2. DEVASTATION is a theme of Joel... Joel 1:2

B. Judgment done by humans

1. Official judgment

a. In the political realm
- –God raised up judges for his people.......... Jdg 2:16
- –Ehud as judge.......... Jdg 3:12–30
- –Deborah as judge.......... Jdg 4:4–16
- –Gideon as judge.......... Jdg 6:11–8:32
- –Jephthah as judge.......... Jdg 10:6–12:7
- –Samson as judge.......... Jdg 13:1–16:31
- –Eli as judge.......... 1Sa 4:18
- –Samuel as judge.......... 1Sa 7:15–17

b. In the legal realm
- –Judges set up by Moses.......... Ex 18:13–26; Dt 16:18–20
- –Approved transactions regarding Ruth.......... Ru 4:1–12
- –Judges set up by Jehoshaphat.......... 2Ch 19:5–7
- –Judges set up by Ezra.......... Ezr 8:25–27
- –Pilate was a judge.......... Mt 27:19; Jn 19:13
- –Paul on trial before Gallio.......... Ac 18:12–16
- –Paul on trial before Felix.......... Ac 24:1–23
- –Paul on trial before Festus.......... Ac 25:6–12
- –Lawsuits among believers.......... 1Co 6:1–8
- –Lawsuits often instituted by the rich.......... Jas 2:6–7

c. In the religious realm
- –Sanhedrin against Jesus.......... Mt 26:57–66
- –Sanhedrin against followers of Jesus.......... Jn 9:22,28–34
- –Sanhedrin against Christians.......... Ac 4:5–21; Ac 5:21–40; Ac 22:30–23:7
- –Judgment done by the church.. 1Co 5:1–5; 1Ti 1:20; Titus 3:10–11

d. Standards for official judgment
- –Two or three witnesses needed.......... Dt 19:15; Mt 26:60
- –Must be impartial.......... Dt 1:17; Dt 16:19; Pr 24:23
- –Must be fair and just.......... Dt 1:16; Dt 16:20; Isa 56:1
- –Oath could be required.......... Ex 22:11; Heb 6:16
- –Decisions made before witnesses.......... Ru 4:9–11
- –Casting lots sometimes used... Pr 18:18

2. The judging attitude
   - –We must not judge others.......... Mt 7:1–5; Ro 14:1–4,13; 1Co 4:5; 1Co 10:29; Jas 4:11–12
   - –We must judge ourselves.......... Mt 7:3–5; Gal 6:1,4
3. Human participation in the final judgment.......... Mt 19:28; Lk 22:30; 1Co 6:2–3

C. Judgment done by God

1. God described as a judge
   - –God as judge of all the earth.......... Ge 18:26; Ps 94:2
   - –Christ as judge.......... Jn 5:22; Ac 10:42; 2Ti 4:1
   - –His judgment is always right.......... Dt 32:4; Job 34:10; 2Th 1:5
2. Temporal judgments

a. Examples of those whom God judged
- –The world in the flood.......... Ge 7:17–23
- –Sodom and Gomorrah.......... Ge 19:24–26
- –The firstborn in Egypt.......... Ex 12:29–30
- –Pharaoh and his army.......... Ex 14:23–28
- –The Israelites in the desert.......... Nu 14:26–35
- –Korah and his men.......... Nu 16:31–35
- –The Israelites during the judges.......... Jdg 2:14–15
- –Ahab and his family.......... 2Ki 9:6–10
- –The city of Samaria.......... 2Ki 17:16–18
- –The Jews in exile.......... 2Ki 24:1–4
- –Proud Nebuchadnezzar.......... Da 4:29–33
- –King Belshazzar.......... Da 5:25–30
- –The city of Jerusalem.......... Lk 19:41–44

–King Herod .... Ac 12:21–23
–The magician Elymas......... Ac 13:9–11

b. Types of temporal judgments
–Drought 1Ki 17:1
–Famine...................... La 2:11–12
–Fire from heaven 2Ki 1:10,12
–Flood....................... Ge 7:17–23
–An invasion of locusts .... Joel 1:2–7
–Earthquake.................. Isa 24:18–20
–Plague 2Sa 24:15–16
–Blight and mildew............ Am 4:9
–Severe storms................ Jos 10:10–11
–Destruction of property....... Eze 33:23–29
–Exile........................ 2Ch 36:20
–Famine of hearing God's word..................... Am 8:11
–Death 2Ki 9:8–10,30–33

c. Purposes of temporal judgments
–To punish sin................. Ge 6:5–7; Hos 5:1,8–11
–To reveal himself as God...... Ex 9:14–16; Eze 5:13
–To purify his people .... Mal 3:2–4; Jn 15:2
–To drive his people to repentance .... Am 5:6,15; Lk 13:2–5

3. The final judgment

a. Names for the final judgment
–The day of judgment.......... 2Pe 2:9
–The day of the Lord........... 1Th 5:2
–The day of God's wrath .... Ro 2:5–6
–The great Day................ Jude 6
–The Day 1Co 3:13

b. The judges of the final judgment
–God as the judge .... Ps 96:13; Ecc 3:17
–Administration given to Christ.................... Jn 5:22; Ac 10:42; Ro 2:16

c. Those who are to be judged
–The living and the dead .... Ac 10:42
–All nations................... Mt 25:31–32
–All people .... 2Co 5:10; Heb 9:27; Rev 20:11–14

d. Time of the final judgment: unknown .... Mt 24:36–42; Lk 12:40; 1Th 5:1–3

e. The basis of the final judgment
–Our faith in Jesus............ Jn 3:16–18; Jn 5:24–26
–Our sincere commitment to Jesus..................... Mt 7:22–23
–Our being heirs of God........ Mt 25:34
–Our names being in the book of life .... Rev 20:15
–Our adherence to God's law ... Ro 2:12–16; Jas 2:12
–What we've done with God's gifts.................. Lk 12:48
–Our actions .... Ecc 12:14; Mt 25:35–46; 1Co 3:12–15; 2Co 5:10
–Our words .... Mt 12:36–37; Jas 3:1–2
–Our inner thoughts 1Co 4:5
–Our perseverance to the end... Mt 24:13
–In God mercy triumphs over judgment .... Jas 2:13

f. The results of the final judgment
–Unbelievers will be punished .... Ro 2:5; 2Th 1:8–9; Rev 20:15
–Believers will receive eternal life................ Jn 3:16; 1Jn 5:11–12
–Believers will receive salvation .... Ro 13:11; Heb 9:27–28
–Believers will receive redemption .... Lk 21:28; Eph 4:30
–Believers will receive a crown.................... 2Ti 4:8; Jas 1:12

g. Attitude toward the final judgment
–Be on your guard............. Mk 13:23,33
–Be alert...................... 1Th 5:6
–Watch .... Mt 25:13

JUSTICE

–Fairness in the treatment of others

A. Related themes
JUSTICE is a theme of Lamentations............................ La 4:13
SOCIAL JUSTICE is a theme of Amos .... Am 5:24

B. Human justice

1. Israelites commanded to exercise justice .... Ex 23:1–3,6; Lev 19:15; Dt 1:17; Dt 16:18–20

2. The prophets and justice
–They called the people to justice....................... Jer 22:3; Hos 12:6; Am 5:24; Mic 6:8
–They spoke against injustice..... Isa 3:15; Am 2:6–8; Mic 3:1–3

3. Christians called to exercise justice......................... Mt 23:23; Col 4:1; Jas 2:1–4

C. The justice of God

1. God is just 2Th 1:6
–His ways are just............. Dt 32:4; Da 4:37; Rev 15:3
–He loves justice .... Ps 11:7; Ps 33:5
–He does no wrong............. Zep 3:5
–He judges justly............... 1Pe 2:23; Rev 16:5,7

2. The nature of God's justice
–He is impartial................ 2Ch 19:7; Job 34:19; Ro 2:11
–He champions victims of injustice..................... Ps 10:17–18; Ps 103:6

3. Expressions of God's justice
–Requires death for sin .... Ge 2:17; Ro 6:23
–Is expressed in his forgiveness 1Jn 1:9

See also RIGHTEOUSNESS

JUSTIFICATION

–Being declared right with God; acceptance by God

A. The basis of justification
- –Christ as our righteousness 1Co 1:30
- –Christ's perfect obedience .... Ro 5:19; 2Co 5:21; Heb 4:15; 1Pe 2:22
- –Christ's death on the cross .... Ro 3:24–25; Ro 5:9
- –Christ's resurrection .... Ro 4:25

B. The manner of justification
- –We cannot earn it by obedience .... Ro 3:28; Ro 9:31–32; Gal 2:16; Gal 3:11; Php 3:9
- –We receive it as a gift of God's grace .... Ro 3:24; Ro 4:16; Ro 5:15–17; Gal 2:21
- –We receive it by repenting .... Lk 18:13–14
- –We receive it through faith........ Ac 13:39; Ro 3:22,26–28; Ro 4:10–12; Gal 2:16; Gal 5:5; Php 3:9
- –Faith must be a living faith......... Jas 2:14–26

C. The results of justification
- –We become children of Abraham ... Ro 4:11–12, 16–17; Gal 3:6–7
- –We are redeemed .... Ro 3:24
- –We receive forgiveness of sins...... Ac 13:38–39
- –We receive the gift of eternal life ... Ro 5:17–18; Ro 8:10; Titus 3:7
- –We are saved from God's wrath .... Ro 5:9
- –We become free from condemnation.................. Ro 8:1,33–34
- –We have peace with God........... Ro 5:1
- –We are blessed by God .... Ro 4:6–9; Gal 3:9,14
- –We are considered to have kept God's law...................... Ro 8:3–4; 2Co 5:21
- –We become free from the law ...... Gal 5:1
- –We share in Christ's sufferings..... Php 3:10
- –We go on to live a life of holiness ... Ro 6:19,22; Gal 2:17–19
- –We will someday be glorified........ Ro 8:30

KADESH, KADESH BARNEA

- –City bordering on Edom.............. Nu 20:14–16
- –God appeared to Hagar near there..... Ge 16:7–14
- –Abraham lived near there .... Ge 20:1
- –Moses sent out spies from there .... Nu 13:1–2,26; Dt 1:19–25; Jos 14:6–7
- –Israelites rebelled against the Lord there .... Nu 14:1–45; Dt 1:26–45; Dt 9:23–24
- –Israelites camped there again for many days .... Dt 1:46; Jdg 11:16–17
- –Miriam died there .... Nu 20:1
- –Moses struck the rock there to get water............................ Nu 20:2–12
- –Joshua conquered that area.......... Jos 10:41
- –Became southernmost town of Judah .. Jos 15:3; Eze 47:19

KETURAH

- –Wife of Abraham after Sarah .... Ge 25:1
- –Also called Abraham's concubine 1Ch 1:32
- –Mother of six sons .... Ge 25:2

KINDNESS

–A hospitable, friendly attitude toward others

A. Related theme
- HOSPITALITY is a theme of 3 John.. 3Jn 8

B. Human kindness
1. Expected of Christians
   - –Commanded .... 2Co 6:6; Gal 5:22; Col 3:12; 2Pe 1:7
   - –One aspect of the fruit of the Spirit.................... Gal 5:22
2. Expressions of kindness
   - –Showing forgiveness .... Ge 50:21
   - –Sparing someone's life .... Jos 2:12–13
   - –Healing the sick .... Ac 4:9
   - –Helping the needy............... 2Sa 9:1–7; Pr 14:21,31; Pr 19:17
   - –Helping victims of injustice ...... Ge 40:14
   - –Helping strangers............... Ac 28:2; Heb 13:1–2; 3Jn 5–8

C. Kindness of God
- –In giving us salvation............. Titus 3:4
- –In being faithful to his promises 1Ki 3:6
- –In watching over us .... Job 10:12
- –In showing compassion to us....... Isa 54:8
- –In providing for needs............ Ge 32:10; Ru 2:20; Hos 11:4; Ac 14:17
- –In helping us in various life situations........................ Ge 39:21; Ezr 9:9

See also MERCY

KING

A. Related theme
- KINGSHIP is a theme of 1 Samuel ... 1Sa 11:15

B. Human kings
1. Examples of non-Israelite kings
   - –Four kings warring against five .... Ge 14:8–11
   - –Melchizedek, king of Salem...... Ge 14:18
   - –List of the kings of Edom .... Ge 36:32–39
   - –Pharaoh, king of Egypt.......... Ex 1:8,15–22
   - –Sihon and Og defeated .... Nu 21:21–35
   - –Various kings in Canaan defeated.................... Jos 8:1–2; Jos 10:1–3,16–42; Jos 12
   - –David defeated various kings 2Sa 8:1–14
   - –The king of Assyria took Israel... 2Ki 17:3–6
   - –King Nebuchadnezzar took Judah 2Ki 25:1–7
   - –King Cyrus allowed return to Judah .... Ezr 1:1–4
   - –Nehemiah served King Artaxerxes .... Neh 2:1
   - –Esther became wife of King Ahasuerus (Xerxes) .... Est 2:1,17–18
   - –Caesar as king.................. Jn 19:12,15
   - –The kings of the earth........... Ps 2:2; Ps 102:15; Ps 138:4
2. The kings of Israel and Judah
   - a. The beginning of kingship
     - –The people asked for a king ... 1Sa 8:4–5

–Samuel warned them........ 1Sa 8:10–18
–Saul anointed as first king 1Sa 10:20–24
1Sa 11:14–15

b. Kings of the united kingdom
–Saul (42 years) 1Sa 13:1
See SAUL
–David (40 years)............... 1Ki 2:11
See DAVID
–Solomon (40 years) 1Ki 11:42
See SOLOMON

c. The kings of Israel (in chronological order)
–Jeroboam (22 years) 1Ki 12:25–14:20
–Nadab (2 years) 1Ki 15:25–31
–Baasha (24 years) 1Ki 15:32–16:7
–Elah (2 years) 1Ki 16:8–14
–Zimri (7 days)................ 1Ki 16:15–20
–Tibni (with Omri)............. 1Ki 16:21–22
–Omri (12 years)............... 1Ki 16:23–28
–Ahab (22 years) 1Ki 16:29–22:40
2Ch 18:1–34
–Ahaziah (2 years) 1Ki 22:51–53
2Ki 1:1–18
–Joram (12 years).............. 2Ki 3:1–8:15
–Jehu (28 years) 2Ki 9:6–10:36
–Jehoahaz (17 years)........... 2Ki 13:1–9
–Jehoash (16 years)............ 2Ki 13:10–25
–Jeroboam II (41 years) 2Ki 14:23–29
–Zechariah (6 months)......... 2Ki 15:8–12
–Shallum (1 month)............ 2Ki 15:13–15
–Menahem (10 years) 2Ki 15:16–22
–Pekahiah (2 years)............ 2Ki 15:23–26
–Pekah (20 years) 2Ki 15:27–31
–Hoshea (9 years) 2Ki 17:1–6

See also entries for each of these kings

d. The kings of Judah (in chronological order)
–Rehoboam (17 years).......... 1Ki 12:1–24
1Ki 14:21–31
2Ch 10:1–12:16
–Abijah (3 years) 1Ki 15:1–8
2Ch 13:1–41:1
–Asa (41 years)................ 1Ki 15:9–24
2Ch 14:2–16:14
–Jehoshaphat (25 years)........ 1Ki 22:41–50
2Ch 17:1–21:3
–Jehoram (8 years) 2Ki 8:16–24
2Ch 21:4–20
–Ahaziah (1 year) 2Ki 8:25–29
2Ch 22:1–9
–Athaliah (7 years) 2Ki 11:1–21
2Ch 22:10–23:21
–Joash (40 years).............. 2Ki 12:1–21
2Ch 24:1–27
–Amaziah (29 years)........... 2Ki 14:1–22
2Ch 25:1–28
–Azariah or Uzziah (52 years) .. 2Ki 15:1–7
2Ch 26:1–23
–Jotham (16 years)............. 2Ki 15:32–38
2Ch 27:1–8
–Ahaz (16 years) 2Ki 16:1–20
2Ch 28:1–27
–Hezekiah (29 years) 2Ki 18:1–20:21
2Ch 29:1–32:33
Isa 36:1–39:8
–Manasseh (55 years).......... 2Ki 21:1–18
2Ch 33:1–20
–Amon (2 years)............... 2Ki 21:19–26
2Ch 33:21–25
–Josiah (31 years)............. 2Ki 22:1–23:30
2Ch 34:1–35:27
–Jehoahaz (3 months).......... 2Ki 23:31–33
2Ch 36:1–4
–Jehoiakim (11 years).......... 2Ki 23:24–24:7
2Ch 36:5–8
–Jehoiachin (3 months)......... 2Ki 24:8–17
2Ch 36:9–10
–Zedekiah (11 years)........... 2Ki 24:18–25:26
2Ch 36:11–21

See also entries for each of these kings

C. God as a king

1. God called a king
–The King of heaven............ Ps 95:3
Da 4:37
–The King of glory .... Ps 24:10
–The eternal, immortal King 1Ti 1:17
–The great King................ Ps 47:2
–He rules over all the earth....... 2Ch 20:6
Ps 99:1–2
Isa 52:7
–He rules from his throne 1Ki 22:19
Ps 9:4,7–8
Isa 6:1–3

2. Christ is a king
a. Prophesied in the Old Testament
–The coming one will have a scepter .... Ge 49:10
Nu 24:17
–He will rule on David's throne .... Ps 132:11–12
Isa 9:6–7
Jer 33:17
–He will rule at God's right hand..................... Ps 110:1
–He will rule eternally .... Da 2:44–45
–He will rule with authority .... Da 7:13–14
–He will rule as a shepherd..... Isa 40:10–11
Eze 34:23–24
Mic 5:2–4
–He will rule wisely............ Isa 52:13
Jer 23:5
–He will rule with justice....... Isa 32:1
Jer 33:15–16
–He will rule humbly .... Zec 9:9
–He will function as a priest.... Ps 110:4
Zec 6:12–13

b. Fulfilled in the New Testament
–He is the king of the Jews ..... Mt 2:2
Jn 19:19–21
–He is the king of Israel .... Jn 1:49
–He claimed kingship.......... Mt 27:11
Jn 18:37
–He entered Jerusalem as king .... Mt 21:1–9
–He came to rule on David's throne .... Lk 1:32–33
Ac 2:29–33
–He now rules at God's right hand..................... Eph 1:20–23
Heb 1:3–8
–He is ruling over his enemies.................. 1Co 15:25–27
–He will sit as a King who judges.................... Mt 25:31–34

KINGDOM

–The rule of humans or God over others

A. Related themes
KINGDOM is theme of:
–2 Samuel...................... 2Sa 5:12
–1 Kings 1Ki 4:21

B. Human kingdoms

1. General kingdoms of Bible history
–Kingdom of Bashan............ Nu 32:33
–Kingdom of the Amorites .... Nu 32:33
–The Aramean kingdom.......... 1Ch 18:6
–The kingdom of Babylon........ Da 1:20
Da 4:36

–The kingdom of Media and Persia .... Est 1:2–4
Da 5:28,30
–Four kingdoms in Nebuchadnezzar's dream ..... Da 2:36–43
–All the kingdoms of the earth .... Dt 28:25
2Ki 19:15,19
Jer 15:4
Mt 4:8

2. The kingdom(s) of Israel and Judah
–The kingdom taken away from Saul 1Sa 13:13–14
–The kingdom united under David 2Sa 5:1–5,12
–The kingdom expanded under David 2Sa 8:11–14
–The kingdom given to Solomon ... 1Ki 1:28–40
–The kingdom to be divided after Solomon........ 1Ki 11:9–13
–The kingdom divided under Rehoboam........ 1Ki 12:16–24
–The kingdom of Israel destroyed ... 2Ki 17:7–23
–The kingdom of Judah destroyed... 2Ki 25:1–21

C. Kingdom of God
1. When and where is that kingdom?
a. The kingdom is present in Jesus
–John preached it was near..... Mt 3:2
–Jesus preached it was near .... Mk 1:15
–Jesus preached the gospel of the kingdom........ Mt 4:23
–Some parables describe its life........ Mt 13:11–52
–Jesus' miracles proved its presence .... Lk 7:18–22
–Casting out demons proved it .... Lk 11:20
–"The kingdom of God is within you"........ Lk 17:20–21
–It comes through Jesus' death .... Lk 23:42–43
–It comes through Jesus' resurrection 1Co 15:20–25
–The apostles preached the kingdom .... Ac 8:12
Ac 19:8
Ac 28:23,28
–Christ brings us into his kingdom .... Col 1:12–13
b. The kingdom is yet to come
–Jesus prayed, "Your kingdom come"........ Mt 6:10
–Some parables describe it as future .... Mt 25:1–34
–It comes with the return of Jesus 2Ti 4:1
–It is something we will inherit .... Mt 25:34
1Co 15:50
Jas 2:5
–It is a heavenly kingdom 2Ti 4:18
Heb 12:26–28
–It is a kingdom we will receive........ 2Pe 1:11
–The millennial kingdom ...... Rev 20:1–6
2. How can we enter the kingdom?
–By experiencing new birth....... Jn 3:3
–By receiving it as a gift from Jesus........ Lk 22:29
–By responding to God's call...... 1Th 2:12
–By repenting of our sins .... Mk 1:15
–By being redeemed through Christ........ Col 1:12–14
–By accepting Christ's righteousness........ Mt 5:20
–By following Jesus .... Mt 19:21–24
Lk 9:61–62
–By loving God .... Jas 2:5
–By persevering in the faith....... Ac 14:22
2Th 1:4–5
–By doing the will of God .... Mt 7:21–23
3. What is life in the kingdom like?
–Described in the Sermon on the Mount .... Mt 5:1–7:27
–Described in the Sermon on the Plain .... Lk 6:17–49
–Described in many parables of Jesus .... Mt 13:11–52
Mt 18:23–35
Mt 20:1–16
Mt 21:28–22:14
–A life of childlike humility .... Mt 18:1–4
–A life of joy and peace .... Ro 14:17
–A life free from sin's control...... 1Co 6:9–11
Gal 5:16–21
Eph 5:3–5
–A life of producing the fruit of the Spirit........ Gal 5:21–23
4. How must we relate to the kingdom?
–We must pray for it........ Mt 6:10
–We must seek it first .... Mt 6:33
–We must preach it........ Ac 8:22
Ac 28:31
–We must work for it .... Col 4:11
–We may have to suffer for it....... Ac 14:22
2Ti 4:16–18

KISS

A. Legitimate uses
–To say hello........ Ge 29:13
Ge 33:4
–To say good-bye........ Ge 31:55
Ru 1:9
1Sa 20:41
–To accompany a blessing .... Ge 27:26–27
–To express deep affection........ 1Sa 20:41
–To express sexual love........ SS 1:2
–To express grief........ Ge 50:1
Ac 20:37
–To demonstrate forgiveness .... Ge 33:4
Ge 45:15
Lk 15:20
–To show honor and respect......... 1Sa 10:1
Lk 7:38
–To express submission........ Ps 2:12
–To show Christian love .... Ro 16:16
1Pe 5:14

B. Pagan use: kissing idols........ 1Ki 19:18
Job 31:26–27
Hos 13:2

C. Hypocritical uses
–Absalom trying to gain popularity.. 2Sa 15:5
–Joab when he killed Amasa 2Sa 20:9
–Judas when he betrayed Jesus........ Mt 26:48–49
Mk 14:44–45
Lk 22:47–48
–A prostitute seducing a man .... Pr 7:13
–Can be used by any enemy......... Pr 27:6

KNOWLEDGE

A. Related theme
KNOWLEDGE is a theme of 2 Peter...2Pe 1:3

B. Human knowledge of God and his ways
1. Source of our knowledge
–God himself........ Pr 2:6
Jer 9:23–24
–Christ .... Col 2:3,8
–The Holy Spirit 1Co 2:9–16

–The world around us .... Ps 19:1; Ro 1:19–20
–God's word...................... Pr 2:1–5; Jn 17:17; 2Ti 3:15–16
–God's mighty acts for his people... Ex 6:6–7; Eze 37:13–14

2. Corruption of human knowledge of God
–First sin: seeking knowledge apart from God .... Ge 3:4–7
–Humans suppress the truth about God...................... Ro 1:18; 2Ti 3:7; Titus 1:16
–Idolatry is evidence of this .... Ro 1:21–23

3. Proper attitude to the knowledge of God
–We must know God .... Jer 9:24
–To know God is to do his will..... Jer 22:15–16
–We must know Christ .... Php 3:8,10
–We must pray for knowledge..... Ps 119:66
–We must grow in knowledge ..... Eph 4:13; Heb 5:12–6:1; 2Pe 1:5–8; 2Pe 3:18
–We must recognize its limitations.................. 1Co 13:8–12
–We must realize love surpasses it................. 1Co 8:1; Eph 3:19
–We must not become proud of it ... 1Co 8:1
–We must not wander away from it 1Ti 6:20–21

4. Benefits of the knowledge of God
–Gives stability to life .... Pr 24:3–6
–Enables us to know the love of God 1Jn 3:1
–Enables us to fight sin and evil 2Pe 1:3–4
–Keeps us from destruction by God .... Hos 4:6
–Essential to eternal life .... Jn 17:3

C. Knowledge possessed by God
–God is all-knowing................. Ps 139:1–6; Isa 46:10; 1Jn 3:20
–God's knowledge of us precedes our birth....................... Ps 139:15–16; Jer 1:5
–God knows what is inside us .... 1Sa 16:7; Ps 44:21
–God knows our needs .... Ps 103:13–14; Mt 6:31–32
–Little things do not escape his notice .... Mt 10:29–30
–God cannot be taught by humans... Job 21:22; Isa 40:12–14
–Jesus knew God's will for him...... Lk 18:31–33; Jn 13:1
–Jesus knows us completely......... Jn 2:25; Jn 4:16–18; Jn 6:64
–All knowledge is hidden in Christ ... Col 2:3

KORAH

–A descendant of Levi................ Ex 6:19,21,24
–Led a rebellion against Moses......... Nu 16:1–3
–Killed by the Lord for this rebellion.... Nu 16:4–35
–His descendants became temple gatekeepers 1Ch 9:17,19; 1Ch 26:1
–His descendants became temple musicians........................ 1Ch 6:31–32,37; 2Ch 20:19
–Sons of Korah wrote various psalms... Ps 44–49,85–88
–His rebellion illustrates God's judgment .... Jude 11

LABAN

–Son of Bethuel....................... Ge 24:24
–Brother of Rebekah .... Ge 24:29
–Father of Leah and Rachel............ Ge 29:16
–Deceived Jacob into marrying Leah ... Ge 29:22–27
–Became Jacob's boss.................. Ge 29:18–20; Ge 30:25–34
–Became jealous of Jacob's prosperity ... Ge 31:1–2
–Disinherited his daughters............ Ge 31:14–16
–Pursued the fleeing Jacob .... Ge 31:22–25
–Made a covenant with Jacob .... Ge 31:43–55

LAMB

A. Uses for lambs
–For food.......................... Dt 32:14; Am 6:4
–For clothing .... Pr 27:26
–For sealing a treaty................ Ge 21:27–31
–For the payment of tribute 2Ki 3:4
–For a sacrifice in place of Isaac ..... Ge 22:8,13
–For a regular burnt offering........ Ex 29:38–42
–For offerings at special feasts ...... Nu 28:27; Nu 29:2
–For the Passover .... Ex 12:3–6; Nu 28:16–19

B. The lamb as a symbol
–Of extraordinary joy .... Ps 114:1–4
–Of innocence 2Sa 12:1–4
–Of weak people .... Isa 40:11; Jn 21:15
–Of peace-loving missionaries....... Lk 10:3
–Of the age of peace................ Isa 11:6; Isa 65:25

C. Jesus as the Lamb of God
–Prophesied by Isaiah.............. Isa 53:4–7
–Fulfilled in Jesus.................. Ac 8:32–35
–Called the Lamb of God .... Jn 1:29,36
–Called the Passover lamb 1Co 5:7
–Shed his blood as a lamb without blemish.......................... 1Pe 1:19
–Receives praise as the slain Lamb ... Rev 5:6–13; Rev 7:9–11
–Celebrates with his 144,000 .... Rev 14:1–5
–Conquers the antichrist............ Rev 17:14
–Marries the church as a bride ...... Rev 19:7,9; Rev 21:9

LANGUAGE

A. Languages mentioned in the Bible
–Hebrew .... Isa 36:11,13
–Babylonian........................ Da 1:4
–Aramaic .... Ezr 4:7
–Ashdod .... Neh 13:23–24
–Lycaonian......................... Ac 14:11
–Latin .... Jn 19:20
–Greek............................. Ac 21:37
–Numerous languages............... Ge 10:5,20,31; Ac 2:5–11

B. Language barriers begun at Babel ... Ge 11:1–9

C. Language barriers removed
–At Pentecost....................... Ac 2:4–11
–Through gift of tongues .... Ac 10:46; Ac 19:6; 1Co 12:10,28–30; 1Co 13:1
–Through the interpretation of tongues....................... 1Co 12:10,30; 1Co 14:5,13,27
–In heaven .... Rev 5:9; Rev 7:9

LAW

A. Related themes
LAW is a theme of:
–Leviticus.......................... Lev 7:37

–1 Chronicles ... 1Ch 22:12
–2 Chronicles ... 2Ch 8:13

B. Meanings of the word "law"
–A general principle ... Ro 7:23
–Rules of conduct in the conscience ... Ro 2:14
–Edicts made by human governments ... Da 6:12
–Rules revealed by God through Moses ... Ex 21:1; Ro 5:13; Ac 15:5
–The first five books of the Bible ... Gal 3:10
–The whole Old Testament ... Jn 15:25; 1Co 14:21

C. The law of God

1. Characteristics
–True ... Ps 119:142,151
–Perfect ... Ps 19:7; Jas 1:25
–Trustworthy ... Ps 19:7; Ps 119:86,138
–Enduring ... Ps 119:91,160; Mt 5:18
–Right and righteous ... Ps 19:8; Ps 119:75,137; Ro 7:12
–Holy ... Ro 7:12
–Good ... Ro 7:12,16; 1Ti 1:8
–Spiritual ... Ro 7:14
–Love is its summary ... Mt 22:37–40; Ro 13:8–10; Gal 5:14

2. Brief history of God's law revealed to Moses
–Spoken directly by God ... Ex 20:1,18–19; Dt 5:4,22
–Spoken by Moses to the Israelites ... Ex 20:22
–Written on tablets of stone ... Ex 24:12; Ex 31:18
–Tablets broken by Moses ... Ex 32:15–19
–Written on tablets a second time ... Ex 34:1–5,27–28
–Repeated in Deuteronomy ... Dt 4:44–46
–Placed in the ark of the covenant ... Dt 31:24–26
–Repeated by Joshua ... Jos 24:25–26
–Honored by David ... 1Ch 16:40
–Disobeyed by God's people ... 2Ki 17:12–20
–Taught by Jehoshaphat ... 2Ch 17:9; 2Ch 19:8
–Honored during Joash's reign ... 2Ch 23:18–19
–Honored during Hezekiah's reign ... 2Ch 31:3–4,21
–Rediscovered during Josiah's reign ... 2Ch 34:14–18
–Studied by Ezra ... Ezr 7:10
–Reintroduced by Ezra to the people ... Neh 8:1–18
–Read in the synagogues ... Ac 15:21
–Fulfilled by Jesus Christ ... Mt 5:17–18

3. Purpose of the law of God
–To show the way to life ... Lev 18:4–5; Dt 30:15–20; Gal 3:12
–To point out our sin ... Ro 3:20; Gal 3:19
–To increase sin ... Ro 5:20
–To show that we lie under its curse ... Gal 3:10,13
–To lead us to Christ ... Gal 3:24

4. The Israelites and the law of God
–Must know it ... Ex 33:12–13
–Must fix it in their hearts ... Dt 11:18; Ps 119:11
–Must teach it ... Dt 4:9–10; Dt 11:19–21
–Must observe it ... Dt 4:1,6; Dt 29:9
–Must remember it ... Nu 15:38–40; Mal 4:4
–Must love it ... Ps 119:47,97
–Must delight in it ... Ps 1:2; Ps 112:1

5. Jesus Christ and the law of God
–Came to fulfill it ... Mt 5:17–18
–Born under it ... Gal 4:4
–Circumcised according to it ... Lk 2:21
–Consecrated according to it ... Lk 2:22–24
–Attended feasts prescribed in it ... Mk 14:12–16; Jn 2:23
–Perfectly obeyed it ... 2Co 5:21; Heb 4:15; 1Pe 2:22–23
–Completed what it pointed to ... Heb 8:5–6; Heb 9:11–15, 23–28
–Bore its curse on the cross ... Gal 3:13
–Ended its burden ... Ro 7:4–6; Ro 10:1–5; Gal 3:24–25
–Gave us freedom from it ... Jn 8:31–36; Gal 5:1

6. Christians and the law of God
–Cannot keep it perfectly ... Ro 3:19–20,23; Ro 7:4–5
–Cannot be justified through it ... Ro 3:20,28; Gal 3:11
–Have met its requirements ... Ro 8:4
–Are free from its condemnation ... Ro 8:2
–Are free from its curse ... Gal 3:13–14
–Are free from its burden ... Gal 2:1–5; Gal 5:1
–Have it written on their hearts ... Heb 8:10–13
–Are under the law of Christ ... Jn 14:15; 1Co 9:21; Gal 6:2
–Must keep the law of love ... Jn 13:34–35; Ro 13:8–10; Gal 5:13–14; 1Jn 3:11–18
–Must keep the Ten Commandments ... Eph 6:2; Jas 2:8–11

7. The Spirit and the law
–Sets us free from it ... Ro 8:2,13; 2Co 3:17
–Enables us to keep its spirit ... Ro 7:6; 2Co 3:6; Gal 5:16–17,22–25

LAZARUS

A. Poor man in Jesus' parable ... Lk 16:19–31

B. Brother of Mary and Martha ... Jn 11:1
–Became sick and died ... Jn 11:2–15
–Raised from the dead ... Jn 11:38–44
–Present at a meal with Jesus ... Jn 12:2
–His resurrection caused a stir ... Jn 12:17–19

LEADER

A. Related themes
LEADERSHIP is a theme of:
–Ezra ... Ezr 7:10
–Nehemiah ... Neh 13:25
–1 Timothy ... 1Ti 4:6

B. Types of leaders
–Moses as God's chosen leader ... Nu 33:1; Mic 6:4

–Joshua as Moses' successor . . . . Dt 1:38
Jos 1:6
–Tribal leaders . . . . Nu 2:3,5,7,10
Nu 7:2
–Judges . . . . Jdg 4:4
Jdg 12:7–14
–Kings 1Sa 8:5–6,20
1Ch 11:2
2Ch 1:10
–Priests . . . . Neh 9:38
–The shepherds of Israel . . . . Jer 25:34–36
–Church officials . . . . Ac 15:22
Heb 13:7,17,24

C. Principles of leadership
1. Positive principles
–Depend on the Lord's strength . . . Jos 1:6
–Obey the law of God . . . . Jos 1:7–8
–Use wisdom and knowledge from God 2Ch 1:10
Jer 3:15
–Exercise justice . . . . Mic 3:1–3
–Live an exemplary life 1Ti 4:12
1Pe 5:3
–Serve the people selflessly . . . . Mt 20:26
Lk 22:26–27
1Pe 5:2
–Govern diligently . . . . Ro 12:8
2. Negative principles
–Do not be rebellious against God . . . . Jer 2:8–9
Hos 9:15–17
–Do not lead the people astray . . . . Isa 3:12–15
Jer 23:30–32
1Jn 3:7
–Do not be a poor example . . . . Ezr 9:1–2
–Do not exert power . . . . Mt 20:25–26
1Pe 5:3
–Do not seek your own needs and wants first . . . . Eze 34:1–6
Am 5:11–13

See also KING
SHEPHERD

D. God as leader of his people
–God the Father as leader . . . . Ex 15:13
Dt 8:2,15
2Ch 13:12
Ps 23:1–3
Ps 139:23–24
–Jesus the Son as leader . . . . Jn 10:2–3,10–14
Jn 13:12–15
–The Holy Spirit as leader . . . . Ro 8:14
Gal 5:18

LEAH

–Older daughter of Laban . . . . Ge 29:16
–First wife of Jacob . . . . Ge 29:22–27
–Not loved by Jacob . . . . Ge 29:31
–Bore six sons and one daughter . . . . Ge 29:31–35
Ge 30:17–21
Ge 35:23
–Buried with Abraham and Sarah . . . . . . Ge 49:31

LEAVEN

See YEAST

LEBANON

A. Location of Lebanon
–Northeast part of the promised land . . . . Dt 11:24
Jos 13:5–6
–Land of mountains and valleys . . . . . Jos 12:7
Jdg 3:3
–Contained Mount Hermon . . . . Jos 11:17

B. Importance of Lebanon to Israelites
–Never totally occupied by Israelites . . . . Jos 13:5–6
–Its wood used in the first temple 1Ki 5:6–10
–Its wood used in Solomon's palace . . . 1Ki 7:2–3
–Its wood used in the second temple . . . Ezr 3:7

C. Lebanon used as a symbol
–Of the majesty of the Creator . . . . Ps 104:16
–Of the power of the Creator . . . . Ps 29:4–6
–Of the fruitfulness of God's people . . . Ps 72:16
Ps 92:12–14
–Of the new world of the redeemed . . . Isa 35:1–2
Isa 60:13
–Of one's beauty and majesty . . . . SS 3:6–9
SS 5:15
–Of the importance of the royal house . . . . Jer 22:6–7
–Of the arrogance of humanity . . . . . . Isa 2:12–18

LEGALISM

See FREEDOM

LEISURE

See REST

LEVI, LEVITE

A. Son of Jacob by Leah . . . . Ge 35:23
1Ch 2:1
–Name means "attached" . . . . Ge 29:34
–With Simeon, avenged rape of sister Dinah . . . . Ge 34:25–31
–Went to Egypt with family . . . . Ge 46:8,11
–Father of three sons . . . . Ge 46:11
–Blessed by Jacob . . . . Ge 49:5–7

B. Tribe descended from Levi
1. History of the tribe
–Moses and Aaron from that tribe . . . . Ex 2:1
–Tribe blessed by Moses . . . . Dt 33:8–11
–Tribe chosen to serve as priests . . . Nu 3:1–4:49
–Made ceremonially clean . . . . Nu 8:5–26
–Numbered . . . . Nu 3:39
Nu 26:62
–Allotted cities, but not land . . . . . . Nu 18:20,24
Nu 35:1–5
–Allotted land . . . . Eze 48:8–22
–One of the tribes of the 144,000 . . . Rev 7:7
2. Duties
–Belonged to the Lord . . . . Nu 3:11–13
–Were Israel's religious leaders . . . . Dt 10:8
–Were in charge of the tabernacle . . . Nu 1:50–53
Nu 4:1–33
–Assisted Aaron . . . . Nu 3:5–9
Nu 18:1–7
–Prepared the sacrifices 2Ch 35:10–14
Ezr 6:19–21
–Gathered tithes and offerings . . . . Nu 18:20–24
Dt 18:1–2
Neh 10:37–39
–Served as judges of the people . . . Dt 17:8–9
1Ch 23:3–4
1Ch 26:29
–Recited the curses of God . . . . Dt 27:14–26
–Supervised the work of the temple 1Ch 23:3–4, 28–32
1Ch 26:20–28
–Instructed the people in the law . . Neh 8:7–9
–Some were gatekeepers 1Ch 23:3–5
1Ch 26:1–19
–Some were musicians 1Ch 23:3–5
1Ch 25:1–31
Neh 12:24,27–43

C. One of Jesus' disciples
See MATTHEW

LIFE

A. Related themes

1. LIFE is a theme of:
–John. . . . . Jn 3:16
–1 John 1Jn 5:20

2. LIFE'S PURPOSE is a theme of Ecclesiastes. . . . . Ecc 12:13

B. God and life
–God is a living God. . . . . Dt 5:26; Ps 42:2; 1Th 1:9
–God has life in himself. . . . . Jn 5:26
–Jesus is the Living One . . . . Rev 1:18
–Jesus is the life. . . . . Jn 11:25; Jn 14:6; 1Jn 1:1–2
–Jesus has life in himself . . . . Jn 1:4
–The Spirit of life . . . . Ro 8:2

C. Physical life

1. Plant and animal life
–Created by God . . . . Ge 1:11–12, 20–25; Ps 104:24–25,30
–Preserved by God. . . . . Ps 104:21,24–28; Ps 145:15–16; Ps 147:8–9

2. Human life
–God is its source . . . . Ge 2:7; Job 33:4; Isa 42:5; Ac 17:26,28
–God preserves it . . . . Job 12:10; Ps 138:7
–God removes it as punishment for sin. . . . . Ge 3:19; Ro 5:12
–Human life should be reproduced. . . Ge 1:28; Ge 9:1,7
–Human life is fleeting and fragile . . . . Job 20:4–11; Ps 90:3–10; Ps 103:14–16
–God's kingdom is more important . . . . Mt 6:25–34; Mt 10:38–39; Jn 12:25
–Taking a human life is forbidden. . . Ge 9:5–6; Ex 20:13; Ro 13:9–10

D. Spiritual life

1. The source of spiritual life
–God, the Father . . . . Eph 2:4–5; Col 2:13
–Jesus Christ, God's Son. . . . . Jn 1:4; Jn 10:10; Ac 3:15
–The Holy Spirit . . . . Eze 37:14; Jn 3:5–6; Ro 8:2,11
–The word of God. . . . . Jas 1:18; 1Pe 1:23

2. Phrases describing spiritual life
–Being born again . . . . Jn 3:3–8
–Being crucified with Christ . . . . Gal 2:20; Ro 6:8–10
–Being raised with Christ. . . . . Ro 6:4; Col 3:1–3
–Being a new creation 2Co 5:17
–Living by the Spirit . . . . Gal 5:16,25
–Having names in the book of life. . . Lk 10:20; Php 4:3
–Already having eternal life . . . . . . Jn 3:36; Jn 6:47; 1Jn 5:11–13
–Not being subject to the second death . . . . Rev 20:6

3. How to obtain spiritual life
–We must choose it. . . . . Dt 30:19–20
–We must hear the word of God . . . Ac 16:14; Ro 10:13–14
–We must be called by God 2Th 2:13–14
–We must repent of our sins. . . . . . . Ac 2:38
–We must believe in Jesus . . . . Jn 3:15–16; Jn 20:31

4. Stages of spiritual life
–The time of birth. . . . . Jn 3:3–8; 1Pe 1:23
–Being babes in Christ 1Co 3:1; 1Pe 2:2
–Growth must take place . . . . Eph 4:14–16; Col 1:10; 1Pe 2:2
–Becoming mature Christians . . . . . 1Co 2:6; Eph 4:13; Heb 5:14–6:1; Jas 1:4
–We must not slip back . . . . Php 3:13–16; Heb 5:12–14

See also GROWTH

E. Eternal life

1. How can we receive eternal life?
–By being appointed to it by God . . . Ac 13:48
–By being called to it 1Ti 6:12
–By reading the Scriptures. . . . . Jn 5:39
–By receiving it as a gift from God. . . . . Ro 6:23
–By receiving it as a gift from Jesus. . . . . Jn 5:40; Jn 10:28
–By taking hold of it. 1Ti 6:12,19
–By realizing Jesus is eternal life. 1Jn 1:2; 1Jn 5:20
–By believing in Jesus . . . . Jn 3:15–16
–By trusting in Jesus . . . . Jn 14:1–3
–By drinking of Jesus as water of life . . . . Jn 4:13–14
–By eating of Jesus as bread of life . . . . Jn 6:48–51
–By eating of the tree of life . . . . Ge 3:22; Rev 2:7
–By dying with Christ 2Ti 2:11
–By knowing God. . . . . Jn 17:3
–By being righteous . . . . Mt 25:46
–By obeying the commands of God . . . . Jn 12:50
–By pleasing the Spirit . . . . Gal 6:8

2. Eternal life begins now
–We have eternal life . . . . Jn 3:36; Jn 5:24
–We are already with Christ in heaven . . . . Eph 2:6; Col 3:3

3. Eternal life is still in the future
–We have been promised it. 1Ti 4:8
–We have hope of it . . . . Titus 1:2; Titus 3:7
–We will rise again to receive it. . . . Jn 5:28–29
–We will receive it as a crown 1Pe 5:4
–We will inherit it. . . . . Mt 19:29
–We will reap it . . . . Gal 6:8
–We will reign in it. . . . . Ro 5:17

- –Jesus will bring us to it .... Jude 21
- –We will someday be in paradise ... Lk 23:43; Rev 2:7

LIGHT

A. God and light
- –God is light 1Jn 1:5
- –He created light .... Ge 1:3; Isa 45:7
- –He is the Father of lights .... Jas 1:17
- –He lives in light .... Ps 104:2; 1Ti 6:16
- –Jesus reflects the Father's light ..... Heb 1:3
- –Jesus is the light of the world .... Jn 1:9; Jn 8:12; Jn 9:5

B. God's word as a light
- –God's word is a light .... Ps 119:105; Pr 6:23; 2Pe 1:19
- –God's word gives light .... Ps 119:130
- –The gospel proclaims light .... Ac 26:18,23; 2Co 4:4
- –In God's light we see light .... Ps 19:8; Ps 36:9
- –God's light guides us .... Ps 43:3; Isa 51:4

C. Believers and the light of God
- –We are enlightened .... Heb 6:4; Heb 10:32
- –We are children of the light .... 1Th 5:5; Mt 5:14
- –We are called into God's light 1Pe 2:9
- –We confess that the Lord is our light .... Ps 27:1; Mic 7:8–9
- –We walk in the light .... Isa 2:5; 1Jn 1:5,7
- –Our path gets ever brighter .... Pr 4:18
- –We put on the armor of light .... Ro 13:12
- –We live as children of light .... Eph 5:8–11
- –We must be light to the world .... Mt 5:14–16; Php 2:15
- –We shall someday enter the kingdom of light .... Col 1:12–13
- –We look for a new heaven of only light .... Isa 60:19; Rev 21:23; Rev 22:5
- –We have no fellowship with darkness .... Lk 11:35; 2Co 6:14; Eph 5:11

See DARKNESS

LION

A. Lion stories in the Bible
- –Samson killed a lion .... Jdg 14:5–6
- –David killed a lion 1Sa 17:34–35
- –A lion killed a prophet 1Ki 13:24; 1Ki 20:36
- –Settlers in Samaria killed by lions ... 2Ki 17:25–26
- –Daniel in the lions' den .... Da 6:16–24

B. The lion as a symbol

1. Characteristics that stand out
   - –Majestic .... Pr 30:29–30
   - –Fierce .... Am 3:8
   - –Stealthy .... Job 10:16
   - –Mean when hungry .... Ps 17:12
2. As a symbol of evil
   - –Of the devil 1Pe 5:8
   - –Of enemies attacking God's people .... Isa 5:29
   - –Of cruel rulers of the people ...... Zep 3:3
   - –Of one's persecutors .... Ps 17:10–12; Ps 22:13,21; 2Ti 4:17
3. As a symbol of God and good
   - –Of Christ, the triumphant Ruler ... Rev 5:5
   - –Of the protecting power of God .... Isa 31:4–5
   - –Of the anger of God against sin ... Hos 5:14; Hos 13:8
   - –Of the powerful Israelites .... Nu 24:9
   - –Of the tribe of Judah .... Ge 49:9; Mic 5:8
   - –Of the bravery of humans 2Sa 1:23
   - –Of the boldness of believers ...... Pr 28:1
   - –Of the victory of believers .... Ps 91:13
   - –The lion lies peacefully with the lamb .... Isa 11:6–9; Isa 65:25

LORD

A. Human lords
- –Used to refer to someone in authority .... Ge 44:16,18; 2Sa 24:3
- –Used as a title of respect .... Ge 23:15; Jdg 4:18; 1Sa 1:15

B. God as the Lord

1. The God of Israel
   - –First revealed as Lord to Moses ... Ex 3:13–14; Ex 6:2–8
   - –Called the Lord of lords .... Dt 10:17; Ps 136:3; 1Ti 6:15
   - –Reigns in majesty and strength ... Ps 93:1; Ps 96:6
   - –Expects trust and reverence as Lord .... Dt 28:58; Ps 96:4; Prov 3:5–6
2. Jesus as Lord
   - –The Lord Jesus Christ 2Co 13:14; 2Th 1:2
   - –Our Lord Jesus Christ .... 1Th 5:9; Eph 6:24
   - –Jesus Christ our Lord 1Co 1:9; 1Ti 1:2
   - –Designated as Lord through his resurrection .... Ro 10:9; Php 2:8–11
   - –He is the Old Testament "Lord" .... Ac 2:21; Ro 10:13; 2Ti 2:19
   - –He is Lord of all .... Ac 10:36; Ro 14:9
   - –He is the Lord of lords .... Rev 17:14; Rev 19:13–16
   - –He is the only Lord .... 1Co 8:6; Eph 4:5
3. Believers confess Jesus as Lord
   - –Confession of Thomas .... Jn 20:28
   - –Confession of early Christians ... Ac 2:36; 1Co 1:2; 1Co 12:3; Col 2:6
   - –Confession commanded of us .... Ro 10:9; Php 2:11

LORD'S SUPPER

–The sacramental meal of God's people

A. Titles for this feast
- –The Lord's Supper 1Co 11:20
- –The breaking of bread .... Ac 2:42; Ac 20:7
- –Participation in body and blood of Christ 1Co 10:16

–Commanded by Jesus......... Mt 22:39
–Commanded by the apostles... Ro 13:9; Gal 5:14; Jas 2:8

b. Love for strangers.............. Lev 19:34; Dt 10:19; Heb 13:2

c. Do good to all humans.......... Gal 6:10

d. Love even for enemies
–Commanded in the Old Testament .... Ex 23:4–5; Pr 25:21–22
–Commanded by Jesus......... Mt 5:43–45
–Commanded by Paul.......... Ro 12:20–21
–Commanded by Peter......... 1Pe 3:9

5. The song of love................. 1Co 13
–Highest of all Christian virtues... 1Co 13:13
–Everything valueless without it .. 1Co 13:1–3
–Central nature is selflessness 1Co 13:4–7
–Endures throughout eternity..... 1Co 13:8–13

C. Love of Christ

1. Love of Christ for the Father....... Jn 14:31

2. Love of Christ for his people
–His love for Mary, Martha, Lazarus..................... Jn 11:3,5,36
–His love for his disciples.......... Jn 13:1,34; Jn 15:9,12
–The disciple whom Jesus loved... Jn 13:23; Jn 19:26; Jn 20:2; Jn 21:7,20
–His love for the church .... Eph 5:25
–His love expressed by his sacrifice..................... Jn 15:13; Gal 2:20; Eph 5:2,25

3. Our relationship to this love
–We must realize how extensive it is .... Eph 3:17–19
–We must remain in it .... Jn 15:9–10
–Nothing can separate us from it... Ro 8:35–37
–It motivates us to love others ..... Jn 13:34; Jn 15:12; Eph 5:2
–It serves as a pattern for husbands.................... Eph 5:25–28
–It motivates us to mission work... 2Co 5:14

D. Love of God

1. God is love 1Jn 4:8,16

2. God loves the Son
–Prophesied in the Old Testament... Isa 42:1; Mt 12:18
–Expressed at Jesus' baptism ..... Mt 3:17
–Expressed at the transfiguration .. Mt 17:5; 2Pe 1:17
–Acknowledged by Jesus .... Jn 5:20; Jn 10:17; Jn 15:9–10; Jn 17:23–24,26

3. God loves the sinful world
–His love for the world stated...... Jn 3:16
–His love in spite of sin .... Ro 5:8; Titus 3:3–4
–His love expressed in sending his Son..................... Jn 3:16; 1Jn 4:9–10

4. God expresses a special love for his people
–In his love for Jesus .... Jn 16:27; Jn 17:23
–In our election.................. Eph 1:4; 1Th 1:4
–In our being called.............. Ro 1:7; Jude 1
–In our receiving his grace........ 2Th 2:16
–In our adoption 1Jn 3:1
–In our salvation................. 2Th 2:13; Titus 3:4–5
–In our redemption............... Dt 7:8; Isa 63:9
–In our forgiveness............... Isa 38:17
–In our being made alive with Christ....................... Eph 2:4–5
–In our receiving the Holy Spirit... Ro 5:5
–In our being disciplined .... Heb 12:5–7
–In our obedience................ 1Jn 2:5
–In our love for others 1Jn 3:17; 1Jn 4:12
–In our receiving eternal life ...... Jude 21

5. Our relationship to this love
–It is everlasting .... Jer 31:3
–We must be directed into it....... 2Th 3:5
–We must keep ourselves in it ..... Jude 21
–Nothing can separate us from it .. Ro 8:35–39

LUKE

–The beloved doctor................. Col 4:14
–Co-worker with Paul .... 2Ti 4:11; Phm 24
–Likely a travel companion with Paul... Ac 16:10–17; Ac 20:5–21:18; Ac 27:1–28:16

LUST

See SEXUAL STANDARDS

LYDIA

–Seller of cloth from Thyatira .... Ac 16:14
–Responded to Paul's preaching .... Ac 16:14
–Invited Paul to stay at her house in Philippi.......................... Ac 16:15
–Church met in her house.............. Ac 16:40

LYING

–Misrepresenting or falsifying the truth

A. Perspectives on lying
–God does not lie................... Titus 1:2
–Denying that Jesus is the Christ is lying 1Jn 2:22; 1Jn 5:10
–Hypocrites are liars .... Ps 62:4; 1Jn 4:20
–The antichrist deceives humanity... 2Th 2:9–10
–Satan is the father of lies........... Jn 8:44; Ac 13:10
–Lying will be exposed .... Pr 12:19

B. The prohibition against lying
–Ninth commandment prohibits lying .... Ex 20:16; Dt 5:20
–Other laws prohibit lying .... Lev 19:11; Eph 4:25; Col 3:9
–Lying is detestable to God.......... Pr 6:16–17
–Pray to be kept from lying .... Pr 30:8

C. The punishment for lying
–Severe punishment for false witnesses .... Dt 19:16–19; Pr 19:5
–God silences liars .... Ps 63:11
–God punishes liars .... Ps 120:3–4
–God destroys liars................. Ps 5:6; Mic 6:12–13
–God excludes liars from heaven .... Rev 21:8,27

D. Examples of lying in the Bible

1. Sinful lying
–Satan in the Garden of Eden ..... Ge 3:4

–Cain to God .... Ge 4:9
–Abram about Sarai.............. Ge 12:10–20
–Sarah to God .... Ge 18:15
–Jacob to his father .... Ge 27:14–25
–Joseph's brothers to Jacob .... Ge 37:31–33
–Gibeonites to Joshua .... Jos 9:1–13
–Saul to Samuel 1Sa 15:1–3, 13–22
–False witnesses about Naboth.... 1Ki 21:11–12
–Lying prophets to Ahab 1Ki 22:6,19–28
–Gehazi to Naaman 2Ki 5:20–24
–False prophets to the people...... Eze 13:1–9
–False witnesses about Jesus...... Mt 26:59–62
–Peter about Jesus .... Mt 26:69–74
–Ananias and Sapphira to God...... Ac 5:1–10

2. Lying with God's approval
–Midwives lie to spare babies ...... Ex 1:15–21
–Rahab lies to save the spies ...... Jos 2:1–14
–Ehud deceives King Eglon .... Jdg 3:15–18
–Jael deceives Sisera .... Jdg 4:17–21; Jdg 5:24–27

See also HYPOCRISY
TRUTH

MACEDONIA

–A Roman province, north of Achaia (Greece)

A. Paul in the main cities of Macedonia
–Paul's vision of man of Macedonia .. Ac 16:9
–Philippi .... Ac 16:12–40
–Thessalonica .... Ac 17:1–9
–Berea .... Ac 17:10–15
See also PAUL

B. Christians in Macedonia
–Suffered persecution .... Ac 17:5–8,13; 1Th 1:6
–Were dedicated believers 1Th 1:7–10; 2Co 8:1,5
–Were poor......................... 2Co 8:1–2
–Gave generously to the poor........ Ro 15:25–26; 2Co 8:2–4
–Helped Paul financially............ 2Co 11:7–9; Php 4:14–18

MACHPELAH

–Cave purchased by Abraham from Ephron .... Ge 23:7–18
–Sarah buried there.................. Ge 23:19
–Abraham buried there............... Ge 25:9–10
–Isaac, Rebekah and Leah buried there... Ge 49:29–31
–Jacob buried there .... Ge 50:12–13

MAGIC, WITCHCRAFT AND SORCERY

A. Terms used
–Divination......................... Dt 18:10
–Sorcery .... Dt 18:10
–Interpreting omens................. Dt 18:10
–Witchcraft .... Dt 18:10
–Casting spells .... Dt 18:11
–Mediums and spiritists .... Dt 18:11
–Consulting the dead................ Dt 18:11
–Magic.............................. Eze 13:18,20

B. Purpose of magic and sorcery
–To determine the future............ Ge 44:15; 1Sa 28:5–7; Da 2:2,27
–To control the future .... Ge 30:14; Nu 23:23

C. Warnings against magic and sorcery
–In the law .... Ex 22:18; Lev 19:26,31; Lev 20:6,27; Dt 18:10–12, 20–21
–In the prophets.................... Isa 2:6; Isa 47:10–14; Jer 27:9; Mic 5:12; Mal 3:5
–In the early church .... Ac 8:9–24; Ac 13:6–12; Ac 16:16–18; Ac 19:13–19; Gal 5:20; Rev 21:8

MANASSEH

A. Firstborn of Joseph................. Ge 41:51; Ge 46:20
–Name means "forget"............... Ge 41:51
–Blessed by Jacob, but not as firstborn............................ Ge 48:12–20

B. Tribe descended from Manasseh
–Blessed by Moses .... Dt 33:17
–Numbered........................... Nu 1:35; Nu 26:34
–Allotted land east of the Jordan .. Nu 32:33,39–42; Jos 13:8–33
–Allotted land west of the Jordan.... Jos 17:1–11; Eze 48:4
–Failed to fully possess the land ..... Jos 17:12–13; Jdg 1:27
–One of the tribes of the 144,000..... Rev 7:6

C. Son of Hezekiah; king of Judah...... 2Ki 20:21; 2Ch 32:33
–Judah's most wicked king........... 2Ki 21:1–11; 2Ch 33:1–10
–Captured by Assyrians 2Ch 33:11
–Repented of his sins............... 2Ch 33:12–13
–Began to clear land of idols 2Ch 33:15–16
–Judah exiled for his sins............ 2Ki 21:10–15

MARK

–Jewish name is John .... Ac 12:25
–A cousin of Barnabas .... Col 4:10
–A close friend of Peter............. 1Pe 5:13
–Believers gathered at his home to pray .... Ac 12:12
–Went to Antioch with Barnabas and Saul .... Ac 12:25
–Did mission work with Barnabas and Saul .... Ac 13:4–5
–Deserted Paul in Pamphylia .... Ac 15:37–38
–Returned with Barnabas to Cyprus .... Ac 15:39
–Later became fellow worker with Paul again .... Phm 24; 2Ti 4:11

MARRIAGE

A. God and marriage
1. God honors marriage
–Established it in Garden of Eden.......................... Ge 2:18,21–24
–Command repeated in New Testament .... Mt 19:5; Eph 5:31
–Regulated it by Old Testament laws .... Lev 20:10–21; Nu 36:1–12; Dt 25:5–10
–Jesus attended a wedding......... Jn 2:1–2
–Marriage must be honored....... Mal 2:15; Heb 13:4

2. Monogamy versus polygamy
–Ideal is monogamy................ Ge 2:24; 1Ti 3:2,12

–Polygamy practiced in Old Testament . . . Ge 29:16–30
1Sa 1:1–2
1Sa 25:42–43
1Ki 11:1–3

–Polygamy often caused friction . . . Ge 30:1
Lev 18:18
1Sa 1:3–8

3. Adultery

–In all cases forbidden . . . Ex 20:14
Lev 18:20

–Excludes one from the kingdom of God . . . Gal 5:19–21
1Co 6:9

See ADULTERY

4. Marriage with unbelievers forbidden

–In the Old Testament law . . . Ex 34:15–16
Dt 7:3–4

–By Old Testament examples . . . Jdg 16:4–21
1Ki 11:1–8
Ezr 9:1–5,10–15
Neh 13:23–27

–In the New Testament . . . 1Co 7:12–16
2Co 6:14–18

5. Permanency of marriage

–Marriage is union for life . . . Mt 19:3–6,9
Ro 7:2–3
1Co 7:39

–God hates divorce . . . Mal 2:16

–Divorce allowed for hardness of heart . . . Dt 24:1–4
Mt 19:7–8

See DIVORCE

B. Being single and being married

1. Remaining single is an option

–It is a gift from God . . . 1Co 7:7–8

–It is preferable in times of crisis . . 1Co 7:25–28

–It frees one to serve God totally . . . 1Co 7:32–35

2. Purposes of marriage

–To inspire human happiness . . . Ge 2:18

–To express love intimately . . . Pr 5:15–20
SS 2:3–7
SS 8:5–7

–To have children . . . Ge 1:27–28
Mal 2:15
1Ti 5:14

–To prevent immorality . . . 1Co 7:2,8–9

C. Weddings in the Bible

–The wedding of Isaac . . . Ge 24:62–67

–The weddings of Jacob . . . Ge 29:21–28

–The wedding of Samson . . . Jdg 14:10–19

–The wedding of a king . . . Ps 45:1–17

–Jesus at a wedding in Cana . . . Jn 2:1–11

–Wedding parables of Jesus . . . Mt 22:1–14
Mt 25:1–13
Lk 14:8–11

D. Duties of marriage partners

–Husband to be devoted to his wife's good . . . Eph 5:25
Col 3:19
1Pe 3:7

–Wife to be submissive to her husband . . . Eph 5:22
Col 3:18
1Pe 3:1

–Equal responsibility . . . 1Co 7:1–5,32–35

E. Marriage as a symbol

–God as the husband of Israel . . . Isa 54:5
Jer 3:14
Hos 2:16,19–20

–Christ as the bridegroom of the church . . . Mk 2:19–20
Jn 3:29

–Christ as the husband of the church . . . 2Co 11:2
Eph 5:22–32

–Church as the bride of Christ . . . Eph 5:22–24
Rev 21:2,9–10

–Heaven begins with a wedding . . . Mt 22:1–10
Mt 25:1–10
Rev 19:7,9

MARTHA

–Sister of Mary and Lazarus . . . Lk 10:38–39
Jn 11:1

–Kept busy preparing food . . . Lk 10:40

–Rebuked by Jesus . . . Lk 10:41–42

–Went to meet Jesus after Lazarus died . . . Jn 11:20

–Confessed the resurrection . . . Jn 11:20–27

–Objected to opening Lazarus's tomb . . . Jn 11:38–40

MARY

A. Mother of Jesus . . . Mt 1:16

–Angel announced her pregnancy . . . Lk 1:26–38

–Visited cousin Elizabeth . . . Lk 1:39–40

–Sang a song . . . Lk 1:46–55

–Her virgin birth announced to Joseph . . . Mt 1:18–25

–Gave birth to Jesus in Bethlehem . . . Lk 2:1–7

–Presented Jesus in the temple . . . Lk 2:21–24

–Fled with Joseph and baby to Egypt . . . Mt 2:13–15

–Returned and settled in Nazareth . . . Mt 2:19–23

–With twelve-year-old Jesus in temple . . . Lk 2:41–52

–Had other children . . . Mk 6:3

–Went to a wedding in Cana . . . Jn 2:1–5

–Questioned Jesus' sanity . . . Mk 3:21

–Observed Jesus' crucifixion . . . Mt 27:55–56

–Entrusted to John at the cross . . . Jn 19:25–27

–Among the disciples after ascension . . . Ac 1:14

B. Mary Magdalene

–Former demoniac . . . Lk 8:2

–Helped support Jesus' ministry . . . Lk 8:1–3

–Present at the cross . . . Mt 27:56
Mk 15:40

–Present at Jesus' burial . . . Mt 27:61
Mk 15:47

–Went to the tomb early on Easter Sunday . . . Mt 28:1

–Saw angel after the resurrection . . . Mt 28:2–10
Mk 16:1–8

–Saw Jesus after the resurrection . . . Mk 16:9
Jn 20:1–2,10–18

C. Sister of Martha and Lazarus

–Jesus visited them . . . Lk 10:38–39

–Went to meet Jesus after Lazarus died . . . Jn 11:28–32

–Listened to Jesus' teaching . . . Lk 10:39

–Washed Jesus' feet . . . Jn 11:2
Jn 12:1–8

–Commended by Jesus . . . Mt 26:6–13
Lk 10:41–42

MATTHEW

–A disciple of Jesus . . . Mt 10:3
Mk 3:18

–A tax collector, called by Jesus to follow him . . . Mt 9:9

–Also called Levi . . . Mk 2:14–17
Lk 5:27–32

–Held dinner for Jesus . . . Mt 9:10–13

–One of the apostles . . . Ac 1:13

MATTHIAS

–Apostle, chosen to replace Judas . . . Ac 1:26

MEDES AND PERSIANS

A. Two related nations . . . Est 1:14; Da 6:8,12,15; Da 8:20

B. Significance for God's people
- –Northern kingdom deported there . . . 2Ki 17:6; 2Ki 18:11
- –Defeated Babylonians . . . Isa 13:17; Jer 51:11,28; Da 5:28,30–31
- –Allowed Jews to rebuild Palestine . . . 2Ch 36:20–23

C. Kings of the Medes and Persians, in chronological order
- –Darius the Mede . . . Da 5:31
- –Cyrus . . . Ezr 1:1–2
- –Darius the Persian . . . Ezr 4:5,24
- –Ahasuerus (Xerxes) . . . Est 1:1
- –Artaxerxes . . . Ezr 7:1; Neh 2:1

MEDIATOR

–Someone who helps bring reconciliation between two parties

A. Related theme
MEDIATOR is a theme of Job . . . Job 9:33

B. Human mediators at work
- –Judah spoke to Joseph for Benjamin . . . Ge 44:18–34
- –Moses spoke to Pharaoh for the Israelites . . . Ex 5:1–5
- –Jonathan spoke to Saul for David . . . 1Sa 19:1–7
- –Abigail spoke to David for her husband . . . 1Sa 25:14–35
- –Esther spoke to the king for her people . . . Est 7:1–6

C. Mediators between God and humans

1. The need for a mediator
   - –Israelites desired one at Mount Sinai . . . Ex 20:18–19
   - –Job cried out for one . . . Job 9:33
   - –Job knew one existed . . . Job 16:19–21
   - –The task of a mediator . . . 1Sa 2:25; Job 33:23–25; Gal 3:20
2. Human mediators between God and his people
   - –Moses . . . Ex 32:7–14; Nu 14:11–20; Dt 5:5; Gal 3:19
   - –Prophets . . . 1Ki 21:17–19; Jer 23:21–22; Da 9:3–19; Heb 1:1
   - –Priests . . . Lev 16:20–21; Nu 6:22–27; Ezr 9:3–15
   - –Kings . . . 1Ki 8:22–53; 1Ch 21:16–17
3. Jesus as mediator between us and God
   - a. Described as a mediator
     - –Our chief mediator with God . . . Heb 8:6; Heb 9:15; Heb 12:24
     - –The only one needed . . . 1Ti 2:5
   - b. His qualifications as a mediator
     - –He is fully God . . . Jn 1:1; Heb 1:3; 1Jn 5:20
     - –He is fully human . . . Jn 1:14; Php 2:6–8; Heb 2:14,17; 1Jn 4:2
   - c. His tasks as our mediator
     - –Isaiah prophesied Jesus' task . . . Isa 53:3–12
     - –Reversed consequences of Adam's sin . . . Ro 5:15–19; 1Co 15:21–22
     - –Reconciled us to God through death . . . 2Co 5:18–21; Col 1:21–22
     - –Intercedes with God on our behalf . . . Jn 17:6–26; Ro 8:34; Heb 7:25; 1Jn 2:1
     - –Brings messages from God to us . . . Jn 12:49–50; Heb 1:1–2

MEDITATION

–Reflecting on God and his word

A. On what are we to meditate?
- –On God . . . Ps 63:6
- –On God's law . . . Ps 1:2; Ps 119:15,48,97
- –On God's promises . . . Ps 119:148
- –On God's unfailing love . . . Ps 48:9
- –On God's works . . . Ps 77:12; Ps 143:5; Ps 145:5

B. What does meditation accomplish?
- –Gives us a sense of peace . . . Php 4:6–9
- –Develops close relationship with God . . . Ps 63:6–8
- –Prepares us for important decisions . . . Lk 6:12–13
- –Gives us strength for Christian living . . . Ps 1:2–3; 2Co 12:7–9
- –Helps give us direction for life . . . Ac 22:17–21

C. When did people meditate?
- –In the morning . . . Ps 5:1–3; Mk 1:35
- –All day long . . . Ps 119:97
- –Day and night . . . Jos 1:8; Ps 1:2
- –In the evening . . . Ge 24:63
- –Through the watches of the night . . . Ps 119:148

D. Examples of those who meditated
- –Isaac . . . Ge 24:63
- –Psalmists . . . Ps 48:9; Ps 119:48,97,148; Ps 143:5
- –Jesus . . . Mt 14:23; Mk 1:35; Lk 5:16
- –Jesus' followers . . . Ac 9:11–12; Ac 10:2,9–16; Ac 22:17–18

MEEKNESS

–The quality of a gentle spirit

A. Human meekness

1. Meekness is required of us
   - –A Christian quality . . . Col 3:12; 1Ti 6:11
   - –An aspect of the fruit of the Spirit . . . Gal 5:22–23
   - –We must act with gentleness . . . Eph 4:2; Php 4:5; 1Pe 3:15
2. Meekness is a powerful force
   - –A gentle tongue is persuasive . . . Pr 25:15
   - –A gentle answer turns away anger . . . Pr 15:1

–A gentle spirit wins people to Christ ... 1Pe 3:1–4

3. The meek are blessed ... Ps 37:11; Mt 5:5

See also HUMILITY

B. God's meekness

–The gentle whisper of God ... 1Ki 19:12

–The meekness and gentleness of Christ ... Zec 9:9; Mt 21:5; 2Co 10:1

MEGIDDO

–Its king defeated by Joshua ... Jos 12:21

–A city given to Manasseh ... Jos 17:11

–Manasseh did not conquer it ... Jdg 1:27

–Deborah and Barak fought there ... Jdg 5:19

–Solomon built it up ... 1Ki 9:15

–King Ahaziah died there ... 2Ki 9:27

–Josiah was killed there ... 2Ki 23:29–30; 2Ch 35:20–27

–Final battle at Armageddon ("hill of Megiddo") ... Rev 16:14–16

MELCHIZEDEK

–King of Salem; priest of God Most High ... Ge 14:18

–Blessed Abram ... Ge 14:19–20

–Called a high priest forever ... Ps 110:4

–His priesthood prophetic of Jesus ... Heb 5:6; Heb 6:20

–His priesthood explained ... Heb 7:1–28

MENAHEM

–King of Israel ... 2Ki 15:17–22

–Assassinated Shallum to become king ... 2Ki 15:14

–Extremely cruel ... 2Ki 15:16

MEPHIBOSHETH

–Son of Jonathan ... 2Sa 4:4

–Shown kindness by David ... 2Sa 9:1–13

–Accused by Ziba of siding with Absalom ... 2Sa 16:1–4

–Explained his story to David ... 2Sa 19:24–30

–Spared from death ... 2Sa 21:7

MERCY

–Underserved kindness and compassion

A. Human mercy

1. The command to be merciful

–Be merciful ... Lk 6:36; Ro 12:8; Jude 22

–Mercy is more important than sacrifice ... Hos 6:6; Mic 6:6–8; Mt 9:13

2. Expressions of human mercy

–Being forgiving ... Mt 18:23–35

–Being kind to the hurting ... Lk 10:30–37

–Being kind to the poor ... Lk 16:19–26

B. The mercy of God

1. A part of his nature

–God is merciful ... Dt 4:31; Neh 9:31; Lk 6:36

–God exercises mercy freely ... Ex 33:19; Ro 9:15–18

–Mercy triumphs over judgment ... Jas 2:13

2. Expressions of his mercy

–Forgiving our sins ... Ps 51:1–2; Da 9:9; 1Ti 1:13–16

–Saving us in Christ ... Eph 2:4–5; Titus 3:4–5; 1Pe 1:3–4

–Being faithful to his covenant ... Dt 4:31; Dt 13:17–18; Neh 9:31

–Receiving us back to himself ... Jer 3:12–13

–Healing us when ill ... Php 2:27

–Sparing his own from destruction ... Ge 19:16; Ps 116:1–6

–Keeping us safe from the enemy ... Ps 6:9–10; Ps 28:6–7

3. Praying for God's mercy

–"Be merciful to me" ... Ps 4:1; Ps 9:13

–"Hear my cry for mercy" ... Ps 28:2; Ps 86:6,16

–"Remember your great mercy" ... Ps 25:6

–"Have mercy on me, a sinner" ... Lk 18:13

–"Jesus, have mercy on us" ... Mt 9:27; Mt 20:30–31

See also GRACE
COMPASSION

MESHACH

–Hebrew deported to Babylon ... Da 1:1–6

–Name changed from Mishael ... Da 1:7

–Refused to be defiled by food ... Da 1:8–20

–Appointed administrator over Babylon ... Da 2:49

–Refused to worship idols ... Da 3:1–12

–Saved from the fiery furnace ... Da 3:13–30

MESSIAH

See JESUS CHRIST

METHUSELAH

–Son of Enoch, father of Lamech ... Ge 5:21–27

–Lived 969 years ... Ge 5:27

MICAIAH

–Prophet of the Lord ... 1Ki 22:7–8

–Warned Ahab of disaster ... 1Ki 22:9–28; 2Ch 18:1–27

MICHAEL

–An archangel ... Jude 9

–Stood against the forces of evil ... Da 10:13,21

–Conducted war in heaven against Satan ... Rev 12:7

MICHAL

–Daughter of Saul ... 1Sa 14:49

–Became wife of David ... 1Sa 18:20–28

–Warned David of Saul's plot ... 1Sa 19:11–17

–Given by Saul to Paltiel ... 1Sa 25:44

–Retrieved by David ... 2Sa 3:13–16

–Criticized David for dancing before the ark ... 2Sa 6:16–23; 1Ch 15:29

MIDIANITES

A. Their identity

–Descendants of Abraham through Keturah ... Ge 25:1–4

–Very wealthy ... Jdg 8:24–26

B. Important Midianites

–Jethro: priest of Midian ... Ex 3:1

–Zipporah: Moses' wife ... Ex 2:21

–Cozbi: killed for marrying an Israelite ... Nu 25:14–15

–Oreb and Zeeb: kings killed by Gideon ... Jdg 7:25–26

–Zeba and Zalmunna: kings killed by Gideon .... Jdg 8:12,21

C. Their interactions with God's people
–Brought Joseph to Egypt .... Gne 37:36
–Allied with Moabites against Israelites .... Nu 22:4,7
–Intermarried with the Israelites .... Nu 25:6
–Were considered enemies of Israel .... Nu 25:16–18
–Defeated by Moses .... Nu 31:1–12
–Oppressed the Israelites .... Jdg 6:1–6
–Defeated by Gideon .... Jdg 7:1–25

MILK

A. Sources of milk
–Cattle .... Dt 32:14
–Cows 2Sa 17:29
–Goats .... Pr 27:27
–Human mothers .... Isa 28:9

B. Importance of milk
1. As a staple food
–For infants .... Isa 28:9
–For adults .... Ge 18:8; Jdg 4:19

2. As a figure of speech
–A land flowing with milk and honey .... Ex 3:8,17; Nu 16:13–14; Dt 6:3
–A special blessing from God .... Isa 7:21–22
–A symbol of whiteness .... Ge 49:12
–A symbol of a lover's charms .... SS 4:11
–A symbol of spiritual blessings .... Isa 55:1; Joel 3:17–18
–A symbol of instruction for the immature .... 1Co 3:1–2; Heb 5:12–13
–A symbol of pure doctrine 1Pe 2:2

MILLENNIUM

MIND

A. What does the mind do?
1. Involved with the human will
–Can be made up 2Co 2:1
–Can make decisions 1Ch 12:38
–Can make plans 2Sa 7:1–3
–Can be willing to do things 1Ch 28:9
–Can give guidance .... Ecc 2:3
–Can sing and pray 1Co 14:15
–Can vacillate (double-minded) .... Jas 1:8
–Can change 2Ki 24:1
–Can plot evil .... Ps 83:5

2. Involved with human intelligence
–Can be opened .... Lk 24:45
–Can think .... Neh 5:7
–Can seek knowledge 1Ki 10:1–2
–Can understand .... Da 5:12
–Can remember .... Ge 37:11
–Can be made dull 2Co 3:14
–Can be blinded 2Co 4:4
–Can be closed .... Isa 44:18

3. Involved with human emotions
–The troubled mind .... Ge 41:8
–A disturbed mind .... Da 7:15
–The anxious mind .... Dt 28:65
–The doubting mind .... Lk 24:38

4. A person can be out of his or her mind .... Mk 3:21; Mk 5:3–5,15; Ac 26:24; 2Co 5:13

B. The believer's mind
1. God and our minds
–God searches them .... Ps 7:9; Ps 26:2
–God tests them .... Jer 11:20
–God puts his law in them .... Jer 31:33; Heb 8:10
–God guards them .... Php 4:7
–Christ searches them .... Rev 2:23
–The Spirit shapes them .... Ro 8:5
–We have the mind of Christ 1Co 2:16

2. Our responsibility to our minds
–They must be made new .... Ro 12:2; Eph 4:23
–We must set them on things above .... Col 3:2
–We must prepare them to serve God 1Pe 1:13
–We must love God with all the mind .... Mt 22:37; Mk 12:30; Lk 10:27
–We must be of one mind as Christians .... Ac 4:32; 1Co 1:10; 2Co 13:11

MIRACLE

A. Related theme
MIRACLES is a theme of Exodus .... Ex 15:11

B. Words used to designate miracles
–Miracles .... Ex 7:9; Jn 7:21
–Miraculous signs .... Ex 4:8; Mt 8:11–12
–Wonders .... Dt 13:1–2; Jn 4:48

C. Purposes of miracles
1. In the Old Testament
–To demonstrate God is Lord .... Ex 9:14; 1Ki 18:36–39; 2Ki 5:8–15
–To designate God's messengers .... Ex 4:1–9; 1Ki 17:17–24; 2Ki 1:10,12
–To confirm one's faith .... Jdg 6:37–40; 2Ki 2:13–14
–To deliver God's people .... Ex 14:21–30; Jos 10:12–14
–To care for God's people .... Ex 17:1–6; Nu 11:31–32
–To care for the needy 1Ki 17:10–16; 2Ki 4:1–7
–To punish sinners .... Ge 19:24–26; Nu 16:28–35

2. In the life of Jesus
–To show compassion .... Mt 14:14; Mt 15:32
–To prove he was God .... Mk 2:8–12; Jn 20:30–31
–To prove he was the Messiah .... Mt 11:2–5; Jn 5:36
–To demonstrate the kingdom of God .... Lk 11:20; Jn 10:37–38
–To secure redemption of believers .... Ro 4:25; 1Co 15:17–20
–Not to dazzle crowds .... Mt 16:1–4; Lk 23:8–9

3. In the early church
–To demonstrate Jesus is Savior and Lord .... Ac 4:8–12; Ac 14:3

–To lead people to faith .... Ac 13:12
Ac 9:42
–To advance the gospel .... Ac 12:1–11
Ac 16:16–18
–To show compassion .... Ac 9:32–41
Ac 20:9–10
–To judge sinners .... Ac 5:1–11
Ac 13:8–11

D. People who performed miracles
–Moses and Aaron .... Ex 7:8–21
Ps 105:26–27
–Joshua .... Jos 3:9–17
Jos 10:12–14
–A prophet of Judah 1Ki 13:4–6
–Elijah 1Ki 17:15–23
1Ki 18:30–38
–Elisha 2Ki 2:19–22
2Ki 4:1–7
–Isaiah 2Ki 20:7–11
–Daniel's three friends .... Da 3:19–27
–Daniel .... Da 6:16–24
–Jesus .... Mt 4:23–24
Jn 20:30–31
–The seventy-two sent out by Jesus ... Lk 10:9,17
–The apostles as a group .... Ac 2:43
Ac 5:12
–Peter .... Ac 3:1–7
Ac 5:15–16
–Stephen .... Ac 6:8
–Philip .... Ac 8:6–7,13
–Paul and Barnabas .... Ac 14:3
–Paul .... Ac 14:8–10
Ac 19:11–12
–One of the gifts given to the church 1Co 12:10,29
Gal 3:5

E. Miracles of Jesus
–Turned water into wine .... Jn 2:1–11
–Healed official's son at Capernaum ... Jn 4:43–65
–Cast out demon in Capernaum .... Mk 1:23–26
Lk 4:33–35
–Healed Peter's mother-in-law .... Mt 8:14–17
Mk 1:29–31
Lk 4:38–39
–Healed leper .... Mt 8:2–4
Mk 1:40–45
Lk 5:12–13
–Net full of fish .... Lk 5:4–11
–Healed paralytic .... Mt 9:1–8
Mk 2:1–12
Lk 5:18–25
–Healed crippled man .... Jn 5:1–9
–Healed shriveled hand .... Mt 12:10–13
Mk 3:1–5
Lk 6:6–10
–Healed centurion's servant .... Mt 8:5–13
Lk 7:1–10
–Raised widow's son .... Lk 7:11–17
–Cast out demon .... Mt 12:22–23
Lk 11:14
–Stilled a storm .... Mt 8:23–27
Mk 4:37–41
Lk 8:22–25
–Cast out demons in Gadara .... Mt 8:28–34
Mk 5:1–20
Lk 8:27–35
–Healed woman's bleeding and raised Jairus's daughter .... Mt 9:18–26
Mk 5:21–43
Lk 8:26–41
–Healed two blind men .... Mt 9:27–31
–Healed mute man .... Mt 9:32–33
–Fed five thousand .... Mt 14:15–21
Mk 6:35–44
Lk 9:12–17
Jn 6:5–13
–Walked on water .... Mt 14:25–33
Mk 6:48–52
Jn 6:19–21
–Healed Canaanite woman's daughter .... Mt 15:21–28
Mk 7:24–30
–Fed four thousand .... Mt 15:32–39
Mk 8:1–9
–Healed deaf man .... Mk 7:31–37
–Healed blind man at Bethsaida .... Mk 8:22–26
–Cast demon out of boy .... Mt 17:14–18
Mk 9:14–29
Lk 9:38–43
–Provided temple tax from fish's mouth .... Mt 17:24–27
–Healed ten lepers .... Lk 17:11–19
–Healed man born blind .... Jn 9:1–7
–Raised Lazarus .... Jn 11:1–44
–Healed crippled woman .... Lk 13:11–17
–Healed man with dropsy .... Lk 14:1–6
–Healed two blind men .... Mt 20:29–34
Mk 10:46–52
Lk 18:35–43
–Cursed a fig tree .... Mt 21:18–22
Mk 11:12–14
–Healed Malchus's ear .... Lk 22:50–51
–Helped disciples catch 153 fish .... Jn 21:1–14

F. Counterfeit miracles
–Performed by Egyptian magicians .... Ex 7:11,22
–Performed by Simon the sorcerer .... Ac 8:9–11
–Performed by false prophets .... Dt 13:1–3
Mt 24:24
–Performed by the antichrist 2Th 2:9
Rev 13:13
Rev 19:20

MIRIAM

–Sister of Moses and Aaron .... Nu 26:59
–Watched over baby Moses .... Ex 2:3–4
–Arranged for Moses' mother to care for Moses .... Ex 2:5–10
–Led dancing at Red Sea .... Ex 15:20–21
–Criticized Moses; struck with leprosy .. Nu 12:1–15
–Her death .... Nu 20:1

MISSION

–*Being sent out on a task*

A. Related themes
WORLDWIDE MISSION is a theme of:
–Matthew .... Mt 21:43
–Acts .... Ac 28:14
–Romans .... Ro 15:19

B. Examples of those sent by God on a mission

1. People
–Abram .... Ge 12:1–3
–Joseph .... Ge 45:5–7
Ps 105:17
–Moses .... Ex 3:10,14
–Moses and Aaron .... Ps 105:26
–Isaiah .... Isa 6:8
–Jeremiah .... Jer 26:16
–Ezekiel .... Eze 3:4–5
–Amos .... Am 7:14–15
–Jonah .... Jnh 1:1–2
Jnh 3:1–2
–Haggai .... Hag 1:12
–Zechariah .... Zec 2:9,11
–Prophets in general .... Jer 7:25
Jer 25:4
Zec 7:12
–John the Baptist .... Mal 3:1
Mk 1:2

–The twelve disciples . . . . . Mt 10:1–10
–The seventy-two messengers . . . . . Lk 10:1–7
–The apostles as missionaries . . . . . Mt 28:19–20
Jn 17:18
Jn 20:21
Ac 13:4
Ac 22:21
Gal 1:1

2. Jesus, God's Son . . . . . Lk 4:18–19
Jn 17:3
Gal 4:4–6

3. The Holy Spirit . . . . . Jn 14:26
Jn 15:26

4. The angels
–To Abraham's servant . . . . . Ge 24:7,40
–To the Israelites . . . . . Ex 23:20–23
–To the inhabitants of Jerusalem . . . 1Ch 21:15–18
–To God's people in general . . . . . Ps 91:11
–To Daniel's three friends . . . . . Da 3:28
–To Daniel . . . . . Da 6:22
–To Mary . . . . . Lk 1:26–38
–To Peter . . . . . Ac 12:6–11
–To all of us . . . . . Heb 1:14

C. For what purpose were they sent?

1. Jesus' unique mission
–To atone for sin . . . . . Mk 10:45
Gal 4:4–5
1Jn 4:9–10
–To preach and to heal . . . . . Mt 9:35–36
Lk 4:18–21

2. Leaders, prophets and missionaries
–To lead God's people 1Sa 12:8
–To prepare the way before the Lord . . . . . Mal 3:1
Mt 11:10
–To bring a message of redemption . . . . . Isa 61:1
Jnh 1:1–2
Mk 3:14
Mt 28:19–20
Ro 10:13–15
1Co 1:17
–To call the people to repent . . . . . Jer 35:15
Jer 42:21
–To heal hurting people . . . . . Isa 61:1–3
Mt 10:8
–To warn God's people . . . . . Jer 26:15
Eze 3:18–21
–To pronounce judgment . . . . . Jer 26:12
Eze 2:3–8
Mt 23:33–36

3. Angels
See ANGEL

MOABITES

A. Their identity
–Descendants of Moab, son of Lot . . . Ge 19:37
–Related to Ammonites . . . . . Ge 19:36–38
–Held land east of the Jordan . . . . . Nu 33:48–49
Dt 2:9
–Served the god Chemosh 1Ki 11:7

B. Important Moabites
–Balak: hired Balaam to curse them . . . . . Nu 22:2–24:25
–Eglon: killed by Ehud . . . . . Jdg 3:12,15–23
–Ruth: married Boaz . . . . . Ru 1:22
See RUTH

C. Their wars against Israelites
–Allied with Midianites against Israel . . . . . Nu 22:4,7
–Allied with Ammonites against Israel . . . . . Jdg 3:12–13
–Defeated by Israelites under Ehud . . Jdg 3:28–30
–Defeated by King Saul 1Sa 14:47
–Defeated by David 2Sa 8:11–12
1Ch 18:11
–Rebelled against Israel 2Ki 3:5
–Defeated by Joram and Jehoshaphat 2Ki 3:6–25
–Allied with Ammonites against Judah 2Ch 20:1
–They and Ammonites destroyed each other 2Ch 20:22–24
–Raided the land of Israel 2Ki 13:20
–Allied against Jehoiakim 2Ki 24:1–2

D. Important data concerning them

1. Before the time of the kings
–Intermarried with Israelites . . . . . Nu 25:1–3
–Israelites did not pass through Moab . . . . . Jdg 11:17–18
–Not allowed to join Israelites . . . . . Dt 23:3
Neh 13:1–3
–Moses died on Mount Pisgah in Moab . . . . . Dt 34:1–5
–Elimelech and Naomi lived there . . . . . Ru 1:1–5

2. During the time of the kings
–David brought his parents there . . . 1Sa 22:3–4
–Solomon intermarried with them . . . 1Ki 11:1
–Israelites worshiped their gods . . . 1Ki 11:7
–Paid tribute to Ahab 2Ki 3:4

3. Numerous Jews intermarried with them . . . . . Ezr 9:1
Neh 13:23–27

4. Prophecies concerning their destruction . . . . . Isa 15:1–16:14
Jer 48:1–47
Eze 25:8–11
Am 2:1–3
Zep 2:8–11

MONEY

See THE RICH AND THE POOR
STEWARDSHIP

MONTH

–*Twelve time segments per year, based on the moon*
–Abib or Nisan, the first month . . . . . Ex 13:4
Neh 2:1
–Ziv or Iyyar, the second month 1Ki 6:1
–Sivan, the third month . . . . . Est 8:9
–Tammuz, the fourth month . . . . . Jer 52:6
–Ab, the fifth month . . . . . Nu 33:38
–Elul, the sixth month . . . . . Neh 6:15
–Ethanim or Tishri, the seventh month . . 1Ki 8:2
–Bul or Heshvan, the eighth month 1Ki 6:38
–Kislev, the ninth month . . . . . Zec 7:1
–Tebeth, the tenth month . . . . . Est 2:16
–Shebat, the eleventh month . . . . . Zec 1:7
–Adar, the twelfth month . . . . . Ezr 6:15

MOON

A. Data concerning the moon
–Created by God . . . . . Ge 1:16
Ps 8:3
–Controlled by God . . . . . Jos 10:12–13
Jer 31:35
–Governs the night . . . . . Ge 1:16
Ps 136:9
–Marks off the seasons . . . . . Ge 1:14
Ps 104:19
–New Moon festivals . . . . . Nu 10:10
1Sa 20:5,18,24
Am 8:5
–Involved in the blessing of productive land . . . . . Dt 33:13–14

–Must praise God ... Ps 148:3
–Believed to cause mental illness ... Ps 121:6
–Worshiped by the heathen ... 2Ki 23:5
Jer 8:2
–No moon needed in heaven ... Isa 60:19–20
Rev 21:23

B. The moon used as a symbol
–Of stability and endurance ... Ps 72:5,7
–Of judgment at the end of time ... Isa 13:10–11
Mt 24:29
Rev 6:12

MORDECAI

–Benjamite exile who brought up Esther ... Est 2:5–10
–Exposed plot to kill Ahasuerus (Xerxes) ... Est 2:19–23
–Refused to honor Haman ... Est 3:1–6
Est 5:9–14
–Gallows made for him ... Est 5:14
–Begged Esther to foil Haman's plot ... Est 4:1–17
–Haman forced to honor him ... Est 6:1–11
–Exalted by the king ... Est 8:1–2,15
Est 9:3–4
–With Esther, established Purim ... Est 9:18–32

MORIAH

–Region where Abraham went to "sacrifice" Isaac ... Ge 22:1–18
–Mountain on which temple was built ... 2Ch 3:1–2

MOSES

A. Family data
–Son of Amram and Jochebed ... Ex 6:20
1Ch 6:3
–Tribe of Levi ... Ex 2:1
–Brother of Aaron ... Ex 4:14
–Name means "drawn out" ... Ex 2:10
–Married Zipporah ... Ex 2:21
–Father of Gershom and Eliezer ... Ex 2:22
Ex 18:2–4

B. His history

1. His youth
–Hid by his parents for three months ... Ex 2:2
Heb 11:23
–Hid in a basket in the Nile ... Ex 2:3–4
–Discovered by Pharaoh's daughter ... Ex 2:5–9
–Brought up by Pharaoh's daughter ... Ex 2:10
–Killed an Egyptian ... Ex 2:11–12
–Fled to Midian ... Ex 2:13–15
–Became a shepherd ... Ex 3:1

2. Delivered Israel from Egypt
–Called by God ... Ex 3:2–4:17
–Explained his call to Israelites ... Ex 4:29–31
–Made demands to Pharaoh ... Ex 5:1–5
–The ten plagues ... Ex 7:14–11:9
–Arranged the Passover ... Ex 12:1–28
–Led Israelites out of Egypt ... Ex 12:29–42
–Led them to the border of the Red Sea ... Ex 13:17–14:4
–Led them across the Red Sea ... Ex 14:21–31
–Sang song of deliverance ... Ex 15:1–21

3. Led Israel to Mount Sinai
–Water at Marah and Elim ... Ex 15:22–27
–Asked God for food; received manna ... Ex 16:1–16
–Brought water from the rock ... Ex 17:1–7
–Raised hands to defeat Amalekites ... Ex 17:8–16
–Delegated judges ... Ex 18:13–27
Dt 1:9–18
–Received law at Mount Sinai ... Ex 19:3–25
Ex 24:12–18
Jn 1:17
–Announced law to Israel ... Ex 24:3–7
–Broke tablets because of golden calf ... Ex 32:19–20
Dt 9:7–17
–Received law a second time ... Ex 34:1–4,27–28
–Saw glory of the Lord ... Ex 33:18–23
–His face reflected glory of God ... Ex 34:29–35
–Supervised building of tabernacle ... Ex 35:4–36:7
–Set apart Aaron and priests ... Lev 8:1–9:24
–Numbered tribes ... Nu 1:1–4:49

4. From Sinai to the border of Canaan
–Left Sinai ... Nu 10:11–13
–Handled the people's complaints ... Nu 11:1–34
–Opposed by Aaron and Miriam ... Nu 12:1–15
–Sent spies into Canaan ... Nu 13:1–33
–Prayed for the rebellious people ... Nu 14:1–25
–Announced forty years of wandering ... Nu 14:26–40
–Opposed by Korah ... Nu 16:1–50
–Struck rock; forbidden to enter Canaan ... Nu 20:1–13
Dt 1:37
–Put bronze snake on a pole for healing ... Nu 21:4–9
Jn 3:14
–Defeated kings in battle ... Nu 21:1–3,21–31
–Numbered tribes a second time ... Nu 26:1–65
–Designated Joshua as successor ... Nu 27:12–23
Dt 34:9
–Gave final address (Deuteronomy) ... Dt 1:5
–Sang a song ... Dt 31:30–32:43
–Blessed the twelve tribes ... Dt 33:1–29
–Saw the promised land ... Dt 34:1–4
–His death ... Dt 34:5–8

C. Titles ascribed to him
–The man of God ... Ezr 3:2
–God's chosen one ... Ps 106:23
–The servant of the Lord ... 2Ch 24:6,9
Ps 105:26
–The lawgiver ... Jn 1:17
–Prophet of the Lord ... Dt 18:15,18
–Intimate friend of God ... Ex 33:11
–Leader of God's people ... Mic 6:4
–Shepherd of God's people ... Ps 77:20

D. Moses in the New Testament
–Appeared to Jesus at the transfiguration ... Mt 17:2–4
–Respected for giving the Law ... Mt 19:7–8
Jn 7:19,23
–Exemplified true faith ... Heb 11:24–28
–Foreshadowed Jesus as the Prophet ... Ac 3:21–23
–His writings prophetic of Jesus ... Jn 1:45
–His lifting up of snake pictured Jesus' death ... Jn 3:14–15
–Crossing the Red Sea pictured baptism ... 1Co 10:1–2
–His veil symbolized the old covenant ... 2Co 3:7–16
–His faithfulness foreshadowed that of Jesus ... Heb 3:1–6
–God, not Moses, gave manna ... Jn 6:30–33

MOTHER

A. Motherhood in the Bible

1. The experience of motherhood
–It is a gift from God ... Ps 113:9
Ps 127:3

–It can be painful .... Ge 3:16; Isa 13:8; Jn 16:21
–Infertility can cause frustration .. Ge 25:21; Ge 30:1; 1Sa 1:1–20

2. Women saved through childbearing 1Ti 2:15
3. Significant experiences of motherhood
–Eve, the mother of the living ..... Ge 3:20; Ge 4:1–2,25
–Sarah........................ Ge 21:1–5
–Rebekah .... Ge 25:21–26
–Leah......................... Ge 29:31–35; Ge 30:17–21
–Rachel .... Ge 30:1–3,22–23; Ge 35:16–18
–Jochabed (Moses' mother) .... Ex 2:1–10
–Samson's mother .... Jdg 13:1–24
–Ruth......................... Ru 4:13–15
–Hannah....................... 1Sa 1:1–20
–Bathsheba 2Sa 12:24–25
–Isaiah's wife.................. Isa 8:3–4
–Hosea's wife.................. Hos 1:2–9
–Elizabeth .... Lk 1:24–25,39–44
–The virgin Mary .... Lk 1:26–38; Lk 2:4–7

B. The mother in the family
1. Duties of a mother to her children
–Loves them.................... 1Ki 3:26; Isa 49:15
–Comforts and cares for them..... Ru 4:16; Isa 66:13; 1Th 2:13
–Protects them .... Ex 2:1–3; Heb 11:23
–With their husbands, educates them........................ Pr 1:8; Pr 31:1,26
–Educates them alone, if necessary 2Ti 1:5; 2Ti 3:15
–Watches over their affairs .... Ge 27:5–17; 1Ki 1:11–31; Pr 31:15,27
2. Responsibility of children to mothers
–Obey them .... Dt 21:18; Eph 6:1–2
–Respect them.................. Ex 20:12; Lev 19:3; Pr 23:22
–Listen to them .... Pr 1:8; Pr 6:20

C. Mother used as a symbol
–God compared to a mother......... Isa 49:15; Isa 66:13
–The church as mother .... Isa 66:10–11; Gal 4:26

MOUNTAIN

A. Mountains mentioned in the Bible
–Mount Ararat..................... Ge 8:4
–Mount Baalah .... Jos 15:11
–Mount Carmel 1Ki 18:19
–Mount Ebal....................... Dt 11:29
–Mount Ephron .... Jos 15:9
–Mount Gaash .... Jos 24:30
–Mount Gerizim .... Dt 11:29
–Mount Gilboa..................... 1Sa 31:1
–Mount Gilead..................... Jdg 7:3
–Mount Halak .... Jos 11:17
–Mount Heres .... Jdg 1:35
–Mount Hermon .... Dt 3:8
–Mount Hor .... Nu 20:22
–Mount Horeb .... Ex 33:6
–Mount Jearim .... Jos 15:10
–Mount Mizar .... Ps 42:6
–Mount Moriah 2Ch 3:1
–Mount Nebo .... Dt 32:49
–Mount of Olives.................. Zec 14:4
See OLIVES, MOUNT OF
–Mount Paran .... Dt 33:2
–Mount Perazim .... Isa 28:21
–Mount Pisgah.................... Jos 12:3
–Mount Samaria .... Am 4:1
–Mount Seir .... Dt 1:2
–Mount Shepher .... Nu 33:23
–Mount Sinai .... Ex 19:11
See SINAI
–Mount Siyon..................... Dt 4:48
–Mount Tabor .... Jdg 4:6
–Mount Zalmon.................... Jdg 9:48
–Mount Zemaraim 2Ch 13:4
–Mount Zion...................... Ps 48:2
See ZION

B. Mountains used in illustrations
–Of God's creative power .... Am 4:13
–Of God's continuing power.......... Ps 65:5–7
–Of God's redemptive power .... Isa 40:4–5
–Of the power of God's judgment .... Rev 6:14–16
–Of God's righteousness .... Ps 36:6
–Of God's glory in the new age ...... Isa 2:2–3
–Of prosperity for God's people...... Ps 72:3; Am 9:13
–Of the strength of human faith ..... Mt 17:20–21
–Of the joy of the redeemed .... Isa 44:23

MOUTH

A. The human mouth
1. Appropriate functions of our mouths
–To praise God .... Ps 63:5
–To sing to the Lord .... Ps 40:3
–To testify concerning God .... Ps 89:1
–To confess Jesus as Lord.......... Ro 10:9–10
–To reveal God's word............. Dt 18:18
–To reveal what is in the heart..... Mt 12:34–35
–To speak words.................. Ps 19:14
–To laugh with joy .... Ps 126:2
–To eat.......................... 1Sa 14:26–27
–To drink .... Jdg 7:6
–To kiss......................... SS 1:2
2. Responsibilities to our mouths
a. Negative
–Keep them from sin .... Ecc 5:6
–Keep them from perversity .. Pr 4:24
–Keep them from flattery .... Pr 26:28
–Keep them from arrogance 1Sa 2:3
–Keep them from lies........... Rev 14:5
–Keep them from unwholesome talk.................. Eph 4:29
–Keep them from cursing ..... Jas 3:9–10
b. Positive
–Speak what is true and just .. Pr 8:7–8
–Speak what is wise........... Ps 37:30
–Guide them properly .... Pr 16:23
–Guard them properly......... Pr 21:23

B. The mouth of God
–God created with his mouth......... Ps 33:6
–God gave his law with his mouth ... Ps 119:13,72
–God gives promises with his mouth . Isa 40:3–5
–God teaches with his mouth......... Dt 8:3
–God pronounces judgment with his mouth...................... Isa 1:20
–God rejects by spitting us out of his mouth...................... Rev 3:16

–God destroys with his mouth . . . . . . Ps 18:8
–Jesus destroys with a sword in his mouth . . . . . . Rev 2:16; Rev 19:15

MURDER

–The deliberate killing of another human

A. The command against murder
- –The sixth commandment . . . . . . Ex 20:13; Dt 5:17; Jas 2:10–11
- –Anger as the root of murder . . . . . . Mt 5:21–22
- –Hatred as the root of murder 1Jn 3:15
- –Murder roots out of a sinful heart . . . Mt 15:18–19

B. What happens after a murder
- –One can be cursed by God . . . . . . Ge 4:11
- –One can be excluded from heaven . . . 1Jn 3:15; Rev 22:15
- –One is subject to capital punishment . . . . . . Ge 9:5–6; Ex 21:12–14,23
- –More than one witness required . . . . Nu 35:30; Dt 19:15
- –Cities of refuge in Israel . . . . . . Nu 35:16–32; Dt 19:1–14
- –Murderers can be forgiven . . . . . . Lk 23:34; Ac 7:60

C. Examples of murder in the Bible
- –Cain killed Abel . . . . . . Ge 4:8
- –Moses killed an Egyptian . . . . . . Ex 2:11–12
- –Abimelech killed his brothers . . . . . . Jdg 9:5
- –David killed Uriah 2Sa 12:9
- –Absalom killed Ammon 2Sa 13:28–33
- –Jezebel killed Naboth 1Ki 21:8–14
- –Hazael killed Ben-Hadad 2Ki 8:14–15
- –Athaliah killed the royal family 2Ki 11:1
- –Herod killed the male babies in Bethlehem . . . . . . Mt 2:16
- –Herod killed John the Baptist . . . . . . Mt 14:6–11
- –The Jews killed Jesus . . . . . . Ac 2:23; 1Th 2:15
- –The Jews killed Stephen . . . . . . Ac 7:57–60
- –Herod killed James . . . . . . Ac 12:2

MUSIC AND SONG

A. Related theme
MUSIC is a theme of 2 Chronicles 2Ch 5:13

B. Musical instruments

1. Begun by Jubal . . . . . . Ge 4:21
2. Types of instruments in the Bible
   - –Bells . . . . . . Ex 28:33–35
   - –Cymbals 2Sa 6:5
   - –Harp . . . . . . Ge 4:21
   - –Flute . . . . . . Ge 4:21
   - –Horn . . . . . . Da 3:5,10,15
   - –Lute 1Sa 18:6
   - –Lyre 2Sa 6:5
   - –Pipe . . . . . . Da 3:5,10,15
   - –Sistrum 2Sa 6:5
   - –Tambourine 2Sa 6:5
   - –Trumpet . . . . . . Nu 10:2
   - –Zither . . . . . . Da 3:5,10,15
3. Used in Israelite worship
   - –Organized by David 1Ch 25:1,6; 2Ch 7:6
   - –Mentioned in the psalms . . . . . . Ps 47:6; Ps 98:5–6; Ps 150:4–5
4. Used when Jesus returns 1Co 15:52; 1Th 4:16

C. Songs

1. In the Old Testament
   - a. Occasions for singing
     - –In sacred processions 2Sa 6:5; 1Ch 13:8
     - –At dedications . . . . . . 2Ch 5:12–13; Ezr 3:10–11; Neh 12:27–28,40
     - –On feast days 2Ch 30:21
     - –At coronations 2Ch 23:13
     - –To celebrate victories . . . . . . Ex 15:1–18; Nu 21:17; Jdg 5:1–31
   - b. The psalmist's intention to sing . . . Ps 27:6; Ps 57:7,9; Ps 61:8; Ps 101:1; Ps 104:33
   - c. Instructions to sing . . . . . . Ps 30:4; Ps 68:32; Ps 98:1; Ps 149:1
   - d. All creation should sing . . . . . . Ps 148:1–12; Isa 44:23; Isa 49:13
2. In the New Testament
   - –Songs at the birth of Jesus . . . . . . Lk 1:46–55, 68–79; Lk 2:14,29–32
   - –Songs in the worshiping church . . . 1Co 14:15; Eph 5:19; Col 3:16; Jas 5:13
   - –Songs in heaven . . . . . . Rev 5:9–10, 12–13; Rev 7:10,12, 15–17; Rev 15:3–4; Rev 19:1–8

MYSTERY

–Secret truths revealed by God

A. Related theme
MYSTERY is a theme of Mark . . . . . . Mk 4:11

B. God and his secret truths

1. God discloses mysteries
   - –To his prophets . . . . . . Ge 40:8; Isa 48:6; Am 3:7; Da 2:18,27–28; Ro 16:25–26
   - –To his apostles . . . . . . Mk 4:10–12; Eph 3:4–5; Rev 1:19–20
2. Only believers understand mysteries . . . . . . Mk 4:10–12; 1Co 2:6–11; 2Co 4:3–6

C. Mysteries revealed to God's people

1. In the Old Testament
   - –Future events revealed to Joseph . . . Ge 40:8–22; Ge 41:1–32
   - –Future events revealed to Daniel . . . Da 2:24–47; Da 4:19–27
2. In the New Testament
   - –Basic teachings about Christ 1Ti 3:16
   - –Basic message of the gospel . . . . . . Col 4:3
   - –All wisdom hidden in Christ . . . . . Col 2:2–3
   - –The nature of the kingdom of God . . . . . . Lk 8:10–15
   - –The union of Christ and his church . . . . . . Eph 5:29–32
   - –Christ's care for his church . . . . . . Rev 1:19–20
   - –What happens at Christ's return . . . 1Co 15:51–52
   - –Inclusion of Gentiles in the kingdom . . . . . . Eph 3:6; Col 1:26

–Plan to reach the Jews with gospel....................... Ro 11:25–26

D. Love is preferable to knowing mysteries....................... 1Co 13:2

NAAMAN

–Aramean general afflicted with leprosy....................... 2Ki 5:1
–Cured by Elisha....................... 2Ki 5:2–14
–Took Israelite soil back to Damascus... 2Ki 5:15–19
–His cure mentioned by Jesus........... Lk 4:27

NABAL

–Wealthy Carmelite; husband of Abigail....................... 1Sa 25:1–3
–Name means "fool"................... 1Sa 25:25
–Refused to help David................. 1Sa 25:4–13
–Abigail pleaded for his life........... 1Sa 25:14–25
–His death........................... 1Sa 25:36–38

NABOTH

–Owner of a vineyard in Jezreel........ 1Ki 21:1
–Refused to sell vineyard to King Ahab....................... 1Ki 21:2–3
–Killed by Jezebel.................... 1Ki 21:4–14
–Ahab's family destroyed for this....... 1Ki 21:17–24
–Joram killed in Naboth's vineyard..... 2Ki 9:21–26

NADAB

A. Firstborn of Aaron.................. Ex 6:23
–Went up Mount Sinai.................. Ex 24:1,9
–Consecrated as priest................. Ex 28:1
–Killed for offering unauthorized fire....................... Lev 10:1–3; Nu 3:2–4
–Had no sons.......................... 1Ch 24:2

B. Son of Jeroboam I; king of Israel.... 1Ki 15:25
–Killed all his brothers................ 1Ki 15:29
–Killed by Baasha..................... 1Ki 15:27–28

NAME

A. Human names

1. Giving a name implied authority... Ge 2:19; Ge 41:45; 2Ki 23:34; Da 1:7

2. Bible names could express
–The feelings of the mother at birth....................... Ge 4:1,25; Ge 29:31–35; Ge 30:4–24
–The feelings of the father at birth....................... Ge 35:16–18; Ge 41:51–52
–Circumstances of the child's conception....................... Ge 17:17,19; 1Sa 1:20
–Circumstances of the child's birth....................... Ge 25:24–26; Ge 38:27–30; Ex 2:10
–Historical situation at time of birth....................... 1Sa 4:19–22; Isa 8:1–4; Hos 1:6–9
–How a person's life would develop....................... Ge 3:20; Ge 27:36; 1Sa 25:25; 1Ch 22:9; Mt 1:21
–A name directly given by God....................... Lk 1:13,60

3. A name change meant a new role
–From Abram to Abraham.............. Ge 17:5–6
–From Sarai to Sarah.................. Ge 17:15–16
–From Jacob to Israel.................. Ge 32:28
–From Simon to Peter.................. Jn 1:42
–Promise of new names for us......... Isa 62:2; Rev 2:17

4. The names of believers
–Are called Christians................ Ac 11:26
–Are known by Christ.................. Jn 10:3–4
–Are acknowledged before the Father....................... Mt 10:32; Rev 3:5
–Are entered into the book of life.. Lk 10:20; Php 4:3; Rev 20:15

B. The name of God and Christ

1. God's name describes him
–It is identical with himself....... 2Sa 7:5,13; Ps 99:6
–It defines his nature................ Isa 9:6
–It defines his power................. Heb 1:4

2. God's name has power
–It delivers us........................ Ex 3:13–15
–It saves us........................... Ps 54:1; Mt 1:21,23; Ac 4:12
–It gives us life....................... Jn 20:31
–It justifies us........................ 1Co 6:11
–It sanctifies us....................... 1Co 6:11
–It protects us........................ Pr 18:10
–It helps us........................... Ps 116:3–4; Jn 14:13–14

3. Our attitude toward God's name
–Praise it............................ Ps 68:4; Ps 99:3
–Glorify it........................... Ps 86:12; Ps 105:3
–Exalt it............................. Ps 34:3
–Hallow it............................ Mt 6:9
–Rejoice in it........................ Ps 89:16
–Love it.............................. Isa 56:6
–Give thanks to it.................... Ps 106:47
–Trust in it.......................... Ps 33:21
–Hope in it........................... Ps 52:9
–Fear it.............................. Ps 86:11; Isa 59:19
–Call on it........................... Ps 116:4,13,17; Joel 2:32
–Declare it........................... Ps 22:22
–Live to reflect it.................... Dt 28:9–10; Ro 2:21–24
–Don't misuse it...................... Ex 20:7; Mal 1:6

4. Our attitude toward Christ's name
–Bow before it........................ Php 2:10–11
–Believe in it........................ Jn 2:23; 1Jn 3:23
–Confess it........................... Ro 10:9; Heb 13:15
–Be baptized into it.................. Ac 10:48
–Call on it........................... 1Co 1:2
–Pray in it........................... Jn 14:13–14; Jn 16:23–24
–Give thanks in it.................... Eph 5:20
–Assemble in it....................... 1Co 5:4
–Preach it............................ Ac 8:12; Ac 9:27–28
–Live to reflect it.................... 2Th 1:12
–Do miracles in it.................... Mk 16:17; Ac 3:16; Ac 4:30
–May have to suffer for it............ Ac 5:40–41; Ac 9:16; Rev 2:3

–Do not covet what is theirs ... Ex 20:17
–Do not deceive them ... Lev 6:2
Pr 26:19
–Do not rob them ... Lev 19:13
–Do not kill them ... Dt 22:26
–Do not plot harm against them ... Pr 3:29
–Do not despise them ... Pr 14:21
–Do not flatter them ... Pr 29:5
–Do not judge them ... Jas 4:12
–Do not commit adultery with neighbor's wife ... Lev 20:10

B. How to treat your neighbors
–Love them as yourself ... Lev 19:18
Mt 22:39
Ro 13:9
Jas 2:8
–Be kind to them ... Lk 10:29–37
–Speak the truth to them ... Eph 4:25

NICODEMUS
–Pharisee who visited Jesus at night ... Jn 3:1–21
–Argued for fair treatment of Jesus ... Jn 7:50–52
–With Joseph, prepared Jesus for burial ... Jn 19:38–42

NIGHT
See DARKNESS

NINEVEH
–A city founded by Nimrod ... Ge 10:11–12
–The capital of Assyria ... 2Ki 19:36
Isa 37:37
–Jonah told to preach against it ... Jnh 1:1–2
Jnh 3:1–3
–The people of Nineveh repented ... Jnh 3:5–10
–The people of Nineveh condemn unbelievers ... Mt 12:41
Lk 11:32
–Prophecies concerning its destruction ... Na 1:8–3:19
Zep 2:13–15

NOAH
–A righteous man ... Eze 14:14,20
–Called to build the ark ... Ge 6:11–22
–Entered the ark ... Ge 7:1–9
–Survived the flood ... Ge 8:15–19
–Worshiped the Lord after the flood ... Ge 8:20–22
–God made covenant with him ... Ge 9:1–17
–Became drunk ... Ge 9:18–23
–Blessed Shem and Japheth and cursed Canaan ... Ge 9:24–27

NUMBERS
A. Numbers used as a literary device
–In poetry ... Ps 62:11
Pr 6:16–19
Pr 30:15–29
–In prophecy ... Am 1:3–2:6
Mic 5:5
–In genealogies ... Mt 1:17

B. Numbers used in a symbolic fashion
1. The number "one"
–One God ... Dt 6:4
1Co 8:6
Eph 4:6
Jas 2:19
–One Lord ... 1Co 8:6
Eph 4:5
–One Spirit ... 1Co 12:13
Eph 4:4
–Father and Son are one ... Jn 10:30
–One body ... Ro 12:4–5
Eph 4:4
–One in Christ ... Jn 17:11,21
Gal 3:28
Eph 2:14–15
–One hope ... Eph 4:4
–One faith and one baptism ... Eph 4:5
–One father of the human race, Adam ... Ac 17:26
Ro 5:12
1Co 15:21–22
–One flesh in marriage ... Ge 2:24
Eph 5:31

2. The number "two"
–Two ways to choose ... Jos 24:15
1Ki 18:21
Mt 7:13–14
–The two-edged sword ... Heb 4:12
Rev 1:16
–Male and female ... Ge 1:27
–Two by two into the ark ... Ge 7:8–9,15–16
–Two tablets of the law ... Ex 32:15
–Disciples sent out two by two ... Mk 6:7
–Two witnesses ... Nu 35:30
Jn 8:17–18
2Co 13:1

3. The number "three"
–Father, Son, Holy Spirit ... Mt 28:19
2Co 13:14
See TRINITY
–Three annual festivals in Israel ... Ex 23:14–17
–Threefold benediction by priests ... Nu 6:24–26
–Job's three friends ... Job 2:11
–Jonah's three days in the fish ... Jnh 1:17
Mt 12:40
–Three temptations of Jesus ... Mt 4:3–10
–Three prayers in Gethsemane ... Mt 26:39–44
–Three denials of Peter ... Mt 26:34,69–75
–Jesus' resurrection on the third day ... Mt 16:21
Lk 24:46
1Co 15:4
–Three questions for Peter ... Jn 21:15–17
–Peter's three visions ... Ac 10:10–16
–Faith, hope, love ... 1Co 13:13

4. The number "four"
–The four rivers in Eden ... Ge 2:10–14
–The four winds ... Jer 49:36
–The four corners of the earth ... Eze 7:2
–Series of fours in Zechariah's visions ... Zec 1:8,18–21
–Four creatures around God's throne ... Eze 1:4–14
Rev 4:6–8
–Four kingdoms seen in a vision ... Da 2:36–43
Da 7:2–7,17

5. The number "seven"
–Creation in seven days ... Ge 1:1–2:3
–The Sabbath on the seventh day ... Ex 20:8–11
–The sabbath year ... Lev 25:1–7
–The Year of Jubilee ... Lev 25:8–12
–Seven lamps on the lampstand ... Ex 25:37
–Feast of Unleavened Bread for seven days ... Ex 34:18
–Feast of Tabernacles for seven days ... Lev 23:34
–Seven sprinklings for a cleansed leper ... Lev 14:7,16
–Seven dippings for leper Naaman ... 2Ki 5:10,14
–Seven days marching around Jericho ... Jos 6:1–16
–Seven deacons ... Ac 6:3–5
–Numerous series of sevens in Revelation ... Rev 1:12–20
Rev 5:1
Rev 8:1–2
Rev 15:1,6–8

OATH

OBADIAH

OBEDIENCE

A. Related themes

1. OBEDIENCE is a theme of:
   - –1 Samuel ... 1Sa 12:14
   - –2 Samuel ... 2Sa 12:10
   - –1 Kings ... 1Ki 9:4
   - –2 Kings ... 2Ki 22:19
   - –Daniel ... Da 1:8
   - –1 Corinthians ... 1Co 7:19
2. TRUST AND OBEY is a theme of Joshua ... Jos 10:25

B. Obedience in the Old Testament

1. Relationships of obedience
   - –Israelites obey the Lord their God ... Ex 19:5; Dt 4:30
   - –Israelites obey the law of God ... Ex 34:11; Dt 11:13,27,32
   - –Citizens obey the king ... 1Ki 2:43; Ecc 8:2
   - –Children obey parents ... Ex 20:12; Pr 1:8–9; Pr 6:20–21
2. Rewards for obedience ... Ex 19:5–6; Dt 28:1–14; Jos 1:7–8
3. Punishment for disobedience ... Dt 28:15–68; 1Sa 12:15; 2Ki 17:7–20; Jer 11:1–3
4. Obedience more important than outward ritual ... 1Sa 15:22; Ps 40:6–8; Pr 21:3; Jer 7:22–23

C. Obedience in the New Testament

1. Relationships of obedience
   - –Christians obey God ... Heb 12:9; Jas 4:7; 1Jn 5:3
   - –Christians obey Christ ... Jn 14:13,23; Ro 1:5; 1Co 9:21; Gal 6:2; Heb 5:9
   - –Citizens obey government authorities ... Ro 13:1–5; 1Pe 2:13–14
   - –Christians obey church leaders ... Heb 13:17
   - –Servants obey masters ... Eph 6:5–8; Col 3:22
   - –Children obey parents ... Eph 6:1; Col 3:20
2. Obeying God precedes obeying humans ... Ac 4:19–20; Ac 5:29

OCCULT

See MAGIC, WITCHCRAFT AND SORCERY

OFFERINGS

See TITHES AND OFFERINGS

OG

- –King of Bashan ... Nu 21:33; Dt 1:4
- –Destroyed by the Israelites ... Nu 21:34–35; Dt 3:1–11
- –Victory sung by the Israelites ... Ps 136:20

OLIVES, MOUNT OF

- –A hill east of Jerusalem ... Eze 11:23; Zec 14:4
- –David climbed it while fleeing from Absalom ... 2Sa 15:30
- –Jesus often went there ... Lk 22:39; Jn 8:1
- –Triumphal Entry began from there ... Mt 21:1–9; Mk 11:1–10; Lk 19:29–40
- –Jesus predicted destruction of Jerusalem there ... Mt 24:3–34; Mk 13:3–31
- –Gethsemane located there ... Mt 26:30,36; Mk 14:26,32
- –Jesus ascended into heaven from there ... Ac 1:9–12

OMRI

- –King of Israel ... 1Ki 16:21–28
- –Father of Ahab ... 1Ki 16:28

ORDER

A. Related theme

ORGANIZATION is a theme of Numbers ... Nu 2:34

CHURCH ORDER is a theme of 1 Timothy ... 1Ti 3:15

B. Order needed among God's people

- –For the Israelites in the desert ... Nu 2:1–34
- –In Christian worship ... 1Co 14:40
- –In the Christian life ... Col 2:5
- –In presenting the truth about Christ ... Lk 1:3

See also CHURCH
DEACON
ELDER

ORPAH

- –Moabitess; daughter-in-law of Naomi ... Ru 1:3–5
- –Remained in Moab ... Ru 1:14

OTHNIEL

- –Nephew of Caleb; married Caleb's daughter ... Jos 15:15–19; Jdg 1:12–15
- –Became a judge ... Jdg 3:10
- –Freed Israelites from Arameans ... Jdg 3:7–11

PAIN

–*Various types of suffering experienced in our lives*

A. Related themes

1. SUFFERING is a theme of:
   - –Job ... Job 2:13
   - –Jeremiah ... Jer 15:18
   - –Mark ... Mk 8:31
   - –2 Corinthians ... 2Co 1:8
   - –1 Peter ... 1Pe 4:12
2. COMPLAINT is a theme of:
   - –Psalms ... Ps 123:4
   - –Habakkuk ... Hab 1:2
3. HARD TIMES is a theme of 2 Timothy ... 2Ti 1:8
4. UNJUST PERSECUTION is a theme of Acts ... Ac 12:2

B. Pain and suffering as a universal experience

1. In humans
   - –The righteous ... Ps 22:1–2,12–18
   - –The wicked ... Pr 10:16; Pr 12:21
2. In creation as a whole ... Ro 8:20–22

C. The problem of pain and suffering for God's people

1. Examples of those who experienced pain
   - –Joseph ... Ge 39:11–20

- –The Israelites in Egypt … Ex 1:8–14
- –The poor … Neh 5:1–5; Am 2:6–7
- –Job … Job 2:7–13
- –David … Ps 22:1–18
- –Asaph … Ps 73:2–14
- –Daniel's three friends … Da 3:13–23
- –Daniel … Da 6:16–17
- –Peter and John … Ac 5:40–41
- –Paul … Ac 14:19; 2Co 11:23–26
- –The Hebrew Christians … Heb 10:33–34
- –Other Christians … 1Th 2:14–15; 1Pe 2:19–21
- –Christians in Smyrna … Rev 2:9–10
- –Saints in John's vision … Rev 6:9–10

2. Christian attitude toward pain
- –We must expect it … Mt 24:9; Jn 16:1–4,33; 2Ti 3:12
- –We may have to endure it … 2Ti 2:3; 2Ti 4:5
- –We must realize not all are delivered … Heb 11:35–38
- –We must be patient in it … Ro 12:12; 1Pe 2:20–21
- –We can rejoice in it … Ro 5:3; Col 1:24; Jas 1:2–3; 1Pe 4:12–14
- –We must overcome it … Ro 8:35–37; Rev 2:10–11
- –We must not become discouraged … Eph 3:13
- –We must not lose heart … 2Co 4:7–10, 16–17; 1Th 3:3
- –We do complain against it … Job 3:3–26; Ps 74:1,10–11; 2Co 12:7–8

3. Why does God allow such pain?
- –To punish sins … 2Sa 12:9–18; 2Ch 33:10–11
- –To test us … Dt 8:2; Job 2:1–6; Isa 48:10
- –To teach us his will … Ps 119:71,75
- –To teach us patience … Ro 5:3; Jas 1:3
- –To humble us … Dt 8:3; 2Ch 7:13–14
- –To discipline us in love … Heb 12:4–11
- –To drive us to repentance … Jdg 6:1–6; Ps 107:4–6,10–13; Hos 5:15
- –To get us to rely on his grace … 2Co 12:7–10
- –To purify us … Zec 13:7–9; Mal 3:2–3; Jn 15:2
- –To promote his glory … Jn 9:1–3
- –To further the gospel … Ac 8:3–4; 2Ti 4:16–17

4. How does God relate to pain?
- –He is in control … Job 1:6–12; Ro 8:38–39
- –He causes good to triumph … Ps 49:13–15; Ps 73:16–20; Ro 8:28
- –He is a refuge for believers … Ps 16:1,8; Ps 46:1; Isa 25:4
- –He shares our pain … Isa 53:2–4; Isa 63:9
- –He walks with us through pain … Ps 23:4; Ps 46:7,11; Isa 43:2
- –He comforts us … Isa 49:13; Zec 1:17; 2Co 1:4–5; Mt 11:28–30
- –He will terminate pain at Christ's return … 2Th 1:4–7; Rev 21:1–4

5. How should believers relate to those in pain?
- –We should pray for them … Ac 12:5; Ro 15:30–31; 2Co 1:10–11; Jas 5:13–16
- –We should comfort them … Job 2:11–13; 2Co 1:6–8
- –We should share their burdens … Job 30:25; Ro 12:15; Gal 6:2; Heb 13:3
- –We should encourage them … 1Th 5:11
- –We should give them help … Isa 58:7; Lk 10:30–37; Php 4:14; 1Jn 3:17–18

PARABLE

–Stories that illustrate spiritual truths

A. The purposes of parables
- –To teach things to children … Ps 78:2–4; Pr 1:1–6
- –To make an important point … Jdg 9:7–20; 1Sa 12:1–7
- –To give a prophetic message … Isa 5:1–7; Eze 17:1–18; Hos 12:10
- –To teach us about the kingdom … Mk 4:2,10
- –To obscure teaching from unbelievers … Mt 13:11–15

B. Parables and fables in the Old Testament
- –The fable of Jotham to Abimelech … Jdg 9:7–15
- –The parable of Nathan to David … 2Sa 12:1–6
- –The fable of Jehoash to Amaziah … 2Ki 14:9
- –The parable of Isaiah to the people … Isa 5:1–7
- –The parables of Ezekiel to the people … Eze 17:1–8,22–24; Eze 20:45–49; Eze 24:1–5

C. Jesus' use of parables
- –He used them regularly … Mk 4:33–34
- –He explained things to the disciples alone … Mt 13:10–13; Mk 4:3–8,14–20; Lk 8:9–10
- –He taught about the kingdom of God … Mk 4:11,26, 30–32

D. Parables of Jesus
- –Lamp under a bowl … Mt 5:14–15; Mk 4:21–22; Lk 8:16
- –Wise and foolish builders … Mt 7:24–27; Lk 6:47–49
- –New cloth on an old garment … Mt 9:16; Mk 2:21; Lk 5:36
- –New wine in old wineskins … Mt 9:17; Mk 2:22; Lk 5:37–38
- –Sower … Mt 13:3–23; Mk 4:3–25; Lk 8:5–15

–Seed's growth .... Mk 4:25–29
–Wheat and weeds .... Mt 13:24–30, 36–43
–Mustard seed .... Mt 13:31–32; Mk 4:30–32; Lk 13:18–19
–Yeast .... Mt 13:33; Lk 13:20–21
–Hidden treasure .... Mt 13:43
–Valuable pearl .... Mt 13:45–46
–Net .... Mt 13:47–51
–House owner .... Mt 13:52
–Good Samaritan .... Lk 10:25–37
–Lost sheep .... Mt 18:10–14; Lk 15:3–7
–Lost coin .... Lk 15:8–10
–Lost son .... Lk 15:11–32
–Unmerciful servant .... Mt 18:15–35
–Shrewd manager .... Lk 16:1–9
–Rich man and Lazarus .... Lk 16:19–31
–Persistent widow .... Lk 18:1–8
–Pharisee and tax collector .... Lk 18:9–14
–Payment of workers .... Mt 20:1–16
–Two sons .... Mt 21:28–32
–Tenants and the vineyard .... Mt 21:33–46; Mk 12:1–6; Lk 20:9–18
–Wedding banquet .... Mt 22:1–14
–Faithful servant .... Mt 24:45–51; Lk 12:42–48
–Ten virgins .... Mt 25:1–13
–Talents .... Mt 25:14–30; Lk 19:12–27
–Sheep and goats .... Mt 25:31–46

PATIENCE

–Long-suffering, perseverance

A. Human patience

1. The command to be patient
   - –Be patient .... Ro 12:12; 1Th 5:14; Heb 12:1; Jas 5:7–8
   - –Bear with others' shortcomings .... Eph 4:2; Col 3:12–13
2. The manner of achieving patience
   - –By dependence on God .... Ro 15:5; Col 1:11
   - –Through hope in Christ .... 1Th 1:3; Jas 5:7
   - –As part of the fruit of the Spirit .... Gal 5:22
3. Examples of patience
   - –Abraham .... Heb 6:15
   - –Job .... Jas 5:11
   - –The prophets .... Jas 5:10
   - –Paul 2Ti 3:10
   - –John .... Rev 1:9

See also PERSEVERANCE

B. Patience of God

1. Statements of God's patience
   - –God is slow to anger .... Ex 34:6; Nu 14:18; Ps 30:5; Ps 78:38
   - –Jesus is patient with us 1Ti 1:16
2. Purpose: to call humans to repentance .... Ro 2:4; 2Pe 3:9,15
3. God's patience at time of Noah 1Pe 3:20

PAUL

A. Related themes

PETER AND PAUL is a theme of Acts .... Ac 19:11
MINISTRY is a theme of 2 Corinthians 2Co 4:1
DEFENSE is a theme of Galatians .... Gal 1:10

B. His background

–Originally called Saul .... Ac 13:9
–From Tarsus .... Ac 9:11; Ac 21:39
–From the tribe of Benjamin .... Php 3:5
–A Pharisee .... Php 3:5
–Educated by Gamaliel .... Ac 22:3
–Unmarried 1Co 7:8

C. His life as a persecutor of Christians

–Assisted in stoning of Stephen .... Ac 7:58; Ac 8:1
–Zealously persecuted church .... Ac 9:1; Gal 1:13–14; Php 3:6
–Cast vote against Christians .... Ac 26:9–10
–Went to Damascus to persecute .... Ac 9:2; Ac 22:4–5
–Converted on the way to Damascus .... Ac 9:3–19; Ac 22:6–21; Ac 26:12–18

D. His life as an apostle

1. From conversion to first missionary journey
   - –Called as missionary to Gentiles .... Ac 22:17–21; Ac 26:16–18
   - –Went to Arabia .... Gal 1:17
   - –Preached in Damascus; escaped in basket .... Ac 9:19–25; 2Co 11:32–33
   - –Went to Jerusalem .... Ac 9:26–29
   - –Went to Tarsus .... Ac 9:30
   - –Brought to Antioch by Barnabas .... Ac 11:22–26
   - –Brought offering to Jerusalem .... Ac 11:29–30
   - –Returned to Antioch .... Ac 12:25
2. First missionary journey
   - –Called by God .... Ac 13:2–4
   - –Preached throughout Cyprus .... Ac 13:5–12
   - –Preached in Antioch in Pisidia .... Ac 13:14–52
   - –Was persecuted in Iconium .... Ac 14:1–7
   - –Preached and stoned at Lystra .... Ac 14:8–20
   - –Preached at Derbe .... Ac 14:20–21
   - –Returned to Antioch .... Ac 14:21–28
3. The Jerusalem council
   - –Sent to Jerusalem .... Ac 15:1–4; Gal 2:1–2
   - –Discussed circumcision privately .... Gal 2:3–10
   - –Open meeting on circumcision issue .... Ac 15:5–22
   - –Letter drafted and sent with them .... Ac 15:23–31
   - –Friction developed with Peter .... Gal 2:11–14
4. Second missionary journey
   - –Split with Barnabas over John Mark .... Ac 15:36–41
   - –Took Silas along .... Ac 15:40
   - –Visited previous churches .... Ac 15:41
   - –Added Timothy to his group .... Ac 16:1–4
   - –At Troas, called to Macedonia .... Ac 16:6–10
   - –Preached to women at Philippi .... Ac 16:13–15
   - –Imprisoned and freed in Philippi .... Ac 16:16–40
   - –Ministered in Thessalonica .... Ac 17:1–9
   - –Ministered in Berea .... Ac 17:10–15
   - –Preached in Athens .... Ac 17:16–33
   - –Ministered in Corinth for eighteen months .... Ac 18:1–11
   - –Attacked by Jews .... Ac 18:12–17
   - –Left Corinth and returned to Antioch .... Ac 18:18–22

5. Third missionary journey
   - –Arrived at Ephesus in Asia ...... Ac 19:1
   - –Ministered for two years there ... Ac 19:2–22
   - –Suffered many hardships there.... 2Co 1:3–10
   - –Visited with leaders from Corinth 1Co 16:17–18
   - –Riot in Ephesus.................. Ac 19:23–41
   - –Left for Macedonia................ Ac 20:1
   - –Met Titus in Macedonia 2Co 7:5–7
   - –Gathered money for Jerusalem..... 2Co 8:1–5; Ro 15:26
   - –Arrived in Greece................. Ac 20:2–3
   - –Gathered more money for Jerusalem .... Ro 15:26
   - –Left Greece for Jerusalem .... Ac 20:3–6; Ro 15:25
   - –Spoke all night at Troas .... Ac 20:7–12
   - –Said farewell to elders of Ephesus....................... Ac 20:17–38
   - –Sailed for Jerusalem .... Ac 21:1–6
   - –Traveled to Jerusalem............. Ac 21:7–17
   - –Reported to Jerusalem leaders ... Ac 21:17–25
6. Paul's period of imprisonment
   - –Attacked and beaten by Jews from Asia .... Ac 21:27–32
   - –Arrested by Roman commander.. Ac 21:33–35
   - –Addressed the Jewish crowd....... Ac 22:1–21
   - –Addressed Sanhedrin .... Ac 23:1–11
   - –Transferred to Caesarea........... Ac 23:12–35
   - –On trial before Felix.............. Ac 24:1–21
   - –Kept in prison in Caesarea......... Ac 24:22–27
   - –On trial before Festus .... Ac 25:1–12
   - –Appealed to Caesar .... Ac 25:12
   - –Spoke before Agrippa............. Ac 25:13–26:32
   - –Sailed for Rome; shipwrecked.... Ac 27:1–44
   - –Stranded on island of Malta....... Ac 28:1–10
   - –Arrived in Rome.................. Ac 28:11–16
   - –Preached to Jews of Rome .... Ac 28:17–28
   - –Remained two years in Rome .... Ac 28:30–31
   - –Freed after trial before emperor .. 2Ti 4:16–17
7. Travels after release from imprisonment
   - –In Macedonia.................... 1Ti 1:3
   - –In Crete......................... Titus 1:5
   - –In Nicopolis .... Titus 3:12
   - –In Miletus....................... 2Ti 4:20
   - –In Troas......................... 2Ti 4:13
   - –Imprisoned again................. 2Ti 2:8–9
   - –Probably killed this time.......... 2Ti 4:6–8

E. Significant issues in Paul's letters
- –His apostleship .... 1Co 9:1–3; 2Co 11:4–12:13; Gal 1:1–2:14
- –Salvation possible only in the name of Jesus............... Ro 3:21–26; Ro 5:1–2; Ro 10:3–13; 2Co 5:18–21; Gal 3:10–14, 24–29; Eph 2:1–22; Php 3:7–14; Col 1:13–23; 1Ti 1:12–16
- –Salvation through faith alone ...... Ro 3:21–5:1; Gal 2:15–21; Eph 2:8–9; Php 3:9
- –Circumcision not necessary for salvation.......................... Ro 4:9–12; Gal 2:3; Gal 5:1–6; Col 2:11–12
- –Christian freedom .... Ro 14:1–15:13; 1Co 8:1–13; 1Co 11:23–33; Gal 4:31–5:13
- –Concern for the salvation of Jews... Ro 9:1–5; Ro 10:1–4
- –Proper use of spiritual gifts .... Ro 12:3–8; 1Co 12:1–14:40
- –Life led by the Spirit of God......... Ro 8:1–17; Gal 5:16–26
- –Proper order needed in the church.. 1Co 11:17–34; 1Co 14:26–40; 1Ti 2:1–3:15; Titus 1:5–2:15

PEACE

–Wholeness and well-being in all areas of life

A. Basic meanings of peace

1. Peace ("Shalom") is a basic greeting
   - –Hello .... Da 10:19; Jn 20:19; Gal 1:3
   - –Good-bye 1Sa 25:35; 2Sa 15:9; 1Pe 5:14; 3Jn 14
2. Peace in a political sense
   - –On the international scene .... 1Sa 7:14; 1Ki 4:24; Ac 24:2
   - –On the national scene 2Sa 3:21–23; 1Ki 22:44; 2Ch 14:1
3. Peace in human relationships
   - –In relationships with others....... Ro 12:18; Heb 12:14; 1Pe 3:11
   - –Among the Israelite people .... Ps 34:14; Ps 122:6–7
   - –In relationships in the church .... Ac 9:31; Ro 14:19; 2Co 13:11; Eph 2:14–17
   - –In relationships in the home...... Ge 44:17; Pr 17:1; Pr 29:17; 1Co 7:15
4. Personal sense of peace
   - –In relationship with oneself .... Ps 4:8; Pr 14:30; 2Co 2:13
   - –In relationship with God.......... Nu 6:26; Isa 26:3; Ro 5:1; Php 4:7–9; Col 1:20

B. The source of peace

1. It comes as a divine gift
   - –From God the Father .... Ro 1:7; Ro 15:33; Php 4:7
   - –From the Lord Jesus Christ .... Isa 9:6–7; Lk 2:14; Jn 14:27; Ro 1:7; Eph 2:14; 2Th 3:16
   - –From the Holy Spirit .... Ro 14:17; Gal 5:22; Eph 4:3
   - –God promises a covenant of peace Isa 54:10; Eze 34:25; Eze 37:26
   - –We must pray to God for peace ... Ps 122:6–7; Jer 29:7; 1Ti 2:1
2. It comes through human effort
   - –We must let peace rule in us...... Col 3:15

- –We must live in peace 2Co 13:11; 1Th 5:13
- –We must seek peace .... Ps 34:14; 1Pe 3:11
- –We must try to live in peace .... Ro 12:18; Ro 14:19; Heb 12:14
- –We must pursue peace .... Ps 34:14; 2Ti 2:22
- –We must obey God to receive peace .... Lev 26:3,6

C. Jesus and our peace
- –Prophesied to be the Prince of Peace .... Isa 9:6
- –Peace proclaimed at his birth .... Lk 2:14
- –Peace promised to his disciples .... Jn 14:27; Jn 16:33
- –Peace achieved on the cross .... Isa 53:5; Col 1:20
- –Began the good news of peace .... Isa 52:7; Ac 10:36
- –He is our peace .... Eph 2:14
- –Enables us to have peace with God .... Ro 5:1
- –Establishes peace within the church .... Eph 2:15
- –Guides us in the way of peace .... Lk 1:79
- –Blesses us with peace .... Nu 6:24–26; Ps 29:11; 1Co 1:3
- –Enables us to die in peace .... Lk 2:29–31

D. The wicked and peace
- –They proclaim a false peace .... Jer 6:14; Eze 13:10
- –They do not know the way of peace .... Isa 59:8; Lk 19:42
- –They hate peace .... Ps 120:6–7
- –They have no peace .... Isa 48:18,22; Isa 57:21

PEKAH

- –King of Israel 2Ki 15:27–31
- –Assassinated Pekahiah to become king 2Ki 15:25
- –Allied with Syria against Judah .... 2Ki 15:37; Isa 7:1–2
- –Inflicted much destruction on Judah 2Ch 28:5–8
- –Destruction of the alliance foretold .... Isa 7:3–9
- –Failed in attempt to take Jerusalem 2Ki 16:5–6

PEKAHIAH

- –King of Israel 2Ki 15:23–26
- –Assassinated by Pekah, an officer 2Ki 15:25

PERFECTION

–Complete and without sin or error

A. Perfection as a human goal

1. The goal stated .... Mt 5:48; 2Co 13:9,11
2. Perfection possible only in the Lord
   - –Animal sacrifice cannot make us perfect .... Heb 10:1
   - –The law cannot make us perfect .... Ro 3:20; Heb 7:11,19
   - –God makes our way perfect 2Sa 22:33
   - –God's strength makes us perfect 2Co 12:7–10
   - –Jesus is the perfecter of our faith .... Heb 12:2
   - –Jesus makes us perfect by his sacrifice .... Heb 10:14
   - –The Spirit helps us attain perfection .... Gal 3:3
3. Perfection requires various human actions
   - –Learning God's wisdom .... Col 1:28
   - –Knowing God's word 2Ti 3:14–17
   - –Pressing forward in faith .... Php 3:12–14
   - –Self-sacrifice .... Mt 19:21
   - –Love .... Col 3:14
   - –Purifying ourselves 2Co 7:1
   - –Controlling what we say .... Jas 3:2
   - –Not being afraid 1Jn 4:18
4. Perfection attained only in the hereafter .... 1Co 13:8–10; Heb 12:22–23

See also HOLINESS
SANCTIFICATION

B. Perfection as the nature of God

1. God the Father
   - –He is perfect .... Mt 5:48
   - –His works are perfect .... Dt 32:4
   - –His way is perfect 2Sa 22:31
   - –His law is perfect .... Ps 19:7; Jas 1:25
   - –His will is perfect .... Ro 12:2
   - –He is perfect in knowledge .... Job 37:16
   - –He is perfect in faithfulness .... Isa 25:1
2. Christ the Son
   - –He is without sin .... 2Co 5:21; Heb 7:26; 1Jn 3:5
   - –He was made perfect through suffering .... Heb 2:10; Heb 5:8–9; Heb 7:28

PERSECUTION

–Oppression because of one's faith

A. Examples of persecution

1. The prophets
   - –Prophets in general .... 2Ch 36:15–16; Mt 5:12; Mt 23:31,37; Ac 7:52
   - –Elijah 1Ki 19:1–3
   - –Micaiah 1Ki 22:9–28
   - –Jeremiah .... Jer 26:1–19; Jer 37:11–38:13
   - –Uriah son of Shemaiah .... Jer 26:20–22
2. The apostles
   - –Persecution prophesied .... Mt 24:9; Jn 15:18–21; Jn 16:1–4
   - –The apostles as a group .... Ac 5:27,40
   - –James .... Ac 12:1–2
   - –Peter .... Ac 12:3–5
   - –Paul .... Ac 14:5–6,19–20; Ac 16:22–24; Ac 22:27–36; 2Co 11:23–26
   - –John .... Rev 1:9
3. Christians in general
   - –Stephen .... Ac 7:57–60
   - –Christians in Judea .... Ac 8:1–3; 1Th 2:14–15
   - –Christians outside Judea .... Ac 9:1–2; Ac 26:11
   - –Christians in Thessalonica 1Th 2:14–15
   - –Christians in Smyrna .... Rev 2:9–10
   - –To be expected for all 2Ti 3:12

B. Attitudes in relationship to persecution
- –Commit yourself to God 1Pe 4:19
- –Persevere under it .... Mk 13:13; Heb 10:32–36; Jas 1:12; Rev 2:10

–Rejoice in it ..... Mt 5:12
Ac 5:41
Php 2:17
Col 1:24
–Flee from it ..... Mt 10:23
Ac 14:6
–Do not be ashamed 1Pe 4:16
–Pray for persecutors ..... Mt 5:44
Lk 23:34
Ac 7:60

PERSEVERANCE

–Remaining firm in our faith

A. Related themes
PERSEVERANCE is a theme of:
–2 Timothy 2Ti 2:3
–Hebrews ..... Heb 10:36

B. God preserves us in our faith
–He draws us firmly to himself ..... Jn 6:37
–He holds us in his hand ..... Ps 37:24
Jn 10:27–29
–He keeps us in his love ..... Ro 8:35–39
–He watches over us ..... Ps 121:3–8
Ps 145:20
–He protects us from the evil one 2Th 3:3
1Jn 5:18
–He keeps our commitment firm 1Co 1:8
2Ti 1:12
–He will keep us until the final day ..... Php 1:6
1Pe 1:4–5

C. We must persevere in our faith
–The command to persevere ..... Heb 10:35–36
Heb 12:2
Jas 1:12
–The command to use spiritual armor ..... Eph 6:10–17
1Th 5:8
–The warning not to turn away from God ..... Heb 3:12
Heb 6:1–6
Heb 10:26–31
Rev 2:4–5
–The possibility of rejecting the faith 1Ti 1:19–20
1Ti 6:20–21
2Ti 2:17–18
Heb 3:16–18

PERSIA

See MEDES AND PERSIANS

PETER

A. Related theme
PETER AND PAUL is a theme of Acts ..... Ac 19:11

B. Background information
–Father's name was John ..... Jn 1:42
–Given name: Simon ..... Jn 1:42
–Brother of Andrew ..... Mt 10:2
–A native of Bethsaida ..... Jn 1:44
–Originally a fisherman ..... Lk 5:1–5
–Uneducated ..... Ac 4:13
–Married ..... Mk 1:30
1Co 9:5

C. Events during Jesus' public ministry
–Let Jesus use his boat to speak from ..... Lk 5:3
–Caught numerous fish at Jesus' command ..... Lk 5:5–7
–Given the name Cephas (Peter) ..... Mt 16:17–18
Jn 1:42
–Called by Jesus to be fisher of men ..... Mt 4:18–20
Mk 1:16–18
–Witnessed raising of Jairus's daughter ..... Mk 5:37–41
–Walked on water at Jesus' bidding ..... Mt 14:28–31
–Confessed Christ as Son of God ..... Mt 16:13–16
Mk 8:27–30
Lk 9:18–20
–Rebuked by Jesus ..... Mt 16:21–23
Mk 8:31–33
–Observed the transfiguration ..... Mt 17:1–8
Mk 9:2–8
–Caught fish that had coin in its mouth ..... Mt 17:24–27
–Inquired about limits of forgiveness ..... Mt 18:21
–Did not want Jesus to wash his feet ..... Jn 13:6–10
–Jesus prayed for him ..... Lk 22:31–32
–His denial of Jesus predicted ..... Mt 26:31–35
Mk 14:27–31
Lk 22:33–34
–Accompanied Jesus to Gethsemane ..... Mt 26:36–45
Mk 14:32–42
–Cut off ear of the high priest's servant ..... Jn 18:10–11
–Denied Jesus three times ..... Mt 26:69–75
Mk 14:66–72
Lk 22:54–62
Jn 18:15–18, 25–27

D. Events between resurrection and Pentecost
–Ran to tomb on Easter Sunday ..... Lk 24:12
Jn 20:2–8
–Jesus appeared to him ..... Lk 24:33–34
1Co 15:5
–Decided to go fishing ..... Jn 21:3
–Had breakfast with Jesus ..... Jn 21:4–14
–Was asked three times, "Do you love me?" ..... Jn 21:15–17
–One of the apostles in upper room ..... Ac 1:13
–Suggested that Judas's vacancy be filled ..... Ac 1:15–22

E. Events after Pentecost
–Preached a sermon on Pentecost Sunday ..... Ac 2:14–36
–Called the people to repent ..... Ac 2:37–40
–With John, healed a lame man ..... Ac 3:1–8
–Preached in the temple ..... Ac 3:11–26
–Arrested with John ..... Ac 4:1–3
–Questioned before the Sanhedrin ..... Ac 4:7–21
Ac 5:27–32
–Spoke judgment against Ananias and Sapphira ..... Ac 5:1–10
–His shadow healed people ..... Ac 5:15–16
–Was sent to new Christians in Samaria ..... Ac 8:14–17
–Through a vision, was sent to Cornelius ..... Ac 10:9–48
–Explained how God was saving Gentiles ..... Ac 11:1–18
–Imprisoned by Herod ..... Ac 12:3–5
–Freed from prison by an angel ..... Ac 12:6–11
–Left Jerusalem ..... Ac 12:17
–Did missionary work among the Jews 1Co 9:5
Gal 2:9
–Had conflict with Paul at Antioch ..... Gal 2:11–14
–Spoke at council in Jerusalem ..... Ac 15:7–11

F. His character and significance
1. Often spoke impulsively
–Asked to come to Jesus on the water ..... Mt 14:28
–Rebuked Jesus ..... Mt 16:22

- –Said he was willing to die with Jesus. Lk 22:33
- –Claimed he would never deny Jesus. Mt 26:33–35
- –Did not want Jesus to wash his feet. Jn 13:6–9

2. A leader among the disciples
- –His name always mentioned first. Mt 10:2; Mk 3:16; Lk 6:14; Ac 1:13
- –Often the spokesman for the rest. Mt 16:16; Mt 26:33–35; Ac 2:14; Ac 4:29

3. One of the major leaders of the church
- –Called "rock" by Jesus. Mt 16:18–19
- –Led the church in Jerusalem. Ac 5:1–9
- –Paul met specifically with him. Gal 1:18
- –Spoke at Jerusalem council. Ac 15:7–11
- –Called a "pillar". Gal 2:9
- –A party at Corinth called by his name. 1Co 1:12
- –Wrote two letters. 1Pe 1:1; 2Pe 1:1

PETITION

–Asking God for personal things in prayer

A. Why must we ask?
- –God commands it. Mt 7:7–9
- –We have needs. Php 4:19
- –We follow the example of the saints. 1Ch 16:4; Da 6:11; Da 9:17–18

B. How must we ask?
- –In faith. Mk 11:24; Jn 14:12–14
- –With thanksgiving. Php 4:6
- –In Christ's name. Jn 14:6,13; Jn 15:16; Jn 16:23–24; Ro 5:2
- –Without worry. Mt 6:25–34; Lk 12:22–31

C. For what may we ask?
- –For daily bread. Mt 6:11
- –For forgiveness. Da 9:19; Mt 6:12
- –For freedom from temptation. Mt 6:13
- –For the Holy Spirit. Lk 11:13
- –For the ability to witness with boldness. Ac 4:29–30
- –For safety in travel. Ezr 8:21–23
- –For healing. Isa 38:2; Mk 1:40
- –For a child. 1Sa 1:11
- –For anything. Jn 14:14

PHARAOH

–The title given to the king of Egypt

A. Pharaohs mentioned in the Bible

1. The Pharaoh at the time of Abram
- –Sarai taken into his palace. Ge 12:14–15
- –Diseases inflicted on his household. Ge 12:17
- –Expelled Abram from Egypt. Ge 12:18–20

2. The Pharaoh at the time of Joseph
- –Put butler and baker in prison. Ge 40:1–4
- –Had dreams, interpreted by Joseph. Ge 41:1–32
- –Made Joseph second in command. Ge 41:37–43
- –Gave Joseph a wife. Ge 41:44–45
- –Invited Jacob to live in Egypt. Ge 45:16–20
- –Greeted Jacob and his family. Ge 47:1–10
- –Settled Jacob and family in Goshen. Ge 47:5–6
- –Allowed Joseph to bury Jacob in Canaan. Ge 50:4–6

3. The Pharaoh at the time of the exodus

a. Oppression of the Israelites
- –Did not know about Joseph. Ex 1:8
- –Turned the Israelites into slaves. Ex 1:9–11
- –Ordered the death of baby boys. Ex 1:15–22
- –Tried to kill Moses. Ex 2:15
- –Increased burden of slavery. Ex 5:1–18

b. Interaction with Moses and Aaron
- –First appearance before him. Ex 5:1–5
- –Second appearance, first miracles. Ex 7:10–21
- –Asked for plagues to be stopped. Ex 8:8,28; Ex 9:27–28; Ex 10:16–17
- –Agreed to let Israelites worship. Ex 8:25–29; Ex 9:27–28; Ex 10:8–10,24
- –Hardened his heart. Ex 7:13,22; Ex 8:15,32; Ex 9:7,12,34–35; Ex 10:1,20,27

c. The exodus
- –His firstborn son killed. Ex 12:29–30
- –Ordered Israelites to leave. Ex 12:31–32
- –Changed mind and pursued Israelites. Ex 14:5–9
- –Followed Israelites into the sea. Ex 14:23–25
- –Drowned. Ex 14:26–28; Ps 106:10–11

4. The Pharaoh at the time of Solomon
- –Alliance between him and Solomon. 1Ki 3:1
- –Solomon married his daughter. 1Ki 3:1; 1Ki 11:1
- –Conquered Gezer and gave it to Solomon. 1Ki 9:16

5. Shishak, at the end of Solomon's reign
- –Befriended Hadad, adversary of Solomon. 1Ki 11:14–22
- –Befriended Jeroboam. 1Ki 11:40
- –Attacked and defeated Rehoboam. 1Ki 14:25–26; 2Ch 12:1–11

6. The Pharaoh in Hoshea's time
- –Possibly called So. 2Ki 17:4
- –Hoshea made alliance with him. 2Ki 17:4

7. The Pharaoh in Hezekiah's time
- –Made alliance with Hezekiah. Isa 30:1–2
- –Advanced against Sennacherib. 2Ki 19:9
- –A weak Pharaoh. 2Ki 18:21; Isa 36:6
- –Unable to save Judah. Isa 30:3–5; Isa 31:1–3

8. Pharaoh Neco
- –Allied with Assyria against Babylon. 2Ki 23:29; 2Ch 35:20
- –Fought and defeated Josiah. 2Ki 23:29–30; 2Ch 35:20–24

–Deposed Jehoahaz . . . 2Ki 23:33; 2Ch 36:3
–Made Jehoiakim king . . . 2Ki 23:34–35; 2Ch 36:4
–Defeated by the Babylonians . . . Jer 46:2
9. Hophra, at the time of the exile
–Zedekiah asked his help against Babylon . . . Eze 17:15
–Marched against the Babylonians . . . Jer 37:5
–Deserted Zedekiah . . . Jer 37:7
–His defeat to Nebuchadnezzar prophesied . . . Jer 44:30; Eze 29:19–20

B. Prophecies against Pharaoh
–By Jeremiah . . . Jer 44:30; Jer 46:14–19
–By Ezekiel . . . Eze 29:1–5; Eze 32:1–15

PHARISEES

–A Jewish party, prominent at the time of Jesus

A. Major characteristics
–Political leaders of the Jews . . . Mt 27:62–64
–Members of the Sanhedrin (Jewish council) . . . Ac 23:6
–Leaders of the synagogue . . . Jn 9:13–16,22
–Official interpreters of the law . . . Mt 23:2
–Strict observers of the law of God . . . Mt 12:2,8–14; Mt 23:23
–Strict adherents of Jewish traditions . . . Mk 7:2–3; Gal 1:14
–Believed circumcision was necessary . . . Ac 15:5
–Believed in the resurrection and in angels . . . Ac 23:8
–Tried to remain separate from sinners . . . Mt 9:11
–Promoted Judaism throughout the world . . . Mt 23:15

B. Prominent Pharisees in the Bible
–Nicodemus . . . Jn 3:1
–Gamaliel . . . Ac 5:34
–Paul . . . Ac 23:6; Php 3:5

C. The Pharisees and Jesus
1. Regularly questioned and tested Jesus . . . Lk 11:53–54
–About eating with sinners . . . Mt 9:11; Mk 2:16; Lk 5:30
–About fasting . . . Mt 9:14; Mk 2:18; Lk 5:33
–About failing to keep the Sabbath . . . Mt 12:2; Mk 2:24; Lk 6:2
–About not keeping traditions . . . Mt 15:1–2; Mk 7:5
–About marriage and divorce . . . Mt 19:3; Mk 10:2
–About a woman taken in adultery . . . Jn 8:1–6
–About paying taxes to Caesar . . . Mt 22:15–17; Mk 12:13–15
–About the most important commandment . . . Mt 22:34–36
–About the kingdom of God . . . Lk 17:20–21
–About the validity of Jesus' testimony . . . Jn 8:12–13
–About their own blindness . . . Jn 8:40
–Asked for a miraculous sign . . . Mt 12:38
–Asked for a sign from heaven . . . Mt 16:1; Mk 8:11
2. Criticized Jesus
–Said he was controlled by a demon . . . Mt 9:34; Mt 12:24
–Said he spoke blasphemy . . . Lk 5:21
–Said he failed to keep the Sabbath . . . Lk 6:6–7
–Criticized his association with sinners . . . Lk 7:36–39; Lk 15:1–2
–Criticized his acceptance of praise . . . Lk 19:38–39
3. Desired to get rid of Jesus
–Tried to arrest him . . . Jn 7:32; Jn 18:1–3
–Sought to kill him . . . Mt 12:14; Mk 3:6; Jn 11:46–50
–Asked for soldiers to guard the tomb . . . Mt 27:62–64
4. Some secretly believed in Jesus . . . Jn 12:42–43

D. Jesus criticized the Pharisees
–For their lack of true righteousness . . . Mt 5:20
–For their questionable teachings . . . Mt 16:6,11–12
–For persecuting God's messengers . . . Mt 21:33–46; Mt 23:33–36
–For failing to understand Scripture . . . Mt 22:41–45
–For their hypocrisy . . . Mt 23:1–32; Lk 11:37–44; Lk 18:9–14
–For their lack of concern for people . . . Lk 14:1–14
–For their love of money . . . Lk 16:14–15

PHILIP

A. Disciple of Jesus . . . Mt 10:3; Mk 3:18
–Brought Nathanael to Jesus . . . Jn 1:44–46
–Jesus tested him at the feeding of five thousand . . . Jn 6:5–7
–Introduced Greeks to Jesus . . . Jn 12:20–22
–Wanted to see the Father . . . Jn 14:8–9
–One of the apostles . . . Ac 1:13

B. One of the seven deacons . . . Ac 6:1–7
–Became an evangelist in Samaria . . . Ac 8:5–13
–Witnessed to and baptized an Ethiopian eunuch . . . Ac 8:26–39
–Continued preaching the gospel . . . Ac 8:40
–Had four daughters who prophesied . . . Ac 21:9

PHILISTINES

A. Their identity
–Descendants of Mizraim, son of Ham . . . Ge 10:6,13–14
–Came from Caphtor (Crete) . . . Am 9:7
–Five main cities . . . Jos 13:3; 1Sa 6:17
–Advanced in culture and war techniques . . . 1Sa 13:5–7,19–21
–Their land not fully taken over by Joshua . . . Jos 13:2; Jdg 3:1–3

B. Prominent Philistines
–Abimelech: wanted Rebekah as wife . . . Ge 26:1,7–11
–Delilah: Samson's lover and deceiver . . . Jdg 16:4–20
–Goliath: giant killed by David . . . 1Sa 17:4,41–49
–Achish: king of Gath, friend of David . . . 1Sa 21:10–15; 1Sa 27:1–7

C. Their wars
1. The period of the judges
a. Defeated by Shamgar .... Jdg 3:31
b. Fought Israel at time of Jephthah .... Jdg 10:7–9
c. Fought Israel at time of Samson .... Jdg 13:1,5
See SAMSON
d. Fought Israel at time of Samuel
–Captured the ark in battle 1Sa 4:1–11
–Returned the ark 1Sa 6:1–12
–Defeated by Samuel at Mizpah 1Sa 7:2–14

2. The period of the kings
a. During Saul's reign
–Attacked by Jonathan 1Sa 13:3–7
–Defeated by Jonathan and troops 1Sa 14:1–47
–Defeated after death of Goliath 1Sa 17:1–53
–Two hundred killed by David 1Sa 18:24–27
–Defeated by David 1Sa 19:8; 1Sa 23:1–5
–Attacked King Saul 1Sa 28:1,4–5
–Defeated Israelites; Saul died 1Sa 31:1–7; 1Ch 10:1–7
b. During David's reign
–God promised to defeat them .. 2Sa 3:18
–David's victories over them 2Sa 5:17–25; 2Sa 8:1; 2Sa 21:15–22; 1Ch 14:8–17; 1Ch 18:1; 1Ch 20:4–8
–Exploits of David's mighty men 2Sa 23:9–17; 1Ch 11:12–19
c. Solomon ruled them 1Ki 4:21; 2Ch 9:26
d. Jehoshaphat ruled them 2Ch 17:10–11
e. They defeated Jehoram 2Ch 21:16–17
f. Uzziah defeated them 2Ch 26:6–7
g. They defeated Ahaz 2Ch 28:18
h. Hezekiah defeated them 2Ki 18:8

D. Important data concerning them
–Isaac made treaty with Abimelech .... Ge 26:26–31
–David hid from Saul among them 1Sa 27:1–7; 1Sa 29:1–11
–Prophecies against them .... Isa 14:28–32; Jer 47:1–7; Eze 25:15–17; Am 1:6–8; Zep 2:4–7; Zec 9:5–7
–Promise concerning their salvation .... Ps 87:4

PHINEHAS

A. Son of Eleazar and grandson of Aaron .... Ex 6:25
–Killed Zimri and Cozbi to end plague .... Nu 25:6–15
–Investigated an altar across the Jordan .... Jos 22:13–31

B. Son of Eli, brother of Hophni 1Sa 1:3
–A wicked priest 1Sa 2:12–17
–Scorned his father's rebuke 1Sa 2:22–25
–His death prophesied as a sign to Eli 1Sa 2:30–34
–Brought the ark into battle 1Sa 4:4
–Killed in the battle 1Sa 4:11,17

PHOEBE

–Christian from Cenchrea commended by Paul .... Ro 16:1–2

PIETY

See MEDITATION
SPIRITUALITY

PILATE

–Governor of Judea .... Jn 18:28–29
–Presided over Jesus' trial .... Mt 27:11–26; Mk 15:1–15; Lk 23:1–5,13–25; Jn 18:28–19:16
–Sent Jesus to Herod .... Lk 23:6–12
–Washed his hands as sign of innocence .... Mt 27:24–25
–Consented to Jesus' crucifixion .... Mt 27:15–26; Mk 15:6–15
–Gave body of Jesus to Joseph and Nicodemus .... Mt 27:57–60; Jn 19:38–42
–Authorized a guard at the tomb .... Mt 27:62–66
–His name forever associated with Jesus' death .... Ac 3:13; Ac 4:27; Ac 13:28; 1Ti 6:13

PITY

See COMPASSION
MERCY

POTIPHAR

–Egyptian official who bought Joseph .. Ge 37:36
–Put Joseph in charge of his household .. Ge 39:1–6
–Sent Joseph to prison, unjustly .... Ge 39:7–20

POVERTY

See THE RICH AND THE POOR

POWER

See AUTHORITY

PRAISE

A. Related theme
PRAISE is a theme of Psalms .... Ps 150:6

B. Praising God is a command
1. Commanded throughout the Bible
–In the law of God .... Dt 8:10
–In the prophets .... 1Ch 29:20; Isa 61:11; Jer 20:13; Joel 2:26
–In the psalms .... Ps 103:1; Ps 104:1; Ps 145–150
–In the New Testament .... Eph 1:3,6,12,14; 1Pe 1:3,7; Rev 19:5

2. Praise is commanded of:
–God's people .... Ps 30:4; Ps 135:1–2,19–21
–Children .... Ps 8:2; Mt 21:16
–The nations .... Ps 67:3–5; Ps 117:1; Ro 15:11
–The angels .... Ps 103:20; Ps 148:2
–Everything that breathes .... Ps 150:6
–All creation .... Ps 98:8; Ps 148:3–12; Isa 44:23

C. Reasons for praise
- –God's greatness.................... Ps 145:3
- –God's splendor and majesty........ Ps 96:4–6
- –God's glory....................... Ps 66:1–2
- –God's holiness.................... Ps 99:3; Isa 6:3
- –God's love and faithfulness .... Ps 57:9–10; Ps 89:1–2
- –God's acts of power .... Ps 150:2
- –God's marvelous deeds .... Isa 25:1
- –God's glorious grace............... Eph 1:6
- –God's salvation .... Ps 106:1–5; Lk 1:68–75; Lk 2:14,20
- –God's benefits to his people .... Ps 103:1–18; Ps 111:1–10; Isa 63:7
- –God's deliverance of us .... Ps 40:1–3; Ps 124:6–8

D. Methods of praise
- –By public worship................... Ps 100:4
- –By singing .... Ps 146:1; Ps 147:1
- –By musical instruments............ Ps 150:3–5
- –By speaking........................ Ps 51:15; Heb 13:15
- –By dancing......................... Ps 149:3
- –By witnessing to unbelievers....... 1Pe 2:9

PRAYER

–Communication with God

A. Related themes
- PRAYER is a theme of Luke......... Lk 11:1
- PRAY AND WORK is a theme of Nehemiah....................... Neh 4:9

B. What is prayer?
- –Calling on the name of the Lord.... Ge 4:26; Ge 12:8; Zep 3:9
- –Calling to God..................... Ps 4:1,3; Ps 17:6
- –Seeking God's face................ 2Ch 7:14; Ps 27:8
- –Seeking the Lord .... Ps 34:4; Isa 55:6
- –Crying out to God................. Ps 3:4; Ps 66:1
- –Lifting up the soul to God.......... Ps 25:1; Ps 86:4
- –Lifting up one's hands to God ...... Ps 28:2; Ps 141:2
- –Approaching God's throne of grace..................... Heb 4:16
- –Drawing near to God............... Heb 10:22

C. To whom should we pray?
- –To God........................... 2Ch 20:5–6; Ezr 9:6; Ac 4:24
- –To the Father .... Eph 1:17; Eph 3:14; Col 1:3
- –To the Lord....................... 2Ch 20:5–6; Ac 4:24; 2Co 12:8
- –To Jesus Christ .... Lk 23:42; Ac 7:59

D. What are the elements of prayer?
- –Praise............................ Ps 150; Mt 11:25–26
  - *See* PRAISE
- –Thanksgiving .... Ps 136; Php 4:6
  - *See* THANKSGIVING
- –Confession........................ Ps 51; Mt 6:12
  - *See* CONFESSION
- –Intercession .... Ps 122:6–9; Jn 17:6–26
  - *See* INTERCESSION
- –Petition.......................... Ps 27:7–12; Mt 26:39,42
  - See PETITION

E. How should we pray?

1. Divine elements
   - –Through Jesus Christ .... Ro 1:8; Col 3:17
   - –In the name of Jesus Christ ...... Jn 14:13–14; Eph 5:20
   - –In the Holy Spirit .... Eph 6:18; Jude 20
2. Human elements
   - –In the fear of the Lord .... Ps 145:19; Pr 1:28–29
   - –In faith.......................... Mk 11:24; Jas 1:6; Jas 5:15
   - –In humility 2Ch 7:14; 2Ch 33:12–13
   - –In repentance.................... 2Ch 6:37; Ac 3:19
   - –With all our heart................ Dt 4:29; Jer 29:13
   - –With a heart free from sin .... Ps 66:18–19; Isa 1:15–16; Jn 9:31
   - –With a life free from selfishness .... Lk 18:9–14; Jas 4:3
   - –With a heart free from doubt..... Mt 21:21; Jas 1:5–7
   - –With a forgiving spirit........... Mt 6:14–15; Mk 11:25
   - –With confidence .... Eph 3:12; Heb 10:19,35; 1Jn 3:21–22
   - –With persistence................. Lk 11:5–10; Lk 18:1–7; 1Th 5:17
   - –With sincerity and simplicity..... Mt 6:5–8; Mk 12:38–40
   - –In accordance with God's will.... Mt 26:42; 1Jn 5:14
   - –By accompanying prayer with obedience 1Jn 3:22

F. Does God answer the prayers of his people?

1. Remarkable answers to prayers
   - –Abraham's servant for a wife for Isaac...................... Ge 24:12–27
   - –Moses for the defeat of Amalek..................... Ex 17:8–13
   - –Gideon and his fleece .... Jdg 6:36–40
   - –Samson for strength .... Jdg 16:25–30
   - –Hannah for a child.............. 1Sa 1:9–20
   - –Elijah for return to life of a dead boy.................... 1Ki 17:19–23
   - –Elijah for fire from heaven....... 1Ki 18:30–38
   - –Elijah for rain .... 1Ki 18:41–45; Jas 5:17–18
   - –Elisha for return to life of a dead boy.................... 2Ki 4:32–35
   - –Hezekiah for healing............. 2Ki 20:1–7
   - –Daniel for safety in the lions' den .... Da 6:10,16–22
   - –Zechariah for a child............. Lk 1:7,11–17
   - –The thief on the cross for salvation .... Lk 23:42–43
   - –Early Christians for Peter in prison .... Ac 12:3–11
   - –Paul and Silas in prison .... Ac 16:25–26

2. God's promises to answer us
   - –In the Old Testament . . . Ps 86:7; Isa 30:19; Isa 58:9
   - –In the words of Jesus . . . Mt 7:7–11; Jn 14:13–14
   - –In New Testament letters . . . Jas 1:5–8; 1Jn 5:14–15

3. The basis of God's answers
   - –God's glory . . . Nu 14:13–16; Jn 17:1–5
   - –God's grace . . . Ex 32:31–32; Nu 14:17–19; Isa 30:19; 2Co 12:8–9
   - –God's faithfulness to his word . . . Ex 32:12–13; 2Ch 20:7–9

4. The manner of God's answers
   - –Sometimes immediately . . . Nu 14:20; 1Ki 17:20–21; Lk 23:43
   - –Sometimes after a delay . . . Lk 18:1–7
   - –Sometimes more than asked for . . 1Ki 18:24,36–38; Eph 3:20
   - –Sometimes different from the request . . . 1Ki 19:1–9; 2Co 12:7–9
   - –Sometimes "No" . . . 2Sa 12:15–20
   - –God requires action on our part . . Neh 4:9

G. Various aspects of prayer

1. Postures of prayer
   - –Standing . . . 1Ki 8:22; Neh 9:4–5
   - –Sitting . . . 1Ch 17:16; Lk 10:13
   - –Kneeling . . . Ezr 9:5; Da 6:10; Ac 20:36
   - –Bowing down . . . Ex 34:8; Ps 5:7; Ps 95:6
   - –Lying on the ground . . . 2Sa 12:16; Mt 26:39
   - –Lifting up hands . . . Ps 28:2; Isa 1:15; 1Ti 2:8

2. Manner of prayer
   - –Alone, silently . . . 1Sa 1:18
   - –Alone, aloud . . . Eze 11:13
   - –With two or three . . . Mt 18:19
   - –In a larger group . . . Ps 35:18

3. Time of prayer
   - –In the morning . . . Ps 5:1–3; Mk 1:35
   - –In the evening . . . Ge 24:63
   - –At fixed times . . . Ps 55:17; Da 6:10
   - –Always . . . Lk 18:1; Ro 1:10; 1Th 5:17

4. Possible places of prayer
   - –In secret . . . Mt 6:6
   - –In bed . . . Ps 63:6
   - –In a family setting . . . Ac 10:1–2
   - –Out in the open . . . Ge 24:11–12
   - –In the battlefield . . . Jos 10:12–13
   - –By the riverside . . . Ac 16:13
   - –In the temple . . . 2Ki 19:14
   - –In the church gathered together . . Ac 4:23–24,31
   - –Anywhere . . . 1Ti 2:8

PREACHING

A. Preachers in the Bible

1. Old Testament saints who preached
   - –Noah . . . 2Pe 2:5
   - –Jonah . . . Jnh 1:2; Jnh 3:2
   - –Isaiah . . . Isa 61:1
   - –Ezekiel . . . Eze 21:2
   - –Amos . . . Am 7:16
   - –Haggai and Zechariah . . . Ezr 6:14

2. New Testament saints who preached
   - –John the Baptist . . . Mt 3:1
   - –Jesus . . . Mt 4:17
   - –Peter and John . . . Ac 8:25
   - –Philip . . . Ac 8:40
   - –Paul . . . Ac 9:27; 1Co 9:16
   - –Timothy . . . 1Ti 4:13
   - –Numerous believers . . . Ac 8:4; Ac 15:35
   - –All Christians . . . Mt 28:19; Mk 16:15

B. The content of preaching

1. In the Old Testament
   - –A message of judgment . . . Eze 20:46; Eze 21:2; Am 7:16; Jnh 3:4
   - –A message of hope . . . Isa 40:1–2,9; Isa 52:7–10; Am 9:11–15

2. In the New Testament
   - –The good news of the kingdom . . . Lk 9:2; Lk 16:16; Ac 20:25
   - –The good news of salvation . . . 1Co 1:21; 1Co 15:1–2
   - –The cross of Christ . . . 1Co 2:1–2
   - –The resurrection of Christ . . . Ac 17:18,31; 1Co 15:12–14
   - –Jesus Christ is Lord . . . 2Co 4:5
   - –Fulfillment of the Scriptures in Christ . . . Ac 2:14–36; Ac 4:12–26; Ac 13:16–41; 1Co 15:3–5
   - –The coming judgment . . . Ac 10:42; Ac 17:31
   - –The call to repent and believe . . . Mk 1:15; Ac 2:38; Ac 10:43; Ac 26:20

PREDESTINATION

See ELECTION
PROVIDENCE

PRIDE

A. Legitimate pride

1. Occasions for such pride
   - –Boasting in the Lord . . . Ps 34:2; Ps 44:8; Jer 9:24; 1Co 1:31
   - –Boasting in the cross of Christ . . . Gal 6:14
   - –Boasting about God-fearing churches . . . 2Co 1:14; 2Co 7:4; Php 2:16

2. The glory of such pride
   - –Must be in God's grace . . . 2Co 1:12
   - –Must be in Jesus Christ . . . Ro 15:17–18
   - –Must be in the Holy Spirit . . . Ro 15:18–19

B. Sinful pride

1. Characteristics of a proud person
   - –Tries to be like God . . . Ge 3:5–6

–Remembers his promises .... Ps 105:42
–Keeps his promises .... Jos 23:15
Isa 38:7
Ac 13:23,32–33
2Pe 3:9
–Is faithful to his promises 1Th 5:24
Heb 10:23
–Fulfills all his promises in Christ ... 2Co 1:18,20
–God's promises never fail 1Ki 8:56

C. Believers and God's promises
–We have them from God 2Co 7:1
–We must believe them .... Ps 106:12,24
Ro 4:16–21
–We must share in them .... Eph 3:6
–We must rejoice in them .... Ps 119:162
–We must meditate on them .... Ps 119:148
–We must not fall short of them .... Heb 4:1

PROPHET

A. Related themes
1. PROPHETS is a theme of:
–1 Kings 1Ki 11:29
–2 Kings 2Ki 6:12
2. FULFILLMENT is a theme of:
–Matthew .... Mt 5:17
–Hebrews .... Heb 7:27

B. How did one become a prophet?
–Called directly by God .... Isa 6:8
Jer 1:4–5
Am 7:14–15
–Inspired by God to prophesy 1Sa 10:6,9–11
1Sa 19:23–24
–Appointed by another prophet 1Ki 19:19–21
–Some joined the company of the prophets 2Ki 2:3,5,7
2Ki 6:1–4

C. What did a prophet do?
1. Spoke messages from God to the people
–God commanded them to speak .. Dt 18:18
Jnh 3:2
–The Spirit moved them to speak .. 2Pe 1:21
–They said, "This is what the Lord says" .... Isa 44:6
Jer 6:16
2. Served as watchmen for the people .... Jer 6:16–17
Eze 3:16–21
3. Pointed out the sins of kings 2Sa 12:1–12
1Ki 18:18–19
4. Pronounced judgment on the people 1Ki 21:20–24
Isa 2:6–21
Jer 4:5–18
5. Predicted the future 1Sa 9:9
–The near future 1Ki 17:1
Ac 11:28
–The distant future .... Isa 65:17–25
Joel 2:28–32
Mic 5:2–5
Lk 24:25–27
6. Called the people to repentance 2Ki 17:13
Jer 18:11
Amos5:4–6,14–15
7. Gave hope to the people .... Jer 23:3–8
Am 9:11–15
Zep 3:9–17
8. Interpreted dreams .... Da 2:17–45
Da 3:9–28
9. Wrote down messages from God ... Jer 30:2
Hab 2:2
Rev 1:11,19

D. Tests for determining the true prophet
–Does the prophecy come true? .... Dt 18:21–22
Jer 28:1–17
–Does it correspond with God's word? .... Dt 13:1–3
1Ki 22:17–28,37
1Jn 4:1–3
–Does the prophet live a God-fearing life? .... Jer 23:9–18
2Pe 2:1–3,13–18

E. Responses to the prophets
1. Positive
–They were to be heeded .... Dt 18:15
–They were to be trusted 2Ch 20:20
2. Negative
–They were often persecuted 2Ch 36:16
Ac 7:52
–They were sometimes put in prison 2Ch 18:25–26
Jer 37:15–16
–They were even killed 1Ki 19:10
Mt 21:35–36
1Th 2:15

F. Jesus Christ as God's final prophet
–He fulfilled God's promise of a prophet .... Dt 18:15,18
Ac 3:21–23
Ac 7:37
–He fulfilled all Old Testament prophecies .... Mt 5:17
2Co 1:20
1Pe 1:10–11
–He is called "The Prophet" .... Jn 6:14–15
Jn 7:40
–He called himself a prophet .... Mt 13:57
Lk 13:33
–He perfectly spoke God's word .... Jn 7:16
Jn 12:49–50
Heb 1:1–2
–He is the Word of God in human flesh .... Jn 1:14

G. Prophets in the New Testament church
1. Names
–Agabus .... Ac 11:28
Ac 21:10
–Judas and Silas .... Ac 15:32
–Twelve men in Ephesus .... Ac 19:6
–Daughters of Philip .... Ac 21:9
–Paul 1Co 13:2
1Th 4:13–17
–Peter 2Pe 3:10–13
–John .... Rev 1:1
2. Prophecy as a gift of the Spirit
–Mentioned by Peter on Pentecost .... Ac 2:17
–Mentioned by Paul 1Co 12:10
1Co 14:1
Eph 4:11
–Distinct from the gift of teaching .... Ac 13:1
1Co 12:28
Eph 4:11
3. Function of prophets in the church
–Served as foundation of the church .... Eph 2:20
–Their gift preferred to tongues ... 1Co 14:1–5
–Message must edify the church ... 1Co 14:4–5,12
–Message must reach unbelievers 1Co 14:23–25
–Message must be tested by other prophets 1Co 14:29–32
1Th 5:19–20
1Jn 4:1

PROVIDENCE

–God's care over creation and his control of history

A. Related themes

1. PROVIDENCE is a theme of:
   - –Numbers .... Nu 21:3
   - –Ruth .... Ru 4:14
   - –Ezra .... Ezr 8:31
   - –Esther .... Est 6:4
2. PLAN OF GOD is a theme of:
   - –Luke .... Lk 16:16
   - –Ephesians .... Eph 1:10
3. GOD'S CONTROL is a theme of:
   - –Jeremiah .... Jer 10:10
   - –Daniel .... Da 4:35
   - –Habakkuk .... Hab 2:13
   - –Zechariah .... Zec 12:1
4. GOD'S FREEDOM is a theme of Job .... Job 40:8

B. God's care for his whole creation

1. Aspects of God's providence
   - –Cares for all his creatures .... Ps 145:9; Mt 10:29
   - –Provides food for his creatures ... Ps 104:14,27–28; Ps 145:16; Mt 6:26
   - –Preserves his creatures .... Neh 9:6; Ps 36:6
   - –Determines the events of history .. Ge 50:20; Ps 33:10–11; Ac 2:22–23
   - –Determines the ways of humans ... Pr 16:1,9; Pr 19:21
   - –Controls everything that happens ... Isa 40:22–26; Da 4:35; Ac 17:26; Eph 1:11
   - –Controls the weather .... Ps 68:9; Mt 5:45; Ac 14:15–17
   - –Controls the smallest details ..... Mt 10:29–30
   - –Controls evil .... Job 2:1–8; Isa 14:24–27; Isa 45:7; Am 3:6
2. Means of God's control
   - –By his powerful word .... Ps 29:3–9; Heb 1:3
   - –By Jesus Christ .... Col 1:17

C. God's special care for his own people

1. General statements .... Ps 91:1–16; Isa 31:5; Ro 8:35–39; 1Pe 3:12
2. Specific statements
   - –Opens hearts to believe the gospel .... Lk 24:45; Ac 16:14
   - –Controls specific events .... Ge 22:8,13–14; Ps 105:5–44; Ps 136:10–24; Isa 38:17
   - –Works for good of those who love him .... Ge 50:20; Ro 8:28

D. Our response to God's providence

- –Acknowledge it 1Sa 2:6–10; 1Ch 29:11–12
- –Rejoice in it .... Ps 4:7–8; Ps 16:7–11
- –Trust in it .... Ps 13:6; Ps 28:7
- –Humble ourselves in the face of it ... Dt 8:2–3; Job 1:20–22; Job 42:1–6
- –Do not worry about tomorrow .... Mt 6:25–34; Mt 10:28–31

PUNISHMENT

–Penalty inflicted because of sin

A. Related theme

CYCLES is a theme of Judges .... Jdg 10:6

B. Human punishment through law

1. Principles of punishment
   - –Power to punish given to government .... Ro 13:4
   - –Eye for eye, tooth for tooth .... Ex 21:23–25; Lev 24:19–20; Dt 19:21
   - –Restitution to be made .... Ex 22:1–9; Nu 5:5–8
   - –Must be impartial .... Lev 24:22; Dt 1:16–17
   - –Innocent must be acquitted .... Dt 25:1
2. Methods of punishment
   - a. Non-capital punishments
     - –Fines .... Ex 21:22; Am 2:8
     - –Confiscation of property .... Ezr 7:26
     - –Beating .... Dt 25:2–3; 2Co 11:23–25
     - –Gouging out eyes .... Jdg 16:21
     - –Imprisonment .... 1Ki 22:27; Ac 12:4
     - –Confinement in a dungeon .... Jer 38:6
     - –Chains .... 2Ki 23:33; Php 1:7,13
     - –Banishment .... Ezr 7:26; Rev 1:9
     - –Excommunication from synagogue .... Jn 9:22; Jn 16:2
   - b. Capital punishment
     - –Stoning .... Dt 22:24; Ac 7:59
     - –Burning .... Lev 20:14
     - –The sword .... Ac 12:2; Heb 11:37
     - –Hanging .... Est 7:9–10
     - –Crucifixion .... Mk 15:20,24
     - –Beheading .... Ge 40:19
     - –Cutting in pieces .... Heb 11:37
     - –Throwing to wild beasts .... Da 6:16,24

C. God's punishment

1. Basic reasons for God's punishment
   - –Human sin .... Am 1:3–2:16; Ro 6:23
   - –Idolatry .... 2Ki 17:14–20; Jer 2:9–13
   - –Disobedience to God's law .... Dt 28:15–68; Neh 9:26–27
2. Methods of God's punishments
   - a. Temporal
     - –Sickness 2Ch 26:19–20
     - –Death of a loved one 2Sa 12:14
     - –Drought 1Ki 17:1
     - –Famine .... La 2:11–12
     - –Violent storms .... Jnh 1:4
     - –Plagues .... Joel 1:2–11
     - –Defeat by foreign armies .... Jdg 2:10–15
     - –Exile 2Ch 36:15–20
   - b. Eternal punishment

QUEEN

A. Queen of Sheba

- –Came to visit Solomon 1Ki 10:1–2; 2Ch 9:1

–Overwhelmed at Solomon's wisdom ... 1Ki 10:3–9; 2Ch 9:2–8
–Gave Solomon many gifts ... 1Ki 10:10; 2Ch 9:9
–Received gifts from Solomon ... 1Ki 10:13; 2Ch 9:12
–Jesus used her as an example ... Mt 12:42; Lk 11:31

B. Queen Athaliah
See ATHALIAH

C. Queen Vashti
See VASHTI

D. Queen Esther
See ESTHER

E. Queen of Heaven (goddess Ishtar) ... Jer 7:18; Jer 44:17–19,25

F. Babylon pictured as a queen ... Isa 47:5–8; Rev 18:7

RACHEL

–Younger daughter of Laban ... Ge 29:16
–Second wife of Jacob ... Ge 29:28
–Loved by Jacob more than Leah ... Ge 29:30
–Bore two sons ... Ge 30:22–24; Ge 35:16–18,24
–Stole Laban's gods ... Ge 31:19,32–35
–Her death ... Ge 35:19–20
–Prophecy concerning her ... Jer 31:15
–Prophecy fulfilled at the birth of Jesus ... Mt 2:16–18

RAHAB

–Prostitute at Jericho who hid spies ... Jos 2:1–21
–Spared when Jericho was destroyed ... Jos 6:22–25
–Mother of Boaz ... Mt 1:5
–An example of true faith ... Heb 11:31; Jas 2:25–26

RAIN

See WEATHER

RANSOM

See REDEMPTION

REBEKAH

–Sister of Laban ... Ge 24:29
–Secured as bride for Isaac ... Ge 24:34–61
–Mother of Esau and Jacob ... Ge 25:19–26
–Abimelech discovered that she was Isaac's wife ... Ge 26:1–11
–Helped Jacob deceitfully get Isaac's blessing ... Ge 27:1–17
–Convinced Isaac that Jacob should leave ... Ge 27:42–28:4
–Buried in cave of Machpelah ... Ge 49:29–31

RECONCILIATION

–Establishing harmony between conflicting parties

A. The need for reconciliation
1. Between humans
–Adam and Eve argued in Eden ... Ge 3:12–13
–Abram and Lot could not agree ... Ge 13:5–11
–Sarai and Hagar could not get along ... Ge 16:3–6
–Jacob fled from Esau ... Ge 27:41–45
–There will always be conflicts ... Mt 24:6
2. Between God and humans
–Adam and Eve hid from God ... Ge 3:8
–Sinners are hostile to God ... Ro 8:7; Col 1:21
–Sinners cannot stand in God's presence ... Ps 5:5–6
–Isaiah fearful of God's presence ... Isa 6:5
3. Between God and nature
–Nature cursed by God ... Ge 3:14–18
–Nature groans because of sin ... Ro 8:20,22

B. The process of reconciliation
1. Only God can reconcile us to himself
–God took the initiative ... 2Co 5:18
–God reconciles sinners to himself ... 2Co 5:19; Col 1:22
–He reconciles all things to himself ... Eph 1:10; Col 1:20
2. Accomplished through the cross ... Ro 5:10; 2Co 5:18–19; Col 1:22; Heb 2:17
3. Reconciliation among humans rooted in Christ
–Christ is our peace ... Eph 2:14–17
–We are one in Christ ... Jn 17:11,22–23; Gal 3:28; Col 3:11
–Harmony experienced in the early church ... Ac 2:44–45; Ac 4:32–35

C. Believers and reconciliation
1. Reconciliation with God
–We must be reconciled to God ... 2Co 5:20
–We must proclaim reconciliation ... 2Co 5:19–20
2. Reconciliation among believers
–Conflicts resolved in the early church ... Ac 15:1–29; Gal 2:1–10
–We may show no partiality in the church ... Jas 2:1–4,9; 1Pe 1:17
–There may be no divisions in the church ... 1Co 1:10–13; 1Co 11:18–22
–We must work for harmony in the church ... Gal 6:1–2; Eph 4:29–32; Php 2:1–5
–We must end personal conflicts ... Mt 5:23–24; Mt 18:15–16; 1Co 6:1–8; Php 4:2–3

REDEMPTION

–Freedom obtained through a price paid

A. Related theme
REDEMPTION is a theme of Isaiah ... Isa 43:1

B. Redemption among humans
1. Redemption of an Israelite slave
–Slave could redeem himself ... Lev 25:49
–Slave could be redeemed by relatives ... Lev 25:48–49
–Slave released in Year of Jubilee ... Lev 25:54
2. Redemption of property
–A person could redeem his own land ... Lev 25:26–27
–A relative could redeem the land ... Lev 25:25,48–53
–Land returned in the Year of Jubilee ... Lev 25:28,39–43
–Land could be redeemed through marriage ... Ru 4:1–12

C. Redemption by God
  1. Natural redemption for Israelites
    –Israelites were slaves in Egypt … Ge 15:13
      Ex 1:11–14
      Dt 5:15
    –Israelites redeemed through the exodus … Ex 6:6
      2Sa 7:22–24
      Ps 106:8–10
      Mic 6:4
    –Price paid was the destruction of Egypt … Isa 43:3
    –Judah redeemed from Babylon … Isa 54:5–8
      Jer 31:10–11
      Mic 4:10
  2. Spiritual redemption from sin
    a. We need redemption
      –We are all slaves to sin … Jn 8:34
        Ro 6:17
      –Humans cannot redeem themselves … Ps 49:7–8
    b. God redeemed the Israelites … Ps 130:8
      Isa 44:21–22
      Lk 1:68–71
    c. Christ redeems us
      –Redemption accomplished in Christ … Ro 3:24
        Col 1:13–14
      –The ransom paid was his blood … Eph 1:7
        1Pe 1:19
        Rev 5:9
      –The ransom paid was his death … Mk 10:45
        Heb 9:15
        1Ti 2:6
    d. The purpose of redemption
      –To justify us before God … Ro 3:24
      –To free us from wickedness … Ro 6:7,22
        Titus 2:14
      –To free us from the law … Gal 4:5
      –To free us from the curse … Gal 3:13
      –To free us from an empty way of life … 1Pe 1:18
    e. The results of redemption
      –We are forgiven … Eph 1:7
        Col 1:14
      –We can now live free lives … Gal 5:1,13
      –We can now serve God … 1Pe 2:16
      –We await our final redemption … Lk 21:27–28
        Ro 8:23
        Eph 1:14

REGENERATION
See BORN AGAIN

REHOBOAM
–Son of Solomon; king of Judah … 1Ki 11:43
  1Ch 3:10
–Had various wives … 2Ch 11:18–21
–Was asked to lighten Israelite yoke … 1Ki 12:1–4
  2Ch 10:1–4
–Refused to ease the Israelites' burden … 1Ki 12:5–15
  2Ch 10:5–15
–Caused division in the kingdom … 1Ki 12:16–24
  2Ch 10:16–19
–Told not to fight to regain ten tribes … 2Ch 11:1–4
–Built up defenses of Judah … 2Ch 11:5–12
–Supported by Levites from Israel … 2Ch 11:13–17
–Led Judah into idolatry … 1Ki 14:21–24
  2Ch 12:1,14
–Fought with Shishak of Egypt … 1Ki 14:25–28
  2Ch 12:2–11
–Humbled himself … 2Ch 12:12
–His death … 1Ki 14:31
  2Ch 12:16

REJOICE
See JOY

REMEMBER
A. Human remembrance
  1. Examples of what humans must remember
    –The day of the exodus … Ex 13:3
    –The Sabbath day … Ex 20:8
    –God's care during forty years in the wilderness … Dt 8:2
    –Rebellion against God … Dt 9:7
    –The power of God … Neh 4:14
    –The miracles of God … Ps 77:11
    –The name of God … Ps 119:55
    –The Creator … Ecc 12:1,6
    –The body and blood of the Lord … 1Co 11:24–25
    –The poor … Gal 2:10
    –The stranger … Heb 13:2
  2. What do humans do when they remember?
    –They celebrate the Passover … Ex 13:3–10
    –They keep the Sabbath holy … Ex 20:8
    –They trust God … Dt 8:17–18
    –They obey and serve God … Dt 10:12–13
    –They fight for the Lord … Neh 4:14
    –They meditate on God and his mighty acts … Ps 77:11–20
    –They keep God's law … Ps 119:55
    –They fear God and obey his commandments … Ecc 12:13
    –They celebrate the Lord's Supper … 1Co 11:26–29
    –They give on behalf of the poor … Gal 2:10
    –They show hospitality … Heb 13:2
B. Divine remembrance
  1. Examples of what/whom God remembers
    –His covenant with Noah … Ge 9:14–15
    –His covenant with Abraham … Ex 2:23–25
      Ps 105:8
    –His promises … Ps 105:42
    –His love and faithfulness … Ps 98:3
    –Noah … Ge 8:1
    –Abraham … Ge 19:29
    –Rachel … Ge 30:22
    –Hannah … 1Sa 1:19–20
    –The wickedness of his people … Jer 14:10
      Hos 8:13
  2. What does God do when he remembers?
    –He spares the world from a flood … Ge 9:14–15
    –He rescues his people from Egypt … Ex 3:7–9
      Ps 105:43–44
    –He saves his people … Ps 98:3
    –He dries up the earth … Ge 8:1
    –He brings Lot out of Sodom … Ge 19:29
    –He gives children to barren women … Ge 30:22–24
      1Sa 1:20
    –He punishes sin … Jer 14:10
      Hos 8:13

See also FORGET

REMNANT
–A small but faithful number of God's people preserved

A. Basis of God's promise to keep a remnant
  –The honor of his name … 1Sa 12:22
  –His promise to Abraham … Ge 17:7
  –His promise to David … 1Ki 6:13
B. God kept his promise to preserve a remnant
  –Remnant kept at the time of Elijah … 1Ki 19:18
    Ro 11:4

–A remnant of Israel joined with Judah.......... 2Ch 30:25; 2Ch 34:9; Isa 10:20–22; Ro 9:27–29
–The entire nation of Judah was a remnant.......... 2Ki 17:18; Hos 1:7
–Remnant preserved from Assyria.......... 2Ki 19:4,29–31; Mic 5:6–8
–Remnant kept after Jerusalem was destroyed.......... 2Ch 36:20; Jer 40:11; Jer 42:2; Eze 11:13
–Remnant returned from the exile.......... Ezr 9:8,13–15; Neh 1:2; Jer 23:3; Eze 34:12–14; Hag 1:12,14
–Believing Jews were a remnant of Israel.......... Ro 11:5

C. God's promise to preserve the church
–Promise of Jesus to Peter.......... Mt 16:18
–Promise of Jesus for the end times.......... Mt 24:21–22
–Remnant preserved in Thyatira.......... Rev 2:24–25
–Remnant preserved in Sardis.......... Rev 3:4–5

REPENTANCE

–Sorrow for sin and turning to God

A. Related themes
REPENTANCE is a theme of:
–Joel.......... Joel 2:13
–Zechariah.......... Zec 1:3

B. The command to repent
–God calls all people to repent.......... Jer 18:11; Eze 18:30–32; Ac 17:30; 2Pe 3:9
–Christ calls people to repent.......... Mk 1:14–15; Lk 13:1–5; Rev 2:5,16; Rev 3:3
–John the Baptist called people to repent.......... Mt 3:2
–The apostles called people to repent.......... Mk 6:12; Ac 2:38; Ac 3:19–20; Ac 26:20
–The call must go out today.......... Lk 24:46–48

C. Essential aspects of repentance
–Acknowledging we are lost.......... Lk 15:3–7
–Expressing sorrow for sin.......... Lk 5:32; Ac 2:37–38; Ac 8:22; 2Co 7:9–10
–Returning to the Father.......... Lk 15:17–20
–Believing in Jesus Christ.......... Mk 1:15; Ac 20:21; Rev 3:19–20
–Doing good works.......... Jer 18:11–12; Mt 3:8; Ac 26:20; Rev 2:4–5

D. The results of repentance
–Escape from disaster.......... Jer 18:7–8
–Forgiveness.......... 1Ki 8:46–50; Ac 2:38
–Salvation.......... 2Co 7:10
–A new heart and spirit.......... Eze 18:30–31
–A knowledge of the truth.......... 2Ti 2:25
–Eternal life.......... Ac 11:18
–Regret without repentance brings death.......... Mt 27:3–5; 2Co 7:10

REPTILES

A. Reptiles mentioned in the Bible
–Adder.......... Isa 30:6
–Chameleon.......... Lev 11:30
–Cobra.......... Isa 11:8
–Frog.......... Ex 8:2–13
–Gecko.......... Lev 11:30
–Lizard.......... Lev 11:29–30
–Serpent.......... Job 26:13
–Snake.......... Ps 58:4
–Viper.......... Ac 28:3
–Worm.......... Jnh 4:7

B. Serpents and snakes used symbolically
–As a symbol of healing.......... Nu 21:8–9; Jn 3:14–15
–As a symbol of shrewdness.......... Mt 10:16
–As a symbol of alcohol's effects.......... Pr 23:31–32
–As a symbol of hypocrites.......... Mt 23:23; Lk 3:7–8
–As a symbol of evil people.......... Dt 32:33; Ps 140:1–3
–As a symbol of God's judgment.......... Nu 21:6–7; Isa 14:28–29
–As a symbol of Satan.......... Ge 3:1–5; Rev 12:9; Rev 20:2

REST

A. Types of rest
–The Sabbath day.......... Ex 20:8–11
–Sleep.......... Pr 3:23–24
–Life in the land of Canaan.......... Jos 1:13
–Absence of war.......... 1Ch 22:9
–Getting away from trouble.......... Ps 55:6–8
–Getting away from people.......... Mk 6:31
–Death.......... 1Ki 2:10; 1Th 4:13,15
–Heaven as the land of rest.......... Heb 4:8–11; Rev 14:13

B. The human need for rest
–Because of six days of work.......... Ex 20:8–10
–Because of fatigue.......... Mt 8:24; Mt 26:43
–Because of overwork.......... Mk 6:30–31
–Because of depression.......... 1Ki 19:3–6
–Because of anxiety.......... Ecc 2:22–23; 2Co 2:13
–Because of the storms of life.......... Job 3:20–26; Ps 55:4–8

C. The realization of true rest
–Through trusting in God.......... Ps 37:3–7; Ps 91:1–2
–Through resting in God.......... Ps 23:1–3; Ps 62:1,5
–Through experiencing God's presence.......... Ex 33:14; Ps 31:19–20
–Through coming to Jesus.......... Mt 11:28–29; Jn 16:33
–Through the Spirit of God.......... Isa 63:14

RESURRECTION

–Resuscitation of a dead body

A. The resurrection of Christ
1. Prophecies of Christ's resurrection
a. The Old Testament in general.......... Lk 24:25–26, 44–46; Jn 20:9; 1Co 15:4

b. Specific prophecies in the Old Testament
–David .... Ps 16:3–11
Ac 2:24–32
–Isaiah .... Isa 55:3
Ac 13:34
–Jonah .... Jnh 1:17
Mt 12:39–40
c. Prophesied by Jesus before his death .... Mk 8:31
Mk 9:9,31
Mk 10:33–34
Jn 2:19–22
2. The event of Christ's resurrection ... Mt 28:1–7
Mk 16:1–8
Lk 24:1–8
Jn 20:1–8
3. The power used to raise Christ
–The power of God .... Ac 2:24
Eph 1:19–20
Col 2:12
–Christ's own power .... Jn 10:18
–Jesus is the resurrection .... Jn 11:25–26
–The power of the Spirit .... Ro 8:11
1Pe 3:18
4. The nature of Christ's resurrected body
a. The same body that died was raised .... Lk 24:39–40
Jn 20:27
b. It was a physical body
–He ate .... Lk 24:41–43
Jn 21:12–13
Ac 10:40–41
–He could be touched .... Jn 20:27
1Jn 1:1
c. It was a glorified body 1Co 15:42–44
Php 3:21
–He passed through locked doors .... Jn 20:19,26
–He ascended into heaven .... Ac 1:9
5. The appearances of the risen Christ
–To Mary Magdalene .... Mk 16:9
Jn 20:10–18
–To several women .... Mt 28:8–10
–To Peter .... Lk 24:34
1Co 15:5
–To two disciples going to Emmaus .... Lk 24:13–31
–To a group of disciples .... Lk 24:36–44
–To the disciples, minus Thomas .. Jn 20:19–25
–To the disciples, with Thomas .... Jn 20:26–29
1Co 15:5
–To disciples at the Sea of Tiberias .... Jn 21:1–14
–To the disciples in Galilee .... Mt 28:16–20
–To a group of five hundred 1Co 15:6
–To James 1Co 15:7
–To all the apostles in Jerusalem .. Ac 1:4–9
1Co 15:7
–To Paul .... Ac 9:3–6
1Co 15:8
–Jesus gave many convincing proofs .... Ac 1:3
6. The significance of Christ's resurrection
–Declares his deity .... Ro 1:4
–Declares his Lordship .... Ro 10:9
–Justifies us .... Ro 4:25
–Forgives us 1Co 15:17
–Saves us .... Ro 10:9
1Pe 3:21
–Gives us living hope 1Co 15:18–19
1Pe 1:3
–Gives us victory over death .... Ro 6:9–11
1Co 15:57
–Guarantees our resurrection 1Co 15:20,23
Php 3:10–11
–Guarantees the coming judgment Ac 17:31
7. The proclamation of Christ's resurrection
–Proclaimed by angels .... Mt 28:5–7
Lk 24:3–7
–Acknowledged by Christ's enemies .... Mt 28:11–15
–Preached by Peter .... Ac 2:24–32
Ac 10:40–41
–Preached by Paul .... Ac 13:30–37
Ac 17:31
1Co 15:3–5

B. The resurrection of humans
1. Resurrection miracles
a. In the Old Testament
–By Elijah 1Ki 17:17–23
–By Elisha 2Ki 4:19–37
2Ki 13:21
b. In the New Testament
–By Jesus .... Mk 5:38–42
Lk 7:11–15
Jn 11:38–44
–At Jesus' death .... Mt 27:52–53
–By Peter .... Ac 9:32–35
–By Paul .... Ac 20:9–10
–In Hebrews .... Heb 11:35
2. The resurrection at the last day
a. Affirmed in the Old Testament ... Job 19:26
Ps 16:10
Isa 26:19
Da 12:2
b. Affirmed in the New Testament
–Believed by the Jews .... Jn 11:24
Ac 23:6
Ac 24:15
–Denied by the Sadducees .... Mt 22:23
Ac 23:7–8
–Prophesied by Jesus .... Mk 12:26–27
Jn 5:28–29
Jn 5:39,44
–Proclaimed by the apostles .... Ac 24:14–15
Ro 2:7–8
Ro 8:11
1Co 15:50–57
1Th 4:13–17
Rev 20:4–5,12–13
3. The nature of the resurrection
a. For believers
–Have already risen to a new life .... Ro 6:3–4
Eph 2:6
Col 2:12
–Will rise first 1Th 4:6
Rev 20:4–5
–Will receive bodies like Christ's .... Php 3:21
1Jn 3:2
–Will receive imperishable bodies 1Co 15:42
–Will receive glorious bodies ... 1Co 15:43
–Will receive spiritual bodies ... 1Co 15:44
b. For unbelievers
–Will go to everlasting contempt .... Da 12:2
–Will be condemned .... Jn 5:28–29
–Will be judged .... Rev 20:14–15

REUBEN

A. Firstborn of Jacob by Leah .... Ge 35:23
1Ch 2:1
–Name means "He has seen my misery" .... Ge 29:32

–Slept with his father's concubine ... Ge 35:22
Ge 49:4
–Attempted to rescue Joseph ... Ge 37:21–30
–Went to Egypt with family ... Ge 46:8–9
–Father of four sons ... Ge 46:9
–Blessed by Jacob ... Ge 49:3–4
B. Tribe descended from Reuben
–Blessed by Moses ... Dt 33:6
–Numbered ... Nu 1:21
Nu 26:7
–Allotted land east of the Jordan ... Nu 32:1–33
Nu 34:14
–Allotted land west of the Jordan ... Eze 48:6
–Failed to help Deborah ... Jdg 5:15–16
–Supported David ... 1Ch 12:37
–One of the tribes of the 144,000 ... Rev 7:5

REVELATION

–God's disclosure of himself and his truth

A. God's revelation in nature
–It reveals God's glory ... Ps 19:1–6
–It reveals God's kindness ... Ac 14:17
–It proclaims his majesty ... Ps 8:1
–It proclaims his righteousness ... Ps 50:6
Ps 97:6
–It proclaims his eternal power ... Ro 1:19–20
B. God's special revelation to his people
1. Direct revelation
–By speaking ... Ge 17:1–2
Ex 33:11
Rev 1:10–11
–By dreams ... Ge 20:3
Nu 12:6
–By visions ... Ge 15:1
Job 33:14–15
2Co 12:1–4
2. Revelation in events of Bible history ... Dt 3:24
Eze 6:13–14
Eze 37:13–14
3. Revelation in his written word
–God revealed to prophets ... 2Ti 3:15–16
2Pe 1:21
–God revealed to apostles ... 1Co 2:10
2Co 12:7
2Pe 3:15
4. His key revelation is Jesus Christ
–Jesus reveals the Father ... Jn 1:18
Jn 14:9
Heb 1:1–2
–Jesus is the Word of God ... Jn 1:1,14
Rev 19:11–13
C. God's continuing revelation to the church
–Revelation is a gift of the Spirit ... 1Co 14:26
Eph 1:17
–Revelations must witness to Christ ... 1Co 12:3
–Revelations must be evaluated by the church ... 1Co 14:29–32
See also DREAMS AND VISIONS
WORD OF GOD

REWARD

–What God has in store for humans

A. In the Old Testament
1. Rewarded according to one's deeds
–Stated in the law ... Lev 26:3–39
Dt 28:1–68
–Stated in the psalms ... Ps 19:11
Ps 28:4
Ps 62:12
–Stated in Proverbs ... Pr 1:29–31
Pr 12:14
Pr 14:14
–Stated in the prophets ... Isa 59:18
Isa 66:6
Jer 17:10
Jer 21:13–14
Eze 9:9–10
2. Cannot always be applied to this life Job 1:1–2:10
Job 9:21–22
Ps 73:1–14
Ecc 9:1–12
3. God does not treat us as our sin deserves ... Ezr 9:13
Job 33:26–28
Ps 103:8–10
4. God's final reward is in the world to come ... Ps 73:16–20
Ecc 12:13–14
B. In the New Testament
1. Whom does God reward with good?
–Those who receive God's grace ... Ro 6:23
Ro 11:6
–Those who believe in Jesus ... Jn 14:1–3
Ro 4:5,16
–Those who have an obedient faith ... Lk 14:12–14
1Co 3:8,12–14
Eph 6:8
Col 3:23–24
Jas 2:14–24
–Those persecuted for Jesus' sake ... Mt 5:11–12
2. Do we earn our reward?
–We inherit our reward ... Mt 25:34
Ac 20:32
Col 1:12
Rev 21:7
–Good works are not done for r
ewards ... Mt 6:1–6,16–18
Lk 17:7–10
3. What is our reward?
–A crown of righteousness ... 2Ti 4:8
–A crown of glory ... 1Pe 5:4
–A crown of life ... Jas 1:12
–A crown that lasts forever ... 1Co 9:25
–The kingdom prepared for us ... Mt 25:34
–A place in heaven ... Jn 14:2–3
2Co 5:1
2Ti 4:8
–Eternal life ... Ro 2:7
Gal 6:8
–Eternal glory ... 2Co 4:17
4. Judgment in store for the disobedient ... Ro 1:18
Ro 2:8–9
Rev 21:8
Rev 22:14–15

THE RICH AND THE POOR

A. Related themes
1. MONEY is a theme of 2 Corinthians ... 2Co 9:7
2. SOCIAL CONCERN is a theme of:
–Deuteronomy ... Dt 26:12
–Luke ... Lk 7:22
B. God is the source of all wealth
–He owns everything ... Ex 19:5
Ps 24:1
Hag 2:8
1Co 10:26
–He gives wealth ... Ge 26:12–13
Dt 8:16–18
1Co 4:7

–He decides who is rich or poor...... 1Sa 2:7
Pr 10:22
Pr 22:2

C. Riches

1. Examples of wealthy people
–Abraham .... Ge 24:34–35
–Isaac .... Ge 26:12–14
–Esau.................... Ge 36:7
–Laban .... Ge 30:29–30
–Jacob .... Ge 30:43
–Nabal.................... 1Sa 25:2–3
–David.................... 2Sa 5:9–13
–Solomon 1Ki 10:14–29
–Jehoshaphat.................... 2Ch 17:5
–Job .... Job 1:1–3
–Joseph of Arimathea .... Mt 27:57

2. Means of gaining wealth
–Prosperity as God's reward to righteous.................. Ps 25:12–13
Ps 112:1–3
Pr 10:22
–The wicked can also be wealthy .... Job 21:7–13
Ps 73:3,12
Jer 12:1–2
–Wealth gained by taking bribes .. Isa 1:23
Eze 22:12
Am 5:12
–Wealth gained by usury and extortion .... Neh 5:1–7
Pr 28:8
Jer 22:17
Eze 22:12
–Wealth gained by exploiting the poor .... Isa 3:14–15
Jer 2:34
Am 2:6–8
Jas 2:6

3. Reactions of the rich to their wealth
a. Unwholesome reactions
–Hoard it for themselves .... Ecc 5:13
Lk 12:16–19
Jas 5:3
–Become greedy and fall into sin.................... Pr 15:27
1Ti 6:9–10
–Trust in it.................... Job 31:24–28
Ps 49:5–6
Ps 52:7
1Ti 6:17
–Become proud because of it.... Eze 28:5
Hos 12:8
Rev 3:17
–Reject God because of it....... Dt 8:12–14
Dt 32:15
Neh 9:25–26
Mt 19:16–22

b. Wholesome reactions
–Use it to help the poor......... Neh 5:14–19
Job 29:11–17
Lk 19:8–9
Ac 4:34–37
2Co 8:1–4
–Use it to help bring about peace .... Ge 32:13–21
Ge 43:11–15
1Sa 25:18–35
Pr 18:16

4. God's commands concerning wealth
–We must acknowledge God as the source .... Dt 8:18
1Ch 29:12
Hos 2:8
–We must use wealth in God's service .... Ex 35:4–9
1Ch 29:3
Mal 3:8–10
–We must help the poor........... Ps 82:3–4
Mt 19:16–21
Eph 4:28
1Ti 6:18
–We must not store up treasures on earth.................... Mt 6:19–21
–We should not trust in wealth .... Ps 62:10
1Ti 6:17
–We should not be greedy......... Eph 5:3
Col 3:5
1Pe 5:2
–We cannot serve God and Money .... Mt 6:24–25

5. Riches are considered
–Fleeting.................... Pr 23:5
Pr 27:24
–Corruptible.................... Mt 6:19
Jas 5:2–3
–Perishable.................... 1Pe 1:18
–Uncertain 1Ti 6:17
–Unsatisfying .... Ecc 4:8
Ecc 5:10
–Deceitful.................... Mt 13:22
–Spiritually dangerous .... Lk 18:18–25

6. Judgments often spoken against the rich
–In the Old Testament .... Isa 1:23–25
Jer 17:11
Am 4:1–3
Mic 2:1–5
Hab 2:6–8
Zec 7:8–14
–In the New Testament .... Lk 6:24–25
Lk 16:13–15
Ac 8:20–23
Jas 5:1–6
2Pe 2:3, 14–15

7. True riches are spiritual
–Having Jesus is worth everything .... Mt 13:44–47
Php 3:7–8
Heb 10:34
–Believing in Jesus brings true wealth 1Pe 1:7
Rev 3:17–18
–God's grace brings spiritual riches .... Eph 1:7,18
Eph 3:8,16
Col 1:27
–All things are ours in Christ 1Co 3:21–23
–We should store up treasures in heaven.................... Mt 6:20
1Ti 6:19

D. Poverty

1. Examples of poor people
–Lot .... Ge 19:23–30
–Naomi and Ruth .... Ru 1:20–2:2
–Widow of Zarephath 1Ki 17:10–12
–Jesus .... Mt 8:20
2Co 8:9
–Lazarus.................... Lk 16:20
–Paul (on occasion) Php 4:12

2. Reasons for becoming poor
a. God's choice for us 1Sa 2:7
b. Exploitation by the rich......... Isa 3:14–15
Jer 2:34
Am 2:6–8
Mic 3:1–3
Jas 2:6

c. The result of
- –Laziness ... Pr 6:9–11
- –Haste ... Pr 21:5
- –Alcohol ... Pr 23:21
- –Greed ... Pr 22:16

3. Laws given to protect the poor
- –There must be no poor ... Dt 15:4
- –Poor must not be taken advantage of ... Ex 22:22–23
- –The poor must be paid daily ... Dt 24:14–15
- –Poor allowed to glean in fields ... Lev 19:10; Dt 24:19–21
- –Laws regarding security on loans ... Dt 24:10–13
- –No interest may be charged to the poor ... Ex 22:25; Lev 25:36
- –The year for canceling debts ... Dt 15:1–11
- –The Year of Jubilee ... Lev 25:5–55
- –Equal justice for rich and poor ... Ex 23:2–3,6; Dt 1:17; Pr 31:9

4. Blessings for those who show kindness to the poor
- –Their throne will be secure ... Ps 72:1–5; Pr 29:14
- –Their righteousness endures forever ... Ps 112:9; Isa 58:6–8
- –God will answer their prayers ... Isa 58:6–7,9
- –They will be rewarded by God ... Pr 14:21; Pr 19:17; Pr 22:9; Pr 28:27
- –They will have treasure in heaven ... Mt 19:21; Lk 12:33; Lk 19:8–9

5. God as the hope of the poor
- –He is their refuge ... Ps 14:6; Isa 25:4
- –He is their protector ... Ps 12:5
- –He is their deliverer ... 1Sa 2:8; Ps 34:6; Ps 113:7
- –He is their helper ... Ps 40:17; Ps 70:5; Isa 41:17
- –He is their provider ... Ps 132:15; Isa 61:1–3; Lk 4:18–19

RIGHTEOUSNESS

–The state of being perfect and without sin

A. Related theme

RIGHTEOUSNESS is a theme of Romans ... Ro 1:17

B. The righteousness of humans

1. In themselves humans are unrighteous
- –No one is righteous ... Ps 14:1–3; Ps 53:1–3; Ro 3:10–12,23
- –Our righteous acts are like filthy rags ... Isa 64:6
- –We deserve God's wrath ... Ro 1:18; Eph 2:3

2. God gives us righteousness

a. Experienced in the Old Testament
- –By Abram ... Ge 15:6
- –By David ... Ps 32:1–2; Ps 103:17
- –By Isaiah ... Isa 45:8,24; Isa 46:13; Isa 61:10

b. Experienced by believers in Christ
- –God declares us righteous ... Ro 3:21–22; Ro 4:1–8; Gal 3:21–22; Php 3:8–9
- –God credits us with Christ's righteousness ... Ro 4:11,22–24
- –His righteousness is a gift ... Ro 5:17
- –We become God's righteousness ... 2Co 5:21

3. Believers are called "the righteous"
- –In the Old Testament ... Ps 1:5–6; Pr 10:3,6–7, 20–22; Isa 26:7; Hos 14:9; Am 2:6
- –In the New Testament ... Mt 25:37,46; Heb 12:23; Jas 5:16

4. Responsibilities regarding a righteous way of life
- –Be servants of righteousness ... Ro 6:13,18–19
- –Long for righteousness ... Mt 5:6
- –Perform righteousness ... Am 5:24; Mt 5:20
- –Pursue righteousness ... Isa 51:1; 1Ti 6:11; 2Ti 2:22
- –Put on righteousness ... Eph 4:24; Eph 6:14
- –Seek righteousness ... Mt 6:33
- –Bring forth fruits of righteousness ... Hos 10:12; 2Co 9:10; Heb 12:11
- –Live for righteousness ... 1Pe 2:24
- –Do what is right ... 1Jn 2:29; 1Jn 3:7
- –Shun wickedness ... 2Co 6:14–15

5. God's word teaches how to be righteous ... 2Ti 3:16–17

6. Our final righteousness
- –Heaven is the home of righteousness ... 2Pe 3:13
- –We receive a crown of righteousness ... 2Ti 4:8

See also JUSTIFICATION

C. The righteousness of God

1. God the Father
- –God is righteous ... Ps 7:9; Isa 45:21; Jer 12:1; Jn 17:25
- –He always acts righteously ... 1Sa 12:7; Ps 145:17; Jer 9:24; Mic 6:5
- –He judges righteously ... Ps 9:4; Ps 98:9; Jer 11:20
- –His commandments are righteous ... Ps 19:9; Ps 119:138,160; Ro 1:32; Ro 7:12
- –His righteousness endures forever ... Ps 111:3; Ps 112:3

2. Jesus is righteous

a. Old Testament prophecies
- –His name is "The Lord Our Righteousness" ... Jer 23:6; Jer 33:16
- –He is the righteous servant ... Isa 53:11

–He is the sun of righteousness . . . Mal 4:2
–He is clothed in righteousness . . . Isa 11:5
Isa 59:16–17
–He loves righteousness . . . Ps 45:7
–He judges in righteousness . . . Ps 72:2
Isa 11:4
–He reigns in righteousness . . . Isa 32:1
Zec 9:9

b. New Testament assertions
–He is the Righteous One . . . Ac 3:14
Ac 7:52
1Jn 2:1
–He fulfilled all righteousness . . Mt 3:15
–He lived a righteous life . . . Ro 5:18
2Co 5:21
1Pe 3:18
–He is our righteousness . . . 1Co 1:30
–He loves righteousness . . . Heb 1:8–9
–He is the righteous Judge . . . 2Ti 4:8

3. Believers and God's righteousness
–They acknowledge it . . . Ezr 9:15
Da 9:7
–They see it . . . Mic 7:9
–They speak of it . . . Ps 35:28
–They proclaim it . . . Ps 22:31
Ps 71:15–16
–They sing of it . . . Ps 51:14
–They exult in it . . . Ps 89:16
–They give thanks for it . . . Ps 7:17
–They are led in it . . . Ps 5:8
–They are upheld by it . . . Isa 41:10
–They pray for it . . . Ps 31:1
Ps 143:11

RIVER

A. Rivers and streams mentioned in the Bible
–Abana . . . 2Ki 5:12
–Ahava . . . Ezr 8:15,21
–Arnon . . . Nu 21:13,24
–Besor . . . 1Sa 30:9,21
–Egypt . . . Ge 15:18
–Euphrates . . . Dt 1:7
See EUPHRATES
–Gihon . . . 1Ki 1:33,38
–Gozan . . . 1Ch 5:26
–Jabbok . . . Ge 32:22
–Jordan . . . Ge 13:10
See JORDAN
–Kanah . . . Jos 16:8
–Kebar . . . Eze 10:15
–Kerith . . . 1Ki 17:3–5
–Kidron . . . Jn 18:1
–Kishon . . . Jdg 4:7,13
–Nile . . . Ge 41:1,3,17
–Pharpar . . . 2Ki 5:12
–Pishon . . . Ge 2:11
–Shihor . . . Jos 13:3
–Tigris . . . Ge 2:14
–Ulai . . . Da 8:2
–Zered . . . Dt 2:13–14

B. How were rivers and streams used?
1. Literally
–For drinking . . . 1Ki 17:3–4
–For bathing . . . Ex 2:5
–For irrigation . . . Ge 2:10
–For transportation . . . Isa 23:3
–For fishing . . . Lev 11:9–10
–For healing . . . 2Ki 5:14
–For baptism . . . Mk 1:5

2. As a symbol
–Of an enemy's strength . . . Ps 124:1–4
–Of God's judgment . . . Ps 88:16–17
Isa 42:15
–Of God's blessings . . . Ps 36:8
Isa 41:17–18
–Of God's peace . . . Isa 48:18
Isa 66:12
–Of wisdom . . . Pr 18:4
–Of life in the Spirit . . . Jn 7:38–39
–Of healing, life-giving power . . . Eze 47:1–12
Rev 22:1–2

ROCK

A. Uses for rocks
–As a pillow . . . Ge 28:11
–As an altar . . . Jdg 6:20–21
–As a landmark . . . Jdg 15:8
–As a memorial . . . Jos 4:1–9
–As a habitat for animals . . . Ps 104:18
–As a hiding place . . . 1Sa 13:6
–As a tomb . . . Mt 27:60
–As a place from which water flowed . . . Ex 17:6
Nu 20:8–11

B. The rock as a symbol
1. Of Simon, named Peter . . . Mt 16:18
Jn 1:42
2. Of the apostles as the church's foundation . . . Eph 2:20
Rev 21:14
3. Of Christ
–The rock in the wilderness . . . 1Co 10:4
–The foundation of the church . . . 1Co 3:11
–The cornerstone of the church . . . Eph 2:20
1Pe 2:6
–A stone over which people stumble . . . Ro 9:33
1Pe 2:8
4. Of God who protects and saves . . . Dt 32:4,15
Ps 18:2
Isa 26:4
Hab 1:12

ROME

–The capital city of the New Testament world

A. The government of Rome
–Ruled the world at the time of Christ . . . Lk 2:1
Jn 18:28
Ac 16:12
–Expelled Jews from the city . . . Ac 18:2
–Gave privileges to Roman citizens . . Ac 16:37–38
Ac 22:25–29

B. Christianity and Rome
1. Jews from Rome in Jerusalem at Pentecost . . . Ac 2:10
2. Paul and Rome
–Paul wrote to the church in Rome . . . Ro 1:7
–Paul wanted to go to Rome . . . Ro 1:15
Ro 15:23–24
–Paul arrived in Rome as a prisoner . . . Ac 28:14–16
–Paul visited with Christians of Rome . . . Ac 28:15
–Paul preached in Rome . . . Ac 28:23–31
Php 1:12–13
–Paul was probably killed in Rome . . . 2Ti 4:6–8
3. Peter may have referred to Rome as Babylon . . . 1Pe 5:13

RUTH

–Moabitess; widowed daughter-in-law of Naomi . . . Ru 1:3–5

–Went with Naomi to Bethlehem — Ru 1:22
–Gleaned in field of Boaz — Ru 2:2–17
–Proposed marriage to Boaz — Ru 3:1–14
–Married Boaz — Ru 4:1–13
–Gave birth to Obed — Ru 4:13–17
–Ancestor of David — Ru 4:17–22
–Ancestor of Jesus — Mt 1:5

SABBATH

–Seventh day of the week, the day of rest

A. The Sabbath in the Old Testament
1. The Sabbath day of rest
a. God rested on the Sabbath — Ge 2:2–3
b. Israel observed it before law was given — Ex 16:23,25
c. Laws concerning the Sabbath
–The fourth commandment — Ex 20:8–11
–No work to be done — Ex 31:14–15; Ex 35:2–3
–A day of sacred assembly — Lev 23:2–3
–A day for special offerings — Nu 28:9–10
2. Purposes of the Sabbath
–To be a sign of the covenant — Ex 31:16–17; Isa 56:6; Eze 20:12,20
–To honor God — Isa 58:13
–To worship God — Lev 23:3
–To remember God's salvation — Dt 5:15
–To rest from work — Dt 5:12–14
3. The Sabbath year — Lev 25:1–7; Eze 46:3
4. The Israelites and the Sabbath
–Disobeyed the Sabbath — Jer 17:20–23
–Desecrated the Sabbath — Eze 20:21,24; Eze 22:8; Eze 23:38–39
–Couldn't wait for Sabbath to be over — Am 8:4–5
–Wanted to work on Sabbath — Neh 13:20–21
–Nehemiah reinstituted Sabbath laws — Neh 13:15–22

B. In the New Testament
1. The Jews and the Sabbath
–Worshiped regularly on that day — Lk 4:16,31; Ac 13:14–15; Ac 17:2
–Used it as a focal point for legalism — Mt 12:2,10; Lk 13:14; Jn 9:13–16
2. Jesus and the Sabbath
–Is Lord of the Sabbath — Mt 12:8; Mk 2:28
–Tried to restore its proper spirit — Lk 13:10–16; Lk 14:1–6; Jn 5:16–18
–Taught Sabbath was for our good — Mk 2:27
3. Symbolism of the Sabbath
–Symbolizes the rest God wants for us — Heb 4:3–4
–Symbolizes the eternal Sabbath — Heb 4:8–11
4. The day of worship in the early church
a. The Sabbath — Ac 13:14; Ac 17:2; Ac 18:4
b. The first day of the week
–Christ's resurrection on that day — Lk 24:1–7; Jn 20:1,19
–Pentecost on that day — Ac 2:1
–Worship on that day — Ac 20:7
–Offerings set aside on that day — 1Co 16:2
–John's vision on the Lord's Day — Rev 1:10

SACRIFICE

A. Related theme
SACRIFICE is a theme of Philippians — Php 2:17

B. Sacrifices in the Old Testament
1. Persons performing them
–Cain and Abel — Ge 4:3–5
–Noah — Ge 8:20–21
–Abram — Ge 12:7–8; Ge 15:9–11
–Jacob — Ge 31:54; Ge 46:1
–Job — Job 1:5
–Regular duties of priests — Lev 1:3–17
2. Types of sacrifices
a. According to substances used
–Various animal sacrifices — Lev 1:2–17; Lev 3:1–4:35
–Grain sacrifices — Lev 2:1–16; Lev 6:14–23
b. According to time performed
–Daily sacrifices — Ex 29:38–41; Nu 28:1–8
–Weekly sacrifices — Nu 28:9–10
–Monthly sacrifices — Nu 28:11–15
–Annual sacrifices — Nu 28:16–29:38
3. Purpose of sacrifices
a. As cleansing for sin
–Burnt offerings — Lev 1:3–17
–Sin offerings — Lev 4:1–5:13
–Guilt offerings — Lev 5:14–6:7
b. As thanksgiving to God
–Grain offerings — Lev 2:1–16
–Fellowship offerings — Lev 3:1–16
4. The insufficiency of sacrifices alone
a. Had to be accompanied by
–A true faith — Heb 11:4
–A humble heart — Ps 51:17; Isa 66:2–3
–A repentant heart — Isa 1:11–16
–A life of obedience — 1Sa 15:22; Ps 40:6–8
–A life of justice — Mic 6:6–8
–A desire to give one's best — Mal 1:6–14
b. Despised if offered by unjust people — Isa 1:11–15; Am 5:21–24

C. Sacrifice in the New Testament
1. View of Old Testament sacrifices
–They cannot take away sin — Heb 9:9–10,23; Heb 10:1–4,11
–They point to the sacrifice of Christ — Heb 9:11–14, 24–26
2. The sacrifice of Christ
–He is the lamb who was sacrificed — Jn 1:29; 1Co 5:7; Rev 5:6
–He is the atoning sacrifice — Ro 3:25; Heb 7:27; Heb 9:28; 1Jn 4:10
3. Sacrifices expected of the Christian
–Total commitment to Christ — Mt 16:24–25
See SELF-DENIAL
–Lives of service to God — Ro 12:1; 1Pe 2:5

–Praising and confessing God. . . . . Heb 13:15
–Deeds of kindness . . . . Heb 13:16
–Gifts of money for use in God's work. Php 4:18

SADDUCEES

–A Jewish party, prominent at the time of Jesus

A. Major characteristics
–Members of the Sanhedrin (Jewish council). . . . . Ac 23:6
–Did not believe in the resurrection of the dead . . . . Mt 22:23; Ac 23:8

B. The Sadducees and Jesus
1. The Sadducees questioned and tested Jesus
–About a sign from heaven. . . . . Mt 16:1; Mk 8:11
–About the resurrection of the dead . . . . Mt 22:23–27; Mk 12:18–23; Lk 20:27–33
2. Jesus criticized the Sadducees. . . . . Mt 16:6,11–12

C. The Sadducees and the early church
–Persecuted the church. . . . . Ac 4:1–3; Ac 5:17–18
–Put the apostles on trial. . . . . Ac 5:21–32
–Put Paul on trial . . . . Ac 22:30–23:6

SALOME

–The mother of James and John, sons of Zebedee . . . . Mt 27:56; Mk 15:40
–Wanted a high position for her sons . . . Mt 20:20–23
–Watched Jesus die on the cross. . . . . Mk 15:40
–Went to the empty tomb . . . . Mk 16:1

SALT

A. Uses for salt
–For seasoning food . . . . Job 6:6
–For seasoning sacrifices . . . . Lev 2:13; Eze 43:24
–For ratifying a covenant . . . . Nu 18:19; 2Ch 13:5
–For rubbing a newborn child . . . . Eze 16:4

B. Symbolism of salt
–Symbol of judgment. . . . . Ge 19:26; Jer 48:9
–Symbol of permanency of covenant. Nu 18:19
–Symbol of preservation. . . . . Mt 5:13
–Symbol of peace . . . . Mk 9:50; Col 4:6

SALVATION

A. Related theme
WORLDWIDE SAVIOR is a theme of Luke. . . . . Lk 19:9

B. Definition of salvation
1. "Save" translated as "heal". . . . . Mk 10:52; Mk 6:56; Ac 14:9; Jas 5:15
2. "Save" as rescue from physical danger. . . . . Da 6:27; Mt 8:25; Lk 23:39; Ac 27:20,31; Heb 5:7
3. "Save" as rescue from personal enemies . . . . Ps 18:3–6; Ps 59:2
4. "Save" as deliverance from political oppression
–Salvation from Egypt. . . . . Ex 14:13,30; Ps 106:8–11
–Salvation from enemies invading Canaan. . . . . Jdg 3:9,31; Jdg 8:22; 2Ki 14:27
5. "Save" as deliverance from sin
a. In the Old Testament
–Asking for salvation from sin. . Ps 39:8; Ps 51:14
–Promise of salvation through Messiah. Jer 23:5–6; Eze 37:23–25
b. In the New Testament, it embraces
–The past: "have been saved" . . . Eph 2:5,8; 2Ti 1:9; Titus 3:5
–The present: "are being saved" . . . . Ac 2:47; 1Co 1:18; 2Co 2:15
–The future: "will be saved" . . . . Ro 5:9–10; Ro 13:11; 1Pe 1:5,9

C. God as the source of salvation
1. Israel's God in the Old Testament
a. He is called "Savior". . . . . 1Ch 16:35; Ps 25:5; Isa 43:11; Isa 45:15,21; Mic 7:7
b. He is Israel's salvation. . . . . Ex 15:1–2; Ps 27:1; Isa 12:2; Jnh 2:9
c. He promised worldwide salvation. . . . . Ps 67:2; Isa 49:6; Isa 52:10
2. Christ as Savior
–Salvation is in his name alone. . . . . . Ac 4:12; Ac 10:43; Ro 10:13
–He is called Savior . . . . Lk 2:11; Eph 5:23; Titus 1:4
–He saves his people from sin . . . . . . Mt 1:21; Ac 5:31; Titus 2:13–14
–He saves the lost . . . . Lk 15:3–10; Lk 19:10
–He saves the world . . . . Jn 3:16–17; Jn 12:47; 1Jn 4:14

D. The process of salvation
1. Salvation required the work of Christ
–His coming to this earth. . . . . 2Co 8:9; Php 2:6–8
–His death on the cross. . . . . Jn 3:14–15; 1Co 1:18; 1Co 15:2–3
–The shedding of his blood. . . . . 1Pe 1:18–19; Rev 5:9
–His resurrection from the dead. . . Ro 10:9; 1Pe 1:3–5
–His ascension into heaven . . . . Ac 5:31
2. Salvation comes as a gift from God
–A gift of his love . . . . Ro 5:8–9; Titus 3:5; 1Jn 4:9–10
–A gift of his grace. . . . . Eph 2:5,8; Titus 2:11
–A gift of his mercy . . . . Titus 3:4–5; 1Pe 1:3

3. Requirements for salvation
–Read the Scriptures ... 2Ti 3:15
–Believe in Jesus Christ ... Jn 3:16; Ac 16:30–31; Eph 2:8
–Repent of our sins ... Isa 30:15; Ac 2:37–38; Ac 3:19; 2Co 7:10
–Accept salvation as a free gift ... Isa 55:1; Rev 21:6
–Realize we can do nothing to earn salvation ... Eph 2:8–9; 2Ti 1:9; Titus 3:5
–Give our all in response to salvation ... Mt 13:44–46; Lk 14:33; Php 3:7–8

E. Our relationship to God's salvation
–We long for it ... Ps 119:81,174
–We wait for it ... La 3:26
–We hope for it ... 1Th 5:8–9
–We pray for it ... Ps 54:1; Ps 85:7; Jer 31:7
–We realize that it is now ... 2Co 6:2
–We must count its cost ... Lk 14:25–33
–We are clothed with it ... 2Ch 6:41; Isa 61:10
–We rejoice in it ... Ps 9:14; Isa 25:9
–We delight in it ... Ps 35:9
–We love it ... Ps 40:16
–We make it known ... Ps 67:2
–We proclaim it ... 1Ch 16:23; Ps 96:2
–We grow in it ... 1Pe 2:2
–We work it out ... Php 2:12

F. Pictures of salvation
–Horn of salvation ... 2Sa 22:3; Ps 18:2
–Fortress of salvation ... Ps 28:8
–Cup of salvation ... Ps 116:13
–Crown of salvation ... Ps 149:4
–Wells of salvation ... Isa 12:3
–Walls and ramparts of salvation ... Isa 26:1
–A rich store of salvation ... Isa 33:6
–Springs of salvation ... Isa 45:8
–Helmet of salvation ... Isa 59:17; Eph 6:17
–Garments of salvation ... Isa 61:10
–Torch of salvation ... Isa 62:1
–Gospel of salvation ... Eph 1:13

SAMARIA

A. Identity of Samaria
–City built by Omri, king of Israel ... 1Ki 16:23–24
–Became capital of northern kingdom 1Ki 16:29,32; 1Ki 21:18
–Became synonymous with the northern kingdom ... 1Ki 21:1; Hos 7:1

B. History in the Old Testament
–Besieged by Ben-Hadad ... 2Ki 6:24–25
–Besieged by Assyria ... 2Ki 17:5
–City taken; people deported ... 2Ki 17:6; 2Ki 18:10–12
–City plundered ... Isa 8:4
–Other people settled in the region ... 2Ki 17:24
–Capital city of Trans-Euphrates province ... Ezr 4:17; Neh 4:1–2

C. History in the New Testament
–Jesus visited it ... Lk 17:11; Jn 4:4–6
–Gospel must be preached there ... Ac 1:8
–Gospel spread there ... Ac 8:1
–Philip preached there ... Ac 8:5–7
–Holy Spirit was poured out there ... Ac 8:14–17
–Simon the magician lived there ... Ac 8:9–13,18–24
–Paul traveled through there ... Ac 15:3

SAMARITANS

A. In the Old Testament
–A mixed race resettled in Samaria ... 2Ki 17:24
–Had a polytheistic religion ... 2Ki 17:25–33
–Wanted to help rebuild the temple ... Ezr 4:1–2
–Offer to rebuild the temple refused ... Ezr 4:3
–Tried to frustrate rebuilding of the temple ... Ezr 4:4–5,24; Ezr 5:3–17
–Tried to frustrate rebuilding of Jerusalem ... Ezr 4:7–23; Neh 4:1–23; Neh 6:1–14

B. In the New Testament
–Jews and Samaritans did not associate ... Jn 4:9
–Jesus told parable of Good Samaritan ... Lk 10:30–35
–A Samaritan leper returned to thank Jesus ... Lk 17:11–19
–A Samaritan town rejected Jesus ... Lk 9:52–53
–James and John wanted to destroy the town ... Lk 9:54–55
–Jesus talked with a Samaritan woman ... Jn 4:7–26
–Many Samaritans believed in Jesus ... Jn 4:39–42; Ac 8:5,12

SAMSON

A. History of his life
–Judge from the tribe of Dan ... Jdg 13:2,24–25
–Birth promised ... Jdg 13:2–14
–Married Philistine woman ... Jdg 14:1–18
–Took revenge on Philistines ... Jdg 15:1–20
–Betrayed by Delilah ... Jdg 16:1–20
–Captured and eyes gouged out ... Jdg 16:21–22
–His death ... Jdg 16:23–31

B. Feats of strength
–Killed a lion ... Jdg 14:6
–Killed thirty Philistines ... Jdg 14:19
–Killed a thousand Philistines with a jawbone ... Jdg 15:13–17
–Carried off gates of Gaza ... Jdg 16:3
–Pushed down temple of Dagon, at cost of his life ... Jdg 16:25–30

C. An example of faith ... Heb 11:32

SAMUEL

A. Early life
–Hannah prayed that God would give her a son ... 1Sa 1:10–18
–Dedicated to God's service ... 1Sa 1:21–28
–Raised by Eli ... 1Sa 2:11,18–26
–Called by God to be a prophet ... 1Sa 3:1–20

B. His life as prophet and judge
–Judged Israel many years ... 1Sa 7:15–17
–Functioned as a prophet ... 1Sa 9:9,19
–Led Israel to victory over the Philistines ... 1Sa 7:2–14
–Israelites asked him to anoint a king ... 1Sa 8:1–22
–Anointed Saul as king ... 1Sa 10:1,17–24; Ac 13:20–21

–The ancient serpent ... Rev 12:9

B. Activities of Satan

1. Activities in the past
–Originally created as good ... Ge 1:31
–Led revolt of angels in heaven ... 2Pe 2:4; Rev 12:7–8
–Tempted Adam and Eve ... Ge 3:1–7
–Incited David to sin ... 1Ch 21:1–2
–Afflicted Job ... Job 1:6–19; Job 2:1–10
–Tempted Jesus ... Mt 4:1–11
–Involved in effort to put Jesus to death ... Lk 22:3; Jn 14:30–31

2. Activities in the present
–Rules a kingdom opposed to God ... Mt 12:25–26; Mt 25:41
–Controls the present sinful world ... 1Jn 5:19; Rev 12:9
–Afflicts people with illness ... Job 2:7; Lk 13:16; Ac 10:38; 2Co 12:7
–Tempts believers to sin ... 1Ch 21:1; Mt 16:23; Ac 5:3; 1Th 3:5
–Tries to keep people from true worship ... Mt 13:19; 1Pe 5:8–9
–Thwarts the spread of the gospel ... Mt 13:19; 2Co 4:3–4; 1Th 2:18
–Wants people to worship him ... Mt 4:9
–Masquerades as an angel of light ... 2Co 11:14
–Uses many schemes ... 2Co 2:11; Eph 6:11
–Persecutes the church ... Rev 2:10; Rev 12:13–17
–Holds the power of death ... Heb 2:14–15

3. Future activities
–Will be bound in the Millennium ... Rev 20:2–3
–Will be set free during the Great Tribulation ... Rev 20:7–9
–Will empower the antichrist ... 2Th 2:9; Rev 13:2–4

C. Victory over Satan

1. God has power over him ... Job 1:6–12; Job 2:1–6; Lk 22:31–32

2. Christ has disarmed him
–Prophesied in Eden ... Ge 3:15
–Christ came to destroy him ... 1Jn 3:8
–Demonstrated in Christ's victory over temptation ... Mt 4:1–11
–Demonstrated by casting out demons ... Lk 10:18; Lk 11:20
–The cross of Christ sealed his defeat ... Jn 12:31–33; Col 2:15; Rev 12:11

3. Believers must fight against him
–We must pray for deliverance ... Mt 6:13
–We must keep busy for the Lord ... 1Ti 5:13–15
–We must resist his temptations ... 1Co 7:5; Jas 4:7
–We must extinguish his flaming arrows by our faith ... Eph 6:16
–We must overcome him ... 1Jn 2:13; Rev 2:10–11; Rev 12:10–11
–Christ prays for the victory of our faith ... Lk 22:31–32

4. Final defeat of Satan
–Prophesied by Paul ... Ro 16:20
–Satan bound in the Millennium ... Rev 20:2–3
–Final victory at Christ's return ... Mt 25:31,41; Rev 20:10,14

SAUL

A. First king of Israel

1. Family data and early life
–A member of the tribe of Benjamin ... 1Sa 9:1–2
–Son of Kish ... 1Sa 9:1–2
–His family ... 1Sa 14:49–50; 1Ch 8:33
–Searched for his father's donkeys ... 1Sa 9:3–4
–Consulted Samuel ... 1Sa 9:5–20
–Anointed king by Samuel ... 1Sa 10:1
–Prophesied ... 1Sa 10:9–13; 1Sa 19:23–24
–Chosen as king at Mizpah ... 1Sa 10:20–26

2. Early events as king
–Defeated Ammonites at Jabesh Gilead ... 1Sa 11:1–11
–Confirmed as king ... 1Sa 11:12–15
–Fought the Philistines ... 1Sa 13:1–7,16–22
–Did not wait for Samuel to offer sacrifice ... 1Sa 13:8–14
–Disobeyed God regarding Amalekites ... 1Sa 15:1–23
–Repented ... 1Sa 15:24–31

3. His interaction with David
–Employed David as musician ... 1Sa 16:14–23
–Approved David's offer to fight Goliath ... 1Sa 17:31–39
–Became jealous of David ... 1Sa 18:1–9
–Tried to kill David, who was playing music ... 1Sa 18:10–11
–Gave David his daughter Michal as wife ... 1Sa 18:20–28
–Again tried to kill David ... 1Sa 19:1–17
–Angry at Jonathan for befriending David ... 1Sa 20:26–34
–Pursued David; killed priests at Nob ... 1Sa 22:6–19
–Went to Keilah and Ziph ... 1Sa 23:7–28
–Spared by David in a cave at En Gedi ... 1Sa 24:1–21
–Spared by David while sleeping in camp ... 1Sa 26:1–25

4. Saul's death
–Sought Samuel's advice through a witch ... 1Sa 28:1–14
–Rebuked by Samuel's spirit ... 1Sa 28:15–20
–Wounded by Philistines; killed himself ... 1Sa 31:1–6; 1Ch 10:1–6
–His death lamented by David ... 2Sa 1:17–27

B. One of Christ's apostles

SEA

A. Seas mentioned in the Bible

1. The Mediterranean Sea
–The Sea ... Nu 34:5
–The Great Sea ... Nu 34:6–7

–The Sea of the Philistines ... Ex 23:31
–The western sea ... Dt 11:24

2. The Red Sea ... Ac 7:36
   –The Sea of Reeds ... Ex 10:19
   –The Egyptian sea ... Isa 11:15
3. The Sea of Galilee ... Mt 4:18
   –The Sea of Kinnereth ... Nu 34:11
   –The Sea of Tiberias ... Jn 6:1
4. The Dead Sea
   –The Salt Sea ... Ge 14:3
   –The Sea of the Arabah ... Dt 3:17
   –The eastern sea ... Zec 14:8
5. The Adriatic Sea ... Ac 27:27

B. The sea used as a symbol
1. Negative
   –Of human sin and restlessness ... Ge 49:4; Isa 57:20; Eph 4:14
   –Of human instability ... Jas 1:6
   –Of the lifestyle of heretics ... Jude 13
   –Of God's judgment ... Jer 49:23–24; La 2:13
   –Of the abode of satanic powers ... Da 7:2–3; Rev 13:1
   –No sea in heaven ... Rev 21:1
2. Positive
   –Of the vast mysteries of God ... Job 11:7–9
   –Of God's presence everywhere ... Ps 139:9
   –Of the wide expanse of a kingdom ... Ps 72:8
   –Of God's great forgiveness ... Mic 7:19
   –Of God's promise of righteousness ... Isa 48:18
   –Of the extension of the gospel ... Isa 11:9; Hab 2:14

See also WATER

SEAL

A. Literal uses of the seal
   –A plate on the high priest's turban ... Ex 39:30–31
   –An item for personal identification ... Ge 38:18,25
   –A mark for identifying correspondence ... 1Ki 21:8
   –A governmental mark warning people ... Mt 27:66
   –A mark securing a title deed ... Jer 32:9–14

B. Figurative use of the seal
   –Circumcision: a seal of t
   he covenant ... Ro 4:11
   –Zerubbabel: a seal of the coming Messiah ... Hag 2:23
   –The Holy Spirit: a seal of salvation ... 2Co 1:22; Eph 1:14; Eph 4:30
   –Christians: a seal of apostleship ... 1Co 9:2
   –God's word: a seal for the church ... 2Ti 2:19
   –The seven seals: Jesus' control of history ... Rev 5:1–6:17
   –The sealed 144,000: God's elect ... Rev 7:1–8
   –The sealed Abyss: God's control of Satan ... Rev 20:3

SECOND COMING

–The return of Jesus at the end of history

A. Terms for the second coming
   –The day of the Lord ... 1Co 1:8; Php 1:6,10; 1Th 5:2
   –The day of God ... 2Pe 3:12
   –The last day ... Jn 12:48
   –The Day ... 1Co 3:13; Heb 10:25
   –The last time ... 1Pe 1:5
   –The appearing of Jesus Christ ... Titus 2:13

B. Prophecies of his second coming
   –By Jesus before the crucifixion ... Mt 24:30–31; Mt 26:64; Jn 14:3
   –By Jesus after the resurrection ... Jn 21:22
   –By two angels at Jesus' ascension ... Ac 1:10–11
   –By the apostles in their preaching ... Ac 3:20; Ac 17:31
   –By the apostles in their writings ... Php 3:20; 1Th 4:14–17; 1Ti 6:14; Titus 2:13

C. The event of the second coming
1. Time of the return
   –It is unknown ... Mk 13:32
   –It will be sudden ... Mt 24:27; Mk 13:36
   –It will be unexpected ... Lk 12:40; 2Pe 3:10
   –It will be after the great tribulation ... Mt 24:29–31; 2Th 2:2–3
2. Characteristics of the return
   –It will be on the clouds ... Mt 24:30; Mk 14:62; 1Th 4:17
   –It will be visible ... Rev 1:7
   –It will be a bodily return ... Ac 1:11
   –It will be with his angels ... Mt 16:27; 2Th 1:7
   –It will be with great glory ... Mt 16:27; Mt 25:31; 2Th 2:8
   –It will be with power ... Mt 24:30
   –It will be with a great noise ... 1Co 15:51–52; 1Th 4:16

D. The purposes of the second coming
   –That he might be glorified in his people ... 2Th 1:10
   –That he might deliver the kingdom to God ... 1Co 15:24
   –That he might reign over all ... Rev 11:15
   –That he might expose the secrets of human hearts ... 1Co 4:5
   –That he might judge the human race ... Mt 25:31–46; Ac 10:42; 2Ti 4:1; 1Pe 4:5
   –That he might complete salvation for believers ... Heb 9:28
   –That he might take his people to be with him ... Jn 14:3
   –That he might gather the elect ... Mk 13:27

E. Believers and the second coming
1. The attitude of believers toward it
   –Should live holy lives until that day ... 2Pe 3:11–12
   –Should long for it ... 2Ti 4:8
   –Should watch for it ... Mk 13:35–37; Lk 12:35–40
   –Should wait for it ... 1Co 1:7; Php 3:20; Titus 2:13
   –Should look forward to it ... 2Pe 3:12–13
   –Should be patient until it ... Jas 5:7–8
   –Should persevere until it ... Rev 2:10–11; Rev 3:11–12
   –Should pray for its fulfillment ... 1Co 16:22; Rev 22:20

–Took the nature of a servant ..... Php 2:7
–Called himself a servant .... Mk 10:45; Lk 22:27
–Compared himself to a servant ... Lk 12:37
–Demonstrated servanthood by washing feet .... Jn 13:4–11
–Demonstrated servanthood by his cross .... Isa 53:4–6; Php 2:7–8
–Exalted as servant .... Isa 52:13

SETH
–Third son of Adam and Eve .... Ge 4:25
–Took the place of Abel .... Ge 4:25
–Made in Adam's image .... Ge 5:3
–His family .... Ge 5:6–8
–An ancestor of Jesus .... Lk 3:38

SEXUAL STANDARDS
A. Sexual sins condemned in the Bible
–Adultery .... Ex 20:14; Pr 5:1–23
–Incest .... Lev 20:19–21
–Sex with animals .... Lev 20:15–16
–Loss of virginity before marriage ... Dt 22:20–21
–Prostitution .... Dt 23:17–18; Pr 7:10–27
–Homosexuality .... Ro 1:26–27; 1Co 6:9
–Obscenity .... Eph 5:4
–Lust .... Mt 5:27–28; 1Th 4:5

B. God's will regarding sexual standards
1. In negative terms
–Laws against illicit sexual behavior .... Ex 20:14; Lev 20:10–21; Dt 23:17–18
–The command to flee immorality ... 1Co 6:18; Eph 5:3; Col 3:5; 1Th 4:3
–Sexual sin excludes one from the kingdom .... 1Co 6:9–10; Gal 5:19–21; Eph 5:3–5; Rev 22:15

2. In positive terms
–Strive for purity 1Th 4:4,7; 1Pe 3:2
–Be faithful in marriage 1Co 7:2–4
–Exercise self-control .... 1Co 7:8–9; Gal 5:23; 1Th 4:4

See also MARRIAGE
ADULTERY
DIVORCE

SHADRACH
–Hebrew deported to Babylon .... Da 1:6
–Name changed from Hananiah .... Da 1:7
–Refused to be defiled by food .... Da 1:8–20
–Appointed administrator over Babylon .... Da 2:49
–Refused to worship idols .... Da 3:1–18
–Saved from fiery furnace .... Da 3:19–30

SHALLUM
–King of Israel 2Ki 15:10–15
–Assassinated by Menahem 2Ki 15:14

SHAME
A. Reasons for feeling ashamed
–Being naked .... Ge 3:7; Eze 23:29
–Experiencing defeat .... Ps 6:10; Isa 29:22–23
–Being humiliated .... Eze 16:63; Zec 13:3–5; 1Co 1:27–29
–Experiencing sin .... Ezr 9:6; Jer 22:22; 2Th 3:14
–Being taunted by one's enemies ..... Ps 44:15–16
–Having an undisciplined child ...... Pr 19:26
–Falsely accusing someone .... Pr 25:8–10; 1Pe 3:16
–Giving less than poorer people 2Co 9:3–4
–Being inconsistent with one's principles .... Ezr 8:22

B. When the Christian need not be ashamed
–When looking to the Lord .... Ps 34:5
–When hoping in the Lord .... Ps 25:3
–When taking refuge in the Lord .... Ps 25:20
–When trusting in the Lord .... Ro 9:33; 1Pe 2:6
–When believing in Christ .... Mk 8:38; 2Ti 1:12
–When believing Christ and his word .... Mk 8:38; Lk 9:26
–When preaching the gospel Rom1:16; 2Ti 1:8
–When suffering for Christ's sake ... 1Pe 4:16
–When obeying God's law .... Ps 119:5–6
–When doing one's best for the Lord 2Ti 2:15
–When the Lord returns 1Jn 2:28

SHAMGAR
–Judge; killed six hundred Philistines .... Jdg 3:31

SHAPHAN
–Secretary during Josiah's reign 2Ki 22:3
–Supervised finances for temple repairs 2Ki 22:3–7; 2Ch 34:8–13,16–17
–Brought newly discovered law to Josiah 2Ki 22:8–10; 2Ch 34:14–17
–Read the law to Josiah 2Ki 22:10; 2Ch 34:18
–With others, visited prophetess Huldah 2Ki 22:14–20; 2Ch 34:20–28

SHECHEM
A. A man who raped Jacob's daughter Dinah .... Ge 34:1–4
–Agreed to circumcision and marriage .... Ge 34:11–24
–Killed by Simeon and Levi .... Ge 34:25–29

B. A city in Canaan
–The Lord appeared to Abram there .... Ge 12:6–7
–Jacob purchased land there .... Ge 33:18–19
–Pillaged by the sons of Jacob .... Ge 34:26–29
–Joseph went there to find his brothers .... Ge 37:14–17
–One of the cities of refuge .... Jos 20:7
–Joshua renewed the covenant there .... Jos 24:1–27
–Gideon's son Abimelech was crowned its king .... Jdg 9:1–6
–Civil war between Abimelech and Shechem .... Jdg 9:22–57
–Rehoboam was made king there 1Ki 12:1

–Jeroboam fortified it as his capital . . 1Ki 12:25
–In New Testament, Shechem is Sychar . . . . Jn 4:5

SHEEP

See LAMB

SHEM

–Son of Noah . . . . Ge 5:32; 1Ch 1:4
–With Japheth, covered his father with a garment . . . . Ge 9:23
–Blessed by Noah . . . . Ge 9:26
–Sons listed . . . . Ge 10:21–31
–Abram came from his line . . . . Ge 11:10–26

SHEOL

See GRAVE

SHEPHERD

A. Related theme
PASTORAL ADVICE is a theme of Titus . . . . Titus 3:8

B. The shepherd as an human occupation

1. Examples of shepherds . . . . Ge 4:2; Ge 29:9; 1Sa 16:11; Lk 2:8

2. Responsibilities of shepherds
–Find pasture for flocks . . . . Eze 34:2,13–14
–Provide water for flocks . . . . Ge 29:2–8; Ex 2:16
–Protect the flocks . . . . 1Sa 17:34–36; Lk 2:8
–Seek lost sheep . . . . Eze 34:16; Mt 18:10–13
–Care for injured sheep . . . . Mt 12:11
–Regularly account for the sheep . . Jn 10:2–5
–Know what happens to the sheep . . Ge 31:38–39
–Shear the sheep . . . . Ge 38:12; 1Sa 25:2,7

C. Figurative use of shepherd

1. Leaders of God's people as shepherds
a. Old Testament leaders
–Joshua . . . . Nu 27:15–18
–David . . . . 2Sa 5:2; Ps 78:70–72
–Cyrus . . . . Isa 44:28
–Selfish shepherds . . . . Isa 56:10–11; Jer 10:21; Eze 34:2–6; Zec 10:2–3

b. Church leaders . . . . Jn 21:15–17; Ac 20:28–31; 1Pe 5:2–3

2. God as a shepherd
–God is called a shepherd . . . . Ps 23:1; Ps 80:1
–We are his sheep . . . . Ps 95:7; Ps 100:3
–God acted as a shepherd in the exodus . . . . Ps 77:20; Ps 78:52; Isa 63:11
–God cares for us like a shepherd . . . Isa 40:11; Eze 34:11–16; Mic 7:14

3. Jesus Christ as a shepherd
a. He is called a shepherd
–The good shepherd . . . . Jn 10:11,14
–The great Shepherd . . . . Heb 13:20
–The Chief Shepherd 1Pe 5:4
–The Shepherd and Overseer . . . 1Pe 2:25

b. He acts as a shepherd
–Old Testament prophecies . . . . . Isa 40:11; Eze 34:23; Mic 5:2–4; Zec 13:7
–He died for the sheep . . . . Jn 10:15
–He has compassion for the sheep . . . . Mt 9:36
–He knows his sheep . . . . Jn 10:3–4,14
–He searches for lost sheep . . . . . Mt 18:12–14; Lk 15:3–7
–He will judge like a shepherd . . . . Mt 25:32

SHILOH

–Located in Ephraim, near Bethel . . . . . . Jdg 21:19
–The first religious center in Canaan . . . Jos 18:1; Jdg 18:31
–Joshua's political center . . . . Jos 21:1–2
–Joshua divided the land there . . . . Jos 18:9
–Benjamites seized women there . . . . Jdg 21:19–23
–Hannah asked for a son there 1Sa 1:3–18
–Eli and sons ministered there 1Sa 2:12–14
–God appeared to Samuel there 1Sa 3:21
–Ark taken into battle from there . . . . 1Sa 4:3–6; Ps 78:60–61
–Eli died there 1Sa 4:12–18
–Prophet Ahijah ministered there 1Ki 11:29; 1Ki 14:2
–City lay in ruins in Jeremiah's day . . . . . Jer 7:12–14; Jer 26:9

SHIMEI

–A Benjamite who cursed David 2Sa 16:5–14
–Spared from execution 2Sa 19:16–23
–Killed on Solomon's orders 1Ki 2:8–9,36–46

SIDON

A. Identity and location
–A chief city of Phoenicia . . . . Isa 23:11–12
–A seacoast city . . . . Ac 27:3
–Often linked with Tyre . . . . Isa 23:1–2; Mt 15:21
–Sidonians were descendants of Ham . . . . Ge 10:6,15
–A peaceful, prosperous people . . . . Jdg 18:7
–Skillful in felling timber . . . . 1Ki 5:6; 1Ch 22:4; Zec 9:2
–Served the goddess Ashtoreth 1Ki 11:5,33

B. Significance of Sidon

1. In the Old Testament
–Territory given to tribe of Asher . . Jos 19:24,28
–Asher did not drive out its inhabitants . . . . Jdg 1:31
–Cut timber for the temple 1Ki 5:6
–Solomon intermarried with them . 1Ki 11:1
–Ahab married Jezebel, a Sidonian 1Ki 16:31
–Elijah stayed with a Sidonian widow 1Ki 17:9–16
–Prophecies against them . . . . Isa 23:2,4,11–12; Eze 28:20–23; Joel 3:4–8

2. In the New Testament
–Jesus ministered there . . . . Mt 15:21–28; Mk 7:24–30
–Paul spent a night there . . . . Ac 27:3

SIDONIANS

See SIDON

SIGN

–An outward event with a spiritual significance

A. Miracles as signs

1. In the Old Testament
–Signs for Israel . . . . Ex 4:29–31; Nu 14:11

–Signs for Pharaoh ... Ex 10:1–2
–Signs for Gideon ... Jdg 6:17–24, 36–40
–Signs for Saul ... 1Sa 10:7,9
–A sign for Jeroboam ... 1Ki 13:3–5
–A sign for Ahaz ... Isa 7:11–14

2. In the New Testament
–Jesus' miracles were signs ... Jn 2:11,23; Jn 12:37; Jn 20:30
–The Jews wanted miraculous signs ... Mt 12:38–40; Mt 16:1–4; Jn 2:18; 1Co 1:22
–The apostles performed signs ... Ac 4:16,30; Ac 8:6; Ac 14:3

B. Signs of the covenant
1. In the Old Testament
–The rainbow with Noah ... Ge 9:12–16
–Circumcision with Abraham ... Ge 17:11; Ro 4:11
–The blood of the Passover at the exodus ... Ex 12:13
–The Sabbath at Mount Sinai ... Ex 31:12–17
–The altar at the crossing of the Jordan ... Jos 4:5–7

2. In the New Testament
–The water of baptism ... Mt 28:19; 1Pe 3:21
–Bread and wine of the Lord's Supper ... 1Co 11:23–26

C. Signs of the end times
1. Jesus is asked to reveal these signs ... Mk 13:1–4
2. Listing of these signs
–Wars and rumors of wars ... Mk 13:7–8
–Persecution of Christians ... Mk 13:9; Jn 15:18–21
–False teachers and false Christs ... Mk 13:6,22; 1Jn 2:18–19
–The worldwide spread of the gospel ... Mt 24:14; Rev 7:9–10
–The antichrist ... 2Th 2:3–4,8; Rev 13:1–9
–The great tribulation ... Mk 13:14–20; Rev 7:14
–Signs in the heavens ... Lk 21:11,25

D. The purpose of signs
–To bring about faith in God ... Nu 14:11; Jn 20:30
–To strengthen faith in God ... Jos 24:16–17; Ro 4:11
–To confirm a message from God ... 2Ki 19:28–29; Lk 2:12,16–20
–To protect God's people from danger ... Ex 12:13
–To bring to mind God's care and promises ... Ge 9:12–16; Ex 13:7–9; 1Co 11:23–26

SIHON

–King of the Amorites ... Nu 21:21; Dt 1:4
–Marched out against Israelites ... Nu 21:23
–Destroyed by Israelites ... Nu 21:24–31; Dt 2:32–36
–Victory sung by the Israelites ... Nu 21:27–30; Ps 136:19

SILAS

–A prophet of the early church ... Ac 15:32
–Delegated to report on council in Jerusalem ... Ac 15:22
–Traveled with Paul on second missionary journey ... Ac 15:40
–With Paul in prison at Philippi ... Ac 16:19–36
–With Paul in Thessalonica and Berea ... Ac 17:1–10
–Stayed behind in Berea ... Ac 17:14
–Came to Paul in Corinth ... Ac 18:5
–Preached with Paul in Corinth ... 2Co 1:19
–Co-writer with Paul ... 1Th 1:1; 2Th 1:1
–Co-writer with Peter ... 1Pe 5:12

SILVER

A. Uses for silver
1. In Israelite worship
–The tabernacle furniture ... Ex 26:19–25; Ex 27:9–11,17
–Offerings ... Nu 7:13,19,25; Ezr 1:4,6,9–11
–The temple building ... 1Ch 29:2–5
–The temple furniture ... 1Ch 28:14–17
2. In crafting idol gods ... Isa 2:20; Hos 8:4; Ac 19:24
3. For personal wealth ... Ge 13:2; Ecc 2:8
4. For gifts ... 1Ki 15:18–19; Ezr 2:69
5. For payment as money ... Ge 42:25–27; Jdg 9:4; Mt 26:15
6. For jewelry ... Ge 24:53; Eze 16:17
7. For royal display ... Ge 44:2; Est 1:6–7

B. Value of silver for God's people
1. Positive: a blessing from God ... Ge 13:2; Isa 60:9,17
2. Negative
–Wisdom worth more than silver ... Job 28:12–15; Pr 3:13–14; Pr 16:16
–Silver valueless in redemption ... 1Pe 1:18

C. Silver as a symbol
–For saints surviving God's testing ... Isa 48:10; Zec 13:9
–For God's dependable word ... Ps 12:6
–For trustworthy spiritual values ... 1Co 3:12–13

SIMEON

A. Son of Jacob by Leah ... Ge 35:23; 1Ch 2:1
–Name means "one who hears" ... Ge 29:33
–With Levi, avenged rape of Dinah ... Ge 34:25–31
–Held hostage by Joseph in Egypt ... Ge 42:24–43:23
–Went to Egypt with family ... Ge 46:8,10
–Father of six sons ... Ge 46:10
–Blessed by Jacob ... Ge 49:5–7

B. Tribe descended from Simeon
–Numbered ... Nu 1:23; Nu 26:14
–Allotted land ... Jos 19:1–9; Eze 48:24
–One of the tribes of the 144,000 ... Rev 7:7

C. A righteous man who blessed Jesus ... Lk 2:25–35
–Sang a song ... Lk 2:29–32

SIMON

A. One of Jesus' disciples
See PETER

B. Another disciple of Jesus
–Called the Zealot ... Mt 10:4
Mk 3:18
–One of the apostles ... Ac 1:13

C. A Samaritan sorcerer ... Ac 8:9–11
–Baptized as a Christian ... Ac 8:12
–Offered Peter money for power to impart the Holy Spirit ... Ac 8:18–19
–Severely rebuked by Peter ... Ac 8:20–23

SIN

A. Related themes
SIN is a theme of:
–Genesis ... Ge 6:5
–Judges ... Jdg 21:25
–Isaiah ... Isa 1:4
–Malachi ... Mal 1:8
–Romans ... Ro 2:12
–1 John ... 1Jn 3:6

B. Words for sin
–Transgression ... Ps 32:1,5
–Iniquity ... Ps 51:2,9
–Wickedness ... Ge 6:5
–Evil ... Ge 8:21
–Rebellion ... Ex 34:7
–Uncleanness ... Lev 16:16
–Disobedience ... Jos 22:22
–Wrongdoing ... 1Sa 24:11
–Guilt ... Isa 1:4
–Unrighteousness ... 1Jn 1:9
–Lawlessness ... 1Jn 3:4
–Depravity ... 2Pe 2:19
–Faults ... Ps 19:12

C. The origin and extent of sin

1. Original sin
–Adam and Eve disobeyed God's command ... Ge 3:1–7
–Their sin passed down to all humans ... Ro 5:12,15
1Co 15:22

2. Present extent of sin
–There is sin in everyone ... Ps 14:2–3
Ro 3:10–20,23
–Present already at conception ... Ps 51:5
–Permeates to the heart of people ... Ge 6:5
Jer 17:9
Mt 15:18–20
–Christ alone was without sin ... 2Co 5:21
Heb 4:15
1Pe 2:22
1Jn 3:5

D. God and human sin

1. His negative reaction
–He is grieved over sin ... Ge 6:6
–He is angry over sin ... Ps 78:19–21, 56–59
Jn 3:36
Ro 1:18
–He hates sin ... Ps 5:5
Pr 6:16–19
–He punishes sin ... Ge 3:15–19
Isa 3:11–26
Am 3:2

2. His positive reaction
–He sent his Son to die for sinners ... Jn 3:16
Ro 5:8
1Jn 4:10
–He forgives sin ... Ex 34:6–7
1Jn 1:9
–He removes sin far away ... Ps 103:8–12
–He sweeps away sin ... Isa 44:22
–He hurls sin away ... Mic 7:19
–He puts sin behind his back ... Isa 38:17
–He no longer remembers our sin ... Jer 31:34

E. Christ and human sin
–He was sinless ... 2Co 5:21
Heb 4:15
Heb 7:26
1Pe 2:22
1Jn 3:5
–He paid the penalty for sin ... Ro 4:25
Ro 8:3
Col 2:13–14
1Pe 2:24
–He forgives sin ... Mk 2:5–12
Lk 7:48
Col 1:13–14
–His blood redeems us from sin ... Eph 1:7
–His blood cleanses us from sin ... 1Jn 1:7
–He takes away the sin of the world ... Jn 1:29
1Jn 2:2

F. Humans and their sin

1. How has sin affected us?
–We are responsible for our sin ... Eze 18:10–18
–We are accountable to God for sin ... Jer 17:10
2Co 5:10
Rev 20:12
–We are subject to death because of sin ... Ge 2:17
Ro 6:23
Jas 1:15
–We cannot atone for our own sin ... Ps 49:7
Mt 16:26

2. What should we do with our sin?
–We should confess it ... Ps 32:1–5
Pr 28:13
1Jn 1:9
–We should repent of it ... Eze 18:30–31
Ac 3:19–20
–We should turn from it ... Ps 34:14
Isa 1:16
3Jn 11
–We should hate it ... Ps 97:10
Am 5:15
Ro 12:9
–We should throw it off ... Heb 12:1
–We should fight against it ... Eph 6:12–13
Heb 12:4

3. What are the blessings after confession?
–We are forgiven our sin ... Ps 32:5
Ac 2:38
Ac 10:43
–God considers us righteous ... Ro 4:5–8
Php 3:9
–We are purified from sin ... 1Jn 1:9
–We are freed from sin ... Ro 6:7,18,22
Rev 1:5
–We are no longer slaves to sin ... Ro 6:6,17
–We do not continue a life of sin ... 1Jn 3:6,9
1Jn 5:18
–We are dead to sin ... Ro 6:2,11
–We pass from death to life ... Ro 6:23

SINAI

A. A desert area where the Israelites camped ... Ex 19:1–2
–Census taken there ... Nu 1:1–4,19
–Passover celebrated there ... Nu 9:1–5
–Israelites stayed there nearly a year ... Nu 10:12

B. Mount Sinai, in the above area
 1. Identity
  –Called Mount Horeb .... Ex 33:6
  –Called the mountain of God...... Ex 3:1; Ex 24:13
  –God came down from Mount Sinai........................ Dt 33:2
  –God is the God of Mount Sinai ... Ps 68:8
 2. History and significance
  –God appeared to Moses there .... Ex 3:1–6
  –God spoke his law from there .... Ex 19:20–20:17; Dt 5:4–21
  –Israelites frightened at the mountain .... Ex 20:18–19; Dt 5:5,22–27
  –Moses received the law there..... Ex 24:15–18; Dt 9:9–11
  –Israelites worshiped a golden calf there........................ Ex 32:1–20; Dt 9:8–17; Ps 106:19–23
  –Moses received the law a second time......................... Ex 34:1–32; Lev 7:38; Dt 10:1–5,10
  –Elijah talked with God there 1Ki 19:8–18

SINGLES
See MARRIAGE

SISERA
–Canaanite commander .... Jdg 4:2
–Fought against Deborah and Barak.... Jdg 4:12–16
–Killed by Jael......................... Jdg 4:21; Jdg 5:24–30

SISTER
See BROTHERS AND SISTERS

SLAVERY
A. Slavery in the Old Testament
 1. Slavery common
  –Abraham had slaves .... Ge 20:14; Ge 21:10
  –Israelites were slaves in Egypt ... Ex 1:11; Dt 6:20–21
  –David had slaves................. 2Sa 6:20,22
  –Solomon conscripted slaves...... 1Ki 9:20–22
  –The Teacher had slaves .... Ecc 2:7
  –Sons were made slaves to pay debts.......................... 2Ki 4:1
  –Israelites were slaves to Babylon ... La 1:1
  –Israelites were slaves to Persia ... Neh 9:36
  –There were slaves among returning Jews............... Neh 5:5
 2. God and human slavery
  a. Delivered Israelites from slavery .... Ex 13:3; Ex 20:2
  b. Regulated slavery in Israel
   –Treatment of slaves............ Ex 21:5–11, 20–21; Dt 15:12–18; Dt 23:15–16
   –Release in the Year of Jubilee... Lev 25:39–55
  c. Gave rights to slaves
   –Were members of the covenant .... Ge 17:12–13
   –Rested on the Sabbath .... Ex 20:10; Dt 5:12–15
   –Included in religious meals.... Ex 12:44; Dt 16:11,14
   –Could expect equal justice..... Job 31:13
   –Could become an heir......... Ge 15:2–3

B. Slavery in the New Testament
 1. Common in Roman society........ Ac 16:16,19; 1Co 7:21; 1Ti 1:10
 2. Messages for Christian slaves
  –Slave and master are equal in Christ .... 1Co 12:13; Gal 3:28; Col 3:11; Phm 15–16
  –Slaves must respect their masters 1Ti 6:1–2
  –Slaves must submit to their masters .... Titus 2:9–10; 1Pe 2:18
  –Slaves must obey their masters... Eph 6:5–8; Col 3:22–25
  –If possible, try to gain freedom ... 1Co 7:21
 3. Messages given to Christian masters
  –Masters must treat slaves kindly .. Eph 6:9; Phm 17
  –Masters must treat slaves justly .. Col 4:1

C. Slavery as a symbol
 –By nature we are slaves to sin ...... Jn 8:34; Ro 6:16–17; Ro 7:14; 2Pe 2:19
 –The Old Testament era saw slavery to the law .... Gal 4:3–5; Gal 5:1
 –We must become slaves to righteousness .... Ro 6:18
 –We must become slaves to God and Christ .... Ro 6:22; 1Co 7:22; Eph 6:6

SNOW
See WEATHER

SODOM AND GOMORRAH
A. Their identity and location
 –Wealthy cities in the Jordan plain .. Ge 13:10
 –Extremely wicked inhabitants..... Ge 13:13; Ge 18:20–21

B. History of Sodom and Gomorrah
 –Lot went to live there .... Ge 13:11–12
 –Cities defeated by four kings .... Ge 14:8–12
 –Abram rescued the cities .... Ge 14:13–16
 –Abraham interceded for the cities .. Ge 18:23–33
 –Sodom and Gomorrah destroyed ... Ge 19:1–29
 –God's promise of restoration .... Eze 16:53–57

C. Sodom and Gomorrah used as symbols
 –A symbol of total wickedness .... Isa 3:9; Jer 23:14; Eze 16:46–50; Mt 10:15
 –A symbol of evil Jerusalem .... Rev 11:8
 –A symbol of God's judgment .... Isa 13:19; Jer 49:18; Am 4:11; Zep 2:9
 –A symbol of eternal punishment.... 2Pe 2:6; Jude 7

SOLOMON
A. Family data
 –Son of David by Bathsheba 2Sa 12:24; 1Ch 3:5
 –Married Pharaoh's daughter 1Ki 3:1
 –Later married numerous pagan women 1Ki 11:1–3

B. His early life as king
- –Appointed as king by David........ 1Ki 1:11–53
- –Given parting charge............. 1Ki 2:1–9
- –Had Adonijah and his supporters killed........................ 1Ki 2:13–46
- –Asked for wisdom................ 1Ki 3:4–15; 2Ch 1:2–13
- –Judged between two prostitutes 1Ki 3:16–28
- –Known widely for his wisdom...... 1Ki 4:29–31,34
- –Wrote three thousand proverbs..... 1Ki 4:32; Pr 1:1
- –Wrote one thousand and five songs.. 1Ki 4:32; SS 1:1
- –Built temple 1Ki 5:1–6–38; 2Ch 2:1–3:17
- –Built palace 1Ki 7:1–12
- –Furnished the temple............... 1Ki 7:13–51; 2Ch 4:1–5:1
- –Brought ark into the temple........ 1Ki 8:1–11; 2Ch 5:2–14
- –Offered prayer of dedication for temple..................... 1Ki 8:22–53; 2Ch 6:14–42
- –Dedicated the temple with sacrifices 1Ki 8:62–66; 2Ch 7:1–10
- –God made promises to Solomon 1Ki 9:1–9; 2Ch 7:11–22
- –Administrated his kingdom........ 1Ki 9:10–28; 2Ch 8:1–18
- –Visited by Queen of Sheba 1Ki 10:1–13; 2Ch 9:1–12
- –Had a glorious kingdom 1Ki 10:14–29; 2Ch 9:13–28

C. His later life as king
- –Wives turned his heart from God... 1Ki 11:1–13
- –Hadad and Rezon rebelled against him......................... 1Ki 11:14–25
- –Jeroboam rebelled against him..... 1Ki 11:26–40
- –His death......................... 1Ki 11:41–43; 2Ch 9:29–31

D. Solomon remembered after his death
- –For his organization of temple service .... 2Ch 35:3–4; Neh 12:45
- –For marrying idolatrous wives ..... Neh 13:26
- –For his splendor.................. Mt 6:29
- –For his wisdom .... Mt 12:42
- –For his building of the temple...... Ac 7:47

SON OF MAN

A. "Son of man" denotes someone merely human
- –God is not a "son of man" .... Nu 23:19
- –"Son of man" means "human"...... Ps 8:4; Ps 80:17
- –"Sons of men" are mortal .... Isa 51:12
- –Ezekiel called "son of man" .... Eze 2:1; Eze 3:1

B. Jesus as the Son of Man
- –Prophesied in the Old Testament ... Da 7:13–14
- –Identified himself as such.......... Mk 2:10; Lk 7:34; Lk 9:58; Jn 9:35–37
- –Died and rose again................ Mk 8:31; Mk 9:31; Mk 10:33–34; Jn 3:14–15
- –Is in heaven .... Mt 26:64; Ac 7:56; Rev 1:13
- –Will return .... Mt 13:41; Mk 13:26; Mk 14:62
- –We must feed on him .... Jn 6:53

SONG
See MUSIC AND SONG

SORROW
See GRIEF

SOUL
–The non-physical element in humans

A. Defining the soul

1. Basic concepts
   - –Humans were created as whole people....................... Ge 2:7
   - –Soul referred to in the context of death .... Ecc 12:7; Mt 10:28; Rev 6:9
2. Soul often synonymous with:
   - –Spirit .... Ecc 12:7; Lk 1:46–47
   - –Heart.......................... Ps 19:7–8; Ps 84:2
   - –Life............................ Ps 26:9; Ps 88:3
   - –One's whole being .... Ps 35:9–10
   - –I (i.e., one's person)............ Ps 130:5
3. Sometimes soul appears distinct from:
   - –Heart.......................... Dt 4:29; Dt 6:5
   - –Spirit .... 1Th 5:23; Heb 4:12

B. What does the soul do?

1. Expresses human emotions
   - –Peace .... Ps 23:3
   - –Refreshment .... Ps 19:7
   - –Joy............................ Ps 35:9
   - –Courage .... Jdg 5:21
   - –Support........................ 1Sa 14:7
   - –Grief.......................... 1Sa 1:10,15; Job 30:25
   - –Sorrow .... Mt 26:38
   - –Bitterness...................... Job 7:11
   - –Anguish .... Ps 6:3
   - –Depression..................... Ps 42:5,11; La 3:20
2. Has spiritual desires
   - –Thirsts for God .... Ps 42:1–2
   - –Yearns for God .... Ps 84:2
   - –Seeks God .... Dt 4:29; 2Ch 15:12
   - –Finds rest in God .... Ps 62:1,5
   - –Waits for God .... Ps 130:5–6
   - –Turns to God .... Dt 30:10; 1Ki 8:48
   - –Takes refuge in God............. Ps 57:1
   - –Loves God .... Dt 6:5; Dt 13:3
   - –Serves God..................... Dt 10:12; Jos 22:5
   - –Obeys God .... Dt 30:2; 2Ki 23:3
   - –Boasts in God .... Ps 34:2
   - –Praises God.................... Ps 103:1–2,22
   - –Cries out to God .... Rev 6:9–10

C. What does God do for the soul?
- –He redeems the soul............... Ps 49:15
- –He delivers the soul .... Ps 56:13
- –He saves the soul.................. 1Pe 1:9
- –Gives hope as an anchor for the soul....................... Heb 4:12

SPIRIT
–An immaterial being

A. The human spirit

1. Defining the spirit
   See SOUL

2. What does the spirit do?
a. Involved with the emotions
–The compelled spirit ... Job 32:18–20
–The stirred-up spirit ... 1Ch 5:26
–The revived spirit ... Ge 45:27
–The stubborn spirit ... Dt 2:30
–The bitter spirit ... 1Sa 30:6
–The fainting spirit ... Ps 142:3
–The longing spirit ... 2Sa 13:39
–The broken spirit ... Ps 51:17
–The troubled spirit ... Jn 13:21
–The anguished spirit ... Job 7:11
–The crushed spirit ... Ps 34:18
–The provoked spirit ... Ecc 7:9
–The proud spirit ... Pr 16:18
–The lowly spirit ... Isa 57:15
–The contrite spirit ... Isa 66:2
–The joyful spirit ... Lk 1:47
–The gentle, quiet spirit ... 1Pe 3:4
b. Involved with the will
–The spirit that follows God ... Nu 14:24
–The spirit that follows itself ... Eze 13:3
–The spirit that guards itself ... Mal 2:15
–The spirit of power and love ... 2Ti 1:7
–The steadfast spirit ... Ps 51:10
–The willing spirit ... Ps 51:12
–The worshiping spirit ... Jn 4:24
–The unified spirit ... Php 1:27
c. Involved with the intellect
–The inquiring spirit ... Ps 77:6
–The understanding spirit ... Isa 29:24
3. What does God do for the spirit?
–He can stir it up ... Jer 51:1
Hag 1:14
–He searches it ... Pr 20:27
–He gives us a new one ... Eze 36:26
–He gives it new birth ... Jn 3:6
–He testifies with our spirit ... Ro 8:16
–It returns to him ... Ecc 12:7
–He receives it ... Ps 31:5
B. The Holy Spirit
See HOLY SPIRIT
C. Spirit beings
1. God sends out spirits
–Angels are spirits he sends out ... Heb 1:14
See ANGEL
–A reporting spirit sent to Sennacherib ... Isa 37:7
–An evil spirit sent to Abimelech ... Jdg 9:23
–An evil spirit sent to Saul ... 1Sa 16:14–15,23
–A lying spirit sent to false prophets ... 1Ki 22:19–23
2. Evil spirits
–Have influence over humans ... 1Ti 4:1
Rev 16:13–14
–Were cast out by Jesus ... Mt 8:16
Mk 1:23–27
–Were cast out by the apostles ... Ac 5:16
Ac 16:16–18

SPIRITUALITY
See HOLINESS
MEDITATION

STARS
A. Data concerning the stars
–Created by God ... Ge 1:16
Ps 8:3
–Controlled by God ... Ps 147:4
Jer 31:35
–Show God's power ... Isa 40:26
–Must praise God ... Ps 148:3
–Were worshiped by the heathen ... 2Ki 21:3
Jer 19:13
Ac 7:43
B. Stars and constellations mentioned in the Bible
–The Bear ... Job 9:9
–Orion ... Job 9:9
–Pleiades ... Am 5:8
–The Star of Bethlehem ... Mt 2:2,9
C. Stars used as symbols
–Of Jesus the Messiah ... Nu 24:17
Rev 22:16
–Of an innumerable number ... Ge 22:17
Neh 9:23
–Of Christians as witnesses ... Php 2:15–16
–Of the saints in heaven ... Da 12:3
–Of angels ... Rev 1:16,20
–Of heretics ... Jude 13
–Of judgment at the end of time ... Isa 13:10–11
Mt 24:29
Rev 6:12

STEADFASTNESS
See PERSEVERANCE

STEALING
–Taking what belongs to someone else
A. The command against stealing
–The eighth commandment ... Ex 20:15
Dt 5:19
Mt 19:17–18
–Fraud and dishonest weights outlawed ... Lev 19:13
Pr 20:10,23
–Theft prohibited in Paul's writings ... Ro 13:8–9
Eph 4:28
–Theft profanes the name of God ... Lev 19:11–12
Jer 7:9–11
–Theft often accompanied by greed ... Ps 62:10
B. The punishment for thieves
–Expected to make restitution ... Ex 22:1–9
Nu 5:5–8
–Are subject to God's judgment ... Hab 2:6
–Can be excluded from the kingdom of God ... 1Co 6:9–10
C. Examples of stealing in the Bible
–Rachel and the household gods ... Ge 31:19,30–32
–Achan and goods from Jericho ... Jos 7:11
–Micah and eleven hundred shekels of silver ... Jdg 17:2
–Ahab and Naboth's vineyard ... 1Ki 21:16,19
See also THE RICH AND THE POOR
D. Theft used as a metaphor
–For gaining admiration (stealing hearts) ... 2Sa 15:6
–For withholding tithes (robbing God) ... Mal 3:8–9
–For claiming to speak God's word (stealing words from others) ... Jer 23:30
–For the unexpectedness of Christ's return ... Lk 12:39–40
1Th 5:2
2Pe 3:10
Rev 3:3

STEPHEN
–One of the seven deacons ... Ac 6:5
–Spoke eloquently ... Ac 6:8–10
–Arrested by the Jews ... Ac 6:11–15
–Gave powerful speech to the Sanhedrin ... Ac 7:1–53
–Stoned to death ... Ac 7:54–60
Ac 22:20

STEWARDSHIP
–How one handles what God has given
A. God's relationship to what we have
1. God owns everything ... Ex 19:5
Ps 24:1
Hag 2:8

2. God is the source of everything
–All our wealth .... Ge 26:12–13
1Co 4:7
–Our personal talents .... Ro 12:3,6
1Co 12:7–11
–Our ability to work.............. Dt 8:17–18
Ecc 2:24–25
–Every moment of our lives .... Ps 39:4–5
Mt 6:27
–Everything we have............... Job 1:21
Jn 3:27

B. Our relationship to what we have
1. Our gifts and talents
–Must use them faithfully......... Mt 25:14–27
1Co 4:2
–Must be trustworthy with them .. Lk 16:10–12
–Must use them for God's glory.... 1Sa 17:45–46
Ro 14:7–8
1Co 10:31
1Pe 4:11
–Must use them to serve others.... Ro 14:19
1Co 12:7
1Co 14:12
1Pe 4:10
2. Our time
–Recognize the brevity of time .... Job 7:7
Ps 89:47
Ecc 9:11–12
–Must be faithful in use of time ... Ps 90:12,17
Eph 5:15–16
3. Our wealth and possessions
a. Basic attitude
–Must believe that God will provide.................. Mt 6:25–34
Php 4:19
–Cannot take credit for what we have .... Da 4:28–35
1Co 4:7
–Must be content with what we have .... Php 4:11–12
1Ti 6:6–8
Heb 13:5
b. Principles of giving to the Lord
–Giving should be proportionate................ Pr 3:9
Mal 3:8–10
1Co 16:1–2
–Giving should be willing .... Ex 25:1–2
1Ch 29:6–9
2Co 8:1–5,11–12
–Giving should be spontaneous.. 2Co 9:2–5
–Giving should be cheerful 2Ch 24:10
2Co 9:7
–Giving should be generous 2Co 8:2
2Co 9:5,11,13
c. Blessings await a giver
–On earth.................... Dt 15:4
Ac 20:35
2Co 9:6,10
–In heaven.................... Mt 19:21
1Ti 6:19

STRANGERS
See ALIEN

SUFFERING
See PAIN

SUN
A. Data concerning the sun
–Created by God .... Ge 1:16
Ps 74:16
–Governs the day .... Ge 1:16
Ps 136:8
–Controlled by God .... Jos 10:12–13
Ps 19:4–6
Jer 31:35
–Needed for crops................. Dt 33:13–14
–Needed for warmth .... Ps 19:6
–Must praise God .... Ps 148:3
–Can harm a person............... Ps 121:6
–Worshiped by the heathen 2Ki 23:5,11
Jer 8:2
–No sun needed in heaven .... Isa 60:19–20
Rev 21:23

B. The sun used as a symbol
–Of God.......................... Ps 84:11
–Of God's glory .... Ps 19:1–6
–Of Christ........................ Mal 4:2
–Of Christ's glory .... Mt 17:2
Ac 26:13–15
Rev 1:16
–Of the future glory of believers ..... Mt 13:43
–Of stability and endurance......... Ps 72:5,17
–Of judgment at the end of time...... Isa 13:10–11
Mt 24:29
Rev 6:12

SWEARING
See CURSE

SYMPATHY
See COMPASSION

SYRIA, SYRIANS
See DAMASCUS

TABERNACLE
A. Related theme
TABERNACLE is a theme of Exodus........................ Ex 40:34
B. Also called "the Tent of Meeting" .... Nu 4:25
Nu 9:17–18
C. The building of the tabernacle
1. Planning the tabernacle
–Extensive plans outlined by God .... Ex 25:8–30:38
–Based on pattern of heaven .... Heb 8:5
Heb 9:24
2. Building the tabernacle
–Material collected............... Ex 35:4–29
Exod36:3–7
–Supervisers chosen .... Ex 35:30–36:2
–Work performed.................. Ex 36:8–39:31
–Inspected by Moses .... Ex 39:32–43
–The completed tabernacle set up... Ex 40:1–33
3. Structure of the tabernacle
a. Contents of the courtyard
–Its construction .... Ex 38:9–20
–Altar of burnt offering .... Ex 38:1–7
–Basin for washing .... Ex 38:8
b. Contents of the Holy Place
–Table for bread of the Presence .... Ex 25:23–30
–Golden lampstand .... Ex 37:17–24
–Altar of incense .... Ex 37:25–29
c. Contents of the Most Holy Place... Ex 37:1–9
Heb 9:4
See ARK OF THE TESTIMONY
d. Two parts separated by a curtain.. Ex 26:33
Heb 9:3

D. History of the Tent of Meeting
–God talked with Moses there....... Lev 1:1
Nu 7:89
–Aaron and his sons were consecrated there................ Ex 29:1–4,10–11
–Filled with God's glory at dedication .... Ex 40:34–35

–Covered by the cloud ... Nu 9:15–23
–Used in Israelite sacrifices ... Lev 1:3–5; Lev 3:2,8
–Placed in the center of the camp ... Nu 2:1–2,17
–Joshua was commissioned there ... Dt 31:14–15,23
–Set up at Shiloh in Canaan ... Jos 18:1; Jdg 18:31; 1Sa 2:14,22
–Located at Nob during Saul's time ... 1Sa 21:1–6
–Located at Gibeon during David's time ... 1Ch 16:37–40
–Brought to Jerusalem during David's reign ... 1Ch 23:25–26,32; 2Ch 1:4,13
–Solomon replaced it with the temple ... 2Ch 5:4–6

E. Symbolism of the tabernacle
1. Symbol of God's presence among the people ... Ex 25:8; Ex 29:43; Ex 40:34–35
2. Its contents symbolized Christ
–He is the tabernacle dwelling among men ... Jn 1:14
–His death is the atoning sacrifice ... 1Jn 4:10
–His body is sacred bread ... Jn 6:27–59
–His body is the curtain ... Heb 10:20
–His blood washes and purifies us ... 1Jn 1:7

TAMAR

A. Wife of Judah's sons Er and Onan ... Ge 38:1–10
–Tricked Judah into fathering children ... Ge 38:11–26
–Gave birth to twins ... Ge 38:27–30
–An ancestor of Jesus ... Mt 1:3

B. Daughter of David, sister of Absalom ... 2Sa 13:1
–Raped by half-brother Amnon ... 2Sa 13:2–21
–Rape avenged by Absalom ... 2Sa 13:23–33

TEACHING

See DOCTRINE
EDUCATION

TEMPLE

A. Related themes
1. TEMPLE is a theme of:
–1 Kings ... 1Ki 6:1
–2 Chronicles ... 2Ch 7:1
2. REBUILDING is a theme of Ezra ... Ezr 5:2

B. The first temple
1. Its construction
–The idea conceived by David ... 2Sa 7:1–2
–David not allowed to construct it ... 2Sa 7:4–13
–Planned by David ... 1Ch 28:11–19
–Gifts collected by David ... 1Ch 29:1–9
–Built by Solomon ... 2Ch 3:1–5:1
2. Its structure based on the tabernacle
–Contained the Most Holy Place ... 2Ch 3:8–14
–Its parts separated by a curtain ... 2Ch 3:14; Mt 27:51
3. Its history
–Ark brought into it ... 2Ch 5:2–10
–Filled with the glory of God ... 2Ch 5:13–14; 2Ch 7:1–3
–Dedicated by Solomon ... 2Ch 6:1–13; 2Ch 7:4–7
–Ransacked by Shishak of Egypt ... 2Ch 12:9
–Refurbished by Asa ... 2Ch 15:8,18
–Joash hidden there ... 2Ch 22:12
–Restored by Joash ... 2Ch 24:4–14
–Furnishings sent by Ahaz to Assyria ... 2Ch 28:21,24
–Purified by Hezekiah ... 2Ch 29:3–19
–Desecrated by Manasseh ... 2Ch 33:3–7
–Purified by Josiah ... 2Ch 34:8–11
–Ransacked by Nebuchadnezzar ... 2Ch 36:7
–Destroyed by Nebuchadnezzar ... 2Ch 36:18–19

C. The second temple
1. Its construction
–Cyrus ordered its rebuilding ... Ezr 1:1–4
–Rebuilding begun under Zerubbabel ... Ezr 3:7–13
–Opposition to its rebuilding ... Ezr 4:1–4
–Work resumed ... Ezr 5:1–2
–Completed ... Ezr 6:13–15
–Dedicated ... Ezr 6:16–18
–Repaired and beautified by Herod ... Jn 2:20
2. New Testament events in the temple
–Zechariah met by an angel there ... Lk 1:8–20
–Jesus presented there ... Lk 2:22,27
–Jesus there at twelve years old ... Lk 2:42–50
–Jesus taught there ... Mt 26:55; Mk 12:35; Jn 7:14,28
–Jesus drove out money changers ... Mt 21:12–13; Jn 2:14–17
–Curtain torn at Jesus' death ... Mt 27:51
–Early Christians worshiped there ... Ac 2:46
–Apostles taught there ... Ac 3:1–4:2; Ac 5:21,42
–Paul arrested there ... Ac 21:27–33; Ac 26:21

D. Prophecies regarding the temple
1. Temple may not give false sense of security
–Jeremiah ... Jer 7:2–8
–Micah ... Mic 3:9–12
–Stephen ... Ac 7:47–50
2. Predictions of its destruction
–The first temple ... Jer 7:14; Eze 24:20–21
–The second temple ... Mk 13:1–2
3. Prophets bemoaned its destruction ... Isa 64:10–11; La 1:9–10
4. Prophets stirred up the people to rebuild ... Ezr 5:1; Ezr 6:14; Hag 1:2–15; Zec 4:8–9
5. Predictions of its future glory ... Isa 60:7,13; Hag 2:3,7–9
6. Ezekiel's new temple ... Eze 40:1–43:27; Eze 47:1–12
7. The new Jerusalem has no temple ... Rev 21:22

E. Symbolism of the temple
1. Symbol in the Old Testament
–Of God dwelling with his people ... 2Ch 6:20,33; Ps 18:6
–Of God's favor to his people ... Ps 65:4
2. Symbol in the New Testament
–Jesus Christ as a temple ... Jn 2:19–22
–The church as a temple ... 1Co 3:16–17; 2Co 6:16; Eph 2:21–22; Heb 3:6
–The human body as a temple ... 1Co 6:19

TEMPTATION

–Enticing one to sin against God

A. The source of temptation
1. God does not tempt us to sin ... Jas 1:1

2. Satan entices us to sin
–Adam and Eve .... Ge 3:1–4
–David 1Ch 21:1
–Job .... Job 1:6–12
–Jesus .... Mt 4:1–11
–Ananias and Sapphira .... Ac 5:1–3

3. Situations tempt us to sin
–Taking the easy way .... Mt 7:13–14
Mt 16:21–23
–The things of the world .... Mt 18:7–9
–Weakness of faith .... Lk 22:31–32
–Sexual desire 1Co 7:3–5
–Pride in one's own strength .... Gal 6:1
–Persecution 1Th 3:4–5
–Riches 1Ti 6:9
–Evil desires .... Jas 1:14–15

B. The fight against temptation
–We must beware of the devil's schemes 2Co 2:11
Eph 6:11
–We must watch out for temptation ... Mt 26:41
Lk 22:40,46
1Pe 5:8
–God helps us overcome temptation ... 1Co 10:13
–Christ helps us overcome temptation .... Heb 2:17–18
Heb 4:15–16
–We must pray for help against temptation .... Mt 6:13

TEN COMMANDMENTS

–Given by God from Mount Sinai .... Ex 20:1–17
Ex 34:28
Dt 5:7–21
–Written on stone tablets .... Ex 34:1
Dt 4:13
Dt 10:4
–Stored in the Ark of the Testimony .... Dt 10:1–2
1Ki 8:9
–Summary of commandments is love ... Mt 22:37–40
Ro 13:9–10
–Ten individual commandments .... Ex 34:28
Dt 4:13

See ADULTERY
CHILDREN
COVETING
CURSE
IDOLATRY
LYING
MURDER
SABBATH
SEXUAL STANDARDS
STEALING
WORSHIP

TESTAMENT

See COVENANT

TESTING

A. Humans' testing
1. Testing God
a. Positive examples
–Gideon testing God's call .... Jdg 6:36–40
–Ahaz invited to test God .... Isa 7:10–12
–Israelites invited to test God ... Mal 3:10
b. Negative examples
–Grumbling over water .... Ex 17:1–2,7
Dt 33:8
Ps 95:9
–Grumbling over food .... Ps 78:17–18
Ps 106:14–15
–Many times of testing .... Nu 14:22
Ps 78:41
–[illegible] tested Jesus .... Mt 16:1
Mt 19:3
[illegible] Mk 8:11
–Ananias and Sapphira test the Spirit .... Ac 5:1–10
c. The command not to test God ... Dt 6:16
Mt 4:7
1Co 10:9

2. The testing of ourselves
–The Teacher tests himself .... Ecc 2:1–11
–We must test our faith 2Co 13:5–7
–We must test our actions .... Gal 6:4
–We must test everything 1Th 5:21
–We must test the spirits 1Jn 4:1

B. God's testing of humans
1. God as a testing God
–God tests our hearts 1Ch 29:17
Pr 17:3
Jer 11:20
1Th 2:4
–His testing refines us .... Ps 66:10
Isa 48:10
Jer 9:7
–We may ask God to test us .... Ps 26:2
Ps 139:23

2. Examples of God's testing
–Abraham, with sacrifice of Isaac .... Ge 22:1
Heb 11:17
–The Israelites, with lack of water .... Ex 15:22–26
–The Israelites, with rules on manna .... Ex 16:4–5
Dt 8:2–3,16
–The Israelites, with thunder on Mount Sinai .... Ex 20:18–20
–The Israelites, with false prophets .... Dt 13:1–3
–The Israelites, with heathen nations .... Jdg 2:20–3:4
–Hezekiah, with envoys from Babylon 2Ch 32:31
–Job, with suffering .... Job 23:10
–Christians, with trials and suffering .... Jas 1:2–3,12
Rev 3:10

3. Purpose of God's testing
–To humble us .... Dt 8:2–3
–To see if we will love him .... Dt 13:3
–To see if we will fear him .... Ex 20:18–20
–To see if we will obey him .... Ge 22:1
Ex 16:4–5
–To see if we will persevere in our faith .... Jas 1:2–3
Rev 3:10–11

THADDAEUS

–Disciple of Jesus .... Mt 10:3
Mk 3:18
–Probably also known as Judas son of James .... Lk 6:16
Jn 14:22
–One of the apostles .... Ac 1:13

THANKSGIVING

A. Related theme
THANKSGIVING is a theme of Psalms .... Ps 100:4

B. Thanksgiving is a command
–A command in the psalms .... Ps 75:1
Ps 107:1
Ps 118:1
Ps 136:1–3
–A command in the prophets .... Isa 12:4
Jer 33:11

–Time ends with final judgment . . . Rev 20:11–15

B. Time as opportunity
–A time for everything . . . Ecc 3:1–8,17; Ecc 8:6
–Our times are in God's hands . . . Ps 31:15
–We must make proper use of time . . . Ps 90:12; 1Co 7:29–31; Eph 5:15; Col 4:5

TIMOTHY

A. Early life
–From Lystra . . . Ac 16:1–2
–From a mixed marriage; uncircumcised . . . Ac 16:1,3
–Brought up as a good Jewish boy . . . 2Ti 3:15
–Taught by mother and grandmother . . . 2Ti 1:5
–Became a believer through Paul . . . 1Co 4:17; 1Ti 1:1
–Circumcised by Paul . . . Ac 16:3
–A young man . . . 1Ti 4:12

B. His life as co-worker with Paul
–Went with Paul on second missionary journey . . . Ac 16:3–4
–Stayed in Berea with Silas . . . Ac 17:14
–Sent to Thessalonica . . . 1Th 3:2
–Came to Paul in Corinth . . . Ac 18:5; 1Th 3:6
–Sent to Macedonia . . . Ac 19:22
–Sent to settle problems at Corinth . . . 1Co 4:17; 1Co 16:10
–Accompanied Paul as he headed to Jerusalem . . . Ac 20:1–4
–Co-writer with Paul . . . 2Co 1:1; Col 1:1; 1Th 1:1
–Ministered to Paul in Philippi . . . Php 2:19–24
–Led church at Ephesus . . . 1Ti 1:3
–A pastor responsible for worship . . . 1Ti 2:1–10; 2Ti 4:2–5
–Spent some time in prison . . . Heb 13:23

C. His character
–A hard worker for the Lord . . . Php 2:19–24; 2Ti 2:15; 2Ti 4:5
–A good follower of Paul . . . 1Co 4:17; Php 2:22; 2Ti 1:13–14
–Somewhat timid . . . 2Ti 1:6–7
–Needed encouragement . . . 1Ti 4:11–16; 1Ti 6:11–14,20
–Tendency to get sick . . . 1Ti 5:23

TITHES AND OFFERINGS

A. Tithes
1. In the Old Testament
–Tithing commanded . . . Lev 27:30–33; Dt 12:6–7; 2Ch 31:4–8
–A tenth of everything required . . . Ge 14:20; Ge 28:22; Dt 14:23
–Tithes used to support Levites . . . Nu 18:21–24; Dt 14:22–27
–Israelites stopped tithing . . . Neh 13:10–12; Mal 3:8–10
2. In the New Testament
–Tithing became hypocritical . . . Mt 23:23; Lk 11:42
–Tithers were self-righteous . . . Lk 18:9–12

B. Offerings
1. In the Old Testament
a. The burnt offering . . . Lev 1:1–17; Lev 6:8–13; Lev 8:18–21
b. The grain offering . . . Lev 2:1–16; Lev 6:14–23
c. The fellowship offering . . . Lev 3:1–17; Lev 7:11–34
d. The sin offering . . . Lev 4:1–5:13; Lev 6:24–30; Lev 8:14–17
e. The guilt offering . . . Lev 5:14–6:7; Lev 7:1–6
f. Freewill offerings
–For the tabernacle . . . Ex 25:1–7; Ex 35:4–9,29
–For the first temple . . . 1Ch 29:6–9; 2Ch 24:8–11
–For the second temple . . . Ezr 2:68
–In the Feast of Weeks . . . Dt 16:10
–As one of the fellowship offerings . . . Lev 7:16
g. Offerings sometimes given hypocritically . . . Isa 1:11–13; Hag 2:14; Mal 1:6–14; Mal 3:8–9
2. Freewill offerings in the New Testament
–Given for the poor . . . Lk 19:8; Ac 11:28–30; Ro 15:25–27
–Given to support Paul . . . 2Co 11:8–9; Php 4:15–18
3. Principles of giving offerings
–Freely . . . Mt 10:8
–Joyfully . . . 2Co 9:7
–In proportion to income . . . Dt 16:17; Pr 3:9; 1Co 16:2
–Generously . . . Ps 37:26; 2Co 9:5–6; 1Ti 6:18

See also THE RICH AND THE POOR
SACRIFICE
STEWARDSHIP

TITUS

–A Christian led by Paul to the Lord . . . Titus 1:4
–Gentile co-worker of Paul . . . 2Co 8:23; Gal 2:1–3
–Sent to Corinth . . . 2Co 2:13; 2Co 8:6,16–18; 2Co 12:18
–Sent to Crete . . . Titus 1:4–5
–Sent to Dalmatia . . . 2Ti 4:10

TONGUES

See GIFTS OF THE SPIRIT
LANGUAGE

TRADITION

–Teachings and religious observances handed down

A. Teachings passed down
–By parents to children . . . Ps 78:3–6; Pr 1:7
–By the Jewish elders . . . Mk 7:3,5
–By the apostles . . . 1Co 11:2,23–26; 1Co 15:3–7; 2Th 2:15

B. Dangers of traditions
–Can obscure God's word . . . Mt 15:1–9; Mk 7:1–13
–Can misdirect a person's life . . . Mic 6:16; Gal 1:14

C. Reactions to traditions
–Consider bad ones to be rubbish .... Php 3:4–8
–Hold fast to good ones 1Co 15:1–5
2Th 2:15

TREE

A. Kinds of trees mentioned in the Bible
–Acacia .... Ex 25:5
–Algum 2Ch 2:8
–Almond .... Ge 30:37
–Apple .... SS 2:3
–Balsam 2Sa 5:23
–Broom 1Ki 19:4
–Cedar 1Ki 4:33
–Citron .... Rev 18:12
–Cypress .... Ge 6:14
–Ebony .... Eze 27:15
–Fig .... Mt 21:19
–Fir .... Isa 41:19
–Myrtle .... Neh 8:15
–Nut .... SS 6:11
–Oak .... Ge 35:4
–Olive .... Jdg 9:8
–Palm .... Ex 15:27
–Pine .... Isa 41:19
–Plane .... Ge 30:37
–Pomegranate 1Sa 14:2
–Poplar .... Ps 137:2
–Sycamore .... Lk 19:4
–Tamarisk .... Ge 21:33
–Terebinth .... Hos 4:13
–Willow .... Eze 17:5

B. Trees used in a symbolic way
1. Significant trees
–The tree of knowledge of good and evil .... Ge 2:17
–The tree of life .... Ge 3:22,24
Rev 22:2
–The tree of the cross .... Ac 5:30
Gal 3:13
1Pe 2:24
2. Comparison to trees
–The righteous are like a tree .... Ps 1:3
Ps 92:12–15
Isa 61:3
–Wisdom is like a tree .... Pr 3:18
–The Branch is a symbol of Christ .... Isa 11:1
Jer 23:5–6
3. Illustrations connected with trees
–Parable of the trees and thornbush .... Jdg 9:7–20
–Parable of the coming new tree .... Eze 17:22–24
–Parable of the tree and its fruit .... Mt 7:17–19
–Parable of the mustard seed .... Mt 13:31–32
–Parable of the barren fig tree .... Lk 13:6–9
Mk 11:12–14
–Cursing of the fig tree .... Mt 21:18–22
–A lesson from the fig tree .... Mt 24:32–33
–Parable of the two olive trees .... Ro 11:17–24

TRIBULATION

See GREAT TRIBULATION
PAIN

TRINITY

–One God in three persons–Father, Son and Holy Spirit

A. There is only one God
–Expressed in the Old Testament .... Dt 4:35,39
Dt 6:4
Isa 45:21
–Expressed in the New Testament 1Co 8:5–6
Eph 4:6
1Ti 2:5
Jas 2:19

B. Hints of a plurality in God in the Old Testament
–God speaks of himself as "us" .... Ge 1:26–27
Ge 3:22
Ge 11:7
Isa 6:8
–Someone coming from God is God .... Isa 7:14
Isa 9:6
See ANGEL OF THE LORD

C. The Son as God
See JESUS CHRIST

D. The Holy Spirit as God
See HOLY SPIRIT

E. Father, Son and Spirit together
–One name for the three .... Mt 28:19
–The three persons mentioned together .... Mt 3:16–17
Jn 15:26
Ro 5:5–6
Ro 8:11,16–17
1Co 12:4–6
2Co 13:14
Gal 4:4–6
Eph 4:4–6
1Th 1:2–5
2Th 2:13
Titus 3:4–6
1Pe 1:2
1Jn 4:2
Jude 20–21

F. Similar divine characteristics for all three
1. Holiness
–Of the Father .... Jn 17:11
–Of the Son 1Co 1:30
–Of the Spirit .... Ro 1:4
2. Eternity
–Of the Father 1Ti 1:17
–Of the Son .... Heb 1:2–3,8
–Of the Spirit .... Heb 9:14
3. All-knowing
–Of the Father .... Mt 6:8,32
–Of the Son .... Jn 2:24–25
–Of the Spirit 1Co 2:10–11
4. All-powerful
–Of the Father .... Ps 135:5–7
–Of the Son 1Co 15:24–27
–Of the Spirit .... Ro 15:13,19
5. Everywhere present
–Of the Father .... Jer 23:24
–Of the Son .... Mt 28:20
–Of the Spirit .... Ps 139:7–10

G. Similar divine activities for all three
1. Creating
–By the Father .... Ge 1:1
–By the Son .... Jn 1:3
–By the Spirit .... Ps 104:30
2. Giving of spiritual life
–By the Father .... Eph 2:4–5
–By the Son .... Jn 10:10
–By the Spirit .... Eze 37:14
3. Performing miracles
–By the Father 1Ki 18:38
–By the Son .... Mt 4:23–24
–By the Spirit .... Ro 15:19
4. Teaching
–By the Father .... Ps 71:17
Isa 48:17
–By the Son .... Jn 13:13
–By the Spirit .... Jn 14:26
5. Experiencing grief because of sin
–By the Father .... Ge 6:6
–By the Son .... Lk 19:41–44
–By the Spirit .... Eph 4:30

TRUST

–Confidence put in someone or something

A. Related themes
  TRUST is a theme of Psalms......... Ps 62:5
  TRUST AND OBEY is a theme of Joshua......... Jos 10:25

B. In whom/what must we trust?
  –In God......... Ps 25:2; Ps 56:3–4,11; Ps 91:2
  –In the Lord......... Ps 4:5; Pr 3:5; Na 1:7; Ac 14:23
  –In Christ......... Jn 14:1; Ro 10:11; 1Pe 2:6
  –In the name of the Lord......... Ps 20:7; Isa 50:10; Zep 3:12
  –In the word of God......... Ps 119:42
  –In God's unfailing love......... Ps 9:10; Ps 52:8

C. What are the results of trusting in God?
  –We become righteous and just......... Ps 37:5–6
  –We are saved......... Isa 25:9
  –We are blessed......... Ps 40:4
  –We experience joy......... Ps 33:21
  –We are released from fear......... Ps 56:3–4
  –We receive direction from the Lord......... Pr 3:5–6
  –We stand firm......... Ps 20:7–8
  –We prosper......... Pr 28:25
  –God keeps us safe......... Jer 39:17–18
  –God delivers us......... Ps 22:4
  –God cares for us......... Na 1:7
  –God surrounds us with his love......... Ps 32:10
  –Jesus prepares a place for us......... Jn 14:1–2

D. In what ought we not trust?
  –In idols......... 2Ki 17:14–15; Isa 42:17; Jer 13:25
  –In other people......... Ps 118:8–9; Ps 146:3; Jer 17:5–7
  –In ourselves......... Pr 28:26
  –In fortified cities......... Jer 5:17
  –In horses and chariots......... Ps 20:7; Isa 31:1–3
  –In weapons......... Ps 44:6
  –In riches......... Job 31:24–28; Ps 52:7; Lk 12:13–21; 1Ti 6:17

TRUTH

–What is accurate and agrees with reality

A. Related theme
  TRUTH is a theme of 1 John......... 1Jn 2:8

B. Of whom/what is truth characteristic?
  1. God
    –The Father......... Ps 31:5; Isa 65:16
    –Jesus......... Jn 1:14; Jn 14:6
    –The Spirit......... Jn 14:17; 1Jn 5:6
  2. God's revelation
    –God's law......... Ps 119:43
    –God's word......... 2Sa 7:28; Isa 45:19; Jn 17:17
    –The testimony of Jesus......... Jn 8:45–46; Jn 18:37
    –The word of the prophets......... 1Ki 18:24; 1Ki 22:16; Jer 26:15
    –The gospel proclaimed by the apostles......... 2Co 4:2; Gal 2:5,14; Eph 1:13
  3. The church, the pillar of truth......... 1Ti 3:15

C. How must believers relate to the truth?
  –Must know it......... Ps 51:6; 1Ti 2:4
  –Must come to a knowledge of it......... 2Ti 2:25; Titus 1:1; Heb 10:26
  –Must seek it......... Jer 5:1
  –Must choose it......... Ps 119:30
  –Must buy it......... Pr 23:23
  –Must believe it......... 2Th 2:13
  –Must love it......... Zec 8:19
  –Must walk in it......... Ps 26:3; 3Jn 3–5
  –Must live by it......... Jn 3:21; 1Jn 1:6
  –Must obey it......... Gal 5:7
  –Must worship in it......... Jn 4:23–24
  –Must speak it......... Ps 15:2; Zec 8:16; Eph 4:25

D. What does the truth do for us?
  –Protects us......... Ps 40:11
  –Guides us......... Ps 43:3
  –Sets us free......... Jn 8:31–32
  –Sanctifies us......... Jn 17:17,19
  –Purifies us......... 1Pe 1:22

E. What do the wicked do with respect to truth?
  –Reject it......... Isa 59:14–15; Ro 2:8
  –Do not speak it......... Jer 9:5
  –Distort it......... Ac 20:30
  –Suppress it......... Ro 1:18
  –Exchange it for a lie......... Ro 1:25
  –Wander away from it......... 2Ti 2:18
  –Oppose it......... 2Ti 3:8
  –Turn away from it......... 2Ti 4:4

TYRE

A. Identity and location
  –A merchant city......... Neh 13:16
  –A seacoast city......... Lk 6:17
  –Often linked with Sidon......... Isa 23:1–2; Mt 15:21
  See SIDON

B. Significance of Tyre
  1. In the Old Testament
    –Territory given to tribe of Asher......... Jos 19:24,29
    –King Hiram sent wood for David's palace......... 2Sa 5:11–12; 1Ch 14:1–2
    –King Hiram sent wood for the temple......... 1Ki 5:7–12; 2Ch 2:11–16
    –Huram of Tyre was a temple craftsman......... 1Ki 7:13–14
    –Prophecies against them......... Isa 23:1–18; Eze 26:1–28:19; Joel 3:4–8; Am 1:9–10
  2. In the New Testament
    –Jesus ministered there......... Mt 15:21–28; Mk 7:24–30
    –Paul spent seven days there......... Ac 21:3–6

UNION WITH CHRIST

A. Related theme
IN CHRIST is a theme of Ephesians .. Eph 2:6
B. Christians are:
–In Christ ... 1Th 2:14
–New creatures in Christ ... 2Co 5:17
–The faithful in Christ ... Eph 1:1
C. Our participation in events of Christ's life
–We suffer with him ... Ro 8:17; Php 3:10; 1Pe 4:13
–We share in his broken body ... 1Co 10:16–17
–We share in his shed blood ... 1Co 10:16–17
–We are crucified with him ... Ro 6:6,8; Col 2:20
–We are buried with him ... Ro 6:4; Col 2:12
–We are raised with him ... Eph 2:6; Col 2:12; Col 3:1
–We sit at God's right hand with him ... Eph 2:6; Col 3:1
–We will return with him ... 1Th 4:14
–We will share in his glory ... Ro 8:17
–We will reign with him ... 2Ti 2:12
D. Our involvement in Christ
–We are chosen in him ... Eph 1:4,11
–We are justified in him ... Gal 2:17
–We who are in him are free from condemnation ... Ro 8:1
–We are baptized into him ... Gal 3:27; Col 2:11–13
–We are babes in him ... 1Co 3:1
–We are found in him ... Php 3:9
–We are one with him ... Jn 14:20; Jn 17:21,23; 1Co 6:17
–We must remain in him ... Jn 15:4–5,7
–We live in him ... 1Jn 3:24
–Our way of life is in him ... 1Co 4:17
–We grow in him ... Eph 4:16
–We pray in him ... Eph 2:18; Eph 3:12
–We are blessed in him ... Eph 1:3
–We are sanctified in him ... 1Co 1:2
–We fall asleep (die) in him ... 1Th 4:14,16; 1Co 15:18
–We will be made alive in him ... 1Co 15:22
E. Pictures of union with Christ
–Vine and branches ... Jn 15:1–7
–Foundation and building ... 1Co 3:10–11; Eph 2:20–21
–Head and members of the body ... Ro 12:4–5; 1Co 12:14–27
–Husband and wife ... Eph 5:23–32
–Shepherd and sheep ... Jn 10:11,14–16

UNITY

A. Related themes
UNITY is a theme of:
–Acts ... Ac 4:32
–1 Corinthians ... 1Co 12:13
B. Expressions of the unity of the church
–One nation and people ... 1Pe 2:9–10
–One body ... Ro 12:4–5; 1Co 12:13,27
–One family ... Eph 2:19
–One bride/spouse ... 2Co 11:2; Eph 5:23–30
–One temple ... 1Co 3:16–17
–One building with one foundation .. 1Co 3:9–11; Eph 2:20–21
–One spiritual house ... 1Pe 2:5
–One field/vineyard ... Jn 15:5; 1Co 3:9
–One flock ... Jn 10:16
–One city ... Heb 12:22–23
C. The basis of unity
–Christ's unity with the Father ... Jn 17:20–23
–Christ's death on the cross ... Eph 2:14–16
–Our unity with Christ ... Gal 3:26–28
–The one Holy Spirit ... Eph 4:3–4
–Our common faith and hope ... Eph 4:4–5,13
D. Demonstrations of unity
–The life of the early church ... Ac 2:42–47; Ac 4:32
–The Lord's Supper ... 1Co 10:16–17
E. Important elements of unity
–Unity is good and pleasant ... Ps 133:1
–Unity makes God's people fruitful .. Ps 133:3
–Unity is a challenge we must strive to achieve ... Eph 4:12–16; Php 1:27; Php 2:1–3; 1Th 5:13; 1Pe 3:8
–Unity requires that we love one another ... Eph 4:15–16
–Diversity in gifts is consistent with unity ... Ro 12:4–8; 1Co 12:7–30
–Diversity in thinking is consistent with unity ... Ro 14:1–6
F. Causes of disunity
–Quarreling ... Ac 15:36–39; 1Co 3:3
–Favoritism ... Jas 2:1–4
–Spiritual immaturity ... 1Co 1:10–12; 1Co 3:1–2
–Hypocrisy ... Gal 2:11–14; 1Pe 2:1

URIAH

–Hittite husband of Bathsheba ... 2Sa 11:2–3
–One of David's brave warriors ... 2Sa 23:39
–Devoted to duty ... 2Sa 11:8–13
–Killed on David's orders ... 2Sa 11:16–25

URIM AND THUMMIM

See CASTING LOTS

USURY

See DEBT

UZZIAH

–Son of Amaziah; king of Judah ... 2Ch 26:1–5
–Also called Azariah ... 2Ki 15:1
–An effective and powerful king ... 2Ch 26:6–15
–Became proud and unlawfully burnt incense ... 2Ch 26:16–19
–Punished with leprosy ... 2Ki 15:5; 2Ch 26:20–21

VASHTI

–Wife of Ahasuerus (Xerxes); Queen of Persia ... Est 1:9
–Refused to display her beauty ... Est 1:10–12
–Deposed as queen ... Est 1:15–21
–Replaced by Esther ... Est 2:17

VICTORY

See WARFARE

VINEYARD

A. Significant vineyards in the Bible
–Noah's ... Ge 9:20

–Those in Canaan . . . . . Nu 13:23–24
Dt 8:8
–Naboth's 1Ki 21:1–16
–Vineyards in Jesus' parables . . . . . Mt 20:1–15
Mt 21:28–31, 33–40

B. Design and care of vineyards

1. The design
–Had protecting walls . . . . . Nu 22:24
Pr 24:30–31
–Had a tower for watchmen . . . . . Isa 5:1–2
Mt 21:33
–Had a winepress in it . . . . . Isa 5:2
Mt 21:33

2. The care
–Clearing the field . . . . . Isa 5:2
–Planting . . . . . Ps 107:37
Ecc 2:4
Isa 5:2
–Cultivating . . . . . Dt 28:39
Isa 7:25
–Pruning . . . . . Lev 25:3
Jn 15:2
–Harvesting . . . . . Lev 19:10
Jdg 9:27
–Treading the winepress . . . . . Isa 16:10

C. Vineyards used as a symbol

1. A symbol of prosperity and security
–To sit in one's vineyard meant security 1Ki 4:25
Mic 4:4
–To eat from one's vineyard meant prosperity 2Ki 18:31
Ps 107:37–38
Isa 36:16

2. Spiritual symbols
–A symbol of the Israelite nation . . Ps 80:8–11
Isa 5:7
Jer 2:21
Hos 10:1
–A symbol of the followers of Jesus . . . . . Jn 15:1–6
–A symbol of the kingdom of heaven . . . . . Mt 20:1–15
Mt 21:28–33

VISION

See DREAMS AND VISIONS

VOICE

A. The human voice

1. Uses of the human voice
–Ordinary communication 1Sa 24:16
–Recognizing a person . . . . . Ge 27:22
1Sa 26:17
Ac 12:14
–Expressing unity (one voice) . . . . . Ex 24:3
–Praying . . . . . Ps 66:19
–Requesting a favor . . . . . Lk 17:13
–Preaching . . . . . Ac 2:14

2. Expressions of the human voice
–The praising voice 2Ch 20:19
Lk 17:15
–The shouting voice . . . . . Isa 40:9
–The complaining voice . . . . . Ps 64:1
–The weeping voice . . . . . Jer 31:15–16

B. The voice of God

1. Expressions of God's voice
a. People called by his voice
–Moses . . . . . Ex 3:4–6
Ac 7:31–32
–Samuel 1Sa 3:1–14
–Isaiah . . . . . Isa 6:8–10

b. The power of his voice
–Accompanied by fire . . . . . Dt 4:33
–Sounds like thunder 2Sa 22:14
Job 37:4–5
Ps 29:3–4
–Accomplishes great things . . . . . Ps 29:5–9
Ps 46:6
–Can come as a gentle whisper . 1Ki 19:12–13

c. Messages of his voice
–His law from Mount Sinai . . . . . Dt 5:22–26
–Affirmation of Jesus as his Son . . . . . Mt 3:17
Lk 9:35–36
–Glorification of Jesus . . . . . Jn 12:28–30

2. The voice of Jesus
–Jesus proclaimed with a loud voice . . . . . Jn 7:37–38
–Jesus cried out with a loud voice . . . . . Mt 27:46,50
–His voice raised Lazarus . . . . . Jn 11:43
–His voice called Paul to be an apostle . . . . . Ac 9:4–6
–His voice revealed things to John . . . . . Rev 1:10–13
–His voice calls his sheep . . . . . Jn 10:16,27
–His voice will raise the dead . . . . . Jn 5:25,28

3. Our response to God's voice
–We must recognize his voice . . . . . Jn 10:3–5
–We must listen to his voice . . . . . Ex 15:26
Dt 30:20
–We must obey his voice 1Sa 15:22
Hag 1:12

VOW

–A solemn promise made to God

A. Significant vows in the Bible
–Jacob's vow at Bethel . . . . . Ge 28:20–22
–The Nazirite vow . . . . . Nu 6:1–21
–Jephthah's vow . . . . . Jdg 11:30–31
–Nazirite vow required for Samson . Jdg 13:1–7
–Hannah's vow regarding Samuel . . . 1Sa 1:11
–David's vow regarding a temple for the Lord . . . . . Ps 132:1–5
–Paul's Nazirite vow . . . . . Ac 18:18

B. The nature of the vow
–Often arose in times of distress . . . . . Ge 28:20–22
Nu 21:1–2
Ps 66:13–14
Ps 116:7–14
–Made only to God . . . . . Lev 27:2,9
Dt 23:21–23
Isa 19:21
–Was completely voluntary . . . . . Dt 23:22
Ecc 5:5
–Had to be fulfilled . . . . . Dt 23:21,23
Ecc 5:4,6
–Should not be made rashly . . . . . Pr 20:25
–Rules for redeeming vows . . . . . Lev 27:1–33
–Could be abused at times . . . . . Mk 7:9–13

WALK OF LIFE

–The Christian way of life

A. Related themes

1. CHRISTIAN LIVING is a theme of:
–Romans . . . . . Ro 12:1
–Ephesians . . . . . Eph 4:1
–Philippians . . . . . Php 1:27
–Colossians . . . . . Col 3:12
–1 Thessalonians 1Th 4:1
–James . . . . . Jas 1:27
–1 Peter 1Pe 5:6

2. RESPONSE is a theme of Deuteronomy . . . . . Dt 13:4

3. ATTITUDE is a theme of Proverbs ..... Pr 10:12

B. What the Christian walk is not
- –Not walking according to the sinful nature ..... Ro 8:4; Gal 5:16–21
- –Not walking in the ways of evildoers ..... 1Ki 15:26,34; Pr 4:14
- –Not walking in dark ways ..... Pr 2:13
- –Not walking in darkness ..... Jn 8:12; 1Jn 1:6; 1Jn 2:11
- –Not walking in the counsel of the wicked ..... Ps 1:1
- –Not walking in pride ..... Da 4:37; Mic 2:3

C. What the Christian walk is
- –Walking with God ..... Ps 56:13; Mic 6:8; Rev 3:4
- –Walking in God's ways ..... Dt 5:33; Dt 10:12; Jos 22:5
- –Walking before God 1Ki 2:4; 2Ch 7:17
- –Walking in truth ..... Ps 26:3; 3Jn 3–4
- –Walking in the light ..... Ps 89:15; Isa 2:5; 1Jn 1:7
- –Walking in the name of God ..... Mic 4:5
- –Walking in the fear of God ..... Neh 5:9
- –Walking in the law of God ..... Ps 119:1
- –Walking in love and obedience 2Jn 6
- –Walking in the Spirit ..... Ro 8:4
- –Walking in the paths of the righteous ..... Pr 2:20
- –Walking as Jesus walked 1Jn 2:6

D. Examples of those who walked with God
- –Enoch ..... Ge 5:22–24
- –Noah ..... Ge 6:9
- –Abraham ..... Ge 24:40
- –Isaac ..... Ge 48:15
- –Levi ..... Mal 2:4–6
- –Jotham 2Ch 27:6
- –Hezekiah ..... Isa 38:3

E. God's promise to walk with us ..... Lev 26:12; 2Co 6:16

WARFARE

A. Related themes
1. CONFLICT is a theme of Revelation ..... Rev 12:7
2. GOD'S HELP is a theme of 1 Samuel 1Sa 17:45
3. GOD'S INTERVENTION is a theme of 2 Chronicles 2Ch 20:17
4. DELIVERANCE is a theme of Esther ..... Est 8:11
5. VICTORY is a theme of:
   - –Joshua ..... Jos 21:43
   - –Daniel ..... Da 6:27
6. CHRIST'S VICTORY is a theme of Revelation ..... Rev 11:15

B. Physical Warfare

1. Wars in the Bible
- a. First recorded war ..... Ge 14:1–17
- b. Israelite wars on the way to Canaan ..... Ex 17:8–13; Nu 21:1–3,21–35
- c. Wars of Joshua
  - –The battle against Jericho ..... Jos 6:1–25
  - –The battle against Ai ..... Jos 7:3–5; Jos 8:1–29
  - –The battle against five kings ..... Jos 10:1–28
  - –The southern cities defeated ..... Jos 10:29–43
  - –The northern cities defeated ..... Jos 11:1–23
- d. Wars in the period of the judges
  - –Deborah and Barak ..... Jdg 4:12–23
  - –Gideon ..... Jdg 7:1–25
  - –Jephthah ..... Jdg 11:4–33
  - –During Eli's judgeship 1Sa 4:1–10; 1Sa 7:2–14
- e. Wars during the time of Saul
  - –Saul rescued the city of Jabesh 1Sa 11:1–11
  - –Against the Philistines 1Sa 13:2–7; 1Sa 14:1–46; 1Sa 17:1–54; 1Sa 31:1–7
  - –Against the Amalekites 1Sa 15:4–9; 1Sa 30:1–20
- f. Wars during the time of David
  - –Gained control of all Israel 2Sa 2:8–4:12
  - –Against the Philistines 2Sa 5:17–25; 2Sa 21:15–22
  - –Against the Ammonites 2Sa 10:1–14
  - –Against the Arameans 2Sa 10:15–19
  - –Civil war against Absalom 2Sa 15:1–18:18
  - –Summary of wars 2Sa 8:1–14
- g. Wars of the northern kingdom
  - –Against the southern kingdom 1Ki 15:16–17,32; 2Ki 13:12; 2Ki 14:9–14; 2Ki 16:5–6
  - –Against the Philistines 1Ki 16:15–17
  - –Against the Arameans 1Ki 20:1–34; 1Ki 22:1–37; 2Ki 6:8–7:11; 2Ki 8:28–29; 2Ki 13:3–7
  - –Against Assyria 2Ki 15:19–20, 29–30; 2Ki 16:7–10; 2Ki 17:1–6
- h. Wars of the southern kingdom
  - –Against the Egyptians 1Ki 14:25–26
  - –Against the Edomites 2Ki 8:20–22; 2Ki 14:7
  - –Against the Ammonites and Moabites 2Ch 20:1–26
  - –Against Assyria 2Ch 32:1–22; 2Ch 33:10–11
  - –Against Babylon 2Ki 24:1–4,10–16; 2Ki 25:1–21

2. Victory for God's people
- a. God is the source of victory ..... Nu 21:3; Dt 20:1–4; Jos 11:7–8; 2Ch 20:15–17; Ps 18:29,34–43; Pr 21:31
- b. Principles of victory
  - –Success when faithful to the Lord ..... Jdg 7:1–25; 1Sa 17:41–50; 2Ch 20:20
  - –Defeat when unfaithful 2Ki 17:5–20; 2Ki 21:10–15
- c. God controls foreign armies ..... Isa 13:3–5; Jer 25:8–9; Eze 21:18–22

C. Spiritual warfare
- 1. God is at war with Satan
  - –At the time of Job .... Job 1:6–12; Job 26:6–13
  - –In the days of Israel .... Isa 27:1
  - –At the time of Christ .... Mt 4:1–11; Lk 10:18
  - –In heaven .... Rev 12:7–9
- 2. Christians are at war
  - –With the devil .... Ge 3:1–15; 2Co 2:11; 1Pe 5:8
  - –With the powers of darkness .... Eph 6:12
  - –With the world .... Jn 15:18–19; 1Jn 2:15–17
  - –With the old self .... Ro 6:6,12
  - –With the sinful nature .... Ro 8:5–9; Gal 5:16–25
  - –With sinful desires .... Ro 7:15–20; 1Pe 2:11
  - –With death .... 1Co 15:26; Heb 2:14–15
- 3. How Christians ought to fight
  - –By depending on God .... Ps 18:29,32; Ps 27:1–2
  - –By being dedicated to Jesus Christ 2Ti 2:4; 1Pe 5:10
  - –By standing firm in the Lord .... Eph 6:10–14
  - –By holding on to the faith 1Ti 1:18–19; 1Jn 5:4–5
  - –By laying hold of eternal life 1Ti 6:12
  - –By being good soldiers 2Ti 2:3
  - –By enduring hardship 2Ti 2:3
  - –By exercising self-denial 1Co 9:26–27
  - –By praying .... Eph 6:18
  - –By resisting the devil 1Pe 5:8–9
- 4. Protection provided by the Lord
  - –The full armor of God .... Eph 6:11,13
  - –The armor of light .... Ro 13:12
  - –God as our shield .... Ge 15:1; Dt 33:29; Ps 115:9–11
  - –The shield of faith .... Eph 6:16
  - –The belt of righteousness .... Isa 11:5
  - –The belt of truth .... Eph 6:14
  - –The breastplate of righteousness .... Isa 59:17; Eph 6:14
  - –The breastplate of faith and love 1Th 5:8
  - –Feet ready to run to bring the good news .... Isa 52:7; Eph 6:15
  - –The helmet of salvation .... Eph 6:17; 1Th 5:8
  - –The sword of the Spirit, the word of God .... Eph 6:17; Heb 4:12
- 5. Victory is certain
  - a. Accomplished by Christ
    - –On the cross .... Jn 12:31–33; Col 2:15; Heb 2:14
    - –In his ascension .... Eph 1:20–21; Php 2:9–11
    - –In his return .... 1Co 15:24–28; Rev 19:11–16
  - b. Our victory given through Christ
    - –God gives us the victory .... Ro 7:25; 1Co 15:55–57
    - –We can do all things in Christ .... Php 4:13
    - –God will crush Satan under our feet .... Ro 16:20
  - c. Victory over sin through the Spirit .... Ro 8:9–13; Gal 5:16–18

WATCHFULNESS

A. God watches over people
- –His protective watch .... Ge 31:49; Ps 121:3–8; Isa 27:2–3; Jer 31:10
- –His watch over good and evil .... Job 7:17–21; Job 13:27; Prov15:3; Jer 31:28

B. God's people must be watchful
- 1. What we must watch
  - –Ourselves and our manner of life .... Dt 4:9; Dt 4:15; Ps 39:1; 1Ti 4:16
  - –For false teachers .... Mk 13:5–6; Ac 20:28–31; Php 3:2–3; 2Jn 8
  - –For those who divide the church .... Ro 16:17
  - –For hypocrites .... Mk 12:38–40
  - –For the second coming of Jesus .... Mt 25:13; 1Th 5:5–6; Rev 16:15
- 2. How we must watch
  - –With prayer .... Mk 14:38; Eph 6:18
  - –With alertness .... Mk 13:33; 1Th 5:6
  - –With care not to fall into temptation .... Mk 14:38; Gal 6:1
  - –With care not to forget what God has done .... Dt 4:9
  - –With hope .... Mic 7:7
  - –With thankfulness .... Col 4:2

WATER

A. Uses of water
- 1. Water for washing
  - a. Simple cleansing
    - –Washing body .... Ru 3:3
    - –Washing face .... Ge 43:31
    - –Washing feet .... Ge 18:4; 2Sa 11:8; Jn 13:4–5
  - b. Ritual cleansing
    - –Washing clothes at Mount Sinai .... Ex 19:10,14
    - –Washing necessary for priests .... Ex 30:17–21
    - –Washing necessary for Levites .... Nu 8:5–7
    - –Washing parts of a sacrifice .... Lev 1:9,13
    - –Washing after a skin disease .... Lev 14:8–9
    - –Washing after uncleanness .... Lev 15:5–13, 21–22; Nu 19:11–13
    - –Various Jewish washing rituals .... Mt 23:25–26; Mk 7:3–4
- 2. Water for drinking
  - a. Water drunk by humans and animals .... Ge 24:11–19; Jdg 7:4–5; Mt 10:42

b. God provided water for his people
- –Hagar ... Ge 21:15–19
- –The Israelites in the desert ... Ex 17:1–6; Nu 20:1–11; Ps 78:20
- –The Israelites in the time of Elisha ... 2Ki 3:15–20

B. God and water

1. God is the source of living water ... Ps 23:2; Isa 55:1; Jer 2:13

2. Christ is the source of living water ... Jn 4:10–14; Jn 7:37–38; Rev 21:6; Rev 22:1–2

3. Water used in judgment by God
- –The flood ... Ge 7:17–24; 1Pe 3:20
- –The destruction of the Egyptians ... Ex 14:26–30; Ps 106:9–11
- –The destruction of the Philistines ... Jer 47:2–5
- –The storm in the story of Jonah ... Jnh 1:3–15
- –Sea storms in general ... Ps 107:23–30

C. Water used as a symbol

1. As a symbol of evil people ... Ge 49:4; Isa 57:20; Jude 13

2. As a symbol of personal affliction
- –Waters overwhelming someone ... Ps 42:7; Ps 69:1–2,14–15; Jer 49:23
- –God protects his people from the waters ... Ps 18:16–17; Ps 124:1–5; Isa 43:2
- –Heaven has no sea ... Rev 21:1

3. As a symbol of cleansing from sin ... Isa 1:16; Eze 36:25; Eph 5:26; Heb 10:22

4. As a cleansing symbol in baptism ... Ac 8:36; Ac 22:16; 1Pe 3:21

5. As a symbol of the Holy Spirit ... Isa 44:3; Jn 7:38–39

6. As a symbol of heavenly peace ... Isa 35:6–7; Isa 43:19–21; Jer 31:11–12; Zec 14:6–9; Rev 22:1–2

WEALTH

See THE RICH AND THE POOR

WEATHER

A. God and the weather

1. God controls the weather
- –He sends sunshine ... Ps 19:4–6; Mt 5:45
- –He sends rain and snow ... Job 5:10; Job 38:22–30; Ps 147:16–17
- –He sends wind ... Ex 10:13; Ps 78:26; Ps 147:18
- –He sends storms ... Ps 107:25–26; Jnh 1:4; Eze 13:13

2. God uses weather elements

a. To exhibit his power ... Ex 19:16

b. To bless his people ... Dt 11:13–15; Ps 65:9–11; Ps 147:7–9

c. To help his people in battle ... Jos 10:11–14; 1Sa 7:10; 2Sa 22:13–15

d. To judge people
- –By withholding rain ... Lev 26:18–20; 1Ki 17:1; Am 4:7
- –By sending floods ... Ge 7:11–24; Isa 8:6–8; Na 1:8
- –By sending violent storms ... Ex 9:22–26; Ps 107:25–27; Na 1:3–4; Hag 2:17

B. Weather elements used as symbols

1. The sun
See SUN

2. Clouds
- –God's presence among his people ... Ex 13:21–22; Ps 104:3
- –The mystery of God ... Ps 97:2
- –Sin and forgiveness ... Isa 44:22
- –Departed Christians who surround us as witnesses ... Heb 12:1
- –God's judgment ... Joel 2:2
- –An advancing army ... Jer 4:13

3. Wind
- –God's presence around us ... Ps 104:3
- –The Holy Spirit ... Jn 3:8; Ac 2:2
- –Meaninglessness ... Ecc 1:6,14
- –False teaching ... Eph 4:14

4. Gentle rain showers
- –The word of God ... Isa 55:10–12
- –God's blessings ... Eze 34:26; Hos 6:3

5. Snow
- –Forgiveness ... Ps 51:7; Isa 1:18
- –Leprosy ... Nu 12:10
- –God's wonders ... Job 38:22
- –Brightness ... Mt 28:3
- –Glory of Christ ... Rev 1:14

6. Hail
- –God's wonders ... Job 38:22
- –God's power and majesty ... Ps 18:12
- –God's judgment ... Rev 8:7

7. Thunder
- –God's voice ... Ps 18:13; Ps 29:3–7; Ps 68:32–33
- –God's majesty ... Rev 4:5

8. Lightning
- –Christ's return ... Mt 24:27; Lk 17:24
- –Satan's fall ... Lk 10:18

9. Violent storms, as God's final judgment ... Eze 38:22; Rev 11:19; Rev 16:18–21

See also HUNGER AND THIRST
WATER

WICKEDNESS

See SIN

WILL OF GOD

A. God's will: what God wants us to do

1. What does God's will include?
   - –His law in general .... Ro 2:18; 1Pe 4:2–3
   - –His word in general .... Ac 20:27
   - –Doing what is good 1Pe 2:15
   - –Avoiding sexual immorality 1Th 4:3
   - –Giving thanks in all circumstances 1Th 5:18
2. How did Jesus relate to God's will?
   - –He came to do God's will .... Jn 4:34; Jn 6:38; Heb 10:5,7
   - –He was obedient to God's will .... Php 2:7–8
   - –He submitted to God's will for him .... Mt 26:39,42
3. How must we relate to God's will
   - –We must know his will .... Col 1:9
   - –We must understand his will .... Eph 5:17
   - –We must choose to do his will .... Jn 7:17
   - –We must do his will .... Ps 40:8; Ps 143:10; Mt 12:50
   - –We must approve his will by obedience .... Ro 12:2
   - –We must stand firm in his will .... Col 4:12

B. God's will: what God plans in history

1. Aspects of God's will
   - –God does whatever he pleases .... Ps 115:3; Ps 135:6; Da 4:35; Ro 9:18–21
   - –Everything occurs according to his will .... Eph 1:11
2. What can we know about God's plan?
   - a. His plan may be kept secret
     - –Hidden in the Old Testament .... Eph 1:9; Eph 3:4–5
     - –Hidden from learned people .... Mt 11:25–26
     - –Even now we may not understand it .... Ro 9:18–24
   - b. Some parts of his plan are revealed
     - –That salvation is in Christ .... Gal 1:4
     - –That God saves both Jew and Gentile .... Eph 3:6
     - –That everyone should be saved 1Ti 2:4; 2Pe 3:9
     - –That all God's children come to him .... Mt 18:14; Jn 6:39–40
     - –That Paul was called as apostle 1Co 1:1
3. God's will and human suffering
   - –His will may include suffering .... Job 1:6–22; 1Pe 3:17; 1Pe 4:19
   - –God works for his people's good .... Ge 50:20; Jer 29:11; Ro 8:28

See also PAIN

4. Our relationship to God's plan for us
   - –Pray that God's will be done .... Mt 6:10
   - –Pray that things happen by God's will .... Ac 18:21; Ro 15:31–32; 1Co 16:7; Jas 4:13–15
   - –Submit to God's plan for us .... Ac 21:14

WIND

See WEATHER

WINE

See ALCOHOL

WISDOM

–Comprehensive knowledge that is put into practice

A. Related theme

WISDOM is a theme of Proverbs .... Pr 2:6

B. Human wisdom

1. Source of wisdom
   - –Received as a gift from God .... 1Ki 3:11–12; Pr 2:6; Ecc 2:26; Dan2:21; Jas 1:5
   - –Received as a gift from the Spirit .... 1Co 12:8; Eph 1:17
   - –Starts with the fear of the Lord .... Job 28:28; Ps 111:10; Pr 9:10
   - –Comes from listening to the wise .... Pr 1:2; Pr 4:1–11; Pr 13:20
   - –Comes from research and education .... Ecc 1:13,17; Ecc 7:25
   - –Comes from discipline .... Pr 29:15
   - –Comes from admonishing one another .... Col 3:16
2. Expressions of wisdom
   - –Serving as craftsman .... Ex 28:3
   - –Following God's law .... Dt 4:6; Hos 14:9; Mt 7:24–26
   - –Writing proverbs and songs 1Ki 4:29,32
   - –Studying God's creation 1Ki 4:29,33
   - –Administering justice 1Ki 3:16–28; 1Ki 10:8–9
   - –Avoiding evil .... Pr 5:1–6
   - –Taking advice Prov13:10
   - –Giving advice .... Da 1:20
   - –Interpreting visions and dreams .... Da 2:23,30
   - –Preparing for the future .... Mt 25:1–13
   - –Exercising patience .... Pr 19:11
   - –Living the Christian lifestyle .... Pr 2:20–21; Jas 3:17
   - –Defending the gospel .... Ac 6:3,10
3. Benefits of wisdom
   - –Makes us blessed .... Pr 3:13
   - –Leads to a long life .... Pr 3:16
   - –Preserves our lives .... Ecc 7:12
   - –Protects us .... Pr 4:6
   - –Exalts us .... Pr 4:8–9
   - –Brings us joy .... Pr 29:3; Pr 27:11
   - –Gives us strength .... Ecc 7:19
   - –Brings us healing .... Pr 12:18
   - –Saves us from evil ways .... Pr 2:12–19

C. Divine wisdom

1. True wisdom centers in God
   - –God has wisdom .... Job 12:13; Job 28:20–24; Da 2:20
   - –Christ is the wisdom of God .... 1Co 1:24,30; Col 2:3
   - –The Spirit is the Spirit of wisdom .... Isa 11:2; Eph 1:17
2. The nature of God's wisdom
   - –Profound .... Job 9:4
   - –Precious .... Pr 8:18–19

–Deep and rich .... Ro 11:33
–Magnificent .... Isa 28:29
–Manifold .... Eph 3:10
–Unsurpassable .... Jer 10:7

3. Activities of God's wisdom
–Operative in creation .... Ps 104:24; Pr 3:19; Pr 8:22–31; Jer 10:12
–Controls nature .... Job 26:12; Job 39:26
–Controls history .... Isa 10:12–13
–Counsels rulers .... Pr 8:14–16

WITCHCRAFT

See MAGIC, WITCHCRAFT AND SORCERY

WITNESS

–One who bears testimony to something or someone

A. Types of witnesses
–God as a witness .... Ge 31:50; Jdg 11:10
–People as witnesses .... Jos 24:22; Ru 4:9–11; Jer 32:12
–Things as witnesses .... Dt 31:19–21; Jos 24:27; Isa 19:19–20

B. Legal witnesses
–Two or three necessary to convict someone .... Dt 17:6; Mt 26:60–61; 2Co 13:1
–No false testimony to be given ...... Ex 20:16; Dt 19:16–18; Pr 24:28–29

C. Witnesses to God's truth and salvation
–Israel as witnesses .... Isa 43:10–12; Isa 44:8
–The prophets as witnesses .... Ac 10:43; Ac 26:22–23
–John the Baptist as witness .... Jn 1:7,15,32–34; Jn 5:33–34
–Jesus Christ as the faithful witness . Jn 8:18; Jn 18:37; Rev 1:5–6
–The Holy Spirit as witness .... Jn 15:26; Ac 5:30–32; Ro 8:16
–Signs and wonders as witnesses ... Jn 2:11; Jn 20:30–31; Heb 2:3–4
–Jesus' followers as witnesses .... Lk 1:2; Ac 1:8; Ac 3:15–16; Ac 5:30–32; Ac 10:41–42

WOMEN

A. Status of women

1. In creation
–Created in the image of God ..... Ge 1:27
–Equal responsibility and blessing .... Ge 1:26,28–30
–Created as a companion for man .... Ge 2:18,20
–Created second, from man .... Ge 2:21–22; 1Co 11:3,7–8,12

2. In and after the fall
–Eve was tempted and sinned first .... Ge 3:1–6; 2Co 11:3; 1Ti 2:14
–Were subordinated to husbands .. Ge 3:16
–Were considered weak and insecure .... Isa 19:16; Jer 50:37; 1Pe 3:7

3. In the covenant of the Old Testament
–Circumcision only for males ..... Ge 17:10–14
–Only males instructed to appear before Lord .... Ex 23:17
–Value of woman was less than that of a man .... Lev 27:1–8
–Sons had priority over daughters .... Nu 36:1–9; Ps 127:3–4
–Women served in the worship of God .... Ex 15:20; Ex 38:8; Ezr 2:65
–Women also expected to keep the feasts .... Dt 16:9–15

4. Jesus' attitude to women
–Healed women as well as men .... Mk 1:30–31; Mk 5:25–34; Lk 13:10–17
–Used women as examples in parables .... Lk 13:20–21; Lk 15:8–10; Lk 17:35; Lk 18:1–8
–Was supported by women .... Lk 8:1–3
–Affirmed women eager to learn .. Lk 10:38–42; Jn 4:7–26
–Praised a poor widow and her gift .... Lk 21:1–4
–Praised Martha's confession ..... Jn 11:24–27
–Women were first witnesses to resurrection .... Mt 28:1–10; Mk 16:1–8; Lk 24:1–11; Jn 20:1–2,10–18

5. In the redemption won by Christ
–In Christ no male or female ...... Gal 3:28
–Salvation came through woman .... Gal 4:4–5
–Woman saved through childbearing 1Ti 2:15
–Spirit poured out on sons and daughters .... Joel 2:28–29; Ac 2:17–18
–Women filled with the Holy Spirit .... Lk 1:41–45; Ac 2:1–4
–Women and men both saved ..... Ac 9:36–39; Ac 17:4,12
–Women prayed and prophesied ... Ac 1:14; 1Co 11:5
–Women were to be silent in the churches 1Co 14:33–35; 1Ti 2:11–12

B. Roles and occupations of women
–Wife
See MARRIAGE
–Mother
See MOTHER
–Shepherdess .... Ge 29:6; Ex 2:16
–Businesswoman .... Pr 31:13–19; Ac 16:14
–Judge .... Jdg 4:4–5
–Prophetess .... 2Ki 22:14–20; Ac 21:8–9
–Teacher .... Ac 18:26
–Workers in the church .... Ro 16:1–2; Php 4:2–3

C. Prominent women in the Bible
- –Abigail........ 1Sa 25:3
- –Anna........ Lk 2:36
- –Athaliah........ 2Ki 11:1
- –Bathsheba........ 2Sa 11:3
- –Deborah........ Jdg 4:4
- –Dorcas........ Ac 9:36
- –Elizabeth........ Lk 1:5
- –Esther........ Est 2:7
- –Eve........ Ge 3:20
- –Hagar........ Ge 16:1
- –Hannah........ 1Sa 1:2
- –Huldah........ 2Ki 22:14
- –Jael........ Jdg 4:17
- –Jezebel........ 1Ki 16:31
- –Leah........ Ge 29:16
- –Lydia........ Ac 16:14
- –Mary the mother of Jesus........ Lk 1:27
- –Mary Magdalene........ Lk 8:2
- –Mary and Martha........ Lk 10:38–39
- –Miriam........ Ex 15:20
- –Phoebe........ Ro 16:1
- –Priscilla........ Ac 18:2
- –Rachel........ Ge 29:16
- –Rahab........ Jos 2:3
- –Rebekah........ Ge 24:29
- –Ruth........ Ru 1:4
- –Salome........ Mk 15:40
- –Sapphira........ Ac 5:1
- –Sarah........ Ge 12:5
- –Tamar........ Ge 38:6

See also entries for each of these women

WORD OF GOD

A. What is the word of God?
- –The word God spoke in creation........ Ps 33:6–9
- –The word God spoke to the prophets........ 1Ki 17:2,8; Jer 1:2,4,11–13; Eze 6:1–3
- –The Old Testament revelation........ Jn 10:34–45
- –The word spoken by Jesus........ Lk 5:1
- –Jesus himself as the Word become flesh........ Jn 1:1,14
- –The word spoken by the apostles........ Ac 13:44; 1Th 2:13; 1Pe 1:25
- –Instructions given by pastors........ Gal 6:6; 2Ti 4:2

B. What power does the word of God have?
- –The power to create........ Ps 33:6; Heb 11:3; 2Pe 3:5
- –The power to sustain all of creation........ Ps 147:15–18; Heb 1:3
- –The power to heal........ Ps 107:20; Mt 8:8
- –The power to judge our hearts........ Heb 4:12
- –The power to give us new birth........ Jas 1:18; 1Pe 1:23
- –The power to lead us to faith........ Ro 10:17
- –The power to save us........ 2Ti 3:15
- –The power to make us holy........ Eph 5:26
- –The power to fight against Satan........ Eph 6:17; Rev 19:13–15
- –The power to destroy the world........ 2Pe 3:7

C. Characteristics of God's word
- –It is reliable........ 2Sa 7:28
- –It is true........ 1Ki 17:24; Jn 17:17
- –It is flawless........ Pr 30:5
- –It is alive and active........ Heb 4:12
- –It is eternal........ Ps 119:89
- –It will endure........ Isa 40:8; Mt 5:18; Mt 24:35
- –It will not return empty........ Isa 55:11

D. Our reaction to the word of God
- –We must hear it........ Isa 1:10; Jer 7:1–2
- –We must understand it........ Mt 13:23
- –We must accept it........ Mk 4:20; Ac 2:41; 1Th 2:13
- –We must hide it in our hearts........ Ps 119:11
- –We must retain it........ Lk 8:15
- –We must let it dwell in us........ Col 3:16
- –We must trust in it........ Ps 119:42
- –We must hope in it........ Ps 119:74,81,114; Ps 130:5
- –We must praise it........ Ps 56:4,10
- –We must live according to it........ Ps 119:9
- –We must obey it........ Ps 119:17,67; Jas 1:22–24
- –We must handle it correctly........ 2Ti 2:15
- –We must preach it........ Ac 8:4

E. Pictures used for the word of God
- –Lamp and light........ Ps 119:105
- –Rain producing fruit........ Isa 55:10–11
- –Consuming fire........ Jer 5:14
- –Destroying hammer........ Jer 23:29
- –Seed........ Mk 4:14
- –Sword........ Eph 6:17; Heb 4:12

F. Scripture as the word of God
See INSPIRATION OF SCRIPTURE

G. Jesus as the Word of God
- –He is the Word of God........ Jn 1:1
- –He is the creative Word........ Jn 1:3
- –He is the Word become flesh........ Jn 1:14
- –He is the Word of life........ 1Jn 1:2
- –He is the victorious Word........ Rev 19:13–16

WORK

A. Related themes
- PRAY AND WORK is a theme of Nehemiah........ Neh 4:9
- DAILY WORK is a theme of 2 Thessalonians........ 2Th 3:6

B. The work of humans

1. Humans in general
   a. Nature of work
   - –Required of Adam before the fall........ Ge 1:28; Ge 2:15,19–20
   - –Required of humans after the fall........ Ex 20:9; Eph 4:28; 1Th 4:11
   - –Became hard work........ Ge 3:17–19; Ecc 3:9–10
   - –Can seem meaningless........ Ecc 1:14; Ecc 2:11,17

   b. God's relationship to human work
   - –He commands it........ Dt 5:13
   - –He expects it........ Ps 104:23
   - –He blesses honest toil........ Pr 14:23; Pr 27:23–27
   - –He speaks against laziness........ Pr 6:6–11; Pr 10:4–5

2. Daily work for Christians
   - –We must earn our daily bread........ 2Th 3:10
   - –We must pray for God to establish it........ Ps 90:17
   - –We must depend on God in it........ Ps 127:1–2; Isa 26:12

WORLD

WORSHIP

–The heavenly hosts ... Rev 5:8–14

D. The day for worship
See SABBATH

E. Characteristics of true worship

1. Principles to follow

–Worship God alone ... Ex 20:4–5
Ex 23:24–25
Mt 4:10

–Love God with all your heart ... Dt 6:4–6
Dt 10:12–13

–Be humble in heart ... Ps 51:17
Isa 66:2
Mic 6:6–8

–Depend on the Holy Spirit ... Jn 4:20–24
Php 3:3

–Formal ritual alone is insufficient ... Isa 1:11–15
Am 5:21–24

2. Specific elements in Christian worship

–Reading Scripture ... 1Ti 4:13

–Preaching ... Ac 20:7
2Ti 4:2
See PREACHING

–Praying ... 1Ti 2:1,8
See PRAYER

–Singing ... Col 3:16
See MUSIC AND SONG

–Giving an offering ... 1Co 16:1–2
See TITHES AND OFFERINGS

–Exercising spiritual gifts ... 1Co 14:26–33
See GIFTS OF THE SPIRIT

–Celebrating the sacraments ... Ac 2:41–42
1Co 11:18–29

WRATH

See ANGER

AHASUERUS (XERXES)

–King of Persia ... Est 1:1–2
–Deposed Queen Vashti ... Est 1:15–21
–Made Esther queen ... Est 2:17
–Signed edict to annihilate the Jews ... Est 3:12–15
–Received Esther without having summoned her ... Est 5:1–8
–Honored Mordecai ... Est 6:1–11
–Furious at Haman ... Est 7:1–8
–Hanged Haman ... Est 7:9–10
–Signed edict allowing Jews to defend themselves ... Est 8:3–14
–Exalted Mordecai ... Est 8:1–2,15
Est 9:4

YEAR OF JUBILEE

See THE RICH AND THE POOR
SLAVERY

YEAST

–A leavening substance for bread

A. Leaven and bread

–Allowed in some offerings ... Lev 7:13
Lev 23:17

–Not allowed in other offerings ... Ex 23:15–16
Lev 2:11
Dt 16:1–8

–The Feast of Unleavened Bread
See FEASTS

B. Leaven as a symbol

–A symbol of corruption and evil ... Mt 16:6,12
Gal 5:7–9
1Co 5:6–8

–A symbol of the penetrating influence of the kingdom ... Mt 13:33
Lk 13:21

YOKE

A. Uses for the yoke

–To use on animals at work ... 1Ki 19:19–21
–To control slaves ... 1Ti 6:1
–To wear as a prophetic symbol ... Jer 27:2

B. The yoke as a symbol

1. Positive

–A symbol of service to God's law ... Jer 2:20
–A symbol of discipleship ... Mt 11:28–30

2. Negative

–A symbol of oppression ... 1Ki 12:4,9–11
Jer 28:10–14

–A symbol of bondage to sin ... La 1:14

–A symbol of legalism ... Ac 15:10
Gal 5:1

–A symbol of union with unbelievers ... 2Co 6:14

YOUTH

A. Characteristics of youth

–Strong ... Pr 20:29
Isa 40:30
1Jn 2:14

–Devoted and zealous ... 1Ki 18:12
Jer 2:2
Gal 1:13–14

–Inexperienced ... 1Sa 17:33
1Ch 22:5
Jer 1:6

–Sinful and foolish ... Job 13:26
1Sa 2:17
1Ki 12:8–15
Ps 25:7
2Ti 2:22

–Lacking in knowledge and judgment ... Ge 37:2–11
Pr 1:4
Pr 7:7

B. Encouragement to youth

–To commit their lives to God ... Ps 119:9
Ecc 12:1
La 3:27

–To seek knowledge from God ... 1Ki 3:7–9

–To enjoy life ... Pr 5:18
Ecc 11:9

–To see visions and to prophesy ... Joel 2:28
Ac 2:17

–To exercise self-control ... Titus 2:6

C. Familiar stories involving youths

–Joseph sold into Egypt ... Ge 37:12–28
–Joseph serving faithfully in Egypt ... Ge 39:1–12
–Gideon called to be military leader ... Jdg 6:15–16
–David killing Goliath ... 1Sa 17:26–50
–Joash repairing the temple ... 2Ch 24:4–14
–Josiah purifying the land and the temple ... 2Ch 34:3–13
–Jeremiah called to serve as prophet ... Jer 1:4–19
–James and John following Jesus ... Mk 1:19–20
–Timothy accompanying Paul ... Ac 16:1–3
–Timothy serving as pastor ... 1Ti 4:12

ZACCHEUS

–Tax collector ... Lk 19:1–2
–Climbed a tree to see Jesus ... Lk 19:3–4
–Welcomed Jesus into his house ... Lk 19:5–7
–Saved by Jesus ... Lk 19:8–9

ZADOK

–A priest in the time of David ... 2Sa 8:17
–Ministered in Hebron after Saul's death ... 1Ch 12:23–28
–Helped bring the ark to Jerusalem ... 1Ch 15:11–13
–Became David's priest ... 1Ch 16:39–40
1Ch 24:6

Map Index and Maps

The Index to Maps will lead you to place names found on the color maps at the end of this study Bible. References are to the map number and the margin markings.

Map 1: **WORLD OF THE PATRIARCHS**

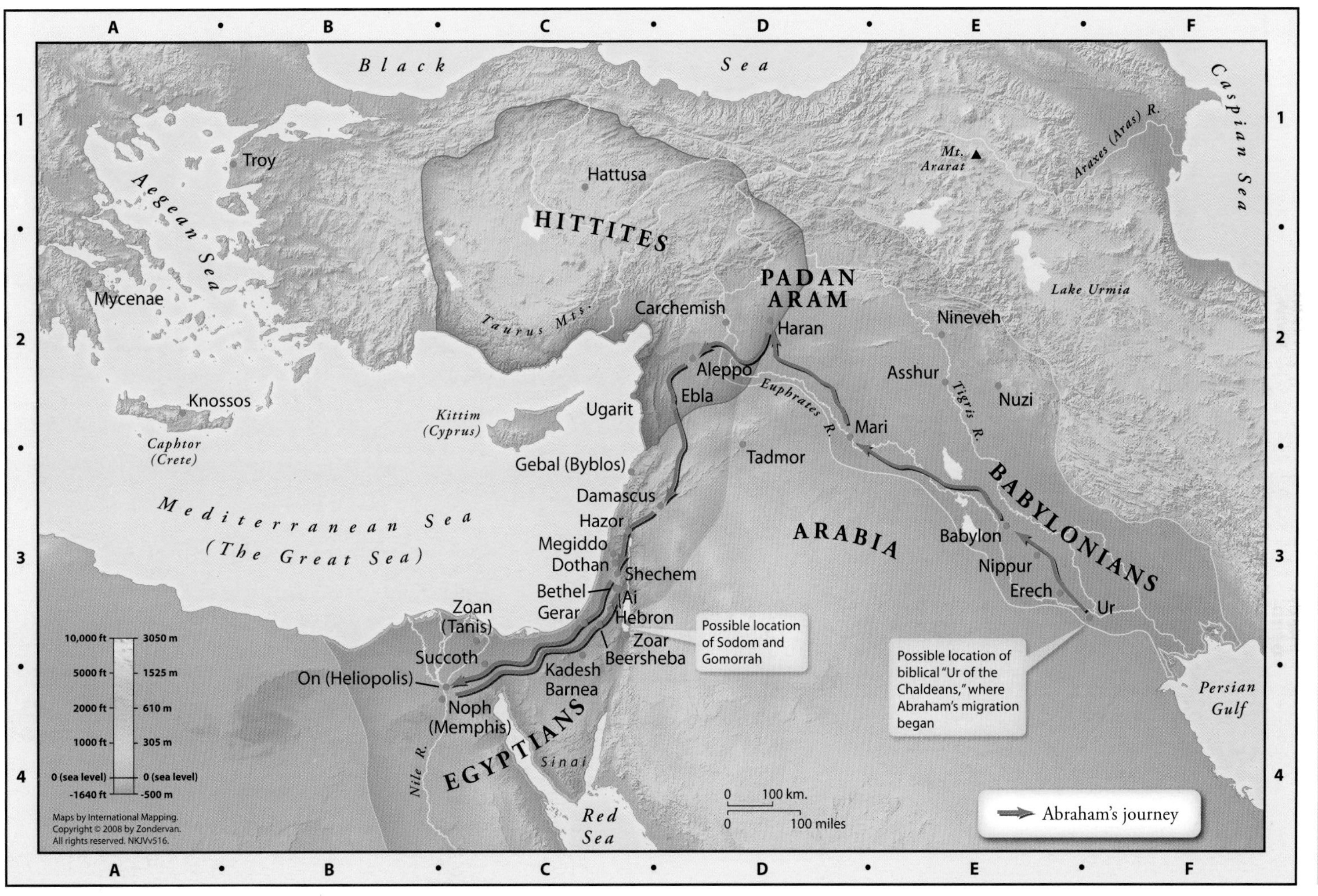

Map 2: **HOLY LAND AND SINAI**

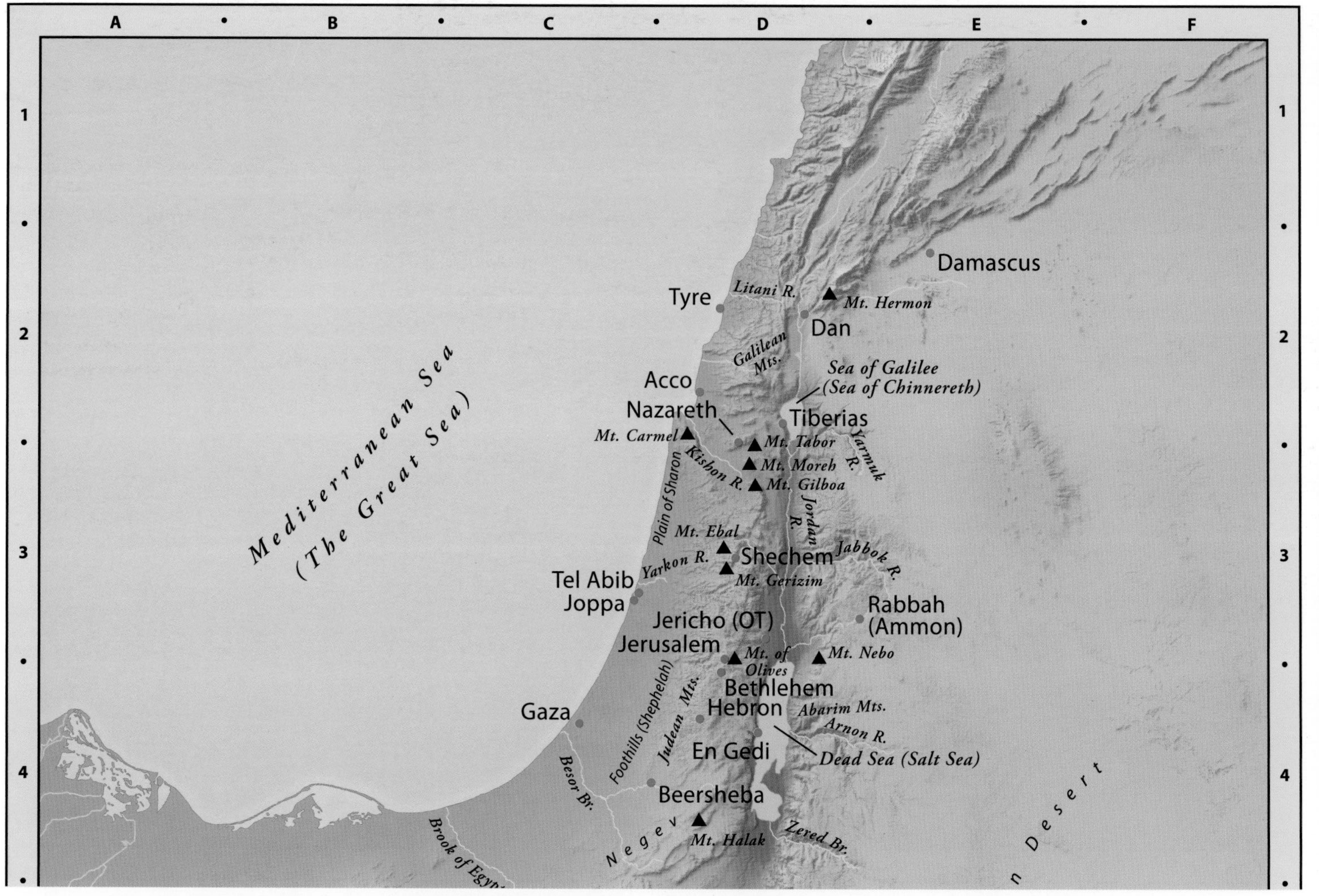

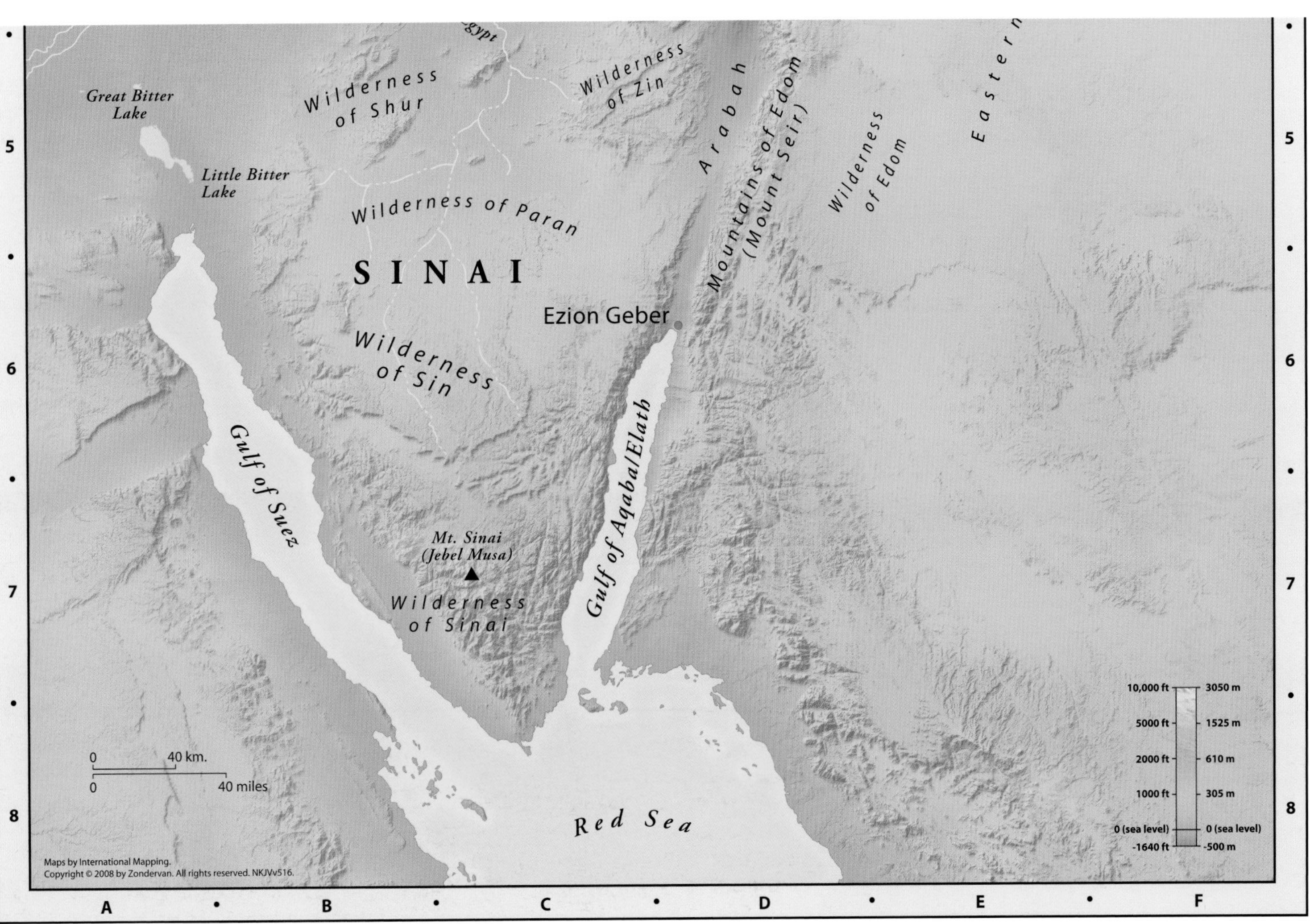
Great Bitter Lake
Little Bitter Lake
Wilderness of Shur
Wilderness of Zin
Wilderness of Paran
SINAI
Wilderness of Sin
Ezion Geber
Arabah
Mountains of Edom (Mount Seir)
Wilderness of Edom
Gulf of Suez
Gulf of Aqaba/Elath
Mt. Sinai (Jebel Musa)
Wilderness of Sinai
Red Sea
0 40 km.
0 40 miles
10,000 ft 3050 m
5000 ft 1525 m
2000 ft 610 m
1000 ft 305 m
0 (sea level) 0 (sea level)
-1640 ft -500 m
Maps by International Mapping.
Copyright © 2008 by Zondervan. All rights reserved. NKJVv516.
A B C D E F
5 6 7 8

Map 3: **EXODUS AND CONQUEST OF CANAAN**

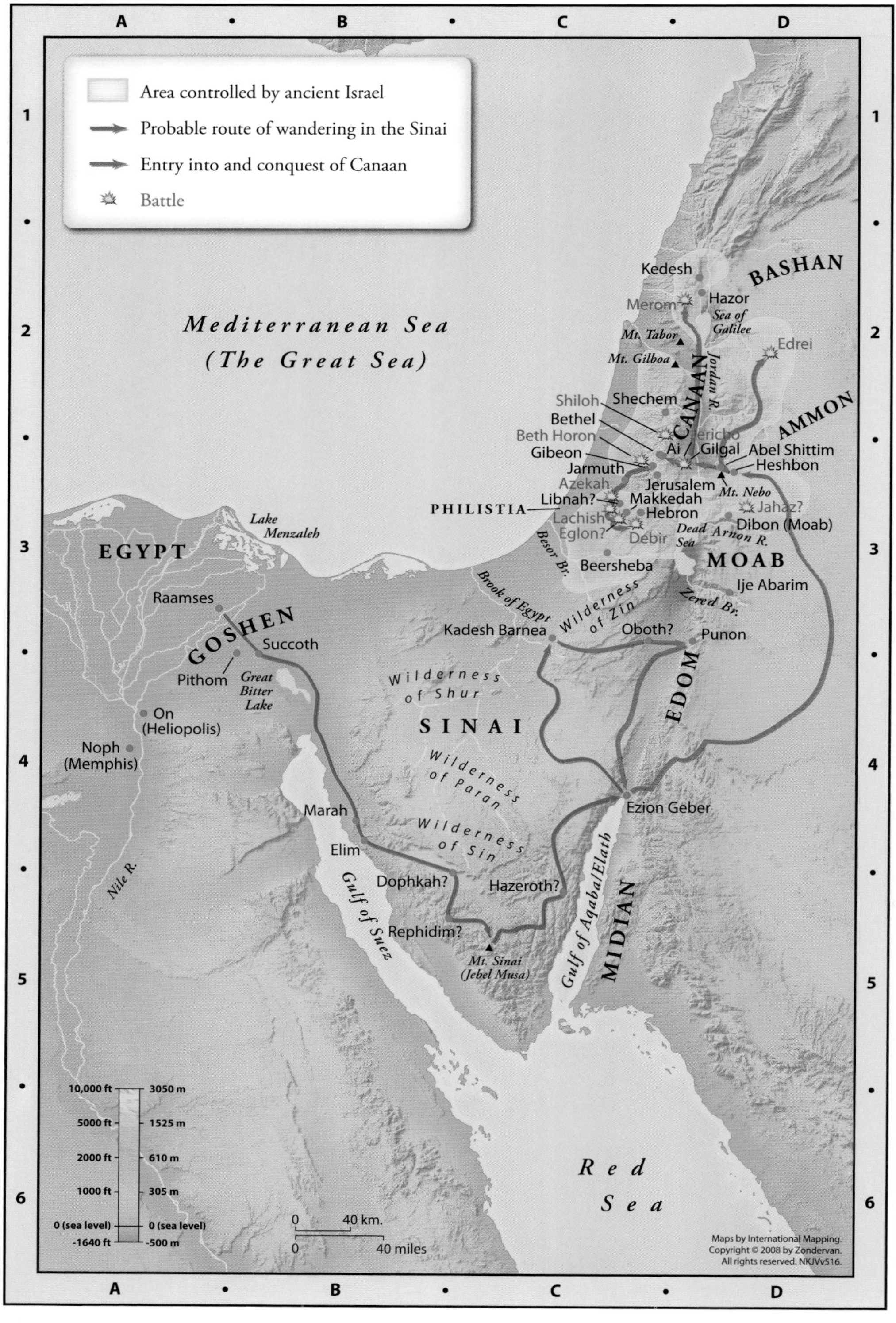

Map 4: **LAND OF THE TWELVE TRIBES**

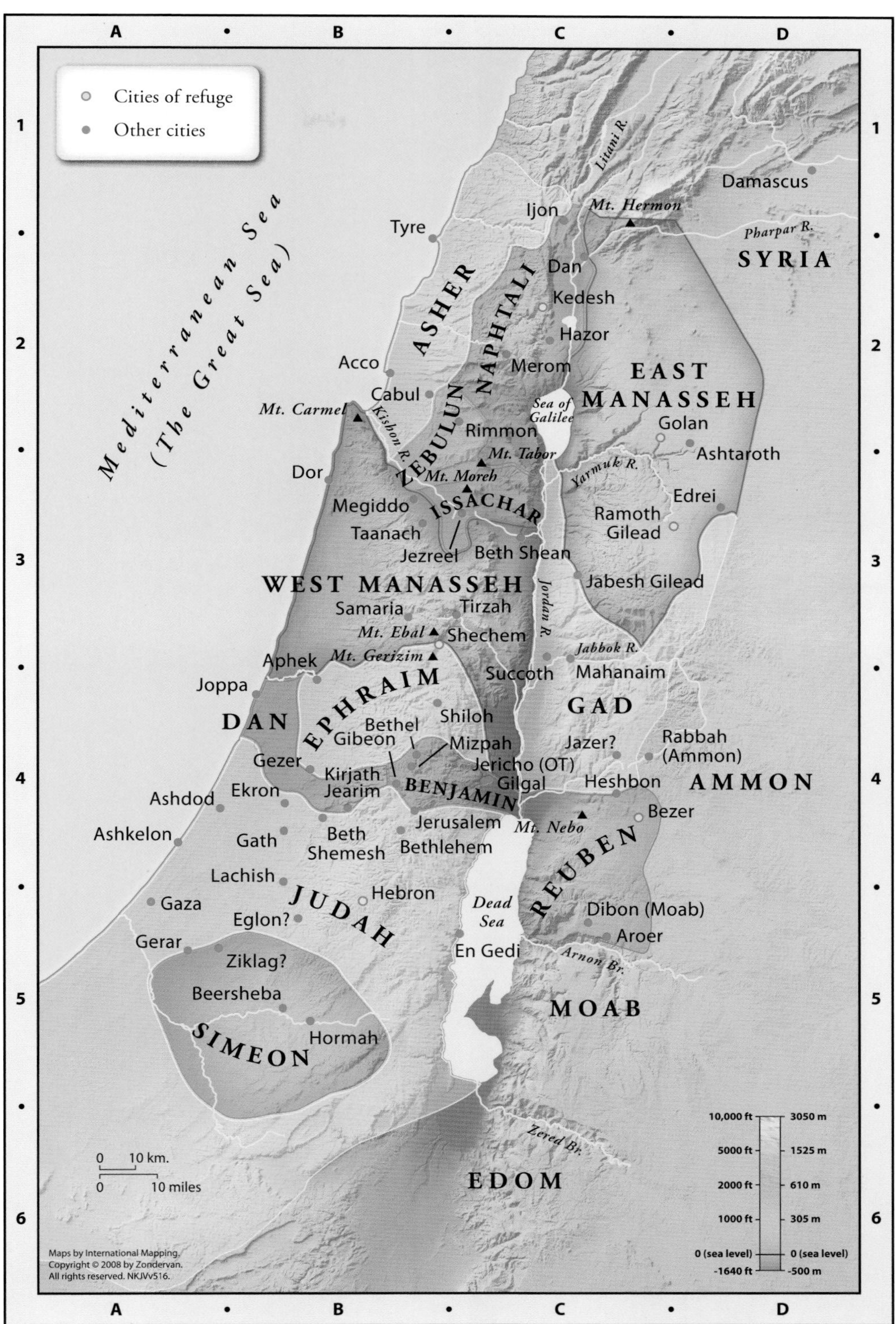

Map 5: **KINGDOM OF DAVID AND SOLOMON**

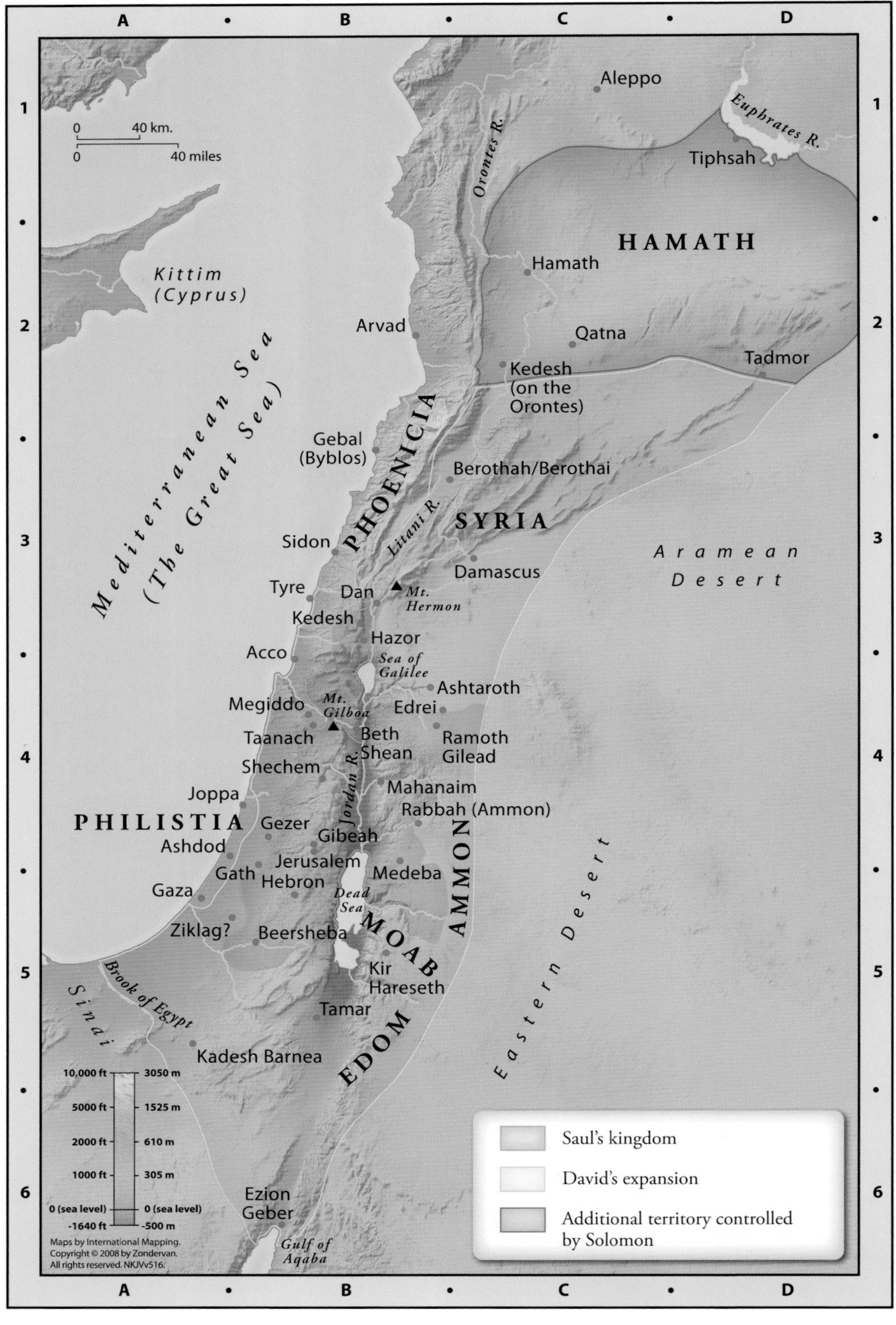

Map 6: **KINGDOMS OF ISRAEL AND JUDAH**

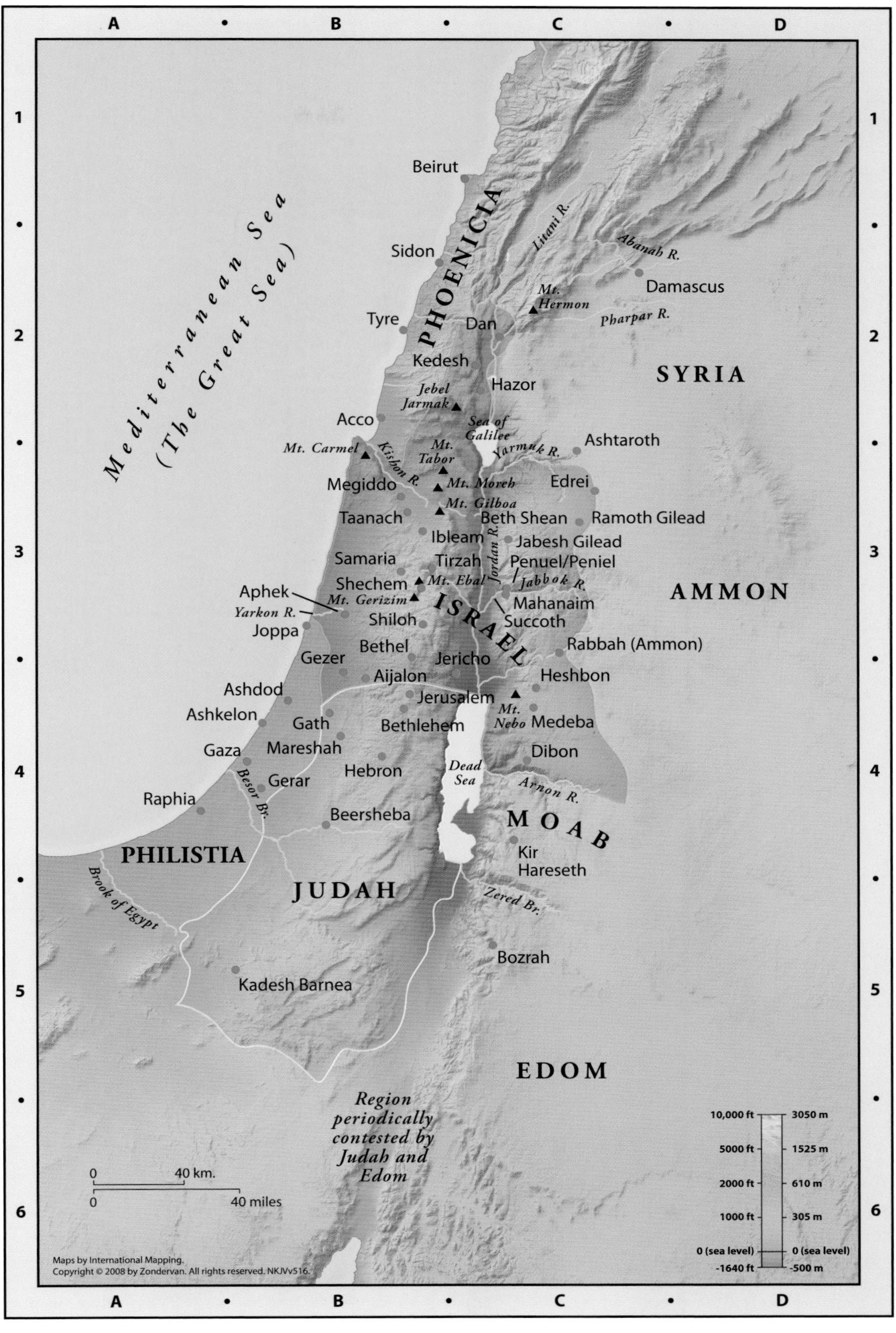

Map 7: **PROPHETS IN ISRAEL AND JUDAH**

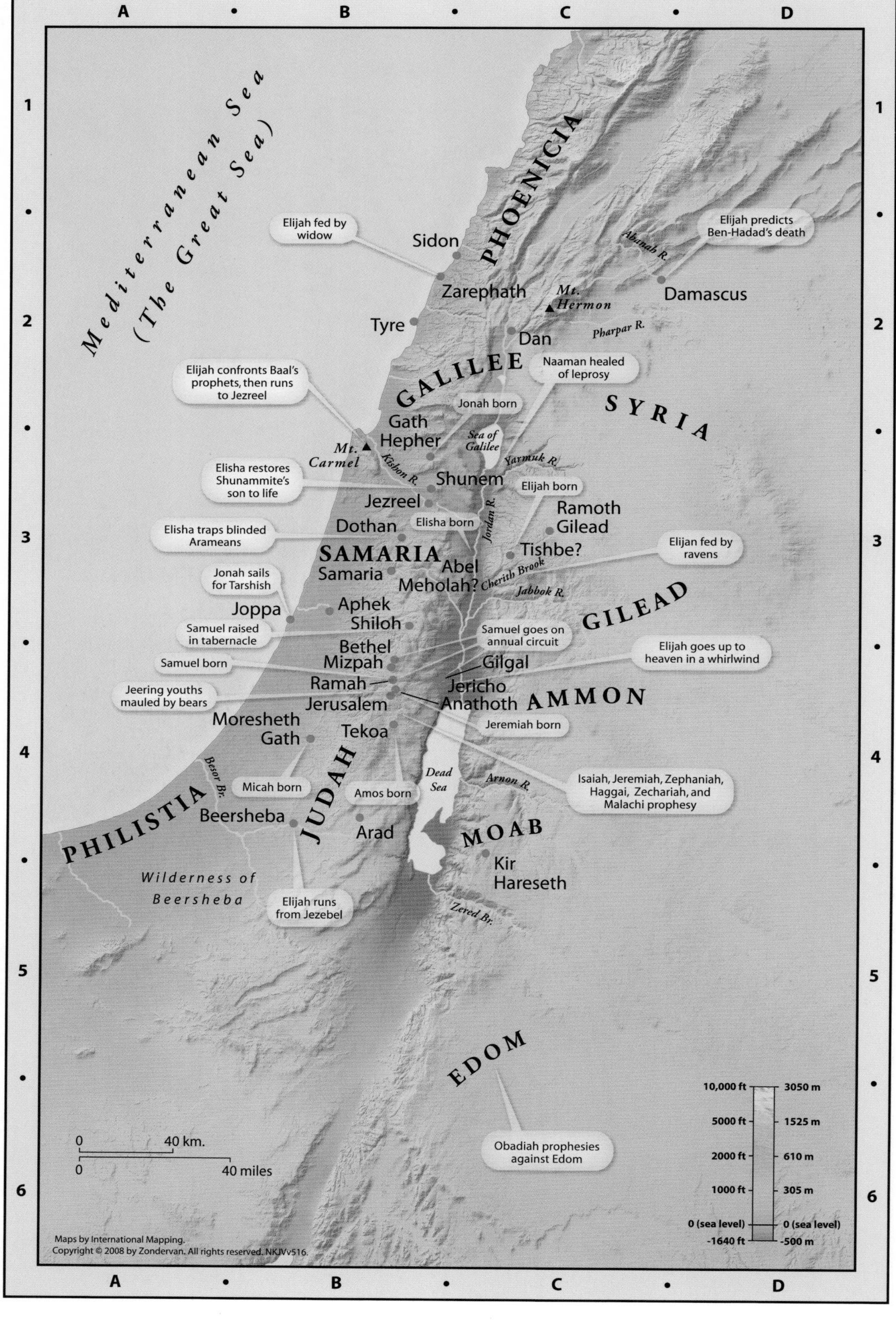

Maps by International Mapping.

Map 8: **ASSYRIAN AND BABYLONIAN EMPIRES**

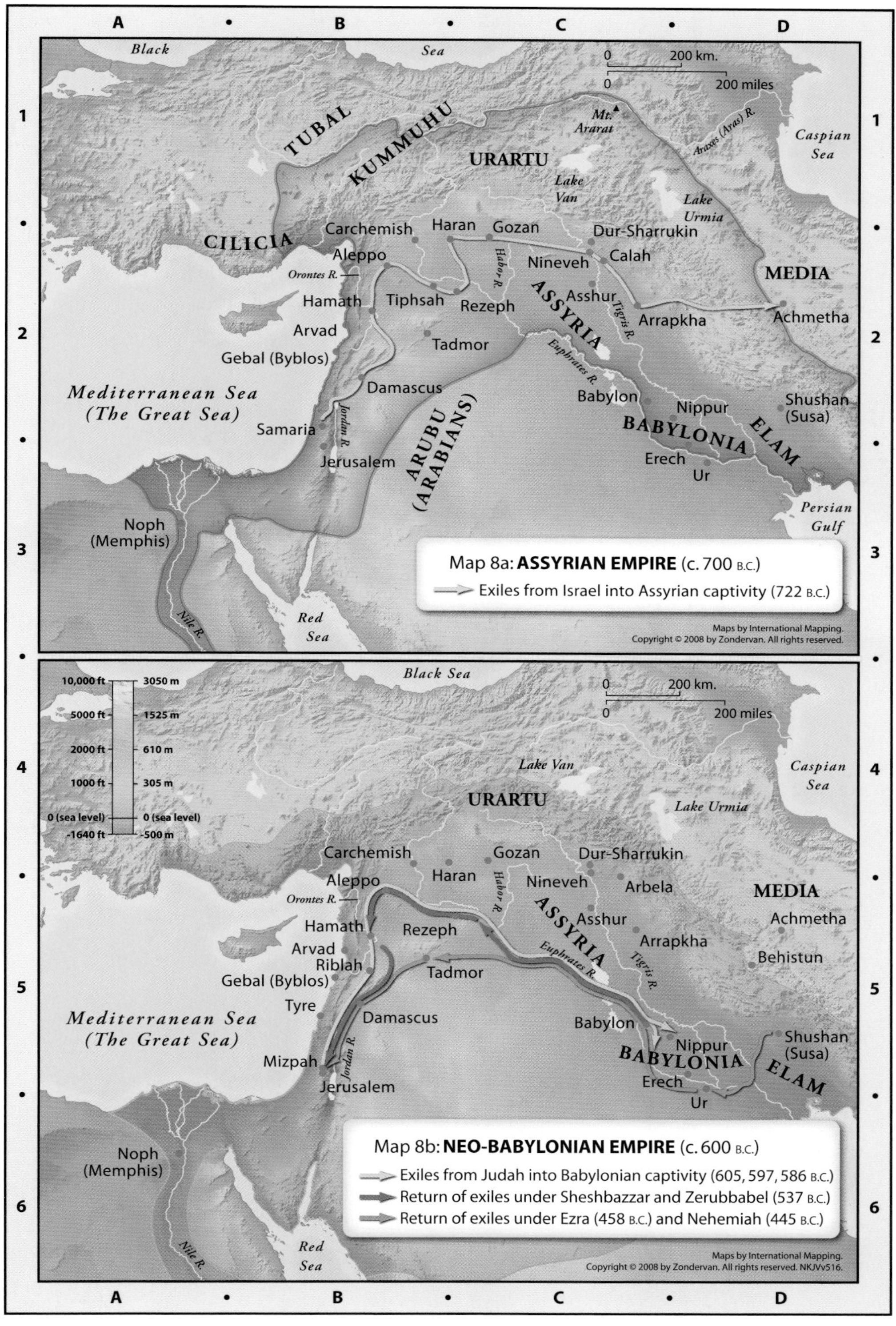

Map 9: **HOLY LAND IN THE TIME OF JESUS**

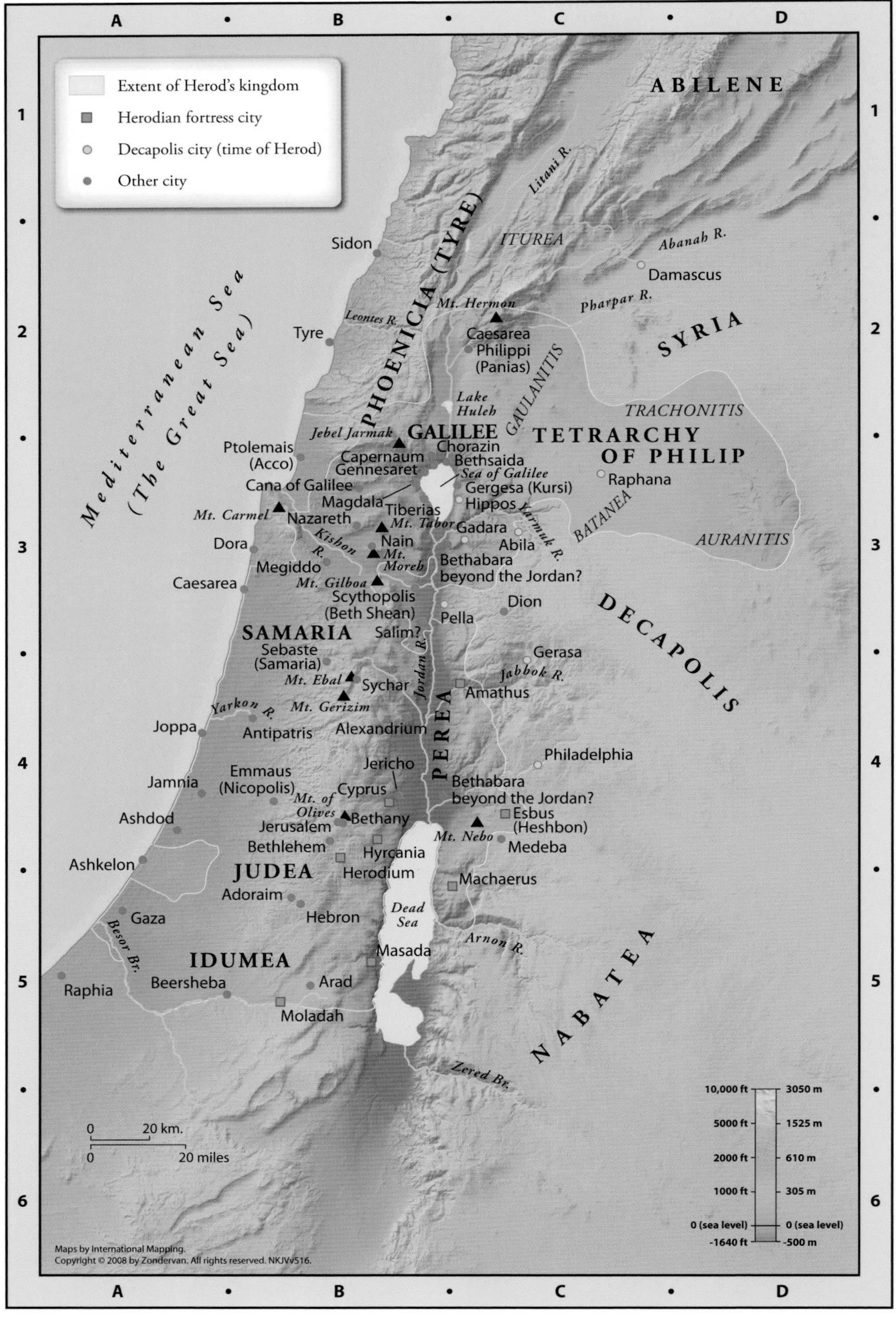

Map 10: **JERUSALEM IN THE TIME OF JESUS**

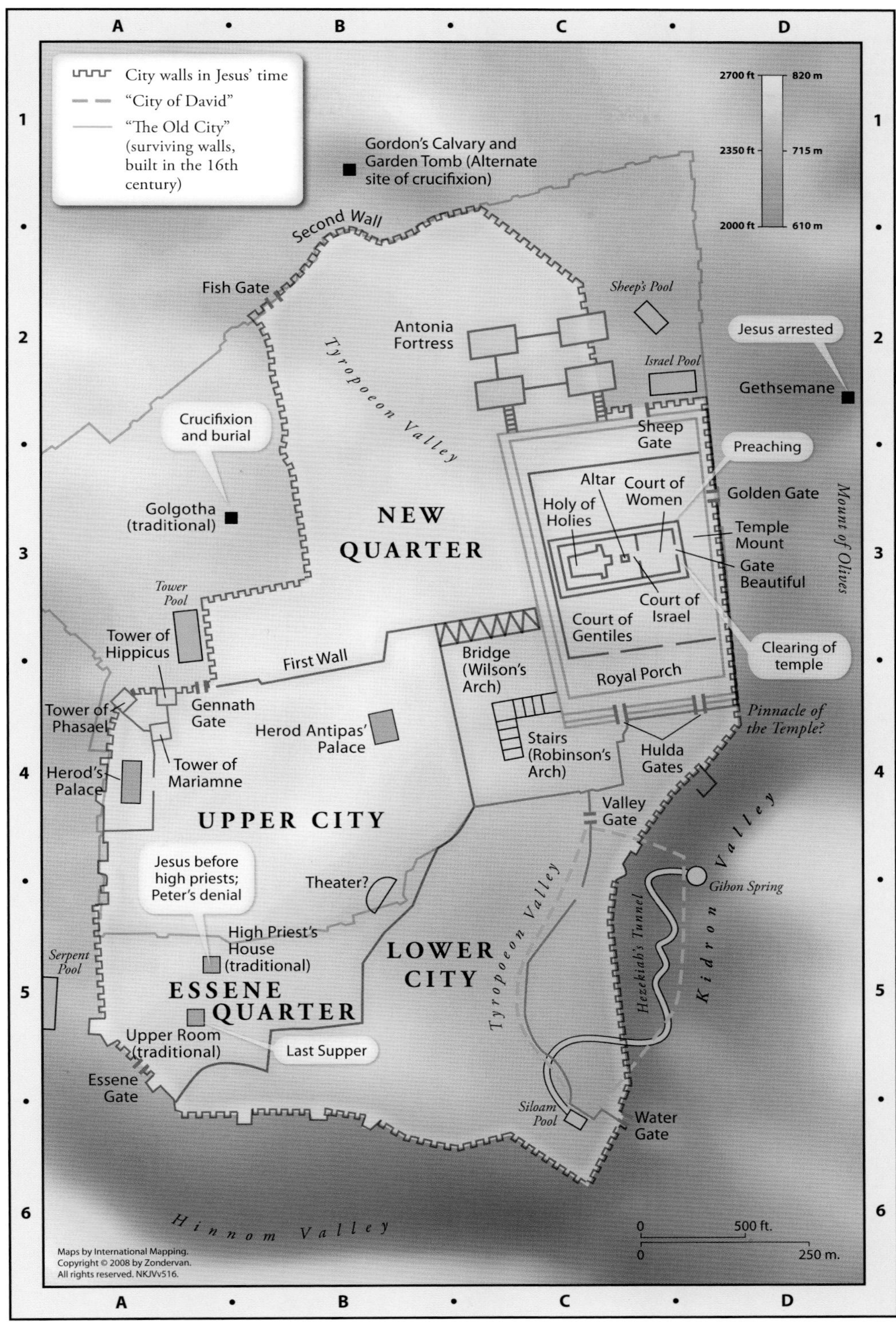

Map 11: **JESUS' MINISTRY**

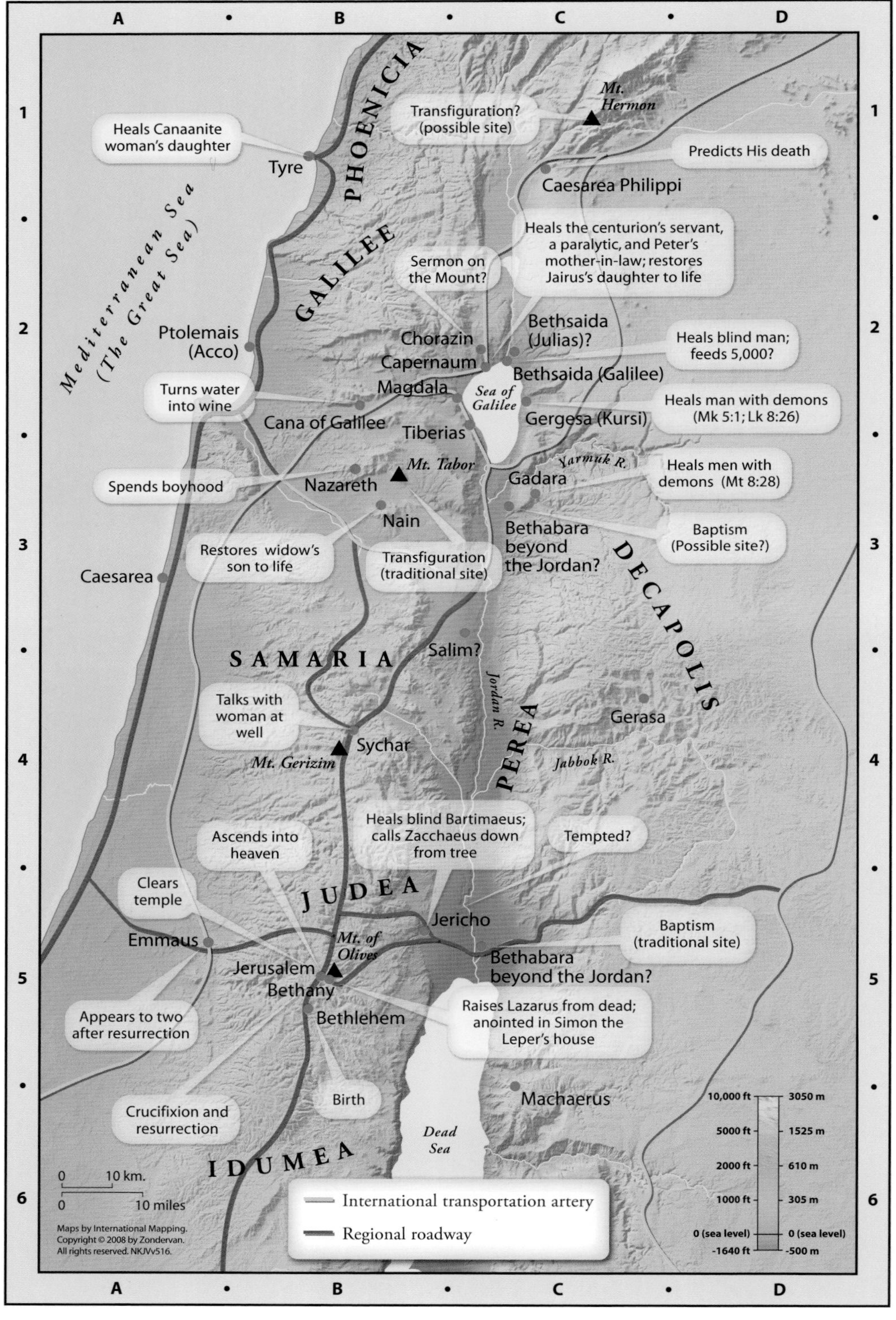

Map 12: **APOSTLES' EARLY TRAVELS**

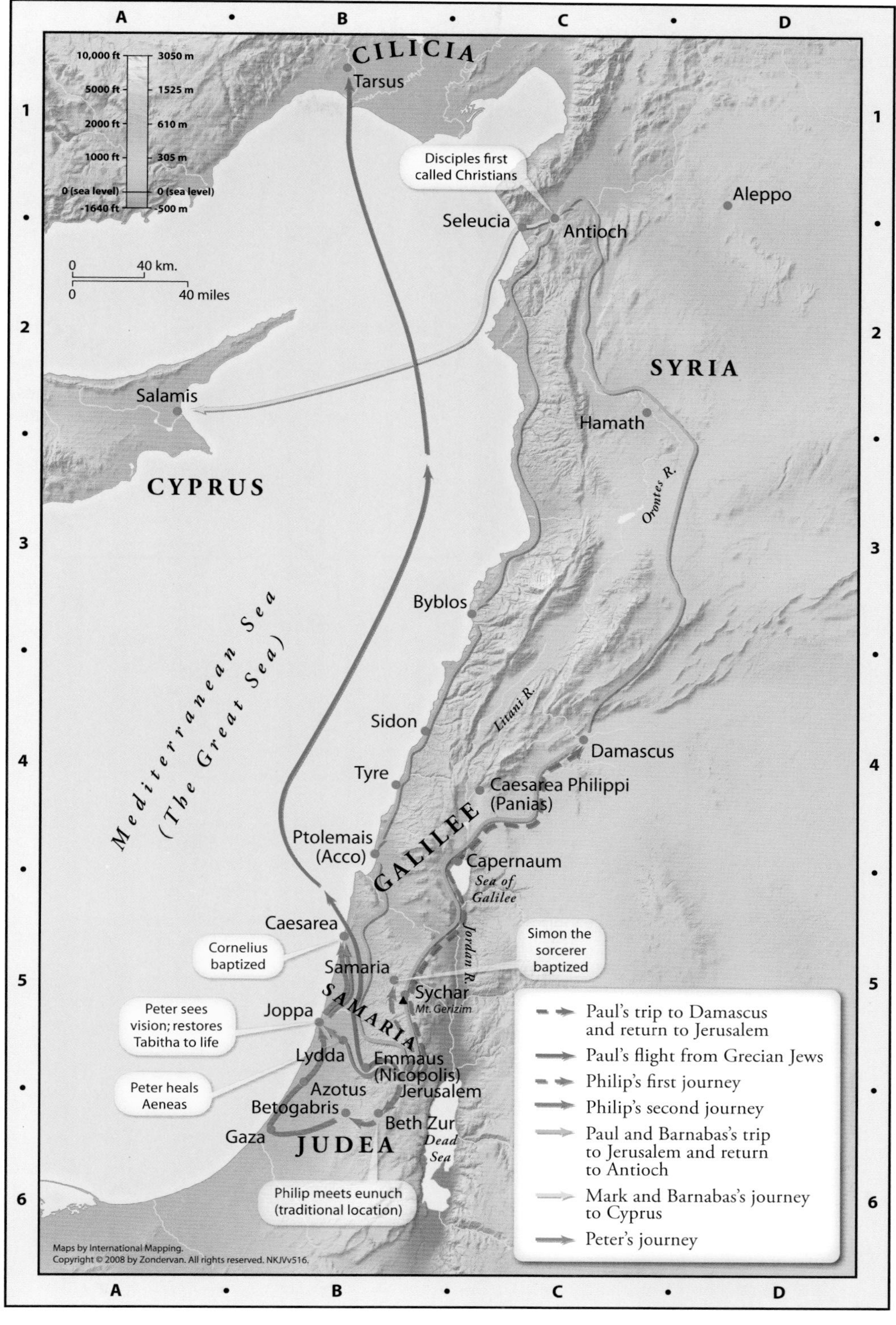

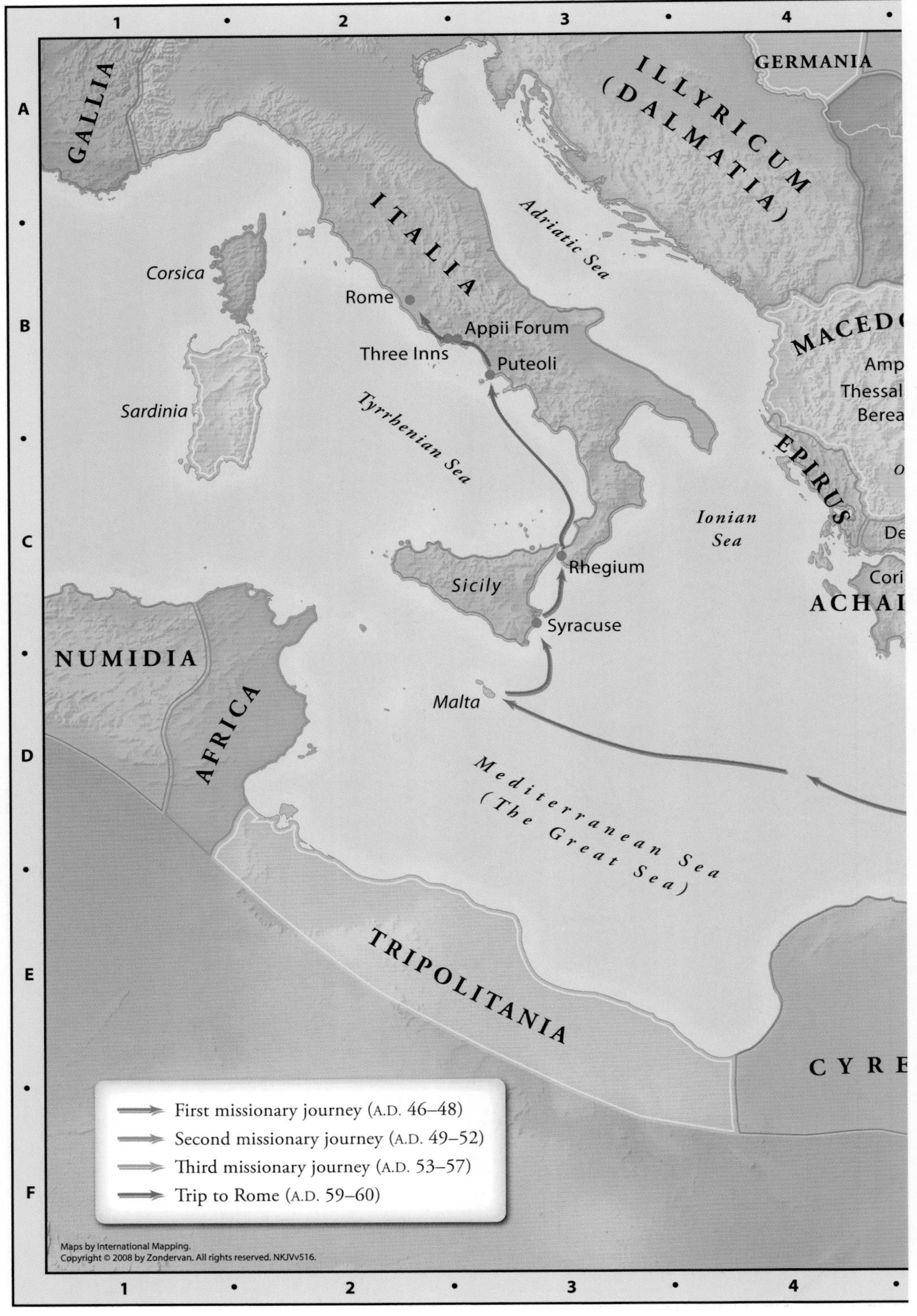
GALLIA
GERMANIA
ILLYRICUM (DALMATIA)
ITALIA
Adriatic Sea
Corsica
Rome
Appii Forum
Three Inns
Puteoli
Sardinia
Tyrrhenian Sea
MACEDO
Amp
Thessal
Berea
EPIRUS
Ionian Sea
De
Rhegium
Sicily
Cori
ACHAI
Syracuse
NUMIDIA
AFRICA
Malta
Mediterranean Sea (The Great Sea)
TRIPOLITANIA
CYRE
First missionary journey (A.D. 46–48)
Second missionary journey (A.D. 49–52)
Third missionary journey (A.D. 53–57)
Trip to Rome (A.D. 59–60)
Maps by International Mapping.
Copyright © 2008 by Zondervan. All rights reserved. NKJVv516.

5
6
7
8
A
B
C
D
E
F
DACIA
MOESIA
THRACE
Black Sea
10,000 ft
5000 ft
2000 ft
1000 ft
0 (sea level)
-1640 ft
3050 m
1525 m
610 m
305 m
0 (sea level)
-500 m
DONIA
Philippi
mphipolis
Neapolis
ssalonica
Samothrace
rea
Apollonia?
Mt. Olympus
BITHYNIA & PONTUS
Aegean Sea
Troas
MYSIA
Assos
ASIA
GALATIA
CAPPADOCIA
Mitylene
Pergamos
Thyatira
Delphi
Chios
LYDIA
Sardis
PISIDIA
LYCAONIA
Smyrna
Antioch in Pisidia
COMMAGENE
Athens
Ephesus
Philadelphia
Corinth
PAMPHYLIA
Iconium
AIA
Samos
Laodicea
Cenchreae
Colosse
Derbe
Euphrates R.
Patmos
Miletus
Lystra
CILICIA
Sparta
LYCIA
SYRIA
Cos
Attalia
Tarsus
Issus
Cnidus
Seleucia Pieria
Patara
Aleppo
Crete
Antioch
Rhodes
Myra
Salmone
Perga
Cyprus
Phoenix
Lasea
Salamis
Claudа
Paphos
Fair Havens
PHOENICIA
ABILENE
Sidon
Mediterranean Sea
(The Great Sea)
Tyre
Damascus
Ptolemais
JUDEA
Caesarea
Jordan R.
Jerusalem
Dead Sea
ENAICA
ARABIA
EGYPT
Nile R.
0
200 km.
0
200 miles
Red Sea

Map 14: **ROMAN EMPIRE**

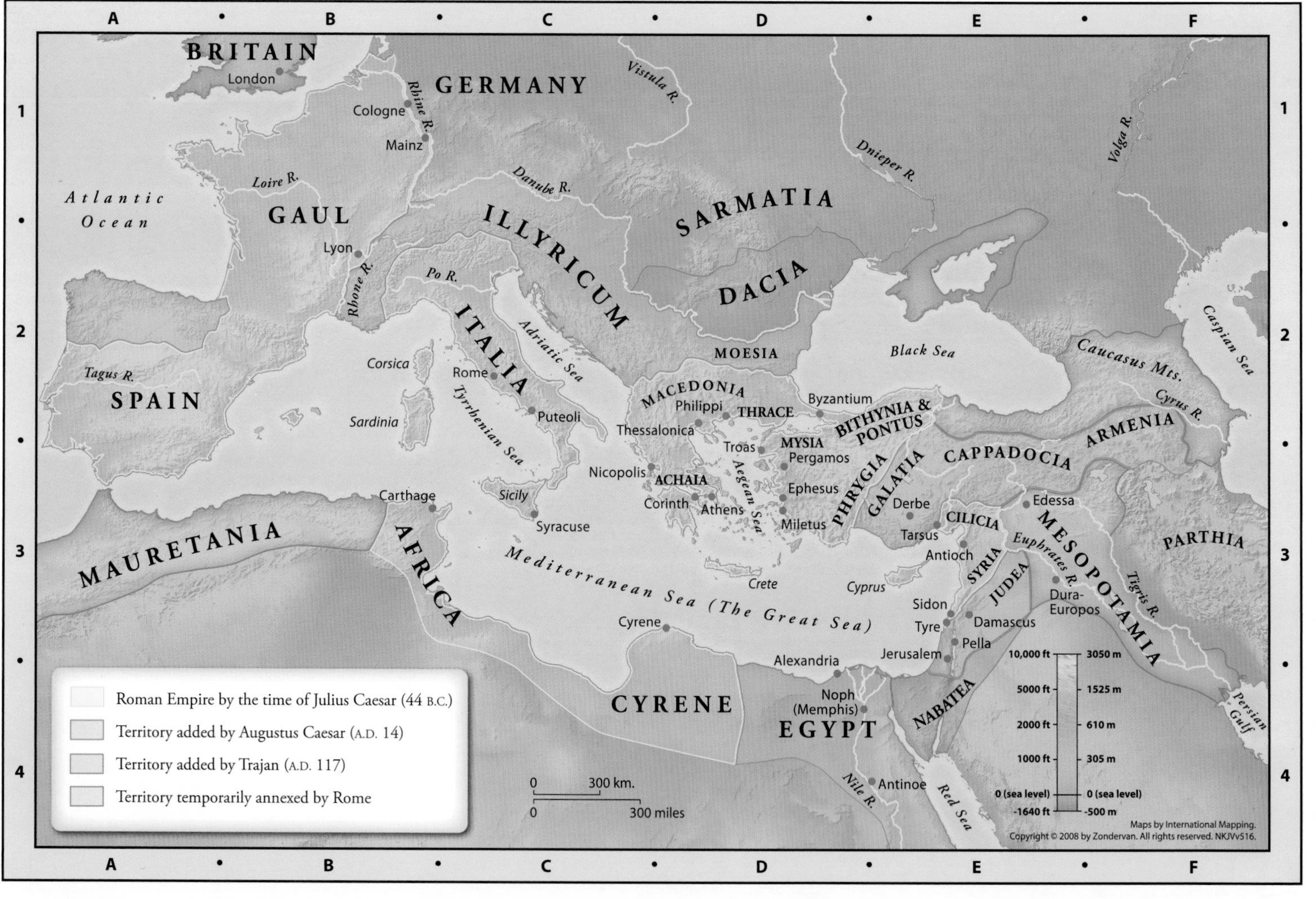